AFRICA BIBLE COMMENTARY

AFRICA BIBLE COMMENTARY

General Editor
Tokunboh Adeyemo

Theological Editors
**Solomon Andria, Issiaka Coulibaly,
Tewoldemedhin Habtu, Samuel Ngewa**

Theological Advisors
Kwame Bediako, Isabel Apawo Phiri, Yusufu Turaki

Published for distribution in Africa by WordAlive Publishers, PO Box 4547 GPO-00100 Nairobi, Kenya
www.wordalivepublishers.com

Distribution in Africa also provided by Oasis International Ltd.
info@oasisint.net

Published for distribution in the rest of the world by The Zondervan Corporation
www.zondervan.com

First published in 2006

Requests for information on all other English editions should be addressed to Zondervan, Grand Rapids, Michigan 49530, USA

Requests for information on translations should be addressed to the Piquant Agency, PO Box 83, Carlisle, CA3 9HZ, UK
abc@piquant.net   www.piquant.net

Library of Congress Cataloging-in-Publication Data

Africa Bible commentary : a one-volume commentary / Tokunboh Adeyemo, general editor
    p. cm.
  Includes bibliographical references and index.
  ISBN-13: 978-9966-805-78-2
  ISBN-10: 9966-805-78-8
  ISBN-13: 978-0-310-26473-6
  ISBN-10: 0-310-26473-1
  1. Bible — Commentaries. 2. Theology — Africa. I. Adeyemo, Tokunbo.

  BS491.3.A47 2006
  220.7096 — dc22

  2006004692

Cover design: Projectluz   projectluz@mac.com
Editorial oversight: Isoword   isoword@sympatico.ca
Proofreading oversight: editorial Suite   www.editorialsuite.com

Printed in China

06 07 08 09 10 11 12 13 14 • 10 9 8 7 6 5 4 3 2 1

CONTENTS

COMMENTARIES

ARTICLES

ADDITIONAL RESOURCES

FOREWORD BY DR JOHN STOTT

The Bible has an indispensable part to play in the church member's personal discipleship and in the pastor's preaching ministry. But this statement assumes that they can understand it. Hence the wonderful provision of the *Africa Bible Commentary*. One of the most significant recent developments in the churches of Africa is the rise of sound biblical scholarship. The church is fortunate indeed to see this resurgence in the continent that gave us such interpreters as Augustine and Athanasius. The *Africa Bible Commentary* is a publishing landmark, and I congratulate contributors and editors on their achievement. Its foundation is biblical, its perspective African, and its approach to controversial questions balanced. I intend to use it myself in order to gain African insights into the Word of God. Indeed, I hope it will have a worldwide readership, so that we may better grasp 'with all God's people' the full dimensions of Christ's love (Eph 3:18).

John Stott
December 2005

FOREWORD BY DR ABOAGYE-MENSAH

The phenomenal growth of the church in Africa brings with it many challenges. One of these challenges is how to sustain the numerical growth while ensuring that the faith of Christians is firmly grounded in the revealed and written word of God – the Holy Bible. Grounding the people's faith in the Bible requires intensifying the teaching ministry of the church. This, in turn, creates a need for appropriate tools to assist pastors, seminarians, theologians, lay preachers and Christian Education teachers to teach effectively. The *Africa Bible Commentary* written by African theologians has come at the right time!

What makes the *Africa Bible Commentary* unique and relevant is the fact that it has been written by African theologians who love the Lord and are committed to the life of the church. They write out of their matured practical experience in teaching the Bible within the Christian community. The content of the commentary can thus be described as tried and tested material that will help others towards Christian maturity when prayerfully used.

In interpreting the biblical text, the authors have also been able to bring together Christian spirituality and the depth of their understanding of African culture and religion.

The *Africa Bible Commentary* will also be useful to Christians outside the African continent who want to enrich their own understanding of the Bible by stepping outside their own culture and experience. In so doing, they will gain insights into their own culture as well, for the African scholars who contributed to the commentary also have a rich and varied experiences of the life of the church outside Africa.

I wish to express my deepest appreciation to all those who contributed to the writing of this commentary and enthusiastically recommend it to Christians everywhere who want to understand the Bible in order to live out and share their faith.

The Most Rev. Dr Robert K. Aboagye-Mensah
Presiding Bishop
The Methodist Church, Ghana
February 2006

GENERAL INTRODUCTION

Everything begins with an idea, a thought, or a concept. As the idea grows, possibilities begin to emerge, riding on the wings of creative thinking. It is like the seed in the parable of the Sower that falls on good soil and yields a bumper harvest (Matt 13:8). In the case of the *Africa Bible Commentary* (ABC), this harvest has sprung from an idea that began to grow in the minds of a number of African church leaders and a cross-section of overseas missionary partners working in Africa.

The History of the ABC

In September 1994, representatives of Protestant churches, both ecumenical and evangelical, gathered in Nairobi, Kenya, for the Second Pan Africa Christian Leadership Assembly (PACLA II). At this historic meeting, Christian leaders identified deficient knowledge of the Bible and faulty application of its teaching as the primary weakness of the church in Africa. They recognized that the church in Africa was a mile long in terms of quantity, but only an inch deep in terms of quality. The Bible needed to be interpreted and explained to the people in familiar language, using colloquial metaphors, African thought-forms and nuances, and practical applications that fitted the African context. After all, God is closer to the people when he speaks in their language, as St Augustine of Hippo once said.

Inspired by the conference, academics set to work and produced many books. But these ended up in the libraries of academic institutions and in the hands of theological students and their professors. These books did not meet the needs of the millions of believers and their pastors who do not have the privilege of a seminary education. So a dream was born among the leadership of the Association of Evangelicals in Africa (AEA). They dreamed of an African Bible commentary produced by seventy African scholars and theologians, male and female, Francophone and Anglophone, who would both explain the text of all sixty-six books in the Bible and apply the Bible's teaching to contemporary Africa. As Professor Bediako stated, such a book would be 'a fundamental resource for the church in Africa: for Christian thought, action and scholarship'.

Many dismissed the idea as no more than a dream. Besides the problem of getting scholars from diverse ecclesiastical traditions and theological viewpoints to cooperate, there were the daunting logistical problems posed by the state of communications across the vastness of the African continent. Could seventy African theologians and scholars work together, keep to deadlines, and produce a mammoth work like the ABC at a reasonable cost?

One of the few to believe that it could be done and to throw its weight logistically and financially behind the project was SIM, which lived up to its name as Serving in Mission. This missionary organization has had an active church-planting ministry in Africa for more than a century. Its literature arm, under the leadership of Jim Mason, has long been conducting pastors' conferences and giving out books to assist pastors in their ministry. They, too, had been contemplating the idea of providing pastors with a Bible commentary written entirely by African scholars.

The Executive Committee of the AEA, the leaders of SIM, and others who had expressed interest in the project thus met on the campus of the Nairobi Evangelical Graduate School of Theology (NEGST), another project of the AEA. Four of those at that meeting from 29-31 January 2001 became the editors of the ABC. Tokunboh Adeyemo (Nigerian), the General Secretary of the AEA, became the General Editor. Samuel Ngewa (Kenyan), a professor at NEGST, assumed responsibility for editing all New Testament commentaries submitted in English. Tewoldemedhin Habtu (Eritrean), also a professor at NEGST, assumed reponsibility for editing Old Testament manuscripts submitted in English, while those submitted in French would be edited by Issiaka Coulibaly (Ivorian), a lecturer at the Faculté de Théologie Evangélique de l'Alliance Chrétienne (FATEAC) in Côte d'Ivoire. In 2002, Solomon Andria (Malagasy), another professor at FATEAC, joined this group and assumed responsibility for New Testament commentaries written in French.

Two of those present at the initial meeting accepted positions as editorial advisors. They were Dr Isabel Phiri (Malawian), Professor of Theology at the University of KwaZulu-Natal and Dr Yusufu Turaki (Nigerian) of the International Bible Society, Enugu, and a Professor at Jos ECWA Theological Seminary (JETS), Jos.

The SIM representatives, Dr Jim Plueddemann, General Director of SIM USA (American) and Mr Jim Mason, International Literature Consultant of SIM Canada (Canadian), were invited to serve as technical partners. Another technical partner was Mr Pieter Kwant, Managing Director of the Piquant Agency, Carlisle, UK (Dutch) and the International Programme Director of Langham Partnership International.

Three other leaders who had expressed interest in the project sent their apologies for being unable to attend. They were Dr Dirinda Marini-Bodho, the initial Old Testament Editor – French, Dr Kwame Bediako and Dr Tite Tienou.

At this first meeting, terms were defined, roles were clarified, terms of reference were spelled out and budgets were approved. It was agreed that the ABC would also include articles on issues affecting the continent, and so a list of these issues was drawn up, as well as a list of writers who could be asked to address them.

Five of the major resolutions passed at this meeting have served as editorial guidelines for this project:

- The ABC should be a readable, accessible and affordable one-volume commentary that pastors, students and lay people can easily use.
- The ABC should be African in terms of its authorship and its content, which must reflect its African context. While remaining true to the biblical text, it must apply biblical teachings and truths to African realities.
- The contributors to the ABC should be chosen to reflect the diversity of Africa as regards denominations and languages, and should include both men and women. The diversity in the contributors should also find expression in their commentaries.
- As part of their contract, contributors to the ABC would be expected to accept the AEA Statement of Faith as a guideline for their work.
- The ABC project should be owned by Africans and should be managed independently, although under the ultimate supervision of the AEA.

After this meeting, possible contributors were approached. They were urged to embark on individual research and to work both from the original Greek and Hebrew texts and also from translations of the Bible into their mother tongues. Writing workshops were organized in different parts of the continent. A number of writers were assisted to take a sabbatical in order to find time to write. Writers from the same area were encouraged to interact in order to encourage each other and critique each other's work.

The Contents of the ABC

The ABC is not a critical, academic, verse-by-verse commentary. Rather, it contains section-by-section exegesis and explanation of the whole Bible as seen through the eyes of African scholars who respect the integrity of the text and use African proverbs, metaphors and stories to make it speak to African believers in the villages and cities across the entire continent. The application is both bold and faithful. Thus the ABC does not speak of a Black Jesus. To do so would be a travesty of the Bible story and cheap scholarship. Instead, the ABC is true to the text and honest to its context both in Bible days and in our day.

The ABC is, in fact, a mini-library that equips pastors and teachers to teach the churches and encourages students and church members to study God's word for themselves.

Of special benefit are the up-to-date specialist articles dealing with burning issues and problems such as poverty, favouritism, HIV/AIDS, refugees, war, politics and so on. And all this information is in one volume, which is easy-to-use, easy to handle, surprisingly light to carry, and very affordable! Even better, it is being published in both English and French, and will soon be translated into several African languages.

Using the ABC

What can the ABC be used for? At the top of my list is personal devotion. As general editor, I had to critique and correct every manuscript. But after completing this task, I began to use the manuscripts for my quiet time. For the shorter books, I first read the entire book in the Bible and then the commentary on the book. For the longer books, I read between five and ten chapters a day and then read the corresponding commentary. My spiritual life has been enriched, and I strongly recommend this approach.

I have also used portions of the ABC for my sermon preparation and pulpit ministry. While doing this, I have learned many new things about African peoples of whom I previously knew nothing. For example, until I read the ABC on Leviticus, I did not know about the Iraqw tribe in northern Tanzania who are of Semitic extraction and have much in common with the Hebrews.

All of the ABC editors are seminary professors. All of them have used some portions of the ABC as part of their class lectures. In fact, some students at the NEGST who interacted with my own manuscript on 2 Peter sent me their comments, expressing their agreement or disagreement with what I had said. Such discussion is beneficial for all of us as we seek to understand and apply God's word. This experience confirms that the ABC will be a powerful resource book for fellowship group discussions and even for Sunday school classes in churches. I expect to find the ABC in every library of every Bible college, seminary, university and other institution of higher learning throughout Africa and beyond.

I also strongly recommend the ABC to every missionary working in Africa or intending to serve in Africa as it will give them insights into the Scriptures and into Africa that can only benefit their ministry

Though the ABC is written by Africans and primarily for Africans, it can be used with benefit by those who are not Africans. In fact, reading the Bible through African lenses may help to inspire others with the dynamism and excitement that is common in African churches.

Acknowledgements

We praise God for all he has accomplished. And it is also important that we acknowledge the significant contributions made by certain organizations and individuals without which the ABC could not have been born.

- The AEA for officially sponsoring the ABC and giving the editorial board the academic and management freedom to function.
- SIM for facilitating the logistics and finances required to move the process forward to its completion.
- NEGST for serving as the academic centre for the ABC, hosting our meetings, and making its library and other facilities available to visiting scholars.
- The Langham Partnership International for providing scholarships to enable many of our scholars to proceed on sabbaticals in order to write.
- Institutions of higher learning (including UNISA, GIMPA and Biola University) and retreat centres for hosting ABC scholars during their sabbaticals.
- Technical teams in Europe and Canada for helping with the administration, copyediting, translation, proofreading, typesetting, tracking down missing writers, and the like.
- The advisors for wise counsel, penetrating academic and theological insights and invaluable contributions.

- The editors for their sound and erudite scholarship with a touch of spiritual anointing, as well as for their selfless, sacrificial service.
- All sixty-nine contributors for making history in our generation by producing the first ever one-volume Bible commentary for the church in Africa.
- Zondervan, WordAlive and Oasis for agreeing to publish, distribute and market the ABC.
- Jim Mason, Pieter Kwant, Isobel Stevenson, Krysia Lear, Maybeth Henderson, Sue Prior and Judy Milasi for your ability to juggle multiple ABC balls without dropping any of them.
- All those individuals and groups in Africa and around the world who have supported this project in prayer.
- All those who have given generously to cover the many expenses incurred in producing the ABC.
- Finally, I would like to thank Dr John Stott CBE for writing a foreword to the ABC and Dr Robert Aboagye-Mensah, Presiding Bishop of the Methodist Church of Ghana, and the many others who have honoured the ABC with their endorsements.

Our prayer is that just as God used his word to ignite the fire of Reformation in Europe in the sixteenth century, he will use the ABC to do the same in Africa today. Amen!

Tokunboh Adeyemo,
General Editor,
Africa Bible Commentary
February 2006

THE VISION

Vision statement for the ABC drafted in January 2001

The Africa Bible Commentary is a one-volume commentary written and edited by African biblical scholars on all the books of the Bible. The general aim of the commentary is to make the word of God speak relevantly to African realities today. More especially, it targets Christian leaders at the grassroots level – pastors, students, and lay leaders – who, under the guidance of the Holy Spirit, can be instrumental in the establishment and nurture of a vibrant church in the continent. A one-volume commentary on the whole Bible is, by its very nature, a major exercise in compression, with a rigorous discipline governing what needs to be included and what needs to be omitted. This volume, therefore, does not delve into critical and exegetical details. Based on the firm conviction of and belief in the divine inspiration and authority of Holy Scripture, it seeks to offer the reader a contextual readable and affordable guide.

The fruit of that vision is now in your hands!

GUIDELINES FOR USING THE ABC

Here are some suggestions to help readers who are unfamiliar with Bible commentaries to find the information they are looking for in the Africa Bible Commentary.

I need information about who wrote a book in the Bible, where, when and why.

Each book starts with a general introduction that attempts to answer some of these questions. Additional information can also often be found in general introductory articles like the 'Introduction to the Pentateuch' and 'Introduction to the Prophets'.

I want to get an overview of a whole book of the Bible.

Read the commentary on that book. The individual commentaries in the ABC were written to be read as a whole, and are not just discussions of individual verses.

I need help preparing a sermon or a Bible study.

1) Read the article on 'Principles of Interpretation' for guidance on how to approach passages of Scripture.
2) Go to the commentary on the book that you will be teaching from.
3) Look at the Outline of Contents to get some idea of how the passage you will be dealing with fits into the whole book.
4) Find the subheading in the Outline of Contents that includes your passage.
5) Turn to that subsection and read it. It can also be a good idea to read the subsections on either side to see the passage in context.
6) Look up any cross-references (marked with 'see' or 'see also') to see what light the rest of the Bible throws on the passage.

The approach taken in the commentary may suggest a structure you can use for your sermon, or it may suggest applications that can be made. If there is one main topic in the passage (for example, marriage) you may also find it useful to read the articles in the ABC that relate to marriage. All the articles are listed in the table of contents.

I don't understand a specific verse.

For example: Why does 1 Corinthians 11:10 say that women must cover their heads 'because of the angels'

1) Find the commentary on the book that verse comes from in the ABC *(Find 1 Corinthians using the table of contents or your knowledge that it comes after Romans, as in the Bible.)*

2) Look at the verse ranges mentioned at the very top of every page except the title pages for commentaries until you find the page that includes the verse you are interested in. *(The page headed 1 Cor 11:2-15 will include commentary on 11:10.)*
3) Scan the page for the reference you are looking for set in bold type (**11:10**). The bold indicates that this is the main place where this verse is discussed. *(The reference to 11:10 stands out in the right-hand column.)*
4) Where specific words in a verse are being discussed, they will be quoted in italics. *('because of the angels' is in italics next to 11:10.)*

I need to know what the Bible has to say about a specific topic.

Scan the list of articles at the front of the commentary and see whether any of them address your topic. *(For example, if you want information about healing, you could look at the article on Healing, and also at related articles on HIV/AIDS, Suffering, Witchcraft, Ancestors and Prayer, all of which may be relevant to your thinking about health and disease.*

The commentary uses a word I don't understand.

We have tried to avoid using technical theological vocabulary, but a few words, such as apocalyptic, could not be avoided. For help with them, turn to the glossary at the back of the ABC.

I have read the commentary, but I want to know more about a book in the Bible.

At the end of each commentary, the author lists books for further reading. You can also consult books from the commentary series listed on the Abbreviations page. These books are sometimes cited in the ABC by their abbreviations. If you have access to the Internet, you may be able to obtain more information from the Web sites listed at the back of the ABC.

I am confused about the difference between references like 5:2-4, which are often used, and just 2–4, which is only used a few times.

All verse references are given with both the chapter and the verses. Where you only see two numbers separated by a long dash, they are chapter numbers, not verse numbers. So 2–4 means chapters two to four of the book referred to.

ABBREVIATIONS

Books of the Bible

Old Testament (OT)

Gen, Exod, Lev, Num, Deut, Josh, Judg, Ruth, 1-2 Sam, 1-2 Kgs, 1-2 Chr, Ezra, Neh, Esth, Job, Ps/Pss, Prov, Eccl, Song, Isa, Jer, Lam, Ezek, Dan, Hos, Joel, Amos, Obad, Jonah, Mic, Nah, Hab, Zeph, Hag, Zech, Mal

New Testament (NT)

Matt, Mark, Luke, John, Acts, Rom, 1-2 Cor, Gal, Eph, Phil, Col, 1-2 Thess, 1-2 Tim, Titus, Phlm, Heb, Jas, 1-2 Pet, 1-2-3 John, Jude, Rev

Translations of the Bible

CEV	Contemporary English Version
GNB	Good News Bible
HCSB	Holman Christian Standard Bible
JB	Jerusalem Bible
KJV	King James Version
Knox	Knox Bible
NASB	New American Standard Bible
NEB	New English Bible
NIV	New International Version
NJB	New Jerusalem Bible
NKJV	New King James Version
NRSV	New Revised Standard Version
RSV	Revised Standard Version

Commentary Series

AB	Anchor Bible Commentary Series
BNTC	Black's New Testament Commentary
BST	The Bible Speaks Today
CBC	Cambridge Bible Commentary
CBSC	Cambridge Bible for Schools and Colleges
CCC	Crossway Classic Commentaries
CC	Communicator's Commentary
DSB	Daily Study Bible
EBC	Expositor's Bible Commentary
EC	Expositional Commentary
EvBC	Everyman's Bible Commentary
FOB	Focus on the Bible
HC	Hermeneia Commentaries
IBC	Interpretation Bible Commentary for Teaching and Preaching
ICC	International Critical Commentary
ITC	International Theological Commentary
NAC	New American Commentary
NBC	New Bible Commentary
NIBC	New International Bible Commentary
NICOT	New International Commentary on the Old Testament
NICNT	New International Commentary on the New Testament
NIGTC	New International Greek Testament Commentary
NIVAC	NIV Application Commentary
PC	Preacher's Commentary
PNTC	Pillar New Testament Commentary
TBC	Torch Bible Commentary
TNT	Tyndale New Testament Commentary
TOT	Tyndale Old Testament Commentary
WBC	Word Biblical Commentary

CONTRIBUTORS

Abate, Eshetu Koyra. Ethiopian. BDiv (Association of Theological Institutions in Eastern Africa), BTh (Mekane Yesus Seminary, Addis Ababa, Ethiopia), STM and PhD in Theology (Concordia Seminary, St. Louis, USA). Former Principal of Mekane Yesus Seminary. Currently Translation Consultant with the Bible Society of Ethiopia.
Philippians

Aboagye-Mensah, Robert. K. Ghanaian. Methodist. Licentiate in Theology (Trinity College, Legon, Ghana), BTh (St John's College, University of Nottingham, England), MA in Christian Education (Virginia Theological Seminary, USA), PhD in Philosophy (University of Aberdeen, Scotland). Former lecturer at Trinity College, Legon, Ghana, and General Secretary of the Christian Council of Ghana. Currently Presiding Bishop of the Methodist Church of Ghana.
War

Adei, Stephen. Ghanaian. BSc (University of Ghana), MSc (University of Strathclyde, Scotland), MTh (University of South Africa), PhD in Economics (University of Sydney, Australia). Former United Nations Development Programme (UNDP) Resident Representative in Namibia, economist and Chief of the Directorate of UNDP Africa Bureau, New York, and Secretary General of the Ghana Missionary Society. Currently Rector of Ghana Institute of Management and Public Administration (GIMPA).
Debt; Wealth and Poverty

Adeyemo, Tokunboh. Nigerian. BTh (Evangelical Church of West Africa [ECWA] Theological Seminary, Nigeria), MDiv and MTh (Talbot School of Theology, Biola University, California, USA), PhD in Theology (Dallas Theological Seminary, Texas, USA), PhD in Philosophy (University of Aberdeen, Scotland). Former General Secretary of the Association of Evangelicals in Africa (22 years). Currently Executive Director of the Centre for Biblical Transformation.
Judges; Daniel; 2 Peter; Jude; Conflict Management; Discipleship; Dreams; Ideas of Salvation in Other Religions; Leadership; Religious Pluralism, Worship and Praise

Adoyo, Bonifes E. Kenyan. BA in Design (Nairobi University, Kenya), MDiv (Nairobi Evangelical Graduate School of Theology [NEGST], Kenya). Former Sales and Marketing Manager of Rank Xerox International. Currently Bishop of Nairobi Pentecostal Church, a ministry of Christ Is the Answer Ministries, Nairobi, Kenya.
Prayer

Afriyie, Ernestina. Ghanaian. Presbyterian. DipTh, BA Hons (Ghana), MTh (Natal), PhD (Natal). Research Fellow with Akrofi-Christaller Memorial Centre, Akropong-Akuapem.
Taboos

Ahoga, Augustin Cossi. Beninese. MSc in Economics (Benin National University), MTh (Faculté Libre de Théologie Evangélique, Vaux-sur-Seine, France), MA in Biblical Studies (University of Gloucestershire, England). Graduate Secretary for IFES in Francophone Africa. Lecturer at the Baptist School of Theology in Lomé, Togo, and at the Benin Bible Institute in Cotonou, where he is also President of the Administrative Council.
Jonah; Nahum

Akanni, Gbile. Nigerian. BEd in Physics and Education (University of Ibadan, Nigeria). Former lecturer at the College of Education, Katsina-Ala, Nigeria. Currently President and Coordinator of Living Seed Peace House, Gboko, Nigeria.
1 Samuel

Andria (Andriatsimialomananarivo), Solomon. Malagasy. BSc in Engineering and Electro-mechanics (Université d'Antananarivo, Madagascar), MTh (Faculté Libre de Théologie Evangélique, Vaux-sur-Seine, France), PhD in Missiology (University of South Africa). Currently Head of History and Theology at the Faculté de Théologie Evangélique de l'Alliance Chrétienne (FATEAC), Abidjan, Côte d'Ivoire.
Colossians; 1 and 2 Timothy; Titus; James; Generosity and Solidarity

Assohoto, Barnabé. Beninese. Baptist. BSc in Electronics (University Polytechnic, Benin), MTh (Faculté Libre de Théologie Evangélique, Vaux-sur-Seine, France), PhD (Strasbourg University, France). Currently Director of the African Research Centre, Cotonou, Benin, and Coordinator of Faith in Action International.
Genesis

Bediako, Kwame. Ghanaian. Presbyterian. BA(Hons) in French (University of Ghana, Legon, Ghana), BA in Theology (London School of Theology (formerly London Bible College), England), PhD in French Literature (University of Bordeaux, France), PhD in Divinity (University of Aberdeen, Scotland). Former Resident Minister at the Ridge Church, Accra, and visiting lecturer at the University of Edinburgh, Scotland. Currently the Director of Akrofi-Christaller Memorial Centre for Mission Research and Applied Theology, Akropong-Akuapem, Ghana.
Scripture as the Interpreter of Culture and Tradition

Bitrus, Daniel. Nigerian. Church of Christ. BA in Theology (United Missionary Theological College [UMTC], Ilorin, Nigeria), MA in Christian Education (Trinity Evangelical Divinity School, Chicago, USA). Served with the United Bible Societies and former General Secretary of the Association of Evangelicals in Africa. Currently Pastor of Bukuru Church of Christ in Nigeria.
Amos

Boniface-Malle, Anastasia. Tanzanian. Ordained Lutheran Minister. BDiv (Makumira Theological College, Tanzania), STM (Wartburg Theological Seminary, Iowa, USA), PhD in OT Studies (Luther Theological Seminary, Minnesota, USA). Former lecturer at Makumira Theological College. Currently Translation Consultant for United Bible Societies.
Numbers

Carew, M. Douglas. Sierra Leonean. BSc (Fourah Bay College, Sierra Leone), MDiv (Nairobi Evangelical Graduate School of Theology [NEGST], Kenya), PhD (Trinity International University, Illinois, USA). Former Professor at Sierra Leone Bible College. Currently Vice Chancellor of NEGST.
Hosea; The Ancient Near East

Chianeque, Luciano C. Angolan. BA in Bible and Theology (University of Durban-Westville, South Africa), MA in Religion and Social Transformation (University of Cape Town, South Africa), PhD (University of KwaZulu-Natal, South Africa). Former Satellite General Secretary of Evangelical Congregational Church in Angola. Currently Country Director of Alfalit, an adult literacy project in Angola.
Deuteronomy; Reward and Retribution

Chingota, Felix Lack. Malawian. BA in French, History and Philosophy (University of Malawi), BDiv (St Paul's United Theological College, Limuru, Kenya), PhD in Biblical Studies (University of Aberdeen, Scotland). Former minister with the Presbyterian Church of Malawi. Currently Senior Professor in the Department of Theology and Religious Studies and Deputy Dean of the Faculty of Humanities at Chancellor College, University of Malawi.
Leviticus; Priesthood in the Bible

Choge, Emily J. Kenyan. BEd in Arts (Kenyatta University, Nairobi, Kenya), MDiv and MTh (Nairobi Evangelical Graduate School of Theology [NEGST], Kenya), PhD (Fuller Theological Seminary, California, USA). Former Deputy Head of St Joseph's Girls High School, Chepterit, Kenya. Currently lecturing at Moi University, Eldoret, Kenya, and part-time lecturer at NEGST.
Hospitality

Cole, Victor Babajide. Nigerian. BTh (Igbaja Theological Seminary, Nigeria), ThM (Dallas Theological Seminary, Texas, USA), PhD (Michigan State University, USA). Former Curriculum Consultant for African Leadership and Management Academy, Harare, Zimbabwe. Currently Deputy Vice Chancellor for Academic Affairs at Nairobi Evangelical Graduate School of Theology (NEGST), Kenya.
Mark; Blood

Coulibaly, Issiaka. Ivorian. MTh, PhD (candidate) in Biblical Exegesis (Faculté Libre de Théologie Evangélique,Vaux-sur-Seine, France). Currently French Translation Publications Manager with the United Bible Societies and lecturer in Old Testament Studies at the Faculté de Théologie Evangélique de l'Alliance Chrétienne (FATEAC), Abidjan, Côte d'Ivoire.
Jeremiah; Lamentations; 2 Corinthians

Datiri, Dachollom C. Nigerian. BD, MA, PhD in Biblical Studies from the University of Sheffield, England. Currently Senior Pastor of the Church of Christ in Nigeria (COCIN), Nassarawa Gwong, Jos, Nigeria; also part-time lecturer at the Theological College of Northern Nigeria (TCNN), Bukuru, Jos, Nigeria.
1 Corinthians

Dembele, Youssouf. Malian. BSc in Applied Sciences (Instituto Superior de Ciencias Agropecuarias de la Habana, Cuba), MTh (Faculté Libre de Théologie Evangélique, Vaux-sur-Seine, France), PhD in Biblical and Systematic Theology (Trinity International University, Illinois, USA). Former lecturer at Reed Bible Institute, Bougouni, Mali. Currently Translation Consultant with United Bible Societies and Pastor of Evangelical Protestant Church of Mali.
Habakkuk

Famonure, Bayo. Nigerian. Diploma in Journalism (London School of Journalism, Frilsham Hermitage, Berks), BA (Hons) in English (University of Nigeria), and Doctor of Divinity (World Link University, Portland, Oregon, USA). Founding member and first Chief Executive Officer of Calvary Ministries (CAPRO); former Executive Secretary of Missions Commission of Association of Evangelicals in Africa. Currently President of Agape Missions in Nigeria.
Indigenous Missions

Gacece, Solomon. Kenyan. Presbyterian. BEd (Kenyatta University, Kenya), DipTh (Presbyterian College, Kikuyu, Kenya). Former lecturer at Kagumo Teachers' College, Kenya. Currently coordinator of street children programme for St Andrew's Church, Nairobi, and Executive Secretary of the Youth and Sports Commission of the Association of Evangelicals in Africa.
Street Children

Githuka, Elias M. Kenyan. BA in Bible and Theology (Pan Africa Christian College, Kenya/ICI University) and completing an MA in Christian Leadership (Global University). Former base manager of Open Doors with Brother Andrew, East Africa Region. Currently Pastor at Nairobi Pentecostal Church, Valley Road.
Persecution

Gotom, Musa. PhD (Claremont). President of TEKAN (Fellowship of Christian Churches in Nigeria). Teaching pastoral counselling at the Theological College of Northern Nigeria.
1 and 2 Kings

Habtu, Tewoldemedhin. Eritrean. Baptist. BA in Business Administration (Addis Ababa University, Ethiopia), MDiv (Nairobi Evangelical Graduate School of Theology [NEGST], Kenya), PhD (Trinity International University, Illinois). Former Pastor of Faith Baptist Church in Ethiopia for over ten years. Currently Associate Professor of OT Studies, NEGST.
Job; Proverbs; Ecclesiastes; Song of Songs; Ezekiel; History of Israel; Introduction to the Wisdom Literature

Isaak, Paul John. Namibian. Evangelical Lutheran Church. MA in Religion (Pacific Lutheran Theological Seminary, California, USA), MTh and PhD (Lutheran School of Theology, Chicago, USA). Head of Department of Religion and Theology, University of Namibia.
Luke

Kantiok, James B. Nigerian. BEd in Social Studies (Ahmadu Bello University, Zaria, Nigeria), MEd in Educational Psychology and MPhil in Teacher Education and Programs Evaluation (University of Jos, Nigeria), MA in Missiology and PhD in Intercultural Studies (Fuller Theological Seminary, California, USA). Former Adjunct Professor at California Lutheran University. Currently Associate Professor at Azusa Pacific University, California, USA.
Christians and Politics

Kapolyo, Joe M. Zambian. Baptist. BA in Theology (London Bible College, England), MA in Social Anthropology (University of London, England), MTh in NT Exegesis (Aberdeen University, Scotland), PhD candidate (University of London). Former Principal of the Theological College of Central Africa, Zambia, and Principal of All Nations Christian College, England. Currently Lead Minister at Edmonton Baptist Church in North London, England.
Matthew

Kasali, David M. Congolese (DRC). MEd in Geography and Education (Institut Supérieur Pédagogique de Bukavu), MDiv and PhD in New Testament (Trinity Evangelical Divinity School, Chicago, USA). Former Vice Chancellor, Nairobi Evangelical Graduate School of Theology (NEGST), Kenya. Currently President of Christian Bilingual University of Congo.
Romans

Kassa, Tesfaye D. Ethiopian. MD (Addis Ababa University, Ethiopia), BTh in Bible and Theology (East Africa School of Theology, Nairobi, Kenya), MDiv (Nairobi Evangelical Graduate School of Theology [NEGST], Kenya). Former medical doctor in Ethiopia and Pastor of Nairobi Pente-

costal Church. Currently pioneering Discipleship Pathway Community International.
Hebrews

Kinoti, George. Kenyan. BSc in Zoology and Chemistry, Postgraduate Diploma in Applied Parasitology and Entomology and PhD in Parasitology (University of London, England). Former professor at Makerere University, Uganda and Nairobi University, Kenya. Currently founder and Director of the African Institute for Scientific Research and Development (AISRED), Nairobi, Kenya.
Christians and the Environment

Kisau, Paul Mumo. Kenyan. BTh (Scott Theological College, Machakos, Kenya), MDiv (Nairobi Evangelical Graduate School of Theology [NEGST], Kenya), PhD (University of Aberdeen, Scotland). Former Deputy Principal for Academic Affairs of Scott Theological College. Currently Assistant Professor at Nairobi International School of Theology, Kenya.
Acts of the Apostles

Kossé, Kuzuli. Congolese. MTh (Faculté de Théologie Evangélique de Bangui [FATEB], Central African Republic), DMiss (Trinity International University, Illinois, USA). Currently lecturer in Missiology at FATEB.
Unity of Believers

Koudougueret, Rosalie. Central African Republic (CAR). BTh in Bible and Theology and MTh in Theology (Faculté de Théologie Evangélique de Bangui [FATEB], Central African Republic). Former Coordinator of Women's Training Program, FATEB. Currently lecturing at FATEB.
1 and 2 Thessalonians

Kunhiyop, Samuel Waje. Nigerian. BA in Theology (Evangelical Church of West Africa [ECWA] Theological Seminary, Nigeria), MA in Exegetical Theology (Western Baptist Seminary, Portland, Oregon, USA), PhD (Trinity International University, Illinois, USA). Former Dean of Student Affairs. Currently Provost and Professor of Theology and Ethics at ECWA Theological Seminary.
Witchcraft

Larbi, E. Kingsley. Ghanaian. BA in Bible and Theology (Pan Africa Christian College, Kenya), MDiv and MTh (Nairobi Evangelical Graduate School of Theology [NEGST], Kenya), PhD (University of Edinburgh, Scotland). Former Vice Chancellor at Central University College, Accra, Ghana. Currently President of Regent University, Accra, Ghana.
Healing

Lasisi, Lawrence Adenyi. Nigerian. BTh (Christ International Divinity College, Erinmo, Nigeria), MDiv (Hons) (Acadia University, Wolfville, Nova Scotia, Canada), MA in Islamic Studies (Hartford Seminary, Connecticut, USA), PhD in Intercultural Studies (Fuller Theological Seminary,

California, USA). Currently Pastor of Springs of Hope Christian Ministries, California, USA, and Adjunct Professor at the School of Professional Studies, Hope International University, Fullerton, California, USA.
Syncretism

Lawanson, Aderemi (Remi) Tesilimi. Nigerian. BSc in Actuarial Science (University of Lagos), MA in Intercultural Studies (Fuller Theological Seminary, California, USA), PhD candidate (Fuller Theological Seminary). Former Executive Director Stewardship and Accountability Commission of Association of Evangelicals in Africa. Currently at Fuller Theological Seminary.
Power and Accountability

Mautsa, Makoto Lloyd. Zimbabwean. BSc in Mechanical Engineering (University of Applied Science, Cologne, Germany), MSc in Agricultural Engineering (University of Zimbabwe). Former Research Engineer with the Institute of Agricultural Engineering, Ministry of Lands and Agriculture, Zimbabwe. Currently Research, Development and Maintenance Manager at Hastt Zimbabwe.
Land

Milasi, Judith A. Kenyan. Diploma in Pastoral Ministry (Grace College of East Africa, Nairobi), BA in Bible and Theology (East African School of Theology, Kenya). Former Registrar of Grace College of East Africa; Personal Assistant to Dr Tokunboh Adeyemo, General Editor of the Africa Bible Commentary. Currently Personal Assistant to the Coordinator of the SIM Pastors Book Set Project, Kenya.
Initiation Rites

Mojola, Aloo Osotsi. Kenyan. Anglican. BA, MA (University of Nairobi); PhD in Philosophy (University of Nairobi), PhD in Linguistics and Philosophy (University of Frankfurt, Germany), studied Hebrew and Biblical Geography (Jerusalem Bible College, Israel). Former lecturer at the University of Nairobi, Kenya, and Translation Consultant for United Bible Societies. Currently Regional Translation Coordinator for Africa for the United Bible Societies.
Bible Translation in Africa

Muriithi, Sicily Mbura. Kenyan. BTh and BDiv (St Paul's United Theological College, Limuru, Kenya), MA in Religion and Social Transformation; PhD (University of Kwa-Zulu Natal, South Africa). Former parish minister with the Presbyterian Church of East Africa, Kenya, and chaplain in secondary schools in Kenya. Currently lecturing at the Presbyterian University in Kenya.
1 Peter; Female Genital Mutilation

Musekura, Celestin. Rwandese. Baptist. BTh (Kenya Highlands Bible College), MDiv (Nairobi Evangelical Graduate School of Theology [NEGST], Kenya), STM and PhD candidate (Dallas Theological Seminary, Texas, USA). Former

Director for Reconciliation Ministries, MAP International. Currently founder and President of African Leadership and Reconciliation Ministries based in Nairobi.
Refugees

Musibi, Patrick Moses. Kenyan. Armed Forces Training College (Lanet, Kenya), Supply Officers' Course (Royal Air Force College, Cranwell, England). Undertaking a degree in Development Economics (Pacific Western University, Los Angeles, USA). Former Commissioned Officer (Major) Kenyan Air Force. Currently independent consultant for Putting Children on the Military Agenda, Nairobi.
The Bible and Authority

Musopole, Augustine. Malawian. BSc in Social Science (Chancellor College, University of Malawi), BDiv (University of London, England), MA (University of Malawi), STM, MPh and PhD (Union Theological Seminary, New York, USA). Former General Secretary, Malawi Council of Churches. Currently Assistant Professor at Chang Jung Christian University, Taiwan.
Obadiah

Mutonono, Dwight S. M. Zimbabwean. BTh in Bible and Theology (University of South Africa), MA in Leadership and Management (African Leadership and Management Academy, Zimbabwe). Former air traffic controller at Prince and Harare airports and Pastor of Administration with Faith Ministries. Currently Director of Administration at African Leadership and Management Academy (ALMA) and Pastor with Faith Ministries.
Land

Ndjerareou, Abel Laoundoye. Chadian. BA in Theology (Faculté Libre de Théologie Evangélique, Vaux-sur-Seine, France), MTh in OT (Trinity Evangelical Divinity School, Chicago, USA), PhD in OT Exegesis (Dallas Theological Seminary, Texas, USA). Former Director of Shalom Evangelical School of Theology in Chad. Currently Principal of Faculté de Théologie Evangélique de Bangui (FATEB) in the Central African Republic.
Exodus; Yahweh and Other Gods; Introduction to the Pentateuch

Ngewa, Samuel M. Kenyan. BTh (Ontario Bible College, Canada), MDiv (Trinity International University, Deerfield, Illinois, USA), MTh in NT and PhD in Biblical Interpretation (Westminster Theological Seminary, Philadelphia, USA). Former faculty member of Scott Theological College. Currently Professor of NT Studies at Nairobi Evangelical Graduate School of Theology (NEGST), Kenya.
Genesis; Deuteronomy; John; Galatians; 1, 2 and 3 John; Intertestamental Period; Legalism; Marriage, Remarriage and Divorce; Principles of Interpretation; The Place of Traditional Sacrifices; Life and Doctrine; What is the Church?

Ngundu, Onesimus. Zimbabwean. BSc in Theology (Philadelphia Biblical University, Pennsylvania, USA), MTh in Biblical Theology and Biblical Languages and ThD in New Testament Theology (Dallas Theological Seminary, Texas, USA), MA in History of Christianity (University of Edinburgh, Scotland), PhD candidate in Church History (University of Cambridge, England). Currently Principal of Harare Theological College, Zimbabwe.
Revelation

Njoroge, Nyambura J. Kenyan. BDiv (St Paul's United Theological College, Limuru, Kenya), MAR (Louisville Theological Seminary, Kentucky), PhD in African Theology and Christian Social Ethics (Princeton Theological Seminary, New Jersey, USA). Former parish minister with the Presbyterian Church, Kenya. Currently Executive Secretary for Ecumenical Theological Education Program of the World Council of Churches, Geneva, Switzerland.
The Role of Women in the Church

Nkansah-Obrempong, James. Ghanaian. BA (Pan Africa Christian College, Kenya), MDiv, and MTh (Nairobi Evangelical Graduate School of Theology [NEGST], Kenya), PhD in Theology (Fuller Theological Seminary, California, USA). Former Regional Director (Africa) of Open Doors International. Currently Professor of Theology at NEGST.
Angels, Demons and Powers; Theological Heresy

Nsiku, Edouard Kitoko. Congolese (DRC). Baptist. BA in Pastoral Psychology and MA in Old Testament (Faculdade Teologica Batista de Brasilia, Brazil), PhD (University of KwaZulu-Natal, South Africa). Member of the Baptist Community Church of Congo River. Has taught in several theological seminaries in Brazil and served with the International Fellowship of Evangelical Students in Mozambique. Currently Translation Consultant for the United Bible Societies, based in Maputo.
Isaiah

Nwankpa, Emeka. Nigerian. Degree in Law (Ahmadu Bello University, Zaria, Nigeria). Former legal practitioner, Lagos, Nigeria, and Founder-President of Africa House of Prayer/Intercessors for Africa, based in Accra, Ghana.
Idolatry

Obed, Uzodinma. Nigerian. PhD in Physics Education (University of Ibadan, Nigeria). Formerly Senior Lecturer, University of Ibadan. Currently International Coordinator, Apostolic Discipleship Movement (ADM) and General Pastor of Glory Tabernacle Ministry, Ibadan, Nigeria.
House Fellowship

Oginde, David. Kenyan. BSc in Architecture (University of Nairobi, Kenya), Certificate in Biblical Studies (Trinity Evangelical Divinity School, Chicago, USA), undertaking an MA in Leadership (Trinity Western University, Langley, British Columbia, Canada). Former General Secretary of the Fellowship of Christian University Students (FOCUS). Currently Senior Pastor of Nairobi Pentecostal Church, Valley Road.
Joshua; Jews and Gentiles

Okaalet, Peter. Ugandan. Anglican. MBChB (Makerere University, Uganda), MDiv and MTh (Nairobi Evangelical Graduate School of Theology [NEGST], Kenya). Former minister in the Anglican Church in Uganda and Kenya. Currently Honorary Professor at African Leadership Development Institute, Pietermaritzburg, South Africa and African Director for MAP International.
HIV/AIDS

Okorocha, Cyril C. Nigerian. Diploma in Theology (Bible College of Wales), BA in Theology (London School of Theology, England), PhD in Theology and Social Anthropology (University of Aberdeen, Scotland). Former Head of Religious Studies and Chaplain of Ahmadu Bello University, Zaria, Nigeria. Currently President of Imo State Christian Association of Nigeria and Presiding Bishop of the Anglican Diocese of Owerri, Nigeria.
Psalms

Okorocha, Eunice Iheoma. Nigerian. BEd (University of Ibadan, Nigeria), MEd in Guidance and Counselling (Ahamadu Bello University, Zaria, Nigeria), PhD in International Education and Intercultural Counselling, University of Surrey, England). Currently ministering with her husband in the Anglican Church of Nigeria and working as a freelance Christian Cultural Awareness Trainer.
Cultural Issues and the Biblical Message

Ouédraogo, Adama. Burkinabe. Graduate in Theology (l'Institut Théologique de Katadji, Côte d'Ivoire). Former President of the Action Missionnaire des Assemblées de Dieu de Côte d'Ivoire, and Principal Pastor of Assemblies of God Church of Adjame, Abidjan, Côte d'Ivoire. Currently Principal Pastor of the Evangelical Church of the Assemblies of God of Riviera II, Côte d'Ivoire, and lecturing at the Institut Théologique de Katadji et Daloa, Côte d'Ivoire.
Faith and the Search for Signs; Prophets and Apostles

Phiri, Isabel Apawo. Malawian. BEd (Chancellor College, University of Malawi), MA in Religious Education (Lancaster University, England), PhD (University of Cape Town, South Africa). Former lecturer at the universities of Malawi and Namibia. Currently Head of the School of Religion and Theology at the University of KwaZulu-Natal, South Africa, and Coordinator of the Circle of Concerned African Women Theologians.
Ruth; The Bible and Polygamy; Rape; Weddings and Lobola

Pohor, Rubin. Ivorian. Advanced Diploma in History, Postgraduate Diploma in Religious Anthropology, PhD in Religious Science (Ecole Pratique des Hautes Etudes,

Sorbonne, Paris, France). Former Deputy Head of the Department of Anthropology and Sociology at l'Université de Bouaké, Côte d'Ivoire. Currently Director of l'Institut Pastoral Hébron, Côte d'Ivoire.
Slavery; Tribalism, Ethnicity and Race

Reggy-Mamo, Mae Alice. African-American. BA in English (Douglass College, Rutgers University, New Jersey, USA), MA in Education (Harvard University, Massachusetts, USA), PhD in Education (University of Maryland, USA). Former literacy consultant for Africa with United Bible Societies. Currently Director of Adult Education at Total Grace Christian Centre and Adjunct Professor at Beulah Heights Bible College, Atlanta, Georgia, USA.
Widows and Orphans; Widow Inheritance

Semenye, Lois Mvuli. Kenyan. Presbyterian. BA in History and the Bible (Covenant College, Tennessee), MCE (Reformed Theological Seminary, Mississippi, USA), EdD and PhD (Biola University, California, USA). Former professor at Daystar University, Nairobi, Kenya and Managing Director of Christian Learning Materials Center. Currently Dean of Instruction and Head of Christian Education at Nairobi International School of Theology.
Esther; Christian Education in Africa

Simfukwe, Joe M. Zambian. Baptist. BA in Theology (Spurgeon's College, London, England), MA in Theology (Australian College of Theology, Sydney), MTh candidate. Currently Principal of Theological College of Central Africa, Ndola, Zambia.
Funeral and Burial Rites

Soungalo, Soro. Ivorian. BA in Theology (Faculté Libre de Théologie Evangélique, Vaux-sur-Seine, France), PhD (Paris). Currently Pastor of Evangelical Baptist Church of Côte d'Ivoire, lecturing in Pastoral Theology at the Faculté de Théologie Evangélique de l'Alliance Chrétienne (FATEAC, Abidjan); and President of Evangelical Training Center for Communication in Africa (CEFCA) in Abidjan, Côte d'Ivoire.
Philemon; Family and Community; Favouritism; New Family Relationships

Turaki, Yusufu. Nigerian. Evangelical Church of West Africa (ECWA). BTh in Theology (Igbaja Theological Seminary, Nigeria), MATS in Theology and Ethics (Gordon-Conwell Theological Seminary, Massachusetts, USA), PhD in Social Ethics (Boston University, Massachusetts, USA). Former Provost of ECWA Theological Seminary, Jos, Nigeria and General Secretary of ECWA, Executive Secretary of Ethics, Peace and Justice Commission of Association of Evangelicals in Africa. Currently Translation Consultant, International Bible Society.
Ephesians; Democracy; Homosexuality; Secularism and Materialism; The Bible; The Church and the State; The Role of the Ancestors; Truth, Justice, Reconciliation and Peace

Weanzana, Nupanga. Congolese (DRC). Evangelical Community Church. MTh (Faculté de Théologie Evangélique de Bangui [FATEB], Central African Republic), PhD in OT Studies (University of Pretoria, South Africa). Former Vice President of FATEB. Currently Academic Dean of FATEB.
2 Samuel; 1 and 2 Chronicles; Ezra; Nehemiah

Yilpet, Yoilah. Nigerian. Anglican. BSc (Hons) in Chemistry (Ahmadu Bello University, Zaria, Nigeria), MDiv and PhD in OT Theology (Trinity International University, Illinois). Former Assistant Minister, Christ Episcopal Church, Waukegan, Illinois, USA. Currently in the Department of Religious Studies at Jos University, Nigeria.
Joel; Micah; Zephaniah; Haggai; Zechariah; Malachi; Introduction to the Prophets

AFRICA BIBLE COMMENTARY

SCRIPTURE AS THE INTERPRETER OF CULTURE AND TRADITION

The Africa Bible Commentary attempts to relate the Scriptures and African cultures and in so doing to seek ways in which the gospel may be seen to be relevant to African cultures. As we do this, we as readers and as writers need to avoid oversimplifications about the nature of this relationship.

What Is Culture?

Culture comprises far more than just music, dance, artefacts and the like. Our culture is our world view, that is, fundamental to our understanding of who we are, where we have come from and where we are going. It is everything in us and around us that defines us and shapes us. When we turn to Christ as Lord, we are turning over to him all that is in us, all that is about us and all that is around us that has defined and shaped us. Thus salvation encompasses not just our 'souls', but also our culture at its deepest level. We need to allow Scripture to become the interpreter of who we are in the specific concrete sense of who we are in our cultures and traditions.

What Is Scripture?

But acknowledging the centrality of Scripture to our identity does not mean that we demonize our own traditional culture or learn to quote certain verses and chapters as proof texts to support particular positions we hold because of our denominational or traditional background. The centrality of Scripture is more fundamental and its significance much larger than that.

Scripture Is a Prism

When light passes through a prism, a rainbow of colours is revealed. Similarly, when our cultures pass through the prism of Scripture, we see them in a new way. The light and shade intrinsic to our cultures are revealed. We are no longer being defined by our traditions, but are allowing Scripture to interpret those traditions.

Scripture Is a Record of God's Engagement with Culture

Scripture is more than just a record of the history and religion of Israel and the early church. Rather, it records God's dealings with his people and with their culture, and is itself the fruit of that engagement. It thus provides a yardstick or a model for encouraging, identifying and controlling all subsequent engagements of gospel and culture in the continuing divine-human encounter that characterizes our faith.

Scripture Is a Road Map

Scripture is the authoritative road map on our journey of faith, a journey that began before we first believed in Christ. This road map reminds us that the journey we are on did not begin at the point when we ourselves received the map. By looking at the map in Scripture, we can see where we have come from and how we got to where we are. It also points us in the direction we are to take if we are to reach our destination. This understanding is one that the early preachers of the gospel stressed when they so often used the phrase 'according to the Scriptures'. Paul reminds Timothy of the guiding role of Scripture (2 Tim 3:16). He demonstrates its use when he recounts part of the history of the Israelites and concludes, 'These things happened to them as examples and were written down as warnings for us' (1 Cor 10:1-11).

Too often, preachers tend to pick a particular text and use it as a launch pad for presenting their own ideas, but apostolic preaching was not like that. It presented the meaning of Scripture as a whole and applied that meaning to the concrete cultural and social situation of the hearers. That is what we have to do if Scripture is to be the road map for getting us to our destination.

Scripture Is Our History

All the references to Scripture in the New Testament relate to the Old Testament, although the majority of those addressed would have been Gentiles, who did not share the Jews' cultural background. Yet, Paul refers to 'our forefathers' when speaking to Gentile Corinthians (1 Cor 10:1). Israel's history had become their 'adoptive' history, for all believers in Christ become children of Abraham (Gal 3:26-29) and are grafted into the original olive tree (Rom 11:7-20). And all believers were slaves who have been set free (Gal 4:7). All of us have been adopted into Christ, with our traditions, and are therefore transformed, with our traditions. The God of Israel is not a tribal God but the God who created all humanity.

Scripture Is the Basis of Our Identity

The earliest church was tempted to see Gentile Christians as second-class Jews, latecomers. But at the Council of Jerusalem (Acts 15) the apostles recognized that God was doing something new. Paul makes the same point when he writes as if there are now three categories of persons: Jews, Gentiles and something new, called the church of God (1 Cor 10:32; 2 Cor 5:17; Eph 2:14-18).

In the early decades of the church, some Christian writers spoke of Christians as a third race. The first race was the Jews; the second, the Gentiles; and the third was the Christians. The basis of this new identity was religious, not ethnic, national, social or cultural in the narrow sense. We have become 'a kingdom of priests to serve God and his father' (Rev 1:5-6; 1 Pet 2:9-10).

Scripture Is Our Story

Scripture is not just a holy book from which we extract teaching and biblical principles. Rather, it is a story in which we participate. When David Livingstone preached in Africa in the nineteenth century, he is said to have always referred to the Bible as the 'message from the God whom you know'. In other words, Scripture speaks to us because Scripture speaks about us. And it speaks about us because we are a part of the gospel we preach. Paul was very aware of this. He emphasized that God had had mercy on him, and now he was called to preach to others (1 Cor 15:8-11).

Africans have a strong sense of their pre-Christian religious journey and should be alive to this participation in Scripture. This was certainly true of the Liberian prophet William Wadé Harris (1865-1929). He was the first distinctive African Christian prophet of modern times, and a man who brought many people into the church. Harris cut himself off from his Grebo life and family in a radical conversion, but he did not live without ancestors or a community. He simply changed his family connections to those based on faith in Christ as known through the Scriptures. His was a spirituality of vital participation totally indigenous to his African way of being within a community. He did not think in terms of what Moses saw or Jesus did in the Bible, but of how his new ancestors, Moses, Elijah, and supremely Jesus Christ, interacted with him. That was how he broke through to many people and they became Christians.

In African culture, participation in a common life constitutes community and marks out an ethnic group. When a libation is poured, the community recites the names of all those who are absent, treating them as present. Traditional believers summon their ancestors, and they believe that these ancestors are present at the ceremony that follows. (Do we have a similar confidence that Jesus is present when we pray?)

In Christian terms, we participate in Christ, and thus also in the resources and powers of the entire community composed of those who are also one with Christ through the Spirit. This community includes both the living and the dead (Luke 20:33-38). It is a transcendent community in which the human components experience and share in the divine life and nature (2 Pet 1:4).

Bringing Scripture and Culture Together

We should not focus on extracting principles from the Bible and applying these to culture. Scripture is not a book existing independently of us. Scripture is the living testimony to what God has done and continues to do, and we are part of that testimony. The characters in Scripture are both our contemporaries and our ancestors. Their triumphs and failures help us understand our own journey of faith (Rom 11:18). Scripture is not something we only believe in, it is something we share in. This is why the people in the Bible will not be made perfect without us (Heb 11:40), nor we without them.

The application of Scripture to our cultures is a gradual process of coming together, of life touching life. Our particular culture encounters the activity of God in building up a community of his people throughout history, a community that now includes us and our particular traditions, history and culture. We will gradually come to share in a family likeness that is not measured by ethnic particularity but

by nothing less than Christ himself (Eph 4:13).

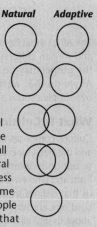

Natural   *Adaptive*

Scripture and culture are like merging circles, gradually coming to have one centre as we increasingly recognize ourselves in Scripture and Scripture becomes more and more recognizable as our story.

The process of bringing the gospel and culture together takes more than one generation. To look for a once and for all biblical 'answer' to a particular cultural problem is to misunderstand the process whereby a community and people come to see themselves as called into the people of God and come to participate in that community.

The process takes several generations, both ancient and modern. All the endeavours of believers from many backgrounds wrestling with gospel and culture are an integral part of our story. To fully understand the impact of the gospel engaging with any particular cultural environment we need to know of the struggle of ancient Israel to come to terms with the uniqueness and the majesty of Yahweh, their backslidings, apostasy, calamity, tragedy and triumphs. We also need to know how African earth shrines relate to God's way. We need to know how the gospel was brought from Alexandria to Axum, how it was taken from Ireland to the English, how it was taken from south-eastern Ghana to the Upper East Region. No part of the story of the people of God is alien to any other part of the story or is more important than any other part. The gospel has no permanent resident culture. It is as we take the experiences and the struggle in one context and funnel them through our own reading and experience of the Scripture in our mother tongue that we find that other Christian stories illuminate our story.

Scripture, Language and Culture

Mother-tongue Scripture has a fundamental place in the engagement of gospel and culture. If people recognize that Onyankopon (as God is called by the Akan of Ghana), the God they have known from time immemorial, is their Saviour, and that the coming of the gospel is what they have looked forward to, then God is continuing to ensure that they will hear him each in their own language so that they can marvel at his majesty and his love for them. Our mother tongue is the language in which God speaks to each of us. He does not speak in a sacred language, but in ordinary language, so that we may hear him and realize that this gospel is about us and that we have been invited to join a company drawn from every people, tribe, tongue, nation and language (Rev 7:9).

Kwame Bediako

(Adapted from Kwame Bediako, 'Scripture as the Hermeneutic of Culture and Tradition', Journal of African Christian Thought, Vol. 4, No. 1 [June 2001], pp. 2-11.)

THE OLD TESTAMENT

INTRODUCTION TO THE PENTATEUCH

The word 'Pentateuch' is a Greek word that was first used in the Septuagint, the ancient Greek translation of the Bible. Literally, it means 'the five rolls', that is, the first five books of the Bible: Genesis, Exodus, Leviticus, Numbers and Deuteronomy. In the Hebrew Bible, these books are known as the Torah, a word that includes the ideas of teaching and law. They tell the history of the people of Israel from their first beginnings till the time they were poised to enter the land God had promised them. During the period covered by this history, the people were given the law at Sinai.

Authorship

The five books are grouped together under one name because they show strong evidence of having been composed as a group. It is possible that they were all written by just one human author. Jewish and Christian traditions have long maintained that this author was Moses. Several passages in the Pentateuch even refer to Moses writing down the law and the history of the people of Israel (Exod 17:14; 24:4; 34:27; Num 33:1-2; Deut 31:9). Later biblical authors also seem to acknowledge Moses as the author of the Torah (Josh 1:7-8; 2 Chr 25:4; 35:12; Ezra 6:18; Neh 13:1). Jesus himself spoke of the Pentateuch as 'the book of Moses' (Mark 12:26) and the 'law of Moses' (Luke 24:44) and stated that 'Moses wrote of me' (John 5:46-47).

However, while we accept that Moses is the author, we do have to admit that some rewriting was done at a later time, bringing up to date things such as words, place names and genealogies. We see an example of this in the reference to Israelite kings in Genesis 36:31. Such changes would have been made for teaching purposes, to enable later generations to understand the text better.

Some commentators prefer to see these changes as evidence that the books of the Torah were written after the time of Moses and are based on oral tradition. However, there is little point in arguing about such things. After all, as with African stories, it is not the author who is important. What matters is the existence of a message that is relevant to the community. Whoever wrote the Pentateuch, it breathes coherence in its text and in its theological content. Its theology is highly relevant to Africa today.

Coherence

The coherence in the writing is evident in the strong links between the five books. Each cannot truly be understood without the others, and all point to the one and only God. It is the same God who is the Creator (Gen 1:1), the God of the patriarchs (Gen 17:1-8; 31:42), the God who liberates the Hebrew people from Egypt (Exod 2:24; 3:6, 15) and the God who sets out his law (Lev 1:1; 26:42; Num 1:1; 32:11; Deut 1:8; 4:32). The book of Genesis in particular lays a

foundation for understanding the next four books, for God's interest in Israel can only be explained in terms of his promise to Abraham.

The law itself can also be understood as deriving from the first principles laid down at creation. For example, humans were assigned the responsibility of ruling over God's creation (Gen 1:26-28). It is thus not surprising that they are prohibited from being in the ridiculous position of worshipping idols representing those things they should rule (Exod 20:4). Similarly, the long lists of rules in Leviticus cannot be understood without a grasp of the idea of sin and the seriousness of its consequences (Gen 3:1-4:15). The rules can then be seen as an object lesson or as a discipline to be observed in order to avoid sinning.

The land of Canaan, the promised land, is itself an echo of Eden. Cleared of those who have been tainted by immorality since the earliest times, it becomes a symbol of a new place of harmony between people, their Creator and creation itself (Gen 2:8; 9:24-25; 17:8; Lev 18:3; Num 33:55; Deut 6:1-3).

This thematic coherence in the Pentateuch is accompanied by a coherence in its theological content. These books are intended to be used for instruction. Like all good teachers, they employ many different literary styles to communicate their message: stories, songs, poetry, treaties and covenants, a code of law and genealogies. All communicate one and the same message about God's nature – he is sovereign, faithful and holy. The history of the Hebrew people describes their apprenticeship as they learn to live in fellowship with this sovereign and holy God, to fully profit from the blessings associated with such fellowship, and to serve as an example to other nations (Gen 18:18; Deut 7:6, 12-13).

The Sovereignty of God

The Torah lays one of the bases of monotheism by affirming the supremacy of God. This supremacy expresses itself in his very name, *Yahweh* ('I am who I am'), which expresses his eternal nature (Exod 3:14-15). Because the Jews were reluctant to pronounce the name of God, we often find it translated as 'LORD' throughout the five books in the NIV and other translations.

The One who is outside of time is also the Creator of all things and has ultimate power over his creation. This is demonstrated in the way he shows himself to be the master of Pharaoh and of the natural elements that were worshipped as gods by the Egyptians (Exod 7:14-10:29).

The Hebrew people were to experience the eternal nature of God by passing on the knowledge of God and his commands from generation to generation. Commemoration and teaching are a constant theme in the Pentateuch (Exod 13:8-9; 20:12; Lev 23; Deut 6:1-9). We should take note of this in our own society, which is still largely oral, with the result that 'the death of an old person is like the loss of a library'. We need to pass on the strengths of our cultures that are in accord with God's nature. The commentary that you are now reading is one example of how this can be done.

The Hebrew people were also to live out God's authority over his creation. Not only were they to refuse to subordinate themselves to created things, but they were also not to be subject to other people. The only one to whom these former slaves should submit was the Lord (Exod 20:3; Deut 15:12-14). This idea also applies to us today. Too often, progress on our continent is paralyzed by natural forces that are endured rather than managed and by a blind reverence for any form of human authority.

The Faithfulness of God

The second major characteristic of God presented in these books is his faithfulness, reflected in his respect for the promise made to Abraham (Gen 24:27). The accounts of the many failures of the Israelites in the desert that make up a large part of these books are all occasions for God to show his patience (Exod 32:9-14; 34:6). The Hebrew people are called to develop the same faithful attachment to the Lord that Moses had (Num 12:7; Deut 6:5; 7:7-11).

The Holiness of God

The holiness of God is shown everywhere in the Pentateuch. This term refers to the difference or the distance between God and sinful humanity (Exod 15:11; 26:34; 28:36). The Hebrew people were also called to resemble the Lord in regard to holiness (Lev 11:44-45; Deut 7:6). Their holiness would be demonstrated by good behaviour in obedience to God's laws and by their carrying out rituals symbolic of their repentance. It was holiness, rather than common land or family ties, that would make Israel distinct from other nations (Deut 26:19; 33:8-10). This invitation to faithfully unite around values that transcend family and ethnic ties is important for African Christians who seek to live in stable, peaceful communities.

While the first readers of the Pentateuch were the Jews of the ot, the message of the Pentateuch is universal. It still speaks to both Jews and Gentiles today. Christians recognize that its teaching about the enmity between the serpent and the woman (Gen 3:15), the faithfulness of the patriarchs, the gift of the firstborn (Gen 22:1-19; Exod 13:12), the offering for sin (Lev 5:14-15), and holiness all foreshadow the person of Christ, his ministry and the life offered to his faithful followers (Matt 26:28; John 1:29; Rom 15:4; 1 Cor 10:1-4; Col 1:15; Heb 11:29; 1 Pet 2:9-10). May we benefit fully from the lessons learned by the people of Israel.

Abel Ndjerareou

GENESIS

Genesis is a book about 'beginnings'. It tells of such things as the beginnings of creation, of languages and of a chosen nation. It also gives us an account of the generations before and after the flood, together with specific details about lineage (5:1-32; 10:1-32). In fact the phrase 'this is the account of', which occurs at key points in the book, could literally be translated 'these are the generations of' (2:4; 5:1; 6:9; 10:1; 11:10; 11:27; 25:12, 19; 36:1; 37:2).

Genesis can also be described as a book about relationships. It shows us relationships such as those between Adam and Eve, Cain and Abel, Seth's descendants and those of Cain, Abraham and Lot, Sarah and Hagar, Jacob and Esau, and Joseph and his brothers.

But above all, Genesis is a book about God: creating (all things), saving (Noah, his family, and certain animals and birds), destroying (with water in Noah's time, with fire at Sodom and Gomorrah), choosing (Abraham), making covenants (with Noah and with Abraham), forgiving (Jacob) and protecting (Joseph).

Genesis and the four books that follow it (Exodus, Leviticus, Numbers and Deuteronomy) are traditionally viewed as a unit known as the Pentateuch. They are all thought to have been written by Moses. Moses was probably born about 1500 BC, and lived for 120 years (Deut 34:7). For the first forty years of his life, he enjoyed the status of Pharaoh's adopted grandson (Exod 2:11; Acts 7:23). The Pentateuch was probably written during his last eighty years, forty of which were spent caring for Jethro's flock in Midian and in God's providence, familiarizing himself with that area (Acts 7:30), and forty of which were spent leading the people of Israel.

Some scholars suggest that the five books were produced by many writers over many years, with the bulk of the writing having been done between approximately 850 BC and 550 BC, and that they were not all put together until as late as the fifth century BC. However, none of the arguments for this view (for example, the use of different names of God in different sections) have been strong enough to overthrow the traditional position that Moses wrote the Pentateuch. This commentary thus assumes Moses to be the writer.

The book falls into two main sections: God's dealing with humans in general (1:1-11:26) and his dealing with those he has chosen to be his special people (11:27-50:26).

Outline of Contents

COMMENTARY

1:1-11:9 God and Humankind

1:1-31 Creation of All Things

The account of God's creation of the world establishes two key points that apply throughout this book and throughout the Bible. The first is that God was uniquely involved in the origin of the earth and the sky. They do not exist by themselves and are not the result of impersonal forces or other spiritual beings. The second is that because the world is God's creation, it reveals him and is subject to his will.

The first verse of Genesis can be read as a summary statement that God created everything – *the heavens and the earth* and everything in them (1:1). The rest of the chapter is then seen as an expansion on this summary. However, it is also possible that these words outline the first step in creation, with the words, *in the beginning* being equivalent to 'first'. The idea then would be that the first thing God did was to create the raw shell (heaven and earth), and then for six days he filled that shell with content. He did not create the whole universe as a finished product in one grand gesture, but worked to create it. This second view fits with the description of the earth as *formless and empty* and of darkness *over the surface of the deep* (1:2). The Spirit of God hovered over the waters to keep them under control until they could be assigned to their place. He was controlling the creation project, with the result that all creation takes place under God's watchful eye and results from his power.

This account of the creation in six days (whether taken literally as twenty-four hour days or figuratively as representing long periods of time) reveals a methodical God who created different things one after another with precise purpose. One by one the Lord puts in place all the elements necessary to sustain the human beings for whom he is creating this world.

As we read this account, we should note that each new stage in God's work begins with his some form of his creative words, *let there be* (1:3, 6, 9, 14, 20, 24, 26). At the end of each of his creative utterances, there is some form of the statement, *and it was so* (1:7, 9, 11, 15, 24, 30). No matter what God ordered to come into being, gather or separate, it came to be. He has the power to create and the power to order his creation. We can rely on this same power in our circumstances. The God of creation is still the God of history. If we listen to his word and submit our plans to his will, he can speak to raise Africa to great heights!

The first thing that God created out of the raw material of the universe was light (**1:3-5**). It was created before everything else because it would be essential for the survival of future plants, animals and human beings. Though the heavenly bodies were not yet created, the light permitted the Creator to give initial temporal structure to his creation: *day* and *night, evening* and *morning.*

During the second phase of his creation, covering days two to four, God provided the material framework to sustain living beings. He created the sky (**1:6-8**), followed by sea and dry land (**1:9**). The dry land would be the main arena for human life and would provide the ingredients for that life (see 2:7). It was only after he had formed the dry ground that God pronounced his creation *good* (**1:10**).

This earth was then blessed with plants that will provide food for human beings once they are created (**1:11-13; 29-30**). Finally, the stars and their movements were specially provided to help the future occupants of the earth to organize time by marking *seasons and days and years* (**1:14-19**). The way the Creator brought together all that was necessary for our survival before creating us reminds us that God was working for our good, not creating us so that we might suffer (Lam 3:33; Ezek 33:11).

The creation of living beings follows the same sequence as the material creation. On day five, God created the creatures that live in sea and sky (**1:20-23**), followed on the sixth day by animals that live on land (**1:24-25**), and finally the culmination of his creation, human beings.

The privileged position of human beings is shown by the fact that our creation required a special decision, presented as if it was made at some great gathering. The plural in *let us make man* indicates the solemnity of the decision and stresses that something new and important is about to happen (**1:26a**). The plural 'let us' also suggests the community of the Godhead, which involves three persons – the Father, Son and Holy Spirit.

Human beings, both male and female, are said to have been made in the *image* of God (**1:26b-27**). Thus humans are different from other created beings like animals, and this fact has important consequences for how we live. First of all, it means that every human being resembles his or her Creator in some way. Consequently, every human being is special and important. We should be able to recognize the Creator in the men and women we see around us. Second, it means that we should not worship any animal (Exod 20:4; Rom 1:21-22). Woe to the person who lowers himself to the level of animals by giving an animal or an image of an animal the place that belongs only to the Creator! Third, because God created both our bodies and our spirits, we must not artificially separate the two and think that we can ignore our bodies while living to God in our spirits. Scripture makes it plain that we must not mistreat our own bodies or those of others (1 Cor 6:19-20).

Both men and women were blessed by God and assigned a two-fold mission: to *increase in number* and *fill the earth* (**1:28a**) and to *rule over* creation and to *subdue* the earth (**1:26c, 28b**). This mission was not a heavy burden but a gift from God. Human beings were to occupy and enjoy, not fear, creation. This mission indicates that the first way in which all of us can glorify and serve God is by caring for his creation.

It is important to note that men and women were permitted to rule only over other living creatures, not over other human beings. Nor were men given authority to dominate women (or vice versa). Our fellow human beings bear the image of the Creator and thus are not to be dominated but to be served (John 13:13-14; Gal 5:13; Eph 5:21). For food God supplied *every seed-bearing plant on the face of the whole earth and every tree that has fruit with seed in it* (**1:29-30**). It thus appears that humans and animals were originally vegetarian. It is only in 9:3 that we are permitted to eat other creatures for food.

The chapter ends with another summary of all God's acts of creation: *God saw all that he had made, and it was very good* (**1:31**; see 1:4, 10, 18, 21, 25). Nothing comes from the hand of God that is not intrinsically good. He is the good God who does all things for good (Mark 10:18; Rom 8:28).

God may have viewed his creation as good because it breathed order. Each element was created at the appropriate time and occupied the place which allowed for the harmony of the whole. It was also filled with rich diversity. God created different species within each vegetable and animal family, each *according to their kinds* (1:11, 12, 21, 24). Each kind was told to multiply (1:11, 20, 22, 28). Finally, his creation was

NEW FAMILY RELATIONSHIPS

Becoming a Christian involves a profound transformation, as was evident in the life of the Apostle Paul. He expressed the difference using the expression 'once ... now': 'You were once darkness, but now you are light in the Lord'. Consequently we are now to 'live as children of light' (Eph 5:8).

The transformation of our lives by Christ affects every aspect of our existence, including our family relationships. Where once we accepted traditional African relationships in the family, now we are to seek for God's style of family relationships. These two styles of relationship are not necessarily contradictory, for, like Africans, God places a high value on a spirit of community. However, some changes may be called for if we are to follow Christ, and there may be areas of conflict. One such area may come with accepting Jesus' insistence that obedience to God comes before blood ties (Matt 12:46-50).

At the core of all family relationships is the union between a man and his wife. The foundational text for the entire Christian philosophy of marriage and the family is Genesis 2:24: 'For this reason a man will leave his father and mother and be united to his wife, and they will become one flesh'. This verse makes it clear that marriage requires leaving one's parents in order to create a new family. It is fine for a man to live with his parents as long as he is single. But when the time comes, he must separate from them and enter into a new relationship with his wife. Doing this requires autonomy, working at a relationship, full responsibility and maturity.

The new husband and wife must then become one flesh. They are no longer two individuals, existing side by side, but must become one entity, sharing each other's lives. This new type of union is very different and very much stronger than that of parents and children. It requires the work of God himself, so that in speaking of this text in Genesis, Jesus says, 'Therefore what God has joined together, let man not separate' (Matt 19:6).

The Apostle Paul's words on the interaction between husbands and wives (Eph 5:22-32) must be interpreted from the perspective of forming a single entity. So must the relationship between parents and children. As the fruit of this new union, the children belong as much to the woman as to the man. Both parents share equal responsibility for training them (Prov 6:20). Given that God is at the core of their union, the parents must train their children in how to live on earth, and also show them the way to heaven (Deut 6:6-7).

Traditional African ideas do not always agree with this biblical concept of the relationship between a man, his wife and their children. At times, in fact, they make a true union almost impossible. For example, in many African cultures, the man does not leave his father and mother. He does not leave them spiritually and, sometimes, not even physically. The husband and his wife are perceived as members of two distinct families, with each family retaining all its rights on their own child. The parents of the woman can reclaim her at any time if they think that their son-in-law has behaved badly. In such a situation, the woman feels obliged to listen to her parents rather than to stay with her husband.

In such a culture, there can be no spiritual unity either, for whenever sacrifices are made to ask protection for the family, the married woman will have to sacrifice to the spirits considered part of her family of origin, and her husband will sacrifice to his family's spirits. In relation to the spirit world, each one is always a member of his or her family. This way of thinking means that the wife is forever a stranger in her husband's home. Among the Senoufo of Cote d'Ivoire, for example, the wife is called 'the foreigner' by her husband's parents and must avoid speaking his name out of respect and shame. When the wife dies in a location distant from her place of origin, no matter how far away that may be, her remains will be transported back to her village, to her own people.

Understandably, such attitudes can lead to conflict within the family. The wife often feels like a foreigner and finds it difficult to integrate, knowing that she is not in her home but in her husband's home. Any visiting relative of the husband's is more at home than the wife. Thus the husband's brother will not hesitate to remind the woman of her foreign origin if her behaviour does not please him. And if the visitor is the husband's mother, the situation becomes still worse, for the mother will believe herself to have full control of her son's home and may attempt to run it. Obviously, such attitudes to marriage can cause problems in the home.

This traditional view of marriage can also have consequences with regard to the status and training of the children. Some traditions regard the children as the offspring of the father and not the mother. She is simply the woman who has borne the children for him. In matriarchal traditions, the children are recognized as belonging solely to the mother. Neither system regards the children as belonging equally to both parents. Either the man or the woman can feel wronged or slighted in the training of the children.

A final consequence of these traditions follows from the fact that a man's inheritance belongs solely to the members of his family. Since the wife is not regarded as a member of her husband's family, she does not inherit anything, and when her husband dies, she may be left destitute. There is no concept of joint property owned by both the man and his wife. Modern legislation may have given women inheritance rights, but conflicts still arise because of the way the relationship is perceived.

One positive aspect of the traditional African concept of marriage is the strength it gives the extended family and the sense of community it encourages. A nuclear family on its own is weak. But the Bible makes it clear that the nuclear family should have a core strength that the traditional concept tends to deny. As Christians, we need to work towards enriching our African culture by integrating into it the new concepts set out in God's ideal for Christian marriage.

Soro Soungalo

full of meaning, for it served the purpose of bringing pleasure to God and to those beings he had created in his image.

We who are in the image of God should imitate his creation in what we create. Thus, for example, we should build a church in Africa that is a place of order, of diversity, of sharing, of meaning rediscovered and of celebration (Matt 28:19; 1 Cor 12:4-27).

2:1-3 God's Rest

On the seventh day, with everything created and in its place, God rested after all *the work of creating that he had done* on the previous six days (**2:1-3**). He was not resting because he was tired, but because the job was done, and done well. God's rest is thus very different from the rest of a lazy man or woman who has produced nothing for the past six days. Unfortunately, the lazy rest is too common in Africa. This must change if Africa is to make progress economically. We need to have a work ethic that is like that of God – working to get our tasks accomplished well so that we can rest with a clear conscience, with nothing left undone.

Moreover, when God rested, it was simply his work of creation that ceased, not all his work. His work of providence never ceases, as he continues to care for his creation. We should be like him in this too. While we may rest from projects that have been completed, we can continue to work in other ways – such as dreaming about our next project or setting goals for the future. Such active rest means that we will not regard 'resting' as involving heavy drinking that makes us incapable of further thought or action. With God's kind of rest, we rest from one activity while we continue in another. We need to start to think about rest in these terms if we are to see personal, institutional and national change across Africa.

2:4-25 Creation of the Human Community

After having told how the heavens and the earth were created, the biblical writer now retells the story, this time concentrating on the creation of human beings and the start of human history. He also establishes the second vital element in human identity: not only are we made in the image of God, but we are also made to live in community. It is in community that we manifest the image of God. That is why God created the first human relationship, establishing a community as an example for us to follow.

The earth in its earliest stages was not suitable for human habitation, for there were no shrubs or plants (**2:4-5**). After God made it habitable by providing streams that watered *the whole surface of the ground* (**2:6**), he proceeded to create human beings. At this stage we are given more details of the creation of men and women, which was touched on briefly in 1:27.

First, God created *Adam,* a Hebrew word that means 'man', and that will later be used as a name (**2:7a**, 20;

3:21). It is clear from 1:27 that the Creator fully intended to create a couple, but he did not create the woman immediately. His purpose may have been to allow the man to realize his need for companionship (see comments on 2:20-23). If God had simply created two individuals without any bond between them, they might have found it difficult to establish a relationship and life would have been painful.

The man was like the rest of creation in being formed of the *dust of the ground,* but what made him different from the rest of creation was *the breath of life* from God that entered the formed dust. This breath transformed the dust into a human being created in the image of God (**2:7b**). The word 'breath' can also be translated as 'spirit'. It is the spirit of God that places human beings in a living relationship with the Creator and makes all the difference between them and other creatures. That is why the Spirit is given anew to those who turn to Christ and receive forgiveness for their sins (Acts 2:38).

God did more than just make the earth habitable for human beings. He also planted a garden in which *he put the man he had formed* (**2:8**). This gift of a garden is a sign of God's love, for it provided a framework in which God could train human beings and give them the reference points they would need to face the vast new universe that lay around them. The garden was not a place of ignorance intended to keep human beings away from science and learning. Rather, it was a place of initiation into life. Human beings would need a model to understand what it meant to subdue the earth (1:28). The garden contained all that they needed to learn at first.

This garden was *in the east, in Eden,* and there God made to grow *all kinds of trees – trees that were pleasing to the eye and good for food.* Special attention is drawn to two trees (**2:9**). The first is *the tree of life,* which was a concrete indication of God's presence and thus was placed *in the middle of the garden.* The relationship with the Creator must be central to human existence. The second is *the tree of the knowledge of good and evil,* which was a sign of the existence of evil and the presence of the evil one before the creation of man (see comment on 3:1, 13). This evil one was certainly the first to disobey the Creator and the presence of this tree warned human beings not to follow his example. It is notable that after this evil one is bound and thrown into the lake of fire at the end of time, there is no further mention of this tree. Only the tree of life grows in the new Jerusalem (Rev 22:2).

God not only made the earth habitable for the man and planted a garden for him, but also took the trouble to water it for him. What a privileged state! The river watering the garden flowed *from Eden* and *separated into four headwaters* (**2:10**). We are told the names of these rivers, *the Pishon, Gihon, Tigris and Euphrates* (**2:11-14**). These names suggest that Eden lay somewhere in the vicinity of modern Iraq.

God placed the man he had made in this well-watered garden of Eden *to work it* and *take care of it* (**2:15**). Work did not come with the fall but was part of God's original plan for humankind. God provides, but he holds us responsible for maintaining what he has provided. This principle applies to us today as it applied to Adam. It is not enough to have been blessed with land. We must maintain that land and control all that could destroy it. Thus we need to stop destructive processes like soil erosion and deforestation and must not use chemicals that are harmful to the soil.

Thus Adam was *free to eat from any tree in the garden* (**2:16**). However, there was one restriction: *you must not eat from the tree of the knowledge of good and evil* and there was a penalty if this command was not obeyed: *when you eat of it you will surely die* (**2:17**; see also comment on 5:1-32). God's approach to teaching is a model for us. He started by showing the man the positive things, the vast number of things offered to him, including what he could eat (2:16). It was only after presenting the positives that God brought up the one restriction. That restriction was justified because its aim was to preserve life.

The forbidden fruit should not be thought of as symbolizing a sexual relationship consummated without divine permission, for the tree of the knowledge of good and evil was already in the garden and the restriction was already given to Adam before the woman was ever created. Moreover the ban was permanent, not temporary, and transgression would prove fatal. Finally, it cannot symbolize a sexual relationship because the man and the woman were invited to enjoy such a relationship before the fall (1:27-28; 2:22-25). Sexuality is not intended as a trap for men and women but as a gift (1 Cor 7:4-5). God is love and does not tempt anyone (Jas 1:13; 1 John 4:8).

Adam had all he needed in terms of food to eat and work to do. Yet one thing was still lacking – companionship (**2:18a**). He was alone. God wanted something better for him. Yes, God was a good friend of Adam, but he was God, Adam's Creator. There were *also all the beasts of the field and all the birds of the air* which the Lord allowed Adam to name, but none of them was a *suitable helper* for Adam (**2:19-20**). The word 'helper' does not mean that the woman was to be the man's servant, parent or keeper. Rather, she was to complement him, working alongside him.

So God did as he had planned (**2:18b**) and made a suitable companion for Adam and *brought her to the man* in what appears to be a wedding ceremony. The process included putting Adam into *a deep sleep* and using one of his ribs to make a woman (**2:21-22**). Note that the woman was not born of the man. She was not the man's child, which would have given him moral authority over her. Rather, God formed her from the man's rib, close to his heart, to establish the intimate link between them in their very creation. The woman will consider the man as part of her very being,

and the man will see the woman as the help he needs, without whom he is incomplete. In this way, the man will help his wife to live up to her potential, with thankfulness for God's gift of companionship. Because of the unity that God had ordained, he did not repeat to the woman the command he had already given to the man. The man was responsible for communicating it to her.

This ideal union ordained by the Creator cannot exist in a polygamous relationship between a man and several women (polygyny) or between a woman and several men (polyandry). Nor can there be perfect complementarity in a homosexual relationship between two men or between two women. God condemns all sexual relationships that involve anything other than one man and one woman (Rom 1:27; 1 Tim 1:8-10).

Amazed at God's act, all Adam could do was exclaim, *This is now bone of my bones and flesh of my flesh* (**2:23a**). He recognized the intimate relationship between himself and the woman. But he did not see her as simply another being exactly like himself, but as someone distinct. Thus he said, *she shall be called 'woman'.* As someone *taken out of man* she is an extension of man, but has a different role (**2:23b**).

On the basis of what the man says here, the writer of Genesis comments: *For this reason a man will leave his father and mother and be united to his wife* (**2:24**). The type of intimacy that God has set up here is so close that it cannot be in competition with the second closest human relationship, that between parent and child. A marriage thus involves leaving one's parents to be united with one's spouse.

Marriage involves more than just the recognition that one's partner is a human being like oneself. It also involves a return to the couple's original unity, captured in the statement *they will become one flesh.* There will be complete sharing, with no boundaries between them. As one flesh, they will constitute a new being that will endure as long as they live, as Jesus confirmed in Matthew 19:6).

When a marriage is in danger of failing because a couple have failed to achieve this unity, they need to look closely to see whether they are failing to recognize what they have in common and that they are partners, not competitors. They also need to consider whether they have truly left all others, which is a prerequisite for being united with one other in marriage.

Complete openness to the other is also one of the secrets of a successful marriage. It was for this reason that the Creator left the first couple naked in the beginning (**2:25**). He did not necessarily intend them to remain that way all their life.

The stress on the marriage of two people and on leaving one's parents does not mean that God does not have a place for the extended family. This is clear from his condemnation of rejection or neglect of parents (Exod 20:12; Lev 19:3; Deut 27:16; 1 Tim 5:4). Obviously the married couple will also be closely connected to the offspring that God encourages them to produce (1:28). But the marriage relationship provides the stable basis from which all other human relationships will develop.

3:1-24 Disobedience of the First Couple

3:1-6 A flaw in the community

At this stage, a fourth character, the serpent, is introduced. He is said to be *more crafty than any of the wild animals the Lord God had made* (**3:1a**), but ends up being cursed 'above all the livestock and all the wild animals' (3:14a). It is not one's intelligence and charm that are important, but what one does with them. The serpent used his abilities to turn the woman, and through her the man, away from God. This pattern has continued down the centuries, as we see the wicked use all sorts of tricks to mislead the unsuspecting. Evil men trick innocent young girls into immoral acts, and unscrupulous people buy valuable items from needy or ignorant people for a fraction of their value.

The fact that the devil took the form of a snake should not be interpreted as meaning that all snakes are evil. It was simply that the devil, who seems to have a spiritual nature (Mark 1:23; Luke 7:21), needed to take on the shape of something familiar to his prey in order to achieve his goal. He chose to take on the form of one of the creatures in the garden, and the one he chose has led to his being referred to in the Bible as the 'ancient serpent' (Rev 12:9; 20:2). But he is also referred to as a roaring lion in 1 Peter 5:8. We would do well to remember that Satan always first approaches us in disguise (2 Cor 11:14). Not trusting appearances is a biblical virtue (1 Sam 16:7).

Satan's first step was to interfere in the communion between the man and the woman. He chose not to speak to both of them, but to only one of them, and encouraged that one to act independently of the other. We do not know why he chose the woman as the one to attack, but the reason may have been that he could take advantage of her having greater sensitivity and openness than the man. These qualities were good, but they could also be exploited for evil.

The serpent's question was a simple and tactful one, apparently asked in respectful tones, *Did God really say, 'You must not eat from any tree in the garden'?* (**3:1b**). But the underlying purpose was to make the woman doubt God's goodness. He was suggesting the possibility that God was not fair to impose this restriction. Satan frequently uses this tactic to stifle spiritual growth. When God does not answer our prayers the way we want or when something unpleasant happens to us, Satan uses the situation to put doubts in our minds about whether the God we serve is really good. He thus prompts us to question the word of the Lord.

The woman corrected the serpent on the issue of 'any tree' as she replied, *we may eat fruit from the trees in the garden* (**3:2**). But then she fell into his trap by adding the words *must not touch it* to what God had told them about the tree in the centre of the garden (**3:3**; 2:17). We must not put words into God's mouth, for that amounts to trying to be wiser than God. Instead we must accurately report what God has in fact said.

Once the woman had shown that she was prepared to add to what God had said, the devil sensed that she might also be prepared to accept that God might tell a lie. So he pushed harder and contradicted God, saying, *You will not surely die* (**3:4**). He then maliciously suggested that God's motive for the prohibition was that he *knows that when you eat of it your eyes will be opened, and you will be like God, knowing good and evil* (**3:5**). Satan was sketching an idyllic vision and suggesting that God was depriving the woman and her husband of some greater blessing than those they were already enjoying. Such an approach is characteristic of false teachers in the church (2 Pet 2:18-19).

The serpent's attack was successful, and in **3:6a** the women gave in to what 1 John 2:16 (NASB) describes as 'the lust of the flesh' (hungering for what seemed *good for food*), 'the lust of the eyes' (the fruit was certainly *pleasing to the eye*) 'and the boastful pride of life' (the desire to gain *wisdom* and be 'like God'). In accepting Satan's suggestion, she acted contrary to the word of her Creator without seeking help or advice from her spouse. Making a major decision alone led her to enter into a relationship with the evil one (a new community), thus abandoning her relationship with God (the primary community) and distancing herself from her relationship with her husband (the secondary community). She was no longer acting in the unity that was supposed to characterize their relationship. Her individualistic outlook led her to abuse her freedom and resulted in sin. It was only after she had eaten the fruit and the situation was irreversible that she turned to her husband and invited him to join her.

But Adam's behaviour was little better. He *was with her* (**3:6b**), but remained silent and passive throughout this entire exchange, prepared to be simply a follower. He did not make any attempt to stop his wife, but simply listened to her and joined her in sinning. He placed a higher value on his relationship with his wife than on his relationship with God. The first couple were thus united in their sin and created a sinful community apart from God.

3:7-19 A new reality

Both the man and the woman had now fallen into the serpent's trap and neither of them could help the other. They were both helpless, as their eyes *were opened* (**3:7a**). God had given human beings the ability to acquire knowledge so that they could gain wisdom. He intended that important experiences would open their eyes and allow them to learn more about how to maintain and cultivate the earth.

Unfortunately their experience of disobedience simply opened their eyes to the possibility of evil.

When the couple *realized that they were naked,* the best they could do was to sew *fig leaves together* and make coverings for themselves (**3:7b**). When we try to be wiser than God by doing what we know is contrary to his will, we end up being very foolish and helpless. Their attempts at covering themselves also indicate the dawning of shame, leading to embarrassment at the very bodies that God had created for them. In their relationship with each other, openness had been replaced by shame, mistrust, instability and superficiality.

God, who is good and full of grace, did not abandon them in their helplessness – even though he was the one whom they had disobeyed. But when he came *walking in the garden in the cool of the day,* the man and his wife no longer welcomed his companionship but *hid from the Lord God among the trees of the garden* (**3:8**). The one who had initiated peace and harmony in their lives had become someone from whom to flee.

God took the first step towards saving sinners, seeking the person confused by shame and calling out, *Where are you?* (**3:9**). The question does not mean that Adam and Eve had managed to hide themselves in a place where God could not see them. Rather, it indicates that he wanted them to bring themselves out. This is what God does with us all the time. He does not enjoy embarrassing us by exposing us, but gives us an opportunity to come to him ourselves and seek his mercy.

Adam admitted that he was hiding and gave the reason for it: *I heard you in the garden, and I was afraid because I was naked* (**3:10**). Until they disobeyed God, Adam and Eve had been covered by the righteousness of God. But now that righteousness was gone – leaving them too exposed to face God's holiness.

God's second question provided another opportunity for Adam and Eve to reflect on what they had done: *Who told you that you were naked? Have you eaten from the tree from which I commanded you not to eat?* (**3:11**). The question was meant to help them recognize their sin.

God did not brutally punish them immediately they admitted their disobedience. He was a model of fairness and questioned the man and the woman individually to determine their responsibility and to allow each of them a chance to repent (Ezek 18:23, 25-30). He did not bother to question the serpent, for it seems that God expected nothing different from him. His disobedience had existed since before creation.

But God's questions only revealed that neither party was willing to accept that they had failed. Each sought to shift the blame onto someone else. Adam no longer spoke of his wife as 'flesh of my flesh' (2:23), but instead blamed her presence on God. She was *the woman you put here with me* (**3:12**). The woman in turn blamed the serpent (**3:13**). While what each said was true (Eve did give the fruit to Adam and the serpent had deceived Eve), they were not facing the situation squarely. This is what we, too, do when we seek to find others to blame for our failures. Thus young people blame their parents for not having created a better home environment for them to grow up in, and their parents blame society in general for a decline in values, and on and on. But each of us must admit the point at which we ourselves have failed before there can be effective change.

God, who holds each individual responsible for their own failure, passed judgment on each of them. His purpose in doing this was to help them understand the gravity of sin and to teach them to flee from it in order to draw near to the Creator and do what was good. But the punishment also included mercy, for God hinted at the coming solution to the curse brought by sin.

The punishment for each of the participants in the sin is given in the same sequence as the temptation had come.

- **The serpent** was given the greatest curse: *cursed are you above all the livestock and all the wild animals* (**3:14a**). This curse is directed in part at the helper the devil had used, as is shown by the statement that the snake will *crawl on* its *belly* and *eat dust* (**3:14b**). We cannot allow Satan to use us and get away with it. If we listen to him, we will share in the punishment reserved for him (2 Cor 11:14-15; Rev 12:7-9). The promise of *enmity between* the snake *and the woman* and her *offspring* applies in part to literal snakes, for they are almost universally feared and hated (**3:15**). However, the statement that the woman's offspring will *crush* the serpent's *head* while the serpent will only *strike* his *heel* applies at a far higher level to the defeat of Satan. He will be crushed by Jesus Christ, the Saviour of humanity and a descendant of this woman (see also Luke 10:19; Rom 16:20; Rev 12). In uttering this promise, God is already hinting at the coming of his new community and the deliverance of human beings and the world from the power of Satan.

- **The woman** was punished with more pain in childbearing and with subjection to her husband (**3:16**). It is important to distinguish between 'subjection' and 'submission'. The former involves being forced to submit to the leadership of another and is a consequence of the fall, and thus not part of God's original plan. By contrast, submission involves willingly allowing oneself to be led by another. A wife's submission to her husband may have a basis in creation (for the man was created first – 1 Tim 2:13), but Christ has done away with the forcible subjection of wives, and Christians should not be guilty of it.

- **The man** was punished with more pain in his work. Unwelcome plants will sprout in his fields, and he will have to work very hard all his life long to obtain the food he needs. All his labours will only end with death, when his body will return to the dust from which it was originally made (**3:17-19**).

3:20-24 Immediate consequences of the fall

In the description of the fall, we saw the perfect unity of the man and the woman start to crumble as they acted independently of each other, ceased to be open with each other, and blamed each other. Now, immediately after God had finished his sentencing, we see Adam asserting his leadership over his wife. In stating Adam's fault, God had said to Adam, 'you listened to your wife and ate' (3:17). Here the word translated 'listened' basically means 'obeyed'. Now Adam asserted his authority over his wife, just as the Lord said he would do (3:16). He took it upon himself to name his wife, an act that is generally done by the senior to the junior (**3:20a**).

The name he gave her was *Eve, because she would become the mother of all the living* (**3:20b**). This name may suggest that from then on he saw his wife more as the mother of his children than as his partner in a conjugal relationship. The unity of the couple suffered yet another blow, one that would scar all the cultures of the world as women came to be valued more as mothers than as wives.

However, the stress on Eve's role as a mother was not solely negative. It was also a sign of hope. Her offspring would bring victory over the evil one who was the source of all their troubles. Moreover, her name was also one of dignity. It is a privilege to be anyone's mother, let alone the mother of 'all the living'. We would do well to take note of the fact that Adam does address her with respect. The principle that wives should submit (Eph 5:22; Col 3:18; 1 Pet 3:1) goes hand-in-hand with the assertion of their dignity. The NT makes this clear when it orders husbands to love their wives and to be considerate towards them (Eph 5:25; Col 3:19; 1 Pet 3:7). In other words, wives should be treated in the same way that their husbands would want to be treated. This is a crucial lesson for many African men even in the twenty-first century. We cannot stop proclaiming it to them until all women are treated with the dignity they deserve as the mothers of all.

The next consequence of the fall was that God acknowledged the shame that Adam and Eve felt at their nakedness and provided them with *garments of skin* (**3:21**). His action shows that God's punishment does not exclude mercy, and that his mercy does not exclude judgment. It is significant that this covering would have required the shedding of blood. This foreshadows God's way of removing sin, which would reach its final fulfilment in the shed blood of Christ.

Finally, God banished Adam and Eve from the Garden of Eden. The Creator God is not only a loving God of grace, but also a holy God of justice. They had committed a serious wrong, and until it was dealt with by way of the internal change brought about by the renewing of the Holy Spirit,

they would only continue to get into bigger trouble by persisting in disobeying God.

Just as creation of human beings involved consultation in the Godhead ('let us make man' – 1:26), so did their banishment, as *the Lord God said, 'The man has now become like one of us, knowing good and evil. He must not be allowed to reach out his hand and take also from the tree of life and eat, and live forever'* (**3:22**). God had created everything very good, and given each thing its place in his created order. Animals had their place, so did humanity, and God himself was the Creator over all. Human beings had tried to break out of their place, and had succeeded only in embarking on a path of destruction.

The seriousness of the expulsion from the garden is evident from God's actions after he drove the couple out. *He placed on the east side of the Garden of Eden cherubim and a flaming sword flashing back and forth to guard the way to the tree of life* (**3:24**). The couple were now kept far from the tree of life. They also lost their access to the model that should have helped them to manage the earth. They left the garden prematurely without having fully benefited from the training that would have prepared them for life in the universe (3:22).

4:1-16 Evil Between Brothers: Cain and Abel

Adam and Eve now began to obey God's command to 'be fruitful and increase in number; fill the earth and subdue it' (1:28). Eve became pregnant and gave birth first to Cain and then to Abel (**4:1-2a**). Each of these two boys had his own interests, and so Abel *kept flocks* while Cain *worked the soil* (**4:2b**). Their interests are reflected in the offerings they bring to the Lord. Cain *brought some of the fruits of the soil* (**4:3**) while Abel brought *fat portions from some of the firstborn of his flock* (**4:4a**). At this juncture, we are told one of the most crucial details in human history: *The Lord looked with favour on Abel and his offering but on Cain and his offering he did not look with favour* (**4:4b-5a**).

We are not told why Cain's offering was not accepted, but it seems likely that God had told them, either directly or through their father Adam, what kind of offering he desired. Abel's offering is close enough to what is prescribed in places like Leviticus 3:16 to suggest that it was not based on a mere guess about what would be acceptable to God. God required that sacrifice involve one life in exchange for another because that would be the only way in which he could ultimately forgive sin (see John 10:11; Rom 5:8; Eph 5:2). It seems that Cain deliberately chose to bring what pleased him, not what pleased God. His parents had been banished from the garden of Eden for disobeying God's explicit command, and it is safe to assume that Cain was doing the same thing. God is not another person with whom we can negotiate what we offer. He is the Creator who owns and gives all things, and his word about offerings is final.

It is terrible not to be accepted by people, let alone not to find favour with God. It must have been a terrible feeling for Cain. When such feelings come, we can respond in one of two ways: we can go back to the drawing board and ask why we did not find favour and then correct the situation, or we can become angry at God and allow envy to make us hate those whom God favours. Cain took the latter route. He *was very angry, and his face was downcast* (**4:5b**).

God does not abandon human beings because they have sinned. It seems that even after having chased Adam from the garden, God continued to talk with him and to show him grace. In the same way as he had sought out Adam and Eve and questioned them in 3:9-13, he sought out Cain, asking, *Why are you angry? Why is your face downcast?* (**4:6**). God knew the answer to his questions, but he wanted to give Cain an opportunity to reflect on his action. The third question was: *If you do what is right, will you not be accepted?* (**4:7a**). If Cain had dealt with the reason why his offering was not accepted and had confessed it, he would have enjoyed the inner peace of forgiveness.

But Cain was not prepared to confess. Nor would he heed God's warning that an unconfessed deliberate sin leads to greater sin: *if you do not do what is right, sin is crouching at your door; it desires to have you* (**4:7b**). He was not interested in God's closing exhortation: *you must master it* (**4:7c**).

Sin now had easy access to human beings, for their hearts were now sinful. Thus the tempter no longer needed to engage in complicated discussions of the type he had conducted with Eve. He had persuaded Cain to prefer his own way to God's way, and now the tempter could exploit the evil tendencies in Cain and lead him into the sin of hate. Cain's anger at God produced envy of his brother, which rapidly turned to hatred, and led him to plot his brother's murder. Sin had damaged the relationship between the man and his wife, and now it entered into the relationship between brothers and affected the family community.

Cain's sin is not unique. When we see the Lord blessing someone else, we tend to become envious rather than asking ourselves whether there is any reason why we have not been blessed. An honest answer to this question would bring us humbly before the Lord to correct all that stands between us and his blessings for us. But when we add one sin to another, the path leads to more murders. What are all the civil wars that Africa has known but Africans murdering their fellow Africans!

Envy, when not dealt with, leads to hatred and where hatred is nurtured, it leads to harming the object of hatred. When the harm purposed is murder, there is always plotting that goes with it. Cain pretended to want his brother's company in the field, and then, *while they were in the field, Cain attacked his brother Abel and killed him* (**4:8**). Cain's evil is as alive among us as it was then. In our cities and towns in Africa, many con men and women lay traps by pretending to be helpful and then robbing the unsuspecting newcomer of all he or she has. Others are invited to join a group that is going somewhere seemingly safe – only to find that they have walked into a death trap. Those who take part in such schemes should expect only the reward of Cain.

Once again, God reached out to Cain, giving him an opportunity to confess. He asked, *Where is your brother Abel?* But Cain's only response was to lie, *I don't know,* and resort to rudeness, *Am I my brother's keeper?* (**4:9**). In his bitterness, he was rejecting the brotherly relationship that is a special gift from God and favouring individualism, just as Eve had done. But God has made us responsible for caring for one another (1 Thess 5:11; Heb 3:13; 10:24-25).

Faced with this denial, the Lord revealed that that he knew exactly what had happened: *Listen! Your brother's blood cries out to me from the ground* (**4:10**). Justice must be done after such a heinous crime against a fellow human being, and so the Lord punished Cain with an even more severe version of the earlier curse in 3:17-24. Cain 'worked the soil' (4:2), but from now on all his work would be unproductive (**4:11-12a**). The Lord who created the soil is able to order it to produce or not to produce. We Africans well know the frustration of tilling the soil year after year yet never getting a good harvest. Cain experienced this because of God's curse. Does any similar reason lie behind the failure of the rains in Africa?

When the questions is asked, 'Is Africa cursed?' some have been quick to deny this and to prophesy that Africa will one day be a shining star. But we must not simply embrace this hopeful vision, for which we all long, but must reflect on the issue carefully. Africa is awash in the blood of civil and tribal conflicts and crime. We need to deal with these problems, which bring elements of a curse on Africa today.

Cain's parents had been driven from Eden, but Cain was now sentenced to a lifetime of restless wandering (**4:12b**). Cain would have nothing of his own on a permanent basis. He would be unhappy about it, but would not know how to correct it. That is the way a curse works. It cannot be removed by mastering situations (that is, by planning how to prevent something or how to improve something else). The only way to deal with a curse is to deal with the situation that led to the curse. When this is done, there will be inner peace and other blessings. Only the ignorant mock the effects a curse can have on individuals, families, clans, tribes and nations.

After hearing the Lord's punishment, the unrepentant Cain asked for mercy: *My punishment is more than I can bear* (**4:13**). He repeated the terms of his punishment accurately, but added one clause: *whoever finds me will kill me* (**4:14**). The Lord promised that this would not happen and pronounced a punishment on anyone who killed him: *if anyone kills Cain, he will suffer vengeance seven times over. The Lord* also *put a protective mark on Cain so that no one who found him would kill him* (**4:15**). There are various views about what this mark was. It may have been a physical mark for others to see or it may have been some sign that Cain could see to give him assurance of God's protection. But the message of the sign was not really a comforting one, for what it meant was 'This is my man to punish, leave him to me!' No wonder Paul warned: 'Do not be deceived; God cannot be mocked. A man reaps what he sows' (Gal 6:7). Let us make sure that what we sow pleases God, for it is a terrible thing to be on the opposite side to God in a battle!

With his mark in place, *Cain went out from the Lord's presence and lived in the land of Nod, east of Eden.* He had lost the most important thing in life: *the Lord's presence* (**4:16**).

4:17-5:32 The First Genealogies

4:17-24 The line of Cain: Multiplication of evil

In the land of Nod, away from the Lord's presence, Cain raised a family. The reader cannot but wonder where Cain found *his wife* (**4:17a**). The only clue we have is in 5:4, where we read that after the birth of Seth, Adam had 'other sons and daughters'. The logical conclusion is that Cain married one of his sisters. Such marriages were not prohibited during these early days because God accepted that they would be necessary for a period of time, even though he later condemned the marriage of brothers and sisters (Lev 18:6-18).

We are also told that Cain built a city and *named it after his son Enoch.* Six generations of Cain's family are given in **4:17b-18**: *Cain, Enoch, Irad, Mehujael, Methushael* and *Lamech.* They are mentioned first not because Cain was special in a positive way but in order to deal with his descendants and get them out of the way at this stage. When it comes to the larger family tree in chapter 5, it is Seth's line that is followed and not Cain's. Sin harms individuals and families by putting them in a place they would not have been in if they had followed the way of righteousness (Ps 1:1-4). Heads of families need to keep this warning in mind. Our actions will affect our children and their children. Nevertheless, we do not need to suppose that all of Cain's descendants lived outside of the Lord's will, for the grace of God supersedes human evil.

It is significant that it is in the line of Cain that God's ideal for marriage takes another blow as polygamy is mentioned for the first time. *Lamech married two women, Adah and Zillah* (**4:19**). God had made Adam only one helper, although he could have made more as Adam still had more ribs. Lamech is acting in defiance of God's plan. His wife Adah gave birth to *Jabal* and *Jubal.* Jabal's descendants were *those who live in tents and raise livestock* (**4:20**) while Jubal was *father of all those who play the harp and flute* (**4:21**). The basic idea is that these men were the first ones to learn these skills. Lamech's other wife, Zillah, had a son and daughter. The son was *Tubal-Cain* and the daughter *Naamah.* Tubal-Cain *forged all kinds of tools out of bronze and iron* (**4:22**).

Lamech seems to have taken pride in following the bad example of his ancestor Cain, for he took pride in his evil accomplishments. He proudly boasted of his violence in response to minor injuries (**4:23**) and claimed that he could do a better job of avenging than God could: *If Cain is avenged seven times, then Lamech seventy-seven times* (**4:24**; see 4:15). With this statement, he was also claiming the protection promised to his ancestor, but was regarding it as an excuse to sin with impunity. His behaviour demonstrates that when sin is not clearly confessed and abandoned, it becomes a trap and poisons an entire community, especially the children for generations to come (Ps 32:3, 6; Prov 28:13; Acts 19:18; Jas 5:16).

4:25-26 The line of Seth: Abel's replacement

The picture we have of Adam's first two sons shows that Abel feared God but Cain did not. Cain killed Abel so that he could be the only one left – with no competitor. But God's power is not limited and his plans are not frustrated by circumstances. When Seth was born, Eve said, *God has granted me another child in place of Abel* (**4:25**). Right after this, we are told that *Seth also had a son, and he named him Enosh* (**4:26a**). The writer is making the point that Seth had a family through which the line continued.

We are also told that *at that time men began to call on the name of the Lord* (**4:26b**). This statement contrasts the attitudes that Seth and Cain passed on to their descendants. Seth and his line feared God and called on his name. Lamech, Cain's descendant, called only on his wives to hear his boasting (4:23). The attitude of Seth and his descendants strikes the first positive note since the tragic events in the garden of Eden. The attitude shown in Abel's sacrifice is starting to take root in his brother's line.

5:1-32 Family tree from Adam to Noah

Chapter 5 is introduced with the words: *This is the written account of Adam's line* (**5:1a**). It presents Adam's line, which strikingly begins with a reference to God as the original father of the entire line (**5:1b-2**; see also Luke 3:37). The genealogist stresses that God created both men and women in his own likeness and blessed them.

The rest of the genealogy is presented following a strict pattern. The name of the man representing each generation is given, followed by his age at the time his heir was born. Then we are told how long the father lived after this first son's birth, that he had *other sons and daughters,* and then his age at his death. The recurrent phrase *and then he died* drives home the point that the death which God had warned Adam about in 2:17 has become the experience of all.

Of course, 'death' in 2:17 meant not only physical death, but also spiritual death, that is, a lack of fellowship with God. The good news is that we can be revived from our spiritual death if we accept God's condition for restoring fellowship with him. That condition is faith in the God of Abraham, Isaac and Jacob and in Jesus Christ. Although we still die physically, we know that we can also anticipate physical resurrection, following Christ who was the first-born from the dead (Rom 8:29; Col 1:15; Heb 1:6; Rev 1:5).

Adam bore Seth at the age of 130, and lived to the age of 930. The relation between Adam and Seth is described in words that recall the relation between Adam and God. Seth is a son in Adam's *own likeness, in his own image* (**5:3**). This description of Seth contrasts him with Cain, who even after he had sinned put on a brave face before God (4:9) and showed no evidence of a desire to set things right. Though Adam's confession had been flawed, in his heart he still honoured God as his Creator. Seth took after Adam in this matter.

Seth lived to the age of 912 and bore a son called *Enosh* (**5:6-8**; see 4:26). Enosh was succeeded by *Kenan* (**5:9-14**), *Mahalalel* (**5:15-17**), *Jared* (**5:18-20**), and *Enoch* (**5:21-24**), who is said to have been a godly man who *walked with God; then he was no more, because God took him.* It seems that he and Elijah (2 Kgs 2:1-12) are the only two people who have ever escaped dying. He is thus listed among the heroes of faith (Heb 11:5).

Enoch's son *Methuselah* (**5:25-27**) lived to be 969 years old. We cannot imagine anyone living to such a great age, but it does not seem to have been remarkable in his time. All of those mentioned in this genealogy lived far longer than people do today. However, this exceptionally long lifespan did not persist, as can be seen by looking at the genealogy in 11:10-26, where the lives are still long by our standards, but nowhere near as long as those listed here. We do not know how to explain these figures. It has been suggested that the flood affected ecology and reduced the span of life, or that God may have changed the characteristics of the human body, particularly given his words in 6:3 ('his days will be a hundred and twenty years'). Whether we live to be eighty, ninety or even one hundred years old, we have nothing to boast of compared to Methuselah! Our duty is simply to thank God for each year he adds to our age.

Methuselah was the father of *Lamech* (**5:28-31**), and Lamech the father of *Noah* (**5:32**). Note that this Lamech is not the same person referred to in 4:19-24. Lamech had not forgotten the events in Eden, for in naming his son, he said, *He will comfort us in the labour and painful toil of our hands caused by the ground the Lord has cursed* (5:29). Noah had three sons: *Shem, Ham* and *Japheth*. We also know from 9:28 that he lived to the age of 950.

The comments noted in the genealogy in this chapter remind us that God, as it were, keeps a diary of our lives,

which includes notes about men such as Enoch. It also reveals that our characters shape the history of our times. We can see the names of three influential and godly men in this list: Enosh, in whose time 'men began to call on the name of the Lord' (4:26); Enoch, who *walked with God* (5:22, 24); and Noah, who received the same praise (5:29; see 6:9.).

God does not force us to follow him, but allows us to choose how we will live before him. But he reminds us of people like Enoch to challenge us to do well.

6:1-8:22 The Flood

6:1-7, 11-13 The cause of the flood

The genealogy in chapter 5 tells us that besides the descendants of Adam and Eve who are specifically named, each of the men had 'other sons and daughters'. Cain, too, had sons and daughters who produced children of their own. Thus by the time of Noah, who is the tenth generation from Adam, the population would have grown substantially, as is indicated by the words *when men began to increase in number on the earth* (**6:1**).

God's ideal for the family had already suffered two blows in that the relationship between husbands and wives was no longer open, for they need to conceal parts of themselves from each other (3:7), or monogamous (4:19). Now it took a third blow that distorted it still further as the *sons of God* married *the daughters of men* (**6:2**). In such a marriage, the husband and wife are no longer both living in the fear of the Lord. They have entered into a covenant between light and darkness, holy and unholy (2 Cor 6:14). In light of this increasing evil, God, who had warned that death was the consequence of sin (2:17) now brings that death even earlier, reducing the length of the human life to *a hundred and twenty years* (**6:3**). Yet this may even have been an act of mercy, for it is hard to live for many years without the peace of God in one's heart.

It is clear that this intermarriage displeased the Lord. However, scholars have struggled with the issue of the identity of those getting married. Some argue that the 'sons of God' are fallen angels, possibly the same ones that Jude describes as having 'abandoned their own home', that is, their state (Jude 6). If this is the case, then the women are being judged as so wicked that they were prepared to marry anyone, even a fallen angel. The angels could have *any of them they chose*. Those who support this view argue that the *Nephilim* (giants – see Num 13:33) of **6:4** were the product of this intermarriage. However, the language does not seem to require that understanding, as all that the text seems to say is that the *Nephilim* existed at the time when this intermarriage was taking place. The reference to them would then simply be an indication that God had blessed humankind not only with long lives and multiplying numbers but also with huge stature.

A more likely possibility is that what is being spoken of here is intermarriage between men from Seth's line (called 'sons of God' because they were descendants of the God-fearing Seth) and women from Cain's line (referred to as the 'daughters of men' because Cain had been sent away from the Lord's presence and followed his own will, as did his descendants like Lamech). The point would then be that the line of Seth, which was supposed to promote the will of God, had lost its values to the point that all that mattered to them was the beauty of the women in Cain's line. While this explanation is not flawless, it does have the virtue of fitting in with the focus of the narrative so far on the differing spiritual values of Cain and Seth. It seems that Enosh's tradition of calling on the Lord (4:26) is dying out. God is displeased when everyone becomes wicked, and there is no longer any distinction between people on the basis of their values.

The increasing *wickedness* of humankind is summed up in the words *every inclination of the thoughts of his heart was only evil all the time* (**6:5**). Human beings are also described as *corrupt* and *full of violence* (**6:11-12**). Unfortunately, many of these words are very applicable to our societies in the twenty-first century. Thus we should be concerned at the Lord's response to these conditions: *I am going to put an end to all people … I am surely going to destroy both them and the earth* (**6:13**).

God does not do this cheerfully or in heedless anger. Rather, in one of the most moving verses in the Scriptures, we are told that God acted in grief and that *his heart was filled with pain* (**6:6**). When children bring their father to this state, they are under a curse, regardless of whether that curse is actually pronounced. This grieving God hates evil and acts to deal with it. That is why we, in Africa, cannot take our plight lightly. Could it be that God's heart is grieved and full of pain due to our corruption and wickedness? If so, we are under the curse of God who gives and sustains life!

This does not mean that there is no escape from the curse. God is a loving Father who gave his Son Jesus Christ to carry the curse for us (Gal 3:13). But he is also a God of justice and righteousness (Mic 6:8), and we are called upon to make right what may be wrong. There are plenty of wrongs to correct in Africa – just as there are elsewhere in the world.

Though the rest of creation had not participated in human sin, it has been contaminated by contact with human beings and will be destroyed along with them (**6:7**). Sin is like yeast, which affects a whole loaf of bread. Human beauty and human community had once been the crown of creation (1:31), but human corruption drew all creation down in ruin. Once again we see the working of the principle

that the behaviour of the head of a household affects not only himself but also his entire household. We saw this in relation to parents and children (Cain and Lamech – 3:19-24), we see it in relation to heads of state and institutions, and we see it in the relations between human beings and nature.

6:8-10, 14-18 An exception

Though the world had sunk deep into sin, there was one person who was an exception and who *found favour in the eyes of the Lord* (**6:8**). He is described as *a righteous man, blameless among the people of his time, and he walked with God* (**6:9**). Many African believers have wondered whether it is possible to prosper if one does business uprightly. Can one stand against the tide and still be successful? We have the answer right here in Noah. He found favour with God. This will be the experience of anyone who glorifies God in his or her generation, no matter how much evil has become part of that society.

God revealed his plans to this exceptional man (6:13) and then gave Noah specific instructions. At first he was given the general command to *make yourself an ark* (**6:14a**), and only after that was he given details about its construction (**6:15-16**). Noah had to decide whether he was going to obey God's overall instruction before the other details were of any significance. In the same way, God today gives us the overall instruction, 'Believe in the Lord Jesus' (Acts 16:31, John 3:16, 36), which must be obeyed before other details are of any importance. It is pointless to debate highly academic theological issues about Jesus before one has obeyed the primary instruction to believe in him. Knowledge of theological or biblical details without the willingness to obey the basic instruction counts for nothing in God's plan of redemption.

The ark was to be constructed *of cypress wood*, have *rooms* within it, and be coated inside and outside *with pitch* to make it waterproof (**6:14b**). It was to be *450 feet* (140 metres) *long*, *75 feet* (23 metres) *wide and 45 feet* (13.5 metres) *high* (**6:15**). It would have a door in the side and *a roof* over it, with an 18-inch (0.5 metres) opening left to allow air to circulate between the walls and the roof (**6:16**). Inside, it would have three decks. God gave such specific instructions because he was the only one who knew such details as how much water would be coming, how long the flood would last, who would be in the ark, and so on. It has been confirmed that an ark of the dimensions given would be able to float.

In 6:13, the Lord revealed to Noah that he was going to destroy all the people, and in **6:17** he revealed how this destruction would come. This explanation must have helped Noah to understand why it was necessary to build an ark. The Lord's statement that *everything on earth will perish* must have been deeply distressing, but neither Noah nor we can question it. As the creator, God also has the right to destroy his creation.

But there is also hope, for God promises Noah, *I will establish my covenant with you, and you will enter the ark – you and your sons and your wife and your sons' wives with you* (**6:18**). God does not indulge in wanton destruction. He destroyed the earth because it was no longer serving the purpose for which he created it. Humanity and all creation were intended to declare not only God's 'eternal power and divine nature' (Rom 1:20) but also his holiness (Pss 19:1; 29:2; Isa 43:7; 51:7). When human beings frustrate this intention instead of promoting it, the Creator has every moral right, just like inventors in our times, to start all over again. Safety is found in upholding God's righteousness as Noah did. The Lord makes a covenant with those who do this, while he destroys the rest. Thus when we preach we should never emphasize God's grace at the expense of his justice. His love and his holiness must be kept in balance, for he maintains both.

Noah's wife, his three sons, and their wives were all saved along with Noah (6:18; 7:13). It can be argued that they were saved because the blessings of Noah extended to his household. Or it may be that Noah's walk with God influenced those around him to such an extent that every member of his household qualified to be in the ark. The former explanation seems more likely, given the general context of the passage. This community principle is certainly applied in other similar situations, as when Lot was told to gather his relatives and leave Sodom (19:12). Once again we are reminded of the importance of the relationship the head of a family has with God, for his or her conduct can result in an overflow of blessings or curses to the rest of the family.

6:19-7:5 The goal of the flood

Though everything that was not in the ark was destroyed (7:21-23), the ultimate goal of the flood was not to destroy all life but to destroy the stronghold of sin. It can be said that the flood did not aim to wipe out creation but to preserve it through all that God had ordered to be put in the ark for safety. Destroying all creation would have signified the defeat of the Creator, but the Lord does not fail in what he does. Not even the initial sin of Adam and Eve had derailed his plan, for he had immediately announced the future coming of the Saviour to crush the devil and bring in a new community that would celebrate his glory (3:15).

Thus God's announcement that he would destroy 'every creature that has the breath of life in it' (6:17) was clearly not meant to be taken literally. Not only did he not destroy Noah and his family, but he also saved representatives of every kind of animal so that life would continue. He had rested from his work of creation (2:2) and even the destruction of the world was not going to make him resume it. So

he instructed Noah to take into the ark a male and female of every kind of bird and animal (**6:19-20a**). Thus God provides both for termination and for continuity. One generation is wiped out, but a remnant survives to raise up a new generation.

God did not tell Noah to set out to hunt and capture these creatures alive. Instead he told him that they would come to him (**6:20b**; 7:9, 15). We would have expected the animals to fear one another and human beings, as animals do today, for this was taking place after the fall, but when God commands it, they obediently present themselves to Noah. But it was not as if Noah had no work to do and could leave it all to God. Besides building the ark, he had to make provision for food to keep these animals and his own family alive (**6:21**).

Just as we would expect given the narrator's description of him as 'blameless' (6:9), *Noah did everything just as God commanded him* (**6:22**). His obedience is also emphasized in **7:5** and 7:16.

Finally God instructed Noah that the time had come for him to go into the ark (**7:1**). Once again he stressed the reason Noah and his family were being saved: *I have found you righteous in this generation.* The purpose of this flood was to destroy sin, and it was the presence or absence of righteousness in people's lives that determined whether they lived or died. This emphasis on righteousness is also evident in the instruction that seven of each type of clean animal and bird, that is, of each type that could be sacrificed to God, should be taken into the ark. This provided three breeding pairs for these animals and at least one for an immediate sacrifice (**7:2-3**; see also 8:20).

The fact that a pair of every creature that God had created was saved is repeatedly emphasized. In 6:19-20 Noah was given specific instructions to save a male and female of each species; in 7:2-3 he is commanded to go into the ark with all of them; and then we are told that these pairs entered the ark (7:7-9, 14-16). The repetition is meant to underline the point that all the animals we see today came from the creative hand of God – whether directly or indirectly through cross-breeding.

7:6-24 The nature and effect of the flood

God had told Noah that *seven days from now I will send rain on the earth* (**7:4**) and he kept his word, for *after the seven days the floodwaters came* (**7:10**). By this time, Noah and his family and the animals were safely in the ark (**7:13-16a**). God did not allow Noah to be in charge of the door of the ark but *shut him in* himself (**7:16b**). He may have done this to make sure it was properly sealed, but it is more probable that he did it in order to spare Noah the sight of the suffering once the destruction began. Only God could endure such sights, for he hates sin perfectly and knew that his punishment was just.

somehow caught a glimpse of *his father's nakedness* (**9:22**). But instead of discreetly covering him and leaving, Ham chose to go and tell his brothers what he had seen. His sin was not that he saw his father naked, but that he did not act to protect his father from shame, and in fact exposed him to the ridicule of others.

His brothers, *Shem and Japheth*, did not share his amusement. Instead they showed proper respect for their father: they *took a garment and laid it across their shoulders; then they walked in backward and covered their father's nakedness* (**9:23**). They carefully kept their faces averted *so that they would not see their father's nakedness*.

God commands us to honour our parents (Exod 20:12) and that means that we will hide their nakedness. This nakedness may be the result of moral weakness or from material poverty or from the physical weakness of illness or old age. Whatever form it takes, we are to act to maintain our parents' dignity. We must not abandon them to misery in our villages nor isolate them in beautiful villas of anguish. Nor must we simply see their needs and talk about them. We must take action to meet their needs (Matt 15:1-5). Often we will find that they long more for our love and our presence than for the things we can offer them.

There are people who are like Ham even in the spiritual realm and within the life of the church. Such people see moral, economic and social problems, talk a lot about them, and may even preach on the subject, but they take no practical and visible steps of love to remedy the situation. We need to learn to combine word and action (Jas 2:14-18; 1 John 3:18).

When Noah was sober and found out what *his youngest son had done to him* (**9:24**), he pronounced a curse, not on Ham, who had humiliated him, but on Canaan, Ham's youngest son (**9:18**; 10:6). Why did he not curse the perpetrator? Some have argued that Noah wanted to curse someone dear to Ham. But if this were the case, then surely Noah would not have singled out only one of Ham's sons, but would have cursed all the sons of Ham. Others argue that Canaan must have done something to draw this curse. He may have reacted inappropriately by laughing when he heard his father describe his grandfather's state, or he may have been with his father when he saw Noah and have encouraged him to tell the others. Such behaviour would indicate a lack of respect for his grandfather. But there is no evidence in the text to support this argument. Yet another possible explanation of the curse can found in chapter 2 of Dr Tokunboh Adeyemo's book, *Is Africa Cursed?* (Nairobi, Kenya: Christian Learning Materials Centre, 1997).

A more plausible solution may be related to the effects of the alcohol Noah had consumed. When he awoke from his wine-induced sleep, he would not have been entirely free of all its effects, and may have mistakenly thought that it was his grandson rather than his son who had betrayed

him. It is likely that the curse was pronounced in haste under the influence of shame and anger when he awoke and learned what had happened, probably from Japheth and Shem (9:24). If this last scenario is correct, then Noah cursed Canaan without first calling him to hear whether he was in fact guilty. The upright and just person had suddenly abandoned the justice of the Lord who questions the accused before pronouncing sentence (see 3:9-13).

By cursing and blessing in the heat of the moment, instead of waiting and considering the facts, Noah divided his house. He called down a curse on Canaan and, indirectly, excluded Ham from fellowship with his brothers. Such lapses in wisdom in someone who is otherwise upright and just are sadly familiar, even among the people of God. This curse was another severe blow to family ties and the fellowship that the Creator intended for human beings.

The curse on Canaan was that he would be *the lowest of slaves ... to his brothers* (**9:25**). The blessing on Shem was *may Canaan be the slave of Shem* (**9:26**), and the blessing of Japheth was m*ay God extent the territory of Japheth; may Japheth live in the tents of Shem, and may Canaan be his slave* (**9:27**). This passage has sometimes been referred to as the 'curse of Ham' and used to justify the enslavement of black people and the material poverty of the African continent as natural results of divine punishments. But this interpretation is clearly wrong. For one thing, the curse was not pronounced on Ham but only on his son Canaan. The genealogy in 10:6-20 shows that Ham's other sons, who were not cursed, included *Cush* (the ancestor of the Ethiopians, and the father of Nimrod, who is praised in 10:8), *Mizraim* (the ancestor of the Egyptians) and *Put* (the ancestor of the Libyans).

It is not God who despises black people, but other people (see Song 1:5-6). Holy Scripture should not be used to justify all historical events. Rather, with faith and respect we should use the word of God to analyse, appreciate and judge events in our history.

So what effect did this curse on Canaan have? We do not know the whole picture. We do know that God later gave the territory of the Canaanites to Abraham and his descendants, which is definitely part of the curse. However, even when he does so, he does not refer to this curse but rather to the Canaanites' immoral and idolatrous practices (Gen 15:16; Deut 18:14). Nor does he tell the Israelites to enslave the Canaanites (which would have been what the curse called for) but to destroy them (Deut 7:1-3). It is, however, possible that the words of rejection and exclusion pronounced by his grandfather aroused scorn and rebellion in Canaan, leading him and his descendants to become distanced from God. A profound and intensified moral degeneration would then be understandable, and hence, God's judgment.

Given this possibility, this incident is a reminder to us of the need to be patient and wise in our judgments. We need to be certain of our grounds for making judgments and to be aware of their possible consequences (Matt 7:1-2). We should not allow anger to lead us into uttering curses on our parents or our children. We are not always aware of the devastating effects of such words.

Noah lived another *350 years* after the flood, to the age of *950 years* (**9:28-29**). Notwithstanding his failure of drunkenness and its evil results, he stands out in history as a model of integrity who followed God's instructions scrupulously and thus saved both himself and his entire household. He was also a model of patience and persevering trust in God through the long years of building the ark, and during the year spent shut up in the ark. He waited for God to deliver him at the right time. Finally, he was a model of thankfulness, whose first action on leaving the ark was to build an altar and to sacrifice to God. The sacrifice showed that Noah understood clearly the causes of the flood and the grace that God had shown him.

10:1-32 Repopulation of the Earth

10:1 Introduction

The author mentioned the repopulating of the earth in 9:19, but now he sets out to show how the human community, composed of the descendants of Japheth, Ham and Shem, organized themselves to 'fill the earth' as commanded by God (1:28; 9:1). The genealogy lists the Japhethites first, followed by the Hamites, and then the Semites. This arrangement does not reflect their order in terms of age, for we know from 9:24 that Ham was the youngest brother. Japheth seems to have been the oldest brother (10:21). We would thus expect to hear them referred to as Japheth, Shem and Ham. But the text actually usually refers to them as *Shem, Ham and Japheth* (**10:1**; see also 5:32; 6:10; 9:18). Why this unusual order? Probably Shem is mentioned first because he was the one from whom the chosen people descended. But why is Japheth last? It may be because in any list the focus falls most on those listed first or listed last, depending on the intention of the writer. Being the chosen line or being the oldest would qualify one for either of these positions. Japheth would, therefore, be listed first if the focus was on age. Shem would be first if the focus was on the chosen line. Since Ham is neither the oldest nor the chosen line, he is consistently given second place.

In discussing each group, the author refers to their 'clans' (10:5, 20, 31). The clan is the family in the larger sense and consists of family cells, united by ties of blood and mutually supporting each other. The clan is meant to provide comfort and stability for children, to educate them, and to train them in the fear of the Lord. But clans can also have negative effects when they harm their members instead of training them in God's way, when they isolate them from the larger community (the nation) and when they encourage them to consider themselves above the rest rather than being willing to serve others. The clan can become a tool of evil and dictatorial dominance.

In these verses the clans are associated with *nations*, that is, the gathering together of the clans of a specific country. The quality of the nations depends on the value of their clans and of the men and women who make them up.

The clans are also associated with *territories*, that is, with a particular piece of land or a geographic area. The Bible recognizes that people need to feel an attachment to a particular location, to become owners of a piece of land that they maintain while respecting one another.

Finally, the clans are also associated with different *languages* after the events at Babel (11:1-9).

In this genealogy each group is shown as independent, and there is no evidence that one group is superior to the others (except that God would work through the line of Shem to bring salvation). But the Lord did not give special intelligence and scientific knowledge to one group while depriving others of those gifts. Each group is responsible before the Creator for the way in which it uses the gifts received from him and for the way in which it deals with the men and women created in his image. Each will give account to him of the skills and activities that it chose or did not choose to develop, because God will judge all our activities as human beings (Luke 12:41-48).

10:2-5 The descendants of Japheth

Japheth's line is listed to the third generation (his grandsons). The writer then makes a general statement that *from these the maritime peoples spread out into their territories by their clans within their nations, each with its own language* (**10:5**; see also 1 Chr 1:3-7). Attempts to relate the names of Japheth's sons and grandsons to what we find in later history suggest that he may be the ancestor of the Indo-European peoples.

10:6-20 The descendants of Ham

Ham's line is listed to the fourth generation (his great-grandsons). The general statement here is that *these are the sons of Ham by their clans and languages, in their territories and nations* (**10:20**; see also 1 Chr 1:8-16). The sons of Ham, who were named Cush, Mizraim, Phut and Canaan, have been related to Ethiopians, Egyptians, Libyans and Canaanites, respectively.

Three of Ham's descendants are singled out for special attention.

- *Nimrod* is said to be a son of Cush, Ham's son (**10:8**). However, his name is not listed with the other sons of Cush in **10:7**. It seems that here *father* means 'ancestor', and not the immediate progenitor. Nimrod is described as *a mighty hunter before the Lord,* a phrase that became a well-known saying (**10:9**). It is also noted that he (and presumably his descendants) built a mighty *kingdom,* beginning in *Babylon* (**10:10**), which he later extended into *Assyria* (**10:11**). Nimrod is given special mention, because Babylon was the site of the tower of Babel (see 11:1-9). Many hundreds of years later, Assyria and Babylon would play important roles in Israelite history.

- *Mizraim* is mentioned because he was *the father of the ... Casluhites (from whom the Philistines came)* (**10:13-14**). These people also played an important role in the history of Israel (see 1 Sam 4:1-11; 5–7; 14).
- *Canaan* became the ancestor of the tribes listed in **10:15-18**. The territory they inhabited is the same land that was later promised to Abraham and his descendants (**10:19**; see Exod 3:8, 17; 13:5; Deut 7:1). It may be that with this detail and the earlier reference to the curse (9:25) are preparing readers for what will come later – the destruction of the Canaanites and the taking of their land.

10:21-32 The descendants of Shem

Shem's descendants are listed to the sixth generation (his great-great-great-grandsons). The general statement here is that *these are the sons of Shem by their clans and languages in their territories and nations* (**10:31**; see also 1 Chr 1:17-27). The larger number of generations covered reflects the interests of the author. Shem's list is the most important line for the narrator and will be continued after the story of the tower of Babel (11:10-32).

At the start of this genealogy Shem is described as *the ancestor of all the sons of Eber* (**10:21**), even though Eber is not mentioned in the genealogy itself until 10:24. The reason he may be singled out for special mention may be that some people explained the name 'Hebrew' as coming from 'Eber'.

Like other biblical genealogies, this list of Shem's descendants is not comprehensive and does not mention every single ancestor. Thus in Luke 3:35-36 an ancestor named Cainan is mentioned between Arphaxad and Shelah, while here *Arphaxad* is described as *the father of Shelah* (**10:24**). In interpreting such differences, we need to remember that in Hebrew 'father' is often used to mean 'grandfather', or even 'ancestor'.

Eber's son Peleg is also given special mention, *because in his time the earth was divided* (**10:25**). This probably refers to the division after the tower of Babel (see 11:8).

11:1-9 The Tower of Babel

After the flood the population was eight people. For some time, as we would imagine, *the whole world* (meaning everyone alive) *had one language and a common speech* (**11:1**). This is an ideal situation if used properly. Language is a good gift from God. Words play a major role in our relationship with God and constitute a marvellous tool for building ties between people. It is therefore necessary to learn to use language wisely (Eccl 5:1-2).

As the population multiplied there was a need for more land, and so they *moved eastward* until *they found a plain in Shinar and settled there* (**11:2**). There they learned to make bricks instead of stone for building (**11:3**), and inspired by this technology they urged each other on: *Come, let us build ourselves a city, with a tower that reaches to the heavens so that we may make a name for ourselves* (**11:4**). The repetition of 'ourselves' and the focus on their 'name' shows that the people have made themselves the centre of life. Not only that, but their desire to avoid being *scattered over the face of the earth* was in opposition to God's command to fill the earth (1:27-28; 9:1). Rather than spreading out horizontally to progressively occupy and manage the whole earth entrusted to them by the Lord, they wanted to act independently, cluster together and rise vertically (climbing towards heaven). Their sin was the same pride and desire to be like God that had caused the fall and the rapid spread of evil (3:5).

The tower of Babel is an example of how not to undertake a project. In building the church in Africa and reconstructing our countries, we must be careful that our unity is not based on grand ideas and the desire to make a name for ourselves, but on the ideals of community communicated by God in the first chapters of Genesis.

The statement that *the Lord came down to see the city and the tower that the men were building* (**11:5**) is an attempt to put God's action into human language that we will understand (see also 3:8; 8:1). The idea is that people were trying to build a tower high enough to reach where God, expressed in human language, lives (11:4), but God 'came down' to where humans live and put a stop to their plans. He forbade it for the good of humankind, to prevent his having to unleash some other event like the flood. Human beings must never forget that they are mortal (6:3) and that God is the Creator, whose position they should not try to usurp. God's words in 11:6 have great relevance to the whole issue of cloning. While he encourages us to advance our knowledge of the world he has created, we must not impinge on his prerogatives. The Creator is a jealous God, who has no equal.

Once again we hear communication within the Godhead: *Come, let us go down and confuse their language, so they will not understand each other* (**11:6-7**; see 1:26). What the people had feared was then brought upon them by their own actions as God *scattered them ... over all the earth* (**11:8**). With the builders unable to communicate properly, work on the city ceased.

The account ends with the words: *That is why it was called Babel – because there the Lord confused the language of the whole world* and *from there the Lord scattered them over the face of the whole earth* (**11:9**). The same Hebrew words is translated both as 'world' and as 'the whole earth' in this sentence. As with the flood of 6:1-8:22, it is possible to debate whether this incident involves all the peoples in the world, or merely those living in this particular area of the known world.

God is never out of options! He chased Adam and Eve out of the Garden of Eden, he opened the floodgates of heaven, he confused languages. Who knows what else he may do to those who oppose him! That is why it is important to be his friend – and in our days this friendship is achieved through belief in the Lord Jesus Christ (John 1:12).

11:10-25:18 Abraham and His Descendants

From here to the end of the OT, the Bible focuses on the history of the descendants of Shem. One of these descendants, Abram, was the one from whom would spring the people whom God appointed as the means of his salvation.

11:10-26 Abram's Ancestors

God had already hinted at the coming of the Saviour, the offspring of the woman, who would be victorious over Satan by crushing the head of the serpent (see commentary on 3:15). But it would be necessary to prepare for his coming and to have people to welcome him before the whole world could benefit. So God, who had used Noah to preserve the human race and all of creation, now started to prepare and train a people so that creation could receive salvation. He chose to start with a man from among the descendants of Shem. Thus we are now given more details about how the line of Shem continued (11:10). The genealogy ends with the *Terah* in the eighth generation after Shem, whose sons are *Abram, Nahor* and *Haran* (11:26). Abram is the one whom the Lord would finally call.

In chapter 5, we are told that those who lived between the times of Adam and Noah reached ages ranging from 365 (Enoch) to 969 (Methuselah). However, in the list given here of those who lived between the times of Shem and Abram, the ages range from 148 (Terah) to 600 (Shem). In general, the ages have been reduced to less than half that of the earlier generation. Put differently, in the first ten generations, the average life span was 858 years, while in the second ten generations it was only 307 years. This difference may be attributed to the effect of the flood on the environment in which people now lived, or God may have acted directly to shorten the human lifespan.

Both Noah and Abram are key persons in God's redemptive history and both end a family tree of ten generations (5:28; 11:26). As observed earlier, the listing is not necessarily of every individual from father to son. There is some selection in the names listed. The author may deliberately have chosen to have only ten generations in each of the lists. He may have been intending to suggest that a complete generation (taking ten to symbolize completeness) was wiped out, and another complete generation brought forth Abram, who was to be the father of a chosen race.

11:27-32 The Move from Ur to Haran

Terah, the father of Abram, had at least three sons: *Abram, Nahor,* and *Haran* (11:27). Haran died, leaving his son *Lot* without a father (11:28). Nahor is dismissed with a few words about his marriage to *Milcah,* while Abram becomes the focus. His wife *Sarai* is also introduced, and described as *barren; she had no children* (11:29-30).

Terah took Abram and Sarai and his grandson Lot and left *Ur of the Chaldeans to go to Canaan* (11:31a). We are not told that this initial move was specifically commanded by the Lord, nevertheless it is quite clear that the Lord was behind their leaving Ur. This comes out clearly later: 'I ... brought you out of Ur of the Chaldeans' (15:7; see also Neh 9:7; Acts 7:2-4).

The travelling group may have included others besides those whose names are given, for the author is focusing on those whose histories will be important in the rest of the book. But it is worth noting that this verse does demonstrate a value Africans should strive not to lose – the place given to the extended family. Lot was an orphan, and Terah took that into account, taking him as his own child. It is also significant that the verse says that Terah took his *daughter-in-law Sarai,* rather than simply that he took Abram and his wife Sarai. Fathers-in-law need to take care to treat their daughters-in-law as their own daughters. This is particularly important if the husband of one of them dies. Too often a widow is forced to live in fear because her brothers-in-law are hungry for their dead brother's property. In such circumstances a father-in-law should step in to protect the interests of his daughter-in-law, including the property her husband owned – whether he inherited it or acquired it in some other way.

Although Terah's destination was *Canaan,* the party halted before they reached there and settled in *Haran,* where Terah later died at the age of 205 (11:31b). Reading ahead and realizing that the land 'I will show you' (12:1) is actually Canaan (12:5, 7), we may draw a lesson from this about settling for less than the final destination. Terah may have decided that Haran was more comfortable, either economically or socially, than continuing his long journey. But it was not the place that he had set out to get to. In the same way, we need to be careful not to settle for less than our original destination when we began our walk with Jesus. The call to Abram in 12:1 comes as an instruction to complete what the group had already began.

12:1-9 Abram Obeys the Lord's Call

There is debate about whether the best translation of the Hebrew text of 12:1a is *the Lord had said* or 'the Lord said'. Those who favour 'had said' argue that Abram was called while he was still in Ur of the Chaldeans and see support for this view in Stephen's speech in Acts 7:2-4. However, it is also possible that Stephen's words in Acts simply indicate that God's providence was at work in arranging for Abram to leave Ur, rather than that God specifically spoke to him while he was there. They then see God's command to 'leave your country' in 12:1b as having been given while Abram was in Haran and obeyed in his departure from Haran, introduced with, 'so Abram left' in 12:4.

Wherever the call was issued, its substance was the same: he was to *leave* and to *go*. He was to leave three things – his *country*, his *people* and his *father's household* (**12:1b**). These are the very things that give anyone a sense of security but Abram is told to leave them. He is not told specifically where he is to go, but is told that his destination will be his inheritance from the Lord. He need have no fear or anxiety about where he will end up, for the Lord's presence will be there for him.

Some who come to faith in the Lord Jesus from Islamic families or from families that are strongly rooted in African traditional religions have also lost everything that would naturally give them comfort on this earth. They should recognize that although their human families have cast them out, they are still members of God's family, and as his children they should have no fear (John 1:12). God's presence is with them. We in the church must give much support to such new believers who have 'lost all' so as to gain Christ. The church must become their new family.

The call to Abram to leave his family did not mean that he was being called to live alone in a monastery. He took his closest family with him, namely *his wife Sarai* and *his nephew Lot*, who had grown up in Abram's family ever since he was orphaned at a young age (**12:5a**). Thus Abram still had his own community, culture and family, which would gradually grow to become the nation who would be the people of God. His example also illustrates the point that God's call to service is not directed to the husband alone, but also to his wife. The two are one before the Lord (Gen 2:24). Sarai, too, will inherit the promise.

God did not beg Abram to leave, nor threaten him if he did not. Nor did he leave Abram guessing about what he was to do. God simply communicated his will to a man who truly feared God. That was all that was needed, for Abram listened with an obedient heart. He provides a model for how we should live and serve God.

While God did not threaten Abram, he did promise him great blessings if he was obedient. In 12:2-3 God utters five 'I wills' (promises), one 'you will' (prediction) and one 'they will' (prediction). The predictions are based on the promises God makes, and so they can be expected without fail. The five 'I wills' are as follows:

- *I will make you into a great nation* (**12:2a**). This promise must have been very welcome, yet very strange to Abram, given that the Lord had not yet been pleased to give him any children. God is saying that Abram is called to be the first ancestor of an entire nation. And this nation will be larger than Abram expects. Not only will he be the human ancestor of most Jews, but he will also be the spiritual ancestor of all Christians, Jews and Muslims. He will thus be the father in the faith for a large part of humanity.
- *I will bless you* (**12:2b**). This blessing will consist of many, strong descendants (also 15:5; 17:5; 22:17) and possession of the land of Canaan (17:8).
- *I will make your name great* (**12:2c**). Abram would become a power to be reckoned with (21:22-31). As the physical ancestor of the Jews and the spiritual father of all believers, his name will be found on the lips of many (see John 8:53; Acts 7:2; Gal 3:6-9).
- *I will bless those who bless you* (**12:3a**). God would stand with Abram and consequently be a friend of Abram's friends.
- *Whoever curses you I will curse* (**12:3b**). Those who would want to do harm to Abram would also have to face his God and endure God's wrath.

The two predictions, *you will be a blessing* (**12:2d**) and *all peoples on earth will be blessed through you* (**12:3c**), make it clear that God's blessings are not for keeping to himself but are to be used to bless others. Supremely, this will take place when his descendant who will be the Saviour is born (Gal 4:4-5). The salvation he offers will not belong to any one nation, as the early Jewish Christians had to learn, but will be passed on by and through one nation (Acts 2:1-11; 10:28-29, 44-48; 11:1-3).

Trusting in the Lord, the seventy-five year old Abram left Haran and *set out for the land of Canaan* (**12:5c**). Not only did he take his wife and nephew with him, but he also took *all the possessions they had accumulated* (**12:5a**). God does not call us to poverty, but we are not to place our possessions before him. If Abram had hesitated to leave because of what he owned (including land that he would have had to leave behind), he would have failed the test and displeased God. It was his obedience – no matter how much he took with him – that showed that he had placed the Lord first.

There is, however, one dark note in this passage. Abram is also said to have taken with him *the people they had acquired in Haran* (**12:5b**). He was not simply employing people to work for him, which is legitimate, but he owned these people as slaves. This evil practice may have been present in the family of Shem ever since the time of Noah, who had cursed Canaan, his grandson, with slavery (Gen 9:25). The fact that Abram followed this evil practice that was widespread in his culture and time shows that he had not been taught the principle laid down by God at the beginning of creation. Then God had stressed that all human beings are made in the image of God and are called to rule animals and things, but not other human beings (Gen 1:29-30).

The nation descended from Abram would continue to practise slavery for many centuries. The Lord, in his love, would gradually undermine this custom over the years. In his law he would lay down principles governing the treatment of slaves and servants, to make sure that they were treated humanely. But it was only after the coming of Christ and his deliverance from the vicious cycle by which sin drags down our societies and cultures that the church set out to eradicate this evil.

Abram moved to *the site of the great tree of Moreh at Shechem* (**12:6a**). There the Lord gave him more information about the land to which he had been directed in 12:1. He tells Abram, *To your offspring I will give this land* (**12:7a**). This specific information is only given after Abram has already acted in obedience. God gives Abram land because he knows that a geographic location is necessary to build and train a people. They need a place where they will gather for worship and with which they can identify.

The land that God promised to give Abram was Canaan, which was then occupied by the descendants of Canaan (**12:6b**; see also 10:15-19). The Lord would eventually give Abram and his descendants the land of Canaan, because of the increasing moral decadence of the Canaanites (Gen 15:16; Deut 18:12-14). This decadence may in part have sprung from the curse pronounced on Canaan (see comment on Gen 9:18-28).

It is noticeable that Abram did not resort to violence to remove the Canaanites from the land that God had told him would belong to his descendants. He left the timing and the method of accomplishing this to the Lord. All he did was to respond in faith by building *an altar there to the Lord, who had appeared to him* (**12:7b**). Moving on, he pitched his tent between Bethel and Ai, and there also he *built an altar to the Lord and called on the name of the Lord (* **12:8**). His action in building altars was an assertion that this land belonged to the Lord, and not to any other god, and thus could be given to him. He then continued *toward the Negev* (the region south of Judah) (**12:9**). Abram, believing in what God had said, did not see the obstacles but saw beyond them. On the basis of God's promise, he took the land as his very own. There is a lesson for us here also. No matter what difficulties there may be, so long as the Lord has given clear indication of his will, there should be no hesitation. What the Lord says is ours will be ours for certain. It may take years, but it will happen.

Abram's behaviour should also show us that we should not use biblical promises to justify our own violence and injustice towards nations, tribes, clans or individuals. We should not take their land, bully them, deprive them of their freedom or hate them for not honouring the Lord or

for abominable practices. God is the sovereign judge and he alone has the right to execute judgment.

12:10-20 The Lord Strikes Pharaoh

Even when we are where God wants us to be, all will not necessarily go well for us materially – no matter what the prosperity gospel teaches. Abram was in the land God had sent him to, but that land was afflicted by *famine* (**12:10**). The Lord does, however, guarantee to provide a way out. While there was famine in Canaan, there was enough food in *Egypt* and so Abram went there to wait till the famine in Canaan was over (**12:11**).

When we praise Abram as a man of faith (as in Heb 11:8-19), we need to remember that his faith was something that developed over time. Especially in the earlier part of his life, when he was still a child in faith, he often seemed to turn to human plans. So when he moved to Egypt, he developed a plan to avoid trouble because of the beauty of Sarai, his wife. He advised Sarai to tell a half-truth (or a half-lie) by claiming to be his sister (**12:13**). She was indeed his half-sister (20:12) but not to mention that she was also his wife was to convey a false impression, and thus to lie. Abram needed to learn to tell the truth and to trust to God for protection. This is a lesson that many of us are still learning!

The strategy worked for Abram – his life was spared and he acquired wealth (**12:16**) but it was at the expense of Sarai's moral purity, for Pharaoh took her as his wife – a statement that may imply that he knew her physically (**12:15**, 19). This immorality did not please God, and so he struck Pharaoh and his house with serious diseases (**12:17**). But Pharaoh was not merely an innocent victim of Abram's deception. He was also someone who abused his position of authority. Abram's fear that his wife would be seized was well founded, and shows that Pharaoh was prepared to exploit foreigners, who are often among the weaker members of society. God condemns such behaviour (Deut 24:17-20; 27:19).

Abram had failed the test the Lord had set him, but the Lord was still in control of the situation. He would not allow Pharaoh to destroy his plans to use this couple to produce a chosen people and eventually the Messiah. It is encouraging to know that the Lord's grace responds to us at the level we are at, and does not demand from us what is beyond us. We ourselves need to cultivate this attitude in regard to others. We are wrong to expect that those who accept Christ today will be mature tomorrow. Maturation in faith is a process through which God graciously guides us.

Pharaoh sensed that the diseases in his household were a punishment, and so after confronting Abram for not telling him the truth, he sent him away with his wife and his wealth (**12:18-19**). Pharaoh was not a believer in Abram's God, but he knew how to read events. If only some of our African leaders were equally sensitive to God! If they were, they might not foolishly keep on ruling even when the Lord is clearly saying that he does not approve of some aspects of their lives and leadership.

13:1-4 Abram Returns from Egypt

When Abram was sent away by Pharaoh he went to *the Negev, with his wife and everything he had, and Lot* (**13:1**). As a further commentary on what he had and in preparation for the next section, we are told that *Abram had become very wealthy in livestock and in silver and gold* (**13:2**). From the Negev, he went to Bethel. He had earlier built an altar there and worshipped the Lord (12:8). Now again, on the same spot, *Abram called on the name of the Lord* (**13:4**).

13:5-18 Abram and Lot Separate

13:5-13 Abram protects family ties

Not having enough is a problem, as we saw when Abram was forced to move to Egypt (12:10). However, having too much can also be a problem. Abram was now a very wealthy man, with large herds of livestock (13:2). His nephew, Lot, had shared in his uncle's prosperity and had his own *flocks and herds and tents* (**13:5**). With the Canaanites and Perizzites occupying much of the land, the area that was available to Abram was too small to provide enough food and water for all their livestock (**13:6**). Consequently, quarrels broke out between those who took care of Abram's livestock and those who took care of Lot's livestock (**13:7a**). These disputes had the potential to harm the relationship between Abram and Lot. They would also affect Abram's testimony for the Lord among the local *Canaanites and Perizzites* (**13:7b**).

In such a situation, it is vital to have the courage and wisdom to analyze the problem in order to reach a godly solution. Abram had failed to do this in Egypt, but this time he got it right by making his decision with reference to his relationship with God and with his family. He decided that while living close together was good in that it provided comfort and protection, it would be better if he and Lot lived apart and were at peace with each other rather than living together and quarrelling (**13:8a**). He was concerned to maintain their family ties, but suggested that a physical separation would be the means to maintain their emotional unity (see 14:8-16). Thus his suggestion that they separate was the appropriate decision, and not a rejection of Lot, whom he spoke of as his *brother* (**13:8b**).

Abram's sensitivity to the emotional needs of those he was responsible for is an example for us today. It is not uncommon for wives to feel crowded by relatives – especially by their husband's relatives. If a wife voices a complaint, her husband typically responds: 'He/she is my brother/sister; I am obliged to help him/her'. While it may sometimes be necessary to take others in under our roof (especially with so many orphans due to HIV/AIDS), it may

sometimes be better to provide for relatives at a distance, rather than creating a situation at home where everyone is unhappy and quarrelling.

Abram shows his generous and unselfish spirit in that he was willing to waive his rights as the older party and let Lot choose whether to take the land that lay *to the left* or *to the right* (**13:9**). Lot was not a man of the same calibre as Abram, and so he chose selfishly, taking *the whole plain of the Jordan,* which was *well watered* (**13:10-11**).

When it comes to the issue of land, many of the stories we hear show attitudes that are more like Lot's than Abram's. Even believers show greed and selfishness as they fight for the better or bigger piece. Arguments over land have even resulted in people being killed! Yet there are examples of those who have followed Abram's example. I know a man of God who told his brother to choose first, even though he knew that his brother would definitely choose the better land. The man of God asked God for strength to work the poorer land he had received, and set to work. Within a few years, his land was as green as *the garden of the Lord, like the land of Egypt toward Zoar* (13:10). With God's Spirit and hard work, a desert can be turned into a beautiful garden! God is looking for other Africans who will be like Abram when it comes to the matter of land.

Lot chose the plain without hesitation and apparently without asking Abram's advice. In using the beauty and fertility of the plain rather than his relationship with the Lord as his criterion for choosing the location of his home, Lot left the land of Canaan and moved to live among the wicked in Sodom (**13:12-13**). Lot chose the plain because of its potential to multiply his wealth without regard to the morality of the people he would live among. His choice would prove disastrous in the long term (18:16-19:29).

Lot's attitude is a common one on our continent. Many believers close their eyes to ethical considerations when they make business deals, seek promotion, or take other actions to advance their prosperity. It is important to take issues of right and wrong into account even as we strive for wealth. A little with the Lord is better than plenty he has not blessed (see Prov 15:16; 16:8).

13:14-18 The Lord reassures Abram

The Lord's response to Abram's choice was to confirm that he had not given away the best land, but that he and his descendants would own all the land in all directions as far as he can see, not just for a time, but for ever (**13:14-15**). Not only that, but the Lord would bless him with offspring as numerous as *the dust of the earth* (**13:16**). The Lord is the comforter and watches out in a special way for those who honour him.

The Lord told Abram *to walk through the length and breadth of the land* as its owner. It was his gift from the Lord (**13:17**). This gift is not like the gifts of public land that some African heads of state give to favoured persons or institutions. Heads of state are only custodians of public land and have no right to give it away. But the Lord owns every inch of the land. Abram was given the land by its true owner.

With this assurance, Abram moved his tents and went to live near the great trees of Mamre at Hebron (**13:18**). There *he built an altar to the Lord*.

14:1-16 Abram Intervenes on Behalf of Lot

Lot had moved close to Sodom (13:12), and he soon found himself in trouble when a war broke out in Canaan that involved the king of Sodom. The reason for the war is that the kings of *Sodom, Gomorrah, Admah, Zeboiim* and *Bela* (**14:2, 8a**), had been subject to *Kedorlaomer* for *twelve years*. In *the thirteenth year* they formed an alliance and rebelled (**14:3-4**). In the *fourteenth year* Kedorlaomer with three allies proved his strength by defeating six people groups – the *Rephaites,* the *Zuzites,* the *Emites,* the *Horites,* the *Amalekites* and the *Amorites* (**14:5-7**). The five kings lined up for battle *in the Valley of Siddim* (**14:8b**). They were, however, no match for Kedorlaomer and his three allies. As the kings of Sodom and Gomorrah and their armies fled, some of the people fell into *tar pits,* for the Valley of Siddim contained many of them (**14:10a**). With Sodom and Gomorrah wide open to them, Kedorlaomer and his allies *seized all the goods of Sodom and Gomorrah and all their food … They also carried off Abram's nephew Lot and his possessions, since he was living in Sodom* (**14:11-12**).

One of those who survived the defeat by fleeing to the mountains brought the news of what had happened to Abram, who is here described for the first time as *the Hebrew* (**14:10b, 13a**). He was *living near the great trees of Mamre the Amorite, a brother of Eshcol and Aner* (**14:13b**). Allied with these three Amorite brothers, Abram swung into action immediately for the sake of his nephew Lot (**14:14**). His rapid response shows clearly that his love for Lot continued after their separation. A relative should always hasten to help another relative who is in need.

Abram organized *318 trained men* and pursued Kedorlaomer and his allies. All of Abram's men were *born in his household* and were loyal to him. They pursued Lot's captors as far as *Dan* where Abram attacked them *during the night* (**14:15a**). They then pursued their fleeing enemies as far as *Hobah, north of Damascus* (**14:15b**). Abram recovered *all the goods and brought back his relative Lot and his possessions, together with the women and the other people* (**14:16**).

Abram with only 318 men routed an army that had defeated five kings and their armies! His victory shows wise choice of men for the task, good planning, and of course the enabling hand of the Lord. It reminds us that a leader does not need a multitude of people to succeed. A good team and wise strategy are the keys to success. This principle applies to all institutions, including governments. It is not the number of staff members or government ministers that matters. Rather, it is who the staff members and government ministers are and how wisely they plan. If African nations could apply this principle, they would be able to solve many of problems that have persisted for years.

14:17-24 Kings' Responses to Abram

Abram's bravery must have been admired by many and his deed appreciated by all the people of Sodom and Gomorrah. What the passage says the king of Sodom did is probably the same thing the king of Gomorrah would have done. *The king of Sodom came out to meet* Abram *in the Valley of Shaveh, that is, the King's Valley* (**14:17**). He offered Abram all *the goods* that he had recovered, telling Abram to give him only *the people* (**14:21**). His attitude is admirable, for he recognized that good deeds must be acknowledged and rewarded. Too often we see a lack of gratitude, as if some people do not even know the word 'thank you'.

Abram refused the generous offer on the basis of having sworn before God that he would not accept *even a thread or the thong of a sandal* (**14:22b-23**). The reason Abram gave for refusing the offered wealth was that he did not want the king of Sodom *to be able to say, 'I made Abram rich'*. He must have feared dulling his testimony and giving the impression that the determination and courage he had shown were motivated purely by a desire for personal gain.

The only gift Abram was prepared to accept was the food his men had eaten as they returned from fighting Kedorlaomer. But he did not object to his allies who had gone with him – the three Amorite brothers Aner, Eshcol, and Mamre – taking their share. They deserved it, and Abram had no intention of imposing his principles on them.

Abram's attitude towards material things is admirable. While many in Africa seek to grab what is not theirs, Abram refused to take even what he rightly deserved. The only one to whom he wanted to owe his prosperity was *the Lord, God Most High, Creator of heaven and earth* (**14:22a**). Abram knew that the Lord was distinct from any other person or image that other nations, including the king of Sodom, might call God. This truth still applies in Africa today. Any other being who seeks our worship is an idol and not God.

The second king who came out to meet Abram as he returned from defeating Kedorlaomer was *Melchizedek king of Salem.* He greeted Abram as a hero or a warrior returning in triumph from battle, according to the conventions of the times, with *bread and wine* (**14:18a**). Melchizedek may have been no more than the local leader of Salem (later called Jerusalem) and a Jebusite (for the Jebusites later controlled Jerusalem – 2 Sam 5:6-7).

But Melchizedek had other attributes that draw attention. For one, he is the first person mentioned in the Bible to whom the title 'priest' is attached when he is described as *priest of God Most High* (**14:18b**). He also *blessed Abram,* praying first for blessings on Abram, and then praising God for delivering Abram's enemies into his hands (**14:19-20a**). His words are a reminder that all our victories are God-given. We should not take the credit for ourselves and see the successful results of an action as our own accomplishments.

Melchizedek seems to have had some understanding of the nature of God for he refers to him as *God Most High* and describes him as *Creator of heaven and earth.* Such descriptions contrast the God he is talking about to the many gods and goddesses worshipped in Canaan and the surrounding nations. If Melchizedek was a Jebusite, his words indicate that not all good values were lost among the Canaanites. He would be a Canaanite in whom something remains of the fear of God despite their estrangement from God.

Abram's response to Melchizedek's blessing was to give him *a tenth of everything* (**14:20b**). Technically, everything was Abram's to give, since he was the one who had recovered it. But what is striking about this act is that by accepting Melchizedek's blessing and giving him this tenth of everything, Abram was implicitly acknowledging Melchizedek as his superior (see Heb 7:4-7).

Given the sudden appearance of a mysterious priest of the true God, and one whose name means 'king of righteousness', it is not surprising that he has fascinated later generations. David speaks of him as the representative of a special order of priests 'in the order of Melchizedek' (Ps 110:4). The NT writers, particularly the author of Hebrews, use him as a symbol of what Christ is like as a priest (Heb 5:6, 10; 6:20; 7:11). The fact that he simply appears and disappears without any further history about him leads the author of Hebrews to describe him as 'without father or mother, without genealogy, without beginning of days or end of life, like the Son of God he remains a priest forever' (Heb 7:3).

These references have led some to wonder whether it is enough to regard Melchizedek as simply the king of Salem, a local chieftain. Thus some think that because 'King of Salem' can mean 'king of peace' (Heb 7:2a), and the name Melchizedek means 'king of righteousness' (Heb 7:2b), what we have here must be Christ himself in a pre-incarnate appearance. Others argue that Melchizedek is a title used for Shem, who may still have been alive if he lived for 600 years, and who comes to meet his descendant Abram. This last view is intended to explain the 'order' of priesthood to which Melchizedek belongs as extending from Shem, through Judah, to Christ.

15:1-21 God Reassures Abram

On returning from his defeat of Kedorlaomer and his allies, Abram may have felt that he had just stirred up a hornet's nest. He may have wondered when they would return to attack him. So it would have been a great comfort to him when the Lord appeared in a vision and said, *Do not be afraid, Abram. I am your shield, your very great reward* (**15:1**). As Abram's shield, God would deal with all those who might plan evil against him.

It is very encouraging to have the Most High as one's defence. I (Dr Assohoto) can testify that there was a time in my own life when those who loved me felt that others were seeking evil power to destroy me. From two different sources I received plaques engraved with the words of Isaiah 54:17: 'No weapon forged against you will prevail'. Whenever my eyes caught these words, I felt a sense of assurance that I was well guarded.

Abram's attention was captured more by the second part of the Lord's promise here, 'your very great reward'. What greater reward could the Lord give him than he had already received? And yet at the same time, he may have had doubts and fears about where his life was heading. Would the Lord keep his promise to give him descendants? So Abram asked the Lord, *O Sovereign Lord, what can you give me since I remain childless?* Like a true African, Abram's greatest need as he saw it was a child. If he remained childless, his only option in the culture of the day was to adopt an heir, and the one he was considering adopting was *Eliezer of Damascus* (**15:2**).

The Lord assured Abram that Eliezer would not be his heir but *a son coming from your own body will be your heir* (**15:4**). An adopted child is a blessing, but there is a feeling of more intimate closeness to a child from one's body. This is what the Lord will give to Abram. He will provide what Abram most desires. And the blessings will not end there. Abram's descendants will be like 'the dust of the earth' (13:16) and *the stars* of *heaven* (**15:5**). The childless Abram will have not only an heir for his estate, but also offspring too numerous to count. Times when we lack what we desire can be discouraging, but only if we have lost sight of the potential of the Lord to provide.

Abram renewed his confidence in God: *Abram believed the Lord, and he credited it to him as righteousness* (**15:6**). This, the most famous statement about Abram's faith, is quoted in Romans 4:3, 9, 22; Galatians 3:6; and James 2:23. It shows that faith involves accepting and clinging to the word of the Lord. The fact that this faith was credited to him as righteousness excludes any idea of merit. He could doubt God, which would be an unrighteous response, or believe God, which is the righteous response to the promise.

Still the list of blessings is not ended. The Lord will also give Abram *this land* (**15:7**). The Lord prefaces this with a reminder of who he is: *I am the Lord, who brought you out of Ur of the Chaldeans.* The idea seems to be that the Lord is telling Abram, 'I brought you from Ur of the Chaldeans for the specific purpose of giving you this land, and will certainly give you descendants to occupy it.'

Although Abram believed God, he still sought further
assurance from the Lord on this matter, asking: *O Sovereign
Lord, how can I know that I will gain possession of it?* (**15:8**).
So as a sign, the Lord provided Abram with a formal covenant ceremony of the kind that would have been familiar
in his culture. Abram was told to slaughter three animals (*a
heifer, a goat, and a ram*) each three years old, and two birds
(*a dove and a young pigeon*). Then he was to cut the bodies
of the larger animals in half and arranged *the halves opposite
each other* (**15:9-10**). The birds were not cut in half, but
the body of one bird was placed in each line. Abram then
waited. While he waited, he watched the pieces so birds of
prey would not eat them (**15:11**). Abram knew that the Lord
cannot be rushed, but that as we wait for him he expects us
to keep watch over what he has entrusted us with.

At sunset, Abram was so tired that he *fell into deep sleep*
(**15:12**). The Lord provided a blanket in the form of *a thick
and dreadful darkness*. At this time the Lord told Abram
three key things:

• His descendants would be *strangers* in a foreign land, be
  enslaved, and *ill-treated* for *four hundred years* (**15:13**; see
  Acts 7:6). The 'four hundred' is an approximate number,
  for the Israelites actually lived in Egypt for 430 years
  (Exod 12:40; Gal 3:17).
• At the end of the four hundred years, the Lord will punish their oppressors and Abram's descendants will go
  out with *great possessions* (**15:14**; see Exod 12:35, 38).
• Abram would go to his fathers (die) *in peace and be buried
  at a good old age* (**15:15**; see 25:8).

The Lord gives direct assurance: *in the fourth generation your
descendants will come back here, for the sin of the Amorites has
not yet reached its full measure* (**15:16**). Because possessing Canaan will not be an act of colonization but an act of
judgment, God alone will decide when it is time to implement that judgment. This promise of judgment on Canaan
reminds us that it is only by obedience to the Lord that
we occupy the land. If we live in sin, we are not fulfilling
the purpose for which he gave it to us, and will be judged
accordingly.

In the years before God's judgment falls on the Canaanites, Abram's descendants will go to Egypt to learn the hard
lesson of slavery. Their experience will leave them better
prepared for the new community, the new brotherhood,
which God aims to establish. God does not give false hope
by suggesting that the process will be easy. He explains
clearly what will be needed and teaches with the aim of
producing solid faith.

The most important part of the covenant ritual took
place *when the sun had set and darkness had fallen* (**15:17a**).
Usually when a covenant was made at the time, both parties would walk between the cut pieces of the sacrificed
animals. It was an acted oath, as if the people were saying,
'May I be cut to pieces like these animals if I do not fulfil

my part of the covenant'. But when it comes to God, there
is no one who is an equal partner who can walk between
the pieces with him. Instead *a smoking brazier with a blazing
torch appeared and passed between the pieces* (**15:17b**). This
represented God entering into a covenant with the watching
Abram (**15:18a**).

The details of the covenant were as follows:

• A restatement of the Lord's commitment: *To your descendants I give this land* (**15:18b**; see 13:14-17).
• A statement about the boundaries of the land: *from the
  river of Egypt* [the Nile] *to the great river, the Euphrates*
  (**15:18c**). The nation of Israel came closest to reaching these boundaries during the days of Solomon (1 Kgs
  4:21; 8:65) and Jeroboam II (2 Kgs 14:25).
• A statement about the current occupants of the land:
  *the Kenites, Kenizzites, Kadmonites, Hittites, Perrizites,
  Rephaites, Amorites, Canaanites, Girgashites and Jebusites*
  (**15:19-21**).

16:1-16 Sarai's Solution to Childlessness

Sarai knew that she should have provided Abram with an
heir but she *had borne him no children* (**16:1**). She was ten
years younger than Abram (17:17), but she was already
seventy-five years old and was 'past the age of childbearing' (18:11). She attributed her barrenness to the Lord of
who *has kept me from having children* (**16:2a**). Like any other
woman (with a few possible exceptions in modern times)
Sarai wanted a family, and she devised a plan to get one.
She told Abram, *Go, sleep with my maidservant; perhaps I
can build a family through her* (**16:2b**). This was a socially
acceptable practice at that time, even as it is in some parts
of Africa today. Any child born to the maidservant would be
regarded as belonging to her mistress.

Abram, meanwhile, must have been getting desperate.
He had obeyed God and come to Canaan, and had been
there for *ten years* already (**16:3a**). But still Sarai remained
barren, and it seemed impossible for the Lord to fulfil his
promise to 'make you a great nation' (12:2a). He had considered adopting his servant Eliezer, but the Lord had said
otherwise (15:2-4) and had insisted that the heir would
come from Abram's own body. But God had not mentioned
Sarai's name, and so Abram decided to try another route
and agreed to her proposal (16:2). Abram made the same
mistake as Adam in following his wife's advice rather than
listening to God. He should first have taken this plan to
God, to see whether he approved of it. By failing to do so, he
failed to play the protective role that God intended for husbands. When the responsibilities instituted in the beginning
by the Lord for the couple are not respected, the home is in
danger of falling into great disarray, and all society with it.

Sarai took Hagar and *gave her to her husband to be his wife*
(**16:3b**). Abram slept with her and she became pregnant
(**16:4**). Hagar viewed her ability to become pregnant as

giving her an advantage over her barren mistress, and she *began to despise* Sarai. Then Sarai, who was the one who had given Hagar to Abram, turns on him and holds him responsible for Hagar's attitude (**16:5**)! We are not told that Abram had done anything to encourage Hagar's misbehaviour. Sarai may, therefore, be saying that Abram should not have listened to her when she suggested he sleep with Hagar. Of course, it is also possible that now that Hagar was pregnant with his child, Abram gave her a status above that of a servant and Sarai felt threatened.

If Sarai had thought that Abram was showing special favour to Hagar, Abram indirectly tells her that she is wrong. Hagar is her servant and she is free to *do with her whatever she thinks best* (**16:6**). So Sarai began to mistreat Hagar until the poor woman *fled from her.* We are not told where she was going, but she was an Egyptian (16:1), and so it is possible that she was hoping to be able to return to her homeland. Certainly, the spring where the angel of the Lord found her was *beside the road to Shur* (**16:7**), so she was heading in that direction.

The angel (thought by many to be Christ in his pre-incarnate state) addressed her as *Hagar, servant of Sarai* (**16:8a**): an immediate reminder of who she was. She had a name of her own, but she needed Sarai for her identity to be complete. She had conceived in order to carry a baby for Sarai, but now she was acting as if she was carrying the baby for herself. She needed to remember who she was.

The angel asks her *Where have you come from and where are you going?* (**16:8b**). It is not that he does not know the answer, but he wants Hagar to think about it herself. Hagar's reply, *I am running away from my mistress Sarai,* is correct but the angel's response focused on why she ran away. The roots of her problem were in her failure to submit to Sarai after she found she was pregnant. The angel of the Lord did not condemn Hagar. But he did tell her to return to Sarai and submit to her (**16:9**). Then he gave her a promise too: she would have *descendants … too numerous to count* (**16:10**). He also told her that her child would be a boy and that he should be called *Ishmael,* meaning 'God hears', reminding Hagar that God had heard her cry (**16:11**).

The angel also told her what kind of a man her son would be (**16:12**): He would be *a wild donkey of a man,* one whose *hand will be against everyone and everyone's hand against him.* He will not accept a subservient position but *will live in hostility towards all his brothers.* This prophecy was fulfilled, for Ishmael is the ancestor of all the Arabs, and the Jews are the descendants of his half-brother Isaac. The conflict between these brothers had spanned the centuries and continues today.

In response to this personal encounter with God, Hagar addressed the Lord as *God who sees me,* saying, *I have now seen the One who sees me* (**16:13**). The name was still used

of the spring located between *Kadesh and Bered* at the time when Genesis was written (**16:14**).

Hagar gave birth to a son as predicted, and following the instructions of the angel of the Lord, Abram called him Ishmael (**16:15**).

The events in this chapter clearly show that wrong choices produce long-lasting problems. Because of Abram's failure, problems arose between himself and Sarai (16:5; see 21:8-21; 25:6), between Sarai and Hagar (16:5-6), and between the children, Isaac and Ishmael, and their descendants (21:8-10).

17:1-27 The Lord's Promises

The events in this section take place thirteen years after the birth of Ishmael (17:25). Abram is ninety-nine years old (17:1) while Sarai is eighty-nine (she was ten years younger than Abram – 17:17b). The Lord appeared to Abram using a name that he had not used before: *God Almighty.* He had told Abram to *walk before me and be blameless* (**17:1**). The Lord had chosen Abram and therefore he had to live a life pleasing to him. The command is not a condition for acceptance but an expression of the need to conform to God's character. For his part, the Lord says, *I will confirm my covenant between me and you and will greatly increase your numbers* (**17:2**).

With Abram lying on his face before him, the Lord expands on the covenant obligations that apply to him, introducing them with the words *as for me* (**17:3-4a**).
- The Lord promises that Abram *will be the father of many nations* (**17:4b**). As a reminder of the Lord's commitment to see this happen, he changes Abram's name to *Abraham,* which means 'father of many' (**17:5**).
- The Lord promises to make Abraham *very fruitful.* Abraham's descendants will be entire *nations* led by *kings* (**17:6**).
- The Lord promises that this covenant will last for ever: *I will establish my covenant as an everlasting covenant between me and you and your descendants after you for the generations to come, to be your God and the God of your descendants after you* (**17:7**). On one level, this promise applies to Abraham's offspring in the flesh, but at a higher level it applies to his spiritual children (Rom 4:16).
- The Lord promises to give Abraham *the whole land of Canaan … as an everlasting possession to you and your descendants after you; and I will be their God* (**17:8**).

What has been said so far deals with the Lord's responsibility under the covenant. Now, however, he turns to what Abraham is expected to do, introducing it with the words *as for you* (**17:9**).
- Every male who is eight days old must be circumcised (**17:10-12a**). Circumcision was the visible sign of the invisible intimacy between God and his people. It was a constant reminder of the covenant with God, and thus a help in keeping the faith.

- The rule regarding circumcision applied not only to Abraham's direct descendants but also to servants and slaves born in the household or purchased from foreigners (**17:12b-13a**).
- Circumcision must be carried on by subsequent generations as *an everlasting covenant* (**17:13b**). The Lord will never cease to be the God of his descendants (Exod 6:7), and they must never cease to wear this God-given 'uniform'.
- Anyone who is not circumcised will be in violation of the covenant and will consequently be *cut off* (**17:14**). Such a person ceases to belong to God – even if born to Jewish parents. The NT refers to circumcision of the heart, which is equivalent to submission to God's saving grace in the Lord Jesus Christ (see Rom 2:28-29, Phil 3:3). This is now the only condition for belonging to God after the incarnation of Jesus Christ.

After the Lord has stated his own commitment and spelled out Abraham's obligation, he went on to reveal Sarai's part in all this. The first thing to be noted here is what the Lord does not say. He does not mention any requirement for Sarai or her any of her daughters to be circumcised. The rite was reserved only for men. Female circumcision cannot be justified from the Bible.

The Lord changed Sarai's name to *Sarah*, saying, *I will bless her and will surely give you a son by her. I will bless her so that she will be the mother of nations; kings of peoples will come from her* (**17:15-16**). Her new name, which means 'princess', makes her suitable for her responsibility – producing kings. She herself would bear only one son, Isaac, but his sons would be the ancestors of the Jews (both Israel and Judah) and of the Edomites.

Abraham had presumably lifted himself off the ground as he heard God's commands, but now at the news about Sarah having a son *he fell face down* again – this time not in reverence but to conceal his amusement. Abraham *laughed, and said to himself, 'Will a son be born to a man a hundred years old? Will Sarah bear a child at the age of ninety?'* (**17:17**). His verbalized response to the Lord focused on Ishmael. He said, *If only Ishmael might live under your blessing!* (**17:18**).

The Lord's response was that Ishmael had his place, but that it was with Sarah's son that he would establish his covenant. He specifies that the boy is to be called Isaac, a name that means 'laughter' (**17:19a**). Each time Sarah says this name, she will be reminded both of the joy he has brought her (21:6) and of the fact that she laughed at the thought of having a son in her old age (18:12). With her son as a living reminder that God can do anything, she will probably never again laugh when God makes such a seemingly impossible promise. God promises to *establish my covenant with him, as an everlasting covenant for his descendants after him* (**17:19b, 21**).

The Lord also responded to Abraham's request regarding Ishmael, promising to *bless him, … make him fruitful and greatly increase his numbers.* Ishmael *will be the father of twelve rulers* (see 25:12-16) and will also become *a great nation* (**17:20**).

When all was done, *God went up from* Abraham (**17:22**) and Abraham swung into action, circumcising every male in his household including himself (at ninety-nine years old) and Ishmael (**17:23-27**). He was aware that even though he had been privileged to be in conversation with the Lord, the Lord remained God. His reverence for God is clear in his falling face down (17:3, 17). He knew that the Lord's words must be taken seriously and acted on without delay, which was why he put the sign of the Lord's covenant with him on every male in his household.

18:1-15 Abraham Entertains Three Visitors

One day Abraham was sitting *at the entrance to his tent in the heat of the day* (**18:1b**). When he saw the *three men standing nearby,* his first instinct was to show hospitality to travellers who must be hot, tired and thirsty, given the hour of the day. He *hurried from the entrance of his tent to meet them and bowed low to the ground* (**18:2**). Then he offered them *water* to wash their feet, a *rest under the tree,* and *something to eat* (**18:3-5a**). The writer to the Hebrews cites this incident when he exhorts his readers to be hospitable (Heb 13:2).

In **8:3** Abraham addresses the apparent leader of the party as *my lord,* which was simply a conventional title of respect. He did not know what the narrator tells us, which is that one of the three visitors was the Lord himself (**18:1a**). What we have here is probably an appearance of the pre-incarnate Christ. His two companions were angels (19:15). The three had taken human form in order to accomplish a task. By the time the men left, however, Abraham must have realized that the person he was talking to was at the very least a messenger of the Lord. He continues to address him as *Lord* (18:27, 30, 32), though now the title is imbued with even deeper respect. In this context, however, it is not necessarily a title of worship.

The three visitors accepted Abraham's offer of hospitality (**18:5b**). While angels do not need to eat, this does not mean that they cannot eat when they are on a mission for which they must take human form. As the visitors ate, Abraham *stood near them under a tree* (**18:8**). His posture was a sign of welcome and respect for the visitors.

Sarah prepared the bread for the meal (**18:6**) while a servant prepared the meat of a *tender calf* (**18:7**). She does not seem to have come out to meet the visitors. Hence the question, *Where is your wife Sarah?* Abraham replied, *There, in the tent* (**18:9**). God then chose to make a startling announcement in this context of a friendly meal: *this time next year … Sarah your wife will have a son* (**18:10a**). Sarah, who was listening *at the entrance to the tent* (**18:10b**),

FEMALE GENITAL MUTILATION

Female genital mutilation (FGM) has been practised on all five continents for several thousand years but is more prevalent in some African and Middle Eastern nations. It is reportedly practised in more than twenty-six African countries.

Different ethnic groups practise different forms of FGM. These include excision, referring to removal of the prepuce and the tip of the clitoris; clitoridectomy, referring to the removal of the entire clitoris and the adjacent labia; and infibulation, consisting of the removal of the clitoris and the adjacent labia and the joining of the sides of the vulva across the vagina, securing them with thorns or with catgut or thread. A small opening is left to allow intercourse on the wedding night and is closed again to secure fidelity to the husband. Other forms of FGM include pricking, piercing or incising of the clitoris or labia, stretching of the clitoris, or cauterization by burning the clitoris and surrounding tissue.

Female Genital Mutilation is performed on girls aged three to sixteen years, usually in unhygienic environments using crude and unsterilized instruments such as a kitchen knife, razor blade, piece of glass or sharp nails. No anaesthetic is administered, and the girl is held down firmly by three or four women for the ten to thirty minutes the operation takes. If the girl struggles, other parts of the body can easily be injured. Physical side effects of the operation include infection, internal bleeding and the transmission of blood-borne infections like hepatitis B and HIV. Thus the operation can be fatal. There is also a potential loss of sexual function.

The psychological side effects of FGM are at least partially dependent on the social context. In some communities, FGM is part of initiation into adulthood and is regarded as strengthening social and political cohesion. In such communities, the women themselves assume that the practice is normal and those who undergo it regard themselves as 'real' women. An uncircumcised woman is considered an immature girl irrespective of her age or socio-economic status. The teaching that accompanies this initiation ritual emphasizes girls' roles in marriage and especially how they should relate to their husband and in-laws.

Possible negative psychological side effects of FGM are a sense of anxiety, humiliation and betrayal, and long-lasting trauma due to the terror experienced during the operation. Ironically, with increasing condemnation of the practice, more women are vulnerable to these responses.

Supporters of FGM defend the practice for reasons of cultural identity and gender identity. It is also believed to reduce women's sexual desire, and thus to reduce instances of sex outside marriage. It is also associated with cleanliness and hygiene. In some communities, uncircumcised women are not allowed to handle food and water.

Numerous international conventions have condemned FGM as a violation of women's sexual, physical and mental health, and thus a violation of their human rights. African theologians, too, need to unite against this scourge which dehumanizes women by seeking to control their bodies. They need to emphasize that God created the human body and female sexuality and declared them both good. Therefore, to abuse the body in a way that destroys the ability to appreciate one of God's gifts is an insult to his creation. Male circumcision, by contrast, is a religious rite that does not interfere with sexual responsiveness. It is also clear that when God instituted circumcision as a sign of the covenant he limited it strictly to men (Gen 17:10-14). God does give instructions regarding Sarah in the very next verse, and these instructions include no mention of female circumcision.

There is an urgent need to break the silence surrounding FGM and to recognize that it, too, is a form of oppression. A number of members of the Association of Evangelicals of Africa (AEA) have already campaigned against it.

Specifically, the church should begin by providing gender training for all church leaders. They need to recognize the problem before they can be in a position to lead others to the light. The message that God created both male and female in his image and gave them both authority over the earth must be preached in support of the equality of all. The church should develop approaches that promote gender complementarity rather than gender competitiveness. It is time we received pastoral statements condemning harmful cultural practices.

Sicily Mbura Muriithi

found this announcement very amusing. Considering that she herself was *past the age of childbearing* (**18:11**) and the advanced age of Abraham, she *laughed to herself as she thought, 'After I am worn out and my master is old, will I now have this pleasure?'* (**18:12**).

Though Sarah had laughed quietly 'to herself', the Lord who sees in secret saw her laughter (see Matt 6:6). He asked, *Why did Sarah laugh … Is anything too hard for the Lord?* (**18:13-14**). Sarah, out of fear, denied that she laughed, but the Lord quietly reprimanded her: *'Yes, you did laugh'*. This exchange reminds us that the child who will be born will be given a name that means 'laughter'.

In the course of time, Sarah would learn that all things are possible with God (Matt 19:26). In fact, the Lord, who is never rushed, planned that both Abraham and Sarah would be well past childbearing age so as to strengthen their faith, and ours as well. Could there be a better proof that nothing is too hard for the Lord?

18:16-33 Abraham Pleads for Lot

After the meal and the conversation about Sarah bearing a son, it was time to move on to accomplish the second mission on the Lord's agenda. The men *looked down towards Sodom, and Abraham walked along with them to see them on their way* (**18:16**). Because of their relationship, the Lord decided to let Abraham know what he was about to do (**18:17-19**). After all, the destruction of Sodom and Gomorrah would be a lesson to be kept in mind by Abraham's descendants. So God told Abraham, *The outcry against Sodom and Gomorrah is so great and their sin so grievous that I will go down and see if what they have done is as bad as the outcry that has reached me. If not, I will know* (**18:20-21**). It was not that the Lord was ignorant of the exact situation in Sodom and Gomorrah. Rather, his justice demanded that proof of sin be demonstrated to the sinner.

While the men (angels) went towards Sodom, Abraham *remained standing before the Lord* (**18:22**). He must have wondered how to approach the subject of his nephew, Lot, who was living in Sodom. So he raised the matter of the righteous and the wicked, asking the Lord, *Will you sweep away the righteous with the wicked?* (**18:23**) and making an assertion, *Far be it from you to do such a thing – to kill the righteous with the wicked, treating the righteous and the wicked alike. Far be it from you! Will not the Judge of the earth do right?* (**18:25**).

Abraham gives us an excellent example of intercessory prayer. It approaches God on the basis of his character, and is made without fear, but with all the appropriate respect for the Lord. Abraham was fully aware that he had the unique privilege of talking with the Lord, and was conscious of the fact that he had no right to be doing this, for he was no more than *dust and ashes* compared to God (**18:27**). His prayer was also audacious, as he modified and reintroduced his initial request. He first asked that the city might be spared if there were *fifty righteous persons* there (**18:24**), and then reduced the number progressively to *forty-five* (**18:28**), *forty* (**18:29**), *thirty* (**18:30**), *twenty* (**18:31**), and finally *ten* (**18:32**). The Lord responded to each of Abraham's petitions, eventually assuring him that he would spare the whole place if there were even ten righteous people there.

Having given Abraham all the time he needed and patiently answered Abraham's questions, *the Lord ... left, and Abraham returned home* (**18:33**). Abraham had made his plea. It was now the Lord's business to do what was right.

19:1-29 The Destruction of Sodom and Gomorrah

Though no doubt still distressed by the immorality of the people of Sodom, Lot had come to feel quite at home there. He had started as a foreigner, pitching his tent near the city (13:12), and only later living in the city (14:12). By now, however, he is *sitting in the gateway of the city* (**19:1**), which implies that he was a respected person in Sodom, or even a leader of some kind, for the city gate was where commercial and legal transactions took place. But though the events in this chapter show that he had succumbed to the evil in Sodom, yet he qualified as one of the righteous for whom his uncle Abraham had pleaded (2 Pet 2:8).

Like his uncle Abraham, Lot immediately offered hospitality to visitors when they arrived in Sodom *in the evening*. He offered them the opportunity to *wash* their *feet and spend the night* at his house (**19:2**). The visitors declined, saying they would spend the night in the public square, probably a place on the street where they would not disturb anyone (compare Judg 19:15). But Lot was insistent, and they agreed to stay with him. He *prepared a meal for them, baking bread without yeast, and they ate* (**19:3**). His actions contrast strongly with the behaviour of the men of Sodom. We can safely assume that he had learnt the values of kindness and hospitality while living with his uncle Abraham.

Before Lot and his visitors went to bed, *all the men from every part of the city of Sodom – both young and old – surrounded the house* (**19:4**). They had no interest in protecting strangers, but wanted to exploit them. Bored with having sex with each other, they now demanded that Lot bring out the strangers *so that we can have sex with them* (**19:5**). Lot was horrified at this breach of the laws of hospitality, which he was so determined to uphold that he even offered to give the mob his *two daughters who have never slept with a man* if they would leave his guests alone (**19:8**). But the men of Sodom grew increasingly violent, attempting to overpower Lot and break down his door. They insulted him, calling him an *alien*, refusing his judgment on the matter, and threatening to treat him *worse than them* (**19:9**). In other words, they were threatening to rape Lot as well – and assuring him that it would be a violent rape. Homosexuality is a detestable sin before the Lord (Rom 1:26-27; 1 Tim 1:10 – the NIV reads 'perverts' but homosexuals are the focus) and to compound it with rape is to invite God's judgment. Even though this rape was not carried out, the intention is as bad as the act (Matt 5:28).

The men of Sodom did not know what kind of visitors were in Lot's house. They had probably done evil to earlier visitors, which may have been why Lot had been so insistent that the men should not sleep in the square (19:3), but this time they were out of their depths. The visitors recognized Lot's concern to protect them, and thus pulled him back *into the house and shut the door* (**19:10**). Then they *struck the men who were at the door of the house, young and old, with blindness so that they could not find the door* (**19:11**; see 2 Kgs 6:18). This must have given them the shock of their lives, though worse was yet to come.

The angels had seen enough of Sodom to understand why *the outcry to the Lord against its people is so great* (**19:13**) and to convince them that this city should be destroyed. But Lot had acted honourably, and in view of this and in response to Abraham's plea (**19:29**), he is given a chance to escape the judgment. He is told to get out of the city with his relatives – *sons-in-law, sons or daughters, or anyone else in the city* who belonged to him (**19:12**). Lot had *sons-in-law, pledged to marry his daughters*, but they thought their future father-in-law was only joking and refused to join him (**19:14**). No more time could be wasted, and so in the morning, Lot was ordered to get out with just his wife and his two daughters (**19:15**). Still Lot hesitated, but the men forced him to act, as they *grasped his hand and the hands of his wife and of his two daughters and led them safely out of the city* (**19:16**). We are told that this was done because *the Lord was merciful to them.*

Having been brought out of the city, Lot and his wife and daughter were given four instructions: flee for your lives; don't look back; don't stop anywhere in the plain; flee to the mountains – or you will be swept away (**19:17**).

By this time Lot had begun to realize the seriousness of the situation. He knew his own physical weakness and judged that he would not be able to reach the mountains before destruction swept over him. So on the basis of the favour and kindness already shown to him (**19:18-19**), he requested to be allowed to flee to a small town that he knew he could reach (**19:20**). The request was granted and Lot was ordered to *flee there quickly* (**19:21-22a**). The reason for the urgency was *I cannot do anything until you reach it.*

Lot had pleaded to be allowed to go to the *very small* town, and his description of it led the town being given the name of *Zoar* which means 'small' (**19:22b**). It was the place where he, his wife, and his two daughters would find safety.

Sodom and its neighbouring city of Gomorrah were now engulfed in a rain of *burning sulphur* that the Lord poured out of heaven (**19:24**), destroying *those cities and the entire plain, including all those living in the cities – and also the vegetation in the land* (**19:25**). As the Creator and righteous judge, God alone has the right to end the life of his creatures.

Lot's wife failed to obey the instruction not to look back, and so she became *a pillar of salt* (**19:26**). There is no favouritism. Judgment comes upon all those who fail to adhere to the Lord's instructions. She was offered the opportunity to escape, but she failed to obey. The grace of deliverance must be lived seriously. There is no place for looking back.

Abraham must have been deeply concerned by what the Lord had disclosed to him about the coming destruction of these cities. He got up early the next morning and looked down toward Sodom. He saw *dense smoke rising from the land, like smoke from a furnace* (**19:27-28**). He did not know what had happened to his nephew and his family, but he could count on 'the Judge of all the earth' having done what was right (18:25).

19:30-38 Lot and His Daughters

The town of Zoar, to which Lot and his daughters had escaped, did not prove to be a permanent home for them. *He was afraid to stay* there, possibly because people might blame him for what had happened to Sodom and Gomorrah, or for some other reason. So he and his two daughters moved to *the mountains* and *lived in a cave* (**19:30**).

His daughters knew that their future husbands had died in Sodom (19:14). Their mother had become a pillar of salt for looking back at Sodom (19:26). They were effectively on their own, without anyone they could turn to for advice. One of the things that deeply concerned them was how they could *preserve* their *family line* (**19:32, 34**), which was not a topic they could easily discuss with their father. They concluded that they would have to have children, and that the only man who was available to father such children was their own father. He would never have agreed to lie with them, but they undermined his defences by getting him so drunk that he did not know what he was doing. First the elder daughter lay with him (**19:33a**) and then the next night the younger daughter lay with him (**19:35a**). In both cases, Lot *was not aware of it when she lay down or when she got up* (**19:33b, 35b**). Both daughters became pregnant. The first one gave birth to a son she *named Moab,* who became the *father of the Moabites,* and the second gave birth to a son she named *Ben-Ammi,* who became *the father of the Ammonites* (**19:36-38**).

This account raises several moral issues: Why did Lot allow himself to become so drunk that he did not know what was going on around him? Were the daughters right in sleeping with their father, given the absence of any other man around them? Was Lot right to be living in a cave with his daughters? Would he not have been wiser to have risked living in Zoar rather than in a cave in such close quarters with his daughters? In today's world and especially in urban areas, there have been cases where a grown girl goes to live with her father in the city to look for a job while her mother stays in the village. Is there a warning here?

Lot's life vividly demonstrates that a godly upbringing and even a righteous life is not enough if one does not keep in contact with the people of God. He chose to live in Sodom, a town known for its wickedness, and presumably married a woman from that town, and planned to have his daughters marry men from Sodom: people who did not know the Lord. He had an opportunity to leave Sodom after he had been rescued by Abraham (14:12), but he chose not to do so. Nor did he return to Abraham when he lost everything after the destruction of Sodom. Consequently, his daughters, who had been raised in a wicked city, acted in terms of the morality that they had learnt from their contemporaries there. He lost everything: his home, his wealth, his wife, and the respect of his daughters, whose behaviour must have covered him with shame. When we allow our freedom to take precedence over our brotherly responsibilities, the end does not glorify God. Let us pay attention to the grace that the Lord gives us through Jesus Christ our Saviour and live it out deeply in such a way that the fear of God in us overcomes our fear of people and events.

20:1-18 Abraham and Abimelech

Abraham now moved on from the place where he had lived for some time, 'near the great trees of Mamre', which was near Hebron (see 18:1). He moved *into the region of the Negev and lived between Kadesh and Shur. For a while he stayed in Gerar* (**20:1**), where Abimelech was king. The name Abimelech seems to have been the standard title for rulers of the Philistines (equivalent to 'president'). Once again Abraham described his wife as his sister, and *Abimelech sent for Sarah and took her* (**20:2**).

What is the relationship of this incident to the similar one described in Genesis 12:10-20? Some suggest that both these accounts refer to the same incident, arguing that the story was passed along in two different forms in the oral tradition before being written down. But such an interpretation ignores the role of the Holy Spirit, who guarded God's word from error. It also ignores the clear differences between the two incidents. One took place in Egypt, the other in Gerar. One involved Pharaoh, the other Abimelech. In one, Abraham was fleeing from famine; in the other he was moving freely, without any external compulsion. All that they have in common is that both involve Abraham saying that Sarah is his sister and both involve a ruler. Abraham's behaviour is the one consistent factor. He had lied in the past to escape danger from a powerful ruler who was attracted to his wife, and he saw no reason to change his tactics.

The Lord uses different ways to communicate his message. In this case, he used a dream that he sent to Abimelech after he had taken Sarah to be his wife. The dream warned of danger: *You are as good as dead because of the woman you have taken, she is a married woman* (**20:3**). This was very frightening to Abimelech, who seems to have had some idea of the nature of the God that Abraham worshipped. He took pains to explain that he had not intended to sin, but had acted *with a clear conscience and clean hands* (**20:5**). The Lord agrees with Abimelech, and points out that he had intervened to keep him from having sex with Sarah and *sinning against me* (**20:4, 6**). We are not told how the Lord did this, but he may have made Abimelech impotent (**20:17**).

The Lord's tells Abimelech, to *return the man's wife, for he is a prophet and he will pray for you and you will live* (**20:7**). Sins of ignorance may find forgiveness before the Lord, but once the sinner learns that the behaviour is sinful, it must stop. The Lord stated the consequences of failure to obey: *if you do not return her, you may be sure that you and all yours will die.* This message should be heard by anyone who, for any reason, treats someone else's spouse as if his or her own. This includes those employers who threaten to fire female employees if they refuse to sleep with them. Such practices are an abomination to the Lord and such men are 'as good as dead'. They cannot expect any good from the Lord. While God may not punish them and all their people with death as he did in OT times, the effects of the death of a father or mother as punishment from the Lord will be felt by the whole family.

God referred to Abraham as a 'prophet' because he communicated with God on behalf of others. The fact that Abraham was chosen by God to be a blessing to the nations (12:3) qualified him as prophet in this sense. As a prophet, he will pray for Abimelech to receive forgiveness from the Lord, and not death.

Abimelech took the matter very seriously and acted *early the next morning* (**20:8**). His officials, too, were gripped with fear once Abimelech had told them of his encounter with the Lord. They knew that any punishment of Abimelech would also affect them. When the Lord blesses a leader, he blesses the whole nation. When he curses a leader, the curse affects the whole nation. In Africa we have had many leaders whose ways do not please the Lord at all. God cannot bless them, and accordingly we also miss God's blessings. We need leaders who fear God and honour his word (whether through the Scriptures or given to them through dreams).

Abimelech *called Abraham in* and asked why he had *brought such great guilt* upon him and his kingdom (**20:9-10**). Abraham explained his fear of being killed for Sarah (**20:11**) and added, *Beside, she really is my sister, the daughter of my father though not of my mother; and she became my wife* (**20:12**). This is the first time we learn that Sarah was Abraham's half-sister. She has previously been spoken of as Terah's 'daughter-in-law' and 'the wife of his son Abram' (11:31). At that time, it was common for relatives to be married (see also 11:29). Once they were married, their status as husband and wife took precedence over their blood relationship.

Abraham may not technically have told a lie, but his excuse did not justify his action. He was just afraid! He is not alone though. We all do similar things when we are in difficult situations. Instead of admitting that we have done wrong, we try to find any excuses that may have some degree of relevance to the situation.

Abimelech who was already repentant about what had happened, gave Abraham *sheep and cattle and male and female slaves … and he returned Sarah his wife to him* (**20:14**). He also told Abraham, *My land is before you; live wherever you like* (**20:15**). What an offer! Abimelech shows respect for God's prophet, even though Abraham had sinned. Things are often very different today! Now we have armed robbers breaking into pastors' houses and mocking them and the gospel they represent. The robbers do this despite the fact that they have Christian names like John, Paul, Peter and James – which suggest they have had some contact with the church and should know better.

The fact that Abimelech had sinned in ignorance did not mean that the Lord had not punished the sin. He had *closed up every womb in Abimelech's household because of Abraham's wife Sarah* (**20:18**). It was only after Abimelech returned Sarah to Abraham and Abraham prayed for forgiveness that the Lord opened their wombs.

We may never know what role the men and women of God among us play in keeping harm from us. But we owe them due reverence, of the type Abimelech showed to Abraham. And we in turn must pray for God to bring those who are guilty of sin to repentance, and to restore those who are penitent.

21:1-7 Isaac, the Promised Son

When Abraham had entertained the three visitors, the Lord had told him that 'about this time next year … Sarah your wife will have a son' (18:10). Sarah did indeed become pregnant (**21:1-2**). When Abraham was *a hundred years old* (**21:5**) she bore him a son whom they named *Isaac* (**21:3**). Isaac was born twenty-five years after the Lord initially committed himself to blessing Abraham (12:4). God's promises never fail, no matter how long the waiting. The Lord is faithful, and his faithfulness enables us to believe in his almighty power and to trust him in all circumstances.

In obedience to the Lord's command, Abraham circumcised Isaac on the eighth day (**21:4**; 17:12).

When Sarah says that the Lord has brought her laughter (**21:6**), she means that he has turned the pain of waiting for a child into great joy. Whereas she had previously mourned her infertility, now she is rejoicing. She was confident that all others who heard about what had happened would rejoice with her.

21:8-21 Hagar and Ishmael

Blessings can also be a challenge. Abraham now had two sons but all was not well. He had to deal with the family complications that are not uncommon in polygamous marriages.

The problems may have been there all along, but they surfaced at the celebration of the weaning of Isaac (probably when Isaac was about three years old). *Abraham held a great feast* (**21:8**), and at this occasion Sarah noticed that *the son whom Hagar the Egyptian had borne to Abraham was mocking* (**21:9**). If Isaac was three, Ishmael would have been about seventeen years of age (see 16:16; 21:5). He could not accept all the attention Isaac was receiving, either because he had enjoyed this attention alone in the past, or because no such celebration had ever been organized for him.

Ishmael and Hagar had names, but Sarah avoided using them, preferring to speak of *that slave woman and her son*. We too sometimes put labels on people to show how much we dislike them. Such a lack of respect is not right, for we are expected to honour everyone (1 Pet 2:17). Sarah failed in this as she told Abraham to *get rid* of Ishmael and Hagar, *for that slave woman's son will never share in the inheritance with my son Isaac* (**21:10**). Notice how Sarah's attitude has changed. When she give Hagar to Abraham, she said, 'perhaps I can build a family through her' (16:2). When Ishmael was born, we are told that 'Hagar bore Abram a son' (16:15). But now Sarah was adamant that Ishmael would have no share in the estate of his father Abraham. No wonder *the matter distressed Abraham greatly because it concerned his son* (**21:11**)!

The Lord, who knows all things and is concerned about the deepest cares of his people, instructed Abraham to grant Sarah's request because *it is through Isaac that your offspring will be reckoned* (**21:12**). It was not that God did not love Ishmael and his mother or that he liked Sarah's attitude. He was acting to bring order out of the disorder caused by the sin of impatience and to protect his plan for our salvation. God knew that no good training in faith would be possible in a family that was full of this type of conflict.

God did not ignore Ishmael's needs. He had plans for him too. Ishmael too would be blessed, for the Lord said, *I will make the son of the maidservant into a nation also* (**21:13**).

God's promise enabled Abraham to do what had to be done. *Early the next morning, he* gave *food and a skin of water* to Hagar and *sent her off with the boy* (**21:14**). Poor Hagar had no idea where to go – either out of confusion or lack of knowledge. So she *wandered in the desert of Beersheba*. When the water Abraham had given her was finished, she was convinced that her son would die and was in great anguish (**21:15-16**). But there was One who knew where she was all the time. *God heard the boy crying, and the angel of God called to Hagar from heaven* and told her to *lift the boy up … for I will make him into a great nation* (**21:17-18**). Hagar may not have known about the Lord's promise to Abraham (21:13), or may have thought that Abraham was simply trying to give her false hope if he spoke of it. But now she has heard it from the Lord himself. He will make Ishmael into a nation. Once the Lord has spoken, there should be no fear of the hardships on the way. His promise will be fulfilled.

The Lord provided water in the desert for her and the boy (**21:19**). He was also *with the boy as he grew up … and became an archer* (**21:20**). He and his mother lived in the *Desert of Paran* (now the Sinai Peninsula), and *his mother got a wife for him from Egypt,* her home country (**21:21**; 16:1).

In due time Ishmael became the father of the Arab nations. But have things changed to the point that God is no longer with the descendants of Ishmael? Certainly not. God is as much the God of the Arabs as he is the God of the Jews. The problem is not with God's attitude but with the failure of his people to appreciate both the blessings and the limitations God has set. The Lord's blessing for Ishmael was to become a great nation, while for Isaac it was to inherit the Abrahamic covenant.

Today, there is much tension between Arabs and Jews in relation to the land of Israel. It cannot be denied that Israel was Isaac's inheritance, but it is also true that it is wrong to expect Ishmael to live in the desert for ever. These two brother nations need to learn to negotiate so that all can share in the abundance that God supplies.

At a spiritual level, Paul uses the tensions between Hagar and Sarah, and between Ishmael and Isaac, to illustrate the tension between the law of the letter and the law of the Spirit (Gal 4:22-31). Believers are 'sons in freedom'. They obey God, not because they must, but because they love to.

21:22-34 The Treaty with Abimelech

Following the incident involving Abimelech and Sarah, Abimelech allowed Abraham to live wherever he liked in his kingdom (20:15). Over time, Abraham became a power to be reckoned with. Abimelech and *Phicol the commander of his forces* attributed this to God being with Abraham *in everything* he did (**21:22**). What a wonderful testimony! Abimelech, therefore, asked Abraham to swear before God that *you will not deal falsely with me or my children or my descendants* (**21:23**). Abraham had no right not to show kindness to his host Abimelech and his offspring, but Abimelech wanted further assurance, which Abraham was happy to give (**21:24**).

This meeting provided Abraham with an opportunity to complain about *a well of water that Abimelech's servants had seized* (**21:25**). Abimelech claimed not to have heard anything about this trouble before (**21:26**). Abraham wanted something more reassuring than words, so he *brought sheep and cattle and gave them to Abimelech and the two men made a treaty* (**21:27**). It is possible that these animals were cut in two and that Abraham and Abimelech passed between the halves (see 15:9-10, 17-18). Abraham did not want there to be any lurking suspicion that he had stolen the wells and so he *set apart seven ewe lambs from the flock* (**21:28**). When Abimelech asked about them, Abraham asked him to accept them as *a witness that I dug this well* (**21:29-30**). Abraham wanted the deal sealed properly. He wanted to be above reproach. The place was then *called Beersheba* [meaning 'well of the oath'] *because the two men swore an oath there* (**21:31**).

After having been reassured by Abraham that his descendants were safe, and after making the treaty about the well, Abimelech *returned to the land of the Philistines* (**21:32**). At Beersheba Abraham *planted a tamarisk tree*, possibly to commemorate the oath that had been sworn, *and there he called upon the name of the Lord, the Eternal God* (**21:33**). He *stayed in the land of the Philistines for a long time* (**21:34**).

The way Abraham handled this dispute about the well shows that a person of God can be a good businessperson. But it also shows that good business practices are not incompatible with worship of God. Many business people in Africa and beyond can learn from Abraham's example.

22:1-19 Another Test of Faith

The Lord had told Abraham to send Ishmael and Hagar away and to concentrate on Isaac, because 'it is through Isaac that your offspring will be reckoned' (21:12). Now comes the most dramatic test of Abraham's faith in God's word.

Some time later, the Lord told Abraham to *take your son, your only son, Isaac, whom you love, and go to the region of Moriah. Sacrifice him there as a burnt offering on one of the mountains I will tell you about* (**22:1-2**). This command must have been very confusing to Abraham, but he had come to believe that God always knows what he is doing. That same confidence will help us to trust him in all circumstances.

The next morning, Abraham set out for Mount Moriah, taking his son Isaac, two servants and a donkey, which helped carry enough wood for the burnt offering (**22:3**). They travelled for two full days, and *on the third day Abraham looked up and saw the place in the distance* (**22:4**). He knew that if he took his servants up the mountain with him, they would be an obstruction to his doing God's will. So he told them, *stay here with the donkey while I and the boy go over there* (**22:5a**). Doing the will of God may at times require extending the meaning of throwing off everything that hinders us from running the race (Heb 12:1) to include people whom we think may stand between us and the will of God.

Abraham assured the servants, *We will worship and then we will come back to you* (**22:5b**). One wonders what Abraham was thinking of when he said 'we will come back'. Was he anticipating the miracle that would take place?

Leaving his servants behind, Abraham had Isaac carry the wood while he *carried the fire and the knife* (**22:6**). The strangeness of having everything needed for a burnt offering except an animal to sacrifice prompted Isaac to ask, *where is the lamb for the burnt offering?* (**22:7**). It was too early for Abraham to let Isaac know what the plan was, and so he replied, *God himself will provide the lamb for the burnt offering, my son* (**22:8a**). There was no other answer he could give except that God knew what he was doing. All that Abraham did was obey the instructions of God whom he trusted.

After this short exchange, *the two then went on together* (**22:8b**). Though what is meant here is that they walked up the mountain together, as the story continues we note that they were also in agreement that God's will must be done. Isaac did not resist or flee from his aged father when he realized that he was to be the sacrificial lamb. Many years later, the prophet Amos asked, 'Do two walk together unless they have agreed to do so?' (Amos 3:3). The answer expected is 'No'. It is a great blessing when a father/mother and son/daughter are of the same mind in serving God.

When they reached the place for the offering, *Abraham built an altar, arranged the wood,* and then *bound his son Isaac and laid him on the altar, on top of the wood* (**22:9**). What faith! In this act of obedience, Abraham was confessing that the Lord was his God even if this meant that he would be deprived of the son he had waited so long for. Though Isaac is described as 'your son' throughout the account, Abraham knew that this was not the whole story. Isaac was his son from God. Were it not for God, he would not have had him. God wants us to have this perspective on everything we have. It is ours, but is on loan to us from God. When we deny him anything he asks for, we are acting as if it is ours and achieved by our own efforts.

Abraham was just about *to slay his son* when *the angel of the Lord called* him by name, *'Abraham! Abraham!'* and gave the most comforting message, *Do not lay a hand on the boy* (**22:10-12a**). The mystery of this test is explained: *Now I know that you fear God, because you have not withheld from me your son, your only son* (**22:12b**). Our response to the will of God is a clear reflection of whether we fear God or not. Our lives are constantly tested in this regard.

As if Abraham knew what would happen when he told Isaac that the Lord would provide the lamb, the Lord did exactly that. Looking up, Abraham saw in a thicket *a ram caught by its horns. He sacrificed it as a burnt offering instead of his son* (**22:13**). Abraham was willing to offer Isaac, but the Lord spared Isaac for Abraham through the miraculous provision of a lamb. We may not know what tests the Lord may have for us, but if we trust him all the way, we can be sure that what he has planned for us is good and not bad. Sometimes the ways in which he leads us may appear to be very strange, but the Lord sees everything from beginning to end, while we can see only our own present and past.

Abraham gave this place a name: *The Lord Will Provide.* This name stands as a reminder of a wonderful truth: *On the mountain of the Lord it will be provided* (**22:14**). We do not need to go to Mount of Moriah to receive his provision. He can give it to us in our room, under a tree, or in a desert place – wherever it is that we have decided to meet with him in prayer. Let us ask God in faith and let us believe his promise, and wait to see how he will provide.

When the angel of the Lord called Abraham a second time it was to reaffirm God's covenant with him (**22:16**). The Lord swore by his own name since there was no one superior to him by whom he could swear. The Lord's reason for blessing Abraham was *because you have done this and have not withheld your son, your only son* (**22:16**; see also **22:18b**). The Lord's favour should never be taken for granted. In love, the Lord reaffirms his commitment to those who obey him, and in love the same God withholds his

commitment from those who disobey him, until they learn to live in obedience to him.

Three aspects of God's commitment to Abraham are repeated here:

- He is promised many offspring: *I will surely bless you and make your descendants as numerous as the stars in the sky and as the sand on the seashore* (**22:17a**; see 13:16; 15:5).
- He is promised victory: *Your descendants will take possession of the cities of their enemies* (**22:17b**; see 13:15, 17; 17:8).
- He is promised that he will be a blessing: *Through your offspring all nations on earth will be blessed* (**22:18a**; see 12:2-3).

With his mission accomplished and fellowship with the Lord renewed, Abraham *returned to his servants* (**22:19**). Though he had not allowed them to come with him lest they hinder him from doing God's will, they were still important to him. Abraham, Isaac, the two servants and the donkey *set off together for Beersheba,* where Abraham then stayed.

22:20-24 Nahor's Descendants

With Abraham and Sarah having been blessed with Isaac, Abraham was interested to know what had happened in the life of his brother *Nahor.* Of his two brothers, Haran had died (11:28) and Nahor was married to *Milcah,* his niece (11:29). Nahor and Milcah had stayed in Ur of the Chaldeans (11:27-31), although he seems to have later moved to Nahor (24:10). Abraham learned that Milcah had given Nahor eight sons (**22:21-22**). The most important of these sons in the story of the patriarchs was *Bethuel,* for he was *the father of Rebekah,* whom Isaac later married (**22:23**; 24:24). In addition to these eight, Nahor had four other sons from his concubine, *Reumah* (**22:24**).

Rebekah was thus Isaac's first cousin once removed, for her father Bethuel was Isaac's first cousin. This is two or so steps further apart than Abraham and Sarah, who were born of the same father but different mothers (20:12).

23:1-20 Death and Burial of Sarah

In 22:19, we were told that Abraham 'stayed in Beersheba', and in **23:2**, we are told that Sarah *died at Kiriath Arba (that is Hebron)* and *Abraham went to mourn for Sarah and to weep over her.* She died at the age of 127 years (**23:1**). We are not told why Abraham was away when Sarah died, but it could have been that he had several places of residence as he had to move about for the sake of his flocks and herds. He probably had homes in both Beersheba and Hebron.

Abraham owned no land in Hebron, and he could not bury Sarah in land that did not belong to him. So he approached the owners of the land, the Hittites, saying *I am an alien among you. Sell me some property for a burial site here so that I can bury my dead* (**23:3-4**). The Hittites honoured him by referring to him as *a mighty prince among us,* and giving him permission to bury his dead in whichever tomb he chose (**23:5-6**). Abraham requested a specific piece of land – that of *Ephron son of Zoar,* specifically, *the cave of Machpelah* at the end of Ephron's field. He asked the Hittites to intercede with Ephron to sell it to him *for the full price as a burial site* (**23:8-9**).

Ephron addressed Abraham as *my lord* (**23:11a, 15a**), giving another indicator of how much honour Abraham enjoyed among the people. He offered to give Abraham both the field and the cave in it, free of charge (**23:11b**), but Abraham insisted on paying for it (**23:13**). It seems that Abraham generally maintained a philosophy of not accepting anything that someone could later claim had made him rich (14:23). Ephron then gave the price of the land as 400 shekels of silver (10 pounds/4.5 kilograms) (**23:15b**) and Abraham paid him that amount (**23:16**). This exchange was done *in the presence of* and *in the hearing of* the Hittites (**23:10, 18**). They were witnesses to this legal transaction.

Abraham now owned a piece of land – *the field of Machpelah, near Mamre (which is at Hebron) in the land of Canaan* (**23:19**). It was there that he buried Sarah.

While this passage shows the Hittite's respect for Abraham, it also shows the respect that Abraham showed to the Hittites. We are told that he *rose and bowed down before the people of the land, the Hittites* (**23:7, 12**). Abraham was aware that God would give him this land, but he saw no reason to hurry. He waited for God's timing. Meanwhile he respected the Hittite's ownership of it. Abraham knew how to wear a crown without pride.

24:1-67 Isaac's Marriage

Abraham was *old and well advanced in years* and *the Lord had blessed him in every way* (**24:1**). But the one task that still remained was to arrange a wife for Isaac. He assigned this responsibility to *the chief servant of his household* (**24:2a**). The seriousness with which Abraham wanted his chief servant to take the matter is shown by his having the servant put his hand under Abraham's thigh, and then *swear by the Lord, the God of heaven and the God of the earth* (**24:2b-3a, 9**). The content of the oath was *you will not get a wife for my son from the daughters of the Canaanites … but will go to my country and my own relatives and get a wife for my son Isaac* (**24:3b-4**). Abraham did not send his servant to just any location, but specified that he had to go to Abraham's birthplace and look for a bride among Abraham's relatives.

Did Abraham lay down this requirement purely because he wanted someone from his own culture for his son? Can this ancient practice of marrying half-sisters (Abraham and Sarah), nieces (Nahor and Milcah) and cousins (Isaac and Rebekah) be used to justify marriages between close relatives today? Certainly, in some African cultures, these marriages would not be tolerated, for even persons from the same clan are forbidden to marry each other. When trying to answer these questions, we need to consider why Abraham was so set on finding a bride for his son from his own family. The answer seems to be linked to the same principle that would later be expressed in the instruction not to be 'yoked together with unbelievers' (2 Cor 6:14). Abraham wanted his son's wife to be a woman who had, or could be easily helped to have, some fear of God, as opposed to a Canaanite woman (24:3). The increasing moral decline in Canaan was bringing the area to the point where it was under the threat of God's judgment. It could be assumed that Canaanite girls would not know the Lord. But God's promise required a community that was faithful to the Lord, and the wife would have to have an important role in passing on this belief. Thus Abraham sought a marriage for his son in which all parties would remain faithful to the promise in order to pass it on.

The chief servant raised the issue of what he should do if the woman refused to come to Canaan – should he then take Isaac to her (**24:5**)? Abraham's response was an emphatic 'no' (**24:6, 8b**). He was confident that God would *send his angel before you* and provide a willing bride (**24:7**). But if it proved to be the case that no woman was prepared to come to Canaan, the servant would *be released from this oath* (**24:8a**).

With this understanding, the servant *set out for Aram Naharaim and made his way to the town of Nahor* in Mesopotamia. He took with him *all kinds of good things* from his master, setting them on *ten of his master's camels* (**24:10**). The narrative stresses that all he took was from his master and he was on his master's mission. If we relate this to our being sent out on a mission by our heavenly master, the focus all the time should be on our master and not on ourselves. We own nothing, and our entire mission is on behalf of our master.

It was towards evening when the servant arrived at the town of Nahor. This was an important time of the day for it was when *the women go out to draw water* (**24:11**). Abraham's servant *had the camels kneel down near the well outside the town.* He then prayed, imploring God to help him find the right wife for Isaac. Those who are single and longing for a spouse should follow his example. Rather than rushing into a hasty choice, we should call on the Lord to lead us to the right person.

The servant's prayer is a model for us in that it is focused, urgent, and selfless. He asks to *show kindness* to his master Abraham (**24:12**). It is also uttered in confidence that the Lord controls all events and that he will order them to bless his servant Abraham. Given this confidence, he asks the Lord for a sign: *May it be that when I say to a girl, 'Please let down your jar that I may drink,' and she says, 'Drink, and I will water your camels too' – let her be the one you have chosen for your servant Isaac* (**24:14**). When there is intimacy with the Lord, we can faithfully ask him for guidance. Such confidence in the Lord will prevent us from assuming something is so when the signs show it is not.

The type of sign asked for was also significant. He did not ask for just any sign, like 'a young woman carrying a black water jug', or 'the woman who greets me first'. The sign he asked for was one that would identify important qualities when it came to married life. The servant was looking for someone who had a heart for hospitality and service to others. She would be eager to serve and would take the initiative, being ready to go further than the minimum requested. Drawing water for ten camels would be a hard task, and by offering to do it the girl would show that she was hard working and not lazy. These were all qualities that the servant wanted in Isaac's wife.

God has promised, 'Call to me and I will answer you and tell you great and unsearchable things you do not know' (Jer 33:3) and has said: 'Before they call I will answer; while they are still speaking I will hear' (Isa 65:24). He fulfilled these promises in this situation, for before the servant had even *finished praying, Rebekah came out with her jar on her shoulder* (**24:15a**). She fitted all of Abraham's requirements (24:4). *She was the daughter of Bethuel son of Milcah, who was the wife of Abraham's brother Nahor* (**24:15b**; 22:22-23). She was also *very beautiful* and *a virgin* (**24:16**). Above all, she met every detail of the test Abraham's servant had set in his prayer. He asked her for water to drink (**24:17**) and *she quickly lowered her jar and gave him a drink,* referring to him as *my lord* (**24:18**). She then went ahead, with no further request from Abraham's servant, to give water to the camels also (**24:19-20**). We are told that Abraham's servant *watched her closely to learn whether or not the Lord had made his journey successful* (**24:21b**). This is a very important element when we are seeking a sign for guidance. Every detail must fit in properly to avoid taking the resemblance of a thing for the thing itself. The servant also did this *without saying a word* (**24:21a**) probably both due to his amazement at the speed at which his prayer was answered and also so as not to influence how things turned out.

When it was all done, Abraham's servant was so convinced that the Lord had spoken that *he took out a gold nose ring weighing a beka* (1/5 ounces, 6 grams) *and two gold bracelets weighing ten shekels* (4 ounces, 115 grams) (**24:22**), and put these on Rebekah (**24:47b**) after finding out who she was (**24:23-24, 47a**). These gifts could probably have been explained as tokens of appreciation for her kind service, but the servant had more than that in his mind.

His question whether there was room at Rebekah's father's house (24:23) was met with expression of great hospitality: *We have plenty of straw and fodder, as well as room for you to spend the night* (**24:25**). There was room not only for Abraham's servant and the men with him (24:32b, 54, 59c), but also for the camels. Everything was so amazing

that Abraham's servant *bowed down and worshipped the Lord,* for his *kindness and faithfulness* to Abraham and for guiding his servant (**24:26-27**). Here is a challenge to all of us. When the Lord answers our prayers, we tend to be so carried away with joy that we forget to worship and praise the giver.

As Abraham's servant worshipped, Rebekah was already on her way home to break the news to her *mother's household* (**24:28**). Laban, Rebekah's brother, hearing the story and seeing the nose ring and bracelets on Rebekah's arms, *hurried out* and found the man *standing by the camels near the spring* (**24:29-30**). This was sensible. He needed someone more senior than the hospitable Rebekah to invite him. Laban did exactly that: *Come, you who are blessed by the Lord. Why are you standing out here? I have prepared the house and a place for the camels* (**24:31**).

The camels were unloaded and straw and fodder given to them, water was given to Abraham's servant and his men to wash their feet, and food was brought (**24:32-33**). Abraham's servant, however, had his priorities right, and refused to eat until he had explained his mission. He told everything, introducing himself as *Abraham's servant,* and then stating how God had blessed Abraham, Abraham's wish to have a wife for Isaac, his meeting Rebekah at the well, including all that had happened there (**24:34-48**), and finished with the words, *Now if you will show kindness and faithfulness to my master, tell me so I may know which way to turn* (**24:49**).

Abraham's servant could not have hoped for better response than the one given by Laban and Bethuel: *This is from the Lord, we can say nothing to you one way or the other. Here is Rebekah; take her and go, and let her become the wife of your master's son, as the Lord has directed* (**24:50-51**). Laban and Bethuel knew that when it is the Lord's doing, we have no business giving our opinion. All there is for us to do is accept it.

After receiving such a positive response, Abraham's servant *bowed down to the ground before the Lord* (**24:52b**), and distributed the gifts he had brought from his master. To Rebekah he gave *gold and silver jewellery and articles of clothing,* and to her brother and mother *costly gifts* (**24:53**). Only then did Abraham's servant and the men with him eat and drink (**24:54a**). What dedication to duty! Their personal needs were ignored until the master's business had been accomplished. They then *spent the night there.*

Getting up the next day, Abraham's servant was ready to return to his master, not only with the good news, but also with the bride he had come to find (**24:54b**). As would be expected for people who love each other, Rebekah's departure would produce feelings of loss, so *her brother and her mother* requested that Rebekah stay with them for another *ten days or so* (**24:55**). But Abraham's servant was anxious to be off (**24:56**) and so Laban and Rebekah's mother suggested, *Let us call the girl and ask her about it* (**24:57**). When she was asked, *Will you go with this man?* Rebekah replied, *I will go* (**24:58**). It was not the wishes of her brother or mother or of Abraham's servant that prevailed here, but those of Rebekah. She had an important role to play in the whole affair. Here is a reminder for parents and guardians that when it comes to the matter of marriage, the wishes of the future wife or husband are of first importance.

It is worth noting that this marriage involves more than just the couple involved. The marriage proposal is presented to the family for approval. It is a matter for the whole community, and it is the parents who give their daughter in marriage – just as the Creator gave Eve to Adam (Gen 2:22). But Rebekah herself has a voice. She, and not her parents, commits herself to the marriage. Parents should listen very carefully to their children when arranging marriages, and allow them to say 'yes' or 'no' and assume responsibility for all the consequences. Forced marriage is a sin before God.

Abraham's servant set out on the road home, accompanied by Rebekah, her nurse, her maids, and a prayer of blessing for many offspring and victory over their enemies (**24:59-61**).

Isaac who was forty years old (25:20) and living in the Negev had *come from Beer Lahai Roi,* the place where God had once met with Hagar (**24:62**; 16:14). He was out in the field meditating when he *saw camels approaching* (**24:63**). Rebekah saw Isaac hurrying towards them and asked, *Who is that man in the field coming to meet us?* (**24:64**). On being told that this was her future husband, she *took her veil and covered herself* (**24:65**). This veil would have covered not only the face but also the rest of her body, and would have been the culturally appropriate dress for a bride when first meeting her husband. She would have to live with this man for the rest of her life, and she wanted to make the correct impression at the outset.

Isaac was told about all that had happened, and then he brought her *into the tent of his mother Sarah, and he married Rebekah* (**24:66-67a**). Here was a marriage that God had been central to, and yet we see no elaborate ceremonies to celebrate it. We need to watch the elaborate marriage customs that we in Africa have adopted lest they become unnecessary financial burdens to many while they are not what matters most. What mattered was that Rebekah *became his wife, and he loved her* (**24:67b**).

It is also worth noting that this marriage was made in sexual purity. Isaac did not have intercourse with Rebecca until after their marriage: the expression *he loved her* is used here to mean the sexual act (24:67b). This was what used to happen in traditional African societies, where the first sexual act took place at the home of the young woman's parents on the evening after the wedding ceremony. If she proved to be a virgin, everyone was happy. If not, there was shame and sadness.

Becoming a wife meant agreeing to live in submission to the husband. Rebekah accepted this, and this in conjunction with Isaac's love made it a happy marriage (see Eph 5:22-33). As a result, *Isaac was comforted after his mother's death* (**24:67c**). Isaac was a fulfilled man, and by implication Rebekah was a happy wife. Many marriages today fail to be like theirs. Unless each party plays his or her role as the Lord would want it, the harmony the Lord desires in marriage is lacking. Instead of comfort, there is stress and unhappiness.

This story of the choice of a partner and a wedding ceremony is presented in a language and with symbolic acts that would have had meaning in the culture of the time. It would have been clear that all that was done was for the glory of God. This key principle would have remained in the memories of all concerned to encourage them to grow in knowing the Lord. May the same be true when we tell the story of our courtships and marriages to our descendants!

25:1-11 Abraham's Death

Presumably, after the death of Sarah (23:2), and not before (although we cannot be certain of this), *Abraham took another wife, whose name was Keturah* (**25:1**). She bore him six sons, and possibly some daughters (**25:3**). With Isaac and Ishmael, therefore, Abraham had eight sons. He *left everything he owned to Isaac* (**25:5**) but *gave gifts to the sons of his concubines* (**25:6a**), who were presumably the sons of Hagar and Keturah (even though Keturah is referred to as his wife in 25:1). Concubines had a lower status than a regular wife. They had no legal rights beyond the right to live with the husband. By contrast, the regular wife and her children were entitled to inherit the husband's property.

Abraham wisely settled the matter of his property while *he was still living* and sent the concubines' sons away *from Isaac to the land of the east* (**25:6b**). Therefore, when he died, *an old man and full of years* (**25:8**), his house was well set to avoid disputes. This is what a good father should do. By giving all that he owned to Isaac, he was not expressing favouritism but doing the Lord's will. The Lord had specified that Isaac was to inherit Abraham's estate (17:19b; 21:13b).

Abraham was buried by *his sons Isaac and Ishmael* (**25:9a**). Though Ishmael was older than Isaac (17:25; 18:10), Isaac is mentioned first because he was the one chosen by God to continue the line of blessings. They buried him *with his wife Sarah* (**25:10**), who had died 38 years earlier, *in the cave of Machpelah near Mamre, in the field of Ephron son of Zohar the Hittite* (**25:9b**). Abraham had bought this field from the Hittites (25:10a; 23:3-20), and so he was buried in his own land. With Abraham dead, the focus now shifts to Isaac, whom God blessed. He lived near *Beer Lahai Roi* (**25:11**; 24:62).

25:12-18 Ishmael's Descendants

Though Ishmael was not the one chosen to be the line of blessing, the Lord had assured both Abraham and Hagar that he would bless him and make Ishmael into a nation (21:13, 18). He lived to the age of 137 years and had twelve sons (**25:13-15**). The twelve sons also represent *twelve tribal rulers according to their settlements and camps* (**25:16**). They settled *in the area from Havilah to Shur, near the border of Egypt, as you go toward Asshur.* There they *lived in hostility toward all their brothers* (**25:18**). The hostility we see between Israel and the Arab world is, therefore, not a new phenomenon.

25:19-28:9 Isaac

25:19-34 Two Sons: Jacob and Esau

The history of a new generation begins with the words: *This is the account of Abraham's son Isaac* (**25:19a**; see 11:27). The details of Isaac's father, wife and her father and brother are repeated (**25:19b-20**, see 21:3; 22:23; 24:29, 67). These details are important in identifying Isaac and his descendants fully – from both paternal and maternal sides. Isaac's clan was 'Abrahamites' and his wife's clan was 'Bethuelites'. Kinship was very important in the biblical world, as it is in Africa. Among the Kamba of Kenya, for example, as soon as a visitor settles down, the first question will be *Wi mwau?* ['What are you?'], asking for your clan. The second question is *Wi mwivwa kwaau?* ['What is your mother's clan']. If there is the slightest link between the visitor and his or her host, it warms up the whole atmosphere. If the two happen to be from the same clan, they regard each other almost as brother or sister.

Like Isaac's mother, his wife was barren. He married when he was forty years old (25:20) and was blessed with his first-born twins only at the age of sixty (**25:26b**). These came as a result of prayer, for we are told, *Isaac prayed to the Lord on behalf of his wife, because she was barren. The Lord answered his prayer, and his wife Rebekah became pregnant* (**25:21**). Isaac had learned a lesson from his father – faith in the God of the covenant. His wait for a child, however, was not as long as Abraham's. The Lord does not allow more than we can endure. And the tests that he gives us aim at different purposes for each of us.

Rebekah had an uncomfortable pregnancy, and she asked the Lord what was going on and why *the babies jostled each other within her* (**25:22**). His reply was that each of the two babies in her womb would become the ancestor of a different nation. One of these groups would *be stronger than the other.* In her culture, as in most African cultures, the older son would be expected to lead the younger, but when it came to Rebekah's children, *the older will serve the younger* (**25:23**). As always happens, in Africa, when the younger asserts himself or herself over the older, there is conflict, and that conflict was already taking place in Rebekah's womb. One wonders whether Rebekah told Isaac what the Lord had told her. If she did, one must also wonder why Isaac later chose to bless Esau and not Jacob.

When her *twin boys* were born (**25:24**), they were given names that derived from the circumstances of their birth, just as many African children are. The first one was named Esau, which means 'hairy', because he *was red, and his whole body was like a hairy garment* (**25:25**). The second one *came out, with his hand grasping Esau's heel* and he was named *Jacob* (**25:26a**). His grasping at his brother's heel was taken as evidence that he would be in hot pursuit of his brother. But figuratively, this expression also means 'deceiver'.

As the two boys grew up, they developed very different personalities. *Esau became a skilful hunter, a man of the open country.* This characteristic appealed to his father, *who had a taste for wild game*, which his hunter son was able to satisfy. Jacob was the opposite: *a quiet man, staying among the tents.* Rebekah probably loved Jacob because the stay-at-home boy was always there to help her (**25:27**). The differences between their sons did not help Isaac and Rebekah's marriage. They became a divided couple, with Isaac loving Esau and Rebekah loving Jacob (**25:28**). God had answered Isaac and Rebekah's prayers and given them what they asked for. But the gift was not wisely managed and sowed division in their household.

Families today can end up with similar divisions. It is important that parents do not simply favour the child who meets their own needs. Instead, 'Isaacs' should love their 'Jacobs' for being of so much help to their mother, and 'Rebekahs' should love their 'Esaus' for giving their 'father' his favourite meal. While it was true that Jacob had been chosen by God, Isaac and Rebekah should not have intensified the rift between their sons.

We are shown one incident in their lives that prepares us for what will come when Jacob gets Isaac's blessing (27:1-29). One day *Jacob was cooking some stew* and *Esau came in from the open country, famished* (**25:29**). Ravenously hungry, Esau immediately asked Jacob for some of his *red stew* (**25:30**). Jacob, recognizing that he had the upper hand, threatened not to give him any unless Esau sold him his birthright (**25:31**). This birthright was probably a double portion of whatever was inherited from their father (Deut 21:17) and the right to assume leadership of the family (27:29). Esau carelessly responded, *Look, I am about to die. What good is the birthright to me?* (**25:32**). Jacob made him swear an oath giving his birthright to Jacob, and then fed him a hearty dish of *bread and some lentil stew* (**25:33-34a**). He had obtained the birthright at a bargain price.

This interaction between the brothers illustrates the way divisions between parents affect relations between children. These two brothers bargain with each other for favours and see each other as rivals, rather than showing the sort of brotherly love the Lord intended families to display.

But the incident also shows that Esau lacked the responsibility to inherit the promise made to Abraham and to pass it on faithfully to his children. He allowed the needs of his stomach to take precedence over the more important things in his life. This choice was immortalized in the other name by which Esau and his descendants came to be known: Edom. Edom means 'red', and Esau sold his birthright in exchange for some 'red stew' (25:30, 36:1).

Though the NT stressed God's free choice of Jacob over Esau (see Rom 9:10-13), this incident highlights the other side of the story – human responsibility. It cannot be denied that *Esau despised his birthright* (**25:34b**; Heb 12:16-17). There is a tension between God's choice of Jacob and Esau's responsibility for freely selling his birthright. In the same way, God's grace draws us to Jesus for salvation (John 6:44), but at the same time, it remains our duty to believe (John 3:16).

We must not think that God needed this sort of conflict in Isaac and Rebekah's home in order to accomplish his plans (25:23). He does not lead us into sin to achieve his ends. God would have fulfilled his plan whatever the conditions in Isaac's home. Whether the family was united or divided made no difference to him, because he is all-powerful and sovereign.

26:1-33 Isaac and the Philistines

The story of Isaac and Abimelech has many similarities with the stories of his father's problems with Pharaoh (12:10-20) and Abimelech (20:1-18). But the author of Genesis is quick to tell us that this was a different incident, stressing that the famine that prompted Isaac's move was a different famine to *the earlier famine of Abraham's time* (**26:1a**; 12:10). Israel is a dry country, particularly in the area around Beer Lahai Roi in the Negev where Isaac lived (24:62; 25:11b), and thus it is not surprising that famine would strike again.

It appears that Isaac considered going to Egypt as his father had done. Egypt was a prosperous country in ancient times, and the abundance of water in the Nile meant that it was spared the worst of famines. However, the Lord explicitly told Isaac not to *go down to Egypt* (**26:2**) but to stay in the land of Canaan (**26:3**). God may have said this to avoid Isaac experiencing the same difficulties as his father had in Egypt. God may have wanted Isaac to stay in Canaan because that would be the place where the promise to give this land to him and to his descendants to be fulfilled. He also reminded Isaac of the importance of obedience: the promise had first been made to Abraham because he *obeyed me and kept my requirements, my commands, my decrees, and my laws* (**26:4-5**). Obedience is an essential part of God's covenant with humanity. God commits himself to fulfil his

promises, but he also expects his people to live in obedience to him. Abraham had done this – to the benefit of Isaac and his descendants (**26:24c**). We, too, should not take our relationship with God carelessly, not only for our own sakes but also for that of our children. While they will not be saved simply because we are saved, they will also enjoy the blessings we are given by God.

So instead of going to Egypt, Isaac *went to Abimelech king of the Philistines in Gerar* (**26:1b, 6**). Abraham had gone to the same place in 20:1, where he too had met with an Abimelech (the standard title for the kings of that region).

Like his mother Sarah, Isaac's wife Rebekah was also beautiful (**26:7**; see 12:11, 14; 24:16). And like his father before him, Isaac was nervous when moving into a new situation with such a beautiful wife (12:12; 20:11). Taking a leaf from his father's book, he felt that the safest way to avoid trouble because of her was to claim that she was a blood relative. In that way, the worst that would happen would be that someone might ask to marry her. There would be no need to murder her husband before doing so (as later happened to Uriah the Hittite – 2 Sam 11). Therefore, when the men of Gerar asked Isaac about Rebekah, he said, *She is my sister* (see 12:12; 20:11). Unlike Sarah, who was indeed Abraham's half-sister (20:12), Rebekah was only Isaac's first cousin once removed.

But there was no need for this deceit. No one tried to take Rebekah as Sarah had been taken in Egypt (12:15b) and in Gerar (20:2b). Isaac lived safely in Gerar for a long time, until one day Abimelech, looking through a window, *saw Isaac caressing his wife Rebekah* (**26:8**). In that culture, such caresses meant only one thing: Rebekah was Isaac's wife, not his sister.

Abimelech summoned Isaac, confronted him, heard his excuses, and expressed his displeasure because such an act could have *brought guilt* to his people (**26:9-10**). But instead of punishing Isaac, he *gave orders to all the people* saying, *Anyone who molests this man or his wife shall surely be put to death* (**26:11**). This must have been the Lord's doing. The hearts of kings are under his control. Thanks be to God for his grace by which he covers over our failures and still watches over us. If the Lord treated us on the basis of our goodness, who would stand!

This disclosure of Rebekah's status and Abimelech's favourable orders, gave Isaac a free hand to do what he wanted without fear. He *planted crops in that land and the same year reaped a hundredfold, because the Lord blessed him* (**26:12**). No matter the weather or other enemies of crops, where the hand of the Lord is, there is bound to be a good harvest. 'Seek first his kingdom and his righteousness, and all these things will be given to you as well' (Matt 6:33) expresses an eternal principle. The Lord blesses those who place their trust in him.

Isaac was at Gerar because the Lord had ordered him to stay there for a while, saying *and I will be with you and will bless you* (26:3a). He is thus in the Lord's place, at the Lord's time and for the Lord's purpose. So the Lord looked after him and *his wealth continued to grow until he became very wealthy* (**26:13**). Isaac might have thought that he would become rich by going to the rich country of Egypt and distancing himself from Canaan. But the Lord gave him far more than he would have found in Egypt because he trusted the Lord and listened to him. It is an important step of faith in a difficult test such as a famine! When tests come, let us be patient (see Rom 12:12) and discern God's ways so as to act wisely rather than rushing to easy solutions.

Isaac acquired *so many flocks and herds and servants that the Philistines envied him* (**26:14**). We should think of how some people might react if someone who came to our country as a refugee rapidly became one of the richest men in it. The Philistines expressed their envy by trying to deprive Isaac of water for his animals. They *stopped up* the wells that Abraham's servants had dug, *filling them with earth* (**26:15**). Besides depriving him of water, their actions would also have checked Isaac's popularity by destroying the wells that reminded the people of Isaac's father, Abraham, and his greatness. Isaac's wealth became such a threat that Abimelech told him, *Move away from us; you have become too powerful for us* (**26:16**). The man who had arrived in Gerar fearing that he would be killed was now 'too powerful' for the people of Gerar as a whole. Small beginnings should never be despised when the Lord's hand is in them.

Isaac was someone whose spirit could not be destroyed no matter how he was handled. So he moved away from the town and settled in *the Valley of Gerar* (**26:17**). There he *reopened the wells that had been dug during the time of Abraham* but which the Philistines had *stopped them up after Abraham died*. As he reopened them, *he gave them the same names his father had given them* (**26:18**). In other words, Isaac kept the memory of Abraham alive. He respected his origins and incorporated them in his own identity.

It seems that the existing wells in the Valley of Gerar did not provide very good water. So with some digging, Isaac's servants *discovered a well of fresh water there* (**26:19**). As would be expected with jealous neighbours, *the herdsmen of Gerar quarrelled with Isaac's herdsmen* claiming that the water was theirs. Isaac *named the well Esek* (**26:20**) which would remind him that it was the 'well of dispute', and looked for another one. He found another one, and the herdsmen of Gerar claimed it too. Isaac *named it Sitnah* (**26:21**), that is 'the well of opposition', and looked for another. At last he dug a well one that no one quarrelled over. This one he called *Rehoboth, which* means 'room', thus 'the well of ample room'. He said, *Now the Lord has given us room and we will flourish in the land* (**26:22**).

We see here a movement from dispute to opposition to the Lord giving room. Dispute is normal given that people are different and perceive things differently. As the Kamba (Kenya) say: *Mathoka me kyondoni kimwe mailea ukalany'a* ['axes in the same basket will not fail to knock each other']. Opposition, however, is an organized attempt to frustrate someone. But Paul reminds us, it is when we are weak that we really see the power of God when he acts (2 Cor 12:7-10). Isaac avoided pointless disputes, concentrated on his work and persevered while facing the difficulties created for him. And despite the opposition, the Lord provided a well that Isaac's herdsmen could use. At times it is pointless to fight over things. It is more honourable to move on and explore new places. The Lord always makes room for those who act for his glory.

From the Valley of Gerar Isaac went to *Beersheba,* where Abraham had also lived (**26:23**; 22:19b). There the Lord appeared to Isaac and assured him of his presence and blessing. At least three things stand out from what the Lord told Isaac:

- *I am the God of your father Abraham* (**26:24a**). God is not just identifying himself; he is also reaffirming his commitment. As the Lord was with Abraham, so he will be with Isaac. As his power was seen in the life of Abraham, so it will also it be seen in the life of Isaac.
- *Do not be afraid, for I am with you* (**26:24b**). Given the opposition that Isaac just received from the herdsmen of Gerar, he had reason to be afraid. However, with the Lord on his side, he had no cause to fear. God had spoken much the same words to Abraham (15:1) after he came from pursuing and defeating Kedorlaomer and his allies (14:13-16). Such moments of tensions are characterized by some fear of what could come next. The Lord visits those he cares for and assures them of his presence.
- *I will bless you and will increase the number of your descendants for the sake of my servant Abraham* (**26:24c**). The Lord reaffirms his promise to Abraham (12:2; 15:5; 17:5-6) and to Isaac also (26:4). He knows our weaknesses, and comes to encourage us when we could easily be discouraged. He does not so much tell us something new as remind us of his promises we already know.

In response, *Isaac built an altar there and called on the name of the Lord* (**26:25**). It was time to worship God, who is always present and reassuring. It is a wonderful thing to 'walk with God'. Isaac *pitched his tent* there and his servants dug yet another well.

As these things were happening, *Abimelech,* escorted by *Ahuzzath his personal advisor and Phicol the commander of his forces* (**26:26**) came to Isaac, requesting him to make a covenant with them for their protection. Abimelech began by saying, *We saw clearly that the Lord was with you* (**26:28a**). They have been observing not only Isaac's increasing prosperity but also Isaac's God in action in his life. This made them fear Isaac, so they said, *There ought to be a sworn agreement between us … Let us make a treaty with you that you will do us no harm'* (**26:28b-29a**). A sworn treaty had unpleasant consequences for anyone who broke the agreement. Abimelech thought this would keep them safe from any possible attacks by Isaac. Abimelech reminded Isaac of what he had personally done for him: *we did not molest you but always treated you well and sent you away in peace* (**26:29b**; 29:11). Abimelech's closing words, *And now you are blessed by the Lord* show that he saw their kind treatment of Isaac as the foundation upon which the Lord had built to bless Isaac.

Isaac's initial greeting to Abimelech: *Why have you come to me since you were hostile to me and sent me away?* (**26:27**) refers to his experience with the herdsmen in Gerar. Abimelech was not without blame, for he was the one who had initially asked Isaac to leave (26:16). But it was true that Isaac had experienced kind treatment as well as hostility. He had received kind treatment when he was a nobody, but hostility when he became a threat. Overall though, Abimelech had been good to Isaac.

Isaac agreed to their request. He made *a feast for them and they ate and drank* (**26:30**). Then *early the next morning the men swore an oath to each other* (**26:31**). When it was done, *Isaac sent them on their way, and they left him in peace.*

Though Abimelech came because he was afraid of Isaac, the Lord planned it so that it would also give Isaac some peace of mind. Just before Abimelech and his team arrived, the Lord had spoken to Isaac and assured him of his presence, encouraging him not to be afraid. The Lord at times uses not defeat of our enemies but peace with our enemies as a way of protecting us. There are many blessings when we live in peace with everyone (Rom 12:18).

The Lord was looking after Isaac not only in his external relationships but also in his daily needs. The same day he made a covenant with Abimelech, his servants came with good news *about the well they had dug.* They said, *'We've found water!'* (**26:32**). Their excitement shows how urgent their need for water was. As the Kamba (Kenya) say, *vala yikaw'a tivo ivalukaa* ['where something (or somebody) is thrown is not where it lands']. The herdsmen of Gerar may have thought that they had forced Isaac out into a dry area, but even there, blessings waited for him. Isaac called this well *Shibah*, which probably means 'oath', and the town that grew up next to it came to be called *Beersheba*, meaning 'well of the oath'(**26:33**).

26:34-35 Esau's Marriage

Esau married two women: *Judith daughter of Beeri and Basemath daughter of Elon,* both Hittites. Isaac had been guided by his faithful father Abraham in his choice of a wife, but Esau did not follow his example. We do not know whether this was because Isaac had neglected to look for

a good wife for Esau, as Abraham did for him (24:1-66), or whether Esau simply desired to be independent and make his own choice, or whether he did it in anger after he had not received the blessing. At the age of forty (**26:34**), a man can be helped by his father only if he is prepared to accept such help (Isaac, too, had been forty when he married – 25:20.)

Esau made a bad choice, not necessarily because his wives were Hittites, but because *they were a source of grief to Isaac and Rebekah* (**26:35**). Their being Hittite may have contributed to this, but their personalities must also have played a role. With so little said on the matter, it is difficult to answer all the questions we may have. But one thing the passage does do is remind us of the importance of living well with fathers- and mothers-in-law. We should strive to be a source of joy and not a source of grief to them.

27:1-29 Esau's Blessing Given to Jacob

The deception recorded in this chapter was possible only because Isaac was *old and his eyes so weak that he could no longer see* (**27:1**). He knew that death was near and wanted to give Esau his blessing before he died. But before he gave the blessing he wanted to have one more taste of his favourite meal (**27:2**). So he told Esau to go out and *hunt some wild game … and bring it to me to eat, so that I may give you my blessing before I die* (**27:3-4**). Esau obediently set off to hunt in the open country (**27:5b**).

Rebekah had overheard Isaac's instructions to Esau (**27:5a**). She was determined that her favourite would receive the blessing (25:28). Her determination may have been strengthened by her memory of the prophecy that accompanied the twin's birth (25:23) and possibly by knowledge about the sale of Esau's birthright (25:29-34). But even if these were factors, she was wrong to assume that God would approve of unethical tactics to accomplish his will.

Informing Jacob of what was going on, she instructed him, *bring me two choice young goats, so that I can prepare some tasty food for your father, just the way he likes it. Then take it to your father to eat, so that he may give you his blessing, before he dies'* (**27:6-10**).

Jacob, who had earlier encouraged Esau to sell his birthright by buying it from him, had no objection to the idea of deceiving his father and cheating his brother. But he did raise one technical problem: *Esau is a hairy man, and I'm a man with smooth skin. What if my father touches me? I would appear to be tricking him and would bring down a curse on myself rather than a blessing* (**27:11-12**). Rebekah confidently dismissed that problem with, *My son, let the curse fall on me* and then insisted, *Just do what I say; go and get them for me* (**27:13**).

Jacob did as he was told, and Rebekah quickly prepared *tasty food, just the way his father liked it* (**27:14**). To complete the deception, she dressed Jacob in Esau's *best clothes* and then smoothed the skin of the slaughtered goat over the only exposed parts of his body (**27:15-16**). As the saying goes, the worst enemy is the one who knows you best. Rebekah certainly knew which details Isaac would notice and planned to address them all. The only problem that she could not solve was the difference between Esau's and Isaac's voices (**27:22**).

This incident reveals a lot about Rebekah's character. We saw her determination, courage and ability to act quickly in her decision to leave immediately with Abraham's servant (24:54-58) and she shows the same characteristics here. She was determined to have her way when it came to the blessing and she acted quickly and with real ingenuity when she realized that Esau was about to get the blessing. She knew that she had to have the meal and the ceremony completed before Esau's returned. She also showed reckless courage in attempting a plan that could have disastrous consequences if anything went wrong (27:13).

Having prepared the food, Rebekah handed it to Jacob who took it to his father, pretending to be Esau (27:14, 17, 19). But several things puzzled Isaac. He asked, *How did you find it so quickly, my son?* (**27:20a**). Jacob, who was already sinning by pretending to be who he was not (**27:19, 24**; Exod 20:16), did not hesitate to lie: *The Lord your God gave me success* (**27:20b**). Not only was this a lie, but he was also misusing the name of God (Exod 20:7). The blind Isaac was aware that there was something odd about the voice he was hearing, but his senses of touch (**27:21-23**) and smell (**27:27**) confirmed that the one before him must be Esau. Probably, Isaac could not even have imagined that his wife would deceive him in such a serious matter. As we read this story we start to ask ourselves, 'Is it safe to trust anyone?' But possibly an even better question might be, 'Can I be trusted?'

Isaac used his senses of hearing, touch, taste, and smell as best he could, but he was still tricked. He heard right – the voice was truly Jacob's – but this was not enough; he touched right – the hands were hairy like Esau's; he tasted right – the food was as he liked it; and he smelled right – the smell was that of Esau. However, what he touched was not Esau's hands but goatskin; what he ate was not wild game but goats from his own flock; and what he smelled was not Esau but Esau's clothes. Any of us can be tricked as Isaac was. What a challenge not to lean on our own understanding (see Prov 3:5)! When we rely on God, who sees through human deceptions, we can be certain of safety. But we should also work to create a culture of honesty among all those with whom we come in contact. The fewer tricksters there are in the world, the less the chance that any one of us will fall victim to them.

Completely deceived, Isaac ate and drank (**27:25**) and then said, *Come here, my son, and kiss me* (**27:26**). Jacob went and kissed him, and then when Isaac *caught the smell of his clothes, he blessed him* (**27:27a**). The blessing took the form of a prayer, for Isaac acknowledged that only the Lord can make any blessing effective. The key blessings he gave to Isaac were

- Satisfaction: the smell of his son is like *the smell of a field that the Lord has blessed* (**27:27b**).
- Provision – material wealth: *heavens dew … earth's richness – an abundance of grain and new wine* (**27:28**).
- Promotion – greatness: *may nations serve you …and may the sons of your mother bow down to you* (**27:29a**).
- Protection: *those who curse you be cursed and those who bless you be blessed* (**27:29b**).

These are blessings that any satisfied and happy father would wish to give to his child, and are ones that the Lord will impart to those who honour their fathers and mothers (Exod 20:12; Eph 6:2-3).

27:30-40 Esau's Despair

After the blessing, Jacob had scarcely left his father's presence when Esau came in from hunting (**27:30**). He prepared tasty food for his father as they had agreed, and then took it to him, saying, *My father, sit up and eat some of my game, so that you may give me your blessing* (**27:31**). Poor Esau! Someone else had said these very words (27:19), received the blessing, and gone. As for Isaac, when he discovered he had been tricked, *he trembled violently and said, 'Who was it then, that hunted game and brought it to me? I ate it just before you came and I blessed him – and indeed he will be blessed'* (**27:33**). Words of blessing cannot be withdrawn. They can only be cancelled by a future 'evil deed' against the one who blessed. So the deceitful Jacob remains blessed.

It was too bitter for Esau. If he had even suspected what it would turn out to be like, he would never have sold his birthright (25:29-34). When he heard what his father said, *he burst out with a loud and bitter cry* and begged Isaac for some blessing at least (**27:34**). But all Isaac could say was, *Your brother came deceitfully and took your blessing* (**27:35**).

Esau now turns his anger on Jacob and says, *Isn't he rightly named Jacob? He has deceived me these two times: He took my birthright, and now he's taken my blessing* (**27:36a**). If we were asked to judge between Jacob and Esau here, we would have to say, 'Yes, your brother has deceived you concerning the blessing. For the birthright though, he was just shrewd and you, stupid!' Esau had obviously not attached any significance to the transaction he had made many years before. He was not someone who took his commitments very seriously. We are often like him in trying to blame others for the consequences of our own actions.

Esau then asked his father, *Haven't you reserved any blessing for me?* (**27:36b**). The situation is so desperate that *Esau wept aloud* (**27:38**). For a grown man to cry like this shows how deeply serious the issue is. The only blessing

Isaac can give him is to spell out the consequences for Esau of the blessing given to Jacob. Esau will have to endure

- Hardships: *dwelling … away from the earth's riches* and *away from dew of heaven above* (**27:39**).
- Danger: *You will live by the sword* (**27:40a**).
- Slavery: *You will serve your brother* (**27:40b**).

These are the opposites of the blessings pronounced on Jacob, and are statements of reality since two people cannot both be masters at the same time. However, Isaac added, *when you grow restless, you will throw his yoke from off your neck* (**27:40c**). Not everything was hopeless for Esau. His descendants will not be slaves for ever, but will have to fight for their freedom.

What are we to make of this sad story?

First, while admitting that Jacob and Rebekah's behaviour was morally wrong, we need to acknowledge that they did act shrewdly. We are reminded of Jesus' parable about the shrewd steward (Luke 16:1-8). Deception is not admirable, but being able to plan and succeed is. Truthful people can learn the need to plan carefully, but to do so for the good of others and for the world in general. Christians cannot afford to be sloppy in their planning, for without their influence the world lacks the light to the morally right path (Matt 5:16).

We also have to acknowledge that in the context of the Lord's promise in 25:13, the blessings went to the right brother. But we also know that God would not have endorsed the sins that Rebekah and Jacob committed to produce this result, for they broke many of his Ten Commandments: Jacob dishonoured God's name, did not honour his father, lied, and coveted his brother's blessing. We do not know how God would have worked to bring out the right situation if Jacob had not acted as he did. In fact, the question is similar to the one, 'What would have happened if Judas did not betray Jesus, given that Jesus' death on the cross was an essential element of his ministry?' The answer to such questions is that we do not know. What we do know is that just as Judas remains responsible for betraying Jesus, so Jacob and Rebekah remain responsible for telling lies. God's ways are infinite and all of them righteous. His plans would not have been frustrated – not even if Isaac had pronounced blessings on Esau.

27:41-28:5 Jacob Flees to Haran

As would be expected, Esau had no love for Jacob who had taken his blessing. He planned to kill him after Isaac's death (**27:41**) but Rebekah learned of his plan (**27:42**). She had plotted to have Jacob get the blessing, and now she plans a strategy to save his life. Her words about losing *both of you in one day* refer to the fact that Isaac's death would immediately be followed by Jacob's death (**27:45b**).

Rebekah knew where to send Jacob for safety. He would have to go to her *brother Laban in Haran* (**27:43**; see 24:29,

50; 25:20). Rebekah would monitor Esau's anger, and hoped that time would make him forget what his brother had done. When it was safe, she would tell Jacob to come home (**27:45a**).

Jacob would need Isaac's consent to leave, and so once again Rebekah schemed to get this. She used the grief caused by Esau's marriage to Hittite women (26:34-35). She said to Isaac, *I'm disgusted with living because of these Hittite women. If Jacob takes a wife from among the women of this land, from Hittite women like these, my life will not be worth living* (**27:46**). Isaac did not know that behind this genuine concern there was a motive deeper than just finding a good wife for Jacob. In fact, it appears that even now Isaac had no idea that Rebekah had been behind the deception to have Jacob take Esau's blessing. He may have ascribed all that had happened to Jacob's wits and planning.

Rebekah continued to carry out her part in this affair with cunning, covering up her role in the problems in their home. She wanted to send Jacob to Laban because of Esau, but she convinced her husband to send him there for a completely different reason: to find a wife. It seems that Rebekah was neither repentant about what she had done nor prepared to give up scheming to get her own way.

Isaac called for Jacob and instructed him not to *marry a Canaanite woman* (**28:1**) but rather to go and look for a wife at Paddan Aram, in *the house of your mother's father Bethuel*. Paddan Aram was a descriptive name, which means the 'plain of Aram' (approximately, present Syria). Haran (11:31; 27:43) was a town in this plain. There, he was to take a wife *from among the daughters of Laban, your mother's brother* (**28:2**).

Isaac then sent Jacob off with his blessings, asking God to give Jacob many offspring (**28:3**) and possession of the land of Canaan, which the Lord had promised to Abraham's descendants (**28:4**).

Jacob then set off *to Paddan Aram, to Laban son of Bethuel the Aramean, the brother of Rebekah, who was the mother of Jacob and Esau* (**28:5**). Modern readers may wonder why the writer gives these details, which are obvious from what precedes. For the Israelites, however, kinship was a very important matter and the writer wanted to make sure that the reader kept in mind all the relationships involving Jacob.

28:6-9 Esau Learns a Lesson

Esau's marriage to Hittite women was 'a source of grief to Isaac and Rebekah' (26:35). Rebekah had used this to convince Isaac that Jacob needed to be sent to Paddan Aram (27:46) and Isaac had specifically commanded Jacob not to marry a Canaanite woman. Although Esau wives were actually Hittites, who were a different group to the Canaanites, it seems that here the term is being used loosely to refer to anyone living in the region of Canaan who was not related to Abraham.

When Esau learned that Jacob was being sent away to get a wife, he *realized how displeasing the Canaanite women were to his father Isaac* (**28:6-8**). In an attempt to have at least one wife who pleased Isaac, he married his cousin *Mahalath,* Ishmael's daughter (**28:9**). He did not want Isaac to die still displeased with his marriage. It was a late attempt to deal with a bad situation, but as the saying goes, 'Better late than never.' Although we may not approve of his multiplication of wives, his sensitivity to his old father's feelings is commendable.

Isaac and Rebekah had many family problems. One of the factors that contributed to them seems to have been a lack of clear teaching of and obedience to God's commands. We must take care to ensure that our children do not merely hear the Lord's word at church, but that they also hear it taught and see it lived out in the home.

28:10-36:43 Jacob

28:10-22 The Lord Meets Jacob

Isaac had settled in Beersheba in the south of Canaan (26:23), and was apparently still living there. So when Jacob *set out for Haran* (**28:10**) he was facing a journey of about five hundred miles (eight hundred kilometres). Depending on how fast Jacob walked, it would have taken him a month or two to cover that distance. At some point on the journey, possibly on the first night, he stopped for the night and had a special experience. As he slept with his head resting on a stone, he had a dream in which *he saw a stairway resting on the earth, with its top reaching to heaven, angels of God were ascending and descending on it* (**28:11-12**). Above the ladder *stood the Lord* (**28:13a**). Many years later, Jesus would refer to this dream when he spoke about the link between human beings and God (John 1:51).

The Lord identified himself clearly to Jacob as *the Lord, the God of your father Abraham and the God of Isaac.* By saying this, he is reminding Jacob of what God had done for his ancestors, and inviting Jacob to follow in their footsteps. After identifying himself, God repeats the promise of the land that he had made to Abraham and to Isaac, saying *I will give you and your descendants the land on which you are lying* (**28:13b**; 17:8; 26:3). He also repeats the promise of many offspring, saying, *Your descendants will be like the dust of the earth* and will *spread out to the west and to the east, to the north and to the south.* Finally, he also repeats the mysterious promise that Abraham's family will bring blessing to many others: *All people of earth will be blessed through you and your offspring* (**28:14**; 22:18).

God's words so far have also been spoken to Abraham and Isaac, but now God speaks specifically to assure Jacob

of his presence and protection (**28:15**). He will have the comfort of knowing that God says, *I am with you.* As he sets out alone on a long journey into the unknown, God promises to be a watchman for him *wherever you go.* Not only that, but he is given a guarantee that he will return to the land he is leaving, for that is where his inheritance lies. Rebekah had promised that she would send word for him to come back (27:45), but he had no guarantee that this would happen – until he learned that the Lord of history was in charge of his movements and was committed to bringing him back. The Lord does not promise him that he will not suffer hardship, but does guarantee that no amount of difficulty or frustration will ever prevent the Lord from fulfilling his promises and carrying out his plans.

The Lord's appearance in this dream was so real and dramatic that Jacob knew beyond doubt that this had been no ordinary dream, but that he had truly seen the Lord (**28:16**). He was afraid and said, *How awesome is this place! This is none other than the house of God; this is the gate of heaven* (**28:17**).

In response to this experience, Jacob took the stone he had been using as a pillow and *set it up as a pillar and poured oil on top of it* (**28:18**). The act of pouring oil on the stone was an anointing that set it apart, as special to God. Jacob would probably have offered a sacrifice if he had had anything he could sacrifice, but he was on a journey and had no animals with him. But the Lord accepts what we give him, no matter how simple, when the offering comes from our hearts.

Jacob gave the place where he had slept a name, *Bethel,* which means 'house of God' to commemorate what had happened there (**28:19**). He also made a vow expressed in a conditional statement. If the Lord did protect and provide for him in the future and what was promised in 28:15 came true, then *the Lord will be my God and this stone that I have set up as a pillar will be God's house and of all that you give to me I will give you a tenth* (**28:20-22**).

Jacob had left home with many problems and living a life that was out of step with God. So God acted dramatically to catch his attention. He knew that Jacob needed to make a firm commitment to follow him. In the same way, God does not speak to us in an unclear way. He gives us clear messages so that we can make informed decisions on how to follow him or serve him better. This decision must be personal and must be made independent of anyone else. It begins with a sincere commitment of one's life to Christ. Considering oneself a Christian and bringing a contribution to church or even wishing to consecrate one's life to being a pastor, evangelist, preacher or teacher of the word of God before knowing Christ personally is of no blessing to the church or even humanity in general. It is our relationship with Christ that enables us to bear lasting fruit.

29:1-14a Jacob Reaches Paddan Aram

Jacob *continued on his journey* until he *came to the land of the eastern peoples* (**29:1**). There he *saw a well in the field with three flocks of sheep lying near it* (**29:2**). The flocks would drink from this well, but only after the large stone that covered the well was moved aside. This stone was so heavy that moving it required a group effort (*harambee* in Kiswahili). So all the local flocks would first gather before *the shepherds would roll the stone away from the well's mouth and water the sheep.* When all the sheep had drunk, the well would be covered again (**29:3**).

Jacob greeted the shepherds waiting at the well as *my brothers* (**29:4a**), even though he had never met them. But his approach would show that he came in friendship, and would make a good first impression. When he asked where they came from, they told him they were from *Haran* (**29:4b**). At last he had reached his destination! He quickly asked, *Do you know Laban, Nahor's grandson?* (**29:5**). They did, and they pointed out that the young woman who was then approaching with her sheep was in fact Laban's daughter, *Rachel* (**29:6**).

Rachel seems to have been some distance away, for Jacob continued to converse with the shepherds until she arrived. He encouraged them to go ahead and *water the sheep and take them to pasture* as the sun *is still high; it is not time for the flocks to be gathered* (**29:7**). The shepherds explained that they needed to wait *until all the flocks are gathered and the stone has been rolled away from the mouth of the well* (**29:8**). They needed to wait and work as a group to make sure that no one was left stranded and unable to open the well if everyone else left.

While he was still talking with them, Rachel came with her father's sheep, for she was a shepherdess (**29:9**). This meeting marked the beginning of something that was going to last Jacob's whole life. His mother Rebekah had been met at a well, and now Isaac was meeting his future wife at a similar well, possibly the same well. Once again, God had led the one searching for a wife to exactly the right place. The God of Abraham and Isaac is a God of miracles. Everything is under his control and he can be trusted for perfect outcomes.

When Jacob saw Rachel, daughter of Laban, his mother's brother, and Laban's sheep, he did what was, to others, practically impossible: he *went over and rolled the stone away from the mouth of the well and watered his uncle's sheep* (**29:10**). Love at first sight is not always recommended, but it can be a powerful motivator!

After the sheep were watered, Jacob *kissed Rachel and began to weep aloud* (**29:11**). Why did he weep? Excitement at meeting a relative? Love? Some other reason? We do not know, but as soon as Rachel heard that he was *a relative of her father and a son of Rebekah,* she did not keep this news to herself but *ran and told her father* (**29:12**). Her excitement

reminds us of the excitement of a Samaritan woman many years later (John 4:28).

Laban, too, was thrilled that his sister's son had come to visit them, and *hurried to meet him, embraced him, kissed him,* and *brought him to his home* (**29:13a**). While this may well have been a typical warm welcome of a relative, we are again reminded of what the Samaritans did after the woman came with the news that she had met the Messiah. They 'came out of the town and made their way toward him' (John 4:30). When good news is received, there should be no waiting. This is a challenge to all of us. What do we do with the good news about Jesus that we receive in numerous ways and places? Do we spread it?

Under Laban's roof, Jacob *told him all these things* (**29:13b**). 'These things' included news about Rebekah and the rest of the family. Laban's response, *You are my own flesh and blood'* (**29:14a**) is a good example of how important kinship was in the OT. Just as in many African societies, the child of a sister is actually a 'son' or 'daughter' to his or her uncle. In fact, among the Kamba of Kenya, when a son or daughter runs away from home, the destination is always 'uncle's house'. That is the child's 'city of refuge'. A bond has been established between Jacob and Laban.

29:14b-30 Jacob Marries His Two Cousins

The Kamba of Kenya have a saying: *Vaii nzau yanasya utumo umwe mbua ili* ['No bull rules the same valley for two seasons'], meaning you cannot assume that you will always have the upper hand. Even the scheming Jacob can be tricked – particularly by a master schemer like his uncle Laban.

For *a whole month* (**29:14b**), Jacob had been working for Laban without any formal salary. Laban was sensitive to this and so he told Jacob, *Just because you are a relative of mine, should you work for me for nothing? Tell me what your wages should be* (**29:15**). Laban was more righteous than many of us in Africa whose relatives come to the towns and cities to stay with us as they look for employment. At times, some of these relatives work for years in our homes with no formal salary at all. We usually justify it by saying that they get food, shelter, water and electricity at our expense and that is enough. But is it actually enough, or are we taking advantage of them because they would be helpless without us? Laban judged that it was not right to use Jacob's labour without paying him for it, and so he offered Jacob an opportunity to name his wages.

Jacob's response was, *I'll work for you seven years in return for your younger daughter Rachel* (**29:18b**). Laban had two daughters: Leah who was older and *had weak eyes,* and Rachel who was younger and *was lovely in form, and beautiful* (**29:16-17**). *Jacob was in love with Rachel* (**29:18a**). He was willing to give seven years of work for the woman he loved. Where there is love, there is no calculation of the cost. There have been cases in Africa where the relatives of the wife-to-be have set a bride price so high that the young man becomes discouraged. But where there is genuine love, there has always been a bouncing back and a struggle to pay the bride price.

Sometimes it is good that 'love is blind'. Jacob in love did not notice as years passed and *they seemed like only a few days to him because of his love for Rachel* (**29:20**).

When the seven years were over, Laban, who had agreed to the deal saying, *It is better that I give her to you than to some other man* (**29:19**), gave Jacob the biggest surprise of his life. After Jacob reminded him that the seven years were over, Laban *brought together all the people of the place and gave a feast* (**29:22**). He fulfilled all righteousness as far as the whole community was concerned. But he *took his daughter Leah and gave her to Jacob* (**29:23**). This was done after evening had come. In the darkness, Jacob thought it was Rachel and so *Jacob lay with her.* The marriage was consummated and could not be annulled.

Laban had been anxious to get Leah married, and to get a good bride price for her. But probably her weak eyes had meant that other men were not interested in her. So he used the appearance of honesty to play a very serious trick on Jacob. He had all the right outward appearance with the big wedding feast, which gave the impression that everything was going as planned, but his heart was dishonest. He had made a deal with Jacob, but he had manipulated things to his advantage without Jacob's knowledge. This is not 'good business' – it is dishonest business. We need to remember that what matters most is not what we have achieved but how we have achieved it. Dishonesty taints everything.

When morning came, Jacob realized that he had been given Leah and not Rachel. He angrily confronted Laban: *What is this you have done to me? I served you for Rachel, didn't I? Why have you deceived me?* (**29:25**). Esau could have asked Jacob a very similar question seven years earlier! Too often we complain about something only when it negatively affects our interests, but justify it when we are the beneficiaries. That is why the Bible frequently speaks of the need to 'love one another' (John 13:34; 15:12; Rom 12:10; 13:8; 1 Thess 3:12; 1 Pet 4:8; 1 John 3:23; 4:11; 2 John 5) and to 'do to others what you would have them do to you' (Matt 7:12).

God knows our self-centredness and he addresses it very clearly. Jacob could have justified his tricking Esau by saying, 'But he sold his birthright to me'. Laban also offered some justification for his action: *It is not our custom here to give the younger daughter in marriage before the older one* (**29:26**). No matter how true both statements were, they did not excuse the conduct that followed. Jacob should have been told about the custom seven years earlier. Even if Laban had hoped that Leah would have a husband of her own by the time the seven years were over, he should

have qualified his agreement with Jacob by saying: 'Yes, provided Leah has found a husband by then'. His failure to clearly state all the terms of the agreement makes Laban a guilty man, no matter what the custom was. At times, some have wondered whether such things as bribery are wrong for Christians to be involved in, because they are also the custom. But custom never makes a wrong right. Honesty is honesty and dishonesty is dishonesty.

Laban then made Jacob another offer: *Finish this daughter's bridal week; then we will give you the younger one also, in return for another seven years of work* (**29:27**). Jacob was in love with Rachel and Laban took advantage of the situation, but there was no turning back as far as Jacob was concerned. After the bridal week with Leah was over, *Laban gave him his daughter Rachel to be his wife* (**29:28**) and Jacob *worked for Laban another seven years* (**29:30**). We are told that Jacob *loved Rachel more than Leah.* While this situation is common in polygamous marriages, it is always the beginning of problems in the family. Every wife should be given her share of love to the point of satisfaction. It may have been difficult for Jacob because he had not chosen to marry Leah. Yet she was now his wife and so she deserved his love also.

Jacob now had two wives, and each of the wives also had a maidservant. Laban *gave his servant girl Zilpah* to Leah (**29:24**) and *his servant girl Bilhah to his daughter Rachel* (**29:29**). The ease with which Jacob became a polygamous person shows how common it was in the ancient world.

The dutiful love of a future son-in-law like Jacob should have been a cause for thanks and praise to the Lord, but Laban saw it as something to be exploited. He profaned marriage by using his daughters to enrich himself. This is not an uncommon problem in Africa. While African parents may not substitute a 'Leah' for a 'Rachel', they still often try to squeeze all they can from a future son-in-law. Such a self-centred attitude is wrong.

29:31-30:24 Life in Jacob's Family

Jacob's family was not a happy one, for it was characterized by injustice with Leah despised and deprived of conjugal love. The focus was on the competition between the two sisters. Their jealousy and envy led to Jacob fathering children on many women, for the sisters used their maidservants to produce children for them. As with Sarah and Abraham, a child born through a maidservant was regarded as the mistress's own child.

29:31-35 Jacob's children from Leah

Since Jacob loved Rachel at the expense of Leah, the Lord filled the gap for Leah. He *opened her womb* (**29:31**). Meanwhile Rachel suffered the same fate as Sarah (11:30) and Rebekah (25:21). She was barren. While she may have been a victim of circumstances to some degree, in that Jacob loved her, while *Leah was not loved,* she does not seem to have encouraged Jacob to change his cold attitude towards Leah (30:14-16). Leah's fertility and Rachel's barrenness are a reminder that God stands with the disadvantaged whenever there is injustice. While Rachel remained childless, Leah gave birth to four sons:

- *Reuben,* whose name means 'God has seen my misery' or 'See, a son' (29:32).
- *Simeon,* whose name means, 'one who hears' (29:33), because God had heard her prayers.
- *Levi,* whose name means 'attached' because she was hoping that her husband would become attached to her (29:34).
- *Judah,* whose name means 'praise', because she said, *'This time I will praise the Lord'* (29:35).

Leah's reasoning is a product of her culture. She was sure that Jacob would love her if she bore him sons. That is why she greeted Reuben's birth with the words, *Surely my husband will love me now* (29:32). That did not happen, and we hear her unfulfilled longings in her words at the birth of Simeon and Levi. But when Judah was born, she changed her focus. Instead of thinking of herself and the misery of not being loved, she focused on God and praised him. Her circumstances remind us of the futility of depending on someone else for happiness (Leah longed for Jacob's love, which never came), the stupidity of focusing on ourselves (as long as Leah focused on herself, she remained miserable), and the joy of focusing on God. A mourning heart was turned into a praising heart.

30:1-8 Jacob's children from Bilhah

As Leah gave birth to son after son, Rachel *became jealous of her sister.* She also placed the blame on Jacob, telling him: *Give me children, or I'll die!* (30:1). Rachel felt that there was something Jacob was not doing as a man that he should do so that she could conceive. Jacob, however, was doing all he could, as his angry words show: *Am I in the place of God, who has kept you from having children?* (30:2). God opens and closes wombs. Those who are barren should look to him, and those who have children should praise him. In Africa, barrenness is seen as a grave misfortune for which a husband blames his wife. But the right thing to do is to look to God as the one who gives or withholds children, and to continue to trust him as a couple.

Rachel was desperate to have children for Jacob. She also reasoned, much like her sister, that Jacob would love the wife who produced the most children. So she told Jacob to sleep with her *maidservant,* Bilhah, *so that she can bear children for me and that through her I too can build a family* (30:3-4). These are familiar words that had earlier led to trouble for Abraham and Sarah (16:2b). But they reflect the fact that one of a traditional woman's strongest desires is to 'build a family', while the traditional man also sees his wife's job as incomplete unless it has been crowned with the birth of a child.

Bilhah gave birth to two sons:

- *Dan,* whose name means 'a favourable verdict', or 'he has vindicated me' (30:6).
- *Naphtali,* whose name means 'my struggle', reflecting Rachel's competition with her sister (30:8).

Competition within polygamous marriages is very common. Rachel is right when she describes it as 'a struggle'. It can divide not only the wives but also their children. It is best avoided. No man is clever when wives compete.

30:9-13 Jacob's children from Zilpah

After Leah gave birth to Judah, 'she stopped having children' (29:35). It appears that God temporarily blocked her womb, or possibly Jacob stopped going in to her. However, Leah was a fighter too. When she saw that Rachel was having children through her maidservant, she decided to use the same tactics. She *took her maidservant Zilpah and gave her to Jacob as a wife* (30:9). Zilpah, like Bilhah, gave birth to two sons:

- *Gad,* whose name means 'good fortune': (30:10-11).
- *Asher,* whose name means 'happy' (30:12-13).

30:14-21 More children from Leah

Leah has now produced four sons of her own and two through her maidservant, Zilpah. One day her eldest son, Reuben, *went into the fields and found some mandrake plants* (30:14). Mandrakes were believed to induce fertility, so Reuben brought them to Leah. Rachel heard about this and asked for some of them, but Leah responded, *Wasn't it enough that you took away my husband? Will you take my son's mandrakes too?* (30:15a). She is saying that Rachel had monopolized Jacob's attention and kept him to herself whenever she could. And Jacob had no love for Leah that would make him resist Rachel's attention.

Rachel was desperate for anything that might help her fall pregnant, and so she offered Jacob to Leah for the night in exchange for the mandrakes (30:15b). A deal was struck. Leah met Jacob as he was coming in from the fields that evening and told him, *You must sleep with me. I have hired you with my son's mandrakes* (30:16). Jacob slept with Leah and God blessed her with pregnancy. Since Jacob had some interest in Leah if she produced children, the Lord blessed her with two more sons and a daughter:

- *Issachar,* whose name means 'reward', and specifically a reward for having given her maidservant to her husband (30:17-18).
- *Zebulun,* whose name means 'honour', because she was sure Isaac would be impressed by the fact that she has now *borne him six sons* (30:20).
- *Dinah,* whose name means 'judgment', was born some time after her brothers (30:21). She is the only one

of Jacob's daughters mentioned, and her name may be related to the judgment her brothers, Simeon and Levi, imposed on the people of Shechem (34:25-26).

30:22-24 Jacob's children from Rachel

So far, Rachel's womb has been closed. But at last *God remembered Rachel; he listened to her and opened her womb* (**30:22**). She gave birth to a son:

* *Joseph*, whose name means 'may he add', expressing her hope for *another son* (**30:23-24**). Her statement that *God has taken away my disgrace* shows how she and others perceived her barrenness.
* As we will see later, the Lord heard her prayer and gave her another son whom she named Ben-Oni (son of my trouble), although Jacob changed his name to Benjamin (35:18), which means 'son of my right hand'.

30:25-43 Jacob Blessed with Flocks

With eleven sons and one daughter, Jacob's immediate family was becoming large. Jacob thought that it was time to return to his home in Canaan. After all, by this time he had worked for Laban for fourteen years (29:20; 30). So he asked Laban to *give me my wives and children, for whom I have served you, and I will be on my way* (**30:26**). Laban, however, was reluctant to let Jacob leave, saying, *I have learned by divination that the Lord has blessed me because of you* (**30:27**) and then adds, *Name your wages, and I will pay them* (**30:28**). Some workers are lazy and do just enough to earn their wages, while others are diligent and work for success. Jacob was one of the latter group. His work ethic had been noticed by others, including Laban, and he was prepared to pay whatever Jacob asked to keep him. All Christians should have the same approach, and see themselves as 'working for the Lord, not men' (Col 3:23). But unfortunately, not many workers in Africa are prepared to do this. If there were a change in our attitudes towards work, there would be a noticeable change on this continent.

Laban did not know the Lord well, and the law against divination had not yet been announced, and thus his report that he had used divination in 30:27 cannot be taken as an endorsement of this practice. Later in the OT, divination is explicitly condemned (Deut 18:10) and those who practise it are said to have forsaken 'all the commands of the Lord' (2 Kgs 17:16-17). It is what false prophets do (Jer 14:14; see also Ezek 12:24; 13:6, 7). Divination is an attempt to tell what will happen in the future by relying not on the Holy Spirit but on other assumed superhuman powers. Because it excludes God, it is a sin for believers to be involved in it.

Jacob reminded Laban of how things had been before he came and how they were now. Before Jacob came, Laban had *little*; now he *has increased greatly* as a result of Jacob's hard work and faithfulness and the Lord's blessing (**30:29-30a**). These three things (hard work, faithfulness, and the Lord's

blessing) are desperately needed in Africa. It is always a mistake to attribute the miseries of Africa to what God has or has not done. God's blessings are most evident when people are working hard and can be relied upon to take very good care of what has been entrusted to them. There has to be a Paul to plant and an Apollos to water before we can expect God to 'make it grow' (see 1 Cor 3:6). While the glory ultimately goes to God, God rewards hard work and faithfulness.

Jacob's next question to Laban, *When may I do something for my own household?* (**30:30b**) is a reminder that it is not only the employer who should prosper as workers work hard and carry out their responsibilities. Too many workers in Africa have suffered unfairly under selfish masters or mistresses, who are quite happy to quote the Bible about the need to obey and to work diligently and wholeheartedly (for example, Eph 6:5-8; Col 3:22-25; 1 Tim 6:1-2) and to ignore the equally strong statements about the need for employers to treat those who work for them well (for example, Eph 6:9; Col 4:1). Such selective use of Scripture is sinful.

Laban had neglected to treat Jacob well. In fact, later Jacob claimed that Laban had cheated him, changing his wages ten times (31:7, 41). Laban knew he has been unfair to Jacob and asked Jacob what he could give him, to which Jacob replied, *Don't give me anything* (**30:31a**). By this time Jacob was well aware that Laban had the bad habit of taking back what he had given. This is another common evil in Africa. The rich, the powerful, and the well-connected prosper at the expense of the poor. There are many Labans. This must change before we can expect God's blessings.

Jacob, however, had a proposal. He was willing to go on tending Laban's *flocks and watching over them* (**30:31b**) in exchange for *every speckled or spotted sheep, every dark-coloured lamb and every spotted or speckled goat* (**30:32-33**). Laban agreed (**30:34**). However, he still remained Laban. He did not want to give many animals to Jacob, and so, *that same day he removed all the male goats that were streaked or spotted, and all the speckled or spotted female goats (all that had white in them) and all the dark-coloured lambs, and he placed them in the care of his sons* (**30:35**). More than that, he *put a three-day journey between himself and Jacob, while Jacob continued to tend the rest of Laban's flocks* (**30:36**). Laban reasoned that, with all the animals that could give birth to the kind that would go to Jacob removed to a considerable distance from the rest of the flock, there was no way for Jacob's animals to increase. There would be no chance of these speckled animals mating with the rest of the flock.

Once again, however, *vala yikaw'a tivo ivalukaa* [Kamba, Kenya – 'where something is thrown is not where it lands']. Laban's scheme did not work out, because God overruled an injustice. Recognizing what Laban had done, Jacob did not pick a fight with him. He was a planner, not a fighter.

Instead, he tried to breed the animals in a way that would increase the likelihood of their producing speckled and striped offspring. He cut tree branches to give a striped effect, and then placed these *in all the watering troughs*. He hoped that when the animals mated near the water, they would be influenced by the markings on the branches in front of them and would produce *young that were streaked or speckled or spotted* (**30:37-39**). He also tried to make the flock look at the animals that were speckled (**30:40a**). And he took care that the strongest animals had the most exposure to these streaked branches when they were in heat (**30:41**). Jacob clearly believed that what animals saw when mating would influence the young they gave birth to. While this belief is not scientifically valid, the Lord honoured it and prospered Jacob. The young ones born to the stronger animals were streaked, and in terms of the agreement with Laban, they belonged to Jacob (**30:42**).

Thus Jacob gradually built up *separate flocks for himself and did not put them with Laban's animals* (**30:40b**). Consequently Jacob, whom Laban had wanted to keep poor and dependent, *grew exceedingly prosperous and came to own large flocks, and maidservants and menservants, and camels and donkeys* (**30:43**). Clearly God, who has more options than we sometimes acknowledge, was working to bless him.

We in Africa need to start to think more like Jacob. Instead of giving in to despair and saying, 'Laban has taken away all the streaked or spotted male goats', we need to consider what our other options are. When the rains fail, do we have other options besides moving on to where there is more food? We must look for alternatives and trust in God – provided, of course, the alternatives are morally right.

Some might ask whether Jacob was morally right to try to manipulate the outcomes here. In response, we can say that he did not steal anything that was Laban's but simply adopted a plan that worked well for him. At the same time, we must admit that Jacob did not claim that the Lord had directed him to use this method, so the question of whether it was right may be left open for debate.

31:1-21 Jacob Leaves Without Telling Laban

First, Jacob had to deal with Laban and his deception. Now he also has to deal with Laban's sons and their envy. Jacob heard that Laban's sons were saying, *Jacob has taken everything our father owned and has gained all this wealth from what belonged to our father* (**31:1**). Though he is their brother-in-law, Jacob is still an outsider. What Laban's sons failed to notice was the hard work Jacob had done for Laban. This is usually the way things turn out when there is envy. The envious cannot be fair judges because they tend to look on one side only and not at the other.

A third problem was that *Jacob noticed that Laban's attitude toward him was not what it had been* (**31:2**). This was bound to happen. If Laban had a good attitude to Jacob

before, it was because he had the upper hand and could use Jacob to make himself richer and richer. However, now that Jacob had applied his shrewdness in the matter of the animals, Laban no longer saw Jacob's presence as beneficial to him.

We do not know the exact context at which the Lord spoke to Jacob – whether it was as Jacob agonized about the matter in prayer or whether it was simply a case of the Lord knowing his needs even before he prayed (Isa 65:24). Earlier, however, the Lord had committed himself to bringing Jacob back to the promised land (28:15). The time had come, and the Lord said to Jacob, *Go back to the land of your fathers and to your relatives*. As before, the Lord assured Jacob of his presence: *I will be with you* (**31:3**).

Knowing that the Lord was on his side, Jacob did what every good husband would do before taking an important step. He *sent word to Rachel and Leah to come out to the field where the flocks were* so he could discuss the situation with them (**31:4**). He needed to be tactful, because he would be commenting on the way their father was treating him.

In speaking to them, Jacob contrasted his circumstances with what God has done:

- Their father was rejecting him, *but the God of my father has been with me* (**31:5**).
- Their father was cheating him, changing his wages ten times in spite of Jacob's hard work for him. *However, God has not allowed him to harm me* (**31:7**) and was in control of what kind of young ones the animals gave birth to (**31:8**). To refute their brother's statements (**31:1**), which might have influenced their thinking, Jacob pointed out that *God has taken away your father's livestock and has given them to me* (**31:9**). This point holds true whether we think that Jacob's strategy for influencing the colouring of the livestock was right or wrong.
- Their father was trying to surreptitiously change the odds in his favour, but God had sent Jacob a dream in which the Lord showed him that the male goats who were mating with the flock were all *streaked, speckled or spotted* like the very ones Laban had removed from the flocks Jacob was tending (30:35). Laban might have hidden these flocks, but the Lord said *I have seen all that Laban has been doing to you* (**31:10-12**).

Here is a deep truth. The God of Abraham, Isaac and Jacob is a God above circumstances. Those who place their trust in him will find that no weapons forged against them will prosper (Isa 54:17). The Lord watches over their interests against all the evil schemes of men and women.

Jacob finished his account of the dream with the statement that the Lord had told him to *leave this land at once and go back to your native land* (**31:13**). Rachel and Leah listened to what Jacob had to say and assured him of their support. They felt that their father was now treating them as outsiders, just as he was treating Jacob. He was also being unfair to them: *Not only has he sold us, but he has used up what was paid for us* (**31:14-15**). They agreed with Jacob, *Surely all the wealth that God has taken away from our father belongs to us and our children,* and agreed to whatever *God has told you* (**31:16**).

Assured of the Lord's presence and of his wives' support, Jacob plans to leave. He is acting in accordance with a very important principle. Any husband who wants to succeed must seek the support of God and of his wife. Many men in Africa conduct their affairs as if what their wife thinks about it does not matter. Yet their success may reflect the degree to which their wife does or does not support them.

Jacob waited until Laban was shearing his sheep in a distant camp (**31:19a**). He must have found some excuse not to accompany him to care for the flock. Then he quickly loaded his four wives and eleven children on camels, and set out with his livestock and *all the goods he had accumulated* to go *to his father Isaac in the land of Canaan* (**31:18**).

When Laban returned to find Jacob and his daughters gone, he must have been deeply disturbed by the deception and that fact that they had left without even saying goodbye. But he must have been even more distressed to find that Rachel had taken his *household gods* (teraphim) with her (**31:19b**). Possession of these gods was closely tied to ownership of the house they represented. Clearly, Rachel's heart was still divided between the God of Jacob and idols. We are once again reminded of why the Lord thought it necessary to have Abraham leave his environment if he were to lay a good foundation for his plan for our salvation.

Jacob and his family crossed the River Euphrates and *headed for the hill country of Gilead* (**31:21**). He is doing what God had told him to do. We did not see any signs of listening to God in Jacob's earlier life, although God had spoken to him at Bethel (28:13-15). While there may have been an incentive for him to leave because of the situation in Laban's house, this is the first time we see him acting explicitly on a command from God.

31:22-32:2 The Lord Protects Jacob from Laban

It was three days before Laban learned that Jacob had left (**31:22**). When he did, he reacted as if Jacob were a thief and gathered his relatives together and *pursued Jacob for seven days* before he *caught up with him in the hill country of Gilead* (**31:23**).

Obeying God's will does not mean there will be no problems or trials. What it does mean is that God in his sovereignty will watch over us and protect us (31:3). That is what the Lord was doing when he appeared to Laban in a dream and said to him, *Be careful not to say anything to Jacob, either good or bad* (**31:24**). The Lord knew that Laban was furious and that he might harm Jacob, and he intervened to prevent this. It seems that this prohibition against speaking to Jacob was probably meant for the day he caught up with Jacob. Laban needed some time for his anger to cool down. There is always wisdom in not handling matters when one is still burning with anger.

When Laban had overtaken Jacob, he and his relatives simply camped at the same place where *Jacob had pitched his tent* (**31:25**). Then, when the time was right, Laban spoke to Jacob. He accused him of having denied him the opportunity to say a proper farewell to his grandchildren and daughters, with a feast and *the music of tambourines and harps* and embraces as they said goodbye (**31:27-28**). Instead, Jacob's behaviour had been more like that of a raider who had abducted them *like captives in war* (**31:26**). Laban reminded Jacob that he and his relatives could punish Jacob and cause him serious harm if they so chose (**31:29**), but that he was not going to do this because of the warning the Lord had given him the previous night.

Jacob responded to these accusations by pointing out that he had been afraid that Laban would not permit his daughters to leave, and *would take your daughters away from me by force* (**31:31**). His concern was probably justified. A schemer like Laban could have used all sorts of tactics to stop Jacob from leaving.

Laban had also raised the question of the missing household gods (**31:30**). Jacob knew nothing of this theft. He swore that whoever had them would be put to death. Jacob could not have imagined Rachel would have taken them. He probably assumed that they had been stolen by one of the male servants, for he used the masculine pronoun when he said, *he shall not live* (**31:32**).

Laban searched thoroughly for his gods. He examined Jacob's tent, Leah's tent, Rachel's tent, and the tent of the two maidservants. He did not find them because Rachel *had put them inside her camel's saddle and was sitting on them* (**31:33-34**). Rachel said to her father, *Don't be angry, my lord, that I cannot stand up in your presence; I am having my period* (**31:35**). The tricky Laban was tricked by Rachel and so for all his searching he *could not find the household gods.*

One of the negative features of Jacob and those around him is their use of lies to achieve their ends. Jacob and his mother Rebekah used lies to get Isaac to bless Jacob (27:1-40). Rebekah then tricked Isaac as to why Jacob needed to leave for Paddan Aram so that Isaac would bless his journey (27:41-28:5), and Rachel now lies to Laban about why she cannot get up. Jacob's father, Isaac, and grandfather, Abraham, also lied to avoid being killed for their beautiful wives (26:7; 20:2; 12:11-12). Yet these people were the ones through whom God had chosen to work. Does this mean that the end justifies the means? Certainly not! Rather, we are reminded of the abundance of God's grace. He receives us as we are and seeks to change our characters so that we become like him.

When assessing their behaviour, there are two things that need to be borne in mind. First, the Bible records these happenings as what the historical people actually did. It does not say that God approved of their actions. Yes, these were people of God – but only by reason of his grace, not because they deserved this status. Second, these people had only a limited knowledge of the will of God. God was just beginning to reveal himself to them. It would be many years before he gave the law to Moses, spelling out his will for almost all aspects of life. These persons cannot be our examples in all areas, for they were still toddlers in their knowledge of God. They had never been given the Ten Commandments (Exod 20), nor had they heard the Sermon on the Mountain (Matt 5–7). Thus we, who have a far fuller revelation of God's will through Jesus Christ, need to respond to the bad behaviour of people like Abraham, Isaac, Jacob and Rachel as we would respond to toddlers who do something that we, as adults, know is wrong. We do not hold a toddler responsible in the same way we would an adult, nor do we think that their behaviour is a model for us to imitate. Rather, we acknowledge that what the child has done is wrong, and then we allow them to experience grace from us as we continue to train them in right and wrong. The end has never justified the means. But God's grace works in imperfect people.

Having said that, we must remember that some of these patriarchs gave unquestioning obedience to the little they did know of the will of God. Abraham, for example, qualified as father of those who believe (Gal 3:7, 9). He was even prepared to offer his long-awaited only son if that was what God commanded (ch. 22). We may have the advantage of knowing more about God's ethical will, but we may know less than the patriarchs did about obedience.

Having been unable to find his household gods, Laban could no longer play the role of an abused victim. Jacob now took the opportunity to set the record straight.

First, he challenged Laban to provide proof of any crime. He asked Laban whether all his searching had turned up anything at all, including the household gods. All of their relatives were present. They could act as judges if there was any disputed property (31:36-37). Laban could not produce any such evidence because Rachel had outwitted him.

Next, Jacob reminded Laban of the excellent service he had given him over the past twenty years, as he served fourteen years for his two wives (29:18, 27, 30) and six years to accumulate his flock (31:38a, 41a). He had taken such good care of Laban's sheep that none of them had miscarried. He had not felt free to eat any of the animals he was caring for, and he had protected them from attacks by wild beasts. If it happened that an animal was attacked, Jacob took it as his responsibility and bore the loss himself (31:38b-39a). And this faithful service had not been easy: *the heat consumed me in the daytime and the cold at night, and sleep fled from my eyes* (31:40).

But Laban had been an unjust employer with no concern for his faithful employee. He had treated him with constant unfairness. If, despite Jacob's vigilance, any animal was stolen from the large flock he tended, Laban showed no mercy but blamed Jacob for the loss and made him pay for it (31:39b). He constantly tried to renegotiate Jacob's wages, so Jacob would get less and he would get more (31:41b). Jacob was convinced that if events had been in Laban's hands, his labour would have been exploited and he would have been left with nothing in return for his years of hard work: *You would surely have sent me away empty-handed* (31:42b).

Fortunately it was God who was in control, not Laban, and it was God who would see that justice was done. He had noted Jacob's *hardship and the toil of my hands, and last night he rebuked you* (31:42c). Jacob refers to the God who has been with him as *the God of my father, the God of Abraham and the Fear of Isaac* (31:42a). He calls God the Fear of Isaac because Isaac served him with reverence.

Laban can offer no excuse for his injustice towards Jacob. So he changes the subject. He insists that everything Jacob has actually belongs to him: Jacob's wives are his daughters, their children are his grandchildren, and Jacob's flocks are all the offspring of his flocks (31:43). What he says is true, up to a point. Jacob had gone to Paddan Aram empty-handed, and he was leaving with almost everything he could ask for. But Laban conveniently ignored the fact that Jacob had worked long and hard to gain every single one of these. Yet Laban also recognized that there was nothing he could do about the situation. Jacob may have been just a useful herdsman to Laban, but the women were his wives and the children were his offspring. They were now part of Jacob's clan. So he proposed that he and Jacob enter into a covenant (31:44).

Jacob was quite willing to make a covenant and took the lead in doing so. As he had done at Bethel (28:18), he took *a stone* and *set it up as a pillar* (31:45). He had his relatives construct a heap of stones and they then ate a covenant meal together next to it (31:46).

The pillar and the heap of stones were physical witnesses to the terms of the covenant (31:48, 52). God, however, was the ultimate witness, as Laban recognized (31:49b).

Laban dictated the terms of the covenant. They were that Jacob would not mistreat his daughters and would not marry any other wives besides his daughters (31:50). The covenant does not refer to the two maidservants, for although they were also Jacob's wives in a way, they had no status as wives independent of their mistresses. Second, neither he nor Jacob would pass the boundary marked by the heap of stones and the pillar in any attempt to harm the other (31:52).

Laban concluded with the words, *May the God of Abraham and the God of Nahor, the God of their father, judge between us*

(**31:53a**). Laban was the son of Bethuel, who was the son of Nahor, Abraham's brother. So Laban was praying to the God of their ancestors.

God's identity never changes. It is only our understanding of him that is partial, imperfect and at times wrong. Many African people groups have descriptive titles that they use when speaking of the person or activity of the Supreme Being, and this Being is the same God of the Bible. His identity is constant, whether we refer to him as the 'God of Abraham' or the 'God of Abraham and Nahor' or, as in NT times, as the 'God and Father of our Lord Jesus Christ' (Eph 1:3).

Jacob took an oath in the name of the Fear of his father Isaac (**31:53b**). He agreed to Laban's demands. Just as he took the lead at the beginning of the ceremony, so he also takes the lead at its conclusion. After taking oath to guarantee his acceptance of the covenant conditions, he *offered a sacrifice there in the hill country and invited his relatives to a meal* (**31:54**).

Given the importance of the events that had taken place to both parties, each gave the place a name. Laban called it *Jegar Sahadutha* and Jacob, *Galeed* (**31:47**). Both names mean 'witness heap', but the first is Aramaic and the second Hebrew. The place was also called *Mizpah* (**31:49a**) which means 'watchtower' or lookout spot.

With the ceremony concluded *they spent the night there* (31:54), and early in the morning *Laban kissed his grandchildren and his daughters and blessed them. Then he left and returned home* (**31:55**). *Jacob also went on his way* (**32:1**). We are told that *the angels of God met him*, which made him view it as *the camp of God*, giving it the name *Mahanaim* (**32:2**).

What could have been a very nasty confrontation, given Laban's anger, ended pleasantly because of the Lord's intervention (31:24) and Laban's fear of God (31:29). In Africa, whenever there is a potential for conflict many of us take it for granted that it will end in a war of some kind. This is the result of past experience of the outcome of disagreements in Africa. We should ask God that at such times he will speak to the stronger party in a dream and tell them to refrain from violence. However, it is probably safe to assume that God does actually speak and command against violence, but that the one spoken to refuses to hear his voice and obey it.

The devastation that has resulted from conflicts in many African countries is part of God's message to us to avoid clashes, to make agreements and to build a strong united Africa. We can recognize that if Laban had disobeyed God and attacked Jacob, he would have been injuring his own family – for Jacob was the husband of his daughters and the father of his grandchildren. Yet many in Africa attack their fellow Africans and destroy them. This cannot be right, no matter what the reason. We need to work to remember that we are each other's keeper.

32:3-21 The Lord Protects Jacob From Esau

With the situation between him and Laban resolved, Jacob had to prepare for another problem. This time it was with his own brother Esau, who was living *in the land of Seir, the country of Edom* (**32:3b**). In regard to Laban, Jacob had been the offended party, but in regard to Esau, he had been the offender. He had taken Esau's blessing and run away. He considered it likely that Esau still held a grudge against him, and so he took precautions. He did not use the fact that the 'angels of God' had met him as an excuse to do nothing (32:1). Instead, he developed a strategic plan.

Jacob took the initiative in seeking reconciliation with the brother he had offended. He did not suggest that he was entitled to return, but presented himself as someone who was in a position of weakness and wanted Esau's favour. He *sent messengers ahead* to Esau (**32:3a**), referring to him as *my master* and *my lord* (**32:4a, 5b**) and to himself as *your servant, Jacob* (**32:4b**). He told Esau that he had been staying with Laban (**32:4c**) and informed him that he was not returning as a beggar but had many possessions: *cattle and donkeys, sheep and goats, menservants and maidservants* (**32:5a**). All he is asking of Esau is *favour in your eyes* (**32:5c**).

When the messengers returned to say that Esau's response to the message was to set out to meet Jacob with *four hundred men* (**32:6**), Jacob was thrown into *great fear and distress* (**32:7a**). He hastily made another plan. He divided the people with him, and all his flocks, herds and camels into two groups. His reasoning was that should Esau attack one group, the other might escape (**32:7b**).

He also assembled a large gift for Esau: 200 female and 20 male goats, 200 ewes and 20 rams, 30 cows with their young, 40 cows and 10 bulls, 20 female and 10 male donkeys (**32:13-15**). He put them in separate herds and sent them on ahead of him. His servants were instructed to make sure that there was a sizeable gap between each herd and the one following it (**32:16**). When Esau met each herd, the servants were to greet him and tell him that all these animals were being sent to him as a gift by Jacob (**32:18**). Jacob hoped to pacify Esau with the gifts before they met (**32:20**).

Jacob did not rely solely on gifts and words to solve the problem; he also prayed to the Lord (**32:9**). In this prayer he humbly admitted his sin and failures: *I am unworthy of all the kindness and faithfulness you have shown your servant* (**32:10a**). He also acknowledged what the Lord had already done for him: *I had only a staff when I crossed this Jordan, but now I have become two groups* (**32:10b**). Then he utters his request for protection: *Save me, I pray, from the hand of my brother Esau, for I am afraid he will come and attack me, and also the mothers with their children* (**32:11**). He bases his appeal on God's earlier promise: *You have said, 'I will surely* *make you prosper and will make your descendants like the sand of the sea, which cannot be counted'* (**32:12**).

His prayer is a model for us. It contains adoration, confession, thanksgiving and supplication (all the elements summed up in the mnemonic ACTS). It also claims God's promise.

With a good strategy in place and an emotional expression of his dependence, in prayer, on a God who cannot lie, Jacob spent the night alone *in the camp* at Mahanaim (**32:21**; 32:2). It was to be a life-changing night.

32:22-32 The Lord Changes Jacob's Name

For safety's sake, Jacob had sent all his family members and *all his possessions* to the other side of the river *Jabbok (32:22-23)*. He was the only one left in the camp. Yet from somewhere a man appeared and *wrestled with him till daybreak. When the man saw that he could not overpower him, he touched the socket of Jacob's hip so that his hip was wrenched* (**32:24-25**). This injury would remain a constant reminder of this strange night.

The man requested Jacob to let him go, *for it was daybreak*, but Jacob asked for blessing first (**32:26**). The man asked, *What is your name?* (**32:27**), and when Jacob answered the man said, *Your name will no longer be Jacob, but Israel* (**32:28**). Jacob means 'he deceives' but Israel means 'he struggles with God'. The man himself gave the reason for the new name: *because you have struggled with God and with men and have overcome.* When Jacob asked for the man's name, but the man would not tell him, but blessed him instead (**32:29**).

Who did Jacob struggle with? He was certainly someone superior to him, for he controlled things and did not follow Jacob's dictates. This is clear from the timing of the blessing (and the refusal to give a direct answer to the request for his name – 32:26, 29). The wrestler also had power over events. Names usually indicated the owner's characteristics, whether displayed at present or as they were predicted to be in the future. Only someone who knew the future could have given Jacob a name that so exactly fitted the future character of the man. The name 'Israel' was a prediction of a change in his character. Jacob himself concluded that the one with whom he had wrestled was God. He *called the place Peniel*, meaning 'face of God', because, as he put it: *I saw God face to face, and yet my life was spared* (**32:30**).

But if the wrestler was God, why is he referred to as *a man* throughout the account and why is it that 'he could not overcome Jacob' (32:25)? The answer is probably that this was God in human form. God accommodated himself to Jacob's context so as to minister to him in a manner that would change him for life. God struggled with him, but did not crush him with a single blow. Instead, he assessed his true value. The senior, stronger, and more powerful one acknowledged the strength of the younger one, even thought it was far less than his own. Jacob needed that encouragement.

With a changed name and a wrenched hip, a limping Israel continued his journey (**32:31**). His injury would serve as a reminder to stay away from sin and as a reminder of his new name. He would no longer be Jacob the deceiver but Israel the God-wrestler. This touch reminds us of our deliverance today. God removes our sins instantaneously when we convert to the Lord Jesus Christ. His severe blow gives us life.

Jacob's experience also gave a permanent practice to his descendants. The Israelites *do not eat the tendon attached to the socket of the hip, because the socket of Jacob's hip was touched near the tendon* (**32:32**). There is no problem in adopting a practice in honour of an ancestor, as the Jews did with Jacob. It becomes a problem only when that practice becomes part of worship. Thus there is nothing wrong with having a totem and abstaining from eating a particular animal. But when that animal becomes elevated to the level of something to bow to, the practice becomes a problem.

33:1-17 The Meeting with Esau

When Jacob finally saw Esau and his men approaching, he arranged his family to meet him. He began by dividing *his children among Leah, Rachel and the two maidservants* (**33:1**). If Esau was hostile, each mother would be able to plead with Esau for her own children. Esau might be willing to listen to at least one of them. Then he arranged these groups of mothers and children with *the maidservants in front*, followed by *Leah and her children*, while *Rachel and Joseph were in the rear* (**33:2**). Jacob was attempting to make sure that his favourite wife and son would be the least exposed to Esau's attack. He hoped that by the time he got to Rachel and Joseph, Esau would have become sympathetic to Jacob's pleading and that of the mothers.

Jacob did not attempt to protect himself by staying with the women. Instead he led the way so that he would be the first to face Esau's anger. As he approached his brother, he *bowed down to the ground seven times* (**33:3**). This was the practice when one met a king. Jacob was acknowledging Esau as the master.

As Jacob bowed, Esau *ran to meet* him *and embraced him; he threw his arms around his neck and kissed him.* At this point *they wept* (**33:4**). Jacob may have been weeping for joy at the unexpected warmth of his brother, and Esau for joy at seeing his brother again after more than twenty years (see 31:38a, 41a).

As might be expected, Esau had many questions for Jacob about his family, who were all introduced to him (**33:5-7**). Then he asked about the gifts of livestock that had been sent ahead (32:13-20). We can assume that Esau already knew the answer to this question, but he wanted to hear it from Jacob himself rather than just from his servants. So

Jacob answered that they were sent so that he could *find favour in your eyes, my lord* (**33:8**).

Esau refused these gifts, saying, *I already have plenty, my brother* (**33:9**), but Jacob insisted that they be accepted as evidence that *I have found favour in your eyes* (**33:10**) and because *God has been gracious to me and I have all I need* (**33:11**). Neither brother had the attitude we often see in Africa of wanting to accumulate more and more wealth beyond what one can possibly need. Jacob, who was serious about giving the gifts, *insisted* and because of that *Esau accepted it.*

Esau was willing not only to accept Jacob warmly but also to provide security for him. He told Jacob, *Let us be on our way; I will accompany you* (**33:12**). But Jacob pointed out that his party could not move rapidly. Reuben, the oldest of his sons, could not have been more than twelve or thirteen years old, as his father had worked for Laban for seven years before marrying Leah (29:20-25), and there were also at least eleven other children. Moreover, as an experienced shepherd Jacob knew if the young animals *are driven hard just in one day, all the animals will die* (**33:13**). So he told Esau to go on ahead to Seir, while *I move along slowly at the pace of the droves before me and that of the children* (**33:14**). Esau offered to leave some men with him to protect him, but Jacob assured him that this was not necessary: *Why do that? ... Just let me find favour in the eyes of my lord* (**33:15**).

Having tried to outdo each other in kindness, the brothers parted. Esau returned to Seir (**33:16**) while Jacob *went to Succoth*, where he *built a place for himself and made shelters for his livestock*. 'Succoth' means 'shelters' (**33:17**).

Esau's willingness to be reconciled with Jacob is striking. When Jacob left, Esau was hoping to kill him (27:41). Now he wants to do everything he can to help his brother. Jacob's attitude may have helped, but would have made no difference had Esau not been willing to forgive.

Esau's attitude is a challenge to the many in Africa who hold grudges for years. We must focus on the fact that we are all brothers and sisters. Christ has given us a perfect model in the unity he has brought to all people of the world by making us all children of God through personal faith in him (Gal 3:26-29). We must see each other as brothers or sisters, forgive past hurts and try to outdo each other in kindness. This same attitude is necessary when it comes to dealing with race issues in America, where black people always remember how white people have treated them, and white people do not show a spirit of humility when dealing with the past. It is also needed by those who have lived with apartheid in South Africa, with the Hutu-Tutsi situation in Rwanda, and with the native-colonialist relationships in many African countries. We should not act as if nothing wrong ever happened; but we should be willing to forgive. And once issues are settled, we should carry on with life

– whether back at 'Seir' or at 'Succoth'. Life needs to continue. We cannot dwell on the past forever.

33:18-34:31 Dinah Dishonoured

Jacob's journey from Paddan Aram ended with his safe arrival at the city of Shechem in Canaan (**33:18**). He bought a plot of land there from the sons of Hamor, the father of Shechem and pitched his tent on it (**33:19**). Here he set up an altar and called it El Elohe Israel (**33:20**), which means 'God is the God of Israel'. Jacob has now been given the name Israel, and he uses this name to declare that his God is the almighty God. This God has kept him, given him food and protected him from every danger, including those that could have come from Laban and Esau.

But trouble came when Dinah (Jacob's daughter from Leah) went out *to visit the women of the land* (**34:1**). She was raped by *Shechem, son of Hamor the Hivite, the ruler of that area* (**34:2**). After he had raped her, he fell in love with her and asked his father to *get me this girl as my wife* (**34:3-4**).

There was nothing wrong about his falling in love with Dinah. What was wrong was the fact that he took her before she became his wife. Such consummation of the marriage covenant before the marriage itself dishonoured Dinah herself and her family. Sexual relations before marriage are an impediment to a wedding celebration, which is meant to crown a period of faithful waiting.

Unfortunately, Shechem is no exception. There are many who truly love someone, would like to marry him or her, but feel that they cannot wait till after marriage to sleep with her or him. Sex before marriage, even when there is mutual consent, is wrong. Sexual abstinence, on the other hand, shows respect for oneself and for one's partner, as well as for God's precious gift of marriage. That is why the writer to the Hebrews says, 'Marriage should be honoured by all, and the marriage bed kept pure, for God will judge the adulterer and all the sexually immoral' (Heb 13:4).

The difference in value systems between the house of Jacob and the people of Shechem is revealed. Shechem was *the most honoured of all his father's household* (**34:19**). While honour is not based solely on someone's morality, it is a problem when the one who is honoured has a completely different value system to ours. This tension between value systems is something that we are acutely aware of in Africa, where influences come from all directions.

When Jacob learned what had happened, he was sad but said nothing about it until his sons came home from *in the fields with his livestock* (**34:5**). But when they did hear the news, they were *filled with grief and fury, because Shechem had done a disgraceful thing in Israel by lying with Jacob's daughter – a thing that should not be done* (**34:7**). It made no difference to them that the offender was the ruler's son. His action could not be tolerated. This uncompromising moral standard compares favourably with the situation in many

African societies today, where helpless women and girls are raped and society does not stand firm against it. It is an unforgivable failure in our societies.

Hamor seems to have agreed with his son's request to marry Dinah, and *went to talk with Jacob* about the matter (**34:6**). Just as in African societies, the father of a young man was the one who went to ask for a wife for his son (**34:8**). This is a healthy aspect of the African culture we need to maintain. It maintains community ideals and holds a larger group (not just an individual) accountable for the way the young girl will be treated once given in marriage.

Hamar proposed that this marriage would be the first of many marriages between his people and the people of Jacob (**34:9**) and offered Jacob land free of charge: *You can settle among us; the land is open to you. Live in it, trade in it, and acquire property in it* (**34:10**). Such an offer would attract many Africans, for we traditionally love land. Jacob, however, needed to consider what would be compromised in exchange for accepting the offer. His father and grandfather had discouraged their sons from marrying into Canaanite families. Should he take the same position? We need to encourage all our people to take ethical perspectives into account when weighing offers that are made to them. Which of the offers will build the kingdom of God?

Shechem also pleaded his case. He spoke to *Dinah's father and brothers,* offering to pay any price they ask (**34:11**). Our reaction to him is ambivalent. On the one hand, he was deeply in love (**34:12**), but on the other, he was speaking like a typical rich man's son, thinking that he can buy whatever he wants. We are called to teach that what matters is not how wealthy a family is, but what values it upholds.

Jacob's sons *replied deceitfully,* concealing their true intentions (**34:13**). They raised only one problem: *We can't give our sister to a man who is not circumcised. That would be a disgrace to us* (**34:14**). They then stated the only condition on which intermarriage between the groups would take place: *You become like us by circumcising all your males* (**34:15**), or *we'll take our sister and go* (**34:17**).

Hamor and Shechem were taken in by this scheme (**34:18-19**). But what they were being told was a half-truth: while it was true that the Israelites' practised circumcision, the brothers had no intention of accepting the marriage. Shechem, for his part, was so head-over-heels in love that he did not stop to think. We see the same pattern in many of our young men and women. Once they have fallen in love, they never pause to reflect on issues. The heart takes over and the mind is not allowed to work. Consequently, pitfalls that could have been avoided give rise to serious problems later in the marriage.

Hamor and Shechem managed to convince all the men of their city that intermarriage with Jacob's family would be to the benefit of the whole community, and they all agreed to be circumcised (**34:20-24**). They had fallen into the trap.

On the third day the circumcision wound is usually at its most painful, and this was when Simeon and Levi, Dinah's brothers, struck. With all the men of Shechem unable to fight back because of their pain, Simeon and Levi *attacked the unsuspecting city, killing every male,* including Hamor and Shechem (**34:25-26**). They took Dinah *from Shechem's house and left.* Then they and the rest of their brothers returned and *looted the city where their sister had been defiled* (**34:27**). They took everything of value, including the animals, women and children (**34:28-29**).

While Simeon and Levi had acted with the rashness of youth, Jacob spoke with the caution of experience. He was concerned that what Simeon and Levi had done would expose the entire family to danger should *the Canaanites and Perizzites, the people living in this land,* join forces against Jacob (**34:30**). If this were to happen, the Israelites would be outnumbered and destroyed.

Simeon and Levi dismissed his concerns because their response had been based on a principle: *Should he have treated our sister like a prostitute?* (**34:31**). Yet no matter how admirable the principle they were upholding, they were wrong to have acted without informing their father of their plans. They had reacted as if they were the only ones affected by the problem, but in reality it would affect the whole group.

This story raises a number of moral and theological issues. To what extent was intermarriage between God's people and unbelievers allowed? Were Simeon and Levi justified in tricking the Shechemites? Does God think it acceptable to kill in order to protect morality? How do we balance the risks that young people take and the caution that older persons exercise in dealing with delicate matters? What are some of the values we have failed to address in Africa because it is too risky? These, and other questions, are worth reflecting on and discussing with others.

35:1-15 Jacob Returns to Bethel

God appeared to Jacob and told him, *Go up to Bethel and settle there and build an altar* (**35:1**). Bethel was the place where God had appeared to the young Jacob more than twenty years ago and had assured him of his protection (28:10-19). Jacob prepared his household for this journey by telling them to get rid of all their foreign gods (**35:2**). There were things that people called gods, but there is only one who is the living God. They were also to purify themselves, for the living God is holy and must be approached with reverence. As a sign of this purification, they were to change their clothes. External confirmation of an internal act of confession was very important to OT people. In NT times, too, repentance that does not show itself forth in the fruit of daily living is no repentance. That is James' point when he argues that faith without works is dead (Jas 2:14-26).

Jacob's people obeyed him and *gave Jacob all the foreign gods they had and the rings in their ears, and Jacob buried them under the oak at Shechem* (**35:4**). The earrings were removed because they could be shaped into idols or were some kind of charm.

There is a tendency, today, to come to God almost as an equal. But preparation is important when we approach him, as traditional Africans well knew. Coming to God required a process of first appeasing him before one dared to make any requests.

Once again, Jacob travelled with God's protection, for God made sure his *terror fell upon the towns all around them so that no one pursued them* (**35:5**). When *Jacob and all the people with him came to Luz (that is, Bethel) in the land of Canaan,* he carried out the instructions God had given him (**35:6-7**; (35:1). *He called the place El Bethel,* which means, 'God of Beth El', because here *God revealed himself to him when he was fleeing from his brother.*

It appears that upon returning from Paddan Aram, Jacob found that his mother Rebekah had already died, for we are told nothing of her death and burial. We are, however, told that Jacob cared for his mother's nurse, Deborah. When Deborah died she was buried *under the oak below Bethel* (**35:8**) and the place *was named Allon Bacuth,* which means, 'oak of weeping'.

The Lord now appeared to Jacob *again and blessed him* (**35:9**). This was the second blessing after he had returned from Paddan Aram (see 32:29). The blessings he was given included a change in his name, from Jacob to *Israel,* a nickname that had already been given to him the night before his encounter with Esau (**35:10**; see 32:28). He was also promised many offspring: *A nation and a community of nations will come from you* (**35:11a**). That promise had first been made to Abraham (12:2; 17:2, 6) and Isaac (26:4), but now Jacob was on the verge of being the father of the nation of Israel. His duty in regard to producing this nation was simple: he was to be *fruitful and increase in number.* That same command had been given to Adam and Eve (1:28) and to Noah (9:7) – but it was one that could be fulfilled only with God's help (30:2).

Jacob was also assured of two other promises that had first been made to his ancestors. He was told that *kings will come from your body'* (**35:11b**; compare 17:6) and that *the land I gave to Abraham and Isaac I also give to you, and I will give this land to your descendants after you* (**35:12**; compare 13:14-15; 26:3).

Then God *went up from him* (**35:13**). This is the mystery of God. He brings himself to our level to communicate with us, but his status is totally different from ours. He who is God by nature (John 1:1) became man (John 1:14) in an act of great humility (Phil 2:6-8), which brought us salvation.

Jacob *set up a stone pillar at the place where God had talked with him* (**35:14**). He then *poured out a drink offering* on the stone and *also poured oil on it,* consecrating it as a holy place. He called the place Bethel (**35:15**; see 28:19).

35:16-29 Rachel and Isaac Die

Moving on from Bethel, Jacob and his household went towards *Ephrath (that is, Bethlehem)* (**35:19**). Some distance from Ephrath, Rachel *began to give birth and had great difficulty* (**35:16**). She gave birth to a son and just before she died, she named him *Ben-Oni,* which means 'son of my trouble'. Jacob, however, *named him Benjamin,* which means 'son of my right hand' (**35:18**). Rachel was buried on the way to Ephrath, and Jacob set a pillar over her tomb (**35:20**).

Jacob moved to *Migdal Eder.* Around this region a shameful thing happened. His eldest son Reuben, who should have been setting an example for his brothers, failed to honour his father. He *slept with his father's concubine Bilhah* (**35:22**). This action, coming so soon after the purification exercise in 35:2-4, shows that ceremonial commitments mean little unless they come from the heart.

Jacob heard about what Reuben had done, but he seems to have waited till he was about to die before he took action (49:4). Like a typical elder, he did not feel rushed to take action, but knew that action would eventually be called for. He may also have been reminded of his own failure to honour his father, to whom he would soon return (35:27).

At this stage, we are given a list of Jacob's sons born in Paddan Aram (although one, Benjamin, was born on the way back from Paddan Aram to Jacob's his father's home near Hebron). Here in **35:23-26** we have a list of the twelve sons who will be the heads of the twelve tribes of Israel. Six of the sons come from Leah, two from Rachel, and two each from Bilhah (Rachel's maidservant) and Zilpah (Leah's maidservant).

Jacob finally moved to stay with his father Isaac in *Mamre, near Kiriath Arba (that is, Hebron)* (**35:27**). This was where Abraham and Isaac had lived. With Jacob at home, Isaac died at the ripe old age of a hundred and eighty years (**35:28-29**). He was buried by his sons, Esau and Jacob, who had reconciled with each other and united to carry out this duty for their father.

36:1-43 The Descendants of Esau

The list of Esau's wives given in **36:1-5** is hard to reconcile with those given earlier (26:34; 28:9). The most likely solution is that the accounts use different names for the same person. Thus a woman may sometimes be referred to by her maiden name and sometimes by a name given after marriage. At times 'father' may mean 'grandfather' or even 'ancestor', as we saw in the genealogies (see 10:1-32). Or different names may have been used for another reason.

The fact that Esau married Canaanite wives suggests that he did not care much about his relationship with the God of Abraham, Isaac and Jacob. His wives, who did not know the Lord, would in all probability have raised children who did not know the Lord. It is difficult, if not impossible, to found a God-fearing family without a wife who fears God, for a mother has a tremendous influence on her children.

But although Esau may have wandered from God, God did not forget Esau. He gave him so much wealth that he and Jacob could not both live in the same territory (**36:6-8**). He also gave him many descendants, some of whom were indeed kings (**36:31-40**).

The reference to kings and other minor details like the record of Moses' own death in Deuteronomy 34 are indications that Moses did not write every single word in the Pentateuch. But these minor additions do not bring into question the traditional position that Moses was the author of the five books.

37:1-50:26 Joseph

37:1-11 Joseph and His Dreams

Jacob lived in the land of Canaan, *where his father had stayed* (**37:1**). It was the promised land (see 17:8; 26:3). *Now Israel loved Joseph more than any of his other sons*, because he had been born to him in old age (**37:3a**). He showed his love for Joseph by giving him a *richly ornamented robe* (**37:3b**). This is where things began to go wrong. Though it may have been natural for Jacob to be especially attached to young Joseph, whose older siblings were grown up and more independent, he openly showed favouritism and so laid rich ground for envy. In fact, the other brothers hated Joseph so much that they could not speak a kind word to him (**37:4**).

Joseph, who was only *seventeen*, did not help the situation when he brought a bad report to his father about his brothers, *the sons of Bilhah and the sons of Zilpah*, with whom he was tending the flock (**37:2**). And then there was the tactless way he spoke of his dreams (**37:5-6**).

Joseph had two dreams. In the first one he and his brothers were binding *sheaves of corn* out in the field, when his sheaf suddenly rose up while his brothers' *gathered around ... and bowed down to it* (**37:7**). His brothers understood the dream as signalling Joseph's intention *to reign over* them, and *they hated him all the more* (**37:8**).

The second dream included not only his brothers but also his parents. Joseph saw *the sun and moon and eleven stars*, all bowing to him (**37:9**). When he told this dream, not only were his brothers jealous of him, but even his father, Jacob, rebuked him, although he *kept the matter in mind* (**37:10-11**). Given Jacob's own experience of dreams (28:12), it is likely that this rebuke was directed at the blunt way in which Joseph reported this dream, given its obvious meaning. Jacob would have been well aware that the dreams themselves come unsought, and that they may be a way of indicating what it is to come in the future and

strengthening one to endure hardships until what God has revealed comes true.

As the story unfolds, however, it will become clear that these dreams were indeed a revelation of what was to come. His brother's interpretation of his dream of the sheaves as meaning that Joseph will rule over them is shown to be right. Jacob's understanding of the dream of sun, moon, and stars as meaning that Jacob and Rachel (though she had and so did not see its realization) and all Joseph's brothers will *come and bow down to the ground* before him (37:10) will also turn out to be so.

37:12-36 Joseph Sold by His Brothers

Jacob seems to have been unaware of the intensity of his other sons' hatred towards Joseph. The sons themselves may have kept it secret. If he had known of it, he might not have sent Joseph from their home near Hebron to *see if all is well with your brothers and with the flock, and bring word back to me* (**37:14**). Joseph first looked for them in the vicinity of *Shechem* (**37:12, 15-16**). On learning that they had moved on from there, he followed them to somewhere near Dothan (**37:17**).

When the ten brothers saw him coming in the distance, they saw their opportunity to get rid of this hated brother whom they refer to contemptuously as *that dreamer* (**37:18-20**). We are not told who originated the plot to kill him, but it is quite possible that it was one of the brothers about whom Joseph had given bad report (37:2). These included Dan, Naphtali, Gad and Asher. Joseph would be vulnerable to them, for he would be one against ten – or rather, one against nine, for Reuben, the eldest, spoke out in his defence.

Reuben proposed a slight change in their plans. The original plot was to kill him and then throw his body into a cistern, that is, a deep hole that had been dug in the ground and was used as a pit to store rainwater (37:20). Reuben suggested that rather than killing him, they should throw him into the cistern alive (37:21-22). While the other brothers might have been thinking of leaving him there to starve to death, Reuben's plan was *to rescue him ... and take him back to his father.*

When wars arise and the whole atmosphere becomes murderous, Christians may well need to become 'Reubens', thinking quickly and coming up with strategies that can be used to save their brothers' lives. Such strategies may, at times, cost their own lives, but it is a risk worth taking.

Because Reuben was the eldest of the brothers, he was listened to. So when Joseph reached his brothers, they seized him, *stripped him of his robe ... and threw him into the cistern* (**37:23-24a**). By God's providence, the cistern was dry (**37:24b**).

Judah brought his brothers to their senses. He reminded them that they would gain nothing by killing Joseph, and that laying hands on him was wrong as he was their own flesh and blood (**37:26-27**). Their hatred had so blinded them that they needed to be reminded that Joseph was actually their brother. Why does hatred at times become so intense that it blinds our eyes to our physical or spiritual connections with other people? It leads one group to dehumanize another group which may be stronger or weaker. It even allowed the brothers to define the sale of their brother into slavery as an act of love – given that it was the alternative to killing him. These accounts are given for our warning. We need to be watchful and not allow any seed of hatred to begin to grow.

The alternative to murder was suggested by the sight of *a caravan of Ishmaelites coming from Gilead*, bound for Egypt with their camels *loaded with spices, balm and myrrh* (**37:25**). Judah suggested that they sell Joseph to these Ishmaelites and the other brothers agreed. When the Midianites (another name for the Ishmaelites) approached, the brothers *pulled Joseph up out of the cistern* and then *sold him for twenty shekels of silver to the Ishmaelites who took him to Egypt* (**37:28**).

Although Joseph may well have thought that God had abandoned him, we can see God's providence working through Reuben's opposition to killing Joseph, through the timely arrival of the Ishmaelites, and through Judah's suggestion that selling their brother will at least produce some gain while killing him will not.

Reuben, who seems to have been absent when the sale took place, returned to the cistern, probably to check on Joseph's well-being. When he did not find him, *he tore his clothes* (**37:29**). Both this and his expression of despair: *Where can I turn now?* show how deeply he cared about Joseph (**37:30**). Obviously not all Joseph's brothers hated him enough to want to hurt him. This should be a comfort for pastors and others who sometimes feel that everyone is against them. Even Elijah knew this feeling (1 Kgs 19:10, 14). But it was not true in regard to Joseph, nor was it true in regard to Elijah. There are always some people who still care for us.

One sin leads to another. Now that Joseph was sold, the brothers had to lie about what had happened. So they *got Joseph's robe, slaughtered a goat and dipped the robe in the blood* so that it would appear that Joseph was torn to pieces by some ferocious animal (**37:31**). They then took the bloodied robe to their father (**37:32**). With no DNA testing, what could Jacob do but believe that the blood on the robe was Joseph's (**37:33**)? His deep grief for his son meant that he *tore his clothes, put on sackcloth and mourned for his son many days* (**37:34**). He refused to be comforted by his other sons and daughters, saying, *In mourning will I go down to the grave to my son* (**37:35**).

But while the human Jacob wept for Joseph, the all-knowing, all-able God was preparing Joseph for the next chapter

of his life. The Midianites *sold Joseph in Egypt to Potiphar, one of Pharaoh's officials, the captain of the guard* (**37:36**). God is always one step ahead of those who seek to harm the people he cares about.

38:1-30 Judah's Sin

Though this section of the book of Genesis focuses mainly on Joseph, we should not forget that the whole Bible is about God and his plan of salvation. So the story of Joseph is interrupted by an account of what was happening in the line of Judah, from which the Messiah would be born.

At that time Judah left his brothers and went down to stay with a man of Adullam named Hirah (**38:1**). The phrase, 'at that time' links Judah's move with the selling of Joseph and the lying to their father. It is possible that he left because of what had happened to Joseph (see 37:26) – a brother sold into slavery and a father in mourning must have been enough to trouble the consciences of people like Reuben and Judah.

But by associating too much with the Canaanites, Judah may have been moving away from the covenant faith of his fathers, which may explain some of the disasters that now came on his family.

While staying with Hirah, Judah married a Canaanite woman (**38:2**). She bore him three sons, *Er, Onan and Shelah* (**38:3-5**). When the boys were grown, Judah, as a good father, arranged for Er to marry, choosing a woman named *Tamar* to be his wife (**38:6**). Er, however, did not live long enough to have children for he *was wicked in the Lord's sight, so the Lord put him to death* (**38:7**). We do not know in what way he was wicked, but it may have been in his treatment of Tamar.

The custom of the time was that when a man died without children, his brother would marry the widow. The first child she bore would be regarded as the son of the dead brother and would inherit everything that would have come to his father (Deut 25:5-6). It thus fell to Onan, Er's immediate younger brother, to produce offspring for his dead brother (**38:8**). Onan, however, would prefer to inherit his older brother's portion himself, and so in order to prevent Tamar from conceiving he *spilled his semen on the ground to keep from producing offspring for his brother* (**38:9**). Such selfishness in regard to his brother and to the widowed Tamar did not go unpunished, and the Lord *put him to death also* (**38:10**).

The principle here is a very important one for African families. The growth of monogamy and the devastation caused by AIDS have led to the abandonment of the idea of widow inheritance in Africa. But that does not mean that we are not under an obligation to support a dead brother's wife. Mistreating a brother's widow is like fighting God himself – a very dangerous thing to do.

With Onan gone, it was now the duty of Judah's youngest son, Shelah, to have children with Tamar. He was, however, still young, and Judah was afraid that he might die as Er and Onan had done. So he instructed Tamar to *live as a widow in your father's house until my son Shelah grows up* (**38:11**).

Shelah grew up, and Tamar waited, but Judah gave no indication that he was ever going to call Tamar to marry him (**38:14b**).

Judah's wife died. After the grieving period, Judah and his friend Hirah, *went up to Timnah, to the men who were shearing his sheep* (**38:12**). The road to Timnah passed through *Enaim* near where Tamar's father lived. Both Enaim and Timnah were small towns not far from Adullam. When Tamar learned that Judah was going to pass the town, she *took off her widow's clothes, covered herself with a veil to disguise herself, and then sat down at the entrance of Enaim* (**38:14a**). When Judah saw her, *he thought she was a prostitute, for she had covered her face* (**38:15**). Tamar's plan worked well, for Judah promptly approached her (**38:16**).

The fact that Judah's use of a prostitute is recorded in the Bible does not mean that it is approved of. The Bible records both the good and the evil that men and women do. And not all evil was punished, for if it were, none would have survived. God graciously overlooks some evil. Judah failed in this matter, but God's grace overlooked it.

Tamar negotiated a price for her services. Judah promised that he would pay her with *a young goat from my flock* (**38:17**). He did not have the goat with him, and so she asked for something as a guarantee that she would be paid. She specifically requested that Judah give her his *seal and its cord,* and his *staff,* and he agreed (**38:18a**). This seal would have been worn on a cord around his neck, and would have been used as his personal signature on any document. Judah, not knowing who she was, slept with Tamar and *she became pregnant by him* (**38:18b**).

When Judah sent his friend Hirah to pay the *shrine prostitute* and give her the young goat, she was nowhere to be found. The people of the area reported that there had never been a shrine prostitute there (**38:19-21**). When he took this report to Judah, Judah said, *Let her keep what she has, or we will become a laughingstock* (**38:23**). This statement implies that though sleeping with a shrine prostitute may have been acceptable, it was not an act that Judah and Hirah would want to advertise. Judah's righteousness, however, is shown in the fact that he did his best to keep his promise. Though the context was not morally pure, there is still the good principle that commitments must be honoured.

About three months later, Judah was told that his *daughter-in-law Tamar* was pregnant and must have been working as a prostitute. He is horrified at such sexual immorality, of which he himself would, of course, never be guilty, and orders that she be *burned to death* (**38:24**). His response is uncomfortably close to what often happens in churches.

Elders pass harsh judgements on people who have committed the same sins that they themselves are guilty of – except that they have managed to keep it secret. This is nothing less than hypocrisy!

God knows the hearts of men and women perfectly, but Judah could have got away with his sin at the human level were it not for the craftiness of Tamar, who had been carefully keeping his seal and staff. As she was being dragged out for execution, Tamar sent a message to her 'holy' father-in-law: *I am pregnant by the man who owns these. See if you recognize whose seal and cord and staff these are* (**38:25**). Judah was as guilty of sexual immorality as Tamar was, for these were his things.

Judah could not deny the evidence of his guilt. But, like many leaders who try to avoid taking responsibility for their sins, he could have tried to excuse himself by saying that the woman he had sex with was dressed as a prostitute and lured him on. Or he could have said that it was quite acceptable for a man to sleep with a prostitute, but not for a woman to be one. But despite his failings, Judah was an honourable man, and so he promptly admitted, *She is more righteous than I* (**38:26a**). He immediately acquitted Tamar on the basis that her act was the result of his own failure to give her his son Shelah.

The statement that Judah *did not sleep with her again* (**38:26b**) is also very instructive. Once a wrong act has been repented of and confessed, it should not be repeated. It is such sins that God's grace passes over – for he knows our hearts perfectly.

Tamar gave birth to twin boys – *Perez and Zerah.* Zerah put out his hand and the midwife tied a scarlet thread around the hand to show which baby had been born first. But it turned out that the baby that was actually born first was Perez, whose name means 'breaking out' because he broke out ahead of his brother (**38:27-30**).

This sad and sordid story, however, does not end in disaster. God takes the disorder sown by the devil and uses it for his purposes. Perez, the son of Judah and Tamar, becomes one of the ancestor's of Jesus Christ (Matt 1:3).

39:1-23 Joseph's Victory over Temptation

The story of Joseph now continues, with Joseph in the household of Potiphar, who bought him from the Ishmaelites or Midianites. Potiphar was an Egyptian and *one of Pharaoh's officials, the captain of the guard* (**39:1**). *The Lord was with Joseph and he prospered* (**39:2**). The Lord's presence always brings blessings. These will not always be material things, for the joy of communing with God is in itself a blessing. In Joseph's case, however, there were material benefits. The Lord's blessing meant that Potiphar recognized Joseph's abilities and made Joseph his attendant, in charge of his household (**39:3-4**). Unlike many employees who are more of a liability than a blessing, Joseph brought blessing to all aspects of Potiphar life – both in his house and in regard to his crops (**39:5**). Eventually Joseph was so trusted that he was in charge of all his master's affairs and the only thing that Potiphar needed to be concerned about was what he would have for dinner each day (**39:6a**)!

Africa today needs many more Josephs, men who can be trusted to work honestly and be channels of blessing to their employers and to others.

But Joseph came face to face with one of the most difficult temptations a young man can face: the temptation to sexual immorality, which his brother Judah had so spectacularly failed in the last chapter. God's blessings on him included the fact that he was *well-built and handsome* (**39:6b**). Like all good things, good looks can be a problem if one does not see them as provided by God to glorify him. Many women, and many men, have fallen into immorality because their appearance made them desirable to others, or gave them the ability to manipulate others.

Potiphar's wife was attracted to the handsome Joseph and made sexual advances to him (**39:7**). Many young people would find it difficult to resist such a temptation, but Joseph refused to sleep with her, insisting that such an action would betray his master who had entrusted him with everything he owned *except you, because you are his wife* (**39:8-9**). More than that, to sleep with her would be a *sin before God*. Given the frequent stories of sexual harassment and affairs between employers or supervisors and their married employees, it seems that many in Africa fail to realize that the Bible strongly condemns such immorality. Not only is it a wicked betrayal of the trust of the betrayed spouse, but it is also a sin before God.

Joseph was able to resist the woman's repeated advances. Not only did he refuse *to go to bed with her,* but he even tried to avoid being left alone with her in any circumstance (**39:10**). Should Joseph have done something more – for example, tell his master? But to do that would be to have caused much trouble for the wife, even assuming that Potiphar was prepared to believe him. He probably hoped that she would eventually lose interest in him.

One day, however, while he was carrying out his duties, Potiphar's wife managed to catch him alone in the house, with no other servants around. She *caught him by his cloak* (**39:12a**) and again forced herself on him. Desperate to escape, Joseph slipped out of his cloak and *ran out of the house* (**39:12b**).

The woman was insulted, and decided to destroy the life of a decent, honest, young man. This is what happens with lust. It is not the other person you love but yourself, and when lust is not satisfied, it turns into hatred.

Potiphar's wife gathered witnesses by calling her household servants to see for themselves that Joseph had left his cloak there. She twisted the truth so that she was not the one mounting the assault but rather the innocent victim whom Joseph had tried to rape. She claimed that he dropped his cloak and ran when she screamed for help (**39:14-15, 17-18**). She also used racism to bolster her case, speaking of *this Hebrew* and *that Hebrew slave* who has insulted her people, the noble Egyptians.

When Potiphar came home, she showed him the cloak as evidence and repeated her story (**39:16**). Potiphar had little choice but to believe her. After all, why else would Joseph's cloak be in his wife's possession? Why would he have taken off his cloak except in the circumstances that his wife described? Like any humiliated spouse, Potiphar *burned with anger* (**39:19**). He had Joseph thrown into the prison, *where the king's prisoners were confined* (**39:20**). There Joseph would have an opportunity to meet others who had served in high capacities.

The Lord knows all things, and no boundaries stand in his way. He did not bless Joseph because he was in Potiphar's house, but he blessed Potiphar's house because Joseph was there. The blessings followed Joseph wherever he was. It is worth noting, however, that the Lord did not cause help to fall down from heaven like the manna in the desert. Rather, he caused Joseph to be appreciated for the work he was doing, which is what brought *Joseph favour in the eyes of the prison warden* (**39:21**). Joseph was put *in charge of all those held in the prison* and made *responsible for all that was done there* (**39:22**).

Joseph achieved the same status in prison that he had in Potiphar's house, and *the warden paid no attention to anything under Joseph's care* (**39:23**; see 39:6). The prison was well run not just because of Joseph's intelligence but *because the Lord was with Joseph and gave him success in whatever he did*. The lesson here is that it does not matter where we serve the Lord. We may serve in a high position or in a low one. God can bless us in either position.

40:1-23 Pharaoh's Two Officials

Some time later two of *Pharaoh's* officials, the *chief cupbearer* and the *chief baker*, offended Pharaoh and he *put them in custody in the house of the captain of the guard*, where Joseph was (**40:1-3**; 39:20). Under God's providence, Joseph was ordered to be a servant to these prisoners (**40:4a**). The way he interacts with them shows that he did this cheerfully and attentively.

One night both of these officials were troubled by dreams (**40:5**). In the morning, Joseph noticed that something was wrong, and in response to his questions they informed him that they had had highly significant dreams, *but there is no one to interpret them* (**40:6-8**). Joseph pointed out that interpretations could be given by God, and asked them to tell him their dreams.

The chief cupbearer's dream involved a three-branched vine that rapidly blossomed, budded and produced ripe grapes. The cupbearer dreamt that he squeezed these grapes into Pharaoh's cup, which he then passed to Pharaoh (40:9-11). Joseph gave a favourable interpretation of this dream. In three days, signified by the three branches (40:12), Pharaoh would restore the cupbearer to his former position (40:13).

Joseph asked the cupbearer not to forget him when he leaves the prison, but to *mention me to Pharaoh and get me out of this prison* (40:14). He insisted that he had done nothing to deserve imprisonment, and would not even be in Egypt were it not that he had been *forcibly carried off* and sold into slavery (40:15). Although he does not mention who was responsible for his imprisonment, his mind must have been full of the harm that his brothers and Potiphar's wife had done to him.

The chief baker was encouraged by the favourable interpretation of the cupbearer's dream, and so he told Joseph his dream. In his dream he had three baskets on his head with all kinds of baked goods for Pharaoh in the top basket. But the birds were eating the food intended for Pharaoh (40:16-17). Sadly Joseph interpreted this dream for him. In three days, represented by the three baskets (40:18), Pharaoh would cut off his head and hang him from a tree, where the birds would eat his flesh (40:19).

Three days later, during Pharaoh's birthday celebrations, the chief baker was indeed hanged (40:22) and the cupbearer was restored to his position, just as Joseph had predicted (40:21). But he *did not remember Joseph; he forgot him* (40:23). Can we assume that Joseph was wrong to try to get himself out of prison through doing a favour for the cupbearer? Was that why the Lord did not prompt the cupbearer to remember him? Or was it simply that the Lord had a better time for him to be delivered from his prison? These questions may be debated, but what is clear is that the Lord intended Joseph to be much more than just another freed slave. We are reminded of the Lord's words to Paul when he, too, wished the Lord to remove something that was making him suffer: 'My grace is sufficient for you, for my power is made perfect in weakness' (2 Cor 12:9).

41:1-40 Pharaoh's Dreams

Though Joseph hoped that the cupbearer's good word would get him out of prison (40:14), this was not to be. For two years the cupbearer forgot Joseph (41:1; 40:23). It was only when Pharaoh himself had dreams that the cupbearer remembered that he had met a man called Joseph who could interpret dreams.

Pharaoh's first dream was about cows. He dreamed he was standing by the Nile. While he was standing there, he saw seven *sleek and fat* cows emerge from the river, followed by seven *ugly and gaunt* cows, who proceeded to eat up the sleek and fat ones (41:2-4).

On the same night that he had this dream, he had a second one in which he saw *seven ears of corn, healthy and good* growing on a single stalk. Then *seven other ears of corn sprouted*

– *thin and scorched by the east wind.* The thin and scorched ears of corn swallowed up the healthy ones (41:5-7).

In the morning, Pharaoh's *mind was troubled* because he did not know what these dreams meant. He sent for *all the magicians and wise men of Egypt* to interpret them, but they could not help him (41:8). It is at this point that the chief cupbearer remembered Joseph. He began by acknowledging his failure to remember Joseph earlier (41:9) and then went on to tell how *a young Hebrew* who was in prison had accurately interpreted his and the chief baker's dreams (41:10-12). What mattered to Pharaoh was not what the young Hebrew was called but what he did.

In the same way, what matters most is not whether people remember our names, but what they remember about us. How would they describe us to someone else? Do we simply have the label of being a Christian, or would people describe us as acting in Christian ways?

The cupbearer bore testimony to the truth of Joseph's interpretations (41:13), and so Joseph was summoned from the dungeon. He was hastily shaved and given better clothes in which to appear in court, and then he was brought before Pharaoh (41:14). When Joseph had asked the cupbearer to mention his case to Pharaoh, he was hoping that Pharaoh would listen and respond to his needs. But God's plan was that the needy one would be Pharaoh, and that Joseph would listen to him and meet his needs! We are reminded of the words in Jeremiah: 'Call to me and I will answer you and tell you great and unsearchable things you do not know' (Jer 33:3).

It is important to pray, but it is equally important to know that God will respond to our prayers in his own time and in his own way. Too often, TV preachers in Africa ask God to act immediately in the way they prescribe – as if they know his will perfectly. If we knew this, he would cease to be God. Preachers sometimes make this mistake because they assume that God will act in the same way for us as he did for some biblical character, like Joseph. But God's ways are limitless, and he has innumerable options for how to handle similar situations. He made each of us with unique fingerprints, and he has unique solutions for each of us. We must let God be God – even when we claim his promises.

Joseph listened as Pharaoh explained that he was helpless because no one could interpret his dream, but that he had heard that Joseph had the gift of doing this (41:15). Joseph did not let this praise go to his head, but humbly replied, *I cannot do it, but God will give Pharaoh the answer he desires* (41:16). Often those who claim that the Lord has given them gifts place God in a secondary role while they display the gift as if it were their very own. This is a very bad mistake. The gift can never be greater than the giver. Joseph gave God the glory from the start.

Pharaoh then told Joseph the content of his two dreams, and repeated that no one had been able to give him an explanation of what they meant (41:17-24). Joseph immediately recognized that these two dreams were the same message in different forms and that God was using them to reveal the future to Pharaoh (**41:25, 28**). The seven sleek and fat cows and the seven healthy ears of corn represented seven years of plenty in Egypt when there would be good harvests (**41:26, 29**). The seven thin cows and the seven shrivelled ears of corn represented seven years of famine that would follow the good years (**41:27, 30-31**). The fact that Pharaoh had been sent two dreams with the same message meant that *the matter has been firmly decided by God, and God will do it soon* (**41:32**). At least one of the purposes of this famine was to elevate Joseph and to bring Jacob and his family to Egypt, as had been prophesied in 15:13.

At this point, Joseph extended his role so that he was not just the one who interpreted Pharaoh's dreams but also his counsellor. In Africa, many preachers who have been privileged to speak before 'kings' have shied away from giving them counsel. They have tended to speak to please the king, rather than to honestly declare the word of truth. In some cases, they have even become so involved in the politics of the day that they have compromised their role as servants of God. We need more people of Joseph's character and courage to stand before our presidents if Africa is to move towards establishing systems that care for the needs of ordinary people. Fairness to all should be at the centre of the counsel our presidents receive from preachers.

Kings always find a way of taking care of their own needs during times of shortage. It is the common people who usually suffer. So Joseph gave advice about how the common people in Egypt could be fed during the years of famine. This was his plan:

- *A discerning and wise man* should be put in charge of arrangements (**41:33**).
- *Commissioners* should be appointed to assist him.
- The commissioners should collect *a fifth of the harvest of Egypt during the seven years of abundance* and store it for the years of famine (**41:34**).
- The collected grain should be stored in the cities, *under the authority of Pharaoh* (**41:35**).
- This food would be distributed during the years of famine.

The plan seemed good to Pharaoh and to all his officials (**41:37**). Who says that a lay person with a discerning spirit, who walks humbly before God, cannot be an advisor to the highest authorities of any land? Joseph the slave became an advisor to Pharaoh.

Pharaoh not only approved Joseph's proposal, but also immediately gave Joseph the role of supervising its implementation. He recognized that this was a man who was led by God (**41:38**), and could think of no one else who would be equally *discerning and wise* (**41:39**). Joseph was given the highest office anyone could hold under Pharaoh (**41:40**). He must now have been grateful for the years of preparation that God had given him as he had learned first to manage a household and then an institution. God had given Joseph intelligence, wisdom and practical training.

Pharaoh, whose knowledge of the Lord was much more limited than ours, stands out as our teacher on how to make political appointments if we are to get through years of famine without everyone starving. The appointment must ignore blood relationships or tribal background and focus on the right person for the job. In Egypt, it was a Hebrew who qualified for the job, and Pharaoh wisely appointed him to it. Thinking in African terms, it is obvious that famines in Africa would not be so disastrous if we had more 'Josephs' in charge. But many African leaders, the majority of whom claim to be Christians, appoint persons for other reasons than their being the most qualified for the job. These people then become 'cows of Bashan' (Amos 4:1) – fattening themselves at the expense of the common people – rather than caring for the people as Joseph did in Egypt. We must strive for change if we do not want famines to ruin our countries year after year. We need to move from dependency on the World Bank to dependency on our own food stores in our cities. But making the change will require changes in attitude and good planning. For example, the water wasted during years of good rains needs to be stored for irrigation during years of drought. And we will have to recognize that it is not just the lack of funds that hampers our projects, but more seriously a lack of wise people in charge of them.

41:41-57 Joseph in Charge of Egypt

While the previous section ended with a statement of Pharaoh's plan to appoint Joseph, the present one begins with a public declaration of his appointment (**41:41**). As a mark of his office, Joseph was given Pharaoh's *signet ring*. Possession of this ring authorized Joseph to make decisions and place his seal and signature on official documents. He was also given *robes of fine linen* and *a gold chain around his neck* (**41:42**). These would serve as constant reminders to others that they were dealing with a man of power. So would the fact that Joseph would be riding *in a chariot as* Pharaoh's *second-in-command* with men shouting, *Make way* before him (**41:43**). Pharaoh retained his position as first in the land, but apart from him, every Egyptian was under Joseph's command. Thus it could be said that *without your word no one will lift hand or foot in all Egypt* (**41:44**).

What a reversal for Joseph! The Lord had transformed all his past humiliations into great honour. No situation, however trying and humiliating, can be an obstacle to the Lord's blessings. When God's presence is with us, the most terrible slavery, the most brutal humiliation, or the worst treatment are nothing. God has the last word.

Joseph was now given an Egyptian name, *Zaphenath-Paneah*. The meaning of this name is not very certain, but it may mean 'the one who furnishes the sustenance of the land'. This would fit well with what Pharaoh saw as Joseph's contribution to Egypt. He was also given an Egyptian wife, *Asenath daughter of Potiphera, priest of On* (**41:45a**). Although he was a foreigner, the Egyptians would see Joseph as one of them because of his name and his marriage. It was a wise political move on the part of Pharaoh, and it also served Joseph well.

Joseph had been about seventeen when he was sold into slavery (37:2) and was thirty when he was put in charge of Egypt (**41:46a**). He then travelled *throughout the land of Egypt* (**41:45b, 46b**) collecting food during the seven years of plenty (**41:47**). In each city, he stored the food grown in *the fields surrounding* that city (**41:48**). He collected so much food that he eventually *stopped keeping records because it was beyond measure* (**41:49**). His well-thought-out strategy was not intended to enrich himself but to save Egypt, and the whole region, from death during the seven years of famine. What a contrast with many African leaders who 'store beyond measure' for themselves in foreign accounts! We have to pray for and elect 'Josephs' into office in Africa.

When the seven years of famine struck, things happened exactly as Joseph had foretold: *there was famine in all the other lands, but in the whole of Egypt there was food* (**41:53-54**). One good ruler can make his or her country appear like paradise while the surrounding ones are like hell. Good planning is crucial! This is what many African nations need. This is a call to all of us who are owners of the land of Africa.

When the Egyptians had consumed their personal stocks of food, they cried to Pharaoh for help. His response was clear and simple: *Go to Joseph and do what he tells you* (**41:55**). Joseph then *opened the storehouses and sold grain to the Egyptians* (**41:56**). The famine was severe in the whole land of Egypt, but because of one man they had enough food for themselves and also enough for the citizens of other countries who also flocked *to Egypt to buy grain from Joseph* (**41:57**).

As he took care of matters of the nation, Joseph did not forget to take care of his family. He had two sons, both of whom came before the years of famine. The first was named *Manasseh*, which means 'forget'. Joseph chose the name because *God has made me forget all my trouble and all my father's household* (**41:51**). Joseph had been healed from the bitterness he must once have felt about how he had been treated by his brothers. God was probably preparing him for the coming reconciliation with his brothers. His second son was named *Ephraim*, meaning 'twice fruitful', because *God has made me fruitful in the land of my suffering* (**41:52**).

The statement that these sons were born before the years of famine may have some significance. There are many in Africa who never plan when to have children. They only worry about whether they will be able to feed them after they have been born. Responsible parenting means having children when we can afford to feed them. It is true

Joseph had plenty of food in store and could have taken as much as he wanted for himself, but he recognized that the whole of Egypt was his to take care of, and that the surrounding world was at the mercy of Egypt. Faith and good planning go hand in hand and are not contradictory.

42:1-38 Joseph Meets His Brothers

The famine affected 'all the world' (41:57), including the land of Canaan (**42:5**) and Joseph's own family. Jacob, Joseph's father, heard of the availability of grain in Egypt and immediately told his sons, *Why do you just keep looking at each other? ... Go down there and buy some for us, so that we may live and not die* (**42:1-2**). His words imply that none of Joseph's brothers had planned as well as Joseph had. It is as if they were content to just sit and wait for the next rain.

Some people tend to give up when traditional ways of meeting their basic needs fail. But instead of allowing such failure to reduce us to the helpless state of beggars, we need to be innovative and explore other morally healthy options for meeting our needs. As has been mentioned before, African countries need to look for alternative ways of feeding their people when the rains fail. Waiting to be fed by the rest of the world in such times is counter-productive. We need to keep our ears and eyes open and be ready to explore other 'Egypts' that may offer other solutions.

All Joseph's brothers, except Benjamin, set off for Egypt. Jacob did not want Benjamin to go *because he was afraid that harm might come to him* (**42:3-4**). While in Egypt, they had to deal with Joseph, *the governor of the land, the one who sold grain to all its people* (**42:6a**). The brothers did not recognize Joseph because he was older and dressed like a leader in a different culture. But he immediately recognized them. However, he did not let them know this. Instead he *spoke harshly to them* (**42:7-8**). He accused them of being spies who had *come to see where our land is unprotected* (**42:9b, 12**). The brothers repeatedly insisted that they were *honest men* who had come only *to buy food*. They were not a group of spies but a group of brothers, *all sons of one man* (**42:10-11**). They explained that there were originally twelve of them, but only ten of them have come to Egypt because *the youngest is now with our father, and one is no more* (**42:13**).

Though we may question the ten brothers' claim to be honest, given the way they had lied to their father about Joseph, so far what they have said about their family is true. They describe the one brother as 'no more' because they are assuming that after this many years as a slave, Joseph is probably dead. But they do not want to admit that they may have caused his death by selling him, because that would raise questions about their characters.

Their dilemma raises the whole issue of how much we should speak of past sins. How should we handle them? When we have committed an offence against other people, it is often good to speak of it openly in case we are talking to the very persons we offended. If we speak as if we have never sinned, those who know our past failure will see us as pretenders.

Joseph *remembered his dreams* (**42:9a**), and the brothers fulfilled them as they repeatedly addressed him as *lord* (42:10) and spoke of themselves as *your servants* (42:11, 13). Also, *they bowed down to him with their faces to the ground* (**42:6b**). Joseph, who had been *distressed* and *pleaded ... for his life* (**42:21a**) when they were selling him, was now the one before whom they were pleading. He was now in the position of strength, while they were in a position of humiliation and weakness, begging him for food and pleading with him to trust them.

One common sense reason for treating people well is that such reversals of fortune are not uncommon. The one in need today may be the one with the upper hand tomorrow, while the one who has the upper hand today may be the one in need tomorrow.

Joseph put his brothers through several tests to find out how much they had changed. He was especially interested in their attitude towards Benjamin. The key condition for proving their honesty was the presentation to Joseph of their younger brother. At first Joseph wanted one of them to go back for Benjamin while the rest remained in custody (**42:15-16**). But after three days he changed his plan in consideration of the ones for whom they came for food and because of his fear of God (**42:17-18**). He detained only Simeon, while the rest left (**42:19, 24**). But he warned the others, *you must bring your youngest brother to me, so that your words may be verified and that you may not die* (**42:20**).

Faced with this apparent hostility, Joseph's brothers concluded that they were being punished for their own merciless treatment of Joseph (**42:21b**). Reuben, who had tried to save Joseph (37:21-22), reminded them of this and insists that *now we must give an accounting for his blood* (**42:22**). We see here the problem of guilty consciences. While the brothers could not undo the selling, they could have undone the concealing of the matter and could have faced the consequences with their father. They had, however, kept it a secret and now it was catching up with them. There is no wrong that never catches up with the doer unless matters are put right. It may appear as if things have been forgotten, but the matter will still come up in one way or another. As long as the sins we have committed are not recognized, confessed to the Lord and abandoned, they will continue to be a great burden, no matter how much we try to hide our suffering. Only Christ's forgiveness relieves us and restores to us the strength and the joy of living to continue our service of faith.

It is also an odd position for Joseph to be in. The brothers discussed these matters in his presence, not knowing that Joseph, who was using an interpreter, understood them

(**42:23**). The memory of the past was very touching and so *he turned away from them and began to weep* (**42:24a**). This, however, needed to be concealed from the brothers till the appropriate time, and so *he turned back and spoke to them again* and then had *Simeon taken from them and bound before their eyes* (**42:24b**). They needed to know that he meant business.

With Simeon detained, the other nine could go. Joseph ordered that their bags be filled with grain, their silver be put back into their sacks, and that they be given provisions for their journey (**42:25**). His care for them is a clear indication that he did not accuse them of being spies to torment them, but to test them. His attitude towards them, hard as it may have appeared, was for their good.

As his brothers loaded their donkeys and left (**42:26**), they did not know what had been done. But when they stopped for the night, *one of them opened his sack to get food for his donkey and he saw his silver in the mouth of the sack* (**42:27**). At this discovery, *their hearts sank and they turned to each other trembling* (**42:28**). Their reaction was quite understandable since the most natural conclusion was that the man over the land of Egypt was planning to accuse them of theft. Their trip had not been a smooth one, and here was another source of trouble for them.

Upon reaching home, they told Jacob all that had happened (**42:29-34**). Needless to say, Jacob was very troubled at the idea that Benjamin would have to go to Egypt. His words, *You have deprived me of my children*, do not mean that he suspected that the brothers had sold Joseph. It was simply that Joseph was dead (as far as he knew) and Simeon was *no more* in the sense that he was no longer present but was in prison in Egypt. There was little hope of his release (**42:36**). The discovery of the pouch of silver in each man's sack must also have intensified Jacob's feeling that something was very wrong. It was no wonder that he and his sons were *frightened* (**42:35**).

Reuben, who had played a key role in trying to save Joseph's life (37:21-22), now played a key role in making sure the conditions for the release of Simeon were met. He even offered to allow Jacob to put his own sons to death if he did not bring Benjamin back to him (**42:37**). Even with such commitment on the part of Reuben, Jacob's response was 'No'. He says, *My son will not go down there with you; his brother is dead and he is the only one left. If harm comes to him on the journey you are taking, you will bring my grey head down to the grave in sorrow* (**42:38**). The problem was not that he did not trust Reuben, but that Reuben was not in charge of circumstances. They did not know what the intentions of the lord over Egypt were. So far, their experience with him had been unpleasant: he had accused them of spying, put them in custody for three days and detained Simeon.

43:1-15 Joseph's Brothers Return to Egypt

Though Jacob at first refused to let his sons take Benjamin to Egypt (42:38), circumstances made him change his mind. The famine continued and the grain that had been brought from Egypt had all been eaten. There was no option but to return to Egypt to buy more food (**43:2**). His sons knew that it would be a pointless trip without Benjamin. Reuben had tried to persuade their father to part with Benjamin before, without success. Now Judah tried. Twice Judah repeated that the man had warned them that they would not be received unless their brother was with them and that they could not go unless Benjamin was with them (**43:3-5**). He was not being disobedient or disrespectful. He was simply stating the situation.

The possibility of losing Benjamin was still very troubling to Jacob. He blamed his sons for ever mentioning Benjamin (**43:6**), but they responded that they had simply answered one of the man's many questions, without any idea of where it would lead (**43:7**). Aware that any longer delay would jeopardize the lives of their families (**43:8**), Judah offered to take personal responsibility for Benjamin and to *guarantee his safety*. He will accept all the blame if anything happens to him (**43:9**).

Judah's commitment was as great as the one offered by Reuben, which was rejected (42:37). But the circumstances were now different. Hunger was biting everyone, including Jacob who was aged and the children who were delicate (43:8). So Jacob reluctantly agreed to send Benjamin with them, with a prayer for his safety and for the safe return of the imprisoned Simeon (**43:14a**). To increase the chances of a favourable reception, he also sends gifts to the man: *some of the best products of the land ... a little balm and a little honey, some spices and myrrh, some pistachio nuts and almonds* (**43:11**).

Risks should be taken only when absolutely necessary. Even then, care should be taken to prepare well so as to minimize the risk. That having been done, there is a need to trust God that things will work out well.

In addition the brothers were to take *double the amount of silver,* enough to pay for the new grain and to *return the silver* that they assumed had been mistakenly put back into their sacks (**43:12**). The older Jacob knew that it was wrong to keep 'lost and found' items before effort had been made to find their owner. Some today think that they are lucky if they find something that someone else has lost, or even interpret it as the Lord's provision, but it is equivalent to theft to keep these things if there is any chance of returning them to the owner.

Jacob's words *If I am bereaved, I am bereaved* show that it was not easy for him to let Benjamin go (**43:14b**). What this brings to mind is the need to be principled, while at the same time having a discerning heart and knowing when to be flexible. To be so principled that one cannot change one's mind when there is danger to human life ceases to be 'an act of principle' and becomes 'an act of stupidity'. While changes of principle may be humbling at times, it is sometimes the way of wisdom. Jacob, examining the situation carefully, changed his mind and took the risk of being bereaved once more.

Reuben earlier, and now Judah, were sensitive to Jacob's emotions and fears. They did not rush him, though they kept on insisting that there was no alternative to taking Benjamin with them (42:37; 43:4-5, 8-10). And when he gave them instructions, they acted accordingly (**43:15**). While Jacob is to be credited with being able to decide when to give in, his sons, and especially Reuben and Judah, are to be credited with being understanding and respectful of their father. Age and experience have their rightful place in bringing success. At times, respect for them may slow things down (**43:10**), but when the younger act with the blessings of the aged, everyone is happy. The Kiswahili saying, *haraka, haraka, haina baraka* ['hurry, hurry, has no blessing'] applies in situations like these. The young need to remember this when they take over key leadership positions from their elders. The aged must be viewed as good resources for counsel if we are to succeed. If they are seen as a nuisance and are swept aside while the younger generation does its own thing, things do not end well. The story of Rehoboam and Jeroboam is a good illustration of this (1 Kgs 12:3-15).

43:16-45:15 Joseph Reveals Himself

One of the most dramatic experiences a person can have is discovering that someone they have been dealing with for some time is someone they once offended deeply. Joseph is now moving towards making this revelation to his brothers.

43:16-34 A meal together

When Joseph saw that his brothers had come back and had brought Benjamin with them, he instructed the steward of his house to *take these men to my house, slaughter an animal and prepare dinner; they are to eat with me at noon* (**43:16**). The brothers could think of no reason why they were being taken to the house of the lord over the land. They thought it was because of the silver and were very frightened. They suspected some plot to seize them and enslave them, and steal their donkeys (**43:18**). As we know, this was far from the truth, but the brothers could have attacked Joseph in self-defence. How many clashes or even wars are the result of wrong conclusions! Waiting till all the facts are clear is the way of maturity.

The brothers, knowing they were outnumbered by Joseph's supporters, did not react violently but tried to sort out what they thought was the problem. As soon as they entered the house, they approached Joseph's steward and explained that they were ready to repay the silver they had found in their sacks (**43:19-22**). Having assured them that all was well and having brought Simeon to them (**43:23**), the steward *gave them water to wash their feet and provided fodder for their donkeys* (**43:24**). Meanwhile Joseph's brothers nervously *prepared their gifts*, because *they had heard that they were to eat there* (**43:25**).

When Joseph came home, the brothers presented him with the gifts they had brought and bowed down before him to the ground (**43:26**; see Matt 2:11). They were doing the very thing that had so offended them when Joseph reported his dreams! And they did it four times, without any hesitation (42:6; 43:26; 43:28; 44:14).

Joseph then politely asked after Jacob's health: *How is your aged father you told me about? Is he still living?* (**43:27-28**) and then asked to be introduced to Benjamin (**43:29**). Joseph greeted him politely, but at this stage his self-control failed: *Deeply moved at the sight of his brother, Joseph hurried out and looked for a place to weep* (**43:30**). As before (42:24a), he did not yet wish to reveal himself to his brothers. So after he had recovered his composure, he returned to them and the meal began (**43:31**).

Those eating this meal sat in three groups. Joseph sat by himself, as was normal for the one in authority. The brothers sat by themselves. The Egyptians who ate with Joseph sat by themselves. They would not eat at the same table as Joseph's brothers, who they looked down on as Hebrews and shepherds (**43:32**; 46:34).

The arrangements for Joseph's brothers were remarkable. They were seated in the order of age, *from the firstborn to the youngest* (**43:33**). However, instead of the youngest getting the smallest portion, he got *five times as much as anyone else* (**43:34**). Everyone had more than enough, but obviously Benjamin was being treated with special honour. The brothers were amazed at what was going on. They were all grown men. How had the governor known their birth order? Why had they been invited to this meal? And why the special treatment of Benjamin?

44:1-34 Benjamin and the silver cup

Joseph gave further instructions to his servants. After filling the brothers' bags with food and returning their money in the bags, they were to put a special silver cup that belonged to him in Benjamin's bag (**44:1-2**). Then, shortly after the brothers had set off (**44:3**), Joseph instructed his steward to accuse them of having stolen *the cup my master drinks from and also uses for divination* (**44:4-5**). He would have used it for divination by filling it with water and observing the shapes formed by things dropped into the water.

Joseph repeats this claim to make use of divination in **44:15**, although the readers will be well aware that it was not divination that had revealed who had the cup. But what are we to make of these casual references to divination? One possibility is that Joseph, who now had an Egyptian name

and was married the daughter of an Egyptian priest (41:45), had also adopted some of the Egyptians customs. But we also need to remember that Joseph lived more than four hundred years before the law was given to Moses. In that law, the Lord clearly forbids divination (Deut 18:9-13). So we should not cite Joseph as an excuse for us to practise it.

The brothers were amazed when the steward caught up with them and made his accusation (**44:7-8**). Convinced of their innocence, they assured him that *if any of your servants is found to have it, he will die; and the rest of us will become my lord's slaves* (**44:9**). The steward, who knew at least partially what was going on, accepted their commitment but with a lesser penalty: *Whoever is found to have it will become my slave; the rest of you will be free from blame* (**44:10**). We might be wise to learn from the brothers' mistake here, and not to be too confident about matters we cannot be a hundred percent sure of – including what is in parcels that we have not personally packed. Nor should we pass judgement on issues about which we are not fully informed.

The sacks were searched one by one, beginning with the sacks given to the oldest brother (**44:11-12**). Just as they were rejoicing that nothing had been found, with only Benjamin's sack left to search – the cup was found. Benjamin knew he had not stolen the cup, but his brothers did not. The evidence was clear, and there was no way out. They *tore their clothes and loaded their donkeys and returned to the city* (**44:13**).

Joseph was still in the house when Judah and his brothers came in. They humbly threw themselves to the ground before him (**44:14**) and heard his accusation (44:15). Unaware that this was all a strategy and thinking that Benjamin had actually taken the cup, Judah admitted the accusation and accepted the punishment: *We are now my lord's slaves – we ourselves and the one who was found to have the cup* (**44:16**).

Joseph's intention with this trick was not to punish his brothers but to discover their attitude to Benjamin. So he insisted that he would not punish all of them, but would keep only Benjamin as his slave (**44:17**). Horrified at this prospect, Judah launched into a most moving plea for his brother's life (**44:18-32**). In these fifteen verses, he humbly referred to Joseph as *my lord* five times, and used *servant* for himself, his brothers or their father ten times. He also describes Joseph as *equal to Pharaoh himself* (**44:18**).

Judah told the whole story about their first encounter with the unrecognized Joseph and the difficulty their father had in parting with Benjamin since *his brother is dead, and he is the only one of his mother's sons left, and his father loves him* (**44:19-24**). Judah's stressed the personal commitment and assurance that he had given to his father that he would bring Benjamin back, and the grief it would cause their father if they went back without him (**44:25-32**). Judah concluded his speech with one of the clearest OT examples of someone taking the place of another as he offered to take his brother's place as a slave (**44:33**). Judah spoke these words thinking that Benjamin was guilty. He was willing to bear the punishment he thought Benjamin deserved. He did this because he cared about his father and wanted to spare him the loss of Benjamin (**44:34**).

45:1-15 Joseph's revelation

When Judah was finished, Joseph needed no further proof that his brothers' attitudes had changed and that they had outgrown their jealousy. He *could no longer control himself* (**45:1**). He ordered everyone except his brothers out of the room. This was a solemn and emotional moment that would not be shared with anyone else. Yet Joseph *wept so loudly that the Egyptians heard him, and Pharaoh's household heard about it* (**45:2**).

After identifying himself, Joseph's first words expressed his concern for his father (**45:3**). But his brothers were stunned and too terrified to answer him. Their terror must have flowed from their awareness of their own guilt and of the power Joseph now had over them. Recognizing their emotions, Joseph did not tell them that they were right to be frightened and ashamed of what they had done, which would be most people's natural response. Instead, Joseph told them not to be distressed or angry with themselves for selling him to Egypt (**45:4-5a**).

Joseph could speak like this because he had access to a supernatural perspective. He encouraged his brothers not to be distressed because God had sent him ahead of them in order to save their lives and the lives of others (**45:5b, 7**). He absolved his brothers from guilt because *it was not you who sent me here, but God* (**45:8**). God had even made Joseph *father to Pharaoh,* that is, one of Pharaoh's most trusted advisors. Joseph did not deny that what his brothers had done was wrong, for they intended to harm him, but he knew that God had used their evil act to produce a good result (50:20).

From Joseph, we learn the lesson of forgiving even the worst of deeds against us. From his brothers, we learn that the tides of life change. The harm we do to others comes round to haunt us; therefore it is wise to do good to everyone at all times. From God, we learn that his ways are above human ways and that humans cannot frustrate his plans. Because he is able to do anything, he can even create good out of evil.

Joseph asked that his father be brought to Egypt. Jacob would learn that Joseph was alive and had a high position in Egypt (**45:9, 13**). The reason he urged them all to move to Egypt, besides his natural desire to see his father, was that there were still five more years of famine to come, and he did not want his father and brothers to become destitute in Canaan (**45:11**).

Joseph expressed his love for his brothers in his actions as he embraced each of them, beginning with his full brother Benjamin, and wept (**45:15**). Up to this point, the brothers seem to have been too paralysed to know what to do. The revelation was too overwhelming. But Joseph's embrace of each them was healing, and afterwards they *talked with him.* We do not know what they talked to Joseph about but we can suppose that they asked his forgiveness.

There is a lesson here: Through the grace of forgiveness, we can turn our hurts into blessings for those who have tried to harm us. When we show kindness to those who have treated us badly, we not only teach them that they were wrong, but also give them the joy and relief of being forgiven. (This, of course, does not apply to those who have hardened their hearts, but that does not appear to have been the case with Joseph's brothers.) Joseph's kind treatment of his brothers gave them great emotional relief (even if they retained some lingering uncertainty about whether he could possibly really have forgiven them – see 50:15-18).

45:16-28 Pharaoh's Support

Though Joseph was certain that Jacob would live near him (45:10), he needed Pharaoh's approval. It must have given Joseph great joy to note how warmly Pharaoh welcomed the arrival of his brothers (**45:16**). What could have made Joseph, who was upright in all his administrative dealings, so appealing to Pharaoh and his officials? His popularity contrasts with the complaints we often hear from Christian government officials, who say that they lost favour because they were too upright in carrying out their duties.

It is possible that governments today are indeed so corrupt that anyone whose work is always clean is hated (see 1 Pet 3:13-14). But it is also possible that we can learn something else from Joseph. No matter how elevated his position, Joseph allowed Pharaoh to be Pharaoh. Joseph was the one who saved Egypt and all the surrounding nations during the seven-year famine, but he never let this go to his head. He did his duties faithfully while not forgetting what his position was. Is it possible that some of those who want to clean up some of the corruption in governments that they are part of throw the baby out with the bath water? In their criticism of the system, they may humiliate their superiors. Christians in government should try to live in submission to the authorities over them even as they make their own positions known. If they can do this, their positions may eventually begin to be accepted by those around them, who would react with great hostility to direct criticism. Gentle criticism that preserves people's dignity can persuade those who know they are wrong to change. But when criticism humiliates the one criticized, the critic will encounter animosity and may well lose his or her position, after which the criticism counts for nothing. If we are to have any hope of changing the system, we need to find ways of remaining within it.

Pharaoh's positive attitude towards Joseph was expressed in his instruction that Jacob and his household be brought to Egypt (**45:17**), in his offer of the *best of the land of Egypt* for them to settle on (**45:18**, **20**) and in the offer to help with transporting any children and wives who would find the journey difficult (**45:19**).

Because of Joseph, Pharaoh extended his favour to Jacob, his other sons and everyone in his household. One person's character can make a difference for many others. One person's character can bless a whole nation. In this case, a whole family was materially blessed through Pharaoh's directive. How much greater the blessing that God could order! God may be looking for only one person like Joseph in a country's government, and then he will pour his blessings on that nation though him or her. No matter what, we should never cease doing what is right – even when it seems to us that we are the only one.

With Pharaoh's full support, Joseph equipped his brothers with transport and provisions (**45:21**). To Benjamin he gave *three hundred shekels of silver and five sets of clothes* (**45:22**). He also sent presents and provisions for Jacob: *ten donkeys loaded with the best things of Egypt, and ten female donkeys loaded with grain and bread and other provisions for his journey* (**45:23**). Knowing that his brothers would talk about what had happened on the way home and blame each other, he told them, *Don't quarrel on the way!* (**45:24**).

When Joseph's brothers gave Jacob the news, he was *stunned; he did not believe them* (**45:26**). However, when he *saw the carts Joseph had sent to carry him back, the spirit of their father Jacob revived* (**45:27**). His focus on Joseph's death (37:33; 42:36, 38) was replaced with the conviction, *My son Joseph is still alive. I will go and see him before I die* (**45:28**).

46:1-47:12 Jacob Moves to Egypt

46:1-4 Jacob's time with God

Though Jacob must have been anxious to get to Egypt and see his long lost son as soon as possible, he did not allow the urgency of the journey to cause him to lose sight of the one who had kept him alive and watched over his son. So, *when he reached Beersheba, he offered sacrifices to the God of his father Isaac* (**46:1**). God rewarded Jacob with a vision in the night that began with his hearing his name called twice, probably to let him know that what he was about to hear was important (**46:2**). The speaker then identified himself as *the God of your father* (**46:3a**). These words would also remind Jacob that God had shown him and his fathers that he is in control of all circumstances.

But this same God has forbidden his father Isaac to go to Egypt (26:2-3) and so Jacob must have worried about how his

journey there would relate to God's covenant with Abraham and Isaac in regard to the promised land. So God assured him that he need *not be afraid to go down to Egypt* (**46:3b**). This journey too was part of God's plan. It would be in Egypt that God would fulfil his promise to turn the descendants of Abraham *into a great nation* (**46:3c**). He would take them there and he would bring him back again (**46:4a**). Canaan would still be the promised land (see 15:13).

God's final promise that *Joseph's own hand will close your eyes* (**46:4b**) was an assurance that Jacob would see Joseph. He would not die on the journey, or miss seeing his son because he had stopped to offer a sacrifice to the Lord.

We, too, need to remember that we will not miss the Lord's good things if we take time to worship him. Students who take some time in their busy schedule to worship God will not miss the desired good grades. Pastors who take time to be with God will never, all other things being equal, miss effectiveness in their ministry. Time spent with God rewards us rather than depriving us of anything.

46:5-27 Jacob's company

Jacob went to Egypt with his sons and grandsons and his daughters and granddaughters (**46:7**), sixty-six persons, which with the two sons who had been born to Joseph in Egypt and Joseph and Jacob himself made seventy in all (**46:27**).

The focus is on Jacob as the respectable old man (*mzee* in Kiswahili), but his sons are the strong ones who drive the carts (**46:5**). So, while on the one hand Jacob *took with him ...* (**46:7**), on the other hand he was taken (46:5). We are reminded of the interdependence of the old and the young. We often see competition or struggle between generations. But we need to remember that without the 'old man', entrance into Egypt (where there is food) will not be so smooth, while without the 'younger ones' we will not get to Egypt. We need each other to get the best for all.

Pharaoh had told Joseph's brothers that they did not need to bring their belongings for all would be provided for them (45:20). However, it is difficult to get rid of things we have become attached to. Joseph's brothers were no exception. *They also took with them their livestock and the possessions they had acquired in Canaan* (**46:6**). There is nothing wrong with this, but it brings to mind how we always carry our presuppositions to a new subject, our old mentality to new political systems, our traditions to our today, and so on. We need to watch lest our baggage hinder us from receiving new blessings.

46:28-30 Jacob meets Joseph

There is deep emotion as Jacob and Joseph meet: *As soon as Joseph appeared before him, he threw his arms around his father and wept for a long time* (**46:29**). Jacob's words are the warmest a father can say: *Now I am ready to die, since I have seen for myself that you are still alive* (**46:30**).

The close relationship between Joseph and Jacob is admirable. But such a relationship should not be at the expense of good relationships with other sons and daughters. Each son and daughter has his or her place, as shown by Judah's role in Jacob's meeting with Joseph (**46:28**). Just being a messenger was important in making the meeting go well.

In some African homes we see a father focus on the son who provides the greater part of his financial support and treat the other children as if they do not exist. This is wrong, for as those who are with him all the time, the other children also do important things, whose absence would be noticed.

46:31-47:12 Pharaoh's welcome

There is no indication of the amount of time between Pharaoh's words in 45:17-20 and Jacob's arrival in Egypt. It was, however, long enough for Pharaoh, who undoubtedly had many other concerns, to need a reminder once they had arrived (**46:31-32**). Joseph now had a lot of experience in dealing with the Egyptians and so he took care to orient his brothers about what they would need to say when they met Pharaoh. They would have to stress that they were shepherds, because if they did this they would be encouraged to settle in *the region of Goshen,* where they would be separate from the Egyptians, for *all shepherds are detestable to the Egyptians* (**46:33-34**).

Joseph then carefully selected five of his brothers to be presented to Pharaoh (**47:1-2**). When Pharaoh asked the predictable question, (**47:3**; 46:33-34), the brothers replied as Joseph had instructed them: *We have come to live here awhile, because the famine is severe in Canaan and your servants' flocks have no pasture. So now, please let your servants settle in Goshen* (**47:4**). There is nothing wrong in being specific about what we want – something many of us Africans tend to shy away from, preferring only to imply it in what is said. Being direct and clear is not an offence, even if the request is not granted. The same principle applies when we approach God in prayer. He takes no offence when we tell him exactly what we desire. Whether he grants it or not, however, must be left to him, and his response must be accepted with appreciation.

Joseph had already found favour with Pharaoh, and consequently Pharaoh was concerned to meet the needs of the people Joseph cared about. He was quite happy to allow them to settle in Goshen (**47:5-6a**; see 45:18). He not only provided land, but also offered them employment, telling Joseph, *If you know of any of them with special ability, put them in charge of my own livestock* (**47:6b**). What a warm welcome by Pharaoh, and all because Joseph had lived such an honourable life! Pharaoh also wanted to use Joseph's brothers in their areas of expertise. In Africa, we have many displaced people from foreign lands living here. How good have we been in providing opportunities of employment for them, so that they can bless their host countries with their expertise? Almost every African country is struggling with the unemployment of her own citizens, but that should not keep us from exploring what special skills the displaced among us may have to offer.

The interview with Joseph's brothers had been a businesslike one, but the aged Jacob's appearance before Pharaoh was more like a courtesy call. When Joseph presented him before Pharaoh, *Jacob blessed Pharaoh* on his arrival and on his departure (**47:7, 10**). Pharaoh did not question his right to bless him, but politely asked him his age (**47:8**). Jacob replied that he was *a hundred and thirty* years old, but that these years *have been few and difficult* (**47:9**). If we recall the years he spent labouring for Laban and the years he had lived believing that Joseph had been devoured by a wild animal, we can understand why he thought that he had a difficult life. His grandfather Abraham had lived to the age of 175 years (25:7) and Isaac to the age of 180 years (35:28). Jacob was still far from attaining their age. He would, however, live seventeen more years before dying at the age of 147 (47:28).

Thus Joseph settled his father and his brothers and their families in Egypt, just as the Lord had sent him there to do. He got them property in the *best part of the land, the district of Rameses,* which was part of Goshen (**47:11**), and he provided them with food (**47:12**).

47:13-26 Joseph's Strategy for the Future

When Jacob and his household moved to Egypt, close to five more years of famine still remained (45:6). Joseph was, therefore, concerned about making sure not only his father and brothers were provided for, but also all of Egypt and the surrounding regions. It is worth noting that Joseph looked after his family affairs without neglecting the duties of his office. In Africa there have been too many cases of embezzlement of public funds, uncalled for absence from duty, and too little effort to do a good job. Christians must pioneer change and show themselves to be good planners who are able to take care of their personal and public responsibilities and meet present and future needs of their families and of society.

Not only did Joseph have a strategy to prepare for this period of famine and to start distributing the food during it, he also had a plan for the future. Once the people had run out of money to pay for food he told them to bring in their livestock in exchange for grain (**47:13-17**). But the following year they had neither money nor livestock, and the famine continued. So Joseph arranged to buy their land in exchange for food (**47:18-20**). By buying all the land (except that of the priests, who did not need to sell since Pharaoh gave them food – **47:22, 26b**), Joseph was able to

AUTHORITY AND THE BIBLE

Authority has been defined as 'the right to choose and to settle one's own course of action without consulting anyone else, and … the right to tell people what to do and what not to do, what to believe and what not to believe on one's own personal responsibility' (Barclay, *By What Authority*, 1974). This is what Jesus is referring to when he declares: 'All authority in heaven and on earth has been given to me' (Matt 28:18). Nothing and nowhere is excluded from his authority. He has the authority to tell us how to live. And he has given us his instructions in the Bible, which is the owner's manual on how to live successfully. It will be the book by which God will ultimately judge all human thoughts, actions and institutions.

God has delegated some of his authority to us, and we need to learn how to exercise this authority appropriately. The first principle to remember is that although the Bible has much to say about the importance of governing ourselves, it also makes it clear that individuals are not responsible only to themselves. If this were the case, we would have the type of anarchy that prevailed in the days of the Judges, when 'everyone did as he saw fit' (Judg 21:25).

Individuals live within the context of other institutions that God has provided, namely the family, the church and the state. All of these institutions are subordinate to God. Thus no institution or group can claim to be the final arbiter of truth and power or claim the right to eliminate all diversity. God thus maintains a balance between individual liberty and the power of groups.

Government, by which we mean direction, regulation, control and restraint, begins with *self-government*. There will be no reform of any other form of government until we ourselves have ceased to be rebels against God and have become his faithful subjects. There can be no love for God and our neighbour, nor true obedience to God, until he gives each of us a new and teachable heart (Ezek 36:26-27).

The next level of authority is *family government*. If you cannot govern yourself, you will not be able to govern in the home, as can be seen in the way King David's personal sins affected his entire family. Thus Paul specifies that an elder must be able to 'manage his own family well and see that his children obey him with proper respect' (1 Tim 3:4). As the authorities in the home, parents are responsible for educating their children (Deut 4:1, 9,10, 40; 6:1-8, 20-25; Ps 78; Eph 6:4); controlling and disciplining their children (Prov 19:18; Exod 20:12; Heb 12:3-11; Ps 89:30-32; Prov 10:13; 13:1, 24; 15:5, 10, 32; 22:6, 15); and for the general welfare of the family (1 Tim 5:8).

The symbol of family authority is the rod (Prov 13:24). Parents have the authority to exercise discipline over a child with a rod of correction (but not with a rod of abuse!).

The next level of authority is *church government*. The family and the church are the training ground for governing or judging the world (1 Cor 6:2; 1 Tim 3:5). We Christians will not be good governors in the civil sphere if we fail to govern well in the church. Thus Paul scolds the church at Corinth both for the immorality that has affected self and family government (1 Cor 5) and for their inability to settle the smallest legal disputes within the church (1 Cor 6:2).

The church has authority to discipline erring brothers or sisters in Christ by using the power of 'the keys' to bar unrepentant members from the Lord's table and finally to excommunicate them if they remain unrepentant (Matt 16:19; 18:15-20). However, it cannot use the rod or wield the sword as punishment.

Civil government is what most people have in mind when they think of 'the authorities'. The symbol of state authority is the sword (Romans 13:4). The state has authority to wield the sword as punishment for both civil and criminal offences, but it cannot use its authority to influence the inner workings of families or the church. These institutions are outside its jurisdiction. When the church disciplines a local church member over an ecclesiastical matter, the state cannot rightly be approached to use its authority to override what the disciplined member might consider an unfair decision. And if the state usurps authority that belongs to God and issues decrees that contradict the law of God (for example, by demanding worship – Rev. 13) the church has every right to disobey (Acts 4:18-20).

The Bible thus sets up a chain of authority in which everyone is responsible to someone else, and all are ultimately responsible to God. This multiplication of authorities means that all earthly authority is delegated and limited, which counters the sinful tendency toward tyranny. But tyranny and corruption do arise when authority structures, from the individual to civil governments at the local, regional, and state levels, break down, and all authority comes to rest in one institution, usually the state.

Too often Christians turn to the state for relief because of the failure of individuals, families, businesses, schools, churches, and civil governments at the local and regional levels. But the state is not the answer for sin, except in its ability to impose temporal punishment for criminal acts. In fact, as recent history proves, the state frequently compounds the ills of society when it claims jurisdiction outside the area of its proper authority.

Individuals must assume their responsibilities under God and thoroughly transform their families. Then, working with other like-minded individuals, they must transform their schools, churches, vocations, local communities and the national civil government. But at each step, it must be remembered that regeneration, the basis of all godly authority, begins with God working in the individual and extends to every facet of life.

Patrick M. Musibi

give directions about how it should be used in the future. His objective was not to enslave the people but to make sure that the land of Egypt was managed well in the future.

When at last the rains came, Joseph gave the people seeds to plant, but he also ordered that one fifth of any crop they harvested would belong to Pharaoh (**47:23-24**). This became a law in Egypt (**47:26a**). Though not stated, the idea was that some of each year's harvest would be kept in storage so that there would always be a good supply of food. The people could keep the remaining four-fifths.

What we see here is an administrator with the people's interest at heart and an awareness of the need to provide for the future. He is the kind of leader that many African nations cry out for. The current generation should not be milked to the last drop by taxation, and some of the income the government gets should be set aside for use by future generations. Some African countries live in debt and do not hesitate to increase those debts for the comfort of today, while not caring about the implications for the next generation. We must make provision for our children, not leave them our debts.

47:27-49:28 Jacob's Final Years

47:27-28 Jacob's circumstances

Jacob's descendants are now for the first time referred to as *Israelites* (**47:27**). Their rapid increase in numbers reminds us that Jacob had seventy direct descendants when he arrived in Egypt (46:26-27), and looks forward to Exodus 1:7, where we read, 'the Israelites were fruitful and multiplied greatly and became exceedingly numerous, so that the land was filled with them'.

Jacob's final years were concerned with preparation for his death (47:29-31) and the passing on of his blessings. He had blessed Pharaoh when he was presented to him (47:7, 10), and later he blessed his own sons and Joseph's sons. It is a good thing for an old man or woman to die blessing rather than toiling! Those who forget to take care of their parents in their old age cause them to be preoccupied with what they will eat, drink and wear, rather than with blessings. The children then miss out on the old person's good wishes.

47:29-31 Jacob plans for his burial

All human beings fear death, and none can escape it. Old age always ends in death. However, some people fear to talk about death, as if by ignoring it they will be able to avoid dying. So they fail to make their wishes known, and this often leads to disputes after their death as the living argue about the wishes of the dead person. Jacob was not like that. When the *time drew near for Israel to die*, he made his wishes known.

He called for his son Joseph to inform him of his wishes (**47:29a**). While this was reasonable as Joseph was prob-

ably the one who would be in a position to make sure that they were carried out, it might have been better if he had called all his sons together. Ideally, everyone involved should know the wishes of the dying person.

Jacob also took the matter very seriously, as is shown by his having Joseph put his hand under Jacob's thigh and promise to carry out his wishes (**47:29b**). A promise made like this was as binding as a vow (**47:31a**; see 24:2b, 3).

Jacob was also quite specific about what he wanted. He did not want to be buried in Egypt, but wanted to be buried alongside his ancestors (**47:30a**). When he talks about this later (49:29-32), he is even more detailed. When the wish is expressed very clearly, it leaves no room for different interpretations that could create divisions in the family. Jacob also took care to express this desire as a request rather than as a demand, prefacing it with *If I have found favour in your eyes … promise you will show me kindness and faithfulness* (47:29). Even for parents who deserve what they are asking for, it is wise to request rather than command. After all, a dead parent is not able to enforce obedience! Jacob requested, and Joseph responded, *I will do as you say* (**47:30b**). A son or daughter who willingly commits himself or herself to the wishes of an aged parent will definitely act accordingly when the parent is dead.

Jacob then *worshipped as he leaned on the top of his staff* (**47:31b**). We are not told specifically what prompted Jacob to worship, but he had plenty for which to thank God. There was his life of 147 years; there was Joseph before him whom he had for many years thought was dead; and there was the land of Canaan, the promised land, where his body would rest, to mention only a few. It is a beautiful thing to die a worshipping person! Long life, and all that goes with it, is a blessing from the Lord.

48:1-22 Jacob blesses Manasseh and Ephraim

Some time later, we do not know how long, Joseph was told that his father was ill and he went to see him, taking *his two sons Manasseh and Ephraim* (**48:1**). When Jacob heard of Joseph's arrival, he *rallied his strength and sat up on the bed* (**48:2**). This was an important occasion and could not be conducted lying down.

Jacob declared that Joseph's two sons *Ephraim and Manasseh* would have the same rights and shares as his own sons (**48:5b**). They would have their full share in what the Lord promised Jacob at *Luz* (Bethel) (**48:3**; 28:19; 35:6, 11-15). The Lord's promises included *a community of peoples* and the land of Canaan as *an everlasting possession to your descendants after you* (**48:4**). This was the reason that Ephraim and Manasseh were allocated a share of the promised land alongside Reuben, Simeon, and their other uncles (Josh 16–17). This may also be part of the reason why the narrator includes them among the seventy said to have been part of Jacob's life when he came to live in Egypt (46:27).

It is possible that Ephraim and Manasseh were not incorporated into Jacob's household as separate tribes but as a single tribe (the tribe of Ephraim and Manasseh), in which case they received a single blessing, that of Joseph (49:22). Later, however, they clearly split into two tribes, possibly because it was difficult for the first-born Manasseh to submit to his younger brother Ephraim. Joseph's other sons, born after Ephraim and Manasseh, would not receive special treatment, and *the territory they inherit will be reckoned under the names of their brothers* (**48:6**).

The mention of his sons reminds Jacob of his favourite wife, Rachel, Joseph's mother, who died *as I was returning from Paddan, … while we were still on the way, a little distance from Ephrath*, which is another name for Bethlehem (**48:7**; 35:19). One can almost feel the pain as Jacob adds, *So I buried her there beside the road to Ephrath.*

Turning back to Joseph, Jacob asked, *Who are these?* (**48:8**), suggesting that he did not recognize Ephraim and Manasseh, possibly because his sight or his memory was failing or because he had not seen them often in his old age. When Joseph identified them as *the sons God has given me here* (**48:9, 5a**) Jacob asked Joseph to bring them *to me so I may bless them.*

The blessing ceremony first involved kissing and embracing them (**48:10b**). As Jacob did this, he rejoiced at the Lord's work, saying to Joseph, *I never expected to see your face again, and now God has allowed me to see your children too* (**48:11**). Of course, the word 'see' here may not be meant to be taken literally, for Jacob's eyes *were failing because of old age, and he could hardly see* (**48:10a**). For many years, Jacob had thought Joseph was dead, but now he was with him and his sons. It was a joyous moment.

Joseph then took Ephraim and Manasseh from Israel's knees, and humbly bowed down with his face to the ground (**48:12**). He then took Ephraim, his younger son, with his right hand, so that Israel's left hand could rest on him, and Manasseh, his eldest, with his left hand so that Israel's right hand could rest on him (**48:13**). Then the unexpected happened: Israel reached out his right hand and put it on Ephraim's head, though he was the younger, and crossing his arms, he put his left hand on Manasseh's head (**48:14**). The right hand was supposed to be placed on the older and the left on the younger, for the older was viewed as the leader of the younger.

Joseph was not happy about this. Thinking that his father must be confused, he took hold of his father's hand to move it from Ephraim's head to Manasseh's head (**48:17-18**). But Jacob was well aware of what he was doing. He foresaw that Ephraim would rise to be greater than his older brother (**48:19**). That was why he mentioned Ephraim before Manasseh in 48:20.

What was happening was nothing unusual in terms of God's plans. Isaac had taken precedence over his older brother Ishmael. Joseph himself will be given Reuben's birthright (48:22; 1 Chr 5:1-3). God's plans are not tied to when one was born, but to his own choice, as he blesses each one individually.

The words of blessing that Israel spoke were a blessing on Joseph and on his sons. The blessing took the form of a prayer committing them to the Lord who is in control of history. This Lord had been the God of Jacob's father and grandfather, and Jacob can say that he *has been my shepherd all my life to this day, the Angel who has delivered me from all harm* (**48:15-16**). It is to this God that he appeals saying, *May he bless these boys.* He then asks for two specific blessings for them: continuity with the past, *May they be called by my name and the names of my fathers Abraham and Isaac*, and continuity in the future, *May they increase greatly upon the earth.*

Israel's second blessing, *In your name will Israel pronounce this blessing: 'May God make you like Ephraim and Manasseh'* (**48:20**), is not as clear as 48:15-16. The best way to understand it is that Jacob changed the focus to Joseph as he said, *in your name* (Joseph), and also changed the focus from himself (Jacob) to Israel (as a nation). As they (Israel) do so, they will mention Joseph's name, and use his sons, Ephraim and Manasseh, as the measure of blessings.

Recognizing that Joseph was the leader of his brothers, Israel assured him of the Lord's presence: *God will be with you and take you back to the land of your fathers* (**48:21-22**). He also gave Joseph a piece of land that was special to him: *the ridge … I took from the Amorites with my sword and my bow.*

49:1-28 Jacob blesses his sons

The blessing of Joseph's sons had happened because Joseph had come to see Jacob (48:1). But now Israel specifically summoned his twelve sons to him: *Gather around so I can tell you what will happen to you in days to come* (**49:1**). Though what Israel says may be merely his wish or prayer for each of his sons, in God's providence he is actually prophesying. He is revealing what will happen to their descendants, rather than determining it. Israel speaks to them one by one, from Reuben to Benjamin. He *blessed them, giving each the blessing appropriate to him* (**49:28**).

One of the details that has proven to be very intriguing, especially for some Western scholars, is the accuracy with which Jacob spoke of his sons' futures (at least, for those for whom we have a fuller account). Some scholars have gone as far as to claim that these statements must have been put into Jacob's mouth after the events. However, most Africans, even those who do not believe that Jacob spoke with God-given prophetic knowledge, do not have a problem with these verses. Africans generally believe that a parent's blessing or curse that is uttered without malice and from a sincere heart will not go unfulfilled. In God's providence here, Jacob spoke prophetically.

JEWS AND GENTILES

Prior to Abraham, all peoples were grouped together without distinction. However, when God entered into a covenant relationship with Abraham and his descendants, this resulted in their becoming known as God's chosen people, everyone else became known as Gentiles.

Originally, Abraham's descendants were called Israelites (Exod 1:9) or Hebrews (Exod 1:15). After the division of the kingdom, the term 'Jew' came into use to refer to the inhabitants of Judah, the southern kingdom. Because the majority of those who returned after the exile were from this kingdom, the meaning of 'Jew' was expanded to embrace all descendants of Abraham (Ezra 4:12; John 18:33). In the NT, the term's meaning changed again, as the Jewish leaders' hostility to Jesus' ministry led some NT writers to refer to those Jews who did not believe in Jesus as 'the Jews' (John 20:19).

A Gentile is simply anyone who is not Jewish. The word is also sometimes translated as 'nation' or 'alien' in the NIV. There is no evidence that God's choice of Abraham's descendants was meant to result in a hostile relationship between Jews and Gentiles. Originally, Gentiles, other than the Canaanites, were treated quite cordially by the Israelites. God commanded the Israelites to show love and sympathy to those Gentiles who lived among them, for the Israelites too had been aliens in Egypt (Deut 10:19). Israelite men like Moses, Joseph and Boaz married Gentile women. The Kenites were treated as equals (Judg 1:16); Uriah the Hittite was a trusted soldier (2 Sam 11); Ittai the Gittite was captain of David's guard (2 Sam 18:2); Araunah, a Jebusite, was a respected resident of Jerusalem (2 Sam 24:16-24)

However, after the Jews returned from captivity in Babylon they developed an exclusivist attitude and discouraged the practice of intermarriage (Ezra 9:12). This exclusivism was intensified by the savage persecution the Jews endured at the hands of those like Antiochus IV (170 BC), who tried to force them to adopt Greek customs. Separation of Jew and Gentile became increasingly strict. By NT times, Gentiles were regarded as unclean and as enemies of God. It was considered unlawful for God's people to have any friendly interactions with them. Even those who became proselytes were not admitted to full fellowship.

With the coming of Christ, a new era began in the relationship between Jews and Gentiles, and in relation to the place of the Gentiles in God's plan. Gentile believers were no longer foreigners and aliens but became fellow citizens with God's people (Gal 3:28-29; Eph 2:19).

The early church struggled to adapt to this change in the status of Gentiles. Christian Jews were offended when Peter broke with tradition by eating with Cornelius (Acts 10:9-48). Some insisted that Gentile believers could not be saved unless they were circumcised. After this question was debated at the Jerusalem Council, Gentile believers were assured that they need not follow the whole Jewish law but should observe some dietary and moral requirements (Acts 15).

The acceptance of the Gentile community into the young church allowed for the rapid spread of the gospel into North Africa and Ethiopia, Europe and Asia. The rest of Africa south of the Sahara received the gospel only centuries later from European missionaries.

At one time, Paul's description of the Gentiles applied to Africans. We were separate from Christ, excluded from citizenship, foreigners to the covenant, without hope and without God (Eph 2:12). But now the phenomenal spread of the gospel on this continent is making Africa the centre of gospel growth in the Gentile world.

The Jews' rejection of their Messiah led to their being oppressed by the Gentiles for an appointed time (Luke 21:24). From AD 70 until the reconstruction of the nation of Israel in 1948, Jerusalem was in the hands of Gentiles. The present day of opportunity for Gentiles, will close with Israel's future restoration (Jer 31:31-34; Rom 11:25-27).

The Gentiles do not share in the Jews' earthly covenant, which even Israel is not now enjoying, but rather they share in heavenly citizenship through the grace of Jesus Christ. The church has not replaced the Jews in God's plan, but the Gentiles have been grafted into the promise that was previously only available to the Jews through the Abrahamic covenant (Rom 11:17-24).

David Oginde

- *Reuben* was Jacob's eldest, who once excelled in honour and power (**49:3**). But he lost his birthright and received what was closer to a curse because he had defiled his father's bed (**49:4**). The incident that was only mentioned in passing in 35:22 totally changed Reuben's future. No matter how old our sins may be, they catch up with us if they have not been dealt with by way of confession and forgiveness. His descendants never provided a national leader that we know of. He certainly no longer excelled in honour and power.
- *Simeon and Levi* were judged for their vices of violence and fury (**49:5-6**), which were shown in incidents like

the one in 34:25-31. Jacob cursed those vices, but not the men (**49:7a**). He wanted them to repent of their violence and cultivate virtues that would be a blessing to others. The price these men would pay for their violence was that their descendants would be dispersed (**49:7b**). But the outworking of this judgment took very different forms. Whereas Simeon's descendants were scattered among the tribe of Judah (Josh 19:1), the descendants of Levi were scattered in the honourable duty of serving as priests all over Israel (Josh 21:1-3; Num 18:20, 23). The Levites found favour before the Lord because of the courage they later showed in confronting sin (Exod 32:26, 29).

- *Judah* is told that *your father's sons will bow down to you* (**49:8**). This may be implying that Judah was being given the birthright due to the eldest that Reuben had forfeited by his immorality, and that the next two brothers, Simeon and Levi, had forfeited by their violence. Judah did not receive this honour because he was particularly virtuous. His marriage to a Canaanite woman and his treatment of Tamar clearly show that he was not. He was chosen solely because of God's grace. However, Jacob also addresses Joseph as *the one over your brothers* in 48:22, which may suggest that Joseph was given the birthright, a position that is supported by the explicit statement to this effect in 1 Chronicles 5:1-3. It may be that the statement about Joseph acknowledged that he was the leader at that time because of his position in Egypt, while that about Judah revealed his permanent status, for his line would be the one in which God had graciously chosen to work. Hundreds of years in the future, David would be the first ruler to emerge from his line, and from then on Judah's descendants would play a prominent role until the birth of the Messiah, the King of kings (**49:9-10**; Matt 1:3).
- *Zebulun* would later be allocated land that, while not directly on the coast, was indeed close to where Jacob said it would be (**49:13**; Josh 19:10-16).
- *Issachar* inherited good land without having to struggle for it (Josh 19:17-23). We do not know enough for us to test whether being strong but lazy became a permanent characteristic of this tribe (**49:14-15**).
- *Dan* was allocated land near the northern boundary of Israel. This tribe was known for preventing enemies from entering the land of Israel. In this way, they kept justice (**49:16**). Their being like a serpent (**49:17**) may relate to their swiftness in wars, or possibly to their introduction of idolatry to Israel (Judg 18:30-31). One of Jeroboam's golden calves was in Dan's territory (1 Kgs 12:28-30).
- *Gad,* who settled east of the Jordan, was exposed to many attacks (**49:19**). The men of Gad were renowned as fighters (1 Chr 5:18; 12:8-15).
- *Asher* settled north of Mount Carmel in very good farm land (**49:20**; Josh 19:24-31).
- *Naphtali* was a tribe that is described in **49:21** as producing either *beautiful fawns* (NIV) or 'beautiful words' (NASB). We know very little about this tribe, but if Barak was a member of it, he certainly contributed to the beautiful words of the song of Deborah and Barak (Judg 5).
- *Joseph* received blessings comparable to those of Judah because he was the one who truly knew God, the Shepherd and the Rock of Israel (**49:22-26**). His descendants provided many leaders. Joshua, Deborah, Samuel and Jeroboam were Ephraimites, while Gideon and Jephthah were from Manasseh. Their land was also very fertile and productive.
- *Benjamin's* future was said to involve strength and success, but also cruelty (**49:27**). Saul, one of his descendants, showed exactly these characteristics. The cruel men of Gibeah were also Benjamites (Judg 19:16-20:48).

Pronouncements of blessings or curses on people's descendants do not imply there will be no exceptions. A descendant who chose a lifestyle different to that which called forth the blessing or curse could be exempt from the pronouncement made. Thus there may have been members of Judah or Joseph who never enjoyed the blessings, while some members of Reuben did. In general terms, however, Jacob's pronouncements were fulfilled. It is always safe to do what calls for blessing and avoid what could call for a curse. God works through such actions to determine the course of our future.

49:29-50:14 Jacob's Death

Immediately before dying, Jacob gave his final instructions regarding his burial. He was to be buried in the family burial plot that the family owned because Abraham had bought it. He repeats this information twice, as if to make sure that his sons know that they are the legal owners of this piece of land (**49:29-30, 32**). There he will rest in the company of five others he cared for: *Abraham and his wife Sarah ... Isaac and his wife Rebekah* and *Leah* (**49:31**; see 23:17-20; 25:9-10; 35:27-29).

After giving these instructions, *Jacob breathed his last* (**49:33**). Overcome with grief, *Joseph threw himself upon his father and wept over him and kissed him* (**50:1**). Death comes without announcement and, therefore, the final parting cannot be simultaneous with the passing on. It can only follow after death has occurred. There is, therefore, nothing wrong with what Joseph did here. For people who love each other dearly, weeping over the body and kissing it is in order. It becomes a problem only when this behaviour is repeated or prolonged.

As would be expected due to his financial ability and social influence, Joseph took the lead in making the burial arrangements. This was also in accordance with Jacob's wishes, expressed in 47:29-31. Jacob's body was embalmed to preserve it (**50:2-3**). This was a lengthy process, which accompanied the seventy days of mourning in Egypt. There would later be an additional *seven-day period of mourning* when Jacob's body re-entered Canaan (**50:10**).

Jacob had made Joseph swear that he would be buried with his fathers and had repeated this instruction to all his sons (47:30; 49:29-32). So Joseph informed Pharaoh of his oath and asked permission for leave of absence to go and bury his father (**50:5**). Permission was granted readily, as is normally the case when one has a good relationship with one's superiors (**50:6**).

Jacob had an impressive funeral procession, attended by *all Pharaoh's officials ... the dignitaries of his court and the dignitaries of Egypt* as well as *chariots and horsemen* (**50:7, 9a**).

All the members of Jacob's household were there too, except *their children* (**50:8**). In summary, *it was a very large company* (**50:9b**). In fact, it was so remarkable that the Canaanites who witnessed the seven days of mourning in Canaan actually recorded it in the name that they gave to the place where it had happened, calling *Abel Mizraim,* which means 'mourning of the Egyptians' (**50:11**).

Should we measure the importance of a funeral on the basis of how many or which people attend? There may be nothing wrong with that, but we need to watch out for excess. In Africa, so much money may be spent on providing an impressive funeral that the living are left without food. This is not necessary. Funeral expenses should not cripple the family budget. Someone in Joseph's position could afford to pay for a large funeral, but in this he should not be taken as a model that we should necessarily follow.

Having fulfilled their father's wish, *Joseph returned to Egypt, together with his brothers and the others who had gone with him to bury his father* (**50:12-14**). After the burial of a dear one, life must continue.

50:15-26 Joseph's Life after Jacob's Death

50:15-21 Joseph's reassurance to his brothers

Though Joseph had assured his brothers that he held no grudge (45:5, 8, 14-15), they seem not to have been convinced that anyone could have enough grace to forgive the things they had done to him. They suspected that it was only Jacob's presence that kept Joseph from taking revenge (**50:15**). Their attitude reminds us of the importance of parents even when they are totally dependent on their children. Many homes disintegrate when both parents die, simply because only the presence of the parents kept the family together.

To protect themselves they sent word to Joseph that Jacob had left him a message asking him to forgive them, and added their own plea for forgiveness to his (**50:16-17a**). It is unfortunate that the brothers waited at least seventeen years before formally asking Joseph for forgiveness (see 47:28), but it is good they were doing so at last. It is also good that they used such explicit terms as 'all the wrongs', 'sins and wrongs', and 'treated you so badly'. There are many people who look for forgiveness without really accepting the depths of their failure.

Joseph, who had truly forgiven his brothers, was deeply touched, and so he wept (**50:17b**). But his brothers, still afraid and still seeking to show the sincerity of their request for forgiveness, *came and threw themselves down before him* and said, *We are your slaves* (**50:18**). Joseph then spoke solemn words of comfort and assurance to them: *'Don't be afraid'* (**50:19a, 21a**). He understood the grounds for his brothers' fear, but was anxious to give them inner peace.

Next, he explained that his response to them was sincere because it was rooted in his beliefs about God: *Am I in the place of God? You intended to harm me, but God intended it for good to accomplish what is now being done, the saving of many lives* (**50:19b-20**). Finally, he assured them that he would continue to support them and their children (**50:21b**).

May the Lord give us more people in Africa who have a kind and gracious heart like that of Joseph. We should not nurture our hurts, but should let them go and live in peace.

50:22-26 Joseph's death

Everyone comes to the point of death. It was now Joseph's turn at the age of a hundred and ten (**50:22a, 26a**). He lived to see *the third generation of Ephraim's children,* and the children of *Makir* son of Manasseh were placed at birth on his knees (**50:23**). In other words, he was not too old to enjoy them.

Just as his father had prepared for his death by telling Joseph his will, so Joseph prepared for his own death. He knew that his brothers and their descendants might be afraid of what would happen to them in this country of Egypt, where they lived as aliens, after Joseph, their protector, had died. So he reassured them that *God will surely come to your aid and take you up out of this land to the land he prophesied on oath to Abraham, Isaac and Jacob* (**50:24**). As a reminder of this, they were to keep his bones and commit themselves to carrying his body with them when they finally left Egypt and returned home (**50:25**). Joseph clearly viewed his time in Egypt as a time of mission and had not adopted Egypt as his home.

When Joseph died, *they embalmed him* and *he was put in a coffin in Egypt* (**50:26b**). Many years later 'Moses took the bones of Joseph with him because Joseph had made the sons of Israel swear an oath' (Exod 13:19).

Joseph died a great man due to two key things: the Lord's presence and his trust in the Lord. The Lord had taken care of him and governed the course of events. Joseph's trust had enabled him to stay patient and faithful even in great trials. He had preserved the community through which God was going to bring his salvation to the world.

Barnabe Assohoto and Samuel Ngewa

Further Reading

Morris, Henry M. *The Genesis Record: A Scientific and Devotional Commentary on the Book of Beginnings.* Grand Rapids: Baker, 1976.

Kidner, Derek. *Genesis: An Introduction and Commentary.* TOT. Leicester: Inter-Varsity Press, 1981.

Waltke, Bruce K. *Genesis: A Commentary.* Grand Rapids: Zondervan, 2001.

Wenham, G.J. *Genesis.* WBC. 2 vols. Nashville: Nelson Reference, 1987, 1994.

EXODUS

Exodus gets its name from two Greek words that mean 'out' and 'way'. It literally means 'way out' or 'departure'. The title captures the content of the book very well, especially its first half. It is the story of the children of Israel's departure from Egypt, where they had been enslaved. The time of the exodus was a defining period in the history of the nation.

Author and Date of Writing

Genesis, Exodus Leviticus, Numbers and Deuteronomy are referred to as the Pentateuch (derived from the Greek, *pente* meaning 'five' and *teuchos* meaning 'volume', with the combination meaning 'a five-volume book') or as the books of Moses. On the basis of both internal and external evidence, Moses is believed to be the author of all of these books. Some have questioned his authorship, but there are no convincing grounds for rejecting the traditional attribution. If we assume that Moses was born around 1500 BC (see the commentary on 1:8 below), and given that he lived for 120 years (Deut 34:9), Exodus would have been written sometime in the late fifteenth or early fourteenth century BC.

Theme

God's presence is the central theme of this book. He guides the people throughout their long pilgrimage towards the promised land. He reveals himself through events and establishes a special relationship with his people. The pivotal events are his deliverance of the people from slavery (1:1-18:27); his establishing of them as a nation under his direct government (19:1-24:18); and his taking up position at the heart of his people (25:1-40:38). His presence is manifest even in the elaborate ordinances that are meant to govern the multifaceted relationship between God and his people. These ordinances are comparable to those found in treaties between kings and their vassals in the ancient Near East and in Africa.

The book of Exodus thus recounts the passionate experience of God's unique relationship with his people whom he liberated from slavery. It places particular emphasis on divine deliverance and on the consecration of the newly formed people of the Lord. It has many historical lessons as well as much prophetic foreshadowing of what God will do in the future.

The events in Exodus must be seen against the background of the book of Genesis, where we learned of God's call to Abraham and the covenant he made with him (Gen 12, 15, 17). As part of this covenant, God promised Abraham that when the right time came, he would be given the land of Canaan (Gen 17:8; 15:13-16). Exodus tells us how God began to fulfil this promise.

Outline of Contents

COMMENTARY

1:1-4:31 Preparation for Deliverance

Throughout this first section of Exodus, God reveals himself as the Lord (3:15; 6:2-7) and as the all-powerful liberator (6:1-3; 7:10). Through his words, deeds and judgments, he reveals his divinity in his relations with the Israelites (6:2-7) as well as with the Egyptians (7:5). Thus the key verse for this whole section is the announcement 'You will know that I am, the Lord your God (6:7). This phrase is often repeated to emphasize the point that God is superior to all the gods of Egypt and to the all-powerful Pharaoh who governed the land.

God deploys his power through the combination of Pharaoh's oppression of the Israelites and the spectacular intervention of Moses, the instrument of the Lord.

1:1-22 The Oppression of the Israelites

The book of Exodus begins with a list of the names of the sons of Israel (**1:1-6**). This brief historical review links the events that follow to the closing chapters of the book of Genesis, which ended with the arrival of Jacob and his family in Egypt. It is easy to grasp the importance of these historical reviews and genealogical records when one remembers the African proverb: 'You may not know where you are going, but you must know where you came from!' Moreover, on our continent, someone whose origins are rather obscure may be given the nickname 'slave'. Israel does not wish to be a slave, still less an illegitimate child, so these genealogies are important.

The reminder of the special origins of the people of Israel also links them all to God's sovereignty and providence. He was the one who chose Israel from among the nations to serve as a channel of blessing for other nations (see also Gen 12:3; Isa 42:6).

By this time, the Israelites had been in Egypt for approximately 400 years (Gen 15:13; Exod 12:40). They had multiplied in this foreign land, as God had promised Abraham, and were exceedingly numerous, so that the land was filled with them (**1:7**; Gen 15:5).

But the Pharaoh who was now in power had a very different attitude to the Israelites than the Pharaoh who had welcomed them to Egypt in Joseph's day (**1:8**; see Gen 47:5). We do not know exactly which Pharaoh this was, for Exodus provides few specific details. Moreover, there is considerable debate about when the exodus took place. Some argue from 1 Kings 6:1, which dates it to 480 years before the fourth year of Solomon's reign (believed to be about 996 BC), that it must have happened around 1445 BC; in that case the *king who did not know about Joseph* would be Thutmose III (1483-1450 BC) and his successor would be Amenhotep II (1450-1424 BC). Others argue that the exodus must have taken place around 1290 BC. They base their argument on the assumption that the mention of Rameses in Exodus 1:11 means that the oppression was happening in the time of Rameses II (1290-1224 BC). His father Seti I (1302-1290 BC) would then be the Pharaoh who did not know Joseph.

Though we cannot be dogmatic about the date, the Bible is clear on two things. The oppression happened because the Pharaoh in power did not know Joseph, and because he saw the multiplication of the Israelites as a threat to the Egyptians. 'Not knowing' Joseph does not mean that he had not heard about him. What it means is that he did not care about what Joseph had done to save Egypt from famine or the commitments that the Pharaoh of Joseph's time may have made to Joseph and his father's house. In Africa, too, the treatment people receive is too often based on who their key relatives are, rather than on their value as fellow human beings. Such attitudes result in nepotism and other vices. It is also common to look at other people groups in terms of whether they pose a threat to us and, if we feel threatened, to find ways to reduce the threat. Once

again, we are failing to honour God, for all human beings, whether 'Hebrew' or 'Egyptian', are made in the image of God, and that should be the principle that governs how each individual or group is treated (Gen 1:26-27). We need to continually seek ways to plant this God-honouring perspective among our African people.

The new Pharaoh had reduced the Israelites to slavery. We are given three examples of the oppression suffered by the people. They were put to forced labour (1:8-14), their midwives were instructed to kill male infants at birth (1:15-21) and, when they refused to cooperate, orders were issued to throw all newborn Israelite boys into the Nile (**1:22**).

The midwives were forced to choose between obeying God and obeying Pharaoh. They chose to obey God, for we are told that they *feared God and did not do what the king of Egypt had told them to do* (**1:17**). They made this choice at the risk of their lives. Their example challenges those who excuse their unethical behaviour by saying, 'I was just following orders from my boss.' God does not accept that excuse. He requires us to obey him, no matter what the risk. If people in Africa had been prepared to take a similar stand, it is likely that we would have been spared many political assassinations and other killings, much diversion of public funds and many other evil practices. We need to take courage and remember that as long as we are on the side of God, we are the majority. We may lose our lives, but not our reward! God even rewarded the midwives in this life, for we are told that *because the midwives feared God, he gave them families of their own* (**1:21**).

God's power is now pitted against Pharaoh's cruelty. God's love for his people leads him to unleash all his power against their oppressors. But this power manifests itself very subtly at first, in that despite these difficulties *the people increased and became even more numerous* (**1:20**).

2:1-4:31 God's Preparation of a Liberator

Chapters 2-4 describe the birth of Moses, his call, his doubts and, finally, the start of his mission to deliver his fellow Israelites from slavery in Egypt.

2:1-10 Moses' early years

The events surrounding Moses' birth clearly demonstrate the powerful working of God's providence. This child's life was given by God, and God used circumstances, people and natural elements to protect it.

Moses was born to ordinary parents, in a very ordinary family, who knew their origins. Both his parents came from the tribe of Levi (**2:1**). We are later told that his father's name was Amram and that his mother's name was Jochebed (6:20). However, it is possible that these are the names of earlier ancestors because Amram is identified as one of 'the sons of Kohath' in 6:16, and Kohath would have been born some 350 years before Moses' time. The family included two other children, Aaron and Miriam, though we do not learn their names until later (6:20; 15:20).

Even before his birth, Moses was threatened by Pharaoh (see 1:16, 22), but he was specially protected for an important mission: (6:26-27). As Stephen pointed out in his summary of Jewish history in Acts 17, Moses was to play a key role when the time came for 'God to fulfil his promise to Abraham' (Acts 7:17-20).

Moses' parents defied Pharaoh's decree by hiding their child for three months (**2:2**). Hebrews 11:23 says they did it 'by faith' because 'they saw he was no ordinary child'. Then in a desperate act which included an element of faith, they entrusted him to God's protection when they left him in a cradle in the Nile. There is a certain irony in the fact that the child who was supposed to be drowned in the Nile was entrusted to the river that the Egyptians worshipped as a symbol of life. God's protection for this helpless child is well expressed in the Ewe proverb from Togo: 'God chases the flies from the animal without a tail.'

But God's protection did not take some supernatural form. Instead he used simple, natural things to provide a safe haven for the child. He used a cradle, ingeniously constructed with love, instinct and maternal desperation (**2:3**). It was coated with bitumen on the outside, just as Noah's ark had been, another vessel that saved a people from disaster (Gen 6:14). Just how ordinary it was is clear from the fact that, even today, it is possible to buy a 'Moses basket' for a newborn infant to sleep in.

Then God drew the people who together would save this child to the Nile and to the cradle wedged between the reeds. Significantly, all of them were women. He used Moses' own mother, who had hidden the child. He used Moses' sister, probably Miriam, who watched from a distance to see what would become of her baby brother (**2:4**). Finally, God used Pharaoh's daughter, who was moved with compassion for this child entrusted to the river (**2:5-6**). She plays a providential role not only in saving the child but also in protecting him and educating him. As a Rwandan proverb says, 'Even if God watches over his flock, he takes care to entrust it to a shepherd.'

The princess would have had to arrange for someone to breastfeed the child, and Miriam, knowing this, took the initiative and offered to *get one of the Hebrew women* (**2:7**). She did not mention that the one she would bring was the child's mother. The princess accepted her offer, and in a delightful mix of God's providence and his humour, arranged to pay Moses' mother to nurse him (**2:8-9**). Thus Moses would have spent his early formative years with his Hebrew mother, who would have taught him about the Lord and his promises to their ancestors, Abraham, Isaac and Jacob.

Pharaoh's daughter adopted the child as her son (**2:10**; see also Acts 7:21). She named him Moses, which means 'drawn from the water'. The name is Hebrew in origin,

not Egyptian, and suggests that the Egyptians must have had some familiarity with the language of the Israelites. The name also shows that the princess was not naive. She knew that the child must be Hebrew and in his name she acknowledged his Jewish identity (2:6). She may also have been playing on the fact that in the Egyptian language *mose* means 'son of' or 'born of', as we see in the names of pharaohs like Thutmose and Ahmose. There is a touch of irony in that the oppressor's own daughter raises the one who will liberate the people humiliated and weakened by Pharaoh.

As the son of Pharaoh's daughter, Moses entered the royal family, which was probably a very large one given the fact that the pharaohs had many wives and numerous children. There, as Stephen reminds us, he would have been instructed 'in all the wisdom of the Egyptians' (Acts 7:22), including their vast scientific knowledge. He grew into a young man who knew what it was like to be in a position of power and who spoke the Egyptian and Hebrew languages fluently.

This whole section is a striking demonstration of what God can do to prepare people long in advance for the task to which he will call them. This child, whom God is so carefully protecting and educating, will have an exceptional destiny. But the long time that is allocated to the preparation of this liberator reminds us that God works at his own pace. The people are enduring oppression, salvation is on the way, but the moment of deliverance has not yet come. It is still decades in the future.

God does not rely on improvisation. He has a detailed script and takes time to get ready for what is coming. He prepares the one who will appear on the stage of history through both the ordinary and the extraordinary events of his life. Moses would become 'powerful in speech and action' (Acts 7:22), because of the training and preparation he had received.

2:11-25 Moses' early acts

Moses was already forty years old before he embarked on the next stage of the preparation for his mission (Acts 7:23). There were three things in particular that directed his new course. These were the suffering of the Hebrew people, a fight between two Israelite men and the mistreatment of Jethro's daughters.

In spite of his royal status and privileged life, Moses must have retained some connection with the Hebrew people. After he *had grown up, he went out to where his own people were* and witnessed their suffering as they did *hard labour* (**2:11a**). One day, something snapped as he watched an Egyptian beating one of the Hebrews. He went to the man's defence, and killed the Egyptian (**2:11b-12**). He then hid the body in the sand. He assumed that his people would understand that God was using him to 'rescue them'

(Acts 7:25). But he was wrong, as an incident the next day revealed.

The day after Moses murdered the Egyptian, he saw two Israelites quarrelling and intervened to plead with them to reconcile (**2:13**). But the aggressor challenged Moses' right to interfere: *Who made you ruler and judge over us?* (**2:14**). The two men did not welcome interference from someone who did not share their lot and who had been raised in luxury in the court of the oppressor. Then the aggressor taunted Moses, asking if Moses was going to kill him too. The day before, Moses might have thought he was safe because he had made sure that no one was around before he struck the Egyptian. However, the Hebrew slave on whose behalf he intervened must have told the story to others, and even the Pharaoh eventually heard of what had happened.

Moses realized that his life was now in danger because he could face a charge of murder and of encouraging insurrection, and so he chose to flee (**2:15**; see also Heb 11:27).

His failure was complete. He was not yet ready for the mission that awaited him. He had assumed that his abilities and his goodwill would be enough to enable him to help his fellow Hebrews. He needed to learn not to trust in himself, and he also needed to learn to wait for God's timing. It was God, not Moses, who would deliver the Hebrews (2:23-24).

Moses found refuge in Midian, a desert country that lay east of the Jordan and the Dead Sea and extended south into the Sinai Peninsula. The region took its name from one of its first occupants, Midian, the son of Abraham and Keturah (Gen 25:1-6).

In Midian, Moses encountered a third situation in which he felt called to intervene. This intervention would lead to the next stage in his training by God (2:16-23). This time, he took the part of seven young sisters who were being mistreated by shepherds at a well (**2:16-19**). His action earned him the gratitude of Reuel (also called Jethro – 3:1; 4:18), the priest of Midian whose daughters these were (**2:20**).

SLAVERY

Slavery exists whenever one human being is thought of as owned by another. Those who are slaves live in total dependence on their owners and may be sold or rented out like horses or oxen.

Africa has a long, sad history of slavery, primarily inflicted by others. The ancient Romans, the Arabs and the Europeans all trafficked in African slaves. But since the nineteenth century, slave trading has gradually been abolished. The practice was strongly condemned in the Universal Declaration of Human Rights in 1948. But the fact that there are laws forbidding slavery does not mean that there are no longer slaves. Here are just a few examples of modern slavery, inflicted on Africans by Africans:

- *Child slavery* is common in countries that have been wracked by civil wars or serious political crises. Too often, children are regarded as the booty of war. In Sudan in particular, tens of thousands of women and children have been snatched in the south of the country and then sold. Daily, these people are victims of all kinds of violence.

- *Prostitution* often involves slavery. No African country is free from this type of slavery, for a country is implicated if the women come from that country, pass through it en route to another country, or are working in the country. Many women are tricked into becoming prostitutes by men who promise them jobs. Yet even those who knew that they would be working as prostitutes did not imagine the violence that they would suffer. Their identity papers are confiscated and the women live in constant fear of their exploiters, of being sent to prison as illegal immigrants, and that their families will suffer reprisals if they report their living conditions.

- *Domestic slavery* traps those who are often innocuously called 'maids' or 'house boys'. Children are sold into this type of slavery by parents who are desperate to repay a debt or simply to survive. These children receive no education. Instead they are expected to do household chores and to care for the children of their employers. Many suffer great abuse.

None of these forms of slavery can be justified, and the church should be in the forefront of the opposition to them. We should be praying for these slaves and taking action on their behalf.

The first step we must take is to boldly proclaim that God is the source of every human life (Deut 4:32; Job 10:12; Acts 17:25, 28). All human beings are made in his image, and thus all must be treated with dignity (Gen 1:27; 2 Cor 3:18; Col 3:10). Women have the same value as men (Gal 3:28), and we have a special responsibility for children (Matt 18:5-6).

Next, we must demonstrate our love in practice. Paul makes it perfectly clear that brotherly kindness, unity in Christ and the message of love overrule the master–slave relationship (1 Cor 7:20-24; Eph 6:5-9; Col 3:22-4:1; Phlm 10-17). We are not to accept oppression but are to work for reconciliation and peace. When confronted by poverty, we are called individually and as communities 'to be rich in good deeds, and to be generous and willing to share' (1 Tim 6:18; see also Lev 25:35; Deut 15:7-11; 1 John 3:17).

Finally, we must encourage our leaders to set up a system that protects every individual, regardless of his or her social status (Exod 22:21-24; Lev 19:13-18; Deut 10:19). Christians should take a stand against all forms of injustice, discrimination and social inequality (Deut 16:18-20; 2 Cor 8:21; Gal 3:28).

Rubin Pohor

The priest invited him to stay with them and *gave his daughter Zipporah to Moses* as his wife (**2:21**). From this union a son was born, whom Moses named *Gershom,* which means 'alien' or 'stranger' (**2:22**). Because of his culture and his origins, Moses, whom the girls had identified as *an Egyptian* (2:19), felt like a foreigner in Midian. The Hebrew root of the name Gershom also has overtones of being forced out or expelled. These ideas link up with Moses' banishment from Egypt, but they may also have been a prophetic sign of what would soon happen to the Hebrews, as they too left Egypt.

This section ends with 2:23-25, which forms an important connection between two situations. On the one hand, there is a terrible helplessness and the looming destruction of the people of Israel and on the other hand there is the liberation that God has long been planning. During *that long period* (it was another forty years) while Moses was in Midian, the oppressive Pharaoh who had known Moses died, but the children of Israel continued to suffer as slaves (**2:23**; see also 1:11). They *cried out* to God and the Lord, who listens to those who suffer, reacted in three phases: *he heard,* he *remembered* and he *was concerned* for them (**2:24-25**).

What God *remembered* was *his covenant with Abraham* (see also Gen 12:1-3; 15:18-21; 17:3-8). Unlike humans, God is faithful. He does not forget the promises he has made. He will fulfil them even if it seems to us that he is taking a long time to do so. Because of his compassionate concern for his people, he will patiently direct the course of human history to accomplish his purposes. He has prepared a hero who will deliver his people, and in chapters 3 to 14, God will display all his power after the long years in which he has seemed absent.

3:1-10 God's call

Moses spent forty years in the Sinai desert, working as a shepherd for his father-in-law, before God called him to fulfil his mission (**3:1**). But those years were not wasted, for he would need his knowledge of the desert when the time came to lead his people through it. Then one day, as he was going about his normal business, God called him. The description of this call is brief, but we are given the essential information: the identity of the one who calls and what Moses is to do. This information is essential not only for understanding the story of Moses, but also for our understanding of the character of God himself.

The place where God chose to reveal himself was Mount Horeb, also known as Mount Sinai (3:1). Later, God would reveal himself to Moses again in the same location and give him his law (see also 19:20; 24:13-18). In fact, God promised Moses such a meeting in 3:12.

Here God attracts Moses' attention by using a strange sight – a bush that burns without burning up (**3:2-3**). The fire is said to represent *the angel of the Lord,* that is, the angelic form in which God at times reveals himself to humans (3:4; see also Gen 16:9). In 19:18, fire will again symbolize the presence of God.

The liberation of the children of Israel was an impossible task from a human viewpoint. But the striking way in which God manifests himself here demonstrates that he would direct everything and that he would do so perfectly, without being subject to human constraints. God is going to demonstrate his omnipotence.

Once Moses' curiosity attracts him to the bush, God calls him twice by name from *within the bush* (**3:4a**). The call is specific and insistent. Moses responds with *Here I am* (**3:4b**). These words are an indication of openness to hear and obey God, and are spoken elsewhere in the Bible by Abraham (Gen 22:11), Jacob (Gen 46:2) and Samuel (1 Sam 3:4).

Because God is present, the ground where Moses is standing is declared to be *holy.* He is told not to come any closer and to take off his sandals as a sign of humility and worship (**3:5**; see also Josh 5:15). God then introduces himself as *the God of Abraham, the God of Isaac and the God of Jacob,* and thus the father of Israel (**3:6**; see also 3:15-16). Moses needs to know exactly which god is speaking. He had been raised in a polytheistic court, and would inevitably have been familiar with the many Egyptian gods, so there is nothing redundant or unnecessary about this repetition. Moreover, this identification is the basis on which Moses will be instructed to make his appeal to the people in 3:15-16.

God then goes on to explain why he has called Moses. He gives two fundamental reasons, both expressed in anthropomorphic language, that is, language that is associated with our human experience. The first reason is that God has seen, heard and reacted with concern to the sufferings of his people at the hands of their Egyptian oppressors (**3:7, 9**). God's attitude is the opposite of that expressed in the saying, 'a neighbour's distress can be like cool water for those who are not suffering!' On the contrary, God knows the pains of his people and has a deep concern for them.

The second reason for calling Moses is that God has decided that it is time to act, and announces that *I have come down* to deliver them and bring them into another land (**3:8a**). For God to 'come down' indicates a very special movement, an exceptional intervention of the Most High in human history. Moses is the instrument, indeed the incarnation, of this divine intervention.

God describes the destination to which he will lead the Israelites as *a good and spacious land.* It will be a place of prosperity, for there will be abundant room to raise flocks. It will also be an ideal environment that can be described as *flowing with milk and honey* (**3:8b**; see also Lev 20:24; Num 13:27; Deut 6:3; 27:3; Josh 5:6; Jer 11:5; Ezek 20:6). This image leaves no doubt that there will be an abundant supply of food in the region.

Then God gives Moses his orders, beginning with a strong imperative: *Go* (**3:10**). The command is precise and there is no way round it. Moses is to confront Pharaoh and *bring my people ... out of Egypt*. He is to be the instrument that God will use to fulfil his promise to deliver the people from slavery. Note, however, that God does not expressly say that Moses will also lead the Israelites into the promised land. By the end of the story, we know that he will not set foot in Canaan with the people whom he leads there (see Deut 32:48-52).

God's call to Moses reveals what sets the God of Abraham, Isaac and Jacob apart from the local gods. He is personal ('your' God), faithful (he keeps his promise to the Israelites' ancestors), compassionate (he identifies with the sufferings of his people), and sovereign (he summons people and gives orders).

3:11-4:17 Moses' doubts and God's reassurance

Overwhelmed by the sheer size of the task he has been given, Moses doubts his ability to perform it. There follows an amazing dialogue between Moses and God as Moses frankly admits his inability and his fears about what God wants him to do. God, for his part, encourages his servant and gives him the assurance he will need if he is to be equal to the mission entrusted to him. Exchanges like this one are what is meant when the Bible later says 'the Lord would speak to Moses face to face, as a man speaks with his friend' (33:11).

Moses voices four objections to God and receives four answers.

3:11-12 OBJECTION 1: AM I THE RIGHT PERSON? Moses' first objection is expressed in a question that in God's sight is neither astonishing nor frivolous: *Who am I?* (**3:11**). This question is any human being's natural response when confronted with the greatness and power of God. But Moses is also aware of his own history: for the past forty years he has been a fugitive, wanted by the Egyptian police and rejected by his fellow Hebrews. He has been reduced to nothing more than the shepherd of his father-in-law's flock. How is he to approach Pharaoh, a powerful monarch who despises all shepherds (Gen 46:34)?

God's response sweeps Moses' objection aside: *I will be with you* (**3:12a**). God is greater than Pharaoh, and he will accompany Moses. What greater guarantee of success could he ask for? But God also offers him a tangible sign. God promises that they will meet again at Mount Horeb once *you have brought the people out of Egypt*, and there all the people will *worship God* (**3:12b**; 19:1-8). There is an important play on words here, for the expression translated 'worship God' literally means 'to be a slave of God' or 'serve God like a slave'. The Israelites will become slaves of God rather than of the Egyptians. But where 'the yoke of

the Egyptians' was heavy (6:6), God's yoke 'is easy and my burden is light' (Matt 11:30).

3:13-22 OBJECTION 2: WILL THEY BELIEVE ME? Moses' second concern is that the children of Israel will not believe him unless he can tell them who has sent him (**3:13**). He knows that the one who is speaking to him is the God of his fathers, but the Israelites are living in a society that worships many gods. They will want to know the name of the specific god who has sent him. A name was also important because in the Hebrew context a name was far more than a mere label. Names both identified those to whom they were attached and gave a clue to their character (see, for example, 1 Sam 25:25). Names have similar importance in Africa, where they often identify both the person and the social group to which they belong.

God responds with a name for himself that is extremely rich in meaning: *I am who I am* (**3:14**). This name is sometimes translated as Jehovah, or more accurately as Yahweh. It is the word that is used whenever we see LORD or I AM in capital letters in our Bibles. But what does this name mean? In Hebrew, it consists of the four letters that form the root of the verbs 'to be' and 'to become'. It is a name that expresses the truth that God has always existed and will always exist. The Lord's emphasis that this will be his name *from generation to generation* is an assurance of his permanent presence among his people (**3:15**).

God's previous response to Moses was an assurance of his personal presence with Moses, but this response is an assurance that he is present not just with Moses but everywhere and always. Moses will bear this news to the people, the elders and even to Pharaoh.

The revelation of God's name also indicates the perfect continuity between the patriarchs and the Israelites, both in the present and in the future. So for the third time God reiterates his ancient promises to the Israelites' forefathers (**3:16-17**). His name, Yahweh, is now associated with God's covenant with Abraham (Gen 15:18-19), his redemption of his people (see 6:6) and his faithfulness (see 34:5-7).

God assures Moses that he will not have to appear before Pharaoh on his own. He will be accompanied by *the elders*, the leaders of the Israelites. The promise that the elders will accompany him is a sign that he will be able to convince them of his mission and of the authenticity of the revelation he has received. Moses will not only speak in the name of the Lord, Yahweh, he will also use another name, *the God of the Hebrews* (**3:18a**; see also 5:3; 7:16; 9:1-13; 10:3,). The use of this name associates God with a particular people and is also a way of distinguishing him from the many Egyptian gods.

Moses can expect Pharaoh to resist the request to allow the Hebrews to go into the desert for three days *to offer sacrifices to the Lord our God* (**3:18b**). But God will act in power to demonstrate his sovereignty over Pharaoh and the Egyptians through judgments and miracles (**3:19-20**). His *mighty hand* will oblige the Egyptians to let the Hebrew people go (see also 6:1; 13:14-16; 32:11; Deut 4:34).

God will further demonstrate his supremacy by ensuring that eventually the Egyptians will be so *favourably disposed* to the Israelites that they will not only allow them to go but will equip them for the exodus by giving them *articles of silver and gold* and *clothing* (**3:21-22**; 11:2; 12:35-36). These gifts will eventually be used for the construction of the tabernacle (35:5-22).

4:1-9 OBJECTION 3: HOW WILL I CONVINCE THEM? Moses' next objection is that he feels incapable of making himself understood and of persuading the Israelites to accept his message (**4:1**). He doubts that what he says will carry conviction. He may be remembering his earlier attempts to help the Israelites, when his actions to defend and reconcile them had only aroused incomprehension and suspicion. One of the Israelites had even challenged him, saying, 'Who made you leader and judge over us?' (2:14).

In particular, Moses fears that the people will not understand or accept his assertion that God has appeared to him. Claims to have seen a vision and received a divine commission can be interpreted as no more than an attempt to gain credibility. Certainly, from what we read later of the magicians at court, they too may have claimed similar miraculous visions. How can Moses prove that he really has spoken with God? After all, God has been silent for more than 430 years (the probable duration of the Israelites' sojourn in Egypt) and they have no reason to expect to hear from him now.

God addresses Moses' concerns by providing three signs he can use to persuade the Israelites that the Lord has truly sent him for a specific purpose.

The first sign involved the transformation of his shepherd's staff into a snake (**4:2-5**). This miracle illustrates both God's power and Moses' courage in obeying God's orders. No one picks up a snake by its tail! This transformation has special significance because snakes played an important role in Egyptian religion. The cobra was a symbol of power and especially of power over life. God uses this miracle to demonstrate that he has power over the natural creation and that his envoy can defy the power of the gods of Egypt and of Pharaoh himself.

The second sign demonstrates that God can heal incurable diseases like leprosy (**4:6-8**). The magicians and snake charmers of Pharaoh's court might be able to imitate changing a staff into a snake (7:11-12), but none of them could cure leprosy.

The third sign relates to the very survival of Egypt itself because it involves the Nile (**4:9**; see also 7:17-21). The Egyptians worshipped this river because it gave life and fertility to their land. But God shows that he is supreme, for he can transform life (the river) into death (blood).

The aim of all these signs is to convince the Israelites that Moses has been sent by God. He is a forerunner of the Messiah and comes to announce the wonderful news of liberation from slavery. The signs also demonstrate that Moses can wield God's power.

4:10-17 OBJECTION 4: I LACK ELOQUENCE Moses then puts forward a fourth objection: he has never in his life been able to speak well (**4:10**). God's answer is clear and direct and provides additional proof of his sovereignty. As the Creator, he is the one who gives human beings all the abilities they need, including the ability to speak, see and think (**4:11**). African proverbs from the Democratic Republic of Congo remind us that God created everything about us: 'God created us with our nails and our fingers' [Batandu] and 'God made us from our hair to our toes' [Yombe]. As Moses' creator and teacher, God will help him and give him the words he wants to speak (**4:12**). He does indeed do this so effectively that Stephen later speaks of Moses as 'powerful in speech' (Acts 7:22).

But when Moses' continues to object, and says *O Lord, please send someone else to do it,* God becomes angry (**4:13-14a**). He makes it clear that although he is ready to dialogue with Moses and to hear his objections, it is not acceptable for Moses to continue to raise unnecessary obstacles to obeying him.

God does, however, make one final concession to Moses' argument that he cannot speak well. He gives Moses a travelling companion and spokesperson who is eloquent and known to him, his own brother Aaron (**4:14b, 16**). God's promise, *I will be with your mouth and with his mouth* (**4:15** NASV) is a further reminder, if Moses needs one, of the sovereignty of God in giving and even controlling what we say. Many years later, the prophet Jeremiah is filled with similar doubts about his capacity to speak in God's name and God gives him the same reassurance (Jer 1:6-9). In the NT we are also told that the Holy Spirit will give believers the words they need both when they are being persecuted (Matt 10:19-20) and when they are recording God's word (John 14:25-26).

Moses' objections and God's answers end with a reminder to Moses to take his shepherd's staff, which will be an instrument of the Lord's power (**4:17**; see 4:20; 7:9, 15, 19-20; 8:5, 16).

In this section God has also modelled for us how to mentor and encourage those we want to develop as leaders. He is patient and gracious with Moses as he responds to his excuses and hesitation (4:1, 10, 13; 6:12, 30). Yet at the same time he is firm about the task Moses has been given and assures him that he will be able to perform it (4:5-9, 14-16).

4:18-31 Confirmation of Moses' call

4:18-20 SETTING OUT ON THE JOURNEY Before leaving Midian to rejoin his *own people in Egypt* and plead the Israelites' cause before Pharaoh, Moses must have told his father-in-law Jethro about his very personal and intimate encounter with God. Jethro gave him his blessing as he set out, implicitly honouring Moses' mission (**4:18**).

God also gave Moses further reassurance by informing him that those who had wanted to kill him were dead (**4:19**). So Moses set out on his journey, taking with him his wife Zipporah (2:21), his two sons, Gershom (2:22) and Eliezer (18:4), and not forgetting his shepherd's staff which is now referred to as *the staff of God* (**4:20**).

4:21-23 WARNING OF PHARAOH'S STUBBORNNESS Before Moses left, God further prepared him for what lay ahead. He warned him that despite impressive demonstrations of the power of God, Pharaoh would resist Moses' demands and would refuse to let the Hebrews leave his land.

We may be startled by God's statement that *I will harden his heart* (**4:21**). God will specifically be said to have done this on a number of occasions later in the book (7:3; 9:12; 10:1, 20, 27; 11:10; 14:4, 8). What does this mean? Did God make Pharaoh stubborn? And yet in other places in Exodus, it is said that Pharaoh hardened his own heart (7:13-14, 22; 8:15, 19, 32; 9:7, 34-35). We are faced with a paradox. On the one hand, Pharaoh hardens his own heart; on the other hand, when Pharaoh seems almost ready to admit the supremacy of God and no longer resist him, God makes him stubborn. The statement that God sovereignly chose to harden the heart of Pharaoh and the statement that Pharaoh freely chose to harden his own heart seem to be mutually exclusive and contradictory. Some might even argue that Pharaoh is innocent of a stubbornness for which he is not responsible, and that the final responsibility for his behaviour lies with God!

But before we accept that argument, there are two facts we need to consider. The first is that we cannot deny that Pharaoh had a free choice. It was his own stubbornness from beginning to end that led to his destruction. This stubbornness was rooted in his awareness of the economic consequences of the Israelites' departure (5:4; 14:5) and was expressed in refusal to acknowledge or submit to the God of the Hebrews (5:2). We must also remember the Egyptians' contempt and hatred for Hebrews (1:8-10) – a hatred that would only increase when the plagues struck the Egyptians and spared the children of Israel. All these elements combined to make Pharaoh blind to reason and led him to persist in his folly.

The second fact we have to acknowledge is the important theological reality that God does not ignore those who close their ears and hearts to him. When God hardens someone's heart, it is because he has begun to judge that person for refusing his light and his purposes. The more one closes one's heart, the deeper one is drawn into disobedience. One's choices have logical consequences.

Thus we cannot blame God for the hardening of Pharaoh's heart; God is simply taking Pharaoh's ongoing disobedience to its logical conclusion. Paul explains this same principle to the Romans: 'Because of your stubbornness and your unrepentant heart, you are storing up wrath against yourself for the day of God's wrath, when his righteous judgment will be revealed' (Rom 2:5). Pharaoh is responsible for his own stubbornness, which will place him under the judgment of God (see also Deut 2:30; Josh 11:20).

It can also be said that God permitted Pharaoh to be stubborn in order to display his glory, to demonstrate his sovereignty and to accomplish his spectacular plan of liberation (see Gen 14:4, 17-18; Rom 9:17-18; 11:9-10). Pharaoh would finally submit after the death of his *firstborn son,* a son whose fate God contrasts with that of *my firstborn son,* namely the people of Israel (**4:22-23**).

4:24-26 CIRCUMCISION OF MOSES' SON Why would God want to kill Moses when he has sent him to Pharaoh on such an important mission (**4:24b**)? Moreover, why would he want to do it now, when up to this point he has been encouraging Moses, promising to be with him to enable him to fulfil his mission?

Some commentators think that the reason was that Moses had failed to observe the law concerning circumcision. They base this on the fact that Zipporah, Moses' wife, managed to 'calm' God by circumcising one of their sons (**4:25a**). This rite was an important sign of the covenant made with Abraham (see Gen 17:9-14) and Moses' negligence may have provoked God's anger. But why would God only address this problem at such a late stage in his plan for Moses? And is this failure enough to explain why God would seek to kill Moses?

Other commentators prefer to focus on the statement that *on the way, the Lord met Moses* (**4:24a**). They argue that this incident is similar to Jacob's meeting with God when he wrestled with the angel (see also Gen 32:22-32). Seen in this light, this episode has to do with initiation. Whereas the angel struck Jacob on the hollow of the thigh, Zipporah put the foreskin at Moses' feet. The two expressions 'hollow of the thigh' and 'feet' may both be euphemistic references to genital organs.

A further difficulty in interpreting this passage is the obscurity of the Hebrew text. It is impossible to say at whose feet Zipporah put the foreskin. Was it at Moses' feet or at the feet of the newly circumcised child? And in what way could Moses be described as *a bridegroom of blood* (**4:25b**). Is Zipporah indicating that she had been opposed to circumcising her child, but that she has finally agreed to do so, while still expressing her opposition to the ritual by disdainfully throwing the foreskin at his feet? Was this incident actually a test of the extent to which Moses' wife would submit to God's plan? But if so, why was Moses the one threatened with death? Or was the problem that Moses had wanted to circumcise his sons, but had not done so because he wanted to keep Zipporah happy? If this was the case, he was failing to honour God above all else.

4:27-31 Arrival in egypt As promised by God in 3:14-15, Moses and Aaron are reunited and Moses faithfully tells his brother Aaron what he has been told by God (**4:28a**). This meeting takes place at Mount Horeb, the same place where Moses has the rare privilege of face-to-face encounters with God (**4:27**; see 3:1; 4:14-17; 18:5; 24:13). Moses explains God's plan and the miracles that he will be able to perform (**4:28b**; see 3:27-28).

Aaron then relays the Lord's word to the Israelite elders, supporting his message with the signs that Moses has been empowered to perform (**4:29-30**). The people react positively to this message and acknowledge Moses' authority as God's envoy, the messiah come to deliver them from their miserable conditions (**4:31**; see 2:24-25; 3:9-10).

An alliance has been made. God will use Moses to honour his ancient promise to save his people, and the people are now ready to listen to this new leader that they have been sent. For his part, Moses is finally ready to undertake his mission. He has been shown that he can trust the word of God. He would agree with the Baluba from the Democratic Republic of Congo, who say that 'God does not discuss things with humans. What he says is right!'

5:1-18:27 The Deliverance of the Israelites

Moses and his brother now stand united, ready to confront Pharaoh. The collaboration and solidarity of these two men will be needed to break the resistance of the king of Egypt. There is a saying that 'one cannot break nuts with one finger' and that 'when jaws meet, they break bones'. These two, working together, become God's instruments to break Pharaoh's arrogance.

5:1-6:27 First Confrontation with Pharaoh

The initial encounter between Moses, Aaron and Pharaoh seems to produce disastrous results, but God instructs them to persevere despite intense opposition.

5:1-21 A request denied

The first confrontation between Moses and Aaron and the king of Egypt begins with a request that the Hebrews be allowed to go and celebrate a *festival* (**5:1**). This festival would involve *a three-day journey*, which evokes the idea of a pilgrimage (**5:3a**). In fact, the Hebrew word 'hag', which is generally translated as 'festival', is closely related to the Arabic word *Haj*, which is used of the pilgrimage that Muslims make to Mecca.

Moses makes it clear that the purpose of the journey is to offer *sacrifices* (**5:3b**). The term used here shows clearly that he is not thinking of presenting an offering of vegetables or fruit but of making an offering that involves the death of a living being (see also 10:26). Since the Egyptians seldom offered sacrifices that involved putting animals to death, they would probably not have approved of what the Israelites were going to do (Gen 8:26). Even some of the Hebrews might have been startled, for they had not yet been given the laws about sacrifices and might have stopped offering them during their stay in Egypt. The three-day journey would thus have served the practical purpose of taking the Israelites far from the view of those who would be offended by these bloody practices.

Moses' request was exactly what God had told him to ask for (3:18), and he makes it clear that he is speaking on behalf of God (5:1). But Pharaoh has no interest in other people's religious practices and sacrifices, and so he sarcastically asks, *Who is the Lord, that I should obey him?* He declares that he will not honour this God whom he claims not to know (**5:2**). God will respond to this insult in the chapters that follow. He will display his power and supremacy over the Egyptian gods that Pharaoh honours, and will even deliver a blow to the ruling dynasty in a culture where the rulers were regarded as gods. The Lord God will reveal himself to Pharaoh and to his people (see 9:1-4, 16, 29; 10:2; 14:4, 18).

Whereas the Pharaoh in 1:8-10 saw the numerous descendants of the children of Israel as a threat, the one with whom Moses meets thinks of them as an abundant source of cheap manual labour (**5:5**). He does not see Moses as an envoy from God but as a troublemaker and a liar (**5:4**, 9). So although Moses had asked him to 'send my people away' (a literal translation of 5:1), it is in fact Moses and Aaron who are aggressively sent away.

To discourage the Israelites from listening to such troublemakers, Pharaoh decides to make their lives even harder than they have been (see 1:8-14). He gives orders to that effect to his *slave drivers and foremen* (**5:6**). These people seem to have been Israelites who were expected to maintain order and discipline among their fellow slaves (5:14). The oppression is evident from the imperatives used: *impose a quota, do not reduce any of it, let the labour be heavier, let them work at it* (**5:7-9** NASB) while the people were *pressed and beaten* (**5:13-14**, NASB). We are reminded of the tragic Ngambaye proverb from Chad: 'Even if a slave has nothing to carry, he must be made to carry a burden because he is a slave'.

The Hebrews are now expected to make as many bricks as before, but without being given the resources they need to make them. They now have to find their own supplies of the straw needed in the process. When they fail to meet their quotas, the Egyptian overseers beat the Israelite foremen (5:14).

Courageously, the supervisors of the Israelites approach Pharaoh in an attempt to get a measure of relief for the slaves. They speak of themselves as *your servants*, thus affirming their loyalty towards Pharaoh, but insist that it is impossible to meet these new demands (5:15).

Pharaoh refuses to listen to them. He dismisses their argument, saying that they are simply being *lazy* (5:17). He will not lessen their load (5:18-19). His attitude is not an uncommon one in employers today, who blame their employees for anything that goes wrong, even when it is obviously not their fault. The assumption that the one who has the upper hand is always right and never wrong makes for injustice – which God hates (Amos 4:1-3).

The dismayed foremen turn on Moses and Aaron and blame them for causing even more suffering by arousing the anger of their Egyptian rulers (5:20). The accusations are harsh and vulgar. They tell Moses and Aaron, God's envoys, *you have made us a stench to Pharaoh* (5:21a). The same expression is later used to describe the smell of the dead fish in the Nile (see 7:18, 21). They think that Moses will bring death rather than deliverance to his people, for he has *put a sword in their hand to kill us* (5:21b).

5:22-6:27 The Lord's encouragement

Dismayed and discouraged, Moses turns to the one he represents and questions him. He freely pours out his heart to God. His question to God reveals his shock at the sufferings of his fellow-Israelites and his impatience to see God intervene powerfully (5:22-23).

God answers Moses by reassuring him that he will act and that Pharaoh will release his people (6:1-2). He reminds him of what he has done for his ancestors in the past. He had revealed himself as *God Almighty* to Abraham, the father of believers, and to his sons Jacob and Isaac (6:3a). He had entered into a covenant with the patriarchs to give them the land of Canaan (6:4). More recently, he had promised to free the people from slavery in order to give them back the promised land (6:5-8). He describes the people as being like oxen, *under the yoke of the Egyptians* (6:6a), and thus forced to carry burdens and do heavy labour for them.

God uses dramatic human images as he speaks of what he will do. He speaks of his *mighty hand* (6:1) and his *outstretched arm* (6:6; see also Deut 4:34; Ps 136:12) and swears an oath *with uplifted hand* (6:8). He reasserts his authority, reminding Moses four times that *I am the Lord* (6:2, 6, 7, 8). He uses the name 'Yahweh', by which he revealed himself to Moses (see 3:13-15), but makes it clear that he is the same God as the all-powerful El-Shaddai, or *God Almighty* who revealed himself to the patriarchs (6:3b).

God promises to *redeem* his people (6:6b). In the OT, the word 'redeem' is used for rescuing someone from a contract or from some evil (as when Jacob speaks of 'the angel who has redeemed me from all evil' – Gen 48:16 NASB). After the crossing of the Red Sea, Moses and the people sang of this redemption, which involves liberation both from slavery and into joy (15:13). Not only will God free the people from slavery; but he will also renew their identity as his people (*I will take you as my own people, and I will be your God* – 6:7) and he will give them a land of their own (6:8).

Strengthened by God's reminders of his past acts and his promises for the present, Moses tries to speak to the Israelites. But they are discouraged by what has happened and refuse to listen to him, despite their previous commitment (6:9; see 4:31).

Then God once again tells Moses to go to Pharaoh and demand that he let the people go from Egypt (6:10-11). But Moses is reluctant to do so. If he cannot even convince his own people that God has spoken to him, how can he hope to touch Pharaoh's heart? (6:12). He complains that he speaks with *faltering lips*, or, in a literal translation, 'uncircumcised lips'. He does not mean that his speech is immoral or impure, but that it lacks eloquence (see also 4:10; 6:30).

At this point, the narrative is abruptly interrupted by a genealogy that quickly skims over the clans of Jacob's two oldest sons, Reuben (6:14) and Simeon (6:15), and then focuses on the tribe of Levi, to which Moses and Aaron belong, and from which the priests will be drawn (6:16-25; see also comments on 2:1). It seems that the genealogy is placed here to emphasize that, despite Moses' doubts, he and Aaron have been appointed the spokesmen and intermediaries between the Lord and Pharaoh. This list is framed by two texts which insist that God sent Moses and Aaron to Pharaoh to bring the Israelites out of Egypt (6:13, 27).

6:28-7:7 New assurance for Moses

In the face of Moses' lack of self-confidence when ordered to approach Pharaoh a second time (6:29-30; see also 6:11-12), the Lord makes an amazing statement about the status and power he has given to him. God declares that Moses, whom he has already said will be like God to Aaron (see 4:16), will also be *like God to Pharaoh*, and Aaron will be his prophet, who will speak in his name (7:1-2). God is not saying that Moses has been deified, nor that he is divine. Rather, God is reassuring Moses that he has been given a position that is superior to that of Pharaoh. In this role, Moses will be able to perform unprecedented miracles and overwhelm the powers of the Egyptian magicians who represent the gods of Egypt. Yet he will remain only God's instrument, though an instrument filled with God's power.

The message that Moses is to deliver to Pharaoh does not change. What is new is the assurance that God will *harden Pharaoh's heart*, thus providing a reason for God to act in judgment against Egypt and its ruler until all acknowledge that Yahweh is Lord (**7:3-5**).

We should note that God gives Moses a clear mission, the authority to carry it out, and even the help he needs to carry it out. In this, God is very different from many leaders who are not clear in the assignments they give to those who work under them, do not provide them with what they need to do the job, and are always interfering in the process.

7:9-13 Second Confrontation with Pharaoh

Encouraged and confident that God is in control even of Pharaoh's hostility, the 80-year-old Moses and the 83-year-old Aaron again appear before Pharaoh (**7:6-7**). This time, as God had predicted, he challenges them to prove that God has really sent them by performing a miracle (**7:8-9**). So Aaron throws down his staff, and to Pharaoh's amazement it turns into a snake (**7:10**). However, this demonstration is not sufficient to convince Pharaoh of God's superiority, for his magicians are able to do the same thing. But when Aaron's snake *swallowed up* all the others, it is a sign that his God is superior to the Egyptian gods (**7:11-12**). Pharaoh is being given a powerful warning of what awaits him, but he refuses to listen.

Many years later, the prophet Ezekiel will prophesy the doom of another king of Egypt, whom he describes as a great crocodile. Ezekiel predicts that this Pharaoh-crocodile will be vanquished by the Lord so that everyone will recognize that God is God (Ezek 29:3-4). Ezekiel may have been remembering the story of Moses when he spoke, for he too predicted disasters for Egypt.

While the episode of the transformed staffs is simply a preamble to what follows, it does illustrate two of God's qualities. First, it shows that he is more powerful than those whose power derives from Satan. The magicians' miracles draw on occult power that imitates divine power (7:11). Satan often operates in this way, for he is a master deceiver and imitator. The NT warns believers not to be tricked by him, reminding us that he can even disguise himself as an 'angel of light' (2 Cor 11:14; see also 2 Thess 2:9-10; Matt 24:24; Rev 13:13-14).

The second quality that is revealed in this incident is God's sovereignty, which is manifested in ways that seem contradictory. It is revealed both through Moses' obedience and through Pharaoh's disobedience, stubbornness and inability to listen. God can use anyone he chooses, even those who are wicked, to accomplish his purposes (Hab 1:6-11). But this does not mean that he will not judge their wickedness (Hab 2:5-17).

7:14-11:10 The Plagues Strike Egypt

God now brings judgment on Pharaoh and the Egyptians through a series of ten plagues. Again and again, we will see the power of God being contrasted with the powerlessness of the local gods to aid those who are suffering. The plagues also humiliate Pharaoh, who was regarded as a god by the Egyptians. Certain commentators have even identified each calamity with an Egyptian god, saying that the fight for the freedom of the Israelites was in reality a combat between the Lord God and the gods of the Egyptians.

Each plague is introduced with the words *Then the Lord said to Moses*, reminding us that it is God who is in control of events. Even though it is possible to explain the plagues and their sequence in terms of natural phenomena, these phenomena are being organized by God. Those who witnessed them, like the magicians, recognized that they were dealing with plagues sent by Moses' God (8:19). When they eventually understood that their magicians were powerless and that they faced ever-increasing threats of destruction, even some of the people at Pharaoh's court began to support Moses and tried to persuade Pharaoh to let the Hebrew people leave (10:7; 11:3).

Although we often speak in general terms of 'plagues', the original Hebrew text uses a variety of terms to describe the special character of these events. Sometimes they are referred to using a Hebrew word that could also be translated as 'blows' (9:14). At other times, they are spoken of as 'signs', or manifestations of God (4:9, 17, 28; 12:13; 13:9, 16). Sometimes they are referred to as 'miracles' or 'wonders' (7:3; 11:9). The word used to refer to the final plague is one that is often associated with a calamity such as being struck with leprosy (11:1). All these terms present different ways of looking at the ten plagues. They were a blow to Pharaoh's pride, they were a sign of the power of God who caused them to happen, and they were wonders because their source lay outside the laws of nature.

The scenario for each of these plagues plays out the same way: Moses and Aaron demand that Pharaoh allow the people to leave, Pharaoh refuses, God responds to the refusal with a plague, Pharaoh repents, God stops the plague, and Pharaoh changes his mind. The situation escalates from minor demonstrations of God's power that affect everyone in the land (the first three plagues), to plagues that fall only on the Egyptians and spare the Israelites, to the manifestation of God's power of life and death when he causes all the firstborn males to die. It is only then that Pharaoh yields.

The Bangala of the Democratic Republic of the Congo say 'You cannot kill an elephant with a single spear'. Pharaoh was like an elephant, and he had to be struck many blows before he yielded.

These events give us four insights into the nature of God:

• God has no rival. His ultimate aim was to bring Pharaoh and the Egyptians, as well as the Israelites, to recognize that he is the only true God, who is able to defeat all the Egyptian divinities (9:14-15; 12:12).

- God is all powerful and uses humans and natural elements to accomplish his purposes.
- God is sovereign. He delivers his people from oppression and ensures that his promises are fulfilled (Gen 15; Exod 12:40-41).
- God is gracious and patient as he tries to bring the most hardened hearts to obedience and repentance.

7:14-25 Water becomes blood

God tells Moses to go and find Pharaoh by the Nile, where he seems to have gone each morning, possibly for some ritual cleansing (7:14-15). He is to remind him that he has been refusing God's command to let his people go (7:16). Here and in other interactions with Pharaoh, God is specifically referred to as *the God of the Hebrews* (7:16; see also 3:18; 5:3; 9:1, 13). This God is superior to the Nile, which the Egyptians worshipped, and to all the other deities that the Egyptians associated with the Nile, such as Apis, Isis and Osiris. These gods will be unable to counteract the action God will take as a result of Pharaoh's refusal, namely changing the water of the Nile *into blood* (7:17). Because of this change, the fish *will die, and the river will stink; the Egyptians will not be able to drink its water* (7:18). This disaster starts when Aaron, at Moses' order, strikes the water of the river, and it is very widespread. Not only the water of the Nile is affected, but also all the water in its tributaries, the water stored in dams and reservoirs, and even water stored in buckets and jars (7:19-21). Unable to drink the available water for an entire week, the Egyptians frantically dig new wells (7:24-25).

Pharaoh, however, is not impressed. When the magicians of Egypt perform the same miracle *by their secret arts*, he dismisses what has happened as unimportant (7:22-23). It does not seem to have occurred to him that his magicians were only capable of imitating God, but were unable to restore the Nile to its normal condition and prevent the fish (an indispensable food) from dying and polluting the river.

8:1-11 Frogs

God can act miraculously, or he can use the natural result of earlier events to accomplish his will. Here, he uses the effect of the first plague to bring about the second plague, as the frogs flee the polluted waters of the Nile. But God is the one who determines the timing and intensity of what happens. Egypt *teems* with frogs. No place is free of them and no one can avoid them. They even penetrate Pharaoh's palace, his bedroom and bed; they infest the houses of his courtiers and all the people, getting into *ovens and kneading troughs* (8:2-4). The plague would have been very difficult to deal with, for the Egyptians identified frogs with the goddess Heqet, who had the body of a woman and the head of a frog. Because Heqet was the goddess of fertility and of birth, frogs were sacred and could not be killed.

The Egyptian magicians are able to duplicate the miracle performed by Moses and Aaron (8:5-7). It would, however, have been more useful had they been able to get rid of the frogs!

Pharaoh can no longer ignore what is happening. So he summons Moses and Aaron and asks them to pray to God to remove the frogs (8:8). He has been forced to recognize that no Egyptian god can deliver the land from this plague. Moreover, he calls God by his name, despite his claim not to know him (see 5:2). If God removes the frogs, Pharaoh promises to let the Israelites go. Moses agrees to intercede for Pharaoh and to ask that the frogs will leave at a specific time, so that Pharaoh will know that *no one is like the Lord our God* (8:9-11).

Pharaoh had asked only that the frogs be taken away, because, for the reason mentioned earlier, he could not ask for their death. But God causes them to die, further undermining the authority of the Egyptian gods and particularly that of the frog goddess who symbolized life (8:12-14).

After enjoying his freedom from the frogs, and no doubt after having second thoughts about his promise, Pharaoh goes back on his word (8:15). He may have been a god to the Egyptians, but he was a god whose word could not be trusted. By contrast, the word of God to him never changed, and was always fulfilled.

8:16-19 Gnats

God responds to Pharaoh's refusal to allow the people to go by changing the dust of Egypt into gnats or mosquitoes (or vermin, which is the literal meaning of the Hebrew word). These gnats annoy both people and animals (8:16-17). The plague begins when Aaron strikes the *dust of the ground* with his staff. This blow can also be seen as a symbolic blow against Set, the Egyptian god of the desert.

The mention of dust reminds us that human beings were made from dust and will return to dust (Gen 2:7), and is thus a reminder of human insignificance before the Creator. There may even be a pun here, for the Egyptian word 'Pharaoh' is similar to the Hebrew word *aphar*, which means dust. The Bible may be implying that this man-god is really as insignificant as dust.

The magicians are unable to reproduce this miracle (8:18) and have to admit to Pharaoh that this plague comes directly from God (8:19). But Pharaoh is still unmoved.

8:20-28 Flies

As with the frogs and mosquitoes, the stinging flies (or gadflies, as the Septuagint says) swarm over Pharaoh, his nobles and the people, getting into their homes and ruining the land (8:20-21, 24). These flies can be seen as symbolic of the sun god Re or the god Uatchit, both of whom were represented by insects.

None of the plagues in this second set of three affects the land of Goshen, the region where the Hebrews live (8:22-23). God thus shows that he is capable of protecting his people, something that the Egyptian gods are clearly incapable of doing as the Egyptians suffer the full effect of each plague.

This time Pharaoh seems to yield. He grants Moses and Aaron permission to take the Hebrew people to sacrifice to their God. But whereas Moses had stated that they wanted to leave Egypt in order to make these sacrifices, Pharaoh specifies that they are to remain *in the land* (8:25). No doubt he wishes to keep an eye on them. But Moses refuses to do this, pointing out that sacrifice of animals such as bulls and rams would be offensive to the Egyptians, to whom the bull represented the god Apis and the ram the god Ammon (8:26-27).

Pharaoh reluctantly agrees to let them travel at least a short distance into the desert and also commands them to pray for him (8:28). His words indicate that the ruler of Egypt has lost faith in his magicians. It must have been difficult for him to admit this, for it means that his belief in his own power is being whittled away little by little. Again Moses prays and again God answers, establishing his absolute power (8:30-31). But, as Moses had suspected would happen (8:29), Pharaoh again breaks his promise (8:32).

9:1-7 Death of domestic animals

The next disaster that follows from Pharaoh's refusal is described as a *terrible plague* (9:3a). We are given a list of the types of animals that died (9:3b). The god Apis was often represented as a bull, the goddess Hathor by a cow, and the gods Khnum and Ammon as rams. We can thus see that this plague can also be interpreted as directed against these gods and goddesses. Horses also died, and their loss would be a severe blow to a nation that derived much of its military strength from its horses (see also 14:23; 15:1). The donkeys and camels that died were pack animals, and the sheep were a source of food and wool. Thus this plague, which may have been anthrax or some other animal disease that God chose to use, affected the religious life, economy and military power of Egypt. We are reminded that the Lord is the only true source of all prosperity. This point is emphasized by the fact that the Israelites' animals do not die, a fact that Pharaoh checks for himself (9:7). Yet he still stubbornly refuses to comply with Moses' request.

9:8-12 Boils

Some commentators interpret the *festering boils* that now break out on the Egyptians as being like the pride that swells human hearts until they are ready to burst, like boils. These boils affect both humans and animals and their pervasiveness is evidenced by the fact that they are mentioned three times in the text (9:9, 10, 11).

This plague starts when Moses tosses *handfuls of soot from a furnace* into the air (9:8). Soot is the residue of combustion, and the Egyptians will be touched by the devouring fire of God. Even their magicians are covered in boils. Physically, they could no longer *stand before Moses* (9:11).

The three Egyptian divinities targeted by this plague are the goddess Sekhmet, who was supposed to control sickness; Sunu, the god of pestilence; and Isis, the goddess of healing.

9:13-35 Hail

Moses gives warning that if Pharaoh does not let the Hebrews leave, God will unleash *the full force of his plagues* on the Egyptians (9:13-14). The plagues that follow will be much worse than those that have preceded them. Pharaoh is reminded that God is actually the one with power, and that it is God who has raised him up and kept him alive through the series of disasters. God tells him that the only reason he has been spared is so *that I might show you my power and that my name might be proclaimed in all the earth* (9:15-16). Paul quotes these words in the NT to develop an explanation of God's sovereignty: who 'has mercy on whom he wants to have mercy, and he hardens whom he wants to harden' (Rom 9:17-22).

The seventh plague will take the form of a hailstorm such as the Egyptians have never seen before (9:18). For the first time, God warns the Egyptians of what is coming and advises them to take shelter. He tells Pharaoh to order the people to bring *your livestock and everything you have in the field to a place of shelter* (9:19). That 'everything' included the Egyptians' slaves. The only ones who would escape harm were those who paid attention to the words of the Lord (9:20-21).

Violent thunder, lightning and hail accompany the *worst storm* in Egypt's history (9:24). God often shows his power through these natural phenomena. As the prophet Isaiah says, 'The Lord will cause men to hear his majestic voice and will make them see his arm coming down with raging anger and consuming fire, with cloudburst, thunderstorm and hail' (Isa 30:30).

At a sign from Moses, the hail begins (9:22-23) and at another sign it stops (9:29, 33). His total control of the storm would have humiliated Nut, the Egyptian goddess of heaven. Osiris, their god of harvests and of the fertility of the earth, is also humbled as the Lord reverses his work. Rather than fertilizing the earth, God destroys the vegetation and the harvests (9:25, 31). Frightened by the power of the Lord, Pharaoh confesses, *This time I have sinned* and admits that *the Lord was in the right* and that he and his people were wrong (9:27). He begs mercy from God, promising that this time he will let the people go (9:28). But again he withdraws his permission. It seems that he is sincere in what he says when the crisis is happening, but that he constantly changes his mind as his circumstances change.

10:1-20 Locusts

This time God gives Moses additional information about his purpose in performing *these miraculous signs*. He wants to make his power known not only to the Egyptians but also to future generations of Hebrews (**10:1-2**).

God again confounds local divinities as well as the Egyptians themselves when he threatens that a plague of locusts will destroy all the crops and vegetation that had survived the hailstorm (**10:3-6**). These insects will often be used in the future as symbols of God's judgment (Joel 1:2-7; Amos 7:1-3).

Those at Pharaoh's court beg him to grant Moses' request. They speak with surprising frankness: *Do you not yet realize that Egypt is ruined?* (**10:7**). The authority of the lord of Egypt is being eroded still more. So Pharaoh summons Moses and Aaron and seems ready to negotiate the departure of the people. However, he insists that only the men may leave Egypt to worship God (**10:8-11**). But this means that he will be holding their wives and children as hostages to ensure that they will return. When Moses insists that everyone must go, Pharaoh refuses to consider this possibility and drives Moses and Aaron away.

Moses then stretches out his hand and the locusts arrive with the east wind. This is the worst invasion of locusts the Egyptians have ever experienced: *Never before had there been such a plague of locusts* (**10:12-15**).

The NIV speaks of the locusts in the plural and refers to them as 'they', but the original Hebrew speaks only of 'the locust' and 'it'. The swarm may comprise millions of locusts, but they act as a unit, like one great army. This idea of many acting as one is also found when the demons inhabiting a man speak of themselves as one, saying 'My name is Legion', but explain the name by saying, 'for we are many' (Mark 5:9).

Faced with this new plague, Pharaoh again admits to having sinned (see 9:27), but this time he asks also for pardon (**10:16-17**). Moses prays, and the wind changes to a very strong west wind, which carries the locusts off to the Red Sea (**10:18-19**). Yet, true to form, Pharaoh once again becomes stubborn (**10:20**). This time, the Lord is said to have *hardened his heart*. For a discussion of what this means, see the comments on 4:21.

10:21-29 Darkness

This ninth plague – *total darkness* – comes without any warning to Pharaoh and lasts for three days (**10:21-22**). God, the one who created light, may have miraculously brought darkness, or he may have used his existing creation to bring the darkness. Thus some commentators suggest the possibility that God could have used a 'khamsin', or a strong

wind to blow a blinding sandstorm in from the desert. The darkness is also a sign of God's superiority to Re, the sun god, of whom Pharaoh was supposedly an incarnation. What makes this sign even more striking is the fact that the Israelites have light while the Egyptians endure a darkness so heavy that *no one could see anyone else or leave his place* while the darkness lasted (**10:23**).

Pharaoh again summons Moses and makes an offer: all the Hebrews can *go to worship the Lord,* as long as they leave their flocks behind (**10:24**). He may have thought that even if he could not guarantee that his slaves would return, he could at least seize their livestock to replace the animals that the Egyptians had lost in the earlier plagues.

Pharaoh may be offering more concessions, but Moses refuses to agree to his terms (**10:25-26**). The negotiations collapse dramatically as Pharaoh forbids Moses to come before him again, threatening, *The day you see my face you will die* (**10:28**). Moses confirms that negotiations are indeed at an end: *I will never appear before you again* (**10:29**).

By not receiving the words of God, humans condemn themselves to darkness. Pharaoh himself is a prime example of the truth of John's words, 'The light shines in the darkness, but the darkness has not understood it' (John 1:5). The exodus from Egypt is near and the people of God will soon leave the darkness of Egypt and move further into the light of God.

11:1-12:30 Death of firstborn and the Passover

Chapters 7 to 10 have told of one plague after another. Now comes a pause and a change of focus. God has Moses announce the last plague, but he does not immediately implement it. Instead, he gives Moses detailed instructions on a new religious observance that the Israelites must follow. Then, while the Israelites are observing the Passover, God strikes the firstborn of Egypt.

11:1-10 A TERRIBLE WARNING Before leaving Pharaoh's presence, Moses, *hot with anger,* tells him of the last and most terrible plague that will come on him and his people – a plague so terrible that the formerly reluctant Pharaoh will not just allow the Israelites to leave but will drive them out of Egypt (**11:1, 8**). In this last plague God will take the life of the firstborn son of every Egyptian family (**11:5-6**). The loss of any child is the most terrible trial a parent can endure, and the firstborn son often has a special position as the privileged heir who carries all the family's hopes. Pharaoh's firstborn would have been the heir to his throne. At the end of each of the previous plagues, the situation had been returned to normal, but for the bereaved parents, things will never again be what they were before.

God's action against the firstborn may seem like cruelty on God's part. But it may well be God's punishment for the Egyptians' cruelty in attempting to kill all the male children born to the Hebrews (1:15-16).

God tells Moses that this will be the last plague and that the people will shortly be leaving Egypt. But he also tells him that the people need to prepare for their journey both materially and spiritually. They are to provide for their material needs by asking their Egyptian neighbours for *silver and gold* (**11:2**). Their requests will be granted because the Lord has influenced the Egyptians' attitude to the Israelites, and even Moses was *highly regarded by* court officials and the people (**11:3**).

The Israelites, however, will only avoid suffering the same fate as the Egyptians if they follow God's directions and observe a new religious feast, which will become known as the Passover.

12:1-28 INSTITUTION OF THE PASSOVER The inclusion of details of the institution of the Passover within the context of the tenth plague proves that the narrator wants to give the death of the firstborn males a meaning that goes beyond it being a sad, cruel event. The Passover will become central to the commemoration of the Lord's deliverance and the exodus from Egypt (see also 12:43-51; 13:1-16). But the blood shed at this first Passover will not only be that of lambs but also that of the firstborn Egyptians. Many years later, the Lamb of God will come to give a new meaning to Passover (see John 1:29).

The institution of the Passover marks the inauguration of a series of religious rituals and ceremonies for the Israelites. The Lord establishes a new religious calendar for his people to follow. It would start in spring, in the first month of the year, Abib or March–April (**12:2**).

The Lord gives Moses precise instructions about what is to be done and about the timetable for action. The Israelites are to select a lamb for sacrifice on the tenth day of the month (**12:3a**) and *take care of it* until the fourteenth day of the month, that is, at the full moon (**12:6a**). God also emphasizes the communal aspect of the celebration. The people are to celebrate in family groups (**12:3b**) and the animals are to be slaughtered by all the *people of the community* at the same time (**12:6b**). This is the first record we have of a sacrifice being offered by families, rather than by individuals, and of the whole community participating in a shared ritual. This had not been done in the times of the patriarchs. The references to the 'community' in 12:3 and 12:6 also suggest the beginnings of the idea of a people, a nation. This idea will come to full bloom with the announcement of God's choice of the nation and his establishment of the covenant with them in chapters 19 and 20.

The requirements for the animal and its preparation are strict. The families can use either a lamb or kid but it had to be a year-old male *without defect* (**12:5**). God requires all sacrifices made to him to be perfect; he will not accept animals with defects (Lev 22:17-31).

When the animals are slaughtered the people are to save some of the blood. God usually required that the blood be drained and buried (Lev 17:10-14), but this time the Israelites were to dip a bunch of hyssop, probably an aromatic plant, into the blood and put it on the doors and the door posts of their homes (**12:7**).

God also specifies how the meat is to be cooked. The people are to roast, not boil, the meat (**12:8a**). Despite the fact that they are to eat the meal in haste, *dressed for their journey* (**12:11**; see also 12:39; Deut 16:3), the meat must not be raw (**12:9**), probably to distinguish this meal from the rites observed by other peoples, who ate raw flesh. The meat is to be accompanied by *bitter herbs* symbolizing the painful experience of slavery, and by *bread made without yeast* (**12:8b**).

In generations to come, when this feast would still be celebrated to commemorate what had happened in Egypt, it would be known as the Feast of Unleavened Bread ('leaven' being another name for yeast – **12:17**). One reason that the bread would be unleavened was that in their rush to leave Egypt, the Israelites would have no time to allow bread dough to rise. But the careful instructions regarding the preparation of this bread (called *matzoh* in Hebrew) and the fact that the people are to eat it for seven days suggests that there must be another reason for its importance. So does the repeated instruction to *remove the yeast from your houses* (**12:15**, **19**; see also 13:7). Even today, observant Jews clean thoroughly before Passover to remove all trace of products with leaven from their homes and businesses.

The emphasis on eating unleavened bread makes sense when we remember that at that time the leaven or yeast that caused dough to ferment and thus to rise was made from a piece of unbaked bread dough left over from the previous batch. This fermented dough worked like the yeast we add to bread dough today. But using it meant that each new loaf of bread contained traces of the former bread. God wants the Israelites to set out on a new life and to make a total break with their old lives as slaves in Egypt, and he uses unleavened bread as a symbol of this new life.

In the rest of the Bible, yeast is often associated with sin, with the traces of our old nature and with the arrogant pride which puffs people up with importance, just as yeast puffs up bread dough. Paul, for example, uses the image of leaven when he writes to the Corinthians: 'Don't you know that a little yeast works through the whole batch of dough? Get rid of the old yeast that you may be a new batch without yeast – as you really are … Let us keep the Festival, not with the old yeast, the yeast of malice and wickedness, but with bread without yeast, the bread of sincerity and truth' (1 Cor 5:6-8).

The instructions about the bread are immediately followed by Moses' explanation of the reason for the sprinkling of blood on the doorframes. *When the Lord goes through the land to strike down the Egyptians,* he will see this bloody sign and spare all those who are inside houses with this marking

INITIATION RITES

Initiation rites are formal ceremonial rites of passage that mark an individual's moves from one stage of life to another, one society to another or one status to another. Different forms of initiation rites are performed by different kinds of groups and communities. Thus secret societies may require candidates for membership to undergo certain rites, while some pastoralist communities like the Maasai of Kenya have initiation rites for *moran* (community warriors) aspiring to become community elders.

Initiation Rites in the Bible

Initiation rites are also found in the Bible. At the age of ninety, Abram and every male in his household were circumcised as a sign of the everlasting covenant God had made with him and his descendants (Gen 17:1). This event marked a new phase in Abraham's life, and also marked the start of the Jewish practice of circumcising every newborn baby boy when he is eight days old. Jewish proselytes also had to be circumcised in order to officially become part of the community (Exod 12:48-49).

In Christianity, baptism is a form of initiation rite. After believing and confessing Jesus Christ as Lord and Saviour, one is required to go through the waters of baptism as commanded by Jesus Christ (Matt 28:19; Mark 16:15). In most denominations this takes place only after one has gone through a series of teachings on major Bible doctrines.

Initiation Rites in Africa

The most common form of initiation in African traditional societies relates to the transition from childhood to adulthood. It is a very important milestone in the life of the youth of most traditional African communities because it marks the end of childhood and the official ushering of teenagers into adulthood. Teenagers are taken through a series of teachings that cover every aspect of life and are intended to shape them into responsible adults. For instance, young girls from the Krobo ethnic group of Ghana spend three weeks preparing for their initiation. During these three weeks they are taught the art of cooking, are encouraged to adopt the stature of a woman, and are taught how to please a husband in every way. At the end of these three weeks, there is a Dipo, a five-day ceremony that publicly declares that the girls are now mature and ready for marriage. Among the Maasai, young men have to live in the bush while taking care of cattle and probably have to perform a heroic act like killing a lion in order to be initiated as a community elder.

Communal initiation rites serve to bring the members of a community together. At such celebrations, parents socialize and may identify good spouses for their children. Thus initiation fosters unity in the community and gives initiates a sense of belonging to it.

But while there is much that is good in traditional initiation, there also are negative aspects. The sacrifices offered to appease community gods and the ancestors and to seek their blessing on the lives of the initiates amount to ancestral worship and spiritism. Moreover, the traditional use of one knife to circumcise a number of initiates is now very dangerous as the practice may transmit infection of HIV/AIDS.

Girls face additional problems when it comes to initiation. The practice of female genital mutilation is traumatizing, deforming and dangerous (see the article on this topic). It is also wrong to assume that girls are automatically ready for marriage after initiation and then to force them into marriage.

Concerns about these negative aspects of initiation have resulted in a decline in the practice of this rite of passage in most African communities and in its being shunned by the African church. Yet the church still recognizes that it is important to prepare children for adulthood. The need for this preparation becomes even more important as social changes and the need to send children away to school greatly reduce the amount of time a child spends with his or her parents. Thus initiation rites should not be allowed to disappear. They offer a forum where teenagers can learn about how to cope with practical life issues as they make the transition from childhood to adulthood.

Initiation Rites and the Church

The African church, therefore, needs to actively revive initiation rites, but in a form that is purged of the evils associated with them. Some churches are already doing this. For example, the Tanari Trust, founded by Nairobi Baptist Church and affiliated churches, is networking with schools, parents and other churches to offer teenagers who are about to enter high school (that is, those aged thirteen years and over) a series of teachings that lasts for one year and culminates in a camp for the initiates during the December vacation. Topics covered in the Bible-based curriculum include relationships, sexuality, responsibility, holiness and purity, handling peer pressure, career choice and other issues recommended by the parents and churches involved.

Christian initiation rites can be a powerful tool in shaping the lives of Christian teenagers as they move into adulthood. With God's help, they can be used to produce responsible, spiritual, vibrant young adults who will bless the church of Christ in Africa.

Judith A. Milasi

(12:23). The Hebrew word *Pesach,* which we translate as Passover, literally means 'pass over' in the sense of 'jump over'. The blood of the lamb causes the angel of judgment to spare those who claim its protection.

For Christians, it is easy to see that the Passover prefigures the coming of the Messiah, Jesus Christ. He himself will be the Lamb without defect (12:5; John 1:29; 1 Pet 1:19). He will be offered as a sacrifice for the deliverance of each person and of the world from their slavery to sin. The Apostle Paul specifically refers to Christ as 'our Passover lamb' (1 Cor 5:7). Just as the blood of the lamb and obedience to what the Lord had commanded preserved the Israelites, so the blood of Christ and obedience to his message preserves believers from judgment for their sin and from eternal death.

The Passover and the festival that follows, the Feast of Unleavened Bread, will last a week and are to be celebrated annually to remind future generations of Israelites of what God did for them in Egypt (12:14, 24-27). These feasts foreshadow the Lord's Supper, at which Jesus becomes the new centre of Passover (see Matt 26:17; 1 Cor 11:23-33).

12:29-30 THE DEATH OF THE FIRSTBORN As the Israelites eat the Passover meal, the Lord kills all the firstborn males in all the houses that were not protected by blood. The tragedy is terrifying in its breadth: *there was loud wailing in Egypt, for there was not a house without someone dead* (12:29-30). Not even Pharaoh's house escapes the angel of death. God deals a final blow to the king of Egypt in the loss of his heir.

12:31-42 The Exodus from Egypt

That same night, Pharaoh calls in Moses and Aaron and orders them to take their people and leave with their livestock (12:31-32a). He wants them to get out immediately because of all the misfortunes that have happened on account of them. The other Egyptians also urge Israel to *hurry and leave the country* because they fear for their lives (12:33). God was right in saying that when Pharaoh finally lets them go, 'he will drive you out completely' (11:1). This time, Pharaoh sets no conditions; instead, he asks Moses for God's blessing (12:32b).

The Israelites hurriedly pack their belongings, including their unleavened bread dough still in the kneading troughs (12:34). Then, as instructed in 11:2, they ask the Egyptians *for articles of silver and gold and for clothing* (12:35). The goods they are willingly given are some compensation for the years in which they had been exploited (12:36).

When the people finally left Egypt, they must have felt like they were living a dream. They left from Rameses (a city they had built – 1:11) heading east towards Succoth. There were a vast number of them, for if we add the probable numbers of women and children to the *six hundred thousand men on foot* (12:37), it is likely that there were at least two million people who left Egypt.

Not everyone who left was an Israelite; there were a large number of non-Israelites (12:38). Some of them were probably members of other minorities who took the opportunity to leave a country where they did not feel welcome or happy. Some may even have been Egyptians who had become dissatisfied with Pharaoh's rule and had become converts to the God of Israel.

The emphasis on the number of years that the Israelites had spent in Egypt (12:40-41) is a reminder that all these dramatic events were the fulfilment of the promise God made to Abram: 'Know for certain that your descendants will be strangers in a country not their own, and they will be enslaved and ill-treated four hundred years. But I will punish the nation they serve as slaves, and afterwards they will come out with great possessions' (Gen 15:13-14).

12:43-13:16 New Regulations

12:43-51 Further regulations for Passover

The instructions for the celebration of the Passover are elaborated primarily for the benefit of all the other groups who have joined the people in the exodus (12:43). The prime requirement for participating in the Passover is simple: circumcision (12:44, 48). This rite was the sign of the covenant between God and Abraham's descendants (Gen 17:10-14). By obediently submitting to it, foreigners and their families can become full members of the community, with the same rights and responsibilities as those who are Israelites by birth (12:49). The Passover feast is not to be shared by those who are merely temporary residents and hired workers, who have not indicated any desire to join the community (12:45).

The fact that God makes provision for welcoming non-Israelites should be noted when it comes to dealing with issues of national purity and national identity. The people who followed Moses and became the Hebrew nation were not only the descendants of Jacob but came from many nations. It is true that they are sometimes referred to in negative terms as 'the rabble' (Num 11:4), but God makes it clear that provided they meet the conditions of the covenant, they are to be welcomed among the covenant people.

Today the only condition for becoming part of the people of God is being covered by the blood of Jesus Christ. Circumcision is no longer required. This point is strongly stated in the NT: 'There is neither Jew nor Greek, slave nor free, male nor female, for you are all one in Christ Jesus. If you belong to Christ, then you are Abraham's seed, and heirs according to the promise' (Gal 3:28-29).

The instructions regarding the Passover also specify that the meal must be eaten inside the home and that none of the animal's bones are to be broken (12:46). The purpose of these instructions may be to ensure that the animal's skeleton remains whole as a reminder that it was a perfect sacrifice, without any defect, offered on their behalf.

The identification of Jesus as the ultimate Passover lamb is heightened by John's reminder that his legs were not broken, unlike those of the criminals crucified with him (John 19:36).

The people respond with complete obedience to the instructions that God gave to Moses (**12:50**). Their new freedom is a freedom to listen to and obey the commands of God. They are now subject to him, and not to the Egyptians. We must be careful not to confuse liberty with licence. Freedom does not mean that we can live as we please, without any religious obligations or beliefs. That was not the goal God had in mind when he rescued his people from slavery in Egypt. Unfortunately, this point was sometimes forgotten in the thirst for freedom and independence in many African countries in the 1960s, with the result that anarchy reigned instead of freedom.

We already see evidence of order rather than anarchy in the statement in **12:51** that the people came out of Egypt *by their divisions* (see comment on 12:41).

13:1-16 Regulations regarding the firstborn

Future generations need to be taught about what God has done in the past. We understand the importance of passing on our history in Africa, for it was the Malian scholar Amadou Hampate Ba who said 'the death of an old man is like the burning of a library'. We also organize Independence Day celebrations to pass on the memory of each country's struggle for freedom from colonial powers. God too arranges for the transmission of the memory of what he had done by instituting two rituals to be observed in the promised land (**13:5**). He describes these rituals as being *like a sign on your hand and a reminder on your forehead* (**13:9, 16**; see also Deut 6:8).

The first of these rituals is the annual Passover and Feast of Unleavened Bread, which has already been discussed at length (13:3-7; see 12:1-27, 43-48).

The second ritual is the dedication to God of every firstborn male, whether human or animal. All of these are to be consecrated to God, that is, regarded as belonging to God (**13:1-2**). The reason God claims them is because he graciously spared all of them when the tenth plague took the life of all the firstborn males in Egypt (13:15). Their dedication to him is a reminder of what the Lord did for the nation when he rescued them from Egypt, and thus also a reminder that the whole nation belongs to the Lord.

An animal that is consecrated to the Lord must be sacrificed to the Lord as a burnt offering, for that is what the expression *give over to the Lord* means (**13:12**). However, if the animal is unclean, like a donkey, and thus unsuitable for sacrifice, it could simply be killed, or a clean animal could be sacrificed in its place (**13:13a**). Numbers 18:14-16 suggests that it could also be redeemed with money.

This principle of substitution is always to be applied when it comes to children (**13:13b**). They are to be symbolically consecrated to the Lord, not sacrificed to him. The God of Israel is rigorously opposed to the human sacrifice that certain peoples of the region may have practised (Lev 18:21; 20:1-5; 2 Kgs 16:3; Jer 32:35). When, centuries before, God ordered Abraham to sacrifice his son and to offer him as a burnt offering, it was a test that God himself stopped before the child died (Gen 22). In this passage, we are not told exactly how a child is to be redeemed, but Numbers 18:16 specifies payment of about two ounces (55 grams of silver to the priests.

This association of consecration and a substitutionary sacrifice to redeem a being who would otherwise be killed is yet another symbol that helps us to understand the meaning of Christ's death for us.

Israelite parents have an important role to play in explaining the significance of these rituals to their children. They are to perpetuate the memories by celebrating the appropriate feasts (13:3-7), telling the children about the events these feasts recorded, and explaining their significance (**13:8-9, 14-15**). They are not to focus on the exploits that they or their families have done, or even on the miracles that Moses has performed, but on *what the Lord did for me* (13:8).

13:17-15:21 God Leads and Protects

13:17-22 God goes before his people

God himself guides the people on a route that he has chosen to ensure that they will have a safe journey. The protection he offers includes protection from themselves, for he knows that if they face war, they may change their minds and return to Egypt (**13:17**). So he does not lead the people by the most direct road, which would have gone up the Mediterranean coast and passed through the land of the Philistines. Had they taken that route, they would soon have faced battle. Instead, he takes them through the desert. He also has another reason for doing this: he wants to meet with them at Mount Sinai, as he promised Moses (3:12).

The route leads the people towards what the NIV translates as *the Red Sea*, but which can also be translated as the Sea of Reeds (**13:18a**). There is disagreement about where exactly this was located, but the most common view is that it was somewhere in the region of the Bitter Lakes that now form part of the Suez Canal. But the name could have been given to any marshy region filled with reeds (see also 2:3).

The NIV states that the Israelites set out *armed for battle* or, as the NKJV says, 'in orderly ranks' (**13:18b**). The expression translated in this way is literally 'by fifties'. It is also used in Joshua 1:14 and 4:13. The idea seems to be that they moved in orderly groups of fifty people, but these groups are unlikely to have been strict military formations because the Hebrew makes no mention of weapons.

Joseph's prediction or prophecy in Genesis 50:25 is now fulfilled as his bones are carried out of Egypt for burial in the promised land, the homeland from which he had gone to Egypt (**13:19**). However, we should not assume that this implies that people's bodies should always be returned to their homeland. The carrying of his bones also does not seem to have any religious significance. All that we have here is the fulfilment of a promise: Joseph had arrived in Egypt as a slave, but he leaves it in freedom, along with his brothers, and his descendants fulfil his request to be buried in his own land.

Christians know that it does not matter where one is buried, as all will be resurrected (Rev 20:4-5, 13). However, many African people are like Joseph in wanting to be identified with their own people even after death. There is normally nothing wrong with such a desire, but it is questionable when the enormous costs of transporting the body home impoverish those left behind.

God manifests his permanent presence with his people in a pillar of cloud that guides them by day and a pillar of fire that guides them by night (**13:21-22**). The book of Exodus will end with the same cloud, the symbol of God's presence, hovering over the Tent of Meeting and signalling when his people are to march and when they are to halt on their long journey to the land of Canaan (40:34-38).

14:1-31 Pursuit and deliverance

God's final victory over the Egyptians and their stubborn Pharaoh at the Red Sea can be said to be like an eleventh plague. Many of the same themes that were heard over and over again in the earlier account of the plagues resurface here: the hardening of Pharaoh's heart (14:4a, 17), the use of Moses' staff (14:16, 21, 26-27), the contrast between the suffering of the Egyptians and the deliverance of the Israelites (14:20; 28-29) and God's insistence that he is taking action so that *the Egyptians will know I am the Lord* (14:4b, 18).

These last words also remind us that God is sovereign and acts to make himself known. He directs the Israelites to wander around and then positions them *by the sea*, where they will be bait for the Egyptians, who will walk into God's ambush (**14:1-3**). The three places mentioned, *Pi Hahiroth, Migdol and Baal Zephon,* cannot be identified today, but some people suggest that they were probably located in the region of the Bitter Lakes towards the middle of what is now the Suez Canal. Pi Hahiroth may mean 'mouth of the canals' and Migdol means 'watchtower' (Ezek 29:10). The name Baal Zephon suggests that this was the site of a sanctuary dedicated to this northern deity.

Pharaoh's change in attitude is caused by God hardening his heart (**14:4**) but also by his second thoughts after the

shock of the death of the firstborn had passed (**14:5-6**). He realizes that he has lost a large part of the labour force for his construction projects. Moreover, in yielding to the God of Israel, he has diminished his own authority. In bowing before Moses and asking for his blessing (13:32), he has allowed himself to act as if he were a subject of the man who represented his slaves! No wonder his wounded pride expresses itself in a desire for revenge.

Pharaoh's words in 14:5 suggest that the Egyptians do not intend to kill the Israelites but to bring them back to Egypt. Nevertheless, on seeing the pursuing army, all the Israelites can think of is that they face death, trapped between their enemies and the sea (**14:10**). They have good reason to fear. Pharaoh's army consists of *six hundred of the best chariots, along with all the other chariots of Egypt* (**14:7**). There were probably three men in each chariot: a driver, a soldier and his squire, who carried the soldier's shield. Such a force would look extremely impressive to the Israelites, who had no weapons and no experience in armed combat. No wonder they cry out, not only in fear but also in rage and incomprehension directed against Moses (**14:11-12**). This is the first occasion on which we see the ingratitude that will characterize the people throughout the long crossing of the desert. God has just stressed the importance of passing on memories (ch 13), but already the people have completely forgotten his spectacular actions on their behalf.

Rather than becoming indignant at the people's reaction and lack of faith, Moses tries to calm the people's fears saying, *Do not be afraid* (**14:13a**). God himself will later say these same words to the people (20:20). They can also be translated as 'stand up straight' or 'stay where you are'. Moses assures them that the Lord will fight for them, and he is greater than any army (**14:14**).

During one of their final encounters, Pharaoh had threatened Moses, saying, 'the day you see my face you will die' (10:28). Here, Moses' words echo those of Pharaoh: *the Egyptians you see today, you will never see again* (**14:13b**). There is a time when dialogue becomes useless and both parties' positions are entrenched. But Pharaoh made a mistake when he threatened Moses with death if they met again. It will be his own army who will die in the coming confrontation.

As the Egyptian army advances, God provides an escape route for the cornered Israelites. He commands Moses to divide the sea with his staff so the people can cross to the other side *on dry ground* (**14:15-16**). These same words are used in Genesis 1:9 to describe the separation between seas and the earth. There they heralded the start of a new stage in God's creation of the world, and here they mark the beginning of a new stage in God's creation of a nation.

We are now told that the cloud that has been leading the people is a covering for *the angel of God* (or, as it could also be translated, 'the messenger of God'). This messenger has already been encountered in 3:2, when he appeared to Moses in the burning bush. The angel now moves from his position in front of the people to take up a position behind them, where the cloud that accompanies him will act as a screen between them and the Egyptians and keep this army in check all night (**14:19-20**).

God uses the east wind to drive back the water so that the Israelites can cross the sea on dry ground (**14:21-22**). Ominously for the Egyptians, this is the same wind that had brought the army of locusts at the time of the eighth plague (10:13). At the end of the plague, God had hurled the locusts into the Red Sea so that 'not a locust was left' (10:19). The same fate awaits the Egyptian army, for *not one of them* will survive (**14:28**).

The Egyptian army follows the fleeing Israelites into the sea, and there God throws them *into confusion* (**14:23-24**). He causes them to have problems with their chariot wheels, which either come off or become jammed in some way, with the result that the chariots are out of commission and cannot be used either for pursuit or for flight.(**14:25a**). And flight becomes uppermost in the Egyptians' minds, for in a flash of enlightenment, they realize that it is *the Lord* who is fighting against them (**14:25b**). Pharaoh had claimed not to know the Lord (5:2), but now all his soldiers proclaim him, using the name God had revealed to Moses, 'Yahweh', translated 'the Lord'.

But their recognition comes too late to save them, and all are engulfed in the returning water and drowned (**14:26-28**). The Israelites are left to marvel at their deliverance. They *feared the Lord and put their trust in him and in Moses his servant* (**14:29-31**).

15:1-21 The song of victory

Led by Moses and his sister Miriam (**15:1a, 21a**), the people now sing a victory psalm that deals with the events they have just witnessed. The poetic form is not only suited to celebration but will also help the people to remember and pass on the story of what God has done for them. Nor was this just a static song, for Miriam, *the prophetess* and sister of Moses and Aaron, led the women in a dance that took up what seems to be the refrain: *Sing to the Lord, for he is highly exalted. The horse and its rider he has hurled into the sea* (**15:1b, 21b**).

The song begins with the words of that refrain, which speaks of what God has done. Then follows a statement of what this means for his people: *The Lord is my strength and my song: he has become my salvation ... I will praise him* (**15:2**). Next comes a celebration of God's strength (**15:3-6**); his greatness and majesty (**15:7-12**); his faithfulness towards his children (**15:13-17**) and finally his eternal kingdom (**15:18**). All these verses contrast the power of God with the final defeat of the Egyptian army. Those who hear it can be left in no doubt concerning God's sovereignty,

his faithfulness, his redemption of his people and his eternal dominion.

The people who have been acquired by this incomparable God are told that they will be planted on *the mountain of your inheritance* and in the *sanctuary* of the Lord (15:17). The Israelites are finally free. They are leaving for a new home, the promised land. But the singers do not know that their own failings will mean that they will end up wandering in the desert for forty years.

15:22-17:7 God Provides for his People

It is one thing to liberate a people from slavery (or from subjection to some dictator or colonial power); it is quite another to govern the freed people (or to run a democracy in Africa). How will the Israelites react now that they have entered a new situation that will place new demands on them? They have witnessed many miracles in the days between Moses' first encounter with Pharaoh and their celebration after crossing the Red Sea. What conclusions will they draw from these miracles and the evidence of God's direct intervention on their behalf? Will they commit themselves to complete obedience to God and to Moses, his instrument? It appears so from the words in 14:31: 'When the Israelites saw the great power the Lord displayed against the Egyptians, the people feared the Lord and put their trust in him and in Moses his servant.' But they still need to learn what this commitment means in practice.

The Israelites' trust is soon tested in situations they have never encountered before. Although they had endured harsh conditions in Egypt, they had not had to worry about what they would eat, or about being attacked by an enemy, or even about who would lead them. Now they need to learn to trust God as they face these new challenges. But they are slow learners, and eventually pay a high price for their lack of faith (Num 14:26-35). Yet, as we look at our own responses to new situations, we can see that we are no different. It takes us a long time to learn to trust God to meet all our needs and not to be anxious during times of crisis (Matt 6:25-34; 1 Pet 5:7).

The first difficulty they run into as their great journey begins is that their supplies of fresh water and food run out. In the chapters that follow, we are told of three occasions on which this happens (15:25-27; 16:1-36; 17:1-7). Each time, the people do not turn to Moses in hope and expectation, but instead turn on him, reproaching their guide and picking a fight with him and with God who has been leading them.

15:22-27 Water at Marah and Elim

After travelling for three days *without finding water*, the people finally find a water source, only to be bitterly disappointed when they discover that the water is undrinkable (15:22-23). It is described as *bitter* (hence the name, Marah, which means 'bitter'). The bitterness may have reminded them that the Passover meal had included 'bitter herbs' to remind them of the bitterness of their slavery (12:8). These memories are still fresh, and that may be why the people do not here speak of their regret at having left Egypt, as they did in 14:11, and will often do so later on when they reproach Moses for having led them into the desert.

The people grumble and ask, *What are we to drink?* (**15:24**). Moses seeks help from God, who gives it immediately. This time, Moses is not to use the staff that has been used in other miracles. Instead he is to throw *a piece of wood* (NIV) or 'a tree' (NASB) into the water, which will then miraculously become drinkable (**15:25**). It is possible that God is here making use of a natural property of this type of wood.

Elisha performed a similar miracle using salt (2 Kgs 2:19-22). But God does not only turn bitter water into sweet water. He can also do the opposite. In Revelation, he acts in judgment to make the waters bitter (Rev 8:10-11).

The people are inconsistent: at one moment they are singing God's praises, and the next they are grumbling about him. This type of behaviour may have been what prompted James to point out that such contradictory things should not come from the same mouth: 'Out of the same mouth come praise and cursing. My brothers, this should not be. Can both fresh water and salt water flow from the same spring?' (Jas 3:10-11).

At the same time as providing a solution to their water shortage, God reminds the people of the importance of keeping the commitment they have made if they are to experience his blessings. He compares these blessings to healing when he says, *for I am the Lord who heals you* (**15:26**). The context is set by the words, *I will not bring on you any of the diseases I brought on the Egyptians.* The Lord is reminding the people that he had not only brought the plagues on Egypt and removed them, but he had also kept them from affecting the Israelites. Now the Israelites lack water, and the Lord provides it as part of his healing ministry. He is promising to watch over his people. If they obey him, they will experience his abundant blessings, here represented by the abundance they find at Elim: *twelve springs and seventy palm trees* (**15:27**).

16:1-36 Manna and quail

About a month into their journey (**16:1**), the Israelites' food supplies are exhausted. They think longingly of the days when they had more than enough to eat in Egypt. Forgetting the hardships they endured as slaves, they start to complain and accuse Moses of having failed them. They insist that they would prefer to have died in Egypt, even if it had meant being struck down as the Egyptians had been, rather than dying of hunger in the desert (**16:2-3**). We Africans can sympathize with their feelings, for many of us are all too familiar with the dreadful suffering that can accompany

famine, and we know that it can lead to irrational behaviour. The Ngambaye (Chad) have a saying that 'one day of hunger can make a wife leave her husband's house'. But the Israelites are wrong to turn on Moses rather than turning to God. They have forgotten the way he has already provided the water they needed.

Moses does not waste his time responding to personal attacks and accusations. He takes the matter to God. When he has received God's response, he confronts the people to remind them that they are not just attacking him, but are also accusing God of negligence (**16:6-8**). We need to remember that God does not make a distinction between the way we treat those he cares about and the way we treat him. Thus Jesus could say, 'whatever you did for one of the least of these brothers of mine, you did for me' (Matt 25:40). Similarly, when Saul of Tarsus persecuted the Christians, Jesus said that he himself was being persecuted (Acts 9:1-5).

God responds to the Israelites' distress by sending them quail in the evening and a sweet, bread-like, granular substance in the morning (**16:11-14**, **31**). The Israelites had seen birds like quail before, but they had never seen anything like this substance. So they ask, *What is it?* **16:15a**). In Hebrew, the words would have been 'Man hu?', and this question is the source of the name given to this substance – 'manna'.

Moses explains that this is the food that God has provided and conveys God's precise instructions about how it is to be collected (**16:15b**). The people are to collect only what they need for a day – which will be about four pints (two litres) per person (**16:4a**, **16-18**). At the end of the day, they are to discard any left uneaten (**16:19**). By making this stipulation, God was both testing the people to see whether they would follow his instructions (**16:4b**, **20**, **27-28**) and teaching them to depend entirely on him for tomorrow, when he would renew his gifts. We are reminded of the prayer Jesus taught us to pray: 'Our Father in heaven [where the manna comes from] … Give us today our daily bread' (Matt 6:9, 11).

There is one exception to the command to take only enough for one's daily needs. On the sixth day, the people are to collect enough for two days, because no manna will be provided on the Sabbath (**16:22-26**, **29**). By making this exception, God indicated the importance of observing the Sabbath as a day of rest on which no work was to be done (16:23, **30**). God himself observed this Sabbath in that he provided no manna on that day.

This miraculous manna would be provided for the entire time the people were in the desert (**16:35**).

Later, the manna will be seen as foreshadowing the coming of the Messiah, Jesus, who refers to these events when he describes himself as the bread of life come down from heaven (John 6:30-35, 48-51). He returns to this symbolism at the institution of the Lord's Supper, where he 'took bread

… and gave it to his disciples, saying, "Take and eat; this is my body"' (Matt 26:26; see also John 6:53-58).

17:1-7 Water from a rock

As the Israelites journey, one of the places where they set up camp is Rephidim, which is in the southern part of the Sinai peninsula. Once again, there is a lack of water (**17:1**). And once again the people turn on Moses and blame him for their plight (**17:2-3**). The situation is so bad that Moses names the place *Massah*, which means 'testing', and *Meribah*, which means 'quarrelling' (**17:7**).

Exasperated by the people's lack of faith, Moses cries out, *What am I to do with these people?* (**17:4**). God replies, telling him to go ahead of the people with the elders and strike *the rock at Horeb* with his rod (**17:6**). This use of the rod with which Moses had already struck the Nile serves to remind the people and the elders, who seem to be regretting ever having left Egypt, of what God had done for them in the past (**17:5**). Moses obeys God and the water flows in abundance.

In a letter, the Apostle Paul recalls this episode in the desert. He reveals that Christ was the source of the water they drank: 'Our forefathers … all ate the same spiritual food and drank the same spiritual drink; for they drank from the spiritual rock that accompanied them, and that rock was Christ' (1 Cor 10:1, 3-4). Christ also offered a Samaritan woman water that would so satisfy all thirst that those who drink it will never be thirsty again (John 4:12-14).

17:8-16 God Defends His People

The Israelites face another terror when the Amalekites attack them (**17:8**; see Deut 25:17-18). These Amalekites occupied the north-east of the Sinai Peninsula (Num 13:29). They were descended from Esau, the brother of Jacob, the ancestor of the Israelites (Gen 36:12). Thus the rivalry of the twin sons of Isaac and Rebekah continues, despite the many generations that have elapsed.

Moses asks Joshua to lead the battle against the Amalekites (**17:9a**). This is the first mention of Moses' successor, the man who will also have the privilege of accompanying him on the mountain of God (24:13). Joshua's role will become more and more important as the Israelites' history unfolds. But even if it is he who leads the battle, he does it with the help of God and of Moses, God's servant.

Moses positions himself on a hill above the battlefield, holding up *the staff of God* with both hands (**17:9b-11**; see 4:20). As long as he holds up this staff, the Israelites are winning the battle, but when fatigue makes him lower it, the tide of battle turns in favour of the Amalekites. So Aaron and Hur support Moses' arms, and the advantage returns to Israel (**17:12-13**). Aaron was Moses' brother, his assistant from the very beginning (4:14), and would later be appointed as a priest (28:1). He came from the tribe of Levi.

Hur was the son of Caleb and came from the tribe of Judah, through Judah's liaison with Tamar (Gen 38; 1 Chr 2:4-5, 19). Hur was not a priest since he was not from the tribe of Levi, but he worked alongside Aaron (see also 24:14). The victory over the Amalekites is won by the cooperation of Moses, Aaron, Hur and Joshua, all working together in obedience to God (17:13). As the Fang of Gabon say, 'The chimpanzee fights because he counts on the help of the gorilla' [meaning that those who are insignificant in themselves can accomplish much when a greater power is on their side].

When the battle is done, the Lord tells Moses to record what has happened 'in a book' (kjv) or *on a scroll* (**17:14a**). This book is not necessarily the book of Exodus. It may have been the Book of the Wars of the Lord mentioned in Numbers 21:14. Moses is to make sure that Joshua knows about this record and about the curse God pronounces on Amalek when he says that he will *blot out the memory of Amalek from under heaven* (**17:14b, 16b**; see also Deut 25:19). The emphasis on Joshua hearing what is said suggests that he is already being prepared for his future role as Israel's leader. The vicious attacks by the Amalekites will not be forgotten and will be avenged in the days of Saul (1 Sam 15:7).

To celebrate this victory, Moses erects an altar in honour of God, calling it Jehovah Nissi, which means *The Lord is my Banner* (**17:15-16a**). What a beautiful name!

18:1-12 Moses Is Reunited with His Family

During the forty years that Moses had spent in the desert of Midian, he had married Zipporah, the daughter of Jethro. She and his two sons accompanied Moses when he first set out for Egypt (4:20-27), but it appears that at some point he judged it best to send her back to live with her father, possibly to protect her from reprisals by Pharaoh (**18:2**). Now Moses has returned to the area where they live, near Sinai, and Jethro sends word that he and Moses' family are coming to meet him. They have heard of all that the Lord has done for him (**18:1, 5-7**; see also 15:14-15).

Jethro is delighted to hear Moses' own account of everything the Lord has done (**18:8-9**). Jethro's words in **18:10** confirm the accuracy of the names that Moses chose for his two sons (**18:3-4**). This priest of Midian declares, *Now I know that the Lord is greater than all other gods* (**18:11**). The role Jethro plays here, and even the language he uses, confirm the truth of Romans 1:20. He and others had heard about what Moses' God had done and could testify to his greatness. In gratitude, Jethro offers burnt offerings to the God of the Israelites.

The meal that Jethro, Moses, Aaron and the elders then share *in the presence of God* is a sacrificial meal, but also indicates that there is a covenant between them (**18:12**; see also Gen 26:30; Exod 24:11).

18:13-27 Jethro's Advice

The *next day* must have been a normal one for Moses. He took up the seated position appropriate for a judge while the people who came before him stood to present their cases. This went on *from morning till evening*, while Moses ruled on one case after another (**18:13**). Moses was acting like any patriarch or head of a large family as he settled various matters and resolved legal disputes. But this family is so large that the task is an impossible one, as Jethro, who is watching, quickly realizes. He advises Moses that he must delegate certain tasks to avoid exhausting himself and wearing out the people's patience (**18:14-18**). Moses must focus on his primary calling, which is to be *the people's representative before God,* and must concentrate on doing this rather than spreading himself too thin (**18:19**).

Later, the apostles would have much the same experience as Moses, and took similar steps to address the problem they faced (Acts 6:1-4). Even today, many pastors make the mistake of being so involved in the details of administration that their spiritual ministry to the people they serve becomes secondary. Pastors who are in this situation need to learn to allow other people to handle some tasks, so that they can maximize their ministry of meeting people's many spiritual needs.

Jethro displays his skill as a leader as he offers Moses wise and practical advice. Moses must teach the people God's laws, so that they do not need to come to him to find out what behaviour God wants (**18:20**). He must also appoint capable and honest men to act as his deputies to handle simple matters, so that only the complex cases will be brought to him (**18:21-23**). Wise leaders take care to multiply themselves in others. No matter how much energy and ability one has, the load is always too great for any one person to carry. Moreover, no one lives for ever. Paul multiplied himself in Timothy and others, and then laid down the principle very clearly in his letter to Timothy: 'the things you have heard me say ... entrust to reliable men [and women in our present day context] who will also be qualified to teach others' (2 Tim 2:2).

Moses recognizes that his father-in-law is giving sound advice that will solve a serious problem, and so he puts it into practice (**18:24-26**). Then, again demonstrating his wisdom, Jethro fades into the background (**18:27**). Both these men demonstrate the humility that goes with true leadership. Moses did not seek to keep all the power himself, but was prepared to share it with others. He seems to have trusted his officials to carry out their duties, for we do not read of him micro-managing them or second-guessing their decisions. This, in itself, must have enabled him to spend more time with God, the source of wisdom and power to lead. As pastors, we need to remember that the more we trust others with responsibilities, the more they will grow

and the freer we will be to spend time with the owner of the flock we serve (1 Pet 5:2).

Jethro has outlined principles for the transmission of knowledge (18:20). These principles will soon be applied when God presents Moses with a large number of directives, laws and ordinances.

19:1-24:18 A People Consecrated to the Lord

We now enter the second part of the book of Exodus, at the heart of which is the statement that *you will be for me a kingdom of priests and a holy nation* (19:6). In these chapters, Israel takes shape as a nation. The slaves who came out of Egypt progressively become a community (or an 'assembly' or 'congregation' – KJV) under the direction of Moses, their God-appointed leader.

The long years in the desert will allow time for a re-orientation, indeed a revolution, in the consciousness of the people who have finally acquired independence and a new identity. When Joseph, his brothers and his father Jacob entered Egypt, they were only a family. Now, they have emerged as a nation, led by a shepherd who has been trained as a prince, as they advance to meet their future. God is going to entrust them with a special mission as well as giving them the land they have long been promised.

We have seen hints of this mission when Moses was first commissioned. God instructed him to tell Pharaoh that 'Israel is my firstborn son' (4:22). As the 'firstborn', Israel has a special place in God's affection and is his 'treasured possession' (19:5). But the adjective may also suggest that their role is to lead other people to God, so that they can become his other sons (Gen 12:3b). Moses refers to the idea of sonship again in one of his final addresses to the people. There he summarizes their history by saying that in the desert 'the Lord your God carried you, as a father carries his son, all the way you went until you reached this place' (Deut 1:31; see also Deut 14:1; 32:6; Hos 11:1). Being called a 'son' implies a very special and privileged relationship between God and his people. Yet a son also owes to his father specific duties. In the case of Israel, the nation is to be entirely dedicated to the service, that is, to the worship of God (19:5-6). Its obligations are set out in a unique covenant that establishes Israel's special status, particularly in relation to other nations (20:1-23:33).

Israel's unique role, its specific mission to other peoples, becomes clearer and clearer throughout the OT, but only becomes fully explicit in the NT. The Apostle Peter summarizes this mission as follows: 'You are a chosen people, a royal priesthood, a holy nation, a people belonging to God, that you may declare the praises of him who called you out of darkness into his wonderful light. Once you were not a people, but now you are the people of God' (1 Pet 2:9-10). Peter is reading the OT texts in the light of the new revelation in Christ when he speaks of Christians enjoying these privileges. But these privileges were originally given to the children of Israel, and they remain in effect even though Israel may not currently be enjoying them. Israel's mission to the world was perfectly and finally fulfilled with the coming of Jesus Christ, but his coming did not mean the end of Israel's calling.

It is now accepted that for a group to be recognized as a nation, it must have its own land, people and a constitution. Problems relating to these factors account for much of the turmoil on the African continent. Colonizers determined the territorial boundaries of many nations without attention to natural divisions of the peoples, and the result has been disunity. The constitutions drawn up for new nations have often been overthrown. The result has been much grief and pain for a divided continent. Many nations are still enduring various forms of the turmoil that the Israelites did in the years following the exodus. It was during those years that God forged a group of loosely associated tribes into one nation, laid down their constitution and laws, and prepared them to occupy the land he would give them.

19:1-25 The Lord Establishes a Covenant

As promised in 3:12, Moses has come back to Mount Sinai to worship God with the liberated people (**19:1-2**). Here, as a mediator, he now works with the elders to prepare the people and everything in the vicinity for an encounter with God.

God summons Moses and speaks of his plan to establish a covenant with his people, whom he identifies as *the house of Jacob* and *the people of Israel* (**19:3**). He reminds the people that he has protected them like an eagle protects its young: *I carried you on eagles' wings and brought you to myself* (**19:4**; Deut 32:10-11). The idea of God bringing the people to himself was also present in the song of Moses and Miriam, where it was said that God would 'plant them' spiritually on 'the mountain of your inheritance' when they arrived geographically in the promised land (15:17).

God then presents Moses with the terms of the covenant that he is to present to the people. Three major points are made:
• Israel is God's property, his own *treasured possession* (**19:5a**; see also Deut 7:6; 14:2; 26:18; Ps 135:4). The same term is translated as 'treasure' in other passages, such as Ecclesiastes 2:8.
• Israel will be a *kingdom of priests* (**19:6a**). A priest has access to God and acts as an intermediary between the people and God. Jethro gave a concise account of a priest's role when he spoke to Moses and pointed out his primary responsibility (18:13-27). Israel, led and taught by God, will become a light to the nations! They will be able to do this because *the whole earth is mine* (**19:5b**). These words would have had a powerful impact at the

time they were spoken, for in those days few had any concept of a universal God. The gods were thought of as local and territorial, and thus limited. But although God would be the God of Israel, that did not mean that Israel would be the only place where he ruled and showed his power.
• Israel is to be a *holy nation* as God is holy (**19:6b**; see also 3:5-6). The people must thus be morally pure and consecrated to the service of God. This consecration compels Israel to be set apart, different from other nations.

Moses passes on God's words to the elders (**19:7**), who pass them on to the people. The people unanimously accept God's terms, which demand obedience and total consecration: *We will do everything that the Lord has said* (**19:8**). We find this beautiful phrase again in Joshua 24:16-24, forty years later! The moment is solemn and the commitment important.

God wants the people to be absolutely convinced that they can trust Moses, because Moses is God's instrument. So he plans to appear to Moses before them all: *I am going to come to you in a dense cloud, so that the people will hear me speaking with you and will always put their trust in you* (**19:9**). God himself insists that the people must 'put their trust' in Moses (see 4:31 and 14:31).

God intends to have a solemn meeting, but he also wants to make it clear that his appearing is not something to be taken lightly. So he lays down requirements for ritual purification. The people are to purify themselves externally by washing their clothes and abstaining from sexual relations (**19:10**, **14-15**). These actions symbolize the attitude of their heart and their total consecration to God. They are also not to come near the mountain where God will appear, for it is now holy, and nothing impure must touch it on pain of death (**19:12-13**). These extraordinary constraints underscore the importance of holiness and the sacredness of the occasion. It takes three days to achieve complete purification. There is nothing superficial about this preparation to meet with God.

After the purification is complete, the Lord thunderously announces his coming before he descends on the mountain (**19:16-18**). In the popular belief of other nations, the gods lived on the mountains, but here it is clearly said that God *descended* to Sinai from some still higher position in the heavens.

The people are invited to approach the mountain to hear God speak to Moses (19:17), but no one should go up onto the mountain. The only exception is mentioned in 19:13, which says that when the ram's horn sounds, they may ascend it. It is reasonable to assume that this means that representatives of the people would ascend the mountain, and not the whole crowd of over six thousand persons.

The idea of God's sacredness is reinforced when Moses again warns the people not to force their way up to see God or they will *perish* (**19:21**, **24**). Approaching God is a serious matter that cannot be taken lightly. When Isaiah was privileged to see something of the Lord's holiness, all he could do was cry 'woe to me' (Isa 6:5a). This is why believers need an advocate before the Father, in the person of the one who died for them (1 John 2:2). It is only 'in Christ' that anyone can approach God's throne (Heb 10:19-22).

20:1-17 The Covenant Terms: Ten Commandments

God now addresses the people directly, speaking what in Hebrew are known as the Ten Words (Deut 4:13; 10:4) or in Greek as the Decalogue (from the Greek *deka logos* meaning 'ten words'). In English, these are referred to as the Ten Commandments. What is happening here is modelled on the treaty texts of the ancient Near East. Ancient treaties were similar to those that were made in ancient Africa between a king of a powerful nation and the ruler of a weaker nation. The written text of a treaty set out the details of the new relationship between the suzerain (the powerful king) and his vassal (the weaker nation). The suzerain imposed duties and taxes and demanded obedience and unconditional allegiance. Sometimes these agreements included specific rules to ensure that the suzerain was protected against future attacks. However, while the form and structure of the covenant that God establishes with Israel is similar to that of human political treaties, the content is quite different from anything in a human treaty.

Like other ancient treaties, this one begins with a reminder of the historical links between the two parties to the treaty: *I am the Lord your God, who brought you out of the land of Egypt, out of the land of slavery* (**20:1-2**). But then it continues with succinct statements that reveal God's nature and set out his will for his people. God has committed himself to them and has acted to fulfil the promises he made to the patriarchs, and he expects a similar commitment from his people. He wishes to have his people serve as a model, communicating his truths to the nations. To be equal to this responsibility and to live as an example of what the kingdom of God can be on earth, they must learn exclusive obedience to the Lord, their liberator. They must learn the right way to worship him and to distinguish him from idols. They must also learn how to love other members of the liberated, redeemed community. The Ten Commandments are a statement of what will be required.

There is some disagreement about how the Ten Commandments should be numbered. Some people argue that 20:3, about having no other gods, is the first commandment and that 20:4-6, condemning idols, is the second. Others argue that all of these verses have to do with one commandment, which is being elaborated at length. Similarly,

20:16-17, which speaks of relations between neighbours, may be considered one commandment or two.

The first four commandments deal with Israel's relationship with God, and the remainder with relationships between people.

20:3 No other gods

The first commandment states that Israel has only one choice when it comes to worship (**20:3**). The people had been slaves for several hundred years in Egypt, where there were many gods. The idea that there was only one God would have been new, introducing a revolutionary approach to worship, and was an innovation that became institutionalized with this commandment.

God's reminder of their slavery in Egypt in 20:2 was also a reminder that he had defeated all the gods of Egypt through the ten plagues. Here God lays claim to the same exclusivity that Jesus speaks of when he says, 'No one can serve two masters' (Matt 6:24). This truth is equally inscribed in African culture. The Dogon of Mali say, 'A man cannot choose two roads at the same time' and the Beti of Cameroon say, 'One cannot chase two pigeons at once'. According to the Lord, it is impossible to truly worship him and any other so-called gods at the same time.

The words of this commandment can be equally well translated 'no other gods against me', or 'besides me' or 'above me'. The wide range of possibilities in the Hebrew covers all the options when it comes to other gods.

20:4-6 No idol worship

The second commandment (20:4-6) is so similar to the first that it seems to be an extension of it, which explains why some people think that the two do in fact constitute one commandment. Whatever the case may be, what we have here is a description of the nature of God and of the way in which he is to be worshipped. Once again, there is a clear break with the gods and style of worship in Egypt.

The Hebrew word translated as *idol* or 'graven image' (KJV) means an image carved in wood or sculpted in stone (**20:4**). It represents something observed in nature that people begin to worship as a deity. It is also an object that the worshippers believe they can manipulate as suits them. God does not wish to be represented in any way that reduces his greatness by making him into an object that people can imagine that they can control in some way. He is invisible, without form, and thus cannot be represented by any object. Moses reminds the people of this when he recounts the events at Sinai: 'The Lord spoke to you out of the fire. You heard the sound of words but saw no form; there was only a voice' (Deut 4:12).

The command that one must not *bow down to them or worship them* (**20:5**) refers to the worship of idols that the people of many nations make to represent their gods and not to any image of God himself, for one must not make any representation of him. We would also do well to remember that an idol is anything that takes God's place in our lives, that is, anything that is given the first place that rightly belongs to the one who created us and gives us life. In our contemporary world, many have replaced God with success, wealth and power. These, too, are idols.

The personification of God by any representation of him leads to false worship. Jesus builds on this idea in his teaching about what constitutes true worship. When a Samaritan woman asks where one should worship the Lord, Jesus answers, 'God is spirit, and his worshippers must worship in spirit and in truth' (John 4:24). He is making it clear that God is invisible and cannot be confined to one location. Later, the Apostle Paul makes the same point when he teaches the Gentiles that 'the God who made the world and everything in it is the Lord of heaven and earth' and is not any idol of 'gold or silver or stone— an image made by man's design and skill' (Acts 17:24-29).

20:7 No misuse of God's name

The third commandment is *You shall not misuse the name of the Lord your God* (**20:7**). Because the Hebrew can also be translated as 'you shall not pronounce the name of the Lord', the post-exilic Jews interpreted this commandment as a prohibition on even saying the name of God ('Yahweh'). Thus they never referred to God by this name, but always replaced it with an alternative term, generally 'Adonai', which is translated as Lord in many Bibles. But this command does not set out to forbid every use of God's name; rather, its goal is to protect the integrity of God's name. That name must be honoured and must not be associated with deceit or lies.

The true targets of this commandment are those who make false promises and seek to give them credibility by invoking an unimpeachable authority. They lard their speech with phrases like 'before God' or 'in God's name'. No one is to invoke God's name with the aim of deceiving someone else. This prescription is made even more explicit in Leviticus 19:12: 'Do not swear falsely by my name, and so profane the name of your God' (see also Deut 5:11; Ps 139:20). In our world today, it is not uncommon, both in political and religious settings, to find people who invoke God's name when making promises that they cannot possibly fulfil, and sometimes do not even intend to try to fulfil. To do this is to profane God's name, which should be held in reverence. Those who try to exploit it for their own selfish purposes cannot expect to go unpunished.

As he so often does, Jesus refines the themes of the OT and extends their applications. When he deals with oaths in the Sermon on the Mount, he advises us not to make any. We should be people of such integrity that a 'yes' or 'no' is

all that is needed to signal our commitment to, or rejection of, some project (Matt 5:33-37).

The significance of God's name is well understood in Africa, where people's names have great importance, not only because they identify individuals but also because they identify them as belonging to particular social and cultural groups. Names are also related to a history and references to particular events. The same is true of the names that humans gave to African divinities. These names shape the nature of the god. Pagans end up believing that they can easily manipulate both the name and the god represented by the name. The name thus becomes a way of controlling, of mastering and of taming the divinity. But the God of Israel refuses to allow his name to be used in this way. He is not an object to be manipulated.

20:8-11 No work on the Sabbath

The fourth commandment introduces another dramatic change from the harsh regime the Israelites had endured under Pharaoh (5:17-19). It insists that one day in seven is to be set apart for worshipping the Lord (**20:8**). This setting apart manifests the sacred character of this day, which is to be a consecrated time of worship and rest (**20:9-10a**). It is to be observed by all, including servants, foreigners and even animals (**20:10b**; compare 20:17). The foreigners or 'aliens' referred to here are those people who had left Egypt with the Israelites (12:42) and who were invited to share in the Passover, provided the men were circumcised.

The Lord had already initiated observance of this commandment when he gave instructions about the gathering of manna (16:22-30). But its roots go much further back, right to God's example at creation, when he also worked for six days and then rested on the seventh (**20:11**; Gen 2:2-3). Humans are to follow his example. In the wisdom of God, he has given us this day to allow us to spend sacred time with him in order to deepen our relationship with him, and also as a time to be refreshed physically, mentally and emotionally.

Respect for this day of rest is so important that God returns to this commandment at the end of his meeting with Moses and insists that disobedience to it will be punishable by death (31:12-17).

The Jews calculate days in accordance with the pattern in Genesis 1 ('there was evening and there was morning') and thus regard each day as beginning at sunset, rather than at midnight. Thus their observance of the Sabbath as the seventh day of the week lasts from sunset on Friday to sunset on Saturday

From NT times on, Christians stopped observing the Sabbath on the seventh day of the week, and instead celebrated the first day of the week, Sunday, the day of Christ's resurrection (see Acts 20:7; 1 Cor 16:2). They did this because Jesus is the true rest of God (Heb 4:3, 11).

During his life here on earth, Jesus made it abundantly clear that keeping the letter of the law does not make anyone closer to God. He stated that he is the Lord of the Sabbath (Matt 12:8; Mark 2:28; Luke 6:5) and demonstrated that meeting human needs takes precedence over the Sabbath observance (Matt 12:11-14; John 5:1-9).

In our time, we need to ensure that in observing our day of rest on Sunday, we do not become like the Pharisees and focus on obeying the letter of the law. We should use the day as an opportunity to draw closer to God and to his people. But we must also beware of spending so much time at church that we have no time to rest our bodies. The principle of the Sabbath excludes any attempt to please God simply on the basis of these externals of our behaviour. Its focus is on our relationship with Jesus Christ, the one sent by God to provide rest for our souls (Matt 11:28).

20:12 Honour your parents

The preceding commandments have dealt with the relationship between God and humans, whereas this commandment and the ones that follow deal with relationships between people. The command *Honour your father and your mother* focuses on the relationship between parents and children (**20:12a**). Here the Hebrew word translated 'honour' could also be translated as 'glorify', which is the same word used of the nation's relationship with God, its father. Thus this verse marks the transition between humans and God. It shows that parents are part of a structure of authority that he has established, therefore, they deserve respect, just as God does. Parents (both father and mother) are God's stewards to produce children and nurture them in the ways of the Lord. God expects each child to give his or her parents the respect they deserve as God's stewards.

Paul calls this 'the first commandment with a promise' referring to the fact that those who obey this commandment will *live long in the land* (**20:12b**; Eph 6:2-3). Those who do not respect their parents are to be punished severely (21:17; Lev 20:9; Prov 20:20).

We have no choice about whether to honour and obey our parents. It is as basic as the fact that 'water in a river always runs downstream' (Nyang, Cameroon). However, as Paul instructed the Ephesians, this is to be done 'in the Lord' (Eph 6:1). As God's representatives, parents are to nurture in us what God wants of us. Parents who do their duty well respect that order of command. But sometimes there is a conflict between what a parent wants and God's will. In such a case, a child is not called upon to obey. He or she must politely and respectfully explain why the thing they are being asked to do is wrong.

20:13 Do not murder

The translation of the sixth commandment in the KJV, *thou shalt not kill* (**20:13**), has led some to argue that this com-

mandment involves a contradiction, for the penalty for breaking it is to be put to death (21:12, 14). But the word translated 'kill' is the one that is used for premeditated murder. All human beings are created in God's image, and no human being has the right to take someone else's life. God, the source of life, is the only one who can rule on whether a life is to be preserved or not (Ezek 18:4)

It is also true that at times someone accidentally kills another. God recognizes the difference between such a death and a murder, and makes provision for appropriate judgments (21:13; Num 35:10-15).

20:14 Do not commit adultery

The seventh commandment, *You shall not commit adultery*, addresses the sanctity of marriage, which adultery flouts (**20:14**). In the OT, it is seen primarily as a sin against one's neighbour. The adulterous man sins against his wife and the deceived husband, and the adulterous woman sins against her husband and the deceived wife. Joseph's description of it as a 'sin against God' (Gen 39:9) shows that it was early recognized to be a violation of God's will.

To commit adultery is to break a covenant and a promise. It shows disrespect for every covenant and every promise. It is thus significant that this commandment is given in the context of the covenant regulations setting out the commitments between God and his people (see comment on 20:1-17).

The punishment for adultery is set out elsewhere in the Pentateuch (see Lev 20:10; Deut 22:22 in the context of marriage; see Deut 22:13-21 when the woman is not married). Generally, the term 'adultery' refers to a sexual relationship involving someone who is married to someone else. Some might thus argue that this commandment does not apply to a sexual relationship in which neither of the partners is married. But 'fornication', which is the word used to refer to such a relationship, is also the word used to refer to all sexual sin, regardless of the marital status of those involved (see 1 Cor 5:1 KJV). God's will is that sex be within a marriage relationship (Heb 13:4), and thus both adultery and fornication are sin before God.

As Jesus makes clear (Matt 19:4-6), the bonds of marriage were originally inviolable. The option of divorce came later because of human sinfulness. The commandment as given here calls for respect for one's spouse and for the commitment made when one married.

20:15 Do not steal

Stealing or robbery makes for social instability. The one who steals is sending a message that he or she is envious and has no respect for other people. This truth applies to thieves who are mere robbers, and to those who use trickery to obtain or retain what belongs to others. An employer steals when he or she does not pay the wages owed to an employee; a shopkeeper steals when he or she uses a false scale to weigh the goods being sold, and so on. The Bible is not concerned simply with spiritual matters, but also instructs us in what makes for healthy relations between people. Thus many biblical texts deal with such everyday matters as the commercial relations between rich and poor, and between bosses and workers. These relations are often bad because one party seeks to make a profit regardless of whether the method causes harm to others.

20:16 Do not lie

The commandment to not lie, like the preceding one, insists that human relations be based on honesty and truth. Here God calls for honesty as regards the reputation of one's neighbours. Giving *false testimony* (**20:16**) does not happen only in a court situation, but occurs whenever we lie about or slander someone else. Such speech is morally wrong because it destroys the integrity of the one telling the lie and the reputation of the one lied about. It can have very serious consequences in the real world, destroying relationships and career prospects, and can even lead to jail terms and suicide. Later, God expands on this commandment: 'Do not spread false reports. Do not help a wicked man by being a malicious witness ... do not pervert justice by siding with the crowd' (23:1-2). It is sobering to remember that false witnesses were even brought in to testify during the unjust trial of our Lord (Matt 26:59-62; John 19:12).

20:17 Do not covet

The tenth commandment, with its emphasis on not coveting or craving what belongs to another (**20:17**), ties in with the eighth commandment about not stealing. It does not mean a person cannot admire something that someone else owns or has done. Rather, it refers to the corrosive desire that undermines good relationships between people and may even lead some to want the person with the desired object or ability to suffer.

This commandment's placement at the end of the list means that it ties up any loose ends as regards human relationships. The commandments have now addressed every possible human relationship – the relationship with God, with one's immediate family, and with the wider society – and have laid a strong and stable foundation for the nation that God is creating. Trustworthiness and respect for others are essential because no society built on false relationships can survive the instability and trouble that flow from such relationships. Deceit, lies, corruption, exploitation, violent relationships, intimidation and a lack of respect have all weakened attempts to build free and independent nations on our continent. If people and nations had heeded the Ten Commandments, we would have avoided many traumas.

20:18-21 The People's Response

The people's response to the presence of God reveals Moses' role as a mediator between them and God. They are afraid even to hear the voice of the Lord with their own ears (**20:18-19**). Moses' response to them may seem contradictory. On the one hand, he says, *Do not be afraid,* and on the other he indicates that God wants them to fear him *so that the fear of God will be with you to keep you from sinning* (**20:20**). Worshippers who approach God need to do so with a sense of awe at his greatness and with a sense of dread because of their own weakness and frailty. Yet the God of the Bible encourages humans to approach him with confidence in his goodness and without irrational fear (Heb 10:19-22). So while Moses encourages the Israelites not to be afraid, he does not want them to forget the fear associated with respect and an awareness of the difference between them and God. Respectful fear leads to confidence and joy (see Ps 40:4; Prov 14:26; Ps 64:10).

20:22-26 Rules Regarding Worship

Before embarking on a more detailed explanation of his laws, God asserts that the people cannot claim to be unaware of their responsibilities to worship and obey him, and him alone, since they have clearly heard him speak from the heavens (**20:22**). Then he restates the fundamental principle embodied in the first and second commandments: because he is the only God, the Israelites are to avoid all contact with other deities (**20:23**). If they do not, they will be betraying the covenant. Moreover, as the Bahaya of Tanzania say, 'if you touch a cooking pot, you get dirty'. The Baha'i of the same region recognize that 'one piece of green wood is enough to prevent the others from burning'. Idolatry will prevent Israel from correctly reflecting the attributes of God, and will thus prevent them from bearing the intended witness to the nations.

God insists that any altar built to him be in a natural state, made either of earth or simple stones (**20:24-25**). None of the stones are to be *dressed*; in other words, they are not to have any engraving or carved images. The same emphasis on what is new, pure and in its raw state is present in other texts. For example, the heifer that is to be used to make atonement for an unsolved murder was never to have been used and the land where it is to be sacrificed is to be uncultivated (Deut 21:3-4). Similarly, in 1 Samuel 6:7, a new wagon is used to carry the ark of the covenant and the cows that draw it have never worn a yoke before. The sacredness of the unpolished or pure state is also evident in the command to sacrifice a year-old lamb without blemish (Lev 9:3).

An altar should not be raised so high that steps are needed to approach it *lest your nakedness be exposed* (**20:26**). This detail is included because men did not regularly wear undergarments under their robes or tunics. Later, God specifies that the priests who serve at his altar must wear 'linen undergarments' (28:42). The instruction served a practical purpose in regard to modesty as well as having theological significance in the sense of suggesting that sins were covered. But where there would be no exposure of the body even when steps were used, the regulation did not apply. Thus in the future temple that God reveals to Ezekiel, the altar is approached by steps (Ezek 43:17). From this we can draw the principle that before we make any of these regulations an absolute, we need to first ask ourselves why it was given in the first place. While some are directly rooted in God's moral nature, others are only indirectly related to it, for it is the principle rather than the exact act that relates to God's character.

21:1-23:19 Details of the Law

21:1 Introduction

Whereas God wrote down the Ten Commandments (see 24:12; 32:15-16; 34:1, 28), Moses wrote down the other laws contained in the book of Exodus, after he had transmitted them to the people (**21:1**; see also 24:3-4; 34:27-28). Chapters 21–23 of the book of Exodus could almost be described as a short manual setting out the regulations that flow from the Ten Commandments. These regulations govern social relations, the relations between God and his people, and relations between individual Israelites. This section may even be the Book of the Covenant mentioned in 24:7.

Just as the God of Israel was very different from the Egyptian gods, so the social and judicial system in Egypt would have been very different from the system that the Israelites are now learning to live under. So God uses laws to reveal his moral character so that his people can imitate him. These laws can be divided into three categories: principles applying to particular situations, moral or ethical legislation and religious legislation.

Some of the regulations in this section seem to echo things previously said, so they may seem to be unnecessary repetitions. But the Lord knows that people are often forgetful, so he reinforces important points by repeating them.

This 'manual' or booklet ends with enthusiastic words about what God will do for the people who have only just begun their journey towards the land he had promised to give them.

21:2-22:16 General case law

This section contains laws related to details of daily life, and applies the laws to particular cases. The laws are presented in the form of a series of situations with the legislation that applies to each case

21:2-11 TREATMENT OF SERVANTS The instructions regarding servants (21:2-11) are intended to give the Israelites a new understanding of how slaves are to be treated. Slaves are not to be forced to endure the sort of victimization that the Israelites had endured in Egypt. Jesus made the same point in his parable of the unmerciful servant (Matt 18:23-35). God wants the Israelites to show to others the same kindness that they have received from him. The same principle applies to all who are in positions of authority, whether as an employer relating to an employee, a supervisor relating to those supervised, or a leader relating to those led. Those who are privileged to enjoy authority sometimes forget that were it not for God's grace, the situation could be reversed. They might be the ones taking orders rather than issuing them. When the grace of God is kept in focus, an employer will treat his or her employees with the dignity that God expects. To fail to treat them well is to displease God.

Exodus gives a specific example of what this principle means: people cannot be kept as slaves indefinitely. If a Hebrew becomes so poor that he has to sell himself, he can only be enslaved for six years and must be set free in the seventh year (**21:2**). This pattern is a reminder of the Sabbath rest and of God's deliverance (see Lev 25:39; Deut 15:12; Neh 5:5).

The attitude of God, who is the Lord and Master of Israel, and was so even when the Israelites were slaves in Egypt, sets the example for how people should relate to any slaves they may own. If they follow his example, it is understandable how a slave can say *I love my master* and continue to serve him in love, and not by constraint (**21:5-6**).

A series of specific rulings are made to protect marriages (**21:3-4**) and especially to protect women from the abuse and social injustice that they endure in many cultures. These rulings make it clear that, in God's eyes, a woman is a person who has her own rights, and that to scoff at a woman or treat her as an object is a sin. Even if a woman is a slave serving a master, her slavery does not deprive her of human dignity, nor does it give her 'owner' the right to treat her unfairly (**21:7-11**).

21:12-36 RESPONSES TO DEATH AND INJURY A number of fatal scenarios are now presented and the sentence laid down. In general terms, any one who kills someone else faces the death penalty (**21:12, 14**). However, if the death was accidental, the killer can *flee to a place I will designate* (**21:13**). This place is later specified to be any one of six cities belonging to the Levites that are official 'cities of refuge' (Num 35:9-15, Deut 4:41-43; Josh 20).

Other crimes that are punishable by death are attacking one's parents (**21:15**), kidnapping someone and either keeping or selling them (**21:16**), and cursing one's parents (**21:17**; see 20:12).

Next, God deals with the legal response to less serious personal injuries that cause permanent or temporary disabilities. Specific cases are given as examples of damage arising from acts committed in anger (quarrelling men – **21:18-19**), acts causing unintended injuries (fighting men injure a pregnant woman – 21:22-25), acts of punishment (a slave is beaten by his or her owner – **21:26-27**), acts of carelessness (leaving a pit uncovered – **21:33-34**), or acts involving one's property (a bull hurting someone – **21:28-32**; **35-36**). The law makes it clear that owners are responsible for injuries caused by their livestock and for causing injuries to another's livestock (21:28-36). The point in all these cases is that someone must take responsibility for what has happened and that the responsible party must be dealt with justly, not excessively.

The law lays down various punishments and reparations. The principle that is laid down here is sometimes referred to as the *lex talionis* or the 'law of retaliation': *life for life, eye for eye, tooth for tooth* (**21:24-25**). This law sets a limit to the penalty that can be exacted for any damage done. It is in marked contrast to the principle of exaggerated revenge that Lamech bragged about (Gen 4:23). Later, Jesus himself speaks about this principle and states that his followers should give up their right to revenge (Matt 5:38).

22:1-15 RESPONSES TO PROPERTY CRIMES The crimes dealt with in the previous section could be covered by the umbrella commandment 'you shall not murder' (20:13). Now the focus shifts to another commandment, 'you shall not steal' (20:15). Thus this section of the book deals with crimes involving people's property. Looking at the various cases that are presented, it is possible to deduce the following principles:

- **Compensation for theft includes a penalty.** A thief will have to pay back five head of cattle for every ox stolen and slaughtered and four sheep for every sheep stolen and slaughtered (**22:1**). If the animal is found alive, he must pay back double; that is, two oxen or two sheep for every ox or sheep stolen (**22:4**). The penalty acts as a deterrent to anyone who is considering stealing, and it also takes into account the fact that a thief causes more damage than merely the value of the property taken. The victim of a theft suffers emotional stress, has to spend time looking for the stolen property, and endures hardship in other ways. Yet in many African countries, armed robbery is committed almost casually. Thieves may greet the victim with 'What have you got for us today?' and may leave saying 'We won't kill you so that you can get some more stuff for us to pick up another day'. God recognizes the emotional cruelty and physical abuse that accompany theft, and thus he demands reparations that are greater than the mere value of the object stolen. Full restitution must be made, even if the only way to obtain the money is to sell the thief into slavery (**22:3b**).

- **A life is not to be taken lightly.** If a thief is killed while in the act of stealing at night, there is no need to impose a penalty on the one who killed him (**22:2**). The thief put his or her own life at risk, and the victim has the right to self-defence. But the Lord does not want this stipulation to be interpreted as meaning that the life of a thief is cheap. Thus he adds the additional clause that

this exemption only applies if the struggle takes place while it is still dark. If the theft happens *after sunrise,* there is no need for bloodshed (**22:3a**). The thief can be recognized and the victim can easily call for help since other people are awake. Thus the Lord does not endorse taking anyone else's life if there is another option available. Yet in many countries that are at war, we see people cheer when many of their enemies are killed and mourn the loss of one of their own soldiers. Their enemies do exactly the same. We have lost our sense of the value of all life, even the life of an enemy. While there are circumstances in which a life may be taken (for example, at night), we should always be looking for other options. Killings done after sunrise are tantamount to murder. God demands justice for those killed in these circumstances. This knowledge should give pause to those who want to resort to war without first exploring all the other options that would spare lives – whether those of their supporters or of their enemies.

- **Everyone must take responsibility for his or her actions or lack of action.** When carelessness in looking after animals or in handling a fire causes damage to others, restitution is called for (**22:5-6**). The Lord does not accept lame excuses when our carelessness has caused harm to others. This is a principle that many African leaders should apply when handling public funds. Poor use or careless handling of such funds calls for restitution. If this principle were applied in the management of African affairs, some of the suffering that is caused by a carefree attitude to public funds would be alleviated.

- **People who offer help to others need some protection.** Those who are willing to help others can sometimes find themselves in very difficult situations of the type described in **22:7** and **22:10**. The person who has previously been grateful for the help may turn on the helper. In such cases, judges must look into the matter (**22:8-9**) or the helper must take an oath before the Lord that he or she had no hand in doing harm to the other person's property (**22:11**). We sometimes see similar situations today, when one person offers another a ride in their car and is then involved in an accident. Some people see this as an opportunity to get rich at the expense of the one who was helping them. Some may even claim false injuries. A just society does its best to protect those who offer help to others from unfair situations. Offering such protection leaves everyone freer to assist others.

- **Those who lend or borrow must be protected.** If a borrowed animal is injured or dies, the owner must be compensated for his or her loss (**22:14**). However, the borrower is protected if the owner of the animal was present when it was injured or died (**22:15**). In that case, it is assumed that no one, including the owner, foresaw what was going to happen or could have done anything to avoid it. The animal simply died while doing its normal work. It would be unfair to expect the borrower to make restitution when it is clear that he or she did nothing out of the ordinary and has paid for the hire of the animal. In this law, too, we see the application of the principle of considering the whole situation. When it is not the carelessness of the borrower but circumstances beyond his or her control that make them unable to return what was borrowed, God expects the loaner to exercise mercy and bear with the borrower. By contrast, the general practice of the world today is to auction whatever the borrower has, regardless of what caused any delay in payment. God's principle is that we should look at the situation fairly. We should neither allow ourselves to be cheated by the borrower nor be without mercy to those who have borrowed from us.

As one reads these rulings, one is struck by the clarity with which each situation is outlined and the appropriate judgment pronounced. The penalties may seem severe, but God wants his people to serve as examples to others. Israel's mission is not only to worship God but also to make him known as a model for social and religious life.

22:16–23:9 Moral law

Most of the laws that follow are no longer given in terms of regulations applying to particular situations. Instead, they are statements of principles that are to be applied in relationships between people, and between individuals and God. 22:16-17; 21-27 RESPONSES TO SINS AGAINST PEOPLE In the section that follows, God gives laws that provide for the protection of four groups of people: virgins, aliens, widows and orphans, and the needy in general.

• **Protection of virgins.** A virgin who was engaged to someone was regarded as that person's wife and the punishment for sleeping with her would be death (Deut 22:23-24). But the *virgin* referred to in **22:16** is one who is *not pledged to be married*. She is a young single girl. The man who seduces her must pay her family the full bride price. He will become her husband, unless the girl's father refuses to allow the marriage (**22:17**). But regardless of whether a marriage takes place, he is required to pay the bride price. God hates the common practice of men destroying young girls' lives by sleeping with them. They are guilty not only of sexual immorality but also of destroying the girl's dignity. God insists that girls have the right to reserve such an intimate relationship for their future husbands.

• **Protection of aliens.** The *alien* referred to in **22:21** is anyone who is not a native of the country. The category would include those whom we refer to as refugees. Aliens tend to be at a disadvantage since they do not have the same rights that natives have. But God forbids mistreatment and oppression of an alien. He bases this command on the Israelites' experience in Egypt. This regulation calls us to reflect on how we treat those who

are refugees among us, or those who for some or other reason are living among us as strangers. God cares about them, and we also must care.

• **Protection of widows and orphans.** The widowed and orphaned have a special place in God's heart. A woman was supposed to enjoy the protection provided by her husband. Children were supposed to be protected by their father. If he died, his widow and his children were left very vulnerable. God firmly states that he will be their protector and that he will hear their cry (**22:23**). Mistreating them will bring death (**22:24**). It is equivalent to asking for one's own wife to become a widow and one's own children to become fatherless. These words should be heeded by those who rush to harm widows and orphans. Far too often, a dead man's relatives seize the land and property that should go to these vulnerable survivors. God observes such action, and he will judge it.

• **Protection of the needy in general.** The poor must not be charged interest by those who lend them money (**22:25**). If a cloak is offered as a guarantee that the loan will be repaid, the cloak must be returned to the borrower by sunset. A cloak was also a blanket, and forcing someone to spend the night without any covering would create great hardship (**22:26-27a**). In our day, it is not uncommon for the needy to be taken advantage of instead of being assisted. Those who cannot take their case to a higher authority (or who have no rich uncle) are sent from pillar to post even when all they are trying to do is to claim what is theirs by right. God's words here should be heard as a reminder that while the needy may not have a rich uncle, they do have a caring father. God says, *when he cries out to me, I will hear for I am compassionate* (**22:27b**).

The rest of the Pentateuch makes it clear that it is not enough to simply avoid harming vulnerable people. We also need to take specific action to meet their needs. Thus harvesters are to leave some of the crop in the field for the poor, aliens, orphans and widows (Lev 19:9; Deut 24:19). 'The aliens, the fatherless and the widows' are to share the tithes with the Levites (Deut 14:28-29; Deut 26:12). In our day, when so many have been left orphaned or widowed by HIV/AIDS and so many are displaced by political instability, wars and natural disasters, we are challenged about what we can do to help them. Every believer needs to accept that God wants us to be concerned about the needs of those around us, and then to act on that belief (Acts 2:45).

22:18-20 SINS DESERVING CAPITAL PUNISHMENT Three specific sins merit capital punishment:

• **Sorcery (22:18).** Sorcery is the invoking of evil powers in an attempt to injure someone we hate or whom we are being paid to harm. Such behaviour involves at least two sins: playing around with evil powers instead of worshipping God alone (20:2; see also Matt 4:10) and seeking to harm one's neighbour instead of loving him or her (20:27; see also Luke 6:27-28).

- **Bestiality (22:19).** The idea of having sexual relations with an animal may have been strange to the Israelites, but it seems to have been practised by the people in the land of Canaan with whom they would soon make contact. We can deduce this from Leviticus 18, where the long list of regulations governing sexual matters (including bestiality – Lev 18:23) begins with these words: 'You must not do as they do in Egypt, where you used to live, and you must not do as they do in the land of Canaan, where I am bringing you. Do not follow their practices' (Lev 18:2). God repeatedly prescribes capital punishment for those who adopt this unnatural practice (22:19; see also Lev 20:15-16; Deut 27:21). Bestiality is a tacit expression of dissatisfaction with God's provision in the matter of sex. He provided Eve for Adam and Adam for Eve. To seek sexual satisfaction in any other way than with a human partner of the opposite sex is an insult to God's intelligence and his good creation (Gen 1:31).
- **Idolatry (22:20).** Sacrificing to any other god is an attempt to put that god on the same level as the Lord. Since the Creator cannot be equal to anything in his creation, and all other gods are created things, the mere attempt to do this is an insult to the glory of God, which also calls for capital punishment.

The common thread linking the sins that deserve the death penalty is a failure to worship, honour and serve God alone. The sorcerer invokes evil powers, the one who practises bestiality denies God's perfect plan to meet our sexual needs, and the one who sacrifices to idols denies God his honour as the only object of worship. God takes all these sins seriously. We must shun them.

22:28-23:9 THE NEED TO HONOUR GOD We are to honour God both in our relationship with him and in our relationship with other people. The golden rule ('Love the Lord your God with all your heart … and love your neighbour as yourself' – Matt 22:37-40) summarizes the will of God, not only in the New Testament time but also during the Old Testament period.

The regulations laid down thus far in this chapter deal with indirect ways of honouring or failing to honour God. But we are also given three specific prohibitions that focus on how we honour God in our relationship with him:

- **Do not blaspheme or curse God or your rulers (22:28).** Blaspheming God makes no sense since he is the Creator who provides for all his creation. As such, he deserves gratitude at all times. Rulers act on his behalf and so they, too, must be respected and not cursed.
- **Do not keep back offerings (22:29-30).** As the giver of all, God deserves what he has prescribed as his offerings, whether these come from the fields or from *your granaries or your vats.* The offerings God demands include the

Israelites' firstborns – whether of their sons or of their animals (see 13:12-16). God as giver is to be honoured with all that we have.

- **Do not eat the meat of an animal that was killed by a wild beast (22:31).** All predatory animals were unclean, and thus any animal killed by one of them would have been rendered unclean (see Lev 11:1-8). Moreover, the blood would not have been properly drained from the carcass (Gen 9:4; Lev 17:13-14). The people must not eat such meat if they want to retain their holy nature as a people set apart for God.

We are also given specific guidance on how we honour God in our relationships with our fellow human beings. The regulations here concern spreading *false reports* (**23:1a**), giving malicious testimony in a lawsuit (**23:1b**), perverting justice by giving in to majority pressure (**23:2**), even when it is the poor who will benefit (**23:3**), withholding needed help (**23:4-5**), depriving the poor of justice (**23:6-7**), accepting bribes (**23:8**) and oppression of aliens (**23:9**). Those who commit any of these offences are failing to follow the principle 'do to others what you would have them do to you' (Matt 7:12). They are failing to recognize the value of human beings in God's sight, as creatures made in his image (Gen 1:26-27).

23:10-19 Religious law

The commandment to observe the Sabbath (20:8) is now expanded to make it clear that it is not only humans who must observe the Sabbath. The land, too, must have a Sabbath rest. However, the rhythm of the land's Sabbaths is different. Land is to be cultivated for six years and is to be allowed to rest every seventh year (**23:10-11**; see also 21:2). The NIV says that the land is to *lie unploughed and unused,* but the KJV is closer to the Hebrew when it says that the land is to *rest and lie still* – using verbs that emphasize the idea of rest. However, this Sabbath command does not mean that the poor and the wild animals are to be deprived of a desperately needed source of food. As Jesus reminded his opponents, 'The Sabbath was made for man, not man for the Sabbath' (Mark 2:27). The Sabbath rest is not intended to impose hardship but is a further sign of the thoughtfulness of God, who recognizes that people and animals grow tired and that the soil can become depleted if too many crops are grown in succession. All need an opportunity to *be refreshed* (**23:12**).

God again insists that the people worship him and him only (**23:13**). As well as honouring him on the Sabbath, the people are to celebrate him at three annual festivals (**23:14, 17**). The first of these is the Feast of Unleavened Bread, which is associated with the Passover (**23:15**; 12:14-17). The second is the Feast of Harvest (or the Feast of Weeks) at which the Israelites offered the first of their produce to God (**23:16a**). In NT times this feast corresponds to Pentecost (Acts 2:1). Finally, there is the Feast of Ingathering (or the Feast of Booths) at the end of the harvest (**23:16b**). These feasts are meant to remind the Israelites that God has not only given them liberty but has also given them all the produce of the soil, although they are still expected to put in the work to grow their crops. (For more information on these festivals, see the commentary on Leviticus 23, Numbers 28 and Deuteronomy 16.)

The list of the main feasts is followed by instructions regarding the offerings made at these feasts. The first instruction is that the blood of a sacrificed animal is not to be offered *along with anything containing yeast* (**23:18a**). In the Bible, yeast is often used as a symbol of evil (see 12:15; 23:15; 1 Cor 5:6-8). It would be inappropriate to associate such a symbol with the symbolism of the sacrificial blood.

In the instruction not to keep any fat of a sacrificed animal until morning, the fat must be understood as representing any part of the animal (**23:18b**; see Exod 12:10). The slaughtered animal is not to be regarded as simply a source of food, which can be stored for another day. It is an offering to God and, particularly at the Passover, a reminder of what God has done for his people. It must thus be treated in a way that reminds the participants of the circumstances of the first Passover meal (ch. 12).

The command that God is to be brought *the best of the firstfruits of your soil* is a reminder that God deserves the best we have, not what is left over after we have kept the best for ourselves (**23:19a**).

Without more knowledge of the period, it is difficult to interpret **23:19b**, which forbids cooking a kid in its mother's milk. Some people suggest that this was a Canaanite custom that the Israelites should not copy. Others think that cooking a nursing kid might dry up its mother's milk and would therefore be unwise. Some Orthodox Jews have greatly extended this rule by insisting that observant Jews may not consume meat at the same time as anything made with milk. They may not even use the same plates and pots for milk products and for meat.

Given the lack of understanding of this command, Christians have not drawn any binding principle from it. However, it could be interpreted as saying that one must not kill both the mother goat who bore the kid and the kid at the same time. To do so would bring to an end part of the cycle of growth that God instituted to allow his creation to continue. It could be argued that we are breaking this command when we treat nature in a way that causes almost irreparable damage to God's creation. Pollution, deforestation and other harmful practices are damaging the environment that supports us. We are already seeing the harmful effects of these practices as deforestation, for example, may be contributing to drought in some parts of Africa. God's creation must be allowed to stay as God planned it, for it was done with the highest degree of wisdom.

23:20-24:18 The Promises of God Reiterated

23:20-33 The promise of land

We now return to the theme of the promise and the conditions on which it will be fulfilled, the most important of which is obedience. God leads his people by sending a messenger (which is what the word 'angel' means) before them (**23:20**; see also 33:2). This angel is God's representative and must therefore be listened to and obeyed as if he is the Lord himself, for he has the ability to punish sin (**23:21-22**). The statement that God's *Name is in him* or 'on him' seems to be echoed in John's record of Christ's high priestly prayer (John 17:11-12).

The angel's mission is not only to lead the Israelites but also to fight for them, wiping out their enemies in order to clear the way for them to advance (**23:23**). But if the Israelites are to be blessed by him, they must demonstrate total faithfulness to God and must refuse to tolerate the presence of other gods. The idols that represent such gods must be destroyed. They must be treated like cities that are burned down by their conquerors (**23:24**).

God speaks of the blessings that will flow from obedience and specifically mentions that faithful worshippers will enjoy *a full life span* (**23:25-26**). This promise may explain the exceptional longevity of some of the people mentioned in the OT. However, the words can also be translated, 'I will fill the number of your days', which could be interpreted as meaning that each day of your life will be full of God's blessing.

In **23:31a**, God himself sets out the boundaries of the promised land. It will extend from the *Red Sea* (see 13:18) *to the Sea of the Philistines,* that is, the Mediterranean Sea. *The River* may be the Euphrates (see also Gen 31:21; Josh 1:4). The occupation of this vast territory will happen progressively (**23:29-30**). Israel will need to settle it gradually, for it is very difficult to cope with a sudden change from owning no land to owning and administering a large area. Most of the time, the Israelites will not have to fight to obtain this land. God himself will spread fear and panic among their enemies and put them to flight (**23:27, 31b**). They will be driven out by *hornets* (**23:28**). This word is rarely used in the Bible and can also be translated as 'bees' (Deut 1:44; Ps 118:12). It seems to be a figurative expression that indicates a plague or something that disheartens the enemy (23:27).

When the Israelites occupy the land, they must resolutely avoid imitating the religious practices of the inhabitants of the conquered lands (**23:32**). The reason that God insists that he cannot be worshipped alongside other gods, or even in the same area as other gods, is that *it will be a snare for you* (**23:33**). As a Ngambaye proverb from Chad says: 'If you try to imitate someone else's walk, you will end up not being able to walk properly yourself'. Christ restates the same principle when he says, 'No one can serve two masters' (Matt 6:24).

The commandment is clear: no covenants with other peoples, and still less with their gods. While God's insistence on this may seem excessive, the later history of Israel confirms why God feared such arrangements and issued these warnings. An Arab proverb from Chad says, 'if you raise a baby elephant in your hut, he will carry away the hut when he sets out to rejoin his herd'. Foreign gods would be like baby elephants that would eventually destroy the house that God was building.

24:1-18 The covenant confirmed

Moses is given specific instructions about the arrangements for the ceremony at which the covenant will be confirmed. The Lord is holy and he is the one who sets the terms on which he is to be approached, even in NT times (Acts 4:12). Only Moses is allowed *to approach the Lord* (**24:1-2**). He is, however, to be accompanied at a distance by Aaron, Aaron's two eldest sons (Nadab and Abihu) and seventy elders of Israel, who may possibly act as witnesses. The seventy elders appear to have been a group who already had some formal position in Israelite society. It is possible that they are the people whom Moses had appointed as officials, following his father-in-law's advice (18:25), or they may have been officials chosen at another time. They represented the people and could bear witness to them about their vision of the majesty and holiness of God (24:10).

The covenant is sealed as the people commit themselves to obeying all the words of God (**24:3**). The formal ratification ceremony involves the building of an altar that represents the whole-hearted commitment of the twelve tribes (**24:4**). Sacrifices are then offered and their blood sprinkled on the new altar (**24:5-6**). The covenant is thus sealed by the shedding of blood. Peter draws on the symbolism of this ritual when he speaks of Christians having been 'chosen … for obedience to Jesus Christ and sprinkling by his blood' (1 Pet 1:2). But he is not speaking of the old covenant but of the new covenant, in which the blood of Christ has even greater significance (see Luke 22:20; 1 Cor 11:25-26).

The *Book of the Covenant* that Moses read to the people (**24:7**) is also referred to in 2 Kings 23:2, 21 and 2 Chronicles 25:4. We cannot be certain of exactly what this book was. It may have been part of Exodus (possibly 21:1-24:18) or Leviticus, but it may also have been some book that has been completely lost.

Moses and several of the Israelite leaders are twice said to *see* God on this occasion. While different verbs are used in **24:10** and **24:11**, both of them can be translated as 'see' and used interchangeably. The problem, however, is that the verb used in 24:10 is the same one used in 33:20, which says that no one can see God and live. Is the Bible contradicting itself? No, for here God is deliberately taking a form

in which he can reveal himself to human beings and have a relationship with them. It remains true that no one can see God in his full glory and live.

The meal that follows the meeting on the mountain is similar to the ritual meal that sealed covenants between two parties in that period.

Moses has always been the intermediary, the privileged mediator between God and the people (24:2, **12**). Now, however, for the second time, we hear of Joshua who is now described as Moses' assistant as Moses prepares to receive the law and commandments the Lord has written for the people (**24:13**). Moses will spend the next forty days in the presence of God, in the midst of the cloud (**24:15-18**). During his absence, Aaron and Hur are appointed to act as his representatives (**24:14**).

We are watching the birth of a nation that will be governed as a theocracy.

25:1-40:38 God in the Midst of his People

The final verse in the book of Exodus is the key verse for this final section: 'So the cloud of the Lord was over the tabernacle by day, and fire was in the cloud by night, in the sight of all the house of Israel during all their travels' (40:38). This verse is significant because this final section deals with God's dwelling place, the tabernacle (25:1-31:18); with Israel's breaking of the covenant and God's threat to withdraw from them (32:1-34:35); and finally with the permanent presence of God in the midst of his people throughout their journey to the promised land. The tabernacle, God's dwelling place, is now the place where he manifests himself (35:1-40:38).

25:1-31:18 Planning the Tabernacle

God issues orders for the construction of a place of worship. Because the people are journeying through the desert on their way to the promised land, this place of worship must be capable of being packed up and transported like the rest of the Israelite camp.

The different names that the Bible gives to this place of worship help us to understand its role among the people. It is called a sanctuary (25:8a), that is, a sacred place that is a visible centre of worship. It is also spoken of as the tabernacle (25:9; 26:1). The word 'tabernacle' comes from the Latin word for 'tent'. It describes what this sanctuary looked like. However, in Hebrew, the word translated 'tabernacle' is closer in meaning to the verb that means 'to dwell', reminding us that this sanctuary symbolizes God dwelling in the midst of them (25:8b). It is at this tent (26:7, 11-14, 36) that God will meet with his worshippers, and this will be where his worshippers assemble. Hence it is also called the Tent of Meeting (27:21). Finally, it is called the tabernacle of the Testimony (38:21), no doubt because the tablets of the law, which were kept there, were themselves called the tablets of the Testimony (31:18).

Moses is given detailed instructions for the construction of the tabernacle and its furnishings. Combining the information given in chapters 25–28, 30 and 35–40, we can deduce that there were two parts to the tabernacle:

- An outer courtyard (27:9-17; 38:9-20) measuring one hundred by fifty cubits (150 x 75 feet/45 x 22.5 metres). This enclosure signified that Gentiles were excluded from the tabernacle. It was open only to Israelites and to those who had identified themselves with the Lord's people by undergoing circumcision. This courtyard contained the bronze laver or water basin (30:17-21; 38:8) and the bronze altar of burnt offering (27:1-8; 38:1-7).
- The tabernacle itself (26:1-37; 36:8-38). This was thirty cubits long, ten cubits wide and ten cubits high (45 x 15 x 15 feet/13.5 x 4.5 x 4.5 metres). These measurements are not plainly stated anywhere, but are deduced from the details given in 26:15-23. (Twenty planks each measuring one and a half cubits give a total of thirty cubits for the length. The planks are said to be ten cubits long.) The tabernacle itself was subdivided into two rooms: a Holy Place measuring twenty by ten cubits (30 x 15 feet/9 x 4.5 metres) and the Most Holy Place (ten by ten cubits (15 x 15 feet/4.5 x 4.5 metres).

The Holy Place was furnished with three objects made of gold: the table of shewbread or of the bread of the Presence (25:23-30; 37:10-16), a seven-branched lampstand or candlestick (25:31-40; 37:17-24) and the altar of incense (30:1-10; 37:25-29). These three items all have significance in the NT. Jesus referred to himself as the bread of life (John 6:32, 35) and as the light of the world (John 8:12). Prayer (represented by incense) is also to be the believer's way of life (1 Thess 5:17).

The Most Holy Place contained the ark of the covenant, which symbolized God's presence (25:10-22; 37:1-9). This chest contained the two tablets of the law. Before the ark were placed a golden pot of manna and Aaron's rod that budded (see Exod 16:33; Num 17:10; also Heb 9:4). The manna and Aaron's rod were a reminder of how God had led and provided for his people. These items are discussed in more detail below.

25:1-9 Assembling the materials

The people are asked to make offerings that can be used to construct this place of prayer and worship. We need to note that these offerings are voluntary, given as the people's hearts prompt them to give (**25:1-2**). This approach is very different from the one we often see today, especially on television, where some preachers' words suggest that they almost want to pronounce a curse on those who do not give. But when we give, we should do so willingly. We should give as much as we are able to, because we are giving to

God, who has given us all that we have. When preachers take this approach, gifts will keep coming in large amounts. While the cursing approach may work for a while, the flow of gifts soon fades or dries up completely.

Moses was to collect the finest materials that people could contribute. These included metals such as gold, silver and bronze, which the Egyptians had probably given to the Israelites at the time of their departure from Egypt (12:35-36). The yarn (spun wool) that had been dyed blue, purple and scarlet would have been very valuable in those days, when the dyes that produced these colours were not readily available. The other fabric that was needed was fine linen (**25:3**). Also needed were goat hair and the skins or hides of rams and sea cows (some type of animal, but it is not certain exactly what the Hebrew word refers to). Acacia wood would have been readily available, for these trees were common in the wilderness. They provide a hard durable wood. Moses also collected oil, spices and precious stones (**25:4-7**). The Israelites may also have obtained the cloths, skins and spices in Egypt, or they may have been able to obtain them from the other peoples who inhabited the desert region they were now in.

The value of these gifts showed the generosity of the worshippers and also testified to the greatness of God.

The instructions regarding the construction of the tabernacle were very detailed and Moses was to take care to follow them precisely. The Lord even speaks of showing Moses what it should look like, almost as if he were providing him with a model (**25:9**, 40). Stephen mentions this detail when speaking about Moses and the tabernacle in Acts 7:44.

25:10-40 Furnishings for the tabernacle

In this section, Moses is given detailed instructions for the essential furnishings of the tabernacle, except for the altars of burnt offering and incense, which will be dealt with later.

25:10-22 THE ARK AND THE ATONEMENT COVER The first object that is to be built is a chest that represents God's presence among his people. This chest is sometimes simply called 'the ark', but it is also referred to as 'the ark of the testimony' (25:21) or 'the ark of the covenant (Deut 10:8). The word 'ark' is a general term for a chest. It is the same word used to refer to Noah's boat. In **25:10**, it is specified that this ark is to be *two and a half cubits long, a cubit and a half wide, and a cubit and a half high* (3.75 x 2.25 x 2.25 feet/ 1.1 x 0.7 x 0.7 metres). It is to be made of acacia wood covered with gold (**25:11**).

The chest will be the place where the two tablets of the law are stored (**25:16**, 21). It seems that at a later date the jar of manna and Aaron's rod that blossomed were also placed inside the ark, although initially they were placed before it (Exod 16:33; Num 17:10; Heb 9:4). More details about the ark are given in 37:1-9.

The chest is to be covered by something called *the atonement cover* (**25:17**). The Hebrew word translated 'atonement' has the idea of covering something, such as a spot or a flaw, in order to erase it. That explains why the same word came to be used for atonement for sin. The atonement cover is to be made of *pure gold*. On top of it, there are to be two *cherubim*, facing each other (**25:18-20**). These cherubim were supernatural beings with both human and animal characteristics, somewhat like the Egyptian sphinx (see also Gen 3:24; 37:7-9; 2 Chr 3:10-13). The Lord designates the space between the cherubim as the place where he will meet with a representative of the Israelites (**25:22**). At the time these instructions were given, that representative was Moses.

25:23-30 The table of the presence Next, Moses is instructed to construct the table on which the *bread of the Presence* is to be displayed (**25:30a**). This table is to be made of acacia wood and, like the ark, it must be covered with pure gold (**25:23-24**). There must always be twelve loaves of bread on it, which are to be replaced with fresh loaves every Sabbath (**25:30b**; see Lev 24:5-9). These loaves served two purposes. They were a symbolic reminder that God dwells among his people and provides their daily bread, just as he provided manna to feed the twelve tribes in the desert (25:8; see also Isa 63:9). The regular replacement of the bread is symbolic of the people's commitment to be loyal to God and their gratitude for his regular provision for their needs.

25:31-40 The golden lampstand Moses is also to make an elaborate golden lampstand with seven branches, each supporting an oil lamp (**25:31-36**; see also Lev 24:2-4; 2 Chr 4:7). The light from these lamps would illuminate the Holy Place for the benefit of the priests serving there (**25:37**) In the nt, Jesus, while teaching in the temple, speaks of himself as being the light (John 8:12, 20). In the book of Revelation, the lampstand is also used as an image of the church (Rev 1:12, 20).

All of these objects are either to be made of or covered with pure gold as a reminder of the purity that must surround service to God (**25:38-40**).

26:1-37 Structure of the tabernacle

The structure of the tabernacle consisted of an inner cover (26:1-6), an outer cover (26:7-14), a framework that supported these covers (26:15-30), a curtain (26:31-35) and a screen (26:36-37).

26:1-6 The inner cover The inner cover comprised *ten curtains* made of spun *linen and blue, purple and scarlet yarn* (**26:1**). These three colours are the colours of the tabernacle. Because they were expensive to obtain, they communicated that the fabric was of the highest quality.

Each curtain is to be *twenty-eight cubits long and four cubits wide* (42 x 6 feet/12.5 x 1.8 metres). They are to be joined together in groups of five curtains to make two long pieces (**26:2-3**). Having them in two pieces probably made it easier to carry them and to hang them when the tabernacle was erected at a new site. The two pieces are to be fastened together using loops and clasps *so that the tabernacle is a unit* (**26:6**). Once again, only the highest quality material is to be used, and the clasps for the inner cover are to be made of gold.

26:7-14 The outer cover Whereas the inner cover required ten curtains, the other cover required eleven (**26:7**). The eleventh curtain covered the entrance to the tabernacle, which was left open in the inner covering (**26:9b**). These curtains are to be made of goat hair, which is more resistant to bad weather than the materials used for the inner cover. The outer curtains are also to be slightly longer than the inner curtains, measuring thirty cubits long and four cubits wide (45 x 6 feet/13.5 x 1.8 metres). They will thus cover and protect every part of the inner cover (**26:8, 12-13**). The outer curtains are also joined together in two sets, one with five curtains and one with six (**26:9a**). The clasps that unite the loops at the end of these sets to make one unit are made of bronze (**26:10-11**). Bronze was not as valuable a metal as the gold that was used for the clasps of the inner covering. This probably indicates the different degrees of importance attached to these layers of the tabernacle. The layer closest to the things that symbolize the Lord's presence was to be of the highest possible quality.

The outer covering is also protected by a covering made of skins and hides donated by the Israelites (**26:14**).

26:15-30 The framework The framework that supports the coverings is to be made of hard, durable acacia wood (**26:15**). It consists of forty-eight planks or *frames* (twenty for each side and eight for the back of the tabernacle – **26:18, 20, 22-23**). According to **26:16**, each plank is to be *ten cubits long and a cubit and a half wide* (15 x 2.25 feet/ 4.5 x 0.7 metres). These planks are to be supported by silver bases (**26:19**). Crossbars passing through golden rings are to be used to strengthen the framework. Once again, the different metals used symbolize the importance attached to different parts of the structure.

26:31-35 The curtain The *curtain* or *vail* (kjv) separates the Holy Place from the Most Holy Place (**26:33**). It is to be identical to the inner cover as regards the fabric and colour and its decoration with cherubim (**26:31**; see 26:1). It is to be supported on golden hooks attached to posts made of *acacia wood overlaid with gold* (**26:32**). The use of only the highest quality materials here stresses that this is an extremely important part of the tabernacle. So does having this area symbolically guarded by angels (cherubim).

The Most Holy Place was not to be entered by the priests, and even the High Priest could not go there whenever he wished (Lev 16:2). It was the place where the ark rested, which symbolized the holy presence of God and was the place where God would meet with a representative of his people (25:22). It was screened off to emphasize the distance between the Holy God and all his worshippers. But through the work of Christ, this separation was done away with (Mark 15:38; Heb 9:12). Every believer in Christ can have access to the Most Holy Place whenever he or she wants to go there.

26:36-37 THE SCREEN The screen or curtain that covers the entrance to the tabernacle is to be made of the same high-quality materials that are used for the inner veil separating the Holy Place from the Most Holy Place. Thus, although the different materials used for different portions of the structure symbolize their relative importance, it is also clear that the whole structure is of high value before the Lord.

27:1-8 The altar and its utensils

The altar described in 27:1-8 stood in the courtyard of the tabernacle, where common people could have access to it (Lev 4:22, 27, 29). It is sometimes referred to as 'the altar of burnt offering', because this was the primary type of sacrifice offered on it (see 30:28; 31:9). However, it is sometimes called 'the bronze altar' because it was covered with bronze (see 38:30; 39:39). The bronze is supported by a hollow frame made of boards of acacia wood (**27:1a**, **2b**, **8**). This construction technique would have made the altar lighter, and thus easier to transport as the Israelites moved through the desert. Poles and rings were also included in the design to help with carrying it (**27:5-7**).

The altar is to be in the form of a square (**27:1b**), measuring five cubits on each side (7.5 feet/2.3 metres) and is to be three cubits high (4.5 feet/1.3 metres). Its form and structure are thus appropriate for its function. The most sacred parts of the altar are the *horns* or projections on its four corners (**27:2a**). The blood of sin offerings was applied to these horns (29:12; Lev 4:30).

Moses is also given instructions regarding all the utensils that will be needed by the priests serving at the altar. These too are to be made of bronze (**27:3-4**).

27:9-19 The courtyard of the tabernacle

The tabernacle is to be erected within a courtyard measuring one hundred by fifty cubits (150 x 75 feet/45 x 22.5 metres). The courtyard is to be marked out by linen curtains – each five cubits wide (7.5 feet/2.25 metres). Their width is not mentioned in the text, but can be deduced from the number of posts required to support them. Since twenty posts are needed on the one hundred cubit side (**27:9-11**) and ten posts are needed on the side that measures fifty cubits (**27:12**), each curtain must cover five cubits. Its entrance is to be on the east side (**27:13-16**) and is to be covered by a curtain of blue, purple and scarlet yarn twenty

cubits (30 feet/9 metres) long. This enclosed area symbolically communicated that the Israelites are a people set apart from the rest of the nations. They are God's own possession (19:5-6).

27:20-21 The supply of oil

The series of instructions ends with details about the supply of olive oil for the lamps placed on the lampstand (**27:20**). Olive oil was the best type of oil used for lighting at the time. The Lord never accepts substandard material for any work connected with him. The oil is needed to make sure that the lamps will shine through the night as symbols of the presence of God (**27:21**). They also provide light for the priests as they do their work in the tabernacle.

28:1-29:46 Provision of priests

28:1-43 THE PRIESTS' CLOTHING Aaron and his four sons are designated as priests (**28:1**). As such, they require special *sacred garments* to indicate their honour and dignity while carrying out their office (**28:2**). The sacredness of the clothing the priests wore when they came into the Lord's presence is brought out even more forcefully in Ezekiel 44:19. That verse specifies that these clothes were to be left in the holy chambers and were not to be taken to the outer court where the people were. If ordinary people were to come in contact with these clothes, the holiness in the clothes would be transmitted to them.

These regulations serve to emphasize the point that anything that comes into God's presence is transformed. Moses' face shone because he had been in the Lord's presence (34:29). In the same way, these clothes will be distinct from ordinary clothes because the priest appears before God in them. While the idea of sacred clothing for priests is not as important in our day, for Christ is the highest of priests, the principle still applies in regard to money that has been set aside for use in God's work through our tithes and offerings. This money is God's property, even though it is used to pay or support men and women. Whatever God has set apart for himself becomes holy, and anyone who misappropriates it invites God's wrath.

The making of suitable clothing for the priests requires people who are specially gifted in the art of making clothing using a variety of materials. The term *skilled* in **28:3** can also be translated 'wise', as in Job 9:4. The materials to be used to make the priest's clothing are also very precious (**28:5**). *Linen* was the finest cloth available, and purple, for example, was a very expensive dye. Its value in NT times is shown by the fact that Jesus was mockingly dressed in 'a purple robe' (Mark 15:17). In the book of Acts, Lydia, who was obviously a woman of some importance, is described as 'a dealer in purple cloth' (Acts 16:14).

The clothes to be made included *a breastpiece, an ephod, a robe, a woven tunic, a turban and a sash* (**28:4**).

- *The ephod* consisted of two pieces made from blue, scarlet and fine linen yarn – one piece covering the back and the other covering the front, that is, the breast and upper part of the body (**28:6-8**). The two pieces were joined at the shoulders with two golden clasps. Each of these clasps included an *onyx stone* with the names of Jacob's sons engraved on it, six on one shoulder and six on the other. Thus the priest symbolically presents and represents all of Israel before the Lord (**28:9-14**).
- *The breastpiece* continues this symbolism, for it had the names of all Jacob's sons mounted on it, each one engraved on a separate precious stone, so that the high priest *will bear the names of the sons of Israel over his heart on the breastpiece of decision as a continuing memorial before the Lord* (**28:15-29**). The breastpiece is called 'the breastpiece of decision' because it contained the *Urim and Thummim,* two unidentified objects that were used to consult the Lord by drawing lots (**28:30**). One of them must have designated a positive response from God and the other a negative response (see Numbers 27:21; 1 Sam 28:6). The high priest would thus be able to guide the nation when it came to making important decisions. His role reminds us of the importance of believers participating in the day-to-day life of a nation. The more believers genuinely get involved in politics, development issues and similar matters, the more just our society will become. This is as true in Africa as it is in any part of the world.
- *The robe* worn by the high priest was decorated with *gold bells* so that he could be heard as he moved around in the tabernacle. Its sound announces when Aaron *enters the Holy Place before the Lord and when he comes out* (**28:31-35**). If he is heard to enter the Holy Place, but no sound is heard signalling his coming out, then he may have died because he was not holy when he went before the Lord. The bells are thus also a reminder to the priest, and to us, that while it is a privilege to serve the Lord, it is also a frightening thing. It cannot be done with a carefree attitude. On a more positive note, the people can participate in prayers with the priest as they hear him move about within the Holy Place. His exit will also be a time of great rejoicing as the people will know that their sins have been atoned for.
- *The turban* was made of linen and had a plate of pure gold attached to it, with the words HOLY TO THE LORD engraved on it. This golden plate rested on Aaron's forehead, where it would be a reminder of the holiness of the Lord and the burden on the priest (**28:36-38**). He comes before a holy God to represent a sinful people and to ask for forgiveness of their sins (see Lev 4-5; Num 18:1). His success in this is a blessing to the people while his failure would be a disaster. It is a delicate ministry and a very crucial responsibility.

- The *tunic,* or outer garment, was tied with a girdle or *sash,* also made by an expert (**28:39**).

Every piece of every priest's clothing, both primary and secondary, was to be specially made (**28:40-42**). As stated in 28:4, *they are to make these sacred garments for your brother Aaron and his sons, so that they may serve me as priests.* The garments are to be sacred as a reminder that without holiness it is impossible to serve the Lord in a way that he approves.

29:1-43 THE PRIESTS' CONSECRATION God, who is holy, demands holiness from those who serve him; and so Moses must anoint and consecrate Aaron and his sons in order to set them apart for his service (**29:1**). The ceremony described in this chapter deals primarily with the consecration of ordinary priests, while that described in Leviticus 8 focuses on the consecration of the high priest. Thus Leviticus mentions more steps in the ritual than the three described here, which are the washing of Aaron and his sons with water (**29:4**), putting official clothing on Aaron (**29:5-6**) and then on his sons (**29:8-9**) and the anointing of Aaron (**29:7**).

The consecration ceremony involved three sacrifices. The first was a sacrifice of purification. In Leviticus, this sacrifice is said to purify a priest who has committed some involuntary sin that would disqualify him from representing the people before God (Lev 4:3-12). Aaron and his sons are to lay their hands on a bull, which is then to be sacrificed and totally consumed by fire, in part on the altar and in part outside the camp (**29:10-14**). The concept of offering a sacrifice for the sin of the priest before he can represent the people before God does not seem to have been known in the worship of the other gods of that period.

The second sacrifice was that of a ram as a burnt offering. Because this offering symbolizes total dedication to the Lord, it too is to be totally consumed by fire, although it can all be burnt on the altar of the tabernacle, and none of it has to be taken outside the camp (29:15-35).

The third sacrifice (29:19-28) involved a second ram, called the *ram of ordination* (**29:22**). Aaron and his sons are to lay their hands on its head, after which it is to be slaughtered and its blood placed on three parts of each priest's body. The blood on the priest's ear signals that he is to hear and obey God, the blood on his right hand signals that he is to serve God, and the blood on his right foot signals that he is to walk with God (**29:20**). The remaining blood is used to consecrate the altar, Aaron and his garments, and Aaron's sons with their garments (**29:21**). In short, everything related to this service – whether persons or things – must be consecrated or made holy.

In the case of this sacrifice, only a portion of the animal has to be burnt. Aaron and his sons are to eat a part of it (**29:27-28, 32-33**). The pieces that the priests can eat are no doubt the salary paid in food that Aaron and his sons receive in exchange for their service. These portions of meat will remain their property after the sacrifice and are intended to be eaten (see also Lev 6:14-18; 7:28-36).

Not only must the priests be consecrated and set apart as holy, but so must objects, most noticeably the altar and all that is attached to it (**29:36**). The need to purify objects implies that just as physical objects are affected by their physical environment, so they are also affected by their moral and spiritual environment. For example, a house that is used for evil becomes polluted by that evil. A new occupant needs to say a prayer (or conduct a more elaborate ritual) asking the Lord to cleanse the house. While inanimate things do not have a will of their own and may be neutral in themselves, the people who work with them, occupy them or own them 'transfer' to them whatever they themselves are. It is in this sense that Moses needs to *make atonement for the altar and consecrate it* (**29:37a**). The ordinary needs to be cleansed and consecrated before the Lord can use it. Once this is done, it shares in the holiness of the Lord and *whatever touches it will be holy* (**29:37b**).

The whole consecration ceremony is to last seven days for both the priests and the objects (29:35-37a)

This long section ends with a restatement of the dealings of God with the Israelites (**29:44-46**). We are reminded that the ultimate aim of the consecration ceremonies was to help the people among whom God had chosen to dwell to remember his requirements and his holiness.

30:1-38 Additional furnishings and supplies

Moses is next given additional instructions about items required for the tabernacle and arrangements that will have to be made with regard to supplying what is needed for the worship there.

30:1-10 THE ALTAR OF INCENSE Detailed specifications are given regarding the shape and role of this altar. It is to be made of *acacia wood* and *pure gold,* both of which have already been used to construct other items for use in the tabernacle (**30:1-5**; 25:10. 29).

When the altar is complete and installed in the tabernacle, Aaron and his sons must burn special incense on it every morning and evening (**30:7-8**). Incense symbolizes prayer ascending to God (Ps 141:2), and the continual burning of it is a symbol that the people are continually grateful to and dependant on God.

Nothing but incense is to be offered on this altar (**30:9**), but once a year there is to be a special ceremony in which the four projections at its corners are anointed with blood as an atonement offering (**30:10**). This ceremony may have taken place on the Day of Atonement (Lev 23:27-28). People's sins pollute their surroundings, and so it was not just the people who needed this annual rite of atonement, but also any objects connected with them. This purification of the altar of incense emphasizes that God is holy and anything associated with him must be clean, beyond question.

30:11-16 A RELIGIOUS TAX The tax that Moses is to levy serves several purposes. For one thing, it is a way of supporting the functioning of the Tent of Meeting (**30:16a**). But it is also *a ransom* for the payer (**30:12a**). A ransom is something that is paid in exchange for someone's life. Here the money is paid in exchange for the life of the one paying the ransom. It is a reminder to the Israelites of their need for atonement (**30:16b**). Those who refuse to pay this tax are symbolically asserting that they are not guilty of any sin before God, which is impossible. Such arrogance invites punishment in the form of a plague (**30:12b**).

Each person is to pay a *half shekel, according to the sanctuary shekel* (**30:13**; see also Lev 5:15). The 'sanctuary shekel' was a standard measure that was used in the context of worship (Num 3:44-51). It was probably an amount that could easily have been earned in a day.

This tax is to be paid by all those over the age of twenty years who *cross over* (**30:14**). This verb is sometimes translated by 'inspect', 'visit' or 'pass in review', which is why it can also be translated as 'numbered', as in the KJV and NASB. The fact that each person has to pay the same amount communicates that the cost of ransom is the same for all, and thus that the value of all lives before God is the same. In our modern society, we sometimes forget that the poor have the same worth before God as the rich and that we should lament the destruction of any life.

30:17-21 THE BASIN FOR WASHING Moses is also instructed to make a large bronze basin to be used for the ritual purification of Aaron and his descendants, who were the priests (**30:17-21**). They had to wash both their hands and their feet before entering the tabernacle or burning the burnt offering. This action was another reminder of the holiness of God. He is to be approached by people who have washed their dirt away. For the believer, this has been done by Christ's blood – through faith in him (Hebrews 10:22).

30:22-38 OIL AND INCENSE Moses must arrange for the manufacture of a special oil, prepared by mixing olive oil with sweet-smelling spices (**30:22-25**). This oil will be used to anoint the tabernacle and everything in it, including the priests (**30:26-30**; see also 40:9-15). The Lord stresses that this mix is to be used only in the tabernacle and only for sacred purposes (**30:31-33**).

Moses is also given instructions for the preparation of the incense to be used in the tabernacle. We cannot be certain of what these ingredients were, but it seems that the one translated 'stacte' in the KJV may be some kind of resinous gum exuded from a tree, hence the NIV translation, *gum resin* (**30:34**). Thus gum is to be mixed with *onycha,* which may have been a substance derived from the shell of a mussel that lives in the Red Sea. *Galbanum* and frankincense were also derived from plants. This final incense is said to be *salted,* an expression that seems to mean that it is 'well prepared', rather than that it tastes salty.

Incense made according to this recipe is to be used only in the Tent of Meeting (**30:37-38**).

31:1-18 Qualified craftsmen

God himself selects two men, Bezalel and Oholiab, to whom he has given all the qualifications they need to make the various objects required. These two men, from two different tribes, are both filled *with the Spirit of God, with skill, ability and knowledge* (**31:3, 6**). The statement that they received their abilities from 'the Spirit of God' is a foreshadowing of the gifts of the Spirit that God will give to all Christians who consecrate themselves to the work of the Lord (see Rom 12:4-8; 1 Cor 12:1-31; Eph 4:7-13).

As these men supervise the production of all the items to be used in the tabernacle, they must take care to ensure that this work is also done in a consecrated fashion. They must not forget the rhythm of life, particularly as regards the Sabbath, which they and all the other Israelites had to observe (30:12-17; see also 20:8-11). Even if there is much work to be done to construct the tabernacle and this work is consecrated to God alone, the Sabbath must not be neglected.

The importance of this command is shown by the emphasis with which it is stated. This does not emerge clearly in the NIV translation and is better communicated by the NKJV, which translates it as *surely my Sabbaths you shall keep*, where the word 'surely' means 'above all, do not forget' (**31:13**). Failure to respect the Sabbath was equivalent to a failure to honour God, and thus was so serious that it was to be punished by death (**31:15**; see comment on 20:8-11).

This long list of recommendations and practical instructions ends with God himself handing Moses the two tablets of stone inscribed with the law (**31:18**; see 24:12).

32:1-33:35 Violation of the Covenant

The covenant between God and the Israelites lasts little more than a month before the people break it.

32:1-6 The nature of the violation

Moses spends forty days and forty nights on the mountain (24:18), and the people become impatient. They *gathered round* Aaron and ask him to *make us gods* (**32:1**; or 'a god', NIV footnote). Their request is a fundamental betrayal of the covenant because they are clearly failing to obey the second commandment. Such disobedience leads to breaking the first commandment too (20:3). In accepting the covenant, the Israelites had promised to worship only one God (24:3). And they had been given frequent reminders of the command they had agreed to obey (20:23; 23:13, 24). But they do not keep their promise. They use Moses' absence as an opportunity to replace the invisible God with a visible image of a calf, before which they prostrate themselves.

Aaron fails greatly and leads the people astray by failing to insist that they observe God's commandments. Instead,

he collects the people's jewellery, melts it down and uses it to make a golden calf (**32:2-4**). However, the translation 'calf' is somewhat misleading, for this Hebrew word suggests a 'young bull' rather than just a calf. Such a bull would be a sign of power and fertility (see 1 Kgs 12:26-32; Hos 8:5; 10:5; Neh 9:18). Aaron probably drew his inspiration from the Egyptian god Apis, who was often shown as a cow or a bull. He tells the people that this golden bull is the god who rescued them from Egypt and arranges a festival at which it will be honoured in the name of Yahweh (**32:5**). But in suggesting that his idol represents Yahweh, he is doing the very thing that God had strongly forbidden (20:4).

The people then celebrate a festival in honour of the god Aaron has made (**32:6**). The psalmist speaks of this episode as being an expression of ingratitude and absurdity: 'At Horeb they made a calf and worshipped an idol cast from metal. They exchanged their Glory for an image of a bull, which eats grass. They forgot the God who saved them, who had done great things in Egypt' (Ps 106:19-21). In his great sermon in Acts, Stephen interprets this incident as an obvious act of disobedience, saying that 'in their hearts, they turned back to Egypt' (Acts 7:39).

Given what God has done for these people, their foolishness can best be described in terms of a proverb: 'As a dog returns to its vomit, so a fool repeats his folly' (Prov 26:11).

32:7-14 God's response

God immediately responds with anger. He sees what is happening as a sign of corruption and of the people deviating from the path he had prescribed (**32:7-8**). By forgetting the commitments they made in 19:8; 24:3 and 7, the people are condemning themselves and placing themselves under the severe judgment of God. He labels them as stubborn (*stiffnecked*) and decides to wipe them all out (**32:9-10a**). He will not forget his promise to Abraham, 'I will make of you a great nation' (Gen 12:2), but he will now fulfil this promise through Moses, rather than through the Israelites (**32:10b**).

Moses immediately acts as an intermediary and an intercessor on behalf of his people. He *sought the favour of the Lord his God*, an expression that can be translated literally as 'Moses caressed the face of the Lord' (**32:11a**; see also in 1 Kgs 13:6; Zech 7:2). Specifically, Moses reasons with God as if to remind him who these people are. They are his own people; the ones he *brought out of Egypt* (**32:11b**). He also reminds God of how his planned course of action will be interpreted by the Egyptians. They will see it as a sign that God was unable to lead the people to the place of blessing that he had promised them, and so he destroyed them in the desert (**32:12**). Finally, Moses reminds God that he promised Abraham, Isaac and Jacob that they would have numerous offspring (**32:13**).

Moses succeeds in making God change his mind, or in other words, the Lord changes his planned course of action in response to Moses' plea (**32:14**). Such a change is consistent with the character of Yahweh. While his nature never changes, his responses do. He is not static (fixed) but dynamic in relation to circumstances, new attitudes of hearts or pleas from his people. Here, he listens to Moses' plea.

32:15-29 Moses' confrontation with the people

Moses hurriedly returns to the camp, clasping *the tablets of the Testimony,* that is, the stone tablets on which the law has been written by God himself (**32:15-16**).

Joshua had accompanied Moses on the mountain (24:13), but apparently he had not been present at Moses' meeting with God. Now he is surprised and worried about the noise he can hear rising from the camp (**32:17**). Moses assures him that what he is hearing is a celebration, not a battle (**32:18**). But it is only when Moses reaches the camp and sees for himself what is going on that he truly becomes angry. God's report of what was happening (32:7) had not had as strong an effect. The sight of the idol and the festival in its honour enrages him. In his anger, he throws down the tablets of the law that God gave him, breaking them in pieces (**32:19**). He then destroys the statue of the bull, reduces it to powder and throws the powder into water. The Israelites are forced to drink the water containing all that remains of their gold and of their god (**32:20**; Num 5:24).

Moses interrogates Aaron about how he as the high priest could allow himself to be so influenced by the people (**32:21**). Aaron's excuse is very weak, but does bring out the fickleness of the people and their tendency to fall into evil ways (**32:22-23**). But Aaron glosses over his own role as he tells the story of the 'birth' of the young bull (**32:24**; compare 32:4).

Moses had begged God to spare the people (32:11), but grace does not mean that they can escape all punishment. To teach both the Israelites and their enemies that Yahweh, the God of Israel, is a jealous God as well as a powerful God, Moses rallies the Levites (the tribe that will later be made responsible for religious ceremonies) and orders them to strike down people in the camp without sparing brothers, friends and neighbours (**35:25-29**). Obedience to God takes priority over family ties (see also Matt 10:37). The punishment seems terrible because three thousand men are killed. But we need to remember that the punishment is far milder than what God had originally proposed, when he threatened to destroy them all (32:10).

32:30-33:35 God and the people

While the Lord decided not to exterminate the people, he did not promise not to punish them severely or curse them. So the next day Moses returns to appeal to him and to confess the people's *great sin.* He tells the people, *perhaps I can make atonement for your sin* (**32:30**). The term 'atonement' conveys the idea of paying what it takes to cover some sin

that has been committed. Moses' words, *blot me out from the book you have written,* seem to imply that if a price has to be paid before the people's sins can be forgiven, he is prepared to pay that price himself (**32:31-32**).

God responds by stating that he will not punish the whole nation, but that *whoever has sinned against me I will blot out of my book* (**33:33**). This declaration is later taken up by the prophet Ezekiel, who focuses on the idea of individual responsibility: 'the soul who sins is the one who will die' (Ezek 18:4). Moses is reinstated as the people's guide and the presence of God is once again guaranteed by this assurance, *my angel will go before you* (**32:34**).

But God does not totally withhold punishment. He strikes the nation with some unspecified plague (**32:35**). He also announces that when the people again set out on their journey to the land he has promised them, he will fulfil his promises but will no longer accompany them in person and dwell among them because they are a stubborn and disobedient people (**33:1-3**). This news greatly distresses the people, to the point where they start to dress in a way that shows they are mourning (**33:4**). It is significant that they choose not to put on their jewellery, because it is their jewellery that was used to make the golden calf. God wants to remind them of what they have done, and thus he calls for the removal of all jewellery (**33:5-6**).

At this point, the author provides evidence of the people's desire to speak with the Lord by referring to the *Tent of Meeting.* The tent is erected outside the camp (**33:7**). This location is a temporary one, for the tabernacle is a movable structure and in Numbers 2:2 it is described as located at the centre of the camp. But at this stage it is *some distance away* because the people's iniquity is incompatible with the presence of God, symbolized by the tabernacle. Yet the tent remains accessible to the people, implying that God has not completely rejected them. It is a holy place where they can go to consult the Lord. It also serves as a place where he can call them together (33:7; 25:22; Num 12:4; Deut 31:14).

The people's desire to be reconciled with God is also evident from the close attention they pay whenever Moses goes *out to the tent* to meet with God (**33:8, 10**). It is impressive that Moses speaks to God face to face, despite the strained relationship between God and Israel as a result of the incident with the golden calf (**33:9, 11a**). God himself stresses how unusual this is in Numbers 12:6-8.

The mention, almost in an aside, of Joshua's presence in the tent is also an indication of his growing importance in the eyes of God (**33:11b**).

The closing scenes in this chapter suggest that Moses is still unsure about what God has in mind for this people. God had threatened to destroy them, but did not do so after Moses pleaded with him (32:9-14). Moses had offered to pay the price for the people to be forgiven, but the Lord had told Moses that he does things his way (32:33-35). Now the tabernacle is located outside the camp as a natural response to what the people did under Aaron (32:6). It is not clear to Moses what God's attitude towards his people is now. It is within this context that Moses pleads with God for several things.

The first thing that Moses asks is who will go with him to help him lead the people (**33:12**). Aaron has failed him. He pleads with God that he cannot act as leader without the Lord's presence and guidance. The Lord's response is *My presence will go with you and I will give you rest* (**33:14**). Moses then asks God to confirm that he will indeed be with his people. He knows what a disaster it will be if the Lord does not go up with them (**33:15-16**). The Lord gives him the assurance that he will *do the very thing you have asked* (**33:17**).

Finally, Moses asks God to show him his glory (**33:18**). The Lord's graciousness is demonstrated in the fact that he mentions the positive aspects of his reply first. He will make his *goodness* pass in front of Moses and will proclaim his name – *the Lord* – in Moses' presence (**33:19**). These words are a guarantee that the Lord will continue to be the covenant-keeping God who will reveal his goodness and compassion in the days ahead. *But,* says the Lord, *you cannot see my face, for no one may see me and live* (**33:20**). These words do not contradict the statement that God spoke with Moses 'face to face' (33:11). The 'face to face' there is an example of figurative language, pointing to the open and friendly relationship between God and Moses. Here, however, *my face* refers to God's hidden nature, his very essence. In spite of the intimacy between God and Moses, the latter cannot see God except through his actions and through his glory. We are reminded of the episode of the burning bush where God spoke directly to Moses, but Moses did not really see him (3:3-6).

The rest of the passage (**33:21-23**) is basically a practical demonstration of the two aspects of God's revelation to Moses. He sees God's back (his manifest actions) but not his face (his hidden nature).

Moses' example teaches us that when we face a dilemma in ministry, we should not despair but should draw near to God and engage in dialogue with him about the issues. We also need to learn from Moses' insistence on being assured that the Lord will go with them. Anything that we attempt to do without the blessing of the Lord will come to nothing, sooner or later.

34:1-35 Renewal of the Covenant

God is ready to renew his covenant and tells Moses to prepare two new stone tablets to replace the tablets that he had broken (**34:1**; see 32:19). At the start of this new meeting, God announces his presence as a herald might proclaim the entrance of a great king. But God does not use a herald, but instead proclaims himself as the Lord (Yahweh). He

describes himself as compassionate, merciful, patient, faithful, loyal, forgiving and a bestower of blessings – although *he does not leave the guilty unpunished* (**34:5-7**). This list of God's attributes reminds us that God's character does not change and that he still cares for his people, even though they are *stiff-necked,* as Moses confesses (**34:9**).

The Lord then confirms the covenant before Moses. The neighbouring nations will bow down before Israel and their God (**34:11**). Then the Lord restates the terms of the covenant, insisting that there must be no compromises with other people, and still less with their gods (**34:12-17**). God does not want the Israelites to lose themselves in the worship of foreign gods who cannot help them. The Lord is the only one who can care for the Israelites.

God then restates the importance of the feasts that are to punctuate the religious life of the people. These feasts are intended to remind future generations that it was solely with God's help that Israel was able to escape slavery in Egypt (**34:18-24**).

Moses, at God's dictation, writes all this down on the new tablets that he made (34:27-28). We are also told that *he wrote on the tablets the words of the covenant – the Ten Commandments* (**34:28b**). It is not clear who the 'he' is, and it is possible that these words were again written by God himself.

As before, it takes forty days, without eating or drinking, to prepare the tablets (**34:28a**). Then Moses comes down the mountain and rejoins the people, shining with divine light (**34:29-30**). It appears that light seemed to flow from him. Some painters and sculptors have tried to represent this by showing Moses as having horns, for rays of sunlight were sometimes spoken of as 'horns'. But it is unlikely that Moses appeared to the people like this, because that would have made him look too similar to the god Baal, who is sometimes represented as wearing a helmet with two horns. God would not have wanted Moses to look like Baal, especially just after the command not to assimilate foreign gods.

Those who see Moses are so amazed at his appearance that he finds it necessary to cover his face with a *veil* or a mask to reduce the brightness that can be seen (**34:33-35**; see also 2 Cor 3:13). It is not clear what exact form this veil took, for the term is only used once in the OT.

35:1-39:42 Constructing the Tabernacle

The previous chapter contained reminders about the destructive effects of idolatry, and this chapter contains similar reminders about Sabbath observance (**35:1-3**). Not only must the people do no work, they must not even *light a fire.* In other words, they must not cook food. This point is emphasized here as a sign of the people's recognition 'that I am the Lord, who makes you holy' (31:13). Once this point has been clearly made, the actual construction of the tabernacle can begin. The specific instructions for what is to be done were given in 25:1-31:11 and are closely followed.

The people's contribution is necessary both to provide the materials needed for the project and to allow each person to participate in a practical way. Both men and women have contributions to make (**35:20-22, 25-26, 29**). Not only do the people donate all kinds of materials (**35:5-9**, 22-24, **27-28**) but they also donate time and skills that can be used in God's service (**35:10**, 25, **35; 36:1, 2, 4, 8**). The passage stresses that these offerings are not demanded from the people, but are given freely as people's hearts are moved and they become willing to give and to serve (35:5, 21, 29). Thus the first thing that the people do when constructing the tabernacle is to give generously and spontaneously, with the right attitude of heart. This way of serving the Lord is part of what distinguishes the Israelites from other peoples, who were sometimes exploited by their gods or who attempted to manipulate their gods. As the Apostle Paul reminds us, the very best offering that we can give to God is our own selves: 'Therefore, I urge you, brothers, in view of God's mercy, to offer your bodies as living sacrifices, holy and pleasing to God – this is your spiritual act of worship' (Rom 12:1).

Above all, God wants the children of Israel to recognize that he is the source of all wealth – material, spiritual and intellectual. That is why Bezalel and Oholiab are described as filled *with the Spirit of God, with skill, ability and knowledge* (**35:31**). Exceptional abilities were required for this exceptional project, and the abilities of these men are listed, showing how they could effectively contribute as individuals and as those who could teach others skills and administer the work of those who were already skilled (**35:32-36:1**). The work would be done effectively and rationally.

These men and the workers they employ are also clearly honest. They can be trusted with all that the people bring. And when they have all that they need, they tell Moses that they have enough and ask him to stop the people from bringing any more gifts (36:2-5). Had they been dishonest, they would have encouraged the people to keep giving so that they could enrich themselves or the tabernacle. We see further evidence of their honesty and of good administration in the statement they present of how the money entrusted to them has been used (**38:21-31**).

The fact that the people have to be *restrained from bringing more* (**36:6**) is a further tribute to their generosity.

God's instructions for the tabernacle and its furnishings in 25:1-31:11 are followed to the letter, as can be seen by the way the passages are repeated word for word. African stories, too, are full of repetition and demonstrate the genius of oral transmission as the art of inculcating truths.

So all the work on the tabernacle, the Tent of Meeting, was completed. The Israelites did everything just as the Lord commanded Moses (**39:32**). This faithfulness in the work is a good sign and gives Moses some satisfaction. After he inspects the work, he blesses the people (**39:43**). We are reminded of how God at creation examined the things he had created, acknowledged that they were good and blessed them (Gen 1:20-31).

40:1-38 Erecting the Tabernacle

Once all the components are ready, Moses assembles the tabernacle, again following God's precise instructions. The emphasis that God is in control of every aspect of the process is a reminder that this tabernacle is not the product of some person's inspiration, like most monuments dedicated to gods and idols. But it is indeed an expression of God's will. The *Testimony* (that is, the Ten Commandments engraved on the stone tablets) is carefully placed in the chest, the ark (**40:20**).

The words *and so Moses finished the work* (**40:33**) remind us of the words at the end of God's creation: 'by the seventh day, God had finished the work he had been doing' (Gen 2:2). Everything is accomplished in the time allotted. The tabernacle is *set up on the first day of the first month in the second year,* which means that it is ready for the celebration of the first Passover in the wilderness, which is celebrated fourteen days later (**40:17**; see Num 9:5). That Passover will be a commemoration of their leaving Egypt as well as evidence that God is indeed in the midst of his people (**40:34-38**; see also 25:8).

The Lord, the sovereign God is present with us through all our travels, just as he was with the Israelites (40:38). He is faithful to his promises. Revelation, the last book of the Bible, reveals his presence right up until the end of the world we know, and then in the new Jerusalem. However, he is no longer present only with the Hebrew people wandering in the wilderness, but with the whole of humanity: 'Now the dwelling of God is with men, and he will live with them.' (Rev 21:3). The NT teaches us that the 'God with us', Emmanuel, is none other than Jesus Christ, who promises to be with us every day (Matt 1:23; 28:20). He is the Way who brings us out of our Egypt of slavery to reach the promised land.

Abel Ndjerareou

Further Reading

Cole, R. Alan. *Exodus*. TOT. Downers Grove: Inter-Varsity Press, 1981.

Durham, John I. *Exodus*. WBC. Waco, Tex: Word, 1987.

Kaiser, Walter C. 'Exodus' in *Genesis, Exodus, Leviticus, Numbers*. EBC. Edited by Frank E. Gaebelein. Grand Rapids: Zondervan, 1990.

LEVITICUS

The authorship of the book of Leviticus is traditionally ascribed to Moses. It deals with matters that concern the priestly tribe of Levi, but it also insists that the information contained in the book is to be communicated to the laity, those who were not priests (1:2; 8:5; 11:2; 12:1; 15:2; 17:2; 18:2; 19:2; 20:2; 23:2; 24:2; 25:2; 27:2). Thus the book may be described as being like a textbook for everyone in Israel. This is significant because it means that every Israelite was called upon to pay special attention to its contents.

The Literary Context

Leviticus is part of the Torah (Pentateuch). The Torah comprises the first five books of the OT, namely, Genesis, Exodus, Leviticus, Numbers and Deuteronomy. It is the story of the Israelites, whom God chose to be his special people because he loved them and also because he stood by the oath which he had made to their forefathers (Deut 7:7-8). The story runs from the creation of the world to the point where the Israelites were on the verge of entering the promised land. It is the story about the creation of the universe. It is the story about God's calling of Abraham and the patriarchs, and the promises of land and children that God gave to Abraham. It is the story of Moses and the deliverance from Egyptian bondage. It is the story of God's covenant with the Israelites in which he spelled out the basis of his relationship with them at Mount Sinai (also known as Mount Horeb). Lastly, it is the story about bitter wanderings in the wilderness. It is no ordinary story. Rather, it is the story of God's dealings with his people, and therefore there is a supernatural dimension to it. In this story God always takes the initiative to reach out to humankind and to reveal himself to them. Knowledge of God is thus revealed through the story. The Torah is the story of God's love. There is no explanation as to why God loved Israel, but the Torah presents the good news of the love of God.

Leviticus is at the centre of the Pentateuch. Its immediate literary context is the deliverance of the Israelites from Egyptian bondage (Exod 1–18). From Exodus 19 through Leviticus to Numbers 10, we read about the events that took place during the time the Israelites were camped at the foot of Mount Sinai. Here Yahweh made a covenant with them, giving them instructions by which to live, instituting the worship of himself as the centre of their life, and ordering their existence around the fundamental fact of his presence in their midst. Thus the whole of Leviticus is part of the story of Yahweh instituting a covenant with the Israelites.

God's instructions for the construction of the Tent of Meeting, which began in Exodus 25, reach a climax in Exodus 40:34-38 when the glory of the Lord descends from the summit of Mount Sinai to rest in and fill the Tent of Meeting. This event is the basic clue to the meaning of the covenant made at Mount Sinai. At its heart is the relationship between God and Israel. By making the covenant, Yahweh was saying to Israel, 'I am with you'.

The book of Exodus ends with the holy God in the midst of Israel. This affirmation of the Holy in the midst of Israel is the presupposition for the instructions from Leviticus 1 to Numbers 10. The instructions answer the question: How should profane and sinful Israel arrange its entire existence around the wondrous Holy One who has come to be in its midst? The answer was critical to Israel's continued existence in the promised land.

African Christians believe that Jesus Christ, the Second Person in the Godhead, is in our midst through the Holy Spirit. For us, too, the question is: How should we arrange our lives in the presence of the holy God who comes to us in the person of the Holy Spirit? The survival of the church in Africa and the survival of African communities will to a large extent depend on the answer to this question. In this respect the answer given by the author of Leviticus is very relevant for African Christianity.

Leviticus is also set within the context of the creation story in Genesis. At creation, God brought order out of chaos; Leviticus is concerned with the maintenance of that order. Any disturbance of God's order, whether cosmic, social, economic or political, provokes the God of justice to intervene to restore that order.

Another important context of Leviticus is God's unconditional promise to Abraham, which revealed his grace as he promised Abraham descendants and land. The issues of land and fertility are also at the centre of Leviticus. Land is an issue in most African countries, and so is fertility, which goes together with the whole issue of human sexuality. Thus in many ways the book of Leviticus deals with current issues in Africa.

Occasion and Purpose

The basis of Israel's relationship with God and the people's hope for the future was obedience to God's will as expressed in the instructions he gave to them at Mount Sinai. For the writer of Leviticus, Israel was basically a worshipping community, and this book sets out the requirements for being a people fit for the worship of Yahweh, that is, a holy people. This transformation would be the work of God and would be achieved solely by his grace (21:8, 15). This message is timeless. It applied to the Israelites in the desert, who had been wrenched from the settled (albeit enslaved) life they knew in Egypt. It could also apply to the uprooted Israelites who were sent into Babylonian exile Many years later Ezekiel would also hold out the hope that after the disruptions of the exile a transformed Israelite community would again centre on the temple and the proper worship of God (Ezek 40:1-47:12).

Like the Israelites, African communities have endured traumatic changes and the destruction and reconstruction of their communities. They have endured colonialism, celebrated independence, suffered again under corrupt rulers, and are currently battling the devastating effects of the HIV/AIDS epidemic. We need to hear the message of Leviticus and recognize that our future does not depend on what politicians attempt to do, but on our becoming transformed societies centred on the reality of the presence of the Lord. Christians whose lives have been transformed by the presence of the Holy Spirit hold the key to the authentic future of African communities.

The Theology of Leviticus

We have noted that the book of Leviticus is at the centre of the five books of the Pentateuch. If we consider these as concentric circles, then Genesis and Deuteronomy form the outermost circle, Exodus and Numbers form an inner circle, and Leviticus forms the innermost circle. This means that the two outer circles are the presupposed background of the theology of Leviticus. Our discussion of the theology of Leviticus can move either outwards from the inner circle to the outermost circle or inwards from the outermost circle to the inner circle. In this commentary I will follow the former direction, or in other words, I will look at the theology of Leviticus primarily in the light of God's revelation in Exodus and Numbers. We will also see how this theology relates to the NT revelation of Christ.

The Presence of the Lord

Both Exodus and Numbers deal with the movements of the people of God. In these movements, God went along with the people. Thus Moses could say to the Lord, 'If your Presence does not go with us, do not send us up from here' (Exod 33:15). In Exodus the cloud was a symbol of God's presence (Exod 19:16), and the book ends with the cloud covering the Tent of Meeting and the glory of the Lord filling the tabernacle (Exod 40:34-35). And so it was from the Tent of Meeting that God spoke to Moses at the start of Leviticus (1:1). Here God is presented as an immanent God, a God who is in the midst of his people. This immanent God was experienced

through worship at the Tent of Meeting and through the everyday duties of life. In the case of worship, it is said that sacrificial ceremonies were done 'before the Lord' (1:5, 11; 3:1) and produced 'an aroma pleasing to the Lord' (1:9, 13, 17; 3:5).

The people also experienced the Lord in their daily life. The phrase 'I am the Lord' is found repeatedly in chapters 18–25 (18:2, 4; 19:3, 10; 20:24; 21:12, 15; 22:2; 23:22; 24:22; 25:17, 55). It reminded the Israelites that every area of their life – their religion (chs. 21–24), their sexual relationships (chs. 18, 20), their interpersonal relationships (chs. 19, 25) – was of concern to the Lord. Leviticus acknowledges that a person's everyday life can even pollute the Tent of Meeting.

For the Christian, God's presence is made known in the person of Jesus Christ. Paul said God was reconciling the world to himself through Christ (2 Cor 5:19). And John, alluding to the OT Tent of Meeting, said that 'the Word became flesh and made his dwelling among us' (John 1:14). Jesus Christ arose from the dead and ascended into heaven so that he can fill the whole universe through the Holy Spirit (Eph 4:10). Furthermore, Paul says that the Christian is God's temple in which God's Spirit lives (1 Cor 3:16). Thus just as the presence of the Lord in the midst of the Israelites affected all areas of their lives, so the presence of the Holy Spirit in Christians should influence all aspects of their lifestyle.

Holiness

The God who was in the midst of the Israelites was holy and his people were to be like him (11:44-45; 19:2). To understand what this means, we need to recognize that the concept of holiness described in Leviticus distinguishes between the holy and the common (or ordinary) and between the clean and the unclean (10:10). These distinctions underlay all of Israel's life as a covenant community.

Something that is common becomes holy when God sets it apart so that it belongs to him. He did this for the nation of Israel, and thus every Israelite was called to be holy (20:26). Ordinary objects could also become holy if they were set aside as belonging to God. Various rituals accomplished this consecration. For example, in 8:10-11 the Tent of Meeting and all its utensils were consecrated. Certain times could also be set aside as holy, as reflected in the religious calendar in chapter 25.

There were, however, also degrees or levels of holiness. Thus the ordained priests were holier than ordinary Israelites, and the high priest was holier than the other priests (ch. 8). Because of their greater holiness, the priests were subject to more restrictions than the rest of the people (see 10:6-7; ch. 21). If they sinned, the effects were far more serious than if the people sinned, and thus greater atonement was required (ch. 4).

The priests' greater holiness meant they could handle holy objects. Ordinary people could not do this, for they would die if exposed to greater holiness. Yet even the priests had to be very careful to observe the conditions laid down for approaching the most holy things and places.

When something common came into contact with something that was most holy, such as the altar, the holy object did not lose its holiness, but the common object became holy (see Num 16:35-38).

Not only was there danger in any interaction between what was common and what was most holy, but there was also danger in interacting with holy things when one was in a state of impurity or uncleanness. God's holiness required that those who approached him be pure. Chapters 11-15 deal with things that caused impurity. These included eating impure animal foods (ch. 11), childbirth (ch. 12), infectious skin diseases (chs. 13-14) and bodily discharges (ch. 15). The one factor that the last three have in common is the risk of death. Thus they are regarded as standing in opposition to the Holy God who is the author of life, and thus they are seen as sources of impurity.

Impurity seems to have been thought of in two ways. On the one hand, it was perceived as something like a substance that could affect both human beings and objects (see, for example, ch. 15). It contaminated by touch and even reached out through solid matter. But the other, and far more important, perception in Leviticus is the recognition that human beings are responsible for generating impurity. We can get some idea of what this means by looking at the way the holy or most holy objects were contaminated in chapter 4. Unintentional sins committed by individual Israelites generated impurity that contaminated only the altar of burnt sacrifices, which was then purified by putting blood on its horns and pouring blood at its base. Unintentional sins committed by the whole community or the high priest generated impurity that contaminated not only the altar of burnt sacrifices but also the altar of incense and the veil. Thus the blood of the purification also had to be sprinkled against the veil and put on the horns of the altar of incense.

Deliberate sins would generate impurity that would penetrate the veil of the Holy of Holies and contaminate the atonement cover (or mercy seat), and thus for such sins purification blood was needed on and before the atonement cover. Personal sacrifices were not enough to remove the impurity resulting from deliberate sin. The nation as a whole had to expiate them in the annual Day of Atonement ritual (ch. 16) when the contaminated Holy of Holies was cleansed with purifying blood and the released impurities were transferred to the scapegoat.

But there was a point of no return when not even ritual atonement was enough. If the people chose to continue rebelling against God, the Tent of Meeting would be polluted to the extent that God would no longer abide in it. He would then leave the Tent of Meeting and leave his people to destruction (ch. 26). There was thus a deep connection between the ethical imperatives and worship.

The NT writers were strongly influenced by the concept of holiness in the book of Leviticus. For example, Peter called upon his readers to be holy just as God is holy (1 Pet 1:15-16) and described Christians as a holy priesthood (1 Pet 2:5). Paul called upon Christians to imitate God (Eph 5:1-2) and described them as God's temple. We are called upon not to pollute that temple (1 Cor 3:17).

Place of Ritual

If Yahweh was to continue to live in the midst of his people and if the Israelites were to continue living in the promised land, the people had to be fit for the worship of Yahweh. The writer of the book of Leviticus challenged his contemporaries to become such people by becoming a worshipping community.

Worship may be either individual or corporate and can be expressed in words or deeds, but in essence it is ritualistic and liturgical, even though the action may be formal or informal, regular or spontaneous. Ritual, that is, the organized repetition of certain symbolic actions, is part and parcel of all religions. The effectiveness of any ritual depends less on the mental state of those performing it, than on whether the worshippers have the right attitude and are committed to the truth symbolized by the ritual. The OT prophets were well aware of this, and condemned the hollowness of people offering splendid sacrifices while violating the law of God in their lives (see, for example, Isa 1:11-15). To honour God in word and not in deed is not to honour him at all. That the attitude of the worshipper is just as important as sacrifices is also shown by the fact that at times repentance on its own is sufficient to secure forgiveness. For example, David, who was guilty of adultery with Bathsheba and of the death of Uriah, confessed his sins when Nathan rebuked him and was forgiven because of this genuine confession (2 Sam 12:13-14).

In order for worshippers to participate meaningfully in a ritual they must have access to an explanation of the meaning of the ritual, for its meaning is not always self-evident. The book of Leviticus thus provides explanations of the rituals of Jewish worship. But we need to remember that sometimes this meaning can change. Thus the Lord's Supper replaces and reinterprets the Passover meal in the light of the death of Jesus Christ.

In Leviticus, rituals were commanded by God to ensure a healthy relationship between himself and Israel. There are founding rituals such as the ordination ritual in chapters 8 and 9; maintenance rituals such as the grain offering in chapters 2 and 6:14-23; and restoration rituals such as that for a new mother (ch. 12), a person healed from an infectious skin disease (chs. 13-14), and the Day of Atonement (ch. 16). Chapters 1-7 describe sacrificial rituals.

The emphasis on rituals in Leviticus helps to correct the imbalance created by an overemphasis on the spirit as against the body found in some brands of Christianity. Leviticus recognizes that a human being is both spirit and body and that the two are so interrelated that they influence each other and cannot be separated. It is only through the body that the spirit finds its full expression and realization.

It is also true that we acquire and transmit knowledge through physical activities. Jesus Christ said, 'If you hold to my teaching ... then you will know the truth' (John 8:31-32). Knowledge of the truth comes only as one obeys the word of Jesus and follows him. In African communities children learn skills by watching the examples set by their elders. Moses inducted Aaron and his sons in their priestly duties through example (ch. 8). It was through participation in ritual activities that one learned to revere the Lord (Deut 14:23). Here we have a philosophy of knowledge different from one that stresses acquiring it through reflection only.

It is also through the body and physical activities that a person locates his or her place in society. For example, people with infectious skin diseases were banned from society and once the disease had healed they could be reintegrated into their families and society through ritual. The rituals were rites of passage through which a person was excluded from society and then reintegrated into it. Because this particular society comprised a people of God, the person was ultimately reconciled with God through the rituals.

The NT writers were influenced by the OT ideas of ritual. Jesus Christ is described as a high priest (Heb 7–8) and Christians derive their priesthood from the priesthood of Jesus (1 Pet 2:9). In Mark 10:45 Jesus is portrayed as offering his life as a 'ransom' (a reparation offering), an idea drawn from Leviticus 5:14-6:7. The death of Jesus is further described as a fragrant offering (Eph 5:2; compare chs. 1–7). In the OT the blood of animals was used to purify objects in the Tent of Meeting for holy use. Similarly the blood of Jesus purifies the defiled consciences of Christians so they can offer perfect worship to God (Heb 9:13-14). Christians are also called upon to offer their bodies as living sacrifices holy and pleasing to God (Rom 12:1). In fact

the whole of book of Hebrews assumes the sacrificial system found in Leviticus.

African Christianity is very ritualistic. Such rituals are an essential part of any religion and need not be done away with. The lesson from the Letter to the Hebrews, as from the OT prophets, is that the external aspects of rituals must be accompanied by worship offered with a purified conscience.

Covenant

Returning to the image of concentric circles, the outermost circle formed by Genesis and Deuteronomy contains background essential to understanding the theology of Leviticus. In Genesis we have God's covenants with Noah and Abraham, and in Deuteronomy the Sinaitic covenant is repeated on the plains of Moab. The covenants with Noah and Abraham were unconditional covenants. God simply promised Noah to protect the Earth and Abraham to give him children and land. In the Sinaitic covenant, those blessings are dependent upon the obedience of the Israelites. We are to regard these two covenant traditions as complementary. The situation is similar to the new covenant announced by Jeremiah (Jer 31:31-34), which was not meant to abolish the Ten Commandments. Rather God was going to write the commandments, which had previously been engraved on tablets of stone, on the hearts of the people. In other words, he was going to so transform the people that they would automatically obey the commandments. Both the bestowal and the conditions under which this new covenant was to be observed depended on the action of Yahweh himself.

The writer of Leviticus has a similar vision of an Israelite community transformed by God (21:8,15). In this book Yahweh not only provides the context for transformation but also controls the process. He provides the Tent of Meeting, the materials for the sacrificial system, and the priesthood as an institution whose various tasks are intended to maintain the relationship between God and the Israelites. Through the provision of these facilities, Yahweh was responding to human need. He will punish his people if they disobey him, but he has promised that he will never ultimately abandon them.

This idea is very significant in the NT understanding of salvation. The NT writers were aware of the sinfulness of human beings. Thus Paul asks, 'Shall we go on sinning so that grace may increase?' (Rom 6:1). His whole being recoiled at the suggestion. How could a holy God be satisfied to have unholy, sin-fettered children? But human beings are by nature sinful. What is the solution? The only way we can cut off our sinful heredity is through death (Rom 6:2). How can we die? Not by trying to kill ourselves but by recognizing that God has dealt with us in Christ. He has put us in Christ (1 Cor 1:30). It is not up to us either to devise a way to enter his presence or to work it out. God has planned it; and he has not only planned it but he has done it. So when Christ died on the cross we died too.

The writer of the Letter to the Hebrews argues that through his death Jesus Christ has become a mediator of a new covenant (Heb 9:15-18), thereby fulfilling Jeremiah's prophecy (compare Heb 8:6-13 with Jer 31:31-34). The word 'covenant' is used there in the sense of a will, which becomes effective after the death of the one who wrote it. The beneficiaries of the will receive their inheritance only after the one who wrote the will has died.

The fact that the new covenant is bestowed purely on the basis of grace does not mean that the beneficiaries are free to do anything with the inheritance they receive. They are duty bound to guard it well. Paul says that when God put us in Christ it means that through Christ's resurrection we received new life, a new life lived only in Christ.

Outline of Contents

COMMENTARY

1:1 Introduction

The Lord who had previously called to Moses from Mount Sinai (Exod 19:3) now calls to him *from the Tent of Meeting*. Previously, Moses had not been able to approach this tent because of the cloud, which signified the glory of God, that had covered it (Exod 40:35).

At times this tent is said to be located in the middle of the camps (Num 2:17; 3:38) whereas at other times it seems to have been outside the camp (Num 11:24-27; 12:4-5). But regardless of where exactly it stood, the point is that Yahweh was now with his people and the Israelites needed to reorganize their way of living and worshipping because of the presence of the Holy in their midst. So the Lord summoned Moses to give him instructions regarding the life that befits a covenant people of God.

1:2-7:38 The Sacrificial System

1:2-6:7 Sacrificial Instructions Directed to the Laity

What is striking here is that the instructions regarding offerings were to be communicated to the people of Israel (**1:2a**). In Mesopotamia or Egypt an ordinary person was not allowed either to participate in any acts of divine service or to view the text of the ritual, but in Israel the priest's manual was an open book, a textbook for all Israel.

Moses' role was to be a mediator between Yahweh and Israel. He was to communicate to the people of Israel that anyone was free to bring offerings to Yahweh. The voluntary nature of the offerings is underlined by the use of the word 'when', which indicates the conditional and optional nature of the sacrificial laws to follow. There were no fixed periods when people had to offer these sacrifices. In this regard they were unlike the appointed feasts or the Jubilee,

which had fixed dates in the religious calendar (see comments on ch. 23). The emphasis was on individual needs, and the instructions about offerings were meant to answer individual needs.

It is noteworthy that God specifies that domestic animals should be offered (**1:2b**). Such animals were easy to come by without any of the risks and uncertainty associated with hunting wild animals. This is an example of the principle that Yahweh will always provide human beings with the means to enable them to fulfil his will. Human beings are not left to obey him unaided. Rather, when he issues commands he also provides the enabling power (grace) to do them.

1:3-17 Burnt offerings

The practice of making burnt offerings was an old one (Gen 8:20; Exod 10:25; 18:12; Num 23:15; Judg 6:26; 13:16; 1 Sam 7:9; 1 Kgs 18:38) and one that was also practised by other nations such as the Moabites (2 Kgs 3:27). Yahweh accepted it as something that could be incorporated into the Yahwistic cult, provided it was regulated.

The ritual for making a burnt offering is presented three times with slight variations (1:3-9, 10-13, 14-17). The steps in the ritual include the preparation of the animal, its presentation, its slaughter, the presentation of its blood, the cutting of the carcass into pieces and the burning of the animal on the altar. In the preparatory stage the offerer chose from the herd a male animal without blemish and brought it to the *entrance to the Tent of Meeting* (**1:3**). This was a sacred place where the divine and human realms intersect.

No particular reason is given for the choice of a male animal for sacrifice. However, according to 2 Samuel 24:24, a burnt offering must be costly. Thus a male animal was chosen because of its economic value. It was also specified that the animal must be without blemish. The prophet Malachi criticized his contemporaries for offering second-rate animals (Mal 1:7, 13). God, being who he is, deserves the best and the most valuable from his people. (In the ritual of the fellowship offering, described in chapter 3, the victim could be either a male or female animal.)

Once at the Tent of Meeting, the offerer laid *his hand on the head of the burnt offering* (**1:4**). At least four different explanations have been offered for this act. Some argue that it symbolizes the transfer of the offerer's sins to the animal. Others have interpreted it as symbolizing the offerer's identification with the animal, so that it became a substitute for the offerer. A third explanation is that this act represented an oath affirming the offerer's purpose or innocence. The fourth explanation is that the act merely represented an assertion that the animal belonged to the one offering it and that it was being presented for sacrifice.

The third and fourth explanations are very close to each other, and thus a number of scholars have argued for them.

These scholars tend to reject the first two explanations on the basis that if this were an act by which the offerer asked God for forgiveness, two hands rather than one would have been laid on the animal (16:10, 21). Furthermore, they argue that there is an unacceptable element of magic in thinking that this act could transfer the soul of the offerer to the sacrificial animal. However, it is clearly stated that God will accept the animal on behalf of the offerer *to make atonement for him* (1:4). The principle of substitution is prominent here, and thus it seems that either one or both of the first two explanations fits the context.

After the presentation the offerer took the animal and killed it *before the Lord* (**1:5a**). Its blood was collected in a basin. Then Aaron's sons took the blood and threw it round about the altar that was at the entrance of the Tent of Meeting. This splashing of the blood against the altar may have symbolized petition (**1:5b**). Next the offerer skinned the animal and cut it into pieces (**1:6**). The entrails and legs were washed with water (**1:9**). Finally the priests, who would have prepared a fire, placed all the pieces of the carcass on the fire (**1:7-8**).

The other two accounts of the ritual deal with different procedures to be followed with different types of sacrificial animals. The procedure is much the same when either a sheep or a goat is offered, except that these must be slaughtered on the north side of the altar (**1:10-13**). When a dove or pigeon is offered, there is no laying on of hands. There was no need for this, for the bird would already be in the hands of the offerer. The priest killed the bird by wringing its neck. Instead of cutting the bird into pieces, it was torn apart by its wings. It was also not washed with water (**1:14-17**).

These acts were not seen as destruction of the animal. Rather the animal was transformed into smoke so that it could ascend to heaven above and become *an aroma pleasing to the Lord* (1:9, 13, 17), something like a gift to the Lord.

Note that the separate roles of the priests and layperson were clearly defined and complementary. The layperson was responsible for choosing the animal for sacrifice (making sure that it was without blemish), slaughtering it, skinning it, cutting it into pieces and washing the remains. Worship was viewed as a corporate event in which one took part. There was no question of laypersons simply being spectators while others performed the worship service – as is too often the case in our churches, where laypersons simply watch what the leaders of worship are doing and do not fully participate themselves.

In considering the significance of the burnt offering, both the human and the divine sides must be taken into account. The goal of the whole ritual is said to be atonement (1:4). The Hebrew word here translated 'atonement' is used in the OT to refer to ransom money. It is the money paid in place of a forfeited life in order to redeem it (Exod 21:28-30;

30:11-12). That is why the offerer of the burnt offering put his or her hand on the head of the victim and the smoke from the burnt offering is described as an aroma pleasing to the Lord. The implication here is that Yahweh had been angered by human sin and something must be done in order to avert his wrath. Thus the burnt offering functioned as a ritual of restoration through which the relationship between Yahweh and the offerer was restored. The symbol of Yahweh's acceptance of the person who submitted to him was the fire that would come out 'from the presence of the Lord and consume the burnt offering' (9:24). A good illustration of the function of burnt offering is found in Genesis 8:21, where we read that God's attitude towards human beings was reversed because of a burnt offering.

Some people have interpreted the burnt offering as giving food to Yahweh, who is then under an obligation to respond. However, to interpret the sacrifice in this way is to think in magical terms and to miss the key point that the victim was a domesticated animal. It was something that Yahweh had already given the offerer (see comments on 1:2b). Herein lies a paradox. Human beings cannot give anything to God that he has not already given to them. Yahweh does not need the sacrifice because everything is his (Ps 50:7-15) and there is nothing automatic about his response. Nor is his response influenced by the size of the offering. A poor person's offering of a dove is as acceptable as the bull offered by a rich man. Yahweh's acceptance of the sacrifice depends entirely on his grace. What Yahweh was interested in was the intention of the offerer.

Paul describes the sacrificial death of Christ in terms of a burnt offering when he urges his readers to 'live a life of love, just as Christ loved us and gave himself up for us as a fragrant offering and sacrifice to God' (Eph 5:2). Furthermore, in the NT, Christian service in church and community is compared to sacrifice (Heb 13:15-16).

Because the death of Christ was a sufficient burnt offering offered up once for all, there is no more need to offer literal burnt offerings. But the legislation in Leviticus reminds us about what the death of Christ means for us. The ritual underlines the importance of a restored relationship between human beings and God, which is achieved through repentance and God's forgiveness.

2:1-16 Grain offerings

The ingredients for the grain offering are specified as fine grain flour, oil and incense, but no specific quantities of these ingredients are mentioned (**2:1**). In preparation for the ritual, the worshipper brings them to the temple. The priests then take a handful of the flour and oil and all the incense and place them on the altar to be burned (**2:2**). The part of the offering that is burned is referred to as the *memorial portion*. What this probably means is that it represents the whole offering. Thus the whole offering becomes holy, even the part that was not actually placed on the altar. This remaining part is referred to as *most holy* (**2:3, 10**), and consequently it can only belong to the priests, who are also holy to the Lord.

The grain offering can be presented raw or cooked in an oven, or pan or on a grill (**2:4-7**). A cooked offering was presented in the same way as the raw offering (**2:8-9**; see also 2:2). However, we are not told how the 'memorial portion' was collected.

Adding leaven or honey to the grain was strictly forbidden (**2:11**). Leaven was forbidden because it results in fermentation, which symbolizes decay and corruption and would thus be a blemish on the grain offering. Honey was forbidden because it, too, was associated with fermentation. (On the other hand, both leaven and honey can be offered as part of a firstfruit offering – **2:12**).

Salt must be used with a grain offering because it symbolizes preservation and durability (**2:13**). It became a symbol of the covenant bond, so that we find references to an 'everlasting covenant of salt', meaning an eternal covenant (Num 18:19; 2 Chr 13:5).

If the grain offering was presented as part of a firstfruit offering, the new grains should be crushed into flour after being roasted (**2:14**). Then it was offered in the same way as the grain offering in 2:2 (**2:15-16**).

The purpose of the grain offering is not mentioned. However, what was offered was the fruit of the land and of human labour. Thus the ritual was done in the context of the daily rhythms of life. In the ritual the people acknowledged that God had given them land in fulfilment of the promise made to Abraham and that they had to work on the land. The ritual therefore reflects a covenantal relationship between Yahweh and the people, a relationship within which God gave the people land and the people reciprocated by giving tribute to God. In this way the people not only gave thanks to God for all their socio-economic and political activities but also dedicated these activities to God. A comparable offering of grain is recorded in Deuteronomy 26:1-10.

Thus after receiving forgiveness through the burnt offering, the worshipper is able through the grain offering not only to thank God for a restored relationship but also to dedicate him- or herself and all he or she has to the service of God. In the NT Paul urged Christians 'to offer your bodies as living sacrifices, holy and pleasing to God' (Rom 12:1). A Chewa proverb *Mwana wa mfulu sagona ndi njala* ['A generous man's child does not go to bed with an empty stomach'] underlines the importance of reciprocating good will.

3:1-17 Peace offerings

There is some debate about the correct name for this offering. The NIV refers to it as a 'fellowship offering', whereas other translations call it a 'peace offering'. The problem arises because of the uncertainty about the exact meaning of the Hebrew word *shelamim*. If this word is related to the verb *shalem*, it means 'to be complete, whole or sound'. A related word, *shalom*, means 'completeness, wholeness, harmony, well-being, prosperity, and peace'. In this case, the focus of the ritual is on achieving harmonious living with God and with other human beings.

However, some people have suggested that the word *shelamim* is related to the word *shillem*, which means 'to complete, pay vows'. If this is the case, this offering can be regarded as 'the concluding sacrifice'. In fact, in 7:37 it comes at the end of the list of sacrifices. This offering can also be used as a way of concluding or reaffirming a covenant (Deut 27:6-7; Josh 8:31).

Given the theology of the book of Leviticus, the translation of *shelamim* as 'peace offering' seems to be appropriate. The focus is not simply on fellowship, but on fellowship within the context of a restored relationship.

The description of the peace offering is in two sections dealing with sacrifices from the herd, that is, cattle (**3:1-5**), and from the flock, that is, sheep and goats (**3:6-17**). The ritual is similar to that of the burnt offering, except that here only parts of the animal, namely all the fat and the two kidneys, were to be burned on the altar. The text does not say what happens to the rest of the animal. However, according to 7:28-36 the thigh and the breast went to the officiating priests. It is possible that the rest was eaten in a fellowship meal by the worshipper and those he had invited. Although such a meal is not mentioned here, there is evidence of it in other places in Scripture (Exod 18:12; 24:3-11; Deut 33:19; 1 Sam 9:13; 16:5). There is also biblical evidence that this type of meal was common among non-Israelites (Exod 34:15; Num 25:2). The difference between this ritual and other offerings is that in the burnt offering, the whole animal was burned up, and in the grain offering, a handful of the offering was burned on the altar and the rest was given to the officiating priests. In the peace offering, something is given to the worshipper.

This ritual was performed during public gatherings to mark the conclusion or renewal of a covenant, or the inauguration of a religious institution (9:18; Deut 27:6-7; Josh 8:31; 1 Sam 11:15; 2 Sam 6:18; 24:25; 1 Kgs 3:15; 8:63; 9:25; 2 Kgs 16:13). However, although the occasions for which we have records of the celebration of this ritual were public, the rite was also done for individuals, as in the case described here. It was a voluntary ritual that could be offered because one chose to (Ezek 46:11-12), or because one wanted to make a vow (Jonah 1:16; Prov 7:14), or simply as an expression of thanksgiving (Pss 22:25-26; 107:22).

The sharing of a meal by worshippers was important because it symbolized God sharing a meal with them. Human beings live in communities with each other, and

God has graciously entered into community with them. Of course, there is no suggestion of any merging of the divine and the human in the ritual. God will always be God and human beings will always be human and finite. However, the privilege of sharing a meal with God evokes the emotions of joy and celebration. This ritual allowed people to express their deep-seated emotions.

Paul says that Jesus Christ is our peace, and that through his life and death he has reconciled God to us and abolished the hostility amongst human beings (Eph 2:13-18). Thus the peace offering foreshadowed the person and work of Jesus Christ. The Lord's Supper resembles the peace offering in many ways. Jesus referred to the cup of wine as 'the new covenant in my blood' (1 Cor 11:25), alluding to the blood of the old covenant. At the conclusion of the Sinaitic covenant, Moses took the blood of the burnt offering and of the peace offering and threw it over the people, saying, 'This is the blood of the covenant that the Lord has made with you' (Exod 24:8). Both at the making of the Sinaitic covenant and the Lord's Supper, there is a sharing of a meal (Exod 24:11; Luke 22:15).

The Israelites used peace offerings to express their thankfulness, to make vows and to give freewill offerings. Christians today can also use the Lord's Supper to thank God for answered prayer, to rededicate themselves to God and simply to praise God for who he is.

The social element in this ritual strikes a powerful note in the African psyche, for in Africa social bonds are very strong. This strength is reflected in the Chewa proverbs from Malawi, *Chibale ndi fupa sichiola* ['Being related is like a bone, it does not rot'] and *Apao ndi mizu ya kachere, akomana pansi* ['Relatives are like the roots of a kachere tree, they converge underground'].

4:1-5:13 Purification offerings

The NIV refers to the offerings described in this section as 'sin offerings', but 'purification offerings' is preferred because of the contexts in which they were offered. They were offered not only by those who had sinned unintentionally, but also by mothers recovering from childbirth (ch. 12), by those who had recovered from infectious skin diseases (chs. 13–14) and by those completing a Nazirite vow (Num 6). Thus these offerings are not prescribed solely for those who have sinned. Moreover the fact that they were also offered when consecrating an altar shows that they were used for objects that cannot sin. The focus is thus on purification of something that has been contaminated rather than on sin as such. When the blood of the purification offering is put on the horns of the altar, what is cleansed is the sanctuary and the holy objects in it, not individuals.

The section starts with an introduction that specifies the situations that give rise to the need for a purification offering. These situations all involve some unintentional

act that violates a prohibition that God has given (**4:1-2**). An error always sets in motion other events that upset the divine ecology and generate impurity that contaminates God's sanctuary and land.

Each of the four sections of chapter 4 begins with a definition of a specific situation that would require a sacrifice and ends with a declaration of the effect of the ritual. While the types of animals to be offered differ, the general outline of the ritual is the same in each case. The result of the ritual is the forgiveness of sins.

Any sin committed accidentally by *the anointed priest*, who represented the whole community, affected the whole congregation (**4:3**). Thus these sins are dealt with first. The priest was to bring a bull to the door of the Tent of Meeting. Then he was to lay his hand on it, just as a layperson was required to do in the ritual of burnt offering (**4:4**; see also 1:3-4). The same anointed priest was to kill the bull and perform the blood rite. The blood rite involved sprinkling some of the blood seven times in front of the curtain that separated the Holy of Holies from the area where the altar of incense stood. Then some blood was put on the horns of the altar of incense. The remaining blood was poured out at the base of the altar of burnt offering, which was at the door of the Tent of Meeting (**4:5-7**). After this the priest performed the fat rite, which was similar to the fellowship offering ritual (**4:8-10**). Lastly there was the carcass rite in which all the parts of the animal that had not been burned on the altar of burnt offering were destroyed in a ceremonially clean place outside the camp (**4:11-12**).

A similar ritual is prescribed for a sin committed by *the whole Israelite community* (4:13-21). Once again, the animal to be killed is a young bull. The purpose of the ritual is given in **4:20** and the ritual was performed so that the congregation might be forgiven. The use of the passive voice, *they will be forgiven*, makes it clear that though the anointed priest is the one who performs the ritual, the actual forgiveness comes from the Lord. There was nothing magical about the ritual. Forgiveness did not depend upon perfect performance of it but on Yahweh's benevolent will.

When *a leader* of the community either recognizes or is told by someone else that he has committed an error, he needs to offer a sacrifice for purification (**4:22-23a**). In this case the purification offering is a goat without blemish (**4:23b-24**). The blood is spread only on the altar of burnt offering, unlike the earlier cases where the blood was also applied to the curtain and the altar of fragrant incense (**4:25**; compare 4:6-7). The fat rite is described in 4:26, but there is no mention of the carcass rite. It may be that the author felt it was unnecessary to repeat these details.

Finally, instructions are given for an error committed by an ordinary *member of the community* (4:27-37). This time the purification offering is either a female goat without blemish (**4:28**) or a female lamb without blemish (**4:32**).

Leviticus 4 shows that the sin of religious and political leaders is more serious than that of ordinary people. The NT also makes it clear that God's judgment on church members is in proportion to their responsibilities (Luke 12:48).

The text moves on to deal with four examples of occasions when a purification offering was needed after a person committed a possibly intentional error. The first is failure to testify when witnesses are called for (**5:1**). The second concerns becoming unclean through touching something unclean such as the carcass of an unclean animal (**5:2**). The third case concerns becoming unclean through contact with human uncleanness (**5:3**). The fourth concerns uttering a rash oath (**5:4**). These cases are different from those dealt with earlier (ch. 4), because here it is possible that the offenders were aware of what they had done or failed to do. The problem was that they had subsequently forgotten about their actions and were now unaware of the problem.

Numbers 15:27-31 makes a distinction between sins committed unknowingly and those committed defiantly or deliberately. Those who committed the latter type of sins were to be cut off from the people (Num 15:30-31). We would have expected a similar ruling if the person committing one of the sins listed in 5:1-4 had acted deliberately. However, what we have is provision for a purification offering. The explanation is that confession of guilt reduces the penalty for sins, although it does not nullify it. The prophets, too, taught that repentance was necessary for God's forgiveness (Amos 5:14-15; Isa 1:16-20; Jer 4:1-4).

The offerings that can be presented to deal with this kind of error are graded to suit the individual's economic ability. A female goat or lamb (**5:6**) is mentioned first. This animal was also specified in 4:27-35. However, if a person could not afford a goat or a lamb, two doves or two young pigeons might be substituted (**5:7**). One bird was offered as a purification offering by wringing its neck, sprinkling some of its blood on the side of the altar and pouring the rest out at the base of the altar (**5:8-9**). The other was offered as a burnt offering, following the procedure outlined in 1:14-17 (**5:10**). A person who could not afford a bird offering could bring a grain offering (**5:11-13**) and offer one tenth of an ephah (that is, about four pints or two litres) of fine flour unmixed with oil or frankincense. The ritual itself was similar to that of the grain offering (ch. 2).

All the purification offerings required a sense of guilt (4:3, 13-14, 22-23, 27-28; 5:5) and confession of sins (**5:5**). The Hebrew word for guilt refers both to the act by which one incurs guilt and the feeling of guilt as a consequence of the act. Thus a person can commit a sin unintentionally and at a later stage come to feel guilt or to recognize the guilt associated with the action, either because the wrong has been explained to him or because it has begun to trouble his conscience. The purification offering is a ritual response for someone who is troubled at heart.

Purification offerings also purified the sanctuary. Two points need to be noted here. First, sins committed unknowingly generate impurity that attaches itself to the sanctuary. The purification offering cleanses the Tent of Meeting of this impurity. If the impurity is not ritually removed, its presence may lead to the departure of Yahweh from the midst of his people, for Yahweh cannot live in the midst of impurity and pollution. The departure of Yahweh would threaten the existence of Israel as a people, as was clear from Ezekiel's vision (Ezek 9–10). Second, the responsibility for the impurity is placed squarely on the people. The ongoing presence of Yahweh in the midst of the people is therefore intimately connected with their behaviour. Ritual thus provides the context for interaction between Yahweh and Israel in their mutual quest for a holy community.

The purification ritual deals with the incurred guilt and the polluted Tent of Meeting by offering both cleansing and restoration. This is reflected in the way blood is manipulated. When the purification ritual involved an anointed priest or the whole community, blood was brought inside the tent. Some blood was sprinkled seven times against the curtain in front of the Holy of Holies, some was put on the horns of the altar of incense, and the rest was poured at the base of the altar of sacrifice. In this way both the curtain and the altar of incense were cleansed and the altar of sacrifice was reconsecrated. When a leader or an ordinary Israelite had committed the unintentional sin, blood was put on the horns of the altar of sacrifice and the rest of the blood was poured at the base. In this way the altar was both cleansed and reconsecrated.

Another element of the ritual that symbolized the complete elimination of impurities was the burning of the skin of the animal, together with its head, legs, entrails and dung, at a clean spot outside the camp. Thus purification, consecration and elimination were part of the ritual process.

The whole concept of sin generating impurity that pollutes the Tent of Meeting has important implications. People often ask why 'good' people perish together with evildoers. The emphasis on unintentional sins in this chapter makes it clear that the so-called 'good' people are not innocent at all. Unintentional sins are as much sins as deliberate ones. Hence John's warning, 'If we claim to be without sin, we deceive ourselves and the truth is not in us' (1 John 1:8).

By allowing sinners to pollute the Tent of Meeting beyond repair, 'good people' are unintentional sinners who contribute to its pollution. The problems that the world is facing today are partly due to the unintentional sinners, the silent majority who by their silence contribute to the pollution of the Tent of Meeting. African politicians have often advised church leaders to keep out of politics. However, the theology of purification in Leviticus leads some church leaders to see it as their responsibility to speak out on political issues.

In Leviticus, the objects that were rendered impure by human behaviour were in the Tent of Meeting. They had to be daubed with blood in order to cleanse them so they could be used in worship. In the NT, the Christian is the temple of God's Spirit (1 Cor 3:16) and so unacceptable human behaviour defiles the conscience, which now has to be purified by the blood of Christ (Heb 9:14).

The function of the purification offering was to deal with the problem of guilt and offer hope through God's forgiveness (4:20, 26, 31, 35; see also 16:21). We have already referred to the ideas of identification and substitution when discussing the burnt offering, and it seems that the purification offering may be a later, specialized development of the burnt offering. But whatever the origins of the ritual, God's forgiveness proceeds from the fact that the offender feels guilt and confesses the sin. The effect of forgiveness is to reorient offenders and allow them to proceed with life as before.

5:14-6:7 Reparation offerings

The NIV refers to what is in this commentary called a 'reparation offering' as a 'guilt offering'. This offering is similar to a purification offering in that the error is unintentional and the offender feels a sense of guilt. However, in this case the offering is occasioned by a breach of faith against the Lord that shows itself in crossing the boundary that separates objects that belong to Yahweh from profane objects (5:14-15). Such an offence calls for restitution, that is, for some reparation or damages to be paid, whereas in the purification offering only cleansing was required. In order to bring out this difference more clearly, this particular offering can be referred to as a 'reparation offering'.

The section is divided into two parts: 5:14-19 and 6:1-7. Each part begins with the words *The Lord said to Moses*. The focus is on those occasions that would require a reparation offering and not on the details of the ritual itself. All

BLOOD

Theologically, blood signifies life (Gen 9:4; Lev 17:11; Deut 12:23) and death. Life is sacred (Ezek 18:4) and thus the shedding of innocent blood needs avenging (Gen 9:5-6).

Blood in the OT:

In the OT, as in African traditional religion, blood sacrifice was known in family worship. The ruptured relationship between God and humans necessitates sacrifice for reconciliation (Lev 16:14-15). The blood (life) of the sacrificial victim was exchanged for that of the worshipper whose sin needed to be atoned for. Consequently, the blood belonged to God exclusively and believers were forbidden to eat it (Lev 7:26-27; 17:10,14; Deut 12:23). Blood was also used to unite the parties to a covenant (Exod 24:6-8) and as a sign of divine deliverance (Exod 12).

The shedding of innocent blood pollutes the land (Num 35:33-34), resulting in corporate guilt (Deut 21:1-9). If not atoned for, it hinders prayers (Isa 1:15). Its expiation can extend even to subsequent generations (Hosea 1:4). We need to remember this when we witness rampant shedding of innocent blood during inter-ethnic blood feuds and clashes, assasinations, robberies and the like. We also need to remember that vengeance for shed blood is a divine matter and is never left to individuals (Lev 19:18; Deut 32:35; Rom 12:19). Rather, God sanctions lawfully constituted civil authorities in these matters (Rom 13:4).

Blood in the NT:

Where OT believers had been forbidden to eat blood, in the NT Christians are instructed to drink or appropriate blood in a spiritual sense to obtain eternal life in Jesus (John 6:53, 56, 57). The Lord's Supper represents a new Passover to celebrate divine deliverance, not from Egypt but from sin. In instituting this sacrament, Christ referred to the wine as 'the blood of the covenant' (Matt 26:28; Mark 14:24) and as 'the new covenant in my blood' (Luke 22:20; 1 Cor 11:25). The earlier covenant, which had been sealed in blood, had been broken, but it had been replaced with a new and effective one as Jeremiah had predicted (Jer 31:32-33). This new covenant is superior to the old one (Heb 7:22) because it is eternal (Heb 13:20) and based on better promises (Heb 8:6; 9:15). Jesus is both its guarantor and its mediator (Heb 8:6; 12:24).

Jesus' blood not only sealed the new covenant but also expiated sin. Animal blood could never finally cleanse anyone of sin or appease God. In the NT it was recognized that the OT sacrifices were shadows of the reality represented by Christ (Heb 10:1). His blood of atonement provides the ultimate covering needed to expiate our sins and appease God (Heb 10:4, 10, 15-16). The blood sprinkled on the Day of Atonement (Lev 16:14-15) foreshadowed Christ, whose blood 'speaks a better word' (Heb 12:24) in heart cleansing (Heb 9:13-14). His shed blood makes possible the forgiveness of sins (1 Pet 1:18-19), daily cleansing (1 John 1:7) and our fellowship around the Lord's table (1 Cor 10:16a). The mercy seat foreshadowed the place of propitiation – the sacrifice of atonement at the cross (Rom 3:25; 1 John 2:2). Where blood was sprinkled on the threshold or doorway in the OT, Christ is now the door through whom all must enter to attain salvation (John 10:7, 9).

Jesus' shed blood has cosmic significance at the end time, providing reconciliation of all things to God (Col 1:19-20). This involves the subjugation of principalities and powers (Col 2:15) so that 'at the name of Jesus every knee should bow' (Phil 2:10-11).

Victor Babajide Cole

that is said is that the *priest … will make atonement for him* (5:16, 18; 6:7).

Two cases are discussed in the first part. In the first case (**5:14-16**) a person unintentionally commits a breach of faith against the Lord *in regard to any of the Lord's holy things*. Numbers 18:8-14 gives a list of 'holy things', which includes animals, grain and fruits. Only Aaron and his family could use these things (22:2-13). If, for example, a layperson ate a sacred offering by mistake, he or she would be punished severely. However, the severity of the offence could be reduced if the offending party felt guilty about what had been done. The confession itself did not remove the offence but reduced it to an unintentional error that could be forgiven if a reparation offering was made. Thus through the reparation offering the Lord provides an answer for a person in torment because of a guilty conscience over an error committed or suspected.

The material for the reparation is a ram without any defect valued in silver shekels *according to the sanctuary shekel* (5:15). This probably means that the sanctuary had its own weights, which the priests would have used to determine the value of the ram. In addition, the person should replace what had been misappropriated and supplement it with an amount equal to one-fifth of the value of the misappropriated holy things. When these were given to the priest, he would perform the expiatory ritual with the ram and the person would be forgiven.

The second case (5:17-19) concerns a person who violates God's commandments not only in regard to holy things but also in relation to any area of life. Such a person may come to feel that he or she may have done something that God forbids and begins to feel guilty about it. In this case a guilt offering is in order if the offence is to be forgiven. Once again a ram *without defect and of the proper value* (presumably also valued in terms of the shekels of the sanctuary) would be brought (**5:18**). It is noteworthy that here there is no mention of restitution and the addition of twenty per cent of the value of the defiled life. How could one replace a defiled life or give one-fifth of one's life to a priest? The only way to do so would be to die. But if the person dies, forgiveness becomes impossible. Instead, the offending party survives purely by the grace of God, which is extended upon completion of the ritual.

The second part of the section on reparation offerings deals with the case of a person who acts inappropriately towards a fellow human being (6:1-7). Such actions are also regarded as a breach of faith against the Lord because they involve lying and deception. In ancient Israel, oaths were made in the context of worship. Therefore, to break such a promise was to violate the sacred and break faith with God (**6:2a**). The first example of something that people may lie about is property that has been entrusted to them (**6:2b**). Those entrusted with the property may eventually claim that it is their own. Another example of lying is that of a person claiming to be the owner of property that had been stolen or obtained by fraud (**6:2c**). The third example is where a person finds something that has been lost and then claims to own it (**6:3**). In all these cases the offending party swears falsely before the Lord. Anyone guilty of such actions must make a reparation offering. As part of the offering, the offending party must restore to the offended party whatever it was that had been misappropriated (**6:4-5**). Furthermore, an additional twenty per cent of the value of the property must also be given to the offended party. Finally, the offending party must bring to the sanctuary a ram *without defect and of the proper value* for a reparation ritual (**6:6**). Only then would the offending party be considered forgiven (**6:7**).

Isaiah 53:10 specifically refers to a reparation offering and throws light on what this offering means. The chapter describes the death of the servant of God, who died because of 'our transgressions' and 'was crushed for our iniquities' (Isa 53:5). The idea of substitutionary atonement is present here. It can therefore be argued that in a reparation offering the ram was put to death instead of the guilty sinner. However, the idea of substitution is present in other sacrifices. What distinguishes the reparation offering is precisely the concept of reparation – the animal was given to compensate God for the loss he has suffered as a result of sin.

The instructions relating to the reparation offering emphasize that people must respect the boundary that separates objects that belong to God from those that belong to them, and the boundary that separates those objects that belong to other people from those that belong to them. The issue of integrity is central here. Community life is impossible without people of integrity, as many Chewa proverbs emphasize: *Mputa samunamiza maso* ['You do not lie to give eyes to a blind person']; *Kumwamba n'kumwamba, pansi m'pansi* ['The sky is the sky, down is down']. Sin has a social dimension. Unfortunately, in many African countries corruption has undermined the whole social fabric and led to poor governance.

Looking at the sacrificial system as a whole, one notices that different images are used to describe the effects of sin and the remedy for it. The burnt offering uses a personal picture. Guilty people deserves to die for their sins, but an animal dies in their place. God accepts the animal as a ransom for them. The purification offering uses an analogy from medicine. Sin makes the world so unclean and unhealthy that God can no longer dwell in it. The blood of the animal cleanses the sanctuary so that God can continue to dwell in the midst of his people. The reparation offering presents a commercial picture of sin. Sin is a debt that a person incurs against God. The debt is paid through the offered animal.

6:8-7:38 Sacrificial Instructions Directed to the Clergy

This section begins with Yahweh asking Moses to speak to Aaron and his sons (6:8-9). The instructions that follow relate to the same types of offering discussed in 1:1-6:7, although the order is different, with the peace offering coming last. But whereas the first section was addressed to the laity, this section is addressed to the priests who were responsible for carrying out the sacrificial rituals. This repetition of material emphasizes the importance of scrupulous attention to the structure of ritual. Observance of the details of sacrificial ritual was a way of showing obedience to God.

6:8-13 Burnt offerings

The particular responsibility of the priests with regard to burnt offerings was to make sure that the fire on the altar of burnt offering was kept burning continually. The importance of this instruction is indicated by the fact that it is mentioned both at the beginning and at the end of the section (6:9, 12-13). Detailed instructions are given on how to clean the altar of burnt offering. In the morning, the priests were to don special garments and remove the ashes from the altar (6:10). After cleaning the altar, the priests were to resume their ordinary clothes and take the ashes outside the camp (6:11). Meanwhile more firewood must be put on the altar so that fire would not go out (6:12). In 1:7 it was implied that a fire was made each time a burnt offering was presented, but it seems that this applies only to individual offerings. A continual burnt offering was to be presented on the altar, with one being offered in the morning and another at twilight, which would burn till the next morning (Exod 29:38-46).

The sacrifices which were offered in the morning and evening were very significant because they marked out a day. In the creation story in Genesis, a day had to be created first before the rest of God's creative work could be done. Here, too, a day is ritually marked out, giving people an opportunity to go about their daily tasks. The ritual responsibility of the priests had the function of maintaining the created order. Secular work is thus viewed as having religious underpinnings.

6:14-23 Grain offerings

The instructions regarding the grain offerings are similar to those in 2:1-2. Here, however, the focus is on the portion of the offering that was reserved for the officiating priests and the manner in which it was to be eaten so as to respect its character as holy to the Lord. The officiating priests were Aaron and his sons – females were not included. Hence the statement in 6:18 that every male amongst the children of Aaron may eat that portion of the holy offering. It must be eaten unleavened and within a holy place (6:16).

The requirements governing the eating of the portion that remained unburned have interesting implications.

The portion is described as *most holy* and therefore not to be taken out of the holy place. God gives it to the priests because they, too, are holy and work within the holy place. The priests' role was to be mediators between God and human beings, embodying both the divine and the human. The view of holiness here has vertical gradations: God is the most holy, and below him are the priests, and then the whole congregation. However, because Yahweh was in the midst of the people, there was also a horizontal relationship with no gradation. Rather, there was a community of equals with Yahweh at the centre. Here is the paradox: the priests were one with the rest of the people, yet different. This has implications for Christian ministry. The ordained minister is one with the rest of church members as the people of God, but he or she has been set apart (ordained) for a special function.

The final section on the grain offering deals with the offering to be made by Aaron and his sons (6:20). There are differences between translations here, with some implying that the priests offered this every day, while others, such as the NIV, imply that it was offered only on the day of their anointing as priests. This grain offering was presented in the morning and in the evening. It was to be cooked (see 2:4-10) and was to comprise a tenth of an ephah of flour (four pints or two litres), half of which to be offered in the morning and the other half in the evening. Because this grain offering was part of the ritual that conferred on them the status of priests, no portion of it was to be eaten; it was to be wholly burned. The ritual was to be performed by the anointed priest, who was the head of the clergy, on behalf of the rest of the clergy (6:22).

The regulation that even the priests were required to offer sacrifices draws attention to the spiritual integrity of the priestly office. The priests were not above the law: just like ordinary Israelites, they had to offer sacrifices for themselves.

6:24-30 Purification offerings

The instructions on purification offerings again deal particularly with the share of the priests. Their duties in regard to sprinkling and smearing blood (4:6-7) are ignored here. After mentioning the place where the animal was to be slaughtered by the offerer and its holy status (6:25), directives are given to the priests regarding the place where it was supposed to be eaten and the persons who were permitted to eat it (6:26). Priests are instructed to burn and not to eat any remains of an animal whose blood was brought into the Tent of Meeting (6:30). There are also directives regarding how to cleanse objects touched by its blood (6:27-28). Conscientiousness in divine ministry is emphasized here.

7:1-10 Reparation offerings

There is a difference between the regulations in these sections and those in 5:14-6:7. Here we find details of the ritual that are not included there. Thus here the emphasis is on the responsibility of the priests. The ritual is similar to that for the purification offering. After the offending party has slaughtered the animal, the priests take the blood and sprinkle it against the altar of burnt offering. Then all the fat is burned. Any males in a priest's family may eat the remaining part of the carcass within the holy place (**7:1-6**).

The priests' portions of the purification and reparation offerings were to go to the officiating clergy (**7:7**). When a burnt offering was made, the officiating priest kept the skin of the animal (**7:8**). Every cooked grain offering belonged to the officiating clergy (**7:9**), but uncooked offerings of dry grain or grain and oil belonged to all the priests (**7:10**).

7:11-36 Peace offerings

The regulations governing peace offerings fall into four sections: 7:11-18, 19-21, 22-27, 28-36, followed by a conclusion in 7:37-38. Those in the first section deal specifically with the reasons for peace offerings and the times when peace offerings can be eaten. A peace offering can be given as an expression of thankfulness, to fulfil a vow or as a freewill offering. One given as an expression of thankfulness should be eaten on the day it is offered (**7:15**). One given to fulfil a vow or as a freewill offering should be eaten on the day it is offered or on the following day. Any food that remains till the third day must be regarded as impure and must be burned (**7:16-17**). Anyone who eats it will be regarded as contracting the impurity (**7:18**).

The types of offerings described in 7:12-15 are similar to those described in 2:4-7. However, **7:13** is rather strange because it allows food mixed with yeast to be offered (an act that is forbidden in **7:12** and 6:17). However, it seems that during the time of the prophet Amos, worshippers brought leavened bread as a thanksgiving offering (Amos 4:5).

The second part of these regulations deals with the eating of sacrificial meat. Any meat that is impure must be burned, not eaten (**7:19**). The clean meat may only be eaten by those who are ceremonially clean. If an unclean person eats clean meat that is offered to the Lord, *that person must be cut off from his people* (**7:20**). The penalty of being 'cut off' from the community was meted out to those who neglected certain ritual duties (Gen 17:14; Exod 12:15, 19; Num 19:13, 20), undertook prohibited worship (Lev 17:3-4, 8-9; 20:2-6), undertook certain prohibited activities (18:29) and undertook improper ritual activities (Exod 30:31-33, 37-38; 31:14; Lev 7:20, 25, 27; 17:10, 14; 23:29-30). God would execute this death penalty.

In **7:22-27** the discussion on peace offerings is interrupted by a brief directive to all Israelites prohibiting the eating of fat and blood, which belong to the Lord (see 3:16-17).

The fat was supposed to be burned on the altar (3:3-5, 9-11, 14-16). This is followed by verses specifying the portions of the peace offering that were allotted to the clergy (**7:28-36**). The officiating clergy were to receive as their perpetual due the breast and the right thigh of the peace offering. The breast was given to the priest after it had been dedicated to the Lord by waving it before the Lord.

7:37-38 Conclusion

This section of the book of Leviticus ends with these verses, which function as a conclusion to chapters 1 to 7. According to **7:38**, God gave these regulations to Moses on Mount Sinai. However, in 1:1 they are described as having been spoken to Moses by God from the Tent of Meeting.

The scrupulous attention to the structure of ritual may seem strange to Christians, who are urged to worship God in spirit and truth. However, we need to remember that the second person in the Godhead became human. His incarnation shows that worship in spirit and truth must be expressed in concrete terms. It is through the body that worship is expressed, and a body has structure. In some ways, the rituals are comparable to the orders of service found in different denominations. Our God is a God of order (1 Cor 14:33) and so attention to the form of our worship is inseparable from its content.

8:1-10:20 Consecration of Aaron and His Sons

The instructions for the ordination of Aaron and his sons are given in Exodus 29:1-37, and Leviticus 8 relates how they were carried out. The manual about sacrificial offerings (Lev 1–7) separates them. This arrangement is probably adopted because the instructions about the sacrificial offerings are presupposed in the ordination ritual.

In the ordination process Moses offered sacrifices that signified the sinfulness of Aaron and his sons. These sacrifices were not offered just once; they had to be repeated annually (16:11, 34). This repetition underlined the continuing sinfulness of the priests. Although Christian ministers do not need to offer animal sacrifices because the blood of Christ cleanses them from all sin, they still need to acknowledge their sinful nature daily and to ask for God's forgiveness.

The repetition of the sacrifices also emphasized their ineffectiveness in removing sin once and for all. The Letter to the Hebrews picks up on this theme, and stresses that Jesus achieved all that the OT priests attempted to do. His sacrifice only needed to be offered once for all (Heb 7:27).

8:1-4 Preparation for Ordination

An ordination ceremony functions as a rite of passage whereby a person moves from one status to another. In this case Aaron and his sons move from the status of being laypersons in the realm of the ordinary to being priests in the divine realm. The ritual is performed at the entrance to the Tent of Meeting (8:3-4). This location is significant because it is the sacred place where the divine and the human meet. It is the place where sacrifices will be made and a place where all the people can be present as participants. The location also makes it clear that Aaron and his sons were still laity and were therefore not allowed to enter the Tent of Meeting. The persons and materials necessary for the ceremony were all brought to the entrance of the tent (8:2).

8:5-36 The Ritual of Ordination

After announcing that what was to be done was in accordance with God's commands (8:5), Moses began the ordination ritual. It involved the following steps.

8:5-9 Washing and robing

Moses washed Aaron and his sons in water (8:6), thereby identifying them as the ones who were going to be ordained. The washing was also a means of cleansing them, for ritual purity was necessary for the movement into the realm of the divine. After the washing, Aaron was dressed in the garments prepared for the high priest, including a coat and a robe (8:7-9; see also Exod 39:1-31). On top of the robe Moses put the *ephod*. This was a short linen garment, held in place by two shoulder straps that were attached to two of its corners and bound at the waist by a band (Exod 39:4-5).

A piece of cloth that was folded to make it into a square flat pouch, called a breastpiece, was tied over the ephod. Attached to this breastpiece were twelve precious stones, arranged in four rows of three each. These stones represented the twelve tribes of Israel (Exod 28:21) and indicated that the high priest represented all the tribes of Israel whenever he entered the Holy of Holies to minister before the Lord. Two small objects known as *Urim* and *Thummim* were put in the pouch of the breastpiece. Drawing these objects from the pouch would indicate whether the answer to a suitably put question was 'yes' or 'no' (Exod 28:30). Through the Urim and Thummim, the high priest represented God before the people.

On his head the high priest wore a turban, fixed to the front of which was a gold plate, the sacred diadem, on which were written the words 'Holy to the Lord' (Exod 39:30). The words implied that Aaron was separated to perform special functions for the glory of the Lord.

8:10-13 Anointing

Moses first anointed the Tent of Meeting and everything that was associated with it (8:10). Next, he anointed the altar of burnt offering and all its utensils (8:11), and lastly Aaron was anointed (8:12). The purpose of this anointing was to make the Tent of Meeting, the altar and Aaron holy,

as Yahweh is holy. Through this ritual, the attribute of holiness become shared by God and Israel.

Moses then dressed Aaron's sons in their priestly garments, marking them off as priests (8:13). However, unlike Aaron, they were not anointed.

8:14-17 Purification ritual

As pointed out in the discussion of 4:1-5:13, a purification ritual presupposes impurity resulting from human behaviour. This was the first time a purification ritual was performed using the altar in the Tent of Meeting. Because it was an inaugural act, it had to be performed by Moses (8:15a) since there were as yet no priests. In this context Moses functioned as a mediator through whom God's forgiveness was extended to Aaron. Moses also functioned as an instructor in an initiation rite, teaching by example. Moses slaughtered the animal for the purification offering, put some of its blood on the horns of the altar in order to purify it, and poured the rest at the base of the altar in order to consecrate it (8:15b). The fat on the entrails, the appendages of the liver and the two kidneys with their fat were burned on the altar of burnt offering. The rest of the carcass was burned outside the camp (8:16-17).

8:18-21 Burnt offering

The purification offering was followed by a burnt offering. As explained in the comments on 1:3-17, a burnt offering was a means through which forgiveness was extended to a worshipper. Here, too, the ritual performed by Moses functioned as a model for Aaron and his sons to learn from. Moses performed the ritual in accordance with the instructions given in 1:3-13 (8:18-21).

8:22-24 Induction rite

The rite of inducting or ordaining Aaron and his sons to their offices involved sacrificing another ram (8:22) and putting some of its blood on the lobes of their right ears, the thumbs of their right hands and the big toes of their right feet. The rest of the blood was *sprinkled against the altar on all sides* (8:23-24). A similar manipulation of blood is found in the ritual restoring of a person who suffered from a skin disease (14:13-14). This ritual involved materials – cedar wood, hyssop, and scarlet yarn (14:4) – that were also used in preparing water to cleanse those defiled by contact with a corpse (Num 19). Anyone suffering from skin disease was considered as good as dead (see Num 12:9-12). It thus appears that the anointing of Aaron and his sons with blood had something to do with a movement from death to life. This understanding of the priest's role is illustrated on the occasion when Aaron took fire in a censer and stood among the people to atone for them and stop the plague God had sent (Num 16:46-49). On that occasion Aaron literally stood between the people and Yahweh, between death and life.

Similarly, we are told that when the people were too afraid to approach the Tent of Meeting (Num 17:13), God chose the family of Aaron to perform the sacred rituals (Num 18:1-7). By the ritual of ordination, Aaron and his sons were located in a dangerous position between the holy God and the sinful Israelites.

8:25-29 Wave offering

Moses then assembled the materials for the wave offering: two cakes of bread (both made without yeast but one made with oil), a wafer, all the fat removed from the ram, and the right thigh (**8:25-26**). He placed these in the hands of Aaron and his sons and together they waved them before the Lord, thereby allowing Aaron to practise performing a wave offering (**8:27**). The ritual was meant to indicate the complete submission of Aaron and his sons to the will of God and the sanctity of their office. Then Moses burned the materials on the altar (**8:28**). Afterwards, Moses also waved the breast, which was his share (**8:29**).

8:30-36 Sprinkling and further instructions

Moses sprinkled Aaron, his sons and their garments with a mixture of the oil and the blood from the altar (**8:30**). Because the blood was from the altar, the rite symbolized their holiness and the connection between their priestly function and the altar.

Finally, Aaron and his sons were given further instructions. The first instructions relate to consumption of the sacrificial meal. This was to be prepared by Aaron and his sons and must be eaten at the entrance of the Tent of Meeting. Any meat that was left over must be burned (**8:31-32**).

Next, Aaron and his sons were instructed not to leave the entrance of the Tent of Meeting for seven days on pain of death (**8:33-35**). This instruction is similar to the practice in a number of African societies where an initiate is required to be in seclusion for a number of days. It was a time for the newly ordained priests to wait upon God, reflect on his attributes and on their new assignment, and die to the old life while rising to the new. The period of seven days symbolizes a complete period of transformation for Aaron that ushered him into the realm of the holy.

Other servants of God have also been called to spend time alone with him. Thus Moses spent forty days on the mountain (Exod 25:18; 34:28), Jesus was led to the wilderness for forty days after his baptism (Mark 1:13), and Paul spent time alone in the Arabian desert (Gal 1:17). What is important is not the length of time but the fact of time alone before the Lord.

9:1-24 The Priests Begin Their Ministry

9:1-7 Preparation

At the end of the week of seclusion, the new priests and the elders of Israel were instructed to prepare for the start of the priests' ministry by assembling the sacrifices needed for the purification, burnt and peace offerings (**9:2-4**). Then they and the people were to assemble before the entrance of the Tent of Meeting (**9:5**). Moses reported that what was being done was in accordance with the will of the Lord (**9:6a**) and that the offering would serve two purposes: the glory of the Lord would appear (**9:6b**) and atonement would be made for the priests and the people (**9:7**).

9:8-14 Purification and burnt offerings for the priests

Aaron began by offering the purification offering (**9:8-11**) and burnt offering (**9:12-14**) for the priests. The procedure followed here, with purification and burnt offerings for the clergy followed by purification and burnt offerings for the people, corresponds to the procedure followed on the Day of Atonement. The blood rite in the offerings for the clergy is different from that outlined earlier, for there is no mention of those aspects of the rite that were to be done inside the Tent of Meeting – the sprinkling of blood seven times in front of the curtain and the putting of some blood on the horns of the altar of incense (4:6-7). These elements are also missing in the purification ritual for a leader or an ordinary person (4:22-35). The burnt offering ritual for an ordinary person also lacks these elements. Thus what we have here are the simplest and most basic purification and burnt offering rituals.

9:15-21 Offerings for the people

Aaron (presumably again assisted by his sons) offered purification and burnt offerings on behalf of the congregation (**9:15-17**). The order of the offerings is the same as in 9:8-14, that is, a purification offering is followed by a burnt offering involving both animals and grain. There is a slight departure from the ritual in chapter 1 in that Aaron slaughtered the sacrificial animals rather than having it done by lay persons. After making the burnt offering, Aaron presented a peace offering for the congregation (**9:18-21**). Here the procedure is essentially the same as in 3:1-16, except that the slaughtering is done by the clergy and that Aaron waves the breast and the right thigh before the Lord as a wave offering to be eaten by the officiating clergy (7:28-34).

9:22-24 Divine approval

After the presentation of the sacrifices, Aaron turned to the people, lifted up his hands and blessed them. Then he stepped away from the altar (**9:22**), and he and Moses entered the Tent of Meeting. When they emerged from the tent, they again blessed the congregation. Immediately, the glory of the Lord appeared: fire came from the tabernacle and consumed the offerings that were on the altar (**9:23-24a**). The glory of the Lord signifies his presence and is symbolized by cloud and fire (Exod 19:9, 18), symbols that had accompanied the Israelites through their pilgrimage in the wilderness (Exod 40:38; Num 14:14). Thus the glory of the Lord was not only the basis of the covenant but also its seal. It was something the Israelites looked forward to. They recognized that if the Lord would not seal the temple ritual by his presence, the worship would be meaningless. The whole worship service was seen as a means to an end, the end being the presence of the Lord.

The congregation's response to the appearance of the glory of the Lord was to shout for joy and fall on their faces (**9:24b**). They recognized that Yahweh was really present with his people, that he had accepted the ordination of Aaron and his sons, and that he had accepted the offerings of both the clergy and the congregation. In other words, the priestly worship in the Tent of Meeting had been inaugurated with divine approval. Hence the joy of the people.

The NT is aware of the emptiness of a ritual where God is not present and insists that worship must be offered in spirit and truth (John 4:24). Jesus Christ manifests the glory of the Lord (1 Cor 2:8; John 1:14) and is present where people gather in his name (Matt 18:20). Just as the fire came out from the Tent of Meeting here, so at Pentecost the Spirit appeared in fire (Acts 2:3).

While one purpose of the event described in Leviticus was to witness the appearance of the glory of the Lord, its other purpose was said to be atonement (9:7). The exact relationship between these two purposes is not made clear. The event, though, is seen as a joyous one. It is not surprising that a peace offering accompanied it (9:18), for this offering evoked joy and celebration (see comments on 3:1-17), allowing human beings to express their deep-seated emotions. The Israelites were happy to see that Yahweh had accepted the ritual as means through which both his presence and forgiveness of sins were guaranteed.

10:1-20 Tragedy and Its Resolution

No sooner had priestly worship begun in the Tent of Meeting than tragedy struck when two sons of Aaron presented unauthorized fire to the Lord. As a result, fire came from the Lord and consumed them. This story illustrates how the Most Holy reacts when in contact with the impure. It also reveals the solemn responsibility of the priests in their ministry before the Lord.

This story is part of a pattern. Unauthorized fire is presented just as the priestly worship is inaugurated with divine approval. Similarly, the Israelites led by Aaron made themselves gods of gold at the same time that Moses was receiving the Ten Commandments from the Lord. Thus chapters 8–10 have a structure that juxtaposes beginnings and disruptions, order and chaos. The co-existence of the divine and the human, the holy and the profane, underlines the awesomeness of priesthood as an institution. Each time the divine presence is juxtaposed with sin, there is a reaction from the Lord. But the purpose of the reaction is not

to abolish the people or the priesthood. Rather, its purpose was to reform the priesthood. A similar thing happened in the flood story, (Gen 6:17) where God's reaction to sin leads to a new beginning.

This chapter has three parts: an account of the tragic event (10:1-7), instructions to the priests (10:8-15) and a resolution of the conflict between Moses and Aaron (10:16-20).

10:1-7 Tragic incident

Nadab and Abihu were performing their priestly duties when they prepared their censers and added incense. However, the fire they used was *unauthorized fire* (**10:1**), that is, fire that was not from the coals on the altar of burnt offerings. This was a violation of the holy, for holy fire must come from within the realms of the holy. Priests who intentionally offer strange fire must bear the consequences – death. Fire came from the presence of the Lord and consumed Nadab and Abihu (**10:2**). The same fire that had come from the presence of the Lord and consumed the offerings as a sign of God's approval now consumes the two priests as a sign of punishment.

Moses tried to explain the incident to Aaron by pointing out that the congregation was supposed to honour the Lord as the priests performed their duties (**10:3**). The welfare of the congregation depended on the priests' ministry, and therefore they bore a solemn responsibility to demonstrate the holiness of the Lord in all that they did. They would do this by taking pains to function within the bounds the Lord had laid down. The Lord himself would also act to protect the holy from improper intrusion

Moses then instructed Mishael and Elzaphan, who were not priests since they were the sons of Uzziel, Aaron's uncle, to carry the bodies of Nadab and Abihu away from the Tent of Meeting (**10:4**). Moses also forbade Aaron and his remaining sons from publicly mourning the two who had been destroyed by fire or leaving the entrance of the Tent of Meeting. However, the rest of the house of Israel could mourn for them (**10:6-7**).

10:8-11 Instructions to the priests

In order to ensure that Aaron and his sons could properly perform the priestly duties listed in 10:10-11, the Lord forbade them to drink wine or any strong drink (**10:8-9**). The reason for this prohibition is not explicitly stated. However, there is awareness in the OT that strong drink may lead to a lowering of one's level of understanding (Prov 20:1). The duties of the priests are defined as being to *distinguish between the holy and the common, between the unclean and the clean* (**10:10a**). The first group – holy and common – will be elaborated upon in chapters 17–26 and the second group – unclean and clean – in chapters 11–16. Any mistake in identifying the category to which something belonged could lead to death. To reduce the risk of such errors, the priests were forbidden to take strong drink before going on duty. Nazirites, too, abstained from taking strong drink as long as they were under their vow (Num 6:3-4; Judg 13:4-5).

The other duty of the priests was to *teach the Israelites all the decrees of the Lord* (**10:10b**). To give instruction properly, one must be in possession of all one's faculties.

10:12-20 Conflict between Moses and Aaron

Moses had instructed Aaron and his remaining sons to eat the remains of the grain offering in a holy place. They and their families were also told to eat the breast and thigh of the fellowship offering in a clean place (**10:12-15**). But when he inquired about the goat for the purification offering for the people, he discovered that it had been burned (**10:16**). He responded with anger because according to 6:30 (and 4:3-21) the purification offering was supposed to be burned only if its blood had been brought into the Tent of Meeting. The blood of this particular goat had not been brought into the Tent of Meeting (**10:18**). It should thus have been treated as a purification offering by a layperson (4:22-26, 27-35; compare 6:24-29) and eaten by the officiating clergy in order to make atonement for the people before the Lord.

Moses angrily asked Eleazar and Ithamar, *Why didn't you eat the sin [purification] offering in the sanctuary area?* (**10:17**). By not eating the purification offering, Aaron had not only violated divine rules, but had also shown disregard for the welfare of the people. Eating the purification offering was a crucial part of the process of divine forgiveness. Aaron responded by asking Moses whether, given that two of his sons had just been killed by divine fire, the Lord would have been pleased if he had eaten the offering (**10:19**). Aaron may have felt that because he was personally affected by the death of his two sons, it would have been improper to eat the offering. Or he may have feared that he too might be struck down like his sons if he ate the rest of the purification offering.

Aaron's response satisfied Moses (**10:20**). Although he did not condone Aaron's failure to eat the offering, he appreciated that Aaron's motive had been fear of God. Moses' satisfaction may also indicate that although we must be careful to obey God's commandments, the context in which we apply them must also be taken into account.

The episode recorded in this chapter illustrates a very important principle – the closer someone is to God, the stricter the standard by which he or she will be judged. Judah and Israel were judged precisely because God had chosen them out of all the nations of the earth to be his own people (Amos 3:2). Jesus said, 'From everyone who has been given much, much will be demanded' (Luke 12:48). The priests were consecrated so that they could draw near to God to offer sacrifices on behalf of the people. Therefore they needed to be extra careful in their performance of their duties knowing that they were serving a holy God.

It is encouraging, though, to note that in spite of this lapse on the part of the priests, God did not reject them outright. He found it fit to speak directly to Aaron and gave him advice. A holy God hates sin, but loves sinners and wants them to reform.

11:1-16:34 Laws regarding Purity

11:1-47 Dietary Laws

The priests had been told that they were responsible for distinguishing between what is unclean and clean (10:10). This chapter now spells out which animals are clean and which are not (11:2-23), and which animals' carcasses can defile through contact (11:24-40). It concludes with a summary of what has been said (11:41-47).

11:1-23 Clean and unclean animals

The introduction in 11:1-2 makes it clear that dietary laws are connected with obedience to God. Various animals living on land (11:2-8), in the seas and streams (11:9-12), and flying in the air (11:13-23) are categorized as either clean or unclean. Clean animals can be eaten and unclean animals must not be eaten.

Various explanations have been offered for why particular animals were declared to be clean or unclean. For example, it has been suggested that the eating of pigs was forbidden because they carried diseases and ate waste matter. Others have argued that the animals that the law declares unclean may have been used as sacrificial animals in other religions or may have been tribal totems. These explanations are flawed because there is no evidence of such totems and because, with the exception of pigs, Israel sacrificed much the same animals as the other peoples in the ancient Near East. Another possible explanation says that the dietary laws were intended to symbolize ethical principles such as restraint, withdrawal, a reverence for life, and moderation in action, thought and feeling. Ecology and the role of specific animals in agriculture play a role in other explanations. Yet another explanation says that the Israelites thought of particular animals as perfect examples of their type and rejected animals that did not fit clearly into a particular class. Finally, it is said by some that the Israelites were allowed to eat only animals that were similar to those offered in sacrifice to remind them that they must be holy because Yahweh is holy.

Clearly, none of the theories outlined above is sufficient to explain all the dietary laws. Instead, the different theories supplement one other, as a closer look at the dietary laws will show.

11:2-8 LAND ANIMALS Members of the covenant community were allowed to eat any land animal that chews the cud and has a split hoof that is completely divided (**11:2-3**). Although we are not given examples of such animals, the definition does cover the main domestic animals, namely, cattle, sheep and goats. Any beast that lacks one or both of these characteristics must not be eaten. The author then goes on to list specific animals that should not be eaten. The camel, the coney and the rabbit are excluded because they do not have split hooves (**11:4-6**) and the pig is excluded because it does not chew the cud (**11:7**). (Camels do not, in fact, have hooves, and coneys and hares do not chew the cud. But these three were excluded, because they did not belong to the group of animals that were recognized as food animals. Thus characteristics that were associated with food animals were applied to these animals.) A person who eats the meat of an unclean animal or touches its carcass is defiled (**11:8**).

Here it seems that the basis for classification is whether the animal could be used for sacrifice or not. This classification can be interpreted theologically by noting that as God had limited the animals that might be sacrificed to him, so he had chosen one nation out of all the peoples on the face of the earth to be his treasured possession and a holy nation (Deut 7:6; Exod 19:6). In this context, it is worth noting that Deuteronomy introduces the dietary laws with a reference to Israel's election (Deut 14:1-2). The classification is therefore symbolic of Israel's covenantal relationship with God.

11:9-12 WATER ANIMALS All aquatic animals are classified on the basis of whether they have fins and scales. Water creatures that do not have these features are unclean and should not be eaten (**11:10-12**). It has been suggested that scales and fins are regarded here as the normal covering and means of locomotion for creatures that live in water. Being told to limit themselves to eating only the 'normal' members of the fish world reminded the Israelites that as a covenant people of God they must lead lives that conform to the moral and spiritual norms of God's world.

11:13-23 CREATURES THAT FLY We are first given a list of unclean birds (**11:13-19**). It has been argued that the common characteristic of the unclean birds is that all of them, except for the hoopoe and the bat, are consumers of either carrion or live prey, or both. These birds were killers, blood-drinkers. The reasoning underlying this law may be that animals owned by Israelites were also supposed to obey the covenant law. Both domestic animals and humans were supposed to obey the law of the Sabbath (Exod 20:10), and the firstborn of both human beings and animals were consecrated to the Lord (Exod 22:29-30). These birds can be said to have violated the fundamental principle of not eating flesh with blood in it, the same principle that applied

to eating 'the meat of an animal torn by wild beasts' (Exod 22:31). For this reason they are declared as unclean.

The discussion of birds of prey is followed by a discussion of insects (11:20-23). Unclean insects are defined as those that *walk on all fours* (**11:20, 23**). The only exceptions are those insects that have *jointed legs for hopping on the ground* (**11:21-22**). The reason why insects that walk on all fours are considered unclean is that they move in a way contrary to nature. Land animals have four legs. These insects, however, fly in the air with their wings, but walk on four feet when they are on the ground. There is a discord between the way they move and the way they appear, and thus they are declared unclean. But insects with jointed legs are declared clean because they hop, which is appropriate for creatures with wings.

The same interpretation applied to the rules on water animals can be applied to the classification of insects. Israel as a covenant people must conform to the norms of the covenant God. The principle of conforming to nature underlines the theological truth that God is a God of order. This order is expressed in sets of opposites that are found in the first creative narrative (Gen 1:1-2:3). God created day by separating darkness from light. He created the firmament by separating the waters above from the waters below. Similarly, in Leviticus the distinction between clean and unclean is a reflection of the concern for order. This order reflected social realities. Just as God separated the opposites of darkness and light at creation, so Israel, too, must make a distinction between herself and other nations. The prohibitions on certain foods in Leviticus 11 can thus be interpreted symbolically as Israel's attempt to preserve the sacred order created by God who made a covenant with them, and to fight against anything that would disturb that order.

11:24-40 Impurity through the flesh of dead animals

The previous verses have classified animals, birds and insects into two groups: those that are unclean and those that are clean. The question though is whether the uncleanness was contagious. The answer is threefold. First, it is said that the carcasses of both clean and unclean creatures are unclean, and this uncleanness is contagious. Second, an unclean creature that is living cannot transmit its impurity to anyone or anything. Third, the impurity that passes to a person or object is temporary and purification mechanisms are available.

The principle behind these instructions is that of order in terms of the binary opposition between death and life. The concern was to maintain the boundary between the realm of death and the realm of life. Every Israelite was made responsible for guarding the purity of the covenanted community against any intrusion of impurity. Here the source of impurity was the touching, carrying or eating of a dead unclean land animal. The passage can be divided into four subsections: 11:24-25; 26-28; 29-38; 39-40.

The first subsection (**11:24-25**) simply introduces 'touching' and 'carrying' as the ways through which a person could contract impurity. When it comes to the requirement for purification, a person needed only to wait till evening (11:24). No mention is made of any ritual for purification, but it may be assumed that washing in water was required. After all, if anything on which a dead animal fell had to be washed (11:32), how much more a human being.

The second section (**11:26-28**) applies the rules to land creatures. The principle found in 11:3-4 is repeated in 11:26. It is repeated yet again in 11:27, but here it is phrased in terms of land animals that walk on their paws. The Hebrew word translated as 'paw' usually means 'hand'. This suggests that animals with paws that appear like hands are behaving abnormally by using their hands for walking. The use of an inappropriate means of locomotion makes them unclean. Anyone touching the carcasses of such animals will be unclean till evening. Carrying the carcass of a dead unclean animal was considered more serious than touching it, and so anyone who carries the dead body of such an animal will have to wash his clothes and be unclean till evening (11:27-28). Whereas touching assumed light contact, carrying implies that the contact was for a longer period or that there was greater intensity of pressure of the carcass on the clothes. Consequently a double act of purification was required: not only must the person wash his or her clothes, but he or she will remain unclean till evening (11:25).

The third section (11:29-38) discusses creeping land animals. The list of animals in **11:29-31** includes most reptiles and small mammals that would infest houses and storerooms. The impurity from the carcasses of these animals affected not only humans but also household objects. If a carcass of any of these animals fell on an article made of wood, cloth, hide or sackcloth, it became impure and must be washed and would be unclean till evening (**11:32**). If the carcass fell in an earthenware vessel, then everything in the vessel, including any water in it, would become polluted and the vessel must be broken (**11:33-34**). If the carcass fell on a cooking utensil, that object became polluted and must be broken (**11:35**). All these instructions reflect the fear that the impurity generated by the carcass of any of these creeping land animals could be transmitted to humans through food and cooking.

Some exceptions to these instructions were allowed. Thus even if a carcass falls in a spring, the water remains clean (**11:36**). However, the carcass itself will still transmit impurity to anything it comes into contact with. Seed that is dry remains clean even after a carcass has fallen on it. However, a carcass will transmit impurity to seed that has had water put on it (**11:37-38**).

The fourth section (**11:39-40**) discusses the impurity generated by carcasses of clean animals that died naturally rather than being slaughtered. Such carcasses, too, are impure and must not be touched, carried or eaten.

11:41-47 Conclusion

In the concluding section, the simplest rule is repeated. *Every creature that moves about on the ground is detestable; it is not to be eaten* (**11:41**). To ignore this rule makes one unclean (**11:43-44**). The state of uncleanness is contrary to the calling of the Israelites. The Israelites were called to imitate the covenant God. They were called to be holy because God is also holy (11:44). The second motive for leading a holy life on the part of the Israelites was their election and deliverance from the Egyptian bondage (**11:45**).

The dietary laws were a cause for great controversy in the NT for two reasons. First, Jews regarded the dietary laws as visible marks of their distinctiveness as the chosen people of God. Second, Jesus seemed to abrogate the dietary laws when he said, 'Nothing that enters a man from the outside can make him unclean … What comes out of a man is what makes him unclean' (Mark 7:18, 20). The evangelist then concluded that 'Jesus declared all foods clean' (Mark 7:19). Jesus broke the rules that distinguish between clean and unclean creatures.

The problem became acute when the gospel was taken into Gentile areas. The story of Cornelius is interesting because in it the food laws are interpreted in social terms. The distinction between clean and unclean animals is seen as representing the distinction between Jews and Gentiles, and one Peter is accused of regarding as unclean what God has cleansed (Acts 11:4-12). Peter used his experience at a religious conference in Jerusalem that was convened to settle the problems arising from missions to Gentile areas. He argued that 'God made no distinction between us (Jews) and them (Gentiles), for he purified their hearts by faith' (Acts 15:9). The conference then agreed to advise the Gentile converts 'to abstain from food sacrificed to idols, from blood, from the meat of strangled animals and from sexual immorality' (Acts 15:29). The Jerusalem Council thus abolished both the requirement of circumcision for Christians and the distinction between clean and unclean animals. The theological basis for the decision of the Jerusalem Council was that whereas circumcision and the distinction between clean and unclean animals applied to the special status of Israel, the prohibition of blood applied to all human beings because its roots could be traced back to the time of Noah (Gen 9:4).

Although the dietary laws have been abolished, Leviticus 11 is still relevant for Christians today. The reinterpretation of the laws by Jesus means that more emphasis must be placed on moral purity than on ritual purity. The dietary laws had reminded the Israelites that they were a chosen people, holy to God. God through Christ has also chosen Christians to be holy. Whereas the Jews strove to express their unique status through obedience to the dietary laws, Christian must express their uniqueness through obedience to God's will as it is revealed in the Bible.

Some African cultures also fear the transmission of impurity through food. Such cultures forbid women who are in an impure state (that is, during their menstrual periods and immediately after giving birth) to prepare food or to add salt to a dish. African Christians need to be reminded about the dangers of moral impurity and the seriousness of sin, which is what truly defiles a person. It is noteworthy in this context that the object of the cleansing work of the blood of Jesus is the conscience. Ritual purity has its place, but it should go together with moral purity.

12:1-8 Impurity and Childbirth

This chapter deals with the impurity generated by childbirth, which was assumed to make the mother unclean. It raises a number of problems for modern readers. For example, why is the purification period longer when the child is female than when it is male? If the child is a boy, the mother's initial period of uncleanness is seven days, as during her menstruation (**12:2-4**; see also 15:19-30). If the child is female, the initial period of uncleanness lasts fourteen days (**12:5**).

During this period of uncleanness, the mother's impurity could be communicated to anything she touched or slept on. This initial period was followed by a further period of uncleanness lasting 33 days or 66 days (again depending on the gender of the child), during which the restrictions imposed upon her were reduced to not being allowed to touch anything holy or enter the Tent of Meeting. She was thus free to conduct domestic activities and even to have a sexual relationship with her husband. These regulations show that purification was a process involving only the woman and the Lord. The whole process was monitored by the woman herself and not by the priest.

After the period of purification was over (40 days for a male child and 80 days for a female child) the new mother brought two offerings to the Tent of Meeting: a burnt offering and a purification offering (**12:6-8**). The purification offering would probably have been given first, for the purpose of cleansing the altar of sacrifice and rededicating it for sacrifices. Through it the altar was restored for holy use. The burnt offering was for atonement, which allowed the woman to participate in religious services once again.

Note that it is only the woman who becomes unclean; the child is not considered unclean, and as a result the child is never subjected to purification ritual. By contrast, in many African societies both the child and its mother are considered unclean and must undergo purification rituals. For example, among the Tsonga of Mozambique, both mother and child are kept in seclusion for a month, after which the infant is taken out and washed in purifying water containing salt. Among the Christians of Garantia Apostolic Church of Zion, this washing is combined with the reading of Leviticus 12:1-5.

The meaning of the ritual is difficult to determine. For example, one wonders why a woman was considered unclean and in need of purification after giving birth when barrenness was considered a curse (Gen 15:1-3; 1 Sam 1) and childbirth a sign of God's blessing (Gen 1:28). It seems that a connection is being made between a woman who had given birth and a menstruating woman. Just as the blood of a menstruating woman makes her unclean, so the bleeding associated with birth makes the new mother unclean. Why is this so? There are several possibilities. One is that since blood was a symbol of life, and life belonged to God, it could only be offered back to God on the altar found at the Tent of Meeting. Any shedding of blood outside the holy premises was abnormal and sacrilegious. However, a woman's shedding of blood was not deliberate, and was thus one of the unintentional sins requiring a purification offering. The flaw in this argument is that if this were the case, one would expect the blood shed when a male child was circumcised would make him unclean. But it clearly did not, for the ritual of circumcision did not involve a purification offering.

Another possible explanation is to regard the whole process in terms of death and life. Blood is a symbol of life and its loss symbolizes death or imperfection. The ritual was then a 'rite of passage' whereby the new woman moved from the realm of death to life, from imperfection to wholeness and perfection.

The context of the passage perhaps provides us with another possible answer regarding the meaning of the ritual. The previous chapter dealt with external sources of defilement. The present one as well as the following chapters deal with internal sources of defilement. God called upon Israel as a people separated to him to be on guard against external threats to their status. In the present chapter, bodily discharge reminded Israelites of internal threats to their status.

13:1-14:57 Infectious Skin Diseases

The NIV uses *infectious skin disease* to translate the Hebrew word *tsara'at* (13:2). It is not clear exactly what 'tsara'at' was, for the symptoms do not correspond to any known skin diseases. From the description in this chapter, we gather that it affects both humans (13:2-46) and inanimate objects such as clothing (13:47-59) and the walls of houses (14:33-53). It is clearly not the same as leprosy. The confusion with leprosy has arisen because tsara'at was translated into Greek as *lepra*, a word that was used by some ancient Greek writers such as Hippocrates as a generic term for various kinds of skin diseases. The translators of the KJV then mistranslated the word 'lepra' as 'leprosy.'

The text of chapter 13 must not be approached from a medical perspective. The priests were not doctors, and those afflicted were not their patients. The focus here is on the religious system of impurity. Counting the words confirms this point. In chapters 13–14, the Hebrew word for 'pure' appears thirty-six times and the Hebrew word for 'impure' appears thirty times, but the Hebrew word for 'heal' appears only four times. We are therefore dealing with ritual rather than medicine. The priest was a specialist in ritual matters.

The view that tsara'at must be discussed within the context of ritual rather than medicine is confirmed by the way it was to be handled (14:1-56). The priest's responsibility was simply to determine whether a person was unclean or not so that the affected person could be isolated. Once the affected person had been isolated, the priest had nothing to do with any treatment offered. It was only when the infectious skin disease had healed that the priest was again involved, as he was called on to certify that the healing had indeed taken place. It was the responsibility of the afflicted person to pray (1 Kgs 8:37-40; 2 Kgs 20:1-2) and fast (2 Sam 12:16) in order to seek God's healing. Thus what is presented in this text is a religious rather than a therapeutic act. It is a symbolic ritual.

Although tsara'at was often believed to be a form of divine punishment (see Num 12:9; 2 Kgs 5:27; 2 Chr 26:18-21), in chapters 13–14 tsara'at is not regarded as such. In fact, the ritual process does not involve any investigation of sin.

In the priestly impurity system, tsara'at was associated with death. Its bearer was considered as a corpse. Thus when Miriam was struck by tsara'at, Aaron prayed: 'Let not her be like a stillborn infant' (Num 12:12). In the book of Job, tsara'at is also identified with death (Job 18:13). The instructions on purity and impurity in these chapters therefore focus on the integrity and wholeness of the body.

13:1-8 First set of tests for diagnosis of skin diseases

The introduction (**13:1**) is followed by instructions on how to distinguish an infectious skin disease from one that is not. Anyone who develops a swelling, a rash or a bright spot on their skin and suspects that they are suffering from such a disease must go to a priest, who will examine the skin to determine whether the suspicion is correct (**13:2**). (Note that the NIV translation 'swelling' may not be altogether correct; a better translation might be 'discolouration', implying that the initial sign of the skin disease is a change in skin colour.) An infectious disease is characterized by the hair on the skin near the sore turning white and the sore itself being more than skin deep (**13:3**). If the person did not exhibit the disease in a sufficiently developed form, he or she could be quarantined for a period of time until a

proper diagnosis could be made. If the disease was found to be spreading, it was regarded as an infectious skin disease (**13:4-8**).

Those found to have skin diseases were declared ceremonially unclean and had to live alone, excluded from the camp. They left their hair unkempt, wore torn clothes and covered the lower parts of their faces (13:45-46).

13:9-17 Second set of tests for diagnosis of skin diseases

The characteristics of a chronic disease include the hair of the skin turning white and the presence of raw flesh (**13:10**). The presence of raw flesh is the fourth of the symptoms for infectious skin disease. If the disease being referred to here is psoriasis, which is a chronic skin disease, then the raw flesh is the tiny reddish patches of various sizes resulting from the rubbing off of the scales caused by the disease. There is no need to quarantine those with these symptoms; they are already unclean (**13:11**). If the skin disease had covered the whole body of the affected person and also turned white, then the affected person was declared clean (**13:12-13**). The presence of raw flesh was determinative for declaring one to be clean or unclean (**13:14-15**). If the raw flesh turned white, then the affected person was declared clean (**13:16-17**).

13:18-28 Tests for skin diseases in cases of boils and burns

A white swelling or a reddish-white spot that appeared on the site of a healed boil had to be examined by a priest (**13:18-19**). If the inflammation was *more than skin deep and the hair in it has turned white,* then it was a skin disease (**13:20**) and the affected person was declared unclean. In cases of doubt, a quarantine period of seven days is prescribed until a proper diagnosis is reached (**13:21-23**).

An infected burn that produced a reddish-white or white spot was potentially unclean (**13:24**). The priest has to examine it to determine whether the basic characteristics of a skin disease – the hair had turned white and the lesion was more than skin deep – are present (**13:25**). In cases of doubt, a quarantine period of seven days is prescribed until proper diagnosis is reached (**13:26-28**).

13:29-37 Tests for skin disease in the head or beard

An infection on the head or, in the case of men, on the chin was potentially unclean (**13:29**). If the priest certified that symptoms of infectious skin disease were present (the sore was more than skin deep, and the hair had turned yellow) then the affected person was declared unclean (**13:30**). The yellowing of the hair is the fifth symptom of an infectious skin disease. In cases of doubt, the affected person could be isolated for two weeks until proper diagnosis was reached (**13:31-34**). If a relapse occurred after someone had been declared clean, then mere spread of the disease in the skin was sufficient to declare the person unclean (**13:35-36**).

On the other hand, the growth of new black hair was a sufficient indication that healing had taken place (**13:37**).

13:38-39 A harmless skin disease

The NIV calls the dull white skin eruption *a harmless rash* (13:37). Unlike the other skin diseases, this one does not go deeper than the skin and the hairs of the skin are not discoloured.

13:40-44 Baldness and skin disease

Ordinary baldness, whether starting from the forehead or the scalp, was clean (**13:40-41**), unless it was marked by reddish-white sores (**13:42**). If it was, the priest had to examine the man, and if he had reddish-white patches like those of a boil (13:19) or a burn (13:24), he was declared unclean (**13:43-44**).

13:45-46 Treatment of those with infectious skin disease

Those who had been diagnosed as suffering from *tsara'at* and were therefore ceremonially unclean and capable of defiling others adopted the posture of mourners. They tore their clothes, allowed their hair to become unkempt, covered their beard or moustache, and cried 'Unclean!' to prevent people from defiling themselves by touching them (**13:45**). Furthermore, they had to go and live outside the camp, either alone or in company with others suffering from similar skin diseases (**13:46**). Those who were unclean were cut off from social and spiritual fellowship with the covenant people of God. They were nothing more than the living dead. In a real sense, being outside the holy camp where God resided, they were without hope. The people of ancient Israel would have understood the Chewa proverb from Malawi *Kali konka n'kanyama, tili awiri n'tianthu* ['What is by itself is a little animal, those that are two are human beings']. Like people in some African societies, they dreaded solitary living.

13:47-59 'Skin disease' in clothing

The two basic symptoms of the presence of an infectious 'skin disease' in clothing are the presence of greenish or reddish spots and whether they have spread over the clothing. Any woollen or linen clothing or anything made of leather that exhibited a greenish or reddish mildew was potentially unclean and had to be examined by a priest (**13:47-49**). If the diagnosis was doubtful, the article was isolated for seven days (**13:50**). If, upon examination on the seventh day, the mildew was found to have spread over the clothing or the leather, then the article was declared unclean and had to be destroyed (**13:51-52**). If the mildew had not spread, the article was washed and isolated for another seven days. If after that period the colour had not changed, even though the mildew had not spread, the article was declared unclean and had to be destroyed (**13:53-55**). If the mildew had not spread and the colour had faded, only the affected parts of the article had to be removed (**13:56**). Should the mildew reappear and spread over the article, it was unclean and had to be destroyed (**13:57**). Finally, if after the second week the mildew had disappeared, the article was washed again and declared clean (**13:58**).

These regulations should be interpreted in relation to the issue of wholeness. Holiness is symbolized by wholeness. Any deformity or abnormality was regarded as unclean. Animals to be used as sacrifices had to be without blemish. Living creatures whose ways of locomotion were abnormal were regarded as unclean. Priests, too, were supposed to be without any defilement if they were to serve before the Lord. The Israelites as people of the covenant were called upon to lead lives that corresponded to their status.

14:1-32 Cleansing rites for those healed

The cleansing rites for a person cured from infectious skin disease involved three ceremonies: one on the first day (14:2-8), another on the seventh day (14:9) and a third on the eighth day (14:10-32). The ritual on the first day was performed by the priest outside the camp from which the stricken person had been banished (**14:3**). Cedar wood, scarlet yarn, hyssop and a wild bird were dipped into a vessel containing fresh water and the blood of a second wild bird. The cured person was then sprinkled with this water seven times, after which the wild bird was set free (**14:4-7**). Then he washed his clothes, shaved off all his hair, and washed his body. After this he was declared clean and was admitted into the camp (**14:8**). The first day of the purification rite rendered the healed person incapable of contaminating persons or vessels by mere proximity. Whereas previously the healed person had been 'socially dead' because he or she had been banished from the camp, he or she is now 'socially alive' after returning to the community. In fact 'life' seems to be the basic theme of this ritual with its use of wild birds, fresh water, and blood and other red materials.

Although the person was now permitted to enter the camp, he or she must not enter his or her tent for a further seven days (14:8). No such restriction was placed on a new mother in chapter 12. It is clear that the impurity of someone with an infectious skin disease was far more severe than that of a new mother. Even after the first rite of purification, a healed person could still contaminate the common by direct contact and the holy by proximity. The exclusion from the home meant that any sacred items there, such as donations to the temple, would not risk being contaminated.

The second stage of cleansing was at the end of seven days. On the seventh day the healed person shaved off all his hair, washed his clothes, and then washed his body in water. After this the person was again declared clean and permitted to enter his tent or house (**14:9**). The washing had reduced the severity of the impurity. The healed person could no longer contaminate any holy item by mere proximity. However, he could still contaminate them by direct touch, and so sacrifices were required on the eighth day in order to eliminate the remaining impurity (**14:10**).

The third stage of cleansing was the offering of burnt, cereal, reparation and purification offerings at the Tent of Meeting. The materials required for this included *two male lambs and one ewe lamb a year old, each without defect, along with three-tenths of an ephah* (about 12 pints or 6 litres) *of fine flour mixed with oil, and one log* (about half a pint or one-third of a litre) *of oil* (14:10).

The ritual started with the priest bringing to the entrance of the Tent of Meeting both the person to be purified and the materials for the ritual (**14:11**). The reparation offering was presented first. The blood of the lamb for the reparation offering was put on the lobe of the right ear, on the thumb of the right hand and on the big toe of the right foot of the one to be cleansed (**14:12-14**). This blood rite is similar to the one used in the ordination of priests (8:23-24). Like ordination, this rite symbolized the transference of a person from death to life. Next, the oil that was used in the wave offering was sprinkled seven times before the Lord and then put on the same extremities as the blood of reparation (**14:15-18**). The oil may symbolize the new life the healed person is experiencing. It is surprising that a reparation offering is used in this instance. According to 5:1-4 and 5:14-19 a reparation offering was required in cases of trespass against sacred property, suspected trespass and false oaths. The person to be cleansed had probably not committed the first and third of these sins, so it seems likely that this reparation offering was given for 'suspected trespass' (see 14:18 where the function of the rite is 'atonement'). After the reparation offering, the priest offered a purification offering to cleanse and rededicate the altar of sacrifice for holy use (**14:19**). Finally a burnt offering was offered for expiation purposes (**14:20**).

The purification ritual for a poor person is described in 14:21-32. He was allowed to bring one male lamb instead of two, and one-tenth of an ephah of fine flour mixed with oil instead of three-tenths. He was also to bring two doves or two young pigeons instead of a ewe lamb (**14:21-22**). The lamb and oil were used for the reparation offering (**14:23-29**). The ritual is similar to that outlined in 14:15-18. One of the two doves or two pigeons that the healed person brought was used for the purification offering and the other for the burnt offering (**14:30-31**).

What did this ritual symbolize? There are at least two points to be noted. First, the Levitical law provided no means of curing infectious skin disease. Sufferers were banished from society and their only hope was in God. Any cure that eventually came was from God. This adds significance to Jesus' healing of those with skin diseases as he came to

seek and save the lost. As God, he dealt with the sufferer's physical problem.

Second, the sufferer's problem was also a social one. Before the priest declared a person clean, he or she lived alone, outside the camp. In effect they were socially dead. The purification ritual started only after the infectious skin disease had healed. Thus the ritual was aimed at socially bringing the 'dead' person back to life and reintegrating him or her into society. The purification ritual was thus a 'rite of passage' marking a transition from death to life. It was also a rite of passage in that the healed person was reconciled with God.

14:33-57 Houses affected by mildew

If the occupants of a house discovered something like mildew in the house, they had to report it to a priest, for it might be an infectious 'skin disease' (14:35). The house had to be emptied of its contents immediately before the priest came to check it, for fear that everything might be declared unclean (**14:36**). The priest looked for the basic symptoms of an infectious skin disease, namely greenish or reddish depressions that were deeper than the surface of the wall (**14:37**). In cases of doubt, the house was closed for seven days until a proper diagnosis was reached (**14:38**). If on the second inspection it is established that the mildew had spread on the walls (**14:39**), the first remedy was to remove all the contaminated stones and throw them into an unclean place outside the town. Any plaster inside must also be scraped off and the scraped material thrown into an unclean place outside the town (**14:40-41**). After this the house should be repaired by putting in new stones and new plaster (**14:42**). Should the mildew reappear, the whole house would be pulled down and the debris dumped in an unclean place outside the town (**14:43-45**).

Anyone who entered the house while it was quarantined became contaminated until evening. Those who slept or ate there also had to wash their clothes (**14:46-47**). The passage is silent about the priest who entered the house. Were the priests immune to contagion, or did the priest, like any layperson, have to bathe and abstain from contact with the sacred until evening?

If the mildew disappeared after the house was replastered, the house was purified and declared clean (**14:48-53**). The ritual for purifying a house involved two birds, some cedar wood, scarlet yarn and hyssop and was similar to the one done for a person healed from skin disease (see 14:4-7).

The fact that the purification rituals for a person healed from skin disease and for a house that had been infected by skin disease are the same gives us an indication of the nature of *tsara'at*. The infectious skin disease has nothing to do with the moral life of the affected persons or things. How could morality be attributed to a house? The statement in **14:34** that God has put the mildew on the affected house does not mean that this was a punishment for a sin committed by the occupants. If an occupant suspected that a 'skin disease' might have infected a house, a priest was called to verify this suspicion. If an infection was diagnosed, the house was destroyed; if no infection was found, the house was purified. Nothing was done to or for the owner of the affected house. The occupant of the house was not even required to bring sacrifices, as was the person infected with skin disease. It is also worth noting that some of Israelites' neighbours believed that demons or occupants of the affected house caused mildew. However, the Israelites attributed its occurrence to neither.

The topics covered in chapters 13 and 14 are briefly listed in **14:54-57**.

15:1-33 Bodily Discharges

This chapter discusses the impurity associated with different types of flows, both normal and abnormal, from the reproductive organs of both males and females. But what is the significance of the regulations in this chapter? In the discussion on clean and unclean animals, a number of possible explanations for this distinction were given. Is it possible to apply any of those theories to the regulations on bodily discharge?

The first point to be made is that the whole issue of purity and impurity is symbolic. Simply looking at the bearers of impurity can support this conclusion. These included persons who committed an unintentional sin (5:2-13), mothers of newborn children (12:1-8), persons, clothing and houses with infectious skin disease (13:1-14:57), males and females with a bodily discharge (15:2-30), one who handles the scapegoat (16:27-28), a corpse-contaminated priest (Ezek 44:25-27), a corpse-contaminated Nazirite (Num 6:9-12), and a corpse-contaminated lay person (11:24-40; 22:4; Num 5:2-3). Not all the cases in the list are associated with disease or disorder. In fact, if it were dealing with diseases, then quite a number have been left out. In some respects, the list appears to be arbitrary. What may, however, link these categories is the issue of death and life, which is handled using the system of impurity and purity. In the context of bodily discharges of semen and menstrual blood, the fluids represent the forces of life and their loss represents death.

Death is a negation of wholeness or perfection. In the priestly laws, anything imperfect was ritually unclean and was unfit for divine service. Blemished animals could not be used for sacrifices. Priests with bodily imperfections were precluded from officiating in the Tent of Meeting. This shows that holiness was symbolized by wholeness or perfection. Because bodily discharges represented death, they were incompatible with holiness.

The rules dealt with in this chapter also locate sexual activity in the wider context of religion and ritual, making it clear that it is not merely a commonplace activity but also has a religious dimension. The reproductive organs are theologically related to creation and to God's promise of many descendants. Thus the human body and sexual activity need to be made subjects of theological reflection and ritual.

15:2-15 Abnormal male discharge

The abnormal male discharge may be either an uncontrollable free flow or an uncontrollable sluggish, thick flow of fluid (**15:3**). The identity of this particular discharge is not clear, but it is certainly not semen. Some people have suggested that it may have been a symptom of gonorrhoea. Whatever it was, this discharge seems to have prevented normal sexual activity, and thus the conception of children. Such a discharge thus negated the divine blessing when male and female were created (Gen 1:28) and the divine promise to Abraham (Gen 15:5). It symbolized the end of community, for without children a community is as good as dead. This is why such a discharge was pronounced unclean, although it was not regarded as having been caused by sin (**15:2**; see the discussion of *tsara'at* at 13:1-14:57).

Unlike someone with an infectious skin disease, a man with an abnormal discharge was not banished from the community. Consequently there was a risk that the impurity associated with his discharge could be transmitted to other persons and objects. The text gives examples of situations in which a man's impurity could be transmitted to other persons (15:5-11). The bed on which he lay and any object he sat on became impure (**15:4**). A person could contract impurity by touching the bed on which the person with a discharge had lain, a seat on which he had sat, or the person himself (**15:5-7**). A person with a discharge could transmit impurity by spitting on someone (**15:8**) or by touching anyone without first rinsing his hands (**15:11**). A person could also contract impurity by carrying something the person with a discharge had sat on (**15:10**). Any clay pot or wooden article that he touched became unclean (**15:12**). The impurity was clearly regarded as being strong enough to affect persons and objects indirectly.

According to 15:11 the person with a discharge did not transmit impurity if he rinsed his hands in water before touching another person. This implies that provided he regularly rinsed his hands in water, he could stay at home without posing a danger to those around him. There was thus no need to banish him from the community.

Two purification processes are outlined for persons and objects that contracted impurity from someone with a discharge. All persons who became unclean through direct contact must wash their clothes, bathe in water and wait till evening to be clean (15:5-11). Any clay pot touched by the unclean person must be broken, and every wooden article they touched must be washed in water (15:12).

After the discharge had stopped, the healed person had to undergo a purification process. We are not told how the discharge stopped. The priests took no part in the physical healing. It would not be wrong to conclude that it was Yahweh who healed the person. This is significant because if the discharge threatened God's creation and promises, it was also God who intervened to redress the situation.

The first step in the purification rite is to wait for seven days. A seven-day period was also observed in the ordination of Aaron (8:33) and in the recovery of a person suffering from an infectious skin disease (14:8-9). It seems to have been a feature of rites of passage in which a person moved from one state to another.

On the seventh day, the man washed his clothes, bathed in fresh water and was clean (**15:13**). Fresh or running water was a symbol of life, just as impurity was a symbol of death. Fresh water was also used in the cleansing of a person suffering from an infectious skin disease (14:5-6).

Although the man was now declared clean, he was still not allowed to enter the Tent of Meeting. He was clean as far as common objects and people were concerned, but not where the holy objects in the Tent of Meeting were concerned. Thus on the eighth day he had to bring two turtledoves or two pigeons to the entrance to the Tent of Meeting, one for a purification offering and the other for a burnt offering (**15:14-15**). In this way the person was finally reconciled with God.

15:16-17 Normal male discharge

The emission of semen referred to here is normal but is not associated with sexual intercourse. The circumstances of the emission are not defined. It may have been deliberate as in masturbation or involuntary as in wet dreams. Whatever the circumstances, any discharge of semen generated an impurity because it meant potential loss of life. The person concerned was barred from entering the Tent of Meeting. Saul may have assumed that David's failure to attend a New Moon festival at the king's court was because he had a wet dream and had not cleansed himself (1 Sam 20:26). In order to be cleansed, the man needed only to bathe the whole body and wait till evening (**15:16**). Any clothing or leather that was impure because it had semen on it had to be washed in water and would be unclean till evening (**15:17**).

15:18 Marital intercourse

The whole of chapter 15 locates sexual activity in the wider context of religion and ritual, where reproduction is theologically related to creation and to God's promise of many descendants. Thus this verse, which is at the centre of the chapter and which focuses on sexual intercourse, is a key verse. Sexual intercourse during which there is emission of semen leaves both the male and female unclean. The emphasis here is on the impurity generated and not on whether the sexual relationship was legitimate or not. The morality of the act is not the focus of the verse. But the question inevitably arises, how does an institution which is a legitimate context for procreation generate impurity? One possible answer is that sexual intercourse creates an ambiguous situation where two incompatible states – life and death – collide, and this generates impurity. While the husband is the source of life, he also loses life through the emission of semen, which generates life. When a woman receives that semen and conceives, she both carries life and is in the realm of death because of the risk of death in childbirth. However, the type of impurity generated by sexual intercourse was not very serious for there was no pollution of the Tent of Meeting and no purification or burnt offerings were required. All that the couple needed to do was to bathe in water and wait till evening, when they would be clean. This explains why sexual intercourse was prohibited the evening before worship (Exod 19:15; 1 Sam 21:4-5).

15:19-24 Normal female discharge

A woman's regular menstrual blood makes her unclean (15:19). It is not clear whether the seven days mentioned in 15:19 refer to the period when she is menstruating or whether this is a purifying period after the flow of blood had stopped, as is the case with abnormal blood flow (15:28). If the former, then we are not told how she is cleansed. Her impurity could be transmitted to other persons and objects either directly or indirectly. Anything she lies on or sits on becomes impure (15:20). Touching her or touching an object she slept on or sat on makes one impure (**15:19, 21-23**).

Why was menstruation regarded as an impurity? The answer may be that menstrual blood is a symbol of both life and death. Thus menstruation represents a clash of two states, and so generates impurity. A similar ambivalence in regard to menstruation is found among the Chewa in Malawi. In Chewa society, there is always rejoicing when a girl has her first menstruation because society is assured of progeny. Thus menstrual blood is a source of joy. However, a number of taboos are imposed on the girl, as if the menstrual blood were something dangerous.

Leviticus requires that those who touch anything the menstruating woman slept on or sat on must wash their clothes and their own body, and then wait till evening. A male who had sexual intercourse with her would be unclean for seven days, and would transmit that impurity to any bed he slept on (**15:24**). Here again we have an example of transmission of impurity indirectly, at second or third remove. The ruling in 15:24 was clearly aimed at discouraging sexual intercourse with a menstruating woman because any emission of semen in this case would not promote procreation. The semen would just be wasted. Thus the principle behind this prohibition was to separate a life-creating process (normal sexual intercourse) from a life-destructive process (intercourse with a menstruating woman).

Because the theme of family and procreation comes up in chapters 12, 15, 18 and 20, and is an issue of concern for all of us, something more must be said. The teaching in Leviticus is consistent with God's commands in Genesis that human beings are to be fruitful and increase in number, and are to fill the earth and subdue it (Gen 1:28; 9:1). These commands have led people to question whether Christians can legitimately use contraception.

In answering this question, one of the points that must be made is that the Scripture recognizes that procreation is not the sole purpose of the sexual act. Human beings were created sexual, for they were created male and female. This is part of being created in the image of God, for to be human is to be in relationship. In the relationship between a man and a woman, both have sexual drives. That is why the law also emphasizes the sexual satisfaction of woman. For example, Exodus 21:7-11 states that if a man decides to marry a second wife without divorcing his former wife, he must not deprive the first one of her marital rights. Similarly, Deuteronomy 24:5 says that a husband is obligated to bring happiness to his wife.

God also gave power to human beings. This, too, is part of being created in his image. Thus, although the divine command is that human beings should be fruitful and increase and fill the earth, human beings have also been given power so that they can cooperate with God to have children within the context of a male and female relationship where there is special regard for one another's sexuality, that is, for one another's feelings, attitudes and values about oneself.

Satisfaction of human sexual desires and considerations of health have been the bases for a number of rabbinic decisions on birth control. For example, it is not disputed that for the sake of their health some women may be advised to use contraception (for example, if they are HIV-positive or if they risk life-threatening complications if they become pregnant again). The question is not whether or not birth control was permitted in the Bible: it was. The real question is whether a particular type of birth control is permissible or preferable and under what circumstances.

15:25-30 Abnormal female discharge

Abnormal bodily discharges make a woman unclean (**15:25**). Her impurity is communicable to other persons or objects either directly or indirectly (**15:26-27**). The purification process for anyone who was contaminated by touching anything she slept on or sat on involved simply washing of clothes, bathing and waiting till evening.

The process for cleansing a woman involved waiting for seven days after the flow of the blood had stopped (**15:28**).

As with the male abnormal bodily discharge, we are not told how the woman was healed. The priest was not involved in the healing process. Yahweh must be the one who healed her. On the eighth day the woman brought two turtledoves or two pigeons to the Tent of Meeting, one for a purification offering and the other for a burnt offering (**15:29-30**). In this way the woman would be reconciled with God and reintegrated into the covenant community.

The laws in this section are relevant to an incident in the life of Jesus Christ, when he met a woman who had suffered from bleeding for twelve years (Mark 5:24-34). The woman was regarded as unclean and was duty bound to avoid contact with other people lest she transmit her uncleanness to them. This is why she was so fearful when she explained to Jesus what she had done (Mark 5:33). She knew that by breaking the Levitical laws she had made other people unclean, and there was the possibility that they would turn against her in anger. However, Jesus reassured her, saying, 'Daughter, your faith has healed you. Go in peace' (Mark 5:34). It is striking, given the Levitical laws, that Jesus touched her without fear of contracting uncleanness (see 15:27). His action here expresses his general attitude to outcasts and sinners. While society isolated such people, Jesus drew close to them, thereby breaking down social barriers. His purpose was to create in himself 'one new man' by uniting all peoples (see Eph 2:14-15).

15:31-33 Motive and summary

The motive given for these instructions applies to all the issues dealt with in chapters 11 to 15. By obeying these instructions, the Israelites would be able to separate themselves *from the things that make them unclean so they will not die in their uncleanness for defiling my dwelling place, which is among them* (**15:31**). Those who were unclean could not participate in divine worship in the Tent of Meeting. If they did, they not only polluted the Tent of Meeting but were also in danger of death. The deaths of Nadab and Abihu served as examples of the fate of those who dared to enter into the Tent of Meeting in an unacceptable condition.

The priests were responsible for teaching the Israelites to distinguish the clean from the unclean in order to avoid serious consequences. During the time of Hosea, God expressed his anger at seeing his people dying for lack of knowledge. Their ignorance was the fault of the priests who ignored the law of God (Hos 4:6).

This chapter is summarized in **15:32-33**.

16:1-34 The Day of Purification (Day of Atonement)

The introduction to the Day of Atonement ritual in 16:1 connects it to the death of Aaron's two sons, Nadab and Abihu, in chapter 10. That chapter did not explain what action should be taken because of the impurity generated by the presence of corpses in the Tent of Meeting. This chapter is partly intended to deal with that circumstance. Furthermore, by linking this text to the incident in chapter 10, the author intends us to note that intervening chapters (11-15) identify impurities that can pollute the Tent of Meeting (15:31) and necessitate a ritual of purification. Thus this chapter functions as a conclusion to the presentation of the purity and impurity system.

The ritual had two main parts. The first part (16:2-19) deals with the purification of the Holy of Holies, the area around the altar of incense and its holy furniture, and the altar of burnt offering. The second part (16:20-28) describes the ritual of atonement.

16:2-28 Purification of the Tent of Meeting

The aim of the ritual presented here was not only to cleanse the Tent of Meeting of all impurities but also to restore it for proper use and for divine habitation. Right at the beginning we are told that certain precautions must be taken. The basic precaution was that Aaron was not allowed to enter the Holy of Holies at just any time he chose (**16:2a**). Familiarity breeds contempt, and if Aaron were to enter the Holy of Holies any time he wished, he might lose his reverence for the Lord. However, he could still enter it when there was an emergency, such as when the bodies of Nadab and Abihu lay there.

The fact that not even Aaron, in theory the holiest man in Israel, could enter the Tent of Meeting without some sacrifices shows that no man can approach the presence of God without appropriate atonement being made. The rituals stressed that even Aaron needed his sins to be forgiven before entering into the Tent of Meeting.

In the innermost part of the Tent of Meeting, God would appear, hidden in *the cloud*, presumably the cloud produced when coal was put into the censer. This cloud appeared over the *atonement cover* (**16:2b**) that was housed in this part of the Tent of Meeting. The atonement cover was a solid gold slab on top of the Ark of the Covenant. At its two edges, made as part of the cover were two golden cherubim, kneeling and facing each other with bowed heads and outstretched wings that touched in the middle (Exod 37:1-9).

Another precautionary measure that Aaron took before entering the Holy of Holies was to don special vestments that included a linen tunic, linen undergarments, linen sash, and linen turban (**16:4**). The high priest's vestments were very simple. Three reasons have been suggested for such simple dressing. First, because angels who minister before the Lord are dressed in linen (Ezek 9:2-3, 11; 10:2; Dan 10:5), the high priest who served before the Lord in the earthly temple must dress likewise. Second, the high priest must indicate his humility. As one involved in a transformation rite, he is stripped of all emblems of his former status. Third, it was to avoid possible accusations of pride. Of these three, the first seems the most acceptable because ordinary

priests wore vestments that were very different from those mentioned here, and because the high priest would remove his vestments as soon as he finished his work in the Holy of Holies.

The high priest's function was fraught with danger. He was engaged in a rite of passage, transforming the Tent of Meeting from a state of impurity to one of purity. He was also engaged in a rite of restoration, restoring the Tent of Meeting to a status in which Yahweh could come and inhabit it. As he passed through the curtain before the Holy of Holies he was to put incense into the censer so that the clouds of smoke it generated would screen the atonement cover from view, in case he saw it and died (**16:12-13**). No one, not even the other priests, was allowed to be in the Tent of Meeting while Aaron was performing the ritual of purification. He himself could not emerge from the Tent of Meeting until he had made atonement for himself, his household and for the whole congregation of Israel (**16:17**). Therefore every precaution had to be taken to enable him to emerge unscathed. Rabbinic tradition from the period of the Second Temple (about 515 BC) prescribed that seven days before the festival the high priest had to separate from his wife and be isolated in a special cell. He would spend the time rehearsing the actions required in the rite. On the eve of the festival, he was not allowed to sleep for fear that he might have a nocturnal emission and thus be deemed impure (15:16). According to later tradition, the high priest held a feast for his friends to celebrate his safe return from the Holy of Holies.

The purification ritual required a young bull and two male goats for a purification offering, and a ram for a burnt offering (**16:3, 5**). There were three steps in the ritual. The first step involved Aaron offering the young bull as a purification offering for himself and his household (**16:6**). The second step was the presentation of the two goats before the Lord (16:7). Lots were cast to determine which goat would be sacrificed to the Lord and which would be the scapegoat (16:8). Bringing the two goats before the Lord showed that God made the selection. The third step was the smoking of the censer (16:12-13; see comment on 16:2). The smoke cloud had to be raised before Aaron entered the Holy of Holies. Then Aaron took some of the bull's blood into the Holy of Holies and sprinkled some of it on the front of the atonement cover and some of it before the atonement cover. This last step was repeated seven times. These two actions represented the purification and rededication of the atonement cover (**16:11, 14**). The blood of the sacrificial goat was manipulated in a similar way (**16:15**). After cleansing the Holy of Holies, the altar of incense was cleansed, and finally the altar of sacrifices was cleansed (**16:18-19**).

The purging of impurities from the Tent of Meeting was not complete until the sins of the people had actually been removed from the camp. A goat was used as the means of transporting the sins of the people into the wilderness. This goat had not been sacrificed but had been *presented alive before the Lord* (**16:7-10**). It was now led forward. Aaron laid both his hands on its head as a sign of transference and confessed over it *all the wickedness and rebellion of the Israelites* (**16:20-21a**). The goat, now laden with these sins, was then sent away into the desert (**16:21b-22**). The person who had been assigned to lead the goat away into the wilderness would wash his clothes and bathe himself in water before returning to the camp (**16:26**). The carcasses of the bull and the goat whose blood had been taken into the Holy of Holies were taken outside the camp and their hides, flesh and offal burned. The person who did this also washed his clothes and bathed himself in water before returning to the camp (**16:27-28**).

The second part of the ritual consisted of offering burnt and purification offerings for both the high priest himself and for the people. For this purpose the high priest had to go into the Tent of Meeting, take off the linen garments he used when ministering in the Holy of Holies, bathe himself and put on regular garments (**16:23-24a**). Then clad in the regular garments the high priest would offer the burnt and purification offerings (**16:24b-25**).

16:29-34 The Day of Atonement

The ritual described in 16:3-28 was to be an annual one, performed on the tenth day of the seventh month (**16:29**). The Day of Atonement was to be characterized by self-denial and abstention from work, that is, rest (16:29, **31**). The purpose is that on this day the people would be cleansed from all their iniquities and the Most Holy Place, the altar of incense, and the altar of sacrifice would be purified, cleansing them from all the impurities generated by the iniquities of the people (**16:30, 33**). This ritual cleansing made the point that the dwelling place of God is polluted by impurities generated by human behaviour. Unless the temple is cleansed, God will bring judgment on his people. However, if the rituals were performed as prescribed, the sins of the people could be forgiven (**16:34**).

The Letter to the Hebrews, especially chapters 9 and 10, draws theological lessons from the ceremonies of the Day of Atonement. For the writer of Hebrews, Christ on the cross achieved what the high priest of the OT had attempted to do on the Day of Atonement. The superiority of Jesus' ministry gives us confidence to enter the sanctuary by the blood of Jesus (Heb 10:19). The writer stresses the superiority of the priesthood of Jesus to that of Aaron by pointing to the differences between them:

- Christ was pure, so he did not need to offer sacrifices for his own sins.
- Christ secured eternal redemption, so that there is no need to repeat the sacrifices regularly.

- Christ's death allowed him to enter into the heavenly sanctuary, not merely the Holy of Holies.
- Christ used his own blood rather than the blood of animals.

Whereas the Day of Atonement was characterized by self-denial, the author of the Letter to the Hebrews does not urge his readers to practise self-denial. Rather he urges them to 'spur one another on towards love and good deeds' and not to neglect meeting together (Heb 10:24-25).

The Day of Atonement was also a day of rest. The practice of resting on holy days is a good one. That is why Christians gather together on Sundays for worship and to meditate upon the salvation which Jesus secured for us on the cross.

17:1-16 Sacrifices and Blood

Chapter 17 can be divided into five sections: 17:3-7; 8-9; 10-12; 13-14; 15-16. The phrase 'any Israelite' opens the first four sections and the fifth section opens with 'anyone'. The instructional material in the first, second and fourth units has motivational or explanatory material added.

Each of the first four units threatens the penalty of *being cut off from his people* (17:4, 9, 10, 14). There are a number of suggestions regarding what this phrase means. It has been suggested that it may mean a) God's direct punishment of the offender, b) capital punishment or c) expulsion from the nation or exile. There are instances where this penalty is attached to secret acts that would be difficult to prosecute in the court of law, for example, the offence of touching something unclean (7:20-21). Blaspheming the Lord is another example of a secret offence, for which only God can punish an offender (Num 15:30-31). Thus the first suggestion seems to be correct. However, the phrase can also be understood as referring to the exile that the Israelites eventually suffered.

The first section (**17:3-7**) forbids any Israelite from slaughtering any clean animal anywhere inside or outside the camp. Instead they are to bring the animal to the Tent of Meeting where it will be treated as a fellowship or peace offering. Failure to do this constituted bloodguilt and would result in the person being *cut off from his people* (17:4).

This command appears to contradict Deuteronomy 12:15-16, which permits the slaughter of animals for food, provided the blood is poured out on the ground. Some scholars explain this contradiction as reflecting different historical situations. The command in Leviticus applied while the Israelites were in one camp in the wilderness, whereas the command in Deuteronomy applies to the situation when they were scattered across the promised land. Others, however, claim that 17:3-7 deals specifically with sacrificial killing, and that by restricting the place where sacrifices could be offered the Israelites were prevented from sacrificing to goat idols. This is certainly the focus of the prohibition in 17:6-7. Whatever these goat idols were, to sacrifice to them was contrary to the first commandment. Exodus 22:20 reads, 'Whoever sacrifices to any god other than the Lord must be destroyed'. According to Deuteronomy, the breaking of the first commandment was what led to the Israelites being sent into exile (Deut 29:24-28).

The NT is also well aware of the danger of fellowship with other gods. Christ warned his disciples that they could not serve God and money (Matt 6:24). Paul warned the Corinthian Christians against participating in pagan worship, because this involved demon worship (1 Cor 10:20-22).

Whereas the first section dealt with the peace offering, the second section (**17:8-9**) deals with the burnt offering. No reason is given for restricting the sacrificing of the burnt offering to the Tent of Meeting. Perhaps the reason is the same as for the peace offering (17:6-7).

The third section (**17:10-12**) prohibits the eating of any blood. The reason for this prohibition is that blood has been set apart by God for the purposes of atonement. Blood can be used in atonement because the life of the animal is in the blood. And since atonement refers to the life of the sacrificial animal being substituted for the offerer's life, the latter's life is in the blood. That is why manipulation of the blood in the context of ritual effects atonement for one's life. The same principle underlies the NT understanding of the death of Jesus Christ. The writer of the Letter to the Hebrews clearly states, 'without the shedding of blood there is no forgiveness' (Heb 9:22).

It needs to be emphasized here that what is forbidden is the eating of blood. Blood played a major role in the divinely ordained arrangements for Jewish sacrifices that foreshadowed the blood of Jesus Christ shed for forgiveness of sin. The author of the passage was clearly not speaking of modern medical procedures like blood transfusion, where blood is used to save a life. Not even the most Orthodox Jews today, who carefully observe all the regulations for kosher butchering and bleeding of meat, have any religious objections to blood transfusion.

The previous sections of this chapter dealt with domesticated animals, especially those that were used in sacrifices. What should happen if someone wanted to kill a non-sacrificial domesticated animal for food? This question is not addressed, for section **17:13-14** deals with non-domesticated animals. It is possible that the ruling for these non-domesticated animals would also apply to non-sacrificial domesticated animals. The ruling is that their blood must be poured out on the ground and covered with earth. The reason given for this law is, once again, that the life of the animal is in its blood.

The care taken to regulate the shedding of the blood of both sacrificial and non-sacrificial animals demonstrates respect for the life of animals and ultimately a respect for

God who created and continues to care for that life. Thus any indiscriminate killing of wildlife for fun, a habit which Westerners have indulged in Africa, or any indiscriminate killing by modern soldiers and guerrillas armed with machine guns should be regarded as sinful.

Whereas the eating of blood is forbidden, the eating of flesh is not forbidden in principle (**17:15-16**). However, it is noted that eating the flesh of an animal found dead or torn by wild animals makes one unclean. A person in that state of impurity must perform a purification ritual. Failure to do this would result in some penalty being imposed.

The prohibition against eating blood was included in the Jerusalem Council's decree to the Gentiles, together with the prohibition against eating the meat of strangled animals (Acts 15:29). The Council also decreed against eating food offered to idols. However, it should be noted that Paul did allow the Corinthian Christians to eat food offered to idols provided the consciences of weak brothers were not wounded (1 Cor 8:4-13). Jesus stated that food does not defile a person (Matt 15:11). It is possible that the same principle applies to the eating of blood. Paul seems to view it as equivalent to eating any other food (Rom 14:2-3).

Another reason why this particular law is not observed by Christians is that Jesus' teaching reaffirmed and reinterpreted the identification of blood with life. The blood in question is now the blood of Jesus. It is his blood that gives eternal life, and anyone who wants to enjoy eternal life must drink the blood of Jesus (John 6:55-56).

18:1-27:34 Holy Living for the People of God

18:1-30 Holiness in Family and Sexual Relationships

This chapter deals with prohibited sexual relations and activities in the context of the Israelite family. It is important to note that these instructions on the issue of human sexuality have divine sanction. The instructions begin and end with the divine self-identification formula: *I am the Lord your God* (**18:2**, 30). Thus there is a theological basis for the family as a social institution.

The chapter begins with an exhortation to avoid imitating the practices of other nations (18:1-5). The exhortation has three parts. The first part is negative, forbidding the Israelites from imitating the practices of either the Egyptians or the Canaanites (**18:3**). The second part is positive: the Israelites are urged to obey God's laws instead (**18:4**). A motivational clause follows (**18:5**). The result of obeying the laws of God is that a person will enjoy life. What is in view here is enjoyment of God's gifts of health, children, friends and prosperity. The OT view of life after death is that of a shadowy, depressing version of life on earth. It is only in the NT that life after death is described as a fuller life than the present one. If anyone can keep all the laws, he or she will enjoy eternal life (Matt 19:16-17; Rom 10:5).

The list of relationships in 18:6-18 describes the social context in which people might be tempted to have sexual relationships. The social context outlined here seems to approximate the extended African family. Where people are related as closely as in an extended family, sexual relationships are forbidden. A man may not marry his mother (**18:7**) or his sister (**18:9**). The blood relationship here is of the first degree. A man should not marry his granddaughter (**18:10**) or his aunt (**18:12-13**). A man should also not marry his stepmother, or his uncle's wife or his brother's wife (**18:8, 14, 16**). The reasons for the prohibitions are given in the motive clauses found in 18:8, 10 and 16. For example, sexual intercourse with one's granddaughter is forbidden because it dishonours the grandfather (18:10). The literal rendering of the Hebrew is 'She is the nakedness of your nakedness', a phrase that can be rendered as 'she is your flesh and blood'. The concept that a child is an extension of the parents is well understood. However, the motive given for not having sexual relations with one's mother is that a wife's nakedness is equivalent to the husband's nakedness (18:8). In other words, marital intercourse makes wife and husband into one flesh. Thus marriage within the extended family setting is forbidden on the basis of consanguinity.

The basic motive for all these prohibitions was the preservation of marriage. Marriage as a social institution is regarded in Scripture as the cornerstone of all other social structures, and so its purity and integrity must be protected at all times. The basic means of achieving this objective was to forbid sexual relationships between close relatives.

Other prohibited forms of sexual relationships are dealt with in 18:19-23. No particular reason is given for these prohibitions, but it is possible that the principle of procreation underlies them. According to Genesis 1:28, procreation is one of blessings God has given to the human family, and thus any sexual relationship that did not contribute to procreation was condemned. Thus a husband was prohibited from having sexual relations with his wife during the latter's monthly period because the husband's seed would be wasted (**18:19**). Adultery is prohibited, probably in order to protect the family, which provides the only context within which a child can be nurtured (**18:20**). Children were so important for the continuation of a family that there was also a prohibition on offering them in sacrifice to the pagan

TABOOS

The word *taboo* comes from the Polynesian word *tapu*. It refers to any act that is prohibited because it will have negative supernatural consequences for an individual or community. These consequences follow because the act offends the ancestors or gods, or because it opens a door for evil spiritual forces. For example, among the Akan of Ghana a man having sexual relations with his own sister would offend the ancestors, who would need to be placated. A taboo is thus much stronger than a mere prohibition. Breaking an ordinary prohibition by, for example, speaking openly about sexual matters does not have supernatural consequences.

Social anthropologists sometimes dismissed taboos as mere superstitions, but to do so is to miss the fact that they reveal much about a people's beliefs about the divine and about life.

In many cases, African taboos are similar to prohibitions found in the Bible. For example, both prohibit incest, and the Akan taboos applying to a woman during her monthly period are similar to those found in Leviticus 15:19-27. These similarities suggest that we should carefully examine taboos to see what they tell us about God and his self-revelation. The laws God laid down in the Bible have been followed by people who were not Jews and who had never seen the Jewish or Christian scriptures. The fact that these people knew that certain acts destroyed their relationship with the divine should make us aware that God does indeed reveal himself to humanity. Paul makes this exact point when he says that the requirements of the law of God are written on people's hearts (Rom 2:13-15).

Because humans were created in God's own image (Gen 1:27), they share something of the nature of God. However, the fall (Gen 3) changed the relationship between God and humanity. Some argue that this resulted in total depravity, citing Paul's statement 'nothing good lives in me, that is, in my sinful nature' (Rom 7:18). They would argue that we have lost all natural knowledge of God's law. Taboos are an indication that this is not the case. Humans still know right from wrong. Total depravity really means that human beings have lost the power, rather than the knowledge, of how to do what is right (see Rom 7:14-24, where Paul says that he cannot do the good he wants to do, and rather does the wrong things he tries to avoid).

It is clear from what has been said above that taboos are not necessarily wrong in themselves. Yet not all taboos are physically or spiritually beneficial. For example, the taboo on children eating eggs (Mamprusi, Ghana) can affect children's health.

The strong link between taboos and the supernatural world also means that those who observe taboos are under bondage. They are afraid of the consequences of engaging in taboo behaviour. Christians should be given proper teaching on the subject to free them from fear. They may also benefit from performance of some ritual that symbolizes their deliverance.

Ernestina Afriyie

god Molech (**18:21**). (Such a sacrifice was also prohibited because it violated the commandment in Exodus 20:3.) Similarly, sexual relations between people of the same gender are prohibited because there is no possibility of procreation (**18:22**). Finally, sexual relations with animals were forbidden for both men and women (**18:23**). Such an act was considered both defilement and confusion of boundaries. Sexual relations between humans and animals were tantamount to crossing the boundary between two realms of existence, blurring the distinction between human beings and animals. Such a mixture of things that should be kept separate was defiling.

In the OT the Canaanites are regarded as particularly licentious and promiscuous and are said to have practised all the unnatural sexual relationships described in this chapter (18:3, 24-28). It was for this reason that the Lord drove them out of the land of Canaan (**18:24, 27-29**). The Israelites, as the people of God, must separate themselves from such practices (18:5, **26, 30**). Anyone who practises any of these unnatural sexual relations must be cut off from the community. The holy God of Israel will not tolerate such behaviour, for it strikes at the heart of the family.

The NT is also concerned about the purity and integrity of marriage. In some cases, such as adultery, the NT imposes even stricter rules than the OT. In the OT it was possible for a man to take a second wife, divorcing the first, and not be accused of adultery. But when Jesus says that 'Anyone who divorces his wife and marries another woman commits adultery against her. And if she divorces her husband and marries another man, she commits adultery' (Mark 10:11-12), he defines these acts as adulterous. He introduced a full reciprocity between the sexes: unfaithful husbands are just as adulterous as unfaithful wives. The saying of Jesus takes seriously the spirit of the legislation in Leviticus 18, for if in marriage a man becomes one flesh with his wife; he cannot later desert her and take another wife.

Jesus' interpretation of the legislation in Leviticus 18 makes the chapter very relevant for situations where polygamy or promiscuity are regarded as acceptable practices.

19:1-37 Miscellaneous Instructions for Holy Living

The chapter begins with a call to the Israelites to be holy because God is holy (**19:2**). Holiness is an attribute of Yahweh that must find expression in the actual life of the community. Thus holiness is not some abstract concept, but one that can be concretized in relationships. In this passage, two types of relationships are explored: first, the vertical relationship between God and human beings and second, the horizontal relationships between human beings.

Holiness in regard to the vertical relationship is exemplified by obedience to such commands as *You must observe my Sabbaths* (**19:3**); *Do not turn to idols or make gods of cast metal for yourselves* (**19:4**); and *a fellowship [peace] offering*

... shall be eaten on the day you sacrifice it or on the next day; anything left over until the third day must be burned up (**19:5-6**). Practices associated with other religions are also prohibited (**19:26-28, 31**). Thus holiness must manifest itself in a total commitment and faithfulness to God.

Holiness in regard to the horizontal relationships between human beings must show itself in the social, economic and political areas of life. In concrete terms, it must manifest itself in respect for parents and the elderly (19:3, **32**) and care for the poor and those with physical disabilities (**19:9-10, 14**). Good neighbourliness is encouraged (**19:16-18, 20-22, 33-34**). Exploitation of those who are economically weak is prohibited (**19:11, 13, 35-36**). The preservation of the ordering of creation is also a practical expression of holiness (**19:19, 23-25**). Political righteousness is manifested in the administration of justice in the courts of law (**19:15**). Thus holiness must manifest itself in human relationships that are characterized by integrity, honesty and love.

What is particularly significant in this chapter is that from the perspective of a life of holiness there is no distinction between 'the religious' and 'the secular'. Holiness must manifest itself even in what we think of as the secular areas of human existence. Holiness must be expressed in public life. Most importantly, holiness must be manifest in the family setting. Charity begins at home.

20:1-27 Activities Punishable by Death

In terms of content, chapter 20 repeats most of the material found in chapter 18. There is also some overlap with chapter 19 – compare for example 20:6 with 19:26, 31; 20:7 with 19:2; 20:8 with 19:19; 20:9 with 19:3; 20:10 with 19:20-22; 20:27 with 19:26, 31. The material in 20:25-26 refers to chapter 11.

A comparison of chapters 18 and 20 shows that the prohibitions in chapter 18 are in the form 'thou shall not ...', and the punishment for disobedience does not immediately follow. The consequences of disobeying the commandments in 18:1-23 are set out in 18:24-29. By contrast, in chapter 20 the consequences are spelled out immediately after every commandment. The punishment for disobedience is death, either at the hands of the community or through some form of punishment initiated by God, who will *set his face against* the offenders and *cut [them] off from their people* (20:5-6).

The two prohibitions in 20:2-6 are applications of the first of the Ten Commandments (Exod 20:3). Both worship of Molech and turning *to mediums and spiritists* are defined as prostitution (**20:5-6**), that is, as acts of unfaithfulness to the covenant God. The community of Israel was a covenant community and owed its existence to the activity of the covenant God who had set them apart from other nations. The penalty for those who ignored the ban was death by stoning (**20:2**). This was to be done by the whole community, perhaps as a deterrent to others. If the people failed to execute the offender, then God would *set my face against that man* (20:3, 5). The motivation for this ban is the holiness of God and of his dwelling place, the Tent of Meeting (**20:3**).

These commands are followed by an exhortation to communal and individual holiness (**20:7-8**). A commitment to keeping the covenant ideals sets the standard for holy living, which is both moral and ceremonial in character.

The legislation in **20:9-21** is similar to that in 18:7-23 and deals with sins against family life. The punishment for these sins is either death or some divine punishment. The sins of dishonouring a parent, adultery, incest, homosexuality and bestiality are punishable by death. The crimes that required some divine punishment include sexual relations with a sister and sexual intercourse with a woman during her menstrual period. Childlessness is a punishment for those who cohabit with an aunt by marriage or a sister-in-law. If a man cohabits with his blood aunt, both the man and the aunt *would be held responsible* (20:19). Perhaps this refers to a penalty that was less severe than *being cut off* but more severe than childlessness.

The majority of the prohibitions in this chapter deal with sexual activities (20:10-21, accounting for some forty-five per cent of the verses in the chapter). Why was the writer so interested in human sexuality? A number of reasons have been suggested. One is that the effort to construct a normative system of sexual partners supported by a set of penalties is part and parcel of the concern for order in Leviticus, defined in terms of categories that must be observed. Confusion of categories leads to disruption of the social order. Therefore only those sexual activities which lead to the creation of legitimate children are approved. The second possible reason is that creation of a child in sexual activity brings one to the boundary between life and death. Yet another option is to read these restrictions on human sexuality in the context of the Levitical system of purity and impurity.

The NT follows the spirit of the OT in condemning adultery, incest, and homosexuality. However, Leviticus 20 goes further by insisting that those who committed such crimes should be put to death. Jesus in the NT did not insist on capital punishment for the woman who was caught in adultery (John 8:1-11). His attitude was consistent with his mission, which was to save the lost rather than to condemn them.

Another question that arises is how far these rules governing sexuality can be applied in our contemporary situation. In reflecting on these issues and on the place of capital punishment in relation to some sexual crimes, we need to remember the context and the importance attached to the institution of marriage in chapter 18. The purpose of the punishments is to protect this institution. The penal codes of many countries now make no provision for capital

punishments for sexual offences, even though the types of sex described here are not approved of.

One particular type of sexual activity that has raised much controversy recently is homosexuality (20:13). The biblical testimony is that this is an improper use of the gift of sex. It must also be emphasized that the predominance of prohibitions relating to human sexuality recognizes the strong destructive potential of the human sexual urge if not controlled. Human sexuality is a divine gift and it must be used in proper ways.

The chapter concludes with a call to the Israelite community to be holy (**20:22-24**). After all, God had set them apart to be his own people. Observance of the food laws, of which they are reminded in **20:25-26**, is a form of concrete expression of the holiness demanded by God.

21:1-22:33 Priestly Holiness

The previous chapters dealt with the holiness of an ordinary Israelite. The following two chapters deal with the holiness of the priests. Chapter 21 defines priestly holiness negatively in terms of taboos. Holiness itself is graded, with restrictions imposed on the high priest (21:10-24) being more stringent than those imposed on ordinary priests (21:1-9). The areas of life where holiness needs to be reflected are funeral rites and marriage.

21:1-9 Funeral and marriage restrictions for ordinary priests

An ordinary priest was permitted to make himself unclean by being involved in the funeral rites of close relatives: his mother, father, son, daughter, brother and unmarried sister (**21:1-4**). Otherwise, he must avoid contamination by any corpse. It is notable here that the corpse of his wife is excluded (21:4). No reason for this is given. Perhaps it is taken for granted that because they were 'one flesh' in marriage, the priest would defile himself because of her. Certainly Ezekiel, a priest, had to be specifically told not to mourn for his wife (Ezek 24:15-17). A non-priest faced no such restrictions.

Although a priest could defile himself by taking part in the funeral of a close relative, he was not allowed to practise certain customs such as shaving his hair or cutting his body (21:5-6). The reasons for this were that priests were separated to God and must be holy (**21:6a**) because they were responsible for performing religious rituals (**21:6b**). Non-priests were also forbidden to observe these customs (19:27-28).

In order to maintain the purity of the priestly line, priests were not permitted to marry a prostitute or a divorced woman (**21:7, 13-15**). The reason may be that any improper sexual relationship would have made it difficult to guarantee that any pregnancy was by the legitimate husband. Apparently a priest could marry a widow, especially the widow of another priest (Ezek 44:22). Once again, the restrictions were imposed on priests because they were holy to God (21:7).

Just as the wife's character reflects on the husband, so too does the character of children. For this reason the children of a priest must exemplify the same holiness as their father. A priest's daughter who became a prostitute was to be punished by death (**21:9**).

21:10-15 Funeral and marriage restrictions for the high priest

The high priest was not permitted to go outside the Tent of Meeting. Thus he could not attend even the funeral service of his closest relatives (**21:11-12**). In addition to having to obey the restrictions imposed on ordinary priests, he was not permitted to leave his hair unkempt or to tear his clothes (**21:10**). The basis for these restrictions was his status. He represented the Israelites before God and represented God to the Israelites (21:10, 12).

Similarly, the high priest could not even marry a widow, but was only permitted to marry a virgin (21:13-14).

Just as the high priest was not allowed to defile himself by burying his father or mother (21:11), so the follower of Jesus Christ is challenged to put union with Jesus above family ties (Luke 14:26). Of course this commitment does not mean that a Christian should use service to God as an excuse for neglecting to support his or her parents. Jesus firmly rejected this attitude (Mark 7:9-13).

21:16-24 Physical impediments to exercising priestly office

Any priest with a physical blemish was barred from serving in the Tent of Meeting (**21:16-21**). He could, however, share in the holy food of God (**21:22**). This prohibition must be viewed in relation to ritual holiness. Just as in burnt offerings and fellowship offerings the sacrificial animals had to be without any physical defect, so, too, the priest representing the whole congregation had to be without any physical defect. There is no suggestion that such a physical defect has anything to do with the morality of the affected person. The motivation for the prohibition is that the God who dwells in the Tent of Meeting is a holy God (**21:23**). Therefore the priests must be holy in terms of bodily integrity.

The NT like the OT, insists on holiness. Jesus Christ is the perfect priest (Heb 7:26) and perfect victim (Heb 9:14). He sanctified the church in order to make a bride 'without stain or wrinkle or any other blemish, but holy and blameless' (Eph 5:27). While holiness is insisted upon in both Testaments, the NT concept of holiness is basically in moral terms and is achieved through redemption, which extends to those with physical disabilities. It is not surprising that Christ invites the maimed, the lame, and the blind to his marriage feast (Luke 14:13).

The concept of 'holiness' in Leviticus did, however, extend beyond ritual purity to embrace moral purity. Priests were expected to behave uprightly and with dignity, and were denounced by the prophets when they were seen to have rejected the law of the Lord (Hos 4:6). Similarly the leaders of the church should be of good character (1 Tim 3:1-12; Titus 1:5-11). Their wives and children should also be well behaved (1 Tim 3:11-12; Titus 1:6).

But the requirement for holiness is not restricted to church leaders. Christians are called 'a holy priesthood' (1 Pet 2:5, 9). Thus all Christians must express the holiness of God in their everyday living.

22:1-33 Holy sacrifices

This chapter follows naturally from 21:16-23, where it was mentioned that a priest with a physical defect could not perform ritual duties but could partake of holy food. This raises the question of whether there were situations where priests could not partake of the holy food. A related question was, who was allowed to partake of the holy food?

The first question is addressed in 22:3-9, in the regulation that a priest can eat the holy food only when he is in a state of ritual purity. The priest, or any other person for that matter, is not permitted to eat holy food in a state of impurity, whether internal or acquired. The basis of this legislation is the holiness of God's name (**22:2**) and the fact that God had separated the priests to himself (**22:9, 16**). God would punish any priest who ignored this legislation (**22:3**).

The second question is addressed in 22:10-16. Only members of the priestly family could share in the holy food. Included in the family circle were slaves and their children. Guests of the priest and hired servants were excluded, as also was a daughter who had married anyone other than a priest. Children born of that marriage would also be excluded. If there were no children and the daughter was widowed or divorced and returned to her parents, then she could again share in the holy food.

A final problem was what to do if someone partook of the holy food by mistake. This issue is addressed in 22:14-16, which lays down the rule that the person must make restitution to the priest for the offering and add twenty per cent of the value to it.

Ultimately it was the priests' responsibility to protect both the holy place and the holy food from contamination. Failure to do so might lead to death (22:9). The sons of Eli died because of their disrespect of the sacred offerings (1 Sam 2:12-33). Priesthood was a dangerous vocation.

The priests were also responsible for ensuring that people were well informed about what type of animals could be presented as burnt or fellowship offerings to the Lord, namely, only unblemished animals (**22:17-28**). They were also duty bound to inform the people that their fellowship offerings must be consumed on the same day that they were offered (**22:29-30**).

The rule against offering an animal before it was eight days old and against sacrificing an animal and its young on the same day (22:27-28) may be related to the practices of other religions.

The main point in this chapter is the holiness of God. It was the responsibility of both priests and ordinary Israelites not to rob God of his dignity and glory. One way of recognizing the dignity of God was by observing the food laws and ensuring that no one who was impure partook of the sacred food. Another was by offering only unblemished animals as sacrifices. The name of the Lord would thus be honoured and not misused (Exod 20:7).

23:1-44: A Calendar of Holy Feasts

The chapter deals with the times in the year when Israelites were called upon to cease from work and to gather together for *sacred assemblies* (**23:2**). Besides for the weekly Sabbath rest, six occasions in the year were set apart for holy assemblies. The purpose of these assemblies is not explained. The writer may have assumed that they were known to the Israelites. The focus here is on specifying the times for each feast, as the writer constructs a temporal framework around which community life could be organized. The pattern is similar to the creation story in Genesis 1:1-2:3, where God's work of creation is organized using a seven-day framework.

The first day to be observed is the Sabbath (**23:3**). The Bible gives two possible reasons for rest on the Sabbath: one is because God rested on the seventh day after creation (Gen 2:2; Exod 20:8), and the other is because God redeemed Israel from Egyptian bondage (Deut 5:12-15).

The next feast to be observed was the Feast of the Passover and of Unleavened Bread (**23:4-8**). The festival started on the evening of the fourteenth day of the first month (which fell in March or April) with a Passover meal (23:5). Details of this feast are given in Exodus 12:1-28. In Deuteronomy 16:1-8 the reason for this feast is given as a commemoration of the acts of Yahweh when he redeemed the Israelites from their Egyptian bondage. The following day, that is, the fifteenth day, was the beginning of the feast of Unleavened Bread (23:6). This festival started with a sacred assembly during which a burnt offering was sacrificed (23:8). More details about the rituals involved are given in Numbers 28:16-25. The festival was to last for seven days, during which the people ate bread made without yeast as a reminder that they had left Egypt in haste (23:6). It seems that burnt offerings were also presented over this seven-day period (23:8).

The Feast of Firstfruits (23:9-14) is associated with the barley harvest, which was also between March and April. The description of this festival parallels the offering of the first fruit of the land in Deuteronomy 26:1-11. People would bring the first sheaf of barley to the priest (**23:10**). Then on the day after the Sabbath (no fixed Sabbath is specified) the priest would wave the sheaves and offer a burnt offering together with a grain offering of two-tenths of an ephah (roughly 7½ pints or 4.5 litres) of fine flour mixed with oil (**23:11-13**). The Israelites could eat the new season's produce only after these offerings had been made (**23:14**).

The next feast was the Feast of Weeks, (23:15-22), which took place in May or June, fifty days after the offering of the first sheaf of barley. This feast lasted for only one day and involved the presentation of two loaves of leavened bread together with sacrificial animals, grain and drink offerings (**23:17-18**). On this day no regular work was to be done. It was a day of rest when people would gather for a sacred assembly (**23:21**). However, the needs of the poor and the alien were also to be remembered at this time. When harvesting, some grains should be left in the fields for the poor and the aliens to gather (**23:22**).

In the seventh month, between September and October, there were three feasts. The first was the Feast of Trumpets (**23:23-25**), which took place on the first day of the seventh month. No regular work was to be done on this day. The people were urged to gather for worship.

Nine days later, on the tenth day of the same month, the Day of Atonement was observed with rest and fasting (**23:26-32**; see also 16:1-34).

The third event in that month was the Feast of Tabernacles (**23:33-43**). It began on the fifteenth day of the seventh month and lasted for eight days. On the first and last days people were supposed to rest from their regular work and gather for sacred assemblies. The feast was closely associated with agriculture, for it was supposed to be held after the crops had been gathered in (23:39; see also Deut 16:13). The months of September and October marked the end of the hot dry summer and the Israelites were looking forward to the coming of the rainy season, which lasted from October to March. In fact in Zechariah 14:17-18 the Feast of Tabernacles is specifically associated with rainfall. The seventh month, therefore, signalled the end of the agricultural year and the beginning of a new one. It is possible that this is the same feast as the one referred to as the Feast of Ingathering (Exod 23:16; 34:22).

The connection of this feast with agriculture is shown by the custom of erecting huts made out of tree branches in the vineyards and orchards while the grapes and fruit were being gathered in. But it was more than merely an agricultural festival, for it affirmed that God is Lord of both nature and history. Thus the Israelites were also commanded to live in booths as a reminder of their stay in the wilderness on their way to the promised land. The feast was thus a ritual re-enacting of the Exodus experience, reminding people of the saving power of God. Thus the whole festival was characterized by the joy of harvest and of salvation, with people waving leafy branches and bringing burnt offerings and choice fruit to the Lord.

Three of the principal OT feasts have been taken over in the Christian church: Good Friday is the equivalent of Passover, Easter the equivalent of the Feast of Unleavened Bread, and Pentecost is equivalent to the Feast of Weeks. Both the Passover and the Feast of Unleavened Bread commemorated the redemption from Egypt. Similarly as Christians celebrate Good Friday and Easter, they are reminded of the redemption achieved through the death of Christ.

24:1-9 Holy Objects: The Lamp and the Bread

Chapter 24 deals with three issues. The first two are related in that they are concerned with the regular service of the Tent of Meeting. It is difficult to see why this material is found at this point in the book, for the following chapter continues the subject of sacred times. One possibility is that this chapter's concentration on symbolic daily offerings is intended to correct any impression that might be drawn from chapter 23 that there are some sacred times during the year and some profane times.

One of the priests' responsibilities was to keep the lamps on the lamp stand in the Tent of Meeting burning continually (**24:2-4**). The oil for these lamps was to be provided by the people. The priests were also expected to use some of the fine grain flour brought to the Tent of Meeting by the congregation to prepare twelve loaves of bread, symbolizing the twelve tribes of Israel (**24:5-8**). These were to be arranged *in two rows, with six in each row, on the table of pure gold before the Lord* (24:6). Some pure incense was also placed in each row. This incense was later burned as an offering by fire to the Lord. The rows of bread were to be renewed each Sabbath. The consecrated bread that David took was from one of these rows (1 Sam 21:3-6; see also Matt 12:1-8).

The lamp and the bread, which are specifically mentioned in Hebrews 9:2, were symbols of the lasting covenant between God and the Israelites. The oil for the lamps and the flour for the bread were products of the land that God had given to them in fulfilment of the promise he made to Abraham. Thus the lamp and the bread symbolized continuous thanksgiving for the gift of land and the daily offering of the everyday duties of the people to God.

24:10-23 Blasphemy and Justice

The final section of the chapter deals with the case of someone who is not an Israelite committing blasphemy. Moses and the people sought a ruling on how to deal with this (**24:12**) and were told that the law must be applied equally to all people, aliens or native born (**24:16, 22**). It is worth noting that the accusers of Jesus and Stephen used the law on blasphemy as part of the justification for the death

sentences passed on Jesus and on Stephen (Matt 26:63-66; Acts 6:11-14).

The law stressed that judgments must be handed out fairly and without favour. Furthermore, the application of the law should be according to the principle of *lex talionis*, that is, an eye for an eye and a tooth for a tooth (**24:17-21**). The context of this principle was the natural human instinct to fight back when attacked, which had led to the practice of vendetta, whereby if one member of a clan was wronged, it was up to the other members of the clan to avenge the wrong. In trying to do this, the injured party often inflicted more harm than had originally been done. The intent of the principle of lex talionis was to control this excess. In particular it was meant to control anger, violence and the desire for revenge and to introduce the principle of justice. Justice is never excessive in its demands. There is a correspondence between the crime and the punishment, the thing done and what is to be done about it. So the aim of the law was not to urge the taking of an eye for an eye, and to insist upon it every time; rather, it was meant to avoid horrible excesses, by checking and holding within bounds the terrible spirit of revenge and retribution.

It should also be noted that this law was not given to individuals but to the judges who were responsible for law and order. It was the judges who were to see to it that it was an eye for an eye and a tooth for a tooth and no more. The law was for them and not for private individuals to take into their own hands.

Jesus discussed the principle of lex talionis in the Sermon on the Mount, in which he declared that he had come to fulfil the law, that is, to give the law its full meaning (Matt 5:17). The principle of lex talionis was part of the law. On this Jesus said, 'You have heard that it was said, "Eye for eye, and tooth for tooth". But I tell you, Do not resist an evil person' (Matt 5:38-39a). The background to Jesus' words was the teaching of the Pharisees and the teachers of the law. They taught that the principle was for personal application and regarded it as a matter of right and duty. Thus they were guilty of two errors: they were turning a negative injunction into a positive one, and they were also carrying it out themselves. Their interpretation of the law was contrary to its spirit.

For Jesus, a correct interpretation of the law would involve a way of living where personal injury is not resisted. Jesus gave two examples to illustrate what he means. The first involves turning the other cheek (Matt 5:39b). Jesus wants us to rid ourselves of the spirit of retaliation, of the desire to revenge ourselves for any injury or wrong that is done to us. In order to understand Jesus' point, it is important to bear two things in mind. The first is that the teaching was addressed to his followers, those who had left everything in order to follow him. In other words, the teaching was for Christians. The second is that the teaching was addressed to Christians in their personal relationships and not in their capacities as citizens of a particular country. Thus Jesus was here urging his followers to forgive those who do them an injury.

The second illustration involves the handing over of a cloak to someone who has taken it as a pledge. According to OT law, no one could take a poor man's cloak as a pledge and keep it overnight (Exod 22:26-27). Thus by handing over his cloak, the poor man was renouncing his rights. In modern times people are very conscious of their rights, and human rights activists fight for them. Jesus' point is that Christians must not insist on their legal rights, even though they may at times suffer injustice as a result. This does not mean that they should not be concerned about law and order. Jesus protested when an officer struck him (John 18:22-23). Paul and Silas insisted that those who had sent them to jail should come and release them openly (Acts 16:37). In both cases the issue was not personal injury but protests for the sake of law and order.

25:1-55 Holy Times: Sabbatical and Jubilee Years

The chapter deals with two related periods, namely, the Sabbath Year (25:1-7) and the Year of Jubilee (25:8-54). Two statements by Yahweh regarding land and people form the basis for the instructions given here. In 25:23 it is stated that the land belongs to Yahweh and that the Israelites are simply tenants on God's land. In 25:38 it is stated that the Israelites belong to Yahweh because he redeemed them from their Egyptian bondage. Consequently, their relationship to the land and to each other must be characterized by the fear of God (25:17, 36). This attitude would find practical expression in both land and people being released and restored to their original state in the Sabbath Year and in the Jubilee Year.

In 25:2-7 the focus is on events to take place every seventh year. In that year the land should be left fallow. It must have *a sabbath of rest* with no planting or harvesting. Two reasons are given for this command: First, the land belongs to God (25:2) and must be restored to him (25:4). Second, anything that the land produces without human aid in the fallow year belongs to everyone, including the poor, livestock and wild animals (25:6-7). The underlying principle behind these two reasons is that God is the supreme provider, and although human beings may assist the process, it is from God alone that all things come. Furthermore, the regulation that after six years of exploitation, the land must be left fallow in the seventh year is a check against overexploitation of natural resources. The legislation encourages good agricultural and ecological practice.

In 25:8-55 the focus shifts to the events that must take place in the fiftieth year. After counting seven times seven years, there would be a Jubilee Year. The Jubilee followed immediately on the forty-ninth year, which was a Sabbath Year, and so here there were two Sabbath Years in succession. God promised to increase crop yields in the sixth year so that there would be enough food to last for three years, that is, until the next harvest (25:18-22).

The instructions regarding the Jubilee Year address issues regarding property, specifically land and houses (25:8-17, 23-34). The legislation in 25:8-13 envisioned a scenario where economic constraints forced some Israelites to be enslaved. The Jubilee Year was a sacred year when the slave population was liberated and allowed to return to their family property and clan.

The legislation also envisioned a scenario where economic constraints forced the head of a family to sell the family inheritance. It is clearly stated that any such transaction must be carried out in the fear of the Lord (25:14-17), that is, with honesty and integrity and in full knowledge that the land belonged to God and that he permitted a particular family to use it. Such an understanding meant that land could not be sold permanently (25:23). The seller had the right to redeem it if he had sufficient funds (25:24, 26-27), or his nearest relative could redeem it on his behalf (25:25). If he could not afford to do this, then the buyer must return it to the family in the Year of Jubilee. (25:28). In pre-colonial Africa, the chiefs owned land on trust and had the right to parcel it out to whoever needed it. That person then owned that land as long as he used it. Commercialization of land, where it is sold to those who can afford it, is foreign to most African societies. Those in favour of commercialization of land argue that it increases productivity. However, this increased productivity must be balanced against the many people who become economically and socially marginalized and impoverished.

The legislation about jubilee release did not apply to a house in a walled city (25:29-31), which belonged permanently to the buyer unless it was redeemed within a year of sale. No reason is given for this exemption. Possibly it was because such a sale did not involve farmland, or because redevelopment was fairly rapid in towns. However, houses in unwalled villages came under the jubilee regulation. Another exception was made in the case of town houses belonging to Levites. These must be redeemed or returned to their owners in the Jubilee Year (25:32-34).

Another possible scenario in 25:35-38 envisioned a situation where an Israelite becomes so poor that he cannot sustain himself. His countrymen are urged to help by lending or selling him food. But they are reminded not to take advantage of the poverty of their brother by either charging interest on borrowed money or selling food at a profit. This behaviour would only put him in a worse situation, with his poverty aggravated by the obligation to service the debt. The creditor should not exploit the poverty of a brother in order to enrich himself. In the Jubilee Year the debt must be cancelled and the debtor freed from his debt-slavery so that he can return to his family.

If things became so bad that an Israelite decided to sell himself as a slave (**25:39-43**), the buyer should treat him simply as a hired servant who sells only his labour but not his freedom. God had redeemed the Israelites from slavery in Egypt and they were not to re-enslave each other. The fear of the Lord, that is, the acknowledgment that the brother belonged to God his redeemer, should motivate them to behave properly. However, non-Israelites could be bought as slaves. They could be redeemed and they could also be bequeathed to one's successors (**25:44-46**).

If an Israelite had sold himself to a non-Israelite, the Israelite could claim his freedom (**25:47-55**). His near relatives might redeem him, or if he were able, he could redeem himself. A person redeemed by God belongs to him and cannot be permanently enslaved.

There are a number of lessons to be learned from this chapter. The first concerns social justice. As members of one stock, human beings should strive to realize of the common good. This common good, rather than individual profit, should be the driving force for all human activities. But the pursuit of the common good should not stifle individual contributions. The individual should be allowed to make his unique contribution to the wider group.

The legislation regarding the Year of Jubilee has been used to campaign for the cancellation of debts owed to rich countries by poor Third World countries. In biblical terms, the jubilee principle means that it is unjust for people of the same stock to enslave or impoverish one another permanently. All economic transactions have to take into account the long-term implications of financial or farming arrangements. Do they treat the parties to the agreement fairly, and in such a way that all commitments entered into can be renegotiated after a certain period of time? Those who campaign for debt cancellation do so on three grounds: first, human beings are one stock, with no distinction drawn between one race and another; second, some of the debt is illegitimate and inequitable; and third, impoverished people should have an opportunity for a fresh start as unburdened as possible.

The principle of justice should also apply to the environment. Just as there are interconnections between human beings, so there is an interconnection between human beings and nature. Consequently, any overexploitation of nature will be only to the disadvantage of human beings themselves. Both human beings and nature need a Sabbath of rest.

Another important lesson concerns the connection between worship and social justice. The Jubilee is presented as an extension of the Sabbath day. This shows that social issues and religion are not incompatible. A good example of this is found in Jesus' outline of his ministry in Luke 4:18-19. His mission was 'to proclaim the year of the Lord's favour', that is, the year of Jubilee. In practical terms, this meant the proclamation of liberty to prisoners, the recovery of sight to the blind, and the release of the oppressed.

26:1-46 Rewards and Punishments

This chapter outlines the blessings associated with obedience (26:3-13) and the punishments associated with disobedience (26:14-39). Yet even after punishment Israelites could still be saved if they confessed their sins and turned to God (26:40-45). Obedience or disobedience is defined in terms of the commandments found in **26:1-2**, which prohibit the Israelites from worshipping other gods (see also Exod 20:3-6). To make an image of God was to misrepresent him and was thus equivalent to worshipping another god rather than Yahweh. Positively, the Israelites were commanded to observe the Sabbaths (see chs. 23, 25) and to show reverence for the Tent of Meeting (see chs.1-16). It is noteworthy that only those commandments that deal with the relationship between God and Israel are emphasized, reflecting the belief that ethics are the product of a proper relationship between God and human beings.

The types of blessings associated with obedience include a bumper harvest (**26:3-5, 10**), peace and military triumph over enemies (**26:6-8**), population increase in fulfilment of God's promise to Abraham (**26:9**), the presence of the Lord in the midst of the people in fulfilment of the covenant at Sinai (**26:11-12**), and the dignity of personal freedom (**26:13**). The covenant at Sinai had been an act of grace by God that initiated a relationship with the Israelites and redeemed them from slavery in Egypt. This redemption should lead to obedience, and obedience to blessings.

In 26:14-39 we have a list of curses. It is significant that the power of the curses intensifies as Israel fails to respond to God's punishments. With each punishment, God gives Israel opportunity to reform. Each time Israel fails to respond to God's correction, the punishment intensifies. The punishments include military defeat and sickness (**26:16-17**), a reduction in soil fertility and productivity because of drought (**26:18-20**), the loosing of wild animals to prey on children and destroy cattle, thereby reducing the population (**26:21-22**), further military defeat resulting in the land being destroyed and the inhabitants sent into exile leaving the land empty (**26:27-35**), and constant fear and anxiety among the exiles, who would eventually die (**26:36-38**). Even those who survived these catastrophes would waste away (**26:39**).

It is important to remember that God was aiming at the reformation of the Israelites and not at their annihilation. He hoped that they would realize their sinfulness and would return to him in confession. Thus the chapter ends with a picture of a God who is anxious to welcome back his straying people (**26:40-45**).

Three issues are relevant here. First, are the blessings and the curses addressed to Israel only, or can they be applied to the church and the whole world? Second, are the blessings and curses to be interpreted simply in material terms or in spiritual terms as well? Third, do the blessings and curses apply only in this world or in the next world as well?

In the NT the nation of Israel is still regarded as God's covenant people and therefore the blessings and curses are still relevant to them. For example, Jesus said he was sent to the lost people of the house of Israel, and Paul says that God did not reject his people (Rom 11:1) and that God's gifts and his call are irrevocable (Rom 11:29). However, there are indications that the blessings and curses also apply to the church, individually and corporately. They are not restricted to Israelites, as the experience of Peter and the resolutions at the Jerusalem Council make very clear (Acts 10:34; 15:13-18). People everywhere are saved by faith alone.

The NT teaches that the blessings and the curses are both material and spiritual. For example, Jesus advised his followers 'to seek first his kingdom and his righteousness and all these things [that is, food and clothing] shall be given to you' (Matt 6:31-33). Paul said that the Christians at Corinth were suffering because God was punishing their misbehaviour at the Lord's Supper (1 Cor 11:27-30). But the NT also teaches that the kingdom of God is spiritual (John 18:36). The African church needs to address many social problems relating to food, security, health and human freedom, but while doing this it must not neglect spiritual issues. The challenge to the church in Africa is how to balance these two aspects of human life.

The question of whether the blessings and the curses are for this world only has been touched on in the previous paragraph. The NT teaches that there is a partial and provisional fulfilment of the blessings in this life. Jesus taught that with his coming the kingdom of God had drawn near and was in the midst of the people, but he also taught that the kingdom of God was something to be expected in future. Here we see things in 'a poor reflection as in a mirror; then we shall see face to face. Now I know in part; then I shall know fully' (1 Cor 13:11-12).

27:1-34 Redemption of Gifts Dedicated to the Lord

This final chapter deals with gifts dedicated to the Lord. These gifts included persons, animals, houses and fields. A person could give money in place of these material gifts, provided the amount of money was equivalent to the value of the gift.

The first section (**27:2-7**) deals with a special vow a person may make to dedicate others to the service of the Lord. The cost of redeeming such persons, given in terms of temple shekels, varied depending on the age and sex of the one dedicated.

Person & Age	Cost of Redemption
Male, 60+	15 shekels
Female, 60+	10 shekels
Male, 20-60	50 shekels
Female, 20-60	30 shekels
Male, 5-20	20 shekels
Female, 5-20	10 shekels
Boy, under 5	5 shekels
Girl, under 5	3 shekels

These figures were probably calculated on the basis of productivity in a labour intensive economy. Those in the highly productive age group were assigned a higher value. If someone was unable to pay the set price, it could be adjusted to a level that he or she could afford (**27:8**).

The situation was different when it came to animal offerings (**27:9-13**). An animal that a person dedicated as an offering to the Lord became holy. No other animal could be substituted for it. If someone attempted such a substitution, then both animals were forfeited to the Tent of Meeting in punishment for the attempted dishonesty. However, an animal could be redeemed by paying its value plus an additional twenty per cent. If the animal offered proved to be unclean and therefore unusable as a sacrifice, a priest would determine its value.

If a house were dedicated as a possession of the Tent of Meeting, the priest would set a non-negotiable value for it. If the person who dedicated it wished to redeem it, he or she must add twenty per cent to its value (**27:14-15**).

The value of a dedicated field (27:16-21) that was part of a family's land had to be calculated in terms of its seed-capacity and yield. The unit of measurement was a homer of barley seed (about 58 gal or 220 litres). The yield was calculated with reference to the Jubilee Year. If the dedication was done during a Jubilee Year, the value set in **27:16** would stand. If, however, the dedication was done after one Jubilee and before the next, the value would be assessed according to the possible yield for the remaining years until the Jubilee (**27:18**). These calculations were necessary in case the original owner wanted to redeem it before the Jubilee Year. If he did, he would have to pay an additional twenty per cent of its value (**27:19**). In a situation where the land that was dedicated to the Tent of Meeting either was not redeemed in one Jubilee Year or had been sold to someone else, then the original owner could not redeem it and it would not be returned to him in the Jubilee Year. Instead it would become the permanent property of the priests (**27:20-21**).

A bought property could be dedicated to the Lord and could be redeemed (**27:22-25**). In that case the value of the property would be computed in relation to the Jubilee Year and must be paid at once rather than in instalments. In the Jubilee Year the property would revert to its original owner.

Leviticus concludes with further observations on dedicated gifts (**27:26-33**). The firstborn of animals could not be dedicated because they already belonged to God. An animal unfit for sacrifice could either be redeemed at a price fixed by the priests plus twenty per cent of its value or sold at the fixed price. Anything dedicated to God, whether a human being or an object, could be sold or redeemed. Tithes belong to God. If a person wanted to redeem his tithe of grain or fruit, then he had to add twenty per cent of its value. If the tithe was of the herd or flock, the owner should not make any substitution, or else both the animal and its substitute would be forfeited to the Tent of Meeting.

Two issues are of interest in this chapter. First, the chapter seems to be concerned with the possibility of people making promises in the heat of a moment and later retracting the promise. The author of Ecclesiastes warns against this when he says, 'When you make a vow to God, do not delay in fulfilling it. He has no pleasure in fools; fulfil your vow. It is better not to vow than to make a vow and not fulfil it' (Eccl 5:4-5). The function of the twenty per cent penalty is to discourage both the making of hasty promises and the reneging on them.

Today, people are apt to make hasty promises to follow Jesus at revival meetings. Yet they soon revert to their old practices. Organizers of evangelistic revival meetings must be very watchful about this happening when people respond to calls 'to offer themselves to Christ'.

The chapter also teaches that both human beings and their property can be offered to God. In other words, holiness involves one dedicating both one's self and one's property to the service of God.

Felix Chingota

Further Reading

Gorman, F. H. *Divine Presence and Community: A Commentary on the Book of Leviticus*. ITC. Grand Rapids: Eerdmans, 1997.

Harrison, R. K. *Leviticus: An Introduction and Commentary*. TOT. Leicester: Inter-Varsity Press, 1980.

Wenham, G. J. *The Book of Leviticus*. NICOT. Grand Rapids: Eerdmans, 1979.

NUMBERS

The book of Numbers was given this name because it contains the records of two censuses: one was of the exodus generation taken at Mount Sinai (Num 1) and the other of the generation born in the wilderness (or 'desert') that was taken on the plains of Moab (Num 26). However, in Hebrew the book is known as *Bemidbar* or 'In the Desert' because most of the major events in this book take place in the desert of Sinai.

Major Themes

Numbers is the fourth book in the Pentateuch, the collection of the first five books of the Bible, which are sometimes called the Books of Moses. These books share two central themes: a) God's activity in bringing the world into being, as described in Genesis 1–11, and b) God's activity in bringing the community of faith into being, which is described in the rest of the Pentateuch.

Also central to the Pentateuch is the relationship between God and human beings that first finds expression in God's creation of men and women in his own image (Gen 1:26-27). Later, God calls certain people – the people of Israel – into a community of faith. God created this community for a special purpose: they were to bear witness to the world about the God who is both creator and judge. They were to testify that he is holy, majestic, transcendent and wholly other. The story of the Pentateuch also reveals that this God is present with his community in all the circumstances of life. He took them out of captivity in Egypt, provided for them in the desert, gave them a stronger identity and prepared them to possess the promised land. He would later be with them when they were invaded by the great nations that surrounded them and during their exile. The community is called to respond to God's mighty deeds in history with obedience and gratitude.

Chapters 12–50 of Genesis begin with the founding of the special community of faith, then tell of its early development through the stories of the patriarchs, from Abraham to Jacob, and end with the community moving to Egypt because of famine. The book of Exodus tells of the oppression that God's community endured in Egypt and of God's intervention and deliverance of them through Moses. The major event of their exodus from Egypt is the crossing of the Red Sea (Exod 14–15).

Exodus narrates God's call to the world and to his special community (Israel), which involves promises that take the form of a covenant. The making of this covenant is at the heart of Exodus. Exodus 20 records the Ten Commandments, and then chapters 21–23 contain laws that expand on these commandments and deal with other relevant matters. Chapter 24 has the culmination of this section, the making of the covenant. The rest of Exodus (25–40, except for 32–34) describes the response of the people through worship. They obeyed by building the Tabernacle and by following all the instructions given to them.

The whole of Leviticus and the first ten chapters of Numbers (up to 10:10) continue this theme of response through worship. This section of the Pentateuch deals with religious laws relating to worship, purity and the like. The rest of the book of Numbers continues the story of the Israelites' journey in the desert until they camp in the plains of Moab, from where they can see the promised land beyond the Jordan. It also tells how Moses divided the land among eleven tribes in preparation for their taking possession of the promised land. The twelfth tribe, the Levites, were given no land of their own. They were set aside to serve in the house of God and were to be supported by offerings brought to the Tent of Meeting by all the other tribes.

Deuteronomy, the final book of the Pentateuch, contains Moses' repetition of the law and his final farewell to the children of Israel.

Purpose of Numbers

The book of Numbers has six main purposes:

- To expand on the details of the events related in the book of Exodus. It gives further details about the historical period from the exodus to Sinai and about Israel's settlement on the borders of the promised land, in the plains of Moab.

- To describe the journey from Sinai to the region beyond Jordan, the preparation of Israel for entry into the promised land and the legal decisions made in the desert.

- To show the great and mighty things that God did for Israel and to stress that the covenant community must respond to God in obedience. Obedience in this context means listening to the word of God and obeying his commands (in the form of his word) and directions. Numbers reveals that Israel's worship and its family life and social life were all to be subjected to God's will.

- To demonstrate that God's laws were given as a gift to govern people's lives. Numbers shows that obedience means life (the people would enter the land and enjoy its blessings) and that disobedience brings destruction (the people and the leaders, including Moses, Aaron and Miriam, learned this).

- To explain why Israel wandered in the desert for forty years, and specifically that this resulted from the faithlessness of the older generation whom God had brought out of Egypt (Deut 1:35-40).

- To show that in spite of Israel's unfaithfulness, rebellion and apostasy, God was still faithful and patient. God's promise to give land to Israel remained binding, even though the rebellious exodus generation died in the desert. God shaped a new generation to be recipients of the covenant promises.

Theological Significance

The Pentateuch's narratives, genealogies, laws and speeches tell of the creation of the world, the origin of the people, the institution of religion and the ordering of family and social life. But these were not recorded simply for their historical interest. Rather, the aim was to lay out the programme for Israel's life in the later periods of settlement, monarchy, exile and reconstruction. Thus, the books of the Pentateuch should not be studied simply as historical documents but as the word of God that directs the religious life of both Israel and the church.

The book of Numbers, in particular, must be interpreted as part of the desert tradition, which is significant and symbolic both for Jewish communities (see the historical Pss 78, 79, 95) and for Christian believers (see 1 Cor 10:11). The covenant had been established at Sinai, and now the people of Israel must live out that relationship in all areas of life and demonstrate what that relationship entails. The desert experience is a prototype of all the experiences that the Israelites would go through in their history. This period stands as a lesson for all.

Relevance to African Christianity

In the book of Numbers, we witness the desert generations struggle with the transition from one way of life to another and with the transmission of their experience to the next generation. We see the possibilities and problems in the passing on of faith and how God and people played their parts.

We too, as Africans, are involved in many transitions as we face issues such as globalization, poverty, epidemics, disease, civil wars, pluralism, interfaith issues and a multiplicity of denominations. How do we deal with socioeconomic, political and religious challenges? How do we define our faith and mission in the world? In other words, how do we apply the biblical message in such a way that

we are enriched rather than impoverished by the challenges our continent faces in this period of transition?

The book of Numbers provides us with some clues as to how to do this because it presents us with a journey based on faith and hope, a journey accompanied by a holy God. The journey is not trouble-free, but God is present with his people as one who leads, provides, loves and punishes as they continue on their spiritual journey.

The Meaning of the Numbers

There has been much debate on the exact numbers recorded in the two censuses and elsewhere in Numbers. Some scholars believe the numbers are to be taken literally, while others argue that they are symbolic. Both interpretations are equally valid ways of reading the Scriptures, and we can learn by looking at them both ways.

First, let us look at the literal meaning. The first census taken in Numbers found a total of 603,550 men over the age of twenty (1:45). But the population would also have included many women and children, as well as elderly men who would not have been regarded as warriors. We can thus estimate that if all the people had been counted, there would have been about three million people there. No wonder Pharaoh said, 'The Israelites have become much too numerous for us. Come, we must deal shrewdly with them or they will become even more numerous and, if war breaks out, will join our enemies, fight against us and leave the country' (Exod 1:9-10). They had indeed become 'a great nation', as God had promised to Abraham (Gen 12:2; 17:5-8).

One of the chief problems with taking these numbers literally is that it is difficult to see how such a large group could have survived in the desert. Such a large nation would also have had no difficulty in later defeating the Canaanites who inhabited the promised land. So those who support a symbolic interpretation argue that these numbers are used to express God's greatness in delivering Israel. God's great army is on Israel's side!

The way the Hebrew language was written adds more uncertainty about what exactly these numbers mean. Since the Hebrew language was initially written without vowels, the word translated as 'thousands' in the KJV may not mean a number but may also mean 'unit', 'clan', 'tribe', 'chieftain' or even 'armed warrior' (see, for example, Judg 6:15). Thus the numbers given may refer either to tribal military units, or to an unspecified number of warriors, or to individual fighting men.

The fact that God tells Israel, 'But I will not drive them [the people of the land] out in a single year, because the land would become desolate and the wild animals too numerous for you. Little by little I will drive them out before you, until you have increased enough to take possession of the land' (Exod 23:29-30) suggests that they were not a vast multitude. So does God's reminder, 'The Lord did not set his affection on you and choose you because you were more numerous than other peoples, for you were the fewest of all peoples' (Deut 7:7). This last quotation implies that Israel was one of the smallest nations in the ancient Near East. This perception is confirmed by archaeological and historical data about the population of the area during the period of the Hebrew exodus.

Structure of the Book

The book of Numbers falls into three major sections, each united by certain common themes.

1:1–10:10 Preparing to Leave Sinai

The first part of the book of Numbers is closely linked to the legislation that is first recorded in Exodus 25–40 and continued throughout the book of Leviticus to the early chapters of Numbers. This part stresses the need to obey Yahweh by listening to his word and following his instructions. The motive for obedience is not fear or legalism, but a response to what he has done to and for them. This section includes instructions about matters such as the census (ch. 1), the holy camp (ch. 2), the separation of the Levites (chs. 3–4), leprosy, wrongs that are not atoned for and suspicions between husband and wife (ch. 5), the separation of the Nazirites (ch. 6), the presentation of offerings (ch. 7) and the separation of the priests from the Levites (ch. 8). Chapter 9:1–14 deals with the celebration of the second Passover by the whole community as an obedient response to God's instruction.

The section concludes with detailed instructions about the preparation for setting out on the march to the promised land. Israel is to obediently follow God's guidance given through the cloud that symbolized God's presence (9:15-23) and communicated to the people by signals sent by silver trumpets (10:1-10).

10:11-21:35 From Mount Sinai to Moab

The second section of the book of Numbers tells of the Israelites' journey from Mount Sinai through the desert of Paran to Kadesh-Barnea and eventually to the plains of Moab. Here the emphasis is on the rebellion of the people and the trouble resulting from this transgression.

The first subsection, 10:11-36, focuses on Yahweh's leadership as the people move from Sinai to Paran. The people move as organized tribal units and there is no reference to failures, needs, difficulties or God's judgments. So far, the people are faithful to God.

However, after this, the picture of the complete faithfulness presented since the beginning of the book begins

to fade. In the second section, the people complain about hardships in the desert and take part in a series of rebellions against God as well as against their leaders. The rebellions are often followed by God's judgment, Moses' intervention and God's mercy and forgiveness. In chapter 12, even the leaders are involved in rebellion against God. This chapter establishes Moses' prestige and authority over his siblings, Aaron and Miriam. Eventually, Israel camps at Kadesh-Barnea (chs. 13 and 14), and Moses sends out spies to investigate the promised land. The rebellious response to the report of the spies causes God to disown the people of that generation and deny them entrance to the promised land. Their desire to return to Egypt is equivalent to a total rejection of Yahweh.

Chapters 15–21 contain further laws and incidents related to the theme of rebellion and its repercussions. The laws include regulations governing cereal offerings (15:1-16), grain offerings (15:16-21), and offerings for sins committed in ignorance (16:22-31). Also presented are the laws covering the violation of the Sabbath (15:32-36) and instructions regarding remembrance of God's commandments (15:37-41).

The earlier rebellion by the people is followed by a rebellion by subordinate Levitical priests (Korah, Dathan and Abiram) and some two hundred and fifty lay leaders. God punishes these rebels, and Moses intercedes with him for the sake of the people. The incident in chapter 16 leads to the need to establish once and for all the supremacy of Aaronic priesthood described in Chapter 17. Chapter 18 demarcates the different roles of priests and Levites.

The rebellions described in the previous chapters have resulted in many deaths. This fact poses a serious threat to the holiness of the camp as people may touch or come in contact with a dead body. Thus the description of the priests' and Levites' duties is followed by a description of the ritual of purification for the unclean in chapter 19.

Chapter 20 tells of a rebellion by the central leaders, Moses and Aaron. This is followed in 21:4-9 by an account of a plague of serpents that God sent because of the people's rejection of the food that he had provided, and an account of how God saved those willing to obey him.

The section ends with an account of Israel's march and of the people's stay in several places before they reach Moab. This account also describes their victories over Sihon, king of the Amorites, and Og, king of Bashan (21:10-35).

22:1-36:13 In the Plains of Moab

The Israelites are now camped on the border of Canaan, anticipating their entry into the promised land. The previous chapters have revealed Israel's shaky relationship to Yahweh because of their failure to obey his commandments. The final chapters of the book hold out some hope of the continuation of that relationship and the fulfilment of the promise.

The first subsection (chs. 22–24) tells of God's blessings of Israel through a foreign prophet, Baalam. King Balak of Moab, a country that bordered the promised land, feared the advancing Israelites and hired Baalam, a professional prophet, to curse Israel. But instead of cursing them he was led to bless them. This incident proves God desires to bless the Israelites and give them the land he had promised to their forefathers.

At the same time, chapter 25 shows that the foreign prophet and his donkey are more obedient than the people of God, who quickly turned against God and worshipped idols and prostituted themselves with Moabite and Midianite women. In this chapter, the last of the generation that came out of Egypt and witnessed the events at Sinai events perishes. A second census is then taken, this time of the new generation that will enter the promised land (ch. 26).

Chapters 26–36 focus on this new generation. They deal with some legal decisions about inheritance (ch. 27), with rituals and legal regulations for the new generation, a systematized program for sacrifices and issues regarding women and vows (chs. 28–30). In chapter 31 the narrator describes Israel's revenge against the Midianites. Chapter 32 records the request of Reuben and Gad to settle on the eastern side of the Jordan and how this was dealt with to avert future trouble. Chapter 33 contains the warnings and encouragement God gives through Moses as the new generation prepares to take the promised land. Chapters 34–36 contain social legislation concerning issues such as boundaries, division of the land and establishment of Levitical cities and cities of refuge.

Outline of Contents

COMMENTARY

1:1-10:10 Preparing to Leave Sinai

This section is divided into two main sections: chapters 1 to 4 deal with the command to take a census and to organize the community, while chapters 5 to 10 deal with commands for the purity of the people. The whole section, in which God orders the people to follow specific rules, involves preparatory activity for entering the promised land. The rules are not an end in themselves; rather, the focus is on listening to the voice of God. Such listening later becomes a key theological focus. In the desert, Israel will either live a life of listening to (obeying) the word of God or a life of disobedience. In other words, the rules show at the outset the nature of relationship between God and the people who are on the move to the promised land. This relationship had been confirmed by the establishment of the covenant (Exod 19–24), which had moved the existing relationship between God and his people to a new level. The people of God are people on the move, but they must move in a constant relationship with God, who made them a people. It is a journey of choice in which they must decide whether to obey God or to follow their own desires. It is also an orderly march, not simply some chaotic, non-directional movement.

1:1-4:49 Organizing the Community

The book of Numbers starts with an account of a census taken in the year after the exodus, while the people camped in the desert of Sinai. This census would help to transform a disorganized mass of former slaves into a unified, organized people. The orderly census of the whole nation (1:54) is followed by instructions for preparing the holy camp for the coming march. The instructions also cover the tribes'

locations around the Tent of Meeting and the order in which they will march (2:1-34). Next come instructions about the Levites and a record of their locations around the Tent of Meeting and of their numbers, responsibilities, and role as a substitute for firstborn Israelite males (3:1-51). Finally, there are details of the number and specific duties of the Levites who served in the Tent of Meeting (4:1-49).

1:1-54 Census of the whole of Israel

By his word, God created the universe (Gen 1; Ps 33:6), by his word, he formed humankind (Gen 1:26-27), and by his word, he gave directives to Moses and the community (Exod 19:3-6). So the first thing that we learn in this book is that *the Lord spoke to Moses* (**1:1a**). By starting with the Lord's word to Moses, the author emphasizes the key role Moses plays in the desert stories. He is the prophet who receives instructions from the Lord and then communicates them to the people. His role is also that of the mediator between God and the people. However, as the details of the census show, Moses does not insist on being the sole leader. He has learned the lesson taught by his father-in-law Jethro in Exodus 18 and acknowledges his own need for help and the fact that God assigns different tasks to different persons. Thus here he seeks the help of the heads of the tribes in conducting the census. Later in this book, he is happy to assign all tasks related to public worship to the priests and Levites. His willingness to allow others to occupy very influential positions is a challenge to African patterns of leadership.

The sense of order in this section on the preparations for leaving Sinai is reinforced by the narrator's specification of the place where God spoke to Moses (*in the Desert of Sinai*) and also the time (*the first day of the second month of the second year after the Israelites came out of Egypt*) (**1:1b**).

God commands Moses, *Take a census of the whole Israelite community* (**1:2**), but in fact the census only covers the men *twenty years old or more* who could *serve in the army* (**1:3b**). Ancient Israel, like most African societies, was a very patriarchal society where political, military and economic power belonged to men.

The need to determine military strength seems to have been a common reason for conducting such censuses (see also 26:4; 2 Sam 24:2). Another reason was to levy taxes to cover the cost of community projects, like building the tabernacle (see Exod 30:11-16; 38:26). A smaller census of a distinct group was used to allocate work assignments in the Tent of Meeting (4:3). Chapter 26 reports on a second census, taken in the fortieth year after the exodus to count the new generation who would occupy the promised land. Later, Solomon took a census to identify able-bodied foreign workers (2 Chr 2:17-18). Ezra also conducted a census, one aim of which was probably to identify individuals who would serve the community as priests, Levites and the like (Ezra 2; see also 8:15).

The above examples show that taking a census was not uncommon in the OT and did not always draw God's wrath, as it did when David took a census (2 Sam 24; 1 Chr 21). It seems that God was angry with David because David had begun to rely more on human power than on the power of God. He had forgotten that he was simply a representative of Yahweh on earth to accomplish God's divine purpose.

Today, a government census still reminds people of their responsibilities to the state, as citizens and taxpayers, and of the state's responsibilities to provide services to them. There are no biblical grounds for objecting to counting people if the purpose is to establish how to offer better services to a community. But we can object if the results of a census are used for selfish reasons and personal gain.

The way the census in Numbers 1 was conducted also fits with the theological theme of obedience to God's instructions. God specifies that Aaron is to help Moses (**1:3a**) and adds that they are to recruit specific assistants, *one man from each tribe, each the head of his family* (**1:4**). From the beginning of their march, God provides the community with the gift of leadership. As the people cross the desert, their future will depend partly on how well these leaders play their role and listen attentively to the voice of God.

Many of our problems on this stricken continent of Africa relate to power struggles. African leaders should keenly listen to the many cries of those living with HIV/AIDS, of those living in abject poverty and of the victims of endless civil wars. But too often leaders seek only to cling to power and to use their power to further their personal ambitions. Yet they are called by God in the same way he called leaders in Israelite society. God knows the name of each African leader, just as he knew the names of the leaders of the tribes of Israel (**1:5-15**) and he calls them to be sensitive to the needs of the people

The names of the heads of the tribes who are to help with the counting are listed in an order similar to that in which the children of Jacob are listed in Genesis 35:23-26. This interest in genealogy is another theological motif that continues through the Bible and is reflected even in the NT books of Matthew and Luke. It resonates with the African tradition, which also places great stress on the original heads of clans and on the preservation of genealogies. African tradition sees one's clan as essential for one's identity within the community. Most Africans believe that it is impossible to exist without a clan.

The number of men in each tribe is listed in **1:17-44**. For a detailed discussion of the numbers given here, see the introduction to this commentary. These numbers can also be compared with the results of the second census to see how each tribe prospered or declined during the forty years in the desert (see the table in the discussion of chapter 26).

It will be noted that Levi, one of Jacob's sons, is not included in this census list, nor in the list in 1:5-15. The Levites were not included because, as **1:45** reminds us, this is a list of those able to serve in the army. The Levites were set aside to provide spiritual leadership and to serve in the Tent of Meeting and were not to be part of the army (**1:47-53**). God again provides a gift of leadership as the people prepare for the journey.

On completion of the census, it was found that 603,550 men were available for the army (**1:46**). Given that the same number is given in Exodus 38:26, it seems that this census was also used to levy taxes to cover the cost of building the tabernacle (see also Exod 30:11-16).

The chapter ends by saying that the Israelites did all this *just as the Lord commanded* them (**1:54**). Once again the importance of obedience comes to the fore, as it will throughout the rest of the book.

2:1-34 Arrangement of the camp

When the people of Israel moved, they travelled with the Tent of Meeting, that is, they travelled with God. The Tent implied that God dwelt in their midst. Because he is a God of order, 'everything should be done in a fitting and orderly way' (1 Cor 14:40), God gave instructions so that the camp would not be disorderly and chaotic. It was to be organized so that the Tent of Meeting, the place that represented God's presence with them, was at the heart of the campsite (**2:1-2**). Their march through the desert was to be marked by holiness because God is holy (Lev 19:2). Once again, God gave Israel the gift of worship to guide them in their desert journey. In this way, the people could maintain their relationship with the Holy God.

The twelve tribes were to occupy particular positions in relation to the Tent of Meeting. The tribes of Judah, Issachar and Zebulun were to camp on its eastern side (**2:3-9**) and those of Reuben, Simeon and Gad were to camp to the south (**2:10-16**). The Tent of Meeting and the Levites were placed in the middle of the camp (**2:17**). The tribes of Ephraim, Manasseh and Benjamin were to take up position to the west of the Tent of Meeting (**2:18-24**) and the tribes of Dan, Asher and Naphtali were to camp on its north side (**2:25-31**).

Thus the whole community of Israelites was divided up into four groups of three tribes each. One of the tribes was appointed as leader of its groups. Judah led the eastern group (2:9a); Reuben, the southern one (2:16a); Ephraim, the western one (2:24); and Dan, the northern one (2:31).

When the time came for the Israelites to move to a different location, they were to set out in the same order as they had been listed. The first to move would be the eastern group under Judah (2:9b), followed by the southern group under Reuben (2:16b). Then would come the Levites, carrying the dismantled Tent of Meeting (2:17; 1:51). They would be followed by the western group under Ephraim (2:24b) and the northern group under Dan would be the rearguard (2:31b).

It is remarkable how the groups of slaves who fled Egypt have become a well-ordered community with God as their leader and with Moses, Aaron and the tribal leaders as God's earthly representatives. They set out on a religious journey, full of anticipation. But the careful attention paid to the preparations for and order of their holy march suggests that Israel would need courage to face future uncertainties. The order and procedures were intended to give them additional hope, but their journey is first and foremost about walking by faith rather than by sight (2 Cor 5:7).

The order in which the tribes were to march is also significant. One might have expected that the tribes of Reuben and Simeon would lead the march, because their founders were the patriarch Jacob's eldest sons and they were mentioned first in the census (1:20-22). But instead Judah's descendants would lead the march. This had been predicted many years before in Jacob's blessing, which promised leadership to Judah (Gen 49:10) and stated that Reuben and Simeon would not enjoy the first place they might have expected from their birth order (Gen 49:3-7). Judah had already begun to show that leadership in the encounters between Joseph and his brothers (Gen 43–44). Both the great king David and the Messiah would be descendants of Judah (Ruth 1:1; 4:18-21; Matt 1:1-16). Such reversals are part of the pattern of the OT understanding of how God works in mysterious and quite unexpected ways. He uses unusual people and events to accomplish his purpose. As God reminded the Israelites, 'My thoughts are not your thoughts, neither are your ways my ways' (Isa 55:8).

Once again, the chapter ends on a note of obedience. In 2:1 the Lord told Moses and Aaron what the Israelites must do, and the chapter ends by saying, *the Israelites did everything the Lord commanded Moses* (**2:34**). In the OT, obedience is not simply following a set of rules. Rather, it is having faith in the one who gives out those rules. The rules and commandments are not meant to burden the people but to enhance a relationship by giving directions as to how best to respond to God. In other words, the rules are a gift that is intended to enhance life. The dominant and recurring theme is that 'God speaks'. Obedience is possible because God gives directives and sets out his purpose clearly. And his purpose is to make sure that Israel succeeds in its journey to the promised land.

3:1-4:49 Arrangements for the Levites

God's purposes sometimes involve setting particular groups apart for a purpose. Israel was chosen to serve a special purpose and to be God's instrument for blessing the whole world (Gen 12:1-3). Within Israel, the tribe of Judah was chosen to produce the leader who would bring salvation to

humanity. The tribe of Levi was also set apart or ordained for a special central function within the community.

3:1-35 THE ROLE OF THE LEVITES The Levites were the descendants of Levi, the third son born to Jacob by Leah (Gen 29:34). They were divided into three groups, each descended from one of the three sons of Levi: Gershon, Kohath and Merari (Gen 46:11). One family from among the Levites, the family of Aaron, were to serve as priests (**3:1-4, 10**). The rest of the Levites were to assist the priests and by doing this serve the community. Their special task was to take care of all the equipment associated with the Tent of Meeting (**3:5-9**).

From a human point of view, the Levites may have held their unique position because Moses needed the support of the members of his own tribe to help him enforce the laws laid down for the community and to encourage allegiance to the new religious institutions being set up. This was what the Levites did when they sided with Moses during the golden calf incident and obeyed his orders to slaughter the idol worshippers, leading Moses to say, 'You have been set apart to the Lord today' (Exod 32:29).

But the appointment of the Levites also had a spiritual dimension. God was entitled to claim the firstborn son of every Israelite woman. He had claimed them for his own on the day when he had destroyed the firstborn of Egypt but had redeemed the firstborn in Israel (Exod 13:12). However, the Levites were to act as substitutes for the firstborn sons and to serve the Lord on behalf of those sons (**3:11-13**). The Levites were to camp closest to the Tent of Meeting, and each clan within the tribe was allocated a position around the Tent and specific tasks to perform (**3:14-39**). Their position as substitutes was made very clear when God had Moses take a separate census of all firstborn males, and by the care Moses took to match the number of firstborn males with the number of Levites, and to collect compensation to make up the difference (**3:40-51**).

4:1-49 THE ALLOCATION OF LEVITES' DUTIES A successful march through the desert would depend on how well each group in the community played its part. And within each group were subgroups among whom the work had to be divided. This chapter gives the division of labour among the three Levitical families mentioned in the census (3:16-37). A separate census was ordered to determine how many were eligible to serve in the Tent of Meeting. All Levite men were expected to serve while they were between the ages of thirty and fifty years old (**4:1-3**). The higher age limit set for starting Levitical service than for starting military service was probably because the seriousness of their duties called for emotional and mental maturity as well as physical maturity. The figures given here differ from those for Levite males in 3:21-39 because that count included all males, even those too young or too old to serve in the Tent of Meeting.

Each of the three Levite clans had to take responsibility for transporting a different part of the Tent of Meeting, under the supervision of one of the descendants of Aaron.

The responsibilities of the Kohathites are set out in 4:4-20. They were to take care of *the most holy things* (**4:4**; see also 3:31). These items were so holy that only the priests might touch and see them. Thus the priests, presumably under the supervision of Eleazar, the son of Aaron (**4:16**) were to carefully wrap these objects before allowing the Kohathite clan to carry them (**4:5-15a**). On pain of death, the Kohathites must neither touch any of these objects directly nor even try to catch a glimpse of the carefully wrapped things they were carrying (**4:15b, 17-20**).

The responsibilities of the Gershonites are set out in 4:21-28. Under the supervision of Ithamar the son of Aaron (**4:28**), they were to carry the Tent itself, the curtains that screened off various areas and the ropes that supported these curtains (**4:25-26**; see also 3:25-26).

The responsibilities of the Merarites are set out in 4:29-33. They were to carry the wooden structure on which the cloth curtains would be hung when the Tent was erected (**4:31-32a**; see also 3:36-37). Each man in the clan was to be responsible for carrying specific items (**4:32b**). Like the Gershonites, the Merarites were supervised by Ithamar the son of Aaron (**4:33**).

The chapter ends with a statement of the total number of men eligible to serve the Tent of Meeting in each of the three clans (**4:34-49**), as determined from the census.

5:1-10:10 Preserving the Purity of the People

So far, the people have responded to God's instructions on preparing for their journey with obedience and anticipation. Now they face another type of preparation, which is discussed in chapters 5 through 10, namely achieving purity as a people. Their journey is not merely a trip to a final destination; on the contrary, it is a journey in which those who have been redeemed offer their whole way of life to God in adoration, praise and thanksgiving for who he is and what he has done.

In Exodus 19:6, God had told the people, 'you will be for me a kingdom of priests and a holy nation', and the idea of holiness is central to the narrative from Exodus 25 to Numbers 10:10. The regulations that follow God's declaration are different expressions of one theological truth: the holiness of the camp depends entirely on how individuals assume responsibility for maintaining that holiness.

5:1-6:21 Preserving the holiness of the camp

This section deals with laws intended to ensure that the people secure and preserve the holiness of the camp.

5:1-4 INFECTIOUS DISEASES Before the march to the promised land starts, certain people must be sent away from the camp, including anyone with an infectious skin disease (not just leprosy, as is often thought) or a discharge of any kind, and anyone who is ceremonially unclean because he or she has had contact with a dead body (**5:1-2**). This rule will benefit the community by preventing infections from spreading. But there is more to it than mere hygiene. In the OT, sickness and suffering are closely associated with sin, and purity involves moral, physical and mental well-being. Consequently, even physical problems were seen as having a spiritual dimension and causing impurity or defilement. So God says that those suffering from these ailments must be sent *away so they will not defile their camp, where I dwell among them* (**5:3**). A priest would determine whether a condition was unclean. He would also determine whether someone could be readmitted to the camp after he or she had undergone the required rituals and had been declared clean (see Lev 13–15).

The Iraqw tribe of northern Tanzania have similar rules regarding anything or anybody who might defile the community. In the pre-Christian era, they refused to allow anyone who had a disease that was thought to be contagious to remain in the community until he or she had undergone a cleansing ritual and some healing interventions. Anyone who had lost a family member was also regarded as unclean until after a period of seclusion in which he or she observed rituals to satisfy communal expectations. Such practices were not egoistic and self-centred but were intended to safeguard the community. Hence, although the separation was undoubtedly difficult, those excluded from the community were not ignored, but special provision was made to meet their needs without defiling the community.

Once again, the Israelites did as God commanded them (**5:4**). Obedience continues to be a dominant theme in this part of the book.

5:5-10 RESTITUTION FOR WRONGS Those who have wronged others, and thus sinned against God, must make reparation for the damage they have done and add an extra one-fifth in additional compensation (**5:5-7**; Lev 6:5). The legislation here expands on Leviticus 5:16 by specifying that if the one who was wronged is now dead and had no relatives, then the payment for restitution must be given to the priest (**5:8**). The expansion makes it clear that laws have to be adapted for each generation and every new context, for laws are designed for the welfare of human beings. Human beings were not designed for the sake of the laws.

African communities are well aware that reconciliation requires more than just words of remorse and contrition; there must be some action and some payment or restitution to the person wronged. They are also aware that this holds true even if the offender or the one offended is dead. The Iraqw of Tanzania expect the relatives, and especially the immediate family, of an offender to make restitution if the offender dies before this can be done. If the person offended is also dead, then his or her relatives will receive the restitution. The Maasai also insist on payment for an offence. They have an established procedure for reconciliation that involves the slaughter of a goat of reconciliation, which the reconciling parties and their families eat in preparation for the day of reconciliation. On that day, there is a ceremony at which the mediator pronounces words similar to those in 2 Corinthians 5:17, 'the old has gone, the new has come!'

Like the Jews and many other Africans, the Maasai believe that the life of every individual is solely grounded in the community. They believe that a person cannot exist without the community, and those who disassociate themselves from it will wither and die like a branch that is cut off from a tree. Reconciliation is vital because it enables the community to keep its relationship with God and maintain relationships with one another. They believe that any one who is not reconciled with his or her neighbour cannot worship *Enkai* (God).

5:11-31 Suspected adultery Preparation for the holy march requires that the people address all the issues that could defile the camp. Such issues go beyond physical purity to include moral purity in the family setting. That is why the next section addresses marital unfaithfulness. Any suspected adultery must somehow be brought to light to vindicate the one who is offended. Thus, if a woman is suspected of infidelity, her husband must bring her to the priest, along with a grain offering for his jealousy (**5:11-15**). The priest will make her drink some bitter water that will bring a curse upon her if she has been unfaithful. If she has not been involved with any other man, the curse will not affect her (**5:16-31**).

This law reflects a double standard in that only women were subjected to this ordeal; men were not tested to see whether they had been unfaithful. This attitude finds resonance in many patriarchal societies where women are stereotyped as being sexually promiscuous, while their male partners are not. This attitude to women is also found in other parts of the social and legal system of ancient Israel. In the Decalogue, a woman is considered part of a man's property, which must not be coveted by another person (Exod 20:17; see also Deut 5:21).

However, it should be noted that the ordeal prescribed here is a relatively mild one, compared to those imposed in other cultures at the time, which were far more likely to produce a guilty verdict. All that the woman had to do was drink a mixture of dust and water, and if she were innocent, this would have no effect on her. Her husband's jealousy would also be allayed, making for a more peaceful home life.

6:1-21 The nazirites After dealing with what making a vow to be a Nazirite entails (6:1-8), this chapter describes the rituals for restoring purity when a Nazirite is polluted by

touching a dead body (6:9-12) and with the rituals the Nazirite observed on completion of his or her vow (6:13-21).

Some men and women within the camp had taken a vow *of separation to the Lord* to become Nazirites. This meant that they were set aside as holy to the Lord (**6:1-2**) and had to abstain *from wine or and other fermented drinks* (**6:3-4**); to allow their hair to grow uncut (**6:5**) and to avoid any contact with a dead body, which would make them unclean (**6:6-8**). The Bible teaches that once vows are made they are binding, therefore they should not be taken lightly (Prov 20:25). Scripture also warns against people who mislead the Nazirites or force them to break their vow (Amos 2:12-13).

While the Nazirites were forbidden to have any contact with a dead body, it was possible that a sudden death might accidentally defile a Nazirite. Thus, 6:8-12 provides a special procedure for restoration when this occurs. The Nazirite will endure the normal period of uncleanness following contact with a corpse, which was seven days (19:14), and then at the purification ceremony on the seventh day have all of his or her hair shaved off (**6:9**). The following day the Nazirite *must bring two doves or two young pigeons to the priest at the entrance to the Tent of Meeting* (**6:10**). The priest will offer one as a sin offering and the second one as a burnt offering to make atonement for the sin of having broken his or her vow by being in the presence of a dead body. The person will then have to resume his or her vow for the full period pledged, without any credit for the days already served (**6:12**).

The Nazirite vow was not a permanent one. When the period specified came to an end, the Nazirite had to come to the Tent of Meeting with a burnt offering consisting of a one-year-old male lamb, a one-year-old female lamb and a ram, together with grain and drink offerings and a basket of unleavened bread and cakes (**6:13-15**). The priest would present these before the Lord and make a sin offering and burnt offering (**6:16**). Thereafter the Nazirite's head was again shaved and the hair offered in sacrifice (**6:18**). Specific parts of the sacrificial animals were then given to the priest (**6:19-20a**). On completion of this ritual, the Nazirite was no longer under the vow and was free to drink wine again (**6:20b**).

The specifications for the sacrifices to be offered did not prevent the grateful Nazirite from offering more, if he or she could afford to do so (**6:21**).

6:22-27 Blessing the community

The account of the preparation for the journey includes what is probably the best-known section of the book of Numbers, the Aaronic or priestly blessing, used by the priests to pronounce God's blessing on the community. The priest's words are framed by the word 'bless': Yahweh commands Aaron and his sons to *bless the Israelites* (**6:23**) and the Lord promises *I will bless them* (**6:27**). The blessing itself is written in poetic style, with three parallel invocations, each beginning with the divine name, Yahweh. This pattern emphasizes that the Lord is the source of blessing, a point that is underscored by the emphatic 'I' when the Lord says, 'And I will bless them'.

The first part of the blessing refers to posterity, the gift of land and of safety on their march, all of which are implicit in the *keep you* (**6:24**). In the book of Psalms, the Lord is referred to as 'Israel's keeper' (Ps 121:4, KJV). The second part of the blessing asks that God's face may *shine upon* the Israelites as they receive his grace (**6:25**). This image of God showing or hiding his face to show his pleasure or anger is a common one in the OT, especially in Psalms (see Pss 13:1; 10:1; 102:2). The last part of the blessing repeats this image, but adds the thought that God's ultimate blessing to the community is his *shalom,* which can also be translated as *peace* or wholeness (**6:26**).

7:1-89 Dedication of the Tent of Meeting

Moses prepared the Tent of Meeting as a place of worship by anointing and consecrating it. Both 'anoint' and 'consecrate' mean the same thing, namely to set something apart for a special function. Moses also *anointed* and *consecrated* all the furnishings of the Tent of Meeting, including *the altar and all its utensils* (**7:1**). This consecration was important because the Tent of Meeting had to be set apart for it to be a sacred place where people could worship Yahweh in the desert.

The Tent of Meeting prefigured the temple that King Solomon would erect. After the Babylonians destroyed that temple, the memory of the Tent and the nation's worship during the desert period became an inspiration for the exiles because it reminded them that it was possible to worship God even without a temple. The prophecy in Isaiah 66:1 is also a reminder that God is present everywhere and cannot be confined in any building: 'Heaven is my throne ...

Where is the house you will build for me?

Where will my resting place be?'

In this chapter, we read about the offerings made to the Lord after the consecration of the temple, offerings that reveal the Israelites' commitment both to Yahweh and to the rest of the community. First we hear of the offerings the leaders gave (7:1-9), then of the offerings each tribe made (7:10-88).

The tribal leaders made the first set of offerings. They offered *six covered carts and twelve oxen* to pull them (**7:2-3**). The Lord specifically instructed Moses to accept these gifts for the service of the Tent of Meeting (**7:4**). So Moses did this and gave the carts to the Levites to be used to help them transport the Tent of Meeting as they travel towards the promised land (**7:5**). The Merarites were given twice as many carts as the Gershonites because they had more to transport than the Gershonites (**7:7-8**; compare 3:36-37

and 3:25-26). The Kohathites were not given any carts because the goods they had to transport were so holy that they had to be carried by hand (**7:9**; see also 3:31).

Besides the carts and the oxen, each tribal leader also brought a special offering on behalf of his whole tribe. This was done in a very orderly fashion, with each tribe allocated a day over a twelve-day period on which to present its offering (Judah – **7:12-17**; Zebulun – **7:18-29**; Reuben – **7:30-35**; Simeon – **7:36-41**; Gad – **7:42-47**; Ephraim – **7:48-53**; Manasseh – **7:54-59**; Benjamin – **7:60-65**; Dan – **7:66-71**; Asher – **7:72-77**; Naphtali – **7:78-83**). This order corresponds to their marching order and to their locations within the camp (see ch. 2). Thus the tribe of Judah presents its offering first, and the tribe of Naphtali is last.

Not only was each tribe given an opportunity to show its support for building the Tabernacle, but each was also asked to show the same level of commitment to its service by bringing the same offering. Each tribe offered one silver plate, one silver bowl full of fine flour mixed with oil for the grain offering; one golden dish full of incense, one young bull, one ram and one male lamb a year old for a burnt offering; one male goat for a sin offering; and two oxen, five rams, five male goats and five male lambs a year old for the fellowship offering. These valuable gifts were a tangible demonstration of the people's unanimous support for the Tent of Meeting and for the priests. Offerings such as the grain offering and the burnt offering were made to signal thanksgiving, while sin offerings and fellowship offerings were meant to restore and maintain the relationship between God and the people.

The total amount offered is summed up in **7:84-88**. The weight of silver offered was about sixty-two pounds (twenty eight kilograms) and the amount of gold offered was three pounds (one and a half kilograms).

The repetition in this chapter would have helped the people to remember what they were supposed to do, so that if one tribe forgot something they would be reminded by their counterparts. But the purpose of the repetition goes beyond simply aiding memory. It also signalled the importance of what was being done and the equality of all the tribes. Every tribe was called to offer the same worship and to accept the same commandments from the Lord. Every tribe had to obey and play its role faithfully to ensure the well-being of the whole community. If one tribe failed to act responsibly, the whole community would be defiled and the holy march would be affected. This concept corresponds to the African ideology of communal accountability through individual participation.

God was present in the Tent of Meeting, and that is where he spoke with Moses and Moses spoke with him (**7:89**). This presence of God in the midst of the people contrasts with the situation in Exodus 33:7-11, in which the Tent of Meeting was put outside the camp because of the incident with the golden calf. God could not dwell in the midst of people who made idols their god. But now the Tent of Meeting is in the centre of the camp and the people can approach God.

8:1-26 Obedience of Aaron and the Levites

The commitment to obedience encompassed the whole community, including the priests, the Levites, the tribal leaders and all those represented by them. The chapter starts by emphasizing the obedience of Aaron, the high priest, as he arranged the seven lamps in the holy place to light the area that God had identified (**8:1-3**) and the obedience shown in following God's design for the lampstand (**8:4**). The details of the design and construction of the golden lampstand had been given earlier (Exod 25:31-40; 37:17-24), but there was no mention of its lights, which are mentioned only here. They were probably lit as part of the dedication of the Tabernacle.

The rest of this chapter deals with the ordination of the Levites as assistants to the priests. The ceremony, which officially dedicated them to carry out their assigned tasks, has some similarities with that prescribed for the ordination of priests in Leviticus 8. However, whereas the priests were made holy, the Levites are merely made clean (**8:5-6**; Lev 8:30); the priests were both washed and anointed, the Levites were merely sprinkled with *water of cleansing* (**8:7a**; Lev 8:6, 12); the priests were given new clothes, but the Levites merely washed their existing clothes (**8:7b**; Lev 8:7-9, 13); oil was applied to the priests for anointing, but was merely mixed with flour for the Levites' offering (**8:8**; Lev 8:12, 30).

Moses was told to bring the Levites before the Tent of Meeting where the whole congregation would lay hands on them (**8:9-10**). Presumably the ritual was carried out by representatives of the entire nation laying hands on representatives of all the Levites. This laying on of hands was a sign that the Levites were substitutes for the firstborn of Israel (**8:16-18**; see also 3:11-13, 40-51). This allusion links this event with the description of the celebration of Passover in Numbers 9, reminding readers of why the Passover was instituted and why the community needed to celebrate it before setting out on its march.

The Levites were to be set apart to serve in the Tent of Meeting as helpers to Aaron and his sons, that is, to the priests (**8:11, 13-15, 19a, 22**). But before they could do this, a sacrifice had to be offered to make atonement for their sins (**8:12**). Later in this chapter, it is also said that the Levites' job is also to make atonement for the people of Israel (**8:19b**). To understand what this means, we have to have some understanding of what is meant by 'atonement'.

In Hebrew, the verb translated as 'atone' literally means 'to cover' or 'to smear over'. Figuratively, it is used to express the idea of appeasing, pacifying or making amends

to someone (Gen 32:20; 2 Sam 21:3; Prov 16:14). Another meaning is 'to forgive' or 'to make expiation' (Deut 21:8; 32:43; 2 Chr 30:18; Pss 65:34; 78:38; 79:9; Prov 16:6; Isa 6:7; 22:14; Jer 18:23; Ezek 16:63). It can also refer to the act of 'covering or abolishing something' (Isa 28:18). Another meaning is 'to perform the ritual of making atonement' (Exod 29:33, 36, 37; 30:10, 15, 16; 32:30; Lev 1:4; 4:20, 26, 31, 35; 5:6, 10, 13).

The ritual of making atonement for the people culminated in the offering on the Day of Atonement (Exod 30:10). This day, which is often referred to in Hebrew as the Day of the Covering of Sins, involved the only prescribed fast in the OT and an elaborate ritual in which the high priest offered sacrifices to atone for the pollution of God's house and of God's people by sin (Lev 16; 23:26-32; and Num 29:7-11). It is this ritual to which the author of Hebrews refers when he speaks of Christ as our high priest, offering atonement for us (Heb 9–10). Jesus can be said to have 'covered' the sins of the world.

The reference to the Levites making atonement for the people (8:19) must not be interpreted as referring to that special ritual but to the word's simpler meaning of covering something. The Levites are to stand as a screen between the people and God, protecting them from the plague that would strike if people who were not holy or set apart for God's service attempted to serve in the Holy Place.

Like the preceding chapters, chapter 8 ends with words that emphasize the obedience of Moses, of Aaron, of the Levites and of the whole community in doing exactly what God commanded (8:20-22).

Because harmony is essential on the journey to the promised land, rules were given in great detail about even minor points such as age requirements. The Levites had to be twenty-five years of age before they were allowed to start serving in the Tent of Meeting (**8:24**). Presumably by this age they were considered mature enough to know how to behave and to make sound judgments. When they reached the age of thirty, they were considered capable of the solemn responsibility of carrying the Tabernacle and its utensils (4:3). Jesus himself started his ministry when he was thirty years of age (Luke 3:23).

The ministry of the Levites terminated at the age of fifty (**8:25**). After that age, they could still assist their brothers, but *must not do the work* (**8:26**). This early retirement meant that the work was done by those who had the strength and energy to do it well, while the older men retired with strength intact and became respected advisors to the younger Levites.

Unfortunately, in many situations in Africa, leaders seem to think that once they have taken office they have to hang on to that office until they die, as if no one else were capable of leading or serving the nation or the church. The pattern that is laid out here in Numbers is a healthier one.

The old retire from active service, but are still viewed as wise consultants and counsellors in view of their experience, while younger people take their place. If this approach to leadership were adopted in Africa, it would make a great difference to our continent.

9:1-14 The celebration of the Passover

The first Passover had been celebrated on the eve of the people's departure from Egypt (Exod 12:25). Now, God reminded Moses of the need to repeat the celebration (**9:1-3**). This second Passover was particularly significant, coming as it did after the episode of the golden calf (Exod 32–33). The first Passover had been defiled by this idolatry, so this second Passover represents a new beginning.

Most of the people obeyed the Lord's command to celebrate the Passover in the desert (**9:4-5**), but some could not because they were ceremonially unclean. The Passover instructions given in Egypt did not address their situation or some others, so the people asked Moses what they should do.

The problem of someone being ceremonially unclean on the day when the Passover was to be eaten had not arisen at the first Passover because the laws on ceremonial purity had not yet been given. Now, however, the command that only those who were ceremonially clean might eat the meat of offerings (see Lev 7:18-20) seemed to conflict with the command to celebrate the Passover (**9:6-7**). Moses was unsure about how to handle this situation, and so he inquired of the Lord (**9:8**). In his answer, the Lord also addressed issues related to travellers, aliens and those who refused to keep the Passover. The Lord says that all who were unclean on the date of the Passover, or who were away from home, should celebrate it exactly one month later, by which time the obstacle to their participation should have been removed. There would have been time to do this, for the Passover was celebrated on the fourteenth day of the first month of the year, and the community moved on from Sinai only on the twentieth day of the second month (10:11). Apart from this concession, the person should follow all the Passover regulations (**9:10-12**).

The problem of some people deliberately refusing to participate in the Passover celebration had not been an issue during the first celebration in Egypt. Along with the Egyptians, such people would have suffered the death of their firstborn. But there would be no such divine punishment on this second Passover. Instead Moses is instructed that such a person must be *cut off from his people* (**9:13**). Being 'cut off' was a serious punishment for the serious sin of disobedience to Yahweh. It may have meant being thrown out of the camp and thus losing fellowship with the community and with God or it may have meant a death sentence. It certainly meant that the offender lost the privilege of entering the promised land. Christians sometimes interpret this

phrase as referring to being excommunicated by the community and by God himself, which leads to eternal death. To be cut off from God is to be condemned and doomed eternally. It means to be denied God's favour, love, grace and mercy.

Finally, God gave instructions on what to do if an alien, or non-Israelite, wished to participate in the Passover celebration. The rule was the same as the one applied to the Passover in Exodus: aliens were free to participate provided they were actually living among the Israelites and were prepared to follow all the regulations governing the Passover celebration (**9:14**; Exod 12:19, 48).

In all these cases, we see the laws being adjusted to meet particular needs and to provide for those who would otherwise have difficulty celebrating the feast. Such reinterpretation of laws from time to time was crucial for Israelites of different generations and is also important for the church today. It is instructive to see how Moses approached problems resulting from changing circumstances or the applications of laws. When he did not know the correct answer to give, he consulted the Lord and waited to hear his answer (9:8). This seems to have been his usual practice, for we see him doing the same thing in the case of the daughters of Zelophehad (27:1-10).

The church too should not unquestioningly uphold existing laws, but must take time to think and pray about modifications that may be needed so that the laws, while not neglecting biblical teaching on particular issues, do not impose undue hardships. Given the rapidly changing circumstances on our continent, it may be unwise to apply old rules to a new community. But we must take care to seek God's guidance as we try to deal with the issues affecting our society.

9:15-23 A sign of God's presence

All the Israelites have done so far is to prepare for their departure from Sinai. Now, the narrator introduces two signals that would indicate when the march to the promised land was to begin. The first sign was the location of the cloud, which symbolized God's presence and power, in relation to the Tent of Meeting (**9:15-16**). (At night, the cloud looked like a pillar of fire.)

In the OT, cloud and fire are closely linked with God's presence. God used the burning bush to reveal himself to Moses (Exod 3:2-3). After the Israelites first left Egypt, they were led by a pillar of cloud in the day and a pillar of fire in the night as a symbol of God's accompanying, protecting and guiding the people in the journey (Exod 13:21-22). The cloud and fire reappeared in the context of the making of the covenant and the giving of the commandments (Exod 19:16-19; 24:15-18). After the golden calf fiasco, the presence of God with the people was also described using the image of cloud (Exod 33:9, 10; 34:5). The use of this image in the book of Exodus reached its climax when the Tent of Meeting was finally set up (Exod 40:34-38). Throughout Numbers and the rest of the OT, God's manifestation of himself is frequently depicted in terms of cloud and fire 'By day you led them with a pillar of cloud, and by night with a pillar of fire to give them light on the way they were to take' (Neh 9:12; see also Lev 16:2; Num 9:14-22; 10:11, 12, 34; 11:25; 12:5, 10; 14:14; 16:42; Deut 1:33; 5:22; 31:15; 1 Kgs 8:10, 11; 2 Chr 5:13, 14; Pss 68:4; 78:14; 99:7; Isa 4:5; 19:1; Jer 4:13; Joel 2:2; Zeph 1:15). In all these references the cloud depicts God's holiness and loving presence as well as his judgment.

The appearance of the cloud settling on the Tent of Meeting, here called the 'Tent of Testimony', on the day it was set up would have reminded the people that God is their leader and his presence was essential on their long and unpredictable journey through the desert. When the cloud was taken up from over the Tent, the people of Israel would set out; when the cloud stayed in one place, so would they (9:17-23). At the start of this section, the narrator does not specifically state that God gave these directions to move, but this point soon becomes clear with the threefold repetition of the words, *At the Lord's command the Israelites set out, and at his command they encamped* (**9:18, 20, 23a**). Once again, the emphasis is on the people's obedient response. At the end of the passage the narrator clearly states that *they obeyed the Lord's order, in accordance with his command through Moses* (**9:23b**).

In the OT, God manifests himself through angels, prophets and various natural and supernatural signs. The culmination of this revelation comes in the NT through the life and the ministry of our Lord Jesus Christ. In him, God is fully manifested, so that we are not only given the gift of salvation but also taught God's will and purpose for humankind. As Christians, we do not have a cloud to guide us, but we do have God's Holy Spirit and the holy Scriptures, which were given to guide us in the way of salvation and direct our journey towards our new 'promised land'. The Bible also gives us new ways of relating to God and to others (including the whole of creation). As a new community in Christ, we have been given a mission of being a blessing to others throughout the world.

10:1-10 Sounding of the silver trumpets

Before the people could set out on their march, they had to obey one final command. God told Moses to make two silver trumpets for the priests to use to issue commands, such as summoning the congregation to get ready for the holy march (**10:1-2**). When the people heard both trumpets, everyone was to assemble before Moses at the Tent of Meeting (**10:3**). If they heard only one trumpet, the leaders of the clans were to assemble before Moses (**10:4**). Long blasts would be the sign for the people to set out on the march;

at the first long blast, those camping on the east were to leave; at the second blast, those on the south were to leave (**10:5-6**).

The trumpets would continue to be used after the march through the desert was over (**10:8**). Once the people had settled in Canaan, the trumpet would be blown for two purposes. They would sound an alarm when Israel went to battle against any group that was oppressing it, so that the Lord would remember and save the Israelites from their enemies (**10:9**). It was not sounding the trumpets itself that would bring them victory, but rather the people's obedience to the instructions of God who brings victory. The trumpets would also be sounded to mark the days of special feasts and festivals, such as the New Moon festival that marked the beginning of each month (**10:10**). They would also be sounded at the start of the Jubilee Year (Lev 25:9). These feasts were occasions when people communed with God, and the sounding of the trumpet prepared them for this.

These trumpets are not, however, the same as those used in the attack on Jericho that led to the collapse of its walls; those were rams' horns, not silver trumpets (Josh 6:4). But the principle is still the same; those trumpets were sounded in obedience to God to summon his help in the battle. Later, we find trumpets used in worship services, along with other instruments in the temple orchestra (1 Chr 16:6). The sounding of trumpets is referred to on many other occasions in the OT.

The trumpets are not alone in having relevance beyond their obvious role. So does the march itself. Israel's journey involved more than merely the physical passage through the desert that culminated in the people's entering the promised land. It was an ongoing journey of relationship with the Lord of the covenant, the God who delivered them from slavery and gave them the gift of land. The book of Numbers makes it clear that this relationship between Israel and its God entailed repeatedly listening to what God said and obeying it. It is thus appropriate that this last section of the preparations for the march begins and ends with the Lord speaking (10:1, 10).

10:11-21:35 From Mount Sinai to Moab

The next major section of Numbers deals with the Israelites' journey through the desert after they leave Mount Sinai. It is a time of trouble, and in the desert the community ceases to be the obedient people described in 1:1-10:10. Instead, this section describes one incident of rebellion after another. Chapter 12 describes the people's complaints about food and Moses' leadership as they camp at an oasis known as Kadesh-Barnea. When spies return from Canaan with fruit that proves the land is bountiful, along with reports of the strength of the inhabitants, the Israelites forget the power of God and are too afraid of the people of Canaan to try to enter the land. God accepts their refusal, but as a result of their rebellion all those in that generation will die in the desert (chs. 13–14). Even some Levites rebel against the roles assigned to them and, under the leadership of Korah, try to assume the prerogatives of priesthood (ch. 16). God performs a miracle to show that Aaron is his chosen priest (ch. 17). When the people continue to complain, God afflicts them with serpents. Moses intercedes and they are healed when they look at a bronze serpent that Moses makes (21:4-9). Then at last, many years after leaving Egypt, as they make their way through the area today known as Jordan, they start to see victory again as they defeat two kings, Sihon and Og (21:10-35).

10:11-36 Departure from Sinai

Finally, Israel broke camp on the twentieth day of the second month of the second year (10:11). The people must have long anticipated this day. The cloud lifted above the Tent of Meeting, signalling the start of the march (10:11). They travelled for three days (10:33), until they again encamped in the Desert of Paran, where the cloud again came to rest on the Tent of Meeting (10:12).

The order of the tribes was similar to that previously assigned, with the additional detail that those Levites carrying the Tent of Meeting marched immediately behind the first group of tribes, so that the tent could be set up and ready by the time the holiest objects, carried by the Kohathites in the centre of the column, arrived (10:14-28; see ch. 2). The emphasis here is still on the people's obedience to the Lord's command (10:13).

Although the Israelites were one covenant community, this community was not exclusive. Other people could be invited to share the blessing. Thus, in Exodus 12:38 we are told that 'Many other people went up with them, as well as large droves of livestock, both flocks and herds.' Moses asked his brother-in-law Hobab, who is said to be the son of Reuel the Midianite, to go with them to the promised land (10:29; see also Exod 2:18). This verse is confusing, for in Exodus 3:1 Moses' father-in-law is called Jethro. But in many parts of the world, it is not uncommon for one person to be called by more than one name. Even in the NT, Peter is also referred to as Cephas and as Simon.

At first Hobab hesitates about accompanying them (10:30), but on Moses' insistence and promise to share the good things promised to Israel, Hobab consents and travels with the Israelites (10:31-32; Judg 1:16; 4:11).

As they travelled, the Israelites were led by the ark of the covenant of the Lord, which contained the stone tablets on which the Ten Commandments were written (10:33; see Deut 10:5). The ark was another symbol of God's presence with the community. It reminded them of the covenant God had made with them at Sinai and of God's promises, including the promise of the land. The ark was also an emblem of war and of God's protection of his people. This is clear from Moses' words whenever the ark set out: Rise up, O Lord! May your enemies be scattered; may your foes flee before you (10:35-36).

11:1-35 Incidents of Rebellion and Judgment

This chapter reports a dramatic change, in which the people suddenly cease to be obedient people of God. The Pentateuch describes two similarly dramatic changes. The first occurred when Adam and Eve abandoned their happy and serene life in a close relationship with God and disobeyed their creator (Gen 2–3). The second occurred after God had delivered the Israelites and made a covenant with them, setting them apart from all other nations (Exod 19–24). Moses had gone to the mountain to receive instructions on the making of the Tent of Meeting (Exod 25–31). Instead of waiting patiently for his return, the people became impatient and forced Aaron to make them an idol to worship and to lead them in their journey. God's awesome revelation on Mount Sinai is thus followed by Aaron's making a golden calf that the people dance around and hail as 'your gods, O Israel, who brought you up out of Egypt' (Exod 32:4). Both in Genesis and in Exodus, God responded to these changes with anger and punished his people.

The Israelites had learned from their punishment at Sinai (Exod 32:25-35) and cooperated with Moses and other leaders to purify the camp and ready themselves for the holy march.

11:1-9 The people's complaints

Yet, immediately after the march started, there were heartbreaking scenes of rebellion and punishment. People became God's enemies and he had to punish them for their sin of discontent and lack of faith.

In 11:1a, we are not told precisely what hardships the people were complaining of. No doubt the desert presented people with all sorts of difficult experiences. But at this point the narrator is not interested in a specific problem. He focuses on the fact that the people complained to God, that God heard their complaints and responded by adding to their distress. Whereas in Exodus 15:22-25 and 17:1-7 the people's complaints are accepted as genuine, here they are seen as a sign of rebellion. This introduces a theme that is central to chapters 11–20, that is, the people's lack of faith and trust in God.

God responded to these complaints by sending fire that burned among the people and consumed part of the camp (11:1b). The people cried to Moses and, acting as an intercessor, Moses prayed to the Lord and the fire died down (11:2). The place was therefore called Taberah, because fire from the Lord had burned among them (11:3).

Then new complaints emerged from the group referred to as *the rabble* (**11:4**). This term may refer to the non-Israelites who had joined the crowd as they left Egypt or who joined them in the desert. Or it may simply mean a group of unsatisfied people in the camp who started a rebellion. Whichever the case, God's reaction implies that all the people participated in disobeying God.

The grumbling focused on the manna that God was supplying as food in the desert. The Israelites gathered this food, which fell with the dew in the evening. They could grind it in mills or beat it in mortars, and then could either boil it or bake it. It is described as being *like coriander seed* and as looking *like resin* (**11:7-9**). In Exodus 16:14 it is described as a 'thin flakes like fine frost', and in Exodus 16:31 we are again told that it was 'white like coriander seed and tasted like wafers made with honey'. It was a unique food for which there is no satisfactory natural explanation. The Israelites ate this food for forty years until they came to the borders of the promised land (Exod 16:35).

The complainers insisted that a daily diet of manna was monotonous, and they reminded the people of all the different types of food they had enjoyed in Egypt, especially the fruit, vegetables and fish. None of these were available in the desert (**11:4-5**). Their discontent spread to others, and the people wept and complained, saying that they would rather be in Egypt in slavery and eat good food (**11:10**). In complaining like this, the Israelites ignored the fact that manna was not simply a physical food but was God's gift to Israel. It illustrated the truth that God would provide for them in the desert until they entered the promised land and could eat the produce of that land (Josh 5:11-12).

Jesus picked up on this theological symbolism when he described himself as 'the bread of life' and 'the bread that came down from heaven' (John 6:35, 41), referring to his own life that he was to give for the salvation of the world. His life was a gift that would sustain people in their journey towards eternal life. As Jesus explained, 'Your forefathers ate the manna in the desert, yet they died ... I am the living bread that came down from heaven. If anyone eats of this bread, he will live forever. This bread is my flesh, which I will give for the life of the world' (John 6:49-51).

11:10-15 Moses' complaint

Moses knew that the people's complaints angered God and he becomes angry at the burden that he himself has to carry (**11:10**). He was tired of having responsibility for the whole community, so he vigorously expressed his feelings to God, asking what he had done to deserve this (**11:11**). He asked God, *Did I conceive all these people? Did I give them birth? Why do you tell me to carry them in my arms, as a nurse carries an infant, to the land you promised on oath to their forefathers?* (**11:12**). Moses was reminding God that Israel belonged to him, and not to Moses. God was the one who would have

to get them to the land of promise. Moses frankly admitted his own inability to meet the people's needs, saying, *Where can I get meat for all these people? They keep wailing to me, Give us meat to eat* (**11:13**). Although Moses was grateful for God's help, he had to acknowledge, *I cannot carry all these people by myself; the burden is too heavy for me* (**11:14**). He needed more human help, as well as divine aid. Totally overwhelmed by his responsibilities, Moses prayed, *If this is how you are going to treat me, put me to death right now – if I have found favour in your eyes – and do not let me face my own ruin* (**11:15**).

This type of lament recurs elsewhere in the OT. The book of Psalms is full of agonized prayers for help for the community and for individuals (see, for example, Pss 3; 4; 6; 13; 44; 69; 74; 80; 102). Hannah laments her barrenness in 1 Sam 1:9-11, and the books of Lamentations and Job consist largely of laments. In Jeremiah 15:18, the prophet complains to God, 'Why is my pain unending and my wound grievous and incurable? Will you be to me like a deceptive brook, like a spring that fails?' These are prayers from the heart of those experiencing deep suffering. They are honest prayers directed to God who is seen as the only one to offer any hope of deliverance from pain. Moses' complaint falls into the category of prayers for help. God recognized that Moses was genuinely weary and exhausted by the hardships of leading a complaining people. Moreover, Moses did not merely lament and complain. He asked for the help that he desperately needed to lead the people.

By contrast, the wailing and complaining of the Israelites in the desert were not part of a prayer directed to God, but were simply a grievance directed against God and their leaders. When the people's plight was genuine, as when they needed water and food, God listened to their groaning (Exod 17:1-7). But in Numbers, the Israelites were rejecting the food God has supplied. Despite an abundant supply of manna, they complained, 'Now we have lost our appetite; we never see anything but this manna' (11:6). Their scorn for God's gift was accompanied by a desire to reject his greater gift of freedom and a promised land, and to return to Egypt, the land of slavery! In short, there is a sharp contrast between prayers of lament and grumbling and complaining.

Moses' prayer offers encouragement to all leaders who are overwhelmed by the burdens of leadership. It brings out the point that leadership is a joint effort by the leader who is entrusted with responsibility and by God himself, who can relieve the burden of leadership.

11:16-31 God's response

The first thing that God did in response to Moses' complaint was to acknowledge that Moses needed human helpers and tell him to select seventy elders from the twelve tribes to share the burden of leading the people (**11:16-17**). This solution underscores the importance of dividing work and involving others in leadership. Leaders today also need to recognize that they cannot do everything themselves but must seek help from others within their community.

In Exodus 18:13-23, Moses was given similar advice by Jethro, his father-in-law, who advised him to appoint elders to settle disputes between people, thus sharing the burden of leadership with others in the community. He did as Jethro advised, but clearly he still carried a heavy burden of leadership on his own.

The second part of God's response was to promise to supply meat (11:18). But the people must first be prepared to receive it. They must be consecrated because they had revolted against God by rejecting the manna he had provided. The giving of meat was both a gift and a punishment. God would give them what they wanted – until they were sick of it! (11:19-20). Unlike the manna, which God would continue to provide throughout the desert journey, he would provide the meat for only one month.

Moses doubted that God would actually be able to supply meat for such a multitude of people for a whole month (11:21-22). Thinking in human terms, Moses asked, *Would they have enough if flocks and herds were slaughtered for them? Would they have enough if all the fish in the sea were caught for them?* (11:22).

God's response reminded Moses of his unlimited power: *Is the Lord's arm too short?* (11:23). This response is somewhat similar to God's words, centuries later, to the exiles in Babylon who may have doubted his message of comfort: 'my thoughts are not your thoughts, neither are your ways my ways' (Isa 55:8-9).

Moses delivered God's message to the people and then obeyed God's command in 11:16 and assembled seventy elders at the Tent of Meeting (11:24). God then kept the promise he made in 11:17. He came down in the cloud on the Tent of Meeting, spoke to Moses, and then took some of the Spirit that was on Moses and puts it on the seventy elders (11:25). This is the same spirit that God gave to the judges of Israel to deliver the people from their enemies, to his servants the prophets, and to some of the kings of Israel.

As the Spirit rested upon them, these elders started to prophesy, probably meaning that they began to speak in tongues or in some other way that was unusual for them (11:25). This was a unique occurrence for these men, for we are told that they never again behaved this way.

For some reason, Eldad and Medad, two of the seventy men who had been chosen, did not go to the Tent of Meeting but remained in the camp. Yet God's Spirit rested on them as well and they too prophesied (11:26). This unusual behaviour caused consternation among observers and Joshua asked Moses to stop them (11:27-28). But Moses reprimanded Joshua and expressed the wish that all God's

people would be endowed with God's Spirit (11:29). He was happy that others could receive the spirit and did not cling to it as a prerogative of leadership. He was not possessive about what had been given to him and wanted to share his experience of God with the rest of God's people, even if this might threaten his leadership.

We need to learn from Moses' explanation that God's spirit is not confined within an institutional setting. In both politics and the church in Africa, there is a greed for leadership because leadership is tied to power. Those who have obtained leadership positions refuse to share that power. They cling to their position and to everything associated with it. Moses, however, humbly recognized that the same God who had given him the spirit of leadership could give that spirit to any other person. God is not bound by our institutional arrangements and he does not always act in conformity with the patterns we are used to. He does as he pleases, for his power and Spirit are unlimited.

This episode with the elders reminds us of the day of Pentecost, when God fulfilled his prophecy in Joel 2:28-29 and poured out his spirit on all people, including Jews and Gentiles, men and women, young and old (Acts 2:1-21).

God next fulfilled the second promise he had made to Moses (11:18-20). He provided an abundant supply of meat by using the wind to blow in a flock of migrating quail that had been flying over the sea, probably the Gulf of Aqabah. The exhausted birds fell on all sides of the camp and the people gathered them day and night (11:31-32).

Although God had given the people what they wanted, he was still angry with them, and as the people began to eat, a plague struck them and many died (11:33). We do not know exactly where this happened, but we do know that the place was called *Kibroth Hattaavah* in Hebrew, a name that literally translates as 'sepulchres of lust' or 'graves of craving' (11:34). No doubt, the people were glad to leave there and travel on to Hazeroth (11:35).

The Hebrew word for the wind that blew in the quails is *ruah*, the word used for God's spirit, as the agent through which God acts. Thus, in 11:24-30, the Lord gave his *ruah*, or spirit, to the seventy elders, and in 11:31-35 God sent forth a *ruah* or wind that brought flocks of quails from the sea to fall on the camp. Jesus similarly linked the spirit and the wind in his discussion with Nicodemus when he said, 'You should not be surprised at my saying, "You must be born again." The wind blows wherever it pleases. You hear its sound, but you cannot tell where it comes from or where it is going. So it is with everyone born of the Spirit' (John 3:7-8).

12:1-16 Rebellion by Aaron and Miriam

The preceding chapter recounted how the people annoyed Moses when they rebelled against God. This chapter describes how Moses becomes angry with his own siblings,

Aaron and Miriam. Whereas Moses has previously faced criticism from without, now the opposition comes from fellow-leaders within his own family – from Aaron, his brother, the high priest, and Miriam, his sister, a prophetess who led the people in a song of victory (Exod 15:20). In Micah 6:4 she is listed among the three leaders of Israel in the desert.

Their ostensible complaint is about Moses' marriage to *a Cushite* (African) woman (**12:1**). Since Moses was married to Zipporah, a Midianite (Exod 2:21), this Cushite woman must have been a second wife. It seems that Miriam and Aaron were using a racist argument to conceal the real source of their resentment of Moses.

The real issue seems to have been jealousy of Moses' supreme role as a channel of God's revelation, as indicated by their complaint *Has the Lord spoken only through Moses? Hasn't he also spoken through us?* (**12:2**).The argument thus concerns whether the gift of prophecy and of leadership is limited only to Moses as the official, institutional leader. All three of them had been given gifts of leadership, but in different areas. It seems that Aaron and Miriam failed to see that their varied gifts enriched the community. If both of them had been given the same gift as Moses, there would have been no priest, no singer and no prophet.

Before reporting God's response to this attack on Moses, the narrator reminds us that Moses was *very humble* (**12:3**), not a person who clung to power and wanted to keep it all to himself. This has been seen in the previous chapter in his request for human helpers and in his delight that others had been given the gift of prophecy (11:14, 29). Thus he did not defend himself to his family, but left the issue to God to settle.

God appeared suddenly to Moses, Aaron and Miriam and ordered them to go to the Tent of Meeting. There the Lord appeared in a pillar of cloud, stood before the entrance of the tent and called *Aaron and Miriam* to him (**12:4-5**). His reprimand to them stressed the unique place of Moses. Whereas God speaks to other prophets through dreams and visions, he spoke to Moses *face to face*. Moses was able to behold God's form and was entrusted with responsibility for all God's house (**12:6-8**).

No one else has ever had such an intimate relationship with God as Moses. Later in the Bible, Moses is frequently referred to as the lawgiver and mediator and as the model for the prophet who is to come. When it comes to the NT, he and Elijah are the two prophets who appear in the transfiguration of Jesus (Mark 9:2-13).

God was angry that Aaron and Miriam had dared to speak against Moses, and he punished Miriam by striking her with a skin disease similar to leprosy (**12:10**). For some unknown reason, Aaron was not punished. It may be that Miriam had instigated the complaint, or that it would have created great difficulty for the worship in the Tent of Meeting if Aaron, the high priest, had been rendered unclean by leprosy. While we believe that God acted in justice and righteousness, Aaron's exemption from punishment does feed into a cultural bias where a double standard is applied based on gender. In many African contexts women are treated differently from men. We see this bias at work in John 8:1-11, where the woman caught in adultery is dragged before Jesus, and her male partner is not.

Aaron was horrified at what had happened to Miriam and acknowledged Moses' superiority by begging him to pray for them both (**12:11-12**). Moses did not hold a grudge and interceded on Miriam's behalf (**12:13**). The Lord agreed to lift his punishment of her, but insisted that she was still unclean and must remain outside the camp for seven days. Miriam's important role in the community is clear from the fact that the congregation did not move on from Hazeroth until she had been brought back into the camp (**12:15**). They then set up a new camp in the Desert of Paran, on the southern border of Canaan.

The whole incident centres on a power struggle within the leadership. We too easily forget that leadership is a God-given gift for the betterment of the community and is not to be sought for personal and selfish reasons. Those who try to assume leadership through coercion or manipulation are going against God's model for leadership.

This passage also indirectly addresses the issue of the diversity of gifts that God, through his Spirit, gives to believers for building the body of Christ. As Paul clearly states in 1 Corinthians 12:4-11, all gifts are given by the same Spirit, but not everyone receives the same gift. If everyone claims to have the gift of prominent leadership, there will be a surplus of presidents and bishops, and the country or church will not thrive. Instead, there will be chaos as different leaders jockey for power and try to implement different plans. But it is not enough to simply say that people must recognize that only some have the gift of leadership. The leaders, in their turn, must also appreciate, affirm and encourage the use of other people's gifts.

13:1-14:45 The Decisive Rebellion

Chapters 13 and 14 are unified around the theme of the death of the old rebellious generation who had left Egypt. God swore that all but two of that generation would die in the desert before entering the promised land. He also promised to bring the next generation, their children, into the promised land.

13:1-25 The spies' mission

With the people now camped on the southern border of Canaan (in the Desert of Paran), all that remained to be done was to take possession of the land of promise. God commanded Moses to send twelve spies, one from each tribe, to spy out the land (**13:1-16**). They were instructed to survey it from the Negev in the south *to the hill country in the north* (**13:17**). Their particular assignment was to determine the strength of the people, the fertility of the land and the strength of the towns. They were also to bring *some of the fruit of the land* back with them (**13:18-20**). The spies set out and spent *forty days* surveying the land and its people (**13:21-25**).

13:26-33 The spies' report

On the spies' return to the Israelite camp at Kadesh, they reported what they had seen and presented the fruit that they had collected (**13:26**). Their initial report was very positive about the productivity of the land, which they described as flowing *with milk and honey* (**13:27**). But their report was far less encouraging when it came to the inhabitants of the land and the strength of their towns. They reported that the people were strong and included *descendants of Anak* (**13:28-29**). From the other references in the Scriptures to these 'descendants of Anak', we know that they were a tall people of remarkable strength (Deut 9:2). The city of Hebron was said to have derived its name Kiriath Arba from an ancestor of the Anakites called Arba (Josh 14:15). Other gigantic people mentioned in the OT are the Nephilim (Gen 6:4) and the Enim (Deut 2:10-11), which explains the spies' later words: *We saw the Nephilim (the descendants of Anak come from the Nephilim). We seemed like grasshoppers in our own eyes and we looked the same to them* (**13:32-33**).

Recognizing that this part of the report was spreading fear among the people, one of the spies, whose name was Caleb, spoke up, urging the people to conquer the land (**13:30**). Later, Joshua would join him in urging this (14:6-9).

But Caleb and Joshua could not persuade the other spies to agree with them. They insisted, *We can't attack those people; they are stronger than we are* (**13:31**). As well, they spread a bad report, claiming that *the land we explored devours those living in it*. The Jewish explanation of these words is that the spies must have witnessed a large number of funerals as they travelled around the land. If this was the case, the funerals could have been part of God's provision for them to move around undetected, but they interpreted them as a sign that the area was not a healthy one to live in – despite the fact that the other inhabitants seemed to be flourishing. What a discouraging report about the land that God had promised to give to the Israelites!

14:1-10a The people's response

On hearing the spies' report, the entire congregation wept and protested against Moses and Aaron, saying, *If only we had died in Egypt! Or in this desert! Why is the Lord bringing us to this land only to let us fall by the sword? Our wives and children will be taken as plunder. Wouldn't it be better for us to go back to Egypt?* (**14:1-3**). Fear led the people to

refuse God's gift of the promised land. They did not want to continue the journey; they would rather go back to Egypt. Though they had seen God's power in the ten plagues he had sent to deliver them from Egypt, in the parting of the Red Sea so they could cross it, in his provision of manna and water in the desert, and in the way he had protected them from many dangers in the desert, they still did not trust God to fulfil his promises.

This rebellion was different from the one involving the golden calf (Exod 32–33). In that incident, the people had not rejected God but had made an image to represent him and lead them on their journey to the promised land. But now the Israelites refused God's offer and denied his promises. In the plain sense of the word, they rejected God. They also rejected the leaders God had given them and suggested choosing their own leader who would take them back to Egypt (**14:4**). The people's desire to go back to Egypt and to choose their own leader aroused God's wrath because it was a total rejection of 'the Lord your God, who brought you out of Egypt, out of the land of slavery' (Exod 20:2).

Every sinful act has consequences. Horrified at the people's disobedience, Moses and Aaron fell on their faces as a sign of their intercession for the people who have rebelled against God (**14:5**). Joshua and Caleb continued to encourage the people to trust God and even tore their clothes as a sign of grief and repentance (14:5-9). They told the people, *The land we passed through and explored is an exceedingly good. If the Lord is pleased with us, he will lead us into that land, a land flowing with milk and honey, and will give it to us. Only do not rebel against the Lord. And do not be afraid of the people of the land, because we will swallow them up. Their protection is gone, but the Lord is with us. Do not be afraid of them* (**14:7b-9**). But the people ignored them and threatened to stone them (**14:10a**).

14:10b-45 God's response

God appeared in the Tent of Meeting and expressed his anger to Moses: *How long will this people treat me with contempt?* (14:11). In the NIV, it says that he would *destroy them*, but the Hebrew word used literally means 'disinherit them' – that is, declare that they were no longer his children. In their place he would raise up a new and greater nation from Moses' descendants (**14:10b-12**).

Moses begged God to forgive the people just as he had done after the incident with the golden calf and on other occasions. He gave two major reasons why God should not destroy the people. The first had to do with God's reputation. The other nations knew that God had brought Israel out of Egypt and had been leading them to the promised land. So Moses argued, *If you put these people to death all at one time, the nations who have heard this report about you will say, 'The Lord was not able to bring these people into the land he promised them on oath; so he slaughtered them in the desert'*

(**14:15-16**). In other words, the death of the people would be taken as implying that God was powerless. Moses' second argument appealed to God's character and specifically to his mercy, steadfast love and forgiveness of the *sin and rebellion* of his people (**14:18a**). Yet Moses knew that God still punishes sin, for he quotes from God's prohibition of idol worship in the Ten Commandments, *Yet he does not leave the guilty unpunished; he punishes the children for the sin of the fathers to the third and fourth generation* (**14:18b**; see also Exod 20:5; Deut 5:9). On the basis of these two arguments, Moses asked God to forgive Israel as he had done in the past (**14:19**).

God responded by promising to forgive the people – but he would also punish them for their disobedience. Israel would wander in the desert for forty years until all of the old generation (those over twenty years of age) perished (**14:20-35**). Of that generation, only Caleb and Joshua would not die in the desert (14:30). The other ten spies, who had brought the evil report about the land, died of plague (**14:36-37**), a symbol of the punishment that would come on all those over the age of twenty.

Moses told the people about God's response to their disobedience and their coming death in the desert (**14:39**). The people admitted they were wrong, but refused to accept their punishment. Instead they continued to disobey. Having initially refused to go into the promised land with God's help, they now decided to enter it without his help (**14:40-43**). Moses refused to accompany them, and the Ark of the Covenant did not leave the camp, but the people advanced north toward the hill country (**14:44**). As Moses had predicted, they were soundly defeated by the Amalekites and the Canaanites (**14:45**). Any human attempt to undertake a journey of faith without God's help and guidance is futile.

15:1-19:22 Rules and Rebellions

At this point, the account of the Israelites' journey is interrupted by a large section dealing mainly with regulations for sacrifices and offerings that, they are told, will apply after Israel has entered the land of Canaan. It may be that this material was strategically inserted here to reassure readers that despite their rebellion and God's threat to disown them, the new generation of Israelites would indeed eventually enter the promised land and worship God there. It may also be intended to make the point that even though the people are still en route to the promised land, they must continue to worship God. God's people are not merely travelling to their final destination; they are on a journey that involves submitting their whole way of life to God.

15:1-31 Laws concerning sacrifices

Chapter 15 deals firstly with animal sacrifices, drink-offerings and grain offerings (15:1-21). Then it speaks of the sacrifices that may be offered to atone for sins committed because of ignorance (15:22-29) and the punishment for the sin of arrogance (15:30-31). Finally, it deals with those who violate the Sabbath (15:32-36) and with tangible reminders of the people's responsibility to obey God's commands (15:37-40).

The opening verses of the chapter specify that these laws concern sacrifices and offerings that the people are to offer to God after they have entered the promised land (**15:1-2**). This statement on its own would have reassured the people that there is hope despite the severe punishment meted out to them.

After they have entered the land, the people of God, who will have experienced his salvation, must remember to give thanks to him through their offerings. Thus the first regulation concerns the burnt *offering from the herd or the flock* (**15:3a**), which is intended to offer *an aroma pleasing to the Lord* (**15:3b**, **7**, **10**, **13**, **14**). The offering also includes a grain offering and a drink offering, the quantity of which varies according to whether the animal being offered is a ram, a bull or a lamb. This offering could be made in fulfilment of a vow to God, as a freewill offering or during a special festivals such as Passover, the Feast of Weeks, the Feast of the Tabernacles, the Day of Atonement, or the like (Lev 23; Deut 16:1-17).

These regulations apply both to Israelites and to the aliens (foreigners) living among them (**15:13-15**). Although the biblical story of salvation focuses on Abraham and his descendants, it is important to note that the people who came out of Egypt were a mixed multitude (Exod 12:38) and that the laws and commandments given in the Pentateuch also applied to them. In other words, the covenant community was a mixed community. God's salvation was open to all humankind from the very beginning, and those chosen are only channels of God's blessing to others (Gen 12:1-3). God's choice and call are not ends in themselves.

The next regulation is a command to offer a cake of ground meal *from the threshing-floor*, that is, to make an offering from the produce of the land (**15:17-21**). Throughout the generations, they are to make these types of offerings as a sign of thanksgiving. The Bible repeatedly reminds us to give thanks for the food that we eat because all that we have comes from the Lord (see also Deut 8:11-18). As Psalm 116:12-14 says, 'How can I repay the Lord for all his goodness to me? I will lift up the cup of salvation and call on the name of the Lord. I will pay my vows to the Lord in the presence of all his people.' In Psalm 24, the psalmist confesses that the world and all that is in it belong to the Lord.

What do these commands mean for Christians today? Many Christians have appropriated the idea of the OT offerings by giving thanks before and after meals. Some Christians go beyond this by giving special harvest offerings once or twice a year, depending on where they live. These offerings may be produce from the land or, for those who do not farm, money or any other income. All count as harvest offerings. Although such an offering is not commanded in Christian churches, believers still give as their response to the gift of salvation through Christ and as a way to serve God through serving humanity.

Offerings are also required when there is an unintentional failure to keep God's commandments (**15:22-23**). When the entire community is guilty of such a failure, they must bring a burnt offering and a sin offering to the Lord (**15:24-25**; see Lev 4). If it is merely an individual that is unaware of one of God's commands and breaks it, a priest must make atonement for him or her by offering a female goat (**15:27-28**). In both cases, this requirement applies both to the Israelites and to any others who are living among them (**15:26, 29**).

The law was far sterner when it came to anyone who deliberately disobeyed God's commandments. Anyone who did this and sinned intentionally was to be *cut off from his people*. Such deliberate sin amounts to showing contempt for God (**15:30-31**).

15:32-36 Punishment for breaking the law

The Sabbath day was very important for the Israelites and its observance as a day of rest was mandated in the Ten Commandments: 'Six days you shall labour and do all your work, but the seventh day is a Sabbath to the Lord, your God' (Exod 20:8-11). God had rested on this day from all his work (Gen 2:1-3). In Deuteronomy 5:12-15, observance of the Sabbath is also linked with remembering God's redemption of the nation from Egypt. The same God who had created the heavens and earth is the one who redeemed his people from slavery (see also Isa 43:1, 14-15).

Given these strong reasons for observing the Sabbath as a day of rest, it is not surprising that the Israelites were upset to find one of their members working by gathering sticks on the Sabbath day (**15:32**). But the people did not take the law into their own hands. They considered the law, and when it appeared that there were no clear guidelines about what to do about someone who deliberately broke it, they brought the issue to Moses and Aaron (**15:33**). They too were not certain how to respond and sought God's guidance (**15:34**). We see a similar pattern of consulting God about difficult legal decisions in the case of the daughters of Zelophehad (27:1-11; 36:1-12).

Rules are not rigid pronouncements that apply to all situations in all times. They have to be reinterpreted, and when the earlier law fails to provide answers, we need to seek guidance as to how the principles should be applied in a new situation. We need to remember that human judgment alone is not enough for discerning the will of God in difficult situations. We need to listen to God through prayer, reading the word of God, and consulting others who share our

faith and hope, especially those whom God has appointed as leaders.

In this case, God pronounced the verdict through the leaders of the community and, unlike on previous occasions, had the community itself carry out the punishment by stoning the man to death outside the camp (**15:35-36**). This punishment was the same as that to be meted out to people who sinned defiantly (**15:30-31**). God sometimes uses leaders, judicial systems and the like to execute justice on his behalf.

It is right to ask the relevance of some of these regulations to our Christian faith. The word of God is always good 'for teaching, reproof, for correction, and for training in righteousness (2 Tim 3:16, RSV). However, with the death of Christ, some laws like that of stoning the offender to death do not hold any more because Christ took upon himself the sin of the world and so offers forgiveness for all. Through his sacrificial death, Jesus redeemed the world from the curse of the law by becoming a curse himself and thus fulfilled the righteous requirements of the law (Gal 3:13; Rom 8:3-4). Consequently, he taught us not to condemn people but to seek to lead them to repentance, forgiveness and reconciliation.

15:37-41 Reminders of God's laws

God then instructs the Israelites to attach tassels to their garments as an outward sign to help them remember that they are God's people and as such have a duty to obey the commandments that he gave through Moses (**15:37-38**). The blue (or purple – CEV) of the cord was also an important symbol. Blue dye was very expensive, and thus it became a colour associated with royalty and with God's kingship. A blue cover was put over the ark of the covenant when it was carried before the people as they journeyed (Num 4:6), and blue was used in the woven screens that covered the entrance to the Tent of Meeting and separated off the Most Holy Place within the Tent (Exod 26:31, 36). Thus the blue cords would also remind wearers that they were to obey and be consecrated to God, because of who God is (**15:41**).

To this day, Orthodox Jews wear fringed prayer shawls with a coloured thread in obedience to this command in Numbers (see also Deut 22:12).

Christians, too, make use of colour symbolism. In the mainline Christian churches, blue and purple are used during the Advent season to remind worshippers of the coming of Christ the King. Many Christians wear symbols that identify them as believers. Thus some wear crosses while others wear bracelets with words like 'What Would Jesus Do?' (or WWJD) engraved on them. Besides identifying them as Christians, these symbols also remind them of their responsibility to obey God and uphold his reputation at all times. But those who choose to wear such symbols must remember that they are not charms that will protect the wearer

– they are merely reminders of the relationship the believer should have with his or her God.

16:1-50 Rebellion by Levites

The glimpse of hope God had given the people when he gave new laws to what was still his covenant community after its devastating rebellion (chs. 13 and 14) is soon overshadowed by yet another rebellion. This time some Levites lead the revolt. Their action shows us one picture of what the defiant sin referred to in 15:30 looks like, and demonstrates what it may mean to be 'cut off from his people'.

Aaron and Miriam had objected to Moses' special role as God's prophet (ch. 12), and now others object to his and Aaron's functioning as priests. Korah, a ringleader of the rebellion, was a Levite, who would have served in the Tent of Meeting. As a descendant of Kohath he would have been one of those caring for the most sacred objects (**16:1a**; see 3:30-31). Korah, however, was not satisfied with this responsibility. He wanted to be a priest.

To achieve his goal, Korah stirred up some of the Reubenites, specifically Dathan, Abiram and On (**16:1b**). They were joined by some two hundred and fifty other leaders of the people of Israel, united in opposition to Moses (**16:2**). Their claim was that Moses and Aaron had *gone too far* in assuming the role of the spiritual leaders of Israel. For them, the whole community was holy (**16:3**). This was a half-truth. Earlier, Israel had indeed been called a holy nation (Exod 19:3-6), but Moses and some others had been set apart from the rest of Israel for a holy function. Korah's greed for power led him to cling to the half-truth and challenge the legitimacy of Moses and Aaron's roles, and indirectly the authority of God who had appointed them to their positions. Even today those who aggressively support half-truths can cause devastating problems for communities of believers.

Korah's action was equivalent to rebellion. Once again, as in 14:5, Moses *fell face down* to express his shame and repentance at this act of rebellion and his submission to God (**16:4**). Then he called for a trial to determine whom God had chosen to be the priests. Aaron and all those taking part in the rebellion were to offer incense the next day. The Lord would make it clear which of them he had chosen to be priests (**16:5-7a**).

Moses did warn Kohath: *You Levites have gone too far* (**16:7b**). God had already given them a special role and it was wrong of them to grumble against Aaron, who here represents the entire priesthood (**16:8-11**).

Moses also summoned the Reubenites Dathan and Abiram, sons of Eliab, who had joined with Korah in rebellion, to come to him (**16:12**). They refused, claiming that Moses had led the people *out of the land flowing with milk and honey* (as if Egypt, the land of slavery and suffering, were the land of promise!) and had not kept his promise to bring them into *a land flowing with milk and honey*. They accused Moses

of being hungry for power and wanting to *lord it over us* (**16:13-14a**). Not only that, but they accused him of trying to blind them to what was actually going on, saying, *Will you gouge out the eyes of these men?* (**16:14b**).

These false accusations angered Moses. But he did not lash out at the people. Instead he turned to God for vindication. He could honestly tell God, *I have not taken so much as a donkey from them, nor have I wronged any of them* (**16:15**). Turning to God for vindication and serving the people faithfully are the qualities of good leadership. Moses' assertion also raises the question of how many African leaders, both in the church and in government, would have the courage to declare before God that they have neither stolen from nor harmed anyone. Given the widespread corruption in Africa, it is unlikely that many would be prepared to do this.

Moses then repeated his order that Korah and all his followers should appear before the Lord the following day (**16:16**). Both they and Aaron would offer incense before the Lord, and God would show which men were to be accepted as God's priests in the holy Tent of Meeting (**16:17-18**).

Rebellion always elicits punishment, and that is what happened. The next day, when the group gathered at the Tent of Meeting, God was so angry that he again threatened to destroy the entire community (**16:21**). Moses and Aaron's prayer for the people gathered at the camp of Korah again displays their true leadership qualities (**16:22**). Then Moses passed on God's warning, telling the rest of the community to move away from the tents of the sinners so that God's punishment would not fall upon them as well (**16:23-27**). He then pointed out God would reveal whether the rebels' attacks on Moses and Aaron were justified or not (**16:28-30**).

God dramatically imposed his judgment, and Korah, Dathan and Abiram and their families were swallowed up as the earth opened beneath their feet (**16:31-34**). The fate of their families reminds us that sometimes one person's sin can affect not only the offenders but also the innocent. For instance, when the environment is polluted or destroyed, both the offender and non-offenders suffer. Similarly, those with self-centred habits may drink excessively and expose their families to poverty and devastation. Or one person's sin may result in HIV/AIDS being spread to innocent spouses and children.

The two hundred and fifty rebellious men who were offering incense were struck by lightning from the Lord (**16:35**). This, however, created another problem. Although the men who waved the censers were guilty, their censers had been used in the service of the Lord and had thus become holy (**16:36-37**). They could not simply be returned to the men's families. So God directed Moses to have these censers melted down and hammered into a covering for the altar, both as a memorial to their folly and as a confirmation that only priests of the family of Aaron were to burn incense there (**16:38-40**).

Instead of learning from the destruction of the rebellious men, the whole community now rose up against Moses, accusing him of being responsible for the death of the rebels (**16:41**). As they gathered to riot against Moses, the cloud covered the Tent of Meeting, displaying God's glory (**16:42**). God ordered Moses and Aaron to get away from the people as he intended to punish them for this new rebellion (**16:43-45**). Once again, Moses and Aaron fell on their faces before God in prayer.

God sent a plague in judgment and, realizing that some action was needed to stop it, Moses told Aaron to take a censer and make atonement for the people (**16:46**). Normally, atonement required a sacrifice, but the situation was so urgent that there was no time to prepare a regular sin offering. The incense that Aaron offered would have to represent such an offering.

Aaron's position, *standing between the living and the dead* is a vivid demonstration of the role of the priest as an intermediary (**16:47-48**). His action prevented further death among the people, but 14,700 people had died before the plague stopped (**16:49-50**).

17:1-13 Vindication of the Aaronic priesthood

The opposition to the Aaronic priesthood described in chapter 16 had been in direct opposition to God's plan to have the descendants of Aaron serve as priests (3:10). Yet it was Aaron who made atonement for the people (16:47). In this chapter, God sends a clear sign to settle the dispute about who the chosen priests are.

God ordered Moses to bring twelve staffs or rods into the Tent of Meeting. Each rod had the name of a leader of one of the twelve tribes written on it. These staffs were then left in front of the Testimony (or the Ark of the Covenant) overnight (**17:4-7**). Aaron's rod, which represented the descendants of Levi, was clearly chosen above all the other rods. Not only did this rod bud, it also *blossomed and produced almonds* (**17:8-9**).

The Lord told Moses to leave Aaron's rod in front of the ark of the covenant as a sign of the Levites' right to be the priests and to bring an end to all rebellion against him and his descendants (**17:10**).

Finally, the people realized their sin in challenging God concerning the Aaronic priesthood (17:12-13). They feared that as a consequence *anyone who even comes near the tabernacle of the Lord will die*, and they pitifully asked, *Are we all going to die?* (**17:13**).This question is answered in the next chapter where the responsibilities and rights of the priests and Levites are again spelled out.

This incident warned the nation that God wants order in leadership, and that those he has appointed as leaders cannot simply be pushed aside because of someone else's ambition. The Israelites were on a holy march, and so they must follow specific rules to avoid chaos and destruction.

18:1-32 Regulations for priests and Levites

Now that the question of Aaron and his descendants' legitimacy as priests has been settled, the author of Numbers describes the rights and responsibilities of the priests and their assistants, the Levites. These instructions had been given to Aaron before, but they are repeated because his priestly office has just been reconfirmed before all Israel, and, in particular, before the subordinate Levitical priests.

Aaron, his descendants and his father's family (that is, the Levites) were told that they would bear the responsibility for offences against the sanctuary. However, only Aaron and his sons were to bear responsibility for offences against the priesthood (**18:1**). This command seems to mean that both the priests and Levites were responsible for maintaining the holiness of the temple, but that protection of the most sacred areas within the temple was, ultimately, the responsibility of the priests, who were to be the descendants of Aaron.

The Levites were to assist Aaron and his sons when they ministered before the Lord in the *Tent of Testimony* and to perform the duties of the Tent (**18:2**). However, the Levites had restrictions on what they were allowed to do: they must not touch any holy objects (**18:3-5a**).

Aaron and his sons were given the services of the Levites as a gift (**18:6**), but they were reminded that their own priestly privilege of approaching the sanctuary and ministering before the Lord was also *a gift* (**18:7**). They were to serve God for the good of the whole people so that God's wrath would not fall on the people (**18:5b**).

God next spelled out how the priests were to be supported. They were not to be allotted any land, and so could not grow rich at the expense of others. God, not property, was to be their inheritance (**18:20**). They and their families would be supported by the regular offerings, such as the offerings of first-fruit and firstborn animals, sin offerings made by the people and the gifts that the people brought to the Lord (**18:8-19a**).

God declared that this arrangement was *an everlasting covenant of salt* (**18:19b**). The Jews and others in the ancient world often included salt in their offerings. At that time, salt was used to preserve food, as it often is today. Thus a 'covenant of salt' was one that was consecrated and permanent (see also 2 Chr 13:5).

Nor were the Levites given an *inheritance* of land; they, too, were to be supported by the tithes that the people of Israel brought to the Lord (**18:21-24**). And from this tithe, they themselves were to pay a tithe to the Lord through Aaron the priest (**18:25-28**), a ruling that emphasized their subordination to the priests, and enabled them to make an offering to the Lord. Obedience to these rules of tithing was also important if the Levites were to escape punishment and death (**18:32**).

PRIESTHOOD IN THE BIBLE

Sacrifices have been offered since the earliest times (Gen 4:3-4; 8:20). The patriarchs, as heads of their families, all offered sacrifices (Gen 12:7-8; 13:4; 15:9; 26:25; 35:3, 7) and some sort of priesthood seems to have developed before the giving of the Law at Sinai (Exod 19:22, 24). In Exodus 19:6, Israel is described as a kingdom of priests (see also Isa 61:6). This means that every member of the Israelite nation, whether male or female, was theoretically part of the priesthood.

Priesthood in the Old Testament

Since it was not practical for a whole nation to officiate at sacrificial rituals, the Levites were chosen to represent the nation (Num 18:21-23), possibly as a reward for their zeal for the Lord (Exod 32:25-29). When the Israelites were in the wilderness, the Levites camped around the tabernacle. Thus they protected it, and simultaneously protected the other Israelites from the wrath of a holy God (Num 1:53; 8:19).

The priests were chosen from among the Levites and were expected to be role models of the holiness required of all God's covenant people because God is holy (Exod 19:6; Lev 19:2). The regulations governing their lives symbolized the sanctity and purity necessary for the service of God (Lev 21:1-9). Their consecration involved a purification rite (Exod 29; Lev 8), their vestments had to be made of fine linen (Exod 39:27-29), and they could have no physical defects (Lev 21:16-23). There were even more restrictions on the high priest, including the requirement that he marry only a virgin (Lev 21:10-15).

The high priest's robes and turban were similar to those worn by a king (Exod 39; Isa 62:3). Whenever he went into the Holy of Holies, he was symbolically taking the whole congregation of Israel with him, for his breastpiece was set with stones engraved with the names of all the tribes of Israel.

Besides offering sacrifices, the priests blessed the people (Num 6:22-27) and summoned them to assemblies (Num 10:8-10; 31:60). They were also responsible for the administration of justice (Deut 17:8-9; 29:5; 2 Chr 19:8-11; Ezek 44:24) and finances (Ezra 8:33-34) and involved in arrangements for battle (Deut 20:1-4; Josh 6:8. 1 Sam 4:3-4).

Although the law laid down that only Levites were supposed to be the priests, priestly functions were also carried out by non-Levites, such as the Ephraimite in Judges 17:5, David's sons who were from the tribe of Judah (2 Sam 8:18 – NIV footnote), and Ira from the tribe of Manasseh (2 Sam 20:26). However, a Levitical priest was preferred to a non-Levitical one (Judg 17:5-13).

Political Developments

A major change in the priesthood occurred when Solomon replaced Abiathar with Zadok as priest in Jerusalem (1 Kgs 2:26-27). This appointment marked the end of one priestly line (as predicted in 1 Sam 2:30-31) and the start of political control of the priesthood. Yet another change was King Josiah's centralization of worship at the temple in Jerusalem (2 Chr 34), which made Levitical priests who served in sanctuaries outside Jerusalem redundant.

During the post-exilic period, the office of high priest became very powerful and was sought by some unscrupulous men, such as Jason (174 BC), who was appointed after promising Antiochus IV that he would promote Hellenistic culture.

The Jewish priesthood that we meet in the Gospels and the book of Acts was Aaronic (Luke 1:5). Jesus accepted its legitimacy and sent healed lepers to priests for confirmation of their healing (Mark 1:44). While the priests, and especially the Sadducees (a priestly party who were opposed to the doctrine of resurrection), were bitterly antagonistic to him, many priests did convert to Christianity (Acts 6:7).

Priesthood of Christ

Gradually Christians separated themselves from Jewish rituals, as shown by Stephen's argument and the decision of the Jerusalem Council (Acts 7:44-53; 15:28-29). Particularly after the destruction of the temple by the Romans in AD 70, Christians exalted the prophetic rather than the priestly tradition of the OT (Matt 9:13).

The rejection of the Jewish priesthood by the church did not mean the concept of priesthood was abandoned. It was seen as fulfilled in the person and ministry of Jesus Christ. The writer of Hebrews presents Jesus Christ as a superior high priest because his priesthood is modelled on that of Melchizedek, who appears in Scriptures without any antecedent (Heb 7:11-28). Whereas ordinary priests all die, Jesus is immortal and his priesthood is established once and for all. He is sinless (Heb 4:15), whereas Aaronic priests were not. Their sacrifices had to be repeated because they were never truly effective. Jesus, by a single sacrifice of himself, put away the sin of his people forever (Heb 10:1-18).

The New Covenant

Furthermore Jesus brings a new covenant (Heb 8:1-13). Under the old covenant, the priests dealt with external pollution by offering animal sacrifices. However these could never remove sin. Under the new covenant, Jesus is the unblemished sacrificial victim who abolishes the barrier between God and his people. The Aaronic high priest ministered in an earthly sanctuary where access to the divine presence was barred by a curtain. Under the new covenant, Jesus exercises his priesthood in the heavenly sanctuary where there is no such barrier between the worshippers and God (Heb 9:1-28; see also Matt 27:51). The writer of Hebrews concludes that the priesthood of Jesus has replaced the Aaronic priesthood.

All the other NT writers also use sacrificial language to describe the work of Jesus. Jesus' mission is described as paying a ransom (Mark 10:45). The words used at the institution of the Lord's Supper are sacrificial (Mark 14:22-25). He is repeatedly described as the sacrificial lamb of God (John 1:29; 1 Cor 5:7; 1 Pet 1:19) whose blood purifies us from sin (Rom 8:3; 1 John 1:7; 2:2; 4:10; 1 Pet 2:24; 3:18; Rev 1:5; 7:14). Jesus sanctified himself as a priest was sanctified (John 17:19) and makes intercession for us like a priest (1 John 2:1).

Priesthood of all Believers

Christ is our high priest, and in baptism an individual is incorporated into him and into the body of Christ, which is the Christian community. In this body, all the members are recognized as priests (Rev 1:6; 5:10; 20:6; compare Exod 19:6), representing God to the world (1 Pet 2:9). There is no separate priestly order or caste, but each individual member has individual and corporate responsibilities to serve God and others.

Like the OT priests, Christians as a community and as individuals offer sacrifices. Christians are told that their spiritual act of worship is to offer their bodies as 'living sacrifices, holy and pleasing to God' (Rom 12:1). Here no distinction is made between Christian living and worship. In fact the bodies of Christians are members of Christ himself and temples of the Holy Spirit (1 Cor 6:15, 19). If Christian living is sacrifice, it follows that the deeds of charity that a Christian performs are also sacrifices (Heb 13:16) and that material gifts are 'a fragrant offering, an acceptable sacrifice, pleasing to God' (Phil 4:18).

The sacrifices offered by Christians also include praise, confession of God's name (Heb 13:15) and prayers (Rev 8:3-4). These can be done both individually and in a community. But the celebration of the Lord's Supper requires a community that thankfully offers God the fruits of its labour, just as the Israelites would do (Deut 26:1-10). These 'fruits' may include some form of sacrificial offering – the people converted through Christians' evangelistic ministry (Rom 15:16; Col 1:18; Rev 14:4).

It is clear that Christian priesthood is corporate in nature and therefore gender inclusive. It was the early church fathers who limited the priesthood to the ordained ministry of the church. However, the biblical witness is that priesthood is the responsibility of every Christian, either as an individual or collectively with others in the body of Christ.

Felix Chingota

19:1-22 Cleansing after contact with the dead

The preceding chapters in Numbers have described many deaths in the camp (see 11:33; 14:37; 14:45; 16:33-35, 49). With so many dead bodies around, there was a strong probability that people would touch corpses, accidentally or intentionally. Such contact was seen as a major threat to the holiness of the camp. The uncleanness resulting from such contact may have been one of the reasons the people expressed fear about coming near the Tent of Meeting (17:13). So God provided a ritual that would cleanse people who had been contaminated and enable them to approach the Tent of Meeting without fear of death.

The ritual for cleaning is described in detail (19:1-22). It involved slaughtering and then burning a red cow (**19:2**). The colour red was highly significant in this ritual. The animal's red blood was to be sprinkled and burned (**19:4-5**) and *scarlet wool* was to be burned with it (**19:6b**). This stress on redness may be meant to emphasize the significance of blood in cleansing the unclean. Other cleansing agents such as *cedar wood* and *hyssop* were to be burned along with the animal (**19:6a**). The priest and his assistant were to purify themselves at the time of this sacrifice (**19:7-10**).

The ashes of the heifer and the things burned with it were then mixed with water to make *water of cleansing* (**19:13, 17, 21**). This water could then be sprinkled over unclean people and furnishings by a ceremonially clean person (**19:18**), using a bunch of *hyssop* dipped in this water. Hyssop was a small bush plant, similar to marjoram, that was frequently used for sprinkling water or blood in ceremonies of atonement and purification (see also Ps 51:7).

The procedures for obtaining ritual purity were effective if they were followed. Their purpose was to ensure the people's safety and holiness. The holy God intends that people who worship him also be holy (Lev 19:2).

The writer of Hebrews refers to this ceremonial purification when he speaks of the cleansing of the consciences of believers from the defilement of sin and futile rituals. He shows that God established a better way: 'The blood of goats and bulls and the ashes of a heifer sprinkled on those who are ceremonially unclean sanctify them so that they are outwardly clean. How much more, then, will the blood of Christ ... cleanse our consciences from acts that lead to death, so that we may serve the living God!' (Heb 9:13-14).

20:1-21 God's Anger Against Moses and Aaron

Once again, a major rebellion occurs. At this time, the Israelites were encamped in Kadesh Barnea, where they stayed for a long time.

While they were there, Miriam died. She had been a key leader, a prophetess and a singer (see Exod 15:20-21). Following her death, Israel faced a still more serious crisis, a lack of water (**20:2**). The people quarrelled with Moses and Aaron, saying that they would have been better off if they had died with their kinsfolk whom the Lord had struck down, rather than dying slowly of hunger and thirst in the desert (**20:3-4**). They complained that the food available in the desert was nothing like the *grain or figs, grapevines or pomegranates* of Egypt (**20:5**).

In response, Moses and Aaron took the complaint to God, and God ordered Moses to take his rod, gather the congregation and tell the rock to give water (**20:6-8**). Moses followed the first part of these directions: he took his staff, and he and Aaron gathered the people together (**20:9-10a**). Then he disobeyed God. First, he spoke to the congregation, *Listen, you rebels, must we bring you water out of this rock?* (**20:10b**) and then, instead of speaking to the rock, he *raised his arm and struck the rock twice with his staff* (**20:11a**). Despite his disobedience, water came out of the rock and the people and their livestock drank (**20:11b**).

God punished Moses and Aaron because they *did not trust him and honour his holiness*. He told them that because of what they had done, they would not bring the *community into the land I have given them* (**20:12**). In other words, Moses and Aaron would receive the same punishment as the rest of the disobedient older generation. The reason for God's anger may be that Moses addressed the people angrily as 'rebels' when God had not been angry with them. But even more significantly, Moses' anger led him to put himself in the role of God, when he said, 'must we bring you water out of this rock?' (20:10). The 'we' here refers to Moses and Aaron, who were putting themselves in the place of God who performs miracles. By doing this, they were encouraging the people to look up to them and give them glory instead of giving glory to God.

In addition, Moses disobeyed God's command to *speak to that rock* (20:8). Instead he struck it *twice with his staff* (20:11). He failed to trust that God's word alone was sufficient to bring the water out of the rock, and so he tried to 'help' God by striking it. In Exodus 14:16, 21, Moses had obeyed God and followed his instructions when he raised his staff over the sea. He had also been right to strike the rock when God told him to do so when the people complained of a lack of water (Exod 17:5-6). But this time, he had not been told to strike the rock, but to speak to it. Moses, however, operated on the basis of his earlier experiences and ignored God's voice in a new situation. We may not understand why God does things in different ways at different times, but he does expect us to follow his guidance.

The place where this happened was called Meribah, which means 'contention' or 'quarrelling', because of what took place there.

Moses continued to act on his own initiative, without taking direction from God (20:14-21). He sent messengers from Kadesh to the king of Edom to ask permission for Israel to pass through Edomite territory. In his message, he stressed that Edom and Israel were closely related by referring to Edom as his *brother* (**20:14**; see Gen 25:20-34). But despite Moses' appeal to the pity of the king of Edom because of Israel's suffering in Egypt (**20:15-16**), and despite Moses'

promise that they would not damage crops or even leave the road and his offer to pay for any water the people drank (**20:17, 19**), Edom refused Israel passage (**20:18, 20**). As a result, Israel had to take a long detour around Edom, leading to another rebellion (21:4).

In Deuteronomy 2:4-8, this detour around Edom is recognized as being God's will. God made it clear that he would not give the Israelites the land of the Edomites, because he had given it to the descendants of Esau. The Edomites were related to the Israelites and were to be left alone. The only thing that God allowed the Israelites to do as they went around the land of Edom was to buy food and water from them.

20:22-29 Death of Aaron

When the Israelites arrived at Mount Hor, close to the Edomite border, the Lord told Moses that the time had come for Aaron to die. He also reminded Moses that Aaron was not entering the promised land because of Moses' and Aaron's disobedience at the waters of Meribah (**20:24**; see 20:12-13). So Aaron died on Mount Hor and was succeeded as high priest by Eleazar, his son (**20:25-28**). The old generation who had lived in Egypt were passing away, and God was raising up a new generation of Israelites.

21:1-35 Incidents on the Journey towards Moab

The Israelites now began to emerge from the desert and approach inhabited lands. To be able to enter the promised land, they would have to conquer the people living on the borders of Canaan. This chapter gives an account of Israel's victories over some kings. But the people were still not fully obedient and were punished for further grumbling.

As the Israelites passed through the Negev Desert on their way from Kadesh to the promised land, they were attacked by the Canaanite King of Arad (**21:1**). So Israel made a vow to God: *If you will deliver these people into our hands, we will totally destroy their cities* (**21:2**). This vow was both a promise and a prayer for help. The Israelites recognized that God was the one who would put their enemies into their hands. Thus by their vow they committed themselves to obeying his command to destroy the cities when they conquered the land. They would make a new beginning in the land that the Lord had promised to give them.

God heard their cry, and Israel completely defeated these Canaanites and destroyed everything, as they had promised (**21:3**). The place in which Israel won victory was called *Hormah*, which in Hebrew means the place of destruction. When Israel remembered to cry to the Lord for help, God made them successful.

However, this victory and closeness to God was short-lived, for soon the people were grumbling again. The people grew impatient on their long detour around Edom and spoke against God and Moses, '*Why have you brought us up out of*

Egypt to die in the desert? There is no bread! There is no water! And we detest this miserable food!' (**21:5**). People's impatience led them to blaspheme the bread God had given them from heaven and to reject God's servant Moses.

Earlier, similar complaints had resulted in a deadly plague in the camp (ch. 11). This time, God punished them by sending poisonous snakes, and many people died after being bitten (**21:6**). The people then realized that they had sinned against God and Moses, and implored Moses to intercede for them (**21:7**). Moses prayed on their behalf, and in response the Lord ordered Moses to make a bronze snake and set it on the pole. Anyone who was bitten and looked upon the bronze snake would live (**21:8-9**). The bronze snake became a symbol of God's healing power. Jesus would later use it as a symbol of his own work (John 3:14-15).

After this incident, Israel set out again and *camped at Oboth,* a place on the eastern side of Seir. From there the Israelites journeyed to Iye Abarim opposite Moab. The journey continued to the Zered valley, which is close to the south-eastern part of the Dead Sea, and then to Arnon between Moab and the Amorite country (**21:10-13**).

The precise locations of these places cannot be determined today because many changes have taken place in the course of history. But the key point is that God led the Israelites throughout their journey and gave them victory as they moved camp from one place to another between the lands of Moab and Edom. We can get only a glimpse of some of their adventures through the poetic excerpt from an ancient document known as *the Book of the Wars of the Lord* (**21:14**). This book is an unknown source that perhaps recorded Israel's (or rather, the Lord's) victories in songs and stories. We know of other such collections, for the OT refers to 'the book of Jashar' (Josh 10:13; 2 Sam 1:18), 'the book of the annals of the kings of Israel' (1 Kgs 14:19) and 'the book of the annals of the kings of Judah' (1 Kgs 15:7). These annals seem to have been records of the history of victories and failure of the kings of Israel and Judah, while the book of Jashar and the book of the Wars of the Lord seem to have been collection of poems recording Israel's victories and troubles.

The meaning of the poems recorded in 21:14-18 is also unclear but the mention of *Arnon* and *Ar* indicates that they focus on the areas that Israel passed through from Edom to the land of Moab. They seem to have been heroic accounts that exhorted the people to march in victory and conquer. The poems are followed by the names of further stops on the journey.

After going around Edom, the Israelites approached the territories that belonged to Sihon, the king of the Amorites, and Og, the king of Bashan. They requested passage through these Amorite territories, but their request was refused (**21:21-22a**). Sihon gathered his army and attacked Israel. He was clearly a powerful king, for it seems that his

armies had earlier destroyed Moab (**21:27-30**). This makes it clear that his complete defeat by the Israelites was God's doing. Israel captured and occupied all the Amorite cities (**21:22b-32**; see also Deut 2:24-37).

Later, Israel defeated Og, the king of Bashan (**21:33-35**; see also Deut 3:1-11). This victory and the one over Sihon are often cited in the Old Testament. They were very significant events that Israel remembered and relived throughout its history (see Judg 11:19-21; Neh 9:22; Pss 135:10-11; 136:18-21; Jer 48:45).

22:1-36:13 In the Plains of Moab

The events narrated in this final section of the book of Numbers took place in the plains of Moab where Israel is camped on the edge of Canaan. From here, the Lord showed Moses all the land of Canaan: 'Then Moses climbed Mount Nebo from the plains of Moab to the top of Pisgah, across from Jericho. There the Lord showed him the whole land – from Gilead to Dan' (Deut 34:1). These final events before Israel occupies the land of promise include Balaam's blessing as they passed through the country of Moab (22:1-24:25) and the final rebellion and the death of the old generation (25:1-18). The book concludes with the rise of the new generation (26:1-65) and with an account of laws and legal decisions intended to guide the people before their final occupation of the land.

22:1-24:25 Balak and Balaam

At certain times the mighty power of God is evident far beyond the borders of the chosen nation of Israel. In a dramatic episode a diviner named Balaam discovers that God's purpose cannot be hindered or interfered with, and that witchcraft and sorcery cannot overcome or twist the divine purposes of God Almighty. Furthermore, the narrative reveals that God's authority cannot be commanded or controlled by any earthly ruler or by materialistic means.

The story of Balaam also shows that although God is holy and perfect, he chooses to use imperfect means such as a non-Jewish diviner and a donkey to accomplish his purposes. Paul might have been thinking of this when he wrote 'But God chose the foolish things of the world to shame the wise; ... the weak things of the world to shame the strong. He chose the lowly things of this world and the despised things – and the things that are not – to nullify the things that are' (1 Cor 1:27). God is the sovereign controller of all history; no human being can thwart his plans.

22:1-22 Balak hires Balaam to curse Israel

King Balak of Moab saw what had happened to his neighbours and realized that without divine intervention he was incapable of conquering the Israelites. Desperate for help, he sought greater power than his army could provide and became convinced that having a truly powerful diviner put a curse on the Israelites could accomplish what his army could not. So he seeks the help of Balaam, a professional diviner who came from near the Euphrates, several hundred miles from Moab (**22:2-7**). He takes great care in composing his request to Balaam, sends a delegation of princes to meet with him and offers payment in silver and gold.

Balaam is interested in the king's offer but waits to hear what the Lord will tell him to do. The Lord tells him that he is not to accompany the messengers and not to put any curse on the Israelites (**22:8-12**). So Balaam sends Balak's messengers away. But Balak is desperate, sends an even more powerful delegation and offers even more money to persuade Balaam to come and curse the Israelites (**22:15-17**). Once again, Balaam refuses to do anything except what the Lord says: *Even if Balak gave me his palace filled with silver and gold, I could not do anything great or small to go beyond the command of the Lord my God* (**22:18**). But it appears that he is tempted by the money, despite his fine words, and so he asks the Lord for guidance again, despite the clear instructions he has been given (**22:19**). This time, the Lord permits him to go with the men, but *to do only what I tell you* (**22:20**). Although God lets Balaam go with King Balak's messengers, he still intends to protect his people. God will not permit Balaam to utter any curse on his people. Instead, Balaam will bless them.

We may be puzzled about why God is angry with Balaam for going to King Balak after he has permitted him to do so (**22:22**). What has Balaam done wrong? The answer may be related to Balaam's decision to consult God again (22:19), even though God has already answered this question (22:12). It is possible that although Balaam claims to be consulting God, he was actually trying to negotiate with the Lord so that God's plan could be adjusted to suit his lust for money. God knew that Balaam was not genuinely seeking to do his will. It is not that God changed his mind when he allows Balaam to go to Balak; rather God permits Balaam to do what he has set his heart on doing.

22:23-35 Balaam, the donkey and the angel

Although Balaam is a diviner who communicates with God, the incident recorded here shows that his donkey is more aware of God's presence than he is because God has expressed his displeasure by blinding Balaam to spiritual realities!

The donkey sees *the angel of the Lord standing in the road with a drawn sword in his hand* (**22:23a**). The word 'angel' means 'messenger' or 'one who is sent', but in the OT 'the angel of the Lord' seems to have been more than a mere messenger. Seeing God himself would have brought death, for as God warned Moses, 'You cannot see my face; for no one may see me and live' (Exod 33:20). So when God wanted to appear to human beings, he was represented by this angel. The angel of the Lord may even be a manifestation of God himself. The appearance of this angel is associated with the birth stories of key biblical figures such as Isaac (Gen 18:9-15), Samson (Judg 13:3) and John the Baptist (Luke 1:11). The angel of the Lord was also sent as a messenger; he spoke with Abraham before the destruction of Sodom and Gomorrah (Gen 18:1) and with Moses when God called him to lead the people out of Egypt (Exod 3:2). The 'angel of Lord' is also associated with the wars that the Israelites fought, for God promised to 'send an angel before you' to 'drive out the Canaanites, the Amorites, the Hittites, the Perizzites, the Hivites and the Jebusites' (Exod 33:2). The angel of the Lord is also associated with judgment in the OT as when Deborah sings, '"Curse Meroz," said the angel of the Lord, "Curse its people bitterly, because they did not come to help the Lord, to the help of the Lord against the mighty"' (Judg 5:23). The angel Balaam encounters is acting in judgment.

When the donkey sees the angel of the Lord, she refuses to attempt to pass (**22:23b-27**). Balaam beats her, until God gives the donkey the power of human speech, which she uses to point out that there is a reason for her strange behaviour (**22:28-30**). Then God opens Balaam's eyes and Balaam sees the angel, who tells him that the donkey has saved his life (**22:31-33**). The donkey's ability to speak and the appearance of the angel remind us that God can use any means he chooses to accomplish his divine purpose of saving and blessing his chosen people.

Balaam, terrified by this encounter with the Lord, offers to return home (**22:34**). But the angel tells him to continue on his journey, but to make sure that he obeys the will of God in what he says (**22:35**). On his arrival in Moab, Balaam is greeted by the king, who again reminds him of the reward he would get for cursing Israel (**22:36-37**), to which Balaam replies that he will *speak only what God puts in my mouth* (**22:38**), which is what the angel had commanded.

Throughout this incident, God has been using someone who is not a Jew as his messenger. This happens again later, when God uses King Cyrus of Persia (a non-Israelite) to issue a decree releasing the Israelites from their Babylonian captivity and sending them back to their homeland to rebuild the temple in Jerusalem (2 Chr 36:22-23). God in his divine wisdom chooses and uses whomever he pleases to accomplish his plan regardless of their gender, nationality, race or status.

23:1-24:25 Balaam's oracles

23:1-26 FIRST AND SECOND ORACLES King Balak and his people (the Moabites) are hoping for a decisive victory over the Israelites that would make it possible to 'drive them out of the country' (22:6). Thus they summon Balaam to curse the Israelites (22:7), and when he arrives they offer sacrifices to get God to agree to this curse (23:1-3). But when God appeared to Balaam (23:4), he told him not to curse Israel. No curse on them would be effective, because God had already promised to bless them and make them a blessing to other nations (23:20; see also 22:12; Gen 12:1-3).

Balaam's statement, *How can I curse those whom God has not cursed?* (23:8), points to the ineffectiveness of any curse that is not upheld by God. His thinking corresponds to that of the Maasai, who believe that the God of justice will protect anyone who is righteous from the effects of a curse. Only wrongdoers will suffer when a curse is uttered.

God's plan to bless Israel could not be thwarted by Balaam's hunger for rewards or by Balak's repeated offering of expensive sacrifices at altars in different locations (23:1, 14, 29). Neither bribes nor geographical location can change God's mind, as is clear from the first two oracles that Balaam utters (23:7-24).

The story of Balaam reveals the vast difference between the true God of Israel and human beings (23:19) who are swayed by greed, and shows the sharp contrast between the true God and false gods. Balak's sacrifices and offers to pay Balaam show that he thinks that the gods are unstable, present more in some places than in others and able to be bribed to persuade them to show favouritism. But the true God of Israel is steadfast and faithful to his people. He honours the covenant he made with them and is the same yesterday, today and tomorrow. The whole of Scripture bears witness to God's constant and unchanging nature.

The blessing of God rests upon Israel because the true God is with them (23:21). The impossibility of cursing those on whom God has bestowed blessings is a clear indication of God's presence in the midst of the people of Israel in the desert.

23:27-24:25 THIRD AND FOURTH ORACLES Next, Balaam surrenders to the will of the Lord for the third time. He has clearly seen that *it pleased the Lord to bless Israel* (24:1a). It is obvious at this point that Balaam is unable to thwart the Lord's plan. Controlled by the Spirit of God, he blesses Israel. Balak was not pleased with Balaam's blessing Israel, but he does not yet give up hope that God could be persuaded to curse the Israelites (23:27-29).

This time, however, Balaam takes a different approach; he *did not resort to sorcery as at other times* (24:1b). Like other ancient diviners, he probably would have relied on interpreting dreams, studying the stars and examining the hearts, livers or other internal organs of animals sacrificed to gods to determine the divine will. But it appears that this time God gives Balaam clear instructions through speech, so that he could describe himself as *one who hears the words of God* (24:4). He also enabled him to speak clearly to Balak about the impossibility of speaking on his own and cursing a nation already blessed by the Almighty God.

Like the first and second oracles, the third oracle speaks of the blessings of prosperity, *How beautiful are your tents ... Like valleys they spread out* (24:5-7a), power, *like a lion they crouch and lie down, like a lioness – who dares to rouse them* (24:8-9a) and fame (24:7b) and ends with the statement, *May those who bless you be blessed and those who curse you be cursed* (24:9b). This echoes God's blessings upon Abraham and his descendants in Genesis 12:3.

By this point, the Lord has so captured Balaam's mind that he is not influenced by Balak's anger or the loss of his promised reward (24:10-11). Free from all external influences, he speaks only what God has revealed to him (24:12-14).

While Balaam's first three oracles reaffirm God's blessings to Israel's ancestors, in the fourth oracle the blessing is set in the future. Balaam speaks of the coming of *a star* and *a sceptre,* both images of a future king and messiah (24:17a). This future leader will enable Israel to conquer its enemies, that is, the nations surrounding the promised land such as Moabites, Edomites, Amalekites (representing the worst enemy of Israel), Kenites and Asshur (24:17b-24). After God has brought the Israelites into the promised land, he begins to fulfil the prophecy with the conquest of Edom and Moab at the time of David (24:18; 2 Sam 8:14; 1 Kgs 11:15-16). But the complete fulfilment of these prophecies awaits the coming of the one predicted in 24:17, who will completely destroy his enemies (24:19). His victory will be so complete that he can be said to be using his enemies as his footstool (Ps 110:1) This prophecy is fulfilled in Jesus Christ whom God sent to redeem the world through death on the cross.

The story of Balaam clearly demonstrates that human beings cannot manoeuvre, twist, change or manipulate God's revelation (prophecy) or its contents to fit their own plans. God warned Balaam to utter only what God would instruct him. And although Balaam cooperated with the princes of Moab, he could not do what they wished, but only what God commanded him to do.

25:1-18 Severe Punishment of Idolatry

One would have expected the people of God, after having escaped the curse of Balaam, to remain loyal to God. But instead Israel fell into a final rebellion. The plague that followed wiped out all the remaining members of the old generation except Moses, Joshua and Caleb.

This chapter combines two stories of rebellion and idolatrous practices in the community, which obviously were deeply disturbing because they are referred to again in 31:15-16. The first is about Israelite men committing sexual offences with Moabite women and participating in idolatrous sacrifices to a foreign god (25:1-5). The second may involve idolatry through the intermarriage between a Midianite woman and a Simeonite man (25:6-15).

Intermarriage was strongly condemned because it would expose the entire community of Israel to the idol worship introduced by a foreign partner. The effects of such marriages can be seen in the lives of Solomon (1 Kgs 11:1-10) and Ahab (1 Kgs 16:31-33).

Israel was defiled by *sexual immorality* when some men had sexual relations *with Moabite women* (**25:1-2**). They became involved in cult prostitution (that is, in fertility rites dedicated to the Moabite gods), thus violating the first of the Ten Commandments, which forbids the worship of any other gods (Exod 20:3; Deut 5:7).

Because of the nature of their sin and their failure to prevent the spread of the sin, God punished them (**25:3-4**). Moses ordered the judges to slay those who joined in worshipping the Baal of Peor (**25:5**). God has previously used plagues, fire and serpents as instruments to carry out his punishments, but as the order reveals, at times he expects people to carry out his judgments. We are reminded that God involves human beings like Moses, the judges and the prophets in his acts of salvation and in his acts of judgment. As God's people, we are expected to discern God's will in a particular situation and respond appropriately.

The second incident of rebellion involved adultery between Cozbi, a Midianite woman, and Zimri son of Salu, an Israelite (**25:6, 14-15**). The strong reaction of *Phinehas son of Eleazar, the son of Aaron,* who was in the line of succession for the office of high priest, suggests that their relationship was introducing idolatry into Israel. He killed Zimri while the Israelite was having sex with the woman, driving his spear *through the Israelite and into the woman's body* (**25:7-8a**). His actions appeased God's anger, and the plague that God had sent upon the Israelites because of their sin ended (**25:8b**).

By the time Phinehas' action stopped the plague, twenty-four thousand people had died (**25:9**); but even more would have perished had he not acted. Those who died probably included the last of the old generation. The severity of the punishment shows that God never allows his people to entertain sin in their midst. He sanctioned the public killing of offenders to emphasize his message about the seriousness of sin and the importance of purity. The punishment would have been a warning to others not to commit the same offence.

Phinehas's action not only averted God's anger, but also reinforced the status of the house of Aaron, because God made a covenant with Phinehas promising that he and his descendants would always be priests (**25:10-13a**). Phinehas is also said to have *made atonement for the Israelites* (**25:13b**). He did this by dealing with sin and so saving the people.

There are parallels between the punishment for sin described here and the practices of some people in Eastern Africa. For instance, the Meru people of Tanzania used to kill those who committed adultery by taking them to crossroads where they were staked to the ground. The intention was that they would die slowly so that everyone in the community had time to see their disgrace and fear this punishment. The Meru believed that such severe punishment would remove the curse and shame of the sin from among the people. The Sharia law associated with the Muslim religion still punishes adulterers, especially women, with death.

This type of punishment is appropriate in a community that had to live in accordance with the laws and rules laid down as part of a covenant. Such a community had to be purged of every evil. But the coming of Jesus and his proclamation of the gospel has broadened our understanding of sin, grace and the love of God. While the church emphasizes purity in all aspects of life and certainly does not approve of or encourage adultery or other sinful acts, it teaches that we are all sinners and should leave judging others to God. We can only exhort, rebuke, correct, teach, guide and forgive as Christ forgives us all.

The final words about the Midianites, *they treated you as enemies when they deceived you* (**25:16-18**), help to explain the revenge later taken on them (31:1-12). There God orders the slaughter of Midianites because they had led the Israelites into idolatry. The incident with the Midianite woman also explains Moses' anger when the people of Israel spare the lives of Midianite women (31:15-18).

26:1-65 Second Census

As noted in the introduction, this book is called Numbers because it tells of the numbering of the children of Israel. The Israelites were first numbered at Mount Sinai (1:2) and are now numbered a second time in the plains of Moab just before they enter Canaan (ch. 26). This chapter not only reports on the census (26:1-51, 57-62) but also gives directions for the division of the land (26:52-56) and reports the death of all of the old generation except for Joshua and Caleb (26:63-65).

The second census has three significant features. First, by numbering the fighting men, it prepares a new generation of Israelites for the last crucial action – conquering the promised land (**26:1-4**). Second, it underscores the absence of the unbelieving generation who had been counted in the first census. All those people who had been approximately twenty years old at the time they left Egypt (except Caleb son of Jephunneh and Joshua son of Nun) had died in the desert because they had sinned against God (**26:64-65**). The new generation that succeeded them would have the blessings and privileges of inheriting the promised land. Third, this census gives the framework for the distribution of the land (26:52-56). God instructs Moses that the division of the land should be determined according to the size of the tribe. *To a larger group give a larger inheritance, and to a small group a smaller one* (**26:54**).

The relative sizes of the different tribes and how each had grown or shrunk in size during the forty years in the desert can be seen from the following table, which compares the results of the first census and the second one.

Population Before and After Forty Years in the Wilderness

	First Census		Second Census	
	Reference	Figures	Reference	Figures
Reuben	1:20-21	46,500	26:5-11	43,730
Simeon	1:22-23	59,300	26:12-14	22,200
Gad	1:24-25	45,650	26:15-18	40,500
Judah	1:26-27	74,600	26:19-22	76,500
Issachar	1:28-29	54,400	26:23-25	64,300
Zebulun	1:30-31	57,400	26:26-27	60,500
Ephraim	1:32-33	40,500	26:35-37	32,500
Manasseh	1:34-35	32,200	26:28-34	52,700
Benjamin	1:36-37	35,400	26:38-41	45,600
Dan	1:38-39	62,700	36:42-43	64,400
Asher	1:40-41	41,500	36:44-47	53,400
Naphtali	1:42-43	53,400	26:48-50	45,400
Total		603,550		601,730

The exact position of the land allocated to each tribe was to be determined by lot, thus ensuring fairness and removing a cause of disputes (26:52-56; see also 33:53-54). This technique was often used to resolve disputed issues. The Israelites were confident that when lots were cast in this way, God determined the outcome. It is important to distinguish this activity, which was designed to achieve fairness and avoid favouritism, from commercial lotteries, which are games of chance where the outcome is sometimes manipulated and which exploit the dreams of the poor and part them from money that they need for other things.

As in the first census, the Levites were counted separately because they were not to serve in the army and were not to receive an inheritance of land (**26:57-62**; see 18:23-24).

27:1-11 Zelophehad's Daughters

Ancient Israelite society, like many African societies, was largely patriarchal and so issues of land, inheritance and power were the domain of men. But this presented a problem when a family had no male children, as was the case in the family of a man named Zelophehad of the tribe of Manasseh.

Patriarchal societies preserve their history by remembering the lineage and names of male figures. So Zelophehad is identified in terms of his male ancestors as the *son of Hepher, son of Gilead, son of Makir, son of Manasseh* (**27:1a**). Some modern translations reflect the same bias when they ignore the fact that in the Hebrew the subject of the sentence in 27:1 is the daughters, not Zelophehad. The NIV translates the sentence correctly, but others, like the CEV translate it as if the father were the subject and thus begin 'Zelophehad was from the Manasseh tribe, and he had five daughters.' The Iraqw translation makes the same mistake: *Selofehadi garmoó Heferi, garmoó Gileadi, garmoó Makiri, garmoó Manase, garmoó Yosefu i dasuú kón. Umer'ín a tí: Mala nee Noa, nee Hogla, nee Milka nee Tirsa.* But the translation in the Maasai Bible (*Biblia Sinyati*) is faithful to the original Hebrew and gives the daughters of Zelophehad their proper place: *Neitoki aanyiku nena toyie e Selofehad olaiyoni le Hefer, olaiyoni le Gilead, olaiyoni le Makir, olaiyoni le Manase, olaiyoni le Yosef.*

Zelophehad's daughters, too, are said to belong to *the clans of Manasseh son of Joseph* (**27:1b**). There is no mention of their mother's name. She may well have suffered shame because of her failure to produce a male heir. Yet she should have been proud of her daughters, who were strong and courageous women who recognized injustice and whose stand against it led to their names being recorded in Scripture alongside those of men. The names of all five daughters are given: Mahlah, Noah, Hoglah, Milcah and Tirzah (**27:1c**; see also 36:11; Josh 17:3). However, the fact that their names also appear in the census data (26:33) indicates that the purpose for which they are mentioned still serves the interests of a patriarchal society. Other men might face the same problem as Zelophehad and die without male heirs. They needed to know what would happen to their inheritance.

The five daughters *approached* the Tent of Meeting and stood before Moses and the elders of the community (**27:1d-2**). The Hebrew word translated 'approached' suggests that the women acted with courage and determination. It shows the courage of these five sisters as they took their own case before the authorities in a culture in which women were expected to submit to custom. How many African women are prepared to move beyond grumbling about something and take the initiative to approach a bishop or church council to voice their demand for a change in the status quo?

These women may have drawn some of this courage from their solidarity. They must have known that they needed to work together if they were to change a system that was biased against them. We see similar examples of what can be achieved by women's solidarity elsewhere in the OT: think of the Egyptian midwives (Exod 1:15-21); Moses' mother and her daughter (Exod 2:1-4); Naomi and Ruth (Ruth), Deborah and Jael (Judg 4:14-21); and Jephthah's daughter (Judg 11:37-39).

But the five daughters may also have drawn courage from their knowledge of all that happened to the Israelites. They knew that plans were being made for land allocation and that so far no laws had been laid down that addressed their position as the representatives of a family without male children. Above all, they were aware of Yahweh's relationship with Israel and knew that his relationship was with the whole community, both men and women, so that their family was entitled to share in God's gift of new land. They knew that even the descendants of sinners like Korah would still be given land, for Korah's line had not died out (26:11). But they were confident that their father was not like Korah (27:3). He had not died as a punishment for some particular sin, but simply as one member of the generation that was not allowed to enter the promised land.

Zelophehad's daughters protested to Moses that it would be unjust if their family were forced to forfeit all claim to land just because their father had not had a son (27:3-4). If the law insisted that only the males would inherit the land, the needs of women and children would be overlooked and their position undermined. Deprived of any means to support themselves, widows and unmarried daughters would be reduced to poverty and possibly even to slavery or prostitution. This pattern is sometimes seen in Africa when widows are evicted from their husband's land because his male relatives claim it.

Moses listened to the sisters' case and then took it to the Lord (27:5). God told him that the women were in the right (27:6-7a). This ruling and the legislation about the jubilee (Lev 25:8-54) reveal that God gives high priority to the equal distribution of economic resources. He recognizes that traditional rules may have to be modified to ensure the well-being of individuals and families among his people. So he ruled that Moses should give the daughters of Zelophehad *property as an inheritance among their father's relatives and give their father's inheritance over to them* (27:7b). The way his ruling is expressed makes it clear that God was not just doing them a favour but was issuing a direct order, a legally binding rule, that must be applied to bring justice to women when question of land inheritance and possessions are raised. Rules were also laid down to cover other cases where the line of inheritance might not be clear (27:8-11a). However, these rulings were not the final word on the subject, for additional legislation affecting the daughters of Zelophehad is set out in chapter 36.

What the daughters of Zelophehad started as a family issue becomes a divine stipulation for the benefit of all and for all generations (27:11b). They used their life-transforming experiences to reconstruct the legal status of women as regards land inheritance and to improve the welfare of all.

The church in Africa needs to learn from this incident about its role as an advocate for laws that resonate with Christian teachings. It should call attention to laws that contradict the gospel message, such as those on widow inheritance (see article on this topic) and those that allow only men to inherit land. Both biblical and social arguments can be advanced for the need to change traditional laws to adjust to a changing society. Our contexts are changing every day, and it is unwise to simply apply old rules to the new community. The church must seek God's guidance in dealing with issues affecting society and seek to provide appropriate guidelines for changes that will promote justice in the community.

27:12-23 Joshua Appointed to Succeed Moses

The Lord warned Moses that the time of his death was approaching. He would permit Moses to see the promised land from a distance, but not to enter it (27:12-14). Moses did not argue with God but was concerned about the question of who would replace him (27:15-17). Like a good pastor, he did not want to leave the people *like sheep without a shepherd* (27:17).

God told him to appoint Joshua as his successor (27:18-21). Joshua had been well trained for this task, for he had long been Moses' assistant (11:28). He and Caleb were the only two members of the old generation who would enter the promised land (14:36-38). Moses did not cling to power, but arranged for a public transfer of authority to Joshua (27:22-23). No leader is irreplaceable.

28:1-29:40 Offerings and Feasts

After reading about the census of the new generation (26:1-51), the instructions about the division of the land (26:52-27:11) and the choice of Moses' successor (27:12-23), we would expect to read about the people making progress towards the occupation of the land, or at least about strategies for conquering it. But this is not what the author of Numbers supplies. Instead, he immediately moves on to issues relating to worship and, specifically, to laws related to offerings. He clearly thought that it was essential to remind this new generation of these laws in case their enthusiasm at the prospect of entering the land at long last made them drift away from the most essential element of their relationship with God: worship. Israel was a worshipping community at the heart of which was the lifelong practice of fellowship in which they remembered the God who had brought them out of bondage, established them as a covenant community and given them the gift of land. And they were to continue to be a worshipping community even after the occupation of the land. So the laws concerning offerings are repeated.

28:1-15 Regular offerings

First, the author deals with the daily offerings that were to be made each morning and evening (28:1-8). Twice a day, the priests were to offer a burnt offering (a male lamb), a grain offering and a drink offering. The procedure and the elements were the same for both the morning and evening offerings.

The second type of offering described was the offering of two male lambs a year old made once a week on the Sabbath in addition to the daily offering (**28:9-10**). These lambs were to be *without defect*, that is, without any blemish or deformity. God must receive the best of what he gives his people. Many years later, Jesus, who was sinless and thus without moral defect, would become 'the lamb of God who takes away the sin of the world' by his death on the cross (John 1:29). He would be the perfect sacrifice for human salvation from sin, the one whose death would fulfil and complete the OT prophecies foreshadowed in these sacrifices.

The Sabbath offering was also accompanied by a drink and a grain offering of twice as much flour as was given in the daily offering.

The third type of offering described was the one offered once a month when the new, or crescent, moon first became visible. This offering is not mentioned in Leviticus 23, but is frequently referred to elsewhere in the OT (see Amos 8:5; 2 Kgs 4:23; Isa 66:23; Ezek 46:1-8). Like the Sabbaths, New Moons were solemn occasions in the Jewish calendar. They were probably intended to celebrate God's creation of time and his providence in giving seasons to regulate human life. The festivals also functioned as a type of calendar, helping people to keep track of time and thus of the activities associated with harvests, appointed feasts and the like.

The offering made at the new moon was considerably larger than the daily and weekly offerings (**28:11-14**). It also differed in that the people were instructed to offer a male goat for a sin offering, *besides the regular burnt offering with its drink offering* (**28:15**). A slightly different New Moon offering is prescribed in Ezekiel 46:6.

28:16-29:40 Special feasts

The difference between the New Moon offerings in Numbers and Ezekiel, and the fact that the Pentateuch contains three festival calendars (see Lev 23; Num 28:9-29:40; Deut 16:1-7) may give rise to questions about how to explain the discrepancies between these calendars. The answer is related to the fact that in different historical periods, worship in Israel took slightly different forms. For example, when worship was centralized in the temple in Jerusalem, all males were expected to go to Jerusalem three times a year for the Feast of Unleavened Bread, at the Feast of Weeks and at the Feast of Tabernacles (Deut 16:16). The mention of only three specific festivals here does not mean that these were the only occasions for worship. Other offerings and feasts may have been observed at home or in other places of worship. This is what would have been done while the Israelites were in the desert, and when they scattered to

the areas allocated to them after their first conquest of the land and during the exile in Babylon. When there was no temple, the people observed all the appointed feasts within their own communities.

Thus, the exact form of worship depended on the historical circumstances of the nation. We need to remember that the way in which we worship and respond to God's deeds in our lives may also have to vary to address the needs of our particular contexts. Christianity has spread rapidly in Africa, but the continent is still beset by social, economic and political predicaments. It is thus appropriate for us to acknowledge the restorative and transformative potential of worship. A worshipping community needs to find appropriate worship forms to suit its needs, with a keen awareness of the needs around it and a willingness to prophetically address the various socio-political structures that perpetuate crises. As a people who gather for worship we live out the reality of God, revealed in Jesus Christ. In other words, by God's grace our worship will bring healing, address suffering and bring reconciliation.

Israel's worship celebrated God's saving deeds in different historical periods through the major religious festivals that commemorated them. Here is a list of the feasts prescribed by the three calendars in the Pentateuch: six feasts are prescribed in Leviticus, seven in Numbers and three in Deuteronomy.

Calendars of Feasts in Pentateuch

Leviticus 23 (six feasts)	Numbers 28:9-29:40 (seven feasts)	Deuteronomy 16:1-17 (three feasts)
Sabbath (23:1-3)	Sabbath (28:9-10)	
	New Moon (28:11-15)	
Unleavened Bread/Passover (23:4-8)	Unleavened Bread (28:16-25)	Passover (16:1-8)
Feast of Weeks (23:15-22)	Feast of Weeks (28:26-31)	Feast of Weeks (16:9-12)
Tabernacles (23:33-43)	Tabernacles (29:12-40)	Tabernacles (16:13-17)
Trumpets (23:23-25)	Trumpets (29:1-6)	
Day of Atonement (23:26-32)	Day of Atonement (29:7-11)	

God's directions concerning these sacrifices and feasts were very detailed because he wanted his regulations to be observed with great care and exactness as a way of exalting his honour and glory. Each feast reminded Israelites of specific things that God had done for them.

As Christians we must also honour God and give thanks to him for his many blessings in our lives. We no longer have detailed instructions on how to do this, but it is still the duty of the church of Christ to teach believers the importance of being a thankful community, so that thanksgiving flows from the heart. We cannot take God's salvation for granted.

28:16-25 PASSOVER The Passover Feast was to be observed on the fourteenth day of the Month of Abib (the first month, equivalent to our March or April) (**28:16**). This feast was combined with the Feast of the Unleavened Bread, which began on the day after the Passover (**28:17**). During this feast the Israelites had to eat unleavened bread for seven days to remind themselves that they had left Egypt in such a hurry that there was no time for them to bake leavened bread (see Exod 12:39-13:16).

On the first day and last day of this feast, people were not to perform regular work but were to attend sacred assemblies, at which they came together to worship (**28:18, 25**). On every day of the feast, the regular daily offering was to be supplemented by a special offering of thanksgiving for their salvation from slavery; they were to offer *two young bulls, one ram and seven male lambs without blemish, as well as grain offering* (**28:19-21, 23**). They were also to offer *one male goat as a sin offering* to make atonement for the people (**28:22**). These offerings, which were *made by fire*, would produce *an aroma pleasing to the Lord* to be offered *in addition to the regular burnt offering and its drink offering* (**28:24**).

To the nation of Israel, the Passover represented the climax of God's salvation. In this decisive event, God's power broke the bonds of slavery and set his people free. That is why the creeds of Israel constantly repeat this fact (see, for example, Deut 26:5-10; Josh 24:5-13; Neh 9:9-12). The historical psalms also make many references to it. Psalm 136 makes its importance clear as it calls on the people to praise God first as the creator (Ps 136:4-9) and then as the deliverer of his people (Ps 136:10-22; see also Pss 77:15-20; 78:10-55; 105:23-45; 136:10-26).

The Christian celebration of Easter generally takes place at the same time as the Passover and is in some ways equivalent to the Passover. The Passover reminded the Jews that God intervened in human history to deliver his people, and Easter reminds us that God broke into human history in a different and perfect way to bring salvation to all of humanity. Jesus became the perfect Passover lamb, sacrificed for us. The Jews were delivered from slavery; Christians are delivered from slavery to sin. Christ's sacrifice fulfilled and perfected the old and inadequate sacrificial system that was repeated yearly (see Heb 9:23-28). God's plan of salvation,

which started with the call of Abraham, is accomplished in the life and work of Jesus Christ, the Son of God.

28:26-31 FEAST OF WEEKS The Feast of Weeks was a harvest festival, similar to those observed in other ancient cultures that also offered the first crops harvested and the first-born animal from a flock as a sacrifice of thanksgiving to a deity. It is described in all three of the calendars of festivals listed earlier, each time with slight modifications. Leviticus 23:16 states that it is to be celebrated fifty days after the Feast of the Unleavened Bread (and so would have fallen in the months we know as May and June). Leviticus also indicates that everyone should participate. It stresses that even the poor and aliens, who would not normally share in the harvest, can participate because those who do own land should not reap their crops to the very edge of the field, but should leave some of the crop for the needy (Lev 23:22). Deuteronomy 16:16 specifies that this is one of the three feasts that must be celebrated at the temple and that entire families, including children and servants (male and female), should take part. It also stresses that this feast must include those – such as Levites, foreigners, widows and orphans – who do not own land from which they can reap harvests (Deut 16:11). All are to come together to celebrate the harvest and give thanks to the Lord. This feast reaches beyond the borders of race, ethnicity, class and gender.

Numbers specifies that the people were not to work on the day of this festival, known as the day of firstfruits, when they made grain offerings; instead the people were to gather for a sacred assembly. In addition to making the regular daily offerings, they were to make a burnt offering, accompanied by a grain and a drink offering (28:27-31). At this feast they were also to offer *one male goat to make atonement* for the people (**28:30**).

The fact that this feast was celebrated fifty days after Passover led to it later being called Pentecost (from the Greek word for 'fifty'). This feast has been carried over in the Christian church, though instead of gathering to celebrate God's gift of a harvest, we celebrate his gift of the Holy Spirit. Just as God's harvest feast was intended as a celebration for everyone to enjoy, so the gift of the Holy Spirit was poured out on all who were present at the feast in Acts 2:1-11, regardless of their race or gender. Pentecost marks the birthday of the Christian church and celebrates the harvest of the fruits of the Spirit.

29:1-6 FEAST OF TRUMPETS Three great festivals took place in the seventh month: the Feast of Trumpets on the first day (**29:1a**), the Day of Atonement on the tenth day (29:7) and the Feast of Tabernacles from the fifteenth to the twenty-first days of the month (29:12).

The Feast of Trumpets received its name because it was to be commemorated with trumpet blasts or a great shout of acclamation (Lev 23:23). This ritual later announced the start of a new religious year (which was different from the civil year, which began seven months earlier). The emphasis on commemoration probably means that it was to be a day on which the people reminded God of their needs and requested that he remember them. On this day, there was to be a sacred assembly and no regular work was to be done (**29:1b**). It was a day of worship. Like other special festivals, this feast also had specified offerings in addition to the daily offerings. The offering included a goat for *a sin offering to make atonement for the people* (**29:2-6**).

Modern Jews celebrate this feast under the name of Rosh Hashanah or the Jewish New Year. Although Christians celebrate a different day as the start of a new year, they too recognize that the first day of the year is an occasion on which to thank God for the past year, praise him for bringing them into another year and ask for his blessings and protection in the year to come. Many Christian denominations have a special worship service on the eve of the New Year and on the morning of the first day of the New Year.

29:7-11 DAY OF ATONEMENT The Day of Atonement, a day of mourning, was observed on the tenth day of the seventh month of the Hebrew calendar. On this day the Israelites were expected to *deny* themselves (or fast) to express their sorrow for their own sins and the sins of the whole community (**29:7**; Lev 16:29-31; 23:26-32). Instead of working, they were to meet for a holy gathering in which the whole community came together for worship. Special offerings were also commanded for that day (**29:8-11**). Whereas Numbers simply lists the sacrifices that are to be made, Leviticus 16 goes into far more detail about the actual atonement ritual, which would 'cover' the sins of the Israelites. This ritual was performed only once a year. It seems that the goats that were offered as sin offerings to make atonement for the people at the other feasts (28:15, 22, 30; 29:11, 22) were reminders of the fuller atonement that would be made at this special festival. (For a fuller treatment of atonement, see comments on 8:19.)

Today, Jews still observe the festival of Yom Kippur, or the Day of Atonement. Christians recognize that this feast foreshadows the reality of Christ, who has atoned for the sins of the world once and for all (Heb 9:24-28).

29:12-38 FEAST OF TABERNACLES Five days after the mourning of the Day of Atonement, the Israelites rejoiced at the Feast of Tabernacles, which, like the Feast of Weeks, was celebrated over eight days. This feast is sometimes called the Feast of the Booths. The 'tabernacles' or 'booths' were temporary shelters made of leafy branches woven together, as is clear from the instructions in Nehemiah, 'Go out into the hill country and bring back branches from olive and wild olive trees, and from myrtles, palms and shade trees, to make booths' (Neh 8:15). These shelters reminded the Israelites of the temporary dwellings when they were wandering in the desert, before they settled in proper houses in the promised land (Lev 23:42-43).

The first and eighth days of the feast were marked by rest from labour and attendance at a sacred assembly (**29:12**, 35). The laws about the observance of this feast in Leviticus 23:33-43 are here expanded to include detailed instructions about the sacrifices to be offered on each day of the feast (**29:13-38**). The number of animals offered decreased on each day of the celebration, as shown in the following chart.

Animals Offered During the Feast of Tabernacles				
	Bulls	**Rams**	**Lambs**	**Goats**
Day 1	13	2	14	1
Day 2	12	2	14	1
Day 3	11	2	14	1
Day 4	10	2	14	1
Day 5	9	2	14	1
Day 6	8	2	14	1
Day 7	7	2	14	1
Day 8	1	1	7	1

The element of repetition in these sacrifices served a purpose. God was teaching the people to be very careful about how they served him and to have the faith to see that each day's behaviour is equally important. The repetition also indicates that when people offer their sacrifices with joyful, grateful and clean hearts, they please God and do not wear him out. God does not object to repetition. What he does hate is lip service and festivals that are celebrated without any desire to truly worship him (see Hos 6:6; Amos 5:21-24). God is not so much concerned about what sacrifice is offered but by the sincerity with which it is offered and by whether the life of the worshipper honours him. This was a truth that the prophets would repeatedly stress (Mic 6:8). In Isaiah, the Lord even goes so far as to say, 'I have more than enough of burnt offerings ... Your incense is detestable to me. New Moons, Sabbaths and convocations – I cannot bear your evil assemblies ... I will not listen. Your hands are full of blood ... Learn to do right! Seek justice, encourage the oppressed. Defend the cause of the fatherless, plead the case of the widow' (Isa 1:11-17).

The people's joy is shown in the abundance of the sacrifices offered in these days as they ate and drank together before God. It was an occasion for the Israelites to immerse themselves in communion with God. Nothing was to hinder their joyful worship (Lev 23:40). Of course, circumstances sometimes meant that not everyone would arrive at the feast with a joyous heart, but they would come to experience joy as they had fellowship with God in prayer and worship, listened to him and shared the rejoicing of their fellow Israelites.

At these major festivals, Israelites were expected to give not only the prescribed offerings but also any offerings they had vowed to give to the Lord, as well as freewill offerings as an expression of individual gratitude to him (**29:39**).

A sacred assembly also took place on the eighth day. It was on this great last day of this feast that Jesus stood up and proclaimed, 'If anyone is thirsty, let him come to me and drink. Whoever believes in me, as the Scripture has said, streams of living water will flow from within him' (John 7:37-38).

30:1-16 Regulations Concerning Vows

Chapter 30 deals in detail with the topic of vows, which were mentioned in passing earlier (29:39). A vow is a commitment made to God under oath to engage or not to engage in some activity (see Deut 23:21-23; Eccl 5:1-7). The fundamental principle laid out in this chapter is that God takes vows very seriously, so that, as Ecclesiastes says, 'it is better not to vow than to make a vow and not fulfil it' (Eccl 5:5). God insists that *when a man makes a vow to the Lord, or takes an oath to obligate himself by a pledge, he must not break his word but must do everything he said* (**30:1-2**).

Often when Scripture speaks of 'man' it is using this term in a general way that refers to everyone, including women. But in 30:2 God is speaking specifically of males. In the ancient world, women were subject to men's authority. This made the situation more complex when a woman made a vow.

Although all women were free to make vows, married women, who were subject to their husband's authority, and young girls, who were subject to their father's authority, were not under any obligation to keep a vow if the male authority figure refused them permission to do so (**30:3-8**). But men were not allowed to use this power to repudiate a vow as a threat to hold over a woman. The man had to decide whether to permit the vow when he first learned of it. Once he had accepted his wife or daughter's vow, whether verbally or by simply remaining silent on the topic, he could not subsequently force her to break it. If he tried to do this, he, and not she, would be held responsible for failing to fulfil the vow (**30:10-15**).

One group of women were not bound to a man's authority: widows and divorced women. Although such women often suffered because they lacked status and property, when it came to vows, they were recognized as having the same authority as men and any vow they made was binding (**30:9**). They had to bear the responsibilities and consequences of their vows, whether good or bad.

The Bible includes accounts of various people who made vows to God. For example, Hannah, the mother of Samuel, promised to devote her son to the Lord (1 Sam 1:9-11). Jephthah, on the other hand, made a foolish vow when he spoke without thinking and promised God, 'If you give the Ammonites into my hands, whatever comes out of the door of my house to meet me when I return in triumph from the Ammonites will be the Lord's, and I will sacrifice it as a burnt offering' (Judg 11:30-31). Unfortunately, his daughter met him first on his return. The seriousness with which a vow was taken is indicated by her response to her devastated father: 'You have given your word to the Lord. Do to me just as you promised, now that the Lord has avenged you of your enemies, the Ammonites' (Judg 11:36). Jephthah was obliged to fulfil his vow and offer his daughter to God (although not necessarily as a burnt offering – see commentary on Judges).

31:1-54 War Against the Midianites

Chapter 31 deals with a war waged in the name of Yahweh. The OT contains other accounts of similar campaigns (Exod 7:4; 12:41; Judg 5:13; 20:2; 1 Sam 18:17; 25:28). These are wars that Yahweh fought for his people, or the wars that Yahweh's people fought in the name of and with the help of Yahweh.

In this chapter, the war is conducted against the Midianites, who were distantly related to the Israelites because they were also descendants of Abraham, by his wife Keturah (Gen 25:2). Some of the Midianites, such as Moses' father-in-law Jethro, settled to the south of Canaan. It seems that he, and probably others in his group, worshipped the God of Israel. However, those who settled east of Canaan seem to have entered into a close alliance with the Moabite people and had fallen into idolatry.

Many years later, this defeat of the Midianites was used to encourage the Israelites by assuring them that Assyria would be punished just as Midian was punished (Isa 10:26).

31:1-24 The campaign

Before he died (for that is what the phrase *gathered to your people* means), Moses had one last assignment to carry out. The Lord ordered him to *take vengeance on the Midianites* (**31:1-2**). We are not told directly what was being avenged, but Moses' words in 31:15-16 strongly suggest that the Moabites and the Midianites were being punished because they had combined to lead God's people into sin. The Moabites had invited the Israelites to worship a Moabite god, the Baal of Peor (25:2-3), and had encouraged the Israelites to visit cult prostitutes. God had punished the Israelites for adultery and idolatry with a plague (25:9), but he also punished those who led Israel into sin. The Israelites were on a holy march and must eliminate anything that blemished the nation's holiness.

Although only the punishment of the Midianites is recorded in Numbers, the Moabites were also punished for this and other sins (see Deut 23:3-6; Judg 3:29-30; 2 Sam 8:2; 1 Chr 18:2). Many centuries later, Ezra will also oppose marriage to non-Israelite women, including Moabites (Ezra 9:1).

A thousand men from each of the twelve tribes of Israel were sent out to wage war on the Midianites (**31:3-5**). Each tribe was represented equally to show that this was a war for all Israelites on behalf of Yahweh. This army of twelve thousand men was considerably smaller than in other campaigns, and possibly small in comparison to the Midianite army. But it was God's war, and 'nothing can hinder the Lord from saving, whether by many or by few' (1 Sam 14:6).

Phinehas led the army (**31:6**). He was an appropriate leader, for it was he who had executed a Midianite woman and an Israelite man in 25:6-8 and stopped the plague. As a priest, he could also take with him *articles from the sanctuary and the trumpets for signalling.* The presence of a priest and of objects from the sanctuary also represented God's presence in this war.

The Lord's orders were duly carried out. The Israelites *fought against Midian … and killed every man* (**31:7**). This statement probably means only that they killed all the men in the group that they attacked, not that they killed every single Midianite male. In the days of Gideon the Midianites were still a powerful and formidable enemy whom God used to punish Israel for its apostasy (Judg 6:1-6).

The dead also included *five kings of Midian* (**31:8a**). These kings are probably identical with 'the elders of Midian' referred to in 22:4. Their names are also mentioned in Joshua 13:21, where they are described as 'princes allied with Sihon' and are lumped together in defeat with other neighbouring kings such as the kings of the Amorites. The king known as *Zur* may be the same one whose daughter Cozbi was slain together with Zimri the Israelite in 25:15.

Balaam was also killed (**31:8b**). We are not told how Balaam came to be in the Midianite camp and to suffer their fate. He may have been hired by the Midianite kings, just as he had previously been hired by the Moabites (22:4-6). His inability to curse the Israelites on that occasion should have made him aware that the Israelites enjoyed God's blessing and should have been a warning to him not to associate with their enemies. But apparently Balaam did not learn his lesson. His presence with the Midianites led to his being punished by God along with them.

The Midianite women and children were taken captive, presumably because it was thought that they would not be able to fight back against the Israelites and because they were wanted as wives or concubines, as often happens to women seized by military groups today. The Midianites' cattle, flocks and possessions were taken as booty (**31:9-11**). Then the warriors returned to the camp (**31:12**). As they displayed all that they had captured, they must have been proud of their victory and would have expected to hear admiring words from Moses and all the people. But they did not.

Moses, Eleazar the priest (the father of Phinehas) and other leaders set out to meet the returning army, presumably intending to congratulate them (**31:13**). But when Moses saw what they were bringing home, he was angry (**31:14**). The commanders had spared the women of Midian, who had contributed to adultery, apostasy and plague at Peor (**31:15-16**; see ch. 25). Moses severely reproved them for saving the women, for he had presumably ordered that everyone should be killed. Now he orders the soldiers to *kill all the boys. And kill every woman who has slept with a man* (**31:17**). Only young girls who were still virgins were allowed to survive because they could be married and integrated into the community without causing further threats (**31:18**).

It is difficult for us to understand how a merciful and loving God could order the killing of the Midianite women and their sons. We know that source and cause of war is human sin, and that war is evil. We also know that the world cannot achieve and maintain peace and tranquillity through waging wars. But at certain times God chooses to use war to punish the wicked. Thus, there are some wars that are called holy wars in the OT. When trying to understand these OT wars and interpret what they mean for us today, there are certain points we need to bear in mind.

- God was the only one who could initiate a holy war, and its sole object was to defeat those who were trying to thwart his purpose. Whenever the Israelites went to war on their own will, they were defeated and punished by God. We cannot use these OT examples to justify wars today.

- God is both saviour and judge; neither of these actions stands on its own. For example, when Egypt was judged, Israel was saved. The idea of holy war illustrates this truth about God.

- God is the Holy One, and holiness was central to the existence of the community he had established. He emphasizes this point in the laws regarding holiness and purity in the book of Leviticus and in Exodus 25–40 and Numbers 1–10. Since God is holy, anything that opposes or defiles this holiness must be destroyed. The order to kill the women and boys reveals how seriously God takes sin, especially the sin of turning his people astray and leading them to worship other gods. Those who resist God's plan and try to hinder God's will and purpose bring judgment upon themselves.

While Christians struggle with the idea of holy war, we cannot simply dismiss it as an error in the Scriptures. But we do know, in light of the NT, that we are not to wage any such wars today. We are to love our enemies, as Christ demonstrated when he did not fight back but loved his enemies to the point of being willing to die for them. The final truth about God is that he is not only a god of justice and holiness, but also a god of love.

31:19-54 Purification of warriors and spoils

While God ordered the destruction of the Midianites, the act of killing was not seen as holy. Therefore, those who had had contact with a corpse, whether they were soldiers or Midianite captives, still needed to be purified before they were allowed back into the camp. All of their clothing and the gear they had used during the war would also need to be purified with fire or water in the way prescribed by Eleazar the priest (**31:19-24**; 19:1-22).

The purification ritual involved their remaining outside the holy camp for seven days, like Miriam when she was stricken with leprosy (12:14). 'Seven' is a significant number in the biblical tradition, where it symbolizes the perfection or completion of something. The seventh day was the day that God sanctified and ordained for worship. The purification ritual was to be done on the third day and repeated on the seventh day.

The purification ritual was followed by the division of the booty, and this too was done under God's direction (**31:25**). In the OT, all spheres of life were dedicated to God, even those areas we might consider too minor or material to concern him. There was no distinction between the sacred and the secular.

The distribution of the spoils of war was done by Moses, Eleazar and the leaders of the community, under God's direction (**31:26-27**). The war had been conducted on behalf of the whole congregation of Israel, and hence the spoils of victory were also to be shared by all, although those who had done the actual fighting received a larger share. Thus, half the girls and cattle were assigned to the twelve thousand men who had done the fighting, while the other half was assigned to the rest of the community (31:27). Moses probably allotted each tribe its share, and then left it to the heads of the tribes to divide this share among themselves, according to their families. This method of division greatly reduced the possibility of discontent in the camp about who got what.

Both the soldiers and the congregation of Israel gave God part of the spoils as a way of giving thanks to the One who had enabled them to win victory. The levy (or *tribute*) on the soldiers' half of the booty was given to the priests (**31:28-29**, **36-41**). The non-combatants had to pay a higher levy than the warriors, and their tribute was given to the Levites (**31:30**, **42-47**). Although the priests and the Levites were not to fight and were not to own land, they too had a right to a share.

The principle of sharing the spoils of war also seems to have been observed at later times in Israel (Josh 22:8; 1 Sam 30:24-25; Ps 68:12). The sharing of benefits is part of the NT story too. The early Christians shared all their possessions for the common good (Acts 2:44-45). Sharing is a biblical virtue that all Christians must practise for the common good. Although Christian churches are in the midst of a world characterized by individualism and selfishness, Christians have not forgotten this duty. Some of the largest charity organizations in the world are operated by churches or church-related institutions. In this way, Christians share the gifts God has given them.

The principle of sharing with non-combatants is also important. We need to remember that those who work for the Lord include not only those who go but also those who stay at home and pray and support the work in other ways.

The spoil that was divided seems to have been only the captives and the cattle. The warriors seem to have been allowed to keep the gold, jewels and other goods that they brought back for themselves (**31:53**). But they did not cling to the booty. Instead the senior officers (captains of thousands) and junior officers (captains of hundreds) brought the gold to Moses as an expression of their thanksgiving to God because not a single Israelite soldier had been killed in the battle (31:48-51). These armlets, bracelets, signet rings, earrings and the like were also offered *to make atonement* (**31:50**), that is, to cover their sins. These leaders set a good example for their men and for future generations by not clinging to the material benefits they could have enjoyed.

The gold weighed about four hundred and twenty pounds (one hundred and ninety kilograms) (**31:52**). All of it was taken *into the Tent of Meeting as a memorial for the Israelites before the Lord* (**31:54**).

It pleases the Lord, even today, when Christians show their gratitude for special experiences of God's goodness and mercy.

32:1-42 A Controversial Request

Chapter 32 contains an account of the request of two of the Israelite tribes to settle in Gilead, across the Jordan from the promised land. It outlines the initial misunderstanding about their request, and then sets out the strict terms on which they and the half-tribe of Manasseh were granted permission to settle there.

The tribes of Reuben and Gad asked Moses for permission to settle on the east side of the Jordan River on the land that the Israelites had captured from the great kings Og and Sihon (**32:1-5**, **33**; see 21:21-35). Moses rejected this request, fearing that allowing the tribes to stay behind and avoid further conflict would discourage their fellow Israelites and lead to disunity among the tribes (**32:6-7**). Not only that, but he interpreted their request as a cover for their fear of entering the promised land and suspected that, like their ancestors, they were pulling back from the brink. Their ancestors' refusal had brought judgment on the nation, and Moses feared further judgment if they repeated the same sin (**32:8-15**). Consequently he denied their request. He believed that all the tribes should conquer the promised land across the Jordan River together and would not tolerate any divisions among Israelites.

The Reubenites and Gadites responded by emphasizing their commitment to the community and their willingness to fight alongside their fellow Israelites until everyone had attained the land they were promised (32:16-19). They were not seeking to avoid conflict so as to pursue their own self-interest. In reacting like this, they were expressing the same belief that prevails in Africa, in which a person's life is so grounded in a community that we can say, 'I am because we are, and since we are, therefore, I am.' Those who separate themselves from the community are like branches cut off from a tree – they will wither and die.

Moses listened to their arguments and eventually accepted the Reubenites' and Gadites' solemn promises to engage in battle for the collective conquest of the promised land before returning to their settlements outside Canaan (32:20-32). God required the whole community to be committed to a common conquest. His promise of the land was intended to unify them, not to promote individualistic interests and isolate people from each other.

After the conquest, the tribe of Reuben and Gad were joined by half the tribe of Manasseh. They all settled east of Jordan and built cities for themselves there (32:33-42).

The importance of unity, of which Moses was so well aware, is captured in the Swahili proverb *Umoja ni nguvu, utengano ni udhaifu* ['Unity is strength, and division is weakness']. Jesus, too, emphasized the importance of unity for his followers. We are to stay united to him, just as the branches of a vine have to stay linked to the main trunk of the vine if the branch is not to wither and die (John 15:1-8) Our unity with God is also shown by our unity with one another. Thus Jesus prayed for his church to be united as his agent of salvation on earth (John 17:26). If the church is to win the world for Christ, it must remain united.

33:1-49 Summary of Israel's Journey

Chapter 33 includes a list of the places where the Israelites camped during their long journey from Egypt to the promised land. This list is not comprehensive, for it does not mention some of the places mentioned in Exodus. It did not set out to be comprehensive, for it is not intended to be used as a geographical map or as a simple historical document. Rather, the list of places has a spiritual dimension and offers a clear indication of God's involvement in human history. Each encampment marked a new milestone in God's daily direction of the people. The list of place names may not make for exciting reading, but by reading this record of the places where they had been, God's people could look back and confess God's leadership in their journey. They could see his plan unfolding as he led them from the land of slavery to the land of liberty.

33:50-56 Command to Drive Out the Inhabitants

The list of camp sites ends with the site where the people are now camped, right on the edge of the promised land (33:50). Here God gave instructions for the conquest of the land. The Israelites were to *drive out all the inhabitants ... destroy all their carved images and their cast idols, and demolish all their high places* (33:51-52). For a detailed discussion of holy war, see the comments on chapter 31. All the original inhabitants of the promised land were to be driven out and their land distributed among the Israelites. If the Israelites were nervous about their ability to do this, they needed to remember God's promise *Take possession of the land and settle in it, for I have given you the land to possess* (33:53). God is the Lord of the land. He created it, he owns it, and he allots it to whomever he pleases (see Gen 1:1; Ps 24:1-2). The exact allocation of the land was to be determined by lot (33:54; see also 26:52-56).

God spelled out clearly the consequences of failure to obey his command: *But if you do not drive out the inhabitants of the land, ... I will do to you what I plan to do to them* (33:55a-56).

Nevertheless, the Israelites did fail to obey and did indeed find that the remaining Canaanites were *barbs in your eyes and thorns in your side* (33:55b). The Canaanites drew the Israelites into worship of their gods and led Israel into apostasy, which later became the reason for the Israelites' being taken to Babylon in captivity.

34:1-29 The Promised Land

34:1-15 The boundaries of the land

The writer's intention in describing the boundaries of the promised land was not so much to give political and geographic details but more to show that God was involved in allotting the land and to demonstrate the greatness of his gift. The people would not reach many of the boundaries described here until long after the time of Joshua (Josh 13:1-7). In Genesis 15:17-20, Abraham was promised a general area, and in Joshua 15–19 there is a more detailed account of the land allotted to particular tribes. All biblical references to land and geographical boundaries are intended to show that God's plan breaks into human history as Israel becomes a nation and takes possession of the promised land. Through Israel's possession of the promised land, God fulfilled his promise to Abraham (Gen 12:7).

34:16-29 Leaders chosen to divide the land

God uses human beings to put his plan of salvation and freedom into effect. Thus, he chose leaders among the Israelites to allot the land. The first two names in the list are well known: *Eleazar the priest* and *Joshua son of Nun* (34:16-17). Their names are followed by a list of the representatives of each tribe (34:19-29). The appointment of Eleazar, representing the priests who could not own any land themselves, Joshua, the successor of Moses, and one leader from each tribe indicated that the land would be distributed equally because every tribe was fairly represented. God was again demonstrating his concern that justice should pervade all spheres of life.

The first name in the list of representatives is *Caleb son of Jephunneh, from the tribe of Judah* (**34:19**). He had been one of the spies sent out many years before (13:6), and he and Joshua were the sole survivors of the earlier generation. The order in which the tribes are listed here, with Judah first, differs from that in chapters 1 and 7. The order is more similar to that used in describing the division of the land in Joshua 19.

35:1-34 Arrangements for Levites

35:1-8 Towns for the Levites

When the land of Canaan was divided among the tribes, the Levites were not allotted any specific area, as had been commanded (18:20-24; see Deut 10:8-9). They had been set aside to assist in the work of the sanctuary, but they would still need some place to live while they served the Lord. Consequently God commanded that the Levites should be given forty-eight towns to live in and sufficient land around the towns to enable them to feed their cattle and other livestock (**35:1-6**). These towns would be scattered throughout the areas occupied by other tribes (**35:7-8**). The towns were

---

THE HISTORY OF ISRAEL

For those who believe in its inspiration and authority – and, therefore, truthfulness – the Bible is the primary source for understanding the history of God's ancient covenant people. This presupposition in no way prevents us from using reliable documents from the ancient Near East to fill in some of the gaps in the biblical account. However, due to the brevity of this article, the focus here will be solely on the Bible. For an Afrocentric reconstruction of the history of ancient Israel, see Adamo's *Africa and the Africans in the Old Testament*.

When we speak about the history of Israel, it is important to remember that what we are talking about is a special kind of history – redemptive history. Thus the Bible should not be read as if it is an ordinary history book or a scientific textbook. Nor is it just a record of events in the ancient Near East that are interpreted so as to reveal God. Rather, it records history in which God is an active participant, shaping the events recorded.

The beginnings of the history of Israel as a nation are present in the history of the patriarchs contained in Genesis 12–50. In fact, it could even be argued that it starts with the earliest history of humankind as a whole, with creation, the fall, the flood and the dispersion (Gen 1–11). However, Israel's distinctiveness and purpose start to emerge more clearly with the deliverance recorded in the book of Exodus.

Although Moses was the human instrument, it is clear that the exodus from Egypt was primarily the work of God: 'the Lord kept vigil that night to bring them out of Egypt' (Exod 12:31-42). Three months after leaving Egypt, the Israelites arrived at Mount Sinai or Horeb (Exod 19:1-2). Here God appeared to them (19:16-25), spoke to the whole assembly (20:1-17, 22-26) and made a covenant with them: 'If you obey me fully and keep my covenant, then out of all nations you will be my treasured possession. Although the whole earth is mine, you will be for me a kingdom of priests and a holy nation' (Exod 19:5-6). The terms, ordinances and institutions of the covenant are outlined in Exodus 19–40, Leviticus, Numbers 1–10 and Deuteronomy. On leaving Sinai,

the Israelites started their journey to the Promised Land (Num 10:11). Rebellion prolonged a journey of eleven days to forty years (Deut 1:2-3); but finally they entered, conquered and occupied the land under the leadership of Joshua (Joshua).

Between the settlement of the land and the establishment of the monarchy the period of the judges, a period characterized by a vicious circle of sin, oppression, sorrow and salvation (Judges and Ruth). The confusion of this period – and especially the failure of Eli and his sons and of the sons of Samuel, along with the oppression of the Philistines – precipitated a request for a king (1 Sam 8). The monarchy had its golden age during the reigns of David and Solomon. However, rebellion against God's covenantal provisions resulted in the division of the nation into a northern kingdom (Israel – ten tribes) and a southern kingdom (Judah – two tribes). Israel fell to the Assyrians in 722/21 BC and Judah fell to the Babylonians about 150 years later, in 587/86 BC. There is no record of the return of the northern tribes. Some of those who were exiled by the Babylonians did, however, return in three stages under the leadership of Zerubbabel, Ezra and Nehemiah. The OT closes with the remnant of the covenant people living under Persian hegemony and worshipping in a rebuilt temple. They were looking forward to the coming of a new age under the Lord's Messiah and had yet to see the fulfilment of a number of the promises given to the patriarchs.

Then came the four hundred years of the intertestamental period before the Messiah (Jesus) and his forerunner, John the Baptist, came, as predicted by Malachi (Mal 3:1-3; 4:1-6; Matt 11:10, 14; Luke 1:76; 7:27). Yet still some of the promises in the OT have not been fulfilled. Clearly the OT points to something beyond itself (Heb 1:1-2) and even beyond the NT.

The re-emergence of the nation of Israel in modern times is a preparation for their end-time acknowledgement of Christ not only as their Messiah but also as the Saviour of the world (Rom 11:25-27; Rev. 1:7). Thus the history of Israel goes beyond the national history of one nation, Israel. Ultimately, it is the history of God's redemption for the whole world through Jesus Christ (John 1:1-14; 3:16-18; Rom 10:11-13).

Tewoldemedhin Habtu

allotted according to the number of towns each tribe had. This meant those who had many would give more and those who had few would give accordingly. Once again, justice was served.

35:9-34 Cities of refuge

Six of the cities given to the Levites were to have a special function as cities of refuge for the people of Israel and for strangers (35:6, 13-15). God's law prescribed the death penalty as a punishment for murder, and thus the relatives of anyone who was killed could seek blood vengeance (34:16-21). However, God knew that some killings are accidental and that some people are likely to be falsely accused of murder (**35:11-12**). Consequently he established these cities as a refuge where an accused killer could be safe until his or her case had come to trial.

God also laid down the criteria for distinguishing intentional murder and accidental death. A murder was deemed intentional if someone died as a result of being struck with a weapon that could kill, such as something made of iron, stone or wood, or by an object thrown with the intention of causing harm. It was also murder if someone died because he or she was punched or pushed in a hostile manner (**35:16-21**). A death could be deemed accidental if someone was bumped or hit by an object that had not been aimed at him or her and had not been intended to cause harm (**35:22-24**).

The task of *the assembly* was to discern which type of death was involved in each case (**35:25a**). Those guilty of deliberate murder were to receive the death penalty (35:21). However, someone who killed by accident was given the protection of a city of refuge, where he or she would have to remain until the death of the high priest (**35:25b, 28**). But if someone granted this shelter chose to leave the boundaries of the city of refuge, he or she could be killed by the avenger of blood (**35:26-27**).

The last verses of this chapter reinforce the points already made. First, murder must not be taken lightly. Anyone who murders deserves death, but the death penalty is not to be meted out lightly. More than one witness to the crime is needed before it can be applied (**35:29-30**). Second, no ransom can be accepted for any murderer (**35:31**). The rich could not use money to escape the consequences of their crimes. Third, no ransom could be paid to allow anyone who had fled to a city of refuge to return to his or her own home before the death of the high priest (**35:32**). The main purpose of this ordinance was to protect the land from defilement through the shedding of innocent blood or through the absence of justice. God told the Israelites, *Do not defile the land where you live and where I dwell, for I, the Lord, dwell among the Israelites* (**35:34**).

36:1-13 Daughters' Inheritance

The laws of inheritance were spelled out in chapter 27. As is often the case when legislation is promulgated, further legislation became necessary when the application of these laws posed a dilemma. If daughters were allowed to inherit where there were no sons, what would happen when those daughters married? If they married someone who was not part of their tribe, the tribe would lose land that rightfully belonged to it. This was the problem with which the male leaders of the Gilead clan of the tribe of Manasseh approached Moses (just as the daughters of Zelophehad had in 27:1-2). These men came to Moses and the elders, but not before the entire congregation as the daughters of Zelophehad had come (**36:1-3**).

The clan representatives tried to justify their concern by relating it to the Year of Jubilee in which all land would revert to its original owner, but their land would revert to the tribe into which these women had married (**36:4**; Lev 25:8-54). At the heart of the problem was the fact that even though a woman might inherit the land, she effectively lost ownership of it as soon as she married, when it became her husband's possession. Independent female ownership of land was as out of question in ancient Hebrew society as it is in many African societies today.

Although the text does not specifically state that Moses presented the case to Yahweh as in 27:5, he presumably did so because he delivered his response as being *at the Lord's command*. He ruled that the daughters had to marry someone from within their own clan (**36:5-6**). This ruling upheld the integrity of clan units as distinct entities within the people of God (**36:7-9**).

The daughters of Zelophehad obeyed Moses and married their cousins (**36:10-12**). Although women had achieved certain rights, they had not yet achieved full recognition as equal recipients of Yahweh's promise with their male counterparts. But that day would come, and Paul writing to the Galatians could stress that in the Lord 'there is neither Jew nor Greek, slave nor free, male nor female, for you are all one in Christ Jesus' (Gal 3:28)

The book of Numbers closes with this ruling on the integrity of tribal lands, an appropriate ending for a book that began with a census of tribes who as yet owned no land, but who were moving in faith towards the possession of the land that God had promised them.

Anastasia Boniface-Malle

Further Reading

Ashley, T. R. *The Book of Numbers*. NICOT. Grand Rapids: Eerdmans, 1993.

Wenham, G. *Numbers: An Introduction and Commentary*. TOT. Downers Grove: Intervarsity Press, 1981.

DEUTERONOMY

Deuteronomy, the fifth and last book in the Torah, begins with the children of Israel temporarily settled in the plains of Moab, opposite Jericho and on the threshold of entering the promised land (1:5; see also Num 33:48-49). At this stage, the story that has been unfolding in Exodus and Numbers pauses while Moses addresses the people in what he knows will be his final words. In a series of speeches that amount to his final testimony he reminds them of their recent history and of all that God has done for them in delivering them from Egypt and bringing them this far across the wilderness. Again and again he emphasizes that Israel is to show total allegiance to God and to obey his law if the people are to enjoy peace and prosperity in their new home. His message can be summed up in the words 'You shall love the Lord your God with all your heart and with all your soul and with all your might' (6:5).

In the course of expounding the Israelites' duty to God, Moses again sets out the details of the law that had been delivered to the people at Mount Horeb (Sinai). This repetition of the law accounts for the name of the book, for the name 'Deuteronomy' is derived from a Greek expression meaning 'the second law'.

Whereas much of the first exposition of the law in Exodus and Leviticus had focused on instruction in the ritual responsibilities of the priests, Deuteronomy is intended to instruct the ordinary Israelites. Hence Moses orders that it is to be read aloud to all the people every seventh year at the Feast of Tabernacles (31:1-13).

Authorship and Date

There has been much debate regarding the authorship of Deuteronomy. Traditionally, both Jewish and Christian scholars have accepted that this book and much of the rest of the Pentateuch were written by Moses. Certainly 31:9, 24 claim that at least certain sections of the book were recorded directly by Moses himself. However, someone else must have added the sections recording Moses' death. Scholars debate whether some other portions also came from another hand.

The date at which Deuteronomy was written has also been the subject of a debate that is strongly influenced by scholars' views on the matter of authorship. There are strong grounds for thinking that much of the book must date from Moses' time, that is, from the late second millennium BC.

Influence of the Book

Despite its Mosaic authorship and the instruction that it was to be read to the entire population every seven years, it appears that the book of Deuteronomy was lost for a time during the tumultuous years of the monarchy. It was rediscovered only during the reign of Josiah, who was endeavouring to restore the worship of Yahweh (2 Kgs 22-23; 2 Chr 34:29-35:19). Josiah was horrified to discover how far the people of Israel had strayed from the law, and instituted even more thoroughgoing reforms.

One of the reasons for his shock may have been the passage regarding the law of the king (17:14-20). The Israelites tended to believe that God had installed the Davidic line of kings that would never be shaken, but Deuteronomy made it clear that without obedience to the requirements of the covenant, there was no guarantee of God's protection. Quite the opposite! Those who broke the covenant were cursed. Josiah pledged that he and his people would again observe the covenant (2 Kgs 23:3).

The book is also often quoted by Christ and by NT writers. In all, the NT contains more than eighty references to this book, signalling its importance. To give some indication of this, just nine passages (6:5; 18:15; 19:15; 21:23; 23:21; 24:1; 25:4; 30:11-14; 32:35) are quoted in sixteen different passages in ten different books of the NT.

Theology of the Book

The theological importance of the book of Deuteronomy is clear from the number of references to it in the NT. It presents Yahweh as Israel's sovereign Lord who demands obedience and will not tolerate the worship of other gods. His grounds for demanding obedience are the saving acts he performed in freeing the Israelites from Egypt, protecting them in the wilderness and defending them from their enemies. Thus his demand for obedience is rooted in the love and mercy he has shown Israel. In response, he wishes the Israelites to love, obey, worship and serve only him. This worship is to be expressed both in personal devotion to him as well as in observance of certain religious festivals and rituals. In return for their obedience, Israel will enjoy peace and prosperity in the land God is giving it, (28:1-14). If it will not obey, punishment will follow (4:26; 27:15-26; 28:15-68).

Israel's response to God is to be the same as that in the Angolan Umbundu saying, *Ocisola uvanga ci sakuiwa locisola cikuavo; onjala lo londunge* ['Love responds to love; only love cures love']. Or as the NT puts it, Israel is to love God, because God has first loved her.

Structure of the Book

There are many similarities between the structure of this book, and of individual sections within it, and the structure of treaties in the ancient Near East, such as the Assyrian vassal treaties of Esarhaddon. Such treaties were common when there was a change in leadership, as when retiring king Esarhaddon demanded that the people swear an oath of allegiance to his successor, Assurbanipal. The treaties always began by stating the names of the parties to the treaty and then gave a historical preamble outlining the history leading up to the treaty (1:1-4:49). This preamble was followed by the specific terms of the treaty and a statement making it clear that these may not be altered (5:1-26:19). Next came an appeal to abide by the terms of the treaty and a list of the consequences of failing to do so (27:1-30:20). The names of witnesses to the treaty were also mentioned, as well as the responsibility of those making the treaty to ensure that future generations were also informed of its terms (31:1-34:5).

Given that treaties were associated with a change of leadership, it is not surprising to find a treaty structure in a book that marks the transfer of power from the elderly Moses, aware that his time is short, to his successor, Joshua (3:23-29, 31:1-8). However, in this case the people are called to swear allegiance not to Joshua, but to God. Where political treaties demanded exclusive loyalty to one king, Deuteronomy demands exclusive loyalty to one God, who is also the only king of Israel (Judg 8:23). This concept of the kingship of God is underlined by modelling the statement of the relations between God and his people on the written political treaties that governed the relations between human kings and their subjects.

Outline of Contents

COMMENTARY

1:1-4:43 Moses' First Address

1:1-5 Introduction

The book opens with a paragraph explaining the content of the whole book and stating when it was produced. Similar paragraphs are found at the beginning of several sections in this book (for example, 4:44-5:1) and also at the beginning of other Old Testament books such as Amos and Ezekiel. They are also, as indicated in the introduction to this book, a normal feature in the preamble to ancient treaties, stating where and when a treaty was made and by whom.

It is clear from the statement *these are the words that Moses spoke* (**1:1a**) that the content of the book was originally a speech. This point is reiterated in 4:45, 29:2, 31:30 and 32:44. However, the book also contains references to the contents of these speeches being recorded in writing (17:18; 31:9).

If anyone is tempted to dismiss this as 'mere words', it is important to note that in Hebrew the noun 'word' had a broad meaning. The Hebrew name for the Ten Commandments, for example, is the Ten Words (4:13; 10:4; see also Exod 34:28). God's revelation is frequently described as the 'the word of God' that came to various prophets (1 Chr 17:3). 'The word of the Lord' was also a technical expression for prophetic revelation. When the speaker is a divinely inspired prophet, 'the words of the prophet' and 'the words of the Lord' can be used interchangeably to describe the message. (see Jer 36:8, 10, 11).

Moses' words were addressed to *all Israel* (**1:1b**), a phrase that is often used in Deuteronomy (see, for example 5:1; 34:12). The words recorded here were intended to apply to the whole nation: those who had first encountered God at Sinai, the generation that had been born in the wilderness and their children who would be born in the promised land (5:3). God's word through Moses had permanent significance for all Israel.

The location where this explanation was given is identified as *the desert east of the Jordan – that is, in the Arabah* (**1:1c**). The 'Arabah' was the dry, low-lying region into which the valley of the Jordan River runs near Jericho before reaching the Dead Sea (1:1; 2:8; see also Josh 12:1; 2 Sam 4:7; 2 Kgs. 25:5). The next words seem to define more particularly the exact spot in the Arabah that Moses was in: *opposite Suph, between Paran and Tophel, Laban, Hazeroth and Dizahab*. The problem for us is that no places with these names are known in that locality, but at least three of the names have occurred in the course of Israel's earlier wanderings. 'Suph' is the Hebrew name of the Red Sea or Sea of Suph, Paran is mentioned in Numbers 10:12 and Hazeroth in Numbers 11:35 and 33:17. Commentators sometimes conclude that not everything recorded here was spoken at one time, but that what this book contains is a summary of various speeches Moses gave while the Israelites were in the wilderness, which culminated in a major speech in the fortieth year of their wandering.

The comment in parentheses that *It takes eleven days to go from Mount Horeb* … (**1:2**) conveys an approximate idea of the distance from Horeb, where the law had been delivered, to Kadesh Barnea, on the southern border of the promised land. It was there that the Israelites had first turned back from entering the land (1:19-40), so there is a stark contrast between the 'eleven days' mentioned here and the fact that this address is finally delivered in the *fortieth year* (**1:3a**).

This speech is Moses' final address to the people he had led through the wilderness, and in it he repeats *all that the Lord had commanded him concerning them* (**1:3b**). The word translated 'command' clearly refers to a superior giving a verbal communication to a subordinate, but can also be used in the more intimate relationship of the instructions a father gives to his sons (Gen 49:29, 33; 1 Sam 17:20).

The exact circumstances of Moses' speech are further defined as being after he had defeated Sihon, the Amorite king, and Og, the king of Bashan (**1:4**; 2:24-3:11). This major victory, the first step in the conquest of the promised land, was still fresh in the people's minds, and there are numerous references to it throughout Deuteronomy. However, the author is at pains to remind his readers that the Israelites have not yet entered the land, and so he repeats the information that Moses spoke *east of the Jordan in the territory of Moab* (**1:5a**).

There *Moses began to expound this law* (**1:5b**), that is, to explain what God has said. The verb here translated 'expound' is a rare one. When used literally, it refers to digging or chopping, or to writing on stone (27:8) or tablets (Hab 2:2). Here it is used metaphorically as Moses digs in to find the core of the law and to engrave it on their memories. Moses is determined that they will hear and understand everything about the law that God revealed to him for them (**1:3c**). This is a goal that we should share with Moses when we preach. Like Moses, we must proclaim his word to our people with a knowledge of their background and of what God has done for them, and a burning desire to see them apply God's word in their daily lives.

1:6-4:40 A Review of God's Mighty Acts

If Deuteronomy is compared to an ancient treaty, then this section of the book comprises the historical preamble. In other words, this is the section of a treaty that presents the history of the relationship between the participants identified in the opening paragraphs. Moses accordingly presents a brief outline of the interaction between God and the Israelites in the days between the people's departure from Mount Horeb and their sins at Beth Peor. It is clear that Israel has consistently failed to obey Yahweh.

The historical information is presented in a series of short scenes, which remind us that Israel's relationship with God was not rooted in mythology or mysticism or in philosophical arguments. Rather, Israel knows God because of his specific historical acts.

1:6-1:46 The first attempt at conquest

1:6-8 ISRAEL AT HOREB In describing the events at Horeb, the order in which the participants are presented is Yahweh, Moses, the people. *The Lord our God* (**1:6**) is referred to by his name, Yahweh, a covenant name that is most often used in connection with his relationship with the nation of Israel. In Hebrew, this name has four letters (YHWH) and is also known as the Tetragrammaton (tetra = four; gramma = letter). The name was considered too holy to be pronounced, and so the Jews generally substituted the word *Adonai* (Lord) each time it appeared in text. This pattern is followed in many modern translations, including the NIV, which set the word 'Lord' in capital letters where this substitution has been made.

At Horeb, God gave the Israelites the law. After they had spent some time there, he commanded them to move on (1:6-7). They were to advance and take possession of the land God had promised to their fathers, Abraham, Isaac and Jacob (1:8; see also Gen 12:1-7; 13:14-17; 15:18-21). The land promised stretches from west (the Arabah) to east (the coast) and from south (the Negev) to north (the Euphrates) (1:7). While not all this area was occupied immediately, much of it was later conquered by David and ruled by Solomon. The details of the area promised will not be discussed in this commentary.

The promises of descendants and of land were basic to Israelite thinking and feature prominently in Deuteronomy. Land is also something that is very close to an African's heart. Sons (and in some groups, daughters too) expect a share of their parents' land. A father who distributes land to others and not to his son is seen as cursing that son and denying his very existence.

1:9-18 ORGANIZATION OF THE PEOPLE God had fulfilled the promise made to Abraham and multiplied the people (1:10; Gen 15:5). While Moses was thankful for this (1:11), it had also greatly increased the burden of leadership (1:9, 12). He recognized that he needed help (1:9; see also Exod 18:13-23) and consequently set out to develop a system of leadership and organization of the people. In setting up this system, he showed the wisdom encapsulated in the Angolan Umbundu proverb *Ukulu wa kulihã ca velapo ovina viomanu okuti ocimbanda ci sule* ['An experienced old person knows better than a diviner']. The elderly are honoured for their experience and treated with respect. Their advice is worth more than a diviner's guesses about the future. Recognizing this, Moses requested that the people choose *wise, understanding and respected men* (1:13) to assist him in governing.

The people accepted this plan and Moses appointed responsible men and gave them authority over *thousands, hundreds and fifties,* terms that denote military groupings, not precise numbers (1:15). The exact tasks of these subordinate officials are not defined, but they administered justice and maintained civil order and military discipline. In appointing these men to their office, Moses impressed on them the duty to be fair and impartial to all, whether Israelites or aliens (1:16-17). It is clear that there was to be no corruption in Moses' government.

1:19-25 SENDING PEOPLE TO SEE THE LAND Although God had commanded the people to undertake the journey, it was clearly not an easy one, as can be judged from the reference to *that vast and dreadful desert* (1:19). It required travelling more than one hundred miles across the forbidding desert of et-Tih. The people had to set out in faith, believing that God means what he says.

Having crossed the desert successfully, the people arrived at the oasis of Kadesh Barnea at the entrance to the promised land, from which they would enter the land. There Moses encouraged the people and told them not to be afraid (1:20-21). God had promised them this land, and they should not allow fear to deprive them of what was rightfully theirs.

But the people were nervous and reluctant to advance, and they requested that spies be sent out to survey the land (1:22). They carefully phrased this in the form of a request to reconnoitre their route. Moses agreed and sent out twelve spies, one from each tribe (1:23). The spies returned, reporting *It is a good land* (1:25). But why did the people need spies to tell them this? 'If they had believed in God's good intentions for them, they would not have needed spies to confirm that the land was good' (*NBC*).

1:26-33 THE FEAR OF THE PEOPLE But while the spies reported that the land was good, they make no comments at all on the route they had supposedly gone to spy out. They had allowed themselves to be distracted from the purpose of their mission, and they brought back frightening news about the people who lived in the land. They described them as Anakites, that is, descendants of giants, and as living in strongly fortified cities (1:28). The people fell into the exact trap that Moses had warned them against (1:21), collapsing into fear and discouragement that were rooted in a lack of faith. Once again the people jumped to the conclusion that God had never meant them any good and that all their journeyings had been solely for the purpose of harming them (1:27).

Moses responded by reminding them again that God had in the past shown himself to be powerful (1:30). If he had known it, he might have quoted them the Angolan Umbundu proverb that says, *Suku upila kapepe onela ku muine womunu u kuonene* ['God removes the ring from the fingers of the giant through his shoulders']. Normally, we would pull down a ring to remove it from our finger, but God has such power that he can do things in a way that humans would never even dream of attempting: pulling the ring up the giant's finger and over his hefty shoulders. God had done equally amazing acts on behalf of Israel, and thus they should continue to trust that he would fight for them.

Not only had God shown Israel that he is powerful, but he had also demonstrated his love for them: *Your God carried you, as a father carries his son* (1:31). He had guided them every step of the way (1:33). But the people chose not to trust, first by sending the spies and then by letting themselves be discouraged by their report. They, like many of us, were too anxious to walk by sight and not by faith.

1:34-46 GOD'S JUDGMENT ON THE PEOPLE The Ovimbundu people of Angola believe that God judges everyone according to what they have done in the universe. This judgment is not remote, but present and actual. It is also communal, in the sense expressed by the proverb *Pokuyenja owanda wa Suku omunu umuamue ka ci kavela ulika* ['When the whole of humankind is carrying God, one person does not become humpbacked' (by bearing the weight alone)]. Everyone shares the responsibilities of the nation or state or family; they do not fall on one person alone. All must share responsibility. Thus all Israel suffered the consequences of their refusal to obey God's command.

God's judgment on the rebels was to give them what they said they wanted: not one of *this evil generation shall see the good land* (**1:34-35**). Even Moses himself would share this punishment, perhaps partly (see also Num 20:11-12) because he had allowed himself to be dragged into a lack of faith that showed itself in the sending out of the spies. God had permitted him to do this (Num 13:1), but it was still an act that showed a lack of faith. He should have insisted that the people move in to occupy the land immediately (**1:37**; see also 1:23). Only Caleb and Joshua, who had not been party to acts of unbelief, were to be exempted from God's punishment (**1:36, 38**).

Yet God had sworn to give Israel the land promised to their ancestors (1:8) and he would keep his promise, but only in the next generation. The very children for whose safety the rebels had expressed fear (**1:39**; Num 14:3) would be the ones to inherit the promise, for they had not rebelled, because they were so young that they did *not yet know good from bad.* God commanded the people to *turn around and set out towards the desert* again (**1:40**). The Israelites had not believed what God promised them, and so they could not proceed.

Realizing that they had done wrong and sinned against Yahweh, the people decided that they would now do what Yahweh had required. However, whereas they had once been told to 'go up and take possession' of the land (1:21), now God's command is *do not go up* (**1:42**; see also Num 14:42). Presumptuously ignoring yet another command, the Israelites attempted to invade the promised land without God's support and were roundly defeated (**1:43-44**). They realized that they could not possess the land unless God gave it to them.

What is clear from this incident is that God's people cannot assume that God will automatically be on their side in war. In modern terms, this means that the mere fact that one side in a conflict calls itself 'Christian' does not mean that it is acting in accordance with God's will.

2:1-23 The journey through Transjordan

2:1-8a ISRAEL TURNS BACK TOWARDS THE RED SEA The Israelites' disobedience had led to them being turned back at the gates of the promised land and to their wanderings in the desert region to the south of the land of Canaan, on the western outskirts of Edomite territory. They wandered *for a long time* (**2:1**). The delay was not a question of months but of years

– a full thirty-eight years – until God's words in 1:35 were ready to be fulfilled (2:14).

It is unlikely that the Israelites were on the move for this entire period. They may at times have spent several years in one place, but they had no permanent homes. During this time God not only punished them for their grumbling and unbelief, but also prepared them to follow him and rely on his leadership and provision (**2:7**). Some of the events in this period are described in Numbers 20 and 21.

At last God gave the Israelites another command to turn northwards towards Canaan (**2:3**; note the repeated use of 'turn' in 2:1, 3, 8 that emphasizes their slow progress). This land through which they would have to pass belonged to *the descendants of Esau,* who Moses referred to as *your brothers* in the sense that they, too, were descendants of Abraham (**2:4, 8a**; see also Gen 25:19, 25-26). Although not mentioned here, it is clear from Numbers 20:18-20 that the ancient enmity (see Gen 27:41-45), between Israel and Edom reasserted itself, and that this is why the Israelites did not go through Edom but walked around it (2:8a; Num 21:4). The important point made in Deuteronomy is that God had given Esau the land of Edom just as he would give Israel the land of Canaan (**2:5**). God's insistence on the need to express their respect for their brother's land by paying for everything they needed is a point that is sometimes forgotten in Africa, where armed bands of government soldiers and rebels sometimes simply help themselves to what they need, without any offer of payment.

2:8b-23 JOURNEY AROUND MOAB Still moving northwards the people came to the region called Moab, which lay to the east of the southern half of the Dead Sea (**2:8b**). The Moabites were also related to the Israelites through their ancestor Lot (**2:9**) and the Lord had given them this land, with the result that Israel was forbidden to conquer it.

The note that is added in **2:10-12** reminds us that both Moab and Edom had also had to overcome great obstacles in order to possess their lands, just as the Israelites would soon be doing. This point is reiterated in Moses' account in 2:18-23 of how these and other groups came to occupy the territories in which Israel found them. None of them were the original inhabitants. The territory held by the Ammonites, who like Moab were descended from Abraham's nephew, Lot (Gen 19:36-38), had once belonged to a group of people who were presumably very tall, for they were described as giants, *as tall as the Anakites,* who had earlier struck fear into the hearts of the spies (**2:21**; see also 1:28 2:10). Similarly, Mount Seir had originally been occupied by Horites, whom the Edomites had dispossessed (2:12, **22**). The Caphtorites, who were related to the Philistines and had come from Crete, had also driven the Avites out of their land and taken possession of it (**2:23**).

The listing of these examples serves several purposes. First of all, it reminds the Israelites that others have been able to defeat giants, so that mere size is no guarantee of success. It also reminded them of how insecure worldly possessions are and how often they change owners. Finally, they must have been encouraged by the realization that if God had done this for other groups, he would surely do the same for them, the people he had specifically chosen and to whom he had promised the land.

The insistence that Edom, Moab and the Ammonites had been given their territories by Yahweh would also have been startling in an age when many gods were worshipped. Moses is making the point that Yahweh is the sole God in charge of history, and he alone has the prerogative to distribute homelands to the peoples of the earth. In our day, as we ponder on the European countries who occupied our land, we need to reflect on whether what happened was caused by God's will or human power. There are no easy answers to this question, but it is one we need to wrestle with.

By the time the Israelites finally crossed the Zered Valley and again encamped on the borders of the promised land, all those who had been adults when they came out of Egypt had died (**2:13-15**). They were the ones who wanted to enter the promised land in their own strength and had been defeated in 1:44. A new stage in the story was beginning, one in which God would give the Israelites victory.

2:24-3:17 The conquest of Transjordan

2:24-25 Order to advance After encouraging the people with his account of the history of related nations, Moses now issues the order to advance across the Arnon Gorge and set foot in the territory that will soon be theirs (**2:24a**). Note that although God assured them of success, he did not deliver the land to them without any effort on their part. His instruction to engage *Sihon, the Amorite, king of Hesbon*, in battle (**2:24b**) clearly indicated that he expected them to take action and fight the enemy. This principle still holds true today. God has given us many promises in his word, but we cannot simply sit back and wait to receive them. We need to work to gain possession of what God has promised us. Yet we will not be fighting alone. Just as God promised to discourage Israel's enemies, making it easier to defeat them (**2:25**), so he will help us in our struggle against evil in the spiritual world, within ourselves and around us.

An Ovimbundu proverb from Angola mirrors God's help here: *Suku eye osulila ombowe ku ukuavita* ['It is God who pounds ombowe for the one-armed person']. When preparing ombowe, a food made from cassava, it is first boiled and then pounded with a pestle. A normal person holds the pestle with both hands, but for the person with only one arm, it is God who helps him or her to pound ombowe. The Israelites may feel weak compared to the nations they confront, but God will be their second arm.

2:26-37 Defeat of sihon The Israelite campaign began with sending a diplomatic mission from *Kedemoth*, where the Israelites were camped. Messengers were sent to Sihon

offering peace and requesting permission to travel peacefully through his territory, which stretched from roughly the Wadi Arnon to the Wadi Jabbok (**2:26-29**). Moses may have been offering to enter into a treaty with Sihon (for examples of such treaties see Josh 9:15; Judg 4:17; 1 Sam 7:14; 2 Sam 3:12; 1 Kgs 5:12). The offer was genuine, even if Moses knew it would be refused, for God had already informed them that they would need to fight Sihon (**2:30-31**). The offer of peace meant that Sihon would have no excuse if violence followed – as it did, for Sihon's response to the offer of peace was to march out to fight, thus beginning the war (**2:32**).

God sometimes ruins his enemies by their own actions, as was the case here, where someone who attacked the people of God suffered the consequences. As the Umbundu proverb says, *Etumba wa lilonga halio liu ku lia* ['He was frying in his own fat'].

What followed is also described in Numbers 21:21-32. Israel was victorious. They executed all the Amorites – men, women and children – *and left no survivors* (**2:33-34**). While they attacked and conquered every single town in Sihon's land, the Israelites were scrupulous about obeying God's command not to attack their own relatives, the Ammonites (**2:35-37**).

The actions of the Israelites here may be partially explained in terms of an Umbundu proverb: *Uwa walingila vakuele omãla wove va kafetiwa ko vaso yoloneke* ['If someone does good, their children reap the benefits after that person's death']. The descendants of a good person reap the fruit of that person's goodness. But the converse is also true: the descendants of an evil person reap the fruits of that person's evil deeds. This may be what is happening here, for the sin of the Amorites may have reached the 'full measure' mentioned in Genesis 15:16.

This passage, and others like it, raise an important ethical question. How could God condone such acts and even give specific instructions such as those in 1 Samuel 15:3, concerning the Amalekites ('totally destroy them … Do not spare them; put to death men and women, children and infants, cattle and sheep, camels and donkeys')? While we may not pretend to understand the mind of God fully, the key to understanding these incidents is possibly found in 7:2-4. There the Lord explains why he commands the destruction of some peoples: 'for they will turn your sons away from following me to serve other gods'.

It is important to remember that Israel was in a unique position. As 7:6 explains, 'you are a people, holy to the Lord your God. The Lord your God has chosen you out of all the people on the surface of the earth to be his people, his treasured possession.' Israel was God's treasure and the means God was planning to use to reveal himself to the whole earth (Gen 12:2; Mic 4:1-2). Thus it was vital that their faith not be corrupted.

We need to remember that God is the source and maintainer of every human being. He is like a farmer who sees a weed growing that is likely to stunt the growth of his crops and decides that the weed needs to be removed so that the other plants can grow to their full strength. But only the farmer is entitled to make such a decision.

What God is doing here is very different from the genocidal massacres we have witnessed in places like Rwanda in Africa. Human beings are not God, and we do not have the right to destroy lives created by God. Those who take part in killings inspired by hatred or mob justice are murderers. These passages should never be cited in support of such actions.

Only God has the right to authority over people's lives, although he has delegated this right to the judicial systems that he has established (Rom 13:1). Such systems he will hold accountable if they become corrupt and do not deliver justice.

3:1-11 DEFEAT OF OG This section of Deuteronomy is almost a word for word repetition of Numbers 21:33-35, the difference being that the pronoun *we* is used instead of the 'they' in Numbers. Here the Israelites meet with another Amorite king, Og of Bashan, who controlled an area to the north and north-east of Galilee that was forested and renowned for its pastures and high hills (**3:1**). He and his people suffered the same fate as the cities of Sihon (**3:3-7**).

These victories were clearly immensely encouraging to the Israelites. They are often mentioned later in the book of Deuteronomy and elsewhere in the OT (Josh 2:10; Ps 135:11; 136:19-20), always in the context of praise to God. These were the first battles in the holy war for the promised land. The people had learned to obey God, and he had given them victory. Not only that, he had given them land in which they could now settle, after hundreds of years of slavery and forty years wandering in the wilderness. No wonder it was a memorable occasion! Moses, too, must have been delighted to see that the goal to which he had been leading them for so long was on the brink of being accomplished.

3:12-17 DISTRIBUTION OF CONQUERED TERRITORY Although Joshua would be primarily responsible for dividing the land after the conquest, Moses had been allowed to witness the start of the conquest and he supervised the first distribution of the land. No doubt some of the land allocated was not yet in Israelite possession, but this was a declaration of intent.

The tribes of Reuben and Gad were allotted the kingdom of Sihon between the wadis Arnon and Jabbok (**3:12, 16-17**). This included *the slopes of Pisgah,* which is the mountain in the Abarim range (Num 27:12) from which Moses looked out over the regions west of Jordan.

The group known as *the half-tribe of Manasseh* was allotted the lands to the north of the Jabbok (**3:13-15**). Later the other half of this tribe would be given another area of land in the territory to the west of the Jordan (Josh 17:7-18; see also Josh 22:7).

The text also includes a note that explains how the names of prominent families in these tribes came to be associated with particular areas (3:14-15; see also Num 32:39-42). The descendants of Makir, one of these subclans of Manasseh, later became so prominent that at times *Makir* was used as the name of the clan, instead of Manasseh (Judg 5:14).

Given the long history of colonial land problems in Africa, we can well imagine the joy the Israelites must have felt in finally having land to call their own. This joy can be compared with what Africans felt as their countries finally obtained independence. Nevertheless, the change from a lifetime of wandering in the wilderness to a settled life in towns and villages would inevitably bring new problems. Moses may well have anticipated some of these problems, and that may be one of the reasons he found it necessary to spell out the details of the law again as they prepared for a new way of life. He wanted them to avoid the experience with which we in Africa are all too familiar, when the joy of independence is swallowed up in the misery of exploitation and tyranny.

3:18-29 Preparing to invade western Palestine

Although the two tribes of Reuben and Gad and of the half tribe of Manasseh had now received their land, they were not free from the obligation to help the other tribes obtain the land promised to them. As the Angolan Umbundu proverb says, *Nda kusole uwa ukuel, love levo uwa waco ku u moli* ['One who does not want someone else (a neighbour) to succeed, also does not succeed']. This reminder that selfishness does not prosper is underlined by Moses' stipulation that the men from these tribes must assist the other Israelites in conquering the lands to the west of Jordan before they could settle down (**3:18-20**). The nation was a united community, under the leadership of Yahweh, and groups could not look after their own interests. Such unity is an important aspect of biblical thinking. Unfortunately, it has not taken deep root in Africa. When the liberation movements started, most Africans hoped that with independence the lives of all would change for the better. But it soon became apparent that many of those in power were content to see their own lives improve, without caring for the entire nation.

After giving instructions to these tribes, Moses turns to his assistant, Joshua, who has already proved himself a leader in earlier battles (Exod 17:9-13). Moses instructs Joshua not to forget what Yahweh has done for them in the battles for Transjordan and assures him that the divine aid will continue on the other side of the Jordan. Yahweh will continue to fight for his people. There is no need for fear (**3:21-22**).

THE ANCIENT NEAR EAST

The nation of Israel did not emerge in a cultural vacuum. By the time Abraham left the city of Ur in Mesopotamia, the kingdom of Egypt in North Africa was at least one thousand years old.

Mesopotamia occupied the area between and immediately around the two great rivers, the Tigris and Euphrates. It was divided into two regions, which were often locked in a power struggle. The Assyrians, with their famous city of Nineveh, were located in northern Mesopotamia, in the general area of modern Iran. Their opponents were the Babylonians, located in southern Mesopotamia, in the general area of modern Iraq.

Egypt covered the territory in North Africa along the banks of the Nile and the Nile Delta, which empties into the Mediterranean Sea. It was also divided into two regions, Upper and Lower Egypt, but these were usually united in a single kingdom.

Between Mesopotamia and Egypt lay Syria-Palestine – sometimes described as the land of Canaan. It was bounded on the west by the Great Sea (the Mediterranean) and on the east by the desert. Its location meant that it often got caught in the power struggles between its powerful northern and southern neighbours. There was no single dominant group in this area. During its early history, the Canaanites occupied the southern area while the Ugarit kingdom was in the north. At later dates, the area was also inhabited by the Phoenicians, Edomites, Moabites, Philistines and others.

A religious world view dominated every aspect of daily life. The central place of religion was reflected in elaborate worship rituals and elegant temple buildings. Polytheism was common, with the gods ranked in a hierarchy. These gods were often associated with elements of nature. Baal was a Canaanite storm and fertility god who was prayed to for a good harvest. Local and territorial deities were also worshipped. Marduk, for example, was the god of Babylon.

The modern separation of religion and state was unknown. The Egyptian king, the pharaoh, was considered to be a god-king, a divine ruler in human form. In Mesopotamia and Syria-Palestine, kings were thought to rule on behalf of the gods. The fact that rulers had both political and religious authority made them extremely powerful. However, the scope of a king's authority was often limited to his own city. Some of these cities grew to become city-states and a few, like Babylon and Assyria, became empires wielding authority and influence over large portions of the ancient Near East. Such territorial expansion often led to wars.

The extended family formed the basic unit of communities. Societies were largely organized on the basis of kinship networks. Land ownership and political patronage were key economic factors as the economy was largely based on agriculture.

Egypt and Mesopotamia made much progress in education and developed methods of writing at an early stage. While Mesopotamia is credited with early developments in mathematics, Egypt made strides in the area of medicine, and produced the engineering skills required to build the pyramids.

M. Douglas Carew

Encouraged by these early victories, Moses now turns to God and begs permission to enter the promised land. He prays passionately to the *Sovereign Lord*, begging permission to cross over the Jordan and witness the end of the great pilgrimage, which had begun under his leadership (Exod 3:10). He feels that he has only begun to see the greatness and the power of Yahweh at work (**3:23-25**). Moses' prayers were powerful and rooted in an intimate relationship with God, as is clear from the reference to his prayers and those of Samuel many years later (Jer 15:1).

Yet even Moses did not always get the answers he longed for. God's reply to him can be paraphrased as 'Enough of that! Never speak to me about this again!' (**3:26b**). But he was offered the opportunity to see the land from the summit of Pisgah (**3:27**) and reassured that Joshua would complete the task he had begun (**3:28**; Num 27:18-23). Like Jeremiah and others, Moses was asked to accept that God will accomplish his purposes, even if he himself does not see this happen. It is a measure of Moses' own faithfulness that he was prepared to commission Joshua and trust him to fulfil his deepest longings for the people.

Moses was forbidden to enter the promised land *because of you* (**3:26a**). Some commentators interpret this as meaning that Moses was in some sense a vicarious substitute for the people, suffering because of Israel's rebellion. Yet Deuteronomy has made it clear that the rebels died in the wilderness and bore their own sins, so Moses did not die instead of them (1:35). While there can be no doubt that Moses suffered in his heart when the people grumbled, it is also true that Moses himself had sinned against Yahweh (32:51; Num 20:12). As a leader, he had been provoked by Israel, but he was still responsible for his own actions and suffered the penalty for wrong actions. Leaders in every age face the awesome responsibility of having to act with integrity and according to God's law despite what others may do to provoke them to act otherwise.

This prayer and the surrounding events are said to have taken place near Beth Peor (**3:29**; 4:46). This is clearly somewhere near Mount Pisgah, but the exact site is not known today. It was probably located in one of the ravines leading down to the Jordan plain (Num 22:1).

4:1-40 The consequences of God's deliverance

Chapter 4 represents the climax of Moses' first address to the nation. Although much of this book shows evidence of a treaty structure, that structure is particularly evident in this chapter. The presentation of the elements is not always in exactly the same order or legal language that a political treaty would use, but all of the elements are included. It begins by stating the names of the parties to the treaty (4:1, 2, 5, 10) and includes some reference to the history leading up to treaty (4:3-4, 10-14, 32-38). There is an insistence that the treaty stipulations cannot be altered in any way (4:2), and on the obligation to transmit knowledge of the treaty to the next generation (4:10-11). This is followed by a statement of the key stipulations of the treaty (4:15-24). The chapter also lists the blessing that will follow from keeping the treaty (4:5-8, 39-40) and the consequences of breaking it (4:25-31). The names of witnesses to the treaty are also mentioned (4:26).

4:1-8 The appeal to listen and obey The words *Hear now* (**4:1a**) refer back to all that has been said so far. It is as if Moses is saying, 'in the light of what God has done for you, you should obey him' (see also 10:12; Exod 19:4-5; Josh 24:13-14). He then urges the people to obey God's *decrees and laws,* pointing them to what is known as the Deuteronomic principle: obedience will result in the blessings of continuing life and possession of the land (**4:1b**). (For comments on **4:2**, see 5:6-21).

Failure to obey brings punishment and death. To remind them that they have already know that disobedience does indeed bring death, Moses reminds them of what had happened at Baal Peor (called Beth Peor in 3:29), where some Israelite men had become involved in idolatrous rites, had worshipped the god Baal and had been judged for it (**4:3**; Num 25:1-9). Those who had remained faithful in the face of that temptation were spared the plague and were alive at the time of Moses' address (**4:4**).

One clear modern example of obedience to God's laws bringing life is in regard to sexual behaviour. Those who engage in promiscuous and adulterous sex are in great danger of contracting HIV/AIDS. Unfortunately, once infected they may spread the plague to innocent victims – their faithful spouses, their children and health workers – so that all Africa suffers.

Moses reminds the people that he has carefully taught them the 'decrees and laws' that Yahweh had revealed to him. These laws reveal the intimacy of the relationship between God and Israel, an intimacy that existed in no other religion (**4:5, 7**). The law of Yahweh, which surpasses all other laws in righteousness, should be the pride of Israel (**4:6, 8**; Ps 119, 147:19). The superiority of Israel's law could be demonstrated by comparison with other law codes of the period and is rooted in the fact that the law that came from Yahweh reflects the righteousness of God himself. If the Israelites obey God's law, not only will they live and inherit the land, but they will also gain a reputation for *wisdom and understanding* that will distinguish them from all the other nations (4:5-8).

Unfortunately, few African states enjoy such a reputation for wisdom and righteousness in government. Is this because our rulers do not obey God's commandments, but are corrupt and concerned only with their own interests?

4:9-14 God's appearance at Mount Horeb The reference to *decrees and laws* inevitably brings memories of God's appearance to the people at Mount Horeb or Sinai (**4:10a, 11**; Exod 19:16-19). The two central features of that experience were, first, that God made known his words to them (**4:10b, 13-14**) and, second, that although God was present at Sinai and spoke from the midst of clouds, he did not reveal himself in physical form (**4:11-12**). The consequence of this, as will be pointed out in 4:15-18, is that no physical representation of God was necessary for Israel's worship (Exod 20:3-6). In this Israel differed radically from its idolatrous neighbours.

There is also great stress on the need to remember what they have heard and seen and to pass it on to their children (4:9-10). That is why God made a point of writing the commandments on stone tablets, so that they would not easily be forgotten (4:13). Moses points out that he, too, is complying with God's command as he teaches the people in the address recorded here in Deuteronomy (4:14).

Like the people of Israel, we in Africa have heard God's commands but sometimes find it difficult to keep them. When everything goes well it is easy to be faithful, but when disgrace, sickness or death comes along we tend to revert to our roots and turn to African traditional religion, which is idolatrous in that it worships something other than Yahweh.

4:15-24 Worshipping god alone The main thing that set Israelite religion apart from the religions of the other nations was that it allowed no image to be made of Yahweh. This prohibition of the worship of images, idols and other gods is clearly and repeatedly stated (**4:15-19**; see also 4:25; 5:6-8; 6:13; 28:14). God was not to be confused with any part of his own creation (4:16-19). His nature is spiritual, not material, and these commands drive it home.

God also stresses that he has provided natural objects for the benefit of *all the nations under heaven* (4:19). They are his gifts, not things to be put in his place. What God has done uniquely for Israel is to take it from the *iron-smelting furnace* of Egypt and shape it, like molten iron would be shaped, to be his very own people (**4:20**). Recognition of Israel's high status in God's sight should have had profound consequences for Israel's behaviour. They may have left the furnace of Egypt, but Moses warns them that Yahweh is *a consuming fire* (**4:24a**), that is, a fire that can destroy what he has made. He is also *a jealous God* (**4:24b**). Here the term 'jealous' does not have the negative connotations of the English word. Rather it indicates God's active determination to maintain his holiness, which means that he will not tolerate Israel's worshipping any other God. Thus idolatry in any form was forbidden. His jealousy is not selfish, like human jealousy, but is rooted in his fervent desire that his people should know him truly and thus live.

4:25-31 THE EXILE FORESEEN There is an Angolan Umbundu proverb that says, *Epuku liocili te eli lioku pukula Suku* ['God's displeasure is the serious thing; that of others can be endured']. This is the point that Moses makes in the next passage when he warns of the consequences of disobedience to God. He foresaw a day in which the descendants of those to whom he was speaking would forget God's commands (**4:25**) – and would then discover that he was indeed 'a consuming fire, a jealous God' (4:24). God assured them that disobedient descendants would not be allowed to enjoy the promised land (**4:26**). Instead, the covenant would be put into reverse, and they would be scattered among other nations with only a few of them surviving (**4:27**; 28:64-68).

This was indeed what happened when Israel's disobedience to the covenant resulted in the loss of their independence and of their land to the Assyrians and Babylonians. Because they had forgotten God, they would turn to idols for help, but would soon find them powerless (**4:28**; Isa 44:9-20). Yet when they turned to God again, they would find him, for God is not merely jealous, he is also merciful (**4:29-31**). Deuteronomy makes it clear that a breach of the covenant will not terminate God's relationship with Israel once and for all. God in his mercy will receive his people again if they seek him in heartfelt repentance.

4:32-40 ISRAEL'S UNIQUE EXPERIENCE WITH GOD Having stressed the need to remain true to God's covenant, Moses returns to the theme that the people are to serve only the Lord because of their amazing, unique relationship with him. The first amazing feature is God's specific choice of them as his own people (**4:34, 37**). While the kings of the nations around them may sometimes have claimed that they themselves or their families enjoyed the specific favour or a deity, such claims were mere propaganda. Yahweh distinguished himself from the other deities of the period by his specific revelation of himself (**4:33, 35**) through his actions in leading them out of Egypt and to the promised land (4:34, 37-38) and by speaking to them directly (4:33, 36) when he gave them the law. Through his saving acts and his revelation God showed them both his love (**4:37**) and his discipline (**4:36**). His love leads him to graciously give them the new land they will soon enter (**4:38**).

The response to this unique revelation of God must be to recognize that he is the only God and to obey his commands. If Israel does this, it will have life (**4:40**).

4:41-43 Cities of Refuge

Moses' first address concludes with some words that are not presented as his own but as reported by someone else. As commanded in Numbers 35:1-14, Moses established three cities of refuge. The purpose of these cities was to prevent blood feuds from developing by providing a place of asylum for someone who had *unintentionally killed* another person. *Then Moses set aside* (**4:41**) three cities named, Bezer, Ramoth and Golan, were distributed across Transjordan, one in the south, another in the centre and the last one in the north.

Africans can well understand the circumstances leading to the establishment of such cities. After all, many of us have left our own countries in fear of our lives. Unfortunately, however, refugees are sometimes treated contemptuously by the people in the places to which they have fled. In Israel, God appointed special protection for such people, and we should follow his example.

4:44-28:68 Moses' Second Address

Moses' second address is the core of the book of Deuteronomy. Like chapter 4, it too is similar to an ancient treaty, although here the parts of the treaty are spread across a longer document. The fact that this is a new speech explains why there is repetition of some information in the historical prologue in which Moses first reminds Israel of Yahweh's deliverance of them in the past before presenting them with the primary demand for total allegiance to Yahweh, first in general terms in chapters 5 to 11 and then in specific details in chapters 12 to 28.

4:44-49 Introduction

The 'treaty' starts with a statement of what it is, *This is the law* (**4:44**), and carefully specifies the place where the treaty is being declared (**4:46**). The mention of the place allows the writer to once again celebrate Sihon's defeat and rejoice in the territory that has been captured from him and Og (**4:47-49**).

The writer is, however, not content to refer to the teaching that has been given as merely 'the law', which is a very broad term. So he breaks it down further into the *stipulations, decrees and laws* (**4:45**). The 'stipulations', which are also translated 'testimonies', are the requirements that must be met because of the covenant between God and Israel. The 'decrees' or 'statutes' were the laws that were written down or recorded formally, while the 'laws' or 'ordinances' were the decisions made by a judge.

5:1-6:25 The Heart of the Covenant Faith

5:1-21 The Ten Commandments

The Ten Commandments given at Sinai are at the heart of Israel's covenant faith. Although these stipulations define the basic demands of the covenant, they represent far more than just a list of demands. Fundamentally, they are an expression of a relationship between Yahweh and Israel.

Moses' words to *all Israel* start with the *Shema,* the solemn formula *Hear, O Israel* (**5:1a**). This formula is used elsewhere in Deuteronomy to mark the start of important sections (6:4; 9:1; 20:3; 27:9). The instruction to 'hear' is followed by two other verbs that demand action: *learn them ... follow them* (**5:1b**).

He then reminds them of the covenant God had made with them at Horeb (**5:2**; Exod 20). But the actual expression used is not *made a covenant,* as the NIV translates it, but literally 'cut a covenant'. This way of referring to a covenant may derive from the ancient practice of sacrificing animals when making a covenant. The bodies of the animals were then cut in two and the parties to the covenant passed between the two pieces (Gen 15:9; Jer 34:17-18). It seems that by doing this the parties were agreeing that if they broke the covenant, they should be cursed and should become like the dead animal.

In reminding them of what had happened at Horeb, Moses stresses that this was not simply a past event involving their ancestors – it concerned every Israelite (**5:3**). All shared the responsibility of identifying with their ancestors and participating in memory and in faith in their experience of God's deliverance.

The statement that at Horeb *the Lord spoke with you face to face* (**5:4**) does not mean that Israel saw God, but instead suggests that the covenant involved a personal relationship rather than merely a legal exercise. In both Exodus 33:11 and Numbers 14:14, 'face to face' seems to mean 'in person'. Yet Israel's fear of the fiery theophany in Exodus 19:16-25 meant that then, as on other occasions, Moses had to act as a mediator between God and Israel (**5:5**).

Having reminded them of the circumstances in which they received the covenant, Moses proceeds to repeat the Ten Commandments to the people (5:6-21). These commandments were first given in Exodus 20:1-1-17, where God commanded the people of Israel to obey them. For a detailed commentary on these commandments, see the commentary on that passage. However, in Deuteronomy, there are differences in the details of the commandments that are worth noting.

The commandments regarding monotheism, the prohibition of idolatry and honouring the Lord's name are identical in Exodus and in Deuteronomy. So are the prohibitions on murder, theft, adultery and false witness.

But in relation to the observance of the Sabbath and honouring parents, Deuteronomy adds the words *as the Lord your God has commanded you* (**5:12, 16**). Moses wants the people to remember that these instructions do not come from him, but from the Lord. In the same way he explains the meaning of the Lord's blessing for honouring parents, which in Exodus is described simply as long life, but which is here expanded to *that it may go well with you* (5:16).

He also relates the commandments to where they are in their history, and thus adds your neighbour's land as a possible object of coveting in 5:12. When the Israelites were first given the commandments at Sinai, none of them would have owned land. The extra stress on not coveting one's neighbour's wife in **5:21** may even reflect incidents that Moses may have had to deal with as he judged the people.

What we see here sheds some light on the Lord's instruction 'Do not add to what I command you and do not subtract from it, but keep the commands of the Lord your God that I give you' (4:2). The key element in this instruction is that we are not to set ourselves up as authorities alongside God. God is not saying that we cannot accommodate his commands to our time. For example, there is no reason why we could not extend the list of things not to covet today and produce a much longer list than the one in Deuteronomy (including cars, computers and the like).

The same principle also applies to the Sabbath. While the Hebrew Sabbath is actually equivalent to our Saturday, the spirit of God's law has nothing against worship on Sundays to honour the day the Lord rose from the dead. In Exodus the command to observe the Sabbath was related to God's rest from the work of creation. In Deuteronomy the people are asked to relate it to the rest they could now enjoy as a result of their release from slavery in Egypt (**5:15**). So also the believer is allowed to look at his or her Saviour as he or she chooses the day on which to worship. Worshipping on Sunday is quite within the will of God.

It is amazing to note that all of these commandments were known in African traditional society. For example, in 1881 the missionary founders of the Evangelical Congregational Church in Angola (IECA) visited King Ekuikui II of Bailundo in order to explain their mission. The missionaries explained the notion of God and the Ten Commandments, but the king pointed out that his people already knew all about this through the local priests at the *Atumbo* (places of worship) of the Ovimbundu kingdom. The missionaries were reminded of Paul's words in Romans 1:19.

One thing that does need to be stressed about the Ten Commandments and the whole book of Deuteronomy is its insistence that God alone is to be worshipped (**5:6-7**; 6:13; 28:14). The Israelites were repeatedly warned not to follow other gods or to have anything to do with them.

5:22-27 Israel's reaction: fear and devotion

After proclaiming the Ten Commandments, *God wrote them on two stone tablets* (**5:22**). It is not clear whether this means that God actually did the writing himself. Certainly he sometimes used agents to do his work (Isa 10:5-6; 44:28; Jer 43:10-13), and when the first tablets were broken and a second set was prepared, the writing was attributed to Moses (Exod 34:28). It is reasonable to suggest that in both cases Moses was God's amanuensis, that is, his scribe.

The people's reaction to this revelation of God was acute fear of the danger associated with seeing God (**5:25-26**). So the representatives of the people, the heads of the tribes and the elders, begged Moses to act as their mediator and represent them before God in all future interactions (**5:27**). Yet despite her fear, Israel recognized Yahweh as her God and committed herself to obeying him.

5:28-31 Yahweh's acceptance of a mediator

Yahweh approved Israel's request and was pleased with their promise to hear and obey (**5:28**). He lovingly longed for this reverent devotion to continue, because it would ensure that things went well for them (**5:29**). The people were permitted to return to their tents (**5:30**), but Moses remained with God on the mountain and received *the commands, decrees and laws* that he was to teach to the people (**5:31**). These would be their guides on how to live in the promised land.

5:32-6:3 The benefit of keeping God's law

Africa has traditionally considered that the wise are those who adhere to the teachings of the elders. Such obedience will bring many benefits and empower them to lead others. Similarly, this section stresses that all the descendants of those who stood at Sinai are also bound to keep God's law. The older generations have a responsibility to teach these laws to their offspring (**6:2**). These laws are to be obeyed without any deviation either *to the right or to the left* (**5:32**). If the people do this, they will prosper as a nation (**5:33**).

In **6:3** and fifteen other times in the Pentateuch, the promised land is described *as a land flowing with milk and honey*, a metaphorical description of the fertility of the land they will be entering. Besides being able to support much livestock (the source of milk) it would also produce much honey. In the Bible, honey is referred to as a luxury item that is worthy of being given as a gift or as an object of trade (Gen 43:11). It could be included in the firstfruit contributions to the priests and Levites (Lev 2:11-12) and was also valued as a high-energy food when engaged in a military campaign (1 Sam 14:29-30; 2 Sam 17:28-29). Honey was considered a source of both health and pleasure, and thus was used to symbolize such things as wisdom, divine guidance and sexuality (Judg 14:18; Prov 16:24; Song 4:11; 5:1).

Milk and honey are also similar in not being crops that are grown in fields; they are natural products that can be obtained from uncultivated land. This is why milk and honey can be used both as symbols of the fertility of the land and as evidence of its poverty when an agricultural economy is destroyed (Isa 7:21-25).

6:4-9 Yahweh is our God; Yahweh is one

The Ovimbundu believe that God, whom they refer to as 'Suku', is essentially a spirit and, like the Jews, they make no visual representations of him. Nor do they have any shrines or temples that could restrict his scope. Suku is everywhere, and the whole universe is the temple of Suku, the Great Spirit, far below whom are lesser spirits.

Suku has unique names and attributes that are not shared by the other spiritual beings in the spirit world. He is the Supreme Being, the Creator and Sustainer of all things, characterized by ineffable majesty and exalted dignity. He is also good, compassionate and kind, a being who is involved in the people's daily lives by providing them with sun and rain. Hence he has the names *Suku Ocimalomata*, giver of everything, and *Suku Ongavi*, giver of rain and water, or the one who causes the rain to fall copiously.

Many of these ideas are also present in the statement of Israel's beliefs known as the 'Shema' (6:4-6:9), which is introduced here with the solemn *Hear, O Israel* (**6:4**). These verses are recited by Jews as a daily prayer, along with 11:13-21 and Numbers 15:37-41.

At the heart of Israel's confession was the belief that Yahweh was not merely one in a pantheon of gods, but uniquely one. This positive assertion is sometimes regarded as the converse of the first two negative commandments in the Ten Commandments. Yahweh was to be the sole object of Israel's faith and obedience.

This text is frequently cited by those who oppose the doctrine of the Trinity, or who ask how Jesus can also be God. But this verse does not contradict the Christian doctrine of the Trinity, for the Trinity is regarded as fundamentally united in one Godhead. It does not consist of competing or separate divinities.

Africans also have to deal with the implications of this verse as regards ancestor worship. There is debate about whether such worship represents a form of pantheism, which this text would lead us to reject, or whether it can be part of a monotheistic system presented by this text.

The Shema starts with a statement of the unity of God, which is followed by a commandment that Jesus himself refers to as the first and great commandment (**6:5**; Matt 22:36-38; Mark 12:29-34; Luke 10:27-28). This command insists that obedience to the law of God involves more than just conforming to an external system of rules; it also involves the attitudes of our hearts and minds (**6:6**). The test of whether we love God is whether we keep his commandments (John 14:21; 1 John 5:2). If we truly love him, we will also pass his commandments on to our children, so that this attitude of love and obedience will be passed on from age to age (**6:7**).

Originally the instruction to tie God's laws on our hands and bind them to our foreheads was a metaphor for how these laws were to be present in every aspect of our lives (**6:8**). Later, however, this command was taken literally and Jews took to wearing phylacteries (Matt 23:5). These were small leather containers containing small scrolls on which were written Deuteronomy 6:4-9, 11:13-21 and Exodus 13:1-10. These containers were then tied on the forehead and the left arm when the Shema was recited. Every male Jew wore phylacteries during morning prayers, except on the Sabbath and on the festival days, which were themselves symbols of the law. On the basis of **6:9**, it also became common practice for Jews to attach a small container for a tiny scroll with these three passages on it to the doorpost of their home.

6:10-25 The importance of remembering

The traditional way of teaching in Africa is based on oral tradition (the telling of stories, myths, legends, folklore, social philosophy, ethical and aesthetic standards). So it is very important to remember what one's elders have taught, in the sense that one's survival and conduct in adult life relies on what one can remember from the past. The same holds true for the Israelites and for all believers. Remembrance of God's past mercies and delivering acts is fundamental to biblical faith. Thus the people of Israel are first exhorted not to forget what the Lord has done for them (6:10-12) and are then commanded to pass these memories on to their children (6:20-25).

Forgetting about God is particularly easy when things are going well, and this would be the case once they had entered the promised land. Whereas they had once been wanderers in an arid wilderness, they would soon be enjoying living in houses in cities and reaping crops from *vineyards and olive groves* (**6:10-11**). Instead of having to search for water, they would be able to draw it from wells – and they would not even have to do the arduous work of digging those wells. Flourishing vineyards and olive trees, cities and houses were all waiting for their possession (8:7-11). Once they had become accustomed to such comfort, it would be very easy for the people of Israel to start to think they were entitled to it and to forget that everything they owned had been given to them by God in fulfilment of the promise he had made to the patriarchs (6:10, **12**).

Forgetfulness would result in Israel starting to serve the gods of the other nations around them. God would not tolerate such divided loyalties, and the result would be misery (**6:13-15**). To remind them of what could happen, Moses referred to the incident at Massah (Exod 17:1-7) in which Israel had tested God (**6:16**). They had asked Moses to supply water as a test to determine whether Yahweh was among them or not (Exod 17:1-7). To try to test God like this is to impose conditions on him and to force him to respond. But it is wrong for us to try to tell God what to do. Moreover, the Israelites had already seen abundant evidence that God was with them. Why were they demanding yet another sign?

Many Christians today are testing God too. Some demand healing, and others demand that he help them to win the lottery to relieve their poverty. When we do this, aren't we acting like the Israelites did at Massah?

When explaining the need to obey the commandments to future generations of children, the Israelites must tell them of God's amazing delivery of their ancestors from Egypt and of his bringing them to the promised land. The story is an exciting one that even a child can understand and makes the point that God is active in human affairs.

7:1-26 The Conquest of Canaan

There is an Angolan Umbundu proverb that says, *Eci okasi lo ku cilã yevelela ka limba oñoma* ['You change your steps according to the change in the rhythm of the drum', meaning that dancers must adapt their pace to the rhythm set by the leading drum, and thus that others also need to respond to different signals]. Up to this point, the Israelites had been told not to attack nations such as Moab and Edom (2:4-5, 9), but now they are explicitly told to drive out certain other nations and to destroy them utterly. What is being envisaged here is a holy war.

It needs to be pointed out that Israel was never in a position to claim that any war was holy simply because God's people were fighting in it. It is clear that the only wars that merited this title were the wars that Israel undertook on God's express command in order to take possession of Canaan, the land God had promised to Abraham long before, and a land whose inhabitants were known for their wickedness. No one today can justify waging war by arguing that it is a holy war.

7:1-5 The rules for the conquest

Chapters 5 and 6 of Deuteronomy have stressed the need to worship God alone, and God's sovereignty in history. In chapter 7, these two forces intersect in relation to the seven nations who occupied the land that the Lord had promised to give to his people, Israel (7:1). These nations worshipped other gods and would have led the descendants of the Israelites astray had they remained in the land. Therefore they were to be destroyed in a holy war.

The specific groups named included the *Hittites*, who may have been an offshoot of the same people who established the great Hittite empire to the north. They had been living in Palestine since the time of the patriarchs

(Gen 25:9-10; 26:34-35). The *Girgashites* are mentioned several times in the OT (Gen 10:16; Josh 3:10; 1 Chr 1:14) and are referred to as allies of the Hittites in some extrabiblical texts. The *Amorites* and *Canaanites* had also been in the land since patriarchal times (Gen 15:16; 24:3) but are difficult to define as groups since the names sometimes seem to be used quite loosely. *Perizzites, Hivites and Jebusites* do not appear to be known outside the Bible. The Hivites may be the same people as the Horites and seem to have lived mainly in the Lebanon hills (Judg 3:3). The Perizzites seem to have lived in unwalled villages both east and west of Jordan. The Jebusites were evidently a Canaanite group that lived in the hill country near Jerusalem (Num 13:29; Josh 15:8). While it may be difficult to determine who these groups were, what is clear is that they were *larger and stronger* than the newcomers, the Israelites (**7:1**). This point is emphasized to underline the fact that no power was greater than that of God, who would fulfil his promise to Israel.

Once the enemy had, with God's aid, been defeated, they were to be utterly destroyed (**7:2-3**). The word translated *destroy them* literally means to set something apart for God. Israel was commanded to surrender everything to God because the victory was his and he alone had the right to decide what to do with the booty. Sometimes this setting aside involved the killing of all the men, women and children and even of their livestock and the burning of their possessions (Josh 6:17-19; 1 Sam 15:3). However, it seems that on other occasions the women, children and animals were spared. This is one way to interpret the instruction forbidding marriage with any survivors of these peoples as such marriages would draw the people away from the worship of Yahweh alone (**7:4**). Their false worship was also to be repudiated by destroying all the sacred places and objects associated with the worship of other gods (**7:5**).

7:6-16 The character of Israel

The reason that Israel had to take such drastic action was that she was in a unique relationship to God. The Israelites had been *chosen out of all the peoples on the face of the earth* (**7:6**) and were now God's *treasured possession*. In case this makes them assume they are innately superior to others in some way, God hastens to remind the people that there was nothing special about them (**7:7**). They were an insignificant bunch, of no importance in world affairs. The only reason that God offered for his mysterious choice of them was that he loved them and was keeping a promise he had made to their ancestors (**7:8**).

The Lord knows that when the Israelites eventually enjoy the blessings of the land they may be tempted to forget how the blessings came about. That is why he both reminds them they were chosen and then reminds them of what he himself is like. At least three things stand out in God's self-description in **7:9-10**. First, he is unique and has no competitor (*God is God*). Second, he is faithful (*keeping his covenant of love to a thousand generations*, a figurative way of saying 'forever'). Third, he responds to us in accordance with how we respond to him, not only blessing those who respond to his love by loving him in return, but also destroying those who hate him.

These words raise the whole question of God's choice of some people over others, which is traditionally known as the doctrine of election. The same mysterious choice is found in the NT, where Christian believers are repeatedly described as chosen by God (John 15:16; Eph 1:4, 10). It is purely by the grace of God that Christ comes to those who are trapped in sin, frees them from the power of darkness and brings them into his kingdom (Eph 2:8; Col 1:13-14).

But what about those who are not chosen? Deuteronomy shows us clearly that God still cares for them. Though Paul in Romans 9:13 can quote Malachi 1:2-3 to the effect that God says 'Jacob I loved, but Esau I hated', God still forbids the descendants of Jacob (the twelve tribes) from attacking or taking the land of the Edomites, who were the descendants of Esau (2:2-6; see also Gen 36:1, 9). They were also not permitted to attack the Moabites and the Ammonites, because these groups were the descendants of Lot, Abraham's nephew (2:9; see also Gen 19:37-38; Deut 2:19). In other words, the fact that God did not choose Lot or Esau as the instruments through which he would bless other nations did not mean that he was not concerned about them and their descendants. In fact, he explicitly states that he had given them certain land.

However, God does punish those who actively hate him and refuse to obey his commandments (7:10). Yet even the chosen are not exempt from punishment if they do not obey God's commands (7:11; 4:25-31) – and it is possible that their punishment may be more severe because they had the knowledge of God that others lacked (Amos 3:2).

It is important to remember that God's choice of Israel was not intended solely to benefit Israel at the expense of others. Rather, God's purpose in choosing Abraham and through him the whole nation of Israel was to shape and teach one nation about himself so that they could proclaim him to the world and provide the context within which the Messiah would come to reveal God's love for the whole world (Gen 12:3; Exod 19:6; John 3:16).

Obviously, humans cannot question why God chose Israel above some other nation (Rom 9:20-21). It was his sovereign choice. This is a lesson that is often missed by nations that have enjoyed the privilege of God's blessings when they relate to other nations that have not yet received them. We saw this in the colonization of Africa. The Western nations brought extended commerce and education to Africa, and above all they brought Christianity, but the good things they brought were tainted by the pride of those bringing them. They should have remembered the principle from Deuteronomy that God blesses one nation so that it can become the instrument through which He blesses others. Western nations had been blessed, not because they deserved it, but purely because of God's love and mercy, and they should have extended a similar love and mercy to others, without pride or a sense of entitlement.

The blessings that flow from obedience are outlined in **7:12-15**. The specific blessings mentioned here are material, not spiritual, making it clear that God has created a good world that people can enjoy. These blessings may also be seen as representing the ideal world that will emerge when God creates a new heaven and a new earth (2 Pet 3:13).

7:17-26 The need for faith

An Angolan Umbundu proverb says, *Epata lepata li kuete ndomo va singa osanji* ['Every country has its way of cooking a chicken']. The proverb teaches that people in different countries do things differently, and that when you go into a new community it is important to take time to learn their ways of behaviour and adjust your behaviour accordingly. While this is generally a wise course of action, it is most definitely not what Moses was advocating for the Israelites in this section of Deuteronomy. Instead, he repeats the points made in 7:2-5, insisting on their need to avoid the danger posed by the Canaanite religion (7:16). He urges the people not to fear the Canaanites, but rather to do three things: remember God's past deeds, count on his promises for the future and obey specific instructions.

God's past deeds include what he *did to Pharaoh and to all Egypt* (**7:18**). Given the great display of his power as he brought the people out of Egypt, it is no wonder he is described as *great and awesome* (**7:21**). He will display the same power in dealing with all enemies of the Israelites (7:19-24). Their victory will be planned by God, but it will not be accomplished all at once. Rather, it will proceed at the pace he sets (7:20-22). Nor will it be accomplished by their fighting strength alone. God will also fight with them by sending panic upon his enemies (**7:23**; see, for example, Josh 10:10; Judg 4:15; 7:21; 1 Sam 7:10; 2 Kgs 9:6-7). They are assured of complete victory in the end (**7:24**).

For their part, they are to separate themselves totally for the Lord their God. They must destroy the images of the heathen gods, regardless of whether these images are made of or decorated with silver and gold. Wealth is not to be allowed to distract them from the worship of God alone. Everything associated with these idols must be burned. Like a good father, God gives them the reason for demanding destruction of all this wealth: they are not to be *ensnared by it* for anything associated with idolatry is *detestable to the Lord your God* and thus should have no place in their homes (**7:25-26**).

8:1-20 The Dangers of Prosperity

Once again Moses returns to the important theme of obeying God (**8:1**), with the motive for obedience being their remembrance of what God done for them in the past. This time, however, he does not refer to the exodus from Egypt, but to their experience of God's care while they were wandering in the wilderness. There God taught them lessons in humility and obedience (**8:2**). He had repeatedly shown them that they were not able to provide for themselves, not even at the basic level of food. They had had to rely on God's supply of the mysterious manna, which they had never encountered before (**8:3**). The lesson that no aspect of human existence can be separated from God's provision is one that Jesus, too, had learned and that he used in his battle with temptation in Matthew 4:4. God had also provided the very clothes they wore and the physical stamina to endure the years of walking (**8:4**). His aim in permitting them to suffer need was not to impose suffering, but to teach them to rely on him, just as a father sets tough goals for a child in order to teach them important lessons for living (**8:5**).

The proof that his discipline had been motivated by a loving desire to prepare them for life is found in the description of the abundance that awaits them in the rich and fertile land they have been promised (**8:6-9**). God intended to give good gifts to his people and wished them to enjoy life in the midst of his good creation.

But the trouble with a life of ease and prosperity is that it is easy to become accustomed to it, and then to assume that one is naturally entitled to it. When this sense of entitlement creeps in, acknowledgment that what one enjoys is God's gift creeps out (**8:10-14**). Pride will lead the Israelites to forget their helplessness when exposed to the dangers of the desert (**8:15-17**). When we forget that we owe even the *ability to produce wealth* to God, we start to think that *my power and the strength of my hands have produced this wealth for me* (8:17-18). God has little sympathy with such arrogance and with the idolatry that often follows it – which in our days may be worship of self, of education, of power, or of money. It is the self-sufficiency that accompanies prosperity that makes it so difficult for the rich to enter the kingdom of God (Luke 18:24).

If the Israelites forget God's commands and turn to idolatry, they should not expect to fare any better than the nations that God has ordered them to destroy (**8:19-20**).

9:1-6 God's Will, Not Israel's Righteousness

Thinking of these nations, Moses again echoes the words of the spies who had earlier discouraged the Israelites (**9:1-2**; see 1:28). In the preceding chapter he had stressed that God had provided for their every need in the desert. In exactly the same way, God will fight for them and give them victory over the enemy. Yet the statement *He will destroy them; he will subdue them before you. And you will drive them* *out and annihilate them quickly* (**9:3**) also calls for action by the Israelites themselves. They cannot simply sit passively and wait for God to bless them.

Just as God's provision for the Israelites' physical needs could eventually lead them to succumb to the illusion of self-sufficiency, so his support for them in battle could lead to the illusion that God was on their side because they were righteous (**9:4**). In that case, their victory would have been their reward for good conduct. This illusion is quickly shattered, and the point is reiterated three times to make sure they heard it (9:4-6). There were only two reasons why Yahweh was blessing them with victory. One was his promise to their ancestors (**9:5**) – a promise that was made freely and that had not been earned. The other was the extreme sinfulness of the people now living in Canaan (9:4-5).

9:7-29 Israel's Own Sinfulness

Comparative righteousness is hard to assess. But in case the Israelites assumed that because they are less wicked than the Canaanites, they are somehow righteous, Moses reminds them that they too *are a stiff-necked people* (9:6, 13). He reminds them of the incident of the golden calf (9:7-21; see also Exod 32) and of a number of other incidents (**9:22-24**) when Israel had been stubborn and rebellious. These incidents had taken place at Taberah where the people complained (Num 11:1-3), at Massah where the people tested God when they lacked water (6:16; Exod 17:1-7; Num 20:10-13), at Kibroth Hattaavah where the people complained about manna (Num 11:31-34) and at Kadesh Barnea where they had refused to obey God when they heard the spies' report (1:21-36; Num 13–14). Israel had constantly questioned God's plans, refused to believe his promises and disobeyed his commands.

But there could be no doubt that the most serious incident was the one at Horeb where the people worshipped a golden calf, breaking the first two of the commandments they had just been given. Effectively, they had destroyed the covenant agreement, a destruction symbolized by the smashing of the stone tablets on which the Ten Commandments had been carved (**9:17**). Such a breach of the covenant meant that Israel was liable to suffer all the curses associated with the covenant. God was indeed angry enough with them to threaten to destroy them (**9:14, 19**). Moses alone stood between the people and God's wrath.

Moses took strong action. He completely destroyed the idol, making it impossible to rebuild (**9:21**). And he devoted himself to prayer and fasting for Aaron, the high priest who had made the calf, and for the people (**9:18, 20**). Four times in this chapter there is a reference to a period of *forty days and forty nights* (**9:9, 11, 18, 25**), a long period of intercession by Moses. The first two references are both to the time Moses spent with God when he first received the Ten Commandments, and the second two both refer to the time

when Moses was interceding for forgiveness for Aaron and for the people.

It is a mark of Moses' character that he did not accept God's offer to continue the line of Abraham through him alone and to destroy all the other Israelites (9:14). Instead, like a true pastor, he not only proclaimed God's word to the people but also wept and prayed for them when they fell. In his prayer Moses reminded God of his loving care and forgiveness of their ancestors, who had also sinned but to whom God had made great promises (**9:27**). He also reminded God of all that he had already done for the people in rescuing them from Egypt and bringing them safely to Horeb (**9:26, 29**). But Moses was concerned not only for his people; he was also concerned for God's reputation. If the people were to die in the wilderness, the nations that had witnessed their delivery from Egypt would be in a position to doubt that God was strong enough to protect them and to deny God's claim that he loved this group (**9:28**). This is an example of what it means to pray, 'hallowed be your name' (Matt 6:9). Moses' prayer is an example to us in his willingness to set aside personal ambition and focus on his love for his people and his love for God and God's reputation.

10:1-11 The Covenant Remade

God's reply to Moses' prayer was to tell him to make two more stone tablets and to prepare a special container for them (**10:1-2**). Whereas the breaking of the first tablets could have signified the ending of the covenant, the making of new ones indicated that the covenant was renewed. Once again, God had graciously forgiven his people.

In this section of the chapter, the perspective constantly moves back and forth across time. Thus the account of the construction of the ark in which the stone tablets were to be kept is described along with the making of the tablets (**10:3-5**). The scene then leaps to the death of Aaron (**10:6**). The reason it is mentioned here may be to underline the fact that Moses' prayer had been heard, so Aaron did not die at Horeb (9:20). The mention of Aaron leads to a comment about his successor, his son Eleazar, and this in turn leads to a discussion of the role of his tribe of Levi and a comment on how their status was related to the coming distribution of land (**10:8-9**). Whereas later a distinction is drawn between the Levites and the priests, it seems that here the term 'Levites' refers to both groups.

The scene returns to Horeb, with God telling Moses to take up again where he had left off and to continue to lead the people towards the land that he would be giving them (**10:10-11**).

10:12-11:32 Religion of the Heart

Many centuries later, the prophet Jeremiah would contrast the covenant engraved on stone at Horeb with a new covenant that God would be instituting, one that would not be written on stone but on human hearts (Jer 31:31-34). While the content of the covenant may remain unchanged, it will no longer be an external law to be imposed but an interior belief to be celebrated. But the seeds of that later covenant are already present here in Deuteronomy, as can be seen in the repeated exhortations in this section to 'love the Lord your God'.

By this stage, Moses' presentation of the broad principles that were to govern the life of Israel is coming to an end, and he is about to embark on a detailed presentation of the laws that would govern everyday life in the promised land. But before going into the details, he once again summarizes the teaching that he has given so far and reminds the people of the important choice that lies before them. They will have to decide whether to obey or disobey God – and will have to live with the consequences of their choice.

10:12-22 What does the Lord require?

This new section is introduced with the rhetorical question *And now, O Israel, what does the Lord your God ask of you?* (**10:12**). The expression 'and now' is commonly used to mark the climax of a speech. There has been a recital of what God has done, and now the listeners need to make some personal response (Exod 19:5; Josh 24:14). The personal response that God requires is summed up in five demands: *fear* him, *walk in all his ways, love him, serve* him wholeheartedly and *observe* his *commands and decrees* (10:12-13). These five verbs occur many times in Deuteronomy (see also 6:4-19). To fear God is to give him the worship that is his due as Lord over all creation. Such fear is not the opposite of love. Rather, it is the type of respect that a child has for its parents, which leads the child to fear causing distress to the parents and to an awareness that the parent is acting for the child's good. Such fear and love combine and find expression in obedience to God's commands, not simply as isolated rules but as representing the way of life that God desires.

Moses' own heart has clearly been caught up in the love of God, and this love pours out in his celebration of the wonder of the Israelites having been chosen by such an awesome being (**10:14-15**, 17, **21**). He recognizes that mere conformity to external signs and rituals such as circumcision is worthless if not accompanied by the right attitude to God (**10:16**). This point is repeated frequently throughout the OT (see, for example, Mic 6:8; Isa 1:11-17). The intent is not to abolish such rituals, which were important symbols of God's special relationship with Israel (Gen 17:9-14), but to put them in perspective.

Yet another implication of love for an awesome and just God is that his followers are to be like him. Like him, they should defend the defenceless and be impervious to bribes (**10:17-18**). Just as God took pity on them and helped when they were strangers in Egypt, so they are to show pity and

care for strangers among them (**10:19-20**). Not the least of the wonders that God has done for them is to take the small group of seventy who entered Egypt in the time of Joseph and make them *as numerous as the stars in the sky* (**10:22**).

11:1-9 Appeal to the past

The parents of the people now listening to Moses had been held responsible for their failure to occupy the land at once and had been punished for their lack of faith (1:35). Moses' audience had been children when God had miraculously led them out of Egypt. They had been witnesses to the power of God in the plagues he had sent on the Egyptians (**11:3**; Exod 7:14-12:30) and in his defeat of the Egyptian army at the Red Sea (**11:4**; Exod 14:5-31). They had also seen God's discipline at work, both in the training he had given in the years spent wandering in the desert (11:5) and in his punishment of people like Dathan and Abiram, who had challenged the leadership of Moses and Aaron and demanded the right to be priests (**11:6**; Num 16:1-3, 8-14). Moses constantly reminds them that they had seen these things with their own eyes (**11:7**) – but that their children had not (**11:2, 5**). Their children would not even have been born when they left Egypt, and many would still be too young to have much memory of the events in the desert. It was up to the generation who had seen these things to communicate their importance to those who had not, and to ensure the obedience to God's commands that was the prerequisite for enjoyment of life in the promised land (**11:8-9**).

11:10-25 Blessings for the obedient

Moses warned the Israelites that farming in the promised land would be a very different from farming in Egypt (**11:10**). There they had worked on level farmland that was irrigated with water from the Nile River. Instead of the flat plains of the Nile Delta, they would be in a land of *mountains and valleys*. Instead of being able to draw water from the Nile, they would be dependent on *rain from heaven* (**11:11**). Consequently the people would have to depend on God to supply their water, which may be why the text says *the eyes of the Lord your God are continually on it, from the beginning of the year to its end* (**11:12**). If Israel loved Yahweh *with all your heart and with all your soul,* he would grant her the rains she needed (**11:13-14a**). He would provide the regular wet and dry seasons, with which we are familiar in Africa. The early rain came in autumn, that is, in October and November and broke the summer drought, making it possible to plough the land and plant crops. The latter rains (KJV) came in spring, that is, during March and April, when the land burst into bloom. In between, there would be scattered showers. The rain would be sufficient to support crops of grain, grapes and olives and to provide grazing for their animals (**11:14b-15**).

However, if Israel started to worship other gods, such as those associated with the fertility religions of the Canaanites, the Lord would respond by sending drought and famine (**11:16-17**; Amos 4:6-10). Unfortunately, both of these disasters are well known in Africa, and this gives rise to the question of why God allows Africa to suffer like this. Is he punishing Africa? To find an answer to this question, it is necessary to look at the whole of the Bible. The Bible makes it clear that God is sovereign over all aspects of creation, including weather, and that he can use weather and other natural phenomena to achieve his purposes (see for example, Gen 6–9; 1 Kgs 17:1; Joel 2:10-11; Hag 2:17). This belief, coupled with the belief that obedience would guarantee prosperity, has led people to believe that all suffering is the result of sin. However, the book of Job and Jesus himself (John 9:2-3) refute this kind of understanding. So does the evidence noted by Job and the psalmist that the unrighteous can enjoy very comfortable lives (Job 21:7-16; Ps 73:3-14). Possibly the best we can say is that the Bible does teach that nature is under God's control and in some way serves his purpose, but that we do not always clearly understand what that purpose is.

Given the importance of obedience to Yahweh and the fact that Moses' audience had not seen God's power demonstrated as their parents had (11:2), it was vital that the details of the covenant govern the daily lives of this generation and be transmitted to the next generation (**11:18-21**). Moses here repeats instruction he has already given in 6:6-9 in order to emphasize the importance of what he is saying. It is only by doing this that they will be in a position to occupy the land for *as many as the days that the heavens are above the earth,* that is, for ever (11:21).

The *if ... then* clause that starts in **11:22** extends all the way to **11:25**. These words make it clear that God will honour his promise only if the people are obedient to his commands. This obedience must not simply be formal and legalistic obedience, but must be rooted in a love for and close attachment to Yahweh. If they do maintain this kind of love, they are promised *every place where you set your foot* (**11:24**). More specifically, they are told that from north to south their land will stretch *from the desert to Lebanon,* that is, from the Sinai area and the Negeb to the mountains of Lebanon. From west to east it will stretch *from the Euphrates River to the western sea,* that is, the Mediterranean. The kingdom did briefly reach this size during the reign of David.

11:26-32 Call for decision

Chapters 5 to 11 had set out the general principles that were to characterize Israel's life, and now the people are faced with a decision. They can choose between obedience, which will lead to blessing, and disobedience, which will lead to cursing (11:26-28). There are no other options.

If Israel rejects Yahweh, it will be giving allegiance to *other gods, which you have not known* (**11:28**). The verb 'know' here refers to more than merely intellectual knowledge. It is the same word used of the intimate acquaintance of marriage partners. Yahweh was the one who had created Israel and cared for it, who knew it most intimately and who was known by the people in a way that no other god could be known.

Moses concludes by reminding the people that this covenant, which had first been entered into at Sinai (Exod 19:1-8), and which was now being renewed as he spoke, would have to be renewed once they had entered the promised land. The people would need to be reminded of the curses and blessings that accompanied the covenant by hearing them proclaimed, with the blessings being proclaimed from *Mount Gerizim* and the curses from *Mount Ebal* (**11:29**). This particular location may have been chosen because these two mountains were close to the centre of the promised land and would be ongoing, silent witnesses to the covenant between God and Israel and the blessings and cursings associated with it.

Finally, Moses repeats the most basic information about their situation: they are about to finish their journey, and once settled in their new land they are still to obey God's commands (**11:31-32**). The details of these commands are set out in the chapters that follow.

12:1-26:19 The Detailed Covenant Stipulations

The laws that are given in these chapters are sometimes referred to as the Deuteronomic Code, using 'code' in the sense of a set of laws that regulate the religious, civil and domestic life of a society. In reading them, it is important to remember that they were designed to apply to a small agricultural community more than three thousand years ago. Thus it cannot be assumed that they will apply in the same way in a modern state. However, the underlying principles behind the laws are of eternal validity.

Some of the laws given here had already been given at Sinai (Exod 20:1-23:19), while others were designed to apply to the new circumstances that would be faced by the Israelites as they embarked on a new life as farmers and no longer led a nomadic existence. By adhering to these laws, Israel would live out its calling to be a holy nation.

A similar pattern is repeated many times in the chapters that follow. First, the basic law or principle is stated. This principle is then explained, and finally there is an encouragement of the hearer to obey this law. This pattern of proclaiming what God has revealed, explaining it and then reminding the hearers of their obligation to respond is one that can be fruitfully followed in contemporary preaching.

12:1-15:23 Laws regarding worship

The detailed law code begins with a restatement of those aspects of Israel's life that will distinguish it from other nations. These include its commitment to monotheism, to observance of dietary laws, payment of tithes, acceptance of the principles of the Sabbath and of Sabbath years, commitment to equality and the observance of sacrifices.

12:1-12 THE PLACE OF WORSHIP Just as the Ten Commandments began with the instruction to worship Yahweh alone, so the detailed laws begin with instructions about the need to worship God alone. Once again, the people are told to destroy all evidence of Canaanite worship (**12:2-3**; 7:5). The destruction is intended not only to desecrate the sites where Canaanite gods were worshipped, but also to wipe out the very memory of their names. The significance of this command is rooted in the ancient view that a name contained something of the being and power of a person.

The *altars, sacred stones ... Asherah poles* and *idols* (12:3) were the cultic objects associated with the Canaanite religion. These were all to be destroyed by those who worshipped Yahweh. Unfortunately, this command is not followed by many church members, who still feel themselves trapped and at the mercy of a multitude of conflicting, fickle powers and spirits invoked in African traditional religion. The desire to pacify these spirits leads to tremendous waste of resources and even of human lives.

While the names of the Canaanite gods were to be wiped out, the Lord would choose a place *to put his Name there for a dwelling* (**12:5**). He does not specifically identify where that place will be. Over the course of Israel's history it moved between a number of places, the most important of which were Shiloh (1 Sam 1:3; Jer. 7:12) and Jerusalem (2 Kgs 21:4). This was the place to which the Israelites were to take all the different sacrifices and offerings that would be part of their regular worship (**12:6**). The entire burnt offering was offered to Yahweh on the altar (Lev 1:9), but the worshippers and priests could eat parts of other sacrifices (**12:7**; Lev 7:15-16). This worship is to be a joyful, communal celebration in God's presence – much like our worship today should be.

These commands can only be fully carried out once the people have been able to escape from their nomadic lifestyle in the wilderness and settle into their new homes (**12:8-10**). Then they would have a *resting place* and enjoy their *inheritance*, free from the threat of enemies.

The instruction to gather at the place God will choose to worship him and to rejoice is repeated in **12:11-12** (see also 12:6-7), but this time there is a stress on the inclusiveness of those who will celebrate. Masters and servants, the poor and the weak, all are to join together in worship and in obedience to the Lord's commands.

12:13-28 SACRED AND ORDINARY MEALS The law carefully distinguishes between the slaughter of animals for burnt offerings, which emphatically must (*Be careful* – **12:13**) be sacrificed only at a central sanctuary in an approved place, and the ordinary slaughter of animals for food (**12:15, 20**). The latter is perfectly legal, provided that no blood is eaten (**12:16**, 23). Domestic animals could be slaughtered and eaten at home as freely as animals killed in the hunt. No restrictions were placed on who could or could not partake of such meals (12:15, 22).

To make sure that there was no confusion about which meals could not be eaten at home, the text supplies a list of the sacred meals that could be eaten only at the central sanctuary (**12:17-18a**). From Leviticus, it is clear that these sacred meals were to be eaten only by those who were ritually pure (Lev 7:20), but there were no other restrictions on who could partake. The meals were to be times of shared rejoicing by the entire household and were to be shared with Levites from their town, who would not have had land on which to raise animals (**12:18b-19**).

The instructions about the eating of meat are repeated for emphasis in the second half of this passage (12:20-25). There is great stress on the need to avoid eating blood (see also Gen 9:4; Lev 17:10-14). The reason for this prohibition is given in **12:23** as *the blood is the life, and you must not eat the life with the meat.* God was reminding the Israelites that all life belonged to him alone. Pouring out the blood on the ground (**12:24**) would mean that it was not available for food and could also not be offered at any pagan altar.

The people are reminded that *consecrated things* may be offered only in *the place the Lord will choose* (**12:26-27**). This, too, would reduce the possibilities for sacrifices being offered to pagan deities.

The constant stress on the need to travel to God's appointed place before offering a sacrifice contrasts strongly with the Christian experience of being able to worship anywhere, provided the worship is offered 'in spirit and in truth' (John 4:23). True worship is no longer associated with a place but with a person, Jesus Christ (John 4:19-26).

12:29-32 PURITY IN WORSHIP This chapter began with a stern instruction to destroy all evidence of Canaanite religion and ends with a warning about the dangers it will pose (compare chapter 7, which has the same structure). Once the Israelites are settled in the land, they must not succumb to curiosity about pagan rites, or decide that it is easier to serve local gods than to make the journey to the sanctuary God will establish (**12:29-30**). Strong language is used to describe the pagan rituals. God is described as hating them, and they are said to involve *detestable things.* The aspect of pagan worship that arouses particular revulsion is the sacrifice of children (**12:31**). This practice was common in the region and obviously persisted despite the attempts of the priests and prophets to stamp it out (2 Kgs 16:3; 17:17; 21:6; 23:10; Jer 7:31; 19:5; 32:35).

13:1-18 Temptation to idolatry Chapter 13 also focuses on the observance of the first commandment. It deals with three ways in which the Israelites might be led astray to worship false gods. The first source of temptation is false prophets and dreamers. An important test is offered to tell whether a prophet is true or not, a test that has nothing to do with his (or her) ability to make correct predictions or to perform miraculous signs (**13:1-3a**). Any prophet who advocates worshipping any other God is a danger to the entire nation, for what he is preaching is rebellion against the powerful God who had rescued them from Egypt and demanded their total love and loyalty (**13:3b-4**). Such a false prophet must be put to death (**13:5**).

Another source of temptation could be a friend or family member who encouraged an interest in another god (**13:6-7**). No matter how near and dear that person was, they must be put to death because they, too, were encouraging rebellion that would undermine Israel's covenant relationship with God (**13:8-10**). Their death would act as a warning to others who were tempted to follow other gods (**13:11**).

In this century, we are seeing noticeable erosion of Christian values and beliefs among many young African people. But no matter who seeks to lead us astray from the Christian faith, we must say 'no' to negative moral and spiritual influences from the global village. Those of us who are Christians must remain true to Jesus who saved us.

We must also be aware of the need to beware of those false prophets who claim to speak in the name of the Lord but who use religion as a cloak to steal money from those who believe them or to promote their own interests by demanding absolute obedience from their followers. God may indeed speak to us through others, but we must always weigh their claims against the truths of the whole Bible.

Deuteronomy even considers the case in which an entire town may be persuaded to abandon God and turn to idolatry (**13:12-13**). In such a case, care must be taken to establish whether what is being reported about the town is in fact true (**13:14**). If it is, the entire town and everything in it must be destroyed (**13:15-17**). The instruction that nothing from the town is to be taken by those who destroy it eliminates any temptation to use accusations of idolatry as means to acquire wealth by falsely accusing others.

The destruction of everyone in a town that is found to be guilty of idolatry is an expression of a belief in corporate responsibility. Individuals advocating idolatry should have been killed before the contamination spread through the town. The community's failure to act against them, and its active involvement in their idolatry, justified corporate punishment for corporate crime. Similar examples of corporate punishment can be found in Exodus 32:26-29, Numbers 25:4-9, Joshua 6:17-21 and Judges 20:42-48.

The statement *The Lord your God is testing you* (13:3b) places these temptations into perspective. God could sur-round his people with a fence to protect them from all distractions from following him, but he chooses not to. He allows us to face these temptations so that as we pass these tests, we will become more established in the faith. This is the principle in operation in 13:3b-4.

14:1-21 Mourning and food The rules about mourning and food consumption are placed in the context of Israel's relationship with God. This relationship is stressed by the syntax in the original Hebrew, where the chapter begins 'children you are' (**14:1**). The pattern is repeated in **14:2**, which begins 'a holy people you are'. Their special status requires them to observe customs that set them apart from the other nations around them.

In the ancient Near East, it was common for mourners to mutilate their bodies by cutting themselves and to shave their heads (Isa 3:24; 15:2; 22:12; Jer 16:6; 41:5; Ezek 7:18; Amos 8:10). But God's law condemns any mutilation of the body that he has made, with the only exception being the rite of male (not female) circumcision, which he commanded (Gen 17:12-14).

The law regarding food is summed up in one sentence: *Do not eat any detestable thing* (**14:3**). This command is then followed by a list of which animals may and may not be eaten (**14:4-20**). It is not always clear what criteria led to specific animals being regarded as clean or unclean. Health reasons may have been a factor, as may religious reasons. But the exact details of the law are less important than the attitude of being willing to submit the details of one's daily life to Yahweh in love and obedience. Jesus made this point when he said that it is not what goes into a man or woman that defiles them, but what comes out (Mark 7:15).

If a dead animal was found, it was not to be eaten (**14:21**). This rule may have been made for health reasons, but the fact that such a corpse could be sold to others suggests that the reason it was forbidden was that the blood had not been drained out of it (12:23-25; see also Lev 17:13-14). The refusal to eat found corpses was a distinctive marker that the Israelites were *a people holy to the Lord your God* (14:21).

The rules regarding dead animals also throw light on the groups with whom the Israelites were in contact, which included resident aliens, who could be given the corpse of the animal, and foreigners, to whom a corpse could be sold for food.

The injunction not to cook a young goat in its mother's milk is a reference to a Canaanite practice. The Israelites are being reminded that they are different from those around them and should not imitate them. It is also possible that there is a parallel here to the prohibition against eating blood because, just as the life of an animal is in its blood, so the life of the kid is in its mother's milk. The command not to destroy both at the same time is an object lesson that God cares about animals too (14:21; see also Lev 17:14-16).

The general principle of this section is that God's people must be sure to separate themselves from everything that is contrary to his word. This principle means that we will have to refuse to have anything to do with some practices associated with African traditional religions. For example, in some cultures women are expected to have sex with certain persons who are not their husbands as a part of mourning for the dead. Christians should not do this. Nor should they agree to the demand that they should kill a goat dedicated to the spirits when celebrating a marriage. At all times, our one standard for behaviour must be the Bible, which calls us to be separate for God. Being separate does not mean that we are to have no contact with or never mix with our own people who still follow traditional religions. Rather, it means that we are to be a light in their midst. Our ability to be lights derives from the Light himself – Christ (John 1:7, 9) – and our guide is the Bible.

14:22-29 Tithes In traditional African society, crops were an important token of God's goodness and were therefore offered in worship, mediated through the ancestors. The Israelite requirement to tithe also recognized that God was the one who owned the land and who made it fertile.

It is clear from 12:6, 11 and 17 that Israel was commanded to bring both tithes and firstborns to the central sanctuary. In **14:22-23** tithes and firstborns are again associated. A tithe is a tenth of what one has obtained in terms of crops, wages, the sale of possessions, or any other source. Jacob promised to tithe when he promised God, 'of all that you give me I will give you a tenth' (Gen 28:22).

We do not know exactly when the tithes were paid. Probably they were taken to the central sanctuary at the time of the harvest festival, known as the Feast of Tabernacles or at the Feast of Weeks (Pentecost) (16:9-17). But given the difficulty of transporting goods over long distances, Deuteronomy included the option of converting the goods into money that could then be used to purchase equivalent goods for offering and for the sacred meal eaten at the central sanctuary by the entire household. These goods included *cattle, sheep, wine or other fermented drink* (**14:24-26**). This provision was used to justify the sale of animals in the temple to which Jesus objected so strongly (John 2:13-17), for the custom had deteriorated into a purely commercial transaction and there was no longer a link between the labour of the offerer and the offering and sacred meal.

The tithe was so much part of Jewish life that the prophets rebuked people when they failed to bring them (Neh 13:10; Mal 3:6).

Many churches treat the tithe regulation as meaning that we should give a tenth of all that we have to God. There is no problem with this if it is taken as a guiding principle. But there is a problem if it is treated legalistically and seen as a rule binding every believer and as a requirement for satisfying the law of God. The NT principle is to give in proportion to how God has blessed us (1 Cor 16:1-2; 2 Cor 8:13-15). This would mean that those who have been richly blessed will be able to give far more than a mere tenth. Christ gave all of himself for us. Why should we keep so much for ourselves and give him so little? But unfortunately church leaders cannot promote this principle while they advocate tithing as a rule. Believers will be content to give only a tenth, when they should be giving more to help meet the needs of the church in Africa. What we should be doing is working with the spirit of the tithe, encouraging believers to give more and not laying a burden of guilt on those who for a time and for good reason are unable to give.

It is also worth noting that God is interested in having the needs of the Levites taken care of (14:28-29; see also 26:12). Money paid to pastors as salaries or allowances is money given to God. We need to keep that perspective before us all the time so that we do not begin to think that we are depriving ourselves to pay our pastors. It is a matter of giving to God because he has blessed us!

Every third year the tithe would not be taken to the central sanctuary but would be stored locally (**14:28**). The supplies would then be used to meet the needs of the poor: *the Levites ... the aliens, the fatherless and the widows* (**14:29**). Clearly, God does not put the needs of the church above those of the poor. Offerings to help the poor are also counted as offerings to him (compare Isa 1:13-17; Hos 6:6; Matt 25:40; Luke 12:33; 1 John 4:20).

A similar principle was applied in some African traditional societies. Every Ovimbundu village in Angola used to include a round hut called the *Onjango,* where the fatherless and the widows could come for a meal and instruction every day. Such daily care for those less fortunate protected children from becoming like the current street children and protected women from having to resort to prostitution in order to survive.

Unfortunately practices like these have been replaced by a high degree of selfishness in many of our African nations. Too often the taxes that are supposed to be used to raise the standard of living of the poor are channelled into selfish causes by our leaders. Deuteronomy is a wake-up call. God is concerned about the poor and the needy.

15:1-18 Remitting debts and releasing slaves In most ancient law codes such as the Code of Hammurabi, the aristocracy, priests, landowners, rulers and military leaders had a distinct advantage over the poor and underprivileged. This was not the case in Israel. Deuteronomy makes it clear that God has a special concern for the poor and that all are called on to provide for the needy.

The year for cancelling debts coincided with the seventh year in which the land was to be allowed to lie fallow (**15:1; Lev 25:3-4**). In that year all loans were to be cancelled and converted into gifts (**15:2**). However, this did not apply to foreigners, who as 14:21 shows were a group distinct from

GENEROSITY AND SOLIDARITY

Poverty has always existed and is found wherever a poor majority lives next to a rich minority – as is the case in most countries of the world. It is defined as the condition in which people lack the basic necessities for a decent life, such as food, clothing and shelter.

Poverty does not come from God, because all that he does is good (Gen 1:25). He created a world that was intended to ensure that all human beings would have everything they needed (Gen 1:29-30). The reason that some people lack what they need is a consequence of the fall, which brought sin into this world (Gen 3). Recognizing this fact is not the same as saying that it is a sin to be poor. Rather, it is saying that sin lies behind all the economic, social, political, environmental and psychological factors that result in poverty.

This sin can take various forms. Many people are condemned to poverty through circumstances that are no fault of their own. Their poverty is made worse by the selfishness of those who think only of themselves, their own family and their own ethnic or social group. Such selfishness widens the gulf between rich and poor, between the great powers and countries in the majority world.

Others may be poor because they are guilty of the sin of laziness (Prov 20:4; 21:25; Matt 25:26) or lack motivation to do the work of caring for the creation that God has entrusted to human beings (Gen 1:28). Some may also fail to use the creativity or initiative that God has given to all human beings.

But if we argue that poverty is rooted in human nature, and that people are naturally sinful, must we give up the attempt to do anything about poverty? Must we give in to Afro-pessimism, accepting poverty as something we cannot change? Of course not! God created every human being, and he is concerned about their well-being.

In the OT, God told the children of Israel to be generous. They were specifically instructed to care for widows, orphans and foreigners (Deut 24:17-22). If such people, who lacked a husband, parents or land, did not receive help, they would be condemned to live in dire poverty.

In the NT, there are many examples of generosity and solidarity among local churches. When a famine afflicted Jerusalem, other churches helped the impoverished church there by sending generous gifts (2 Cor 8). It was in the context of helping others that Paul encouraged the Christians, 'Each man should give what he has decided in his heart to give, not reluctantly or under compulsion' (2 Cor. 9:7).

Not only must churches help each other, but believers must also show practical concern for the destitute in their local church. James, whose letter focuses on Christian behaviour, clearly considers solidarity and generosity to be essential parts of faith in action. He recognizes that while faith alone is enough for salvation, action must flow from our faith. As he says, 'Show me your faith without deeds, and I will show you my faith by what I do' (Jas 2:18). Thus he argues that it is a totally inadequate to simply say, 'Go, I wish you well; keep warm and well fed' to a brother or sister who has nothing (Jas 2:16). We must go beyond words and must clothe and feed them if we are to demonstrate the authenticity of our faith in Christ.

Generosity is not foreign to Africa; it is part of our culture. And we know that one does not need to be rich to be generous. We share what little we have. There is even a proverb, 'In friendship, even a crust of bread is shared.'

The African Christian should be the most generous of all Africans, for our generosity should not merely be cultural but should also be rooted in a heartfelt response to God's generosity to us. We should model our generosity on the generosity of the Heavenly Father, who promises to provide our daily bread (Matt 6:11). But this bread he supplies does not normally drop from heaven, as the manna did in the wilderness (Exod 16:4). Nor is his generosity limited to sharing a crust of bread, which merely staves off hunger. He created a world that would meet our needs for food (Gen 1:30). Following his example, we must not just provide emergency food supplies, but must act to change the situation. We must empower the person who receives help to help others (2 Cor 1:4). And we must not insist on our own preconceived ideas as to how help is to be offered. Rather, we must support the poor in the use of their own creativity and imagination to find a way out of their poverty. Experience has shown that people can be very resourceful.

African solidarity and generosity go together at the family level, in the clan and in the community. For the African Christian, solidarity in the church is even more important. This solidarity is not rooted in blood relationships but in faith and obedience to God, who asks us to love our neighbour as ourselves (Matt 22:39). We should be inspired by the example of Christians in the apostles' time. There were no needy people among them because they had everything in common (Acts 4:32-35). That was the best way to deal with the poverty in their context. Today, the church can help its poorer members by encouraging them to be creative in thinking of solutions and helping them to obtain the training and equipment they need both technically and spiritually.

Unfortunately, generosity and solidarity can easily be corrupted by selfish motives. When this happens, these cultural virtues can lead to tribalism, nepotism or the clinging dependence of parasitism. These evils have resulted in there being more poor people than rich people in Africa. But when the gospel guides our generosity and solidarity, these virtues become strong tools with which to build a better world (Matt 5:43-48).

Solomon Andria

the resident aliens who lived amongst the Israelites (**15:3**). Their exclusion may have been intended to protect the Israelites' generosity from being exploited by people who had no ties to the community. God reassures those who are worried about the financial implications of this arrangement that it will not be burdensome, for if they obey his law there will be very few poor and needy people requiring help (**15:4-6**).

However, the law is also realistic in recognizing that disobedience is likely and that there will probably always be some who require help (15:11). So the Israelites are exhorted to be generous and to meet the needs of others (**15:7-8, 10-11**). In fact, failure to do so is labelled a sin (**15:9**).

Extreme poverty might lead some to sell themselves into service as slaves (**15:12**). The Israelites' treatment of such slaves was to be conditioned by their own experience of slavery in Egypt (**15:15**). It was certainly very different from our modern conception of slavery. Slavery was not a permanent condition, but would end every seventh year. Not only that, but upon regaining their freedom slaves had to be given a generous allowance of food and livestock by their former master to enable them to survive on their own (**15:13-14**). However, slaves did not have to be forced to leave if they wished to remain in a family's service (**15:16-17**). Once again it is stressed that generosity will bring God's blessing (**15:18**).

A similar pattern of behaviour is found among the Ovimbundu people. There a male or female slave who had worked for his or her master for some time would marry a family member and become a member of the family with the same rights as any biological family member.

15:19-23 Firstborn animals Firstborn animals have been mentioned in passing in 12:6-7 and in 14:23, but now explicit instructions are given in regard to them. The law specifies that firstborn male animals are to be set apart for the Lord (**15:19**). This means that they are not to be used for mundane work like ploughing and are not to be used for economic gain by shearing their wool. Instead they are to be sacrificed and eaten in a ritual meal (**15:20**). However, no animal with a defect was an acceptable sacrifice – to offer such an animal would be an insult to God (**15:21**; Mal 1:7-8). So any firstborn animals that were defective in some way could be eaten in ordinary meals, as if they were hunted game such as gazelles or deer (**15:22**; 12:15, 22). As always, none of the blood was to be eaten (**15:23**; 12:15-16).

16:1-17 Laws regarding annual pilgrimages

The Israelites were expected to observe three annual feasts that required a pilgrimage to the central sanctuary, namely, the Feast of Passover and Unleavened Bread, the Feast of Weeks and the Feast of Tabernacles. Details about these feasts had been given earlier in Exodus 23:14-17, Leviticus 23 and Numbers 28. The details given here in Deuteronomy supplement the information given there.

Even in this section there is an interesting parallel with ancient Near Eastern treaties. Many such treaties required those signing the treaty to report to their overlord at regular intervals, at which time they were expected to offer tribute and to renew their oath of allegiance (compare 16:16-17).

16:1-8 The passover The instruction to *observe the month of Abib and celebrate the Passover of the Lord your God* is phrased much like the instruction regarding the Sabbath in 5:12. Like the Sabbath, it is associated with the deliverance from Egypt (**16:1**). The month in which it is to be celebrated is referred to by its Canaanite name of 'Abib' (which means 'the time when the corn is green'). Later, Israel adopted Babylonian names for months, and this became known as Nisan. Abib/Nisan falls in approximately March-April, that is, in the spring. Besides being the month in which they had actually been delivered, this was also an appropriate time to celebrate the start of a new life for the nation.

Although the original Passover sacrifice was a lamb (Exod 12:3-5), here the command is to sacrifice either a sheep or an ox (**16:2**; see also Num 28:19). The feast of Passover was immediately followed by the seven-day Feast of Unleavened Bread, mentioned in Exodus 23:15 (**16:3-4**; Exod 12:14-15; Lev 23:5-6). Both of these festivals coincided with the time of the barley harvest, which was also in spring.

The purpose of the Passover feast was to remember what God had done for the nation and to make sure that each new generation was informed of the covenant between God and Israel. The feast of unleavened bread also reminded them that they had *left Egypt in haste,* with no time to wait for bread to rise (Exod 12:34).

The Passover was to be celebrated at one central place (**16:5-6**). The time of the sacrifice is also specified as *in the evening, when the sun goes down.* This was the same time at which the exodus had begun.

By New Testament times the Passover was again celebrated in homes, although many Jews made considerable effort to get to Jerusalem for the festival. Thus Jesus ate the Passover with his disciples in Jerusalem in a specially prepared upper room (Matt 26:17-19; Luke 22:7-15). The narrative in Exodus 12:8-9 indicates that the flesh was to be roasted in the fire, but not eaten raw or boiled with water. The Deuteronomic law appears to authorize a change in **16:7**, where it states that the Passover sacrifice was to be boiled. However, the problem here is one of translation. The same word can mean either 'roasted' (niv) or 'boiled' (rsv). The decision about which term to use is often determined by whether there is any mention of water or pots in the context.

The people were told that on the morning following the Passover they were to *return to your tents.* Clearly, such an instruction could only be obeyed literally when Israel was living a nomadic existence and dwelling in tents (16:7).

Presumably, after settling in the promised land, they would return to their temporary places of accommodation in Jerusalem where they would remain for the whole week before returning to their homes. The seventh day of the festival was a day of solemn assembly (**16:8**).

16:9-12 THE FEAST OF WEEKS The Feast of Weeks took place on the fiftieth day after the Sabbath that had marked the beginning of the Passover (**16:9**), and thus in the NT this feast is referred to as Pentecost (from the Greek word for fifty; see Acts 2:1). In the OT it is also known as the Feast of Harvest (Exod 23:16) and as the Day of Firstfruits (Num 28:26). Whereas Passover took place at the time of the barley harvest, this feast in May or June was associated with the wheat harvest, and was one of the main dates in the agricultural calendar of the time.

This feast is not associated with God's deliverance of Israel but with gratitude for his ongoing blessing in providing a bountiful crop (**16:10**). It was an occasion for joy and feasting that was to be shared not only by the family but also by their entire household, landless Levites, and any who were in need (**16:11**). The memory of their own poverty in Israel should spur them on to gratitude and generosity (**16:12**).

16:13-17 THE FEAST OF TABERNACLES Like the combined Passover and Feast of Unleavened Bread, the Feast of Tabernacles lasted a full week (**16:13**). It is also referred to as the Lord's feast (Lev 23:34) and as simply 'the Feast' (Ezek 45:25), indicating its great importance. In some translations it is also referred to as the Feast of Booths (KJV, RSV). It was celebrated after the hard work of threshing the grain and pressing the grapes had been completed, and thus fell during the autumn months of September and October. Like the other feasts, it was to be celebrated at the central sanctuary and the keynote was to be joy and thanksgiving for the harvest (**16:14-15**). The Feast was to be shared with all. Elsewhere it is also treated as an opportunity to remember the temporary shelters the Israelites had lived in during their wanderings in the wilderness (Lev. 23:40-43). The NT records Jesus' teaching in the temple during this feast (John 7–8).

The section on festivals concludes with a reminder that all men must attend all three festivals and that they should always bring a gift with them that is commensurate with the extent to which God has blessed them (**16:16-17**). As pointed out at the start of this section, such a requirement would have been a familiar one in treaties of the period.

16:18-18:22 Laws regarding leadership

The next section of the law code deals with Israel's leaders, namely its judges (16:18-20), law courts (17:8-13), kings (17:14-20), priests (18:1-8) and prophets (18:9-22). While 16:21-17:7 may appear to belong in the previous section, which contains the regulations governing worship, it is not entirely unrelated in that it does contain rules for investi-

gation and for witnesses. It may also have been put here to remind the people that in all circumstances their overwhelming loyalty must be to God.

16:18-17:13 JUDGES Moses had been the Israelites' first judge and had been assisted by judges drawn from each of the tribes (1:12-18; Exod 18:13-27). However, as the people scattered throughout their new land, they would need some other system of justice. Consequently they are instructed to appoint judges *for each of your tribes in every town* (**16:18**). Presumably difficult cases would still be referred to the religious leadership, as had been the case previously (1:17; 17:8; Mal 2:7).

The judges were given strict instructions to *follow justice and justice alone* (**16:20**). This is explained as meaning that their judgments are not to be affected by bribes, friendships or personal biases (**16:19**).

Because justice and correct religion are inextricably linked, the initial instructions to judges are immediately followed by a reminder of the need to be faithful to Yahweh. There is to be no tolerance of syncretism, with worship being offered to symbols of Canaanite religion alongside worship of Yahweh (**16:21-22**). This command is a direct condemnation of the practices we often see or hear of, where God's people involve themselves with things of the world of spiritual darkness. Some place charms on their children or carry charms on their own bodies so as not to be bewitched. Others place certain objects under their seats to protect their jobs, or in a private part of the house to make their business prosper. All such practices are a form of idolatry. If we practise them, we cannot expect God's blessing. God demands total allegiance from his people.

Nor is the worship of God to be treated lightly. A sacrifice of a blemished animal is a cheap offering of one's second-best, not a statement of love that shows one's appreciation of what God has done (**17:1**). Real worship always has an element of self-sacrifice (Mal 1:6-8).

Those found guilty of idolatry were subject to harsh punishment, because this evil would break the covenant between God and Israel and result in the destruction of the nation (**17:5**). However, this punishment is not to be meted out casually. There must be a thorough investigation to determine whether the accusation is true (**17:4**). To avoid such accusations being used to settle individual grudges, it is specified that there must be more than one witness to the offence (**17:6**). Nor can the witnesses escape the consequences of their allegation: they must confront the person they have accused and be in the forefront of those putting the idolater to death (**17:7**). The sentence must be carried out at the *city gate* because that was where the law court was located in this period.

The care with which justice is to be executed clearly shows that God does not take the loss of innocent lives lightly. Although at times for moral reasons he may have to order the death of men, women and children, such behaviour is not central to his nature. He loves justice and righteousness and seeks to uphold them. This aspect of God's nature needs to be taken more seriously in Africa, for here justice is often corrupted. Many have been killed merely because of suspicion or one person's false accusation. Many others have suffered because the wealthy have been able to bribe the officials who should administer justice. Such actions rouse God's displeasure and definitely will not bring blessings to a nation. Everyone should be treated fairly within our judicial systems.

Inevitably, local judges will be confronted with some cases in which they are not sure how the law applies, or whether an offence was deliberate or accidental. All such cases should be referred to a 'Supreme Court' that was associated with the central sanctuary and was presided over by priests and judges (**17:8-9**). The ruling of this court was binding (**17:11**). In order to maintain respect for this court, the penalty for showing contempt for it was death (**17:12-13**).

17:14-20 KINGS IN AFRICA, kings were invested with political, religious and divine powers that gave them the authority to exercise the functions of mediation and intercession with ancestral spirits and *Suku,* the Almighty Being. In Angola, the Ovimbundu king was responsible for social and economic administration, diplomacy, the dispensing of justice and wisdom, and guarding and incarnating the philosophy, ethics and traditions of the people. He always had the last and the final word in the dispensation of justice. For this the Ovimbundu people have a proverb that says, *O popia onganji, o malapo osoma* ['The advocate speaks; the king concludes or decides']. The king was seen also as possessing spiritual powers. Because he was also seen as the magician, he lived in the realm of witchcraft and divination to protect himself and his people from evil forces, calamities, diseases and misfortunes. He was the guardian, the protector of his people and the unifier of the nation.

Deuteronomy clearly assigns a king a far more restricted role. Rather than being the mediator with God and wielding spiritual powers, he is to subject himself to the authority of the priests and the written law of God (**17:18-20**).

The ideal king must be an Israelite (**17:15**) and must not consider himself superior to his fellows (17:20), particularly as regards the temptation to imagine that God's laws apply only to ordinary citizens and not to those in power. The reference to not acquiring horses means that he must also not be set on building up a large army (**17:16**), for at that time cavalry was becoming important in warfare, and the Egyptian horses were famed. Nor must he want to accumulate wealth for himself or to display it ostentatiously through the number of his wives (**17:17**). Having a large number of wives will tend to make him forget the requirements of God's law.

Solomon fell into all these sins. In fact, it has even been argued that this passage must have been added to the text later to reflect the actual behaviour of the kings of Israel and Judah. However, none of these failings were unique to these kings. Moses had grown up in the courts of power and had met many kings as the people travelled in the wilderness. He would have been well aware of the temptations of power and was in a position to issue a warning against them. While the type of rule he envisaged for Israel was one in which God was their king, he was probably realistic enough to admit the possibility that at some stage a human monarch would be appointed (17:14-15). It was thus important that he lay down the bounds to that monarch's authority in order to ensure that the covenant with God, the supreme monarch, was upheld.

18:1-8 PRIESTS AND LEVITES Unlike the book of Leviticus, Deuteronomy pays little attention to priests. Nor does it distinguish between priests and Levites, with the former being the descendants of Aaron (Exod 28:1) and the latter the other members of the tribe of Levi with supporting duties in the tabernacle (Num 3:5-10). Instead the book focuses on the obligations that rest on the people as a whole and not on specific groups.

In this passage, however, the focus does fall on the priests and Levites. This tribe would not be allocated land, like the rest of the Israelites, but were to be supported by specific portions of the offerings of their fellow Israelites (**18:1-4**). This regulation may have been intended to prevent those who were supposed to be devoted solely to the service of Yahweh (**18:5**) from being bribed by offers of land and coming to devote their attention to secular matters, as has happened in the church in the past. The assertion that *the Lord is their inheritance* (18:2) means that they have nothing else to rely on except him. Should the Israelites cease to be faithful to the covenant, the Levites would have nothing to live on. Although the Levites would be scattered in various cities across the land (Num 35:1-8), any one of them who chose to come to serve at the central sanctuary was to be welcomed and given the portions to which his membership in this tribe entitled him (**18:6-8**).

Churches should look to the principle that underlies the rules regarding the support of Levites when considering how to support pastors and others who devote themselves to work in the churches or in Christian organizations. Clearly the members of the church should be committed to providing properly for such people. They are to be given the *firstfruits* (18:4), not the leftovers.

18:9-13 FALSE LEADERS People are always anxious to know the future and to have supernatural help in making decisions or in affecting what happens in the future. The nations around Israel had developed various techniques for obtaining such help. These techniques ranged from child sacrifice to witchcraft, sorcery and spiritualism (**18:9-10**). Moses stresses that God detests all of these practices; his hatred of them is so deep that these are among the reasons he is permitting the Israelites to drive out those who practise them (**18:12**). Although no explanation is given of why God hates these practices, one probable reason is that human sacrifice is both cruel and usurps God's prerogative over life and death. Another is that those who practise witchcraft or act as mediums open themselves to manipulation by demonic powers

Since the believer has been called to relate to God in all aspects of his or her life, this instruction leaves no room for any consultation with anyone in opposition to God – whether in the spiritual or physical world. The Holy Spirit is the believers' teacher and guide in all things (John 14:26). There is no room in the life of believers for either the consultation with the dead or witchcraft.

18:14-22 THE PROPHET Whereas the Canaanites used a range of techniques in attempts to determine or manipulate the will of the gods, Yahweh acknowledged only one way to hear from him. That way was through the words of a prophet (**18:14-15**). Moses had been the first prophet in Israel. At Mount Horeb he had been the one to transmit Yahweh's message to the people when the people had been terrified at God's presence (**18:16**). But now Moses is old and about to die. To whom will the people turn to hear God's word? Moses reassures them that God will raise up a successor to him (**18:17**). While this reference does not necessarily exclude all the subsequent OT prophets (who, like Moses, spoke on God's behalf), in the NT this prophecy is interpreted as referring to Jesus. That is why John the Baptist (who was a prophet) denied being 'the prophet' (John 1:21). The reference to this verse in the sermons in Acts 3:22-23 and 7:37 makes it plain that the speakers understand Jesus to be this prophet, a prophet far greater than any of those who had preceded him. He is 'the Holy and Righteous One' (Acts 3:14; 7:52), 'the author of life' (Acts 3:15) and 'the Christ' (Acts 3:18) whom the other prophets foretold. Yet he is more like Moses than any prophet of the OT in that just as Moses was central to the giving of the old covenant (the commandments) on Mount Sinai, so Jesus is central to the new covenant.

Naturally, the people are concerned about how they can distinguish a true prophet from someone who is merely claiming to be a prophet (**18:21**). The simple answer is that a false prophet's word will not come true (**18:22**). However, this is not the only test, for the warning in 13:1-3 must also be remembered.

One problem that prophets have faced is that the fulfilment of their prophecies may be a long time in coming. Jeremiah, for example, had to wait many years before his words came true. Thus it may take time to establish whether a prophet does indeed have a word from the Lord. Today in Africa there are dozens of new denominations

founded on the basis that a leader heard the voice of God or had a revelation. Care must be taken to assess whether these leaders are truly speaking God's word, or whether they are running the churches for their own financial gain and trapping the unwary.

19:1-26:15 Assorted laws

The next section of the book of Deuteronomy consists of brief statements of an assortment of laws. Sometimes laws relating to a similar topic are grouped together, but this is not always the case.

19:1-13 HOMICIDE AND CITIES OF REFUGE In dealing with a situation where someone is killed, the law is careful to distinguish between accidental homicide (**19:4-5**) and deliberate murder (19:11). In both cases, someone is likely to want revenge for the killing, but such revenge is not justified if the killing was not deliberate (**19:6, 10**). Consequently the law laid down that a number of cities of refuge were to be established, to which those accused of homicide could flee. Moses had already established three such cities in Transjordan (4:41-43), and now he specifies that a further three must be created once they have entered the promised land (**19:2**). These cities must be easily accessible from anywhere in the land (**19:3**). Consequently, if the land area occupied by Israel grows, a further three cities will be needed (**19:8-9**).

However, there was always the possibility that some of those who sought refuge in these cities were in fact guilty of murder. So the law allows the elders of the city to expel someone from the city if they judge that he or she did indeed commit a deliberate murder (**19:11-12**). Presumably they would take this action only after some form of legal trial had been conducted (Num 35:12).

Those found guilty of murder received the death penalty, since murder broke a basic law laid down in the Ten Commandments (5:17). Applying it was necessary to free Israel of the pollution caused by this breach of the covenant (**19:13**).

19:14 BOUNDARY MARKERS In an agricultural society without surveying instruments and fences, a boundary stone was vital to the protection of property rights. Removing one would be equivalent to stealing land that Yahweh had given to a particular family. Greedy and powerful people could easily be tempted to take this action, and that is why God strictly forbids it.

This concern for protecting land ownership has great resonance in Africa today, where the scars left by colonial land policies run deep. But attention also has to be paid to the protection of the land inherited by AIDS orphans and widows. Their right to land ownership must also be respected.

19:15-21 WITNESSES AND EVIDENCE The Ten Commandments forbade the bearing of false witness (5:20), but prohibition alone is not enough to stop this evil, which is known in all ages and societies. Accordingly the law insisted that all accusations be presented before a court composed of priests and judges and that more than one witness was needed to convict someone of a crime (**19:15**). This explains why there was so much effort on the part of the Jewish leadership to get witnesses who agreed on an accusation against Jesus (Matt 26:59-61). Jesus also supported the application of this law when resolving disputes (Matt 18:16) and cited it in support of his own claims (John 8:17). Paul also cites it (2 Cor 13:1).

A harsh penalty was imposed for false witness (**19:19**) with the aim of deterring others from attempting the same behaviour (**19:20**). The penalty was determined in accordance with the law of retaliation (Exod 21:23-25; Lev 24:17-19), that is, *eye for eye, tooth for tooth* (**19:21**). Presumably, this could even go so far as the death penalty if this was what the one bringing the charge had hoped to achieve (see, for example, Haman's fate in Esther 7:3-10). The law of retaliation should not be seen as a barbaric system of punishment. What it actually achieved was to limit punishment. Vengeance was limited to what was appropriate for the crime committed.

When Jesus criticized this law in Matthew 5:38-42, he was not rejecting it as a principle to be applied in the law courts. Rather, he was objecting to it being used to govern all relationships between individuals. Individuals should work to show love and brotherhood, two concepts that recur repeatedly in the book of Deuteronomy.

20:1-20 REGULATIONS FOR WAR Given that the Israelites are poised on the edge of the invasion of the promised land, it is not surprising that the book of Deuteronomy pays considerable attention to the topic of war. Given, too, that this was a war that God had explicitly commanded, it is not surprising that they can be confident that God will fight on their side (**20:1-4**). However, Deuteronomy has already made it clear that not every war is sanctioned by God (see 1:41-45). A holy war could be undertaken only after consulting Yahweh (1 Sam 28:5-6; 30:7-8; 2 Sam 5:19, 22-23) and the men involved must be holy (23:9-14). Thus it is appropriate for the priest to address the army before it went into battle and to remind them that the God who was with them was the same one who had delivered them from Egypt (**20:1-2**). However, as the experience of Eli's sons showed, God's promise of support did not apply when the people's lives were not holy (1 Sam 3:13-14; 4:1-10).

Because victory would be given by Yahweh, there was no need to draft every available man into the army (Judg 7:2-4; 1 Sam 14:6, 17). Thus anyone who had recently built a house, planted a vineyard or become engaged was excused from military service (**20:5-7**). So was anyone who was fearful, who might discourage his comrades (**20:8**). Yahweh

had promised his people that they would enjoy the land, and he provides opportunities for them to do so.

It was only after these people had departed that officers were appointed, making it clear that this was not a standing army like the one Solomon assembled (1 Kgs 10:26) but one that had been specially assembled to meet a particular need (**20:9**).

Rules are also laid down for the conduct of a war, both as regards offers of peace and the disposal of captured people and livestock. These rules differed depending on whether the city being attacked was on the borders of Israel (**20:10-15**) or specifically part of the promised land (**20:16-18**). In the latter case, the danger of contamination of Israelite belief was so great that no mercy could be shown.

Although these laws seem harsh at first sight, they do conceal certain principles that apply even to this day. There is the principle of restraint, where diplomacy is to be tried before violence (**20:10-11**). There is also the principle of mercy to non-combatants, that is, the women, children and livestock (**20:14**). And there is also the principle of respect for the environment, which forbids random destruction of trees that may have taken generations to grow (**20:20-21**). Fruit trees are always to be spared, and other trees should be cut only if needed for the siege. The principles outlined in this passage could definitely be applied in parts of Africa that are ravaged by wars. Unfortunately, they are not

We need to exercise caution, however, when trying to apply other details of this chapter to modern war. No other war has the same status as the holy war that God permitted to give Israel the land he had promised them. At that point in history, God was establishing a people to whom he would reveal himself and from whom he would bring the Messiah. No other nation can make similar claims to justify a war. But today God's kingdom is no longer associated with a political unit. He has drawn all nations into his church, and the church has no mandate to fight wars. Consequently no nation can claim that God will fight on its side, even if its cause seems just.

21:1-9 COMPENSATION FOR ANONYMOUS MURDER Where 19:1-13 dealt with the fate of the perpetrators of accidental homicide and deliberate murder, this passage lays out the procedure to be followed if it is not known who perpetrated the crime (**21:1**). In such a case the murderer could not be punished and the whole community was regarded as contaminated by bloodguilt. Consequently some sort of ceremonial execution was required to satisfy the demands of justice and purge the land of guilt. (Purging is referred to numerous times in Deuteronomy – see 13:5; 17:7; 19:13.)

The responsibility for performing the ceremony fell on the elders of the city nearest to the scene of the crime (**21:2**). They are to take a young heifer to a place near a stream that has also not been used for agriculture. There it is to be killed ritually (**21:3-4**). The procedure for the killing makes it clear that this is not a sacrifice, although the priests are present in their role as judges (**21:5**). The elders then ritually wash their hands over the slaughtered heifer and solemnly proclaim that they know nothing about the crime or the perpetrator (**21:6-7**). In their prayer, they ask God to clear the nation of this crime (**21:8**).

Presumably, if the murderer was later identified, he or she would still be put to death in terms of the requirements in 19:11-13.

An important principle that underlies this ritual is that of corporate guilt. Communities and nations cannot deny all responsibility for the evil within them. Thus we need to take seriously such issues as racial and tribal discrimination, tribal wars and genocides, neglect of the underprivileged by governmental institutions, discrimination against those suffering with HIV/AIDS, and the failure of our governments to eradicate preventable diseases such as polio, malaria and measles. We cannot simply avert our eyes and claim that we have no responsibility for social evils with tragic consequences.

21:10-14 FEMALE PRISONERS OF WAR The first words of this section repeat those regarding the holy war in 20:1: *when you go forth to war against your enemies ...* (**21:10**), but in this case the topic is what to do with women who are taken as booty in war (see also 20:10, 14). On the basis of the laws laid down in 7:3 and 20:16-18, these women are presumably not Canaanite women but come from other areas. An Israelite man was permitted to marry such a woman (**21:11**). This may seem odd, as she too would have worshipped foreign gods, but it may have been felt that because she was coming from some distance, she would be less inclined to continue to worship those gods. Surrounded by Israelites, and given that the Israelite man would take the lead in the home, she might come to worship their God.

Before the marriage, she was to be allowed a month in which to mourn the loss of her parents (**21:13**). This was the same period of mourning awarded to honoured leaders (34:8; Num 20:29). Her father would probably have been killed in the war (20:13). Even if her mother had survived, they would now belong to different owners and might never meet again.

The instruction that the woman was *to shave her head, trim her nails and put aside* her foreign garments may be related to her mourning for her own people from whom she will now be separated (14:1). It may also symbolize her leaving the past and transferring her life to a new setting. However, the most important element seems to be that this was part of a purification ritual (see Lev 14:8; Num 8:7). Yahweh had set the children of Israel apart as a holy people for himself, and these actions symbolized that the woman, too, was being set apart. When the month of mourning was over, the man could go to her because she was now rightfully his wife (21:13).

Should the marriage turn out to be an unhappy one, the woman enjoyed legal protection (**21:14**). She could not simply be given the status of a slave or sold to someone else. She was free to go wherever she wished.

21:15-17 THE RIGHTS OF THE FIRSTBORN The presentation of this law differs from the previous ones in being in an impersonal legal style ('a man', 'he') whereas most of the previous ones are addressed to 'you'. It also differs in containing no references to God, which almost all the other laws do. However, it is similar to the previous law in that it deals with an individual whose rights may be violated within a family. In this case the individual is the son of the wife who is less favoured in a polygamous marriage (**21:15**). If this son is the firstborn, he is entitled to the privileges that traditionally accompanied that position regardless of his father's attitude to his mother (**21:16**).

The situation where a polygamous husband preferred one wife to another was not uncommon (Gen 29:30-31; 1 Sam 1:4-5). But the right of the firstborn to a *double share* had a long tradition behind it (**21:17**; see also Gen 27; 48:14) and was not to be set aside for reasons of favouritism. Interestingly, however, the OT does supply a number of examples of cases where a younger son was preferred above his older brother. These cases include Jacob and Esau, Isaac and Ishmael, Ephraim and Manasseh, David and his elder brothers, and Solomon and his elder brothers. But these cases were clearly marked as exceptions to the general custom.

In modern times, the firstborn may no longer enjoy quite such a special status, but the principle that parents should not favour one child above another still applies. All children should inherit what is due to them.

21:18-21 A STUBBORN AND REBELLIOUS SON A father who passed over his firstborn son was abusing his authority. But a son could also abuse his parents (**21:18**). The behaviour described here represents a serious breach of the fifth commandment (5:16) and undermines the ability to pass on the covenant to the next generation. From the description of the son as *a profligate and a drunkard* (**21:20**), it is clear that the behaviour went far beyond the normal conflicts that sometimes occur between parents and children. It is also clear that the behaviour was not just representative of a conflict with one parent, for both parents were to act together in reporting their child to the elders (**21:19**). It was then the responsibility of the elders to decide what further action should be taken, and thus they too acted as a check on unreasonable accusations. If the elders agreed with the parents that the man was guilty, the men of the town were to stone him to death (**21:21**). In other cases where a death sentence was imposed, the witnesses were required to participate in the stoning. This was not the case here. It has been suggested that the reason for this was not only respect for the parents' feelings but also to remind parents that they did not possess the power of life and death over their children. Only the community was entitled to impose such a severe penalty.

21:22-23 THE BODY OF AN EXECUTED CRIMINAL In ancient societies it was common practice to expose the corpses of those who had been executed as a warning to others (**21:22**). The bodies might be hung from a tree or impaled on a pole. The Philistines also displayed the bodies of their enemies (1Sam 31:10) and so did the Assyrians. The Israelites were forbidden to follow this practice for more than a few hours. The corpse of an executed criminal was not to be left on display overnight, but was to be buried on the same day he died (**21:23**). The reason for this was that such a corpse was an object accursed of God and would defile the land, just as contact with a dead body would defile a person (Num 19:11-13). Many years later Paul would draw an analogy between this law and Christ's having become accursed by being exposed on a cross (Gal 3:13).

22:1-4 RESTORATION OF LOST PROPERTY This law addresses both what must not be done and what must be done regarding lost property. What must not be done is to ignore a situation (**22:1, 3, 4**), in this case a straying animal, which will cause loss to a neighbour. What must be done is to take action to prevent the neighbour from suffering loss. These laws apply even when one does not know the neighbour whose property one finds (**22:2**). Property that is found must be kept in trust until the true owner appears.

Thus when one picks up money from the floor, or a goat joins one's flock with no clear sign whose it is, the situation, or any other like it, is not to be interpreted as an unexpected blessing from the Lord. Rather, it is one's duty to look for the owner till he or she is found. This is the practical outworking of the instruction to love your neighbour as yourself (Lev 19:18; Luke 10:27).

22:5 WEARING THE CLOTHES OF THE OTHER SEX It is likely that the law against wearing the clothes of the other sex (**22:5**) is related to aspects of Canaanite religion. Some claim that the worship of the goddess Astarte sometimes involved women dressing as men and vice versa. However, it is also possible that it is related to the Israelites' distaste for anything that went against nature.

Given that the style of dress was very similar for both men and women at the period when this law was given, and the wide differences in cultural perceptions of what constitutes appropriate dress for men and women, this law needs to be interpreted sensitively in today's world. Certainly, it is a gross oversimplification to say that it simply means that women should never wear trousers! Rather than focusing on particular items of clothing, the principle here may be that there is value in preserving some differences in dress between the sexes. Such differences do not deny the fact that all Christians have a common status in God's sight, regardless of sex (Gal 3:28), but simply acknowledge God's

creation of two sexes. The Creator made us different, and we can honour that difference.

22:6-7 SPARING A MOTHER BIRD The Israelites did not keep domesticated fowls, but were permitted to eat certain birds (14:11) and their eggs. Finding a nest would thus be an opportunity to obtain food. However, the law lays down that while the eggs or young may be taken, the mother bird must not be harmed (**22:6-7**). The reason for this instruction is probably not some sentimental associations with motherhood, but the fact that by preserving the mother bird she would be in a position to lay another clutch of eggs and raise more young, thus protecting the species and supplying more food. What we have here is an example of early conservation legislation!

22:8 A SAFETY PRECAUTION IN HOUSE BUILDING The flat roofs of Middle Eastern houses were used for many purposes, including sleeping, performing household chores and entertaining. There was thus a real danger that someone might fall off the roof. Consequently the law required that a low wall be built round the outside of the roof to prevent this from happening (**22:8**). If there was no wall and someone fell and injured himself or herself, the owner of the house could face charges or manslaughter or have to pay compensation for any injury suffered.

This law makes it clear that God values safety legislation that is intended to protect the lives of people he has made. Too often, such precautions are ignored in the pursuit of profit, but God will hold employers and owners responsible for preventable injuries. Believers should also ensure that the vehicles they drive are roadworthy and not likely to cause injury to others. In Africa, reckless driving is a common cause of death. Those responsible for the deaths are often the drivers of public service vehicles who are speeding in order to make as many trips and as much money as possible. God condemns all such behaviour. The value of human life must be guarded..

22:9-11 PROHIBITION OF CERTAIN MIXTURES It is not clear why certain mixtures were prohibited. One possible reason is to maintain distinctions that God has created. Another is to avoid cruelty to animals. Another is to remind the people that the worship of God cannot be mixed with pagan worship and that he must be worshipped single-mindedly. But none of these explanations is fully satisfactory, and some commentators argue that these practices may have been associated with some elements of pagan religion that have been forgotten today. It is also possible that there is no one answer that applies to all three of the prohibitions in this section.

22:12 WEARING TASSELS The prohibition against mixing fabrics in 22:11 is followed by the positive command to attach tassels, or twisted lengths of thread, to *the four corners of the cloak you wear* (**22:12**). Numbers 15:37-41 explains that these tassels are to remind the people of their relationship with God and the need to obey his commands.

22:13-21 ALLEGATIONS CONCERNING A NEW WIFE The law makes it clear that pre- and extramarital sex have serious consequences for all parties. The law does not have a double standard. Both men and women are held to account for their behaviour. If a husband found that his wife was not a virgin at the time of their marriage, he was entitled to have her stoned to death for having premarital sex and bringing shame on the community (**22:21**). However, the law recognized that a husband might use such an accusation to try to get rid of a wife he had decided he did not like (**22:13-14**). The woman's parents were thus encouraged to provide proof of her virginity, which would be a sheet or clothing used on the night of the wedding that was stained with blood or else some proof that the daughter was menstruating until the time she married (**22:15-17**). The lying husband was then subject to a heavy fine (**22:19**) and he was forbidden ever to divorce her. This ruling may seem hard on the woman, who is forced to stay with her accusing husband, but may reflect the reality that once her reputation has been slandered, she might well not find another husband, and in that period there was no place for a single woman. The ruling may thus have protected the woman from a life of extreme poverty and forced her husband to support her.

Given that divorce was permissible in ancient Israel (24:1), it is puzzling why the husband would be tempted to lie about his wife's virginity in order to get rid of her. The answer may be that ancient laws required that if he divorced her, he had to return any dowry she had brought with her, and the woman and her family would keep any gifts he had given them. However, if she was found guilty of premarital sexual relations, she would be executed and he could keep all these objects for himself. Thus greed would have been an incentive for lying about his wife.

22:22-29 ADULTERY AND RAPE The section that follows deals with other examples of sexual immorality. The first is adultery, which is defined as extramarital sexual intercourse with a married woman (**22:22**). Adultery was prohibited in the Ten Commandments (5:18), and both parties to it were to be put to death (an instruction that was ignored when Jesus was presented with only the woman caught in adultery: John 8:3-5). Adultery was regarded as polluting the whole land: *you must purge the evil from Israel.*

The prohibition on adultery extends to the position of a woman who is engaged to be married. In Israelite culture, a betrothal was a formal agreement to marry, accompanied by the exchange of goods. A betrothal signified that a man and a woman had entered into a contract to be faithful to one another. Thus having sex with someone else was tantamount to being unfaithful to one's marriage partner. Once again, the penalty was death for both parties (**22:23-24**).

However, this penalty applied only in the case where the sex took place in the city, as it was judged that in the close quarters of an Israelite town it would have been easy for the woman to summon help had she not consented to the sex (22:24). Thus what took place was not judged to be an act of rape.

However, if the betrothed woman was in a defenceless position in the country, where screams would not have brought any aid, the incident was judged to be a case of rape, and only the man was to be put to death (**22:25**). His act was seen as similar to murder.

If a girl was raped before she was betrothed, the rape was regarded as establishing a marriage. The man must pay a fine to the woman's father and must marry her, without any option of divorce (**22:28-29**). This ruling protected the woman and any children born as a result of the rape.

This insistence on sexual responsibility in these passages contrasts with the often casual attitude to sexual violence that destroys many women's lives in Africa today. The church needs to speak out on this issue.

22:30 STEPMOTHERS AND STEPSONS The final ruling on illicit sexual relations deals with a man's desire for his stepmother, presumably after she is widowed or divorced. Such attraction could easily occur given the sometime wide differences in age between husbands and wives and the proximity that the family relationship would force upon them. But the law is adamant that marrying one's father's wife will *dishonour the father's bed* (**22:30**; see also 27:20).

23:1-9 ADMISSION TO THE ASSEMBLY The *assembly of the Lord* seems to refer to the covenant people of God, gathered in his presence. In later years the same expression would be used to refer to a congregation or church, in the sense of a group of people gathering together to worship God. Thus the prohibitions in this section refer to who may and may not share in the worship of the Lord.

A man who *has been emasculated* was not allowed to enter the assembly of the Lord (**23:1**). This prohibition probably applied to those who had mutilated their bodies as part of the worship of another god, rather than to those who had suffered an accident or illness.

No one *born of a forbidden marriage* was allowed to enter the temple of the Lord (**23:2**). In some versions, this word is translated 'bastard', which means any illegitimate child. However, that scope is too wide. It seems that the focus here is on those born as a result of incestuous relationships, such as that between a man and his mother referred to above. The term may also refer to the children born to cult prostitutes, actively involved in the worship of another god. Whatever the meaning, any such prohibition has been removed by Christ's offer of salvation to all. It is not our backgrounds but our response to Jesus that matters (John 3:16; Gal 3:26-29). The prostitute's child who believes in

Jesus is welcomed with open arms while the pastor's child who does not believe remains under condemnation.

The Ammonites and Moabites are prohibited from access to the assembly of the Lord *to the tenth generation* (**23:3**). The instruction never to seek peace with them (**23:6**) may be related to the fact that these groups were believed to be descended from the incestuous relationships between Lot and his daughters. Moses, however, relates their exclusion to their failure to offer hospitality to the Israelites and to their unsuccessful attempt to use Balaam to bring down the curse of God on the Israelites (**23:4-5**; Num 22-24).

The descendants of Edomites and Egyptians would, however, ultimately be allowed to enter the assembly of the Lord (**23:7-8**). The Edomites were granted this respect because they were the descendants of Esau, Jacob's brother, and thus cousins to the Israelites (2:1-8; see also Gen 36:1-19). Although the Egyptians had later enslaved the Israelites, they had originally treated them with kindness and given them refuge in their land. Thus God's willingness to welcome these people was related to their attitude to his chosen people.

While it cannot be the basis for salvation, God does notice kindness extended to his people (see Matt 25:40). Humans have a moral humanitarian duty to help each other. This applies not only to Christians but to all the people of the earth. Here is a call for all of us in Africa to extend a helping hand to all who need it. God rewards such kindness in one way or another.

23:9-14 PURITY IN THE MILITARY CAMP This section is linked with the earlier regulations governing warfare (see ch. 20). Here the instructions do not deal with avoiding moral impurity but with avoiding anything that is unclean (**23:10**). A nocturnal emission made a man ritually unclean. He was required to remain outside the camp till evening, when he could wash himself and return to camp (**23:10-11**). A similar regulation applied in all cases of emission of semen (Lev 15:16-18) although it is only in the case of a military camp that the man is required to go outside the camp. This law probably reflects the religious significance attaching to life and reproduction.

The legislation also lays down rules relating to hygiene. A specific area outside the camp must be set apart to be used as a toilet and must be kept clean by burying excrement (**23:12-13**). Such cleanliness was necessary to avoid offending the Lord God who *moves about* inside the camp (**23:14**). The camp was to be kept holy in his honour and to prevent him from leaving. This regulation would also contribute to the health of soldiers by removing one possible source of infection.

23:15-16 ESCAPED SLAVES Ancient treaties, like many modern ones, allowed for the extradition of fugitives who had fled from one party to the treaty and sought refuge with the other party. Deuteronomy clearly states that there was to be no extradition of slaves who had run away from foreign masters and sought refuge in Israel (**22:15**). They were to be welcomed and allowed to settle wherever they wished (**22:16**). No rule is given regarding the treatment of escaped Hebrew slaves. This may be because the regulations in 15:12-18 made it clear that the maximum time for which an Israelite could be a slave was seven years.

23:17-18 SACRED PROSTITUTION The type of prostitution being discussed here is not the type to which people are sometimes driven by desperation, as expressed in the Angolan Umbundu saying *Nda ndi mola epuluvi ndiya ndi kakuela, pole nda sia kuelele ñala ño o cipuepue* ['If I get a chance, I will marry; if I fail I will live by prostitution'].

Israelite men and women were forbidden to become shrine-prostitutes (**23:17**). These prostitutes worked in the temples associated with Canaanite gods, where sexual intercourse was associated with the fertility of the land. This behaviour was labelled detestable both because it involved the worship of foreign gods and because it violated the commandments regarding sexual purity.

Then, as now, prostitutes probably made good money, and it was possible to envisage a situation where a prostitute or a relative of theirs had made a vow to give money to the house of the Lord, or temple, and wished to use the money earned in prostitution to discharge the debt (**23:18**). All such money is to be rejected. God does not need money. The gift associated with a vow was meant to be a token of gratitude for what God had done for the person. But God refused to accept the implication that he had provided for their need through the sinful path of prostitution. They would have to find some other means to pay their vow.

A question arises here about what money Christian churches are prepared to accept. Should the church be prepared to accept money given to it if the money is the proceeds of corruption, crime, or gambling, or should we refuse to finance God's work with money that is earned in sin? When weighing what to do about such a gift, we need to be careful about jumping to wrong conclusions. It is not necessarily true that a man accused of corruption has earned every cent of his money by corruption. And a loose woman may have obtained money from sources other than prostitution. What is important is that every believer be taught that God desires our hearts before our money. In cases where money is obviously the proceeds of corruption or some other sin, the church should refuse to accept it, for to do so would be to compromise the purity of the gospel.

23:19-20 LENDING MONEY ON INTEREST The Angolan Umbundu proverb says, *Olombongo vi kuete ovolu* ['Money has legs']. It can disappear rapidly, leaving one in a position where one has to borrow money to stay alive. This was the situation in ancient Israel, where loans were needed to alleviate poverty and help fellow Israelites in times of crisis. Such loans are not the same as modern bank loans, mortgages and commercial loans that are needed to provide capital to cover major expenses and are paid back at a fixed rate over a number of years. Modern loans and banks have no equivalent in the economic structure of the time of Deuteronomy.

The reason that interest was forbidden on Israelite loans (**23:19-20**) was that such money was lent only in a time of crisis, and having to pay additional money in interest would only exacerbate the crisis that created the need for the loan. Moreover, the attitude of someone demanding interest would be wrong in a covenant community. The only reason someone was wealthy enough to make a loan was because God had blessed him or her. All possessions were given by God and were to be used for the good of the whole community, including blessing those who were in need. Loans should be made freely, without interest, to reflect the lender's own thankfulness to God. In return, the giver would continue to receive God's blessing. Israelites were, however, allowed to lend on interest to foreigners, since they were not members of the covenant community (23:20).

23:21-23 MAKING vows God did not require any vows from the Israelites other than a commitment to love and obey him. However, if someone chose to promise something to God, then it was important to be true to one's word and carry out the vow (**23:21, 23**). What is being called for here is complete honesty before God. This is the point Jesus underscores in his comments on vows in Matthew 5:33-37.

23:24-25 A NEIGHBOUR'S CROPS African societies traditionally allowed visitors to eat cassava from the field as well as sugarcane and corn, for, as the proverb puts it, *Ukombe elende o pita ombamba* ['A visitor is like a cloud that soon disappears']. The ancient Israelites had the same obligation to show hospitality to passersby. A visitor was allowed to satisfy his immediate appetite from his neighbour's vine or from his grain, but was not allowed to carry away supplies to be eaten later. Thus Jesus' disciples were not stealing from a farmer when they ate grain that they had picked as they walked through his field (Mark 2:23).

24:1-4 DIVORCE AND REMARRIAGE Two earlier passages have indicated that divorce was forbidden in certain circumstances (22:19, 29), implying that it was possible in others. This passage does not discuss what those circumstances are, but speaks vaguely of *something indecent about her* (**24:1a**). By the time of Jesus, the exact meaning of this phrase has become a topic of debate, which is one reason why the Pharisees raised this topic with Jesus (Matt 19:3).

The text in Deuteronomy does not focus so much on the reasons for the divorce as on the administrative arrangements involved. In Jewish culture, divorce proceedings were initiated only by the husband. There was, however, some protection for the woman in that he had to give her a *certificate of divorce* (**24:1b**), which proved that she was no longer married and was free to remarry. This is the provision that Jesus refers to in Matthew 5:31 and Mark 10:4.

If she did remarry and then found herself widowed or again divorced, the first husband was forbidden to remarry her (**24:2-4**). Thus he cannot help himself to any wealth she may have acquired through her second marriage (see comments on 22:19). Gomer, Hosea's wife whose story is told in the book of Hosea, was able to return to him despite her unfaithfulness because he had refused to divorce her. God used Hosea's love and mercy as an example of his own mercy and faithfulness to Israel despite her unfaithfulness to him (see also Jer 3:1-8).

It is, however, not clear why remarriage to a former wife was considered so offensive. Various explanations have been offered, ranging from the claim that it is only natural to be repulsed by such a remarriage to the argument that the ban on remarriage was meant to discourage impulsive divorce or second thoughts after a second marriage.

While this passage permits divorce, in the NT Jesus taught that it was only permitted by God, not approved of. Marriage was intended to be a lifelong commitment between one man and one woman (Matt 19:1-9; see also Gen 1:27; 2:24).

The comment that such remarriage of a previously divorced husband would *bring sin upon the land* indicates that this was another case in which improper sexual relations would affect far more than just the couple involved. This is certainly the case with HIV/AIDS, a disease that spreads rapidly where sexual purity is not maintained, affects the innocent who are infected by the guilty, and spreads death, grief and poverty across the land.

24:5 EXEMPTION FROM MILITARY SERVICE This law is similar to that in 20:7. A recently married man was exempted from military and other civic duties for a year. This gave the marriage time to settle and made it likely that the man would have descendants should he die in battle. One principle that can be drawn from this ruling is that God is interested not only in a pastor's ministry in the church, but also in his or her ministry to his or her spouse. Those who neglect their families because they are too busy at or for the church will not get a 'well done' from the Lord.

24:6 MILLSTONES NOT TO BE TAKEN IN PLEDGE In ancient Israel and throughout the Middle East, the grain that was used to make the staple food was ground between two stones, with the top one moving over the bottom one. Taking the whole mill or even just one of the stones as security for a debt would deprive a family of the means of preparing food. Once again the law demonstrates its concern to protect the poor from abuse.

24:7 KIDNAPPING The kidnapping described here is not the one that involves taking someone and threatening to harm them unless a ransom is paid, although it would apply to such situations. The situation is closer to the one in Africa, where children or adults are abducted and forced to live as slaves, sometimes having to carry supplies, prepare food, or even fight on behalf of their captors. Whether the thief keeps the person abducted as his personal slave or sells him or her into slavery to someone else, the penalty is the same – death. (**24:7**)

24:8-9 LEPROSY The disease referred to as 'leprosy' here is not the same as the modern disease with the same name. We are not told what the exact regulations are regarding people with this disease. Instead, readers are referred to some other instructions already given on the topic. Such instructions can be found in Leviticus 13–14. The people are simply exhorted to follow the instructions given by the priests (**24:8**). This reference to Miriam's leprosy may be intended to remind them that this disease can strike anyone in the community, regardless of rank, and may be a sign of God's displeasure (**24:9**; see also Num 12:9-16).

24:10-13 LEGISLATION RELATING TO PLEDGES This verse returns to the topic of security for loans, already discussed in 24:6. Loans were also discussed in 23:19-20, where Israelites were forbidden to charge interest on a loan. However, they were permitted to take some kind of security for the loan. But the dignity and property rights of the one requesting the loan were preserved. The person lending the money or property could not simply walk into the house and specify what possession he or she wished to take (**24:10**). Instead, the person had to wait outside and let the borrower produce whatever he wanted to offer as security (**24:11**). Often this was an article of clothing. If keeping it would cause severe hardship by depriving the poor person of the ability to keep warm at night, the lender was to return it in the evening (**24:12**). Such action would evoke gratitude and would be approved by God.

The principles underlying these restrictions on those making loans are still relevant today, both on the personal and the national level. Many African nations are burdened by heavy debts to the West, and campaigns such as Jubilee 2000 have been mounted to have these debts written off because they impose an intolerable burden on the poor. So far, little has been achieved.

24:14-15 PROTECTION FOR EMPLOYEES God is concerned for the just treatment of the poor. In an agricultural society, all those whose land could not support their families and who were forced to hire themselves out to others were necessarily poor. Regardless of whether the labourer was a fellow Israelite or a resident alien, he was to be given his wages promptly at the time appointed, which at that time was every evening. Should the employer renege on the promised payment, the labourer was entitled to cry out to God about such sinful neglect. The principle expressed here should guide employers and employees in Africa. Any employer who fails to pay employees what is due to them needs to be reminded that God is on the side of the employee and will discipline the employer for injustice. And employees who reach a dead end while trying to obtain what is due to

them should cry out to God and believe that He will act on their behalf.

24:16 PERSONAL RESPONSIBILITY Family solidarity was taken for granted in Semitic society at the time of Moses. Thus there are times when we see entire families being killed for the sins of individual members (Josh 7:25-26). However, this verse makes it clear that such group punishments were not to be the norm. We find special praise of King Amaziah, many years later, for his refusal to execute the families of those who had murdered his father (2 Kgs 14:6), which suggests that the Israelites had not always applied this principle. The view also contradicts the argument put forward by some that individual responsibility was a late concept in Israel. The Pentateuch clearly recognized the principle of personal responsibility.

24:17-18 PROTECTION OF THE WEAK AND DEFENCELESS Many ancient law codes insisted that the king must provide justice for defenceless people such as resident aliens, orphans and widows. The OT insists that this is also the responsibility of every member of society. The Israelites were reminded of what they had suffered when they were defenceless in Egypt. God had shown mercy to them, and they were to show mercy to others. They were not to have the attitude reflected in the Angolan Umbundu proverb *Po lofa via cimboto omanu va siya* ['People spit when a frog dies']. The implication of the proverb is that the poor are so unimportant that even their deaths go unnoticed. This is not to be the case in Israel.

24:19-22 GLEANING The concern for the poor extends to ensuring that they have access to some food supplies. Thus a farmer is not to be meticulous about harvesting every single head of corn, grape or olive in his field. After the reapers have passed though the field once, anything that is still there should be left for the destitute. This practice was followed in the days of Ruth, when she set out to glean food for herself and the widowed Naomi (Ruth 2). This instruction is repeated twice in the book of Leviticus (Lev 19:9-10; 23:22), each time with the comment 'I am the Lord your God'. God may have been making the point that such gifts to the poor were equivalent to offerings to him.

The repeated instruction to *remember you were slaves in the land of Egypt* (**24:22**) is made despite the fact that those Moses was addressing must have been over forty years old, and must have been young children at the time of the exodus. Their memories of slavery were likely to be hazy, but nonetheless the experience was not to be forgotten. Each generation had to identify with the nation's history and see how it should affect their present conduct.

25:1-3 CORPORAL PUNISHMENT Disputes between people are not to be solved by violence but are to be brought before the courts (**25:1**). If someone is judged to be in the wrong and deserving of corporal punishment, the courts will supervise its administration (**25:2**). This requirement also prevented individuals from meting out an inappropriate degree of punishment. The maximum approved level of punishment was forty lashes (**25:3**), a number also found in other legal codes from this period. In later Jewish law, the maximum was set at thirty-nine lashes to avoid any possibility of accidentally giving more than forty (see 2 Cor 11:24).

While a public beating was undoubtedly humiliating for the victim, it did not degrade him provided the number of lashes was kept within the set limits. The principle at work here is the same that is expressed in the Umbundu proverb *Ci longa longa omolã ohombo utue wahe vombia* ['A fool must be treated roughly to do him any good'].

25:4 Muzzling an ox In the ancient Near East, oxen were used for ploughing the soil when planting grain and for threshing the harvested grain. Threshing was done by spreading the stalks of the harvested crop over a threshing floor and then having an ox drag a threshing-sledge, that is, a board to which sharp stones were attached, round and round over the crop. The sledge separated the heads of grain from the stalks. The mix of grain and stalks was then separated by throwing it up into the air with a broad, flat winnowing fork, so that the wind would blow away the useless chaff while the heavier grains fell to the floor.

The same compassion that led to concern for the poor and the insistence that they be allowed to collect gleanings of the crop (24:19-22) was also extended to animals. The ox was not to be forced to work surrounded by food that it could not eat (**25:4**). Kindness was to be extended to all God's creatures.

In the NT, Paul quotes this verse to make the point that those who work for the church are entitled to be supported by the church (1 Cor 9:9; 1 Tim 5:18). A similar point is made by the Umbundu proverb *O munu apa a talavaya hapo aliya* ['Where someone works is where his bread comes from'].

25:5-10 Levirate marriage Because the Israelites had little concept of an afterlife, they looked for immortality through their sons, who would continue the family line and ensure that their names were not forgotten. Dying without a son was considered a disaster, and so legal arrangements were made to avoid this fate if at all possible through a levirate marriage, in which the dead man's wife married the man's brother (**25:5**). The first son born to this union would be regarded as the son of the dead man and would inherit his property (**25:6**). This arrangement also provided for the security of the widow. We see an example of how this worked in practice in the story of Ruth, who entered into a levirate marriage with Boaz.

But the brother was not always an enthusiastic participant in such arrangements, for the child, who would be regarded as his brother's son, would inherit land that might have come to his own family. If the dead brother had been the oldest, that child would be entitled to share of the firstborn, which would substantially reduce the amount the surviving brother would inherit. There is an example of this reluctance in the story of Tamar in Genesis 38:1-11. But whereas Tamar had to trick Judah into carrying out his responsibilities, Deuteronomy provided another option for a woman in this situation. She could summon the reluctant brother before the elders and there shame him by removing his sandal and spitting in his face (**25:7-9**). Thereafter, his family would be known as *The Family of the Unsandalled* (**25:10**), as a reminder that they had not cared for a brother and his widow. Presumably, this stigma would affect the willingness of other families to marry into this family.

In relating this to the African context and the practice of widow inheritance, we need to remember the dangers of possible transmission of HIV/AIDS. The practice is now dangerous for men and women, and so the church needs to consider other ways of providing for widows. These could include helping those without income start some form of business, helping to pay children's school fees, or some other forms of support possible. Some African churches have begun fellowship to offer emotional support to widows. All these creative ideas need to be blessed and encouraged by the church, for the challenge of AIDS will remain with us for years to come.

25:11-12 Grabbing a man's private parts Like the preceding law, this one is also related to the issue of having heirs. Presumably, the woman who takes this action to break up a fight could cause serious damage to the man and affect his ability to produce children. So even though she was acting in support of her husband, she is to be punished by having her hand cut off.

25:13-16 Weights and measures The law on using accurate weights relates to a situation that was common in the past (Amos 8:5; Mic 6:10-11) and still occurs today. Goods customers are buying are measured with a weight that is said to be a one-pound weight but is actually slightly lighter, so that a customer paying for a full pound of, say, sugar gets slightly less than a pound. However, when that same sugar was delivered to the merchant, he used a heavier 'one-pound' weight and received more than the one pound of sugar he paid for.

The principle behind this law relates to all commercial transactions. People should be given what they have paid for, without any attempt to cheat them.

25:17-19 The Amalekites to be exterminated Many of the laws in this section of Deuteronomy have focused on God's concern for the weak and exploited. The final injunction in this chapter expresses his judgment on those who do not share this concern. The Amalekites had apparently harried the rear of the long procession of Israelites and had killed the old, the weak and the ill who were lagging behind (**25:17-18**). They were guilty of crimes against humanity, and thus God instructed the Israelites to destroy them

(**25:19**; see also 1 Sam 14:48; 15:1-8). Later, he would issue similar threats against others guilty of similar cruelty (Amos 1:3-2:3) and would promise to use Israel as an instrument of divine punishment (Ps 149:7; Isa 41:14-15).

26:1-15 Two rituals accompanying offerings

The purely legal material of Deuteronomy has now ended, and this section of the book concludes with detailed instructions regarding the performance of two rituals: the presentation of firstfruits (26:1-11) and the presentation of the tithe of the third year (26:12-15). Because these two rituals were closely associated with agriculture, they may have been in particular danger of being contaminated by elements of Canaanite worship, which was focused on maintaining the fertility of the land. This may be why such careful attention is paid to the exact words to be spoken. Another reason for the careful explanation may be that the Israelites would not have an opportunity to celebrate these festivals under the eye of Moses. They would start to be celebrated only after the people had settled in the promised land (**26:1**).

26:2-11 LITURGY FOR FIRSTFRUITS The instructions for this liturgy start by stressing that what is offered are fruits of *the land that the Lord your God is giving you* (26:2). The constant references to 'the Lord your God' in this section (26:1, 2, 3, 4, 5, 10, 11) emphasize that it is not the pagan god Baal who is responsible for the fertility of the land and their present prosperity.

The firstfruit in the basket was obviously only a sample of the various agricultural products that had been grown on the land (**26:2**). This sample was to be presented to *the priest in office at the time* (**26:3**), meaning the chief priest at the central sanctuary. On handing the basket over to the priest, worshippers were to solemnly acknowledge that they were living in a land that had been promised to them by God. The ceremony would later conclude with the assertion that the gift of firstfruit was a grateful acknowledgment of this gift (26:10).

The priest was to *take the basket ...* and *set it down in front of the altar* (**26:4**). In 26:10, it seems to be implied that it is the worshipper who places the basket at the end of the ceremony. However, there is no real contradiction here, for the ceremony is so brief that the words and the actions would go together, and only the priests were permitted to go near the altar, so that the reference to the worshipper placing it there refers to the action done on his behalf by the priest.

While the basket is being placed, the worshipper makes a confession of faith (**26:5-10**) that summarizes the history of the people so far, from the days of the patriarchs to the exodus and entry into the promised land. Surprisingly, there is no reference to the need to obey God's commands, an instruction that is embedded in the similar historical review

in 6:20-25. The reason for this may be that in chapter 6 the focus is on passing the faith on to the next generation. Here, however, the focus is on the personal act of a worshipper who has accepted that faith and who is already acting in obedience to God's command.

While the ceremony is solemn, it is not sombre. It is followed by an instruction to *rejoice in all the good things* they have been given. This rejoicing is to be shared by the entire household and by Levites and resident aliens. It seems likely that this means that the offering of the firstfruits was followed by a special celebratory meal.

26:12-15 LITURGY FOR THE THIRD-YEAR TITHE Every third year the tithe was to be kept in the villages and used for the relief of the poor (**26:12**; see also 14:28-29), here specified as *the Levite, the alien, the fatherless and the widow,* and was thus outside the control of the priests at the central sanctuary. These priests would have had no way of knowing whether this offering had been made or not, and so people had to make a solemn declaration that they had complied with the law (**26:13**). At the same time, they had to assert that they had *not eaten of the tithe any of the sacred portion* while in mourning, had not *removed any of it while ... unclean, nor ... offered any of it to the dead* (**26:14**). The activities denied here may be associated in some way with Canaanite worship. The declaration closes with a prayer that God will bless Israel and her land.

26:16-19 A concluding exhortation

The entire section from 5:1 through these verses constitutes Moses' second address to the people. He has set out both the general principles of the covenant law and its specific requirements. He closes his speech with a reminder of God's call for wholehearted obedience (**26:16**) and with a reminder of two declarations that have been made. The first was that Israel had declared that it would accept the terms of the covenant that God offered them (**26:17**). The second was that God had declared the special status of Israel as *his people, his treasured possession* (**26:18**). This status carried with it the obligation to obey him, but it also would be accompanied by blessings that would bring the Israelites *praise, fame and honour* and by God's promise that they would *be a people holy to the Lord your God* (**26:19**). Here 'holy' means 'set apart for God'. God would ensure that this setting apart for himself was also manifested in a separation of the people from sin. Note that this promise is made to the people as a whole: it does not mean that every individual would receive 'praise, fame and honour'.

27:1-26 Covenant Renewal in the Promised Land

This chapter differs from those that precede and follow it by sometimes speaking of Moses in the third person, rather than presenting him as the main speaker that he has been up to this point. The other unusual feature of this chapter is that it describes two ceremonies that will need to be performed only once. All the other instructions in Deuteronomy refer to practices that are to be continued from generation to generation.

27:1-8 The final stipulations of the covenant

The direct reference to Moses (**27:1**), the first one since 5:1, indicates that this verse marks the start of another section of the book of Deuteronomy. This time Moses is joined by the elders, who will be responsible for ensuring that these commands are carried out once the people have crossed the Jordan, an event that still lies in the future (**27:2**).

Once the people have entered the promised land, they are to *set up some large stones and coat them with plaster* and write *all the words of the law* on them (**27:2-3**). The practice of recording important information on standing stones was common in the ancient Near East. Some of the inscriptions that have been found by archaeologists are as long as the second discourse in the book of Deuteronomy. However, it is also possible that 'all the words' does not refer to the complete text from 5:1 to 26:19 but to a summary of it. Clearly the law existed in written form from a very early age.

The stones were to be erected on Mount Ebal (**27:4**). In the same vicinity, the people were to build an altar. The instruction that no iron tools were to be used in shaping the stones of the altar (**27:5**; see also Exod 20:25) may be intended to prevent any carving of images on the altar, an act that would violate the second commandment (5:8). Burnt offerings and fellowship (peace) offerings were to be made on the altar. The burnt offerings would be totally consumed by fire (Lev 1:1-17), but parts of the fellowship offerings would be consumed in a joyful sacred meal (**27:6-7**). This conjunction of burnt offerings and fellowship offerings is common in the OT.

The erection of an altar on Mount Ebal even though there was already an altar in the Tent of Meeting, which was the central sanctuary, indicates that altars could also be erected in other places (see also 1 Sam 9:12). However, the main centre of worship was the altar associated with the Tent of Meeting.

27:9-10 A challenge

Once again, Moses speaks to *all Israel*, demanding the people's full attention. By accepting the terms of the covenant, they *have now become the people of the Lord your God* (**27:9**). The consequence of this is that they are to hear and obey God's words, including all the decrees that Moses issues in regard to the covenant renewal ceremony once they have entered the promised land (**27:10**). These verses underline the relationship between the covenant and obedience. The covenant came first and obedience was to be the people's grateful response to being chosen to be God's people.

27:11-26 The ceremony on Mount Ebal

The ceremony that Moses envisaged was impressive. The tribes, or representatives of them, were to take up positions on two mountainsides, facing each other across a narrow valley along which the road ran. Six of the tribes, namely, Simeon, Levi, Judah, Issachar, Joseph and Benjamin, all descendants of Jacob's wives Leah and Rachel, were commanded to stand on Mount Gerizim on the south. These tribes were *to bless the people* (**27:12**). The other six tribes, Reuben, Zebulun, Dan, Naphtali, Gad and Asher, the descendants of Leah and of Jacob's other wives, were to stand on Mount Ebal to the north peak *for the curses* (**27:13**). It seems that their positions symbolized the radical difference between the two possible fates that awaited the people, blessing if they obeyed, cursing if they did not (see also Matt 25:31-46).

Once the people were standing in the correct places, the Levitical priests on Mount Ebal recited the first of the curses in 27:15-26. Then *all the people* replied *Amen* (**27:15**), signalling that they agreed with this curse. The same pattern of proclamation and response was followed for each of the subsequent twelve curses. The number twelve may have been chosen to match the number of tribes in Israel.

The first curse falls on anyone who *carves an image or casts an idol*, encompassing any image made of wood, stone or metal. Making such an image would break both the first and the second commandment. The text stresses that this image is *the work of a craftsman's hands*, underlining the distance between such an artefact and the living Lord. The law had specified that anyone who did this should be put to death (ch. 13), but the curse here refers to anyone who does this *in secret*, implying that even though society would not know of and punish the crime, the person would still be under God's curse for doing something that the Lord detests.

The second curse relates to the one who dishonours his or her father and mother, an action that would violate the fifth commandment (**27:16**; see also 5:16). This curse would apply even if the punishment laid down in 21:18-21 was not implemented.

Whereas the first curse had related to God and the second to family relationships, the third one relates to neighbourliness and property rights (**27:17**; see also 19:14). The reason for moving a boundary stone would be to try to steal land from a neighbour. Boundary stones found in Mesopotamia that date from this period are inscribed with details of property rights and reminders about divine sanctions and protection.

The fourth curse is directed against anyone who *leads the blind astray on the road* (**27:18**). This curse reflects God's concern for the weak and disadvantaged. It may be meant literally, but it may also refer to any behaviour that takes advantage of or is cruel to someone with a disability.

The same theme is continued in the fifth curse, which is directed against all those who seek to take unfair advantages of weaker members of society such as *the alien, the fatherless or the widow* (**27:19**). Those who exploit the vulnerable need to remember that God is aware of their actions.

The next four verses deal with sexual offences. Those who commit such offences in secret may also escape judicial punishment, but they are nonetheless under God's curse. A curse rests on anyone who has sexual relationships with his father's wife (**27:20**); who has sex with an animal (**27:21**); who commits incest with his sister or half-sister (**27:22**); and who has sex with his mother-in-law (**27:23**).

The tenth and eleventh curses relate to someone who breaks the sixth commandment. Anyone *who kills his neighbour secretly* is cursed (**27:24**) and so is any hired assassin, who kills for money (**27:25**). Both of these people may seem to get away with their crimes, but are still under God's curse.

The twelfth and final curse is less specific than those that have preceded it. It is intended to make sure that no one finds a loophole in the list of curses and so feels free to sin. So the twelfth curse is all-inclusive; cursing anyone who *does not uphold the words of this law* (**27:26**). This verse makes it clear that any action that breaks God's law brings a curse on the one committing it (Gal 3:10-14).

28:1-68 Blessings and Curses

African people recognize God's warnings. There is an Angolan Umbundu proverb that says, *Vombela, vo vi kelu viombela lo va lende momo ame ndi lungowala omanu vange* ['I have warned you (of the coming rainy season) with lightning and with thunder; do you think that I have a sickle with which to cut the grass and thatch your roofs?']. People are to heed the signs and take the necessary action. For the Israelites, the action needed was a decision to obey God in order to avoid the curses mentioned in this chapter.

The previous chapter had given instructions for a future ceremony to take place in the promised land at which the covenant would be renewed and blessings and curses would be declared to the people. Now the focus returns to the present, and the style returns to that of an ancient Near Eastern treaty, in which the statement of the stipulations (5:1-26:19) is followed by a lengthy declaration of the consequences of obeying or breaking the treaty. The former will result in blessings, the latter in misery.

The blessings and curses are an important part of this book, for they teach that the world is rational and moral. We do not have to live in a world of turmoil, but can know the good things that God delights to give. On the other hand, evil will not go unpunished.

28:1-14 The blessings

The blessings that will follow from obedience are closely related to the basic human fears of political instability and famine. God assures the people that they and their offspring, whether living on the land or in the cities (**28:2b**), will enjoy prosperity and will be victorious over their enemies (**28:7**). They will not suffer crop failures but will be blessed with bountiful harvests (**28:4-5, 8, 11, 12**). In a region that was dominated by the worship of Baal and other fertility gods, it will be abundantly clear who is the real source of nature's bounty. Their prosperity will not go unnoticed by those around them, who would look up to them and seek their aid (**28:1, 10,** 12-13).

All these promises are firmly rooted in a covenant setting. Israel is reminded that God has chosen them (**28:9**) and that it is he who will give them this peace and prosperity – provided they do not turn to idolatry. They are reminded that all these blessings are conditional on obedience three times in this section: at the beginning, in the middle and at the end (**28:2a, 9b, 13-14**).

The blessings and curses are an important part of the teachings of this book that Yahweh's universe is rational and moral. Humankind is not left in a sea of doubt and danger. They can have confidence about the fundamental things in life because they know what Yahweh is like.

28:15-68 The curses

The curses are introduced with a section that exactly parallels 28:2-6, except that everything that was blessed there is cursed here because where the former deals with the results of obedience, this passage deals with the results of disobedience – the loss of all the benefits God had promised (**28:15-19**).

The picture of the life that follows disobedience is one of abject misery. Both humans and plants will be afflicted by disease and drought (**28:20-24**). The nation will be defeated by its enemies and bodies will be left to rot in the fields (**28:25-26**). God will be actively hostile to them and will afflict them with physical and mental ailments (**28:27-29**). He had protected them from these ailments when he had used them as plagues on the Egyptians (Exod 7–11) but now he will expose the Israelites to their ravages.

Whereas he has promised them good things in the land (wives, houses, vineyards, livestock and offspring), and had issued laws to protect the enjoyment of these things, disobedience will result in the loss of all pleasure in them and of the fruits of their hard work (**28:30-35, 38-42**). Women will be raped, houses seized, crops and livestock stolen or killed by diseases and insect plagues, and children will be marched away into slavery, never to return. They will not even have their own physical health (28:35).

The Israelites who were listening to Moses would still have had vivid memories of their years as slaves in Egypt, which would have increased their horror at the threat of renewed servitude in **28:36-37**. If they were disobedient, they would be deported from the promised land. They would not be taken to a nation that they knew, like Egypt, but to *a nation whom neither you nor your fathers have known*. Rather than serving the living God, they would be forced to serve lifeless gods of wood and stone. The people would have even lower status than the *resident alien* whom they were frequently exhorted to care for because they were underprivileged (**28:43-44**; compare 28:12-13).

At this point, the writer again pauses to remind his readers that the reason the nation will suffer such terrible disasters is because the people have not obeyed God wholeheartedly (**28:45-48**). Their fate will serve as a warning to others.

The text then returns to a prophetic description of the nation that God will use as his instrument of judgment. It is described as being *like an eagle swooping down* on its prey – an image that conveys the speed and strength of the enemy (**28:49**). This enemy nation will neither respect the old nor pity the young (**28:50**). They will take all that the land produces and leave no livestock, grain, wine and oil for Israel's consumption (**28:51**).

Once they have stripped the land, they will turn and besiege the cities (**28:52**). The Israelites will cower within them, forgetting that their own experience has shown that city walls offer no protection if God is angry with the inhabitants. The inhabitants of the cities will suffer such hunger that they will resort to cannibalism, eating their own children (**28:53**). More than that, they will refuse to share their terrible food even with those they love (**28:54-55**). Even the most fastidious of women will be reduced to regarding her babies as food to be kept for herself alone (**28:56-57**). These predictions came true in the sieges described in 2 Kings 6:28-29 and Lamentations 2:20.

The law had forbidden infant sacrifice and had called for food to be shared with the needy. Clearly, turning one's back on Yahweh leads to a terrible reversal of values.

The curses that accompany a failure to *carefully follow all the words of this law, which are written in this book* (**28:58**) and to honour the awesome name of Yahweh are summarized again in 28:58-62. Then the text moves on to the most terrible threat to a people who have been promised land – the threat of exile and a return to the slavery they had known before (28:63-68). Israel will then know no security (**28:65-67**). God himself will take the initiative in punishing the people and sending them *back in ships to Egypt* (**28:68**), presumably as captives in the slave trade. Once there, they will face the ultimate ignominy in that they will be so worthless that the Egyptians will not even be interested in buying them.

Sadly, many of the curses described in this text are all too familiar in Africa. Africa's peoples dreamed of a better future when their countries obtained independence, but the reality has not matched their dreams. Many have seen their lives and prosperity destroyed in ongoing civil wars. May God help our leaders to realize that leadership should not come from the barrel of a gun!

29:1-30:20 Moses' Third Address

Some scholars regard chapters 29 and 30 as a summary of the material contained in chapters 1 to 28, which means that they repeat the words of earlier chapters. Such duplicate copies of the texts of treaties were not unusual in the ancient Near East. Other scholars regard chapter 29 as a summons preceding the final taking of the covenant oath, in 30:11-20. Whichever view is taken, it is clear that chapter 29 is also patterned on a Near Eastern treaty. It begins with a review of the Lord's works in the past (29:1-8), issues a call to enter into the covenant (29:9-15), warns that the curses of the covenant will fall on rebels (29:16-29) – although ultimate restoration is intended (30:1-10) – and ends with a call to a firm decision to accept the covenant (30:11-20).

29:1-8 Historical Review

The opening words of the third address are similar to those at the start of this book (1:1-5). The covenant that will be made in the land of Moab is contrasted with the one made at Horeb (**29:1**; 1:5, 5:2-3). As the phrase *in addition* suggests, the covenant of Deuteronomy 5–26 is very similar to that given in Exodus 19–24, but also contains numerous new regulations.

As mentioned above, the text starts with a historical review (29:2-8) and a brief reference to the *great trials ... miraculous signs and great wonders* that Israel has been privileged to see. Yet despite these and other evidences of God's power and care, the people still lacked insight into God's nature and a deep love for him (**29:4**).

In **29:5-6** God himself speaks to the people, reminding them that he had led them for *forty years in the desert*. The 'you' here clearly refers to the nation as a whole, which had shared in these experiences even if many of Moses' audience may have been too young to remember all of the events in the wilderness. There God had provided them with clothing, food and drink that had not been prepared with human resources. Instead of having to patch their clothes or weave new cloth, their clothes and shoes had lasted well. Instead of having to bake their own bread, they were fed with manna, and instead of having to brew wine or beer, they drank the water that God supplied (29:5-6). Then Moses resumes the speech in **29:7-8**. He cites further evidence of Yahweh's help in conquering the area in which they now live, and from which they will be moving on into the promised land.

29:9-15 Exhortation to Commitment

Now comes the appeal to enter the covenant, beginning with the words *Carefully follow the terms of this covenant*. We are entering the final stage of the covenant ceremony, immediately preceding the taking of the oath. That is why the entire covenant community is assembled *in the presence of the Lord your God* (29:10). Those assembled include tribal heads and other leaders, ordinary Israelite men, women and children, and resident aliens who are their servants (29:10-11). (The phrase he *who chops your wood and he who draws your water* seems to have been a standard way of referring to those performing menial tasks.) The purpose for which they had assembled was *to enter into a covenant with the Lord your God ... that he may be your God* (29:12-13a). The covenant was to be confirmed with a solemn oath. In terms of this covenant Yahweh confirmed that Israel were his people and that he himself was their God, as he had promised the patriarchs (29:13b). The covenant was being entered into not only with the people who were present at the time but also with those who were not present, including those yet to be born (29:14-15). We may ask how one generation can enter into a covenant that is binding on future generations. But the answer is that one of the participants in this covenant does not change. The Israelites' descendants had no inalienable right to be parties to the covenant; rather they were granted that right because God is faithful to his promise to bless those who love him and obey his commandments. Each new generation has to be taught of God's saving actions, and must in turn accept their responsibility to love and obey him.

29:16-21 Warning Against Hypocrisy

During their time in Egypt and wanderings in the wilderness, the Israelites had observed the idols that were worshipped by other nations (29:16-17) – and had even been tempted to engage in idol worship themselves (Num 25). Moses stresses that these idols are mere constructs of wood, stone, or metal, and points out that the desire to worship them is like the root of a plant that will, when grown, produce only poisonous fruit (29:18; see also 32:32; Hos 10:4).

The type of person who is tempted to idolatry may listen to the recital of the blessing and curses accompanying the covenant, but ignore them, thinking, *I will be safe, even though I persist in going my own way* (29:19). Such an attitude can lead only to disaster, for both fertile and arid land, and will bring ruin first to the individual and then to the nation. The seriousness of this disobedience is underscored by the fact that God will never pardon the offender and that *his wrath and zeal will burn against that man.* (29:20). He will suffer all the curses that have been recorded in Deuteronomy and will endure the ultimate disaster of having his very name forgotten (29:20-21).

29:22-28 A Lesson for Posterity

Moses now reminds the people of what the land will be like should all the curses in the book come into effect. He does this by describing what it will look like to their descendants and to foreigners in that future time. It will be a wasteland, with its soil ruined by salt and sulphur, so that nothing will grow there. It will be as thoroughly destroyed as Sodom and Gomorrah (Gen 19). Given that the Dead Sea was on the border of Moab, the Israelites would have had a vivid idea of what such a landscape might look like. When foreigners ask what had provoked Yahweh to such destruction, the answer will have to be *this people abandoned the covenant of the Lord ... and went off and worshipped other gods* (29:25-26). In response, the land had been destroyed and the people exiled (29:27-28). 'The modern reader of these verses who knows something of the suffering of the Jews over the many centuries since these verses were written may ask again and again: *why has Yahweh done thus to this land?* In terms of Deuteronomy, the answer would be *it is because they forsook the covenant of Yahweh*' (TOT).

29:29 Secret Things and Revealed Things

The final verse of this chapter makes the point that although there is much about God and his actions that we do not know or understand, there are certain things that have been clearly revealed. We are not to worry ourselves about *the secret things*, which are God's concern. Instead we are to concentrate on what has been revealed, particularly the law as given in this book, and are to make sure that we and our descendants live in obedience to what we do know of God's will.

30:1-10 Repentance and Forgiveness

Yet even if the people of Israel fail to obey God and are scattered among the nations (30:1), that will not be the end of the story. If they wholeheartedly return to God again (30:2, 10), he will restore all that they have lost, and more (30:3-9). They will again enjoy all his blessings, and he will somehow work to make them love him more deeply by circumcising their hearts (30:6). This promise offers hope even when the nation sinks into times of dark despair.

30:11-20 A Solemn Appeal to Choose Life

The time has now come for the final appeal to the people to make a clear decision in regard to the covenant. Moses starts by reminding them that all the terms and conditions have been spelled out very clearly. They cannot say that they lack knowledge of the terms, or that it is too difficult to grasp. The terms are clear and comprehensible and all that is still needed is their commitment to keeping them (30:11-14; see also Rom 10:6-8). They are faced with a simple choice between *life and prosperity* or *death and destruction* (30:15-18). Moses urged the people to choose the route of love for God that led to life, pointing out that *the Lord is your life* (**30:19-20**). His appeal still rings in the ears of Christians, for we are called to love the one who described himself as 'the way, the truth and the life' (John 14:6).

31:1-34:12 Moses' Last Acts and Death

The first thirty chapters of the book of Deuteronomy comprise three long discourses by Moses. But from chapter 31 on, the focus is on the closing days of Moses' life and his final instructions. Even these instructions contain some feature of ancient treaties, such as the instructions on where the treaty document is to be kept (31:24-29), who is to be the leader of the community that is subject to the terms of the treaty (31:1-8, 14-23) and a promise of the blessing to be enjoyed by the tribes (ch. 33). The book concludes with an account of the death of Moses (ch. 34).

31:1-8 The Presentation of Joshua

Moses' final words are addressed to the people (31:1-6), to Joshua (31:7-8) and to the priests (31:9-13). He starts by reminding the people of his advanced age, which is making it impossible for him to lead them any more (**31:2a**). He is a hundred and twenty years old – ten years older than the age the Egyptians considered the traditional life span of a wise man. The extra ten years may be yet another symbol of Moses' superiority to the wise men of Egypt. He was aware that his time as leader was coming to an end but reminds them that he is not their true leader – Yahweh is. Moses would not cross the Jordan, but *the Lord your God himself will cross over ahead of you* (**31:2b-3a**). Their human leader, who would act as God's deputy, would now be Joshua (**31:3b;** see also 1:38; 3:28; Josh 14:11). This would have come as no surprise to the people, for Joshua had already been set apart as their future leader (1:38; Num 27:18-23). He would lead them in the next stage of the advance into the Holy Land. The people are not to be afraid, as they had been earlier (1:26), but are to advance with confident obedience (**31:5-6**).

Joshua is then addressed specifically and is told to be strong and resolute (**31:7**) – an encouragement that is repeated many times (31:8, 23; Josh 1:6-9, 18), suggesting the difficulty of the task he faced. His source of confidence is the fact that God had promised them the land (31:7) and to be with him at all times (**31:8**). Christ made a similar promise to believers when he commissioned them for their task, which was not merely to occupy a country but to go into all the world (Matt 28:20).

31:9-13 Covenant Renewal Ceremony

Moses' upbringing in Egypt had clearly given him the gift of literacy, and so here he commits the law he had been presenting to the people in his discourses to writing. The written text is then handed over to the priests and elders, who are to care for it (**31:9**). The reference to the priests as carrying *the ark of covenant of the Lord* is a reminder that the ark contained the stone tablets on which the Ten Commandments had been inscribed. (Exod 25:16; 1 Kgs 8:9). Moses' law is to be kept safe next to the ark. However, it is not to be kept safe by being shut away from the people. Every seventh year, *in the year for cancelling debts, during the Feast of Tabernacles,* which was one of the set feasts for which the people had to travel to the central sanctuary, the law would be read aloud to the entire nation (**31:10-11**). Knowledge of the law was not to be restricted to the small group of 'experts', the priests; nor was it something that could be known only by adult men. It was to be read to everyone: men, women, children and resident aliens (**31:12**). All were to know their rights and their responsibilities. The period of seven years between readings was also enough to ensure that every child should hear the entire law read at least once in their childhood.

This passage reminds us of the importance of obeying the law of the Lord from generation to generation and of passing on knowledge of the law to the whole population. It would be wonderful if those African nations in which there is a significant Christian influence used one of their days of national celebration primarily for hearing Scripture read. Yet even if a nation does not organize such a day, churches could do so themselves. While doing so, they would have to take care that the whole law is read and not just some favourite portions of Scripture. A nation that keeps the law of God before it is blessed by God.

31:14-23 Divine Charge to Moses and Joshua

The Tent of Meeting was the place where the Lord often met with people when an important announcement was to be made. Thus a divine summons to the Tent of Meeting was always a solemn matter, even if it had not been accompanied by a warning that Moses' death was imminent (**31:14**). It is also striking that in the past it had been only Moses who met with Yahweh at the Tent (Exod 33:9), but now Joshua, his successor, is ordered to accompany him. Once again the Lord appeared as a pillar of cloud at the entrance to the tent (**31:15**).

The Lord speaks first to Moses, telling him that despite all the work he has done and his careful presentation of the covenant, the people will soon forget their words and break the covenant (**31:16**). Their unfaithfulness is described in vivid language: *they will prostitute themselves to the foreign gods.* Given the sexual element in Canaanite religion, this may refer to literal prostitution, but it may also simply be a symbolic way of referring to unfaithfulness in general. God will be angry and will be forced to punish them, and the people will begin to question whether he is with them at all (**31:17-18**). So God has one last task for Moses. To make sure that the people will understand what is happening and why, God commissions Moses to write a song that will explain the covenant and that will be a witness, so that the people cannot deny that they know the terms of the covenant (**31:19-21**). The mere reading of the law every seven years would not be enough to keep the people faithful to God. Nor could a song. But a song that would be easily remembered and passed on from generation to generation was a way of helping people remember who God was and what he had done for them. Our hymns in church should fulfil the same function and should not merely be fun to sing but should help our congregations remember the truths they hear proclaimed from the pulpit. This way of passing on knowledge by incorporating it in a song is by no means foreign to Africa, where the events of one's life are remembered in the form of songs and sayings.

Then God turns to Joshua. His commission is brief and does not look to the distant future but to the immediate situation. It repeats the call for courage and determination and assures him that God will be with him in the days that lie ahead (**31:23**). This is a promise that God has given to many of his servants over the centuries.

The fact that the instruction to Moses to write the song and the song itself are separated by the words of Joshua's commissioning in 31:23 may be deliberate. The song warns Israel of the dangers of disloyalty. In the time that follows, they are to be loyal to Joshua and to God.

31:24-30 The Place of the Law

Some commentators see the instruction in **31:24-26** as an expansion of what was said in 31:9-13, where Moses is also described as writing down *this law* and giving it to the priests for safekeeping. Others argue that 31:24 should be read as 'this song' rather than 'this law', and that the song, too, was kept beside the ark. They would make a similar change in 31:26. While the second approach is attractive in that it ties this whole section together by focusing exclusively on the song, there is no evidence of another reading in the Hebrew manuscripts. It seems more likely that the aim in referring to the law here was to establish the credibility of the song as a *witness against you* because of their failure to keep the law.

Moses argues that the need for the witness of the song is because the people have already rebelled against God while he was their leader and are even more likely to do so after he has died (**31:27**). So he summons all the elders and officials of the tribes (**31:28**) to hear the words of the song, which will be a witness against them when God puts Israel on trial. He calls *heaven and earth* as witnesses to the fact that the people had been warned of the consequences of disobedience. The image of God launching a court case against his unfaithful people is one that is repeated in other OT passages, such as Psalm 51, Jeremiah 2 and Micah 6:1-8.

Moses repeats what the Lord has told him in 31:16-18 about Israel's future failure (**31:29-30**), before launching into his song, which was an indictment of Israel's unfaithfulness. The words of this song could be applied to Israel at many times in her long history.

32:1-43 The Song of Moses

This was not the first song Moses had written. The first had been written near the start of his ministry and was a song of triumph after the crossing of the Red Sea (Exod 15:1). This song is a song of warning, a valuable farewell gift for, as an Angolan Umbundu proverb says, *Waku lungula, waku telekela ohombo longombe* ['A warning is equivalent to the gift of a goat or an ox']. The song is written in a literary form that would have been familiar to at least some of the Israelites. Moses had probably encountered it himself while at pharaoh's court. The form is that of an official complaint by an overlord about a rebellious vassal. The king's messenger starts by summoning witnesses and recounting the benefits the king has given to the vassal, before moving on to recount the ingratitude of the vassal that has sparked the rebellion.

This song begins with a summoning of heaven and earth as witnesses (**32:1**; see also 4:26; 31:28; Isa 1:2; Mic 6:1-2). Then, thinking in terms of the rain that falls from heaven and the earth that absorbs it, Moses prays that his teaching will be as life-giving and refreshing as *dew, like showers on new grass, like abundant rain on tender plants* (**32:2**).

The song itself then moves into a summons to praise God (**32:3-4**). Here God's faithfulness and uprightness are described in general terms. By the final verse of the song, the summons to praise will be rooted even more in Israel's experience of living as God's people. One of the key images used for God here is *the Rock*. This image recurs several times in this passage alone (32:15, 18, 30, 31) and is repeated throughout the OT (see 1 Sam 2:2; 2 Sam 22:47; Ps 18:2, 31, 46; 19:14; 28:1; 31:2, 3; 42:9; 89:26; 95:1; Hab 1:12). A rock is a place of stability in a flood and a place of refuge in war, when one can hide behind a rock, or fight with a wall of rock preventing attack from the rear. It represents God's unchangeableness and the security he offers in a dangerous world. The image has universal appeal and has been picked up in many hymns such as 'Rock of ages, cleft for me' and 'O safe to the rock that is higher than I'.

The declaration of God's goodness is followed by an accusation. God *does no wrong* (32:4), but his people have *acted corruptly;* where he is *upright*, his people are *warped and crooked* (**32:5**). The contrast leads to a passionate question: Is this the way to repay a Father and Creator for his care? (**32:6**).

Moses then goes on to outline God's care for his people through the years (32:7-14). The older generation were supposed to have passed on a knowledge of this care to the succeeding generations (**32:7**). Moses reminds them that God had chosen them (**32:8-9**), had cared for them in the wilderness (**32:10-12**) and had brought them into the fertile land of Canaan with its abundance of food (**32:13-14**).

But Israel had abused the goodness of God. The nation is referred to as *Jeshurun*, a name that literally means 'the upright one' (32:15; see also 33:5, 26; Isa 44:2), but had ceased to be upright and had begun to behave like an animal that was spoiled by having too much rich food. God's kindness had resulted in the people becoming fat, lazy and reluctant to serve God. Comfortable in their fields and with their stomachs full, they no longer saw a need for a Rock and turned to worshipping other gods, even though such gods had done nothing for them in the past and were in fact demons rather than divinities (**32:15-17**). This is gross ingratitude to the one who had both fathered them and been the mother who gave them birth (**32:18**).

God responds by pronouncing his judgment on children who treat their parent in this way in 32:19-25. Instead of blessing them, he will turn his face away from them as they suffer the curses associated with breaking the covenant (**32:20**). The people had decided to worship what was *no god*, and so he will respond by allowing them to suffer so much that they will even be envious of those who are *not a people* (**32:21**). (A similar wordplay occurs in Hos 1:9, 2:23.) There will be no escape from the fire of divine wrath, for it will burn even *to the realm of death below and* will *devour the earth and its harvests, and set on fire the foundations of the mountains* (**32:22**). The curses listed in **32:23-25** are similar to those listed in chapter 28: famine, pestilence, wild beasts, violence and death.

Yet although Israel merits annihilation (**32:26**), God cannot bring himself to take the final step and *blot out their memory from mankind.* His reason is that if he were to do this, Israel's enemies would take the credit, saying, *Our hand has triumphed: the Lord has not done all this* (**32:27**). The nations need to recognize that God is in control.

Moses laments that Israel is a nation *without sense* (**32:28**). They will not heed his warning and avoid the bitter fate that he foresees (**32:29**). They need to consider that it is possible for a small force to overcome a whole nation only if God abandons that nation (**32:30**). They will find this true

WORSHIP AND PRAISE

Worship and praise are inseparable in Christian experience. To praise is to offer thanks and honour to God – to glorify him, especially in songs and with dancing. It can be as simple as the everyday greeting *Bwana Asifiwe* meaning 'Praise the Lord'. It can also be as elaborate as a three-hour festival of praise featuring presentations by Christian artists and choirs. In a typical African church, worship also includes acts of homage such as bowing down, kneeling with hands raised above one's head and prostrating oneself before God (Neh 8:5-6; Rev 4:9-10).

African traditional religion (ATR) has no tradition of corporate worship in a building like a church or mosque. Rather, worship takes place in the open at a sacred place such as a particular tree or stream. But these places are not used for weekly congregational worship. A congregation is involved only during annual or seasonal festivals. At home, the head of a family regularly performs simple worship by chanting the praise-names of a god or ancestor and pouring a daily libation to a household idol. Whether simple or elaborate, worship in ATR is incomplete without sacrifices and offerings.

ATR also differs from Christian worship in that it rarely worships the Supreme Being directly. Instead sacrifices are offered to the divinities and ancestors believed to be mediators between God and people. This worship is utilitarian: 'African peoples do not thirst after God for his own sake alone. They seek to obtain what he gives, be that material or even spiritual; they do not seem to search for him as the final reward or satisfaction of the human soul or spirit' (John Mbiti).

In ATR, the gods exist for humans and the main goals of worship are to restore the balance between humanity and the spirit beings, to ward off evils such as sickness, failure and barrenness and to enhance success.

Many of these traditional concepts have been brought into Christianity, as illustrated in a Nigerian TV drama in which a couple consult a herbalist about money that is owed to them. The herbalist gives the man a concoction and assures him that the money will arrive soon. When the cheque comes, the couple dance, singing "He is a miracle-working God!" They have one foot in Christianity and the other in ATR. This type of syncretism is forbidden in the Bible.

The key to the meaning and purpose of worship in the OT is found in Exod 20:1-8. Jesus quoted this passage when the devil tempted him with an offer of all the kingdoms of the world in exchange for worship. Jesus responded with 'Away from me, Satan! For it is written: worship the Lord your God, and serve him only' (Matt 4:8-10). It is clear that the object of biblical worship is God alone.

Biblical worship is rooted in redemption, relationship and representation. All three are included in Christ's definition of worship: 'God is spirit and his worshippers must worship in spirit and in truth' (John 4:24). Worshippers of Yahweh have been redeemed by the blood of the Lamb. They have a dynamic relationship with him as his sons and daughters (John 1:12) and represent him in the world as his ambassadors (2 Cor 5:20). Worship flows from gratitude (Rev 5:9-10), proclaims God's greatness and glory (Ps 19:1) and anticipates Christ's return (1 Cor 11:26).

Tokunboh Adeyemo

in their own history, as they enter Canaan and drive out the nations that live there, but they will also find themselves being judged if they turn from their Rock and start to worship the inadequate gods of their enemies (**32:31**). Even these enemies are prepared to concede that Israel's God is very different from their own and that he has acted powerfully (Exod 14:26; Num 23, 24; Dan 4:34-35).

Israel's enemies are depicted as vines, drawing their sustenance from things that God hates, as did Sodom and Gomorrah, and thus their fruit is bitter and poisonous (**32:32-33**). They should not think that they will escape judgment, for God has stored up their evil fruit in his storehouse (**32:34-35**). At the proper time, he will punish them. God states that *it is mine to avenge.* This verse is quoted in Romans 12:19 and Hebrews 10:30 to support Paul's point that Christians ought to live at peace with all others and should never seek revenge. While governments may sometimes punish wrongdoing (Rom 13:4), no individual should assume that he or she is entitled to exact the revenge that belongs only to God. In the original context, God's vengeance was directed against Israel's enemies, who reaped what they had sown.

While God is zealous in punishing evil, he is also anxious to forgive and save those who repent of their sin (**32:36**). His judgment of the wicked enemies of Israel will be accompanied by compassion for his people (32:36) who will recognise the futility of serving false gods (**32:37-38**). God himself announces that he is the sole ruler of the universe: *I myself am he! There is no god besides me* (32:39). Only he can *put to death and ... bring to life,* wound and heal, and no power can resist him (**32:39-42**).

Caught up in his vision of the majesty of God, Moses tells the nations of the world to rejoice along with Israel in this God who *will avenge the blood of his servants* and bring judgment on his enemies. The RSV states that God will *make atonement for his land and people* (**32:43**). The word translated 'make atonement' literally means 'cover' and presents an image of God drawing a cover over the guilt of his people. He will not only forgive them but also remove from view the wrong they have done. It is with this promise that the song ends.

32:44-47 Moses' Final Exhortation

After Moses and Joshua had recited this song to the people, Moses charged them to take these words to heart and to see to it that their children obeyed the law of God (**32:44-46**). The song and the law are treated as intimately connected, but the law is the most important – so important, in fact, that Moses takes pains to remind them that it is more than just words. The law is the very life of Israel (**32:47**). If they obey it, they will have a long and blessed life in the promised land.

32:48-52 Command to Ascend Mount Nebo

On the same day that Moses delivered his final address, God told him to go *up into the Abarim range* and to climb Mount Nebo, where he would die (**32:48-50**; Num 27:12-14). Aaron, his brother, had died on Mount Hor (Num 33:37-39), and now Moses, too, was to die on a mountain top (32:50). Moses is reminded that the reason he will die before entering the promised land is that he *broke faith* with God at Meribath Kadesh (**32:51**; see also 1:37; 3:26; 4:21; Num 20:10-12; 27:14). It is not clear exactly what Moses did that was wrong, although several suggestions have been made. Some argue that Moses struck the rock twice, thus displaying anger; others that Moses and Aaron made arrogant claims for themselves by asking, 'Shall we bring water forth for you out of this rock?'; still others that Moses allowed the people to provoke him to speak rash words (Ps 106:32-33); and others that Moses and Aaron failed to provide proper leadership when the spies brought back their report. Whatever the exact sin, the result had been a failure to uphold God's holiness and thus a lessening in God's authority among the Israelites. Consequently God had forbidden them entrance to the promised land, showing that not even his chosen leaders were exempt from his judgment. But he did permit Moses to see the land from a distance (**32:52**).

33:1-29 Moses' Blessing

An Angolan Umbundu proverb says, *O vinga olonjila o kava; o vinga omanu ka kavi* ['Be not weary in well doing; in trying to get people to do right']. It is common in Africa for the elderly to give instructions to their close family in the last days of their life. These instructions include blessings and guidance on how each individual is supposed to behave in the group. Metaphors, proverbs and wise saying as well as some catch songs are used to help the family to understand what they ought to do and how to live in harmony.

Moses, too, issues his final blessings and guidance to the tribes of Israel as his death approaches (**33:1**). In this he is like the patriarchs, whose dying blessings are recorded in Genesis 27:7, 49:1 and 50:16. As is clear from those accounts, such blessings were powerful and would be fulfilled. Moses himself is here referred to as *the man of God*, a title that clearly became closely associated with him (see Josh 14:6). Elsewhere in the OT the same phrase is used to refer to a prophet (1 Sam 9:6, 10; 1 Kgs 13:1, 8; 2 Kgs 4:7, 9, 16).

The blessing is presented in the form of a psalm that starts with a description of the majesty of God (33:2-5), a theme to which Moses will return in 33:26-29. Verse **33:2** is very similar to Deborah's song of triumph (Judg 5:4-5), Habakkuk 3:3 and the war song in Psalm 68. God is shown as leading his people in triumph from Sinai to their present location and as having given them the law in love (**33:3-4**).

He thus deserves the position of king over the Israelites (**33:5**; Exod 15:18; Judg 8:23). Here the nation is referred to as 'Jeshurun', the poetic term that means 'the upright one' and emphasizes the high calling of the people of Israel.

The opening words of Moses' blessing thus sketch out the realities that underlie the blessing he is about to give: the people have already been delivered and protected by God, they have been given the laws they will need to govern themselves and a government in which God is king over the leaders of the people. If they are to enjoy the blessings, they need to remember these facts.

Moses then goes on to bless each of the tribes individually, but leaves out the tribe of Simeon. This tribe may have been omitted because Moses could not pronounce a blessing on a people God has just punished with a plague. A man from the tribe of Simeon had been the chief culprit in the incident described in Numbers 25:6-14. The very low numbers for the tribe of Simeon in the census recorded in Numbers 26:5-62 (ten thousand fewer men than any other tribe) suggest that most of the twenty-four thousand who died from the plague were from that tribe. These events took place towards the end of Moses' life and may account for Moses' refraining from blessing them.

The tribe of Reuben is blessed with life and numbers (**33:6**), perhaps in contrast to the deaths the tribe had suffered when Dathan and Abiram had rebelled (Num 16:1-30).

God's help is requested for the tribe of Judah in its conflicts with its enemies (**33:7**). Levi, too, is blessed with God's blessing on his work and protection in the smiting down of his enemies (**33:11**). The Levites' blessing is far more detailed than that of most of the other tribes. They were placed in charge of the Urim and Thummim, which seem to have been two flat stones used for finding guidance (**33:8a**). The implication of being in charge of these stones is that this group are to have a special role as the teachers and priests of Israel (33:10; 18:1-8; 27:9-26; 31:24-25). In this case, *the man you [God] favoured* must be Levi.

The interpretation of **33:8b** is difficult because Scripture contains no record of the role that this tribe played at Massah (see 6:16) and Meribah (32:51; see also Num 20:13; 27:14). The individual whose faith was tested at these places by the grumbling of the people was Moses himself, as the people showed their lack of faith that God would provide (see Ps 81:7; 95:8). However, Moses was himself from the tribe of Levi (Exod 6:16-20), so it is possible that he is here seen as representative of the whole tribe. It is also possible that the text is implying that the whole tribe of Levi was tested like the rest of the Israelites by the shortage of water, but that this tribe remained faithful to God's covenant, no matter what their external circumstances.

The zeal of the tribe of Levi for the Lord was demonstrated in the incidents described in Exodus 32:25-29 and Numbers 25:6-13, when others had abandoned the covenant. It was on occasions like these that they had put their faithfulness to the Lord's covenant even above the claims of family (**33:9-10**). Those who are faithful to God's word are best placed to proclaim it and administer it.

The tribe of Benjamin was assured that it could trust God, for it was carried between his shoulders, just as a shepherd might carry an animal needing care (**33:12**; see also Luke 15:5).

The tribe of Joseph, which comprised the two subtribes of Ephraim and Manasseh (**33:17b**), also received a lengthy blessing, with a detailed description of the fruitfulness of their land in the hill country and the blessings they would enjoy from *him who dwelt in the burning bush* (**33:13-16a**; see also Exod 3:2). These tribes will clearly be powerful both among the Israelites and in relation to other nations (**33:16b-17a**).

The tribes of Zebulun and Issachar are assured of prosperity. Whereas Joseph enjoyed the fruits of the hill country, they will enjoy the fruits of the sea, in the form of both seafood and trade (**33:18-19**).

The tribe of Gad had chosen to take over part of the region that had belonged to Sihon (3:12, 16) and had defended their choice before *the heads of the people* (**33:20-21**; see also Num 32). They would need to be fierce and strong as lions in the position they had chosen on the border of Israel.

If the tribe of Gad was like a lion, the tribe of Dan was like a lion's cub, strong and vigorous and coming from an area that was known for the quality of its livestock (**33:22**; see also 32:14).

The tribe of Naphtali was promised God's blessing in the fertile land around the Sea of Galilee (**33:23**).

Last, but not least, for it is described as *most blessed* is the tribe of Asher, which was given land famous for its olive oil, whence the reference to bathing *his feet in oil* (**33:24-25**). Asher's territory was on the northern borders of the promised land and so would be vulnerable to attack, but the tribe was reassured that their defences would be strong and that they themselves would have all the strength they needed.

All of these blessings anticipate the life that will be theirs once they occupy the promised land, where they will enjoy God's gifts of material prosperity and physical protection. The specific blessings mentioned by Moses represent the details of the benediction given in Numbers 6:22-27.

Moses concludes his blessing in the same way he began, with a triumphant celebration of God's power and of his wonderful goodness to Israel. He speaks of God as being above his people (*he rides on the heavens*), under his people (*underneath are the everlasting* arms), in front of his people (*he will drive out your enemy before* you) and around them (as their *refuge*) (**33:26-27**). With such a God on their side, it is no wonder that the people can anticipate a new life of peace and prosperity (**33:28**). It is no wonder that Moses, reminded of what a saviour and defender his people enjoy, cries out: *Blessed are you, O Israel!* No wonder, too, that he can end with a confident assertion of victory over all Israel's enemies (**33:29**).

The whole of the book of Deuteronomy has dealt with the question of how the people of Israel will live after they have entered their own land. They have been constantly reminded that the Lord is the one who will bless them if they obey the laws that he has given them. Moses' blessing is a catalogue of the blessings they will enjoy provided they remain faithful to the Lord who has been and will be their deliverer.

34:1-12 Farewell to Moses

In Moses' final act of obedience he ascends Mount Nebo (**34:1a**; see 32:49). He climbs to the top of *Pisgah*, a word that denotes the mountain's highest peak. From this peak it is possible on a clear day to see all of the land of Israel, the land that the Lord had promised to show Moses but had forbidden him to enter (**34:1b-4**). There is some evidence that this viewing of the land may even have had an element of legal significance, in the sense of a man viewing a property that he was to possess. This land had first been viewed by Abraham; now Moses was seeing it; and soon it would belong to the people whom God had prepared to live there.

Moses died alone and was buried on the mountain. The words *He buried him* (**34:6a**) have been taken to mean that Yahweh himself buried Moses. No attempt was made to venerate his tomb. His memory would be forever honoured, but no object would become a place of pilgrimage and possibly of idolatry (**34:6b**).

Moses is described as having been a vigorous 120-year-old (**34:7**). In Egypt, reaching the age of 110 was regarded as the reward for an exceptional life and was assigned as an accolade no matter what age a person might have been at death. By reaching 120, Moses demonstrated his superiority over all others.

The people mourned Moses' death for thirty days in the plains of Moab (**34:8**). His role would now be assumed by Joshua, to whom Moses had formally passed on the spirit of wisdom that would be required for the arduous task ahead.

In a further act of obedience, the people honoured the new leader Moses had appointed at God's command (**34:9**).

Moses' final epitaph is contained in 34:10-12. He is described as the greatest of Israel's prophets (18:15-22; Num 12:6-8). The first of the things that made him great was his intimate, personal knowledge of God, whom he had met *face to face* (**34:10**). Next was the fact that God had enabled him to perform unequalled *signs and wonders* in delivering the people from Egypt (**34:11**). He was 'God's chosen charismatic leader in Israel, God's spokesman, God's agent. In him were concentrated all the great offices of Israel: prophet, ruler, judge and priest' (*TOT*).

Conclusion

The end of the book of Deuteronomy marks the close of the Torah, the first five books of the ᴏᴛ, which describes how God chose his people, shaped them into a nation and gave them his law. Now they are ready to embark on a new stage of their history, as they enter into and settle the promised land. It is a time of great hope, as shown in Moses' blessings. But is also the time when the people will have to put into effect the laws that Moses has given them and live by them even though they will soon be scattered in small communities across the land. They will no longer have one leader of the calibre of Moses to urge them to obedience; obedience is now their own responsibility, one that they have to pass on to their descendants. If they fail to love and serve the Lord, the blessings they anticipate will evaporate, and they will be left with the curse that they accepted in Moab. Should that come upon them, however, they can still hope in the faithfulness of a loving God who will eventually return to restore them and will send them one even greater than Moses in the form of his Son.

Luciano C. Chianeque and Samuel Ngewa

Further Reading

Driver, S. R. *A Critical and Exegetical Commentary on Deuteronomy*. ICC. Edinburgh: T & T Clark, 1999.

Thompson, J. A. *Deuteronomy: An Introduction and Commentary*. TOT. Downers Grove, Ill: Inter-Varsity Press, 1974.

JOSHUA

Joshua is the person whom God chose to bring about the fulfilment of his promises to Abraham to make his descendants into a great nation and to give them their own land.

In about 2000 BC, the Lord called Abraham from Ur of the Chaldeans, showed him the land of Canaan, and said, 'To your offspring I will give this land' (Gen 12:7). Later he told him, 'Know for certain that your descendants will be strangers in a country not their own, and they will be enslaved and ill-treated four hundred years. But I will punish the nation they serve as slaves, and afterwards they will come out with great possessions ... In the fourth generation your descendants will come back here' (Gen 15:13-15).

The first part of this prophecy was fulfilled when Jacob led his whole family from famine-stricken Canaan to Egypt to join his son Joseph, who had been sold into slavery there but who had risen to become prime minister. A temporary journey in search of relief turned into four hundred years of slavery for the Israelites. Yet Jacob's family still believed that a day would come when God would fulfil his promise and lead Israel into the promised land. At the close of Genesis, Joseph is so confident of the reliability of God's word that he can say, 'I am about to die. But God will surely come to your aid and take you up out of this land to the land he promised on oath to Abraham, Isaac and Jacob.' He insisted that his descendants must take his bones with them when they eventually left (Gen 50:24-25). Even though Abraham, Isaac and Jacob had died, Joseph held on to God's promise, determined to partake of it even after he was long gone. He was determined to enter the promised land even if only as his bones!

God did not forget his promise to Abraham. He appeared to Moses in the burning bush and said to him, 'the cry of the Israelites has reached me, and I have seen the way the Egyptians are oppressing them. So now, go. I am sending you to Pharaoh to bring my people the Israelites out of Egypt' (Exod 3:9-10). Moses went to Egypt, and with God's help led Israel out. Unfortunately, the Israelites were an obstinate people, and thus their journey to the promised land took forty years. Moses himself did not live to enter the promised land.

God then picked Moses' assistant, Joshua, to lead God's people as they realized a dream that they had clung to for hundreds of years. The book of Joshua attests to the fact that God's promises never fail, that God's word is utterly dependable. So, even when everything seems to indicate otherwise, be not afraid! 'Though it tarry, wait for it; because it will surely come' (Hab 2:3 KJV).

In this book, we see God as the promise-giver who revealed himself to Abraham, Isaac and Jacob, and also as the promise-keeper who revealed himself to Joshua

Outline of Contents

COMMENTARY

1:1-9 The Call and the Promise

1:1a The Passing of a Servant

Moses had been an outstanding leader, endowed with great strength and stamina. He had possessed exceptional spiritual qualities, and also enjoyed a special relationship with God. After his call at the burning bush, Moses became God's spokesman and the mediator between God and his people, whom God spoke to 'face to face, clearly and not in riddles' (Num 12:8). Moses was a truly special *servant of the Lord* (**1:1a**).

The Israelites must have been amazed that despite Moses' stature and special relationship with God, he was forbidden from entering the promised land. Now the unimaginable had happened: Moses was dead. He had been the only leader they knew and now he was gone.

We all fear the mysterious power that is death. Perhaps because of the fear of death, human beings have often chosen to either not think about it or to wish it away. We think of it as something that comes to somebody else but not to us. The constitutions of some African countries state that it is treason to even imagine the death of a president!

However, death is a reality of life. It is no respecter of persons. Death takes the king, and will not spare the beggar.

Death will ignore and break through every barrier to visit the rich in his mansion, and it will stalk the poor man on the streets. Death will outwit the best professor and not argue with the fool. It will snatch away the medical doctor and bewitch the medicine man. Death flies with you in the aeroplane and rides with you in the *matatu* (a Kenyan taxi). It swims with you in the pool and sails with you on the sea. It walks with the pedestrian and drives with the motorist. Death will snuff out the life of a 120-year-old, and not spare a newborn. Death cannot be avoided or evaded. No wonder Job cried out, 'Man born of woman is of few days and full of trouble. He springs up like a flower and withers away; like a fleeting shadow, he does not endure' (Job 14:1-2).

Part of the reason Africa faces such difficulty during leadership transitions is that leaders tend to view themselves as immortal. They never envisage the possibility of their own death, and therefore do not prepare others to carry on their work. In Africa, it seems that leadership positions are held 'until death do us part'. When death deals its blow, the gap it leaves is difficult to fill.

The Bible declares that we are 'destined to die once, and after that to face judgment' (Heb 9:27). Death is an appointment that cannot be postponed or missed. It finally caught up with Moses, the servant of the Lord.

1:1b-2 The Promotion of an Assistant

Upon the death of Moses, the Lord turned to Joshua to carry on the mission to the promised land. This Joshua is introduced as *Joshua son of Nun, Moses' assistant* (**1:1b**).

Joshua's first appearance in the history of Israel is as a warrior whom Moses tells to 'choose some of our men and go out to fight the Amalekites' (Exod 17:9). He is also mentioned as an aide who accompanies Moses when he sets out to meet with God on the mountain (Exod 24:13); who is with him when he returns and finds the Israelites worshipping the molten calf (Exod 32:17); and who remains in the tent after the Lord had spoken to Moses face to face (Exod 33:11).

But the most significant story about Joshua by far is about his role as one of the twelve men sent to spy out the promised land (Num 13:2). In the list of these men, he appears as 'Hoshea son of Nun' (Num 13:8). Later in that same chapter it is recorded that 'Moses gave Hoshea son of Nun the name Joshua' (Num 13:16). Joshua is the English form of the Hebrew name Jehoshua meaning 'Yahweh is deliverance' or 'Yahweh is salvation'. The Greek form of this name is Jesus – the name of our Lord, Deliverer and Saviour.

When the twelve spies returned from exploring the land, ten of them reported that while the land might be 'flowing with milk and honey', it was also full of fierce giants and fortified cities, so that the Israelites would have no hope of conquering it (Num 13:27-29; 31-33). But Joshua and Caleb

son of Jephunneh brought a different report. 'The land we passed through and explored is exceedingly good. If the Lord is pleased with us, he will lead us into that land, a land flowing with milk and honey, and will give it to us. Only do not rebel against the Lord. And do not be afraid of the people of the land, because we will swallow them up. Their protection is gone, but the Lord is with us. Do not be afraid of them' (Num 14:7-9).

With this report, Joshua and Caleb distinguished themselves as a different breed of men, full of faith and courage. It is not surprising that Moses had chosen Joshua to be his personal aide. This mentoring relationship developed so that just before the end of his life and ministry, Moses summoned Joshua, and told him in the presence of the people of Israel that God had chosen him to lead them into the promised land (Deut 31:1-8).

The African continent is in a serious leadership crisis. Almost every change of leadership is accompanied by strife. Either there is no suitable successor or the handover is full of fights and struggles. This is true not only in national politics but also in the corporate world and most certainly in the church. It is rare to hear of a smooth handover of leadership or, even better, a gradual one in which new leaders build on the foundation of their predecessors and move the nation, organization or church to greater heights of growth and development. Men like Julius Nyerere of Tanzania and Nelson Mandela of South Africa, who have voluntarily handed over leadership of their nations, stand out as lighthouses in a dark night, not because what they did was unusual, but because it is unusual in Africa.

With Moses gone, the Lord called on Joshua to take over his mantle: *Now then, you and all these people, get ready to cross the Jordan River into the land I am about to give to them – to the Israelites* (**1:2**).

1:3-5 Divine Promises

As Joshua stood on the verge of the Jordan ready to enter the promised land, it must have been an overwhelming experience. He knew that the promise of this land had been made hundreds of years earlier to Abraham, who never saw its fulfilment. Isaac, Jacob, Joseph and Moses were all dead. Joshua may have wondered who he was that he should be the one to see the realization of this age-old dream. So God reassured Joshua with three promises.

1:3-4 A promise of fulfilment

God makes a very special promise to Joshua concerning the certainty of possessing the land: *I will give you every place where you set your foot, as I promised Moses* (**1:3**). Joshua was going to experience the fulfilment of the promise for himself. His own feet, and the feet of all the people he was leading, were going to determine what he would get. The people would be able to occupy all the land *from the desert to*

Lebanon, and from the great river, the Euphrates … to the Great Sea (**1:4**). The area described is similar to that which the Lord promised to Abraham (Gen 15:18-20).

In terms of current political boundaries, the promised land would thus cover modern Israel, the whole of Jordan, a large part of Saudi Arabia, half of Iraq, the whole of Lebanon, part of Syria and the whole of Kuwait! But Israel occupied only a tiny portion of this land even when its kingdom was at its largest under David and Solomon. Arabs, who also claim a right to the land, occupy the rest. So the question arises, who has the legitimate claim to this land? Was Israel's rebirth legitimate after two thousand years? If Israel has a right to exist, should its boundaries be extended to match those originally promised? What about the Arabs, who are also Abraham's descendants through Ishmael? Do they have any right to the promised land? These questions are part of the firewood fuelling the fire boiling the pot of the conflict in the Middle East.

1:5a A promise of victory

If there is something that scares any leader, it is the prospect of failure. Moses, despite all his weaknesses and difficulties, had successfully brought God's people right to the banks of the Jordan River, the verge of the promised land. But now Joshua must have wondered whether he was going to be able to complete the task. Did he have the courage to fight all the groups living in the land? What about opposition from among the Israelites? Were the people going to rebel against him? No! God said, *No one will be able to stand up against you all the days of your life* (**1:5a**). God promised Joshua victory over everybody who would come up against him. What is more, it was a lifetime promise; Joshua was going to experience victory in all his battles!

1:5b A promise of God's continuing presence

God had been with Moses in an extraordinary way. He had performed miracles by the hands of Moses. He spoke to the people through him. He encouraged him in times of disappointment. Was Joshua likely to have the same experience? Yes – *As I was with Moses, so I will be with you* (**1:5b**). Though Moses was dead, the God of Moses was more than alive!

It was Moses who told God, 'If your Presence does not go with us, do not send us up from here. How will anyone know that you are pleased with me and with your people unless you go with us? What else will distinguish me and your people from all the other people on the face of the earth?' (Exod 33:15-16). In other words, Moses felt that he would rather dwell in the desert with the Lord than go into the land flowing with milk and honey without him. He recognized that the only difference between God's people and any other people is God's presence with them, that is, the evidence of his favour upon his people.

Without God's presence, we are like everyone else, our homes are just like those of others, and our businesses are just like other businesses. But when the Lord is present with us, then we become 'a chosen people, a royal priesthood, a holy nation, a people belonging to God' (1 Pet 2:9-10). No wonder Moses insisted that he needed God's presence! The Lord granted Moses' request and said to him, 'I will do the very thing you have asked, because I am pleased with you and I know you by name' (Exod 33:17). It is of great significance, therefore, that God now took the initiative to reassure Joshua that his presence was going to be with him wherever he went. God would be there to direct, to sustain and to assure success: *I will never leave you nor forsake you* (**1:5b**).

Armed with these promises of fulfilment, victory and God's presence, Joshua was ready to obey God's command to set out, confident of the continuity of God's blessings from one generation to the next.

1:6-9 Demands of the Promise

God's reassuring words to Joshua did not mean that Joshua had no part to play in realizing God's promise. God expected him to display courage and strength and to devote himself to the Book of the Law.

1:6-7a, 9 'Be strong and courageous'

Since God knows and understands every human heart, he must have known that Joshua was afraid to embark on the task at hand. This fear is odd considering that Joshua, together with Caleb, had made a very powerful and confident statement about God's power after they had surveyed the land with the ten other spies. So why would Joshua now be in need of exhortation to be strong and courageous? There are at least four possible reasons why Joshua might have been afraid of the task ahead of him.

- **The people he was to lead.** Joshua knew the Israelites well. As Moses' assistant, he knew the mental and spiritual anguish that Moses had experienced as he led them. He knew that Moses had once been so tired of them that he almost disowned them (Num 11:11-15). God himself had once become fed up with them and told Moses, 'Go up to the land flowing with milk and honey. But I will not go with you because you are a stiff-necked people and I might destroy you on the way' (Exod 33:3). Now, it was Joshua's turn to lead these same people. If even God found them difficult, how would Joshua cope? Leadership of such a group was a dreadful prospect. So God reassured Joshua, *Be strong and courageous, because you will lead these people* (**1:6a**).

- **The land he was to possess.** The land they were entering was indeed flowing with milk and honey, but Joshua's fellow spies had been right when they reported that the people who lived there were powerful and the cities fortified and very large. Their conclusion had been unanimous: 'We can't attack those people; they are stronger than we are' (Num 13:31). Even though Joshua had disagreed with the other spies, he was now faced with the grim reality of actually going to face the Canaanites! This must have been a scary prospect. So God told him, *Be strong and courageous, because you will lead these people to inherit the land I swore to their forefathers to give them* (**1:6b**).

- **The man he was to succeed.** Moses was a man who could plead with God until God, in his grace, changed his course of action (Num 14:11-23). He had displayed wisdom, patience, tolerance and great strength in dealing with the people. For forty years, he had been an untiring mediator between God and his people. It is difficult to take over from such a man. Joshua must have feared constantly being compared with Moses and being found inadequate. He must have dreaded comments like 'If only Moses was still alive', or 'If Moses were here, he would …'. In other words, Joshua may have feared walking in the shadow of Moses all his life. So God reassured him, *Be strong and courageous. Be careful to obey all the law my servant Moses gave you … that you may be successful wherever you go* (**1:7**).
- **The God he was to serve.** Another possible reason for Joshua to be afraid was the God he was to serve. Yahweh was an awesome God. In his anger he had caused the ground to open and swallow people alive (Num 16:31-32)! He had caused the children of Israel to wander around in the wilderness until they all died and a new generation was raised up. He had forbidden Moses from entering the land after labouring so much for him simply because he hit a rock instead of speaking to it as he had been instructed (Num 20:7-12). Surely, dealing with this God was a fearful thing. So God reassured Joshua *Be strong and courageous …, for the Lord your God will be with you wherever you go* (**1:9b**).

For Joshua to accomplish the task God has given him, he will need to be a leader who displays strength and courage. No wonder the words 'be strong and courageous' are repeated three times (1:7, 9, 18). And the addition of the phrase *Have I not commanded you?* (**1:9a**) made it abundantly clear to Joshua that this was God's command, not a request.

There is a similar call to all Christians in the NT: 'Do not throw away your confidence; it will be richly rewarded. You need to persevere so that when you have done the will of God, you will receive what he has promised. … "my righteous one will live by faith. And if he shrinks back, I will not be pleased with him." But we are not of those who shrink back and are destroyed, but of those who believe and are saved' (Heb 10:35-39).

1:7b-8 Study and commitment

The second demand upon Joshua was complete and total devotion to the law of the Lord. By the time of Joshua, Moses had put in writing all the laws that God had given him. Moreover, Moses had compiled a careful record of all that had taken place from the beginning of creation until Israel was about to enter the promised land. The five books of the Pentateuch – Genesis, Exodus, Leviticus, Numbers and Deuteronomy – were together known as the Law. Deuteronomy 31:9 records, 'So Moses wrote down this law and gave it to the priests, the sons of Levi, who carried the ark of the covenant of the Lord, and to all the elders of Israel.' Deuteronomy 31:26 says, 'Take this Book of the Law and place it beside the ark of the covenant of the Lord your God. There it will remain as a witness against you.'

As Joshua is commissioned to lead the people into the promised land, he is commanded, *Do not let this Book of the Law depart from your mouth; meditate on it day and night, so that you may be careful to do everything written in it* (**1:8a**). In other words, he is to study it carefully, meditating on its teachings and their implications and applying them in all his activities. Presumably, as he does these things, he will also pass on these teachings to those he leads.

Ezra, too, 'devoted himself to the study and observance of the Law of the Lord, and to teaching its decrees and laws in Israel' (Ezra 7:10). The same charge is given to Timothy as Paul prepares to hand over the mantle of leadership to him: 'Continue in what you have learned … Preach the Word; be prepared in season and out of season; correct, rebuke and encourage – with great patience and careful instruction' (2 Tim 3:14-4:2). The charge to study, practise and teach the word of God applies to any leader who desires to walk in the will of God.

This command to Joshua marks a major turning point in the communication between God and his people, especially with regard to knowing God's will. Up to this point God had revealed his will to his people through dreams, visions, angels, prophets and even directly in person. But it appears that God is telling Joshua that whatever he may need to know has already been revealed and put down in writing by Moses in the Book of the Law. Joshua was therefore not to wait for dreams and visions, angels and prophets, or God's personal appearance. Instead he was to study and meditate on the Book of the Law and faithfully put it into practice.

The fact that God's main emphasis was on the Book of the Law – the Holy Scriptures as developed thus far – did not mark the end of God's special revelation through other means. When Joshua had been officially appointed as Moses' assistant, God had indicated that he was going to be receiving special instructions through Eleazar the priest, who would inquire for him from the Urim (Num 27:18-21). In other words, God was still going to speak through special revelation, but the emphasis had started shifting to the written word of God, and Joshua was to be totally committed to this written word.

With the charge, Joshua is given a great promise of success and blessing: *that you may be successful wherever you go* (1:7). *Then you will be prosperous and successful* (**1:8b**). This echoes what God had promised through Moses: 'If you fully obey the Lord your God and carefully follow all his commands that I give you today, the Lord your God will set you high above all the nations of the earth. All these blessings will come upon you and accompany you if you obey the Lord your God' (Deut 28:1-2).

1:10-2:24 Planning and Preparation

While there is no record of Joshua's response to God's call and promise, his actions from here on indicate that he was committed to following God's command. Unlike Moses in Exodus 3:11-4:1, Joshua did not hesitate to accept God's commission. Instead he took God at his word and set out to accomplish the task at hand. In this section we see his planning and preparation for leading God's people to possess the land. One of the biggest mistakes believers often make in responding to God's call is to embark on a task without giving careful thought and consideration to how it is to be accomplished. A spiritual call does not mean intellectual impotence.

1:10-18 The Plan

Joshua had just been given a job description and an appointment letter from God. His task was to lead the people of God across the Jordan and take possession of the land. So Joshua launches a three-point plan to mobilize the people to capture the land. This plan involves passing on the word, planning the details, and getting the people's response. As he implements it, we see Joshua demonstrating strength and courage as he gives authoritative commands to the leaders, clear instructions to the people, and reminds special groups of their obligations to their brothers and sisters.

1:10-11 Passing on the word

1:10 SELLING THE VISION TO THE LEADERS In order for Joshua to accomplish the task at hand, he needed to communicate his plan and strategy to those under him. The first group who needed to know about it were the leaders. So he spoke to *the officers of the people* (**1:10**). These 'officers' correspond to today's staff officers, who manage the details of the orders given by the leader, who cannot see to every detail himself. The same term is used to refer to Pharaoh's slave-drivers (Exod 5:6-19), the tribal leaders appointed by Moses to judge the people (Deut 1:15) and the officers who served in King David's army (1 Chr 27:1).

The officers to whom Joshua spoke may have been the same team established by Moses on the advice of his father-in-law, Jethro. Moses had chosen 'capable men from Israel and made them leaders of the people, officials of thousands, hundreds, fifties and tens. They served as judges for the people at all times' (Exod 18:24-26). If these are the same officers, then it means that Joshua used existing structures to pass on the word to the people. Here is another great lesson in leadership. In Africa it appears that every leader who takes over comes in with a totally new structure, and it therefore takes a while before progress can be made.

1:11 SELLING THE VISION TO THE PEOPLE If Joshua was going to be successful, he also needed to let all the people know what was happening. They needed to prepare their supplies and be ready to move. So Joshua sent word to all in the camp to let them know that the time had come for them to realize the promise of God. Having received authority from the Lord, Joshua communicated to the people with that authority. He did not beg and plead with them but *ordered the officers* (1:10) to *go through the camp and tell the people* (**1:11a**). This is one of the first signs of Joshua acting courageously as the Lord had instructed him to do.

Joshua's message to the people was short, precise and clear: *Get your supplies ready* (**1:11b**). Up to this point God had been the direct source of food for Israel, providing manna on a daily basis (Exod 16:14-31). But manna could not be kept for more than one day, so it is unlikely that Joshua was asking the people to gather food for the journey. The 'supplies' referred to here were primarily their personal belongings and their livestock. However, manna was probably not the only food that was being eaten by this point, and the supply of it would cease when the host crossed the Jordan (5:12; see Exod 16:35). So there may have been some preparation of food supplies too.

His message was also delivered with great conviction and left no room for doubt, argument or negotiation: *Three days from now you will cross the Jordan here to go in and take possession of the land the Lord your God is giving you for your own* (**1:11c**). The message communicates Joshua's certainty about the final result of this call – the Lord will give them the land.

It is amazing, but people will often follow a person of conviction whether they are being led or misled! That is why dictators, gang leaders and cults rouse such unswerving devotion among their followers. A man who is apologetic, uncertain, and unconvinced should not be surprised if the queue behind him is empty. To rally people behind your vision, you must be convinced and convincing. Joshua was not only convinced, but also very convincing in his rallying call to the people, and with his deep conviction he inspired them to prepare to occupy the land.

1:12-15 Involving special groups

There was a special group that also needed to be addressed in the plans – *the Reubenites, the Gadites and the half-tribe* of Manasseh (**1:12**). On the way to the promised land, Israel had conquered Sihon and Og, kings in the land of the Moabites east of the Jordan (Num 21:21-35). The tribes of Reuben, Gad and the half-tribe of Manasseh had requested that they be allowed to occupy this land since it offered good pasture for livestock. Moses had granted their request on condition that they promise to help the other Israelites when the time came to enter the promised land (**1:13-15**; Num 32:1-33). They may have hoped that their promise would be forgotten now that Moses was dead. But Joshua was clearly studying the Book of the Law, and knew of Moses' words to them. So he sent them a reminder: *Your wives, your children and your livestock may stay in the land that Moses the servant of the Lord gave you east of the Jordan, but all your fighting men, fully armed, must cross over ahead of your brothers* (1:14). In other words, they were not only to fulfil their pledge but also had to be at the front of the battle.

1:16-18 The people's response

Because Joshua looked and sounded convinced about the mission to possess the land of Canaan and because the Lord's favour was upon him, his rallying call met with resounding support. The people gave Joshua a unanimous vote of confidence. No one stood up against him, just as God had promised. This must have been more than Joshua could have expected from this obstinate crowd. Not only do they support him, but they reiterate God's promises:

- God had transferred leadership from Moses to Joshua (1:1); the people promise to transfer their loyalty from Moses to Joshua: *Just as we fully obeyed Moses, so we will obey you* (**1:17a**).
- God had promised to grant Joshua everywhere he placed his foot (1:3); the people now promise *whatever you have commanded us we will do, and wherever you send us we will go* (**1:16**).
- God had promised to be with Joshua just as he had been with Moses (1:5a); now the people echo the same words as they pray for the Lord's presence in all Joshua does (**1:17b**).
- God had told Joshua, 'No one will be able to stand up against you all the days of your life' (1:5); now the people reiterate this promise by pronouncing the death penalty upon anyone who dares rebel against Joshua (**1:18a**).
- God had specifically told Joshua to display strength and courage if he was going to see victory (1:6, 7a, 9); the people too make strength and courage Joshua's personal responsibility and requirement (**1:18b**). Just as God told Joshua that he would keep his part of the bargain if Joshua kept his, so the people tell Joshua to play his part and they will play theirs.

What a beginning for Joshua! Such unanimous support is clear evidence of God's favour. With this combined promise

from his God and his people, Joshua must have been even more confident that he would see the promise fulfilled.

But we must also observe that Joshua started right. He began the task with a positive attitude, he communicated clearly and appropriately with the people, and he set out a clear and definite plan of action. It is generally believed in management circles that a leader's effectiveness is judged by his initial three months, and especially his first day at work. Joshua seems to have passed the test.

Richard Hess observes, 'This opening chapter of Joshua teaches that leadership of God's people must be recognised by the people as God's choice. The test for all such ministry is found in the knowledge of and obedience to God's word, something that can meet the practical needs of God's people' (*TOT*). God's call will often (but not always) be confirmed by a positive response from the people being lead. God will often watch over his word and confirm it with positive signs.

2:1-24 The Preparation

With God fully on his side and with a unanimous vote of confidence from his leaders and followers, Joshua was now ready to face the enemy. He was ready to do battle to take possession of the promised land.

But like a good leader, Joshua knew that spiritual anointing and popular support are no substitute for careful preparation when undertaking a major task. Many Christian leaders have made the mistake of coming from the prayer room under the definite power of God, and then, after sharing their thoughts with the people and receiving unanimous support, have gone ahead to embark on their mission without careful planning. The results have at times been disastrous. Joshua was not that kind of person. He, like Nehemiah, set out careful plans and preparations and undertook some very practical steps.

2:1-7 Surveying the land

The first thing Joshua did was to assess the magnitude of the task before him. He *secretly sent two spies from Shittim* (**2:1a**). Shittim is a Hebrew word, which means 'acacia trees'. According to Numbers 33:49, Shittim was on the plains of Moab, facing Jericho across the Jordan. The first-century Jewish historian Josephus in his book *The History of the Jews,* places the camp 'near Jordan where the city of Abila now stands, a place full of palm trees'. Shittim was the last camping-ground of Israel before they crossed the Jordan to begin the conquest of Canaan.

Joshua's instructions to the spies were *Go, look over the land … especially Jericho* (**2:1b**). Jericho was a well-fortified city at an oasis supplied by springs of water, and was located about five miles (eight kilometres) from the Jordan. It was therefore the most logical city to attack first.

So they went and entered the house of a prostitute named Rahab and stayed there (**2:1c**). Why the house of a prostitute? Some historical, non-biblical records refer to Rahab as an innkeeper. An inn or a lodge is certainly the perfect choice for spies, because all manner of visitors can come and go without raising eyebrows. The terrorists who bombed the American embassy in Nairobi in 1998 assembled the bomb in one of Nairobi's down-market hotels. The high flow of all kinds of hotel patrons meant that they could move in and out of the hotel with all manner of things without drawing any attention.

It seems likely that Joshua's spies also chose to use a local inn. There is no evidence from the text that they went there for immoral purposes. Otherwise the text would have said something like 'They went in to Rahab the prostitute' without mentioning 'the house of'. We can thus safely assume that they chose the house as a place where they would not be obviously noticeable.

Another possible reason for their choice of residence is that an inn, lodge, hotel, bar or restaurant is a good place to pick up the latest gossip in a city or country – just the kind of information a spy may require. You can ask an innkeeper direct questions about the city or country without betraying yourself as a spy.

On the other hand, an inn is also the place where government informants could be strategically placed to pick up any information touching on state security. Someone like this must have noticed Joshua's spies. *The king of Jericho was told, 'Look! Some of the Israelites have come here tonight to spy out the whole land'* (**2:2**). Yes, word reached the highest level of Jericho's government, and Rahab was ordered to hand the men over (**2:3**). But she hid them on the roof. She then tricked the police and security men to chase them with blaring sirens outside the city gates in pursuit of nothing but the wind! (**2:4-6**). *The men set out in pursuit of the spies on the road that leads to the fords of Jordan, and as soon as the pursuers had gone out, the gate was shut* (**2:7**).

2:8-21 Support in the land

Why did Rahab risk her life this way? The fact that the king himself knew about the spies' visit put her in grave danger. But she had good reason to take the risk. Before the spies lay down for the night, she went up on the roof and said to them, *'I know that the Lord has given this land to you and that a great fear of you has fallen on us'* (**2:9**). How did she know this? She told them, *We have heard how the Lord dried up the water of the Red Sea for you …, and what you did to Sihon and Og, the two kings of the Amorites … When we heard of it, our hearts sank and everyone's courage failed because of you, for the Lord your God is God in heaven above and on the earth below* (**2:10-11**). Here was a 'heathen' woman who, because of what she had heard, was willing to abandon her Canaanite gods and confess total faith in the God of Israel.

This is the reason why Rahab is listed among the heroes of faith in Hebrews 11:31. Her confession of faith in the Lord is astounding for a non-Israelite.

The great irony is that whereas Israel was still surveying the land to see whether the Lord 'could' give it to them, here was a Canaanite woman stating that she knew, as a matter of fact, that God had already given the land to Israel.

The Bible says that 'faith comes by hearing' (see Rom 10:17). Rahab had heard and had believed. What's more, her faith was not just a verbal confession. It was combined with action, and risky action at that. It was faith she was ready to die for. If the spies had been found in her house, she would have gone straight to the gallows! But because of her faith in God, Rahab was willing to take the risk. Her confession of faith in the God of Israel in 2:11 was unwavering and without doubt.

Rahab knew that her life was not in the hands of the king of Jericho, but in the hands of the Lord. So in assisting the spies, Rahab was not really taking any risks. The real risk would be to be found on the wrong side of the Lord. She made arrangements with the spies and asked them to swear that they would spare her life, and those of her family, when they came to take over the city (**2:12-13**). For Rahab, the taking of Jericho by Israel was but a matter of time.

It is amazing that we, as believers, often remain blind to the victory that is ours in Christ, and while we go around in fear and fret, unbelievers' eyes are opened to see the opportunities that God has placed before us. They are the ones who come in to encourage us to be bold, to be confident, to move forwards and possess our possession.

Recognizing that Rahab was an asset in their strategy, the spies swore to her, *Our lives for your lives* (**2:14**). With this agreement, she let them down the wall to safety (**2:15-16**). They asked her to tie a *scarlet cord* in the window, and to bring her whole family and anyone else she wished to protect into the house for safety (**2:18-21**). Their vow and the use of the scarlet cord remind us of the Passover when the Lord struck down the firstborn in those houses that were not protected by blood on the door-frames (see Exod 12:7, 13, 22-23). Then the spies went away, having found support in the land.

The hymn writer John Henry Sammis was absolutely right when he wrote:

When we walk with the Lord,
In the light of His word,
What a glory He sheds on our way!
While we do His good will,
He abides with us still,
And with all who will trust and obey!

When we are committed to walking in the light of God's word and seeking to do his will, he will place on our way people who will be favourable to our course. Even in enemy territory, God will provide someone who will identify with us. No wonder David declared, 'You prepare a table before me in the presence of my enemies' (Ps 23:5). The Lord placed Rahab in Jericho to prepare a table for the spies.

2:22-24 Report of success

Joshua must have been waiting anxiously for the spies' report. Good news was on its way, but Joshua had to wait at least three days before he got it. The spies went into the hills and stayed three days until the pursuers had searched all along the road and returned empty-handed (**2:22-23a**).

When the spies returned, they told Joshua *everything that had happened to them* (**2:23b**). They reported Rahab's words, 'I know that the Lord has given this land to you' (2:9). These words were now the spies own words too: *The Lord has surely given the whole land into our hands* (**2:24a**). These words confirm God's 'I will give you ...' to Joshua in 1:3, when he assured him that he would fulfil his promise.

The God of Joshua is a promise-keeping God. He had told Joshua that no one would stand up against him, and he was committed to ensuring that promise came true. Hence the spies reported that *all the people are melting in fear because of us* (**2:24b**). When God has spoken, he ensures that his word is confirmed. He told Jeremiah, 'You have seen correctly, for I am watching to see that my word is fulfilled' (Jer 1:12).

Has God called you to a task? Do it in faith and confidence. Step out in faith and begin to see him open doors before your very eyes. The God who did it for Joshua is the same God today as he was yesterday, and as he will be for ever. Sit down and with the guidance of the Holy Spirit, lay out a strategy of how you may take possession of that which is yours. Then arise and spy out the land!

3:1-6:27 The Great March

With the land surveyed and a good report obtained, Joshua was ready to march into the promised land. This was going to be one of the most significant events in the history of Israel. A promise that had been made to Abraham almost eight hundred years earlier was about to be fulfilled (Gen 15:13-15). It was certainly a momentous time for Joshua. But this march into the promised land meant overcoming at least three significant challenges that stood in his way: the barrier of the Jordan, the reproach of Egypt and the stronghold of Jericho.

3:1-4:24 Marching Across the Jordan

Between God's people and the promised land lay the River Jordan, which was in full flood (3:15). The river was a visible, physical barrier to the fulfilment of God's promise. It is noteworthy that thus far, nothing had been said about the challenge that the swollen river would pose to Joshua and the people as they prepared to enter the land of Canaan. The spies are reported to have forded the river without difficulty

(2:23). But getting the whole multitude of people across, including women, children, animals and other belongings, was a different matter. However, Joshua was about to see God do the impossible right before his eyes!

3:1-4 Watch the ark

In preparation for the great crossing, Joshua and the Israelites set out from Shittim and camped by the Jordan (**3:1**). *After three days the officers went throughout the camp, giving orders to the people* on how they were to proceed. The people were told, *When you see the ark of the covenant of the Lord your God, and the priests, who are Levites, carrying it, you are to move out from your positions and follow it* (**3:2-3**). This instruction meant that the people could not be concerned with any other activities or they would be at risk of being left behind. Their full attention was to be on the ark and those carrying it. When the ark moved, they were to move. The same is true for anybody who is waiting on God for guidance – they must be alert to the movement of the Holy Spirit. The people were to keep up with the ark. Wherever it went, they were to follow. In this way they would *know which way to go,* since they had never been that way before (**3:4**). Those who walked out of step with the ark did so at their own risk and were on their own. Thus it is for all those who seek God's guidance. They must keep in line and in step with the Holy Spirit.

The people were warned that they had to *keep a distance of about a thousand yards* (nine hundred metres) between them and the ark. The fact that God was willing to lead them did not diminish his holiness – his otherness. Through the ark, he was dwelling in their midst, but they were not to be overly familiar with him and to treat the ark casually. This lesson was bitterly learned when David tried to move the ark to Jerusalem. Uzzah 'took hold of the ark of God, because the oxen stumbled' (2 Sam 6:6), and the Lord 'struck him down and he died' (2 Sam 6:7).

Familiarity breeds contempt, and sometimes even our familiarity with God breeds contempt. We treat God as if he were merely a fellow human being. It is a sad fact that many believers do not even consider how they enter God's house of worship on a Sunday morning, or how they partake of God's sacraments. Paul warned the Corinthians, and indeed all believers, against partaking of the Lord's table in an unworthy manner. He told them that whoever 'eats the bread or drinks the cup of the Lord in an unworthy manner will be guilty of sinning against the body and blood of the Lord' (1 Cor 11:27). Everyone ought to examine him or herself 'before they eat of the bread and drink of the cup. For anyone who eats and drinks without recognizing the body of the Lord eats and drinks judgment on himself' (1 Cor 11:29). Paul told the Corinthians that such behaviour was the reason many among them were weak and sick, and a number had died. Yet, as Paul emphasized, if we judge ourselves, we will not come under judgment. We must keep a reverential distance from the ark.

3:5-6 Watch your life

Joshua was obviously excited at the prospect of finally taking the people across the Jordan. This great man of God was ready to see God do amazing things. He was expecting the unexpected.

But first, the people had to consecrate themselves (**3:5**). The details, however, are not given. But a similar command given by God to Moses meant that the people purified themselves, washed their clothes, and abstained from anything that would contaminate them (Exod 19:10). Perhaps the same was required of the people now. They were to prepare themselves to receive amazing things from God.

After hundreds of years, the time had come. The Lord would fulfil his promise *tomorrow.* Indeed God's time always comes. Solomon was later to declare that 'there is a time for everything, and a season for every activity under heaven' (Eccl 3:1). God's time of salvation for his people was to be the very next day! When Habakkuk could no longer stand the sight of evil in his community and felt as though God was taking too long to act on his promised judgment, God asked him to exercise patience: 'Though it linger, wait for it; it will certainly come and will not delay' (Hab 2:3).

Perhaps more than any other people, Christians in Africa stand exactly where Habakkuk stood – where evil, oppression and poverty abound. And most of us wonder when God will come through for us. But a day is coming when a voice will be heard, *Consecrate yourselves, for tomorrow the Lord will do amazing things among you* (3:5).

It is often possible that we may hear God's voice, we may do our groundwork, we may even see God's favour and yet not expect God to do what he has said or to perform miracles on our behalf. Joshua expected God to do amazing things in the sight of the people. Like a good preacher, Joshua built up the people's faith to receive that which God had in store for them.

Then Joshua instructed the priests, *Take up the ark of the covenant and pass on ahead of the people* (**3:6**). The ark of the covenant represented the presence of God. By having it lead the way, Joshua put God first in this faith venture. His faith is also demonstrated by the fact that he issued the order to advance before God revealed to him how he was going to handle the waters of the Jordan. It is after Joshua had asked the priests to carry the ark and lead the way, and after he had called on the people to consecrate themselves that God appears to him with further details. Joshua's attention was not on the Jordan, but on the Lord his God. He was not focusing on the barriers, but on the God who was able to remove them. Furthermore he did not tell the people to look to him but to God. All he required was that the priests do their duty of bearing the ark and leading the way and

that the people consecrate themselves, so that they were clean before the Lord.

With those prerequisites in place, Joshua was certain that the Lord was going to do amazing things among them.

3:7-11 A step upward

It was not long before Joshua's faith was rewarded. God told Joshua, *Today I will begin to exalt you in the eyes of all Israel, so they may know that I am with you as I was with Moses* (**3:7**; see 4:14). Joshua had exalted the Lord by his act of faith, and now God was going to exalt Joshua by doing amazing things through him. By removing the barrier of the Jordan, God would vividly demonstrate to everybody that he was with Joshua as he had been with Moses. Joshua's role in this miraculous passage would bring him honour and give him high credit with the people. From now on his authority was established, and obedience to him fully secured.

Whenever we exalt the Lord, the Lord not only exalts himself by doing amazing things in and through us, but also exalts us in the eyes of the people. Yet the opposite is equally true. If we are ashamed of the Lord, he will be ashamed of us 'when he comes in his glory and in the glory of the Father and of the holy angels' (Luke 9:26). No wonder Paul prays, 'I eagerly expect and hope that I will in no way be ashamed, but will have sufficient courage so that now as always Christ will be exalted in my body, whether by life or by death' (Phil 1:20). To exalt the Lord must be the believer's utmost desire.

Joshua called the people together, saying, *Come here and listen to the words of the Lord your God* (**3:9**). But what he tells them are not God's actual words but his own words of faith. He draws their attention to God's divine acts and demonstrations of his presence in their midst. He also instructs them to observe carefully the movements of the priests (**3:10-11**).

3:12-13 A step in unity

Joshua called on the assembled people to choose *twelve men from the tribes of Israel, one from each tribe* (**3:12**). It is not clear exactly what role these men were to play, but it seems that Joshua wanted a witness from each tribe to participate in this miracle and behold the wonder of God's amazing works. Because these men had been chosen by the people, they would be credible witnesses whose report would be believed. Later we see these men build an altar of remembrance at the banks of Jordan with stones carried from the middle of the river (4:4-9). Once again, it appears that Joshua takes a step of faith and anticipates what the Lord is about to do before it actually happens.

3:14-17 A step of faith

When the people broke camp to cross the Jordan, the priests carrying the ark of the covenant went ahead of them. As soon as the priests reached the Jordan, the water upstream stopped flowing, while the water downstream flowed away. The priests then stood on *dry ground in the middle of the Jordan* while all the people crossed (**3:17**).

To the people of the ancient Near East, this miracle would have an additional significance that we may miss today. At that time, someone accused of a crime was often tried by being thrown into a river. If the accused drowned, the gods had found them guilty; if not, the gods had declared them not guilty. Many African cultures had similar practices. For example, people accused of some wrongdoing might be required to jump over a puddle of water or over a strand of grass with a magician's saliva on it, knowing that doing so would invite serious consequences if they were guilty. In crossing the Jordan, the God of Israel accepts this trial, as it were. Not only does he not drown, he causes the water to flee! His priests stood in the middle of a dry river until all his people had passed. Thus Yahweh, the God of Israel, 'proved' his stake in the land of Canaan over and above every other god. His claim to the land was justified to everybody who heard about what had happened.

This miracle would also have had special significance to the people of Israel. Just as God had parted the waters of the Red Sea before Moses (Exod 14:21-22), so he now parted the waters of the Jordan before Joshua. It seems certain that God wanted to emphasize to his people that he was with Joshua as he had been with Moses. All those who passed over would only have heard about the parting of the Red Sea from their parents or grandparents. But they now witnessed the parting of the Jordan. God was setting his signature and seal to Joshua's certificate of leadership.

What is also significant is how the waters were parted. The Jordan was *in flood* (**3:15a**), and therefore at its highest. Yet as soon as *the priests' feet touched the water's edge* (**3:15b**) – as soon as they acted in obedience to God's word – *the water from upstream stopped flowing and piled up into a heap a great distance away at a town called Adam in the vicinity of Zarethan* (**3:16a**), while down stream the water was *completely cut off* (**3:16b**).

Archaeologists have identified both *Adam* and *Zarethan* as ancient towns along the Jordan. In fact, *Adam* is said to have been a convenient point to cross the Jordan when it was in flood because the river was narrower and shallower there. What is more, geographical studies have shown that earthquakes could cut off the Jordan at this point.

The first time I read this in a commentary as a young Christian, I was quite disturbed. I thought that these scholars were trying to show that the parting of the Jordan was not a miracle but a natural occurrence. Then it suddenly hit me: even if it is true that the Jordan was occasionally cut off by earthquakes, on this particular occasion it was not due to an earthquake – it was cut off when the priests' feet touched the water. It was parted by a literal step of faith!

Regardless of how God made the water stop flowing, the miracle here was that God stopped it as soon as the priests' feet touched the water. A miracle is not necessarily an unusual occurrence. It could be a usual occurrence happening in an unusual way. The miracle here was that the barrier of the Jordan was removed at God's word, at God's time and in God's way.

The human mind tends to try to explain away God's acts through logical reasoning. Healing is explained by medical treatment; God's provision is attributed to a secondary source. For example, if you were praying for some money to meet an emergency need, and then a friend or relative gave you some money, that friend is only a secondary source. The primary source of that money is God. Yet so often we fail to recognize that he is at work through others.

4:1-24 A step of remembrance

Once the miracle was done, God told Joshua to pick twelve men, *and tell them to take up twelve stones from the middle of the Jordan from right where the priests stood* (**4:1-3**). These stones were to be set up as a memorial to the people of Israel forever and as a witness to future generations of the great and amazing things God had done (**4:6-7**).

Joshua set up the twelve stones that had been in the middle of the Jordan at the spot where the priests who carried the ark of the covenant had stood (**4:9**). This is a difficult verse to understand for it is not clear exactly where Joshua set up the memorial. It could also be translated as 'Joshua also set up twelve stones in the middle of the Jordan'. Some commentators thus believe that there were two memorials – one in the middle of the Jordan and another in the camp at Gilgal (**4:20**). They argue that the twelve stones in the bed of the Jordan might have been placed on a base of strong stonework, high enough to be always visible, marking the very spot where the priests had stood with the ark. The twelve stones set up at Gilgal would then stand as a monument to the place of the first encampment after this miraculous crossing. Others believe that there was only one memorial at Gilgal, constructed from stones taken from the middle of the Jordan where the priests had stood.

Whether there was one or two memorials, what is significant is that the stones came from the middle of the Jordan. They must have been well-worn and smoothed by the water and the sand of the riverbed, making it clear that they could not have come from anywhere else. The stones could not be faked. This is also true of God's miracles. Whether in the midst of the Jordan or in the camp at Gilgal, these stones were set up to serve as a permanent reminder of the wondrous works of God.

The human mind has a tendency to forget even the great things that God has done. When God answers our prayers and does a miracle, we are very excited. But we soon forget, and when we face another challenging situation, we doubt God's goodness and his ability to act on our behalf. God wanted to ensure that these people did not forget his powerful work in parting the Jordan. If they were tempted to grumble and complain against God, the stones stood as a witness against them.

Africans are very familiar with memorials. Perhaps more than any other people, Africans set up all manner of memorials as reminders of significant events. Trees are planted or marked to signify a great victory. A mountain or river is named in honour of a mighty warrior. A rock or altar is dedicated to a great god or goddess. In some African communities, as in ancient Israel, even the names of children can be memorials to signify a special event that took place around the time of the birth of the child. Thus across Africa there are many people named after Nelson Mandela because they were born either when Mandela, the great hero of South Africa, was arrested or when he was released.

We should also set up memorials in our minds whenever God does something great or significant in our lives. These mental memorials will remind us of God's faithfulness and his unchanging power and love. David was returning to such a memorial when he assured Saul that he could defeat Goliath because God had helped him overcome lions and bears. His memories of those events gave him confidence as he faced a new challenge.

The same must have been true of Joshua, as he saw God establish his credibility and leadership with the people (**4:14**; see also 3:7). But the memorial that Joshua set up at Gilgal was not just a reminder to himself or to the Israelites of the greatness of God: *He did this so that all the peoples of the earth might know that the hand of the Lord is powerful and so that you might always fear the Lord your God* (**4:24**). God does not perform miracles for us to boast about, but to glorify his holy name, to let people know that there is a God in heaven who rules over the affairs of the earth. Jesus made the same point when he said that a man had been born blind 'so that the work of God might be displayed in his life' (John 9:3). Controversy followed his healing of the man, but there could be no doubt that the man's opened eyes were a testimony and a memorial to what God had done in his life, forcing everyone to reckon with who Jesus actually was.

When the book of Joshua was written, the stones were still standing there for anyone to see: *they are there to this day* (4:9). This fact was not disputed; nor was the fact of the miracle. The account of the building of this memorial in the Bible means that there is a sense in which those stones are still there today, for we remember them and what they stood for.

God's total control of all that happened is evident from the fact that he gave Joshua specific instructions even about when the priests should leave the centre of the Jordan (**4:16**). The chain of command was clear. What Joshua heard from the Lord, he passed on to the priests: *Come up out of the Jordan* (**4:17**). The priests moved at Joshua's command, and the people watched them. Each party had an obligation to watch and listen if they were to move within God's will. There is a Kiswahili saying, *'Ngoja niongoze na la kwangu', huchelewesha mazungumzo* ['"Let me add my bit" delays the conversation']. In other words, if a conversation is to move forward, there must be speakers and listeners. If everybody wants to express their own opinions, little progress will be made. The priests and the people had to listen to Joshua and follow his instructions if they were to succeed.

No sooner had the priests come up out of the river *than the waters of the Jordan returned to their place and ran in flood as before* (**4:18**). Though the Jordan could occasionally be parted or cut off by strong winds or earthquakes, on this particular day there could be no doubt that it was God's work. The priests' stepping into the waters had started the miracle that parted the waters, and as soon as their feet left the riverbed, the Jordan returned to its place. God was the one who controlled its flow.

The people set up their first camp in the promised land *on the tenth day of the first month* (**4:19**). On the same day, forty years before, Israel had begun to prepare to go out of Egypt by setting apart the Passover lamb to be slain on the fourteenth day (Exod 12:3). God had said, 'For forty years – one year for each of the forty days you explored the land – you will suffer for your sins and know what it is like to have me against you' (Num 14:34-35). Exactly forty years after leaving the land of enslavement, they entered the land of promise. God had kept his word. And at the same time, he had mercifully arranged that they should enter the promised land just in time for the Passover lamb to be slain to atone for their sin and rebellion (5:10).

5:1-12 Marching from the Reproach of Egypt

5:1 Sinking hearts

The Israelites' crossing of the Jordan sent shivers throughout the land of Canaan: *Their hearts sank and they no longer had courage to face the Israelites* (**5:1**). This is exactly what Joshua had predicted earlier in his report to Moses after they came back from spying the land. 'Do not be afraid of the people of the land … Their protection is gone, but the Lord is with us' (Num 14:9). In a real sense, Israel actually had a head start against their enemies. The Canaanite kings did not dare attack them.

5:2-7 Flint knives at Gilgal

There is suddenly a dramatic change in the flow of the story. The enemy is terrified – but now it is the Israelites who are facing flint knives. Why did God not allow Joshua to just move in and conquer these fear-filled kings? The answer is that God's covenant with Abraham had been marked by circumcision (Gen 17:10). All the males who came out of

Egypt had been circumcised according to the covenant. But they had rebelled against God and had all perished in the desert without inheriting the land (**5:5-6**). The new generation that was now being led into the land of promise had not been circumcised according to the Abrahamic covenant (**5:7**), and so were not entitled to its full blessings. If they were to face their enemies with confidence, they had to be certain of their complete acceptance into God's covenant with Abraham.

Thus God instructed Joshua, *Make flint knives and circumcise the Israelites again* (**5:2**). Some argue that the word 'again' may mean that they may have already been circumcised, according to either traditional Egyptian or Jewish rites. This is not clear from the text. What is explicit is that God wanted them circumcised according to the covenant.

The implication here is that mere ritual does not bring us into a covenantal relationship with God. For example, there are many who claim to be Christians simply because they were baptized in their childhood. The Bible makes it clear that baptism is meaningless without personal faith in the Lord Jesus Christ. 'Repent and be baptized!' (Acts 2:38) was the message of the early church. Ritual without relationship cannot be depended on in the spiritual battle. Flint knives must be applied again whether or not there was an earlier cut.

The same is true in many African cultures. Marriages, burials and other major social activities are not recognized unless and until the appropriate rites have been performed. In some communities these are even done posthumously to appease the gods and protect the community from the consequences of their not having been performed properly.

5:8 A patient wait

After having been circumcised, the Israelites were in no state to move any farther in their journey. *They remained where they were in camp until they were healed* (**5:8**). This must have had an amazing impact on their lives. Being already in the promised land, they must have been anxious to explore the land and begin to enjoy its fruits. But not yet! Being in the vicinity of their enemies, they must have felt extremely vulnerable. But they just had to be still and wait. They must have wondered what this was all about.

As they nursed their wounds, these people had a unique moment to reflect on their relationship with the God who had brought them across the Jordan – a moment in which they could consider the significance of the circumcision they had just undergone.

5:9-12 The reproach of Egypt

Once the people were circumcised, God told Joshua, *Today I have rolled away the reproach of Egypt from you.* So the place was called *Gilgal,* a Hebrew word meaning 'to roll' (**5:9**). It

is as if God were telling these people, 'Today I have dealt with your past. Let's start afresh. Forget the past.'

Israel's history included slavery in Egypt, oppression by the Egyptians, and disobedience to their God. Even though the group that Joshua now led had not experienced the slavery and oppression, nor participated in the disobedience of their fathers, they knew about it and understood why their parents had died in the wilderness.

The Israelites knowledge of their background must have caused them to lose their sense of self-worth, their self-confidence and their confidence in God. Even though they had seen mighty works of God in their lives, their past stood as an obstacle between them and the promised victory. God therefore saw the need to deal with it before he could send them to battle the giants of Canaan. If they were going to be confident enough to face their enemies, then the reproach of Egypt needed to be removed. This past had to be dealt with.

Through the circumcision at Gilgal, God rolled away the cloud of guilt and fear that hung over these people's heads. He completely separated them from their past and gave them a new beginning. They were able to regain their confidence and start off anew as the people of God. In fact it was at Gilgal that the manna stopped flowing as they celebrated the first Passover in the promised land (**5:10-12**). From then on, they ate of the fruit of the land. The old had passed away and the new had come. They were 'born again' into God's covenant of faith with Abraham.

For many believers, the past can be a major stumbling block to a victorious Christian life. Some may be tempted to doubt that God can deal completely with their pagan past, which may include idolatry or witchcraft. Those with a history of failure may be afraid to accept success even if success comes their way. They fear that it may not last and do not want to risk disappointment. So they are very afraid when God suddenly ushers them into the realm of victory and success. Others are weighed down by guilt. They feel that they do not deserve anything good from God. If any prayer is not answered or if some evil befalls them, they think that God is punishing them for their sins, and they feel that they deserve it. Still others are crippled by a broken past. A woman who has been raped may find that every time the husband approaches her in bed, she remembers the pain of the rape and freezes in fear. Those who grew up in abusive homes, where the adults fought or the children were physically abused, may end up either being abusive themselves or becoming very passive in their relationships. Children of divorced parents may also bear deep scars.

As with the Israelites, these are 'reproaches' that can render success unattainable. If we suffer any such oppression from our past, we must come to Gilgal and allow God to use the flint knives of the Spirit to circumcise our hearts. Old methods, old sins, old habits and generational problems must be left at Gilgal. Real and imaginary fears must be dealt with.

Obviously, this gives rise to the question: what is our equivalent of Gilgal? To adequately answer this question, we must understand the spiritual significance of the practice of circumcision. In Genesis 17, circumcision signalled the ratification of the covenant between Yahweh and Abraham. Yahweh undertook to be the God of Abraham and his descendants. Abraham was to be the father of a multitude of nations and the founder of a line of kings. Abraham and his descendants were to inherit Canaan. This agreement was permanent. But to be included in the covenant it was necessary that every male child should be circumcised on the eighth day. Similarly, a foreigner who had attached himself as a slave to a Hebrew household had to undergo the rite. Non-fulfilment of circumcision led to death or excommunication. No uncircumcised male could take part in the celebration of the Passover (Exod 12:48).

Circumcision therefore became the one and only basis for being considered a member of the commonwealth of Israel. It was the distinguishing mark that separated Jews from Gentiles, the people of God from the people of the world. So important was this practice among the Jews that even after Christ's death some of the disciples insisted that for anybody to truly belong to Christ they must be circumcised (see Acts 15). At the Council of Jerusalem, it was finally agreed that Gentile believers should not be burdened with the yoke of Jewish laws and practices. What made these early believers shelve such a significant practice was their grasp of what Christ had accomplished through his death on the cross. His death and resurrection had ushered in a new covenant that comes by faith and not by circumcision.

Paul wrote to the Galatians, assuring them that Jesus fulfilled all that was required by the Abrahamic covenant and that 'in Christ Jesus neither circumcision nor uncircumcision has any value. The only thing that counts is faith expressing itself through love' (Gal 5:1-6). Paul also told the Colossians, 'you were also circumcised, in the putting off of the sinful nature, not with a circumcision done by the hands of men but with the circumcision done by Christ, having been buried with him in baptism and raised with him through your faith in the power of God, who raised him from the dead' (Col 2:11).

When dealing with the problems carried from our past, we need to remember that Jesus has done everything necessary for settling the burdens of our past; we no longer need any form of circumcision. Figuratively, therefore, the cross of Christ is the new Gilgal for all pilgrims entering God's new land of Canaan. When we come to Christ in repentance and accept him as our Lord and Saviour, we hear him say to us, 'Today I have rolled away from you the reproach of Egypt' (5:9). At that point every sin, habit, oppression or curse is rendered absolutely powerless and useless as we come under the cleansing blood of Jesus Christ by faith.

If you feel weak and helpless, remember the case of Gideon. The circumstances of his day and of his family had given him a poor self-image, so that he described his clan as the weakest in Manasseh, and himself as the least in his family (Judg 6:15). Yet he was chosen to show the Israelites and the Midianites that God does not operate like human beings. In fact throughout Scripture, God has picked the most unlikely individuals to carry out his mission so that no one should take the glory due to him. This is the truth that Paul told the Corinthians, 'God chose the weak things of the world to shame the strong. He chose the lowly things of this world and the despised things – and the things that are not – to nullify the things that are, so that no one may boast before him' (1 Cor 1:27-29).

God will in most cases choose weak vessels to accomplish his plans, as such people will be the most likely to trust in him for their success. The fact that you feel weak and inadequate may be the very asset that qualifies you for God's service.

Another concern for many Christians, especially in Africa, is the question of heritage: can our success be affected by what our forefathers did? This issue has occupied the minds of many believers as they come to terms with their cultural past. The problem has been compounded by preachers and teachers who emphasize the passing on of blessings and curses from one generation to another. We hear categorical assertions: 'Curses can be inherited. They can be passed down from generation to generation.' This point may be illustrated by the example of the Canaanite woman who came to Jesus seeking help (Matt 15:21-28; Mark 7:24-30). It is claimed that Jesus referred to her as a dog because there was a curse on the Canaanites (Matt 15:26), and that they looked like dogs in the spirit realm. While it is true that Canaan was cursed many generations earlier, nowhere is it recorded that they were made to look like dogs whether spiritually or physically. However, at the time, the Jews called all Gentiles dogs. Most scholars understand that what Jesus was saying was that his ministry was primarily to the Jews and not to the Gentiles (see also Matt 10:5-6). If the curse of Canaan had been on the woman, then Jesus would have dealt with it before answering her prayer, instead of simply acceding to her great faith.

Even if we suppose that the curse of Canaan stood between this woman and her blessing, it should still come as great encouragement to us that no matter what curse may be upon us, it cannot prevent us from receiving God's blessings if we come to him in faith. Either way we are winners! The woman did not have to go back home and break the curse before she could receive blessings from the Lord. In humility she reached out right there and then, and received the desires of her heart from the Master!

However, it is true that the effect of sin can spread beyond the individual sinner to his or her family, fellowship, church or even nation. It therefore follows that there are times when the sin of one man or woman can affect many innocent people. Achan's sin led to the defeat of the whole of Israel (7:1-26). Jonah's disobedience led to a storm that affected the whole ship in which he was a passenger (Jonah 1:3-4). This means that if we are aware of sin, it must be confessed and forgiven. The Bible promises that when we confess our sins, God is willing to forgive us. We should not continue to live under the curse of sin. It must be readily brought to the cross and nailed there.

But does God hold us accountable for the sins of our forefathers? God told Moses, 'I, the Lord your God, am a jealous God, punishing the children for the sin of the fathers to the third and fourth generation of those who hate me, but showing love to a thousand generations of those who love me and keep my commandments' (Exod 20:5-6; see also Exod 34:7; Num 14:18; Deut 5:9).

These and similar scriptures have been used by many to explain that God does indeed visit the sin of the fathers upon the children, in fact, to the third and fourth generation. They also say that curses pronounced upon parents may be passed on to their children. We must consider one or two ideas that should inform our life regarding this.

It is an undeniable fact that under the old covenant, the law of Moses, God did visit the sins of the fathers upon the children. This can be seen, for example, in King David's family. Because David committed adultery with Bathsheba and murdered her husband Uriah (2 Sam 11), God decreed that 'the sword shall never depart from your house' (2 Sam 12:10). So David's sons also fell into sexual sins and murdered others – and were punished for their wicked acts.

However, if the words of Exodus 20:5 about punishing sin 'to the third and fourth generation' are true, what about Exodus 20:6, where God promises that he will show love 'to a thousand generations' of those who love him and keep his commandments? Did God mean only the first part and not the second? Or are there people who, because one of their forefathers loved God and kept his commandments, are blessed to a thousand generations irrespective of what kind of lives they live?

In anticipation of the new covenant in Christ, God spoke through the prophet Ezekiel, quoting the popular proverb: 'The fathers eat sour grapes, and the children's teeth are set on edge' (Ezek 18:2; see Jer 31:29). The Lord declares, 'you will no longer quote this proverb in Israel. For every living soul belongs to me, the father as well as the son – both alike belong to me. The soul who sins is the one who will die' (Ezek 18:3-4; see also Jer 31:27-33). God is very specific about what he meant. 'Suppose there is a righteous man who does what is just and right … He follows my decrees and faithfully keeps my laws. That man is righteous; he will surely live' (Ezek 18:5, 9). But, how does this righteousness affect the next generation? 'Suppose he has a violent son, who sheds blood or does any of these other things (though the father has done none of them) … Will such a man live? He will not! Because he has done all these detestable things, he will surely be put to death and his blood will be on his own head' (Ezek 18:10, 13). Then comes the third generation, how are they affected? Here is a case where their grandfather was righteous but their father was wicked. How does God treat this third generation? 'But suppose this son has a son who sees all the sins his father commits, and though he sees them, he does not do such things … He keeps my laws and follows my decrees. He will not die for his father's sin; he will surely live. But his father will die for his own sin' (Ezek 18:14, 17).

This message is straightforward and clear. Yet God anticipated that the people of Israel would have difficulties with the new form of justice because they were used to the order in which God visited the sin of the father on the children. So he explained, 'The son will not share the guilt of the father, nor will the father share the guilt of the son. The righteousness of the righteous man will be credited to him, and the wickedness of the wicked will be charged against him' (Ezek 18:20).

This is an extremely important fact to consider when dealing with the reproach of our past. We must not dwell too much on the sins of the past, especially if we were not directly responsible for them! The new covenant provides for the punishment of an individual for his or her own sin.

If we were accountable for the sins of our ancestors, we should also be able to obtain salvation for them. But only those who call upon the name of the Lord shall be saved. You may love your father with the greatest love that is humanly possible, but unless he accepts Christ as his Saviour, he is destined for eternal judgment. Likewise, you may love your children dearly, but unless they make a personal commitment to Christ, they are destined for eternal death. The reverse is also true. You may be the most wicked man who ever lived, but if your children choose to follow Christ as Lord and Saviour, they are going straight to heaven!

The prayers of Nehemiah and Daniel have often been used to justify repenting of the sins of one's ancestors (Neh 1:5-11; Dan 9:4-19). But, both Nehemiah and Daniel included themselves in their confessions, not because they themselves were under God's curse, but because they recognized that the sins of their people had come between them and their God. These are therefore intercessory prayers rather than personal confessions.

Some people have been known to take the idea of generational sin and curses so far as to dig into their backgrounds to find out if there were any unconfessed sins of their parents and grandparents that they could repent of. Some have even gone to the graves of their parents to confess the parents' sins. There is nowhere in Scripture where this is taught or encouraged. Sin can only be confessed while one is alive! Otherwise this would mean that we can confess the sins of our ancestors and somehow attain righteousness for the dead. Too often, all this looking into the past seems more like an escape from reality than a genuine search for divine sanctification.

Instead of trying to understand or explain the source of your problems, like Job's friends who thought all of life's problems can only come as a result of our sin against God (see Job 4:7; 8:20), why not simply bring them to the foot of the cross and leave them there. Jesus did not say, 'Check into your past and find out the source of your sorrows.' He simply said, 'Come to me, all you who are weary and burdened, and I will give you rest' (Matt 11:28-30). These words are echoed by Peter, 'Humble yourselves, therefore, under God's mighty hand, that he may lift you up in due time. Cast all your anxiety on him because he cares for you' (1 Pet 5:6-7).

We must let our past rest. We must not continue to fish in God's sea of forgetfulness. Paul declared, 'Forgetting what is behind and straining towards what is ahead, I press on towards the goal to win the prize for which God has called me heavenwards in Christ Jesus. All of us who are mature should take such a view of things' (Phil 3:14-15). Dwelling on your past is a sure way to paralyse yourself on your journey to reaching your destiny. You must choose to forget the past, and like Paul press on towards the future. If there is anybody whose past should have haunted him, it was Paul. When he was known as Saul, he had vigorously persecuted the church (Acts 8:3). When Stephen was stoned to death, Saul was there full of approval (Acts 8:1). And yet once Paul accepted the saving grace of the Lord Jesus, he moved forward in boldness and confidence in full appreciation that the blood of Christ had cleansed him from all unrighteousness and broken every chain that had bound him!

5:13-6:27 Marching Against Jericho

Jericho was one of the physical barriers to the Israelites' divinely ordained conquest of the promised land. Therefore, Jericho had to be overcome, its gates had to be opened. But Jericho also represents every form of stronghold that stands against the advance of God's plan, whether individuals who have closed their minds to God's word or evil powers holding down God's people and hindering their progress in life. On the outside they may appear strong and fortified, but our very presence causes them to tremble with fear. Sometimes all we can see are mighty walls and closed gates. But the God who brought down Jericho is able to bring them down.

5:13-15 A man with a sword

When Joshua was standing near Jericho, he suddenly saw a man, *with a drawn sword in his hand* (**5:13**). He wondered whether an enemy had ambushed him. *Are you for us or for our enemies?* he asked. The answer was as unexpected as the man's presence, *Neither, but as the commander of the army of the Lord I have come* (**5:14**). The man was saying that he was not on their side, as if the battle belonged to Joshua and Israel. The battle belonged to the Lord. So really it was for Israel to be on God's side and not vice versa! God is not a mercenary who is summoned to fight battles on behalf of others. He is the eternal commander-in-chief in all battles against the forces of evil.

The Christian community faces the forces of evil in society. Civil wars, poverty, illiteracy and disease are overwhelming challenges for Africa. At times we may seem helpless, but God's assurance is that the battle belongs to him, and it is up to us to make sure we are on his side. As Paul puts it, 'If God is for us, who can be against us?' (Rom 8:31).

Realizing whom he was dealing with, Joshua fell down in reverence. He was told, *Take off your sandals, for the place where you are standing is holy* (**5:15**). Sandals were not worn indoors, so putting them on was a sign of readiness for some activity. That is why Paul, when describing spiritual armour, talks of the shoes as a sign of readiness to engage in battle (Eph 6:15). For Joshua to be commanded to remove his sandals at such a crucial moment not only disarmed him, as it were, but also further reminded him that he was not dependent on his own armour or his own strength. He was to look up to God in worship and reverence, even in the face of war. Joshua, like Moses (Exod 3:5), removed his sandals with no further argument. Though a mighty warrior, Joshua realized that the battle before him could only be won under the direction of God. It is only in submitting to God's will that we can realize victory. Having humbled himself before God, Joshua received instructions on how Jericho was to be taken.

Another leader to whom the Lord sent a similar word of encouragement was Zerubbabel, who was appointed to rebuild the temple after the exile. God reassured him that the temple was going to be rebuilt, not by human power, but by the divine providence, authority, power and energy of the Most High (Zech 4:6). In the same way the church must be raised and preserved. No secular power, no human prudence, no earthly policy, no lawsuits can ever be used for the founding and preservation of the church of Christ.

6:1-5 Trumpet blasts and human shouts

Jericho was an impregnable fortress, and it *was tightly shut up because of the Israelites. No one went out and no one came in* (**6:1**). This great fortress was actually shut up because of Israel! It is evident that what Rahab had told the spies was true: the hearts of the people had melted with fear and their courage had failed (2:11). They had retreated like a tortoise into its shell. It is also possible that the king of Jericho, finding that the spies had escaped, may have taken precautions to prevent anything of the kind happening in future. Keeping the city shut both day and night, he was determined to defend himself to the uttermost.

But nothing can be 'shut up' to God. Jericho was an open opportunity for God to demonstrate his power. He said to Joshua, *See, I have delivered Jericho into your hands, along with its king and its fighting men* (**6:2**). What foolishness when men attempt to shut themselves up against God! The communists in Europe tried for many years, but the walls came tumbling down in the 1990s. The animists and traditionalists of Africa have tried, but the Spirit of God is sweeping across the continent like a whirlwind!

Jesus told his disciples, 'I will build my church, and the gates of Hades will not overcome it' (Matt 16:18). In other words, when the church chooses to rise up in Jesus' name, nothing can stand in opposition and prevail against it. Even the most fortified stronghold must give way.

God had a special plan for conquering Jericho. It was to be taken in style, by a grand march round the city, once every day for six days, and seven times on the seventh day. As in the march across Jordan, the priests carrying the ark of the covenant had the central role, along with seven other priests carrying rams' horns. God told Joshua, *On the seventh day, march around the city seven times, with the priests blowing the trumpets. When you hear them sound a long blast on the trumpets, have all the people give a loud shout; then the wall of the city will collapse and the people will go up, every man straight in* (**6:4-5**).

God has given us the weapons to pull down every stronghold that stands in our way. But 'the weapons that we fight with are not the weapons of the world. On the contrary, they have divine power to demolish strongholds. We demolish arguments and every pretension that sets itself up against the knowledge of God, and we take captive every thought to make it obedient to Christ' (2 Cor 10:4-5). But as with Jericho, the pulling down of strongholds requires patience and faithfulness to God's word. Some strongholds require marching around in spiritual silence for a period of time until they come tumbling down. At times we give up on strongholds on the first round, or the second or the third. Joshua's team had to go round once a day for six days and seven times on the seventh day!

Jesus told his disciples who had failed to drive out an evil spirit, 'This kind can come out only by prayer' (Mark 9:29). Just as very serious medical cases are taken to an intensive care unit (ICU), so very serious spiritual cases must be taken to the Lord's ICU through prayer. Prayer is one way of encircling the strongholds of Jericho. It is one way of expressing our total dependence upon God and his mighty power. In prayer, we cast our hope on the only one who is able to bring the walls of the fortress crashing down before us.

6:6-10 Keeping in step

Though God had promised to deliver Jericho into Joshua's hands, there were detailed instructions that he and the people had to follow if they were going to experience victory (**6:6-9**). They had to keep in step with God's command. They were to shout, but only as directed. So Joshua commanded the people, *Do not give a war cry, do not raise your voices, do not say a word until the day I tell you to shout. Then shout!* (**6:10**).

Spiritual victories can only be realized if we keep in step with the Spirit and follow his instructions carefully. Joshua and his team had to observe God's instructions. Only when God commanded them were they to shout. A major tragedy confronting the church in Africa is that although everybody knows that we should shout the message of Christ in order to win the continent for the Lord, our shouting is absolutely uncoordinated. At the continental level, there seems to be no leadership able to coordinate the shout. At the country level, there are too many shouts from too many quarters. Even at the local church level, clear leadership is often lacking, and therefore our shouts bear little or no fruit. Until a new Joshua comes to coordinate our shouts, the walls of evil in the continent will not come crashing down.

6:11-14 Return to camp

Joshua had the ark of the Lord carried around Jericho, circling it once. Then the people returned to camp and spent the night there (**6:11**). At the end of this first day, the people went back to camp with no evidence of any success or progress. Everything was as it had always been. Of course everybody was a little more tired than when they began, but there was nothing tangible to show for what they had done that day. But they had done what the Lord had told them to do. What was crucial was that they had acted in simple obedience to the word of God. The walk with God will not always make sense, but we must walk in full obedience if victory is to be ours.

Their faith and obedience were tested in the next five days as they woke up each morning, went around the wall and returned to the camp with no evidence of God's divine intervention (**6:14**). This must have required very special corporate faith on the part of all involved: Joshua as the leader, the seven priests carrying the seven trumpets marching before the ark of the Lord, the armed men ahead of them and the rear guard behind – a united team of faith waking up every morning and taking a walk of faith every day for six days!

The walk of faith has always required unquestioning obedience to the voice of God no matter how ridiculous the instructions may seem. It is not always easy. When the prophet Elisha told Naaman how he could be healed of his leprosy, this great commander of the army of the king of Aram was angry. He found Elisha's instruction ridiculous and offensive (2 Kgs 5:1-12). It is thus of great significance that at Jericho the people obeyed Joshua and completed this march for the six days with no resistance, questioning or discouragement. It shows that they had developed total confidence in Joshua as their leader and in Yahweh as their God.

The other notable contrast between the Naaman account and those who marched at Jericho is that Naaman could make his decision on his own and affect only only himself. But at Jericho there was a need for corporate faith and action. It can be difficult to mobilize others to rally behind such an act of faith. The leader may convince the followers to go for the first round and possibly for a second round. But to be consistent followers for six unfruitful days requires a special leap of faith that is not common.

6:15 The seventh day

The seventh day was a significant day in the siege of Jericho. The seven days' march of the seven priests blowing seven trumpets round the walls of Jericho now culminated in seven circuits of the city (**6:15**). While it is not clear whether Joshua had disclosed to the people that the seventh day would be the day of victory, it must have been a day of great anticipation, for the seventh day in particular and the number seven in general bore special significance in the Jewish mind. What is immediately noteworthy is the repetition of the number seven in the narrative of this grand march around Jericho.

There is clear evidence that the Babylonians regarded seven as the number of totality or completeness. The Sumerians, from whom the Babylonians seem to have borrowed the idea, equated the word 'seven' with the word 'all'. For example, 'seven gods' at the end of a list meant 'all the gods'. Seven was thus the expression of the highest power, the greatest conceivable force.

The number seven is referred to in one way or another in nearly six hundred passages in the Bible, as well as in many passages in other Jewish literature. In many of these references, it simply means the number seven, but in many it also has symbolic significance. It symbolizes perfection, fullness, abundance, rest, and completion. In Scripture, the number seven plays a conspicuous part in many passages giving rules for worship or purification or recording ritual actions. The seventh day of the week was holy (Exod 20:8-11; Deut 5:12-15), there were seven days of unleavened bread (Exod 34:18) and seven days of the Feast of Tabernacles (Lev 23:34). The seventh year was the sabbatical year (Exod 21:2). Jacob served seven years for Rachel (Gen 29:20) and bowed down seven times to Esau (Gen 33:3). There were Joseph's seven years of plenty and seven years of famine in Egypt (Gen 41:53-54), the seven daughters of Jethro (Exod 2:16), the seven sons of Jesse (1 Sam 16:10), the seven sons of Saul (2 Sam 21:6) and the seven sons of

Job (Job 1:2; 42:13). The number must no doubt be understood literally in many of these passages, but even then its symbolic meaning is probably hinted at by the historian. When a man was said to have had seven sons or daughters, or an action was reported as done or to be done seven times, the number was noted, and its symbolic force remembered.

The symbolic use of numbers is not uncommon in Africa. In many communities, funerals for various categories of people run for a specific number of days to symbolize the honour due to them. In other African communities, births are celebrated for a specified number of days. Among the Luo of Kenya for example, a baby girl is not to be taken out of the house until three days after she is born, while a boy is kept indoors for four days.

It can therefore be assumed that when Joshua got up at daybreak on the seventh day and commanded the people to march around the city seven times, it must have created a sense of anticipation in the minds and hearts of the people. Moses had promised them that if they were obedient, the Lord would grant that their enemies would be defeated. He assured them, 'They will come at you from one direction but flee from you in seven' (Deut 28:7). And now it was the seventh day of surrounding their enemies. Their patience was about to bear fruit. The Éwé of Ghana have a proverb: 'If you are patient enough you can cook a stone and it will become soft.' These people had cooked their stone for six days – and on this seventh day it was getting soft!

6:16, 20 The shout

A simple act of obedience to God's instructions was to bring the walls of Jericho tumbling down. The seventh time around, when the priests sounded the trumpet blast, Joshua commanded the people, '*Shout! … When the trumpets sounded, the people shouted, and … the wall collapsed; so every man charged straight in, and they took the city* (**6:16, 20**). As Abraham's obedience was accounted to him as an act of faith, so this shout is recorded as an act of faith: 'By faith the walls of Jericho fell, after the people had marched around them for seven days' (Heb 11:30).

Faith is an act of obedience to the voice of God irrespective of whether or not his instruction makes sense. To shout when God says to do so is an indication that we believe in God and trust in his wisdom and ability to do what he says he will do. Jesus told his disciples, 'if you have faith as small as a mustard seed, you can say to this mountain, "Move from here to there" and it will move. Nothing will be impossible for you' (Matt 17:20).

An Éwé proverb from Ghana says, 'If you keep water in your mouth for too long, it turns into saliva.' In other words, whatever you are to do, do it promptly because if you delay you may lose interest in it or miss the moment. Joshua and his team had to shout at the right moment or they would not only have lost the opportunity, but they would also have disobeyed God. God had put water into their mouth, and they had to swallow it before it turned into saliva.

It was not the noise that the people made that brought down the walls of Jericho. Joshua made it clear that *the Lord has given you the city!* The shout was a mere act of obedience to God. Many have tried to replicate these shouts without God's express instructions, and they have been greatly disappointed.

6:17-19; 21-25 Keeping their word

The instructions for taking the city were clear. The inhabitants were to be totally destroyed. This instruction should be viewed in light of Deuteronomy 20:18. If the nation of Israel were to be true witnesses to the Lord's glory, they had to be guarded from all influences that would turn them away from serving him. Only Rahab was to be spared. *The city and all that is in it are to be devoted to the Lord* (**6:17**). All the silver and gold and the articles of bronze and iron were sacred to the Lord, and had to go into his treasury (**6:19**). The people were to keep away from the things devoted to God, otherwise they would bring judgment upon themselves (**6:18**).

Some Bible scholars view this demand as being connected to God's requirement that the firstfruits be devoted to him. Moses had told the people that when they had taken possession of the land, they were to take some of the firstfruits of all that they produced and bring it to the Lord as a special offering (Deut 26:1-4; see also Exod 13:2). It is argued that since Jericho was the first city to be conquered in the promised land, the Lord required that it be devoted to him as the firstfruit of the land.

Here was another great test of obedience. The people had lived in the wilderness for forty long years, and a rich city such as Jericho with all its gold and silver must have presented very real temptations. People must have longed to take some articles for themselves. But God forbade them to do so and instead instructed them to devote everything to him.

After the walls fell down, Joshua ensured that the people obeyed the Lord's instructions. First, *they devoted the city to the Lord and destroyed with the sword every living thing in it* (**6:21**). Then *they burned the whole city and everything in it, but they put the silver and gold and the articles of bronze and iron into the treasury of the Lord's house* (**6:24**). He also told *the two men who had spied out the land, 'Go into the prostitute's house and bring her out and all who belong to her, in accordance with your oath to her'* (**6:22-23**). Thus Joshua kept the word of the men he had sent as spies into Jericho.

The ability to keep one's word is a rare gift, especially among leaders. Many of us make empty promises that are never fulfilled. A Kiswahili proverb says: *Neno la mtawala halilingani na mlio wa ngoma* ['The word of a leader is not like the voice of a drum']. In other words, the word of a leader must be reliable, not like the empty sound of a drum. A leader must be able to keep his or her word. Ecclesiastes warns, 'It is better not to vow than to make a vow and not fulfil it. Do not let your mouth lead you into sin' (Eccl 5:5-7).

After the fall of Jericho, Rahab lived among the Israelites (**6:25**). A Canaanite turned Israelite! A simple act of faith in the God of Israel counted as righteousness. 'By faith the prostitute Rahab, because she welcomed the spies, was not killed with those who were disobedient' (Heb 11:31). Jesus said, 'Anyone who gives you a cup of water in my name because you belong to Christ will certainly not lose his reward' (Mark 9:41). Rahab granted safety to God's people, and she was granted safety by God's people. She did not lose her reward.

6:26-27 A solemn oath

With the city utterly destroyed, Joshua placed a curse upon Jericho: *Cursed before the Lord is the man who undertakes to rebuild this city, Jericho* (**6:26a**). Many believe that this curse was meant to preserve the ruins of Jericho as a reminder to all of the power of the God of Israel. Any attempt to rebuild it would be an attempt to tamper with this evidence of the mighty works of God.

God's ultimate aim in all that he does is that his glory might be displayed for the appreciation of those who embrace it, and the desolation of those who do not. Therefore, he rewards acts that confess human helplessness and express hope in God, because these acts call attention to his glory. When Jericho fell, there was no doubt in anybody's mind as to who had done it – not in the minds of the people of Jericho, nor in the minds of Israel.

Another possible explanation for the curse can be found in the Lord's command, 'If you hear it said about one of the towns the Lord your God is giving you to live in that wicked men have arisen among you and have led the people of their town astray … you must certainly put to the sword all who live in that town. Destroy it completely … as a whole burnt offering to the Lord your God. It is to remain a ruin forever, never to be rebuilt. None of those condemned things shall be found in your hands, so that the Lord will turn from his fierce anger' (Deut 13:12-13, 15-17).

Joshua declared of whoever attempted to rebuild the walls of Jericho, *at the cost of his firstborn son will he lay its foundations; at the cost of his youngest will he set up its gates* (**6:26b**). This may be because Jericho was the firstfruit of the land (see comment on 6:18). Whoever wanted to rebuild it would have to 'redeem' it with his firstborn son!

The curse proved effective: 'In Ahab's time, Hiel of Bethel rebuilt Jericho. He laid its foundations at the cost of his firstborn son Abiram, and he set up its gates at the cost of his youngest son Segub, in accordance with the word of the Lord spoken by Joshua son of Nun' (1 Kgs 16:34). Is it possible that when we do not obey the Lord by bringing the firstfruits into his house, we too repay with something more dear to us?

Israel's destruction of Jericho was without doubt a major breakthrough, for Jericho was a major fortress that must have been a serious worry for Joshua. Because of the pulling down of that stronghold, his fame spread throughout the land (6:27).

7:1-9:27 Defeat and Deceit

7:1-8:29 Ai – A Strategic City

Joshua's next step was to take Ai, a name that means 'the ruin'. It was in central Palestine, just east of Bethel (modern Beitin), about ten miles (sixteen kilometres) north of Jerusalem. During Abraham's first journey through Canaan, he had built an altar between Bethel and Ai (Gen 12:8; 13:3). Ai was much smaller than Jericho, but it occupied a strategic position at the top of the hill country. The capture of this city would give Israel a command post from where they could easily take control of major portions of Canaan.

7:1 Achan's sin – a false start

After describing the great victory at Jericho and God's clear command on how to deal with the city and its loot, the writer opens chapter 7 with *But*. Readers are being warned to brace themselves for a totally different story.

Israel acted unfaithfully and disobeyed Joshua's command not to touch any of Jericho's loot. However, not all of Israel committed this sin. It was only one of them, *Achan, son of Carmi, the son of Zimri, the son of Zerah, of the tribe of Judah* (7:1). Because of what he had done, *the Lord's anger burned against Israel.* Thus, although only one man sinned, all Israel was held liable. Achan's sin forms the backdrop to Joshua's attempt to capture Ai.

7:2-26 Trouble at Ai

7:2-3 HUMAN ANALYSIS Unaware of what had happened, Joshua set out to take Ai. As he had done with Jericho, he sent spies to assess the city (7:2). Within no time, the spies came back with an extremely encouraging report. They told Joshua, *Not all the people will have to go up against Ai. Send two or three thousand men to take it and do not weary all the people, for only a few men are there* (7:3). The spies were confident that Ai was going to be a walkover. There was no need to waste human resources on this simple project. A few men would be adequate to take the tiny city.

7:4-5 HUMAN STRATEGY The battle of Ai was a sorry affair. The Israelites *were routed by the men of Ai, who killed about thirty-six of them* (7:4). They then chased the rest from the city and struck them down on the slopes. As would be expected, *the hearts of the people melted and became like water* (7:5).

What had happened? After the previous victory, Ai must have seemed like a minor affair. But it seems that the spies' report was not a statement of faith and confidence in God,

but one of pride and confidence in themselves. The Israelites assumed that because Jordan had been crossed and Jericho had fallen so easily, Ai was no big deal. A few men would be enough to take it.

Unfortunately, such thinking was presumptuous self-deception. We see no evidence of the Israelites turning to God for guidance and direction, as they had done at the crossing of the Jordan and the taking of Jericho. Taking things for granted, they did not ask the Lord how they ought to handle Ai. They must have thought, 'This is a small city, we can take it by ourselves, we do not need to bother God.' The result – a great defeat!

The Lord had previously given specific instructions that Jericho was to be totally destroyed with everything in it. They were not to plunder the city, but to dedicate the precious articles to the Lord. But Achan had not obeyed this command. If only the leaders of the Israelites had paused for a moment to contemplate and seek God's guidance concerning Ai, God would have revealed to them that they needed to do some housekeeping before embarking on the battle against the city. But these men and women of God were perhaps too elated after Jericho to be spiritually alert.

This is a very important lesson. It is often after a major victory that we are most vulnerable. It is at that moment when we think we have God on our side that we can easily become arrogant and proud. 'If you think you are standing firm, be careful that you don't fall' (1 Cor 10:12).

Just when Joshua and his team thought they were the invincible army of Israel, they found themselves fleeing from the tiny army of Ai. Just when they should have mounted the podium to be crowned the undisputed conquerors of the great fortresses of Canaan, they found themselves fleeing for safety from the underdogs of Ai. Before the national anthem could be played to mark their victory, they found themselves running, not the lap of honour, but for dear life!

7:6-7 HUMAN RESPONSE Joshua could not believe what had happened. This was perhaps the most humiliating moment of his life. He was utterly distraught and could not contain himself. He *tore his clothes and fell face down to the ground* (7:6). He had no choice but to prostrate himself before the Lord, and with the elders doing the same, they entered into a corporate petition.

But instead of trying to find out the root cause of their problem and repenting and seeking God's forgiveness, Joshua complained to God saying, *Ah, Sovereign Lord, why did you ever bring this people across the Jordan to deliver us into the hands of the Amorites to destroy us? If only we had been content to stay on the other side of the Jordan!* (7:7).

Joshua questioned God's wisdom in bringing them across the Jordan! Is it not amazing how quickly we shift blame and see the source of our troubles anywhere else but in ourselves? How easy it is for us to blame God for the blessings he has given us, as if they were the root of our sorrows.

When Adam and Eve sinned and were confronted with their disobedience, instead of falling down in repentance, Adam stood up to God and said, 'The woman whom you put here with me – she gave me some fruit from the tree, and I ate it' (Gen 3:12). Adam was implying that God had made a mistake! If he had not given the woman to Adam, everything would have been just fine. Yet is this not the same woman of whom Adam had exclaimed in excitement, 'This is now bone of my bones and flesh of my flesh' (Gen 2:23)?

Similarly, the same Joshua who had celebrated God's parting of the waters of the Jordan and breaking of the walls of Jericho was now blaming God for performing those miracles and bringing them into the promised land. How often we behave in a similar manner. When we meet with trouble and difficulties, we blame God for his blessings. We wish he had never interfered in our lives. We blame him for having given us a wife or a husband, a child or a friend, a job or a business, a car or a house, not remembering that we have perhaps received a particular blessing after much prayer and petition. Proverbs 10:22 says, 'The blessing of the Lord brings wealth, and he adds no trouble to it.' It follows that if a blessing seems to bring sorrow with it, there is need for introspection. In most cases the problem lies neither with the blessing nor the Blesser, but with the blessed!

7:8-9 HUMAN CONCERN As Joshua continued his prayers, another concern hit him. He cried out, *O Lord, what can I say, now that Israel has been routed by its enemies? The Canaanites and the other people of the country will hear about this …. What then will you do for your own great name?* (**7:8-9**). Beyond just his own shame and embarrassment, Joshua felt that God's reputation was also at stake. He reminded God that, unless he did something to get them out of this shameful situation, God's name was going to be irreparably defamed. The Canaanites and the other people of the country, upon hearing about it, were going to take advantage of the opportunity, surround God's people and wipe them out.

Joshua was pushing God to protect his own reputation. But what Joshua did not realize is that the Lord needs no defence. Usually one needs to maintain a reputation if one's reputation is at stake or if one is competing against equals. But the Lord stands alone as God in the whole universe. He is the great I AM and owes nothing to anybody! In any case, whatever he does is done in absolute perfection and can never fail under any form of scrutiny.

7:10-13 A DIVINE REBUKE God answered Joshua's prayer with a sharp and direct rebuke: *Stand up! What are you doing down on your face? Israel has sinned; they have violated my covenant* (**7:10-11**). The Lord tells Joshua the problem and the solution. He tells him to tell the people, *Consecrate yourselves in preparation for tomorrow; for this is what the Lord, the God of Israel, says: That which is devoted is among you, O Israel. You cannot stand against your enemies until you remove it* (**7:13**).

The greatest impediment to our success is usually not the many obstacles we encounter. The real enemy to living a victorious life is never the strongholds that Satan may hold against us. For as long as we are obedient to God's word, even the strongest barrier will have to give way, the highest wall will come tumbling down! The one thing that will most certainly spell doom to every effort we may seek to make on our way to the top is unconfessed sin. The psalmist was absolutely right when he declared, 'If I had cherished sin in my heart, the Lord would not have listened' (Ps 66:18). With unconfessed sin in our hearts, we open ourselves and others to defeat. Sin must be dealt with before we can expect God's blessings and victory.

7:14-18 A DIVINE PRESCRIPTION God's prescription for identifying the source of the sin was long and tedious. God told them, *In the morning, present yourselves tribe by tribe. The tribe that the Lord takes shall come forward clan by clan; the clan that the Lord takes shall come forward family by family; and the family that the Lord takes shall come forward man by man. He who is caught with the devoted things shall be destroyed by fire, along with all that belongs to him* (**7:14-15**). What was the idea behind all this? I believe that God wanted to get everybody involved in this purging exercise, to let everyone know that despite his grace, he does not tolerate sin. He wanted to make it abundantly clear to them that his word was to be strictly adhered to if success was to be realized. After this long process, Achan was identified as the culprit.

7:19-21 A DIVINE EXPOSURE Achan thought that he had done everything in total secret, but he was finally found out. Joshua said to Achan, *My son, give glory to the Lord, the God of Israel, and give him the praise. Tell me what you have done; do not hide it from me.* Achan replied, *It is true … This is what I have done …* (**7:19-20a, c**). One wonders why Achan waited until the lot fell on him. Why did he not come forward at the start and confess? He was perhaps hoping that his sin would not be discovered. But unfortunately for him, it was. The Bible says, 'Be sure that your sin will find you out' (Num 32:23). Interestingly, after Achan was discovered, he confessed: *I have sinned against the Lord* (**7:20b**). But was this a genuine confession? No! If he were sincere, he would not have waited so long.

By his own admission, Achan had stolen the beautiful, precious things that belonged to God (**7:21a**). This man, out of evil desire, had chosen to possess that which was not his. He had sacrificed the greater for the lesser, the eternal for the temporal. But was he enjoying them? No, they were hidden under the ground inside his tent. (**7:21b**). The things that cost this man his destiny lay buried inside his tent! He was not even enjoying them.

That is the deceit of sin! It looks pleasurable while you are being enticed. But in the end it brings neither pleasure nor joy. Instead it stings once you taste it. Achan could not enjoy what he had stolen. In fact, when he was discovered, he lost all his personal possessions!

7:22-26 A DIVINE JUDGMENT Joshua sent messengers to bring Achan and his family, with all his belongings and all that he had stolen, to the Valley of Achor (**7:22-24**). Joshua said to him, *Why have you brought this trouble on us? The Lord will bring trouble on you today* (**7:25**). Then all the people of Israel stoned him and his family, burned their bodies and piled rocks over them. What a painful end for a man who was destined to better things in the land of Canaan. Here was a man who chose to take a shortcut to gain material goods, and lost everything in the process. Here was a man who had survived the hardships of the wilderness, and yet died without enjoying the pleasure of Canaan!

Jesus once asked, 'What good will it be for a man if he gains the whole world, yet forfeits his soul?' (Matt 16:26). And yet the temptation to take shortcuts to achieving our dreams is very real, especially when it seems that God's promise is taking for ever to come true. The world, the flesh and the Devil, the unholy trinity, are ever present to assist us in this path to destruction. Businesspeople have sold their souls at the market of corruption in order to gain quick profits. Young women, tired of waiting for God's chosen husbands, have surrendered their chastity to cunning men who have promised them heaven only to deliver them hell. Many believers are living in deliberate sin thinking that nobody knows and that they are safe. While no one may know what is going on in our inner lives, we cannot hide anything from him before whom everything is laid bare. He saw Achan as he took the devoted things. He sees you as you walk in secret darkness or as you engage in underhand deals.

We cannot afford to tolerate sin in our lives if we want to make progress. God allowed the Israelites to be defeated at a crucial hour, and he will not walk with us in dark corridors. Sin is the greatest cancer that can eat at a human soul, and the worst obstacle to possessing your possessions. Isaiah said, 'Surely the arm of the Lord is not too short to save, nor his ear too dull to hear. But your iniquities have separated you from your God; your sins have hidden his face from you, so that he will not hear' (Isa 59:1-2).

The other truth about sin is that it often affects not only the sinner, but it spreads its consequences to their family, fellowship or the whole church. Achan's sin led to the defeat of the whole of Israel and the death of his family! It is not enough just to pray about sin. It must be identified, confessed and repented. When Joshua tried to pray about it, God told him to stand up and call for repentance and consecration. Sin must be dealt with ruthlessly and expeditiously. For to be sure, your sin will find you out! Achan perhaps thought and hoped that he would not be found out. But he was.

Yet God's gracious promise is that 'if we confess our sins, he is faithful and just and will forgive us our sins and purify us from all unrighteousness' (1 John 1:9). If we are to experience the blessings of the Lord, we must deal with sin in our lives as individuals and as a fellowship. But if, like Israel, we abuse God's grace, he can let us suffer defeat. Israel took God's grace and guidance for granted, and paid dearly.

8:1-29 Defeat of Ai

When Ai sent Israel fleeing, the people of Ai could not believe it. They had heard of the great slaughter Israel had inflicted upon Jericho, a much larger and more heavily fortified city, but they had put on a courageous face and tried their luck defending their own city. To their surprise they had won, and quite easily! This was certainly a great victory for Ai. To their delight, they found that Israel was actually not as invincible as the reports had made them to appear. There must have been great celebration in Ai.

What the people of Ai did not know was that Israel's victory over Jericho was based on their obedience to God's commands and not on their military might or experience in conventional warfare. The only reason that Israel ever won a battle was because their God was a mighty warrior who could never be defeated. On the day they were defeated at Ai, God had left them on their own because of Achan's sin. Thus although Ai had defeated Israel, they had not defeated the God of Israel. And the Lord was not about to take this humiliation of his people lying down. He laid out a strategy for conquering Ai.

Having dealt with the sin in the camp, God was ready to give victory to his people. His assurance of forgiveness was spoken straight to Joshua. *Do not be afraid, do not be discouraged* (**8:1**). He was not to be afraid of any possible defeat, nor was he to be discouraged by the previous failure. Unlike humans, God forgives totally. He does not despise a broken and contrite heart. Once we come to him in true repentance, he is ready and willing to allow us back into his fold and to restore us to ministry. Discouragement from past failures and fear of possible future blunders must not cripple our call and mission.

The spies had told Joshua, 'Not all the people will have to go up against Ai' (7:3), but this was a human analysis and a human strategy. The Lord said, *Take the whole army with you, and go up and attack Ai* (**8:1a**). When fighting God's battles, it is imperative that we seek his way and follow it. *For I have delivered into your hands the king of Ai, his people, his city and his land* (**8:1b**). God re-emphasizes that the battle for Canaan is his and not theirs. In the case of Ai, these people who had sent Israel running were now going to face the God of Israel and none of them was going to escape.

Just as Joshua had totally destroyed Jericho and killed its king, so he was to do the same to Ai and its king. However, unlike in the case of Jericho where the people were forbidden to take any plunder, in Ai the people were free to carry off plunder and livestock for themselves (**8:2a**).

God is rich in his designs and strategies, and he does not follow a formula. Every challenge is a unique opportunity to display his wisdom. So the strategy he provided this time was totally different from that used at Jericho. Joshua was commanded to *set an ambush behind the city* (**8:2b**). Part of the army was to hide, while the other part lured the people of Ai out of their city. Having sent Israel fleeing in the previous battle, the defenders of Ai would come out confidently believing that Israel was no more than a bunch of cowards. But in God's scheme, Israel's flight, which the army of Ai thought was a sign of Israel's weakness, was to be their strength (8:3-8). It would deceive the people of Ai into thinking that just as they had won easily before, they would win again.

Some have questioned whether it was worthy of God to employ such a strategy in warfare. Calvin deals with this objection. 'Surely,' he says, 'wars are not carried on by striking alone; but they are considered the best generals who succeed through art and counsel more than by force … Therefore, if war is lawful at all, it is beyond all controversy that the way is perfectly clear for the use of the customary arts of warfare, provided there is no breach of faith in the violation of treaty or truce, or in any other way.'

Contrary to what the spies had initially advised, Joshua now musters a large army in accordance with God's instructions. He tells some of them to lie in ambush behind the city (**8:4**). There is a problem regarding exactly how many men were assigned to this ambush. While **8:3** and **8:9** talk of thirty thousand being moved into position *between Bethel and Ai*, **8:12** talks of five thousand men *between Bethel and Ai*. We cannot simply say that these were two different groups, because both seem to be in the same location. It is possible that a later scribe copied one of these numbers incorrectly. Alternatively, the thirty thousand men in 8:3 may have had some other role in this mission while the specific ambush group numbered only five thousand.

Joshua sent these men out at night, and under cover of darkness they took up a position *behind the city*, not *very far from it* (8:4).

Having been defeated by Ai because of Israel's failure to seek God's mind, Joshua was keen to move only according to God's instructions. He listened carefully to God's instructions and required that the people obey his commands. True success in any venture, and especially in spiritual assignments, will be realized only if careful attention is paid to God's word. 'Blessed is the man who does not walk in the counsel of the wicked or stand in the way of sinners or sit in the seat of mockers. But his delight is in the law of the Lord, and on his law he meditates day and night … Whatever he does prospers' (Ps 1:1-3). This is important to note because even as they followed God's instructions, it is the Lord God who was to give Ai into their hands (**8:7-8**).

With God's instructions carefully relayed, the plan was in place. The story reads like the script of an action movie, full of suspense and intrigue. With the trap set to the west of the city, Joshua mustered his men, and *set up camp north of Ai, with the valley between them and the city* (**8:11**). Then he and his army moved down into the valley. As anticipated, the king of Ai hurried out to fight Israel. *But he did not know that an ambush had been set against him behind the city* (**8:14**). He was so blinded by his previous success that he never imagined that Israel could be up to anything. He took the bait, hook, line and sinker!

Joshua allowed his men to be driven back, and *all the men of Ai were called to pursue them* (**8:16**). *Not a man remained in Ai or Bethel who did not go after Israel. They left the city open and went in pursuit of Israel* (**8:17**). Just as God had planned, the people of Ai were lured out of their city. Being overconfident from their previous victory, they all went out, leaving their city empty and totally unguarded.

The town of Bethel was near Ai, which is why its inhabitants were fighting alongside the men of Ai. They had probably entered into a treaty to help each other against the advancing Israelites. The men of Bethel may only have come to the help of Ai for the first time on the day of the battle itself, although it is more likely that they had been stationed in the town in expectation of a second attack by the Israelites. The king of Bethel is included in the list of the kings killed by Joshua (12:16).

At the Lord's command, Joshua *held out his javelin towards Ai* (**8:18**). At this moment the men in the ambush attacked. Later we are told that *Joshua did not draw back the hand that held out his javelin until he had destroyed all who lived in Ai.* (**8:26**). This is reminiscent of the time when Aaron and Hur held up Moses' arms when the Amalekites attacked the Israelites at Rephidim, and 'as long as Moses held up his hands, the Israelites were winning, but whenever he lowered his hands, the Amalekites were winning' (Exod 17:8-12). God's promise to Joshua to be with him as he was with Moses is again affirmed and confirmed.

When the Israelites set the city on fire the men of Ai were caught completely unawares. They looked back only to find their city going up in smoke (**8:19-20**). What is more, they found themselves trapped between two Israelite armies with no way of escape. The Israelites who had been fleeing towards the desert turned back against their pursuers, and the men of the ambush came out of the city against them. The trap had been sprung!

The Lord has a way of mounting ambushes for those who oppose the plans of God and are proud of their own wisdom and power. At the moment of apparent victory, such people will find themselves not only caught between the lion and the bear, but will look back only to see the source of their pride going up in smoke.

As believers, the greatest mistake we can make is to fight those who oppose us with our own strength or wisdom. Like Israel, we are not acquainted with or experienced in conventional warfare. If we are to survive the Ai onslaught, we must allow God to set out the strategy, otherwise we will be vanquished. We must always remember that every battle a believer faces belongs to the Lord. And it shall be won: 'Not by might, nor by power, but by the Spirit of the Lord' (see Zech 4:6)!

Israel experienced a great victory over Ai that day. *Twelve thousand men and women* (**8:25**) were killed. Destruction such as this should not be used to justify slaughter in our day (see comment on 6:17-19). Only God has the right to take lives as he wishes, for he created life and all life belongs to him.

Israel carried off much plunder (**8:27**). Joshua then burned Ai and left it a permanent heap of ruins, a desolate place *to this day* (**8:28**). This was the worst disgrace that could be brought upon a city. The king of Ai, who had been captured alive, was brought to Joshua. *He hung the king of Ai on a tree and left him there until evening* (**8:29**). The Jews regarded being hung or crucified as a disgraceful death. Joshua was following the law carefully, as instructed in 1:7-8, and thus he obeyed the command in Deuteronomy 21:22-23: 'If a man guilty of a capital offence is put to death and his body is hung on a tree, you must not leave his body on the tree overnight. Be sure to bury him that same day, because anyone who is hung on a tree is under God's curse.' So *at sunset, Joshua ordered them to take his body from the tree and throw it down at the entrance of the city gate.* They buried it under *a large pile of rocks* (**8:29**).

8:30-35 The Law Read on Mount Ebal

It is not quite clear how the next part of the narrative follows the conquest of Ai. *Then Joshua built on Mount Ebal an altar to the Lord* (**8:30**). Some have considered that this section may be misplaced, or even a later addition. Mount Ebal is about thirty miles (forty-eight kilometres) north of Ai, and considering the crowd that was with Joshua, it would have taken at least two days to get there. It is possible that the fall of Ai gave the Israelites access to the heart of Canaan, as Bethel and the other towns in the vicinity seem to have yielded without a struggle. This would have given them easy passage to Mount Ebal.

Moses had told Israel that once they had crossed the Jordan, they were to take some large stones, coat them with plaster and then 'write on them all the words of the law'. These stones were to be set up on Mount Ebal (Deut 27:1-5). They were also to build an altar to the Lord there. Joshua moves quickly to fulfil this command after the conquest of Ai.

It would seem that this ceremony was not only an expression of thanksgiving on the part of the covenant nation for its entrance into the land, but also a practical acknowledgment of God's help. Their victories so far were a strong pledge of the conquest of the foes that still remained. The ceremony served to stamp their mark of ownership of the land through their conquering King, Yahweh.

Joshua takes this first opportunity in Canaan to remind the people of the word of the Lord by reading *all the words of the law* (**8:34**). Since a majority of this crowd had not been in the wilderness in the days of Moses, it was important that a proper foundation be laid before they settled in the land, so that no one had any excuse for going against God's law. *There was not a word of all that Moses had commanded that Joshua did not read to the whole assembly of Israel, including the women and children, and the aliens who lived among them* (**8:35**).

Too often believers, and even leaders, only read the word when they seek God's opinion about something. Once the crisis is past, few turn back to read the word of God. Nehemiah and Ezra, like Joshua, led the people in reading the word at the peak of victory and success (Neh 8).

9:1-27 Israel's Gullibility

9:1-2 An armed alliance

The news of the defeat of Jericho and Ai spread rapidly and produced fear in many Canaanite kings (**9:1**). They naturally began to work on survival strategies. Some of them chose to come together to stop the Israelite army. The kings of the Hittites, Amorites, Canaanites, Perizzites, Hivites and Jebusites set aside their differences and agreed to form a united alliance against Israel.

9:3-15 A deceitful alliance

However, not everyone agreed with this warlike strategy. The Gibeonites, knowing that they had no hope of defeating Israel, opted for a different approach. They tried a clever trick. Unfortunately, the Israelites fell for it and found themselves saddled with Gibeon as extra baggage for the rest of their lives. The Israelites were deceived by sight, flattery and pride in victory.

9:3-6 Deceived by sight The delegation the Gibeonites sent to meet the Israelites were wearing worn and patched sandals and old clothes. Their donkeys were loaded with worn-out sacks and old wineskins, and they carried dry and mouldy bread (**9:4-5**). They said to Joshua, *We have come from a distant country; make a treaty with us* (**9:6**). They showed Joshua their worn-out clothes and mouldy bread as evidence of the long journey they had taken to seek Israel's help. And they were believed! No wonder Paul says that we must live 'by faith, not by sight' (2 Cor 5:7). The Christian walk must never be dependent on what we see, for there is great deceit in sight.

9:7-13 DECEIVED BY FLATTERY The next trick that Gibeon used was flattery. When the Israelites seemed inquisitive about where the Gibeonites had come from (**9:7-8**), they diverted attention from themselves to the fame of Israel's God. They said they had come *because of the fame of the Lord your God. For we have heard reports of him: all that he did in Egypt* (**9:9**). They also said, *This bread of ours was warm when we packed it at home on the day we left to come to you. But now see how dry and mouldy it is. And these wineskins that we filled were new, but see how cracked they are. And our clothes and sandals are worn out by the very long journey* (**9:12-13**).

First, the Gibeonites offered Joshua praise and flattery concerning how far the fame of his conquests had spread, and offered what looked like evidence to back up their words. Second, they appealed to the logical reasoning of Joshua's team. These two psychological weapons have brought down many leaders. Anyone who relies on the flattering words of those who seek his favour is headed for certain ruin.

Paul also had to deal with flattery in Philippi. A slave girl who had a spirit that predicted the future followed Paul shouting, 'These men are servants of the Most High God, who are telling you the way to be saved.' Instead of saying 'Amen!' to this flattery, Paul became so troubled that he turned around and said to the spirit, 'In the name of Jesus Christ I command you to come out of her!' (Acts 16:16-18).

Daniel prophesies that when the anti-Christ comes in the last days, 'with flattery he will corrupt those who have violated the covenant, but the people who know their God will firmly resist him' (Dan 11:32).

9:14-15 DECEIVED BY PRIDE IN VICTORY The men of Israel sampled the provisions that supported the Gibeonites' story, but they did not inquire of the Lord (**9:14**). Whereas Joshua had previously been careful to seek God's guidance, now he was misled by human praise and fell into the Gibeonite trap. He was deceived, conned and defeated by them. He made a peace treaty with them, agreeing to let them live, and the leaders of the assembly ratified it by an oath (**9:15**). Moments of victory and success are very dangerous times in our spiritual walk. It is often after successful exploits that we are most prone to imagine that we have everything under control. It is at such moments that we are prone to embark on projects without seeking God's will.

9:16-27 Discovery of deceit

Three days after they made the treaty with the Gibeonites, the Israelites heard that they were neighbours, living near them. So the Israelites set out and on the third day came to their cities (**9:16-17**). But it was too late. The Israelites could not attack these people, because of the oath their leaders had sworn. Upon discovering that the Gibeonites had tricked them, the people of Israel grumbled against their leaders for entering them into a false treaty (**9:18**). They pleaded

with the leaders to get them out of the situation, just as they had brought them into it. But things were not as easy as they seemed, because the leaders of the assembly had sworn an oath to them by the Lord, the God of Israel.

But was Israel bound by an oath that was based on deceit? Some argue that since Israel had been absolutely forbidden to make any treaties with the Canaanites, the Israelite rulers were under no obligation to observe the treaty which they had made in good faith but in which the other party had lied. From the standpoint of strict justice, this argument appears correct.

However, the leaders of Israel shrank from breaking their oath, not because they assumed that it had an absolute binding force, but because they had sworn it by Yahweh, the God of Israel (**9:19**). Breaking this oath would bring the name of Yahweh into contempt among the Canaanites, and would also make the Israelites guilty of breaking God's command not to use his name in vain. They were therefore bound to observe the oath, if only to preserve the integrity of the God by whom they had sworn. To invoke the name of the Lord is an awesome thing. No wonder Paul told Timothy, 'Everyone who confesses the name of the Lord must turn away from wickedness' (2 Tim 2:19).

Bound by their oath, the worst that Israel could do to the Gibeonite con men was to make them their servants, *woodcutters and water-carriers for the entire community* (**9:20-21**). The Gibeonites thus secured their safety by deceit. And even though they were made into servants, they became Israel's responsibility for hundreds of years thereafter.

During the reign of David, there was a famine for three years. David sought help from the Lord, who said, 'It is on account of Saul and his blood-stained house; it is because he put the Gibeonites to death' (2 Sam 21:1). In other words, God brought judgment upon Israel in the time of David, hundreds of years later, simply because Saul had disregarded this oath and sought to destroy the Gibeonites. The psalmist was later to ask, 'Lord, who may dwell in your sanctuary? Who may live on your holy hill?' He then listed several categories of people who qualified, among them is the one 'who keeps his oath even when it hurts' (Ps 15:1, 4).

Joshua confronted the Gibeonites with their lie: *Why did you deceive us by saying, 'We live a long way from you,' while actually you live near us?* (**9:22**). The Gibeonites, like most con men, had done their homework and knew how to answer. Their excuse was that having heard of God's command that all the Canaanites were to be destroyed, they had feared greatly for their lives (**9:24**; Deut 7:1; 20:16-17). Again these heathens appealed to Israel's God and to his word. And then, in a show of great humility, they readily submitted to whatever verdict Joshua came to: *We are now in your hands. Do to us whatever seems good and right to you* (**9:25**). *That day Joshua made the Gibeonites woodcutters and water-carriers for the community and for the altar of the Lord*

(**9:27**). These con men, even though slaves, found themselves serving at the very altar of God because of Israel's blunder!

Jesus once said, 'the people of this world are more shrewd in dealing with their own kind than are the people of the light' (Luke 16:8). With ruthless shrewdness, the Gibeonites secured their future not only from an Israelite attack but also from any other attacks. Thus when Adoni-Zedek king of Jerusalem joined forces with other cities to attack Gibeon for making the treaty with Joshua, the Gibeonites appealed to Joshua for help (see commentary on 10:1-8).

Some of the worst con men are those who pretend to be born again, when their real intention is only to win a Christian wife. These men work patiently and cunningly to achieve their objective. They attend Sunday services regularly, learn the right language, speak in tongues, attend midweek prayer meetings and *keshas* (overnight prayer vigils) and other fellowships and, if possible, become involved in ministry! An unsuspecting Christian lady will be thoroughly deceived by such a man's charm, charisma and unusually loving style. By the time the long-awaited question, 'will you marry me?' is asked, the dear sister, like Joshua and the Israelites, sees no reason to bother the Lord about such an obvious matter.

But as soon as the marriage certificate is signed and they are pronounced husband and wife, she will be dismayed to find that this brother's mouldy bread and worn-out clothes and sandals are not from long-distance travel with the Lord. She will discover that this 'spirit-filled' brother is actually filled with a completely different spirit – a Gibeonite spirit! Unfortunately by this time, as in Joshua's case, the oath will have been sworn and the treaty signed 'until death do us part'! She may choose to console herself that she will turn the man into her own woodcutter and water-carrier, providing for her every need because such men are often materially well off, but he will be a burden for the rest of her life. He will be her unspoken prayer request at every miracle service, the first item on her prayer list at every *kesha,* and often the subject of discussion among her close confidantes.

We should never sign any treaty without first seeking God's opinion. Seek God before you enter into any contract, and especially at that vulnerable moment when you are in desperate need and the deal sounds too good. The wisest man who ever lived gave this timeless advice: 'Trust in the Lord with all your heart and lean not on your own understanding; in all your ways acknowledge him, and he will make your paths straight. Do not be wise in your own eyes; fear the Lord and shun evil. This will bring health to your body and nourishment to your bones' (Prov 3:5-8). The biggest mistake that Israel made when the Gibeonites came to Joshua was their failure to enquire of the Lord (9:14).

They leaned on their own understanding and became wise in their own eyes. They paid the price, as will anyone who trusts in their own discernment.

Listen to what the Lord says: 'Cursed is the one who trusts in man, who depends on flesh for his strength and whose heart turns away from the Lord. He will be like a bush in the wastelands; he will not see prosperity when it comes. He will dwell in the parched places of the desert, in a salt land where no one lives. But blessed is the man who trusts in the Lord, whose confidence is in him. He will be like a tree planted by the water that sends out its roots by the stream. It does not fear when heat comes; its leaves are always green. It has no worries in a year of drought and never fails to bear fruit' (Jer 17:5-8).

10:1-12:24 Taking the Land

10:1-27 A Coalition of Five Kings

10:1-5 The coalition against Gibeon

The next major city on Joshua's list was Jerusalem, whose name means 'the foundation/possession of peace'. In the time of Abraham, it was called Salem (Gen 14:18), equivalent to Kiswahili *Salaam* as in Dar es Salaam (Harbour of Peace). The king of Jerusalem was Adoni-Zedek or 'lord of righteousness'. Some believe his name was based on the name of an ancient king of this city, Melchizedek (Gen 14:18), which means 'king of righteousness'. His people were the Jebusites (see 9:1; Num 13:29; 2 Sam 5:6-9).

Before Joshua could lay out a strategy for taking this 'city of peace', word reached Adoni-Zedek that Jericho and Ai had been totally destroyed. What is more, he was also informed that Gibeon had signed a peace treaty with Israel. The 'lord of righteousness' realized that the peace of his city was at stake! Adoni-Zedek and his people were greatly alarmed. Why?

Jericho and Ai were not only strategic cities, but very well fortified. For them to be taken so easily and destroyed so totally was a terrifying sign. If those two cities could fall, then so would other cities. The king of Jerusalem was therefore understandably alarmed. But what was even more alarming to Adoni-Zedek was that Gibeon, an important city in the region, had signed a peace treaty with Israel without even trying to put up a fight! *Gibeon was an important city* (**10:2a**) because it guarded the Beth Horon pass, which was on a major trade route to the coastal lowlands to the west. It was also *like one of the royal cities* because it provided a safe haven for royal leaders.

Gibeon was even stronger than Ai, whose walls Israel did not breach. It also had good fighters, and therefore was one of the best allies to be depended upon in times of war (**10:2b**). Adoni-Zedek could not understand how Gibeon had surrendered to Israel without even putting up a fight. He was not only alarmed, but also obviously furious at Gibeon. He decided to teach the Gibeonites a lesson.

It is clear that Adoni-Zedek considered Gibeon a force to be reckoned with, for he did not propose to attack it alone. Instead he appealed to Hoham king of Hebron, Piram king of Jarmuth, Japhia king of Lachish and Debir king of Eglon: *Come up and help me attack Gibeon … because it has made peace with Joshua and the Israelites* (**10:4**).

Hebron was situated in the mountains, about thirty miles (forty-eight kilometres) south of Jerusalem. There were two cities with the name Jarmuth. One was given to the tribe of Issachar (21:29); the one mentioned here fell to the tribe of Judah (15:35). It is thought to have been about eighteen miles (twenty-nine kilometres) from Jerusalem. Lachish is mentioned several times in Scripture. Amaziah, king of Judah, was slain by conspirators there (2 Kgs 14:19). It was also besieged by Sennacherib, king of Assyria (2 Kgs 18:14, 17; Isa 37:8), and Nebuchadnezzar, king of Babylon (Jer 34:7). In Joshua's conquest, Lachish fell to Judah (15:39). It is not clear where the city of Eglon was situated, but it too fell to the tribe of Judah (15:39). The five Amorite cities combined forces, moved all their troops to Gibeon and attacked it.

10:6-8 Rescuing the Gibeonites

While Adoni-Zedek called out to his neighbours, 'Come up and help me attack Gibeon', the Gibeonites called out to Joshua: *Do not abandon your servants … Help us, because all the Amorite kings from the hill country have joined forces against us* (**10:6**). They believed that even though 'all' the Amorite kings were ganged up against them, Israel was capable of countering the attack. They also hoped and believed Israel would honour the treaty signed in the name of the Lord and come to their rescue.

These people, who had basically conned their way into Israel's life, now saw themselves as Israel's responsibility. Their battles were now Israel's battles; their problems were now Israel's problems. And when they called on Joshua for help, it was with confidence and a sense of urgency – *Come up to us quickly and save us!* They were not pleading for a favour, they were asking for their right according to the treaty. These friends of Israel had now become the burden of Israel. This must be exactly what Joshua had feared all along – the Gibeonites being perennially dependent upon Israel, and having Joshua fight battles that were not his own. This call must have been a stark reminder to Joshua of the grave mistake he had committed in signing a treaty without first seeking God's judgment. It must have felt like a recurring wound in Joshua's flesh. Yet he had no choice but to honour the terms of the treaty he had made. So he marched up from Gilgal with his entire army, including all

the best fighting men – perhaps ready to pay for his own mistake (**10:7**).

But amazingly, *the Lord said to Joshua, 'Do not be afraid of them; I have given them into your hand. Not one of them will be able to withstand you'* (**10:8**). What great news for a man who was suffering from the guilt of his mistake! Yet this is the greatest privilege we have in placing our faith in God's grace. Whereas Joshua might have thought that if he died on the battlefield, he would have deserved it, God had greater plans for Joshua: plans for prosperity and not harm, plans to give him a future and a hope (Jer 29:11).

One of the characteristics that distinguishes Christianity from all other religions is its doctrine of grace. God's grace allows sinners like you and me to be in a relationship with an absolutely pure and holy God. In all other major religions, worshippers must perform acts of merit to gain access to the divine. Specific requirements must be fulfilled if one is to enjoy the blessing of the gods. The requirements vary from one religion to another. Some are more stringent than others. Some require severe discipline, others great sacrifices. Violating any of the requirements stirs the wrath of the gods, with grave consequences.

In traditional African religions, for example, the gods required strict adherence to customs and practices. Failure to observe these practices would result in suffering the wrath of the gods, unless they are offered certain prescribed sacrifices to appease them. One constantly has to walk circumspectly for fear of angering them. It is this fear that has kept many African societies enslaved to their traditions and cultures.

Christianity, on the other hand, offers a relationship with God with no strings attached. This arrangement is made possible through God's grace. As the psalmist declares, 'The Lord is compassionate and gracious, slow to anger, abounding in love. He will not always accuse, nor will he harbour his anger forever; he does not treat us as our sins deserve or repay us according to our iniquities. For as high as the heavens are above the earth, so great is his love for those who fear him; as far as the east is from the west, so far has he removed our transgressions from us' (Ps 103:8-14). The grace of God offers the sinner a second chance, an opportunity to start again. It also allows us to continue to enjoy the goodness of the Lord, despite our having offended him through our folly and our mistakes. But, as Paul asks, 'Shall we go on sinning so that grace may increase? By no means! We died to sin; how can we live in it any longer?' (Rom 6:1-2).

Thus, God in his grace came to Joshua and assured him of victory over the coalition of kings arrayed against Gibeon.

10:9-21 Shattering the coalition

With assurance from the Lord, Joshua confidently marched out against the coalition. He marched all night from Gilgal to Gibeon. This was about a twenty-mile (thirty-two kilometres) uphill journey, and therefore Joshua's arrival took the kings by surprise (**10:9**). But it was not just the unexpected arrival of Joshua's army that threw the coalition forces into terror and panic; God was also at work to spread confusion. Instead of putting up a fight, the coalition took to flight, with Israel in hot pursuit (**10:10**). The Lord obviously took over the battle. As the coalition army fled before Israel, *the Lord hurled large hailstones down on them from the sky, and more of them died from the hailstones than were killed by the swords of the Israelites* (**10:11**). Some argue that what fell were actually stones, and that they are referred to as hailstones only because of the way they fell and the number of them. Historical evidence shows that showers of stones have indeed fallen in various parts of the world. But regardless of the exact nature of the stones, there can be no doubt of the fact that God has the power to hurl down stones like this, for his power is unlimited.

To see God fighting on their behalf must have been such a wonderful sight for Joshua and Israel that Joshua seems to have wanted it to last longer. He prayed: *O sun, stand still over Gibeon, O moon, over the Valley of Aijalon.* And, miracle of miracles, *the sun stood still, and the moon stopped, till the nation avenged itself on its enemies* (**10:12-13a**). The sun stopped for *about a full day* (**10:13b**). This miracle has been the subject of much discussion. The author of the book of Joshua has taken this passage from *the Book of Jashar* (**10:13c**), which celebrates the mighty acts of the Lord. This has led some to believe that the record of this miracle was a later addition to the narrative. But such an attempt to explain away this miracle may be motivated by the inability of the finite mind to comprehend how such an occurrence could have taken place without affecting the whole course of the created universe.

The objection that a sudden stoppage of the revolution of the earth on its axis would have hurled the earth and the moon out of their orbits and destroyed everything on the earth's surface does not prove anything. Not only does this argument imply that there is only one way that God could have achieved this effect, it also ignores the fact that the omnipotent God, who created the stars and makes them revolve with regularity in their orbits, and who upholds and governs all things in heaven and on earth, is powerful enough to guard against any such disastrous consequence.

This was not the only time that God suspended the laws of nature in response to the pleadings of his own. Sarah conceived and gave birth to Isaac when she was well past the natural childbearing age (Gen 17:15-17; 18:10-14; 21:1-3), Elisha made an iron axe head float on water (2 Kgs 6:4-7), and Jesus and Peter walked on the water of the Sea of Galilee (Matt 14:25-29). It is clear that when God chooses to intervene, he is not limited by anything, for nothing is impossible with him.

The author of Joshua declares that *there has been never a day like it before or since, a day when the Lord listened to a man* (**10:14a**), and stopped the universe in its tracks. God is not in the habit of suspending his laws in order to intervene in human affairs. He operates within the normal course of events. That is perhaps why many of us constantly miss what God is doing around us daily. But when God supernaturally steps in to deliver his people, everyone will notice. When the sun and moon stopped at Joshua's command, and hailstones hit Israel's enemies, everybody recognized that *the Lord was fighting for Israel* (**10:14b**).

When the five kings realized what they were up against, they did the natural thing – they fled and hid in a cave (**10:15**). But they were found and their hiding place was reported to Joshua (**10:17**). He promptly laid siege to their position by ordering that large rocks be rolled up to the mouth of the cave, and men posted to guard it (**10:18**). Meanwhile, he continued to pursue the enemy and destroyed them almost to a man – only a few reached the safety of fortified cities (**10:19-20**). Having seen how totally Joshua and his army had defeated the five cities, *no one uttered a word against the Israelites* (**10:21**). Their enemies were silenced!

It is abundantly clear that God is able to turn our mistakes into blessings. He can turn the weapons directed towards us against the enemy. Gibeon had tricked Israel into signing a treaty with them, but still God used Gibeon to help Israel shatter a coalition of five other kings, enabling Joshua to conquer five cities in one battle!

10:22-27 Stepping on necks

Instead of staying with their men and fighting bravely, the five kings had gone into hiding as soon as defeat threatened. Joshua had confined them in the cave while he pursued their armies, but then he returned to punish them by parading them in public (**10:22-23**). He summoned all the men of Israel to watch as his army commanders placed their feet on the necks of these kings (**10:24**). This ritual humiliation emphasized his supremacy and their lack of power and strength. Joshua then used them as examples of what would be done to anyone who dared stand up against Israel, telling his leaders, *Do not be afraid; do not be discouraged. Be strong and courageous. This is what the Lord will do to all the enemies you are going to fight* (**10:25**). After this public humiliation of the kings, he ordered them killed and their bodies hung on trees. At nightfall, he buried their bodies in the same cave where they had hidden (**10:26-27**).

10:28-43 The South – Easy Victories

Joshua's breakthrough did not end with the defeat of the five kings. With the great coalition broken, the narrative takes us quickly on a swoop through the southern cities of Canaan. Joshua moved to Makkedah and *put the city to the sword and totally destroyed everyone in it* (**10:28**). He then moved to Libnah and put everyone to the sword (**10:30**). When he went down to Lachish, he also put the city to the sword (**10:32**). Horam, king of Gezer, one of the most powerful kings in the area, came to assist Lachish, but he must have regretted it, because Joshua defeated him and vanquished his army (**10:33**). Next came Eglon, Hebron and Debir, all destroyed and all put to the sword (**10:34-39**).

Like a mighty bulldozer clearing a forest, Joshua moved across the land unhindered. He *subdued the whole region, including the hill country, the Negev, the western foothills and the mountain slopes* (**10:40**), leaving no survivors. Joshua conquered the land from *Kadesh Barnea to Gaza and from the whole region of Goshen to Gibeon* (**10:41**). The Israelites had occupied all of Canaan south of Jerusalem. The land had been cleared of its inhabitants. Other than Jericho and Ai, the other cities conquered were not destroyed, only the people were put to the sword.

Joshua was able to defeat all these kings and capture their cities in one campaign because the Lord, the God of Israel, fought for Israel. God had promised victory, and he was there to give it. This was a time of great success for Joshua. There will be moments like this in believers' lives, when we will experience unhindered success. When this happens, we must remember to return thanks to God, for it is out of his grace and for his purposes that he grants it.

But even though we may experience great victories, we are not to settle down. We must press on in the Lord and take full possession of our promised land. Many have settled down at the first sign of success and thus missed the full blessing that God may have had in store for them.

11:1-23 The North – Opposition and Victory

The fact that you experience an exceptional victory in the Lord does not mean that there will be no opposition. In fact, the bigger the opposition, the greater the success.

Once the southern campaign was finished, Joshua returned with the Israelites to the camp at Gilgal. Meanwhile, word had spread up north about the havoc Israel had visited on the south. *When Jabin king of Hazor heard of this,* he set in motion plans for a mighty alliance of forces to repulse Israel (**11:1a**). He may have taken the lead in doing this because Hazor was formerly the head of all the kingdoms of northern Canaan (**11:10**). Hazor was perhaps the largest and best fortified city in Canaan. It covered about a hundred and seventy-five acres (seventy hectares); much bigger than Jericho, which was only seven. Some think that Jabin was probably the hereditary title of the kings of Hazor (see Judg 4:2). The name means 'one who is discerning', and is equivalent to 'the wise one' or 'the intelligent one'. It seems that Jabin sought to apply his 'wisdom' to the crisis

at hand by setting up a strong coalition to oppose Israel (**11:1b-3**). He mobilized the north, and came out with *a large number of horses and chariots – a huge army, as numerous as the sand on the seashore.* These northern kings *joined forces and made camp together at the Waters of Merom, to fight against Israel* (**11:4-5**).

Jabin's ability to mobilize the whole region shows that he must have been a man of influence and great power. Israel's first three battles had been waged against seemingly insignificant opponents, but Hazor offered a totally different challenge to Joshua. This coalition was the strongest political and military adversary they had ever faced. The author of Joshua seems to go out of his way to emphasize their numerical and technological strength.

The sight of such a strong opposing army must have sent shock waves through the camp of Israel. But once again the Lord assured Joshua, *Do not be afraid of them, because by this time tomorrow I will hand all of them over to Israel, slain* (**11:6**). This is exactly what happened. Joshua struck this mighty army unexpectedly, and the Lord gave him victory. He hamstrung their horses and burned their chariots (**11:7-9**). After defeating the strong and the proud, Joshua *turned back and captured Hazor,* burned the city and put to death everything and everyone in it (11:10-11). This was the third city to be destroyed.

Each of the royal cities that had come out against Joshua was captured. He put their kings and all the inhabitants of each city to death (**11:12**). The Israelites carried off great plunder (**11:13-15**).

Joshua's wars against all these kings lasted for a long time (**11:18**). Yet, no one except the Gibeonites tried to make a peace treaty (**11:19**). The author, in an attempt to explain why the kings did not bother seeking peace with Israel, says that God *hardened their hearts ... so that he might destroy them totally, exterminating them without mercy* (**11:20**). These people had rebelled against God. He took his time to allow them an opportunity to repent, but they did not. Therefore God used them to fulfil his promise to Abraham.

Finally there is a brief mention of a people whom the Israelites seem to have feared the most – the Anakites. These were the people who had caused Israel to 'look like grasshoppers' (Num 13:33). The victory over them is mentioned only in passing: *Joshua went and destroyed the Anakites from the hill country* (**11:21-22**).

Most of the land was now vacant and available for settlement, and *Joshua took the entire land, just as the Lord had directed Moses, and he gave it as an inheritance to Israel according to their tribal divisions* (**11:23**). God fought for Israel throughout and granted them the promised land. The faithfulness of the Lord was thus clearly demonstrated to his people.

Joshua's experience gives us a clearer idea of what the Lord means when he says through the prophet Isaiah, 'All who rage against you will surely be ashamed and disgraced; those who oppose you will be as nothing and perish. Though you search for your enemies, you will not find them. Those who wage war against you will be as nothing at all … See, I will make you into a threshing sledge, new and sharp, with many teeth. You will thresh the mountains and crush them, and reduce the hills to chaff. You will winnow them, the wind will pick them up, and a gale will blow them away. But you will rejoice in the Lord and glory in the Holy One of Israel' (Isa 41:11-12, 15-16).

12:1-24 The Conquered Land – The Final Tally

In the detailed historical account of Joshua's wars in Canaan, the only kings mentioned by name as having been conquered by the Israelites were those who had formed a league to make war on them. We are, however, also told that Joshua had subdued all the kings in the south and north, and taken possession of their towns (10:40; 11:17). To complete the account of these conquests, a detailed list is given of all the kings who were defeated, first by Moses (12:1-6) and then by Joshua (12:7-24). This list gives a complete picture of the victories that Israel had gained with the help of its omnipotent God.

13:1-19:51 Dividing the Land

In the previous chapters, God led his people under Joshua in battles that saw most of Canaan fall into the hands of Israel. These campaigns basically cleared the land of its Canaanite inhabitants. The land however was not immediately occupied by Israel, who probably still operated from Gilgal. Chapters 13 to 19 form the second section of the book and provide details of the division of the land among the twelve tribes, who were the descendants of the sons of Jacob (Gen 29:32-30:24; 35:16-18). The sons of Leah were Reuben, Simeon, Levi, Judah, Issachar and Zebulun. The sons of Rachel were Joseph and Benjamin. The sons of Bilhah, Rachel's maidservant, were Dan and Naphtali, and the sons of Zilpah, Leah's maidservant, were Gad and Asher. Rachel's son, Joseph, had two sons, Manasseh and Ephraim. Jacob blessed both of Joseph's sons before he died (Gen 48:20), but would this blessing have any bearing on the lives of the children of Israel four hundred years later? To answer that question, we have to look at how the land was allocated.

13:1-7 Unconquered Land

Chapter 11 ends 'So Joshua took the entire land' (11:23), and yet chapter 13 opens with the Lord telling Joshua, in his old age, that there are still very large areas of land to be taken over (13:1). How do we explain this?

It seems that 11:23 is a summary at the end of the detailed report of the conquest. Some of the land, however, remained either unconquered or unpossessed even by the time Joshua was old. The details of this land that remained unconquered are given in 13:2-5. In other words, although the Israelites had captured the main strongholds of Canaan, they were still surrounded by people who were not of the Lord. Joshua had done his part in leading the major campaigns, but age had caught up with him before all the land was conquered. What was going to happen?

The Lord promised Joshua that he himself was going to take care of the situation. *I myself will drive them out,* he assured Joshua (13:6). Yes, although Joshua was old and advanced in years, his God was still alive and well, ever ready to do battle for his people. God does not age or grow weary. He is the same yesterday, today and for ever! Thus the unconquered land was going to be conquered by God himself (although this conquest did not take place until King David's time.) So God instructed Joshua to go ahead and allocate the land to Israel even though it was still inhabited by his enemies.

No reasons are given for Joshua's inability to conquer this land, but the principle laid down in Deuteronomy 7:22 may have been in play here. Judah was not able to take Jerusalem, so the Jebusites dwelled with Judah *to this day* (15:63). *The Manassites were not able to occupy these towns for the Canaanites were determined to live in that region* (17:12). However they were later subjected to forced labour.

The Israelites were thus faced with some people whom they simply could not dislodge from their midst and had to live with. Even when the Israelites became strong enough to dislodge them, they chose to subject them to slavery rather than drive them out. There were also other areas that remained unconquered for unknown or unspecified reasons, but which God promised to conquer eventually.

Their situation mirrors that of Christians. Every believer faces at least three enemies to spiritual growth and development – the world, the flesh and the Devil. Each of these poses a different kind of challenge to the believer's spiritual journey:

- The world is like the Jebusites. We cannot dislodge the people of the world and their ungodly ways, but must dwell with them. So, while we live in the world, we are not of the world. We must not conform to the world. Indeed, we are called to be the salt and the light in it. The Jebusites will always be with us, but they must never influence us.
- The flesh, however difficult, can be conquered. It is like the Canaanites who were determined to live in the region of Manasseh. Yet there was a time when Manasseh had enough strength to drive out these people. Did they do it? No! Instead they simply made slaves of them. Many of us are like that. We do not want to conquer the flesh

completely. Paul says, 'Put to death the misdeeds of the body' (Rom 8:13). Yet we are content merely to put them to sleep.

- The Devil is an enemy that will, for us, remain unconquered. We cannot get rid of him no matter how earnestly we may pray. But God has promised that a day is coming when he shall deal Satan one final blow and send him to the bottomless pit (see Rev 20:10).

13:8-33 The Eastern Lands

Before he died, Moses had allocated the land east of the Jordan to Reuben, Gad and half of the tribe of Manasseh (**13:8**). These tribes had come to Moses and requested that they be allowed to occupy this land since it was good for livestock. Moses had granted their request on condition that they join their brothers across the Jordan in the battle to capture the promised land (1:12-15; Num 32:1-5; 16-22). It should be noted that the land east of the Jordan was not part of the promised land, but was granted to the two and a half tribes on their request.

14:1-19:51 The Western Lands

14:1-5 Division of the land

The land west of the Jordan, which had been promised to Israel as an inheritance, was divided among the remaining nine and a half tribes of Israel. The division was not done arbitrarily by Joshua, but also involved *Eleazar the priest* and *the heads of the tribal clans*, who represented the people (**14:1**). Very precise details are given of the boundaries of each area. The actual allocation was done by casting lots in the presence of the Lord, so that it was God who decided who got what (**14:2**). No one could complain of being discriminated against or of others being favoured. It is therefore safe to say that it was God who conquered the land and God who distributed it among the tribes of Israel.

14:6-15 Caleb's lot

The only exception to this allocation of the land by lot appears to have been made in the case of Caleb, son of Jephunneh. He was the other spy who, with Joshua, gave a positive report on the land (Num 13:30; 14:7-9). He approached Joshua and said to him, *I brought [Moses] back a report according to my convictions, but my brothers who went up with me made the hearts of the people melt with fear. I, however, followed the Lord my God wholeheartedly. So on that day Moses swore to me, 'The land on which your feet have walked will be your inheritance and that of your children forever, because you have followed the Lord my God wholeheartedly'* (**14:7-9**). What do these words reveal about Caleb?

- **Caleb believed that God's word is reliable despite the passage of time.** God keeps his promises. The fact that God's promise to him forty-five years earlier had

not yet been fulfilled did not mean that God had forgotten about it, or gone back on his promise. Caleb believed that 'God is not a human being, that he should lie, nor a son of man, that he should change his mind. God does not speak and then not act on his word. Neither does he promise and fail to fulfil' (Num 23:19).

- **Caleb did not follow the crowd, but followed his personal convictions.** The fact that everybody else seemed to agree about an issue did not mean that he had to go along with them. He spoke and acted according to his convictions (14:7). Where other people saw problems, Caleb saw possibilities. When people said, 'This is impossible', Caleb said, 'All things are possible', and believed it. Even now as people scrambled for the already conquered land, he wanted something different. Something in line with his convictions. So he asked, *give me this hill country that the Lord promised me that day* (**14:12**).
- **Caleb was not ready to settle for less than what God had promised him.** Moses had promised him 'the land on which his feet had walked' and that was what he wanted (14:9). Nothing more, nothing less! He was not ready to settle for less, when he knew he should get his just share. He was aware that the good is always the enemy of the best, and that the available is always a barrier to the possible.

Jabez was a man of a similar spirit (1 Chr 4:9-10). His mother named him Jabez, meaning 'pain', but he was not content to accept the destiny implicit in his name and cried out to the Lord, 'Oh, that you would bless me and enlarge my territory! Let your hand be with me, and keep me from harm so that I will be free from pain.' As a farmer or herdsman, Jabez looked over the land his family had passed down to him, ran his eye down the fence lines, visited the boundary markers, calculated the potential – and made a decision: 'Everything you've put under my care, O Lord – take it, and enlarge it!' The Scriptures tells us that the good Lord granted his request.

The hard fact is that if we are already satisfied with what we have, we cannot desire more, just as we do not change what we can tolerate. Too often, people simply put up with unsatisfactory jobs or live as beggars with no work without making any attempt to change their circumstances. Or they may tolerate a poor relationship or a leaky roof without making any attempt to fix it. Caleb would not have tolerated any of these!

The same is true in the spiritual realm. We will not desire more from God until we develop spiritual dissatisfaction. As long as we are at ease in Zion, the fire of God may burn around us, but we will be completely oblivious to it. Many of us Christians backslide not by becoming involved in any sinful acts but by being satisfied with the status quo. As we become busier, we become less and less interested in spiritual things, devoting our time to what we deem to be more urgent matters. We lack personal spiritual ambition to rise beyond the ordinary and any drive to reach for the skies.

As crowds stream into churches Sunday after Sunday, we go too, to be handed a piece of the land already conquered by the preacher! There are many Christians who neither read the word of God, nor have time for personal prayer. They are dependent on spiritual morsels handed down to them by preachers, some of whom are themselves spiritually dead. Such people are happy with the crumbs, when they ought to be feeding on buttered loaves.

Caleb decided that he was not going to wait for a handout from Joshua. He was not going to settle for less when he could fight for his fair portion. He stepped out of the queue and went up to Joshua to ask for what he felt was his, in view of the Lord's promise in Numbers 14:24. He was now ready to possess his possession. His different spirit showed in his dissatisfaction with the ordinary. It also showed in his awareness that it is never too late to realize your dreams! Many of us are younger than Caleb who was then eighty-five years old. He challenges us to strive, in God's strength, towards our life goals.

But because he is dissatisfied does not mean that Caleb does not appreciate what God has given him. He expresses his appreciation of God's gift of life, saying, *just as the Lord promised, he has kept me alive* (**14:10**). Everyone else who had started out with him from Egypt had died in the wilderness, including Moses. Only he and Joshua had survived. That was something worth thanking God for! How often we overlook 'little things', such as the gift of life. Many of us keep complaining about how disadvantaged we are because we do not have this or that, not realizing that the very fact that we are alive is an asset that we can make use of. How many of your classmates in school or at college have already died? Yet you are alive today!

Caleb also thanks God for the gift of strength. Not only is he still alive, he is still strong, claiming *I am still as strong today as the day Moses sent me out* (**14:11a**). Men of eighty-five are not usually known for their strength. Caleb considered this a blessing from God, and another great asset for his mission. There are many strong men and women doing nothing with their energies. Even worse, some abuse their strength by using it in robberies, fights and rebellion. Caleb was ready to put his strength to good use to improve his circumstances.

Caleb also thanks God for the gift of agility. He says, *I'm just as vigorous to go out to battle now as I was then* (**14:11b**). Not only was he strong physically, he was also strong for battle. He was agile enough not only to go into battle, but also to emerge victorious from the battle!

Having evaluated himself and found that God had blessed him with life, strength, ability and agility, Caleb told Joshua, *Now give me this hill country that the Lord promised me that day* (**14:12a**). That bold declaration shows a determination to go beyond the ordinary, a readiness to pursue the impossible and surmount the insurmountable. Victor Hugo, the great nineteenth-century French writer, once wrote, 'There is nothing as powerful as an idea whose time has come.' When we realize the time of our opportunity has come, we must seize that opportunity and get the very best out of it.

But Caleb's confidence was not just in his own abilities. He was moved by faith! It is probable that as Caleb spoke to Joshua, Joshua stared at him in disbelief. Joshua may have responded by saying something like, 'Caleb, I know you were a great warrior. But do you know what you are asking for? Do you remember what kind of people we saw, when we went to spy the land? I know you were a man of great faith and a mighty warrior, but you are no longer a young man my friend. You are eighty-five years old, not twenty-five! Eighty-five! Give up these youthful ambitions.' But listen to Caleb, *'You yourself heard then that the Anakites were there and their cities were large and fortified, but, the Lord helping me, I will drive them out just as he said'* (**14:12b**). Here was a man determined to achieve his destiny, and nothing was going to stop him! He had his eyes focused on the goal, and was determined to get it. The obstacles were not going to discourage him. The Anakites were among the most feared of the Canaanite tribes. Compared to the Israelites, they were giants, and many believe that the 'giant' Goliath was descended from their race. But Caleb was not intimidated by them – not by their strength, and not by their fortified cities. He believed that with God's help, he was going to drive them out and take their land for his inheritance. And he did (see 15:14).

But Caleb was not too proud to accept help. Because occupying his land was so important to him, he offered his daughter Acsah to the one who helped accomplish it. Othniel did, and Caleb kept his word (15:16-17). Caleb's good relationship with his daughter is shown both in her freedom to ask him for land with water, and in his giving her 'the upper and lower springs', that is, a piece of land with springs of water at both the higher and lower levels (15:18-19).

What did Caleb's dissatisfaction lead him to? Determination. Dissatisfaction without determination leads to mere frustration. If you cannot get up and do something about your situation, you might as well settle down and enjoy yourself under the current state of affairs. There are many of us who are dissatisfied with our current circumstances, but the only thing we do is complain or criticize. There is an unfortunate culture prevalent in Africa – that of criticizing, complaining and blaming. We are always finding fault, blaming someone else for our own shortcomings. If it is not the school we went to, it is the English teacher who taught us, the pastor of our church, the poverty of our parents, the colonialists, the corrupt leaders, the donors, the economy, the IMF, the World Bank … the list goes on and on. This attitude is aptly illustrated in Joshua 17.

15:1-63 Judah's lot

The first lot in the allocation of the western lands was *the allotment for the tribe of Judah* (**15:1**). Jacob had set aside Reuben's rights as the firstborn because he had sexual relations with Bilhah, Jacob's concubine (Gen 49:4). Simeon and Levi had also been set aside because of their fierce anger when they massacred the Shechemites for defiling their sister Dinah (Gen 49:5-7; see also Gen 34). Jacob felt that they had dealt too harshly and treacherously with Shechem. This left Judah in first place. When Jacob blessed Judah, he said that Judah would be praised by his brothers (Gen 49:8). So the tribe of Judah received the first share of the promised land west of the Jordan. Judah's share consisted of all the southern land from the Mediterranean Sea to the Dead Sea. It included Caleb's portion, which was the largest portion of all. Judah also received Jerusalem, the city that was to become David's capital, although the Israelites did not capture it until David's reign (**15:63**; see 2 Sam 5:1-7).

16:1-17:18 Joseph's lot

The next lot fell on the house of Joseph, another of Jacob's favourite sons. Once again, Reuben, Simeon and Levi had to await their turn. Not only that, but Joseph's two sons, Ephraim and Manasseh, were treated as two different tribes in the allocation because Jacob had adopted them as his children (**16:4**; see Gen 48:5). But, there is something even more intriguing about how they were allocated land. Jacob had blessed the younger Ephraim before the older Manasseh (Gen 48:11-20) and now once again, the younger is preferred to the older, and the lot falls on Ephraim before Manasseh. Thus Ephraim is given the central portion of the land.

Manasseh, Joseph's firstborn, is allocated land to the north of Ephraim. Half of the tribe of Manasseh had already been allocated land on the east of the Jordan (13:8), so this land was for the other half of the tribe of Manasseh. Manasseh was unable to dislodge the Canaanites from this land. Even when they became strong, they preferred to use them as slaves rather than expel them (**17:12-13**).

As Jacob had predicted in his blessing, Ephraim and Manasseh had become *a numerous people* (**17:14**). It was because of their large herds of livestock that some of them had chosen to settle east of the Jordan. But now they complained that the land that they and Ephraim had been given was too small for them. It seems that Joseph's family were like spoiled children, always looking for special treatment.

These people were saying that because of their large numbers, they deserved a larger portion than had been given to them. What is more, they tried to spiritualize their problem: *We are a numerous people and the Lord has blessed us abundantly* (17:14). Yes, it was God's fault for making their tribe so large! And so, in their view, Joshua ought to have sympathized with their plight by giving them a larger allotment of land.

What was Joshua's response to this 'spiritual' complaint? He told them, *If you are so numerous ... and if the hill country of Ephraim is too small for you, go up into the forest and clear land for yourselves there in the land of the Perizzites and Rephaites* (**17:15**). What a fitting rebuke to a spoiled lot! If they were so many, why could they not use their numerical strength to conquer more land for themselves? Why did they turn to Joshua for more of the already conquered land?

But they did not even comprehend Joshua's rebuke. They were too engrossed with their problems to even realize that he was being sarcastic. Such people have a beggarly attitude. They replied, *The hill country is not enough for us, and all the Canaanites who live in the plain have iron chariots, both those in Beth Shan and its settlements and those in the Valley of Jezreel* (**17:16**). What were these people saying? That despite their numbers, they were not strong enough to fend for themselves. That they wanted the land already cleared. That all they were interested in were handouts. While Caleb at eighty-five was ready to take on the fortified cities of the Anakites (11:12), the people of Joseph, despite their numbers, were afraid to tackle the Canaanites of Beth Shan. Why? Because the Canaanites had iron chariots! This was utter nonsense.

Joshua was furious. I can imagine him pacing up and down and walking away in anger from this parasitic lot, telling them as he did so, *You are numerous and very powerful. You will have not only one allotment but the forested hill country as well. Clear it, and its farthest limits will be yours; though the Canaanites have iron chariots and though they are strong, you can drive them out* (**17:17**). Case closed!

If we are to enjoy life, we must be ready to arise and clear the land. Nobody owes any of us anything. Your destiny is in your own hands. Get into some unexploited territory and, as Joshua told Joseph, 'Clear it, and its farthest limits will be yours.' In other words, the sky is the limit to what we can achieve if we are ready to take risks and get our hands dirty. The Anakites may be huge and tall, their cities large and fortified, but with God on our side, we will drive them out! Someone once said, 'You are where you are because that is where you have subconsciously chosen to be.' Indeed while some of us sit and complain about the size of our pieces of land, the Calebs of our day are crying out, 'Give me this mountain!' We should not be satisfied with or simply complain about the status quo, but should aim for greater things, no matter the hardships on the way. When it is God's will, there will always be a way.

18:1-19:51 The rest of the land

After Judah and Joseph had been apportioned land, things seemed to settle down. Joshua moved the camp from Gilgal to *Shiloh* (**18:1**). Seven tribes still had no land, and Joshua asked them *'How long will you wait before you begin to take possession of the land'* (**18:2-3**). So men were sent out to survey and map the land (**18:4-5, 8-9**). Lots were cast to divide the land among the seven remaining tribes (**18:10**).

Benjamin was the first to receive a portion. They were allocated a place between Judah and Joseph (**18:11-21**). Moses had prophesied; 'Let the beloved of the Lord rest secure in him, for he shields him all day long' (Deut 33:12). Benjamin was going to have a special closeness to the Lord. When the northern tribes later turned away from the Lord, it was Judah and Benjamin that stood fast.

The next lot fell on Simeon. Jacob had said that Simeon and Levi would be scattered among Israel (Gen 49:7) and this prophecy was fulfilled as the inheritance of the Simeonites was taken from the large share of Judah (**19:1-9**). As such Simeon had no real portion. The Levites, too, were scattered when the land was distributed (see 21:1-45).

Then lots were drawn for Zebulun (**19:10-16**), Issachar (**19:17-23**), Asher (**19:24-31**), Naphtali (**19:32-39**) and finally Dan (**19:40-47**).

With all the tribes settled, it was time for Joshua to be given some land. They gave him the town he asked for – *Timnath Serah in the hill country of Ephraim* (**19:50**). It is worth noting that Joshua as the leader got his portion last. What a contrast with many of our leaders who prefer to be served first! The land-grabbers of Africa are often the first to allocate themselves public land. But Joshua appropriately came last.

And so they finished dividing the land (**19:51**).

20:1-24:33 Mission Accomplished!

All the tribes of Israel had received their share of land, but there still remained a few administrative matters that needed to be sorted out before the task of settling the people in the new land could be considered complete. There were the special allotments for the cities of refuge and for the Levites. Then there was the return of the two and a half tribes to the east of the Jordan.

20:1-21:45 Special Allotments

20:1-9 Cities of refuge

During Israel's journey from Egypt, God gave the Israelites a set of laws to govern their relationships with him and with one another. One of the evils that God regards most seriously is murder. This is because humanity is created in God's image, and anybody who takes the life of another has tampered with God's image.

In the time of Moses God commanded, 'Anyone who strikes a man and kills him shall surely be put to death' (Exod 21:12). There was therefore no mercy for a murderer. Nevertheless, for a person who mistakenly or unintentionally killed another, God made a concession: 'If he does not do it intentionally, but God lets it happen, he is to flee to a

place I will designate' (Exod 21:13). This was explained further: 'Six of the towns you give the Levites will be cities of refuge, to which a person who has killed someone may flee … These six towns will be a place of refuge for Israelites, aliens and any other people living among them, so that anyone who has killed another accidentally can flee there' (Num 35:6, 15).

Now God reminds Joshua of this special provision: *Tell the Israelites to designate the cities of refuge, as I instructed you through Moses, so that anyone who kills a person accidentally and unintentionally may flee there and find protection from the avenger of blood* (**20:1-3**). Who exactly was the 'avenger of blood'? God had set a law of retribution in the case of murders, 'Whoever sheds the blood of man, by man shall his blood be shed; for in the image of God has God made man' (Gen 9:6). Therefore if a person killed another, the murderer was to be put to death by a near relative of the dead person chosen by the family. He was to avenge the blood of the murdered relative. This person was known as the avenger of blood.

An avenger of blood would go after the killer regardless of whether the killing was intentional or accidental. Therefore the killer had to flee to a city of refuge. Provided that a fair trial in that city concluded that the killing had happened unintentionally and without malice aforethought, the accused would not be handed over to the avenger of blood. However, the killer would have to stay in the city until released from it by the death of the high priest (**20:4-6**).

Since the only way to escape an avenger of blood was to flee to a city of refuge, the cities of refuge had to be within easy reach of everyone throughout the land. In fact, God had commanded, 'Build roads to them … so that anyone who kills a man may flee there' (Deut 19:3). So Joshua established cities of refuge in different areas of the land. To the west of the Jordan, these cities were Kedesh in the north, Shechem in the centre and Hebron in the south; to the east of the Jordan, they were Bezer in the south, Ramoth in the centre and Golan in the north (**20:7-8**; see Num 35:14).

These cities of refuge were open to all: to the Israelite and the alien (**20:9**). Though it is not stated in the passages that talk of these cities of refuge (Josh 20:7-8; Num 35:6, 13-14; Deut 4:41-43), it is probably safe to assume that the gates of these cities were never locked so that anyone could run into them at any time. Because these cities belonged to the Levites, who received tithes from the Israelites, they would have had adequate food supplies (Num 18:21).

We can draw parallels between the cities of refuge and Christ as our refuge:

- **Jesus Christ is easy to reach.** In fact he is far easier to reach than any city of refuge. We may cry to him at any moment in any place. The Bible says, 'everyone who calls on the name of the Lord, will be saved' (Joel 2:32; Rom 10:13).

- **Christ is open to all.** The Jew, the Gentile, the Greek, the barbarian, the black, the white – all may come under his wings.
- **The gates to Christ are never locked.** For he neither sleeps nor slumbers. Day or night, anytime, any place, even in the depths of despair – Christ is open to receive any who run to him for refuge.
- **Christ is completely sufficient.** He does not just rescue from eternal death, but he also supplies the needs of the moment. What's more, once you are in him you are completely safe from any harm or danger for 'your life is hidden with Christ in God' (Col 3:3).
- **Christ is a haven for us all.** However, a city of refuge was only a haven for the innocent person who accidentally killed another, Christ is for all. The worst of sinners can run to him and find total forgiveness. Why? Because, at the cross, the great 'avenger of blood' shed the blood of Christ, and he has paid the penalty. Hallelujah! What a Saviour!

21:1-42 Towns for the Levites

The next special provision in the promised land was towns for the Levites. Jacob, in his final blessing, had cursed the anger of Simeon and Levi and said, 'I will scatter them in Jacob and disperse them in Israel' (Gen 49:7). We saw the effects of this curse in the area allotted to Simeon (19:1-9).

What about Levi? Did Jacob's words have any effect on him and his descendants? Before answering that question, we need to observe a significant development in the tribe of Levi before they came into the promised land. In Exodus 32, Moses came down from the mountain to find God's people eating, drinking, dancing and offering sacrifices to a golden calf that Aaron had made at their request. God was extremely angry and ready to wipe every one of them from the face of the earth. But Moses pleaded with God and the Lord relented.

When Moses cried out, 'Whoever is for the Lord, come to me', all the Levites rallied round him and then at his command went through the camp killing those who were worshipping the idol. Then Moses said, 'You have been set apart to the Lord today, for you were against your own sons and brothers, and he has blessed you this day' (Exod 32:26-28). Because of their stand for the Lord, the Levites were later set apart as the caretakers of the tabernacle and aides to the priests.

However, when it came to the distribution of land, the curse pronounced by Jacob still stood. But God turned it into a blessing because they had chosen to be on God's side. The Lord commanded that the Levites should be given towns to live in with pasture-land around them for their livestock (Num 35:2-5; see also Num 18:20-24). The Levites were thus to be spread throughout the land both east and west of the Jordan.

The family heads of the Levites now asked for the towns they had been promised (**21:1-2**). Levi had had three sons Gershon, Kohath and Merari. When Joshua distributed the towns to the Levites, he allotted them on the basis of these three family units. Kohath got the first lot, receiving twenty-three towns of which thirteen went to the descendants of Aaron and ten to the rest of the family (**21:4-5, 9-26**). Gershon received thirteen towns (**21:6, 27-33**), and finally Merari received twelve from Reuben, Gad and Zebulun (**21:7, 34-40**). This totalled forty-eight towns, just as God had commanded Moses (**21:41-42**; see Num 35:7).

21:43-45 Mission Summary

With the special allotments finalized, the author concludes by asserting that *the Lord gave Israel all the land he had sworn to give their forefathers, and they took possession of it and settled there* (**21:43**). What's more, *the Lord gave them rest on every side* (**21:44**). In other words, the mission was now accomplished. Israel was finally established in the land. Joshua had succeeded in seeing God's people settled in the promised land. *Not one of all the Lord's good promises to the house of Israel failed; every one was fulfilled* (**21:45**).

22:1-34 The Eastern Tribes Return Home

22:1-8 Blessings for the journey

It is estimated that the war in the west may have taken about seven years. So for all this time, the eastern tribes had faithfully fought alongside their brothers in the west, leaving the comfort of their own homes on the east side of the Jordan (**22:1-3**). No wonder the psalmist said, 'How good and pleasant it is when brothers live together in unity!' (Ps 133:1). Joshua now tells them that they have fulfilled their commitment, reminds them to stay close to the Lord, and gives them his blessing as they return home (**22:4-7**). The Lord bestowed many blessings on the eastern tribes because of their solidarity with their brethren. They returned home with *great wealth – with large herds of livestock, with silver, gold, bronze and iron, and a great quantity of clothing* (**22:8**).

It is clear that with the same measure they had given to their brothers, they had received full measure, 'pressed down, shaken together and running over'! Africans should learn from these tribes to pool our resources for the common good. We should unite in fighting our common enemies of disease, illiteracy, poverty and civil war. Too often, we are content to enjoy our own prosperity without concern for others.

22:9-34 The altar of witness

Reuben, Gad and half of the tribe of Manasseh left the Israelites at Shiloh in Canaan to return to Gilead. But on arriving at Geliloth (which is probably another name for Gilgal), they

LAND

Over the centuries, many wars have been fought over land. We therefore need to develop an understanding of how God views land.

In the OT, the concepts of land and covenant are closely related for the nation of Israel. God promised Abraham and his descendants land in a particular area (Gen 12:1, 6-9; 13:14-18; 15:18-21; 17:8) and later he gave that land to them (Deut 1:8; 5:31; 9:5-6; 11:17). The prophets looked to a time when the nations would come to Israel to worship God (Mic 4:1-5) and when the Messiah would set up his righteous kingdom there and continue the line of David (2 Sam 7:8-17; Isa 9:1-7; 11:1-16).

In more general terms, the Bible makes the following points:

- *God owns the land* because he created it (Ps 24:1; see also Gen 1:9-10; Lev 25:23; Ps 50:12). He gives and takes away land as he chooses (Gen 3:23-24; 4:11; Deut 2:5, 9; Ps 125:3).

- *God's laws govern life on the land.* If those who live on God's land are sinful, God will punish them as he did the people in the time of Noah (Gen 6:7) and the Canaanites (Lev 18:25-28). The Israelites were warned that they could only live in the land and enjoy prosperity if they did not defile it through similar sinful practices (Deut 4:25-27; 11:8-25; Josh 23:12-16, 15; 1 Kgs 9:6-7). When they did disobey God, they were exiled from the land (2 Kgs 17:7-23).

- *God desires that land benefits its inhabitants.* God instituted the year of Jubilee, when debts were to be forgiven and all land returned to its original owners (Lev 25:8-34). His purpose was to ensure equitable distribution of land and thus of wealth and resources. Social injustices such as the oppression of the poor and the affluence of an elite minority at the expense of the poor were condemned. The prophets were particularly outspoken on such issues (Isa 1:17; 3:14-15; 10:1-4; 11:4; 25:4; 58:1-14; Jer 2:34; 7:5-7; 22:13; 25:4; Ezek 9:9; 16:49; 18:5-9, 16; 22:29; Hos 12:7; Amos 2:6-8; 4:1-2; 5:11-12; 8:4-8; Mic 2:2; Zech 7:10).

African tradition agrees with the Bible in asserting that land belongs to the high god. However, specific areas are seen as the property of revered ancestral spirits who control the fertility of the land and care for their descendants. When a child was born in Zimbabwe, the umbilical cord was buried, symbolically uniting the baby to the ancestral spirits. Consequently Zimbabwe's liberation struggle was seen as a type of holy war to regain the sacred land of the ancestors that offered the people identity, history and a livelihood.

Traditionally African land belonged to the community and could not be owned by an individual. Chiefs and headmen were its custodians and members of the community were expected to be stewards, nurturing the land, not plundering it. Selling land or amassing land while others had none was considered a sign of unfaithfulness to God.

The traditional view of land still persists even though it has been fundamentally affected by colonialism. With the dismantling of traditional social structures came an increasingly commercial view of land, with a focus on prosperity. Thus the Zimbabwean media express their support for the land reform program by relentlessly stressing that 'Our land is our prosperity.'

African Christians need to embrace the African tradition as regards the equitable distribution and stewardship of land. However, some traditional beliefs will lead us astray. For example, the belief that prosperity comes from the land is a fallacy. Lasting prosperity does not come from the land but from God. We should not seek our identity in the land but in God. Obeying his commands will ensure his blessing (Deut 28:1-13). Moreover the notion that prosperity comes from the land leads to an excessive focus on natural resources and a neglect of human resources. But people are a nation's most important resource. Countries like Japan have managed to industrialize despite a lack of natural resources.

At times, traditional attachment to land has also meant that instead of being used productively for cultivation or mining to benefit those who live there, the land is worshipped and left uncultivated.

Christians should not forget that our citizenship is in heaven (Phil 3:20). Rather than getting entangled in a scramble for land, we should take a stand as stewards of the land and present a Christian response to land issues.

D.S.M. Mutonono and M.L. Mautsa

decided to build an imposing altar on the western side of the Jordan (**22:10**). They had not said anything about doing this before, and their action alarmed the western tribes, who prepared for war against their brothers (**22:11-12**). But before they set out to fight, they sent a high-powered delegation to verify the information and establish why the eastern tribes had erected the altar (**22:13-14**).

The delegation explained the fears that the eastern tribes were neglecting Joshua's warning in 22:5 and had set up an altar to some other god (**22:16-18**; see also Lev 17:1-9). If it was, there would be war to nip this apostasy in the bud. Throughout the conquest of the land, great emphasis had been placed on complete obedience to God. It was feared that any rebellion by the eastern tribes would bring punishment upon the whole community, just as had happened when Achan disobeyed God (**22:20**; 7:1). So serious was their concern that the delegation offered the eastern tribes land in the west if the land in the east was defiled (**22:19**).

Now it was the turn of the eastern tribes to be alarmed. How could anybody even imagine that they could turn from their one and only God? They broke into shouts of *The Mighty One, God, the Lord! The Mighty One, God, the Lord! He knows!* (**22:22**), calling as their witness the very God whom they were alleged to have betrayed. This shout combined three names of God: *El*, the strong one; *Elohim*, the Supreme Being; and *Yahweh*, the truly existing One, the covenant God. These people took the matter equally seriously. They must have been acutely aware of the danger of calling on the name of the Lord in vain. They would not have invoked the names of God in this way if they were not certain of their innocence (**22:23**).

Contrary to what the rest of Israel thought, the altar had been built to serve as a constant reminder to future generations that 'the Mighty One is God!' and that the God of the west was equally the God of the east. The eastern tribes had feared that with the passage of time, the two groups of Israelites, separated by the Jordan, might forget that they were one nation under one God. They feared that their descendants might one day be excluded from the worship of Yahweh simply because they lived on the east side of the Jordan (**22:24-25**). Thus far from abandoning the worship of Yahweh for another god, these tribes were actually seeking to preserve and secure it for their descendants. This was why they had built the altar according to the pattern of the altar before the tabernacle, and had built it not in their own land, but on the western side of the Jordan, where the dwelling-place of Yahweh was. It was to be a witness that the tribes on both sides of the Jordan worshipped one and the same God (**22:26-29**).

No wonder the delegation was satisfied about the other group's commitment to God (22:23-33).

This whole misunderstanding arose simply because of a lack of communication. The eastern tribes should have shared their thoughts with the western ones before embarking on this noble project. They should at least have notified Joshua, their leader, of their concerns and the possible solution. This would have saved both parties from this unnecessary confrontation. The western tribes, too, acted prematurely on unconfirmed reports and were too hasty in passing judgment on the others. If reason had not prevailed so that they moved quickly to check the facts, they would have shed innocent blood.

This incident should be a warning to us. Too often there has been internal strife and conflict within the body of Christ because we have rushed to implement noble ideas without due consultation.

On the positive side, this incident shows the western tribes' zeal for the Lord. Even though these were their brethren who had for seven years helped them fight and conquer the land, and though they certainly had developed comradeship and love for one another, when it came to defending the name of the Lord, they were ready to go to war against them. Their love for God superseded their comradeship. How often we condone the sins of those we love because we do not want to offend them.

The eastern tribes were equally concerned about the name of the Lord. Even though they had settled outside the promised land, they wanted a permanent witness that they too belonged to the Lord.

The manner in which the matter was solved is an excellent example of how Christians should handle misunderstandings. In the end, they all became witnesses to the Lord (**22:34**).

23:1-24:33 Whose promised land?

After Israel was settled in the land under the leadership of Joshua, a period of about twenty-five to thirty years elapsed during which God's people enjoyed the good of the land without any trouble. They enjoyed land on which they did not toil, and cities they did not build, they ate from vineyards and olive groves they did not plant (see 24:13). It was truly a land flowing with milk and honey.

But when everything is going fine, there is a tendency to forget the really important things. Moses had warned the Israelites, 'When the Lord your God brings you into the land he swore to your fathers, to Abraham, Isaac and Jacob, to give you … be careful that you not forget the Lord, who brought you out of Egypt, out of the land of slavery' (Deut 6:10, 12). As Joshua realized that he was growing old and that his life might soon end, as a good *mzee* [Kiswahili: 'respected elder'], he decided to remind the children of Israel of a few things before his departure.

23:1-8 The land of the promise

Joshua, by then old and well advanced in years, summoned all Israel (**23:1-2**) in order to remind them where they had come from and what God had done for them. He especially wanted to re-emphasize certain facts about the promised land.

23:1-4 Its extent Joshua had allotted all the land between the Jordan and the Mediterranean Sea (**23:3-4**). However, not all this land was in the hands of Israel. Although Joshua had already conquered it, parts of the land were still unoccupied. Moreover, God had earlier promised that the promised land would extend 'from the desert to Lebanon, and from the great river, the Euphrates … to the Great Sea on the west' (1:4). In Exodus, God had described the extents of the land as 'from the Red Sea to the Sea of the Philistines and from the desert to the River' (Exod 23:31). The Israelites' task was not yet completed.

23:5-6 Its possession So, what was going to happen to the portion that was not yet occupied?

Joshua told the people, *The Lord your God himself will drive them out of your way* (**23:5**). However, God had told

Moses, 'But I will not drive them out in a single year, because the land would become desolate and the wild animals too numerous for you. Little by little I will drive them out before you' (Exod 23:29-30). In other words, it was not a mistake that parts of the land remained unoccupied. Though the land had been conquered and subdued, God in his divine wisdom had planned that the original inhabitants would remain in the land to take care of it so that it did not become desolate. Then at the appropriate time, when Israel had multiplied in numbers, God would drive out the people from the land to make room for Israel!

23:7-8 ITS PEOPLE The people who remained in the land did not worship the Lord. Therefore, the Israelites were warned not to associate with them. They were not to invoke the names of their gods or swear by them. They were not to serve these foreign gods or bow down to them. Israel was to hold fast to the Lord their God.

23:9-16 The promise-keeping God

The second matter that Joshua reminded the people about was the promise-keeping God.

23:9-13 HIS MIGHT The nations that had come up against Israel were powerful and skilled in warfare, but God showed his power and might as he drove them out (**23:9-10**). No one could, can or ever will be able to withstand him. In return Joshua called upon the people to be very careful to love the Lord their God (**23:11**). If they aligned themselves with foreigners, they would fail to overcome these nations. Instead the nations would become snares and traps for them, whips on their backs and thorns in their eyes, until they perished from the land (**23:12-13**).

23:14 HIS FAITHFULNESS Joshua reminded the people of God's faithfulness to his promises. Whatever God had promised, he had brought to pass. They could not deny this fact because, as Joshua told them, *You know with all your heart and soul that not one of all the good promises the Lord your God gave you has failed* (**23:14**). Whatever God promises, he brings to pass. The prophet Balaam declared that 'God is not a man, that he should lie, nor a son of man, that he should change his mind. Does he speak and then not act? Does he promise and not fulfil?' (Num 23:19).

23:15-16 HIS JEALOUSY God's love and mercy for his people are often demonstrated by his faithfulness in fulfilling his promises. But God's grace and mercy cannot be taken for granted. As Joshua points out, he is also faithful in carrying out his threat to punish those who disobey him (**23:15**). Israel could not afford to take God's promises and blessings for granted. This is the same message Paul communicates to Christians who imagine that a gracious God cannot punish sin. He asks, 'Shall we go on sinning so that grace may increase? By no means!' (Rom 6:1-2).

Many of God's followers live according to the Kiswahili saying, *Asante ya punda ni mateke* ['The donkey's thank-you

is a kick']. They abuse God's grace, and indulge in all that God has expressly forbidden. Joshua warned the Israelites that such behaviour means *You will quickly perish from the good land he has given you* (**23:16**).

24:1-13 The people of the promise

As Joshua brought his leadership to a close, he *assembled all the tribes of Israel,* as represented by their leaders, at Shechem for a final reminder of their covenant relationship with the Lord (**24:1**).

It is significant that Joshua chose to hold this solemn assembly at Shechem and not at Shiloh, where the Lord's sanctuary stood (see 18:1). But considering the significance of his speech, Shechem was a natural choice. It was here that Abraham received the first promise from God after his migration into Canaan, and built an altar (Gen 12:6-7). Jacob had settled at Shechem on his return from his time with his uncle in Mesopotamia, and it was here that he had purified his house from foreign gods, burying the idols under an oak tree (Gen 33:19; 35:2, 4). Joshua may have chosen the same place for the renewal of the covenant, because this act involved a practical renunciation on the part of Israel of all idolatry. The leaders standing before him must have been acutely aware of this fact as they listened to his words.

Joshua opens his speech by declaring that what he was about to tell them was not merely his words but those of the Lord. *This is what the Lord, the God of Israel, says* (**24:2**). In the whole speech Joshua is but a mouthpiece of God.

Joshua begins by tracing the origins of the promise of land, and to whom this promise was made. The promise of the land was not a general or universal promise. It was a promise made to a specific people at a specific time. Who were these people of the promise? Abraham and Terah, his father, were not originally believers in Yahweh. They were worshippers of other gods, and were far from God (24:2). But God by his grace and divine plan called Abraham from beyond the Euphrates, and brought him to Canaan (**24:3a**). Later, God made a promise to him, 'To your offspring I will give this land' (Gen 12:7).

Abraham had two lines of descendants: the Jews are his descendants through his son Isaac, whose mother was Sarah; the Arabs are his descendants through his son Ishmael, whose mother was Hagar. Thus both Jews and Arabs are descendants of Abraham, and hence both should have legitimate claims to the land.

But no! Here God simply says, *I gave him Isaac* (**24:3b**). This leaves Ishmael out of the 'many descendants' God gave to Abraham. This is significant, because when Abraham had tried to get God to bless Ishmael, God had told him 'As for Ishmael, I have heard you: I will surely bless him; I will make him fruitful and will greatly increase his numbers. He will be the father of twelve rulers, and I will make him into a great nation. But my covenant I will establish with

Isaac, whom Sarah will bear to you by this time next year' (Gen 17:20-21).

Therefore though God promised to bless Ishmael, he was categorical that his covenant was with Isaac. This covenant is reported in Genesis 26:2-4. There was another parting of ways between Esau and Jacob, the two sons of Isaac. God *assigned the hill country of Seir to Esau, but Jacob and his sons went down to Egypt* (**24:4**). In Gen 36:6-8, we are told that 'Esau … moved to a land some distance from his brother Jacob. Their possessions were too great for them to remain together; the land where they were staying could not support them both because of their livestock. So Esau (that is, Edom) settled in the hill country of Seir.' Thus Esau voluntarily chose to move from Canaan to Seir, but his steps had been arranged by God so that Jacob might receive Canaan for his descendants as a sole possession. Having been left in Canaan, Jacob was later led into Egypt, and many years later his descendants were led out of Egypt by Moses (**24:5-7a**). After they had *lived in the desert for a long time* God finally led his people into land he had promised them and drove out their enemies before them (**24:7b-13**). The promised land thus did not belong to all of Abraham's descendants but only to the people who came out of Egypt.

24:14-27 The renewal of the covenant

24:14-18 THE CHOICE TO BE MADE God's promise of the land was not unconditional. Joshua had warned the people that if they did not obey God, 'the Lord's anger will burn against you; and you will quickly perish from the good land he has given you' (23:16). The most important condition for continuing to enjoy the land was that they continue to worship the Lord.

The Israelites could choose between a number of different gods. There were the gods that Abraham had once worshipped when he lived beyond the Euphrates. There were the gods of Egypt, whom they had come to know when they were slaves. And there were also the gods of the Amorites, among whom they now lived in the promised land (**24:14**). Joshua called on the people to make a clear choice about which god they would serve (**24:15a**). This choice was important because the God of the promise is a jealous God and will not share his worship with others. But the worship must also be voluntary. Unlike other religions, where adherents are often forced into devotion, the worship of the Lord must be free and voluntary. Jesus later underlined this fact when he declared 'true worshippers will worship the Father in spirit and truth, for they are the kind of worshippers the Father seeks' (John 4:23). The price to be paid for peaceful enjoyment of the promised land was faithful worship of the Lord.

As a humble leader, Joshua had been the last to lay claim to any piece of the promised land; but as a true spiritual leader, he was the first to declare his uncompromising stand on the matter of the worship of the Lord: *As for me and my household, we will serve the Lord* (**24:15b**). Taking their cue from Joshua, the people responded positively and enthusiastically. They assured Joshua, *Far be it from us to forsake the Lord to serve other gods!* (**24:16-18**).

Joshua's reference to 'my household' may refer to his military aides, servants and relatives, for we have no indication that Joshua was married or had any descendants. The Bible, unlike many in Africa, does not insist that marriage and children are prerequisites for leadership.

24:19-27 COMMITMENT TO THE LORD Joshua knew that promises are easily made without real consideration of their implications, so he took the matter a step farther. He reminded the Israelites that true worship must express itself in obedience and commitment, and he warned them not to expect things to be easy. They would not be able to keep this promise by their own efforts: *You are not able to serve the Lord*. Because God is holy and jealous, he will not be content with mere lip service. (**24:19**). If they turned and forsook the Lord for foreign gods, he would turn and bring disaster upon them and make an end to their nation (**24:20**).

This truth has not changed since the days of Joshua. Jesus still has harsh words for those who pay mere lip service to God: 'Woe to you … you hypocrites!' (Matt 23:27). 'Not everyone who says to me, "Lord, Lord," will enter the kingdom of heaven, but only he who does the will of my Father who is in heaven' (Matt 7:21).

The people pledged to fulfil the conditions of the promise and thus ensure that they lived in the promised land for ever: *We will serve the Lord* (**24:21**). Joshua sealed their pledge by leading them through a solemn commitment before the Lord (**24:22-24**). Once the people had pledged to follow the Lord, Joshua made them a covenant and *there at Shechem he drew up for them decrees and laws* and recorded them in the Book of the Law (**24:25-26a**). *Then he took a large stone and set it up there under an oak near the holy place* as an eternal reminder of the renewed covenant (**24:26b-27**).

24:28-33 Joshua's Death

After these things, Joshua son of Nun, the servant of the Lord, died (**24:29**). He died in the promised land. God took him to himself, being one hundred and ten years of age; exactly the same age as the patriarch Joseph. Here was a man who had served the Lord faithfully to his death. Like Paul, Joshua could have declared, 'I have fought the good fight, I have finished the race, I have kept the faith. Now there is in store for me the crown of righteousness, which the Lord, the righteous Judge, will award to me on that day – and not only to me, but also to all who have longed for his appearing' (2 Tim 4:7-8). Joshua had literally fought the good fight in driving the Canaanites from the promised land, and an even greater fight of keeping Israel on the narrow path of spiritual commitment to their God, for *Israel served the Lord throughout the lifetime of Joshua* (**24:31**).

Joseph had desired to be buried in Canaan and had given strict instructions that his bones were to be carried back from Egypt (Gen 50:25; Exod 13:19). That desire was fulfilled hundreds of years after his death. He was buried *at Shechem in the tract of land that Jacob had bought for a hundred pieces of silver from the sons of Hamor, the father of Shechem* (**24:32**; see also Gen 33:18-19). This tomb became the possession of his descendants as their inheritance.

Finally, we are told of the death of *Eleazor son of Aaron* (**24:33**). He had been Joshua's spiritual advisor (Num 27:18, 21, 22).

The death and burial of Joshua (24:29), the burial of the bones of Joseph (24:32), and the death and burial of Eleazor (24:33) marked the final closing of one chapter in Israelite history, that of Egypt and the exodus, and the beginning of a new one with the people at last living in their new land.

The book closes on a very positive note, with its reference to the obedience of the people until the end of Joshua's life. But sadly it was not long before the people broke the pledge they had made in 24:22-24. The book of Judges reports that 'after that whole generation had been gathered to their fathers, another generation grew up, who knew neither the Lord nor what he had done for Israel' (Judg 2:10). That new generation marked the beginning of the trouble in the promised land that has persisted through the centuries up to today. The current conflicts between Israel and its Arab neighbours are based on all the issues that Joshua reminded Israel of before he died: the land of the promise, the God of the promise, the people of the promise and the conditions of the promise.

God had warned the Israelites that if they departed from his ways, 'the Lord's anger will burn against you; and you will quickly perish from the good land he has given you' (23:16). Israel did depart from God, and they were accordingly completely removed from the land. Modern Israel only became a sovereign state on 15 May 1948, after being non-existent for nearly two thousand years. The Romans, who renamed it Palestine, had obliterated it from the map in AD 135. For most of the two thousand years that Israel did not exist, Palestine was occupied mainly by Arabs.

Even today, the restored nation of Israel does not enjoy the full extent of the land promised to and conquered by Joshua. But God, who is rich in grace and mercy, has promised that one day he will fully bring Israel back to its own land and will establish a new Jerusalem for all who have lived according to the conditions of the promise.

In the book of Revelation, John declared, 'Then I saw a new heaven and a new earth, for the first heaven and the first earth had passed away, and there was no longer any sea. I saw the Holy City, the new Jerusalem, coming down out of heaven from God, prepared as a bride beautifully dressed for her husband. And I heard a loud voice from the throne saying, "Now the dwelling of God is with men, and he will live with them. They will be his people, and God himself will be with them and be their God. He will wipe every tear from their eyes. There will be no more death or mourning or crying or pain, for the old order of things has passed away"'(Rev 21:1-4).

Are you living in hope of this new promised land, and are you drawing others to Christ, the only gate to enter this new land?

David Oginde

Further Reading

Hess, Richard. *Joshua*. TOT. Leicester: Inter-Varsity Press, 1996.

Butler, Trent C. *Joshua*. WBC. Nashville: Nelson, 1983.

JUDGES

Reading Judges is like reading the neo-colonial post-independence history of Africa. By 2004, approximately forty years after independence for most African nations, Africa has recorded over sixty successful military coups and numerous unsuccessful attempts at coups. Justice is trampled upon, corruption thrives and insecurity is rampant.

Judges covers a period of more than three hundred years, the period between the death of Joshua in about 1390 BC (assuming that the exodus from Egypt took place in 1446 BC) and the coronation of Saul as Israel's first king in about 1028 BC. During these years, the new nation experienced political instability and suffered from internal turbulence, paralysis, defeat and external oppression. Once Joshua's generation passed away, the promised peace and prosperity of a land flowing with milk and honey disappeared, giving way to chaos and confusion. The recurrent refrain in the book of Judges is, 'In those days Israel had no king; everyone did as he saw fit' (17:6; 18:1; 19:1; 21:25). The primary cause of Israel's tragedy was a leadership vacuum.

Unfortunately Joshua had failed to mentor a successor as Moses had mentored him. He had left the nation without a strong central government or a human head of state. It was a confederacy of twelve independent tribes without any unifying force except God. This form of government is called a 'theocracy', meaning that God rules over the nation either directly or through a religious group.

The people's sins, primarily their worshipping of foreign gods, repeatedly angered the Lord, who would then allow other nations to gain supremacy over them. The people would cry to the Lord who, in turn, 'raised up judges who saved them out of the hands of these raiders' (2:16). During the period covered by the book, twelve such judges were raised up: six major ones (Othniel, Ehud, Deborah, Gideon, Jephthah and Samson) and six minor ones (Shamgar, Tola, Jair, Ibzan, Elon and Abdon). The major judges are those who brought high-profile deliverance from six significant occupations by enemy forces.

The judges all had three things in common:

- God raised them up.

- God's Spirit empowered them to function in an extraordinary way.

- Their work led to victory, times of rest, peace and civility.

When we pray for godly leaders for our nations, this is the kind of leader we should have in mind.

It is depressing to note that no sooner had a judge died than the nation lapsed into rebellion. Consequently the Lord would again allow them to endure a yoke of oppression. They would then cry to the Lord, who in compassion would raise up another judge to deliver them. This vicious cycle is similar to the experience of many African nations, which has given birth to the infamous saying: 'The road to development is always under construction, never completed'. The nation had wandered around for forty years in the desert, and the Israelites wandered for even longer in the promised land. No development and no progress for over three hundred years! The book has been preserved to enable us to learn to avoid making the same mistakes as the Israelites, both as nations and as individual Christians. The lives of too many believers are also characterized by a cycle of sin and repentance, without much sign of progress towards spiritual maturity.

Authorship and Date

The book does not specify who wrote it. According to a Jewish tradition, Samuel, Israel's last judge, was the author. Some contemporary scholars see Judges as the work of a team of three prophets, namely Samuel, Nathan and Gad (see 1 Chr 29:29).

The date of compilation is also unknown, though the repetition of the words 'in those days Israel had no king' (17:6; 18:1; 19:1; 21:25) indicates that it was produced during the monarchy. Another clue to the dating is the statement that the Jebusites live in Jerusalem 'to this day' (1:21). These words must have been written before David conquered Jerusalem in about 990 BC (2 Sam 5:6-10). Consequently, it is likely that Judges was written at some time during the reign of Saul, somewhere between 1025 and 1000 BC.

Moral Lesson of Judges

The central theme of Judges confirms the spiritual law that obedience to God's laws brings his blessing, while disobedience results in punishment and curses (see Exod 19:5-6; Lev 26:3-28; Deut 28:1-68). Throughout the book, the sin of the people is followed by suffering, just as night follows day. But whenever they pray, God responds and pardons them. These realities are indissolubly wedded. We reap what we sow. Sin and suffering cannot be divorced. Similarly, supplication and salvation are joined.

The individual incidents described in the book also address many of the major problems facing Africa. It vividly presents the harm that can flow from tribalism, nepotism, incompetent leadership, corruption, bad governance, poverty and oppressive external economic forces. It shows how these forces were dealt with, or not dealt with, in ancient Israel.

But Judges also presents us with many moral problems, as it shows God-appointed leaders like Gideon, Jephthah and Samson failing to act in accordance with the laws God had laid down in the Pentateuch. Yet God still worked through them to deliver his people. Faced with this conundrum, all we can do is thank God that he is prepared to use less than perfect people as his servants. If he did not, we too would not be able to serve him! But that recognition should not lead us to complacency. Instead, it should drive us to prayer. Are we complacently enjoying God's blessing while indulging in behaviour or nursing attitudes that do not bring honour to God? Are we causing others to turn away from him because he is so poorly represented by us?

Outline of Contents

COMMENTARY

1:1-3:6 Prologue: Incomplete Conquest

1:1-36 The Political Background

1:1-20 The incomplete faith of Judah

Readers are notified that Israel is entering a period of transition by the words *After the death of Joshua* (**1:1a**). Every change involves some degree of uncertainty, but in this case the uncertainty is exacerbated because Joshua had not left the people with any clear leader. To his credit, however, he had taught them to know God and seek his will (Josh 24:14-28). So they probably asked the priest to use Urim and Thummim (Exod 28:30) to answer the question they asked the Lord, *Who will be the first to go up and fight for us against the Canaanites?* (**1:1b**).

In Joshua 21:43-45 we were told that the Israelites had already taken possession of the land, so why are they asking this question in Judges 1:1? To understand the situation, we need to remember our own African situation and our struggle for independence from colonial powers. That independence often came in two stages. After years of negotiation and armed struggle, colonies were given *madaraka* (self-rule), which was a trial government. If they were successful at governing themselves, they were then given *uhuru* (independence). Similarly, Joshua initially conquered Canaan and, together with Eleazar the priest and the tribal leaders, he apportioned the land by lot (Josh 14:1-21:42). But it was still the responsibility of each tribe to dispossess the local inhabitants in their own territory and complete the conquest.

In response to the people's question, the Lord assigned Judah to lead the way with the encouraging words, *I have given the land into their hands* (**1:2**). The Lord speaks with the authority of ownership (see Ps 24:1). He will do whatever it takes to secure the land for Judah. It is surprising, therefore, to read of Judah asking the *Simeonites their brothers* for assistance (**1:3**). Some see this as a good spirit of cooperation, but it is actually an expression of incomplete faith in God. It is easier for Judah to go to war alongside the Simeonites, whom they can see, than alongside God, whom they cannot. We will see more of this in Judges (4:8-9; 6:16-17). Ultimately, every Christian battle belongs to the Lord (2 Chr 20:15, 20), and we do well to put our trust in him and do whatever he tells us in any given situation.

When, in partial obedience, Judah took on the Canaanites it was the Lord, not the Simeonites, who *gave the Canaanites and Perizzites into their hands* (**1:4**). Ten thousand foot soldiers were struck down as well as their fleeing king, *Adoni-Bezek* was later captured and died in Jerusalem (**1:7**). The men of Judah extended their victory into the Judean mountain range, capturing Jerusalem (**1:8**). It seems that they were content to burn Jerusalem, but did not occupy the site, for in 1:21 we are told that the Benjamites could not dislodge the Jebusites from that city (see also 19:10-12). They also took Hebron and advanced into the lowlands towards the western coast (1:8-11).

At this point the author repeats an older story about Joshua's contemporary, Caleb, who offered to give his daughter Acsah in marriage to anyone who could attack and capture Kiriath Sepher (**1:12**; see Josh 15:16-19). His nephew Othniel took up the challenge and won. He was given a wife who secured him an abundant supply of water through her father's generosity (**1:13-15**). It is not clear why this story about Othniel was repeated here, but we will hear more about Othniel's exploits as a judge in 3:7-11.

The Simeonites had helped Judah, and now Judah keeps its promise to help them in return (1:3, 17). Together they destroyed the Canaanites living in *Zephath* and renamed it *Hormah,* meaning 'destruction' (1:17; Num 21:3). They also captured *Gaza, Ashkelon and Ekron,* all in the coastal region of modern-day Palestine (**1:17-18**). As far as the author was concerned this was all part of Judah's victory procured for them by the Lord (**1:19a**). However, once again they did not hold onto all the towns they captured, for Gaza, Ashkelon and Ekron soon reverted to Philistine control.

The reason for the incomplete victory over the plains is said to be that the Canaanites *had iron chariots* (**1:19b**). But this was not the first time that the Israelites had faced opponents who had iron chariots. The Egyptians had had them, and their army was probably more sophisticated and better organized than that of the Canaanites. But with the Lord fighting for Moses, Pharaoh's chariots and horsemen drowned in the Red Sea (Exod 14:23-31). The Lord could equally well have defeated the Canaanites for Judah if his terms and conditions had been met.

It is no accident that the account of Caleb's victory in **1:20** is sandwiched between two stories of failure (1:19b, 21). The message is clear: when we follow the Lord with our whole heart as Caleb did, we are guaranteed victory and success as Caleb was. When, like the men of Judah, we do not follow the Lord, our victories will be less than total (see also Num 13:1-31; 14:24; Josh 14:6-15).

1:21-36 A catalogue of failures

Seven other tribes did not take full possession of their inheritance. They are the tribes of Benjamin (**1:21**), Manasseh (**1:27-28**), Ephraim (**1:29**), Zebulun (**1:30**), Asher (**1:31-32**), Naphtali (**1:33**) and the Danites (**1:34**). (Note that the 'house of Joseph' in **1:22** and **1:35** is not another tribe, but is simply a generic name for the whole of Israel, focusing on the one who had originally saved the nation by bringing them to Egypt.)

Apart from the statement that *the Canaanites* (1:27) and *the Amorites* (1:35) were *determined to live in that land,* no reason is given for their failure to take all the land. The narrative implies that it may have been because originally they were too weak. This would be in keeping with the earlier promise, 'The Lord your God will drive out those nations before you, little by little. You will not be allowed to eliminate them all at once, or the wild animals will multiply around you' (Deut 7:22). However, once these nations had been conquered, they should not have been allowed to remain in the land. The Israelites disobeyed this instruction when they subjected their enemies to *forced labour* (1:28, 30, 33, 35). This failure to drive out the Canaanites (a name often used to mean all the original occupiers of the promised land) not only contravened God's command (Deut 7:1-5; 20:16-20), but also limited God's power. It was a tragedy.

God requires every one of his children to be totally obedient. When we are not, we displease him and suffer the consequences. And even when we confess that we have done wrong and are forgiven according to his mercy, there are cases where the damage that has been done cannot be undone. We would be wise to remember the Yoruba proverb: *Ro ohunti o fe se lekan, sugbon abo re l'emeji* ['Think of what you are about to do once, but think about its consequences twice'].

2:1-3:6 The Spiritual Background

2:1-5 The angel of the Lord visits the Israelites

The angel of the Lord who speaks in **2:1a** is none other than Jesus Christ, who was with God 'in the beginning' (John 1:1-2; see also John 8:58; Rev 1:8; 21:6). When he chooses to appear in the OT, it is often in the form of the angel of the Lord (see Gen 16:7, 11; 22:11, 15; Exod 3:2). That is why this angel does not speak as a messenger, which is what the word 'angel' means, but as God himself. He identifies himself by what he did for them in the past: *I brought you up out of Egypt and led you into the land that I swore to give to your forefathers* (**2:1b**). He underscores his faithfulness by referring to the covenant he made with Abraham, Isaac and Jacob to give them the land of Canaan (Gen 15:18-21; 26:2-6; 28:13-15). In the same breath, he expresses his disappointment at their disobedience in not driving out the inhabitants of the land, and asks sadly, *Why have you done this?* (**2:2**).

The Israelites had broken their part of the covenant, and no one walks away from such an agreement without facing some penalty. We know this even in our own politics, for whenever African politicians break their promises to the electorates, chaos and confusion ensue at the expense of peace, stability and progress.

The consequences of their choice to disobey will be those predicted in Numbers 33:55. First, his military assistance is withdrawn. Secondly, the Canaanites will be *thorns in your sides,* that is, sources of irritation and annoyance. Thirdly, their gods will cause the Israelites to stumble (**2:3**). The consequences of this judgment will be similar to the current ongoing problems between Israelis and Palestinians.

Following the verdict, *the people wept aloud, and they called that place Bokim* (**2:4-5**), which literally means 'Weepers'. Probably in penitence, they offered burnt and sin offerings to the Lord as required by the law (Lev 1:1-17; 4:1-34). He would respond in mercy by raising up judges, but the judges were not in God's original plan. They were his second-best option.

2:6-15 Historical interlude

After presenting the visit of the angel of the Lord, the author steps back in history in order to sketch the spiritual point of departure from the covenant. He identifies the problem as stemming from a failure to pass the faith on from one generation to the next. Joshua's generation knew God, saw his mighty acts both in Egypt and in the wilderness and, though not perfect, they generally served him (**2:6-7**). The next generation was the exact opposite. It was characterized by ignorance of God and of what he had done for Israel in the past (**2:10**). Clearly Joshua's generation had failed to discipline and mentor their children as commanded by the Lord (Deut 6:6-9).

The Baganda of Uganda say, 'Don't despise history, for without it there will be no anchor for our present and no compass for our future.' The truth of this saying is apparent from the behaviour of this ignorant generation as they forsook God and instead worshipped false gods (2:11-13). Such behaviour is *evil in the eyes of the Lord* (**2:11**) and provoked him to anger.

The Lord's judgment is described in three different ways in **2:14-15**: he *handed them over,* he *sold them to their enemies,* his *hand … was against them.* Once people are given up by the Lord, the enemy takes over and they experience defeat, depression, disgrace and distress (Rom 1:18-32).

2:16-19 A deeply entrenched problem

Disobedience can become a deeply entrenched habit, making it impossible for people to do good when they 'are accustomed to doing evil' (Jer 13:23). The more the Lord raised up judges to save them, the more they *prostituted themselves to other gods* (**2:16-17**).

Before embarking on the stories of specific judges and their achievements, the author gives a summary of the entire period:

- *Whenever the Lord raised up a judge for them, he was with the judge and saved them out of the hands of their enemies as long as the judge lived* (**2:18**).
- *But when the judge died, the people returned to ways even more corrupt than those of their fathers* (**2:19**).

Thus begins a depressing cycle of disobedience, oppression and deliverance.

2:20-3:6 The people of the land

The Israelites had broken the covenant by failing to drive out the people of the land, and so the Lord allowed the people of the land to remain there (**2:20-21**). The eight nations that the Lord did not drive out are listed: *Philistines, Canaanites, Sidonians and Hivites … Hittites, Amorites, Perizzites … and Jebusites* (**3:3, 5**). Faced with eight big nations with numerous warlords (the Philistines had the five lords of Ashdod, Ashkelon, Ekron, Gath and Gaza), Israel had enough to keep it busy.

The Lord had two reasons for allowing these nations to remain: to test the obedience of the Israelites (**2:22; 3:1, 4**) and to teach warfare to those without any experience of it (**3:2**). Those without war experience were all members of the generation who had only been children when the people first entered the promised land, or who had been born since then.

While the Israelites probably learned the lesson about warfare and acquired military skills, they failed miserably in the test of obedience. Two closely related areas of disobedience are mentioned: marriage to those who did not share the Jewish faith and worship of false gods (**3:6**; Deut 7:2-4). Both of these are evil acts that contaminate their purity and lead them away from the Lord.

3:7-16:31 Oppression and Deliverance

3:7-11 Othniel Defeats Mesopotamia

The Israelites did evil in the eyes of the Lord (**3:7a**) is the refrain that introduces the story of each of the major judges (3:12; 4:1; 6:1; 10:6; 13:1). The evil is here spelled out as forgetting God and following after *the Baals and the Asherahs* (**3:7b**). This is a flagrant violation of the first commandment (Exod 20:3; Deut 5:7). Nothing angers God more than our turning our backs on him and giving his glory to idols.

This act of rebellion is followed by retribution as *he sold them into the hands of Cushan-Rishathaim king of Aram Naharaim … for eight years* (**3:8**). The name 'Cushan-Rishathaim' literally means 'double wickedness' and suggests the cruel and impious character of this king. He ruled over the area between the Euphrates and Khabour rivers in north-west Mesopotamia.

Brought to their knees in repentance by his oppression, the Israelites *cried out to the Lord* who, in compassion, raised up *Othniel* to deliver them (**3:9**). This is not the first time we have met Othniel (1:11-13). His military experience qualified him for the work. But over and above that, God qualified him by pouring his Spirit upon him (**3:10a**). This seems to be God's standard procedure whenever he commissions a leader for a great task (Gideon, 6:34; Jephthah, 11:29; David, 1 Sam 16:13), including the greatest leader of all, Jesus Christ (Matt 3:16-17; Mark 1:10-11; Luke 3:22; John 1:32). Leaders thus anointed are rightly called 'charismatic' and often perform extraordinary feats because God's Spirit empowers them.

God delivered Cushan-Rishathaim into Othniel's hands and he *overpowered him* (**3:10b**). Othniel's forty-year rule was characterized by peace and stability. The phrase used to describe it, *so the land had peace* (**3:11**), also becomes a refrain in the book of Judges.

Reading the account of Othniel's rule, we are left with one lingering question: Why had Joshua not identified Othniel as his successor and mentored him to succeed him in the first place?

3:12-30 Ehud Defeats Moab

It is disheartening to read that, after forty years of rest, *once again the Israelites did evil in the eyes of the Lord* (**3:12**). This time, no specific evil actions are reported. But whatever they did, it was bad enough to bring the axe of God's wrath down upon the nation. This time it was the Moabites and Ammonites who were the instrument of his wrath. These peoples were the descendants of Lot, Abraham's nephew (Gen 12:4-5; 19:30-36), who had settled on the eastern side of the River Jordan. To ensure complete victory over Israel, *Eglon king of Moab* secured an alliance with *the Ammonites and Amalekites* and invaded Israel, recapturing the ruins of Jericho, here called *the City of Palms* (**3:13**). The Israelites were subject to him for *eighteen years* (**3:14**).

In frustration and desperation, *the Israelites cried out to the Lord*, who raised up *Ehud, a left-handed man* from the tribe of Benjamin on the western side of the Jordan (**3:15**). We have no military record of Ehud before this time. Nor is it explicitly stated that God poured his Spirit upon him, as in the case of Othniel. However, given the intelligence he displayed and his great exploit, one cannot deny that it was the Lord who wrought the victory for his people. Ehud himself testified to this: *the Lord has given Moab, your enemy, into your hands* (**3:28**).

Ehud realized that leadership is critical to the rise and fall of any nation so he found a way to remove Moab's king. Since he was left-handed (a common feature among the Benjamites –20:15-16), he strapped his short *double-edged sword* to his right thigh both for concealment and easy access. This detail is significant because it may have contributed to his success. The Moabites would have expected any weapon to be on his left side and to be wielded with his right hand.

After delivering the tribute he had brought, he obtained a private audience with the king (**3:17-19**). During their brief moment together, Ehud stabbed and fatally wounded Eglon. Then he escaped without rousing any suspicions among the king's attendants (**3:20-26**). God must have intervened to prevent the king from being suspicious of Ehud and to make him curious to hear the *secret message* that Ehud claimed to bear (3:19), even though Eglon was not a worshipper of Yahweh (3:19, 26).

With Eglon dead, Ehud wasted no time in marshalling an Israelite army, probably made up of Benjamites and Ephraimites, their immediate neighbours (**3:27**), and *struck down about ten thousand Moabites* (**3:29**).

Ehud, whose name means 'union', brought victory and unity to Israel, *and the land had peace.* He led his people for *eighty years,* the longest period of all the judges (**3:30**).

3:31 Shamgar

Shamgar is the first of the six minor judges. The other five are Tola (10:1-2), Jair (10:3-5), Ibzan (12:8-10), Elon (12:11) and Abdon (12:12-15). They are regarded as minor not because their achievements were insignificant or their characters uncharismatic, but because of the very brief accounts of their activities in the book of Judges. *Shamgar,* for instance, is dealt with in one verse (**3:31**).

Shamgar seems to have been a contemporary of Deborah (5:6). Because he is said to be the *son of Anath,* some commentators have concluded that his family worshipped Anath, Baal's sister, who was a goddess of war. However, others claim that the expression merely means that he came from the town of Beth Anath (1:33). If this interpretation is correct, it indicates that Shamgar belonged to the tribe of Naphtali. A third interpretation treats the expression as a military title, meaning 'warrior'. In context, it seems most likely that the phrase simply states that Shamgar's father was Anath, who was probably a fairly well-known local chief from the tribe of Naphtali (see 1:33; Josh 19:38). No definite years are assigned to his judgeship. However, by single-handedly striking down *six hundred Philistines,* he prepared the way for the greater deliverance of Israel under Deborah and Barak.

There is nothing special about his choice of an *ox-goad* as a weapon. It was an ordinary farm implement, in common use. But when the ordinary is placed in the hand of God, he uses it to perform extraordinary feats. Other examples include Moses' rod (Exod 4:2-5), Jael's tent peg (4:22), Gideon's jars and torches (7:20), the woman's millstone (9:53) and Samson's jaw-bone of a donkey (15:15).

He too saved Israel is a significant statement. Many Christian leaders in Africa complain about their lack of special buildings and of sophisticated communication equipment such as is common in the West. Shamgar's success shows that these are not always necessary. We simply need to start where we are, do what we can, and use whatever we have to. It has been said, 'little is much, when God is in it'.

4:1-5:31 Deborah (and Barak) defeat Canaan

4:1-3 Twenty years of Canaanite oppression

After the death of Ehud, the second major judge, the Israelites forsook Yahweh and followed the foreign gods of Canaan. They *once again did evil in the eyes of the Lord* (**4:1**), which caused God to turn his back on them for twenty years as they suffered under the tyrannical rule of *Jabin,* a Canaanite king with headquarters at *Hazor* (**4:2**). That city had been captured by Joshua some one hundred years earlier (Josh 11:10-11), but the Israelites had not been able to hold on to it. Jabin's army was equipped with sophisticated military hardware including *nine hundred iron chariots* (**4:3**).

The extent to which Jabin's oppression has disrupted normal life in Israel is evident from 5:6-8, which describes a helpless nation, too afraid even to travel on the main roads.

4:4-10 Deborah commissions Barak

Deborah, whose name means 'bee', was the only woman among the twelve judges. She was a contemporary of Shamgar (compare 3:31; 4:1; 5:6), but was more prominent than he was. Despite living in a male-dominated culture, she served as head of state, commander-in-chief and chief justice (**4:4-5**; 5:7). Her achievement should put an end to debates about whether women can provide leadership.

Deborah was the only judge out of the twelve who was also a prophetess. She performed prophetic functions such as speaking for God (**4:6**), foretelling (**4:7, 9**) and urging Barak to action (4:14). Other prophetesses in Scripture are Miriam (Exod 15:20), Huldah (2 Kgs 22:14), Noadiah (Neh 6:14), Anna (Luke 2:36), and Phillip's four daughters (Acts 21:9). Their example, combined with that of Deborah, clearly indicates that leadership in the church and society is ultimately God's gift and is gender-neutral (Rom 12:8). Like all other gifts it is mediated by the Holy Spirit to whomever he chooses (Joel 2:28; Acts 1:14; 2:1-4, 17-18).

As commander-in-chief, Deborah summoned her chief of staff, General Barak, whose name means 'thunderbolt'. The military chain of command is set out clearly in the charge to Barak: *The Lord, the God of Israel,* [the supreme commander] *commands you* [through me, your commander-in-chief]: *Go, take with you ten thousand men of Naphtali and Zebulun and lead the way to Mount Tabor* (4:6). God had already determined the number of troops Barak should take, which tribes they should come from, where the army should be positioned, and what the outcome would be – for he promised Barak a victory. In spite of all that, Barak's response smacks of hesitation: *if you don't go with me, I won't go* (**4:8**). Deborah agreed to go with him, but not without pointing out the consequences of his failure to trust God (4:9; see 4:21). It is surprising that Barak, not Deborah, is listed among the heroes of faith in Hebrews 11:32.

In contemporary Africa, gender is still a major issue, particularly as regards political leadership. Yet, Africa already has its first woman president with the election of Ellen Johnson-Sirleaf in Liberia. The story of Deborah shows that a woman can be as effective as any male leader, provided she has divine backing, and combine charisma with character, courage with competence, and conviction with commitment.

4:11-16 Confrontation and defeat

The account of the confrontation between Barak and Sisera begins with a parenthetical note introducing the family of Jael (**4:11**), into whose hands Sisera would be delivered (4:17-21). The Kenites had been allies of the Israelites at the time of Moses (1:16). Although they were not among the twelve tribes, some of them had embraced Judaism and had been assimilated into the Jewish nation. Heber had separated himself from the rest of the Kenites, moved from the south to the north and become an ally of Jabin (4:17).

Acting on a tip-off from the Kenites about the movements of the Israelite army (**4:12**), Sisera gathered his troops and those of his allies, supported by his invincible iron chariots, and advanced on the Israelite army (**4:13**). The Israelites were in a strong strategic position, for they had taken up position on Mount Tabor, overlooking the plain and the river Kishon. Nevertheless, Barak must have been nervous about facing such a superior force. Deborah roused him to action with two assurances. First, she assured him of Sisera's defeat: *the Lord has given Sisera into your hands* and, secondly, she assured him of God's direct involvement, which guarantees victory: *Has not the Lord gone ahead of you?* (**4:14**).

Encouraged by her words, Barak and his men moved out to attack the Canaanites. Their task proved much easier than they expected because the Lord had thrown Sisera and his troops into confusion, disabled their chariots and scattered them (**4:15**). The way in which he did this emerges from Deborah's song of victory. There she describes the enemy forces and sings that 'the river Kishon swept them away' (5:19-21; see also 5:4). The bed of the river Kishon is usually dry, but after heavy rain it becomes a torrent, and this is presumably what trapped Sisera's army. The heavy iron chariots would have bogged down and become stuck in the mud, which is why Sisera is said to have *fled on foot*.

Barak pressed home his victory, taking the battle into the enemy's territory and pursuing Sisera's fleeing troops all the way back to their home base at Harosheth Haggoyim (**4:16**; 4:2). He killed them all *by the sword*. But his victory would only be complete when Sisera himself was captured or killed.

4:17-24 Death of Sisera

Barak's victory can be explained in terms of military strategy and weather conditions, but no natural explanation is adequate to explain the drama that took place in *the tent of Jael*. Sisera sought refuge there because its owners were friendly (**4:17**). Why would an ally suddenly turn into an enemy? And how could a woman muster sufficient courage and strength to drive a tent peg through the temple of a sleeping warrior? (**4:21**; 5:24-27). It is one thing to pitch a tent; it is quite another to kill a man. All this happened to fulfil Deborah's prophecy (4:9). God was at work, bringing his plan and purposes to pass, as we are reminded in **4:23**: *On that day God subdued Jabin the Canaanite king, before the Israelites*. Having lost his best general, Jabin grew weaker and weaker, while the Lord made the Israelites *stronger and stronger against Jabin until they destroyed him* (**4:24**). For the next forty years, there was peace in the land (5:31).

5:1-31 Celebration in song

Following their victory, Deborah and Barak burst into song (**5:1**), just as Moses, Aaron and Miriam did after the destruction of the Egyptian forces at the Red Sea (Exod 15:1-21). Their song repeats the story told in chapter four, but what had previously been presented as prose is now told in poetry.

The prologue to the song is an invitation to praise the Lord (**5:2-3**). It is followed by a celebration of God's power, spoken of as revealed in a violent storm approaching from the direction of Sinai, where God had long before revealed himself to his people in clouds and thunder (**5:4-5**; Exod 20:18). The statement that *the clouds poured down water* foreshadows the means God will use to achieve victory.

But before celebrating the victory, the song deals with why it was needed, setting out the problems that faced the nation (5:6-9). Those of us who live in war-torn regions of Africa will recognize the type of disruption of normal life that is described (**5:6-7a**). Moreover, the people were helpless, without any weapons to defend themselves (**5:8b**; see also 1 Sam 13:19-22). The reason for their plight is not glossed over: *when they chose new gods, war came to the city gates* (**5:8a**).

The *Jael* mentioned in 5:6 should not be confused with Jael, the wife of Heber the Kenite (**5:24-27**). It seems likely that the Jael in 5:6 is some unrecorded minor judge, who was a contemporary of Shamgar and Deborah.

In this distressing situation, it was a woman who took the lead to rescue the nation (**5:7b**). And it is to Deborah and to Barak that the people in the song appeal for help (**5:12**). Their status as leaders is evident from the mounts on which they ride (**5:10**). The people still sing the songs about God's deliverance of their people in the past (**5:11**), and they want to see him acting for them again. But the words also look forward to the new song of deliverance that is being sung as a result of Deborah and Barak's victory.

A coalition of Israelites combine forces to oppose Jabin and Sisera. In 5:13-18 we have a description of how the different tribes responded to the call to unite against their common enemy. Some enthusiastically reported for duty (**5:13-15a, 18**). Others debated what to do (**5:15b-16**), and others did not come at all (**5:17**).

The battle itself is described in **5:19-23** and is followed by an account of Jael's heroism as she kills Sisera (**5:24-27**). Her actions contrast with that of another woman, Sisera's mother, who sits waiting vainly for his return, looking anxiously out the window, thinking up reasons why he may have been delayed, and anticipating what gifts he will bring her (**5:28-30**). But he will never come again.

The epilogue of the song prays that the hopes of all God's enemies will be similarly dashed, but that the hopes of his people will flourish (**5:31**).

The story of Deborah and Barak ends with the report that the *land had peace for forty years* (5:31).

6:1-8:35 Gideon Defeats Midian

6:1-10 The conditions under Midianite oppression

Forty years of peace and prosperity under the leadership of Deborah and Barak were soon gone and forgotten. Deborah's generation passed away, and again *the Israelites did evil in the eyes of the Lord.* For seven years, God allowed the *Midianites* to oppress them (**6:1**).

The Midianites were nomads, like the Maasai of East Africa. Just as the Maasai roam across the national boundaries of Kenya, Uganda and Tanzania, so the Midianites roamed the northern frontier of Palestine, through Transjordan, crossing the Jordan and penetrating as far west as Gaza (**6:4**). Because they were not a large enough group to wage war against the Israelites single-handed, they often formed coalitions with others (**6:3**; including with the Moabites, see Num 22:4-6). Since their home area was largely desert, the Midianites would normally move into Israel's territory during harvest time, when they could feast on farm produce, livestock and wildlife.

They were merciless. The text states that *they invaded the land to ravage it* (**6:5**). In terms of their numbers and destructiveness, they could be compared to *swarms of locusts*. They plundered the country just as some colonial powers plundered Africa. As Walter Rodney reminds us in *How Europe Underdeveloped Africa*, directly or indirectly, the carefree, opulent bourgeois lifestyle of the rich has a harmful effect on the poor. The Midianites made life unbearable for the Israelites, who could not sustain any economic development and had to hide in the *mountain clefts, caves and strongholds* (**6:2**). They became poverty stricken (**6:6**).

So the Israelites cried to the Lord, whose first response was to send them *a prophet* to reprimand them for their disobedience (**6:7-10**).

6:11-24 The call and commissioning of Gideon

God's love for the Israelites would take him beyond the reprimand. Just as he went down to Egypt to redeem them (Exod 3:1-8), so he came personally to Gideon, their next leader, in the form of *the angel of the LORD* (see comment on 2:1-5). When he appeared to Gideon, he assumed the posture of someone who is in control, sitting down under an oak tree just as Deborah had sat under a palm tree (**6:11**; see 4:5). Gideon, by contrast, was so afraid of the Midianites that he was hiding and disguising what he was doing, *threshing wheat in a winepress.*

The Lord's greeting affirms his presence with Gideon: *The Lord is with you, mighty warrior* (**6:12**). But who is this 'mighty warrior'? Some claim that God is saying that he himself is the mighty warrior who is with Gideon. But God does not normally introduce himself in this way, and the occasion does not seem to call for it. Rather, Gideon was being addressed as a potential warrior, even though he dismisses this title and focuses on the first words of the angel's greeting (**6:13**). But the greeting foreshadowed the assignment Gideon would be given (**6:14**).

The dialogue that ensued between Gideon and the angel of the Lord reminds us of the similar encounter between God and Moses (Exod 3–4). Moses gave many reasons why he was not suited to be a leader, and Gideon did the same (**6:15**; see Exod 3:11; 4:10). In both cases, God's answer is the same: *I will be with you* (**6:16**; Exod 3:12). God's presence with any servant of the Lord makes all the difference (Gen 26:12-14; 39:2-5, 21-23; Mark 16:20; Acts 18:9-10; 2 Tim 4:16-17).

Words alone were not enough for Gideon. He asked for a sign, and the angel of God condescended to give him one, just as he had given signs to Moses (**6:17-21**; Exod 4:2-7). Some have taken Gideon's request as a sign of unbelief, but that seems unlikely, for God does not respond to unbelief (see Heb 11:6). Asking for a sign to confirm God's word or any particular promise to us is as legitimate and valid as praying in Jesus' name (see Matt 7:7-8; Luke 11:9-10; John 14:13-14; 15:7).

Gideon's request to bring an *offering* (6:18) uses a term that would be very unusual if used to describe a meal, but one that is appropriate when presenting something to a divine being. It seems that he recognized that the one he was speaking to was some kind of divine messenger, although he had not fully grasped who he was. It was only when *the meat and the bread* were consumed by fire as a sign of divine acceptance of Gideon's *offering* (6:21; see Lev 9:24) and the angel of the Lord disappeared that Gideon suddenly realized who he had been talking to (**6:22**). Terrified, he

FAITH AND THE SEARCH FOR SIGNS

In religious thinking and in popular opinion, a 'sign' is a supernatural event that enables one to believe some claim, statement or promise made by or about God. Many Africans have an avid interest in signs. Signs are the foundations for traditional beliefs and for many new movements that claim to represent an African Christianity.

The Bible contains many accounts of miraculous signs. They are one of the means by which God chooses to reveal himself to humans (Exod 3:1-4; Ezek 1:1-28; Acts 9:1-7). He is all-powerful and nothing is impossible for him. But can one insist on a sign as a precondition for faith in God or to prove that someone has been sent by God? Are signs essential as a proof of one's faith? Is it normal to look for signs from God, or are there dangers in doing so? What does Scripture have to say on this subject?

The first point that must be made is that not all supernatural events are necessarily of divine origin. As the saying goes, 'All that glitters is not gold'. Non-believers such as Pharaoh's magicians were able to produce counterfeit miracles (Exod 7:20-22). Scripture warns us to be suspicious of signs. Faced with the proliferation of prophets and prophetesses who claim to work miracles, it is important that we discern whether they are indeed faithful to God and his word (Deut 13:1-5). After all, Christ warns us that certain signs are deceptive and serve only to turn us away from true faith and to enslave us (Matt 24:24).

The second point to emphasize is that individuals who sought signs in the Bible wanted them for a specific purpose – to confirm a prior call from God to a particular mission. Thus Moses, for example, received a sign from God to confirm his call to liberate the people (Exod 4:1-5). Gideon requested a miracle in order to be sure he was to fight the Midianites

(Judg 6:36-40). The disciples received signs that confirmed Christ's command to them to proclaim the gospel (Mark 16:20). Above all, many miracles were performed to support Jesus' principal mission – that of forgiving sins and granting eternal life (see Mark 2:9-12; John 20:30-31).

The purpose of all these signs was to lead people towards God and his word, not to glorify one individual and set him or her above others. The apostles refused to fall into this trap. In spite of the power that had been given to them, they wanted neither special treatment nor honour paid to their own names (see, for example, Acts 14:8-15 and 1 Cor 3:4-9).

The third and final point concerning the quest for signs is that they are neither necessary for faith nor able to create it. Pharaoh saw many signs and yet did not believe (Exod 7:9-13). Similarly, in Jesus' time many people did not believe in him in spite of his many miracles (John 12:37). On several occasions Jesus even refused to respond to requests for signs because he knew that signs alone are ineffective in producing a change of heart (Matt 12:38-39; 16:1-4).

Signs are only one of God's gracious gifts. They are granted to some of God's people, but are not the best way (John 20:29; 1 Cor 12:28-13:1). Thus they cannot be taken as a proof of strong faith and should not be sought as evidence of faith. Rather, a sign is a gift from God that confirms an already existing and living faith.

We must not sit back and wait for our hearts and lives to be transformed by some miraculous sign. If we wish to be delivered from the powers of darkness in Africa and elsewhere and to live a life of faith, we should not pursue miracles, as many people do today. Instead, we should devote ourselves to the word of God, which is the only infallible source of true Christian faith.

Adama Ouedraogo

expected to die (see Gen 32:30; Exod 33:20). But the Lord calmed his fear, pronouncing *shalom – Peace!* – upon him (**6:23**). Overflowing with gratitude, Gideon responded by naming the altar he built at the site of the offering, *the Lord is Peace* (**6:24**). By this action, Gideon signalled that he had accepted the call of God upon his life.

Many across Africa and in the world at large are struggling with the call of God upon their lives. Like Gideon in 6:13, we may not be able to understand where God is in our predicament. But, again like Gideon, we can ask him tough questions and even ask for signs, as long as we do so in faith. Ultimately each of us must build an altar for him in our heart and enthrone him as *the Lord is Peace*.

6:25-32 God's command to Gideon executed
God now gave Gideon an explicit command: the *altar to Baal* and *the Asherah pole beside it* that belonged to Joash, his father, must go (**6:25**). In their place a *proper kind of altar* as stipulated by the law (Exod 20:25) was to be constructed

to the Lord, and a burnt offering for sin was to be made with his father's *second bull* (**6:26**). Gideon passed the test, but not without fear and trembling (**6:27**).

It is surprising that the people of the city would contemplate killing Gideon for destroying idols (**6:28-30**). By law, they should have done this themselves (Exod 34:13; Deut 7:5). Joash protected his son with an irrefutable argument: a God who cannot save himself is not worth worshipping (**6:31**). The same principle applies today. When enduring religious persecution, believers have to learn to leave vengeance to God and not take the law into their own hands (Rom 12:19; Heb 10:30).

On the day Gideon tore down Baal's altar, he was given a new name, *Jerub-Baal*, meaning, *Let Baal contend with him* (**6:32**). His original name, Gideon, means 'one who cuts down'. As a Yoruba proverb says, *Oruko nima ro omo* ['our destiny is driven by our names']. This was certainly true for Gideon.

6:33-40 Confirmation of Gideon's call

When individuals take up any divine assignment in the OT, God implicitly or explicitly pours his Spirit upon them (**6:34**; see 2:18; 3:10; 11:29; 14:6, 19; 15:14-15; Exod 31:1-5; Num 11:17; 1 Sam 10:6). This divine act, which is theologically referred to as anointing, empowers the recipients to know, see, say and do things beyond their natural ability. It is the evidence of God's presence with them. So it was that as the enemy forces advanced (**6:33**), God anointed his servant Gideon for action (**6:34**).

Immediately, the one-time coward from the weakest family in Manasseh (6:15), took the bold step of rallying thirty-two thousand men from four tribes: *Manasseh, Asher, Zebulun* and *Naphtali* (**6:35**). This is awesome! It is extraordinary. Yet Gideon was human, with limited capabilities. His limits are clear in the drama that followed, as Gideon asked for yet more signs (**6:36-40**). He did this not once but twice, and again God did not condemn him for it.

Young believers often want to know whether it is wrong to put out a fleece before God in order to determine the choice of a career, a college or a spouse. From this text, and the use of the ephod (1 Sam 30:7-8) and of lots (Prov 16:33; Jonah 1:7; Acts 1:26), one can conclude that there is nothing wrong with asking God for a sign. However, caution must be exercised that we do not manipulate the sign to suit our own wishes. One safe principle is this: God will never give a sign or an answer to a specific question that contradicts his general principles as revealed in the Bible.

7:1-8:32 Gideon's conquests

With his call reconfirmed, Gideon was ready to move forward into battle. What followed was further proof that God was with Gideon. There is no other way to explain how an untrained individual with three hundred unskilled men and no military weapons could defeat and destroy coalition forces of 135 000 warriors (see 8:10) with their two kings and two princes. Like politics, warfare is a game of numbers in terms of both soldiers and weaponry (Luke 14:31-32). However, the equation changes radically when God takes sides, as seen in Gideon's story.

7:1-8 SELECTION OF GIDEON'S ARMY Right from the outset, the Lord proved who was in charge. He gave two tests that reduced Gideon's thirty-two thousand men to a mere three hundred. First, he let the fearful and the trembling turn back voluntarily (**7:3**). The trembling were those whose bodies were visibly shaking, like leaves being blown by the wind, or whose teeth were chattering or their knees knocking together. Twenty-two thousand men took advantage of the opportunity to leave, which was made in compliance with an established law (Deut 20:8).

God stated that the remaining ten thousand were still too many for him, hence the second test. Dogs do not need to *kneel down to drink* because of the short distance between

their mouths and the water (**7:5**). Consequently, even while it is drinking, a dog is ready for action if danger threatens. Not so a man who is down on his knees drinking. The men who did not bury their faces in the water but brought the water *with their hands to their mouths* were similarly alert. Only the three hundred men who drank like this passed the test.

God assured Gideon that such a small army would be adequate to defeat the Midianites (**7:7**). The point God was trying to make is clearly stated in **7:2**: *or else Israel might brag, 'I did it myself'* (HCSB).

7:9-14 SUPPLY OF INTELLIGENCE INFORMATION Knowing that Gideon was afraid to attack (**7:9**) and would probably ask for another sign, the Lord gave him vital information about a state of affairs that Gideon could never have imagined: the Midianites feared him! He learned this when he obeyed God's instruction to *get up, go down against the camp, because I am going to give it into your hands* (**7:9**). Obediently, he crept into the vast Midianite camp and listened to what they were talking about (**7:10-12**). He overheard one of them telling another about his dream, a dream that the Midianite's companion interpreted as foretelling Gideon's victory (**7:13-14**). The Lord had already given Gideon the same message of victory seven times before (6:14, 16, 17-23, 36-38, 39-40; 7:7, 9), but none of the previous messages had galvanized him to action as this one did. Hearing this truth from an enemy's mouth was a turning-point in Gideon's career.

7:15-25 SURPRISE ATTACK Having bowed in worship to thank God, Gideon moved into action. His attack is a model of how to launch a surprise assault:

- Secrecy: No one, except possibly his bodyguard Purah, knew that he was going to attack that night.
- Suddenness: No time was wasted as he returned to camp and commanded his men, *Get up!* (**7:15**).
- Simplicity: He gave no complicated instructions, simply telling his men to *do exactly as I do* (**7:17**) and shout: *For the Lord and for Gideon* (**7:18**).
- Strategic timing: He and his men arrived at the enemy camp at *the beginning of the middle watch* (**7:19**), about midnight, when the change of guard was more likely to cause havoc.

Gideon's men, armed only with trumpets and torches hidden in jars (**7:16**), sneaked up to the Midianite camp and *blew their trumpets and smashed the jars* and shouted out the war cry: *A sword for the Lord and for Gideon!* (**7:20**). The sudden sounds of destruction and the flare of lights on all sides confused the sleeping Midianites, who assumed that the camp was being attacked by a large army and *ran, crying out as they fled* (**7:21**). While the strategy was effective, it was the Lord who brought victory, for in the confusion he caused the Midianites *to turn on each other with their swords* (**7:22**).

Gideon called out more Israelites from *Naphtali, Asher and all Manasseh* to help him pursue the fleeing army (**7:23**).

He gave a special assignment to *the men of Ephraim*. They were to take up position at the places where the Midianites would attempt to ford *the waters of the Jordan* (**7:24**). The Ephraimites obeyed him and captured and *killed two of the Midianite leaders, Oreb and Zeeb* (**7:25**).

8:1-21 Pursuit and death of Zebah and Zalmuna The Ephraimites, however, were discontented (**8:1**). It rankled that they had not been among those Gideon had initially summoned to join his army (6:35). This grievance had the potential to turn the victory into a tragic loss as the Israelites argued amongst themselves. Rather than engage in argument with them as Jephthah would do years later (12:1-6), Gideon wisely gave them more credit than they deserved and thereby quelled their resentment (**8:2-3**). A lot of the border conflicts tearing African nations apart could be resolved and effectively managed if political leaders in places such as Burundi and Rwanda were as level-headed and shrewd as Gideon.

Knowing that the war was not over as long as *Zebah and Zalmuna, the kings of Midian* were alive with about fifteen thousand men (**8:5b, 10**), Gideon and his three hundred kept pursuing them, despite being exhausted. Gideon did not allow himself to be discouraged by the sarcasm and refusal of the men of *Succoth* and *Penuel* to give him any food for his troops (**8:5a, 8**). Instead he stayed focused and, by faith, spoke of his assured victory and eventual return (**8:7, 9**). After capturing the two kings and *routing their entire army*, Gideon returned as promised and disciplined the men of Succoth and Penuel (**8:12-17**).

Before putting the two kings to death, Gideon asked them: *What kind of men did you kill at Tabor?* (**8:18**). He informed them that those they had killed were his own full brothers. In retaliation for this killing, he would kill them, and to add to their humiliation and disgrace he would have the killing done by a young boy, his son, Jether. When Jether quailed at the task, they challenged Gideon to do the job himself, and he did (**8:21**).

8:22-35 Gideon's legacy After the war Gideon started out well by refusing the people's demand that he establish a monarchy: *I will not rule over you, nor will my son rule over you. The Lord will rule over you* (**8:23**). His attitude contrasts with that of many African presidents who want to be president for life and attempt to establish family dynasties.

Unfortunately, Gideon's next move was disastrous. He made a golden *ephod*. In the Pentateuch, an ephod was a garment worn by the high priest (see Exod 28:6-13; 39:2-7; Lev 8:7). However, Gideon's ephod, which was made with 43 pounds (19.5 kg) of gold, is unlikely to have been a garment that could easily be worn. The high priest's ephod was associated with the Urim and Thummin, which were used to determine God's will, so it is possible that Gideon intended his golden ephod to be used for a similar purpose. But this ephod *became a snare* to him and his household *as all Israel prostituted themselves by worshipping it* (**8:24-27**; see 17:5; 18:14, 17). Consequently, it was easy for this gullible people to return to Baal worship soon after Gideon's death (**8:33**).

Gideon started well by pulling down the altar of Baal and the Asherah pole (6:25-27). But he ended poorly by putting up a golden ephod that became a snare for generations to come. In the twilight of his life, Gideon and his household were trapped in a form of spiritual backsliding and lukewarmness. One of the moral consequences was Gideon's indulgence in many wives, including a Canaanite concubine in Shechem who bore him a son named Abimelech (**8:30-31**). This sad spiritual drifting had far-reaching consequences for Gideon's family and the nation as a whole immediately after his death.

Although *the land enjoyed peace for forty years* during his reign (**8:28**), one is shocked to read that the Israelites *did not remember the Lord their God who had rescued them from the hands of all their enemies on every side* (**8:34**).

9:1-57 Abimelech's Tyranny

Merely three years after Gideon's death (9:22), there was hardly any trace of his religious reform (6:25-32), no remembrance of his gallant victory against the Midianites, nor any reward for his family after forty years of peaceful rule (9:16-20). How did all this come about?

9:1-6 Abimelech's intrigue

Abimilech seized power. The name *Abimelech* means either 'the father is king' or 'the father of a king'. In the OT it was a title of Philistine kings (see Gen 20:2; 26:1), but here it seems to be used as a personal name (9:1). This Abimelech had close ties to Shechem, a city in the hill country of Ephraim in north-central Palestine, because that was where his mother lived (8:31), although Gideon himself lived in Ophrah, a town some distance away in the territory of Manasseh. Shechem was an ancient city – the first place in Canaan to be mentioned in connection with Abram's arrival in the land. Following God's appearance to him, Abram built his first altar there (Gen 12:6-7). It was selected by Joshua as one of the six cities of refuge (Josh 20:7) and was where he gave his farewell address (Josh 24:1).

After his father's death, Abimelech conspired with his maternal uncles in Shechem to kill his seventy half-brothers so that he could be king. Here is a striking instance of the evils of polygamy and nepotism. He asks, *Which is better for you: to have all seventy of Jerub-Baal's sons rule over you, or just one man?* Before they answered he threw in this tribalistic line: *Remember, I am your flesh and blood* (**9:1-2**). Similar nepotistic tribalism is among the major problems retarding the development of Africa.

Abimelech gained the support of his relatives, who got him money from the temple of Baal to hire idle *reckless adventurers* as mercenaries (**9:3-4**). Using mercenaries to achieve political or military goals was a common strategy in ancient times, as it still is in Africa today. In the OT mercenaries were used by Jephthah (11:3), David (1 Sam 22:1-2), Absalom (2 Sam 15:1), Adonijah (1 Kgs 1:5), Rezon (1 Kgs 11:23-24) and Jeroboam I (2 Chr 13:6-7).

Abimelech slaughtered all his half-brothers like sacrificial animals *on one stone* and set himself up as king, a position that his father had vehemently refused to accept (**9:5a**; 8:23). But the youngest of his brothers, *Jotham*, managed to escape the massacre (**9:5b**). (Thus, strictly speaking, only sixty-nine brothers were murdered, but the author has used a round number. Abimelech certainly intended to execute all seventy).

Abimelech's ambition was achieved when he was crowned king in the ancient city of Shechem (**9:6**).

9:7-21 Jotham's indictment

Jotham, the sole survivor of Gideon's other sons, was indignant at the honour being paid to Abimelech. So he climbed to the top of *Mount Gerizim,* the hill that overlooks Shechem on the south-west (Mount Ebal is on the other side). There he raised his voice and shouted a parable to the citizens below (**9:7**).

In the parable, the trees are looking for a king. They approach three fruit-bearing trees, *the olive tree* (**9:8-9**), *the fig-tree* (**9:10-11**) and *the vine* (**9:12-13**), asking each of them in turn to become king. But these trees refuse to leave their important productive duties in order to become king. But an insignificant *thornbush*, which bears no fruit at all, brags of what it cannot offer, saying *come and take refuge in my shade* (**9:15a**). Thorns burn easily, and this thornbush threatens to consume with fire the far more precious *cedars of Lebanon* (**9:15b**). The moral of the parable is that foolish and wicked people will boldly usurp positions of power and influence that wise and good people tend to avoid.

Jotham condemned the action of the citizens of Shechem in no uncertain terms (**9:16-18**). He invoked a curse on them, saying, *let fire come out from Abimelech and consume you, citizens of Shechem and Beth Millo, and let fire come out from you, citizens of Shechem and Beth Millo, and consume Abimelech* (**9:19-20**).

Having delivered his indictment, Jotham fled to Beer, where he would be safe from Abimelech (**9:21**).

9:22-25 God's intervention

Although Abimelech *governed Israel for three years*, he is never referred to as a judge (**9:22**). His rule must have been a reign of terror. There is no record of any war he waged against any of Israel's enemies and, of course, no record of any victory. Whereas we are told that God's Holy Spirit came upon other judges (2:18; 3:10; 6:34; 11:29; 14:6, 19), we are told that *God sent an evil spirit* [a demon] *between Abimelech and the citizens of Shechem, who acted treacherously*

against Abimelech (**9:23**). Those who had put him in power now turned their backs on him. The citizens of Shechem revolted against Abimelech and reverted to highway robbery and a state of lawlessness (**9:25**).

The Yoruba of Nigeria have a saying, *Ohun ti aba gbin l'aokore* ['Whatever we sow, we are bound to reap']. The Bible repeatedly makes the same point (see Job 4:8; Prov 11:18; 22:8; Hos 8:7; 10:12; Gal 6:7-8). Jesus himself put it this way: 'all who draw the sword will die by the sword' (Matt 26:52). The truth of this law is revealed in the subsequent fate of Abimelech and his supporters.

9:26-55 Gaal's insurrection

Out of the blue, there arose a self-appointed captain of a band of robbers by the name of *Gaal son of Ebed* (**9:26**). He fanned into flame the fire of rebellion against Abimelech that was already simmering among the citizens of Shechem. They trusted him and followed him and his band in revelry (**9:27**). Gaal, who was probably drunk after the feasting, bragged of his ability to remove Abimelech from power, challenging him to *call out your whole army* (**9:28-29**). Rebels and politicians have one thing in common – they both crave recognition.

Zebul, the governor of the city was *very angry* with Gaal (**9:30**) and secretly reported his bragging to Abimelech (**9:31**), who apparently was not living in Shechem at this time. Zebul advised Abimelech to ambush the city and deal with Gaal and his followers (**9:32-33**). Abimelech did as advised (**9:34**). The ambush, with the troops divided into four companies, was successful (**9:35-39**). Gaal and his men were put to rout and driven out of the city (**9:40-41**). The resistance put up by the citizens of Shechem was ruthlessly put down by Abimelech. He tore down the city and *scattered salt over it* (**9:42-45**). Sowing an area with salt would make the land infertile. Abimelech may not have had enough salt to be able to do this literally, but scattering salt over the city was a symbolic ritual that punished the city for having broken its covenant with Abimelech and cursed it with infertility. (The city of Shechem was later rebuilt by Jeroboam I – 1 Kgs 12:25).

But bloodthirsty Abimelech was not yet satisfied. When he heard that the citizens of Shechem had taken refuge inside the temple of *El-berith* (a variant form of 'Baal-berith' – 9:4), he and his men set the tower on fire, killing about one thousand men and women (**9:46-49**). Still not satisfied, he turned his rage against *Thebez*, a dependent town of Shechem. He *besieged it and captured it* (**9:50**). But this was where he met his end. While he was attempting to storm the strong tower in which the people had taken refuge, *a woman dropped an upper millstone on his head and cracked his skull* (**9:50-53**). He could not survive the blow. Nevertheless, out of his pride he told his servant: *Draw your sword and kill me, so that they can't say, 'A woman killed* him' (**9:54a**). What an arrogant man! He died anyway (**9:54b-55**), and history remembers that he was killed by a woman (2 Sam 11:21).

9:56-57 Author's inference

The author of Judges drew a twofold moral conclusion. First, the God of justice would not let evil go unpunished. God punished Abimelech for killing his seventy brothers (**9:56**). Secondly, the curse that Jotham pronounced upon him and the citizens of Shechem was also fulfilled (9:20). Those around them must have learned the lesson that crime doesn't pay.

10:1-2 Tola

The next forty-five years after Abimelech passed relatively quietly under two minor judges, Tola and Jair. They were regarded as minor judges partly because they fought no major enemy and have no mighty deeds recorded. Nevertheless, they also saved Israel and consolidated the gains made by their predecessors such as Gideon and Deborah.

Tola was from the tribe of Issachar and made Shamir in the hill country of Ephraim his headquarters (**10:1**). Tracing his ancestry through Puah, his father and Dodo, his grandfather, helped to confirm his roots. For twenty-three years he performed leadership functions such as managing conflict and maintaining peace and stability (**10:2**). Though he did not wage any wars, his presence kept would-be aggressors at bay. He must have led with justice and righteousness to be in office for twenty-three years (see Prov 29:4, 14).

10:3-5 Jair

Jair, whose name means 'he enlightens', ruled for twenty-two years in Gilead (**10:3**). His leadership style was more flamboyant than that of his predecessor, and he showed his wealth in the types of gifts he gave to his *thirty sons* (**10:4a**). Opinions are divided as to whether he got these thirty sons from one wife, from many wives, or through sequential marriages. Since the text is silent about it, it is best not to speculate.

Jair's leadership focused on building rather than on fighting. He established *thirty towns* for his thirty sons in Gilead. These towns became known as *Havvoth Jair* that is 'the settlements of Jair' (**10:4b**). In all probability, his sons served as administrative chiefs of those towns, helping their father to administer justice and maintain peace. This is a beautiful legacy.

10:6-12:7 Jephthah Defeats the Ammonites

10:6-18 Israel's rebellion and repentance

Surprisingly, none of Jair's thirty sons rose up to fill the leadership vacuum after his death. It may be that none of them possessed the military skill and capability needed at

the time. This seems likely given the words of the leaders of the people of Gilead: *Whoever will launch the attack against the Ammonites will be the head of all those living in Gilead* (**10:18**). It is worth noting that a leader who is capable of managing and maintaining peace and economic growth is not necessarily the best leader in a time of war. Nor is a leader's son necessarily the best person to succeed him.

Meanwhile, the Israelites *did evil in the eyes of the Lord,* and sank back into their usual despicable state of forsaking God and following *the Baals and the Ashtoreths* (**10:6**). This time around, they sank deeper and worshipped other foreign gods: *the gods of Aram,* including Rimmon (2 Kgs 5:18); *the gods of Sidon,* including Ashtoreth (1 Kgs 11:33); *the gods of Moab,* including Chemosh (1 Kgs 11:7); *the gods of the Ammonites,* including Molech (1 Kgs 11:33); and the *gods of the Philistines,* including Dagon (16:23).

The grossness and universality of this apostasy exceeded that of earlier times. It made God angry, and so he sold them to two enemies, *the Philistines and the Ammonites* (**10:7**). Their combined forces demoralized and shattered the Israelites in just one year. For the next seventeen years they could not rise (**10:8**). The scale of oppression, which began on the eastern side of the Jordan, escalated and was extended by the Ammonites across the Jordan to the west, suppressing Judah, Benjamin and the house of Ephraim. *Israel was in great distress* (**10:9**). Their rebellion had brought them God's wrath. We, too, need to remember that sins have consequences: 'the wages of sin is death' (Rom 6:23).

In their distress, the Israelites cried out to the Lord: *We have sinned against you, forsaking our God and serving the Baals* (**10:10**). Crying and confessing sin is the first step of repentance. God however, was not impressed. He would not help them unless they recognized that repentance needs to be accompanied by a willingness to obey him in future (**10:11-14**). The people listened to his reprimand and pleaded for rescue: *Do with us whatever you think best, but please rescue us now* (**10:15**). This is the second step. Then they went further and took the third step; *they got rid of the foreign gods among them and served the Lord* (**10:16a**). Whenever sinners turn to God in genuine penitence like this, mercy flows. Then *he could bear Israel's misery no longer* (**10:16b**). God's grace surpasses his wrath.

Though the Israelites had repented of their sin and turned to God, no leader had yet emerged (10:17-18). But one would soon come, for in spite of his earlier words, God was now set to raise up a deliverer for them, Jephthah.

11:1-3 Jephthah's background

Jephthah, whose name means 'opened' or 'opener', would have seemed an unlikely leadership candidate for Israel. His story could be entitled: 'From rejection to election'. He was a descendant of Manasseh (1 Chr 7:14-17) who was born out of wedlock by a prostitute mother, whose name is not given, to a prominent man by the name of Gilead. Gilead, meaning 'rugged', was originally the name given to the vast region east of the Jordan that Moses allocated to Reuben, Gad and half of the tribe of Manasseh (Deut 3:13). All the Israelites who settled in this region came to be known as 'Gileadites'. Jair, too, had been a Gileadite (10:3).

Jephthah was a Gileadite both from his place of birth and because of his father's name. But being born of a prostitute made him a social outcast. His brothers, who were born in wedlock, drove him from the paternal home and refused him any share in their father's inheritance (**11:2**). He fled to *Tob,* somewhere in Syria, where he made a name for himself through military adventurism and surrounded himself with *a group of adventurers* (**11:3**).

11:4-11 The choice of Jephthah

Over a period of time, no volunteer stepped forward to take up the offer made by the leaders of Gilead in 10:18. So they decided to ask Jephthah to lead them. They went to him in the land of Tob and begged him for help, saying: *Come, be our commander, so we can fight the Ammonites* (**11:4-6**). Jephthah's response implies that some of his brothers, who had hated him and driven him away, might have been part of the delegation (**11:7**). He forced them to eat humble pie before agreeing to lead them (**11:8**). Jephthah and Israelites then made a covenant in the presence of the Lord at Mizpah (**11:9-11**).

There is in this a certain similarity between Jephthah and Christ. Both are like a stone that was rejected by the builders, but which nevertheless became the capstone (1 Pet 2:6-7; see Ps 118:22).

11:12-28 Jephthah's attempt at negotiation

Jephthah brought to Israel's leadership a combination of intelligence, knowledge and military prowess that had not been seen in any of the judges before him. He appealed to reason as he asked the king of the Ammonites to come to the negotiation table and enter into a dialogue: *What do you have against us that you have attacked our country?* (**11:12**). On receiving the king's response (**11:13**), Jephthah gave an informed reply, getting his facts right. He refuted the king's claims with historical and biblical facts as he reviewed the history of the Israelites from their emancipation from Egypt to their occupation of the land that was now in dispute (**11:14-22**).

Jephthah's argument was straightforward: Israel did not take away your land. The Lord God of Israel drove you away and gave us what we now possess. Will you drive us out? (**11:23-24**). His words acknowledge that the right of ownership to any land belongs to God or gods, and that he or they can dispose of it as they please (11:24; Ps 24:1).

He also appealed to a three-hundred-year history of peaceful coexistence and tolerance (**11:25-26**), urging the king to 'live and let live'. He concluded his statement with an appeal to God as the supreme judge (**11:27**).

The king of the Ammonites refused to listen to Jephthah's argument (**11:28**). As so often happens in international negotiations, when words fail, the sword takes over.

11:29, 32-33 Jephthah's anointing as judge

Up to this point, Yahweh had been a passive partner, although Jephthah had been careful to involve him all along (11:11, 21, 23, 24, 27). With the Ammonites refusal to back down, God moved to take an active role by anointing Jephthah with his Spirit (**11:29**). As in 3:10 and 6:34, the outpouring of the Holy Spirit unleashed a supernatural force that transformed Jephthah and empowered him to do extraordinary things. With the Spirit upon him, he advanced into the enemy's territory (**11:29, 32**). Before he did so, he did two other things. First he made a vow to the Lord (11:30), which we will look at later. Secondly, he probably solicited Ephraim's assistance (12:2).

The text does not tell us how many men Jephthah had with him. It does not matter. What mattered then (and now) was the power of the Lord upon him and the presence of the Lord with him. The bottom line is that *the Lord gave them into his hands* (11:32). He devastated twenty towns *from Aroer to the vicinity of Minnith as far as Abel Keramium. Thus Israel subdued Ammon* (**11:33**). It was an incredible expedition!

11:30-31, 34-40 Jephthah's vow

A vow is a voluntary promise to perform some service or give something back to God in return for some anticipated benefits (see, for example, Gen 28:20-22; Num 30:1-2). In the OT, people were not required to make vows, but once made they became binding obligations (Deut 23:21-23; Ps 66:13). One could not simply walk away from a vow without paying some penalty. Vows could be redeemed with money, with the amount involved being determined by a priest (Lev 27:1-31). In the NT, Jesus discourages us from making vows (Matt 5:33-37).

Jephthah promised that *whatever comes out of the door of my house to meet me when I return in triumph from the Ammonites will be the Lord's, and I will sacrifice it as a burnt offering* (**11:31**). He did not specify whether he meant an animal, a chicken or a human being. From his reaction when his only daughter met him, we realize that he had never anticipated this possibility (**11:34**). As a man of honour, he felt bound to keep his word, and his amazing daughter cooperated, making only one final request (**11:36-38**).

This story raises the difficult question: what does the text mean by *and he did to her as he had vowed* (**11:39**). There are two schools of thought. One states categorically that he offered her as a burnt offering. The other suggests that she was redeemed in keeping with the provisions in Leviticus 27:1-8, but that instead of paying with money, she was required to forfeit the option of marriage. I would argue for the second position on the basis that her mourning of her virginity and the yearly commemoration would be uncalled for and meaningless if she was actually sacrificed as a burnt offering (**11:38, 40**).

12:1-7 Conflict with Ephraim

Once again the Ephraimites decided to cause trouble, just as they had when Gideon won his victory over the Midianites (8:1-3). Jephthah, however, was not as tactful as Gideon, and simply denied the charge brought against him (**12:1-3**). The hostility escalated and the derogatory remarks made by the Ephraimites about the Gileadites provoked Jephthah and his people to take up arms (**12:4**). In the resulting conflict, the Gileadites defeated the Ephraimites and captured *the fords of the Jordan* that the defeated men would have to cross to return home (**12:5**). They demanded that anyone who wanted to pass pronounce the word *Shibboleth*. The Ephraimites could not pronounce the 'sh' sound in this word, but instead said *Sibboleth*. When they were identified by their accents, they were killed. Sadly, some forty-two thousand of them suffered this fate (**12:6**).

It is tragic that the Israelites, who should have been united against their common enemies, were at war with each other and that so many lives were lost. Their resulting weakness would have played into the hands of their enemies. It may be one of the factors that accounts for the absence of any statement that the land was at peace during the six years in which Jephthah judged Israel (contrast 3:11, 30; 5:31; 8:28).

In Africa today, we need to work to avoid seeing nations divided on tribal lines, or believers being divided on regional lines, or in any other way. As believers, we have a common enemy, the devil, and if we stand united, we are better able to resist his attacks.

12:8-10 Ibzan

The next three judges after Jephthah: Ibzan, Elon and Abdon, were all minor judges. What was said about Shamgar (3:31), Tola (10:1-2) and Jair (10:3-5) applies to them as well.

Nothing spectacular happened in Israel during the seven years of Ibzan's reign. However, he was remembered for breaking the tribal taboo about marriage. Though the text is silent about his marital status, he must have been a polygamist and have had concubines to be able to have *thirty sons and thirty daughters*. His good practice of inter-tribal marriage is something Africa can learn from. God only condemns marriages between believers and unbelievers, not marriages across racial, cultural and tribal lines.

12:11-12 Elon

Elon was the tenth judge of Israel. The only information we are given about him is that he came from Zebulun and was a judge for ten years (**12:11**). His tenure must have been marked by peace and stability.

12:13-15 Abdon

Abdon, the eleventh judge, was a flamboyant leader and a happy family man. He had *forty sons and thirty grandsons* (**12:13**). Josephus, the first-century Jewish historian, says this about him: 'He is only recorded to have been happy in his children: for the public affairs were then so peaceable and in such security that he had no occasion to perform glorious action.' Abdon is also said to have enjoyed marching in state with his seventy offspring, all mounted on donkeys (**12:14**). After leading Israel for eight years, he died a happy man and was buried at his home town of Pirathon in Ephraim in central Canaan.

13:1-16:31 Samson Defeats the Philistines

13:1-23 Announcement of Samson's future role

The thirty-one years of peace and quiet between the reign of Jephthah and that of Abdon came to an end. Once *again the Israelites did evil in the eyes of the Lord,* and in consequence he handed them over to the Philistines for *forty years* (**13:1**). Then, without any reference to remorse or repentance on their part, God chose to deliver them.

God's method of deliverance was also new, for of all the twelve judges, Samson was the only one born to lead. His mission to *begin the deliverance of Israel from the hands of the Philistines* was announced to his sterile and childless mother before his conception. She was given a set of restrictions to observe during her pregnancy. The reason for these restrictions was that her son was to be a *Nazirite* from his birth (**13:3-5**). A Nazirite was someone who was dedicated to God. Consecration to God's service was marked by abstaining from wine and all alcoholic beverages, not using a razor to cut one's hair at all, and avoiding all contact with dead bodies (see Num 6:1-21). There were two forms of Nazirite vow: the temporary one, which individuals took for various reasons (see Acts 21:23), and the perpetual one. Scripture records only three cases of people being Nazirites from birth, namely Samson, Samuel (1 Sam 1:11) and John the Baptist (Luke 1:15).

Once the announcement had been made, the angel withdrew and the woman went to tell her husband (**13:6-7**). We do not know why God did not choose Samson's father, Manoah, to become a judge immediately, rather than waiting for a child to grow. Nor do we know why God chose to announce Samson's birth to his mother, rather than to his father.

The woman described the awe-inspiring appearance of the angel of the Lord, although she did not fully recognize him (**13:6**; see commentary on 2:1-5). Manoah was moved to pray for further guidance about how to raise such a special child (**13:8**). God heard his prayer, and the angel appeared again to Manoah's wife, rather than to him (**13:9**). She hurriedly fetched her husband to meet him. Manoah repeated his question (**13:12**), but instead of answering it, the angel simply reminded him of the restrictions his wife must observe (**13:13-14**).

Manoah, like his wife, thought that the angel was simply *a man of God* and invited him to a meal (**13:15**). The angel declined, but suggested that Manoah instead offer a burnt offering (**13:16**). While preparing this, Manoah politely asked this 'man', *What is your name so that we may honour you when your word comes true?* (**13:17**). Jacob had asked the same question of the mysterious stranger with whom he wrestled, but had received no answer (Gen 32:29). Manoah was privileged to receive an answer: *It is beyond understanding* (NIV) or 'It is wonderful' (NASB) (**13:18**; see Isa 9:6). Semitic and Arabic cultures as well as African culture believe that names are highly significant. A name can encapsulate someone's character, career, destiny and behaviour. That is certainly true in this case. Everything about the angel of the Lord was wonderful! He could appear and disappear at will (**13:19-20**), and he could predict a child's future before it was even conceived (13:5; Jer 1:5).

When Manoah finally realized whom he had been speaking to, he cried out, *We are doomed to die! … We have seen God!* (**13:22**). He was right, for no one can see God and live (6:23; Gen 32:30). The angel he had seen was probably the pre-incarnate Christ (see comment on 2:1). But his wife had a better grasp of God's dealings with human beings. She gave him three reasons why God would not kill them (**13:23**): he had accepted their sacrifice, he had spoken with them, and he had revealed that they would be the parents of one who would bring deliverance.

13:24-25 Birth of Samson

The word of the angel of the Lord came true. Manoah's wife gave birth to a baby boy and named him *Samson*, which means 'little sun' or 'brightness' (**13:24a**). She may have given him such a name because of the joy and brightness he brought to her sterile life. Here again we see the importance of a name.

The boy developed normally, with God's favour upon him (**13:24b**; see Luke 2:52). Over and above that, God's anointing, which marked the judges and the prophets, *began to stir him while he was in Mahaneh Dan between Zorah and Eshtaol* (**13:25**). Zorah, his hometown, was halfway between Jerusalem and the Mediterranean coast, along which the Philistines lived.

14:1-20 The beginning of Samson's task

The text says nothing about Samson's age when he began to pursue his mission. Like Ehud, the second judge (3:12-30), Samson was a lone ranger. He had no army around him and went about his mission in a most unusual way. He seemed to be given to sexual passion and lacked the strict discipline expected of a Nazirite. His behaviour must have baffled his parents.

After visiting *Timnah*, a Philistine town about three miles (five kilometres) from Zorah, Samson demanded that his parents get as his wife a *young Philistine woman* whom he had just met (**14:1-2**). They were astounded, and had no idea that God was involved in this decision (**14:4**). (It was certainly an exception for God to do this, given his prohibition of marriages with non-believers – Deut 7:3-4). They asked, *Isn't there an acceptable woman among your relatives or among all our people? Must you go to the uncircumcised Philistines to get a wife?* (**14:3**). The term 'uncircumcised' was a derogatory way of referring to people held to be inferior to the circumcised Israelites.

Samson could not be persuaded to change his mind, and so they set out for Timnah (**14:5a**). On the way there, Samson stepped aside, probably to answer a call of nature. Suddenly he was attacked by *a young lion*. With the help of the Spirit upon him, he tore it apart like a *young goat* (**14:5b-6**). Then he rejoined his parents for their first visit to his future in-laws (**14:7**).

Things went smoothly and a wedding was arranged. While on his way to the wedding with his parents, he stopped to see *the lion's carcass* and scooped some *honey* from it, an action that violated his Nazirite vow, which forbade contact with a corpse (**14:8-9**). This may explain his reluctance to tell his parents about the source of the honey.

In the ancient Near East, as in the Horn of Africa today, it was common for a bridegroom to organize a party at the bride's home (**14:10**; Gen 29:22). In Ethiopia, such a feast can last for several weeks. However, in Samson's case, it lasted for only a week. During the feast he challenged the company of thirty Philistine men with a riddle, wagering with them for thirty changes of clothing (**14:11-14a**).

Try as they might, they could not solve the riddle (**14:14b**). But as the Yoruba of Nigeria say: *Bi ãse gbon nine oko ni ãse gbon ni ile alarina* ['Just as they are smart on the groom's side, so are we on the bride's side' – the implication is that one needs one's wits about one when negotiating a dowry or lobola]. When the Philistines could not solve the riddle, they threatened to kill the bride unless she found out the answer (**14:15**).

The technique she used to get the answer is still common. The demand that one proves one's love or that some action shows *you don't really love me* (**14:16**) is often used to manipulate the unwary. Many Christian girls have been seduced into premarital sex by men who falsely claim that sex is proof of love. This claim is not true, and girls must beware of such deceivers.

Through incessant nagging, the young woman finally extracted an answer from Samson and conveyed it to the young men (14:16-17). Realizing that he had been tricked, Samson left in a fury (**14:18**). He was still obliged to keep his part of the bargain, and so he went down to *Ashkelon*, about twenty-three miles (37 km) away on the Mediterranean coast, and *killed thirty of their men* and passed their clothes on to the young men. The only reason he could perform such a feat was that the Holy Spirit *came upon him in power* (**14:19a**).

It is worth noting that during the time of the judges, as in the time of the OT prophets, the Holy Spirit played a special role. Though believers today have the Holy Spirit resident in them (Luke 24:49; John 14:16-17; Acts 1:8; 1 Cor 12:13; 2 Tim 1:7), his power is no longer displayed in the same way. To say this is not to deny the supernatural and the miraculous (for we still see signs and wonders and miracles) nor is it to diminish the Holy Spirit (for his power cannot increase nor decrease). But today he has a different style of operation.

Samson went back home in rage and without a wife (**14:19b**). To add insult to injury, his wife was given to another man who had been at the wedding (**14:20**). We can expect Samson to retaliate.

15:1-20 Samson's revenge

15:1-8 A CYCLE OF REVENGE A West African folk tale tells of neighbour A smashing a number of eggs laid by a hen belonging to neighbour B, claiming that the hen had spilt A's milk. Neighbour B then remembered that neighbour A's goat had eaten some of his yams during harvest, and so he killed some of A's calves. Then neighbour A … And then neighbour B … And so on and on. The cycle of revenge never ends – and no one wins.

So it was with Samson and his wife's family, the Philistines. Samson's move towards reconciliation turned sour when he learned that his wife had been given to another man (**15:1-2**). The offer of her younger sister was unacceptable (Lev 18:18). So he decided to get even by torching the Philistine's grain fields, vineyards and olive groves with his circus-like stunt with foxes and fire (**15:3-5**). He caused massive destruction. In retaliation, the Philistines burned the woman and her father to death (**15:6**).

It seems that up to this point, Samson's actions had been local, involving primarily his wife's family and relatives. The burning of the Philistines' farms, however, affected a larger group. Their revenge on his wife further angered Samson, who turned on them, *and slaughtered many of them* before withdrawing to *a cave in the rock of Etam*, not to hide but to rest (**15:7-8**).

15:9-20 SAMSON'S LEADERSHIP OF THE NATION The scope of the conflict now widened, for the Philistines refused to back down. They invaded *Judah* and raided *Lehi* (**15:9-10**). To make their point about the unacceptable behaviour of this upstart, they did not attack Dan, Samson's tribe, but Judah, a much bigger and more central tribe in Israel. But in doing this, they gave Samson a national platform and risked making him a national hero.

Surprisingly, Samson's fellow Israelites did not recognize his potential role as a deliverer, but simply accepted the Philistines' domination (**15:11**). However, they did recognize his strength, and so some *three thousand men from Judah* went to capture Samson. They were successful, but only because Samson yielded himself to them after making them promise not to kill him themselves (**15:12-13**). We are also surprised that Samson did not seize the occasion to sound the trumpets and mobilize these three thousand Israelites against the Philistines, just as Deborah, Gideon and Jephthah had done.

The men tied Samson up and marched him off to hand him over to the Philistines. But as they were approaching the Philistine camp and the Philistines were baying for vengeance, the Spirit came upon Samson again (**15:14**). He easily snapped the ropes binding him, and *finding a fresh jaw-bone of a donkey, he grabbed it and struck down a thousand men* (**15:15**). There was nothing magical about this weapon. He could as easily have used something else, or even his bare hands as he had when tearing the lion (14:6) or killing the thirty Philistines at Ashkelon (14:19) or the Philistines at Timnah (15:8). The power of the Spirit was upon him.

Samson exultantly made up a rhyme to celebrate his victory (**15:16**), and then he tossed the jaw-bone aside (**15:17**). What a contrast with what many an evangelist or pastor or miracle worker in our day would do! They would probably sanctify that jaw-bone and eventually commercialize it! Too often, leaders cling to the evidence of some particular miracle that God accomplished through them, build their ministries around it, and claim incredible titles because of it. But God does not mean us to cling to past victories, but to put them behind us while we move on to the next task he assigns.

Although Samson had won a miraculous victory, he was still human and had human needs. He suffered severely from thirst (**15:18**). His thirst drove him to make his first recorded prayer. Significantly, he did not speak of himself as 'superman' but as God's *servant*. As Paul says, 'we have this treasure in jars of clay to show that this all-surpassing power is from God and not from us' (2 Cor 4:7). Whatever God may accomplish through us, we must be careful to give him all the glory.

Not until he acknowledged God's leadership over his life could Samson lead others. Thus it is only at this point that we are told that *Samson led Israel for twenty years in the days of the Philistines* (**15:20**). But the phrase 'in the days of the Philistines' indicates that Samson did not have absolute control of the whole nation. The Philistines remained a force to be reckoned with.

16:1-31 Samson's ruin

A popular Yoruba saying aptly describes the life of Samson: *Alagbara mo mero, ni baba ole* ['A strong man who lacks sense is the father of a lazy fool']. One would expect Samson to have learned from his experiences and to change his behaviour and his strategy in relation to the Philistines. Instead, he allowed himself to become enslaved to his passions and lost his sense of direction and purpose. It is no wonder that the NT uses very strong words to warn against sexual immorality (see 1 Cor 6:9-10, 18).

16:1-3 IN GAZA WITH A PROSTITUTE Gaza was a Philistine stronghold and a port city. Therefore it contained many prostitutes. Having failed in his attempts to marry a Philistine wife, Samson now turned to a prostitute (**16:1**). But he had forgotten that he was at the top of the Philistines' list of 'most wanted men'. The Swahili-speaking community of East Africa say, *Usiambie Hawara siri Zako* ['Never share your secrets with a prostitute']. It soon became known that he was in the city and the Philistines laid a trap to kill him *at dawn* (**16:2**). But Samson outwitted them. Getting up at midnight, he escaped dramatically by using his enormous strength to pull out *the doors of the city gate together with the two posts* and carrying them a quarter of a mile to *the top of the hill that faces Hebron* (**16:3**).

16:4-20 IN DELILAH'S LAP Samson took a break, but did not permanently stop his escapades. Soon he turned up at the house of *Delilah*, whose name means 'a devotee' (**16:4**). Her name is Semitic, but as the story unfolds her nationality is revealed as undoubtedly Philistine. Some commentators have suggested that she could have been of mixed blood: half Philistine and half Israelite. If so, that may be the reason why Samson felt at home with her. Though she may not have been a prostitute like the woman in 16:1, her mercenary character and her heartlessness give reason enough to believe that she was a profligate woman. Samson is said to have fallen in love with her (16:4), but this must have been an infatuation. The text never says that Delilah loved Samson.

The *Valley of Sorek*, where Delilah lived, was under the control of the Philistines. On hearing that Samson was going there, the five rulers of the Philistines joined together in a loose confederacy in an attempt to eliminate their common enemy (see 3:3). Their previous strategy of open confrontation and ambush had not worked. So now they swallowed their pride and hired Delilah to act as an agent for them. They each offered to pay her *eleven hundred shekels of silver* for any intelligence information she could glean about the secret of Samson's Herculean strength (**16:5**).

Accepting this offer of the enormous sum of 5500 pieces of silver, Delilah went to work. She acted as if it were a game. In a relaxed romantic atmosphere, she tried three times to extract the secrets of Samson's strength from him, and three times he lied to her about it (**16:6-14**). But she never gave up. Finally, she appealed to his weakest point, his heart. She said: *How can you say 'I love you', when you won't confide in me? This is the third time you have made a fool of me and haven't told me the secret of your great strength* (**16:15**).

Delilah's words should have set off alarm bells in Samson's mind after what had happened the last time a woman had attempted to manipulate him in this way (14:15-17). Had Samson been a Yoruba man, he might have remembered the proverb: *Ife aja-ode ati okete kodenu* ['the love between a hunting dog and a wild rat is not heart deep']. If he had, he would have run for his life. Unfortunately, he did not flee as Joseph did (Gen 39:12; 1 Cor 6:18). He was too comfortable on Delilah's lap. Eventually he yielded to her nagging and disclosed his secret (**16:16-17**).

Delilah wasted no time. Just as Jael had lulled Sisera to sleep (4:17-21), so she lulled Samson into a deep sleep, and then got a man to shave his dreadlocks, thereby rendering him powerless and helpless (**16:19**). Once again, she woke him with the cry that he must previously thought was part of a game, *Samson, the Philistines are upon you!* (**16:20**). He woke with a start, assuming, *I will go out as before and shake myself free*. Alas, it was too late. He did not realize that *the Lord had left him*. The romantic comedy has become a tragedy of betrayal.

16:21-31 IN THE HANDS OF THE PHILISTINES The first thing the Philistines did when they had seized Samson was to gouge out his eyes (**16:21**). The 'little sun' was consigned to darkness (see comments on 13:24-25). This is what living in sin does to believers. It renders them powerless, joyless and lifeless, and may eventually kill them if not dealt with quickly by confession, contrition and repentance (Pss 32:1-5; 66:18; 139:23-24; Isa 59:1-2; Rom 6:1-14; 1 Cor 10:1-14).

The Philistines bound Samson, took him down to Gaza and forced him to grind grain in the prison. The text doesn't say how long he endured this torment, but it was long enough for his hair to begin to grow back (**16:22**). This was evidence of God's mercy. The Lord had started to prepare him for his final showdown with the Philistines.

The final scene could be poetically described as the final battle between Yahweh and Dagon. All the Philistine leaders and about three thousand spectators, both men and women, gathered at a large temple to offer a sacrifice to their god Dagon. It was a great feast, and when the people were drunk they called for Samson to be brought in to entertain them, presumably with feats of strength, as well as by being mocked (**16:25**). The people crowded onto the roof to get a good view of his performance, while their leaders probably had a good view from inside the temple.

Samson was eventually allowed to take up position between two of the main pillars supporting the roof of the Philistine temple (**16:26**). Standing there, he silently offered God his second and third recorded prayers (**16:28, 30a**; see 5:18). He prayed for vengeance, and he prayed for death. God answered both prayers. Samson *pushed with all his might, and down came the temple on the rulers and all the people in it. Thus he killed many more when he died than while he lived* (**16:30b**).

The question is often asked: Did Samson fulfil the mission that was announced before his birth (13:5)? Some think he did; some think he did not. I think he did – partially. For twenty years he brought some relief to Israel, but he did not bring full release from their bondage to the Philistines. After the victories of Othniel (3:11), Ehud (3:30), Deborah (5:31) and Gideon (8:28), the land is said to have enjoyed peace, but Samson's twenty-year tenure is not described as peaceful. He was the only judge who died at the hands of the enemy. Nevertheless, he did judge Israel, and amazingly he is listed with the heroes of the faith in Hebrews 11:32.

17:1-21:25 Epilogue: Apostasy, Atrocity, Anarchy

Technically the story of the judges, as recorded in the book of Judges, ends with the story of Samson in chapter sixteen. Their story begins again with the story of Samuel, who served as the last judge before the introduction of the monarchy.

The last five chapters of Judges (17–21) plus the book of Ruth recount various events that took place at some time during the period of more than three hundred years between the death of Joshua and the coronation of Saul. These events are not chronologically arranged, but they do give insights into Israelite life during the period of the judges.

In his book, *The Trouble with Nigeria* (1983), Chinua Achebe writes: 'The trouble with Nigeria is simply and squarely a failure of leadership. There is nothing basically wrong with the land or water or air or anything else. The problem is the unwillingness or inability of its leaders to rise to the responsibility and challenge of personal example which are hallmarks of true leadership'. The author of Judges came to this same baneful conclusion as he writes again and again in these chapters: 'In those days Israel had no king' (17:6; 18:1; 19:1; 21:25).

17:1-8:31 Religious Apostasy

17:1-6 Micah's idolatry

The story of Micah is set in *the hill country of Ephraim* (**17:1a**), which has featured prominently in the stories in Judges (7:24-8:3; 12:1-6). *Eleven hundred shekels of silver*

had been stolen from Micah's mother by none other than her son (**17:1b**). Fearing the curse she had placed on the thief, *Micah* confessed and returned the money. His mother cancelled the curse with a blessing, *The Lord bless you, my son!* (**17:2**).

She then dedicated the money to the Lord for the benefit of Micah and ordered that *a carved image and a cast idol* of solid silver be made for him. Both were made by a silversmith, a maker of idols (Isa 40:19; Jer 10:9; Acts 19:24), and *put in Micah's house* (**17:4**). Micah set apart a special room called *a shrine* in which he kept these images plus *an ephod* (used for divining) and other household *idols* (**17:5a**). With these, Micah and his mother were violating the second commandment that categorically states: 'You shall not make for yourself an idol' (Exod 20:4; Deut 5:8; 13:1-18). Moreover, by installing one of his sons to be his priest (**17:5b**), Micah was disobeying God's command that worship should be centralized (Deut 12). Instead of going to the priests at Shiloh, Micah was privatizing his religion. But the statement *in those days Israel had no king, everyone did as he saw fit* (**17:6**) implies that such departures from the standards of conduct enshrined in the Ten Commandments and the statutes were not uncommon.

17:7-13 Micah's private priest

Micah met up with a roving *young Levite*, who had come from *Bethlehem in Judah* (**17:7-8**), which was not one of the forty-eight cities given to the Levites. Since Levites could connect themselves to other tribes in Israel by marriage, it is possible that this Levite's mother belonged to the tribe of Judah, which would account for his living in Bethlehem. Since he was not part of the Levite establishment, whose needs were met by tithes and offerings, this young Levite had to fend for himself.

Many pastors, evangelists, prophets and other Christian workers in contemporary Africa find themselves in this young man's position. Many who are called into the ministry, and who may even be ordained, have to look for alternative avenues of service outside the denominational establishment. They run the risk of going wrong or of taking a commercial approach to their calling, as this Levite did. Micah, not God, became his employer when he responded positively to Micah's offer: *Live with me and be my father and priest, and I'll give you ten shekels of silver a year, your clothes and your food* (**17:10**). Such commercialization of the priesthood is unbiblical and wrong. (Note that the Levite's behaviour should not be confused with a Christian making a living by working for a Christian organization.)

Micah was also wrong to consecrate the Levite as his private priest, for the priests and the Levites were intended to be two separate groups (**17:12**; see Num 8:5-26; 18:1-7). But now that he had been able to replace his son (17:5) with what he thought was a 'real priest', Micah superstitiously expected God to bless him (**17:13**).

Micah is not alone in assuming that God can be manipulated into blessing someone by setting up objects or associating with certain types of people. Nor is he alone in his adoption of syncretistic forms of worship. Similar beliefs are widespread across Africa. But Micah was wrong, and so are those who share his attitudes.

18:1-31 Migration of the Danites to Laish

The tribe of Dan took some time to settle down in the Promised Land. The migration recorded here is also reported in Joshua 19:47, where Laish is called Leshem. According to Judges 1:34, the Amorites forced the Danites to move, when they refused to let the Danites settle in the fertile valley in the Danites' original land allotment.

18:1-6 THE DANITES SCOUT FOR LAND Samson, the twelfth judge, was a Danite from Zorah (13:1-5). Having grown too large for the territory allocated to them by Joshua and suffering pressure from the Amorites and the Philistines, some of the Danites decided to move away from the trade highway of *Zorah and Eshtaol* and into the remote countryside. A delegation of *five warriors* was sent to *explore the land* (**18:2**). As they travelled north through the hill country of Ephraim, they arrived at Micah's house, where they met the Levite-turned-priest. After getting acquainted with him, they asked him to find out whether their mission would be blessed with success (**18:3-5**). He was happy to assure them that it would be, using God's name to give credibility to his words (**18:6**).

18:7-10 THE DANITES' SPIES ARRIVE AT LAISH *Laish* was a small colony of Sidon in the upper Jordan Valley. It was a safe and secluded place, self-sufficient with regard to food and everything else needed to sustain life. In the eyes of the spies, this *land lacked nothing* and would be a perfect place for the tribe (**18:7**). In addition, the Laishites did not suspect any trouble was coming and were thus very vulnerable to external aggressors. The spies were elated. They concluded that God had given the land to them and reported this back to their people (**18:9-10**).

The Laishites are a reminder that we should not have a false sense of security when living in isolation and neutrality in an island of plenty that is surrounded by poor, landless and oppressed people.

18:11-29 INVASION AND OCCUPATION OF LAISH Upon receiving the spies' report, the Danites wasted no time in beginning their journey. Six hundred well-equipped soldiers led the way (**18:11-13**). Passing by Micah's house, they emptied his shrine and conscripted his private priest, the Levite (**18:14-18**). Although the Levite resisted initially, their logic overwhelmed him: *Isn't it better that you serve a tribe and clan in Israel as priest rather than just one man's household?* (**18:19**). Unsurprisingly, given the commercial motivation

for his ministry in the first place, he quickly jumped at the offer (**18:20**). Micah's own resistance was silenced by a show of force. The Danites threatened to kill him and his household if he raised any objection (**18:22-26**).

There was no justice in the land. The rich and the powerful acted with impunity (just as the world's superpowers do in our time). No one spoke for the voiceless; no one defended the rights of the most vulnerable. Since there was no king in Israel, everyone did whatever he wanted! The picture looks very similar to what we see in neo-colonial Africa.

Upon their arrival in Laish, the Danites found a quiet and unsuspecting peace-loving people who put up almost no resistance. It was a walkover. *They attacked them with the sword and burned down their city. There was no one to rescue them … The Danites rebuilt the city and settled there. They named it Dan after their forefather Dan* (**18:27-29**).

As one reads this text, one is inevitably reminded of how Africa was colonized in the late nineteenth century. In some parts of Africa, the process was violent and the programme dehumanizing. In other parts, the colonizers were more humane and progressive. The effects of these two approaches to colonization can still be seen in Africa in the twenty-first century.

18:30-31 THE DANITES DRIFT INTO IDOLATRY After rebuilding Laish and renaming it Dan, the next strategic step taken by the Danites was to establish a place of worship. Using the idols seized from Micah's house, a place of worship was set up. To give it some credibility and recognition, Jonathan, the grandson of Moses, was invited to be the first priest. His descendants served as priests for the Danite tribe until *the captivity of the land,* that is until the ark was captured and taken away from Shiloh in the eleventh century BC (**18:30-31**; 1 Sam 4:11). Some commentators think that this Jonathan was the same person as Micah's private priest, but the text does not imply this. In all probability he was not, because Micah's priest was a Levite and not properly a priest, whereas Jonathan came from the main priestly family.

What began as a tribal centre of worship in the northern extremity of the land was later given national prestige by Jeroboam I, who chose Dan to be the location of one of the two national shrines for the northern kingdom (1 Kgs 12:28-30).

The closing statement underscores the Danites' departure from the centralized worship at *Shiloh* and their drift into idolatry (18:31).

19:1-30 Moral Atrocity

The last three chapters of the book of Judges deal with the story of a Levite and his concubine. What started as a domestic feud ended up as a national tragedy. Centuries later, this case would still be referred to as an example of national moral corruption and wickedness (Hos 9:9; 10:9).

19:1-10 A Levite woos back his concubine

That a Levite would take a concubine (a woman legally living with him but considered to be of a lower status than his wife) was in itself a lowering of God's marriage standard for Levites (see Lev 21:7, 13-15; Ezek 44:22). To make matters worse, the woman *was unfaithful to him* and *left him* for *her father's house* (**19:2**). Contrary to what the law requires, namely divorce (Deut 24:1), the Levite followed her to her father's house in Bethlehem in Judah and successfully wooed her back (**19:3-4**). The rapport that developed between the man and his father-in-law delayed his return with his wife and led to his only leaving his in-law's house on the evening of the fifth day (**19:5-10**). He was unwise to set out that late, because it meant he had to break his journey when night fell.

19:11-28 The Levite's concubine raped and killed

As the man, his concubine and his servant with their two donkeys drew near Jebus (Jerusalem –19:10) about six miles (10 km) from Bethlehem, his servant advised, *Come let's stop at this city of the Jebusites and spend the night* (**19:11**). This comment and the reply that follows confirm that Jerusalem was still in Jebusite hands at the time this incident took place (1:21). Influenced by fear of the unknown aliens, the Levite resisted the advice and travelled about four more miles (seven km) to *Gibeah* (**19:12**), which was under the control of the Benjamites. Sadly the reception he received from his fellow Israelites was barbaric and inhospitable.

Under normal circumstances, spending a night in a city square could be risky and dangerous for travellers, but this appeared to be the Levite's only option, for nobody offered to take them into his home (**19:15**). However, eventually a non-Benjamite Israelite, *an old man from the hill country of Ephraim,* stopped to talk with him (**19:16-17**). Upon learning who they were, where they came from and where they were going, he welcomed them into his house. Though the Levite and his team were fully prepared (*we don't need anything* – **19:19**), the old man refused to be denied the joy of hosting them for the night. His warning, *don't spend the night in the square* (**19:20**), must have been derived from his knowledge of the behaviour of some in that town. The Levite yielded, and they had a joyous evening, eating and drinking and probably getting acquainted since the Levite had come from the same area of Ephraim as the old man (**19:21, 18**).

This man's hospitality reminds me of traditional African hospitality, where a meal could always be shared with any visitor or passer-by who might drop in without notice.

Unfortunately the happy moment was short-lived, as some wicked men of the city descended on them demanding to have sex with the Levite. Apparently, homosexuality was common among the Canaanites, but God unequivocally forbade it for his people, saying: 'Do not lie with a man as

one lies with a woman; that is detestable' (Lev 18:22). This sin is called 'sodomy' because the similar episode that took place at Sodom led to the destruction of the twin cities of Sodom and Gomorrah (Gen 19:1-8).

The moral atrocity of the period becomes even more evident when the old man seeks to protect his guest by offering his virgin daughter and the Levite's concubine to be used by the wicked men in whatever way they pleased (**19:23-24**). Rather then defending the women and proving themselves men by fighting it out with the attackers, the two cowardly men shamefully remained indoors while the concubine was subjected to gang rape. We are right to be outraged by this moral decadence and sexual perversion.

The text does not give the number of attackers. What it does say is that *they raped her and abused her throughout the night* (**19:25**). Consequently, she died by the morning (**19:26-28**).

19:29-30 The Levite's concubine dismembered

This ugly story has presented a series of shocks. The lack of hospitality to a fellow Israelite was shock number one (19:15). This was followed by attempted sodomy (19:22). The old man's offer of his virgin daughter for abuse was shock number three (19:24 – even though she seems ultimately to have been spared). The rape and death was a shock (19:25). But the greatest shock waves were caused by the dismembering of the Levite's concubine into twelve parts, to match the twelve tribes of Israel, and the distributing of these parts to all areas of Israel as a call to action (**19:29**; see 1 Sam 11:6-7). The Levite may have seen such a gruesome action as the only way to get a response in the absence of a central government and any judge. It was certainly effective. It got everybody's attention (**19:30**) and aroused the entire nation to respond – 'All the people rose as one man' (20:1, 8, 11). The only group who did not respond were the Benjamites (20:3). It is possible that as the tribe of the perpetrators they had not been sent part of the concubine's body, but that instead two parts were sent to the Manassites – one to those east of the Jordan and the other to those west of the Jordan.

20:1-21:25 Political Anarchy

Though the period of Judges was marked by religious apostasy, moral atrocity and general political anarchy, there was still a pervading national sense of justice and unity. The Israelites maintained their national identity as a people redeemed from Egypt (19:30).

20:1-7 Calling of a national assembly

Facing a crisis that was not caused by an attack by an external enemy but by an internal calamity, leaders from eleven tribes gathered at Mizpah. They came from all over Israel, *from Dan to Beersheba,* meaning from the northernmost part

TRIBALISM, ETHNICITY AND RACE

Race can be thought of as simply the biological phenomenon whereby someone from Nigeria looks very different from someone from France or from China. But cultural understandings of race involve far more than these surface differences. When we speak of someone's race, we are often assigning them to specific categories on the basis of their social relationships, that is, who they associate with, and their economic status.

Attempts to categorize and separate people of different races inevitably lead to racism, for they encourage stereotyping and attempts to prove that one's own group is superior to any other group. Thus we find that racism draws heavily on the type of vocabulary used to promote nationalism, with references to 'blood', 'land', 'our roots', ' our identity' and 'our homeland'. Stereotyping slogans emerge: 'Whites are soulless'; 'Civilization comes from the West'; 'The White world is the Free World'; 'Blacks are so demanding'; and so on. Racism that is expressed in this way in daily newspapers and conversation becomes part of our everyday thinking and sometimes prompts bloody confrontations within multiracial communities.

Race is a very broad way of classifying people, but there are also smaller categories we can use such as ethnic group and tribe. The word 'ethnic' comes from the Greek 'ethnos', which means nation' or 'people'. An ethnic group shares a common national or cultural tradition and usually a common language. A large tribe may be identical to an ethnic group, but in many cases a tribe is a smaller family grouping within the ethnic group. Its members are linked by blood ties, real or imaginary, going back to a common ancestry and geography, and by linguistic, political and social factors.

Those who are members of a tribe are entitled to expect to be protected by that tribe. They can also expect to be united with others in the tribe by a network of responsibilities within which members work together, helping each other and sharing resources.

Belonging to a tribe does offer many benefits, and there is nothing wrong with recognizing that we belong to different races, ethnic groups and tribes. But the danger comes when we move beyond acknowledging our differences and embrace racism, ethnocentrism or tribalism. These -isms are the result of the entry of sin into the world, which has affected all civilizations and all social structures (Jer 17:9-10; Mark 7:21-22). Sin can distort the strong sense of community that is fostered by belonging to a tribe so that it has the negative effect of reducing a sense of individual responsibility and individual worth. But the Bible stresses that every human being has intrinsic value and personal responsibility to God.

The protection offered by a tribe is distorted when it is used as an excuse to show favouritism to those who belong to one's own family, tribe or ethnic group. It is also distorted when protection of one's own group leads one to despise other groups, tell them to 'go home', and even to resort to violence against them.

Unfortunately, tribal and ethnic problems exist within the African church. One of the historical reasons for this is the fact that missionary organizations tended to work in particular regions and focused on particular linguistic groups. When a mission works mainly with one ethnic group, it establishes an ethnic church composed of a majority of Christians of one ethnic group.

Not only do religious groups and denominations tend to be regional, but each also has its own particular doctrines, its own understanding of church government, and of the division of responsibilities and ways of exercising power. This characteristic of African Protestantism, in conjunction with the linguistic realities of the continent, has served to reinforce the differences between groups, whether these are institutional, doctrinal or organizational, and whether they appear in terms of our pastoral ministry, our academic emphasis, charititable work or our social action. We urgently need to rediscover the unity for which Christ prayed in his high priestly prayer (John 17:20-23).

The Bible insists on the divine origin of all races, for we are all descended from our first parents, Adam and Eve (1:28; Acts 17:26-28). At the same time, it recognizes the differences represented by the sociological categories of race, for it sees the world as divided into Jews and non-Jews, or Gentiles. However, the NT stresses the equality and unity that Christ has brought between these races. In Christ, the church is a community composed of people from all races, all ways of life and all social conditions (Gal 3:28-29). No matter what their race, ethnic group or tribe, the members of the church form one family (Eph 2:14-19). All who are in the church can rejoice in being 'a chosen people, a royal priesthood, a holy nation, a people belonging to God' (1 Pet 2:9). John's vision of the cultural diversity and multiplicity of people groups that will be found around the throne of the Lamb should be enough to show the folly and sinfulness of tribalism, ethnocentrism and racism (Rev 7:9-10).

Rubin Pohor

of the country to the southernmost part (**20:1**; 1 Sam 3:20; 2 Sam 3:10). The author of Judges, who was probably writing in the time of the monarchy (see the introduction to this commentary), might well have used this common phrase even if Dan had not yet been founded at the time these events took place (18:11).

The fact that the assembly included *four hundred thousand soldiers armed with swords* (**20:2**) implies that they were ready to go to war against the Benjamites if a political solution failed. It would seem that the Benjamites had not been invited to the assembly (**20:3**, 12).

The Levite who had used shock tactics to summon the assembly (19:29-30) presented his case clearly and convincingly (**20:4-6**). At the end, he demanded a verdict (**20:7**).

20:8-15 Unanimous response to atrocity

The people were united in their disgust and anger at the horror of the rape and death of the woman, and were equally united in their commitment to punishing those responsible (**20:8, 11**). So they worked out a plan for supplying their soldiers in case of war – one out of every ten would provide food for the nine at the battlefront (**20:9-10**). Then they sent envoys throughout the area occupied by the tribe of Benjamin to demand that some action be taken in response to this horrendous crime (**20:12**). They were hoping that there would be no need to go to war against their own kinsmen. All that they wanted to do was to punish the rapists and thereby *purge the evil from Israel* (**20:13a**; Deut 13:5; 17:7; 19:19-20).

Unfortunately *the Benjamites would not listen* (**20:13b**). Instead of handing over the handful of wicked men from Gibeah who had committed the crime, their tribal pride led them to mobilize an army of 26 700 men and come together at Gibeah (the scene of crime) to fight their fellow Israelites (**20:14-15**). Many African nations such as Uganda, Sudan, Somalia and Ivory Coast have suffered from civil war for years simply because their leaders failed to negotiate a political solution, which often calls for 'give and take'. The peace offer was rejected; the Benjamites took up arms.

20:16-46 War against the Benjamites

It seems that the Benjamites had too much confidence in the prowess of their elite troops armed with slingstones as their small army of just over twenty-six thousand men faced an army of four hundred thousand men (**20:16-17**). We are not told that they offered any prayer to God. The united Israelite army, on the other hand, consulted with God before this confrontation (**20:18**), as they did on two other occasions in the story (20:1, 28).

Prayer expresses our dependence upon God. Unfortunately, many believers only pray after they have tried something and failed. This is like taking 'medicine after death' as the saying goes. The best time to offer prayer is before the event – but we should not assume that such prayer will automatically bring success. God is sovereign, and he is free to answer our prayers in any way that pleases him. In this case, his answer brought defeat to the Israelites. Twenty-two thousand of them were cut down on the first day (**20:19-21**).

When we fail after we have prayed and done our best, we should not be discouraged and curse God, as many do. We can learn from the Israelites. They *encouraged one another, took up their positions*, went back to God and even *wept before the Lord* (**20:22-23**). They changed their question to

God from *who of us shall go first to fight?* (20:18), which is a bit presumptuous, to *shall we go up again to battle against the Benjamites, our brothers?* (20:23). Yet this second time they still suffered a defeat with eighteen thousand casualties (**20:25**).

This should have demoralized them completely. But they refused to be dejected. Instead they went up to Bethel, which had been a major religious centre in the days of Jacob (Gen 28:10-22; 35:7, 15) and continued as such for many centuries. It would be where Jeroboam I would set up the second of his national shrines for the northern kingdom (1 Kgs 12:28-30). At Bethel, they sat and wept before God as they had before. But this time they added two more religious disciplines: they fasted all day and presented burnt offerings and fellowship offerings to God (20:26-27). By fasting they humbled themselves before God (2 Chr 7:14; Joel 1:14), and by their offerings they repented of any sin and restored their fellowship with God (Lev 1:3-17; 6:8-13; 7:11-21). Fasting is taught and encouraged in the NT (Matt 4:1-2; 6:16-18), while repentance and restoration is carried out by confessing and believing (1 John 1:5-2:2).

The presence of the ark of the covenant in Bethel instead of its more permanent location at Shiloh and the mention of Phinehas as the presiding priest (**20:27-28a**; Josh 22:13) indicate that the events described in this chapter happened early in the period of the judges.

Not wanting to be presumptuous, even after performing all the religious duties, they asked God again: *Shall we go up again to battle with Benjamin our brother, or not?* (**20:28**). God's answer was more definite than before: *Go, for tomorrow I will give them into your hands.* This is the first time he promised them a victory. And he kept his promise.

This time, the Israelites adopted a different strategy, the one that God had first given to Joshua in his battle against Ai (Josh 8). On the third day, the Israelites *set an ambush around Gibeah* (**20:29**). Their attack on the Benjamites seemed to follow the same pattern as the two previous attacks, but this time the Israelites allowed themselves to be driven back while suffering the loss of only about thirty men (**20:30-32, 39**). As the Benjamites pursued them, another group assaulted and took the city of Gibeah and set it on fire (**20:33-34, 37-38**). As soon as the Israelites saw smoke rising from the city, they stopped pretending to withdraw and vigorously attacked the Benjamites (**20:40-41a**). The Benjamites were trapped with no way to escape, for behind them their city was on fire and before them the swords devastated. Terrified, they broke and fled, pursued by the victorious Israelites (**20: 41b-45b**).

The writer leaves no doubt that *the Lord* gave them this victory (**20:35**). With the help of God, the Israelites defeated the Benjamites. Justice was upheld and evil was purged from Israel, albeit at a very high price in terms of the human casualties on both sides and the destruction of property. Besides the Israelites casualties in the previous battles, 25 100 Benjamites were struck down (20:35, **46** – this last verse gives a round number, not an exact number).

20:47-21:12 Wailing for the missing tribe

The slaughter of the Benjamite men in battle was followed by the destruction of all in their towns (**20:48**). The sole survivors were the *six hundred* Benjamite men hiding at *the rock of Rimmon* (**20:47**). There were no more of them than the Danite warriors in 18:11-31. But the Danites had still had wives and children, whereas the Benjamites had lost theirs. Not only that, but the Israelites had taken an oath at Mizpah that they would not give their daughters in marriage to Benjamites (**21:1**). The tribe faced extinction.

As this reality sank in, the people wailed bitterly at the loss of one of their tribes (**21:2-3**). They were confronting the consequences of foolish oaths and unrestrained vengeance. Once again, they gathered for prayer and sacrifice (**21:4**) and began to think how they could *provide wives* for the six hundred Benjamites who were left without directly violating their vow (**21:6-7**).

As they discussed the problem, they discerned one possible way to escape their dilemma. Their oath at Mizpah had included a vow that anyone who had not obeyed the summons to the great assembly was to be put to death (**21:5**). An investigation revealed that no one from *Jabesh Gilead* had come to the camp for the assembly (**21:8-9**). This gave them grounds to send twelve thousand warriors to kill every male in Jabesh Gilead, as well as every female who had slept with a man, but to bring back the virgins alive (**21:10-11**). The mission was successful, although it only produced four hundred virgins, rather than the target of six hundred (**21:12**). Two hundred more virgins were needed.

21:13-25 Rebuilding the Benjamite tribe

With four hundred virgins on hand, a peace envoy was sent to the six hundred Benjamites hiding at the rock of Rimmon (**21:13**). The offer of peace was accepted, and the four hundred girls were delivered to them, but there was still the problem of finding wives for the remaining two hundred men (**21:14**). Once again, a plan was drawn up (**21:15-22**). With the approval of the elders, the Benjamites ambushed girls at the annual feast of the Tabernacles at Shiloh: *while the girls were dancing, each man caught one and carried her off to be his wife* (**21:23a**). This mass kidnapping meant that no one could be said to have given his daughter to a Benjamite, and thus the vow was circumvented. *Then they returned*

to their inheritance and rebuilt the towns and settled in them (**21:23b**). The tribe would survive.

There are a few aspects of this sorry account that we can learn from. The first is the Israelites' concern and care for the remaining Benjamites. One translation reads: *The people had compassion on Benjamin* (21:15, HCSB). The way of compassion is far more effective than setting up tribunals to apportion blame. The second lesson is that in order to solve problems, we may have to approach them from a different angle, as the Israelites did as they worked out a way to solve the problem without violating their oath. In conflict management, wisdom is much in demand as it is important to consider alternative courses of action, which may not be immediately obvious. The third lesson is the community collaboration witnessed in the rebuilding exercise (21:23). It would appear that the reconstruction of the houses and essential infrastructure of the Benjamite community was done cooperatively rather than individually. Thus out of the ashes of ruin a new strong and vibrant community developed. This tribe would provide a united Israel with its first king, Saul, son of Kish, a Benjamite (1 Samuel 9–10).

But much in the story is an example of what not to do. The solution adopted by the Israelites did uphold the principle that marriage involves one man and one woman (21:23; Gen 2:24; Matt 19:5). But God's plan for marriage does not intend women to be treated as objects to be manipulated by men, with no voice in what happens to them. Yet that is how African women are often treated by men who regard them as existing purely to satisfy male sexual needs and to create comfortable homes. Such an attitude results in abuse of women and does not provide the loving, supportive marriage that models Christ and the church and is characterized by love and respect (Eph 5:22-33).

Given the sordid story with which the book of Judges ends, it is no surprise that the book ends with the condemnatory words, *In those days Israel had no king; everyone did as he saw fit* (**21:25**).

Tokunboh Adeyemo

Further Reading

Cundall, Arthur and Leon Morris. *Judges and Ruth.* TOT. Downers Grove: Intervarsity Press, 1981.

Davis, Dale Ralph. *Judges: Such a Great Salvation.* FOB. Fearn, Ross-shire: Christian Focus Publications, 2000.

Wilcock, Michael. *The Message of Judges.* BST: Downers Grove: Intervarsity Press, 1993.

RUTH

The book of Ruth is more than just a good story. It also has moral teaching about God and about the resilience of women when they work in solidarity. While it was written in a patriarchal (male-centred) society, it presents women as using patriarchal structures to their advantage as they seek to survive.

In this commentary, I will concentrate on what this book has to say about relationships, for its teaching has important implications for relationships in modern Africa. We will look at the relationships between women, between women and men, and between a foreign woman and David, the king of Israel.

It is clear from the way the story is narrated that it existed in an oral form before it was written down. For example, the end of each chapter introduces what is coming in the next chapter, creating a sense of anticipation in the listeners. This oral background is one reason that the story is very appealing to the oral society of Africa, where storytelling is a familiar form of communication.

Some scholars argue that the story of Ruth has no basis in historical events because the names of the characters match their actions or character. For example, *Mahlon* means 'sickness', while *Chilion* means 'failing'. *Orpah* means 'she who turns back'. *Naomi* means 'sweetness'. *Boaz* means 'in him is strength'. *Ruth* means 'friendship or female companionship'. This argument is not convincing to Africans, who are accustomed to children being named for events around the time of their birth. One of my sisters was named Manzunzo (suffering) because she was born two months after the death of my father.

Authorship

We do not know who wrote the book of Ruth. Some biblical scholars have even suggested that it may have been written by a woman because it presents women characters in a way that was very unusual in the patriarchal Jewish society. For example, it has the name of a woman as its title and is an account of the experiences and initiative shown by two women. The book of Esther is the only other book in the Hebrew Bible that bears the name of a woman. It is also striking that this is the only book in the Bible in which the women talk more than the men. The author has allowed women to speak in thirty three of the fifty-five verses in which characters speak.

Other scholars disagree with the argument for female authorship on the basis that at the time of writing women were not prominent enough to author a book. Some explain the dominance of female characters by saying that while the author may be male, the voice of the narrator of

the story is female. In other words, the author of the story is separate from the character who tells the story.

Certainly the presentation of women is unusual, even as regards the language used. For example, in chapter 1:8, Naomi instructs her daughters-in-law to return to their mothers' home instead of sending them to their fathers' home, as would be expected in a patriarchal society. The women of Bethlehem tell Naomi that Ruth is worth more than seven sons, despite living in a society that valued sons more than daughters. And when Obed is born, it is the women who name him and speak of him as belonging to Naomi, rather than as a continuation of the line of Elimelech, which would have been the goal of a levirate marriage. Young men draw water for Ruth to drink (2:9), not normally the case in a patriarchal society.

Date

According to 1:1, the story takes place in the period when the judges ruled Israel. Some scholars dispute this date. They argue that the events of the story seem to take place during a period of political peace, with no evidence of the evils that are described in the book of Judges. Secondly, they argue that the need to include an explanation of the legal reasons for taking off sandals in 4:7 suggests that the audience for the story was beginning to forget the Mosaic laws, which would mean that the story was written long after the time of the judges. Thirdly, the genealogy at the end of chapter 4 suggests that the book was written after David became king. These scholars would argue that the book must date from the post-exilic period.

It is important to remember that while the story may first have been written down in the post-exilic period, the content could be much older. Hence the period in which the Bible sets the story may fit with the events described, rather than with the time when these events were written down. The absence of war could indicate that it was written during a period when the Hebrew people enjoyed rest from their enemies. Examination of the lives of individual judges shows that God identified them as good people in the midst of evil. One should avoid making generalized statements that deny that there were ever periods of tranquillity during the time of the judges. The story of Ruth should be located among one of the pockets of good people during that period.

Purpose

In order to see a story in its context, it is important to consider why it was written. This truth is enshrined in the saying *umanena chatsitsa dzaye kuti njobvu ithyoke nyanga* [Chewa, Malawi –'You have to mention what caused the fruit to fall and break the elephant's tusk'].

Biblical scholars have suggested several possible reasons for the existence of the book of Ruth. One is just to tell a good story. Others suggest that the aim was both to tell a good story and to raise the image of women in a patriarchal society. Still others mention the need to tell a story that improves the image of the Hebrew people as regards the way they treated those who worshipped God differently from them. In Ezra 10 and Nehemiah 13: 23–27, God is presented as being opposed to Hebrew men marrying foreign women, but in the book of Ruth God is seen as blessing a foreign woman, Ruth, and enabling her to conceive a child who became the grandfather of David, the king of Israel. Still other scholars have argued that the purpose of the book is to show the kindness of God towards any person who shows trust in God, regardless of gender, race or ethnic and religious background.

Theology

In the book of Ruth, one encounters a God who is concerned about the day-to-day affairs of ordinary people. God is behind the 'chance' encounter between Ruth and Boaz in the field. God is the one who directs Ruth, a simple woman, to glean in the field of the kinsman-redeemer of Elimelech. God is also behind the 'chance' arrangement that Boaz slept away from everyone else so that Ruth could sneak into and out of the threshing floor without being noticed by other men. God is also involved in finding a husband for Ruth and her immediate conception of a child, called Obed, who later become the grandfather of King David. God made a simple, faithful, foreign woman, Ruth, part of the royal line of Israel that went through King David, and thus one of the human forebears of Jesus Christ.

Although Naomi initially blames God for her loss of her husband and two sons, she ends with a God who provides for her needs through Ruth and Boaz. God is the one who protects widows. God rewards faithfulness with goodness. God is generous even to Gentiles.

Outline of Contents

COMMENTARY

1:1–22 The Solidarity between Naomi and Ruth

The forces that brought Ruth and Naomi together were beyond their control. Naomi had moved from Bethlehem in Judah to the foreign country of Moab because of famine (**1:1**). Such displacement by famine is very familiar to Africans. Being a refugee is a stressful experience for anyone, but it is particularly difficult for women and girls because it can lead to sexual abuse and the spread of HIV/AIDS. The second force that brought Naomi and Ruth together was marriage. They were mother-in-law and daughter-in-law.

In the ten years of their relationship in Moab, both went through tragic experiences. Naomi's husband, Elimelech, died (**1:3**). There is a saying that *Mvula ikakuona litsilo sikata* [Chewa, Malawi – 'When the rain sees dirt on you it does not stop, meaning that often one problem follows another']. This was certainly true for Naomi: besides having the status of a refugee in Moab, her husband died, and then so did her two childless sons, Mahlon and Chilion, who had married Moabite women, Orpah and Ruth (**1:4–5**). The proverb also applies to Ruth's life, because she had become a childless widow. In patriarchal societies where having children is valued, Ruth's position was very bad. Her cultural oppression tripled when she relocated to Bethlehem with Naomi, for there she was not only a widow who was childless but also a foreigner.

In Africa the relationship between mother-in-law and daughter-in-law is generally sour, especially in patrilineal societies. The young woman is overworked and is treated like an outsider. Yet the wedding songs tell her that no matter how difficult life may be, she cannot leave her marriage. Women are made to feel that they are trapped by marriage. Yet Orpah, Ruth and Naomi had a good relationship, as is clear from Naomi's blessing of her daughters-in-law: *May the Lord show kindness to you as you have shown to your dead and to me. May the Lord grant that each of you will find rest in the home of another husband* (**1:8–9**). Naomi's blessing reflects a society where the personhood of a woman is attached to her having a husband. She wishes good husbands for her daughters-in-law because she knows that she cannot supply them (**1:11**).

Orpah accepted Naomi's instructions and returned to her mother's home (**1:14**). Her choice should be respected. In a patriarchal society, choices are made for women, but in this story, the women made bold choices for themselves that shaped the rest of their lives.

Ruth's response to Naomi's instructions was an oath that epitomizes the good relationship between the two women: *Don't urge me to leave you or turn back from you. Where you go I will go, and where you stay I will stay. Your people will be my people and your God will be my God. …* (**1:16**). Ruth was declaring that her commitment to Naomi was final. She had decided to change even her religious and cultural identity in order to stay with Naomi. This was a powerful decision by a young woman, even without taking into account the fact that she might be choosing a life of singlehood in a society that valued marriage and children. The oath reveals a loyalty to another human being that is of the highest order because it is a lifetime binding of two individuals of the kind that is usually seen only in marriage. It is not surprising that it silenced Naomi completely, and the two women then journeyed to Bethlehem together at the end of the famine (**1:18–19a**). Some Western readers of the text see a gay relationship between Naomi and Ruth. However, no such relationship comes to mind when one is reading the text with African eyes.

Ruth's attitude is well expressed by the Chewa saying *Madzi akatayika saoleka* ['You cannot collect spilled water, meaning that once something has happened, you cannot reverse it']. As far as she was concerned, the past was gone and it was time to look to the future. Naomi, on the other hand, returned to Bethlehem with bitterness because she felt that *the Lord's hand has gone out against me* (**1.13d**). She regarded the deaths of her husband and two sons as a punishment from God. She repeats this view in **1:20–21** when the women of Bethlehem greet her. Some scholars have echoed Naomi's interpretation, insisting that God was punishing her family for having gone to live in a foreign land that worshipped other gods. These are the same scholars who see HIV/AIDS as a punishment from God. This interpretation does not concur with the experiences of other Hebrew people who sought refuge in foreign lands during

REFUGEES

In 2004, some three and a half million Africans were refugees outside their own countries, and some ten million others were refugees within their own countries. Most were not fleeing natural disasters but internal political violence and power struggles that feed on religious, tribal and ethnic differences.

The Bible is familiar with immigrants, aliens, wanderers and refugees. Cain became a fugitive following his murder of Abel (Gen 4:12). Drought contributed to Jacob and his sons settling in a new area (Gen 47:3-4). Jesus himself was a refugee in Egypt (Matt 2:14).

God cares about refugees. He even cared for Cain, whose circumstances were the result of his own sin (Gen 4:15). He established cities of refuge where accidental murderers could escape those seeking revenge (Exod 21:12-14, Num 35:9-34; Deut 4:41-43; 19:3-13; 1 Chr 6:42-55). There was provision for those forced from their homes by wars, economic hardship and famine (Lev 25; Isa 16:1-4; Ezek 47:21-23). Strangers and aliens within Israel were to be treated with respect, love, dignity and equality, like fellow citizens or blood brothers or sisters (Lev 19:33-34).

The NT emphasizes hospitality, brotherhood, love and care for strangers and the poor and suffering (Matt 25:31-40). The distinction between a brother and a stranger was removed by the new law of love that governs all disciples of Christ (John 13:34), by the unity of all believers (John 17:20-23), and by the brotherhood and universality of humanity (Acts 17:24-26)

In ministering to refugees, the African church must start by meeting their immediate needs for security, love, food, shelter, water, medicine and clothes, remembering that what differentiates the sheep from the goats is the way they provide for strangers (Matt 25:31-46). Without such ministry, refugees will never hear the gospel, for as a Rwandan proverb says, *inda irimo ubusa ntigira amatwi* ['an empty stomach has no ears'].

Not only should we minister to refugees' spiritual and pastoral needs, but they should be encouraged to minister to us by sharing in our worship, fellowship, service and ministries. Their insights can enrich our own Christian experience and they can become missionaries in our communities, just as the early Christians did in similar circumstances (Acts 8:1-4; 18:1-2). Such recognition will start to restore their dignity and hope.

The church must, however, go beyond providing refugees with 'a cup of cold water' and teach them how to dig their own wells, that is, help them to learn skills and trades that will sustain them while they wait to determine whether they will be returning to their homeland or finding permanent asylum elsewhere. The church will need to investigate the expertise and skills of refugees and match them with jobs and market opportunities. New programs may be required to teach profitable skills. To put it differently, the church must work towards including foreigners in the social and economic structures of the community.

The church in Africa must also be involved in searching for solutions to the problems that produce refugees. This may involve supporting initiatives for democracy, peace and justice, human rights, reconciliation and leadership, and the reconstruction of the physical and economic infrastructures of the countries from which the refugees were expelled. Host churches, the refugees' national churches and other church-based ministries will have to work side by side with local, regional and international humanitarian, government and non-governmental organizations. Some evangelicals may complain that this is to stress social rather than spiritual ministry. But both types of ministry are needed, and the African church must seek to put its faith into practice by ministering to the whole person.

Celestin Musekura

times of famine (see the stories in the book of Genesis). God is able to take care of people who show faith in God even in strange lands.

2:1–23 Ruth Meets Boaz

The relationship between Boaz, a wealthy landowner, and Ruth started in Boaz's field through God's intervention. When Ruth and Naomi arrived in Bethlehem at the time when the barley and wheat were being harvested, Ruth did not wait to be told to go and look for food (**2:2**). She initiated the move because *wanva Mmimba ndiye atsekula chitseko* [Chewa, Malawi – 'the one with diarrhoea opens the door', meaning that the one with a problem goes to seek help]. Ruth had a problem. She needed to find food for herself and Naomi if they were to survive. Ruth is typical of many rural African women who spend most of their time looking for food to feed their families. It is wrong to describe an African woman as 'a housewife who just stays at home'. There is no rural African woman who 'just stays at home'. They work long hours for their families, but their labour is unpaid.

Ruth knew about Israel's law that widows and foreigners were allowed to glean in the fields (Lev. 19:9–10). This law was God's provision for people in Ruth's situation. The divine hand is also seen when Boaz visited his field on the day that Ruth was gleaning there. When Boaz enquired about who Ruth was, he did so in a patriarchal way: *Whose young woman is that?* (**2:5**). Such a question assumes that every woman must belong to a man, either a father or a husband. This is also true in the African construction of the identity of African women. It is this mentality that makes it difficult for single women to take up leadership in some churches.

In the first contact between Ruth and Boaz, Boaz showed kindness to Ruth (**2:8–9**). He explained that he had heard her story and had been impressed by her kindness and commitment to Naomi (**2:11–12**). It can truly be said of Ruth, *mbiri sigonela* [Chewa, Malawi – 'good news travels fast'].

Another Chewa proverb says *Wakutsina kutu ndi nansi* ['the person who gives you advice is your relative for they wish you well']. That is the image that Boaz presented of himself to Ruth as he advised her to glean only from his field in order to protect her from sexual molestation: *I have told the men not to touch you* (**2:9c**). Naomi echoed this advice when she said: *It will be good for you, my daughter, to go with his girls, because in someone else's field you might be harmed* (**2:22**). Such advice emphasizes the dangers faced by foreign women.

In modern Africa, women live in constant fear of being raped both at home and outside the home. The silence of the church on this issue is disturbing. Men and women need to work together to break the silence that surrounds the rape of children and women. When the church remains silent, it gives the impression that it is okay for women and children to be raped.

3:1–18 Ruth and Boaz at the Threshing Floor

Wakwatila kwa mphenzi saopa Kung'anima [Chewa, Malawi –'when you marry in the family of lightning, you do not fear its brightness', meaning that once you have decided on a course of action that you are convinced will solve your problem, you do not fear whatever you meet on the way]. This proverb describes Ruth's mindset once Naomi had made a plan that she should ask Boaz to redeem her according to the patriarchal practice of levirate marriage (**3:1–4**; see also Deut 25:5–10). When Ruth committed herself to Naomi, she showed that she chose to take care of Naomi in a foreign land rather than returning to her own people to seek a husband. Now she was prepared to accept a levirate marriage because she would be able to raise children for Naomi. Her commitment to Naomi did not change.

As Ruth went to meet Boaz at the threshing floor, she must have known that this was dangerous, for she could not predict that no one would see her or that Boaz would not molest her. She risked being thought a prostitute by going to the threshing floor where only men slept. She followed Naomi's plan, uncovering Boaz's feet while he was sleeping and waiting for him to wake up from the cold. When he did eventually waken, the startled Boaz's question to Ruth changed. It was no longer 'whose young women is she' but *who are you?* (**3:9**), indicating an interest in Ruth's identity as a person and not as someone's property.

The fact that Ruth could have been mistaken for a prostitute had she been discovered by other men at the threshing floor raises the problem of prostitution in Africa. The poverty that the majority of Africans live with has forced many girls and women into prostitution. This is an issue that the church cannot just wish away. Serious reflection that leads to action is required because of the dangers to which prostitutes expose themselves. Any effective way of dealing with this issue must also take account of the clients who keep the trade going.

Ruth did not wait for Boaz to tell her what to do, as Naomi had instructed (**3:4**). She directly asked for marriage because he was the kinsman-redeemer of Elimelech (**3:9**). In terms of Chewa proverbs, Ruth was saying to Boaz *Nzako akati kozu, nawenso umati konzu* ['one good deed deserves another']. Ruth had been good to Naomi and people praised her for it. Boaz was being asked to rise to the occasion by providing for Ruth and Naomi just as he had prayed that God would do in 2:12. Naomi and Ruth showed shrewdness in proposing marriage to Boaz rather than waiting for Boaz to initiate it.

Boaz accepted the proposal, but explained to Ruth that he was not the nearest kinsman-redeemer for he knew of

WIDOW INHERITANCE

In the OT, levirate union was an ancient custom sanctioned by practice (Gen 38:6-10) and by law (Deut 25:5-10). A dead man's brother or closest male relative was required to marry his brother's widow and raise up children in the dead man's name. This ancient levirate law underlies the story of Ruth. Boaz, her dead husband's relative, was righteous enough to support the legitimate claims of a widow, including her right to glean and to contract a levirate union (Ruth 4:13).

It is significant that levirate unions are not mentioned in the NT. It appears that an order of widows came into being (1 Tim 5:9-11). Older widows of good character served the church and were compensated for their labour (1 Tim 5:3-16). It seems that the early church found new ways of caring for widows that respected their dignity and personal freedom.

In the African tradition, several types of marital unions are open to a widow. In one of them, a widow becomes the legal wife of a close relative of the dead husband. The children of this union inherit through the new husband, who is their legal father. This custom is called widow inheritance. It is different from a levirate union because the widow is still regarded as the wife of the dead husband. A close relative of the dead husband cohabits with her, but he is merely a substitute husband and any children born of the union are considered the children of the dead husband, who continues to be the legal father.

Widow inheritance conflicts with the Christian belief that death ends the marriage union. Romans 7:2 states that 'A married woman is bound by the law to her husband, as long as he lives, but if he dies, then she is free from the law that bound her to him.' In a Christian marriage, the contract is absolutely and completely dissolved by the death of one of the partners, whence the phrase 'until death do us part' in the Christian marriage ceremony. Allowing a widow to be taken over by an in-law constitutes a denial of that Christian belief because such an action is based on the view that the marriage contract continues even after the death of the husband.

Since the care of widows has long been an important task of the church, widows have good reason to turn to the church as the resource most likely to extend comfort, emotional support and spiritual guidance. Many widows have been disappointed, and not without reason. Although widows comprise nearly one-third of some congregations in Africa, the churches have neglected to deal with issues that affect them. For the most part, churches have kept silent on issues such as widow inheritance. Christian widows need affirmation and support. Otherwise, they may give in to cultural pressures and agree to widow inheritance. In an era where HIV/AIDS is widespread, such a practice can lead to death.

Mae Alice Reggy-Mamo

someone else who was closer. He promised to approach him first. If he was not willing to marry Ruth, Boaz would do so himself (**3:12–13**). This may explain why Boaz had not offered to marry Ruth earlier in the story.

Boaz raises the issue of older men marrying young women in his comment to Ruth: *The Lord bless you my daughter . . . this kindness is greater than that which you showed earlier: You have not run after the younger men, whether rich or poor* (**3:10**). Boaz did not consider the age difference a problem but took it as a compliment, for indeed there is prestige for an older man in marrying a young woman. However, such marriages are a big issue in Africa, where young women are married off by their parents to rich older men as second, third, fourth or fifth wives. Boaz may have been in the same age group as Ruth's father-in-law, Elimelech. Naomi should have been the one offering herself to have children with Boaz for Elimelech. The reason she did not may be that she had already passed the stage of having children or being able to attract a husband (**1:11–12**).

Ruth was a willing participant in this kind of marriage arrangement. Ruth was quite capable of saying 'no' to Naomi, as she had done when Naomi tried to stop her from following her to Bethlehem. Ruth also went to glean in the fields on her own initiative. Naomi did not force her to go. At the same time, it must be admitted that she did not have much choice about marrying Boaz because of the desperate poverty of widows. Poverty dehumanizes people by depriving them of the ability to make free choices.

4:1–12 Boaz Marries Ruth

The legal transaction between Boaz and the nearest kinsman-redeemer in the presence of the elders at the gate is a typical male-centred arrangement in which women are regarded as men's property. Ruth was being traded off as Elimelech's property and as an instrument to continue the line of the deceased men (**4:5**). While the kinsman-redeemer was willing to take the property that belonged to Elimelech (**4:3–4**), he declined to marry Ruth (**4:6**).

In the end, things worked well for Ruth because she ended up marrying the person of her choice, Boaz. Because this was a levirate marriage, the first-born child would be regarded as belonging to Elimelech's family. This child would inherit the property that had belonged to Elimelech (**4:6, 9–10**).

Most African societies practise levirate marriage or widow inheritance, and most African churches accommodate such marriages by approving the union of a single kinsman-redeemer with a widow. Yet such arrangements seldom work out in practice as most men want to marry virgins even though they themselves may not be virgins.

In the era of HIV/AIDS, a levirate marriage can be a death trap for a woman.

4:13–22 The Genealogy of David

Pasamba nfulu, kapolo asambira pomwepo [Chewa, Malawi – 'Where the freeborn washes, there the slave washes too', meaning the poor thrive on the better off]. This proverb was true for Ruth. On the social scale of the people of Israel, she was at the bottom because she was a foreigner, a woman and a widow. However, by the grace of God she moved up the social ladder to be associated with King David, and in the gospel of Matthew she is mentioned as an ancestor of Jesus Christ. Thus, whether the genealogy of David was a later addition or whether it was part of the original story, it makes a very powerful statement that Ruth became part of the history of Israel.

It is not clear why Ruth had no children with Mahlon but conceived with Boaz, other than the fact that *the lord enabled her to conceive, and she gave birth to a son* (**4:13**). In the patriarchal societies of Africa, male inability to have children is carefully concealed. However, arrangements are made for the man to father children with his wife. Yet in the case of a woman, infertility is regarded as a major problem justifying divorce or polygamy.

When Ruth's son was born, he was given his name, Obed, by the women of Bethlehem, which was unusual in that culture where the men usually assigned names. It is also significant that the child was not referred to as the child of Elimelech, as was supposed to be the case in a levirate marriage, but as Naomi's child. He was a blessing for Naomi who had come empty from Moab and had been made full (**4:14–15**). God is seen to be on the side of the living and not the dead by making Naomi full again.

Conclusion

In the book of Ruth, one finds a story that starts with sadness ending in wholeness and well-being. Women show initiative despite male-centred social structures. After the death of their husbands, life would have been very hard for Ruth and Naomi. However, they took matters into their own hands to find ways to survive and formed an alliance that was solid until death. Naomi carefully hatched a plan and Ruth put it into action, skilfully using the male-centred tradition of levirate marriage to their advantage. With the help of God, who is on the side of the oppressed, their plan worked.

The narrator of the story considers that Ruth's strength lies in marriage and motherhood. Theologians agree that those qualities are highly appreciated in African women. However, it is also important that African theologians seek to understand marriage and motherhood in ways that bring out the wholeness of both male and female humanity, without discriminating against women who are single or childless.

Isabel Apawo Phiri

Further Reading

Dube, M. W., ed. *Other Ways of Reading: African Women and the Bible.* Atlanta: Society of Biblical Literature, 2001.

Nadar, S. 'Subverting Gender and Ethnic Assumptions in Biblical Narrative: Exploring the Narrative Voice of Ruth.' *Journal of Constructive Theology* 6 (2) (2000).

Oduyoye, M. A. *Daughters of Anowa: African Women and Patriarchy.* Maryknoll: Orbis, 1995.

1 AND 2 SAMUEL

In the Hebrew Bible, the two books of Samuel (which were originally one book) form part of a group comprising the books of Joshua, Judges, Samuel and Kings. These books cover a well-defined period of Israel's history, from the military conquest of Canaan under the leadership of Joshua to the military loss of Israel's territory and the deportation that followed. In other words, in the book of Joshua, Israel gains possession of its territory, and at the end of Kings, Israel loses its land. Unfortunately, this pattern is less apparent in our Christian Bibles, where the continuity of this history is broken by the inclusion of the book of Ruth after Judges and where we are distracted by the book of Chronicles appearing immediately after Kings. This arrangement of the books of the Bible can be traced back to the ancient scholars who translated the Hebrew Bible into Greek (the Septuagint Version).

The Jews refer to this set of books as the Former Prophets, whereas Christians refer to them as the Historical Books. The difference in what we call them has a marked influence on how we understand and interpret them. If a book is said to be prophetic, readers will look for the word of God passed on by a prophet. However, if a book is said to be historical, readers will look first for history. But none of these books were written primarily as histories. They do not set out to provide a more or less objective account of events, but to present the facts from God's point of view. They interpret events as resulting from obedience or disobedience to the word of God in each particular situation. Thus any distinction between historical books and prophetic books is somewhat arbitrary. There is prophecy in the historical books, just as there is history in the prophetic books.

The books known today as 1 and 2 Samuel follow directly on the book of Judges. Judges ends with the words: 'In those days Israel had no king; everyone did as he saw fit' (Judg 21:25), and Samuel tells how Israel obtained a king.

Author and Date

Jewish tradition regards Samuel as the author of the book of Samuel. Though certain parts of the book were probably written by him, he cannot have written it all, for some of the events presented take place well after his death, which is recorded in 1 Samuel 25:1. But the fact that Samuel is regarded as the author testifies to his stature as the most important person in the OT after Moses. He dominates the entire book and is the one who set Israel on the path towards monarchy, anointing first Saul and then David.

The date of the writing of the book is not known. We know only that this book covers a period of about a century, from the installation of the monarchy to the final days of David's reign (1030-970 BC).

Purpose

The book states no purpose for its writing. However, we can deduce something of the author or authors' intentions from the scope of the books of which it forms a part. The Former Prophets end with the catastrophe of 587-586 BC when the temple in Jerusalem was destroyed and much of the population was deported to Babylon. Presenting these painful events in the light of the covenant blessings and curses in the book of Deuteronomy enables readers to recognize that Israel had failed to obey the stipulations of the covenant and was suffering the consequences spelled out in Deuteronomy 28. The aim of the author or authors was thus to use the past to teach the new generation the importance of obedience to God, which was the sole guarantee of prosperity and long enjoyment of the territory given as an inheritance to the patriarchs.

The further purpose of the book of Samuel, however, was to answer the question of why God chose Saul and then rejected him because of his sin, while David also sinned but was not rejected. The choice of stories about David addresses this concern. The book shows that David's sin is also punished, as when the child born of his adulterous affair with Bathsheba dies. This perspective must be maintained while reading this book.

Theology and Content

God is presented as the one controlling the history of individuals and nations. Behind sometimes ordinary events, there is the hand of God working to accomplish his purposes. For the author or authors of this book, nothing takes place that is not planned by God, and disobedience to his law yields bitter fruit.

Three important themes with strong theological content provide the framework of the book of Samuel:

- The end of the period of the judges (1 Sam 7)

- The installation of the monarchy (1 Sam 12)

- The start of the Davidic dynasty (2 Sam 7)

We are shown the choice and then rejection of Saul, the first king of Israel, and then the choice of David, to whom an eternal dynasty is promised. Samuel, the last judge, Saul, the first king, and David, the king par excellence, are the three main characters in this book.

2 Samuel and 1 Chronicles

The book of 2 Samuel deals with the events from the death of Saul to David's sinful census. David's reign is described with unprecedented honesty. Despite his faults, he is recognized as the greatest king of Israel, one to whom an eternal dynasty was promised. This promise fed the messianic hopes of the people of Israel, so that in the NT Jesus Christ is called the Son of David.

The book of 2 Samuel parallels 1 Chronicles. Both of these books offer a synopsis of David's reign, but they present it from different points of view. Attempts to harmonize these accounts are misguided because they fail to take into account the intention of the author or authors. Samuel is written from the perspective of catastrophe; Chronicles from the perspective of re-establishment after the exile.

The Book of Samuel in Africa

The book of Samuel is regularly read and preached on in Africa. However, too often the African reading of this book seeks a spiritual lesson in every historical detail. While such a reading is legitimate, it also impoverishes the text and hinders many Africans from delving into the riches of the book. The book of Samuel should be read as a vivid history of individuals with strengths and weaknesses, but also as the story of a nation with its highs and lows. Reading the book from this perspective will help many Africans to understand their own situation. In the book of Samuel we meet situations quite similar to those on our continent: hunger for power, social exploitation, sexual abuse, intrigues in the centres of power, political alliances that are made and unmade, political assassinations, and the like.

The book of Samuel also recounts two significant changes in the life of the people of Israel. First, Israel moves from a theocracy to a monarchy; second, under David's rule, Israel changes from a loose confederation of twelve tribes to a centralized state with a well-organized administration. Such changes have important consequences in the life of the people and determine their future. Africa has undergone similar changes as it has experienced the slave trade, colonization, the rise of independent autocratic states and democratization.

Nupanga Weanzana

Outline of Contents

COMMENTARY

1:1-2:11 Samuel's Dedication to the Lord

1:1-8 Conflict in Samuel's Family

The child who would grow up to be the last of the great judges of Israel was descended from the family of Kohath that was part of the tribe of Levi (1 Chr 6:33-38). This descent is important given his future role, for God had appointed the tribe of Levi to serve in the sanctuary (Num 1:50).

Samuel's father, Elkanah, is described as an Ephraimite in **1:1** because he lived in *the hill country of Ephraim*. He was a devout man who every year went to worship and to sacrifice to the Lord in Shiloh, which was where the Tent of Meeting had been set up after the conquest of the promised land (Josh 18:1). His faithfulness in doing this is all the more remarkable because the priests there were *Hophni and Phinehas, the two sons of Eli* (**1:3**). The bad character of these men must have brought the sanctuary into disrepute in the eyes of the people (2:12-17). Because 'there were not many visions' and 'the word of the Lord was rare' (3:1), attendance at the yearly feasts was probably dwindling, for worshippers would have received few spiritual benefits. But Elkanah faithfully attended the annual feasts, and endeavoured to take all his family with him every year. He overlooked the priests' behaviour and sought to serve the Lord.

Hannah, one of Elkanah's two wives, was barren. Despite this, he loved her and tried to assure her of his loving care (**1:5**). In this, he resembled Isaac in his love for Rebekah (Gen 25:21). But no amount of special treatment could lessen Hannah's grief about her barrenness. The statement that *the Lord had closed her womb* does not mean Hannah was being punished for some sin. It simply states that the Lord had not given her children. He is the one who gives or withholds these blessings (Gen 15:3; 25:21; 29:31;

30:17, 22). The fertile Peninnah shows no signs of holiness nor any particular closeness to the Lord that would have encouraged him to bless her with children (**1:4**). Rather, she was happy to add to Hannah's misery by showing off her sons and daughters (**1:6**). The description of her as Hannah's *rival* (**1:7**) indicates the problems that result when we depart from God's original requirement of monogamy. The word 'rival' can also be translated 'adversary', showing that Peninnah acted as an agent of the believer's adversary, the devil. Her behaviour was a calculated attempt by the enemy to provoke Hannah to jealousy, hatred, despair and discouragement, so that she would lose her faith because God seemed unfaithful, uncaring and unloving. It is also typical of Satan that this attack went on year after year. The annual family feast became such a time of torment for Hannah that she wept profusely and lost her appetite (**1:8**).

1:9-18 Hannah's Response

Hannah's response to Peninnah's provocation and to her own barrenness provides a model for all of us, and particularly for women in cultures where polygamy is rampant and where a first wife may have to learn how to handle a second or third woman in her husband's life.

Hannah could have responded to Peninnah's provocation by simply continuing to feud with her. Or she could have turned on her husband like Rachel did when she told Jacob, 'Give me children, or I'll die!' and then insisted, 'Here is Bilhah, my maidservant. Sleep with her so that she can bear children for me and that through her I too can build a family' (Gen 30:1-3). Or she could have turned to witchcraft, either as a way to have children herself or to harm or kill Peninnah's children. Or she could have stopped loving and serving the Lord because her prayers had not been answered. But she did none of these things.

Instead, she prayed fervently to the Lord (**1:10**). In this prayer, she did not curse the day she was born or the day of her wedding. She did not curse her rival or her husband. She did not ask the Lord to revenge her or vindicate her. Instead, she humbly addressed God as *O Lord Almighty* (**1:11**). She knew him to be all-powerful and knew that if only he would look on her affliction, all her misery would come to an end. She saw herself as the Lord's *servant*, born to fulfil God's pleasure. And so she did not selfishly seek a child purely for her own satisfaction or focus on the need for someone to look after her in her old age. She was willing to dedicate her child to God as a Nazirite, set aside like Samson for God's service (Num 6:2-5; Judg 13:5).

As Hannah prayed, her lips moved but no words were heard (**1:12-13a**). She wanted only God's attention, not human sympathy. She also did not beg the man of God to pray for her, because she knew how to go beyond priests to meet God directly. She was not one of these 'pray for me' Christians who go from one house of prayer to another,

seeking prophecies from the professional and commercial prophets of our time. Hophni and Phinehas were the type of men who would eagerly have swindled a needy soul and offered superficial prayers for a fee of the type that is now often called 'seed faith' or a 'prophet's offering' or a 'divination or revelation offering'. Hannah sought God for herself and found him.

Eli, the father of Hophni and Phinehas, seeing her emotions and silent muttering, assumed that she had had too much to drink and reproached her for drunkenness (**1:13b-14**). The old priest may have seen so many ungodly women with his sons that he could no longer discern who came to the temple to pray and who came to mess around. Yet Hannah did not take offence at his words but replied politely (**1:15-16**).

Eli pronounced a benediction on her (**1:17**) and Hannah left with an assurance that God would handle her case. So she *ate something, and her face was no longer downcast* (**1:18**). She knew her prayer had been answered, and so she set about living as if she had no problem. Like the patriarchs, she believed God's promises even if she had not yet received them. So she did not wait until she became pregnant before she began to rejoice and eat. She did this as soon as she had a breakthrough in the place of prayer and knew that the matter was in the Lord's hands. Peninnah must have been very surprised by this sudden change of outlook.

1:19-20 Birth and Naming of Samuel

The Lord's blessing brings results. Elkanah must have lain with Hannah many times without her conceiving, but this time the result was different (**1:19**). God acted in response to Hannah's selfless prayer. The medical condition that had caused Hannah's barrenness was miraculously cured. Nothing is too difficult for God, and nothing is too ordinary to be used by him to bring a blessing. So a child was born to Elkanah and Hannah (**1:20a**).

God acted for Hannah and for Sarah (Gen 18:13-14), Rebekah (Gen 25:21), Manoah's wife (Jud 13:2-3) and Elizabeth (Luke 1:7, 13), and he can do the same for us. He is not limited by age or physical condition, or by what others think of us. He is the Lord of all and his power knows no limit. Like Hannah, we need to pray to him as the one who alone can help us.

Hannah was the one who named her child (**1:20b**). In Israel, as in most of Africa, the father usually chose the name, although occasionally the mother might announce the name, but usually in conjunction with her husband (Luke 1:57-63). But Hannah seems to have been allowed to name this child, possibly because her husband may not have been as desperate for a child as Hannah was.

She named him Samuel, a name that means, *I have asked him of the Lord* (**1:20c**). Every time she said his name, she would be reminded of her vow in regard to this child. His name would be a sufficient answer to questions like 'Why must you leave him in the temple when he is still so young?' 'Why can't he work for the family?' 'Why is his life so different from that of Elkanah's other children?' The name would also remind the boy himself of his divine destiny. He lived in the consciousness and fulfilment of that name all the years of his life.

In many African cultures, names have specific meanings. They may refer to some ordeal the parents were enduring at the time or their expectations for this child, or they may honour a deity or some important person who has influenced the parents. The Yoruba of Nigeria are particularly careful when naming their newborns. They may even consult oracles to find the appropriate name, for they believe that *oruko nro omo*, meaning that what you call a child influences what he or she will become.

Names are important in the Scriptures too. Abigail noted that her husband's name, Nabal, means foolishness, and that although he was rich and successful, his actions were foolish (1 Sam 25:25). Similarly Jacob lived up to his name as 'supplanter', for he struggled with his brother from the womb, grew up to struggle with others, and even struggled with God, until God changed his name to Israel (Gen 32:28). At times, God names children while they are still in the womb to indicate who they will be and what they will do in their lives (Matt 1:21). Jesus changed the names of some of those he called to reflect the new things he would be doing with their lives (John 1:42).

Given these precedents, Christian parents should think carefully about what they name their children, although we do not have to name a child after some Bible character for them to have a godly name. But we do need to remember that the names we call our children give them their first identity. Naming may be prophetic and set the direction of the child's life. In view of this, we ought to be prayerful and deliberate in seeking God's face in naming our children.

What are believers to do if the name their parents gave them invokes some traditional god or an oracle? Some have chosen to change such names, but this is not essential, unless they feel specifically commanded by God to do so.

1:21-28 Fulfilling the Vow

The law of Moses sets out the principles governing vows (Lev 27; Num 30), but here we have examples of what these principles meant in real life.

Elkanah always went to Shiloh for the yearly sacrifice *and to fulfil his vow* (**1:21**). The Bible is silent about the circumstances of his vow. Hannah too had made a vow before the Lord. She may not have told Eli about it, but Elkanah must have known, for she told him, *After the boy is weaned, I will take him and present him before the Lord, and he will live there always* (**1:22**). He did not raise any objection to her having made this vow, and thus the vow was binding

(Num 30:10-15). The vows we make must not destroy our marriage relationships. Some wives today use church activities as an excuse to disobey their husbands, but God makes it clear that this is not acceptable to him.

Elkanah respected his wife's wisdom, and told her, *Do what seems best to you*. At the same time, he confirmed their obedience to God: *only may the Lord make good his word* (**1:23**). So the woman stayed at home and nursed her son until she had weaned him, possibly at around three years of age.

Finally, the right time came, and Hannah took her son to Shiloh (**1:24**). She could have offered sacrifices to redeem the boy from being the actual offering. But she was not seeking a way out of her vow by paying a token ransom, as others might do (Lev 27:1-8). She had counted the cost and knew that she must prepare herself and her son for offering his life to God. So, after presenting a sacrifice, she presented her son to Eli, reminding him of what had happened some years before in case he had forgotten about her vow or had never known about it (**1:25-27**). Clearly she was doing this willingly. She had not been exhorted to make a vow by some speaker. Nor had her vow been of the type that is announced publicly, as some churches today advertise the pledges made by their members. No priest had been requested to follow up to see that she was keeping her vow. Biblically, a vow is a private matter between God and the person who makes it.

Hannah's account of the past leads up to the words, *So now I give him to the Lord* (**1:28a**). Her gift was her response to God's own faithfulness to her – as all of our gifts should be as we return to him what he has first given to us.

The NIV translates the verb Hannah uses as 'give', but the KJV and other translations have 'lent', a word that suggests a temporary transfer on condition that the borrower will return the object to the owner. Hannah is clear that Samuel was a permanent loan to the Lord, but the word 'lent' reminds us of the humility of our God. He created and thus owns all things, but he gives them to us and allows us to choose whether to return them to him. And when we do voluntarily return his gifts, he will forever acknowledge it, as if we actually owned what we offered. Thus it will always be on record that Hannah gave her son to God, that women were generous to Elijah and Elisha (1 Kgs 17:7-16; 2 Kgs 4:8-10) and that Mary of Bethany anointed Jesus (Mark 14:1-9). God makes our gifts a part of his purpose on earth. And he blesses the giver (2:20-21).

Samuel's dedication to the Lord was permanent: *For his whole life he shall be given over to the Lord* (**1:28b**). For Hannah, there was no turning back. Samuel would abide there forever. What a resolve to please God!

Many in Africa appear before the Lord on Sundays, but also appear before the oracle or the gods in their community because their family ties are stronger than their faith in

Jesus. Consequently, nominalism, syncretism and idolatry bedevil the church on our continent. Christians must come to know that living for Jesus demands that we abide in him and in his will for the rest of our lives without going back to serve family ambitions, ancestral spirits, idols or anything else that is contrary to our faith in Christ Jesus.

At the end of this chapter, we might expect to read, 'And they worshipped the Lord there', but instead we find *he worshipped the Lord there* (**1:28c**). Samuel saw his dedication to the Lord as a privilege that called for worship. This is the spirit in which we should offer our lives to the Lord's service (Rom 12:1).

2:1-11 Hannah's Prayer

In 1:13, Hannah prayed in her heart, 'with groanings which cannot be uttered' (Rom 8:26 KJV). Her lips moved, but no words were heard. Now, however, she prays aloud with praise and adoration for all the Lord has done for her. The contrast reminds us that prayer comes in many forms, including thanksgiving and praise, petition, intercession and confession.

Hannah's prayer was not meaningless repetition of bogus statements, nor a carefully written speech to be delivered at a conference, nor a presentation about God to the priests. Hannah prayed directly to God from her heart (**2:1a**). She demonstrates what Paul means when he tells believers to 'speak to one another with psalms, hymns and spiritual songs. Sing and make music in your heart to the Lord' (Eph 5:19). Mary's Magnificat expresses a similar joy to Hannah's as she declares 'My soul glorifies the Lord and my spirit rejoices in God my Saviour' (Luke 1:46-47). Like Mary and Zechariah (Luke 1:68-75), Hannah was filled with the Spirit and burst out in praise and prophecy, demonstrating that a godly woman is free to exercise her spiritual gifts even in the sanctuary.

Hannah's prayer is similar to Christ's pattern for prayer (Luke 11:2) in that she begins with adoration and worship of God. Though the dedication of Samuel was the occasion for this prayer of thanksgiving, Samuel is not specifically mentioned. She was rejoicing in the giver, not the gift. She somehow knew there could and would be several 'Samuels', but that the one who had given him to her was the one and only God, who has no equal, for *there is no one holy like the Lord* (**2:2a**). Thus every verse of her prayer begins with the Lord and focuses on him.

Africans can be highly expressive and emotional in worship, but usually we focus on describing what God has done, rejoicing in his gift and losing sight of the giver. But Hannah's joy was not in the miracle God had done for her, in Eli who had blessed her, or in her friends and sympathizers; it was in the Lord himself. This is the only way our joy can be constant and remain fresh and full. 'Samuels' may come

and go; gifts may fade away or be damaged or stolen, but our God, the author of life, remains the same for ever.

All through Scripture, a horn is a symbol of strength, just as it would be for a bull facing a rival or a predator. In some African cultures, a horn is also a symbol of unconquerable power. Yoruba mythology describes a very powerful demon as having many horns. Bowing one's head (or one's horn) is a sign of shame and defeat, but lifting one's horn, like a bull tossing its head, is a sign of victory. This is the image behind Hannah's words, *in the Lord my horn is lifted high* (**2:1b**). She came from a community where a woman's only pride was in the children she bore for her husband, and especially in her sons. We are familiar with this attitude in Africa. That is why the names Ijagbemi ('I am victorious'), Omodamilare ('the child has vindicated me'), Adeponmile ('my crown') are common, all pointing to the fact that this son saved his mother from shame and abuse. But Hannah did not say that her horn was lifted high by her son, but by her Lord. She knew where her hope should rest: *My mouth boasts over my enemies, for I delight in your deliverance* (**2:1c**). Her confidence and release from a sense of inferiority and personal shame did not come from her son but from God's deliverance and the knowledge that *there is no one besides you; there is no Rock like our God* (**2:2b**).

God has no equal – whether in power, in holiness or in any other respect. He is a God of knowledge, as Hannah reminds us when she says *the Lord is a God who knows, and by him deeds are weighed* (**2:3**). He needs no light to see, no X-ray to perceive. He knows our very thoughts. We may be able to deceive other people, but God knows the truth about us. It is he, and not public opinion, who will determine the rightness or wrongness of every action we take.

Hannah's prayer focuses on the sovereignty of God, that is, his absolute power to do what he wants. He breaks the weapons of warriors, leaving them powerless, and strengthens those who were previously weak and stumbling (**2:4**). He reverses people's situations, so that those who had everything and saw no need to acknowledge God are now desperate for any work that will enable them to get some food, whereas those who previously went hungry now have enough to eat (**2:5a**). Those who prided themselves on having many children have collapsed in shame and become feeble, while those who were barren and in despair, like Hannah, have borne many sons (**2:5b**).

The catalogue of reversals continues in the contrast of death and life, riches and poverty, and high and low status (2:6-8). God controls them all. None are so low that God cannot lift them up. None have fallen so far that God cannot reach down to them. And there is no height from which God cannot bring someone down!

Given that God is the one who gives people their positions, even setting some *among princes* (**2:8a**), we should not enviously scheme to get ahead and begrudge any brother or sister his or her position. Rather, we must patiently and faithfully carry out the work he has given us, using the gifts he has given us (1 Cor 12:28). Wherever he has put us in life and in ministry, this particular place has been given to us by God.

God's power is so great that the very *foundations of the earth* belong to him. In fact, he was the one who *set the world* on these foundations (**2:8b**). He bears the entire world in his hands, and it is by him that everything holds together. Science has created nothing; it has only discovered a little of what God has done. Should he shake the foundations, the entire structure of the earth would immediately collapse.

Hannah recognized the vast difference between God's power and human power. She saw beyond what can be seen with ordinary eyes and declared, *It is not by strength that one prevails* (**2:9b**; see also Eccl 9:11). The believer's greatest comfort and source of strength is the knowledge that God *will guard the feet of his saints* (**2:9a**). Once you acknowledge Jesus as your Lord and Saviour, you belong to God and he fights your battles and your adversaries become his enemies (see 1 Chr 16:22). They will be *shattered*, that is, broken in pieces. When Hannah says that the Lord *will thunder against them from heaven* (**2:10a**), she may have been thinking of incidents like the one described in Joshua 10:11. The battle is the Lord's. What a comforting thought for anyone who believes and wholly follows the Lord.

When the Lord appoints people to positions, he also gives them the power needed to fill that position: *he will give strength to his king and exalt the horn of his anointed* (**2:10b**). This certainty is the basis for effective ministry, whether in the sanctuary or in the marketplace.

At the time Hannah was speaking, Israel had no king. Her words are thus prophetic and point to the King of kings and Lord of lords who will reign for ever. He has broken Satan, the enemy, and destroyed his weapons. This Lord will ultimately take his seat and *judge the ends of the earth* (**2:10c**).

Hannah's spontaneous prayer reveals her heart (Matt 12:34). The depth of her knowledge of God and her deep understanding of human weakness and insufficiency show that Hannah was a woman who meditated on the law of her God day and night.

The dedication was completed with Hannah's prayer. Then she had to face the reality of her vow. Hannah and Elkanah *went home,* leaving Samuel to face his destiny and to be trained in the Lord's service by Eli (**2:11**). What a challenge to us to release our treasures to the Lord rather than clinging to them.

2:12-4:1a Samuel's Ministry in the Temple

2:12-17 The Wicked Sons of Eli

Although living at the temple, Samuel was exposed to ungodly influences through Eli's *wicked* sons (**2:12**). In the KJV they are described as 'sons of Belial', an expression used to describe evil men throughout the Scriptures. 'Belial' seems to have been the name of a demon. Hophni and Phinehas came from a privileged background, but they squandered their opportunities. The chief reason for their wicked lifestyle is that *they had no regard for the Lord.* They knew about him, and knew the duties and routine of the temple, and the dates and the seasons for the offerings and annual feasts. They even knew the requirements of the law concerning each kind of offering. But they did not know the Lord. Their knowledge of him was all head knowledge, not heart knowledge. They knew the catechism and could offer stereotyped prayers, but they had no personal encounter with God. Consequently they *treated his offerings with contempt* (**2:17**).

True knowledge of the Lord comes out of deep interaction with him through perceiving daily the wonder of who he is. It is having such communion with him that his preferences and desires become the watchword in a growing relationship. Such knowledge of him is built cumulatively with time. It begins with the first encounter at conversion, but it does not stop there (see Hosea 6:3; John 17:3). The sons of Eli may never have had any initial encounter with God, or they may have allowed themselves to become focused on their ministry rather than on the Lord. Ministry on its own cannot make us spiritual. It can actually make us immune to the condition of our own hearts, and even immune to the fear of the Lord. Ministry can make us presumptuous about our personal growth and relationship with God as we throw all our efforts into external activities and programmes. That is why Jesus warned those who only claim to act in his name that he may disown them (Matt 7:22-23).

Greed and immorality are rampant among ministers in our day because many have stagnated in their knowledge of God. They neglect the ministry of the word and instead seek to make a good living out of the ministry. Like Eli's sons, they take the best portions of peoples' offerings for themselves (**2:13-16**).

2:18-21 Samuel's Childhood

Despite the corrupting influence of Eli's sons, *Samuel was ministering before the Lord* (**2:18**). His behaviour may reflect the training he had earlier received from Hannah, who must have told him to obey God's word and Eli's instructions no matter how others behaved. If his half-brothers and sisters were as unpleasant as their mother, Peninnah, he would also have learned not to automatically imitate those who were older than he was.

The secret of growing in holiness and in the knowledge of God is to make sure that all of our service is dedicated to the Lord and is done in obedience to him. Every doctrine, no matter how wonderful, becomes dry and deadly unless it is held up and quickened before the Lord. The word we minister must be sustained and kept fresh and alive before the Lord, otherwise it will become merely the letter of the law that kills. Teaching that does not bear the stamp of God's presence is always dry. It may appear accurate, factual and strong; yet it is lifeless. Moses knew this when he said that he would not go on without God's presence with him (Exod 33:15) and Paul emphasized that his ministry was done in the sight of God (2 Cor 2:17; 4:2).

Though Hannah and her husband had given Samuel wholly to the Lord, they still supported him every year by bringing him *a little robe* (**2:19**). Such a gift would not distract him from his call. It seems that they never asked him to come home even for a holiday. He was given to the Lord completely, and Hannah trusted God to keep him.

What will you do if God calls any of your children into Christian ministry? Will you encourage them or will you saddle them with problems from home to make them feel irresponsible because they answered God's call? Hannah's example reminds us that the Lord blesses us when we allow our children to respond to his call. He gave Hannah and Elkanah another *three sons and two daughters* (**2:21a**). This was what Eli had prayed for in appreciation of Hannah's deed (**2:20**).

While Samuel's mother looked after his brothers and sisters at home, *Samuel grew up in the presence of the Lord* (**2:21b**). He did not yet have any public ministry, but he was putting down his roots in the Lord. While the sons of Eli grew in wickedness, Samuel grew in his personal communion with God.

2:22-25 Eli's Weak Rebuke of His Sons

Eli became *very old* (**2:22a**) and reached the point where he should have been able to look back and see what he had accomplished for the Lord and enjoy watching the ministry of his spiritual sons. But the story of Eli is the sad story of all men or women of God who are too busy to give attention to their families. Ministry does not come before the family in God's scale of priorities (1 Tim 3:4-5, 12).

Eli must have been bombarded with reports about the behaviour of his sons (2:16, 22). They disgraced him in the eyes of those he had ministered to. He would have understood the African proverb, 'The child you did not train well will sell the house and the business you were so busy building'. His children seemed poised to destroy his life's work.

His rebuke to his sons suggests something of what the problem may have been. Instead of taking firm action to stop their behaviour, he despairingly asked, *Why do you do such things? I hear from all the people about these wicked deeds of yours* (**2:23**). He appears to be focusing more on what people are saying than on their actual behaviour (**2:24**). Instead of demanding repentance, he used a hypothetical example: *If a man sins …* (**2:25a**).

Not surprisingly, his sons ignored his words. Their wickedness had not become full-blown in one day. It had started with their removing some of the sacrificial meat (2:13-14), and progressed to forceful collection of the best meat before anything was offered to the Lord (2:15-16). Now it had gone as far as immorality with *the women who served at the entrance to the Tent of Meeting* (**2:22b**). Eli should have stopped them earlier. At the first sign of trouble, he should have denounced them and suspended them from sanctuary service for a while. As the proverb says, 'It is when the Iroko tree is still tender that you trim it and straighten it, but once it is grown, its shape is permanent' (see Prov 13:24; 19:18).

Parents and Christian leaders must keep an eye on their children and their spiritual children to make sure that they are standing firm in the faith. Do you also pamper those who are not walking with the Lord with positions at the altar? Do you insist on keeping them on the music team even though you know their lives are not right with God? Do you allow your children to use church property as if it were family property? Do they use your official car for their private business? Do those who respect you because of God's anointing on your own life give your children special treatment, rather than insisting that they must behave themselves and be taught like other children in the congregation? Eli's sons did not know the Lord before they knew the rewards of temple service, and consequently, they were corrupted.

The reason Eli's sons *did not listen to their father's rebuke* was that *it was the Lord's will to put them to death* (**2:25b**). Hophni and Phinehas had sinned past the zone of grace. They had entered the zone of judgment, where the Lord's activity hardens the heart rather than convicting of sin. This is what had happened to Pharaoh (Exod 4:21) and is similar to what Paul is speaking of when he says 'God gave them over' (Rom 1:24, 26) and to what John means when he speaks of the 'sin that leads to death' (1 John 5:16). It is a terrible situation to be in! But it is only reached through deliberate and persistent sin by one who already knows the truth (Rom 1:18).

2:26 Samuel's Growth

While Eli's sons were growing increasingly wicked, Samuel was continuing *to grow in stature and in favour with the Lord and with men* (**2:26**). While bodily growth is almost automatic, spiritual development needs greater diligence. It is easy to stop growing and to rely on glorious experiences of the Lord in the past. But our growth, like Samuel's, should be continuous. Past burnings can only produce ashes; they cannot kindle a fresh flame.

As Samuel grew, he experienced the favour of both God and the people. Anyone who is to succeed in ministry must enjoy both. But God's favour must be our first priority and must count for more than the favour of others. It is more important to pursue right standing with God than to mount a public relations campaign (see Prov 16:7). The latter is easier to do. All it requires is to be kind and sociable, although this may sometime require us to compromise our standard of holiness. Spiritual growth is more difficult. It requires becoming more and more conformed to God's image so that he can express himself through us. Samuel grew to become someone whom God could visit and whom he could even trust to announce his future judgment on Eli's family (3:11-14).

2:27-36 The Lord's Rebuke of Eli and His Sons

Eli was so reluctant to act that God had to send a messenger to rebuke him (**2:27**). This *man of God* is to be commended for having the courage to obey God and bring unambiguous words of rebuke and judgment from the Lord to an older leader.

2:28-29 God's favour and Eli's failure

Eli owed his position to the covenant that God had made with Aaron and particularly with Phinehas, Aaron's grandson who had used his spear when Israel was sinning (**2:28a**; see Num 25:5-8). Eli and his sons were thus squandering a relationship that had been established by bold obedience and consecration to the Lord. They were also squandering the many privileges they enjoyed as priests: *to go up to my altar, to burn incense, and to wear an ephod in my presence* (**2:28b**). God pointed out that he had provided for the upkeep of Eli and his household, giving him *all the offerings made with fire by the Israelites* (**2:28c**).

Eli and his sons enjoyed these privileges because God had graciously chosen them. All who are called to ministry should remember that it is a trust we have been given (1 Cor 4:1-2; 2 Cor 4:1-2; Gal 1:15-16). Consequently, we should approach the altar with fear and trembling, and not treat our service for the Lord as if it were ordinary employment that we have earned through our academic qualifications or our superior abilities.

God states exactly what is wrong, so that Eli will not think he is being accused arbitrarily: *Why do you scorn my sacrifice and offering that I prescribed for my dwelling?* (**2:29a**). Eli was insulting God rather than worshipping him. God did not see Eli's sons' behaviour as mere youthful exuberance. He saw Eli's timidity to discipline them as placing their personal pleasure above God's commands (**2:29b**). Moses and Aaron had made the same mistake at the waters of Meribah

and God had reproved them for not honouring the Lord and upholding his holiness before the people (Num 27:14).

God is jealous about his glory. We need to take care that no act of ours draws his name into the mud. We must honour him in the way we conduct our ministry, and fear him more than we fear our children or anyone else. We should not fail to rebuke members who are disobeying God's word, regardless of whether they will leave the church. We should not keep people in positions because we need their votes to stay in office, when their lives contradict God's written word. All such compromises amount to honouring people more than God.

God was also angered by the way offerings were being handled. Eli and his sons were *fattening yourselves on the choice parts of every offering* (**2:29c**). God had given the priests a particular portion of the offering (2:28c). As one who cared even for animals and insisted that his people should 'not muzzle an ox while it is treading out the grain' (Deut 25:4), he had provided sufficient food for his servants. He knew, as did Jesus, that 'the worker deserves his wages' (Luke 10:7). Paul uses these two statements together to point out the need to support those who teach God's word (1 Tim 5:18). Yet Eli and his sons were not content with their wages, but were fattening themselves with the best of all the offerings of God's people.

There are still ministers who abuse the offerings of believers. Some take every offering anywhere they preach. Others declare that all tithes belong to the high priest – and appoint themselves to that office. Others take the tithes offered by their congregations, so that some pastors and founders of ministries are now richer than the entire church they preside over. They even devise additional offerings: prophet's offerings, revelation offerings, new anointing offerings, seed-faith offerings, thank offerings, healing offerings, and so on, and pocket the proceeds. They become fat and parade their cars, expensive clothes and jewellery. The error of Eli can still be found in our sanctuaries today! It is unacceptable for God's work not to get adequate funding, for the widows and the poor to be neglected, and for a church to meet in a rented property while a so-called man of God draws a large salary, rides in an expensive car and lives in a mansion.

We must be faithful in the way we manage church finances. We must never grab the best for ourselves and leave the crumbs for God and his work. We are not called to operate a business venture but to offer sacrificial service.

2:30-34 God's judgment

God's judgment is introduced with the word 'therefore'. God does not punish anyone without an adequate reason, nor does he remove someone from a ministry without several warnings.

God started with a reminder of the promise he had made: *I promised that your house and your father's house would minister before me for ever* (**2:30a**). He does not forget his promises even when those to whom he originally made them have died. He continues to honour his word with their descendants.

Yet while God honours family heritage and covenants, he punishes individuals who misbehave and *despise me* (**2:30b**). This is what he did with Eli and his descendants. God continued to honour his covenant with Phinehas and Aaron, but he removed Eli and his descendants from that lineage.

Just as Phinehas' obedience brought a blessing to his descendants long after him, so Eli's disobedience brought death, poverty and sorrow to his own descendants. Every one of the curses that God pronounced on him in **2:31**-36 came to pass (see also 4:17; 1 Kgs 2:27).

We must be careful lest our misbehaviour jeopardize the destiny of our children.

This pattern of reward and punishment appears throughout Scripture. All of humanity fell with Adam, and all of us have access to redemption through the obedience of one man, Jesus Christ (Rom 5:14-19). Yet while Christ's sacrifice is sufficient for all our sins, we must personally appropriate it if we are to benefit from it. Those who despise what Christ has done for them will die. Our personal walk with God counts for more than any blessing we might inherit from our ancestors.

2:35-36 Eli's replacement

The Lord had already started to prepare a replacement for Eli in the person of the young boy, Samuel, who came from the family of the Kohathites, descendants of Phinehas (1 Chr 6:33-34). God was still keeping his promise.

The priest whom God would raise up would be *a faithful priest* (**2:35a**), that is, one who would be trustworthy and faithful in little things as well as in big things.

Today, faithful priests are those who faithfully present God's message. They esteem Scripture as the final authority, even when it judges their own lifestyle. They do not use preaching as an opportunity to speak about themselves rather than about God, and they do not avoid certain topics to avoid upsetting sinners on the church board.

Faithful priests must also be faithful to those who work with them. They must show themselves dependable and considerate to all, and must take care that their own behaviour does not detract from the glory of God. Thus they will not cheat or exploit desperate members of their congregations. Nor will they seek to intimidate them with the trappings of their office or to lure them into illicit sex. They will watch their own behaviour in all areas and at all times, including when they are with their families, so that they will not spend so much time counselling others that they neglect or become unfaithful to a spouse and children. They will be

aware that refusing to delegate tasks to others may be a sign of personal ambition rather than of godly dedication.

Finally, faithful priests are faithful to themselves. They will not live in hypocrisy, pretending to be in good shape when they are actually backsliding. They will confess their sins quickly and seek the help of others in dealing with them. Such honesty with oneself means that one is not soft on oneself while harshly condemning the mistakes of others. It also involves listening to the criticism that comes from those whose motive is not to undermine someone else's ministry but to build it up. Constructive criticisms deserve a hearing, for they contribute to developing godly character.

God himself summarizes what it means to be a faithful priest when he says that the one he will raise up *will do according to what is in my heart and mind* (**2:35b**). A faithful priest will not pursue his own desires or personal convenience, but will live solely for God. To be able to do this, he will need to know God personally, so that he knows what is on God's heart and in his mind. This personal and growing knowledge of God will be his first priority, regardless of the other demands made on him in his ministry. He will be led by God's Spirit, for no one can know what is in another's heart unless he interacts with that person's spirit.

If we are to be faithful servants of God, we must gaze daily at the Lord so as to see what he is doing in heaven so that we can do the same here on earth (see Matt 6:10). God does not want servants who treat his name as a rubber stamp for their personal ambitions or projects. God looks for those whose only reason for being in the ministry is to please him and to pursue his will, even if that is at the expense of their own lives.

God also says that this faithful priest *will minister before my anointed one always* (**2:35c**). Who is God speaking of here? Some argue that the faithful priest is Samuel, who carried out prophetic and priestly duties during the times of Saul and David, both of whom he had anointed (10:1; 16:13). However, given the stress on 'my' in the phrase 'my anointed one' and the manner in which Saul became king (8:4), it seems likely that the anointed one is actually David. In this case, the faithful priest is Zadok, who served as priest during David's reign (2 Sam 8:17). His service and that of his descendants is described as 'faithful' (Ezek 44:15; 48:11). In Ezekiel's vision, they are seen as the only priests (Ezek 40:46; 43:19).

In the NT, Christ is the ultimate 'anointed one' who combines in himself the offices of prophet, priest and king. In the long term, he qualifies as the 'faithful priest' (Heb 5:5-6) and as 'my anointed', but it seems that in this message to Eli, God was speaking of Zadok's service to David.

3:1-3 Results of Priestly Backsliding

The personal backsliding of the priests affected the ministry in the sanctuary, for we are told that *the word of the*

Lord was rare in those days (**3:1**). God only speaks through channels that are clean and open to him. The people came eagerly to hear the word of the Lord, and they went away empty-hearted and disappointed. Attendance at the yearly feasts and at the offerings must have dwindled.

Our personal walk with God determines how much God can entrust to our hands. If we preach without a fresh anointing from the Holy Spirit, we will have nothing to offer but sermons, stories and philosophies. The hearts of our hearers will be poisoned and our churches will die.

Eli's eyesight was almost gone (**3:2a**). This blindness may be associated with old age, for Eli was ninety-eight when he died (4:15). But his physical condition was symbolic of the state of his heart. He had lost the sight of both his physical and spiritual eyes.

Eli is said to have been *lying down in his usual place* while the lamp of God went out in the temple (**3:2b**; for details of the lamp, see Exod 25:31-40; 27:20-21; Lev 24:2). This darkness too is symbolic. Physical and spiritual darkness were taking over the entire temple. God's habitation was growing darker and emptier, except for the presence of Samuel (**3:3**).

We each need to examine the state of the light in our own church. Do people receive illumination each time they come to services? Is the lamp of God, which is the word of God (Ps 119:105), still burning brightly? Is it carefully trimmed with prayer so that it can burn more brightly in the hearts of those who hear it? Is there oil to keep the lamp glowing? Or is the oil of the Spirit dried up, so that it is the wick that burns as people hear only the letter of the word and have their eyes blinded by smoke?

3:4-10 The Call of Samuel

God's judgment on Eli's household (2:31-34), does not mean that he will leave himself without a witness. Though Samuel was young, *the Lord called Samuel* (**3:4**).

God's voice sounded exactly like that of Eli, calling the boy to run some errand for him. Consequently, Samuel responded by going to Eli each time (**3:5-8a**). He would not have made that mistake three times if God had spoken with an earthquake or with fire and smoke. But God's call often comes without fanfare. It may seem to be no more than ordinary thoughts. Or it may be in a human voice, as Samuel heard it. Or it may sound like thunder, as when the voice spoke to Jesus (John 12:29). The way to judge whether what we have heard is God's voice is to consider whether the content of the message honours God and agrees with the whole counsel of God's word.

God, who had not spoken in vision or dream in Shiloh for many years, waited until Eli perceived that it must be God who was reaching out to Samuel (**3:8b**). Eli advised Samuel to respond with *Speak, Lord, for your servant is listening* (**3:9**). Once Samuel listened attentively, God spoke (**3:10**).

God does not speak until he is sure we are ready to hear. When he called Moses, he did not speak until Moses came over to 'see this strange sight – why the bush does not burn up' (Exod 3:3-5). He did not deliver his full message to Saul on the road to Damascus until he was praying and ready to listen (Acts 9:11). God's voice may be becoming scarce in our generation because we are too busy to pause to listen to him. We are so overbooked that we have no time to hear God speak.

3:11-18 God's Message

God did not use his first appearance to Samuel to tell him anything about his own future or his own ministry. Those who are called to the ministry today should not focus too much on what God says they will become in the future.

What God did was confide in Samuel and tell him what he was doing: *I am about to do something in Israel that will make the ears of everyone who hears of it tingle* (**3:11**). That knowledge made Samuel a prophet.

God told Samuel about his coming judgment on Eli and his entire household. Though God said nothing about Samuel's own ministry, this message must have stayed with him when it became his turn to lead. When God allows us to see the faults of our elders, we are not to ridicule them. Rather, we are to take precautions to avoid repeating the same fault in our own lives. God will not punish someone else for a wrong and then tolerate it in us, especially if he has warned us against it.

All that God said to Samuel was a confirmation of what the Lord had repeatedly said to Eli himself, either through his own heart or through another man of God (2:27-34). God stressed this repeatedly, as he spoke of *everything I spoke against his family … I told him … I swore that …* (**3:12-14**). This is in keeping with God's way of dealing with his servants. He first speaks to us directly before sending others to confirm the message. Most of the time, prophets are sent to confirm something rather than to inform us of something. Modern prophets do not take the place of the Holy Spirit within a believer. They only speak to confirm what the Lord has said to someone either by the Spirit within or through the Scriptures.

Samuel's response to his first vision of God was to lie down until morning (**3:15a**). He probably did not sleep. He must have pondered the implications of the message for his own life and been sobered by the fact that God had bypassed his master to talk to him directly. Samuel's response is a model of how we ought to respond to God's word. We should not become overexcited by what we have heard, but should ponder it till it mixes with faith in our hearts (Jas 1:19).

Samuel must also have been seeking wisdom on how to deliver the message to Eli. Such wisdom is needed so that the message will be conveyed accurately and will evoke the right response from the hearers.

The next morning, Samuel *opened the doors of the house of the Lord* as was his normal duty (**3:15b**). His vision of God in the night did not go to his head and make him neglect his duties. He kept the whole encounter in his heart until Eli compelled him to reveal it, for *he was afraid to tell Eli the vision* (**3:15c**). This is understandable, for he was still a child. Eli has been his master and mentor. Eli had been kind and helpful in the way he guided Samuel to respond to the Lord in the night, but Samuel could not be sure how Eli would react to this terrible news.

Samuel was not happy to announce judgment on his master's family; judgment that could not be averted since God had sworn that *the guilt of Eli's house will never be atoned for* (3:14; see comment on 1:25). Clearly Samuel was compassionate and not ambitious to take over the leadership.

It took a lot of persuasion from Eli to get Samuel to reveal the entire vision to him (**3:16-17**). But when Samuel did, he told *Eli everything, hiding nothing from him* (**3:18a**). He did not play down the bitter part of the message so that he could stay in Eli's good books.

The comprehensive delivery of the message shows how carefully Samuel had noted in his heart all of what God said, without writing it down on paper. He did not fumble and jumble the message, but delivered it clearly. What a challenge to preachers today! Are you faithful to proclaim God's entire word, even when it hurts?

Eli's response was *He is the Lord; let him do what is good in his eyes* (**3:18b**). He did not argue with the messenger. He could not deny that Samuel had heard the Lord, for this message was only a confirmation of what the Lord had already told him (2:27-36). This fact must have been an affirmation of Samuel's first experience of hearing God. It must have reassured him that it was not a demon that he had heard and have taught him to take seriously all that God would say to him in the future.

Despite his failings, Eli knew that God is the Lord and has authority to do as he pleases. Since God had sworn to an oath on this matter, the decision was irreversible. Eli must have known that Samuel would sooner or later become the priest and prophet in place of his own sons, and he did not do anything to put an obstacle in his way. In this, Eli honoured the Lord and esteemed the word of the Lord above his personal pleasure.

3:19-4:1a Samuel Established As a Prophet

Samuel's early years can be summed up by the words, *the Lord was with Samuel as he grew up* (**3:19a**). He grew constantly in grace and in wisdom. The same words are used of other heroes who did great things for the Lord in their times (Abraham – Gen 21:22; Joseph – Gen 39:2, 21-23). It was God's presence in their lives that made all the difference.

God confirmed every word of prophecy he gave to Samuel (**3:19b**). It is God who makes our words carry weight in the hearts of others. This was the testimony of the early apostles (Mark 16:20), and it will be no different for us. We may preach and teach, but it is only when God confirms what we say that we see conversions, miracles of healing and deliverance, and fulfilment of prophecies.

God gave Samuel a divine introduction *from Dan to Beer-sheba,* that is, throughout the entire land from north to south (**3:20**). Samuel did not have to launch a publicity campaign with posters to inform people that he was now the anointed prophet. Instead, he allowed God to speak about him. And soon *all Israel ... recognized that Samuel was attested as a prophet of the Lord.*

The sanctuary at Shiloh had been dead and dry for many years (3:1), but now at last it revived as the Lord continued to reveal himself there (**3:21a**). When a church leader has no personal communion with God, God will not bless the church, no matter what gimmicks may be used to attract people. But when the right person is in place, the Lord will appear and the people will be blessed.

It is worth noting that the Lord revealed himself *to Samuel* (**3:21b**). God does not reveal himself in the furnishings of the temple (no matter how beautiful), nor in programmes and projects. He only reveals himself to people. If Samuel had been in Ramah, God would have revealed himself there. Church buildings may be intended to communicate a sense of God's glory, but God dwells only in human hearts. If people with God in their hearts come together in a building, God's presence will be there. But if a group of careless and unspiritual people gather in a sacred sanctuary, it will become no more than an ordinary building.

The method by which God revealed himself was *his word* (**3:21c**). We are often eager to have visions, dreams and extraordinary experiences, but the basic way in which God reveals himself is by his word. No revelation is dependable until God's word authenticates it. It is not enough to stand in the pulpit and describe your dreams and visions. You must let God reveal himself to you by his word if the faith of God's people is not to be based on human wisdom. As God told Jeremiah, 'Let the prophet who has a dream tell his dream, but let the one who has my word speak it faithfully. For what has straw to do with grain?' (Jer 23:28).

Many people in Africa tend to favour prophecies, visions, dreams, feelings and elaborate demonstrations of spiritual gifts rather than settling for God's infallible word. Churches are sometimes built solely on the visions and dreams of one individual. The word is so rare that it is no wonder there is so much vagueness and false doctrine.

The opening line of chapter 4 seems to be part of chapter 3, for its declaration that *Samuel's word came to all Israel* (**4:1a**) fits in with the earlier statements that the news of what God was now doing in Shiloh came to be widely known. Those who had lost interest in the feasts and offerings at Shiloh must have come back eagerly. They did not hate God; it was the dryness, the deadness and the corruption at the altar that made them stay away. All Israel began to seek the Lord again.

Even today, people will turn to God (even in sophisticated societies) when those who know God's presence are back in our pulpits. People leave when God's presence leaves. If it comes back, the churches will be full again.

4:1b-7:1 The Ark of the Lord

4:1b-11 The Capture of the Ark

The Philistines had long been enemies of Israel. Joshua had been supposed to root them out completely, but he had left some of the 'sons of Anak' in Gath, Gaza and Ashdod (Josh 11:22). These groups had become a thorn in the side of the children of Israel. They had oppressed Israel all through the days of Samson, who had failed to deliver his people from them. Their oppression continued throughout the forty years that Eli judged Israel (4:9).

Given the backsliding in Israel in these years, it is not surprising that there is no indication that the Israelites sought the face of the Lord before they launched an attack on the Philistines (4:1b). The result was tragic. Four thousand Israelites were killed (4:2).

The Israelites knew that as long as their God was with them, they always conquered their enemies. So now they asked, *Why did the Lord bring defeat upon us today?* (4:3a). Joshua had asked this same question when Israel was defeated before Ai (Josh 7:5-9). But whereas Joshua and the elders had torn their clothes and fallen on their faces before God, the elders and teachers in the days of Eli were dry-eyed and arrogant. They believed that God ought to fight for them, no matter how they lived. They did not humble themselves to seek his face, turn from their wicked ways and pray for mercy (2 Chr 7:14).

The people took another presumptuous step in the wrong direction when they sent for the ark of the covenant, hoping that a symbol of God's presence would be enough to help them on the battlefield (4:3b). They were confusing a symbol of God's presence with the reality of God. They spoke as if the ark was saving them, rather than God. During the exodus, 'whenever the ark set out, Moses said, "Rise up, O Lord! May your enemies be scattered; may your foes flee before you." Whenever it came to rest, he said, "Return, O Lord, to the countless thousands of Israel"' (Num 10:35-36). But Moses knew that it was God, not the ark, who scattered their enemies (see also Josh 6:4, 8). By Eli's day, the people were putting their confidence in a form of religion while denying the God behind the forms.

The same mistake is common in Africa. People carry bottles of anointing oil in their bags, believing that it has power to save them from every disaster. Some drink it. Others rub it on their wares in the market. Others place their trust in a handkerchief or cloth that has been anointed or prayed over. Still others spray their homes with kegs of water or blackcurrant juice that symbolizes the blood of Jesus in order to drive away demons. All these practices point to idolatry in the heart, for those who practise them want to hold a visible god to assure them of safety. And some preachers give these tokens to the people rather than pointing them to Jesus the Saviour.

If it had been Samuel who had brought the ark, it is possible that the Lord would have listened to his prayers for the Israelites. But the ark was carried by Hophni and Phinehas (4:4), the same sons of Eli who had abused their duty.

The Israelites' fetching of the ark must have given the Philistines the impression that the Israelite God was no different from their own god, Dagon, who could only move when carried. Clearly, the Israelites did not believe that their God was omnipresent and omnipotent. They thought that they could not pray to him in Shiloh and expect him to act in Ebenezer. What an insult to the One who created the heavens and rules the affairs of earth! Yet in some parts of Africa, Christians are being told that they have to go to the graves of their dead parents to pour out anointing oil or to sprinkle the blackcurrant 'blood of Jesus' before their prayers will be heard!

When the ark was brought into the Israelite camp, there was such a loud shout from all Israel that the earth shook (4:5). The hearts of the ignorant in the army were lifted up as if it were a real revival. They danced around the ark as if it could do something on its own. It is amazing to see how we will dance and get excited about a mere form of religion and yet feel so cold towards the reality of God's word and God himself. Much noise may accompany meetings where the focus is solely on tokens and forms. But if the people are confronted with the principles of Scripture, they fall asleep. They would rather keep a vigil for a whole night, chanting empty songs and crying around symbols, while Christ is obscured from their minds.

The Israelites' shouting created fear among the Philistines (4:6-7). They must have heard something of the wonders the God of Israel had done in the past (4:8). They probably remembered how they had suffered at the hand of Samson. But one among them challenged them to be courageous and to fight to the last drop of their blood lest they become slaves of the Hebrews (4:9). So they fought with all their strength – and discovered that the God they had heard of was not with his people! There was a great slaughter and Israel was defeated (4:10). Hophni and Phinehas, Eli's sons, were killed and the ark was captured (4:11). The Philistines must have thought that they had actually captured the God of Israel!

The church must learn that empty noise when the power of God is not with us will only set the enemy in fierce array against us. Instead of crying out at the crusade ground, we should be crying out for God to visit us again and forgive our sins and backsliding.

Unbelievers recognize when our speech is empty and cease to respect the church and the things of God. They steal church property and have no respect for God's people. They seem to know that we have no power and that our prayers will not be heard. Sin and hypocrisy have brought us to this valley of shame.

4:12-22 Fulfilment of the Prophecy About Eli's House

Eli was restless because the Holy of Holies stood empty without the ark. His heart must have been filled with fear and longing as he sat on a seat beside the road watching for its return (**4:13**). When the news finally came from the battlefield, the whole city was in uproar. Eli grew increasingly agitated until finally the news was broken to him (**4:14-17**). He took the news of his sons' death fairly calmly. He may even have anticipated it given the prophecies he had been given (2:34). But what really concerned him was the fate of the ark. When he heard that the Philistines had captured it, he fell backwards off his seat, broke his neck and died (**4:18**). Thus forty years of ministry both as a priest and as a judge of Israel came to a sorry end.

Eli did not die simply because of shame or sorrow for his children. He died because of the disaster that the capture of the ark represented. How would he replace it? What would people gather to do in the temple when the ark was no longer there?

Eli's daughter-in-law, Phinehas' wife, was pregnant and went into premature labour when she heard that *the ark of God has been captured and that her father-in-law and her husband were dead* (**4:19**). Her labour went badly and she was dying when the midwives told her that she had delivered a boy, hoping to encourage her to fight for her life (**4:20**). She ignored them. When asked to name the child, the only name she would give him was *Ichabod,* meaning *The glory has departed from Israel* (**4:21**).

This woman probably feared God. She had suffered great personal loss, yet she still had a deep concern for the glory of God. Her dying words summarize the life and ministry of Eli and of Israel at that time. It was not so much the ark as an object that she mourned, but the fact that its loss symbolized the departure of God's glory from the land. The Israelites would now worship before an empty Holy of Holies, without any symbol of God's presence.

This situation continued for many years, even during Samuel's ministry, for he inherited the ruin left by his old master.

5:1-12 The Ark Among the Philistines

While the children of Israel mourned, the Philistines rejoiced that they had captured the God of Israel. But the events that followed proved that God does not need the help of a priest or an army. Jesus made the same point when he said that if we will not praise him, even stones will do so (Luke 19:40). If we will not prophesy for him, even a donkey will speak on his behalf (Num 22:28). If Jonah would not obey him and go to Nineveh, a fish was ready to do the Lord's bidding (Jonah 1:17). No one is indispensable.

The Philistines took the ark of God to Ashdod and set it beside their god, Dagon, They were probably happy to have another god, even if, in their eyes, he was subordinate to Dagon (**5:1-2**). But the next morning, they found that the idol of Dagon had fallen on its face before the ark of the Lord (**5:3**). Assuming that this was just a coincidence, they lifted up the idol and stood it in its place again. But the next morning, not only had the idol again fallen on its face before the ark of the Lord, but this time the head and hands had also been broken off from the trunk (**5:4**). The invisible but invincible hand of God had pushed down their god.

Despite this display of the weakness of their god, the people of Ashdod continued to assume that Dagon was powerful and that they must not touch anything that he had touched. So thereafter they refused to step on the *threshold* where the idol's head and hands had lain (**5:5**; see also Zeph 1:9)

The mere fact that their idol had been broken did not prompt any action from the people of Ashdod. So the Lord sent them further trouble in the form of *tumours* (**5:6**). Given that the Philistines included gold rats in their offerings when they returned the ark (6:4), it seems likely that the Philistines were suffering from bubonic plague, which is spread by rats and produces huge swellings in the groin.

This time, the people of Ashdod got God's message and concluded that *the ark of the god of Israel must not stay here with us* (**5:7**). The Philistine rulers gathered to discuss what to do next. They decided that the problem lay in Ashdod and decided to send the ark to Gath (5:7). But there, too, the people broke out in tumours (**5:9**), and it was decided to move the ark again, taking it to Ekron (**5:10**). But by this time the people had concluded that the association between the ark and tumours was not a coincidence, but was God's work. So the people of Ekron protested strongly when the ark arrived, crying out, *they have brought the ark of the god of Israel round to us to kill us and our people.* And its arrival was indeed accompanied by death (**5:11b-12**).

God was fighting against the Philistines without help from the Israelite army. Because of their disobedience, God's people had missed out on the help they could have had.

The Philistines concluded that it was time to *send the ark of the god of Israel away* and return it to *its own place* (**5:11a**). They still thought of God as associated with one place. But God actually rules over all the earth.

6:1-12 The Ark Returned to Israel

The ark stayed *in Philistine territory for seven months* (**6:1**). It must have been a bleak time for the people of Israel, who mourned Eli for the first month, but had to mourn the departure of the glory of God for seven full months. It was also seven months of distress for the Philistines, during which they learned the power of the God of Israel, the same power that had been manifested in the ten plagues in Egypt (**6:6**; **4:8**).

After seven months, the Philistines were brought to the point of surrender, asking their priests and diviners, *What shall we do with the ark of the Lord? Tell us how we should send it back to its place* (**6:2**). Today, people need to come to the same point where they honestly ask 'What must I do to be saved?'

The Philistines' priests and diviners were not entirely ignorant of spiritual things. They had lived alongside the Israelites for long enough to know something of how they worshipped God. So they prescribed that the ark must not just be sent back by itself, but should be accompanied by a guilt offering (**6:3**). Note that they do not speak of returning the ark to the Israelites, but of returning it *to him,* that is, to God.

However, the priests' advice about what would be an appropriate guilt offering and how the ark should be carried were not in accordance with the laws God had given to Moses. They sent two female cows to pull the cart and later to be used as a burnt offering (**6:7**), where the law prescribed that the offerings should be males (Lev 5:14-18). They also set the ark on a new cart (**6:8**), rather than carrying it by hand using the supporting poles (1 Chr 15:15). Many years later, Uzzah would lose his life because he touched the ark while it was being carried on a cart (2 Sam 6:6). The Philistines did not suffer similar punishment because God may permit ignorant unbelievers to get away with things that he will not excuse in a believer who has been taught his laws. He recognized that the spirit behind their advice was commendable, for they instructed the people to *pay honour to Israel's god* (**6:5**). They interpreted any sluggishness in making these offerings to hardness of heart, and reminded their countrymen about what had happened to Pharaoh when he opposed the Israelites (**6:6**).

The Philistine priests proposed a test to see whether their diagnosis of the source of their troubles was correct (**6:9**). They received clear confirmation that it was God who had brought trouble upon them and that he is a living God as the cows went straight to Beth Shemesh, (**6:12**). The cows were not driven along this route, but were again proving that animals will obey God while humans struggle to do so (see Isa 1:3). *The rulers of the Philistines,* that is, the governors of the five Philistine cities of Ashdod, Gaza, Ashkelon, Gath and Ekron (**6:17**), simply followed them in amazement and watched as the cows stopped where God commanded, at Beth Shemesh in the territory of Israel.

6:13-18 The Ark at Beth Shemesh

The choice of where the ark returned to Israel was God's. All the Philistines wanted was that it leave their territory. God chose to direct it to the field of a man called Joshua of Beth Shemesh (**6:13-14**), once again choosing to reveal himself to the humble.

Beth Shemesh was a border town. The people's joyous response when the ark suddenly arrived among them shows that they maintained this border both physically and spiritually (**6:13**). They had been longing for the ark's return. They also knew the appropriate way to welcome it back. Though they might have welcomed a new cart and cows to convey their harvest to market, it was clear to them that these gifts were meant for the Lord and were not for their personal use. So they broke up the cart and used it for firewood as they offered the cows as a burnt offering to the Lord (**6:14**).

Beth Shemesh was also one of the cities of refuge allotted to the Levites (Josh 21:16). These Levites now came forward to perform their ordained ministry of caring for the ark (Num 1:50-51). They carefully placed it and the chest containing the Philistines' guilt offerings on the large rock next to which the cart had stopped (**6:15**). God, their true Rock, had provided this stone as a platform on which to place the ark while the Tent of Meeting was still far away. Then the people of Beth Shemesh offered burnt offerings and made their sacrifices to the Lord. They were prepared and ready to serve the Lord at any time and at any cost.

By doing all these things in the sight of the Philistine rulers (**6:16a**), they were witnessing to these unbelievers about how the God of Israel should be worshipped. The Philistines must have noted how they cherished and honoured their God. They may also have been amazed that the ordinary people carried out this celebration and did not wait for the official leaders of Israel. This was how things should have been from the beginning, with everyone in Israel a worshipper, every head of every family a spiritual leader (Exod 12:3; 13:8) and every firstborn dedicated to the service of the Lord. Disobedience had resulted in the Lord's service becoming the exclusive preserve of the Levites (Exod 32:26, 29)

But what the Philistines had seen was not enough to make them abandon their gods and worship the Lord God of Israel. Instead *they returned that same day to Ekron* (**6:16b**). We need to remember their behaviour when we are tempted to think that some change in the way we are doing things will make a difference to the way the world sees us. The world has never changed its commitment to the prince of this world (Jer 2:11) and while it may be impressed by what we do, it does not change its allegiance.

6:19-7:1 The Ark Moves to Kiriath Jearim

The Lord wants people to serve him according to the pattern he has shown. The people of Beth Shemesh had done this when they allowed the Levites to handle the ark. But then they became too bold and opened the ark to look inside it – something that was clearly forbidden in the Law of Moses (Num 1:51). The Philistines may have looked inside the ark without being struck down, for they did not know the law of the Lord. But this was not the case with the people of Beth Shemesh. God held them accountable on the basis of the greater revelation they had received (see Luke 12:47-48), and seventy of them died (**6:19**). (Some manuscripts give the number who died as 50 070, but that is impossible for Beth Shemesh was not a great city.)

In **6:20a**, the heart of the matter emerges in their cry of inadequacy: *Who can stand in the presence of the Lord, this holy God?* The answer to this age-long question can be found in Psalms 15:1-5 and 24:3-5. The requirement for standing and ministering to and for the Lord has not changed in our day. Preachers may downplay the issue of personal holiness, but the Bible clearly states that 'without holiness no one will see the Lord' (Heb 12:14). Our Lord made the same point when he said, 'Blessed are the pure in heart, for they will see God' (Matt 5:8). In God's rating, your character comes before your charisma.

Their second question, *to whom will the ark go up from here?* (**6:20b**), should have been asked earlier. The fact that they only now notify the inhabitants of Kiriath Jearim that *the ark has returned from the land of the Philistines* (**6:21a**) suggests that the people of Beth Shemesh may initially have wanted to keep the ark for themselves. They had not broadcast its return to the whole nation of Israel so it could be taken to its proper and permanent place. The temptation to hang on to privileges and roles leads to much competition and rivalry among God's servants today. But we need to remember that God has not called us to perform every task in his vineyard, and that he may have someone else whom he wants to carry out a specific ministry. We should constantly be asking the Lord for discernment as to who should do which task if we are not to cause disorder in the family of God and in his service.

The people of Beth Shemesh told the inhabitants of Kiriath Jearim to come and fetch the ark (**6:21b**). This message may seem selfish, as if they were anxious to get rid of the ark now that it had begun to bring trouble to them. But it brought the ark to the place where God wanted it and where it would remain for the next twenty years.

Archaeological discoveries suggest that the reason that the ark was sent to Kiriath Jearim rather than Shiloh, where it had been kept in the past, was that the Philistines had burnt Shiloh after defeating the Israelites.

The men of Kiriath Jearim came and took up the ark of the Lord (**7:1**). They did not leave it on a rock exposed to the sun and rain, but brought it into the house of a man named Abinadab. Eleazar, the son of Abinadab, was set apart to look after it.

7:2-8:22 The Ministry of Samuel

7:2 The Years of Silence

The focus now returns to Samuel, who would be a priest, an intercessor, a prophet, and a judge of Israel. The time between 4:1, when we last heard of Samuel, and 7:2 when he reappears, must have been years of testing, training and spiritual growth. Samuel had once been recognized as a prophet (3:20) but no one seems to have even considered making him the custodian of the ark. But while Samuel was serving God in obscurity, God was preparing the hearts of the people for his ministry as *all the people of Israel mourned and sought after the Lord* (**7:2**). They were no longer mourning for the ark, but for the Lord himself.

7:3-4 Samuel's First Message

When Samuel finally emerged from the shadows, it was to deliver a powerful message calling on the people to repent and turn from their idolatry (**7:3**). He knew that God must be the Lord of all, and that he will not tolerate rivals or half-measures. So he made it perfectly clear what action was required if the people were to hope for God's deliverance. He boldly addressed specific issues, and confronted the people about their worship of *foreign gods* and the *Ashtoreths* (fertility goddesses).

His sermon was no mere story about a tortoise and an elephant, nor a message about himself, nor a promise that prosperity would follow if the people gave offerings. Instead he issued a clear and unambiguous call to repentance and told them what they should do. All effective ministry follows the same pattern, as shown by the ministries of Ezra (Ezra 9-10), John the Baptist (Matt 3:1-12), Jesus Christ (Matt 4:17-25), Peter and the apostles (Acts 2:36-41, 3:11-26), Stephen (Acts 7:44-57) and Paul (Acts 17:30-31).

7:5-14 Samuel's Priestly and Intercessory Ministry

Samuel did not only summon the whole congregation to public fasting and prayer (**7:5-6**), he also prayed for them privately, as the people of Israel recognized when they begged him to continue praying for them (**7:8**; see also 12:23). So powerful were his prayers that many centuries later the Lord would say, 'Even if Moses and Samuel were to stand before me, my heart would not go out to this people' (Jer 15:1). These men stood before God on behalf of their nations until God responded in mercy. They are models of the place that prayer should occupy in our own ministries.

Because of the people's repentance and Samuel's prayers, God repelled a Philistine attack (**7:7, 10-11**). Samuel humbly acknowledged that his help came from the Lord. To remind the people of this, he erected a stone memorial that he named Ebenezer, which means 'stone of help' (**7:12**). He was providing a record for future generations of what the Lord had done, not of what Samuel had done.

As long as Samuel prayed for Israel before God, *the hand of the Lord was against the Philistines* (**7:13**). The territory that the Philistines had taken from Israel was restored to the nation and there was peace between Israel and the Amorites (**7:14**), for 'when a man's ways are pleasing to the Lord, he makes even his enemies live at peace with him' (Prov 16:7).

7:15-17 Samuel's Prophetic Teaching Ministry

Samuel continued to judge Israel all the days of his life (**7:15**). In those days, judges were expected to do more than merely settle disputes and deliver the people from their enemies. They were also responsible for teaching the people the principles of the law and deciding difficult matters of doctrine, lifestyle and worship, as Moses had done (Exod 18:16, 19-20). Samuel is ranked with the judges whose names are recorded in the book of Judges (12:11).

It appears that Samuel's ministry focused on building the lives of the people. He spent more time raising disciples and mentoring others than he did on the usual ceremony of the temple. Eli had been content to sit at Shiloh and let the people come to him, but Samuel set out to bring the word of the Lord and justice to the people. So every year he travelled to Bethel, Gilgal and Mizpah (**7:16**). But he always returned to his home at Ramah, where he judged Israel and built an altar to the Lord (**7:17**).

8:1-9 The Demand for a King

Samuel's ministry was so strenuous that it seems he grew old earlier than his predecessors like Eli. Though he retired early from his public office as judge due to the change of government in the land, he remained the prophet, the priest and the father of the nation. It was he who anointed two successive kings.

Like Eli, Samuel had two sons, named Joel and Abijah (**8:2**). Samuel must have been careful in the training of his children, and he considered them competent to take his place as judges at Beersheba when he could no longer keep travelling there himself (**8:1**). But his faith in them proved misplaced (**8:3**). Samuel himself had never *accepted bribes and perverted justice,* and his personal integrity was acknowledged by those who trusted him enough to complain openly to him, *Your sons do not walk in your ways* (**8:5**; see also 12:4). That the children of such a righteous leader should turn from the way of integrity is evidence that it is only grace that can ensure that our children follow the Lord.

These young men succumbed to temptation and in doing so they brought disgrace to the ministry of their father. They gave people with ulterior motives an excuse for satisfying their desire to have a king like other nations did (8:4-5).

Samuel must have been deeply hurt by the elders' request to change the system of government, especially seeing that it was his long ministry of prayer and fasting, preaching and teaching that had brought Israel back to God so that they could now enjoy peace and deliverance from their enemies. Why were they asking for a king now, rather than in the corrupt days of Eli and his reckless sons? But instead of lashing out in anger, Samuel took the matter to God in prayer (**8:6**). God had appointed him to his office, and God would know if that office should now end. His reaction is a model for us when we face provocation and seeming rejection.

The Lord reassured him that the request for a king was not a no-confidence vote and not a judgment on him because of some sin he had committed. Rather, the people were rejecting their heavenly king (**8:7-8**).

Only after Samuel had listened to the Lord did he have something to say to those who had demanded a king. God would grant their request, and Samuel would agree to find his own replacement (**8:9a**). Doing this would not be pleasant, but Samuel was never ambitious for position and would not cling to power. Yet he solemnly warned them about what it would be like to be ruled by a king (**8:9b**). He was not trying to threaten or intimidate them to get them to change their minds, but simply warning them what to expect.

8:10-22 The Nature and Behaviour of Kings

Obediently, Samuel repeated *all the words of the Lord* to those who had come requesting a king (**8:10**). He then gave them a clear and accurate prophecy of what would come to pass (**8:11a**). Most of the things the king would do were contrary to what was prescribed in the Law of Moses in Deut 17:14-20. But that was what the people wanted. Had they waited for God to give them a king, or asked his advice about when they should have a king, they would have been given a leader like David, who would have obeyed God.

Samuel warned them that a king would impose himself on them in a way that none of their previous leaders had done. In the past, they had never really served one man. They had voluntarily taken their tithes into the storehouse in the temple. Their daughters or sons had never been servants or slaves. But they did not appreciate the liberty and dignity they enjoyed when God was their king.

By contrast, a human king would require their sons to look after his chariots and horses and to run ahead of him (**8:11b**). No judge or prophet had ever had such a retinue. Labourers would be required to plough the king's farms and to reap the king's harvest, rather than their own (**8:12**). Others would be employed to make him weapons and equipment for his chariots. He would confiscate their best fields and vineyards for himself and his officers, as happened to

Naboth (**8:14-17**; see 1 Kgs 21:1-16). And there was no guarantee that he would actually win their battles.

God solemnly warned them of what was coming and added that *when that day comes, you will cry out for relief from the king you have chosen, and the Lord will not answer you in that day* (**8:18**). Despite this opportunity to think again, the people were obstinate. They refused to listen to God's clear warning. Instead they insisted, *we want a king over us* (**8:19**). They had already made up their minds that they wanted to be like other nations and to have a visible leader in battle, no matter what the cost (**8:20**). They had forgotten all the victories that God had given them in the past. Rebellion closes our eyes to the danger ahead.

Samuel acted as a faithful priest and intermediary and repeated what the people had said to the Lord (**8:21**). Then he waited to hear God's final instruction.

God granted the people's request (**8:22**). This was, however, his permissive will rather than his perfect will. Israel was again on a downward journey spiritually, just as they had been in the wilderness. We, too, need to be aware that just because God is graciously meeting our needs does not guarantee that we are in his perfect will.

9:1-10:27 Appointment of the First King

9:1-17 The Choice of Saul

Saul's genealogy is given in **9:1**. His father is described *as a man of standing,* probably because of his wealth. Saul himself was tall and handsome (**9:2**) – but these are the only characteristics mentioned. We are given no insight into his character or spirituality. He also does not appear to have been too involved in the public matters of his nation, for he had never met Samuel before. Once again, we see God choosing someone who is lowly rather than one of the mighty.

The journey that would bring Saul to Samuel began with an instruction to go and search for some lost donkeys (**9:3**). Saul set out and conducted a thorough search of the surrounding area (**9:4**). God must have noted his faithfulness in carrying out an unglamorous task on behalf of someone else. He was a man who could be sent on an errand and who would do his best to accomplish it. These were quiet qualities that contributed to making him fit to be a leader of his people.

He was about to give up his search, when the servant suggested they consult the man of God who lived in the city they had now reached (**9:5-6**). Although the servant did not know Samuel's name, he had heard of his fame.

Saul knew that in his culture it was not polite to approach a man of God without offering him some gift, but he had nothing left to give (**9:7**). His words reveal his humility. God is not interested in someone who boasts of what he has to give God. Nor does he want someone who thinks that he can have whatever he wants because of his outward appearance, his power of speech, or even his family heritage. He is attracted to those who recognize that they have nothing to offer God.

Saul was also humble in relation to other people. He was prepared to take advice from his own servant, and even to accept a gift from him (**9:8-10**). He certainly started well, though like many he became arrogant after unexpectedly tasting the grace and power of God.

Saul and his servant set out to find Samuel (**9:11-14**). They did not know that God, the great coordinator, was organizing things to suit his own purpose. God had already told Samuel, *I will send you a man from the land of Benjamin* (**9:16**). Saul thought he was looking for donkeys. His father thought he had sent him on an errand. His servant had suggested a plan. But God was working through all these people.

Many times God may use simple errands for parents or others as a way to get someone to a place of divine appointment. He did this with Joseph (Gen 50:20; Ps 105:17-21) and David, who was on an errand to his brothers when he defeated Goliath (17:1-58). Even Saul's long search was part of God's plan to have him arrive at the right time. Do not fret if God is leading you on a winding path. He will make everything beautiful in its own time.

As Saul and Samuel met, there was joyful confirmation in the heart of the old man of all the Lord had told him (**9:17**). We should all pray for similar accuracy of ministry and of insight.

9:18-27 Saul's Talk with Samuel

Saul would be ill at ease until he knew what had become of the donkeys. So Samuel immediately established his reputation with Saul as a true prophet by telling him that the donkeys had been found, before Saul even mentioned them (**9:18-20**).

Samuel also told Saul not to be in too much of a hurry. He must first have a meal with Samuel and thirty others before he could speak to Samuel on his own. Eating with Samuel was a privilege for the thirty guests invited. Saul must have been dumbfounded when he discovered that not only were two seats of honour reserved for him and his servant, but that he was also the one served the best cut of meat (**9:22-23**). When God has made a plan for you, your seat is reserved. You need not take another man's place.

Saul was baffled about why Samuel, whom he had never met before, took such a keen interest in him (**9:21**). Saul knew he was not worthy of all this attention.

After the meal, Samuel took Saul to his own house, where they talked at length on the flat roof (**9:25**). Samuel must have been seeking to impart spiritual wisdom to Saul before he entered into his new responsibilities.

The next morning, Samuel instructed Saul to send the servant on ahead so that he could speak to him in private and deliver *a message from God* (**9:26-27**). We often need to be alone in order to hear God's message and discern the depth of his purpose for our lives.

10:1-16 Saul Anointed King

As soon as Samuel and Saul were alone, Samuel anointed him with oil (**10:1a**). Very often in Scripture, a public announcement that someone has been appointed to an office is preceded by a secret anointing. This was certainly the case with David, who was secretly anointed before he came to confront Goliath (16:13). It will also often be the case in our own ministries.

Samuel explained that the reason he was anointing Saul was *because the Lord has anointed you commander over his inheritance* (**10:1b**). Israel was God's inheritance, and he wanted Saul to know this from the very start. Anointing would not make him the owner of God's people, but would only make him a trustee who must care for them. Paul makes the same point when addressing church elders: 'Keep watch over yourselves and all the flock of which the Holy Spirit has made you overseers. Be shepherds of the church of God, which he bought with his own blood' (Acts 20:28).

Samuel gave Saul an amazingly detailed prophecy of what would happen on his way home (**10:2-7**). When this prophecy was fulfilled in every detail (**10:9-11**), Saul must have been convinced that God was indeed calling and anointing him through Samuel.

Samuel was not the only prophet to achieve such intimacy with God as to know minute details of what God is doing. Elisha had supernatural knowledge when he rebuked Gehazi for taking gifts from Naaman (2 Kgs 5:26) and when he revealed the war strategies of the king of Syria (2 Kgs 6:8-12). Isaiah too made detailed prophecies that were fulfilled. Nor was this gift restricted to OT prophets. Ananias in Damascus was given a clear vision of where Saul of Tarsus was and what he was doing (Acts 9:10-17). The Holy Spirit is still at work in the church today and may grant us this gift too, if we will make ourselves available for him to use and are truly people of prayer. Such a ministry will bring as much assurance to the hearts of our congregation as it did to Saul's heart then.

The most important of the things that would happen to Saul on his way home was that *the Spirit of the Lord will come upon you in power ... and you will be changed into a different person* (10:6). A changed heart and an outpouring of the Holy Spirit are prerequisites for effective service in God's vineyard. They are given to all NT believers when they are born again.

After Saul had been filled with the Spirit, he prophesied among the prophets, as Samuel had predicted (10:6, 10).

Since this incident was intended to be a sign, it was most likely a momentary gift of prophecy rather than a permanent endowment.

The prophets he met were probably a group who congregated around a leading prophet (19:20; 1 Kgs 18:4). Saul's joining with a group like this caused some stir among those who knew him already (10:6, 11) but passed unnoticed in society as a whole. God deals with individuals in private before he puts them in the public eye. Saul had to wait until God chose to introduce him to the nation, for otherwise he would have been faced with the familiar question 'Who made you a leader over us?'

Samuel instructed Saul to go down to Gilgal and wait there for him for seven days. Then Samuel would come and offer a burnt offering of consecration on his behalf as well as a peace or fellowship offering that is eaten in fellowship in the presence of the Lord (**10:8**). God's training of his servants includes a period of waiting during which the fire on the altar of burnt offering must be kindled and kept aglow, and they must learn how to share in fellowship with other believers. Saul was guided through this by his godly mentor.

Although Saul knew beyond doubt that he had been chosen to be king, he did not tell his family his secret (**10:14-16**). He waited for God to reveal it.

10:17-27 Saul Proclaimed King

Saul did not force himself on the nation, but humbly attended the meeting Samuel summoned in Mizpah (**10:17-19**) and waited throughout the process whereby the Lord made his appointment clear to others (**10:20-21**). Even then, he did not push himself forward (**10:22-24**).

Samuel reminded the people of the implications of having a king over them (8:11-17) and then wrote his words down on a scroll that he deposited before the Lord (**10:25a**). The people were left in no doubt about what their choice would mean for them, even as Samuel dismissed them to return to their towns (**10:25b**).

After his coronation, Saul was content to return to Gibeah, his old home (**10:26a**). He did not strike out at those who refused to acknowledge his position and scornfully asked, *How can this fellow save us?* He waited for God to vindicate him and his call (**10:27**). Even when it came to his own escort, he waited for God's selection and relied on *valiant men whose hearts God had touched* (**10:26b**).

Leaders of our time should learn from Saul that it is not self-proclamation that makes one a leader in God's work. Education or social achievements, and even the gifts of the Spirit, should not be used to intimidate people into accepting you as a leader. Genuine leaders must learn to wait for a divine introduction.

11:1-12:25 The Young King

11:1-15 Saul's First Challenge

Saul's first challenge was to battle the Ammonites to rescue Jabesh Gilead (**11:1-3**). The news that the city was under attack reached Saul as he was coming in from the fields. Clearly, he was still living simply and carrying on his normal work (**11:4-5**). But when he heard of the cruel bargain being proposed, *the Spirit of God came upon him* (**11:6**) just as it came on Samson, on Isaiah, on Ezekiel and on others. He was ready to go into battle to defend the Lord's people.

Sacrificing his own oxen, Saul sent out a summons to all the Israelites to join with him and Samuel in battle (**11:7**). He invoked Samuel's authority because he did not presume that his own status was sufficient to make people obey. The response proved that God was at work, for *the terror of the Lord fell on the people, and they turned out as one man*. God mobilized the people to create an army of 300 000 men from Israel and 30 000 from Judah (**11:8**). The people came as the fear of God (not of Saul) came upon their hearts. The same should be true as we summon others to serve the Lord in our churches.

Saul's battle plan involved dividing his troops into three companies and launching an attack very early in the morning. It was completely successful and the siege of Jabesh Gilead was lifted (**11:9-11**). Those around Saul urged him to use this victory as an occasion to punish those who had not accepted him as king (**11:12**; 10:27). But Saul was gracious and meek, and insisted that *No one shall be put to death today, for this day the Lord has rescued Israel* (**11:13**). We should not be found bragging or boasting about work that the Lord himself has done or using God's work as an opportunity to settle old scores.

Saul was also not the one who threw a party to celebrate his coming into his kingdom. Samuel was the one who had summoned the people to Gilgal (**11:14**), where Saul was confirmed as king *in the presence of the Lord* (**11:15**). So far in his reign, Saul had indeed walked humbly before the Lord.

12:1-5 Samuel's Stewardship

At Gilgal, Samuel arranged a service at which he transferred the leadership of the Israelites from himself to Saul. There he delivered a farewell speech to the people he had served since childhood. Moses too had given a farewell speech when he was about to depart as leader (see Deuteronomy 32–33). But whereas Moses knew that he would soon die, Samuel knew that he would still be around for some time to pray for, guide and help the new king.

Samuel provides a model of how we should handle any change of leadership in our churches in Africa. Africa is bedevilled by leaders who hold tenaciously to power until death steals them away, with the baton of leadership still in their bedroom. They leave no instructions for their successors, and so set them up to fail. By contrast, Samuel created a time of transition, where both he and Saul could work together. In this way, Samuel's name and influence helped to mobilize the people behind Saul. Then he gradually faded out of the picture and allowed the new leader to assume full leadership.

Not only was Samuel mindful of his successor, but also of those he ruled. Thus he could honestly say, *I have listened to everything you said to me and have set a king over you* (**12:1**). Though he was personally hurt by their desire for a king and disagreed with it as a policy, he did not simply dismiss it. He took it to the Lord, and then agreed to do what the people wanted. But he does remind the people that they must accept responsibility for the outcome of the process.

The people's excuse for demanding a king was that Samuel was old (8:5). He did not deny it (**12:2**). Leaders must accept the limitations that old age imposes upon them graciously and be willing to let fresh hands come in. In God's work and even in political leadership, we must recognize that it is not a defeat to grow old and to step aside.

Outgoing leaders should give a transparent account of their stewardship to stamp their integrity on the minds of those they led and to lay a firm foundation for the incoming young leaders. So Samuel presents his life for public scrutiny, saying, *Testify against me in the presence of the Lord and his anointed* (**12:3a**). Few leaders have the courage to do this. Many are so secretive about their affairs that no one can make any comment on their tenure in office. Nor was Samuel asking only for the judgment of the elite. He was opening his life up for everyone to scrutinize. Though we know that it is God's measurement of our lives and ministries that counts most, listening to the way our fellow believers see us will make us more effective in our ministry among them.

The leadership issues that Samuel specifically mentions as the grounds for evaluation are those that God had earlier spoken of (**12:3b**; Deut 17:14-17). Saul, the new leader, will face temptations to use his position to amass wealth or to take advantage of his followers by taking their properties for his personal use. Samuel had acted with integrity in the financial area. He had defrauded no one. Nor had he failed in the area of equity and justice, where many leaders fall into favouritism and tribalism. He had not oppressed anyone or denied anyone a fair hearing of his or her case. He had never accepted a bribe.

The people's response to Samuel's challenge is testimony to a life of integrity and transparent holiness (**12:4-5**). The power of Samuel's ministry was the power of his life. The word being preached had become the flesh of the preacher himself. No ministry can be more effective than this. Samuel's example here may even have influenced Paul many years later, when he issued similar challenges to the churches (Acts 20:33; Phil 4:11-12; 2 Thess 3:7).

Samuel set the seal on his accountability by calling on the Lord God and Saul to be his witnesses. Samuel knew that people might be afraid to speak up. But God knows what no one else may know. He is the righteous judge and the one who will make the final judgment on the integrity with which we have worked.

Samuel was acting as role model for Saul, a young man just coming into leadership. He was setting the standard that Saul should maintain.

12:6-15 Samuel's Message

Samuel's personal integrity gained him a position from which he could further instruct the people by reminding them of the history of God's past faithfulness to Israel. Note that he did not use himself and his own integrity as the basis for showing the people how unfaithful they had been to God and even to him, his servant. Samuel would not preach about himself, but about the Lord. No matter how much evil has been done to us, the sin against us must not be the subject of our message. Instead we must help others to see their sin against the Saviour who died for them.

Samuel started at the very beginning, with Israel's deliverance from Egypt. He stressed that it was the Lord who had raised up leaders like Moses and Aaron at that time (12:6, 8).

Whenever their ancestors forgot the Lord and abandoned his ways, he brought trouble on them from their enemies, including the Philistines, the Moabites and the Midianites (12:9-10). God used these enemies to discipline them and bring them back to him (Jdg 2:2-3; 2:12-15). Whenever they cried to the Lord in penitence, he raised leaders and deliverers for them – leaders like Gideon (also known as Jerub-Baal), Barak (along with Deborah), Jephthah and even Samuel (12:11). This cycle of rebellion and rejection, repentance and restoration had characterized the history of the nation ever since they left Egypt under Moses.

Samuel's point is that having or not having a king will make no difference to the people's prosperity. That will depend on their relationship with the Lord. Asking for a king like the other nations when they saw how Nahash the king of the Ammonites led the battle against them was actually a misjudgment of the cause of their troubles. Jehovah has been their king (12:12) and would remain the invisible but invincible power behind them. They would only face defeat when they disobeyed their God (12:14-15).

We too need to remember that if we walk closely with the Lord our God, he will fight our battles. We should not hastily blame our predicaments on other people or on the environment, for at times our troubles may be the direct result of our broken communion with the Lord (Eccl 10:8-9).

12:16-25 God's Testimony to Samuel

God bore witness to Samuel's ministry when he responded to Samuel's prayer by sending thunder and rain, which was most unusual at harvest time (12:16-18). The purpose was not to destroy them or their harvest, but to bring them to an awareness of their sins and of their need for the Lord's mercy (12:19). When they cried out, Samuel exhorted them to serve the Lord with all their hearts and assured them of God's commitment to them (12:20-22). Samuel was a preacher who would not minimize God's severity against sin, and yet also one who never missed an opportunity to point those around him to the saving grace of our God.

As for himself, Samuel was not vindictive and would not stop praying for the people despite the way they had treated him and his sons. He would actually regard it as *a sin against the Lord* if he were to stop praying for and teaching God's people (12:23). Praying and teaching were the pillars of his ministry, just as they would later be for the apostles (Acts 6:2-4).

Samuel continued to engage in this ministry behind the scenes until his death many years later. Retirement from public ministry should not terminate a leader's calling. We need leaders in Africa, both in the church and in society, who will work behind the scene to bring matters before the Lord in prayer and who will make themselves available to be consulted by current leaders.

13:1-14:52 Saul's Fall from Grace

13:1-7 Saul's Self-Reliance

Saul soon began to deviate from the purpose for which he had been placed over the Lord's people. Whereas he had rallied 330 000 men for the fight at Jabesh Gilead (11:8), he now reduced his army to 3000 men and sent the rest of the people home (13:2). We are not told what criteria he used for making this selection, or whether he sought God's guidance in selecting those who would be with him, as Gideon did (Judg 7:1-8). When we make choices of who will serve with us, we should be careful to be guided by the Lord.

Whereas once Saul had been moved to action by the Spirit of the Lord (11:6), he now resorted to propaganda. His son Jonathan led a minor skirmish with the Philistines (13:3a), and Saul quickly grabbed the credit, blowing trumpets all through the land and saying, *Let the Hebrews hear* (13:3b). Whereas Moses had urged the people into action with 'Rise up, O Lord! May your enemies be scattered' (Num 10:35), the news was now 'Saul has attacked a garrison.'

Mobilization for the work of God must not centre on our achievements but on the Lord. We should not seek centre stage, but should remain humble and ensure that none but Christ is seen, known and heard.

Saul may have wanted to focus attention on his exploits and what he was doing as king, but his action intensified the Philistines' animosity towards Israel, so that Israel became *an offence to the Philistines* (**13:4**). When the Lord is no longer in the centre of our actions, our work for him will not draw others to him but will merely cause them offence.

The effect of the attack was simply to provoke the Philistines to mobilize against Israel in huge numbers (**13:5**). Saul had foolishly exposed Israel to a battle they were not prepared for. Recognizing this, many Israelites fled and hid, while others moved across the Jordan to safer territory (**13:6-7a**).

Even Saul's own presence at Gilgal was not enough to calm the fears of those who followed him (**13:7b**). He had acted without waiting for God's advice, and now had no encouragement to offer them.

13:8-15 Saul Usurps the Priest's Office

Saul attempted to rally his troops by stepping into a role that was not his and acting as a priest (**13:8-9**). By doing this, he trivialized the priesthood and diminished the sacredness associated with the burnt offerings. We must learn to stick to the ministry to which God has called us and not try to usurp what others have been equipped to handle.

Samuel was indignant at what Saul had done, and told him that because of his foolish act, he had lost the Lord's favour on his family. His kingdom would pass on to someone else, who was *a man after his* (God's) *own heart* (**13:13-14**). This is the first reference to David, although his name is never mentioned.

Now Saul was faced with two battles, one internal and the other external. The external battle against the Philistines would be easy compared to the internal battle, which Saul was losing. To know that God had rejected him and would no longer go with him into battle was a defeat greater than any the Philistines could inflict. Not only did Saul lose the joy of God's presence, he also lost the fellowship of Samuel. He was left alone on his own to face his enemy. The three thousand men he had chosen had dwindled to a mere six hundred unarmed and frightened troops (**13:15b**).

Though Samuel had spoken emphatically, there might still have been room for repentance and restoration if Saul had sought it. But Saul did not cry out to the Lord like Hezekiah did (2 Kgs 20:1-5). Nor did he plead with the Lord as Moses did (Exod 33:3). Moses prayed for forgiveness for the people, and they were pardoned. But instead of seeking forgiveness, Saul carried on with his preparations for battle. Yet what was the use of his counting his men when the One who truly counts in the battle had already withdrawn? (**13:15a**).

13:16-22 Philistine Raids

The Philistines recognized that Saul's depleted army no longer represented a serious threat and sent out three raiding parties in three different directions (**13:17-18**). Saul's broken communion with God had left Israel as defenceless as a city without walls. The same happens in our lives when we fail to walk with God in daily obedience. We are left defenceless without the sword of the Spirit, the spear of praise and the goads of courage.

Not only were the people demoralized, they were also unarmed. There was no blacksmith in the whole of Israel who could make or sharpen swords and spears (**13:19**). They had coped without these weapons at the battle at Jabesh Gilead (11:11), but then the Lord had been with them and had given them sufficient weapons to win all their battles. At times he had even used the swords of their enemies on their behalf (Judg 7:22). But now their divine help was gone.

The only ones who were able to sharpen Israelite tools were their Philistine enemies (**13:20-21**). And they charged high prices for their services! What a defenceless position! Like the Israelites, we believers too often rely on the world's smith to sharpen our instruments of war against the world, whereas we should be sharpening our spiritual swords, vision and hearing in the presence of God.

The result of this failure to arm was that *on the day of the battle not a soldier with Saul and Jonathan had a sword or spear in his hand* (**13:22**).

13:23-14:23 Jonathan's Victory

Defeat and gloom filled the whole land of Israel. While the Philistines raided at will and set up garrisons at strategic points like Michmash (**13:23**), the king of Israel simply sat under a pomegranate tree in the outskirts of Gibeah (**14:2**). Interestingly, he was accompanied by Ahijah, a great-grandson of Eli, wearing an ephod as a mark of his office and as a means of seeking God's guidance (**14:3**). Apparently the ark of the covenant was also in the camp, for in **14:18** Saul sends for it. Saul still wanted the Lord to be present with him as he faced the enemy. Yet he did not even wait to hear from Ahijah before he rushed into battle (**14:19**).

Each time the roll was called, Saul must have learned that one or more of his six hundred men had left to join the Philistines, or to go into hiding, or to flee across the Jordan River. But faith arose in the heart of Saul's son Jonathan. He was a bold and daring young man, who drew up a plan of action. He did not share his plan with others because he did not want to commit the whole army to battle before he had proved the faithfulness of the Lord in his life. Nor did he share his vision with Saul, for his father had lost touch with God (**14:1**). Saul would have put out the little flame of faith glowing within Jonathan. He might either have discouraged him from trying or have made the plans too public, as he had after the previous raid (13:3).

When others come to us with plans, we must take care not to discourage them because of our own unbelief. We must also not be the types who would rather speak and publicize others than pray for them and support them.

Jonathan's plan involved climbing the steep cliffs that the Philistines thought protected their position (**14:4-5**). But Jonathan was not concerned that these cliffs would be a barrier. He saw the Philistines as *uncircumcised*, that is, as men without a covenant with God, and he trusted in God's power rather than in human strength (**14:6**). If God is at work, then the battle is as good as won. But if God is not fighting for us, we are wasting our time and energy. The issue is not whether we are many or few. Nor is it the state of our facilities, or our excellent organization, or even our politeness that will win over the hearts of men. We need to rely on God to accomplish his purposes. We must not be presumptuous and demand that God act but, like Jonathan, we must rather act in faith in the ability of God to save and deliver.

Although Jonathan did not tell his father of his plan, he did tell his armour-bearer, who was a faithful and daring companion. His response was *Go ahead; I am with you heart and soul* (**14:7**). We all need partners like this to stand by us as we carry out our calling.

Amazingly, Jonathan's daring plan succeeded! Two men climbing on their hands and knees were able to take on and defeat the well-equipped Philistine garrison (**14:8-14**). They proved the truth of the words, 'One of you routs a thousand, because the Lord your God fights for you' (Josh 23:10).

The entire Philistine army was thrown into confusion by the fall of this key garrison (**14:15a**). Their panic was heightened when an earthquake struck (**14:15b**), and some even ended up fighting each other (**14:20**). Those Israelites who had collaborated with the Philistines rejoined their brothers in Israel (**14:21**). Even those who had been in hiding rushed out to share in the victory (**14:22**). *So the Lord rescued Israel that day* (**14:23**).

14:24-46 Saul's Rash Oath

Backsliding often has the effect of producing legalistic rules rather than gracious instruction. Saul, having lost his personal communion with the Lord, became arbitrary in his leadership. He made the people swear a foolish oath (**14:24**). How does fasting help warriors in a battle? It left them with no reserves of strength to pursue the enemy or to engage in physical combat. And it caused them emotional distress as they were all afraid of incurring a curse if they broke their oath and tasted a little water or honey.

Looking at the oath itself, it gives no evidence of arising from commitment to the Lord. It certainly did not inculcate fear of the Lord, but only *fear of the oath* (**14:26**). It seems

to spring from Saul's personal ambition and be all for his own glory. It even prevented the people from enjoying both the victory and the honey that God provided (**14:25**).

Legalism never produces genuine holiness. It only creates fear and encourages hypocrisy, as people live a double life. We must employ the means of grace by the power of the Holy Spirit to bring people into obedience to the word of God, rather than rules and regulations that 'lack any value in restraining sensual indulgence' (see Col 2:20-23).

Jonathan, who had not heard about the oath, tasted some of the honey. The effect was like serving glucose to a long-distance runner. He was refreshed and ready to carry on (**14:27**). There was no question of greed or anything wrong in his desire to eat it.

One of the army immediately informed Jonathan of what his father had forced everyone to do and how it was weakening them. He was obeying the oath, but was clearly bitter about it. This is what happens when people are subjected to rules that do not come from the conviction of their own hearts.

Jonathan's response to the news was *My father has made trouble for the country* (**14:29**). Saul's thoughtless words had resulted in the people missing a golden opportunity (**14:30**). Not only did they have to give up the pursuit at Aijalon (**14:31**), but they immediately fell into more serious sin. Once released from the arbitrary oath, they fell on the spoil in hunger and ate meat with the blood still in it, which was specifically forbidden in God's law (**14:32**; see also Lev 17:10-14). Legalism always leads people to commit more sins than the ones we were creating rules about. It encourages them to focus on things of minor importance and forget the more important issues (Matt 23:23).

When alerted to what was going on, Saul took prompt action (**14:33-34**). He immediately erected an altar to offer sacrifices to atone for this sin (**14:35**). This is said to be the first altar that Saul erected. He had not erected an altar to show his own repentance after offering sacrifices illegally (13:9-13). He had not erected one when he was first chosen to be king. His first altar was public, not private and personal. While his response here was a good one, he should also have been building his private relationship with the Lord. Public ministry should not precede our personal walk with the Lord.

Having exhausted his men, Saul next wished to launch an all-night battle (**14:36a**). His men did not attempt to argue, but simply said, *Do whatever seems best to you* (**14:36b**). Fortunately, the priest was not so ready to encourage action without seeking God's will. It pays to make it our practice to seek his face before taking any action so that we can be sure that we are in the centre of his will. Then he will reveal to us what is wrong in our lives and needs to be fixed.

Saul asked the Lord, '*Shall I go down after the Philistines? Will you give them into Israel's hand?*' but he received no reply (**14:37**). He recognized that this was because of some sin, for sin always blocks the Lord's response to our prayers (**14:38**). The sin in this case was the oath that Jonathan had unknowingly broken. This case epitomizes the problem with a rash vow. It is better not to rush to make a vow, for once it has been made, you make yourself a sinner if you do not honour it (Eccl 5:1-6).

But Saul had still not learned this lesson, for he made a second foolish vow about what he would do to the perpetrator: *As surely as the Lord who rescues Israel lives, even if it lies with my son Jonathan, he must die* (**14:39**). Thoughtless and hasty vows have always made leaders lose their integrity when they find out that they cannot keep them. A vow is binding, regardless of whether it is reasonable or not. Thus we must be careful not only in what we vow to the Lord but also in the promises we make to other people around us. Once we have made a promise, the right thing to do is to fulfil it, no matter how costly it becomes.

If it had not been for the intervention of the people who refused to allow Jonathan to be slaughtered because of a frivolous oath and a careless vow, he would have died a useless death (**14:40-45**). It was not that God particularly held Jonathan to be an offender, but that Saul could not hope to apply one standard to other people and a different one to his own family.

Jonathan was prepared to die (14:43). He did not argue with his father about the rightness of the oath in the first place, or point to the victory that he had won for Israel that day. He was willing to be the scapegoat for the troubles his father had been inflicting on the people of God. This may be the reason why God allowed the people's plea to prevail in sparing Jonathan's life. And he did not allow the Philistines to benefit by Israel's loss of a great leader, as well as by the cessation of the pursuit (**14:46**).

14:47-52 Summary of Saul's Reign

This section seems to be a summary of the way Saul ruled Israel before things went so wrong that Samuel and even the Lord mourned him as though he were already dead (15:35). Before that time, God used Saul to protect Israel from her many enemies (**14:47**).

The details of Saul's family given in **14:49-51** help us interpret the many later references to Saul and his relatives.

Saul's reign can be summarized as follows: *All the days of Saul there was bitter war with the Philistines, and whenever Saul saw a mighty or brave man, he took him into his service* (**14:52**). His mode of recruitment never changed till he died. He chose men simply on the basis of whether they appeared strong and brave, without asking about the condition of their hearts and their relationship with the Lord.

15:1-35 Saul Rejected

15:1-3 A New Commission

Samuel reminded Saul that God did not anoint him to serve his own pleasure and interests, but to carry out God's instructions (**15:1**). It seems that Samuel also felt a need to re-affirm his authority to bring this instruction to Saul, because he began, *'I am the one the Lord sent to anoint you'*.

Before giving Saul his commission, God explained why he was being ordered into battle against the Amalekites (**15:2**). Saul was to contribute to the fulfilment of prophecy rooted in their historical treatment of the people of Israel (Exod 17:8-16; Deut 25:17-19).

We may wonder how God could possibly order the destruction of all the Amalekite *men and women, children and infants* and all their animals (**15:3**). We need to remember that we are all God's property. Just as we have the right to dispose of the things we own, so God has the unquestionable right to dispose of what he owns. However, this incident should never be used to justify our treatment of some other group. No nation or people can own another, and so no nation or people has the right to destroy another. That is solely the prerogative of the owner of all, God himself.

15:4-21 Partial Obedience

Saul obeyed God's instruction to attack the Amalekites (**15:4-5**). While doing so, he took care not to harm the Kenites who lived among them, who had shown kindness to Israel (**15:6**; Judg 1:16). But when God gave Saul total victory over the Amalekites (**15:7**), he did not carry out God's command. Instead he let King Agag of Amalek live (**15:8**). His love of material things led him to destroy only what was useless or worthless, and to keep the best of the sheep and cattle (**15:9**).

In his joy at having won the battle, Saul went to Carmel to erect a monument in his own honour (**15:12**). What a change from the humble man he had been in chapter 11! Now he is quick to erect a memorial to himself, rather than to God who had given him the victory.

But God knew about Saul's instruction to his men to spare the best of the sheep and calves. He knew that Agag was still alive. So the Lord sent a message to his servant, Samuel, beginning with the lamentation: *I am grieved that I have made Saul king*. God was not the only one who was grieved, *for Samuel was troubled, and he cried out to the Lord all that night* (**15:11**). He must have been pleading for mercy and for another chance for Saul. But God's mind had been made up, just as it had been in Noah's time (Gen 6:6).

Early the next morning, Samuel set out to find Saul (15:12). It did not appear that Saul was anxious to meet with him. He may even have been avoiding him. Saul now preferred being with his enthusiastic supporters to being with his teacher and those who would confront him with the truth. When you notice a similar preference in yourself, it is time to check whether you are not going the same way that Saul went.

When Samuel finally caught up with Saul, Saul was defensive. He insisted that he had obeyed God, even if the evidence was against him (**15:13-14**). Then he tried to cover up his disobedience by making it look as if he had a religious motive (**15:15**), although his lack of personal conviction may be evident in his reference to *the Lord your God* rather than 'the Lord our God'.

But God knows our motives, and he had revealed Saul's motives to Samuel (**15:16**). Samuel's opening words lay bare the root of the problem. The young Saul had been a humble and unassuming man whom God had called to serve him (**15:17**; see chs. 9–10). But now he had acquired an inflated opinion of himself and no longer saw any need to take instruction from an old prophet like Samuel. Pride is at the root of all disobedience, for a proud person will not follow anyone else, not even God.

Many of those whom God raises to prominence forget where they were when God picked them up. They start to advertise themselves and their accomplishments more than the God who anointed them for his service.

If pride was the first cause of Saul's downfall, greed was the second cause, as he *pounced on the plunder* and did not destroy everything as he had been commanded (**15:18-19**). Greed for cash or material goods, or even for honour and respect, has destroyed many who have been in God's work.

Saul had also fallen prey to the misconception that he could substitute activities and offerings for personal consecration and commitment to the Lord. We do this when we increase the amount of money we give while decreasing our attendance at services of worship, prayer and Bible study. Saul thought that God would overlook his disobedience if he simply offered a sacrifice (**15:20-21**).

15:22-23 God's Judgment

Samuel promptly put an end to Saul's delusion: *To obey is better than sacrifice* (**15:22**). This principle was the foundation for Samuel's integrity, and ignoring it produced corrupt and greedy priests and prophets like Eli's sons. The point is underscored in the NT (Heb 10:5-7). God seeks those who will obey him implicitly and promptly, rather than those who bring expensive sacrifices to atone for deliberate sin (Isa 66:1-3).

God sees disobedience as more than just a refusal to carry out an instruction. It is an indicator of the state of our heart, and of whether God is indeed the one we serve. Disobedience is thus equivalent to rebellion, and sluggish or incomplete obedience reveals unspoken rebellion. God does not tolerate rivals, and so he acts strongly against disobedience.

Saul had been given opportunities to confess and repent of his sin. But instead he had simply argued about it with Samuel. So he is confronted with God's judgment. This judgment is not arbitrary, but comes *because you have rejected the word of the Lord* (**15:23a**). Saul had acted as if a direct message from the Lord was a minor matter that deserved no deep consideration. Such behaviour was a rejection of the message, of Samuel who had delivered it, and of God who had sent it.

Saul would have known that the universe had been created by the spoken word of God (Gen 1:1). Thus in rejecting that word, Saul was also resisting the spirit and life of God and God's rights as his creator (see also Isa 45:9-10). He had forgotten that 'man does not live on bread alone but on every word that comes from the mouth of God' (Deut 8:3). Rather than treating God's word as a lamp for his feet and the light on his path in life (Ps 119:105), he was seeking to find his own way without it.

Because Saul had rejected the Lord, the Lord had rejected him (**15:23b**; see also 2:29-30; Gal 6:7-8). Saul could no longer count on God's support as he sat on the throne of Israel. His prayers would not be heard. He would not enjoy God's presence. Little things would overwhelm him. God did not strike Saul dead immediately. Instead Saul lived for many years, tormented by the agony of rejection, without communion with God or with his mentor Samuel. He would be reduced to consulting diviners and witches when he sought light and direction (28:7). Saul's fate should lead us to a deep fear of disobedience.

15:24-33 A Partial Repentance

Saul begged for forgiveness, but God refused to give it to him and repeated his rejection of Saul (**15:26b**). Why did God, who repeatedly declares his compassion and mercy in Scripture, refuse to listen to Saul? The answer must be that Saul's repentance was superficial. Samuel had described the offence as 'rejecting the word of the Lord', but Saul saw what he had done as merely a minor violation of one command and of Samuel's instruction (**15:24a**). Fake repentance seeks to reduce the seriousness of sin by speaking as if God's messengers who preach holiness of life are merely seeking to impose their personal will on the people of God.

Moreover, Saul was still seeking to shift the blame. He did not accept responsibility for his action but explained, *I was afraid of the people and so I gave in to them* (**15:24b**). This argument seems implausible, given the people's earlier obedience to Saul's whims (14:24, 36). He had shown no evidence of listening to them or fearing them before.

Saul's final words reveal that he was actually pleading with Samuel, and not with the Lord: *Now I beg you, forgive my sin and come back with me so that I may worship the Lord* (**15:25**). He spoke as if it was only Samuel's pardon that he needed, not God's. It was as if he has decided that if God will not go with him anymore, Samuel's company will be sufficient.

Like Samuel, we need to exercise discernment when dealing with those who claim to be repenting of sins. We must not allow ourselves to be appeased with gifts and praises, as if that is all that is needed, rather than the Lord's forgiveness. We must not lend our blessing to those who are not really repentant by associating with them in a way that suggests that all is well. To act like this brings conflict to the hearts of simple saints who know the word of the Lord and walk daily in his fear. Our response must be like Samuel's *I will not go back with you* (**15:26a**).

In his desperation at Samuel's rejection of him, Saul caught hold of the hem of Samuel's robe, tearing it (**15:27**). This gesture too reveals a fundamental problem with Saul's repentance. He thought that he could force Samuel to do what he wanted. Rather than tearing his own robes and repenting in dust and ashes, he turned his anger outwards.

Samuel used the torn robe as an object lesson to reiterate God's judgment (**15:28-29**), and Saul's response indicates that Samuel had judged his repentance correctly. It was not the horror of sin or the loss of God's favour that bothered Saul. All he was worried about was his possible loss of honour and dignity before his people (**15:30a**). He did not want anyone else to know what had happened between him and God and between him and Samuel. He is like those who want their photograph taken with a prominent person to show how close they are to them. Saul wanted to be able to say, 'Look, Samuel and I worshipped the Lord together.'

Leaders and pastors in Africa are often more concerned about receiving honour and respect than about maintaining a proper relationship with God. They will not be afraid to commit immorality, but will fear having it exposed to others. They will bring in great preachers from abroad, so that they can bask in their reflected glory. Or they will hide their spiritual emptiness under great titles and honorary degrees.

Saul's slide from the Lord is evident in the words he uses. In 15:25 he asked 'that I may worship the Lord', but now all he says is that I may worship the Lord thy God (**15:30b**). God is no longer his God, but Samuel's God.

Saul's shallow repentance was not enough to reverse the judgment, but nevertheless, Samuel agreed to accompany him at this point (**15:31**). Why? Possibly because God does not support rebellion as a means of dealing with anyone he has placed in authority, even when that person has derailed in life. Thus the conversation between Samuel and Saul took place in private, rather than in the public eye. This privacy also gave Saul space to seek genuine restoration if he truly desired it.

In the meantime, no one else in Israel knew that God had rejected Saul, and Samuel kept the secret. In the eyes of the nation, Saul was God's appointed leader, and Samuel knew that he had to be prepared to worship with him until God found a replacement. Even when that replacement had been found and anointed, Saul would remain God's anointed till he died. Samuel rebuked Saul, but he did not publicly flout his authority. In fact he upheld it, which is why he was afraid to go to the house of Jesse to anoint David (16:2). Samuel must also have taught David that he must not touch the Lord's anointed, no matter what the provocation.

It is difficult to resist those who are in authority without tampering with their authority, which was given to them by God. The person may be rebuked, but their authority must still be respected. Like Samuel and David, we may need to exercise patience while waiting for the Lord to remove them or deal with them as he sees fit.

There may also have been another reason why Samuel accompanied Saul. While not revealing the private message he had given Saul, Samuel still needed to publicly put right Saul's disobedience so that no one else would follow in his footsteps. He thus summoned Agag, the king of the Amalekites, whom Saul should have put to death (**15:32a**).

Saul's disobedience meant that Agag had no suspicion of what was coming, and thus had no time to prepare for death (**15:32b**). He certainly had not learned to fear the Lord. This is what disobedience in God's people does to the unbelieving world. It hardens them against the word of God and against his judgment.

Samuel confronted Agag with the fact that God's judgment is not arbitrary, but that one reaps what one sows (Job 4:8). So he told Agag, *As your sword has made women childless, so will your mother be childless among women* (**15:33**). He then executed Agag in front of Saul and all the people – and *before the Lord*.

Though Agag was put to death, some of his sons may have survived. One of them may have been an ancestor of Hamedatha, the Agagite, who was the father of Haman, who planned to slaughter the Jews in the days of Esther and Mordecai (Esth 3:1).

15:34-35 The Parting of Samuel and Saul

Samuel returned home with a heavy heart. Though he would not broadcast God's judgment in order to discredit Saul, he never again sought to see him (**15:35a**). He had lost all influence with him, and his only ministry now would be the private one of prayer. But Saul did not lose his place in Samuel's heart. Samuel wept and grieved for him, probably begging the Lord to bring him to true repentance. He did not rejoice that his prophecies about the problems a king would bring were coming true. Instead, he grieved as he watched the struggles of the nation because it was no longer led by a godly man. Eventually God had to tell him to let go and to move on to anoint another man as king (16:1).

We too may sometimes find ourselves in a situation where it seems that our ministry has been brought to an abrupt end and we mourn unfulfilled hopes. At such a time, we should be like Samuel and focus on prayer and intercession for our fellow believers including those who have let us down.

Saul returned to his own home in Gibeah (**15:34**). He went on with life, but it was empty and his rejection must have weighed on his spirit. His old teacher Samuel would not come to him, and Saul was too arrogant to humbly go to him. He was merely filling the throne while God prepared his replacement.

God too was filled with regret at what had become of Saul (**15:35b**). For many more years God would feed Saul, protect him and provide for him, but Saul still lived under God's judgment. His situation was like that of the people wandering in the wilderness for forty years, until one generation had died and a new one had arisen (Deut 1:34-40). We may wonder why God did not kill him immediately. We have no way of knowing the answer, but we do know that God is patient and kind, and that if Saul had truly sought to return to him, God would have been there for him. Saul's son, Jonathan, certainly won the affection of the Lord, and he might have helped Saul to repent and at least die in God's favour if Saul had listened to him. But Saul grew worse and worse in his rebellion against God.

Yet even in his backsliding, Saul was still an instrument that God used. Saul's persecution of David trained him and produced godly character in him. God can still overrule and use human misbehaviour to produce something glorious. He did this with Pharaoh and he also did it with Saul (Rom 9:17-23).

16:1-23 Introducing a New King

16:1-13 The Anointing of David

While Samuel was clinging to Saul and pleading for restoration of a dying order, God had a different plan. So he told Samuel to stop his mourning for Saul (**16:1a**). He had given Joshua a similar message when it was time for him to stop mourning Moses and move on with God's work (Josh 1:2). Individuals come and go, some by death and some by disobedience, but God's work must go on. Sometimes the successor may not appear immediately, but God will be preparing another person for the task.

It was now time for Samuel to act. He had to fill his horn with oil and set out to anoint one of the sons of Jesse of Bethlehem (**16:1b**). The first time Samuel anointed a future king, God had brought Saul to him (9:16), but this time Samuel was to go to David. God does not always use the same methods, and we must learn to listen for different instructions for different stages of our ministries.

The journey to Bethlehem would not be a problem for Samuel. He had travelled around the country for many years. His question *How can I go?* related more to the changed political environment. He had a legitimate fear that Saul would kill him if he heard that Samuel had anointed a replacement king (**16:2**). He needed to learn new strategies to cope in a new situation.

In changing times we too may be tempted to stay with the way things have been done in the past. We need to remember that while God's message has not changed, the means of presenting it may change. Africa needs a ministry that is relevant in our changing society and yet faithful to the faith of our fathers. We must keep asking the Lord, 'How should I go?' rather than simply copying foreign methods from America, Europe or anywhere else.

Samuel waited for God's strategy for carrying out this assignment, and God directed him to use an ordinary sacrifice (**16:3**). While we must be prepared to change, we must not despise the usual routines if they are the means God wants us to use at this time.

Samuel did what the Lord said, and went to Bethlehem (**16:4**). Obedience is the key to a fruitful ministry (John 2:5). The fear and trembling of the elders of Bethlehem when Samuel arrived tells us that they feared the judgment of God. For them, however, all was well. There was no sin in the picture (**16:5**).

All that the Lord had told Samuel was that he had chosen one of Jesse's sons to be the next king (16:1). When Samuel met these sons, he was so impressed by the appearance of the eldest, Eliab, that he was about to anoint him to be the next king. But God intervened and reminded Samuel that the heart is far more important than looks when choosing someone for a divine assignment (**16:6-7**).

Samuel must have become confused as one after another each of the sons of Jesse was rejected as a potential king (**16:8-10**). Eventually he turned to Jesse and asked, *Are these all the sons you have?* (**16:11**). It turned out there was another brother, the youngest, considered so insignificant that he was not even invited to the sacrifice at the family house.

The Lord sees the end from the beginning. David might still be an insignificant – though handsome (**16:12**) – shepherd boy. But God saw his potential and his heart, and knew that many years in the future he would be the next king. God may also have seen in David that faithfulness that led him to stay with his sheep rather than try to be invited to the celebration at his home. He was prepared to put up with discomfort and danger to carry out his duties. Faithfulness in small things is a prerequisite for all who long to serve God greatly.

Samuel sets us an example in his willingness not to overlook someone simply because they are young. We should not be blinded by people's looks, wealth or status, or even by their education when appointing people to positions in

God's work. These things may all be good in themselves, but a heart to serve God is even more important.

Samuel heard God telling him to anoint David, and this is what he did *in the presence of his brothers* (**16:13a**). Though this action risked causing jealousy, it was important that David begin his life of service to the Lord at home, among his family. Our Lord Jesus first served at home (Luke 4:16-20). Too many are willing to make great claims in foreign lands, where they are not known and where no one can attest to their character. It is far more difficult to have a good testimony among one's family and those who live around one. Yet that is what David was called to do as he went back to looking after the sheep after his anointing (16:19).

The symbolic significance of the anointing oil is revealed in the next words, *and from that day on the Spirit of the Lord came upon David in power* (**16:13b**). The oil on his head would soon dry up, but the Holy Spirit had found a dwelling in his heart. Even in the OT, the oil was only a symbol, and no one is expected to cling to the symbol when the reality is available. That is why in the NT we do not find anyone being anointed with oil for ministry, for now the Holy Spirit comes directly to those whose hearts are right with God. Instead, all that is done is the laying on of the hands of others in the church (for example, Acts 13:3). Going about with bottles of oil, anointing people, trees, cars, carpets, soups and all sorts of things is a bastardization of the meaning of anointing and completely out of keeping with NT theology (except in the type of situation specifically referred to in James 5:14). In the days of our ignorance, we used to wear charms around our waist. These days, the 'charm' may take the form of a bottle of anointing oil that we carry for emergencies. But relying on any such charm is a return to idolatry.

In the OT, the Spirit of God usually came on someone to empower them for a specific task, after which the Spirit would leave them. But David enjoyed the Spirit's presence 'from that day on'. His task of being king over Israel would continue all his life. His awareness of the joy and enabling that the Spirit's presence brought caused him to pray 'do not cast me from your presence or take your Holy Spirit from me' when he sinned (Ps 51:11).

As NT believers, we need to keep in mind that the Spirit of the Lord is not just a good feeling or a powerful emotion, a momentary outburst of uncontrollable force. He is a person who has come to live within us. He does not come and go but remains in our hearts, empowering us to serve the Lord acceptably.

David, though now anointed, was still a very young man. It would be many years before he became king. In those years, he would be shaped and trained to fulfil his calling.

16:14-23 David Plays for Saul

Saul had known the abiding Spirit of God when he was anointed (10:6). But he had turned his back on God, and had become an easy prey for the enemy. Not only had *the Spirit of the Lord … departed from Saul* but an evil spirit came into his life (**16:14**). This spirit made him depressed and prompted him to act wickedly and violently. To walk away from the presence of God is to walk into darkness.

Saul's servants recognized his distress and suggested a way to relieve it (**16:15-16**). The person they identified as best qualified to treat Saul's misery was none other than David (16:18-19). God uses ordinary people to put those he wants to use in the right place of training at the right time. God was making a way for David to be introduced to the palace, to gain the confidence of the people and to develop his gifts and grace.

What Saul required was a skilful harpist (**16:18a**). David had not been practising the harp for some concert or for a career, but because he enjoyed it. He used his talent to compose some psalms that expressed his own heart to God. We should not allow ourselves to lose skills God has given us because of disuse. God may be planning to use them as the bridge that will link us to our destiny.

David was described as *a brave man and a warrior* (**16:18b**). David had not yet faced an army to prove that he was a warrior, but he had faced 'the lion and the bear' (17:36). These feats would have been talked about in the village of Bethlehem, where his skill as a musician would also have been praised. But he was not simply a man of action or an artist, for he was also praised for what he said: *He speaks well.*

Being described as *a fine-looking man* means more than just that David was handsome (**16:18c**). He must have taken care of his body as well as his soul. He was not unkempt but trimmed his beard and kept his clothes clean. All these ordinary things recommended David to the palace and to the king.

But skill in music and good looks are given to many who are not believers. The most crucial quality that made David stand out from all the other talented, handsome young men was mentioned last: *the Lord is with him* (**16:18c**). The servants may have left this characteristic till last from fear that Saul would not want to employ someone who would remind him of what he had lost (16:14). Yet this was the one factor that would make David's service effective. No gadgets, no equipment, no good planning, or good appearance will help us if God's presence is not with us.

David, like Joseph before him and Daniel after him, proved the truth of the saying, 'Do you see a man skilled in his work? He will serve before kings' (Prov 22:29). He entered into Saul's service and became so trusted that he lived at court as one of Saul's armour-bearers, close to the man whose position he would inherit (**16:19-22**).

God positioned David in a place of training where he could be quietly introduced to Israel. He would learn what it is like to serve a king who is not kind. He would learn how to handle success as a subordinate. He would learn how not to be corrupted by the court. He would learn to preserve his own anointing while working with someone whose heart had turned away from the Lord.

Though David was primarily in the palace for spiritual training, God granted him a ministry to Saul. When David played his harp, Saul felt relief from the oppression of the evil spirit (**16:23**).

17:1-58 David and Goliath

17:1-11 The Philistine Attack

Saul was having internal battles with demons, and the Philistines saw this as an opportune time to strike. The enemy will often attack us when we are in a time of spiritual dryness and backsliding; he knows when we are at our weakest.

Each side occupied a hilltop, with the Valley of Elah between them. The Philistines were confident in their weaponry, leadership and strength, and because they had been the victors in the past. The Israelites, by contrast, were demoralized and afraid. Their leader was defeated from within. God was not with him, and Samuel was not present to offer a burnt offering and to deliver God's message before the battle.

So confident were the Philistines that they nominated one champion to lead them in this battle. Goliath from Gath was a huge man, not only in height and size but also in pride (**17:4-7**). He was so confident that his people agreed that he alone should engage in battle, and that in the unlikely event that he was defeated, they would surrender to the Israelites and become their subjects (**17:9**). They were sure that no one in Israel would be a match for their champion.

Goliath bellowed out his challenge to the armies of Israel, boasting of his nationality while dismissing the Israelites as mere 'servants of Saul' (**17:8**). Then he demanded that they send out a man to fight with him (**17:10**).

No one took up his challenge, for *Saul and all the Israelites were dismayed and terrified* (**17:11**). None of them remembered that Dagon, the god of the Philistines, had been broken in pieces before the ark (5:1-4). They did not remember the exploits of Jonathan, who had single-handedly attacked a whole garrison (14:6-15). Because of the sin in Saul's heart, he had lost an awareness of God's power and exaggerated the power of those opposed to God. And his own discouragement had been communicated to his army. The life of a leader affects all those who follow him!

For forty days Goliath was able to bellow defiance at the Israelites twice a day, without eliciting any response other than fear (17:16).

17:12-27 David Comes to the Camp

The spotlight now returns to the family of Jesse. Jesse, who was the grandson of Boaz by Ruth (Ruth 4:21-22), was too old to fight himself, but the three oldest of his eight sons were in Saul's army (**17:12-14**).

The youngest son, David, had last been seen as a musician, playing the harp for Saul (16:21-24). Presumably, he had been sent home when the war broke out. He had humbly returned to caring for his father's sheep (**17:15**). He did not insist that after being at the palace he could no longer be expected to perform such a menial task. Like him, we should not attach such importance to the companionship of powerful people that we forget our primary duty of caring for our sheep.

David may have thought that his position in the palace would eventually lead to his being recognized as the next king. He might have expected that as one of Saul's armour-bearers he would go to the battle with him. But when that did not happen, David was prepared to wait for another divine introduction to the king and to the people of Israel. It is important to learn to wait for divine introductions and not to just grab at every opportunity that crosses our path. If David had refused to leave Saul, he might have been permanently thought of as a musician. It was because he was prepared to withdraw into obscurity that he was able to emerge and be seen with fresh eyes as a warrior.

David had served the king, but he was also prepared to obediently serve his father and to obey his instruction to deliver some bread and cheese to his brothers and their commander (**17:17-18**). So, like Saul (9:3), he set out on an errand without knowing that this was part of God's plan. Jesse certainly had no idea he was sending David into battle and gave him no weapon. But David had the whole armour of God, which has nothing to do with bronze or iron weapons and armour. He bore the presence of God everywhere he went.

David's responsibility in carrying out his duties is apparent even in the minor details of this story. He set out early in the morning. He did not leave his sheep unprotected but made arrangements to leave them in the care of another shepherd (**17:20**).

By God's own timing, David arrived at the army camp at much the same time that Goliath issued his twice-daily challenge (**17:21-23**). Goliath's words aroused fear in others, but they stirred up faith in David. While the others fled, David was lost in thought: Who is this uncircumcised Philistine to defy the host of God? Why can't I go against him in the name of our God?

Saul had promised a rich prize to anyone who was willing to fight Goliath, but no one had dared to take the risk (**17:25**). The soldiers were so sure that whoever challenged him would be killed that they were not tempted by the promise of riches, marriage to the king's daughter and freedom from taxes.

David asked about the reward, but it is clear that what moved him most was not the reward but the insult that *this uncircumcised Philistine* was being permitted to *defy the armies of the living God* (**17:26**). Where others saw an invincible giant, David saw an 'uncircumcised Philistine' – a man who was not in a covenant relationship with God. God would not defend him and he was destined to be driven out of the promised land. The armies of Israel were not merely 'servants of Saul', but the host of the Living God!

We must learn to be like David and see things with the eyes of faith. We must hear things with ears tuned to the frequency of heaven. We must not look at what the eyes can see before we see the invisible. God's presence and communion with David sharpened his eyes (see also Num 13:31-33; 14:9; 2 Kgs 6:15-17).

17:28-31 David Faces Opposition

Like many leaders, David faced opposition, disdain and misunderstanding from those who were closest to him. Eliab, his oldest brother, possibly jealous because God had chosen to anoint David rather than himself, led the attack. He misjudged David's motives and accused him of pride and of neglecting his duty (**17:28**). He never bothered to check his facts, or to enquire whether David had made arrangements for the care of his sheep (see 17:20).

If David had been careless in leaving the sheep without a keeper, it would have provided a platform for the enemy to attack and discredit him. We must be aware that it is not only important to watch the great points of our calling, it is equally crucial to look after the smaller matters that concern our families.

David was humble in dealing with this attack. He did not argue or seek to defend himself. Nor did he insult his brother. He simply replied, *Now what have I done?* and turned to speak to others (**17:29-30**). We must not allow ourselves to be bothered by those who have written us off in advance, but should turn from them to others.

As David spoke, the atmosphere in the camp changed. The men began to rally around David, as if he were their champion, like Goliath was for the Philistines. They reported what he was saying to Saul (**17:31**). God had made a way for David to be brought before Saul, not as a musical shepherd boy but as a warrior bold enough in his faith to confront the arrogant Philistine. It is a good principle for us to wait for God to open the doors to a ministry for us, rather than trying to force them open ourselves.

17:32-37 David Represents God's People

David was demonstrating leadership as he spoke words of courage and faith to Saul: *Let no one lose heart on account of this Philistine* (**17:32**). His words touched the root of the trouble – people's hearts. They had forgotten their heritage in God, and spoke only of Goliath's height, his helmet, his shoes, and his shield. But David spoke of who he was – a mere Philistine! A leader must inject courage into the hearts of his followers by giving them a balanced analysis of the situation.

Saul was nervous because David was still a very young man (**17:33**). To counteract Saul's fears, David shared with him how God had helped him in other private battles. He did not need to exaggerate or make up stories of wars that he never fought. He simply told what God had done in his life. Alone and with no army to back him up, he had fought off attacks by hungry wild animals (**17:34**). His story of killing a lion may have reminded Saul of Samson, the great enemy of the Philistines, who had killed a lion with his bare hands (Judg 14:4-6). We are reminded that anyone who seeks to lead God's people in any way must have an authentic personal history with God. A leader can only take others where he has gone before.

David presented his struggle with the lion vividly, right down to describing how he caught it by its mane and killed it (**17:35**). The mane, the symbol of the lion's strength, became the means of its defeat. David was reminding those listening to him that an enemy's strength may actually be his undoing if God is on our side. David's words must have temporarily distracted the attention of those listening to him from the shouts of Goliath. David, like a true leader, was providing an alternative to gloom and despondency by painting a picture of hope and victory.

In laying out his plans for battle, a leader must not be vague about strategies and must not appear mystic and arbitrary when speaking of divine intervention. It is too simplistic just to say 'God will do it'. So David stressed his courage and skills and outlined the basis of his faith that God would enable him to defeat the Philistine. His first point was that Goliath was an *uncircumcised Philistine* (**17:36**). The reference to circumcision reminded them that they were the covenant people of God, whereas the Philistine's god was the work of a sculptor or blacksmith! Second, this man had *defied the armies of the living God*. He had challenged the living God to battle. God surely must arise to defend his name! Finally, David alluded to the unfailing faithfulness of God. The same Lord *who delivered me from the paw of the lion and the paw of the bear will deliver me from the hand of this Philistine* (**17:37a**). He could speak with great confidence in God because of his personal relationship with him.

David's words inspired even Saul. He immediately gave his approval: *Go, and the Lord be with you* (**17:37b**). As a true leader, David had lifted others up from the valley of depression to the mount of faith and vision.

17:38-47 The Right Armour for the Battle

Saul was eager to assist David in fighting Goliath. But it would have been a disaster had David accepted the offer of Saul's armour and weapons (**17:38**). For one thing, the glory of the victory would then have been shared between God and Saul's equipment, and the miraculous deliverance would have been reduced to a normal battle. But that was not the reason David gave when he politely but firmly declined Saul's offer. He refused them *because I am not used to them* (**17:39**). They may have fitted him well enough, but they were unfamiliar.

As God's servants, we should not jump at a chance to use other people's armour and methods that we have never proved in our own walk with God. Rather than becoming fascinated with the latest equipment, we should be using the equipment with which God has trained us. The battlefield is no place to be learning how to operate a weapon! Too many African leaders are eager to discard what God had used to raise and train them as soon as they meet others from abroad who use erudite language and speak through microphones in air-conditioned rooms. These African leaders then try to sound like Westerners and try to use weapons that are alien to their spirit, weapons that are not the ones God has given us for our particular battle.

David's first victory was in choosing the right weapon for the battle: his staff and his sling (**17:40a**). He made no attempt to disguise the fact that he was trained as a shepherd and had never been in the army. The only ammunition that David needed was five smooth stones from a stream. He had probably long been in the habit of carrying such stones in his shepherd's bag. They did not need to be sharp, for their strength did not derive from their edges but from the power of God that can drive a stone into a hard skull.

David approached the Philistine *with his sling in his hand* (**17:40b**). Note the pronoun here. It was his sling. It had been with him before this battle and was not newly purchased. It was not crafted just for Goliath. Too often, we construct new weapons just for the battle we will face in the coming week. We arrange a hasty program of training counsellors for a crusade. We put together a large choir and fly in teams of strangers to officiate at the crusade. Millions of dollars are spent just to put on a show for a weekend. But the enemy will not be conquered with new untested weapons. He himself knows better than to rely on them, for he uses long-tested temptations that have brought down many believers.

Confident in the invisible but invincible God, David *approached the Philistine.* Goliath responded with his usual tactics of intimidation and ridicule (**17:41-43**). He mocked David's age and his weapons, and *cursed David by his gods,* not knowing that they were powerless against the God of Israel. He boasted of feeding David to the birds.

Such empty talk may frighten those who do not know their God, but David put the battle in the right perspective. He knew that 'the battle is the Lord's' (**17:47**). Like David, and Joshua before him (Josh 5:14-15), we must never forget that God is the worker and we are simply the channels through whom he works.

David started out by declaring that he had come *in the name of the Lord Almighty* (**17:45**). The enemy may come with weapons of iron and brass, and with a spear, sword and shield, but the servant of the Lord knows that 'the name of the Lord is a strong tower; the righteous run to it and are safe' (Prov 18:10). By coming in the name of the Lord, David came as God's own delegate. He is no mere 'servant of Saul' (17:8) but God's representative in the battle. Jesus used the same idea when he taught his disciples to use his name to confront the power of darkness and to heal the sick, saying 'I will do whatever you ask in my name' (John 14:13; see also Acts 3:6, 11-16; 4:9-12). God's servants must only go in the name of the Lord, a truth that David celebrates in Psalm 20:5-8.

David also referred to the Lord as the *God of the armies of Israel* (17:45). The plural 'armies' is odd, for Saul had only one army. But David may have been making the point that Israel had several armies: the visible one that Goliath could see, and the invisible legions of angels who are at God's command.

David approached this battle with clear understanding of who would do the work: *This day the Lord will hand you over to me* (**17:46a**). The secret of victory in every spiritual battle is recognizing that it is the Lord who will deliver the enemy into our hands. This point is made repeatedly in the book of Judges (see, for example, Judg 3:10) and David repeats it in Psalm 60:12.

Goliath had boasted about what he would do to David. David retorted that he would be doing the same to Goliath (**17:46b**). But whereas the Philistine based his boast on the contrast between his own strength and experience and the youthfulness of David, David's boast was based on his confidence in the name of the Lord and his motivation was very different from Goliath's. He ought to win this battle so that *the whole world will know that there is a God in Israel* (**17:46c**). When someone is working purely for God and not for himself, God will surely act.

There was a second lesson David wished to teach. The Israelites had forgotten that *it is not by sword or spear* that the Lord saves (**17:47a**). They had been taught this in the days of Moses and Joshua, and had been reminded of it in the days of Samuel and even in the early days of Saul and Jonathan. But their memories were short. David wanted to use this combat with Goliath to restore confidence in the God of Israel. Rather than making a great investment in weapons of war, the Israelites needed to invest their hearts in personal communion with their God.

David concluded his speech to Goliath with a ringing restatement of his main theme: *the battle is the Lord's* (**17:47b**). This theme would be taken up again in the days of Jehoshaphat (2 Chr 20:15-17). David was basically saying, 'this is not my battle. At best, I am God's errand boy. He may use my hand to throw a stone or whatever, but God is the owner of this battle.' What peace we would know in our ministries if this truth were deeply engraved in our own hearts.

David had started his speech as if speaking for himself. But he ended it with a phrase that made it clear that his victory would also be a victory for the entire people of God, for he uses the plural when he says, *he will give all of you into our hands* (**17:47c**). Whatever God does through any of us is not for our personal benefit but for the benefit of the body of Christ.

17:48-54 David and Goliath in Battle

The two champions advanced towards each other (**17:48a**). As Goliath strode forward, there must have been a great shout from the praise singers in his camp. They did not know that Goliath was up against the invisible forces of the Most High. Instead they rejoiced, thinking that it was to their advantage that Israel had chosen to send a lightly equipped young man like David against their champion. The Philistines must have known that Israel had some expert slingers, who could sling stones at a hair and not miss (Judg 20:16), but they never imagined that this youth could have been one of them. God has chosen 'the weak things of the world to shame the strong' (1 Cor 1:27).

David for his part ran quickly towards Goliath (**17:48b**). He was bold and ready to die for the glory of the God in whom he believed. The Israelites watching him must have been amazed by his courage. But faith in the heart puts strength in the feet of God's servants. David was not on the defensive, but on the offensive. He was out to win, not just to survive. Most Christians do not seek victory. They make do with survival mentality, thinking that we shall only be victorious in heaven. But victory is meant for us here. There is no battle to fight in heaven.

With his sling, David flung a stone that struck Goliath on the forehead. Stunned, he slumped to the ground. David then rushed upon him, seized Goliath's own sword, and cut off his head (**17:49-51a**). In an instant, the battle turned and the Philistines fled. Without their champion, they had no courage to fight Israel (**17:51b-53**).

David cutting off Goliath's head reminds us of how important it is to work for total victory in our spiritual warfare. Partial victory over any vices we may be struggling with is not enough. We should aim at pulling them up by the roots.

If we merely wound the enemy, he will recover and regroup for battle.

David took the head of the Philistine to Jerusalem and not to Bethlehem. This action may imply that Israel had some degree of control of the city. Judah had once conquered it (Judg 1:8), but it had never been brought totally under Israel's control (Josh 15:63) until David's conquest of it (2 Sam 5:6-10). David may even have taken Goliath's head to Jerusalem as a sign to the Jebusites that one day they too would be conquered.

David also took Goliath's weapons (**17:54**). We are reminded of how Christ disarmed powers and authorities and made a public spectacle of them (Col 2:14-15). Later we learn that David gave Goliath's sword to the temple as an offering and as a memorial, and that it was kept there wrapped in a cloth (21:9). By doing this, David avoided using the sword for his own glory and attracting attention to it rather than to the God who had won the victory.

17:55-58 A Divine Introduction for David

The questions in **17:55-58** may seem odd because David had played the harp for Saul (16:21-23). But Saul was now seeing David in a very different light from before. The David he had known was a boy who played the harp, not a valiant warrior. And the David who had set out to meet Goliath was not dressed for the court, but was still in the clothes he would have worn as a shepherd. He still smelled of sheep and carried a shepherd's bag and staff.

But Saul was not the only one to be seeing David in a new light. Even his father and his brothers would have been surprised by this new David. There comes a time in the life of anyone God intends to use for his service when God shows them to their close acquaintants in a new light. Each of us must wait on the Lord for that introduction, rather than shouting out to try to attract the attention of others.

Saul's question about David's family is very significant. He seemed to think that David's family could account for the type of person David was. But while David did have a great genealogy, that was not what made the difference. David's three brothers, who were in Saul's army, shared his ancestry but showed no signs of greatness. What made David great was not his earthly father but his Father in heaven.

18:1-19:24 David at Saul's Court

18:1-5 The Friendship of David and Jonathan

The last chapter brought David into a closer relationship with Saul, and also into a relationship with Jonathan, Saul's son. Jonathan was someone who had earlier demonstrated the same kind of faith and courage as David (14:6).

He would have expected to inherit the kingdom from his father (were it not for Samuel's prophecy – 13:14). He was loved by the people, who had once rescued him from death (14:45). A young man like this might easily have seen David as a rival for the throne and for the affection of the people.

Instead of resenting David's success, Jonathan entered into a deep friendship with him. Their love went beyond that of a woman for her husband, as David would later say in his oration after Jonathan's death (2 Sam 1:26). In that oration, David also spoke of Jonathan as his brother. He may have experienced more love from him than he did from his blood brothers. Jonathan is said to have *become one in spirit with David* (**18:1**). It was as if they were one soul but in two bodies.

Jonathan and David entered into a covenant to remain loyal friends till death (**18:3**). As a sign of this covenant, Jonathan gave David his own robes and his weapons (**18:4**). This act was prophetic, for Jonathan was giving David all that could have been his on the throne. Jonathan was willing to lay down his all for the sake of a friend, who could have been his rival. What a contrast to the attitude of Cain, who killed his brother because Abel's offering was preferred (Gen 4:3-9). What a contrast to the later attitude of Saul to David. Jonathan's attitude was not something he had inherited – it was the fruit of his personal encounter with God.

In refusing to see his father's throne as something to be grasped, Jonathan reflects the lifestyle of our Lord Jesus Christ. He also models the type of love God desires to see in the church (Phil 2:1-8). Such love is without hypocrisy and is prepared to allow each child of God to use his or her gifts without jealousy and competition. In fact, it prompts us to use our resources to help others fulfil God's purpose for their lives.

Do we see such deep relationships among God's servants in Africa? Or are rivalry and competition the reason why we have so many denominations and personal ministries on our streets today? Does the desire to outshine one another lead friends to pull in different directions, so that they end up preaching and speaking against one another?

Jonathan's friendship was God's gift to David. Every leader needs a friend to whom he or she can speak openly about what God is doing in his or her heart.

Saul did not at first see David as a threat, for he did not sense any ambition or greed in him. Instead he saw David as someone who would be useful to him and so he insisted that he remain at court and not return home (**18:2**).

David continued to do whatever Saul told him to do. He went out wherever Saul sent him and behaved wisely, so that his missions were successful (**18:5**). Consequently Saul gave him *a high rank in the army.* Promoting such a young man might have led to resentment from other officers, but instead they were *pleased.* They saw in David, a leader raised by God. No one will struggle with someone who comes in humility but with a definite anointing and wisdom from God.

18:6-9 Praise Singers: A Test for the Heart

A crucial test of the hearts of Saul, David and Jonathan came when the women from all the cities of Israel came out to welcome the victorious army home. Their joy at their safe return was expressed in *singing and dancing* (**18:6**). They sang with naïve enthusiasm, and did not think about how their words might be interpreted by those whose hearts were not pure and selfless (**18:7**).

As Saul heard the words, emotions that had been stirring deep in his heart erupted in jealousy (**18:8**). He was a man with an inferiority complex, a desire to be noticed and pride that did not tolerate anyone else being recognized.

Praise is a good test of the purity of a person's heart (Prov 27:21). Saul was self-centred. He loved praise. He wanted trumpets blown and monuments erected in his honour (13:3-4; 15:12). He would have preferred the song to show him in the most favourable light, even if that meant distorting the facts about the battle.

Brooding jealously on the praise given to David, Saul must have remembered Samuel's prophecy that God would give the kingdom 'to one of your neighbours' (15:28). Could David be that neighbour? From that moment on, *Saul kept a jealous eye on David* (**18:9**).

18:10-30 Saul's Jealousy

The rage and jealousy that was sparked by the women's song continued to eat at Saul until he finally died in battle. His story shows what jealousy can do.

Saul had been behaving quite normally, but the very day after he opened his heart to bitterness and envy, the evil spirit that tormented him came back (**18:10**). The devil seeks avenues of hatred and bitterness in which he can operate freely, and he found those in Saul (see also Jas 3:14-16).

Saul became reckless and determined to eliminate David. He saw an opportunity one day while *David was playing the harp* and Saul was *prophesying.* This prophecy was not a proclamation of the will of God but was probably some kind of ecstatic utterance made under the influence of the evil spirit that now possessed him. He attempted to strike David with his spear, but David escaped injury (**18:11**).

The fact that David was still content to report for duty and play the harp for Saul shows that he had not attached much importance to the women's songs. When Saul attacked him, he did not defend himself or attack Saul. He demonstrates what Jesus had in mind when he spoke about his followers being 'as shrewd as serpents and as innocent as doves' (Matt 10:16).

David walked daily in the presence of God and bore that presence in all he did. But the more Saul saw the presence of the Lord with David, the more he feared him (**18:12**). Backsliders are always in fear of anyone who enjoys the presence of God, for they are reminded more acutely of what they have lost. Thus David's humility, integrity and holiness did not earn him Saul's admiration but his fear.

Saul next attempted to get rid of David by having him killed while fighting the Philistines (**18:13**). But this plan backfired, for David's campaign was so successful that both David's popularity and Saul's fear of him grew (**18:14-16**).

Saul tried to neutralize David, using a mixture of bribery and force. He suggested that he would allow David to marry Merab, his eldest daughter, if he promised loyal service to Saul (**18:17**). In making this offer, Saul was conveniently forgetting that Merab had already been offered as the reward for killing Goliath (17:25). But David was not ambitious and had not demanded that she be given to him. When offered the opportunity to marry Merab, he protested that he was unworthy of such an honour (**18:18**), a protest that he later repeated when asked to marry Saul's other daughter, Michal (18:22-23).

Saul, however, could not overcome his hostility to David, and instead of giving Merab to him in marriage, he married her to another man (**18:19**). But not even this deliberate insult was enough to make David rebel or cease to serve Saul.

On discovering that his younger daughter, Michal, was in love with the handsome young commander, Saul saw her love as yet another opportunity to trap David (**18:20-21**). David's objection to the marriage was partly that he could not possibly afford to pay the bride price required to marry the daughter of a king. Saul insisted that the only price he would want was one hundred dead Philistines. David could prove they were dead by bringing their foreskins to Saul (**18:24-25**). To Saul's chagrin, David was not killed while attempting to collect these. Instead, he easily slaughtered twice the required number of Philistines (**18:26-27**). This time, the frustrated Saul had no option but to allow David to marry Michal.

All these attempts to dispose of David were cloaked in deception. Such deceit is typical of the devil, who at times likes to appear as an angel of light. Thus Saul spoke as if the battles he was asking David to fight were 'the battles of the Lord' (18:17; see 17:47). He had his other servants approach David with supposedly private messages, *the king is pleased with you* (**18:22**). The devil can use many strategies to lure and destroy those who are upright in heart.

While jealousy made Saul restless and harmed his relationships with others, David became increasingly popular (**18:30**). The message that was being hammered home to Saul was that *the Lord was with David* (18:12, 14, 28). Rather than welcoming God's blessing on another, Saul merely feared him more and more (18:12, 15, 29). Thus he

comes to the pathetic conclusion described in **18:29**, where Saul is described as *David's enemy for the rest of his life*.

But David was not Saul's enemy. He never rebelled against his master despite all the troubles he faced, but defended his kingdom against Philistine attacks. And he proved that God defends those who serve him from every evil, a truth that he celebrated repeatedly in his psalms.

In the midst of wolves, we must walk victoriously. Conflicts and enemy attacks are the tools God has always used to shape the character of his saints. Do not shudder if he places you in the furnace. Paul reminds us that 'our light and momentary troubles are achieving for us an eternal glory that far outweighs them all' (2 Cor 4:17). For David, this 'moment' lasted several years and landed him in several caves in various deserts. But through all this process he was being refined into a king who could govern the way God wanted.

19:1-10 Saul's Persecution of David

In chapter 18, Saul was disguising his hatred of David, but in **19:1** he throws caution to the winds and tells all his attendants to kill David. He even told Jonathan to do this, ignoring the covenant relationship that existed between the two men (18:3). He does not give any cogent reason for his order, or take into account all the benefits that David has brought to Israel by stopping the Philistine attacks. His behaviour is typical of those who are drunk with power and the desire for personal vengeance. They act arbitrarily and unreasonably.

Saul's behaviour shows how the enemy progresses when someone surrenders to him. Saul had turned from God and allowed a demon to gain control of his heart. Now he was actively opposing God's purposes and had lost his fear of shedding innocent blood.

Whereas Saul was rash and impulsive, his son Jonathan was calm, thoughtful, patient and a faithful friend. He would not allow his relationship with his father to jeopardize his spiritual relationship with God and with David. The love in his heart could not allow him to 'walk in the counsel of the wicked' (Ps 1:1). So he warned David of Saul's plot and advised him to hide (**19:2**). He also developed a strategy for finding out how deep his father's hatred for David was and what safety precautions should be taken (**19:3**). But even when opposing his father's plans, Jonathan was still a dutiful son who did not insult his father, but spoke of him respectfully.

Jonathan is a wonderful example of an intercessor who maintains relationships with opponents so as to be able to break down the wall that divides them. In the same way, servants of God ought to stand between God and other people. Like Jonathan, they must stand beside the Father and hear what the Father says about people and what he is doing or feeling. Then they must report only what they have seen and heard and advise others on how to act. But, unlike Saul, our Father is loving and does not desire the death of a sinner. Our task is to bring people home to a Father who is eager to receive them. Jonathan had the more difficult task of standing with a furious father, who uttered death threats. Yet Jonathan still stood up for the one who was going to take his own place and crown!

Jonathan argued David's case in a clear and systematic way that got his father's attention. He did not flatter his father, nor did he insult him. But he did tell him frankly that he was doing wrong to David (**19:4**). He showed wisdom in the way he marshalled his argument. First, he highlighted the risk that David had taken when he was the only one prepared to face Goliath (**19:5a**). He was reminding Saul that, rather than seeking the throne, David was prepared to die on his behalf. Saul may also have remembered that David had not insisted on receiving the rewards that should have been given to the one who killed the Philistine (17:25).

Second, Jonathan corrected the error in the songs of the women who had credited the victory to either Saul or David. He stressed that it was the Lord who *won a great victory for all Israel* (**19:5b**; see also 17:47). In his hunger for more credit for the victory than David, Saul had forgotten that the Lord was the one who had directed events (see also 1 Cor 3:3-9).

Third, Jonathan reminded Saul of his initial glad reaction to David's victory, before he heard the songs of the women (**19:5c**; see also 18:7-9). Some conflicts will only be resolved if we remember where we were coming from and what we did before the interruption. Saul had been glad and had embraced David and demanded that he stay with him. Why should the songs of some ignorant women change his emotions?

Finally, Jonathan raised a searching question, *Why then would you do wrong to an innocent man like David, by killing him for no reason?* (**19:5d**). Jonathan ended his argument with a question. He had not relied on emotional arguments, but had carefully addressed the issues and set his father the task of justifying his actions. Then he fell silent and waited for a response.

There is much to learn from Jonathan's strategy in our ministry of reconciliation today. Moses had employed a similar approach when pleading with God to reconsider his decision to wipe out Israel (Exod 32:10-14).

Saul listened to what Jonathan said and recognized the truth of his words. But he did not stop to think about the real answer to Jonathan's question. Instead, impulsively as always, he simply swore, *as surely as the Lord lives, David will not be put to death* (**19:6**). It seems that Saul had still not learned how serious it is to make a vow with the name of the Lord. He had not yet confessed his sins against the Lord and against David. Nor had he faced his fear that the Lord was with David whereas God had departed from

him. Instead, as at Gilgal, Saul pretended that everything was right between himself and God (15:30-31). Because the roots of his sin were not dealt with, it would spring up again, no matter how great his vow. We should beware of this trap as we seek to reconcile people to God with the gospel. Nothing can be accomplished without genuine confession and repentance.

Saul's vow was enough to convince Jonathan, and so he brought David back to the court (**19:7**). But David must have returned with caution in his heart. He had learned that Saul was like a chameleon, who could change dramatically and unexpectedly.

For a while, Saul seemed calm, for life seems to have been quiet and there was nothing to arouse his old jealousy. But as soon as war broke out again and David was again successful, all his old emotions returned (**19:8**). Instead of rejoicing in the victory, he must have been asking himself, 'Why David and not me? Why is God always working through him and not me anymore? Soon everyone will forget me and think David is the leader.' At this, the evil spirits came upon him again as he was tempted by his own desires (**19:9**; see also Jas 1:13-14). He slipped back into his depression again, and David returned to playing the harp for him. What a waste of his precious anointing! David's ministry could only bring temporary relief, for Saul was not ready to deal with the root cause of his problem. And that is precisely the kind of ministry we see in many congregations today.

The old demon had come back, and Saul again attempted to spear David. But God helped David to evade the spear (**19:10**). David could have used his popularity and denounced what the king had done, but instead he chose to flee that night. He knew that Saul would not be concerned about breaking his vow. Those who do not fear God cannot stand by their word.

Saul's behaviour must not be excused as madness. A drunkard only does what has been in his heart to do before getting drunk. Saul in his so-called madness still knew whom to target with the spear. If he had been truly mad and acting under the influence of the evil spirit, he would have attempted to kill others in the house, including his sons. But David was his chosen target.

19:11-17 Michal's Rescue of David

Even in his own home, David was not safe, for Saul had sent messengers to watch for him and kill him in the morning (**19:11**). Michal, David's wife, warned him of this. Saul had intended her to be 'a snare to David' (18:21), but her love for him made her choose to side with him rather than with her father. It seems that no one was on Saul's side in his hostility to David.

Michal used the same technique as Rahab the harlot of Jericho and the believers in Damascus: she let down her husband through a window (**19:12**; see also Josh 2:15; Acts 9:25). David thus escaped with his life, but he lost the comfort of his home and marriage and set out on the lonely road of an outcast. Many followers of God have had a similar experience (Joseph in Gen 37:28; Moses in Exod 2:15). God uses conflicts and difficulties to set our feet on the narrow path that leads to glory and the fulfilment of his call on our lives.

Michal cleverly kept David's departure a secret for as long as possible (**19:13-14**). She was prepared to risk the king's anger at her deception (**19:17**). Michal was not as virtuous as her brother, for she kept an idol and lied to her father, rather than telling him the truth as Jonathan had done (19:13, 17). But she did save David's life. Their separation would be a long one, for David could not return to her without her father's permission.

19:18-24 David Finds Refuge with Samuel

David was now a fugitive. Where could he go? Should he go to his old home in Bethlehem or seek refuge in one of the cities he had recently rescued? He decided that the right thing to do was to go to Samuel, the old prophet who had first anointed him and so turned his life upside down (16:13). In his distress, he did not go to his earthly father nor his friends but to his spiritual father (**19:18**). He told Samuel all that happened between him and Saul.

Samuel may not have been surprised, for he was well aware that Saul would kill those who threatened him (16:2). But Samuel was still prepared to provide shelter for David at the hill of Naioth, where a group of prophets lived (19:18). It would have been a similar group to the one in whose company Saul had earlier been filled with the Spirit (10:10).

David's fellowship with Samuel must have been refreshing. Psalms 27 and 91 may even have been written at this time to express his confidence in God despite adversity. Samuel may also have reminded David that Saul was still the Lord's anointed and that, no matter what the provocation, he must not be harmed. He may also have counselled David to stay at a distance from Saul, for he knew that Saul could not be trusted. But God was trustworthy and would bring David to the throne in his own time and in his own way.

Saul sent out informants to track down David. When he heard that he was at Ramah, he promptly sent messengers to capture him (**19:19-20a**). Saul had clearly lost his fear of Samuel and of God's house.

But God has the power to deliver his own. When the squad sent to arrest David met the company of prophets prophesying under Samuel's leadership, the Spirit of God came on them and they also prophesied (**19:20b**). They were swept off their feet into some kind of divine ecstasy.

Under the influence of the Holy Spirit, they acted as if they were prophets themselves.

Saul waited in vain for their return. When he was told what had happened, he must have been furious at seeing yet another example of God's blessing on David. He sent another group of men to arrest David, with the same result (**19:21**). The same thing happened to a third group of men he sent.

Saul decided that the only way to deal with the situation was to go to Ramah himself (**19:22**). Once again he was going to seek Samuel, but this time his aim was not to ask his advice or to worship, or repent. Nor was it to seek to renew the covenant that had brought him to the throne, or even to eat a meal with Samuel again. This time, his goal was to disrupt the work being done there.

There were no security guards on the hill, for none were needed. God was arresting all those who came to cause problems on that day. The Spirit of God fell on Saul and he too started to prophesy as he walked along the road (**19:23**). He is an example of someone who has God's gifts but does not show God's grace in his life and character. Such people may be violent at home, but eloquent in the pulpit; great interpreters of tongues in meetings, but womanizers in the city; great evangelists on crusade grounds, but thieves when it comes to money in the purse. They are charismatic, yet lack character. Such people have brought the faith into such disrepute that unbelievers see us as mere performers and stage managers.

But Saul was not performing, for God had arrested him. He was so caught up that he forgot himself and stripped off his royal robes as he prophesied (**19:24a**). Without his robes, he was reduced to a mere man, or even less if he was naked or nearly so. God was driving home the point that it was not Saul's own merits but solely the mercy of God that kept him on the throne. God had no need to pin down Saul with a spear, as he had tried to pin down David. Instead, he simply had him lie prostrate on the bare ground all night and all day.

It appears that Saul may have remained unconscious until after David left Samuel and returned home to speak with Jonathan. Certainly there is no indication of any interaction between Saul and Samuel or Saul and David. Most likely, when Saul woke he was ashamed to find himself awake naked and humbled for having confronted the power of the Almighty directly.

When Saul first encountered God and was filled with the Holy Spirit, people asked in amazement, 'Is Saul also among the prophets?' (10:11). They were filled with admiration that an ordinary man was granted the Holy Spirit. But here the same words were spoken in ridicule (**19:24b**). Is the wicked Saul also among the prophets? Doesn't he know that he has no part there any longer?

David went to Naioth and found refreshment and fellowship; Saul went there and found only disgrace and ridicule. God knows how to handle people – and how to preserve them. The aged Samuel did not rely on a security guard to keep him safe, as many church leaders do today. Like Elisha and Elijah, he relied on the power of God (2 Kgs 1:9-12; 6:8-23). Jesus too was able to walk calmly among those who wished to arrest or stone him until the time came when he willingly handed himself over to the soldiers in the Garden of Gethsemane. We need to learn to trust God and know his closeness like Samuel did.

20:1-21:15 David's Flight from Saul

20:1-9 Jonathan's Commitment to David

Leaving Saul at Naioth, David set out to meet his friend Jonathan to share with him what was going on. He began their discussion by asking the same question that Jonathan had asked Saul: *What have I done?* (20:1).

Apparently Jonathan did not know of the series of attacks on David at court and at home, nor about the attempts to arrest him at Ramah (19:9-22). He was confident that he would know his father's intentions in advance (20:2). But Saul was no fool. He knew of the relationship between David and Jonathan, and he knew that this son would not tolerate evil. Darkness usually hides from light, and so Saul hid his wickedness from Jonathan. David pointed this out to his friend and showed the seriousness of his concerns by swearing an oath: *as surely as the Lord lives and as you live, there is only a step between me and death* (20:3). He was right, but that step would never be taken until the Lord had finished all he wanted to accomplish in David's life.

Though David was secure in God, he also knew that he needed to act wisely as he accepted Jonathan's offer to do whatever David asked (20:4). This open offer shows that Jonathan was confident that David would never ask him to do anything wrong or to rebel against his own father.

David asked for permission to be absent from the New Moon meal with the king (20:5). Though a backslider, Saul had not reduced his religious activities and he expected all his officers to join him for this monthly religious festival. Such behaviour is typical of nominal Christians, who enjoy the ceremonies but do not care about issues of the heart. David's excuse for being absent would be that he had gone home for a family sacrifice (20:6). Saul's reaction to this news would enable Jonathan to gauge his true attitude to David (20:7).

In confronting his father, Jonathan was risking his own life for the sake of his friend. And David was prepared to lay down his life too. He reminded Jonathan of their covenant relationship, and the obligation it placed them under to be honest with each other. As part of that honesty, he was willing to be killed by Jonathan if he actually deserved death (20:8). If only all our friendships were as honest and as unwilling to condone sin.

20:10-23 Jonathan's Covenant with the House of David

David and Jonathan agreed that because David could no longer enter the palace, Jonathan would be his eyes and ears, and represent his interests, speak for him and keep him informed of what was happening there (20:10-13a). Jonathan's task is similar to that of faithful supporters who pray for missionaries and keep their names before the church at home to mobilize support for them. Those who have to leave home for the sake of the gospel are often desperately lonely and feel the lack of news from home. But David could know that he was not forgotten, and that he had a faithful friend who would tell him all that he needed to know. What a service!

Both men knew that they would soon have to part, but before separating, they renewed their commitment to each other with a covenant that was much more profound than their earlier one, for they had a clearer view of the future (18:3). Jonathan no longer saw David as simply a friend; he now saw him as a man with whom God would walk for many years, just as God had been with his father in the beginning of his reign (20:13b). Thus he asked David to promise to show kindness to him and to his descendants after him (20:14-15a). He was tacitly acknowledging that David would become the next king of Israel. Jonathan did not resent the fact that God was not going to allow him to succeed his father. Instead of working to hinder the divine plan, he did all he could to encourage and help David to fulfil his destiny.

When Jonathan twice spoke of the Lord cutting off *every one of David's enemies from the face of the earth,* it would have been impossible not to think of his own father's hostility to David (20:15b-16). He was ready to be identified with righteousness, even if it was at the expense of his own father's interests, and thus of his own interests.

It was love that led Jonathan and David to renew their oath (20:17). And because their relationship was born in the presence of God and in the love of God, it stood the test of time.

20:24-42 Jonathan's Discovery

Jonathan must have waited anxiously to see how his father would react to David's vacant seat at the table the next night. He would have been relieved the first night, when Saul did not appear upset at David's failure to appear (20:24-25). But in reality, Saul was merely thinking that there was some mundane explanation for David's absence, such as his having done something or touched something that made him ceremonially unclean until evening, and so unfit to attend a religious feast (20:26). Saul did not stop to consider whether his own murderous thoughts might render him unclean as well! Hypocrites are always more anxious to see uncleanness in others than in themselves.

On the second day of David's absence, Saul grew suspicious. He asked Jonathan pointedly, 'Where is your friend?' (**20:27**). When Jonathan admitted that he had given David permission to be absent (**20:28-29**), Saul turned on him in fury, verbally attacking both him and his mother (**20:30**). His attitude is often found in African men. They are happy to claim that every good son is theirs, but any son who causes shame is denounced as the son of his mother. The mother receives no glory when her children do well but is blamed if there is any conflict between them and their father. This situation should not exist in a Christian home. If a man and his wife are indeed one flesh (Gen 2:24), then no such distinctions can be drawn. Both the husband and the wife share responsibility for the successes and failures of their children.

As so often happens when words are spoken in anger, Saul revealed more of his heart and his marital life than he may have intended. He openly revealed his fears that David would supplant him (**20:31**).

Jonathan endured the anger that was meant for David, an anger that even endangered his own life (**20:32-33**). Deeply grieved and ashamed of his father's behaviour, he left the table and did not eat at all that day (**20:34**).

The next morning Jonathan went out to keep his appointment with David (**20:35**; see also 20:19-22). He was a covenant-keeping friend, whom David could trust. Neither of them betrayed the other's secrets, and their relationship transcended family ties. They understood each other's language and symbols of communication (**20:36-40**).

The message David received determined what he would do next. It is thus not surprising that their greeting and their parting were emotional (**20:41**). It was the last time they would ever be able to meet and talk freely, but in spirit they remained loyal friends.

Jonathan's parting words were, *Go in peace, for we have sworn friendship with each other in the name of the Lord, saying, 'The Lord is witness between you and me, and between your descendants and my descendants for ever'* (**20:42a**). Absence and distance would not alter anything between them. Hearts knitted together in love, spirits bound together in the will of God, though they must part for now, there is the hope of meeting again where friends do not part any more, at the feet of him, whom they both loved.

Jonathan went back to the city to remain an ambassador for David even though he knew that his father would never trust him again (**20:42b**). David set off for the wilderness.

21:1-9 David and Ahimelech at Nob

Saul's jealousy had reduced David to an outlaw and a fugitive. David went in search of a place of refuge, and decided to begin at the temple, which was then at Nob. His arrival alone aroused fear and suspicion in Ahimelech, who knew that David normally travelled with his soldiers (**21:1**).

The rift between David and Saul was still not public knowledge, and David did not want it known yet. He did not want to stir up support for himself against the king, nor did he want to risk the priest's refusal to help someone who had lost the king's favour. So David lied about why he was there alone (**21:2**). He should have known from his previous experience that such lies were unnecessary, and that God would have provided for him had he told the truth.

David had probably not eaten or slept properly for three days, for he had been hiding in the fields waiting to hear from Jonathan. So he must have been hungry. If he had companions and was not lying about them too, they would also have been hungry. In his hunger, he did not steal food but instead went to the house of the Lord and asked, *Give me five loaves of bread, or whatever you can find* (**21:3**). He was specific in stating what he needed, but left it to the priest and to the Lord as to how that need would be met. In this, his request is a model for our own prayers.

Ahimelech's response shows that he was meticulous in the discharge of his calling. His first words were, *I don't have any ordinary bread on hand* (**21:4**). Even with a person of David's status, he would uphold the law and not lower the standard of holiness. But he did have *consecrated bread, … provided the young men have kept themselves from women*. Although this may refer to the young men having avoided immorality, it may simply be a reference to the stipulation that any emission of semen, even within a marriage, left a man impure until evening (Lev 15:16-18). When David assured him that all his men were ritually pure, Ahimelech let him take the consecrated bread (**21:6**).

The consecrated bread was the twelve loaves known as 'the bread of the Presence' (Exod 25:30; Lev 24:5-6), which reminded the Israelites of the Lord's daily provision for them. Only priests were allowed to eat this bread (Lev 24:9). David and his men were not priests, but they were in danger of dying from hunger. Jesus referred to this incident when speaking to the Jewish leadership about the difference between the spirit of the law and the letter of the law (Matt 12:3-4). Adherence to the letter of the law leads to legalism. God is more interested in obedience to the spirit of the law, which is intended to be a blessing rather than something that would condemn David's men to starvation.

An ominous note is introduced by the quiet mention of the presence of an Edomite, Saul's head shepherd, Doeg, who was *detained before the Lord* that day (**21:7**). This probably means that he had to stay there for a day to be cleansed of some ritual impurity. As an Edomite, Doeg was a member of a group who had traditionally been Israel's enemies. His later behaviour in killing all the priests (22:18-19) shows that Doeg's spirituality was merely skin deep, a matter of ritual, and had nothing to do with any conversion of his heart.

The fact that Doeg is referred to as being 'detained' at the temple also reveals much about Doeg. He had not come there to worship but to perform a religious duty, and was counting the hours till it would be over. We see similar attitudes in many people today. This type of fulfilment of religious activity produces no lasting fruit of holiness. It only creates a legalistic fear of other people and not a true fear of the Lord.

In the circumstances in which David had left, he had not even been able to take a weapon with him. Knowing that he would need one, he politely asked whether any weapon was available at the temple (**21:8**). He may even have forgotten that the sword of Goliath had been left there (**21:9**). He had not used that sword as a trophy he could show off, but had dedicated it to God. Now God returned it to him in his time of need.

21:10-15 David in Gath

Meeting Doeg at the temple would have convinced David that he could not be safe there, and so he fled further, this time to *Achish king of Gath* (**21:10**). He was seeking refuge in the camp of the enemy! It seems that in his haste and fear, David had not waited for divine guidance but was struggling to protect himself.

David may have hoped that the Philistines would not recognize him, but they did so immediately (**21:11**). The camp of the enemy is probably always more aware of the presence and conduct of believers than their Christian brothers and sisters are, and is always seeking to catch them out and discredit them.

This recognition meant that David now had reason to fear both Saul and the king of Gath (**21:12**). One wrong step born of fear always leads to another and another. Once again, David had to resort to lying to escape from the Philistines. He pretended that he had lost his mind (**21:13**). His deception worked. The king was happy to let him go, thinking that the man they so feared had been reduced to *a madman* (**21:14-15**). God again overruled and delivered his servant, but the deception was unnecessary for God could have delivered him had he waited for the heavenly wisdom.

Although David's actions here left much to be desired, God judged that David's heart was right. But if someone like David could make such serious errors, then we need to be aware that we too may fail when under pressure. It is only the grace of God that will preserve us.

22:1-26:25 David in the Wilderness

22:1-5 From Adullam to Hereth

David still needed further training before he would be fit to lead Israel, and that training could only be given by suffering. He had to learn how to lead not only the rich and successful but also the poor, who were in trouble, distressed or in debt (**22:2**). He had known how to care for and feed his father's flock in the wilderness, but now he had to learn how to care for his own followers. And he had to learn how to do this even while he himself was in distress at the loss of his position and of his young wife.

The men who came to join David were not warriors. Their main qualification was that they were in distress. David became their captain. He slept among them, ate with them, restrained them from evil and poured grace into their lives. He sang his psalms and hymns to them, and taught them until they were a force fit to take their place at a king's side. This is discipleship: taking unqualified believers and training them to take their places in the service of the kingdom. We must teach them how to live and train them to handle the weapons of spiritual warfare. This cannot be done in a one-month programme in a Bible school, nor even in a degree programme. It requires coming alongside others and standing beside them day after day. And those we train will not only be pastors and evangelists but also artisans, laboratory assistants, shop assistants, mechanics, market women – all need to be trained to serve their God and King.

Saul's vindictiveness made it likely that David's family would suffer because of his hatred for their son and brother. So they fled to join him (**22:1**). David recognized that the hard life of a fugitive would be too difficult for his aged parents, and so he arranged a place where they could live in safety (**22:3-4**). He may have sent them to Moab because his father's grandmother had come from there (Ruth 1:4; 4:13, 21-22). David's example, like that of Jesus on the cross (John 19:26-27), reminds us that we must not let the pressure of our lives distract us from filial responsibilities.

In his haste to escape from Saul, David had not waited for the Lord's instructions. But he did not make that mistake this time. When the prophet Gad told him to *Go into the land of Judah* (**22:5**), he obeyed immediately. He did this even though God gave him no explanation of why he should leave the safety of the stronghold, secure among the rocks, and go to the forest where danger could threaten from any direction.

God was training David to be perfect in obedience. This is the quality God looks for in anyone with whom he wishes to share his authority over others. Disobedience had been Saul's downfall.

22:6-19 Saul's Rage Against the Priests

Saul now made no secret of his hatred of David, but declared it openly to all his officials (**22:6**). The fact that he addressed these officials as *men of Benjamin* shows that he was now willing to destroy the fragile unity between the twelve tribes by pitting his own tribe of Benjamin against the tribe of Judah, to which David belonged (**22:7**). He appealed to their self-interest, greed and desire for status, and played on their sympathy, presenting himself as a betrayed father (**22:8**). To do this, he had to exaggerate and fabricate lies against David and Jonathan. His strategy is a common one among those who seek to create division in the body of Christ or in a community.

One of those who heard him, although not a member of Saul's tribe, still saw an opportunity to get ahead. Doeg had seen David at Nob (21:7) and knew that Saul would appreciate being able to take his anger out on someone. So he reported what he had seen, but phrased it as if Ahimelech was consciously in league with David against Saul, rather than merely ignorant of the change in David's status and fooled by the lie David told him (**22:9-10**; see 21:1-2).

Saul sent for Ahimelech and all his relatives, who were the priests at Nob, and confronted them with what Doeg had said (**22:11-13**). Saul was enraged and they had no hope of a fair hearing. But Ahimelech bravely stated the truth that Saul was denying: *Who of all your servants is as loyal as David, the king's son-in-law, captain of your bodyguard and highly respected in your household?* (**22:14**). Once again, Saul was being judged by the life of David. Saul's religious failings were also judged, for Ahimelech makes it clear that David had frequently been to the temple (**22:15**). In ministering to him, Ahimelech had simply been carrying out his normal duties as a priest to a man he knew to be godly.

Saul would not listen and ordered all the priests killed. But none of his men were prepared to carry out such a wicked command against holy men (**22:16-17**). They feared God and mistrusted Saul. Doeg had no such scruples, even though these same priests had served him. Not only did he kill eighty-five priests but he went beyond his commission and destroyed their entire community (**22:18-19**). This massacre was a partial fulfilment of the prophecy that had been made against the house of Eli (2:31-32), yet Doeg is still to be condemned for his slaughter of God's anointed priests.

22:20-23 David's Response

At least one person managed to escape the slaughter. He was *Abiathar, son of Ahimelech, son of Ahitub*, and he fled to join David (**22:20**). With characteristic honesty, David recognized how his own actions had contributed to this massacre. If he had told the truth, Ahimelech would at least have been prepared for trouble and Doeg might not have been allowed to witness what went on (**22:22**). David also realized that he should have taken his own concerns about Doeg's presence more seriously. This guilt must have haunted David for a long time. Deep scars are left when our action or inaction gives an enemy a chance to wreak havoc in the lives of others.

But David did not seek to avoid Abiathar as someone who would rouse unpleasant memories. Instead he welcomed him into his company and promised him safety (**22:23**). Abiathar's ministry would prove to be a blessing to David and his small group in the wilderness, for he had brought with him the ephod, which was used to determine God's will (23:6)

23:1-6 David Saves the City of Keilah

On hearing the news of the Philistine attack on Keilah, David did not simply leap into action, assuming that because he had fought this type of battle in the past, he must do so again. Instead he asked God: *Shall I go and attack these Philistines?* (**23:1-2a**). Like him, we must wait to hear God's voice before starting any new course of action. We must not be content to rely on a general vision or past experience, but must wait for a fresh command.

David received a very clear answer: *Go, attack the Philistines and save Keilah* (**23:2b**). But as so often happens when God tells a leader to do something that looks unfamiliar and possibly dangerous, he immediately ran into objections from his followers: *we are afraid* (**23:3**). They had been nervous about leaving the stronghold at Adullam and moving to the more open country of Judah (22:5). Now David wanted to antagonize another group, so they would have to beware of both Saul and the Philistines. Did they need two enemies rather than one?

Their objections were sound and David took them seriously, as we should when others point out problems with our plans. David went back to the Lord to check that he was not wanting to go into battle merely to satisfy his private ambitions. Once again, he received a clear instruction to fight the Philistines. Coupled with this was a promise: *I am going to give the Philistines into your hand* (**23:4**). This certain word from the Lord was more than enough for David. He went back to his men and injected courage into their hearts because he himself had received courage. Many will not catch a glimpse of divine possibilities awaiting them until their leader acts to lead them in obedience to the will of God.

As promised, God gave David victory and delivered the people (**23:5**).

23:7-14 God Delivers David from Saul

David's obedience to the Lord did not make his own life any easier, for Saul increased his attacks. Sometimes we feel that God does not care and is letting our enemies have their own way. But he knows what he is doing. Until he decides the time to deliver us has come, we must learn to wait, to endure and to grow in the grace and character that only such trials can produce.

Saul was delighted to hear that David was now in Keilah. Like David's men, he thought that the attack had made David more vulnerable and that he would be able to capture him by mounting a siege of the town (**23:7-8**).

David did not assume that because he had helped the people of Keilah, they would protect him. The only one he trusted was the Lord. So he asked the Lord, first, whether Saul would attack, and second, whether he could count on the loyalty of the people of Keilah. God answered yes to the first question and no to the second (**23:9-12**).

We too should not make assumptions about how other people will behave based on their present response. Only the Lord knows how people will react in the face of pressure, and that is why we need to consult him when making decisions.

David did not blame the inhabitants of Keilah. He simply acted on the wisdom that God had given him and left with his men, who now numbered about six hundred (**23:13**). They kept on the move so as to avoid Saul. As soon as David left, Saul abandoned his plan to besiege Keilah.

Had David relied on his own wisdom and stayed in Keilah, the town would have been burned and many innocent people would have died. He would have kept himself alive, but he would have created enmity between the inhabitants of Keilah and Saul, and between them and himself as the cause of their troubles. None of that had been in his plan when he fought the attacking Philistines.

Too often, opposing leaders allow their self-interests to divide the flock. Each asks believers to commit to their side and join in their battles. But David would not allow his personal struggle with Saul to escalate into a civil war within the nation. That would have poisoned both the present and the future.

David also did not assume that just because he was influential and had brought blessing to Keilah, he was entitled to recruit them to fight his personal battles. No civil war must be allowed in the church because of leadership struggles.

Instead of attacking Saul, David withdrew far to the south in the Desert of Ziph. There he could hide in the mountains until the Lord saw fit to introduce him to Israel again. Meanwhile, *day after day Saul searched for him, but God did not give David into his hands* (**23:14**). David did not escape because he was cleverer than Saul or had a stronger fortress. His safety came from God.

23:15-18 Jonathan's Encouragement

David still had one loyal friend, Jonathan. He came from the palace to the desert and *helped him find strength in God* (**23:15-16**). Jonathan knew that David needed more than

just human sympathy. He needed someone to point him to the Rock that will protect us in all storms (Ps 61:2).

Even David, the great warrior, needed to be given comfort and told, *Don't be afraid* (**23:17a**). Fear would make him forget God and the promise he had been given in his anointing. But Jonathan had no doubt that the promise would be fulfilled: *You will be king over Israel, and I will be second to you. Even my father Saul knows this* (**23:17b**). Saul may have thought that he was fighting for Jonathan to succeed him, but Jonathan knew and accepted the will of God. He was prepared to take the second place if that was where God put him.

As at each of their previous meetings, Jonathan and David entered into a covenant before they separated (**23:18**). Each of these covenants was made *before the Lord*. Because their covenant extended beyond themselves to include their descendants, it had to be made before the Lord, who keeps covenants for countless generations.

We need God's help to be faithful not only to him but also to all those with whom we are in a covenant relationship. For many, the primary human covenant will be with their spouse. But we may also be in close covenant relationships with others because we worship the same God. We must show our integrity in our faithfulness to such brothers and sisters in the Lord.

When they parted, Jonathan *went home*. His father was out searching for David, but he would not trust his son to command the army in such a search. All Jonathan could do was stay at home and pray for the safety of both his friend and his father.

23:19-29 The Ziphites' Conspiracy

The Ziphites tried to get into Saul's good books by betraying David to him (**23:19-23**). David did not seek revenge for this betrayal, because he knew they were simply being loyal to their king.

Once again, God demonstrated his power to protect his own – and that we do not understand his ways. He could have stopped the Ziphites from betraying David and stopped Saul from pursuing David. He could have caused Saul to die in his sleep. Instead, God allowed David to feel that all was lost and the chase was closing in before he diverted Saul's attention by permitting a Philistine raid (**23:24-27**). God never comes late to any situation. He comes to our rescue at the right time.

In memory of his great deliverance, David named the rock where it had taken place *Sela Hammahlekoth* (**23:28**), which could be translated as 'rock of escape' (NASB, focusing on God's wonderful protection of David) or 'rock of parting' (NIV, focusing on the separation of Saul and David).

After this narrow escape, David moved further south into the region of the Dead Sea and set up camp at En Gedi (**23:29**).

24:1-2 Saul Resumes the Chase

Having chased off the Philistines, Saul returned to his pursuit of David. Satan is no less vigorous in his attempts to trap believers, no matter how many times he has suffered defeat.

Saul must have had informants who tracked David's movements and monitored his hideouts (**24:1**). Some of these informants were like the people of Ziph (23:19-20). Others may even have pretended to be David's friends. In every team, the enemy seeks to plant a traitor. It is not the exclusion of such informants that guarantees our deliverance, but God himself, who keeps our soul. We must not waste our energy trying to identify or deal with informants, but must focus on doing what God has called us to do.

Saul set out with 3000 chosen men to find David and his 600 men, who had not been chosen for their expertise as soldiers but were simply men who, for various reasons, had fled to be with him (**24:2**; see also 22:2). David was outnumbered five to one – except that God was on his side!

24:3-6 A Test for David's Heart

God may have brought Saul into David's hands to test his heart and to see whether it would be overcome with hatred and bitterness. He was training David to develop a heart of forgiveness and love, like that of Jesus.

The means God used to bring Saul to David was very ordinary. Saul needed to relieve himself and used a cave as a makeshift toilet so that he could maintain his privacy (**24:3**). He must have been partially undressed and have laid down his weapons.

David's men saw how vulnerable Saul was and urged David to strike him down. They even quoted Scripture to back up their position (**24:4**). It can be hard to resist such advice from friends. But David did not yield to them, and all he did was to quietly cut off a corner of Saul's robe.

After having done this, *David was conscience-stricken* (**24:5**). We, too, need to maintain a heart that is sensitive, not one that is seared and dead. David could have rationalized his action and explained the provocation. He could have pointed out that what he did was minor compared to Saul's attempts to kill him. But David knew that two wrongs will never make a right, and that it is not sufficient to be merely better than some others. We will have to give account of our personal walk in this life, rather than a group analysis of what was done in our generation.

Because David was sensitive to God's law, he identified what he had done as a sin. In exposing Saul to possible ridicule, he was attacking an authority that God had put in place. It was wrong to do this, regardless of whether the one in authority was behaving well or badly. Those to whom God has given authority are his representatives, and to assault them is to assault the one they represent. That is why, despite everything Saul had done to him, David still referred to him as *my master, the Lord's anointed* (**24:6**). He did not focus on the fact that the Spirit had departed from Saul or exploit the fact that he had in the past used his music to drive away demons from Saul. Nor did he make pronouncements about Saul's private relationship with God in an attempt to undermine his position. He knew that God would deal with Saul in his own time and in his own way.

David also spoke as if Saul were the only one whom God had anointed. He did not boast that the same man who had anointed Saul had anointed him. David was humble and prepared to make 'himself of no reputation' (Phil 2:7 KJV). He knew that his anointing would only come to fulfilment at a later date. So he was happy to downplay his own role, honour Saul, and prevent others from harming him. This behaviour was not put on for show but came from his heart, as can be seen in his grief at the deaths of Saul and Jonathan (2 Sam 1).

Humility comes from a deep conviction of our nothingness except for the grace of God. It makes us see the grace of God in others and submit to the slightest trace of that grace in them. Humility is the understanding of the boundaries we need to observe in relation to anyone to whom God has given authority. It will lead us to respect the authority that goes with any spiritual gift that God gives.

24:7-16 The Power of the Spoken Word

Rebellion against constituted authority is usually mobilized by inflammatory words that highlight the weaknesses, omissions and faults of the leaders. But words can also quench the flame of rebellion: *With these words David rebuked his men and did not allow them to attack Saul* (**24:7**).

Words can inspire or discourage; they can lead others to faith or turn them away from it. We must take care that our words are always wholesome. When we speak about those in leadership positions, we must focus on their strengths rather than their weaknesses. We must speak from a peaceful and loving heart if we are to be able to restrain those under our charge from becoming rebellious.

Are we not called to work for righteousness in the church and society? We are, but we must not speak so much of the evils within the leadership of the church and society that leaders become objects of scorn. Those who listen to such talk will come to despise all leadership and will not grow in holiness and humility. The Lord must teach us how to use words that can heal and restore the church and society.

We see the effect of wrong words in **24:9**: *Why do you listen to the words of men, saying, 'Behold, David seeks to harm you?'* It was the words of songs and of gossips and flatterers that had made Saul jealous of David and led to this ignoble chase.

Words are powerful. They can build up or tear down a whole community in a matter of days. Rumours may cause more harm than machine guns. God must help us to speak discreetly so that our words honour the Lord and build up people and the church (Jas 1:26; 3:2-6). We must learn to speak the truth, but in a spirit of love. What makes words pleasant or rebellious is the spirit in which they are uttered.

David's spirit is revealed even by his body language, for he *bowed down and prostrated himself with his face to the ground* (**24:8b**). It is also evident in the titles he used to address Saul: *My Lord the king!* (**24:8a**), *my father* (**24:11**), and in the way he humbly speaks of himself as *a dead dog* and *a flea* (**24:14**).

This approach produced a remarkable effect. Saul's hatred and anger melted when David spoke with grace from his heart (**24:16**). Our leaders too might listen if we spoke to them as considerately.

24:17-22 Meekness Wins the Battle

David's refusal to take personal vengeance led Saul to see himself in a new light. He was not convicted by argument or by accusation but by the testimony of David's life. He confessed: *You are more righteous than I … You have treated me well, but I have treated you badly* (**24:17-19**).

Saul ended with an even more remarkable admission: *I know that you will surely be king* (**24:20**). He was not forced to admit this by physical combat but by humble kindness and service. Such service is what the church should be offering.

Saul then began to plead with David not to *cut off my descendants* (**24:21**). David again in the grace of God and with love in his heart, promised that he would not take vengeance on them. Unfortunately, this promise was not kept to the letter, for David played a role in the killing of seven of Saul's male descendants (2 Sam 21:6, 8-9).

Saul's words must have made a deep impression on all who were following him, confirming to them that David was the man God had raised to deliver Israel.

After this meeting, Saul stopped hunting David and returned home, seemingly repentant. But David did not assume that he was safe and returned to the stronghold with his men (**24:22**). In spiritual warfare, one victory does not preclude another battle.

25:1 The Death of Samuel

Samuel fulfilled his mother's vow and served the Lord 'all the days of his life' (1:11). He had served with integrity, courage and love for his people and their leaders. When his public ministry ended, he devoted himself to a life of prayer that God himself noted (Ps 99:6; Jer 15:1). But all lives must end, and eventually Samuel died. So great had been his influence that *all Israel assembled and mourned for him* (**25:1a**). His death drew the land together again in a way that had not been seen for many years. As is so often the case, his ministry was probably more appreciated after

his death than it had been while he was alive, when his critics were probably legion. Fortunately, it is God who is the ultimate judge of his faithful servants.

Samuel was buried *at his home in Ramah*. As a priest, Samuel had not been permitted to accumulate lands and property. God was his true inheritance (Num 18:20). His tombstone might well have read: 'Here lie the remains of a man of prayer; a selfless intercessor; an incorruptible judge and a fearless preacher of righteousness, who entered into the sanctuary service of his Lord at the tender age of three years and there remained until his very last breath at old age.' May we leave a similar legacy to the coming generation.

The conflict between Saul and David may well have ceased during the days when they both mourned Samuel, their mentor. But thereafter David thought it wise to remain in the desert near Maon rather than to trust Saul (**25:1b**).

25:2-44 David and Nabal

25:2-8 David's request

Maon lay close to Hebron in the part of the promised land that had been given to Caleb. In this area, there lived a very wealthy man named Nabal, which means 'Fool' (25:2). His name seems to have fitted him. Nabal was called a fool daily by his parents and colleagues, and even his wife said, 'He is just like his name – his name is Fool, and folly goes with him' (25:25; see comment on names at 1:20).

Nabal was a descendant of Caleb, a man who had wholeheartedly followed the Lord (see Deut 1:36; Josh 14:12-14). But Nabal was nothing like his ancestor. He was rich in cattle and goats, but not in grace and faith (**25:2-3**). By contrast, his wife, Abigail, *was an intelligent and beautiful woman*. How could such a woman have been married to a man so unlike her? Had she been attracted to him by his wealth? Had he deceived her before their marriage or had his character changed over the years? Or had her parents forced her into this marriage? We do not know, but all women should take warning about choosing carefully when it comes to marriage, and parents should beware of pressuring their daughters to marry simply because the man has wealth or worldly influence.

News reached David that *Nabal was shearing his sheep* (**25:4**). David had been a shepherd, and he knew that this would be a time of feasting and celebration at which Nabal would be expected to share food with his neighbours. So he sent ten of his men to go and greet Nabal in David's name (**25:5-6**). The greeting was a standard one in Israel and would be friendly and non-threatening, like the greeting Jesus told his followers to give when entering a house (Matt 10:11-13).

The young men were then instructed to remind Nabal of the services David and his men had provided for his shepherds. The shepherds could confirm that David and his men had not raided their flocks or harassed them in any way. Moreover, they had protected them from attack by others, so that *nothing of theirs was missing* (**25:7-8**). Given the size of his band, David could simply have helped himself to what he wanted, but he had not. However, he was not too proud to ask Nabal for a gift of food for his men. He did not specify how large this gift should be, but left that to Nabal's sense of goodwill.

25:9-13 Nabal's response

Nabal's response reveals much about the man. *Who is this David? Who is this son of Jesse?* was not a request for information but a disdainful dismissal (**25:10a**). It was like asking, 'Why should I give *him* any food?'

But the problem went deeper than that. There was no need for Nabal to know who someone was or where they came from when someone asked for food at harvest time. The law of Moses insisted that some of the crop should be set aside for strangers, the poor and widows (Deut 15:7-11; 24:19-22; Prov 19:17). At harvest time, anyone passing through the land of Israel should be given food. By refusing David's request, Nabal was showing that he did not obey God's laws.

Nabal went on to accuse David of being no more than a rebel who had broken away from his master (**25:10b**). He sided with Saul against the innocent (Prov 17:15). He did not bother to check his facts with his own servants, who had met David and his men (**25:15-16**). They could have told him that David still regarded Saul as his master (24:6, 8) and that Saul recognized David as a future king (24:20).

Nabal's self-centredness is clearly evident in the string of 'I's and 'my's that follows: W*hy should I take my bread and water, and the meat I have slaughtered for my shearers?* (**25:11**). He claimed total ownership of all that God had graciously blessed him with and did not acknowledge that it was a gift from God. He was like the rich fool of Luke 12:16-21. Not surprisingly, his own servants regarded Nabal as *a wicked man* with whom no one could reason (25:17). He would not listen to advice or godly counsel, but acted arbitrarily, without much thought.

Nabal's insults provoked David into making his own foolish decision. He had spared Saul who was seeking to kill him, but set out to kill a man who had simply insulted him (**25:12-13**). He was acting in anger, but 'man's anger does not bring about the righteous life that God desires' (Jas 1:20).

25:14-39a Abigail: A woman in the gap

Abigail demonstrated the intelligence referred to in 25:3. In many ways, she resembles the woman described in Proverbs 31:10-31. Though married to a fool, she maintained her personal character and remained approachable even by the servants. Despite her wealth, she was humble enough

to listen to them (**25:14**). Though beautiful, she was not too proud to kneel down and plead with David (**25:23**). She was also a generous woman, who was horrified by her husband's meanness and hastened to make up for it by providing a large quantity of food (**25:18** – a seah was equivalent to about nine gallons or thirty-seven litres). She must have been hard-working and organized to be able to do all this without the support of her husband.

A quick thinker, Abigail recognized the likely consequences of her husband's behaviour and sprang into action to avert the danger that now threatened her entire household. It was night, but she did not let darkness deter her from doing the right thing at the right time. She also knew that this was not the right time to speak to her unreasonable husband (**25:19**). She knew him well enough to be able to put up with his foolishness without having to quarrel with him incessantly. What a lesson for many wives whose husbands are not believers!

Abigail intercepted David as he was coming down from the mountain of holiness into error (**25:20**). It was a timely intervention, as David himself confessed (25:32-34).

When Abigail saw David, she dismounted from her donkey and bowed before him (**25:23**). Despite being a strong and competent woman, she knew how to submit. Humility and submission were the tools that gave her victory, just as they had given David victory over Saul in 24:8. Yet Abigail's submission to David meant that she was not submitting to her unwise husband. Her example shows that women are to submit to their husbands to save or build up their families. But when submission will harm the family, a wife may have to take the lead for the sake of everyone else in the family, including the unreasonable husband.

Abigail interceded passionately for her husband and her entire household. She needed to do this, for David was enraged and she had to find some way to make him stop and think. She addressed him as *my lord,* not simply to flatter him, but also because she recognized the grace of God in his life. Her next words reveal her to be a true intercessor ready to take the punishment of the one for whom she intercedes, for she says, *let the blame be on me alone* (**25:24**).

Her plea that Nabal's behaviour be ignored because he is foolish and cannot act otherwise reminds us of the Lord's prayer on the cross and Stephen's prayer just before he was martyred (**25:25**; Luke 23:34; Acts 7:60). Abigail wanted David to see Nabal as a fool who was not worth being noticed by someone as wise as David. Her words could be paraphrased like this: 'My husband is not as wise as people think. His name has actually followed him. Folly is with him. He is not just being foolish now. He wakes up and sleeps with folly every day. We cannot expect him to be able to make wise decisions. I did not see the young men, whom you sent. If I had, I would have taken them aside and handled the matter without him knowing about it. It was all my fault because I failed to intercept the young men.'

Abigail's final point was much more spiritual than the first two. She pointed out that David should not seek vengeance himself, but should let the Lord deal with David's enemy as he saw fit (**25:26**). If David did not do this, his conscience would forever be burdened by this rash action (**25:31**). She noted that it was the Lord who had prevented him from taking revenge in the past. At this stage in her speech, Abigail was not standing in the gap for her husband but for David, and was protecting him from sinning against the Lord who said 'You shall not avenge' (Lev 19:18; Deut 32:35; Rom 12:19-20). Abigail begged David to let the Lord handle Nabal, as he had handled all David's other enemies.

Abigail did not present the gift of food as if this was David's main concern. She only presented it when she saw that he was seeing the spiritual reasons why Nabal's misbehaviour should not be allowed to damage his walk with the Lord. In presenting it, she made light of all she had brought, as if it were only good enough for the young men who followed David (**25:27**). Her repeated plea for forgiveness suggested that she was giving a trespass offering, and not something that David should be indebted to her for.

Unlike her husband, Abigail recognized that God was working in David's life. She noted that David had been fighting *the Lord's battles,* whether with Goliath or in other encounters with the Philistines (**25:28**). She was not deceived by the rumours that Saul had been spreading about him, but prayed that no evil would ever be found in David.

Abigail repeated the truth that David was clinging to, that God was watching over his life. She used a metaphor that David could identify with when she spoke of God using a sling to fling away his enemies (**25:29**; see also 17:49). She also spoke with certainty, almost prophetically, about David's future reign, using the phrase *when the Lord* … not 'if the Lord' (**25:30**). She did not want him to start his reign with a sin on his conscience (25:31). She ended her intercession in much the same way that Jonathan had: *remember your servant* (25:28).

David's response to Abigail's plea was a shout of praise. He saw the Lord at work again, using his servant Abigail to guide him on the right path (**25:32**). He gratefully acknowledged the wisdom of her words that had stopped him from committing murder (**25:33-34**). Then he accepted her gift and told her that she could go home in peace (**25:35**). Abigail's intercession had saved her own life and the lives of her family and employees, and had also saved David from committing sin.

On her return, she found her husband presiding over a feast, as if he were a king, totally unaware of the doom he had so narrowly escaped (**25:36**). He was like many in our day who are oblivious of the wrath of God. Nabal was happy,

not because he was at peace with God but because he was drunk. He had not been prepared to help the needy, but was happy to throw a party for his friends.

Abigail knew that it was useless trying to tell him what had happened that night, so she waited till the next morning. When he learned of the danger he had been in, Nabal became *like a stone,* which may mean that the shock of the news led to a stroke that left him paralysed. Ten days later, he died (**25:37-38**). He had refused to share what he had, and had been left with nothing (see also Luke 12:20). God had indeed avenged his insults without David having to do anything (**25:39a**).

We must learn to let God fight our battles, rather than taking matters into our own hands. If he does not seem to act while an enemy attacks us, it may be because their sin 'has not yet reached its full measure' (Gen 15:16).

25:39b-44 Abigail becomes David's wife

Abigail had asked David to remember her, and that was what he did on hearing of Nabal's death. He sent for her and asked her to become his wife (**25:39b-40**). Abigail humbly agreed (**25:41-42**). While becoming David's wife was an honour, it also involved considerable sacrifice. She would have to leave her comfortable home to live with David in caves and deserts. Instead of being in charge of servants and running a large farm, she would be the wife of a fugitive, whose life would be full of uncertainties. There were no sumptuous meals in those caves. She would often be left alone in the camp while David went off to fight the Lord's battles. She would even have to endure being captured by the raiders who burned Ziklag (30:3-5). Yet Abigail consented because she saw this invitation as an opportunity to serve and to contribute to the future of Israel.

David himself had not fared well in terms of marriage. The woman he should have married after killing Goliath had been given to someone else (18:17). He had then been allowed to marry Michal, but only after killing two hundred Philistines (18:27). But after he had been forced to flee, Saul had forced Michal to marry someone else (**25:44**). There seems little doubt that Abigail was wiser and more beautiful than either of these women.

The Bible reports that David had another wife, called Ahinoam of Jezreel (**25:43**). While the Bible does not condemn him for this, and his wives appear to have accepted the situation, we know from the rest of his history that this fondness for women would be a weakness that would affect the rest of David's life (2 Sam 11:2-4) and would be passed on to his son, Solomon. We must watch our hearts and not rush to fill our lives with women (or men) simply because we are experiencing some trial at home.

26:1-25 David Again Spares Saul's Life

26:1-12 David and the sleeping Saul

Saul's repentance was never deep, for while he confessed his sin he made no attempt to root it out of his heart (24:17-21). He had made David swear that he would not destroy Saul's family (24:22), but had given no similar promise in return. Thus it is not surprising that he leapt into action as soon as the Ziphites came with news of David's whereabouts (26:1).

When discord is allowed to linger between leaders, their subordinates tend to try to seek the favour of whichever one they consider the winning side. Saul may not have publicly acknowledged the repentance he expressed to David (24:17-21), and that may be why the Ziphites were still supplying him with information. Alternatively, their previous betrayal of David (23:19) may have left them fearing the consequences if David eventually became king. One sin leads to another.

Again Saul set out with three thousand men to hunt for David (26:2). David was well aware of his movements (26:3-4). He not only kept a watch over Saul's camp (26:5), but like Gideon he actually went inside the enemy camp (Judg 7:9-11).

David asked two of his friends to accompany him on what must have seemed a suicidal adventure (26:6-7). His nephew Abishai responded, *I'll go with you* (26:6). So they set off, trusting in the Lord's protection. God would show them another dimension of his power, when he put three thousand armed men into a deep sleep (26:12b).

Inside the camp, David and Abishai found Saul fast asleep, with his officers and men sleeping around him (26:7). Abishai urged David to kill Saul while he slept (26:8). This was how Jael had delivered Israel from an enemy (Judg 4:21) and Abishai was sure that God had given David a similar opportunity.

But David refused to let Abishai kill Saul. It was not that David was afraid that Abishai would bungle the blow and wake the whole camp. Rather, David's heart had become even more sensitive to God. His encounter with Nabal and Abigail had taught him that it was better to wait for God's vengeance than to take revenge himself (26:10). He would not allow the hatred and bitterness that controlled Saul to rouse those same qualities in himself. Moreover, David was still acutely aware that Saul had been anointed by God and should thus be treated with special honour (26:9, 11a).

Instead of taking back Saul's head as evidence of God's miraculous help for them that day, as Abishai would have liked to do, all that David took back with him was the spear and the water jug that were beside the sleeping Saul (26:11b-12a). Displaying them would provide evidence of how easily David could have killed Saul if he wished and would reprove Abner for his failure to protect his master.

26:13-20 David's speech rouses Saul

David took the spear and jug and quietly carried them to the top of a hill that was far enough away from the camp for him to be safe. Then he shouted to attract the attention of Abner and all Saul's men (26:13-14).

The deep sleep that had taken Abner and his men earlier must have been sent by God, for Abner was easily woken by the distant call. David knew that God had been at work, but he still used the opportunity to reprimand Abner for his poor security arrangements (26:15-16). Such carelessness was a blot on his professional reputation! Having been a soldier in Saul's army, David knew what punishment Abner deserved. His words can be paraphrased: 'You are the one who is actually worthy to die, not me. You all pretend to be the King's friends, but you slept while he was in danger. I was actually the one who protected him from harm!' To prove his point, David displayed the spear and water jug.

Saul suddenly recognized David's voice, and addressed him as *David my son* (26:17). The words, 'my son' acknowledged that Saul's heart had been touched by David's grace and forgiveness. David's response, in which he addressed him as *my lord the king* also underscored David's submission to Saul. David's question, *Why is my lord pursuing his servant? What have I done, and what wrong am I guilty of?* (26:18) is the same one that had been asked by Jonathan (20:32) and Ahimelech (22:14). Every honest person in Israel was asking the same question, but Saul was not ready to answer it because he knew the fault lay within himself.

David did not push the point that the problem lay in Saul's heart. He gave Saul a chance to save face in front of his troops by offering some other options that might explain his hostility. One was that the Lord might have *incited you against me* (26:19a). But if this were the case, then God would accept an offering and pardon a sinner who genuinely repents. And surely the fact that David had twice refused to harm Saul showed that he had repented of any evil he might ever have thought.

The other possibility was that other people were stirring up trouble for David (26:19b). If so, David cursed them for what they had done to him. This curse did not apply to the women who sang David's praises (18:7). They had not intended to make trouble for David, but there may have been others, like Doeg (22:9), who enjoyed fomenting trouble.

The thing that troubled David most was not his loss of position at Saul's court but the fact that he could no longer *share in the Lord's inheritance* (26:19c). He did not claim the land as his own possession but as something that had been given to the nation by God. To drive him away from the land was to drive him away from God. Being deprived of any opportunity to worship at the temple was equivalent to being told, *Go, serve other gods* (26:19d). For a man after God's own heart, this would be the greatest punishment (Pss 27:3-9; 42:1-4; 63:1-3).

David's words must have reminded Saul of his own back-sliding. Rather than wanting to worship in the temple, he had murdered the priests who served there. He had no particular concern about bringing the ark back to the temple. He had not bothered to seek the Lord in repentance after hearing Samuel's judgment. Though he could worship in the temple whenever he wanted to, he could not do it with praise in his heart.

David concluded with a reminder of his own insignificance and how ridiculous it was that the king of Israel spent so much of his time and energy looking for him (**26:20**). While his troops searched for David, the country's borders were left unguarded and other government business was left undone.

26:21-25 Convicted but not converted

David's words prompted Saul to make three confessions. The first was, I *have sinned* (**26:21a**). But once again, his confession was vague. He did not identify the specific sins he had committed and get to the root of the problem. Real confession must be particular and definite. Because Saul does not confess specific sins, he does not promise to stop trying to harm David because what he is doing is sinful, but merely because David has spared his life.

Saul's second confession, *I have acted like a fool* (**26:21b**), also conveys no sense of repentance. It is more a confession of embarrassment than a renunciation of sin. His third statement, I *have erred greatly* (**26:21c**), fails the same tests as his other confessions. None of them seem to have led him to pray or to ask David for forgiveness.

David knew that he could not depend on Saul's confession as a guarantee of safety, so he ignored Saul's request, *Come back, David, my son.* All he did was return the goods he had taken from Saul, even though he was under no obligation to do so (**26:22**).

David ended his last speech with Saul with a statement of his conviction that *The Lord rewards every man for his righteousness and faithfulness* (**26:23**). He transferred the case between him and Saul to the Lord's court, where he was sure justice would be done at the appropriate time.

He made it clear that he expected no reward from Saul. He simply prayed that the Lord would have the same respect for his own life as he had shown for Saul's (**26:24**). We too should not expect a reward for service from anyone other than God.

Saul left David with a parting benediction: *May you be blessed, my son David; you will do great things and surely triumph* (**26:25a**). While he recognized the blessing that would come to David, he refused to contribute to it.

The two men separated (**26:25b**). They would never meet again. But David left in the knowledge that he had done right and would be blessed, while Saul returned humiliated in front of his men, who must have come away with increased admiration for David and increased awareness that he was their future ruler.

27:1-31:13 David's Alliance with the Philistines

27:1-4 David's Move to Gath

David had spoken boldly and acted in faith, but inwardly he was besieged by doubts. His thoughts must have been full of the troubles he faced, the treachery of the Ziphites and the unreliability of Saul's promises, to the point that he ended up thinking, *One of these days I shall be destroyed by the hand of Saul* (**27:1**). He seems to have forgotten all the goodness the Lord had shown to him.

In this state of depression, he decided to go and live among the Philistines. There is no indication that David consulted Abiathar and looked for God's guidance about this step. He had simply had enough! He reasoned that there he would at least be safe from attack by Saul. But he did not take into account the cost of living with the Philistines, and all the lies and deceit he would have to engage in. It is significant that the name of the Lord and prayer are never mentioned in this chapter. It seems that for sixteen months (27:7), David lived without deep fellowship with God.

Human nature is very weak. One day, we may be triumphant and jubilant, and the next we may be overwhelmed by anxiety as if we had never heard the word of the Lord. We see this in Elijah's flight from Jezebel after triumphing over the prophets of Baal (1 Kgs 18–19). We see it in Peter, who one moment could walk on water and the next minute was sinking (Matt 14:25-31). This same Peter one day confesses 'You are the Christ, the Son of the living God (Matt 16:16) and soon afterwards tells a young girl, 'I don't know what you're talking about' (Matt 26:68-70). Whatever we become in God's hands is always by his grace. Nothing is based on our fluctuating strength.

David put his thoughts into action and he, his men and their families all went to Gath and offered to serve *Achish son of Maoch king of Gath* (**27:2-3**).

David's thinking was right on one point: when Saul heard that David had moved out of his territory and was now among the Philistines, he stopped searching for him (**27:4**). Achish, for his part, was pleased to see division among the Lord's people and was happy to provide accommodation for David (27:5-6). He was hoping that this great warrior would forget his nationality and settle down as a Philistine.

The enemy still loves to encourage disunity in the church today. He is happy to make arrangements that help to sustain it and hopes to recruit God's people to fight on his side.

27:5-12 David Settles in Ziklag

David may have been uneasy living in one of the main Philistine towns, and so he asked the king of Gath for permission to settle in *one of the country towns* (**27:5**). This modest request signalled that David was not ambitious or anxious to be seen as a rival to those who had served the king in the past. He knew the danger that can be unleashed by jealousy. He may also have remembered how dangerous too close an association with the Philistines had been for Samson (Judg 14–16).

Achish allocated the border town of Ziklag to David and his men (**27:6**). Achish did not know it, but he was fulfilling the statement that this portion of the promised land would be part of the inheritance given to Judah (Josh 15:31). The Israelites may not have been able to drive out the earlier inhabitants, or the Philistines may have occupied it, but whatever had happened to the town in the past, God was giving David back a portion of his inheritance.

Living in Ziklag kept David out of the public eye. He was able to get news about what was happening in Israel and was free to fight the battles of the Lord. He no longer had to sit by in idleness while his people were oppressed. So he and his men went and attacked the Geshurites, Girzites and Amalekites, who were ancient enemies of Israel (**27:8**). To keep what he was doing secret from the Philistines, they killed off every single inhabitant of the areas they raided (**27:9, 11**). In doing this, he was certainly not following God's will. But the slaughter enabled him to bring back loot for Achish and to report that he had taken this loot from areas that belonged to Judah (**27:10**), giving the impression that he had truly turned against his own people.

These lies won David the confidence of Achish, who believed that David had *become so odious to his people, the Israelites, that he will be my servant for ever* (**27:12**). The enemy would like this to be true of all God's servants.

28:1-2 David's Dilemma

The most difficult moment in David's life must have been when Achish ordered David to accompany him to fight against Israel (**28:1**). How could he fight against the Lord's people? Yet how could he betray the trust Achish had in him and his kindness in granting him asylum? He must have cried out to God for help. What conflict we sometimes bring ourselves into because we have made compromises with sinners rather than waiting for the Lord to help us.

David gave the only answer he could: *You will see for yourself what your servant can do* (**28:2a**). This answer was deliberately ambiguous. David had never fought any battle solely in his own strength. Would the Lord turn away from him this time and make him a liability to the army of the Philistines? David must have been praying desperately for God to help him out of his predicament.

Achish, not realizing the turmoil in David's heart, promised him a reward, *I will make you my bodyguard for life* (**28:2b**). But David had been promised the throne of Israel! Many times the devil offers a child of God appointments that look lucrative at the moment, but which will make him unable to fulfil his true destiny.

The story pauses with David left in suspense, while we are shown what is happening in the camp of Israel.

28:3-25 Saul Seeks the Witch of Endor

An African proverb says, 'Every day is for the thief, but one day is that of the owner'. Someone may seem to get away with something for a long time, but there will be a day of reckoning when all the pleasure that trickery bought will evaporate. That day had now come for Saul.

He was facing a major battle on his own. The Philistines had boldly crossed his borders and come into Shunem at the centre of the country (**28:4**). They knew that Samuel, whose prayers had opposed their enemies, was dead (**28:3a**). They knew that David, the national champion, had been chased out of the land. What better time to invade? No wonder Saul was afraid (**28:5**). The memory of all the wrongs he had done must have weighed heavily on his heart. He badly needed a word from the Lord, but received none (**28:6**). He could not go to Samuel, for he was dead. And their last contact had been in the context of his vicious search for David (19:23-24). He could not go to the priests, for Doeg had killed all of them (22:17-19). All the spiritual channels for getting a word from the Lord had been blocked.

In the days when Saul followed the Lord, he had thrown all the mediums and spiritists out of the land (**28:3b**; see also Lev 20:27). Back then he had not recognized that the rebellion in his own life was as bad as the sin of witchcraft. But now in his desperation he contemplated seeking a medium if he could not get a priest or a prophet of the Lord (**28:7**). The dog returns to its vomit and the sow to its wallowing in the mud (2 Pet 2:20-22). How terrible it is when preachers return to the same sins they preached against, and reassure sinners that they do not matter any more.

Saul's journey to see the medium at Endor must have been dangerous, for it was an eight-mile (13 km) journey over difficult terrain that would have involved skirting the Philistine camp at Shunem. Saul also had to disguise himself before setting out, for otherwise the woman would have strongly denied that she was involved in any illegal activity (**28:8-10**).

The type of divination in which this medium engaged was common in Palestine and the Middle East and is still common in Africa. Here the spirits of the ancestors are often invoked in times of trouble or difficulty, or by those who want to know what the future holds. The spirits consulted are demonic, but they usually take the shape of someone familiar, impersonating that person in order to oppress others

WITCHCRAFT

Belief in witchcraft is approaching epidemic proportions in Africa. While it is easy to understand how nominal Christians can cling to this deep-seated belief, it is disturbing that it is widespread among Christians too. Christian rituals are sometimes seen as little more than a form of protection against witchcraft. Thus mothers 'cover' the beds of their children with the blood of Jesus to ward off witches and evil spirits before putting them to bed. It is also 'poured' on roads to ward off the witches who cause accidents.

The Bible does not support the doctrines of demons, evil spirits and witchcraft that derive from traditional beliefs, but many professing Christians are unaware of what the Bible teaches on this subject. One reason for this is the tendency to interpret the Bible in terms of established opinions and beliefs. Church leaders and missionaries have also tended to dismiss witchcraft as mere superstition, rather than developing an adequate understanding of it rooted in the doctrine of evil. There is an urgent need for the culturally postulated reality of witchcraft to be addressed pastorally with seriousness, sensitivity and respect.

In most African societies, witchcraft is the traditional way of explaining any untimely death, particularly that of a young person. Even if the immediate cause of death is disease or a traffic accident, these are regarded as merely material instruments. Similarly, witchcraft is held to be ultimately responsible for such things as infertility, the break-up of a friendship or a marriage, failure to win promotions, and political setbacks.

There are scores of stories about the activities, powers and confessions of witches. Many young Christians can recount such stories, and many live in fear of being bewitched by envious relatives or friends.

When such stories are told, we need to ask two questions. The first is whether the actions described are metaphorical or physical. For example, even Christians have been accused of eating human flesh and drinking human blood in the Lord's Supper. Are some of the activities of which witches are accused equally symbolic? The second question we need to ask is how we are to judge the truth of the stories. Did the person confessing to using witchcraft only do so under duress? Some stories should be interpreted more as proof that there is a profound belief in witchcraft than as proof of its power.

Yet while we need to clarify these issues, we also need to accept the reality of demonic powers, which are clearly known in both the OT and the NT (see, for example, Acts 13:6-11; 16:16-18). The people of God are warned to have nothing to do with anything related to demonic activity (Exod 22:18; Lev 19:31; 20:26; Deut 18:14; Gal 5:19-21). The Galatians are referred to as bewitched because they were denying their previous beliefs about salvation (Gal 3:1 – although in this verse 'bewitched' may simply mean deceived or deluded). Believers who have dabbled in demonic activities have suffered serious consequences (1 Sam 28; Acts 8:18-23).

The story of Job makes it clear that evil spirits or demons not only exist but also afflict human beings (Job 1–2). Yet Satan or evil spirits can inflict suffering on believers only with God's permission and to achieve his special purposes (Gen 50:20; Acts 2:23). Assurance of this provides security in a world that is full of misery and trouble (Rom 8:31, 35, 37-39). The child of God must say along with Job, 'though he slay me, yet will I hope in him' (Job 13:15; Rom 8:38-39). Ultimately, God will abolish evil, and he already sets limits on it (Job 19:25-27; Heb 9:27).

Believers also need to understand that evil is always a result of sin for which we all share responsibility (Rom 5:12). The consequences of the fall include death, pain and suffering (Gen 3:19), and all are doomed to die (Ps 90:10). Christians should live in such a way that they are ready to die at any moment (Ps 90:10-12). God has not promised that because we are believers we will not die a violent death or suffer disaster (Job 21:22-25).

Suffering may also be the product of bad moral choices that set in motion laws of cause and effect which God has established. Those who are promiscuous have only themselves to blame if they contract HIV/AIDS.

In the face of suffering, it is vital that believers understand that God is sovereign. If witchcraft has power, it is far surpassed by the power of God (I John 4:4). The cross has disarmed demonic forces and stripped them of their power (Col 2:15; Jas 4:7). Christians also need to remember that God is always present with them (Exod 3:14; 2 Kgs 6:16; Matt 28:20) and that he is good and loving, and extends his grace, love and mercy to all his creatures. We need to remind ourselves of this when faced with disaster (Lam 3:21-25). Evil is temporal, but God's love for his children is everlasting.

The Christian does not live as if there are no evil spirits and witches, but lives with the full conviction that the devil and his forces have been conquered. The joy of being a Christian is that our God is sovereign over all evil forces. The clear teaching of the Scriptures is that the Christian has victory in Christ over witchcraft in all its forms (1 John 4:4; 5:4).

Samuel Waje Kunhiyop

or demand a sacrifice. The spirits also play a role in fortune-telling through astrology and palm reading, and in the Yoruba masquerades of Nigeria and other nations. Their presence is felt in the belief in reincarnation that underlies some names we give babies, as if a deceased parent has returned. They are also invoked in ceremonies to call forth the dead at critical times of war in our various cultures. But the Bible strictly forbids any attempt to consult the dead (Deut 18:9-14). God is the only spirit we may seek.

A session with a medium is described in **28:11-14**. A familiar figure appears, who may genuinely have been the spirit of Samuel, but who could equally well have been a demon taking on his appearance. The spiritual world is real and full of activity, but the child of God in Christ has victory over it because at Calvary Christ 'disarmed the powers and authorities' and gave us victory over them (Col 2:14-16). As John reminds us, 'the one who is in you is greater than the one who is in the world' (1 John 4:4).

The words, *Why have you disturbed me by bringing me up?* (**28:15**), are a reminder that it is wrong to disturb the rest of those who have walked with the Lord and are now with him, waiting for the rest of us (Rev 6:9-11).

The devil had no message of comfort for Saul. Saul had not listened to Samuel while he was alive and had not heeded the message taught by David's life. How could he hope that calling Samuel from the dead would make any difference? He had no need to consult the dead to know what he should do (28:15).

The spirit confronted Saul with his sins and reminded him that the Lord had departed from him (**28:16-18**). It foretold his death in the coming battle (**28:19**). While its words came true, we must not treat this as proof that the devil is capable of speaking the truth. He does, but he uses the truth for evil ends. This judgment on Saul totally sapped his strength (**28:20**). His only emotions were grief and fear. The spirit offered no hope of mercy and did not suggest that Saul could still repent.

He left for the battlefield with physical food but sapped of spiritual strength (**28:21-25**).

29:1-11 The Philistines Reject David

The combined Philistine armies were mobilized for a major war against the Israelites. David, still waiting for the Lord to deliver him from this situation in which his lapse of faith had landed him, was at the rear with his men (**29:1-2**).

When the commanders of the Philistine army noticed David's men, they were deeply unhappy about it. *What about these Hebrews?* (**29:3a**) they demanded, meaning 'what are they doing here?' Achish immediately leapt to David's defence, and explained that David had quarrelled with Saul and had been on his side for a year already. Since David had been lying about what he was doing, Achish did not know what David was thinking, and that his heart was still with Israel.

Achish's testimony to David was *I have found no fault in him* (**29:3b**). All believers should receive similar praise from the world – but they should not earn it with lies and deceit as David did! Any testimony we gain by dubious means is not acceptable in the sight of the Lord.

The other Philistine rulers were less trusting than Achish. They insisted that he send David back to Ziklag (**29:4-5**). They were not prepared to trust an ex-enemy in

their army. They knew that blood is thicker than water and that family ties are not easily broken. David might be a saboteur who would turn against them or reveal their weaknesses to his people. They, too, had a vivid memory of the popular song that had started David's troubles (18:7).

God used the Philistine commanders to rescue David from his predicament. Achish obeyed their orders and apologetically summoned David and discharged him from the army (**29:6-7**). David pretended to be upset that his services were being rejected and humbly asked if he had done anything wrong (**29:8**). Achish reaffirmed his personal respect for David: *you have been as pleasing in my eyes as an angel of God* (**29:9**). In his brief acquaintance with David, something of the grace of God in David had become apparent even to this Philistine. Could non-believers say the same about us as we go about our daily lives? Do they see us as angels or as crooks to be avoided? In very hard circumstances, David still maintained some of his integrity. He was careful not to destroy the trust the king of Gath had in him.

Early the next morning, David obeyed Achish and led his men out of the camp (**29:10-11**). God knew that it would have ruined David's reputation with many Israelites if he had opposed them in battle. That was why he intervened to deliver David from another costly mistake that would have done major damage to his career.

30:1-31 David and the Amalekite Raiders

30:1-6 The Amalekite raid

David and his men must have been rejoicing on the three-day journey back to their homes in Ziklag (**30:1a**). But as they approached the city, they grew anxious. There was a smell of burning. They passed some destroyed buildings on the outskirts of the town. And then they saw their homes – reduced to ashes. There had been a raid by the Amalekites. Desperately, they searched for bodies, and the realization dawned that there were none. But there was also no one there. What had happened to their families? Had they been massacred somewhere else? Raped and molested? Taken as slaves? No one was there to give them a clue! As the reality of their loss dawned on them, the warriors wept uncontrollably (**30:1b-4**).

The Amalekites had long been enemies of Israel, who attacked whenever God's people were off guard. Saul had been instructed to wipe them out (15:2-9), but he seems to have done a half-job, either because he was disobedient (as was definitely the case with Agag) or because the Amalekites were spread out over a number of regions.

The Amalekites' hostility to David would have been sharpened by his raids on them (27:8). So Ziklag would have been a target as soon as the city was left defenceless when David and his men marched off to join the Philistine army. But they had also plundered Philistine and Israelite settlements, knowing that the men would be away preparing for battle (30:14).

Everyone who goes out for God in battle for souls must be aware of the need to maintain a garrison at home. Too often, our carelessness has allowed the spouses and children of God's servants to fall prey to temptations. Our enemy does not only attack from the front but also from the rear, where he seeks to cut off our supports.

It seems that David and his men had begun to take the grace of God for granted and were no longer regularly seeking the Lord's guidance. The Lord may even have permitted this attack to call him back to his senses. Or he may have planned to use it to summon David back if he had insisted on staying to fight for Achish. Moreover, this raid ensured that David was completely occupied while the battle between the Philistines and Saul was raging. He could neither participate in the battle nor be blamed for not having participated. Here we have another example of how 'in all things God works for the good of those who love him' (Rom 8:28).

An African proverb says, 'There is nothing God allows on our way without leaving us a space for gratitude'. God did not allow the Amalekites to kill any of the women or children (30:2). Property was stolen, but not destroyed (30:19). It was as if they were restrained by an invisible hand.

But David and his men did not yet know the condition of their loved ones. They wept until they could weep no more. They were so distressed that they turned on David and spoke of stoning him, even though he too had suffered the loss of his wives (30:6a). How often we give in to despair and fail to look up to see God's provision for us.

David did not lash out at the angry men, reminding them of what he had done for them in the past and threatening those who threatened him. Instead he accepted responsibility and *found strength in the Lord his God* (30:6b). He cast all his cares and burdens upon the Lord (Ps 121:1-2).

Leaders need to know how to seek personal encouragement in the presence of the Lord in turbulent times. Weeping over a loss with our subordinates is not enough. We need to be able to comfort them with the comfort we ourselves have received (2 Cor 1:4).

David must have reminded himself of God's promises and his past faithfulness, as he did in his own psalms (Pss 42:5; 103:1-5). Then he wiped away his tears and sought God's wisdom and guidance on what to do next. As an African proverb says, 'In weeping, a leader must still open his eyes to see the road'.

30:7-19 The pursuit of the Amalekites

David called on Abiathar to help him discern the will of God (30:7-8a). He needed clear direction on whether he should pursue the Amalekites or wait for God to restore things in his own way. We may think that the course of action was obvious, but David knew that it was important to listen. We are often too ready to assume that we know the will of God, and we tell him what to do rather than listening for his voice. David was not wasting time by listening to the Lord, as our impatience would suggest, but was saving time. Divine guidance will save us from costly trial-and-error approaches to situations we confront in our families and even in the church. David would not move an inch unless he had heard from the Lord. And God graciously answered him. What a contrast with Saul, who also sought God but received no answer (28:6). Like Saul, David had make mistakes, but God knew that David would repent and turn to him again.

God told David to *pursue them* (30:8b). David was not to sit back passively and wait for God to act, but was to embark on a vigorous and exhausting chase. We should be prepared to put as much effort into pursuing revival and winning back those who are drifting from the faith – including ourselves. Like David, we can be confident that our chase will not be in vain, for God has promised us ultimate victory (Rom 14:11).

David and his six hundred men, who were probably still tired from their three-day march, set off immediately. They ran so fast that by the time they reached the Besor Ravine, two hundred of this fit group of fighting men collapsed with exhaustion. But David did not allow this loss of one-third of his army to discourage him, just as we must not be discouraged when our helpers grow weary. Leaving the exhausted men there, he and the rest pressed on (30:9-10).

David would have had only a general idea of which direction the Amalekites would be taking. So he must have been grateful when God led them to a young Egyptian slave, whose master had callously abandoned him to die of hunger when he became ill (30:11, 13). This is typical of Satan! He repays no one with good. David and his men could simply have killed this straggler from the raiding party or left him to die. But they showed him compassion and gave him the food and water he so desperately needed (30:12). It is no wonder that he was prepared to offer to lead David to the Amalekite camp (30:15-16a).

This incident reminds us not to be so focused on the big things we want to do for God that we neglect the small things and the seemingly unimportant people. God has a place for them in his plans as well, and our success may hinge on their contribution.

As David and his men crept up on the Amalekite camp, there could not have been a greater contrast between their grief and the celebration going on in the camp (30:16b). The enemy celebrates every time God's people suffer loss. And this loss need not simply be material loss. It is also the loss of principles of righteousness and holy living as prosperity, greed and covetousness are preached. It is the loss as believers marry unbelievers, and as ministers seduce and are seduced by church members.

But in their exhilaration, the Amalekites had let down their guard. The Lord had lulled them into complacency, and so David and his men were able to launch a sudden counter-attack. As always happens, for those who live outside the kingdom of God, their joy turned to sorrow.

The ensuing battle lasted from *dusk until the evening of the next day* (**30:17**) and the entire raiding party was wiped out, except for four hundred young men who were able to escape because they rode camels and could outrun their pursuers. But all they escaped with was their lives. They left behind all the goods and people that they had stolen – including David's two wives (**30:18-19**). God is able to restore to us far more than we ever expected (Ps 60:12).

30:20-31 The division of the spoils

Like most battles, this one brought great spoils to the victors (**30:20a**). But spoils of war can spoil lives, as happened to Saul (15:9-11), Balaam (Num 22), Achan (Josh 7), Gehazi (2 Kgs 5) and Judas Iscariot (Matt 26:14-15). Many men then and now have allowed their desire for material goods to harm the work of God.

The simple statement, *This is David's plunder* (**30:20b**) reminds us how easy it is to assume that what comes to us is our due. After all, we have worked hard and long for it, and possibly even risked our lives, as David did. But to allocate all the plunder to the leader is to ignore the contribution of all his co-workers. The leader of a revival may be showered with attention and gifts, some of them large gifts like cars and houses, as if he or she were alone in the battle. But behind every leader stand those who provide administrative help, and who, while they may not be gifted to carry the sword, can still carry cups of water to refresh the exhausted leader.

David's men were prepared to give him all the plunder, assuming he would share it with them. All was joy and rejoicing until the actual division of the plunder began. As so often happens, money reveals what people are really like. These men were comrades until the issue of money arose. Then it became apparent that there were *evil men and troublemakers among David's followers* (**30:22a**). They were unwilling to share the captured goods with the men who had collapsed from exhaustion before the battle (**30:21**).

Are we like this when money matters are discussed? Will we destroy the unity of the church to benefit ourselves? And will we also look down on those to whom God has given different work and different strengths that are less in the public eye, and regard them as less deserving than we are? Such a 'survival of the fittest' ethos has no place in the kingdom of God. Paul reminds us, 'What do you have that you did not receive? And if you did receive it, why do you boast as though you did not? (1 Cor 4:7). Those who had

been able to carry on had only been able to do so because God had given them extra strength

The troublemakers suggested that everyone they thought were not entitled to rewards should just *take his wife and children and go* (**30:22b**). They were happy to dismiss one-third of David's army, as if there would be no more battles to fight. They were happy to wave away all the years of their training and service that these men had put in, and all the gifts God had given them as unimportant in comparison with their own self-interest.

To what lengths will we go to eliminate rivals for rewards or honour? Do we scheme to keep them out of the limelight? Do we set traps for them, hoping to lure them into sin? Or do we encourage our supporters to gloss over our failings and to sing our praises, so as to leave others in the dust? Do we insist on being on the platform at every meeting? We need to remember that God is building his church, not our personal empires. He looks for those who will stand shoulder to shoulder as comrades as they declare his glory to the nations.

David was aware of the need to work cooperatively, and thus his response was *No, my brothers* (**30:23a**). He was actually their captain, the one who had welded this group of men into a fighting force, the one who led them in combat. Yet he addressed them as his brothers. He did not support a spirit of hierarchy by calling them 'my boys' or 'my sons', or 'my children'. His attitude exemplifies the teaching of our Lord Jesus on the matter of titles and hierarchies in the church (Matt 23:8-12). The apostles also applied this teaching, and thus in the Epistles their fellow believers are often referred to as brothers. We have human fathers whom we acknowledge as such, but in spiritual matters, God is our only father and we are brothers. Even Christ calls us by that name (John 20:17). We are not called to make disciples for ourselves, but to train our fellow heirs, with whom we sit side by side as sons and daughters of one Father.

David's firm statement, *You must not do that* (**30:23b**), has credibility because he had overcome his own desire for plunder. If he had been a greedy leader who hoarded the plunder, his men would have had no respect for his rulings. The same applies to us. If we expect our followers to live frugally and sacrificially, we must do no less. If we expect people to serve in poor areas for low wages, we must be prepared to work there too. If we expect them to be honest when they claim expenses, we must not claim for hotel bills when we stayed at the homes of other believers. No one could challenge David's ruling on the basis that it was not consistent with his life. None could object when this ruling became *a statute and ordinance for Israel* (**30:25**).

David's attitude to the plunder is neatly summed up in the phrase *what the Lord has given us* (**30:23c**). What they had was given to 'us', to the whole team, and not to 'me'. He also knew that the Lord had enabled them to acquire these goods. They were gifts, not payments. We should show the same attitude when dealing with honoraria, special donations, love offerings and other incidental spoils – including honour. All are to be shared for the benefit of the whole church.

David knew that it was God who had *protected us and handed over to us the forces that came against us* (**30:23d**). Once again, he sees this as a group matter, not an individual one. And he recognizes that the victory and their very lives are God's gift. Without his protection, some of them would surely have died in battle. Some of you may secretly think that you should have more of the spoil because you prayed the most. You forgot that it was the grace of God that inspired you to pray. And your prayers would have had no effect if God had chosen not to answer them.

As David firmly ascribed the glory to the Lord, he was doing the opposite of Saul, who blew a trumpet and built a monument in his own honour to celebrate his incomplete victory over the Amalekites (13:3; 15:12). David is the model for how we should behave when God enables us to perform some exploit (see also Acts 3:12-16).

Because the victory was a gift from God, the plunder was to be shared equally among the whole army (**30:24**). This became a law in Israel (30:25), and should also become the principle by which we live. Each of us should gather and receive strictly in accordance with our needs (Exod 16:16-18; Acts 2:44-45; 4:34-35; 2 Cor 8:13-15).

David's personal generosity is also evident in his actions after the men returned to Ziklag. He sent portions of the spoils to friendly elders of Judah, who had not even participated in the battle, saying, *Here is a present for you from the plunder of the Lord's enemies* (**30:26-30**). His motive may partly have been to remain in their good books, but his action shows that he did not use all his wealth for himself. He showed his gratitude to those who had helped him while he was in hiding in the wilderness areas of Judah before he fled to Philistine territory (**30:31**).

31:1-13 The Tragic End of Saul and His Sons

Saul's visit to the medium at Endor had left him shattered and heartbroken (28:20). But he still had to lead the people in battle. The result was predictable (**31:1**). The Israelite army crumbled before the massive Philistine attack. Many fell on Mount Gilboa.

The Philistines were intent on wiping out the leadership of Israel. The enemy has always known that if he can strike the shepherd, the sheep will scatter (Matt 26:31). Thus they made a point of attacking Saul and his sons. *They killed his sons Jonathan, Abinadab and Malki-Shua* (**31:2**) but did not stop to celebrate, for they wanted to kill Saul too. Eventually, he was badly wounded by Philistine archers (**31:3**). Knowing that death was near, Saul begged his

armour-bearer to kill him rather than leave him for the Philistines to torment before they killed him (**31:4a**). But his armour-bearer refused to kill the Lord's anointed. He may have been influenced by David's words in 24:10 or 26:23. So Saul committed suicide by falling on his own sword (**31:4b**). As death approached, he was more scared of what the Philistines would do to him than of meeting the Lord. There is no evidence that he repented of his sins before dying.

Saul's armour-bearer committed suicide next to him (**31:5**). Leaders do not die alone, but take many of their followers along with them. The faithful and godly Jonathan died simply because he was standing by his father in the battle. His brothers and many other Israelites also died (**31:6**). As leaders in God's church, we need to tremble when we lead our innocent followers into danger because we have fallen away from God.

As a result of this defeat, *the Israelites along the valley and those across the Jordan* abandoned their towns to the Philistines (**31:7**). They lost land that had been hard won under the leadership of Joshua and the judges. The fall of a leader is always a setback for the purpose of God as the enemy regains ground. Fresh battles will be needed to reclaim them for the Lord.

Saul was not even given a decent burial. The Philistines found his body, cut off his head and stripped off his armour. They sent his armour to an idol temple, just as David had put Goliath's sword in the temple at Nob, and celebrated their victory as a defeat for the God of Israel (**31:9-10**; see also 21:8-9). They fastened Saul's body to the wall of Beth Shan, one of their major cities. It was an ugly way to treat a king.

Saul's first act as king had been to rescue the people of Jabesh Gilead (11:1-11). They remembered that kindness and were determined not to let his body be insulted. So they made a risky night-time journey to remove the bodies of Saul and his sons from the wall of Beth Shan (**31:11-12**). Having recovered them, they burned them and then took the bones and buried them (**31:13a**).

When Samuel died, the whole nation attended his funeral and mourned him (25:1), probably for thirty days, as this had been the mourning period for Moses and Joshua. But only a small town fasted for the loss of Saul and his sons, and their mourning lasted only seven days (**31:13b**). It was a tragic end to a tragic and wasted life as Saul reaped what he had sown.

God had cleared the way for David to ascend the throne without blame for Saul's fate. But David did not rush in to claim it. He still had to wait on God's divine timing. He received the news of Saul's death while still in exile, and his reaction was not jubilation. He and all who were with him sincerely mourned the deaths of Saul and Jonathan and all the others who had fallen. David demonstrates the love for our enemies that Christ would later teach (Matt 5:43-48).

The books of 1 and 2 Samuel were originally one book. Thus the first chapter of 2 Samuel follows immediately on the events described in this chapter.

2 Sam 1:1-4:12 The Fight to Succeed Saul

This first section of 2 Samuel recounts the events following the death of Saul in 1 Samuel 31, including the death of Abner, the protector of Saul's family (3:27) and the murder of Saul's son Ish-Bosheth (4:7). In recounting the events that led David to the throne (beginning in 1 Sam 16), the author or authors of the book of Samuel wanted to show clearly that David had never sought Saul's throne and that he was not responsible for Saul's death – either directly or indirectly. Instead, David condemned the one who brought him the news of Saul's death (1:15).

This first section of 2 Samuel deals especially with the question of David's right to be king of Israel, rather than the next king being one of Saul's descendants. It is interesting to note that in 1 and 2 Chronicles, there is no record of the fight for the throne after Saul's death. This is possibly because Chronicles was written after the return from the Babylonian exile – that is, during a time when unity among the people of Israel was especially important. At that point in Israel's history, the authors preferred not to emphasize past disunity.

1:1-16 David Learns of Saul's Death

2 Samuel opens by continuing the story of Saul's death – but from the point of view of David. 1 Samuel ended with a description of Saul's death in battle against the Philistines. In this battle the royal family was almost entirely wiped out: 'So Saul and three of his sons and his armour-bearer and all his men died together that same day' (1 Sam 31:6).

David himself could have become involved in Saul's death and the destruction of Saul's family, but as the Philistines' alien lackey, he was not permitted to go into battle against his own people, the Israelites (1 Sam 29:4-5). Instead, David and his troops had been sent back to Ziklag (1 Sam 29:10). David was there when an Amalekite messenger came to tell him that Saul had died. Ironically, David had just returned from fighting a group of Amalekites who had pillaged Ziklag and captured David's two wives (1:1; 1 Sam 30).

When told that Saul was dead (1:4), David was not eager to believe the news. Instead he asked for confirmation: *How do you know that Saul and his son Jonathan are dead?* (1:5). He needed to be certain that the throne was truly vacant before he would even consider claiming it for himself.

The details of Saul's death remain controversial. According to the account in 1 Samuel 31:4, Saul fell on his own sword when his armour-bearer refused to kill him. Here, however, the Amalekite messenger claims to have killed the first king of Israel (1:6-10a). It is possible that this

young man was presenting his own version of events in an attempt to enhance his own reputation and earn a great reward. Like the pillaging Amalekites of 1 Samuel 30, he had stripped Saul of his royal regalia (1:10b). He now delivered these to David.

Those who were with David were likely waiting to see his reaction to the news of the death of the man who had often tried to kill him. However, David's response was appropriate: he mourned the death of one who was God's anointed (1:11-12). He had acknowledged Saul's anointed status on several occasions when he had refused to take Saul's life himself (1 Sam 24:7; 26:23-25).

David and his men also mourned the death of Jonathan, the legitimate heir to the throne (1:12). The young Amalekite, who had thought he was bringing good news to the next king, was put to death because he had not been afraid to lift his *hand to destroy the Lord's anointed* (1:13-16).

David's behaviour is a model to all those who are tempted to rejoice at the death of their enemies. David had suffered under Saul, and had even become a fugitive among the Philistines because of him. Yet he did not rejoice at Saul's death but sang a funeral dirge for him.

In Africa death is often considered an opportunity for reconciliation between individuals. In many cultures, there are sayings which emphasize that death silences quarrels and soothes ill feeling. Brothers and sisters who were not on speaking terms are sometimes reconciled at the death of their parents.

1:17-27 David's Laments for Saul and Jonathan

The funeral dirge sung after the death of Saul and his son Jonathan is one of the first of David's poems to be recorded. The idea of singing such a song is a familiar one in Africa, where specific songs are sung when death strikes a family. These days, families tend to invite a choir to come and sing or they install an audio system to play religious music.

It is quite possible that David's lament was composed by the future king himself, although some commentators deny this by arguing that it is written in a style typical of a later period. But it is certain that David and his men sang a lament for Saul (1:17), and some form of this lament may well have been incorporated in the anthology known as the Book of Jashar under the title 'Song of the Bow' (1:18; see also Josh 10:13).

The lament expresses David's pain at the death of the first king of Israel and of Prince Jonathan and at Israel's defeat at the hands of the Philistines. The song's refrain expresses the depth of the loss suffered by Israel: *How the mighty have fallen!* (1:19, 25, 27).

Although the closing chapters of 1 Samuel had shown Saul's growing hostility towards David, David's lament says nothing negative about the former king. Instead it praises him as a great warrior. We find this practice in many cultures. When a person dies, we often forget all the evil that individual has done, and remember only the good things.

David did not see Saul's death as only the death of an individual but as the humiliation of the nation of the circumcised before the uncircumcised Philistines. The pain of defeat was made worse by the fact that it would cause the Philistines to rejoice publicly, just as the women throughout Israel had rejoiced at David's victory over the giant Goliath (1 Sam 18:7). David does not wish the Philistines to do the same, and thus he begs those who know of Saul's death not to mention it in *Gath* and *Ashkelon,* that is, in the cities of the Philistines, *lest the daughters of the Philistines be glad* (**1:20**). David even curses the mountains of Gilboa, which were witnesses to the death of Saul (**1:21**).

Though this song is sung in honour of both Saul and Jonathan (**1:22**), the closing verses celebrate the deep friendship between David and Jonathan. David even goes so far as to say that Jonathan's love was *more wonderful than that of women* (**1:26**). He may have been thinking of the love of a woman for her husband or of a mother for her child.

The fact that God is not mentioned anywhere in this song may give the impression that Saul died only because of the Philistine's military superiority. Nothing could be farther from the truth. When David spared Saul the second time, he realized that God's hand alone would strike Saul: 'As surely as the Lord lives … the Lord himself will strike him; either his time will come and he will die, or he will go into battle and perish' (1 Sam 26:10). The account of Saul's last battle in 1 Chronicles 10:14 clearly states that 'the Lord put him to death'.

David's response to the death of his enemy should lead us to reflect on our own attitudes. Like the Philistines, some people are pleased by the many civil wars that are destroying the African continent and even seek to profit from them. But the godly response is to lament as David did. Like the *men of Judah* (**1:18**), we should weep for 'the mighty' who have fallen – including all the innocent children who will never achieve their full potential and whose loss is not only a tragedy to those who love them but also a loss to all humanity.

The end of this lament marks the end of the reign of the first king of Israel. David has observed a period of mourning (1:12), and composed this lament (1:17-27), and now he needs to turn to other things. The death of Saul was not the end of life. In Africa, where death has such devastating effects, we sometimes act as if that is the case. Long periods of mourning (even extending to 40 days) can result in businesses being ruined, herds decimated, and economies entirely destroyed. Like David, despite our grief, we need to move on to what needs to be done.

Saul's death also marked the start of a new era in the history of Israel as it opened the way for David to gradually ascend to the throne. The only remaining obstacle was one of Saul's sons, Ish-Bosheth.

2:1-4a David Anointed King of Judah

In spite of his faults, Saul had forged a real but fragile unity between the tribes of Israel. Upon his death, however, that unity disappeared. Consequently, David's rise to become king took place in two stages. Initially, he was anointed king over Judah, and only later did he become the king of all Israel.

Unlike Saul, who sometimes acted without consulting God, David always sought God's guidance. So he asked God where he should move to (**2:1a**). We do not know the details of how he asked for guidance, but it would probably have involved the use of lots, and specifically of the Urim and Thummim, which were stored in the ephod that Abiathar had brought with him (1 Sam 23:6). In some way, the positions of these objects indicated whether God's answer was 'yes' or 'no'.

Seeking God's will in everything is recommended in God's word. Unfortunately, in Africa today, we see questionable practices in the way God's will is sought. There are many who call themselves 'prophets' who specialize in determining the will of God for every area of life. We hear of homes that have been destroyed because God's will pointed to another husband or another wife for someone already married. Some of these false prophets mimic speaking in tongues and pour out a stream of incomprehensible words of their own choosing, pretending these give guidance from God. We do not mean to say that God cannot speak directly to us by his Spirit, for he does (Acts 8:26; 9:10-16; 10:1-6; 13:1-3; 16:6-10; 18:9-10; 1 Cor 12:8). However, we need to remember that God's will is clearly expressed in the Bible. Any so-called prophecy that contradicts Scripture comes from the evil one.

God directed David to go to Hebron (**2:1b**) so he and all his followers moved to that town (**2:2-3**). This move indicated that he was separating himself from Achish, the Philistine lord who had allowed him to stay in Ziklag in exchange for his services (1 Sam 27). The city of Hebron was well chosen. It was situated about eighteen miles (thirty kilometres) south-west of Jerusalem in the heart of Judah's territory. It had strong associations with the patriarchs (Gen 13:18; 23:19; 35:27; 37:14) and was in territory assigned to the great hero Caleb when Israel entered the land.

The elders of Hebron were no doubt more than happy to welcome David, as he had sent them booty from the war after his victory over the enemies of the Lord (1 Sam 30:26-31). It was here that David was anointed king for the second time, and this time publicly (**2:4a**; 1 Sam 16:13). But he was king only over Judah. The northern tribes remained faithful to Saul's family.

In the account of this ceremony in 1 Chronicles 11:1-3, it is described as making him king over all Israel, and not just Judah. The author of Chronicles thus combines this anointing with the later one in 5:3 because he seeks to affirm the unity of the people of God. This unity would have been especially important to him because, at the time he was writing, the Israelites had just returned from exile.

2:4b-7 David's Message to the Men of Jabesh

David was now king of Judah, but if he was to become king over all Israel he had to gain the sympathy of those who had sided with Saul. He started by sending a message to *the men of Jabesh Gilead who had buried Saul* (**2:4b**; see 1 Sam 31:11-13). In burying Saul and Jonathan, they had done them a great kindness, for in ancient times great importance was attached to honourable burial (**2:5**).

Honourable burial is still of great concern to many African families today. At times, this can lead to wrong priorities. Families may be reluctant to help a sick family member to pay for medicine or even to get to a doctor, but for the sake of their own reputation they will spend a lot of money on the funeral. They will provide an expensive coffin, a luxurious hearse, lots of flowers, and so on. The church should be teaching people that it is even more important to show love while the person is alive.

The people of Jabesh Gilead may have been moved to honour Saul by their gratitude because he had delivered them from an Ammonite attack (1 Sam 11:1-11). But while their action showed commendable loyalty to Saul, it could also be interpreted as a rejection of the new king installed by the people of Judah. So David gently reminded them that their former king is dead, and that they should be saying, 'Long live the king' (**2:7**). He was asking for their allegiance and promised to show them the same *kindness and faithfulness,* as Saul had done before him (**2:6**). He does not want to have to resort to violence. He also knows that his right to rule might soon be challenged by the surviving sons of Saul and Jonathan.

David knew that God had chosen him to reign over Israel, yet he showed wisdom in seeking to gain the support of those who were faithful to Saul. His policy should inspire Christians to realize that carrying out God's will does not require us to ignore human wisdom and diplomacy. God seldom acts in a miraculous way to bring about his purposes. Rather, he gives us the skills and intelligence we need to achieve his goals. Thus we should act, and not simply sit passively and wait for him to do things for us.

2:8-11 Ish-Bosheth Proclaimed King of Israel

The fragile unity of the tribes fell apart immediately after Saul's death. While David was being crowned by the people of Judah, Abner, Saul's cousin and the *commander of Saul's army* (**2:8**), was working to install Saul's son Ish-Bosheth as king of Israel (**2:9**). For two years, Ish-Bosheth reigned over the tribes of the north from Mahanaim, a town which was north-east of Hebron, on the east side of the Jordan River (Hebron was on the west side). Abner may well have chosen this place deliberately because it was far from the threat of the Philistines.

The coronation of Ish-Bosheth was very different from that of David. Where the entire house of Judah chose David, Ish-Bosheth was installed by Abner alone, as is clear from the statements that Abner *had taken* him and *brought him* over to Mahanaim (**2:8**). Although Abner gave Ish-Bosheth a vast territory (2:9), the real power lay with Abner. Ish-Bosheth was just his puppet.

The account indicates that David reigned *seven years and six months* (**2:11**) at Hebron, whereas Ish-Bosheth reigned over Israel for only two years, starting at the age of forty (**2:10**). The difference of about five years probably includes a period during which Abner held power directly before installing Ish-Bosheth on the throne.

David waited patiently for God's promises to be fulfilled. He knew he was to be king over all Israel, but he did not force events to bring that about. Divided Christian communities in Africa can learn from him. Impatience – wanting everything right now – is causing great strife and goes against Christian teachings about the fruit of the Spirit (Gal 5:22). Impatience is also far too common among African politicians.

The coronation of the puppet king foreshadowed the complete division between Judah and Israel that would follow Solomon's death. But it also triggered a civil war.

2:12-3:1a War Between David and Saul's House

A sad episode in the history of the people of Israel followed the country's fall into civil war. The rivalry between Judah and Israel escalated into a major conflict between two groups, each faithful to a crowned king. It began when Abner led his army to Gibeon, about halfway between Mahanaim and Hebron, but on Judah's side of the Jordan (**2:12**). Joab and David's men met them at *the pool of Gibeon* (**2:13**).

Abner suggested to Joab, the commander of David's army, that a representative fight be staged involving twenty-four men, which would spare the lives of many others (**2:14**). (A similar proposal was made in the incident involving David and Goliath – 1 Sam 17) This time, however, the formula did not work because all twenty-four combatants were killed, and a battle began between the two armies (**2:15-17**).

While the battle itself served little purpose and did not settle the issue of the divided kingdom, it did produce one result with lasting consequences. In his determination to kill Abner, Asahel one of Joab's brothers, pursued him relentlessly until Abner reluctantly struck him down (**2:18-23**). Asahel's death enraged his two brothers, Joab and Abishai, and generated deep animosity between Joab and

Abner, the effects of which would be felt until the end of David's reign.

Asahel died because he refused to follow the advice of the more experienced Abner (2:14, 21-22). His fate reminds us that we should recognize our limits and commit ourselves to activities for which we are really qualified.

Joab and Abishai pursued Abner to avenge their brother's death (2:24-25). They only stopped at dusk, when Abner took up a defensive position and asked, *Must the sword devour forever? Don't you realize that this will end in bitterness? How long before you order your men to stop pursuing their brothers?* (2:26). His words may seem surprising in the midst of an armed conflict, but they were a poignant reminder that the combatants are all members of the same family. And his pursuers actually stopped, realizing the wisdom of what he had said (2:27-29).

Abner's words should be heard by all Africans thirsty for war. The end of a conflict, even through a ceasefire, always leaves a bitter aftertaste. We need to remember that we are all brothers and sisters.

In the end, David's men were the victors. Although they lost twenty men (2:30), Abner's followers lost 360 men (2:31). But the victory was hollow. It settled nothing, and there must have been many subsequent battles for we are told that *the war between the house of Saul and the house of David lasted a long time* (3:1a).

3:1b-5 Sons of David Born in Hebron

This biographical note about David's family recalls a similar passage about Saul in 1 Samuel 14:49-51 and shows the growth of David's house in Hebron as *David grew stronger and stronger* (3:1b). In the OT, a growing family is always a sign of God's blessing (Ps 127:3-5), and several of the sons named here – Amnon, Absalom, and Adonijah – will play significant roles later.

The comments on the growth of David's family remind us that in Africa many marriages break up if there are no children. We should not minimize the importance of this problem for barren couples by merely giving them a formulaic response such as, 'If you have no physical children, try to have spiritual children'. As God's servants, we should try to help sterile couples, both by praying constantly for them and also by directing them to medical services (modern or traditional) that will help them to conceive. It is a tragedy that some pastors in Africa take advantage of couples in this situation, presenting themselves as the only source of help and offering to spend time in prayer and fasting for them, often with the hope of getting some financial reward from the barren couple.

3:6-39 Abner's Story

The rest of this chapter describes a dramatic turn of events as Abner withdrew his support from Ish-Bosheth, and offered it to David. Unfortunately, he was then murdered.

Abner's defection is an example of the political disloyalty that we often see in Africa where alliances are constantly shifting, sometimes with bitter results. Personal interests are often the principal cause of political changes. Yet these events, which seemed to be directed solely by human rivalries and ambition, were nevertheless used by God to accomplish his will in uniting all Israel under David (see Rom 8:28).

3:6-21 Abner's defection to David

Abner knew that he was the real holder of power in the north (3:6). He thus took it upon himself to have sexual relations with Rizpah, one of the concubines of the late King Saul. In ancient times, this act would have been interpreted as showing a desire to take the throne, as we can see from Solomon's reply to his mother when she asked Solomon to let one of David's concubines marry his brother Adonijah: 'Why do you request Abishag the Shunammite for Adonijah? You might as well request the kingdom for him' (1 Kgs 2:22). Not surprisingly, Ish-Bosheth confronted Abner about what he had done (3:7). But from Abner's point of view, his affair with Rizpah was minor compared with the privilege he had conferred on Ish-Bosheth by installing him on his father's throne (3:8). In response to Ish-Bosheth's perceived ingratitude, Abner shifted his loyalty to David, swearing that he would *do for David what the Lord promised him on oath … and establish David's throne over Israel and Judah* (3:9-10). No wonder Ish-Bosheth feared Abner (3:11).

In Africa, having sexual relations with a married woman is not just a question of an illicit love affair but is also perceived as an underhanded way of controlling her husband. It is thus not surprising that sexual relations can exert a great influence on politics. Such matters can determine the future not just of individuals but also of an entire nation, for we see people being appointed to positions on the basis of sexual advances, and political decisions being made on the basis of how they will contribute to the fulfilment of sexual desires. In the case of Abner and Ish-Bosheth, the result was good for David and his supporters. But such an affair can also have very negative effects.

After his break with Ish-Bosheth, Abner decided to make good on his threat. He sent messengers to David saying, *Make an agreement with me, and I will help you bring all Israel over to you* (3:12). This message started negotiations between the two kingdoms. David accepted the proposal but insisted that one of the conditions was that his wife, Michal, Saul's daughter, be restored to him (3:13-14; see 1 Sam 25:44). In his letter to Ish-Bosheth demanding Michal's return, he mentioned the bride price he paid to emphasize that she was still his wife because the bride price had never been returned (1 Sam 18:27). This act was also a calculated political move. His marriage to Saul's daughter would help attract the support of the tribe of Benjamin and justify his claim to the throne.

Michal was taken from her second husband by force and sent back to David, causing great grief to her husband (3:15-16). Abner also began to meet *with the elders of Israel* reminding them that for some time they had *wanted to make David ... king* (3:17). Abner reinforced the point by reminding them of the Lord's promise to use David to *rescue ... Israel from the hand of the Philistines and from the hand of all their enemies* (3:18). He sees David's kingship as ordained by God.

Abner's words to the elders of the northern tribes are similar to those Samuel received from God about Saul in 1 Samuel 9:16. David is, therefore, the one who will replace Saul.

Abner, the clever politician, also spoke to the Benjamites in person (3:19). Once he had the agreement of all the elders of the north, he and twenty of his men went to meet David at Hebron. David, ever the diplomat, arranged a special feast in their honour (3:20).

3:22-39 Abner's murder

Unfortunately, Abner would not live to see the fruit of his negotiations. He was assassinated by Joab, the commander of David's army (3:24-27). Joab had two reasons to eliminate Abner. First, he wanted to avenge the death of his own brother Asahel, whom Abner had killed (3:30; 2:18-23). Second, he probably wanted to eliminate a powerful rival. The experienced Abner might well have replaced Joab as the commander of David's army.

As with Saul's death, the author takes pains to emphasize that David was not responsible for Abner's death. Three times he mentions that David allowed Abner to depart in peace (3:21, 22, 23). He also makes it clear that David did not know that Joab had pursued Abner (3:26) and that he only learned of the murder some time after it had happened.

On hearing of Abner's death, David immediately set out to prove that he was not involved in it in any way (3:28). He ordered an official funeral for Abner and ordered Joab, the killer, and all the army to tear their *clothes and put on sackcloth and walk in mourning in front of Abner* (3:31-32). The king himself sang a lament for Abner, just as he had for Saul and Jonathan. In this lament he grieved the fact that Abner had not died as a war hero but *as the lawless die ... before wicked men* (3:33-34). He refused to eat anything on the day of the funeral (3:35).

This official funeral publicly demonstrated David's innocence with regard to Abner's death (3:37). The northern tribes would have rejected the treaties made if they had believed that David had arranged it. The people understood the king's message and approved of his behaviour (3:36).

From this time on, David is referred to as *King David* (3:31) or as *the king* (3:37).

Abner's story reminds us of the feuds between different political groups in Africa. One group will demonize another and each will be prepared to use any means to eliminate its rivals. This is what Joab did when he killed Abner, whom David recognized as a *prince and a great man* (3:38), one whose advice might have begun to outweigh that of Joab.

David cursed *Joab's house* for his actions (3:29, 39b), but he did not act to punish Joab immediately, probably because he was still politically too weak to do so (3:39a). Many years later, however, he did instruct his son Solomon to punish Joab (1 Kgs 2:5-6, 28-35). As Jesus reminded us, 'all who draw the sword will die by the sword' (Matt 26:52).

4:1-12 Death of Ish-Bosheth, Saul's Last Son

The only remaining obstacle between David and sovereignty over all of Israel was Ish-Bosheth. The death of Abner had plunged both him and the rest of Israel into a state of fear (4:1). Ish-Bosheth was weakened both by the death of the one who had been his protector, and by the support that the elders of the northern tribes had given to the agreement Abner had negotiated with David.

Ish-Bosheth was assassinated and decapitated by two of his own officers (4:2, 5-7), who then took his head to David in Hebron (4:8a). We do not know exactly what motivated them to kill him, but their words leave no doubt that, like the Amalekite who had killed Saul, they were hoping for a substantial reward from King David (4:8b). But David gave them the same reward he had given the Amalekite (4:10). He condemned them to death, with their feet and hands cut off and their corpses exposed publicly beside the pool in Hebron (4:9-12). David, always the diplomat, then arranged for proper burial of Ish-Bosheth's head in Abner's tomb (4:12).

David has been cleared of responsibility for the deaths of Saul, Abner and Ish-Bosheth. This is a king whose hands are clean of innocent blood.

Mentioned in passing at the start of this chapter is Mephibosheth, Jonathan's sole remaining son, who was still alive and thus could also lay claim to the throne (4:4). But he had been crippled since early childhood, and therefore could not take on royal responsibilities. With no other claimants, the throne was truly vacant and a new royal line could begin.

David's ascension to the throne clearly reveals the brutality of power which so often involves intrigues, broken alliances and assassinations. African politicians who are Christians are called to act as salt and light in the political realm (Matt 5:13-16). The church should also pray for all those who exercise political power so that 'we may live peaceful and quiet lives in all godliness and holiness' (1 Tim 2:1-2).

2 Sam 5:1-8:18 David, King over All Israel

From 2 Samuel 5 on, the story parallels the account beginning in 1 Chronicles 11. This section begins with David being crowned king over all Israel, and ends with the consolidation of his royal administration. The kingdom that began so uncertainly under Saul will reach maturity under the new king. At the same time, we also see a change in David. The man who knew he would become king had waited patiently for the right time to ascend the throne. Now, however, we see him as a politician, doing his utmost to stabilize and secure his throne. At the heart of this section lies God's promise, delivered by Nathan, that David's kingdom will become a dynasty (7:1-17). This promise can be considered one of the most important events in the whole history of Israel.

Surprisingly, these four chapters are the only ones that really describe David's reign. Given the long build-up to his coming to power, we might have expected a far more detailed account of his doings once he became king. Instead, from chapter 8 on, we are presented with the account of the long fight to succeed him.

5:1-5 David Proclaimed King over Israel

Verses 1-5 conclude the long account of David's ascension to the throne. With the deaths of all its other leaders, Saul, Jonathan and Abner, the nation became acutely aware of its weakness and of its need for a courageous leader to protect it. Thus the elders of all the tribes came to David at Hebron and mentioned three reasons why he should become their king. First, all the Israelites, both in the north and the south were of the same *flesh and blood*, and thus were related (**5:1**). Second, David had demonstrated his military prowess during Saul's reign, and had thus met an important requirement for kings at that time (**5:2a**). Third, God had promised David that he would *shepherd … Israel, and … become their ruler* (**5:2b**). The shepherd metaphor would have reminded David of his youth, when he literally cared for sheep (1 Sam 16:11), an experience that he immortalized in Psalm 23. This metaphor for kingship is a powerful one. A king who is a true shepherd will not become authoritarian, oppressive, or exploitative like the bad king described in 1 Samuel 8:10-18 (see also Ezek 34:23-24).

Seven years and six months after the death of Saul, Israel and Judah were at last reunited with the anointing of David as *king over Israel*, and not just over Judah (**5:5**). But there was not a true bond between the northern and southern tribes; rather, it was as if two separate states had entered into an alliance under a common sovereign. This alliance would dissolve after the death of Solomon. David, however, worked hard to create a durable union by establishing a neutral capital (5:6-10), a national sanctuary (6:1-19) and a dynasty (7:1-17).

David was thirty years old when he was anointed at Hebron (**5:3b**), the same age at which Levites were first allowed to serve in the Tent of Meeting. It was thus regarded as the age at which one had reached a level of maturity that qualified one for high responsibilities (Num 4:3).

David's life was always directed by two main forces: theology and politics. God had chosen him as king, but his human qualities also suited him to this role. Similarly, those God chooses for spiritual leadership today will have the ability to carry out responsibilities he gives them. As the saying goes, God equips those he calls.

The behaviour of the northerners was also admirable. They recognized David's good qualities and did not seek to prolong the civil war needlessly. Even though David did not belong to any of their tribes, they recognized that he was capable of governing and of protecting them against their enemies.

It is important to note that the tribes of Israel did not offer David unfettered power. Rather, they entered into a *compact* with him when they asked him to be their shepherd (**5:3a**). The contents of the agreement are not given, but it would presumably have imposed obligations on both parties. The existence of this compact also throws light on why the elders of the northern tribes felt entitled to make demands of Rehoboam, Solomon's son. Even though the northern tribes trusted David, both they and David knew that it was important to define what we could call the 'rules of the game'.

We could learn from their example, for problems arise in many Christian communities today because leadership responsibilities are not well defined. A pastor may be assigned to a parish but given no job description. Deacons do not always know what the community expects of them. Christians are baptized without knowing anything about their responsibilities as members of a local church.

The shepherd model is often presented as one that pastors can use when reflecting on their ministry. However, this metaphor does not always work well. In many regions of Africa, herds of sheep and goats are basically expected to take care of themselves when it comes to finding food, water and protection. All that the owner does is slaughter one occasionally for meat. Thus when we tell a pastor that his title means 'shepherd', he does not have any concrete reality with which to associate it, and the metaphor fails to communicate the concepts we intend it to.

5:6-10 David Captures Jerusalem

David's first act as king was to *march to Jerusalem to attack the Jebusites* (**5:6a**). This city was located at the border between Judah (David's tribe) and Benjamin (Saul's tribe). Thus by having his capital here, David could have better control of two tribes that had been influential in his coronation. Moreover, the city belonged to neither group, which meant that it was politically neutral. David's choice of it is further evidence that he recognized the fragility of the unity achieved at Hebron and was working to cement it.

Jerusalem occupied an extremely strong defensive position, which was why it was still in Jebusite hands. Its strength also explains the defenders' mocking claim that even the disabled could defend the city against David (5:6b). Nevertheless, the city was captured by *the king and his men*. These men would have been those who had been with him while he was a fugitive. Thus there could be no objection when David called the captured city *the City of David*, for he had taken it in battle (5:7, 9). Calling it his city also meant that no individual tribe could claim ownership of the new capital.

David's concern for the unity of his new kingdom reminds us that unity is a form of wealth that needs to be worked for and maintained. David's example should inspire all those who are working toward unity in their church communities, their wider community, or their countries as a whole.

This section closes with further confirmation that David's kingship was part of God's plan: *he became more and more powerful, because the Lord God Almighty was with him* (5:10).

5:11-12 Envoys from Hiram, King of Tyre

David also began to enjoy international recognition as ambassadors from Hiram, king of Tyre, arrived in his new capital. The port city of Tyre was famous for its flourishing trade and for the supply of cedar wood that was used in construction. The king of Tyre sent David both the materials and the manpower he would need to construct a palace (5:11). The new king in his new capital recognized the hand of God in all that was happening (5:12).

Although the text makes no further comment on this alliance between David and a pagan king, we know that this sort of alliance often led to the temptation to be self-sufficient and to follow other gods (Deut 17:17; Isa 2:6-8).

Wealth is here recognized as a sign of God's blessing. But some who preach only a gospel of prosperity have abused Scripture verses like these. It is true that in his love the Lord does bless his people, but this should not lead us to blur the line between salvation in Jesus Christ and material prosperity. The prosperity gospel has had destructive effects on the African continent. Rather than working to transform their lives, people are content to pray and fast, hoping that God will one day make them rich. God blesses his children in their work, not in their idleness!

5:13-16 Sons of David Born in Jerusalem

In 3:2-5 we learned that David had several wives and a number of sons born while he was at Hebron. Once he had become king of Israel, his harem grew even larger. Not only did he take several more wives, but he also took concubines (5:13). Some of these marriages were probably entered into for diplomatic reasons, to seal alliances between royal houses. We are not told the names of any of these wives. Of the eleven sons mentioned in 5:14, only Solomon is later given any prominence. However, it is likely that the Nathan here is the ancestor of Jesus who is mentioned in Luke 3:31.

Some African political leaders also have concubines who, in some circles, are called 'second ladies', the 'first lady' being his legitimate wife. It sometimes costs the man more to maintain his second wives than it does to maintain his true wife, resulting in his dipping his hands into the country's coffers.

5:17-25 David Defeats the Philistines

The Philistines were Israel's traditional enemies and had been responsible for the death of King Saul. David had been their vassal, but the Philistines did not believe that this situation would continue once David had taken Saul's place as the leader of a united Israel. So they set out to attack him (5:17).

The *Valley of Rephaim*, where the Philistine forces established themselves on two separate occasions, was in the territory of Benjamin (5:18, 22). They may have chosen this location in hopes of exploiting any lingering resentment of David by some members of Saul's tribe.

As a soldier who placed his confidence in God, David twice asked for a plan of attack from God, who was his real commander-in-chief (5:19, 23). Using two different tactics supplied by God, David defeated the Philistines (5:20-21, 22-25). David succeeded where Saul had failed because he acted in perfect obedience to the plans he had received from God. These victories were decisive and from then on the Philistines ceased to be a serious threat to Israel.

God does not always act in the same way as shown when he gave David two very different battle plans, both of which led to victory. We often have a tendency to put God in a box, thinking that he is always going to act in the same way. But God's intervention is more like the advice that doctors give patients. Even if two patients have similar symptoms, they will not necessarily receive exactly the same treatment. Each patient needs to be diagnosed and treated individually. We cannot insist that because God has done something for us in one way, he will follow exactly the same pattern for everyone else.

6:1-23 The Ark Goes to Jerusalem

Having laid the foundations for unity by establishing a neutral capital, David continued to pursue the consolidation of his realm by establishing a national sanctuary. He recognized that religion is also an element that unites a nation. Consequently, he decided to move the ark of the covenant to the new capital, Jerusalem. This transfer takes place in two stages. The first effort failed (6:1-11), but the second was successful (6:12-19).

The ark of the covenant was a potent symbol of national unity because it dated back to the time of Israel's wandering in the desert, and thus reminded the different tribes that they were all descendants of Jacob. It was not a symbol that belonged to any particular tribe. Rather, it belonged to all Israel, and was the supreme visible symbol of God's presence among his people.

Many years before, the Philistines had captured the ark (1 Sam 4:10-11). They had eventually returned it to Israel, and it had ended up in the house of Abinadab in Kiriath Jearim (1 Sam 6:1-7:1). There it remained, almost completely forgotten, throughout Saul's reign. David's victory over the Philistines now allowed him to seek it out without fear of being attacked.

6:1-11 First attempt

The first attempt to bring the ark to Jerusalem takes on the appearance of a military operation as David and thirty thousand of his best men set out from Kiriath Jearim *to bring up from there the ark of God* (**6:1-2**). The passage does not say why he took so many men with him, but it may have been a precaution against interference by the Philistines. The thirty-thousand figure also reveals that David had ten times as many men as the three thousand often associated with Saul (1 Sam 13:2; 24:2; 26:2). The author may have chosen to emphasize this number to confirm that David was ten times greater than Saul. The same view was expressed by the women who sang, 'Saul has slain his thousands, and David his tens of thousands' (1 Sam 18:7).

Despite the precautions taken, including using a *new cart* to transport the ark (**6:3a**), and despite the joy that accompanied the ceremony (6:5), the first effort at transferring the ark of the covenant to Jerusalem was a terrible failure. It ended tragically with the death of Uzzah, one of the men who was guiding the cart (**6:3b-4**). The episode was dramatic. *David and the whole house of Israel* had been *celebrating with all their might* (**6:5**). Then the oxen pulling the cart stumbled and Uzzah *reached out and took hold of the ark of God* (**6:6**). The Lord was angry because of Uzzah's *irreverent act* (**6:7**) and struck him dead. Uzzah thus suffered the same fate as the men of Beth Shemesh who had 'looked into the ark of the Lord' (1 Sam 6:19).

We do not know exactly what it was that Uzzah did wrong, but according to the Jewish historian Josephus, a popular interpretation was that Uzzah was not a priest and therefore had no right to touch the ark of the covenant. According to the writer of the book of Chronicles, this first effort failed because no Levites were present (1 Chr 15:2). They were the group who were authorized to carry the ark, though not to touch it (Num 4:15).

David was angered and frightened by Uzzah's death, and decided not to risk trying to carry the ark any further (**6:9**). So instead of being taken to Jerusalem, it was taken to the house of Obed-Edom the Gittite, where it remained for three months (**6:10-11**). It has often been claimed that Obed-Edom was a descendant of the Philistines, since the description of him as a Gittite means that he lived in Gath. However, there were several places known as Gath, not all of them in Philistine territory, and it is quite possible that this man was an Israelite.

6:12-19 Second attempt

David learned that God was blessing the family of Obed-Edom because of the ark (**6:12**). This news probably gave him the courage to try again to take it to Jerusalem. This time, however, the ark of the covenant was carried, as prescribed in Numbers (Num 4:15, 7:9) instead of being placed on a cart. Moreover David *sacrificed a bull and a fattened calf* after the carriers had taken only six steps (**6:13**). And *the entire house of Israel brought up the ark of the Lord with shouts and the sound of trumpets,* while David danced *before the Lord with all his might* (**6:14-15**). What had initially been planned as if it were part of a military campaign is transformed into a worshipping procession.

But there is one sour note in this atmosphere of rejoicing. Saul's daughter Michal was disgusted by David's unrestrained behaviour and despised her husband *in her heart* (**6:16**).

The ark was placed inside a tent that David had erected for it (**6:17**). Its presence there united Israel and Judah in worship in the new capital. The fact that it reached the city without further mishap was seen as an expression of God's consent to make this city his new home. We can thus understand David's joy at the end of this ceremony as he blessed the people and distributed food to all who were present (**6:18-19**). With the arrival of the ark of the covenant, Jerusalem became not only the political capital but also the religious centre of all Israel.

In moving the ark to Jerusalem, David showed that he was not afraid to make religious changes when the change was in accordance with God's will. He did not just leave the ark where it was, but brought it to his new city. There is a lesson here for us as Christians. Although the gospel of the death and resurrection of Jesus Christ remains unchanged, there will be changes in how it is communicated and applied in different contexts and circumstances.

We are also reminded that the presence of God is not something to be taken lightly. His presence brought death to Uzzah, but blessing to the family of Obed-Edom.

6:20-23 Michal Despises David

The religious procession also provides an opportunity to reassert the legitimacy of David's reign through the quarrel it provoked between David and his wife Michal. This disagreement was not just personal, but was also political and reflected the conflict between the house of Saul and the house of David. Michal is behaving like her father, which may be why she is referred to as *the daughter of Saul* rather than as the wife of David (**6:20a**). Michal believed that a king should be strong and dignified, and so she was disgusted by David's dancing *as any vulgar fellow would* in front of everyone (**6:20b**). As the daughter of the former king, Michal may have thought that she conferred some legitimacy on David's reign and could thus tell David what to do. But David reminded her that his status had nothing to do with her. He was chosen to be king by God, *who chose me rather than your father or anyone from his house* (**6:21**).

The statement that Michal was barren is a statement about the end of Saul's dynasty (**6:23**). Since Jonathan's brothers including Ish-Bosheth were now dead, the only hope for Saul's line to retain power was through Michal, but she died without offspring.

David's joyful dancing should also not be used to argue that all kinds of dancing are equally acceptable in church. Worship through dance has been become more and more important in African Christian communities. Some Christian musicians have, however, taken to imitating the style of dancing of popular musicians, which sometimes involves inappropriate exposure of women's bodies. While the Bible does not give us any particular model for dance in church, the leaders in each Christian community must take care to ensure that no indecent dances are performed.

The capture of Jerusalem, the building of David's palace, and the transfer of the ark of the covenant to Jerusalem are all events that lead into the account of the construction of the temple and the associated promise of a dynasty.

7:1-17 The Promise of a Dynasty

Chapter 7 deals with David's plans to build a permanent and durable home for the ark. But the most important element in this chapter is undoubtedly Nathan's prophecy that David's dynasty will endure for ever. This prophecy may be the high point of Israel's history as told in the books that the Jews called the Former Prophets (Joshua to 2 Kings), and marks the high point of David's reign. It also foreshadows the NT, where Jesus is presented as a descendant of David, continuing his dynasty (Luke 1:32).

The content of this entire chapter closely parallels 1 Chronicles 17.

7:1-4 David's desire to build a temple

Once the turmoil around his coming to the throne had subsided and the Philistines had been defeated, King David was able to turn his attention to an issue that could only be addressed in a time of peace. He was disturbed by the discrepancy between his own splendid *palace of cedar* and the humble tent that housed the ark of God (**7:1-2**). The situation should be the opposite because God deserves more honour than an earthly king. However, he knew that he could not proceed with such a massive project without the Lord's approval. So he sought advice from his spiritual advisor, Nathan, who replied positively to the king's request: *The Lord is with you* (**7:3**). That night, however, God told Nathan otherwise, probably in a vision or a dream (**7:4**).

7:5-17 Nathan's prophetic declaration

This prophetic word may be divided into several parts: a rejection of David's proposal (7:5-7); a reminder of David's past and ascent to the throne (7:8-11a); and the promise of an eternal dynasty (7:11b). It answers one of the questions that would have arisen as anyone scanned the history of Israel: Why was it Solomon and not David, the greatest king of Israel, who built the temple?

Although God appeared to be rejecting David's project, the focus of the message was not so much on the project as on David himself. The rhetorical question in 7:5 could be translated: *Are you the one to build me a house to dwell in?* (**7:5**). God reminded David that he had long been content to move *from place to place with a tent as my dwelling* (**7:6**). He had never asked any ruler to build him a permanent temple (**7:7**).

The Lord restrained David's ambitions by reminding him of the circumstances of his ascent to the throne. David might want to do something great for God, but through God something great had already been accomplished. God had raised him from being no more than a young man looking after a flock of sheep to being king over the entire nation (**7:8**). David was also reminded that God had disposed of all his enemies (Saul, Abner, Ish-Bosheth, the Philistines) and that he had given David the time of peace he was now enjoying (**7:9**). Rather than David exalting God, God had and would continue to exalt David! But the Lord's purpose was not to bless only David, but also to bless the entire nation (**7:10-11a**).

Instead of David building a house for God, God would *establish a house* for David (**7:11b**). In Hebrew, the word 'house' has a wide variety of meanings. It can refer to a physical dwelling but also to a family, and, as in this case, to a royal family, David's dynasty. This promise of a dynasty will echo throughout the Bible and reach its culmination in Jesus, born of David's line.

God made it even clearer that David was not to build the temple by specifying that this task would fall to one of his sons (**7:12-13a**). He made many promises to this descendant of David: his throne would be established forever (**7:13b**), he would be a son to God (7:14), and most importantly, unlike the case with Saul, God would never withdraw his blessing even in the event of disobedience (**7:14-15**). Saul lost the throne and God's gracious favour, but David and his descendants would not lose these things. God also made a solemn promise to David: *Your house* [that is, your family] *and your kingdom shall endure for ever before me; your throne shall be established for ever'* (**7:16**). The parallel pronouncement is given differently in 1 Chronicles 17:14, although there the focus is not on David's house but on 'my house' (that is, God's house, the temple) and 'my kingdom'.

It is striking that God's promise of a long-lasting dynasty had already been hinted at by Abigail in 1 Samuel 25:28.

God's choice of David and his descendants marked an important turning point in the spiritual life of God's people. From then on, the future of God's people was linked to solidarity with the family God had chosen. This is why the northern tribes who later separated from Judah were considered apostate, even though they represented the majority of the Israelites. Their separation from and rejection of David's dynasty was seen as a refusal to submit to the will of God.

7:18-29 David's Prayer of Thanks

The promise of an eternal dynasty on the throne of Israel led David to open his heart before God. David's prayer of thanksgiving expressed both gratitude and a request. But nowhere in the prayer was there any mention of the temple. David had taken God's message to heart. Instead of complaining about God's non-endorsement of his building plans, he readily accepted the revelation. He focused solely on his successors.

In the first part (7:18-21), David praised God for the grace that he was being shown in the present. He humbly recognized that he did not deserve God's generosity: *Who am I, O Sovereign Lord,* he says, *and what is my family, that you have brought me this far?* (**7:18**). This was no fake humility intended to flatter the giver. David was well aware that neither he nor his ancestors had any claim to the throne. By rights, he should have remained a shepherd. Now not only had God graciously given him a throne, but he had also promised him a dynasty (**7:19**)! David further emphasized his humble position by repeatedly referring to himself as a *servant,* a term that is repeated ten times in the prayer.

In the second part of his prayer (7:22-24), David moved beyond thoughts of his own family to consider the generosity God had shown to the entire nation of Israel in the past. His use of the plural pronouns when he says that *we have heard with our own ears* (**7:22b**) makes it seem that he was inviting all Israel to celebrate God with him as he recalled the events of the exodus from Egypt (**7:23**). David remembered that the God of Israel is incomparable: *There is no God but you* (**7:22a**).

In **7:24**, the fate of the nation of Israel is implicitly linked with that of David's dynasty. God has established the people of Israel as his own forever, in the same way as he has established David's throne for ever.

Having looked to the present and past, David, in the third part of his prayer, turns to the future of his dynasty (7:25-29). Although he marvelled at the promise God had given him, he was not afraid to ask his Lord to make good on the agreement: *Do as you promised,* he says, *so that your name will be great for ever* (**7:25-26**). He pushes the promise of a dynasty as far as it will go: *be pleased to bless the house of your servant, that it may continue for ever in your sight* (**7:29**).

David's courage in this prayer shows his intimacy with God (**7:27**). He did not hesitate to take God at his word, and to remind him of what we could even call his 'obligation' to bring about what he has promised. Christians need to remember that God is our loving father, which means that we can approach him without fear, opening our hearts to him.

However, even when we take God at his word as David did, it is also important to remember that God is sovereign in his decisions. Despite God's promise to David, the earthly dynasty of David did come to an end. The dynasty was suspended for a time with the destruction of Jerusalem and the deportation that followed. It was not that God's promise had failed, but rather that David's human descendants were not faithful to the covenant. It was only in Jesus Christ, himself a descendant of David, that this promise was truly fulfilled.

8:1-18 David Consolidates His Kingdom

Chapter 8 tells the story of how King David set about consolidating his kingdom. Externally, he waged wars to strengthen it, and internally, he set up an administration system.

8:1-14 David's wars and victories

David now embarked on wars and expanded Israel's territory by defeating four of his neighbours. First, he defeated the Philistines and took Metheg Ammah from them (**8:1**). The name of this city means 'the bridle of the mother' which suggests that it may be a symbolic name for their leading city. After this, David had no more troubles with the Philistines (the mention of them in 2 Sam 28 dates from a time before David was established as king).

David also defeated the Moabites (**8:2**), the king of Zobah (**8:3-4, 7-8**), the Arameans (**8:5-6**), and the Edomites (**8:13b-14**). His victory over the Arameans is recounted in slightly more detail than the others – perhaps because of the amount of booty he captured from them. These spoils of war, along with the items captured from others, may have become part of the temple treasure because David dedicated these articles to the Lord (**8:11-12**).

By this time, David had become famous for his military prowess (**8:9, 13a**), and King Tou of Hamath, an enemy of the king of Zobah, sent his son Joram to King David with gifts of silver and gold and bronze to congratulate him on his victory over Hadadezer (**8:9-10**).

The wars fought by David were the Lord's wars, for *the Lord gave David victory wherever he went* (**8:6, 14**).

8:15-18 David's royal administration

Every kingdom seeks peace and economic growth (although these remain no more than dreams without the justice and righteousness that exalt a nation – Prov 14:34). To achieve these, a nation needs a competent administration. This is what David now proceeded to set up, appointing well-qualified men to assume the daily operation of the kingdom.

David himself, as the head of the administration, was responsible for law and justice, *doing what was just and right for all his people* (**8:15**). The story about Mephibosheth, which follows in chapter 9, is probably intended as an example of his justice, showing him as a model king who sought the well-being of his people. *Joab,* David's nephew, was commander of the army, which provided physical protection (**8:16**). The civil administration under Seraiah cared for the well-being of the people, while the priests and Levites, who were responsible for worship, cared for their spiritual well-being, that is, for the relationship with the Lord (**8:17**).

It is interesting to note that David is often shown as surrounded by a group of foreigners, *the Kerethites and Pelethites* who made up his personal bodyguard (**8:18**). He may have employed these men so that he was not seen as too closely associated with any one of the twelve tribes.

Similar groups exist in many African countries. Often when a new president assumes power, a brigade or special division is immediately created for his personal protection. Generally, this group receives its orders not from the regular army, but directly from the president. Its members generally come from the same ethnic group as the president, and they are well trained and well equipped. They are also often well paid, because if they were not, they could be tempted to become disloyal to their president. Even if teachers or other military personnel are not paid, those who protect the president are paid regularly. As in David's case, rather than counting on popular support, the president counts on the abilities of his brigade or division for protection.

Many African presidents also appoint a wide variety of counsellors to deal with every aspect of the nation's life. Some even appoint spiritual counsellors. But all these counsellors are expensive, for all of them are well paid, at the people's expense.

While bureaucracy is important for maintaining any kingdom, it also presents many temptations and dangers for those who are in powerful positions. Ultimately, the cost of maintaining a growing number of officials and a professional army would become a heavy burden for the people of Israel. Although David's bureaucracy was small, it would grow under his successor until complaints about the taxes, duties and forced labour resulted in the northern tribes revolt against Rehoboam (1 Kgs 12:1-24; 2 Chr 10:1-19).

2 Sam 9:1-20:26 David's Decline

The third part of 2 Samuel is often thought of as dominated by the struggle to determine who would succeed David on the throne. This assessment, though correct in some ways, does not totally reflect the contents of this section. Rather, we could say that up until this point, the author has been presenting the high point of David's reign. From now on, however, we see David begin to decline. Whereas so far he has been presented as an ideal king, and readers may have assumed that a monarchy is the ideal form of government, now we will see the darker side of monarchy. David has to deal with internal struggles, palace intrigues, and the moral ambiguities inherent in the exercise of power. While superficially everything may seem to be going smoothly, beneath the surface there is growing conflict.

9:1-13 David's Generosity toward Mephibosheth

As noted in the comments on 2 Samuel 8:15-18, the story about David's generosity toward Mephibosheth was probably included as proof that David administered justice in a righteous way. That is probably why it is presented here rather than in chapter 21 with the other events involving Saul's family. Those events, too, are not presented in their chronological position in David's life, but in the position that best suited the author's purposes.

David's mercy toward Mephibosheth was unusual in the context of the times. Normally, when a new king ascended the throne, his family would acquire all the land that had belonged to the former dynasty. We also know from the history of the Near East that members of a dethroned royal family were often treated severely. They might escape execution, but would certainly be stripped of all their possessions. Unfortunately, examples of this type of behaviour are still common in Africa. After a coup d'état, the new regime often confiscates the property of the officials of the former regime.

Jonathan probably had just this type of situation in mind when he had asked David to enter into a covenant to 'show me unfailing kindness like that of the Lord as long as I live, so that I may not be killed, and do not ever cut off your kindness from my family' (1 Sam 20:15). The word 'kindness' in that covenant is echoed several times in this chapter as David shows kindness to Jonathan's son (9:1, 3, 7). He starts by asking one of Saul's servants, Ziba, whether there were any survivors of Saul's family to whom he could *show God's kindness* (**9:1-3a**). Ziba identified *a son*

HOSPITALITY IN AFRICA

In Africa and in the Bible, hospitality is about welcoming strangers and not just friends. In fact, in the NT, the Greek word for someone who practises hospitality means 'lover of strangers'. Interestingly, in most African languages the same word is used for both 'stranger' and 'guest'. Hospitality is rooted so deeply in African societies that meals are not prepared for the exact number of people in the household, for there is always the possibility that someone may drop in to share the meal. It goes without saying that when strangers come into the house they must be offered something, even if only a cup of water.

In the OT those who show hospitality to strangers are rewarded, while those who do harm to them are liable to judgment. Positive examples of the practice of hospitality include Abraham welcoming the strangers by the oaks of Mamre (Gen 18:1-5), Lot welcoming the strangers before the destruction of Sodom (Gen 19), Rebecca (Gen 24), the daughters of Jethro (Exod 2:16-20) and Abigail (1 Sam 25). Those who withheld hospitality include the men of Sodom who wanted to assault Lot's guests (Gen 19), the men of Gibeah (Judg 19), the Ammonites and Moabites who failed to show hospitality to Israel on their way from Egypt (Deut 23:3-6) and Nabal (1 Sam 25).

Mosaic law required that strangers be respected and given fair treatment: 'The alien who resides with you shall be to you as a citizen among you; You shall love the alien as yourself, for you were aliens in the land of Egypt' (Lev 19:33-34).

The NT also values hospitality highly. Jesus was both a host who received strangers and a guest who received hospitality. He welcomed all at his table: feeding the hungry, healing the sick and receiving social outcasts such as tax collectors and prostitutes. He instructed his disciples to give a blessing wherever they were received to show that he built hospitality into his mission.

In the Epistles it is clear that both church leaders and church members were expected to show hospitality (Rom 12:13; 1 Tim 3:2; 5:9-10; Titus 1:8; Heb 13:2; 1 Pet 4:9; 2 John 10-11). This hospitality contributed to the spread of the gospel. During the early days of the church, inns were not safe places to stay and so travelling Christians stayed in the homes of believers. There they also interacted with non-believers and the gospel was spread by word of mouth. It is said that when Papias, Bishop of Hierapolis (AD 60–125), offered hospitality he inquired diligently about the lives of the early apostles because he could learn more this way than from books.

The instructions given in the *Didache*, an early church manual, included guidelines to check abuse of hospitality: 'Everyone who comes in the name of the Lord is to be welcomed … And if the one who comes is merely passing through, assist him as much as you can. But he must not stay with you more than two or if necessary three days. However, if he wishes to settle among you and is a craftsman, let him work for his living.' Similar guidance is provided in the Swahili proverb *Mgeni siku ya kwanza, siku ya pili mpatie jembe* ['A visitor comes for one or two days; after that, give him a hoe']. Heeding these guidelines helps to prevent people from preying on a host's generosity.

In contemporary Africa, social, political and economic pressures make it difficult for Christians to practise the ancient tradition of hospitality. In urban areas especially, it can be difficult to tell which guests are genuine. The church needs to develop realistic ways to continue this practice. One option is to practise communal hospitality, so that the burden is shared within the body of Christ rather than being carried by one individual. To help our brothers and sisters who have been displaced by war, we need to encourage our governments to adopt just and humane refugee policies. Most of all, we need to pray that our hearts will not be hardened by the abundance of needs around us so that we turn a deaf ear to a needy brother or sister on our doorstep. We need to remember Jesus' words: 'I was a stranger and you invited me in' (Matt 25:35).

Emily J. Choge

---

of Jonathan, but pointed out that he was crippled in both feet and thus presented no threat to David (**9:3b**). David then sent for Mephibosheth to appear before him (**9:4-5**).

Mephibosheth must have been very afraid at this development. His fear is understandable if, as seems likely, this incident took place shortly after the massacre of most of Saul's other descendants described in chapter 21. Thus before any words were spoken, he bowed down to pay David *honour* (**9:6**). His attitude is better conveyed by the NASB translation, *Mephibosheth … fell on his face and prostrated himself … And he said, "Here is your servant!"*. He must have been greatly relieved at David's response, *Don't be afraid* (**9:7a**).

David then promised to treat Mephibosheth with kindness *for the sake of your father Jonathan* (**9:7b**). His kindness is shown in restoring to Mephibosheth *all the land* that had belonged to Saul but which had been confiscated. Mephibosheth was also told that henceforth he would have a place of honour at the king's table, as if he were one of David's sons (**9:8, 11**). Now that David has defeated all his enemies, and established his throne and his kingdom, he no longer fears treating Saul's house with kindness.

David also orders Ziba, one of Saul's servants, to farm Mephibosheth's land and *bring in the crops* for him (**9:10**). The story closes with a reminder of Mephibosheth's handicap, perhaps to re-emphasize the fact that he posed no threat to David's reign (**9:13**). Nor did his son (**9:12**), probably because he was too young when David was first crowned, and by the time he had grown to adulthood, David's kingship was well established.

Regardless of the political benefits that David could have received from this act of kindness, people would have been astonished that the king could give such honour to a person who was crippled. In African society, and especially in our cities, the disabled are excluded from society. In some families, people will even ask a disabled child to stay away from the house when a visitor is expected. Being disabled is sometimes even perceived as a curse. As a result, it is rare for disabled people to complete their schooling or even training program.

However, in contexts where intellectual or artistic achievements are more important than physical strength, the disabled can make a great contribution to society and to the church. Christian communities should be places where the disabled are welcomed and supported. Like David, we should welcome them to our tables.

10:1-19 David and the Ammonites and Arameans

Besides showing faithfulness and kindness to Mephibosheth, David also showed his faithfulness to Nahash, king of the Ammonites. Unfortunately, the court officials misinterpreted this act of faithfulness. Their maltreatment of David's ambassadors led to war.

10:1-5 Humiliation of David's ambassadors

Scripture does not tell us about any alliance between David and Nahash, or about the kindness that Nahash showed to David. All we know is that the Ammonites were Saul's enemies (1 Sam 11). But David and Nahash must have had some agreement, for when Nahash died, David thought to *show kindness to Hanun son of Nahash just as his father showed kindness to me* (**10:1-2**). He thus sent a delegation to express his condolences to the new king.

But Hanun and his nobles were suspicious of David's motives. One can understand why. As happens today, the arrival of the delegation from another country at the funeral of a head of state is never simply a gesture of sympathy but is also an attempt to ensure that there is a cooperative relationship with the new leader. Before we condemn such political behaviour at a funeral, we need to remember that in Africa too, some people have come to see times of mourning as opportunities for commerce. While pretending to offer consolation, they seize the opportunity to sell pieces of cloth or jewellery or some expensive services.

Hanun and his nobles, however, did not simply see some political motive in David's delegation. They decided that they were spies, taking a look around the city so that David could attack it (**10:3**). So instead of treating the official delegation with the respect that would have been expected, they manhandled them. Fortunately, Hanun was not as cruel

as his father, who had wanted to gouge out the right eyes of the inhabitants of Jabesh Gilead (1 Sam 11:2). Rather than killing the men, he shamed them. Shaving off half the beard and cutting off their clothes *at the buttocks* was extremely humiliating (**10:4-5**).

Hanun's counsellors led their new king in the wrong direction by labelling the delegation as spies. It is possible that they deliberately set out to provoke a war with Israel if they were subject to Israel in any way. If so, their actions were successful, for David immediately recognized that this humiliation of his envoys was tantamount to a revolt.

10:6-14 Joab and Abishai's victory

Both parties knew that conflict was now inevitable and began preparing for war. The Ammonites, who were weak, recruited Aramean mercenaries, as well as soldiers from *the king of Maacah* and *men from Tob* (**10:6**). David sent his army commander *Joab* against this coalition, with the entire Israelite army (**10:7**).

The Ammonites and their allies took up positions in two separate places near the Ammonites' city (**10:8**), so Joab divided his troops into two (**10:9-10**). He led the battle on the Aramean front, while his brother *Abishai* took on the Ammonite front. Joab's words of encouragement to Abishai blended faith and patriotism: *Be strong and let us fight bravely for our people and the cities of our God* (**10:11**). He ended his instructions by expressing complete trust in the will of God: *The Lord will do what is good in his sight* (**10:12**). The outcome of the battle depended on the Lord and not on the combatants. Joab's humility contrasts markedly with the attitude of some who engage in what they call 'spiritual warfare'. These people sometimes leave God no option in regard to the outcome but announce their victories to us before the time. No human being, a mere creature, is able to oblige the Creator to act in a particular way.

Joab's strategy gave Israel victory (**10:13-14**). The Arameans were of no help to the Ammonites, as they fled as soon as they saw Joab's troops coming (10:13).

10:15-19 David's victory

The defeated Arameans later regrouped and brought up reinforcements (**10:15-16**). When David heard this he led the battle against them himself (**10:17**). To judge by the number of soldiers killed, David was fighting an army that was roughly twice as large as the one defeated by Joab (compare **10:18** and 10:6). Unlike Joab, who expressed his dependence on God, David says nothing of the kind – although it is true that we do not hear David say anything on this occasion. David's victory ends with the Arameans becoming subject to him.

11:1-12:25 David, Bathsheba, Uriah and Nathan

Chapters 11 and 12 deal with David's affair with Bathsheba, the murder of her husband, Uriah, and then Nathan's confrontation of David with what he has done. These tragic events devastated not only the family of the greatest king of Israel but also the lives of the entire nation. Interestingly, this sordid tale does not appear in Chronicles. 1 Chronicles 20:1 is similar to 11:1, but the verses that follow in 1 Chronicles pick up the story at 12:29-31, leaving out everything contained in 11:2-12:28.

11:1-5 David seduces Bathsheba

Chapter 11 opens with a clear condemnation of David's position: *In the spring, at the time when kings go off to war, David sent Joab out with the king's men and the whole Israelite army* (**11:1**). The war in question was the war with the Ammonites described in the preceding chapter. This war, precipitated by the ill-treatment of David's ambassadors, would drag David himself into sin. And it would do so because David chose not to carry out his royal responsibilities to lead his army, but instead chose to remain in Jerusalem while sending his men into battle.

While walking on the roof of his house, the king was seduced by Bathsheba's beauty while she was bathing (**11:2**). The king made enquiries and was told that this beautiful woman was *Bathsheba … the wife of Uriah the Hittite* (**11:3**). We will soon learn that Uriah is on the battlefield with Joab (11:6).

What happened next is told with remarkable rapidity. David sent for the woman and slept with her (**11:4**). The verb that is employed regularly in the first five verses of this chapter is 'sent'. It is David who sends, and this is a sign of his power and authority. He sends Joab to battle, he sends to ask the identity of this woman who is bathing, and he sends for her.

No dialogue is recorded between David and Bathsheba, and there is no indication of love. The liaison appears to be one-sided, with David exercising his power in a corrupt way, in order to please himself. Bathsheba's situation reflects the plight of many African women who are subject to the whims of those who hold power or have weapons. In fact, the verb used in Hebrew to express David's command could be translated as 'take by force', strongly suggesting that Bathsheba was virtually abducted. In many war-torn regions of Africa, married women and young girls are similarly taken by force and often used as sex slaves by those who are fighting leaders. Moreover, many women in Africa die of AIDS because they are given no choice about sexual relations, and cannot insist that their partner or husband be faithful to them alone, or even ask that he use a condom.

The first time we hear Bathsheba's voice is when she sends word to the king that she has conceived (**11:5**). In Hebrew, this message is only two words long.

11:6-25 David orders the murder of Uriah

Anxious to cover up his sin, David ordered Joab to send Uriah back from the battlefield. We once again see the power of the king in the constant repetition of forms of the verb 'to send' in **11:6**. The king pretended to consult Uriah about the progress of the war, and then sent him home to his wife with an encouragement to have sexual intercourse, couched in the Hebrew euphemism – *wash your feet* (**11:7-8**). David was hoping that Uriah would sleep with Bathsheba without realizing that she was already pregnant (for the pregnancy was still in its very early stages), and would then assume that he was the father of her child. But Uriah was a conscientious soldier. He did not go home. Instead, he slept *at the entrance to the palace with all his master's servants* (**11:9**). Unlike David, he did not want to enjoy the comforts of home while the rest of Israel was on the battlefield. There are two contrasts with David here. David did not go into battle, and he slept with someone else's wife. Uriah did go into battle and refused to sleep even with his own wife.

David's informants reported that Uriah had not gone home that night, and so David resorted to Plan B. He invited Uriah to eat with him and offered him a great deal of wine, hoping that when he was drunk, Uriah would forget his scruples and go home to sleep with his wife (**11:10-13**). David's recognition of the probability that excess consumption of alcohol would lead to sex reminds us that alcohol contributes greatly to the spread of HIV/AIDS in Africa. Someone who is drunk will easily forget all about morality and practising safe sex

Yet despite being drunk, Uriah refused to go home. Instead, he again slept *on his mat among his master's servants.* We may wonder whether Uriah had become suspicious about David's sudden interest in his domestic life. It is also possible that he was simply obeying some taboo on sexual relations when waging war. In Africa, similar taboos exist among certain tribes, who associate sexual relations with bad luck. Thus they will avoid them before setting out on a hunting or fishing expedition. Similarly, many football (soccer) teams expect players to avoid sexual relations before a big game. But sexual relations within a marriage should not be seen as bringing misfortune to anyone.

Uriah spent three days and nights in Jerusalem without visiting his wife. Meanwhile, the pregnancy was advancing. David decided that the only way out of his predicament was to have Uriah killed. It was not that he feared prison for what he had done, but rather he feared that the public shame he would be exposed to would erode support for his throne. Accordingly, he gave Uriah a letter for Joab that would seal Uriah's fate (**11:14**). Joab was to put Uriah *in the front line where the fighting is fiercest* and then those around him were to fall back, leaving him to *be struck down* (**11:15**). This time, the plan worked. Uriah died in the battle

RAPE

Rape is sexual intercourse that one of those involved does not want. Although men can be raped, the victims are generally women and children. The rapists may be strangers, as with Shechem and Dinah (Gen 34) or they may be trusted friends and family members, as in the case of Amnon and Tamar (2 Sam 13).

Some say that rape happens because women are inherently morally weak. This argument is false, for both men and women are equally affected by sin. The argument that women are raped because their revealing clothing excites men is also simplistic, for if that were the case, why are women of all ages raped? The story of Tamar shows that rape has nothing to do with what a woman is wearing, for she is specifically said to have been wearing 'a long robe with sleeves' (2 Sam 13:18 NASB). Beauty should be celebrated as a gift from God, not as an excuse for rape.

Women are sometimes raped to punish them for not respecting men's authority. Many men believe that they can demand sex because women are there to serve them sexually. They refuse to listen when women and girls say no to their sexual advances. The same type of thinking leads some men to see women as just toys to provide fun for them, as happened in the gang rape of the concubine in Judges 19. Such men have no concern for the woman's feelings or whether she is injured. Women are created in the image of God. They are not toys to be used for the amusement of others.

Other men rape virgins and children (including infants) because there is a myth that sex with a virgin will cure someone who is HIV positive. There is no truth whatever to this belief, and all that happens is that an innocent victim is infected with HIV/AIDS.

During war, rape is often used as a weapon, to show contempt and assert one group's power over another.

Sadly, the court systems of some countries do not take rape seriously and impose very light sentences on those who perpetrate it. This encourages rape, because men know that they can get away with it. It also discourages people from reporting rapes to the police, because they know that they will be humiliated and blamed for what happened by the police, the law, their family and their community. Such attitudes are incompatible with our belief that God is a God of justice.

Society minimizes the effects that rape has on those who survive it. But Karen Buckenham, who has written a resource manual for those dealing with violence against women, reports that 'rape has the same effects on a victim as torture: intense degradation, inability to trust, constant fear, psychological problems, anger, feelings of guilt and shame'. Some women who were raped as children or young adults are unable to lead a normal married life. The self-esteem of others is so destroyed that they turn to prostitution.

David's lack of response to his son's rape of Tamar reminds us that while only a few men rape, many men are silent about it. Silence encourages rape, and so the church needs to break its silence by preaching constantly against the abuse of women and children. We need to create an atmosphere of trust so that survivors of rape can have the courage to talk about it. We need to declare the church and our homes to be zero tolerance zones for any form of sexual abuse. We need to direct rape survivors to professional counselling. If such counselling is not available, we need to set up shelters where it is available. At the very least, all pastors should have some training in counselling rape survivors. These survivors include the families of victims, because as the history of Tamar, Amnon, King David and Absalom shows, rape wounds a whole family.

Jesus Christ came to redeem humanity from evil. He restores broken-hearted survivors, and he can also restore those who perpetrate rape. The church should report rapes to the police, but it should also seek to confront perpetrators of abuse and lead them to confession, deliverance and counselling.

Finally, the church needs to preach a message that helps men and women to develop relationships of respect and trust. It should encourage men to take responsibility for their sexuality and make it clear that anyone who abuses another has lost a sense of dignity and integrity. The church should clearly and consistently proclaim that true love protects others from all that is harmful. We show our love for God by the way we treat others (John 13:34-35).

Isabel Apawo Phiri

(11:16-17). It could be said that 'anything goes in politics, including murder!'

David's commander Joab sent a full report about the battle (11:18). He knew that David would be angry that men had been lost in battle because the attackers had gone too close to the city wall. The dangers of doing this were well known (11:19-21a; Judg 9:52-53). Joab also knew that in the past an angry David had killed messengers who brought bad news (1:13-16). So he told the messenger to add the words that would immediately calm the king's anger: *Your servant Uriah the Hittite is dead* (11:21b).

Joab's message was faithfully reported to David (11:22-24). On hearing of Uriah's death, David did not reproach Joab for his recklessness, but instead sought to salve Joab's conscience about what had happened with the platitude that deaths were to be expected in battle (11:25).

11:26-27 Conclusion

Events moved swiftly after Uriah's death. Bathsheba went into mourning at the death of her husband. As soon as that period of mourning was over, David took her as his wife and she bore him a son (**11:26-27a**).

Throughout this account, we have heard no word of reproach from God. This may give the reader the impression that God accepted everything David had done. Why had he not condemned David's adultery?

But the final words of the chapter express God's condemnation of David's actions: *the thing David had done displeased the Lord* (**11:27b**). David might attempt to dismiss what had happened as a minor incident, but in God's eyes he had committed great sin.

By the end of this chapter, we see David in a very different light from the way we saw him at 8:15. The man who had previously done 'what was just and right' has become a despot who murders a faithful subject.

12:1-14 Nathan confronts David

God revealed his displeasure with David through the prophet Nathan. This man of God must have known that it was dangerous to speak to the king, particularly when rebuking him. So he presented his rebuke in the form of a story. It is about a poor man and a rich man, which focuses particularly on the situation of the poor man. He owned only one lamb, which he had bought and which he loved as if it were his child (**12:1-3**). The rich man had many sheep and cattle, yet when he wanted to offer a meal to visitors he did not slaughter one of his own animals, but took the poor man's lamb (**12:4**). The verb 'took' reminds us of how David took Bathsheba. In the same way that the rich man had numerous sheep, David the king had numerous wives. Just as the poor man had only one sheep, Uriah had only one wife. Yet rather than being content with his many wives, David had stolen the only wife of one of his soldiers. It is also worth noting that in the story the rich man did not organize the death of the poor man as David had done with Uriah.

David failed to recognize the analogy between this story and what he had done, but his sense of justice was aroused and he immediately responded in anger, stating that *the man who did this deserves to die!* Not only that, but he must make restitution and *pay for that lamb four times over* (**12:5-6**). This reminds us of the amount Zacchaeus vowed to pay to those he had cheated (Luke 19:8; see also Exod 22:1).

David's response gave Nathan the opportunity he needed: *You are the man!* he said (**12:7**). He then delivered God's verdict on David's actions. But first the Lord (through Nathan) reminded David of his goodness toward him. Particular stress is laid on the number of wives God had given David, because it was David's attraction to women that had caused the problem. Here, for the first and only time in the Bible we are told that David had also taken over Saul's wives

(**12:8**). This would not have been an uncommon practice in the Near Eastern culture of that time, where a king often inherited the harem of his predecessor. The Lord's mention of all these wives emphasizes David's extreme selfishness in taking another man's only wife. The accusation is clear: you took Uriah's wife and you assassinated Uriah (**12:9**).

The judgment was now delivered: *the sword will never depart from your house* (**12:10**), *before your very eyes I will take your wives and give them to one who is close to you* (**12:11**; see 16:21-22) and *the son born to you will die* (**12:14b**). Though David acted in secret, the Lord saw everything. And David will be punished publicly, over time (**12:12**). The abduction of Bathsheba will be the cause of death and misery that will descend on David's house. It is important to note that David was not being punished just for what he had done to Bathsheba and Uriah, but because his sin had *made the enemies of the Lord show utter contempt* (**12:14a**). Although David is king, he cannot just do as he pleases. He has to listen to the Lord's message of justice, delivered by his prophet.

Nathan's example reminds us that the African church needs to play a prophetic role when it comes to defending the poor. In a number of countries, the rights of the poor are not respected. The law is applied especially severely against the poor, and courts and tribunals sometimes deliver unfair verdicts against those who have less money. The property of the poor may be expropriated, or villagers' crops may be seized by men in uniform. Those who have more than enough (the rich) take what little the poor have scraped together.

The story also reminds us that in many countries in Africa and around the world, extreme wealth exists beside extreme poverty. In the big cities we often see hovels next to luxurious villas.

Recognizing the seriousness of his situation, David confessed what he had done and begged for pardon (**12:13**). As the saying goes, acknowledging one's sin is the first step to having it pardoned. Nathan was able to assure David that he would be forgiven, but the death penalty that he deserved would be transferred to Bathsheba's child, who would die.

12:15-25 Death of the child

We are never told the name of the child born to David and Bathsheba, for the focus of this section is not so much on the fate of the child but on David's reaction to the child's illness and death. He was filled with grief and remorse (**12:15**). In spite of Nathan's prophecy, David pleaded with God for the child, fasting and spending the nights lying on the ground (**12:16-17**).

But when David's servants plucked up the courage to tell him the child had died (**12:18-19**), his response surprised them. Instead of being prostrate with grief, he got up from the ground, put on fresh clothes, went into the house of the

Lord to worship, and resumed eating (**12:20-21**). David's explanation for the change was that death is irreversible. A sick child might recover if God were moved by its father's repentance, but once the child was dead, there was no hope, and no point in continued prayer and fasting (**12:22-23**). His words *I will go to him* are often used by African preachers to console those who have lost loved ones.

At the start of this section, Bathsheba was referred to as *Uriah's wife* (12:15) but now that David has suffered his punishment, she is referred to as his wife (**12:24a**). The second child that she bore to David was named Solomon (**12:24b**). To mark the fact that David had been restored to favour, God again sent Nathan to him with a message of comfort (**12:25**). This message is summed up in the instruction to give the newborn the additional name of *Jedidiah* (meaning 'loved by the Lord').

12:26-31 End of the war with the Ammonites

The chapter finishes with an account of the end of war against the Ammonites that had been sparked by the insult to David's ambassadors in 10:1-5 and that dragged on during the affair with Bathsheba and Uriah. Joab had effectively captured the city of *Rabbah* by taking its water supply, but he did not want to claim this victory for himself (**12:26-28**). So he summoned David to come from Jerusalem and lead the final assault (**12:29-30**). The Ammonites were now subject to David and were condemned to forced labour (**12:31**).

13:1-19:43 The Story of Absalom

The saga of Absalom, David's third son, begins in chapter 13 and continues until chapter 19. In these chapters, we see the consequence of David's sin with Bathsheba.

13:1-22 The rape of Tamar

David had shown a lack of sexual restraint when it came to the wife of one of his soldiers, Uriah; Amnon, one of David's sons, showed a similar lack of restraint when he raped his half-sister Tamar.

Amnon's infatuation with Tamar was the spark that ignited the events that would bring disaster on David's family. Tamar was very beautiful and Amnon was obsessed with her *to the point of illness* (**13:1-2**). Yet he could not get near her because the princesses were raised separately from their brothers and were watched over by one or more chaperones. One reason for this was to protect their virginity, which was highly valued in Israel. A young woman who was not a virgin was often not considered marriageable. This custom helped to restrain debauchery and immorality. Unfortunately, some young women today take completely the opposite view and regard virginity as something to be ashamed of! Even the church no longer stresses the importance of virginity for all those who are entering into a first marriage.

Jonadab, Amnon's cousin, decided to help his friend satisfy his lust. Together they worked out a plan whereby Amnon would pretend to be very ill and would beg that Tamar be allowed to come and feed him (**13:3-5**). The ruse worked, and King David sent Tamar to nurse Amnon (**13:6-10**). Seizing the opportunity, Amnon raped Tamar, despite her desperate pleas for mercy (**13:12-14**). She clearly struggled against him for it is said he was successful because *he was stronger than she* (13:14). His lust overrode all thoughts about family honour and concern for what would become of Tamar.

Tamar's situation is sadly similar to that of the many girls and women who are raped each day on the African continent. Some of them are lured into situations where they cannot resist their attacker, while others are simply subjected to violent rape.

The emotion that had been characterized as love in 13:4 proved to be nothing more than fleeting lust. After having had sex with her, Amnon wanted nothing more to do with Tamar and had his servant throw her out of his apartment (**13:15-18**). Having lost her virginity, she had lost her honour and likely any chance of security, love and marriage. No wonder she tore her robe and *put ashes on her head* in a sign of mourning (**13:19**).

Tamar's brother Absalom saw her distress and learned of what Amnon had done. He offered her shelter in his own home (**13:20**). But he hated Amnon for what he had done to his sister and planned revenge (**13:22**).

David too *was furious* when he heard how Amnon had abused his sister (**13:21**). But he remained passive and took no action to punish Amnon. His own abduction of Bathsheba and murder of her husband may have shaken his confidence in his authority to rebuke Amnon.

13:23-39 Absalom's revenge and flight

Both rape and sexual relations with a sister were forbidden by Israelite law (Lev 18:9, 11). So Absalom probably waited for his father to act. When he did not, Absalom decided to take matters into his own hands.

We see similar situations in Africa today, where many women and girls have been raped and have no recourse to justice. The result is that they internalize their anger and grief. Justice has the power to heal grief, but the lack of justice will produce more violence, as it did in David's family.

Absalom nursed his anger for a whole two years before avenging his sister's rape. His revenge would be the second consequence of David's sin and the beginning of the fulfilment of Nathan's prophecy that the sword would never depart from David's house (12:10).

Absalom was a cunning man who disguised his intentions while carefully planning his revenge. He finally decided that the appropriate time had come and invited the king, his officials and all his half-brothers to a feast at Baal Hazor

(**13:23-24**). This would not have aroused any suspicion, for sheep-shearing was always accompanied by feasting (see 1 Sam 25:4, 36). When David declined to come, Absalom requested that Amnon be sent as the king's representative, for Amnon was the heir to the throne (**13:26**; see also 3:2). Finally, the king gave in to Absalom's persistent pleading and sent Amnon to the feast (**13:27**).

Amnon and *the rest of the king's sons* assembled at Baal Hazor. There Absalom instructed his servants to kill Amnon when he was in *high spirits from drinking wine* (**13:28**). Like his father, Absalom was using alcohol as a tool to manipulate others (see 11:13). Although Absalom did not tell his servants why he wanted Amnon dead, they probably knew the reason, for the disgraced Tamar now lived in Absalom's home. So the servants did *to Amnon what Absalom … ordered* and Tamar's rape was avenged (**13:29**).

Not only did the death of Amnon settle a debt of honour, it also removed David's firstborn son, who would have been ahead of Absalom in the line for the throne (3:2). By killing Amnon, Absalom became the heir apparent.

Absalom had chosen the site for the murder because it offered a quick escape route. He took to flight and found refuge with his maternal grandfather, the king of Geshur (**13:37-38**).

Meanwhile, all the king's sons fled back to Jerusalem. Before they arrived, a rumour reached the palace that all of them had been killed by Absalom. David must have thought that Nathan's promise about his continuing dynasty would now never be fulfilled (**13:31**; 7:12-16). But Jonadab, who had helped set up Tamar's rape, guessed what had happened. He assured David that only Amnon would have been killed, because of what he had done to Tamar (**13:32-33**). Jonadab takes care not to mention his role in those events.

Eventually the king's surviving sons rejoined their father and joined him in mourning (**13:34-36**). We are told that King David *mourned for his son every day* (13:37) – but it is not always clear whether the son he mourns is Amnon or Absalom (**13:39**).

14:1-33 Absalom's return

We are next given an account of Joab's manoeuvrings to enable Absalom to return to favour and to the royal court. One of the reasons he was anxious to bring this about may have been that Absalom was now David's legitimate successor (assuming that his older brother Kileab, the son of Abigail, had died – 3:3). It was therefore undesirable for him to remain in exile.

Absalom's return took place in two stages. In the first, Joab arranged for him to return to the court but without any access to the king. In the second stage, Absalom pressured Joab to intervene to have his full rights as heir to the throne restored.

14:1-24 Joab's intervention for Absalom Absalom remained in exile for three years (13:3). During this time, Joab, the commander of David's forces, must have worked closely with the king, and he noticed that *the king's heart longed for Absalom* (**14:1**). So he carefully staged an appeal to the king that would lead to amnesty for the murderer. The one who would make this appeal would be a *wise woman* from the town of Tekoa, which would later be the birthplace of the prophet Amos (**14:2a**). Joab carefully chose the right moment and the right spokesperson to achieve his goal.

Joab coached the woman in how to act and what to say as she approached the king (**14:2b-3**). His strategy was similar to that of Nathan's in 2 Samuel 12. Once again a story was used to awaken the king to his own situation. The details of the story remind us of Cain's murder of Abel (Gen 4:1-15).

The woman of Tekoa pretended to be a widow, who had only two sons. During a dispute between these sons, one had struck the other and killed him. Now the community court had imposed a death penalty on the sole surviving son. If this sentence were carried out, her husband's family line would be wiped out, which would be a tragedy for an Israelite (**14:5-7, 16**). Not only that, but she herself would be left destitute – for as sometimes happens in Africa today, a widow with no sons to protect her could be evicted from the family property. So she appealed to the king for an amnesty for her son (14:5-7).

David granted her appeal, saying that he would *issue an order* on her behalf that would prevent the *avenger of blood* from exacting vengeance (**14:11-12**).

The woman then took the opportunity to point out that David's judgment in her case also applied to his own relationship with Absalom. Just as she would be left desolate if her sole surviving son was killed, so the nation would be left desolate if the heir to the throne was not brought back from exile (**14:13**). Amnon was dead and there was nothing that could be done about that (**14:14a**). Absalom was a murderer, but that did not take away his rights as the king's son. God had been merciful to Cain (Gen 4:13-15), cannot David be equally merciful to his son? (**14:14b**).

The woman concluded her appeal by praising David's discernment (**14:17**), which he promptly demonstrated by asking the woman whether she had been sent by Joab (**14:19-20**). David does not seem to have reproached Joab for manipulating him. It is likely that he was hoping for some excuse to recall Absalom, but had not wanted to be the one to take the initiative (see 14:1). By framing events in this way, David cannot be accused of not punishing Absalom for the murder of his brother. It was not David who arranged for him to return to court, but Joab.

While Joab was the one who set up this meeting, we should not underestimate the woman's contribution to its success. Joab could not have predicted exactly how the king would reply to her, and she would have had to rely on her own wisdom when it came to directing the course of the dialogue between them.

This passage raises the question of whether murderers should be granted amnesty. Such amnesties are becoming increasingly common in Africa. Each time a new regime is installed, one of its first acts is to issue a general amnesty because those who have seized power by force are anxious to avoid being hauled into court to account for their actions. Similarly, whenever there is a peace treaty between enemy factions, one of the clauses is an amnesty for all the combatants.

But as Absalom's subsequent history demonstrates, peace cannot be built on the basis of amnesty for the guilty. Amnesties do not result in true peace and true reconciliation. Only justice can produce that.

Similar situations may arise within the church, where a member may be encouraged to pardon another for harm done to them. But in encouraging forgiveness, the church should not ignore the damage done. If, for example, a Christian brother or sister borrows someone's vehicle, and then drives it carelessly and has an accident, that brother or sister should be pardoned – but they should also be expected to compensate the owner of the vehicle for the damage they caused (unless the owner refuses such compensation).

David granted Absalom only a partial amnesty. The heir to the throne could return to the court, but he was not to appear before the king.

14:25-33 Absalom takes action This section begins with a description of Absalom (**14:25-26**). His good looks remind us of the young Saul (1 Sam 9:1-2) and David (1 Sam 16:12), and prepare us for what will follow as he starts to plot to become a king. Absalom also had sons and daughters, and he named one of his daughters Tamar, in honour of his raped sister (**14:27**).

Absalom had been banished for three years, and another two years elapsed without direct contact with his father (**14:28**). Then Absalom himself decided it was time to act, and tried to contact Joab to intercede for him again (**14:29**). But Joab was surprisingly reluctant to be allied with Absalom. We do not know why there had been this change in his attitude, but it may be that he had begun to be concerned about Absalom's ambition. For whatever reason, Joab kept his distance from Absalom.

Following Samson's example (Judg 15:4-8), Absalom set fire to Joab's field, which immediately got him Joab's attention (**14:31**). The prince demanded that he either be given a full pardon or be condemned to death as a murderer (**14:32**). He was tired of being excluded from power, and knew that David could not bring himself to execute him. Joab conveyed Absalom's message to the king who at last agreed to receive Absalom, a meeting that was equivalent to granting him complete amnesty (**14:33**). Five years after

the death of Amnon, Absalom was reinstated at court as the heir apparent.

Tamar had been raped, Amnon murdered, Absalom banished and then reconciled with his father. But there was still more trouble in store for David's family. Absalom's return to favour would put David's life and throne in danger.

15:1-12 Absalom's coup d'état

By this time, David must have been an elderly man, and people must have been thinking about who would succeed him. As noted in 14:25-27, Absalom had characteristics that would make him a very attractive candidate. And even though the throne was not yet vacant, the ambitious Absalom was anxious to occupy it.

Absalom began to behave like a king. He obtained a *chariot, horses* and a large personal bodyguard *to run ahead of him* (**15:1**). He also embarked on a campaign to win the hearts of the people. He did this by presenting himself as a friend to all, refusing to let people *bow down before him,* and vigorously criticizing the inadequacies of David's administration of justice (**15:2-6**). He promised that if he were the chief justice (which in those days was equivalent to being king) he would ensure that everyone could obtain justice. Given the frequent lack of access to justice in Africa, and the extent to which judges are swayed by tribal and regional loyalties, we can well appreciate the appeal of such a promise.

While Absalom may have exaggerated the extent of the problem, there seems to be little doubt that his words did reflect something of the reality of the system of justice in David's day. Justice had not been done in the case of Bathsheba, when it was the king himself who had broken the law. David had also not stood up for justice with regard to the rape of Tamar or the murder of Amnon.

Four years after his return to favour, Absalom decided that the time was ripe to stage a *coup d'état.* He quietly set off for Hebron, pretending that he had a vow that he had to fulfil (**15:7-10**). Hebron was symbolically important, for it was not only his birthplace but also the place where his father David had been anointed king.

He did not invite his father or his brothers to accompany him. His brothers might well have been reluctant to accept any invitation from him after what had happened to Amnon (13:23-29). He was, however, accompanied by *two hundred men* from Jerusalem, who had no idea of what Absalom was planning (**15:11**). But not everyone was in the dark, for Absalom had sent out secret messengers to all the tribes of Israel, who would rise in support of him when the time came, saying, *Absalom is king in Hebron* (15:10). And he had also managed to obtain the support of one of his father's counsellors, *Ahithophel* (**15:12**).

But no matter how much support Absalom rallied, there could be no doubt that he was seizing the throne by force. The legitimate king, David, was still alive; thus any other authority was illegitimate. But as we often see in Africa, when people cannot obtain power by the legitimate route of the ballot box, they turn to other means. Power is seized by the army, or with the help of the army. We need to remember that, while it is true that the Bible does not endorse any one system of government, democracy, the expression of the will of the people, is still a sound way of establishing a legitimate government.

15:13-37 David flees Jerusalem

An informant, probably one of those who had been tricked into attending the coronation at Hebron, rushed to inform David that *the hearts of the men of Israel are with Absalom* (**15:13**). The balance of power had shifted, and the people were no longer with David but with the new king.

Fearing that Jerusalem would quickly be overrun, David ordered his supporters to leave the city immediately. He recognized that the forces loyal to him would not be sufficient to resist the army raised by Absalom. He also feared that a battle in Jerusalem might lead to the destruction of the city and the loss of many lives (**15:14**). David was still concerned for the welfare of his people in the city of his God. The interests of the nation and the people took precedence over his personal political interest.

What a contrast with the attitude of those who have led many of the wars in Africa! Our cities have been pillaged and great structures destroyed. Factories have been ransacked and homes demolished. Those who put their thirst for power before the interests of the nation cannot claim to be concerned about the welfare of their people or city.

Although Absalom's support was growing rapidly, David still had faithful men, ready to follow him wherever he went (**15:15**). He left the city, leaving only ten of his concubines behind *to take care of the palace* (**15:16**). This information prepares the ground for what will happen in 16:21-22.

After putting some distance between himself and the city, David stopped to check who was with him (**15:17**). His main supporters appear to have been his personal bodyguard, *the Kerithites and Pelethites*, who were foreigners (**15:18**). We do not know why David did not trust his brother Israelites for his protection. David was also accompanied by six hundred men who came from Gath, led by a man called Ittai. It is possible that David had come to know Ittai when he found refuge with the Philistines (1 Sam 27). In a test of Ittai's loyalty, David suggested that he should remain in Jerusalem, where he had recently arrived, but Ittai insisted that he and his men would stand by David (**15:19-22**).

David might be fleeing from Absalom, but that did not mean that he did not think of the future. He instructed *Zadok and Abiathar* to return to Jerusalem with the ark of the covenant, which the Levites had brought with them when they fled (**15:24-25**). He knew what he would need

most in the desert was not priests but his army. The priests would be more useful to him if they remained in Jerusalem. There they would be his secret agents, his informants, with their sons carrying messages to him without Absalom knowing anything about it (15:27-28).

David's words of farewell as he sent the priests back to Jerusalem remind us that this king was fully obedient to the will of God. He did not manipulate God. He did not try to force God to act in his favour (**15:25-26**).

The people who were with David and those who were watching him and his men leave felt deep compassion for him (**15:23, 30**).

Not only had David been betrayed by his son, but one of his trusted counsellors had abandoned him and joined with Absalom (15:12). On learning of this, David was moved to pray that God would *turn Ahithophel's counsel into foolishness* (**15:31**). But another of his counsellors, *Hushai*, was faithful to David and offered to accompany him (**15:32**). Instead, David asked him to return to Jerusalem along with Zadok and Abiathar to strengthen the information network (**15:33-36**). Hushai was to offer his services to Absalom, and then to use his privileged position to pass information on to Zadok and Abiathar. These two priests would then pass on the information to their sons, who would carry it to David.

King David was a practical politician. He trusted in God, but he also did everything humanly possible to control the course of events. He did not simply sit back and passively wait for God to intervene to bring him back to Jerusalem. He would have agreed with the great Saint Benedict, whose slogan was 'Pray and Work'. In Africa today, some people treat God as a magician. They do nothing but sit around, pray and wait for a miracle from God. They are encouraged to do this by many preachers who destroy lives and drain energy. One such preacher told a group of Christians that each of them should bring him a large sum of money if they wanted to get ten times as much in return. In their naivety, some brought their entire savings. Months passed and nothing happened. God cannot be treated as a counterfeiter who multiplies money in a miraculous way. The money we get should be money we earn. God blesses us in our work, not in our idleness.

Hushai, who was David's friend as well as his counsellor, obeyed David's instructions and returned to Jerusalem just *as Absalom was entering the city* (**15:37**).

16:1-14 Meetings on the road from Jerusalem

As David was fleeing from Absalom, he met two men who were associated with Saul's family, Ziba and Shimei.

16:1-4 DAVID AND ZIBA Ziba was one of Saul's servants whom David had entrusted with the care of Mephibosheth's estate (9:9-10). Mephibosheth remained in Jerusalem, probably because his disability would have made it difficult for him to accompany David. Ziba, however, hurried out to meet David, to signal that he was on David's side (**16:1**). He had brought much needed food and wine for David's troops, who had probably not had time to assemble provisions before leaving the city.

David was always suspicious of the loyalty of Saul's descendants, and so he asked Ziba a question in order to find out Mephibosheth's views about the political upheaval in Jerusalem (**16:3**). Ziba's response (which may or may not have been true) revealed that Saul's descendant still aspired to the throne. According to Ziba, Mephibosheth thought that the civil war that was now raging would provide an opportunity for his family to regain power. Angered by Mephibosheth's ingratitude after all the kindness he had been shown (ch. 9), David stripped him of all the land he had been given and gave this land to Ziba (**16:4**).

Once again, we see a king using his power to allocate land to reward his supporters. The problem is that such allocations take no account of people's legal rights, but simply reflect what the king wants to do.

16:5-14 DAVID AND SHIMEI Shimei's hostility to David is understandable when we note that he was from *the same clan as Saul's family* (**16:5**). His words and actions reveal how Saul's supporters, who were clearly still active, interpreted Absalom's revolt. They saw David as a *man of blood*, meaning that David had killed others himself, or had caused them to be killed (16:8). The biblical account clears David of any involvement in the death of Saul and his family, but Saul's party probably still held David responsible for the deaths of Saul, Ish-Bosheth and Abner. They thus regarded Absalom's *coup d'état* as God's punishment of David. Thus Shimei had no respect for the king who was fleeing from his own son, and he cursed him and threw stones at him (**16:6-8, 13-14**).

Abishai, the brother of Joab, David's general, was ready to kill Shimei, but David stopped him (**16:9**). David left everything in God's hands. He did not respond to Shimei's allegations but accepted the curse if this was part of the trouble God was sending him (**16:10**). Moreover, as he pointed out, *My son, who is of my own flesh, is trying to take my life. How much more, then, this Benjamite!* (**16:11**). David was well aware that Saul's descendants were still hostile to his rule.

16:15-23 Absalom in Jerusalem

The narrator now turns attention away from the king and back to Jerusalem. In 15:33-36, David had sent Hushai back to act as his agent and to counter any good advice given by the traitor, Ahithophel. We now see how Hushai accomplished his mission.

16:15-19 HUSHAI'S DECEPTION When the new king made his entry along with his troops, Hushai came before him and expressed his allegiance, saying, *Long live the king!*

(**16:15-16**). Absalom was sceptical, and questioned him about his loyalties (**16:17**). Hushai's response was convincing, but also ambiguous. He stated that he would always serve the true king (but did not specify whether this was David or Absalom – **16:18**). He also argued that swearing allegiance to Absalom was not treachery against David (which was true, because he was doing as David had instructed him). Hushai insisted that serving Absalom was no different from serving David because the new king was the son of David. Serving the father or the son amounted to the same thing (**16:19**).

16:20-23 AHITHOPHEL'S ADVICE Once he had arrived in Jerusalem, the new king was not sure what he should do next. So he consulted his father's counsellor (**16:20**). Ahithophel advised him to sleep with his father's concubines, who had been left to look after the palace (**16:21a**). Some have interpreted this act as an attempt to claim that he was David's legitimate successor (see 12:8, which speaks of David inheriting Saul's concubines). But this was not the reason that Ahithophel gave for doing this. He saw it as a way to make a public statement that there was a total break between Absalom and his father, with no hope of reconciliation: *all Israel will hear that you have made yourself an offence to your father's nostrils* (**16:21b**). Absalom's supporters could be sure that he would not go back on what he had done and expose them to trouble. The break with his father would be as definite as that of Reuben, who forfeited his position as the first-born when he slept with Bilhah, the concubine of his father Jacob (Gen 35:22; 49:3-4).

A tent was accordingly set up on the roof of the palace, probably very near the place from which David had seen Bathsheba bathing. Absalom then publicly went in to be with his father's concubines, making sure that *all Israel* knew about it (**16:22**).

The story ends with a note concerning Ahithophel. For David and Absalom, Ahithophel's advice had the same authority as God's word delivered by a prophet (**16:23**). David and Absalom might sit on the throne, but the real power lay in the hands of their counsellor.

In some Christian communities, there are people whose word is treated as if it were 'gospel truth'. This is always dangerous. We may trust advice given by a human being, but we should always remember that human beings are fallible and may sometimes be wrong. Only God's word is never in error.

17:1-14 Absalom's advisors

Absalom was given conflicting advice by his two most senior advisors. As we read their advice, we should remember David's prayer against Ahithophel (15:31) and that Hushai was acting as David's agent (15:33-36).

17:1-4 AHITHOPHEL'S ADVICE Ahithophel's advice to Absalom to have sex with his father's concubines had helped to consolidate Absalom's power (16:20-21) and so Absalom again turned to this man, who was regarded as the greatest of counsellors (16:23), for advice on what to do next. Ahitophel proposed a plan to eliminate David, thus ensuring that Absalom would have no rival. He recommended that Absalom take a thousand men from each tribe and pursue the king immediately, before he had time to recover from his long march and rally support (**17:1-2**). A surprise attack on this disorganized group would enable Absalom to minimize loss of life, thus reducing any hostility towards him. The focus should be on killing David, because once he was dead, his troops would transfer their allegiance to Absalom (**17:3**). Ahithophel proposed that he himself should lead this army.

Ahithophel's plan was a good one (see also 17:14) and was accepted by Absalom and his counsel (**17:4**). Yet Absalom was still nervous and wanted a second opinion.

17:5-14 HUSHAI'S ADVICE The advisor to whom Absalom turned for a second opinion was Hushai who, unbeknown to Absalom, was working to promote David's interests (**17:5-6**). Hushai's advice was presented in a persuasive and well-organized way. He acknowledged that Ahithophel was usually a wise counsellor, but insisted that on this occasion his advice was wrong because he was ignoring one important fact (**17:7**). David was an experienced warrior who had been in this type of situation before when he fled from Saul. He would not be taken by surprise, or even be found with his men. Moreover, given that the troops who were with him were brave battle-hardened men, he might even have set up an ambush for pursuing troops. If Absalom's attack failed, his supporters would be demoralized (**17:8b-10**). Hushai used a popular metaphor to make his point that David and his men would have become even more dangerous during their flight: they would be as brave and aggressive as a *wild bear robbed of her cubs* (**17:8a**; see also Prov 17:12; Hos 13:8).

Hushai proposed an alternative plan to the one put forward by Ahithophel. His plan contrasted with the other at every point. Whereas Ahithophel proposed immediate action, Hushai suggested that they wait and gather their forces *from Dan to Beersheba* (**17:11**). Instead of a small army of twelve thousand men, Hushai suggested that all Israel should be mobilized. The army should also not be led by Ahithophel but by Absalom himself, and the goal should not be a surgical strike to take out only the king, but rather the slaughter of all David's men (**17:12-13**).

Hushai knew that David and his troops were exhausted (16:14) but hoped that, in the time it would take to assemble the full Israelite army, David would have time to choose a refuge and to reorganize. The suggestion that Absalom lead the army meant that Absalom himself might be killed. The goal of eliminating David's entire army would ensure

a pitched battle, in which Absalom's death would be more likely, and would also alienate the relatives of those killed.

Earlier David had prayed, 'O Lord, turn Ahithophel's counsel into foolishness' (15:31). That prayer was answered as Absalom found Hushai's argument more convincing than Ahithophel's. Ahithophel's advice might have been regarded as 'like that of one who enquires of God', but on this occasion God worked against him (**17:14**; 16:23).

There is a lesson here for those who ask advice. The advice we receive may not be in our best interests, but rather in the interests of the one giving the advice. Ahithophel's advice was actually far better than that of Hushai, but Absalom failed to realize that Hushai's objections to it were designed to protect David.

17:15-29 David crosses the Jordan

Not certain which plan would be adopted, Hushai hurriedly sent a message to David telling him not to *spend the night at the fords in the desert,* which was where Ahithophel planned to attack him (**17:15-16**). Obviously Hushai could not deliver this message himself, and so he arranged to have a servant girl deliver the message to *Jonathan* and *Ahimaaz,* the sons of the priests, who would then pass it to David (**17:17**). Unfortunately, the two sons of the priests were seen and followed. But their lives were saved by a quick-thinking woman who hid them in a well (**17:18-20**). When they reached David with their information, he and his troops quickly crossed over the Jordan by night (**17:21-22**).

This episode ends with the suicide of Ahithophel (**17:23**). He may have felt disgraced, in that for the first time in many years, his counsel had not been followed. Or he may have realized that Absalom's rejection of his plan would inevitably lead to the failure of his revolt and committed suicide before he could be executed as a traitor. Before he died, he *put his house in order,* that is, he issued orders about who was to inherit his property and how it was to be distributed. As the most powerful counsellor at the royal court, Ahithophel must have been a very wealthy man.

Though habits are starting to change, many Africans die without setting their own houses in order by leaving either a legal will or clear instructions to the village elders about what is to happen to their property. When a man fails to do this, it can cause great hardship for his wife. The husband's relatives may seize everything that he expected would be used to support his wife and children. One of the reasons that people die without a will is that they are afraid to think about their own death. But Christians should not be afraid to do so. Christ defeated death. Our lives are safe in Christ, even when we die. So we have no reason not to prepare for death.

Joab, the army commander, had fled with David, so Absalom now replaced him with a man named Amasa, who was

Joab's cousin (**17:24-25**). Absalom's army assembled *in the land of Gilead* (**17:26**).

Meanwhile David had set up camp at Mahanaim (where Ish-Bosheth had been installed during his reign – 2:8). There he and his tired and hungry men received welcome supplies of equipment and food (**17:27-29**). Those who provided the help included an Ammonite leader, *Shobi son of Nahash*, who was probably the person David has appointed as governor after he had conquered Rabbah (12:29). Those welcoming him also included *Makir,* who had first given shelter to Mephibosheth (9:4), and a man called *Barzillai* who will be mentioned later (19:31-39).

18:1-33 Absalom's defeat

The scene is now set for the decisive battle between the armies of Absalom and David.

18:1-18 THE DECISIVE BATTLE Once safely installed on the far side of the Jordan, David set about organizing his troops for the coming battle (**18:1**). He divided his men into three groups led by Joab, Abishai and Ittai (**18:2**). Once again, the king did not accompany his troops to battle (see 11:1), a fact that reminds us of the introduction to the account of his sin with Bathsheba, and thus of the fact that Absalom's revolt is in part a consequence of that sin. But this time David had a good reason for not going into battle: his men were concerned for his safety and asked him to stay behind (**18:3-4**). His absence also freed him from any responsibility for the death of his son.

David's order to his troops to *be gentle with the young man Absalom for my sake* also makes it clear that David did not seek his son's death, just as he had not sought the deaths of Saul, Ish-Bosheth and Abner (**18:5a**). But we notice that in this address to his troops he did not refer to Absalom as his son, but simply as 'the young man'. His words revealed his inner conflict. He was simultaneously a king who was fighting to defend his life and his throne and a father fighting against his son. No wonder his dearest wish was that the rebellion could be brought under control without it having to cost Absalom his life.

The author of 2 Samuel obviously considered this order very important, for the account of the battle focuses primarily on whether it was obeyed. We are left in no doubt that it had been heard: *all the troops heard the king giving orders concerning Absalom to each of the commanders* (**18:5b**).

Two chapters have been devoted to the events leading up to this battle, but the account of the battle itself is very brief. The opponents are named: the *army of Israel* (allied with Absalom) and *David's men* (**18:7**). The site of battlefield is also given as *the forest of Ephraim* (**18:6**). The forest contributed to David's victory, for although the Israelite army was defeated by David's men (18:7), *the forest claimed more lives that day than the sword* (**18:8**). The forest did not literally kill men, but Israel's soldiers were not accustomed to fighting in a forest, and may have become lost in it as they fled, so that they died there of thirst and hunger.

Absalom found himself face to face with *David's men* and tried to flee on *his mule* (**18:9a**). But as the mule ran through the trees in the forest, Absalom's head caught in a tree and he was swept off his mule and remained hanging in the tree, literally *between heaven and earth* (**18:9b** NASB). Pictures of the scene often show Absalom suspended by his hair (probably because of the reference to his hair in 14:26) but the Bible does not mention his hair here.

One young man who saw Absalom hanging there went and told Joab (**18:10**). Once again we are reminded of the order David had issued regarding the treatment of Absalom. The man's attitude shows his loyalty to the king through strict obedience to the king's command. He insists that even if someone weighed *a thousand shekels* of silver into his hands, he would not disobey the king's order (**18:12**).

His attitude contrasts with that of many in Africa, who will sell their consciences for money. The temptation to do this is very strong, for the continent's severe economic crises push people towards unethical behaviour. Thus we find police officers accepting bribes to free known criminals. Teachers give passing grades to students who do not merit them, but who have money. Money can deaden the conscience and corrupt the righteous.

The young man's attitude also contrasts with that of Joab, who deliberately murdered Absalom in defiance of the king's orders, of which he has just been reminded (**18:11-15**). Why did he do this? One possibility is that he still resented the fact that Absalom had manipulated him by burning his field (14:29-32). But it is also possible that he was showing the same cynical attitude that David had done when he responded to the news of Uriah's death by saying 'the sword devours one as well as another' (11:25). Joab had obeyed the king's command to eliminate Uriah because it was politically expedient to do so. Now he knew that only Absalom's death would end the rebellion.

With Absalom dead, Joab sounded a trumpet to recall his troops (**18:16**). Absalom was given a hurried burial. (**18:17**). His rebellion was over. His line had also ended. The three sons mentioned in 14:27 must have died before Absalom erected his memorial pillar (**18:18**).

18:19-19:8a DAVID'S REACTION TO ABSALOM'S DEATH The battle was over, Absalom dead – but the king still had to be informed of the outcome. Ahimaaz, the son of Zadok, who had been the agent who carried Hushai's warning to David (17:1-21) was eager to be the one to report the good news of the end of the rebellion (**18:19**). In his eyes, God had justly meted out punishment to the rebels.

Joab did not think that Ahimaaz was making a wise move, for although there had been a victory, the king would not be glad to hear that his son was dead (**18:20**). Joab knew how David had reacted in the past to those who thought they were telling him good news about an enemy's death (4:9-11). So Joab sent a *Cushite*, an African, to take the news to the king (**18:21**).

The problem with Eurocentric interpretations of the Bible becomes clear when we look at how Western scholars treat this incident. Some writers have suggested that Africans can run fast, and that is why this black man was chosen as a messenger. Others have been more blatantly racist, saying that a black man was chosen because black is the appropriate colour for someone bringing bad news. Still others assume that this man must have been a slave. None of these assumptions can be justified from the OT. This man was probably just another soldier in David's army. Despite attempts to downplay their role, Africans have participated in the history of God's people. Moses was even married to a Cushite, or Ethiopian, woman (Num 12:1).

Ahimaaz insisted that he would still like to take the news to the king, and so two envoys set off. Ahimaaz took the shorter route and reached David first (**18:23**). The sentinel watching from the wall recognized Ahimaaz' way of running at a distance (**18:24-27**). As a spy, he must often have brought news to the king. Ahimaaz praised God as he announced the news of the victory, but the king was more interested in the fate of his son (**18:28-29**). Ahimaaz, mindful of Joab's warning, pretended not to know what had become of him.

The Cushite then arrived. He, too, attributed to the Lord the victory of David's troops over *all who rose up against* him (**18:31**). Again David asked about the fate of Absalom. This African was a wise man. He indicated that Absalom was dead without actually using the word: *May the enemies of my lord the king and all who rise up to harm you be like that young man* (**18:32**). King David understood what he meant, and began to weep. Whereas he had questioned Ahimaaz and the Cushite about the 'young man Absalom' (18:29, 32), now he is overwhelmed with grief for *Absalom, my son*. The words *my son* echo five times in **18:33**. David's emotions as a father outweighed his emotions as a king.

David had casually ordered the death of Uriah, but now he had to endure the deep grief that only those who have suffered the death of a loved one can understand. The description of his grief is deeply moving and astonishingly frank. If any African journalist were to give a similarly honest report about the tears of a head of state, he would probably be charged with defamation!

Rather than celebrating the victory of his army, David was plunged into deepest mourning. The army crept back into town, as if they had been vanquished rather than victorious (**19:1-4**). But in his bitter grief for his son, David was neglecting the well-being of his troops and denying the people any chance to celebrate the end of the *coup d'état*.

In his intervention on Absalom's behalf many years before, Joab had used a woman from Tekoa to speak for him (14:1-3).

But there was no time for any such indirect approach now. Immediate action was necessary, and so Joab confronted the king and scolded him for his behaviour that risked alienating all those who had supported him and who had been prepared to risk their own lives on his behalf. David's behaviour was sending the message that the lives of his soldiers meant nothing to him in comparison with the life of his son (18:5-6). Unless David sent a different message to these men, he would face a new revolt (**19:7**).

David recognized the truth of Joab's words. So he *got up and took his seat in the gateway* (**19:8a**). He did not speak, but his followers were reassured that he was still able to govern.

19:8b-15 Preparation for David's return

After the battle, the nation was still divided. David's supporters had gathered around him, and Israel (Absalom's followers) had scattered to their homes (**19:8b**; see 18:10). David's return to the throne was not automatic. Absalom's revolt was no minor matter. He had turned the hearts of the people away from David, and he had been accepted and anointed as king in David's place (**19:9-10a**). That was why David could not simply march back into Jerusalem, and why he had to develop a strategy for regaining power.

The restoration of David, like his initial coronation, took place in two phases. The northern tribes, who had been Absalom's supporters, were the first to express an interest in David's return (**19:10b**). But David wanted to return to Jerusalem in the south. So he used the priests to deliver his political message to the elders of Judah, appealing to family ties as he asked the people of Judah (his own tribe) to bring him back before the Israelites (Absalom's allies) did so (**19:11-12**). The fact that David had to make this plea is proof that some of the inhabitants of Judah had supported Absalom's revolt. In his concern to appease his enemies, David went so far as to offer Amasa the commander's position to replace Joab (19:13).

Several rebel leaders in Africa have obtained high positions in the army or in government as rewards for laying down their arms and entering into an alliance with the governing party. Some military personnel who were not even officers in the regular army have suddenly become generals through agreements that ended fighting. King David, who wanted to win the favour of the people of Judah at any price, was even prepared to sacrifice one of his most loyal warriors, Joab, in favour of a traitor.

It is also possible that David was still angry with Joab for having killed Absalom against his orders, a murder that would undoubtedly have reminded David of Joab's earlier murder of Abner (3:26-29). His anger may also have contributed to the decision to demote Joab.

David's strategy was effective. The men of Judah invited him to return and even set out to meet him and lead him across the Jordan (**19:13-14**). This was the first step towards restoring David as king over a united Israel. But David is playing a dangerous game as he pits the north and south against each other, rather than seeking to have both groups welcome him simultaneously.

19:16-40a Meetings on the road to Jerusalem

As David proceeded along the road back to Jerusalem, he encountered a number of people he had met during his flight, including Shimei, Mephibosheth and Barzillai.

19:16-23 DAVID AND SHIMEI Shimei was the man from the tribe of Benjamin who had cursed David and thrown stones at him as he fled from Absalom (16:5-14). He now hurried to meet David, desperate to prove his new loyalty to him (**19:16**). He was accompanied by a thousand men of Benjamin. The repetition of the word *Benjamites* reminds us that these men belonged to Saul's tribe. Shimei had called the king a 'man of blood' (16:7), now he begged for the king's mercy, acknowledging his sin and asking forgiveness for it (**19:19-20**). Abishai, Joab's brother, felt that Shimei deserved only death for having cursed the king, the Lord's anointed (**19:21**). But David refused to take vengeance, possibly because he was seeking the allegiance of the people of Benjamin and could not afford to provoke them by executing one of their leaders (**19:22-23**). However, David did not forget what Shimei had done, and had his son take revenge for it many years later (1 Kgs 2:8-9, 36-46).

19:24-30 DAVID AND MEPHIBOSHETH The encounter between David and Mephibosheth is presented as if it took place during the journey back to Jerusalem, but it must actually have taken place in Jerusalem. It is probably presented where it is because Mephibosheth's former servant, Ziba, who had helped David as he was fleeing, was among those who met David as he crossed the Jordan (19:17). Ziba had accused Mephibosheth, the son of Jonathan, of treason, saying that he was sympathetic toward Absalom's rebellion. David had responded to the accusation by taking all the property that he had restored to Mephibosheth and giving it to Ziba (16:3-4). But when David reached Jerusalem, he met Mephibosheth himself. He gave the impression that he had been in mourning since the departure of the king (**19:24**). When David asked him why he had not accompanied him into exile, Mephibosheth defended himself by pointing to his lameness, and claimed that Ziba had abandoned him and slandered him (**19:25-28**). With two different but equally plausible versions of events, David could not decide who was telling the truth. So he settled on a compromise, telling them to share the property between them (**19:29**).

19:31-40a DAVID AND BARZILLAI Barzillai had been among those who welcomed David to Mahanaim (17:27). He was a rich man, who had supported David while he was in exile (**19:31-32**). David proposed that Barzillai accompany him to Jerusalem, promising to be good to him. But Barzillai was already an old man of eighty, and he had no interest in leaving home and going to court. His age would mean that he would not be able to appreciate the king's fine food, or hear the music played at court, or tell what was good or what was bad (**19:34-36**). So he suggested that his son, Kimham, go in his stead (**19:37**; see also 1 Kgs 2:7).

In the Democratic Republic of Congo, people often use the expression *kosalela âge* ['act your age']. They use it when speaking of people who do not admit to their age and who insist on behaving as if they were youngsters. These are the older men who run after young girls and the older women who wear the tight-fitting clothes intended for younger women.

The king accepted Barzillai's offer, and so Kimham accompanied David to Jerusalem (**19:38-40a**). We do not know what sort of reward he was given, but it may have been a high position in the royal court.

19:40b-44 Rivalry between Judah and Israel

The rivalry between the people of Judah and the rest of Israel that David had provoked (19:9-15) now became more obvious. The men of Israel were unhappy that the men of Judah had crossed the Jordan with the king, while half the troops of Israel were excluded from the king's escort (**19:40b-41**). To justify themselves, the people of Judah put forward a tribal argument: *The king is closely related to us* (**19:42**). This annoyed the people of Israel, who boasted about their superior numbers in relation to Judah. They were ten tribes, whereas Judah was only one (**19:43**). The people of Judah responded with increased hostility. There is no indication that this rivalry was resolved in any way. It would continue to grow until the northern tribes broke away from the southern ones in the days of Rehoboam (1 Kgs 12:1-16).

Similar regionalism is a problem in many African countries. Most of the conflicts on the continent take place between northerners and southerners, or between those who live in the east and those who live closer to the centre of the country, and so on. Like David, many African leaders use these rivalries to strengthen their hold on power. In some cases they even foster these divisions for their own political benefit.

20:1-22 Sheba's Revolt

What began as a simple dispute between the northern and southern tribes about the return of the king soon escalated into a serious threat to the unity of Israel.

Sheba, who was a *Benjamite*, was among the delegation that came to meet the king on his return. Responding to the hostility of the men of Judah (19:43), he *sounded the trumpet* and shouted the secessionist slogan: *We have no share in David, no part in Jesse's son! Every man to his tent, O Israel!* (**20:1**). He was calling on Israel's troops to desert David's ranks, and that is what they did. David, the king who had just returned, was left with only the people of Judah to accompany him to Jerusalem (**20:2**).

On arriving there, David dealt with the concubines that he had left to take care of the palace and with whom Absalom, on Ahithophel's advice, had had sexual relations (16:21-22). They had been left to guard the palace (15:16) and were now placed in a guarded house (**20:3**). David had no further sexual relations with them, and they lived the rest of their lives as if they were widows (Deut 24:1-4).

In an attempt to gain the confidence of the people of Judah, David had put Amasa, who had been one of Absalom's supporters (17:25), in command of the army instead of Joab (19:13). David now assigned him the task of suppressing Sheba's rebellion, asking him to muster the men of Judah within three days (**20:4**). It seems that David suspected that his own men might not be sufficient to put down Sheba's revolt.

Unfortunately, Amasa did not return before the king's deadline. David must have begun to consider the possibility that Amasa had defected to Sheba, and urgently asked Abishai to set off in pursuit of Sheba. The situation was so serious that David commented that *Sheba son of Bicri will do us more harm than Absalom did* (**20:6**).

Amasa had not defected, he had merely been delayed. But when he met up with the troops under Abishai, Joab, who was part of this group although not the one in command, killed his cousin Amasa by thrusting a dagger into his belly (**20:7-10a**). We are reminded of Ehud's assassination of Eglon (Judg 3:20-21). As when Joab murdered Abner (3:27), his victim suspected nothing before Joab struck.

Having eliminated the rival who had taken his place, Joab resumed his position as commander of the army, and he and his brother Abishai resumed their pursuit of Sheba (**20:10b-11**). Sheba eventually took refuge in a city named *Abel Beth Maacah* (**20:14**). Joab and his troops besieged the city to destroy it, but a wise woman saved it. This woman must have been somewhat famous or have occupied some prominent position in the city, for she was able to get Joab and the people in the city to listen to her (**20:15-17, 22**). She described her city to Joab as *a mother in Israel* (**20:19**), which had taken no part in the revolt and therefore did not deserve to be destroyed. Joab was happy to agree to spare the city – provided they handed Sheba over to him (**20:20-21**). The woman accepted Joab's terms and spoke to the people of Abel. Sheba was killed, and his head was cut off and thrown over the wall to Joab, who sounded the trumpet to end the war and lift the siege (20:22).

This woman's wisdom saved the city and all its inhabitants. Her story gives the lie to the currently accepted opinion that the ot always offers a negative image of women. This woman's wisdom is honoured, and it is clear that she occupied a position of leadership. The ot cannot be used to argue for the domination and subordination of African women.

20:23-26 David's Administration

The list of David's civil and military leaders given here parallels the one given in 8:16-18. There are, however, a few differences. In both lists, Joab is named first. His success in putting down the various revolts that threatened David's reign made him the most important person in the royal administration. But the reader should not think that David had forgotten the wrongs that Joab had done. The security of David's throne rested in large part on the army, and that is why David made no move to punish Joab. But before his death, David entrusted this responsibility to Solomon, his successor (1 Kgs 2:5, 28-34).

In this new list, the first two officials are paired. Joab was the commander of the army, but Benaiah was in charge of David's bodyguard, which was composed of foreign mercenaries. This division was probably a deliberate strategy to counter Joab's power (**20:23**).

For the first time, an official is mentioned as being in charge of *forced labour* (**20:24**). Some commentators rush to affirm that this labour must have been done by non-Israelites. But this practice would be at the root of the schism that would eventually tear the kingdom of Israel apart after Solomon's death. It is, therefore, reasonable to think that even during David's reign, some Israelites were consigned to forced labour. If so, this might explain the popular success (especially in the north) of the various revolts against David. The list also names two priests, who had earlier acted as David's agents (15:27-29). By appointing two of them, David ensured that each of them would keep an eye on the other (**20:25**).

These new administrative arrangements for the kingdom reveal David's lack of confidence in his officials. He was now wary, for he had been betrayed by one of his most trusted advisors, Ahithophel, and had been actively disobeyed by Joab in regard to Absalom's death. So he set up duplicate officials, just as the leaders of many African countries do. Today we often find two parallel security services, two parallel political arms, and two parallel chiefs-of-staff in the army. All these parallel services carry out surveillance and report on each other for the good of the leader, but not, unfortunately, for the good of the people.

Sheba's revolt was just another in the long line of events that had disturbed David's reign since the day he made himself doubly guilty before God by abducting a married woman and arranging the murder of her husband. The sentence pronounced by the prophet Nathan was literally fulfilled (12:10). The sword was never far from David's household. His own son, Absalom, took his father's concubines and slept with them in full view of all Israel. For a time, David lost his throne and the support of Israel. The king had to leave Jerusalem as a fugitive. The consequences of his sin were like a swelling river.

The series of misfortunes also raises questions about the forgiveness that Nathan had announced in 12:13. David acknowledged his sin, but the consequences followed him for the rest of his long reign. God pardons our sin, but does not necessarily remove the consequences, which may continue to trouble us for the rest of our lives. The account of David's eventful reign is therefore an illustration for the people of God. This king, who began his reign in humility and total trust in God, ended by giving in to pride in his own power, to the point of neglecting God's law. But God remains faithful. The entire account of the life of David is a testimony to God's faithfulness, which is not dependent on our behaviour but rather on his grace.

If God were to repay David for what he had done, this powerful king would have been killed for having organized the assassination of his faithful soldier, Uriah. But God kept his covenant and his promises (7:12-16). David was punished, but God did not withdraw his love from him as he had done in the case of Saul (1 Sam 15:26).

The book of 2 Samuel does not present David as an ideal king but as a real person with human strengths and weaknesses. He was a man who knew how to depend on God's grace. David's reign is described from a different perspective in the book of Chronicles. There he is presented as a near perfect king. Except for the episode of David's sinful census, which ended with his locating the site of the future temple, David is faultless. There is no account of any revolt, nor any conflict about who is to succeed him, and no mention of the affair with Bathsheba. The reason he is presented in such a different light is that the book of Chronicles was written after the return from the exile in Babylon. At that time, the returned exiles needed a strong positive figure to encourage them and restore their hope.

2 Sam 21:1-24:25 The End of David's Reign

The last four chapters of the book of 2 Samuel form a sort of appendix. The events that are mentioned here are not in any clear chronological relationship to those in chapter 20. Rather, they are fillers that separate the end of Sheba's revolt and the last days of King David. The royal history will continue in 1 Kings 1:1, where we meet the elderly David, in the royal court.

These chapters are organized according to an elegant literary plan: two accounts of plagues, one at the beginning and one at the end (21:1-14; 24:1-25), two lists (21:15-22; 23:8-39) and in the middle two songs (22:1-51; 23:1-7).

21:1-14 Three Years of Famine

At some stage in David's reign, there was a three-year famine, about which we know very little, for the writer is not as interested in the famine itself as he is in the way in which David reacted to it.

The famine probably occurred around the time of the events related in chapter 9, where an account of David's dealings with the house of Saul is also preceded by a list of David's officials. A similar list is found at the end of chapter 20. The author probably presents the incident at this point in the book because it fits with the theme of the preceding section, which deals with God's punishment for disobedience.

As the famine persisted, David came to understand that it was the result of some failure relating to God's law, and consulted the Lord to find out what it was. We do not know in what way this consultation occurred. But God informed him that the famine was a punishment for Saul's bloody attack on the Gibeonites (**21:1**). We do not have any record of this particular event in the tumultuous reign of Saul. But we do know that Saul had been guilty of other massacres, such as that of the priests at Nob (1 Sam 22:19), so the accusation is quite plausible.

We also know that a treaty had been signed with the Gibeonites in Joshua 9 (**21:2b**). Saul's violation of that treaty would have serious consequences, just as David's sin in murdering Uriah had serious consequences. David would thus have understood the Gibeonites's attitude.

David did not suggest what should be done to atone for this evil. Instead he asked the Gibeonites what should be done to appease their anger and remove the curse from his kingdom (**21:3**). The Gibeonites were not interested in any material compensation (**21:4**). All that they wanted was the deaths of seven of Saul's male descendants to make up for all the men they had lost (**21:5-6**). Some commentators suggest that they specified seven men because seven was the symbol of completeness, and would indicate a complete revenge.

David is again presented as a man who keeps his word. He acceded to the Gibeonites' request, thus restoring the covenant between Israel and Gibeon. But he also kept his promise to Jonathan by not handing over Jonathan's son, Mephibosheth (**21:7**; 1 Sam 20:14-17). The men who were handed over were the sons of Saul's concubine, Rizpah (see 3:7), and of Saul's daughter, Merab (**21:8**). David had made no covenant with their families.

We are astonished to read of these men being killed *before the Lord,* as if in a human sacrifice to end the drought (21:6, 9). The suggestion of human sacrifice is strengthened by the explicit linking of their killing to *the first days of the harvest* and by the fact that their bodies are left there until the rains come (**21:9-10**). It may be that the Gibeonites, who were not Israelites (**21:2a**), were carrying out an Amorite ritual even if they claimed to be doing it before the Hebrew God. Certainly, the law strictly forbade human sacrifice (Deut 12:31).

It was a great dishonour to leave someone's body to be eaten by animals and birds. Rizpah, as a devoted mother, refused to allow her sons to suffer this final indignity (21:10). Her devotion moved David to provide a respectable tomb for Saul, Jonathan and the seven men *in the tomb of Saul's father, Kish* (**21:11-14**). This was where Saul would have wanted to be buried. The Israelites prized being buried near their homes, as can be seen from Jacob's insistence that Joseph take his body back to the family burial site (Gen 47:29-31) and Joseph's request that his bones be taken back to Canaan (Gen 50:25).

Many in African cities have a similar desire. There may well be a modern cemetery nearby, but people want to be buried in the village from which they came or in their own fields. This practice sometimes imposes an enormous financial burden on the grieving family.

The section ends with the return of the rains. The Lord's anger had been appeased (21:14).

21:15-22 David's Brave Men

This section mentions various battles in the long war between the Philistines and Israel, possibly the one mentioned in chapter 5. But the narrator is not interested in the war so much as in the exploits of David's mighty men. Each battle is introduced with some variation on the formula *once again there was a battle between the Philistines and Israel* (21:15, 18, 19, 20). In each battle, a hero in David's army kills a Philistine champion.

David no longer appears to be the warrior he had been when young. His life was threatened by a Philistine warrior and he had to be saved by Abishai (**21:15-17a**). Following this incident, the men of Israel forbade David to go to war with them. They describe him as *the lamp of Israel* (**21:17b**), an image that reminds us of the lamp in the temple (Exod 27:20). The lamp may also represent David's dynasty. But whatever the exact symbolism, the king was clearly precious to the nation.

One of the Philistine heroes was named Goliath, like the man David had defeated in 1 Samuel 17. It is possible that more than one man bore this name, which may even have been a sort of nickname or title (**21:19**). This second Goliath also taunted Israel, suggesting that such taunts were common in the wars of that time (**21:20-21**).

22:1-51 David's Song

We have already come across David's artistic gifts in the elegy he composed for Saul and Jonathan (1:19-27) and in his prayer in response to the promise of a dynasty (7:18-29). This psalm, which dates from a later time in his life, is longer than all the others. It can be found in a slightly different form in Psalm 18.

The title of this song, like that of Psalm 18, refers to the days when David was delivered from the hand of all his enemies, including Saul (**22:1**). This may explain its position here, immediately after the account of victories over Philistine champions. The Philistines were the traditional enemies of Israel and David's deliverance from them took many years under God's direction. The song is thus a reminder of God's goodness to David and his house over time.

David uses several vivid metaphors that simultaneously express his praise and his confidence in God. The Lord is described as a *rock* (**22:2, 3**), something that is solid and unshakeable and on which we can find a firm footing. David had found refuge among the rocks when he fled from Saul (1 Sam 23:25-28). The strength of a rock is expressed even more clearly in Psalm 125: 'Those who trust in the Lord are like Mount Zion, which cannot be shaken' (Ps 125:1). Such a rock cannot be overturned!

In the OT, a *shield* represented protection and a *horn* represented strength (22:3; see 1 Kgs 22:11). David and his men had experienced both God's protection and his strength in their victories over the Philistines in many different battles.

David remembered his desperate calls for help. He had almost lost his life in the *torrents of destruction* and *the snares of death* (**22:5-6**), but he had called to God and God had answered (**22:7**). David's life had often been in danger from the Philistines, from Saul, from Absalom and from the other nations he had defeated in battle. But prayer is effective. It changes situations. That is why Paul asks Christians to pray without ceasing and gives prayer a special place among the weapons wielded by Christians (Eph 6:10-19). Without prayer, Christians cannot use their other weapons effectively.

God's response to David's prayer takes the form of a theophany, that is, an impressive appearance by God on earth. His coming is described as shaking the cosmic order and is accompanied by *smoke* and *fire* (**22:9**), storms and *lightning* (**22:12-13**). God is presented as riding on the *cherubim*, who are great winged angels (**22:11**; Ezek 1:5-28) and as a warrior (**22:14-15**). All these images are intended to show how impressive it is when God comes to the rescue of someone who trusts in him.

David uses a human image to describe God's aid to him, saying that God was like someone who stretched out his hand to him while he was struggling in *deep waters* and rescued him from drowning (**22:17**). The expressions David uses to describe who he was rescued from remind us of various adversaries. The *powerful enemy* was probably Saul (**22:18**), whereas *the day of my disaster* was probably the time of Absalom's rebellion (**22:19**).

David argues that God has helped him because he is a man of integrity (**22:21-25**). If we ignore the incident with Uriah and Bathsheba, we can agree that David had nothing to be ashamed of in relation to his enemies. Saul had died by his own hand (1 Sam 31:4), Absalom was killed by Joab despite David's orders to spare him (18:5, 14-15).

David's view of justice here is based on the principle that God's justice obeys the law of retribution, meaning an eye for an eye, and a tooth for a tooth (**22:26-28**; see Exod 21:24; Lev 24:20; Deut 19:21). But in Matthew 5:38-39, Jesus overturns this law.

The final verses of this long psalm highlight a point that has become clear throughout David's reign, namely that God's actions and David's actions go hand in hand. David sings of God's victory and of the help he received from God (**22:29-37**), but also of how he, as king, defeated his enemies (**22:38-43**). The establishment of David as king, so that other nations became subject to him, was also God's work (**22:44-49**).

The closing words of the psalm remind us of the covenant between God and David (7:12-16). It is now time for God to take steps to fulfil his promise of a dynasty, for David is approaching the end of his life. But David has confidence in God's promise to be with *his descendants for ever* (**22:50-51**).

David, the warrior, took time to contemplate the goodness of God and to thank God for the many blessings he had received. Many Christians are so caught up in the busyness of life that they do not take time to notice all that God has done for them. His acts of kindness and mercy often pass unnoticed because we do not take the time to stop and contemplate God's greatness. We would do well to remember the old hymn, 'Count your many blessings, name them one by one, and it will surprise you what the Lord has done.'

23:1-7 David's Last Words

This song and the previous one occupy a central place in this final section of the book of Samuel. Here the song is introduced with a few words in praise of David. He is described as a man who has been *exalted* by God and *anointed by the God of Jacob*. He is a poet, and *Israel's singer of songs*. And more than that, he is portrayed as a prophet who declares an *oracle* and speaks words given to him by *the Spirit of the Lord* (**23:1-3a**).

Once again, the eternal covenant between David and his God is at the heart of the psalm (**23:5**). David's reign and his dynasty cannot be interpreted as simply a historical era in the life of the people of Israel. They must be seen as an expression of God's beneficent love. The king was not appointed to reign so that he could enjoy wielding power but so that he could exercise justice (**23:3b-4**). Those who oppose God's will as expressed in the eternal covenant with the house of David are like thorns that a farmer removes from his field to burn. These thorns have to be moved carefully with an iron rake or *the shaft of a spear* so that they do not pierce the farmer's hands before they are thrown into the fire (**23:6-7**). This will be the fate of all those who are

enemies of David and his dynasty. But like thorns, these enemies can cause harm if they are not removed.

Those who practice justice are rewarded, whereas the wicked will be punished and wiped out. That is why Jesus insisted that righteousness was a defining characteristic of the kingdom of God, saying that we should 'seek first his kingdom and his righteousness' (Matt 6:33).

23:8-39 David's Mighty Men

All those who had helped David to consolidate his kingdom are now honoured. The information given here parallels that in 1 Chronicles 11:10-28, where it is placed at the beginning of the account of David's reign rather than at the end.

First, we are given the names of the three bravest of David's men, who were honoured more than all the others (**23:8-12**). These three performed amazing feats. But the text is careful to remind us twice that it was *the Lord who brought about a great victory*.

The author then relates an incident from the past that illustrates the devotion and bravery of some of David's other mighty men, without giving their names. At the risk of their lives, three men crossed Philistine lines simply to draw water for David from the well he remembered drinking from at the gates of Bethlehem. David considered their gift so precious that he could not drink it, but rather offered it to God (**23:13-17**).

Despite Joab's position as David's general and the frequent references to him elsewhere in the book, he is not mentioned as an outstanding warrior. That honour is held by his brother, Abishai, who has also been referred to on several occasions (see, for example, 1 Sam 26:6-11; 2 Sam 10:10-14; 20:7).

The second list (**23:18-39**) is of the thirty soldiers who were highly honoured in Israel but whose exploits did not compare to those of the first three. These military men came from various places. The greatest number came from the tribe of Judah, David's tribe, but there were others from the tribe of Benjamin, which was Saul's tribe, as well as some foreigners. Some of the names in the list are familiar to us. *Benaiah* was the commander of David's bodyguard (23:23; see 8:18; 20:23). *Asahel*, the brother of Joab and Abishai, had died early in David's reign (2:18-23). We know nothing about the other warriors, except for the one mentioned last in the list: *Uriah the Hittite* (23:39). Again, we are reminded of the extent of David's betrayal when he had Uriah murdered.

24:1-25 David's Sinful Census

The introductory word *again* makes it clear that this incident parallels the one involving the Gibeonites in 21:1-14. Both incidents involve divine judgment on Israel during David's reign, and in neither case do we have access to detailed information about the cause of God's anger. In the parallel account in 1 Chronicles 21, it is not the Lord but Satan who incites David to make the offending census. If we are puzzled by this, we need to remember that it is possible to have both God and Satan involved in events, as happened in the case of Job (Job 1:6-12). Without God's permission Satan could not have come near Job.

24:1-9 The census

We are not told why *the anger of the Lord burned against Israel* (**24:1**). Because of his anger, the Lord prompted David to order *a census of Israel and Judah* that would provide the obvious reason for the plague (**24:1**). This census would count how many men were capable of bearing arms (**24:2**). Even Joab tried to persuade the king against taking this step, but David would not listen to him (**24:3-4**).

The census took *nine months and twenty days* to complete (**24:8**). During this time, a team of military personnel travelled to all the cities of Israel, and beyond Israel into Hittite territory (**24:7**). They identified 800 000 men in Israel and 500 000 in Judah who could serve in the army (**24:9**).

24:10-25 The punishment

By the time David was given the results of his census, he recognized that it had been prompted by sinful motives. It seems that he had not simply trusted God to multiply his people, but had wanted to know exactly how many he could command in order to satisfy his own pride. He was relying on his army rather than on God for protection.

The question of motive is what is important here. It is not that conducting a census is wrong in itself. In fact, in the book of Numbers God instructs Moses to take a census (Num 1:2; 26:2).

When David recognized his sin, he begged for forgiveness (**24:10**). God responded by sending *Gad the prophet, David's seer* to announce his judgment (**24:11**). This prophet had once saved David's life when he was fleeing from Saul (1 Sam 22:5). Once again, as after the murder of Uriah, God accepted David's request for pardon but still insisted that his actions had consequences and would be punished. David was offered a difficult choice between three scourges of different lengths: *three years of famine, three months of fleeing from enemies* or *three days of plague* in the land (**24:12-13**).

David avoided making an explicit choice. His reply simply excluded the second option, that of falling into the hands of his enemies (**24:14**). David knew what it was like to suffer at the hands of an enemy. He had endured this himself when pursued by Saul, and had himself subjugated many enemies. He would prefer to leave the choice to the Lord because his *mercy is great.*

God sent a great plague, which killed 70 000 people (**24:15**). The plague was about to destroy Jerusalem when the Lord's anger abated (**24:16**). But a sacrifice was needed to bring an end to the plague. The prophet Gad brought a message telling the king to build another altar on the threshing floor of Araunah the Jebusite (**24:18**).

Araunah was willing to give his threshing floor to the king as a gift, but David refused to accept this gift and insisted on paying for it. While doing so he uttered one of the most beautiful sentences in the Bible: *I will not sacrifice to the Lord my God burnt offerings that cost me nothing* (**24:24**). After David had sacrificed *burnt offerings and fellowship offerings*, the Lord's anger subsided (**24:25**; see 21:14).

The end of the book of 2 Samuel does not coincide with the end of David's reign, which continues through 1 Kings 2:1-11. But the succession of distresses at the end of the reign are a prelude to the further struggle to succeed David.

Conclusion

King David, though described by God as a *man after my own heart* (Acts 13:22), has been presented as a man with very human characteristics. He was a man who knew how to place his trust in God, but also knew how to use human wisdom. He was a man who desired to obey God in everything, but at times failed to do so. When he failed, he was not too proud to ask God's forgiveness. Though he was the greatest king of Israel, he was prepared to humbly accept a rebuke from the prophet Nathan.

Unfortunately, David's successors were not like him. They turned away from God's covenant and in so doing risked the end of the Davidic dynasty. But that dynasty would not end, for David was also the ancestor of Jesus Christ, the King of kings. Thus the opening verse of Matthew's gospel declares that it will tell the story of 'Jesus Christ the son of David' (Matt 1:1).

1 Samuel – Gbile Akanni
2 Samuel – Nupanga Weanzana

Further Reading

Baldwin, Joyce G. *1 & 2 Samuel*. TOT. Leicester: Inter-Varsity Press, 1988.

Evans, Mary J. *The Message of Samuel: Personalities, Potential, Politics, and Power*. BST. Downers Grove, Ill: InterVarsity Press, 2004.

1 AND 2 KINGS

Kings was originally one book, but was divided into two because it was too long to fit onto one scroll. In the ancient Greek translation of the OT, called the Septuagint, 1 and 2 Samuel are grouped with 1 and 2 Kings under the title *Basileiai,* meaning Reigns or Kingdoms. These books tell the story of Israel's kings, from Saul, the first king, to the last king who was carried off to exile in Babylon. The last two of these books are known as Kings because they focus more on the kings who ruled than on any of the other important people, whereas the books of Samuel also include much information about the prophet Samuel and about David before he became king.

At times, the books of Kings are also grouped with Joshua, Judges and 1 and 2 Samuel. Taken together, those books tell the history of Israel from the time the people entered the promised land of Canaan to the date they were taken away into exile.

The book of Deuteronomy, which immediately precedes these books, briefly outlines the religious history of Israel from their exodus from Egypt under Moses until the time when they were poised to enter the promised land. It also contains the laws, commandments and decrees of God about how they were to live in the land. In Kings, we find that individual kings are condemned if they fail to follow these laws, and are commended if they keep them.

Date

Kings closes with King Jehoiachin's release from prison by the Babylonian king Evil-Merodach, who became king of Babylon around 560 BC (2 Kgs 25:27-30). The book probably took its final form shortly after that date. However, parts of it were probably written before that date. The evidence for this is the repeated references to the annals of the kings of Judah and the annals of the kings of Israel. The royal annals would not have been easily available for reference if Kings had been written during the exile in Babylon. Moreover, the phrase 'to this day' crops up regularly and shows that certain situations and conditions in the land of Israel were still the same at the time when that section of the book was written.

Authorship

Kings gives no indication of who wrote it. But the author must have been very familiar with the general events in the history of Israel as a whole, with the histories of the monarchies of Israel and Judah and with the stories of the prophets. He himself, like many prophets of the OT, calls the kings and people of Israel back to the Lord of the covenant, whose requirements are given in the book of Deuteronomy.

Early traditions say that Jeremiah wrote Kings. Certainly, he lived in a very literate community and he himself wrote freely. He wrote to the people of Israel who were in exile (Jer 29). He hid his personal written documents in safe places (Jer 32:11-14). He had a secretary, Baruch, to whom he dictated his prophecies (Jer 36:4, 32). Jeremiah's writings also reveal an intimate knowledge of the events leading up to the fall of Jerusalem (Jer 32:17-25; 40–44, 52). But none of this evidence is sufficient to prove conclusively that he was the writer.

All that can be said with certainty is that Kings must have come from the community of true prophets that was in existence at the time of the fall of Jerusalem. The book evaluates the reign of each king and explains why Israel and Judah had to be taken into exile (2 Kgs 17; 21:10-15; 22:15-20).

Sources of Information

The events recorded in Kings cover a period of some four hundred years. So the writer must have drawn on various sources of information, including detailed information on numbers and weights and the dimensions of buildings and the kinds of foreign gods that were introduced into the Jerusalem temple and Samaria. Some of these details suggest that the author must have been an eyewitness to some of the events recorded.

The writer also had access to written records. He knew the history of Israel before the death of David, and is also familiar with the laws of Moses and especially the book of Deuteronomy.

In addtion to these biblical sources, he used other books, specifically the annals of King Solomon and the annals of the royal houses of Judah and Israel. These annals (or chronicles) are not the same as the biblical books we know as 1 and 2 Chronicles. The annals were like royal libraries or archives that kept a record of the activities and events in the reigns of different kings. They were kept in the royal palaces of the two kingdoms. It is clear that the writer did not use all the information in these historical records, for he directs those who were sceptical of what he says or who want more information to look for it in the annals.

Besides these official sources, the writer must have had access to other sources outside the palaces, that recorded what the prophets had said to the kings. Thus we hear that Ahijah prophesied that Jeroboam would become king, and later condemned him (1 Kgs 11:29-39; 14:4-16). Of all the prophets mentioned, many of them unnamed, the major ones are Elijah and Elisha, whose activities are recorded in great detail. The information about them and the other prophets must have come from sources that were kept in the 'schools' or communities of prophets.

With such a range of sources to choose from, the writer must have relied on the spirit of the Lord to choose what he would include in his history, a history that continues to speak the word of God across the ages.

Relation Between Kings and Chronicles

The biblical books of Kings and Chronicles were written at different times. Whereas Kings was probably written about the time of the fall of Jerusalem, Chronicles was probably written during or after the exile in Babylon. The two books address different theological concerns. Kings answers the 'Why?' questions of the exiles: 'Why did this happen? Did God fail to keep his end of the covenant? Did Marduk, the Babylonian god, overcome Yahweh?' The answer given in Kings is that God's chosen people failed to obey him and so were punished. Chronicles, on the other hand, answers the community's question, 'What now? – Do Yahweh's promises still apply to us?'

Style

The writer is not like secular historians who give details of cultural, social, political and economic developments in the period of each ruler. For that kind of information, he would refer the reader to the royal annals. He has, therefore, left out a lot that would be of interest to a secular historian. For example, from other sources we know that King Omri was a great king who did many things to develop Israel as a nation. But this writer tells the story of Omri in just a few verses because Omri did not consider it important to follow the God of Israel. This author is seeing history from God's point of view. He wants to make the point that it is God, not political and economic successes or foreign gods, who saves Israel, and he chooses his information to answer the theological question, 'Why are God's beloved people in exile?'

The history of each king begins with a summary that tells us how long he reigned. In the case of the kings of Judah, the name of the king's mother is sometimes mentioned. Each king is evaluated in a statement specifying whether he did what was right and pleasing to the Lord, or what was evil and therefore displeasing to the Lord. A king was judged as good if he followed and obeyed the covenant of the Lord like King David. Those kings who freely allowed the worship of foreign gods were described as making the God of Israel angry.

Of the kings judged to be good, only Hezekiah and Josiah measured up to David's record. They excelled because they insisted that the temple in Jerusalem was the only place of worship and served only the covenant God of Israel (Deut 12). Others described as good kings were against foreign gods but permitted people to freely worship on the high places.

In general, those kings who did what was good in the eyes of God receive more attention. However, in the cases of Jeroboam I, Ahab, Ahaz and Manasseh, we are given detailed accounts of the evil they committed. Ahab, for example, led Israel away from worshipping their God into worshipping other gods. His reign is treated at more length than that of any of the other kings of Israel, and he also received more warnings and advice from prophets than any of the other kings.

King Solomon's reign also received much attention, mainly because he started well, loving and serving the Lord. He was the builder of the temple in Jerusalem where the ark of the covenant was kept. Without these achievements, Solomon would have had less attention. But he was found to have made the Lord angry because he loved foreign wives and not only built places for them to worship their gods but also worshipped there himself.

Message

The book of Judges concludes, 'In those days Israel had no king; everyone did as he saw fit' (Judg 17:6; 21:25). Gradually, a strong belief emerged that the problems created by a lack of order would be solved only if they had a king to rule over them and unite all of Israel (Judg 18:1; 19:1). The people had forgotten that with God as their leader, they could get order and power if they obeyed his laws and commandments. So they asked Samuel to choose a king to rule them like other nations.

Many years before, God had instructed the people that if they did have a king, he was to be different from the kings of other nations (Deut 17:14-20). He must be chosen by God and not just be a random choice (Deut 17:15). The anointed king must also keep and read a copy of the book of the law (Deut 17:18-20). He must not regard himself as greater than his fellow citizens (Deut 17:20). King David was the only one who came near God's ideal. Under his rule, Israel gained political power. Wherever they turned, God gave them victory. In his religious life, David followed God with all his heart.

The book of Kings looks at David's successors and the whole process of existing as a nation and finds that without God even kings could not make Israel a stable nation. The kingdoms of the earth will never be as perfect as the kingdom of heaven. They come short of the standard that God sets and are not to be depended on to bring any permanent salvation to individuals or society.

Most of the kings did not measure up to what God expected of them. Even Solomon, who made a good beginning with the Lord approving of him and giving him wisdom, wealth and power (1 Kgs 3; 9:1-10) and who built a temple in the capital city, found that those achievements were not what God was asking for. The condition God gave for his presence with Israel was this: 'If you follow my decrees, carry out my regulations and keep all my commands and obey them, I will fulfil through you the promise I gave to David your father. And I will live among the Israelites and will not abandon my people Israel' (1 Kgs 6:11-13; see also 1 Kgs 2:3-4; 11:38). Solomon failed this test and so did his successors.

No human king was without fault before God, not even King David (1 Kgs 15:5; see also Ps 130:3). The influence of faithful kings like Hezekiah and Josiah was not enough to cause the people to return to serve God faithfully. Thus Israel ceased to exist as a nation. The Israelites had no king in the days of Samuel and they again had no king as they went into exile. But God was still their leader and king of those who remained faithful and sought him.

Despite the people's disobedience, God remained loving, gracious and faithful. He continued to show them mercy for the sake of their ancestors Abraham, Isaac and Jacob, for the sake of David, and sometimes just for his own name's sake (2 Kgs 13:4, 22-23). Even though Ahab provoked the Lord to anger, God did not easily give up on him but sent prophet after prophet to speak to him. Thus Ahab was confronted by Elijah (1 Kgs 18:1; 21:17-18), an unnamed prophet (1 Kgs 20:13, 22, 39), and Micaiah (1 Kgs 22:14-23). God also noticed when Ahab humbled himself and repented (1 Kgs 21:27-29). God heard the prayers of Hezekiah (2 Kgs 19:14-19, 35-37), Josiah (2 Kgs 22:11, 18-20) and Jehoahaz (2 Kgs 13:4-5). He is presented as the one in charge of all the kingdoms and powers of the earth.

This great God expects the people of Israel who know him to follow him humbly, even if they fail to do so perfectly. Why? Because he loves them, especially the common people who humbly, obediently and faithfully serve him. But God gets angry with and punishes people who deliberately worship other gods or commit sin. He is a jealous God, and when angry, he punishes severely (see also Amos 3:2). Yet the Lord has a tender heart for those who truly humble themselves and repent before him.

God's great plan of salvation is not for Israel alone, but for all of humanity. In implementing this plan, he follows his own timetable, not that of Israel. But he worked with Israel as a people as part of his plan to bring salvation to the whole world.

The book further teaches that a leader influences a nation and its people. As such, it issues a call to Christians in Africa to be more involved in the political life of the continent than they have been in the past. Almost no nation in Africa meets the requirements God set out in Micah 6:8 – to act justly, love mercy and walk humbly with God. Instead tales of corruption, nepotism, the theft of public funds and murder still dominate the headlines in our newspapers. The situation calls for African Christians to criticize evil practices and to be at the centre of activity in politics – whether vying for public office (if called to do this) or voting in every election.

Those who have been appointed to positions of leadership must also take warning from this book that God expects them to be even more faithful to him than they were before.

History of the Period

Israel did not exist in isolation. Other nations and peoples were struggling for power, and their struggles affected the history of Israel. But the Lord God of Israel, the Creator, is the Lord over history. He brings nations to power and then removes them in his own time, though these powers may not always know him. God knows when each king and world power will come and go (2 Kgs 19:26-27).

The writer of Kings organized his material into three periods. The first section covers the time of Solomon, about 970-930 BC (1 Kgs 1–11). During this period, Israel was at the peak of its power. David had conquered the neighbouring peoples who were hostile to Israel. Egypt on the southern border was an ally, and Solomon married Pharaoh's daughter in order to strengthen this alliance (1 Kgs 3:1). To the north, Hiram of Tyre was also a friend, and there was peace with Syria and the north-eastern nations. But by the end of Solomon's reign, things had begun to change. There was a new pharaoh in Egypt who willingly gave asylum to Solomon's enemies (1 Kgs 11:14-19; 1 Kgs 11:40), Aram (Syria) in the north was beginning to give trouble (1 Kgs 11:23-25) and Hiram, too, was growing discontented (1 Kgs 9:10-13).

After Solomon's death in about 930 BC, his kingdom broke up into the two kingdoms of Israel and Judah. The second section of Kings deals with the history of these two kingdoms up to 721 BC when Israel went into exile. The divided kingdom was poorly equipped to face others in struggles for power and as soon as the kingdom divided, Judah was attacked by Shishak (1 Kgs 14:25-26). Instead of seeing each other as brothers and natural allies, the kings of Judah and Israel forgot the prophecy of Shemaiah (1 Kgs 12:24) and were constantly at war with each other (1 Kgs 14:30; 15:7, 16; 2 Kgs 14:11-14). Thus we find Asa of Judah entering into an alliance with Ben-Hadad of Aram against Baasha of Israel (1 Kgs 15:18-19).

KINGS OF ISRAEL AND JUDAH

The chart below lists the kings from the time when Israel split into two kingdoms after the reigns of Saul (1028-1013), David (1013-973), and Solomon (973-933 BC).

The dates for the kings are only approximate because it is not easy to reconcile all the details in the books of Kings and Chronicles to get a smooth chronology. For example, calculations based on the reigns of the kings of Israel (the northern kingdom) would indicate that Solomon died in approximately 948 BC. However, if we base our calculations on the dates for the kings of Judah (the southern kingdom), his death would have taken place in approximately 964 BC. To further complicate matters, the latest date for Solomon's death is generally held to be 933 BC.

These discrepancies should not shake our firm faith in the accuracy of Scripture. The differences can be accounted for in several ways. First, one year may be included in the dating for two kings, because a part of a year was regarded as a full year. Thus, if a king died in May of a certain year, that year would be counted as the last year of his reign, and also as the first year of his successor's reign. Second, it was not uncommon for the heir to the throne to begin ruling alongside his father. The years in which they reigned together would be counted as part of each one's reign, so that each of these years would be counted twice.

In trying to sort out the chronology, we do, however, have some fixed dates to work with. The Assyrians brought an end to the northern kingdom in 722 BC; the Babylonians attacked the southern kingdom and took its people into captivity in 586 BC; and Uzziah died and Isaiah was commissioned in 740 BC. We also know that Ahaziah of Judah and Joram of Israel died at about the same time, since Jehu killed both of them.

Kings of Israel (Northern Kingdom)	Dates BC	Foreign rulers	Kings of Judah (Southern Kingdom)	Dates BC
Jeroboam I – 22 yrs (1 Kgs 14:20)	933-912	Shishak of Egypt 945-924 (1 Kgs 11:40; 14:25)	Rehoboam – 17 yrs (1 Kgs 14:21)	933-917
			Abijah (Abijam) – 3 yrs (1 Kgs 15:2)	917-915
Nadab – 2 yrs (1 Kgs 15:25-26)	912-911		Asa – 41 yrs (1 Kgs 15:9, 10)	914-874
Baasha – 24 yrs (1 Kgs 15:33, 34)	911-888	Ben-Hadad of Syria 890-843 (I Kgs 15:18, 20)		
Elah – 2 yrs (1 Kgs 16:8)	888-887			
Zimri – 7 days (1 Kgs 16:15)	887			
Tibni – (1 Kgs 16:21)	887-884			
Omri – 12 yrs (1 Kgs 16:23)	887-876	Ashurbanipal II of Assyria 883-860		
Ahab – 22 yrs (1 Kgs 16:29-33)	876-854		Jehoshaphat – 25 yrs (1 Kgs 22:41)	874-850
		Shalmaneser III of Assyria 859-825		
Ahaziah – 2 yrs (1 Kgs 22:51-53)	854-853			
Joram – 12 yrs (2 Kgs 3:1, 2)	853-842		Jehoram – 8 yrs (2 Kgs 8:17)	850-843
Jehu – 28 yrs (2 Kgs 10:36)	842-818	Hazael of Syria 841-796	Ahaziah – 1 yr (2 Kgs 8:26)	843-842
			Athaliah – 6 yrs (2 Kgs 11:3)	842-837

Kings of Israel (Northern Kingdom)	Dates BC	Foreign rulers	Kings of Judah (Southern Kingdom)	Dates BC
Jehoahaz – 17 yrs (2 Kgs 13:1)	818-805		Joash – 40 yrs (2 Kgs 12:1)	837-798
Jehoash – 16 yrs (2 Kgs 13:10)	805-791		Amaziah – 29 yrs (2 Kgs 14:2)	798-770
Jeroboam II – 41 yrs (2 Kgs 14:23)	791-753	Shalmaneser IV of Assyria, 783-773	Azariah (Uzziah) – 52 years (2 Kings 15:2)	792-740
Zechariah – 6 mths. (2 Kgs 15:8)	753		Jotham – 16 yrs (2 Kgs 15:33)	740-735
Shallum – 1 mth (2 Kgs 15:13)	753	Tiglath-Pileser III, of Assyria 745-727 (2 Kgs 15:29; 16:7, 10)		
Menahem – 10 yrs (2 Kgs 15:17)	753-746			
Pekahiah – 2 yrs (2 Kgs 15:23)	746-745		Ahaz – 16 yrs (2 Kgs 16:2)	735-720
Pekah – 20 yrs (2 Kgs 15:27)	745-728	Rezin of Syria 735-732 (2 Kgs 15:37; 16:5-9)		
Hoshea – 9 yrs (2 Kgs 17:1)	728-722	Shalmaneser V of Assyria 727-722 (2 Kgs 17:3; 18:9)	Hezekiah – 29 yrs (2 Kgs 18:2)	720-692
		Sargon II of Assyria 722-705		
		Sennacherib of Assyria 705-681 (2 Kgs 18:13; 19:16, 20, 36)		
			Manasseh – 55 yrs (2 Kgs 21:1)	692-638
		Esarhaddon of Assyria 681-669 (2 Kgs 19:37)		
		Ashurbanipal of Assyria 669-626	Amon – 2 yrs (2 Kgs 21:19)	638
		Nabopolassar of Babylon 626-605	Josiah – 31 yrs (2 Kgs 22:1)	638-608
		Neco II of Egypt, 609-593 (2 Kgs 23:29)		
			Jehoahaz – 3 mths (2 Kgs 23:31)	608
		Nebuchadnezzar of Babylon 605-562 (2 Kgs 24:1)	Jehoiakim (Eliahim) – 11 yrs (2 Kgs 23:36)	608-597
			Jehoiachin – 3 mths (2 Kgs 24:8)	597
			Zedekiah (Mattaniah) – 11 yrs (2 Kgs – 24:18)	597-586

The kings of Judah continued to come from David's family, but the kings of Israel came from several families, and often succeeded to the throne by staging a coup d'état or by assassinating their predecessor. Aram caused a lot of trouble to Israel until the rise of Assyria around 750 BC. The Assyrians weakened both Judah and Israel and made them pay taxes. Eventually, in 721 BC, the Assyrians conquered the Israelites (2 Kgs 17:6). Almost all the people of Israel were deported from their native land, which the Assyrians resettled with people from other nations (2 Kgs 17:24).

The third section of Kings covers the period when Judah alone survived in the land of Canaan as the people of God. During the reign of Ahaz, Judah came under the rule of Assyria (2 Kgs 16:7-8). But when Hezekiah came to the throne, he rebelled against Assyria. Sennacherib of Assyria invaded Judah, capturing forty-six of its strong cities and deporting two hundred thousand people as slaves. Jerusalem was saved by a special act of God (2 Kgs 19:35-36). By the time of Josiah, Assyrian power was weakening, but that of Babylon was growing. Josiah supported Babylon against Pharaoh Neco of Egypt, who supported Assyria. Josiah was killed in a battle against Neco at Megiddo in 609 BC, and for a short period Judah was under Egyptian power. The defeat of Neco at Carchemish resulted in Judah becoming not a friend but a subject of Babylon. It made unsuccessful efforts to gain its freedom, and the people of Judah were taken to the land of Babylon in 558 BC.

Outline of Contents

COMMENTARY

1 Kgs 1:1-11:43 The Kingdom under Solomon

When the people of Israel left Egypt, their human leader was the prophet Moses (Exod 3:10). After his death, he was succeeded by Joshua (Deut 31:14; Joshua 1:1-3), the judges (Judg 2:16) and Samuel (1 Samuel 7:15-17). God was understood to be the supreme leader and was closely consulted by the human leaders (see, for example, Exod 19:3; Josh 7:6-8; Judg 2:18; 1 Sam 7:3b). But in the days of Samuel the people asked for 'a king to lead us such as other nations have' (1 Sam 8:5). God directed Samuel to anoint first Saul (1 Sam 10:1) and later David (1 Sam 16:1-3, 11-13) as kings over God's people. On David's death, his son Solomon assumed the throne and became the last king to rule over a united Israel (2:10-12).

1:1-2:46 Solomon's Throne Established

1:1-4 Abishag, the last of David's wives

David had become very old, possibly more than seventy years old, and could no longer keep himself warm (**1:1**). So *his servants*, who may have been the palace medical officers, searched the whole kingdom for a young virgin to take care of the king as a nurse and to keep him warm by lying beside him (**1:2**). They found Abishag, a girl from Shunem in the north of Israel (**1:3**). The fact the she was from Shunem does not necessarily mean that she was the Shunammite girl mentioned in the Song of Songs.

Abishag became the last of David's wives, though he did not have sexual relations with her (**1:4**). Although her presence in the palace may seem a minor matter, it is actually very important. For while she took care of the king's physical needs as a nurse, she would have listened to those who came to speak with him and would have become well informed and aware of what was going on in the palace.

1:5-10 Adonijah, the would-be ruler

Adonijah, the eldest of David's surviving sons, put himself forward and said, *I will be king* (**1:5**). His words were unwise and did not reflect the wisdom spelled out in Proverbs 25:6-7 and the teaching of our Lord in Luke 14:7-10. Adonijah's story is a good lesson for the African continent, where in both political and church settings we frequently see a craving for power and manipulation of many factors in order to achieve it. But those who take power by force or manipulation cause much suffering. While ambition to serve is not bad in itself, God can only bless it when it is pursued in line with his will in a God-fearing manner. Adonijah was self-centred and so failed miserably. Where there is fear of God, there is wisdom and success.

Adonijah's *father had never interfered with him* (**1:6a**), meaning that Adonijah had never been rebuked for any wrong he did. It seems that this was true of many of David's sons, as is clear from the behaviour of Amnon (2 Sam 13:1-21) and Absalom (2 Sam 13:22-29). Their behaviour not only points to a weakness in David himself, but also to the problem of raising children in a polygamous family. With his numerous political responsibilities and his numerous wives, the king would have had little time for his children.

David's family situation raises the topic of a father's role in any family. David, good man as he was, became so busy with public life that he failed in his own family affairs. The same is true of many African pastors. Their children may not be well nurtured because the father of the home (the pastor) is always out at church meetings or engaged in some kind of ministry, day in and day out. While the situation has improved in our generation, all those in ministry need regular reminders that failure in the home is an indication of poor administrative skills in public. A failed home life gives the gospel a poor reputation. Paul stressed this point when advising Timothy and Titus about church leadership at Ephesus and Crete (1 Tim 3:4; Titus 1:6).

Adonijah's human qualifications for kingship were that he was *very handsome and born next after Absalom* (**1:6b**; see also 2 Sam 3:2-4). But God does not look at outward appearance but at the heart (1 Sam 16:7). Where there are many sons of many wives, what counts for leadership is not only age and looks but gifts and maturity (Gen 37:5-8; 1 Sam 1:2; 3:1). Moreover in Israel it was the Lord who should identify who would succeed to the throne (Deut 17:15).

The recognition that both gifts and age are important would minimize the tension in some African homes where a younger brother outshines an older one. While the younger brother must still show his older brother the respect he deserves, the older brother is called upon to support his younger brother and to enable him to shine even more.

Unfortunately, too often the older brother seeks to apply the brakes to the progress of a younger brother. Such behaviour reveals a failure to recognize that God has given each of us different gifts and that when we bring them all together what we have is not one brother who is a star and another who is not, but rather an entire family that shines. This principle applies both to the exercise of our talents and abilities within our families and to the exercise of our spiritual gifts within the church (1 Cor 12:21-26; Eph 4:11-13).

Adonijah was able to gain the support of Joab, the commander of the army, and of Abiathar, the priest who had been loyal to David during Absalom's uprising (**1:7**). The two of them were carried away with the idea and did not consult the king, nor even God, though a great number of animals were sacrificed (**1:9**).

A faction loyal to David was against this move. Their refusal to join the celebration party shows they may have been approached but did not support Adonijah (**1:8, 10**). Among those who were not approached was Nathan, the prophet who had faithfully delivered God's messages to David in the past (2 Sam 7:1-17; 12:1-25).

1:11-27 Nathan and Bathsheba's move

Knowing that Adonijah was assembling his supporters, Nathan took action. He approached Bathsheba and informed her of what was happening, and of the risk that she and Solomon would face if Adonijah became king (**1:11-12**). He wanted her to approach the king and let him know what is going on, but he advised her to start with a question, *Did you not swear to me?* (**1:13**). David must at some stage have made a vow to her that Solomon was to succeed him. It is normal for aged rulers to name their successors and for a mother to hope that her son will succeed his father. But this time, the need was particularly urgent, for Bathsheba knew that if Adonijah succeeded, *I and my son, Solomon, will be treated as criminals* (**1:21**). Adonijah would no doubt want to eliminate any possible rivals to the throne and would see Bathsheba and Solomon as a threat.

Bathsheba took Nathan's advice (1:15-21). While she was still speaking, Nathan arrived, as planned (**1:14, 22-23**). He confirmed what Bathsheba has just said (**1:24-26**) and then, in his usual shrewd way (see also 2 Sam 12:1-10), asked, *Is this something my lord the king has done without letting his servants know?* (**1:27**). He is making the point that Adonijah and his supporters had not consulted other leaders properly.

Nathan and Bathsheba's questions roused the old king to take urgent action to prevent disaster and confusion. As Bathsheba had reminded him, *The eyes of all Israel are on you* (**1:20**). Even in his very old age, David had so much respect from his people that whomever he supported would be acceptable to them.

How wonderful it would be if more African leaders enjoyed such respect! By the time most of them have been in power for several years, those they rule have become tired of them and start crying for change of any kind. They feel this way because so many leaders accumulate wealth and power at the expense of the very people whose prosperity they should be promoting. Such leaders respond to any threat to their power with more injustice, with some even being prepared to kill all their political enemies. While David did have some vices, he is still an admirable example of a ruler who enjoys honour and respect both when he assumes power and when he lays it down.

1:28-53 David's action

The king was old and weak, but he could still act as quickly when action was needed. Bathsheba, who must have left the room when Nathan was announced, was recalled and David repeated his oath that Solomon would be his successor, which he swore before *the Lord the God of Israel* (**1:30**). Oaths were binding promises that had to be kept. Abraham kept his oath to the king of Sodom (Gen 14:22-23), Joshua kept his promise to the Gibeonites (Josh 9:15, 19), Ruth kept hers to Naomi (Ruth 1:17), and Elisha his to Elijah (2 Kgs 2:2). Even God considers himself bound by an oath (Heb 7:20-22). Bathsheba responded by bowing *low with her face to the ground* (**1:31**) in a gesture of respect and appreciation (see also Nathan in 1:23).

Next the king called *Zadok the priest, Nathan the prophet, and Benaiah*, the commander of his bodyguard, the Kerethites and Pelethites (**1:32**; 2 Sam 8:18). He instructed them to place Solomon on the king's own mule (**1:33**). Mules were peaceful animals used by kings and princes (2 Sam 13:29; Esth 6:8-9; see also Matt 21:5). Mounted on the mule, Solomon was to be led to the spring of Gihon, the main source of water for the entire city of Jerusalem, and thus an important public space. There Zadok and Nathan were to anoint him as king using holy oil (**1:34**). These two men represented two key offices in Israel: the prophet communicated the will of God to the people, and the priest communicated the needs of the people to God. The priest and the prophet together were to anoint Solomon to emphasize the unity of their choice.

After anointing Solomon, they were to blow the trumpet and start the shout of acclaim, *Long live King Solomon!* (**1:34**). Thereafter, Solomon would take his place on David's throne (**1:35**). This ceremony and Solomon's taking the throne would send the message that he was now the legitimate king.

David's instructions were duly obeyed (**1:36-37**). Solomon was escorted down to the Gihon spring by an escort of *the Kerethites and the Pelethites* (**1:38**), the king's own bodyguards whose first loyalty was to the king and not to any tribe or clan. They were led by the three leading men in the kingdom as the inauguration ceremony that David had ordered was carried out (1:38-40). All the people (except

those at Adonijah's feast) followed Solomon and the ground shook with the sound of joyous cheers and music (**1:40**). Some nine hundred years later, there would be similar celebration as Jesus Christ, the Son of God, rode through Jerusalem on a mule (Matt 21:6-11; Mark 11:1-10; Luke 19:29-38). Then, too, those supporting the king rejoiced, while his opponents were unhappy.

David received the congratulations of his *royal officials*, who expressed the wish that Solomon's throne might be *even greater than yours* (1:36-37, 47-48). These words were a common expression of hope for better future government. David's reign had been good, but even when earthly kingdoms are good, we can still expect an even better one to follow. We will continue to pray this prayer and nurture this hope until the promised ruler from the 'branch of Jesse' arises (Isa 11).

The noise of the celebration reached Adonijah and his supporters (**1:41**). When they learned what was going on, they were understandably dismayed and afraid, and dispersed rapidly (**1:42-46, 49**).

Meanwhile David praised the Lord for allowing him to see his successor safely installed on his throne (**1:48**). He no longer had to worry about the succession, which must have been a relief after the uncertainties following Absalom's rebellion.

Adonijah knew that his own life would now be in danger, and so he fled to the temple, where he took *hold of the horns of the altar*, which was a traditional place of safety (**1:50-51**; Exod 21:14). Solomon, assured of his power, now spoke firmly and gave conditions for peace with his brother: *if he shows himself to be a worthy man*, that is, if he becomes loyal to Solomon (**1:52**). But the conditions of his release include the instruction, *Go to your home* (**1:53**), making it clear that Adonijah must now consider himself an ordinary man, and no longer a powerful force in government.

2:1-12 David's charge to Solomon

David's last advice to Solomon is equivalent to a verbal handing over of power and is intended to help the young ruler start off his reign well (**2:1**). David must already have given Solomon much advice before this time. For example, 1 Chronicles 28 records in great detail his instructions to the elders of Israel about the plans for the building of the temple. But Solomon was still young (probably only about twenty years old) and had not much experience. The last words recorded here were meant for Solomon's ears only, but secrets of the palace do leak out into public records.

David's opening words (**2:2-4**) are similar to the Lord's charge to Joshua (Josh 1:6-9). Faithful obedience to the law of Moses would bring prosperity to Solomon and keep the kingship in the house of David. Solomon is, however, exhorted to do more than just obey the written laws and commandments, which were written and given to Moses while in the wilderness, as is clear from 1 Chronicles 28:9-10. David presents him to the living God, the Lord of the covenant, and issues a call to love the Lord and to whole-heartedly 'walk in his ways'. To walk in the Lord's ways is to keep in constant consultation with him and to seek his guidance in making any major decisions (Exod 20:4-5; Deut 6:4-5).

David next turned his attention to those who must be eliminated before the kingdom could take firm root (2:5-9). This part of David's instructions sounds very harsh and unloving to Christian ears. But it must be viewed within the context of God's progressive revelation of his will. Now that we have full revelation, God expects us to love even our enemies (Matt 5:43-44; Rom 12:14). However, at the level of revelation that David had, he understood that all those who stand against God and his chosen are to be destroyed together with their evil, while those who bless the Lord and his anointed will receive favour from the Lord. Thus David is not a pattern for us to follow here, since we enjoy the totality of God's revelation, the OT completed by the words of Jesus in the NT in Hebrews 1:1.

The first person on David's list was Joab, a close rela-tive of David's who had stood by him and fought for him in the most difficult times of his rule. However, he had killed Abner (2:5a), the commander of Israel's army during the reign of Saul, just after Abner had agreed to bring the army of Israel over to David (2 Sam 3:17-30). Later, David had planned to replace Joab with Amasa as the commander of Israel's army (2:5b; 2 Sam 19:13). Joab had effectively pre-vented this by killing Amasa while he was carrying out the king's orders. David had been forced to put up with this 'son of Zeruiah' (2 Sam 19:21-23), but he knew that shedding innocent blood could bring disaster on the whole nation. When Saul had killed the Gibeonites, Israel had suffered afterwards (2 Sam 21:1-3). The guilt of shedding innocent blood had to be removed (2:6; Deut 19:13; 21:9).

But not all of David's final commands were unpleasant. Solomon was also commanded to reward the sons of Barzil-lai for the kindness of their father (2:7; 2 Sam 17:27-28).

At the same time as Barzillai was showing kindness to David, another man, Shimei, was insulting him (2 Sam 16:5-14; 19:21-23). Cursing the ruler of the people was a serious wrong that was punishable by death (Exod 22:28; Deut 17:12-13). David had chosen to ignore this insult to himself, but he could not let Solomon take this risk, and so he ordered Solomon to eliminate him (2:8-9).

After giving these instructions, David died and *rested with his fathers* (2:10). Ordinarily he would have been buried in Bethlehem along with his ancestors, but instead he was buried in his own city, the city of David. His burial marks the beginning of the clan settlement in Jerusalem, without abolishing the one in Bethlehem.

He had reigned for a long time, forty years (2:11; see also 2 Sam 5:4), and had been glad to see his son Solomon firmly in control on the throne.

2:13-46 Solomon takes control

The rest of chapter 2 relates how Solomon carried out his father's instructions in dealing with possible opponents. Adonijah had not been one of those slated for punishment, but he drew attention to himself with the request that he sent to Solomon via Bathsheba. He admitted that the Lord had given the kingdom to Solomon, but he still felt that he had a strong claim to the throne and that the people had expected that he would be the next king (2:13-16). So he requested that he be given Abishag as his wife (2:17-21).

This may look like an innocent request, but in the cul-ture of the time it was the new king who had the right to marry and so inherit all the wives, and especially the young wives, of the previous king. Abishag was not just a beautiful woman of good character; she also had important symbolic status as David's last wife. Moreover, because she had nursed him in his last days, she would be very well informed about what was going on at the court. Adonijah's request could thus be interpreted as showing disrespect for the new king. Solomon was deeply offended by it (2:22a), and prob-ably saw it as implying that Adonijah was not obeying the terms on which he was pardoned (1:52). Accordingly, he ordered him executed (2:23-25).

If Adonijah still represented a threat, so did his sup-porters (2:22b). Accordingly, Solomon also considered it necessary to remove Abiathar the priest from his office. Because of Abiathar's faithful support of David, Solomon did not execute him, but he lost his job as a priest in fulfil-ment of the word of God by an unnamed prophet (2:26-27; 1 Sam 2:27-36). Joab, the army commander, saw what was happening and concluded that he was next on the list of those to be killed. Like Adonijah, he took refuge at the altar of the Lord. Like Adonijah, he was killed, and so the blood guilt for the death of innocent men was removed (2:28-35). Shimei was restricted to his home in Jerusalem as if under house arrest. When he broke the conditions of his sentence, he too was executed (2:36-46). These executions must have created much fear in the hearts of others who may have had thoughts of rebellion in these early days. For now, the kingdom was firmly in Solomon's hands.

There is no indication that the Lord condoned these kill-ings, but there is also no condemnation of them. As said earlier, they were done at a time in God's progressive rev-elation when standing with God and his anointed brought blessings while all that stood against God and his anointed (whether systems or persons) deserved to be destroyed. Solomon was God's anointed and therefore his enemies were also God's enemies. Their destruction was seen as serving a positive purpose in promoting God's will. In the

NT, such action has been replaced by the call to pray for the salvation of our opponents (Matt 5:44b).

3:1-4:34 Solomon's Wisdom and Greatness

3:1-15 Solomon given wisdom

Solomon married Pharaoh's daughter (**3:1a**). Neither Saul nor David had married non-Israelites. In fact, such marriages were forbidden to all Israelites (Deut 7:3; 20:17; see also Ezra 9:1-2; Neh 13:26). There were, however, a few cases of Israelites marrying people from other groups. Moses married a Cushite (Num 12:1) and Boaz, David's ancestor, married Ruth the Moabite. In such cases, the wives became believers and worshipped the God of Israel (Ruth 1:10-18; 4:13). The case of Pharaoh's daughter was different, for this was a political marriage, intended to strengthen a political alliance. This marriage was Solomon's first mistake. His priorities were wrong, and he was ignoring internal matters that would have strengthened the nation of Israel. Ahab was later to follow his example, which would draw Israel away from the Lord (16:31).

As yet, Jerusalem had no temple or palace (**3:1b-2**). The *high places* at which the people were worshipping would not have been very different from those of the Canaanites, except that the God of Israel was worshipped there. In the early stage of his reign, Solomon loved the Lord, which means he was seeking after God. Love for the Lord is the first commandment (Exod 20:3-6; Deut 6:4-5; 11:1; Matt 22:37). It is characteristic of those who seek to serve the Lord and be successful (Josh 23:15-17). However, the summary comment on Solomon in **3:3** not only acknowledges his obedience, but also his major act of disobedience: *he offered sacrifices and burned incense on the high places.* The writer later associates this behaviour with Solomon's many wives.

The bronze altar made in the days of Moses (Exod 27:1-8) was at Gibeon, about six miles (ten kilometres) from Jerusalem (2 Chr 1:3-5). Solomon went there to consult the God of Israel and offered numerous burnt offerings (**3:4**). But it was not the offerings that made the Lord listen to Solomon, but the fact that Solomon was seeking God as David his father had advised him to do (1 Chr 28:9).

The Lord appeared to Solomon *in a dream,* saying, *Ask for whatever you want* (**3:5**). Such an open-ended offer is both generous and confusing. Solomon first responded to God's generosity by remembering the kindness that the Lord had shown to his father and to him (**3:6**). But then he turned to his confusion. Like the tax collector at prayer, he was very aware of his real weakness (Luke 18:13). He remembered that he was still a very young man, without experience in life, and facing a daunting task (**3:7-8**). So Solomon asked for a *discerning heart* – heart knowledge is better than head knowledge – to know the difference between good and evil and truth and falsehood (**3:9**). When a leader cannot see the difference between right and wrong, the people suffer. In a similar situation in the past, Moses had asked for the presence of the Lord (Exod 33:14).

The Lord was pleased that Solomon was not selfish but was concerned for the welfare of his people. He gave him what he requested and also the riches and honour he might have requested but had not (**3:10-13**). The Lord left him with the promise that if he walked in the ways of the Lord and obeyed him as David his father had, he would receive the blessing promised to obedient children, namely, long life (**3:14**; see also Deut 5:16; Eph 6:2-3). Solomon's obedience to God was in agreement with the central theme of David's charge to him (2:2b-3). By obeying the God of his father David, he was also honouring his father (Exod 20:12). The Lord is happy with all those who obey (1 Sam 15:22).

Then Solomon awoke – and he realized it had been a dream (**3:15a**). But this does not mean that it was a delusion, for among the Hebrews, the same word is used to refer to a dream and a vision. But while it is true that God does, at times, speak through dreams (see also Matt 1:20; 2:12-13, 19, 22; 27:19), not every dream is God speaking. Discernment is needed to be able to distinguish between those dreams that are merely a natural result of our own thoughts and experiences and those that are the voice of the Lord. Those that are from the Lord will never contradict or add to what God has said in the Scriptures, but they will confirm it. It is also important to note that dreaming is not specifically included in the list of spiritual gifts in 1 Corinthians 12:7-10, 28 and Ephesians 4:11. While this does not mean that dreams are not part of God's program (see Joel 2:28; Acts 2:17), it indicates the degree of importance we should attach to them.

Solomon's experience of meeting with the Lord was a real one. So he returned to Jerusalem and continued his habit of worshipping at the altar before the ark of the covenant in the city (**3:15b**; see 2 Chr 1:4). There he offered burnt offerings, which were sacrifices showing personal devotion, and fellowship offerings, which involved others in the worship.

3:16-28 Solomon demonstrates wisdom

It is interesting that the case that is used to demonstrate Solomon's wisdom involves two prostitutes (**3:16a**). Like most cities of the world, African cities and towns have prostitutes. We tend to leave them to the mercy of those who use them to satisfy their evil sexual cravings and of the police who arrest them from time to time. Yet in God's program, they are as important as any other citizen. Yes, their deeds are evil, but their lives are precious. This story shows very clearly that Solomon was a judge not only for the righteous but also for the unrighteous. In the same way, the church is called to minister to all.

The prostitutes' case would probably have been tried in the lower courts and then referred to Solomon because they could not reach a decision in such a difficult case. (Contrast this with the pitiful case in 2 Kings 6:26-30, when the woman appeals directly to the king.) The king allowed each of them to present her argument and may have guessed which was the rightful mother (**3:16b-22**). He may also have remembered the ancient law in Israel relating to a situation where there were two owners and one dead ox and one live one. In that case, the oxen were to be equally shared between the interested parties (Exod 21:35). So he suggests that a similar principle be applied here (**3:23-25**). As he expected, the true mother could not bear the thought of her son being killed and identified herself by her response (**3:26-27**).

As news of this case spread, all the people not only feared the king but became convinced that he had wisdom from the Lord (**3:28**).

4:1-19 Solomon's officials and administrators

All the twelve tribes of Israel were under the rule of Solomon, as **4:1** emphasizes, and the tribal leaders and leaders of clans and families were powerful (8:1). However, Solomon also had his own officials, and the names of the eleven people we might call his cabinet ministers are listed in 4:2-6. It is possible that some of these people held office in succession, rather than simultaneously.

The list includes a number of priests: Zadok, Azariah his son, Abiathar and Zabud. Besides being a priest, Zabud was also the *personal adviser to the king.* In 2:26-27, we were told that Abiathar had been banished to Anathoth, so it may be that he was later pardoned and again allowed to serve among the priests.

But the list includes no prophet either as an official or an adviser. During the time of Samuel, the offices of prophet and priest had been combined in the one who led the nation. With the appointment of Saul, there was a separate king, but he was guided, at least at first, by a priest and prophet. David had the prophet Nathan as an advisor (2 Sam 12; 1 Kgs 1:10-38), and later Hezehiah consulted Isaiah (2 Kgs 19:1-7). But most of the kings ignored the office of the prophet. In fact, the appearance of prophets in the palace was often unwelcome – for as a last resort God often sent them to the palaces to pronounce his judgment. Solomon does not seem to have made room officially or unofficially for receiving counsel from a mentor with prophetic vision, and his reign may have suffered because of this. So does the rule of our African leaders who claim to be Christians but who do not respect and listen to people with genuine Christian vision.

Two of those listed (Azariah and Zabud – **4:5**) are said to be sons of Nathan, who may be the prophet who served David, or Solomon's brother Nathan (1 Chr 3:5), or some other man of the same name. There were also two secretaries (Elihoreph and Ahija – **4:3a**) and a recorder (Jehoshaphat – **4:3b**), who was responsible for recording not just the royal history but also the wisdom of Solomon. Benaiah was commander-in-chief of the army and Ahishar was in charge of the palace (**4:4, 6a**). Ominously, the last official mentioned, Adoniram, is said to be *in charge of forced labour* (**4:6b**) – the labour that led to much unhappiness and finally to rebellion and the breaking up of the kingdom

We thus find that Solomon's cabinet included a priest who would serve as chaplain, secretaries who may have been in charge of supervising the keeping of records and all correspondence, a recorder who may have been responsible for matters to do with protocol, a commander-in-chief to oversee the affairs of the army, a supervisor of civil servants (district officers), an overseer of all royal property, and a money man (overseeing labour and probably also taxes). It was a carefully chosen group, small in number but covering all the important areas. Having four priests in the cabinet (Azariah, Zadok, Abiathar and Zabud) may reflect how much Solomon desired to seek direction from the Lord.

While it would be foolish to copy Solomon's practice exactly today, there is an important principle here for many African presidents who favour large cabinets that have to be maintained at the taxpayers' expense. A small but well organized cabinet can do the job. The principle of having religious leaders among the officials should also not pass unnoticed. African presidents would do better if they kept close to and listened to people with genuine Christian vision as they seek to discern how to lead or make important decisions. For administrative purposes, Solomon divided Israel into twelve districts each under its own governor. The districts were responsible for supplying the food and other needs of the palace, with each district being responsible for one month of the year (**4:7**). This was the beginning of raising taxes from the people. The borders of the districts did not match the tribal settlements of the people of Israel, but were drawn up so that minority settlers and non-Israelites could fit in. This arrangement also had the effect of weakening tribal solidarity. The land of Judah seems to have been omitted in the division. The names of the governors of the various districts are listed in **4:8-19**.

It appears that there was a sound reason for having twelve districts. It distributed the load of meeting the physical needs of the king and his household across society, so that each district was responsible for only one month of the year. This was a tidy solution to what could otherwise have been a difficult problem.

Unfortunately, in Africa administrative districts are not set up for functional reasons but serve merely to multiply the number of members of parliament from a particular location for political convenience. Such management of affairs for selfish ends has also invaded the church in some places.

The creation of new administrative divisions, whether in the political or the church context, is wrong when it is not governed by the need to serve the people better and meet a legitimate need.

4:20-28 The size of Solomon's kingdom

It is significant that this description of Israel under the rule of Solomon begins by speaking of the *people of Judah and Israel* (**4:20a**). The kingdom was united, but there were traces of the division that dated back to the early days of David's reign. He had been king of Judah alone for seven years before moving to Jerusalem and becoming ruler of a united Israel for thirty-three years (2 Sam 5:5; 1 Kgs 2:10-11).

The combined population of Israel was now as *numerous as the sand on the seashore* (**4:20b**). This phrase had been used in God's promise to Abraham (Gen 13:16) and to Jacob (Gen 32:12). That promise had now been fulfilled. And despite the large population, there was no poverty (**4:20c**). The people were happy and there was such peace in the land that it could be described using the proverb that spoke of *each man under his own vine and fig-tree* (**4:25**; Deut 8:8; Mic 4:4; Zech 3:10). This peace stretched over the whole traditional expanse of Israel, *from Dan to Beer-sheba*. These were prosperous years for the whole of Israel.

Solomon's kingdom stretched from the river Euphrates in the north-east to Lebanon, Tyre and Sidon and the Mediterranean Sea in the west (**4:21, 24**). His marriage to the daughter of Pharaoh had extended the southern border to Gezer (9:16). There was peace with Egypt and with Hiram of Phoenicia. The palace was well supplied on a daily and monthly basis with what it needed to support its people (**4:22-23**) and its horses, of which there were twelve thousand (**4:26-28**).

4:29-34 The breadth of Solomon's wisdom

Once again, the author reminds us of the extent of Solomon's wisdom. It was greater than that of any of the other famously wise people of the day (**4:29-31**).

Much of his wisdom would be general knowledge and information acquired by his own intelligence, but it would also have been informed by his knowledge and fear of God (Prov 1:7). His intimate relationship with God enabled him to discern the will of God (the way of wisdom) as he governed the people. His *three thousand proverbs* would have been short sayings each of which expressed a truth about life (**4:32**). Many of them are included in the books of Proverbs and Ecclesiastes. His song as we have it in Song of Songs is a beautiful celebration of the true depths of love – whether one takes it as applying to a man and a woman, Yahweh and Israel, or Christ and the church. He also produced books on plant and animal life (**4:33**; see also Eccl 2:4-6). Most of his work has not survived, except those that came to be included in the Hebrew Scriptures.

People from many parts of the world came to listen to and learn from Solomon (**4:34**). Rulers like the Queen of Sheba (10:1-10) came and consulted him about the problems they faced.

5:1-9:9 Solomon's Temple and Palace

While King Solomon probably undertook a number of building projects, the most significant ones were the construction of his own palace and of the temple of the Lord. The process of building the temple is described in the most detail because the temple had a special place in the spiritual life of the people and the nation. It was to be the final resting place of the ark of the covenant.

The real preparation for this building had started when David told the prophet Nathan that he intended to build a temple (2 Sam 7:1-2). Long before Solomon came to the throne, plans for the temple building had been drawn up and the cost of the building estimated (1 Chr 28:11-18). David had accumulated money and gold, silver, bronze and iron for the work (1 Chr 22:2-4, 14-16). He had also called a large gathering of the leaders of Israel to raise money to build the temple (1 Chr 29:2-9).

5:1-18 Final preparations

Hiram, the king of Tyre from 970-935 BC, was friendly with David and Solomon. He had supplied David with cedar wood and craftsmen to build his house in Jerusalem (2 Sam 5:11). Tyre and its neighbour Sidon were good sources of materials, for they were situated on the Mediterranean Sea in Lebanon, to the north of Israel. They were both great markets where the nations of the west and east met to trade. Moreover, Lebanon was famed for its forests and the high quality of the cedar wood that grew there.

On hearing that Solomon had succeeded his father as king, Hiram sent messengers to congratulate him (**5:1**). Solomon's reply spoke of his father's dream of building a temple. David had been fully occupied in fighting the enemies of Israel, but the Lord had *put his enemies under his feet* (**5:3**), an idiom that expressed the idea that defeated enemies were under the feet of the victor. It was the Lord who had brought this about (Ps 110:1-3; Heb 1:13). Now, however, Solomon can say that through David's work *My God has given me rest on every side* (**5:4**). It was true that at the beginning of his reign and throughout the period of building the temple, there was no war with the neighbouring nations. Solomon was right to recognize that it is the Lord who gives such peace.

In this time of peace, Solomon proposed to carry out his father's dream and to build a temple *for the name of the Lord my God* (**5:5**). God himself had described it in the same words when he prophesied that *your offspring ... will build a temple for my name* (2 Sam 7:12-13). Solomon recognized that what he was building was not a place where God would live (8:30; Acts 7:48-50), for he knew that the God of Israel was too great to be confined to a building. After all, not even the heaven and earth could contain him (8:27). Jesus underscored this point when he said that we do not need an earthly worshipping place (John 4:19-24). Believers are the temple of God (1 Cor 3:16; 6:19).

Solomon placed an order for cedar wood from Lebanon, promising to supply men to help Hiram's skilled woodcutters and to pay for both the labour and the materials (5:6). He also requested skilled craftsmen and masons to work alongside his builders in Jerusalem (2 Chr 2:3-16).

Hiram was delighted to agree to Solomon's request (5:7-9) and the two kings entered into a good business relationship (5:12). Unfortunately, it appears that the treaty they signed, like the treaty with Egypt, also involved other relationships as Solomon is later reported to have married Sidonian women (11:1).

The terms of the business deal required Solomon to provide food for Hiram's household (5:9). This requirement imposed an added burden on Israel. In addition to raising the support required for the palace in Jerusalem (4:22-23), they also had to supply wheat and oil to Hiram and his workers. This was not a temporary requirement but one that went on *year after year* for the twenty years it took to complete the temple and the palace (5:11).

When Israel opted to have a king to lead them like other nations, they had been warned that their attention would end up being focused on meeting the material needs of the monarchy and not on their own spiritual lives (1 Sam 8:9-18). This prophecy came true as Solomon conscripted workmen to work with the men of Tyre (5:13-14) and put Adoniram in charge of forced labour (4:6). Thirty thousand men were drafted into this forced labour. They worked in shifts of ten thousand. Each shift spent one month in Lebanon and two months at home. Besides this group, there were another seventy thousand men who worked as carriers and eighty thousand who worked as stonecutters. These labourers were supervised by 3300 foremen. According to 2 Chronicles 2:17-18, the 153 600 who were carriers, stonecutters and foremen were aliens, but the writer of Kings seems to lump them together with the thirty thousand Israelites who were also conscripted. With so many people engaged in a building project that lasted at least twenty years (6:37-7:1), their farms and personal jobs must have been neglected. Yet at the same time the nation had to feed this workforce and the workmen from Tyre, and pay the cost of materials. It is no wonder that there was much dissatisfaction.

The number of people involved in the building reminds us of Israel in the land of Egypt. But this time Israelites were being forced to build in the land of promise, as Samuel had warned them (1 Sam 8:10-18). The comment that all this work was done at the *king's command* (5:17) shows that Solomon himself insisted on the forced labour.

The agreements between Israel and Tyre that began with David and were continued by Solomon must have had other effects besides the erection of some magnificent buildings in the capital city. The work brought the people of Israel and the Sidonians together. There must have been cultural exchange of ideas and learning, not only of building skills but also of other religions. Though Israel was supposed to be unique and separate, it was very open to foreign influences of all kind.

6:1-7:51 Building the temple and the palace

The writer of Kings gives much space to and goes into great detail about the building of the temple. The palace was a larger building, but its construction is described in only a few verses (7:1-12). Then he goes on to give more details about the furnishings of the temple to make it clear that his main interest is in the house built to honour 'the name of the Lord' (5:5).

6:1-38 BUILDING THE TEMPLE The actual building of the temple began about four hundred and eighty years after the Israelites left the land of Egypt and in the fourth year of Solomon's reign (6:1). If he came to power in 960 BC, then the exodus can be dated to around 1440 BC. At that time, the Lord had announced that he would choose a particular place where his name would dwell (Exod 20:24; Deut 12:5), but it took four hundred and eighty years before that place was identified. The Lord's promises never fail, but sometimes there is a long wait before they are fulfilled.

Over the four hundred and eighty years, Israel had become a strong power with its capital in Jerusalem. There David had built a house for himself, but had been unhappy because the ark of the Lord was still housed in a tent. Thus when Solomon came to the throne, one of the first things he did was to start work on building the temple. Thereafter, he built his own palace.

The broad details of the temple are described in 6:2-13, with its dimensions being given in cubits. One cubit is equivalent to roughly eighteen inches (just under half a metre). The temple was ninety feet (twenty-seven metres) long; thirty feet (nine metres) wide and forty-five feet (thirteen and a half metres) high (6:2). Narrow windows were set high on the temple walls (6:4). The *portico* was an open porch in front of the temple that made the building thirty feet (nine metres) wider (6:3). The *side rooms* that were added to the structure may have been used as storerooms for the priests who ministered in the temple (6:5-6).

A striking feature of the building site was that there was no noise of hammers or chisels on stone while the building was going up. All the stones were shaped at the quarry and then simply fitted into place in the building (6:7). This procedure was probably adopted in obedience to the command that no iron tools were to be used when constructing God's altar (Exod 20:25; Deut 27:5).

The details of the interior of the temple are given in 6:14-36. The insides of the stone walls and the ceiling of the temple were completely covered with cedar wood (**6:15, 18**), which would not only make the building look beautiful but would help to keep it cool. Cedar was also used to create a partition that would separate the Most Holy Place where the ark of the covenant would be placed from the holy place where the altar would stand (**6:16, 19**).

The ark of the covenant was the box that God had instructed Moses to make. Inside it Moses had placed the two stone tablets with the commandments of the Lord on them. On top of the ark were two cherubim (Exod 37:1-9). We do not know exactly what a cherub was like ('cherubim' is the plural of the Hebrew word 'cherub') but it was clearly some winged creature like an angel.

The design of the Most Holy Place echoes that of the ark, for it includes two gigantic cherubim, each with one wing touching the wall and the other wing towards the centre of the room touching the wing of the other (**6:23-28**). The ark of the covenant would be placed under the point where the wings of the cherubim touched in the middle. The ark, which symbolized the presence of the Lord, would thus be under the wings of the two cherubim.

The inner walls of the temple and the outer rooms were decorated with carvings of cherubim, palm trees and open flowers. These walls were then covered in gold. So were the statues of the cherubim, the altar, the furniture, the utensils, the floors and the ceiling. In using this much gold, Solomon was following the pattern seen in other ancient temples from the period.

With its beautiful carvings and gleaming gold, the finished temple must have looked very rich and impressive. The expensive wood, stone and metal were intended to show the devotion of Solomon and the people to the God of Israel. But it could have another effect on ordinary people. There was the danger that they might direct their devotion to the gold and not worship the true God of Israel, as Exodus 20:4 warned. In the days of the prophets Jeremiah and Ezekiel, the temple itself had become the object of worship. People thought that the mere presence of such an expensive building in Jerusalem was enough to give them security and protection (Jer 7:4-8). They had forgotten the need to walk humbly in the ways of the Lord and to obey his commands (Mic 6:8). That is why the writer inserts a message about what the Lord required of Solomon and the rest of us before giving a detailed description of the temple (**6:11-13**). The presence of God with his people would depend on their following his decrees and keeping and obeying his commandments (2 Chr 7:12-14).

To fear God and to shun evil are equal to wisdom and understanding, which cannot be bought with gold or precious stones (Job 28:12-19). Gold, precious stones and metals are poor measures of human devotion to God. God looks at people, not at their riches. Thus the gift of the poor widow was appreciated more than the money of the rich (Luke 21:2-4).

The description of the temple ends with an account of the time it took to complete. Construction began in the fourth year of the reign of Solomon and ended in his eleventh year, meaning that it had taken seven years to build (**6:37-38**).

When it comes to constructing a church, the place of worship in our time, we can admire Solomon's temple, but we also need to remember that it was destroyed by the Babylonians in 586 BC. In 20 BC, Herod the Great began to build another magnificent temple, which took over forty-six years to finish (see John 2:20), but it was destroyed in AD 70 by the Romans. As Jesus told the Samaritan woman, the most meaningful worship comes from the heart (John 4:23). So when we erect church buildings, we would be wise to be guided by the principles of decency and affordability. The church building should be of the same quality as the house of the average rich believer (neither the richest nor the poorest member of the congregation). It must also be a building the congregation can afford to build, so that the work of the church is not crippled by a huge debt. And it should not be wholly financed by one person or by a few businesspeople or politicians.

7:1-12 Building the palace Solomon's palace took thirteen years to complete, much longer than the seven years spent on the temple (**7:1**). His main palace was called the *Palace of the Forest of Lebanon* (**7:2**), most likely because of the amount of cedar and pine from Lebanon on display (5:6, 8-9) but also possibly because the workmen and the woodworkers were from Lebanon or the style imitated Lebanese palaces. Besides the main building described in 7:2-5, there was also a colonnaded *Hall of Pillars* (RSV) (**7:6**) and a *Hall of Justice* with a special throne from which the king could pass judgment (**7:7**). He also built a palace for Pharaoh's daughter (**7:8**). This last must have aroused jealousy in his other wives, leading each to ask for special treatment for themselves, which he seems to have granted (11:1-6).

The palace buildings were all built of special stone, but did not have as much gold as was used as in the temple. The description of this massive complex is very brief because the writer considered the palace a private project of the king and not central to the national religious history. Although the temple of the Lord was smaller in size, it was more important. It was intended to unite the nation in the worship of Yahweh of Israel.

7:13-51 Furnishing the temple In Exodus, God had filled Bezalel and Oholiab with the Spirit of God and given them artistic gifts that contributed to the building of the tabernacle (Exod 31:1-6). But God had not prepared an Israelite to carry out a similar task in the building of his temple. Instead Solomon employed the services of a man called

Huram (or Hiram) who must have been one of the specialists who had come to Jerusalem to build the temple (2 Chr
2:13). He was half Israelite, for his mother was an Israelite and his father a Phoenician, who was gifted in working
bronze (**7:13**).

Huram's first task was to construct two huge bronze
pillars, each about twenty-seven feet (eight and a quarter
metres) tall and eighteen feet (five and a half metres) round
and skilfully decorated with rows of pomegranates (**7:15-21**).
Both pillars were erected in front of the temple. The pillar
on the south side was called *Jakin*, meaning 'Established',
while the pillar erected on the north side was called *Boaz*,
meaning 'Strength'. The function of these pillars is not
known. Perhaps they and their names were intended to
remind the people that God had established and strengthened the nation by placing the temple in Jerusalem.

Huram's second major project was to build a large water
container called the Sea (**7:23-26**). It was about fifteen feet
(four and a half metres) across and could hold ten thousand
gallons (forty-four thousand litres) of water for the purification of the Levites who served in the temple. This vast
basin was mounted on the backs of twelve bronze bulls. It is
strange that bulls should be used in the temple of the Lord
after the commandment in Exodus 20:4 and considering
how easily the fathers of Israel had been carried away into
worshipping the calf in the wilderness (Exod 32:1-8).

However, given God's implied acceptance of the building, it does not appear that these bulls had any religious
meaning. Bulls were the animals of labour, and so it makes
sense that they would be the ones to carry the Sea on their
backs.

Huram's third task was to make ten moveable stands on
wheels that could support basins to carry water for use by
the priests (**7:27-39**). Huram also made many other smaller
bronze utensils for use in the temple (**7:40**). The chapter
concludes with a list of all the objects Huram had made
(**7:41-45**) and of other furniture that Solomon had made in
gold (**7:48-50**). All these items were installed in the temple and any leftover bronze, silver and gold were carefully
stored there (**7:51**).

8:1-66 The dedication of the temple

This chapter describes a national worship service that was
one of the most important political and religious gatherings in Israelite history. Jerusalem had been the capital of
the whole of Israel for over forty years, and this ceremony
marked the official recognition that the city was now spiritually and officially the place where the God of Israel had
chosen to set his name.

David had longed for this celebration, but had only been
able to take the first steps towards it by bringing the ark
of the covenant to be sheltered in a tent in Jerusalem. But

his son Solomon had achieved David's dream and built a
magnificent temple.

8:1-11 THE CEREMONY Solomon summoned the elders of
Israel, all the heads of the twelve tribes and their chiefs to
Jerusalem (**8:1a**). It was a historic gathering of people who
came from the length and breadth of the whole kingdom,
from Lebo Hamath on the northern border to the Wadi of
Egypt in the south (8:65a). The gathering provided effective
publicity in a culture where news was spread by eyewitnesses and word of mouth. The fact that the king, rather
than the priests, played a central role in this ceremony
underscores the point that this was not just a religious
occasion but also had a political aim.

The celebration was far more than a one-day event. To
encourage all Israel to attend, it was planned to take place
in the seventh month at the same time as the Feast of Tabernacles (**8:2**), which was one of the three major feasts for
the nation of Israel. (The other two were Passover and Pentecost, which fell in the first and third months of the Jewish
calendar.)

The celebration also took account of the special significance of the number seven in the Bible. Thus for seven days
the people celebrated the Feast of Tabernacles (8:65a) and
then there were another seven days of celebration, making a total of fourteen days of celebration (8:65b) before
people were sent away (8:66). Most of those invited would
have stayed in Jerusalem or in its vicinity throughout the
celebration.

The announced purpose of the gathering was to bring *the
ark of the Lord's covenant* from its tent in the *City of David*,
that is, the area of Jerusalem also known as Zion (see
2 Sam 5:7, 9) to the temple (**8:1b**). The ark was a reminder
to Israel that God had both chosen them as his special people and chosen to be among them.

Solomon and all the others present accompanied the ark
as it was carried from its tent in the City of David to the
Most Holy Place in the new temple, and numerous sacrifices
were offered (**8:5**). The account in the book of Chronicles
shows that there was also a choir and orchestra taking part
in the worship (2 Chr 5:11-13). The ark itself and the holy
furnishings from the tabernacle were carried solely by the
priests and the Levites (**8:3-4**). The experience at Perez
Uzzah had not been forgotten (2 Sam 6:6-9).

The ark already had small cherubim on its lid, but it was
now placed under and between the bigger cherubim of gold
that Solomon had placed inside the Most Holy Place (**8:6-7**;
see also 6:23-28; Num 17:8-10; Heb 9:4). The ark had once
been associated with 'the gold jar of manna, Aaron's staff
that had budded, and the stone tablets of the covenant'
(Heb 9:4; see also Exod 16:33-34; 25:16, 21-22; Num 17:10;
Deut 10:1-5), but by this stage it contained only the two
stone tablets on which the Ten Commandments were written (**8:9**). Knowing the living God and obeying his laws

were what distinguished the Israelites from the people of other nations.

As the priests completed this part of the ceremony, a cloud filled the temple as a sign that the Lord was present with his people (**8:10**). The cloud was a symbol of the presence of God, as it had been in the days of Moses (Exod 40:34-35). Ezekiel's vision of the departure of the cloud (Ezek 10:3-4, 18-19; 11:23) meant that the glory of the Lord had left the temple because Israel's sin could no longer be forgiven.

As the cloud filled the temple, the priests could not continue their work (**8:11**). When the Lord is present, the work of priests is no longer needed.

8:12-21 Solomon's address Solomon now spoke to the people about the faithfulness of God. On three occasions in this speech, he quotes the word of God, presumably from a book that had already been written (8:12, 16, 18-19).

Solomon began by referring to the cloud that all could see had filled the Holy Place (**8:12**). The cloud was a reminder that God is too great to live with ordinary people. While Solomon described the temple he had built as *a place for you to dwell for ever* (**8:13**), his later prayer shows that he was well aware that it was not the temple that had brought God among them but his grace. He also knew that he could not expect the Almighty God to actually live in his temple permanently.

Solomon now turned to face the people, blessed them, and then shouted the praise of the Lord who had fulfilled his promise to David (**8:15**). God had chosen the house of David and had promised David that his son would accomplish his vision of *building a temple for the Name of the Lord* (**8:16-19**). The Lord had kept his promises – Solomon now sat on the throne and he had built the temple and provided a place for the ark that reminded them all of the covenant God had made with their ancestors during the exodus (**8:20-21**). The ark was thus a symbol that united all Israel.

8:22-61 The prayer of dedication Solomon's prayer was uttered while he was standing in front of *the altar of the Lord* (**8:22**). This standing posture was common when praying in those days, as many illustrations from the period show. It marked the king as inferior to the deity, who was thought of as seated on a throne, like a king listening to a subject's request. By the end of the prayer, Solomon had changed his posture and was *kneeling with his hands spread out towards heaven* (8:54).

Solomon's posture before the Lord expressed his awareness of his own unworthiness. Though some may argue that worship comes from the heart, our posture does communicate our attitude to God to those around us. In Africa, we would never speak to a superior with our hands in our pockets, and we should not address God with less respect. Others need to see that he is a great God, and while we have joy in his presence, this does not mean that we should

act as if we have lost all sense of our own unworthiness to come before him.

The prayer of dedication began with praise to God who has no equal in heaven or on earth (**8:23**). Whatever God says, he is able to carry out. He has shown his faithfulness to the house of David, but he is also faithful to all who walk faithfully before him (8:23-24). Solomon prayed that the faithfulness God had shown to David in the past would continue in the future (**8:25-26**).

Solomon was aware that even his magnificent temple was far too small for such a great God, *for even the high heaven cannot contain you* (**8:27**). Nevertheless, he prayed that God would be merciful and would listen to the prayers offered from the temple or *towards this place* (**8:28-30**). The majority of the people of Israel, especially the common people, could not travel to Jerusalem for worship or prayer. Instead, they would pray facing towards the city and the temple, just as Daniel did when he prayed with his windows open towards Jerusalem (Dan 6:10).

Though Christians do not need to face in any particular direction as they pray, there is a need to maintain an awareness of the presence of God. Now that we have fuller revelation of God, we know that God is not in one place (John 4:21, 23-24) and therefore wherever we face, he is there. Some Christians make a practice of lifting up their eyes to heaven as a symbolic expression of where their help comes from (Ps 123:1). This is not to be discouraged; but those who choose to do this should not seek to impose their practice on others. No one particular posture is acceptable for Christians, but our posture should express our awareness that when we come before the Lord, we are before the King of all kings. The same attitude should be shown to others around us who face a particular place when they pray. Their external expression of humility before God is to be appreciated, even as we pray that those of them who do not actually know God through his saving grace in Christ will come to that knowledge. Above all, we need to remember Jesus' words that 'God is spirit, and his worshippers must worship in spirit and in truth' (John 4:24).

The rest of the prayer is divided into seven parts:

- Solomon prayed that in the temple, the guilty and the innocent might be revealed (**8:31-32**). He knew that in the presence of God, nothing is hidden. God is a God of justice and righteousness, and he will protect the innocent and punish the guilty. Here is a good principle for those who have been unjustly treated and have not found (or have not chosen to pursue – maybe in view of 1 Cor 6:1-8) justice in the courts. The Lord is the ultimate court of appeal, and if we leave things in his hands, we can take comfort in the knowledge that he will act, even if his ways are sometimes mysterious to us.

- Solomon prayed that when the people confessed their sins, they would be forgiven and again given victory over their enemies (**8:33-34**).
- Solomon prayed that in times of drought, God would forgive the people when they repented of their sins and would send rain (**8:35-36**). Droughts were common then, as they are now, and just as Solomon acknowledged that drought could come as punishment from God, so we too should include a time of confession in our prayers for rain.
- Solomon prayed that God would forgive and restore them in time of national disaster, such as disease, crop failure, agricultural pests or human enemies. Clearly, he believed that all such disasters were a result of sin in the nation (**8:37-40**). It is interesting that he asked God to *hear from heaven your dwelling place* (8:39). He knew that God does not dwell in any human temple.
- Solomon prayed that God would also answer the prayers of foreigners who believe in him (**8:41-43**). These foreigners were expected to pray *towards this temple* rather than in it, for there seems to have been no place for foreigners in the temple at that time. This prayer agrees with God's intention all along. When he chose Abraham, he told him, 'all peoples on earth will be blessed through you' (Gen 12:3b). While this ultimately meant blessings through Christ, it also meant that as others came to know and accept the God of Abraham as their God, they would be blessed. Thus God accepted people like Ruth (who told Naomi, 'your God [will be] my God' – Ruth 1:16) and Rahab the harlot who told the spies sent by Joshua that, 'the Lord your God is God in heaven above and on the earth below' (Josh 2:11). God did not choose Israel so as to exclude other peoples forever, but so that others will be blessed through 'blessing Abraham' (Gen 12:3a) and accepting Abraham's God. In the NT, we also find proselytes and God-fearers who were acceptable among God's chosen people, the Jews, even before they became born again members of the church. For example, there is the Ethiopian eunuch (Acts 8:27) who had gone to Jerusalem to worship, and Cornelius (Acts 10:2) who was devout, God-fearing and generous to the needy).
- Solomon prayed that when the people went to war, God would hear when they prayed towards his temple (**8:44-45**). But this prayer does not apply to any war, but only to those that are against God's enemies and that are embarked on following God's orders.
- Solomon prayed that should God have to punish the Israelites by handing them over to their enemies who would take them into exile, he would still hear when they repented and prayed towards the temple from the land of their exile. God is asked to forgive them and to move their conquerors to show them mercy (**8:46-51**).

Solomon concluded his prayer with a final plea that God would hear all the prayers offered by his servants because he had graciously chosen them to be his special people (**8:52-53**).

Rising from his knees, Solomon blessed the assembly while standing and facing the people (**8:55**). Once again he praised the Lord who had fulfilled all this promises. *May the Lord our God be with us ... so that all the peoples of the earth may know that the Lord is God and that there is no other* (**8:56-60**). The purpose for which he was asking for these blessings was so that Israel would be a witness to the world – that the world would come to know the true God through Israel, as God had promised to Abraham (Gen 12:3).

There are some important lessons we can draw from this account of the dedication of the temple. First, it is important for people to have a place that they can identify as somewhere that they 'come before the Lord'. The place may be a big church building, a garage, someone's living room, or even under a tree. Second, believers must consciously remember that though such a place may be referred to as the Lord's, he does not live there. Even the earth and the heavens cannot contain him (8:27; 2 Chr 2:6a; 6:18). It is simply the place the believers meet to worship (2 Chr 2:6b). Third, a place built for God needs to be known by all as such, and a dedication is one way to declare its function. Thus dedication services for church buildings are quite in order. The focus in such dedication services should be on declaring who God is and on reminding the people of their responsibility before God. Solomon's prayer and exhortation to the people may be a good model to follow on such occasions.

8:62-64 CONSECRATION OF THE TEMPLE The final step in the consecration of the temple was the sacrifice of thousands of cattle, sheep and goats (**8:62-63**). David had offered similar sacrifices when the ark was first brought to the city (2 Sam 6:17). Solomon would have provided the sacrificial animals and the priests would have offered them. Grain offerings were also made (**8:64**). Most of these offerings would have been eaten by those who were attending the celebration because this was permitted for fellowship offerings.

At the end of the celebration, all the people went home feeling impressed and joyful because of what they had seen and participated in (**8:65-66**). Even today, this is the experience of those who have been to a worship centre. Those who have met with the Lord do experience great joy. We see this in the shepherds (Luke 2:20), the wise men from the east (Matt 2:10-11) and in Jesus' disciples (John 1:41-45).

9:1-9 THE LORD APPEARS TO SOLOMON A SECOND TIME This section should be regarded as part of the ceremony of dedication of the temple. It is the Lord's response to Solomon's prayer on behalf of the people. However, it appears to be dated after the completion of both the temple and the palace buildings (**9:1**), which would imply that the Lord responded only thirteen years after the prayer had been prayed. What is happening is that the writer of Kings, who wrote many years after both events, is working from the principle that the Lord's response, which stresses that obedience takes precedence over all merely physical achievements, applies to all that Solomon achieved. It was relatively common at that time to group a lot of related items together without bothering with details of their exact relationship. A similar pattern is evident in Mark 1:2, which reads, 'It is written in Isaiah' and then quotes a combination of words from Malachi 3:1 and Isaiah 40:3. Isaiah is a major prophet, and Malachi a minor one, and so everything is lumped together under Isaiah's name. The writer of Kings recognized that the principle the Lord laid down at the dedication of the temple applies to all Solomon's achievements, and so he listed them at this point.

The Bible writers were not writing biographical history, but theological history. The former gives dry details of history, while the latter takes the same details and shows how they tie in with the person's relationship with God. So where someone writing a biographical history might have said, 'after the building of the temple but before … ', the one who is writing theological history lumps both the major and minor events together.

Once again, *the Lord appeared to him* in a dream, as he had at Gibeon (3:4-5). The Lord told Solomon that his prayers had been heard and his requests granted (**9:3a**). But in case Solomon should think that he is the one who has consecrated the temple, the Lord stressed that *I have consecrated this temple* (**9:3b**). Human rituals cannot control God. He is the only one who can make anything sacred. But he has agreed to make the temple his own, *putting my Name there for ever.* The Lord's identification of himself with the temple was visibly seen when the cloud filled the temple during the dedication. When he says that *my eyes and my heart will always be there* (**9:3c**), the Lord is saying that he sees and appreciates this place and cares for it. He will be the watchman for this building that he cares about.

Although the Lord's words in **9:4** were directed specifically to Solomon, there can be no doubt that the way of gaining the Lord's blessings remains the same for all of us – we are to walk with integrity before the Lord, be righteous like David, and obey God's laws and commandments. We are reminded of Deuteronomy 6:4-5 and Exodus 20:1-6, which are not a summons to legalism but to a life committed to a special relationship with the living God. The general application of the Lord's response is even clearer from the words recorded in 2 Chronicles 7:14: 'if my people who are called by my name will humble themselves and pray and seek my face and turn from their wicked ways, then I will hear from heaven and will forgive their sins and heal their land'.

If Solomon lived the type of life God requires, his sons would inherit God's promise to David that his dynasty will endure *for ever* (**9:5**). However, there was also the possibility that Solomon and his sons might reject God. Here the word 'sons' does not refer only to Solomon's physical descendants but to all the people of Israel then and in the future. If they failed to maintain the right relationship with the Lord, and instead chose to enter into relationships with other gods, they would receive the curses promised in Deuteronomy 28:15-68 (**9:6-7**). The impressive temple building would not protect them, for God would destroy it too (**9:8-9**).

Solomon and his sons did indeed fail to keep God's commands and drew the wrath of a jealous God. But God kept his promise to David, by raising up another son who would be the true 'stem of Jesse' who will rule with perfect justice and carry out the will of God (Isa 9:2-7; 11:1-9).

9:10-10:29 Solomon's Greatness

9:10-28 Solomon's economic programme
After twenty years (**9:10**; see also 6:38; 7:1), the temple and the palace buildings were completed, although no doubt improvements and additions continued to be made. Solomon was still in debt to Hiram of Tyre for all the labour, materials and gold he had supplied, and thus he gave him twenty towns in northern Galilee as partial payment (**9:10**). It is possible that Solomon's taxes had not been able to raise all the grain and oil to pay for the labour (5:11) and that the towns were in compensation for the outstanding balance. Hiram was not happy with the towns he was given because he found them to be poor and neglected (**9:12-13**).

The temple and palaces were not Solomon's only building projects. He also built the walls of Jerusalem, Hazor, Megiddo and Gezer. This last had been conquered by Pharaoh and given to Solomon as a wedding gift (see 3:1), but needed extensive rebuilding (**9:15-17a**). Some desert towns were rebuilt (**9:17b-18**) and fortresses, storehouses and towns for horses and chariots were constructed (**9:19**).

Not all of the original inhabitants of the promised land had been wiped out by Israel in the days of Joshua (**9:20-21a**). Solomon turned those who remained into slaves (**9:21b**); their situation was similar to that of the Israelites in Egypt. This act must not be viewed as approved by God, although he does make allowance for it with the statement, 'your male and female slaves are to come from the nations around you' (Lev 25:44). But the focus of that passage in Leviticus is that no Israelite should ever enslave another Israelite (Lev 25:39). They all have equal status before God. Yet at times manual work has to be done, and in that case, other nations will serve the 'royal nation' – not because they deserved it but because God in his grace had chosen to bless Israel.

These days, the equality that prevailed among Israelites is enjoyed by all believers because of their spiritual status, no matter what their nationality, race or origin. So when Christians find themselves in an employer-employee relationship, with one Christian employing or being employed by another Christian, both must remember that they are equal before God. Such an attitude transforms the attitude of the employer and the employee, so that they conform to Paul's teachings in Ephesians 6:5-9.

In obedience to the law, Solomon did not enslave Israelites. Instead he conscripted them into his army or appointed them as overseers of his projects (**9:22-23**).

Because of his economic strength, Solomon was able to build a separate house for his wife, the daughter of Pharaoh, because he did not want an outsider to live in a place where the holy ark of the Lord had been (**9:24**; see also 2 Chr 8:11). To fulfil his religious obligations, he offered burnt offerings and fellowship offerings three times a year (**9:25**). He also had ships constructed and manned by sailors from Tyre. He sent these ships on business ventures, trading with the Arabs to the south on the Red Sea, and possibly even going south along the east coast of Africa and even as far as India.

10:1-13 Visit of the Queen of Sheba

We have already read that Solomon had become famous. Many rulers and leaders had heard of him and came to consult him (4:29-34). One such visitor was the Queen of Sheba. The exact location of Sheba is not known. On the basis of the gifts she brought (**10:2a**, **10**), some have claimed that she came from somewhere in Asia (south Arabia, India or Yemen) or from somewhere in Africa (the East African coast or the Horn of Africa). Regardless of the exact location of Sheba, it was a wealthy, distant land that had heard of Solomon's wisdom and business ventures. Its queen came to see Solomon for herself and to personally consult the king about matters that could not easily be resolved (**10:1, 2b**). All her questions were answered, and she herself was amazed by all she heard from him and what she saw of his lifestyle (**10:3-8**). As a state visitor, she would no doubt have seen the magnificent temple and recognized that Solomon's wisdom and material riches were signs of blessing from the God of Israel. So she praised the Lord God who showed *eternal love for Israel* (**10:9**). But, like all the other rulers, she did not meet in person the one greater than Solomon (Luke 11:31).

When rulers meet, they commonly exchange gifts. Thus the Queen of Sheba gave Solomon much gold and quantities of spices, and probably received gifts of equal value in return (**10:13**). She and Solomon probably also used this meeting to arrange future trade between their kingdoms.

At this point, there is an interruption that lists the typical goods that might be imported by Solomon around the time of the queen's visit. Hiram's ships, not those built by Solomon at Ezion Geber, brought in cargoes of gold, rare almug wood and precious stones (**10:11-12**).

10:14-29 Solomon's splendour

Solomon accumulated great wealth, as described in the rest of this chapter. The 420 talents (31 000 pounds / 14 280 kilograms) of gold referred to in 9:28 were a one-time import. Annually, more than 666 talents (49 950 pounds / 22 644 kilograms) of gold were imported, in addition to the regular income received from taxes on traders who had to pass through the land held by Solomon (**10:14**). The trade route that passed through Israel also presented opportunities for trade with people on their way to trade with other countries.

Solomon stored his gold by making two hundred large golden shields and three hundred smaller ones for display in his palace (**10:16-17**). He also used it to cover a magnificent throne, which was inlaid with ivory (**10:18-20**). The twelve lions ornamenting the steps up to the throne represented the twelve tribes of Israel as well as strength and royalty (Prov 30:30). Gold was so abundant that it was used to make many of the utensils in the palace (**10:21**).

Yet even though the king amassed great wealth (**10:22-27**), we know that he discovered that the pleasure it brought was only 'chasing after the wind' and of no ultimate purpose (Eccl 2:4-11). The reason why he became so dissatisfied may be hinted at in **10:28-29**. Solomon traded in horses and chariots, repeatedly buying them in Egypt and selling them to others. In doing this, he was disobeying the command in Deuteronomy 17:16. In the eyes of the world he was making great progress, but he was beginning to act outside the law and was therefore regressing.

Our Lord warns that it is hard for a person who is rich to enter the kingdom of heaven (Matt 19:23-24) and the Apostle Paul urges contentment (1 Tim 6:5). The hidden danger of riches is clear from Proverbs 30:8-9: 'give me neither poverty nor riches … otherwise I may have too much and disown you … or I may become poor and steal, and so dishonour the name of my God'. Wealth, which is good and essential for supporting the work of the kingdom, can also be a snare through which Satan will work our downfall. We see this danger more and more in Africa as the gospel of prosperity becomes the sermon of almost every evangelist, and as congregations start to relate a minister's walk with the Lord to the material blessings the Lord has given to him or her. When we start to focus on things and not on God, Satan is given a stronghold. Instead of preaching the word and applying it so that people can grow in their walk with God, preaching and application may end up being geared towards getting another pound, dollar, shilling, naira, kwacha or rupee from the people's pockets and into the offering basket. Wealth has its place, but it should not take the place of the more important matter – a close walk with God.

THE BIBLE AND POLYGAMY

There are two definitions of polygamy. According to the *Advanced Oxford Dictionary,* polygamy refers to marrying many wives or husbands at the same time, or many wives one after the other. In the Bible and in many African cultures, polygamy refers to one man having many wives. It is this practice that will be examined here.

When considering the issue of the Bible and polygamy, it is important to start by recognizing that the Bible contains the gospel, but that this gospel was revealed in the context of human cultures. One, therefore, needs to distinguish between the gospel that leads to salvation and the culture of the people that God was dealing with. Polygamy was a feature of the culture within which the gospel was revealed.

The first biblical incident of polygamy is Lamech's being married to two women, Adah and Zillah (Gen 4:19-24). The passage does not explain why Lamech diverged from God's original plan in which he created one man and one woman (Gen 2:18-24). Many Western scholars have mentioned Lamech's display of pride and his lack of dependence on God as the reason for his marrying two wives. Yet while the author of Genesis does show the flaws in Lamech's character, he does not explicitly condemn him for his marriages.

The case of Abram, Sarai and Hagar is not presented as polygamy, although in some translations of the Bible it is said that 'Sarai his wife took her Egyptian maidservant Hagar and gave her to her husband to be his wife' (Gen 16:3). However, in the rest of the story, Hagar is still referred to as Sarai's servant and not Abram's wife. The desire for a male child to inherit his father's property was the driving force behind Sarai's action, which was an accepted cultural practice in Assyria. As a slave woman, Hagar is treated as having no value, but God came to her aid and protected her and her son (Gen 16:7-12; 21:17-20).

Jacob found himself in a polygamous relationship when his father-in-law, Laban, tricked him into marrying two sisters, Leah and Rachel (Gen 29:15-29). His marriage to the two sisters is described as rife with jealousy and competition. Rachel, who proved barren, gave her maidservant, Bilhah, to Jacob so that she could have children through her. Leah gave her maidservant, Zilpah, to Jacob too, so that she could have even more children. The four women produced thirteen children, twelve of whom were sons. The maidservants were known as Jacob's concubines, a word that is difficult to translate into most African languages because the concept of a concubine is foreign to most African cultures. Therefore, most African translations of the Bible refer to all four women in Jacob's life as his wives. Although Jacob tried to treat all his children equally, when he was faced with a possibility of an attack from his brother, Esau, he arranged his family in such a way that the maidservants and their children were put at the front while his favourite wife, Rachel, and her child,

Joseph, were put safely at the rear (Gen 33:1-2). Esau, too, was polygamous (Gen 36).

It is even possible that Moses practised polygamy. Some scholars have argued that Moses only married his Cushite wife (Num 12:1) after the death of his wife, Zipporah (Exod 2:21). Others maintain that Moses was married to both women at the same time.

Because of the cultural emphasis on having many children, and preferably sons, the Hebrews had laws that seem to accommodate polygamy. For example, polygamy could result from the levirite marriages entered into to raise sons for a brother or relative who had died without leaving an heir (Deut 25:5-10; Ruth 5:5-10). Another law that could have resulted in polygamy was the requirement that a man who raped a virgin must pay the bride price for the girl and then marry her even if he was already married (Deut 22:29).

Samuel, the great prophet, came from a polygamous home. His father, Elkanah, was married to Hannah and Peninnah. Penniah had children, but was not loved by Elkanah, while Hannah was loved by him, but was barren (1 Sam 1:2, 5). Jealousy between the two women over the love of their husband and the ability to have children caused a lot of turmoil in this family. With the help of the Lord, Hannah conceived and gave birth to Samuel, whom she gave back to the Lord.

Polygamy was widespread in the time of the Judges. Gideon was said to have had many wives and seventy sons (Judg 8:30). Abdon had 'forty sons and thirty grandsons, who rode on seventy donkeys' (Judg 12:14). Daughters were not considered worth mentioning, but a large number of wives and sons displayed wealth and political power. This held true even during the time of the kings. David married eight different women, mostly for political reasons (1 Chr 3:1-9). His marriage to Bathsheba stands out because of the way he connived to have Uriah, Bathsheba's husband, killed in battle. Thereafter, David was faced with constant problems with his children. Solomon, Bathsheba's son, became a famous king of Israel after his father David. He married 'seven hundred wives of royal birth and three hundred concubines' (1 Kgs 11:3). These wives led Solomon astray, and 'as Solomon grew old, his wives turned his heart after other gods' (1 Kgs 11:3-4).

The New Testament is quiet on the issue of polygamy. The nearest Jesus came to addressing the issue of different types of marriages are his comments on divorce (Mark 10:1-12). There Jesus refers back to the creation of one man and one woman as representing God's ideal for marriage (Mark 10:6).

In the early church, Paul's discussion of the qualifications for elders or overseers and deacons includes the requirement that they must be in a monogamous marriage (1 Tim 3:2, 12; Titus 1:6). This suggests that polygamy may still have existed at that time, but was not acceptable for someone wanting a leadership position. However, polygamy cannot have been common because the Greeks were monogamous.

From what has been said, it can be concluded that God's original plan at creation was for the marriage of one man and one woman. Polygamy only appeared after the fall. The patriarchs in Genesis were polygamous, but it should be noted that this was not their first choice. Like Africans, the Jews associated marriage with having children. Barrenness led Jewish men to take a second wife. So did a culture that valued sons more than daughters. A male child was needed to inherit his father's property. A woman who gave birth only to girls, was blamed for it. Thank God that science has now revealed that it is the father, not the mother, who determines the sex of a child. We have also noted that having many wives was a symbol of wealth and political power.

Polygamy does not promote partnership between a husband and the wives. The biblical examples show that polygamous families were full of quarrels among the wives, and in some cases among the children too. The peace of the Lord was not in polygamous marriages. However, nowhere in the Bible does God explicitly condemn a person for polygamy. Yet those who practise it are shown to suffer the consequences of their decision.

Jesus upheld God's original plan of marriage as involving one man and one woman. The lack of attention to polygamy in the NT may reflect the fact that Greek society was monogamous.

The majority of African women theologians do not support polygamy because it dehumanizes women. It shows a lack of respect for the dignity of women as full human beings, created in the image of God. Polygamy does not value a woman as a person, but only for what she can produce for her husband.

Most evangelical denominations encourage monogamous marriage as God's ideal form of marriage. Nevertheless, they are prepared to baptize converted polygamists and accept them as members of the church who are free to partake of Holy Communion. The most controversial issue is whether a converted polygamist can hold a position of church leadership or not. Some argue from 1 Timothy 3:2-7 that no polygamist may lead a church.

Isabel Apawo Phiri

11:1-43 Solomon's Downfall

Despite his wisdom and the fact that the Lord had appeared to him twice (3:5; 9:2), Solomon was ultimately not found to be obedient to the Lord. It is only those who remain faithful and obedient to the end who receive the Lord's approval (Rev 2:10).

11:1-13 Solomon's wives

In a display of his economic and political strength, Solomon married seven hundred wives of royal birth (**11:3**). These marriages were intended to strengthen relations between the kingdom of Israel and surrounding nations (**11:1**). Besides these official wives, he also had three hundred concubines, women who were part of his household but had lower status than wives.

The foreign wives had a bad influence on Solomon. He loved them and *held fast to them in love* (**11:2**), whereas previously he is said to have loved the Lord (3:3). Solomon was proving the truth of God's prediction in Deuteronomy 7:3-4 (11:2) and of Paul's words that the unmarried person is concerned about pleasing God, but the married person is concerned about the affairs of the world and how to please his or her marriage partner (1 Cor 7:32-33). Solomon wanted to keep his foreign wives happy. They were not believers in the God of Israel. As he was ageing, he gave in to their wishes to worship the gods of their own peoples (**11:4**). Thus he ended up worshipping Ashtoreth, a goddess of fertility and love who was widely worshipped by the Canaanites and the Sidonians and who had seduced the Israelites in the days of the judges and in the days of Samuel (**11:5a**; Judg 2:13; 10:6; 1 Sam 7:3-4; 12:10). Now

the king himself was involved in such worship. He also worshipped Molech, the god of the Ammonites, whom God hated because children were sacrificed to him (**11:5b**). The law laid down that those who sacrificed their children to Molech were to be put to death (Lev 18:21; 20:2-5).

Solomon's wives persuaded him to use his resources to build places of worship for each of them. Thus in addition to the great temple in Jerusalem, he also built temples to gods like Molech and Chemosh, the god of the Moabites, whose worship was very similar to that of Molech (**11:7-8**). By introducing these practices, Solomon was no longer being faithful to the God of Israel as commanded in Exodus 20:1-7. He could no longer be thought of as loving the one God of Israel wholeheartedly (Deut 6:4-5). Moreover his support for such worship affected others, and by the days of Jeremiah, these gods were very popular (2 Kgs 17:31; 23:10; Jer 32:35)

Solomon's story here is a warning to those who marry unbelievers. It is impossible to please an unbelieving spouse who is set in his or her ways and God at the same time. There will be moments of conflict. God, who led Paul to instruct believers against being yoked with unbelievers (2 Cor 6:14), knows that unbelievers make it impossible for believers to surrender fully to God's will. When believers get opposition rather than support from their spouses, it becomes very difficult to serve God freely.

The Lord responded with anger because Solomon knew the will of the Lord but had chosen not to follow it (**11:9-10**). Solomon preferred listening to his wives to listening to God. So the Lord spoke to him for a third time, but this time he uttered words of judgment, not blessing. Solomon's dynasty would not thrive. After his death, the whole kingdom, except for one tribe, would be torn away from the house of David (**11:11-13**). This retention of one tribe was a sign that even when God is angry, he still remembers his promises. He had promised David that his sons would rule and he had promised that his name would dwell in Jerusalem, and he kept that promise.

11:14-40 Solomon's enemies

Solomon had started his reign in peace, without enemies (5:4). But with God's judgment of him, the situation changed. Israel was no longer at ease – and the nation that had been peaceful and prosperous now had enemies both outside and within. We are reminded that the nations of the world are at the service of the Lord God of Israel. He chooses to raise up some nations in order to put others down (Dan 2:20-21).

This time God raised up two enemies of Israel, one in the south and one in the north. The enemy in the south was an Edomite prince called Hadad, who had grown up in Egypt after fleeing from David's army, and who now sought to regain his territory (**11:14-22**). Hadad enjoyed the support of the Egyptian pharaoh, suggesting that the pharaoh whose daughter Solomon had married had died and that the new leaders of Egypt were less inclined to befriend Israel. The enemy to the north was a man called Rezon, who had become the leader of a band of rebels after David defeated Hadadezer (2 Sam 8:3) and captured the city of Damascus and used it as a base to attack Israel (**11:23-25**).

Besides his external enemies, Solomon also had to contend with internal rebellion in Israel. Jeroboam, an able and ambitious young officer, was put in charge of a large part of the labour force (**11:26-28**). He met Ahijah who acted out a prophecy for him by tearing his new cloak into twelve pieces, representing the twelve tribes of Israel. The prophet then offered ten of these pieces to Jeroboam, explaining that the Lord was going to make him king over ten of the twelve tribes of Israel (**11:29-31**). The one tribe left to the house of David seemed to be the house of Benjamin, as Judah was already counted as supporting David (**11:32**). The reason for the Lord's judgment on Solomon was also explained (**11:33**). Ahijah did not anoint Jeroboam, as Samuel had done with David, but his words carried conviction.

The description of the charges against Solomon is also a warning to Jeroboam. If he wants to continue to enjoy God's blessing, he must meet the same conditions and obey God as David did. If he does this, his kingdom will be established, although David's house will still ultimately be greater. God's continuing faithfulness to his promises to David, despite Solomon's sin, is evidence that Jeroboam, too, can trust him and obey him (**11:34-39**). Obeying the Lord means keeping his commandments as well as loving and being loyal to the one God of Israel. Jesus said that those who love him will keep his commandments (John 14:15).

We do not know exactly what happened next. It is possible that Jeroboam tried to organize a coup, or that Ahijah's prophecy, although given in private, became known, or the people may have become so tired of the forced labour and the rule of Solomon that they were looking for another leader and favouring Jeroboam. Whatever the case, Solomon tried to kill Jeroboam (**11:40**), just as Saul had tried to kill David. But God's plans cannot be thwarted. Jeroboam escaped to Egypt, where he enjoyed the protection of Shishak, a pharaoh usually identified as Sheshonq I, who founded a new Egyptian dynasty between 945 and 924 BC.

11:41-43 Solomon's death

The writer of Kings makes it clear that he has merely summarized Solomon's reign. The full story of his life and achievements during his forty-year reign was recorded in the official records (**11:41-42**).

Death came to Solomon as a rest from the labour of life (**11:43**). He also enjoyed the blessing of being buried with his ancestors. This was what Jacob had requested when he asked that his bones be taken from Egypt to Canaan and buried beside Sarah, Abraham and Isaac (Gen 50:13). Joseph, too, had given instructions that his own bones should be taken from Egypt and buried in the land of promise (Gen 50:25).

There is nothing wrong about wanting to be buried next to one's ancestors, which is a common African tradition. However, there should not be any religious reason for this desire, for both the ancestor and his or her descendants only rest there as they wait for resurrection – either to blessedness as a result of their having believed in Jesus Christ when they were alive, or to eternal damnation for those who did not invite Jesus into their lives.

1 Kgs 12:1-2 Kgs 17:41 The Two Kingdoms

12:1-14:20 The Kingdom Divided

David had been able to advise his son on how to govern (2:1-9), but Solomon did not see his son ascend to the throne. His son, Rehoboam, lacked the advice of a God-fearing father. Yet it is also true that all the wise and foolish decisions that led to the break up of the unified kingdom were taken as part of the Lord's plan that he had already declared to Solomon and to Rehoboam (11:11-13, 31-32).

12:1-24 Israel rebels against Rehoboam

Even before the death of Solomon, there were signs of discontent (11:27, 40) and these signs multiplied with his death. It seems that Israel had already distanced itself from Jerusalem, for the people did not gather in the capital city that Solomon had built but at Shechem, a city in the hill country of northern Israel (**12:1**). Rehoboam did not immediately ascend his father's throne, but had to travel to the gathering convened at Shechem in order to be crowned.

Not only that, but when he arrived in Shechem he found that the rebel Jeroboam had returned from Egypt (**12:2**). Nor had he merely returned, he had been *sent for* because he had become a recognized leader who could speak on behalf of the rest of Israel (**12:3**). He seems to have been the spokesman for a delegation of the chiefs of Israel who went to negotiate better conditions for all Israelites (**12:4**).

Wisely, Rehoboam did not answer them immediately but asked for time to think about their request (**12:5**). He consulted with the elders who had been his father's advisors. They advised him to grant the people's request (**12:6-7**). But Rehoboam was not happy with this advice and turned to consult his age-mates, who advised him to 'talk tough' and refuse to negotiate at all (**12:8-11**). Foolishly, he chose to follow their advice (**12:12-15**). Putting this in today's terms, the elders advised Rehoboam to be a servant-leader to his people, while the young advised him to be a dictator. Rehoboam missed the blessings of wise counsel. For us today, servant-leadership is more than just a model that glues the leader to his or her people. It is also a sign of obedience to Jesus, who left his home in glory to become part of humanity (Phil 2:6-8) and washed his disciples' feet, giving them an example that they should follow (John 13:14-15).

Rehoboam's reply was not well received by *all Israel,* here referring to the ten tribes other than the tribe of Judah, who accepted Rehoboam as one of their own. The Israelites took up the cry first uttered by Sheba Ben Bicri during unrest in David's day (2 Sam 20:1) and returned to their homes without acknowledging Rehoboam as king (**12:16**). Only one tribe continued to support the house of David (**12:17**).

The gathering at Shechem ended in confusion and violence. The sending of Adoniram, the minister of forced labour, to negotiate or to force the people to accept Rehoboam was not a wise move. He was stoned to death and the mob then turned on Rehoboam, who had to scramble into his chariot in order to escape to Jerusalem (**12:18**). Israel had now rebelled and separated from Judah for good (**12:19**). They summoned Jeroboam and declared that he was now their king (**12:20**).

Rehoboam attempted to rally his followers from the tribes of Judah and Benjamin and launch an attack to end the rebellion (**12:21**). The Lord, however, put a stop to these plans by sending a message through Shemaiah that they were not to fight against their *brothers* (**12:22-24**). It seems that the Lord intended the two kingdoms to exist together as brothers under his rule.

From then on, the kingdom centred on Jerusalem in the south was known as the Kingdom of Judah, while the ten tribes in the north were known as the Kingdom of Israel. Over the years, Judah and Israel continued to drift apart, sometimes at peace and sometimes at war with each other.

12:25-33 Jeroboam's golden calves

Jeroboam now established his capital at Shechem (**12:25**). Then he turned his attention to the problem of maintaining power. His worries reveal that he had forgotten God's promise that he would become king (11:38). Instead, he was afraid that the people would kill him and return to King Rehoboam (**12:26-27**). Those who are in the Lord's plan need not fear because the Lord is with them (Josh 1:9; Jer 1:8, 17). Saul was rejected by the Lord because he was afraid and gave in to the people's demands (1 Sam 15:24). Fear is evidence of the sin of unbelief in the God who sends people out to do his will.

If Solomon, with all his religious background and experience of God, could become disloyal to Yahweh the Lord God of Israel, then Jeroboam had little chance of obeying God's command and receiving the blessing offered in 11:37-38. Clearly, he himself did not attach much importance to the ark of the Lord's covenant in Jerusalem, but he was concerned that his people would continue to do so. There was historical precedent for this. The two and a half tribes who resided to the east of Jordan had placed great stress on building an altar similar to the Lord's altar in Israel to remind their children and all of Israel that, although the Jordan separated them from their fellow Israelites, they still had a share in the covenant of Israel (Josh 22:21-30).

In an attempt to break this link to Jerusalem and the temple, the leaders of Israel advised the king to set up two other centres of worship, one in Bethel and the other in Dan. Bethel was an attractive location because it was on the route to Jerusalem, and travellers stopping there instead of carrying on to Jerusalem would save themselves twenty-two miles (thirty-five kilometres) of travel (eleven miles/seventeen kilometres each way). The expression 'from Dan to Beer-sheba' had previously been used to refer to the whole of Israel. Now the Israel of Jeroboam would consider itself as stretching from Dan to Bethel (**12:29**).

Jeroboam made two golden calves, one to be located at Dan and the other at Bethel, and introduced them to the people, saying *Here are your gods, O Israel, who brought you up out of Egypt* (**12:28**). His words echo those of Aaron when he led Israel into sin (Exod 32:4-8, 18-25; Deut 9:16-21), except that this time there is not just one calf but two.

Calves and bulls were commonly used to represent gods in Egypt and throughout the Near East. Israel was in the midst of a culture where Baal worship was common, and where Baal was often represented as riding on the back of a bull, which was itself a symbol representing agricultural fertility and the power to bear children. Solomon may even have drawn on this symbolism when he approved the design of the giant basin, the Sea, which held water for use in the temple, with its stand made in the form of twelve bulls that carried the basin on their backs (7:25). Perversion of the faith came gradually but effectively through images that were accepted as normal.

By discouraging the Israelites from going to Jerusalem to worship and be taught the ways of the Lord of the covenant, Jeroboam was making it easy for the people to identify these calves with the Baal of the Canaanites' religion. Consequently, *this thing became a sin* (**12:30**) – the people were no longer worshipping and sacrificing to the Lord God of Israel but to the golden calves (**12:32**). The first and second commandments (Exod 20:2-4) were broken. The Israelites could not remain the people of God while worshipping these calves.

To strengthen his grip on the kingdom, Jeroboam went on to build more shrines and high places. No true Levite would agree to serve at them, and so Jeroboam appointed anybody who wished to serve as priest (**12:31**). He also chose dates for his religious festivals that would clash with those in Jerusalem and so discourage the people from going there to worship (**12:33**).

13:1-34 The man of God from Judah

The Lord did not easily give up Israel. He sent messengers to warn them of the dangers of adopting a form of worship he had not approved. *By the word of the Lord* an unnamed man of God was sent to Bethel (**13:1**). It is not clear whether he received his message directly from the Lord or he was sent by a more senior prophet with strict instructions on what to do and how to deliver the message.

The message was not directed against Jeroboam, nor the golden calf, nor the worshippers, but against the altar at Bethel. The man of God denounced it and foretold its final destruction. A son born to the house of David would one day destroy the priests of the high places *who now make offerings here*. Burning *human bones* on the altar would desecrate it so that it was no longer fit for any more sacrifices (**13:2**). This prophecy was fulfilled by King Josiah, some three hundred years after it was uttered (2 Kgs 23:15-16).

The man of God gave a sign to support the truth of his prophecy: he announced that the newly constructed altar at Bethel would split apart and that ashes would pour out of it (**13:3**). Jeroboam reacted angrily and called for the arrest of the man of God. But as he stretched out his hand to point to him, his hand *shrivelled* and could not be pulled back. At the same time, the altar did indeed crack and ashes poured out (**13:4-5**).

The king must have been shocked both at the damage to his altar and by the damage to his own body. So he asked the man of God to pray for him, and the Lord healed his hand (**13:6**). But despite seeing these evidences of God's power, and having heard Ahijah's prophecy and seen that fulfilled as well (11:29-38), Jeroboam did not repent and obey the Lord. Instead he simply asked the man of God to come and eat with him and to accept a gift (**13:7**).

Politicians and others who want to become popular often try to attract the people of God by offering gifts and hospitality. This is a snare a servant of God must always watch out for.

The man of God refused this offer. He had been instructed not to eat or drink while on his mission, and he was also not to return home by the same route (**13:8-9**). Other messengers in the OT were given similar instructions. For example, when Elisha sent his servant to Shunem he was told not to speak to or greet anyone on the way (2 Kgs 4:29). Jesus gave similar instructions to his disciples when he sent them out on a preaching mission (Luke 10:4). The reason for the prohibition was to show that the errand was serious and true. Thus if the man of God had accepted the king's invitation, it would have meant that he was not convinced about his proclamation or the serious position Israel was in.

The man of God overcame the first temptation to disobey the word of God (**13:10**), but he may have relaxed too soon. Another temptation was coming, this time from someone who appeared to be a godly man, for he is described as *an old prophet* (**13:11**). He may indeed have been a man of God, or he may simply have been someone with some psychic powers like Balaam of old, who was able to receive words from the Lord but was corrupted by deceit and thirst for gain (Num 22–24; 31:8, 16). This old prophet was determined to get the young man to eat with him in Bethel. Like Balaam, he set out on a donkey in pursuit of the man of God (**13:12-13**). He found him resting under a tree by the wayside and tried to persuade him to come home with him for a meal. Initially, the young man refused to return, citing his instructions (**13:14-17**). But the old man was determined, and so he told a lie, framing it in religious language – *an angel said to me* (**13:18**). The younger man failed to recognize a temptation when it was phrased in religious language, and so he set aside the word from the Lord that originally came to him and started following other instructions (**13:19**). We are reminded of Paul's warning to NT believers that 'even if we or an angel from heaven should preach a gospel other than the one we preach to you, let him be eternally condemned' (Gal 1:8-9). John also warns us, 'Dear friends, do not believe every spirit, but test the spirits to see whether they are from God, because many false prophets have gone out into the world' (1 John 4:1).

Another important lesson that may be learnt here is that when Satan notes that we are watchful when he tempts us on matters that are clearly sin, he changes his strategy and tempts us on matters where the lines are not so clear. The old man could possibly have been a messenger from God. However, the young man should have reflected on the matter and, recognizing that what was being said contradicted his earlier instructions, he should have decided to abide by what he had been told by his original source, a prophet whom he knew he could trust. When two ways seem right at the same time, it is always best to choose the safest and not the more convenient one.

During the meal, the old prophet suddenly received a message of judgment condemning the disobedience of the younger man (**13:20-22**). Being buried away from *the tomb of your fathers* implies dying far from home, which was regarded as a great misfortune. The prophets of Israel spoke out strongly against disobedience to the word of God, and the fate of the younger prophet shows that such disobedience is punished, even in believers (**13:23-28**).

The older prophet was deeply distressed by the unexpected results of his glib lie. He brought the body of the man of God home, mourned him like a brother, and buried him in his own tomb. He even insisted that on his death he should be buried next to this man (**13:29-31**).

God's prophecy about the altar at Bethel was not altered by the disobedience of the man of God. In fact, the old prophet announced his support of the message (**13:32**). Nevertheless, the death of the man of God must have helped to undermine people's belief in the message they had heard at Bethel, and the old prophet had contributed to this confusion. Jeroboam for one did not repent but persisted in his sinful ways in Bethel and Dan, appointing anyone who wanted the job as a priest (**13:33-34**). The appointment of non-Levites meant that the people of Israel were led further and further away from the covenant Lord.

This incident was not the last time that prophets preached in Bethel. Many years later, Amos, the farmer, also prophesied there, and was opposed by the priest Amaziah (Amos 7:10-17).

14:1-20 Ahijah's prophecy against Jeroboam

Jeroboam does not seem to have sought the advice of Ahijah, the prophet who predicted the separation of the ten tribes with Jeroboam as their king. He did not consult him about his plans to gain political and religious independence from Jerusalem, and the prophet does not seem to have sought him out either. It may be that Ahijah was getting old, and that age restricted his movements. Or he may have been bitterly disappointed in the new king's religious policy and may have avoided contact with him.

Eventually, Jeroboam's son became seriously ill. Jeroboam must have prayed to his calves, the new gods that he claimed had brought Israel out of Egypt. He must have asked his priests to pray for his son at the high places of worship. The boy's condition did not improve, and at last Jeroboam remembered the old prophet Ahijah, whose word had come true (11:29-38). But Jeroboam had done many things against the God of Ahijah and he and his wife were ashamed and felt guilty about now beginning to pray to the God he had long deserted. To avoid embarrassment, he told his wife to disguise herself and pretend to be some other woman. She was to take with her the normal presents for a prophet – some cakes and a jar of honey. Jeroboam's words, *he will tell you what will happen,* indicate that he still believed in the prophet and the God of Israel, although he no longer obeyed him (**14:1-4a**).

By this time, Ahijah was so old that he could no longer see. But the Lord was still with him and he still received words and visions from the Lord. True visions or dreams are received through the ears and eyes of the spirit and heart. The Lord let him know who his visitor would be and how he was to answer her request (**14:4b-5**).

His opening words to Jeroboam's wife, *Why this pretence?* (**14:6**) must have embarrassed her, but must also have impressed her with his insight. Instead of answering her question immediately, Ahijah launches into a strong condemnation of Jeroboam, something the unnamed prophet in chapter 13 did not do. The king of Israel is rebuked for the way he has led God's people. He is reminded of his humble beginnings, just as Nathan reminded King David of his roots (**14:7-8a**; see also 2 Sam 12:7-8). But Jeroboam is not like David, for David had repented instantly when Nathan confronted him. David followed the Lord with all his heart; Jeroboam, by contrast, had *done more evil than all who lived before you* (**14:8b-9a**). He had prevented Israel from going to Jerusalem to worship the covenant Lord of all Israel, and had set up other gods, the calves made of metal. He had thrust God behind his back, like something he was ashamed of (**14:9b**).

In 11:38, God had promised to establish Jeroboam's dynasty if he obeyed him. But Jeroboam had not, and thus he faced judgment and disaster. All of his male children would die, meaning the end not only of his reign but also of his family. Not only that, but their deaths would be shameful. They would not receive a proper burial and would not be mourned by relatives or friends. Instead their bodies would be eaten by dogs or birds of the air (**14:10-11**).

Ahijah now turns to the fate of the boy whose illness was the reason for the visit – *the boy will die.* But his death would in fact be a sign of God's mercy to him, because he would be the only one in the family to receive proper burial and mourning. He was the only one in that royal family who the Lord saw as having any good qualities (**14:12-13**). His death would spare him much sorrow. We are reminded of the psalmist's words, 'precious in the sight of the Lord is the death of his saints' (Ps 116:15).

Ahijah's prophecy is not yet over. Jeroboam's sinful example would affect the whole nation, and in time the whole kingdom of Israel would be removed from their land to a land beyond the River, that is, beyond the river Euphrates (**14:14-16**). Those who are in positions of leadership should take warning that their evil decisions and actions can bring disaster on entire nations.

The woman left with this terrible prophecy. As soon as she reached their home in Tirzah (Jeroboam had apparently moved his capital from Shechem) the first part of the prophecy was fulfilled, for the boy died and Israel buried him and mourned for him (14:17-18).

Jeroboam ruled Israel for twenty-two years and was succeeded by his son Nadab. The history of his reign is recorded in greater detail in the now-lost royal history books of Israel (14:19-20).

14:21-31 Rehoboam, King of Judah

Rehoboam was forty-one when he came to the throne and took the bad advice of his age-mates. The fact that his mother, Naamah, was an Ammonite is mentioned twice (14:21, 31) because in polygamous homes, mothers play an important part in moulding the character of their own children. Solomon, busy with his studies, his royal duties and his seven hundred wives, would have had no time for his many children. Thus Rehoboam would not have been properly taught the fear of the Lord but would instead have been taught by his Ammonite mother to worship Molech. As a result, he made no attempt to stop the *detestable practice of the nations the Lord had driven out*. In fact, things became even worse, for shrine prostitutes were now introduced in the land. People indulged in practices that were hateful to the God of Israel (14:22-24).

As a result, God permitted Shishak, the pharaoh of Egypt who had previously sheltered Jeroboam (11:40), to attack Jerusalem. He seized all the treasure and the golden shields of Solomon, reducing Judah to a shadow of its former glory (14:25-28). This is the last we learn of the reign of Rehoboam, except for the final note that reveals that the words of Shemaiah the prophet were not heeded for long (12:24). There was *continual warfare* between the closely related kingdoms of Israel and Judah (14:30). The same relationship would continue for years to come. A kingdom divided against itself cannot stand (Mark 3:24), and these conflicts made the two kingdoms weaker and unable to face the attacks of enemy nations.

On Rehoboam's death at about the age of fifty-eight, he was succeeded by his son Abijah (14:31).

15:1-8 Abijah, King of Judah

The short three-year reign of Abijah of Judah is dated in relation to that of Jeroboam (15:1-2). Like his father, he was not faithful to the Lord as David had been (although the writer reminds us that even David was not perfect and had sinned in the case of the murder of Uriah the Hittite) (15:3-5; see also 2 Sam 11). Throughout Abijah's reign, there was war with Israel (15:6-7). He was succeeded by Asa, his son (15:8).

15:9-24 Asa, King of Judah

Asa was a good king and one of the longest reigning kings of Judah – he ruled for forty-one years (15:9-10). He is compared to David in terms of his devotion to the Lord (15:11). Although he did not remove the high places that had been built in Judah, he did get rid of the idols that his father had introduced. He even deposed his grandmother from the position of queen mother, cutting down her Asherah pole (15:12-14). Such poles were sacred to the fertility goddess Asherah, who was often presented as the wife of the Canaanite god Baal. Asa also brought gold and silver into the temple treasury to fulfil his vow to the Lord (15:15).

During his reign there was war between Judah and Israel. It seems that the war was not started by Judah but by Israel, which moved to prevent people from either leaving or going to Judah. To do this, Baasha, king of Israel, fortified the border town of Ramah (15:16-17). To counteract this attack, Asa requested help from Ben-Hadad of Aram, sending him a large gift that was only put together by emptying the temple of its remaining treasure (15:18-19).

Ben-Hadad agreed to the alliance and started attacking Israel from the north, forcing Baasha to leave Ramah in the south and move to defend his northern border (15:20-21). Asa then swooped down on Ramah and took the building materials brought there by Baasha, using them to strengthen the defences of Geba and Mizpah (15:22).

The constant warfare between the two kingdoms of Israel, who should have been united in their worship of the Lord, weakened them both. Judah's gold and treasure were used to pay Aram, and Israel too suffered financial loss as Ben-Hadad attacked its towns. Moreover, it is possible that by making an alliance with Ben-Hadad, Judah came under his rule and protection. None of this was the will of the Lord, who was opposed to the wars and to foreign alliances (see 11:2; 2 Chr 19:2).

Towards the end of his long reign, Asa had foot disease even though he had been a God-fearing king. He sought help only from his doctors and not from the Lord (2 Chr 16:12). He was succeeded by his son Jehoshaphat (15:23-24).

15:25-16:20 Struggle for the Throne of Israel

We now turn to the kings of Israel. Six different kings ruled in Israel during the reign of Asa of Judah. Their reigns were often short and were marked by bitter power struggles and assassinations. Eventually, Omri emerged as a strong king, and was succeeded by his son Ahab.

Nadab, the son of Jeroboam, reigned for only two years. He did evil before the Lord by continuing in the sin of his father (15:25-26). Nadab was assassinated by Baasha while Israel was fighting to take Gibbethon from the Philistines (15:27-28). Baasha then eliminated all potential rivals by wiping out *Jeroboam's whole family*. In doing this he was fulfilling Ahijah's prophecy and God's judgment on Jeroboam (15:29-30; see 4:10-11).

We are not told much about the wars between Israel and Judah during Baasha's reign because those have already been touched on in 15:16-22 (**15:32**).

Baasha was no better than those he had deposed, and he did not learn from Jeroboam's fate but continued in the same sins for the twenty-four years of his reign (**15:33-34**). So the Lord sent him a message through the prophet *Jehu son of Hanani* (see also 2 Chr 20:34). Jehu pointed out that Baasha had been a nobody whom the Lord had permitted to become a leader, but that he had sinned against the Lord, just like Jeroboam, and consequently his family would suffer the same fate as Jeroboam's (**16:1-4, 7**). The fact that he had been used by God to destroy Jeroboam's family should have caused him to stay away from the evil practices of that family. But instead he had adopted their practices, and thus showed that his killing of Jeroboam's descendants was done merely to serve his own purposes, not to serve the Lord.

Baasha was succeeded by his son Elah (**16:6, 8**). His reign was not memorable, and all that we are told is that it lasted approximately two years and that he was drunk when he was assassinated by Zimri, one of the officers in his army (16:8-10). Zimri then proceeded to fulfil the prophecy of Jehu and wiped out all of Baasha's male family members, relatives and friends (**16:11-13**).

But Zimri's reign was very short – a mere seven days (**16:15**). The army refused to accept a junior officer as king, and rallied around Omri, the general in command of Israel's army. The army then marched on the capital at Tirzah. Recognizing that he had lost, Zimri set fire to the palace and died in the flames (**16:16-18**). Zimri, too, is dismissed as a king who did what was displeasing to the Lord and led Israel into sin (**16:19**).

16:21-28 Omri, King of Israel

Omri might command Israel's army, but he was not automatically accepted as the next king. Two factions emerged, some supporting Omri and others his rival Tibni (**16:21**). The ensuing civil war must have lasted about four years (compare the dates in 16:15 and 16:23). Eventually, Omri emerged victorious (**16:22**).

Omri might be king, but the kingship must have lost respect because of these power struggles. Ambitious people must now have begun to see the throne as something that they could try to gain. Such a situation is very bad for a nation, as the numerous *coups d'état* in Africa have shown over the years. Those with power in the army tend to long for leadership while the one on the throne tends to protect it with all might, and the outcome is suspicion and violence.

But Omri proved not just an able commander in the army but a good administrator who started a new dynasty. During his twelve-year reign, he erected many buildings and moved his capital from Tirzah to a new site named Samaria after the man, Shemer, from whom he bought the hill on which his new capital was situated (**16:23-24**).

We know from the records of other nations that Omri was famous for his many achievements. For the writer of the book of Kings, however, none of these achievements are worth mentioning because he followed the example of Jeroboam who brought *worthless idols* into the land (**16:25-26**). The land may be developed and properly governed, but the people can still be very poor spiritually, and far from God.

Omri was succeeded by his son Ahab (**16:28**).

16:29-22:40 Ahab, King of Israel

16:29-34 Ahab's rule

Ahab reigned in Samaria for twenty-two years and did more evil before the Lord than the kings who ruled before him (**16:29-30**). Not only did he repeat the sins of his predecessors, but he married Jezebel, the daughter of the king of Sidon, and worked with her to make Baal worship almost the state religion. He built a temple for Baal in Samaria and, as will become clear in subsequent chapters, installed hundreds of prophets of Baal there, in addition to the priests who had been employed to minister before the calves and in the high places since the days of Jeroboam (**16:31-33**). Many prophets of the Lord were killed (18:4). Compared to Ahab's sin, the sin of Jeroboam was only a small matter.

As an individual, Ahab seems to have had some fear of God and some conscience. He listened to Elijah (18:16-21). He was not angry with Elijah for killing the 450 prophets of Baal (18:40-46). When confronted about the killing of Naboth, he repented and humbled himself fasting in sackcloth (21:27). His weakness was that he was dominated by Jezebel, who must have been a very aggressive woman. He could not restrain her and instead joined her in having a temple built for Baal in Samaria. His life reminds us that both men and women should be very careful about whom they marry!

The writer of the book of Kings would not have devoted so much space to Ahab were it not for the stature of the prophets like Elijah who opposed him. More prophets were sent to him than to other kings – 'where sin increased, grace increased' (Rom 5:20). The prophets who were sent to him were ministers of the grace of God.

The rebuilding of Jericho was another sign of the religious decay in Israel during Ahab's reign. Joshua had condemned any attempt to rebuild it after its conquest (Josh 6:26), but one Hiel of Bethel ignored Joshua's curse. Nevertheless, what Joshua had predicted came true as the two sons of Hiel were sacrificed, one for laying the foundations and the other for completing the gates of the city (**16:34**). It seems that Hiel was acting like those in some parts of Africa who appeal to *majini* (evil spirits) for wealth. These spirits may supply wealth, but in return they demand blood

– the blood of animals or even of wives, sons and daughters. It may be costly to please God, but it is even costlier to please Satan. We must walk in the ways of the Lord and not play with the world of Satan. Our call is to overcome it, not to befriend it.

17:1-19:21 Ahab and Elijah

17:1-6 ELIJAH'S PROPHECY TO AHAB
Like most of the other prophets mentioned in this book, Elijah simply appears, without any introduction. He must, however, have already been well known in Israel at the time he appeared to announce the judgment of God for the sins of Ahab and Israel (**17:1**). The judgment was that there would be no rain or dew for some years as a punishment for the sins mentioned in the previous verses. Elijah must not be thought of as similar to African rainmakers. Stopping or making rain was not his main work. Rather, as a true prophet, Elijah could see or hear what the Lord was planning to do. James says that the rains stopped because the prophet prayed in faith (Jas 5:17-18).

The closing words of Elijah's prophecy, *Except at my word* left some hope that if the king and the people repented, the situation might change. But they did not, and Elijah had to leave and settle east of the Jordan River (**17:2-3**). By doing this he escaped death with the other prophets (see 18:4; 19:10) and had a supply of water from the Brook Kerith, which continued to flow for some time despite drought. The Lord took charge of meeting his need for food (**17:4-6**).
17:7-24 ELIJAH TO ZAREPHATH When the drought became so severe that the brook dried up, the Lord told Elijah to move from the east of Jordan to the region of Sidon to the north-west of Israel (**17:7-9**). There may have been more water in that region because it was near the sea, but the famine had spread from Israel to other lands. Grain was in short supply throughout the region. As before, Elijah was staying in a foreign country, outside Ahab's territory. But the Lord has people who do his will in the most unexpected places.

On arriving at Zarephath, Elijah met a widow near the town gate. Just as Eliezer had asked Rebecca for a drink outside the town of Nahor (Gen 24:17), so Elijah requested a drink from the widow, as well as something to eat (**17:10-11**). The widow told him of her poverty and that she and her son were down to the last of their food. But the prophet reassured her, *Don't be afraid* and promised that the Lord would sustain her till the end of the drought (**17:12-14**). The widow did as she was told. She believed the word of God and was obedient to it (**17:15-16**). Many years later, Jesus would mention her as an example of someone with faith (Luke 4:26). Her supply of oil and flour lasted to the end of the famine.

After a time, the son of the widow became ill to the point of death (**17:17**). It was the general belief then, as often today, that suffering is always a result of sin. So the

widow felt that the presence of a man of God must have drawn attention to some sin she had committed (**17:18**). Elijah does not seem to share this view. He took the child, stretched himself on the child three times, and prayed for the boy's life. God responded by allowing life to return to the child (**17:19-23**). This story is similar to the one in which Elisha brought the son of the Shunammite back to life (2 Kgs 4:8-37).

Jesus later explained that suffering and death are not always a result of an individual's sin. Some illness happens to allow God to show his power of healing and to receive glory from people (John 9:3; 11:4). This was certainly the case here. The widow was overjoyed and her faith turned into knowledge and greater trust that Elijah's words were true, because they were the words of the Lord (**17:24**).

The fact that she commends Elijah for speaking the word of the Lord without changing its meaning suggests that there must have been lying prophets even in those days.
18:1-15 ELIJAH AND OBADIAH Towards the end of the dry years, the Lord directed Elijah to go to Ahab (**18:1**). The Lord was now planning to send rain on the land, as he does on the righteous and the unrighteous alike (Matt 5:45). As Elijah was on his way to see Ahab, he met Obadiah, *a devout believer in the Lord*. Obadiah was an officer in the court of Ahab and had secretly hidden away a hundred prophets of the Lord in caves to save them (**18:2-4, 13**). The Lord has his faithful servants planted in the places they are least expected so that they can carry out the work of God where it is most opposed. Moreover, Obadiah's actions show that the faithfulness of God was not just extended to Elijah but to many other prophets. Just as the ravens and the widow took care of the Elijah's needs, so Obadiah met the needs of others.

Obadiah told Elijah about what had been happening during his absence, but was afraid to take Elijah's message to Ahab. Elijah clearly had a reputation for disappearing without a trace, and he was worried about Ahab's reaction if this happened again (**18:11-12, 14**). Unlike Elijah, Obadiah was not a prophet and made no claims to receiving divine revelation, as is clear from his statement, *I do not know where the spirit of the Lord may carry you* (18:12). He was merely a man who had worshipped the Lord for many years.

Elijah had to make a promise invoking the name of the Lord Almighty to convince Obadiah to bring the king to meet him (**18:15**).
18:16-46 ELIJAH ON MOUNT CARMEL Ahab regarded Elijah as simply another rainmaking priest, like those in Africa, who could make or stop rain. Where Obadiah had greeted him respectfully as *my lord Elijah* (18:7), Ahab curtly addressed him as the *troubler of Israel* (**18:16-17**). Because Elijah was sent by the Lord, he had no fear of the king. He defended himself and delivered the word from the Lord. It was not he who had brought trouble on Israel, but Ahab and his father's

house. They were the ones who had *abandoned the Lord's command and have followed the Baals.* Elijah used the plural to make the point that there were numerous shrines dedicated to Baal. The extent to which this is true is revealed in Elijah's words that there were 450 prophets of Baal and 400 prophets of Asherah *who eat at Jezebel's table,* meaning that the queen was providing for their upkeep (**18:18-19**).

Elijah told Ahab to bring people *from all over Israel* as well as the prophets of Baal and of Asherah to a meeting on Mount Carmel, a high mountain overlooking the Mediterranean Sea (**18:20**). The king may have been angry with the prophet, but he respected the power the Lord had given him and obeyed the prophet's instructions and summoned the prophets and the people.

When the large crowd had assembled, Elijah addressed them: *How long will you waver between two opinions* (**18:21a**). The root of the problem was that the people were wanting to have things both ways. They wanted to serve both God and Baal. But God requires absolute devotion, not partial worship (Exod 20:3-4), the same sin condemned as being neither cold nor hot (Rev 3:15-16). The people were not able to respond, probably because the king was present (**18:21b**).

Elijah pointed out that he is *the only one of the Lord's prophets left* (**18:22**). He did not reveal that there were other prophets of the Lord who had survived in hiding (18:4). Certainly, he was the only prophet who took a public stand.

The unequal contest between 450 prophets and one prophet would involve two bulls. The prophets of Baal were to select one bull, and the other bull would belong to Elijah, who was representing the Lord God of Israel. Each party would offer their bull as a burnt offering, but neither could light the fire themselves. The god being worshipped would have to prove himself by providing fire for the offering (**18:23-24**).

Elijah allowed the prophets of Baal to start (**18:25**). They shouted their prayers, *O Baal answer us!* and danced around the altar. They went on shouting and dancing their prayers till noon, and even slashed themselves to let blood flow. Elijah mockingly asked them to shout louder but he knew very well that no answer was coming: Baal had failed to provide fire for his followers (**18:26-29**).

Elijah then called all the people to come to him. Because of neglect, the altar of the Lord has fallen into ruin and needed to be repaired (**18:30**). He used twelve stones to rebuild the altar and to remind the people of Israel of how the nation had begun with the twelve tribes. It would remind them that the God they were now praying to was the God who had made a covenant with Jacob, the father of all Israel. The altar was built *in the name of the Lord* (**18:32**) to show that he depended on the Lord. To allow God to show his power, he asked that water be poured on the sacrifice and the altar (**18:33-35**). The odds against Elijah were that he was only one against 450 prophets of Baal backed by a very powerful ruler before an altar that was soaked with water. The only point in his favour was that the God of Israel had sent him and that he had trusted and followed obediently.

In his prayer to the God of Abraham, Isaac and Jacob, Elijah did not draw any attention to himself. The purpose for which he prayed was s*o these people will know that you, O Lord, are God and that you are turning their hearts back again* (**18:36-37**). He did not need to shout, dance or gash himself to please the Lord and so persuade him to act. The fire of the Lord came and burnt the sacrifice, the altar stones and the water (**18:38**).

This miracle led the people to believe in the covenant Lord of Israel. They all fell down, shouting, *The Lord – he is God! The Lord – he is God!* (**18:39**). It is not clear whether the prophets of Baal also fell down to confess the Lord of Israel as God. Elijah then gave orders for all the prophets of Baal to be killed in the Kishon Valley as part of a religious cleansing (**18:40**). Those who witnessed the occasion saw for themselves how the Lord God of Israel showed himself powerful and Baal powerless. Ahab, too, saw for himself and could not speak against Elijah.

The impression we are left with here is that God approved the killing of the prophets of Baal. This and other passages in Kings and elsewhere raise the question of whether it is right to kill for religious purposes. We need to see this question in perspective. God has spelled out his will in natural revelation (his creation, including our consciences) and in his word (Scripture and Christ). He clearly states the results of obedience and warns that the punishment for deliberate and continuous disobedience is death. In the OT, this is physical death, for God was shaping a people to be the custodians of his covenant, and obedience was closely related to the attitude a person or group of people had towards the covenant and commandments of God. In the NT, the emphasis shifts from physical death to eternal punishment in hell (Matt 25:46; Rev 20:15). We may at times wonder whether such punishment is fair, but the question is, 'fair to whom?' Everything that exists was created by God to glorify God. He brings to life and he takes life. While he has given human beings authority over everything else he has created (Gen 9:3), he has reserved the right to give and take life as his private prerogative, and his alone. Consequently, he alone has the authority to take life, even for religious purposes as we see in the OT. When a human being takes life, as Elijah and Jehu and others later in this book do, it should be only at his explicit direction. Our duty is not to kill but to bear witness about him so that many will come to faith and be spared the death they deserve for disobedience to the giver of life.

While the battle on Carmel had been won, there still remained the problem of the drought. But Elijah had faith that God would hear his prayers again. So he *put his face between his knees* and requested rain on the land to prove conclusively that it was God and not Baal who controlled the rain and that it was not Asherah who was in charge of the fertility of the land. His prayer of faith was heard and granted by the Lord (**18:41-44**). The death of the prophets meant that those who taught sinful ways had been removed, and the Lord could now withdraw his judgment and bring rain. In fact, Ahab was told to hurry back to the city of Jezreel some eighteen miles (thirty kilometres) away before heavy rain brought flooding and made the roads impassable.

Elijah did not head off into the wilderness after this victory, but accompanied the king to Jezreel as a loyal subject. Like Elijah, ministers must leave no doubt that they love the political leaders they criticize. We must hate the evil that they do, but not the person who does it.

Despite the heavy rain, Elijah was able to run to the city ahead of Ahab's chariot. He got the strength for this gruelling marathon after a dramatic day from the power of the Lord (**18:45-46**).

Elijah had killed the prophets of Baal and believed that the land of Israel was now rid of Baal worshippers. The people had witnessed the work of the God of Israel and believed. Elijah must have felt that he had effectively countered the sin of Jeroboam son of Nebat and of Ahab which had led the majority of the people away from the Lord.
19:1-18 Elijah's flight to horeb Elijah must have been in very high spirits as he ran back to Jezreel. He must have thought that his troubles were over, that his hopes had been fulfilled, and that the worship of the Lord had been restored to Israel. Even the king must have been convinced by what he saw of the Lord's power. But when Ahab told Jezebel about the Lord's victory and the killing of the prophets, she was furious and vowed to kill Elijah. Ahab does not seem to have been able to restrain her (**19:1-2**).

Once again Elijah had to run for his life This time he headed south, over a hundred miles (one hundred and sixty kilometres) past Beersheba and into the desert (**19:3**). After travelling all day in the desert, he was tired and cried to the Lord, *Take my life* (**19:4**). Life had become meaningless. He had expected that the victory on Carmel would lead to religious reforms in Israel, but Jezebel was determined that it would not. Elijah is not alone in feeling this way, for it is not uncommon for a period of depression to follow a very uplifting religious experience.

The Lord graciously did not rebuke Elijah for his fear, exhaustion and depression, but instead sent an angel to provide for his physical needs (**19:5-7**). Strengthened by a good meal and sound sleep, he was strong enough to travel for *forty days and forty nights* – the same length of time Moses had fasted on Mount Sinai. Elijah was seeking some guidance and he felt he could get it more easily on Mount Horeb (Sinai) where Moses had received the laws and where the covenant had been made with Israel (**19:8**).

The Lord had not directed Elijah to come back to Mount Sinai, so he asked him, *What are you doing here, Elijah?* (**19:9**). God asked Elijah this question to remind him that he could have looked to the Lord anywhere in Israel. If the Lord could hear and answer his prayers on Mount Carmel, he could hear him anywhere. Elijah wanted to seek the Lord of the covenant where he had met with Moses and Israel. But the Lord of Israel is not a local God who is more available at Sinai than anywhere else.

Elijah presented his complaints to the Lord: Israel had rejected the covenant, broken down the altars and killed the prophets of the Lord (**19:10**). His claim to be the only one left is not proper after what Obadiah has told him (18:13).

The Lord responded by telling him to stand on the mountain before the Lord, just as Moses had when God appeared to him in the wilderness (Exod 33:12-23). This command was followed by three signs: first a strong wind that shattered the rocks, then an earthquake, and then a fire. The fire was followed by the sound of a quiet voice. Elijah knew that it was the Lord speaking and he came *and stood at the mouth of the cave* (**19:11-13**). The gentle quiet voice shows that the Lord uses ordinary ways to speak – he does not always need to use powerful events to bring his words.

The Lord repeated the question in 19:9, and Elijah repeated his complaints (19:10, **14**). God did not immediately respond to his complaint, but instead gave him new orders. Elijah was to go back to the area north of Israel and anoint Hazael as king over Aram, Jehu as king over Israel, and Elisha son of Shaphat of Abel Mehola as prophet who would continue his work (**19:15-17**). Anointing an unbeliever is not common in the Bible, but here the Lord commands it to make it clear that even among unbelieving nations, it is the Lord who decides who will lead. The Lord's plan, as revealed to Elijah and Elisha, was that Hazael would become king, even though he would bring suffering on the people of Israel (2 Kgs 8:13).

Then the Lord told the self-pitying Elijah that there were still up to seven thousand people who feared and served the Lord in Israel (**19:18**). Most of these would be secret believers like Obadiah. The believers were a small minority, but they were there and Elijah was not alone.

19:19-21 The calling of elisha It seems Elijah was not able himself to anoint Hazael and Jehu as kings. Elisha, possibly at Elijah's instruction, would later arrange for the anointing of Jehu (2 Kgs 9:1) and would inform Hazael of his future, even if he did not physically anoint him (2 Kgs 8:13).

When Elijah found Elisha, it must have been apparent that Elisha was a very successful farmer. Anyone who needed *twelve yoke of oxen* to plough his land must have had a very large farm (**19:19**). It seems that he also had labourers or neighbours working for him, driving the other eleven pairs of oxen while he himself drove the twelfth pair. Elijah did not literally anoint Elisha. Instead he threw his cloak over him, a gesture that Elisha obviously understood as a call to discipleship. Elisha responded happily but asked permission to say goodbye to his parents before leaving to follow Elijah. Elijah's words, *Go back,* indicate that he gave him permission to do this, although his next words, *What have I done to you?* may indicate that he also wonders why Elisha, who has just begun to run after him, would want to go back. What had he done within that short period of relationship to make Elisha want to return home? (**19:20**).

Elisha's words here may remind readers of Jesus' quite different response to a similar request from the men who came to him in Luke 9:57-62, one of whom wanted to bury his father while the other wanted to say goodbye to his family. The different response may be because the underlying attitudes were very different. Elisha genuinely asks for permission to have a smooth departure from his family, but the men who came to Jesus were making excuses for not following Jesus yet. It is quite likely that the one who asked for time to bury his father was actually asking to be excused from following Jesus for however long it would take before his aged father died. The urgency of the call to which the men were responding is also quite different. Elisha was being called to ministry, but the men Jesus was dealing with were making a choice about their eternal destiny.

Elisha burned the ploughing equipment to prevent any thought of ever returning to this occupation. His slaughtering of his oxen and giving the meat to the people meant that they ate, blessed him, and wished him well in his new work for the Lord (**19:21**). Elijah then set out with Elisha as his *attendant,* that is, as his disciple and servant. Elijah would have had other servants like the one he left at Beersheba (19:3), but Elisha was the only one chosen to succeed him.

20:1-43 Ahab and Ben-Hadad of Aram

The constant wars between Israel and Judah had weakened both countries. Thus Judah had been invaded by Egypt (14:25-28), and Aram (in modern Syria) under Ben-Hadad had attacked Israelite territory during the reign of Asa (15:18-20). The Ben-Hadad referred to in chapter 20 is probably the son of the king who had formed the alliance with Asa.

It appears that Ben-Hadad had formed alliances with the kings of a number of other city-states and had conquered most of Israel and gone on to attack Samaria (**20:1**). His main interest seems to have been in gaining wealth: the silver, the gold and the best of the wives and children of Samaria (**20:2**). Ahab was prepared to make this payment in order to end the war. But Ben-Hadad wanted more. He wanted to humiliate Ahab and loot the city by sending his army in to search for and remove the booty themselves (**20:5-6**). The elders of Samaria advised Ahab not to submit and informed the king of Aram that his final terms for peace were not accepted (**20:7-9**). Ben-Hadad responded by threatening to destroy the city completely. Ahab's retort sounded confident, but he knew very well that he had no army to match the huge one assembled by Ben-Hadad (**20:10-12**).

While the defenders of Samaria were preparing for the coming battle, an unnamed prophet appeared with a word of encouragement from the Lord. Ahab had seen what God could do on Mount Carmel, and now he would have another chance to *know that I am the Lord* (**20:13**). The Lord did not give up easily on Ahab as he had with the other kings before him.

Ahab knew that he had no standing army to count on, so he asked the prophet, *But who will do it?* (**20:14**). The prophet then outlined how the battle was to be fought. Ahab was to start the battle. The 232 officers of *the provincial command* would do the fighting; the remaining seven thousand men in the army would follow the officers to the attack, which would take place at noon, when the enemy was not expecting it.

The attack duly took place and was successful. The army of Aram was defeated and Ben-Hadad had to escape on horseback (**20:15-21**). The victory was the work of God, not Ahab, because the army of Israel was far smaller than that of their opponents. The Lord often wins his battles with only a few people, as he did with Gideon and his three hundred soldiers. Ahab believed what the prophet had told him and went out trusting the Lord, not Baal. But the problems with Ben-Hadad had not yet ended. The prophet of the Lord returned to warn Ahab to prepare for another war with Aram the following year (**20:22**).

The Arameans, too, knew that it was only with God's help that they had been defeated. They, however, thought of God as a territorial god, who could only defend his own area, the hill country. So they raised another huge army to fight with Israel on the Plain of Aphek (**20:23-26**). Their army was so large that it *covered the countryside,* while by comparison the tiny army of Israel looked like *two small flocks of goats* (**20:27**).

The man of God came again and assured Israel that the Lord was not just a god of the hills but of the plains as well, and that they would be victorious. The Lord would defeat the Arameans to make Israel know the Lord (**20:28**). In the battle, Aram was again defeated, their soldiers scattered, and their king forced to hide (**20:29-30**).

Recognizing that they had no other hope of escape, Ben-Hadad's officials went together in sackcloth to beg Ahab to spare his life (**20:31-32**). Ahab showed mercy and did not kill his enemy, but instead made a peace and trade agreement with him. Aram was to return the Israelite cities taken in past wars, and Israelites would be allowed to set up stalls in the market at Damascus (**20:33-34**).

Ahab had recognized God's hand in his victory over Ben-Hadad, but he still did not trust God enough to consult him about the decisions he made. He was more interested in getting a trade agreement than in following the Lord. Thus the Lord sent a message to him, a message that was delivered in a special way by *one of the sons of the prophets* (**20:35a**). Though the Bible tends to focus on particular prophets like Elijah and Elisha, this does not mean that they were the only prophets who were serving the Lord at a given time. There were groups of prophets like those Obadiah hid in caves (18:40; see also 2 Kgs 2:3-7; 4:1, 38; 5:22; 9:1). They are referred to as 'the Lord's prophets' and are contrasted with the other prophets who served Baal, other heathen gods, or even Ahab.

This prophet asked his companion to strike him. The companion refused to obey a command that came from the Lord, and was killed by a lion for his disobedience (**20:35b-36**). His fate is similar to that of the unnamed prophet in chapter 13. Another man was, however, prepared to wound the prophet. The prophet then presented himself to the king, pretending to be a soldier wounded in the battle who had neglected his duty and allowed an important prisoner to escape (**20:37-40a**). When Ahab pronounced the sentence for doing this, the prophet answered with words similar to those that Nathan had spoken to David (**20:40b-42**; see also 2 Sam 12:7). Ahab should not have *set free the man I have determined should die.* His failure to execute Ben-Hadad would lead to many more deaths, including Ahab's own. The war would continue. There are certain things that God wants to be done completely, not halfway, and it is up to us to carry out his plans. When we fail to complete a task he has given us, we are storing up trouble for the future.

David responded to Nathan's criticism with profound repentance (2 Sam 12:13), but Ahab was not like David. Instead of admitting his mistake, he became sullen and angry, as we see him do at other times (**20:43**; see 21:4; 22:8). It takes grace for powerful people to accept criticism from common people. Those who receive criticism, repent and change their ways will continue to excel in life. But Ahab was not really concerned to know and serve the Lord who was favouring him.

21:1-28 Ahab and Naboth

Some time later, Ahab asked a neighbour to trade or sell him a piece of land (2:2). Naboth had a vineyard situated in Jezreel near Ahab's country palace (his other palace was in Samaria) (**21:1**). However, the farm was the property of Naboth's extended family. Although he may have been the oldest male or the person then farming the land, he could not on his own make a decision about selling or exchanging it. Such a major decision might destroy the future security of the children of his clan. Moreover, the law in Israel was intended to keep the ownership of farmland within a family (Lev 25:25-28; Num 27:1-11; 36:7). In cases of extreme poverty, land could be leased, but it would revert to its origi-

nal owner in the year of the jubilee (Lev 25:10, 13, 28). Ahab may have been ignorant of this law since the Levitical priests had lost their position in Israel. But he should also have recognized the possibility that any exchange of land might lead to trouble, for the land that Naboth would be given must have already belonged to some other clan. Naboth had many reasons for responding to Ahab's request with, *The Lord forbid that I should give you the inheritance of my fathers* (**21:2-3**).

Ahab reacted to this refusal like a spoiled child. He went home sad and angry and refused to eat, until his behaviour attracted the attention of his wife, Jezebel (**21:4-5**). She was a Sidonian princess, probably from a culture where all the land belonged to the king and was only leased to the people. She either did not know or refused to accept the law of Israel that clearly stated that the king 'must not consider himself better than his brothers' (Deut 17:18-20). So when she heard Ahab's story, she took action (**21:6-7**).

Jezebel took a deceitful and violent approach to solving the problem. She sent letters stamped with the king's seal to the elders in the town where Naboth lived. Ahab even allowed her to use his seal and name so that it would appear the letters came from him. Her letters asked the elders to trump up charges against Naboth (**21:8-10**). Then, as now, there were people who would go to any length to please someone in a position of leadership. A covetous leader can usually get people to give him what he wants. So the elders broke the law (Exod 23:1-3), carried out Jezebel's plot and notified the palace, *Naboth has been stoned and is dead* (**21:11-14**). It appears from 2 Kings 9:26 that his sons were also killed.

Far from protesting that Jezebel had usurped his authority, broken the law, and had an innocent man and his family killed, Ahab simply accepted what she had done (**21:15-16**). He had surrendered his conscience and his will to hers. He set out to enjoy his new possession.

Once again, the Lord sent Elijah to confront Ahab, this time at Naboth's farm (**21:17-18**). Ahab had already received a prophecy of doom from another prophet: *your life for his life* (20:42). Now Elijah added detail to this judgment: *dogs will lick up your blood* (**21:19**).

All the meetings between Elijah and Ahab were hostile. Ahab saw Elijah as his enemy, not as a messenger from God (**21:20**). And the message this time was one of judgment on the house of Ahab: it would end in the same ways as the houses of Jeroboam and Baasha. No male child would be left to succeed him. Jezebel, too, received her sentence of judgment (**21:21-24**).

On hearing Elijah's words, the king repented, tore his clothes, put on sackcloth and fasted (**21:27**). True repentance in humility never goes unnoticed, and so the Lord showed mercy to Ahab as he would later to the people of

Nineveh (Jonah 3:10). God promised that the coming disaster will take place after Ahab's death (**21:28-29**).

22:1-28 Ahab and Micaiah

The peace agreement between Israel and the Arameans (20:34) lasted only three years. It appears that during this time relations with Judah were also friendly, so that King Jehoshaphat of Judah was able to make a state visit to Samaria (**22:1-2**). It is unfortunate that such peace came so late, after both kingdoms had been weakened by years of conflict, and only in the days of the evil Ahab. He would have a bad influence on the religious life of Judah.

During this visit, Ahab brought up the topic of Ramoth Gilead (**22:3-4a**). Apparently Ben-Had had not handed over this town despite his promise to return all captured towns to Israel (20:34). Jehoshaphat agreed to go with Israel to war – *I am as you are, my people as your people* (**22:4b**). His people would fight alongside the people of Israel. There was, however, a difference between the two kings. Ahab was confident that Israel could defeat Aram because of the two previous victories described in chapter 20. But he had forgotten that it was the Lord who had given him these victories. Now he was making plans without consulting God, relying solely on the support of Judah. Jehoshaphat, on the other hand, suggested they should consult the Lord before taking action (**22:5**).

Ahab called his prophets together. It appears that he had recruited another large group of prophets, presumably to replace those killed on Mount Carmel (18:22, 40). These prophets, however, claimed to consult the Lord, not Baal. But in reality they were ready to say whatever the king wanted to hear, and so were no better than palace praise singers. They were only too happy to encourage Ahab to go to war and promised that the Lord would give him victory (**22:6**).

Jehoshaphat recognized that these prophets were more interested in pleasing the king than in listening to God, and so he asked to hear from a genuine *prophet of the Lord*, not merely a prophet of the king (**22:7**; see also 2 Kgs 3:11). Ahab grudgingly admitted that there was one other prophet who could be consulted: Micaiah. But Ahab disliked Micaiah because he was prepared to criticize the king's actions *and never prophesies anything good about me* (**22:8a**).

Even today, political leaders seem to appreciate pastors only when the pastors approve of their behaviour and reject them when they are critical. But pastors must remember that they are the prophets of our day. They must not compromise and allow moral decay to take root in the nation. Their duty is to speak up against all that is contrary to God's will.

Jehoshaphat gently rebuked the king for not being prepared to listen to God's prophet, and insisted on hearing from Micaiah. A messenger was sent to fetch him (**22:8b-9**).

Once again, we have a dramatic scene, with one true prophet of the Lord confronting a large number of false prophets. The writer sketches the scene vividly, with the two kings sitting outside the gate of Samaria, surrounded by the palace prophets, all prophesying victory. Zedekiah the leader of the prophets had even decided to act out his prophecy, making a pair of iron horns to symbolize the way the kings would gore and overcome the enemy (**22:10-12**).

The messenger who had gone to fetch Micaiah advised him to make his prophecy match that of the other prophets (**22:13**). But Micaiah refused to accept the common belief that 'the voice of the majority is the voice of God'. The truth of God is not necessarily what the majority think. The word from the Lord does not originate from people but from God himself. Micaiah vowed to speak only the word that he received from the Lord (**22:14**). A person sent from God has no other message than the word of God, which is spoken as the Spirit of God carries the prophet along (2 Pet 1:20-21).

Much to Ahab's surprise, Micaiah's first answer to his question was identical to what was being said by the other prophets (**22:15**). But there must have been an overtone of sarcasm in his words, for Ahab recognized that this was not his true message (**22:16**). So Micaiah presented Ahab with his real vision: Israel was going to be defeated (**22:17**). Micaiah went on to describe the vision he had seen. There was a council in heaven with the Lord presiding. At this council, the suggestion was adopted that a lying spirit would be sent from the Lord to deceive Ahab's prophets (**22:19-23a**). Thus, in one sense, both the prophecies of the prophets and that of Micaiah came from the Lord.

God's use of beings whose ways are contrary to his to accomplish his purpose baffles the mind. Although Habbakuk was a prophet, he struggled with this as he wondered why God would plan to use the Chaldeans, who were even more evil than Israel, to punish Israel. It seems that we are asked to view all creation as God's instrument to accomplish what he needs done. For some, he may send an angel of light to show them the way, while others may receive a lying spirit to harden their hearts.

Micaiah's message that ultimately *the Lord has decreed disaster for you* was not an easy one for Ahab to accept (**22:23b**). But it was one that could have saved Ahab if he had believed and humbly repented, as he did in 21:29.

This passage also raises the question of how to discern who are true prophets and who are false prophets. In **22:24-28**, Micaiah's answer to Zedekiah and Ahab, who accuse him of being a false prophet, is similar to that given in Deuteronomy 18:22 (see also 13:1-2). We can also learn from Micaiah's vision of the council of the Lord, which is similar to that in Job 1:6-12 and 2:1-6. In Jeremiah, God states that true prophets are those who stand in the council of God. They will receive a complete vision that will help others to serve the Lord. False prophets have no such privilege. They sit outside the council of God and receive only second-hand or incomplete messages (Jer 23:21-22, 30-32).

But being a true prophet is no guarantee that one will escape suffering. Micaiah, like Jeremiah, suffered for giving the exact message from the Lord (22:24, 27). So did our Lord Jesus Christ.

22:29-40 Ahab's death

Ahab was clearly still between two opinions (18:21). He followed the voice of the majority and his own desires in going to war. But deep in his heart he believed Micaiah, and tried to thwart his prophecy by going into the battle in disguise (22:29-30). Had he gone into battle in his own robes, he would probably have been killed, as Jehoshaphat discovered (22:31-33). But no disguise can thwart the word of the Lord: Ahab was killed at Ramoth Gilead by an arrow shot at random that pierced his armour (22:34-37). Israel was defeated and lost its king as Micaiah and the unnamed prophet had foretold (22:20; 20:42). As Elijah had predicted, dogs licked up Ahab's blood (22:38; 21:19).

In the eye of the world, Ahab was a success. He built a palace *inlaid with ivory* and fortified many cities (22:39-40). But the Lord was angry with him and would later subject his family to a terrible judgment (2 Kgs 10:6-11).

22:41-50 Jehoshaphat, King of Judah

The twenty-five year reign of Jehoshaphat is summarized briefly. For part of this time, he may have reigned beside his father. He was a good king because he followed the example of his father Asa (22:41-43a; see 15:11). He got rid of the remaining shrine prostitutes (22:46). However, because the high places were not removed, the people continued to worship in them (22:43b). There is also a brief discussion of his foreign policy. As we have seen, he maintained friendship with Ahab and with Ahab's sons, Ahaziah and Joram (2 Kgs 3:7; 2 Chr 20:35). The unsuccessful attempt to build a trading fleet was initially a joint venture, but when Jehoshaphat realized it was not the Lord's will, he refused the trade partnership with them (22:48-49).

1 Kgs 22:51-2 Kgs 1:18 Ahaziah, King of Israel

The final verses of 1 Kings summarize the two-year reign of Ahaziah of Israel. He followed the example of Ahab his father and did evil before the Lord. Like his predecessors, he caused Israel to continue to sin (22:51-53).

The events of Ahaziah's reign are presented in 2 Kings 1:1-18. He was faced with a rebellion by Moab, which we know from other sources had been conquered by Omri, Ahab's father. The Moabites hoped to take advantage of the confusion resulting from a change in the ruler and the installation of a young king. Ahaziah was unable to take action to stop the rebellion because he had suffered serious injuries in a fall from the top of his house (1:1-2a). Ahaziah must have heard of the events on Mount Carmel where the Lord had proved himself superior to Baal (1 Kgs 18:16-45). He must also have known that the Lord had given his father victory over Ben-Hadad and the Arameans (1 Kgs 20:1-34) and that Micaiah, a prophet of the Lord, had correctly prophesied his father's defeat (1 Kgs 22:23). But instead of consulting Micaiah or Elijah about his prospects for recovery and asking them to pray for him, Ahaziah sent messengers to consult Baal-Zebub at Ekron and probably to ask him for healing (1:2b). This god's name means 'Baal of the flies', and he may have been a fly god. But it is also possible that his name was originally Baal-Zebul (meaning 'Prince Baal'), and that the Hebrew writer punned on this name, changing Zebul to Zebub. By the days of Jesus, the name Beelzebub had come to be applied to the prince of demons (Matt 12:24; Mark 3:22; Luke 11:15).

The angel of the Lord sent Elijah to meet the messengers sent to Baal-Zebub (1:3). It is worth noting that Elijah did not usually take action without the Lord or an angel sending him. Elijah's message was one of judgment: because the king was consulting Baal-Zebub instead of the God of Israel, he could expect death, not healing (1:4). The messengers do not seem to have recognized Elijah, but they must have believed that he was a man of God and quickly returned to their master with his message (1:5-8).

Ahaziah's response to this message was not repentance but confrontation. He sent a captain and a squad of fifty men to arrest Elijah (1:9). The king was declaring his opposition to God, not just to Elijah. If Elijah had obeyed the captain's command, he would probably have suffered the same fate as the many prophets of the Lord who were killed during the days of Ahab. After all, Jezebel was still alive. So Elijah called down fire that consumed the captain and his men (1:10).

Still the king did not repent, but sent another squad who suffered the same fate as the first one (1:11-12). We do not know whether Elijah took this action because of his own fear or whether he was directed to do it by God. But God responded to his call for fire, supporting him in his action. Many hundreds of years later, Jesus' disciples wanted to do the same thing after they had merely been refused lodging. They had the power that Elijah had and could have done this, but the Lord rebuked them and led them to another town where they were received (Luke 9:51-55).

Ahaziah then sent a third group, but the captain of this group was more careful. He realized that he was dealing with the Lord's powerful representative, and he begged that their lives be spared (1:13-14). The angel of the Lord reassured Elijah that it would be safe to go and meet the king (1:15). When the Lord sends a person, he is sure to be with them if they obey. Characteristically, Elijah fearlessly obeys the Lord's command.

Ahaziah heard the message of doom from the prophet with his own ears and then died. He had reigned only two years. He had no male child and was succeeded by Joram, his brother (**1:16-18**).

2:1-8:15 Elisha's Ministry

2:1-18 Elijah taken up to heaven

Elijah's ministry had been as important as that of Moses. When Israel was drifting away from the faith, he was the one who reminded them of the covenant made with their fore-fathers in the wilderness of Sinai. At Mount Sinai (Horeb), he met with the Lord God of Israel just as Moses had met him there (compare Exod 33:12-33 and 1 Kgs 19:11-18). Elijah's importance is underscored by Malachi's prophecy that he would return before the final events of the end time (Mal 4:5). Jesus states that John the Baptist fulfilled that prophecy (Matt 17:10-12; Mark 9:11-13). Elijah was the one who appeared with Moses and spoke with the Lord at the time of his transfiguration (Matt 17:1-7; Mark 9:2-9). Like Moses, Elijah would die alone in a mysterious way (Deut 32:48-52; 34).

As Elijah and his successor Elisha set out on their final journey together, Elijah makes three attempts, at Gilgal, Bethel and Jericho, to persuade Elisha to leave him (**2:1-2, 4, 6**). In the past, he had left another servant at Beersheba when he hoped to die (1 Kgs 19:3-4). But Elisha refused to leave him, each time swearing an oath to that effect. Three attempts were enough, and Elijah did not try to stop Elisha from accompanying him again.

The companies of prophets whom they met as they journeyed warned Elisha of what was coming, but he already knew it (**2:3, 5**). He was a faithful servant to his master and stayed with him to the very end. Those who continue to the end enjoy greater privileges and blessings.

Finally, Elijah himself spoke of what was about to happen: *Tell me, what can I do for you before I am taken up from you?* (**2:9**). The man of God had no material property to be inherited, but Elisha could have requested a special prayer for himself or for the nation of Israel, with the prophet laying hands on him to confer some final blessing. But what Elisha asked for was a *double portion of your spirit*. He may have been asking that he would become twice as great as Elijah, or that the spirit that would rest on him would be two times greater in power or quantity than it had been for Elijah. But it is also possible that he was simply requesting that the spirit at work in Elijah's life and generation would continue in his own life for another generation, so that two generations would be blessed. This last interpretation may be supported by the fact that some of the works of Elisha seem to repeat those of Elijah (compare 1 Kgs 17:14 and 2 Kgs 4:3-6; 1 Kgs 17:17-23 and 2 Kgs 4:32-37).

This was a gift that Elijah could not give, because it was dependent on God (**2:10**; see also Jesus' answer to the sons of Zebedee – Matt 20:20-23). Yet he could say that this request would be granted if Elisha could still see him while he was being taken up. It would appear that he is making the point that a man of God must be able to see the whole picture, both physically and spiritually, if he is to benefit from heavenly gifts.

Suddenly a *chariot of fire* came between them, separating them (**2:11**). Elijah was taken up into heaven in a whirlwind, leaving Elisha to weep, *My father! My father! The chariots and horsemen of Israel* (**2:12**). The meaning of the reference to chariots is not clear. Elisha may have been lamenting the pitiful position of Israel's army at that time, or he may have been saying that Israel was left defenceless with the loss of its great prophet. The same lament is offered at the time of Elisha's own death (13:14). Yet another possibility is that Elisha is speaking of the chariot he has just seen, the evidence that the Lord is defending Israel. He would again see these chariots that were invisible to many when they surrounded his house at the time when the Arameans attempted to capture him (2 Kgs 6:17).

As a mark of mourning Elisha tore his clothes (**2:12**). He then picked up Elijah's cloak that had fallen off. He used this cloak to strike the water of the River Jordan (**2:13**). His next words, *Where now is the Lord, the God of Elijah?* suggest that at first nothing happened. His question reveals his recognition that the power to stop the river flowing was not embedded in any magic in the cloak but came from God, who had granted him a double portion of Elijah's spirit. When Elisha realized this, God showed his presence and the River Jordan divided, as it had in the days of Joshua (**2:14**; Josh 3:7). We hear nothing more of Elijah's cloak.

Pastors must never forget that there is no magic in following a ritual or some order of worship. Our faith must not depend on the ritual but on the living God who provides the ritual as a means of grace.

This power to divide water was with Moses at the Red Sea, with Joshua at the Jordan, and had just been exercised by Elijah (**2:8**). When the company of prophets at Jericho saw Elisha do this, they understood that the same spirit that had been with Elijah was now with Elisha and immediately acknowledged him as their leader (**2:15**). But they did not believe that Elijah had simply been taken up to heaven – they thought that the Spirit of the Lord would have put him down on some high hills or in some other place. A search party was sent out, but found no trace of Elijah (**2:16-18**).

2:19-25 Elisha's first miracles

Elisha responded to an appeal from people whose *water is bad* (**2:19a**). From their words and those of Elisha, it seems that the water was causing deaths and harming crops (**2:19b, 21b**). Elisha healed the water by throwing a bowl of salt into the spring, but it was not the salt itself that restored the water supply but the miraculous hand of God, as is clear from his words, *This is what the Lord says* (**2:21a**).

The word of God has power to heal (**2:22**), but it also has power to destroy, as is evident from the incident described in 2:23-25. This story lacks enough detail for us to tell exactly what was going on. It is not clear why the large mob of youths (there were at least forty-two of them – 2:24) started to shout insults at Elisha. There must have been some reason for such shockingly disrespectful behaviour in a culture that respected elders (**2:23**). Elisha turned it around, looked at them and called down a curse on them (**2:24a**). Curses do not usually take effect except where they are deserved. This curse must spring in part from the prophecies of judgment spoken against Jeroboam, Ahab and other kings. Because of their ungodly lives, the Lord was bringing disaster on the lives of those living in the land, including these youth, who were mauled by bears (**2:24b**).

This incident, and others like it, prove that there must have been many wild animals in the land of Israel at that time (Deut 7:22; 1 Kgs 13:23-24; 20:36; 2 Kgs 17:25-26).

3:1-27 Elisha and the rebellion of Moab

Ahaziah had been unable to deal with Moab's rebellion against Israel (**3:4-5**; see also 1:1) and so the task fell to his brother Joram, who assumed the throne and reigned for twelve years (**3:1**). Although he removed the sacred stone of Baal, he continued in the sins of Jeroboam. Yet he was not as bad as his father and mother (**3:2**).

Relations between Jehoshaphat of Judah and Joram of Israel were good, and thus they agreed to join forces against Moab. Jehoshaphat expressed his support using the same words he had used to Ahab when they set out to attack Ramoth Gilead (**3:6-7**). They also seem to have enlisted the support of the leader of Edom, and thus planned to attack through that country (**3:8**). Before long the combined armies of the kings of Judah, Israel and Edom were in trouble for they found no water for their troops and horses (**3:9**).

Joram saw the water shortage as the Lord's doing, setting them up for defeat by Moab (**3:10**). But once again, as before the attack on Ramoth Gilead, Jehoshaphat advised that they consult the Lord (**3:11**). Jehoshaphat had not forgotten the covenant Lord of Israel. He used this opportunity to witness to the God of the ancestors of the united Israel. Joram had little choice but to agree, particularly when it was pointed out that Elisha, who had been Elijah's servant, was nearby. Jehoshaphat greeted this news with enthusiasm: *The word of the Lord is with him* (**3:12**). He knew that Elisha would tell them the real word of God.

Elisha made no attempt to hide his distaste for Joram, whose father Ahab had encouraged so many false prophets (**3:13**). However, he had time for Jehoshaphat, and agreed to consult the Lord because he was with the other kings (**3:14**). He asked for a harpist to play some music to assist him. It seems that music was often associated with the prophets (see 1 Sam 10:5-13). While the music was playing, Elisha heard the word of the Lord (**3:15**). The Lord was going to provide plenty of water for the army and the animals even though it was not going to rain where they were. With the Lord nothing is impossible. The Lord would also give victory over Moab (**3:16-19**): all the cities and towns would fall to the kings.

The following morning there was some kind of flash flood and water flowing from Edom filled the land (**3:20**). When the defenders of Moab saw the red reflection of the early morning sun in the water, they assumed that what they were seeing was blood and thought that there must have been fighting within the attacking army (**3:21-23**). They advanced, not expecting serious resistance, and were soundly defeated (**3:24**). The armies of the three kings destroyed the Moabite towns and spoiled their farmlands. Destruction of farmland was specifically forbidden in the law (Deut 20:19). It thus seems likely that God does not endorse this action, but that the text is merely stating what victors do (**3:25**).

The king of Moab gathered seven hundred swordsmen and tried to break through the advancing forces, but could not. In an act of desperation, he offered his first-born son, who would have been his heir, on the city wall as a burnt offering to his god (**3:27**).This action may have inspired the Moabites to fight fiercely, even suicidally, and the Israelites broke off the fight and withdrew to their own land.

The Lord may possibly have permitted this defeat because the Israelites had broken his laws when they destroyed farmlands (see 3:25). An important theological point to note is that God is not threatened by beliefs in other gods. He allowed Israel to suffer heavy casualties at a time when it would appear that this defeat was the result of an offering made to Chemosh. His existence and honour do not depend on anything outside himself.

4:1-44 Various miracles

We are now told of some other miracles associated with Elisha that resemble those worked by Elijah. The miraculous supply of oil is similar to the supply of flour for the widow of Zarephath that did not run out till the end of the famine (1 Kgs 17:8-16). The raising of the dead child of the Shunammite woman resembles that of the child of the widow in Zarephath (1 Kgs 17:17-24).

One thing that should be noted about all these miracles is the faith and obedience of those who benefited. None of them doubted the ability of the prophet – they did as the prophet told them and they saw the power of the Lord working to meet their needs.

4:1-7 THE WIDOW'S OIL In OT times, widows were among the most needy and powerless groups in society. Elisha met the widow of a prophet who had died before he could repay a debt he owed. Now creditors were threatening to take her two boys as slaves to raise the money to pay the debt (**4:1**). The widow had nothing in the house except a little oil (**4:2**). But that was all that was needed to solve her problem. Elijah told her and her sons to collect as many empty bottles as they could from her neighbours and then to close the door behind her and her children. Then they were to fill all the bottles they had until none were empty. Thereafter she could sell the oil and pay off the debt, and she and her sons could live on the rest of the money (**4:3-7**).

This incident is a reminder to us to be sensitive to the problems that widows face and to actively seek ways to meet their needs. It also serves as an assurance to widows that they can trust the Lord to provide for them.

4:8-37 THE SHUNAMMITE'S SON A couple in Shunem, a village a few miles north of Jezreel, showed hospitality to Elisha whenever he was passing that way. They even prepared a furnished room for his use (**4:8-10**). Showing hospitality to a man of God has its own rewards (Heb 13:2), but Elisha wanted to do something to show his appreciation for what they had done (**4:11-13**). She and her husband had no ambition to go to the court, or to be given a commission in the army, but what they did lack was a son (**4:14**). As they had no child of their own, it would be a great blessing if they were to have one. The prophet promised that, like Sarah, she would have a son despite the age of her husband (**4:15-16a**).

The woman did not want to have her hopes raised only to be disappointed (**4:16b**). But the words of the prophet were fulfilled, and the next year she gave birth to a son (**4:17**). The boy grew, but tragically one day he was struck down by some disease that caused an acute headache. He died in his mother's arms (**4:18-20**). Devastated, the mother laid her dead son on the bed of the man of God and set out to find Elisha. She may have hoped that there was still something he could do to bring the child he had given her back to life (**4:21-22**).

Her husband was puzzled about why she was looking for Elisha on that day, seeing *It's not the new moon or the Sabbath* – possibly the only two occasions on which Elisha could be found at home. But the wife insisted on going (**4:23-24**). It is strange that it was the mother and not the father who set out on this journey. But it may be that as a mother she felt more for her child than the father did. He may already have accepted his death, whereas the mother was still in denial. However, there are also other possibilities. The wife may not even have told her husband about what had happened, believing that if she could get to the prophet, he could still heal her son. Alternatively, the description of the husband as *old* in 4:14 may suggests that he was far older than his

wife, and less able to stand up to a long and hurried journey than his young wife. Whatever the case, she had faith and her faith moved her to action.

She covered the twenty-five miles (forty kilometres) from Shunem to Mount Carmel as fast as possible. Elisha saw her coming in the distance, and sent his servant, Gehazi, to ask what was wrong, but she refused to divulge her mission until she was clinging to Elisha. Nor was she content with having his servant attempt to revive the boy. Elisha must come himself (**4:25-30**).

Gehazi was sent ahead with instructions to run to the boy on a mission that was so urgent that he was not to greet anyone along the way. But he could not help the child.

When Elisha arrived he first prayed to the Lord before stretching himself out over the body of the dead child. Life returned to the boy, whom Elisha returned to his overjoyed mother (**4:31-37**). This life was not the resurrection life, but an ordinary life that would ultimately end in death.

It is important to note that this story merely tells us what actually happened, and not what should happen. The Scriptures show that very few of God's servants have had the power to raise the dead, namely Elijah (1 Kgs 17:17-24), Elisha (1 Kgs 32–37), Jesus (Matt 9:18-26; John 11:43-44), Peter (Acts 9:40-41) and Paul (Acts 20:9-12). Anyone today who seeks to do the same must be very certain the Lord has spoken before making the attempt. To say this is not to downplay the power or faith but to remind us that the Lord is the one who actually does the raising. Prophets, or pastors for that matter, are not all-able or all-discerning, except as the Lord chooses to use them and grants them these gifts. Even Elisha had limitations on his knowledge, as we see in this incident where he did not know what was wrong until the woman told him (4:27b).

4:38-41 THE POISONED POT The next miracle described happened during a time of famine, which would have made the loss of edible food even more disastrous (**4:38**). It appears that someone accidentally gathered some poisonous plant along with edible ones when searching the countryside for food. It would be death to eat the food in that pot (**4:39-40**). Elisha added flour to the pot, and the poison was miraculously neutralized, leaving food that was safe to eat (**4:41**).

4:42-44 FEEDING ONE HUNDRED PEOPLE A man came to Elisha to present him with some loaves and the firstfruit of his farm (**4:42**). Moses had prescribed that the firstfruits should be given to the priests and Levites (Deut 18:1-5). However, this ruling would not have been followed strictly because the Levitical priests had been neglected since the days of Jeroboam, who had appointed priests who were not Levites (1 Kgs 12:31; 2 Chr 11:13-16). By the days of Elisha, the faithful in Israel would have been content to take their firstfruit to anyone they believed was a man of God. While this may not be in accordance with the letter of the law, it is in harmony with its spirit, for the principle behind the regulation seems to have been that the gifts would free the priests to concentrate on their spiritual ministry.

By a special directive from the Lord (4:43), all those present, who were probably Elisha's disciples, were permitted to eat of this firstfruit. The directive was also in accordance with the spirit of the law, which laid down that everyone who was ceremonially clean in the priests' houses might eat it (Num 18:12-13).

When Elisha told the man to use this food to feed a hundred people, he knew it would not be enough. But he obeyed and his small gift fed so many people that they had enough and there was some left over (4:43-44). This story resembles the Lord's feeding of the multitude (John 6:1-14) and may explain why the people were so ready to hail Jesus as a prophet (John 6:14).

5:1-27 Naaman healed of leprosy

We have no indication of the names of the kings of Israel or Aram in whose time this incident took place. It may well have been after the reign of Ahaziah. The presence of Israelite slaves in Aram (5:2) and the Israelite king's reaction to the letter (5:7) suggest that there was a very uneasy peace between the two nations.

Naaman is introduced as the successful commander of the Aramean army (5:1a). But there was one victory he could not win – he suffered from an incurable skin disease (5:1b). This disease is described as *leprosy* – but this word was used for many serious skin diseases and may not have been what we today know as leprosy.

The slave girl who referred Naaman to Elisha must have been especially capable and of good character, for commanders usually kept the best of any captured slaves for their own household. Because she was female and a slave, not much is said about her. But we know that her witness to the saving power of the God of Israel was powerful and convincing. Naaman came to believe that there was a cure in Samaria for his leprosy (5:2-3). Her role in this story may be of some comfort to the numerous young girls in

---

HEALING

In traditional African cosmology, God is the ultimate source of sickness and of health, as expressed in the proverb *Onyame ma wo yarewa a, oma wo ano aduru* [Akan, Ghana – 'If God gives an ailment, he also provides the cure']. Divinities and ancestors are mediators of health. While diseases are regarded as having both natural and supernatural sources, ultimate causality is assigned to the supernatural. God can send disease, but more commonly diseases are understood to be caused by evil forces (such as witchcraft and sorcery) or to be a result of one's own evil deeds.

This traditional view means that treatments based solely on scientifically observed cause-and-effect relationships are not perceived as meeting the health needs of the sick. A permanent cure requires a redemptive ritual to deal with the spiritual factors that made someone vulnerable to the disease. Hence the office of the traditional priest has always been associated with divination, diagnosis, healing and exorcism.

According to the Bible, all sickness is ultimately a result of the fall. Diseases may be a punishment for violations of God's laws (Exod 15:26; Deut 28:22), while continued obedience to God may ensure good health (Exod 15:26; Deut 28:1-14). The book of Job, however, makes it clear that disease does not always represent divine punishment. Healing is the manifestation of God's goodness and compassion in response to human suffering (Exod 15:26).

Only a few healing miracles are recorded in the OT, most of them clustered around the exodus and the ministries of Elijah and Elisha. Those healed include Miriam (Num 12:9-16), Jeroboam (1 Kgs 13:4-6), the widow's son (1 Kgs 17:17-24), the son of the Shunammite woman (2 Kgs 4:1-37), Naaman (2 Kgs 5:8-14) and Hezekiah (2 Kgs 20:1-11).

Jesus threw light on the understanding of sickness as punishment (John 9) and also recognized that some sicknesses are demonic in origin (Mark 9:17-27). He cured the blind (Mark 8:22-26; 10:46-52), lepers (Luke 17:11-19), the disabled and the paralysed (Matt 9:2-7; Mark 2:3-12; Luke 5:18-25). His healing activities manifested God's compassion towards the sick and the oppressed (Matt 9:35-36; 14:14; 15:29-34; Mark 1:40-42; Luke 4:18-27). They also established his status as the Christ (Matt 9:1-8; Mark 10:46-52) and had an evangelistic purpose (John 20:30-31). Jesus expected his disciples to continue the ministry of healing (Mark 16:9-20; John 20:21; see also Acts 3:6-10, 12-16; 14:8-10).

In dealing with the subject of healing, we must avoid two extremes: first, the claim that godly Christians do not fall sick (contradicted by Phil 2:25-30), and second the denial that there can be faith healing (Acts 28:3-6; 1 Cor 12:9).

The traditional understanding of the cause of disease has survived in African Christianity, as is clear from the popularity of prophets and faith healers. The clergy are expected, whether justifiably or not, to authenticate their ministry by exercising powers traditionally credited to religious persons, such as healing, unveiling hidden things, predicting the future, and being able to bless and curse effectively. When such powers are not present, members drift to other churches, attend other healing services, and consult spiritualists and fetish priests.

African Christians must realize that God reserves the sole prerogative to heal. Not all the sick in the days of Jesus were healed, nor were all the dead raised to life like Lazarus. Whether Jesus chooses to heal or not does not change the fact that he is Saviour and Lord. Consequently, we must seek him for who he is and not merely for healing.

Kingsley Larbi

Africa who have been abducted from their homes and forced to serve soldiers or others against their will. Even in such situations, they can be used by God to make a difference in the lives of individuals and nations. They should not give in to despair but should rather look for opportunities for doing good.

Naaman told the king of Aram about what the girl had told him, and was sent off to Samaria to look for healing. He took princely gifts with him – 750 pounds (340 kilograms) of silver, 150 pounds (70 kilograms) of gold, and *ten sets of clothing* – as well as a letter addressed to the king of Israel (**5:4-6**).

The king of Israel had no idea what to do when he received this letter. He was sure that the king of Aram was looking for an excuse to start a war. In desperation, he tore his clothes (**5:7**). Unlike the slave girl, he either did not know or did not believe that the prophet of the Lord could cure leprosy.

As soon as Elisha heard of the king's predicament, he sent word that Naaman should come to him so that *he will know that there is a prophet in Israel* (**5:8**). Elisha was not calling attention to himself but was concerned that people of other nations would come to know that the God of Israel was the only true God.

When Naaman arrived at Elisha's house, the prophet did not even bother to go out to address him in person. He simply sent out a messenger telling Naaman to go to the Jordan River and wash himself seven times (**5:9-10**). Naaman was an important man and was used to being treated with great respect, so he was angry about receiving so little care and attention. After all, he reasoned, if all that was needed to heal him was river water, he could bathe in the bigger rivers in Damascus (**5:11-12**). We, too, often want to design God's salvation to suit us. The message of the gospel of salvation often sounds like foolishness to those who are perishing. But what was needed was not earthly wisdom but faith and obedience to the word of God through his prophet. God had said that he would heal Naaman if he bathed in the River Jordan. Namaan would not be healed if he bathed in another river.

Fortunately, Naaman was humble enough to swallow his anger, accept the advice of his servants and obey the word of God. He did exactly as the man of God had said, and he was healed (**5:13-14**). Where Naaman had once thought that the God of Israel was only one among many territorial gods, now he could say, *there is no God in all the world except in Israel* (**5:15**). He now believed the God of Israel to be the true God. He returned to Elisha's house, and this time he met the prophet face to face. Full of gratitude, he offered him rich gifts.

But Elisha would not accept any gifts (**5:16**). The mark of a true man of God is that he is not out to make money or acquire possessions but seeks the welfare of others. Paul makes the same point when he reminds the Ephesian elders that he had not wanted to take anyone's money or goods, but had supported himself (Acts 20:33-35; see also 1 Cor 9:11-16; 2 Thess 3:7-10; Phil 4:15-19). He also tells Timothy that a church leader should not be someone who loves money (1 Tim 3:3).

Naaman was so impressed with his healing and with Elisha's attitude to wealth that he asked for another gift for himself. He wanted to take some soil from Israel to Damascus (**5:17**). It was not that he wanted to worship the soil as such, but he wanted a souvenir that would remind him of his experience and of his miraculous healing by the God of Israel whom he would now serve. In the same way, some of us who have had the privilege of visiting Israel may want to keep a small bottle of water from the Jordan River to remind us that we have been where Jesus was.

Naaman knew that in the course of his official duties he would have to accompany the king of Aram to the shrine of their god Rimmon and bow down with other officials. He would not be able to avoid doing this in future, even though he was a believer in the God of Israel (**5:18**). Elisha understood Naaman's problem and assured him of pardon – *Go in peace* (**5:19**). In saying this, Elisha was not accepting that Rimmon was worthy of worship but was recognizing Naaman's level of growth. Naaman had just realized that only Yahweh is God, and Elisha was now letting the rest play out as Naaman grew in understanding of what that meant. When we deal with people, it is important to remember that spiritual growth is gradual and that we should not expect perfection as soon as someone comes to faith. In situations where we are closer to the new believers than Elisha would have been to Naaman upon his return to Syria, follow-up ministry is vital.

Throughout the OT, there are secret believers in the service of unbelieving rulers. These believers include Obadiah who served Ahab (1 Kgs 18:3), Nehemiah who served Artaxerxes (Neh 2:1), and Mordecai and Esther in the book of Esther.

But Gehazi, Elisha's servant, was not as mature as Elisha. He gave in to greed and ran after Naaman, told him a lie and got himself some money and two gowns (**5:20-24**). Greed leads people into telling lies and into other sins. After hiding the gifts he received, Gehazi returned to serve Elisha as if nothing had happened (**5:25**).

But the Lord had revealed what Gehazi had done to Elisha, and Elisha accused him: *Is this the time to take money?* (**5:26a**). The question implies that at this time all the glory should go to God. He was the one who had made the healing possible and he was already being glorified by Naaman. It was a time to rejoice that someone from a nation other than Israel was taking home the message that the God of Israel is able to heal.

Unfortunately, we all too often focus on what we can gain rather than on the glory God must receive, and so fail like Gehazi. We must strive to make sure that we always put God at the centre. Like Elisha, we must be prepared to refuse any gift that lessens someone's focus on what they have just discovered about Yahweh. Our hold on all our possessions is very precarious, and so we should live like pilgrims on this earth (Gen 47:9-10; 1 Chr 29:15), and not seek to accumulate *vineyards, flocks, herds or menservants and maidservants* (**5:26b**).

Gehazi gained silver and gowns, but he also gained Naaman's leprosy (**5:27**). Those who try to accumulate material riches dishonestly will always live with spiritual and mental unease.

6:1-7 The floating axe head

The *company of the prophets* in Gilgal has been mentioned earlier (4:38). Here Elisha appears to be associated with this community, who lived in their own settlement under his leadership (**6:1**). Their reference to meeting with Elisha suggests that this was some kind of residential school, and their building plans indicate that the buildings were made of wood or of wood and mud (**6:2**).

Elisha accompanied them as they started their project (**6:3**). While they were cutting the trees, the metal head of an axe came loose from its shaft and fell into deep water. This was a disaster, as the axe had been borrowed. It may have been borrowed because the prophets could not afford to purchase their own axe head, for iron was very expensive at the time (**6:4-5**). Elisha was summoned and threw a stick into the water, after which the heavy iron axe head floated on top of the water where it could be retrieved (**6:6-7**). There is no way to explain how this happened without mentioning the power of God through Elisha. The God who created the law of gravity to make things fall down can also make metal float.

6:8-8:15 Israel, Aram and Elisha

6:8-6:23 ARAMEAN SOLDIERS MISLED Once again there was war between the unnamed king of Aram and an unnamed king of Israel. The Arameans became very frustrated, because it appeared that the Israelites always anticipated their movements. The king became convinced that one of his officers must be a traitor who was revealing his plans to the enemy (**6:8-11**). But he was wrong. It was God who was revealing their plans to Elisha, who would then issue warnings to the king of Israel. The Aramean officers informed their king of what Elisha was doing (**6:12**). Determined to put an end to this, the king sent an army with chariots and horses to capture Elisha (**6:13-14**). But this attempt would be no more successful than Ahaziah's attempt to arrest Elijah (1:9-12).

If Elisha knew all the king's plans, he must have known of the army coming to arrest him. But he was not disturbed

and remained calmly in Dothan. His servant, on the other hand, was overcome with fear when he saw the encircling troops and cried out, *What shall we do?* (**6:15**). The reason Elisha could remain calm was that he knew that God's army, who were on his side, were not only more in number but also more powerful than the Aramean forces. He prayed for the eyes of his servant to be opened so that he could see that they were surrounded by a protective army of horses and chariots of fire – the army of the Lord (**6:16-17**). It may have been one of these same chariots that had appeared when Elijah was taken away (2:11). The Lord's army was there not to fight for the whole of Israel but specifically for Elisha and his servant. Elisha must have understood the truth 'if God is for us who can be against us?' (Rom 8:31).

Elisha had prayed that his servant's eyes would be opened, but he prayed the opposite for the Arameans. He asked God to strike them with blindness (**6:18**). Clearly, this was not a physical blindness but a mental blindness that prevented them from recognizing what was actually happening. Then Elisha himself led them into the city of Samaria, where they were greatly outnumbered (**6:19-20**). Imagine their horror when they realized where they were (**6:20**)! The king of Israel wanted to take advantage of the situation and kill the Aramean soldiers, but Elisha forbade it. After all, the king would not kill helpless captives he had taken in battle, and he was not to kill men whom God had captured and handed over to him, almost completely disarmed and at a disadvantage (**6:21-22**). Instead Elisha advised that they be treated in a way Jesus would have approved, for he told us to show love to those who persecute and ill-treat us (Matt 5:44) and to overcome evil with good (Rom 12:21). Thus the Aramean soldiers were given a feast and then set free to return to their master (**6:23**). Probably because of this good treatment, Aramean raids on Israel stopped for some time. The people of Samaria had solved this conflict by returning good for evil. God was pleased to use this approach to give a time of peace to Israel.

God's positive use of Elisha's statement in 6:19 does not necessarily mean that God approves the use of lies. Rather, it shows that in spite of lies, he watches over his people. Elisha is to be judged within the context of the level of revelation at his time, when what mattered most was the honour of Yahweh and the protection of his people. We cannot take the ethical standards of OT characters such as the midwives in Exodus 1:19, Rahab in Joshua 2:4-7, and Elisha as our standards since we have the full revelation of God. However, one aspect of their behaviour that we can emulate is that they did not act in a spirit of self-centredness but were focused on the honour of God and the welfare of people he loved.

It is also possible that Elisha was not telling a deliberate lie. The first time that the king of Syria had contacted Elisha on behalf of Naaman, he had followed the proper diplomatic channels, writing a letter to the king of Israel. Elisha may have been insisting that the same route must be followed again. It is also true that Elisha's approach was actually the one that was most favourable to the Arameans. Had he told the bare truth and let the Arameans attack him, they would have clashed with the horses and chariots of fire that were already on guard.

6:24-7:2 THE SIEGE OF SAMARIA We do not know how long after the peaceful solution described in 6:22-23 this episode took place. The war between Israel and Aram had resumed, and the army of Ben-Hadad was camped around Samaria, trying to capture the city. People could not go out or come in, and there was great famine (**6:24-25**). Food was so scarce that people were prepared to eat the head of a donkey, even though a donkey was unclean and should not have been eaten (Lev 11:3). Some people were so desperate that they even killed and ate children (**6:26-29**). The king was inspecting the fortifications when he learned of this, but he clearly was not in control and was unable to offer any solution. In despair and grief at what had happened, he tore his robes, revealing that he was wearing sackcloth underneath, probably to express his own humble repentance before the Lord (**6:30**).

The account of cannibalism was the last straw and the king turned on Elisha, swearing to kill him (**6:31-32**). He may have felt that Elisha should have been able to get the Lord to deliver his people before things got this bad, or he may have felt that it was Elisha's bad advice that had led to his predicament. Certainly, he blamed Elisha and Elisha's God for not bringing help, and demanded *Why should I wait for the Lord any longer?* (**6:33**).

But the time of waiting was over, and Elisha had a message from the Lord. Within twenty-four hours the famine would be over and food prices would return to normal (**7:1**).

The king's bodyguard did not believe Elisha and scoffed at his words. So he was told that he would live to see the plenty, but would not enjoy any of it (**7:2**).

7:3-20 THE LIFTING OF THE SIEGE The law of Israel stated that lepers must not be admitted into the camp of Israel (Lev 13:45-46). So during the siege some lepers had taken refuge from the Arameans close to the city walls, but not actually inside the city. They decided that they faced death wherever they were, and with nothing to lose they took the risk of going into the Aramean camp (**7:3-4**). They found it deserted! (**7:5**). What had happened was that the Arameans had heard what they thought was the sound of a great army approaching, with chariots and horses. They knew the Israelites were wily enemies who had often escaped them in the past (6:8-10, 19-20). They began to suspect that they had somehow managed to summon help and that the large armies of the Hittites and the Egyptians were getting ready to attack them from the rear (**7:6**). They fled in terror, leaving all their belongings behind so that there was plenty of

food and money available for the citizens of Samaria (**7:7**). This confusion was brought about by the Lord, who may have sent the same chariots and horses that had protected Elisha (6:17) or who may simply have made the Arameans imagine a noise.

After the starving lepers had eaten and taken supplies for themselves, they realized that they needed to share this good news with those in the city (**7:8-11**). Their news rapidly reached the palace, and the king sent out a reconnaissance party to see if this was merely an attempt to lure them out and ambush them (**7:12-14**). These soldiers returned to inform the king that there was no sight of the Arameans over the many miles between Samaria and the River Jordan, except for equipment that they had dropped as they ran (**7:15**).

The city gates were opened at last and the starving people rushed out to plunder the Aramean camp. In the rush through the gates, the king's unbelieving bodyguard was trampled to death. Thus he saw God's deliverance, but did not share in it (**7:16-20**). Lack of faith prevents people from participating when the Lord does eventually send relief.

8:1-6 RESTORATION OF THE SHUNAMMITE'S FARM This story seems to be a continuation of the earlier story (4:8-41). It probably took place before the incident with Naaman, because Gehazi was not yet a leper. The Shunammite's hospitality to Elisha meant that her family enjoyed easy access to the word of God. Elisha advised them to move away because of a famine that was going to last for seven years (**8:1**). Years earlier, Elimelech and Naomi had gone to Moab in similar circumstances (Ruth 1:1), and now the Shunammite family went to the land of the Philistines, who were not Israelites (**8:2**). At the end of seven years, they returned and had some problem reclaiming their property from others who had taken possession of it. Once again the woman is the main character, as she and her son arrive to ask for the king's help just as Gehazi was telling the king about the miracles Elisha had done and specifically about the raising of the boy from the dead (**8:3-5**). The king spoke to the woman about her experience and restored all her property and the income from her land (**8:6**). Once again, the Lord had met her need.

8:7-15 HAZAEL BECOMES KING OF ARAM When Elijah was at Mount Horeb, the Lord had told him to anoint Hazael as king of Aram (1 Kgs 19:15). Elijah did not get to carry out this instruction before he died. The books of Kings being historical, and all history being selective, the author does not tell us why Elijah did not carry out this instruction. However, we may assume that it was not due to disobedience for we are not told that he was rebuked by the Lord for not having done it.

Consequently, it fell to Elisha to tell Hazael that he would become king. Elisha had travelled to Damascus at a time when King Ben-Hadad was very ill (**8:7**). Ben-Hadad must have come to some belief in the power of the God of

Israel and of Elisha after Naaman's healing, and so when he heard that Elisha was nearby, he sent Hazael, one of his officers, with rich gifts to consult the Lord. His gift of *forty camel loads* of the best products in Damascus was very large for a consultation (**8:8-9**). As shown with Naaman, the costliest gifts from the Lord are always given freely and Elisha could be freely consulted.

The answer that the Lord gave to Elisha was that the king would not die from his illness. But while his illness would not kill him, murder would (**8:10**). Elisha foresaw what Hazael was going to do and all the future evil that Hazael would do to Israel, and he started crying. He did not anoint Hazael, but told him that he would become king of Aram (**8:11-13**). True prophets can see what the Lord had ordained to happen in the course of time. As always, Elisha's prophecy came true. Hazael smothered the king by pressing a wet cloth over his face to cut off his breathing. Hazael then succeeded Ben-Hadad (**8:15**).

8:16-24 Jehoram, King of Judah

Jehoram king of Judah began his reign in the fifth year of Joram king of Israel, about three years before the death of Jehoshaphat his father. His disastrous reign illustrated the truth of the saying that 'bad company corrupts good character' (1 Cor 15:33). Jehoshaphat had long been friendly with the house of Ahab, and Joram, his son, continued this friendship and married Ahab's daughter and Omri's granddaughter, Athaliah (**8:16-18**, 26). This friendship brought no gain to Judah. God had wanted Israel and Judah to be friends at the time when Israel could still be regarded as the covenant people of God (1 Kgs 12:24). But Israel had long since failed to keep its part of the covenant.

Jehoram was an evil king who killed all his brothers, men who were better than he was (2 Chr 21:1-4, 13). He misled Judah into religious prostitution, introducing them to other gods (2 Chr 21:11, 13). During his reign, Judah lost control over Edom and over Libnah. Jehoram barely escaped from the Edomites with his life (**8:20-22**). Not only that, but he lost his goods, his wives and his sons to attacking Arabs and Philistines (2 Chr 21:16-17). Only Ahaziah his son escaped capture, along with his mother Athaliah. When Jehoram died, Ahaziah succeeded him (**8:23-24**).

8:25-29 Ahaziah, King of Judah

Ahaziah became king of Judah on the death of his father Jehoram. He reigned for only one year and did evil before the Lord (**8:25-27**). He was no doubt influenced by his mother Athaliah, the daughter of Ahab, who brought bad influences to Jerusalem and Judah. Ahaziah is said to have *walked in the ways of the house of Ahab*, meaning that Baal worship was introduced to Judah and the king was serving Baal in Jerusalem (8:26-27). The two kingdoms now were living as

brothers, which is why Ahaziah went to Jezreel to greet his uncle Joram who was seriously wounded (**8:28-29**).

9:1-10:36 Jehu, King of Israel

9:1-13 Anointing of Jehu

Elijah had been instructed to anoint Jehu as king of Israel (1 Kgs 19:16), but that task was delegated to Elisha, who did not carry it out in person. Instead the ageing Elisha sent another prophet with instructions to anoint Jehu and to run away immediately afterwards (**9:1-3**). (Note that this Jehu is not the same person as the prophet of that name who had prophesied against Baasha in 1 Kings 16:1-4.)

The young prophet found Jehu at Ramoth Gilead, where he had been left in command of the army after Joram was wounded (**9:4-5**; see also 8:28-29). He took Jehu aside from the other officers and hurriedly anointed him king over Israel, while instructing him to carry out the prophesied destruction of the house of Ahab (**9:6-10**). When the other officers heard of what the prophet had done, they spread their clothes on the ground for Jehu to walk on and blew the trumpet as they proclaimed him king of Israel (**9:11-13**).

Jehu was following in the footsteps of Omri, who had also been an army commander who rose to power with the support of the army (1 Kgs 16:16). The enthusiasm with which the other officers greeted Jehu as king suggested that they were not happy with the way Joram was reigning.

9:14-29 Jehu kills Joram and Ahaziah

While Jehu was being proclaimed king at Ramoth Gilead, Joram was in Jezreel receiving treatment for his wounds and entertaining his nephew Ahaziah, king of Judah. Jehu's first concern was to prevent the king from hearing what had happened and to carry out the prophecy. He thus got into his chariot and set out for Jezreel (**9:14-16**).

When the two kings saw troops in the distance, they were nervous and tried to find out what was going on. Were the approaching troops friends or enemies of Israel? (**9:17-19**). Eventually, they recognized Jehu and set out to meet him to hear what news was bringing him from the battle in such haste (**9:21a**). They had not heard that the officers of Israel's army had accepted Jehu as king. Jehu and the two kings met at a place with ominous memories for any descendant of Ahab – the farm that had belonged to Naboth (**9:21b; 25b-26**; see also 1 Kgs 21:19, 29).

Jehu's answer to Joram's greeting revealed his treachery, and the kings tried to flee. Joram was killed instantly and his body was thrown on the farm of Naboth in Jezreel (**9:25a**). Ahaziah, who was also a descendent of Ahab through his mother, was pursued and seriously wounded. He escaped to Megiddo where he died (**9:27-28**). Those who associate with evil people suffer with them.

9:30-37 Death of Jezebel

Jehu went on to Jezreel, where Jezebel the queen mother was still alive. She knew what was coming, and put on a brave face (**9:30**). As Jehu entered the city gate, she insulted him by calling him *Zimri*, recalling the earlier rebel whose reign had survived a mere seven days (1 Kgs 16:9-20) and who had been overthrown by her husband's father, Omri (**9:31**).

Jezebel was thrown down from the wall (**9:32-33**). Dogs devoured her and she did not receive the burial due to a king's daughter and a queen mother (**9:34-37**). The word of the Lord against Jezebel was fulfilled (see 1 Kgs 21:23).

Jehu showed no pity as he killed Ahab's son, Jezebel and the rest of Ahab's family. Their deaths illustrate the truth that we reap what we sow (Gal 6:7). We need to remember that God will not show mercy to us on the day of judgment. The time to receive mercy is now, before the axe of judgment is applied to the root of every tree that bears no fruit (Matt 3:8-10).

10:1-17 Killing of Ahab's family

After Joram had been killed, Jehu wrote a letter to the elders and officials in Samaria, challenging them to appoint one of the king's sons as king of Israel and then to meet him in a battle (**10:1-3**). The officials in Samaria knew how powerful Jehu was and were afraid to take this step. Instead they submitted to Jehu (**10:4-5**). As a peace settlement, Jehu demanded that they present the heads of the seventy sons of the king, meaning the heads of all male descendants of Ahab, for the instructions in 9:7 were to destroy the house of Ahab completely. So all the king's sons were beheaded and their heads were sent to Jezreel in baskets the following day. Jehu left these heads piled outside the gate overnight to be seen by everyone (**10:6-8**).

In his speech the next morning, Jehu acknowledged that he had killed the king, but claimed to be innocent of the deaths of the princes. He insisted that he had nothing to do with their deaths! Rather, it was a fulfilment of prophecy (**10:9-10**). But Jehu went much further than God commanded. He killed all the friends, priests and leaders who were close to Ahab (**10:11**) and also massacred some forty relatives of Ahaziah who had not heard about the revolt and who were arriving to visit Jezebel and Joram (**10:12-14**). God was displeased about this, as is clear from Hosea 1:4. Disobedience does not only involve failure to do what God commands, but can mean going beyond it. When that happens, we become our own masters rather than following the Lord's instructions.

One man who was an eyewitness to some of Jehu's murders was Jehonadab son of Recab, whom Jehu welcomed into his chariot (**10:15-16**). Jeremiah refers to this man as 'our forefather' (Jer 35:6). He seems to have been a prophet among his people, the Recabites, who were the descendants of someone called Hamath (1 Chr 2:55). They were a Jewish sect who did not build houses but lived in tents, drank no wine, and did not plant vineyards or keep gardens. They viewed the simplicity of their lifestyle as springing from their devotion to Yahweh (Jer 35:6-10, 18-19).

Clearly, Israel and Judah had begun to come together as one people with a common origin, but the Lord of the covenant had not been at the centre of their union.

10:18-36 Destruction of followers of Baal

Having completed the destruction of the house of Ahab, Jehu turned his attention to those who worshipped Baal. He pretended to be a worshipper of Baal, and summoned the priests and prophets of Baal from all over Israel to Samaria for a great sacrifice (**10:18-20**). So these priests and prophets assembled to worship Baal and put on their special robes. Jehu reminded them to make sure that only those who served Baal were present – there must be no doubt of the god to whom they owed allegiance (**10:21-23**). Jehu offered a burnt offering to Baal, and then he turned on the priests and ordered his troops who were stationed around the temple for this purpose, to kill them all (**10:24-25**). The Hebrew word for 'sacrifice' also carries the idea of 'slaughter', and both happened on this occasion The temple of Baal was destroyed and its property desecrated. It was turned into a public latrine (**10:26-27**).

It is not easy to say how much Jehu's action contributed to any reduction in the worship of Baal. Jehu himself appears to have enjoyed the destruction. He was not completely devoted to the Lord and did not put an end to the worship of the golden calves that Jeroboam had erected (**10:28-29, 31**).

The Lord did, however, reward Jehu for having carried out his instructions in regard to the house of Ahab. He was promised that four generations of his own house would rule in Samaria (**10:30**). Yet because of the continuing sinfulness of Israel, God allowed portions of Israel to fall under the control of other nations. All the territory east of the Jordan came under the rule of Aram (**10:32-33**).

Jehu reigned over Israel for twenty-eight years and was succeeded by his son Jehoahaz (**10:34-36**).

11:1-12:21 Joash, King of Judah

11:1-21 Athaliah and Joash

The close association between the house of Jehoshaphat and the family of Ahab had resulted in a marriage between their children. Jehoram the son of Jehoshaphat married Athaliah, the daughter of Ahab and Jezebel (8:18). Their son was Ahaziah, who succeeded Jehoram but within a year was killed by Jehu. Jehu seized the throne of Samaria, but the throne of Judah was vacant. So Athaliah, the queen mother in Judah, proceeded to kill all her grandchildren and took the throne herself (**11:1**). We know little about her six-year reign, but there must have been a lot of unhappiness during that period judging by how her overthrow was welcomed.

If Athaliah's plan had been successful, she would have eradicated the line of David. But the Lord had promised to keep the sons of David on the throne of Judah (8:19). So Jehosheba, the sister of Ahaziah, somehow got wind of the plan and had just enough time to steal away Ahaziah's son Joash, who was only one year old. Jehosheba was the wife of Jehoiada the priest (2 Chr 22:11). Joash was hidden away in the temple under the charge of his nurse and not his rightful mother lest the secret be discovered (**11:2-3**).

Jehoiada the priest must have known of this throughout the six years that Athaliah was on the throne and must have been planning prayerfully as he carried on with his ordinary duties. This story is one where the people of God did what they believed to be best in the course of their normal everyday work. God was working even in the ordinary but secret plans of his people.

When Joash was seven (**11:21**), Jehoiada swore the commanders of various units of guards to secrecy and then revealed that Joash had survived the massacre (**11:4**). Then he revealed his plan for installing him as king. Even the guards who were not officially on duty would be armed and at the temple that Sabbath for a coronation (**11:5-11**). They were issued with the *spears and shields that had belonged to King David* (11:10) as a visual reminder to the people that David's house still lived on.

That Sabbath, Jehoiada presided over a two-part coronation ceremony. In the first part, the king's son was brought out, a crown was put on him, he was given a copy of the covenant and was proclaimed king. Then he was anointed. The people celebrated by clapping their hands and shouting *Long live the king!* (**11:12**). The copy of the covenant must have been a copy of the most official document kept in the temple in the custody of the priests, and must have contained the covenant of the Lord for the people and the king. The giving of such a document to the king is prescribed in Deuteronomy 17:18-20.

At this stage, the proceedings were interrupted by the arrival of Athaliah, who had heard the commotion and came to investigate it. The scene she witnessed sounds similar to the one that accompanied the crowning of Solomon (1 Kgs 1:34-35). At Solomon's coronation, there had been no temple, but by now the custom has developed that the new king should stand by one of the great pillars that Solomon had erected before the temple (1 Kgs 7:15-22). Athaliah's cry of *Treason* did not elicit any help from her guards. So Jehoiada, in full command of the situation, ordered that Athaliah be led out of the temple and put to death outside (**11:13-16**).

The second part of the coronation ceremony involved the renewing of the covenant between the Lord, the king and the people (**11:17**). The people were reminded *that they would be the Lord's people* who belonged to the Lord and served him, and who thus had certain rights and respon-

sibilities to the Lord and the king. The king, too, made a covenant to serve the Lord and his people.

Once the covenant had been renewed, all the people went and tore down the temple of Baal. They destroyed all the idols and the altars to false gods and killed the priest of Baal (**11:18**). Athaliah would have encouraged worship of these foreign gods, but once a people have decided to serve the Lord, they must destroy the idols and symbols of their former religion. Those things must be permanently put away so that they do not draw people back to false religion.

Finally, the king was escorted from the temple to the palace to take up the royal throne (**11:19**). The people were liberated from the reign of Athaliah and *the city was quiet* (**11:20**). It was a time of happiness and relief as Jerusalem was again at peace and free from Athaliah's threats.

12:1-16 Joash repairs the temple

Joash is formally introduced in 12:1-3. It is clear that Athaliah's six-year reign was regarded as an interruption and not a continuation of the rule of the house of David. The writer of Kings does not evaluate her period of rule in Jerusalem in the same way as he does that of other rulers. There can be little doubt that her reign represented a period of testing of those who were true worshippers of the Lord.

Joash was one of the longest reigning kings of Judah and, at seven, the youngest to ascend the throne (Josiah, his descendent, would be eight years old at the start of his reign – 22:1). For such a young boy to hold onto power, the royal administrators and palace and religious officers must have been very loyal and committed to working together. They were people who believed and did the will of the God of Israel, and made sure that wise decisions were made and wise policies adopted. It is clear that the spirit in Jerusalem and Judah was very different from that in Samaria and Israel, where kings were regularly overthrown. The credit for this smooth reign must be given to the high priest Jehoiada, who was the spiritual and political power behind the throne. He instructed the young king (**12:2**). Because he was so young, the king was still able to be taught to do what was right in the Lord's eyes.

Since the time of Solomon, the temple had been emptied of its treasures several times and had fallen into disrepair. Joash ordered that steps be taken to repair it. The money for this would come from a head tax, from personal vows and from voluntary offerings (**12:4**). But fifteen years after he came to the throne, by which time Joash was twenty-three years old, no progress had been made (**12:5-6**). The money was not being spent in the way he intended (**12:7-8**).

Joash did not give up because of this setback. Instead he set up a system to ensure that all the money collected went into the building fund, and that two senior administrators, namely the royal secretary and the high priest, counted it when it came in and oversaw payments to the workmen and suppliers (**12:9-12**). They made sure that the money was not spent on utensils and equipment for the temple but on structural repairs (**12:13-14**). They also made sure that all the workmen who were employed were completely trustworthy so that they did not need to keep extremely detailed accounts. The work was seen to be carried out *with complete honesty* so that there were no grounds for suspicion (**12:15**).

Complete honesty should always be the mark of the people of God. The care taken to set up a system that would make it impossible for anyone to pilfer money and that would ensure honest work is in keeping with the principle that the people of God must be able to give an account of whatever has been entrusted to them. Paul showed a similar concern to avoid any possibility of accusations of fraud when he made the arrangements to deliver the churches' gifts to Jerusalem (see 1 Cor 16:3).

The system also made sure that sufficient money remained for the priests' needs. They received whatever was brought as guilt and sin offerings.

12:17-21 The reign of Joash

Joash's reign was not all peaceful. Hazael of Aram captured Gath and attacked Jerusalem. Joash bought him off by giving him all the treasures in the temple and the palace (**12:17-18**). More information is given about Joash in 2 Chronicles 24, from which it appears that he listened to bad advice after the death of the high priest Jehoiada. He went astray into idol worship, which was why God allowed this attack.

After forty years on the throne, Joash was assassinated by some of his officials, and his son Amaziah took the throne (**12:19-21**).

13:1-9 Jehoahaz, King of Israel

Jehoahaz of Israel began to rule in the twenty-third year of Joash of Judah. He followed the religious traditions of his fathers – the sins of Jeroboam (**13:2**). The Lord was not happy with Israel and so he allowed Hazael and Ben-Hadad of Aram to overpower them to such an extent that many of the Israelites fled their homes (**13:3, 5b**). Their army was reduced to only ten chariots, fifty horsemen and ten thousand foot soldiers (**13:7**). The number of foot soldiers was similar to what it had been in Ahab's day (1 Kgs 20:15), but the ten chariots compare poorly with the 1400 chariots that Solomon commanded (1 Kgs 10:26) and even to the thirty-two that the Arameans commanded in the battle where Ahab died (1 Kgs 22:31). Israel suffered at the hand of Hazael throughout the reign of Jehoahaz. The only reason the nation was not destroyed was because of the covenant of the Lord with their ancestors Abraham, Isaac and Jacob (**13:22-23**).

As in the days of Judges, Israel must have found that the Baals were useless. Jehoahaz now sought the Lord and the Lord listened to him and even provided a saviour for Israel

(**13:4-5a**). Those who humble themselves and wholeheartedly seek the Lord will find that he responds. The name of the saviour and what he did are not mentioned. It is possible that the Lord led some other power to attack Aram on a different border, and so provided some relief for Israel. Once again the Israelites were able to sleep in their own homes, but the threat of Aram remained throughout Jehoahaz' seventeen-year reign. On his death, he was succeeded by his son Jehoash (**13:8-9**).

13:10-25 Jehoash, King of Israel and Elisha's Death

Jehoash succeeded his father Jehoahaz in Israel. He did not please the Lord. The writer of Kings would have ended his account of the history of this reign at **13:13** were it not for the meeting between Jehoash and Elisha.

By this time, Elisha would have been a very old man. He was near death when Jehoash went to greet him and lament his coming death, which marked the closing of the major channel that God had used to communicate with Israel. Jehoash must have remembered how Elisha's visions and spiritual intelligence had kept Israel informed and saved them from the attacks of Aram (6:8-10). Now, in words similar to those Elisha himself had used when Elijah was taken away into heaven, Jehoash laments the desperate state of Israel's army, which had been reduced to almost nothing by Hazael.

Elisha took the king to a window and asked him to shoot an arrow. As the king obeyed the prophet, the action was interpreted as predicting the victory of the Lord (**13:17**). Small acts of humble faith and obedience result in victory in great things

Elisha next gave an open-ended instruction. The king was to take arrows and strike the ground. He struck the ground three times, believing that three defeats of an enemy should make the victory complete. Elisha had expected that the king would strike more often, up to six times, which would have signalled the complete destruction of the Arameans (**13:18-19**). Sometimes the Lord allows future events to depend on the action or non-action of human beings. People's actions can thus sometimes shape the present and the future.

Elisha's final prophecies were fulfilled as Jehoash defeated the Arameans three times and recaptured some towns that had been taken from his father (**13:25**).

Elisha's death was not as dramatic as that of Elijah, for he died in his bed and was buried (**13:20**). But the power of the Lord still resided in his bones, as is evident from the incident recorded in **13:21**. This miracle must have occurred some years after his death to allow time for the body of Elisha to decompose and the bones to become exposed.

14:1-22 Amaziah, King of Judah

Amaziah is introduced as a good king, but not as good as his ancestor David. Like his father Joash, he took no action against the high places where sacrifices and incense were offered to other gods (**14:1-4**). His obedience to the law is underlined by the fact that while he executed those who had assassinated his father Joash, he spared their children (**14:5-6**; see Deut 24:16).

Amaziah also defeated Edom, although it is not clear whether Edom then came under the power of Judah (**14:7**). However, after the defeat Amaziah started worshipping the idols he had captured from Edom (2 Chr 25:14). The campaign against Edom also resulted in increased tension between Israel and Judah, as Amaziah initially hired one hundred thousand troops from Israel and then sent them home before the battle, on the advice of a Judean prophet. The mercenaries were angry and took out their anger on some Judean towns (2 Chr 25:6-13).

Amaziah's invitation to Jehoash of Israel *come meet me face to face* (**14:8**) may have been intended to provide an opportunity to discuss the bad relationship, or it may have been a declaration of war. Certainly, Jehoash assumed the latter and sent back an insulting reply advising Amaziah to remain at home in Judah and not allow his victories over Edom to lead him into trouble (**14:9-10**). Israel must have regained some of its military strength and was no longer in the condition described in 13:7.

In the ensuing war, Israel defeated Judah at Beth Shemesh. Amaziah was captured. Jehoash marched against Jerusalem and broke down about six hundred feet (one hundred and eighty metres) of the city wall. He took away what was left of the temple treasures and the royal treasures, as well as captives, and returned to Samaria (**14:11-14**). After these achievements, Jehoash died and was succeeded in Samaria by his son, Jeroboam II (**14:15-16**).

Amaziah continued to rule in Jerusalem for fifteen years after the death of Jehoash (**14:17**). Things were not easy. Eventually, for reasons we are not told, a conspiracy against him led him to flee to the strong city of Lachish, where he was killed (**14:18-19**). The kingdom of Judah was not as turbulent as that of Israel, and thus David's dynasty continued, with the king's sixteen-year-old son Azariah (Uzziah – Isa 1:1; 6:1) taking the throne rather than the conspirators (**14:20-21**). *All the people of Judah* welcomed him as king.

14:23-29 Jeroboam II of Israel

The longest reigning king of Israel was Jeroboam II, the son of Jehoash, who ruled Israel for forty-one years. Jeroboam II did not do anything different in religious matters from the other kings of Israel (**14:23-24**). But he did produce substantial political and military achievements by restoring the borders of Israel from Lebo Hamath in the north to the Dead Sea (**14:25**). These successes had been prophesied by

Jonah the son of Amittai, the same prophet who was sent to Nineveh.

The Lord was merciful to Israel because he saw the suffering of the people in spite of the fact that there was no evidence of repentance (**14:26**). He had not yet pronounced his final words of judgment (**14:27**). Sometimes the Lord shows mercy to his people for a long time for no other reason than that he is a gracious God. Such times should be used to set things right and to bring people to repentance.

15:1-7 Azariah, King of Judah

Azariah has already been introduced briefly in 14:21-22. He came to the throne at the young age of sixteen and ruled for fifty-two years – the second-longest reign of any of the kings of Judah (Manasseh would have the longest reign). Azariah was a good king, although the high places were still used as alternative places of worship (**15:1-4**). He was successful politically, although the only one of his achievements mentioned in Kings is that he rebuilt Elath, a town on the north-east corner of the Gulf of Aqabah (14:22). More details of his reign are given in 2 Chronicles 26, where his name is spelled Uzziah. He was instructed by Zechariah (not the prophet who wrote the book of Zechariah, but possibly a descendent of the Zechariah who was the son of Jehoida (2 Chr 24:20), the high priest who had protected the young Joash. 'As long as he sought the Lord, God gave him success' (2 Chr 26:5). Fearing, respecting and seeking the will of the Lord brings success.

Azariah trained and maintained a strong army and supplied it with the latest equipment (2 Chr 26:11-15). He regained lost lands for Judah and rebuilt many places (2 Chr 26:3-11). But eventually his pride led him to attempt to perform a role reserved for priests and like Saul (1 Sam 13:8-13) he was punished. Azariah's punishment was to be afflicted with leprosy (**15:5**; see also 2 Chr 26:16-21). Because of this disease, he had to live apart *in a separate house* while his son Jotham took charge of the day-to-day affairs of government, but with the advice and strong direction of Azariah. The situation was similar to that when Solomon began his reign, and could still consult his father David.

Judah lost a great achiever when Azariah died (**15:6-7**), and the nation may have feared for the future after so many years under one ruler. It is thus significant that it was 'in the year that King Uzziah died' that Isaiah saw the Lord, still seated 'high and exalted' on the throne that would not pass away (Isa 6:1).

15:8-31 Upheavals in Israel

While Judah was enjoying a period of stability under the reign of King Azariah, things were very different in the northern kingdom of Israel. Within a period of just seven months, two kings were assassinated. The manner in which power changed hands in that kingdom inevitably caused internal conflict resulting in hostility and disloyalty, so that the kingdom was greatly weakened. The prophet Hosea complained that Israel 'set up kings without my consent, they choose princes without my approval' (Hos 8:4). These kings neither knew nor followed the law of the Lord as set out in Deuteronomy 17:15, and the leaders and the advisers of Israel were without foresight. Where there is no fear of the Lord, people cannot plan and take action with proper foresight.

15:8-12 Zechariah, king of Israel

Zechariah succeeded his father Jeroboam II, and like his father, he worshipped the calves at Bethel and Dan (**15:8-9**). He reigned for a mere six months before he was assassinated by Shallum *in front of the people.* His death marked the fulfilment of the prophecy to Jehu that *'Your descendants will sit on the throne to the fourth generation'* (**15:10-12**; see 10:30). Prophecies of judgment in Israel were often carried out in brutal ways.

15:13-15 Shallum, king of Israel

Shallum's assassination of the son of a powerful and competent ruler like Jeroboam must have aroused much public anger. Shallum seized the throne (15:10) but managed to hold on to it for only one month before he in turn was assassinated by Menahem (**15:13-15**).

15:16-22 Menahem, king of Israel

Menahem imposed his rule, showing great cruelty to anyone who opposed him (**15:16**). For the ten years of his rule, he continued in the traditional sin of Israel (**15:17-18**).

In the first sign of the coming fate of Israel, the Assyrians under King Pul, who is also known as Tiglath-Pileser, invaded the land. Rather than opposing him, Menahem paid him a tribute of about thirty-four tons (thirty-one tonnes) of silver by exacting this money from the wealthy. In return for this Pul recognized him as the ruler of the region and withdrew his troops (**15:19-20**).

On his death, Menahem was succeeded by his son Pekahiah (**15:21-22**).

15:23-26 Pekahiah, king of Israel

Pekahiah reigned for only two years, during which he did not please the Lord (**15:23-24**). He too was assassinated by one of his officers, a man called Pekah (**15:25-26**). This assassination took place in the year that King Azariah of Judah died after fifty-two years on the throne. It is no wonder that the people of Judah, including Isaiah, were nervous about the future with a new king on their own throne, a new enemy to the north, and Assyria preparing to attack.

15:27-31 Pekah, king of Israel

Pekah did not do what was good before the Lord (**15:27-28**). The Lord allowed Tiglath-Pileser to take many towns in Galilee and Transjordan and to deport their inhabitants to Assyria (**15:29**). Isaiah refers to this deportation and to a separate attack on Jerusalem by Pekah (Isa 7:1).

Hoshea son of Elah probably thought be could manage the affairs of the land better in the face of the attack of Assyria because he was fond of diplomatic intrigue (see 17:4). So he assassinated Pekah and took the throne (**15:30-31**).

15:32-38 Jotham, King of Judah

Jotham's reign must have started while his father was still alive but suffering from leprosy. His mother was the daughter of Zadok, implying that she had some link to the priestly family (**15:32-33**). Jotham must have had good advisers, for he continued the good work of his father. *He did what was right in the eyes of the Lord* (**15:34**). The high places were, however, not removed. People continued to offer sacrifices and burn incense there. He also *rebuilt the Upper Gate of the temple of the Lord,* an addition to the building done by his father (**15:35**; 2 Chr 26:9).

During Jotham's reign, Pekah of Israel and Rezin of Aram formed an alliance against Judah (**15:37**). It is surprising that the Lord would send them against Judah at this time when Judah was closer to the Lord than those nations were. The ways of the Lord are beyond our understanding and sometimes the Lord permits such evil to happen so that his people will cry out and come closer to him. In a similar situation, Habakkuk prophesied that the just have to live by their faith in God (Hab 2:4).

On Jotham's death, he was succeeded by his son Ahaz (**15:36, 38**).

16:1-20 Ahaz, King of Judah

We do not know who was the mother of Ahaz the son of Jotham, but it is clear that he was influenced by evil people. He was the complete opposite of his ancestor David and did even worse things than Athaliah had done (**16:1-2**). He went so far as to sacrifice his son with fire, *following the detestable ways of the Canaanites* who had done this before Israel was given the land. God had strictly forbidden such sacrifices (**16:3**; Deut 18:10-12). He worshipped freely wherever he wanted to, in the high places, on hilltops and in forested places (**16:4**). The writer of Kings does not specifically state that the Lord was angry with him and with Judah, but the events that follow show the extent of the Lord's anger (see also 2 Chr 28).

Rezin and Pekah, who had started to harass Judah during the reign of Ahaz father's, now stepped up their attack (**16:5-6**). The two nations were in alliance against Assyria and may have wanted Judah to join them (2 Chr 28). For unknown reasons, Ahaz may not have been willing to do so. They defeated Judah and took many of its people captive, although these captives were later allowed to return after a prophet rebuked the people of Israel (2 Chr 28:8-15). Judah was being humbled by the Lord and many of its towns were in the hands of its enemies

Isaiah 7:1-6 shows that the people of Judah and their king were terrified as the joint forces of Rezin and Pekah approached Jerusalem. The two kings had threatened to replace Ahaz with a son of Tabeel. Isaiah encouraged Ahaz to trust in the Lord and not to seek the help of any foreign powers. But Ahaz refused to listen. In a desperate move, he sent messengers to Tiglath-Pileser, the king of Assyria, offering to serve him if he would come to his rescue. He again emptied the temple and the palace of their treasures in an attempt to buy this support (**16:7-8**). Assyria agreed and attacked Damascus, the capital of Aram, forcing Rezin to break off the attack on Judah. In the ensuing conflict, Rezin, the king of Aram, was killed (**16:9**).

Ahaz then went to meet the king of Assyria, his new overlord, in Damascus. While there, he admired an Assyrian altar and sent plans for such an altar back to Uriah the priest, who had it constructed before Ahaz returned to Jerusalem (**16:10-11**). The king ordered that this Assyrian altar should replace the original bronze altar made in the days of Solomon. The old altar would be moved to the side and used only for *seeking guidance,* that is, for special consultation of the God of Israel by the king alone (**16:12-15**). His actions are a sign of real confusion, for the law of the God of Israel forbids the worship of other gods (Exod 20:2-6; Deut 6:4). But Ahaz had become a worshipper of many gods and saw the God of Israel as just one among many alternatives. He worshipped at the Assyrian altar because he thought that the gods worshipped in Assyria must be stronger than the Lord God of Israel (2 Chr 28:23). His failure to keep the law and to worship the living God exposed him to trying many gods. To make matters worse, he had a priest who agreed with him in every move against the Lord (**16:16**).

Ahaz made many other changes in the temple. He removed the basins and the gigantic Sea from their rightful places and designated stands (**16:17-18**). No reasons are given for the changes except to show how far the king had gone from the covenant Lord of Israel. The removal of the Sabbath canopy and the royal gateway to the temple show that Ahaz himself had become distant from the Lord.

When Ahaz died, he was succeeded by his son Hezekiah (**16:19-20**).

17:1-41 The Fall of Samaria

17:1-6 Hoshea, king of Israel

The royal houses of Israel, the northern kingdom, had never been stable and the kingdom had been plagued by assassi-

nations and changes in leadership. The last king to occupy the throne, Hoshea, also gained power by assassinating his predecessor (15:30). Hoshea was not considered to be as evil as *the kings of Israel who preceded him* (**17:1-2**). This is not to say that he sought the Lord in any particular way or carried out any religious reforms to return Israel to the Lord of the covenant.

Menahem paid tribute to Assyria (15:19), and much of the land had been seized by Tiglath-Pileser in Pekah's day (15:29). Hoshea was supposed to continue paying tribute to the next Assyrian king, Shalmaneser, but he eventually decided to make an attempt to free himself from this by entering into an alliance with Egypt. Shalmaneser moved to put down this rebellion, and Egypt did nothing to help. Hoshea was put in prison (**17:3-4**). It is not clear whether he was imprisoned before or after the three-year siege of Samaria (**17:5**). When the city fell to the Assyrians, many Israelites were deported and settled in lands far from Palestine, in what is today northern Iraq and Iran (**17:6**). Politically, Israel was no more. Religiously, too, the Israelites seem to have vanished. They had rejected God for so many years that they had no faith in the living God to take with them into the land of exile.

17:7-23 Explanation of Israel's fate

Hoshea was the last king of Israel and Samaria. After him, the Israelites were taken into exile and ceased to exist as a nation with their own king and in a covenant with the Lord God of Israel. They had tested the patience and the kindness of the Lord for too long, and so he finally thrust them out of the land, as he had threatened long before (Deut 28:58-65).

The author of Kings now explains why this terrible fate has befallen the chosen people whom the Lord had brought out of Egypt (**17:7**). The Lord had made a covenant with them. This covenant was an agreement that Israel would belong to and worship God alone, and in return God would bless and protect them as a special nation belonging to him alone. Because of this covenant, God had driven other nations out of the land of Canaan so that the Israelites could settle there (**17:8**). These other nations were driven out because of their evil and ungodly customs (Deut 18:12), but instead of adopting good and godly customs, Israel drifted into worshipping other gods and idols just like the people they had displaced. Israel ceased to worship God alone (**17:9-12**).

The Lord had fulfilled his side of the covenant. He encouraged his people to keep theirs, sending prophets to Israel and Judah to point out their sin and call them back to their God to keep his laws and commandments (**17:13**). But the people had refused to listen (**17:14**). They had chosen to worship *worthless idols* and had *themselves become worthless* (**17:15**; see also Ps 115:8). Those who reject the living

God to worship man-made idols do eventually become fools in the process, for the Lord gives them up to chase after wind (Rom 1:21-25).

A key element in Israel's departure from the Lord was the making of the calves in the reign of Jeroboam I (**17:16**; see 1 Kgs 12:28-30). This marked a separation not just from Jerusalem and Judah but also from the covenant Lord of all Israel. The calves and the setting up of an Asherah pole broke the first and second commandments (Exod 20:3-6). Departure from these basics developed into sorcery, divination and human sacrifice. They *sold themselves,* meaning that they knowingly and willingly gave themselves to do evil (**17:17**).

While God is a God of love (1 John 4:16), he does become angry with those who know his laws but refuse to obey them. No one can stand his fierce anger that burns like fire (Nah 1:6). No one can stand in God's day of judgment (Rev 6:17). So God removed the nation of Israel *from his presence,* leaving them to the idols that could not save (**17:18**). *Only the tribe of Judah was left.* But Judah adopted the same practices as the Israelites, and their fate would be the same as that of their brothers (**17:19-20**).

The writer concludes this theological review with a brief summary of what he has said (**17:21-23**).

17:24-41 New settlers in the land

It was Assyrian policy to deport conquered people from their own native lands and resettle them in foreign lands. This policy reduced the chances of rebellions. They adopted the same policy in Israel, and resettled the land with captives from other nations that they had conquered (**17:24**). The depopulation of the countryside probably meant that wildlife thrived, and the Lord allowed lions to attack the new settlers (**17:25**). The king of Assyria attributed this to a lack of knowledge of the local god, and so he sent one of the captive Israelite priests back to teach the settlers the ways of the Lord. This must have been a futile effort, a case of the blind leading the blind (**17:26-28**). The result was that instead of these settlers learning to serve the Lord, as he may have intended when he sent the lions, they chose to serve him and their traditional gods (**17:29-33**). They thus ignored the heart of the covenant law, summarized in 17:34-41 (see Exod 20:2-4; Deut 6:4).

While these settlers introduced their gods to Israel, those who had been deported from Israel cannot be said to have carried any good things of the Lord to the places they were resettled. They had lost the faith of their ancestors and had already parted ways with Yahweh the Lord God of Israel.

Many today in Africa are familiar with the experience of being forced out of their country against their will. Unlike the Israelites, however, the displaced in Africa take their culture and religious faith with them. Those who have been given opportunities to minister in the churches of their host countries have been a source of much blessing.

The words of **17:39,** *worship the Lord your God; it is he who will deliver you from the hand of all your enemies,* stand true for all people all over the world for all generations.

2 Kgs 18:1-25:30 The Kings of Judah until the Exile

18:1-20:21 Hezekiah

18:1-16 Hezekiah's faithfulness

Hezekiah became king over Judah at the age of twenty-five. He was very different from his father Ahaz, who had certainly not served the Lord (16:10-18). Ahaz had been more interested in pleasing the Assyrians and had made many changes in the temple to impress them. One would expect that with such a father, Hezekiah would have been influenced to do worse things. His mother, Abijah, must have been a God-fearing woman who taught him about the covenant God of Israel (**18:1-2**). Other servants of the Lord must also have helped to bring up this prince in the fear of the Lord. They included the prophet Isaiah (19:2) and Micah of Moresheth, who uttered warnings to which Hezekiah listened (Jer 26:18-19).

Hezekiah receives praise that is equal only to that of King Asa (1 Kgs 15:11). He did what was right in the eyes of his God, just like David his ancestor (**18:3**). More than that, he trusted the God of Israel wholeheartedly. No past or future king of Israel followed the Lord as he did (**18:5-6**). His religious reforms led him to remove the high places (**18:4**). The sacred stones and the Asherah poles were destroyed. Hezekiah even destroyed the bronze serpent that Moses had made many years before (Num 21:8-9). This bronze serpent was a reminder of God's salvation, but snakes are symbols of cultic forces in many cultures, and so the serpent had become an object of worship. Hezekiah ruthlessly destroyed it, calling it *Nehushtan,* a word that simply means 'that thing of brass'. The removal of so many places of worship would have helped the people of Judah to focus their undivided faith on the God of Israel.

Hezekiah's actions remind us that while it is good to have presentable church buildings furnished with objects that remind us of God's goodness, we must avoid anything that can distract people from keeping their eyes on God alone. Today, the distraction often comes not so much from material objects as from an undue focus on a person, such as the founder of a church, the charismatic leader of a congregation, or some other person of influence. But God must remain at the centre if there is to be true worship.

Because of Hezekiah's relationship with God, the Lord was with him. He had success in whatever he did (**18:7a**). The presence and blessings of the Lord strengthen the faith of a believer to attempt higher things. One of the things in which Hezekiah was successful was the same thing that had brought destruction on Israel under Hoshea: he refused to pay tribute to Assyria (**18:7b**; compare 17:4-6). Whereas Ahaz's troops had been defeated by the Philistines (2 Chr 28:18-19), Hezekiah defeated the Philistines as far as Gaza (**18:8**). Because that area was also under the control of Assyria, attacking it would mark Hezekiah as a rebel.

The danger of Hezekiah's policy is underlined by the repetition in **18:9-12** of the information about the fate of Israel already given in 17:3-6. Assyria was a world power, and it was dangerous to oppose it. With Israel scattered and deported by Shalmaneser, his successor Sennacherib now had an open route to Judah. He captured all the strong cities of Judah, and Hezekiah had to apologize and request a peaceful settlement (**18:13-14**). He was expected to pay a heavy fine for his rebellion, and to meet it took all the silver and gold from the temple and the royal treasury and even the gold on the temple doors (**18:16**).

18:17-37 Sennacherib threatens Jerusalem

The events recounted in the next few chapters are also recorded in Isaiah 36–39.

It appears that Hezekiah's payments to Sennacherib must have been inadequate, or he may have rebelled in some other way. Certainly, he did not throw open the gates of Jerusalem to the advancing Assyrians. Nor did he go to meet the great ruler, as his father Ahaz had done (16:10). So from his base in Lachish, Sennacherib sent three of his top officers *with a large army* in a show of force to terrify Hezekiah and make him surrender (**18:17**). The three officers met with three officials from Jerusalem to deliver Sennacherib's message (**18:18**). The Assyrian officers delivered their messages speaking loudly in Hebrew. They were questioning the reasons why Hezekiah refused to submit to Assyria (**18:19-20**). They warned him that it was foolish to hope that Egypt would help him, for Egypt was not strong enough and disappointed those who trusted in it (**18:21**). Was Hezekiah depending on the God of Israel? Sennacherib thought no help would come from that source because Hezekiah had removed so many places where he was worshipped (**18:22**). To unbelievers, Hezekiah's reforms simply meant that less worship was being offered. They failed to realize that the Lord is not interested in the amount of outward show in worship and sacrifices. What he really wants from the faithful is broken, humble, repentant hearts (Ps 51:17), not dozens of sacrifices to many idols.

The officer's third argument was an attempt to persuade Judah's army not to follow Hezekiah (**18:23-24**). If they were so weak as to need Egypt's help, why not take help from Assyria?

Finally, the commander ended his open-air message by claiming that his army had been sent against Jerusalem by the Lord himself (**18:25**). Such claims are easy to make, but it would be surprising if the same Lord who was happy with Hezekiah would be the one to send the Assyrians against Jerusalem.

Hezekiah's officials tried to limit the damage this speech could do by asking the envoys to speak in Aramaic, a language that had come to be used for trade and diplomatic communication, but which many of the ordinary inhabitants of Jerusalem would not understand (**18:26**).

The Assyrians refused to cooperate, and instead their commander deliberately spoke in Hebrew, addressing his message to the people watching this meeting from the city walls (18:27-28). He warned them not to believe Hezekiah when he said, *the Lord will surely deliver us* (**18:29-30, 32**). The Assyrians thought that the Lord of Israel was a territorial god, like the gods of other nations, who could not protect their people (**18:33-35**). But the boastful claim to be stronger than God, *How then can the Lord deliver Jerusalem from my hands?* was made prematurely. The Lord was going to deliver Jerusalem. The people did not have to accept the Assyrian offer of survival at the cost of exile (18:28-32).

As instructed by the king, the people did not respond to what they heard but remained quiet (**18:36**). Silence is sometimes the best response to blasphemers. But Hezekiah's officials returned to him with their clothes torn in sorrow (**18:37**).

19:1-13 Deliverance of Jerusalem foretold

Hezekiah and his representatives decided to pray to the Lord and to ask the prophet Isaiah to pray for them too. By tearing their clothes and wearing sackcloth, they were humbling themselves and repenting of any sin they might have committed (**19:1-2**). Hezekiah asked Isaiah to join them in prayer for the remnant that survived, that is, for the remaining few who continued to trust the Lord and serve him (**19:3-5**). The book of Isaiah talks of the remnant, not the whole nation, as the hope of Israel, and Isaiah had even named his son Shear-Jashub, which means 'a remnant will return' (Isa 7:3; 10:20-22). The Lord would work out his purpose for Israel and the world through a remnant, not the majority.

Isaiah brought two messages of deliverance from the Lord. The first word was given just after the first appearance of the Assyrian envoys. Hezekiah was told that he should not fear (**19:6-7**). The Lord was going to make Sennacherib return home and be destroyed.

And that is exactly what the Lord did (**19:8-9**). The Assyrians received a report that Tirhakah, an African king, had come from Egypt to fight against them. The Assyrian field commander heard that his king had left Lachish and was now fighting at Libnah, so he withdrew from Jerusalem, but not before sending a threatening letter to Hezekiah. The content of the letter is a summary of the message earlier presented aloud outside the city walls of Jerusalem (**19:10-13**). He was urging Hezekiah not to be deceived by the God of Israel whom the Assyrians considered no different from the idols of the other nations they had conquered.

19:14-19 Hezekiah's prayer

The king promptly took this letter to the temple. It had become a common practice to pray in the temple during hours of distress, as Solomon prayed (1 Kgs 8:33-34) and as Isaiah himself had done in the year that King Uzziah died (Isa 6:1). Hezekiah spread the letter before the Lord, as if to let the Lord read it too (**19:14-15**). The faithful cast all their heavy burdens on the Lord. In his prayer, Hezekiah declared his firm belief that the gods of the other nations the Assyrians had defeated were only idols, but that the God of Israel is the creator of heaven and earth and has power over all the kingdoms of the earth (**19:17-19**). He is enthroned between the cherubim, who are angels who guard and proclaim his glory and majesty.

19:20-37 Isaiah's prophecy

The Lord heard the prayers of Hezekiah and answered through Isaiah (**19:20**). The answer was in the form of a poem, the first part of which was addressed to the king of Assyria (19:21-28). *The Virgin Daughter of Zion* and *the Daughter of Jerusalem* would soon be mocking him. By putting it this way, the prophet was saying that Sennacherib would not even have the respect of young girls, let alone of the other people in Jerusalem who had all heard his boasting (**19:21**). Sennacherib was accused of insulting the God of Israel (**19:22-23a**). Sennacherib may boast of all the victories he has won (19:10-13) but the Lord has quite a different interpretation of world events. He demolished Sennacherib's pride by quietly saying, *Have you not heard? Long ago I ordained it* (**19:25**). All that Sennacherib had achieved was to carry out the plans of the God of Israel. He may have thought that he was performing magnificent feats as he boasted of cutting down the *tallest cedars* (**19:23b**) but God said that his achievements were as easy as pulling up tiny plants or removing dead grass from a roof, because God had weakened his opponents (**19:26**). Assyria's conquests were fulfilling what the God of Israel had planned long ago. None of the gods of the other nations could so plan history.

Now the Lord had had enough of the arrogance of this little man, and he sent him back to his home, back the way he came (**19:27-28**). He would be led home like a domestic animal, with *my hook in your nose and my bit in your mouth*.

The final part of the prophecy (19:29-31) was addressed to Hezekiah and the people of Jerusalem. They would eat what grew by itself for the first two years, but in the third year they would sow and reap crops (**19:29**). This was a message of hope. Much of Judah had been destroyed (18:13), but those who were left in Jerusalem would be the remnant who survived (**19:30-31**). Sennacherib would not even attack the city (**19:32-33**). The Lord was going to save Jerusalem for the sake of his own name and that of David (**19:34**). Here the Lord showed his kindness and love to Israel for the sake of David.

The example of David reminds us that an ancestor's devotion to God can be a source of blessing for generations to come. While our children cannot inherit salvation, we can leave them an inheritance of good, in the general sense, if we have lived faithfully before God. The faithful devotion of God's people benefits people in many places all over the world.

Of course, the ultimate example of an inheritance received for the sake of another is the way God shows his saving love to us because of the faithful life of Jesus Christ.

The prophecy was fulfilled and the Assyrians never set foot inside Jerusalem or even shot an arrow against it. Without any delay, that night an angel of destruction, like the one in Egypt during the first Passover, went through the camp of the Assyrians. Thousands of their soldiers died (**19:35**). With the loss of his troops, Sennacherib was unable to continue the war. Humiliated, he returned to Nineveh, where he was assassinated by his own sons (**19:36-37**). Truly, a defeat of an arrogant man that would make even the youngest of girls laugh!

20:1-11 Hezekiah's illness

Hezekiah's illness must have struck in his fourteenth year on the throne, for 18:2 says he reigned for a total of twenty-nine years, and in **20:6** he is given fifteen more years to live after his illness. This was the same year in which Sennacherib attacked Judah (18:13). It is likely that his illness came before the encounter with the Assyrian officers described in chapter 18.

When Isaiah came to see Hezekiah in his illness, it was not to bring him comfort but to inform him that he was going to die (**20:1**). This was a grim message, and a startling one. Hezekiah had been a good king and had received the high praise of being considered as faithful as David (18:3). Moreover there was then, as there sometimes is today, a general belief that death and suffering comes as a result of sin. Those people who were opposed to Hezekiah's reforms would have interpreted his early death as punishment from Baal or from the strange gods that his father had introduced because he had destroyed their altars.

Hezekiah's illness raises the question of why misfortune comes to good people. We do not always know why God allows this. The book of Job and Jesus tell us that some misfortunes happen 'so that the work of God might be displayed' (John 9:3) or so that God's son may be glorified (John 9:3; 11:14-15). All that we know is that some people of faith gain victory over their enemies, while others, equally faithful, are not delivered in this life (Heb 11:33-38).

Hezekiah was greatly distressed at the news that he would soon die. In a similar situation, King Asa did not seek the Lord in prayer but relied only on medical people, who treated only his physical body and not his spirit (2 Chr 16:12). But Hezekiah turned to God in prayer (20:2). He reminded God of all that he had done for him, mentioning his good works as reasons why the Lord should heal him (20:3). But the faithful are not saved by their good works of righteousness but by the grace of God.

The Lord responded graciously to Hezekiah's prayer and promised healing, another fifteen years of life and deliverance from the Assyrians (20:4-6). The simple healing mixture that Isaiah applied was not what cured Hezekiah (20:7). It was simply a means of conveying the power of the Lord where other treatments had failed.

Weakened by his illness, Hezekiah found it hard to believe that God would answer his prayer so rapidly. After all, Isaiah had not even left the palace before he received God's answer to Hezekiah's prayer (20:4). So Hezekiah asked for some further assurance that what Isaiah had said was the truth (20:8). The Lord was willing to give him a sign, and performed a miracle similar to that when the sun stood still in the days of Joshua (Josh 10:12-14). The shortening of the shadow made it appear that time had been reversed (20:9-11).

We are not able to see into the eternal plans of God to know whether Hezekiah's recovery for an extra fifteen years was for the better or not. It was during these years that he met the messengers from the king of Babylon and that the wicked Manasseh was born.

20:12-21 Visitors from Babylon

Merodach-Baladan, the king of Babylon, sent messengers to greet Hezekiah. They pretended that they had come to congratulate him on his recovery, but that was not their only motive (20:12). Like Judah, Babylon was struggling against the rule of Assyria and was seeking an alliance with Judah, and perhaps with other neighbouring nations as well. Hezekiah received them gladly and allowed them not only to inspect his guard of honour but also his treasury and the armoury (20:13). He showed them everything in his palace and in all his kingdom. Such openness was unwise, for it gave the Babylonians information about the strengths and weaknesses of Judah that they could use against it in the future. Leaders who have faith in God also need to be as wise as the children of the world when it comes to administrative planning for the state or community. They need to combine foresight with faith in the Lord of history.

Isaiah recognized that Hezekiah had not acted wisely (20:14-15). He himself had consistently urged the kings of Judah to have faith in the Lord and not to make alliances with other nations. With God-given insight into the future, he informed Hezekiah that one day the Babylonians would carry away all the treasure they had been shown and many of the people of Jerusalem to their land (20:16-18).

Hezekiah was not particularly disturbed by this news. He was more concerned about whether there would be peace during his lifetime (20:19). In this, his attitude is similar to that of some leaders today. He was not sorry for his wrong actions and the suffering it would cause future generations. God-fearing leaders must see themselves as the Lord's stewards for future generations as well as just for their own lifetimes.

The summary of Hezekiah's reign in 20:20 includes a reference to a tunnel he had dug to bring water into Jerusalem. This tunnel is still in existence today.

When Hezekiah died, he was succeeded by his son Manasseh (20:21).

21:1-26 Manasseh and Amon

Chapter 21 records the reigns of two kings who took decisive steps to reverse all Hezekiah's reforms.

21:1-18 Manasseh

Manasseh had the longest reign of any king of Judah and Israel. He became king at the age of twelve, suggesting that he must have had strong advisers and teachers to direct the course of affairs (21:1-2). These must have been drawn from a group who supported Ahaz's policies and opposed those of Hezekiah. However, since this book focuses on the kings, little is said about the activities of political and religious parties that supported or resisted royal policies in the kingdom. What is clear is that Manasseh led Judah into adopting the type of sinful life that was practised by the Canaanites whom Israel had displaced (21:3). The pendulum swung to the extreme opposite of Hezekiah's position. All that Hezekiah had done was reversed (21:4a, 5-7a).

Manasseh's actions clearly violated the covenant God had made with his chosen people and had repeated in his promises to David and Solomon (21:4b, 7b-8). The people of Judah were also held responsible for allowing Manasseh to mislead them (21:9). Their behaviour was condemned by prophets who announced the Lord's judgment on Israel (21:10-11). The Lord's attitude to Israel would now be reversed. They would no longer be able to count on his protection (21:12). Two vivid images are used to express the Lord's judgment. One is of the Lord holding a measuring line used to determine whether a wall was built straight or would have to be knocked down and rebuilt (21:13a; see also Amos 7:8). Samaria had already failed this test. There was no doubt that Judah would also fail it. The second image is of the Lord doing the dishes! He cleans a bowl, wipes it and turns it upside down (21:13b). The meal is over, the action completed. Judah and Israel are finished (21:14-15).

When God says that he will *forsake the remnant of my inheritance* (21:14-15) he is not speaking of the faithful few who would survive the fall of Judah and would later return to rebuild Jerusalem (see, for example, Ezra 9:13; Isa 10:22). Rather, he is speaking of what remains of what had once been a mighty kingdom united under David and Solomon.

Although the writer of Kings focuses on Manasseh's religious crimes, these were not the only evil aspects of his long reign (21:16). The very length of this reign must have been disturbing to people who were faithful to the Lord. They believed that long years are a reward that God gives to his faithful followers, yet Manasseh was permitted to reign for fifty-five years. Part of the answer to this problem may be found in 2 Chronicles 33:10-20, which reports that the Lord allowed the Babylonians to take Manasseh captive to Babylon. There he repented of the evil he had done and humbly asked the Lord's forgiveness, which he received. He was then allowed to return to Jerusalem to continue his reign and died in peace. His repentance may, however, have come very late in his reign, for his change of heart certainly had no effect on his son who succeeded him (21:20).

The Lord forgives those who truly repent. But the negative effects of their sin do not disappear. Manasseh's counter-reforms caused irreversible suffering and damage to Judah. The people continued to serve other gods.

When considering Manasseh's long reign, we need to remember that it is not the length of days that one spends on earth that counts but the quality of the life lived. Our Lord Jesus Christ did not live long on this earth. He died as a young man of thirty-three years, but he carried out the task God had given him (John 13:1; 17:1). To our Lord, death meant returning to God (John 17:11-13). The way of the God-fearing is still the best (Eccl 8:12), for we shall all eventually be judged according to what we have done on earth (2 Cor 5:10).

On Manasseh's death, he was succeeded by his son Amon (21:17-18).

21:19-26 Amon

Amon, the son of Manasseh, came to the throne at the age of twenty-two but ruled for only two years (21:19). Like his father, he did what was evil to the Lord (21:20-22). For some unknown reason, his officials assassinated him (21:23). But the people would not accept their behaviour and executed the assassins. Then they appointed Josiah, Amon's eight-year-old son, as king (21:24-26). The fact that those who assassinated the king did not assume the throne contrasts with what had frequently happened in Israel and reveals the stability of Judah. The country was still united and under control, and prepared to accept that the next ruler must be the child of the deceased king.

22:1-23:30 Josiah

22:1-2 Introduction to Josiah's rule

Josiah was eight years old when he came to the throne (22:1). He must have received good training from God-fearing leaders in the palace and priests of the temple, for he is introduced as one who *walked in all the ways of his father David* (22:2a). Of all the kings of Judah, only Hezekiah and Josiah received this high commendation. The description of him as *not turning to the left or right* (22:2b) reminds us of the charge given in Joshua 1:7-8, where the new leader was advised that if he closely followed the Book of the Law he would be sure of success.

22:3-20 The finding of the Book of the Law

At the age of eighteen, Josiah turned his attention to the house of the Lord in Jerusalem (22:3). The long reign and counter-reforms of Manasseh and Amon must have left the temple in need of repair. Josiah ordered that finances be made available and men appointed to oversee the repairs (22:4-6). The instruction that *they need not account for the money* showed that the quality of their work would be a witness to their faithfulness (22:7). This statement does not mean that faithful people should not be checked or audited, but it does mean that they should be encouraged to use money wisely, negotiating to get the best materials for the lowest price.

In the course of the repairs, the contents of the temple must have been cleaned and rearranged. One item caught the attention of the high priest. It was *the Book of the Law* (22:8a). This book must have been either the whole or a section of the book of Deuteronomy, which had been there for a long time but had been ignored and forgotten during the fifty-five year reign of Manasseh. The priest and the secretary read the book and found that the content challenged their lives and the attitude of the people of Judah (22:8b). The king was informed of the discovery and the book was read to him too (22:10). On hearing its contents, Josiah was greatly shocked and *tore his robes,* a response that shows true repentance and humility before the Lord (22:11). He was grieved not just for himself but also for the whole people of Israel. The book must have condemned the religious life of Judah and the presence of the strange gods that were being worshipped. Josiah realized that God's anger must be burning against the king, his people and all of Judah because *our fathers have not obeyed the words of this book* (22:13). Since the period before Manasseh and throughout his long reign, the people had been living in disobedience to the law of the Lord. God's people had so acted against the word of the Lord that their judgment was already spelled out in the Book of the Law.

Josiah instructed his officials to *go and enquire of the Lord for me,* that is, to go and pray for mercy and forgiveness and to find out how Israel stood before the Lord (22:12-13). So they went to consult Huldah, a prophetess who was the wife of a temple official (**22:14**). The fact that they went to consult a woman must have some bearing on the way we interpret NT passages such as 1 Corinthians 14:34 and 1 Timothy 2:11-15 that have been used for years in Africa to keep women from active service in the church.

Other prophets like Jeremiah were around in Jerusalem at this time, but it is possible that they chose to consult a woman because they hoped she would deliver a more comforting message than the types of prophecies that Jeremiah was delivering (Jer 15:1-6). But they were wrong.

Huldah did not defer to the king. She told his messengers to take back her prophecy to *the man who sent you to me,* without any mention of his title as king. She is letting him know that her message comes from a far greater authority, the Lord (**22:15**). The message she gave about the impending judgment of Judah confirmed what the other prophets of the Lord were saying about the fate of Judah. The Spirit of the Lord ensured that the prophets spoke with one voice, and did not contradict one another. They did not speak words of comfort because the axe of judgment was poised to strike. The sin of Judah had reached such a point that her fate could not be reversed, even if, as Jeremiah said, the great prophets Moses and Samuel were to pray for the nation (**22:16-17**; see also Jer 15:1)

But while the judgment was decided, God was merciful in regard to the way in which it would be carried out. He sent a special message addressed personally to Josiah: *Tell the king of Judah* (**22:18**). The Lord does not ignore the king's humble cry of repentance. True repentance, turning to the Lord with a humble and broken heart (Ps 51:16-17), moves the heart of God. We have seen this with Ahab (1 Kgs 21:27-29), Hezekiah (20:2), and the people of Nineveh (Jonah 3:7-10). Because the king had been moved *when you heard what I have spoken* in the book of the law (**22:19**), he would be spared the sorrow of having to see *the disaster I am to bring on this place* (**22:20**). The disasters of the future would not come just by chance but because the Lord himself would cause them to happen.

23:1-3 Renewing the covenant

The king had heard the content of the book of the law and had believed that it was the word of God. Now he called together *all the elders of Judah* (**23:1**). These elders would have been all the chiefs, tribal heads and titled members of each community in all Judah. Then he led them to the temple along *with the priests and the prophets,* representing the spiritual leaders in the land (**23:2a**). *The people of Jerusalem,* that is, those who lived there, were also present, enjoying the privilege of those who live in cities to witness important events.

Once the crowd had assembled, they were read the contents of the *Book of the Covenant,* that is, the Book of the Law that Hilkiah the high priest had found in the temple (**23:2b**; 22:8). It is now called the Book of the Covenant because it was a record of the covenant that should guide the religious lives of the people from then on. This was why the people needed to hear the content of the book for themselves.

The king took his place *by the pillar* in the temple, the site where the kings of Judah were traditionally anointed (see 11:14). Standing there was an assertion of his willingness to act with authority. Then, like Joshua of old (Josh 24:15), the king publicly *renewed the covenant,* that is, he publicly promised to follow the teaching of the book (**23:3a**). These teachings are referred to as *the commands, regulations and decrees* of the Lord, the same phrases that were used to describe the law of Moses as summarized in the book of Deuteronomy (Deut 6:17).

The leaders then promised that they, too, would live by the teaching of the book, making a pledge on behalf of the people whom they represented (**23:3b**). The promise was made for themselves and their families, clans and all the people under their care.

23:4-28 Josiah's religious reforms

The leaders of the people had heard the words of the Book of the Covenant and had promised to be guided by it. The king and the elders had all taken the oath or promised to be guided by the book. Now their task was to cleanse the land spiritually by getting rid of all that was condemned by the book.

Just as the Jews could not be faithful to God with so much idol worship among them, so also we in Africa cannot be true to God without leaving behind all that is contrary to the Bible in our traditional beliefs and practices. At times, we need Josiahs to lead such reforms. We should also be reformers of our own selves. God wants all, not partial dedication. We cannot serve two masters (Matt 6:24).

The king personally directed the actions of the priests and the doorkeepers (**23:4a**). The priests would have no fear in handling objects sacred to idols, for they knew that these things really had no power to harm anybody. The Asherah, the Baal and all the things associated with them and their priests were destroyed as commanded in the book of the law (Deut 12:2-3). Everything associated with a foreign god was burned, to destroy and defile it and so to break whatever power their worshippers believed these sacred objects to have. Those who worshipped them would no longer expect them to represent any powerful spirits. The ashes were taken to Bethel in a symbolic removal of cursed things to a distant land that was now occupied by non-Israelites (**23:4b**).

The amount of stuff removed from the temple shows how much the people of Judah had sinned and how far they had gone from the law of the Lord. The temple itself had become crowded with things that the Lord hated (**23:6-7, 11-12**).

The religious cleansing was not restricted to Jerusalem but was taken to the rest of Judah. Even the high places where the Lord was worshipped were destroyed. The Levite priests of the Lord serving in these places were not given jobs in the temple in Jerusalem but were allowed to share the temple food with those priests who were serving in and around the temple (**23:8-9**; see also Deut 18:6-8).

Josiah destroyed Topheth, the fireplace where human sacrifices took place, in the valley of Ben Hinnom (**23:10**). Jeremiah also mentions Topheth and says that the place where it is located will be called a Valley of Slaughter (Jer 7:31-32). Josiah desecrated it to discourage any further human sacrifice.

The housetop altars erected by Ahaz and Manasseh were destroyed (23:12). So were the high places that Solomon had put up for his wives to worship the gods they brought along from the lands of their people (**23:13-14**; 1 Kgs 11:7-8). These were located on what had come to be called *the Hill of Corruption* because their presence in Jerusalem drew people to corrupt worship habits.

The reforms were taken as far as Bethel at the border of the northern territory, which was now occupied by non-Israelites. The notorious altar in Bethel set up by Jeroboam the son of Nebat was finally demolished, fulfilling the prophecy of the unnamed prophet from Judah (**23:15-16**; 1 Kgs 13:1-3). Bones dug out from graves were burned on the altars to make them unfit for any religious worship. However, the tomb of the unnamed prophet and the old prophet in Samaria were not disturbed (**23:17-18**; 1 Kgs 13:30-32). After doing this, Josiah extended his reforms further into the territory of Samaria (**23:19-20**).

The religious cleansing culminated in the celebration of the Passover, the old festival that reminded Israel of their last days in Egypt (**23:21-23**; see Exod 12; Deut 16:1-8). This festival had once been celebrated in people's homes, but now it had become a national celebration in Jerusalem. This Passover eclipsed even the one celebrated in the days of Hezekiah, when some of the northern tribes had come to Jerusalem for the feast (2 Chr 30).

Josiah's reforms extended to rooting out household idols and spiritualists, that is, people who communicate with the dead (**23:24**). Such activities are also condemned in Deuteronomy (Deut 18:10-13).

Josiah loved God with all his heart, soul and strength (**23:25**), as commanded in Deuteronomy 6:4-5 and by Christ (Mark 12:30). As an individual leader, Josiah did more than all those who ruled before or after him. King David may have been more devoted to the Lord, but he did not have as much heresy and false worship to fight against. Yet for all

Josiah's fervour, he could only reform the surface of things. The evils encouraged by Manasseh and Amon (ch. 21) had taken deep root in the society, and people had not truly repented (Ezek 8:9-18). The Lord's sentence of judgment on Jerusalem was waiting to be carried out. The heat of the Lord's fierce anger would burn against Judah (**23:26-27**; see also 22:16-17).

23:29-30 Josiah's death

While Josiah was ruling and carrying out his reforms, the Lord was raising up Babylon as the next world power. Friendly relations between Judah and Babylon had begun during the reign of King Hezekiah (20:12). In about 609 BC, Pharaoh Neco of Egypt had to pass through the territory of Judah on his way to join the Assyrians in fighting against Babylon at Carchemish. Josiah went out with his forces to intercept Neco (**23:29a**). What happened is described in detail in 2 Chronicles 35:20-27. Neco claimed he was going to attack the Babylonians at God's command. Josiah could have consulted Huldah or Jeremiah, both of whom were prophesying at that time. But he did not seek the will of the Lord like David (1 Sam 23:9-13; 30:7-8; 2 Sam 2:1; 5:19) or Jehoshaphat had done. He insisted on going into battle, where he was wounded and died (**23:29b**).

Josiah's death again raises the question of why the righteous suffer. One possible answer in this case is that the Lord was fulfilling his promise to Josiah through the prophetess Huldah that he would be buried in peace and would not have to see the disaster that was coming to Judah (22:20). The Lord was taking Josiah to his fathers before that happened. Moreover, we need to remember that righteousness does not guarantee that we will not suffer. The sinless Son of God had to endure a shameful death in order to glorify the Father (John 13:27-32; 17:2).

Josiah was buried in his own tomb, not 'with his fathers' as so many of his predecessors had been (**23:30a**). It is possible that the graveyard in the city of David was already overcrowded. This possibility is suggested by the fact that Manasseh and Amon had been buried in their own graves in the garden of Uzza (21:18, 26).

For the last time, the king-makers of Judah had the chance to choose their own king, and they anointed Jehoahaz, the son of Josiah (**23:30b**).

23:31-24:20 The Last Kings of Judah

23:31-35 Jehoahaz

Jehoahaz seems also to have been known as Shallum (1 Chr 3:15; Jer 22:11). It is possible that Shallum was his given name and Jehoahaz his throne name. In the three months of his reign, he did evil before the Lord (**23:31-32**). With the death of Josiah, Judah had come under the rule of the Egyptians. Neco was not happy with the choice of Jehoahaz as king and replaced him with his brother Eliahim, whom he renamed Jehoiakim (**23:33-34**). Jehoahaz was carried away in chains to Egypt where he later died. Neco also made the country pay a large tribute to him (**23:35**).

23:36-24:7 Jehoiakim

Both Jehoahaz and Jehoiakim did evil in the eyes of the Lord. This means that the reforms carried out by Josiah did not change even his own children. Jehoiakim showed no respect for the words of the Lord. Unlike Josiah, who tore his garments when he was read the Book of the Law (22:11), Jehoiakim burned the word of the Lord when it was read to him, despite the officials in the palace who urged him to listen to it (Jer 36). He also had the prophet Uriah brought back from Egypt and killed (Jer 26:20-23). The prophet Jeremiah and his scribe Baruch had to hide to save their lives.

Jehoiakim had been put on his throne by the Egyptians, but during his reign Babylon defeated Pharaoh Neco at the battle at Carchemish in 605 BC and severely weakened Neco (**24:7**). The balance of power in the area shifted, and Judah was invaded by Nebuchadnezzar (**24:1**). This first attack came in the third year of Jehoiakim, and it was at this time that Daniel and his friends were taken to Babylon (Dan 1:1-6). Judah also struggled with attacks by other groups, including the Arameans, Ammonites and Moabites (**24:2a**). The reason for all this turmoil was that the Lord planned to destroy Judah as a nation, and *was not willing to forgive* (**24:2b-4**). Neither the prayers of Jeremiah (Jer 11:14; 14:11) nor even the prayers of saints like Moses and Samuel (Jer 15:1) would make the Lord change his mind.

The writer of Kings does not give the details of Jehoiakim's death, which Jeremiah 22:19 prophesied would be a very shameful one. He appears to have died a captive (2 Chr 36:6), although he may not yet have been deported from Jerusalem. He was succeeded by his son Jehoiachin (**24:6**).

24:8-17 Jehoiachin

Like his uncle Jehoahaz, Jehoiachin ruled for only three months (**24:8**). Within that short time, he did evil before the Lord (**24:9**). He suffered the consequences of his father's rebellion against Nebuchadnezzar (24:1). He surrendered to Nebuchadnezzar, and the king, his mother and the royal family gave themselves up to the Babylonians as the prophet Jeremiah had advised them to do (**24:10-12**; see also Jer 13:18). Jerusalem was not destroyed, but Nebuchadnezzar took away all the treasures from the palace and the temple (**24:13**). He also took the king, the royal family and the chief officials and advisers of Jerusalem away to Babylon (**24:15**; see also Jer 22:24-30).

It was the practice of Babylon to move conquered people away from their native lands and settle them elsewhere to prevent any rebellion from the colonies. So in the case of Judah, all the people with useful skills were taken into exile, along with seven thousand military personnel (**24:16**). All together ten thousand people went into slavery. This was the second group of exiles to leave Judah and go to Babylon. They would have been surprised to know that Jeremiah regarded them as blessed compared to those left behind, who were the poorest in the land (Jer 24:5-10).

Jerusalem had not been destroyed, but it had been made so politically, materially and spiritually weak that it could not mount any rebellion. Zedekiah, the king's uncle, was appointed king over a nation that would soon fall apart (**24:17**).

24:18-20 Zedekiah

Zedekiah did evil before the Lord (**24:19**). He was not a man of strong will. It is clear from Jeremiah 37–38 that he sought to hear from the Lord, but he lacked the courage to obey what he heard. Judah was on the brink of disaster, but the prophets gave conflicting messages. Jeremiah prophesied judgment and disaster. He advised surrender to Nebuchadnezzar and even wrote to those in exile to tell them that Babylon was going to be in power for seventy years (Jer 29). But false prophets assured Zedekiah and Judah that Jehoiachin and those in exile would soon return and reoccupy the throne (Jer 28:1-4). Zedekiah must have felt like a transitional ruler.

The book of Kings does not give all these details, but summarizes this whole period of confusion and bad counsel by saying that the Lord's judgment was hanging over Judah as *he thrust them from his presence* (**24:20**).

25:1-26 The Fall of Jerusalem

25:1-7 The end of the kingdom of Judah

Early in the reign of Zedekiah, Jeremiah had made it clear that the Lord intended to give all the land, the people and the animals to Nebuchadnezzar (Jer 27:4-7). The prophet had advised Zedekiah not to resist but to submit to the Babylonians and so save his life and the city of Jerusalem (Jer 27:12-14). At the beginning of his reign, Zedekiah was loyal to the Babylonians and even visited Nebuchadnezzar in Babylon (Jer 51:59). Later he must have listened to the false prophets and to bad advice. He joined forces with Amon, Edom, Moab, Tyre and Sidon to rebel against Babylon (24:10b; Jer 27:3-7).

Nebuchadnezzar responded by again attacking Judah. He surrounded the city of Jerusalem for almost two years (**25:1-3**) and then managed to break through the city wall (**25:4a**). Jeremiah described how the Babylonian officers went into the city and sat in the Middle Gate. Recognizing defeat, Zedekiah and his troops fled the city, heading south *towards the Arabah,* that is, towards Jericho in the Jordan Valley (**25:4b-5;** Jer 39:3-4).

But the attempt to escape failed. Zedekiah was captured and brought before Nebuchadnezzar at Riblah. His sons were killed before his eyes and then his eyes were put out (**25:6-7**). Thus there was no hope that he would have any successor on the throne of Judah in Jerusalem.

25:8-22 The destruction of the city and the temple

With no king in Jerusalem, events were now dated according to the dates of Nebuchadnezzar's reign (**25:8**). Nebuzaradan, the Babylonian commander, set out to destroy the city so that it could not cause trouble again. He burned down the temple of Solomon, the royal palace and all the important buildings (**25:9**). He had his troops break down the city wall (**25:10**). Another group of 4600 people were carried away to exile in Babylon (**25:11;** see Jer 52:28-30). These were in addition to the ten thousand carried away with King Jehoiachin (24:14-16), and the first group taken in the days of Jehoiachin (Dan 1:1-6). The bronze pillars and bronze Sea that Solomon had asked Huram of Tyre to make for the temple were broken up and carried away, along with all the gold and silver utensils from the temple (**25:13-17**).

The high priest, other senior priests and all the officials still in the city were arrested and brought before Nebuchadnezzar, who ordered them killed (**25:18-21**). Only the very poor were left in the land to look after the farms (**25:12**).

The kingdoms of Judah and Israel in the promised land had come to an end. Amos's prophecy was fulfilled: '"Are not you Israelites the same to me as the Cushites? ... Surely the eyes of the Sovereign Lord are on the sinful kingdoms. I will destroy it from the face of the earth – yet I will not totally destroy the house of Jacob," declares the Lord' (Amos 9:7-8).

25:22-26 Gedaliah, governor of Judah

The Babylonians knew that some leaders would still be needed, and so they appointed Gedaliah the son of Ahikam the son of Shaphan as governor (**25:22**). The events of his governorship are described in detail in Jeremiah 40:7-41:3. Gedaliah was an educated man and not simply an ignorant and incompetent administrator.

Those who were scattered by the war started gathering around him and, like Jeremiah the prophet, he assured all who came to him that if they submitted to the Babylonians, they would have peace (**25:24;** see also Jer 27:12-14).

He set up his new capital at Mizpah to replace Jerusalem, which had been destroyed (Jer 40:8-12). But there was still resistance to the Babylonians, which the king of Ammon encouraged. He helped a man named Ishmael to assassinate Gedaliah. Those who had gathered around him were also killed, as were the Babylonians in Mizpah (**25:25;** Jer 40:14). Fearing Babylonian retribution for these killings, many people fled to Egypt and set up Jewish settlements there (**25:26;** Jer 41:16-18). Only the poorest and weakest of Judah remained. Without a leader, they soon lost their Jewish identity. They are not mentioned as rejoining the exiles who eventually returned to Jerusalem in the days of Ezra and Nehemiah (Ezra 2:2-67; Neh 7:6-73).

25:27-30 Jehoiachin Released

The author of Kings does not, however, end his book on a note of despair. There is still hope for Israel. The promise of a messiah still stands. In 562 BC a king called Evil-Merodach freed King Jehoiachin from prison and set him above all the kings from other lands who were also in exile in Babylon (**25:27-30;** Jer 52:31-34). He would be one of the ancestors of Jesus, the Messiah (Matt 1:11-12; Luke 4:27).

The Lord was still with his people, even in exile. The Babylonians were very open to using the best talents in their administration (Dan 1:19; 2:48-49) and people like Ezra, Zerubbabel, Nehemiah, Daniel and his friends, Mordecai and Esther fared well. Those exiles who were God-fearing and faithful did gain their freedom. It was only those who were without faith in God who became lost and separated from the people of God.

The reign of the kings had come to an end in Israel and Judah, but God remains the King of kings. He raises one earthly king to power and deposes another (Jer 27:4-5). The kings of Israel had failed to save the people of God, but God himself saves those who believe, love, respect and faithfully obey him.

Musa Gotom

Further Reading

Montgomery, James A. *A Critical and Exegetical Commentary on the Book of Kings.* Reprint. ICC. Edinburgh: T & T Clark, 1976.

Provan, Iain W. *1 and 2 Kings.* NIBC. Peabody, Mass.: Hendrickson, 1995.

Wiseman, Donald J. *1 and 2 Kings.* TOT. Downers Grove, Ill.: InterVarsity Press, 1993.

1 AND 2 CHRONICLES

How many times in a year is a verse from the book of Chronicles used as a sermon text? This book is among the most neglected in the Bible. Many books, articles and commentaries about the OT never mention it. Pastors, evangelists and lay people read only selections from it. In many Christian congregations, the book of Chronicles is read only on certain special occasions such as at the dedication of a new church building or of a new house.

However, Chronicles is as much the word of God as the other books of the Bible. It should not be so neglected. In his preface to the translation of the books of Samuel and Kings into Latin (the Vulgate), Jerome said that those who think they know the sacred Scriptures but ignore Chronicles are deluding themselves. So we encourage Christians, preachers and students of the Bible in particular to take Chronicles seriously.

Contents

The book of Chronicles offers a short summary of the OT. It is a Bible within the Bible. It tells the sacred story from the creation of humanity to the return of the exiles from Babylon and covers a wider sweep of history than any other book in the OT. Its main focus, however, is on the period of the monarchy in Israel. Of the sixty-five chapters which make up the book, fifty-six deal with that period (1 Chr 10:1-2 Chr 36:21).

The history that preceded the institution of the monarchy in Israel is presented in an abridged form of genealogical and geographical information (1 Chr 1:1-9:44). The position of all these lists at the beginning of the book discourages many Christians from reading further. Someone has compared the first nine chapters of Chronicles to nine lions guarding the entrance, discouraging less determined readers from discovering the treasures to be found farther on. While there is some truth in this image, it is flawed because these early chapters themselves contain treasure. At first glance, the long lists may seem unimportant, but they lay the foundations for the history that follows.

The different subjects and themes developed in the body of the book are rooted in the genealogies. The important place given to the tribe of Judah in the genealogies prepares us for the major role David's dynasty will play. The same is true of the major place given to the genealogy of the descendants of Levi. The Levites are a very important class in the book of Chronicles.

A list of all the kings of Judah is given in 1 Chronicles 3:10-16, but in telling the history of the monarchy, the author of Chronicles lays particular stress on the reigns of David (1 Chr 11:1-29:30) and of his son and immediate successor Solomon (2 Chr 1:1-9:31). The reigns of the other kings of Judah are covered more briefly (2 Chr 10:1-36:21), with particular attention to the reigns of Asa (14:2-16:14), Jehoshaphat (17:1-21:1), Hezekiah (29:1-32:33) and Josiah (34:1-35:27), because these were kings who were faithful to God and his temple.

Unlike the books of Samuel and Kings where the history of the two kingdoms of Israel and Judah is told in parallel, the book of Chronicles focuses solely on the kingdom of Judah. It refers to the northern kingdom only when events there affect the southern kingdom. From the perspective of the writer of Chronicles, the northern kingdom is apostate and rebellious because it revolted against the house of David and the temple in Jerusalem.

It is almost certain that the two accounts of the monarchy of Israel in the Bible, the books of Samuel and Kings on the one hand and the book of Chronicles on the other, were written at different times. They deal with different concerns, which we must consider in interpreting them. Whereas the books of Samuel and Kings were written from a perspective that justified the catastrophe of 587-585 BC (the end of the Davidic dynasty and the destruction of the temple), the book of Chronicles is more concerned with the restoration of the people and the reconstruction of the temple. In other words, the books of Samuel and Kings tell a history ending in catastrophe while Chronicles is a story that ends with hope and restoration. Thus we find that 2 Chronicles starts with the construction of the temple and ends with the decree of Cyrus authorizing the construction of another temple.

Name and Divisions

Chronicles is the third longest book in the OT after Psalms and Isaiah. In the Hebrew Bible, it is grouped with the Writings (the other two Hebrew categories are the Law and the Prophets).

The book of Chronicles was not originally separated into two parts; it was one book called 'The Events of the Days', meaning that it records events that were considered significant in the annals of the time. The Bible does not have any word that means 'history' as such.

In the third century BC, the Hebrew Bible was translated into Greek (the Septuagint). The translators called the book of Chronicles *Paraleipomenon,* which means 'things omitted' or 'things passed over'. This Greek title implies that the material in Chronicles supplements the account in Samuel and Kings. The Septuagint also moved away from the three-section division of the Hebrew Bible and located the book of Chronicles among the Historical Books after Samuel and Kings.

Probably the name *Paraleipomenon* and the location of the book right after Samuel and Kings contributed to the failure to appreciate the intrinsic value of the book of Chronicles. It came to seem insignificant compared to the books of Samuel and Kings, which were regarded as the primary history of Israel. The fact that many of the stories in Chronicles resemble those in Samuel and Kings certainly led the Septuagint translators to consider Chronicles as a sort of filler or complement to the books of Samuel and Kings. A superficial reading can, in fact, give the impression that the book of Chronicles is simply a repetition of the books of Samuel and Kings. However, a deeper reading will show that this is not the case. We would advise readers of this commentary not to use this book only to fill in details missing in the books of Samuel and Kings. What is happening here is somewhat similar to what happens with the Synoptic Gospels in the NT. Matthew, Mark and Luke give us three parallel but different versions of the ministry of Jesus Christ. The same events are retold from different angles for a specific purpose. Chronicles does the same in regard to Samuel and Kings.

The translators of the Septuagint also divided the single book of Chronicles into two parts, now 1 and 2 Chronicles. Unfortunately, they divided it at the place where its author would have least wanted any division, that is, between the reigns of David and his successor Solomon. In this commentary, we will largely ignore this late division of the book into two because there is perfect continuity between their reigns. David undertook the preparations for the construction of the temple, while Solomon faithfully carried out his instructions when building it.

The name 'Chronicles', by which the book is currently known, originated with Jerome (347-420 AD) who translated the Bible into Latin. He regarded this book as a chronicle of the whole of sacred history. Luther used the German form of the same word in his translation of the Hebrew Bible into German, completed in 1534, and ever since the book has been widely known as 'Chronicles'.

However, we must not be misled by the English word 'chronicles', which means a record of the events in the order in which they occurred. The author of the book of Chronicles is less concerned with the exact chronology of the events than with their significance. This can be clearly seen in 1 Chronicles 11:4-12:40. There it appears that the conquest of Jerusalem occurred in the middle of David's coronation ceremony. If we assume that the order is strictly chronological, we get the impression that, in the middle of the ceremony, David and those who had come to attend his coronation went off to conquer Jerusalem,

and that the coronation was only completed after the city had been taken. Such a scenario is highly improbable.

Time Frame and Context

The book of Chronicles itself does not mention when it was written. The last event recorded in the book is the decision of Cyrus, King of Persia, to authorize some Jewish exiles in Babylon to return to Jerusalem to rebuild the temple. This temple had originally been built by Solomon, but had been destroyed in 587 BC when the Babylonians conquered the capital of the kingdom of Judah. At that time, the cream of the population (the royal family, priests, scribes, nobles and military personnel) were all deported to Babylon.

Cyrus conquered Babylon in 539 BC and established one of the greatest empires of antiquity. This Persian Empire was known for its stability. Despite internal and external conflicts, the Achaemenid dynasty ruled 'the whole world', or what was known of it at that time, for at least two centuries (539-331 BC). Cyrus was the only pagan king to received positive mention in the OT. The prophet Isaiah even gave him the title 'Messiah' (Isa 45:1).

The Persians treated conquered peoples somewhat differently from their predecessors. Whereas the Assyrians and Babylonians had practised massive, systematic deportation of conquered peoples, the Persians only resorted to deportation in cases of extreme necessity, for example, when there was a revolt. They recognized that the extent of their empire meant that they could not hope to rule it solely by force. Thus they granted a certain autonomy to some groups under their control. They did not impose their religion on those they conquered. Instead, the empire's treasury financed the repair, construction and maintenance of local temples. However, for all that, their policy could not be described as one of non-intervention, and it would be wrong to think of them as practising religious tolerance as we understand it today. The relative autonomy and religious tolerance went only as far as served the interests of the empire and contributed to the control of the population without the use of much force. The Persian kings practised what is today called *realpolitik*. The Persian authorities did not hesitate to use force when it was necessary to wipe out a revolt, especially when the interests of the empire were at stake.

Despite various obstacles which delayed the start of the work, the temple would be rebuilt under the direction of Zerubbabel, a descendant of King David, and dedicated in 515 BC during the reign of Darius I.

Examination of the contents of the book of Chronicles, such as the post-exilic genealogies, enables us to deduce that the book of Chronicles was written some time during the Persian period, although the exact date is difficult to pinpoint. Some commentators think that it was written immediately after the return from Babylon, while others suggest that it was written towards the end of the Persian Empire (in the fourth century BC). The purpose and themes of the author, however, leave little doubt that it was written after the return from exile, the rebuilding of the temple, and the renewal of religious activities in Jerusalem.

Author

We do not know who wrote the book of Chronicles. Ezra the scribe has often been said to be the author, but there is no specific mention of this in the text itself. The unknown author is identified as the 'chronicler'. Because of the interest he shows in the Levite singers, some think that he may have been a member of this group.

Recognition of Ezra as the possible author is strongly tied to how commentators interpret the relationship between the books of Ezra and Nehemiah on one hand and Chronicles on the other. About thirty years ago, there was general agreement that there was a degree of unity among the three books, and the historical survey they offered was known as 'the Chronicler's history'. Recently, however, this unity has been questioned by many commentators and the majority now favour different authors for these books.

The arguments about authorship revolve around linguistic differences (for example, the fact that part of Ezra is written in Aramaic, rather than in Hebrew) and the treatment of some theological subjects. In Chronicles, David plays an important role, the Levites are represented in all the ceremonies, and the prophets are influential. In the books of Ezra and Nehemiah, however, David is not mentioned, the Levites play only a minor role, and the prophetic word is marginalized.

An even more striking difference is noticeable as regards the attitude to foreign nations. Chronicles is somewhat conciliatory, whereas the books of Ezra and Nehemiah are more exclusivist (Ezra 9:1-10:44). Thus Nehemiah uses the example of Solomon to condemn mixed marriages (13:23-28), but no such judgment is expressed in Chronicles, where Solomon is presented as a faithful king. In fact, Chronicles does not contain any criticism of Solomon.

However, the differences between the book of Chronicles and those of Ezra and Nehemiah should not be exaggerated, for both reflect the concerns of the post-exilic community. They should be thought of as complementary, not contradictory.

One of the benefits of the new approach is that now the book of Chronicles is treated independently, whereas in the past its treatment depended entirely on the books of Ezra and Nehemiah.

Sources

The book of Chronicles reads like a historical account, even if the word 'history' is defined differently today. So questions arise as to what sources the author used, for it was written long after the events, when the people had returned from exile. What was the source for the patriarchal history condensed in the genealogies? And what was the source for the history of the monarchy?

The author himself gives no indication of what sources he used. Nor does he claim to have received a specific revelation. But what strikes the attentive reader is the resemblance between the book of Chronicles and other books of the Bible, mainly Genesis, Samuel, Kings and Psalms. The name *Paraleipomenon* to which we have already referred, may be an indication of the sources. The author of Chronicles used the books of Samuel and Kings as his principal sources. Today, some commentators have suggested that rather than his having borrowed from the books of Samuel and Kings, these two books and the book of Chronicles all had a common source. But most commentators do not agree with this position, and insist that the books of Samuel and Kings are the principal source of the book of Chronicles. This commentary, too, argues that the author of the book of Chronicles did use other books of the Bible, whether in their canonical form or not, to write his history. His principal source for the genealogical material was the Pentateuch, and for the history of the monarchy, it was the books of Samuel and Kings. The Psalms are also quoted extensively in 1 Chronicles 16:8-37.

At the end of his account of the reign of each king, the author of Chronicles provides the reader with additional sources without saying whether he himself had used these documents as a basis for his account. These sources are official documents such as the royal records and the writings of certain prophets. Many of the prophets mentioned in these sources played an active role in the events recorded in Samuel and Kings, but are not mentioned in Chronicles. Their work is not mentioned because their ministry did not directly affect the kingdom of Judah or relate to themes dear to the author, such as the temple, the Davidic monarchy and worship.

Readers will find some discrepancies between the books of Samuel and Kings and the book of Chronicles. As indicated, some differences result from the author of Chronicles having his own agenda. Other discrepancies may reflect that the author used different documentary sources than the author or authors of Samuel and Kings. Changes may have also occurred during the transmission process.

Relevance to Africa

The main purpose of the author of Chronicles is to retell a history that was well known to the people of Israel in the light of their new circumstances.

The circumstances included the return from exile, the reconstruction of the temple and the resumption of religious services, the return from the exile, the reconstruction of the temple and the resumption of religious service, the lack of a king descended from David, and the fact that Judah was now a province or district of the Persian Empire. There are themes here that strike a chord with our continent.

The book of Chronicles offers Africa a positive example of how past events can be used to consolidate a nation, a people and even a continent. Without compromising the facts, the author has selected and retained those acts and facts that will contribute to the unity of the nation after the exile. In the case of David, for example, the book of Chronicles leaves aside all that could tarnish the image of this great king. Thus it does not mention his affair with Bathsheba, the incest of his children, or the blood and fratricide of the struggle to succeed him. Nor does Chronicles report the failings of King Solomon. He is presented as the perfect king, without faults. The sad memory of the destruction of Jerusalem is dealt with very briefly.

As Africans, we are often too attached to our painful past: the slave trade, colonialism and post-colonialism. Without minimizing the consequences of these periods in our history, we should look for what can rekindle hope among our people. Pastors, theologians, evangelists and other leaders will find in the book of Chronicles the basis for their task in the church and the community of making the word and marvellous acts of God in the past meaningful for Africa in the here and now. The book of Chronicles offers several paths to this goal.

The Kingdom of God

David's reign and that of his son and successor, Solomon, are regarded as the high point of Israel's history. But David and Solomon are not elevated because of their military prowess or political success, but rather because of their religious commitment. If the author ignored the many stories that could have tarnished David's image, he also silently passed over stories that could have contributed to his glory. Chronicles does not present David as the invincible warrior who killed Goliath and conquered foreign armies. Rather, he is the pious king who dedicated his whole reign to planning and preparing for the construction of the temple: bringing back the ark of the covenant, purchasing the site, providing the plans, preparing materials and assigning personnel for the temple service. Solomon is not the extravagant king of the book

of Kings. He is the son who followed scrupulously the instructions of his father. He was divinely chosen to be David's successor and is praised for his role as builder of the temple.

All the other kings of Judah are judged according to their faithfulness or lack of faithfulness to the temple. The book ends with the edict of Cyrus authorizing the Jews to return to Jerusalem to rebuild the temple. In other words, the history of Israel in the book of Chronicles starts and ends with the temple.

In focusing on the temple, Chronicles is more concerned with its spiritual and religious aspects than with its physical aspects. The author is well aware that the rebuilt temple at Jerusalem was not as spacious as Solomon's had been. Hence the book gives fewer details of the materials used to construct the temple but deals at length with its spiritual dedication. The temple is seen as a symbol of the presence of the kingdom of God in the midst of his people. The absence of a king in the post-exilic community led the author of Chronicles to stress the kingdom of God. The kingdom in Chronicles is not the Davidic kingdom but the kingdom of God. Thus we find statements like these: 'I will set him over my house and my kingdom forever' (1 Chr 17:14; 28:5); 'So Solomon sat on the throne of the Lord as king in the place of his father David' (1 Chr 29:23). The monarchy had long vanished and now it is God who is king, and the temple is his palace in the midst of his people.

Chronicles is the only OT book to have this focus on the 'kingdom of God'. That theme would, however, become central in the preaching of Jesus in whom the kingdom is present today. He, too, links the kingdom of God and the temple when he says, 'Destroy this temple, and I will raise it again in three days' (John 2:19).

Like the temple at Jerusalem, the church of Christ in Africa should be a symbol of the presence of the kingdom of God on the continent. This kingdom, we know, is a kingdom of peace, of joy, of justice and of love. So the church should mobilize its people to promote these virtues. As long as this continent is synonymous with war, famine and poverty, the church is failing in its mission of anticipating the kingdom of God.

The Role of the Levites

Though the book of Chronicles mentions both 'priests and Levites', the latter are more prominent. The genealogy of the tribe of Levi in 1 Chronicles 6:1-6 is the longest after that of Judah. The word 'Levites' appears more often in the book of Chronicles than in any other book of the OT, the book of Leviticus included. The first attempt to transport the ark of the covenant to Jerusalem failed because of the absence of Levites (1 Chr 15:2, 12-13).

On some occasions, they were more appreciated than the priests because they were more concerned with consecrating themselves (2 Chr 29:34). For this reason, the Levites did not share in the responsibility for the destruction of Jerusalem and the exile, whereas the priests did. In fact, the Levites were not included in the list of guilty parties (2 Chr 36:14). It is possible that the special attention given to the Levites in the book of Chronicles reflects their importance after the return from exile.

Chronicles focuses on the role of the Levites as musicians in ritual worship. Under King David, this group who had carried the ark of the covenant became the leaders of services in the temple. The Levites were chosen by God himself for this function. But this was not their only function. In the book of Chronicles, the Levites also play a role outside the temple as prophets, teachers of the law, and religious and civil administrators (1 Chr 23:28-32).

King David himself specified the functions of the Levites well before the construction of the temple. The kings of Judah whose reigns were successful (Jehoshaphat, Hezekiah and Josiah) were those who set a high value on the Levites and respected their contribution.

All in all, Chronicles presents the Levites as an indispensable group within the community and as a group that was committed to holiness. They were responsible for religious services, but were also present at all the great events in the life of the people and participated in civil life.

Statistics show that Africa is the most Christianized continent. Unfortunately, this bright record is not reflected in the everyday life on this continent. Too often, there is a dichotomy between religious life and everyday life. Those who attend church also consult a *nganga* or an *nkisi*, leaders in African traditional religions, when there is a crisis. The book of Chronicles rejects this type of dichotomy. It shows that worship in the temple was important, but not more important than obedience to the law. It reminds us that everyday life and religious exercises are two sides of the same coin.

'All Israel'

The expression 'all Israel' appears more than forty times in the book of Chronicles. It expresses the unity of Israel. From the beginning, Israel is presented in the genealogies as one family composed of the twelve sons of Jacob. Jacob is, in fact, constantly called 'Israel' in the book of Chronicles. This unity of Israel became a reality during the reigns of David and Solomon. 'All Israel' was united around David at major ceremonies, David was crowned king by 'all Israel', David and 'all Israel' conquered Jerusalem and 'all Israel' participated in transporting the ark of the covenant to Jerusalem (1 Chr 11:1, 4; 13:6).

The reigns of David and his successor, Solomon, offer a model of democratic relations between the king and his people. David included 'all Israel' in his projects. He was a king who discussed, or even better conferred, with his co-workers (1 Chr 13:1). He called his fellow-citizens 'my brothers' (1 Chr 28:2). The book stresses the subordination of the king to the authority of God. He is, in a real sense, the 'first among equals'. Today, the understanding of democracy in Africa has often been reduced to meaning little more than elections. The imposition of the Western concept of democracy in Africa has not gone smoothly, and some other form of democracy may be preferable. What is important is the active participation of the people as a whole.

The author's preoccupation with the unity of Israel led him to omit any mention of the political history of the northern kingdom. Even though that kingdom took 'Israel' as its official name, the book of Chronicles insists on using 'Israel' with a broader meaning. Despite the division into two kingdoms, the author regards Israel as one society. Hezekiah invited the people from the northern kingdom to come to Jerusalem to celebrate Passover (2 Chr 30:1). Josiah's reform included the northern kingdom (2 Chr 34:6-7).

The unity sought was not solely a sociological unity but especially a unity of faith. This is the reason that the people of the northern kingdom are not thought of as belonging to an independent political entity but are invited to the temple at Jerusalem.

The unity and identity of Israel were of prime importance for this people who were living in a territory without fixed or guarded borders in the heart of the vast Persian Empire. However, the concern for the unity of Israel did not hinder the author of the book from presenting Israel in its relationships with its neighbours. The genealogies in 1 Chronicles 1–9 include interactions between Israel and other nations and peoples.

In Chronicles, unity is associated with rejoicing. On numerous occasions 'all Israel' assembled for a feast (see, for example, 1 Chr 12:39-41). Joy, music, dance, feasting and drinking were part of these occasions.

The liturgy in Christian communities should use all the resources of the African culture to express our joy. Casio or Yamaha keyboards should not automatically replace our own xylophones and other traditional instruments that can be made at little cost. These instruments were banned from church by early Christian missionaries, who considered them pagan because they were also used at other gatherings. But the guitar and piano can be criticized for the same reason, for they are also used to produce worldly music.

A few years ago, traditional African dance in the church was widely condemned. But now, some congregations incorporate it in their worship. Igbo Christians of Nigeria often quote 1 Chronicles 25:1-31 to justify the place of music and dance in the celebration of worship. Dance, joy and shared meals should again find their place in the liturgy. Our membership in a particular Christian tradition should not prevent us from worshipping in an authentically African way. Doing so would reinforce our unity.

Seeking the Lord

The importance of 'seeking the Lord' is frequently emphasized in Chronicles. Unfortunately, the English language does not have a perfect translation for the Hebrew verb *darash*. 'Seek' is only part of its meaning; the other part conveys the idea of total obedience and submission, and even of repentance (2 Chr 7:14).

This obedience and submission are expressed especially in terms of ritual worship. The kings who succeeded were those who sought the Lord and who introduced reforms to put an end to idolatry (1 Chr 13:3; 2 Chr 14:3-4; 15:2; 17:4; 31:21; 34:3). David's first act as king after taking Jerusalem was to seek the Lord. This seeking expressed itself in his interest in the ark of the covenant, the symbol of the divine presence in the midst of his people. Thus 1 Chronicles 13:3 can be literally translated as 'Let us bring back the ark of our God to us, for we did not seek it in the days of Saul.' In some cases, the verb 'seek' in the book of Chronicles means 'repent' (see, for example, 2 Chr 7:14).

But this 'seeking' is not limited to the realm of institutional worship. When enemies, attack the king who is seeking the Lord also places his confidence in God, rather than in his army. And this reliance involves more than simply consulting the Lord in the hopes of receiving an oracle from him.

King Saul died because he did not consult the Lord and was unfaithful to him (1 Chr 10:13-14). The word *ma'al*, translated 'unfaithful', is the opposite of *darash*. It is the main word used for sin in the book of Chronicles (1 Chr 2:3; 5:25; 9:1; 10:13; 2 Chr 12:2; 26:16; 28:19; 29:19; 33:19; 36:14). Although it applies first to the religious realm, it also encompasses other areas of the relationship between God and his people.

We get the impression that much of the experience of the people of God was marked by unfaithfulness. The first time we encounter this word in Chronicles, it is applied to the tribe of Judah, David's tribe. The last time we encounter it, it is also applied to Judah.

In Chronicles, the sin of unfaithfulness is often accompanied by another action, abandoning God. Those who sin abandon God and are swept into idolatry, which results in neglect of the legitimate worship in Jerusalem and the corruption of the people. Unfaithful people are those who do not depend on the Lord, do not trust him, and count on their own strength. They deserve punishment. It was because of their unfaithfulness that the inhabitants of the northern kingdom were carried away captive by the Assyrians. Later, the kingdom of Judah was destroyed by the Babylonians and its inhabitants were deported for the same reason (1 Chr 5:25-26; 9:1).

Retribution

Retribution is one of the characteristics of the theology of the book of Chronicles. Faithfulness to the Lord brings blessing (victory in battle, riches, descendants, health and a good reputation), while the result of unfaithfulness is punishment (death, defeat, sickness, exile). The book of Chronicles presents us with a God who intervenes in the affairs of the world. In the NT, we also find examples of immediate punishment. Ananias and Saphira died suddenly when they sinned (Acts 5:1-10). And Christians are warned of the judgment reserved for the end of the world (2 Tim 4:1).

The modern and postmodern tendency to separate God from the sphere of human activity is not present in the book of Chronicles. Rather, its view is similar to the African view of divine involvement in human life. Our ancestors believed that the gods were involved in everyday life, and we still believe that. That is why a catastrophe or a defeat was interpreted in terms of the will of the tribal or clan divinity. While not allowing ourselves to abdicate our human responsibilities, we should live in a way that expresses our hope in God. He is the one who intervenes to change the course of history. He is the one who brought the exile of his people to an end. He is also there to bring an end to the sufferings of our continent.

However, the connection between obedience and blessing, or disobedience and punishment, should not hide the fact that God is also presented in the book of Chronicles as the source of pardon. The connection is not always automatic. Disobedience does not always call for punishment. David understood this well when he said, 'Let me fall into the hands of the Lord, for his mercy is very great; but do not let me fall into the hands of men' (1 Chr 21:13). He had grasped God's compassion.

There are many Christians in Africa who do not experience a life of joy because they continue to assume an automatic link between their life and punishment for sin. In Africa, any premature death or sterility in the family has always been attributed to some unfaithfulness towards a tribal or clan god, or even towards the ancestors. Even in today's Africa, the tendency is always to attribute an illness to wicked conduct.

If a person is sick, and especially if the illness continues after several days of fasting and prayer, people begin to look for the unconfessed sin. In many healing campaigns on the continent, the lame who cannot walk, the blind who cannot see and the sick who are not healed after powerful prayers for deliverance are often forced to confess a hidden sin which is hindering God from acting.

But not all illness originates in sin. Nor do all disabilities. Jesus' disciples thought that these were linked when they asked Jesus, 'Rabbi, who sinned, this man or his parents, that he was born blind?' (John 9:2). Jesus replied that neither had sinned, but that the man's blindness presented an opportunity to reveal God's glory.

Outline of Contents

COMMENTARY

1 Chr 1:1-9:44 Genealogies

In the OT, we also find genealogies in the books of Genesis and Ruth, but those of the book of Chronicles are the most extensive. They occupy the first nine chapters of the book. The relation between these chapters and the rest of Chronicles has often been disputed. Some commentators think that the two parts do not belong together. However, the fact that the themes of the second part have their roots in the genealogies suggests that the two parts are a unit.

While the first nine chapters of Chronicles are commonly classified as genealogical lists, it is important to recognize that these lists are not like modern genealogies. They include a historic dimension and deep theology.

In the past, genealogies were considered to be of purely historical interest. But it has now been recognized that they serve many purposes. In ancient societies the function of a genealogy was not limited to simply drawing up a family tree of those descended from a common ancestor and related by blood. Genealogies were also used to define an individual's social status, property rights, economic relations or position in the religious hierarchy.

In pre-colonial Africa, for example, the chief of the clan was supposed to belong to a particular family. The right of succession was limited to this particular family. Someone else might have all the qualities of a chief, but as long as he did not belong to the chief's family, he could not lay claim to the chieftaincy. The genealogy also served to support property rights on a piece of land, a river or a water source. Consequently the genealogy was carefully passed on orally from one generation to another.

Research into genealogies has also revealed another feature that would not have seemed at all odd to those in pre-colonial African societies. The terms 'father' and 'son' do not necessarily imply direct descendant. A son, a grandson and a great-grandson, in fact any male member of a particular clan, may be termed a 'son' of a common ancestor. This pattern can also be seen in the genealogies in Chronicles. For example, in 4:1 the sons of Judah are said to be Perez, Hezron, Carmi, Hur and Shobal, whereas 2:4, 5, 7 (see also Josh 7:1), 19 and 50 clearly show that these people are not related to Judah as father and son.

Genealogies also have a geographical dimension. People's names are frequently associated with place names. Hur is the firstborn of Ephrathah and the father of Kiriath-Jearim (2:50); Salma is the father of Bethlehem (2:51). Ephrathah, Kiriath-Jearim and Bethlehem are known as place names. The families of the scribe lived at Jabez the name (2:55) which is also of a person (4:9). The tribes mentioned in the lists each occupy a specified territory.

The genealogies of the first nine chapters begin with Adam and continue through Abraham, Israel (Jacob and his descendants), Judah and David up to the post-exilic period. Some authors suggest there is a geographical element in this presentation, with the scope narrowing from the world to the territory of Israel and Jerusalem to the temple.

The tribes of Judah, Levi and Benjamin receive special attention in these genealogies, particularly as regards the number of words allotted to each in the text. This suggests that these three tribes were the most important in the post-exilic community. The genealogy of Judah, the tribe of David, is presented first. The genealogy of Levi, the tribe of the Levites, is presented in the middle of the genealogies, while the very last genealogy is that of Benjamin, the tribe of Saul. It seems that the genealogies of the royal families and of religious leaders were well preserved at the time these lists were recorded.

The lists of those who returned from the Babylonian exile serve to create continuity between the communities before and after the exile. They show that the community living in the land of Judah under Persian rule still has an ongoing connection with the Israel of the monarchical period. At a time when all the territorial ties which would have supported tribal identities have lapsed into ancient history, and when the people of Israel are scattered throughout the Persian Empire, the genealogies in Chronicles are reminders that their unity is not territorial but the product of their descent from a common ancestor, Jacob.

Despite the emergence of large cities, most African societies still function on the basis of family ties. Unfortunately, unlike the genealogies in Chronicles, the rich genealogies in Africa are not used to unite but to divide. But we should not allow our ties to our family, clan, tribe and even country to obscure the fact that we all descend from a common ancestor created by God. Moreover, the history of African migrations shows that most tribes have not arrived at their present locations by deliberate choice but as a result of war or a natural disaster. Thus we find that the Ngbaka language spoken in the north-west section of the Democratic Republic of Congo (DRC) is very similar to the Mandja language spoken in the Central African Republic (CAR). The ethnic Bassa group is scattered across Cameroon, Nigeria, DRC, Mozambique, Liberia, Togo and Sierra Leone. Careful study might reveal that all the members of this ethnic group are descended from a common ancestor, Bassa. Today, Africa is the victim of its narrow nationalism. The genealogies in the book of Chronicles should help us to understand, based on our own genealogies, that we are all brothers and sisters. The African Union, formed at Durban in July 2002, could thus find fairly solid theoretical support.

1:1-2:2 Genealogy from Adam to Israel (Jacob)

Though the focal point of the author of the book of Chronicles is the twelve tribes of Israel, he wants to show that despite Israel's election by God, the Israelites are linked to the first human being, Adam, and also to the rest of humanity. Luke 3:23-38 makes a similar point when it gives the genealogy linking Jesus to Adam, and we should not forget that we Africans are also linked to the rest of humanity through Adam.

This genealogical list presented here is, however, very selective. After briefly listing the descendants of Japheth and Ham (1:5-16), attention turns to the line of Shem (1:17-23) to which Abraham, the father of the nation of Israel, belonged.

1:1-3 From Adam to Noah

This list is a shortened version of the list in Genesis 5:1-32. The lines of parentage and the length of each life are not given here. Cain and Abel, the first two sons of Adam, are not mentioned. *Seth*, Abel's replacement, takes their place (Gen 4:25).

1:4-23 The sons of Noah

The Hebrew Bible does not include the phrase *The sons of Noah* (1:4), but this relationship is implicit in the lists of the descendants of the sons of Noah that follow. The order in which these lists are presented is the reverse of their birth order, for although Shem is first in the list in 1:4, his descendants are mentioned last because of the link that the author wishes to create with Abraham.

Africa is not ignored in these genealogies, for the genealogy of Ham clearly mentions *Cush, Mizraim* and *Put* (1:8). Cush could be considered the ancestor of Africans. The area known as Cush comprised modern-day southern Egypt and northern Sudan. In the Septuagint the inhabitants of Cush are referred to as 'Ethiopians', a Greek word that was applied to people with dark skin living in southern Egypt (this area is to the north of modern Ethiopia, which was known as Abyssinia in the past). According to Esther 1:1 and 8:9, the Persian Empire extended from India to Cush.

Jeremiah 13:23 is referring to the Cushites when it asks, 'Can the Ethiopian change his skin?' The Greeks and Romans had a similar expression, 'washing an Ethiopian white' to refer to the futility of trying to change the unchangeable.

Egyptian culture had a considerable influence on Cush, although at times the situation was reversed and a Cushite king ruled over Egypt. In our time, the Cushite language includes some four hundred different groups of languages spoken throughout the Horn of Africa in Sudan, Ethiopia, Djibouti, Somalia, Kenya and Tanzania.

Mizraim is a reference to Egypt, whereas Put seems to refer to Libya. *Nimrod*, an African, is presented in the Bible as someone who was one of the first to become *a mighty warrior on earth* (1:10; see also Gen 10:8-10).

In the book of Chronicles there is no reference to the curse on Ham, which has often been taken as applying to Africans (Gen 9:18-27). This interpretation of the curse comes from a falsified ethnological theory that was used in the past to justify the slave trade and colonialism. It is completely wrong. African peoples are not cursed, but belong to God and are made in his image, just like the rest of humanity.

The African continent has always had a place in God's plan. The ot contains some 680 references to Egypt, some of them positive and others negative. Egypt had a negative reputation as the place where the children of Israel were enslaved (Exod 13:3; Deut 4:20). However, Egypt also made several positive contributions in the history of the people of God. Abraham – Abram at the time – stayed in Egypt when he needed to escape a famine (Gen 12:10). He received a large part of his riches from Pharaoh (Gen 12:16). It was in Africa (Egypt) that Jacob and his family found refuge during a later famine. It was also in Egypt that Jacob's family became numerous (Gen 46:3). The people of Judah took refuge in Egypt when they were fleeing from the Babylonians (2 Kgs 25:26; see Jer 44:1). Jesus' parents fled to Egypt to save the infant Jesus from Herod's massacre (Matt 2:13-15). Men from Egypt and Libya were present at Jerusalem on the day of Pentecost (Acts 2:10). One of the most celebrated conversions was that of an Ethiopian (Acts 8:26-38). No, Africa is not a cursed continent.

One of Eber's sons mentioned in **1:19** was named *Peleg*, which means 'division' in Hebrew. The explanatory note given about this name says, *because in his time the earth was divided*. This probably alludes to the division of humanity after the events at the Tower of Babel (Gen 11:1-9).

1:24-27 From Shem to Abraham

This section gives the genealogy of *Shem* to whose line the Israelites belonged. All of the sons of Shem are named in 1 Chronicles 1:17, but here only the genealogy of the line of *Arphaxad* is given (**1:24**), because it produced *Eber*, the father of the Hebrew race. The name Eber in **1:25** has often been thought to be the root of the word 'Hebrew'. The explanatory note in **1:27** is included to show that *Abram* is the same person as *Abraham*. He is the one who connects all the lists that follow. Not only that, but the author of Chronicles also intends to remind readers of God's promise to Abraham that he would be the father of a multitude of nations (Gen 17:5).

1:28-33 The sons of Abraham

Abraham is introduced, but his line of descendants through his wife Sarah is not presented at length here, because information on them will be presented in the following chapter. In the original text, neither Hagar nor Sarah is mentioned by name. Their names are added before 1:29 and 1:34 in the niv to make the lists easier to understand.

Chronicles does not look down on the descendants of Abraham through Hagar and Keturah (Gen 16:1-16). It lists

the descendants of Ishmael, the Arab people, for they are also among the 'many nations' that God promised would descend from Abraham (**1:29-31**). Unfortunately, because the Christian religion sprang from Judaism, Christians often do not treat Abraham's other descendants with respect.

1:34 From Abraham to Israel

This verse picks up from 1:28, reintroducing the progeny of Abraham in order to better prepare for the genealogy of Esau/Edom that follows and then for the genealogy of the sons of Israel.

1:35-54 The sons of Esau

Abraham's descendants are grouped according to their mothers, but this pattern is not followed with *the sons of Esau* (**1:35-37**), compare Gen 36:9-14. The genealogy of Esau is followed by that of his neighbours, *the sons of Seir* (**1:38-42**). This group was incorporated into Esau's line because *Timna*, the sister of *Lotan*, a son of Seir, became the concubine of Eliphaz, Esau's son (Gen 36:12). The list of the kings who reigned over *Edom* before the beginning of the monarchy in Israel (**1:43-50**) is followed by that of the subjugated *chiefs of Edom* (**1:51-54**).

2:1-2 The sons of Israel

Having dealt with the sons of Esau, the author now returns to the genealogy from which he branched off in 1:34. He began the genealogies with that of humanity in general, and has gradually pruned away side shoots so that he can focus on the group in which he is really interested, *the sons of Israel* (**2:1**). Jacob, the father of the twelve tribes, is consistently called Israel in the book of Chronicles. The only exception is found in 16:17, which is quoting Ps 105:10.

This list in (**2:1-2**) may be considered an introduction to the whole of 2:3-8:40. It lists the sons of Jacob in the same order that is usually followed in the book of Genesis (Gen 29:31-30:24; 35:16-26; 46:8-27).

2:3-8:40 Genealogy of the Sons of Israel

The detailed genealogies of each tribe that follow are not in the same order as the introductory list in 2:1-2. Because of the importance of the tribe of Judah as the tribe from which King David came, it starts with this tribe. It also focuses on that line within the tribe that leads directly to David: the line of Jesse. The genealogy of the tribe of Benjamin is given last, because it is the tribe of the unfaithful king Saul. Despite their inclusion among the sons of Israel in 2:1-2, the tribes of Dan and Zebulun are not mentioned. Either the author of the book of Chronicles wanted to replace their genealogies with those of Ephraim and Manasseh to retain the number of tribes as twelve, or their genealogies had simply been lost.

2:3-4:23 Genealogy of Judah

2:3-8 THE SONS OF JUDAH The genealogy of Judah starts with the names and a short genealogy of the five sons of Judah: *Er, Onan* and *Shelah* by the daughter of Shua and also *Perez* and *Zerah* by *Tamar,* Judah's daughter-in-law (2:3-8).

Judah is not presented as an ideal tribe. Its pre-eminence in the book of Chronicles is not due to merit but is a demonstration of the grace of God. The father of the tribe married *a Canaanite ... the daughter of Shua. Er, Judah's firstborn,* is said to have been *wicked in the Lord's sight* (**2:3**). Still worse, Judah had two children by his daughter-in-law, Tamar, an ancestor of Jesse, the father of David (**2:4**). The author of the book of Chronicles makes no judgment on the marriage of Judah with a non-Jewess, nor on his incestuous union with his daughter-in-law. Unfaithful *Achar,* called Achan in Joshua 7:1-26, also belongs to the tribe of Judah (**2:7**).

2:9-55 THE SONS OF HEZRON The author then moves on to concentrate on the genealogy of the three sons of *Hezron,* a descendant of Perez: *Jerahmeel, Ram* and *Caleb.*

Ram is not the firstborn but his genealogy is given first because of his relationship to Jesse, the father of David (2:9-17; see also Ruth 4:19-22). The book of Chronicles shows its interest in Jesse's family by mentioning the birth order of his children. The high point is reached in **2:15** with *David.* He is said to be the seventh child, whereas in 1 Samuel 16:10-13 he is eighth (it is possible that one of his brothers died young). We are also told that David's sister, *Abigail* married *Jether,* an *Ismaelite,* instead of an Israelite (**2:17**).

The genealogy of *Caleb* is given in 2:18-24. It will also be repeated later in 2:42-55. This family or clan is presented in terms of the children of each of his wives or concubines, two of whom were *Azubah* (**2:18-19**) and *Ephah* (**2:46**). The author's interest here is in introducing *Bezalel* (2:20), who was the craftsman who constructed the Tent of Meeting (Exod 31:1-5). The appearance of his name establishes that the tribe of Judah has long had an interest in the building of the temple. The others mentioned in **2:21-24** are associated with place names.

The genealogy of *Jerahmeel,* the third son of Hezron, is given in **2:25-41**. The names of his descendants are unknown throughout the rest of the OT. In another example of intermarriage in the tribe of Judah, *Sheshan gave his daughter in marriage to his servant Jarha,* who was an Egyptian (2:34-35).

The second list of Caleb's descendants in 2:42-55 probably incorporates descendants through wives who are not mentioned in the preceding genealogy (2:18-24). Once again there is a mingling of the names of people and places such as *Hebron* (**2:42-43**), *Haran* (2:46), *Ephrathah* (**2:50**), *Bethlehem* (**2:51**) and *Kiriath Jearim* (**2:52-53**).

3:1-24 DAVID'S DESCENDANTS Chapter 3 is totally devoted to the genealogy of David's family (3:1-24). He is, in a sense, the epicentre of all the genealogy of the tribe of Judah and

perhaps also of all the genealogies of the book of Chronicles. The genealogy of David's descendants is arranged according to three distinct periods: the sons of David, the kings of Judah and the post-exilic generation.

The sons of David are arranged according to whether they were born in Hebron or in Jerusalem (3:1-9). Even if the author asserts that in principle David was favoured by all Israel from the beginning of his reign (11:1-3), here he admits that David reigned first in *Hebron* before he ruled all Israel (**3:4**). The list of David's sons born in Hebron is also found in 2 Samuel 3:2-5.

The list of David's sons born at *Jerusalem* differs from that of 2 Samuel 5:14-16. In a totally unexpected way, *Solomon* appears as the fourth child of *Bathsheba.*

The list of David's sons who reigned on the throne of Judah (3:10-16) follows the order of succession used in the book of Kings, with the exception of *Johanan* who is introduced here as the first son of Josiah instead of Jehoahaz (**3:15**). Athalia, the usurper of the throne, is not mentioned (2 Kgs 23:31; 2 Chr 22:10-12).

The post-exilic generations are introduced in 3:17-24. *Zerubbabel,* the leader of the rebuilding of the temple, is here called the son of *Pedaiah,* although elsewhere he is called the son of Shealtiel (Ezra 3:2; Neh 12:1; Hag 1:14). There are several possible explanations for this discrepancy. For example, he may well have been Pedaiah's grandson. The names given the children of Zerubbabel are significant: *Meshullam* means 'restored'; *Hananiah,* 'the Lord is merciful'; *Shelomith,* 'peace'; *Hashubah,* 'the Lord has considered it'; *Ohel,* 'tent'; *Berekiah,* the Lord has blessed'; *Hasadiah,* 'the Lord has made a covenant of love'; and *Jushab-Hesed,* 'the covenant of love is re-established' (**3:19-20**). These different names contain the seeds of the restoration.

4:1-23 OTHER CLANS OF JUDAH The information about Judah ends with several lists that complete the genealogy of Judah. Many names in this section are unknown in the rest of the OT. The interest seems more geographical. The list also contains names of people as well as places. The term 'father' followed by a place name appears ten times. Ephrathah is the father of Bethlehem (**4:4**). Ashhur is the father of Tekoa (**4:5**), the home village of the prophet Amos (Amos 1:1).

The introduction to the section beginning in **4:1** revisits chapter 2 after the parenthesis of chapter 3. *Perez, Hezron, Carmi, Hur* and *Shobal* are mentioned in 2:4, 5, 7, 19-20, and 52 respectively. The section ends with a reference to Judah's son *Shelah* (**4:21-23**; see also 2:3).

The name *Jabez* means 'pain'. His mother called him that because *I gave birth to him in pain* (**4:9b**). These words remind us of Eve's punishment (Gen 3:16). The habit of giving a name related to the circumstances of a child's birth was current in Africa before the introduction of what is today called the 'surname' or 'family name'. But in many traditional societies there are no family names, and each child is given a special and significant name. My own name, Nupanga, derives from the Ngbaka language spoken in the north-west of the DRC and means 'May the earth become bitter'. Before my birth, my mother had had a stillborn child. Hence my name expressed my parents' desire that the ground would become bitter (compact) so that it could not receive me as it had received the other child at his burial. In the same way, the name Epaso (equivalent to the English 'surgery') indicates that the person was born by Caesarean section. We have lost great cultural richness by adopting a system of naming that is foreign to our understanding of families and the community.

Jabez' unpleasant name might have been seen as a curse. But his prayer changed his destiny. Despite his name, Jabez was honoured more than his brothers (**4:9a**). The first mention of the name of God in this book appears in the statement that he *cried out to the God of Israel* (**4:10**). This expression is dear to the author of Chronicles. It suggests a request for help from the Lord. After their return from exile, the Jewish community was anxious to *enlarge their territory*. Jabez did not depend on his own power to accomplish this, but turned to God in trust. His other request, *keep me from harm* is similar to what we ask of God in the prayer beginning 'Our Father': 'Deliver us from the evil one' (Matt 6:13).

Someone called *Joab* is mentioned as the father of craftsmen (**4:14**). Their occupations, which in general receive little honour, became very important in the context of the construction or reconstruction of the temple.

4:24-43 Genealogy of Simeon

The tribe of Simeon is dealt with immediately after that of Judah because of its territorial proximity to the south of Judah. Of the five sons of Simeon (see Gen 46:10; Exod 6:15), only Shaul's line is given (**4:24-27**). It is certainly the most important. This *Shaul* is not to be confused with King Saul, David's predecessor, who belonged to the tribe of Benjamin.

An explanatory note informs us that the tribe of Simeon was not as numerous as that of Judah (4:27). The association of the weak tribe of Simeon and the powerful tribe of Judah probably led to the assimilation of the first by the second. This fits with Jacob's prophecy that this tribe would be scattered among the people of Israel (Gen 49:7).

In 4:28-33, Chronicles describes the location occupied by the tribe of Simeon. The expression *until the reign of David* (**4:31**) indicates that these locations no longer belonged to the tribe of Simeon but to Judah. Their dispersion in the land and their relation with neighbouring groups is further outlined in **4:34-43**.

5:1-26 Genealogies of Reuben, Gad, Manasseh

The genealogies of the three Transjordan tribes are presented together. Though the descendants of each tribe are listed separately, their history is tackled collectively. The pattern followed here is similar to that followed for the tribe of Simeon. We are given the names of their descendants, their territories, and a few historical notes.

The genealogy of Reuben is given in 5:1-10. It begins with a note explaining the reason why Reuben, though the firstborn of Jacob's sons, does not appear first in the list of the tribes (**5:1**). Reuben lost his birthright because he had an incestuous relationship with his father's concubine (Gen 35:22). This loss of this right is predicted in Jacob's blessing, or rather, curse: *you will no longer excel, for you went up onto your father's bed, onto my couch and defiled it* (Gen 49:3-4). These words remind us that in some African cultures, incest is also considered to bring a curse of sterility or madness, and even death.

Acknowledging that the birthright had passed to *the sons of Joseph*, Chronicles points out that Judah is the most powerful tribe. This tribe was also promised royalty in Jacob's blessing: 'The sceptre will not depart from Judah, nor the ruler's staff from between his feet' (Exod 49:10).

After the explanatory note, which interrupts the train of thought, the genealogy picks up again (**5:3**). The genealogy of Reuben focuses on his descendants through Joel, a little known figure in the OT and one whose line of descent from Reuben is not identified here (**5:4**). The brief genealogy of the descendants of Joel quickly ends at the exile and the fate of one of his descendants, Beerah (**5:6**). This tragic end of the Reubenites contrasts with their territorial expansion during the reign of Saul (**5:9-10**).

The genealogy of the tribe of Gad follows immediately after that of Reuben because of their geographical proximity (**5:11-18**). There is no continuity in this genealogy. The various descendants are not introduced in chronological order. They live in Bashan, Gilead and Sharon. These territorial identifiers lend historical precision to Chronicles.

The genealogy of the Transjordan tribes is now interrupted by the story of the war by the Transjordan tribes against *the Hagrites and all their allies* (5:18-22). The Hagrites were descendants of Hagar, the Egyptian servant of Sarah, the wife of Abraham (Gen 16:1-16). They were briefly mentioned in 5:10. The account of this first war in Chronicles serves as a model for the accounts of other wars and victories in this book. The author makes it clear that the outcome of the war depends entirely on God. The number of troops and their armaments does not matter. The coalition of Transjordan tribes was victorious because at the crisis point of the war, they cry to God and depend on him. The author uses the passive voice to emphasize God's intervention: *they were helped in fighting them* (**5:20**). As a further sign of God's blessing, enormous quantities of goods were acquired: fifty thousand camels, two hundred fifty thousand sheep, two thousand donkeys, and one hundred thousand prisoners of war (**5:21**). The Hagrite lands were also occupied (**5:22**).

The account of the war is not followed by a complete genealogical list of the descendants of the half-tribe of Manasseh that lived to the east of the Jordan. Their proliferation is only hinted at (**5:23**). The bravery of the family heads is contrasted with their unfaithfulness to God. They follow the gods of the peoples of the country despite God's clear intervention during the battle (**5:24-25**).

In the logic of Chronicles, such unfaithfulness can only lead to exile and the loss of lands. The expression *the God of Israel stirred up the spirit* (**5:26**), common in the post-exilic period, suggests God's intervention in human activities (see also 2 Chr 21:10; 36:22-23). All three of the Transjordan tribes were taken into captivity by Tiglath-Pileser, king of Assyria.

6:1-81 Genealogy of Levi

At eighty-three verses, the genealogy of the tribe of Levi is second only to that of Judah (one hundred verses) in length. These two genealogies are the only ones traced from the ancestor of the tribe right to a descendant who went into exile. The importance of this tribe is also shown by the fact that it is given a central place in the genealogies, with five tribes being listed before it and six after. It receives this honour because of its role in the service of the temple, which had an important place in the life of the community, at least in the eyes of the author of Chronicles. But the Levites were more than just a religious order; they were also an integral part of the tribes of Israel. Chronicles is therefore concerned with the genealogy of the descendants of Levi (6:1-53) as well as their territory (6:54-66).

6:1-53 The descendants of Levi The genealogy of Levi begins by naming the three sons of Levi: *Gershon, Kohath and Merari* (**6:1**). It then immediately focuses on the family of Kohath, which produced the high priests (6:2-15). These were the only priests allowed to enter the Holy of Holies in the tabernacle, and later in the temple. The genealogy shows the continuity of the high priestly ministry right up until the time of the exile. Chronicles traces the line of the high priests from Aaron to *Jehozadak,* who was the high priest during the captivity under Nebuchadnezzar (**6:15**). However, this record of the line of high priests is very selective. Amariah and Jehoiada, for example, are not mentioned (2 Chr 19:11; 22:11). At the end of the section, speaking of the exile, Chronicles deliberately reminds us once again that it is the Lord who *sent Judah and Jerusalem into exile* (**6:15**).

After the very specific list of 6:2-15 in which only the descendants of Kohath are mentioned, Chronicles deals with all the descendants of Levi in 6:16-29. It traces the lineages of the three sons of Levi: *Gershon, Kohath and Merari* (**6:16**). For Gershon (**6:17, 20-21**) and Merari (**6:19; 29-30**), only the line descended from the eldest son to the seventh generation beyond the father is given. The genealogy of Kohath is longer than that of either of his two brothers and is given the central place to indicate that this is the most important branch of the family. It does not include Kohath's eldest son, Amram, because his genealogy has already been given in the line of high priests (6:2). Here the focus is on the line of *Amminadab* (**6:22**), who is not mentioned among the sons of Kohath in 6:2. The author traces this line because he wishes to show that the prophet Samuel belongs to the line of Kohath (**6:26**). It is important to him to prove that Samuel, who officiated as priest in Israel, belonged to the tribe of Levi and the line of the priests.

The next genealogy is that of the Levites who were in charge of the music in the worship services (6:33-47). The genealogy of these singers is prefaced by a note regarding their legitimacy. The singers, like the other Levites, were assigned to this service by David when the ark of the covenant arrived at its place of rest long before the construction of the temple (**6:31**). Three groups of singers were formed under the command of Heman, Asaph and Ethan. The genealogy of these three leading musicians is traced backwards to the second son of the three ancestors of the tribe of Levi: the musician *Heman* descended from Izhar, the second son of Kohath (**6:33-38**); *Asaph,* responsible for the second group, descended from Shimei, the second son of Gershon (**6:39-42**); while *Ethan,* the leader of the third group, descended from Mushi, the second son of Merari (**6:44-47**).

Heman, of the family of Kohath, was in overall command of the singers. His genealogy is the longest (going back to Jacob/Israel) and leads the list. Heman alone is designated specifically as *the musician* (6:33). He is presented as standing in the middle with Asaph on his right (6:39) and Ethan on his left (6:44).

Other Levites, called their *kinsmen* (NASB) were given other responsibilities in the temple service (**6:48**), but only the priests, the sons of Aaron, offered the *sacrifices in accordance with all that Moses the servant of God had commanded* (**6:49-53**).

6:54-81 The levite settlements Unlike the other tribes, the Levites have no specific area allocated to them, but live throughout Israel in the midst of the other tribes (Josh 14:4). So the next section gives precise geographical information about the settlements occupied by Levites (6:54-80). Once again, the settlements of the priests, the descendants of Aaron in the family of Kohath, head the list (**6:54-61**). These settlements consisted of towns and the surrounding pasture-lands.

7:1-5 Genealogy of Issachar

Four sons of Issachar are mentioned (**7:1**). This list corresponds with that in Numbers 26:23-24. However, only the descendants of the eldest son are listed, from *Tola* to the sons of *Izrahiah* (**7:2-3**). The other descendants of Issachar are not specifically named but referred to as *relatives* (**7:5**).

The list of the descendants of Issachar focuses on their military might. The descendants of Tola are described as *fighting men* (**7:2**) while those of Izrahiah are said to have been *ready for battle* (**7:4**). These genealogies probably came from a military source, such as the census initiated by David (21:2).

7:6-12 Genealogy of Benjamin

Three sons of Benjamin are mentioned with their respective descendants. Of the three, only *Bela* is mentioned in the list of the sons of Benjamin in Numbers 26:38-41. Like the genealogy of Issachar, that of Benjamin is of a military nature. Expressions such as *fighting men* or *fighting men ready to go out to war* are used (**7:7, 11**).

The genealogy of the tribe of Benjamin given here is quite short, and Benjamin is treated as simply one of the tribes that make up Israel. Longer versions are found in 8:1-40 and 9:35-44, where Benjamin is treated as the tribe that produced Saul, the first king of Israel.

In lists of the tribes of Israel, Benjamin is generally flanked by Zebulun and Dan. However, these two tribes are not mentioned in the genealogies in Chronicles. The reference to the Hushites in **7:12** comes at the end of the genealogy of Benjamin at the place where that of Dan could be expected. Hushim is mentioned as a son of Dan in Genesis 46:23.

THE ROLE OF THE ANCESTORS

Belief in and reverence for the ancestors is fundamental to traditional African thinking. It is believed that those who die at a mature age do not cease to be members of the community but continue to play an active role in the lives of their descendants. Thus those who are dying are sometimes asked to take messages to those who have died before, and are expected to continue to communicate with the living. If burial ceremonies and rituals are not properly observed, the spirit of the ancestor is believed to be capable of haunting the living in unpleasant ways.

Ancestors are believed to be the custodians of kinship, religion, morality, ethics, and customs and are expected to bless the community when traditional customs and beliefs are upheld. This belief meant that when, on the morning of the 2002 elections in Kenya, presidential candidate Uhuru Kenyatta went alone to his father's mausoleum to offer prayers, there was much speculation about whether this reverence for his ancestor would give him victory.

In the majority of cases, ancestors are male. There are, however, a few exceptions such as among the Kikuyu of Kenya and the Yoruba of Western Nigeria. Male or female ancestors are either the progenitors of a whole tribe, clan or community, or they are national liberators and defenders of the nation. They are symbols of tribal and ethnic unity, community cohesiveness and perpetuity of traditions. Many liberation fighters including Jomo Kenyatta (Kenya), Kenneth Kaunda (Zambia), Kwame Nkrumah (Ghana), Mnamdi Azikwe (Nigeria), Samora Machel (Mozambique), Walter Sisulu and Nelson Mandela (South Africa) will qualify as national ancestors. As fathers, these heroes suffered and sacrificed their lives to free their people. They are held in high esteem and some of them are sometimes venerated almost as gods.

It is believed that ancestors are capable of influencing the destinies of the living for good or ill, depending on how the living have treated them. This belief has given impetus to ancestor worship, which ranges from a simple pouring of palm wine accompanying a petition to elaborate animal sacrifices with festivities. For instance, when the Yoruba in western Nigeria experience a drought, the people say: 'The ancestors are angry therefore they have withheld the rain.' Consequently a national day of repentance is observed, not in sackcloth, but with animal sacrifice. Stories abound of heavy downpours of rain once the ancestors have been placated.

Given the power and influence wielded by the ancestors, some African theologies have proposed that Jesus be presented as an African ancestor. This idea is not without merit, for Jesus is like the ancestors in that people can take their problems to him and he does guarantee a better future for those who follow him. But there is a danger that making him an ancestor may be tantamount to reducing his post-resurrection elevation as Lord of lords (Phil 2:9-12) and may cause people to lose sight of his status as God.

The best approach may be modelled on the one taken in the book of Hebrews, which was written against a religious background similar to that found in traditional African religions. Taking this approach, it can be said that Jesus has come to fulfil our African ancestral cult and has taken the place of our ancestors, replacing them with himself. He has become the mediator between God and African society. Consequently, African veneration, worship and respect for the ancestors should now properly be addressed to Jesus as the mediator. All the 'intermediaries' of African theology or of any other religion or culture are inferior to the person and work of Christ. He is the superior mediator by virtue of this deity and his work of redemption. And just as he fulfilled, transformed and supplanted the Jewish religious system, so he has fulfilled, transformed and supplanted the ancestral cult and traditional religions of Africa.

Yusufu Turaki

7:13 Genealogy of Naphtali

The genealogy of Naphtali is the shortest of any tribe in Chronicles. Only the first generation is mentioned. The sons of Naphtali are designated as descendants of *Bilhah*, Rachel's servant, whom she gave to Jacob. Bilhah is known as the mother of Dan and Naphtali (Gen 35:25).

7:14-19 Genealogy of Western Manasseh

The part of the tribe of Manasseh situated on the east of the Jordan was already mentioned in 5:23-26. The descendants of Manasseh who are discussed in chapter 7 are those living to the west of the Jordan.

In another case of intermarriage that is not condemned in Chronicles, *Asriel*, son of Manasseh had an *Aramean* (Syrian) concubine who bore him *Makir, the father of Gilead* (**7:14**). (The Hebrew here is difficult to interpret, so some translations associate the concubine with Manasseh himself). The genealogy of Manasseh is linked to that of the Judean clan of Hezron through Makir, whose daughter was married to Hezron (see 2:21). Makir himself took a wife from among the Huppite and Shuppite peoples (**7:15**), who are mentioned in the genealogy of the tribe of Benjamin (**7:12**). Here we see interrelationships developing between Judah, Benjamin and Manasseh.

Another important descendant of Manasseh is *Zelophehad* whose name does not sound Israelite. The author tells us that this man *had only daughters* (7:15). This remark is important. Often in biblical genealogies the names of daughters are not given because the lineage did not pass through them. But the genealogy of the tribe of Manasseh shows how women contributed to maintaining the family lineage. Nine women are mentioned in 7:14-19 if we include the five daughters of Zelophehad who are not named in Chronicles but who received special attention in the OT. They appear in four passages (Num 26:33; 27:1-11; 36:2-12; Josh 17:3-6). They obtained lands by the same right as the men and had the right to freely choose a husband from among the members of their tribe.

Unfortunately, in many African countries, daughters are not considered to have the same value as sons. In Ngbaka, the name *kpala boko* (literally, 'feminine seed') is given to a female child born into a family with a number of girls and not wanting another girl. A woman who conceives only girls will not be loved, especially by her in-laws. Inheritance is thought to be transmitted through sons because when daughters marry, they will belong to the family of their husbands. The desire for a son leads some men to become polygamists. Fortunately, science has today shown that it is not the woman who determines the sex of a child. African women have a big contribution to make to the building up of the body of Christ in the same way as men. The African church should value women and encourage them to take up important positions at the heart of the church.

7:20-29 Genealogy of Ephraim

This genealogy includes two relatively short lists (**7:20-21a; 7:25-27**), separated by a historical anecdote (**7:21b-24**). The first lineage is traced from Ephraim to the son of *Zadab* who is not mentioned anywhere else, while the second list seems to be the genealogy of *Joshua*, son of Nun, successor of Moses (Josh 1:1).

The episode where Ephraim gave his son the name *Beriah*, which means 'misfortune' is similar to that involving Jabez (7:23; see 4:9-10). However, unlike Jabez, who was from the favoured tribe of Judah, Beriah does not seem to have shaken off the misfortune associated with his name.

The remaining verses give information concerning the lands occupied by the two sons of Joseph, Ephraim and Manasseh (**7:28-29**).

7:30-40 Genealogy of Asher

The list of the sons of Asher (**7:30**) corresponds to that in Genesis 46:17. As with the genealogies of Issachar and Benjamin, this genealogy results from a military census (**7:40**).

With the genealogy of Asher, the author of Chronicles has dealt with twelve tribes descended from the sons of Israel. His introduction of 'all Israel' is now complete. However, he returns to the genealogy of Benjamin.

8:1-40 Second genealogy of Benjamin

This chapter is the longest treatment of the descendants of Benjamin in the OT. The tribe of Benjamin is the one, along with that of Judah, that formed the southern kingdom, and remained faithful to the temple and to the Davidic tradition after the kingdom split in two. Judah and Benjamin are often mentioned together because of this (for example, see 2 Chr 15:2, 8). The tribe of Benjamin was also that of Saul, the first king of Israel. With Judah and Levi, Benjamin was therefore one of the principal tribes in the genealogies of Chronicles.

As with preceding lists, the author combines geographical details and historical events. From a strictly genealogical point of view, there is no direct and clear link between the descendants of Benjamin mentioned in 8:1-28. They are referred to as *heads of family* (8:6, 10, 13, 28). The interest here is probably more geographical.

Section **8:1-7** introduces those Benjamites who were *living in Geba* (8:6). They are the descendants of *Ehud* (8:6), who was probably the judge who was the son of Gera, a left-handed Benjamite, as mentioned in Judges 3:15.

Section **8:8-12** introduces those Benjamites living in *Moab* and in *Ono and Lod,* that is, outside the tribal lands. They are mentioned as being descendants of *Shaharaim,* an unknown person in the rest of the OT (8:8).

Finally, section **8:13-28** introduces the descendants of Benjamin living at *Aijalon* and *Gath* (8:13) and in *Jerusalem* (8:28).

After these considerations of places, **8:29-40** introduces the genealogy of the father of Gibeon. This lineage leads to Saul, the first king of Israel and the greatest member of the tribe of Benjamin.

9:1 Conclusion of the Genealogies

This verse marks the conclusion of the genealogies of the sons of Israel that began in 2:2. The exact nature of *the book of the kings of Israel* mentioned as a source or supplement is unknown. Unfortunately, the perfect picture of *All Israel* (**9:1a**) is offset by the mention of the exile of Judah to Babylon (**9:1b**). Here, the word 'Judah' represents the whole of the southern kingdom. Because of its unfaithfulness to God, this kingdom suffered the same fate as the ten northern tribes. 'All Israel' was unfaithful to God. This mention of the captivity is a foreshadowing of the events recorded in 2 Chronicles 36:14, 20.

While this verse is a conclusion, it also introduces the period following the captivity when Jerusalem was repopulated.

9:2-34 List of Returned Exiles

Chronicles presents the repopulation of Jerusalem as starting with the first inhabitants taking possession of their tribal or family properties (**9:2a**). The territorial occupation in the post-exilic period is thus presented as part of a continuum with the situation before the exile. In a way, those who returned from the exile were simply taking back what they had possessed in pre-exilic times.

The new arrivals are grouped in four distinct categories: the Israelites (laity), the priests, the Levites and the temple servants (*nethinims*) (**9:2b**). The exact nature of these servants' function in the temple is not clear (Ezra 8:20). The word used for them comes from a root word that means 'give', and suggests that these may have been those who were dedicated by their parents to the service of the Lord.

The list of the new inhabitants of Jerusalem is parallel to that of Nehemiah 11:1-36, with the exception of the mention of the descendants of Ephraim and Manasseh in Chronicles (**9:3**). In introducing the new inhabitants of Jerusalem, the author once again testifies to his interest in 'all Israel'. Jerusalem is not only the capital of Judah, as it became at the time of the separation of the kingdoms, it is the capital of all Israel, which overrides tribal differences just as it did during the time of David and Solomon. *Judah* and *Benjamin* represent the south while *Ephraim and Manasseh* represent the ten tribes of the north.

The descendants of Judah (9:4-6) are presented in terms of the three principal clans of the tribe: the Perezites (**9:4**), Shilonites (**9:5**) and Zerahites (**9:6**). The Perezites receive pre-eminence because David belonged to their clan.

Section **9:7-9** lists the descendants of *Benjamin*. There is no link between this list and the list of the Benjamites living in Jerusalem before the exile (8:14-28).

The remaining verses in the chapter concern the different categories of temple personnel. The *Levites* (**9:14-34**) receive more treatment than the priests (**9:10-13**). Among the Levites, particular attention is paid to the Levite *gatekeepers*, the temple guards (**9:17-32**). Their designation and assignments, like those of the Levite singers, date back to David and Samuel (**9:22**). They form a distinct group at the heart of Korah's clan.

What characterizes the list of temple personnel is the diversity of their functions. They all had different gifts that they used to keep the temple functioning. Similarly, Paul reminds the Corinthians, 'There are different gifts, but the same Spirit. There are different kinds of service, but the same Lord. There are different kinds of working, but the same God works all of them in all men. Now to each one the manifestation of the Spirit is given for the common good' (1 Cor. 12:4-7). The list in Chronicles and these verses from Paul underscore two important things that contribute to the good health of the body of Christ. First, the Spirit of God gives gifts to all. The church of God is not divided into actors and spectators. Every single member should participate in ministry. The community should be organized in such a way that all the gifts may be placed at the service of building up the body of the church. The phenomenon that some people assume too many functions in the church sometimes hinders others from developing their gifts. The second point that should be clear is that different gifts are not in competition or hierarchical. They are all important and each should contribute to the building up of the body as a whole.

9:35-44 Genealogy of Saul

The author now returns to the genealogy of Saul, which was given in 8:29-40. At first glance, this list seems to be a simple repetition of the first one, with minor differences. In chapter 8, the genealogy of Saul included nineteen generations and extends beyond the exile. In chapter 9, the lineage stops at the sixteenth generation, that of the exile. Verses 8:39-40 are not repeated after **9:44**. This list serves as a transition to what follows in Chronicles, namely the history of the monarchy.

1 Chr 10:1-14 The Extinction of Saul's Dynasty

From this chapter onward, Chronicles focuses on the story of Israel's monarchy. However, the first king of Israel, Saul, receives little attention; his reign is not reported. Whereas the book of Samuel gives a detailed account of the beginning of the monarchy in Israel, God's designation of Saul as king and his anointing (1 Sam 8:1-12:25), Chronicles retains only the story of Saul's last and fatal battle against the

Philistines on Mount Gilboa. But the author of Chronicles was well aware that Israel was not originally a monarchy. He knew that their neighbours, the Edomites, had kings long before there were kings in Israel (1:43).

The story of the death of Saul is intended to make it clear that his entire house was wiped out when his dynasty ended. The climax of the story is found in **10:6**, *So Saul and his three sons died, and all his house died together.* This verse differs from 1 Samuel 31:6, which reads, 'So Saul and three of his sons and his armour-bearer and all his men died together that same day.' The words 'all his house' are particularly important for the author of Chronicles because he wishes to show that the throne passed peacefully from Saul to David. David is not implicated in any way in the death of Saul. A Sechuana (Botswana) proverb says, *Bogosi boa tsalelo, ga bo loeloe* ['no one fights for royalty, you are born to it']. The author of Chronicles regards David as born for royalty (5:2), and thus neither the brief two-year reign of Ish-bosheth, Saul's son, nor the struggle between the house of Saul and that of David (2 Sam 2:1-4:12) are mentioned. For Chronicles, the battle on the mountain of Gilboa ended Saul's dynasty. All those who could aspire to succeed Saul died in that battle.

Chronicles concludes the story of the death of Saul with a theological evaluation: *Saul died because he was unfaithful to the Lord* (**10:13**). His going to *a medium for guidance* is only one example of the unfaithfulness that characterized his entire reign.

Chronicles emphasizes that the death of Saul was not brought about by war or circumstances, but by God. Saul committed suicide (**10:4**), but the text says, *So the Lord put him to death* (**10:14**). It was also the Lord who transferred the kingdom to David, the son of Jesse. Unfaithfulness to God always leads to disaster.

The OT records at least six cases of suicide (Judg 9:50-57; 16:21-31; 1 Sam 31:1-7; 1 Chr 10:4-5; 2 Sam 17:23; 1 Kgs 16:15-20). The reason for all these suicides is the refusal to accept shame. However, the only case of suicide clearly considered heroic is that of Samson, who is said to have *killed many more when he died than while he lived* (Judg 16:30). In 10:4, Chronicles does not mention that Saul committed suicide because he wanted to avoid being killed by uncircumcised men (see 1 Sam 31:4). The author does not want Saul's suicide to appear heroic.

Suicide is becoming increasingly common in Africa. As in the OT, the motive is often a refusal to live with shame. Many suicides would not happen if the community showed a little more compassion towards those who have done wrong. But a lack of support often leads people to adopt the easiest, most desperate and most immediate way out – suicide. Many young women who become pregnant before marriage commit suicide to avoid shame and punishment by their parents. The church should be the place where those who have

lost their reason to live can find new hope through Jesus Christ, who took our shame on himself and faced ignominy courageously even while dying on the cross. It is a great pity that churches in Africa have not put ministries in place to help those tempted to commit suicide.

1 Chr 11:1-29:30 The Reign of David

David's origins are given in the genealogy (2:10-17) but nothing is said of David's youth. Chronicles makes no mention of his anointing by Samuel (1 Sam 16:1-13). He only becomes important when he becomes king. David's reign dominates Chronicles and serves as a standard to evaluate the reigns of the various kings who succeeded him on the throne of Israel. It is stressed that, in contrast to his predecessor, Saul, David devoted his whole reign to seeking the Lord. Thus the focus is on David's role as initiator of the construction of the temple and organizer of the worship there. The sinful relationship between David and Bathsheba is not mentioned. Nor is David presented as the young man who killed the giant Goliath or the hero who won all his wars and organized the administration of his empire. Even though Chronicles includes a few stories of David's victories in battle, it is primarily interested in his establishing a period of peace in which it would be possible to construct the temple.

David's reign is not presented as flawless. He fails in his first attempt to bring the ark of the covenant back to Jerusalem. He orders a census of which the Lord does not approve. Yet even in these failures, Chronicles evaluates David more favourably than does the book of Kings. The failed first attempt to bring the ark back to Jerusalem becomes an occasion to underline the importance of the Levites and to describe the first worship before the ark (without parallel in 2 Samuel 6:1-23). The unapproved census ends with the choice of the site for the construction of the temple (without parallel in 2 Samuel 24:1-25).

David's real failure lay in his being disqualified for the construction of the temple, an honour that was reserved for his son Solomon (17:1-27; 22:7-8; 28:3).

11:1-12:40 David Becomes King

These chapters describe the circumstances of David's becoming king of Israel.

11:1-3 David's coronation

Chronicles gives us the impression that David became king immediately after the death of Saul. 'The king is dead; long live the king.' The genealogy of David in 3:1-9 avoided mentioning that David was crowned on two separate occasions. In 2 Samuel 5:1-3, we are told that David was king of Judah for only seven years before reigning over both Israel and Judah (after the death of Ish-Bosheth) for thirty-three years.

Chronicles, however, presents all the people without exception as participating in the crowning of David as king and speaks as if David reigned over *all Israel* from the beginning of his reign (**11:1**). The writer is preoccupied with the unity of Israel around the new king anointed in accordance with the will of God.

In the theological evaluation of Saul's reign (10:13-14), the author has already stated that David was not chosen to be king by the Israelites but that God handed the kingdom to him. Here, too, the crowning of David is not presented as simply a fact of political history. David had been chosen by God to be king, even during Saul's lifetime (**11:2**). He is anointed as king following God's promise delivered by the prophet Samuel (**11:3**). The emphasis that everything is occurring *as the Lord had promised* is also reaffirmed in 11:10.

11:4-9 The conquest of Jerusalem

The capture of Jerusalem is presented as David's first act as king. It even interrupts the description of the coronation ceremony (which the author will return to in 12:24).

In 2 Samuel 5:6-9, the capture of Jerusalem is presented primarily as a military conquest, prompted by political concerns. Jerusalem would provide a neutral capital because it did not belong to any tribe in particular and was situated near the border between the north and the south. Moreover, from a military standpoint, it was easily defensible because it was situated on a hill.

In Chronicles, on the other hand, Jerusalem is thought of primarily as a religious capital. It seems that David already sees the role of Jerusalem as the place of residence of the ark of the covenant and the future site of the temple. As well, David conquered Jerusalem, not with *his men*, meaning with his private militia as in 2 Samuel 5:6, but rather with *all Israel* (**11:4**). We get the impression that all the people assembled for the coronation of David march with him against Jerusalem.

From this perspective, Jerusalem belongs to all the people of Israel. Thus whereas in 2 Samuel 5:9, 'David … called it the City of David', in **11:7** we are told, *and so it was called the City of David,* implying that others were also involved in giving it that name.

Unlike 2 Samuel 5:6-10, Chronicles says nothing about 'the blind and the lame' in **11:5**. Moreover, Joab, who is absent from the account in Samuel, occupies a prominent place in the account in Chronicles. He is the one who takes the city and plays an active role in restoring it (11:6-8).

11:10-12:23 David's supporters

At this point we are given a list of the names of David's fighting men, interrupted by a few explanatory notes praising their exploits. The introduction to the list in **11:10** explains why these names are being given here. The author wants to show his readers again that David fought for the kingdom with people coming from *all Israel* according to God's will. The bravery of the men who offered their total support to David is a sign of the accomplishing of *the word of the Lord.*

The list in 11:11-47 parallels that in 2 Samuel 23:8-39, except for 11:41-47, which is not found anywhere else in the OT. What is most different about the two lists is the context in which Chronicles places its list. In the book of Samuel, the list comes as an appendix to the account of David's reign; that is, at the end of his career. Its purpose was to exalt the reign of David through the exploits of these different war heroes. In Chronicles, on the other hand, the list appears right at the beginning of David's reign. It is put there in order to show us that David became king thanks to the unity and heroic support of the people. These war heroes are introduced introduced in three groups: the Three (11:11-19), three individuals (11:20-24), and the Thirty (11:26-47).

In 1:12, Chronicles speaks of *three mighty men,* but at this point only two names are given: Jashobeam and Eleazar. The name of the third, Shammah (2 Sam 23:11), is not mentioned. These men are singled out because of their extraordinary feats of arms. *Jashobeam,* whose name means 'let the people return', killed three hundred men with his spear in one encounter (**11:11**). *Eleazar,* whose name means 'God helps', along with only David, struck down a troop of Philistines (**11:12-14**). In Samuel, this exploit against the Philistines is attributed to Shammah. The Three were brave both individually and collectively. At the risk of their lives, they crossed the camp of the Philistines to draw water for David (**11:15-19**).

Two other chiefs are mentioned in 11:20-25, apparently belonging to a second list of three. Abishai, the brother of Joab, killed three hundred men with his spear (**11:20-21**). Benaiah killed a lion (or three lions, depending on how one translates the Hebrew here) and an Egyptian who was about two and a half metres (seven and a half feet) tall (**11:22-24**). Despite their exploits, these other chiefs did not measure up to the first three (**11:25**).

David's support was not limited only to his own tribe of Judah. The list in 11:26-47 includes men from Benjamin, Simeon, Dan, Ephraim, Reuben and the tribe of Manasseh on the east of the Jordan. Even foreigners from Ammon and Moab supported David's kingship (**11:39, 46**). *Uriah the Hittite,* known in the book of Samuel as the husband of Bathsheba (1 Sam 11:3) is listed here as one of David's mighty men (**11:41**).

This list is followed by another list of the Israelite warriors who join David before he becomes king (12:1-38). Whereas in 1 Samuel 22:2, the first men to come to join David are described as 'all those who were in distress or in debt or discontented', Chronicles presents him as surrounded by *warriors* from an early date (**12:1**).

These men are said to have come to David at Ziklag and in the desert. Mention of these places recalls, the hostility between Saul (who was king at the time) and David, as well as the years of David's wandering before his coronation as king (1 Sam 27:1-2 Sam 4:12). In his flight from Saul, David had found refuge among the Philistines and had fought alongside them. For his allegiance, David had received the city of Ziklag as payment from Achish, king of Gath (1 Sam 27:6).

The first warriors to be mentioned are the mighty ambidextrous men of the tribe of Benjamin (12:1-7b). They were *kinsmen of Saul* (12:2). Mention of them makes it clear that well before the death of Saul, some of those in his own tribe had given their support to David, recognizing in him the king chosen by God.

David also received support from a more distant tribe, Gad, on the east of the Jordan (12:8-15). The Gadites crossed the Jordan when it was in flood to join him (12:15). There may be some word play in the name of their chief, *Ezer*, which is related to the Hebrew verb meaning aid or support. Variants of this word are also found in the names Ahiezer (12:3), Azarel and Joezer (12:6) and Ezer (12:9)

A second wave of Benjamites as well as men from Judah came to assist David (12:16-19a). However, David was not certain of their sincerity. Were they traitors or friends? The prophecy of Amasai, one of the leading officers, reassured him. It is said that *the Spirit came upon Amasai*, or literally, that 'the Spirit then clothed himself with Amasai' (12:18). The expression reminds us of the call to Christians today to be 'clothed with Christ' (Gal 3:27).

Verses 12:20-22 tell us that men of the tribe of Manasseh joined David when he went to fight against Saul on behalf of the Philistines. The Philistines sent David back, and thus he could not be accused of having fought against his own people (12:19b; see also 1 Sam 29:1-11).

12:24-40 The celebration of David's coronation

After the diversions into the capture of Jerusalem and events preceding David's coronation (11:4-12:23), Chronicles again takes up the story of his coronation at Hebron.

The preceding lists show that David receives support from several tribes, but only to a limited extent. Now in 12:23-38, all twelve tribes are present at Hebron for the coronation. The sequence of the tribes is unparalleled in the OT. Even Levi is presented as a secular tribe, rather than a religious one (12:26).

The number of members of each contingent shows that the tribes farther away provided more troops than those nearby. Judah and Benjamin supplied six thousand eight hundred and three thousand men respectively (12:24; 29a), whereas the Transjordan tribes of Reuben, Gad and Manasseh provided one hundred and twenty thousand men (12:37) and the most distant tribe, Dan, sent twenty eight

thousand six hundred men (12:35). Verse 12:29b explains the small representation from Benjamin: most of them had remained loyal to Saul's house.

The men of Issachar are described as having a particular ability, they *understood the times and knew what Israel should do* (12:32). Jesus reproached the Pharisees and Sadducees for their inability to discern the signs of the times (Matt 16:2-3). The tendency among Christians is to act the same way at all times. However, each situation calls for an appropriate response.

The reader of these lists will certainly be struck by the fact that these different groups came with *undivided loyalty* (12:33) and were *fully determined* to accomplish their goal (12:38). The church in Africa often goes to battle in disarray. To fight the powers of evil that keep the continent in darkness, the church must put aside its internal differences, form a unified camp and fight the enemy as one.

This point is reinforced by the overall agreement on the coronation of David implicit in the expression *of one mind* (12:38). In Hebrew, the expression is literally 'of only one heart'. This particular expression is also present in many African languages and signifies agreement and involvement. Work well done is described as *mosala na motema moko* ['work done with one heart'] in Lingala (DRC), and as done *be oko* ['with a single heart'] in Sango (CAR).

The constant focus of Chronicles on the unity of Israel highlights the fact that the church of Christ in Africa is weak because of its divisions. It has been reduced to groups of church members with no connection to one another. The roots of the division are often a thirst for power, a search for money and tribalism. But Paul told the Galatians, 'There is neither Jew nor Greek, slave nor free, male nor female, for you are all one in Christ Jesus' (Gal 3:28). Paraphrasing Paul, we could say, 'There is no longer either Hema or Lendu (DRC); there is neither Tutsi nor Hutu (Rwanda/Burundi, Uganda); there is neither Zulu nor Xhosa (South Africa); there is no longer either Baule or Senufo (Ivory Coast), because you are one in Jesus Christ.'

The chapter ends with the feast that followed the coronation of the new king of all Israel (12:39-40). The feast lasted three days, during which those present ate and drank. Each tribe, even those from farthest away such as Issachar, Zebulun and Naphtali, contributed to the feast bringing provisions which *their families had supplied*. In many African villages, a feast is often organized with contributions from everyone, each one according to his particular area of work. The hunter brings game, the winemaker brings beverages, the women contribute produce from their fields. It is because everyone contributes that the village feast can be considered as belonging to everyone. There is no need to receive a personal invitation to attend.

David's coronation brought *joy in Israel* (12:40). The theme of joy is important in the eyes of the author of

Chronicles (see also 1 Chr 15:16; 29:9, 17, 26; 2 Chr 15:15; 20:27; 23:13-18; 24:10; 29:30, 36).

13:1-17:27 History of the Ark of the Covenant

The ark of the covenant, the chest containing the tablets of the law given by Moses, was one of the most sacred objects of the Jewish religion. Thus David wanted it brought to Jerusalem. The transport of the ark in 2 Samuel 6:1-23 is presented as a continuous story. In Chronicles, this event is separated into two parts. The story of the transfer of the ark of the covenant reaches its peak when David finally decides to build a permanent shelter, a temple, for it at Jerusalem.

13:1-14 Attempt to bring the ark to Jerusalem

Chronicles presents the transportation of the ark as David's first official act after his installation at Jerusalem. In the book of Samuel, the story of the construction of the palace of the new king, the growth of his family and his double victory over the Philistines precedes the transportion of the ark. Chronicles, however, structures the information to show that the ark was David's primary preoccupation after taking the throne. In other words, we could say that David sought first the kingdom of God (Matt 6:33). In that respect he was different from Saul whose negligence with regard to the ark is remembered here, again using the Hebrew verb *darash,* meaning 'seek' (**13:3**; see also 10:13-14). Because the ark was the symbol of the presence of God in the midst of his people, neglecting the ark was equivalent to neglecting God himself.

The introduction in 13:1-4 is not found in the parallel account in 2 Samuel 6. These verses make the transport of the ark a more important event than the crowning of David. In the book of Samuel, the transport of the ark to Jerusalem is presented as almost a military enterprise led by David and his own thirty thousand men (2 Sam 6:1). But in Chronicles, the transport is more a religious enterprise in which *all Israel* took part. Those who had not attended David's coronation, that is, *the rest of our brothers throughout the territories of Israel,* were invited to join in transporting the ark. A special invitation was extended to the priests and Levites (**13:2**), although they played no major part in this first effort to bring the ark to Jerusalem.

The initiative behind bringing the ark to Jerusalem was David's, but the final decision to proceed with it was made in consultation with all the leaders of Israel (**13:1**). This *whole assembly* of Israel is referred to using a term that is usually used of a religious congregation.

David is here presented as a democratic king who refuses to impose a unilateral decision on his people. After the consultation with the chiefs, what had been David's personal concern became a national matter, an affair of state. He understood that there is strength in unity, as a Mongo-Nkundo (DRC) proverb stresses when it says 'one person

alone cannot break a branch'. David gives the African church an example of what makes a good leader. He avoids making unilateral decisions, the root of much frustration and lack of support.

The active participation of the people in this ceremony of bringing the ark of the covenant to Jerusalem is shown by the repeated use of the plural: *Let us send word far and wide to the rest of* our *brothers ... to come and join us. Let us bring the ark of* our *God back to us* (13:2-3). This wide mobilization of the people is also supported by the geographical facts. The people who assembled at Jerusalem had come from places as far apart as Shihor in Egypt (perhaps in the Nile delta) and the entry of Hamath in Syria (**13:5**). They had gathered to bring back the holiest item in Israel, the ark of *the Lord, who is enthroned between the cherubim* (**13:6**). The cherubim were winged beings who guarded access to the presence of God (Gen 3:24).

But the ark of the covenant did not make it to Jerusalem. The unfortunate death of Uzzah put an end to the joyful procession (**13:7-10**). He had touched the ark in an attempt to steady it and prevent it from falling when the oxen shook it. His tragic end plunged Israel into great agitation as to how such a holy object could be safely moved (**13:12**).

David directed that the ark of the covenant should be temporarily stored in the house of Obed-Edom, who lived at Gath, which may have been a town with the same name as the Philistine town. Its presence in his home brought him blessing (**13:13-14**). It is worth noting that the presence of God is simultaneously a source of death and of blessing. In the case of Uzzah, he died trying to prevent the ark of the covenant from falling. For Obed-Edom, the ark was a source of blessing, for his family and for everything that belonged to him. In trying to understand this, we can use the illustration of an electric current. When the current is put in contact with a light bulb, it produces light. But when it is brought in contact with a human body, it can produce death. Like electricity, the presence of God is dangerous if he is not treated carefully.

The disastrous end of this ceremony shows that joy and praise cannot replace obedience. For the last few years Christian congregations in Africa have given particular importance to songs and to praise in the liturgy of the church. Hours are spent in dance and cries of joy are mixed with prayers and other prophecies. These things are good, but they become useless if our lives are not in conformity with the will of God.

We will see later that while David had been keen to serve, he had been wrong to attempt to transport the ark in an ox cart instead of on the shoulders of the Levites. In our congregations, there are many people who are keen to help in any way to show their service to God. But it is important to check that any actions taken are in conformity with the word of God.

14:1-17 David's prosperity

This section interrupts the story of bringing the ark of the covenant to Jerusalem. We may thus get the impression that it is describing what happened during the three months during which the ark stayed at the home of Obed-Edom (13:14). But it would be impossible for David to build a palace, father a large family and defeat the Philistines twice, all in the space of three months. In 2 Samuel 5:11-25, these events are all reported directly after the conquest of Jerusalem. Probably the purpose of this section is to make it clear how David's fame is spreading (**14:17**) and to show that he continues to be blessed by God despite his first failure to bring back the ark.

David received material and manpower for constructing his palace from Hiram, king of Tyre. David sees in this the confirmation of his kingdom by God (**14:1-2**). In any era, a king must have a palace. The recognition of God as king meant that he too should have his palace, the temple.

The list of David's sons born at Jerusalem is not included for genealogical purposes (14:3-7). The emphasis here is indicated by the repetition of the word 'more': *David took more wives and became the father of more sons and daughters* (**14:3**). At that time, such a large family was, in fact, a sign of divine blessing, as it still is in many traditional African societies. One of the sons of David mentioned before Solomon in verse **14:4** is Nathan. In the genealogy of Luke 3:23-38, Nathan is the only son of David through whom the family lineage passes. Solomon is set aside.

We are also told of David's double victory over the Philistines (14:8-16). The Philistines were considered the traditional enemies of Israel. The first king of Israel, Saul, dies fighting them. The Philistines attack David because they have learned that their former vassal has now become *king over all Israel* (**14:8**; note that 2 Sam 5:17 simply says 'king of Israel'). As long as David was only king of Judah, he had not been regarded as a threat by the Philistines. But although the reason for the Philistine attack was political, the author of Chronicles also sees it as having a spiritual dimension.

David's double victory over the Philistines is in marked contrast to Saul's defeat. Twice, David proves a model of perfect obedience to God. He consults (*darash*) God before each battle whereas Saul had not done so (**14:10, 14**). As a mighty warrior, God gave David two different battle strategies (14:10, 14) and each victory is a result of God's help (**14:11, 15**). We should seek the will of God on every occasion. Each new situation demands a new strategy.

When the Philistines defeated Saul and his army, they put his armour in the temple of Dagon (10:10). In **14:12**, the situation is reversed when the Philistines abandoned their gods. But David does not bring them to the sanctuary: instead he burns them.

The conclusion of this section tells of David's renown (14:17). David is blessed, not for his personal benefit, but for the benefit of the people of God (14:2).

15:1-16:43 Bringing the ark to Jerusalem

The insertion of chapter 14 left the ark in limbo. No reason was given for the failure of the first effort to bring it to Jerusalem. But in this chapter, Chronicles returns to the ark. The account of the second effort to bring it back to Jerusalem is very different from that given in Samuel. New themes are introduced, notably the organization of the Levites and their permanent assignment well before the construction of the temple. There is also a long introduction devoted to the preparations of a place for the ark, the means of transport and the personnel needed for moving it (15:1-25).

In 2 Samuel 6:12, David went to fetch the ark from the house of Obed-Edom because he had learned of how God had blessed him and all that belonged to him. It could thus be said that it was a form of envy that prompted David to attempt to move it again, despite the first failure. Chronicles allows no room for envy as a motive, because it has just informed us of how richly David was blessed.

The three-month delay between the first and second attempts permitted David to prepare an appropriate place to shelter the ark (**15:1**). While doing this, David identified the reason for the failure of the first mission: the Levites are the only people authorized to carry the ark (**15:13**). They have been chosen by God *to carry the ark of the Lord and to minister before him forever* (**15:2**).

As at the first attempt to move the ark, *all Israel* assembled at Jerusalem (**15:3**). The priests and Levites had to consecrate themselves for the occasion (**15:12, 14**) which involved washing their clothes and abstinence from sex (Exod 19:10, 14-15). The ark was not placed on a cart but *the Levites carried the ark of God with the poles on their shoulders, as Moses had commanded in accordance with the word of the Lord* (**15:15**). On this occasion, David initiated a new class of Levites, the singers and musicians, who were to provide music to accompany the movement of the ark (**15:16**).

The ark was transported to Jerusalem with joy, dance, music and sacrifices (**15:25-29**). And whereas Uzzah had been struck down by God, the Levites are helped by him (15:26).

The reference to Michal, introduced here as the *daughter of Saul* reminds us of the proverb 'like father, like son (or like daughter)'. In the same way as her father had neglected the ark, the daughter does not participate in Israel's joy when the ark of the covenant enters Jerusalem (15:29).

We next have an account of the first service before the ark of the covenant at Jerusalem (16:1-43). In principle, the arrival of the ark in Jerusalem should have put an end to the ministry of the Levites because there would be no more need to carry the ark. But in Chronicles David assigns the Levites a new and permanent ministry before the ark: *to make petition, to give thanks, and to praise the Lord, the God of Israel* (**16:4-7**).

The *psalm of thanks* sung by the Levites (16:8-36) proclaims God's royalty (**16:31**), a theme dear to the author of Chronicles. This song is made up of three songs found in the canonical book of Psalms: **16:8-22** corresponds to Ps 105:1-15; 16:23-33 corresponds to Ps 96:1-13; and **16:34-36** corresponds to Ps 106:1, 47-48. There are some changes in the new psalm thus formed, changes that suit the context of Chronicles. For example, the ending of the original psalm in 106:48-49 says, 'Praise be to the Lord, the God of Israel, from everlasting to everlasting. Let all the people say, "Amen!" Praise the Lord.' The call to respond in the book of Psalms becomes in Chronicles a spontaneous response of the people to the song of the singers.

The new ministry assigned to the Levites, now that the ark is in Jerusalem, marks the beginning of regular services well before the construction of the temple (**16:37-42**).

17:1-27 David forbidden to build the temple

This chapter is one of the most important in the presentation of the history of Israel in Chronicles. It also lays the foundation of the author's theology, which centres on the temple, and marks the beginning of a long process that culminates in the construction and dedication of the temple by Solomon in 2 Chronicles 6–7.

The chapter begins with a description of David's situation and his interview with Nathan (**17:1-2**). It is quite similar to 2 Samuel 7:1 except that the sentence *The Lord had given him rest from all his enemies around him* does not appear in Chronicles. As will be clarified later, the 'rest' is the prerequisite for the construction of the temple. Since David did not build the temple, his reign could not be said to be a time of rest.

The arrival of the ark at Jerusalem and its installation in a tent (15:1) made David recognize the disparity between his palace built with cedar wood and the poor housing provided for the ark (17:1). Because the 'Lord reigns' (16:31), he merited the honour due a king. David informed his spiritual counsellor, Nathan, of his intention to build a temple to correct the situation. Nathan's spontaneous response to David's desire was yes.

However, in **17:3-4** God gives a negative response to David's project. The apparent contradiction between Nathan's 'yes' and God's 'no' has often been emphasized. But Nathan's response to David after having received God's instructions is not a rejection of David's project. Though God minimizes the importance of the temple construction, he does not oppose it (**17:5-6**). The question here is not whether God accepts the idea of the project but whether now is the right time to pursue it. In God's eyes, the period of rest favourable to the construction of the temple, has not yet come (**17:8-10a;** 1 Kings 5:35). David is not to build the temple but one of his sons (Solomon, not mentioned by name here) will be designated to build it (**17:12**).

Nathan's message in 17:4-15 is sometimes called 'the dynastic oracle' because in it God takes back the initiative. David had sought to build him a house, and now God promises David a 'house', which means a dynasty (although the same word can also mean a habitation or a family) (**17:10b**). The oracle should be interpreted in the light of the various repetitions and elaborations of it recorded in 1 Chronicles 22:6-10; 28:1-10 and in 2 Chronicles 6:14-17; 7:17-18.

There are some differences between the form of the promise given here and that in 2 Samuel 7:14. Chronicles does not include the warning that David's successor will be punished if he disobeys, for Chronicles presents Solomon, the temple builder, as a perfect king, without any flaw. There is also a more subtle difference. In 2 Samuel 7:16 we read, 'Your house and your kingdom will endure forever before me; your throne will be established forever.' Chronicles **17:14** reads, *I will set him over* my *house and* my *kingdom forever; his throne will be established forever.* The author of Chronicles is not focused specifically on the house, the kingdom or the throne of David. As was stressed in the introduction to this book, he is focused on Israel as the kingdom of God. The angel who speaks to Mary uses similar words to announce to Jesus' mother that the child who will be born to her will receive the throne of his father David (Luke 1:32).

One final interesting difference between Nathan's message in Samuel and in Chronicles relates to 17:5. In 2 Samuel 7:6 there is a specific mention of God having brought the Israelites out of Egypt. In Chronicles, the NIV has added the word *Egypt* in its translation of the verse, but what the Hebrew actually says is, *for I have not dwelt in an house since the day that I brought up Israel unto this day* (KJV). While it is reasonable to assume that the place from which Israel was brought was Egypt, the omission of the specific word would enable the first readers of Chronicles, the Jews who had returned from exile in Babylon, to identify with the liberation to which he refers.

David's response to the oracle is given in 17:16-27. The expression *then King David went in and sat before the Lord* means that he went and sat before the ark of the covenant (**17:16a**). His reply is in two parts: thanksgiving and a request.

First of all, David exalts the greatness of God. The expression *Who am I?* in the Bible expresses humility (**17:16b**). David repeatedly refers to himself as simply a servant (**17:17, 18, 19, 23, 24, 26, 27**). He speaks of God's gracious acts towards his own family (17:16b-17, 25-27). He recalls the power of God manifested in the events of the exodus (**17:21-22**). He also willingly accepts the role of preparing for the construction of the temple. His request is simply that the word that the Lord had said might be fulfilled: *Let the promise you have made ... be established forever* (17:23-24). David's prayer is his 'Amen' to God's promise. The word translated 'let it be established' is in fact equivalent to 'let it be so', which is what 'Amen' means.

Like David, we should accept what God asks us to do. David accepted his role in preparing for the construction of the temple with joy. He accepted it in such good faith that he put much effort into assembling the materials and manpower that would be required for the project (see ch. 28).

18:1-20:8 David's Wars

One after another, David defeated the Philistines to the east (18:1), the Moabites to the west (18:2), the Syrians to the north (18:3), the Edomites to the south (18:12), and Ammonites to the west (19:1-20:4). These were Israel's main enemies who surrounded the country.

David's wars are mentioned at this point in Chronicles to prove the fulfilment of God's promise to David, *I will also subdue all your enemies* (17:10). The same verb is used in 18:1 and 20:4. The wars also confirm that David's reign was not a period of peace conducive to the building of the temple. These times of trouble and bloodshed justify the disqualification of the king as builder (22:7-8; 28:3). Though David was deprived of this honour, he was not rejected by God, who blessed him in giving him victory over his enemies. Finally and especially, Chronicles shows that, through these wars and victories, David was creating the peaceful conditions that would enable his successor to construct the temple. Thus David could later say to Solomon, *Is not the Lord your God with you? And has he not granted you rest on every side?* (22:18). The victories also permitted the accumulation of booty which would be used as material in the construction work.

This section falls into three parts, each beginning with the same expression: *in the course of time* (18:1; 19:1; 20:4).

The first part in 18:1-17 mentions several wars, the first of which is against the Philistines, the traditional enemies of Israel. David took the city of Gath and the territory surrounding it from the Philistines (**18:1**). These were Israelite cities that the Philistines had occupied since the death of Saul (10:7). David also defeated the Moabites (**18:2**), the Syrians (**18:3-10**) and the Edomites (**18:12-13**). The details of these different battles are not given because the focus is on the plunder that David consecrated to God. For example, 18:8 indicates that Solomon used the bronze that David had taken from Hadadezer to make the bronze Sea, the columns and other objects for the temple (see 1 Kgs 7:13-51). All the victories are attributed not to David's prowess but to God. Twice we find the sentence, *The Lord gave David victory everywhere he went* (18:6, 13).

David is described as reigning *over all Israel, doing what is just and right for all his people* (**18:14**). The words suggest that David was made king for the well-being of God's people, not to satisfy his personal interests.

In **18:15-17** we are given a first draft of the administrative organization of the kingdom with the names of the chief officers, counsellors and religious leaders. This list represents an important step in consolidating a nation that has now abandoned the tribal model. This list differs from the one in 2 Samuel 8:18 in that Chronicles categorizes David's sons as *chief officials* (18:17) and not as 'royal advisors', or literally 'priests'. The author of Chronicles is very concerned to maintain the distinction between the priests and the laity.

In 19:1-20:3, the author goes into more detail about the wars against the Ammonites that were briefly mentioned in 18:11. An account of these wars is also found in 2 Samuel 10:1-12:31, with a few minor differences. As in previous wars, the result is spreading peace in the country and the defeat of Israel's enemies. In the first war against the Ammonites, David also defeated the Syrians who had been called to help Ammon.

The war against the Ammonites was sparked by the humiliation of David's ambassadors. When Nahash, the king of the Ammonites, died, David sent a message of condolence to Hanun, his successor. This message also expressed David's hope for continuing good relations between the two kingdoms (**19:1-2**). David's intentions were misunderstood by the Ammonite king's advisors, who saw these ambassadors as spies. David's men were humiliated as if they were slaves or prisoners of war: their beards were shaved and their clothes cut off *in the middle of their buttocks* (**19:3-5**). 2 Samuel 10:4 states that 'half of each man's beard' was shaved, whereas in 19:4 the 'half' is not mentioned. Possibly, Chronicles wishes to make the affront suffered even more serious.

Such humiliation of ambassadors was tantamount to a declaration of war, and so the Ammonites prepared for David's retaliation. With a thousand talents of silver (not mentioned in the book of Samuel), the Ammonites proceeded to buy the Syrians' support (**19:6-7**). David himself did not take part in the battle but relied on Joab, the commander of his army (**19:8**).

Finding himself trapped between the Ammonite and the Syrian (Aramean) armies, Joab divided his army in two. The elite troops, who were better trained in combat, were to fight the Syrians under Joab's leadership, while Abishai, his brother, would lead the remaining troops against the Ammonites (**19:9-12**). Joab's instructions contain not only military strategy but, even more importantly, deep theology regarding the final outcome of the battle: *Be strong and let us fight bravely for our people and the cities of our God. The Lord will do what is good in his sight* (**19:13**). In the book of Chronicles, military victory does not depend on the size or strength of the army but only on confidence in God and faithfulness to him. The expression *be strong* is characteristic of the language of battle (Deut 31:6, 23; Josh 1:6, 7, 9).

God's response was not long in coming. Joab routed the Syrians, causing panic in the camp of their allies, the Ammonites. Seeing themselves defeated, the Syrians went looking for reinforcements (**19:14-16**). This time David himself rallied *all Israel* to attack the Syrians. In 2 Samuel 10:17, it is the Syrians who prepared to meet David and set up the battle, but in **19:17**, it is David who forms the battle lines. David's name is honoured in this passage through the repetition of *When David was told ... David formed his lines ... David killed seven thousand of their charioteers and forty thousand of their foot soldiers* (19:17-18). The Syrians were finally defeated (**19:19**).

The final capitulation of the Ammonites is described in 20:1-3. David is crowned as king of the Ammonites with the crown of their king placed on his head. This story is condensed from 2 Samuel 11:1-12:31. The line *in the spring, at the time when kings go off to war* (**20:1**) recalls the introduction to the story of David's adultery with Bathsheba as well as the death of Uriah, her husband, which followed. This unfortunate incident in David's reign is not mentioned in Chronicles. As we have noted, the author does not want to tarnish the image of the one who is at the heart of the construction of the temple.

Yet another war with the Philistines is recounted in 20:4-8. This section on David's wars began with war with the Philistines and it ends with the same. As has been noted, this nation was the traditional enemy of Israel. The period of rest for Israel that was promised in 17:10 could not begin without the total subjugation of the Philistines, which is why **20:4** stresses this point (in contrast to 2 Samuel 21:18).

Three different hand-to-hand battles between mighty Israelite warriors and Philistine giants are described (**20:5-8**; compare 2 Samuel 21:15-22). However, the story of David's weakness before Ishbi-Benob (2 Sam 21:15-17) is not told. The author of Chronicles does not want to include something that would suggest weakness at the time when David is consolidating his kingdom.

The Philistine giants are like descendants of the people who aroused fear in the spies sent by Moses and whose report spread fear in the camp of the Israelites during their march towards the promised land (Num 13:31-32). In the eyes of the author of Chronicles, it is only during the reign of David that these giants were finally defeated. One of these giants, who had six fingers on each hand and six toes on each foot, was like Goliath in 1 Samuel 17 in that he came from Gath and *taunted Israel* (20:7). These words make it clear that what is being described here is not just a combat between different armies or individuals, but a war

between the gods. The stronger god would give victory to his worshippers or followers.

The total defeat of the Philistines meant that one of the prerequisites for the building of the temple had been achieved: a period of peace for the people of Israel. From now on, the author of Chronicles focuses on the temple.

21:1-29:30 Preparations for the Temple

The final chapters of the first book of Chronicles as well as the end of David's reign are taken up with various preparations for the construction of the temple. Matters dealt with in this preparatory phase include the choice of a site, the appointment of key personnel, the stockpiling of materials, and advice to Solomon, who will be responsible for carrying out the construction. Though David was prevented from doing the actual building, Chronicles credits David with making all the preparation for it. In the book of Samuel, however, scant attention is paid to David's contribution.

21:1-22:1 Choice of a site

This section of Chronicles has often been entitled 'the census', because that is the main event of the story. But the census itself is only a pretext leading up to the choice of the site for building the temple. Whereas in Samuel the story of the census peters out without a strong conclusion, 22:1 states, *The house of the Lord God is to be here, and also the altar of burnt offering for Israel*. Other differences between the story in Chronicles and that in Samuel show that the author's main concern is not the census. For example, the details about the route followed by the census takers (2 Samuel 24:5-8) are not reported in Chronicles.

In Africa, we are accustomed to censuses. Before important elections, there is a census to learn how many people can be expected to vote and to gather information so that electoral lists can be drawn up. A census may also be conducted to gather information needed for economic and social planning. In ancient times, a census had three main purposes: maximization of taxes, determination of the number of men who could be summoned to work on great building projects, and recruitment for military service. It was for this last reason that David ordered his census. Two facts confirm his intention. First, the people counted are all introduced as *fighting men ... who could handle a sword* (**21:5**). Also, it is Joab, the army commander, who is in charge of this huge task.

Unlike 2 Samuel 24:1 where it is God who *incited David* to carry out the census, in Chronicles it is *Satan* who incited David to do it (**21:1**). The word 'Satan' appears in only two other places in the OT: Job 1:6-2:7 and Zechariah 3:1-2. In each case, Satan is the one who incites to evil. The ancient Greek Bible translates the Hebrew word *satan* meaning 'accuser' or 'adversary' with the word *diabolos* (meaning 'slanderer'), from which we get the word 'devil'. The NT identifies Satan more clearly, presenting him as the dragon, 'that ancient serpent, who is the devil' (Rev 12:9; 20:2). By attributing the census to Satan rather than to God, the author of Chronicles is probably trying to avoid presenting God as both the instigator of evil and the one who punishes it. He is making the same point that James does when he says, *no-one should say, 'God is tempting me. For God cannot be tempted by evil, nor does he tempt anyone'* (Jas 1:13).

This census displeases God (**21:7**). Until now in Chronicles, David has not committed any error except in his first abortive attempt to bring the ark of the covenant back to Jerusalem, and for that he was not directly responsible. The exact reason why the census was wrong in God's eyes is not mentioned. There is no condemnation of other censuses in the ot (for example, Num 1:3; Exod 30:11). It is possible that the problem here is that the census followed immediately on the record of David's victories. If David had already won these victories, why did he need a military census? His decision to hold one to determine the size of his army at this time betrays a lack of confidence in God.

Joab's opposition makes this point clearer: *May the Lord multiply his troops a hundred times over. My lord the king, are they not all my lord's subjects?* Joab then argues that the census is sinful and asks David, *Why should he bring guilt on Israel?* (**21:3**). Joab's reluctance to carry out the task and God's explicit displeasure mentioned in **21:6** are not mentioned in the parallel passage in 2 Samuel 24:3. David's guilt is thus affirmed more strongly in Chronicles.

However, the author of Chronicles also strongly presents David's responsible behaviour in accepting full blame for what he has done. The words *Was it not I who ordered the fighting men to be counted?* (**21:17**) do not appear in the book of Samuel. Though Chronicles does not include the story of David's adultery, the account of the census shows that David is not a perfect king. In the case of the census, as in the story of Bathsheba, David says, *I have sinned greatly by doing this* (**21:8**). Like him, we should be ready to acknowledge our faults. As John says, *If we claim to be without sin, we deceive ourselves and the truth is not in us* (1 John 1:8).

Through Gad, the seer, God gives a David a choice between three punishments (**21:9-12**). These punishments strongly resemble those mentioned in Leviticus 26:25-26 in relation to the breaking of the covenant. David rejects only the second punishment at the hands of his human enemies, stating that he prefers to *fall into the hands of the Lord, for his mercy is very great* (**21:13**). His words indicate that the ot, as well as the nt, knows God as a God of compassion and pardon. This is in contrast to current opinion which regards the God of the ot as a legalist who demands 'an eye for an eye', and who offers no pardon. But from eternity to eternity, God has been the God of compassion. The compassion of God to which David refers is the unconditional love of God. Finally, on behalf of David, God chooses the third plague, which kills seventy thousand men of Israel (**21:14**).

Satan is not the instrument God uses to punish Israel. He uses his angel of destruction, here referred to as the angel of the Lord (21:15-17), a title that reminds us of Exodus 12:23.

David accepted full responsibility for his sin (21:17), and is instructed to build an altar (**21:18**). He therefore sets out to buy the threshing floor of Araunah, which is the place God has designated for the sacrifice.

The transaction between David and Araunah is recounted in more detail in Chronicles than in the book of Samuel. David insists on paying the full price for the property though Araunah offered it to him as a gift (**21:23-24**). This attitude reminds us of the story of Abraham when he bought the cave of Machpelah as a sepulchre for his wife Sarah (Gen 23:1-20). A sacrifice is not really a sacrifice if it does not cost something. In Chronicles, the price of the threshing floor is six hundred shekels of gold (**21:25**) whereas in the book of Samuel it is fifty shekels of silver. Some commentators see in the number six hundred the fifty shekels of Samuel multiplied by the twelve tribes of Israel.

David then proceeds to offer the sacrifices (**21:26**). God's acceptance of the sacrifice is shown by the fire coming down from heaven, a miraculous intervention that reminds readers of Gideon (Judg 6:21-24), and also of the prophet Elijah on Mount Carmel (1 Kgs 18:36-38). David's guilt is removed. The plague is stopped and the angel of destruction sheaths his sword (**21:27**).

The author then adds an aside explaining why David did not go to Gibeon to worship, and preparing the way for David's statement about the site of the future temple (**21:29-30**).

Chronicles establishes a strong link between the pardon of David's sin and the temple that will be built on this site (**22:1**). The temple will ultimately become the place par excellence for the forgiveness of sin. For Christians, Jesus, by his death and resurrection, accomplished in a perfect way the act of pardon that was formerly the function of the temple (Rom 3:24). If we come to him and confess our sins, as King David courageously did, we will also be forgiven.

Now that the site of the temple has been indicated by divine choice, the next step is to assemble the materials and choose a builder.

22:2-19 Organization of the construction

At this point, the parallels with the books of Samuel and Kings end, at least as far as the reign of David is concerned. Those books give David a minor, almost non-existent role in the construction of the temple, but that is not the case in Chronicles. This section, which falls into three parts, is dominated by the phrase *build a house for the name of the*

Lord and the verb *provide,* which appears repeatedly in different forms.

The first section, 22:2-5, tells of the preparation of the material necessary for the construction and the recruitment of labourers. The reason David undertakes this huge preparation is given in **22:5**: *My son Solomon is young and inexperienced, and the house to be built for the Lord should be of great magnificence and fame and splendour in the sight of all the nations.* David wants the temple to be a magnificent structure that will bring glory of God, and he is not sure that his young successor will have the necessary political base to engage the people in such work. So David gathers the foreigners living in the country and orders them to start preparing the stone, metal and wooden materials for the building of the temple (**22:2-4**). In the ancient Near East, prisoners of war were regarded as a plentiful and free labour force for the heavy work of construction. In Egypt, the children of Israel themselves had participated in the construction of the cities of Pithom and Rameses (Exod 1:11).

The second section, 22:6-16, contains the instructions that David gave to Solomon concerning the building of the temple. He shows far more concern for this task than for the future reign of his son. These verses supplement Nathan's oracle in 17:1-15.

In 17:1-15 no reason was given as to why David was not permitted to build the temple. In **22:8** some of God's words that are not mentioned in the earlier account of Nathan's prophecy are reported. David was prevented from building the temple because he had *shed much blood and ... fought many wars.* Opinion is divided as to how this objection is to be interpreted. Some commentators think that shedding blood had made David ritually unclean for the construction of the temple. The holy temple required a holy builder. However, what follows in the story tends to suggest that the lack of peace and rest during David's reign was a more important consideration.

In 17:1-15, there is also no indication which of David's sons will build the temple, but here it is made clear that God chose Solomon as the builder even before his birth (**22:9-10**). Solomon's very name supports the direct link between a period of rest and the favourable time for building the temple. Chronicles plays on the similarity between the name Solomon, *Shelomoh* in Hebrew, and the Hebrew word for peace, *shalom.* A contrast is created between David, the man of war, and Solomon, the man of peace. Israel is promised tranquillity during Solomon's reign (22:9).

David's exhortation to Solomon (**22:13**) reminds us of the instructions that God and Moses gave to Joshua (Deut 31:7-8; Josh 1:7-9). The resemblance is striking, and the words *Be strong and courageous. Do not be afraid or discouraged* are found in all three texts. Moses did not lead the people right into the promised land; that honour was reserved for his successor, Joshua. In the same way David will not build the temple; that honour will fall to Solomon, his successor.

David finished his instructions to Solomon by assuring him that preparations have been made so that Solomon would have access to inestimable riches, top quality materials and the services of highly skilled craftsman (**22:14-16**).

The third and final section, 22:17-19, contains the instructions David gave to *the leaders of Israel* (**22:17**). He knows that the young Solomon will need all the princes of Israel to recognize his legitimacy and to advise him in the building of the temple. Once again he emphasizes that peace is a precondition for the construction of the temple (**22:18**). David asks especially that the leaders seek the Lord (again using the Hebrew verb *darash*). The construction of the temple for the Lord will be the sign that they have done this faithfully (**22:19**).

David's attitude should inspire the leaders of churches in Africa. Too often, churches face crises during and after a time of transition between two pastors or two boards of elders. David knew that the end of his reign was near, and he undertook all the preparations to assure the success of his successor. He not only prepared materials and personnel for the temple, but he also prepared what we would today call public opinion to accept and help Solomon in the exercise of his responsibilities. A good leader is one who prepares the way for his successor without any spirit of competition. He should be like Paul, who could tell the Corinthians, *I planted the seed, Apollos watered it, but God made it grow ... The man who plants and the man who waters have one purpose* (1 Cor 3:6-8). We could apply these words to this situation by saying, 'David planted, Solomon watered.' For the good of the body of Christ, a leader should prepare for his succession.

23:1-26:32 Appointment of personnel

23:1-32 THE LEVITES Besides arranging for the construction of the temple, David also makes arrangements for its functioning. However, before dealing with this, the author of Chronicles announces that *David was old and full of years* (**23:1**). This description honours the king by placing him in the same category as other great personalities of the OT, such as Abraham (Gen 25:8) and Isaac (Gen 35:29). Unfortunately, the words also recall the painful episode of the family feud about who was to succeed David, for the description of these events in 1 Kings 1:1-53 begins with the same words. But Chronicles does not mention any dispute. It has already stated that Solomon was designated by God as David's successor and the builder of the temple well before his birth (22:9-10). There is, therefore, no controversy about the succession. The verse even gives us the impression that Solomon may have ruled alongside his father as a co-regent.

The fact that the public proclamation of Solomon as David's successor is immediately followed by a section on the role of the Levites suggests that these two events are linked. It was certainly at a gathering of leaders of Israel that David installed the Levites in their positions well before the building of the temple. They will be ready to start their ministry as soon as the temple is complete. It is also worth noting that on this occasion, the priests are already regarded as a distinct group (**23:2**) separate from the Levites, their brothers (23:13, 32). The other Levites, though they have an important role, are aides to the priests, the sons of Aaron.

David makes arrangements for the roles of the Levites in general, and then specifically for the priests, the Levite singers and the Levite temple guards. The organization of the Levites starts with counting them (**23:3**). This census is not condemned in any way by God. It reveals that there are thirty-eight thousand Levites aged thirty years old and over. They are divided into four groups, each with specific functions: twenty-four thousand are to act as supervisors in the temple, six thousand are to be magistrates and judges, four thousand are to be gatekeepers and four thousand are to be musicians (23:3-5).

The Levites are divided into different classes according to their descent from one of the three main branches of the sons of Levi: Gershon (**23:7-11**), Kohath (**23:12-20**) and Merari (**23:21-23**). Aaron and Moses were descended from Amram, son of Kohath. However, whereas Aaron and his sons were set aside as priests, the sons of Moses were considered simply as members of the tribe of Levi (**23:13-14**).

While the book of Numbers specified that Levites would begin to serve at the age of thirty (Num 4:3), David moves the age at which they can start work back to twenty (**23:24-27**). The requirement that they be thirty years of age was probably introduced because of the weight of the loads the Levites were required to carry as they moved the ark of the covenant and the tent of meeting. Now that the ark will be taking its place in a permanent structure, there will be no need to carry it, and so much younger men can enter the temple service. Their services would certainly be needed given the immensity of the task of overseeing the construction and functioning of the temple.

David adapts here to the realities of his time and offers a model for the church of Christ in Africa. The church, too, sometimes needs to adapt to the changing realities of our world without compromising the essentials of the faith. However, some Christian groups in Africa cling to traditional practices in their denomination as if these practices are at the heart of the gospel. The foundation of our faith and our salvation in Jesus Christ are fixed, but the manner in which these are expressed and lived out in our community should be adapted to our surroundings. A clear example of this relates to the elements used in communion.

In villages far from commercial centres, it can be difficult to obtain supplies of grenadine, a blood-red syrup made from pomegranates that is used to represent Christ's blood, and of the bread that represents Christ's body. Consequently, months may pass without any celebration of communion even though local products could be used to replace the bread and wine. Fortunately, not all groups are so bound by tradition, and thus sometimes, even in cities, red sorrel (a type of hibiscus tea) replaces grenadine.

The responsibilities of the Levites are described in detail in 23:28-32. They were to purify the temple utensils, prepare bread for the offerings, preserve the standard of weights and measures, offer praise when sacrifices were made and sometimes even offer the sacrifices (see KJV translation of 23:31; also 2 Chr 30:17) and guard the house of God. Their role could be summarized as preserving the holiness of Israel. The tent referred to in **23:32** was in use during this transitional period before the building of the temple.

It is very important that the Christian community be well organized. Most Christian groups in Africa consist of a small number of actors and a large number of spectators. A large part of the congregation does not participate in any active way in the life of the group. But the church, as the temple of God, needs to be organized in a way that encourages participation by every member of the congregation. If, as the apostle Peter says, all Christians are 'living stones' (1 Pet 2:5) in God's house, then each Christian has a role to play in the construction of that spiritual house. Pastors and church leaders should take pains to ensure that their church is set up in a way that permits all members to express themselves and be active in the life of the community. There is room for everyone and work for one and all in the house of God. This reminds us of the expression that is well known to African hunters, 'It takes more than one person to cut up an elephant.' There are as many things to be done in God's house as there are pieces of meat to be cut off an elephant! One person alone, or a small group of individuals, cannot do all that has to be done in an effective manner.

24:1-31 THE PRIESTLY ROSTER The author of Chronicles includes a comment to explain why there are only two main clans of priests even though Aaron had four sons (**24:1-2**). Two of Aaron's sons, Nadab and Abihu, died without leaving any descendants (see also Lev 10:1-3; Num 3:4). Thus all the priests were descended either from Eleazar or from Ithamar, Aaron's two remaining sons. The leaders of these clans in David's time are Zadok, a descendant of Eleazar, and Ahimelech, a descendant of Ithamar (**24:3**). Zadok had probably officiated at Gibeon (16:39) while Ahimelech had served before the ark of the covenant in Jerusalem. However the construction of the temple and the closing of the sanctuary at Gibeon would have brought all the priests to Jerusalem. The descendants of Eleazar were more numerous than those of Ithamar, for Eleazar had sixteen heads of family while Ithamar had only eight (**24:4**).

The functions of the priests, already summarized in 23:13, are not repeated here (see also 6:34). Instead Chronicles explains how they were organized into groups to serve at different times. David had been the one exercising authority in delegating tasks to the Levites, but he does not do this in relation to the priests. The organization of the rotation between the different families of priests is done according to a rule established by Aaron, the content of which is not known (**24:19**). Nor does David act alone in setting up the roster. He is assisted by the two chief priests, Zadok and Ahimelech (24:3). Their role is implied in the use of a plural verb in 24:4, which contrasts with the singular *David said* in 23:4.

The order in which the twenty-four families would serve in the temple is decided by lot (**24:5**). Due to the two-to-one ratio of the size of the families (24:4), lots were drawn alternately for one family and then for the other (**24:6**). The author then provides a list showing the order of families that emerged (**24:7-18**).

Lots were also used to determine the order in which the other Levites will serve (24:20-31). The list of the Levites given here includes the Kohathites (**24:20-25**) and the Merarites (**24:26-30**). The Gershonites are not mentioned, though 23:7-11 describes their lineage.

At this period in time, drawing lots was a means of ensuring an impartial division of responsibilities. Otherwise, Eleazar's clan, which was twice as large as that of Ithamar, would have taken all the jobs. The church can learn from how this situation was handled, for the fair division of labour within Christian communities in Africa remains a crucial problem. Too often, decisions are based on tribal lines or other social criteria, and result in the groups that feel neglected leaving the church to form their own congregations.

The leaders of congregations should actively seek to make choices that remove all suspicion and give everyone confidence. Elections alone are not enough, because sometimes they do not favour fair representation. People may cast their votes on the basis of candidates' tribal or regional affiliations rather than on the basis of their competence for a position. It may sometimes be necessary to have the courage to simply appoint people who really fill the conditions set out clearly in the NT (1 Tim 3:1-13) to responsible positions without any consideration of tribe or politics.

25:1-31 THE LEVITE SINGERS As with the priests, the service of the temple singers was organized by drawing lots to set up twenty-four rotations. But before reporting the results obtained by lot, the author reminds his readers that the singers had been *set apart* for this role (**25:1**). The expression 'set apart' is often used in the Bible. For example, it is used of the separation of the priests and Levites from the rest of the Israelite community (Num 16:9; Deut 10:8). In the case of the Levite singers, its use indicates the value attached to this new position. These singers are placed on a par with the other members of the clergy and enjoy the same status as the other Levites. The importance of music in the temple service has already been touched on in Chronicles 15:16-24 when the ark of the covenant was relocated and in 16:37-42 when the singers were assigned *to minister ... regularly* before the ark in Jerusalem.

The assignments of the singers are made by *David together with the commanders of the army* (25:1). Although the OT sometimes speaks of relations between the Levites and the military, for example in relation to a holy war (see 2 Chr 20:21), it is difficult to establish a relationship between the two here. It seems likely that these 'commanders' are not the military leaders of Israel. The term 'army' may be used here to refer to all of the Levites, in which case the commanders are the same as the leaders of the Levites mentioned in 15:16 who have the authority to assign the singers.

The singers for whom lots were drawn came from three families. The largest group was that of Heman with his fourteen sons and three daughters (**25:4-5**). Heman is described as the *king's seer* and his family was given to him through the promises of God to exalt God (25:5). The next largest group was Jeduthun with his six sons (**25:3**) and finally Asaph with four sons (**25:2**). The sons of Asaph prophesied according to the instructions of the king, while those of Jeduthun prophesied under the direction of their father.

Their music is regularly associated with *prophesying*, which some commentators see here not as preaching but as uttering words of praise. Certainly 25:3 seems to indicate that the purpose of prophecy here is for *thanking and praising the Lord*. However the OT offers other examples of prophecy linked to music. In 1 Samuel 10:5, Saul is told that he 'will meet a procession of prophets coming down from the high place with lyres, tambourines, flutes and harps being played before them, and they will be prophesying'. Before prophesying, Elisha asked a harpist to be present. It was only when the harpist played that 'the hand of the Lord came upon Elisha' (2 Kgs 3:15).

In Africa, it is not uncommon for music to be associated with prophecy or preaching. This linkage is characteristic of some African religions. It is often to the sound of music that a person goes into a trance and pronounces 'prophetic' words.

Music received special attention in Chronicles. It was seen as an integral part of worship that David was concerned about even before the building of the temple. And music also plays an important role in African culture. Unfortunately that has not carried over into our religious services, where music either has no role or has only a secondary role in relation to something like preaching. Far too often, the importance of music is downplayed by remarks like 'Let us sing while waiting for the others to arrive', or 'Let us sing before listening to the message.' Music's role is far greater than simply minimizing lateness in arriving for worship or preparing 'hearts' to listen to the message!

But while the church needs to take music seriously, it is also important to beware of music that lacks valuable content and that is mainly concerned with the financial interests of the musicians. It is also important to avoid the situation, which is sometimes seen, where music and dance tend to supplant the preaching of the word. People sing and dance for hours and sleep during the sermon. Both extremes should be avoided.

26:1-28 THE TEMPLE GATEKEEPERS AND TREASURERS The gatekeepers for the temple are all Levites and are all given assignments by David before the construction of the temple (26:1-19). They come from three different families: Meshelemiah's (26:1-3), Obed-Edom's (26:4-8); and Hosah's (26:10-11). The family of Obed-Edom receives special attention. The reference to God's blessing in 26:5 reminds us of the blessing reported in 13:14 when he guarded the ark after the failure of the first attempt to transport it to Jerusalem. This blessing here takes the form of a large family. It is also expressed in the quality of his sons and grandsons, who are described as *leaders ... very capable men ... with the strength to do the work* (26:6-8). Obed-Edom himself appears to have been both a musician and a guard (15:21-24; 16:5, 38).

The gatekeepers guarded the four gates into the temple that were situated at the different points of the compass. Their task was to assure the security of the temple and also to preserve its holiness by preventing idolatrous practices and by preventing unclean persons from entering it (2 Chr 23:19).

Each family was assigned to a particular gate by drawing lots (26:13). Shelemiah received the East Gate (26:14a), which was the most important because it gave access to the royal palace and was probably the gate by which the king entered the temple (see 9:18). Six guards are assigned to this gate, but only four to each of the others (26:17-18).

Since there were only three major families and four gates, Zechariah, the eldest son of Shelemiah (a variant spelling of Meshelemiah), who is described as a wise counsellor, was given the task of guarding the North Gate (26:14b). Hosah received the West Gate and Obed-Edom, the South Gate.

The Levite treasurers (26:20-28) are dealt with next because their responsibilities overlap with those of the gatekeepers (9:26). A distinction is made between *the treasuries of the house of God* and *the treasuries for the dedicated things* (26:20). The former contained the sacred objects in the temple (such as the utensils for offering sacrifices) and were to be cared for by the sons of Ladan, the Gershonite

(26:21-22). The latter contained the spoils of war that had been consecrated to the Lord and were to be cared for by the Kohathites (26:23-28; see 23:12). It is interesting to see a favourable reference to Saul in 26:28. He too had dedicated things to the Lord.

26:29-32 OTHER LEVITE OFFICIALS Finally, in a transition to the next section on the administration of the kingdom, Chronicles introduces the Levites who carried out their tasks outside the temple. They handled the tasks of civil administrators, magistrates and judges (26:29; see also 23:4). We are also given information about their jurisdiction, which shows that their responsibilities covered the whole territory of Israel, both to the west and to the east of the Jordan River (26:30-32).

27:1-34 Military and civil organization

David knew that successful construction of the temple would require more than just men and materials; it would also require stability in the country and rest for its people. Military leaders and civil authorities would be required to achieve this peace, and so these leaders are dealt with in chapter 27.

In Chronicles, there is no distinction between the sacred and the secular, for the two domains intersect. This pattern does not always apply in the life of the church in Africa. Here the pastor or minister is regarded as having been 'set apart', while the rest of the congregation are referred to as the laity and are considered of lesser importance. But all the ministries in the church are of equal importance. Outside the church, the Christian who works in the civil service is also serving God. We should not act as if the church and everyday life are in two separate spheres.

The heads of families and army commanders are listed in 27:1-15. This army is divided into twelve divisions, each with twenty-four thousand men under a commander. Its total strength was thus two hundred and eighty-eight thousand men (a number much smaller than that identified by Joab in the census in 21:5). The nature and tasks of these divisions are not known. Each division served for a month each year. If these divisions represented the regular army, this rotation supposes a period of peace, for in a time of war, all the soldiers would be on duty.

Of the twelve division commanders, at least six are from Judah (27:3, 7, 9, 11, 13, 15), two from Ephraim (27:10, 14), one from Levi (27:5-6), one from Benjamin (27:12) and two are of unknown origin (27:4, 8). The presence of sons of priests in these divisions is not surprising because 12:26-28 indicates that the Levites were not exempt from military service. The division commanders include heroes who have already been mentioned elsewhere. One such is Jashobeam, the commander of the first division for the first month, who had killed three hundred men during one battle (27:2-3; see also 11:11). Another was Benaiah, son of the priest Jehoiada, who we were told had killed a lion in a pit on a snowy day (27:5-6; see also 11:22).

The *officers over the tribes of Israel* who are introduced in 27:16-24 are undoubtedly the political leaders of each of the tribes. Many names are unknown. These men were appointed for their work by the king rather than for occupying hereditary positions. The list does not include officers for the tribes of Joseph, Gad and Asher; instead, these groups are replaced by the two tribes of Ephraim and Manasseh. The tribe of Manasseh is divided into two, one branch living to the west of the Jordan and the other to the east of it, which retains the ideal number of the tribes at twelve. The comment about not numbering the men in **27:23-24** is an explicit reference to the census of 21:1-6. There is also an allusion to God's promise to Abraham that he would multiply Israel as the stars of the sky (Gen 15:5; 22:17; 26:4). Joab must have been referring to this promise when he told the king, *May the Lord multiply his troops a hundred times over* (21:3).

The list of public officials is followed by another list for which there is no parallel in the OT. It gives the names of twelve of David's officials, a number that is highly symbolic (27:25-31). These officials are in charge of agricultural matters, including the production of wine and oil and the raising of livestock. The royal estates were scattered throughout the country. The regions mentioned include areas in Shephelah where crops were cultivated and the Plain of Sharon where livestock were pastured. The officials included foreigners, notably Obil the Ishmaelite who cared for the camels (**27:30**) and Jaziz the Hagrite who was in charge of the sheep (**27:31**). These foreigners probably received these positions because of their competence in their respective areas of responsibility.

The wise management of church property is an indispensable component of church growth. The establishment of what are often known as 'development services' has often led the church in Africa to initiate projects with the aid of foreign financing. In general, these projects have not survived once the foreign funds are exhausted. One of the reasons why such projects have failed to become self-sustaining is poor management. Projects have often been managed by incompetent people who are appointed on the basis of the wrong criteria. The property of the church community should also be quite distinct from the property of church leaders. At this time when there is much talk of good governance in Africa, the church should provide a model in the way it manages its finances and property.

We are given a few details about the men who were in close contact with the king. Jonathan is described as *a man of insight;* Jehiel *took care of the king's sons;* Ahithophel, Jehoiada and Abiathar were the king's counsellors; Hushai the Arkite *was the king's friend,* perhaps something like his

aide-de-camp, and Joab *was commander of the royal army* (**27:32-34**).

28:1-29:20 David's final recommendations

The final two chapters of 1 Chronicles form a unit and describe without a break the last events of David's reign. Readers who are familiar with the account of this period in the book of Kings will notice a distinct difference between that account and the one given here. In 1 Kings 1:1-2:46, the end of David's reign is characterized by internal fighting within the palace about who is to succeed him. Hastily, the prophet Nathan and Solomon's mother, Bathsheba, intrigue to persuade the old bedridden king to order the coronation of Solomon, while one of David's other sons, Adonijah, is already celebrating his own coronation. David's last words to Solomon are instructions to wipe out the enemies of the kingdom (1 Kgs 2:1-9). None of these events are mentioned in Chronicles. It records neither rivalries, nor in-fighting for the succession, nor David's weakness due to old age. Instead it presents David as standing firmly as he makes his final recommendations, which here focus on the building of the temple. This topic is not even touched on in the account of David's death in Kings.

28:1-10 CHARGE TO THE NATION AND TO SOLOMON David calls a public gathering that brings together what we would call the power brokers of the nation. The detailed description of the make-up of this gathering is unique in Chronicles: *the officials of Israel … the officers over the tribes, the commanders of the divisions, … of thousands, of hundreds, … the officials in charge of all the property and livestock, … palace officials, the mighty men and all the brave warriors* (**28:1**). Though the gathering ended with the crowning of Solomon, its real purpose was to promote the future building of the temple. This gathering changed the building project from a private matter for royal family into a public project that required the participation of all the people.

This method David chose to move this project forward has something to teach us. When important decisions are made for the Christian community, it is important that all the members participate. Without such participation, the support for any project will be weak.

David's speech to the assembly is recorded in 28:2-10. Unlike the old man of the book of Kings, he rises to speak. Then he addresses those assembled there as *my brothers and my people* (**28:2**). He is appealing to them both in terms of the tribal system, in which he is their fellow-Israelite, and in terms of the monarchical system, in which he is a ruler and they are his subjects. If only all leaders in the Christian community would also remember that they are, above all, brothers and sisters of the other members. If they did, it would have a profound effect on relationships within the church.

The speech refers back to 17:1-27 and 22:6-16 as David publicly and in more detail presents the content of Nathan's prophecy and his own private message to Solomon. He begins by stating that God had overruled his desire to build a temple: *I had it in my heart to build a house … But God said to me, You are not to build a house for my name* (28:2-3). The words 'But God said to me', which are echoed in **28:6**, imply that God was in direct communication with David, a fact that is not mentioned elsewhere in the Bible.

David speaks of his temple project as building a *place of rest for the ark, … for the footstool of our God* (28:2).These two expressions indicate his desire to maintain the presence of God at Jerusalem.

In designating Solomon as his successor, David makes it clear that this is no arbitrary decision, nor one dictated by circumstances. It is a continuation of a long process that stretches back to the choice of the tribe of Judah to be the royal family (Gen 49:10), passes on through the choice of Jesse's family, and resulted in the choice of David as king from among all his brothers (**28:4**). In the same way, from among all the sons of David, God has chosen Solomon both to sit *on the throne of the kingdom of the Lord* (**28:5**) and to be the builder of the temple (28:6).

David urges the assembly, here referred to as *the assembly of the Lord*, to accept this choice and to obey God so as to be able to enjoy a peaceful life in the promised land (**28:8**).

Then, David turns to speak to Solomon. Previously he had spoken to him in private (22:6-16), but now he publicly instructs him to accept the responsibility laid on him in being chosen to build the temple and to act accordingly (**28:10**). No advice is given to Solomon concerning the enemies who have tried to weaken David's power (1 Kgs 2:1-9). Instead David concentrates on urging Solomon to obey God: *If you seek him, he will be found by you; but if you forsake him, he will reject you forever* (**28:9**). Jesus said much the same thing in his day: 'Seek and you will find' (Matt 7:7). Solomon will have to recognize the scope of the task that falls to him because he has been chosen to construct the temple and will have to act accordingly (28:10).

David's words here make it clear that election does not exclude obedience, just as salvation by faith is not a reason to live carelessly. In the same way as election calls for obedience, so too does salvation by faith (see also **28:7**).

28:11-21 BLUEPRINT FOR THE TEMPLE After this brief exhortation, David gives Solomon a document that deals not only with the architecture of the building but also with the details of its furnishings, utensils, objects for use in worship, and staffing. It amounts to a detailed plan of the temple and its services (**28:11-18**).

David indicates that he received this plan from God himself (28:12, 19). The temple being God's house, its plan, its architecture could only come from him. Chronicles, unlike the book of Kings, places the architecture of the temple in the context of divine revelation. There is a clear analogy between David, who received the plan of the temple and passed it on to Solomon, and Moses who received from God the plan of the tabernacle and passed it on to Bezaleel (Exod 25:31). Just as the plan or model of the tabernacle and its utensils had been given by God himself, so too had the plan of the temple and its utensils.

One of the weaknesses of the church in Africa is that we often think of the church as the work or property of a person. We should think of it as the work of God himself, the perfect architect, and act accordingly.

After giving Solomon the plan of the temple, David immediately exhorts him to start the work of building the temple (**28:20-21**). His words are almost word for word the same as in 22:13 and are very similar to the encouragement Moses gave to Joshua in Deuteronomy 31:5-8. He will need to be strong, to be courageous and not to be afraid.

In 28:20, the emphasis is placed on action. The words *do the work* are added (see also 28:10). Solomon can be sure that God will be with him until all the work is accomplished. We are reminded of the name 'Emmanuel' that was given to Jesus, a name that means 'God with us' (Matt 1:23). We are also reminded of Jesus' promise to his disciples: 'And surely I am with you always, to the very end of the age' (Matt 28:20). What assurance!

29:1-9 PLEA FOR FINANCIAL SUPPORT David now stops speaking to Solomon and turns to address the whole assembly. He reminds them that Solomon is *young and inexperienced* and that the house to be built is to be *palatial* (**29:1**). A young king will have neither the wealth nor the experience needed to tackle such a project on his own. It will not be completed without the contributions and support of others.

David informs the assembly of all the provisions that he has made for the building, drawing both on the spoils of war and on his own treasures (**29:2-5a**). But still there is not enough. So he asks the leaders to make freewill offerings to support the work (**29:5b**). This appeal to the leaders of all Israel to make offerings for the building of the temple is similar to the appeal made by Moses for the construction of the tabernacle (Exod 25:1-9). The Hebrew expression is literally 'to consecrate his hand to Jehovah', and is used of a freewill gift or when someone dedicates himself to someone (2 Chr 17:16). It shows that this offering is the sign of the dedication of the assembly to God, and especially to the building of the temple.

David's request receives a positive response. The leaders give voluntarily, *wholeheartedly* and with joy (**29:6-9**). Their attitude was like that prescribed by Paul: 'Each man should give what he has decided in his heart to give, not reluctantly or under compulsion, for God loves a cheerful giver' (2 Cor 9:7).

This positive result came because David did not just ask the leaders to give, but also set an example by giving himself. The leaders followed their king's example. In churches, preachers often speak about offerings or tithes, but they need to demonstrate such giving themselves. How can anyone ask the members of the congregation to give a tithe when the leader of the community is not giving a tithe? Teaching must be done by example.

The freewill offering organized by David also resembles the practice of many churches in Kinshasa in the DRC. When facing a major expense such as the construction of a new building or the purchase of new furniture for the church, they organize what is called a *matondo* ['thanksgiving']. The congregation is informed of this ahead of time, and prepare to bring a special offering. The collection of this offering is accompanied by music, dancing and joy. Sometimes there is even a competition between the women and the men as to who can give the most. Such services enable congregations to collect all the money needed in just one service. This practice should be encouraged, while taking care to avoid the giving becoming like a show. The offering must come from hearts entirely dedicated to God.

29:10-20 DAVID'S PRAYER The joy that accompanies the freewill offering leads David to launch into a psalm of praise. It starts with a doxology in which David exalts the grandeur and the sovereignty of God in all things (**29:10-13**). He contrasts God's greatness with the humbleness of the human condition. He expresses this humility in relation to himself and to all the people, *But who am I, and who are my people?* (**29:14a**). David presents what has been offered to God, but insists that the size of the offering is not an occasion for pride because everything that he and the people have given for the work of building the temple is what they have received from God (**29:14b**).

David is acutely aware of the brevity of human life on earth: *Our days on earth are like a shadow* (**29:15**). He knows that he will soon die. If only all of us were aware of the brevity of life, it would change our relationship to the world. As the book of Ecclesiastes reminds us: 'Be happy, young man [or young woman], while you are young, and let your heart give you joy in the days of your youth … but know that for all these things God will bring you to judgment' (Eccl 11:9). Human beings long to live forever, but the end of all flesh is death.

Finally, David brings two requests to God (29:18-19). One is for the people and the other for Solomon. For the people, David asks God to maintain in them the same attitudes that led to their freewill offering (**29:18**). For Solomon, he asks for *wholehearted devotion to keep your commands, requirements and decrees and to do everything to build the palatial structure for which I have provided* (**29:19**). In both requests, David does not mention either strength or power but focuses on the attitude of the heart. This is how we should pray for our

successors. David knows that obedience to God is the prerequisite for the success of the building of the temple.

David concludes his prayer by inviting all the assembly to praise the Lord (**29:20**).

29:21-25 Solomon's coronation

David had already established Solomon as king of Israel in 23:1, and so **29:22** clarifies that the ceremony described here is a second coronation. This comment confirms that Solomon must earlier have reigned as regent alongside his father. However, at this ceremony Solomon is anointed, which is not mentioned in the earlier ceremony. At the same time, Zadok is anointed as priest.

The description of the coronation ceremony picks up various themes from earlier in the book, and specifically the theme of *all Israel*. Sacrifices are offered for *all Israel* (**29:21**), *all Israel obeyed* Solomon (**29:23**), and the Lord blesses him *in the sight of all Israel* (**29:25**). Another theme that is brought up is that of the kingdom of God. Whereas 1 Kings 2:12 speaks of Solomon sitting *on the throne of his father David*, Chronicles has him sitting on *the throne of the Lord* (22:23).

To show that this coronation is peaceful and there is no opposition to Solomon's authority, Chronicles specifically mentions that *all the officers and mighty men, as well as all of King David's sons, pledged their submission to King Solomon* (**29:24**). The literal meaning of the Hebrew is that 'they placed their hands under Solomon's feet' as a sign of allegiance. Anticipating what is to follow, 29:25 exalts the reign of Solomon, which has not yet begun. This ceremony is in stark contrast to the bloody settling of accounts that followed the coronation of Solomon in 1 Kings 2:13-46.

29:26-30 David's obituary

The first book of Chronicles ends with a brief survey of David's reign. It offers an historical summary of it and mentions additional sources where more information about David may be found. We are again reminded that David, presented as the *son of Jesse*, ruled over *all Israel* (**29:26**). This expression recalls the similar words at the beginning of his reign (10:14). Consistent with what has gone before, Chronicles closes its account of the reign of David by affirming the unity of Israel.

David is said to have ruled for forty years. The seven years in which he reigned in Hebron over Judah alone are not ignored, but are presented as a transition from a provisional capital to a more permanent one (**29:27**).

It is also said that David *died at a good old age, having enjoyed long life, wealth and honour* (**29:28**). This happy ending of David's life differs from that in 1 Kings 2:1-11, where David's final recommendations to Solomon relate to the assassination of his enemies and suggest that many enemies remained. Chronicles does not mention where David was buried.

Finally, **29:29-30** gives information about other documents containing records of David's reign. The three prophets mentioned all played an important role in David's life. Although Samuel does not play an important role in Chronicles, he is known as the one through whom God designated David as king to succeed Saul (11:3). Nathan is known for the oracle concerning the dynasty that he pronounced in 17:3-14. Gad is the one who announced to David both the punishment and the way to end it after the census in 21:18.

The first book of Chronicles ends on a positive note. The kingdom is not David's kingdom but God's. The throne on which Solomon is seated is not David's throne but God's. The author of Chronicles wants to show his people that the end of David's kingdom does not mean the end of the kingdom of God. Even if Judah does not have a king, its God remains on the throne in the temple that will be built.

Another son of David will fully accomplish this ideal. It is Jesus who reigns eternally. He is the son of David, but at the same time, he is the Son of God (Matt 22:41-46).

2 Chr 1:1-9:31 Solomon's Reign

The theme of the temple dominated 1 Chronicles from the start of David's reign and it remains central to 2 Chronicles. The book of 1 Chronicles ended with Solomon being chosen as king specifically so that he could erect this temple (1 Chr 28:5-6), and with David's exhortation to him, *Be strong and do the work* (1 Chr 28:10). Hence, of the nine chapters devoted to Solomon's reign, six tell of the construction and dedication of the temple.

This book describes the history of the monarchy from the reign of Solomon to the decree of Cyrus. In other words, 2 Chronicles starts with the construction of the temple and ends with the authorization of the construction of another temple. The author's preoccupation with the temple is also evident in his references to both the beginning and the end of the construction work (3:1-2; 5:1; 8:16).

The construction and inauguration of the temple mark the start of a new stage in the history of Israel's monarchy. From now on the kings of Judah and of Israel will be judged by their concern or lack of concern for the temple, its services and its personnel. The temple becomes a measuring rod for the king and also for the entire nation. The kings who undertake reforms in favour of the temple are given more attention in the book of Chronicles than the others. These kings are Asa (14:2-16:14), Jehoshaphat (17:1-21:1), Hezekiah (29:1-32:33) and Josiah (34:1-35:27).

The forty-year reign of Solomon recorded in Chronicles is divided into two periods of twenty years each, but the treatment of these two periods is not equal. The first twenty years, during which the temple is built, receive more attention (1:1-7:22).

In the book of Kings, Solomon's reign is also divided into two parts. The first part of his reign is the period of obedience and prosperity, whereas the second is that of disobedience. Solomon's reign ends on a negative note of infidelity and of rebellion in the kingdom (1 Kgs 11:1-43).

The book of Chronicles, by contrast, presents Solomon as a perfect king with no negative notes. Some commentators have concluded that the author of the book of Chronicles is presenting an idealized, and thus false, portrait of Solomon. However, it is not just Solomon's faults that are not mentioned, but also certain other facts that would have contributed to his renown. The most notable example is the omission of any reference to his famous judgment in the case of the two prostitutes (see 1 Kgs 3:16-28). In Chronicles, Solomon's wisdom is not primarily linked to good governance but to the building of the temple (2 Chr 2:12)

In selecting which events of Solomon's reign to record, the author has focused solely on facts relating in some way to the construction and service of the temple. All other events are considered of only minor importance. Solomon's legendary wisdom is revealed only through the success of this building project. What the author of the book of Chronicles wants to show is that Solomon was the son who meticulously followed his father's instructions regarding the construction of the temple.

Chronicles also emphasizes the peaceful character of Solomon's reign. He had earlier been identified as a 'man of peace' and one whose reign would be a time of peace and tranquillity for Israel (1 Chr 22:9). This promise was fulfilled from the moment Solomon ascended the throne.

Chronicles presents Solomon as an example of how a good leader should fulfil his responsibilities. He scrupulously accomplishes the tasks for which he was appointed king. He does not allow himself to be sidetracked by other preoccupations. He committed all his heart and all his soul and all his strength to the building of the temple.

The narrative brings out marked similarities between the story of David and that of his son Solomon. For example, like David, Solomon was chosen to be king by God. This was not the case for the other kings of the Davidic dynasty. Like David, Solomon received the support of *all Israel* from the beginning of his reign. Like David's, Solomon's reign began with an assembly of all the leaders of Israel. During the times of both David and Solomon, there was worship, an appearance by God (in fire descending from heaven), prayer and answers to prayer.

Hence it is with good reason that some commentators have seen Solomon as a second David, even though it is true that like all comparisons, this one has its limits. Chronicles clearly shows that there are more complementary points between David and Solomon than there are similarities.

David transported the ark of the covenant to Jerusalem, but Solomon installed it in the temple. Nathan's prophecy was addressed to David but concerned the reign of Solomon. David made all the preparation for the construction of the temple, but it was Solomon who built it. Solomon may even be said to be greater than David because the account of his reign contains nothing blameworthy, whereas David's first attempt to bring the ark to Jerusalem failed (even though the fault was not directly said to be his) and the census he organized led to God's judgment.

1:1-17 Solomon Established as King

2 Chronicles begins by indicating the consolidation of the kingdom: *Solomon son of David established himself firmly over his kingdom* (**1:1a**). Even though Chronicles glosses over the rivalry associated with Solomon's ascension to the throne, there are still hints of it. The assertion here is almost identical to that in 1 Kings 2:46, 'The kingdom was now firmly established in Solomon's hands.' In Kings, this affirmation comes after a series of acts of vengeance carried out by Solomon on the final instructions of his father. These acts eliminated all competition for the throne. The idea of consolidation after a period of troubles or conflicts menacing the throne is also implicit in the Hebrew verb translated 'established' in 2 Chronicles (12:1, 13; 15:8; 13:21).

Solomon is referred to as the 'son of David' in order to stress the continuity with his father. David had promised Solomon, 'the Lord God, my God, is with you' (1 Chr 28:20). This statement is confirmed in the words of **1:1b**: *the Lord his God was with him.* The God of David was thus also the God of Solomon *and made him exceedingly great.* As in 1 Chronicles 29:25, the author points out the exceptional character of his reign before giving any details of it.

After his father's death, Solomon's first act as king was to go to the high place at Gibeon (1:3-6). In 1 Kings 3:4, this visit by Solomon is described as an act of personal piety. In Chronicles, it is a national matter. Solomon went there with *the whole assembly* of Israel (**1:2-3**). The Hebrew word translated 'assembly' is *qahal*, which refers to a religious assembly. This same word is used in 1 Chronicles 13:2 when David assembled Israel to bring the ark of the covenant to Jerusalem. So, just like David at the beginning of his career, Solomon is surrounded by *all Israel.* This sort of assembly aims at involving all the people and the new king. Clearly **1:5** says that Solomon and the people inquired of the Lord there. The text does not specify in what way the people and Solomon inquired of him. It simply says that important sacrifices were made: a thousand burnt offerings (**1:6**).

Why was the high place at Gibeon chosen for this ceremony when the ark of the covenant was at Jerusalem? Probably because at the beginning of Solomon's reign, the presence of the ark in Jerusalem had not yet made this city an official sanctuary. David had not closed the high place at

Gibeon. In fact, he had assigned priests to it (1 Chr 16:39). It is described as *the most important high place* in 1 Kings 3:4. Chronicles explains why Gibeon enjoyed this status by adding the information that *God's Tent of Meeting was there, which Moses the Lord's servant had made in the desert* (1:3). The sanctuary at Gibeon thus had official status, so it was important that Solomon visit it.

Gibeon was also the location of the bronze altar that Bezalel had made (1:5). The only places in the Bible where this man is mentioned are in Exodus and Chronicles (see Exod 31:2; 35:30; 36:1-2; 37:1; 38:22; 1 Chr 2:20). The reference to his work as an artisan anticipates the role of Solomon as the architect of the new bronze altar in the temple (4:1).

During that night, *God appeared to Solomon* (**1:7a**). In Africa, we know that strange things happen in the night. That is when sorcerers are at work. Thus in Lingala (DRC), people will say *ndoki ya moyi makasi* ['daytime sorcery'] when someone acts with cruelty during the day, for sorcery is associated with the late night. But African Christians should not fear the night for God's power is also at work then. It was at night that God spoke to Solomon, and at night that the prophet Nathan received the message from God for David about the temple (1 Chr 17:3). Jesus' example shows that night can even be an ideal time for seeking God's presence (Matt 14:22-27).

The account of this incident in Kings mentions that God appeared 'in a dream' (1 Kgs 3:5). The author of Chronicles does not mention a dream, perhaps because he wishes to emphasize the dialogue between Solomon and God. God said to him, *Ask for whatever you want me to give you* (**1:7b**).

Solomon begins his reply by acknowledging God's goodness to his father David and to himself in making him king (**1:8**). In 1 Kings 3:6 the goodness of God towards David is said to have been conditional – 'because he was faithful to you and righteous and upright in heart'. Chronicles makes no reference to this condition. Solomon then asks God for two things.

The first thing he asks for is the fulfilment of the promise made to David (**1:9**). This promise concerned the creation of a dynasty and the construction of the temple (1 Chr 17:11-12). The first part of the promise had already been fulfilled because Solomon has succeeded his father, but the temple had not yet been built.

The second thing Solomon asked for was wisdom to rule over *a people who are as numerous as the dust of the earth* (1:9-10). In 1 Kings 3:7, this request for wisdom is accompanied by a reference to Solomon's youth: 'But I am only a little child and do not know how to carry out my duties.' However, in Chronicles, it is David who comments on Solomon's youth, and he makes the comment in relation to the building of the temple and not to wisdom (1 Chr 29:1).

The reference to the vast number of people whom Solomon will be ruling reminds us of Joab's words to David:

'May the Lord multiply his troops a hundred times over' (1 Chr 21:3). Whereas the account of Solomon's words in 1 Kings 3:8 links up with God's promise to Abraham in Genesis 13:16, the form used in Chronicles is closer to God's promise to Jacob, the father of the twelve tribes in Genesis 28:14. This slight difference reflects the focus of the chronicler on the rebuilding of the nation of Israel.

God is impressed by Solomon's unselfish request. Normally, what a king wants first is security for his realm, long life for dynasty and victory over his enemies. Solomon has asked for none of these. What he was interested in was the ability to govern wisely and well. His request for wisdom picks up his father David's longing, *May the Lord give you discretion and understanding* (1 Chr 22:12). God responds favourably to Solomon's request. In fact, he promises Solomon even more than he asked: *wealth, riches and honour, such as no king who was before you ever had and none after you will have* (**1:12**).

Jesus instructs us to 'seek first his kingdom and his righteousness, and all these things will be given to you as well' (Matt 6:33). It is because Solomon asked for the most fundamental thing that God gave him riches and honour. Unfortunately, many African leaders are looking for riches rather than wisdom. Our African countries are rich, but because of poor governance the riches do not contribute to the well-being of the great majority of the population. Too often, a small minority monopolize everything. There is much talk in Africa today about the importance of good governance, and it is one of the objectives of New Partnership for Africa's Development (NEPAD). Unfortunately, the church itself is sometimes an example of poor governance and does not offer an example to governments or other associations. Good governance should start in our homes and our local churches before reaching the summit of the state.

God's reply also confirmed that Solomon's monarchy is of divine origin. The expression *my people over whom I have made you king* (**1:11**) is not found in 1 Kings 3:11.

The following verses tell of Solomon's return to Jerusalem (1:13-17). According to 1 Kings, on his return from Gibeon, Solomon offered sacrifices before the ark of the covenant and then demonstrated the wisdom he had just been given by God in the way he handled the case of the two female prostitutes (1 Kgs 3:15-28). Instead of mentioning these events, the author of Chronicles deals with the fulfilment of God's promise of riches. He describes Solomon's military power: one thousand four hundred chariots and twelve thousand horsemen (**1:14**). He stresses the abundance of materials. In Solomon's time, silver and gold became so common that they lost their value as precious metals and were thought of as just another stone! Cedar, which was an expensive imported wood, became as common as the wood of the common sycamore trees so familiar to Israelites (1 Chr 27:28). The statement that Solomon's horses and chariots were imported from Egypt reminds us that at that time the African continent was an important trading partner of Israel (1:16-17).

In Kings, this description of Solomon's wealth comes only at the end of his reign (1 Kgs 10:26-29) and therefore has no direct link with the visit to Gibeon. Chronicles establishes the link because Solomon's riches and honour contribute to his ability to construct a majestic temple. The building of this temple now becomes the focus of the account of the rest of Solomon's reign.

2:1-18 Further Preparations for the Temple

2:1 Solomon's contribution

Although David had undertaken much of the preparation for the building of the temple, Solomon also made a contribution. David himself had recognized that his supply of building materials might be insufficient, and had told Solomon 'you may add to them' (1 Chr 22:14). This chapter in Chronicles shows Solomon's determination to start the construction work. We are told that he *gave orders to build a temple for the Name of the Lord* (**2:1**). He began his preparations as his father had done, by assembling a work force and materials.

2:2 The labourers

The following verse is devoted to the work force (**2:2**). In our day, big work projects are undertaken with the help of machines that mix the concrete and move and lift heavy loads. At that time, everything was done by hand. Solomon had seventy thousand men who worked as carriers and eighty thousand who were *stonecutters in the hills*. A further three thousand six hundred were foremen.

Most of these labourers were conscripts, that is, prisoners of war or others who had been reduced to slavery. All of them were foreigners (2:17-18), a detail that is lacking in 1 Kings 5:13-18. The Israelites themselves had provided slave labour when they built the cities of Pithon and Rameses in Egypt (Exod 1:11).

Solomon's example should not be used as an excuse for a government or a people to enslave or mistreat foreigners who live among them. Jesus told us to welcome foreigners (Matt 25:38, 43-45). Yet fear and hatred of foreigners is increasing in African countries. We even sometimes hear the word 'stupid' being used when they are spoken of. In South Africa, for example, foreigners are mocked and rejected when they are referred to as *makwerekwere*.

Not all that long ago, foreign communities lived peacefully alongside nationals in their host countries in Africa. Now foreigners are accused of all kinds of evils. Rather than holding their own governments responsible for a lack of employment and the dropping standard of living, nationals accuse foreigners of taking their jobs. Governments blame foreigners for crimes and thefts. While it is true that a few foreigners have committed crimes, they cannot be held responsible for all the crime in a country. Very often, the hostility to foreigners is actually rooted in jealousy, for foreigners, living far from their homelands, may work harder and achieve more success than those around them.

The church should be concerned about the treatment meted out to foreigners in African countries. We can draw on African cultural values and especially on the virtue of hospitality as we seek to teach the gospel values of love and protection of foreigners. Yet the church must also exercise discernment, for there are some foreigners who do abuse the hospitality offered to them and who do oppress and exploit the nationals.

2:3-18 Materials and artisans

The second phase of Solomon's preparation involved special materials and artisans, and is presented to us in the form of correspondence between Solomon and Hiram (or Huram) king of Tyre. Though this correspondence is about the building project, it also contains some key theological statements about the nature of God, the temple and the kingdom.

This exchange of letters is also recounted in 1 Kings 5:15-32, but there are significant differences. In Kings, the first letter is from Hiram and is purely a diplomatic response to Solomon's coronation. The request from Solomon for materials is a response to Hiram's congratulations. In Chronicles, it is Solomon who initiates the correspondence, and the main purpose of the letters is to place an order for materials and a qualified workman (2:3, 7-10). The omission of any reference to the first letter indicates the central place that the author of Chronicles gives to the construction of the temple. He does not show Solomon as waiting for any correspondence from Hiram before he asks for materials.

There are also other differences between the account in Kings and that in Chronicles. Whereas 1 Kings 5:3 refers to David's intention to build the house of God and the state of war which prevents him from carrying out his plans, **2:3** refers solely to Hiram's helpfulness in assisting David to build his palace. 1 Kings 5:4-5 mentions the rest God has given to Solomon as well as the promise of his succession and his role as the builder of the temple. None of this is mentioned in the correspondence in Chronicles, although the same points are made elsewhere (see, for example, 1 Chr 17:22).

What Chronicles does have that is not mentioned in 1 Kings 5 is a description of the temple and its operation (2:3-5). This remarkable description reinforces the central place of the temple in Chronicles. The list supplements the list of temple activities in 1 Chronicles 23:28-31 by indicating that the temple is a place of sacrifice.

Solomon emphasizes the grandeur of the temple that is to be built *because our God is greater than all other gods*

(**2:5**). However, the grandeur of God is also shown in the fact that the temple cannot contain God since even *the highest heavens cannot contain him* (**2:6**). Thus on the one hand, the temple is truly God's house; but on the other hand, it is simply a place of sacrifice. God is simultaneously immanent (dwelling in the temple) and transcendent (far greater than the temple). The words *who then am I* indicate Solomon's humility when faced with the task of erecting a worthy temple for such a God (see also 1 Chr 17:16; 29:14).

It is only after this theological introduction that Solomon presents two concrete requests, each one introduced with the words, *Send me.* The first request is for a qualified artisan, described in **2:7** as a man skilled in working with most of the materials to be used for the construction. He will not work alone but with other qualified workers whom David had brought to Jerusalem (see 1 Chr 28:21). This request is not included in the parallel passage in Kings. A specialist is mentioned in 1 Kings 7:13, but he is only brought in after the construction of the temple and his contribution is limited to works in bronze.

The second request (**2:8-9**) is for the wood necessary for the construction. Solomon asks for cedar wood, pine and algum. The servants of the king of Tyre were specialists in working with wood.

At the end of his request, Solomon states what he is prepared to pay for these supplies: *twenty thousand cors of ground wheat, twenty thousand cors of barley, twenty thousand baths of wine and twenty thousand baths of olive oil* (**2:10**). One 'cor', used for solid measurements, corresponded to about forty-six gallons (two hundred and twenty litres) and one 'bath', used for liquid measurements, was about six gallons (twenty-two litres). The trade goods that Solomon offers here are very similar to those mentioned in Ezekiel's prophecy against Tyre, which states that Judah exported wheat, honey, oil and balm to Tyre (Ezek 27:17).

The king of Tyre's response to Solomon's request is given in the letter presented in 2:11-16. In 1 Kings 5:8 we get the impression that Hiram's response was delivered verbally by his emissaries. By presenting it as a letter, the author of Chronicles confers a solemn tone on this reply. This letter follows the same pattern as Solomon's request, and thus it does not merely respond to the request for material but also makes significant theological points.

First, this foreign king recognizes that Solomon's kingship comes from the Lord and that it is a sign of God's love for his people (**2:11**). Then Hiram praises the Lord, the God of Israel. He recognizes in him the Creator *who made heaven and earth* and also as the one who gave David an intelligent son who is going to build the temple (**2:12**). Once again, the important role of the temple is emphasized. The parallel text in 1 Kings 5:7 says simply that God 'has given David a wise son to rule over this great nation'.

The second part of Hiram's letter replies to the Solomon's specific requests. A qualified artisan, Huram-Abi will be sent to Solomon (**2:13**). Hiram confirms that, as Solomon has requested, Huram-Abi will be able to work with the other qualified workers whom David had gathered (**2:14**). Huram-Abi's father was from Tyre, but his mother was from the tribe of Dan, and thus an Israelite. This reference to his parentage reminds us of another skilled craftsman from the tribe of Dan, namely Oholiab, who assisted Bezalel of the tribe of Judah in building the tabernacle (Exod 31:6; 34-35). Thus Chronicles treats the construction of the temple as following on the construction of the tabernacle, for once again a member of the tribe of Dan (Huram-Abi) is going to help someone from the tribe of Judah (Solomon).

The king of Tyre accepts the terms of the trade suggested by Solomon and asks that the goods mentioned be sent in exchange for the wood (**2:15-16**). Hiram's reference to Solomon as 'my lord' has led some commentators to assume that he is Solomon's vassal, that is, a king who is subordinate to Solomon. But the fact that he expected Solomon to pay for the supplies and the craftsman suggests that this form of address is simply a mark of respect and does not imply subordination.

3:1-5:1 Construction of the Temple

Finally, the long-awaited moment arrives when Solomon begins to construct the temple. The start of the work is reported in 3:1 and its conclusion in 5:1. What strikes the attentive reader is the brevity with which the author of Chronicles reports the actual work. After such long and laborious preparations, we expect a long description of the construction but there is nothing of the sort. The author is more interested in the attitude towards the temple than in its actual walls.

The account of the construction is dominated by the frequent use of *he made* which occurs some fourteen times (for example, see 3:14, 15, 16). This expression recalls the account of the building of the ark of the covenant and the other furnishings for the tabernacle by Bezalel in Exodus 37:1-38:20. There the words 'they made' recur frequently.

The site of the temple is specified first. It is being erected on the site of the threshing floor that David designated as the site of the temple after the Lord responded to his penitent sacrifice by sending fire from heaven (1Chr 21:26; 22:1). But now the site is identified not only as the threshing floor of Araunah but also as Mount Moriah (**3:1**). This name recalls the place where the angel of the Lord appeared to Abraham to prevent him from sacrificing Isaac, although Genesis 22:2 does not specifically mention Mount Moriah but rather one of the mountains in 'the region of Moriah'. (The Samaritans in fact identified Moriah with Mount Gerizim – Deut 11:29; Josh 8:33; John 4:20). By associating Abraham's sacrifice of a ram in place of Isaac

and David's sacrifice to stop the plague, the author underscores the role of the temple as the place where sacrifices are to be made. The account of the start of construction in 1 Kings 6:1 makes no mention of the site of the temple in the same way that the account of the census did not conclude with the identification of the site (2 Sam 24:25).

The date of the beginning of the work was the second day of the second month of the fourth year of Solomon's reign (**3:2**). In Kings the date of the beginning of the construction work on the temple is fixed in relation to the exodus: the four hundred and eightieth year after the children of Israel left the country of Egypt (1 Kgs 6:1). It is clear that Chronicles is more interested in the covenant between David and the Davidic dynasty than in the events of the exodus.

The outer structure of the temple is described in the following five verses. The measurements given in **3:3-4** indicate that it was not a large building. It was sixty cubits long (about ninety feet / twenty-seven metres) and twenty cubits wide (about thirty feet / nine metres). Thus it was smaller than many churches in Africa. The reason is simple. The temple was not intended to receive crowds as are our buildings. It was the house of God, and did not need to be very large because, as Solomon had already said, 'even the highest heavens cannot contain him' (2:6).

Even though Christians sometimes call their churches 'the house of God', the parallel has its limits. Our buildings are first of all for us to meet in, even though we are assured of God's presence by his Spirit when we meet (Matt 18:20). Twice, Paul told the Corinthians that it is the Christian community as a whole that forms the temple of God (1 Cor 3:16-17), and he also stated that the body of each believer is the temple of the Spirit (1 Cor 6:19).

The use of gold to cover the inner walls is remarkable. Each verse from 3:4 to 3:10 refers to the use of gold. Solomon obviously made use of the one hundred thousand talents of gold David had set aside for use in the temple (1 Chr 22:14).

The interior of the temple is described in 3:8-14, with priority given to the Most Holy Place, where the ark of the covenant would rest. This room was a square thirty feet (nine metres) on each side. The weight of the gold used to overlay the interior of the Most Holy Place is given with precision: six hundred talents of gold or about twenty-two tons (20 tonnes) (**3:8**). This number recalls the six hundred shekels given by David to Araunah for the purchase of the place that became the site of the temple (1 Chr 21:25). The wings of the two cherubim, covered with gold, stretched across the Most Holy Place (**3:10-13**).

We could say that the Most Holy Place represented 'God's private room' in his house. Only the high priest entered that room once a year on the Day of Atonement. The author of the letter to the Hebrews draws on this tradition when he describes Jesus as the high priest of the new covenant. It is he who entered into the Most Holy Place once for all, not with the blood of goats and calves, but 'by his own blood, having obtained eternal redemption' (Heb 9:11-12).

A curtain separated the Most Holy Place from the rest of the temple (**3:14**). This curtain (or rather its later replacement) was what was torn when Jesus died on the cross. Matt 27:51; Mark 15:38; Luke 23:45).

In front of the temple stood two massive pillars of bronze (**3:15-17**; see also 1 Chr 18:8).

The furniture and equipment of the temple are described in chapter 4. This description shows how carefully Solomon followed the instructions and plan of his father, as set out in 1 Chronicles 28:11-19. The objects made included the *altar* that would be used for sacrifices (**4:1**), the great iron basin called *the Sea* where the priests would wash themselves as part of their ritual purification (**4:2-5, 6b**; see Exod 30:17-21), *ten basins* to hold water to wash the various parts of the sacrifice (**4:6a**; see Lev 1:9, 13) and *ten lampstands* (**4:7**). The lampstands gave light, but also symbolized the permanent presence of God in the temple (Exod 25:31-40; 27:21). In the NT, Jesus proclaimed himself to be the light of the world (John 8:12). He is the living and eternal lampstand. There were also *ten tables* on which the consecrated bread was displayed (**4:8a**; see Exod 25:23-30; Lev 24:5-9). The symbolism of the bread is also picked up in Jesus' teaching in the gospels when he says, 'I am the bread of life' (John 6:35). There were also a further one hundred gold bowls (**4:8b**) and *the courtyard of the priests* (**4:9**).

Huram had a finisher's role; he finished the works of bronze and their decorations and made tools to be used for the sacrifices (**4:11-17**). Solomon himself provided tools of gold (**4:18-22**).

The final step in the building was naturally the installation of the inner and outer doors of the temple (4:22). At this stage, *all the work Solomon had done for the temple of the Lord was finished,* and Solomon marked the end of the construction by bringing into the temple the treasure that David had dedicated to the Lord.

Solomon's completion of his building project is a challenge for church leaders. In far too many African countries, towns and villages, we find projects that the government, or a church or an individual has failed to complete. There are half-built houses, churches, offices, airports, roads, bridges and the like. The reason they were never completed was that proper preparation had not been done or that the head of the project did not know how to go about finishing the job. Sticking to a plan, a well-thought-out schedule, and good management of resources are the keys to success. It is reason for pride and also a good Christian testimony when we complete a project we have begun.

For the author of Chronicles the construction of the temple, while a necessary step, was not the most important one. The most important thing from his perspective was the solemn dedication of the temple when the ark of the covenant finally arrived in its home.

5:2-6:42 Dedication of the Temple

5:2-3 Gathering for the dedication

There was certainly a time lapse between the end of the construction work and the inauguration ceremony, if only because time would be necessary for the heads of the different tribes and families to make the journey to Jerusalem, sometimes from distant parts of the country. These leaders represented all of Israel, and they gathered in Jerusalem to carry the ark of the covenant from the tent where it had rested to the newly built temple (**5:2**). The dedication of the temple coincided with the Feast of Tabernacles in the seventh month (**5:3**) and had the atmosphere of a national holiday.

5:4-14 Installation of the ark in the temple

David had charged Solomon: 'Begin to build the sanctuary of the Lord God, so that you may bring the ark of the covenant of the Lord and the sacred articles belonging to God into the temple that will be built for the Name of the Lord' (1 Chr 22:19). With this ceremony, Solomon completes the task.

In 1 Kings 8:3 the priests are said to carry the ark of the covenant. However, Chronicles, faithful to the role of the Levites as the only authorized carriers of the ark, says that it is the Levites who carried it (**5:4**). It will, in fact, be the last time that they perform this duty, for with the building of the temple, the ark has finally found its resting place and will no longer need to be carried. As when David transported the ark to Jerusalem, numerous sacrifices were offered (**5:6**; see also 1 Chr 15:26, 16:1). Using hyperbole, the author of Chronicles states that they sacrificed *so many sheep and cattle that they could not be recorded or counted.*

The Levites carried the ark to the temple, but it was the priests who placed it in the Most Holy Place (**5:7**). As has so often been said, 'To each his own'. Only the priests were permitted to enter the Most Holy Place. Even if Chronicles favours the Levites, that does not mean that it confuses their functions with those of the priests.

A detail is added about the purpose of the wings of the cherubim, described in 3:10-13. Their outstretched wings covered the ark of the covenant (**5:8**). It is also made clear that the ark of the covenant contained only the two tablets of the Law, testimony to the covenant between God and Israel (**5:10**).

The details given in **5:12-13** are not found in the description of the ceremony in 1 Kings 8, which focuses solely on the role of the priests. These verses are intended to emphasize the presence of the Levites and their participation in the ceremony. Levite singers accompany the ceremony with their instruments and their words. Their music marks the actual beginning of the ministry in the temple that they had been assigned by David (1 Chr 23:25-32). The words of praise they sang, *He is good; his love endures forever* (5:13) remind us that Heman and Jeduthun were appointed to 'give thanks to the Lord, 'for his love endures forever' (1 Chr 16:41). We are reminded that it is not because of Solomon's ability and foresight that the construction is finished, but because of the mercy of God.

Whereas in 1 Kings 8:10 the cloud filled the house when the priests left the Most Holy Place, in Chronicles, the cloud did not fill the house until after the departure of the priests and the praise of the Levites. This cloud is a symbol of the presence of God. The link between the cloud and the praise is clearly marked by the word *then* (5:13).

The priests could not fulfil their roles because *the glory of the Lord filled the temple* (5:14). This appearance by the Lord is similar to what happened at the dedication of the tabernacle in Exodus 40:34-35. In both cases, a cloud of glory was present. And just as Moses had not been able to enter into the Tent of Meeting, so the priests were not able to remain in the temple for their ministry. Despite their consecration, mentioned in 5:11, the priests could not stand before the glorious presence of God.

From this time forward, God was present in this temple. Moses and David had each built a temporary residence for God, but with the temple built by Solomon, God had a permanent place of residence among his people. However, the happiness of the people would not depend solely on the physical presence of the temple. What follows in this section will stress the necessity of obedience and faithfulness.

6:1-11 Solomon's prologue

With its forty-two verses, chapter 6 is the longest in 2 Chronicles, which underscores its importance in the entire book. The only other chapter of similar length also deals with an inauguration, namely the inauguration of ministry before the ark in 1 Chronicles 16. The chapter consists almost exclusively of the words of Solomon.

The exact meaning of the first verse is not clear, for we do not know what is meant by *a dark cloud* in 6:1. But Solomon's blessing is quite clear as it concentrates on God's expressions of goodness. In a sense, what is said is a summary of the history of the temple. The exodus is mentioned (6:5), but only in passing as the focus is on God's choice of Jerusalem and of David (6:6). David's name is mentioned five times in 6:4-10. In the parallel passage in 1 Kings 8:16, the choice of Jerusalem is not mentioned.

God is the one who accomplishes his purposes (6:4). Solomon starts by recalling David's desire to build the

temple (6:7) and God's earlier commitments to David concerning his successors and the building of the temple (6:8-9). He then points out that God's promise to David has been fulfilled: Solomon has succeeded him as king and he has built the house of the Lord to provide a shelter for the ark of the covenant (6:10).

In 1 Kings 8:21, the ark is described as 'the ark, in which is the covenant of the Lord that he made with our fathers when he brought them out of Egypt'. Chronicles says, *the ark, in which is the covenant of the Lord that he made with the people of Israel* (6:11). The slight difference between these two versions is important, for the latter involves the present generation, *the people of Israel*, whereas Kings associates the covenant more with a past generation. The author of Chronicles stresses God's covenant with David and 'plays down' the covenant at Sinai. He presents his material in a way that stresses the importance of the presence of the ark in the temple for the people of Solomon's day.

6:12-42 Prayer of dedication

The third part of the dedication ceremony is Solomon's prayer, which is the longest of the prayers recorded in Chronicles. As he offered this prayer, Solomon stood *before the altar,* but not in a place reserved for the priests (6:12). Chronicles avoids crediting Solomon with priestly privileges and makes it clear that he is first standing and then kneeling on a platform specially constructed for the occasion (6:13a).

In front of the whole assembly of Israel, Solomon kneels with his hands outstretched towards the sky (6:13b). The Bible does not dictate any specific position for prayer, but Solomon's posture testifies to his humility and reverence before God. In certain African cultures we kneel to show respect when addressing an elderly person or a dignitary. Without falling into formalism, it is sometimes necessary for our own sake to adopt this posture before our great and perfect God.

Solomon's long prayer can be divided into four parts. The first part is an exaltation of God's greatness. Solomon does not start his prayer with an immediate list of requests. Instead he praises God for who he is and what he does (6:14). The God of Israel has no equal. His unique character is revealed in the fact that he keeps his promise just as he kept his promise to David regarding Solomon and the temple (6:15). We are often in such a hurry in our prayers that the requests come first. But Jesus himself in the prayer that he taught the disciples did not start with requests. The Lord's Prayer begins *Our Father in heaven* (Matt 6:9). It begins by recognizing the greatness of God.

The second section of the prayer contains two precise requests. First, Solomon asks God to keep his promise towards the Davidic dynastic (6:16-17). God's words quoted by Solomon, *You shall never fail to have a man to sit before me* on the throne of Israel, *if only your sons are careful in all they do to walk before me according to my law as you have done* (6:16), do not appear elsewhere in this form, either in Kings or in Chronicles. They are however, implicit in 1 Chronicles 17:11, 23-27. In 1 Kings 8:25 it says, 'if only your sons are careful in all they do to walk before me as you have done'. It is clear that the author of Chronicles insists on the importance of obedience to the law.

Then Solomon returns to the purpose of the temple as a place of prayer (6:18-21). His words in **6:18** are similar to those in his letter to Hiram in 2:6 and restates the impossibility for God to *really dwell on earth with men.* The word 'men' is not mentioned in 1 Kings 8:27. By using that word, Solomon wants to stress the importance of prayer as the only means of entering into contact with God. Therefore, the king asks God to answer the prayers that were addressed to him in the temple (**6:19**). Speaking as if God were a human being, Solomon says, *May your eyes be open towards this temple day and night* (**6:20**). The end of Solomon's request, … *and when you hear, forgive* (**6:21**), unveils another important characteristic of the temple: it is a place of forgiveness. Earlier, David had chosen to 'fall into the hands of the Lord, for his mercy is very great' (1 Chr 21:13). God's pardon is not only a NT privilege, as is often thought. Ever since the garden of Eden, God has been the one who forgives.

Solomon's awareness of the greatness of God should remind us of the need for humility. God is so great that we cannot squeeze him into the confines of our congregations or denominations. Too often, churches and denominations in Africa run each other down by accusing each other of lacking God's presence. When we read Solomon's prayer, we are reminded that our attitudes of pride should be replaced by ones of humility.

The third part of Solomon's prayer mentions seven types of prayers that may be offered in the temple and for which Solomon asks God's grace:

- prayers for justice (**6:22-23**)
- prayers offered when sin has resulted in defeat by an enemy (**6:24-25**)
- prayers offered when sin has resulted in a drought (**6:26-27**)
- prayers offered when threatened by famine, plague, blight or mildew, locusts, enemies or any other disaster (**6:28-31**)
- prayers offered by foreigners (**6:32-33**)
- prayers offered when the Israelites are involved in a war initiated by the Lord (**6:34-35**)
- prayers offered when sin has resulted in exile (**6:36-39**).

These seven areas for prayer represented huge challenges that the people of Israel would face. The key element in Solomon's prayer remains forgiveness. Solomon recognizes that without God's forgiveness, Israel cannot continue to exist as the people of God for there is no one who does not

sin (6:36). This phrase is echoed in Romans 3:22-23: 'there is no difference, for all have sinned and fall short of the glory of God'.

Some of the circumstances mentioned by Solomon are of direct concern on the African continent. Take, for example, the issue of famine. Many Africans do not have enough to eat. Despite its fertile soil, for the past few years this continent has suffered serious shortages of food. The reasons for the shortage are multiple and complex. But too often it is the result of numerous pointless wars that have forced sections of the population into refugee camps where they can only survive with the help of international aid. Drought, too, is sometimes brought on by human error, particularly in the wanton destruction of the environment. The African church has a role to play in these situations of crisis and drought that harm men, women and children who are created in the image of God.

Solomon also mentions the prayers of foreigners (6:32). The church should be a place where everyone is welcome. Jesus underscores this when, quoting Isaiah 56:7, he speaks of the temple as 'a house of prayer for all nations' (Mark 11:17).

Another important element in Solomon's prayer is his confidence that although God is present in the temple, he hears the prayers addressed to him from distant locations (6:37; see also John 4:21-23). Solomon had already mentioned the transcendence of God, and now he appeals to this transcendence, saying, *from heaven, your dwelling place, hear their prayer and their pleas, and uphold their cause* (6:39). This aspect of Solomon's prayer is a great comfort to us African Christians, because we can know that when we pray to God regarding the condition of our continent, he listens to us.

The conclusion of the prayer is a final solemn appeal to God. Once again, God is addressed as if he has a human body: *Now, my God, may your eyes be open and your ears attentive to the prayers offered in this place* (**6:40**; see also 6:20).

Solomon next invites God to take possession of his house, *his resting place* (**6:41**). This invitation, is not mentioned in Kings. There Solomon's prayer ends with an allusion to the exodus from Egypt and God's choice of Israel at that time (1 Kgs 8:51, 53). But these are not the reasons advanced for why God should answer Solomon's prayer in Chronicles. Here the ultimate appeal to God is *Remember the great love promised to David your servant* (**6:42**).

7:1-22 God's Response

God responds to Solomon's prayer in two ways. He responds during the ceremony (7:1-11) and during a night-time visit to Solomon (7:11-22).

7:1-11 God's response during the ceremony

God gives a positive response to the prayer offered by Solomon. As had happened when his father first sacrificed on the future site of the temple, the fire of God descends from heaven and consumes the sacrifice (**7:1**; 1 Chr 21:25-26). This fire confers legitimacy on the temple as the new place of worship. As had happened when the ark arrived in the Most Holy Place, the glory of the Lord (the cloud) fills the house, preventing the priests from entering (**7:2**; see also 6:14). *All the Israelites saw the fire* and *the glory of the Lord* over the temple. Then *they knelt on the pavement with their faces to the ground, and they worshipped and gave thanks to the Lord* (**7:3**). This scene strongly resembles the one where the fire consumed the sacrifice at the dedication of Aaron and his sons to the priestly ministry (Lev 9:23-24). When the cloud first appeared in 6:14, it was the Levites who expressed praise; but this time it is all the Israelites who praise God saying, *He is good; his love endures forever.*

There follows a huge ceremony involving the sacrifice of *twenty-two thousand head of cattle and a hundred and twenty thousand sheep and goats* (**7:4-7**). This in turn is followed by days of rejoicing as the people celebrate the festival (**7:9**).

Those who were present at the ceremony had come from as far away as Lebo Hamath and the Wadi of Egypt (**7:8**). People had come from the same distances when David gathered the Israelites to Jerusalem to bring up the ark (1 Chr 13:5). Each one returned home happy and content. But whereas 1 Kings 8:66 says that they were all grateful *for all the good the Lord had done for his servant David and his people Israel,* the author of Chronicles adds in Solomon's name after David's (**7:10**).

7:12-22 God's response during the night

The second part of God's response to Solomon's prayer comes in God's appearing to him during the night. Whereas in 1 Kings 9:2 this appearance is placed close to the one at Gibeon, the author of Chronicles does not link the two appearances. What we have here is a separate and fundamental encounter.

God tells Solomon that he has accepted the temple as a place of sacrifice. His response makes specific reference to Solomon's prayer in 6:24-39 and includes what is perhaps the best-known verse in Chronicles: *if my people, who are called by my name, will humble themselves and pray and seek my face and turn from their wicked ways, then will I hear from heaven and will forgive their sin and will heal their land.* (**7:14**). God assures Solomon that, as he has requested, God has accepted the temple as the place for his name to reside and promises that *my eyes and my heart will always be there* (**7:16**).

But God's promise is not a blank cheque. God clearly spells out the conditions on which he makes it. The conditions in **7:17-18** are introduced by *as for you* (singular) and are addressed to Solomon personally. They make it clear that obedience is required if his dynasty is to continue. The conditions in **7:19-22** are addressed to a plural *you,* and thus apply to all the people. They too must be obedient. If

they are not, they will face consequences. The first consequence is exile, which Chronicles mentions in passing. The second consequence affects the future of the temple, a subject dear to the author of this book. Despite having chosen the temple as his place of residence, God is prepared to *make it a byword and an object of ridicule among all peoples* if his people turn away from him (7:20). The parallel passage in 1 Kings 9:7 mentions the people rather than the temple as the object of sarcasm and mockery. The scenarios presented by God are played out in the history of the monarchy in Judah that is recorded in chapters 10–36.

8:1-9:28 Solomon's Other Accomplishments

The section begins with chronological information. The construction of the temple and of the palace took some twenty years (**8:1a**). The final two chapters dedicated to Solomon cover the other twenty years of his reign. It was noted earlier that Chronicles divides Solomon's reign into two twenty-year periods, but pays far more attention to the first period. A total of one hundred and fifty-two verses deal with that period, whereas the second period is dealt with in a scant forty-nine verses. The focus in chapters 8 and 9 is not so much to provide information about Solomon's accomplishments but to enhance the glory of this king who devoted his reign to the construction of the temple. There is already an example of this in **8:1b**, which mentions that Solomon built a palace as well as the temple. However, we are given no information about the building of the palace. The author of Chronicles is interested only in Solomon's building of the temple.

8:1-11 Construction projects

In antiquity, the glory of a king was measured by his building projects. The great kings were builders of great cities. Without spending time on it, the author wants to show that Solomon was also a great king, and so in 8:2-11 he lists the great projects undertaken by Solomon. The verbs 'built' or 'rebuilt' are repeated in **8:2, 4, 5, 6,** and **11a**.

The only reference to war during Solomon's reign is found in **8:3**. He was a man of peace. So the reference to his military victory is not intended to exalt Solomon's military prowess but to show his success in all the areas considered to be proof of God's blessing. In Chronicles, a military victory is always interpreted as a sign of blessing.

On the social level, Solomon contributed to the happiness of his people. During his reign, the people of Israel were not forced into slave labour. On the contrary, they served as his military men and officials (**8:9**). Foreigners were, however, used as slave labourers (7:8; see comments on 2:1)

Solomon is also said to have built a separate house outside the City of David for Pharaoh's daughter whom he had married (see 1 Kings 3:1). The reason given is respect for the holiness of the ark (**8:11b**). It was probably not because of her sex that this woman had to live there, but because of her pagan origin. Other wives of Solomon stayed near the temple.

This situation reminds us of the way in which the church sometimes treats African women in general and Christian women in particular. On the one hand, the church values their participation and contribution, but on the other hand, because they are women, the church refuses to allow them to hold certain positions. Like this Egyptian, women are kept at a distance from 'the city of David' in a separate 'house' that the church has built for them and are only assigned secondary responsibilities. And yet they are not pagans and do not deserve such treatment!

8:12-16 A functioning temple

Although Chronicles is here dealing with other accomplishments of Solomon, it never loses sight of the temple. So in the midst of reporting on these various building projects, it suddenly gives details of Solomon's sacrifices and the organization of the temple. The author tells of the regular daily, weekly, monthly and annual services of worship (**8:12-13**). Solomon is shown to be carrying out all the requirements laid down by Moses. Special mention is made of functions David has assigned to the Levites (**8:14-15**). They were to praise the Lord, assist the priests in service and guard the doors of the temple and its treasure. David is referred to as *the man of God* in 8:14, a designation that places him on an equal footing with Moses, who is described in the same way in Deuteronomy 33:1.

For the author of Chronicles, the real climax of the building work is the holding of regular temple worship. It is after reporting on this that he declares *the temple of the Lord was finished* (**8:16**).

8:17-9:12 International renown

Solomon's accomplishments include a joint commercial enterprise undertaken with Hiram, king of Tyre (**8:17**). International contacts such as this must have spread Solomon's fame abroad and resulted in the visit of the Queen of Sheba (**9:1**). The identity of this queen remains controversial. It is possible that she came from Africa, and specifically from Ethiopia, which was the name given at that time to the territory on the border between Sudan and Egypt. There is a legend that Solomon had a child with the Queen of Sheba. This legend is based on a sexual interpretation of 9:12, which says, *King Solomon gave the queen of Sheba all she desired and asked for.* However, the queen's primary purpose was to test Solomon with difficult questions (9:1). She found *nothing was too hard for him to explain to her* (**9:2**). The queen was also impressed by the palace and the temple that Solomon had built (**9:3-4**).

This meeting between Solomon and the Queen of Sheba was recorded to glorify Solomon's wisdom and to contribute

to the international prestige of the king who had built the temple (9:5-8). The Queen of Sheba praised Solomon: *Indeed, not even half the greatness of your wisdom was told me; you have far exceeded the report I heard* (**9:6-7**). Like Hiram, king of Tyre, had done before her, she also praised the Lord and recognized that Solomon's kingdom had been given to him by God (**9:8**). The gifts that the Queen of Sheba brought to Solomon were insignificant compared to those that he gave to her (**9:9, 12**). His ability to give such gifts is underscored by the aside in **9:10-11**, which stresses his wealth.

9:13-28 Solomon's riches and authority

Solomon's riches are further described in **9:13-21**. The pinnacle is reached in **9:22**: *King Solomon was greater in riches and wisdom than all the other kings of the earth.* God's promise to Solomon in 1:11-12 had been fulfilled to the letter. Wisdom and riches had been given to Solomon 'such as no king who was before you ever had and none after you will have'.

This little section is closely linked with chapter 1 and the riches accumulated for the building of the temple. It is said in **9:27** as in 1:15 that the king made *silver as common in Jerusalem as stones and cedars as plentiful as sycamore-fig trees in the foothills.* Even Jesus recognized Solomon's glory, although he mentioned that it could not be compared to that of the lilies of the field which God had created (Matt 6:29).

Solomon also exercised authority over all the kings from the Euphrates to Egypt (**9:23-24, 26**).

9:29-31 Conclusion of Solomon's Reign

The final verses dealing with Solomon refer to the existing records of the events of his reign (**9:29**), its length (forty years – **9:30**), his death, the place of his burial and the name of his successor (Rehoboam – **9:31**). In Kings, this conclusion is preceded by a long chapter (1 Kgs 11) that tells of the events towards the end of his life that ruined the reign of this king. These included his numerous wives, his worship of other gods and the enemies that God raised up against him. Though the author of Chronicles does not wish to spoil the reputation of the temple builder, he does mention, among the archives, *the visions of Iddo the seer concerning Jeroboam son of Nebat* (9:29). This Jeroboam was one of the enemies mentioned in 1 Kings 26:40 and would become a major player after Solomon's death.

2 Chr 10:1-36:21 The Kings of Judah

After Solomon's death, the monarchy in Israel experienced a crisis that left indelible marks in the life of God's people. Solomon and David had reigned over a unified Israel. The expression 'all Israel' was frequently used in both their reigns. But the union of the twelve tribes forged by David and maintained by Solomon would be destroyed. Bible historians would call the new era that followed 'the divided monarchy' in comparison to the united monarchy of David and Solomon. The kingdom would be split in two. The northern kingdom with its ten tribes would henceforth take the name Israel because it included the larger number of tribes. The other two tribes, Judah and Benjamin, would form the southern kingdom or the kingdom of Judah. These two kingdoms would sometimes be allies and sometimes enemies.

The southern kingdom remained faithful to the Davidic dynasty and the temple services at Jerusalem. The northern kingdom rejected these two institutions set up by God. For this reason, Chronicles tells nothing of the northern kingdom's history. Whereas in Kings the parallel history of the two kingdoms is told alternately, Chronicles presents an uninterrupted account of the history of the kingdom of Judah. It expresses no hatred of the northern kingdom, but does not consider it to be legitimate.

The kings who reigned in Jerusalem, in order of succession, were Rehoboam, Abija, Asa, Jehoshaphat, Jehoram, Ahaziah, Joash, Amaziah, Uzziah, Jotham, Ahaz, Hezekiah, Manasseh, Amon, Josiah, Jehoahaz, Jehoiachin and Zedekiah. The faithfulness of these different kings is judged in relation to the faithfulness of their ancestor David. They were either good like David, as was Hezekiah ('he did what was right in the eyes of the Lord, just as his father David had done' – 29:2) or they were evil like Ahaz ('unlike David his father, he did not do what was right in the eyes of the Lord' – 28:1).

10:1-12:16 Rehoboam's Reign

The account of Rehoboam's reign in Chronicles is longer than that in Kings. He was king when disaster struck and the ten northern tribes set up a kingdom independent of the Davidic dynasty.

10:1-19 Secession of the ten northern tribes

Rehoboam went to Shechem for his coronation (**10:1**). This town is far from Jerusalem and is in the northern part of the kingdom. The reason Rehoboam went there instead of to Gibeon or Jerusalem for the coronation is not given. But we can understand from the delegation that met him there that the death of Solomon had raised hopes of liberation in the northern tribes. They had not dared to revolt before because of Solomon's stature.

Jeroboam represented the people at this assembly (**10:2-3**). He had once been one of Solomon's officers responsible for the slave labour force, but he had rebelled (1 Kgs 11:27-28). His presence as a spokesman for the people probably indicates that one of the reasons for his revolt against Solomon may have been his opposition to slave labour. The people requested that the workload that Solomon had imposed should be eased, particularly as regards his building projects (**10:4**). Chronicles had stressed that Solomon had used only foreigners as forced labour (8:9) but the complaint here shows that Israelites too had been forced to work for him. Their complaint shows that they would not unconditionally accept the Davidic dynasty. The king would have to negotiate with them.

Rehoboam asked for three days to consider their request (**10:5**). During this time, he consulted his advisors. Those who had worked with his father Solomon recommended that he give in to the people's request and lighten their burden (**10:6-7**). The advice reveals that these elders knew the characteristics of a good leader: *be kind to these people … please them … give them a favourable answer* (10:7). But when Rehoboam sought the advice of the young men of his own generation, they advised him to take a hard line. Their suggestions were rude and confrontational rather than conciliatory (**10:8-11**).

Unfortunately, the young king chose to take the advice of the young men. When the delegates returned to him on the third day to hear his answer to their request, he took the position advocated by his young advisors (**10:12-14**). Chronicles, like Kings, states that behind the king's decision was the hand of God who was fulfilling the prophecy made to Jeroboam (**10:15**; 1 Kgs 11:29-39). But the author of Chronicles does not report that this prophecy was given in response to the excesses of Solomon, and so places all the blame for the break-up of the kingdom on Rehoboam.

This story reminds us that in Africa the 'elders', as older people are affectionately called, are considered a source of wisdom and their word is listened to with attention. Our folktales include many stories that teach that caring for an elderly person brings good fortune. The elders are more than just living libraries, they are also a source of wisdom (Prov 16:31). Too many conflicts between young and old in the churches start because young people do not want to listen to the wise advice of older people.

The monarchy had been appointed to bring justice and happiness to the people of Israel. When the king's rude reply made it clear that these were no longer his concerns, there was a secessionist outcry: *What share do we have in David, what part in Jesse's son? To your tents, O Israel! Look after your own house, O David!* (**10:16**). The cry threatened the eighty years of unity and of the reign of the Davidic dynasty over all Israel. What a contrast with the prophecy of Amasai: 'We are yours, O David! We are with you, O son of Jesse!' (1 Chr 12:18).

The secession had taken place, and Rehoboam now ruled only the cities of Judah. (**10:17**). However, it seems that he only realizes the gravity of the situation when he sends Adoniram, the newly appointed head of his labour force, to meet the Israelites only to have them stone him to death. Rehoboam recognized that he, too, was threatened with death in this distant area of Shechem and hurried back to his base in Jerusalem (**10:18**).

The permanence of the division is stated in **10:19**: *So Israel has been in rebellion against the house of David to this day.* Though God was behind the secession, on the human level the representatives of the northern tribes complained of the burdensome yoke that weighed them down. By contrast, Jesus said, 'Take my yoke upon you and learn from me, for I am gentle and humble in heart, and you will find rest for your souls. For my yoke is easy and my burden is light' (Matt 11:29-30). Life at the heart of a Christian community should not be experienced as a heavy burden. But sometimes the demands imposed on Christians make it seems like a burden. This may be because church discipline is applied without love, gentleness, goodness and humility.

The account of the division of the kingdom should also draw the attention of church leaders. We deplore the divisions in the body of Christ in Africa. Although in some cases, a division is brought about solely because of the ambitions of one group, there are other cases where a division is the result of the intransigence of a leadership team who refuse to acknowledge the complaints of those who feel wronged.

11:1-23 Consolidation of the kingdom of Judah

As soon as he returned to Jerusalem, Rehoboam wanted to use his military power to bring the northern secessionists back under his control. He assembled his best troops, a hundred eighty thousand men from the two tribes who remained faithful to him (**11:1**). But before he could send them to battle, God sent the prophet Shemaiah to dissuade him (**11:2**). The message was addressed not only to Rehoboam, but also *to all the Israelites in Judah and Benjamin* (**11:3**). These words are missing in 1 Kings 12:23, and expresses the spiritual ideal of the author of Chronicles. Despite the division and the secessionist slogans, Israel and Judah remained *brothers* and should not fight. God announces that *this is my doing* and should therefore not be opposed (**11:4**). Rehoboam and his people obeyed the prophetic word and abandoned their plan to fight (**11:5**).

In the overall scheme of Chronicles, obedience to the prophetic word always brings blessing. For Rehoboam, this blessing was expressed in the construction projects that he undertook (11:5-12). The same Hebrew verb is used three times in this chapter, but in the English it is variously translated as 'fortified', 'strengthened' or 'made strong' (**11:11, 12,** 17). The cities fortified by Rehoboam were all located in the south, east and west of the kingdom, suggesting that he may not have feared an attack from the north. These building projects are not mentioned in the parallel text in 1 Kings 12, which pays more attention to Jeroboam.

In 11:13-17, the author returns to the central theme of the temple. Jeroboam had been concerned that if the people from the northern kingdom went there to worship, they might be tempted to return to Rehoboam's rule. So Jeroboam set up his own altars and appointed his own priests. Jeroboam's apostasy is described in even stronger terms in Chronicles than in Kings, for he is accused of having set up not only a golden calf but also goat idols (**11:15**). Jeroboam and his sons (his dynasty) hindered the priests and Levites from carrying out their functions. They were cut off from the temple in Jerusalem and from the Davidic dynasty to which they had probably remained faithful. They, therefore, left their property to go to Judah (**11:13-14**). Their example was followed by all those living in the ten tribes of the north who *set their heart on seeking* (Hebrew – *darash*) *the Lord* (**11:16**).

For three years, Rehoboam's reign was strengthened because he was *walking in the ways of David and Solomon during this time* (**11:17**). Rehoboam was the first king of Judah after the kingdom was divided in two. Therefore his reign constituted a test of God's promises to the Davidic dynasty. These promises were clearly fulfilled. Rehoboam's obedience to the prophet's message and especially his faithfulness to the temple brought blessing that was publicly manifested in his building projects and in the growth of his family.

The information that follows about the growth of the royal family must not be read independently from what went before, because it is part of the blessing resulting from Rehoboam's obedience. A large family is a blessing according to Chronicles. Rehoboam had eighteen wives and sixty concubines who bore him eighty-eight sons and sixty daughters (**11:18-21**). As in many polygamous marriages on the African continent, precedence was given to one of the wives. Rehoboam's favourite wife was Maacah, though she was not his first wife. He named Abijah, one of her sons, as his successor (**11:22**). This decision could have caused internal fighting within the royal family because Abijah was not the eldest son. However, Rehoboam was able to keep the opposition to the future reign of Abijah in check by setting up his other sons in leadership positions in distant cities of Judah and Benjamin (**11:23**). Rehoboam prepared Abijah for succession just as David had prepared Solomon who, like Abijah, was not the eldest son.

12:1-16 Rehoboam's disobedience

During the last part of his reign, Rehoboam no longer followed the example of David or Solomon as he had been said to do in 11:17. Once the kingdom was established, *he and all Israel with him* abandoned the law of the Lord (**12:1**).

Rehoboam's behaviour is like that of many Christians in Africa. In times of distress, we remain close to God, begging his mercy. But once it is delivered, we quickly forget about him. Similarly, a man may be an active member of a church, living peacefully with his wife until he is named a cabinet minister. Then the power, the money and the glory ruin him. He is seen less and less frequently in Christian circles, becomes unfaithful to his wife and has multiple marriages. In a sermon to new priests, the late Cardinal Malula of Kinshasa, Congo warned them that money and power were among the dangers they faced. But these dangers threaten not only priests but the entire church of Christ in Africa. The Apostle Paul recognized the danger associated with money (and all that accompanies it) when he told Timothy, 'the love of money is a root of all kinds of evil. Some people, eager for money, have wandered from the faith and pierced themselves with many griefs' (1 Tim 6:10). In Paul's terms, we could say that Rehoboam 'wandered from the faith'.

Just as obedience had brought prosperity, so disobedience led to ruin. The ruin took the form of an invasion of Judah by Shishak, king of Egypt (**12:2b**). Egypt was allied with Jeroboam because it was there that he had taken refuge during the reign of Solomon (10:2). The Egyptian attack took place during the fifth year of Rehoboam's reign. The author states that the reason for this attack was the nation's unfaithfulness to the Lord (**12:2a**). He applies the same Hebrew word used to describe Saul's unfaithfulness (1 Chr 10:13) and to justify the exile (1 Chr 36:14). The parallel text in Kings states, 'Judah did evil in the eyes of the Lord' (1 Kgs 14:22). Kings gives more details about the form this evil took (1 Kgs 14:22-24). Unfortunately, Judah was acting just like the people in the northern kingdom.

The cities that Rehoboam had fortified were captured by Shishak, who advanced as far as Jerusalem (**12:3-4**). Loss of territory was always regarded as a punishment from God. In 1 Chronicles 10:7, Saul's unfaithfulness resulted in the loss of territory to the Philistines.

For a second time, the prophet Shemaiah brings the word of God to the king and the leaders of Judah taking refuge in Jerusalem. The words of the prophet are clear: *You have abandoned me; therefore, I now abandon you to Shishak* (**12:5**). Rehoboam and the leaders reacted positively again to the prophetic word: *The Lord is just* (**12:6**). They humbled themselves (**12:7**), which means that they acknowledged their guilt and asked God's pardon. We are reminded of the words in 7:14: 'If my people, who are called by my name, will humble themselves, ... [I] will forgive their sin'.

But Rehoboam's humility resulted in only a partial deliverance (**12:8**). Probably, king Rehoboam and his people had not completely turned from their sins. Rehoboam was not killed, but he was humiliated by Shishak, king of Egypt. The treasures of the temple and the palace were taken (**12:9**). Rehoboam had to replace the golden shields put there by Solomon with shields of bronze, a much less valuable metal (**12:10-12**).

Rehoboam's reign is summed up in 12:12-16. Things had not turned out as badly as they might have: *there was some good in Judah* (12:12). But Rehoboam *had not set his heart on seeking the Lord* (**12:14**). His reign lasted seventeen years

(**12:13a**). Once again, the importance of God's choice of Jerusalem is stressed, as it was in 6:6 (**12:13b**).

Abijah, the successor chosen during his father's life, succeeded him on the throne of Judah (**12:16**).

13:1-22 Abijah's Reign

The transition from Rehoboam to Abijah had been prepared in advance and did not occasion a grand assembly. The account of his monarchy given here differs from the account in Kings. In Kings, his name is often given as Abijam and he is said to have been unfaithful to God: 'he committed all the sins his father had done before him' (1 Kgs 15:3). Chronicles gives a longer version of the reign of Abijah, for this author regards him as a faithful king to whom God gave victory. The major feature of his reign is his long discourse, a real 'sermon on the mount' delivered to Israel and Judah. This discourse covers the most important points in the theology of Chronicles: the dynasty of David, the temple, religious practices, sacrifices and the position of the Levites. However, Chronicles does not totally ignore the fact that Abijah also acted badly, as the account of the reign of his son Asa will show.

The introduction to the reign of Abijah (13:1-2) includes one of the rare references in Chronicles to dates in the kingdom of Israel: *in the eighteenth year of the reign of Jeroboam* (**13:1**). This introduction also indicates the brevity of the reign of Abijah and hints at his evil behaviour (**13:2a**). A reign of only *three years* is far shorter than the average reign recorded in Chronicles and is a bad sign, for a good king was normally rewarded with a long reign.

The end of this introduction mentions the civil war between Abijah and Jeroboam (**13:2b**). Indeed, this is the only event that the author of Chronicles records in Abijah's brief reign (13:3-19). Skirmishes in this war had already been fought during the reign of Rehoboam (12:15). The reasons for the major attack in Abijah's reign are not given. Probably it was simply an attempt by Jeroboam, king of Israel, to exploit the death of Rehoboam and the coming to power of his young son in order to take control of *all Israel*. Abijah fielded an army of four hundred thousand elite troops, but Jeroboam had twice that number: *eight hundred thousand able troops* (**13:3**). Judah was outnumbered and Israel's victory seemed certain. The battlefield was at Zemaraim in the land of Benjamin. Having taken up a defensive position on the mountain, Abijah launches into a speech that is also presented as more defensive than offensive (13:4-12).

Abijah's speech is addressed to Jeroboam and all Israel (**13:4**). This speech concentrates on two differences between the two kingdoms. The first difference concerned the concept of the monarchy (13:5-8). Israel had rejected the Davidic dynasty whereas Judah had remained faithful to a dynasty that had been established by God. According to Abijah, God had given the *kingdom to David and to his descendants for ever by a covenant of salt,* meaning an unchangeable alliance (**13:5**).

Abijah attributes responsibility for the division that took place in chapter 10 to Jeroboam's rebellion. He speaks of the king of Israel as merely an *official of Solomon,* who thus has no legitimate right to rule as king (**13:6**). Those who followed him are referred to as *worthless scoundrels.* Abijah attributes their success to Rehoboam's youth, indecision and lack of firmness (**13:7**), ignoring the fact that his father was forty-one when he became king (12:13).

Abijah presented the civil war between Judah and Israel as an effort by Jeroboam *to resist the kingdom of the Lord* (**13:8a**). He gives a spiritual character to the rebellion.

The second difference between the two kingdoms relates to worship (13:8b-12). Abijah reproaches the northern kingdom for having come to battle with golden calves (**13:8b**). His words are intended to remind those listening to him of another golden calf and of Israel's disobedience in Exodus 32. The northern kingdom had also driven out *the priests of the Lord, the sons of Aaron, and the Levites.* The new priests do not serve God and the method by which they were appointed was subject to corruption (**13:9**).

Judah, however, had remained faithful. The priests who served daily in the temple in Jerusalem were sons of Aaron and they were assisted by Levites. The ritual worship in Jerusalem was the only one that was valid in the eyes of the Lord because *we are observing the requirements of the Lord our God. But you have forsaken him* (**13:10-11**).

Abijah's words position David's dynasty in a close relationship with temple worship. They imply that support for the Davidic dynasty would guarantee ongoing worship at Jerusalem.

Unlike Jeroboam and his army, Judah was led by God himself and had God's priests with their trumpets sounding the battle-cry. These words remind us of Numbers 10:5, 9 and 31:6 and give even more legitimacy to Judah's army. The war against Judah is, in fact, described as a war against the Lord, presented to the northern kingdom as *the God of your fathers* (**13:12**). No one can succeed in such a war against God. In the NT, Gamaliel also understood that no one could destroy what came from God (Acts 5:39).

An account of the battle itself is given in 13:13-19. Jeroboam and his army were deaf to Abijah's urgent appeal and the many reasons he has given for avoiding war. Confident in the size of his army, Jeroboam surrounded Judah, which found itself caught in an ambush. Their desperate situation added to the significance of the victory that God gave to Abijah.

Instead of throwing themselves into battle, the men of Judah cried to the Lord in an act of faith and the priests sounded the trumpets (**3:14**). This complete dependence on God was the key to victory according to the author of

Chronicles. The kings who won military victories were those who placed their trust in God and not in men and their weapons. The battle cry of the men of Judah prompted God to act. It was God himself who defeated *Jeroboam and all Israel* (**13:15**). The behaviour of the Judeans in this chapter strongly resembles that of the Reubenites, the Gadites and the people of Manasseh who cried out to God in their fight against the Hagrites (1 Chr 5:20).

This was major defeat for Israel's army, for some five hundred thousand elite troops fell (**13:17**). As a further sign of divine blessing, Abijah extended his territory by taking cities from Jeroboam (**13:19**). The power of the king of Israel was weakened for the rest of Abijah's reign; by contrast, Abijah *grew in strength.* Another sign of God's blessing on him was the large size of his family. He had fourteen wives, twenty-two sons and sixteen daughters (**13:21**).

Abijah's victory over Jeroboam was a prelude to the ultimate victory of God's kingdom over the kingdom of darkness. Jesus is the other son of David who came to inaugurate the new era of the kingdom of God. Speaking of the church which represents his kingdom, Jesus Christ said to Peter: *the gates of Hades will not overcome it* (Matt 16:18). Jesus' message is centred on the kingdom of God and is an invitation to enter into this kingdom, just as Abijah's discourse was an invitation to reunite the kingdom of God under a legitimate king of the Davidic dynasty.

Abijah's victory is a message of comfort for all those in Africa who are confronted with wars of various kinds. God delivered Abijah, just as he had previously delivered his people in Exodus 14:14, when God himself fought for them. What reassurance to have such a combatant who goes into battle on our behalf! All that he asks is that we trust him.

14:1-16:14 Asa's Reign

The account of Asa's reign is more detailed than the accounts of the reigns of Rehoboam and his son Abijah. Once again, the perspective in Chronicles differs from that in Kings. In Kings, Asa's reign is dealt with in a few verses and receives a positive evaluation (1 Kgs 15:9-24). Chronicles, however, divides his reign into two periods. The first thirty-five years of his reign are characterized by Asa's obedience and the blessing that follows (14:1-15:19). A second, briefer period is characterized by his disobedience and defeat (16:1-14).

14:1-15:19 Asa's obedience and blessing

Asa's reign started on a positive note: *he did what was good and right in the eyes of the Lord his God* (**14:2**). Though Chronicles has not mentioned it, it appears that idolatry was present during the reign of Abijah. He must have permitted the erection of altars to strange gods, the high places, the statues and the idols (**14:3**). Their destruction showed Asa's concern to maintain the temple as the only place chosen and authorized by God for worship. This material reform was accompanied by a spiritual reform. Asa's instructions to his people conformed to the Davidic message traced in Chronicles: *seek the Lord ... and obey his laws and commands* (**14:4**). These are the two conditions for success. This exhortation to his people is not mentioned in the account of Asa's reign in Kings.

The first fruit of this faithfulness was the rest God gave to Judah (**14:1, 6**). This rest is not mentioned in Kings, which states that 'there was war between Asa and Baasha king of Israel throughout their reigns' (1 Kgs 15:16). Rest is a sign of blessing in Chronicles. It permitted the building of the temple. It permitted Asa to begin large construction projects, another sign of God's blessing. The blessing on Asa is also seen in the size of his army, even if the number is mentioned as a prologue to the account of the war that followed (**14:8**).

After this period of rest given by God, the kingdom of Judah suffered an attack by Zerah the Cushite (14:9-15). It is not clear exactly who this man was, although the reference to him as a Cushite suggests that he came from Ethiopia. In the reference to this invasion in 16:8, the Cushites are said to have been allied with Libyans. Zerah was probably an African who led a band of mercenaries in service to the king of Egypt. The reasons for this war are not clear, but one of the issues was certainly control of the area around Marashah (**14:9-10**).

This war too has all the characteristics of a holy war: the Judeans are outnumbered, they pray to God and God gives them victory by striking down the people's enemy. Zerah's army was twice the size of Asa's, as had been the case with Abijah (14:8-9). Asa was faithful to the policy laid down by Solomon (6:34-35). Rather than relying on military strategy, Asa turned to God in prayer, a sign of humility. He placed his confidence in the Lord and not in his army: *we rely on you, and in your name we have come against this vast army* (**14:11**). In the same way as God had intervened to strike Israel and Jeroboam (13:15), God struck Zerah and his army (**14:12**). The same verb is used in Hebrew for God's intervention in both cases.

All that Judah's army had to do was simply to pursue and destroy the fleeing enemy. They collected large quantities of booty, much of which was offered as a sacrifice (**14:13, 15; 15:11**). The Judeans were also able to loot the nearby villages because *the terror of the Lord had fallen upon them* (**14:14**).

After the war, Asa received a message of encouragement and a call to obedience from the prophet Azariah, son of Oded (**15:1**). This prophet's name means 'God has helped' and he is not mentioned elsewhere in the Bible. It is likely that he was not a professional prophet but an occasional one, as 15:1 seems to indicate: *the Spirit of God came upon Azariah son of Oded*. He spoke to *Asa and all Judah and*

Benjamin (**15:2a**). Elsewhere in the Bible, this sort of prophecy is given as an exhortation to repent after a defeat or after the people have been scattered. It is thus surprising that this prophet came forward after a victory to offer encouragement and to impress on Asa and Judah the danger of abandoning the Lord. He may have done this because of the natural human tendency to let down our guard after a great victory. Satan can use this as an opportunity to lead us astray.

His message is well summarized in **15:2b**: *the Lord is with you when you are with him. If you seek him, he will be found by you, but if you forsake him, he will forsake you.* These prophetic words repeat David's words to Solomon before the assembly of Israel: *If you seek him, he will be found by you; but if you forsake him, he will reject you forever.* (1 Chr 28:9; see also Jer 29:13-14). The central part of the prophecy briefly recalls the history of Israel in order to show that God had let himself be found by his people (15:3-6). The reference to 'distress' may refer back to the time of the judges (**15:4**). This brief reminder of their history served to encourage Asa and all Judah to persevere in the ways of God. They can be sure that their *work will be rewarded* (**15:7b**). The Apostle Paul said much the same in his encouragement to the Corinthians: 'therefore, my dear brothers, stand firm. Let nothing move you. Always give yourselves fully to the work of the Lord, because you know that your labour in the Lord is not in vain' (1 Cor 15:58).

The prophet's message was accepted by the king. The prophet told him to *be strong* (**15:7a**), and in response Asa *took courage* (**15:8**). He consequently went even further with his reforms than he had in 14:2-5. This time, his purification of worship extended to the territory of Ephraim, too (15:8). Many residents of the northern kingdom even left their homes and moved to Judah when they learned what the Lord had done for Asa (**15:9**).

These reforms were followed by a grand assembly at Jerusalem (**15:10-11**). There the people make a covenant to *seek the Lord, the god of their fathers, with all their heart and soul* (**15:12**). The death penalty was pronounced on those who would not respect the terms of this covenant, *whether small or great, man or woman* (**15:13**). Asa even deposed his own mother (or grandmother) to keep his promise (**15:16**). Again, the results of this obedience to the Lord is rest; peace is restored until the thirty-fifth year of Asa's reign (**15:15, 19**).

The type of commitment made by Asa and all Judah is sometimes lacking in Christian communities in Africa. This sort of renewal of the covenant may at times be needed to rekindle the flame of faith. There could be a service in which all the members of the Christian community renew their faith and declare their commitment to Jesus Christ and to doing his work. Our initial confession of Jesus as Saviour needs to be reaffirmed periodically.

16:1-14 Asa's disobedience and defeat

Chapter 16 follows the same pattern as chapter 15, with a war followed by a prophetic message. But this time the events illustrate the second part of the principle laid down by Azariah: *if you forsake him, he will forsake you* (15:3).

This time, the war was against the northern kingdom. Baasha, king of Israel, had built fortifications at Ramah, in the territory of Benjamin to hinder the movement of people between the northern and southern kingdoms (**16:1**). Faced with this provocation, Asa forgot how he had acted at the time of the first war. Instead of praying, he hastily sought to make a human alliance with Ben-Hadad, king of Syria. Worse still, he offered him part of the treasures of the temple to persuade him to break his alliance with the king of Israel (**16:2-3**). From a tactical standpoint and in strictly human terms, this was a winning strategy, for Ben-Hadad's military intervention on behalf of Asa led Baasha to cease his building (**16:4-6**). However, from God's point of view, this alliance was evidence of unfaithfulness, as the intervention of the prophet showed.

The prophet Hanani, who is also not mentioned elsewhere in the Bible, brought a negative judgment of Asa's behaviour when faced with Baasha's threat (**16:7-8**). His reasoning was as follows: If the Lord had been able to deliver Asa from Zerah's huge army, could he not have done the same when it came to Baasha? Asa had behaved unwisely, preferring to trust a pagan nation. The prophet pronounced judgment against him: *from now on you will be at war* (**16:9**). Thus, the thirty-five years of rest, which had resulted from Asa's obedience, came to an end. Hanani's reproof is not mentioned in 1 Kings 15:17-22. Nor does Kings condemn Asa for this alliance with a pagan nation.

When he heard Azariah's prophecy, Asa was obedient. However when he heard the prophecy of Hanani, Asa did not repent. Instead, he became angry and imprisoned the prophet (**16:10**).

The end of Asa's reign is described in 16:11-14. In the logic of Chronicles, the illness that struck in his thirty-ninth year must have been a punishment for disobedience to God (**16:12**). Worse still, in his illness, Asa did not seek the Lord but consulted only doctors. Recourse to doctors is not a sin, but the problem was that Asa was neglecting the real cause of his illness: his disobedience.

Despite this final negative note, the comments on Asa's tomb and his burial testify to the esteem in which the author of Chronicles held this king (**16:14**). Asa was buried in the royal cemetery in Jerusalem and the spices and perfumes and fire that accompanied his burial are all signs of respect.

The reign of King Asa contains a lesson for African Christians. The Christian life is an ongoing fight against the forces of evil. Victory today does not mean that we will not face battles tomorrow. We do not build up immunity against sin! Asa had begun well but he finished badly. We constantly need to remind ourselves of the message of 15:7: 'as for you, be strong and do not give up, for your work will be rewarded'.

17:1-21:1 Jehoshaphat's Reign

17:1-19 A good beginning

The fact that four whole chapters are devoted to the reign of Jehoshaphat indicates the importance of this king in the mind of the author of Chronicles. Little is said about his reign in Kings, where he appears as subject to Ahab, king of Israel (1 Kgs 22:1-51). Chronicles on the other hand, regards Jehoshaphat as one of the great kings of Judah along with Hezekiah and Josiah, his successors. His reign was not perfect, however; it had both highs and lows. The lows included two alliances with the kings of Israel, each of which was denounced by a prophet. As during the reign of Asa, obedience to the law and faithfulness to the temple brought blessing while disobedience and alliances with other nations brought disaster.

At the very start of his reign, Jehoshaphat is introduced as a king who was independent of the kingdom of Israel. This independence was first of all military. He *strengthened himself against Israel* (**17:1**). He protected his people against the menace from the north by stationing troops in all the fortified cities and in the cities of Ephraim that his father had taken (**17:2**). His independence was also spiritual. He rejected the Baals and adopted the faith of his ancestor David, the founder of the dynasty, *rather than the practices of Israel* (**17:3-4**).

As a result, the Lord gave him *great wealth and honour* (**17:5**). This blessing encouraged him to go farther in his fight against idolatry. The Hebrew expression translated *his heart was devoted* (**17:6**) can also be translated 'he took great pride in the ways of the Lord' (NASB). In the Bible, pride is generally seen as leading to ruin (see 26:16). This is one of the few positive references to it in the Bible.

Jehoshaphat understood that the teaching and respect for the Law were important for the life of the nation as a whole. He therefore set up a team of itinerant teachers that was composed mainly of priests and Levites. They were accompanied by royal officials who gave this mission official status and guaranteed its authority (**17:7-8**). The OT is familiar with the role of the priests as teachers of the law (Lev 10:11). The Levites, however, only generally took up a teaching ministry after the post-Babylonian exile.

Jesus' final command to his disciples was not only that they should 'make disciples of all nations', but also that they should be involved in 'teaching them to obey everything I have commanded you' (Matt 28:20). The African church preaches, but too often does not teach. There is much talk of revival and sometimes the impression is given that revival comes suddenly like a roll of thunder. But the Bible, and the example of Jehoshaphat's teachers who took with them *the Book of the Law of the Lord* (**17:9**), show that teaching is the best way to bring revival to a nation.

Other blessings also flowed from Jehoshaphat's conduct. First among them was peace because *the fear of the Lord fell on all the kingdoms of the lands surrounding Judah* (**17:10**). The Philistines, long-time enemies of Israel, even brought gifts to Jehoshaphat (**17:11**). Construction projects along with the formation of a large and well-trained army were also traditional signs of God's blessing (**17:12-19**).

18:1-19:3 A bad alliance

The ideal picture of Jehoshaphat's reign is tarnished by his association with King Ahab of Israel. An account of this alliance is also found in 1 Kings 22:1-38, but there Ahab is the principal actor and the focus falls on his inability to escape the prophetic judgment announced by Elijah. Chronicles, by contrast, places Jehoshaphat at the centre of the story and does not mention Elijah.

The story opens on an ironic note. We are reminded of Jehoshaphat's riches and glory (17:5), which makes us wonder why he would bother to enter into an alliance with Ahab (**18:1**). Such an alliance was not necessary for a king who was already blessed and protected by God. The alliance between Jehoshaphat and Ahab was sealed by the marriage of Jehoram, Jehoshaphat's son, to Athaliah, Ahab's daughter (21:6). This marriage would later prove to be a threat to the Davidic dynasty and the purity of worship in Jerusalem.

Maintaining the alliance, Jehoshaphat visited Samaria in the northern kingdom. After a large celebration, Ahab asked his ally to join him in a campaign to recapture *Ramoth Gilead,* a city that had fallen into Syrian hands (**18:2**). The verb used in the statement that Ahab *urged him* to action is the same one used in 1 Chronicles 21:1 where Satan 'incited David to take a census of Israel'. This same verb is used in Deuteronomy 13:6 with the idea of inciting others to apostasy. But Jehoshaphat does not really have a choice. His reply reflects the seriousness of the alliance: *I am as you are, and my people as your people; we will join you in the war* (**18:3**).

Though Jehoshaphat was compromised, he continued to behave as a worthy descendant of David. He urged Ahab, *first seek the counsel of the Lord* (**18:4**). So four hundred prophets, probably all Baal worshippers, were assembled and asked whether the kings should attack Ramoth Gilead. They all promised victory: *Go, … for God will give it into the king's hand* (**18:5, 11**). Zedekiah, one of the prophets, even went so far as to act out his favourable prophecy by waving a pair of iron horns that symbolized the strength of the two kings' armies that would *gore* their opponents (**18:10**). Such symbolic behaviour by the prophets was not unusual (see Jer 27:1-28:17).

Jehoshaphat was sceptical about the reliability of these four hundred prophets. They were probably maintained by the court and it was their job to confirm what the king of Israel said or did. The king of Judah wanted to hear from a real prophet of the Lord (**18:6**).

Hesitantly, Ahab sent for the prophet Micaiah. Like Elijah, Micaiah had no doubt already delivered unpopular messages to this king (**18:7**). He was encouraged not to do this again by the messenger sent to him by the king of Israel (**18:12**). But Micaiah refused to be corrupted or to compromise: *As surely as the Lord lives, I can tell him only what my God says* (**18:13**).

Micaiah's first response to Ahab was ironic. He repeated almost word for word the message of the four hundred prophets (**18:14**). But the king of Israel recognized that Micaiah was mocking him. He knew in advance that Micaiah's word would not be exactly the same as that of the others (**18:15**). Finally, Micaiah describes two different visions, both of which tell of the fatal outcome of the battle of Ramoth Gilead.

The first vision describes Israel as a flock of sheep without a shepherd (**18:16**). It symbolically announced the death of the king in battle. The theme of sheep without a shepherd is also found in Numbers 27:17, Isaiah 13:14 and Zechariah 10:2. The second and longer vision supported the first. In the same way that Ahab had urged Jehoshaphat to go with him to battle, a spirit from the heavenly courts had incited the prophets to lie so as to cause the death of the king of Israel (**18:18-22**).

Zedekiah, one of the most fervent of the large group of prophets, felt that this vision insulted him, and so he slapped Micaiah (**18:23-24**). Ahab then put Micaiah in prison until such time as he would return from the war (**18:25-27**). Jehoshaphat, who had specifically requested to hear from a prophet of the Lord, did not defend him.

In our cities, there are many prophets who pretend to speak for God. They claim to predict what will happen in someone's life. While it is true that God continues to give gifts of prophecy to his church, we should be aware that there are also false prophets. As Christians, we need to distinguish true prophets from false, prophets who speak for God from those who are only expressing their own ideas. Many families and many couples have been destroyed by prophecies given to them. A false prophecy may lead a man to leave his wife because the prophecy states that she is not the wife God has chosen for him. The Bible reminds us: *Do not treat prophecies with contempt. Test everything. Hold on to the good* (1 Thess 5:20-21).

Despite Micaiah's words, the two kings go to battle (**18:28**). King Ahab, however, disguised himself to avoid being recognized, thus hoping to escape the prophecy (**18:29**). The fact that Jehoshaphat agreed to remain in his royal robes indicates that Ahab was the stronger influence in this alliance. The battle centred on Jehoshaphat, who was mistaken for the king of Israel. So Jehoshaphat *cried out, and the Lord helped him* (**18:30-31**). 1 Kings 22:32 simply says that *Jehoshaphat cried out*. In Chronicles, the cry of the king of Judah was really a prayer. After hearing his cry, his enemies realized that he was not the king of Israel and withdrew from him (**18:32**). As for Ahab, he was hit by an arrow shot at random and fatally wounded (**18:33-34**).

In Kings, the account of the death of Ahab is followed by a conclusion that presents this event as the result of the prophetic message (1 Kgs 22:38). In Chronicles, attention is turned to Jehoshaphat who was confronted by the prophet Jehu, son of Hanani, on his return to Samaria (**19:1**). The alliance with Ahab was denounced as giving help to the wicked. However, in his anger, God remembered the good things about Jehoshaphat's conduct, notably his destruction of idols and his desire to seek the Lord. So the prophet did not pronounce any punishment (**19:3**).

By allying himself with Ahab, Jehoshaphat had been gravely unfaithful to the Lord. The words *should you ... love those who hate the Lord?* carry the same meaning as *should you help the wicked?* (**19:2**) Paul makes the same point in his letters to the Corinthians, when he speaks of relationships between Christians and unbelievers; *you must not associate with anyone who calls himself a brother but is sexually immoral or greedy, an idolater or a slanderer, a drunkard or a swindler. With such a man do not even eat* (1 Cor 5:11). Elsewhere he wrote, *What harmony is there between Christ and Belial? What does a believer have in common with an unbeliever* (2 Cor 6:15)?

There is a Lingala (DRC) proverb that says, *lisoloya mwasi oyo abala na mwasi ya nduma ebongaka te* ['a friendship between a married woman and a prostitute will not end well']. This proverb is often quoted by parents when they advise their children that 'bad company corrupts good morals'. A married woman and a prostitute have very different interests and there is a huge risk that the prostitute, who is known for her greed, will influence the behaviour of the married woman, leading her into marital unfaithfulness that may result in divorce. While we should not treat those who are not Christians as enemies, we should exercise great caution about whom we enter into relationships with.

19:4-11 Judicial reforms

After receiving Jehu's warning, Jehoshaphat undertook a tour of his entire kingdom. His purpose was to encourage the people to turn *back to the Lord, the God of their fathers* (**19:4**) The verb 'to turn back' implies repentance.

Among those called to repentance were the judges, for Jehoshaphat now initiated judicial reform (**19:5-11**). This was an appropriate action for him to take, for in Hebrew his name means 'the Lord judges'.

Jehoshaphat appointed judges in all the main towns of the kingdom (**19:5**) and set up an appeal court in Jerusalem (**19:8-11**). The judges of this appeal court were Levites (who are mentioned first), priests and heads of families (**19:8**). This appeal court was especially intended to turn aside God's wrath in the event of a bad judgment at a first hearing before a lower court (**19:10**). This court comprised two chambers: one for religious matters and one for civil matters (**19:11**). This judicial reform was made with reference to the law of Moses (see Exod 18:17-26; Deut 1:16-17; 16:18-20).

His speech at the installation of the judges reveals that the judicial system of Judah was not being put in place for the satisfaction of humans but for God: *you are not judging for man but for the Lord, who is with you whenever you give a verdict* (**19:6**). Though named by the king, the judges were agents working for the application of justice whose basis was the justice of God. Thus the judgments were not to be delivered in the name of the king or the kingdom but in God's name. Hence the judges were to do their task in *the fear of the Lord* (**19:7, 9**). Jehoshaphat particularly warned the judges against corruption and partiality, evils that are not in keeping with God's character. This charge to the judges repeats instructions given in Deuteronomy 10:17 and 16:19.

Matters of justice are a challenge to African churches. We live in countries where justice is perverted by corruption and partiality. The rich and the poor receive different verdicts. In most African countries, delays in paying the salaries of government employees mean that judges are tempted to accept bribes. Although not all gifts are bribes, it is also true that in all eras gifts have corrupted the heart (Prov 17:23; Eccl 7:7). The church must fight for true justice and, failing that, must denounce cases of corruption and perversion of justice. Like the judges whom Jehoshaphat addressed, we must *act with courage* (19:11).

20:1-21:1 War, prayer and deliverance

The account of Jehoshaphat's judicial reforms is followed by an account of his victory over a coalition formed by the Moabites, Ammonites and other inhabitants of southern Edom (**20:1; 10**). This victory is similar to that of Asa (14:8-14). However, more detail is given in this case.

The enemies were *a vast army* that arrived from the south (**20:2**). Informed of this impending menace, Jehoshaphat became fearful, but he did not let himself be carried away by fear. He sought the Lord (**20:3**). As a worthy descendant of Solomon, he knew God's promise contained in 7:14-15. He therefore called for a national fast, an evidence of humility, and called representatives of the people to the temple to pray (**20:4-5**).

Jehoshaphat offered a prayer that can be a model for us when we face fear, as we all do. All of us have been afraid at some time. The disciples of Jesus were afraid when they were caught by the storm (Matt 8:23-27). We, too, as African Christians experience fear almost every day. Fear of death, fear of war, fear of famine, fear of losing our job, fear of evil spirits. Let us remember this prayer of Jehoshaphat that invites us to turn our eyes to God.

Jehoshaphat started his prayer by praising the power of God: *Are you not the God who is in heaven? You rule over all the kingdoms of the nations. Power and might are in your hand, and no one can withstand you* (**20:6**). He reminded himself of God's actions and promises in the past. The land itself is a gift to them from God in accordance with the promise given to them by Abraham, the friend of God (**20:7**). In this land they had built a temple to honour God and as a place where prayer could be offered and heard (**20:8-9**). This type of appeal will touch the heart of God and influence him to intervene.

To encourage God to act, Jehoshaphat then stressed the sinful ingratitude of the invaders who had previously been spared (Num 20:14-21) and the threat to God's gift, the land of Israel (**20:10-11**). In a way, the enemies were attacking God. There was, therefore, reason for God to judge them.

Jehoshaphat was anxious to touch God's heart, and so in his final appeal he speaks of the weakness of the kingdom of Judah. He very simply says, *We do not know what to do, but our eyes are upon you* (**20:12**).

He did not have to wait long for a reply to this prayer. *The Spirit of the Lord came upon Jahaziel* (**20:14**) just as he had come on Azariah in 15:1. The expression shows that Jahaziel was not a professional prophet. Like Azariah, he was a Levite. The prophetic message he delivered began with an appeal for attention: *Listen*. This appeal was followed by encouragement: *do not be afraid* (**20:15**) and finally by an invitation to action: *tomorrow march down against them* (**20:16**). The main theme of the message is that God himself will fight for Judah. *You will not have to fight this battle. Take up your positions, stand firm and see the deliverance the Lord will give you* (**20:17**).

Judah responded by expressing its gratitude and faithfulness to the word of God given by Jahaziel through an outburst of praise. King Jehoshaphat and the assembly prostrated themselves while the Levite singers loudly celebrated the Lord (**20:18-19**).

The next day, Jehoshaphat and Judah set out to meet the enemies. Before they left, the king addressed the people, encouraging them to believe the prophetic message (**20:20**). As a sign of confidence in God, the front line of the army was not led by soldiers but by singers praising God (**20:21**). It was at that precise moment that the Lord himself began the battle. First the Moabites and the Ammonites wiped out the inhabitants of Mount Seir in Edom. Then the Moabites and Ammonites turned on each other (**20:22-23**). The destruction was complete, *no one had escaped* (**20:24**). The prophet's word was fulfilled to the letter. The army of Judah did not have to fight. Its only task was to gather the booty from the battlefield, and that took more than three days since there was so much to be collected (**20:25**).

As a sign of gratefulness, a praise service was held at the site of the victory. The place was given a commemorative name: *Beracah*, which in Hebrew means 'blessing' (**20:26**). Another service of praise was conducted in the temple on their return to Jerusalem (**20:27-28**). The most important result of this victory was peace, the peace resulting from the fear of the Lord that had taken possession of all the neighbouring kingdoms (**20:29-30**; see 1 Chr 14:17).

A summary of Jehoshaphat's life follows in 20:31-34. It reports his age when he came to the throne, the length of his reign, the name of his mother and sources of further information about his reign. It appears that his campaign to remove *the high places*, which was reported in 17:6, had not been completely successful (**20:33**). Nevertheless, the general tone is positive: Jehoshaphat *did what was right in the eyes of the Lord* (**20:32**).

The summary is followed by a brief report of one other incident in his reign: an attempt at reconciliation between Jehoshaphat and Ahaziah, king of Israel. Kings and Chronicles differ in their presentation of this incident. Kings suggests that Jehoshaphat built ships to do trading with Tarshish but that the expedition failed. Ahaziah then offered help, which Jehoshaphat refused (1 Kgs 22:48-49). This account sees Jehoshaphat's role in a positive light.

Chronicles, however, indicates that Jehoshaphat and Ahaziah were allied in constructing the ships (**20:36**). This alliance, like the one with Ahab, was denounced by a prophet. It is only following this condemnation that the ships were destroyed (**20:37**). The author cannot accept any relationship with a king *who was guilty of wickedness* (20:35).

21:2–20 Jehoram's Reign

Jehoram's reign plunged the kingdom of Judah and the Davidic dynasty into torment. The alliance between Jehoshaphat and Ahab that was sealed by the marriage of Jehoram to Ahab's daughter produced bitter fruit, the worst of which was the very real danger that the royal line of David would be extinguished. In Kings, the reign of Jehoram is dealt with very briefly (2 Kgs 8:16-24) and is preceded by the long account of the death of Elijah and the prophetic ministry of Elisha (2 Kgs 2:1-6:15). Chronicles is only interested in the legitimate monarchy in Judah, and so does not mention these events. It offers a longer account of Jehoram's reign.

As a good king, Jehoshaphat had prepared for his succession. He had established his various sons in fortified cities across Judah; that is, far from Jerusalem the centre of power, and had given them sufficient gold and silver to meet their needs. Jehoram, the first-born, could expect a peaceful succession (**21:2-3**). But Jehoram was greedy, and when he had *established himself firmly* in power, he killed all his brothers and some of the princes of Israel (**21:4**). He probably wanted to retake all the property willed to them by their father. These murders were the first threat to the Davidic line, which was now maintained by only one descendant. A first judgment is brought against Jehoram in the mention of the length of his reign (**21:5**). This short reign of eight years was a bad sign from the perspective of Chronicles. Good kings had long reigns.

The negative evaluation continues with the condemnation of the marriage between the house of Judah and the house of Ahab. The influence of Ahab's house on Judah was great and evil. King Jehoram *did evil in the eyes of the Lord* (**21:6**). He is credited with nothing good. This total unfaithfulness on the part of Jehoram could have led the Lord to reject the house of David according to the conditions laid down in 7:18-20. However, *because of the covenant the Lord had made with David, the Lord was not willing to destroy the house of David* (21:7; see 1 Chr 17:10-14). Kings makes no reference to the covenant made between God and David and simply says, *for the sake of his servant David, the Lord was not willing to destroy Judah* (2 Kgs 8:19). Kings is more concerned with the preservation of Judah than with the preservation of David's dynasty.

However, Jehoram's infidelity had consequences. Edom to the south revolted against his authority (**21:8**). Though Jehoram survived a battle against them, the author of Chronicles specifies that this rebellion was still continuing in his time. This remark implies that disputes continued throughout the reign of this king (**21:9-10a**). The city of Libnah, situated to the west on the Philistine border, also revolted (**21:10b**). These rebellions contrast with the fear of the Lord that had restrained all the surrounding kingdoms during the reign of Jehoshaphat (20:29). The loss of these territories should be seen as divine punishment. Whereas 2 Kings 8:22 simply states what happened, Chronicles gives a theological reason for these two revolts. They happened *because Jehoram had forsaken the Lord* (**21:10c**). The principle stated by Azariah remains true: *if you forsake him, he will forsake you* (15:2).

Jehoram's abandoning of God is shown by his abandoning of the temple. He preferred to build *high places on the hills* and caused the spiritual decline of his people (**21:11**). This verse offers additional proof of the evil influence of the house of Ahab on Jehoram.

At the height of his infidelity, Jehoram received a letter from the prophet Elijah. It is the only mention of this northern prophet in Chronicles. The letter has all the hallmarks of a prophetic message of judgment. Jehoram is accused first of having sinned by omission in not having done what he should have done. He had strayed from the way of his fathers Jehoshaphat and Asa, who were worthy members of the house of David (**21:12**). Chronicles considers it important that we live up to the heritage we have received from our ancestors and often speaks of the Lord as the 'God of your fathers'.

Jehoram is next accused of sinning by modelling his reign on that of the kings of Israel, represented by the house of

Ahab. Following their example had led to idolatry and the murder of his brothers (**21:13**).

The last part of Elijah's letter announces God's judgment on the people, the royal family in general, and the king in particular. The people and the royal family will be struck a terrible blow (**21:14**). The exact nature of this blow is not specified but it will clearly be a divine punishment. The king himself will be struck down by a painful and fatal disease (**21:15**).

The judgment pronounced by Elijah came swiftly. The heavy blow to the people and the king's family took the form of an invasion of Judah by Philistines and Arabs. These groups had previously been at peace with Judah and are mentioned among those who brought presents to Jehoshaphat, Jehoram's father (17:11). Chronicles says that *the Lord aroused* them, an expression that is used when God uses outsiders as instruments to accomplish his will (see 36:22). They captured all the king's wealth and carried off his wives and almost all his sons. Only the youngest prince, Ahaziah, escaped (**21:16-17**). Jehoram had killed all his brothers and now he would experience the same sad treatment of his children (22:1).

The second judgment was on Jehoram himself. He was struck down by an incurable disease that worsened from day to day. He did not die in peace but *in great pain.* Worse still, this unfaithful king was not considered worthy of a good tomb and no perfumes were burned in his honour, as had been the case for his fathers. Whereas Chronicles frequently says of other kings that 'he slept with his fathers', no such euphemism is used for Jehoram. All that is said is that *he passed away, to no one's regret* (**21:18-20**).

Jehoram's reign confirms the evil influence of evil companions. Paul rightly warned the Corinthians: 'Bad company corrupts good character' (1 Cor 15:33). In the case of Jehoram, his marriage was an important source of the problem. While it is true that marriage is primarily a matter for two people, a man and a woman, their families can have a profound influence on them. The richness of African culture thus recognizes that marriage is not just a matter of two individuals, but also involves two families, two clans, two villages. For this reason, parents pay great attention to the reputation and the quality of the family into which their child (whether son or daughter) is going to marry. They will not, for example, allow their daughter to marry a young man whose family members are known to be thieves. Our ancestors acknowledged the strength of the influence that an individual's family can have on a marriage.

22:1-9 Ahaziah's Reign

The reign of Ahaziah, whose name means 'the Lord has upheld' or 'has helped' was like that of Jehoram, his father. The danger of extinction of the Davidic dynasty became even more acute.

As with Jehoram, the formula introducing Ahaziah's reign is preceded by the account of the circumstances of his ascension to the throne and a brief historical summary. Ahaziah was established as king of Judah by *the people of Jerusalem* (**22:1**). The exact makeup of this group is not clarified, but their intervention was necessary because of the lack of preparation for the succession. Besides, their choice was very limited for Ahaziah was the only son of the royal dynasty who had not been killed.

Ahaziah's reign was extremely brief: one year. His mother, Athaliah, was the daughter of Ahab king of Israel, and thus the granddaughter of Omri (**22:2**). The identity of his mother suggests that there will be a negative judgment of Ahaziah, so we are not surprised to be told that, like his father (21:6), he followed the evil conduct of the kings of Israel. He chose to follow them because of the bad advice given by his mother (**22:3**). The queen mother occupied an influential position in the ancient Near East. For example, in 1 Kings 2:17 Adonijah was convinced that King Solomon could not refuse a request from Bathsheba, his mother.

But Ahaziah was not only influenced by his mother, he also received advice from his counsellors *to his undoing* (**22:4**). These counsellors seem to have come from the northern kingdom. All these comments regarding bad advice are not recorded in 2 Kings 8:27. The very first verse of Psalms warns us against bad advice when it says, *Blessed is the man who does not walk in the counsel of the wicked* (Ps 1:1). Job said the same thing: *I stand aloof from the counsel of the wicked* (Job 21:16; 22:18).

On the basis of this bad advice, the King of Judah went to fight alongside Joram, king of Israel, against the Syrians at Ramoth Gilead (**22:5**). We are reminded of the earlier coalition between Jehoshaphat and Ahab (18:22-34). Ahaziah and Joram are fighting the same enemy, in the same location, and the result of the battle is similar. The king of Israel was wounded in battle and withdrew to Jezreel for medical care. Ahaziah went to visit him (**22:6**). At this point in the narrative, Kings inserts a long section concerning the intervention of the prophet Elisha, the anointing of Jehu as king, and the destruction of the house of Ahab (2 Kings 8:29). The death of Ahaziah was not the main concern in Kings.

In Chronicles, however, the death of Ahaziah is at the centre of the story. The author reports that this visit of the king of Judah was part of God's plan for his downfall (**22:7**). Far from Jerusalem, Ahaziah, of David's lineage, his relatives and his counsellors suffered the end destined for the house of Ahab (**22:8-9a**). It was humiliating for a descendant of David to hide and then to die in Samaria, the rebel capital, rather than in Jerusalem. Kings reports that the body of King Ahaziah was carried to Jerusalem for burial (2 Kings 9:27), but the author of Chronicles remains silent on this point, and rather gives the impression that the king of Judah was buried where he died. He was given a funeral only out of respect for his grandfather Jehoshaphat and, like Jehoram his father, was certainly not buried in the royal tomb (**22:9b**).

After a century of dynastic succession, the Davidic line runs the risk of extermination: *there was no one in the house of Ahaziah powerful enough to retain the kingdom* (22:8-9). God's promise to David and Solomon seems to be on hold. This situation was almost the same as had been the case with the house of Saul in 1 Chronicles 10:4-6.

The reigns of Jehoram and Ahaziah are clear evidence of the serious effects of the alliance made between Jehoshaphat and Ahab. Though the signatories of this alliance were no longer alive, its negative effects were still felt. The consequences of our actions outlast the acts themselves. Jehoshaphat had believed that he was making an alliance that would strengthen Judah, but instead it had almost brought it to ruin.

22:10-23:21 Athaliah's Reign

The word 'reign' could be inserted between quotation marks because Chronicles regards Athaliah as a usurper. The classic introduction formula stating the year of accession to the throne and the length of the reign are not given. Her power was illegitimate. David's dynasty ruled over Judah for four centuries, except for the six years of Athaliah's rule. She was rejected because she was not a descendant of David and because of her behaviour, not because she was a woman. Indeed, it was through another woman, Jehosheba, that the Davidic dynasty was saved from extinction.

The queen mother, Athaliah, seized the throne after the death of her son Ahaziah. After having been a bad counsellor, she became a bad queen. To secure her throne, she *proceeded to destroy the whole royal family of the house of Judah* (**22:10**). However, Jehosheba saved a baby of David's line, Joash. She hid him away, probably keeping him in areas of the temple reserved for priests. Chronicles does well to name this woman and give her a place of honour: she was *the daughter of King Jehoram*, and thus *Ahaziah's sister* (**22:11**). The historian Josephus thought that she was Jehoram's half-sister, sharing the same father but not the same mother. The relationship might also explain her opposition to Athaliah's diabolical plan.

For six years Joash was raised in the temple by his nurse and by Jehosheba. His story reminds us of that of Moses in Egypt and of Jesus, also in Egypt, and also in Africa (Exod 2:1-10; Matt 2:13-15). In one way or another, the African continent has at times played the same sheltering role as the temple did here for Joash. Africa contributed to the preservation of another descendant of David: the Lord Jesus. This role played by Africa in the history of salvation is not often stressed.

The manner in which Joash was saved also brings out the link between the Davidic dynasty and the temple. In fact, the restoration of the throne of Judah into the hands of Joash will be accompanied by religious reform.

The restoration took place in the seventh year of Athaliah's reign. The delay was probably to allow Joash, who was one year old at the time of his rescue (see 24:1), to grow a little older before becoming king. The management of the restoration is in the hands of Jehoiada, the high priest and husband of Jehosheba. His first step was to form an alliance with the military commanders (**23:1**).

Although this story also appears in 2 Kings 11:4-20, additional details are included in the account in Chronicles. Thus Chronicles places Jehoiada's undertaking in a more national context. We are told that, like David and Solomon, Jehoiada called a religious assembly in Jerusalem. Then he reminded those present of God's promise to the Davidic dynasty (**23:2-3**). These details are not mentioned in Kings, which also does not mention the role of the Levites in the assembly.

Jehoiada issued precise instructions on what role each group was to play in the coronation (**23:4-10**). Once again, the Levites have important roles. The plot would be put into action on a Sabbath day so as not to draw attention in advance. Presumably Athaliah, a follower of Baal, had little interest in what went on in the temple.

When everything was ready, Jehoiada brought out the young boy from his hiding place, presented him before the assembled people and crowned him (**23:11**). An important detail that is mentioned is that *a copy of the covenant* was given to the young king. This document was probably a copy of the law (Deut 17:14-20). The cry, *Long live the king!* declared the people's support for the kingship of Joash (see 1 Sam 10:24).

The noise of the crowd drew Athaliah's attention (**23:12**). Hurrying to the temple, she found Joash standing beside the pillar surrounded by the military commanders and the rejoicing people. The Levite musicians were also leading the people in praise. She shouted, *Treason! Treason!* but the crowd and the guard rendered her powerless to harm the young monarch (**23:13**). 'Those who kill with the sword will die by the sword', says the proverb. Jehoiada ordered Athaliah be taken from the temple and executed (**23:14-15**).

The restoration of the Davidic dynasty was not an end in itself because, with the disappearance or at least the interruption of David's line, the temple and its worship had also been corrupted. The alliance between the house of David and the house of Ahab had deprived Judah of its status and of its special relationship with God. Jehoiada proceeded to renew the covenant between the people, the king, and the Lord (**23:16**). The first physical result of this commitment was the destruction of the temple of Baal and of his altars and images. The priest of Baal, Mattan, suffered the same fate as Athaliah (**23:17**). Jehoiada next re-established the proper form of worship in the temple by the priests and Lev-

ites (**23:18-19**). These two verses are not found in Kings. They reflect Chronicles' preoccupation with temple worship, and include all the favourite themes of the author of Chronicles: the priests and Levites, the law of Moses, David's assignment of roles in the temple, and praise.

No one seems to have opposed Joash's entry into the royal palace (**23:20**). The people throughout the realm rejoiced at the death of Athaliah and the peace reigning in Jerusalem (**23:21**). This period of tranquillity should be seen as a blessing from God. It was given to faithful kings of the Davidic dynasty. Here Jehoiada and the people acted in accordance with David's heritage by maintaining appropriate worship.

The Davidic line was not maintained by the merit of David's successors but by the faithfulness of God. Were it not for God's mercy to David and respect for his promises, David's dynasty would have suffered the same fate as Saul's family. God is faithful. In speaking of the faithfulness of God, the Letter to the Hebrews says, 'Let us hold unswervingly to the hope we profess, for he who promised is faithful' (Heb 10:23). This text about the promise of God speaks also of another high priest, Jesus Christ, established over the house of God and the one by whom the covenant with God may be renewed (Heb 10:21).

24:1-24:27 Joash's Reign

The author of Chronicles follows the same pattern in his account of Joash's reign as he does for those of Amaziah and Uzziah, Joash's successors. The description starts with a period of obedience that brings blessing, describes an important event that unleashes a change in attitude, and then presents a period characterized by disobedience and resultant punishment. For Joash, the crisis was the death of Jehoiada, the priest (24:15-16); for Amaziah, it was his victory over the Edomites (25:14-15), and for Uzziah the crisis came when he became powerful (26:16).

The lives of these three kings remind African Christians of the need to persevere. All three of them did good things and were obedient, but unfortunately all finished in disobedience. We often discuss whether it is possible to lose our salvation. Even if salvation in Jesus Christ is by faith, there is a need to persevere because our faith is in danger of dying every day. The letter to the Hebrews underscores this need for perseverance: *We have come to share in Christ if we hold firmly till the end the confidence we had at first* (Heb 3:14).

24:1-16 Obedience and blessing

The account of Joash's reign begins with the usual introduction that tells his age when he came to the throne (seven years), the length of his reign (forty years) and the name of the queen mother (Zibiah). Chronicles presents Joash as a king who was faithful to God during the life of Jehoiada. This detail warns of the sad change to come in the life of the king of Judah. However, Chronicles is less negative in its assessment of Joash than Kings is. The author does not mention the continuation of the high places (2 Kgs 12:3).

Jehoiada chose two wives for Joash and daughters and sons were born of these marriages (**24:3**). These children were a sign of blessing, and were also of vital importance given what had happened to David's family. These marriages were necessary to rebuild the dynasty as quickly as possible. David's line has escaped extinction. However, the fact that Joash (and Abraham) were polygamous should not be used as a justification for polygamy. God's plan from the beginning is for monogamy, for he said 'a man will leave his father and mother and be united to his wife, and they will become one flesh' (Gen 2:24).

The faithfulness of Joash is revealed by his loyalty to the temple and its worship. During the reign of Athaliah, the temple had been degraded and pillaged for the benefit of Baal worship (**24:7**). Joash thus decided that repairs were needed (**24:4**). He gathered the priests and Levites and instructed them to collect the money necessary for the work (**24:5**). In principle, in the ancient Near East, the responsibility for maintaining the temple was that of the king alone. Joash's initiative marks a change. He introduced the idea that the people were also responsible for the maintenance of the temple.

The parallel account in 2 Kings 12:4-16 differs widely from the Chronicles version in certain details. In 2 Kings 12:5, the king asked the priests to use the cash offerings made by the faithful in the temple for the repair work. Chronicles specifies that the money was to come from a collection to be made in 'all Israel' by the priests and Levites. The author links this offering to the tax instituted by Moses in the desert (**24:6, 9**; see Exod 25:1-9; 38:25-31).

As is his habit, the author of Chronicles also mentions the Levites, who are not mentioned in Kings. Here, they play an important role. It was the Levites and not the priests who were responsible for neglecting the collection of the funds (24:5-6). This comment is the only negative remark about the Levites in the entire book of Chronicles.

In 2 Kings 12:10, Jehoiada the priest had the idea of placing a chest in the temple for the collection. In Chronicles, the king ordered the construction of the chest. Finally, 2 Kings 12:13 specifically states that the outstanding balance of the money brought for the repairs to the temple was not used for making utensils. According to Chronicles, it was used for this purpose (**24:14a**).

All these differences serve to indicate greater involvement by Joash in the restoration of the temple and greater faithfulness to the law that had been given to him at his coronation. Moreover, once the work was completed, the author emphasizes the continuity of the temple worship during the life of Jehoiada (**24:14b**).

Sadly, the high priest died. Having saved the temple and the Davidic dynasty, he deserved the greatest honours. He died *full of years* as had David, Abraham and Isaac (Gen

25:8; 35:29; 1 Chr 29:28). His exceptional life is reflected in its long length – one hundred and thirty years (**24:15**), longer than the lives of even Moses or Joshua (Deut 34:7; Josh 24:29). He was honoured as a king and buried in the royal tomb (**24:16**).

24:17-27 Disobedience and punishment

Jehoiada's death was the prelude to a period of disobedience for Joash (24:17-27). The high priest had no doubt acted as his tutor. Without his wise counsellor, the king followed the bad advice of the officials of Judah and idolatry returned in full force (**24:17-18**). The influence of the northern kingdom must have continued among the leaders despite the death of Athaliah.

God sent his prophets to warn them, but the king and all Judah with him did not listen to them (**24:19**). So Zechariah, the son of Jehoiada, was seized by the Spirit of God. He repeated Azariah's message during the reign of Asa: *Because you have forsaken the Lord, he has forsaken you* (**24:20**; 15:2). Not only did the people refuse to listen to this prophet, but, on orders from the king, Zechariah was executed (**24:21**). The author of Chronicles expresses his sorrow at this murder by saying, *King Joash did not remember the kindness Zechariah's father Jehoiada had shown him* (**24:22a**). Jesus may have been referring to this murder in Matthew 23:35, although there the father's name is given as Berekiah rather than Jehoiada as in Chronicles.

The logic of Chronicles dictates that refusing to listen to a prophetic message brings punishment. As he died, Zechariah asked that God *call you to account* (**24:22b**). The Syrians were the instrument chosen by God to carry out his judgment on Joash and the people of Judah. As had happened in the wars won by faithful kings, divine intervention enabled an army *with only a few men* to triumph over *a much larger army* (**24:23-24**). But this time, Judah was the one who was defeated. Weakened by this defeat, Joash was killed in his bed by his officials who were angry about the death of Zechariah. Joash was not buried in a royal tomb, a sign of the negative judgment of Chronicles on this king (**24:25-26**).

25:1-28 Amaziah's Reign

25:1-2 Introduction to Amaziah

The account of the reign of Amaziah starts with the classic introductory formula of giving his age at succession (thirty-five years), the length of his reign (twenty-nine years) and the name of the queen mother (Jehoaddin) (**25:1**). The author then specifies this king was faithful to God *but not wholeheartedly* (**25:2**). Kings is more precise, saying that 'he followed the example of his father Joash' (2 Kgs 14:3). This wording announces a reign in two parts, like that of his father.

25:3-13 Obedience and blessing

Amaziah started by showing signs of obedience. As with Joash, Chronicles makes no reference to the continued presence of the high places that is recorded in 2 Kings 14:4. It replaces that verse with one referring to another painful event, but one that gives testimony to Amaziah's respect for the law. He ordered the execution of the officials who had murdered his father, but obeyed the law in not extending the punishment to include their children (25:2-4; Deut 24:16; Ezek 18:20).

He also demonstrated obedience in his conduct of the war against Edom. Before setting out for the campaign, Amaziah recruited mercenaries from Israel, probably because of the small size of his army (**25:5-6**). This association with Israel was condemned by an anonymous prophet simply called a *man of God*. He told the king of Judah to send these mercenaries back home. The reason was simple: *the Lord is not with Israel* (**25:7**). These prophetic words remind us of those of King Abijah (13:4-12). Associating with an army that did not enjoy God's presence would also distance God from Judah's army. The prophet explained the choice before Amaziah, saying *God has the power to help or to overthrow* (**25:8**). Amaziah was willing to follow the advice of the man of God, but regretted the large amount of money he had already paid for the mercenaries' services. The prophet reassured him: *The Lord can give you much more than that* (**25:9**). As a faithful king, at least at this stage, Amaziah sent the mercenaries from Israel back home, much to their discontent (**25:10, 13**).

Amaziah's obedience to the prophetic word resulted in establishing his power and a crushing defeat on Edom. However, unlike the case with the wars of totally faithful kings, there was no particular intervention by God here, nor was there any booty (**25:11-12**). We do, however, see cruel treatment of prisoners of war (25:12). And the angry mercenaries raided and destroyed, much as we see happening in some parts of Africa today (25:13).

25:14-28 Disobedience and punishment

Amaziah's victory led him into disobedience. He carried his defeated enemies' gods back to Jerusalem, and he *bowed down to them* (**25:14**). In antiquity, victory over an enemy was interpreted as also a victory over their gods. That was why the victorious Philistines in 1 Samuel 5:2 took the ark of God and put it in the temple of Dagon, their god. Amaziah did not follow the example of David who, when he defeated the Philistines, not only did not carry away their gods, but burned them (1 Chr 14:12). By worshipping the gods of Edom, Amaziah made himself hateful in the eyes of the Lord.

Another anonymous prophet was sent to him with a message from God. The prophet pointed out that it was stupid to bow to gods who had not even been able to save their own people (**25:15**). Unfortunately, this time, the king was not prepared to listen to the prophetic message. He told the prophet to stop and threatened to strike him down. The words of the prophet as he withdrew sealed the fate of the king: *I know that God has determined to destroy you* (**25:16**).

God's judgment came during the war that Judah fought with Israel. King Amaziah was the one who provoked the conflict by sending a message to Jehoash, king of Israel: *Come, meet me face to face* (**25:17**). The king of Israel replied with a beautiful fable that reminds us of the fable told by Jotham in Judges 9:8-15. This fable denounced Amaziah's pride following his victory over Edom. The king of Israel warned his adversary that this conflict would result in his own ruin and that of his people (**25:18-19**).

But the king of Judah would not listen. Unlike the parallel passage in 2 Kings 14:8-14, Chronicles specifies that God made him deaf to reason in order to deliver Judah into the enemy's hands because of their idolatry (**25:20**). Jehoash, king of Israel, therefore responded to the challenge by the king of Judah and entered the southern kingdom with his army. Judah was utterly defeated (**25:21-22**). Amaziah was captured by the king of Israel and taken to Jerusalem. The walls of the city were destroyed, and the royal treasury and that of the temple were pillaged. Jehoash also took hostages and carried them off to Samaria (**25:23-24**).

In one of the rare linkages of the history of Judah and Israel, **25:25** specifies that, despite his defeat, Amaziah outlived Jehoash, king of Israel. However, like his father, he ended up being assassinated by his own people and was not buried in the royal tomb (**25:26-28**).

In Chronicles the events of Amaziah's reign represent the exact opposite of the blessings traditionally enjoyed by faithful kings: Amaziah did not undertake any building projects; on the contrary, the walls of Jerusalem were damaged. He did not experience material plenty; on the contrary, he worried about the money given to the mercenaries and his own treasure was taken. In place of peace, his reign was one of war and conspiracy. Rather than him being surrounded by a large family, his family was taken hostage.

26:1-23 Uzziah's Reign

Uzziah is the final one of the three kings in Chronicles who follow the pattern of obedience during the early years of their reign and disobedience during later years.

26:1-15 Obedience and blessing

This king of Judah was said to be as faithful as his father Amaziah (**26:4**), a statement that foreshadows the sad end of this king who started so well. Uzziah's reign is introduced in a very positive way, with the author twice repeating the favourite expression, *he sought God* (**26:5**). This seeking lasted as long as the prophet Zechariah lived and his advice guided the king. We are reminded of the situation of King

Joash before the death of the priest Jehoiada. As a result of this seeking, *God gave him success*.

God's blessing on Uzziah found concrete expression in three areas. In war, it meant that Uzziah enjoyed victories over the Philistines, the Arabs and the Meunites. Like David, Uzziah owed his success to God's help (**26:6-7, 15**; see also 1 Chr 12:18). These victories contributed to Uzziah's fame. The Ammonites brought him gifts. As a prelude to **26:16**, it is said that *he had become very powerful* (**26:8**).

Building projects, too, are always regarded as indications of divine favour in Chronicles. Uzziah repaired the walls of Jerusalem that had been damaged by Jehoash, king of Israel (**26:9**; 25:23). He also built cisterns to provide water for his livestock and for crops, *for he loved the soil* (**26:10**).

The third sign of divine favour was the improved security of his kingdom. He had a large, well-trained and well-equipped army (**26:11-14**). Using the best technology available at the time, he hired an engineer to install war machines on the walls of Jerusalem that could hurl arrows and large stones at any attackers (26:15).

26:16-23 Disobedience and punishment

Uzziah's power led him to become proud. The KJV gives a literal translation of the original when it says that 'his heart was lifted up', for this was the metaphor the Hebrews used when speaking of pride. In Lingala (DRC), however, when we speak of a proud person, we say *Azali mutu monene* ['he has a big head']. This *pride led to his downfall* (**26:16a**). It is interesting to note that Chronicles distinguishes between pride and power. Jehoshaphat became powerful, but he did not become proud. On the other hand, Uzziah's power led him to sinful pride.

This pride must have grown after the death of Zechariah (25:5). It led Uzziah to be *unfaithful to the Lord his God*. The word here translated 'unfaithful' is the same as that used of Saul in 1 Chronicles 10:13-14. This word has not been used of any king since the reign of Rehoboam (12:2). Thus its use here to describe the action by King Uzziah underscores the gravity of his act in God's eyes.

Uzziah's unfaithfulness took the form of interference in matters related to worship. He took it upon himself to enter the temple and *burn incense on the altar* (**26:16b**). Only the sons of Aaron were entitled to burn incense to the Lord and so this usurping of functions reserved for the priests and Levites roused the opposition of *Azariah the priest* and *eighty other courageous priests*. They asked Uzziah to leave the temple on pain of punishment from the Lord (**26:17-18**; see also Num 16:40).

The burning of incense did not bring immediate punishment by God. But punishment came when Uzziah became angry with the priests, and probably refused to obey the order to leave the temple. He was struck with leprosy (**26:19**). This punishment reminds us of the punishment of Miriam, who had also been guilty of pride (Num 12:10). The law forbade anyone suffering from a skin disease from even entering the temple, and so Azariah and the other priests hurried the sick king (who was now also ritually impure) out of the temple (**26:20**). Uzziah remained ill until his death and lived in isolation from others as laid down by the law (Lev 13:46; Num 5:1-3).

The author's concluding statement about Uzziah's reign is given in **26:22-23**. The events of his reign are said to have been recorded by the prophet Isaiah, son of Amoz – the same Isaiah whose name is attached to one of the books of the Bible. Uzziah was buried as close as possible to his ancestors but not in the royal tomb because he was a leper.

At the start of chapter 24, it was pointed out that the lives of the three kings just discussed remind us of the need to persevere in the faith. They also have something to teach us about prosperity. For all three, prosperity was a consequence of obedience. Does their experience support the prosperity gospel that is spreading more and more in Africa? The prosperity gospel claims that there is a direct relation between faith in God and material prosperity. When faith does not produce material prosperity, believers are suspected of hidden and unconfessed sin. While the NT does not deny that God blesses the faithful, verses like Philippians 4:12 show that the equation is not as automatic as it is made out to be in the prosperity gospel. Our greatest blessing is Jesus Christ himself, and the quality of our faith can never be measured by our prosperity.

Uzziah sets a good example for us. Although his prosperity came from God, Chronicles shows that king Uzziah also worked hard to achieve it. The references to his raising cattle and cultivating vineyards should lead us to recognize that we must, in a sense, contribute to God's blessing. The prosperity gospel teaches a passive waiting to acquire wealth. It presents God as a banker who pays interest if we simply deposit faith in our account. But God's blessing on our work is the true measure of prosperity.

27:1-9 Jotham's Reign

Jotham's three predecessors may have all followed the same pattern, but with Jotham, Chronicles returns to individual responsibility following the principle laid down during the reign of Amaziah (25:3-4). Thus the reigns of Jotham and his successors, Ahaz and Hezekiah, present great contrasts. Jotham was obedient; his son Ahaz was one of the worst kings; Ahaz's son, Hezekiah, was the greatest reformer of all the kings of Judah. The way they are presented matches the teaching of the prophet Ezekiel, who disagrees with the common saying after the destruction of Jerusalem: 'The fathers eat sour grapes, and the children's teeth are set on edge' (Ezek 18:1-20). This proverb means that the present generation suffers the consequences of the failures of past generations. For the prophet and the author of Chronicles, each generation is responsible for its own destiny.

The description of the reign of Jotham is one of the briefest in Chronicles. The main point that the author wants to make is that, unlike his father, Jotham was not carried away by pride brought on by power. The comparison is clear: *after Uzziah became powerful, his pride led to his downfall* (26:16), but Jotham *grew powerful because he walked steadfastly before the Lord his God* (**27:6**). A person may be powerful and remain true to God.

The usual formula is used to introduce Jotham's reign. He is said to have ascended the throne at the age of twenty-five, and to have reigned *for sixteen years* (**27:1**). For some of these 'sixteen years' he may possibly have been as regent during his father Uzziah's illness (26:21). Jotham did what was right in the eyes of the Lord in that, unlike his father, he did not enter the temple. Although the people are accused of corruption, Jotham is not held responsible for his people's behaviour (**27:2**). The people's corruption may have included their maintaining of the high places that are mentioned in 2 Kings 15:35 but not in Chronicles.

The blessings Jotham received are in line with those given to his father. He completed the building projects. In particular, he repaired the Upper Gate of the temple, which had probably been damaged by Jehoash, king of Israel (**27:3-4**; see also 25:24). Jotham also received a large amount of tribute from the Ammonites after his victory over them (**27:5**).

Jotham was entitled to be honoured at his death: he *rested with his fathers and was buried in the City of David* (**27:9**). Chronicles does not mention the start of the invasion of Judah by Syria and Israel (see 2 Kgs 15:37), but deals with all these events during the reign of his successor, Ahaz.

28:1-27 Ahaz's Reign

The reign of Ahaz is one of the darkest moments of Judah's monarchy for during it God would be deprived of his residence, the temple. Ahaz was twenty when he became king and his reign lasted sixteen years. His mother's name is not given in the introduction, as was normally the custom. The evaluation of the reign of Ahaz is totally negative when compared to the standard set by David (**28:1**).

The depth of Ahaz's infidelity is evident in the description of him as living according to *the ways of the kings of Israel* – nothing worse could be said of a king of Judah (**28:2a**). Ahab, king of Israel, and his dynasty were regarded as representatives of the worship of the Baals. Following their example, Ahaz made idols, burned incense at alien altars and even *sacrificed his sons in the fire* (**28:2b-4**; note that 2 Kgs 16:3 mentions only 'his son'). In doing these things he was acting like the nations that the Lord had dispossessed at the time of the conquest of the promised land (Deut 12:29-31).

God's punishment took the form of an invasion by the Syrians and the northern kingdom. Kings presents this as a joint attack by the two countries (2 Kgs 16:5), but for Chronicles, it is a matter of two distinct attacks. The first, quite short, was by the Syrians. Judah was defeated and a large number of prisoners of war were taken to Damascus (**28:5**). But the only effect of this defeat was that Ahaz chose to accept the popular belief that the victory of an army corresponded to the victory of its god, and so he chose to sacrifice to the gods of the Syrians (**28:22-23**).

The second attack, described in detail in 28:5b-15, was by Pekah, king of Israel. The defeat was total. Many men of Judah were killed because they *had forsaken the Lord, the God of their fathers* (**28:6**). The king's son and the officer in charge of the palace were among the victims (**28:7**). No doubt with deliberate irony, the author of Chronicles tells us that the Israelites took many prisoners from their *kinsmen* and plundered their belongings (**28:8**). King Abijah had inflicted a similar defeat on Israel (13:2-20), but now the situation was reversed.

The prisoners of war were saved by the intervention of the prophet Oded. He met the returning army outside Samaria and reminded the Israelites that they themselves were as guilty before God as the people of Judah (**28:9-10**). He therefore told the Israelites to return the prisoners of war so as to calm God's anger (**28:11**).

This section is the only one in Chronicles to give a positive impression of the northern kingdom. Some of the Israelite leaders paid attention to the prophet's words and persuaded the army to release the booty and the prisoners (**28:12-14**). These leaders then acted as good Samaritans. They *took the prisoners, and from the plunder they clothed all who were naked. They provided them with clothes and sandals, food and drink, and healing balm. All those who were weak they put on donkeys. So they took them back to their fellow countrymen at Jericho, the City of Palms,* just as their successor would do in the story Jesus would tell in Luke 10:30-36 (**28:15**).

Africa is a continent where there are many who have been taken prisoner or who have been displaced by war and famine. These people endure all kinds of violence. Displaced women and girls become vulnerable and are often raped or sexually exploited in exchange for a bit of food. The African church in general should be proclaiming and demonstrating this message of care for those afflicted by war. They are our brothers, our sisters, people created in the image of God.

King Ahaz responded to these two military defeats by seeking an alliance with Assyria (**28:16**). He pillaged the temple treasures and those of the royal palace to provide gifts for Tiglath-Pileser, the Assyrian king (2 Kgs 16:8). Unfortunately, Tiglath-Pileser did not help Ahaz when the Edomites and the Philistines attacked (**28:17-18**). Worse still, he himself attacked Judah (**28:20-21**). Chronicles does not want readers to miss the cause of all these problems, and so spells it out plainly: *the Lord had humbled Judah* (**28:19**).

But the king of Judah did not repent. Not only did he worship the Syrian gods, but he ended up removing all the furnishings from the temple and closing the door of the Lord's house. In its place, he set up altars *at every street corner in Jerusalem* (**28:24**). Not only had he shut up God's house, but he was actively promoting idolatry. No wonder God was angry! (**28:25**).

We know nothing of the circumstances of Ahaz's death. We are only told that he was not buried in the tomb of the kings of Israel (**28:27**).

29:1-32:33 Hezekiah's Reign

Hezekiah is the author's 'favourite' after David and Solomon. He surpasses Asa, Jehoshaphat and Josiah (who was one of his descendants). He reopened the temple that Ahaz had closed and re-established worship. Kings also gives a detailed account of his reign (2 Kgs 18:1-20:11), but the perspective of Chronicles is different. For this author, the most important aspect of Hezekiah's reign was his reform of worship. Of the four chapters that Chronicles devotes to the reign of Hezekiah, three are devoted to this aspect. In Kings, only one verse hints at the reform (2 Kgs 18:4).

29:1-36 Re-establishment of temple worship

Hezekiah's reign started with repairs and re-establishment of what his predecessor had abandoned. This son who distanced himself from the evil ways of his father reminds us of the words of the prophet Ezekiel: 'But suppose this son has a son who sees all the sins his father commits, and though he sees them, he does not do such things ... ' (Ezek 18:14). Hezekiah's faithfulness is compared to that of David, his ancestor (**29:2**). This comparison is important because Hezekiah's actions for the temple and its worship ceremonies correspond to those of David, whose name appears several times in this section (29:25, 26, 27, 30).

The young king's determination to restore the temple is seen in *the first month of the first year of his reign*. This means that from the very start of his reign Hezekiah recognized the importance of the temple and worship. Indeed, he immediately opened and repaired the doors of the house of the Lord (**29:3**).

As a worthy successor of David and Solomon, he then began his reign by calling together the priests and Levites (**29:4**). He spoke particularly to the Levites (**29:5**). He asked them to consecrate themselves so that they could consecrate the house of the Lord after Ahaz's abominations. Hezekiah recognized that Judah has been unfaithful: *they turned their faces away from the Lord's dwelling-place and turned their backs on him* (**29:6-7**). He knew that this was the reason Israel had suffered grief and humiliation (**29:8**).

The captivity to which Hezekiah referred is the one mentioned in 28:6 (**29:9**).

This consecration of the temple is necessary because Hezekiah intends to make a covenant with the Lord, the God of Israel (**29:10**). Hence he asked the Levites not to be negligent (**29:11**) and reminds them of their calling by God as David had done (1 Chr 15:2).

The Levites take responsibility for the organization and purification of the temple (**29:12-15**). However, the author does not forget that the law stated that only the priests might enter the temple, and so it is the priests who clean the interior, with help from the Levites once goods have been moved into the courtyard (**29:16-17**). The mention of the utensils in **29:18-19** is important because they are proof that present and ongoing worship is possible. They are a sort of link between the old and new generation. In the second temple, built after the return from exile in Babylon, the utensils were once again a sign of continuity (Ezra 5:13-15).

In Africa, we are aware of the importance of this idea of passing on a heritage that guarantees continuity. In certain families, dishes have served several generations.

Once the temple was restored, the king of Judah proceeded to offer the first sacrifice for the forgiveness of sins (**29:20-23**). He ordered that this sin offering be made for *all Israel* (**29:24**). The Levites took an active role, accompanying the priests with music *in the way prescribed by David* (**29:25**) *with David's instruments* (**29:26**) and using words composed by David (**29:30**).

The final sacrifices offered after the consecration were thank offerings (**29:31-35**). The author of Chronicles again shows his preference by stating that *the Levites had been more conscientious in consecrating themselves than the priests had been* (**29:34**). In his earlier exhortation (**29:11**), Hezekiah had stressed the great responsibility that falls on those who serve God: there is to be no carelessness in their work. Yet some leaders do not take their work seriously and are not even prepared for it. Although the prophet Jeremiah was speaking in specific circumstances when he declared 'a curse on him who is lax in doing the Lord's work' (Jer 48:10), the statement still applies today!

The renewal of temple worship brought great joy in Judah (**29:36**).

30:1-31:1 Celebration of the Passover

This account of the Passover, which is characterized by its concern for the unity of *all Israel*, does not appear in Kings.

For the good kings of Judah, great religious celebrations were to be held by a unanimous decision of the assembly. Hezekiah called on *all Israel and Judah* to meet at Jerusalem (**30:1**). The date of the celebration is settled at this meeting (**30:2-4**). Unfortunately, it could not take place at the time prescribed in the law (Lev 23:5-6). The festival was proclaimed to *all Israel, from Beersheba to Dan* (**30:5**). These two points were the traditional borders of the territory occupied by Israel before it split into two kingdoms. The reference to them shows the author's great concern for the unity of the people of God.

It was during the reign of Hezekiah that the northern kingdom was destroyed by the Assyrians and a large part of its population was deported. Thus by this time the northern kingdom was only an Assyrian province. The letter inviting the people from the north to come to the ceremony did not contain anything to encourage revolt against the Assyrians, but was simply a call to repentance (**30:6-9**). The invitation was not warmly received in the old northern territories where *the people scorned and ridiculed* the messengers (**30:10**). However, a few people from the north did respond positively and travelled to Jerusalem (**30:11**). In the southern kingdom of Judah the response was far more enthusiastic, as the people responded with *unity of mind* (30:11-12) so that a *very large crowd of people assembled in Jerusalem* (**30:13**).

The celebration itself was preceded by the removal from Jerusalem of all the altars and incense altars to other gods (**30:14**). This task was done by the people, who acted just as the Levites and priests had done when cleaning in the temple. The priests and the Levites may have been *ashamed* because of the way the zeal of the people contrasted with their own failure to play a leading role in this religious reform (**30:15**). Unfortunately, in the Christian community, we still find some leaders who are like barriers preventing revival in the church.

The people who had come from the north were not properly consecrated, and were thus ritually impure. They could not sacrifice their own animals, but the Levites sacrificed them on their behalf. If the law were strictly applied, these people would not have been allowed to participate in the Passover, but Hezekiah prayed for these people that God would not punish them. Their willingness to make the long journey to Jerusalem after so many years showed that they were indeed seeking God. As when Solomon had asked (6:18-24), God listened and answered Hezekiah's prayer (**30:17-20**).

There was so much joy (**30:21, 23, 25-26**) that the whole assembly decided to prolong the celebration for seven days. The king and leaders contributed generously, providing many animals (**30:24**). Chronicles emphasizes the general joy at celebrating the Passover, but the celebration may also reflect the joy of being reunited with formerly distant relatives (30:25).

The feast ended with the people being blessing by the priests and Levites. The author of Chronicles again insists on the role of the temple as the place where God heard and answered prayers: *for their prayers reached heaven, his holy dwelling-place* (**30:27**).

When the pilgrims returned to their towns after the feast, they broke down the altars to foreign gods, just as they had done at Jerusalem (**31:1**). The purification that Hezekiah had begun thus reached not only Judah and Benjamin but even the territories of Ephraim and Manasseh, which were part of the northern kingdom.

This celebration of Passover introduced an important change. Normally, the Levites would not have sacrificed animals, but because of the lack of preparation of those who had come from the north, the Levites sacrificed the Passover animals for those who were not consecrated. New situations sometimes demand adjustments in the way we do things. For example, in many isolated communities of Africa, life is regulated by the big weekly markets. One day each week, merchants come from all around to a certain place to meet and sell their goods. For the villagers, it is the only favourable time to buy and sell. Unfortunately, this day may be Sunday. Rather than the pastor scolding the people from his pulpit about worldliness and quoting texts about preserving the holiness of the Sabbath, the church council should work to find a solution that will take into account the needs of everyday life. For example, the hour of the worship service could be changed. Rather than having it in the morning, why not meet in the afternoon after the market has finished?

31:2-21 The re-organization of temple worship

For the author of Chronicles, a good king is one who supervises the organization of the temple personnel. David did it (1 Chr 23–26), Solomon did it (2 Chr 8:14) and now it is Hezekiah's turn. In this section, only 31:20-21 are parallel to 2 Kings 18:6-7. But the rest of this section underscores a point that is very important in Chronicles: maintaining worship is not solely the responsibility of the crown but also involves all the people.

Hezekiah follows the example of his ancestors David and Solomon in appointing priests *to offer burnt offerings and fellowship offerings* and Levites *to minister, to give thanks and to sing praises* (**31:2**).

Before asking the people to give towards the support of worship, Hezekiah himself set the example: *the king contributed from his own possessions ... as written in the Law of the Lord* (**31:3**). Then he ordered the people to do likewise (**31:4**). The response was more than generous, a point that is emphasized by the use of the words *generously* and *a great amount* (**31:5-7**). Both the speed with which the people gave and the quantity given led Hezekiah and his ministers to praise the Lord (**31:8**).

Azariah the high priest responded to the king's question in **31:9** by saying *since the people began to bring their contributions to the temple of the Lord, we have had enough to eat and plenty to spare* (**31:10**). This response suggests that the earlier idolatry had meant that the income of the priests and Levites could not be guaranteed, as ordered in the law. Hezekiah wanted to use the gifts that had now been brought in to provide income for temple personnel.

The king of Judah took measures to assure an equitable distribution of the offerings to all the temple personnel. The role played by the Levites in the storing and distribution of the goods was important. It is also important to note the repetition of the word 'faithful', which characterized this distribution: *they faithfully brought in the contributions* (**31:12**); they *assisted him faithfully* (**31:15**); *they were faithful in consecrating themselves* (**31:18**).

The church in Africa needs faithful servants and stewards. The church's goods must be entrusted to several faithful people who can ensure their careful management. As in Chronicles, the community's money should be looked after by more than one person to avoid any temptation for the person handling the money to keep some for himself or herself.

This section is also a reminder to each member of the church of our responsibility for the smooth operation of the church, and for the material support of the pastor. Even though he was king, Hezekiah asked for a contribution from everyone. The financial support of God's servant should not be left to a few in the community, as is sometimes the case. The apostle Paul clearly told the Corinthians: 'Don't you know that those who work in the temple get their food from the temple, and those who serve at the altar share in what is offered on the altar? In the same way, the Lord has commanded that those who preach the gospel should receive their living from the gospel' (1 Cor 9:13-14).

The last verses of this chapter praise Hezekiah's faithfulness: *doing what was good and right and faithful* (**31:20**). There are three reasons for his success: his seeking God, his zeal for the temple, and his obedience to God's commands.

32:1-23 The siege of Jerusalem

In Kings, two chapters are devoted to the Assyrian invasion of Judah (18:9-19:37; see also Isa 36:2-20). Once again, Chronicles has a different perspective on this event. Many of the elements included in Kings are omitted. For example, there is no mention here of Hezekiah's humiliation and the heavy tribute he paid to the Assyrian king (2 Kgs 18:14-16). On the other hand, Chronicles is the only book to report two speeches with strong theological overtones, one by Hezekiah (32:7-8) and the other by Sennacherib (32:10-15).

The period of faithfulness and joy referred to by the clause *after all that Hezekiah had done* was succeeded by one of trouble (**32:1**). Like Asa and Jehoshaphat, Hezekiah experienced a military threat despite having been faithful.

When he learned that Sennacherib, the king of Assyria, was heading for Jerusalem (**32:2**), Hezekiah did not make an immediate and unilateral decision. He first held a counsel

with *his officials and military staff* (**32:3**). His first steps were practical ones. He *blocked all the springs* to reduce the water supply for the Assyrians (32:3-4); he repaired or reinforced the walls of Jerusalem (**32:5a**) and finally, he reorganized and equipped the army (**32:5b-6**).

Hezekiah then set about spiritual preparation of his people. He encouraged his soldiers by a rousing speech with strong theological overtones. Though he had prepared his army, he knew that victory does not come from the power of the army but from God. The content of his speech is similar to the prophetic message given by Jahaziel when the Ammonites and Moabites wanted to fight King Jehoshaphat (20:15-17). The same theme is repeated: *Do not be afraid or discouraged because of the king of Assyria ... for there is a greater power with us than with him* (**32:7-8**).

The king of Assyria's message is the opposite of Hezekiah's and is full of offensive propaganda. It was read near Jerusalem by envoys sent by the king of Assyria and was intended to discourage the army so that it would surrender without a fight (**32:9**). Sennacherib's speech is also deeply theological. He claimed that Hezekiah was destined for defeat because he had destroyed all the altars outside the temple (**32:10-12**). Sennacherib misinterprets Hezekiah's pious acts as acts of impiety that will have made him obnoxious to God, who will now punish him by allowing him to be defeated. To discourage the army even more, the king of Assyria speaks of his previous victories and questions the power of the God of Israel (**32:13-16**).

The author of Chronicles characterizes the speech as an insult to the God of Israel (**32:17**). He contrasts it to Hezekiah's speech by noting that its purpose was *to terrify them and make them afraid* (**32:18**) and that it spoke of God as if he were just another idol (**32:19**).

The king and the prophet Isaiah went to pray (**32:20**) and God answered their prayer and responded to the insults to his name. He sent an angel who destroyed the Assyrian army without any help from the army of Judah, which did not even have to fight. Sennacherib did not die in battle but, ironically, was killed in the house of his god by his own sons (**32:21**). This victory contributed to Hezekiah's renown and to the respect for his monarchy (**32:22-23**).

Hezekiah's response to his situation gives us practical and spiritual lessons: practical, because he took concrete steps when facing the imminent danger of the Assyrian army; spiritual, because he did not place his confidence in these preparations but in the Lord who would decide the outcome of the battle. The prayer of faith does not exclude practical action. This attitude should inspire African Christians who pass nights in prayer for peace in Africa and their own countries. This sort of faith commitment should not exclude practical steps to bring about peace. Let us pray and act!

32:24-33 Hezekiah's flaws

In the last section, the author of Chronicles acknowledges, but only briefly, two events which were not to Hezekiah's credit: his pride about his healing from a fatal disease (**32:24-26**) and his mistake in showing off his riches to Babylonian envoys (**32:31**). These events are given in more detail in Kings (2 Kgs 20:1-19). This author prefers to emphasize the material blessings received by the king of Judah (**32:27-30**).

The comment regarding the funeral is exceptional: *Hezekiah ... was buried on the hill where the tombs of David's descendants are* (**32:33**). The KJV translation states that he was buried in 'the chiefest of the sepulchres', a translation that underscores the high esteem that the author of Chronicles has for Hezekiah, regarding him as above all the other kings of Judah.

33:1-20 Manasseh's Reign

Manasseh's reign lasted fifty-five years (**33:1**) and was the longest of any of the kings of Israel and Judah. Whereas in Kings Manasseh is considered the worst of the kings of Judah and is held responsible for the exile of Judah (2 Kgs 21:1-18), Chronicles presents him as the model of a repentant king. The author probably seeks to explain this exceptionally long reign, which would normally be interpreted as a sign of divine blessing.

But there is no doubt about Manasseh's early unfaithfulness. He really *did evil in the eyes of the Lord* (**33:2**). He rebuilt the high places, profaned the temple, sacrificed his sons in the fire (2 Kgs 21:6 speaks of one son), practised divination and occultism and refused to listen to the prophets (**33:3-10**). However, unlike Kings, the author of Chronicles does not go so far as to compare Manasseh's behaviour with that of the house of Ahab, as he did in the case of Ahaz (28:2; 2 Kings 21:3). Though Manasseh was not without fault, Chronicles does not consider him the worst king of Judah.

The consequence of infidelity is God's punishment. The king of Assyria attacked Judah. Manasseh was taken prisoner and escorted to Babylon (**33:11**). The account in Kings does not mention his capture.

In exile, Manasseh's behaviour conforms to that called for by Solomon in his prayer (6:36-39). The king of Judah *humbled himself greatly before the God of his father ... he prayed to him* (**33:12-13a**). God enabled him to return to Jerusalem and Manasseh *knew that the Lord is God* (**33:13b**). Manasseh offers a good example of repentance. Whatever our sins, God welcomes us if we return to him. David recognized this truth when he wrote in Psalms: 'as far as the east is from the west, so far has he removed our transgressions from us' (Ps 103:12).

On his return, the king changed his behaviour. He undertook construction work, a labour that Chronicles always

regards as a sign of blessing (**33:14**). As far as religion was concerned, the repentant king removed all the foreign gods from the temple and re-established worship there (**33:15-16**), but he did not succeed in changing the idolatrous behaviour of the people (**33:17**).

At his death, Manasseh was buried *in his palace* (**33:20**). That may mean that he did not have the honour of being buried in the tomb of the kings.

33:21-25 Amon's Reign

Amon's brief reign of two years is not reported in detail. Amon is presented as worse than his father. Not only did he sacrifice to idols, but *he did not humble himself before the Lord* as his father had done (**33:22-23**). His punishment did not take the form of a foreign invasion but of conspiracy among his own servants who killed him (**33:24**). His burial is not even recorded.

34:1-35:27 Josiah's Reign

The sequence of events during Josiah's reign differs in Kings and Chronicles. For Kings, a priest's discovery of the law in the temple set in motion a cultural reform (2 Kgs 22:1-23:30). For Chronicles, on the other hand, it is because of the cultural reform initiated by the king that the law was found.

The author of Chronicles regards Josiah as one of the best of Judah's kings. Like Hezekiah's, Josiah's faithfulness is compared to that of David, his ancestor. The expression *not turning aside to the right or to the left* underscores his perfect obedience to the law (**34:2**). This expression was used in the same way by Joshua (Josh 23:6).

34:1-33 Josiah's reforms

Josiah's acts of faithfulness are divided into two parts according to a chronological formula marking the eighth and the eighteenth years of his reign.

From the eighth year of his reign, when Josiah was sixteen, *he began to seek the God of his father David* (**34:3**). When he was twenty, he undertook the purification of the kingdom of Judah. He removed all traces of false gods from Jerusalem and Judah: the high places, carved idols and images. Not only that, but he desecrated the sites of idolatrous worship, so that they could not be used again (**34:4-5**). This purification even reached the ruined cities of the kingdom of Israel, from which the people had already been deported (**34:6**). Josiah travelled through the country to ensure that these reforms were carried out (**34:7**).

From the eighteenth year of his reign, Josiah devoted himself to repairing the temple (**34:8**). Hezekiah had already set the precedent of mobilizing popular support for the temple, and Josiah too was not going to pay for the work from the royal treasury. He used money that the Levites *had collected from the people of Manasseh, Ephraim and the entire* *remnant of Israel and from all the people of Judah and Benjamin and the inhabitants of Jerusalem* (**34:9**). This detailed list underscores both the unity in Israel and the popular support for the work of repairing the temple. Once again the Levites were at the forefront of the work, supervising the repairs (**34:10-13**).

During this work, they discovered the *Book of the Law that the Lord had given through Moses* (**34:14-15**). Was this a copy of Deuteronomy or of the entire Pentateuch? The exact identity of the book is not known, nor are the contents of the book mentioned. But we are told that when it was read to the king, he tore his clothes as a sign of grief and repentance (**34:16-19**). Josiah asked the prophetess Huldah to consult the Lord on their behalf (**34:20-22**). She reported that God had irrevocably made up his mind to send *all the curses written in the book* because of the conduct of the people (**34:24-25**). She was probably referring to the curses mentioned in Deuteronomy (28:15-68). However, she announced to Josiah that, because of his humility before the Lord, these events would not take place during his reign (**34:26-28**).

Huldah's position as a prophetess who advised kings is all the more striking when we consider how often the African Christian community refuses to allow women to occupy positions of responsibility, despite the large number of women in the church.

After receiving this prophecy, Josiah assembled all the elders of Judah and Jerusalem (**34:29**). He also summoned all the people to this assembly in the court of the temple. There he read *The Book of the Covenant* to them (**34:30**), and then renewed the covenant with God (**34:31**). For the rest of his reign, Josiah required the people living in all Israel to respect it (**34:32-33**), including, no doubt, the foreigners settled in the area by the Assyrians after the deportation of the northern kingdom (2 Kgs 17:24-41).

35:1-27 Passover and Josiah's death

Kings devotes only three verses to the celebration of the Passover that followed the renewing of the covenant (2 Kgs 23:21-23). But the author of Chronicles regarded this Passover as very important because it was the last major celebration of this festival before the destruction of the temple and the exile of the people. He gives details of its organization for the sake of his readers, the Jews who had returned from exile. Josiah's Passover, unlike that of Hezekiah, conformed to the rules laid down in the law. This concern for orthodoxy is indicated by the date of the ceremony: the fourteenth day of the first month (**35:1**; compare Exod 12:6; Lev 23:5; Num 28:16). This date will be respected in Ezra's time after the return from captivity (Ezra 6:19).

Preparation for the Passover started with appointing temple personnel. Josiah appointed priests, set out their duties and encouraged them (**35:2**). Then he addressed the Levites in more detail. As usual in Chronicles, they had an important role to play.

Josiah's first order to *put the sacred ark in the temple that Solomon son of David king of Israel built* (**35:3**) is hard to understand. It is possible that the apostate kings who preceded Josiah had removed the ark of the covenant from the temple. Josiah repeated the new responsibilities of the Levites as modified by David, Solomon and Hezekiah when the ark had reached its resting place. There are seven imperatives: *put, serve, prepare, stand, slaughter, consecrate yourselves and prepare* (**35:4-6a**). Everything must be done according to *what the Lord commanded through Moses* (**35:6b**), which means in conformity with the Law of Moses.

The leaders of the kingdom (King Josiah, his ministers, the Levite leaders and the priests) provided the animals to be sacrificed at this Passover. In all, they supplied thirty-seven thousand six hundred lambs or goats and three thousand eight hundred cattle (**35:7-9**).

The celebration of Passover took place as king Hezekiah had ordered. Indeed, the expression *as the king had ordered* appears twice, thus framing the feast (**35:10; 16**). Josiah himself made sure his instruction matched what was *written in Moses* (**35:12**). First of all, the sacrifices were offered (35:10-12). Then came the communal meal. Care was taken to see that the meat was distributed fairly so that no one would go without. Even those who were on guard duty were served and did not have to leave their posts (**35:13-15**). This celebration was said to be without equal in all the history of the monarchy in Israel. The only possible comparison could be with the period preceding the monarchy under Samuel (**35:18**).

Then came an unexpected event. This expression *After all this* reminds us of 32:1 and the Assyrian invasion after Hezekiah's acts of faithfulness (**35:20a**). However, in this case, there was no invasion. Pharaoh Neco of Egypt was simply passing through Judah on his way to join his Assyrian ally and cut off the advance of the Babylonian army. *Josiah marched out to meet him* (**35:20b**). This pagan king then spoke on behalf of God. For Chronicles, he was like a prophet: *stop opposing God, who is with me* (**35:21**). These words remind us of King Abijah's speech to Jeroboam's army (13:4-12). However, Josiah did not listen to Neco. We do not know why he should have paid attention, but the account teaches us that God can use anyone and anything to accomplish his purposes or to announce his wonderful acts.

The account of how Josiah fought and the circumstances of his death are very similar to the account of Ahab's death (18:29, 33-34). The king of Judah disguised himself (**35:22**). *Archers shot King Josiah, and he told his officers, 'Take me away; I am badly wounded'* (**35:23**). Back in Jerusalem, he finally died. He was buried with his ancestors (**35:24**).

The laments composed for Josiah by Jeremiah (**35:25**) should not be confused with the book known as Lamentations, which does not deal with the fate of an individual but with the destruction of Jerusalem and its temple.

The final comment on Josiah's reign insists on the conformity of his *acts of devotion* to *the Law of the Lord* (**35:26**).

36:1-4 Jehoahaz's Reign

Jehoahaz and his three successors each in turn suffered exile. Through their weakness or their behaviour, each contributed to the eventual destruction of Jerusalem and of the temple and the exile of the population. However, the author of Chronicles minimizes the severity of the catastrophe. Many events recorded in Kings are passed over in silence.

Jehoahaz only ruled for three months after the death of his father Josiah (**36:1-2**). His coronation by the people did not please Neco, the pharaoh who had defeated his father, who may have seen in it the seeds of independence from Egypt. So Neco headed for Jerusalem, deposed the helpless king of Judah, and imposed a heavy tribute on the people (**36:3**). He set up Eliakim, an older brother of Jehoahaz, as king, and changed his name to Jehoiakim in order to clearly indicate his subject status. He carried Jehoahaz off to Egypt (**36:4**).

36:5-8 Jehoiakim's Reign

Jehoiakim reigned for eleven years. He *did evil in the eyes of the Lord* and did *detestable things* (**36:5, 8**). As a result, God sent Nebuchadnezzar, king of Babylon against him. He took Jehoiakim captive to Babylon, and took with him many articles from the temple (**36:6-7**). Unlike Kings, Chronicles does not tell of the arrival of the Babylonians, the subjection of Judah for three years, and the reprisals of the Chaldeans after the king of Judah revolted (2 Kgs 24:1-4).

36:9-10 Jehoiachin's Reign

Jehoiachin reigned three months and ten days. Like his father, *he did evil in the eyes of the Lord* (**36:9**). Hence, he suffered the same fate. He too was taken to Babylon along with valuable articles for the temple (**36:10**). Nebuchadnezzar set up Zedekiah, the brother of Jehoiakim, as king of Judah.

36:11-21 Zedekiah's Disastrous Reign

It was during Zedekiah's reign that Judah ceased to exist as an independent nation with well-defined borders. This reign lasted eleven years. Not only did Zedekiah do what was *evil in the eyes of the Lord* as his three predecessors had done, but he refused to listen to the prophet Jeremiah and broke the oath made in God's name, revolting against his master, Nebuchadnezzar (**36:11-13**). He probably refused to pay tribute.

Zedekiah was not the only one responsible for the disaster. The leaders of the priests and the people profaned the house of the Lord (**36:14**). Before the disaster, the Lord had warned his people through the prophets (**36:15**). Unfortunately, *they mocked God's messengers, despised his words and scoffed at his prophets* (**36:16**). God's anger was aroused and there was no other solution. Exile, the destruction of Jerusalem and of the temple were God's ultimate punishment following the ever-increasing disobedience of his people (**36:17-20**). Chronicles interprets the exile as a Sabbath period for the land of Judah. The seventy years of rest correspond to the prophecy of Jeremiah (**36:21**; Jer 25:11-12).

36:22-23 The Edict of Cyrus

Unlike Kings, Chronicles does not end in despair. The last two verses indicate the end of the exile under the reign of Cyrus, the Persian king, who authorized the rebuilding of the temple and the return of anyone who volunteered for the work. The author of Chronicles sees in this the hand of God; *the Lord moved the heart of Cyrus king of Persia* (**36:22**). These two verses find their parallel in Ezra 1:1-3.

Throughout the book of Chronicles, the temple is presented as playing an important and beneficial role in the life of the people of Israel. The author's aim was to show that when all other institutions had disappeared, only the temple could assure continuity between the generations that had lived before the exile, and those who came after it. Thus when he recorded the start of people's contributions to support the temple during the reign of Hezekiah, for example, he was also speaking to his own contemporaries about their support of the temple. His concern for continuity is evident throughout the book, beginning with the genealogies.

Chronicles is therefore a book that deals with the events of the past for the benefit of the new generation. It does not end by gazing into the distant past or the distant future, but with the affirmation here and now of the end of the exile and the restoration of the community. Thus the book of Chronicles ends with a message of hope. The mention of Cyrus' edict softens the impact of the account of the deportation and exile on the life of the readers. The exile and the return are both recorded.

The African continent is now enduring a difficult time of war, famine, drought and poverty, but there is hope. This hope is not based on any human edict, but on the Lord's mercy through Jesus Christ.

Nupanga Weanzana

Further Reading

Selman, M.J. *1 and 2 Chronicles*. TOT. Downers Grove, Ill.: Intervarsity Press, 1994.

Tuell, S.S. *First and Second Chronicles*. Interpretation. Louisville, Ky: Westminster John Knox Press, 2001.

EZRA

In the Jewish tradition, the two books we know as Ezra and Nehemiah are combined in one book known as Ezra. This book is placed before Chronicles in the third section of the Hebrew Bible, which is known as 'the Writings'.

In our Bibles, Ezra and Nehemiah are categorized as Historical Books, and are placed after 1 and 2 Chronicles. This change in the order in which the books are listed may have been imposed for chronological reasons because they are regarded as historical books. Ezra and Nehemiah follow logically on the proclamation recorded in 2 Chronicles 36:22-23 – verses that are repeated in Ezra 1:1-2.

Context and authorship

The books of Ezra and Nehemiah tell the story of the restoration of the people of Israel after the Babylonian Empire fell to the Persian Empire. Whole sections of the book of Ezra are, in fact, written in Aramaic, the official language of the Persian Empire (4:8-6:18; 7:12-26). This is also the case for the book of Daniel, which was written in the same period,

Ezra and Nehemiah give no indication of their sources for the history of the restoration. However, several official documents are mentioned: various decrees or Persian royal edicts, some letters, and lists of exiles. The official decree issued by Cyrus following the takeover of Babylon was the key factor determining the course of events described in Ezra and Nehemiah (1:1-4).

The books of Ezra and Nehemiah provide no details about the author and the date of writing. Despite the fact that these books tell of the work of the two main heroes of the Jewish rebirth, tradition holds that Ezra, whose name means 'aid' and 'help', wrote both of them. This argument is based on the description of him as 'a teacher well versed in the law of Moses, which the Lord ... had given' (7:6, 10-11). As a descendant of Aaron, he was also a priest (7:1-5). In uniting the functions of a priest and a scribe, Ezra combined two very important functions in the post-exilic community. He is said to have 'devoted himself to the study and observance of the law of the Lord, and to teaching its decrees and laws in Israel' (7:10). He had read the Law in front of those who had returned from exile (Neh 8). This role, and the his arrival in Jerusalem in 458 BC, means that Ezra is considered the father of Judaism.

Nehemiah, by contrast, was a member of the laity. He was a leading official of the royal court during the reign of Artaxerxes who later became governor of Judea. In the Bible, he is known for his role in the reconstruction of the walls of Jerusalem. He was a man of great piety who often fasted and prayed and confessed the sins of the people.

He made two trips to Jerusalem, the first in 445 BC, the second at an unknown date.

Contents

These two books constitute the main biblical source of knowledge about the era of the return from the Babylonian exile. They tell the story of a triple reconstruction:
- The reconstruction of the temple at Jerusalem under Zerubbabel (Ezra 1-6).
- The reconstruction of the Jewish community under Ezra (Ezra 7-10).
- The reconstruction of the walls of Jerusalem under Nehemiah (Neh 1-6).

The order of events shows the importance given to the temple. It is the foundation of the new community.

In Ezra and Nehemiah, the triple reconstruction signals continuity with, or more precisely a return to, what had been before. Both books repeatedly stress the echo of the preexilic community in the life of the postexilic community. Certain themes bring this point out strongly:
- The altar of sacrifices is re-established on its ancient site (3:3).
- The rebuilt temple is not really new; it is the re-establishment of the temple built by Solomon (5:11).
- This new temple is built on the site of the ancient temple (5:15; 6:7).
- The articles used in the temple are the same as those used in the ancient temple of Solomon (1:7-11).
- The sacrifices and the feasts are conducted in accordance with the law of Moses (3:2-3; Neh 8:14).
- The temple personnel are reinstated in accordance with the ancient decree of King David (Neh 12:24, 45).
- The new community which has returned to Israel traces its lineage back to pre-exilic times: Ezra is a descendant of Aaron (7:1-5); the Levites are sons of Asaph (3:10); those who have returned are the descendants of those who were deported (Neh 7:6). A genealogical register offers proof of these claims (Neh 7:5).

The books of Ezra and Nehemiah thus show how God was faithful in fulfilling the promises made long before through Jeremiah the prophet (1:1; Jer 29:10). However, the restoration was only partial. Israel was not restored to its status as an independent kingdom, which it had been in pre-exilic times. It remained a province of the Persian empire.

Like Chronicles, Ezra and Nehemiah contain numerous lists: of the articles returned to the temple (1:9-11); of the exiles who returned to Jerusalem (2:1-70; Neh 7:6-7); of the genealogy of Ezra (7:1-5); of the heads of families

(8:1-14); of those who were part of mixed marriages (10:18-43); of those who helped in the reconstruction of the walls of Jerusalem under Nehemiah (Neh 3); of those who made a binding agreement (Neh 10:1-27); of the inhabitants of Jerusalem and its surrounding area (Neh 11:3-36) and of the priests and Levites (Neh 12:1-26). The genealogies were particularly important for the population who were seeking to reclaim land that had once belonged to them.

Relevance to Africa

The books of Ezra and Nehemiah are not among the ot books that African pastors most often turn to when preaching or conducting Bible studies. However, they are the source for what African theologians have for some years been calling the theology of reconstruction. This approach sees the present situation of the African continent as comparable in varying degrees to that of the Jewish community on their return from exile. These books tell the story of God's people at a critical time in their history. They describe the rebirth of the people of God after the disastrous consequences of the fall of Jerusalem in 587 BC, which included the end of the Davidic monarchy, the loss of national independence, the destruction of the temple and the deportation of an important segment of the population to Babylon.

In Africa, the slave trade deprived the continent of human and economic resources, and colonization often had a devastating effect on the structure and functioning of traditional African society. Although various countries regained their independence in the 1960s, the African continent has not been able to achieve political, social or religious cohesion. It is still influenced and fascinated by foreign nations that are regarded both as models to emulate and scapegoats to blame for all problems. Consequently, this continent needs reconstruction in the spiritual, social and economic spheres. The books of Ezra and Nehemiah contain some guidelines on how to achieve this.

In these books, the community itself is more important than its religious or political leader. Though there are strong leaders such as Zerubbabel, Ezra and Nehemiah, they take second place to the overall community. Nehemiah especially provides a model of good governance. The strategy he employed in his mission to rebuild the walls of Jerusalem in the face of opposition is at the heart of many training sessions for pastors and committed lay leaders. There is even a Bible school in South Africa called Nehemiah Bible Institute. Traditional African society, too, is known for its community spirit that calls on everyone to contribute to the common good.

The books of Ezra and Nehemiah also present the interaction of divine and human activity in the process of reconstruction. This equilibrium is often skewed, forgotten, or even denied in Christian preaching in Africa. While it is true that God is at work, he also needs men and women resolutely working with him to accomplish his purposes. In our day, we have a tendency to passively wait for God to intervene miraculously. But the books of Ezra and Nehemiah mention no miracles. God moved the heart of Cyrus (1:1) and he prompted King Artaxerxes (7:27-28; Neh 2:4-6), but these were still ordinary humans whom God used to accomplish the great task of rebuilding his people. Whereas in Exodus God freed his people by striking the Egyptians, in Ezra and Nehemiah, he accomplishes his purpose through human actions taken by the kings of Persia, Zerubbabel, Ezra, Nehemiah and others.

Though God has the power to do anything by simply speaking the word, he will not come down in person to build hospitals, repair roads, bring an end to tribal conflicts and wars, stop the HIV/AIDS epidemic, and so on. God needs men and women of this continent who will take the initiative in his name to mobilize the entire community to work to rebuild Africa. A theology that simply waits to see miracles is harmful. Ezra and Nehemiah were men of prayer and men of faith and holiness (7:10, 27-28; 9:3; 10:6; Neh 1:5-11; 2:4-5), but they were also and especially men of action. The African church needs men and women of their calibre today.

Outline of Contents

COMMENTARY

The book of Ezra tells the story of two waves of returnees, the first led by Zerubbabel (1–6) and the second by Ezra (7–10). Reading the whole book in the light of 1:1 makes the author's purpose clear: to show how God directed the re-establishment of his people in the land given as an inheritance to their ancestors, and thus fulfilled his promises. The God of Jesus Christ is worthy of trust (2 Tim 2:13).

As Africans, living on the continent considered to be the poorest in the world, we are sometimes tempted to believe that we have no future. Let us remember that after four centuries of painful work God delivered his people from slavery in Egypt, and that after decades of dispersion and exile, he gathered his people again in the promised land.

1:1-6:22 Return and Rebuilding under Zerubbabel

The first part of the book of Ezra covers one generation. It recounts the events from the conquest of Babylon by Cyrus, king of Persia in 539 BC to the dedication of the temple in 515 BC during the reign of Darius. The author does not deal with everything that took place but focuses on the theological and religious dimensions of the story. Thus the proclamation of Cyrus, for example, is understood as the fulfilment of prophecies by Jeremiah.

1:1-2:70 Return from Exile

The first chapter of Ezra tells of the circumstances that surrounded the return from exile, while the second, the longest in the book, is a list of those who responded to the appeal of King Cyrus.

1:1-11 The circumstances of the return

Chapter 1, which is an introduction to the book, is divided into two distinct parts. The first (1:1-4) contains a copy of the decree authorizing the return of the exiles to rebuild the temple in Jerusalem. Part two (1:5-11) deals with the response of the exiles to the decree and the return of the articles the Babylonians had taken from the temple in Jerusalem.

1:1-4 CYRUS' DECREE The first part of the book of Ezra is dominated by the theme of the rebuilding of the temple, and 1:1-4 indicates that the events that made it possible did not come about by chance. The arrival of Cyrus, king of Persia started the process. Cyrus had ruled over Persia since 558 BC, but only conquered Babylon in 539 BC. The *first year of* Cyrus mentioned in **1:1a** is not the first year of his reign, but rather the first year after this conquest.

The events that follow are set in relation to Jeremiah's prophecy about Cyrus (**1:1b**; Jer 25:11-12; 29:10). There is

also a prophecy about Cyrus in Isaiah (Isa 44:28; 45:1-13). The author of the book of Ezra wishes to emphasize the continuity between the God who punishes (by exile) and the God who blesses (preparing for the return from exile by working in the heart of Cyrus).

Cyrus was the one who acted, but it was the hand of God that produced the action. The combination of divine and human action is clear in the statement, *the Lord moved the heart of Cyrus* (**1:1c**). Twice before, in the books of Chronicles, God is said to *have done* the same thing with foreign kings (1 Chr 5:26; 2 Chr 21:16). We need to remember that although many Christian communities frantically search for revival, the coming of revival is ultimately dependent on God's sovereign action.

Cyrus' decree was not only put in writing, it was also proclaimed by heralds in the various cities of the Persian empire (**1:1d**). Few in the ancient world could read or write, and heralds were thus the best way to get the message out. Oral communication functioned in much the same way in Africa before the arrival of writing. There were always heralds to communicate instructions and orders, or simply to summon villagers to a meeting. Without denying the benefits of writing, oral communication is still a good means of communication in our villages, especially given its power and relational quality. Our churches should not ignore it.

Even though the decree concerned all the Jews scattered throughout the Persian empire, the author of Ezra centres his attention on the exiled community in Babylon. In his eyes, this community now constitutes the 'sons of Jacob'. Nothing at all is said regarding the fate of the exiles outside of Babylon, especially those in Egypt (2 Chr 36:4).The contents of Cyrus' decree are given in 1:2-4 (the Aramaic version is found in 6:3-4). The text of the decree given here is similar to that quoted in 2 Chronicles 36:22-23, but is more detailed. It even includes details about the provision of materials for the work of reconstruction (**1:4**).

Cyrus speaks of the Lord as the *God of heaven* (**1:2a**). While this way of referring to God was common among the Persians, it is the first time that this title is used in the Bible for the God of Israel. It reappears in the post-exilic books, especially in Ezra, Nehemiah and Daniel. For Africans, this way of speaking is familiar; it is the way several people groups speak of God.

From the very beginning of the book, special importance is attached to God's house (the temple) and to God's city (Jerusalem). They are frequently mentioned in the decree: *he has appointed me to build a temple for him at Jerusalem in Judah* (**1:2b**), *let him go up to Jerusalem ... and build the temple of the Lord* (**1:3**); *freewill offerings for the temple of God in Jerusalem* (1:4). It is the desire to rebuild the temple that makes the return possible.

Cyrus' instruction to rebuild the temple should not be interpreted as meaning that he was practising the Jewish religion. Cyrus probably had political goals in mind when he drafted this decree. As proof of this, theologians point to another ancient document, known as the cylinder of Cyrus, in which the king credits his victory over Babylon to the support he received from Marduk, the chief Babylonian divinity. For political reasons, Persian kings adopted the religions of conquered peoples and pretended to act in the name of local divinities. As long as the practice of the local religion did not threaten the stability of the empire, these kings did not impose their own religion. But whereas Cyrus may have thought he was using God, God was using him. God had often used pagan nations to punish Israel (2 Chr 36:17). This time, however, God prompted a pagan king to contribute to the well-being of the chosen people.

Cyrus' political manoeuvrings should not escape the notice of churches in Africa. Political leaders will often try to rally religious leaders to their cause. This presents a great temptation to church leaders who appreciate the support of powerful people. However, there is a great danger that by associating with them the church will risk losing its freedom of speech and its prophetic role of identifying or even denouncing issues (Matt 6:24).

The decree also asked for contributions to assist those Jews who were embarking on this journey. David and Solomon had collected contributions for the building of the first temple (1 Chr 29:1-9), and now everyone, including those who would remain in the land of exile, was invited to contribute to the building of the second temple (1:4).

1:5-11 THE EXILES' RESPONSE This response to Cyrus' decree mirrors the two main concerns in that decree: reconstruction of the temple and provision of the materials needed for that task.

The Jews who set out to return were led by *the family heads of Judah and Benjamin, and the priests and Levites* (**1:5**; 1 Chr 9:1-3). Judah and Benjamin were the two southern tribes who had remained faithful to the temple in Jerusalem and to the Davidic dynasty when the kingdom split in the reign of Rehoboam (1 Kgs 12; 2 Chr 10). With the priests and Levites, these two tribes now form the nucleus of the post-exilic community.

Those who returned did so because, as with Cyrus, God had *moved* their hearts. Some of the second and third generation exiles must have decided to remain in their colony in Babylonia. They did not know the country from which their parents and grandparents had been deported and had no yearning for it. They had prospered during this time and did not want to abandon their possessions to start a new life from nothing, even if it was in their country of origin. It seems, in the eyes of the author, that those who stayed did not do so because of unfaithfulness to Jerusalem but rather because God had not touched their spirits.

A similar situation exists in relation to certain African countries such as South Africa and Angola. Before these countries achieved independence, some of the colonized peoples had sought refuge in neighbouring countries. When independence finally came, some of these displaced people preferred to continue to live in the country that had welcomed them.

The response to the second part of the decree concerning provisions for the house of the Lord is described in 1:6-11. The description of events reminds us of what happened immediately before the Israelites left Egypt under Moses' leadership. Then they had been told to ask their neighbours for objects of gold and silver (Exod 12:35-36). Now they once again receive voluntary gifts as they set out to return to the promised land (**1:6**).

King Cyrus himself contributed provisions, restoring objects related to worship that King Nebuchadnezzar had carried to Babylon (**1:7**). At that time, it was common for the victors in a war to destroy the temple of the vanquished people and sometimes to carry away the national god to symbolize the nation's subjection (1 Sam 5:1-2). Since there was no representation of God in the temple at Jerusalem, it was the utensils and sacred articles that had been carried off (2 Kgs 24:13; 25:13). These objects were finally placed in the hands of Sheshbazzar, the man who would lead the first group of exiles back to Jerusalem (**1:8**).

An inventory of these articles is given in **1:9-11a**. It seems that scribes must have prepared a meticulous list of the spoils of war, and this list no doubt originated from such an inventory. There is a lesson here for African churches regarding the care of church property. Unfortunately, there is often no similar inventory of what belongs to a congregation, with the result that sometimes when church leaders change, there is no formal handing over of property, still less an inventory of what should be there. But care should be taken to keep an inventory of church property and to distinguish it from a leader's personal property.

Whereas the end of the books of Kings and Chronicles repeatedly spoke of a movement from Jerusalem to Babylon, in **1:11b** the movement is in the opposite direction. Operation Return has begun as God reverses his people's destiny and they set out *from Babylon to Jerusalem*.

In this chapter the author of Ezra has made it clear that with the accession of Cyrus to power, God was offering his people an opportunity for restoration. If we as African Christians believe in the sovereignty of God, we may also try to read the events on our continent or on our planet in such a way as to discern the opportunities that God raises up to show his glory. For example, in recent years the concept of globalization has entered the world economic system. Rather than simply criticizing this system, Africans should devote a lot of thought to discerning the opportunities gobalization may provide for our continent.

2:1-70 List of the returned exiles

In 1:5 there was a summary statement about who returned to Jerusalem, but here in chapter 2 there is a detailed list giving names and numbers of those involved. This list is similar to that found in Nehemiah 7:6-69, although there are some differences in the spelling of family names. The chapter is framed by the references to the exiles settling in their own towns in 2:1 and 2:70. This theme of returning to their own towns and ancient properties continues with the concern for continuity in relation to the pre-exile situation that was noted in regard to chapter 1.

The narrator provides no details of the journey, nor of the arrival of the exiles in Jerusalem. He does, however, reveal his focus on the community of exiles living in Babylon. The decree of Cyrus concerned 'anyone of his people' (1:3), but only those who had lived in Jerusalem and in the Kingdom of Judah and who were deported by Nebuchadnezzar are mentioned in this chapter (**2:1**).

The author begins by listing the leaders responsible for the community of exiles returning to Jerusalem (**2:2a**). Eleven names are mentioned, but the parallel list in Nehemiah 7 includes twelve names, perhaps to suggest a link to the twelve tribes of Israel. The name Nahamani (Neh 7:7) does not appear in the list in Ezra. Some of the people mentioned in this list appear in Ezra and Nehemiah, and elsewhere. *Jeshua,* for example is mentioned in 3:2; 4:3; 5:2; in Nehemiah 7:7; 12:1, 10; and in Haggai 1:1, where the spelling is Joshua.

Zerubbabel is also mentioned in 3:8 and in Haggai 1:1. This name originates from the Babylonian *zer-babili,* meaning 'seed of the exile'. It is certainly a reference to his birth in Babylon. Many African names are similar. For example, in the Ngbaka language spoken in the Democratic Republic of Congo, the root *kpala* or 'seed' forms part of many names.

It is not certain whether the *Nehemiah* and *Mordecai* who are mentioned in this list are the same people as appear in the books of Nehemiah and Esther (Esth 2:5, 21; 3:2; 4:1; 5:14; 6:3; 7:9; 9:20; 10:3). It is possible that this list actually gives the successive leaders of the post-exilic community.

The rest of this chapter is made up of various lists of those whom the author calls *the men of the people of Israel* (**2:2b**). The first list is of the different families who returned (**2:3-20**). Each family group is identified as *the descendants of....* This way of referring to people is common in many countries of the Near East and Africa. For example, in Douala in Cameroon, some people are referred to as 'Bonabéri' which means 'the sons of Béri'. Many of the family names on this list appear elsewhere in Ezra and Nehemiah (chs. 8, 10; Neh 10).

Whereas in Chronicles the priests and Levites are usually named first, here, surprisingly, priority is given to laymen. This change suggests that although the presence of priests and Levites is important, the task of rebuilding the temple fell to these ordinary people. African laymen have long been considered as inferior in the hierarchy of the church. But a new wind is blowing in many communities where the laity are now taking responsibility and organizing themselves. In this, we recognize the priesthood of all believers that the NT develops further (1 Pet 2:5, 9).

The next list groups the people according to the name of the town or village they came from (2:21-35). *Bethlehem* and *Netophah,* the first two towns mentioned, are in Judea (**2:21-22**). All the other towns mentioned are in the territory of Benjamin. *Anathoth* is the home town of Jeremiah (**2:23**; Jer 1:1). The towns mentioned in these verses strongly suggest that the majority of the returning exiles had originally come from places within the borders of the ancient Kingdom of Judah.

The names of the founders of families in 2:3-20 and of the cities listed in 2:21-35 certainly date back to the time before the exile. The towns referred to as 'their towns' in 2:1, 70 must refer to the towns they had occupied since the time of the conquest of Canaan under the direction of Joshua (Josh 12-21). The continuity implicit in this repossession of property confirms that the promises made to Abraham remain true (Gen 12:1-3).

After listing the families and towns, the author lists the various categories of temple personnel (2:36-58). This list is very important since the main reason for their journey is the rebuilding of the temple at Jerusalem. This temple would need sufficient legitimate personnel in order to function properly.

The *priests* are arranged in four classes: the sons of *Jedaiah,* of *Immer,* of *Harim* and of *Pashhur* (**2:36-39**). The first three names are mentioned in 1 Chronicles 24:7-18.

Only one verse is devoted to the *Levites* and their number is reduced to 74 (**2:40**). We cannot help noticing the author's lack of interest in this category of temple personnel. The *singers* are simply referred to as *descendants of Asaph* (**2:41**). Asaph was the choir director appointed by David when the ark of the covenant was installed in Jerusalem (1 Chr 16:1, 5).

The *gatekeepers* were those who guarded the entrances to the temple to prevent it from being desecrated (**2:42**). They also guarded the temple treasury. In Chronicles, both the singers and the gatekeepers are listed among the Levites.

The *temple servants* (**2:43-54**) are referred to as the Nethinims in the KJV. This word comes from a Hebrew root that means 'give'. It is possible that they were 'given' to the Levites in the same way as the Levites were 'given' to the priests (Num 3:9). This group is not mentioned among the temple personnel before the exile (1 Chr 9:2, 25-26). On the other hand, in 7:24 this group is listed as being among the temple personnel benefiting from tax exemptions. They also participated in the construction of the walls of Jerusalem (Neh 3:26).

The names of *Solomon's servants* indicate that they are all of foreign origin (**2:55-58**; see also 1 Kgs 9:20-21; 2 Chr 8:7-8).

The final list gives the names of those among the population and priests who could not verify their genealogical connection with the deported Jews (**2:59-61**). The rigorous verification of recognized genealogies was a way of avoiding the desecration of the temple. Though these verses are often understood as indicating Jewish exclusivity, the main purpose is to safeguard the perfect continuity of the chosen people after the parenthesis of the exile.

While nothing is said about the laity who could not prove their family connections, the priests with a questionable genealogy were excluded from service by order of the governor (**2:62**). This exclusion was temporary until the *Urim and Thummim* could be consulted about what was to be done with them (**2:63**). Today, we do not know what the Urim and Thummim looked like or exactly how they functioned. All we know is that they were sacred objects kept in the ephod of the high priest. At one time, these objects were certainly considered necessary for drawing lots or interpreting the divine will. Moses was initially commanded by God to use them (Exod 28:30), but the practice of consulting them, which could resemble some practices associated with sorcery, totally disappeared after the building of the second temple.

In Africa, we still today know of surprising practices such as those involving cowry shells. This shell, originally used as money, has become a magic object associated with amulets and other fetishes. Some people think that the future can be foretold by randomly throwing cowries (or bones) and then reading their positions. Similar occult practices are found in many cultures. As African Christians, we should allow ourselves to be led by the Holy Spirit (Gal 5:16-25). Depending on cowries and other so-called lucky means has ruined many individuals and entire families.

The final section of this chapter recapitulates the total number of people returning: 42 360 (**2:64**). This number does not include the 7337 male and female servants of those who returned (**2:65**). The large number of servants suggests that those who made the journey from Babylon to Jerusalem were relatively wealthy. There were also musicians, who are not to be confused with the Levite singers. The exiles also returned with a considerable quantity of livestock (**2:66-67**).

The rebuilt temple would be erected on the site of the former one (**2:68**). The financial contributions towards this project (**2:69**) remind us of other similar offerings reported in the Bible. At the time of the exodus, the Israelites gave gifts to be used for making the ark and the tabernacle (Exod 25:2-7; 35:21-29). During David's reign, their freewill offerings contributed to the construction of the temple (1 Chr 29:6-9). What is different about this incident is that the initiative came from the entire community. Obviously, in the eyes of the author, the rebuilding of the temple was the responsibility of the whole community.

In conclusion, we should note that in ancient times, genealogies were very important as they allowed others to identify people's origin and the group to which they belonged. They set out people's relationship to others, and their rights and duties in relation to those who were not of their group. They were a vital part of their identity.

But today the question of identity is at the heart of many conflicts on the African continent. The term 'xenophobia' has slipped into everyday use. The African continent is itself the victim of its politics of exclusion. Numerous wars are prompted by the desire of one tribe (or group of tribes) to exclude another group. Pride leads certain tribes to consider themselves as superior to others.

Before God, there is no racial or tribal superiority; we are all created in his image. No race or tribe can have any image greater than that! The body of Christ, the church, is made up of men, women and children of all races and all tribes, of all languages and of all levels of society. As God's creatures, we have a common identity. Moreover, as Christians, we are given our identity by Jesus Christ. This identity in Christ does not lead to exclusivity, but to love and care for all, especially for outsiders and foreigners. The apostle Paul wrote to the Colossians: 'you have … put on the new self, which is being renewed in knowledge in the image of its Creator. Here there is no Greek or Jew, circumcised or uncircumcised, barbarian, Scythian, slave or free, but Christ is all, and is in all' (Col 3:9-10).

3:1-13 The Rebuilding of the Temple

Shortly after settling in Israel, those who had returned from exile turned to the task of rebuilding the temple. In the next section of the book, the author gives a detailed account of the different stages in the rebuilding: the re-establishment of the altar, the resumption of sacrifices, the laying of the foundation of the temple, and the rebuilding of the actual temple. Later, he reports the opposition to this project from various sources.

3:1-6 Restoring the altar and sacrifices

Little time elapsed between the return of the exiles and the beginning of work on the temple: in *the seventh month … the people assembled as one man* (**3:1**). The book of Ezra seeks to show that the whole community gives priority to the rebuilding of the temple. We get the impression that those who had just arrived thought this more important than restoring their own homes. The same scene is described in Nehemiah 7:73-8:1a, which gives the added detail that they met 'before the Water Gate'. Ezra is content simply to mention Jerusalem as the place where they met, because he seeks to encourage the social unity by reminding his readers of the gathering in the capital of Judah.

It is also significant that they assemble in 'the seventh month', which was one of the most important months in the Jewish calendar. It had been the first month of the year during the days of the kings, before Israel came under the strong influence of the Babylonian calendar. Yom Kippur, the Day of Atonement, was on the tenth day of this month (Lev 16).

The reconstruction of the altar takes place under the direction of Jeshua and Zerubbabel (**3:2a**). Here the order of their names is the opposite of that in 2:2, for when it comes to a religious celebration Jeshua, who was of the family of the priests, is given precedence. Each person has a role to play. No title is given to either Zerubbabel or Jeshua in this verse, although in the book of Haggai, Jeshua (or Joshua) is referred to as the 'high priest' and Zerubbabel as the 'governor of Judah' (Hag 1:1). The restoration of the altar was a project supported by the whole community. Though Jeshua and Zerubbabel were the religious and political leaders, their importance fades in relation to that of the community. Seeking titles does not advance the work of Christ. The Lord Jesus does not look at our titles; he looks at our faithfulness to his call and our commitment to the holy task he has given us (2 Cor 10–12).

The altar was established *on its foundation* (**3:3a**). It is possible that those who had remained in Jerusalem had continued sacrifices, but for the author of this book, the only legitimate community to perpetuate this worship is the one that has returned from the Babylonian exile. The author gives two reasons why they reconstructed the altar. The first is their desire for an immediate return to *what is written in the law of Moses the man of God* (**3:2b**). This same expression is used in Chronicles (2 Chr 30:16). The second reason is obscured by the NIV translation, which reads *despite their fear of the peoples around them.* The Hebrew is more accurately translated 'for they were terrified because of the peoples of the lands' (NASB). We are not told why they feared them, but the expression may indicate their determination to set themselves apart from these people. Daily sacrifices were resumed *on the first day of the seventh month* (**3:6**). These sacrifices would have involved *burnt offerings* and *morning and evening sacrifices.* One lamb a year old was sacrificed each morning, and another each evening, and there were also offerings of flour, oil and wine (**3:3b**, **5-6a**; see Exod 29:38-42). The calendar of feasts was also resumed in accordance with the law of Moses. The *Feast of Tabernacles,* which was a harvest festival, would have been celebrated from the fifteenth to the twenty-second day of the month (**3:4**). It reminded the Israelites of their journey through the desert when they had lived in tents (Lev 23:42-43). The other sacrifices and festivals were also reinstated.

Even though the altar had been rebuilt, the foundations of the temple had not yet been laid (**3:6b**). The altar was a structure separate from the temple. In David's time, sacrifices had also been made before the construction of the temple by Solomon (1 Chr 21:28-22:1).

3:7-13 Laying the foundation of the temple

The process of constructing the second temple is similar to that followed in constructing the first one. The preparation involved is described in terms that recall the construction of Solomon's temple (**3:7**): the stonemasons and the carpenters probably came from Tyre and Sidon (1 Chr 22:4); the cedar wood is imported from Lebanon (1 Chr 22:4; 2 Chr 2:8) and the materials are transported by sea as far as Joppa (2 Chr 2:15).

Construction work started in the second month of the second year after their arrival in Jerusalem (**3:8**). Solomon had started construction of his temple in exactly the same month (1 Kgs 6:1-2; 2 Chr 3:2).

The words *when the builders laid the foundation* (**3:10a**), may give the impression that they laid a new foundation. However, the original Hebrew text can be interpreted as meaning 'when they repaired or restored the foundations'. The Babylonians had burned Solomon's temple, but it is unlikely that they had broken up its foundation. Thus, the stones of the new temple were laid on the same foundation as the old building.

But despite all these similarities to the construction of the first temple, there is a major difference. Here, the rebuilding of the temple is not the king's responsibility, but that of the whole community. David and Solomon had contributed substantially to the construction of the first temple (1 Chr 29:1-5; 2 Chr 2:8-9); here, the people take responsibility for the costs (see the commentary on 2:3-20 and 2:69). Many projects in churches fail because of a lack of sufficient support, either because the Christians do not identify with the project or because they are not well informed about it. Too much involvement by one leader can stifle and discourage community participation. But for a ministry to succeed, it must have the support of the whole community.

The celebration of the laying of the foundation makes us think of the one in Solomon's time. The praise is led according to David's instructions (**3:10b**; 1 Chr 16:7). The Levite singers, known as *the sons of Asaph,* reminded the whole community of the Lord's faithfulness by singing the refrain, *He is good; his love to Israel endures for ever* (**3:11**). This refrain is repeated several times in the Bible (1 Chr 16:34; 2 Chr 7:3; Pss 100:5; 106:1; 107:1; 118:1; 136:1). The event in which this community is participating must remind them of God's faithfulness in fulfilling his promises. Sometimes, God may keep us waiting before he does this. But while we wait, we can hum this refrain and remember that God is the same yesterday and forever (Heb 13:8).

It is not easy to understand why those who had seen the first temple should weep (**3:12-13**). Was it from joy or sadness at the sight of a less glorious temple (Hag 2:3)? Whatever the reason, the weeping is mentioned here to show that among the returned exiles were some who had known Solomon's temple. They were a connection, a bridge, with the past generation.

In Africa, loud weeping is an expression of pain or anxiety. When there is a death in a Christian family, church leaders sometimes do not allow the grieving family to express their pain in tears. But weeping was acceptable on this occasion described in Ezra, and is not a sin. Jesus himself wept (John 11:35). What the Bible, and especially the NT, asks us to avoid is being sad like non-believers who have no hope (1 Thess 4:13).

4:1-6:13 Opposition to Rebuilding the Temple

The return from Babylon was interpreted as the fulfilment of prophecy: God himself had moved the heart of Cyrus and touched those who returned (1:1, 5). We might think that with such divine support, nothing could hinder the reconstruction. But opponents soon arrive on the scene.

4:1-5 Opposition during the reign of Cyrus

Those who first opposed the rebuilding of the temple are here introduced as *the enemies of Judah and Benjamin*, the two tribes that formed the ancient southern kingdom (**4:1**). The Hebrew word used for *enemies* is the same word from which we get the name 'Satan'. Satan is the one who always opposes the plans of God's children. Christians will experience opposition and sometimes even apparent failure (see, for example, 2 Cor 12:7-10). But God is always there to help those who rely on him.

The returned exiles encountered opposition because of their refusal to accept the help of those who had remained in the country or who had been brought there by the Assyrians (**4:2-3**; see 2 Kgs 17:24-41). This hybrid population with syncretistic practices would later be known as the Samaritans. Zerubbabel's position is surprising because we would have thought that such cooperation would have made the work of reconstruction proceed more rapidly. However, Zerubbabel probably understood that cooperation with such people might harm the holiness of the temple, which they had been at such pains to protect, even refusing to accept as priests anyone whose genealogy was at all suspect (2:61-63). How could they then accept people whose religious practices were doubtful? The lesson here is that not all offers of cooperation are to be welcomed. The church must remain cautious when it receives unsolicited offers of assistance. Those making the offer sometimes have harmful hidden motives.

Zerubbabel's response was diplomatic. Though his decision was based on a religious principle, his stated reason for rejecting their offer was that he was acting in absolute obedience to the terms of Cyrus' decree.

Angered by this rejection, the local population set out to disrupt the project. They use many different tactics: discouragement (the Hebrew expression literally means 'weakening the arm'), intimidation and corruption of imperial officials (**4:4-5a**). The Letter to the Hebrews deals with the issue of being discouraged. After giving examples of those who have preceded us in the faith, the author urges Christians to imitate their perseverance. He reminds us that when our eyes are fixed on Jesus, there is no place for discouragement and despair (Heb 12:1-3).

Because of this opposition, the rebuilding of the temple was not completed during the reign of Cyrus (559-530 BC) but only during that of Darius (522-486 BC) (**4:5b**).

Here the account of the rebuilding of the temple is interrupted and only resumes in 4:24, after a description of other opposition that the community of returned exiles faced as they set out to rebuild Jerusalem and its walls.

4:6-23 Opposition under Xerxes and Artaxerxes

As noted earlier, this section is something of a parenthesis in the story of the rebuilding of the temple. It shows how the opponents of the rebuilding of Jerusalem as a whole attempted to hinder the work. Their tactic was to send letters to successive Persian rulers. The first letter was addressed to Ahasuerus, better known as Xerxes (486-465 BC). The identity of the enemies and the contents of the letter are not given (**4:6**).

We are given more details about the second letter, destined for Artaxerxes (464-423 BC). As **4:7** indicates, the letter was written in Aramaic, the official language of the Persian Empire. In fact, from 4:8 to 6:18, the book of Ezra was originally written in Aramaic rather than in Hebrew.

The main author of the letter is Rehum, the governor of Samaria (**4:8-11** – see comments on 4:2 for details regarding the Samaritans). Rehum told the king of Persia that if the Jews were to finish the reconstruction and fortification of Jerusalem, they would rebel and no longer pay taxes (**4:12-13**). He then invited the king to consult the archives to verify the tense relations between Jerusalem and previous Babylonian kings (**4:14-16**; 2 Chr 36:1-21). From the perspective of those in charge of the empire, the accusations presented here were very serious. Two things are essential to maintaining an empire: receiving revenue and stability. Refusal to pay taxes threatened the functioning of the royal bureaucracy, while the secession of a colony would put the stability of the empire in jeopardy. These concerns probably explain the prompt response to this letter.

The king drafted a meticulous reply to the accusers' letter. After giving the name and address of the recipient, he addressed each of their demands, in reverse order. The investigations had been carried out by the administration and they confirmed Rehum's accusations. The king therefore ordered that the work be stopped (**4:17-22**).

The king's order was enforced immediately. Rehum and his colleagues even *compelled them by force to stop* the work (**4:23**).

This chapter shows clearly that the fact that we are doing what God wants does not mean that we will not face difficulties. The same was true during the exodus. After showing the strength of his arm when he freed the Israelites from Egypt, God allowed them to experience hunger and thirst in the desert, as well as the hostility of some of the nations they encountered. These difficulties are part of God's teaching method. The opposition experienced by the returned exiles undoubtedly contributed to strengthening their faith and increasing their confidence and dependence on him. This newly re-established community needed to relearn how to rely on God and live constantly in fellowship with him.

4:24-5:2 Resumption of the work under Darius

After telling of these hostile letters, the author takes up the theme of the rebuilding of the temple in the reign of Darius (**4:24**; 4:5). In chapter 5, we see how God took charge after his 'absence' in the preceding chapter. Indeed, in chapter 4 there is no mention of divine intervention at the time of the interruption of the work. When we face resistance or rejection, God's silence at that moment in our life does not signal his absence. He always intervenes in his own time (Eccl 3:11). The catastrophes that Africa is suffering today do not mean that God has abandoned this continent.

The return to constructing the temple is said to be the direct result of a word of prophecy (**5:1**). At the instigation of the prophets Haggai and Zechariah, the returned exiles resumed work despite Artaxerxes' decree. The words that galvanized the people into action are found in the book of Haggai and in Zechariah 1–6. These two men exercised a marvellous ministry of encouragement in God's name. The people must certainly have been discouraged by the royal decree that stopped the work and by the intimidation they faced from others living in the region.

All too often, the African church preaches a message of judgment. While it is true that judgment and condemnation need to be part of Christian preaching, circumstances and events should also prompt pastors and evangelists to deliver a message of encouragement. African people feel beaten down and afflicted. They can see no bright spot on the horizon. They need to be encouraged to persevere in the assurance of God's intervention. In Ezra's day, the prophetic message had that effect. Under the dual influence of Zerubbabel (the political leader) and Jeshua (the religious leader), the exiles returned to the work and the prophets *were with them, helping them* (**5:2**).

5:3-17 Tattenai's letter to Darius

The resumption of the construction work on the temple drew the attention of Tattenai, governor of the province of Trans-Euphrates, which is Samaria (see 4:9-10). He was responsible for making sure that things ran smoothly in his province. We know from other sources that the start of Darius' reign was accompanied by many revolts in various parts of the Persian Empire. Hence the governor probably feared that the rebuilding of the temple would eventually result in a revolt in this area close to Egypt.

This governor's approach to the problem was far fairer than that of Rehum (4:8-23). In fact, he sets an example of good governance. First, he set out to establish whether the Jews had a building permit (**5:3**). Taking care not to lump everyone together, he specifically asks for the names of those participating in the building project (**5:4**).

In view of the importance and place of the temple in Jewish society at that time, the governor also wanted convincing proof of a royal decree. It seems that the Jews could not produce such a document, and so he wrote to the king of Persia for information. Giving the Jews the benefit of the doubt, the governor did not insist that work be stopped while he awaited the king's reply. The author credits this favour to the fact that *the eye of their God was watching over the elders of the Jews* (**5:5**). The 'eye of God', an expression used here for the first time in this letter, means the same thing as 'the hand of God' (7:6, 9), and refers to divine providence (Deut 11:12; Ps 33:18).

It is also a sign of Tattenai's good governance that the Jews seem to have received a *copy of the letter* sent to the king (**5:6**).

In his letter, the governor informs the king of this building project in the province of Judah and gives a detailed account of the materials being used – an account that illustrates the *diligence* with which the exiles have responded to the prophets' call (**5:7-8**).

Scrupulously fair, the governor allows the builders to speak in their own defence by quoting their replies to his questions (5:9-16). Their reply is rich in teaching. They introduced themselves as *servants of the God of heaven and earth* (**5:11**; see the commentary on 1:2). The building that they are constructing is not a new one; they are simply restoring a building that the Babylonians had destroyed. The question that inevitably arises is how the house of such a great God could ever have been destroyed. Was this God defeated? The response is negative. The builders acknowledge that the reason for its destruction and their exile was the sin of the people (**5:12**).

Tattenai does not close his letter with an expression of distrust and vague fears about a movement towards independence (4:15). Instead, he simply asks that the archives be searched to verify whether the Jews were speaking the truth when they said that what they were doing had been authorized by Cyrus (**5:13-17**).

6:1-13 Darius' response

Chapter 6 is very important because it deals with a series of events that are finally going to allow the rebuilding of the temple, the rallying point of the Jewish community. It starts with Darius' order to search the royal archives, and the discovery of a copy of Cyrus' decree (**6:1**).

The copy of the decree was found at *Ecbatana,* (or Achmetha – KJV) the capital of Media and one of the Persian kings' summer residences (**6:2**). This Aramaic copy is slightly different from the version of the decree recorded in 1:2-4 in that it gives a few extra details and theological observations. It specifies that the temple is to be *a place to present sacrifices* (this detail strongly suggests that no other place may be used for this purpose), gives the dimensions of the temple and instructs the imperial treasury to contribute to the costs (**6:3-4**). The restoration of the utensils and other articles used in the temple is already mentioned in 1:7-11, but this copy specifies that these objects are to be *returned to their place in the temple ... to be deposited in the house of God,* again underlining the concern for continuity (**6:5**).

The record of the decree is followed by Darius' reply to Tattenai's letter. He authorizes the work to continue (**6:6-7**). He also grants additional favours to the exiles: the royal treasury is to provide all that is needed for the sacrifices *daily without fail* (**6:9** – we should recall that the altar was already built according to 3:2). In return, Darius asks that the Jews pray for the well-being of the royal family (**6:10**). Finally, he threatens anyone who *lifts a hand* against his orders (**6:11-12**).

On receiving this definite statement of support for the building work, Tattenai, still acting fairly, *carried it out with diligence* (**6:13**).

6:14-22 Completion and Dedication of the Temple

This section starts with a reference to the providence of God in the course of events; he is responsible for the success of this enterprise. King Artaxerxes is mentioned in anticipation of his later role (**6:14**; 7:21-26).

The work was completed on a date that corresponds to March 515 BC (**6:15**), almost exactly seventy years after the destruction of the first temple by the Babylonians. The new temple is inaugurated *with joy* – there were no more tears (**6:16**; see commentary on 3:12-13). Because of the precarious economic and political situation of the inhabitants of Jerusalem, the number of sacrifices offered was small compared to the offerings listed in 2 Chronicles 30:24 and 35:7. They offered twelve goats *one for each of the tribes of Israel* because the returned exiles consider themselves representatives of the twelve tribes (**6:17**).

After 6:18, the text ceases to be written in Aramaic and reverts to Hebrew, the language in which it was written up to 4:8.

The building of the new temple was not a waste of effort. The inauguration was accompanied by the renewing of ritual worship as specified in the law of Moses (**6:18**; Exod 12:18). The community's celebration of the first Passover feast since their return from exile has profound significance when we remember that in Exodus the first such feast symbolized deliverance from slavery in Egypt (**6:19-20, 22**; Exod 23:15). The book of Ezra is often accused of stressing Jewish exclusivity, but here an invitation is issued to all who wish to join the community to participate in the celebration (**6:21**).

With the reconstruction of the temple, the first stage of the restoration of the community ends. The foundations have been laid. Those who returned from exile have understood the reasons for God's judgment. In NT language, they have sought first the kingdom of God. Jesus promised that if we do this, 'all these things will be given to you as well' (Matt 6:33). The first step in the rebuilding of Africa will be the reconciliation of individual Africans with their God.

7:1-10:44 Rebuilding the Community under Ezra

Ezra, the hero of this book, is first introduced in this chapter, which speaks of his person and his mission. Chapter 8 tells us about his own journey from Babylon to Jerusalem, while chapters 9 and 10 dealt with the practical task of reconstructing the Jewish community by denouncing those who have married outsiders.

7:1-28 Introduction of Ezra and His Mission

The long genealogy of Ezra connects him with Aaron, the first high priest (**7:1-5**; Exod 28:1). During the era of the new temple, when there was no royal dynasty, the high priest played an important political role at the heart of the community. Some commentators even speak of the system of government as being a hierocracy, that is, government by priests. The priests exercised executive and judicial powers, and were leaders and judges of the observance of the law of Moses. This genealogy therefore legitimates Ezra's role in the rebuilding of the community.

Though Ezra was of the high priestly line, he was also a scribe, or as the NIV translates it, a teacher (**7:6a**). During this period, scribes were not simply those who made copies of the law of Moses but were also teachers of that law, which they recognized had been given by God (**7:6b**).

The priest-scribe Ezra enjoyed favour with the king because *the hand of his God was on him* (**7:6c**). In the preceding chapter, the author spoke of 'the eye of their God' (5:5), but from now he speaks of God's 'hand' when speaking of divine action (see 7:9, 28; 8:18, 22, 31; Neh 2:8, 18).

Ezra and those who accompanied him set out from Babylon to journey to Jerusalem on the first day of the first month (**7:7-9**). The date is significant because that was the month of the Passover and thus of the exodus from Egypt (Exod 12:2). It is even more significant in light of the fact that **7:10** positions Ezra not just as a physical descendant of Aaron, but as a spiritual descendant of Moses. Like Moses, he was a zealous teacher of the law who functioned as an intermediary between God and the community. In Jewish tradition, Ezra is, in fact, often regarded as 'the second Moses'.

The author now gives the reasons *that the gracious hand of his God* was on Ezra. Not only did he teach the law but more than that he studied it and put it into practice (7:10). All three elements are important for a successful Christian life. Many Christians do not experience a deepening life because they have not made these things priorities. Too often in Africa, we know how to preach the word, but not how to put it into practice.

Ezra's life offers a model for our teaching on this continent. The reason he came to Jerusalem was to apply the law of the Lord. Such a mission could not succeed unless he applied this word in his own life. This was the price he had to pay in order to earn credibility and respect. Pastors, evangelists and Christian teachers must, above all, practise the word that they teach.

After this introduction to Ezra, the author tells us more about why he came to Jerusalem by providing us with a copy of the commission Ezra received from King Artaxerxes (7:11-26). This commission takes the form of a letter addressed to Ezra and written in Aramaic, since it is a Persian administrative document (**7:11-12**). Ezra's main tasks are as follows: to inspect Judah and Jerusalem to see that the people there are obeying God's law (**7:14**); to carry freewill offerings from the king and his counsellors for the work of the temple (**7:15**); to gather any freewill offerings made by the Jews remaining in Babylon (**7:16**); and to deliver all these offerings to the temple (**7:17-20**). In addition, Ezra was to inform *the treasurers of Trans-Euphrates* of the tax exemption granted to temple personnel (**7:21-24**) and he was to appoint judges and magistrates to give justice according to the law of the Lord and to teach the law (**7:25**).

We do not know exactly what part of the Law this priest-scribe had in *[his] hand* (7:14) and was to teach in Jerusalem, but it was most probably the entire Torah, that is, the first five books of the OT, also known as the Pentateuch. Whatever it was, Ezra also received extensive authority since he could impose the death penalty on those who did not obey the law of the Lord (**7:26**).

All of these responsibilities are similar to those carried by Moses (Exod 18:24-26; 35:4-5, 21-22).

This section ends with a psalm of thanksgiving written by Ezra in the grand tradition of the exodus (**7:27-28**; Exod 15:1-18). Ezra did not seek his own glory; he attributed his success to God without pretension and without pride. He would agree with Psalm 127:1: 'Unless the Lord builds the house, its builders labour in vain.'

8:1-36 Ezra's Journey to Jerusalem

The priests, Levites and leaders of Israel who left with Ezra have already been mentioned in passing (7:7, 13, 28). The story of his journey begins with details about these people who accompanied him (8:1-14). The list begins with two very familiar names. *Phinehas* and *Ithamar* were the names of the sons of Aaron (Exod 6:23-25). Phineas' son, *Gershom,* has the same name as Moses' son. (Exod 2:22). The fact that in **8:1** the descendants of priestly families are listed before the descendants of King David (see 1 Chron 3:22) confirms the importance of the priests during the post-exilic period. The rest of the list is composed of common people similar to those listed in 2:3-39.

While preparing to set out on the journey, Ezra and his companions camped near the Ahava Canal for three days (**8:15**). Ezra was disturbed to discover that there were no Levites in the group and so he called for some (**8:16-20**). The presence of the Levites was important for the operation of the temple, and also for the journey itself since the law specified that they should be the ones to carry any holy objects (Num 3:5-8; 1 Chr 15:2).

Before setting out on the journey, Ezra proclaimed a fast. The purpose of this fast was to commit the trip to God and thus to be assured of divine protection (**8:21, 23**). Ezra had told the king of God's great power, and did not want to ask him for an armed escort for fear that would weaken his testimony (**8:22**).

God honoured Ezra's fast (**8:31-32**), but it should be pointed out that God does not always respond to fasting with some miraculous intervention. Though fasting is recommended in the Bible, it is not the only way of having our prayers heard. Nor should it be a basis for pride (Matt 6:1, 16-18). It is regrettable that in Africa today fasting has come to be regarded as a type of magic that even replaces the need for God. Sometimes it feels as if we are present at a sort of fasting competition. Christians seek to break records for the number of days they fast. They speak of Esther's fast (3 days – Esth 4:16) or of Daniel's fast (3 weeks – Dan 10:2-3). Fasting has become such a standard that those who do not fast are considered to be less spiritual.

Nehemiah also fasted, but he did not hesitate to have a military escort (Neh 1:4; 2:9). God's grace does not exclude human intervention; the same faith acts in both cases. As the apostle Paul wrote: 'He who eats meat, eats to the Lord, for he gives thanks to God; and he who abstains, does so to the Lord and gives thanks to God' (Rom 14:6).

We are given a detailed account of how Ezra entrusted the money and other objects belonging to the temple to the care of the priests and Levites (**8:24-27**). They were held accountable for them (**8:28-30**). On their arrival in Jerusalem, the goods were again counted to make sure that the full amount entrusted to them had been delivered: *everything was accounted for by number and weight* (**8:33-34**). We are again reminded about the importance of proper management of church property. Failure to manage it properly hinders the growth of the church (see commentary on 1:9-11a).

9:1-10:44 Mixed Marriages

The last two chapters of the book of Ezra deal with the issue of marriages between Jews and the other people in the region.

A short time after his arrival, Ezra was informed that both laymen and temple personnel had taken foreign wives (**9:1**). There are echoes of Deuteronomy 7:3 in **9:2**, a verse that identifies the danger that results from such unions: corruption of what should be a holy family line. And in this matter, it was leaders who were the first to be guilty of this sin!

Some of the patriarchs had married foreign wives (Abraham, Gen 16:3; Joseph, Gen 41:45; Moses, Exod 2:21), but the Lord had pointed out to the people of Israel that intermarriage with the inhabitants of Canaan would lead to apostasy (Exod 34:10-16). According to 1 Kgs 11:1-8, it was his foreign wives who turned Solomon's heart and led him to be unfaithful to God. The consequence of his unfaithfulness was the break-up of his kingdom. The NT also prohibits Christians from being 'yoked together with unbelievers' (2 Cor 6:14).

Africa, like other countries in the world, is seeing a rise in religious pluralism. If we do not pay attention, we risk losing our identity for the sake of tolerance. But note that we are speaking here of our personal and spiritual identity, and not of our societies, in which we should tolerate pluralism (see the commentary on 2:68).

Ezra expresses his grief by going into mourning. He adopts traditional expressions of grief: tearing his clothing and pulling hair from his head and beard – still very African ways of expressing pain (**9:3-4**). He then prays for the people (**9:5-15**).

Ezra's prayer reveals that he is a true successor of Moses (see the commentary on 7:27-28; Exod 32:11-13). The focus of the prayer is on confession, and so Ezra makes no requests. He simply recognizes the just judgment of God, although he is also aware of the grace that accompanies this judgment (9:13).

Sincere confession calls for concrete change. Seeing Ezra's pain and hearing his prayer, the community unites around him (**10:1**). In the name of the whole community, Shecaniah approaches Ezra (**10:2**). The community recognizes its guilt and decides to act; it is the people who decide to send away all the foreign wives and their children (**10:3-17**). It seems that as a good teacher, Ezra did not impose this decision on the people. He did his work of teaching the law, and thus reminded the people of their responsibilities. Imposed solutions are not easily accepted; it was by example that Ezra was able to change his community.

The book of Ezra closes with a list of those who sent away their foreign wives (**10:18-44**), thus honouring these men.

This decision to send away the pagan women was taken in the context where the very survival of the Jewish community was at stake, and should not be taken as rule for the church. The apostle Paul specifically opposes this (1 Cor 7:12-14). However, in a general way, the book of Ezra ends by stressing the purifying of the community. It is this new community founded on obedience to God that guaranteed the future of the people then – and now (1 Pet 1:13-16).

Nupanga Weanzana

Further Reading

Brown, Raymond. *The Message of Nehemiah: God's Servant in a Time of Change.* BST. Downers Grove, Ill: InterVarsity Press, 1998.

Rossier, H. L. *Ezra, Nehemiah, Esther.* H.L. Rossier Commentaries. Sunbury, Pa: Believers Bookshelf, 2003. Also available at http://www.biblecentre.org/commentaries.

Stedman, Ray C. and James D. Denney. *Adventuring Through the Bible: A Comprehensive Guide to the Entire Bible,* Discovery House, 1997.

NEHEMIAH

As noted in the introduction of the commentary on Ezra, the books of Nehemiah and Ezra originally formed one book. That introduction has information about the possible author, the historical context and the relevance of these books to Africa.

Unlike the book of Ezra, where the main hero appears for the first time only in chapter 7, Nehemiah, the hero of this book, is introduced in the first verse. The relationship between the two heroes who united the post-exilic community is quite difficult to establish. Ezra's ministry began in the seventh year of the reign of King Artaxerxes (Ezra 7:8), whereas Nehemiah arrived on the scene in the twentieth year of the reign of the same king (1:1). They were, therefore, contemporaries. However, the biblical narrative gives the impression that the two men worked independently and did not know each other well. It is difficult to confidently identify the exact time frame in which each of them operated, for the original author was not particularly interested in the chronology of events. His narrative is driven more by specific themes. Some have even argued that he dealt with Ezra first because he felt that Ezra, a scribe and priest, should take precedence over Nehemiah, a mere layman.

The name 'Nehemiah' means 'the Lord comforts', a meaning that can shape our approach to the whole book. Nehemiah's work brought healing and reassurance to the returned exiles.

The book of Nehemiah deals primarily with the reconstruction of Jerusalem's protective walls, which the Babylonians had destroyed when they captured the city (2 Chr 36:19). The first exiles, who had returned under the leadership of Zerubbabel and Jeshua, had been more concerned about rebuilding the temple than the walls. When they did attempt to repair the walls, progress was blocked by King Artaxerxes (Ezra 4:12, 21-22). This book describes the second and successful attempt to rebuild them. Even though Nehemiah acknowledges the grace of God in the success of this enterprise, it is clear that his own personality was a determining factor in its accomplishment. Thus the book of Nehemiah gives insight into the characteristics of an effective leader.

As one reads the book, one is impressed with the character of this man who efficiently supervises the reconstruction of the walls of Jerusalem, despite repeated opposition. But he is more than just a man of action; he is also a man of prayer. The entire story is wrapped in prayers (long, short, over a long period, or in haste in a particular situation). Nehemiah believed in the power of prayer. Yet,

while he had absolute confidence in the God to whom he prayed, he also knew that God works through people. He saw no contradiction between divine action and human initiative. For instance, even though he knew how to depend on God, he asked for an escort to protect his convoy on its journey to Jerusalem. He was also a leader who led by example, in any and all circumstances. Finally, he knew how to plan for the important task to which he had been called. When he asked the king for permission to rebuild the walls, he had done his homework. He could specify how long the project would take and the materials he would need to accomplish it.

As pointed out in the introduction to the book of Ezra, African theologians have forged a theology of reconstruction from this episode in the history of Israel. The qualities displayed by Nehemiah are sorely needed for the reconstruction of our continent today.

Outline of Contents

COMMENTARY

1:1-7:72 Nehemiah's Mission to Jerusalem

The first important section of this book deals with Nehemiah's repair of the fortifications of Jerusalem. It begins with a reminder of the desperate state of the city and its inhabitants and then carries on to describe the course of the reconstruction and the opposition that the builders experienced.

1:1-4 The Situation in Jerusalem

The book is introduced with an emphatic statement: *The words of Nehemiah* (**1:1a**). These words give the impression that what we will be reading is a personal story or an autobiography. But the book is more than this, for while it begins in the first person (I, me), later it moves on to speak of Nehemiah in the third person (he).

When the book opens, Nehemiah is at Susa, the winter residence of the Persian kings (**1:1b**). Climate was a major factor when these kings chose a location to establish their headquarters. Ecbatana, in the cooler mountains, was their summer residence. Similarly, some African countries have two capitals; in this case an official administrative capital and a 'private' capital, often the village from which the head of state came, which has been transformed by the building of luxury hotels and the like.

A long period of stability enforced by imperial Persia had made travel possible between the Empire's capital and its provinces. Thus Nehemiah was able to meet with Hanani and other men who had arrived from Judah (**1:2a**). Nehemiah describes Hanani as *one of my brothers*, which could mean they were close relatives, but which could also be understood in the larger sense, as it often is in African culture. A missionary who did not understand the system of African family ties was very surprised when his cook informed him that he had lost more than one father during the same year. The missionary understood that the cook's birth father had died, but was puzzled by the reference to other fathers. The cook had to explain, 'The oldest and youngest brothers of my father are also my fathers!'

Nehemiah questioned Hanani and his companions about how *the Jewish remnant* was doing (**1:2b**). This is the first time the word 'Jews' is used in the Bible. The word would become the generic name for God's people after the exile. It is not completely clear whether Nehemiah is asking about those who had returned from Babylon to Jerusalem after the exile, or about those few Jews who had escaped being deported and were living in a ravaged country. His question probably concerned both groups.

The men's answer is not given in detail. What we have in **1:3** is a summary of their report on the state of the people and the city. The survivors of the exile were in great

distress and faced scorn and ridicule. Meanwhile the walls of Jerusalem were still in ruins, meaning that the city was completely defenceless against any enemy. In their focus on rebuilding the temple, Zerubbabel and Ezra had neglected the problem posed by the lack of a wall (Ezra 1-8).

Nehemiah's immediate reaction to this news was to mourn and weep (**1:4**). His way of expressing sadness is identical to that of many African tribes: we too sit and weep. But it is worth noting that he is grieving for the sorrows of others. More and more, African society is abandoning its traditional sense of community and is adopting an individualism that makes us insensitive to the sufferings of others. But the Letter to the Hebrews reminds us to 'remember those in prison as if you were their fellow prisoners, and those who are mistreated as if you yourselves were suffering' (Heb 13:3).

1:5-11 Nehemiah's Prayer

Nehemiah's concern for his people did not end with mourning. The mourning was followed by intercession for the people. This passage presents the first prayer of lamentation in Nehemiah.

The opening words of the prayer remind us of three important facts: the greatness and power of God, God's faithfulness to the covenant he made with Israel, and the mercy of God (**1:5**). Using vivid language, Nehemiah appeals to God to hear him as he prays *day and night* (**1:6a**). The expression does not mean that Nehemiah prayed all night and all day. If he had, he would not have been able to do his work in the king's court. Rather, the words express the fervency with which Nehemiah prayed.

Some believers in urban centres of Africa (rural areas are often sheltered from this sort of excess) have been inspired by what they take to be Nehemiah's example and a few other examples in Scripture, as well as the instruction to 'pray continually' (1 Thess 5:17). So they have taken to organizing long prayer vigils that cause problems for those who have to go to work early the next day. Often, those who encourage such prayer vigils can go home afterwards to sleep, while the others must go to their places of employment. The exhausted Christians then cannot carry out their professional responsibilities properly, and some have run into serious difficulties and have even lost their jobs! We need to remember to imitate Nehemiah in showing balance in everything we do. We must be people of prayer, but also people of action.

The tone and the form of the prayer show Nehemiah's solidarity with his people (**1:6b**). In 1:5 he had spoken of God as faithful to his covenant, and in **1:7** he admitted that the people have not been equally faithful. The exile was the result of the nation's sin and lack of obedience to God.

When he invited God to *remember* the details of the covenant (**1:8**), he was not implying that God had forgotten the terms he set out in Deuteronomy 30:1-4. God cannot forget his people (9:31, 33-34). Rather, he was speaking in human terms as he called on God to intervene to change the situation (**1:9**). He reminded God that he had redeemed his people in the past (**1:10**), first in the exodus from Egypt (Exod 6:1; 9:16; 32:11), and then in the second exodus when the exiles returned to Judah from Babylon (Ezra 1:1-2:70).

Nehemiah made a specific request in **1:11a**: he asked God to give him *favour* and *success* before the king, although he did not use the word king, but simply referred to him as *this man.*

At the end of the prayer, Nehemiah informs his readers of his position at court: he was *cupbearer to the king* (**1:11b**). The cupbearer was a trusted servant, responsible for tasting the king's wine to make sure that it was satisfactory and had not been poisoned before offering the cup to the king. He thus had easy and direct access to the monarch. Clearly, exiles such as Nehemiah had integrated in Babylonian society and occupied high positions.

Nehemiah's position and attitude remind us of Moses. Despite the privileged position Moses enjoyed in Pharaoh's court, he had a real concern for his people who had been reduced to slavery (Exod 2:10-11).

2:1-8 Royal Authorization to Go to Jerusalem

After prayer came action. In his prayer (1:5-11), Nehemiah had asked God to cause the king to look on him with favour. This section tells how God answered that prayer as Nehemiah carried out his duties as cupbearer.

The month of Nisan (**2:1a**) came four months after Nehemiah had received information about Jerusalem (1:1). It was the first month of the Babylonian year, a month for doing favours. Similarly, in several African countries, the month of January has often been the occasion for heads of state to grant amnesties to some prisoners and to ease the conditions of others.

Nehemiah's evident sadness as he carried out his duties may have been due to his many months of fasting and prayer, or it may simply have been because he was all too aware of the contrast between the celebration around him and the terrible situation of his people in Jerusalem. As Proverbs 15:13 says, 'A happy heart makes the face cheerful, but heartache crushes the spirit.' When the king asked the reason for his solemn face, Nehemiah was seized with fear. He could be punished for appearing sad in the king's presence. But he was also seized with fear because the moment had finally come to speak of what was in his heart (**2:1b-2**). It took courage to ask Artaxerxes to authorize work that he had earlier ordered to stop (Ezra 4:1-24). Simply presenting the request might endanger Nehemiah's life.

Nehemiah gave a careful reply to the king's question in verse **2:3**. He spoke of Jerusalem not in political terms but in terms of the Jews strong attachment to the tombs of their ancestors. He may have given the impression that he was only concerned about restoring the graveyards.

Nehemiah's fear may slowly have begun to evaporate as the king asked him what it was that he wanted. For the second time, Nehemiah prayed. This prayer was probably a silent one, no more than a quick thought, but God listens even to this kind of prayer (**2:4**). Then he clearly stated his request. Again speaking of Jerusalem as the city *where my fathers are buried,* he asked the king for permission to rebuild Jerusalem (**2:5**).

The king's third question concerned how long the project would take (**2:6**). Nehemiah's answer to this question is not recorded. However, we know that he was gone for at least twelve years (5:14). Clearly, in the four months that had preceded this interview, Nehemiah had put a lot of thought into this project. He had anticipated what steps would be needed and could lay a plausible plan of action before the king. Nehemiah was not a leader who acted on impulse; he drew up detailed plans before acting. By contrast, several projects begun by African churches have never been completed because they were begun hastily without due planning. After four months of thinking and praying about what needed to be done, Nehemiah could present all the details of his project when the appropriate opportunity presented itself. Prayer does not exclude planning.

His first request was that he be given letters to the governors of the provinces beyond the Euphrates River ordering them to give him safe conduct through the areas they controlled (**2:7**). In addition, he asked for a letter to Asaph, the *keeper of the king's forest,* because he would need wood from this forest to repair the city gates, the wall and his own residence (**2:8**). The king granted these requests – a fact attributed to *the gracious hand of my God.* Like Ezra (Ezra 7:27-28), Nehemiah gave all the glory to his Lord. Armed with these letters and a military escort, he set out for Jerusalem (**2:9**).

2:9-20 Arrival in Jerusalem and the First Opposition

Before Nehemiah even reaches Jerusalem, we are informed of the hostility he will face from *Sanballat the Horonite and Tobiah the Ammonite* (**2:10a**). (The -iah in Tobiah's name represents the word *Yah,* a short form of God's name, Yahweh). These two men were probably local officials who regarded Nehemiah as a direct threat to their own authority. They were annoyed that someone *had come to promote the welfare of the Israelites* (**2:10b**). The use of the name 'Israelites' is significant, for it shows that the author of the book considers the exiles who have returned to Jerusalem to be God's people and representatives of the twelve tribes (7:6; 12:1).

On his arrival, Nehemiah rested for three days before beginning any activity (**2:11**). Earlier, Ezra and his team had profited from a three-day rest on their arrival in

LEADERSHIP

Many traditional African ideas about leadership are embedded in the Kikuyu legend about the despotic king Gikuyu who was overthrown because of his tyrannical rule and replaced by a council of elders, chosen from the older men of the community who had previously been warriors. Most traditional African societies were governed by a council of older men who had established their prowess in warfare. Africans have always responded to strong leaders who demand obedience, as can be seen from the rapid rise to power of the Zulu king Shaka. This stress on military power has meant that councils were male dominated (despite the occasional rise of women leaders with exceptional qualities). The military model also meant that traditional leadership was hierarchical, with orders passed down from above.

Leaders are also expected to possess sufficient economic wealth to provide for those around them. They establish their authenticity by caring for others and are supposed to practise *ubuntu,* putting people first. Thus it is not uncommon for the compounds of clan leaders, school principals or successful businesswomen to be packed with people seeking their help.

Besides power and wealth, African leaders are also expected to have knowledge. A Masai proverb says, 'When an elder dies, a whole library is buried with him.' Elders are repositories of African history. Not only that, but they are expected to have magical knowledge too. A leader such as a chief or king is expected to be in contact with the ancestors. As a result of their knowledge, leaders are expected to have wisdom, that is, the ability to resolve community conflicts. A leader is regarded as a problem solver and peacemaker.

Leadership is often hereditary, even though the new leaders may not possess the same leadership qualities as their predecessors. However, in cases where no one stands out as possessing the qualities identified above, or where a leader has fallen out of favour with the people, power is vested in a council of clan elders. Julius Nyerere, the late president of Tanzania, popularized the concept of *ujamaa,* which emphasizes leadership by a fellowship or partnership, where a leader is one among equals.

Western Influences

The colonization and Christianization of Africa brought tremendous changes to the concept and structures of leadership. Age and eldership were pushed aside as a Western education, and especially command of a European language, took centre stage. Leadership became more inclusive, involving men and women, young and old. The introduction of a monetary economy and the modern military system challenged leadership derived from mystical powers. With the growth of new government structures, large corporations and elaborate infrastructure came demands for new forms of leadership. Unfortunately, some of the strengths and values of the old systems, such as their emphasis on seasoned knowledge of life, wisdom, *ubuntu,* and *ujamaa,* were discredited or lost and replaced with pride and arrogance. Leadership became focused on position, privileges, power and *pesa* ('money' in Swahili). By and large, leadership came to be understood in terms of a secular Western model. But this 'hand in pocket' style of leadership is neither biblical nor African.

Biblical Leadership Qualities

The Bible uses six major metaphors when speaking of a good leader.

- A leader is a servant who waits on others (Mark 10:35-45; Luke 22:24-27).

- A leader is a scapegoat who carries others' burdens and punishment (Lev 16:10-26; John 11:50).

- A leader is a shepherd who cares for and protects the sheep (Ps 23:1-5; John 10:1-15; Acts 20:28; 1 Pet 5:1-4).

- A leader is a steward who takes care of others' valuables (Luke 19:11-26; Acts 20:35; 2 Tim 1:11-14).

- A leader is a student, scholar and scribe, who listens to and learns from others (Ezra 7:10; Acts 20:17-21; 2 Tim 2:15).

- A leader is a salesperson, who motivates and inspires others (Num 14:6-9, 24; Josh 14:8; 2 Tim 1:6-7).

Jesus epitomizes all of these qualities, and more. This is why he uses himself as an example of leadership in Matthew 20:26-28.

Christlike leadership is needed in both the church and society in Africa. Such leadership will require purity of heart (God looks at the heart, not the head), passion for people, power to serve through prayer, a pioneering spirit, practical wisdom to solve problems and perseverance. Christlike leaders will be imaginative, visionary, knowledgeable, wise, caring and responsible – leaders of integrity. Needless to say, they will also be humble. They will be known for their character, competence, courage, commitment and compassion.

Tokunboh Adeyemo

Jerusalem (Ezra 8:32). Rest is necessary, but it is also a time for observation as we see with Jonah in Nineveh and Paul in Athens (Jonah 4:5; Acts 17:16). Many African pastors do not allow themselves time to rest. Some even think that resting represents neglect of their pastoral responsibility, and so they work with an agenda that is always too full. However, their refusal to rest affects their health and hinders their effectiveness in ministry.

Before undertaking any work, Nehemiah familiarized himself with the state of Jerusalem and of its inhabitants. This inspection confirmed what he had heard (1:3) and enabled him to draft a realistic plan of action.

Having sensed opposition, it seem necessary for him to be prudent. So Nehemiah inspected the walls by night, accompanied by several trusted men. He rode his own mount because, being accustomed to its master, it would make no noise. Discretion in the smallest details is an important element in the success of any undertaking (2:12-16).

On seeing the ruined condition of Jerusalem, Nehemiah, who had wept at Susa, remained stoic. The time for tears was past; it was time for action. As Africans, we need to learn more about such an attitude. Nehemiah mourned when he learned the condition of the city, but set aside his mourning when there were was work to be done. African Christians should not let themselves be paralyzed by despair. We should, of course, show sorrow in difficult situations, but our grief should not preclude action (Heb 10:36, 39).

After his rest and inspection tour, Nehemiah reminded the Jews of the disgraceful state of the city (referring back to 1:3) and shared his vision for rebuilding the walls (2:17-20). We wonder why the Jews, who must have been conscious of their sorry situation, had done nothing. Did they lack a leader? Whatever the reason, the impetus to rebuild the walls came from an outsider.

Nehemiah had done careful planning, but he attributed his mission and the success he has achieved thus far to God's support for this project (2:18). The Jews' response, *Let us start rebuilding,* is no doubt the most quoted verse in the book. It is frequently the theme of meetings on our continent, and is a challenge that Africa needs to hear. Our continent has suffered repeated wars and pillaging. Each time troubles break out, its people destroy, plunder and burn. It is time that the African church started echoing Nehemiah's call to action and initiating peace and reconstruction.

The theme of opposition, first encountered in 2:10, soon returns. A third adversary, Geshem the Arab, joined Sanballat and Tobiah (2:19). Their strategy involved mockery, ridicule and lies. Like Nehemiah, those serving God may encounter opposition despite their prayers.

One of the accusations levelled against the Jews was that they were planning to rebel against the king (Ezra 4:12-13).

This dishonest political argument was a powerful one because Jerusalem was in a strategic geographical location on the road between Egypt and Persia. Consequently, Persian rulers were alert to any signs of disloyalty in Judah. This was particularly the case because in Nehemiah's time Egypt was a rebellious Persian colony, so the Persian king needed to be able to intervene there quickly, without any obstruction from Jerusalem.

Nehemiah refused to become involved in an argument with his opponents. He simply stated his case and left the outcome to God (2:20; Rom 12:19).

3:1-32 Reconstruction of the Walls of Jerusalem

Chapter 3 names those who participated in rebuilding the walls and specifies where they worked. Nehemiah organized the project in such a way that each participant worked on a section in front of his or her home.

The record begins with those working on the north side of Jerusalem (3:1-7), then moves to those in the west (3:8-13), from there to those in the south (3:15-32), and from there back to the north. The first and last location mentioned is the Sheep Gate (3:1, 32). It seems that this gate gave entry to the place where the sheep destined for sacrifice were washed, an interesting symbolic point because Nehemiah's work involved repentance (9:7-37).

The list of builders begins with the priests, men regarded as examples: *Eliashib the high priest and his fellow priests went to work and rebuilt the Sheep Gate* (3:1). Eliashib, who is mentioned in Ezra 10:6, will be mentioned again in 3:20-21. The high priest's involvement was particularly significant, for after the exile his position was supremely important because their faith was the only link that united the Jewish people scattered across the multicultural Persian Empire.

The priests' involvement was a powerful response to the exhortation of 2:18: 'Let us start rebuilding'. Unlike these priests, some of God's servants in Africa take the title of priest, preacher or pastor in order to be served, not to serve. Such an attitude is harmful because the teaching Christians retain best is what they learn from their pastor's example and attitude. Pastors carry great responsibility (1 Tim 3:1-13).

Meremoth was the treasurer into whose hands the silver, gold and temple utensils had been entrusted (3:4; Ezra 8:33). He is noteworthy because his grandfather, Hakkoz, is mentioned in Ezra as one of the priests whose genealogy was questionable (Ezra 2:61).

Tekoa (3:5) was the little town south of Jerusalem, better known as the hometown of the prophet Amos (Amos 1:1). The verse notes that its nobles *would not put their shoulders to the work* (literally, 'would put not their necks to the work' – KJV). Their attitude could be described as 'stiff-necked' (see also 9:15-16, 29; Exod 32:9; Acts 7:51). We find various forms of this idiomatic expression in African languages. For example, someone who will not obey may be said to have a hard head.

Shallum's daughters also helped rebuild the wall (**3:12**). We might have thought that such a work environment would exclude women and girls, but that was not the case. Women in Africa are often marginalized by society, and even more so by the church, where they may be allowed to exercise only secondary responsibilities. We need to learn from the role of these women when reading the book of Nehemiah.

The long list of workers shows what God's people are capable of doing when they work together. These Jews came from different families, social and professional classes and both sexes; yet they all worked together, with perfect cooperation and coordination. Almost forty different groups are mentioned, and all agreed on the necessity of raising the walls. But their unity on this issue did not erase the differences between them. We too as believers should remember that while our practices may be different, we share a common aim: the proclamation of the Kingdom of God (John 17:21). It is not normal that the church in general, and the church in Africa in particular, nurses the divisions inherited from different traditions. The enemy, who knows the power of unity and knows that God blesses it (Ps 133), seeks to destroy it. Let us not give him the opportunity! The account in Nehemiah shows that, despite hostile forces, the construction work was completed thanks to the unity of the people.

4:1-23 New Opposition

This section picks up on the theme of opposition, previously introduced in 2:10, 19-20. It describes a series of attacks on Nehemiah and the builders by the same enemies, who again intended to stop the work.

The opposition now intensifies. In 2:19 it had merely involved scorn and mockery, but now emotions are stronger. When Sanballat learned that the builders were busy and that the wall was rising, he became angry and was greatly incensed (**4:1**). Whereas he previously mocked the builders in private, now he scorned them in public, in the presence of his associates and the army of Samaria (**4:2**). He ridiculed the weakness of the builders, claiming they were feeble Jews. But on what basis could he say they were weak? Because they were only returned exiles? People without a king? Too few in number for the task to be accomplished? Whatever the case, God's power is made perfect in weakness (2 Cor 12:9).

When we pause to think of the immensity of the task confronting us, we can become discouraged and feel weak. Today, Africa is enveloped in a cloud of pessimism, with many assuming that its fate is sealed. But the Christian church should bring hope, and renewed energy for the task of reconstruction. Africa is weak in the new economic order known as globalization. But the continent is also weak because it lacks men and women of Nehemiah's stature, people capable of rising up to empower communities and get them to work, people who do not seek their own interest, but rather the welfare of the whole community (2:10).

Tobiah joined in Sanballat's mockery. He claimed the Jews' construction work would crumble because of the materials they were using (**4:3**).

In reaction, Nehemiah prayed what is called an imprecatory prayer, that is, a prayer directed against one's enemies. Similar prayers are found in a number of Psalms (for example, Pss 69:21-27; 79:12; 109:14-15). These prayers should not lead Christians to think that the OT gives them permission to curse anyone. After all, in the book of Proverbs we read, 'If your enemy is hungry, give him food to eat; if he is thirsty, give him water to drink' (Prov 25:21). Nehemiah was not actively bringing a curse on his enemies, but he was committing his cause to God, the righteous judge. He recognized that their opposition to the building was not really directed at him but sprang from their hostility to God, the one who was truly in charge of the work (**4:4-5**).

The Gospel law is a law of love, not of vengeance. Jesus commanded: 'Love your enemies, do good to those who hate you, bless those who curse you, pray for those who mistreat you' (Luke 6:27-28; see also Matt 5:44). In Romans, Paul wrote, 'Bless those who persecute you; bless and do not curse' (Rom 12:14).

Once again, Nehemiah identified with his people in prayer. Despite his own privileged position, he included himself with them when he said, we are despised (**4:4**). This expression is similar to one Hanani used in his report (1:3).

Despite the opposition, the construction work went ahead and all the gaps in the walls were soon being filled (**4:6-7**). The key to the success lies in the words *the people worked with all their heart*. They put their hearts in the work, as we Africans say.

But as the work moved forward, the opposition grew. Arabs, Ammonites and the people of Ashdod joined Sanballat and Tobiah. The enemies' tactics changed too: whereas previously they had merely mocked and expressed contempt for the builders, now they planned an attack to demolish what had been built (**4:8**). They hoped that such an attack would undermine the morale of the builders.

Nehemiah was forced to adopt a different approach to repelling these attacks. People's lives were now in danger, and it was time to take practical steps. Nehemiah did not stop praying (**4:9**), but he also prepared to resist force with force, if that became necessary. His compatriots were becoming discouraged (**4:10**) and fearful (**4:11-12**), but Nehemiah, a man of faith, encouraged them to stand their ground and put their trust in God (**4:13-14**). His words recall the words in Exodus: 'The Lord will fight for you' (Exod 14:14).

The show of force was enough to discourage the enemies' initial attack, and the people returned to work (**4:15**). Confident that God was with them, Nehemiah divided the people into two groups: one to work and the other to stand guard. Those who carried supplies to the builders did so with only one hand because they held a weapon in the other. Nehemiah also set up a warning system with a trumpet to sound the alarm if there was an attack (**4:16-20**).

Nehemiah is an example of a leader who has a clear strategy for handling each new situation. As the opposition changed, so did his response. At first, he relied on prayer and work, then on prayer and a guard, and finally on prayer and weapons and fighters. His strategy, which combined prayer with action, set up a partnership between heaven and earth.

This chapter also speaks of the importance of perseverance. We will always face obstacles as we seek to serve the Lord, but we should not give up or abandon our work. This chapter calls us to pray and act in dependence on God.

5:1-19 Social and Economic Crises

Until now, Nehemiah has only faced external hostility. But in this chapter, he is confronted with internal opposition brought about by a social and economic crisis that rocked the city (**5:1**). Although the construction work on the walls may have resulted in social inequality, it is more likely that the roots of this crisis were present before the construction began. The burden imposed by the work merely accentuated the divisions within the community.

The social crisis took several forms. There was a food shortage, with some people not having enough food for their large families (**5:2**). Famine is a recurring problem in Africa. Until recently, we could grow enough food to feed ourselves, but now we too often have to rely on international charity, with the dependence that entails. In some countries, the climate is responsible for this situation, but for the most part it is due to wars and political unrest that interfere with food production.

The lack of food produced another crisis (5:2). Hungry people complained that they were being obliged to mortgage (or pawn) their belongings (their homes, fields and vineyards) to moneylenders in exchange for food. To their voices were added the voices of those who had to borrow money to pay the heavy taxes collected by the Persians to support the administrative and military needs of their empire (**5:4**).

This swelling volume of complaints begins to sound like a speech on equality: ... *we are of the same flesh and blood as our countrymen and* ... *our sons are as good as theirs* (**5:5**). The Bible did not wait for the Universal Declaration of Human Rights to announce the equality of all!

The people have had to endure indignities themselves, but even worse is what is happening to their children, especially the girls: *some of our daughters have already been enslaved* (5:5). The Hebrew makes it clear that the slavery that these girls are enduring may include sexual abuse (in Esther 7:8, a similar expression is translated 'molest'). They were being expected to provide sexual favours to repay their parents' debt! This type of violence against women is all too common in the wars that take place on every continent. Not only do the women suffer sexual violence, but they and the entire society suffer through the spread of sexually transmitted diseases, including HIV/AIDS. A crisis that may appear to be only social and economic has far-reaching consequences and poses a serious threat to people's lives. Solutions are urgently needed!

Nehemiah has appeared to be a calm man, responding without anger to those who oppose him. But faced with such a crisis, he could not contain himself and became *very angry* (**5:6**). Certain situations rightly elicit a strong response. After the anger, came the solution. He proposed a series of measures to address the problem. First, though, he identified the people truly responsible for these abuses – *the nobles and officials* (**5:7**). He addressed them directly and accused them of injustice and of violating God's law (**5:8-9**). It was behaviour like theirs that had led God to punish the nation and take it into exile in the first place (1:7-8).

Nehemiah then presented his own behaviour as a model for the others. He too was lending money and grain, but he set an example for the other wealthy citizens by not charging interest on these debts. He ordered the nobles and magistrates to restore what they had taken from their fellow citizens (**5:10-11**). Zacchaeus the tax collector made similar restitution when Jesus came to his house (Luke 19:8).

The solution that Nehemiah proposed was accepted. To make sure it was carried out, he made the nobles and officials swear to abide by it before the priests (**5:12-13**).

This crisis reminds us that we are not only fighting against forces from without; the enemy may also be within our ranks. Even when everything seems to be going well, we need to remain vigilant! When Nehemiah started the building project, he had no idea of the crisis that was brewing at the heart of the community. The more victories we score over our external enemies, the more likely it is that the next attack will come from within (see also 1 Cor 10:12).

The verses in **5:15-19** continue the theme of the wise and just use of resources that has been at the heart of this chapter. Nehemiah tells how he gave up the prerogatives and privileges that were his as governor, especially in relation to his own income. Let us preach by example, teach by example, evangelize by example! Such is the great principle that Governor Nehemiah gives us today.

6:1-19 Work Completed Despite Growing Opposition

Chapter 6 starts with the news that the walls have been rebuilt, and all that remains to be done is the installation of the doors (**6:1**). Once again, the opposition changed its target, this time focusing on Nehemiah himself. The enemies remained the same: Sanballat, Tobiah, Geshem and others who resented the growing strength of the Jews (2:10, 19; 3:33; 4:1, 3, 7).

The enemies invited Nehemiah to a meeting without specifying its purpose. They wanted to meet him at *one of the villages on the plain of Ono* (**6:2**). This plain, which is mentioned in 7:37 and in Ezra 2:33, is located north-west of Jerusalem in a neutral area between Samaria and Ashdod. The people of Ashdod had opposed the rebuilding of the walls (4:7). His opponents were thus attempting to lure Nehemiah to a potentially hostile area some distance from Jerusalem. Nehemiah would be in real danger.

The enemies' intentions were left vague, but they may have been planning to assassinate him. Nehemiah was not prepared to run the risk and declined the invitation four times. He did not let them know about his concerns, but excused himself on the grounds that he was busy with the work (**6:3-4**). In face of this uncertain menace, Nehemiah adopted a conciliatory position, even a seemingly naïve one. He needed to find good reasons for declining an invitation from Sanballat, who was an authority figure.

Frustrated, his enemies raised the stakes. This time, they sent a written message (**6:5**). Ordinarily, a sensitive matter such as an accusation of sedition would have only been mentioned in a confidential, sealed letter. Sending an open letter indicated their contempt for Nehemiah and forced him to reply publicly because the letter (and the accusation) was public. Nehemiah was trapped!

The accusation was very serious. According to Sanballat, it was being rumoured that the purpose for constructing the wall was not the protection of Jerusalem but its fortification so that it could launch a rebellion against the king of Persia. Nehemiah was accused of preparing to set himself up as a king (**6:6-7**). Any actions that might destabilize the Persian empire would be viewed with deep suspicion by the Persian authorities.

The enemies had revealed their tactics, and Nehemiah no longer held his peace. He gave them a blunt reply: *you are just making it up out of your head* (**6:8**). He still wisely refrained from accepting their invitation to meet to discuss the rumours.

Nehemiah gave his own reading of what was going on, and closed his analysis with a short but appropriate prayer: *Now strengthen my hands* (**6:9**).

With their plans thwarted yet again, Nehemiah's enemies tried a new approach. This time, they worked through an accomplice and attempted to discredit Nehemiah on the religious level, and thus to disqualify him as a leader of the people. The traitor was Shemaiah, a man about whom we know little beyond his association with Sanballat and Tobiah. He was probably one of the Levites who was also regarded as a prophet (2 Chr 20:14). As such, he would

have had access to the temple and could speak to Nehemiah as a godly man wanting only the best for the governor. Yet what he actually said was a false prophecy intended to trick Nehemiah into going to the temple to save his life (**6:10**).

Even though Shemaiah was supposedly a prophet, Nehemiah used discernment in weighing his proposal. He identified two fundamental reasons why he could not agree to hide in the temple. First, he recognized that it would be shameful for him as governor to run away and hide in the temple, a place of refuge. Such an action could also be interpreted as an admission of guilt (**6:11a**). Second, he recognized that it would be inappropriate for someone like himself to *go into the temple to save his life* (**6:11b**). The law insisted that only those who worked in the temple were allowed to enter the sacred place (Num 18:6-7). King Uzziah had been punished with leprosy because he had entered the holy place of the temple to offer incense (2 Chr 26:16-20). The law of God could not be broken because of a prophecy, even a prophecy intended to save one's life. Nehemiah could not believe that such a prophecy could truly have been sent by God.

The Bible deals with the problem of false prophecy. Even a prophet like Balaam understood that prophecy should not be exchanged for money or any other goods (Num 22:18). Today, the African church also has to deal with the phenomenon of prophecy. Many Christian communities include prophets who reveal the future and hidden things. Unfortunately, sometimes these prophets abuse the trust of church members by uttering false prophecies that contradict the word of God. We can refer to the tests laid out in two OT texts when it comes to discerning whether a prophecy is genuine. The first is whether the prophecy comes true (Deut 18:14-22). But that is not the sole factor to be considered. A prophecy that predicts something which then takes place does not necessarily come from God. Any prophecy that from God must conform to the law of God (Deut 13:1-5).

The episode of Shemaiah's treachery ended with a new prayer by Nehemiah, again beginning with the familiar formula used elsewhere in the book: *Remember … O my God* (1:8; 5:19; 6:14; 13:14, 22, 31). We do not know why this prayer does not contain the name of Shemaiah, but instead mentions the prophetess Noadiah. However, Shemaiah is certainly included among *the rest of the prophets who have been trying to intimidate me* (**6:14**).

Three other prophetesses are mentioned in the OT: Miriam, Moses' sister (Exod 15:20), Deborah (Judg 4:4) and Huldah (2 Kgs 22:14; 2 Chr 34:22). Contrary to widely held opinion, women were not excluded from religious life. Even if there were no priestesses in the OT, women still played an important part in various areas of religious life. Our current practice seems to contradict the Bible in this area. Women have often been excluded from certain ministries at the heart of the African church. There is, of course, considerable

CONFLICT MANAGEMENT

On 21 November 2005 over six million Kenyan voters went to the polls in a national referendum to adopt or reject a new draft constitution. This constitution provoked heated debate and deep disagreements. But rather than resorting to bullets to resolve this national constitutional conflict, Kenyans took up their ballots and voted. What a welcome development in the political history of a continent riddled by internal insurrections, border conflicts, violent *coups d'etat* and civil unrest! If other African nations learn from Kenya's example, many innocent lives will be saved and we will see progress, peace and prosperity.

This example reminds us that conflict itself is less important than how we resolve it. For conflict is inevitable in any ongoing relationship, whether at home, at work, in business, nationally or internationally. It arises wherever some incompatibility between opinions and principles results in serious disagreement or argument. At its worst, it escalates into a prolonged armed struggle.

But conflicts do not only arise between people. We also experience conflict within ourselves, when we go through an inward personal struggle or restlessness of the soul. Such struggles can be thought of in terms of the healthy competition in which athletes do their utmost to develop all their skills in order to excel at what they do (1 Tim 6:12; 2 Tim 4:7; and Hebrews 12:1).

The pressures of the external and internal conflicts are often made worse by what we could call 'foreign intervention': we face not only human adversaries and our own selves, but also spiritual foes (Col 2:1; Phil 1:30; 1 Thess 2:2; Eph 6:12; Heb 10:32).

Given the spiritual dimension to conflict and the unhappiness that conflict can generate, we might be tempted to assume that all conflicts are bad and should be avoided at all costs. But this is not the case. Indifference to what is going on is a far greater danger than conflict itself when people care deeply about something (Rev 3:16). Spiritual conflicts within and demonic confrontation without have a way of keeping us alert so that we do not slip into complacency. Conflict also spotlights problems that require attention. It may force clarification of issues and challenge leaders to question the status quo and search for better solutions. Good handling of the conflict between the Hellenized Jews and the Hebrew Jews in Jerusalem resulted in the exponential growth of the early church (Acts 6:1-7).

But when conflicts are not well handled, they can seriously damage a relationship, divide a nation (as is the case in many African nations), destroy an organization and demoralize the people involved. Improper handling of the conflict between Barnabas and Paul in regard to John Mark led to the division of their missionary team (see Acts 15:36-41).

Management is an art that can be learned and a skill that can be acquired. When we manage a conflict, we simply organize, regulate and take charge of it in order to make it serve a good cause, whether that be in a business, a household, a team, an institution or in one's career. While this may not be easy to do, the results are worthwhile.

In resolving any conflict, there are three key questions to ask: What are we agreeing or disagreeing about? Why are we agreeing or disagreeing? And how can we get past this and move forward?

In answering these questions, we need to keep the following principles in mind:

- *Honest communication.* Silence and isolation only deepen misunderstanding, which fuels conflict. In Genesis 13:1-18, Abram did not gloss over the potential for quarrels between his herdsmen and those of Lot. He discussed it openly with Lot and developed an appropriate strategy to deal with it.

- *Getting beneath surface issues and unseen motives.* Often the apparent cause of a conflict is not the real issue. Instead the conflict is rooted in people's underlying motives and beliefs, which they may not have clearly identified. We see an example of this when Isaac was driven away from one well after another in Genesis 26:19-32. On the surface, the conflict was about water supplies, but Abimelech's meeting with Isaac revealed that the real problem was that the local people of Gerar felt threatened by Isaac's increasing prosperity and power.

- *Negotiation.* The best way to find peace is through a process of give and take, in which neither party to the conflict insists on being the winner. The events of 1 Kings 12 show the disastrous consequences of Rehoboam's unwillingness to negotiate.

- *External intervention.* The parties involved in a conflict may be so caught up in it that they have difficulty talking to one another and reaching any agreement. In such a case the assistance of a neutral person such as a marriage counsellor or an organization like the United Nations may be sought. When Paul and Barnabas became involved in a 'sharp dispute' about circumcision, they and their opponents took the case before the Council at Jerusalem (Acts 15:1-2).

- *Divine intervention.* The majority of conflicts among believers involve an unseen malevolent spiritual influence. Thus in resolving them we need to involve God by seeking his mind in his word and praying for his assistance. This is how the Council at Jerusalem resolved the crisis that would have permanently divided the church into Jews and Gentiles (Acts 15:23-29).

These five principles can be applied as we prayerfully follow the Lord's prescription for resolving conflicts among believers (Matt 18:15-17). He tells us first to approach the other party directly but privately, seeking honest communication. If there is no willingness to negotiate, we can then seek external help in the form of two or three witnesses who can help to uncover the real sources of the disagreement and suggest compromises or creative solutions to the problem. If all these steps fail, we are to take the conflict to a larger body, the church, for its mediation. If the conflict persists, the root of the problem must be identified as a sinful attitude, which means that the party who refuses to work for reconciliation must be treated as an unbeliever. This last step may involve temporary separation, but we should continue loving and praying for the one who is being disciplined.

Tokunboh Adeyemo

variation from one denomination to another: in some churches, the ordination of women is accepted, while in others they are not even permitted to pray in public.

The work on the wall was completed in just fifty-two days (**6:15**). This remarkable achievement was probably due to the large work force. Nehemiah's enemies were amazed that all their attempts to thwart the project had failed (**6:16**). They finally understood that God's hand had been evident in all that had happened. The glory was not Nehemiah's, but God's.

A third and final attempt at treachery is alluded to in **6:17-19**. Tobiah's spies were keeping him informed about the situation in Jerusalem and the progress of the work. Even within the community of those who had returned from Babylon, there were influential agents of the enemy.

7:1-73 Repopulation of Jerusalem and Judah

The construction of the walls of Jerusalem was not an end in itself. Nehemiah's aim was to reunite the people. His enemies had suggested that he wanted to build the walls in order to unite the people for an attempt to secede, but this was not the case. Nehemiah was only interested in the well-being of the Israelites (2:10). In keeping focused on this purpose, he is again a model for some churches, where the administration, the hierarchy and the organization have become ends in themselves, and the leaders have forgotten that their objective is to serve their community.

Chapter 7 falls into two parts. The first deals with measures for protecting the community (7:1-3), and the second deals with the resettlement of Jerusalem and Judah and includes details from a census of the population (7:4-72).

Though the construction work was finished, Nehemiah's mission had barely begun. As governor of the province, he recognized the need for vigilance and watchfulness, and thus made important appointments to ensure the security of the city. Many years before, David had appointed gatekeepers from among the Levites to guard the entrances to the temple (1 Chr 26:1-19), and now the combined reference in this context to the *gatekeepers and the singers and the Levites* suggests that these temple personnel were assigned the additional task of guarding the gates of the city (**7:1**). It may have seemed a natural extension of their existing responsibilities, particularly in the absence of a local regular army.

It is possible that the same Hanani who first informed Nehemiah about the disastrous situation of Jerusalem (1:2-3) was appointed to oversee the Levites and assume the function of 'mayor' of the city (**7:2a**). If so, he was certainly someone who had already shown his concern for the city. It is also possible that this Hanani, a member of Nehemiah's family, is the same person as the Hananiah, referred to as *the commander of the citadel,* although they may have been two different men with the same name.

Hanani was appointed to his position because of his personal qualities. He was a man of *integrity* (certainly towards Nehemiah and the king of Persia) and one who *feared God* (**7:2b**). This raises a sensitive issue as regards the poor management that has ruined many churches and Christian ministries in Africa. Too often, people are appointed to positions because of favouritism, without consideration of their real competence. We should never allow family, regional or ethnic considerations to take precedence over aptitude and integrity.

Nehemiah issued security orders regarding the times for opening and closing the city gates. Normally, these would have been opened at sunrise, but Nehemiah ordered that they remain shut until the sun was high. This measure limited the time the gates were open. He also ordered that residents be appointed to guard the walls, preferably in the immediate vicinity of their own homes (**7:3**).

With the end of the construction, it would have been easy to relax, but vigilance was still necessary. The same is true for Christians, for the Apostle Peter warns of the need for constant watchfulness: *Be self-controlled and alert. Your enemy the devil prowls around like a roaring lion looking for someone to devour* (1 Pet 5:8).

The walls were up, but the city still needed more inhabitants, for as **7:4** explains, *there were few people in it.* Nehemiah knew that God had promised to bring the people back (1:9) and he sees God as directing his moves to repopulate it (**7:5a**). He used the results from an earlier census to guarantee equitable distribution of land, while respecting pre-exilic property rights (**7:5b**). This point is supported by **7:73,** which concludes the list of the people who had returned to Jerusalem. There it is stated that the Jews *settled in their own towns.* This expression means that each Israelite lived again on ancestral land.

With a few variations, the list in **7:6-72** is the same as the one found in Ezra 2:1-70.

8:1-10:39 Renewing the Covenant

8:1-18 Reading the Law and the Feast of Tabernacles

The theme of the resettlement of Jerusalem is now interrupted until the start of chapter 11. Nehemiah had taken on the huge double task of rebuilding the wall and repopulating Jerusalem, yet these actions would have no meaning if they did not have a religious dimension. So Ezra the scribe comes on the scene for the first time in this book and Nehemiah fades into the background for a while. He does this because he recognized that as a layman he had no real authority in the religious realm. This same point had been made earlier when he refused to enter the temple because he had neither the right nor the law's authority to do so (6:11). God's work on the African continent sometimes suffers because leaders lack Nehemiah's humility. They think that they have all the gifts and can do everything, and that nothing can be done without them. Nehemiah, by contrast, knew his limitations and respected them.

The whole of chapter 8 is dominated by the theme of God's law. The first part deals with the solemn reading of the law under the leadership of the scribe Ezra (8:1-12), and the second with the celebration of the Feast of Tabernacles (8:13-18).

Neither rebuilding the wall nor resettling Jerusalem could guarantee the religious rebirth of the people of God after the exile. The exile had been a punishment for their lack of respect for God's law (1:6-10), and now the people had to demonstrate their obedience to this law if they were to enjoy divine blessing and a new quality of life.

It is a sign of their restored unity that *all the people assembled as one man* (**8:1a**; Ezra 3:1). If only the Christian church presented the same image to the world! Different denominations often work as if we are involved in a competition, rather than all serving the same master, the Lord Jesus Christ. Our challenge is not to form one great church, but rather to be united in love despite doctrinal and denominational labels.

We do not know who organized this gathering, but it is clear that it was the people who spontaneously requested Ezra to read the law to them (**8:1b**). The choice of Ezra as the reader was not accidental. As a scribe, he was expected to have devoted himself to the study, practice and teaching of the law of God. And Ezra had certainly done this (Ezra 7:10). The request for a public reading of the law was understandable, for at that time not many people were literate and only a small group would have had the privilege of having access to a written document. It was only with the invention of the printing press that it became possible for ordinary people to have access to the written word.

Ezra read before an assembly composed of men, women *and all who were able to understand,* that is, children who had reached a suitable age (**8:2**; Deut 31:11-12). The mention of women is significant. They were not excluded from the assembly.

The date on which this assembly took place was *the first day of the seventh month* according to the Babylonian calendar. In the Jewish calendar, this was the first day of the month of Tishri (September-October in our calendar) in which the Jews celebrated the great Day of Atonement ('Yom Kippur') as well as the Feast of Tabernacles ('Sukkot') (Lev 23:26-44). It was also the first month in their year, meaning that the first day of Tishri was equivalent to our New Year's Day in January. It was thus a highly significant day on which to meet. This gathering near the newly completed wall marked the beginning of a new era. The people were well aware of this, as the sealing of the new covenant in chapter 10 indicates.

Ezra and those who were assisting him read aloud from the *Book of the Law of Moses* (**8:1c, 3-5**). This may have been the whole Pentateuch, or just one of its books, such as Deuteronomy. The reading lasted from morning until midday. Despite the length of this reading, the people stood and *listened attentively.*

The reading of the law started with words of praise to God, to which the people responded with *Amen! Amen!,* which means 'So be it' (**8:6**). The Hebrew word 'amen' comes from a root that means 'solid' or 'firm', and testifies that listeners agree with what they have just heard. Unfortunately, it has become so overused in our Christian assemblies that it has lost its significance. When we meet a fellow-believer on the road, we now say, 'amen' as if it were a greeting. In church, the liturgy is punctuated with 'amens' even at times when no assent is required. Many preachers now use 'amen' to introduce a pause during their message before moving on to a new point. Moderation is important in everything – including the use of 'amen'!

The reading of the law was accompanied by explanations of what was being read (**8:7-8a**). These explanations were needed because most of the exiles spoke Aramaic and did not understand the Hebrew in which the law was written. The care taken to help them understand it reminds us of the importance of the translation and distribution of the Bible. People need to read God's word in a language that is familiar to them.

But reading or hearing the word and understanding it are two different things. Thus explanations were also needed to help the people understand what the law meant. That is why this section is full of words like *understand* (8:2, 3) *making it clear and giving the meaning* (**8:8b**) and *understood* (8:12). While it is true that the word of God speaks directly to us, it still needs to be interpreted and explained. One of the reasons there is so much religious heresy on our continent (with so many unfortunate consequences) is that many think that they do not need to study the word of God before dispensing it to others. Such people mistakenly assume that all that is required to understand God's word is openness to the Holy Spirit. But normally we benefit from the help of others. This is illustrated in the Acts of the Apostles, when Philip, one of the seven deacons named in Acts 2, asked the Ethiopian eunuch who was reading in the book of Isaiah: 'Do you understand what you are reading?' (Acts 6:5; 8:30). That good question opened the door to guided study.

The scribes of the OT, who were the learned men of the time, were above all permanent students of the law. To guarantee the faithful transmission of this law, they were trained in schools attached to the temple. Pastors should be equally concerned that they are understanding and faithfully transmitting God's word.

When we truly understand God's word, we will always respond to it. The people's response was clear: they were plunged into mourning. They wept while listening because they became aware of their own guilt (**8:9**).

Ezra and Nehemiah are clearly presented as contemporaries in 8:9 (and 12:26). Together with the Levites, they reminded the people that this was intended to be a day of celebration, not of lamentation (Lev 23:24; Deut 31:9-13). The call to feast was accompanied by an encouragement to share within the community: *send some to those who have nothing prepared* (**8:10-12**).

The leaders of the post-exilic community were acutely aware of social problems. Nehemiah had addressed some of these problems that were ruining the society (5:1-19). The African Christian community needs to redirect its gaze toward community solidarity and to seek to cure the gangrene of the present – individualism and a selfish search for personal success. We need to rediscover the sense of community that was present in the early church (Acts 2:42-47).

On the second day, only the heads of families, the priests and the Levites gathered to hear Ezra continue to read and explain the law for the benefit of this smaller but influential audience (**8:13**). They were still seeking to rediscover the law that God gave through Moses. As they listened, they learned that they were supposed to observe the Feast of Tabernacles (**8:14**), mentioned in Leviticus 23:34-43. Though this was an agricultural celebration (which was why it was also called the Feast of Firstfruits), the Israelites were required to live in tents and booths as a reminder of their time in the desert. Although this feast had been rediscovered by the elite, it became a feast for all the people. A proclamation was issued in Jerusalem and in all the villages, calling on everyone to celebrate it for seven days as the ancient law prescribed (**8:15-16**).

The reference to days of Joshua in **8:17** suggests that the Jewish community regarded their return from exile as a historic and theological parallel to the return from Egypt.

During the feast, the law was read each day (**8:18**). Such reading of the word along with its systematic explanation is not often part of our liturgy. Of course, the word is read and preached each week, but do we really spend the time needed

to understand it in depth? Without a clear understanding of the word, we cannot hope for perfect obedience. In addition to gathering to listen to preaching on Sunday, the community should have the opportunity to meet together on other occasions. Thus Bible study groups are to be encouraged in our congregations.

9:1-37 Fasting and Confession of Sins

According to Leviticus 23:27-28, the New Year's festival was to be followed on the tenth of the same month by Yom Kippur, the Day of Atonement. The Israelites, who were still rediscovering what the law commanded, had not celebrated this at that time, but had instead celebrated the Feast of Tabernacles. But the new gathering that took place *on the twenty-fourth day of the same* month (**9:1**), even though it was fourteen days late, was an appropriate expression of national repentance for sin. The atmosphere is totally different from that of chapter 8. Then there had been rejoicing; now there is mourning. This mourning had begun in 8:9, but had been set aside for a while because it was inappropriate at a time of celebration (8:9).

This chapter deals with preparation for the renewal of the covenant that will take place in chapter 10. It begins with a time of confession and fasting (9:1-6), which is followed by a long prayer of repentance (9:7-37).

As the people gathered once again, they were in mourning, symbolized by the ritual wearing of sackcloth and the sprinkling of dust on head and body (9:1; see also Jonah 3:5, 8; 1 Chr 21:16). These signs of humility and repentance are similar to mourning customs in Africa.

We do not know exactly what led to this new assembly. The fact that **9:2** speaks of their separation from foreigners has led some commentators to think that this chapter follows on the events described in Ezra 10. However, that chapter in Ezra speaks specifically of marriages with foreign women, which the text in Nehemiah does not mention.

The ceremony was introduced by the reading of the law for three or four hours (**9:3**); after which the people begin their actual confession. The Levites who, on Ezra and Nehemiah's prompting, had previously exhorted the people to rejoice (8:11) now played another important role: they called the people to prayer (**9:4-5**).

The prayer from 9:5b-37 is one of the longest prayers of confession recorded in the Bible and has been incorporated in the liturgies of some churches. It begins by presenting the history of the people of God from the creation (**9:6**) up to Nehemiah's time, with references to Abraham (**9:7-8**), the years spent in Egypt (**9:9**), the exodus and the conquest of Canaan (**9:10-25**), and the time of the judges, the kings and prophets (**9:26-31**). This history emphasized the ongoing faithfulness of God and his compassion, when faced with people who were always rebellious and disobedient.

Verses **9:32-35** form the heart of this prayer. They concern the present generation and its repentance of its own failures. The contrast between the faithfulness of God (*you*) and the disobedience of the people (*we*) is emphasized. The prayer ends abruptly on a deep note of despair (**9:36-37**).

With their alternating sadness and joy, rejoicing and fasting (8:9, 17; 9:1-2), chapters 8 and 9 offer a model for the liturgy of the African church. This alternation is in marked contrast with the present liturgy of many communities in which only dances and rejoicing fill the worship. We should rejoice in God's grace, but at the same time we need to be aware of our failures and to allow ourselves to be in an attitude of mourning.

9:38-10:39 Renewal of the Covenant with God

The repentance in chapter 9 (*all this* – **9:38**) is followed by the renewal of the covenant as the people make a commitment to follow the law of God. Even though the word 'covenant' does not appear in this chapter, the Hebrew verb in the phrase translated *making a binding agreement* is one normally used to signify entering into a covenant (**10:1**).

The commitment to the law was made in writing, in a document on which all the important officials stamped their seals to indicate that they were bound to obey it. The names of those who took part in this ceremony are listed in 10:1-27. Curiously, we do not find Ezra's name in this list, despite the key role he played in chapter 8. As indicated in 9:38, the signatories fell into three categories: *our leaders, our Levites and our priests*. Evidently, those who signed the agreement did so in the name of the groups to which they belonged (**10:28-29**).

Next come details on the commitment they were making. The first pledge, to avoid mixed marriages, represented the culmination of Ezra's ministry (**10:30**). The mission he had been given by Artaxerxes was to make the law of God known and to ensure that it was followed (Ezra 7:25-26). In Ezra 10, he addressed what the law had to say about mixed marriages. His teaching and this pledge involve a reapplication of the ancient law in the Pentateuch that forbade the Israelites from marrying any of the Hittites, Girgashites, Amorites, Canaanites, Perizzites, Hivites and Jebusites (Deut 7:1-6). These peoples were no longer in existence during the Persian period, but the scribes recognized that the law now applied to *the peoples around us* (10:30), that is, those who were outside the Jewish community and who had been moved into the area by the Assyrians and Babylonians (2 Kgs 17:24). Mixed marriages would be a threat to a people who were still searching for their identity in a multicultural empire. It is important to note that the goal of this law is the preservation of the faith, not the purity of any racial or ethnic group (Col 3:11).

Although the Apostle Paul does not specifically mention mixed marriage, he does tell believers not to 'be yoked together with unbelievers' (2 Cor 6:14), an instruction that seems also to apply to marriage. Marriage is a serious commitment for life. When a couple want to give their love precedence over their faith when making the decision to marry, people will often argue that after the marriage, the Christian partner will lead the other to faith. There is little likelihood of that! If you cannot lead your partner to faith while you are engaged, you are unlikely to succeed later.

The second pledge made by the people concerned respect for the Sabbath, Israel's holy day (**10:31**). At a time when many foreigners lived in and around Jerusalem, the market was open even on the Sabbath day. But the Jewish community now committed itself to buying nothing on that day, as an extension of the principle laid down in Exodus 20:8-11. Respect for the Sabbath went hand in hand with respect for the sabbatical year, which occurred every seven years. During this year, all debts were cancelled (Deut 15:1-2).

Today, Christians no longer observe the Jewish Sabbath, which extends from Friday evening until Saturday evening. Instead we observe Sunday, the day of Christ's resurrection, as a day of rest. However, we hear Christians asking whether they can work or buy or sell on Sunday. In answering this question, we need to remember that observing the Sabbath or Sunday is more than just an opportunity for physical rest. It is also an act of faith. Those who rest are confessing that they do not live only for work, but for God.

Other commitments that were made concerned the temple tax (**10:32-33**; Exod 30:13); the wood for sacrifices (**10:34**) and the firstfruit offering (**10:35**). The 'firstfruit' was regarded as including all firstborn males, who thus belonged to the Lord (**10:36**). But while firstborn animals were sacrificed, a firstborn son was not. Instead an animal was offered in his place (Exod 34:19-20). The people also promised to pay a tithe of their crops to the Levites (**10:37**; Num 18:21). The Levites, in turn, were obliged to give a tithe of the tithe, as laid down by the law (**10:38**; Num 18:26).

The covenant document ended with a firm commitment by the people not to abandon God's house, that is, the temple (**10:39**). That this was a real danger is clear from the words of prophets such as Haggai, Zechariah and Malachi, who ministered at about that time (Hag 1:1-2:9; Zech 6:9-15; Mal 1:6-14).

This chapter describes a practice that could be useful for African Christian communities: the renewing of commitments. Our Christian commitment always needs to be revitalized; if not, it will fade. Those who accepted the Lord and became involved in his work many years ago need this sort of renewal. What is being spoken of here is not the type of call issued during an evangelistic campaign or after a sermon on commitment, but a ceremony in which Christians are led to remember God's faithfulness throughout their ministry and to renew their commitment to the work of the Lord.

11:1–13:31 Final Steps in the Recovery

11:1-12:26 More on Repopulation

In chapter 11, the book returns to the theme of resettlement, picking up where it broke off in chapter 7. There we were told that although the city 'was large and spacious', it was underpopulated – 'there were few people in it, and the houses had not yet been rebuilt.' (7:4). Chapter 11 tells the story of the repopulation of Jerusalem and the resettlement of those who had returned from exile.

Two approaches were used to resettle Jerusalem. First, the exiles decided that a 'tithe' (one-tenth) of the population would settle there, and then drew lots to see who these would be (11:1). Casting lots was one means used in Israel to learn God's will. Joshua had used this method at the first settlement of Canaan (Josh 14:2; Prov 16:33).

In addition, some volunteers chose of their own free will to reside in Jerusalem (11:2). In the Hebrew, it is clear that the first group were described in religious terms as a tithe, and another religious term was used to describe the volunteers, the word normally used for freewill offerings. That is why the volunteers were *commended* by the people.

The text then proceeds to list the people who settled in Jerusalem (11:3). This list is similar to the list of the first inhabitants of Jerusalem after the exile found in 1 Chronicles 9:3-21. However, the list in Nehemiah is shorter. The list covers only the three tribes that constituted the heart of the post-exilic community: Judah, Benjamin and Levi.

The descendants of Judah (11:4-6) were related to King David, and are thus mentioned first (1 Chr 9:3-6). They are described as *able men*. The language is military and reflects a concern for the security and defence of Jerusalem.

The descendants of Benjamin (11:7-9a) were related to King Saul, and were those who had remained faithful to the kingdom of Judah (1 Chr 9:7-9; 2 Chr 11:1). This tribe seems to have exercised a more administrative role (11:9b).

The list of *the priests* and other temple personnel (11:10-23) is the longest, indicating that they were the most important group, and thus the importance of the temple in this community. Their ministry of music and of guarding the temple dated back to the time of David (11:17, 19, 22-23; 1 Chr 15; 2 Chr 5:4). This continuity was extremely important, as was noted in the commentary on Ezra. For the first time in the book of Nehemiah, Jerusalem is called *the holy city* (11:18).

Despite his interest in Jerusalem, the author does not forget the population outside the city. This list focuses on the same three tribes mentioned in the list of the inhabitants of Jerusalem: Judah (11:24-30), Benjamin (11:31-34) and Levi (11:36).

Following the list of the priests and Levites who lived in Jerusalem (11:10-23), the author gives a full list of all the priests and Levites going back to the days of Zerubbabel

and Jeshua, the two leaders of the first wave of exiled Jews who returned to Jerusalem immediately after Cyrus' decree (12:1-26a; Ezra 2:1-2). The author is concerned to maintain continuity between the present generation, in the time of Nehemiah and Ezra, and the first community that had returned to Jerusalem at an earlier date. That is why the list begins with a reference to the returnees under the leadership of Zerubbabel and Jeshua and ends with a reference to the new leaders: Nehemiah, the governor and Ezra, the priest and scribe (12:26b).

The Jews who returned from exile carefully preserved the genealogical record of their ancestors. Sadly, the African church has not been as conscientious about preserving its history. The names of the African pioneers, pastors and evangelists who laboured to evangelize this continent, have vanished without a trace. If the younger generation does not turn its attention to recording this information, the African church may suffer a regrettable lack of knowledge of its roots.

12:27-43 Dedication of the Walls of Jerusalem

This section is the high point of the book of Nehemiah. It reports the re-establishment of Jerusalem as the religious centre of the nation. At the same time, it signals the success of Nehemiah's mission, despite opposition. The work has been completed. We remember the mockery of the enemies: 'What are these feeble Jews doing? Will they restore their wall? Will they offer sacrifices? ... Can they bring the stones back to life from those heaps of rubble – burned as they are?' (4:2). The dedication of the walls is the answer to each of these mocking questions. The city was restored and sacrifices were offered.

There were two important steps in the preparations for dedicating the walls. First, all the Levites were called together to lead the celebration (12:27). The Levites' responsibilities included serving as musicians who led the people in praise and thanksgiving (12:24) hence their presence at the dedication was essential. (David had called them together for a similar purpose when the ark of the covenant was carried to Jerusalem –1 Chr 15:16-24.) But many of them lived in the villages around Jerusalem (12:28-29). They came to the temple when it was their turn to be on duty and then returned home. There were not enough Levites actually living in Jerusalem to perform the dedication ceremony, hence the need to summon the other Levites to the city.

The second step in the preparation was ritual purification. The priests and Levites were purified first, and they purified the people and then the walls (12:30). The method of purification is not indicated, but it is likely that the purification of the religious leaders included such things as ritual washings, abstaining from sex, laundering of clothing and making of sacrifices (Exod 19:10-15). The laity were probably required to wash their clothes and their bodies (or certain parts of their bodies). The walls were probably purified by some symbolic actions such as sprinkling. Many years earlier, King Hezekiah had purified the temple after King Ahaz defiled it (2 Chr 28:21, 25; 29:3-24). The rebuilt walls needed similar purification because the dedication ceremony would symbolically transfer what the people had built into the hands of the holy God (even if God had been the chief architect of this work – 6:16). The dedication would make God the owner of the object dedicated.

This ceremony is described in detail in 12:31-43. The people were divided into two groups, each arranged in the same order. Each group was led by seven priests and Levite musicians. The two groups set off from the same point but marched in opposite directions in a procession along the top of the ramparts until they met again in an open space opposite the temple. There, many sacrifices were offered and all those present, including the women and children, rejoiced. The joy on this occasion is evident in the fact that *joy* and variations of 'rejoice' are used four times in **12:43** alone. This verse sets the seal on the success of Nehemiah's mission. He had come to Jerusalem to 'seek the welfare of the people' (2:10), and the people were now rejoicing before the temple. Through perseverance, prayer and wisdom, he had reached his goal.

We always experience joy when we successfully complete a task – but unfortunately, we do not often see this in Africa. Our cities and villages, and even our churches, are full of unfinished projects. Church buildings and pastors' homes sit unfinished; projects intended for the good of the community are abandoned for lack of leaders of Nehemiah's calibre. We need more leaders like him, who will place their trust in God and persevere despite difficulties and opposition.

12:44-13:31 Nehemiah's Other Reforms

In the thirty-second year of King Artaxerxes, several years after the rededication of the walls, Nehemiah returned to Babylon, which he had left twelve years earlier (5:14). We do not know the purpose of this trip. Had he been recalled because of the accusations of Tobiah and others? Was his term as governor completed? Whatever the case, Nehemiah needed new permission to return to Jerusalem (**13:6-7a**).

On his return, he found that in his absence things had changed. The final section of the book of Nehemiah is devoted to the reforms he undertook to correct the abuses that had arisen. There is a strong link between his actions here and the commitments made in chapter 10 after the reading of the law by Ezra. These commitments are now addressed one after the other. We can thus state that Nehemiah came back to enforce the law dictated by Ezra. Ezra, the priest and scribe, had been invested with the emperor's authority to see that God's law was respected (Ezra 7:14-26),

so in reinforcing these measures, Nehemiah was not going against the law of the empire.

The administrative procedures discussed in 12:44-47 are best understood in the context of 13:10-14, and thus this passage will be discussed there.

Despite the expression *on that day* (**13:1a**), it is not certain that the events of **13:1b-3** occurred immediately after the ceremony of dedication. What is clear is that they follow after a reading of *the Book of Moses*. Although this expression could refer to the entire Pentateuch, here it refers specifically to Deuteronomy, for it is in that book that we find the statement that Ammonites and Moabites are to be excluded from the assembly of the Lord (Deut 23:3-6). Accordingly, a decision was made to exclude all foreigners from *the assembly of God*, that is, from the worshipping community (13:3). The issue of divorcing foreign wives is only addressed later (13:23).

Part of the background to this decision may be the behaviour of Tobiah, the great enemy of Nehemiah, who was an Ammonite (2:10). During Nehemiah's absence and with the complicity of a priest named Eliashib, Tobiah had settled into a large room in the temple reserved especially for the grain offerings destined for the Levites and priests (**13:4-5**). Nehemiah was not a man to tolerate such a thing. He immediately put an end to this desecration of the temple. He did this without hesitating, seeking an intermediate solution, or compromising. That room was reserved for a specific purpose and no one, not even Tobiah, could change that fact. Nehemiah immediately restored the room to its original purpose (**13:7b-9**).

Steps had been taken to permanently guarantee the provision of clergy and services for the temple (**12:44-46**). At one time, the Persian king had provided for their needs (11:23), but that arrangement would not have continued indefinitely. As in Zerubbabel's time, the Israelites would need to provide for the needs of the Levites. The Levites, in turn, would give a tithe of the tithe they received to the priests (**12:47**). Maintaining the temple services would enable the temple to function as it had in the golden days of Israel under David and Solomon (12:45-56).

The tithe promised to the Levites (10:37; 12:44-47) had been neglected during Nehemiah's absence (**13:10**). Tobiah's presence may have been one of the causes of this neglect. Nehemiah rebuked the officials for allowing God's house to be abandoned. He clearly and unmistakably reminded them of the commitment the Israelites had made: 'We will not neglect the house of our God' (10:39). In spite of that promise, the Levites had abandoned their posts. Nehemiah gathered the Levites to remind them of their responsibilities. The people also brought the tithes that were due (**13:11-12**).

To guarantee good management of the storerooms, Nehemiah appointed supervisors (**13:13**; 12:44). Their calibre should be noted: *these men were considered trustworthy.* The ability to inspire confidence is certainly a quality that we expect of a leader. The African continent is passing through a severe crisis of confidence in which scepticism reigns and the churches are not spared. We no longer know to whom we may entrust the money or the goods of the church because sometimes those in charge have diverted them from their intended use. Reading the book of Nehemiah should prompt us to exert more control in this area.

The amount of space given to the question of the Sabbath shows that its observance had become an important issue for the Jews who had returned to Jerusalem. The commitment made in 10:32 had not been kept. Jerusalem's position in the Persian Empire meant that it was open to people of other nations, who did not respect the holiness of the Sabbath as the law of Moses required. The Jews were tempted to do likewise, and were working and selling that day. It was also the day on which the people of Tyre, who lived on the coast, came to sell fish to the inhabitants (**13:15-16**).

Nehemiah reminded the Jewish leaders that non-observance of the Sabbath was one of the reasons for the destruction of Jerusalem and the exile (**13:17-18**). He then took practical steps to stop commerce on that day. He set guards to watch the gates on the evening when the Sabbath began so no one could bring in goods for sale, and he ordered the Levite gatekeepers to ensure that the law was respected (**13:19-22**).

Marriage to foreign women continued to be a serious threat to the community. This issue had been treated at length in Ezra 9-10. At the renewal of the covenant, the people had promised: 'We promise not to give our daughters in marriage to the peoples around us or take their daughters for our sons' (10:30). But because Judah was part of the Persian Empire, the Jews had contact with many nations and multicultural marriages had become common (**13:23-24**). Such marriages may even have been undertaken for political or material gain.

These unions were a threat to the integrity of the Jewish faith, for there was always the danger that the women would win their husbands over to their own non-Jewish faith (see also commentary on 10:31). Nehemiah reminded the people that Solomon's foreign wives had dragged him into idolatry (**13:25-27**; 1 Kgs 11). The consequence of his sin had been the splitting up of the Jewish nation. Women from the very nations mentioned in the book of Nehemiah, Ammon and Moab, were among Solomon's wives (1 Kgs 11:1).

In Ezra 10:18-44, it was noted that even the priests, the keepers of the law, were sometimes in mixed marriages. This practice, which defiled the priesthood, had not ceased

(**13:29-30**). So Nehemiah took action, even against such important people as Joiada, a grandson of the high priest, Eliashib (13:28). Nehemiah drove him away because of his marriage to a foreign wife, none other than the daughter of the Horonite Sanballat, a fierce enemy of Nehemiah. This action also got rid of a possible enemy agent.

The last chapter of the book of Nehemiah focuses on the need to remain vigilant to ensure that the commitments made in chapter 10 were kept. We, too, should reflect on the various commitments we have made. Earlier in the chapter, the issue of confidence was mentioned (13:13). Confidence is linked to keeping commitments. When commitments are broken, confidence evaporates. The financial weakness of the African church is in part due to broken commitments. We meet at conventions and make decisions and take on commitments, but afterwards too few Christians act on these decisions. When collections are taken up, men and women promise to give substantial sums in order to enhance the prestige of the group to which they belong, but then they do not deliver on what they promised! The book of Nehemiah reminds us that we should take our commitments very seriously.

African reconstruction cannot be successful without God. That is why it is worth noting that the book ends with the words, *Remember me with favour, O my God* (**13:31**; see also 13:14; 22; 29). In 1:8, Nehemiah had asked God to 'remember' his words to Moses when he was appealing to God to act to change a situation. At the end of the book, however, he is simply seeking God's blessing. He has fulfilled the mission he was sent to achieve. Paul says much the same thing when he triumphantly ends his last letter to Timothy with the words, 'I have fought the good fight, I have finished the race, I have kept the faith. Now there is in store for me the crown of righteousness, which the Lord, the righteous judge, will award to me on that day' (2 Tim 4:7-8). Paul was facing death, but Nehemiah may also have been asking God for his guidance and support as he turns to the next task that God will have for him to do. That task was not recorded for posterity, yet we can be confident that Nehemiah carried it out faithfully before the Lord.

Nupanga Weanzana

Further Reading

Brown, Raymond. *The Message of Nehemiah: God's Servant in a Time of Change.* BST. Downers Grove, Ill: InterVarsity Press, 1998.

Rossier, H. L. *Ezra, Nehemiah, Esther.* H.L. Rossier Commentaries. Sunbury, Pa: Believers Bookshelf, 2003. Also available at http://www.biblecentre.org/commentaries.

ESTHER

The book of Esther tells a fascinating story that has all the drama of a good novel. It gives insight into human nature and current life. It introduces us to three outstanding characters: a beautiful heroine who saves the day; a hero who saves the king's life; and a villain, rotten to the core, whose plot is discovered and foiled. This book is a favourite in Jewish communities, where it is read every year at Purim.

The book is unique in being one of only two books in the OT named after a woman (the other is Ruth). More significantly, it is the only book of the Bible in which the name of God is not mentioned. Nor does it mention prayer. Yet its running theme is the sovereignty of God working quietly to shape events and protect his people. The lack of mention of God's name may imply that God was not directly speaking to the Israelites during their exile. He had hidden himself, and revealed himself only through his providence.

Early Jewish commentators had difficulty categorizing the book of Esther. Did it belong among the books of the law because it gave guidance on how to observe Purim? Or was it simply a history? Or did it belong in both groups? Christians, too, have not been certain what to do with it. After all, most Christians do not observe Purim. Even today there is some debate about the genre of this book.

The events recorded in the book took place in the capital city of the Persian Empire early in the reign of King Xerxes (486-465 BC) at a time when a few thousand Jews were returning to resettle Judea and rebuild the walls of Jerusalem. Other Jews were scattered throughout the Persian Empire, which stretched from India to Ethiopia or Cush, which included southern Egypt and Sudan.

We do not know who wrote the book. Some have thought that Mordecai may have been the author. Whoever the writer was, he must have lived close to the time of the events recorded here. He is very familiar with Persian culture and customs and may have been an eyewitness of the events described.

The original purposes of the book were to encourage Jews, to help them understand the origins of the Feast of Purim, and to teach them that adherence to their traditions would help them survive in the midst of the pagan world. But the book of Esther has many lessons for today. It shows God's sovereignty at work and demonstrates his commitment to protecting and caring for his people. It also reveals God's ability to use various people to influence the affairs of nations. Finally, it shows the consequences of ethnic hatred and strife and the possibility of living and communicating God's truth in an alien world.

Outline of Contents

COMMENTARY

1:1-21 The Deposing of a Queen

1:1-9 Xerxes' Banquet

King Xerxes ruled a vast empire stretching from northern India to the Upper Nile (**1:1**). But he was not content with his 127 provinces and still planned to invade Europe and destroy Greece. So in the third year of his reign he invited a wide range of leaders to gather at his court. Those invited included nobles from the various provinces, officials of lower rank and military leaders. The king displayed his wealth, power and trophies at festivities that lasted for six months (**1:3-4**). It is safe to assume that the gathering was also used to take an inventory of the empire's resources and to plan future military campaigns.

The fact that the invitees came from all the provinces means that the invitations cut across tribal lines. In doing this, Xerxes set an example. Africa has many nations and tribes and leaders should not rely solely on support from their own tribes. Rather, they should encourage people from different areas to unite for a common cause.

The strategizing was followed by a lavish banquet at which guests were allowed to drink whatever they wanted. The guests overindulged for a whole week (**1:5-8**). The king seems to have known that the way to a man's heart is through his stomach! Even today, leaders will dish out food to win the favour of their followers.

While this lavish banquet was going on, Queen Vashti held a separate banquet for women (**1:9**). Persian law did not require men and women to celebrate separately, but the women may have felt uncomfortable with the drunken men and may also have disliked the military tone of the discussion. Alternatively, Vashti may not have wanted to mingle with the common people, who were also attending the king's banquet.

1:10-22 Vashti's Disobedience and Banishment

On the seventh day of the banquet King Xerxes sent his personal servants to fetch the queen so that he could display her beauty *for she was lovely to look at* (**1:10-11**). But Queen Vashti refused to be paraded in front of drunken men. Although some would condemn her disobedience, most can sympathize with her and admire her courage in sticking to her principles. She did not want men to lust after her.

Vashti was a strong character who did not fear the wrath of an angry king (**1:12**). Xerxes is known to have had a violent temper. In fact the Greek historian Herodotus records that when his planned invasion of Greece failed, he commanded the soldiers to whip the ocean.

Like Vashti, African women should have self-respect and be women of principle, with their principles derived

from the word of God. This may be costly but it is worth the price. Men, too, need to learn not to exploit women's beauty for their own pleasure.

Queen Vashti's refusal caused consternation. To refuse the king was to humiliate him. So the king turned to his trusted advisors: What was the appropriate punishment for a queen who had committed the crime of disobeying the king? (**1:13-15**). It seems that the king made no attempt to ask Vashti why she had not come. This suggests a certain arrogance, which is also not unknown in Africa. Men should not only ask advice from their friends or counsellors but also from the ones who are closest to them, their wives. Vashti may have had good reason for refusing to appear – she herself may even have been drunk and reluctant to appear before important guests in that state.

Xerxes was, however, wise to take counsel from others rather than lashing out in anger. Proverbs 15:22 states that, 'Plans fail for lack of counsel but with many advisers they succeed.' But the important question is, who counts as a wise advisor? What makes a good counsellor? The criteria must include honouring and respecting God and having the gift of discernment. African leaders should seek counsellors with these qualifications.

Memucan, one of Xerxes' counsellors, reminded the king that no individual in a high position can act without affecting many other people. Leaders need to know they are on a pedestal and that they set the norm for their followers. Hence, African leaders need to be chosen wisely. They must be men and women of integrity, who will set high moral standards. Memucan feared that many women in the provinces would hear about how Queen Vashti had defied her husband and would copy her behaviour (**1:16-18**). He, therefore, urged the king to banish Vashti from her throne for good and to prevent her from ever regaining her royal station (**1:19**). Her punishment was to be a warning to others.

One can, however, wonder why the advisers were so insistent that Vashti should never be reinstated. The answer may be that if the king had any residual love for her, and if he ever reinstated her, the counsellor's lives might have been in danger. So they pressed the king to issue an irrevocable decree.

We are reminded of the care we need to exercise when evaluating rules, regulations and laws. Rules should be based on the good of the majority, not on selfishness, which is contrary to the Lord's norm. Africans need to carefully consider why particular laws are enacted and why there are demands for the review of national constitutions.

Xerxes' new law stated that every man must be master of his own house (**1:22**) – something that is not easily legislated. While this law was in accordance with the NT, which teaches that the husband is the head of the family (Eph 5:23), Xerxes himself did not love his wife as a husband is commanded to in the NT. If he had loved her, he would have given her an opportunity to explain her actions.

Another lesson to be learned from this scene is that disobedience costs. It cost Vashti her queenship. Yet God was working behind the scenes. He had seen far ahead and Vashti's banishment had a place in his plans.

2:1-17 The Search for a New Queen

No attempt was made to replace Vashti, and eventually the king became lonely. His thoughts must have dwelt on her (**2:1**). He may have been uncomfortable with continually remembering his ex-wife whom he had banished by an irrevocable decree. We are reminded of the danger of acting out of anger and humiliation. He could not reverse the decree that he had issued after consultation with his wise men.

Xerxes' servants noted the change in his mood. Someone who is depressed can make a servant's life miserable. These servants knew their master's moods. They wanted peace. Like them, those who are serving people in leadership positions need discernment in order to avoid unnecessary suffering.

To deal with his discontent, these servants advised the king to find a beautiful replacement for Queen Vashti (**2:2**). Accordingly a search was launched in all the provinces. It is likely that the task of finding beautiful girls was tackled with some enthusiasm. Suitable girls were brought to Susa where they were placed under the care of Hegai, the eunuch who was in charge of caring for the king's women. He would give them a year of beauty treatment before each one was taken to spend a night with the king (**2:3**).

We do not know how many women were taken to the king, but what we do know is that the Bible frowns on such a lifestyle. Although the kings in the Bible had many wives and concubines, it is clear that God's model for marriage involves one man and one wife. Africans should not excuse polygamy on the grounds that it is part of their culture, but should conform to the norms of the Bible.

2:5-11 Esther Enters the Contest

We are introduced to Esther through her uncle Mordecai, a Jew. His great-grandfather Kish was among the Israelites who had been carried into captivity by Nebuchadnezzar (**2:5-6**). Mordecai may have been a minor official in the Persian government, but he plays a great role in the book of Esther and can indeed be referred to as the hero of the book.

Mordecai was a sensitive, caring man. He had adopted an orphaned younger cousin whose Hebrew name was Hadassah (**2:7**), which means myrtle. The myrtle is a small tree known for its delicate fragrance. However, the Persian name by which the girl was known was Esther, which

means morning star, and may refer to her radiance. She is described as beautiful, with a lovely form and features. She may have gone by her Persian name because Mordecai, who was like a father to her, had instructed her not to reveal her background (**2:10**), possibly because he wanted her to fit into the new land and blend in with the culture.

She, too, was brought to the harem to enter the beauty contest. There she immediately won the favour of Hegai, who was in charge of the harem. He quickly noticed that there was something special about her, and gave her a special room and seven servant girls to wait on her (**2:8-9**).

While not all women can be as radiantly beautiful as Esther, one's aim in raising one's daughters can be to give them the security and love that Esther received from her uncle. Christian women, too, can strive to be well groomed, to have a gentle and quiet charm, and to have the wisdom shown in Esther's quick obedience to her uncle's instructions. These qualities opened a door for her to play a part in God's plans.

Mordecai, too, sets an example as a foster parent who treats his foster child as if she were his own. Indeed, we are told that Mordecai was so concerned about his cousin that he checked on her daily and kept watch over her (**2:11**). War, civil strife and AIDS have left Africa full of orphans. Many more Mordecais are needed to devotedly look out for their welfare.

2:12-14 Preparation for the Contest

We do now know exactly what went on in the harem during the year of preparation. The beauty treatment included six months of care with oil of myrrh, a fragrance extracted from several plants found in East Africa. A further six months of treatment with perfumes and cosmetics followed (**2:12**).

After the twelve months, the virgins were taken to the king for a night. The girl could take whatever she wanted with her to enhance her beauty (**2:13**). The next morning, she would be transferred to the home of the concubines. She would never see the king again unless he specifically asked for her (**2:14**).

2:15-20 Esther Wins the Contest

Hundreds of virgins may have spent a night with the king before Esther's turn came. As we consider this, many questions arise. How could Mordecai, a Jew, allow his cousin to go to a king who was not a Jew? How could he allow his cousin to give her virginity to a king who would probably not even marry her? God values virginity (Deut 22:13-21). The answer may be that Mordecai may have hoped that having her in the king's palace would help his own career. But it is equally likely that he had little choice in the matter. Esther's beauty may have been noticed by others, and so she may have been taken from his home by royal officials. We also need to remember that becoming the king's concubine was not equivalent to sleeping with someone one was not married to. Concubines were not regarded as immoral women, but rather as wives with less status than those who enjoyed the title of 'wife'.

When Esther went to the king, she took with her only what Hegai suggested (**2:15**). This shows that Esther was prepared to learn from those who were in authority or senior to her. She had obeyed her uncle and now she listened to Hegai's advice. Her wisdom was rewarded. She won the beauty contest, for *the king was attracted to Esther more than to any of the other women* who had been brought for his pleasure (**2:17**).

Esther was thus enthroned as queen of the Persian Empire. Gifts were distributed to celebrate her coronation (**2:18**). Yet, although he had taken Esther as his wife, the king had a second wave of virgins brought to the harem (**2:19**). Maybe he still craved sexual variety. Old habits die hard. Women need to be careful whom they marry, as they cannot assume that their love will stop a man's cravings for promiscuous sex. Only God can do that. The leaders of Africa also need to take note that sexual orgies have consequences and do not please God.

Meanwhile, Mordecai continued to hang around the citadel, keeping a watch on his orphan girl who was now the queen. Esther had never revealed her background although she was the queen, for she continued to obey Mordecai (**2:20**).

2:21-23 An Attempted Assassination

The king obviously needed a large number of attendants. When some of them became dissatisfied, there would be plots against him. Somehow Mordecai learned of an assassination plot involving two of the king's eunuchs, Bigthana and Teresh. He reported it to Esther who then informed the king, carefully giving credit to Mordecai for the discovery (**2:21-22**). The king had the would-be assassins hanged and the whole case was written up in the records of the kingdom (**2:23**). Our African leaders need trustworthy attendants, and those who learn of coups or other dishonest plans should not hide their knowledge.

3:1-15 Haman's Plot

3:1-6 The Offence

Once Esther was crowned queen she and Mordecai might have assumed that the rest of their lives would flow smoothly. For a number of years things did go well, but unbeknown to them a storm was brewing that would result in a plot to annihilate the Jews. African Christians, too, need to be careful not to be lulled into contentment when things appear to

be going very well. Our enemy is always plotting his next attack.

For some reason King Xerxes chose Haman the Agagite to be the prime minister of Persia and ordered everyone to bow before him in honour of his new position (**3:1-2**). The need for such an order may suggest that Haman was not from a noble family. Respect that comes without threats or force is the only kind worth having.

As in our society, there were many busybodies in Susa. Some of them noticed that Mordecai did not bow down to Haman, and they hurried to report this to him (**3:3-4**). It is strange that Mordecai, who had told Esther to remain silent on the topic, here declared his Jewish nationality. That stirred even more trouble. Haman decided that all the Jews would suffer because of Mordecai's refusal to pay him homage. Only this would soothe his injured pride (**3:5-6**).

The reason for Mordecai's refusal to bow was not that he despised Haman, but that he had to obey God. The Jews were forbidden to bow down to other gods (Exod 20:5). Haman was certainly not a god, but in his pride he may have presented himself as if he were one. If this was the case, Mordecai's refusal to bow was symbolic of the refusal of all Jews to bow to Haman, and thus all Jews were exposed to Haman's hatred.

Haman's wounded pride surfaced as hatred. He could not control Mordecai, and so he hated him and generalized his hatred to include all Jews. In his racial hatred he is another in the long line of those who have persecuted the Jews in the past and in the present. Much of our tribalism in Africa and the racism that was so prominent in South Africa are also rooted in anger and in wanting to control everyone and everything. Racial hatred tries to bolster itself with the myth that one tribe is superior to others. But no race, nationality or tribe is superior to any other. God has created all for a purpose. We need to remember that God is against all unfair discrimination (Jas 2:1-4) and opposes the ethnic fighting that destroys rather than builds the continent.

3:7-15 The Revenge

In presenting his plan to the king, Haman used exaggeration and lies. He pointed out that Jewish customs were different, which was true, but then moved on to the false generalization that none of the Jews obeyed the king's law (**3:8**). Haman even offered to pay for the annihilation of the Jews out of his own pocket. The sum he was prepared to pay was amazing – close to 350 tons of silver (**3:9**). It is difficult to translate this into current money, but we can get some idea of its value from the fact that some commentators say that this was equivalent to two-thirds of the annual income of the Persian Empire. It is clear that Haman himself was not short of money, yet he still wanted to plunder the Jews. Even today we need to be wary of greedy men and women who selfishly promote and even fund tribal wars.

Haman won favour with the king who, on the spur of the moment, without even consulting the wise men or verifying what he had heard, handed Haman his signet ring. This was equivalent to giving Haman a signed cheque. It signalled that Haman would be acting with the king's approval. Xerxes also waved away Haman's offer of money and authorized his government to fund the destruction (3:10-11).

There are lessons to learn here for Africa. Leaders must have people of integrity around them if there is to be any hope of peace. Moreover, even with trusted counsellors, leaders should verify information, particularly when it affects many people. King Xerxes was not ruling wisely. Nor was he wise in delegating his power by handing over his signet ring without appropriate consultation.

Haman had now been given the power he craved. He now took pains to ensure that his orders were communicated to officials at all levels of authority within each of the 127 provinces: to the satraps, provincial governors, and the leaders of smaller people groups (3:12). The message to all was *to destroy, kill and annihilate all the Jews – young and old, women and little children – on a single day* (3:13-14).

As the news of these orders spread through the city of Susa, the Jews were devastated, but the king and Haman sat at ease, drinking (3:15). They may have been avoiding thinking about what their decrees would actually involve. Leaders who drink are not ruling well or focusing on the needs of their people.

4:1-17 An Appeal for Help

4:1-3 Mordecai Leads the Mourning

When Mordecai learned of the plot to annihilate all the Jews, he tore his clothes and put on sackcloth and ashes, the traditional signs of mourning. He went out into the streets of the city, wailing loudly (4:1). As the news of Haman's orders reached all the provinces, the Jews there joined Mordecai in mourning, fasting, weeping and wailing. Many of them, too, wore sackcloth and ashes (4:3). What a contrast between the mourning Jews and the carousing king!

Mordecai came as close to the gate of the king as the law would allow (4:2). He wanted to let Esther know about the agony of the Jews. Living in the seclusion of the palace, she was not aware of what was going on in Susa. Her ignorance is a reminder of another danger facing those in leadership positions. They may become so remote from their followers that they do not know what is going on in the daily lives of those followers, and hence may make wrong decisions. Leaders need to keep in contact with real life.

4:4-17 An Appeal to Esther

Mordecai needed to get a message to Esther to persuade her to approach the king on behalf of the Jews. He was hoping that Esther would hear that he was at the gate dressed in mourning and would investigate. Esther did hear that he was there, and was distressed that he was in mourning. She sent him proper clothes to replace his sackcloth, but Mordecai refused to stop mourning and would not put on the clothes (4:4).

Esther now suspected that something must be seriously wrong. She sent Hatach, one of the eunuchs, to get more information. Mordecai told him all about Haman's plot and even sent Esther a copy of Haman's orders. He made it clear that he wanted her to approach the king on behalf of her people (4:5-9).

Esther pointed out that this was not as simple as it sounded. The law specified that one could only enter the presence of the king by invitation. To go to see him uninvited was to risk one's life. And it had been thirty days since she had last seen the king, suggesting that she was no longer his favourite (4:10-11). Not surprisingly, Esther was afraid to act.

In response, Mordecai reminded her that she was also a Jew and would be killed. It she failed to act, God would deliver the Jews in some other way, but there was no doubt that she and her family would die in the massacre. Her only hope lay in action. He also pointed out that it was providential that she was queen at a time when such danger threatened. There was a reason she was in the palace (4:12-14).

Mordecai's response to the bad news is a model for us. His initial response was deep concern not only for himself but also for his people. His mourning led to fasting, which would have been accompanied by prayer, and to involving others in prayer and fasting. He did not simply seek to protect himself by using his connection with Esther, nor would he accept comfort from her when others were facing death. He stood by his Jewish people. But he was not solely a man of prayer. In encouraging Esther to go to the king and present their case he showed that he was also a man of action.

Esther responded that she would act, even if it cost her life. But she did not rush into action. She asked Mordecai to gather all the Jews in Susa and have them fast for three days, while she and her maids also fasted. Then on the third day she would approach the king (4:15-16).

Esther was willing to step into the unknown and risk her life. She would do her part, not knowing how the king would respond. She, Mordecai and their fellow Jews would pray and fast, but the outcome would be in God's hands. Although God is not mentioned by name, it is clear that he is the one before whom the Jews were fasting and to whom they were praying.

5:1-8 Esther's Appeal to the King

Esther did not rely only on fasting and prayers; she also put thought into how she would approach the king. She dressed formally for the occasion in her full royal robes, as if she were appearing at a state function (**5:1**). This also suggests that she adorned herself in a way that she knew would please the king

Esther then took the biggest risk of her life. She defied the protocol that dictated that no one appeared before the king without his invitation. She put her life on the line in a desperate attempt to save the Jews, for she knew that only the king's intervention could save her people. Her courage and faith are admirable.

King Xerxes was seated on the throne when Esther appeared. He must have been surprised to see her, and Esther must have been terrified as she awaited his reaction. To her great relief, he was pleased to see her and extended his sceptre to welcome her. Even before he knew her request, he offered her *up to half the kingdom*. He had pardoned her for coming uninvited (**5:2-3**).

Although the king claimed to be ready to grant Esther anything she wanted, she did not immediately make her real request. Instead she invited the king and Haman to a banquet (**5:4**). Esther was following Middle Eastern custom, where business deals traditionally followed meals. She may have felt that this was not the right time to make her request. She wanted the right time, God's time. Dramatically, this delay also increases the tension as we read the story.

Esther provides a good example of risk-taking as a believer. She did not act casually, but put in many hours of prayer and fasting before risking her life. When it was time to act, she used the resources and skills she had in determining the best way to act. She had beauty, she knew the king loved good food and good wine, and she was able to organize a banquet. We, too, need to consider how we can most effectively use the skills and resources the Lord has given us to serve his kingdom.

The banquet for three was a great success, but Esther did not rush to make her request. She created suspense within the king by promising that she would reveal her request if he and Haman would come to a second banquet the next day (**5:5-8**).

5:9-6:14 Unexpected Developments

5:9-14 Haman's Pride

Haman was highly honoured by having been invited by the queen to attend a private banquet with the king. And this invitation had been extended not once, but twice! Hence he left the palace in high spirits. He felt on top of the world. He called his wife, Zeresh, and friends together and boasted about the favour that he was enjoying, cementing his place as the number two person in the kingdom (**5:10-12**).

However, despite all his success and honour, he felt very angry that Mordecai would not pay homage to him (**5:9**). Haman had everything he wanted, and yet one person could make his life miserable. He was quick to focus on the one negative point and let that spoil his enjoyment of his blessings. He told his friends and wife that his pride could no longer tolerate the sight of Mordecai: *all of this gives me no satisfaction as long as I see that Jew Mordecai sitting at the king's gate* (**5:13**).

Haman should have focused on the privileges he had rather than on the small irritants. But he could not do this, and so he sought advice on how to deal with the issue. He was advised to build very tall gallows that would be visible across the city and to seek the king's permission to have Mordecai hanged (**5:14**).

Within a day the gallows were ready. Haman was really pleased with himself. Soon he would be rid of Mordecai, and then nothing would disturb his enjoyment of his second banquet with the king and queen.

6:1-3 A Sleepless King

After Esther's first banquet, the king had a bad night. He could not sleep (**6:1**). Maybe his mind was on the military situation or on what Esther could possibly require of him and Haman. But those were the human causes; the ultimate cause was the providence of God.

Unable to sleep, the king decided to pass the hours of the night by having his attendants read him the records of his reign. By God's providence, the particular record that they read concerned Mordecai and how, five years earlier, he (and Esther) had exposed an assassination plot against the king (**6:2**).

The king being unable to sleep, this particular record being read, and the king pausing to wonder whether Mordecai had ever been rewarded for his faithful act (**6:3**) – these were not mere coincidences. God was at work. He knew that Haman was preparing to hang Mordecai. God was going to use these coincidences to save his chosen people, proving 'that in all things God works for the good of those who love him and who have been called according to his purpose' (Rom 8:28).

God uses and controls natural events, so that nothing happens by mere chance. He uses each individual with his or her own character, values and beliefs.

6:4-11 Honour for Mordecai

As the king reflected on what would be a fair reward to Mordecai for having warned him of the assassination plot, he decided to call for advice. By yet another 'coincidence', Haman happened to be in the court. He had come early to request permission to kill Mordecai (**6:4-5**). But the king knew nothing of this. Haman, too, knew nothing of the king's night. So when he was called in and asked for advice about how to honour someone, Haman's pride could not imagine that the one honoured would be anyone other than himself. (**6:6**). So he recommended the honour he himself would most like.

The honoree should be dressed up in royal robes and mounted on one of the king's own horses. Then he should be paraded through the streets of the city. A very important official should lead the way, shouting, *This is what is done for the man the king delights to honour* (**6:7-9**). Haman was not interested in a financial reward, because he was planning to get rich by plundering the Jews. Wearing the king's own robes and riding the king's own horse, led by the noblest official, was the clearest way he could imagine of signalling that he was second in importance only to the king. He must have been thrilled to hear the king telling him to go and *get the robe and the horse* – only to discover that he was getting them, not for himself, but for Mordecai! Rather than hanging Mordecai from the newly constructed gallows, Haman would have to lead him through the streets, proclaiming that Mordecai was more honoured than he was (**6:10-12**). What a humiliation!

God instructs us about how he should view others and ourselves. We are told to 'do nothing out of selfish ambition or vain conceit, but in humility consider others better than yourselves' (Phil 2:3). Haman certainly did not consider anyone else better than himself, and particularly not Mordecai, even though he had saved the king's life. God humiliated Haman's pride, reversing the situation so that one who had been put down and had his hours on earth numbered was elevated to the highest position (see also Luke 1:52). God does not consider anyone worthless. All are important and special to him. Furthermore, God does not look at our outside but at our heart.

6:12-14 A Warning from Haman's Wife

Following his humiliation, Haman returned in shame, with his head covered. He had been forced to honour the man he had hoped to hang. He shared his pain with his wife and friends, but received little comfort from them as they predicted his downfall. It is interesting to note that Haman's wife and friends now realized that he was playing with fire. They recognized that as a Jew Mordecai was a special person from a unique people: *Since Mordecai, before whom your downfall has started, is of Jewish origin, you cannot stand against him* (**6:13**).

Why had they not seen this before? Earlier, they had encouraged him to kill Mordecai. No answer can be given, but their comment focuses on the central point of the story of Esther. God had chosen the Jewish nation. The Jews were a special people and God was going to protect them and deliver them from the hand of their enemies.

This is a great lesson for believers. God is at work in our daily lives, even if we often do not recognize his providence until after the event. We may wonder where God is when we face difficult situations, but we can be assured that he is working behind the scenes. What happens is no accident but is allowed by his sovereign will.

While Haman was still talking to his wife and friends, the king's eunuchs arrived to fetch Haman for Esther's banquet (**6:14**). He would never see his wife and friends again. He must have set out feeling that his joy at his invitation to this second banquet had evaporated with the elevation of the man he hated.

7:1-7 Esther's Request

After the king and Haman had enjoyed the meal that Esther had provided, the king repeated his question for the third time: *What is your petition?* Again he was prepared to offer the queen *up to half the kingdom* (**7:1-2**). This offer must have been encouraging to Esther, for it suggested that she was still in the king's favour.

It is instructive to see how Esther goes about presenting her request. She could simply have been angry with the king and Haman and demanded that the orders be revoked. She did not. Her tactic was not to assign blame but to plead for her life (**7:3**). When we launch straight into accusations, the person accused often becomes defensive and nothing is accomplished. Nor did she make demands, even though she was the queen. Instead she pleaded, with great politeness and formality: *If I have found favour with you, O king, and if it pleases your majesty, grant me my life … And spare my people.* Stam notes that 'Even after a meal, with much wine, when people sometimes let down their guard and become a bit loose, Esther still carefully preserves the proper style'. He also notes that Esther was careful to avoid Vashti's mistake of trying to lay down the law for the king. Esther knew that she had to be extremely careful.

Esther's first request was for her own life. The king must have been puzzled. Who was intending to kill the queen? This request touched on the king's power and ability to protect those who were close to him. Esther was his wife, and not only that, she was the one he had chosen out of many women to be made queen.

Esther had to explain herself. Given her silence about her origins (2:10, 20) it is probable that neither the king nor Haman knew that Esther was a Jew. Neither of them would have immediately thought of the edict against Jews when she presented her petition. So Esther must have embarked on her explanation with some trepidation, for she did not know how the king would react when she revealed her nationality. Would he be angry that she and Mordecai had kept this information from him?

Note the care with which she stated her case. She starts with the prospect of destruction, slaughter and annihilation, and makes it clear that it is only because the threat is so devastating that she has brought it to the king's attention. If it had been a minor matter, *if we had merely been sold as male or female slaves, I would have kept quiet, because no such distress would justify disturbing the king* (**7:4**) Again, Esther's wisdom and grasp of etiquette are clear. She emphasizes her great respect for the king.

It is no wonder that the king was outraged and demanded to know who was responsible for this dreadful plan to kill his wife, the Queen of Persia, and her people (**7:5**). Now Esther's response was quick and to the point: *the adversary and enemy is this vile Haman* (**7:6a**). Haman was exposed as utterly evil. His attack on the queen meant that he was a traitor, who should not be close to the king.

Furious, the king stalked out into the garden so he could get some fresh air and digest what he had just heard (**7:7a**). He had fully trusted Haman, giving him his signet ring, and now he was discovering that the power he had delegated had been misused. Clearly he had not been given full information when asked to approve the edict. But what could be done now, for an edict was irrevocable?

Leaders need to beware of the danger of being used by those they think they can trust. Too often in Africa, leaders have been fed false information by those close to them. Wise counsel from honest people is necessary if leaders are to get to the heart of the problem before acting. And such people can be found. Mordecai was one of them. If only the king had earlier elevated the one who had saved his life from the assassination plot rather than Haman, of whose record we know nothing.

7:8-9:17 Role Reversals

7:8-10 Haman's Death

Haman must have been shocked at the sudden disastrous turn of events. He must not have known about the connection between the queen and Mordecai. Realizing that his life was in danger, he did not rush out after the king but remained behind to appeal to Esther for mercy (**7:7b**). No longer could he appeal to the highest authority – the king. But his appeal to the queen did not help him. When the king returned a few moments later, he found Haman *falling on the couch* where Esther was reclining, as was the custom at meals. The king immediately misinterpreted Haman's actions: *Will he even rape the queen right here in the palace, before my very eyes?* (**7:8** LB). His wrath knew no bounds.

As soon as the king spoke, the attendants covered Haman's face, a sign that he was to die. Haman is now to be pitied. He had enjoyed a rapid rise to power and to be being (as he thought) a favourite of both the king and the queen, but his downfall was even swifter. Within minutes he becomes a convicted criminal awaiting execution. We need

to be aware that any position and powers we are entrusted with are fleeting so that we do not put our trust in them.

Haman does not seem to have had many friends. His pride may have alienated those around him. No sooner was his face covered than an attendant named Harbona informed the king about the gallows Haman had erected for Mordecai. The king promptly ordered that they be used to hang Haman (**7:9-10**). Haman's life ended on the gallows he himself had built. Not only that, he had built them right outside his own house, so he was hanged in full view of his family and friends.

A popular proverb says 'the bigger they come, the harder they fall'. Scripture makes the same point: 'Pride goes before destruction, a haughty spirit before a fall' (Prov 16:18). Haman's pride evaporated in total humiliation. In fact, his pride was what brought about his downfall. If he had been prepared to ignore the fact that Mordecai was not paying homage to him, he would never have plotted against the Jews and we would be reading a different story. God makes it clear that he hates pride and arrogance: 'To fear the Lord is to hate evil; I hate pride and arrogance, evil behaviour and perverse speech' (Prov 8:13). Humility is a great virtue that can save people and nations.

8:1-2 Mordecai's Promotion

Haman, who had wanted to destroy the Jews and gain their property, had himself been destroyed. His own property had been given to a Jew (**8:1**). No one would have imagined that events would have turned out this way. Esther, the new owner of Haman's estate, would probably willingly have given it to her uncle Mordecai, but because of her respect for the king, she instead appointed Mordecai the administrator (**8:2b**).

This was not his only new responsibility. The king also needed a replacement for Haman, and he handed over responsibility for the administration of his empire to Mordecai on the same day that Haman died. Mordecai was even given the same signet ring that Haman had used (**8:2a**). Mordecai thus joined the seven wise men who gave the king advice (1:13-14). It is ironic that the same signet ring used to seal the edict to annihilate the Jews was now worn by a Jew! Mordecai rose from mourning to sharing the authority and power of the king.

This serves to remind us that no one should despise another, even if the person appears unimportant. Things can change suddenly. Those who seem to look down on this continent of Africa should remember that God can choose to elevate it at any time.

8:3-14 A Massacre Averted

One problem remained. The king's edict against the Jews still stood, for no one had the right to revoke it. Esther and

Mordecai had won a victory, but their people were still in danger of annihilation.

Esther again used her wisdom and courtesy. She pleaded and wept for her people. She begged that the evil scheme of Haman the Agagite should be stopped (**8:3, 5-6**). The king was sympathetic (**8:4, 7**), but faced a legal problem. Once a decree had been issued, it could not be repealed. The king did not want it to appear that he did not know his own mind or that he made impulsive decisions. He was probably unsure how to handle the situation. But once again, God was in control. When Esther came to plead for her people, her uncle stood nearby, offering moral support. The king turned to him, and delegated the problem to Esther and Mordecai to solve (**8:8**).

Esther and Mordecai tackled the task of writing and distributing the new edict. It had to be carefully phrased, for it had to counteract but not annul the first decree. So where Haman's decree had given the enemies of the Jews the right to kill all of them and their children and plunder their property, the new decree made it clear that the Jews were entitled to organize and defend themselves against their enemies (**8:11**). Stam observes that, in the new edict, 'The Jews have the right to organize a defense league. They have the right to set up headquarters in every region. They have the right to purchase or make weapons. These are the kind of things they normally would not be permitted to do. They may carefully prepare their defense'.

God was defending his own. Stam comments, 'The Lord God often uses the laws of the land – some laws foolish or even ungodly in themselves – to defend his people. Here again we see the sovereign grace of God. He does not say to his people; "Rebel and break the yoke of Persia." That would be revolution. But he leads the king of Persia to decree that self- defense is allowed and facilitated.'

8:15-17 A Celebration

What a change! The Jews who had been dreading the coming of the 13th day of the month of Adar now celebrated with great joy. All the people of Susa joined in the celebration (**8:15-17a**). They were glad that Mordecai had been promoted. It is surprising to read that many many *people of other nationalities* became Jewish proselytes at this time (**8:17b**). Some may have done this on the basis of genuine convictions, but others may merely have jumped on the bandwagon as the Jews under Mordecai moved into positions of leadership.

The psychology is similar to what we see during election campaigns. Today, the crowds hail one candidate; a day later his opponent receives an equal welcome. People enjoy being associated with people in power, and often act in crowds without regard to their true convictions. Jesus was well aware of this phenomenon: 'Many will say to me on that day, "Lord, Lord, did we not prophesy in your name,

and in your name drive out demons and perform many miracles?" Then I will tell them plainly, "I never knew you. Away from me, you evildoers!"' (Matt 7:22-23). Christians, too, can succumb to crowd psychology when they gather in megachurches or are prepared to follow great men and women of God without themselves having come under proper conviction. The Lord Jesus needs to convict us and we must receive him as our personal Saviour.

Mordecai's new status was clear in his dress. He had worn sackcloth and ashes. Now he wears *royal garments of blue and white, a large crown of gold and a purple robe of fine linen.* He had risen from humble beginnings to become one of the greatest men in the land. Leaders need to humble themselves and see what the Lord can do on their behalf.

9:1-16 The Jews' Revenge

The enemies of the Jews had no doubt been looking forward to the 13th of Adar, when they were sure they would easily overpower the Jews by sheer force of numbers. Haman's decree had merely given official sanction to a hatred that had long been building, and plans would have been laid for the destruction of the Jews.

But now, with this second decree, the Jews were free to respond by arming themselves with all manner of weapons. They gathered together, prepared to attack their enemies (**9:1-2**). We may wonder how they knew whom to attack, but presumably they had their own sources of intelligence.

The great fear among the Persians (**9:2**) may have been because the Jews were God-fearing people – hence behind this fear of the people lay the fear of the Lord. However, it may also have been because the Jews were now enjoying the support of all the nobles, satraps, governors, and administrators, and were quite ready to strike *down all their enemies with the sword* (**9:5-10**).

The news of these killings even reached the palace, and on hearing about the many deaths in the city of Susa, the king wondered what had been happening in other places. He also asked the queen if she was now satisfied, or whether she had a further request (**9:12**). Esther's response was to request another day of killing in Susa, and that the bodies of Haman's ten sons, who had already been killed, be hung from the gallows. It is difficult to justify this request. It may be that she wanted to purge the city of all enemies of the Jews, including those who were still in hiding.

Esther's actions are not easily explained biblically. However, Stam observes, 'we must not see the slaughter described as just another bloody page of which there are so many in the Bible, especially in the Old Testament. This is nothing less than another battle in an ongoing war, not caused by God but certainly waged by him, which will not end until the final Day of Judgment.' But not all commentators agree. Baldwin, for example, considers it despicable to respond to the grace of God with hatred of those who oppose us. Sadly, this is a trap that Christians have some-times fallen into, in Africa and elsewhere in the world.

The Jews' victory was immense. Eight hundred people were killed in the capital city and seventy-five thousand in the provinces. But where Haman's decree had encouraged the plundering of the Jews' possessions, the Jews *did not lay their hands on the plunder* (9:10, 15, 16). Their goal was not to enrich themselves or to impoverish the families of their enemies.

The Jews' victory was rooted in the humility and integrity of Mordecai and in their willingness to band together. Humility, integrity and unity are what give a people strength. The African church should build people of integrity to lead us, and we should unite behind them. We should not be working for our own selfish goals but for the glory of God. 'We need each other badly to stand united against the world and the devil. To others we shall show gentleness and respect, keeping a clear conscience. The result is a united church, and a world that is kept wondering about the power of Christ' (Stam).

9:18-22 The Institution of Purim

After the passing of the dreaded day, the Jews had good reason to celebrate (9:18). The terror had passed. They had victory over their enemies. Indeed their sorrow had been turned into joy and their mourning into a day of celebration. Although the name of God is never mentioned, he has clearly been at work in the background.

Mordecai carefully recorded all that had happened and sent letters to all the Jews in all the provinces to instruct them to commemorate their deliverance (9:20-22). The Jewish celebration was quite different from the feast described in chapter one. There the guests were feasting and overindulging in wine. By contrast, the Jewish celebration was one of home and family. Those who had material wealth were not to forget those who did not, but were to distribute gifts and food to them (9:22). In many parts of Africa, there are great differences between the haves and the have-nots. In our many celebrations, we need to remember the instruction to give gifts and share our feasts with those who live in the slums.

The feast commemorating the Jewish victory came to be known as Purim. The name derives from the plural of the Assyrian word *pur*, which means 'lot' (9:26). Haman had cast lots to determine a favourable day for annihilating the Jews (3:7), but the day he had chosen turned out to be one of the most favourable days for the Jews in many years.

Purim is still celebrated with feasting by many orthodox Jewish synagogues. The Book of Esther is read aloud. Haman is still hated, and there is loud jeering each time his name is mentioned.

Africans, like the Jews, can celebrate their deliverance from their colonial masters. But we should not stop with celebration; we should also acknowledge the Lord who can and has intervened to change the course of events for his glory.

10:1-3 The Greatness of Mordecai

The Jews, who were to have been exterminated, were now managing the kingdom. Mordecai the Jew now ranked second to the Persian king (10:3). We, too, need to learn to ignore tribal borders when selecting our leaders, and we need to choose leaders who do not use their position to promote their personal interests but to champion the welfare of others. Mordecai, unlike Haman, was a true statesman.

What had seemed like an utterly hopeless situation had been turned around by the dedication of a few people who devoted themselves to God. The same can be true for Africa. God can change the state of affairs on this continent.

In conclusion, the book of Esther encourages us to realize that God is involved in all of our dealings. This is a book in which God is never mentioned, yet he is overwhelmingly present through his control of events. His providence is also at work for us today, both in the church and in our continent as a whole.

Lois Semenye

Further Reading

Baldwin, G. Joyce. *Esther*. TOT. Downers Grove, Ill.: InterVarsity Press, 1984.

Bitrus, Daniel. *Making the Right Choices*. Nairobi, Kenya: CLMC, 2002.

Huey, F. B. Jr. 'Esther', in *1 & 2 Kings, 1 & 2 Chronicles, Ezra, Nehemiah, Esther, Job*. EBC. Grand Rapids, Mich: Zondervan, 1988.

Stam, Clarence. *Regina Dei Gratia: The History of Queen Esther*. Winnipeg: Premier Publishing, 1999.

INTRODUCTION TO THE WISDOM LITERATURE

The OT contains a group of books with a distinctive literary style that are collectively referred to as the Wisdom literature. This type of writing is also found in other texts from the ancient Near East, such as the ancient Egyptian instruction manual called *The Teaching of Amenemope*. In fact, it was the finding of that text in 1923 that led to the identification of Wisdom literature as a separate genre. Here, however, we will focus only on the Wisdom books in the Bible.

Scholars disagree on exactly which books of the Bible fit into this category. The list can be shorter or longer, depending on whether one's perspective is Jewish and Protestant or Catholic and Orthodox. For our purpose here, we understand the Wisdom literature as comprising Job, Proverbs, Ecclesiastes, Song of Songs and some wisdom psalms. These psalms have similar content to the teaching of the Wisdom books and include Psalms 1, 10, 12, 15, 19, 32, 34, 36, 37, 49, 50, 52, 53, 73, 78, 82, 91, 92, 94, 111, 112, 119, 127, 128 and 139.

Environment of Religion

The greatest bone of contention among biblical scholars has been the relationship of the theology of the Wisdom literature to that of the rest of the OT. There are those who say that since the teaching of this block of books fails to agree with the redemptive approach of the rest of the OT, it is foreign to the world of the OT and, therefore, an illegitimate source for theology. Others go to the other extreme and see creation theology – which they think is the main thrust of the teaching of these books – as the core theology of the entire OT, rather than the history of God's saving acts. A third group of scholars tries to hold a mediating position, either by demonstrating that the discrepancies are only apparent or by bringing the seemingly disparate tendencies under a unifying umbrella.

Much of the polarization around the theology of the Wisdom literature and of the rest of the OT is due to the imposition of a secular or rationalistic mindset on the authors of this type of literature. This is contrary to the realities of the biblical and ancient Near Eastern contexts, which were nothing but religious. Whether in the monotheistic world of the Bible or the polytheistic world of the ancient Near East, religion was the environment in which people lived and worked. People did not rely solely on human reason, but constantly sought the help of the deity or deities they worshipped. There was no such thing as a secular mindset.

In this respect their attitude was similar to that of the traditional African worldview, which is holistic and does not draw a sharp line between the material and the spiritual. This holistic perspective is encapsulated in the story about an elderly African mother who denied that a passport-size photograph represented her son because his arms and legs were missing. Similarly, to deny the spiritual elements of the Wisdom literature is to present a truncated version of reality.

Essence of Religion

The message of the Wisdom literature can be summarized by looking at the books that form the backbone of this corpus in the Bible – Job, Proverbs and Ecclesiastes – and focusing on the theme that brings them together. (See the individual commentaries for more extended treatment of each of these books.)

On reading the book of Proverbs – especially chapters 1–9 – one is struck by the contrast between the wise person and the fool and the rewards and punishments their respective lifestyles bring. The contrasting of these two ways of life continues in chapters 10 and following, where wisdom is equated with righteousness and folly with wickedness. The theme verse of the book (Prov 1:7) encapsulates the two lifestyles as follows: 'The fear of the Lord is the beginning of knowledge, but fools despise wisdom and discipline' (see also Prov 9:10 and 31:30). As far as Proverbs is concerned, the presence or absence of the fear of the Lord divides humanity into two camps. This belief pervades the book. In addition to the verses already cited, see Prov 8:13; 10:27; 14:2, 26, 27; 15:16, 33; 16:6; 19:23; 23:17 and 24:21.

The main character of the book of Job is described as 'blameless and upright; *he feared God* and shunned evil' (Job 1:1 – emphasis added). We hear this testimony about the life of Job twice from the very mouth of God (Job 1:8; 2:3). Job went through all the suffering and affliction described in the book because he feared God. But he was also vindicated and restored by God because he feared him. The main theme of the book is captured in the beautiful poem in Job 28, which speaks of the search for wisdom. After describing human ingenuity in extracting precious minerals from the belly of the earth (Job 28:1-11), the writer asks 'But where can wisdom be found? Where does understanding dwell?' (Job 28:12). We scan the earth, the sea and the heavens but cannot find wisdom. Nor can we buy it with all the gems we possess (Job 28:13-19). The query is repeated (Job 28:20) and the absence of wisdom in the created universe underscored. The end of the human search for wisdom is intimated in the words 'God understands the way to it and he alone knows where it dwells' (Job 28:23). And then God articulates the essence of wisdom: 'And he said to man, "*The fear of the Lord* – that is wisdom, and to shun evil is understanding"' (Job 28:28 – emphasis added). That is the message of the book, as incarnated in and exemplified by Job.

The book of Ecclesiastes depicts the folly of seeing life solely from an earth-bound perspective, that is, from 'under the sun'. The refrain that brackets what is being said about such a secular lifestyle is '"Meaningless! Meaningless!" says the teacher. "Utterly meaningless! Everything is meaningless"' (Eccl 1:2; 12:8). Then, having summarized the gist of his book, the writer says: 'Now all has been heard; here is the conclusion of the matter: *Fear God* and keep his commandments for this is the whole duty of man' (Eccl 12:13 – emphasis added). He adds, 'For God will bring every deed into judgment, including every hidden thing, whether it is good or evil' (Eccl 12:14). The fear of God is mentioned at crucial points in the body of the book (Eccl 5:7; 7:18; 8:12-13; 12:13). It is clear that it is this perspective on life that will enable a person to avoid the folly of a meaningless earth-bound life and instead live with eternity in mind.

It is sometimes difficult to articulate what is meant by 'fear' in the encounter between God and human beings. The phrase 'the fear of the Lord' or 'of God' does not refer to the dread of the unknown or of the mysterious. Nor does it refer to the terror induced by the wrath of God. In the context of the covenant people, of whom the Wisdom writers were a part, this fear is the reverent and humble submission of the whole of life to the revealed will of Yahweh. It manifests itself in worshipful adoration of the Creator of heaven and earth and the sovereign Lord of history. The psalm which reproduces the statement 'The fear of the Lord is the beginning of wisdom' is a great song of praise and adoration to the covenant Lord (Ps 111:10; see also Prov 1:7, 9:10; Job 28:28).

It is clear that the theme of the Wisdom literature, as summarized in the preceding statement, captures the essence of religion. In other words, it is a vital and life-encompassing relationship with the Creator and Redeemer of humankind – as presented in the rest of the OT. Thus the degree to which we submit our lives with abandon and adoration to the will of our Creator and Redeemer is the degree to which the wisdom that comes from heaven can be said to be the guide of our lives.

Tewoldemedhin Habtu

JOB

The book of Job, though ancient, is amazingly relevant given the suffering that has been and is being experienced in Africa. The study of it, though challenging, is deeply rewarding. It is in a class by itself both for the depth of its message and the complexity of its literary forms.

Scholars are unsure when this book was written, with the suggested dates ranging from patriarchal to postexilic times. The early date is supported by the fact that Job performs priestly functions in relation to his family (1:5) and his friends (42:8-9), indicating that the Levitical sacrificial system promulgated by the Mosaic law was not yet in place. As for authorship, Job or someone else with personal knowledge of the events – both on the human and divine levels – could have written the book.

There is general consensus that the structure of the book consists of a major poetic middle section sandwiched between introductory and concluding prose sections.

Outline of Contents

COMMENTARY

1:1-2:13 The Prose Prologue

Some biblical scholars regard these two chapters as mythological, rather than as records of actual events. They would happily discard both the prologue and epilogue to the book as inferior and retain only the poetic middle section and the great truths it explores. Their views reflect a world view fostered by the European Enlightenment, with its insistence on erecting a wall between the empirical world and the spiritual world.

Yet in terms of the African world view, which seems to be closer to the biblical world view, such traffic between the world of humanity and the spirit world is nothing strange, but rather to be expected. Africans are thus quite at home with the alternation of heavenly and earthly scenes in these two chapters. Scene one (1:1-5) describes the man Job, his family and his wealth; scene two (1:6-12), in heaven, tells of a conversation between God and Satan; in scene three (1:13-22), back on earth, we read of a series of catastrophes that come upon Job; in scene four (2:1-6), in heaven, there is a second conversation between God and Satan; in scene five (2:7-13), on earth, we read of a terrible attack on Job's body and of his own response and that of his wife and of the three friends who come to console him.

A full understanding of the message of the book of Job requires one to come to grips with both the prose narrative and the poetic dialogue. In his book *Disappointment with God*, Philip Yancey confesses that he, like many of us, had always read the book from the perspective of chapter 3 – in other words, from Job's perspective. But when he started to take the opening chapters seriously, he came to realize that God, not Job, is the central character, and that the theme of the book is faith, not suffering. Rather than dismissing the opening chapters as an embarrassing representation of God and Satan using people as pawns in a game, Yancey argues that these chapters serve to remind us that what happens in the everyday world around us may reflect far greater conflicts in the spiritual world. Actions that seem ordinary to us may have extraordinary effects in that world: 'a short-term mission assignment causes Satan to fall like lightning from heaven (Luke 10); a sinner's repentance sets off celestial celebration (Luke 15); a baby's birth disturbs the entire universe (Revelation 12). Much of that effect, however, remains hidden from our view.'

1:1-5 Job, the Man

After giving Job's place of origin and his name, the writer describes him as the epitome of godly character: he was *blameless and upright; he feared God and shunned evil* (1:1). Blameless implies that he was a man of integrity; upright implies that he was completely fair and honest in his dealings;

that he feared God implies that he was committed to obeying the will of God above all else; while the fact that he shunned evil shows he took trouble to avoid anything of which God would disapprove. God twice repeats this description of Job's sterling character (1:8; 2:3), showing that he regards Job as his 'best representative of his purpose for man on earth' (*CC*). It is important to remember this when reading the dialogue between Job and his friends.

We are also told about Job's children, the extent of his wealth, his many servants, and his meticulous care for the spiritual welfare of his family. The number seven represents perfection, so the references to *seven sons* (1:2) and *seven thousand sheep* (1:3) underscore the perfection of his blessings. Add to this the joy and unity his children manifest in feasting together regularly, and we exclaim, 'Job is indeed a blessed man!' Not only this, but Job was also *the greatest man among all the people of the East* (1:3). Righteousness, wealth, a perfect family, assured continuance of his family line, and fame were the jewels that adorned his crown of life. These are the indicators of a life blessed by God in the context of the OT – and in a traditional African context.

1:6-2:13 Job's Trials

Job has it all, he is living the ideal life as far as his job and his family are concerned, but this ideal life is threatened by the impending conflict in heaven.

1:6-22 The first trial

1:6-12 SATAN'S ACCUSATION The idea of God sitting on his heavenly throne with the angels presenting themselves before him is not unique to the book of Job (see 1 Kgs 22:19-22; Isa 6:1-3; Dan 7:9-10; Rev 4 and 5). Although the NT gives the impression that Satan and his hosts have been cast down from heaven (Luke 10:18; Rev 12:7-9), in the OT Satan and other evil spirits have access to the heavenly council. Not only that, but God has conversations with them. Whenever Satan appears before God, it is to accuse the people of God – whether individually or corporately (see also Zech 3:1). That is why Satan is called 'the accuser of our brothers' (Rev 12:10). How and why God allows this we do not understand.

God asks Satan where he is coming from. Satan answers *From roaming through the earth and going back and forth in it* (1:7). Although he works behind the scenes and is not simultaneously present everywhere like God, Satan is not a figment of the imagination – he is alive and well on planet Earth. God then mentions Job, stating that Job's character and lifestyle are pleasing to him. Satan responds with the accusation that Job has ulterior motives for behaving the way he does: *Why shouldn't Job be faithful to you seeing that you have showered him with so many blessings?* Satan's reference to a protective hedge around Job (1:9) may suggest his frustration at not being able to find any way into Job's life. Be that as it may, Satan suggests that Job *will surely curse you to your face* if you *stretch out your hand and strike everything he has* (**1:11**). In order to prove Satan a liar and vindicate himself and his servant Job's authentic piety and disinterested righteousness, God allows Satan to test Job to the limit.

1:13-22 The attack on Job's property and family Having received the go-ahead from God – though with some limitations (**1:12**) – the adversary goes at it with gusto. Most commentators try to categorize the four disasters that destroyed Job's family and property into human disasters (the attacks by the Sabeans and Chaldeans) and natural disasters (lightning and a tornado). However, if the conversation between God and Satan is taken seriously, there is no question that all these disasters are from a supernatural source. Note their timing and the breathless way in which they are reported: *While he was still speaking another messenger came and said …* (**1:16, 17, 18**); *… and I am the only one who has escaped to tell you* (1:16, 17, 18). The final devastating blow is the loss of his ten children. Job's initial reaction to the catastrophes that have befallen him and his family is shock and boundless sorrow. He expresses this by tearing his robe and shaving his head (**1:20**), which was the mourning custom of the day.

There is no doubt that Satan is intent on dislodging Job from his faith and causing him to curse God. However, to the chagrin of the adversary, that does not happen. Scripture says, *In all this, Job did not sin by charging God with wrongdoing* (**1:22**). Instead he confesses in worship and in absolute surrender to the Lord that he did not bring anything with him when he came into this world – it was all God's gift – and that he will not take anything with him from this world – he would depart naked (**1:21a**). There is no duality in Job's faith – everything that happens comes from God: *The Lord gave and the Lord has taken away; may the name of the Lord be praised* (**1:21b**).

How do we as Christians respond to calamities? David Atkinson concludes his comments on this section with a pastoral note: 'How difficult it is to worship at such a time! Yet worship is Job's reaction … Would that we could learn to make that our first reaction to crisis – to pray. How important in pastoral ministry to seek to lead others who are in pain to place their needs before God' (*BST*).

2:1-10 The second trial

Why was it necessary for Job to go through another trial? That was the choice of neither God nor Job himself. It was simply that the adversary would not give up. That is why the Apostle Peter admonishes believers: 'Be self-controlled and alert. Your enemy the devil prowls around like a roaring lion looking for someone to devour' (1 Pet 5:8). Even when he tested our Lord during his earthly sojourn, the

Scriptures tell us 'he [the devil] left him until an opportune time' (Luke 4:13).

2:1-6 Satan's accusation Back in heaven, the next encounter between God and Satan is almost identical to that in chapter one. There are slight differences though. This time Satan is not only among the angels, but he also *presents himself* before God (**2:1**). Not only is Job's piety described again, but God adds, *he still maintains his integrity*, indicating that Job has passed the first test with flying colours (**2:3**). Finally God indicts the adversary with the words *you incited me against him to ruin him without any reason* (2:3).

But Satan shows no respect for God and focuses on his opposition to Job. His response to God's praise for Job's steadfastness is *skin for skin* (**2:4**). These words are probably a proverb, meaning that a man will be happy to sacrifice someone else to save his own skin. The meaning of the proverb is clarified in Satan's elaboration: *A man will give all he has for his own life.* He challenges God, *stretch out your hand and strike his flesh and bones* (**2:5**). As in the first encounter, he unashamedly claims that Job would then *surely curse you to your face.* Once again Satan is granted permission to do his worst, on one condition: *you must spare his life* (**2:6**). Knowing Satan's nature, it is easy to predict that intense suffering will follow.

2:7-8 The attack on Job's health Satan promptly *afflicted Job with painful sores from the soles of his feet to the top of his head* (**2:7**). Opinions about the exact nature of his ailment range from it being open sores to boils to malignant cancer to leprosy to elephantiasis. He is in such pain that he scrapes himself with broken pottery (**2:8**). He is also rejected by his community, for *he sat among the ashes* (2:8). This probably means that he was treated like a leper and consigned to the garbage dump or ash heap outside his town or village. The picture that we have of Job is of a man who is 'physically afflicted, loathsome in appearance, and isolated from the warmth of human fellowship' (Gordis).

2:9-10 The responses of Job and his wife Job's wife is mentioned here for the first time. Satan appears to have succeeded as far as she is concerned. She can no longer stand the catastrophes that have befallen her family and her husband, and therefore tells Job: *Are you still holding on to your integrity? Curse God and die!* (**2:9**). God has told Satan that Job *still maintains his integrity* (2:3). While God has been confident that Job would maintain his integrity even in the present horrible situation, his wife insists, 'It is sheer folly to maintain your integrity under the present circumstances.' It is possible that Satan is launching his final attack through her, as she urges her husband to utter the curses that Satan has predicted would follow such suffering.

Job rebukes his wife: *You are talking like a foolish woman* and then reminds her what the proper response should be: *Shall we accept good from God, and not trouble?* (**2:10**). With those words Satan's defeat is sealed and God and his servant are vindicated. Scripture adds: *In all this, Job did not sin in what he said.* Not only in this book bearing his name, but in the NT as well, Job is mentioned as a great example of perseverance (Jas 5:11).

2:11-13 Job's three friends

The descrption of the visit by Job's three friends is a further part of the preparation of the readers for the major poetic section of the book. The text implies that these friends did not live close to Job, and that his suffering must have lasted from some time for them to have been able to arrange a meeting. Scholars differ as to the identity of these friends, but it seems likely that they were Edomites because their names are similar to names in the genealogy of Esau in Genesis 36.

Job's friends *saw him from a distance* (**2:12a**), which confirms that Job is no longer in his home but has been relegated to the open ash heap of the village or town. He is indeed a public spectacle. Their immediate reaction, like his when he received the news of the loss of his property and family (1:20), is one of utter shock: *they could hardly recognize him, they began to weep aloud and they tore their robes and sprinkled dust on their heads* (**2:12b**). Their initial shock is followed by a significant action: *Then they sat on the ground with him for seven days and seven nights. No one said a word to him, because they saw how great his suffering was* (**2:13**). While such behaviour may seem unusual in some cultures, it is perfectly appropriate in an African setting – particularly given the magnitude of Job's loss. In my culture, when a person dies the bereaved family sit in mourning for seven days, with community members constantly coming to console them. With the pressures of modern life, these days of mourning have now been reduced to three.

And what of the silence! Words are not of much help in situations like this. Silent empathy is the best a wise friend can offer. This paragraph is one of the most moving in the whole book of Job for some readers, and a model for us when we have to minister to the bereaved. Silence can sometimes be more eloquent than words.

Yet the sympathetic silence does not continue long enough. The attitude it expresses is terribly missing in the poetic section of the book where there is so much verbosity, talk and argument. No wonder the imagery of *wind* recurs so frequently (6:26; 8:2; 15:2).

3:1-31:40 The Poetic Dialogue

The poetic section of the book of Job clearly begins here in chapter 3 and ends in 42:6. It is also clear that the silence that prevailed for *seven days and seven nights* (2:13) is broken by Job. However, we are not told that in breaking the silence, Job intended to start the debate that follows.

3:1-26 Job's Lamentation

A question that has baffled biblical scholars is how to reconcile the Job of the prologue with the Job of the poetic dialogue, especially when one comes to the present chapter where he is cursing the day of his birth. We will return to this problem as we examine the text.

3:1-10 He curses the day of his birth

In this lamentation, Job is not addressing God, his friends, or anyone else for that matter. He is just giving vent to the grief and pain that have been building up within him. Like Jeremiah (Jer 20:14-18), he curses the day and the night on which he was born, the start of his existence. Those of us who have been affected by the West, and especially our children, cherish the celebration of our birthdays, but Job has no such feelings. 'His prolonged suffering on the borders of death intensifies because of depression and loneliness … Righteous anger, at once the hottest and the coldest of human emotions, consumes him. Directly, he curses the day of his birth; indirectly, he protests injustice; and, inferentially, he accuses God, his last friend' (*CC*).

The Hebrew word translated *cursed* in **3:1** is different from the word translated as 'curse' in chapters 1 and 2 (1:5, 11; 2:4, 9). The word used here is the exact word for cursing, whereas in the earlier chapters the word actually used was 'bless'. A literal translation would show that Satan predicted that Job would 'bless God' in 2:4, and in 2:9 Job's wife told him to 'Bless God and die'. Cursing is a dreadful thing when it is directed at humans, and even more so when directed at God, and so the euphemism 'bless God' was used instead. The Hebrew perspective seems to chime with the African.

In **3:8**, yet another Hebrew word is used for curse. This verse is difficult to understand, with its references to *those who curse days* and *Leviathan*. The background is probably some myth that we no longer know, but what is clear is that 'Job invokes the creatures of chaos to emerge and destroy his "day"' (Gordis).

We do not have to interpret Job's cursing of the day he was born as implying that God was mistaken in bringing him into this world. What he seems to be saying is that if the condition he finds himself in is the result of being born, then it would have been better not to have been born at all.

3:11-19 He longs for death

Questions about why, if he had to be born, he could not have died at birth (**3:11-12**) create a transition from the cursing of his day of birth to Job's consideration of death as a better option. 'Sometimes life is so bad that death can begin to look like a friend, a way out, an escape. Though certainly an unknown, it cannot be worse than what is known' (Simundson).

Reactions to Job's expectation of finding peace and rest in or beyond the grave vary depending on one's interpretation of the teaching of the OT about life after death. Those who believe that the OT does give a glimpse of life after death argue that Job is thinking of rest in heaven. Others argue that such an idea is foreign to the OT, which holds out no hope of a happy future life. However, even though the idea is not as clear as in the NT, there are indeed passages that suggest life after death and even the hope of resurrection in the OT. Such passages include the ones here: *I would be lying down in peace* and *I would be asleep and at rest* (3:13), *the weary are at rest* (3:17), *captives also enjoy their ease* (3:18). Later in the book Job himself speaks very clearly about the resurrection life (19:25-27). Thus in the midst of his darkness, Job sees a ray of hope.

3:20-26 He laments life in general

Job expands his questions and his lament to the level of humanity at large – although at times it is difficult to isolate the personal from the general. The intensity with which death is sought is quite alarming: people *search for it more than for hidden treasure* (3:21) and *are filled with gladness and rejoice when they reach the grave* (3:22). If 3:23 is speaking about Job – and a close look at the following verses seems to indicate that it is – then we witness a reversal of the perspective in chapter 1. The word 'hedge' is used in both situations, but with diametrically opposite meanings. In chapter 1, Satan accuses God of having *put a hedge around him* [Job] *and his household* (1:9) – clearly a sign of protection and care. Here, however, Job feels *hedged in*, deprived of his freedom, like a bird in a cage. Job would have very much appreciated release by death. Is that not how we feel in times of trial? Hear how Job bewails his predicament: *For sighing comes to me instead of food; my groans pour out like water* (3:24); *I have no peace, no quietness; I have no rest, but only turmoil* (3:26). But no! Death will not come. Why? Because the Almighty has decreed that Job will not die, even under the fiercest attacks of the enemy (2:6).

Commentators are puzzled by 3:25: *What I feared has come upon me, what I dreaded has happened to me.* What did Job fear? The fear of death may be ruled out because he is longing to die as a way out of his suffering. Gordis thinks that 'the fear to which Job refers is the natural sense of insecurity felt by any sensitive human being with regard both to his actions and to his fate.' Others think that his fears are a reflection of the anxiety expressed in 1:5 regarding the spiritual condition of his children. Fear of something happening to them may have afflicted him throughout his life. Still others argue that his fear is that he will be abandoned by God. It is difficult to pinpoint a specific cause for his fears. Some combination of the reasons mentioned above may be valid given Job's lamentation in this chapter and his complaint that he is being punished unjustly.

4:1-27:23 Three Rounds of Debate

Job's lamentation not only breaks the silence that has prevailed for 'seven days and seven nights' (2:13) but also triggers a heated discussion – although that may not have been intentional on the part of Job – between him and his three visiting friends. It all starts with *a word* (4:2) that opens a floodgate of words simply because the parties are entrenched in their respective theological positions and do not want to consider each other's point of view. A Tigrigna proverb from Eritrea captures the emptiness of too many words: *zereba adam hamed gdam* ['the speech of humankind is like the dust of the ground']. We have three rounds of speeches. In the first two rounds, Eliphaz, Bildad and Zophar each exchange views with Job. In the final round, only Eliphaz and Bildad speak to and are answered by Job.

4:1-7:21 First round: First exchange

The sequence in the first round of speeches goes as follows: Eliphaz speaks (chs. 4 and 5) and Job responds to him (chs. 6 and 7); Bildad speaks (ch. 8) and Job answers (chs. 9 and 10); Zophar speaks (ch. 11) and Job answers (chs. 12–14).

The first of Job's friends to speak is Eliphaz. In the context of the ancient Near East, it is generally understood that this is an indication that he is the oldest and the wisest in the group (15:10). Atkinson represents the consensus of biblical scholars when he says 'Eliphaz seems to be the oldest, profoundest, gentlest and generally nicest of the three friends' (*BST*).

4:1-5:27 ELIPHAZ'S FIRST SPEECH Eliphaz begins politely and some scholars think he is upholding Job's innocence in this first speech. His first considerate question is: *If someone ventures a word with you, will you be impatient?* (4:2). However, in the same verse there is a clue that this 'word' will multiply many times before long: *But who can keep from speaking?* Eliphaz reminds Job that he has been an encourager and source of comfort for many in his life, and challenges him not to be terrified by his predicament (4:3-5). It is difficult to be sure whether Eliphaz is being sarcastic or sincere when he tells Job, *Should not your piety be your confidence and your blameless ways your hope?* (4:6). Whichever is the case, he goes on to affirm that no innocent person has ever perished, but that *those who plough evil and who sow trouble reap it* (4:7-11; see also 5:1-6). The 'it' mentioned in 4:8 is the destruction referred to in the preceding verse.

It is worth reflecting on the theological position crystallized in 4:8 – that people or individuals reap what they sow. This idea is crucial to our understanding of the dispute that flares up between Job and his friends and to the doctrine of rewards and punishments that is encountered throughout the Scriptures (see, for example, Ps 1; the Sermon on the Mount; Mark 4:24; 1 Cor 3:10-15; Gal 6:7; 1 Pet 3:12). 'Behind this theological principle is a view of the world as an ordered moral universe. God is a just God and a good

God. Virtue will be rewarded, and the way of the wicked will perish' (*BST*).

It is thus strange that some scholars try to dismiss this position as they defend Job and challenge his friends' position. What needs to be attacked is not the teaching itself but rather the wrong way of applying it to Job's case. Eliphaz turns the biblical teaching on its head by claiming that because Job is reaping disaster, he must have sown iniquity. 'Eliphaz seems unable to allow God to be the judge of rewards and punishments, or even to allow that some principle other than rewards and punishments may be in operation … As Psalm 73 makes clear, God's actions and providences do not necessarily fit in with our immediate experiences' (*BST*).

Modern versions of Eliphaz can be found in the prosperity movements within Christian churches, which 'argue that because God blesses the righteous, material prosperity is therefore a sign of divine blessing, and therefore something we should seek. We do not have to travel very far before we find the quest for material prosperity replacing the quest for godliness and righteousness of life' (*BST*).

Eliphaz claims he has received a divine revelation in support of his doctrinal position (4:12-21). The gist of the message is given in **4:17**. The vision also comes with a warning for *those who live in houses of clay* (**4:18-21**). Assuming Eliphaz did indeed see some vision in the night, we need to ask who the spirit is that *glided past* his face (**4:15**), that *stood before [his] eyes* in some form (**4:16a**) and in *a hushed voice* (**4:16b**; see also 4:12) gives him this message (4:17-21). It is possible that Eliphaz and his friends are receiving the message that Satan wants conveyed. No wonder Scripture instructs us not to believe every spirit, 'but test the spirits to see whether they are from God' (1 John 4:1).

Eliphaz is telling Job to acknowledge the sins that have landed him where he is and to take responsibility for them. After all *hardship does not spring from the soil, nor does trouble sprout from the ground* (**5:6**) and, in any case, *man is born to trouble as surely as sparks fly upward* (**5:7**). He then goes on to give Job advice of the 'If I were you' -type, and again reiterates his basic theology (**5:8-16**) which, though true, is out of place when it comes to Job. He states the truism *Blessed is the man whom God corrects* (**5:17**). What he appears to be saying is that Job should accept his chastisement and experience the restoration of God (**5:18-26**). As far as Eliphaz is concerned, what he has said is authoritative: *We have examined this, and it is true. So hear it and apply it to yourself* (**5:27**).

6:1-7:21 JOB'S RESPONSE Eliphaz starts his first speech with the remark, *Who can keep from speaking?* (4:2) implying that he cannot help but speak in the light of Job's outburst in chapter 3. In his response to Eliphaz, Job seems to say, 'If you have reason to speak, I have even more'. And he goes on to say *no wonder my words have been impetuous* (**6:3**; see also 7:11). In 6:2-7 Job gives a justification for what may have appeared to be an impetuous speech. He says that there is no comparison between the weight of his anguish and misery and the weight of his words. His suffering is beyond measure. God (the Hebrew has *the Almighty*) has pierced him with his arrows and his spirit is drinking their poison (**6:4**). Just as a wild donkey will not bray if it has grass to eat, nor an ox if it has fodder, so Job would not complain were it not for his unbearable physical and spiritual anguish (**6:5**). Continuing to use food imagery, he accuses his friends of speaking words that are unappetizing because they are not sensitive to his situation (**6:6-7**).

Then Job again turns his attention to God and to the hopelessness of his current situation. The only hope he has is to die and exit this life (**6:8-9**). He affirms his innocence (**6:10**) and complains that he does not have the strength of stone or bronze to be able to continue to bear such extraordinary suffering (**6:11-13**).

Turning back to his friends, he accuses them of not fulfilling the purpose for which they came – they have turned out to be useless comforters. He has looked to them for comfort and encouragement in his troubles (**6:14**), but they have failed him. He uses the illustration of a stream that flows only during the rainy season but is dry the rest of the year (6:15-23). Trade caravans hoping to find water in the wadi of such a stream are disappointed, just as Job is disappointed in his friends. Instead of being a help to him, they take fright at the sight of his affliction (**6:21**). Yet their reaction is unjustified because Job did not ask them to deliver him or stand surety for him (**6:22-23**).

In the last section of the chapter Job expresses his willingness to be taught and to listen to *honest words*, but not to the kind of false, empty words that Eliphaz has spoken (**6:24-27**). He challenges them to look at him and see if there is anything false in his case (**6:28-30**). 'In the Middle East, business transactions are conducted at close quarters. Honesty or dishonesty is read by "eye language" … To attest his innocence, Job challenges his friends to a duel between the eyes as well as a debate over the facts. Once and for all, he wants these questions settled' (*CC*).

Having stated that his case is just, Job concludes with the challenge: *Is there any wickedness on my lips? Can my mouth not discern malice?* (6:30).

In chapter 7 Job directs his complaints mainly to God. He feels that his life is as futile as that of *a slave* or *a hired man* waiting for relief that is slow in coming (**7:1-3**). He can enjoy no rest by day or night (**7:3-4**). He graphically describes the disintegration of his body (**7:5**) and says *My days are swifter than a weaver's shuttle, and they come to an end without hope* (**7:6**).

The futility of his life reminds Job of how ephemeral life is, and he reminds God of this: he will soon pass away *as a cloud vanishes and is gone* (**7:9**) and never again experience happiness or return to his home. *Remember, O God* (**7:7**) he exclaims (although *God* does not appear in the Hebrew). Having reminded God of how brief his life is, Job asks God to show him mercy and leave him alone (7:11-16). He refuses to exercise restraint in expressing the agony of his soul (**7:11**). He tells God, 'I am not your enemy. Why do you then *put me under guard* like the monster of chaos?' (**7:12**). Again Job mentions his sleepless nights, but this time it is God who is terrifying him through dreams and visions (**7:13-14**). Even death by strangling is preferable to the life he is now enduring (**7:15-16**).

In the final verses of the chapter (7:17-21) Job's words seem to contradict the message of Psalm 8. Both ask the question: *What is man that you make so much of him?* (**7:17**; Ps 8:4) but while the psalm says that God seeks to glorify humans, Job says that God targets them for evil. It is important to remember that Job is thinking of his own situation when he asks this question, for we hear him saying, *Will you never look away from me or let me alone even for an instant?* (**7:19**). Appearing to admit his sinfulness, he continues: *If I have sinned, what have I done to you, O watcher of men? Why have you made me your target? Have I become a burden to you?* It is safe to say that Job is generalizing about humanity from his own experience, rather than the other way round. His words are not the taunts of a rebellious infidel, but the questions and struggles of a man of faith. For we hear him say, *Why do you not pardon my offences and forgive my sins? For I will soon lie down in the dust; you will search for me, but I will be no more* (**7:21**). In addition to the plea for mercy, Job is telling God 'You'll miss me when I'm gone' (7:21; see also 7:8). The words testify to the close fellowship God and Job enjoy. Yet they appear quite strange to us who live on this side of the cross of Christ. We ask, 'Why does Job think that his fellowship with God will be interrupted?' Is Job thinking only of earthly fellowship? If he leaves this life, where would he go if not to the place where God is?

8:1-10:22 First Round: Second exchange

The next interaction is between Bildad the Shuhite and Job. Although Bildad's speech is much shorter than that of the elderly Eliphaz, it is devastating and therefore invites an equally uncompromising response from Job.

8:1-22 BILDAD'S FIRST SPEECH Job asked his friends to evaluate his explosive language against the backdrop of his suffering and not to 'treat the words of a despairing man as wind' (6:26). But that plea means nothing to Bildad. He opens his mouth with an accusation, *Your words are a blustering wind* (**8:2**), and takes the moral high ground as he defends the justice of God (**8:3-4**). But his approach is callous, as is clear from his harsh words about Job's children: *When your children sinned against him, he gave them over to the penalty of their sin* (8:4). By contrast, Eliphaz made only

passing references to Job's children (5:4, 25). It is no wonder that God later tells Eliphaz: 'I am angry with you and your two friends, because you have not spoken of me what is right, as my servant Job has' (42:7). Having rubbed salt into Job's wounds, Bildad goes on to pontificate about God's restoration of Job. He says: *if you will look to God* (**8:5**), *if you are pure and upright,* God will *restore you to your rightful place* (**8:6**) – as if Job had not been looking to God and as if God himself had not already testified that Job is indeed *pure and upright*.

Bildad invokes tradition in support of his position (**8:8-10**). While tradition has a valuable role in giving continuity and stability to society, Bildad's appeal to tradition is false because he uses it to support an inflexible and rigid interpretation of the doctrine of retribution. In the rest of the chapter he gives illustration after illustration of how God always punishes the wicked and rewards the righteous. Papyrus does not *grow tall where there is no marsh* and reeds do not *thrive without water* (**8:11**). Without water, *they wither more quickly than grass* (**8:12**). *Such is the destiny of all who forget God* (**8:13**) – by inference, the destiny of Job. The things that the *godless* person depends on are as fragile as *a spider's web* (**8:14-15**). Such a person is *like a well-watered plant in the sunshine* which spreads rapidly, but withers even more rapidly when removed from its place (**8:16-19**) and is soon forgotten. Bildad concludes his tirade with an appeal to Job to return to God (**8:20-22**).

9:1-10:22 JOB'S RESPONSE In these chapters, Job's attention appears to be focused on God rather than on his friends – although he is keenly aware of what they have been saying to him. There is a lot of repetition from now on, and fewer and fewer new points will be raised.

Job begins his response to Bildad by admitting, *Indeed, I know that this is true* (**9:2a**). The NASB rendering is clearer and closer to the Hebrew: *In truth I know that this is so*. What part of Bildad's speech is Job referring to here? Commentators are uncertain. All we can say is that from **9:2b** to 9:13, Job seems to take up the theme of God's justice and man's righteousness – an issue that Eliphaz touched on (4:17) and Bildad hammered on (8:3). After stating the problem (**9:2b-3**), Job says that God's wisdom and creative power are clearly demonstrated by the works of his hand (**9:4-10**). This appears to be a foreshadowing of Yahweh's speeches in chapters 38 to 41. Yet in spite of this reality, Job says: *'When he passes me, I cannot see him; when he goes by, I cannot perceive him* (**9:11**). His person and his ways are mysterious. When he wants to do something, no one can ask him, *What are you doing?* (**9:12-13**).

Job then picks up his opening argument (9:3) to underscore the point that no creature can dispute with the Creator and win (9:14-24). Reflecting on his own situation, he says that he cannot find words to argue with or answer God (**9:14-15**). His only option is to plead for mercy. Continuing with the law court imagery, Job claims that even if he were to summon God, God would not respond. With a note of hopelessness, he says, God *would crush me with a storm and multiply my wounds for no reason* (**9:16-18**). He again stresses the hopelessness of getting justice (**9:19-20**). Frustrated by the injustice he is experiencing, he gives the adherents of the wisdom school – and his friends who uphold an inflexible doctrine of retribution – the shock of their lives when he says, *He destroys both the blameless and the wicked* (**9:22**). He extends his sense of injustice from his own experience to the experience of all humanity (**9:23-24**).

Using images of papyrus boats and swooping eagles, Job laments that his life will pass very swiftly without any joy (**9:25-26**). He has no hope of establishing his innocence. If God is the prosecuting attorney, jury and judge, where can justice be found? (**9:27-31**). The only hope for justice would be if God were a man like Job (**9:32**): *If only there were someone to arbitrate between us, to lay his hand upon us both, someone to remove God's hand from me, so that his terror would frighten me no more* (**9:33-34**). In those circumstances, Job says, *I would speak up without fear of him* (**9:35**). But as things stand now, Job can do nothing.

Coming to chapter 10, Job again reiterates his determination to speak out (see 6:3; 7:11). But this time not against his friends but against God (**10:1**). He says he will challenge God to tell him what the charges against him are (**10:2**) and ask why God seems to enjoy the oppression of one of his creatures, as a human being might (**10:3-7**). Job gives a beautiful account of how God created him – and all of us (**10:8-12**; see also Ps 139:13-16). However, he implies that God had an evil motive for doing this: *But this is what you concealed in your heart, and I know that this was in your mind* (**10:13**). And then Job piles up his 'if' statements – about his sins, his guilt, his innocence, his attempt to lift up his head – and accuses God of stalking him *like a lion* in order to *again display your awesome power against me* (**10:14-17**). Coming full circle, both in terms of what is said in this chapter and in chapter 3, Job again asks: *Why then did you bring me out of the womb?* (**10:18-19**). He concludes with a plea to God to give him a reprieve before he passes on to the land of gloom and darkness (**10:20-22**). It is interesting to note that here Job describes the realm of the dead in negative terms, whereas he had earlier referred to it as a place of rest from affliction.

11:1-14:22 First round: Third exchange

The third exchange is between Zophar and Job. Since Zophar speaks last in the first two rounds and not at all in the third round, he is thought to be the youngest of the three. He is also the least sympathetic. McKenna puts it graphically: 'Like a leopard springing from ambush upon its unsuspecting prey, Zophar enters the debate clawing and

scratching for Job's jugular vein' (*CC*). This may be why his speech receives a more elaborate response from Job.

11:1-11:20 ZOPHAR'S FIRST SPEECH All the disputants accuse each other of 'windy' words, but Zophar's rebuke of Job is the most wordy (**11:2-3**). Rodd understands him as saying 'Job's speeches are a spate of words, he possesses a glib tongue, his talk is endless. Such irreverence must be rebuked.' Zophar proceeds to do exactly that in a very brutal manner (**11:4-6**). First of all, he misrepresents Job when he says, *You say to God, 'My beliefs are flawless and I am pure in your sight'* (**11:4**). What Job had said was that he was innocent and not conscious of any sin that could have precipitated his suffering. Zophar then wishes that God would reveal Job's secrets so that the latter would understand that *God has even forgotten some of your sin* (**11:6**). Zophar seems to be saying that God has not even bothered to punish him for some of his many sins. He has not suffered as much as he deserves. Not enough suffering! Is this the way to comfort a friend who is going through excruciating pain and anguish of soul? And for reasons of which the 'comforter' knows nothing?

Not only are Zophar's words cruel, but they undermine his own argument. McKenna points this out clearly: 'If Job's suffering is less than his sin, his sin may also be less than his suffering! In his zeal to shame Job, Zophar has fallen into the trap of "situational ethics" by opening up an exception to a truth he held to be absolute' (*CC*).

There are two possible interpretations of Zophar's words *for true wisdom has two sides* (**11:6**) in the context of his desire for God to speak to Job. One interpretation takes the two sides as being the human and divine perspectives, while the other takes the two sides as being the principles governing the universe and God's moral law, with no human reference.

Zophar speaks of the unfathomable knowledge and power of God (**11:7-12**), something that Job himself has touched on earlier (9:4-20). Zophar's intention is to belittle Job. As far as he is concerned, a wild donkey will sooner give birth to a human being than a stupid man (an implicit reference to Job!) become wise (11:12). He speaks as if he knows exactly why Job is suffering. Finally, with the 'if' and 'then' of conditional statements, Zophar offers Job the (by now, almost trite) prescription for restoration (**11:13-19**), concluding with a warning that the only alternative for the wicked is *a dying gasp* (**11:20**).

12:1-14:22 JOB'S RESPONSE Whereas Job took two chapters to respond to Eliphaz and Bildad, his response to Zophar spreads over three chapters. It is, however, possible that Job is winding up the first exchange here, and that his response is not only addressed to Zophar but also to all three friends. In these chapters he is also speaking to God and musing to himself. His thinking oscillates between hope and despair.

As he begins (**12:2-3**) he reminds his three friends that he also knows what they know and that he is not inferior to them (see also 13:2). In fact he is quite sarcastic when he says this: *Doubtless you are the people, and wisdom will die with you!* (12:12). He then reverts to his usual complaint, this time mentioning that he has become *a laughingstock* to his friends, whereas 'the *tents of marauders are undisturbed* (**12:4-6**). He once again reminds us of the unfairness of his situation. A proverb captures Job's sense of his fall from a position of respect: *zwedeqe gereb msar yibezho* [Tigrigna, Eritrea – 'axes multiply on a fallen tree']. Once a big tree falls, axes – large and small – congregate to chop it into pieces. Job is right when he says that *men at ease have contempt for misfortune* (12:5). We fail to empathize with people who are suffering because we really do not understand what they are going through until we experience it ourselves. Although Job's friends started well (2:11-13), their initial sympathy has evaporated in the heat of the debate.

There are various translations of the last part of 12:6, which speaks about wicked people. The NIV has *those who carry their god in their hands*, while the NASB has *Whom God brings into their power* (but 'He who brings God into his hand', a literal translation of the Hebrew, in the margin). It seems that the NIV and the marginal reading of the NASB are correct in understanding this as saying that the wicked, *those who provoke God*, are either idol worshippers or those who think they have God under their control.

Having earlier said, *Who does not know all these things?* (12:3) with regard to the wisdom and power of God, Job proceeds to remind his friends that animate creatures and even inanimate creation will tell them of his power (**12:7-10**). In the light of Job's assertion that God holds *the life of every creature and the breath of all mankind* in his hands, it is ironic that the wicked people mentioned in the previous paragraph think they can 'carry their god in their hands'. Admonishing his friends – and especially the likes of Zophar – Job says, first of all, that he is in a position to weigh what they are saying, and second that in any case wisdom is found *among the aged* (**12:11-12**).

He appears to link the wisdom he has just talked about with the wisdom of God when he begins the next section by saying: *To God belong wisdom and power; counsel and understanding are his* (**12:13-25**). Job is speaking about the wisdom and power of God, just as he did in 9:4-10. He 'seems to be saying that everything that happens must be God's doing, whether it be giving authority or taking it away, whether it be something that involves whole nations or individuals' (Simundson). Some commentators, however, are of the opinion that Job is giving God's power a negative slant this time. Rodd, for example, after mentioning that this could have been 'a hymn in praise of God's power', asserts that here it is actually 'a fierce arraignment of God for the cruel use he makes of his omnipotence. He pulls down, imprisons, produces drought and devastating flood, destroys the reason of counsellors, judges and priests, and makes kings powerless. He leads people astray and destroys them, leaving them without effective rulers.'

To prevent his friends from forgetting what he had said at the beginning of chapter 12, Job repeats it at the beginning of chapter 13: *My eyes have seen all this, my ears have heard and understood. What you know, I also know; I am not inferior to you* (**13:1-2**).

And then, as if telling his friends, 'I do not expect any justice or consolation from you,' he says, *But I desire to speak to the Almighty and to argue my case with God* (**13:3**). Before speaking to God directly, however, he elaborates on the injustice and falsehood of Eliphaz and company (13:4-19). He upbraids them as *worthless physicians* and says that they would be of more help if they remained silent as they had done in the beginning and were willing to listen to him (**13:4-6**). He accuses them of trying to defend God falsely (**13:7-12**). Rodd makes the point that despite the friends' zeal to defend God, 'it is not the friends who pray to God but Job'. This should not surprise us. Job is vulnerable in the context of his suffering, whereas the friends who are *at ease* are full of contempt for his misfortune (12:5).

It is instructive how often Job asks his friends to keep silent and listen to him in this section (13:5-6, 13, 17). He gives his reasons for being adamant on this issue: *Though he slay me, yet will I hope in him* (**13:15**). After asserting that he would surely defend his ways to God's face (13:15), he says *Indeed, this will turn out for my deliverance* (**13:16**) and *I know I will be vindicated* (**13:18**). He says this because he has prepared his case, otherwise he would have kept silent as he is asking his friends to do (**13:19**).

It is only after this preparation that Job speaks to God (**13:20-27**) as he said in 13:3 he was going to do. His first step is to ask God to meet two conditions. First, he asks God to withdraw his hand (that is, to stop torturing him) and to stop terrifying him. Then he asks God to call him in to present his case. Only then will Job be able to state his case or reply to God's accusations. After presenting his case to God, Job concludes with the words: *So man wastes away like something rotten, like a garment eaten by moths* (**13:28**).

Job's reflection on the brevity of human life and its futility, which started in 13:28, seems to spill over into the beginning verses of chapter 14. He then resumes his discourse with God in 14:3-22. In his conversation with God here, Job appears to move from despair (**14:3-12**) to hope (**14:13-17**) and then back to despair (**14:18-22**). Some scholars try to rearrange the order of parts of Job in order to eliminate these mood swings and make it fit better with Western concepts of logic and coherence, but this approach 'fails to do justice to the passionate and impetuous change of theme and mood characteristic of Semitic poetry in general and of Job in particular' (Gordis).

In an eloquent speech, Job contrasts the life and death of a tree and of a human being (14:7-10). A tree that has been cut down may sprout again *at the scent of water*, but there is no such hope for us: *As water disappears from the sea or a riverbed becomes parched and dry, so man lies down and does not rise* at least *till the heavens are no more* (14:11-12).

15:1-17:16 Second round: First exchange

Each of Job's friends has had a turn to speak. Job has also had an opportunity to respond to each of them. However, the problem that triggered the debate is far from being resolved. Instead, the level of conflict and hostility has increased.

The sequence in the second round of speeches is as follows: Eliphaz speaks (ch. 15) and Job responds to him (chs. 16 and 17); Bildad speaks (ch. 18) and Job answers (ch. 19); Zophar speaks (ch. 20) and Job answers (ch. 21).

Once again, it is Eliphaz who speaks first.

15:1-35 ELIPHAZ'S SECOND SPEECH Although Eliphaz was polite and sensitive in his first speech, he sees no reason for that now, and he too abuses Job and speaks violently. Why the change? Simundson speculates that at first Eliphaz was 'troubled by the apparent goodness of Job and he struggled to reconcile this with his view of suffering as retribution for sin'. But after the first round of speeches, 'Eliphaz had seen a display of Job's nastiness, hostility, nearly blasphemous statements about God, and sharp criticism of his three friends. Job has given himself away by his own words and there is no need to be so gentle with him any more.'

Eliphaz begins rhetorically by asking, *Would a wise man answer with empty notions or fill his belly with the hot east wind? Would he argue with useless words, with speeches that have no value?* (**15:2-3**). The answer Eliphaz expects is a resounding 'no', thereby labelling Job as a fool and not as the wise man he thinks he is. Commentators have argued about the precise meaning of 'the hot east wind', but it seems likely that this is not a reference to what we could call 'hot air' but rather focuses on the wind as something light and elusive. As far as Eliphaz is concerned, Job's 'windy' speeches not only prove that he is a fool, but also destroy the fear of God – which is the essence of religion – and become a stumbling block to others (**15:4**). He is bringing condemnation on himself (**15:5-6**).

Eliphaz then accuses Job of putting himself on a pedestal (**15:7-13**). He hurls questions at him: *Are you the first man ever born?* (**15:7**); *Why has your heart carried you away and why do your eyes flash, so that you vent your rage against God and pour out such words from your mouth?* (**15:13**). Although people wiser and older than him have given him *God's consolations* and *spoken softly* (**15:10-11** – most likely a reference to Eliphaz's advice to Job in chapters 4 and 5), Job has rejected them. Add to this the 'blasphemous' words he has uttered against God, and the only possible conclusion is that Job is a condemned man.

After this barrage of questions meant to cut Job down to size, Eliphaz goes on to belittle humanity as a whole – but of course his target is always Job (**15:14-16**). The fact that Eliphaz is here repeating what he said earlier (4:17-19) indicates that he is running out of ideas. It is a relief to realize that Eliphaz's views do not represent the way God values those he created in his own image (see Ps 8:3-6).

In a long and windy passage (**15:17-35**) – repeating the very error of which he accuses Job – Eliphaz tells Job 'that pain, dread, darkness, trouble, anguish, desolation, ruin, loneliness, and futility are the automatic and inevitable wages for wickedness'(*CC*). Although this passage may be understood to refer to the destiny of wicked people in general, one cannot help but note the subtle indicators that suggest it applies to Job's situation. Eliphaz prefaces this passage with a claim that this is what he himself has seen and *what wise men have declared*, who in turn trace this knowledge to their ancestors right at the beginning *to whom alone the land was given when no alien passed among them* (**15:17-19**). There is thus no admixture to this pure knowledge. Having claimed special revelation for what he said in his first speech, Eliphaz now cites the lore of the wise and the ancients in support of his views.

16:1-17:16 JOB'S RESPONSE Deserted by God and incessantly attacked by his friends as a hypocrite, we see Job's moods fluctuating even more in these chapters. Yes, he is still adamant about his integrity, but his physical, emotional, social and spiritual suffering are taking a toll. In his references to *you* (16:2-4) he mixes both singular and plural forms. He speaks to all three when he accuses them of being *miserable comforters* (**16:2**). He specifically responds to Eliphaz when he asks, *Will your long-winded speeches never end? What ails you that you keep on arguing?* (**16:3**). The word translated by the NIV as 'what ails you' is translated by the NASB as 'what plagues you'. It comes from a root that can mean 'be ill', although some commentators prefer to translate it as 'compel' or 'force'. Whatever is driving Eliphaz to speak as he does, Job says that if he and his friends were to exchange roles, *I also could speak like you* (reverting to the plural) … *I could make fine speeches against you and shake my head at you* (**16:4**). But to do that would be to come down to their level, and so Job insists: *But my mouth would encourage you; comfort from my lips would bring you relief* (**16:5**).

Simundson clearly identifies where Job's friends have gone completely astray. Job is approaching the problem of suffering as 'the actual sufferer. When he talked about suffering he was talking about *himself* in relationship to God. He was very much on the "feeling" level, even as he raised his "Why?" questions.' By contrast, his friends see suffering as an intellectual problem, requiring a rational answer. 'When Job made disparaging remarks about God's justice, he was hoping for compassion. Instead he got arguments, along with condemnation for getting himself into trouble and for daring to question it once it had come.'

After a transitional statement that neither speaking nor being silent makes any difference to his pain (**16:6**), Job resumes his complaint with regard to his human and divine enemies – sometimes speaking to God directly and at other times indirectly (16:7-17). The language he uses to depict God's cruel attack on him is quite graphic. *God assails me and tears me in his anger and gnashes his teeth at me* (**16:9**). *All was well with me, but he shattered me; he seized me by the neck and crushed me. He has made me his target, his archers surround me. Without pity he pierced my kidneys and spills my gall on the ground. Again and again he bursts upon me; he rushes at me* like a warrior' (**16:12-14**). Consequently, Job puts sackcloth on his skin and buries his brow (**16:15**; 'horn', NASB, in line with the Hebrew) – an external manifestation of sorrow, shame and destitution. Yet he does not deserve all this (**16:16-17**). He therefore pleads with the earth not to cover his blood (**16:18**). Though he appears to see a glimmer of hope on the horizon (16:19-21), the last words on his lips as the chapter comes to a close concern the brevity of human life (**16:22**).

Going back to the hope mentioned by Job, we see that he speaks of a *witness*, an *advocate* and an *intercessor*. Elaborating on the intercessor, the text says *on behalf of a man he pleads with God as a man pleads for his friend* (**16:21**). Who is this witness or advocate or intercessor? Or the umpire or mediator mentioned in 9:33? Or, for that matter, the Redeemer mentioned in 19:25? In the context of the monotheistic faith of the OT, this cannot be any other than God himself. But looking at Job's accusation of God's injustice, how can God be the enemy and deliverer at the same time? How can he appeal to God against God? He has already accused God of being the prosecuting attorney, jury, judge and executioner, and now he seems to regard him as the defence attorney too!

It seems that Job is torn between different perceptions of God. Some commentators find it difficult to reconcile the different roles Job ascribes to God, but the problem may really be with Western categories of thought, with its clear delimitation of roles. We need to be sensitive to the biblical world view in order to interpret the Scriptures correctly.

There is no break between chapters 16 and 17. Job's comment on his life in 16:22 flows right into 17:1-2. Then, in a verse that appears to return to the law court imagery of 16:19-21, Job asks God to give him *the pledge*. What he is asking for is the type of guarantee given on behalf of a debtor or someone accused of a crime. Job demands that God give this because no one else will put up security for him (**17:3**). Having mentioned the friends turned enemies in verse **17:2**, he reverts in **17:4-5** to them and the judgment that awaits them. He again laments his condition (**17:6-8**), though seeing a glimmer of light: *Nevertheless, the righteous*

will hold to their ways, and those with clean hands will grow stronger (**17:9**). We observe the usual fluctuations of mood in 17:10-16. In thinking about his enemies, all Job sees is darkness (**17:10-12**). After several 'if' statements that seem to dampen his hope, he asks: *Where then is my hope? Who can see any hope for me? Will it go down to the gates of death? Will we descend together into the dust?* (**17:15-16**).

18:1-19:29 Second round: Second exchange

Once again, Bildad speaks, and his words do not help the situation at all. He is the foremost and harshest advocate of the traditional theology of retribution.

18:1-21 BILDAD'S SECOND SPEECH In his first speech (ch. 8), Bildad had been harsher to Job than Eliphaz. True to form, he speaks even more harshly this time. The picture that he paints for Job is dark. There is no hint of the earlier option of restoration provided Job is willing to confess his sin.

In his introductory remarks in the first four verses, Bildad's tone is harsh: *You who tear yourself to pieces in anger, is the earth to be abandoned for your sake? Or must the rocks be moved from their places?* Bildad seems to imply that Job's suffering is self-inflicted, although Job has clearly asserted that God had brought it on him (16:7-14). Bildad also seems to imply that Job is pushing his claim of innocence out of proportion, expecting the very laws of nature to be changed to suit him (**18:4**).

Bildad devotes the rest of his speech (18:5-21) to lecturing Job once again on the doctrine of retribution in its bleakest form, leaving no opening for restoration through repentance. McKenna describes Bildad as 'the traditionalist with the barbed tongue. His blunt and violent language has a way of escalating conflict beyond resolution … Under the guise of defending the faith, he would not hesitate to send Job to the stake and wield the torch himself' (*CC*).

Job has confessed that God had worn him out: 'you have devastated my entire household' (16:7). Bildad seizes on this as if it were a confession of guilt and insists that this is God's punishment: *The lamp of the wicked is snuffed out* (**18:5-6**, 18). We feel the impact of this image more when we remember that there were no matches to light fires in Job's day. Once lit, a lamp or a fire would be kept burning permanently.

Next, Bildad uses imagery of hunting, speaking of *a net, a mesh, a trap, a snare,* and *a noose* (**18:8-10**) that will catch an evil man. He describes the predicament of the hunted man: *Terrors startle him on every side and dog his every step. Calamity is hungry for him; disaster is ready for him when he falls* (**18:11-12**). Can Job possibly doubt that he is the one Bildad has in mind? Not at all – particularly when Bildad stresses that the 'disaster' he has just mentioned *eats away parts of his skin; death's firstborn devours his limbs* (**18:13**). Not only does the evil man suffer during life, but after death *the memory of him perishes from the earth; he has no name* *in the land* (**18:17**) for the reason that *he has no offspring or descendants among his people, no survivor where once he lived* (**18:19**). Bildad had earlier implied that Job's children deserved the judgment that had come on them (8:4), and here he rubs in the fact that they are all dead. Not only will the memory of a wicked man not be preserved, but all those who hear of his fate, *men of the west* and *men of the east* will be *appalled* (**18:20**). Bildad cannot have forgotten that Job was himself one of the people of the east (1:3). These idiomatic expressions might also mean that past and future generations will only know of Job as an example of the terrible fate of the wicked. Yes, *surely such is the dwelling of an evil man; such is the place of one who knows not God* (**18:21**). Job has indeed become 'a byword to everyone' (17:6).

Bildad does not seem to consider the effects of his words on Job. Rather, he seems to relish describing the disasters that will come on an evil man. He enjoys the picture of suffering that he paints. There is a warning here about our attitude towards people who are experiencing difficulties. Are we judgmental? What efforts do we make to try to understand their situation and help them? Words can be weapons, and we need to wield them with great care. We should be extremely circumspect with our words in situations such as this.

19:1-29 JOB'S RESPONSE Bildad began his first speech with 'How long will you say such things?' (8:2), and his second speech with 'When will you end these speeches?' (18:2). In his response to his friends, Job picks up this word, and demands to know *How long will you torment me?* (**19:2**). He accuses them of having tormented him with their words *ten times now* (**19:3**). This is a Hebrew idiom that means 'many times'. *If it is true that I have gone astray*, Job says, *my error remains my concern alone* (**19:4**; see also 7:20). If they insist on trying to prove that they know more than he does, he tells them point blank, *know that God has wronged me* (**19:6**).

Job's complaint is that his cry for justice has received no response whatsoever (**19:7**). Atkinson illustrates Job's desperation by citing Romanian pastor Richard Wumbrand's experience as 'a prisoner of conscience in gaol under a repressive totalitarian regime. He illustrated the cry of fellow-believers, heard daily from the cells, as one or another was tortured for their faith. He threw back his hands, and threw back his head and gave a long, loud, agonized, terrifying scream' (*BST*).

Referring to God in the third person, Job complains that he is the cause of all his suffering. In the past God had *blocked my way*, *shrouded my paths*, *stripped me of my honour*, and *removed the crown from my head*, while in the present God *tears me down*, *uproots my hope*, and *counts me among his enemies* (**19:8-12**; see also 16:7-17). Not only that, Job has been completely cut off from society, from *brothers*, *acquaintances*, *kinsmen*, and *friends*. Not even his servants respond to

his call, and his breath is offensive to his wife (19:13-18). It is not clear why both the NIV and NASB translate the second half of **19:17** *my own brothers* when the Hebrew has 'my own sons' or 'children'. It may be that the decision is based on the logical argument that the narrative prologue states that all Job's children have died, so there are no children to whom Job can appear *loathsome*. The translation in my mother tongue (Tigrigna) follows the Hebrew, probably on the basis that there is no need to force consistency between every detail in the prose portion and every detail in the poetry. Semitic literature does not insist that there should never be any apparent contradictions within a text.

Job summarizes the afflictions God has brought on him as follows: *All my intimate friends detest me, those I love have turned against me. I am nothing but skin and bones; I have escaped with only the skin of my teeth* (**19:19-20**). Turning to his friends, Job utters a cry of dereliction: *Have pity on me, my friends, have pity, for the hand of God has struck me* (**19:21**). Reminding them that they do not have to play God, Job asks them, *Why do you pursue me as God does? Will you never get enough of my flesh?* (**19:22**). Before the chapter closes, however, he will also tell them that the tables will be reversed and God's judgment will be meted out to them (19:28-29).

Bracketed by the plea and challenge (19:21-22) and the warning (19:28-29) is a passage that has baffled biblical scholars and theologians (19:23-27). McKenna links his understanding of it to the spiritual principle expounded by Paul, 'If we endure [with him], we shall also reign with him' (2 Tim 2:12). Job has just recognized the troubling possibility that he may die before he is vindicated. Consequently he has to try to interpret his position in the light of eternity. We can clearly trace his growth in understanding. In 7:7-10 he thought of Sheol, the world of the dead, as just an 'impersonal suspension between worlds'. Later, he began to hope that some traces of his personhood would remain, and even dared to suggest that God would miss him (7:21). Then in 17:13-16 'another flash of insight lets him see the potential of personhood even in death'. But 'not until Job touches the bottom of the pit of humiliation, however, do the eyes of his faith open wide' (*CC*).

What exactly is Job saying? He is facing the annihilation of death without any hope of vindication in this present life. It is a mark of his emotional and spiritual maturity that he can accept the postponement of his desire for instant answers (which we all share) and can face up to this stark reality. Now he exclaims, *Oh, that my words were recorded*. Note the increasing intensity of his desire for a permanent record of his words. He moves from *were written on a scroll*, to *were inscribed with an iron tool on lead*, to *engraved in rock forever* (**19:23-24**). Bildad has told Job that he would be forgotten or remembered only with horror (18:17-20); Job's desire was to leave a written record for posterity.

Which words did Job want to have recorded? It may have been his words proclaiming his innocence, or it may have been 19:25-27. However, it does not seem necessary to debate which exact words he was referring to. The biblical record incorporates both the record of his innocence and of his revelation.

Next, Job makes a giant leap of faith and asserts that there is no doubt that he will ultimately be vindicated (19:25-27). As we try to understand this passage, it is important not to overspiritualize Job's words or to get bogged down in minor details.

There has been much discussion of the identity of the *Redeemer* in **19:25**. The concept is linked to the ot idea of a kinsman redeemer, whose responsibilities included redemption from bondage or slavery (Lev 25:47-49), redemption of property (Lev 25:25; Ruth 4:4, 6), marrying the childless window of a deceased brother (Ruth 3:4, 6, 13; 4:5-6), and avenging the blood of a family member who has been murdered (Num 35:16-28; Deut 19:6, 12; see also Gen 4:10; 9:6 and 16:18-19 here in Job). Yet although this may be the type of redeemer Job is thinking of, it is clear from the context that he is not speaking of a human redeemer. So what does he have in mind?

Three main possibilities have emerged. Some commentators say that Job is referring to the words he wanted recorded in 19:23. This record will restore his reputation and lead to his being declared innocent. Others say that Job must be referring to some heavenly being other than God who will plead his case before God. A third view, which has long been the most common interpretation in Jewish and Christian circles, is that the redeemer is God himself. God would redeem Israel from slavery in Egypt and from the Babylonian Exile, and he will eventually redeem Job.

Examining this passage in the context of the entire biblical revelation, McKenna comments that in saying *I know that my Redeemer lives* (19:25a) Job is recognising that, despite his earlier pleas for an independent umpire, he 'cannot stand before God in his own righteousness … A brother who is willing to shed his blood on Job's behalf is his only hope. He dares to believe that such a brother exists and will vindicate him in the future. Job foresees the Atonement' (*CC*). Not only that, but in saying that *in the end he will stand upon the earth* (19:25b), Job also foresees the incarnation. He also expresses the hope of personal resurrection: *I myself will see him with my own eyes – I, and not another* (**19:26-27**).

The idea of a go-between, a mediator, is not new to Africans. In African traditional religion, the ancestors – 'the living dead' – have played that role. In the Catholic and Orthodox churches, saints (living or dead) and angels are said to have mediating roles. But in the light of the divine revelation that was given to Job and its fulfilment in the incarnation, death and resurrection of Jesus Christ, the Son

of God, we know that there is only 'one mediator between God and men' (1 Tim 2:5) and that 'salvation is found in no one else, for there is no other name under heaven given to men by which we must be saved' (Acts 4:12) but the Name that is above all names (Phil 2:9).

20:1-21:34 Second round: Third exchange

In this last exchange of the second round of speeches, it is Zophar and Job who are speaking. This will be the Zophar's last speech, unless – as some scholars do – we try to carve out another speech for him in chapter 27.

20:1-29 ZOPHAR'S SECOND SPEECH Zophar is agitated, speaking of *My troubled thoughts* and saying *I am greatly disturbed* (**20:2**). The source of his discomfort is that he takes all that Job has said as having been directed at him personally: *I hear a rebuke that dishonours me* and insists that *my understanding inspires me to reply* (**20:3**). Given the agitation in his soul, he would have been wiser to have remained silent. Some commentators also understand this statement as a claim that he has received a special revelation, like his elder companion, Eliphaz (4:12-16).

The rest of the chapter is taken up with Zophar's elaboration of the fate of the wicked – a topic already addressed by Eliphaz and Bildad in previous chapters. As mentioned earlier, these men have nothing new to say. Zophar introduces his topic with *Surely you know how it has been from of old, ever since man was placed on the earth* (**20:4**) and then proceeds to catalogue the woes that await the wicked. He mentions that the joy of the wicked will not last (**20:5**). The wicked may try to reach heaven in his pride and boasting, but his fall will be great (**20:6-7a**). He will disappear, so that people will ask, *Where is he?* But he will be nowhere to be found (**20:7b-9**). His children will suffer the consequences of his sinful life and he will die while still young (**20:11**). Though he may try to hide his evil, like a person sucking a sweet candy under his tongue, it will finally be like the venom of a snake and poison his entire life (**20:12-16**). He will not enjoy the wealth he has unjustly accumulated (20:17-19). Instead his children will use it to pay back to the poor he has defrauded (**20:10**). While this whole catalogue of retributions is expressed in general terms, there can be no doubt that it is targeted at Job. Yet the accusation that he has *oppressed the poor* (**20:19**) is an outright lie. Even Eliphaz admitted that Job had cared for the poor (4:3-4).

Continuing with his barrage of punishments, Zophar says that distress and God's anger will be the lot of the wicked man in the midst of his prosperity – he cannot escape (**20:20-26**). What is more, *the heavens will expose his guilt* and *the earth will rise up against him* (**20:27**). These realms, usually used as witnesses by God and his holy messengers, will all testify against the wicked. Having introduced his sermon with 'Surely you know' (20:4), now Zophar sweeps to an end with *Such is the fate God allots the wicked, the heritage appointed for them by God* (**20:29**).

McKenna labels Zophar's speech in this chapter 'The Almost-Perfect Sermon' (*CC*). He gives it that label because although perfect in style and content, it is delivered with the wrong motive and to the wrong audience.

21:1-34 Job's RESPONSE Zophar has argued that God always punishes the wicked. Actually, that has been the thrust of most of the friends' speeches. But in what they have been saying recently there is no mention that God would restore Job if he repented, nor any mention of the other side of retribution – that God rewards the righteous.

Job flatly dismisses their argument. He begins by telling them that they would do a better job of consoling him if they really listened to what he was saying (**21:2-3**). He sees what they have been saying as a form of mockery (21:3). His complaints are not directed to them but to God (**21:4**) and the friends should have simply put their hands over their mouths and shut up – reminding them of their initial shock when they first saw his suffering (**21:5**). In fact, when he thinks of the extent of his suffering, he himself is *terrified* and *trembling seizes* his body (**21:6**). How can an innocent man suffer so much when the wicked are at ease? Atkinson reminds us that originally 'Job would no doubt have shared [his friends'] view that God's moral universe is one in which righteousness is rewarded and wickedness punished ... But Job's whole experience contradicts that. Not only does *he* suffer in his *innocence*, but the wicked actually have quite a good time!' (*BST*). So he tells his friends that their argument that God always metes out the punishment the wicked deserve is a lie (21:7-13). Contrast the punishment that Zophar and his companions have described with the actual lives of the wicked: they grow old and increase in power (**21:7**), their children are established around them (**21:8**), their homes are safe and secure (**21:9**), their cattle multiply without any miscarriages (**21:10**), they and their children rejoice (**21:11-12**), and, finally, *they spend their years in prosperity and go down to the grave in peace* (**21:13**).

The surprising thing, as far as Job is concerned, is that these people even go to the extent of confronting God and nothing happens to them (21:14-15). These are 'fools' – the characterization of the wicked in the terminology of the Wisdom books (Ps 14:1). Hear what they say to God: *Leave us alone! We have no desire to know your ways. Who is the Almighty, that we should serve him? What would we gain by praying to him?* (**21:14-15**). What an affront! And what a misunderstanding of what prayer is about. Their attitude is similar to that of some Americans who responded to our request for intense, sacrificial prayer (rather than formal, superficial praying) with 'It's not surprising that you pray a lot in Africa, for you have all those natural and man-made catastrophes to deal with. But here in America we have everything we need at our fingertips, so why should we pray?' To say this is to forget that prayer is, first of all, worship of

the God who has created and redeemed us. Praying is far more than just presenting him with our own shopping list of needs. Even we believers need to guard against such an attitude in our prayer life and in our relationship with God.

While admitting that the destiny of powerful and wealthy wicked persons is not under their own control but is in God's hands (**21:16**), Job fires off a series of questions, hammering on *How often ... ?* as he challenges his friends' assertions about the fate of the wicked (**21:17-18**). Then he moves on to Zophar's statement (20:10) that the children of a wicked man suffer the consequences of his sin. Job would rather that the wicked person himself reap what he has sown, since he does not care about the welfare of the family after he is gone: *Let his own eyes see his destruction; let him drink of the wrath of the Almighty. For what does he care about the family he leaves behind when his allotted months come to an end?* (**21:19-21**).

Some commentators treat **21:22**, *Can anyone teach knowledge to God*, as a gloss added by a later hand, but there is no need to see it as such. Job is criticizing his friends' presumption in assuming that God will act in the way they find appropriate and uphold their limited understanding of the doctrine of justice. Job insists that there is no distinction between the righteous and the wicked when it comes to death. *One man dies in full vigour, completely secure and at ease, his body well nourished, his bones rich with marrow* (**21:23-24**; see also 21:13). *Another man dies in bitterness of soul, never having enjoyed anything good* (**21:25**). If life were fair, there should be some difference between the two, yet *side by side they lie in the dust and worms cover them both* (**21:26**). Ecclesiastes underscores the point Job is making (Eccl 8:14; 9:2-3).

Turning to his friends, Job stresses that he understands their thinking but does not agree with it: *I know full well what you are thinking, the schemes by which you would wrong me* (**21:27-28**). Then, going over the ground he has already covered, he tells them to consult those who have travelled widely and have rich experience (21:29-33). No one reprimands or pays back the wicked for their evil conduct (**21:30-31**). On the contrary, they are given a respectful burial and rest at peace in the grave (**21:32-33**). Having made his point, Job gives his logical conclusion: *So how can you console me with your nonsense? Nothing is left of your answers but falsehood* (**21:34**).

22:1-24:25 Third round: First exchange

One would have expected that Job's responses would have silenced his friends, or that they would have run out of arguments. But that is not the case, although Bildad is flagging and Zophar opts out of the discussion.

McKenna summarizes the situation as a stalemate as Job and his friends move into their third and last cycle of speeches: 'Their arguments have been pushed to opposite extremes and neither will concede a point. Confusion is represented by the fact that the arguments are now partial and disjointed' (*CC*). Yet it is clear that by this stage. 'Eliphaz and Bildad do not hesitate to indict Job, not just as a sinner who has rebelled against God but as the epitome of evil who wreaks havoc upon the most helpless of creatures – the poor, the widows, and the orphans' (*CC*).

The sequence in the third round of speeches is as follows: Eliphaz speaks (ch. 22) and Job responds to him (chs. 23 and 24); Bildad speaks (ch. 25) and Job answers (chs. 26 and 27). Zophar does not speak at all in this round.

As has been the pattern throughout, it is Eliphaz who speaks first.

22:1-30 ELIPHAZ'S THIRD SPEECH Without any preliminaries, Eliphaz plunges into a set of rhetorical questions (22:2-5). What he wants to impress upon Job is that whether Job is wise or righteous is of no concern to God (**22:2-3**). How blasphemous to say this of the holy God who has established a moral order in his universe! And is not the belief that God does care the basis for this endless debate?

Whether Eliphaz realizes it or not, God has spoken directly to the adversary in the presence of the heavenly hosts, saying: 'Have you considered my servant Job? There is no one on earth like him; he is blameless' [the very word used by Eliphaz in 22:3] 'and upright, a man who fears God and shuns evil.' And God has said this not once, but twice (1:8; 2:3). Yes, it does please the Almighty when people he has created in his own image live lives worthy of the one who created them and redeemed them. Yes, it is indeed because of his *piety* that Job is suffering (**22:4**) – even if Eliphaz's rhetorical question is meant to elicit a negative answer and thereby condemn Job.

Eliphaz's final question (**22:5**), which serves as a transition to the next three verses, clearly betrays his intention. Having labelled Job's sins as *great* and *endless*, Eliphaz proceeds to articulate them: *You demanded security from your brothers* and left them naked at night (**22:6**); you withheld water from the weary and food from the hungry (**22:7**); *you sent widows away empty-handed and broke the strength of the fatherless* (**22:9**). Eliphaz reminds Job of the power

SUFFERING

Everyone who reads the Bible, whether regularly or only occasionally, must have noticed the important role suffering plays in it. We cannot miss the sufferings of the people of Israel, of the prophets, of Jesus Christ himself and of the apostles.

The subject is so common that we get the impression that the Christian life cannot be separated from suffering. But what is even more astonishing is that suffering and joy are so often mentioned together that it seems that joy flows naturally from suffering.

In the OT, the prophets announce that, after a time of testing, God will wipe away the tears from the faces of his people and remove their disgrace (Isa 25:6-9). The NT likewise emphasizes the triumph of joy over sorrow. We see this in the Beatitudes, especially those relating to the persecuted: 'Blessed are you when people insult you, persecute you … Rejoice and be glad' (Matt 5:11-12). We find the same idea in Paul's letters (Rom 8:18; 2 Cor 4:17) as well as in Peter's (1 Pet 4:13; 5:10).

Should we conclude from this that the Bible calls believers to go out of their way to attract unfair treatment and persecution? Does it encourage them to seek out suffering in the hope of gaining some benefit?

No! None of what has been said suggests that suffering is good in itself. No one can tell the sick that their sickness is a blessing because something good will come of it. Nor can we tell refugees that they should be happy to have experienced war because God can and will change their situation. No, suffering is an evil that we should fight with all our strength! This is why the Bible teaches that there will be no pain and

suffering in the new world order that God will set up at the return of the Lord Jesus Christ (Rev 7:17b; 21:4).

The sufferings that the Bible describes as followed by joy and gladness are those we do not deserve and that we experience because of our faith in Jesus Christ (1 Pet 2:20-21; 4:15-16). They are not troubles that a believer seeks as an expression of special spirituality. Besides, we know that some of the trials we experience have nothing to do with whether we belong to the Lord. Many terrible events on our continent affect both believers and unbelievers alike. What is important is to know how the Bible encourages us to face them.

Faced with suffering, we need to affirm our confidence in the love and tenderness of our God and Father. It is he who allows us to experience these tests. For our good, he also provides a way of escape from these trials. He does not allow them to last too long or to be too hard for us to bear (1 Cor 10:13). This is true even if, humanly speaking, today's circumstances and the forecast for the future leave us fearing the worst for our continent.

It is clear that we cannot say, 'Blessed suffering!' Such a statement would be a contradiction of the word of God. However, in God's hands, trials can become a tool to purify, to mature and to strengthen his children. Forgetting that, some people teach that we should not suffer at all. These people seem to see only the evil of the suffering, rejecting altogether its usefulness.

Let us accept willingly all the trials through which we pass, never forgetting that the testing of our faith produces perseverance. But let us be sure that this perseverance is allowed to finish its work so that we 'may be mature and complete, not lacking anything' (Jas 1:2-4).

Issiaka Coulibaly

and wealth he enjoyed (**22:8**), in contrast to the plight of the groups he mistreated: the poor, widows and orphans. All the sins Eliphaz lists invite God's fiery judgment (Exod 22:22-27; Deut 24:12-17; 26:12-13; 27:19; Isa 1:17, 23; 10:1-2; 58:7; Ezek 18:7; 22:7; Zech 7:10). But what we find amazing is that Eliphaz is completely contradicting his own earlier evaluation of Job's character (4:3-4).

Eliphaz assumes that the gross sins he has just described are the reason why Job is suffering (**22:10-11**). Bringing God into the picture (22:12-18) by first stating that he lives in the *heights of heaven* (**22:12**), Eliphaz accuses Job of having said, *What does God know?* (**22:13-14**). While it is true that Job has spoken about the hiddenness of God and his injustice in his own case, one wonders where or when he made a statement such as Eliphaz alleges. Reverting to the issue of the wicked, he again asks Job, *Will you keep to the old path that evil men have trod?* (**22:15**) and elaborates the point (22:16-18) – to the dismay of Job and us readers. Eliphaz is no longer original. Speaking about the wicked – with whom Job is lumped – Eliphaz says, *They said to God, 'Leave us alone! What can the Almighty do to us?'* (**22:17**). Not only is he snatching Job's very words from his mouth (21:14-15) but he is using those words to describe Job himself. Eliphaz's disclaimer: *so I stand aloof from the counsel of the wicked* (**22:18**) is, in fact, exactly what Job had said (21:16). Job, too, had raised the issue of mockery (21:3), which Eliphaz takes up (**22:19-20**). He has indeed run out of ideas!

Finally, Eliphaz pleads with Job to confess his sin and experience God's restoration (22:21-30). This is truly a beautiful passage, full of hope in a hopeless world. It speaks about submission to God with the promise of restoration of peace and property (**22:21-23**), trusting in God rather than in earthly riches (**22:24-25**), finding joy in the Almighty (**22:26**), answered prayer and guidance (**22:27-28**) and becoming an instrument of reconciliation for others (**22:29-30**). But again, it is being delivered to the wrong audience.

These final words mean that Eliphaz must still be seen as comparatively more sensible than his two friends. Whereas the other two in their anger made no mention of any possibility of restoration, Eliphaz, wrong as he may be, has at least offered that option in captivating words.

23:1-24:25 JOB'S RESPONSE Job does not want to dignify Eliphaz's speech with a direct response. Instead of beginning with the usual address to his friends, he ignores them – as he had earlier said he would (13:3; 21:4) – and focuses on God. Thus we do not see him answering Eliphaz directly in these two chapters. Instead, we see him speaking of God immediately. First, he expresses his longing for a meeting with God, so that he can state his case before him, or at least hear what accusation God would bring against him (**23:2-5**). Then, to our surprise in the light of his earlier outbursts against God's injustice, he says that God will acquit him (23:6-7). The revelation of a coming Redeemer appears

to have given Job hope. Listen to his words: *Would he oppose me with great power? No, he would not press charges against me. There an upright man could present his case before him, and I would be delivered from my judge* (**23:6-7**). This is the exact opposite of what Job said in his previous speeches. Of course, as we have already seen, Job's moods fluctuate, but from now on these fluctuations will be less dramatic.

Next, Job again speaks of the hiddenness of God (**23:8-9**; see also 9:11). Job searches for him in all the directions of the compass, but cannot find him anywhere. *But*, says Job – and this is further evidence of his changed attitude – *he knows the way that I take; and when he has tested me, I will come forth as gold* (**23:10**). No longer is Job complaining that God is unjust, a torturer with a sadistic enjoyment of Job's suffering. A positive belief that the outcome will, after all, be for his good has begun to set in. Once again, Job mentions his faithful walk before God as the basis for this hope (**23:11-12**).

But Job cannot sustain the confidence he shows in 23:6-7 and 23:10-12. Once again he slides into an ambivalent state of mind (23:13-17). In a passage that reflects our own bafflement as we try to understand Job's and our God, we hear Job saying, *he stands alone, and who can oppose him? He does whatever he pleases* (**23:13**). The God that Job and we have to deal with is the Almighty God – unique, incomparable, majestic! Although Job, along with his friends, believes that God rewards the righteous and punishes the wicked, he also realizes that God can do anything he wants with his creatures and no one can ask, 'What are you doing?' (9:12-13). Applying this insight into who God is to his own situation, Job says, *he carries out his decree against me, and many such plans he still has in store* (**23:14**). While Job longs to meet God, he is also in awe of his power and of the mystery of his acts. Job cogently explains his feelings as he anticipates an encounter with this awesome God: *That is why I am terrified before him; when I think of all this, I fear him. God has made my heart faint; the Almighty has terrified me* (**23:15-16**). Despite this storm of reverence and uncertainty within his soul and mind, Job speaks with determination: *Yet I am not silenced by the darkness, by the thick darkness that covers my face* (**23:17**; see also 22:12-14). Here the 'darkness' is not just Job's suffering but all that hides God and his ways from Job and thus leaves him ambivalent about the outcome of the encounter he is looking forward to. Simundson points out that Job 'wants that judgment and yet he doesn't. He still trusts God and yet he doesn't. He loves God and yet he is terrified of God. But, when all is said and done, there is no place else to turn.'

In chapter 24 Job returns to the vexing problem of why the wicked seem to escape God's retribution (24:1-17). He asks: *Why does the Almighty not set times for judgment? Why must those who know him look in vain for such days?* (**24:1**). Why are wicked people allowed to carry out their evil schemes without any intervention from the governor of the universe? He then goes on to identify three categories of wicked people. McKenna labels these three groups the renegades against the helpless, the profiteers against the poor, and rebels against the light (*CC*).

Who are the 'renegades against the helpless' described in 24:2-8? They are described in **24:2** as *men* (NIV) or *some* (NASB – although it has *they* in the margin), neither of which is found in the original. The third person masculine plural is built into the verb in Hebrew, and the text does not specify who these people are. From the context, however, there is no doubt that the people referred to are the wicked. These people *move boundary stones* and *pasture flocks they have stolen* (24:2), they *drive away the orphan's donkey and take the widow's ox in pledge* (**24:3**) and they *thrust the needy from the path and force all the poor of the land into hiding* (**24:4**). As the result of such atrocities, the poor and helpless are forced to forage for food in *the wasteland* (**24:5**), to *gather fodder in the fields and glean in the vineyards of the wicked* (**24:6**), to *spend the night naked* because they have no clothes (**24:7**). *Drenched by mountain rains,* they *hug the rocks for lack of shelter* (**24:8**). This is a graphic picture of deprivation. McKenna underlines the immensity of such wickedness in the context of a subsistence economy of the type that existed in the OT: 'Mutual respect is given to the boundaries of the scrubbiest farms, the sustenance value of the smallest flocks of sheep, the carrying power of a single donkey, and the working power of a cumbersome ox. To violate this code is a crime punishable by death' (*CC*).

The next group of wicked people, the 'profiteers against the poor', are described in 24:9-11. These people snatch the fatherless child *from the breast* and seize the infant of the poor *for a debt* (**24:9**). The purpose is to exploit them as slaves. The lot of these slaves is described for us in vivid language: they *go about naked* due to lack of clothes (**24:10**); *they carry the sheaves, but still go hungry* and they *crush the olives* and *tread the winepress, yet suffer thirst* (24:10-11). Job says that *the groans of the dying rise from the city, and the souls of the wounded cry out for help. But God charges no one with wrongdoing* (**24:12**). It is as if God turns a deaf ear to the plight of these poor and helpless people.

The third group are those who are said to *rebel against the light* (24:13-17). These people literally shun daylight and emerge under cover of night to kill and steal from *the poor and needy* (**24:14, 16**). Under cover of darkness, when no *eye will see* them, they commit adultery (**24:15**). These nocturnal criminals are like beasts of prey, prowling in the night (**24:17**).

Yet although all those perpetrating these evils may imagine that no eye sees them, God does (**24:23**) and hence judges them.

Some commentators find it difficult to accept that 24:18-25 is part of Job's speech. Consequently, they try to assign this passage either to Bildad (whose speech in the third round is quite brief) or to Zophar (who does not speak at all in the third round). Their reason for doing this is that Job, who has been arguing that his friends' position is untenable because the wicked enjoy life rather than being punished, would not have changed his mind at this point. Yet although Job has fiercely opposed his friends' position that there is exact and immediate retribution here and now, he has never said that the wicked would not be punished in the long run (see, for example, 21:19-21). Moreover, we have noticed a change in Job's attitude since his confession that a Redeemer will come. Once he has positively affirmed that God will acquit him as a righteous person, can he not, by the same token, affirm that the wicked will be punished?

Job says that the apparent success of the wicked is temporary (24:18-19). They are like *foam on the surface of the water* (**24:18**), which soon disappears. *As heat and snow snatch away the melted snow, the grave snatches away those who have sinned* (**24:19**). Then they will be remembered no more (**24:20**). After reminding the reader of the wicked's brutality to the poor and helpless (**24:21**), Job affirms that they have no security, though they appear well established for a season (**24:22-23**). *For a little while they are exalted, and then they are gone* (**24:24**). Job's testimony here resembles that of the psalmist who confessed that 'as for me, my feet had almost slipped; I had nearly lost my foothold' (Ps 73:2). Why? 'For I envied the arrogant when I saw the prosperity of the wicked' (Ps 73:3). But his attitude began to change once he 'entered the sanctuary of God' (Ps 73:17). There he confessed to God: 'Surely you place them on slippery ground; you cast them down to ruin. How suddenly are they destroyed, completely swept away by terrors! As a dream when one awakes, so when you arise, O Lord, you will despise them as fantasies' (Ps 73:18-20). Job would add his 'Amen' to this: *If this is not so, who can prove me false and reduce my words to nothing?* (**24:25**).

25:1-27:23 Third round: Second exchange

As mentioned earlier, there is a lot of debate among scholars in relation to the last exchange in the third round of speeches. Part of it relates to the change in Job's attitude that was discussed in the comments on chapter 24, and part to the fact that Bildad's speech consists of only five verses. Some say that what we have is a mutilated text and try to locate parts of Bildad's speech in the chapters that follow, which are said to have been spoken by Job. Rather than going into details about this debate, I will accept what is before us as the authentic text.

25:1-6 BILDAD'S THIRD SPEECH It is possible that Bildad is exhausted and has used up all his ideas. He has little left to offer at the end of the debate. As McKenna says, 'His view of God, man, and creation not only summarizes the position of the three friends but dead-ends the debate' (*CC*).

In his final utterance, Bildad seems to be taking his cue from Eliphaz, who earlier spoke of God's *servants* and *his angels* (4:18) and *his holy ones* and *the heavens* (15:15).

One cannot gainsay Bildad's beautiful doxology reminding us of the majesty of God. *Dominion and awe belong to God; he establishes order in the heights of heaven* (**25:2**). The word translated 'order' is actually the Hebrew word *shalom*. While this is often translated by the English word 'peace', its range is much broader. It covers the whole range of personal, social, spiritual, material, physical and emotional provision and satisfaction – the all-round tranquillity that prevails as a result of God's rule. But when Bildad says that God establishes this order *in the heights of heaven*, he locates God far from earth – far from the situation of Job. But the God who is beyond the heavens and the highest heavens is also the God who is here to help the people who trust in him. Indeed his hosts cannot be numbered and there is no place or person upon whom his light does not shine (**25:3**). Bildad is right to say that God is incomparable. But what does that have to do with the unspeakable suffering of Job?

He then goes on to assert that *if even the moon is not bright and the stars are not pure in his eyes* (**25:5**), what hope is there for Job? Driving his point home, Bildad says, *How then can a man be righteous before God? How can one born of woman be pure?* (**25:4**). Eliphaz has twice mentioned this before (4:17-19; 15:14-16). The debate is becoming increasingly repetitive. Not only that, but in their desire to demolish Job's arguments his friends are becoming increasingly hostile to all humanity. Eliphaz started by describing humankind as *those who live in houses of clay, whose foundations are in the dust, who are crushed more readily than a moth* (4:19). Later he spoke of *man, who is vile and corrupt, who drinks up evil like water* (15:16). In our present chapter, Bildad speaks of *man, who is but a maggot – a son of man, who is only a worm* (**25:6**). This 'worm theology' slams the door of hope in Job's face.

26:1-27:23 JOB'S RESPONSE Job actually carries on speaking up to the end of chapter 31, but chapters 26 and 27 seem to contain his response to Bildad and his two companions. Chapter 28 represents a break between this response and the last three chapters of Job's speech (chs. 29-31), in which Job reflects on his life as a whole.

The first part of Job's response is clearly addressed to Bildad, for he uses the singular form of *you*. He speaks with biting sarcasm (**26:2-3**), and the person he refers to as *powerless*, *feeble* and *without wisdom* in these verses is clearly himself. We hear him tell Bildad: *How you have helped the powerless! How you have saved the arm that is feeble! What advice you have offered to one without wisdom! And what great insight you have displayed!* Though there is nothing wrong in what Bildad has said about God in his speech, he had made him so removed from the human scene that Bildad's God is of no practical help to Job. Questioning his theology, Job

asks: *Who has helped you utter these words? And whose spirit spoke from your mouth?* (**26:4**).

The remaining verses of the chapter (26:5-14) speak about the greatness of God. That is why some scholars speculate that these verses must be a continuation of Bildad's speech in chapter 25 (see the brief discussion preceding the commentary on chapter 25). But who said that describing God's majesty in creation was the sole preserve of Job's friends? Job has already spoken on this very topic in 9:2-13. McKenna is of the opinion that Job has a better understanding of the power of God than his companions: '[his] knowledge goes far beyond the teaching of his friends, who speak of God's power in heaven and on earth but seem baffled by the dark underworld beyond Sheol and the sea' (*CC*). By contrast, Job describes Sheol and Abaddon (translated 'Death' and 'Destruction' in the NIV) as *naked* and without covering before the power of God (**26:5-6**).

Job goes on to speak of how God *spreads out the northern skies over empty space* and *suspends the earth over nothing* (**26:7**). The greatness of his power is clear from the waters and the clouds (**26:8**), from the full moon and the horizon (**26:9-11**), and from his destruction of the forces of chaos (**26:12-13**). (Note that the Rahab referred to here and in 9:13 is not the same as the prostitute Rahab of Joshua 2, but a mythological female monster.) Job humbly admits that he has not even started to scratch the surface of the unfathomable mystery of who God is: *And these are but the outer fringe of his works; how faint the whisper we hear of him! Who then can understand the thunder of his power?* (**26:14**). If what Job and his friends have described in these chapters is 'the whisper we hear of him' – and a faint one at that – then indeed his omnipotence must be far greater than we can ever imagine.

In 27:2-6 Job states his determination to uphold his innocence in the strongest words so far. He confirms his resolve with an oath: *As surely as God lives, who has denied me justice, the Almighty, who has made me taste bitterness of soul* (**27:2**). But how can Job make an oath in the name of the God who has treated him in the way he describes? (We asked a similar question when Job expressed his belief in a coming Redeemer – 19:25.) The answer is that as far as Job is concerned, the God he believes in is the sovereign ruler of heaven, earth, the seas and the 'underworld' (described in 26:5-6) and all that are in them. Nothing happens without his knowledge and outside of his will. Job has made this conviction clear by his arguments with and complaints to God about his suffering. One swears by the highest authority one believes in, and for Job God is that authority – although he is also the source of his suffering.

He makes this resolution not only in the name of the highest authority in the universe but also for life: *as long as I have life within me, the breath of God in my nostrils* (**27:3**). Job will not budge – neither in the presence of the Almighty nor before his friends. He says *my lips will not speak wickedness, and my tongue will utter no deceit* (**27:4**). He recapitulates the essence of the entire dialogue when he says, *I will never admit you are in the right; till I die, I will not deny my integrity. I will maintain my righteousness and never let go of it; my conscience will not reproach me as long as I live* (**27:5-6**). His words could not be clearer nor his resolution stronger!

Although talk of the judgment of the wicked has been more frequent on the lips of Job's friends in their futile attempt to convince him that he is a sinner, there is no reason to doubt that 27:7-23 represents Job's own words. He is turning the tables on his judgmental friends: *May my enemies be like the wicked, my adversaries like the unjust* (**27:7**). He has warned them that this was coming (19:29). What is new here is that now he utters an imprecatory prayer, similar to those in the psalms. Giving as good as he got, he tells them *For what hope has the godless when he is cut off, when God takes away his life?* (**27:8**). He goes on to add: *Does God listen to his cry when distress comes upon him? Will he find delight in the Almighty? Will he call upon God at all times?* (**27:9-10**). The mention of prayer in times of distress is a challenge to Job's friends, who have specialized in debate rather than prayer. Not once do we hear them praying, whereas Job is always praying and bringing his complaints to God.

Prefacing his words with *I will teach you about the power of God; the ways of the Almighty I will not conceal* (**27:11-12**), Job elaborates on the final destiny of the wicked (27:13-23). *Here is the fate God allots to the wicked, the heritage a ruthless man receives from the Almighty* (**27:13**): his children perish by the sword, he will have no survivors (**27:14-15**), the wealth he has accumulated will be divided among the righteous (**27:16-17**), his house will be deserted and his wealth will disappear overnight (**27:18-19**). There is no escaping the destruction that will overtake him (**27:20-23**).

Some commentators find it difficult to believe that these words are coming out of Job's mouth and therefore assign this section to Zophar. However – at the risk of repetition – the Scriptures, as we have them now, assign them to Job and that is the way we should understand them.

28:1-28 Poem on Wisdom

Job 28 is a beautiful and serene poem, far removed from the heated debate we have witnessed in the preceding chapters. But why is it here? Who wrote it? How does it relate to what has gone before and what follows? Commentators tend to divide between two positions.

Some believe that these cannot be the words of Job himself, arguing that the tone is so different from what precedes and follows the poem that it must have been inserted by the author of the book of Job and is not intended to represent Job's own words. They see its purpose as giving the reader

a breathing space in which to reflect before Job plunges on with his discourse in the next three chapters.

McKenna counters this argument by asserting that the contrasts in the rest of the book give us abundant evidence that we should not impose 'our Western way of thinking upon the Eastern mind of Job'. He argues that 'the strongest case can be made that Job himself sings as a poet, speaks as a philosopher, and sees as a prophet in this Hymn to Wisdom' (*CC*). Since the chapter is tacked between chapters clearly labelled as spoken by Job (27:1 and 29:1), this commentary will assume that it, too, represents his words.

The hymn to wisdom is in three sections. The first section (28:1-11) speaks about the ingenuity of humankind in exploiting the resources of the earth – more specifically the precious minerals stored in the belly of the earth. The poem begins *There is a mine* and goes on to speak of the mines that are the source of silver, gold, iron and copper (**28:1-2**). Human technological skill penetrates the deep darkness and farthest recesses of the depths of the earth where these minerals are hidden *far from where people dwell* and *in places forgotten by the foot of man* (**28:3-6**). So deep are the mines where these minerals are found that *no bird of prey knows that hidden path, no falcon's eye has seen it. Proud beasts do not set foot on it, and no lion prowls there* (**28:7-8**). This passage tells us something about what was a high-tech industry at the time of Job – an industry that evoked the same type of admiration for human ingenuity that we sometimes feel in relation to space exploration.

After expressing his admiration for the skill and dedication involved in extracting precious metals from the deep recesses of the earth's crust, the writer makes a transition to the next section (28:12-22) with the query *But where can wisdom be found? Where does understanding dwell?* If there is *a mine for silver*, where is the corresponding mine for wisdom? The same question is asked in 28:20. The search for wisdom is at the heart of this entire poem. It would not be too much to say that it is also the theme of the entire book of Job.

But the search for a place where wisdom can be mined is fruitless. *Man does not comprehend its worth; it cannot be found in the land of the living* (**28:13**). It cannot even be found in the deepest oceans (**28:14**).

What is more, wisdom cannot be bought – not even with all the wealth that humanity has accumulated from its mining of the earth (28:15-19). The list of precious metals and gems is long: gold and silver (**28:15**); the gold of Ophir, onyx, sapphires (**28:16**); crystal and jewels of gold (**28:17**); coral, jasper, rubies (**28:18**); topaz from Cush and pure gold (**28:19**). But all of this wealth is *not worthy of mention* compared to wisdom. (Scholars are still arguing about which gems the Hebrew words refer to, and their disagreements are reflected in the different translations of this passage. Fortunately, the poet's point that wisdom is beyond price does not depend on whether the gems referred to are pearls, as in the KJV, or jasper.)

So the question is repeated: *Where then does wisdom come from? Where does understanding dwell?* (**28:20**). Human ingenuity and curiosity, which have discovered all the minerals the poet has listed, have failed to find wisdom. Not even the keen eyesight of birds, scanning the entire earth from a great height, has been able to find it: *It is hidden from the eyes of every living thing, concealed even from the birds of the air* (**28:21**). If the desperate search extends even beyond this life, all that is learned is that *Destruction and Death say, 'Only a rumour of it has reached our ears'* (**28:22**).

At last, in the third section of this chapter, a source of wisdom is found (28:23-28). Wisdom comes from and dwells in God. God is the one who understands the way to wisdom and knows where it dwells (**28:23**). The reason is that *he views the ends of the earth and sees everything under the heavens* (**28:24**) – unlike his creatures, who are finite and limited. God's knowledge of the sources of wisdom dates from creation *when he established the force of the wind and measured out the waters* (**28:25**) and *made a decree for the rain and a path for the thunderstorm* (**28:26**). At that time God also *looked at wisdom and appraised it; he confirmed it and tested it* (**28:27**). The NASB says *He saw it and declared it; He established it and also searched it out.* Andersen captures the meaning for us when he points out that wisdom is not located solely in God's mind. 'Wisdom is what God understands when He looks to the ends of the earth. Wisdom is observable in the universe because God embodied it in His creation … Men can see this for themselves, but only when God himself shows it to them (Rom 1:19)' (*TOT*).

After this, God *said to man, 'The fear of the Lord – that is wisdom, and to shun evil is understanding'* (**28:28**). Andersen makes the surprising statement that 'Many commentators do not like this verse … They dismiss it as a platitude that replaces a noble agnosticism with a banal moralism' (*TOT*). 'Banal moralism' or not, human beings can become beneficiaries of wisdom only through *the fear of the Lord*. Job himself is an exemplar of wisdom – an upright and moral man, devoted to God, shunning evil (1:1).

29:1-31:40 Job's Account of His Life

The three friends of Job have long stopped speaking. Job, too, has long stopped speaking to them and has turned his attention to God alone. In chapters 29-31 we see Job on his own. He reflects on his past life (ch. 29) and his present condition (ch. 30) and in chapter 31 'positions himself between his magnificent past and his miserable present with an oath of innocence' (*CC*). One is constrained to ask, 'Why is Job behaving this way again?' What happened to the vision of a redeemer and vindicator in chapter 19 and the serene search for wisdom in chapter 28?

29:1-25 His past life

In this chapter Job is reflecting on 'the good old days'. Simundson reminds us that it is natural for human beings to think nostalgically of the good life they enjoyed in days gone by: 'As people get older, as their various losses accumulate, they look back on their days of strength and happiness. Often, the past begins to look better and better as we increase our distance from it.' While remembering the past may help us to come to terms with it, Simundson warns that 'if remembering becomes nostalgia, overly sentimental and yearning for a return to a past that is no longer recoverable, then it has moved from a healthy remembrance to an unhealthy attachment to the past.'

Job begins by recounting the wonderful relationship he had with God and the blessings with which God showered him (29:2-6). He speaks of *the days when God watched over me* (**29:2**), *when his lamp shone upon my head* (**29:3**), when he was in the prime of his life, *when God's intimate friendship blessed my house* (**29:4**), when his children were around him (**29:5**) and *when my path was drenched with cream and the rock poured out for me streams of olive oil* (**29:6**). Those were indeed glorious days. The path 'drenched with cream' and the rock pouring out 'streams of olive oil' are figurative expressions of the wealth of Job. Among my people, a person who had a large herd of cattle used to demonstrate his wealth by bathing himself in the milk his cows produced.

Job also remembers the honour that his community used to accord him (29:7-11). When he went to the gate of the city – the place where legal and business matters were transacted – *the young men … stepped aside and the old men rose to their feet* (**29:8**) out of respect for him. The chiefs and nobles were hushed in his presence and spoke highly of him (**29:9-11**). He received this respect because of his advocacy for the poor and lowly in society (29:12-17). He *rescued the poor* and *the fatherless*, helped the dying and widows, took up the cause of the needy and strangers, and broke the stranglehold of the wicked who oppressed the poor. He expresses his stand for justice dramatically, saying, *I was eyes to the blind and feet to the lame* (**29:15**). To crown it all, he says, *I put on righteousness as my clothing; justice was my robe and my turban* (**29:14**).

The next section (29:18-25) appears to be an elaboration of verses 29:9-11, with additional thoughts about his hopes for how his earthly life would end. Job had hoped to die in his own house with dignity and honour (**29:18**); now it appears that he will die on the ash-heap to which he has been consigned because of his physical affliction. Verse **29:19** reminds us of the description of the blessed man in Psalm 1, who 'is like a tree planted by streams of water, which yields its fruit in season and whose leaf does not wither' (Ps 1:3). Job's presence and favour used to spread confidence and comfort among the members of his community (29:24-25). He ascends to poetic heights as he explains his previous role among his people (29:24-25). His smile was *precious to them* and he dwelt among them *as their chief, as a king among his troops.* 'Here is the picture of a benevolent father, almost kingly in his dignity, yet kind and caring for the needs of others' (Simundson).

30:1-31 His present life

The *But now* of **30:1** is an emphatic marker of how Job's past life, described in chapter 29, contrasts with his present situation. Where he had once been praised, he is now mocked by the dregs of his society (30:1-8). Job's characterization of his mockers, who *are men younger than I* (30:1), is extremely insulting when he says that they are men *whose fathers I would have disdained to put with my sheep dogs.* Dogs were not pets in Job's society, but were considered filthy and vicious animals. To say that someone was not even fit to keep company with dogs was the ultimate insult.

Job goes on to describe the fathers of these mockers as a spent force (**30:2**), *haggard from want and hunger,* who roamed the desolate places and *gathered salt herbs* and *the root of the broom tree* for food (**30:3-4**). They were *shouted at as if they were thieves* and were banished from society and forced to live in dry river beds *among the rocks and in the holes in the ground* (**30:5-6**). These *brayed among the bushes and huddled in the undergrowth* (**30:7**). Job goes on to describe them as *a base and nameless brood* who *were driven out of the land* (**30:8**). And these men were the fathers of those who were now mocking Job: *And now their sons mock me in song; I have become a byword among them* (**30:9**). The 'song' referred to by Job must have been a taunt song, biting into his mind and soul. As if that were not enough, Job says, *they detest me and keep their distance; they do not hesitate to spit in my face* (**30:10**). Job now suffers continual abuse (30:11-14).

Some may feel that Job's description of these people is rather cruel. He does not show any evidence of the compassion mentioned in 31:16-20. Rodd says, 'The only excuse for showing such contempt for such wretched outcasts is that Job has sunk so low that even the most despised rejects of society now feel able to taunt him.'

It is not easy to interpret the meaning of **30:11**, for there is a tangle of pronouns and possessives, and the word *God* does not appear in the original Hebrew. But it seems that Job is accusing God of having initiated this torrent of abuse. We find the clue in the phrase *Now that God has unstrung my bow.* The word that the NIV interprets as the string for a bow could, according to Gordis, also be interpreted as referring to a tent rope or the cord with which one tied one's girdle. If girding one's loins is a sign that one is ready for action, then having one's girdle fall loose is a humiliating sign of weakness. God has exposed Job to the ridicule of this rabble by weakening him, that is, by removing the honour and respect he had in society. Job describes himself as if he were a city

with a 'gaping breach' in its walls through which these people advance to abuse him (**30:12-14**).

Then Job reverts to a description of his terrors and bone-racking pain (30:15-19). Again, it is difficult to determine the referent of the pronouns in **30:18**. The word *God* is not in the original. Nevertheless, as Rodd has put it, 'Without naming him, Job blames God for his misfortunes.' Job laments: *He throws me into the mud, and I am reduced to dust and ashes* (**30:19**).

In the remaining verses of the chapter (30:20-31), Job takes his lament directly to God: *I cry to you, O God, but you do not answer* (**30:20**). The silence of God must have pierced even deeper into Job's soul than his physical pain and isolation. Yet he does not stop pleading with God. That is the apparent contradiction of faith – it is 'a leap in the dark' at its starkest: 'Now faith is being sure of what we hope for and certain of what we do not see' (Heb 11:1).

Instead of answering his cry, God *ruthlessly* pursues him with all his might, as the wind does a dry leaf and a storm the waters of the sea (**30:21-22**). Nothing remains for Job but to die (**30:23**). But how can God be so cruel to Job? *Surely no one lays a hand on a broken man when he cries for help in his distress* (**30:24**). Should he not have been rewarded for his good deeds? (**30:25**). But as for Job, *when I hoped for good, evil came; when I looked for light, then came darkness* (**30:26**). And what darkness! The *churning* (**30:27**) may refer to the fever produced by the excruciating physical pain he is enduring. Job's skin is turning black, *not by the sun* but because of the fever burning within him (**30:28, 30**). His associates are now the jackals and owls in their 'melancholy cry' of loneliness and deprivation in the wilderness (**30:29**). Where Job had once enjoyed feasting and music, now *my harp is turned to mourning, and my flute to the sound of wailing* (**30:31**).

31:1-40 An oath of innocence

After reviewing his happy past and his current dark straits, Job proceeds to uphold his integrity. He begins with a statement regarding the injustice that has befallen him (31:1-4). Basically, he is asking, *Should not the kind of calamity that has overtaken me be the lot of the wicked?* (**31:2-3**). Why has the Almighty allowed such a miscarriage of justice in Job's case? *Does he not,* says Job, *see my ways and count my every step?* (**31:4**).

Confident of his innocence, Job then presents his case in a moving series of 'if' (conditional) and 'then' (consequence or result) clauses, which make up the rest of the chapter. There are more conditional clauses than result clauses, for sometimes two or three 'if' clauses are lumped together ending with one consequence clause. Each conditional clause mentions a specific sin, often mentioning who might have been wronged by the sin, and then states what the consequence should be if Job is guilty of that sin.

The background to Job's oath of innocence lies in the ancient Near Eastern custom in which an accused person could take an 'oath of clearance'. This involved listing each of the crimes of which the defendant was accused in an 'if' clause, and clearly spelling out the negative consequences if he or she was guilty in a 'then' clause – 'then let me be cursed by man and God'. The defendant signed the document which contained these clauses, and 'the document was then posted in public as a call for the persons who were wronged to come forward and testify against the accused. If none came forward, the judge accepted the "not guilty" plea and announced acquittal' (*CC*).

In this chapter, Job is going public before both God and his community. He says, *If I have walked in falsehood or my foot has hurried after deceit* then *let God weigh me in honest scales and he will know that I am blameless* (**31:5-6**). Next he mentions the sins of turning away *from the path* or of having allowed his eyes to mislead his heart or of having defiled his hands (**31:7**). If he has done this, Job says, *then may others eat what I have sown, and may my crops be uprooted* (**31:8**). Next he mentions the sin of adultery (**31:9**; see also **31:1**) with the 'then' of the result clause. He elaborates on how grievous this sin is: *For that would have been shameful, a sin to be judged. It is a fire that burns to Destruction, it would have uprooted my harvest* (**31:11-12**). With the 'if' of **31:13**, Job introduces a list of ways in which he could have committed the sin of mistreating the underprivileged: denying justice to his servants; failing to meet the needs of the poor, the widow and the fatherless; using his influence to deny justice to the lowly (31:13-21). This is followed by *then let my arm fall from the shoulder, let it be broken off at the joint* (**31:22**; see also the further elaboration of **31:23**). Job's confession that he and his servants are equal before God (**31:14-15**) is unique – especially in the context of the stratified society of the ancient Near East.

In 31:24-28 Job moves on to the sins of trusting in one's wealth and of idolatry. Since Job was the greatest and wealthiest man among all the people of the East (1:3), he could easily have fallen into the trap of putting his confidence in this fame and wealth, as Eliphaz had accused him of doing (22:24-25). Job spells the sin out clearly, saying, *If I have put trust in gold or said to pure gold, 'You are my security' and if I have rejoiced over my great wealth, the fortunes my hands have gained* (**31:24-25**). He does not immediately produce the 'then' clause, but moves straight on to the related sin of idolatry. Job speaks about the possibility that he might have looked at *the sun in its radiance* or *the moon moving in splendour*, and have felt his heart being secretly enticed, leading him to offer them *a kiss of homage* (**31:26-27**). 'While Job could never be charged with substituting the sun and the moon for the Almighty ... the temptation might be to curtsy to the lesser gods while bowing to the one God' (*CC*).

In rejecting the charge of offering even minor reverence to other deities, Job has something to say about the syncretism we encounter among African Christians. For example, although Zionist churches claim dependence on the power of the Holy Spirit and on Jesus Christ rather than on the ancestors, they attempt to combine traditional and Christian methods of healing. McKenna warns that pluralism, or tolerance of various denominations and religions, can sometimes be twisted into 'a subtle rendering of the word *syncretism*, which means the dilution of doctrine in order to accommodate various theological views and promote cooperation among religions and denominations' (*CC*).

The 'then' for the conditional clauses in 31:24-27 comes in **31:28**: *then these also would be sins to be judged, for I would have been unfaithful to God on high*. In line with the Mosaic law – although it appears he lived before it was given – Job recognizes no gods other than the true and living God. 'Moreover, he refuses to greet other gods by such a customary and presumably innocent gesture as kissing his ring to acknowledge their presence' (*CC*).

The next sin mentioned is the sin of rejoicing over an *enemy's misfortune* and *invoking a curse against his life* (**31:29-30**). This is followed by the failure to extend hospitality to strangers (**31:31-32**). Another sin appears to be the very opposite of what Job is doing in this oath of innocence – the sin of hiding one's guilt out of fear of public contempt (**31:33-34**).

Some commentators consider that 31:35-37, the passage that captures Job's final plea, is misplaced and should come at the end of the chapter. Others, however, regard the final 'if ... then' in 31:38-40 as an afterthought on the part of Job. The sin mentioned in those verses relates to both the land and its tenants. The conditional clauses figuratively speak about the land crying out against Job, with *all its furrows ... wet with tears* (**31:38**). The other sin that Job says he could have committed is to *have devoured its yield without payment or broken the spirit of its tenants* (**31:39**). The sin here is twofold: depletion of the land (the OT made provision for restoration through leaving land fallow) and stealing from the tenants or farmers what is due to them. Job continues, *then let briers come up instead of wheat and weeds instead of barley* (**31:40**). This sounds like the curse on the land after the Fall (Gen 3:18).

To underline his point that he is completely innocent of all the sins he has enumerated using the 'if ... then' pattern, Job now gives his oath of innocence (31:35-37). As in previous chapters, he expresses his eager desire for someone to take up his case: *Oh, that I had someone to hear me!* And then, most surprising of all, he issues a confident challenge: *I sign now my defence – let the Almighty answer me; let my accuser put his indictment in writing* (**31:35**). Job goes on to say: *Surely I would wear it on my shoulder, I would put it on like a crown* (**31:36**). The twice repeated 'it' is a reference to the bill of indictment Job is challenging his accuser to present. Such an indictment would, mostly likely, involve the sins Job has covered in this chapter. And Job is confident that the verdict will be 'not guilty', for he says, *I would give him an account of my every step; like a prince I would approach him* (**31:37**; see also 31:4).

What is our attitude to Job's overconfidence here? Our answer may be a measure of our own spirituality, rather than Job's!

32:1-37:24 Elihu's Speeches

Suddenly, without any warning, another figure appears on the scene. Elihu is not among the three friends mentioned at the end of the narrative prologue (2:11-13), nor is he included in God's condemnation of Eliphaz and his two companions because they have not spoken what is right about him as his servant Job has done (42:7). He is an enigma. Who is he? Where does he come from? Why was he not mentioned until this moment? Some information is provided in 32:1-5, the only narrative passage in the book of Job other than the prologue and the epilogue, but it fails to satisfy our curiosity.

32:1-5 Elihu, the Man

Elihu is introduced to us in the short narrative passage prefacing his speeches (32:1-5). However, before introducing Elihu, the passage has this to say: *So these three men stopped answering Job, because he was righteous in his own eyes* (**32:1**). We have had earlier indications that Job's friends had stopped answering him. Although commentators have given various reasons why they stopped, here for the first time we are told that the reason was 'because he was righteous in his own eyes'. The mention of this as a prelude to the speeches of Elihu is quite significant, as we shall soon discover.

The man is identified as *Elihu son of Barakel (Barachel in some versions) the Buzite, of the family of Ram* (**32:2a**). It is interesting to note that he is introduced to us as an angry man right at the outset. His anger is mentioned four times in four verses: he *became very angry with Job* (**32:2b**; Elihu's anger is mentioned twice here in the Hebrew; see also the NASB and Tigrigna translations); he *was also angry with the three friends* (**32:3a**); and *his anger was aroused against the three men* (**32:5**). Is this righteous anger? Maybe! He is angry with Job *for justifying himself rather than God* (**32:2c**). He is angry with the three friends first because *they had found no way to refute Job* (**32:3b**; see also 32:5 where *had nothing more to say* is the wording) and second because, despite their failure to refute him, they *had condemned him* (**32:3c**).

The passage also tells us that Elihu is younger than the other three. In explaining why he did not speak prior to this point, the text says: *Now Elihu had waited before speaking to Job because they were older than he* (**32:4**).

32:6-37:24 Elihu's Speeches

Not only is the arrival of this man enigmatic, but so are his speeches. Scholars argue about their structure, theology, style and language. What purpose do they serve after Job has thrown down the gauntlet with his oath of innocence, when logic leads us to believe that God's answer is just around the corner?

Some commentators go to the extent of affirming that we would not even notice it if these chapters were left out of the book of Job. But they are there in our Bible. And if, as the apostle has put it, 'All Scripture is God-breathed and is useful for teaching, rebuking, correcting and training in righteousness' (2 Tim 3:16), then – no matter how obscure it may appear to us – there must be a reason for the inclusion of Elihu's speeches in the book of Job.

In fact, Elihu's speeches are not a cumbersome appendage but have a role to play in the unfolding drama of the book. They serve both a theological and a dramatic purpose. Their theological significance is that they return to the theme of wisdom, which Atkinson describes as 'a theological bridge in the story between Job's experience and his hearing the Lord' (*BST*). Dramatically, this scene serves to keep us waiting for God's reply, which we are sure is imminent: 'These chapters give us a space between Job and Yahweh. They illustrate, just by being there, that Yahweh is not forced into a quick reply by the intensity of Job's entreaties. God acts in his own time, he is not at human beck and call' (*BST*).

Elihu's contribution is generally divided into four speeches, based on the four times Elihu is mentioned as the speaker (32:6; 34:1; 35:1; 36:1).

32:6-33:33 The first speech

Elihu begins by expanding on the reasons – given in the narrative introduction – why he did not speak before now (32:6-10). Mentioning his youth, he says *that is why I was fearful, not daring to tell you what I know* (**32:6**). He had also thought that *age should speak; advanced years should teach wisdom* (**32:7**). But he had come to realize – and this is his encouragement to speak now – *it is the spirit in a man, the breath of the Almighty, that gives him understanding. It is not only the old who are wise, not only the aged who understand what is right* (**32:8-9**). Elihu is claiming inspiration here, as Eliphaz had earlier claimed special revelation – though for different reasons. Hence, having discarded his fear, Elihu exhorts his elders, *Listen to me*, adding *I too will tell you what I know* (**32:10**).

In the next passage (32:11-22) he appears apologetic and goes over ground already covered in the narrative introduction – with more repetition. He tells the three: *I waited while you spoke, I listened, I gave you my full atten-tion* (**32:11-12a**). *But,* says Elihu, *not one of you has proved Job wrong; none of you has answered his arguments* (**32:12b**). Admonishing them for their resignation, he says, *Do not say, 'We have found wisdom.'* Wisdom in what? In saying *let God refute him, not man* (**32:13**). When and where did Job's friends say these words? Or is Elihu inferring them from their silence?

Elihu then discloses the way he proposes to deal with Job, telling them, *Job has not marshalled his words against me, and I will not answer him with your arguments* (**32:14**). He continues to expand on their failure – speaking about them in the third person – and prepares the ground for his own devastating attack on Job (**32:15-17**).

He can no longer wait to speak: *Inside I am like bottled-up wine; like new wineskins ready to burst. I must speak and find relief; I must open my lips and reply* (**32:19-20**). Alluding to the inspiration mentioned earlier and to his present sense of being almost at bursting point, Elihu says: *For I am full of words and the spirit within me compels me* (**32:18**). Speak he must. But he gives a firm commitment to be objective: *I will show partiality to no one, nor will I flatter any man* (**32:21**). He gives his reason for this affirmation: *for if I were skilled in flattery, my Maker would soon take me away* (**32:22**). Job had accused his friends of defending God 'deceitfully' (13:7-12). Could Elihu correct this imbalance? In addition, in his search for fair judgment, Job had said, 'If only there were someone to arbitrate between us, to lay his hand upon us both' (9:33). Elihu promises to play that role effectively. As the chapter ends, we wait to see whether he is capable of fulfilling such bold promises.

Turning his attention to Job, Elihu once again appears pompous and presumptuous (33:1-7). What is more, he continues to waste time and words on preliminaries, rather than going to the heart of the matter. He urges Job to *listen to my words; pay attention to everything I say* (**33:1**). If it is true that he is bursting to speak (32:19), why does he not say what is inside, rather than keeping people in sus-pense? He carries on: *I am about to open my mouth; my words are on the tip of my tongue* (**33:2**). It is this sort of beating about the bush that has given rise to the proverb *zereban mashelan kekab ksadu* (Tigrigna, Eritrea – 'talk and sorghum [are best] when chopped from the neck', meaning that just as the best way to harvest sorghum is to chop off the ear and not the whole stalk, so speech is best when one goes straight to the point rather than being long-winded). Elihu affirms the sincerity of his speech next (**33:3**) and again refers to *the breath of the Almighty* (**33:4**). After challenging Job to be able to answer him (**33:5**), he appears to be too condescending when he says, *I am just like you before God; I too have been taken from clay. No fear of me should alarm you, nor should my hand be heavy upon you* (**33:6-7**).

At long last Elihu comes to the point, indicting Job for his accusation of God (33:8-11). The indictment here is two-pronged. First, as Elihu puts it, *you have said in my hearing – I heard the very words – 'I am pure and without sin; I am clean and free from guilt'* (**33:8-9**). Second, Job has accused God: *Yet God has found fault with me; he considers me his enemy. He fastens my feet in shackles; he keeps close watch on all my paths* (**33:10-11**). Elihu adds a third accusation in the course of pointing out Job's mistakes: *Why do you com-plain to him that he answers none of man's words?* (**33:13**). So, Job's faults, as summarized by Elihu, are saying that he is pure, that God has turned into his enemy for no reason, and that God does not answer his prayer.

Elihu is exaggerating what Job has said. While Job has said that he does not deserve the suffering that has been thrust on him and that he is innocent of the sins of which his friends accuse him, he has not claimed to be totally *pure and without sin*. Elihu's response to what he thinks Job has said continues to the end of the chapter (33:12-33). He starts off with a general answer: *But I tell you, in this you are not right* simply because *God is greater than man* (**33:12**). Implicit in this statement is the truth that God is not accountable to any of his creatures. Then Elihu takes up the last of the sins of which he accused Job. He demands to know: 'Why do you complain to him that he answers none of man's words?' (33:13). As far as Elihu is concerned *God does speak – now one way, now another – though man may not perceive it* (**33:14**). Though Elihu may be faulted for his confrontational *in this you are not right*, he may have a constructive point here. It is possible that Job is crossing the line in trying to tell God how he should answer him. McKenna comments: 'Job not only complained about the silence of God, but set the ground rules for his speaking. He insisted upon a personal audience with the privilege of cross-examination just as if he and God were equals' (*CC*).

Elihu's reminder that God has many ways of speak-ing to people is appropriate. One of these ways is through dreams and visions in the night (33:15-18) which *speak in their ears and terrify them with warnings* (**33:16**). Could Job have missed the message of the 'dreams' that were meant to frighten him and the 'visions' that should have terrified him (7:13-14)? God's intention in sending messages such as these is *to turn man from wrongdoing and keep him from pride, to preserve his soul from the pit, his life from perishing by the sword* (**33:17-18**).

It is also true (although this truth may be misused – as it has been by Job's friends) that affliction itself may be God's means of chastising us to teach us something (33:19-22). Elihu's description of a lack of appetite (**33:20**), the wast-ing away of the body (**33:21**) and the approach of death (**33:22**) vividly remind us of Job's own experience. We can almost hear Elihu saying to Job: 'Have you ever tried to be still and hear God's voice in all of these?'

In 32:23-28 Elihu offers a ray of hope to Job, indicating that he is indeed an honest and helpful counsellor. Once again we meet the 'if ... then' statement in a passage full of consolation (33:23-25). This *angel*, this *mediator* may be *one out of a thousand*; but if he is found he will be a beacon of hope in the present darkness. Elihu lists the things this angel/mediator does for the suffering one. He tells him *what is right for him* (**33:23**). He behaves graciously towards him in that he pleads for mercy on his behalf, saying, *Spare him from going down to the pit; I have found a ransom for him* (**33:24**). Though God is not mentioned, he is clearly the one to whom the prayer is addressed, for the context makes it very clear that what is going on here is between a suffering man and God. It seems that this angel may be the arbitrator, mediator or redeemer for whom Job had been longing. The mediator found a ransom, and a price is paid on behalf of the prisoner so that he can go free.

Alluding to the sores that cover Job's body, and thinking in OT terms, Elihu says that when someone is restored *his flesh is renewed like a child's; it is restored as in the days of his youth* (**33:25**). The one who is restored *prays to God and finds favour with him, he sees God's face and shouts for joy; he is restored by God to his righteous state* (**33:26**). If this is not the gospel of redemption, what is! But this redemption is not earned by works of righteousness but is a result of God's mercy. For the redeemed one *comes to men and says 'I sinned, and perverted what was right, but I did not get what I deserved. He redeemed my soul from going down to the pit, and I will live to enjoy the light'* (**33:27-28**). Note that the 'pit' or 'grave' is mentioned here for the fourth time in this section (the other mentions were at 33:18, 21, 24). The grave was all that Job was waiting for. Elihu is preaching the gospel to Job. Will he accept it and have this restoration, this song, this light – instead of ashes? That is the crux of the matter.

True as Elihu's speech is, there is still a problem with it: 'Job was not an unregenerate sinner who needed to hear this message. Like many a good gospel message, it was wasted, as it were, on the saved rather than being well invested and preached to the lost' (*NAC*).

By way of concluding this section of his speech, Elihu reminds Job: *God does all these things to man – twice, even three times – to turn back his soul from the pit, that the light of life may shine on him* (**33:29-30**; see also 33:18). Elihu ends this chapter with the usual exhortation to Job to listen (33:31-33). But the purpose of this relentless exhortation to listen is that Job may sense the gospel message here and appropriate it. Elihu says this to Job in so many words: *for I want you to be cleared* (**33:32**).

34:1-37 The second speech

Elihu is quite generous with his invitation to listen. This time, however, it is the *wise men*, the *men of learning* being invited to listen (**34:2**, 10, 34). The purpose of the invitation is to consider the matter together so that they may join him in condemning Job (**34:3-4**). The proverb in 34:3 was actually used by Job earlier (12:11; see also 25:11). It is disappointing to see Elihu turning against Job in this speech, after his fairly helpful counsel in the first speech.

He states Job's position first: *Job says, 'I am innocent, but God denies me justice. Although I am right, I am considered a liar; although I am guiltless, his arrow inflicts an incurable wound'* (**34:5-6**). Then comes the threefold indictment. First, *What man is like Job, who drinks scorn like water?* (**34:7**). Second, Job *keeps company with evildoers; he associates with wicked men* (**34:8**; reminding us of Ps 1:1). Finally, Job is accused of saying that there is no benefit in trying to please God (**34:9**). As before, Elihu tries to reproduce what Job has said, but adds his own insinuations and exaggerations to achieve his purpose.

There is some disagreement about what he means when he says that Job 'drinks scorn like water' (34:7) Some interpret this as implying that Job is the object of the scorn, and that Elihu is saying Job is impervious to criticism, that is, he simply ignores it. But since this comment comes immediately after what Job has said about God (and may include what he has said against his friends), it seems more likely that Elihu is accusing Job of enjoying scorning God and man as one enjoys drinking water when one is thirsty.

Though Elihu may be exaggerating to some extent, he has a point in that some of what Job has said borders on blasphemy. However, his accusation that Job is a companion of evildoers does not hold water in the light of the testimony of God and Holy Scripture about Job's blameless life. In the context of his suffering and his struggle with the doctrine of retribution, Job may even have come close to saying that it is useless to serve God, as Elihu charges (34:9), but he has not said this in so many words (see 9:29-31). McKenna says, 'Job may have come close to claiming pristine innocence for himself and injustice on the part of God, but he studiously avoided the conclusion that righteousness is unprofitable' (*CC*).

Invoking the attention of his fellow wise men once again (34:10), Elihu proceeds to justify God (34:11-15). He says that God cannot do evil or pervert justice at all (**34:10, 12**); he repays people according to their deserts – giving us a classic restatement of the doctrine of retribution (**34:11**). Since God is the Creator, he is accountable to no one and can even *withdraw his spirit and breath* precipitating the annihilation of humankind (**34:13-15**).

Elihu has summoned wise men to listen, but now he uses a singular form in **34:16** to challenge Job directly in light of what has gone before (34:11-15) and what follows (34:17-30): *Will you condemn the just and mighty One?* (**34:17**). Starting with the rhetorical question *Can he who hates justice govern?*, expecting the answer 'no', Elihu goes on to elaborate God's righteous involvement in the governments of this world (34:18-20). He *says to kings, 'You are worthless'* *and to nobles, 'You are wicked'* (**34:18**), he *shows no partiality* *to princes and does not favour the rich over the poor* (**34:19**), when he judges them *they die in an instant* and *are removed* *without human hand* (**34:20**).

God's administration of human affairs, described in the preceding paragraph, is just because no one can hide from the all-seeing eyes of God (**34:21-22**). God does not need to follow due process of law because he knows everything beforehand (**34:23**). Consequently, *without inquiry he shat-* *ters the mighty* (**34:24**), *he overthrows them in the night and* *they are crushed* (**34:25**), *he punishes them for their wicked-* *ness where everyone can see them* (**34:26**). Why? Because *they turned from following him and had no regard for any of* *his ways* (**34:27**) and *caused the cry of the poor to come before* *him, so that he heard the cry of the needy* (**34:28**).

Elihu then carries on, most likely with Job's complaint in mind, *But if he remains silent, who can condemn him? If he* *hides his face, who can see him?* (**34:29a**) for *he is over man* *and nation alike, to keep a godless man from ruling, from laying* *snares for the people* (**34:29b-30**). Although Elihu's argument is true in general, the problem is that he does not bother to ask whether this is what Job is experiencing in his personal life or whether it matches the reality of human experience.

Elihu moves on to imagine a scenario where an individual is repenting (**34:31-32**). He presents a model prayer to encourage Job to confess his sins and receive God's restoration on God's own terms. We are left in no doubt that he has aimed this at Job when he says, *Should God then reward* *you on your terms, when you refuse to repent?* (**34:33a**). Then, using words almost identical words to those of Eliphaz, he leaves the choice with Job: *You must decide, not I; so tell me* *what you know* (**34:33b**).

Having finished his indictment of Job, he once again invites *men of understanding* to join him in condemning Job (**34:34**). He puts words into their mouths when he has them say: *Job speaks without knowledge, his words lack* *insight* (**34:35**). Seemingly dismissing the suffering Job is already enduring, Elihu prays: *Oh, that Job might be tested* *to the utmost for answering like a wicked man* (**34:36**). He concludes the chapter by alleging that Job is adding rebellion to the sin that is the reason for his suffering (**34:37**). In 34:7 he said that Job 'drinks scorn like water'; in 34:37 he says that Job *scornfully claps his hands* in their midst. His judgment is sealed.

McKenna contrasts the Elihu of the first and second speeches. In the first speech, where he speaks 'under the inspiration of the Spirit, he is a compassionate equal who serves as a mediator for the purpose of justifying Job', but in the second speech he is 'posturing on behalf of human reason' and 'represents a cold-hearted superior who is bent on defending God and condemning Job' (*CC*).

35:1-16 The third speech

Elihu begins his third speech by asking Job, 'Do you think this is just?' (**35:2a**), and then quotes two things Job has said – and two contradictory things at that. The first is Job's confident statement: *I will be cleared by God* (**35:2b**), answered by Elihu in 35:9-16. The second is, *What profit is* *it to me, and what do I gain by not sinning?* (**35:3**), which is the converse of the question he ascribed to Job in 34:7. The contradiction between these two statements is indicated by the *Yet* of 35:3 – Why does Job bother whether or not God finds him innocent if it makes no difference to his life? Elihu invites Job's friends to listen as he demolishes these statements (**35:4**).

He begins with the last question first (**35:5-8**). But he actually has very little to say. None of his listeners has disputed the greatness of God. In fact, almost all he says in this passage is a repetition of previous speeches. Statements about *the heavens* and *the clouds so high above* (**35:5**) were made in 9:8-10, 11:8 and 22:12. The question in **35:6** has already been asked by Job (7:20) and the question in **35:7** is similar to the one asked by Eliphaz (22:3). Elihu is here asserting that God is not affected by Job's sin – no matter how many individual sins he may have committed (note the *If you sin* and *If your sins are many* – 35:6). Nor does God benefit in any way by Job's righteousness.

Nothing can be further from the truth than Elihu's assertion here! The rest of Scripture teaches us that God's heart is broken when his creatures stray from him. And earlier in the book of Job we heard God speak approvingly of his servant Job.

The only statement that Elihu can claim as his own is this: *Your wickedness affects only a man like yourself, and your* *righteousness only the sons of men* (**35:8**). He has a point here, although it may not have been the one he intended to make. Sin is not only personal but social as well – it affects an entire community, as we in Africa are well aware.

Elihu then devotes the rest of the chapter (**35:9-16**) to a critique of Job's first statement 'I will be cleared by God' (35:2). What he says elicits various responses from commentators. Some think that it merely shows how callous Elihu is. Others, however, see this denial that God will bother to speak as indirectly starting to prepare the way for God's direct intervention in chapter 38.

Elihu's first point is that *men cry out under a load of* *oppression, they plead for relief from the arm of the powerful* (**35:9**). Despite this cry for release, they are not heard. Elihu gives several reasons for this. First of all, *no one says,* *'Where is God my Maker, who gives songs in the night, who* *teaches more to us than to the beasts of the earth and makes* *us wiser than the birds of the air?'* (**35:10-11**). The idea seems to be that people should first seek God for who he is before they ask him to meet their needs. This idea is also expressed in Jesus' words in the Sermon on the Mount,

'But seek first his kingdom and his righteousness, and all these things will be given to you as well' (Matt 6:33). If we have him in our lives, he *gives us songs in the night*. This is a beautiful thought and a great encouragement for the suffering. Despite the night of darkness, suffering and tribulation, God makes us rejoice in him. He is the one who set us above the animals and the birds, not only by creating us in his own image but also by teaching us and giving us wisdom.

The second reason the cry of the oppressed is not answered is because of their pride (**35:12**), and the third reason is because their plea is *empty* (**35:13**). Here the word 'empty' may include the idea that their motives are wrong, but the main emphasis is on the fact that they do not really know what they are asking for – they are asking in ignorance (just as Elihu accuses Job of doing in **35:16**, where he uses the same word.)

The cruelty of Elihu comes to the surface when he applies what he has been saying to Job himself, telling him *How much less, then, will he listen when you say that you do not see him, that your case is before him and you must wait for him* (**35:14**). Moreover, he accuses Job of having said that God's *anger never punishes and he does not take the least notice of wickedness* (**35:15**). Not only does Elihu say that Job's repeated plea to the Lord is even more empty than that mentioned in 35:13, but his very talk is empty – a multitude of words, meaning nothing (35:16).

36:1-37:24 *The fourth speech*

By way of introducing his fourth and final speech, Elihu tells Job that he is not yet done (36:2-4). He, therefore, requests him to *bear with me a little longer* (**36:2a**). Yet he carries on at length, ranging far and wide, for he wants to show Job *that there is more to be said in God's behalf* (**36:2b**) Elihu insists – even more forcefully than he has done up to now – that he will *ascribe justice to my Maker* with knowledge that he has fetched *from afar* (**36:3**). But he sounds very pompous when he claims that he has unique knowledge (**36:4**) (what a contrast with Job, whom he has just described as *without knowledge* – 35:16). In chapters 36 and 37, Elihu basically restates the doctrine of retribution (36:5-21) and describes the glory of God in nature (36:22-37:24).

He begins his further explication of the doctrine of retribution by asserting that God is mighty and firm in his purpose (**36:5**). God *does not keep the wicked alive but gives the afflicted their rights* (**36:6**). Moreover *he does not take his eyes off the righteous; he enthrones them with kings and exalts them forever* (**36:7**). Turning to the wicked again, Elihu explains why God brings suffering their way. The suffering that God inflicts upon them is because they *have sinned arrogantly* (**36:8-9**). However, the purpose is not just to make them suffer but to help them learn from the suffering their sin has precipitated and return to God in repentance (**36:10**). There are two possible outcomes. *If they obey and serve him, they will spend the rest of their days in prosperity and their years in contentment* (**36:11**). On the other hand, *if they do not listen, they will perish by the sword and die without knowledge* (**36:12**).

He then goes on to utter a stringent warning to these in the latter group (36:13-14) and encouragement to those who will listen to God (36:15). He warns of the fate of those who refuse to repent: *The godless in heart harbour resentment; even when he fetters them, they do not cry for help* (**36:13**). Earlier, Elihu had said that God does not answer this group of persons when they cry (35:12). Now he says that they themselves *do not cry for help*. He warns that these people *die in their youth, among male prostitutes of the shrines* (**36:14**). Several commentators believe that the point he is making here is that those who are insensitive to God's chastisement die young and in shame. Alden's comment links both the ancient Near Eastern context and the present: 'A prostitute could serve worshipers at the shrine of a fertility deity for only a limited number of years, and it is likely that sexually transmitted diseases claimed the lives of many, then as now' (*NAC*). The encouragement to the group who are prepared to repent is that *those who suffer he delivers in their suffering; he speaks to them in their affliction* (**36:15**; see also 35:10).

Elihu has been speaking in general terms, but now he turns to Job and admonishes him in the light of what he has been saying (36:16-21). Scholars are agreed that the Hebrew text of this passage is extremely difficult, which is why there is such diversity in the different translations. But the general thrust of the passage is that Elihu is expressing hope that Job will turn out to be among those who understand the disciplinary purpose of suffering and listen to what God is saying. *He is wooing you*, he tells Job, *from the jaws of distress to a spacious place free from restriction, to the comfort of your table laden with choice food* (**36:16**). The reference to 'a spacious place' is relevant to Job, who had felt hemmed-in by God (13:27). But, like Job's other friends, Elihu insists that Job is suffering because of some wickedness in him: *But now you are laden with the judgment due the wicked; judgment and justice have taken hold of you* (**36:17**). What a contrast between a 'table laden with choice food' (36:16) and a person 'laden with the judgment due the wicked'.

Elihu draws a similar contrast between the way God is trying to 'woo' Job (36:16) and the enticement of riches (**36:18**; the Hebrew root of the words translated 'woo' and 'entice' is the same). Elihu is trying to be helpful, but his words do not apply to Job who no longer has any wealth in which to seek security, nor any power which might lead someone to offer him a bribe (36:18-19). Moreover, even in his heyday Job was a righteous man, not one whose security was in riches, nor one who took and gave bribes. Nor are Elihu's warnings about the night and being dragged away from home in **36:20-21** any more relevant (note that the sense of the Hebrew – and the Tigrigna translation – is that it is *the night* that is dragging people). Job has already been dragged away from his home (36:20), unless Elihu is here referring to death.

In accusing Job of *turning to evil, which you seem to prefer to affliction* (36:21) it seems that Elihu is warning Job that his insistence on arguing his case before God rather than taking his suffering as a learning experience could finally lead to blasphemy and rebellion against God. It is interesting to note that although what Job has said about God in the bitterness of his suffering may have bordered on blasphemy, this was not a sin of which God accused him.

Elihu then moves on to speak of the greatness and power of God in creation. He prefaces his words with three questions and three statements. The questions come first: 'Who is a teacher like him'? (**36:22b**; see also 35:11). *Who has prescribed his ways for him?* (**36:23a**). Who said to him, *You have done wrong?* (**36:23b**). All three are rhetorical questions, expecting the answer 'no one'. God acts on his own initiative and is accountable to no one.

Elihu exhorts Job (and us): *Remember to extol his work, which men have praised in song* (**36:24**). He adds *All mankind has seen it; men gaze on it from afar* (**36:25**). Elihu's exhortation reminds us of Psalm 19: 'The heavens declare the glory of God; the skies proclaim the work of his hands' (Ps 19:1). And then, the exclamation: *How great is God – beyond our understanding! The number of his years is past finding out* (**36:26**). God is indeed *exalted in his power* (**36:22a**).

What Elihu is saying here and in what follows is true, and has already been spoken of by Job and his three friends. But Elihu's presentation of it is at least unique in the way it is framed. That is why some commentators believe that this part of the speech prepares Job for the coming divine encounter.

Elihu focuses on God's control of the intricacies of nature (36:27-37:13). He speaks of the water cycle that produces rain (**36:27-28**), using it as an example of how God superintends the operations of nature and provides us with food (**36:31**). He marvels at God's inscrutable role in this: *Who can understand how he spreads out the clouds, how he thunders from his pavilion?* (**36:29**). No one can understand it! And yet, as Job has said before *these are but the outer fringe of his works* (26:14).

There is a wonderful transition from the thunder of a rainstorm to the voice of God in 36:32-37:5. The thunder announces both the coming of the storm and the coming of God, and animals (**36:33**) and humans like Elihu respond to its approach. Elihu describes his response as follows: *Listen! Listen to the roar of his voice, to the rumbling that comes from his mouth. He unleashes his lightning beneath the whole heaven and sends it to the ends of the earth* (**37:2-3**). True to our human experience, the thunder, *the sound of his roar* (**37:4**) comes after 'his lightning' in 37:3.

Verse **37:5** serves as a transition between what has gone before and what follows: *God's voice thunders in marvellous ways; he does great things beyond our understanding*. Elihu proceeds to describe areas of God's marvellous work that have not been mentioned before or to expand on ones that have already been mentioned (37:6-13). It is he who *says to the snow, 'Fall on the earth,' and to the rain shower, 'Be a mighty downpour'* (**37:6**). Daily work is interrupted and animals go into hibernation because of the snow and driving rain (**37:7-8**). *The tempest comes out from its chamber* and *the cold from the driving winds* (**37:9**). Not only that: *The breath of God produces ice, and the broad waters become frozen. He loads the clouds with moisture, he scatters his lightning through them* (**37:10-11**). All this is done *so that all men he has made may know his work* (37:7). *At his direction they* [the clouds] *swirl around over the face of the whole earth to do whatever he commands them* (**37:12**).

As far as Elihu is concerned, God's retributive justice is made manifest even in his direction of the forces of nature: *He brings the clouds to punish men, or to water his earth and show his love* (**37:13**). 'God is behind it all, either for punishment or correction (if one is at the wrong end of the thunderbolt or suffering from lack of rain or washed away in a flood) or for love (God provides the cloud which produces the rain which makes possible the food which we need to survive)' (Simundson).

In the last section of his last speech, Elihu turns to Job and directs several rhetorical questions to him (37:14-24). Intriguingly, these questions are similar to those the Lord will ask Job from the whirlwind. Elihu challenges Job to *listen to this* and to *stop and consider God's wonders* (**37:14**). He asks: *Do you know how God controls the clouds and makes his lightning flash?* (**37:15**). Next he asks: *Do you know how the clouds hang poised, those wonders of him who is perfect in knowledge?* (**37:16**). The exact function of Elihu's reference to *you who swelter in your clothes when the land lies hushed under the south wind* (**37:17**) is not clear. Of course, there is a contrast between the sweltering heat indicated in this verse and the cold weather described in 37:6-13 above, but why does Elihu make this contrast? One explanation is that he may be driving 'home the point that man has absolutely no control over the weather (let alone in the moral ordering of human affairs), unlike God, who changes it at his will' (*TOT*). He is preparing Job for the sarcasm of 37:19-20.

Continuing with his rhetorical questions, Elihu asks Job: *Can you join him in spreading out the skies, hard as a mirror of cast bronze?* (**37:18**). He then sarcastically invites Job to *tell us what we should say to him; we cannot draw up our case because of our darkness. Should he be told that I want to speak? Would any man ask to be swallowed up?* (**37:19-20**). The Hebrew of the second half of 37:20 is very difficult to interpret, as is clear from any comparison of different translations. But it is clear that what Elihu is saying is something like this: 'Job, you think you're wise enough to be able to speak to God? You don't know what a risk you are running!' Alden comments, 'the tangled character of the syntax of this verse ... betrays the unclear thinking and frustration of Elihu who, so confident at the beginning, was now running out of arguments and eloquence ... The point of the two questions is that it would be certain death to contest God' (*NAC*).

The Hebrew of **37:21-22** is also difficult, but it seems that what Elihu is saying is that the splendour of God's coming is even more dazzling than the reappearance of the sun after the winds have swept the sky clear of clouds. No one can look at it, and even less can one look at him.

The concluding verses of Elihu's speeches remind Job and us of the awesome majesty of God and of what our response to him should be. All that the interminable debate between Job, his three friends and Elihu has accomplished is to remind us that it is not possible to know all about God and his ways. The point is driven home in **37:23-24**, where Elihu for the last time stresses God's power, justice and *great righteousness* and the fact that *he does not oppress*. The only response to such a God is reverent fear – a characteristic of the wise (37:24; see also 28:28).

38:1-42:6 God's Speeches and Job's Response

Finally God speaks *out of the storm* – some versions have 'whirlwind'. Although Elihu was the one speaking in the immediately preceding chapters, God speaks directly to Job. He speaks in his own time and in his own way. He speaks on his own terms, not in the courtroom terms Job has been demanding, and he is never on the defensive.

Some scholars complain that God does not appear to give a direct answer to Job's questions, and especially to the challenge Job issued when swearing his oath of innocence (31:35-37). We will look at that problem as we examine the text, but at this point it is worth pointing out that the fact that God speaks at all already addresses Job's fear that God is totally ignoring his need. Both what God says and the fact that he bothers to say anything at all are a response to the questions Job has been asking.

God's speech comes in two parts, separated by Job's first response. The second speech is also followed by a response from Job. The first speech begins at 38:1 and goes up to 40:2. The second speech begins at 40:6 and ends at 41:34. Job's responses to God are found in 40:3-5 and 42:1-6.

Scholars have compared the two speeches in terms of literary style and content. Some say that the first speech is a beautiful and well-structured poem, with superb content. But they are less enthusiastic about the second speech, labelling it as dull and uninteresting. Some even go to the extent of cutting it out of the book. These complaints, too, will be addressed in the text.

38:1-40:5 The First Encounter

38:1-40:2 God's first speech

After appearing *out of the storm*, God begins with hard-hitting words: 'Who is this that *darkens my counsel with words without knowledge?* (**38:2**). Then the challenge: *Brace yourself like a man; I will question you, and you shall answer me* (**38:3**). God then proceeds to bombard Job with a series of questions about his creation.

God begins with the earth (**38:4-7**). *Where were you when I laid the earth's foundation? Tell me, if you understand. Who marked off its dimensions? Surely you know! Who stretched a measuring line across it? On what were its footings set, or who laid its cornerstone – while the morning stars sang together and all the angels shouted for joy?* Does Job understand? Does he know? The fact that Job has spoken *words without knowledge* is being exposed.

Next comes the sea (**38:8-11**). *Who shut up the sea behind doors when it burst forth from the womb, when ... I said, 'This far you may come and no farther; here is where your proud waves halt'?* This is followed by an interrogation about dawn and the morning (**38:12-15**). *Have you ever given orders to the morning, or shown the dawn its place, that it might take the earth by the edges and shake the wicked out of it?* Then come the deep and the gates of death (**38:16-18**). *Have you journeyed to the springs of the sea or walked in the recesses of the deep? Have the gates of death been shown to you? Have you seen the gates of the shadow of death?* What about light and darkness (**38:19-20**)? God adds a sarcastic note: *Surely you know, for you were already born! You have lived so many years* (**38:21**).

Snow and hail come next (**38:22-23**). *Have you entered the storehouses of the snow or seen the storehouses of the hail, which I reserve for times of trouble, for days of war and battle?* The elaboration may seem strange, but we know from experience and the historical accounts of the Bible that God does use the weather to accomplish his purposes (see Josh 10:11). Thunderstorm, lightning, rain, dew and ice are mentioned together (**38:24-30**). *What is the way to the place where the lightning is dispersed ... ? Who cuts channels for the torrents of rain, and a path for the thunderstorm, to water a land where no man lives ... and make it sprout with grass? From whose womb comes the ice? Who gives birth to the frost from the heavens?*

God then turns to the stars (**38:31-32**). *Can you bind the beautiful Pleiades? Can you loose the cords of Orion? Can you bring forth the constellations in their seasons or lead out the Bear with its cubs?* The point God is making is: *Do you know the laws of the heavens? Can you set up God's dominion over the earth?* (**38:33**). Job has nothing to do with administration of the earth, which is under divine superintendence.

In 38:34-38 God comes back to clouds, lightning and water. He interrupts his questions about these with a question about wisdom. *Who endowed the heart with wisdom or* gave understanding to the mind? (**38:36**), emphasizing the wisdom that is needed to make the clouds (and the moisture they contain) water the scorched earth.

Now God turns to animals and birds and continues his interrogation of Job (**38:39-41**). *Do you hunt the prey for the lioness and satisfy the hunger of the lions...? Who provides food for the raven when its young cry out to God and wander about for lack of food?* God asks Job if he knows anything about the reproduction of the mountain goat and how its young grow and thrive in the wilderness (**39:1-4**). The freedom of the wild donkey is amazing (**39:5-8**). *Who let the wild donkey go free? Who untied his ropes?* Then comes the strength and untameable nature of the wild ox (**39:9-12**). *Will the wild ox consent to serve you? ... Will you rely on him for his great strength?*

Can Job make sense of the fast but foolish ostrich (**39:13-18**). As to the beauty, strength and fearlessness of the horse (**39:19-25**), what was Job's input? *Do you give the horse his strength or clothe his neck with a flowing mane? Do you make him leap like a locust striking terror with his proud snorting?* The first speech concludes with a mention of another group of birds (**39:26-29**). *Does the hawk take flight by your wisdom and spread his wings toward the south?* – referring to the hawk's migration to its winter home in Africa. *Does the eagle soar at your command and build his nest on high?* The nature and behaviour of each species is brought to light in these chapters that focus on the marvel and order of God's creation.

Although God may not have answered Job's questions directly, what these chapters tell Job and us is that 'God is purposeful in his creation, pervasive in his control, and personal in his care' (*CC*). Then the challenge at the beginning of chapter 38 is repeated – though in a different form. *Will the one who contends with the Almighty correct him? Let him who accuses God answer him!* (**40:1-2**).

Some commentators give the impression that it is not fair for God to bombard a man who is suffering for no fault of his own with such questions. However, in stating this, they too may be liable to condemnation as darkening counsel 'with words without knowledge' (38:2). We do not know why God chose to respond to Job in this way. But we do know that God was teaching his servant great lessons – as Job himself acknowledges. Questions are an effective way of teaching, because they force the learner to think for himself. Earlier, Job had described God's power in similar terms (9:4-10), but the questions force him to move beyond mere descriptions to profound meditation on what this power is and how God uses it.

40:3-5 Job's first response

The impact of what God has said about himself produces a profound change in Job. He finally stops defending himself. First, he says, *I am unworthy* (**40:4a**). Second, he confesses,

I have no answer (**40:4-5**). Note the repeated sense of his inability to answer God: *how can I reply to you* (**40:4b**), *I put my hand over my mouth* (**40:4c**; the exact thing he had repeatedly urged his friends to do!). *I spoke once ... twice, but I will say no more* (**40:5**). This last is a Hebrew idiom, meaning 'I have spoken once too many times already' (*NAC*).

The eloquent speaker and indefatigable disputant has been silenced. Putting it in the context of Job's unyielding stance of innocence, McKenna says, 'The snowman of self-righteousness melts before God in the confession, "I am unworthy," and in the admission, "I don't know"' (*CC*).

40:6-42:6 The Second Encounter

If God's revelation of himself has led Job to accept his unworthiness and admit his ignorance, why does God need to continue speaking? 'Is this overkill on God's part', as Simundson puts it, 'or does Job still need more convincing?' As usual, scholars give diverse opinions. However, since the second speech is part of the Bible – and we cannot simply use our finite human rationality to excise it from the text – there must be a purpose for it in God's mind. Simundson offers the possible explanation that the first speech has merely left Job feeling 'pressured from the outside. The insight of his own human limitations has not quite penetrated to his being. It is not yet completely congenial to him. He is still fighting it and holding out for something else. So he can use another dose of God's medicine.'

McKenna agrees: 'He is learning to listen to God, but hearing alone is not healing. God has more to say and Job has more to learn' (*CC*). It is worth noting that Job's first response, unlike the second one (see 42:6), does not include the word *repent*.

Once again, I will not make any substantial comment on the text of God's speeches. These wonderful texts can speak for themselves.

40:7-41:34 God's second speech

God again tells Job: *Brace yourself like a man; I will question you, and you shall answer me* (**40:7**; see also 38:3). In the first speech the accusation was 'Who is this that darkens my counsel with words without knowledge?' (38:2). Now it is *Would you discredit my justice? Would you condemn me to justify yourself?* (**40:8**). Even though Job has accused his friends of having a narrow theology, he himself appears to suffer from the same mindset. He argues that because he has not committed any sin that deserved the affliction he is going through, God must be acting unjustly.

God's response is neatly summarized by Simundson: 'Since Job complained about God's execution of justice, God invites Job to try it himself' (40:10-14). But before he presents that challenge, the Lord asks Job: *Do you have an arm like God's and can your voice thunder like his?* (**40:9**).

The question arises, why does the Lord speak about himself (God) in the third person in this verse? Gordis's explanation for this is that the writer, that is, the person recording what God said, 'momentarily forgets that he is speaking in the name of the Lord and refers to him in the third person.' We see similar patterns in the writing of the prophets. At one point, a prophet may speak in the name of God and use the first person, 'and then, as his human individuality comes to the fore, [he] speaks of God in the third person'.

God is presenting Job with the ultimate challenge in these verses (40:10-14) – that is, to take over and see if he can perform better than God if he is not satisfied with the way God is running his universe.

God first invites Job to put on the divine regalia. *Then adorn yourself with glory and splendour, and clothe yourself in honour and majesty* (**40:10**). Glory, splendour, honour and majesty are among the unique attributes of God (see Pss 21:5; 93:1; 96:6; 104:1). Once Job has assumed these attributes, he is to *unleash the fury of your wrath, look at every proud man and bring him low, look at every proud man and humble him, crush the wicked where they stand* (**40:11-12**). The second half of verse eleven and the first half of verse twelve are identical, except for the minor difference between *bring him low* and *humble him*. Since Job had complained that the wicked go scot-free, God challenges him to use his usurped power to humble the twice-repeated 'every proud man' with just a glance. Not only is he to bring down every proud man, he is also to 'crush the wicked where they stand' (40:12) and, finally, *bury them all in the dust together; shroud their faces in the grave* (**40:13**). Can Job do this? If he can, God adds, *Then I myself will admit to you that your own right hand can save you* (**40:14**).

The inference is that Job has been asking for the impossible! According to Alden, 'God was demonstrating to Job that he was not God and could not do what God does. Therefore Job should not presume on God or lay charges at his door' (*NAC*). Andersen rightly describes 40:8-14 as 'the heart and pivot of the Lord's reply' (*TOT*). In asserting his integrity, Job has been accusing God of acting unjustly. Now God challenges Job to run the universe better. The problem is that if Job were to usurp the role of God, 'he would become another Satan. Only God can destroy creatively. Only God can transmute evil into good. As Creator, responsible for all that happens in his world, He is able to make everything (good and bad) work together into good' (*TOT*). God is making the point that 'the reality of his goodness lies beyond justice ... the categories of guilt and punishment, true and terrible though they are, can only view human suffering as a consequence of sin, not as an occasion of grace' (*TOT*).

Next, we have God's interrogation of Job about two aquatic monsters: behemoth (40:15-24) and leviathan (41:1-34). These two animals are described at much greater length than any of the animals mentioned in God's first

speech. God is focusing on these two to further underscore his governance of creation, mentioned in the preceding passage (40:6-14).

God begins by telling Job: *Look at the behemoth, which I made along with you* (**40:15**). It is amusing to see the human Job placed on a par with the immense 'behemoth', which most commentators believe to be the hippopotamus. But what does God mean when he says 'which I made along with you'? Maybe God is telling Job that the hippopotamus is as much his creature as Job is.

Job is no longer bombarded with questions. Instead he is asked to observe the physical details of this animal (40:15-19), its habitat (**40:20-23**) and its strength (**40:16, 24**). The only question is found in 40:24 and does not appear to be directed to Job.

With regard to **40:19**, Alden is of the opinion that *first* does not necessarily mean that 'chronologically the behemoth was the first to be created but that it is the chief or mightiest of the animals' (*NAC*). Only his Maker can overpower him. This interpretation fits with the context and the question in 40:24.

The description of leviathan in 41:1-34 is far longer than the earlier description of behemoth (40:15-24). The English names of both these creatures are merely transliterations of the Hebrew. Most commentators believe that leviathan is to be understood as the crocodile. Some biblical passages (for example, Job 3:8; Ps 74:14; Isa 27:1) give the impression that leviathan may be a mythological figure of chaos and evil. Here, however, it seems to refer to the literal crocodile, even though some aspects of the description involve figurative language (for example, the *flashes of light* and *sparks of fire* in 41:18-21). This language is used to emphasize how terrifying the animal is, and the image may arise from the impression created by his steaming breath and red eyes, which suggest that there is flame within. As in the first speech, God again starts with a barrage of questions. He stresses the uncontrollable nature of this animal through a series of question directed to Job (41:1-11). Can Job catch leviathan as he would a fish (**41:1-2**)? Can he tame him and use him for service (**41:3-4**)? *Can you make a pet of him like a bird or put him on a leash for your girls?* (**41:5**). The reference to girls here is not the same sort of cruel reminder of Job's dead children that his friends had given. Rather, the image of 'a girl leading on a leash a crocodile that may weigh as much as a ton is a whimsical if not absurd scene' (*NAC*). Even traders cannot bargain for leviathan (**41:6**). Harpoons and spears are useless on him (**41:7**). God elaborates on the folly of trying to control him: *If you lay a hand on him, you will remember the struggle and never do it again. Any hope of subduing him is false; the mere sight of him is overpowering. No one is fierce enough to rouse him* (**41:8-10a**).

Suddenly, in the middle of this passage on the invincible power of leviathan, God says, *Who then is able to stand* against me? Who has a claim against me that I must pay? Everything under heaven belongs to me (**41:10b-11**). Has Job any answer for this – since these questions are directed at him?

The body of leviathan is described in greater detail in the next section (41:12-24). We read of the strength of his limbs (**41:12**), his tough *outer coat* (**41:13**), his mouth *ringed about with his fearsome teeth* (**41:14**), his back like tightly fitted row of shields *that no air can pass between* (**41:15-17**), his breath like that of a fiery dragon (**41:18-21**), the strength of his neck (**41:22**), the folds of his flesh (**41:23**), his chest – *hard as rock* (**41:24**).

This description is followed by more evidence of leviathan's power – this time with more emphasis on its terrifying nature (41:25-34). Even *the mighty are terrified*, and so *they retreat before his thrashing* (**41:25**). Iron, bronze and wooden weapons such as swords, spears, darts, javelins, arrows and clubs have no effect on him. Nor do slingstones. Note the phrases *have no effect, he treats like straw – like rotten wood, like chaff, but a piece of straw* (**41:26-29a**). He is so fearless that *he laughs at the rattling of the lance* (**41:29b**). He is terrifying when he moves on land – *his undersides are jagged potsherds, leaving a trail in the mud like a threshing sledge* (**41:30**). He is even more terrifying in the water, where his ferocious thrashing *makes the depths churn like a boiling cauldron and stirs up the sea like a pot of ointment. Behind him he leaves a glistening wake; one would think the deep had white hair* (**41:31-32**). The chapter concludes with these words: *Nothing on earth is his equal – a creature without fear. He looks down on all that are haughty; he is king over all that are proud* (**41:33-34**).

Can Job even dream of controlling the raw power of these monsters? God does not even bother to give Job a final challenge, as he did at the conclusion of his first speech!

42:1-6 Job's second response

Job answers spontaneously. He is a different man now: *I know that you can do all things; no plan of yours can be thwarted* (**42:2**).

In 42:3 and 42:4, the *You asked* (**42:3a**) and *You said* (**42:4**) of the NIV are not in the original Hebrew. Consequently some scholars say that these verses are misplaced variants of 38:2-3 and 40:7, that is, different formulations of the question that God was asking at that point. But the majority of scholars agree that while these are variants, they are not misplaced. Rather, Job is quoting God in order to answer him. Job is admitting his ignorance: *Surely I spoke of things I did not understand, things too wonderful for me to know* (**42:3b**). In Andersen's words, 'This is the cry of a liberated man, not one who has been broken and humiliated' (*TOT*). Following his second quotation of God's words, Job says: *My ears had heard of you but now my eyes have seen you* (**42:5**).

It is clear that not only has Job seen God, he has also seen himself, as is clear from his next words: *Therefore I*

despise myself and repent in dust and ashes (**42:6**). His experience is similar to that of Isaiah (Isa 6:1-5). As in Job's experience, so in ours. It is only when we meet God that we can understand who we are.

Job's words in 42:6 are the climax of his reply to God and the last statement in the poetic dialogue. But what exactly does Job mean? The crucial point involves the understanding of the two Hebrew roots translated here as 'despise' and 'repent'. The word 'despise' is much stronger than the mere 'unworthy' of 40:4. Does it mean that Job hates himself? It is worth noting that the word 'myself' is not in the Hebrew of the phrase translated 'despise myself' in English. It seems that Job is not despising everything about himself, but rather the sin of his arrogant talk against God. Job's deep contrition is implied in the second phrase as well – he repents 'in dust and ashes'. 'Dust and ashes' are regularly associated with mourning and humbling of oneself in the OT (2:12; Josh 7:6; Esth 4:1).

What needs to be emphasized here is that the 'I despise … and repent' are not related to any one particular sin which might have precipitated Job's suffering – as his friends insisted. Andersen points out that 'Job confesses no sins here. And, even if this is implied, it is one thing to repent before God and another thing to disown one's integrity before men' (*TOT*).

42:7-17 The Epilogue

The book of Job began with a prose prologue and concludes with a prose epilogue. Just as we were left with many unanswered questions in the prologue, so we are left with many unanswered questions in the epilogue. For example, why isn't Satan mentioned? What about Job's wife? Why is Elihu not mentioned – for good or bad? Yet even with all these questions, the book ends with a gratifying resolution of the problem of Job the man, and with a great theme of reconciliation and restoration.

However, reactions to this 'grand finale' are mixed. Simundson displays a certain ambivalence when he asks what our response would be if Job had continued to suffer from chronic illness, even if restored in all other respects. He reminds us that not all stories like Job's have happy endings. 'Would it have been enough for Job to be assured of God's presence and care for him? … It has been enough for many sufferers who have found that God was with them in the depths even though the suffering did not go away.'

Others say that the restoration of Job's fortunes spoils the beauty of the story, that it is an anticlimax. Some even go to the extent of saying that in rewarding Job for his integrity the author of the epilogue misses the entire point of the dialogue, and so they wish to excise the epilogue from the book. While they might agree that the Bible teaches that God does reward good and punish evil, they would say that this happens only in heaven: 'God will adjust the balances there, but he will not do so in this life.' But don't we sometimes see this happen in this life too? Alden suggests we look at the facts from a different perspective: 'In the long run God really did not forsake his 'servant Job' ... The Satan expected and hoped that he would. ... The felicitous resolution of the story is also the final ignominy to him who would destroy God's servants by luring them into sin and urging them to deny their Lord' (*NAC*).

Andersen, too, sees nothing wrong with the conclusion, and argues that it is artistically and theologically appropriate that 'Job's vindication be not just a personal and hidden reconciliation with God in the secret of his soul, but also visible, material, historical, in terms of his life as a man. It was already a kind of resurrection in the flesh, as much as the Old Testament could know' (*TOT*).

The text of the epilogue falls basically into two sections: God's judgment of the trio (42:7-9) and his restoration of Job (42:10-17).

42:7-9 Judgment of the Three Friends

God has to deal with Job first before he turns to his friends – but turn he does: *After the Lord had said these things to Job, he said to Eliphaz the Temanite, 'I am angry with you and your two friends, because you have not spoken of me what is right, as my servant Job has* (**42:7**). When the Lord says, 'I am angry' something very serious must have happened. There is no need to repeat the debate that went on between Job and his three friends. In explaining the reason for his anger against the three, the Lord twice says, 'because you have not spoken of me what is right, as my servant Job has' (42:7 and 42:8). In trying to uphold a very narrow doctrine of retribution and defend God's righteousness, Eliphaz and his friends spoke wrongly of him. By contrast, Job who – though he did not discard the doctrine in general – rejected its relevance to his situation and in the heat of the argument even said things about God which bordered on blasphemy, did speak *what is right*. What a sudden turning of the tables! Those who think they are upholding God and his justice are condemned, while the man they think deserves God's judgment is justified.

So, they are told, *now take seven bulls and seven rams and go to my servant Job and sacrifice a burnt offering for yourselves. My servant Job will pray for you, and I will accept his prayer and not deal with you according to your folly* (**42:8**). What an irony! They have to 'sacrifice a burnt offering', but their sin will not be forgiven until the man they thought deserved God's wrath prays for them. In the wisdom tradition, wisdom corresponds to righteousness and folly to wickedness. So the three – who thought of themselves as wise men par excellence – were the ones who were exhibiting folly, not the man they called stupid and without knowledge. God was gracious in opening the way for their

restoration to divine fellowship. The good thing is that they are obedient: *So Eliphaz the Temanite, Bildad the Shuhite and Zophar the Naamathite did what the Lord told them; and the Lord accepted Job's prayer* (**42:9**).

42:10-17 Restoration of Job

It is interesting to note that it was only after Job had prayed for his friends that the Lord *made him prosperous again* (**42:10**). Although his sickness is not mentioned, we can safely assume that this phrase, together with **42:12a** – *The Lord blessed the latter part of Job's life more than the first* – includes the restoration of his health. The Lord *gave him twice as much as he had before*. Then **42:12b** elaborates on this as far as the animals are concerned. *And he also had seven sons and three daughters* (**42:13**). While some may be puzzled as to why the number of his sons and daughters does not also double (compare 1:2), Alden interprets this merely a problem of perception. Job does now have two sets of seven sons and three daughters: 'the first set, to be reunited with him when he died, and the second set, born after his tragedies and trials (compare 2 Sam 12:23; 1 Thess 4:13; 1 Cor 15:54)' (*NAC*).

The naming and special attention given to Job's daughters is quite unusual. Although the writer may not have intended to communicate anything by the names of the three daughters (**42:14**), what follows appears to take the restoration of Job to new levels. *Nowhere in all the land were there found women as beautiful as Job's daughters, and their father granted them an inheritance along with their brothers* (**42:15**). Nothing similar is said about the first set of daughters, none of whose names are known. The naming, their unsurpassed beauty and the *inheritance along with their brothers* mark them off as remarkable women. In granting them an inheritance, Job was doing something unheard of at that time and in his culture. True, in the absence of living male heirs, daughters were allowed to inherit (Num 27:1-11). But daughters inheriting *along with their brothers* was quite unique. Simundson comments: 'In our day, it is tempting to look at a passage like this and see it as an early glimmer of hope for equal rights for women – certainly not the common practice, but a reminder that sex roles are not as stereotyped in the Bible as we might think.'

McKenna goes further: 'Why then does Job break with tradition ... his daughters neither expect an inheritance nor, according to tradition, deserve one. Grace has to be the answer. As God has blessed Job with double wealth that he doesn't expect or deserve, he in gratitude shares his fortune with all whom he loves' (*CC*).

As one reads 42:11 with its catalogue of those who now come to comfort him, one is tempted to ask, 'Where do these people come from?' Where were they when Job was going through all that suffering and deprivation? Were they among those Job mentioned in 19:13-19 as having deserted him during his season of affliction? Have they now returned to him because God has restored him to a double portion of his previous glory? We do not know. But human nature being the way it is, we can have our reservations about these fair-weather friends. Simundson thinks so. 'Now that his life has improved, everything is looking up, and his wealth has been restored, he is suddenly surrounded by empathetic well-wishers. Had these people been waiting for his recovery before they showed their faces?' A proverb captures the unreliable nature of such friends: *feqren teqmen tsehay ziweqo tesmen* (Tigrigna – 'love and advantage and butter exposed to the sun', meaning that just as butter exposed to the sun melts away, so love based on taking advantage of someone else or on self-interest disappears when circumstances are not favourable).

All his brothers and sisters and everyone who had known him before came and ate with him in his house. They comforted and consoled him over all the trouble the Lord had brought upon him, and each one gave him a piece of silver and a gold ring **(42:11)**. Is not the comforting and consoling a little too late? Again the Tigrigna saying *dehri mai nab beati* ('moving into the cave after the rain') must have originated in a situation similar to the one we have here – doing something after the event. Another proverb makes the same point: *jib kehede behwala wusha chohe* (Amharic, Ethiopia – 'the dog barked after the hyena had left'). The motive for their gifts may even be more to curry favour for themselves than to aid Job.

Yet even this inadequate consolation may still have been necessary, for Job would still have been mourning the loss of his children. And, as McKenna reminds us, 'grace holds no grudges' (*CC*) and therefore Job forgives and receives them – as he did his debating friends when he prayed for them so that their relationship with God might be restored. Gordis interprets the eating and socializing together positively when he says that 'his kinsmen and friends give public testimony that he is no longer a pariah or a leper'.

The final paragraph in the book starts with the words: *After this* and proceeds to report on the *hundred and forty years* for which Job enjoys life after his restoration. The man who faced the bleak prospect of dying without any offspring *saw his children and their children to the fourth generation* **(42:16)**. When he eventually dies, he is *old and full of years* **(42:17)**. The man who had wanted to die and was only waiting for the exit of death during his trial lives for many more happy years. Die he does – as all of us must when our time comes, but all the commentators agree with Andersen when he says, 'The simple, dignified ending (42:17), which reminds us of the peaceful deaths of the patriarchs in Genesis, completes the fulfilment of the Israelite ideal' (*TOT*).

Conclusion

The doctrine of retribution, or rewards and punishments, is taught in the Bible. A person does, indeed, reap what he or she sows. Job, a man after God's own heart, loses all that he has – property, children, even his health – suddenly and for reasons that he cannot fathom. But we know those reasons, for although Job and his friends are not aware of chapters 1 and 2, we are. His friends, who adhere to a very literal, narrow interpretation of the doctrine of retribution, conclude that some hidden sin on Job's part must have precipitated this calamity. Job, knowing his own heart, protest that he is innocent and holds his ground to the very end. As the debate between Job and his friends grows more heated, positions become entrenched. Job accuses his friends and God of injustice, while the friends accuse Job of trying to justify himself and of arrogance towards them and God. Elihu tries to address the issue objectively, but to no avail. All this time, God is silent.

The resolution comes when God speaks to Job from the storm or whirlwind. Job repents – confessing his finiteness, unworthiness and ignorance. God accepts his confession and restors Job to full fellowship with himself, with a double portion of his blessings. The friends are also admonished and restored after Job has prayed for them. God and his servant Job are vindicated and Satan is proved to be 'the father of lies' and the enemy of righteousness.

Tewoldemedhin Habtu

Further Reading

Gordis, Robert. *The Book of Job: Commentary, New Translation and Special Studies*. New York: The Jewish Theological Seminary of America, 1978.

Rodd, C. S. *The Book of Job*. Philadelphia: Trinity Press International, 1990.

Simundson, Daniel J. *The Message of Job: A Theological Commentary*. Minneapolis: Augsburg, 1986.

PSALMS

The worship team led the congregation, largely of young people, in singing: 'I will enter his gates with thanksgiving in my heart, I will enter his courts with praise; I will say, this is the day that the Lord has made, I will rejoice for he has made me glad.' They sang with gusto, clapping and dancing. Another chorus followed: 'This is the day that the Lord has made, that the Lord has made, I will rejoice and be glad in it.' For thirty minutes the jubilant worshippers kept singing songs that were extracts from different parts of the Psalms. Few of them would have had any idea of what specific chapter and verse they were singing.

This congregation's practice reflects the fact that the psalms lend themselves easily to memorization, recitation and singing. Using them in this way is commendable. But it is possible to simply repeat individual verses over and over and lose track of their original meanings. The study of the Psalms will help to counter this abuse of them.

Title and Purpose

The ancient Hebrews, who probably used this portion of Scripture in the same way as Africans do now, referred to it as The Book of Praises. The Septuagint (the Greek translation of the OT, which was the earliest Christian Bible) called it 'The Book of Psalms', from the Greek word *psalmoi,* which means 'poems sung to the accompaniment of musical instruments'.

These psalms were born out of divine-human encounters over more than a thousand years and under diverse circumstances. Their central theme is worship. The psalmists (of whom at least seven are named) impress upon their readers that God is worthy of all praise because of who he is, what he has done and what he will do. Throughout the Psalms, God is presented as being on the side of the righteous and those who truly seek him. Whatever situations they may find themselves in, he will see them through and will show himself worthy of praise. This presentation of God as a caring elder brother is part of the appeal of the psalms to Africans. The songs reflect many of the circumstances we face in life: difficulty and danger, sickness and the fear of death, failure and sin and defeat. But they also sing of joy, deliverance, victory and triumph, always with an awareness of God's attributes of love, goodness and power. The psalms inspire us to trust him as much as they draw us to him in surrender and worship.

Authorship and Date

David, who lived from about 1011 to 941 BC and was a shepherd boy, musician, warrior and king, wrote 73 of the 150 psalms (3–9; 11–32; 34–41; 51–65; 68–70; 86; 101; 103; 108–110; 122; 124; 131; 138–145). If Psalms 2 and 95, usually classified as anonymous, were also written by David, that would make him responsible for fifty per cent of the psalms.

Inspired by David and under his instruction, Asaph, a priest who headed the music ministry in the temple, collected twelve psalms (50; 73–83), while a guild of singers, the sons of Korah, composed a further eleven (42–49; 84; 87). Two psalms are attributed to Solomon (72; 127), while Moses, Heman and Ethan contributed one each (90, 88 and 89 respectively). The psalm by Moses must have been composed around the time of the exodus from Egypt (in about 1410 BC), but collected during the reign of David. This leaves forty-seven psalms whose authors are unknown. Most of these remaining psalms seem to have been produced during the time of national reformation under the leadership of Ezra and Nehemiah in the fifth century BC.

Because of David's direct contribution and indirect influence, the book was known as 'The Psalms of David' for several centuries. Islamic scholars, who also regard the psalms as inspired, refer to the book by that name.

Nature and Classification

The psalms are poetic in form, like the songs and hymns we sing in Christian worship. Today they are often read responsively, an approach that reminds us that much Jewish poetry was based on parallelism and rhythm. In some ways, the rhythm of Hebrew poetry is similar to the traditional Afro beat, called *raara* by the Yoruba of West Africa, which is still found among those of African descent in the West Indies.

Ancient Hebrew poetry makes much use of a technique called 'parallelism' in which the poet states an idea in the first line and then reinforces it by various means in the succeeding line or lines. There are three main types of parallelism in Psalms:

- *Synonymous parallelism,* where the second line essentially repeats the idea of the first (3:1; 103:10).

- *Antithetic parallelism,* where the second line contrasts with the idea of the first (1:6; 37:16).

- *Synthetic parallelism,* where the succeeding line or lines add to or develop the idea of the first (1:1; 42:1).

Repetition is also important in ancient Hebrew poetry. It can be used for emphasis (22:1; 118:10-12), or as a refrain, as in Psalm 80 where the prayer is punctuated three times with the expression: 'Restore us, O Lord; let your face shine, that we may be saved' (80:3, 7, 19). Sometimes the last line of a psalm repeats the first and binds the whole together (8; 118).

Alphabetic acrostics are used in certain psalms, including 25, 34 and 119. In an acrostic psalm, each line or section begins with one of the twenty-two letters of the Hebrew alphabet, arranged in alphabetic order. Thus Psalm 119 has 176 verses, in twenty-two groups of eight verses. The first eight verses all begin with the first letter of the Hebrew alphabet, the next eight verses all begin with the second letter, and so on.

The psalms also contain rich imagery. Perhaps most striking are the many different descriptions of the Lord. God is a shepherd (23:1), a vineyard owner (80:8-16), a builder (127:1) and a father (68:5). He is a shield (3:3), a refuge (14:6), a rock (28:1) and a fortress (18:2). He is righteous (5:8), merciful (6:2) and just (9:8), but also angry (6:1), unrelenting (7:12) and a warrior (68:7-8). He rides on the clouds (68:4), is enthroned between the cherubim (99:1) and is in heaven (115:3). The Lord is King of Glory (24:10), the Most High (7:10) and the Lord Almighty (46:7). These and many other examples show the psalmists' attempts to describe in mere human language everything that God meant to them.

There are many different categories of psalms, and some psalms may belong to more than one group. Some of these categories are:

- Thanksgiving or praise psalms, offered either by an individual (18; 30; 116), or by the community (65; 66).

- Psalms expressing trust or hope in God (5; 7; 42).

- Wisdom psalms, which give guidelines for godly living (1; 37; 119).

- Laments or petition psalms, containing cries to God for help. These can be individual (3; 10; 13) or communal (44; 60; 74).

- Testimonial psalms, which tell others what God has done (115–118; 124–130).

- Pilgrim psalms, which were sung during pilgrimages to the holy city of Jerusalem. These include the Songs of Zion (46; 48; 76; 84; 87; 122) and the Songs of Ascents (120–134).

- Penitential psalms, which deal with sorrow over sin (6; 32; 51).

- Nature psalms, which tell of God's handiwork in creation (8; 19; 36).

- Historical psalms, which look back on God's merciful dealing with the nation of Israel (78; 135–137).

- Enthronement psalms, which describe the Lord's sovereignty over all (47; 93; 96–99).

- Royal or Messianic psalms, which survey the reigns of earthly kings and look forward to the promise of the heavenly king, who would be Jesus Christ, the Messiah (2; 18; 20; 21; 45; 72; 89; 101; 110; 132; 144).

- Imprecatory psalms, which ask for judgment on the wicked, usually the perceived enemies of the psalmist (7; 35; 55; 58; 59; 69; 79; 109; 137; 139; 140).

The psalms in this last group are the most controversial as they call down curses on the psalmist's enemies. Eight of the eleven imprecatory psalms were written by David and reflect his emotions as he was hunted and persecuted even though he was innocent of any crime. While the emotions are real, it is difficult to reconcile the content of some of these psalms with Christ's teaching about forgiving our enemies and turning the other cheek (see Matt 5:38-44).

In studying these imprecatory psalms, it must be noted that a) they call for divine justice rather than human vengeance (58:11); b) they ask God to punish the wicked in order to vindicate his righteousness (59:13); c) they call upon the wicked to seek the Lord (83:16); and d) God's righteous judgment causes people to praise him (7:17).

Believers in Africa must not yield to the temptation to use these psalms as an excuse for contending with those who contend with us and returning fire for fire. This is what happened in the early 1990s when church buildings were being burned and believers killed by Muslim fanatics in northern Nigeria. Some Nigerian theologians developed what became known as 'a theology of the third cheek'. This so-called theology argued that when an enemy had slapped a Christian on both the right and left cheeks (see Matt 5:39), the church should strike back. Though this approach did bring some immediate respite, in the long run the weapon of love and prayer for our enemies has brought far more people into the kingdom of God (see Matt. 5:44).

Headings and Technical Terms

The psalms are divided into five books (1–41, 42–72, 73–89, 90–106, 107–150), each ending with a doxology (41:13; 72:19-20; 89:52; 106:48; and 150:6 or Psalm 150 itself). All but thirty-four of the psalms have headings or superscriptions. These are editorial titles, added after the Psalms were written, but are historically accurate. They include information such as who wrote or collected the psalm (17; 79; 90), when or why it was written (3; 34; 51) and musical directions (69; 80; 88).

A common technical term is *Selah,* which occurs seventy-one times in the Psalms and three times in Habakkuk 3. It is probably a musical notation, signalling an interlude or some change of musical instrument. The other technical term is *For the choir director,* which is attached to fifty-five psalms. It suggests that there was a collection of psalms for the choir director to use on special occasions.

Christian Use of the Psalms

The Psalms obviously meant a great deal to Jesus. Words from Psalm 2:7 assured him of his place as Messiah and Son, both at his baptism and as he set out on his ministry (Mark 1:11). On the cross he used the prayer that begins Psalm 22 (Mark 15:34). We read in Luke 24:44 that after his resurrection he told his disciples, 'everything must be fulfilled that is written about me in the Law of Moses, the Prophets, and the Psalms'.

Christians use the psalms, along with the rest of the Scriptures, for 'teaching, rebuking, correcting and training in righteousness' and inspiration, so that we 'may be thoroughly equipped for every good work' (2 Tim 3:16-17).

Psalms are read in many mainstream Protestant churches across Africa each Sunday, as one of the three readings from Scripture. Besides this use in corporate worship, they are also often used in individual worship, in small group fellowships, in Bible studies, and in family devotions at home. They have a special place in our hearts because they are easy to study, to preach and teach from, and to store in our hearts. They are enjoyable to recite and sing as hymns, songs and choruses. They are practical and down to earth. While most of the Bible speaks to us about God and God's ways, the psalms help us to speak to God. They are not given to be used as magic formulae. Rather, they draw us near to God and help us to cry out to him in our times of need and to praise him as he deserves. Praise the Lord!

Outline of Contents

BOOK ONE: PSALMS 1-41

Psalm 1: The Two Ways
Psalm 2: The Lord's Anointed
Psalm 3: Prayer in a Time of Trouble
Psalm 4: How to Face Difficulty
Psalm 5: Trusting God When Facing Opposition
Psalm 6: A Prayer from the Depths of Distress
Psalm 7: Facing Injustice
Psalm 8: God's Creation and Our Place in It
Psalm 9: God's Rule over the Nations
Psalm 10: Times When God Seems Far Away
Psalm 11: Foundations for Life
Psalm 12: Three Kinds of Words
Psalm 13: Pain – Prayer – Praise
Psalm 14: The Way of Fools
Psalm 15: The Life That Pleases God
Psalm 16: The Results of Trust in God
Psalm 17: A Just Cause
Psalm 18: Deliverance
Psalm 19: God's World and God's Word
Psalm 20: Prayer Before Battle
Psalm 21: The Way of Victory for a Ruler
Psalm 22: Out of Deep Distress
Psalm 23: The Shepherd Psalm
Psalm 24: King of Glory
Psalm 25: Waiting on God
Psalm 26: Godly Ambitions
Psalm 27: Confidence and Prayer
Psalm 28: A Cry for Help and Justice
Psalm 29: The Majesty of God
Psalm 30: Experiences of Life
Psalm 31: Trusting Life into God's Hands
Psalm 32: Sadness and Joy
Psalm 33: The Word and the Works of God
Psalm 34: Praise, Encouragement And Teaching
Psalm 35: War on Injustice
Psalm 36: The End of the Way
Psalm 37: The Test of Time
Psalm 38: A Sinner's Prayer
Psalm 39: Life Is Short
Psalm 40: The Pilgrimage of Faith
Psalm 41: Healing, Forgiveness and Protection

BOOK TWO: PSALMS 42–72

Psalms 42-43: The Way of Encouragement
Psalm 44: The Cry of a Besieged Nation
Psalm 45: The Marriage of a King
Psalm 46: Our Refuge and Strength
Psalm 47: Worship the King
Psalm 48: The Glory of the City of God
Psalm 49: Facing the Reality of Death
Psalm 50: 'You Who Forget God'
Psalm 51: The Prayer of a Penitent
Psalm 52: The Fall of the Proud
Psalm 53: No God – No Hope
Psalm 54: The Name of God – Great and Good
Psalm 55: Oppression, Corruption, Betrayal
Psalm 56: Faith Instead of Fear
Psalm 57: God's Glory over All the Earth
Psalm 58: Banish Injustice
Psalm 59: God of Justice and Mercy
Psalm 60: A Prayer of Hope after a Defeat
Psalm 61: Trust in God in a Time of Need
Psalm 62: Trust in God at All Times

COMMENTARY

BOOK ONE: PSALMS 1-41

Psalm 1: The Two Ways

This psalm gives us no indication of who wrote it or when it was written. But there was good reason for putting it first in the book of Psalms. In six verses it tells us briefly what many of the psalms and many parts of the Bible tell us: there are two different ways in which people can live their lives. Each person has to choose, and each of us is responsible for the way we choose.

Jesus too speaks of these two ways of living and describes the outcome of the life that enjoys God's blessing (Matt 5:3-12; Luke 6:20-22) and of the life of those who reject God (Matt 6:19-24; 7:13-14, 24-27). His words can be profitably compared with those in this psalm.

1:1-3 The Way of the Godly

The psalm begins by saying *blessed*, that is, happy, are those who reject the ways of evil (**1:1**). Their rejection is shown by their refusal to *walk ... stand ... or sit* with those who reject God. These three verbs may indicate different stages of association with people, as do the accompanying three nouns: *counsel ... way ... seat*. Those who choose evil rather than good are also described in three ways, as the *wicked ... sinners* and *mockers*. Mockers are those who laugh at people who serve God and strive to do what is true and good.

The godly seek to know and follow the ways that God has shown. For the Jewish people in OT days, this meant *the law of the Lord* (**1:2**). This is what Joshua was commanded to study if he wished to enjoy God's blessing (Josh 1:6-9). Today, it is the whole of Scripture that gives us guidelines for life. We should be so deeply grateful that we have God's word that we should *delight* to study it (see also 112:1; 119:14-16), spend time meditating on it, and seek to live by its teaching.

The results of living in this way are set out in **1:3**:
- The believer's life will bear fruit. The fruit will be seen in the believer's character, in good works and in helpful service to others (see also John 15:1-8; Gal 5:22-23)
- The believer's life will not wither. It will be renewed day by day by God's word and by the Holy Spirit.
- The believer's life will be truly prosperous. The prosperity may not be in material things, for godly people often have to suffer for their faith. But real prosperity is found in life and work that is worthwhile and deeply satisfying, however hard it may be.

Jeremiah may have known this psalm and may be quoting 1:3 in Jeremiah 17:7-8.

1:4-6 The Way of the Wicked

When we are tempted to 'follow the advice of the wicked' (1:1a, NRSV) or 'take the path that sinners tread' (1:1b, NRSV), we need to remember the outcome of their ways:
- They produce nothing that is of lasting good to themselves or to others. They are *like chaff that the wind drives away* (**1:4**). 'Chaff' is what is left when the good corn or grain has been threshed out and taken away. It is of no use for food or for anything else (compare Isa 17:13; Hos 13:3; Matt 3:12).

- They have no place *in the assembly of the righteous* (**1:5**), that is, among those who are truly God's people and confess that fact in the world.
- When such people appear before God to give an account of their lives, as all of us must do (see 2 Cor 5:10), they will not be able to stand.

The final verse of the psalm sums up the different outcomes of the two lives: while the wicked will perish, the children of God will enjoy the blessing of living under God's care, for *the Lord watches over the way of the righteous* (**1:6**; see also 2 Tim 2:19).

Psalm 2: The Lord's Anointed

This psalm is similar to other psalms such as 21, 45, 72, 110 and 132 that are known as royal psalms because they are about Israel's king. It was probably written for a time when someone was anointed with oil (as Saul and David were in 1 Samuel 10:1 and 16:13) and crowned king (like Joash in 2 Kings 11:12) to rule over the people of Israel.

2:1-6 King in Israel

One who had been anointed as king could be spoken of as 'the Lord's anointed' (2:2; see also 1 Samuel 24:6). He could trust God to support him even though there were enemies in neighbouring countries who wanted to overpower him (**2:1-3**). These enemies are described as despising both the king and the God whom Israel's king worshipped and served.

God responds with a comment on the foolishness of human pride (**2:4**; see also Isa 2:11). Powerful men and women may think that they can do what they like and oppose God's purposes, but all that they do deserves only to be laughed at. As someone has put it, it is like a fly attacking an elephant or like a man trying to take the sun out of the sky. Oppressive rulers often seem to have great power over others, but history has shown that their power does not last long.

God's scorn is followed by his righteous anger against those who oppose him and oppress his people. He asserts that *I have installed my king on Zion, my holy hill* (**2:5-6**). Zion was the hill on which the temple stood in the centre of Jerusalem. The one anointed to be king over Israel had been put there by God. It is foolish to oppose God and his servants.

2:7-9 God's Anointed

In **2:7**, the king asserts that God has declared him to be his son. In the same way that Israel could be called God's son (as in Hos 11:1), each king of Israel could be called God's son (see 2 Sam 7:14; Ps 89:26-27). However, OT history shows that most of Israel's kings failed to live up to God's ideals and purposes for their people. The prophets gave the people the hope that one day a king, an Anointed of the

Lord, a true Son of God, would come and rule in righteousness and bring salvation and peace to Israel and the world. So although this psalm referred originally to a historical king of Israel, it came to be interpreted as speaking of the Messiah. This is seen in the pre-Christian writings found in the Dead Sea scrolls and in the *Psalms of Solomon* of the first century BC.

In the NT, the words of this psalm are applied to Jesus (Mark 1:11; Luke 3:22; Acts 4:25-26; 13:33; Heb 1:5; 5:5). In the fullest and deepest way, God could say of Jesus, *You are my Son.* It is far truer of him than of any king of Israel that the nations of the world have been given to him and that he rules over them (**2:8**). Today people from almost every nation on earth gladly confess that 'Jesus is Lord' and willingly serve him.

The statement that he will smash nations *like pottery* (**2:9**) draws on a custom of the time. When an Egyptian king was crowned, the names of foreign nations were written on pottery that was then smashed. Mesopotamian rulers had a similar custom. Thus what we have here is the use of poetic language to describe the power of God's rule, a power that will be fully revealed at the end of time (Rev 12:5; 19:15).

2:10-12 God is King

Whether we are insignificant people in the eyes of the world or whether we have authority over others in any way in church or state, in larger or smaller communities, there is only one way to *be wise* (**2:10**). That is to realize that God is King over all and that we can never succeed if we try to work against his purposes. His ways are always wisest and best for us and for all people because he loves and cares for us and has perfect wisdom.

Having been warned of the foolishness of opposing God, we need to serve him with *fear* and *trembling* (**2:11**). This does not mean that we are to be afraid of God, but rather that we are to recognize both 'the kindness and sternness of God' (Rom 11:22) and are to approach him with humility and reverence. Thus we are also told to *kiss the Son* (**2:12**). Because these words are difficult to translate, there are differences in our English translations, with the NEB having 'kiss the King' and the NRSV, 'kiss his feet'. The GNB probably catches the meaning with its freer translation, 'bow down to him'. When we acknowledge God's greatness and holiness, we will serve him with joy and *take refuge in him* in every difficulty and danger (**2:12**).

Psalm 3: Prayer in a Time of Trouble

The heading of this psalm is *A psalm of David. When he fled from his son Absalom* (see 2 Sam 15-18). (The headings of the psalms are discussed in the introduction to this commentary.) Although this link to that particular event in David's life may have been added some time after the

writing of the psalm, the feelings expressed mirror those of David and of others who are in the midst of great trouble.

3:1-2 My Need

The psalmist has many, many enemies. He uses the words *many* three times in **3:1-2a** and in **3:6** he speaks of *tens of thousands* against him. Worst of all, they laugh at his trust in God, and say openly, *God will not deliver him* (**3:2b**). But the psalmist knows that those who mocked his faith were wrong, and in the remainder of the psalm he tells us of four ways in which he looked to God.

This statement of his troubles is followed by the word *Selah*, which recurs at the end of 3:4 and 3:8. See the Introduction for a discussion of the meaning of this word, which is found in many psalms.

3:3a My Shield

In biblical times a soldier carried a large shield that protected him from the spears and arrows of the enemy. But it could protect him on only one side at a time. The psalmist knew that God's presence was like a shield all around him (**3:3a**). God's word to Abraham was, 'Do not be afraid, Abram, I am your shield' (Gen 15:1). The NT speaks of 'the shield of faith, with which you can extinguish all the flaming arrows of the evil one' (Eph 6:16). We may not use shields today, but we know that if we have faith in our living Lord, we can find protection from evil in whatever forms it comes against us.

3:3b-4 My Glory

The Scriptures often speak of God's glory, meaning his greatness and goodness as they are revealed to us. Our glory is what we most rely on, take pride in, and are thankful for. If we say that God is our glory, we are saying that for us the greatest thing in life is to know God and his presence with us. As Jeremiah 9:23-24 states, 'This is what the Lord says: Let not the wise man boast of his wisdom, or the strong man boast of his strength, or the rich man boast of his riches, but let him who boasts boast about this: that he understands and knows me.' The same idea is repeated in 1 Corinthians 1:31: 'Let him who boasts, boast in the Lord'. The Lord is the giver of all that is good and of all that we will ever need. If we are discouraged or depressed and feel put down, we can trust God to lift us up (**3:3b**; see also Luke 18:9-14).

God is said to answer the psalmist's prayer *from his holy hill* (**3:4**). The temple was built on the hill of Zion in Jerusalem, and there God's presence was especially felt by the people. 'The holy hill' or the temple also represented the heavenly dwelling place of God.

3:5-6 My Security

There are many things that can make one afraid. Many fear the darkness of night and what can happen in it. Many fear magic and the occult and forces of evil that can be used against them. Many fear what powerful people may be able to do to them, perhaps in secret. Yet whatever fear comes to us, we can always say, *I lie down and sleep; I wake again, because the Lord sustains me* (**3:5**).

Jesus told his disciples not to fear those who could only kill their bodies. He said that not a sparrow could fall to the ground without the heavenly Father knowing it. 'So do not be afraid; you are of more value than many sparrows' (Matt 10:31; see also Matt 6:25-34). He gave a perfect example of such trust in his heavenly Father by sleeping in the boat in the midst of the terrible storm on Lake Galilee (Mark 4:35-38). When Peter was condemned to be put to death, he slept peacefully in his chains the night before he was due to die, knowing that his life was in the Lord's hands (Acts 12:6). We may at times know that people are trying to harm us, but with the Lord's help we can say, 'I will not fear' (3:6; see also Phil 4:6-7). Jesus has conquered all the powers of evil and death itself (Heb 2:14-15).

3:7-8 My Salvation

The psalms often contain prayers like that of **3:7a**: *Arise, O Lord!* (see 7:6; 9:19; 44:26; 68:1). The words probably go back to the ancient battle cry of the people of Israel when they took the ark, the sign of God's presence, with them into battle. As they lifted it, they prayed, 'Rise up, O Lord! May your enemies be scattered, may your foes flee before you' (Num 10:35). It was not that they thought God was asleep, but when they were in trouble and it seemed that God had not acted on their behalf, they prayed that they might know him to be active by seeing him use his great power to defeat the enemies who opposed his rule.

The language in **3:7b** is poetic rather than literal. When we as Christians pray for God's victory, our attitude must be the one Jesus taught in Matthew 5:45-48. We are not to have hatred towards any person, nor to seek revenge for wrongs done to us, nor are we to use the psalms or any other part of the Scripture against people. It is God's victory that we are to seek and not our own.

Sometimes what we need most is God's salvation, that is, the deliverance that comes from the Lord (**3:8a**). The Israelites knew the truth of that, for God had set them free from slavery in Egypt. Jesus came to be our Saviour (see Matt 1:17), to save us from the guilt and power of sin. He has given his Spirit, more powerful than any power of evil, so that the words of 1 John 4:4 are always true: 'The one who is in you is greater than the one who is in the world' (see also Heb 2:14-18).

When we know personally that God is our shield, our glory, our security and our salvation, we can pray in confidence

(for others as well as for ourselves) the closing prayer of the psalm, 'May your blessing' – your blessing in all these ways – 'be on your people' (**3:8b**).

Psalm 4: How to Face Difficulty

The heading at the top of this psalm associates it with David and gives directions that the musical accompaniment should be 'with stringed instruments'. (See the comments on headings in the introduction to this commentary.)

This psalm begins and ends with trust in God expressed in prayer. There were several different kinds of difficulties that David found he could meet with trust in God and prayer to God.

4:1-4 Dishonesty, Corruption and Lies

The Bible speaks out strongly against the bribery and corruption in business dealings and in politics that we still experience today (see, for example, Amos 5:12; 8:4-6; Prov 17:23). Sometimes those who lead us seem to be speaking dishonestly. Some people also lie when they try to tell us the way we should live. So in **4:2b** the psalmist bursts out with *how long will you love vain words, and seek after lies* (NRSV). In the OT, the words translated '*vain words*' and '*lies*' are often used for idols and for all objects of worship other than the true and living God. We may be tempted to put our possessions or our position first and God second. To do so is to follow a lie, and to change what is honourable for what is shameful (**4:2a**). We are then very easily led into corrupt practices.

We need to cultivate an awareness of the 'vain words' and 'lies' that we constantly hear around us. When we are tempted to fear or follow these lies, we need to remember that *the Lord has set apart the godly for himself* (**4:3**). We are to treasure God's word in our hearts so that we may not be led into any kind of sin (119:11). We belong to God and should put him first in our lives in all things. Then we can be sure that the Lord will hear us when we call. Remember the words of Jesus: 'seek first his kingdom and his righteousness, and all these things will be given to you as well' (Matt 6:33).

4:4-5 Anger

The command *In your anger, do not sin* (**4:4a**; see also Eph 4:26-27) indicates that it is not always wrong to be angry. Jesus was angry when those responsible for the temple in Jerusalem were neglecting to make sure that it was used as a place of worship (see Mark 11:15-18). We may be angry at the evil that goes on around us. We must take care, however, that our anger does not lead us to hate and despise people, for that is sin in God's sight.

When we are tempted to let anger grow to resentment and bitterness, we are wise to be quiet. As we lie on our beds at night, we should think quietly of God's ways, trust in the Lord and give ourselves to him (**4:4b**). We need to ask the Holy Spirit to fill our hearts with the love of Christ and, realizing that God has forgiven us much, be forgiving and patient with other people.

When we give ourselves to God, we will be offering *right sacrifices* (**4:5**). While Exodus and Leviticus give many directions about the sacrifices that the Israelites should offer to God, the ot also speaks of spiritual sacrifices as being the most important of all. The sacrifice acceptable to God is 'a broken spirit; a broken and contrite heart … Then there will be righteous sacrifices, whole burnt offerings to delight you' (51:17, 19). The nt too speaks of the sacrifices that God seeks to receive from us (Rom 12:1-2; Hebrews 13:15).

4:6-7 Discouragement

Often people think that there is more evil than good in the world and say, *Who can show us any good?* (**4:6**). In response, we should pray that God will 'make his face shine upon you' (Num 6:24-26). If we stop to think, we will realize that the light of God's presence has shone on us. God has been good to us. His presence with us is the greatest blessing in life.

Farmers all over the world rejoice at harvest time as they gather in the fruit of their labour in planting and caring for the crops. It was the same in the land of Palestine, where the Bible often speaks of the great joy and celebration when the grapes and other crops were harvested (see Ps 126:6; Isa 9:3). But the writer of this psalm knows a gladness of heart that is even greater than the joy when there is abundant harvest (**4:7**).

Do we know this joy? Can we be like the prophet Habakkuk and say, 'Though the fig tree does not bud and there are no grapes on the vines, though the olive crop fails and the fields produce no food, though there are no sheep in the pen and no cattle in the stalls, yet I will rejoice in the Lord, I will be joyful in God my Saviour. The Sovereign Lord is my strength' (Hab 3:17-19)? When we face discouragement, we should think of the love and goodness of the Lord that we have known in our lives. That will help us to give thanks and rejoice despite what is happening to us. He has promised that nothing can separate us from his love, and the sufferings of the present cannot be compared with what he has in store for us (Rom 8:18, 37-39).

4:8 Anxiety

We are often tempted to be anxious when we face great difficulties and problems. But such anxiety is a waste of our strength and time. Instead of lying awake at night and worrying, we should memorize **4:8** so that we can say with the psalmist, *I will lie down and sleep in peace; for you alone, O Lord, make me dwell in safety.* When we are fearful, worried, troubled or discouraged, we should meditate on that verse, as well as on Jesus' words to his disciples: 'Peace I leave with you; my peace I give you … Do not let your hearts be troubled, and do not be afraid' (John 14:27). Other passages we can turn to as we search for inner peace include Psalm 37:1-4, Proverbs 3:5-8, Isaiah 26:3 and Philippians 4:6-9.

Psalm 5: Trusting God When Facing Opposition

This psalm has the same heading as Psalm 4, except that here the musical direction is 'for the flutes' instead of 'stringed instruments'. We read of the use of flutes in worship in 1 Samuel 10:5 and Isaiah 30:29.

The psalm is the prayer of a godly person surrounded by the ungodly, a righteous person surrounded by the unrighteous. While there is no place for self-righteousness before God (Rom 3:10, 23), Jesus says that great spiritual benefits come to those who 'hunger and thirst for righteousness' (Matt 5:6) and that we are to 'seek first his kingdom and his righteousness' (Matt 6:33) in every situation in life. But that way is not easy, as Jesus made clear to his disciples (Matt 10:22; 24:9; John 15:18-21; 16:1-4). It is only possible by relying on a God who is loving, righteous, faithful, caring and almighty, as shown in the five sections of this psalm.

5:1-3 Help from a Loving God

The evil in the world around us often seems very powerful, and we sigh over the things that go on. But we can be sure that God hears and pays attention to our *sighing* (**5:1**). Like the writer of this psalm, we can address God as *my King and my God* as we pray to him (**5:2**).

It is possible that the person praying this psalm spent the night in the courts of the temple, and then in the morning offered a sacrifice and prayed to God. We too can turn to God in the morning of each new day for help in our struggle against injustice and wrong, and for strength in facing our temptations and weaknesses. The Scriptures often speak of the need to pray to God in the morning and to bring our needs to him as the day begins (**5:3a**; see also 55:17; 57:8; 59:16; 88:13; 92:2; 119:147; Mark 1:35). Then once we have presented our requests to him, we are to watch or wait for God to act (**5:3b**; see also 25:5; 27:14, 33:20-22; 40:1; 62:1-2; Isa 30:18; 40:31; Lam 3:24-26; Rom 8:18-25; 1 Cor 1:7; Gal 5:5).

5:4-6 Justice from a Righteous God

We can be completely sure that God, who is holy and righteous, has no *pleasure in evil* (**5:4**). We cannot cling to anything that we know is evil and refuse to repent and at the same time live in fellowship with God (see Ps 15). In particular, God hates all human pride and boasting (**5:5**), all that is untrue and deceitful, and all that harms other people (**5:6**). We all need of forgiveness for the wrong that we have done, and once we are forgiven and accepted, we are called to take God's commandments as the guidelines for our living.

5:7-8 Guidance from a Faithful God

It is by the abundance of God's steadfast love that we can come to worship him (**5:7a**). The psalmist speaks of bowing down toward the temple (**5:7b**; see also 28:2; 138:2). It may have been that worshippers came to the entrance of the temple, faced the inner sanctuary and worshipped (see 134:2). When devout Jewish people were far from the temple, they turned towards the temple to pray (Dan 6:10), just as Muslims today face Mecca.

For Christian people, no place on earth is in itself more holy than any other. Jesus has 'tabernacled' among us (John 1:14, literal translation) and fulfilled the deepest meaning of the temple of OT days. Since the Holy Spirit has come and made our lives and the fellowship of God's people his temple (see 1 Cor 6:19-20; 2 Cor 6:16), we can no longer think of a building in the way that OT people thought of the temple. A building can be set aside as a place of worship and prayer, but we worship 'in spirit and in truth' (John 4:19-24) and our lives are to be God's living temple (Eph 2:19-22).

In worship we can know God's presence and we can pray for his guidance in our lives. The writer of this psalm knows that he is surrounded by people who will lead him astray from the ways of God. So he earnestly prays, *make straight your way before me* (**5:8**). His deep desire is to know the right way and to keep walking in it. God always honours that desire, and those who wish to follow will be guided and guarded in God's ways (see John 8:12).

5:9-10 Judgment from a Caring God

Sometimes we think of God's judgment as opposed to his love. Yet it is because of his love for all people that he cannot allow those who oppose his ways and oppress others to go on as they like for ever. The psalmist knows that there are many whose words cannot be trusted. Their speech is flattering rather than sincere, while in their hearts they plan *destruction* (**5:9**). Paul uses this verse in Romans 3 as he sets out his teaching about sin and righteousness.

We who have learned the way of Christ must pray for the conversion of evil people rather than for their destruction. But **5:10** should teach us to be concerned for the victory of righteousness, and we certainly should pray that people may not continue to rebel against God and despise his people.

5:11-12 Protection from a Mighty God

Because God is not only righteous but loving and strong, those who seek to serve him and 'hunger and thirst for righteousness' (Matt 5:6) can trust him to guard them in difficulties, dangers and temptations. We can use **5:11-12**

as a prayer for those who are facing great difficulty or opposition, those who are persecuted for Christ's sake, and those who are tempted or greatly discouraged. We can ask that they too will find *refuge* in God and ask God to *spread your protection* over them and surround them *as with a shield*. Those who find this help from a mighty God can *be glad ... sing for joy ... and rejoice* in the Lord.

In 5:11 the psalmist speaks of *those who love your name*. This is the first of more than a hundred references to the name of God in the psalms. Often the expression simply refers to God as he has revealed himself to be. To love God's name is to love God for all he is. To praise his name is to praise him as he has revealed himself to us.

Many different names are used for God in the Bible. These names often describe his attributes. However, the most important personal name of God in the OT is the one that used to be mistakenly translated as 'Jehovah'. The Jewish people felt that the name of God was too holy to speak, and so whenever they found it written in their holy books, they replaced it with the word *Adonai* (meaning Lord or Master). Where this word is found in Hebrew, the NIV and most other English translations translate it as LORD, written in capital letters. The result of never saying God's name was that there was uncertainty about how to pronounce it. However, we can guess the first part of the pronunciation from words like 'Allelu-ia' or 'Hallelu-jah', both of which mean 'praise Yah' or 'Jah'. Thus these days God's personal name, the name that he announces in Exodus 3:13-15, is normally translated as 'Yahweh'.

Psalm 6: A Prayer from the Depths of Distress

This psalm has the same heading as Psalm 4, but adds, *According to sheminith*, which may refer to the tune to be used or to a type of music. Like Psalms 38, 41, 88 and 102, it is the prayer of a very sick person. Like many who are sick, the psalmist also had many other troubles to bring to God.

6:1-2 Sin

This psalm encourages us to reflect on the relationship between sin and suffering. Jesus makes it clear that not all sicknesses are a direct result of sin (John 9:1-3), but he does not deny that it can sometimes be a factor (see Mark 2:1-12; John 5:14). The writer of this psalm clearly saw his suffering as a rebuke from God, probably because of some sin he knew he had committed. He knew he had failed and sinned against God, and felt that if God rebuked him in anger and disciplined him in his righteous wrath, he could not stand (**6:1**). His experience shows that suffering can indeed be God's discipline (see Prov 3:11-12 – quoted in Heb 12:5-11; Jer 10:23-24).

Yet the psalmist knew that he could ask the Lord to be gracious to him and give healing, both of body and spirit (**6:2a**). Thank God that we know the love and mercy that will accept us when we turn from sin in repentance and turn to God in faith. Through the coming of Jesus Christ, and because of his death and resurrection, we know this even more clearly than people in ot days (see 1 John 1:7-9; 2:1-2).

6:2b-3 Suffering

The psalmist had been suffering for a long time and, like many others whose prayers we have in the psalms, he asked God, *How long?* (**6:3b**). When would he be freed from his sickness? He felt that death might be near and his bones were *in agony* (**6:2b**). It is interesting to see that Jesus uses the same words as **6:3a** in John 12:27. He understands our suffering.

The psalmist asked God to act in steadfast love to save him and deliver him (**6:4**). He saw this present life as the only opportunity he would have to praise God (**6:5**). In ot times there was little knowledge or hope of life after death, although a few passages (such as Isa 26:19; Dan 12:1-3) speak clearly of such a hope. But it is through the resurrection of our Lord Jesus Christ that we know that death has been conquered and that those who believe in him are assured of life beyond death. The Christian does not mourn like those without hope (1 Thess 4:13-18).

6:6-7a Sorrow

As often happens in times of sickness and physical weakness, the psalmist was deeply discouraged. In his depression, he wept bitterly (**6:6-7a**). All the joy was taken out of life. He felt that no other human person could understand and share his sorrows. So he did the best thing that anyone can do in such trouble. He turned to the only one who could really help and honestly told God about his situation. We can do the same (Phil 4:6-7; 1 Pet 5:7).

6:7b Enemies

The psalmist's many enemies added to his grief (**6:7b**). Perhaps they were glad to see his troubles. Perhaps, like Job's friends, they kept telling him that he was suffering because of his sin. They did evil rather than good as far as he was concerned, and in looking to God for help he could only say to them, *Away from me* (**6:8a**). He wanted to make sure that he was not associated with the way that they lived and what they did. These words are echoed in Matthew 7:23 and Luke 13:27, where God is the speaker. He too wants nothing to do with sin.

6:8-10 Deliverance

Up to the end of 6:7, the psalm is all trouble, trouble, trouble – sin, sickness, sorrow and enemies. Then suddenly there is a change. Perhaps the psalmist remembered past experiences of answered prayer, or perhaps a messenger came from God (as happened when Eli spoke to Hannah in 1 Sam 1:9-17). However it came about, the psalmist could suddenly say with great certainty: *the Lord has heard my weeping. The Lord has heard my cry for mercy; the Lord accepts my prayer* (**6:8b-9**). We too can be sure that sin can be forgiven, sickness can be healed, sorrow can turn to joy, and enemies can be turned back (**6:10**), all because our God answers prayer (Jas 5:14-16).

Psalm 7: Facing Injustice

The heading of this psalm includes the word *shiggaion*, found again in the Bible only in Habakkuk 3:1. It may mean a certain kind of song, perhaps a lamentation. We have no knowledge of the *Cush* who is mentioned. He was probably one of the many people who unfairly criticized David or opposed him – just as people criticize and oppose us today.

When we read this psalm, we should not assume that the writer was being self-righteous and saying that he had never done anything wrong. Rather, in this particular situation, he knew that he was being dealt with unjustly. He was sure that right was on his side. Many Christian people face similar situations today as they are persecuted because of their stand for the truth and because they have preached the gospel of Christ with their words and life. Others of us may not face such persecution, but we may often face criticism. Sometimes the criticism is just and deserved. Then we should take notice and accept correction for the ways that we have spoken and acted wrongly (Prov 3:11-12; 5:7-14; 9:7-10; 13:1, 18; 17:10; 27:5-6; 29:15). However, if the criticisms are unjust, we must trust God as the one who sees with perfect understanding. We are called to react as Jesus himself did: 'When they hurled their insults at him, he did not retaliate; when he suffered, he made no threats. Instead he entrusted himself to him who judges justly' (1 Pet 2:23).

7:1-2 Rely on God

The psalmist felt that people's criticisms of him and his persecution by enemies were like attacks of a lion – fierce, cruel and frightening (**7:2a**; see also 10:9; 17:12; 22:13, 21). Humanly speaking there was *no one to rescue me* (**7:2b**). He turned to God to find refuge and asked God to save him from all who were pursuing and attacking him (**7:1**).

7:3-5 Be Open to God's Correction

This part of the psalm is sometimes referred to as an 'oath of innocence', possibly similar to the one referred to in 1 Kings 8:31-32. A similar claim of innocence is made in Job 31. It is as if the person who is being accused says, 'I know that I have done no wrong in the matter of which you accuse me, but God is the judge, and I leave my case in his hands.' We must ask God to show us if we have returned evil for good or done harm to other people, even to those who have made themselves our enemies (**7:4**). We should always be willing to pray, 'Search me, O God, and know my heart; test me and know my anxious thoughts. See if there is any offensive way in me, and lead me in the way everlasting' (139:23-24). God is certainly with the thoughts of our hearts as well as our words and actions (Matt 5:21-30).

The Apostle Paul is a good example of someone who tried to act with a good conscience and then entrusted his situation to God, however much people misunderstood and criticized his actions (1 Cor 4:1-5; 2 Cor 1:12-24).

7:6-11 Trust in God as the Just Judge

The words *Arise, O Lord* (**7:6a**) recall the shout that went up when the sacred ark, which symbolized the presence of God, was taken out to lead the people, 'Rise up, O Lord! May your enemies be scattered; may your foes flee before you' (Num 10:35; see also Ps 3:7). The psalmist wants God to move in power against the forces of evil and to act in judgment. He is confident that God is the judge of all. God is lifted up over all (**7:6b-8a**). All stand before God who *searches minds and hearts* (**7:9**), that is, who judges the very thoughts of our hearts (1 Sam 16:7; Heb 4:12-13; Rev 2:23). He is *a righteous judge* (**7:11a**).

As God's people, we pray, *bring to an end the violence of the wicked and make the righteous secure* (**7:9b**). But God himself is far more troubled about the evil in the world and the oppressive actions of powerful people than we could ever be. This is what **7:11b** means when it says that God *expresses his wrath every day*. He gives people an opportunity to repent and turn to him for salvation (see 2 Pet 3:9), but there will come a time when he will *decree justice* (7:6). We have a clear statement of this in the NT, which says that 'he has set a day when he will judge the world with justice' (Acts 17:31). The judge will be Jesus Christ, whom God has sent to be the Saviour of all who turn to him in repentance and faith.

7:12-16 The Seriousness of Refusal to Repent

There is a difficulty in the translation of **7:12-13** since it is not clear from the Hebrew whether the 'he' referred to here is God or a wicked person who is sharpening his sword and making his arrows ready to attack others. Most translations, and this commentary, hold the view that the 'he' refers to God, who takes action against those who refuse to repent.

All through the Bible, we read of God's offer of forgiveness to all who repent and turn from evil. It is a very serious thing, however, to refuse his offer. The NT gives very strong warnings against doing this (Heb 2:1-4, 10:26-31; 12:25-29). Those who *are pregnant with evil* and who conceive *trouble* must be prepared to face the consequences

(**7:14**). Experience shows that the prosperity of evil people is short-lived. But whether the world sees it or not, evil will be judged. It never brings lasting satisfaction or true happiness, but only sorrow and loss. That is why the psalmist compares it to someone who digs a pit to catch others and falls into it himself or to someone who throws something into the air only to have it fall on his own head (**7:15-16**).

7:17 In the End – Praise

The psalm ends with praise. Since God is a just judge who is merciful to all who turn to him in repentance, and since he is a refuge for all who ask his help, we can truly say *I will give thanks to the Lord because of his righteousness and will sing praise to the name of the Lord Most High* (**7:17**). As surely as day follows night, justice will prevail in the end because God rules.

Psalm 8: God's Creation and Our Place in It

The heading of this psalm is the same as that for Psalm 4, except that instead of referring to musical instruments it says *According to gittith,* which probably refers to the tune to be used.

The psalm itself is a beautiful hymn of praise. As we read it, we should ask the Lord to help us appreciate the greatness of his creation, and should thank him for his care for all of us, including those who may seem insignificant in the eyes of the world.

8:1a, 9 The Greatness of God

The psalm begins and ends with God himself. *O Lord, our Lord, how majestic is your name in all the earth!* (**8:1a, 9**). The psalms often speak of the name of God, not meaning a particular name like 'Father' or 'Almighty' or 'Lord', or even some so-called 'secret name' known only to superspiritual people or prophets (see comments on 5:11). No, God's name simply means God's essential nature, now revealed to us in Jesus Christ, and his glory is all that is great and wise and loving in God's nature as that has been made known to us. In this psalm, the wonder of God's creation is seen in three types of things.

8:1b, 3 Sun, Moon and Stars

The beauty of the moon at night amazes us. The light of the sun by day is so powerful that we cannot look at it directly without seriously injuring our eyes. We cannot count the stars we see in the heavens on a clear night, and scientists have discovered that there are countless suns and moons and stars that our human eyes have never seen. Isaiah 40:26 says, 'Lift your eyes and look to the heavens: Who created all these? He who brings out the starry host one by one, and calls them each by name. Because of his great power and mighty strength, not one of them is missing.'

CHRISTIANS AND THE ENVIRONMENT

Although the Bible does not use the word 'environment', it does have a great deal to say about creation. It tells us that God made everything that exists (Gen 1) and that he made if for himself (Col 1:16). He rejoices in its beauty in the same way that an artist rejoices over a finished masterpiece (Gen 1:31; Ps 104:31; Matt 6:28-30).

Creation also praises its creator (Ps 148; Rev 5:13-14) and reveals his glory to people of every culture and language (Ps 19:1-4). The vastness and orderliness of the universe speak of his glory and power (Isa 40:25-26). So does the intricacy of atoms and microscopic life forms. God's glory is also shown by the love and care he lavishes on his creation (Ps 104; Matt 6:26).

God's creation fulfils all our human needs, including our material needs for food, shelter, medicine and clothing (Gen 1:29-39; 3:7, 21), our aesthetic need for beauty (Gen 2:8-9), and our intellectual need for stimulation (Gen 2:19). Study of creation satisfies our desire for knowledge and provides solutions to practical problems such as hunger and disease. Solomon, that wisest of men, was also a student of nature (1 Kgs 4:29-33; Prov 6:6-8).

The natural world is important to God. He took care to protect animal life when he sent the flood, and he entered into a covenant not only with Noah but also with 'every living creature' (Gen 9:8-17). The final redemption we await is not just for humans but also for the whole of creation (Rom 8:18). The creation needs this redemption because it too has been damaged by human sin (Gen 3:7).

God commanded human beings to care for and protect his precious creation (Gen 1:28; 2:15). Thus believers cannot ignore what is happening to it today. Three factors in particular are harming God's creation: rapid population growth, especially in the Majority World (Africa's population more than doubled between 1972 and 2000); an enormous increase in the consumption of resources, especially in rich countries; and the use of polluting technologies. These factors affect our lives and the environment in various ways:

- *Overuse of land*. As the population grows, land has to be farmed more intensively. In drier areas, this results in a loss of soil fertility and soil erosion, which in turn reduces crop and livestock production and thus increases poverty. Overgrazing can even turn land into a desert, as has happened in the Sahel region.

- *Loss of forests*. Cutting down trees to sell the wood or to clear land for cultivation results in many of the plants and animals that live in forests becoming extinct. We also lose the firewood, medicinal plants and other products that come from the forest. With trees and other vegetation gone, rain runs off the land faster, leading to devastating floods.

- *Water pollution*. Growing human populations have reduced the amount of water available per person and increased pollution of drinking water. More than 5 million people die each year from diseases caused by unsafe drinking water and a lack of water for sanitation and washing. When rainwater carries fertilizers and pesticides from farms into lakes and rivers, fish and other creatures may die.

- *Loss of species*. God created a world of great variety. Human activities that destroy habitats or overexploit resources can result in many species of plants and animals becoming extinct. When this happens, we lose wild plants, animals and micro-organisms that are important for developing new varieties of animals or crops or medicines.

- *Loss of fish*. Fishing provides food and a livelihood for millions of people. But pollution, overfishing and the use of fishing methods that damage fish habitats or disrupt breeding patterns are reducing the number of fish in the sea and bringing poverty to many.

- *Climate change*. So much coal, oil, wood and gas are being burned that the earth's atmosphere is changing, and this causes changes in the earth's climate. The result will be that some will suffer devastating hurricanes and floods, while others will suffer from terrible droughts. Some species of plants and animals will become extinct, and malaria and other diseases will spread more widely.

- *Loss of earth's shield*. Some of the chemicals we use are damaging the ozone layer in the atmosphere, which protects us from the harmful part of sunlight, called ultraviolet radiation. As more of the sun's dangerous rays reach earth, people will start to suffer from more skin cancer and cataracts, which cause blindness.

- *Pollution by chemicals*. Some of the chemicals used in pesticides (such as DDT and dieldrin) and in industrial processes have long-term harmful effects, and can cause cancers, birth defects and infertility.

If we are to be obedient to God and look after his creation, we must not ignore what is happening. Like Noah, we must work to rescue all creatures in danger of extinction – whether the danger comes from pollution, habitat change, overfishing, poaching or any other cause. Christians should be encouraged to take proper care of their own fields or gardens and to participate in community protection of common water and grazing resources. Christians should also support national and international policies and laws to govern the care of the environment and the use of natural resources. We should be working alongside people like Wangari Maathai, the Kenyan woman who was awarded the Nobel Peace Prize because of her work to preserve Africa's environment.

George Kinoti

8:2 Little Things and Little People

Different translations link the end of 8:1 with **8:2** in slightly different ways. For example, the JB has *Above the heavens is your majesty chanted by the mouth of children, babes in arms. You set your stronghold against your foes to subdue enemies and rebels.* But all translations retain the central idea of God's glory in creation, the praise of little children, and the certainty that the enemies of God will be silenced.

Scientists have not only seen the greatness of God's creation in the big things he has created, like the countless stars far greater than our sun, but they have also seen it in little things, in atoms and electrical particles and in the cells that make up all living creatures. The little things matter to God as well as the great. Jesus said that a sparrow does not fall to the ground without God knowing it and that the hairs of our head are numbered (Matt 10:29-31). He said that little children are important in God's sight, and he took them in his arms and blessed them (Mark 10:13-16). In 8:2 the psalmist says that the faith of a little child is more powerful than those who may seem to be strong enemies opposing God's purposes. The truth expressed in a little child's praise silences the enemies of God (compare Matt 21:16; 1 Cor 1:26-29).

8:3-8 God's Human Creation

All the wonders of creation are described as merely the work of God's *fingers* (**8:3**). Given God's greatness, even more of which is revealed by the discoveries of modern science, we have reason to join the psalmist in saying, *When I consider your heavens … what is man that you are mindful of him?* (**8:4a**) The second half of the verse makes the same comment about *the son of man*. The psalmist is not speaking of the Son of Man, as Jesus calls himself in the gospels. Rather, this is an example of the parallelism often found in the psalms, where the two halves of a verse express the same thought in slightly different words. Here the psalmist is expressing his awareness that we humans are so small and the universe is so big. Yet there are three ways in which God's human creation is special:

- God is *mindful* of us and cares for us (**8:4b**). Jesus made this even clearer in his teaching (Matt 6:25-30), and supremely in the fact that he was willing to die for us.
- We are made only *a little lower than the heavenly beings* (**8:5a**). This phrase is also translated 'a little lower than God' (NRSV). The Hebrew word used in the original may mean 'angel' or 'divine being', or simply 'God'. Many prefer the translation 'angels' here because that was how it was translated in the Septuagint, the ancient Greek translation of the OT, which is the version quoted in Hebrews 2:7. However, the translation 'God' also makes sense, for although we are certainly far, far less than God, we were made in his image. As such, we are crowned *with glory and honour* (**8:5b**). We are like

crowned kings and queens. We have been given powers of thinking, making and discovering that no animals have. Above all, because we are made in God's image (Gen 1:26), we can hear God's word and speak to him in prayer.

- God has made us rulers over *the works of [his] hands*, that is, over everything else he has created (**8:6-8**; compare Gen 1:28). This does not mean that we can do what we like with the rest of creation. It does mean that God has given us responsibility to care for creation. We may use animals for meat, but we may not be cruel to them, nor hunt and fish to the point that some kinds of animals or fish become extinct. We may use trees to construct buildings and furniture and for firewood, but if we destroy and do not plant, we will suffer in the future and our countries will become deserts. We can use the resources of the earth as a blessing to all, or we can turn them into weapons or drugs or poisons that destroy people's lives. We have not been given freedom to do as we like with creation, but to see that it is used well and for the benefit of all.

This psalm is also cited in Hebrews 2:5-18, where it is used to show that Jesus has perfectly fulfilled God's purpose for humanity. We are restored to our true position and worth through what he has done for us.

Psalm 9: God's Rule over the Nations

In some early manuscripts, Psalms 9 and 10 are combined in one psalm. In favour of this, it can be pointed out that Psalm 10 does not have a separate heading and that the instruction *Selah*, which usually comes in the middle of a psalm, is put at the end of Psalm 9. Moreover, there is an acrostic structure running from Psalm 9 to Psalm 10, meaning that in Hebrew each verse begins with a different letter of the Hebrew alphabet. Yet there are also differences between the two psalms. In the long run, it makes little difference to our understanding whether we read them as one psalm or two.

The heading of Psalm 9 is similar to those of surrounding psalms, except that it specifies the tune to which it was to be sung. The tune was *The Death of the Son* ('according to Muth-labben' in the KJV).

Justice and love go together. Our God rules in justice and love over the nations of the world. This means that in his own time God will bring down the powerful nations who cruelly oppress others and deliver those who are oppressed. Like the song of Mary in Luke 1:46-55, this psalm celebrates both these things. It may have been written at a time when Israel had just been delivered from powerful enemies, such as the Egyptians, the Philistines, the Assyrians or the Babylonians. The twin realities of God's justice and love should lead us to praise him and to remember that we can always turn to him in prayer.

9:1-2, 11 Praise

Because we can see that God judges the nations and defends the oppressed, we can give praise to him. We can thankfully tell of all his wonderful deeds in the past (**9:1**). However, to be able to do this, we need to think about the ways in which the judgment of God is indeed seen in past history, both in biblical times and closer to the present. When we have done this, we will be able to be like the psalmist and *be glad and rejoice* in the Lord and *sing praise* to the name of the *Most High* (**9:2**). Israel in particular was called to *sing praises to the Lord, enthroned in Zion,* to appreciate his presence in the temple in Jerusalem, and to *proclaim among the nations what he has done* (**9:11**).

9:4-8 God Judges the Nations

From what the psalmist himself has experienced of God he can say, *For you have upheld my right and my cause; you have sat on your throne, judging righteously* (**9:3-4**). But he recognizes that some nations seem to be very powerful and that some rulers make themselves rich at the expense of their people whom they oppress without pity. It seems as if their power will last for ever and that no one can humble them. When we feel like that, we need to look back at history. Powerful nations have fallen. Their cities have become ruins, and *even the memory of them has perished* (**9:5-6**). God has judged them, and ultimately he is Lord over all: *The Lord reigns for ever … He will judge the world with righteousness* (**9:7-8**).

9:9-12, 15-18 God Defends the Oppressed

God's justice and judgment are bound up with his mercy and love. There is no contradiction between them. God judges the powerful oppressor because he is concerned for the poor and afflicted: *The Lord is a refuge for the oppressed, a stronghold in times of trouble* (**9:9**). Again the psalmist can speak of his own knowledge of God's actions: *you, Lord, have never forsaken those who seek you* (**9:10**). God *does not ignore the cry of the afflicted* (**9:12**) and he avenges blood that is shed in acts of aggression (9:12; see also Gen 9:5-6; Matt 26:52). That is why *those who know your name,* that is, God's character (see 5:11; 7:17; 8:1), *will trust in you* (9:10).

Sometimes people may suffer for a long time at the hands of the powerful, for God is patient and long-suffering before he brings judgment on those who make themselves his enemies. But *the needy shall not always be forgotten, nor the hope of the afflicted ever perish* (**9:18**). The people of Israel faced long years of slavery and oppression in Egypt, but the Lord finally said, 'And now the cry of the Israelites has reached me, and I have seen the way the Egyptians are oppressing them' (Exod 3:9). So the Lord set Israel free and

the powerful Egyptians were defeated. Many other nations in the course of their history *have fallen into the pit they have dug; their feet are caught in the net they have hidden* (**9:15**). We need to remember this as we look for God's judgment and overruling in the affairs of nations today.

The meaning of *Higgaion* at the end of **9:16** is not certain, but it probably refers to a kind of music to be used at this point.

9:13-14; 19-20 Prayer

While we are thankful for what God has done in the past in judgment of the oppressor and deliverance of the oppressed, we still live in a world where there are oppressors and oppressed. So with the psalmist we pray that God will continue to act in mercy and in judgment. We may need to pray for ourselves, *O Lord, see how my enemies persecute me!* (**9:13**). It is worth noting that the psalmist does not here pray for personal triumph over his enemies, but rather prays that he may *declare your praises in the gates of the Daughter of Zion* (**9:14**). Here and elsewhere in the OT, Israel is spoken of as a person 'whom God loved as his daughter, even as God loved the king as his "son"' (2:7, DSB).

We may also need to pray on behalf of others, especially those in countries where there is great injustice and persecution: *Arise, O Lord, let not man triumph; let the nations be judged in your presence. Strike them with terror, O Lord; let the nations know they are but men* (**9:19-20**). This prayer should supplement our regular prayer that the rulers of the nations of the world may be humble, live in reverence before God, and truly serve their people (1 Tim 2:1-2).

Psalm 10: Times When God Seems Far Away

A number of psalms deal with the same problem as this one: Why is it that evil people seem so powerful? This was often a problem in Israel, and it is still a very real problem today. People ask, 'Why doesn't God do something about this?' But in the end, people of faith find the answer to their question.

In some parts of this psalm it is not completely clear whether the persecuted or the persecutors are being described. In 10:2 the NRSV translation takes the second part of the verse as a prayer that the wicked will be caught in the traps they have prepared for others, while the NIV takes it as meaning that the weak are caught by the plots of the wicked. Similarly, 10:10 can be interpreted as describing the wicked stooping and crouching to attack the weak (NRSV) or as meaning that the 'victims are crushed, they collapse' (NIV). The main meaning of the psalm is not affected by these differences in the interpretation of details.

10:1-11 Evil People are Very Powerful

When we look around us in *times of trouble,* it often seems that the wicked have everything going their way while those who serve God feel weak and oppressed (**10:1**). The wicked think so too, as is clear from this description of their thoughts, words and actions. In arrogance and pride, *the wicked man hunts down the weak* (**10:2**). They boast that they can do whatever they want (**10:3**). They think that God will not see. In fact, they act as if there were no God at all (**10:4**). Despite this, it seems that they are *always prosperous* (**10:5**). Their confidence that *nothing will shake me* (**10:6a**) is a parody of the confidence of those who trust in God saying 'I will not be shaken' (16:8; see also 112:6-8; Luke 12:13-21; James 4:13-16).

But while the wicked expect to *always be happy* (**10:6b**), they make others miserable with their *curses, lies and threats* (**10:7**). They oppress the innocent, the helpless and the poor (**10:8-9**). They are as dangerous and stealthy as lions hunting their prey, and as ruthless as hunters catching animals in their nets (10:8-10). They act with impunity because they believe that God does not see what they are doing (**10:11**).

While it is easy for us to sit back with the psalmist and condemn such people, we also need to be aware that greed, pride and a desire for status can easily tempt us to commit similar sins. When we condemn others, we need to check that we are not doing the same things. We also need to check whether our security is rooted in God or in our own pride in our abilities.

10:12-13, 15 Question: Does God Do Nothing?

While evil people remain powerful and prosperous, those whose hearts are set on serving God are weak and oppressed. They suffer as they are dragged off and overwhelmed by the power of their evil oppressors (**10:9-10**). They seem to be unable to do anything to change their situation. Not surprisingly, the unchallenged power of evil people and the undeserved suffering of those who serve God drives the psalmist to ask, 'Why? Why? Why?' *Why, O Lord do you stand far off? Why do you hide yourself in times of trouble?* (**10:1**). *Why does the wicked man revile God? Why does he say to himself, 'He won't call me to account'?* (**10:13**; see also Hab 1:4). Surely God must act.

The psalmist then prays the kind of prayer that was prayed in the wilderness when the sacred ark was taken out before the people of Israel as they went to battle (see Num 10:35): *Arise, Lord! Lift up your hand, O God. Do not forget the helpless* (**10:12**). *Break the arm of the wicked and evil man; call him to account for his wickedness that would not be found out* (**10:15**).

We too need to be faithful in our prayers and support for the oppressed, the very poor, the hungry, refugees, and those who suffer because of bribery and corruption in society.

We need to pray that they may know the strength of trusting in the almighty and ever-loving God.

10:14, 16-18 Answer: 'The Lord Is King'

There is an answer to the question and to the problem. It is the certainty that God is in control. God rules, and in the end God's purpose will triumph. The psalmist says, *You, O God, ... do see trouble and grief* (**10:14a**). Evil men and women may think they can act without God seeing (10:11), but God does see. God does hear prayers (**10:17a**). In fact the verbs in 10:14 and 10:17 could be translated as, 'You have seen', and 'you have heard'. This has been shown in the past and so we can be sure that it will be seen again in the future.

Because God listens when victims commit themselves to him and because he is *the helper of the fatherless* (**10:14b**), he strengthens those who trust him (**10:17b**). In his own time and in his own way, he will act to defend *the fatherless and the oppressed, in order that man, who is of the earth, may terrify no more* (**10:18**). Yes, God answers. His delays are not denials. But it is important for us to remember how he has helped and delivered us in the past and not give up faith when new problems come our way.

Psalm 11: Foundations for Life

This psalm is not a prayer addressed to God, but (like Psalms 23 and 27) is a psalm of confidence addressed to anyone who will listen. It answers the question posed in **11:3**: *When the foundations are destroyed, what can the righteous do?* This psalm can encourage Christians when it seems that there are no foundations or law and order in society and when injustice, bribery and corrupt practices seem to prevail. At such times we need to draw encouragement from psalms such as this one, as well as from the record of people in the Bible who faced great opposition, including Moses, Nehemiah and the leaders of the early church.

11:1-4a The Foundations of the Godly

When we face trouble or sorrow, the death of loved ones, financial problems or discouragement in our work, it may seem that the very foundations of our lives are being destroyed. In the days of the psalmist, when bows and poisoned arrows were the most fearsome weapons of war, it could be said, *For look, the wicked bend their bows; they set their arrows against the strings to shoot from the shadows at the upright in heart* (**11:2**). Today powerful people threaten violence in many ways, and nations keep their armaments, including nuclear weapons, ready for use. There is great political insecurity in many parts of the world. In these times too people may well say, *Flee like a bird to the mountains* (**11:1b**, NRSV). In other words, 'Run away and escape from it all'. Psalm 55:6-7 expresses a similar thought: 'Oh, that I had the wings of a dove! I would fly away and be at rest – I would flee far away and stay in the desert.' But that is not the right answer to the challenge of difficulties and trials.

The foundations of godly people – those who truly love God – are in God alone (see Matt 7:24-27; 1 Cor 3:10-15). Whatever other people say or suggest, they can say, *In the Lord I take refuge* (**11:1a**). When we know the Lord's promise, 'Never will I leave you; never will I forsake you', we can say with confidence, 'The Lord is my helper; I will not be afraid. What can man do to me?' (Heb 13:5-6). Even though the people opposed to the psalmist might seem very powerful, he could say, 'The Lord is in his holy temple; the Lord is on his heavenly throne' (**11:4a**). In the temple in Jerusalem, he could sense God's presence. He knew that God also has a heavenly throne. In other words, God is Lord and King over all creation. God rules over all the nations of Earth.

11:4b-7 The Foundations of the Ungodly

Those who reject God's ways also have foundations that they try to rely on. In OT days, their confidence was in bows and arrows. Today, people may rely on weapons of mass destruction. Some trust in their riches and their economic strength. Others trust in their position of importance. Such people often seem very powerful. But what happens to them when trouble or sorrow comes? What foundations do they have for their lives? The question of 11:3 might be turned on them, 'if the foundations are destroyed, what can the wicked do?'

An even more important question that we all face is how they (and we) will stand before God as judge. *He observes the sons of men; his eyes examine them. The Lord examines the righteous, but the wicked and those who love violence his soul hates* (**11:4b-5**). The judgment of God is what matters most in the end.

In 11:6, God's judgment on the wicked is described in terms that may be drawn from his judgment on Sodom and Gomorrah (Gen 19; see also Luke 17:28-32; 2 Peter 2:6-9). If this is the case, the suggestion to *flee like a bird to the mountains* (11:1, NRSV) may also be an allusion to Lot and his family being told to 'flee to the mountains' (gen 19:17). however, it is not necessary to read it this way, for throughout history people have taken to the hills when danger threatened.

The phrase that the NIV translates as *their lot* in 11:6 can be translated more literally as 'the portion of their cup' (NASB). These words are often used to refer to the blessings that God gives to those who trust and serve him (see 16:5; 23:5; 116:13). However, they are also used for what must befall the wicked in God's judgment (as in 75:8; Isa 51:17; Jer 25:15-26; Ezek 23:33). Jesus also spoke of his suffering as his cup that he had to drink and of the suffering of his disciples as their cup (Matt 20:20-23; 26:39-42).

11:7 The Ultimate Foundation

No human being can claim to be completely righteous, for we have all failed to keep God's commands, to do God's will and to live in love towards others. But as we turn to Christ in repentance from our wrongdoing, and as the Holy Spirit gives us God's strength to do what is right, then we will be able to *see his face* (**11:7**). Jesus said, 'Blessed are the pure in heart, for they will see God' (Matt 5:8). We can know his presence with us in this life, find joy in worshipping him (27:4; 63:2) and look forward after this life to seeing him face to face (1 John 3:1-2).

Psalm 12: Three Kinds of Words

This psalm has the same heading as many of the other psalms. The words *According to sheminith* may refer to a tune or a style of music.

The world is full of words, which are often empty. The Yoruba in West Africa have a proverb, 'Many words do not fill a basket.' Often people's words are deceitful, either direct lies or promises that cannot be fulfilled. But words spoken in truth and in love encourage and bless others. Most important of all, God in his grace speaks his words to us. This psalm speaks of three different kinds of words.

12:1-4 False Words

The writer of this psalm felt like the prophet Elijah when it seemed to him that he was the only person left in the land serving God (1 Kgs 19:10). There seemed to be no *godly* or *faithful* people left (**12:1**; see also Jer 5:1-5; Hos 4:1-3; Mic 7:2-7). Human relationships are ruined because *everyone lies to his neighbour;* no one can be trusted. People have *flattering lips*, meaning that they will say good things about you to your face but speak very differently when you are not present (**12:2**). In the Hebrew, the words in 12:2 that the NIV translates 'with deception' and the NRSV as 'a double heart' are literally 'a heart and a heart'. People are trying to follow two ways at the same time (compare Matt 6:24). By contrast, the Bible calls us to serve God with one heart, that is, single-mindedly (Jer 32:39; Ezek 11:19-20; Acts 4:32).

Those who seek to manipulate others with their words are *boastful*, saying, *with our words we get what we want. We will say what we wish, and no one can stop us* (**12:4** GNB). We as Christians need to have a very different attitude, for our lips are not our own. We respond to the scornful question, *Who is our master?* by affirming that Christ is our master (1 Cor 6:19-20). And he has warned us to watch how we speak and to speak only words that can be trusted (Matt 5:33-37; see also Eph 4:25; Jas 3:2-12). We need to pray, 'Set a guard over my mouth, O Lord; keep watch over the door of my lips' (141:3) so that we speak only words that are true, sincere and helpful to others.

12:5-6 God's Word

The words and actions of evil people cause suffering to those poorer and weaker than they are. Yet in this world full of lies, truth can be found. God has spoken, and he still speaks. We hear his voice, perhaps speaking through a prophet, *'Because of the oppression of the weak and the groaning of the needy, I will now arise,' says the Lord. 'I will protect them from those who malign them'* (**12:5**; see also Isa 33:10). There are a number of psalms like this one, where the word of God, probably revealed though his messenger or in some other way, breaks into what is being said (for example, 50:5, 7-23; 81:6-16; 95:8-11).

The last word is always God's, and that word of promise is always sure and certain. Compared to a metal like silver that is merely purified, the promises of God are *like silver refined in a furnace of clay, purified seven times* (**12:6**). There is nothing impure, nothing worthless in God's word that he graciously brings to us through his servants and that we find in so many different ways in the Bible (19:7-11; 119:105; Matt 24:35; Heb 4:12-13).

12:7-8 Trusting Words

Because of God's word and God's promises, although *the wicked freely strut about when what is vile is honoured among men* (**12:8**), believers can be confident in God's protection. Not only will they cry, *Help, Lord* (12:1), but they will also say with assurance, *O Lord, you will keep us safe and protect us from such people for ever* (**12:7**). The Christian can be even more confident in light of the prayer Jesus made and makes for all his disciples, 'My prayer is not that you take them out of the world but that you protect them from the evil one' (John 17:15). The evil in the world around us does not suddenly change. Yet we know God has given us the Holy Spirit to be in us, and so we are sure of the truth of the words, 'the one who is in you is greater than the one who is in the world' (1 John 4:4).

Psalm 13: Pain – Prayer – Praise

Many people have been perplexed when God does not seem to answer their prayers. There is no sign of the desperately needed rain. Prayers for the gift of a child go unanswered. A sickness drags on and on (6:3). God does not provide clear guidance for the way ahead, despite faithful prayers. Wicked people seem to flourish at the expense of the weak (94:3). Sometimes 'How long?' is the cry of a nation or ethnic group who have spent long years under powerful oppressors or dictators (as did Israel – 74:9-10; 79:5-6; 80:4; 89:46). Sometimes it is the distressed cry of a long-persecuted church (Rev 6:10). It was certainly the cry of the psalmist.

13:1-2 Pain

This psalm begins with four anxious questions, each beginning with *How long … ?* We do not know what painful experiences the writer of this psalm had endured, but it seemed that God had forgotten him for a long time. God's blessing in the past had been like the light of his face shining on him, but now it seemed as if God had hidden his face (**13:1**; compare Num 6:25-26). There was nothing but pain and sorrow, and in his struggles against enemies the psalmist seemed to be defeated. He found it hard to understand why this should be so, and go on for so long. But he knew that the best thing, and indeed the only thing, to do was to bring his situation frankly to God in prayer.

13:3-4 Prayer

Although the psalmist cannot understand the ways of God, he still says, *O Lord, my God* (13:3a). He prays, *Look on me,* meaning 'think of me in my trouble'. He asks God to *give light to my eyes* (**13:3a**). God is the giver of light, and without his presence in the world, and in our lives, all would be darkness. God is the giver of life, and without him there is only death.

In the Bible, death is often spoken of as *sleep,* as in **13:3b**. The OT often describes a person's death by saying as it does of David that he 'slept with his ancestors' (1 Kgs 2:10, NRSV). Yet in OT days there was little understanding or hope of life after death. In the NT that hope is clear, but death is still spoken of as sleep (by Jesus – Matt 9:24; John 11:11-13; by Paul – 1 Cor 15:20, 51; 1 Thess 4:14). Death means the end of consciousness of life in this world, but for the Christian there is the certainty that after the sleep of death we will wake up in the presence of Christ (Phil 1:21-24, 1 Cor 15).

The enemies that plagued the psalmist (**13:4**) may have been people or they may have been discouragement, doubt and temptation. In either case, God alone can give victory over them. The psalmist's prayer in these verses can be our prayer in times of trial and perplexity.

13:5-6 Praise

As in so many of the psalms, prayer turns into praise. Why? The psalmist can say, *I trust in your unfailing love* (**13:5**). This is what he had done in the past, and he had not been disappointed. The Bible and our own experience suggest various reasons why there may be delays in God bringing blessing to us or answering our prayers (see Isa 59:1-2; John 11:1-15; 1 Pet 1:3-9).

But there are also many things that we, with our present knowledge, may not understand of the ways of God with us. What we can be sure of is that God is unchanging. We can probably also say with the psalmist that he has often shown his 'unfailing love' to us in the past. We can trust him to do so again, even when we cannot see immediate answers to our prayers. We have known his salvation, and we can be sure that in the future we will be able to say, *my heart shall rejoice in your salvation* (13:5) – salvation from the guilt and power of sin, and freedom from every power of evil that opposes God's will for us. God *has dealt bountifully* (**13:6b**, NRSV) with us, and he will do so again. Given this confidence, we can say, *I will sing to the Lord* (**13:6a**). Pain can give place to prayer, self-pity to trust, and prayer can lead to praise.

Psalm 14: The Way of Fools

This psalm, is almost exactly the same as Psalm 53. The reason for this is that there seem to have been a number of different collections of psalms (like our different Christian hymn books), and this particular psalm was in two collections that were later joined in the book of Psalms.

This psalm cannot be said to be either a prayer or thanksgiving or a hymn of praise. It is more like the type of admonition we find in the prophets, namely a rebuke of people's godlessness, a warning of what God will do in judgment, and direction to the way of true joy and gladness.

14:1-3 Foolishness in Life

The world may think someone very clever and wise, but in the end that person may prove to be a fool. This is a recurring theme in the book of Proverbs, which has much to say about the fool and the wise person (Prov 12:15; 13:16; 14:7-8; 17:21, 24; 18:6-7; 30:32). The form in which their foolishness manifests itself is in their saying, *There is no God* (**14:1a**). Today some people take this position, arguing that there is no God who is Lord and Creator of all. Yet, as Psalm 19:1 puts it, 'How clearly the sky reveals God's glory! How plainly it shows what he has done!' (GNB) The apostle Paul says that we can know the reality of the unseen God from creation (Rom 1:20). We must respect the doubts and problems of those who say they are atheists and cannot believe in God. But at the same time, we may say for ourselves that the more we see of creation, the more we read the Scriptures, the more we see the lives of those who sincerely believe in God, the more we are convinced that there is a God over all, who made us, cares for us and is also our judge.

More numerous than atheists are people who believe in their hearts that there is a God but act as if God does not see what they do and would never call them to account for their actions (10:4, 6, 11). The psalmist calls such people 'fools' too, and says that their lives are marked by three things:

- A refusal to do the greatest thing that any human being can ever do, namely seek to know God and to live day by day in a personal relationship with him (**14:2**).

- A lack of moral control. *They are corrupt, their deeds are vile* (**14:1b**); they go astray and do what is perverse and wrong (**14:3**).
- A willingness to oppress others, thinking they can do as they like to the weak and the poor (14:4, 6).

But this psalm is not just speaking of unbelievers and the ungodly. As *the Lord looks down from heaven* on humankind (14:2), how many good and godly people does he see? The answer is *not even one* (14:3). For which of us truly seeks after God with our whole heart? Which of us has not gone astray and failed to do what is good? In Romans 3:9-18, Paul uses this and other OT verses (like 5:9) to show that 'all have sinned and fall short of the glory of God' (Rom 3:23). But that passage goes on to show that we can be forgiven and accepted by God through what Jesus Christ has done for us. So we who have been fools like others can turn to God and do what is wise and right. We will then *seek God* (14:2), *call on the Lord* (14:4) and make God our *refuge* (14:6).

14:4-7 Foolishness Shown Up

Will evildoers never learn? (**14:4a**), the psalmist asks. Do these people think that they can oppress the weak, eating them up as easily *as men eat bread?* (**14:4b**). The metaphor of eating is a common one in the OT to express the idea that some people are making themselves rich at the expense of others (Isa 3:14-15; Jer 10:25; Amos 5:11; 8:6; Mic 3:1-2; Hab 1:13).

Those who do this are foolish to think that they can get away with it. In the very place where they act wrongly towards others, they will be *overwhelmed with dread* (**14:5**). There they will discover that God is with the righteous, and where they try to *frustrate the plans of the poor* (**14:6**), they will find that the Lord is the refuge of the poor.

When we are tempted to act in the foolish ways of which this psalm speaks, we should take the advice in 2:10-12, 'be wise; be warned, you rulers of the earth. Serve the Lord with fear … Blessed are all who take refuge in him.' The fear of the Lord takes away the dread of which 14:5 speaks. True wisdom prays, 'Deliver us from evil'.

The last verse of the psalm widens the prayer for deliverance. All too often the people of Israel acted as if there were no God. Or they turned from the Lord to worship other gods that were not truly God. They suffered defeat and exile. When they prayed for deliverance (**14:7a**), God did *restore the fortunes of his people* and renewed their joy (**14:7b**). The same principle still applies. Whenever we turn from the foolishness of our sin and return to the ways of God, we too are restored and can *rejoice* and *be glad* (**14:7c**).

Psalm 15: The Life That Pleases God

This psalm, like the previous one, is neither a prayer nor a song of thankfulness and praise, but a description of the way of life that God calls us to follow. We should study these guidelines, and supplement them with the directives in the NT, especially in passages such as Colossians 3:12-17.

15:1 Vital Questions

The *holy hill* spoken of in 15:1 is the temple on Mount Zion in Jerusalem. Before that temple was built in the time of Solomon, there had been the Tent of Meeting in which the presence of God was specially known from the time when the people wandered in the wilderness. It is sometimes helpful to be reminded of that Tent of Meeting lest we start to imagine that God's presence depends on there being some beautiful and mighty structure built by human hands (see 1 Kgs 8:27; Acts 7:44-50).

It is possible that as people approached the temple hill in Jerusalem to worship God, they asked the question, *Lord, who may dwell in your sanctuary? Who may live on your holy hill?* (**15:1**; see also 24:3). This question asks, 'Who can be God's guest in his house? Who can truly worship him? What type of life makes one worthy to do this?' The prophets too asked and answered the question, 'How shall I come before the Lord?' (Mic 6:6-8, NRSV; Isa 33:13-15).

If the approaching people asked the question, then the priests in the temple may have answered with the rest of the psalm. Or the rest of the psalm may simply have been the answer the priests gave when worshippers asked these questions. Whatever the case, it is important to notice that the answer did not involve making the right offerings and sacrifices or being ceremonially clean. All the things mentioned relate to being pure in word and action and to caring for people. We are reminded of Micah's words, 'And what does the Lord require of you? To act justly and to love mercy and to walk humbly with your God' (Mic 6:8).

The ten requirements listed in the answer (15:2-5) may be compared with the Ten Commandments (Exod 20:2-17; Deut 5:6-21). We will discuss these ten points under six headings.

15:2 Doing What Is Right

Plainly and simply, we are called under all circumstances to do what we know is right. That is to walk blamelessly (**15:2a**), to have the highest standards for our lives. The same word is used in the legislation specifying that only animals without blemish could be offered in sacrifice to God. In the words of Jesus, we are called to be 'pure in heart' (Matt 5:8), or as it is put later in the Sermon on the Mount, 'Be perfect … as your heavenly Father is perfect' (Matt 5:48).

15:2c-3 True in Words

God's standard for us is also that we speak the truth, and do so from our hearts (**15:2b**). Our words should be sincere and trustworthy. We should also refuse to *slander* other people, that is, to speak evil of them (**15:3**). In other words, we should not tell the worst about other people. Before speaking about others, we should always test ourselves with the questions, 'Is it true? Is it loving? Is it helpful?' Zechariah 8:16-17 puts it well: 'Speak the truth to each other, and render true and sound judgment in your courts; do not plot evil against your neighbour, and do not love to swear falsely.'

We can harm people by our words and by what we do – or fail to do. If we want to live in God's ways and in fellowship with God, it must be our simple rule to 'do no evil' to others.

15:4a Honouring Those Who Deserve Honour

When 15:4 speaks about despising the wicked, it does not mean that we must reject some people as beyond hope. These words need to be read in conjunction with the next part of the verse, which calls us to honour *those who fear the Lord* (**15:4a**). This means that in our community we must honour and support those who put God first, rather than those who seek to lead people in the opposite direction. As the Apostle Paul says, love 'does not delight in evil, but rejoices in the truth' (1 Cor 13:6).

15:4b True to Promises Made

We all make promises, and sometimes it is hard and hurts –**15:4b** to carry out what we promise. We promise to serve the Lord, and it is often hard to be true to that promise. Many of us have made promises to be true to our marriage partner, 'in sickness and in health … till death us do part'. We should stand by the oaths and promises we make.

15:5 Right Attitude to Money

Two wrong uses of money are condemned in 15:5: receiving interest and receiving bribes. The OT had a law against lending money to gain interest from it (see Exod 22:25; Lev 25:35-38; Deut 23:19-20). This is rather different from our putting money in the bank today and receiving interest, as the bank lends our money to others to get more interest for itself. What the OT forbade was lending money to a poor person in order to make money out of someone in desperate need. We should be prepared to help those in need without expecting anything in return.

Bribery is condemned in the OT (Exod 23:8; Prov 17:23; Amos 5:12). It involves using money to gain an unfair advantage over someone else. Some people demand bribes just to do their everyday job. And some will be prepared to perpetrate an injustice if they are paid enough. Christians need to take to heart what this psalm says about bribes.

15:6 The Outcome of a Righteous Life

Becoming aware of all that God requires of us, if we are to worship him, should lead us to humility and repentance. We should thank God that we can come and receive his forgiveness through Jesus Christ. But the guidelines given here do not apply only when we worship; they should also govern our entire life. To follow them is to know true security and to be like the one in Jesus' parable who builds a house on a solid foundation (Matt 7:24-25): *He who does these things will never be shaken* (**15:5**).

Psalm 16: The Results of Trust in God

The heading of this psalm is *A miktam of David.* A 'miktam' seems to be some particular kind of psalm, but the exact meaning of the word is uncertain.

This psalm, like Psalms 1 and 23, expresses confidence in the Lord and joy in the path of life in which he leads those who trust in him. Passages in the NT that express a similar confidence in the gifts and blessings of God include Romans 16:25; 2 Corinthians 9:8; Ephesians 3:20; Jude 24-25. In taking refuge in the Lord, the psalmist has found great blessing and five strong reasons for feeling content.

16:1-2 Prayer

It may be that the psalmist had not always believed in God, but he can now say *in you I have taken refuge* (the perfect tense is a more accurate translation of **16:1b**). The psalmist has proved the reality and the power of prayer and that there is no one apart from the Lord to whom he can turn as the source of all that is good (**16:2**). So in every time of difficulty and danger, he knows that he can pray, *Keep me safe, O God* (**16:1a**). He could share the great confidence that is expressed in Psalm 46:1: 'God is our refuge and strength, a very present help in trouble'.

16:3-4 The People of God

The psalmist found support in *the saints in the land,* that is, among those who sought to serve God. They were *glorious* because of their way of life and their care for others, and he could *delight* in them (**16:3**). On the other hand, he resolved to have no part with those who turned aside to other gods who required *libations of blood* (**16:4a**). These 'libations' may have been drink offerings to gods who demanded human sacrifice (Isa 57:5), which was completely forbidden to Israel. Or the libations may have been offered by people whose hands were 'full of blood' (Isa 1:15), that is, people who had committed violent crimes. Following other gods, whether ancient ones or those more frequently worshipped today like money and pleasure, also involves thinking of them and taking *their names upon my lips* (**16:4b**).

16:5-6 Possessions from God

From the time of Joshua, the land of Israel had been divided up between the tribes, with each family being given their *portion,* or *lot,* with clearly marked *boundary lines* (**16:5-6**). There was, however, one exception to this rule. The Levites were not given a tribal area as they had to serve in the temple. Instead they were told that the Lord himself was their inheritance (Deut 10:9). It may be that this is what the author of 16:5 had in mind. People of faith are like the Levites. In God they have all the inheritance and all the possessions that they could ever hope for.

The psalmist certainly sees life in this way. He describes blessings, his spiritual possessions, as being like having land in *pleasant places.* This is indeed *a delightful inheritance.* These blessings can also be described as a cup of rich wine at a feast (23:5).

16:7-8 The Presence of God

Above all, the psalmist can rejoice in God's presence with God to guide him. Even at night, God speaks to him in his heart to teach and instruct him (**16:7**). God's presence also means security. If we always remember that God is present with us, and can truly say, *I have set the Lord always before me,* then we will also be able to say that, whatever problems life brings, *I shall not be shaken* (**16:8**).

16:9-11 The Prospect for the Future

Even in the face of death, there can be joy (**16:9**). The words of **16:10** can be translated using the Hebrew words for death and the grave, *you do not give me up to Sheol, or let your faithful one see the Pit* (RSV). This confidence may have been the result of being spared from death in a very serious illness. Yet it was more than just that. It was also a confidence that God had led him into *the path of life*, and to the joy in the unfailing presence of God that is described as *eternal pleasures* (**16:11**).

We cannot tell how much the writer knew of life beyond death and what exactly he meant by his words in 16:11. There are some OT passages (Isa 26:19; Dan 12:2-3) which express a clear hope of life beyond death. For Christians the words of 16:11 certainly have deep meaning, as Jesus taught that lives brought into a living relationship with God cannot be overpowered by death. As he put it, if God is the God of Abraham, Isaac and Jacob, they cannot be thought of as just dead (Mark 12:26-27). Above all, Jesus himself has risen from the dead and 'destroyed death and has brought life and immortality to light through the gospel' (2 Tim 1:10). Peter on the day of Pentecost (Acts 2:25-32) could say that these words in Psalm 16 found their fullest reality in the resurrection of Christ. So in Christ we can say with great thankfulness and praise, *You have made known to me the path of life; you will fill me with joy in your presence, with eternal pleasures at your right hand* (16:11). Peter expresses similar thanksgiving in NT terms: 'Let us give thanks to the God and Father of our Lord Jesus Christ! Because of his great mercy he gave us new life by raising Jesus Christ from death. This fills us with a living hope, and so we look forward to possessing the rich blessings that God keeps for his people. He keeps them for you in heaven where they cannot decay or spoil or fade away' (1 Pet 1:3-4, GNB).

Psalm 17: A Just Cause

In the heading, this psalm is called a 'prayer'. This is also the heading of Psalms 86, 90, 102 and 142, although, many more psalms are actually prayers to God.

In many countries, when people feel they have been unjustly treated in court, there is no higher court of appeal that they can turn to for justice. The Israelites were very familiar with this type of situation. They had endured oppression in Egypt. David was in a situation of oppression when Saul persecuted him and tried to take his life (1 Sam 22-24). Christians too have often suffered unjustly. That is why peoples and individuals have often had good reason to make this psalm their prayer, for it is an appeal to God to uphold justice in his own way. The prayer is divided into three parts (17:1-5, 6-12,13-15), each of which begins by calling on the name of God.

17:1-5 A Prayer for Justice

Hear, O Lord, my righteous plea (**17:1**) is the psalmist's first prayer. He goes on, *may your eyes see what is right* (**17:2**). This was his cry to God. When he speaks of his lips as being free from deceit and says, *I have resolved that my mouth will not sin* (**17:3**), *I have kept myself from the ways of the violent* (**17:4**) and *my steps have held to your paths* (**17:5**), he is not trying to say that he has never said or done anything wrong. What he is doing is uttering an oath of innocence (see 7:3-5). He is telling God that he has been unjustly persecuted and oppressed by his enemies. These enemies were people who neither cared for God nor for others, while he was sincerely trying to keep God's word and follow God's ways.

The Apostle Paul was certainly conscious of his own sins and failures, but when he was unjustly opposed by his own people, he insisted that he had tried to live with 'a clear conscience before God and man' (Acts 23:1; 24:16). So he appealed for justice like the psalmist did, and as we also can do when we are treated unjustly. But, like the psalmist, we must be prepared for God to test us and search our hearts, and to speak to us in the silence of the night when there are no other voices to influence us (**17:3**). He will help us to discern when our cause is just, and when others are justified in their criticism of us.

17:6-12 A Prayer for Protection

Just as the psalmist saw God as his court of appeal against the injustice of his enemies, so he believed that as he turned to God in prayer, he would find help and protection. He could say with complete confidence, *I call on you, O God, for you will answer me* (**17:6**). The psalmist knew that God is the Saviour of all who turn to him for refuge (**17:7**). He could be sure of the *great love* the Lord would show him.

He was sure of this despite his enemies showing no pity and boasting of what they could do (**17:10**). They surrounded him and threatened to throw him to the ground (**17:11**). They attacked him as fiercely as a lion (**17:12**).

He uses two beautiful pictures to express God's protection, possibly drawing on the images in Deuteronomy 32:10-11. He asks God to keep him *as the apple of your eye* (**17:8**). This 'apple' is the pupil at the centre of the eye, which the eyelids keep from harm by reacting to any danger to it. Next, he prays, *hide me in the shadow of your wings* (**17:8**). The picture is of a mother bird caring for her young ones and protecting them from danger under her wings. Jesus too uses this picture in Matthew 23:37.

17:13-15 A Prayer for Deliverance

In **17:13** the psalmist's prayer becomes more urgent. He needs not only defence against injustice but also protection from his enemies. They even threaten to take his life, and so he prays for deliverance: *Rise up, O Lord, confront them, bring them down!* (**17:13**). Many psalms have similar prayers for victory over enemies. We understand that in Christ it would be better to pray for our enemies to be converted to the ways of God so that they seek to live in justice and peace with others rather than oppress them. Yet we should recognize that the psalmist was not asking for personal revenge. He wanted God to act in justice, to uphold the right and to conquer evil.

The verse referring to those *whose reward is in this life* (**17:14**) is very difficult to translate. The psalmist may be praying that those who seek only the things of the world may have just those things and nothing else for themselves, their children and their grandchildren. Or he may be praying that these people and their children and grandchildren may have what God has stored up for them, namely his judgment. A third option is that he is praying that those who serve God will find their hunger satisfied and that their children and grandchildren will have plenty. My own position is that he is praying that these people will get what they want, and that their children and their children's children will have material things in abundance. Yet despite having all this, they will miss true life.

What the psalmist wants for himself more than anything else is to live close to God and, as **17:15** puts it, to see his face. To understand what the Bible means by this, we need to read passages such as Numbers 6:25-26, Deuteronomy

5:4, 34:10, Psalm 27:8-9, 2 Corinthians 4:6 and Revelation 22:4. The psalmist would understand the prayer, 'One thing I ask of the Lord, this is what I seek: that I may dwell in the house of the Lord all the days of my life, to gaze upon the beauty of the Lord' (27:4).

The psalmist expects to see God's face *when I awake*. It may be that the psalmist is thinking of seeing God's face when he awakes from the sleep of death (see comments on 16:11). Or he may simply be praying that he will awake after a night of sleep (perhaps in the temple where he has come to pray to God), and be sure of the Lord's presence with him.

This is a blessing which neither unjust accusations, nor persecution, nor death itself can take away. We, with the NT as well as the OT to guide us, can set alongside 17:15 the words of the Apostle Paul, 'For I am convinced that neither death, nor life ... neither the present nor the future, nor any powers ... nor anything else in all creation, will be able to separate us from the love of God that is in Christ Jesus our Lord' (Rom 8:38-39).

Psalm 18: Deliverance

18:1-30 Personal Deliverance

This psalm has a heading that does more than just link it with the name of David. The whole psalm is found in almost exactly the same words in 2 Samuel 22. Even the introduction is virtually identical: *Of David the servant of the Lord. He sang to the Lord the words of this song when the Lord delivered him from the hand of all his enemies and from the hand of Saul.* The first part of the psalm deals with David's sense of personal deliverance especially in the days when Saul was trying to kill him. It is a good idea to read the record of these events in 1 Samuel chapters 18–24 and 26 while reading 18:1-30 in order to see how this part of the psalm would be true to David's experience in those times. The second part of the psalm (18:31-50) speaks of national deliverance such as David experienced after he had become king over Israel.

18:1-3 The God who delivers

The psalm begins with praise. The metaphors used to describe God's protection may have been drawn from David's experience as a shepherd boy in the mountains of southern Palestine and later as a young man escaping from danger. God was like a solid *rock*, like a *fortress*, like a great cliff beside which he could shelter in a storm, like a *shield* to protect him, or like the *horn* of an ox that signalled the animal's strength (18:2). From his experience David could certainly say God *is worthy of praise* since he had called on the Lord for help and had found deliverance from his enemies (18:3).

18:4-6 The need for deliverance

David had certainly been in great need and in real danger of death. He refers to this as he speaks in 18:4 and 18:5 of *death* and *destruction* and *the grave*. He pictures himself as being tied up with cords, or being drowned in torrents of water, or being like an animal trapped in a hunter's snare. In his great distress there was only one thing he could do: he called on God and God heard him (18:6).

18:7-19 Deliverance brought

In graphic poetic language, these verses powerfully describe the way God comes to help those who call on him. He is the great God of creation, able to use the storm clouds, the mighty wind, thunder and lightning as his servants. His anger against those who oppress his people can be described as smoke from his nostrils and fire from his mouth (18:8). His coming to help those in need is like heaven coming down to earth (18:9) and like God's showing himself in power as he did when he saved his people at the Red Sea when they came out of Egypt (with 18:15, read Exodus 14).

The OT often speaks of God's power revealed in the forces of nature (see Pss 29; 77:16-19; 104), but particularly in what happened at Mount Sinai in the days of Moses (Exod 19:16-25). When the law was given, a storm and a volcanic eruption seem to have given evidence of God's presence and mighty power. The people in later generations often looked back to that event and spoke of Sinai (or Paran) as involving a revelation of the power of the Lord as he came to his people (Deut 33:2; Judg 5:4-5, Ps 68:8, 17; Hab 3:3-16).

When we pray, we should remember that we are calling on the one who is Creator and Lord of the universe. We should think of him when we see the awesome power of a storm, of thunder, lightning and earthquake. But we also need to remember that these are not the only ways in which God's greatness is made known to us (1 Kgs 19:11-18). Similarly, when we see the thick dark clouds gathering and being pierced by brilliant flashes of lightning, we need to remember that the Bible often uses this phenomenon as a metaphor for God's glory. The clouds obscure it because it is too bright for human eyes to see, but the flashes of lightning indicate that it is there, behind the clouds (1 Kgs 8:12; Ps 97:2-4).

Because of the mighty power at his disposal, the Lord is able to reach down to help us. The Hebrew words used in the clause, *he drew me out of deep waters* (18:16) are often used in the OT, but are also found in Exodus 2:10. The verbal link may be a reminder that as Moses was drawn from the water and saved from death that threatened him, so God saved the psalmist. God can deliver us from forces that are too strong for us (18:17). He delights in those who turn to him (18:19) and willingly becomes their support (18:18).

18:20-30 Those whom God delivers

We need to read **18:20-24** not as a claim to perfection but as expressing determination to sincerely follow the ways of God and to keep clean from evil (see comments on Pss 7 and 17). Those who are single-mindedly faithful to God will find God faithful in coming to their help (**18:25-26a**), but those who are *crooked* in their ways will find that God works against them and brings their plans to nothing (**18:26b**).

Those who feel that the claims made in 18:20-24 represent arrogant pride should note the words, *You save the humble but bring low those whose eyes are haughty* (**18:27**). Those who are humble and faithful are like lamps that manage to stay alight, or like lights waiting to be switched on (**18:28**). When they are lit by the Lord, they can become lights to others (Matt 5:14-16; John 8:12). Those who rely on God and trust in God's promises will find that they are helped to do things that may have seemed almost impossible in human terms (**18:29-30**).

18:31-50 National Deliverance

The psalm began with praise of God – 'my rock, in whom I take refuge' (18:2) – and returns to this theme in **18:31** – *who is a rock besides our God?* But where the subject of most of the first half of the psalm has been personal help and deliverance, now it is national deliverance. It is help for the king to win victories over his enemies so that, as the very last verse says, *He gives his king great victories; he shows unfailing kindness to his anointed, to David and his descendants for ever* (**18:50**). In 2 Samuel we have a record of the triumphs of David and his followers. It would be a good idea to read about these in 2 Samuel chapters 2 to 8 when reading the last half of the psalm.

Although David had his failures – his adultery with Bathsheba (2 Samuel 11) and the weaknesses that led to Absalom's rebellion – he had many victories, and the generations that followed looked back on David as a great king and spoke of the Lord's 'steadfast, sure love for David' (Isa 55:3, NRSV).

18:31-45 David's victories

David had been anointed by Samuel while King Saul was still alive. So David waited patiently for the time when God would make him head over the nation. He was patient until all the tribes of Israel (and not just Judah in the south) accepted him as king (see 2 Samuel 2:1-4; 5:1-5). Then he conquered the Philistines who had threatened the people of Israel and their land for so long. Later he was given victories over other nations also (see 2 Samuel 8). As 18:31-45 shows, it was God who gave David victory. It was he who equipped his soldiers with strength and agility. Like the deer, they could move quickly but surefootedly on rocky hills, without stumbling (**18:33**).

When David says, *You stoop down to make me great* (**18:35**), he recognizes his humble position in regard to God. But God's stooping was even greater than David realized, as we can see in the light of Christ's humbling of himself (2 Cor 8:9; Phil 2:6-8).

It was by the Lord's strength that David had power over other nations. So in singing their psalms and telling the stories of their people's history, Israel recalled God's blessings on David. Then because David was a great king, and God's special promises had been given to him, the prophets led the people in later years to expect another 'David', one even greater than this David.

18:46-50 Victory for God's people

David celebrated his victory over human enemies, but we who belong to Christ must apply what is said here about military battles in to the spiritual battles that we have to fight. We are not to see other people as our enemies. Our real enemies are the spiritual powers against which Jesus did battle, and which we also can conquer in Christ's strength (Rom 16:20a; Eph 6:10-18). With even greater assurance than David or any other person in OT times, we can say, *The Lord lives!,* and we can surely add, *Praise be to my Rock! Exalted be God my Saviour!* (**18:46**). The NT also quotes **18:49** in relation to taking the gospel to all peoples (see Rom 15:9). Once again we, more than David or any other person in OT times, have reason to say, *Therefore I will praise you among the nations, O Lord; I will sing praises to your name* (18:49). Jesus has given us the task of teaching and preaching his name in all the world and making disciples of all nations (Matt 28:18-20; Acts 1:8).

18:50 Great David's greater Son

We who read the OT in the light of the NT know that the hope of another David was fulfilled in Jesus. The ideal of a Shepherd-King that was partly realized in David's reign was perfectly expressed in the life and work of Jesus. He also fulfilled the promises given to David and his descendants (18:50; see 2 Sam 7:8-16; Ps 89:19-37) as the true Anointed of God, the Messiah, the Christ. The wars celebrated in the psalm, like other wars between nations then and now, were fought with weapons that were intended to overthrow the opposition physically. The battles Jesus fought were with spiritual enemies, the forces of sin, evil and death. He won those battles through his death and resurrection.

Psalm 19: God's World and God's Word

Psalm 19 may have been two psalms that were joined. The first, 19:1-6, is like Psalm 8 in that it speaks of creation and refers to God using the Hebrew word *Elohim*. The second, 19:7-14, speaks of the Lord (Hebrew *Yahweh*), as revealing himself in his word.

This psalm celebrates two ways we can know God: through creation and through revelation (in the law). This celebration leads to humble prayer.

19:1-6 God's Wonderful Creation

The Apostle Paul said, 'For since the creation of the world God's invisible qualities – his eternal power and divine nature – have been clearly seen, being understood from what has been made' (Rom 1:20). The psalmist would agree as he advises us to look up to the *heavens* both by day and by night (**19:1**). *Day after day* and *night after night* they proclaim an unending chain of praise (**19:2**). Their testimony is not in human speech (**19:3**), yet it is a silent but magnificent witness to the Creator's power and wisdom. The countless stars in the night sky pour forth their witness (**19:2**), and modern science has taught us even more amazing things about them than those in OT days could ever have known. We have even more reason to let our knowledge of creation turn our thoughts to the wonderful wisdom and care of the Creator.

The sunrise witnesses to God's glory. Gradually light breaks in on the darkness of the night, and then suddenly the sun bursts forth. We can understand how the psalmist thought of it as being like a gloriously dressed bridegroom, or like an athlete ready to run his race (**19:4-5**). To our eyes, the sun moves across the heavens in the course of the day. We sense its warmth, and fortunately *nothing is hidden from its heat* (**19:6**), for without the sun nothing on earth could live.

In many parts of the world in the past, and in some places today, people worship the sun, the moon and the stars, and look to them to guide and protect their lives. Such worship of stars, either directly or through astrology or horoscopes (reading one's stars), is idolatry in God's sight (Deut 18:9-14; Rom 1:25). The psalmist has greater wisdom; he recognizes that *the heavens declare the glory of God* (**19:1**). We too should look to the heavens, and readily say, 'My God, how great thou art!' But we do not have to restrict our admiration to the heavens. We should look at other aspects of creation such as plants, birds, animals and human life, and allow our increasing knowledge of these things to bring us to a still greater appreciation of the greatness of the Creator.

Yet from creation alone we cannot know God's purpose for our lives and that we ought to live in fellowship with God and in peace and justice with our fellow human beings. Thus God has sent us human messengers to make his way known and has given us the law, the prophets and finally his son Jesus, as his living word (Heb 1:1-3).

19:7-11 God's Wonderful Law

The second part of the psalm begins *The law of the Lord is perfect* (**19:7a**). Often when people think of law, even the law of God, they think of it as something that restricts their lives. Instead we should think of God's love as giving us guidelines to help us to live wise and happy lives. God's law, and all of God's word to us in the Scriptures, is good and life-giving. It brings wisdom to our minds and joy to our hearts (**19:7b-8**). Like the psalmist, we can say that the law of the Lord is more precious than gold and sweeter than honey (**19:10**). The law directs, corrects, warns and restores us (2 Tim 3:16-17). Thus we should study it and seek to know it better.

Jesus taught that the law has an important purpose (Matt 5:17-20) and always aimed to focus on its spirit and purpose. He summed it all up in the words, 'Love the Lord your God with all your heart and with all your soul and with all your mind', and 'Love your neighbour as yourself' (Matt 22:37-39). His coming also meant that God gave use the gospel (good news) as well as the law. We have all failed to keep the law, and so we need the good news of God's forgiveness through Christ crucified and risen. We also need the revelation that we have been given through the Holy Spirit now living in us (John 1:16-18).

19:12-14 Prayer to the Revealed Creator

Thinking about the greatness of God as revealed in nature and the purpose of God as revealed in the law should lead us to pray. Like the psalmist, we should ask three things of God:

- God's forgiveness, even for faults that we do not yet recognize (**19:12**).
- God's protection from insolent and proud people or from the attitude of pride and selfishness that is indeed a *great transgression,* because we are acting as if we are more important than God (**19:13**).
- God's guidance so that our thoughts and words may be good in the sight of God, our great *rock* and *redeemer* (**19:14**).

Psalm 20: Prayer Before Battle

This psalm seems to be a prayer for a king of Israel as he sets out for battle against some enemy that threatens the land. An account of a similar prayer offered by Jehoshaphat is found in 2 Chronicles 20:6-21. This psalm may have been written for David or for some other king, perhaps Jehoshaphat or Hezekiah (2 Kgs 20).

We need to remember that in many ways our world is very different from the world in which the people of Israel lived. Moreover, as Christians, we should be seeking grace and forgiveness, not revenge and retaliation. Understanding that, we can then pray the prayer in this psalm.

20:1 Israel's God

This prayer is directed to the *God of Jacob* (**20:1**). Jacob had also been given the name Israel (Gen 32:28) and thus his descendants are referred to either as 'Israel' or as 'Jacob'. When God is spoken of as the *God of Jacob*, we are reminded of how God was with Jacob and showed great patience, love and grace to him, in spite of all his human weaknesses and failings. This same *God of Jacob* is our God.

The psalmist repeatedly stresses the *name* of God in this psalm (20:1, 5, 7). To understand what he means by this, see the comments on Psalms 5 and 8.

20:2 Israel's Temple

The temple that Solomon built on Mount Zion in Jerusalem was God's sanctuary. Because God's presence was felt there, the psalmist said that God's help and support came from Zion (**20:2**). But it could also be said that God answered prayer *from his holy heaven* (**20:6**). God is both present with us and above and beyond us.

Jesus Christ came to take the place of the temple, making real God's presence in our world (John 2:18-22). Now the Holy Spirit seeks to make our lives and the fellowship of Christian people God's temple, where the presence of God is known in the world (1 Cor 6:19-20; 2 Cor 6:16-18).

20:3 Israel's Offerings

Leviticus 1–7 and other parts of the law tell us about the different kinds of offerings and sacrifices that the people were to bring to God. Such sacrifices were also offered to express their dependence on God before going into battle (1 Sam 7:7-11; 13:8-12). These are probably the *offerings* and *burnt sacrifices* that are referred to in **20:3**.

The meaning of all those sacrifices was fulfilled when Jesus made the sacrifice of himself for our sins on the cross. We no longer need sacrifices. We come to God through the sacrifice Christ offered once for all (Heb 10:10, 14).

20:4-5, 7-8 Israel's Battles

As we have seen in Psalm 18, the Israelites had to fight battles to keep their land and people secure. Often they turned to God for help and in reliance on God set up their *banners* (**20:5**). These banners were like flags that showed who they were during the battle and that were waved in celebration of victory.

The enemies of Israel were confident of victory because of their superior weaponry – they had greater numbers of horses and fast horse-drawn chariots that we might compare to the tanks of modern warfare. Where the psalmist said, *Some trust in chariots and some in horses* (**20:7**), today we might say, 'Some trust in missiles and some in nuclear weapons'. And while we may not be involved in actual wars, we are all facing troubles of some kind, and may be tempted to put our trust in material things or in human relationships

rather than in the living God. But, especially in our spiritual battles against evil, we must learn to *trust in the name of the Lord our God* (20:7) and to use the weapons for spiritual warfare described in Ephesians 6:10-18 (see also 2 Cor 10:4).

20:6 Israel's King

The psalmist prays especially for God's *anointed* (**20:6**), who is *the king* (**20:9**), to have victory over his enemies. The NT teaches us to pray that our national rulers may rule justly and with true care for their people, 'so that we may lead a quiet and peaceable life in all godliness and dignity' (1 Tim 2:1-2). We should also pray for our Christian leaders.

Whenever we are *in distress* (**20:1**), we can humbly and sincerely pray for victory over all the forces that work against God in our lives. Then we can confidently say, *Now I know that the Lord saves* (20:6). This confidence may come from clear revelation or from an inner assurance because sincere prayer has been offered (Phil 4:6; 1 John 3:19-22).

Psalm 21: The Way of Victory for a Ruler

This psalm (like 2, 45 and 72) refers to the king of Israel and to the battles in which he led the Israelites in fighting for their freedom and their land. Sometimes it has been thought that Psalm 20 was the prayer before battle and Psalm 21 the thanksgiving after victory had been obtained. But it is also possible that this psalm was written for a coronation ceremony (21:3), in which a king and his people together thank God for his blessings.

21:1-7 Blessings on the King

In Israel, the king was anointed with oil by a prophet, as Saul and David were by Samuel (1 Sam 10:1; 16:13). This anointing signified that God had set him apart for his work and was willing to give him the strength and wisdom needed to rule well. Even when Saul was hunting David and trying to kill him, David would not do any harm to Saul because Saul was the Lord's anointed (1 Sam 24:6). This psalm speaks of the blessings God gives to his anointed one.

It starts by saying, *the king rejoices in your strength* (**21:1**). God answers the king's prayers and grants him his heart's desire (**21:2**; see also 37:3-4). God comes to meet him with rich blessings (**21:3**). God gives the king glory and majesty that reflects something of his own glory (**21:5**). The king's part was to trust in the Lord and be faithful to him. Then he could be sure of being kept strong and secure through *the unfailing love of the Most High* (**21:7**).

But even the greatest and best kings of Israel – men like David, Hezekiah and Josiah – failed in many ways. So the prophets held out the hope of God's special Anointed – the Messiah, the Christ, the ideal king – who would come and save his people and rule in righteousness. Thus first the

Jewish people, and later the Christians, came to read many of the psalms as applying to the Messiah. What is said in a psalm like this finds its deepest fulfilment in the coming of Christ. His glory is the most perfect reflection of God's glory. He literally has *length of days, for ever and ever* (**21:4**). The psalmist was probably thinking of patriotic expressions like 'Long live the king' or 'May the king live for ever!' (1 Kgs 1:31; Neh 2:3). There may also have been the idea that the king would live on in his descendants after him, for God had promised to bless the house of David and make it 'continue for ever' (2 Sam 7:29). But, as noted above, we find the greatest fulfilment of such words in the Christ, the eternal Son of God.

21:8-13 The Battle of the King

The second part of the psalm speaks of the battles that Israel had to fight under the leadership of the king. These battles were understood to be God's battles. The people trusted God for deliverance and victory as they fought for their freedom and their land. They were convinced that if they trusted God, their enemies' evil plans would not succeed (**21:11**). God would give victory to his people and put their enemies to flight (**21:12**).

The overwhelming majority of Christians do not pray in the same way today, although there are a few who do. Jesus teaches us to love our enemies, to pray for those who persecute us, and never to retaliate, bear grudges or become vindictive (Matt 5:44). Yet in some countries Christians face very difficult questions when one people or one nation oppresses another, or when a ruler assumes power as a dictator and oppresses his people. Is there such a thing as a just war? Are there times when it is right for Christians to fight for their country or to be involved in a revolution to overthrow oppressive rulers? Every Christian must seek the guidance of the Holy Spirit in facing such situations. We must also take care to distinguish between a patriotic attitude in support of a just cause and personal vindictiveness against other groups.

What we all are certainly called to is a spiritual battle against the forces of evil (2 Cor 10:3-5; Eph 6:10-18). In these battles, the only way of deliverance and victory is reliance on the mighty power of God.

We also need to remember that our prayers for deliverance and victory over evil should not be just for our own help and comfort, but so that God's name will be exalted as we praise him (**21:13**).

Psalm 22: Out of Deep Distress

The heading of the psalm is similar to that of many other psalms, but includes what is probably a reference to the tune used, *The Doe of the Morning*.

22:1-21 Suffering

This psalm is written out of an experience of great suffering and deep distress, and is thus one that people turn to in times of great trial. It is a very special psalm for Christians because its opening words were on the lips of Jesus on the cross, and other parts of this psalm seem to express vividly what he suffered. We will think first of what the psalmist suffered and then of the suffering of Christ.

The psalmist endured four different kinds of suffering:
- He was despised by other people, so that he felt like *a worm* rather than a human being (**22:6**). People laughed at him for his trust in God when it seemed that God did not deliver him out of his trouble (**22:7-8**).
- He had enemies who were like the *strong bulls* that came from *Bashan* (**22:12**), like *lions* (22:13, 21), or like *dogs* in their attacks on him (22:16, 20). Those enemies were *a band of evil men* who had surrounded him and oppressed him (22:16).
- He suffered great weakness and pain. All his bones seemed *out of joint,* his mouth dried up, perhaps with fever. He felt death was near (22:14-15). His enemies, thinking that too, divided up his clothes among them (22:18).
- Worst of all, it seemed that God had forsaken him, remaining silent when the psalmist called on him in prayer. *Why? ... Why?* he asked (22:1), and he pleaded, *Do not be far from me, for trouble is near and there is no one to help* (22:11).

Yet even though God seemed far away, the sufferer still prayed. He still remembered that *you are enthroned as the Holy One; you are the praise of Israel* (**22:3**) or as the NRSV has it, 'you are holy, enthroned on the praises of Israel'. The latter translation shows that by our praise we exalt the Lord as King on the throne of the universe. The sufferer reminded himself of how other believers before him had called on God, and God had not failed them (**22:4-5**). For himself he knew that God had watched over him from his birth (**22:9-10**). He still addressed God as *My God ... my God ... my God* (**22:1, 2,** 10) and called *O my Strength, come quickly to help me* (**22:19**). In **22:20** he begs God to save *my life,* but literally the Hebrew reads 'my only one', perhaps meaning 'the one and only life I have'.

The NT descriptions of the sufferings of Jesus use the words of this psalm in four ways:
- Jesus prayed from the cross, *My God, my God, why have you forsaken me?* (22:1; Matt 27:46; Mark 15:34). He lost his sense of the Father's presence as he bore the guilt and filth of the sin of the world, but still he prayed, 'My God, my God'.
- His enemies mocked, saying 'He trusts in God; let God deliver him now, if he wants to' (22:8; Matt 27:39-44).
- The soldiers divided his clothes among themselves, and cast lots for his tunic (**22:18**; John 19:23-24).

- His hands and feet were pierced (**22:16**; John 20:27). This verse is translated in different ways in different versions, but it is clear that, whatever the psalmist experienced, his description of his sufferings in **22:14, 15, 17** could well be applied to a person being crucified.

22:22-31 Beyond Suffering

The psalmist's prayer was answered. He was rescued. As for Jesus, suffering and death were followed by resurrection as God the Father raised him from the dead. The psalm ends with praise as the psalmist records that God answered him in his affliction (**22:24**). He would thus fulfil the vows he had made when suffering. To understand **22:25-26**, read the description of the regulations in relation to vows in Leviticus 7:16 and Deuteronomy 12:10-11, 17-18. Deuteronomy 16:11 and 26:12 stated that the poor were to share the feast of rejoicing at sacrificial meals.

Notice those whom he wanted to hear his praise:

- His own people, *in the great assembly* of Israel, whom he wanted to tell what God had done.
- People all over the world, who needed to know the greatness and goodness of God (**22:27-28**).
- Past generations who had died (**22:29**) and future generations (**22:30**). There is some disagreement about the translation of 22:29a. Literally, the Hebrew means that all the rich or fat ones of the earth shall eat and worship, but a minor change in the Hebrew gives a translation that retains parallelism and makes both parts of the verse refer to those who have died.

We can join the psalmist in singing: 'I will praise you, O Lord, among the nations; I will sing of you among the peoples. For great is your love, reaching to the heavens; your faithfulness reaches to the skies' (57:9-10).

Psalm 23: The Shepherd Psalm

All over the world, this psalm is known and loved. Children often learn it before they learn to read; old people die with its words on their lips. Even in countries where sheep and shepherds are not known, and in our cities far from fields with sheep in them, people love this psalm. Why? Its words are beautiful and easy to remember. But most important is the fact that it expresses trust in God as the one who is with us in all the experiences of life, restoring us when we go wrong, guiding us, providing for us, watching over us in the dark places of life, near us from the day that we are born till the day we die.

23:1-2 The Shepherd

The life of a shepherd in Palestine was not easy. They had to be with their sheep day and night, leading them in the daytime to good grass to eat and to places where they would have water to drink. They might have to defend them from the attacks of wild beasts. Genesis 31:38-41, 1 Sam

17:34-35 and John 10:11-15 give us some idea of what a shepherd's life was like.

The OT often says that the leaders in Israel were supposed to be like shepherds in the way they cared for their people, though they often failed to do this (2 Sam 5:2; Jer 23:1-4; Ezek 34:1-10). Christian ministers too are often spoken of as 'pastors', a word that means 'shepherd', because their work is similar to that of a shepherd (1 Pet 5:1-5; John 21:15-17). But above all, God is spoken of as the true Shepherd of his people, and we have beautiful expressions of his care for them, like that in Isaiah 40:11, 'He tends his flock like a shepherd: He gathers the lambs in his arms and carries them close to his heart; he gently leads those that have young' (see also 77:20; 78:52, 70-72; 80:1; 100:3; Ezek 34:11-31). But here the psalmist says very personally, *The Lord is my shepherd* (**23:1**). Because he could say that, he could add, *I shall not want*. This does not mean that he would have all that he might selfishly desire, but all he needed. Sheep basically need two things: *green pastures* to feed on (**23:2**), and places where they can drink *beside quiet waters* (23:2). As we look to God as our Good Shepherd, we can trust all our needs to him. In the NT this is promised in Matthew 6:33 and Philippians 4:19. We are also promised that Christ cares for us as the Good Shepherd (Luke 15:3-7; John 10:1-18, 25-30).

23:3-4 The Guide

The reference to *your rod and your staff* (**23:4c**) reminds us of the club that a shepherd would use to protect his sheep from the attacks of wild animals and the staff or crook he would use to guide them in the right way. Then the focus of the psalm moves on from the idea of a shepherd to that of the Lord as our guide through all the experiences of life. First, he restores us, bringing us back to himself when we have taken the wrong way. The paths along which he leads us are *paths of righteousness* (**23:3**) – that is, ways that are right with God and right in terms of our relationships with other people. He does this not just for our own sake but *for his name's sake* (see comment on 5:11).

In **23:4a** some translations have *the valley of the shadow of death*, while others translate it as *the darkest valley*. We can think of all the dark valleys through which we pass – troubles, trials and sorrows that seem to us as dark as death. If we know God as our Good Shepherd, we can say in all of these, *I will fear no evil; for you are with me* (**23:4b**). And when at the end of our days on earth we go finally through death itself, we can still say the same words. This is the greatest comfort we could ever have.

23:5-6 The Host

The scene changes to one where we are guests staying with a host who meets all our needs. As a good host, God provides a table set with nourishing food (**23:5**). A good host also protects his guests from any enemies. As they come in from the hot and dusty countryside, he greets them with anointing oil, which expresses his welcome as it honours and refreshes his guests. So God anoints his people with his Spirit and gives them an overflowing cup of blessing (compare this with the references to the 'cup' that the Lord gives in 16:5). All the days of their lives they can know the *goodness and love* of the Lord (**23:6a**).

Some have thought that the *house of the Lord* in **23:6b** means the temple, and that the table was spread for a meal following sacrifices offered in the temple. However, it is more likely that the picture is of a host and his guests, enjoying the welcome and blessings that the Lord in 'goodness and mercy' offers us as long as we live. Life has its problems, difficulties and sufferings. We cannot avoid them, but we can face them with courage when we realize that the presence of God with us makes us like guests in the house of the Lord all our life long.

As noted in Psalm 16, it is hard for us to be sure how much the psalmists knew of life beyond death. Certainly those of us who know that Jesus Christ has conquered death can say with confidence and trust that the Lord will be with us not only all the days of our lives, but beyond our life on earth, so that we *shall dwell in the house of the Lord forever* (**23:6**).

Psalm 24: King of Glory

This psalm may first have been sung when David took the ark of the covenant, that special symbol of God's presence, up to Jerusalem, where Solomon later built the temple (2 Sam 6; 1 Chr 13). Or perhaps the psalm reminded people in later days of that event. Or it may have been written to be used during a special annual celebration when people went up to the temple in Jerusalem to worship. Whichever scenario is correct, the psalm shows us how the people worshipped, and the three parts of the psalm tell us three important things about worship.

In the worship of the Christian church, this psalm, and especially 24:7-10, is often used to celebrate Jesus' ascension into heaven when God raised him from the dead and 'seated him at his right hand in the heavenly realms, far above all rule and authority, power and dominion' (Eph 1:20-21; see also Phil 2:6-11).

24:1-2 The Greatness of God

When we worship, we should always remember how great God is. When we think of our world, its mountains and valleys, its rivers, oceans and underground water, the vast variety of plants, trees, flowers, birds and animals, we realize how wonderful creation is. But as we think of creation, we should turn our hearts and minds to the Creator, for *the earth is the Lord's, and everything in it* (**24:1**). We ourselves belong to God as his creatures. The land we live in belongs to him. We are like tenants who have use of it,

and God entrusts the care of it to us (Gen 1:28). Today we think of the dry land of the continents and the islands of the world as surrounded by sea. The psalmist thought of the dry land as floating on the seas and the waters under the earth (**24:2**). What matters most, however, is that we see the world and all of us who live in it as really belonging to God – though we often rebel against him and try to be independent of him.

24:3-6 The People God Wants to Worship Him

The psalmist asks a question similar to the one asked and answered in Psalm 15 and in Isaiah 33:14-15: *Who shall ascend the hill of the Lord?* (**24:3**). Which people are fit to go up to the place where the temple stands and worship there, or in other words, what does God ask of those who worship him? The answer, given in **24:4**, speaks of four things:
- *Clean hands* – hands that do good and not evil.
- *A pure heart* – not only must our actions and words be right, but so must our thoughts and motives.
- No idolatry – we must have no selfish ambitions or worldly goals in our lives. That is what is meant by lifting up our souls *to what is false* (NRSV). We do that when our values and ideals are controlled by the world or by contemporary fashions rather than by God's word and God's Spirit (see Rom 12:1-2; 2 Cor 5:9).
- Truthful speech – we must not *swear by what is false,* but must be truthful and honest at all times.

If we test ourselves by these four things, we will probably realize that we have failed in all four areas. We are not worthy to approach God in worship. We become even more acutely aware of this as we look at other passages that speak of the kind of life God calls us to live (for example, Mic 6:6-8; Matt 5:3-10). Thankfully we can ask his forgiveness for the past, but we must also desire to be people who live by these rules. The God who saves us from our sins will then give us his *blessing* and his *vindication* (**24:5**), which means that he will accept us.

24:7-10 God as Lord of Our Lives

These verses may describe what happened as this psalm was used by people going to the temple to worship. As we read it, we should remember that today our lives and the fellowship of Christians are God's temple (1 Cor 6:19-20; 2 Cor 6:16-18) and reflect on what it means to welcome God into the temple and worship him there.

As a procession of worshippers came to the temple gates, they demanded admission for the *King of glory* (**24:7, 9**). Then the question was asked, *Who is this king?* 'Who is the One who is honoured and worshipped, the One to whom people should always open the gates?' The answer came back: He is *the Lord, strong and mighty* (24:8), able to conquer all the forces of evil; *the Lord, mighty in battle* (**24:8**); *the Lord Almighty* (**24:10**), Lord over all the hosts of earth and heaven. Five times in these verses, God is spoken of as the *King of glory.* God's glory is God's greatness as revealed to us, and that means God's love, truth, goodness, power and wisdom. The first two verses of the psalm speak of God's glory in creation. We also can often see his glory in human lives. But the place where we see it best is in his son, Jesus Christ, for 'the Word became flesh and made his dwelling among us. We have seen his glory ... full of grace and truth (John 1:14).

Because God is such a wonderful *King of glory,* we should open the doors and gates of every part of our lives to receive him as Lord and to worship and serve him. We should pray that his glory may be seen in our lives and that his glory may be 'over all the earth' (57:5, 11).

Psalm 25: Waiting on God

Like Psalms 9 and 10, this psalm is an acrostic, in which each verse begins with a different letter of the Hebrew alphabet (although in two lines this pattern is not kept). The pattern would have helped people to remember the words of the psalm so that they could reflect on them.

25:1 A Faithful Worshipper

The previous psalm stated that those who come to worship God must not lift up their souls to an idol (24:4), and this psalm demonstrates what it actually means to have trust and confidence in God. It begins, *To you, O Lord, I lift up my soul* (**25:1**). This means that the psalmist turns fully to God, trusts him (25:2) and looks to him for help (25:15). He repeats this idea three times in the psalm when he speaks of putting his hope in the Lord (25:3, 5, 21). Clearly he relies on God patiently and trusts him to answer prayer, to help and guide and protect him in his own time and in his own way. He knows that God's attitude to him means he can have confidence in praying. He also shows us what should be our true attitude to God as we pray.

25:2-7, 11, 15-20 Needs Brought to God

The psalmist brings three special needs to God in this psalm. They are the types of things for which we also always need to pray.

25:2-3, 15-21 Deliverance

The psalmist feels the forces of evil against him as he tries to live his life in the service of God. There are enemies who want to boast of their power over him (25:2), and who *are treacherous without excuse* (**25:3**), that is, they cannot be trusted in what they say and do. They try to catch him as a hunter would catch an animal or a bird in a net (25:15). Without the help of God he will remain *lonely and afflicted* (**25:16**).

Different translations render **25:17** in different ways. The NIV has *the troubles of my heart have multiplied,* but it

may also be right to take it as a prayer, as in the NRSV, 'Relieve the troubles of my heart'. Whichever the case, it is clear that the psalmist is deeply unhappy. So in 25:16-20 he asks God to take note of his situation and of his enemies, to guard and deliver him and not to allow him to be *put to shame* (25:2, 3a, 20). Those who should *be put to shame* are his enemies (25:2, 3b, 20).

In his appeal for protection in **25:21**, the psalmist speaks as if *integrity* and *uprightness* are two guardian angels standing beside us. He may mean that God's truth and righteousness guard us, or that when, with God's help, we act in integrity and uprightness, we are kept in the right way. Certainly 'truth' and 'righteousness' are essential elements in a Christian's armour (Eph 6:10-17).

25:4-5 Guidance

The psalmist knows that he needs direction and guidance for the future. Hence he prays that God will teach him so that he will know the path in life that the Lord wants him to follow (**25:4a, 5**). He is acutely aware of the need to walk in the ways of the Lord (**25:8, 9, 12**). Christians can make this prayer with added confidence because of Jesus' promise, 'I am the light of the world. Whoever follows me will never walk in darkness but will have the light of life' (John 8:12).

25:6-7, 11 Forgiveness

The psalmist knows that he is not perfect and does not deserve God's help. He remembers only too well the sins of his youth and what have often been his *rebellious ways* (**25:7**). He can only pray that God in his mercy will not remember them and will overlook his past sins (**25:6**). *Forgive my iniquity,* he asks, *though it is great* (**25:11**).

25:8-11 Reasons for Confidence in God

The psalmist has confidence that God will hear him, for he knows God as *my Saviour* (25:5). God has saved him from sin and evil in the past and can be trusted to continue to save. His mercy and steadfast love *are from of old* (25:6). In other words, the psalmist is not just relying on his own experience, he knows that people in ages past have found that God's love and faithfulness have never failed them (**25:10**). Steadfast love is one of God's main attributes (25:6, 7, 10), and so the psalmist can appeal to God using the expression that we have often found in the psalms, *For the sake of your name,* or in other words, 'because of your character, because of who you are' (**25:11**).

25:9, 12-14 The Results of Prayer

Those who humbly fear the Lord and live in the ways that he approves will enjoy *prosperity* (**25:13a**). This should not be interpreted as meaning that they will necessarily enjoy earthly riches. As the experience of the psalmist shows, those who serve God often face trouble, difficulty and opposition. The meaning of this promise and of the promise that *his descendants will inherit the land* (**25:13b** – a promise that is often repeated in the OT) may need to be interpreted in the light of Jesus' words: 'Blessed are the meek for they will inherit the earth' (Matt 5:5).

But even better than the promise of prosperity is God's amazing willingness to enter into a covenant relationship with us (**25:14**), offering us his *friendship* (RSV), or confiding in us, as the NIV puts it. We weak and sinful people can become friends of God Almighty! The only requirement for enjoying this great privilege is that we *fear him* (25:14). We can have intimacy with God, but we must also reverence him as Lord of our lives and Lord of all the universe, and be *humble* before him to let him teach us his ways (25:9).

25:22 Conclusion

This is a very personal psalm, expressing an individual's trust and devotion. Each of us can make it our own prayer. But it ends with a reminder that we should not pray only for ourselves. This prayer should be extended to all of God's people, and so the psalmist concluded with the words, *Redeem Israel, O God, from all their troubles!* (**25:22**).

Psalm 26: Godly Ambitions

This psalm teaches us three important things about what it means to be determined to live a godly life in dependence on the steadfast love of the Lord.

26:1-2 Trusting and Tested

When we first read this psalm, we may think that the psalmist is very self-righteous. His first words are *Vindicate me, O Lord* (**26:1a**). The GNB translates this verse as 'Declare that I am innocent, O Lord, because I do what is right'. We need to understand that he was in a situation in which, like the authors of Psalms 7 and 17, he felt wrongly criticized and accused. He needed the Lord to defend him.

He wanted never to waver in his trust in the Lord (**26:1b**). In the NT, James speaks of that kind of trust when he says, 'If any of you lacks wisdom, he should ask God, who gives generously to all without finding fault, and it will be given to him. But when he asks, he must believe and not doubt, because he who doubts is like a wave of the sea, blown and tossed by the wind. That man should not think he will receive anything from the Lord; he is a double-minded man, unstable in all he does' (Jas 1:5-7).

Yet the psalmist's trust does not mean that he is overconfident. He is willing to be tested by the Lord in heart and mind (**26:2**). When we pray the way he does, it means that we are willing for God to show us our failings, and then make our lives more what they ought to be. It means praying the prayer of Psalm 139:23-24, 'Search me, O God, and know my heart; test me and know my anxious thoughts. See if there is any offensive way in me, and lead me in the way everlasting.' An effective prayer life requires a character that is honest, truthful and humble.

26:3-5, 9-10 Hating Evil and Loving Good

Leading a blameless life, or as the NRSV translates this, 'Walking in integrity' (26:1, 11) means going consistently in God's ways as we move step by step along the journey of life. God is faithful, and so we who profess to serve him must walk in faithfulness (**26:3**). This means a refusal to compromise in any way with evil. We have to live among people of all shades of character, and we are called to lovingly bear witness to the truth before those who deliberately follow an evil course in life. But we must not associate with them in what they do and plan. Thus we are not to *sit with*, nor *consort with*, nor enjoy the company of *deceitful men* ... *hypocrites* ... *evildoers* or *the wicked* (**26:4-5**). These verses reminds us of Psalm 1 and other Bible passages that speak of the two ways which we may follow in life. In every situation, we are called to hate and reject the evil and to love and choose the good. Jesus spoke of the narrow gate, the way that leads to life, and the broad gate, the way that leads to destruction (Matt 7:13-14).

Nor are we to associate with *sinners* and *bloodthirsty men* (those who are guilty of crimes of violence) or those who have *wicked schemes* (**26:10**), an expression that is used in the OT to speak especially of idolatry and of sexual immorality. It is striking that the psalmist puts these violent and sexual crimes in the same category as taking bribes (26:10). Bribery is not a new problem; it was common in OT times (1 Sam 8:3; 12:3; Isa 1:23; 33:15; Amos 5:12; Mic 3:11). God condemns it as an evil in the life of a nation (Exod 23:8; Deut 16:19; Prov 17:23; Isa 5:22-23).

The psalmist prays from his heart, *Do not take away my soul along with sinners* (**26:9**). He is determined by God's grace to live a God-centred life. True faith must be shown in righteous conduct (Jas 2:14-26). In order to cultivate such purity, we must take Paul's words to heart and, rather than associating with what is evil, we must focus our attention on things that are excellent or praiseworthy: 'whatever is true, whatever is noble, whatever is right, whatever is pure, whatever is lovely, whatever is admirable' (Phil 4:8).

26:6-8 Worship and Witness

Washing one's hands represented a claim to be innocent of a crime of which one might be accused (**26:6**; see Deut 21:6; Matt 27:24). But it was also an outward symbol of the desire to purify oneself from all evil and defilement (see Exod 30:17-21). Thus the prophet Isaiah could say, 'wash and make yourselves clean. Take your evil deeds out of my sight! Stop doing wrong, learn to do right' (Isa 1:16-17). The psalmist sincerely sought this type of cleansing for himself, and thus he delighted in going to the temple and feeling God's presence there (**26:8**).

In the ᴏᴛ the temple is often spoken of as the place where God's *glory dwells* (**26:8**), because of the ways in which God's presence was specially revealed there (see 1 Kgs 8:10-11). In the ɴᴛ God's glory was revealed perfectly in Jesus Christ (John 1:14), who fulfils the meaning of the temple (John 2:19-22). Now the Holy Spirit makes Christians God's temple (Eph 2:19-22) and so we must always glorify God in our bodies and in our lives. What good news – and what a challenge!

Not only did the psalmist love to go to the temple, but he also loved to worship with God's people. With them, he would sing songs of thanksgiving to God and let others know of God's *wonderful deeds* (**26:7**). Christians should have a similar attitude to meeting for worship with other believers (see also Heb 10:24-25).

26:11-12 Conclusion

The psalmist concludes by reiterating his innocence: *I lead a blameless life* (**26:11a**), but he also clearly recognizes that this does not mean that he is sinless, for in the very same verse he prays, *redeem me, and be merciful to me* (**26:11b**). But he is confident that his life is on a sure footing, and that the one to be praised for this blessing is God (**26:12**).

Psalm 27: Confidence and Prayer

This psalm is a prayer for God's light to guide us and God's power to save us – a prayer of the kind that we often need to make. Some commentators have suggested that it was once two different psalms, for the first half expresses strong confidence (27:1-6), while the second is an anxious prayer (7-14). While it is possible that two psalms have been combined, it is also possible that the psalmist thinks first of his strong reasons for trust in the Lord and then brings his needs to God. We see the same pattern in Psalm 40.

27:1-6 Confidence in God's Salvation

The psalmist knew he had many enemies, who told lies about him and threatened him with violence (**27:2, 12**). Yet he could say, The *Lord is the stronghold of my life – of whom shall I be afraid?* (**27:1**). And *though an army besiege me ... even then I will be confident* (**27:3**). He knew what it means to face difficulty and trouble, yet he could trust God, saying, *in the day of trouble he will keep me safe in his dwelling* (**27:5**). In the psalmist's time, it was a matter of honour for those who lived a nomadic life to protect a guest from attack. In the same way, the Lord will take the psalmist into his tent and conceal him *in the shelter of his tabernacle* (27:5). Using a different picture of security, he said, God will *set me high upon a rock* (27:5). Because he realized the greatness of the Lord's power to lift him up, to protect and keep him, he said

that he would *joyously offer sacrifices in the tabernacle* and *sing and make music to the Lord* (**27:6**).

27:7-14 Prayer for God's Salvation

27:7-10 Seeking God's face

The psalmist knows that he can be confident in God, but he also knows that he is in desperate need of help. This is why he seeks the Lord's face. Different translations express **27:8** in slightly different ways, but all involve an invitation and a response to it. The ɢɴʙ puts it very simply, *When you said 'Come worship me,' I answered, 'I will come, Lord.'*

In his anxiety, the psalmist fears that he may not be able to find the one he seeks (27:9). He knows that sin can lead to God's face being hidden from his people (Isa 59:1-2). This is why his prayer speaks of the need for God's mercy and grace (**27:7**).

He also knows that there are times in life when we do not receive help even from those closest to us. Even our parents may neglect us or turn against us (**27:10a**; see also Isa 49:14-16). Or they may die, leaving us alone in the world. But God is a helper who never sleeps (121:3-4) and who does not change with passing years (Heb 1:10-12). The psalmist knew the living God as the One who would never fail. His anxious prayer, *Do not reject me or forsake me, O God my Saviour* (**27:9**) is replaced with the confident statement, *the Lord will receive me* (**27:10b**).

27:11 Living in God's light

The Bible is full of promises that God will guide those who trust him and seek his direction. God's word in Scripture is given as a lamp to our feet and a light to our path (119:105), but the psalmist also describes God himself as *my light* (27:1). And Jesus said, 'I am the light of the world. Whoever follows me will never walk in darkness, but will have the light of life' (John 8:12). God has also given his Spirit as the Spirit of truth to guide us into all the truth that we need to know (John 16:13). We can, therefore, have great confidence in praying *teach me your way, O Lord* (**27:11a**). Because there are many who try to tempt us to go a very different way, we can ask, *lead me in a straight path because of my oppressors* (**27:11b**).

Confidence in prayer is linked with walking in God's light. If we do not do that, we cannot pray honestly, for 'God is light, in him there is no darkness at all' (1 John 1:5).

27:4, 13 Enjoying God's presence

There is something that is even more important to know than God's salvation and God's light – namely God himself. More than all God's gifts and God's blessings, we should desire to know God and enjoy his continued presence with us. Nothing is greater or more wonderful than that. The psalm puts this in two ways. It is like being *in the house of the Lord,* in the temple of the Lord all our days (**27:4**). None of us can live in a temple or a church building all day and every day, but we can know God near to us wherever we are. Secondly, it is like having the *face* of God turned towards us and not hidden from us because of our failures and sins (27:9, see also 13:1).

We cannot literally see the face of God, but we can feel he is near and that is like seeing *the beauty of the Lord* (27:4) and *the goodness of the Lord* as long as we live (**27:13**). The priestly blessing bestowed by Aaron and his sons included the words, 'the Lord make his face shine upon you and be gracious to you' (Num 6:24-26). We as God's people should respond by seeking God's face, that is, his presence more than anything else in life (27:4). We have two examples of people who sought this single-mindedly in Mary (Luke 10:38-42) and Paul (Phil 3:12-14).

Psalm 28: A Cry for Help and Justice

This psalm begins with a cry for help. Then it continues with a cry for justice. It concludes with thankfulness and praise that the cry has been heard. It is an example for us of how to 'approach the throne of grace with confidence, so that we may receive mercy and find grace to help us in our time of need' (Heb 4:16).

28:1-3 A Cry for Help

To you I call, O Lord my Rock (**28:1a**). The psalmist knew that there was no other to whom he could turn in his need and so he pleaded, *do not turn a deaf ear to me* (**28:1b**). His words *if you remain silent* (**28:1c**) suggest that God has not answered his recent prayers, possibly because of sin (see Isa 59:1-2) or because God may have been testing him and teaching him to wait for him (Deut 8:2-5; Heb 12:3-11).

The psalmist recognizes that if God does not answer his prayer, he will *be like those who have gone down to the pit* (**28:1c**). As we have seen in the study of earlier psalms, people in OT days called the place of the dead 'Sheol' or 'the Pit', and had no clear hope of life after death. So the psalmist means that he will be without hope if God does not answer his prayer.

As he prays, the psalmist lifts up his hands (**28:2**). This gesture is also reported in other parts of the Bible (63:4; Lam 2:19; 1 Tim 2:8). It represents our looking up to God for his blessing, just as bowing our knees before God in prayer expresses our humility in coming to him (Eph 3:14). The psalmist's hands were lifted up towards *Your Most Holy Place* (**28:2**), that is, the holy of holies in the temple, where it was felt that God's presence was specially known (see comments on 5:7).

We are not told what the psalmist's particular need was. It may have been a crisis in the life of his country, for he

feared that godly people would have to suffer along with those who had no regard for God (**28:3**).

28:4-5 A Cry for Justice

The prayer of **28:4-5** is not a truly Christian one. The Lord Jesus teaches us to love our enemies and to pray for those who persecute us (Matt 5:44). The good news of salvation in Christ and our calling to share the good news means that we, being forgiven sinners ourselves, must seek to turn other sinners to the Saviour.

We should, however, read 28:4-5 as evidence of the psalmist's concern for justice. He does not want the world to think that God does not distinguish between those who seek to serve God and those who do evil. Those who speak words of peace but actually do harm to others should be brought to realize that they have cut themselves off from the blessing of God. He is praying, in effect, that trouble-makers will be repaid for their crimes and that God will prevent them from destroying the faith of other people.

One of the characteristics of the people he describes as evil is that *they show no regard for the works of the Lord* (28:5). The Bible often speaks of the consequences of people not taking notice of the works of God in creation, in human lives and in judgment (see Isa 5:11-12; 18-19; Rom 1:20-22).

28:6-9 Thankfulness that the Cry is Heard

Many times the psalms teach us the lesson of thankfulness. Often we pray for God's help in time of need, but when God answers our prayer, we forget to thank him. The psalmist says, *Praise be to the Lord, for he has heard my cry for mercy.* He confesses with gratitude that the Lord is his strength and shield (**28:7**). He determines to give thanks to the Lord with song and with a praising heart.

We may sometimes wonder how the psalmist can move so rapidly from an urgent cry for help and justice to a song of confidence and praise like that in 28:6-8. It may be that something specific happened to assure him that his prayer had been heard (**28:6**), just as Eli the priest assured Hannah that her prayer in the sanctuary was heard (1 Sam 1:17). Or his circumstances may have been like that of the writer of Psalm 73, who was troubled because ungodly people seemed to prosper in life. Then he 'entered the sanctuary of God' and came to realize that the end of the ungodly was not a good one (73:16-19). When we pray for God to intervene, we also need to wait on God and listen for him to speak through his word and through our fellow Christians.

Finally, this psalm, which has been a personal cry for help and justice that God graciously answered, becomes a prayer for the nation and for the king as the Lord's anointed (**28:8-9**). The NT teaches us to pray for our rulers (1 Tim 2:1-2). If they rule justly and well, all will benefit. Above all, the nation and its people will find blessing as God answers the prayer to *be their shepherd and carry them forever* (**28:9**).

Psalm 29: The Majesty of God

Anyone who has experienced the violence of a tropical thunderstorm can appreciate this psalm that describes the greatness and majesty of God as the Creator of all. It ends with a prayer for God's people to experience his peace, as well as his power.

We can compare what is said here about God's power revealed in creation, in wind and in fire with the signs of the coming of the Holy Spirit in Acts 2:1-4.

29:1-2 The Call to Worship

The psalmist summons heaven and earth to respond to what they see, hear and know of God by worshipping him. As the Nicene Creed puts it, God is 'Maker of heaven and earth' and of 'what is seen and unseen'. So the psalm begins by calling on the *mighty ones* (**29:1**), that is, heavenly beings, to *ascribe to the Lord glory and strength* (**29:1**). This means that they should acknowledge that God is indeed strong and mighty.

The glory due his name (**29:2**), which we are called to proclaim in worship, is all that God has made known to us about himself. We are created to know God and to praise him (see Isa 43:21).

Different translations treat the end of 29:2 differently because the Hebrew does not make it clear whose holiness is being referred to. Thus some translations such as the NIV focus on the splendour and beauty of God's holiness. Others, however, focus on the holiness of the worshippers. Thus the NRSV speaks of worshipping God in 'holy array', possibly referring to the garments of priests, and the NEB speaks of 'the splendour of holiness'. Both interpretations are possible, for not only is God's holiness beautiful, but so is a human life when it shows the holiness of seeking to serve and please God.

29:3-9 The Mighty God of Creation

One of God's attributes is his power, which is revealed in his creation. It may be that the writer of this psalm had just experienced a great thunderstorm. He describes it as having arisen over the sea, stirring up great waves (**29:3**). As it advanced over the land to the north of Palestine, it felled magnificent cedar trees (**29:5**, see 92:12; 104:16; Isa 2:13 for the way that people in Bible times thought of the great cedars of Lebanon). The high mountains of the Lebanon range, including Sirion (or Mount Hermon as it is better known – see Deut 3:9) seemed *to skip like a calf*, as in an earthquake (**29:6**). With thunder crashing and lightning flashing, the tempest swept down to the wilderness in the south and created a great dust storm (**29:8**).

The idea that the storm moves from north to south is based on the identification of Kadesh in 29:8 as the place by that name in the wilderness where Israel wandered (see Num 13:26). There were, however, other places with the same name in more northern parts of Palestine. The site in the south is preferred because the people of Israel remembered God's power revealed in the wilderness, particularly in the thunder, lightning and earthquake at Mount Sinai when the law was given (Exod 19:16-20).

Two very similar Hebrew words mean that **29:9** can be translated in two ways. The reference may be to the storm causing the boughs of the great oak trees to thrash in the wind, or it may be to the storm making the deer give birth before their time.

All of these effects are produced by *the voice of the Lord*, which is mentioned seven times in the psalm (29:3-5, 7-9). God's power can be known in all that he has created, from the mighty waters of the sea to the grandeur of the mountains. The raging wind, the thunder and lightning are like his voice speaking with immense power and signalling his presence.

In view of the NT reference to Jesus as the Word of God (John 1:1-3), it is worth noting that in 29:3, 5, 8 the Lord is described as doing what *the voice of the Lord* does.

29:10-11 Lord of Heaven and Earth

We can indeed be thankful that the 'voice of the Lord' not only tells of God's power but also speaks to us. The Hebrew people often thought of the God of creation, but they thought even more of the God of history and of God's actions all through their past history. Thus when God is described as *enthroned over the flood* (**29:10**), there may well be a reference to the great flood of Genesis 6–8, where God used the forces of nature in judgment. In fact, this is the only place in the Bible where the same Hebrew word for 'flood' is used. The forces of nature are always under God's control, as *the Lord is enthroned as King forever* (29:10). The same point may have been made with the reference to Kadesh in 29:8.

This psalm speaks of the voice of God being heard in the mighty things of creation, but he also speaks in quietness and stillness (1 Sam 3:1-14; 1 Kgs 19:11-18; Isa 30:15). He can rouse storms, and he can calm them (see Matt 8:23-27). He does this because his aim is not to terrify us with storms or earthquakes but to give us strength every day of our lives and to bless us with his peace (**29:11**).

Psalm 30: Experiences of Life

The heading of this psalm states, *For the dedication of the temple.* It seems that what began as a personal prayer in a time of great sickness came to be used as a national prayer. It was sung at the Feast of Dedication (referred to in John 10:22), which commemorated the rededication of the temple after it had been defiled by the enemies of the Jews in the second century BC. The nation had then been seriously sick and in danger of death, but had been restored and its enemies had not been allowed to triumph over it.

This psalm begins with praise of God for having answered the psalmist's prayer and healed him (30:1-3). The psalmist calls others to join him in thanking God (30:4-5), and then he tells his story (30:6-12). It is not a story that is unique to him, for King Hezekiah had a similar experience (Isa 38) and so have many Christians today. The psalm demonstrates the right attitude in facing trouble and difficulty, whether caused by our own errors and pride or caused by others. While reading it, we should also remember that the NT teaches that there are sufferings that Christians must endure in this life, but that these are small compared with the future glory for which we hope (Rom 8:18; 2 Cor 4:16-18).

30:1-3 Healing

The psalmist had been afraid that he would die and go down to the grave ('Sheol' and 'the Pit', mean death and the grave). His enemies would then boast that his trust in God had been useless (30:1; compare 13:2-4). But he had prayed to the Lord, and God had answered his prayer, restoring him to life. It had been like being lifted up out of a deep pit.

30:4-5 Praise

He summons his fellow believers to praise God, reminding them that for a moment it had seemed that God was angry, but that the Lord wants his grace and favour toward us to last for a lifetime (see also Isa 54:7-8). There is a night of weeping, of sorrow and distress when God seems far away, *but rejoicing comes in the morning.*

30:6-7 Overconfidence

The psalmist had felt that God had established him like a strong mountain (30:7). Such faith and confidence in God are good. But when difficulties are removed, confidence can easily become self-confidence, when a person boasts, *I shall never be shaken* (30:6). When we become self-confident and proud, we can easily fall. We lose the sense of God's presence and help and protection.

In the prayer of Aaron, God's blessing is spoken of as God making his face to shine on his people, being gracious to them and giving them peace (Num 6:24-26). The results of our sin and pride, on the other hand, are often spoken of as God hiding his face (as in 30:7; Isa 59:1-2). When the psalmist experienced that, he said, *I was dismayed* (30:7), or, as the GNB puts it, 'I was filled with fear'.

30:8-10 Prayer

When God seemed to hide his face, the psalmist knew that all he could do was repent and pray. It was earnest prayer,

no doubt in a spirit of repentance and humility: *To you, O Lord, I called; to the Lord I cried for mercy* (30:8). Unlike us, he knew of no hope of life beyond death, and thus he cried, *What gain is there in my destruction, in my going down into the pit? Will the dust praise you? Will it proclaim your faithfulness?* (30:9) He could only plead, as we must in our troubles, *Hear, O Lord, and be merciful to me; O Lord, be my help* (30:10). We have no other helper than God to turn to in such times.

30:11-12 Transformation

God heard that humble prayer. Though the psalmist had been sad and mourned, since God answered his prayer, he has been joyful and dancing (30:11). People in those days dressed themselves in sackcloth as a sign of mourning. Now, it is as if his mourning clothes have been removed and he is clothed with joy.

When we know the joy of answered prayer, we should make sure that we turn back to thank God. We should not be silent about it (30:12), but should tell others the great things the Lord has done. We should reflect on God's blessings, so that we can say what the psalmist says in 30:12, *O Lord my God, I will give you thanks forever.*

Psalm 31: Trusting Life into God's Hands

Many of the psalms are prayers to God spoken out of experiences of great trouble and difficulty. This one is the prayer of a servant of God who had to suffer because of his faithfulness to God's calling. It makes us think especially of the prophet Jeremiah, who was rejected by his own family because he faithfully preached God's word. There were plots to kill him. He so often proclaimed that there was 'terror on every side' (31:13) that he was given the nickname 'terror all around' (Jer 20:10). Jeremiah turned to God in faith and trust for the help that he needed (Jer 11:21; 12:6; 18:18; 20:1-13; 26:11; 38;1-6).

But this psalm also applies to other situations some of us are in today. It could be prayed by many who suffer from HIV/AIDS, especially those who have been infected by a spouse or by a blood transfusion. They too suffer physical wasting and may have to endure the undeserved scorn of friends and neighbours. They too need to take refuge in the Lord.

31:1-5 A Cry for Help

Facing trouble on every side, the psalmist took refuge in God (31:1, 4) whom he trusted to be his rock and refuge in the future (31:2). He begged God to lead and guide him for the sake of his name (31:3), that is, because of God's character. Only with God's help would he escape his enemies, who were like hunters setting nets to trap animals or birds (31:4).

His prayer surrendered all the uncertainties and difficulties of life into the hands of a loving and powerful God, as he prayed, *Into your hands I commit my spirit* (**31:5**). This was the last prayer on the lips of Jesus as he died on the cross (Luke 23:46), and countless Christians also have made it their dying prayer. So it should be, but it can also be our prayer every day we live.

31:6-8 A Statement of Faith

The psalmist makes it clear that God was the only one he trusted. Those who opposed him served *worthless idols* instead of the living God (**31:6**). They opposed all that he said and did, as those with worldly and immoral values will always oppose and ridicule those who follow Christ. (Note that some translations, such as the NRSV, interpret 31:6 as *You hate those who cling to worthless idols,* rather than *I hate.* Both versions give good meaning.)

Despite his suffering, the psalmist knew he was not alone, for God *saw my affliction and knew the anguish of my soul.* God had delivered him in the past and could be trusted to do so again, and so despite everything that has happened to him, the psalmist could still give thanks to God and rejoice in God's steadfast love (**31:7-8**).

31:9-18, 21b-22a Persecuted and Abandoned

We feel with the psalmist as he tells of the distress that his opponents cause him: *My eyes grow weak with sorrow, my soul and my body with grief. My life is consumed by anguish and my years by groaning; my strength fails because of my affliction, and my bones grow weak* (**31:9-10**, GNB). His sufferings included being treated with contempt by all his neighbours (**31:11a**). Even his friends were anxious to avoid association with him (**31:11b**). He is utterly alone, with no one standing by him, and both he and his beliefs are laughed at. He is regarded as no more important than a broken pot that could simply be thrown away (**31:12b**). He might as well have been dead for all the notice his friends and neighbours took of him (**31:12a**).

But he was not forgotten by his enemies, for he constantly heard the rumours they spread with *lying lips* and *with pride and contempt* for one who stood for what was right (**31:13a, 18**). They were the ones who deserved judgment, but he was the one who was suffering! (**31:17**). He knew that they were plotting to kill him (**31:13b**) and that he could easily fall into their hands (**31:15**). No wonder he felt like *a besieged city,* surrounded and attacked from all sides (31:21). There were times when his faith and trust failed, and God seemed far away. Thinking more of the power of his enemies than the power of God, he became alarmed and said, *I am cut off from your sight!* (31:22a).

31:19-24 Recovered Faith

When we are tempted to think like the psalmist, we need to also imitate him in remembering God's goodness (**31:19-20**). When he did this, he could reject his fear that God had left him and confidently claim *you heard my cry for mercy* (**31:22**). Faith is not just a matter of assurance for the future. It is remembrance of the past. It is constantly remembering and acknowledging God's deeds for us in the past and thanking him. Such remembrance strengthens faith and also pleases God. In our part of Africa, people say that a ruler will always give favour to those who acknowledge previous favours. Trust triumphs over fear and anxiety when we remember who God is and what he has done for us.

Reassured by this remembrance, the psalmist could say *You are my God* and acknowledge that *my times are in your hands* (31:14-15). He was sure that ultimately God was in control of whatever happened to him. He could also summon others to join him in trusting God. God will bring justice (31:23), and therefore the faithful can *be strong and take heart* (**31:23**). They are in no danger of ultimately being 'put to shame' (31:1).

Psalm 32: Sadness and Joy

This is the first of twelve psalms that are referred to as *Maskil.* The meaning of this word is not certain, but because it is linked with the verb that means 'understand' or 'be wise' it is thought that it may mean a psalm that is intended to teach, or one on which to meditate and be wise.

This psalm begins and ends with joy: *Blessed is he ... Blessed is he ...* (**32:1, 2**) and *Rejoice in the Lord and be glad, you righteous; sing, all you who are upright in heart!* (32:11). Other passages that also speak of the blessed life are 1:1; 2:12; 34:8; 41:1; 84:4-5, 94:12 and Matthew 5:3-11. This psalm sets out three cases in which sadness and sorrow are contrasted with true joy and happiness.

32:1-5 Sin and Forgiveness

A number of different words are used to describe sin in 32:1-2. It is a *transgression,* which means a rebellion against God. The word translated as *sin* means missing the mark, failing to reach the true goal in life. It is *iniquity* (RSV), that is, inner corruption. It is also *deceit,* something dishonest and insincere.

Someone who has realized his or her sin but has not turned from it cannot find peace of mind. They suffer distress, lose energy and feel as drained as one does in a hot dry summer (**32:3-4**). But what a change when that person does as the psalmist does in **32:5** and turns from all dishonesty, sincerely confesses the sin to God and repents of it! Then the transgression is *forgiven,* a word that implies that a burden is lifted. *Sins are covered* (32:1), so that the forgiving Lord sees them no more. The Lord no longer counts the wrongdoing against the sinner (32:2). Nothing brings greater peace and joy in life than knowing God's forgiveness.

The Apostle Paul quotes 32:1-2 in Romans 4:7-8 where he sets out the good news that God offers us forgiveness because of the sin-bearing sacrifice of Jesus Christ on the cross, so that our sins are covered and we are no longer considered guilty of them. The words of 1 John 1:8-9 are also relevant: 'If we claim to be without sin, we deceive ourselves and the truth is not in us. If we confess our sins, he is faithful and just and will forgive us our sins and purify us from all unrighteousness.'

32:6-7 Trial and Deliverance

Forgiveness is the gift of God that restores us to a right relationship with him and helps us to have the knowledge of his presence with us. Yet we are not promised that everything in life will be easy simply because we have God's forgiveness and acceptance. We need to establish our relationship with him now, in times when life is relatively peaceful (**32:6a;** Isaiah 55:6), before we face the storms of distress and difficulties that are like *the rush of mighty waters* threatening to overpower us (**32:6b,** NRSV).

Yet even in distress, we are not left sad and sorrowful. We can turn to God and he will be our *hiding place* (**32:7**). Trouble will not overwhelm us. Jesus told his disciples that they would face trials, but he also promised them, 'you will rejoice, and no one will take away your joy' (John 16:22). They could have this calm confidence because he had assured them, 'I have overcome the world' (John 16:33). Other passages that we can turn to for comfort in turbulent times include 18:16, 124:1-5, 144:7-8, Isaiah 43:1-2 and Romans 8:35-39.

32:8-11 Disobedience and Obedience

God offers us his guidance on how he wants us to live (**32:8**). We need to be careful to make sure that we are not *like the horse or the mule* (**32:9**). Mules have a reputation for being stubborn and unwilling to do what humans want, and horses require firm control with a *bit and bridle* otherwise they will do what they want rather than what the rider wants. We should not be like them but should have a willing spirit (51:12) that rejoices that God is willing to direct us. Our trust and obedience will prove the truth that *the Lord's unfailing love surrounds the man who trusts in him* (**32:10**).

By contrast, the wicked will have many troubles (32:10). It may sometimes seem that those who give God no place in their lives prosper (see Ps 73), but they lack the peace of mind and real happiness that belong to those who have been restored to a right relationship with God. In the NT, 1 Timothy 6:10 states that those who love the things of this world and wander away from God 'pierce themselves with many griefs' (see also 1:3-6).

There is joy when we allow God to instruct and teach us the way we should go (32:8). Those who want to be righteous and who truly desire to live an upright life can surely join the psalmist in saying, *Rejoice in the Lord and be glad, you righteous; sing, all you who are upright in heart!* (**32:11**).

Psalm 33: The Word and the Works of God

The first three verses as well as the last three of this psalm tell us what should be our attitude to God. In between, we are given four reasons for this attitude.

33:1-3 A Call to Praise God

We are called to use our voices (**33:1**) and instruments of music (**33:2**) in the worship of the Lord. We can rejoice in every *new song* composed to praise God (**33:3**), but our praise itself should also be new every day, as there are indeed always new reasons for praising and thanking him.

33:4-5 The Character of God

Five aspects of the character of God are revealed in all his words and works. He is right, true and faithful, and he loves righteousness and justice. The first three mean that he is utterly reliable (**33:4**). His love for *righteousness and justice* means that he always acts rightly and fairly – and expects us to do the same (**33:5a**). He does not practise favouritism. His *unfailing love* is shown in his kindness and goodness towards all creation. We are especially aware of this in relation to his human creation, but it fills the whole earth (**33:5b, 18, 22**).

33:6-9 God of Creation

The psalm says that the heavens were made *by the word of the Lord* (**33:6**), or, as a later verse put it, *he spoke, and it came to be* (**33:9**). That is how his creative work is described in Genesis 1:3: 'God said, "Let there be light," and there was light.' Again, in Genesis 1:9: 'God said, "Let the water under the sky be gathered to one place, and let dry ground appear." And it was so.' This is what the psalmist thinks of when he says that God *gathers the waters of the sea into jars* (**33:7**). Another translation could be that he gathers them 'as a heap', as when the water piled up so that the people of Israel were able to cross the Red Sea (Exod 15:8). God can gather up the waters of all the oceans as easily as we can fill a bottle. Isaiah speaks in similar terms when he says, 'Surely the nations are like a drop in a bucket' (Isa 40:15). When we realize God's greatness and our smallness, we should *fear the Lord*, not by being terrified and afraid of him, but with a sense of wonder and reverence (**33:8**). In our joy and celebration in Christian living, in our witness and worship, we should always remember how small and weak we are when compared to his greatness. We depend entirely on him for life itself and for all we have and are.

33:10-12 God of History

To us, the great nations in the world seem very powerful, but this is not how they appear to God. They may have *plans* and *purposes* (**33:10**), but the *plans* and *purposes* of the Lord are far greater (**33:11**). He brings their plans to nothing, but his own plans *stand firm forever.* History has often shown that nations that seem invincible are not. So it was with Egypt in the days of Moses (Exod 7–15), and with Assyria and Babylon in later generations (see Isaiah 37, 47). As nations, we should realize that there are more important things than economic wealth and military power. We need to get closer to God. *Blessed is the nation whose God is the Lord* (**33:12**).

Proverbs 19:21, Jeremiah 29:11-13 and 1 John 2:15-17 also speak of the plans of God and the will of God for our human lives. We need to reflect on how this teaching applies to God's people today, both individually and corporately.

33:13-19 Lord of All Humanity

God is enthroned as King over all (notice how 'all' is used three times in **33:13-15**). He made us – hearts and minds as well as bodies. He knows all our thoughts and observes all our deeds. He knows what we rely on most in life. In those days, the military strength of a people was in horses and chariots. Today a nation thinks of nuclear weapons, warplanes and tanks. But salvation is not found in any of these 'great' things (notice the word 'great' is used twice in **33:16-17**). They are not to be relied on, nor are they to be feared. The Lord watches over *those who fear him* (33:18). Those who hope *in his unfailing love* know that the living God, the Creator and Lord of all, is ultimately the only one who can *deliver them from death* (**33:19**).

33:20-22 An Attitude of Trust

Given God's character and power, the right attitude is for us to *wait in hope for the Lord,* to *rejoice* in him, and to *trust in his holy name.* Then we will find that *he is our help and shield* (**33:20-21**). When we thus rely on him, we will be able to pray with confidence, *May your unfailing love rest upon us, O Lord, even as we put our hope in you* (**33:22**).

Psalm 34: Praise, Encouragement And Teaching

Like some of the other psalms, this psalm is acrostic in form, with each of the verses beginning with a different letter of the Hebrew alphabet. The heading links it to the incident described in 1 Samuel 21:10-15, although the ruler's name there is given as Achish. It is likely that Abimelech, the name used in the psalm, was a royal title, for it means 'my father is king'.

This psalm is appropriate for use when a person proves the goodness of God in answering prayer for a special need.

34:1-7 Words of Praise

The psalmist is determined that all his life will be filled with thankfulness to God: *his praise shall always be on my lips* (**34:1**). Praise means *boasting in the Lord,* that is, not boasting in what we have or are, but in God who is the Source and Giver of every good gift (**34:2**; see 1 Cor 1:31). It also means that we *glorify the Lord* (**34:3**). We cannot, of course, make God any greater than he is, but we can show his greatness to other people. This is what Mary the mother of Jesus did when she spoke of glorifying the Lord (Luke 1:46). The Apostle Paul also said he wanted the Lord to be exalted by his life or his death (Phil 1:20). In this psalm, praise is offered especially because the Lord answers the prayers of all who turn to him (**34:4-5**). Those who look to him as the light of their lives are made *radiant* with his peace and joy (34:5, and see 2 Cor 3:18). It does not matter to him that we may be very poor (**34:6**), for God does not give special advantages to the rich and powerful. Rather he specially cares for those who honestly rely on him for their needs (**34:7**; see Isa 57:15).

A number of passages in the Bible speak of the angels of God protecting those who turn to God in their need and in times of danger (34:7; Gen 32:1-2; 2 Kgs 6:15-17; Ps 91:11; Matt 18:10). There are other passages that speak of a particular angel (Exod 14:19; Josh 5:13-15) or of a special manifestation of the presence of the Lord himself (see Isa 63:9).

34:8-14 Words of Encouragement

Because of the help that he has found in the Lord, the psalmist speaks words of encouragement to others, calling them to prove for themselves the goodness of the Lord by taking refuge in him (**34:8**) and trusting him to meet all their needs (**34:9-10**).

His good advice to people of every age and in every situation is quoted in 1 Pet 3:10-12. The question is, *Which of you desires life, and covets many days to enjoy good?* (**34:12** NRSV). In our hearts, we all do. Then what must we do to enjoy the good life? The answer is not to seek riches or power or popularity in the world. Rather we need to follow these four principles (**34:13-14**):

• Watch your words; do not speak what is evil or untrue.
• Forsake all that you know is evil in your life.
• Give yourself to doing good.
• Actively seek and pursue peace in your relationships with others, even when it is very difficult.

34:15-22 Words of Wisdom

Like many of the psalms and the book of Proverbs, this psalm shows that we must choose between two ways of life. God's attitude to us depends on the choice we make. If we choose to do what is right, we can be sure that his eyes are on us for good and his ears are open to our prayers (**34:15**).

We will still have troubles and we may be broken-hearted because of our failings or our disappointments (**34:17-18**); but he knows and understands, he is near to us and will deliver us from them. On the other hand, *the face of the Lord is against those who do evil* (**34:16**); *the foes of the righteous will be condemned* (**34:21**). All of us have done evil in many ways, but if we turn from evil, ask God's forgiveness and give ourselves to do what is right, then we can have confidence in God's mercy. In the closing words of the psalm, *no one will be condemned who takes refuge in him* (**34:22**).

Psalm 35: War on Injustice

This is one of those psalms (like Psalm 10) that pray for the overthrow of ungodly and evil people. If we live in a country where there is peace and where justice is given in the law courts, we should remember that, both in the days when the psalms were written and now, many people live in situations where they face violence for doing good and can find no justice in the courts. Even so, as we have seen in the study of earlier psalms, we should not simply pray for the defeat of all our enemies, but also that they may turn to God and come to live justly and with concern for others. So the psalm should lead us to ask not solely for the downfall of our human enemies but also for the victory of truth and justice in the world. It should also move us to pray for all who suffer under unjust and oppressive governments and for those who are persecuted for their faith.

In the three sections of this psalm, we see three ways in which people who reject God's ways are oppressive.

35:1-10 Seeking Evil rather than Good

Using the imagery of the weapons of warfare of those days, the psalmist prays that God would, as it were, take up his *spear and javelin* and his great defensive *shield* and come and fight on his behalf (**35:1-3a**). He wants to hear the Lord say, *I am your salvation* (**35:3b**). He feels that his opponents deserve only disgrace and shame (**35:4**) and that they should have the angel of God's judgment pursuing them along paths that are *dark and slippery* (**35:5-6**). He feels this way because the evil people have tried to catch him just as a hunter would try to catch a wild animal in a net or in a pit. He prays that they might be caught in their own net or in the pit they had dug (**35:7-8**). Then God would have the honour and deserve the praise of all who see him as able and willing to *rescue the poor from those too strong for them, the poor and needy from those who rob them* (**35:9-10**).

35:11-18 Returning Evil for Good

Not only did these enemies accuse the psalmist of wrongs of which he knew nothing (**35:11**), they had also repaid him evil for good (**35:12**). When they had been sick and in trouble, he had cared for them and prayed for them. He had

grieved over their difficulty, fasting and wearing sackcloth as people in mourning did in those days. He had treated them as close friends and brothers and had felt the same sympathy for their sorrows as he would have felt when grieving for the death of his own mother (**35:13-14**).

Yet when he encountered problems, these same people had not sympathized with him, but had rejoiced in his troubles and attacked him like lions (**35:15-17**). Like so many who endure long periods of persecution or physical sufferings, the psalmist is reduced to crying out, How long will this go on? (35:17 NRSV). The same question, 'How long will you allow this to continue? is also asked in 6:3: 74:10; 90:13-14; 94:2-3; Rev 6:10. In such circumstances, Christians have to turn to passages such as Hebrews 13:6-8, Romans 8:18 and 2 Corinthians 4:16-18.

All the psalmist can say is that when the Lord delivers him from them, he will give thanks to God at a time when all the people meet to worship in the temple (**35:18**).

35:19-28 Pretending that Evil can Win

The psalmist is confident that he has given his attackers no reason for their virulent hatred. This statement was certainly true of Jesus, who quoted this psalm in John 15:25. When we suffer at the hands of others, we need to take care to discern whether it is indeed without reason or whether they are treating us badly because of our own wrong actions or foolishness (1 Pet 2:19-25; 3:14-18).

The enemies of the psalmist were confident that they would win. Their words were *false accusations against those who live quietly in the land* (**35:20**). They claimed that they had seen things that would give them an advantage no one could take from them (**35:21**). They boasted, *We have swallowed him up* (**35:25**).

The psalmist responded with the assurance that God had seen all they were doing (**35:22a**). Although it seemed that God was taking no action, he prayed earnestly that his enemies would not continue to be able to rejoice over him (**35:22b-26**).

The praise that ends this section and the two earlier sections shows that the psalmist does not pray for and celebrate his victory over his enemies, but the triumph of God's righteousness and God's care and concern for those who rely on him: *May they always say, 'The Lord be exalted, who delights in the well-being of his servant'* (**35:27-28**).

Psalm 36: The End of the Way

The heading of this psalm refers to the same two collections as do many other psalms, that of *the director of music* and that *of David*. But this heading adds that David was *the servant of the Lord*, a description used of Moses and Joshua (Josh 1:1; 24:29) and of the prophets (Amos 3:7).

A number of the psalms (like Psalm 1) show us the difference between two ways, the way of the godly and that of the ungodly. This psalm begins with a picture of the way of the ungodly (36:1-4) and then has words of praise for the way of God (36:5-9). The closing verses (36:10-12) tell of the sad end of evildoers who have made great boasts for themselves.

36:1-4 The Ways of Sin

There are difficulties in translating the opening words of this psalm. The original Hebrew has 'my heart', so the NIV translates it as *An oracle is within my heart concerning the sinfulness of the wicked* (**36:1a**), meaning that what the psalmist has to proclaim is a word from the Lord. However, an ancient translation reads the Hebrew to mean 'their hearts', and thus the NRSV translates this as 'transgression speaks to the wicked deep in their hearts', meaning that *the wicked* choose to listen to the voice of evil rather than to the voice of God.

But all versions are in agreement that at the root of wickedness is the lack of *fear of God* (**36:1b**). Instead of having a respect for God, the wicked have an overwhelming respect for themselves, and proudly *flatter themselves* (**36:2**). The GNB translation is, 'Because he thinks so highly of himself, he thinks that God will not discover his sin and condemn it.' So they freely indulge in evil and deceit and *they have ceased to act wisely and do good* (**36:3**). Even at night, rather than resting or reflecting on God they spend their time planning evil against others (compare Mic 2:1).

36:5-9 The Ways of God

Like Paul in Romans 11:33-36, the psalmist struggles to find words to describe the love, faithfulness, righteousness and justice of God (**36:5-6**). They are as high as the heavens, or as a later psalm says, 'as the heavens are high above the earth, so great is his steadfast love toward those who fear him' (103:11). They are stronger and more enduring than the mighty mountains, deeper than the deepest sea. Because of what we know from our own experience if we have trusted in God, we can say, *How priceless is your steadfast love* (**36:7a**). God protects us and cares for us as a mother bird shelters her chicks (**36:7b**; see also Matt 23:37). A person who trusts in God may have many difficulties, but because of God's presence and love, the person may enjoy the peace of God. This is like having a feast of good things (**36:8a**). It is like having our need for water met by a mighty river or by a spring or fountain that never dries up (**36:8b-9a**; see also 46:4; Ezek 47:1-12; John 4:7-15; 7:37-39). It is like always having light on our path no matter how dark and stormy the night (**36:9b**; see also John 1:4-5, 8)

36:10-12 Conclusion

The psalm ends with two prayers and a confident statement. The prayers are that the Lord's people may always continue to know his steadfast love, and that they may be delivered from the evil that the proud and arrogant seek to do them. The psalmist securely states that those who continue to do evil and refuse to turn from their ways will be *thrust down, unable to rise* (**36:12**).

Psalm 37: The Test of Time

This psalm does not contain praise or prayer addressed to God. It is teaching addressed to all who will hear. To help them remember, it is written in the form of an alphabetic acrostic. In this psalm, each section is roughly two verses long. The material is presented like that in the book of Proverbs, with a number of separate thoughts loosely organized around a central theme.

37:1-8, 34 How to Live in the Present

The theme of this psalm is given in the opening words: *Don't be worried on account of the wicked* (37:1, GNB). When ungodly people seem to prosper, we are not to *fret*, or in other words, we are not to get hot with worry and anger (**37:1a, 8**). Such fretting and anger can easily lead to evil. Nor are we to copy or try to catch up with the kind of prosperity that ungodly people have (**37:1b**).

These are the positive things we should do: *Trust in the Lord, and do good* (**37:3**), *delight yourself in the Lord* (**37:4**), and *commit your way to the Lord* (**37:5**). What this means is that we are to pass the burdens that we feel to the Lord, thus leaving our worries with him (see 1 Pet 5:7). When we are *still before the Lord, and wait patiently for him* (**37:7**), we wait for him to act in his own way, for we can be sure he will. The psalmist returns to this theme in **37:34**, where we are again told to *wait for the Lord, and keep his way.*

37:9-15, 20-21, 32, 35-38 Future of the Wicked

In every age and in every land, there have been those who set out to harm others. They plot against those who try to live honest and upright lives (**37:12**). They use force to take advantage of the poor and needy (**37:14**). They crave money, and when others lend it to them they neither repay the loan nor share their own money with others in need (**37:21**). In the most extreme cases, they *lie in wait for the righteous, seeking their very lives* (**37:32**). They seem to be able to get away with doing what they like.

This psalm emphasizes that ultimately power is not in the hands of the wicked. God is a God of justice. He is able to bring down those who do evil. The wicked may seem very strong and secure, standing firm like a mighty tree (**37:35**), but *like the grass they will soon wither* (**37:2**) and vanish away like smoke (**37:10, 20, 36**). God's timing may not be the same as ours, and his way of acting may not be as we might expect or hope, but we can be completely sure that the evil will not triumph in the end. The time is coming when power and life itself will be taken from those who do evil. They may now laugh at those who seek to live godly and upright lives, but *the Lord laughs at the wicked, for he knows their day is coming* (**37:13**). They have no hope for the future (**37:9**, 10). In fact, *the future of the wicked will be cut off* (**37:38**). This contrasts with the promise in the previous verse that *there is a future for the man of peace* (**37:37**).

37:16-19, 22-33, 39-40 Future of the Righteous

In contrast to the lies and plots of the wicked, *the mouth of the righteous man utters wisdom, and his tongue speaks what is just* (**37:30**). However, those who seek to live righteous lives will not be saved from all troubles in this life. The psalm makes this clear, but it also makes clear that they will never be forsaken by God (**37:17-19, 25, 28, 33**). They may be wrongly accused by others, but as surely as day follows night, they will be upheld (**37:6**). They may stumble, but they will not fall, because the Lord holds them by the hand (**37:23-24, 31**). He will be their refuge and will save and rescue them (**37:39-40**).

Many times this psalm speaks of the righteous inheriting the land (**37:9**, **11**, **22**, **29**; see also 7, **27**, 34). For Israel in oт days this meant that God would uphold them as a nation and keep them in their land if they trusted in him and sought to obey his commandments. Jesus, however, took up the words of **37:11** and said to his disciples, 'Blessed are the meek, for they will inherit the earth' (Matt 5:5). What does this mean? Rich and powerful and ungodly people seem to have the greatest possessions in the world. But do they really enjoy God's gifts with peace and contentment as they live their selfish lives? Those who are content with what they have and who know the presence of God with them are the ones who really enjoy all the gifts of God and their inheritance on the earth. For them **37:16** is true (see also Phil 4:11-13; 1 Tim 6:6).

Psalm 38: A Sinner's Prayer

The heading of this psalm is *A petition*. The Hebrew can literally be translated as 'to bring to remembrance'. The meaning may be that the psalmist is bringing his trouble to God's remembrance. Prayer is sometimes described in this way in the Bible.

38:1-14 The Suffering Brought by Sin

Many of the psalms are prayers of people who have tried to live uprightly but have found that others have taken advantage of them, opposed them and oppressed them. So they prayed and asked the Lord to defend their just cause. Other psalms, such as this one (and 6, 32, 51, 102, 130, 143), are prayers of those who realize their failure and sin, and the trouble and suffering it has caused them. While it is clear from the teaching of Jesus in John 9:1-5 that not all suffering is the direct result of someone's sin, there are cases where suffering is directly caused by people's wrongdoing or foolishness. But whatever the cause of suffering, God can use it to bring us closer to himself (1 Pet 1:3-7; Heb 12:3-11

The psalmist brings three dimensions of his trouble God.

38:1, 4, 10 The Guilt of Sin

The psalmist realizes that he deserves only the righteous anger and wrath of God (**38:1**). His guilt for what he has done is like a flood of water that goes over his head (see also 69:1-2, 15), or like a burden too heavy for him to carry (**38:4**). All his joy has gone from him and there is no light in his eyes (**38:10**).

38:2-3, 5-8, 17 Physical Suffering

His sin has resulted in God's punishment, which he describes as like *arrows* or like God's hand resting heavily on him (**38:2**). His physical suffering is taken as God's punishment for his sin (**38:3**). We do not know exactly what disease he was suffering from, but it was something very unpleasant that left his bones and flesh pitifully weak (**38:3**). He was a mass of foul festering wounds (**38:5**). He felt crushed and broken and his body was full of pain (**38:6, 17**). The word used for *wounds* in **38:11** may mean that he suffered from leprosy, which would explain why people kept away from him. Another suggestion derives from his words in **38:7**, which the NIV translates as *my back is filled with searing pain*. However, this can also be translated, 'my loins are filled with burning' (NRSV). Taken with his words that he is suffering because of his *sinful folly* (38:5), this symptom may suggest that he was suffering from a sexually transmitted disease. Whether or not this interpretation is correct, there can be no doubt that many people do suffer in their bodies because of the misuse of drugs or alcohol or because of sexual immorality.

38:9, 11-16 Other People's Attitudes

Perhaps because of the nature of his disease, friends and neighbours kept away from him (38:11). Enemies took advantage of his suffering and depression (**38:12**). He felt powerless to defend himself against their plots and attacks (**38:13-14**). He knew he had done wrong, but now he was suffering at the hands of those to whom he had done good (**38:20**).

38:9, 15-22 The Remedy for Sin

Fortunately the psalmist knew the one way to deal with all his troubles, the way of true repentance and prayer.

- He told God exactly how he felt, realizing that God knew all his sorrow and the longing of his heart (**38:9**).

- He addressed the Lord as *my God* (**38:15**), confident that he would answer prayer in his own time and way.
- He made no attempt to defend himself from the hurts that others caused him (38:13-14). He just told God about them (38:12, 16, 19, 20).
- He expressed genuine sorrow for his sin and asked for forgiveness (**38:18**).

The last two verses sum up the earnest prayer of the psalm. The one who prays knows that he does not deserve the help of the Lord, but only his righteous anger (38:1). Yet he cries out, *O Lord, my salvation*, and throws himself on God's mercy. He pleads that the Lord will not *forsake* him (**38:21**), or be far from him, but will come quickly to help him (**38:22**). That can always be the sinner's prayer. Once we have prayed it, we can rejoice in the promise of God's forgiveness, for 'If we claim to be without sin, we deceive ourselves and the truth is not in us. If we confess our sins, he is faithful and just and will forgive us our sins and purify us from all unrighteousness' (1 John 1:8-9).

Psalm 39: Life Is Short

The *Jeduthun* mentioned in the heading of this psalm is probably the person referred to in Chronicles as sharing responsibility for the music in the temple (1 Chr 16:41-42; 25:1; 2 Chr 5:12.

39:1-4 A Time of Silence

When a family member or close friend dies, or when we ourselves face serious illness, we begin to think of the uncertainty and shortness of life. The writer of this psalm seems to have been faced with a life-threatening illness. His attitude can be compared with that of King Hezekiah when he faced a similar situation (Isaiah 38). The psalmist was puzzled as he struggled to understand the purposes of God. He decided not to speak of his questions or his complaints about the ways of God, so as not to give wicked people an opportunity to criticize or raise their voices against God (**39:1**). Yet his worries distressed him more and more and came to be like a fire burning inside him (**39:2-3**). At last he felt that the time for silence was over and that he must speak (see also Eccl 3:7), but wisely his words were words of prayer addressed to God.

39:4-6 The Shortness of Life

He asks God: *Show me, O Lord, my life's end and the number of my days* (39:3). He is not wanting to know exactly how long he has to live. What he wants is to understand the reality of the shortness of life (see also 90:12). James 4:14 makes the same point as **39:5**, when it says, 'Why, you do not even know what will happen tomorrow. What is your life? You are a mist that appears for a little while and then vanishes.' People rush here and there, but what do they gain for all their effort? Wealth and many possessions – but no matter how much they accumulate, they cannot predict what will happen to it after they die (**39:6**; see also Matt 6:19-21; Luke 12:13-21).

What do I look for? the psalmist asks (**39:7**). In what can he have confidence? He knows he must answer that his hope is in God, the only one who never changes, who can always be trusted, and who will never leave those who trust him.

39:7-13 The Failures in Life

Although the psalmist says his only hope is in God, he recognizes that he has no right to demand favour from God. So he does not complain or protest, but remains silent in the face of what God is doing and has done (**39:9**), accepting that God must be chastising him for some wrong he has committed (39:10-11). Yet he does make three requests. First, he asks that God will forgive him – *save me from all my transgressions* (**39:8a**). Second, he prays that he may not be laughed at by fools who take no notice of God (**39:8b**). Finally, he asks that in mercy God will remove from him the suffering he deserves (**39:10**), even if it is only a temporary relief before his short life comes to an end (**39:13**). The earnestness with which he turns to God is shown by the references in **39:12** to his *prayer,* his *cry for help* and his *weeping.*

We can learn a great deal from this psalm's emphasis on the shortness of life and the fact that we are just aliens and strangers, or *passing guests* as the NRSV puts it, in this world. Yet because of 'our Saviour, Christ Jesus, who has destroyed death and has brought life and immortality to light through the gospel' (2 Tim 1:11), we do not need to share this psalmist's pessimism as he thinks of departing to be no more (39:13).

Psalm 40: The Pilgrimage of Faith

The short Psalm 70 is almost identical with 40:13-17. It could be that the writer of Psalm 40 used Psalm 70 as a model, but it seems more likely that at some stage this prayer from the psalm was used separately from the other verses.

Many psalms begin with earnest prayer in a situation of great difficulty and end with thanksgiving that God has heard the prayer and given help and deliverance. This psalm begins with the experience of deliverance and goes on to earnest prayer for help in the face of many evils and iniquities. That order is true to life. We may experience great blessings from God, but we still have to face life's day-to-day problems and our own weaknesses and failures. We can say that this psalm shows us six aspects of life as a pilgrimage of faith.

40:1-3 Salvation

Life had been like being in a *slimy pit.* This may be because of illness, or depression and discouragement, or failure and wrongdoing. But those who turn to the Lord in prayer find that he hears and lifts them out and, as it were, sets their *feet on a rock* (**40:1-2**). Given new life, they have a *new song* of praise to sing (**40:3a**). Moreover, others see what God has done for those who depend on him, have a sense of awe and wonder, and are helped to trust in the Lord for their own deliverance (**40:3b**).

40:4-5 Commitment

People who find God's saving help can say confidently, *Blessed is the man who makes the Lord his trust* (**40:4a**). And if people are committed to the Lord, it means they do not *turn aside to false gods* (**40:4b**). They can rejoice in the great things that God has done, more than could ever be counted. They can be grateful for his thoughts and loving purposes for his people. The NRSV translates **40:5** as *None can compare with you,* expressing the feelings of someone who has proved the goodness of God.

40:6-8 Obedience

The OT speaks of the offerings and sacrifices the Hebrew people brought to God as part of their worship. But this psalm says what the prophets often said, that such sacrifices are of no value without true obedience to the Lord (**40:6a**; see also 1 Sam 15:22; Isa 1:11-17; Jer 7:21-23; Hos 6:6; Amos 5:21-24; Mic 6:6-8).

What the Lord seeks of us all is an open ear to hear his word. The words *my ears you have pierced* (**40:6b**) can be translated literally, 'ears you have dug for me'. Some people have understood this to be related to the ceremony described in Exodus 21:1-6 by which a person agreed to be a slave for the rest of his or her life. However, it is more likely that it refers to God making our ears hear, and seeking ears that are open to hear his voice (see Isa 50:4-5).

If we do hear his voice, we will recognize that his words *in the scroll* apply directly to each of us (**40:7**). The scroll referred to here could be either a scroll containing all or part of God's law, or the book of the covenant that was given to a king when he was anointed (see 2 Kgs 11:12; Ps 132:12). However, the writer of Hebrews sees the words *it is written about me in the scroll* as applying ultimately to Jesus Christ (Heb 10:4-10). In quoting these verses from Psalm 40, he uses the ancient Greek translation of the OT, in which the words 'my ears you have pierced' are translated as 'a body you have prepared for me' – a translation that applies even more specifically to the incarnate Christ.

When we take God's word seriously so that it moves from the scroll into our hearts, then we will say, *I desire to do your will, O my God* (**40:8**), and we will act on our words. In short, it is not enough to hear God's word, sing our hymns and recite our creeds. It is important that we put the word of God into practice (Jas 2:18-26).

40:9-10 Witness

People who have proved the goodness of God and want to serve and obey his will also want to tell others about what he has done in the *great assembly* (**40:9**), where those who seek to worship the Lord will be encouraged. Notice the words in these verses that we often find relating to God in the psalms: *righteousness ... faithfulness ... salvation ... love.* God's work and God's purposes are such good news that they should not be hidden from others.

40:11-15 Opposition

Even when we have known the steadfast love and saving help of God, life does not proceed smoothly. Job rightly said, 'man is born to trouble, as surely as sparks fly upward' (Job 5:7). We may encounter three types of problems: *troubles* in the sense of trials and difficulties and sufferings (**40:12a**), *sins* that are our own wrongdoings (**40:12b**), and the opposition of those who try to hurt us or laugh at us (**40:14-15**). Sometimes these troubles seem to be more in number than the hairs of our head (**40:12c**). Our heart sinks within us, and we can no longer think clearly (**40:12d**). At such times our prayer could be, *Be pleased, O Lord, to save me; O Lord, come quickly to help me* (**40:13**).

40:16-17 God-centred Living

The psalm ends with a confession of weakness and distress, *I am poor and needy* (**40:17**), but also with the prayer, *may the Lord think of me,* and the assurance that he will again prove to be a *help* and a *deliverer.* For those who live a God-centred life, prayer for help and joyful praise are never far apart. Let us say continually, *The Lord be exalted!* (**40:16**).

Psalm 41: Healing, Forgiveness and Protection

There are three parts of this psalm that fit under the headings of promise, prayer and praise.

41:1-3 Promise

Those who show concern for the poor are here called *blessed* by God (**41:1**), as they are in such NT passages as Matthew 5:7 and 25:31-46 (for further comments on Christian care for the needy, see Acts 2:44-47; 4:32-37; 6:1-6; Jas 1:27; 1 John 3:16-18). Protection, deliverance in trouble and support in sickness are promised to them (**41:2-3**). We need not take this to mean that they are promised a life free from trouble. The psalms, as well as other Scripture and human experience, show that this is not the case. But the promise means that whatever difficulties they face, they will know the presence of the Lord and his care for them. Hebrews 6:10 says, 'God is not unjust; he will not forget your work and the love you have shown him as you have helped his people and continue to help them.' Hebrews 2:14-15 and 1 John 4:4 also remind us that God is greater than the forces of evil that confront us.

41:4-10 Prayer

The psalmist cannot say he is without sin or that he deserves God's favour and goodness. He can only ask God to be *merciful* to him (**41:4**), heal him and forgive. At the same time he has enemies who are trying to harm him without cause. They want evil to happen to him. They want him to die and his name to be forgotten (**41:5**). Those who visit him in his sickness *speak falsely* (**41:6**) while they are with him and then whisper evil things about him after they have left (**41:7**). What is spoken of in **41:8** as *a vile disease* can also be translated as a *deadly thing* that has *fastened* on him (see NRSV). The words may reflect the suspicion that his enemies have been using witchcraft against him.

What he found hardest of all to bear was that a close friend, whom he had even welcomed to eat at his table, had turned against him (**41:9**). David may have been thinking of his betrayal by his trusted counsellor, Ahithophel, who joined Absalom's rebellion against his father (see 2 Sam 15–17). Jesus too experienced such betrayal, and he quotes this verse in John 13:18.

Many of us too have faced sickness, the unfaithfulness of friends, the desertion of relatives, and fear of the forces of evil. Prayer is the only way to face these difficulties. How true are the words of the hymn, 'What a friend we have in Jesus!' (see Matt 11:28).

However, there is one part of the psalmist's prayer that we cannot pray. The words *raise me up, that I may repay them* (**41:10**) express a desire for personal vengeance, and we must realize that the way that we learn in Jesus Christ is a higher way. We are to leave justice for God to bring about, and are taught to forgive, love and pray for our enemies. But we also need to remember that in OT times, the ruler was responsible for seeing that those who sought to harm others were brought to justice. That may have been the psalmist's concern. What we should always remember is that we know a judge whose justice never errs and whose mercy and love never fail.

41:11-13 Praise

After he had prayed, the psalmist may have been given an assurance that his prayer would be answered (as Hannah was in 1 Sam 1:9-18). He may have experienced the answer. At least he could say with confidence that God had not allowed his enemies to triumph over him. When he speaks of his *integrity* (**41:12**), he does not mean that he is sinless (41:4 shows that). Yet he had been sincere in his desire to do what was right, to care for those in need, and to

serve God. The greatest blessing we can ask of God is to be upheld by him, and to be in his presence for ever (41:12).

The psalm closes with great words of praise like those that conclude each of the books of the Psalms (**41:13**; see 72:19; 89:52; 106:48). We should also note that 'Amen' is not just a word to be said easily at the end of a prayer. It is a strong statement like saying, 'yes, this is indeed true', 'I agree completely', or 'so be it'.

BOOK TWO: PSALMS 42–72

Psalms 42-43: The Way of Encouragement

Psalms 42 and 43 were probably one psalm originally, for there is no heading to Psalm 43, and we have the same refrain or chorus in 42:5, 42:11 and 43:5. The theme and situation of the writer also seem to be the same in both psalms.

Psalm 42 (like Psalm 32 and eleven others) is called a *maskil*. The exact meaning of this word is not certain, but because it is linked with the verb that means 'understand' or 'be wise', it may mean that this psalm is intended to teach, or one on which to meditate to be wise. The heading of the psalm also mentions *the Sons of Korah,* who were responsible for 'the service of song' in the temple (1 Chr 6:22, 31-48).

This psalm was written by someone who felt great loneliness and depression. As such, it summons us to identify those in our community who feel this way, and to take action on our own and along with our families and churches to help them.

42:3-4, 6-7, 9-10 Discouragement

The psalmist felt lonely and disheartened because he was far away from his home and his place of worship. He had loved the worship of the temple in Jerusalem and being with the crowds who came to praise God. He had led their processions and dances, especially during the great festivals (**42:4**). Now he is far away near Mount Mizar (**42:6**). We do not know exactly which mountain he is speaking of, but it was somewhere near Mount Hermon in the north of Palestine, where the river Jordan begins its course. When the rains came and the water poured down the Jordan River, he realized the great power of the water in the *roar of your waterfalls* (**42:7a**). He thought of the even greater power of the water of the deep ocean, and his troubles seemed like the waves of the sea rolling over him. He was powerless under them and his life was in great danger (**42:7b**). The situation seemed hopeless.

Worst of all, the people around him laughed at him for his trust in God (**42:3**). It certainly seemed that not only was Jerusalem far away, but God was far away and had forgotten him. When people said to him, *Where is your God?* it was like being struck and wounded in his body (**42:10**).

42:1-2, 5, 8, 11, 43:5 Encouragement

But the psalmist did not allow hopelessness to destroy his faith altogether. Deep in his heart he was sure that God could not change. God could not fail. He is the *living God* (**42:2**). The psalmist could speak of him as *my stronghold* (43:2) and as *my Saviour and my God* (42:5). He recalled his past experiences of God and how he had felt the presence of God in the temple (42:4). Why should he not know the presence of God somewhere else? In the past God had often shown his steadfast love, as the psalmist remembers when he says *the Lord directs his love, at night his song is with me* (**42:8**). So in the quietness of the night, when people are tempted to worry about the things of the day, he reminded himself of God's mercies to him in the past. In this way his worry was turned into praise and prayer. Of course, his words do not mean that God only answers prayers made in the night or at some special hour of the day or night. When one thinks of God's mercies and prays at any time, faith is revived.

The psalmist rebukes his drooping spirits, plucks up his courage, and addresses himself, *Why are you downcast, O my soul? Why so disturbed within me?* And he gives himself the answer: *Put your hope in God and I will yet praise him, my Saviour and my God* (**42:5, 11;** 43:5). Like a thirsty animal longs for streams of water, so he could truly say that he longed for God (42:2; see also Jer 2:13 and 17:13).

Problems and difficulties in life have a way of driving us back to God, and they help us to reorder our priorities and to see that the only thing that really matters in life is to be pleasing God at all times. So here, as a result of his problems, the psalmist concluded that to enjoy God's presence was what mattered to him more than anything else in life (42:1-2; compare 63:1; 143:6). For the person of faith, difficulties and problems are blessings in disguise.

43:1-5 The Power of Prayer

In most of Psalm 42 the writer is either talking about himself and his discouragements, or he is talking to himself about the way he should trust in God. In Psalm 43 he prays directly to God. He tells God about the people who were laughing at him, an *ungodly nation* made up of *deceitful and wicked men* and begs God, *vindicate me* and *rescue me* (**43:1**). He tells the Lord, *You are God my stronghold* (**43:2**) and asks for God's light to guide him and his truth to teach him (**43:3a**). His highest hope and the most important goal in life is to get back to God's *holy mountain* (**43:3b**), that is, to the temple in Jerusalem, and so to *the altar of God* where sacrifices were brought and worship offered (**43:4**).

As Christians, we should have a similar burning desire to worship God together with our fellow-Christians. However, we are not dependent on a place or a building to be able to worship God. Jesus told the Samaritan woman at the well, 'a time is coming when you will worship the Father neither on this mountain nor in Jerusalem' (John 4:21). What God does seek is 'worship in spirit and in truth' (John 4:23). Thus prayer is still the way for us, as it was for the psalmist. When we pray in faith and according to God's will, we can repeatedly remind ourselves, 'Put your hope in God, for I will yet praise him, my Saviour and my God'. Furthermore, when we learn to remember God's mercies in the past, we will stop panicking when we face new problems and challenges, and will start praying and praising God in hope. And we will find increasingly that our difficulties draw us closer to our loving and unchanging God.

Psalm 44: The Cry of a Besieged Nation

The heading of this psalm is almost identical to that of Psalm 42.

Many of the psalms tell of the deeply personal experiences of those who wrote them. Others, like this one, speak about the experiences of the nation. Israel was facing difficulty and defeat that the Israelites found hard to understand, because they knew what God had done for his people in the past and what he had promised for the future. The spiritual problem raised by the suffering of a godly person, which Job wrestled with, was now faced by the nation.

Much of this psalm uses 'we' and 'us' and speaks for the whole nation, but 44:4-6 and 15-16 have 'I' and 'me'. Perhaps one person led in those parts of the prayer and then others joined in the rest.

44:1-3 What God Had Done in the Past

It was the duty of all Hebrew parents to pass on to their children the story of what God had done for them in the past (see Exod 12:25-27; 13:7-10; Deut 6:20-25; Joshua 4:5-7). Christian parents are under a similar obligation to teach their children and pass on the faith to them. This is a special challenge to parents in these days when children listen to peer groups rather than parents. Yet we must not give up. Because of his parents' faithfulness, the psalmist could say, *We have heard with our ears, O God; our fathers have told us* (**44:1**).

What he had heard was how God had given them the land and made it possible for them to possess it. Their ancestors had been people who were like a fruit-bearing vine planted in good soil (**44:2**; see 80:8-11; Isa 5:1-4). It was not because of their military power that they had been successful. It was because of God's power helping them, and God's loving purpose for them (**44:3**).

44:4-8 Trust Learned from the Past

Because they knew the great things that God had done for them in the past, they could say, *You are my King and my God* (**44:4**). God had given victories in the past, and so they could expect him to help them to overcome all the enemies who threatened them in the future (**44:5**). They had learned that they should not trust in military power: *I do not trust in my bow, my sword does not bring me victory* (**44:6**). They knew that the Lord was always willing and able to save them, and so they boasted in him, saying, *we will praise your name forever* (**44:7-8**).

Yes, faith comes from remembering God's past blessings. But God has no grandchildren. Saving faith has to be a first-hand experience. While hearing of other people's experiences may help us learn to trust God, it is our own experience of God that will help us in the day of trouble. We need to make sure that our faith is not second-hand.

At the end of 44:8, we find the word *Selah*. This may originally have indicated a pause, perhaps to allow people to think about the meaning of the words while musical instruments played.

44:9-26 The Problems of the Present

The people could learn lessons of trust in God from the past, but it was the present that was a problem to them. It seemed now that God was not acting for them as he had done in the past. He had gone out with their armies then, but not now (**44:9**). Now they were defeated by their enemies and terribly humbled (**44:10**). They were like sheep taken to be slaughtered for meat (**44:11**). They were like people sold as slaves – and so little valued that they did not even fetch a high price (**44:12**). The surrounding nations laughed at them (**44:13-16**). Their towns and villages were ruined and made places where only jackals would live (**44:19**). Jackals are wild animals that live away from places inhabited by humans. Another translation of this verse could be, 'you left us helpless among wild animals; you abandoned us in deepest darkness' (GNB).

The law told them that if they did not keep true to God's covenant, they would suffer defeat and be scattered far and wide (see Deut 28:32-37), as happened at the time of the fall of Jerusalem and the exile of the people to Babylon in 587 BC. But at this time this psalmist felt that they had not turned aside from the covenant and served other gods (**44:17-18, 20-21**). They felt that God had no good reason to make them suffer and die on his behalf (**44:22**).

King Hezekiah had faced a similar situation (Isa 36–37). So did the Jews in the second century BC, when their faith was under severe attack. So did the early Christians. Paul quotes 44:22 in Romans 8:36, a passage that gives great comfort to those who are suffering great persecution.

The psalmist found no satisfying answer to his question. He could only pray. Though the faith of his people was

in a God who 'will neither slumber nor sleep' (121:4), it seemed to him that God was sleeping, that his face was hidden from them instead of being turned towards them in blessing (**44:23-24**). It seemed that God had forgotten the trouble they were in. Yet the psalmist kept on praying, *rise up and help us* (**44:26**). *Redeem us*, he pleaded, *because of your unfailing love*.

Although things happened that the psalmist could not understand, he knew from all the experiences of the past that *unfailing love* was so much part of God's nature that he would not finally abandon them. There are two special lessons for us here:

- When we meet problems in our lives or in the lives of others, we should not be too quick to jump to conclusions. Sometimes the wicked may prosper for a while (see Ps 73). Prosperity is not always a sign of godliness, nor is suffering always evidence of sin.
- When problems come our way, we should take time to meditate on the Lord, on his word and his ways, and in the attitude of prayer, to know God's will about the situation. This is what the psalmist did. Psalm 37:7 puts it 'Be still before the Lord, and wait patiently for him'. 'Be still, and know that I am God!' (46:10).

Psalm 45: The Marriage of a King

The heading of the psalm is similar to the headings of earlier psalms. *Lilies* seems to be the name of the tune to which it was sung (as were also Pss 69 and 80). It is understandable that a marriage should be celebrated with a love song.

Marriage customs differ from society to society, with some customs being compatible with a truly biblical and Christian understanding of marriage, while others are not. Christians may have to make difficult decisions when there are conflicts between cultural practices and biblical revelation. However, one thing that is a constant across cultures is that marriage is a time of celebration.

45:1-9, 12-16 The Setting

The writer of this psalm rejoiced as he found words to celebrate the marriage of the king (**45:1**). We do not know which king of Israel it was, but he is described as richly blessed by God. He was *handsome* (NRSV) in appearance and spoke words of grace and kindness (**45:2**). Like all kings at that time, he was ready to fight, but his battles were in the cause of truth and justice (**45:3-5**). Similarly, his *sceptre*, the rod or staff that was the symbol of his authority, was wielded with justice (**45:6**).

The OT often emphasizes the responsibility of rulers in Israel to uphold justice and defend the cause of the poor and oppressed (see Deut 17:18-20; Isa 1:23) – a challenge to political leaders today, and to the church to be faithful to its prophetic ministry. And just as the king had to be ready to fight if called upon to do so, the Christian has to be prepared to fight spiritual battles (Eph 6:10-20) and battle for social justice (Amos 5:24).

On the wedding day the fragrance of beautiful perfume, *myrrh and aloes and cassia* (**45:8**), and the loveliness of music added to the joy of the celebration. Daughters of kings of other nations were among the bridal attendants (**45:9**), and gifts were brought from near and far (**45:12**). The bride was arrayed in robes *interwoven with gold* and *embroidered garments* (**45:13-14**). *With joy and gladness* she and her companions *enter the palace of the king* (**45:15**).

The psalmist predicts that the king and his bride will produce sons who will continue their noble family line into the future (**45:16**). The marriage of a king could influence the whole nation and its life for generations to come, as is well illustrated by the story of Solomon.

45:10-11 Advice for Marriage

While the marriage described in this psalm is a royal one, every marriage is a special time of joy and celebration. However, marriage should not be entered into lightly. It should always be preceded by the counselling and good teaching vital for those choosing a wife or husband and preparing for marriage.

The reason this is necessary is that marriage links two lives, two families, and two communities and marks a new beginning. Genesis 2:24 speaks of a man leaving his father and mother and coming to cleave to his wife. In this psalm, the same principle applies to the bride, for she is instructed to forget her people and her father's house (**45:10**). The past is left behind, and the link with parents and the extended family cannot be the same as before (45:16). Responsible care for the extended family, especially aged parents and other needy persons in the family, is not to be neglected (see Matt 15:3-6), but the thought must be for the future, as a new family unit is established (see the marriage blessings of Gen 24:60 and Ruth 4:11-12).

Happy is the husband who can rejoice in the God-given beauty of his wife (**45:11a**), but Proverbs 31:30 says something important about true beauty. As the Igbo (Nigeria) put it, *agwa bu mma* ['true beauty is in a person's character']. Similarly, happy is the wife who not only has a 'most excellent' (45:2) and well-spoken husband, but one whom she can respect for his striving for truth and justice, for his love of righteousness and hatred of wickedness (**45:11b**; 45:7). It takes more than physical beauty or material wealth to make a happy marriage (see Prov 19:14).

45:6-7, 17 The Messiah

The words of **45:17**, *the nations will praise you for ever and ever,* cannot ever fully apply to any earthly king in Israel. Nor could any of those kings truly live up to the description in this psalm. The Jewish people therefore came to hope

that its words would be fulfilled in their expected Messiah. In a similar way, they took the words to the king in Psalm 2:7, 'You are my Son; today I have become your Father' as also applying to the Messiah.

Christians came to see that verses and passages such as **45:6-7** were fulfilled in Jesus (see Heb 1:8-9). Certainly no one has loved righteousness and hated wickedness like him. No one rules and acts in perfect truth and justice as he does.

There are various translations of 45:6. The NEB has 'your throne is like God's throne', the NJB 'your throne is from God', and the GNB speaks of 'the kingdom that God has given you'. The NIV translates the verse as *Your throne, O God,* which sounds odd when addressed to the king. But the word here translated 'God' (Hebrew *Elohim*) can be used of human beings in special positions (as John 10:34-35 shows). However, when it is applied to Jesus, it receives its fullest meaning, as he is uniquely 'Emmanuel, God with us.' God has indeed rewarded him for his love of justice and hatred of wickedness by setting him *above [his] companions* (Phil 2:9-11).

The words of the psalm gain added resonance when we remember that the NT speaks of the church as the bride of Christ (Eph 5:23-32; 2 Cor 11:2), and compares the final union of Christ and his church in heaven to a wedding (Rev 19:6-9; 21:2; 22:17).

Psalm 46: Our Refuge and Strength

The unusual element in the heading to this psalm is *According to alamoth.* The same expression is found in 1 Chronicles 15:20. It may indicate that this psalm was to be sung by young women.

In both 46:7 and 11, the word *Selah* marks a pause to reflect after the chorus, 'The Lord Almighty is with us; the God of Jacob is our fortress.' It is possible that this chorus was once sung after 46:3 as well. Certainly, the chorus is a great statement of faith that sums up the message of the psalm.

The people of Palestine in OT days were often oppressed by fear of two things: the forces of nature and the forces of foreign nations. Prophets and psalmists showed them the way to overcome fear: faith in the living God. This is also the way in which we must overcome our own fears of the powers of evil, the forces of nature, or the actions of others.

46:1-5 The Forces of Nature

Few things are more frightening than an earthquake. It is terrifying to feel that the ground beneath one's feet is no longer secure. The earth trembles and the mountains shake (**46:2b**). The Jewish people were not seafarers but were greatly afraid of the sea, with its roaring and foaming waters (**46:3**). Yet in the face of all these things, when they trusted in God they could say, *we will not fear* (**46:1-2a**). What an encouragement that is still! Some problems we face are familiar and commonplace. Others are different from anything we have experienced. But this psalm assures us that our unchanging God is greater than any problem we face now or may face tomorrow (see Heb 13:6, 8).

The Israelites relying on God could indeed feel that their city was *the city of God* (see also 125:1-2). Though the rest of the world was in turmoil, God protected it, and continued to refresh it as if it were beside a beautiful river (**46:4**; see also Ezek 47:1-12; John 4:1-15; 7:37-39). God was present there, and so they could say, *she will not fall* (**46:5a**).

Some of the words of this psalm seem to echo the song of Israel's triumph over Egypt in Exodus 15:1-18. Then, and at many times since then, after what seemed a dark night of trouble, the morning of God's salvation dawned (**46:5b**; see also 30:5).

46:6-9 The Forces of Nations

Other psalms and many of the OT narratives show that the Israelites often had to face foreign invaders whose forces were vastly greater than their own. But they could always look back in their history and see what God had done for them. As in the days of Hezekiah when the Assyrians were turned back after besieging Jerusalem in vain (see Isa 37), they could say that *the God of Jacob is our fortress* (**46:7**).

Nations may rage and roar like the mighty ocean. Dictators and oppressive regimes may trample on us, but let us remember that our God is greater than them all. At his word their power can melt away (**46:6**). The most powerful enemies can be left desolate (**46:8**), and their weapons of war destroyed (**46:9**).

46:10-11 The Power of God

In the face of this turmoil, God tells his faithful ones to *be still and know that I am God; I will be exalted among the nations, I will be exalted in the earth,* that is, in the world of nature (**46:10**). He is saying, 'Relax, don't panic. I am in control, I am in charge of this difficult situation!' If only we can learn to turn our anxieties and worries over to this caring, ever present, and almighty God in prayer, then no matter what happens, we will be able to show a calmness which the world will envy, and which may draw others, including even our enemies and oppressors, to trust God. As the hymn puts it, 'With Christ in the vessel, I smile at the storm' (see also Isa 30:15; 1 Pet 5:7; Phil 4:6-7).

Psalm 47: Worship the King

Psalm 47 is one of a number of psalms (like Pss 93; 95–99) that celebrate the fact that God is King and Lord over all. In describing OT worship, it challenges us to assess the extent

to which our own personal worship and that of our congregations expresses similar joy and reverence.

47:1-2 Worship of the King of All Kings

This psalm starts by teaching us two things about what the worship of God's people should be like. First, it should be worship with joy. The people are called to *clap your hands* (an activity that may have included jubilation and dancing) and to shout loud praise to God (**47:1**). Second, it should also be worship with reverence, for the *Most High* is *awesome,* and we should always remember that he is Creator of all, Lord of all, *King* of all (**47:2**, 7). It is amazing that we as believers can approach such a great God with confidence (Heb 4:12-16).

47:3-7 Reasons for Rejoicing

The people have good reason to worship for they have seen that the Lord rules over all and had *subdued nations under* them as they looked to him for help (**47:3**). In giving the Israelites victory over their enemies, God had blessed them with a beautiful land, *the proud possession of his people, whom he loves* (**47:4** GNB). The Bible sometimes speaks of God 'coming down' to help his people (as in Isa 31:4), and so **47:5** might reflect rejoicing in the fact that he has done his victorious work, and then *ascended amid shouts of joy,* (compare 68:18). A land of plenty and freedom, with peace and justice to enjoy it, is a great blessing from the hand of God, enabling us to say, 'The boundary lines have fallen for me in pleasant places; surely I have a delightful inheritance' (16:6).

Alternatively, this psalm may be associated with David taking the symbol of God's presence, the ark of the covenant, to Jerusalem (see 2 Sam 6:17-19). That event could well have been spoken of as God going up into Jerusalem with 'shouts of joy', and might have been remembered year by year in a drama when God was, as it were, enthroned afresh in Jerusalem just as kings were crowned and enthroned (47:5; 2 Kgs 9:13; 11:12). However, God was not just king over Israel but *over all the earth* (47:2).

This psalm reminds us that we should learn to praise God for his goodness and attribute to him all the victories and successes and achievements that come our way. There is great blessing also in making special records of God's unique blessings on our lives, remembering them from time to time in special anniversaries or annual thanksgiving services.

God's people are called to praise him with cries of joy, clapping, shouts of acclamation, music and singing (**47:6**). However, the psalm makes it clear that our praise and thanksgiving must not be just emotional outbursts of the kind described in Matthew 13:20-21, but should include our minds as well. When **47:7** says *sing to him a psalm of praise,* the word that is translated 'psalm' is the word *maskil* that is also found in the heading of Psalm 42. Because it probably means 'wise' or 'understanding', some older translations read, 'sing praises with understanding'. The Apostle Paul made a similar point when he spoke about praising God 'with the mind' (1 Cor 14:15; see also Rom 12:1-2). We are to remember what Jesus has done for us, and so realize that we have every reason to praise God and to do so at all times (see 34:1; Matt 13:44-46; Luke 15:11-24).

47:8-9 The Kingdom, Present and Future

This is God's world, God's universe, that we live in, and we know God is King and Lord over all. So when we pray, as Jesus taught us, 'your kingdom come' (Matt 6:10), we are asking that God will truly rule in our lives, and in the lives of others where we are, and throughout the world.

Some translations of **47:9b** speak of 'the shields of the earth', but the NIV is probably correct to translate this as *the kings of the earth,* for the image is one of leaders protecting their people just as a shield protected a soldier in those days (compare 84:9). The image makes us ask how much of a 'shield' the leaders of today's world are, and should encourage us to pray for our own nation and its leaders.

All the rulers of other nations are described as *the people of the God of Abraham,* that is, as Israel (**47:9a**), and as together acknowledging the one God as their King and as Lord over all. The prophets often expressed the hope that the nations would unite like this in worship. Isaiah, for example, writes, 'Many peoples will come and say, "Come, let us go up to the mountain of the Lord, to the house of the God of Jacob. He will teach us his ways, so that we may walk in his paths"' (Isa 2:3). There was a wonderful fulfilment of this in the NT. It is also fulfilled in the life of the Christian church today, as people of all nations are drawn to know Jesus Christ as Lord and Saviour (think especially of Acts 2). We are also praying and looking forward to that day when we will be able to rejoice and say, 'The kingdom of the world has become the kingdom of our Lord and of his Christ, and he will reign for ever and ever' (Rev 11:15).

Psalm 48: The Glory of the City of God

Psalm 48 tells us something of what Jerusalem must have meant to Jewish people in OT days, and should encourage us to reflect on what the Christian church should be to its members and to the world today. The psalm should also spur us on to think of the hope that we have of a heavenly city, the new Jerusalem, in which the temple of God will be physically present with us.

48:1-2 The City of the Great King

To Israel in OT days, the land of Palestine was the holy land that God had given them. The temple was the holy place where they came to meet with God and to worship. Jerusalem was the city of God. It stood high up in the mountains in a beautiful spot, *the joy of the whole earth* (**48:2a**). Other people, like the Phoenicians, might think that Mount *Zaphon* in the far north was the place where the gods lived (**48:2b**), but for the Israelites Zion was the place where they felt the living and true God was especially present. Similarly, some people might call their supreme ruler 'the great king' as the Assyrians did (2 Kgs 18:28). Some might speak like that of the gods whom they worshipped. But to Israel Yahweh (Jehovah) their God, the one true God, was beyond all other 'great kings' and Jerusalem was *the city of the Great King* (**48:2c**) who was *most worthy of praise* (**48:1**).

Jerusalem is still a very special place for Jews and Christians, as well as Muslims. Yet we should not be depressed if we have no money to go on a pilgrimage there, nor feel proud if we can make such a visit. Jesus told the Samaritan woman that there was no one place on earth that was a special place beyond all others for knowing God's presence and worshipping him (John 4:19-24). He said that true worship was rooted in 'spirit and truth' and that he is present whenever and wherever people meet to honour his name (Matt 18:20). He sends his Holy Spirit into every heart that opens to him in grateful and humble surrender (John 14:22-23). Thus for those who truly believe in God through Jesus Christ, access to God is not confined to special seasons or geographical locations. For those in Christ, every place is holy ground.

This is not to say that the history (or geography for that matter) of the Christian faith is not important. But it is to say that to make an idol of that history and especially of that geography can be dangerous hypocrisy. The Christian church, the fellowship of the people in whose lives God is present, is now God's city. God's temple is the universal fellowship of all who believe that Jesus is 'the Christ, the Son of the living God' (Matt 16:16). But this honour also lays on us the obligation to live holy lives, for we ourselves are now the holy temple of the living God (1 Cor 6:15-20).

48:3-7 The City Defended

This psalm may have been written at a time when Jerusalem, by the help of God (**48:3**), had been saved when threatened by powerful enemies. It may have been in the days of King Hezekiah and the prophet Isaiah, when the great Assyrian general, Sennacherib, came against it (2 Kgs 18–19). Or it may have been earlier, in the days of King Jehoshaphat, when the Moabites and Ammonites came against the city and were defeated and turned back. On that occasion, the people 'returned joyfully to Jerusalem, for the Lord had given them cause to rejoice over their enemies. They entered Jerusalem and went to the temple of the Lord with harps and lutes and trumpets' (2 Chr 20:27-28). Or it may have been written on some similar other occasion.

The psalm says that kings came against the city, but when they saw it, they took to flight (**48:4-5**). They were thrown into confusion as when a powerful wind shatters the *ships of Tarshish* (**48:7**). 'Tarshish' is probably Tartessus in Spain, at the other end of the Mediterranean Sea from Palestine, about the farthest that people in Israel could think of travel by sea. The ships of Tarshish, which are mentioned several times in the OT, were thus ocean-going ships, large ships for those days.

48:8-14 God's People Encouraged

When the enemies who had threatened their city were overcome, the Israelites could see what great things God had done. What they had heard in the past about the mighty works of God, they had seen now in their own time and they recognized that he was indeed the *Lord Almighty* (**48:8**), their 'Great King' and 'most worthy of praise' (48:1-2). We, too, should be able to say that we have heard and seen the Lord at work in our world and in our own lives, so that we and our churches can tell the world about him and proclaim his praise *to the ends of the earth* (**48:10a**). As we do this, Jerusalem will truly become 'the joy of the whole earth' (48:2; Isa 2:2-4).

The people's gratitude for their deliverance would take them to the temple, where they would *meditate on God's unfailing love* (**48:9**). They had recognized that their city would not be great and glorious apart from the blessing and *righteousness* of God (**48:10b**). In praising God's righteousness, they were seeing a truth that is also preserved in Proverbs 14:34: 'Righteousness exalts a nation, but sin is a disgrace to any people.' Righteousness in this sense means justice on the part of leaders and social justice among the people.

The deliverance did not only send the people to the temple to give thanks, it seems to have driven them to march in procession around the city, thanking God for its towers, ramparts and citadels (**48:12-13**). This may have been done regularly year by year in Jerusalem. It is possible that the meditation in the temple referred to in 48:9 also involved the people watching a dramatic re-enactment of what God had done for them.

We, too, need to record and keep special symbols of God's goodness to us, and tell our story to encourage others, especially our children, that they may trust our God, a God who never fails nor deserts his people (48:13). He is our God and our Guide, not just part of the way, but all the way through life, to its very end (**48:14**). The next generation should learn to trust him as their *guide* (48:14) and their fortress (48:3) as well.

The towers and ramparts that defended the city the psalmist loved have now been thrown down. However, we need to remember that Jesus has laid a solid foundation for his church that can be trusted because not even death will ever be able to overcome it (Matt 16:18). Paul speaks of Christians as 'built on the foundation of the apostles and prophets, with Christ Jesus himself as the chief cornerstone' (Eph 2:19-22). Thus God's church is the new temple, and in a way also the new city of God, the new Jerusalem. We can eagerly await our heavenly home in 'the Holy City, the new Jerusalem' (Rev 21:2), with 'the river of the water of life' (Rev 22:1) flowing through it, and 'the tree of life' bearing fruit constantly – as it is pictured in Revelation 22:1-5 – 'and the leaves of the tree are for the healing of the nations' (Rev 22:2).

Psalm 49: Facing the Reality of Death

This psalm offers neither prayer nor praise. It is teaching, like the wisdom writing of the books of Proverbs and Ecclesiastes. It does make use of some Hebrew expressions that are difficult to translate, and this is why there are differences between various English translations, especially in 49:8-9, 13-14 and 18. However, the main point that is being made is quite clear.

49:1-6 A Summons to Attention

The teacher starts by calling people of all races and nations to listen to his message (**49:1**). It applies to rich and poor alike (**49:2**). It is true wisdom and shows the way of understanding (**49:3**). The problem that he sets himself the task of addressing is this: *Why should I fear when evil days come?* (**49:5a**). 'Evil days' are those when wickedness seems to triumph (**49:5b**) and those who are wicked *trust* in and *boast* about their wealth (**49:6**), instead of trusting and boasting in God (34:2; Jer 9:23-24; 2 Cor 10:17).

49:7-14, 17-20 Death Comes to All

The psalmist finds his answer in looking at the reality of death. People speak of death as 'the great leveller', because we are all level or equal when it comes to death. Whether we are rich or poor, uneducated or highly educated, with great authority in the world or with no authority, we will all die (**49:10**). No one can avoid or bribe death. There is nothing that any of us can do for our dearest friends or loved ones, or indeed for ourselves, to prevent or avoid death, when their time or our time has come to die. If we had all the money in the world *no payment is ever enough* to buy off death, no amount sufficient to ensure that we *should live on forever and not see decay* (**49:7-9**). Life and death are ultimately in the hands of God (see also 89:48).

To emphasize his point, the psalmist speaks of those so famous and powerful that they have *named lands after themselves* (**49:11**). Their modern equivalents would be those who own several mansions, control much wealth, and who have had streets or cities named after them. But when they die, *their tombs will remain their houses for ever,* and they will have nothing more. This applies even to rulers like those of ancient Egypt who were buried with great riches and great quantities of food and drink, along with representations of their favourite wives and slaves (in some cultures, actual wives and slaves were buried with the ruler) – but all to no purpose.

We all are mortals facing death, and in this respect we are no different from other creatures, however great we think we are. So as the refrain, repeated with slight variations in **49:12** and **20,** puts it, *man … is like the beasts that perish.*

Death takes by surprise those whose lives have been centred on themselves and their possessions. They may have become richer and richer in this life, but *he will take nothing with him when he dies, his splendour will not descend with him* (**49:17**). They have thought only of their bodies and not their souls, but these bodies *will decay in the grave* (literally, in *Sheol*) (**49:14**). The grave will be their home, not their *princely mansions.*

49:15-16 The Difference Trust Makes

Until our Lord Jesus Christ breaks into human history again at his coming in glory, we all must die. Yet there is a difference in the way that those who trust God face death. The psalmist, living before Christ's coming and his resurrection, was limited in the hope he had, yet he was given wise insight to pass on to others. He had earlier insisted that no one 'can redeem the life of another', (49:7). But God is not subject to human limitations, and so he can say, *God will redeem my life from the grave* (**49:15a**), and, best of all, *he will surely take me to himself* (**49:15b**). The word translated 'take' is the same one used for God 'receiving' or 'taking' Enoch and Elijah to himself at the end of their lives on earth (Gen 5:24 and 2 Kgs 2:3). It is also used in Psalm 73:24, 'You guide me with your counsel, and afterward you will take me into glory.'

When Jesus was speaking to the Sadducees who had no belief in resurrection, he quoted God as saying, 'I am the God of Abraham, the God of Isaac, and the God of Jacob', and added, 'He is not the God of the dead, but of the living' (Mark 12:26-27). If we know that the Lord is our God, and that in Christ we are accepted by him, death does not have the last word. God receives us. Death is the door to life eternal in God's presence. The truth that OT men and women saw only dimly is clear to us in Jesus Christ who has conquered death for us and risen from the grave. He has 'destroyed death and brought life and immortality to light through the gospel' (2 Tim 1:10). Through his own death and resurrection, he has delivered us who trust in him, from the fear of death (Heb 2:14-16) that makes for a miserable life. Jesus frees us from fear. Again and again, he said to his followers, 'do not be afraid' … for 'I have overcome the world' (John 16:33).

So we can conclude that we have much greater reason than the psalmist to say to ourselves, 'Why should I fear when evil days come?' (49:5). And to others we can say, *Do not be overawed* when people seem rich and powerful in this life (**49:16**). We should not be envious when people become rich suddenly or through dubious means. We must not join them, but must instead recognize the impermanence of earthly possessions (see Matt 6:19-21; Luke 12:13-21; 16:19-31; 1 Tim 6:6-10, 17). If our hand is in the hand of God, and if God's hand is on us, there is nothing in time or in eternity that we need fear.

Psalm 50: 'You Who Forget God'

Psalm 50 is the first of a number of psalms that belong to an *Asaph* collection (the others are Pss 73–83). Asaph was one of the chief musicians leading worship in the time of David (according to 1 Chr 15:17-19, 16:7, 25:1-2).

This psalm is a challenge to those who profess to be God's people and to have a special covenant (50:5) relationship with him, but in fact forget God (50:22). They know the reality of God and yet do not give him his rightful place in the centre of their lives. They are like those referred to in the NRSV version of 2 Timothy 3:5 as 'holding to the outward form of godliness but denying its power'. They live lives that contradict the saving and sanctifying power of the religion they profess with great fervour. Such people are challenged in three ways by this psalm, and we can also apply these things to ourselves today.

50:1-5 Realize God's Greatness

The psalm starts with *the Mighty One, God, the Lord,* who speaks and calls the whole world to hear his word, *from the rising of the sun to the place where it sets* (**50:1**). These words look back to the experience of God's showing himself to the people of Israel in great power and glory on Mount Sinai when the law was given to them (see Exod 19). Deuteronomy 33:2 says, 'The Lord came from Sinai, and … he shone forth from Mount Paran', but after the temple was built on Mount Zion, the Israelites came to think of that as where God's presence was specially known, and so they said that it was from that beautiful place that *God shines forth* (**50:2**). Fire and storm always show the power and greatness of God as creator (**50:3**), as they did on Mount Sinai. The mighty Creator God revealed in such ways is judge of all (**50:4**), and he judges with perfect knowledge and absolute justice (50:6).

The summons to gather *my consecrated ones* (**50:5**) may be a summons to those with whom God had entered into a covenant to appear as witnesses in the court case he will conduct. It is, however, more likely that the people are being summoned to renew their covenant with God. The people did this in the time when King Josiah called them back to fresh obedience to God's law (2 Kgs 23:1-3). It is also possible that there was an annual festival when the people of Israel were called back to God to renew their covenant with him. The psalm would certainly be very appropriate for such a ceremony.

50:6-15 Outward Devotion Is Not Enough

The reference to *sacrifice* in **50:5** is a reminder that the covenants that God made with Abraham and with the people in the days of Moses were all accompanied by the offering of sacrifices (see Gen 15 and Exod 24). This practice still continued in the days when this psalm was written, for the Lord could say, *I do not rebuke you for your sacrifices or your burnt offerings, which are ever before me* (**50:8**). They felt that their many offerings showed that they were very religious. They felt that they were pleasing God by giving him these things, as if they were supplying him with food and drink that he needed. Such sacrifices could have been the outward expression of sincere worship of their hearts and lives, but they were not. So the word of the Lord in this psalm rebuked them, as the prophets also often did (see 1 Sam 15:22-23; Pss 40:6-8; 51:16-17; Isa 1:11-17; Jer 6:20; 7:21-26; Hos 6:6; Amos 5:21-24; Mic 6:6-8).

God was not complaining that they failed to offer enough sacrifices (50:8), but was criticizing their assumption that he needed any of those sacrifices. The world and everything in it is God's (**50:9-12**). What he wanted (and still wants) was that his people would show that they were truly thankful for all his gifts, and would acknowledge that they depended completely on him for help in all their needs (**50:14-15**; see also 116:12-14).

The ministry of giving such things as tithes and offerings is important in the life of the believer and in the mission of the church. Yet this psalm reminds us that only the giving that comes out of a pure heart and a sincere appreciation of God's love for us and his supreme gift to us in Christ brings lasting blessing to the giver. Paul commended the Macedonians for giving *themselves first to the Lord* (2 Cor 8:1-5). Their giving of material resources was an outflow of that totally selfless act of surrender to God's love and will.

50:16-23 Obedience Means More Than Words

The people God refers to as *the wicked* had learned God's commandments so well that they could *recite* (**50:16a**) them. They spoke about his covenant (**50:16b**) as if they respected it, but in actual fact they rejected God's words and hated his discipline (**50:17**). The commandment said, 'You shall not steal', but they made friends with thieves (**50:18a**). In church life today, Christians may do this by encouraging donations for personal support and church projects from people known to be thieves or whose sources of sudden wealth are very dubious. Another commandment said, 'You shall not commit adultery', but they found pleasure

in the company of adulterers (**50:18b**). The counterpart today is enjoying pornographic films and videos and reading obscene literature. Another commandment said, 'You shall not bear false witness', but even their close family could not trust their words. They were liars and wicked gossips (**50:19-20**).

These people thought that God cared as little about their sinful actions as they did themselves (**50:21**). They were very mistaken. As the Law gave warning about the results of disobeying God's commandments (Deut 28:15-46), so a serious warning is given here (in **50:22**). As the Law gave promise of the blessings of obedience (Deut 28:1-14), so the end of the psalm gives the assurance that those who bring a sincere offering of thanksgiving to God, and who choose to follow the honest way, will surely find the salvation of God (**50:23**). The church that preaches God's word faithfully and seeks to impact society through the lives of its members inspired by the Holy Spirit will come to experience the blessing of God's revival in its land (see 2 Chr 7:14). We must take the warning in James to heart, and do what the word says, not merely listen to it (Jas 1:22).

Psalm 51: The Prayer of a Penitent

This is a psalm that expresses the terrible reality of our human sinfulness, the marvellous reality of God's pardon, and the life of thankfulness and humble but courageous witness that the pardoned sinner should live. The note that came to be attached to the psalm as its heading links it with King David and his sin of adultery with Bathsheba and the way Nathan the prophet came to him (see 2 Sam 11 and 12). We can certainly understand it as expressing what David must have felt then. He came to confess, 'I have sinned against the Lord' (2 Sam 12:13). He had sinned as an adulterer, but he had also been guilty of bloodshed (51:14) in causing the death of Bathsheba's husband, Uriah. All down the ages, many a penitent sinner has felt like the writer of this psalm, and it has helped countless people to turn to God for pardon.

51:1b-6 The Reality of Our Human Sinfulness

This psalm opens with a desperate appeal for mercy, using three different words to describe the psalmist's sin: *transgression* speaks of sin as rebellion against God (**51:1b**); *iniquity* speaks of sin as turning from the right path, the corrupt inclination of the human heart (**51:2a**); and the third word, *sin* has the meaning of missing what should be one's aim in life (**51:2b**). We are created to serve God and enjoy fellowship with him at all times. When we put ourselves in a position where that fellowship is broken and the 'joy of the Lord' forsakes us, we have 'missed the mark' (see Rom 3:23).

Even when our sin is against other people, it is also, fundamentally, against God (**51:4**, see also Gen 39:9). We are deliberately breaking God's law. He sees such behaviour as malicious and insulting and is offended by it. So God is always right when he judges us for the wrong things we do, and when we fail to do the right things (51:4, which is quoted in the NT in Rom 3:4). God wants us to have truth in the very thoughts of our hearts, and he teaches us the wisdom of his ways (**51:6**). But we turn aside from that truth.

Our trouble is that we have a sinful nature. When the psalmist says, *Surely I was sinful at birth, sinful from the time my mother conceived me* (**51:5**), he is not implying that sexual relationships in marriage and conception are evil. Both sexual relationships and conception are gifts from God, and the crown of married love (see Heb 13:4). What the verse means is that because we are human, and members of a sinful race ever since Adam and Eve's sin, we have an inborn inclination to do wrong. Paul speaks of the sin factor in each of us from which no human effort or religious observances can free us (Rom 7:21-24; Col 2:16-23). Only the blood of Jesus can cleanse us from all sin, and only the power of the Holy Spirit can keep us from the inclination to sin and selfishness (Rom 7:24-8:3).

51:1a, 7-12 The Blessing of God's Forgiveness

Happily the psalmist could speak not only of the reality of sin, but also of the reality of God's forgiveness. We deserve only his judgment, and that he should turn his face from us rather than towards us in blessing. But he is willing to *have mercy* on us. He wants to show us his *unfailing love* and *great compassion* (**51:1a**). Notice the ways in which the psalmist asks that he may know that love and grace, and the pardon of God:

- *Blot out all my iniquity* (**51:9**; see 51:1). The idea here is that a record of sins was written down, but was then completely wiped out so that it can no longer be read. God's great generosity is such that when he forgives, he remembers the sins no more. He forgives and forgets. What a Saviour! The devil taunts and intimidates us with the thought of our past failures. He is the accuser of the brethren (Rev 12:10). But these verses remind us that after God has forgiven our sins, he erases them from his book and tears out the page. We should remember this especially if we are among those Christians who seem to enjoy the torment of digging up the past.
- 'Wash away all my iniquity' (51:2a). God is able to make a filthy life clean again, *whiter than snow* (**51:7**; see also Isa 1:18).
- 'Cleanse me from my sin' (51:2b). The word translated 'cleanse' is sometimes used to speak of purifying metals, as well as in connection with ceremonies of purification. In some of these ceremonies the *hyssop* plant (51:7)

was used to sprinkle water or sacrificial blood for ritual cleansing (Lev 14:1-7; Num 19:17-18).

- *Let me hear joy and gladness; let the bones you have crushed rejoice* (**51:8**), and *restore to me the joy of your salvation* (**51:12a**). Those who are burdened with failure and sin know no joy, and the psalmist compares their suffering to that of a person whose bones have been crushed.
- *Create in me a pure heart, O God* (**51:10**). In asking God to make him a new person, he uses a word that is only used in the OT for God's work of creation (as in Gen 1:1). By the help of God's Spirit (a truly *holy spirit* – **51:11**) – he wants to have *a willing spirit* (**51:12b**).

This is one of only two passages in the OT that use the compound form 'Holy Spirit' (the other is Isa 63:10-11). Although the personal Holy Spirit was only given to all believers at Pentecost, he had already been active in the OT. David knew that Saul's sin had resulted in God's Spirit leaving Saul (1 Sam 16:14) and in Saul being removed from his kingship. David was asking that God not take away his Spirit and depose him too.

The psalmist longs for his own spirit to be holy. He desires a humble and penitent disposition, what he describes elsewhere in the psalm as a 'broken and contrite heart' (51:17), rather than an arrogant one. In order to hear God, to repent or to change one's attitude to others, there must first be a holy, or humble, spirit or attitude.

The psalmist wants to be a totally different person from what he has been in the past. Instead of rebelling against God, he wants to serve him gladly and willingly. The NT says that in Christ a person becomes 'a new creation; the old has gone, the new has come!' (2 Cor 5:17). The most fundamental mark of genuine repentance and conversion is that our ways of thinking and our values change completely (Rom 12:1-2). That is why Jesus described it as being like rebirth when he told Nicodemus that he must be born again to see the kingdom of God (John 3:3-6). We all need a life- and value-transforming encounter with God again and again in the course of our Christian life. That is how the Holy Spirit transforms us from one degree of glory to another – making us more like Jesus as a result of each fresh encounter (2 Cor 3:18).

51:13-19 A Life of Thankfulness

The psalmist knows that powerful praying or personal faith are not enough to bring about all of the things that he has prayed for. He is totally dependent on the love and goodness of God. So he knows the debt that he owes to the Lord for his forgiveness. He wants to tell others about it by opening his lips to praise God (**51:15**), and using his tongue to sing aloud of his deliverance (**51:14**). In this way he will seek to lead others who are sinners like he has been back to God (**51:13**). He knows now what God seeks from his people more than anything else. This is something more important than sacrificial offerings (**51:16**; see 50:8-15). For us, there is something more important than outward religious practices such as attending church, giving money to the church, serving on church committees and councils, singing in the choir, assisting in the services, or earning titles from the church. True religion means having a heart that is right with God, a humble heart that grieves over sin. As the psalmist says: *a humble spirit, O God; you will not reject a humble and repentant heart* (**51:17**, GNB).

The last two verses of the psalm may have been added at a later time, probably before all the psalms were brought together in this one book. The personal prayer of the psalmist came to be used as a prayer for the whole nation. After Israel had suffered defeat and exile because of their sins, God brought them back to Jerusalem again. Then their prayer was for the rebuilding of the city (**51:18**), as happened in the time of Nehemiah. Then the people with repentant and pardoned hearts would bring offerings that would be acceptable to God (**51:19**).

When we return to God in humility, true repentance and faith, and make restitution to our fellow human beings, what peace we enjoy and how acceptable to God our prayer and worship become!

Psalm 52: The Fall of the Proud

This psalm pictures the rise and fall of a proud man who had no respect for people nor any regard for truth in word or action.

The heading added later to the psalm links it with the action of Doeg the Edomite who was in charge of Saul's servants. When Saul was seeking to kill David, Doeg told him that David had been seen at the sanctuary at Nob and that the priests there had given him a sword and food. Saul then ordered Doeg to kill all the priests of the Lord in the sanctuary (see 1 Sam 21–22). But what this psalm says could apply to many other boasting men of whom we read in the Bible – like Shebna (Isa 22:15-20), Pashhur (Jer 20:1-6), Hananiah (Jer 28) and Herod (Acts 12:20-23) – and powerful oppressors in the world in every generation.

52:1-4 The Boaster Revealed

The person about whom this psalm is written is described as a *mighty man*. Certainly this was how he saw himself. He boasted of his power over others, and no doubt also in the riches that he had gained. The psalmist, however, challenges him by asking, *Why do you boast?* (**52:1a**) What do you really have to boast about? Think of what you are doing. You plot to destroy people. You do evil to those who serve God. In fact, you *are a disgrace in the eyes of God* (**52:1b**). This last phrase is translated as 'the goodness of God endureth continually' in the KJV. While this translation is possible, the NIV translation fits the context better.

The psalmist also accuses the man of doing harm with his tongue and trying to deceive people by the words that he speaks. His tongue is said to be as dangerous as *a sharpened razor* (**52:2**) and the source of deceit. The Bible often reminds us of the evil that can be done by the tongue (see 50:19; 55:21; 57:4; 64:3; Jas 3:1-12).

The law says that you should love God with your heart and soul and strength, and love your neighbour as yourself, but the psalmist tells this man, *You love evil rather than good* (**52:3**). You love words that devour (**52:4**). 'Why do you boast?' Do you think that you can go on like that forever, and that nothing will happen to stop you?

52:5-7 But God …

The proud man thinks that he can do and say what he likes and get away with it. But God has the last word. There are three things that the psalmist says that God will do in **52:5**: *God will bring you down to everlasting ruin,* like a house is broken down in a great storm; *he will snatch you up and tear you from your tent* and you will no longer be able to live in peace and have a position of power; *he will uproot you from the land of the living,* just as a great tree is uprooted and dies (37:35-36).

The righteous will see the fall of the proud with a mixture of fear and laughter (**52:6** see also Job 22:19-20). Proverbs warns us that it is never right to rejoice over the fall of an enemy (Prov 24:17-18), and Jesus teaches us to seek the conversion rather than the judgment of even the worst of sinners and oppressors. Yet it is understandable that people of faith feel both awe and thankfulness when they see the fall of unrepentant oppressors or murderous dictators such as Hitler or Idi Amin, who have caused the suffering and death of countless people. The proud have refused to take refuge in God (**52:7**), and instead have foolishly trusted in riches and worldly power (see Ps 49).

There is a pun in the statement *Here now is the man* (52:7). The Hebrew word used for 'man' here is *Geber.* He is no longer the *mighty man,* or *Gibbor,* referred to in 52:1. Once he was 'superman', but now he is just 'a man' when God acts in judgment.

52:8-9 But I …

What the psalmist sees of the power and then the humbling of the proud makes him determined that his own life will not be like a great tree uprooted, but *like an olive tree flourishing in the house of God* (**52:8**). The olive was and still is one of the best-loved trees in Palestine. It is an evergreen tree that can live for hundreds of years and still bear fruit. Its fruit has long been used for food, and olive oil has been used in cooking, in lamps, in soaps and in ointments for many centuries. Israel as a nation was intended to be as 'a thriving olive tree with fruit beautiful in form' (Jer 11:16) – versatile and always available and ready to serve. The individual members of the people of God should want to be like that too (see also 1:3), and to *trust in God's unfailing love for ever and ever.* We should be able to say, expressing our heart's desire, *I will praise you forever for what you have done* (**52:9a**). By contrast with the harm done by the tongue of the evil man, the tongue of the righteous brings encouragement and help to others (**52:9b**; Prov 12:18).

The psalmist declares, *in your name I will hope* (52:9a). The word used here for 'hope' is often translated 'wait'. The 'name' of God reflects the character of God, as he is revealed through his word. So to hope in God's name or to wait on God's name speaks of sincere trust in God himself.

Psalm 53: No God – No Hope

This psalm is almost word for word the same as Psalm 14. However, here the heading adds what is probably the tune to which it is to be sung: *according to mahalath* (see also Ps 88). The heading also adds that this psalm is a *maskil*. The meaning of this term is discussed in relation to Psalm 42.

This psalm may have been included in two of the early collections of psalms, which would explain its similarities to and differences from Psalm 14. For example, whereas Psalm 14 regularly speaks of 'the Lord', using a word that represents the special personal name of God, *Yahweh,* this psalm refers to God using the Hebrew word *Elohim.* This reflects a difference between books 1 and 2 of Psalms. In Book 1 (Pss 1–41), Yahweh is used 272 times and Elohim 15 times; whereas in Book 2 (Pss 42–72) Yahweh is used 30 times and Elohim 164 times.

The psalm as a whole tells us what happens in the lives and to the lives of those who reject God. It applies strongly to any of us anywhere if we try to live our lives as though God did not exist.

53:1-3 The Lives of Those Who Reject God

When people turn away from God and in effect say, *There is no God* (**53:1a**), then there is nothing to stop their lives becoming more and more evil. They become *corrupt,* and their ways become *vile* (**53:1b**). Their corruption means that they have no desire at all for what is good (**53:3**). They also become oppressors of others, who *devour my people as men eat bread* (53:4; see also Mic 3:1-4). We can see these patterns in the life of nations and societies.

53:4-6 God's Response to Those Who Reject Him

Whatever our sin, if we turn from it and turn to God, we will always find him willing to accept and forgive us (John 6:37). But those who refuse, and continue to reject him, need to realize that God will reject them. The NT gives the same solemn warning in Romans 1:18-32.

God does not ignore those who reject him and who act as if there is no God to whom they would have to give account

for their lives. He 'looks down from heaven' (53:2) and he sees the good and evil of every person's life and hates those who oppress other people who are his creatures. So he speaks to challenge them: *Will the evildoers never learn – those who ... do not call on God?* (**53:4**). His words are followed by action, as he sends them into a terror and panic that they have never known before. They are defeated on the battlefield where God scatters *the bones of those who attacked you* (**53:5**). Those who were so proud in their own strength and wisdom are put to shame. No wonder these evildoers were called *fools* (53:1). They had heard about God's punishment of evildoers in the past, and yet continued to do evil themselves.

The reference to a battle in 53:5 marks another difference between Psalm 14 and Psalm 53. It seems that while Psalm 14 applied to those in Israel who gave no thought to God in their lives, Psalm 53 applies a similar message to the nations that threatened Israel – but did not succeed. In spite of their boasted power, terror and panic struck them and many perished in battle (see, for example, 2 Kgs 7:1-8; 19:1-7; 2 Chr 20:1-30).

The psalm ends with a prayer that the people of Israel must often have prayed in times of difficulty. Most of all, in the time when they were defeated by Babylon and sent into exile, they prayed for deliverance and for God to *restore the fortunes of his people* (**53:6**) And God answered that prayer so that they rejoiced and were glad. While those who turn from God face fear and shame, those who trust in him can rejoice even in the midst of difficulties and trials (see also Rom 5:1-5). They have no need to give in to panic like their enemies do, as we see from the examples of Isaiah in 2 Kings 18–19 and Paul in Acts 27 (see also Ps 46; Matt 10:28-29; John 16:33; Phil 4:6-7; 1 John 4:4).

Psalm 54: The Name of God – Great and Good

In the heading, this psalm too is labelled a *maskil* (see Ps 42) and directions are given that it is to be sung to the accompaniment of *stringed instruments.* The heading also associates it with the time when David was escaping from the jealous Saul, who was trying to kill him, and his location was betrayed by the people of Ziph, which is near Hebron in South Palestine (see 1 Sam 23:15-29; 26:1-25). But the psalm is appropriate to the situation of all who find themselves opposed by ruthless enemies.

This psalm begins and ends with a reference to the 'name' of God. *Save me, O God, by your name* is the prayer of 54:1. *I will praise your name, O Lord* is the psalmist's decision in 54:6. Sometimes people, perhaps influenced by psalms like this one and verses like Proverbs 18:10, feel that they can use names, especially divine names, in a magical kind of way and so gain control over spiritual forces. Such practice is unbiblical and can lead to dangerous occultism. The name of God or the name of Jesus is not a talisman or a magic word that we may invoke to ward off fear and evil. Some people expect power to emanate to their advantage if they repeatedly shout, 'Jesus! Jesus!' or 'Jah! Jah!' or 'Blood of Jesus!' Our Lord gave a warning about this kind of religious behaviour that mixes superstition with faith (Matt 6:7-8; see also Acts 19:13-17).

The name of God means the character of God, God as he is, as he is made known to us by his word, by what he does, and now especially in Jesus Christ. To call on or 'swear' by God's name means to be faithful to God in utter dependence and obedience. It means to honour God, as we pray, 'Hallowed be your name' (Matt 6:9) and as we celebrate the fact that God has given Jesus 'the name that is above every name, that at the name of Jesus every knee should bow, in heaven and on earth and under the earth, and every tongue confess that Jesus Christ is Lord, to the glory of God the Father' (Phil 2:9-11).

54:1-3 Prayer

The psalmist in his need turns to God who alone can save him. Where he is in the right, he asks that God will *vindicate* (**54:1**) him, showing that he has worked for what is true and just. He has enemies whom he describes as *strangers* (**54:3a**). In some versions, this word is translated as 'arrogant', which is how it is also translated in Psalm 86:14. In Isaiah 25:2-5 the same Hebrew word is used when speaking of foreigners who are ruthless oppressors. It makes little difference which translation we choose, for God-fearing people in Israel and people today often face oppression both from foreigners and from proud and powerful people of their own nation and race.

The psalmist's enemies are also *ruthless* (**54:3b**) – cruel in the way that they act towards others who are weaker than themselves. They think that they can do what they like and no one will stop them. They are *men without regard for God* (**54:3c**), that is, men who give no thought to God, unlike the psalmist, who can say 'I have set the Lord always before me' (16:8).

54:4-5 Confidence

Because of what the psalmist knows of God, and because of what God has done for him in the past, he can say, *Surely God is my help* (**54:4a**). He can face difficulty and danger and the oppression of others because he believes *the Lord is the one who sustains me* (**54:4b**).

Although this may appear unpalatable to us (**54:5**), it is right to pray that evil will be shown up for what it is, that God's righteousness and justice will triumph, and that oppression will be brought to an end.

54:6-7 Thankfulness

The psalm ends with thanksgiving to God. A *freewill offering* was not a legalistic obligation, but one that a person offered out of sheer gratitude to God. It is not clear whether **54:6a** is speaking of an actual offering or of a general attitude of thankfulness. Whichever the case, the verse speaks of a thankful heart and a willingness of spirit resulting in an offering to God (see also 40:6-10; 116:8-19).

When the psalmist says, *I will praise your name, O Lord, for it is good* (**54:6b**), that one little word 'good' says so much about God. God is good in his character, in his nature, and in his loving purpose for us all (see also 34:8; 52:9). All that this psalm says is based on faith in the goodness of God, and submission to the sovereignty of God. We should be in awe of the majesty or transcendence of God, and filled with reverent gratitude for his matchless love (Rom 8:31-39; 12:1-2).

The psalmist is grateful for deliverance and victory (**54:7**). Christian believers should be equally grateful for God's forgiveness because of what Christ has done for us. He has given us victory over temptation and every kind of evil that threatens us and tries to prevent us from living for the service of God and others.

Psalm 55: Oppression, Corruption, Betrayal

The heading of this psalm is identical with that of Psalm 54, except that it does not attempt to identify a setting for this psalm in the life of David. However, an ancient Aramaic translation of this psalm associates it with Ahithophel, the close friend who betrayed David (see 2 Sam 16–17). David must have had the feelings expressed in this psalm at the time when his son Absalom led a revolt against him and Ahithophel was unfaithful. But many others in positions of leadership have faced similar circumstances where troubles beset them on all sides.

55:1-8 Oppression

This psalm is a prayer asking God urgently to *listen to my prayer,* to *hear me,* and *answer* a cry from the heart of one who is deeply troubled (**55:1-2a**). *My cares give me no peace* is the NEB translation of **55:2b**. The hatred of powerful enemies was more than the psalmist could bear. *They bring down suffering upon me* (**55:3**), he says, and his words paint a picture of enemies rolling stones down on him from a height above. His life was in great danger, so that he felt *the terrors of death* (**55:4**), with *fear and trembling* and *horror* overwhelming him (**55:5**).

His one thought was to try to escape from it all. If only he had wings like a dove and could fly to a lonely place in the wilderness where there would be no people at all to worry him! He would find a place that would be as secure as a great rock that offers a desert traveller shelter, *far from the tempest and storm* (**55:6-8**). He is not alone in his desire to run away from opposition and difficulties. The great prophets Elijah and Jeremiah would have sympathized with him (Jer 9:1-9; 1 Kings 19). So do we as we face problems in our own lives.

But he had no wings, and there was no possibility of escape. The only way in his need and danger, and of course the best way, was to turn to God in prayer.

55:9-11 Corruption

The corruption within the city where he lived deeply disturbed the psalmist. He felt that he could only pray that God would *confuse* those who were wicked, and *confound their speech* (**55:9a**), as had happened at the tower of Babel (Gen 11:1-9). In Psalm 43:3, God's light and truth are pictured as personally guiding the psalmist to God's city to worship. But in **55:9b**, there are two very different guides to the city. They are *violence* and *strife,* and they are going round the walls of the city day and night. Crime – including robbery, bribery and all kinds of sexual immorality, *malice and abuse* – is operating inside the city all the time (**55:10**). Destruction is there, and *threats* and *fraud* (**55:11** GNB). We may feel that this describes many of our cities today. Hence the psalmist's experience helps us to trust our great unchanging God. His reliability in times of trouble is constantly emphasized throughout the psalms (see, for example, Ps 46).

55:12-21 Betrayal

The third and hardest thing that the psalmist had to face was the fact that he had been betrayed by one who had been as close to him as a brother or sister. They had even worshipped together in the house of God (**55:13-14**). Facing such betrayal was worse than having open enemies (**55:12**). This person had attacked him and broken the covenant of friendship with him. Though the betrayer had spoken smooth words of loyalty, he had *a heart set on war* (**55:21**, NRSV).

We can understand the psalmist's anger as he faced injustice and opposition everywhere, from those whom he knew to be his enemies, from the forces that controlled the city, and even from one whom he had thought to be a close friend. In anger he prays, *Let death take my enemies by surprise* (**55:15**). He was sure that God *will humble them, because they do not change, and do not fear God* (**55:19**, NRSV). Such a bitter outburst is very natural. But Jesus teaches us a higher way. He was betrayed by one of his specially chosen twelve disciples (John 13:1-30), and yet his prayer for the forgiveness of his enemies is the supreme example of forgiving love and the height of moral strength: 'Father, forgive them; for they do not know what they are doing' (Luke 23:34).

The psalmist did not know Jesus' way, nor do very many people around the world, both past and present. What a challenge to us who do know! And who can expect to face similar difficulties (see Matt 10:21-22). But having said this, we should still realize that it is true that 'bloodthirsty and deceitful' (55:23) people, who refuse to turn from their corrupt and violent ways, will come under God's judgment.

There are several places in this psalm where various English translations differ. This is because the original Hebrew of the psalm, or its meaning, has been hard to determine. In 55:19, for example, where the Hebrew says literally 'there are no changes with them', the RSV has 'because they keep no law', while others take it to mean there is no change to their fortunes. The NIV says they are *men who never change their ways.* This fits with what follows: they *have no fear of God.*

It is unusual to have *Selah* in the middle of a verse as in 55:19, because it is thought to indicate a pause, perhaps while music plays and people can think about the words that have gone before. In this case, it may have been misplaced as the psalm was copied.

55:22-23 Trust

The best lesson that we can learn from the psalmist is the way that he turned to God in prayer at all times: 'evening, morning and noon I cry out in distress' (55:17). His confidence was in the words of encouragement of **55:22**: *Cast your cares on the Lord and he will sustain you; he will never let the righteous fall.* So the final words of his prayer to the Lord were *I trust in you* (**55:23**). Whatever other people might do to him, he was determined to keep trusting in God and serving him. We as Christians should always remember that in forgiving our enemies we find release for them and for ourselves. In trusting God we find peace (see John 14:1; 16:33; Phil 4:6-7; 1 Pet 5:7).

Psalm 56: Faith Instead of Fear

This psalm was to be sung *to the tune of 'A Dove on Distant Oaks'.* The heading links it with David's experience in the hands of the Philistines (1 Sam 21:10-15 or 29:1-11).

This is another psalm that was written out of the experience of great trouble and trial that was met by faith in God. It can profitably be compared with Psalm 116, which also speaks of how God delivers those who turn to him and of the gratitude owed to God by those who pray.

56:1-2, 5-6 Endless Trouble

There seemed to be no end to the psalmist's troubles at the hand of those who oppressed him. Three times he says, 'all day long': *All day long they press their attack* (**56:1**); *my slanderers pursue me all day long* (**56:2a**); *all day long they twist my words* (**56:5**). Those who were fighting against him were *many* and they were attacking him *in their pride* (**56:2b**). Some translations, like the KJV, interpret these words as an exclamation addressed to God, 'O Most High' rather than as a description of the high opinions his enemies have of themselves. But all translations are clear about the extent of the psalmist's suffering.

The enemies' purpose was to harm him (56:5). He wanted to live in peace, but they stirred up strife, kept watch for him and tried to take his life (56:6).

56:3-4, 7-12 The Way to Meet Trouble

The psalmist knew, however, that the one way to deal with trouble was to turn to God in prayer, and to have faith in God when he was tempted to fear. So he began with words that begin many psalms, *Be merciful to me, O God* (56:1; see 4:1, 6:2, 51:1 and 57:1). He could pray that prayer because he believed in God's word. He speaks of this in 56:4 and repeats it in 56:10. God had promised to help those who turned to him, and he relied on that promise.

There are several possible translations of 56:8a: the NIV has *Record my lament,* the NKJV has 'You number my wanderings', while the NRSV has 'You have kept count of my tossings'. The psalmist may be referring to his sleepless tossing in bed at night, or to his wanderings as he tries to escape from his enemies. But regardless of the exact translation, it is clear that he was confident that God knew and perfectly understood his trouble. This point is reinforced in the second half of the verse: *list my tears on your scroll – are they not in your record* (56:8b). Other translations say *put my tears in your bottle* (NRSV). The word translated 'bottle' really refers to a 'skin' that was used for holding liquids in those days. We have no evidence that 'tear bottles' were used in OT times to collect the tears of mourners. So it seems likely that what is being referred to is a skin used to write on. The psalmist is saying that God has a written record of his sorrows, meaning that all his sorrows and distresses are known perfectly to God.

So he says, *When I am afraid I will trust in you* (56:3), and *Then my enemies will turn back when I call for help* (56:9). Because he knew that God was with him to help him, he could say, *What can mortal man do to me?*(56:4) and *What can man do to me?*(56:11). In other words, although the people against us are many and evil and seem very powerful, their strength is very small and of no account before God (see also Isa 2:22; 31:1-3; 40:6-8; Jer 17:5-8; Heb 13:5-6). One person and God are stronger than all the rest put together! But we can only be sure that God is on our side if we are on God's side, doing his will and working for him and for his honour in the world.

There are two other things the psalmist did in his trouble. The first was that he prayed for God's judgment to come on his enemies (56:7). We should understand this in the same way as we do other prayers like it in the psalms. It is not so much a prayer for personal revenge as a prayer that God's justice will prevail and oppression will end. It can also be seen as a prayer for freedom from fear and anxiety, either by the removal of the sources of fear and anxiety, or by God giving courage and fortitude to go through those difficult situations victoriously and without sinning (see 1 Cor 10:13). Unlike the psalmist, we have heard Jesus' teaching to forgive and to pray for our enemies, but to be able to do this we need the grace and power of the Holy Spirit (see Phil 4:13).

The second thing that the psalmist does is to determine to thank God for what he has done. Because of the constant blessings of God on our lives we should want to praise him constantly. For special blessings of help and deliverance, there should be special acts of thanksgiving, as 56:12 speaks of in terms of *vows* and *thank-offerings.* The last verse vividly describes what God had done for the psalmist, and we know how he does the same for us: our souls have been delivered from death, our feet kept from falling, so that we *may walk before God in the light of life* (56:13).

Psalm 57: God's Glory over All the Earth

The heading associates the psalm with the difficulties that David experienced in the days when he was hiding in caves to escape Saul (see 1 Sam 22:1-5; 24:1-22).

This psalm teaches us that however overwhelming our situation or deep our problem, the glory of God must be our ultimate motive in our search for help. Thus any solution we find must be in accordance with God's word and God's law. He must be the only one in whom we trust (121:2).

57:1-4, 6 Need for God

This psalm begins with the picture of a person in great need, turning to God in trust. His enemies are strong and terrifying, but he knows that he can turn to God. Although he realizes he has no right to God's help, yet he knows that God is merciful. He probably remembered the Levitical injunction to meet with God at the 'mercy seat', the place of God's special presence in the temple. He clings to that, as a Christian would to the teaching of grace, and cries, *Have mercy on me, O God, have mercy on me.* He has turned to God for refuge before, and, thinking of a mother bird sheltering her young ones with her wings, he can say, *I will take refuge in the shadow of your wings until the disaster has passed* (57:1 – compare Deut 32:11-12; Ruth 2:12; Matt 23:37).

The reason for his trouble is that his enemies are pursuing him (57:3). They are like lions wanting to devour him (57:4a – compare 10:9 and 17:12). They are like people coming against him with *spears and arrows,* and their threatening words are like *sharp swords* (57:4b). They are like hunters who use nets and pits to catch their prey (57:6 – compare 35:7).

The psalmist knows that what he needs – and what God will supply – is God's steadfast love and faithfulness, sent like two guardian angels to help him (57:3). So he can say with confidence that God's purpose for him will not fail to be fulfilled (**57:2**; see also 37:3-5; Rom 8:28; Phil 1:6), as he trusts and obeys his God. The evil people who pursue him will not continue to prosper, but will be caught in their own net, and fall into the pit that they have made to catch others (57:6).

57:5, 7-11 The Glory of God

It is good that this psalmist was not content just to find help and deliverance for himself. By the end of this prayer, he is thinking more of the greatness of God than he is of his own need. God's steadfast love is as high as the heavens, his faithfulness reaches to the clouds (**57:5, 10**). In other words, these qualities are greater than any human person can realize or words can describe. So his desires go beyond just being delivered out of his difficulties to wanting God's greatness to be realized by others. For himself he was determined to sing God's praise. The harp and lyre referred to (**57:8a**) were both stringed instruments regularly used by Hebrew people, especially in their worship. The psalmist would start praising God so early in the morning that he, as it were, would wake up the dawn rather than the dawn waking him (**57:8b**). He wanted God's glory – God's greatness and truth and lovingkindness – to be known among all the nations of the earth. He wanted people of all nations to hear of his great God and to come to trust and serve him (**57:9**).

The psalmist's refrain in 57:5 and **57:11** could profitably be the prayer of our own hearts. In many ways, it resembles the beginning of the Lord's Prayer (Matt 6:9-13) and thus is a model for us in our own prayer. It also challenges us to consider the missionary implications of such a prayer and what it means for us as individuals and as congregations to declare God's praises among all the nations on earth.

Some of the verses in this psalm are repeated elsewhere: 57:7-11 are almost identical to 108:1-5, and 57:10 is the same as 36:5. When people realized that the words used in prayer and thanksgiving in one situation were appropriate to another, they felt free to reuse them. We do the same in the hymns and songs that we sing, and we do the same with the Scriptures, which we should constantly be applying to the different situations that we face in life.

Psalm 58: Banish Injustice

The heading of Psalm 58 is similar to that of Psalm 57 and other psalms.

When we read this psalm, our first thought may be that it is very bloodthirsty and full of thoughts of vengeance. But we need to remember that its language is often the exaggerated picture language of poetry, and we are not expected to literally bathe in the blood of the wicked (58:10), or break

the teeth of the ungodly. Nor are the ungodly literally lions that kill and tear up those they have taken as prey (58:6).

This psalm is a prayer for God's justice to be seen by his acting in judgment. Such prayers come from those who have been oppressed by powerful and evil rulers, enemies of God and of justice. These oppressed people have suffered at the hands of those who have ruled over them, and they have found no justice in the courts of the land. David had this experience, so did people in Jesus' time (Luke 18:1-8) and so do many people in the world today. There is no human hand to help them, no one to defend them or to seek justice for them so as to prevent their sufferings.

God cares about injustice and that is abundantly clear from the warnings in this psalm and those issued by the prophets (see especially Isa 1:21-28; 3:10-11; 10:1-4; Jer 5:20-29; Amos 5:6-12; Mic 3:9-12). This concern, and the prayer uttered in this psalm, should encourage us to pray and work passionately for justice and fairness in God's world.

We need to also consider the psalm's underlying note of selflessness in the desire for God's glory. In our prayer and work for social justice, we must not become selfish, vindictive or unjust ourselves. This is the difference Christ makes in the lives of those who believe and trust in him. He prevents those who were once oppressed from themselves becoming oppressors.

58:1-5 When Injustice and Corruption Flourish

The psalm starts by addressing the rulers: *Do you rulers indeed speak justly?* (**58:1**). The word translated 'rulers' can also be translated as 'gods'. This translation reflects the ancient belief that rulers, and especially kings and queens, were given divine powers or divine authority. As a result such rulers often felt that they had a right to rule despotically, and could do as they wished (see 82:1, 6-7).

Regardless of whether we translate 58:1 with the word 'gods' or 'rulers', it is clear that the psalmist was concerned with the unjust and oppressive actions of those in power. He accuses them, *In your heart you devise injustice* (**58:2**). Justice is often spoken of as being 'weighed out', as in a just balance (see Job 31:6). But what these men weigh out is violence rather than justice. In fact they appeared to be totally evil, going astray more and more ever since they were born (**58:3**).

They were like poisonous snakes, dealing out death to those whom they attacked. Speaking of snakes led the psalmist to speak of snake-charmers, well-known by Hebrew people in those days (**58:4-5**; see also Jer 8:17), as they are in many parts of Africa and Asia today. Just as a snake may appear deaf to the charmer's music, so these wicked rulers were deaf to any words of truth that called them to change their ways. Jeremiah, in his time, spoke of the refusal of the leaders of Israel to hear the word of the

Lord (Jer 6:10; 7:13; 11:7-8). How does this compare with politicians – especially military dictators – in our own day? By contrast, our ears should be open to God's word (see 1 Sam 3:1-10; Ps 40:6-8; Isa 50:4-5; Matt 7:24-25).

58:6-9 Injustice and Oppression Judged

Because these people are like poisonous snakes that kill others, and because they refused to listen to any voice that cautioned them, the psalmist prayed for God to act. They were like *lions* on the attack, and so the psalmist prayed that their teeth might be broken so that they would not be able to tear into their victims any more (**58:6**). He prayed that they might disappear like a stream that flows only in the time of rains and vanishes in the dry season (**58:7a**).

The NRSV translates **58:7b** as referring to evil rulers being trodden down and withering like grass in the heat. However, the NIV translation is closer to the original Hebrew in changing the metaphor, so that the verse now reads, *when they draw the bow, let their arrows be blunted.* The psalmist also thought of a snail or slug that leaves a trail of slime but which soon seems to dissolve away. So he hoped that such evil people would come to an end. He thought too of the sad circumstances of a baby born too soon to be able to survive and enjoy the light of day, and he wished that fate on the oppressors.

The last picture in **58:9**, a verse very difficult to translate, may be of people who gathered thorns or weeds for a fire under their cooking pot, that a storm swept away. So may these unjust rulers be swept away.

58:10-11 The Attitude of Those Who Fear God

The psalmist asserts that *the righteous will be glad when they are avenged* (**58:10**), that is, when justice is upheld. Can Christians rejoice in God's judgment or the downfall of those who have opposed the purposes of God and caused suffering to many people? In one way, the answer is 'No', if by 'downfall' we mean their personal destruction or death as opposed to the fall of the system or ideology or prejudice they represented or upheld. While their personal destruction may bring temporary relief to those they oppressed, there is a better option. Like our Lord Jesus Christ himself, we should always seek not the death of sinners, but that they should repent, turn to God for forgiveness, and come to live a new life. In that sense our prayer and expectation should be that their repentance will show itself in a new life, characterized by the fear of God and gracious concern for the welfare of others, letting the oppressed go free (Isa 58:6).

In another way, however, we can rejoice that a day is coming when wrongs will be righted, justice will be upheld, and the reign of terror and persecution will be at an end. But that rejoicing is not personal or vindictive. It is the desire to see an end to evil, and especially that God will be glorified as human dictators are brought to an end. God

is then given his rightful place as almighty and sovereign Lord in his world by politicians, whether military or civilian, religious or atheistic. Then people will be able to say, *Surely the righteous still are rewarded; surely there is a God who judges the earth* (**58:11**). Through such divine interventions, the righteous are encouraged: the wicked are restrained, and justice and respect for human dignity with fear of God reign. Such judgments are seen in the world from time to time when God surprises powerful oppressors, and brings their splendour to an end.

Above all, there is a final judgment, and the message of the last book of the NT, addressed to a persecuted church, is that persecutors who seem all powerful do not have the last word. They will have to give account to God as their judge. The words of Revelation 19:1-2 are a jubilant psalm: 'Hallelujah! Salvation and glory and power belong to our God, for true and just are his judgments.' This is the final triumph of good over evil and the ultimate reign of God for which we eagerly work, pray and wait.

Psalm 59: God of Justice and Mercy

The heading of Psalm 59 is similar to that of Psalms 57 and 58, except for the reference to David's situation when Saul was watching his house in an attempt to have him killed (see 1 Sam 19:8-17). He certainly was in desperate need of God's protection and deliverance at that time.

The psalmist is surrounded by enemies, but he directs his thoughts to God. His awareness of God's justice and mercy enables him to trust God, and in the end his trust turns to thankfulness and praise. His words encourage us to reflect on our attitude to injustice in the world, in our country, or in our own community. How should we react when we feel the hatred or attacks of evil people in our neighbourhood, our extended family, our workplace, or even our church? How should we pray about it? What actions should we take?

59:1-7, 12, 14-15 A Cry for Help

This psalm begins an urgent cry for help in the face of danger and difficulty: *Deliver me … protect me … save me* (**59:1a, 2**). He cries out like Jesus' disciples in the storm on Lake Galilee (Mark 4:38): *Arise … Rouse yourself* (**59:4-5**).

The psalmist's enemies are all too real to him. They *rise up against* him (**59:1b**). They are *evildoers* and *bloodthirsty* (**59:2**). They secretly *lie in wait* to take his life, and *conspire* against him (**59:3**). They are like wild dogs that roam about the city, barking, biting, causing fear and spreading disease (**59:6-7, 14-15**). They feel that they can say and do what they like, and that no one will call them to account (**59:7**). That is their arrogant boast, and *curses and lies* are constantly on their lips (**59:12**). In many parts of the world, people – and especially Christians – feel the reality of enemies like these.

59:8-10, 16-17 The Reality of God

The psalmist's appeal to God for protection in the opening verses shows his trust in God. As the psalm proceeds, he reminds himself who God is, and that God is more real and much stronger than any force that can ever be brought against us. The psalmist reminds himself that he is addressing the 'Lord God Almighty, the God of Israel' (59:5) and addresses him as *my strength* and *my fortress* (59:9). He returns to these attributes again in **59:16-17**, where he praises God as *my refuge in times of trouble.* The man or woman of faith can be sure that God sees their plight. Evil and oppressive people may think that they can do what they like, but such pride and arrogance are laughable in the sight of God (59:8, see also 2:1-4). Those who are oppressed can trust in the justice of God, and also in his steadfast love to all who turn to him in their need (59:10).

59:11-13 A Prayer for Judgment

The psalmist does not only pray for deliverance, he also wants to see God's judgment on his enemies. He realizes that he is not the only one to suffer like this, but that the nation is affected by the actions of *wicked traitors* (59:5) against others. Thus his prayer, *do not kill them* in **59:11** is not a request for mercy on his enemies but rather a prayer that God's judgment will take place over time, so that the nation will notice and learn from what happens to these evildoers. He wants people to remember seeing them *wander,* a word that may recall the judgment of Cain, who was condemned to be 'a restless wanderer on the earth' because he murdered his brother (Gen 4:12-14). But ultimately he wants God to *consume them till they are no more* (59:13).

Here, as in other psalms, this psalmist's prayer is not a truly Christian one. It does not show the spirit of our Lord Jesus Christ, who prayed for the forgiveness of his enemies, nor the spirit of evangelism that seeks the repentance and conversion of even the most desperate sinners. Yet it is a cry for justice and not for personal vengeance, for the vindication of the cause of the oppressed, and for the triumph of God's cause over human arrogance. The psalmist wants God to act in such a way that *it will be known to the ends of the earth that God rules,* that he rules *over Jacob* (that is, the nation of Israel), and that he rules in justice everywhere else as well (59:13).

59:16-17 Prayer and Praise

The psalmist had recorded that his enemies surrounded him *at evening* (59:6, 14), but he knows that he will survive the night, and thus he says, *But I will sing of your strength, in the morning I will sing of your love* (59:16). The Bible often encourages us to do the same and turn to God in praise

and prayer at the beginning of the day (see, for example, Pss 5:3; 55:17; 88:13; Isa 50:4-5; Mark 1:35).

The last part of the psalm is prayer and praise that we can always offer. We can always think of ways in which our Lord is our fortress and our *loving God* (59:17), and then thank him for it. This is important. Many of us know how to cry to God for help when we are in pain or danger, but very few remember to shout his praise and, in gratitude, to work for his glory when the danger is over and pleasure comes our way!

Psalm 60: A Prayer of Hope after a Defeat

The heading given to Psalm 60 is similar to many of the others. It refers not only to the collection, the type of psalm and the tune it should be sung to, but it adds that it was also intended *for teaching.* Then it refers to the time when David fought against Syrian kingdoms (2 Sam 8:9-12). Edom lay to the south of Israel, and it may be that the Edomites attacked and defeated Israel while David was involved in campaigns in the far north. Ultimately, however, the Edomites were decisively beaten (2 Sam 8:13-14).

Like Christian people today, the people of Israel in OT days knew times of failure and defeat, as well as times of success and victory. They had to learn, as we must learn, what may be the causes of failure and defeat. We need to learn to discern whether our own desperate times are meant to test and strengthen our faith, or whether they have come because of our own wrong attitudes, words or actions.

Once again, some verses of this psalm are used in a different psalm. Thus 60:5-12 is the same as 108:6-13. For comments on such borrowing, see the comments on Psalm 57.

60:1-4 The Experience of Defeat

In this time of failure the people realized that God had allowed things to happen as they did. Instead of helping them, he had let them be defeated by their enemies. They had turned aside from trusting and serving God, and so his righteous anger was against them (60:1). Consequently their land had suffered a great upheaval like an earthquake (60:2) and the people were enduring *desperate times* (60:3). The pattern we see here had also been the experience of the people at Ai in the days of Joshua (Josh 7), of Ahab in his battle against the Arameans (Syrians – 1 Kgs 22), and of Judah before the Babylonians (2 Kgs 24–25). The image of their having been given wine to drink (perhaps drugged wine) that made them reel (60:3) is similar to the image that Isaiah uses, when he says that Jerusalem had 'drunk from the hand of the Lord the cup of his wrath' (Isa 51:17, 22). But when the people turned back to him, that cup was taken away and God supported and helped them once more.

The Hebrew of **60:4** is difficult to translate, and various English translations render it in different ways. It may mean that those who fear the Lord find that he is their defence even in the time of defeat and failure.

60:5-8 Hope in Time of Defeat

Israel had to learn the causes of their failure, so that they could learn also the way of renewed victory by turning back to God. The psalmist here pleaded God's love for his people, and asked for their prayer to be answered, and that they would know rescue and victory by the power of God's mighty *right hand* (**60:5**).

He reminds the Lord of a prophecy or promise that may have come from long before and that expressed God's purpose for his people (in 60:6-8). God's words were spoken *from his sanctuary* (**60:6**). However, the words here could also be translated as saying that God has spoken 'in his holiness' – in other words his holy word has been given.

The prophecy stated that the land of Israel belonged to God. He had given them Shechem in the west and Succoth in the east. So also he had given them the good land of Gilead east of Jordan and the territory of the tribe of Manasseh. The tribe of Ephraim in the north and Judah in the south were his. These areas were like the *helmet* and *sceptre* of the Warrior King (**60:7**).

It could be said that the nations that threatened Israel were actually just God's servants. People could look out on Moab with its hills surrounding the Dead Sea and think of that nation as the Lord's *washbasin* (**60:8**). Edom could be described as merely the slave to whom he threw his shoes when he returned home. (It is also possible that this refers to God's possessing Edom, for a ceremony that involved casting a shoe is mentioned in Ruth 4:7.) The Lord would also triumph over the Philistines who had so often tried to invade and conquer Israel.

60:9-12 Confidence for the Future

It seems that the people were experiencing defeat at the hands of the Edomites in the south. They were Israel's enemies in the time of David, and they often tried to take advantage of Israel and especially of Judah in the south. When Jerusalem fell to the Babylonians in later times, the Edomites rejoiced (Obad 11-14). They seemed all-powerful in their mountain kingdom. So the question was, *Who will bring me to the fortified city? Who will lead me to Edom?* (**60:9**). There was only one answer to that question. There was only one way to gain victory: pray to God and acknowledge that *the help of man is worthless* (**60:11**). When people truly realize that in all the circumstances of their lives, and sincerely and wholeheartedly rely on God, they can then say with confidence, *With God we will gain the victory, and he will trample down our enemies* (**60:12**; see also 2 Chr 7:14). The Apostle Paul in the NT said much the same thing to tempted

and tested Christians: 'The God of peace will shortly crush Satan under your feet' (Rom 16:20).

While there is a place for seeking human help and support in times of trouble, we must learn never to rely on it rather than on God (see Isa 30:1-7; 31:1-5; Jer 17:5-8).

Psalm 61: Trust in God in a Time of Need

The particular feature of the heading of Psalm 61 is the instruction that it is to be accompanied by *stringed instruments* (see also Pss 4, 6, 54, 55).

This is another psalm that is a prayer in time of need. It shows how prayer is the cure for anxiety, and when we have confidence in God, prayer leads to praise.

61:1-2 Great Need

The psalmist is not simply uttering a prayer to God, but a *cry* that rings out with the earnest plea that God will hear (**61:1**). He is far from home and from friends on whose support he has relied in the past. He feels that he is calling to God from *the ends of the earth* (**61:2a** – compare the feelings expressed in Psalm 42.) His *heart grows faint* (**61:2b**) – in other words he is discouraged and depressed as he thinks about his enemy (61:3), and his utter need of God's defence and protection.

61:3-4 Great Security in God

All the psalmist's circumstances make him feel insecure. But he knows that God is the source of true security. He expresses this confidence using five different images, many of which are also found in other psalms.

- **God is like a 'rock'** (61:2c). A great rock in the wilderness offers protection from storms and shade from the burning heat of the sun. As Psalm 18:31 asks, 'Who is the rock except our God?'
- **God is like a** *refuge* (61:3a). A refuge is a place of protection in times of danger. 'God is our refuge and strength, an ever-present help in trouble' says Psalm 46:1.
- **God is like a strong tower** (61:3b). A tower is a place in which people can be safe from their enemies.
- **God is like a** *host* (61:4). When the psalmist says, *I long to dwell in your tent forever,* he may mean that he wants to stay in God's sanctuary or temple, which was originally the Tent of Meeting that the people carried with them as they wandered in the wilderness and then took into the land of Canaan. But it may also imply that he can rely on receiving the hospitality of a God who prepares 'a table before me in the presence of my enemies. You anoint my head with oil; my cup overflows' (Ps 23:5).
- **God is like a mother bird** (61:4). The wish *to take refuge in the shelter of your wings* may possibly be associated with taking refuge under the outstretched wings of the cherubim that were in the inner sanctuary of the temple.

However, it is more likely that here, as in Psalm 57:1, it refers to the way young birds find protection under the wings of their mother (see Ruth 2:12 and Matt 23:37). All of these images express the same thought found in Psalm 91. In order to find rest and peace and security in God in a world full of troubles, we need to learn to appreciate and totally rely on the love and power of God. We need to *dwell* (or 'abide') and *take refuge* in God. In the NT the Apostle Paul reminds Christians of the total security that is ours in Christ, especially in relation to spiritual warfare, when he says, 'your life is now hidden with Christ in God' (Col 3:1-3). God offers full protection to those who are humble and courageous enough to depend entirely on him.

61:5, 8 Great Cause for Praise

Answered prayer should always lead to praise. Psalm **61:5a** speaks of praise for *vows* being heard. People often made vows when they prayed to God in the face of some great difficulty or danger, as we can tell from 66:13-14 and from Jephthah's vow in Judges 11:29-31 (though that was a foolish vow as Judg 11:34-35 shows). Vows were not necessarily bargains with God as Jacob's vow (in essence, 'If you do this for me, then I will serve you') in Genesis 28:20-22 seems to have been. One of David's vows, of which Psalm 132:1-5 speaks, was an expression of a desire to honour the Lord and worship him. In thankfulness to God we should make vows or promises to serve him, but it is most important that we keep the vows that we make (**61:8;** see also Eccl 5:4-5).

The psalmist also gave thanks for his *heritage of those who fear your name* (**61:5b**). For Israel in OT days their 'inheritance' was the land that God gave them. The inheritance of Christians is the spiritual wealth that we have in Christ, which Hebrews 9:15 speaks of as an 'eternal inheritance', and 1 Peter 1:4 as 'an inheritance that can never perish, spoil or fade' (see also Eph 1:11, 14; Col 1:12; 3:24). For such an inheritance of life and hope, Peter says, 'praise be to the God and Father of our Lord Jesus Christ' (see also Eph 1:3 which speaks of God as the source of 'every spiritual blessing' that is offered to us 'in Christ').

61:6-7 A Prayer for the King

If we understand **61:6** as a prayer for an individual king, there is clearly exaggeration in the request that his years may *endure to all generations* (NRSV). It may be right to understand this as a prayer that the whole line of Davidic kings would continue from generation to generation. Such psalms, however, came to be understood to refer to the Messiah, and their perfect fulfilment is in our Lord Jesus Christ, whose 'years will never end' (Heb 1:12, quoting Ps 102:27).

The king needed to realize that he was on his throne *enthroned in God's presence* and under God's watchful eye, and to know that he needed God's *love and faithfulness to protect him* (**61:7**). When rulers govern their people in the

fear of God and with a concern for justice, a country can prosper and be at peace. The NT teaches us the duty of praying for our rulers that this may be so (see 1 Tim 2:1-3).

Psalm 62: Trust in God at All Times

Jeduthun was one of those who assisted in the music of worship in Jerusalem (1 Chr 16:41-42), but the words *for Jeduthun* in the heading of Psalm 62 probably refer to the tune to which it was sung.

62:1-7 Confidence in God in the Face of Difficulties

This psalm starts, as it will end, with a confident statement of trust in God: *My soul finds rest in God alone* (**62:1**). This quiet resting in God and the pouring out of our hearts to him (62:8) are both valid aspects of our own praying (see also Matt 6:3-8; Rom 8:26-27; Eph 6:18).

The word 'alone' is emphasized in the original Hebrew by the same word being repeated six times in this section of the psalm, in verses 1, 2, 4 (where it is translated as 'fully'), 5 and 6.

There is also repetition in 62:1-2 and **62:5-6**. Both speak of God as a number of the psalms have done as a *rock* and a *fortress* (see Psalm 61:2). In 62:1 he speaks of God as *My salvation*, and in **62:7** he says *my salvation and my honour depend on God.* Here 'salvation' means being rescued from the evil that threatens. Its meaning is similar to what the apostle Paul meant when, facing imprisonment and death for his faith, he wrote, 'The Lord will rescue me from every evil attack and save me for his heavenly kingdom. To him be the glory forever and ever' (2 Tim 4:18).

The evil that the psalmist faced was that he was surrounded by those who professed to bless when *in their hearts they curse* and who *take delight in lies* (**62:4**). Their only aim was to attack their victim, who was like a *leaning wall, this tottering fence,* so that they would bring him down to the ground.

Although these enemies were so strong and the psalmist felt so weak, yet he could say that he would 'leave it all quietly with God' (as Moffatt translates 62:1). Because he did this he could say with confidence that although his enemies may see him as a 'tottering fence', *I will never be shaken* (see also 16:8; 46:5).

62:8-10 Confidence in God Rather Than in Humans

We do have to trust other people, and often we are helped by the support that our friends give us. We, in turn, should offer that kind of help to those around us who are in need. But in the deepest sense our trust must be in God and not in other people (**62:8**). All human beings are frail, and we ourselves often fail even to do the kindness that we intend to do for others. This is the point of **62:9** when it says that in comparison with God, people are *like a puff of breath ... Put them*

HIV AND AIDS

According to the United Nations, more than 41 million people globally are living with HIV/AIDS. Some 75 per cent of them (30 million) live in Africa. All fifteen countries where HIV/AIDS has infected between 11 per cent and 38 per cent of the population are in Africa, and particularly in East and Southern Africa.

Since the beginning of the epidemic in the early 1980s, more than 21 million Africans have perished from AIDS, and the average life expectancy in Sub-Saharan Africa has dropped to forty-seven years from sixty-two years. More than 15 million children have become AIDS orphans.

The church in Africa, and globally, has failed to provide the resources in terms of personnel, leadership and materials required to deal with this pandemic. There have been sins of commission, in that the church has often been responsible for communicating negative social and cultural attitudes, alienating and stigmatizing those infected and affected by HIV/AIDS. There have also been sins of omission, in that the church has failed to talk about sex and sexuality, and has sometimes considered it unholy to discuss these topics on church premises. The church has also underestimated the scope of the problem.

It is now time for the church to break its silence in the face of this pandemic. We need to inculcate moral and spiritual values into our children, youth, men and women, but more than this, we need to develop policies and guidelines on how to respond, as well as having people and pastors committed to dealing with AIDS. There is also a need for resources – money, books, manuals and other materials – to equip the church with the needed skills.

On the local level, health committees should be established in each congregation to work towards making congregations healing communities. These committees should focus on prevention education and awareness-raising, home-based care and support for those infected or affected, care for orphans and advocacy at all levels of society.

Many factors can make the church a powerful force in the fight against HIV/AIDS. These include its long history of presence, proclamation and persuasion and its well-developed structures. The church is also self-sustaining; has a loyal audience that meets every week; has predictable leadership; cuts across geographic, ethnic, national, gender and other barriers; and has grassroots support and understands the language at the grassroots level. More than this, it can offer hope beyond the grave and it has the Bible, a sacred manual that has been tested and proved effective in changing behaviour and morals.

In a time of despair, people need to hear that the message of the Bible is about hope, love and the future and to meditate on such passages as Ps 9:18; 30:5; 62:5; 71:5; Prov 23:18; Rom 12:12-13; 2 Cor 1:7; 2 Tim 2:22. The church can then lead by *understanding hope,* knowing the facts about HIV/AIDS; *discovering hope* in the HIV/AIDS epidemic through our biblical foundation; *spreading hope* by mobilizing the church to perform HIV/AIDS ministries; *developing hope* by changing feelings and attitudes about HIV/AIDS; *sharing hope* through pastoral care to families and communities affected by HIV/AIDS; *offering hope* through HIV/AIDS pastoral counselling; *giving hope* to parents and youth for AIDS-free living and *ministering hope* through home-based care to people with AIDS.

In September 1999, representatives of Christian development organizations and the United Nations gathered in Gaborone, Botswana, to discuss collaboration in HIV/AIDS issues. The gathering adopted an Affirmation of Presence and Continuity that states in part:

> We are in an evolving epidemic of HIV/AIDS.
> Loss and death are real for all of us. Through
> the strength of fellowship we must face our fear
> of death. Only then can we celebrate life fully
> – now, and after death.
> We have a vision of the Church as a servant with
> the courage to truly participate in communities
> so as to realize shalom. We look forward to
> rethinking and reworking the relationships and
> ethos of participating in community, care and
> change. We also look forward to a movement
> beyond ourselves and beyond our boundaries.
> We together are on a JOURNEY INTO HOPE!

Peter Okaalet

---

on the scales and they weigh nothing, they are lighter than a mere breath (GNB). The same point is made in Psalm 118:8-9, Isaiah 40:6-8 and James 4:14.

Some people trust in wealth, which they may have taken violently from others by extortion or robbery (**62:10a**). But even if riches are earned honestly, it is foolish to trust in them instead of in the living and unchanging God (**62:10b**; see also Mark 10:17-27; Luke 12:13-21). We are called to be 'rich towards God' (Luke 12:21).

62:11-12 Confidence in God's Power and Love

The Hebrews often expressed proverbial sayings in the form, 'Once … twice', or 'three times … four times' (see, for example, Prov 30:18-19; Amos 1:3). God's word had come to the psalmist a number of times and in a number of ways (**62:11a**). That word from God was consistent and reliable (compare what is said about God's word in Mark 13:31 and 1 Pet 1:24-25.) That word told what God is like, and, like God, it is utterly dependable. We need always to remember the three things that are said here about God:

- **God is powerful** (**62:11b**).
- **God is also** *loving* (**62:12a**). We can trust God to help in all our needs and in every situation because he is both almighty and all-loving. Humans may seem powerful. Demonic and occult forces may seem powerful – but they are powerful and evil. God is powerful and loving.
- **God is also just**. He knows when people are acting unjustly and oppressively. *Surely you will reward each person according to what he has done* (**62:12b**). Those words should humble us all, because all of us are guilty of doing what is sinful in God's sight. But when we turn to him in repentance, he forgives and restores us to his blessing.

The psalmist would have understood the words recorded in Jeremiah: 'Let not the wise man boast of his wisdom or the strong man boast of his strength or the rich man boast of his riches, but let him who boasts boast about this: that he understands and knows me, that I am the Lord, who exercises kindness, justice and righteousness on earth, for in these I delight' (Jer 9:23-24).

Psalm 63: Thirsting for God

The heading of Psalm 63 suggests that it was written by David *when he was in the desert of Judah.* This could have been when he was escaping from Saul (1 Sam 23:14; 24:1-2) or from Absalom's rebellion (2 Sam 15:14, 23).

The Lord our God is the Creator of the whole universe and the God of the nations, but he is also the One who is concerned for each of us individually, so we can know him and respond to him personally. This psalm is a very personal response to God, which repeatedly uses the words 'I', 'me' and 'my'. Three times it speaks of 'my soul', that is, the inner life, what we really are in our thoughts and deepest wishes. These three statements are the main points of the psalm. We need to examine ourselves to see whether our love for and trust in our Lord matches that of the psalmist.

63:1-4 'My Soul Thirsts for You'

God was first in the psalmist's life – this relationship mattered more to him than anything else. As a very thirsty person wants water more than anything else, so he longed for God. He thought of life apart from God as being like *a dry and weary land where there is no water* (**63:1**) – a land similar to the one where he now found himself, according to the heading. 42:1-2 uses a similar picture of a person's longing for God, 'As the deer pants for streams of water, so my soul pants for you, O God. My soul thirsts for God, for the living God.'

Jesus recognized this thirst, and spoke of it as a 'hunger and thirst for righteousness' (Matt 5:6). He also provides the means to quench it: 'If anyone is thirsty, let him come to me and drink. Whoever believes in me, as the Scripture has said, streams of living water will flow from within him'

(John 7:37-38). This promise of Jesus is fulfilled by the Holy Spirit in the lives of those who sincerely believe.

The most wonderful experience of the psalmist's life had been seeing God in the sanctuary (**63:2a**). The word used for 'see' here is the same one used when a prophet is referred to as a 'seer'. It may refer to a vision that he had of God, or simply to the experience of feeling God's presence and having a sense of his power and glory during times of worship (**63:2b**).

Most people value life itself more than anything else, and it is natural for us to cling to life, but the psalmist says that God's *love is better than life* (**63:3**). Indeed, as the NT often emphasizes, to know God in the personal way of which this psalm speaks, is real life, life in all its fullness, eternal life (see John 3:16; 10:10; 17:3).

63:5-7 'My Soul Will Be Satisfied'

Realizing the wonderful love and goodness of God, the psalmist says, *my lips will glorify you* (63:3) and *I will praise you as long as I live* (63:4). He sings praises to God because it is in an intimate relationship with God that he finds his deepest satisfaction. Although the psalm goes on to speak of difficulties and of enemies, the psalmist insists that a life lived close to God is like being satisfied at a feast with *the richest of foods* (**63:5**; compare 23:5; 107:9; Isa 55:1-2).

When he lies awake in the night, the psalmist thinks of God's goodness (**63:6**). Some people are kept awake at night by fear: fear of death, fear of enemies, fear of armed robbers and thieves, and even fear of bad dreams and nightmares. But those who put their trust in God can rest assured that their Keeper will never let them down whether they are awake or asleep (see 4:8; 121:1-3). God has never failed to help those who trust him in times of need.

Using the picture that other psalms have used, the psalmist speaks of being in the shadow of the wings of the Almighty (see comments on 61:4). In that secure place he says, *I sing for joy* (**63:7**, NRSV; see also 91:1-2).

63:8-11 'My Soul Clings to You'

In saying *my soul clings to you* (**63:8a**), the psalmist uses a word that is used of a husband and wife linking their lives together (Gen 2:24), and of the way the people of Israel were called to keep close to the Lord (Deut 10:20; 11:22; 30:20). Those who want to keep close to the Lord, and remain faithful to him in this way, find that they can also say, *your right hand upholds me* (**63:8b**).

When we read **63:9-10**, we need to remember that we are not to seek harm and retribution for those who oppose us, but rather that they should turn to know the truth and the redeeming love of God. At the same time those who trust in God can be sure that deceit and injustice will not triumph in the end. Those who oppose God's will, and try to stop God's people from fulfilling the purpose of God, will surely face a day of reckoning. Our task is to do right, to seek peace and justice for all, and to commit our cause to God. That means that in the struggle for social justice in the world we must not become frustrated and try to take justice into our own hands, whether by our actions, our thoughts or even our prayers. Jesus was eventually vindicated by God because he committed his cause entirely to God, and harboured no bitterness or ill will towards his enemies (1 Pet 2:21-23). We must learn to forgive, and to leave our vindication in the hands of God. He is just and fair, and he is almighty.

In the last verse of the psalm, as in many other psalms, we have a reference to the king. There can be no doubt that a God-fearing king or ruler should *rejoice in God,* turn from all evil and deceit, and lead his people also to *praise* God and gladly serve him (**63:11a**).

We are commanded not to use oaths today as people did in OT days (Matt 5:33-37), but this is not what is meant by *swear by God* in **63:11b**. Here what is meant is acknowledging God's perfect truth and righteousness and affirming that there is no other like him (Deut 6:13; Isa 45:23).

Psalm 64: Spiritual Battle

Psalm 64 describes the spiritual battle that is going on all the time all over the world. There are those working to oppose the will of God in the world and to make life difficult for those who try to serve God. Anyone who wishes to do God's will and live honestly for God's kingdom in our world must be prepared to experience opposition, intrigue and ridicule (see 2 Tim 3:12). In those OT days the normal weapons of warfare were swords and bows and arrows, so the psalm speaks of the arrows used on both sides of the battle.

64:1-2 A Cry for Help

The psalmist felt that he was in the midst of the battle, and he was greatly distressed. Enemies were very near and very threatening. Yet he knew that God was against all evil and that he could turn to God and cry to him, *Hear me, O God* (**64:1**). Literally, he is asking, 'save my life from the fear of the enemy'. Those enemies were trying to hide what they were doing and thus surprise him, but he could ask God, *hide me from the conspiracy of the wicked* (**64:2**).

When we, like the psalmist, fear that the forces of evil against us are very strong and threatening, we can turn to this psalm and to passages such as Acts 4:23-31, Philippians 1:12-14 and 1 John 4:18.

64:3-6 The Weapons of the Opposition

The *evildoers* (64:2) were making *evil plans* (**64:5**) against others. Their tongues were like swords sharpened for battle (**64:3a**). Their *bitter words* (NRSV) may have been hurtful slander of godly people, or they may have been curses that

were intended to bring trouble on those against whom they were directed. Whatever the case, they were like arrows used to cause deep hurt and injury to those who feared God (**64:3b-4**).

The evildoers themselves showed no fear of any human being, nor yet of God. They thought that they could make their plans secretly and carry them out, without anyone being able to stop them. *Who will see them?* (64:5) they asked. The differences between the various English translations show how hard it is to understand the Hebrew here. It may be the boast of cunning people who think that they *have devised a perfect plan* (**64:6**) that God does not see and will not prevent. Or it may be, as the NJB puts it, a question and answer: 'Who will see us, or will penetrate our secrets?' 'He will do that, he who penetrates human nature to its depths, the depths of the heart'.

These words remind us of other passages in the Bible that show the foolishness of people thinking that God does not see what they are doing (for example, Pss 10:1-11; 59:6-8; 73:1-11; 94:1-11; 139:1-16; Isa 29:15-16).

64:7-8 The Weapons of God

There was a response to their hurtful words and their actions – in the words and actions of God. Though *the mind and heart of man are cunning* (64:6), God knows the secrets of every human heart, and from him nothing that we think or say or do can ever be hidden. Though evil people *aim their words like deadly arrows* (64:3), the last arrow is God's (**64:7a**). They may attack *from ambush* and do harm to godly people (64:4), but God, too, will act *suddenly,* and the wicked will be unprepared for his action (**64:7b**). They may use the words of their tongues as swords against others, but those same tongues will bring them to ruin (**64:8**).

All this means that all the powers of evil in the world will be broken in God's time and way. Those who use their strength and their positions to harm, oppress and humiliate others may sometimes seem to have great power. But God looks on and patiently waits for his own time to judge them and to vindicate his people. In our own times there have been many powerful dictators who have caused immense suffering to millions of people. But all such dictators in history have been overthrown, or have died, powerless against death itself. Only those who trust God and want to do his will in their lives can rest unafraid.

64:9-10 In the Midst of the Battle

The psalmist believed that God would win the spiritual battle. It would be seen that in the end evil could not conquer. *All mankind will fear,* he says confidently. *They will proclaim the works of God, and ponder what he has done* (**64:9**). Inasmuch as we seek to be *righteous* and to rely on God, we can truly *rejoice in the Lord and take refuge in him* (**64:10**). God does fight and win the battle for us if we refuse to avenge ourselves, and if we set his glory and honour before our eyes no matter how much we are provoked.

The most painful thing to many of us is when the opposition we face is personal, and carried out by people close to us – colleagues at work, leaders in the church, or even a spouse or family member. We must be ready to see where there are faults in our own lives and address these. Then we must pray that those who are opposing us may change their minds in repentance. There is always true security for those who trust in the Lord and put his will first in their lives.

One who faces danger or fear can often do nothing but pray. One can always pray, and the person who prays is never helpless because God answers prayer.

Psalm 65: Pardon, Power and Provision

Psalm 65 is often used in harvest thanksgiving services today. It may have been written for one of the Hebrew festivals at which they gave thanks to God for the harvest, perhaps the Festival of Unleavened Bread or of Tabernacles. It is also possible that it was written after a drought, when the people had prayed and made vows to God and then experienced the blessing of rain, as described in 65:9-13. Yet another possibility is that verses 9-13 are prayers for rain and for God's blessing on the land, suggesting that this psalm may have been sung at the beginning of the rainy season rather than at the time of harvest.

It begins with the words *Praise awaits you, O God* (**65:1**), and as we go through the psalm we can see many reasons why we should praise God. We can think of them under the three headings of pardon, power and provision. It also speaks of fulfilling our vows to the Lord, a topic that was discussed in relation to Psalm 61:5 and 8.

65:2-4 Pardon

God is addressed as *you who hear prayer* (**65:2**). He hears the prayers of *all men,* that is, of everyone who has put their trust in him all down the ages and all over the world. Yet he is the great Creator and Lord of the universe, and we are weak and sinful people, who have no right to come to him. Our sins are a barrier between us and God. It is amazing that he is prepared to hear our prayers. But all through Scripture, and above all in Jesus Christ, we are shown that God is willing to hear and to forgive those who turn to him. So we need never continue to think that we are *overwhelmed by sins* (**65:3**). God pardons us and sets us free from the failures and wrongs of the past.

Not only may we ask for God's forgiveness, but we can rejoice in the fact that even before we ask, God has chosen us (**65:4a**) and has drawn us so that we desire to live close to him (see John 15:16). This psalm captures both sides of the truth that James expresses when he says, 'Come near to God, and he will come near to you' (Jas 4:8).

For the people of Israel in OT days, the temple on Mount Zion in Jerusalem was God's *holy temple* or dwelling place (**65:4b**). As they thought of that, devout Israelites could say, *we are filled with the good things of your house* (65:4b). How much more is this true for us today! Now we know that we can meet God in any place and that God seeks to make our bodies and the fellowship of Christian people his temple (see 1 Cor 6:19-20; 2 Cor 6:16).

65:5-8 Power

We praise *God our Saviour* (**65:5**) because he not only forgives but he also saves us from the power of sin. Not only that, but he performs *awesome deeds of righteousness* (65:5) as he delivers the weak and poor (see 45:4; 47:2-4; 76:7-9). People have often felt overwhelmed by strong oppressors, but history records the fall of one oppressor after another.

God's power is also seen in creation. He has made and established the mighty mountains (**65:6**). God controls the wild sea as he also controls wild people (**65:7**). From one end of the earth to the other, people feel a sense of awe at God's *wonders* (**65:8**). They are signs of power at work in creation and in human history, but also signs of wisdom and love.

The NRSV describes *the gateways of the morning and the evening* as shouting for joy before the Lord (**65:8**). What does this image mean? The psalmist may be thinking of the beauty of sunrise and sunset. Or of the worship of people at first light in the morning and last light in the evening. Or of the fact that God in wisdom gives the day to work in and the night to rest. Or that the people in furthest east and furthest west alike bring their joyful praise to God, so that the NIV translates this as, *where morning dawns and evening fades you call forth songs of joy.* All these interpretations are true causes for joy. And we should be looking out for other signs of God's presence and power, wisdom and love, so that we can join those all over the world who are awed by the wonders of God's work.

65:9-13 Provision

What would the earth be without rain? Whatever land we live in, we know the blessing of the rain. Without it our crops could not grow, and none of us could live. Those who live in countries where there are months of dry weather know best the transformation that comes to the earth when the rain comes. When God gives the rain as from a heavenly river (**65:9**), the ploughed earth is softened, plants are able to grow, and so in due time there are the crops that God gives us to enjoy (**65:10**).

God's *bounty* (**65:11**) crowns the year in the sense that we know the blessing of the passing seasons, according to the promise of Genesis 8:22, 'seed time and harvest, cold and heat, summer and winter'. The psalmist uses the image of God passing over the land in a chariot in the clouds, and wherever he passes his *carts overflow with abundance* (65:11). Where there had been wilderness or desert before, there are rich pastures (**65:12**). The fields with their sheep, the valleys with their crops, are like people dressed in great beauty for a happy celebration. The psalmist thinks of them, and feels almost that the fields are shouting and singing their praise to God (**65:13**).

As all nature praises God, how much more should we! There is beauty, as there is praise, in a life that is committed to God in faith and love through Jesus Christ and enjoys 'the unsearchable riches of Christ' (Eph 3:8).

Psalm 66: Come and See – Come and Hear

Psalm 66 is a song of praise. The psalmist pictures first what God had done among the nations of the world, then what he had done for Israel, and he says, *Come and see what God has done* (66:5). Finally he says, *Come and listen, all you who fear God; let me tell you what he has done for me* (66:16). It is like many services of worship in Nigeria, and perhaps in other parts of the world, which start with worship and praise of God by all and then give opportunities for individuals to come with their family and friends to publicly express their personal thanksgiving for God's special blessings on them. It is important to praise and thank God in our hearts privately, but there is special blessing and added joy in praising God by giving public testimony to his goodness in the presence of his people.

66:1-4 Lord of All Nations

The psalm begins with *all the earth* (**66:1**) being called to worship God. Everyone should worship because of God's glory and God's name, that is, because of who he is, and for the way that he has revealed himself in greatness and power, in holiness and love. The leaders of powerful nations often think that they can do as they please and oppress others, but God's 'eyes watch the nations' (66:7; and compare 11:4; 33:13-15). So this is the warning to them, *let not the rebellious rise up against him.* When powerful nations do exalt themselves and rebel against God's ways, what happens and indeed has often happened in history, is that they are brought down. Such are God's judgments in the world, what the psalmist calls the 'awesome deeds' of the Lord (**66:3**, 5; compare 46:8-9; 47:2-3; 65:5).

66:5-12 God of Israel

The OT tells especially the story of God's dealings with Israel. At their annual festivals (like the Passover) and in their worship at other times, the people of Israel would look back to what God had done for them as he led them out of Egypt and into the promised land. *Come, and see what God has done* (**66:5**) they said, and after hearing it they said *let us rejoice in him* (**66:6**). They spoke as if God was doing

that great work of salvation before their eyes. In the same way, Christians recall the death and resurrection of Christ in worship, and especially as we celebrate the Lord's Supper, the Holy Communion service.

The Israelites remembered how God had set them free from slavery in Egypt, and that when it seemed they would be captured by the Egyptian army, *he turned the sea into dry land* (66:6); so they went free (see Exod 14). Then, so that they could come into the land that God was giving to them, *they passed through the waters* (the river Jordan) *on foot* (66:6, see Josh 3). They could say, the Lord *has preserved our lives and kept our feet from slipping* (**66:9**).

But having favour with God did not mean that they would enjoy his favour no matter what they did. When they turned away from him, they had to suffer being chastened and disciplined, as a child is disciplined by wise parents. That meant *burdens* (**66:11**) on their backs, and the nations around them gaining victories over them (**66:12**). It was like going *through fire and water*, but the fire and water did not destroy them (see Isa 43:2). They were brought out safely, but the experience was a testing of their faith in God. As silver is refined and purified by being heated to very high temperatures, so God refined and purified them through what they had to suffer (**66:10**). But at the end he brought them into *a place of abundance* (66:12).

Fiery trials make our characters nobler. Problems sent to us from God, or resulting from our commitment to the will of God and our desire to reflect the character of Christ can be 'spiritual promotions'. The story of Job expresses this (see especially Job 42:10-12), and the NT abounds with teaching on patient endurance, and the blessing of not avenging ourselves or retaliating (Rom 12:14-21; 1 Pet 3:8-17; see also Isa 48:10; Jer 9:7; Zech 13:9; Mal 3:2-4; 1 Pet 1:6-7).

66:13-20 My God

It is a great thing when a person regards God not only as the Lord of all nations and the God of Israel, but can also say 'You are my God' and 'the Lord is my Shepherd'. In Israel, and perhaps in many situations today, people often recognize the existence of God. Some even go as far as addressing him as 'our God', or thinking of him as 'the God of our religion' or 'church'. But to know and address the Almighty as 'my God' – with filial, yet holy, affection – results from the personal experience of, and encounter with, God that Jesus describes as being 'born again' (John 3:3-5; John 1:11-12).

The psalmist speaks here of such a personal experience. In a time of trouble he had called on the Lord and made a vow (**66:13-14**; for the meaning of such vows, see the comments on 61:5, 8). Now he could celebrate the fact that God had been very good to him. He did this by sacrificing animals to the Lord. Christians today do not make such sacrifices, but we express our vows and offerings by giving God our lives (see Rom 12:1-2).

There were two things that the psalmist saw as special causes for thanksgiving:

- He knew that sin always separates a person from God and is a hindrance to prayer (**66:18**; see also Isa 1:12-17; 59:1-2; John 9:31; 1 John 3:21-22). But he knew that God had forgiven his sin when he turned to him.
- He knew that when he *cried out* (**66:17**), God had heard and answered his prayer (**66:19**). So the psalm ends on a note of joyful confidence in God: *Praise be to God,* he affirms, because he *has not rejected my prayer or withheld his love from me!* (**66:20**). Trials and difficulties drive us back to God in prayer and meditation, to understand him better and more deeply, and to trust him with greater confidence for the future.

There is one final thing that we should notice about this psalm. Its writer wants other people to know what God has done. So in relation to God's mighty acts in the world he says, *Come and see what God has done* (66:5). In relation to God's loving acts towards him he says, *Come and listen, all you who fear God; let me tell you what he has done for me* (**66:16**). If we know God's power and love, we should want others to come to that knowledge too. After all, we were chosen 'to declare the praises of him who called you out of darkness into his wonderful light' (1 Pet 2:9).

Psalm 67: All Nations to Praise God

In the heading added to Psalm 67, it is called *a song.* Like Psalms 4, 54, 55, 61 and 76, it is to be accompanied by *stringed instruments.* Once again we are reminded of the role of music in worship.

This psalm has sometimes been thought of as a song of thanksgiving for the harvest, but this is a minor element as the harvest is mentioned only in 67:6. The psalm is primarily a prayer for the full realization of God's blessings in all the world and for people of all nations to praise God.

The words of the psalm recall two OT passages. The first is Genesis 12:1-3 where God promises to bless Abraham and make him a blessing, so that 'all peoples on earth will be blessed through you.' The second is Numbers 6:24-26, where the priests are told to pray for God's blessing on the people by saying: 'The Lord bless you and keep you; the Lord make his face shine upon you and be gracious to you; the Lord turn his face towards you and give you peace.'

67:1 The Blessing of God

The psalmist asks for three things:

- **For the grace of God.** It is always right to make this the first thing that we ask from God. We come to him as sinful people, and we should come as the tax-collector rather than as the Pharisee in Jesus' parable (Luke 18:9-14),

praying 'God, have mercy on me, a sinner!' Hebrews 4:16, speaking of the privilege of prayer, says that we can come to God's 'throne of grace with confidence', first to 'receive mercy', and then to 'find grace to help us in our time of need'.

- **For God to bless us with his gifts** that will meet both our physical and spiritual needs.
- **For his face to shine on us.** This image is often used in the psalms (see 4:6; 80:3, 7, 19; 119:135), and is heard in the priestly blessing in Numbers 6:24-26. Proverbs 16:15 speaks of the light of a king's face indicating that he is showing favour to his people. Thus when God's face shines on us it means he looks with favour on those who turn to him. But his face is 'hidden' when we have sinned against him and have not repented (see Deut 31:17-18).

67:3 The Praise of God

The praise of God was what mattered most to the psalmist. *May the peoples praise you, O God; may all the peoples praise you* is a refrain that is repeated in **67:3** and 67:5. There is a difference between thanksgiving and praise. We thank God for the blessings that he has given to us. We praise him when we think more of the Giver than of the gifts, and realize that he is the Creator and Lord of all; he is holy, all-powerful and all-wise, our heavenly Father, our loving and gracious Saviour. We praise God when in our thoughts, our words and our lives we truly worship and serve him. The psalmist ends with these words: *May all people everywhere honour him* (67:7, GNB).

67:2, 4-7 The Knowledge of God

The psalmist wants the Lord to be known in all the world and among all nations. He mentions four things that can be known about God.

- **God's way** (**67:2a**). God has not left us ignorant of how he wants us to live. The people of Israel, who were given the law and the prophets, were to be a light to other nations showing them God's way (Isa 42:6; 49:6). Similarly the NT asserts that Christians are the light of the world to show people the way to God (Matt 5:16), to proclaim by word and deed the good news of the One who has called them 'out of darkness into his wonderful light' (1 Pet 2:9). The early Christians actually referred to themselves as those who followed the Way (Acts 9:2; 19:9, 23; 22:4; see also John 14:6). All nations should have the opportunity to follow that way.
- **God's salvation** (**67:2b**). God has shown his love in his willingness to save us from the guilt of our sins as we turn to him. He also shows us his power to save us from all the attacks of evil and all our temptations to do what is wrong. So in Christ we come to a Saviour who is able to save thoroughly, completely and entirely, and to keep us safe permanently (Heb 7:25).

- **God's justice** (**67:4a**). God is judge of all as well as Saviour, but we know that he is perfectly just. Nations and their leaders who acknowledge him can see that God rules *the peoples justly*, that is, with perfect fairness. So they in turn are called to act justly towards all. The principle here is that 'righteousness exalts a nation, but sin is a disgrace to any people' (Prov 14:34).
- **God's guidance** (**67:4b**). As shepherds lead their sheep, so God guides all those who look to him. Anyone who trusts God for guidance in this way can testify from experience and say, 'he guides me in paths of righteousness for his name's sake' (23:3). But also the nation that looks to God for direction will be able to say as Israel did, 'In your unfailing love you will lead the people you have redeemed. In your strength you will guide them to your holy dwelling' (Exod 15:13).

The most important message of this psalm is that we who know the blessing of God (**67:6-7**) should live to praise God and to share with others all over the world the wonderful good news of Jesus Christ that has transformed our lives and that can transform theirs as well (see Matt 28:18-20; Acts 1:8; Rom 10:13-17).

Psalm 68: The Victories of the Lord

Psalm 68 is so rich and inspiring that it is worth reading over and over again. Yet in some ways it is hard to understand. It reads like a lot of little pieces of other psalms brought together. Parts of it are actually very similar to other passages in the OT, which we will see as we study it. In a few places it is difficult to know what the original Hebrew language of the psalm meant. Some of the words used are found nowhere else in the OT. Yet one great theme runs through it all. It is that the Lord God rules over the nations. When he comes to his people, he comes in power. Those who oppose him cannot win in the end. So all peoples of the earth should realize his power and majesty, and worship him.

The psalm can be divided into eight main sections, dealing with what God has done in the past and looking forward to what he will do in the future.

68:1-4 'Let God Rise Up'

The first verse comes from the words of Numbers 10:35. The people of Israel had the ark of the covenant that was the special symbol of God's presence with them. It was like a large box, and contained the stone tablets on which the Ten Commandments were written (see Exod 25:10-16; Deut 10:1-5). It was carried ahead of the people as they travelled in the wilderness or went into battle. And as it was carried out they prayed, *May God arise, may his enemies be scattered* (**68:1**). Israel made that prayer with the assurance that those who reject God cannot have true and lasting power,

but they are like smoke driven away by the wind, or wax melting near a fire (**68:2**).

Because the use of this prayer is associated with the ark, some people think that this psalm may have been composed to be sung as David brought the ark to Jerusalem to make that city the centre of Israel's worship (see 2 Sam 6). We have no such ark today, but if we seek to serve God, we, too, can be encouraged by his presence, and so can sing and rejoice (**68:3**).

God is described as riding *on the clouds* (**68:4a**) or riding 'the ancient skies above' (68:33) – a vivid image that is used in the OT to describe God as like a warrior, riding in his chariot as he comes to the help of his people (see Exod 19:9; Deut 33:26; Pss 18:9-10; 104:1-4).

God is celebrated by his holy name, which is here translated as *the Lord* (**68:4b**). Literally, the text says 'his name is Yah', the name that is part of the word Hallelu-jah ('praise Yah') and of many Hebrew names that end in -iah. It is the shortened form of the personal name of God, Yahweh.

68:5-10 God Frees and Provides

Powerful people in the world often oppress the weak, but God cares for the weak, protects widows and orphans who have no human help, and comes to the aid of the lonely and desolate. 68:5 is particularly relevant and comforting for people who live in situations where widows and orphans are subjected to oppression and deprivation. In some cases their oppression comes from close relatives such as brothers-in-law and uncles. The psalm encourages those who suffer to take heart because God is the *father to the fatherless, a defender of widows* (**68:5**). As God's children, we should share his concern for them (Exod 22:22-24; Deut 24:17-22; Isa 1:16-17; Jas 1:27).

The psalm also speaks of the way the Lord came to the people of Israel when they were *prisoners* in Egypt and set them free (**68:6a**). The fate of the *rebellious* who have to *live in a sun-scorched land* (**68:6b**) may be a reminder that the rebellious people in Moses' time had to live for forty years in the wilderness and were not allowed to enter the promised land.

God led them as they went through the wilderness, and made himself known to them at Mount Sinai (**68:7-8**; see also Judg 5:4-5; Exod 19). Then he brought them into the land of Canaan and provided for them (**68:9-10**). So those who feel abandoned by everyone, or lonely and oppressed, may rely on the goodness of our great unchanging God.

68:11-14 Battles Won

When Israel came into Canaan there were battles to be fought and victories to be won (**68:11-12**). The book of Judges tells how when the people relied on God, enemy kings were scattered and took flight, and spoils were divided, whether among the men *in the camps* (NIV) or the *women at home* RSV (**68:12**).

The next two verses are very difficult to interpret. Thus some interpret the doves referred to in **68:13** as objects taken as plunder, while others argue that the dove is a symbol of Israel, or even of the women of Israel dressed in the finery that has been taken.

It is not known exactly where Zalmon was (**68:14**). It was probably the place of a battle in the days of Judges, and it may be that the flight of the army is likened to snow driven by the wind.

68:15-20 The Temple Mount

There are majestic mountains in the area of Bashan in northern Palestine (**68:15**). But to Israel, Mount Zion in Jerusalem was far greater, because that was where the ark of the covenant had been taken, and there the temple was built where they met with God and worshipped him (**68:16**). Just as God had previously made his presence known on Mount Sinai, so he made his presence known in the temple on Mount Zion (**68:17**). It was right that people should bring their gifts there, and know the living God as the One who gives salvation, saves from death and bears his people up (**68:18-20**). But God does not only receive gifts, he also distributes them as is clear from the use of 68:18 in Ephesians 4:7-13.

68:21-23 Victory over Evil Enemies

The expressions used in these verses are an OT way of telling how the living God brought down those who wanted evil to triumph (**68:21**). Such people would not be allowed to escape either in the highest mountains or the deepest seas (**68:22**). Their fate would be like that of the wicked Ahab and Jezebel (**68:23**; see also 1 Kgs 22:29-38; 2 Kgs 9:30-37).

68:24-27 A Procession to Worship

These verses suggest that this psalm was written for special celebrations at a festival in the temple in Jerusalem when the worshippers remembered the great acts of God in their past. What we have here is a vivid description of a procession to the temple, with singers and musicians leading the people in praising God (**68:24-26**). This group is followed by representatives of the different tribes in Israel (**68:27**) making up what the psalmist calls *the assembly of Israel*. The NRSV translates this last expression as 'you who are of Israel's fountain', implying that God is like a never-failing supply of thirst-quenching water (compare Jer 2:13).

As we read about this procession, we should be reminded of the great triumphal procession of Christ described in 2 Corinthians 2:14.

68:28-31 Enemies That Threatened

The power of God had been shown in the help he gave to Israel in the past. Kings of other nations had brought tribute to them (**68:28-29**). Yet enemies still threatened. *The beast among the reeds* was probably the Egyptians, and the *bulls* and *calves* were possibly their soldiers or those of other nations (**68:30a**). With God's help, those who delighted in war would again be scattered (**68:30b**). The Egyptians would bring tribute, and even distant Cush (or Ethiopia – NRSV) would *submit herself to God* (**68:31**).

68:32-35 All Nations to Worship

The true God, the living God, is the God of all the earth, and so all nations should *sing praise* to him (**68:32**). We can be thankful that God has spoken and made his ways known. He is awesome in *power* and *majesty* (**68:33-34**), but those who submit to him find *strength* for their lives (**68:35**). Those who know God in Jesus have an even greater reason for praising God than the psalmist and can give a much deeper meaning to the words (see Eph 1:3). For them the closing words of this psalm can indeed come from the heart.

Psalm 69: A Cry Out of Deep Distress

In the heading of Psalm 69, *To the tune of 'Lilies'* is probably a reference to the tune to which the psalm is sung. The same tune is referred to in the headings of Psalms 45 and 80.

This psalm is a cry from the heart of one who was in great trouble. Not even his closest family stood with him, pitied him or comforted him. Such suffering was the fate of many who served God in the OT – Jeremiah could certainly identify with this sufferer (Jer 12:6; 20:1-2, 7-10; 36:1-38:28). There was also another even greater servant of God who suffered like this – the Lord Jesus Christ. Except for the other psalm of suffering, Psalm 22, this psalm is quoted in the NT more than any other. We, too, may have to suffer insults or opposition from others because of our faith. This psalm can become our prayer too, as we pray for ourselves and others: 'Lord, because of our many failures we need your forgiveness; because we are weak in ourselves we need your strength and guidance; but help us to live in thankfulness to you and to seek that all your people may find blessing, through Jesus Christ our Lord'.

69:1-3, 14-15 Distress Described

Sometimes the crises of life become so overwhelming that it feels as though one is being sucked into a deep ditch or into choking mud. This is how the psalmist felt when he described his distress as like being in deep water that had come up to his neck and threatened to flood right over the top of him (**69:1-2**). He may be speaking metaphorically, but Jeremiah faced such a situation in reality when he was put into a well with deep mud at the bottom, in which he could find no foothold (Jer 38:1-6).

He returns to this sensation of drowning in troubles in **69:14-15**. There he also speaks of *the pit* closing over him, meaning that he is in fear of death and of being enclosed in a grave.

In the midst of this flood of troubles, the only thing that is dry is his parched throat as he calls frantically for help, but receives no answer (**69:3**). At such times it is not easy to keep trusting in God. We can easily think that everyone, including God, has forgotten us, but God does not fail (see 23:4; 27:10).

69:4-12 The Cause of Distress

The reason the psalmist felt as he did was that he was surrounded by enemies who hated him without reason, accused him of things that he had never done, and even tried to take his life (**69:4**; see also John 15:25). He knew that he had sometimes acted foolishly and done what was wrong (**69:5**), and he sincerely prayed that others might not stumble in their trust in God because of what he had done (**69:6**). But he could honestly say that he was not guilty of what his enemies accused him of doing. In fact he had suffered reproach and unending criticism from them because he had tried to serve God (**69:7**). Worse still, his tormentors included his own family (**69:8**). When he had turned to God humbly with prayer and fasting and sackcloth (the sign of mourning), they and other people had only laughed at him and insulted him (**69:10-12**).

The psalmist speaks of being attacked because of his zeal for the house of God (**69:9a**). This zeal may have been his concern that there be true worship of God in the temple (a zeal shared by Jeremiah) or a more general concern for God's people and his work. The words can also be taken as referring to a zeal for rebuilding the temple after the people came back from exile (a zeal shared by the prophets Haggai and Zechariah). This last interpretation also fits with 69:35-36, which may have been part of the original psalm, or which may have been added later to make the prayers of the psalm applicable to that time. The disciples' interpretation of this verse as applying to Jesus fits both of the first two interpretations (John 2:17).

69:9b is also cited by Paul in Romans 15:3 as a reminder that we are to stand by our fellow believers and share their suffering for the sake of God, even if we are mocked for it. After all, Christ himself did no less.

69:13, 6-18 Help in Distress

In his deep distress the psalmist knew that he could turn to God, and that indeed God was the only one to whom he could turn. His first and constant prayer was *Save me* (69:1), *Come near and rescue me; redeem me because of my foes* (**69:18**). Why could he pray like this? Because he knew the truth of God's very nature as love and compassion. He could say, *'in your great love, O God, answer me with your sure salvation* (**69:13**). *Answer me, O Lord, out of the goodness of your love; in your great mercy turn to me* (**69:16**). He knew that 'the Lord hears the needy' who turn to him (69:33). The God whom the psalmist knew was the God who made himself known to Moses as 'the compassionate and gracious God, slow to anger, abounding in love and faithfulness, maintaining love to thousands, and forgiving wickedness, rebellion and sin' (Exod 34:6-7). The message here is that God can be trusted. We may have difficulty praying for ourselves when in the heat of a crisis, but we need no long prayers or many words to make our need known to God. We can just pour out our hearts before him (see, for example, 1 Sam 1:15-16). We can also draw encouragement from the ministry of the Holy Spirit who intercedes for God's people with sighs too deep for words (Rom 8:26-27). Above all, let us remember that we have a Saviour who 'always lives to intercede' for us (Heb 7:25).

69:19-29 Another Sufferer

This psalm is often quoted in the NT in relation to the sufferings of Jesus. As we have seen, 69:4 is quoted of Jesus in John 15:25, and 69:9 is quoted in John 2:17 and Romans 15:3. The writers of the Gospels probably had **69:21** in mind when they spoke of Jesus being offered vinegar and gall on the cross (Matt 27:34, 48; Mark 15:36; Luke 23:36; John 19:29).

Yet there was one great difference between the psalmist in his sufferings, and Jesus in his. The psalmist prayed for judgment on his enemies in ways that they deserved if they received justice from God (**69:22-28**). Jesus prayed for his enemies, 'Father, forgive them, for they do not know what they are doing' (Luke 23:34). He offered his enemies life, rather than praying like the psalmist, *may they be blotted out of the book of life* (69:28). The OT refers a number of times to such a book in which the names of God's people are recorded (Exod 32:32-33; Isa 4:3; Ezek 13:9; Dan 12:1) and the idea is also taken up in the NT (Luke 10:20; Phil 4:3; Heb 12:23; Rev 3:5; 13:8; 20:12; 21:27).

69:30-36 Prayer Turns to Praise

We are not told how or when the psalmist's distress was dealt with. Was it before he ended his prayer, or after a long period of waiting? In any case, as in the similar Psalm 22, he praises God in the last few verses. This indicates that this psalmist, like others before him, proved for himself in his own situation, that God answers prayer. *The Lord hears the needy* (**69:33**). All who trust in him can be encouraged, and when people who are depressed praise him, they find their spirits revived (**69:32**).

Thanksgiving offered to God means more than religious observances, as did the sacrifice of animals in OT days

(69:30-31). The psalmist rejoices so much in the goodness of God that he says, *Let heaven and earth praise him, the seas and all that moves in them* (69:34).

This psalm is not dominated by one individual's distress and his rescue from his troubles. It shows concern for all of God's people, for the well-being of the land and the nation, and for the restoration of Zion and the cities of Judah. The final prayer is for those who love God's name to live in the land (69:35-36).

Psalm 70: Say Evermore, 'God Is Great'

In the heading, Psalm 70 is described as *a petition,* or a *memorial offering* (RSV). Memorial offerings were regularly made in the temple, possibly as a reminder to God of the person bringing the offering, and of his or her need. Isaiah 62:6 also speaks of prayer to God as reminding him – not that God forgets, but in prayer we express our constant dependence on God, bringing before him our needs, the needs of others, and our concern for the work of his kingdom.

This psalm is almost the same as the last five verses of Psalm 40. We do not know whether these verses were composed separately and then someone thought it appropriate to add them to the earlier part of Psalm 40, or whether the whole of Psalm 40 was composed first, and the last five were then taken and used as a prayer.

Something similar seems to have happened with other psalms too. For example, Psalms 14 and 53 are almost exactly the same, and so are 31:1-3 and 71:1-3, as well as 57:7-11 and 108:1-5. Some phrases are used again and again in praise and prayer in the psalms. Such phrases include, 'Hear my cry, O God', 'be gracious to me, O God', 'do not hide yourself from me', 'I am poor and needy', 'O God, I put my trust in you', 'make a joyful noise to the Lord', 'let all peoples praise you', 'sing to the Lord a new song', 'his unfailing love endures forever'. Sometimes whole verses are almost the same in different psalms. Thus 27:14, 'Be strong, and take heart and wait for the Lord', is almost identical to 31:24. In Psalm 98:9 the psalmist calls all the earth to rejoice, saying 'let them sing before the Lord, for he comes to judge the earth. He will judge the world in righteousness and the peoples with equity', and 96:13 is almost the same. There are many more examples of this.

At a time when there were no printed books, these songs of prayer and praise would have been in people's minds and memories. Sometimes someone would recall and reuse the exact words of a psalm they knew. At other times, they might introduce small differences, such as those found in this psalm, where different names are used for God, slightly different Hebrew words used for *help* (70:1) and *salvation* (70:4), and a few other minor differences occur.

All this repetition is a reminder that psalms, hymns and songs speak to us in all sorts of different situations. They are worth memorizing as they will help us to express our own prayer and praise in the situations in which we find ourselves. It is no wonder that Paul advised believers to 'Speak to one another with psalms, hymns and spiritual songs. Sing and make music in your heart to the Lord, always giving thanks to God the Father for everything, in the name of our Lord Jesus Christ' (Eph 5:19-20).

70:1-5 Prayer and Praise

This psalm, like the last one, is a prayer to God made in a situation of great need. The psalmist prays urgently to be delivered: *O Lord, come quickly to help me* (70:1) he cries. There are those around him who are mocking him, trying to hurt him, even to take his life. He has no help but God. To God alone he can say, *You are my help and my deliverer* (70:5). He is indeed the kind of person that Jesus would describe in Matthew 5:3 as 'poor in spirit'.

Yet the psalmist's plea is not just a prayer that he will be helped in his time of need and find relief and comfort from God. He wants people to see and joyfully acknowledge, *Let God be exalted!* (70:4b). And he wants it to be seen that those who seek God and rely on him can *rejoice and be glad* (70:4a), and that in the end those who seek evil and to harm others are put to shame and frustrated in what they try to do.

Psalm 71: A Prayer in Old Age

Psalm 71 has no heading, and it is thought that it may originally have belonged together with Psalm 70, but we cannot be sure of that.

Old people frequently look back on the earlier years of their lives. Godly old people can look back and recall many ways in which they have known the help and blessing of God. Clearly this psalm was written by someone who looked back like this, but who also courageously faced the present with its difficulties and had hopes for the future. It was also written by someone who was steeped in prayer and songs of praise, as we can see by comparing the words of this psalm to Psalm 22:9-11; 30–31; 33:1-3; 35:4, 10, 22, 26, 28; 36:5 and 38:21-22. He is an example to us in the way he has made these words his own and uses them in his prayers and thanksgiving to God.

71:1-4 A Cry for Help

The psalmist was not enjoying a peaceful old age. He still needed God as a refuge (71:1) and suffered the attacks of *evil and cruel men* (71:4). But what he had learned in his life was that God is *my rock of refuge, to which I can always go* (71:3a). So he could confidently approach God, saying *save me, for you are my rock and my fortress* (71:3b). The fact that God is righteous gave him confidence that those who trusted in him would *never be put to shame* or be disappointed (71:1). He would be delivered *from the hand of the wicked, from the grasp of evil and cruel men* (71:4). He also trusts God because of his experience of what God has done for him in the past.

71:5-9 Looking Back to the Past

The psalmist's thoughts go right back to the beginning of his life, as he says, *you brought me forth from my mother's womb* (71:6). He knew that from his birth he had been dependent on God. His earliest memories were of relying on God and finding him faithful: *For you have been my hope, O Sovereign Lord, my confidence since my youth* (71:5). He repeats this idea later, when he says to the Lord, 'Since my youth, O God, you have taught me' (71:17).

It is hard to be sure what is meant in **71:7** by the psalmist being *a portent to many*. A 'portent' was often something that served as a sign that trouble was coming, and the psalmist may be asserting that no matter what he endures, God is still his refuge. Alternatively, this verse may mean that the psalmist's life is a testimony to God's help and grace. The GNB translates this verse, *My life has been an example to many, because you have been my strong defender.*

Not all the psalmist's memories were pleasant, for he had had to face 'troubles, many and bitter' (71:20), but he had been brought through them all. We have been learning from many of the psalms that remembering God's help in the past is a great booster to faith amidst present difficulties and future uncertainties. The question is, do we remember?

71:10-11 Looking Around in the Present

The memories of the past were wonderful and continued to be an inspiration and encouragement to the psalmist. But he faced a difficult situation in his old age, such that he had to say, *Do not cast me away when I am old; do not forsake me when my strength is gone* (71:9). He may have been sick. He was certainly weak, and his enemies took advantage of his weakness. Some of them were like Job's friends and said that his weakness meant that God had forsaken him, and so they could do what they liked to him (**71:10-11**).

71:12-13 Looking Up to God

The words of prayers often used in the past, and the words of earlier psalms, came to the psalmist's mind, *Be not far from me, O God; come quickly, O my God, to help me* (**71:12**; see also 22:11; 35:22; 38:21-22).

71:14-24 Looking to the Future

What then was the psalmist's hope for the future? Five times in the psalm he speaks of God's righteousness (71:2, 15, 16, 19 and 24). Because God is just and fair, he knows God *will restore my life again* (**71:20-21**). His enemies will

perish in shame (71:13) and will be covered in *shame and confusion* (**71:24**).

The psalmist himself wants to live to the end of his life praising God more and more because of all that God has done for him (**71:14-16**). He states that he does not know the *measure* of God's salvation (71:15), meaning either that God has done more for him than he can possibly count up, or that God's salvation is so wonderful that he cannot even begin to describe it.

He asks the Lord never to leave him till he has had the opportunity to tell the coming generation of God's power and righteousness (**71:18**). The importance of passing on the message of what God has done from parents to children, and from one generation to the next is frequently stressed in the OT (see, for example, Exod 12:25-27; Deut 6:20-25; Josh 4:4-7; Pss 44:1-3; 78:1-8). We, too, should pass on God's message to those who come after us.

Looking back on God's mercies in the past, and trusting God in the present, should give us hope for the future and lead us always to the desire to sing praises to our loving, righteous and mighty Lord (71:22-24). With the author of this psalm and the authors of the rest of Scripture, we should be able to say, *You who have done great things. Who, O God, is like you?* (**71:19**; see also Exod 15:11; Pss 35:10; 86:8; 89:6, 8).

Psalm 72: The Reign of Righteousness

Psalm 72 and Psalm 127 are the only two psalms that have the heading *Of Solomon*. It is possible that this heading was added because the psalm contains the kind of prayer that David might have made for Solomon, his son, who would succeed him as king. Certainly, the psalm is a prayer for the king of Israel, and we can take many of its verses and make them our prayers for our own political leaders today. We need to remind them of the truth implicit in the British coronation service, in which the newly-crowned ruler is given a Bible and is told, 'This is the most precious thing the world affords' with the desire that he or she should rule according to God's word.

Some things in the psalm, however, can never be true of any human political leader. So it is easy to see how the Jewish people took them as applying to the Messiah whom they expected, and how Christians saw them as fulfilled in Jesus, our Christ.

The psalm does, however, point to virtues that politicians who desire peace and prosperity must aspire to, and it shows the political practices that will allow righteousness to reign. In this sense, the prayer is similar to the practice of setting 'the regulations of the kingship' before the king at the beginning of his reign (see 1 Sam 10:25).

72:1-4, 12-14 Justice and Mercy

The first prayer is that by God's help the king will uphold justice and live a righteous life, always judging people fairly (**72:1-2**). In particular, as the ot often emphasizes, it was the duty of the king to uphold the rights of the poor and put down those who oppressed the weak (**72:4**; see also Isa 1:23; 3:14-15; 10:1-2; 32:1-2; Jer 22:15-17; Amos 8:4-6). This theme is so important that the psalmist returns to it in **72:12-14,** saying that the good ruler cares for the *needy*, the *afflicted*, the *weak* and those *who have no one to help*, because their lives (*their blood*) are precious to him. Can the same be said of our rulers? Can it be said of us in our relationships with other people?

72:6-7, 16 Peace and Plenty

The ot often emphasizes that blessing comes to the land when righteousness is allowed to flourish. Hebrew people used the word *shalom,* which has come into many African and Asian languages in words like *salaam* or *salamu*. In **72:7**, it is translated as *peace* (nrsv) or as *prosperity*. That simple word captures the greatest welfare and highest well-being of a person or nation. It expresses a blessing that is like rain coming to a dry and thirsty land (**72:6**).

It is not wrong to pray that God's blessing may be on our crops, and to ask God's provision for our people both in our rural areas and our cities (**72:16**). We need to have the attitude of the woman who prayed wholeheartedly about everything, as though everything in life depended on prayer. She would kneel on the farm praying over a large heap of yams (the main food crop among the Igbo people of Nigeria) and maize, pouring out her heart in prayer and thanksgiving. God truly gives us all that we have.

Godliness will not always make us prosperous in material things. But a close walk with God brings a wealth of peace and serenity that money cannot buy. Christians are sometimes called to suffer for their faith, but experience shows that the peace of God rules their hearts in the face of great uncertainties, so that they can say: 'I fear no evil, for you are with me' (23:4). At the national level, history shows what a difference the rule of humble and unselfish leaders can make to a country or a community.

72:5, 8-11, 15, 17 Long Life And Far-Reaching Rule

Long may he live! is the prayer of **72:15**, and of the national anthems of many countries. It is the language of poetry to ask for a ruler to live as long as the sun and moon continue to exist (**72:5**), even if the prayer is interpreted as being for the whole ruling house and not just for one person. It would also have been poetry to ask that the king might rule *from sea to sea and from the River to the ends of the earth* (**72:8**). 'The River' was the Euphrates River, thought of as the north-eastern limit of the land of Israel as 1 Kgs 4:21 shows. It was also a poetical prayer that the kings of Tarshish

in the west and Sheba and Seba in the south would bring tribute to the king (**72:10**). Tarshish is thought to be Tartessus in Spain, Sheba in the area of modern Yemen, and Seba in the area of Ethiopia. The thought, however, was probably of the extent of God's rule, and the king of Israel was God's representative.

Some people read these verses as a prophetic reference to the millennium when the universal Messiah, God's chosen King, will rule the world for a thousand years, and there will be no more wars (Rev 20:4-6; 22:3). However, it can also be interpreted in less literal terms. It is not just a prayer that the king will conquer and dominate many nations, but it is a prayer that the promise to Abraham will be fulfilled (Gen 12:1-3; 22:18; 26:4) and that all nations will be blessed (**72:17**). The words express the deep longing of a person of faith who is fed up with the evils and bad leadership around him. It is the longing that the perfect rule of God may become a reality on earth, the longing expressed in the prayer, 'your kingdom come' (Matt 6:10).

No human king can be the answer to all these prayers. But there was a great hope that began in the time of King David (2 Sam 7:12-16) and that continued as one prophet after another spoke of the one who would come from the house of David to rule in righteousness and peace (see Isa 9:6-7; 11:1-5; Jer 23:5-6; Ezek 34:23-24; Mic 5:2-5). Those hopes and prophecies were fulfilled in the coming of Jesus, the one who remains the same *through all generations* (72:5), and who will rule over all nations. Where he is allowed to rule in people's lives and communities today, there is true shalom, abundant blessing.

72:18-20 Conclusion

These verses should probably be seen not just as the conclusion to this psalm, but as the conclusion to Book 2 of Psalms. Similar high praise of our great and glorious God is found at the end of Books 1, 3 and 4 of Psalms (see 41:13; 89:52; 106:48). The final verse, **72:20**, shows that before the final collection of psalms in the Bible was made, there must have been a collection that had the title, 'The Prayers of David Son of Jesse'.

BOOK THREE: PSALMS 73–89

Psalms 73 to 83 are part of what is known as the Asaph collection, as is also Psalm 50. For more information about Asaph, see 1 Chronicles 25:1-8.

Psalm 73: The Mystery of Suffering

The questions asked in this psalm are still asked today: Why do the righteous suffer? Why do the wicked prosper? Why doesn't God remove the wicked from the earth? Why does he look on as though he is unwilling or unable to deal with them the way they deserve? How is the Lord good to the godly? Is it merely by giving them pleasurable experiences?

73:1-2 Faith and Doubt

The psalm begins with a statement of faith, *Surely God is good to Israel, to those who are pure in heart* (**73:1**). But the psalmist found that his experience did not seem to match this truth, and his faith was tested so greatly that he was stumbling in the way (**73:2**).

73:3-15 The Tests of Faith

The test of the psalmist's faith took three forms.

73:3 A temptation to his spirit

The psalmist was tempted to say, 'That's not fair.' Why should people who have no desire to be *pure in heart* be so prosperous (73:1)? He found it hard to understand the ways of God and to persevere in serving him. In particular he was tempted to be jealous of the wicked when things seemed to go so well with them (**73:3**). This will always be the difficulty of those who make the mistake of thinking of God's goodness only in terms of pleasurable experiences. Like the psalmist in 34:1-2, we have to say, 'I will extol the Lord at all times' and under all circumstances. God is good, absolutely good, and he gives what is truly good to those who love him. It is a dangerous error to hold to a prosperity theology that expects material blessings in direct proportion to good conduct or religious activities such as giving or church attendance.

73:4-12 A problem for his thinking

The wicked seemed to have no physical or material problems. Although they had no regard for God or concern for others, everything seemed to go well for them. They seemed to have none of the troubles that others had. They had wealth, health and strength and faced no pain in life (**73:4-5**). In fact, they wore their pride as if it were a necklace and their *violence* or aggression was as obvious as the clothes they wore (**73:6**). In today's language, they were fast guys, go-getters whose *minds are filled with wicked schemes. They make fun of others and speak of evil things; they are proud and talk about oppressing others. They speak evil of God in heaven, and give arrogant orders to men on earth* (**73:7-9** GNB). They thought that they could do whatever they wanted without God doing anything to stop them (**73:11**). Their credo was 'money is power', and they believed that their wealth would always protect them. And they seemed to get away with things. No one stopped them; they were even popular. The NIV translates **73:10** literally as *their people turn to them and drink up waters in abundance*, perhaps meaning, as the JB puts it, people 'lap up all they say'.

The psalmist sums up his impressions of their lives in **73:12**: *This is what the wicked are like – always carefree, they increase in wealth.*

73:13-14 A challenge to his feelings

By contrast, the psalmist, who feared God and tried to serve him, had a hard life. He confessed to almost believing that his trials were in vain and that his attempt to live with a clean heart and with hands innocent of evil was pointless (**73:13**). Where the wicked were carefree, he seemed to have been *plagued* with troubles and even *punished* as he endured God's discipline in his life (**73:14**). He was tempted to feel bitter about his life. He would have identified with the feelings expressed in Malachi 3:14-15.

73:15-26 How Faith Wins Through

73:15-17 Adopting the right approach

As the psalmist faced this challenge to his faith in God's goodness, he decided on two things. First, he would not talk about his doubts in a way that could hurt others and cause them to stumble (**73:15**). It is a mark of Christian maturity to use one's tongue wisely, to encourage rather than discourage others (Prov 12:18). While it is healthy to share our burdens openly with others for prayer and counsel, we must be careful not to discourage others with an attitude of grumbling and complaining, especially if we are in a leadership position or have others who look up to us. Yet there is great blessing in the gift of friends with whom leaders, who are often lonely people, can bare their hearts and experience God's holy refreshing (see Malachi 3:16).

Second, despite his doubts and his inability to understand God's ways (**73:16**), he decided to seek the presence of God in *the sanctuary* (**73:17**) and to ask the Lord for wisdom and guidance. The NT teaches us to see Jesus Christ as a friend who understands perfectly, and whose invitation is, 'Come to me, all you who are weary and burdened, and I will give you rest' (Matt 11:28). We can cast our anxieties on him because he cares for us (1 Pet 5:7).

73:18-20 Thinking straight

In the sanctuary, in the presence of God, the psalmist saw things more clearly. He realized that the end of evildoers was not a happy one. He could see many examples that showed him their path ran through *slippery ground* and ended in trouble (**73:18**). They had no lasting strength (**73:19**). They were just like a dream that fades away when a person wakes up (**73:20**). What this affirms is that the psalmist realized that evil could not endure in the presence of God who is righteous and just. Its triumph is only temporary, because real 'power belongs to God' (62:11, NRSV).

73:21-22 Recognizing temptation

The psalmist now realized that he had been utterly foolish when he listened to the temptation to be jealous of wicked people. In giving in to bitterness (**73:21**), he had been *senseless and ignorant,* more like *a brute beast* (**73:22**) than a person made in the image of God, and a child of God. Bitterness hinders the work of the Holy Spirit in us, and we must take the words of 37:1-3 to heart: 'Do not fret because of evil men; or be envious of those who do wrong ... trust in the Lord, and do good.'

73:23-26 Dealing with his feelings

The psalmist found that when he allowed his thoughts to dwell on the imagined prosperity of the wicked, he became very upset. But when he turned his thoughts back to God, he found peace and could say, *Yet I am always with you; you hold me by my right hand* (**73:23**). All through life he could ask God to guide him, and in the end know that he would be received in glory (**73:24**; see also Mal 3:17-18). It is not certain whether the psalmist was speaking of his future in this life when God would receive him *with honour* (NRSV), or whether he was expressing a hope of life after death (see comments on 16:11). But he knew that God's presence and support would never fail him. In times of great weakness, God would be the strength of his heart and his richest possession (**73:26**). There was no one like the Lord among the spiritual beings in heaven, and there was nothing and no one on earth to be desired more than him (**73:25**).

The psalmist might still not understand why God acts as he does, but he had come to a wiser understanding of God's discipline in our lives (see also Heb 12:3-11).

73:27-28 Renewed Faith

His revelation in the temple reassured the psalmist, so that he could say to the Lord, *Those who are far from you will perish; you destroy all who are unfaithful to you* (**73:27**). When the psalmist met the test of faith and dealt with his jealousy, envy and bitterness, he finished up with the same faith with which he began, *Surely God is good to Israel, to those who are pure in heart.* So he made two resolutions. The first was that it was always *good to be near God,* to trust him and to have him as *my refuge* (**73:28a**). The second resolution could be expressed as follows: 'I see so much of God's wisdom, love and power that, even though there are things I do not fully understand, I will tell others of his deeds' (**73:28b**).

Psalm 74: The House of God Destroyed

This psalm is described as a *maskil* (see comment on Psalm 42). It was written after the people of Israel had been conquered by their enemies. These invaders had destroyed the beautifully carved woodwork of the temple with hammers and axes, and then set the temple itself on fire. God seemed to be silent.

Even today, there are many Christians who know what it is like to have their churches destroyed and their copies of the Bible taken from them and burned. Their experience is similar to losing the temple and having no prophets left, and they can identify with the emotions expressed in this psalm.

74:1-3, 10-11 God's Purpose Questioned

As in Psalm 73, the psalmist asks why God has allowed all this to happen. The prophets Jeremiah and Ezekiel had prophesied the defeat of the Jewish people by the Babylonians because they had turned away from God and had not trusted him in their need. But the years had passed, and it seemed that God had rejected his people *for ever* (**74:1**) and that the ruins of the temple were *everlasting ruins* (**74:3**).

He returns to this question in **74:10**, asking *How long ... O God?* (see also 4:2; 6:3; 79:5; 89:46). *Why have you refused to help us? Why do you keep your hands behind you?* (**74:11**, GNB).

We need to remember that God's delays are not always denials. The triumph of evil is short-lived. But while we are in the thick of the battle, we need patience: 'Wait for the Lord; be strong and take heart and wait for the Lord' (27:14).

74:4-9 God's Name Dishonoured

The deepest distress of the psalmist was not so much for his own suffering or the defeat of his people, but because God's house had been destroyed. He speaks of it as *the place where you met with us* (**74:4a**) and *your sanctuary* (**74:7**). Not only had they destroyed the place where God was worshipped, but they had set up their own *standards* there as signs of their conquest (**74:4b**). Whether these standards were military or religious, they profaned the house of God. Thus it was not so much the loss of the beautiful building described in 1 Kings 6 and of all the beautifully carved woodwork within it that disturbed the psalmist, although he mourned this too (74:5-7). But what upset him most deeply was that the name of God, that is, his reputation in the world, had been brought into disrepute. He returns to the insult to God's name repeatedly in the psalm (74:7, 10, 18, 21). He was concerned lest the living God should be thought to be powerless because he had not defended *the sheep of your pasture* (74:1), *the people ... whom you redeemed* (74:2) against your *foes* and your *adversaries* (74:4, 23).

This prayer challenges us to reflect on whose honour or glory we are concerned for when we pray or struggle for justice. Do we think in terms of God letting us down, rather than in terms of our not upholding God's reputation? We are reminded of this each time we say the prayer that

Jesus taught us to pray, 'Hallowed be your name' (Matt 6:9; Luke 11:2).

The psalmist also mourns that *they burned every place where God was worshipped in the land* (**74:8**). Some translations speak of 'all the synagogues' being destroyed. There were no synagogues at the time of the fall of Jerusalem to the Babylonians. So if this translation is correct, the psalm may be referring to the time in the second century BC when Antiochus Epiphanes defiled the temple. Yet another disaster is that *no prophets are left* (**74:9**). Not only were the places of worship destroyed, but God seemed to be silent and was not communicating with his people. The usual queries, *how long?* and *why?* resurface in 74:10-11.

74:12-23 God's Power Trusted

The psalmist was distressed and perplexed, but he turned back to God. The temple was destroyed. The signs of the worship of God were removed. There were no prophets left. Yet the psalmist said, *But you, O God, are my King from of old* (**74:12a**). When the going is tough, let us remember the times 'of old'. There is no greater encouragement to faith in the dark hours than remembering God's mercy and acts of deliverance in the past.

God was the one who was known to *bring salvation upon the earth* (**74:12b**). He had done this at the dawn of the history of Israel as a nation, when he had set them free from Egypt, led them across the Red Sea and through the wilderness, and made a way for them to cross the River Jordan (**74:13-15**). He describes these events using the language of the ancient Babylonian and Canaanite stories of creation, though the OT writers did not believe the ideas behind them. These stories told of the *monster in the waters* and the great Leviathan being conquered as the world was created. The psalmist knew that the one living God had conquered chaos and brought all things into being and into their order in the universe. He also recognized that the old stories could be applied both to creation and to the work of God in saving his people from Egypt and bringing them to their land (see also Isa 51:9-11). Both events show the mighty power of the living God. That is why the psalmist goes on to express his trust in God as the mighty Creator. He who had established the sun, moon and stars, fixed the boundaries of land and sea and ordered the seasons could never be said to be powerless (**74:16-17**).

The psalmist calls on God to *remember* (**74:18**) and *not forget* (**74:19**) the situation of his people and to *have regard* (**74:20**) for his covenant. These words suggest that true prayer involves reminding both ourselves and God of the promises we have been given and claiming them in faith (see also Isa 62:6-7). Though the land was dark and full of violence (74:20), the psalmist knew he could pray that the enemy would not be allowed to blaspheme God's name for ever. He could ask that the people would not remain powerless like a little dove at the mercy of wild animals (74:19). He could pray that poor and downtrodden people might have cause to praise God for his salvation (**74:21**). *Rise up, O God* he could say, *and defend your cause* (**74:22**).

Truly it was God's cause. Such prayer to the living God is never made in vain. But God asks us to refrain from violence and not to avenge ourselves (see Rom 12:19). This may be hard for believers who are oppressed by business or workplace colleagues, or even by other believers. Does God forget such people? No, for Jesus says, 'he will see that they get justice, and quickly' (Luke 18:8).

Psalm 75: The Proud and the Humble

The heading of this psalm includes the words *Do not destroy*, as in the heading of Psalm 57 (see comments on that psalm). This psalm is about both judgment and salvation.

75:1 Thanksgiving

This psalm begins by praising God because his *Name is near* (**75:1a**). God's name means his nature, his attributes and his very presence. The presence or nearness of God means more to the psalmist than anything else in life. He could rejoice in his nearness because 'the Lord is near to all who call on him, to all who call on him in truth' (145:18).

All people have reason to speak about God's *wonderful deeds* (**75:1b**). There are God's mighty deeds in creation, and his loving kindness towards us that has resulted in our salvation. We need to realize, however, that in the world God's work of salvation and of judgment must go together. Some people are oppressed, and their situation can only be changed when their oppressors are defeated and no longer have power to use against others.

75:2-3 The Time for Judgment

Sometimes it may seem to us that everything is going wrong in the world. Morally and spiritually, it seems that the earth is like a tottering building with shaky foundations (**75:3a**). But we can be sure that God is still in control. Continuing to use the metaphor of a building, God says that he is the one who keeps *its pillars firm* (**75:3b**). Though it seems that evil has been allowed to have its way and oppressors are very powerful, God's response is, *I choose the appointed time; it is I who judge uprightly* (**75:2**). When God judges we can be sure that it will be done with perfect fairness.

75:4-8 The Strong and the Proud Brought Down

In the OT, a horn is often used as a symbol of strength. The horn of an animal, especially one like a wild ox (see 92:10), is very powerful and can do much harm to other animals or to human beings. In the same way that an aggressive animal tosses its head to display its horns and threaten others, so oppressors boast in their power and what they can do to others. But the Lord's word to such arrogant people and to all who try to get to the top by fighting or bribing is *Boast no more* (**75:4**). Oppression of those who are weak or of a minority race or tribe is an offence against God, as is shown by the words *do not lift your horns against heaven* (**75:5**). Proverbs 14:31 puts it this way, 'He who oppresses the poor shows contempt for their Maker'. A similar point is made in Acts 9:4, where the Lord's words to Saul of Tarsus indicate that in persecuting Christians he was persecuting Christ. We need to take seriously God's concern that we not be harsh with, or marginalize those under us in the workplace or in any other relationships (see also Isa 58:1-9 and 1 Pet 5:5).

No one should boast about how important they are, for God is the only one who can ultimately determine someone's position. This truth applies regardless of whether the people concerned come from east or west, from the *desert* to the south or from the mountains in the north (the Hebrew word that is translated *exalt* may also be translated as 'mountains', **75:6**). Today, instead of speaking of the geographic directions of east, west, south and north, we might say that this applies regardless of whether the people are European or African, Asian or American – they are not to boast and use their power or position to harm or marginalize others. God is the one who judges whom to lift up and whom to bring down (**75:7**; see also Hannah's song in 1 Sam 2:1-10; Mary's song in Luke 1:46-55).

One of the ways in which judgment is often described in the Bible is as a drink that causes a person to stagger about, out of control. God offers those who trust him a cup of blessing (see 16:5 and 23:5), but those who reject that cup of blessing and work against God, and against God's people, have to drink another kind of cup (see Jer 25:15-29; Hab 2:15-16). They will have to drink it *down to its very dregs* (**75:8**; see also Isa 51:17), meaning that they receive the full consequences of their wrongdoing.

75:9-10 The Humble Lifted Up

The final verse of the psalm brings us God's assurance, *I will cut off the horns of all the wicked, but the horns of the righteous will be lifted up* (**75:10**). In other words, the time will come when the power of wicked people will be broken. Proud people, proud nations, proud empires in history have all fallen, while those who trust in God find unfailing strength even though they suffer. Those who are weak in themselves but rely on God can *rejoice forever* (NRSV), and *sing praises to the God of Jacob* (**75:9**). They can confess, 'you are a shield around me, O Lord; you bestow glory on me and lift up my head' (3:3).

Psalm 76: Victory over the Forces of Evil

The directions in the heading of this psalm, like those in Psalm 4, say it is to be sung to the accompaniment of *stringed instruments*. It is thought that this psalm may have been written after the Assyrian forces retreated from Jerusalem with great loss in the days of Hezekiah and Isaiah (see 2 Kgs 19).

The Bible – OT and NT alike – is full of witness to the love of God and the offer of forgiveness and new life to all who turn to him. But the Bible is also realistic about evil in the world – the fact that people rebel against God and seek to use power to oppress and crush others. This psalm makes it clear that God will not allow evil to continue to triumph. As some of the psalms that we have already studied have emphasized, the triumph of evil is short-lived. This is a constant theme in the Scriptures, and the death and resurrection of Jesus Christ are the strongest witness to this truth. Jesus also taught his disciples to live fearlessly, knowing that God alone is almighty (see Matt 10:28-31; 28:18-20).

76:1-6 God's Power Displayed for Israel

The psalm begins by describing how God has made himself known in Israel (**76:1**). His presence has been specially known in the temple in Jerusalem and in the life of the people of Judah (**76:2**). Powerful rulers and nations like Sennacherib have come against the people with swords and arrows intending to crush them, but God is able to overthrow the most powerful of human rulers and to frustrate their weapons (**76:3**). Psalm 46:9-10 makes a similar statement when it says that 'he makes wars to cease to the end of the earth; he breaks the bow and shatters the spear; he burns the shields with fire.' In our days, we can replace the references to swords and arrows with references to such things as economic muscle, bombs, landmines and missiles.

In **76:4**, the psalm praises God's majesty with words that recall the song celebrating his victory over Pharaoh, 'Who among the gods is like you, O Lord?' (Exod 15:11). There are differences in the translation of the last part of this verse. The Hebrew literally means 'the mountains of prey', and that is why the NIV translates this as 'mountains rich with game'. The NRSV translation follows the ancient Greek translation and speaks of 'the everlasting mountains', while the GNB interprets the words symbolically and translates them as 'the mountains where you defeated your foes'.

The psalm then mentions other examples of God's deliverance. Thus **76:5** may refer to the events described in 2 Kings 19:35-37, as also may **76:6**. However, that verse may also refer to what happened at the beginning of Israel's history as a nation when the Israelites escaped from Egypt, and Pharaoh's chariots and horses were overwhelmed in the Red Sea.

76:7-9 God's Justice for the Oppressed

God is not only a warrior who can conquer the powerful who boast in their weapons of war. He is also a judge and his righteous anger is directed against all oppressors. He acts to establish justice and to *save all the afflicted of the earth* (**76:9**). As we saw in the study of Psalm 75, judgment and salvation belong together. God judges proud persecutors so as to save those who suffer at their hands. Those who see God's work in this way can only confess, *You alone are to be feared. Who can stand before you when you are angry?* (**76:7**).

The description of the land as having been reduced to silence by God's judgment (**76:8**) reminds us of his earlier command, 'Be still, and know that I am God! I will be exalted among the nations, I will be exalted in the earth' (46:10; see also Zech 2:13).

76:10-12 God's Overruling of Human Plans

The NIV translates **76:10a** as *your wrath against men brings you praise,* implying praise given to God for his punishment of oppressors. However, another possible translation, which many versions prefer, is 'human wrath serves only to praise you' (NRSV). The history of God's people in the Bible, and indeed all human history, is full of examples of the way that powerful men and women have angrily planned to do harm to others, but God has overruled their purposes. Often when evil people have had a plan to bring evil on others, God has used the plan to bring good to and through the victims. For example, Joseph's brothers sold him as a slave because they were jealous of him, but God overruled so that many years later Joseph could tell his brothers, 'You intended to harm me, but God intended it for good to accomplish what is now being done, the saving of many lives' (Gen 50:20).

This illustrates Paul's great statement that 'in all things God works for the good of those who love him' (Rom 8:28). No matter what happens, there is an almighty God with a most loving purpose for our lives. Thus when people and circumstances threaten to push us over the edge, we should not fear. We should rest assured that 'underneath are the everlasting arms' (Deut 33:27). The greatest example of this was in the crucifixion of Jesus. Judas betrayed him, the Jewish leaders rejected him, the Romans put him to death, but God raised him from the dead. Thus God's wonderful redeeming purposes were fulfilled. We can believe that God still works in the world and in our own lives to bring good out of evil.

It is difficult to be sure of the meaning of **76:10b**. Most likely *the survivors of your wrath are restrained* means that whatever rebellious intent remains, God prevents it from causing further harm. Because God is all-powerful and the judge of all, able to frustrate human plans and bring his own

plans to pass, all people everywhere should pay due reverence to him. *The kings of the earth* should realize the limits of their power, and *rulers* should know that their lives are in his hands (**76:12**). Those of us who confess him as our Lord and Saviour should *make vows* to serve him and gladly carry out those vows (**76:11**).

Psalm 77: Remembering the Past

Like Psalm 39, this psalm is associated not only with *Asaph* but with *Jeduthun,* who shared responsibility for the music in the temple (1 Chr 16:41-42; 25:1; 2 Chr 5:12).

There are different ways in which we can remember the past. The effects of these different ways are well illustrated by this psalm.

77:1-9 Discouragement

The psalmist was in great trouble. Whether the trouble was personal or that of his nation, it affected him very deeply. He *cried out to God* (**77:1**). In the night as well as in the day, he stretched out his hands to God in earnest prayer (**77:2-3**). Yet he found no comfort. He was unable to sleep, and he blamed God for that (**77:4**). He said he was so troubled that he was unable to speak.

In his misery, the psalmist *thought about the former days, the years of long ago* (**77:5**). But all that he could think of was that things were much better in the past. As he lay awake at night, he remembered the songs he had sung when his meditations had brought joy and praise to his lips (**77:6**). If only he could go back to those times! Now it seemed as if the Lord no longer showed his *unfailing love.* The promises of God seemed no longer to have any meaning (**77:7-8**). Had God become so angry with his people that they could never again know his compassion? (**77:9**).

In this first part of the psalm, the pronoun 'I' is prominent. The psalmist allowed himself to be filled with self-pity. Although he was trying to pray, he was not really looking up to God, but inwardly to himself, and he was just thinking of all his troubles and disappointments.

77:10-20 Encouragement

In the first half of the psalm, the psalmist has thought about how things used to be and felt sorry for himself. But in **77:10-11** he seems to give himself a shake, and to remind himself again that God is powerful. Not only is God powerful, but his ways are *holy* (**77:13a**). Because they are God's ways, they are always wise and true. He is appreciating the truth that 'my thoughts are not your thoughts, neither are your ways my ways, … As the heavens are higher than the earth, so are my ways higher than your ways and my thoughts than your thoughts' (Isa 55:8-9).

Someone who thinks about the ways and works of God in those terms will say that there is none *so great as our God*

(**77:13b**). That leads to thinking of the past in a different way, and to finding encouragement from the past because God does not change. The God who has done great things in the past is still *the God who performs miracles* (**77:14**). He is a God of love and mercy who redeemed his people, setting them free from their slavery in Egypt (**77:15**). And he still has the same power, as can be seen in the storm, in thunder and in the lightning flashes that are like God's *arrows* (**77:16-18**).

God showed both his power and his love when, though himself unseen, he led them across the Red Sea to freedom and across the Jordan into their land (**77:19**; Exod 15:1-13). As a shepherd caringly leads his flock, he led his people *by the hand of Moses and Aaron* (**77:20**).

The prophet Habakkuk, who lived in a time that made him long to see God's salvation, also found encouragement in remembering what God had done in the past (Hab 3:2-16). We need to remember these things, and to remember above all what Jesus Christ has done for us (1 Cor 11:23-26). The knowledge that God never changes means that there is always encouragement and never discouragement in recalling the past, although God may choose to act in the future in ways different from the ways in which he has acted in the past.

Psalm 78: Learning from History

This psalm is described as a *Maskil* of Asaph (see comments on Ps 42).

Like many other peoples, the Hebrew people loved to recall the story of their ancestors, and especially the stories of what God had done for them. Judges 5:11 shows that when people met at their 'watering places' (their wells) to draw water, they talked and sang of 'the righteous acts of the Lord'. Their stories told what God did in love and power for his people, how they forgot and turned away from him, and how he responded with both judgment and mercy.

78:1-7 The Call to Remember

The psalmist describes the history he is going to teach as *parables* (**78:1a**) because his aim is not just to teach about the past, but to use the stories from the past to give guidance about how to live in the present (78:7-8). He also says that he will speak of *hidden things* (**78:1b**), making the point that the pattern of history is not self-evident but needs to be discerned by the eye of faith. He is convinced that the story of the wonderful acts of God has a meaning and that each chapter in the history and experience of God's people has lessons for future generations (**78:3-4a**). So he uses Israel's history to teach lasting lessons about God's guidance, protection and provision for those who have taken the risk of responding to his call in faith.

Trouble begins when we refuse to learn from history (note the words of Paul in 1 Cor 10:11-12). In telling his children of *the praiseworthy deeds of the Lord, his power and the wonders he [God] has done* (**78:4b**) the psalmist is also ensuring that he obeys God's command to pass on the law from generation to generation (**78:5-6**).

Christian parents today need to continue to teach their children God's ways. It is not enough to expect them to learn Bible stories in church. They need to hear history made personal as their parents tell them what God has done in the past and how they should serve him (Exod 13:3-10; Deut 4:9-10; 6:4-9).

78:8-16 The Results of Forgetting

When people do not keep in mind what great things God has done in the past, they lose sight of the power and love of God and the importance of trusting him and obeying him. This can happen to an individual, and it can happen to a whole community. Sadly Israel, forgetting what God had done for them, became *a stubborn and rebellious generation, whose hearts were not loyal to God, whose spirits were not faithful to him* (**78:8**).

Among those guilty of this sin were *the men of Ephraim* (**78:9**). Ephraim was the largest of the northern tribes. We do not know what specific incident of cowardice is being described here, but the tribe is referred to again, as in 78:67, as being passed over for leadership.

God had given the people of Israel his special covenant, but they did not keep it. He had made his ways known, but they *refused to live by his law* (**78:10**). They forgot the miracles they had seen (**78:11**). They even forgot what he had done for them in Egypt, in *the region of Zoan*, near where the River Nile enters the sea (**78:12**). Zoan had been Egypt's capital at the time when the Hebrews were oppressed in Egypt and was where they had worked as slaves before God delivered them. God had helped them to cross the water to freedom, making the waters stand *firm like a wall* (**78:13**) and he had led them by a pillar of cloud in the daytime and a pillar of fire at night (**78:14**; see Exod 13:17-14:30). They also forgot that God had provided them with the water that they needed in the wilderness (**78:15-16**; Exod 17:1-7; Num 20:1-11).

Instead of remembering, the people wanted to go their own way, *rebelling in the desert against the Most High* (**78:17**). One wonders why people do not learn the obvious lessons from history. Are they unable to learn? Or do they distort or misread history? In country after country we see people exploited by unscrupulous politicians, and we witness the shameful end of these same dictators and oppressors. Surely the leaders of today should learn from the errors of the past. Yet while new leaders are quick to condemn those who have gone before, they soon become even worse and more evil themselves. The same applies to individuals. A man ruins a family by committing adultery with another woman. Is he likely to remain faithful to her? We are frail humans, and our history should teach us to depend on God or we shall surely fall.

78:17-39 Judgment And Mercy

History is meant both to warn us against arrogance and unbelief and to teach us to trust God. 'Don't you remember?' Jesus asked his disciples (Mark 8:18). Doubt begins when faith forgets God's goodness in the past. Thus even though God provided the Israelites with water when there seemed to be none in sight, they doubted his power and love and said, *Can God spread a table in the desert?* (**78:17-20**). In other words, 'is he able to give us the food we need'?

It is no wonder that at one point God said to Moses, 'How long will these people treat me with contempt? How long will they refuse to believe in me, in spite of all the miraculous signs I have performed among them?' (Num 14:11). God was angered by their lack of faith (**78:21-22**). Yet he gave them the food they needed in the form of manna, poetically described here as the *bread of angels* (**78:23-25**; see Exod 16) and drove in a flock of quail (**78:26-29**; see Num 11:31-32). But he also judged them, as is clear from the events described in **78:30-31** (see Num 11:33-34).

Through the years, both Jews and Christians have repeated the story of how the generation who came out of Egypt died in the wilderness and were not able to go into the promised land because they forgot God's goodness and his judgment (**78:32-34**). The NT tells this story in Hebrews 3:7-18 and 4:1-13, and warns us: 'Take care, brothers and sisters, that none of you may have an evil, unbelieving heart that turns away from the living God' (Heb 3:12).

There were times when *they repented and sought God earnestly* (78:34-35, NRSV). Yet all too often, even when the Israelites professed to turn to him, it was not with sincere repentance or genuine faith, but *they would flatter him with their mouths, lying to him with their tongues* for *their hearts were not loyal to him, they were not faithful to his covenant* (**78:36-37**). By doing this they added to the catalogue of sins described in various terms throughout this psalm (78:8, 10, 11, 17, 18, 22, 32, 36, 37).

Nevertheless, God was still merciful to them, even though there were times when he had to punish them. His aim was always to lead them back to a true trust in him. *Yet he was merciful; he forgave their iniquities and did not destroy them. Time after time he restrained his anger and did not stir up his full wrath. He remembered that they were but flesh, a passing breeze that does not return* (**78:38-39**; see also 103:13-18).

78:40-55 God's Faithfulness

Still amazed at the people's ingratitude for what God has done for them (**78:40-42**), the psalmist returns to all that God did when he set his people free from their oppression in Egypt. The *signs* and *wonders* he displayed included plagues of blood, of flies, of frogs, of locusts and of hail (**78:43-50**; see also Exodus 7–10). The culminating act was the killing of the firstborn (Ps 78:51), and the delivery of the Israelites, which is still celebrated by the Jewish people in the Festival of the Passover. The reference was made to Ham in 78:51 because the Egyptians were considered to be descended from *Ham* (Gen 10:6). God also led them through the wilderness, across the Red Sea (see 78:13), and then helped them to settle *in their homes* in what was to be their land (**78:52-55**).

78:56-64 Israel's Unfaithfulness

Those whom God had settled in the promised land proved to be no better than their ancestors (**78:57**). They are described as being like *a faulty bow.* The bow was an important weapon in those days, but if it was twisted the owner could no longer shoot straight and the bow became unreliable. God's people could no longer serve his purpose.

Their sin is described as testing (or challenging) God and rebelling against him (**78:56**). Similar words are used to describe sin in 78:17-18 and 78:40-41 (see also Exod 17:1-7; Deut 6:16; Matt 4:5-7). Such rebellion grieved God, but it also provoked his righteous anger (**78:58-59**; see also Num 14:20-25). With their idols and their high places, the Israelites tried to combine the worship of Yahweh, the true God, with the worship of other gods.

In **78:60-64**, the psalmist describes God's punishment of the rebellious people at the time when Samuel was born. The worship of God was corrupt, and God allowed the Philistines to conquer Israel. The Tabernacle or house of God was at Shiloh, but God abandoned it and allowed the ark of the covenant to be captured (78:60-64; see 1 Sam 3–4). He was reminding the people that they were not safe simply because they had a sanctuary or a temple or a church. Many generations later, the prophet Jeremiah reminded the people of Jerusalem of what had happened to Shiloh, and warned them of what could happen to them and to their temple (Jer 7:1-15). Judah needed the warning, as we still do today, that only those who keep faithful to the Lord can enjoy his ultimate salvation.

78:65-72 God as Shepherd to His People

Of course God never sleeps (121:3-4), but when it seemed that he had not been active on behalf of the people, the psalmists sometimes prayed as if he did. Thus, speaking poetically, they would ask God to rise up to help them (68:1; 74:22). The psalmist continues that image here, saying the Lord may have seemed to be as deeply asleep as a drunkard while the terrible events described in 78:59-64 were happening, but now he is awake and ready for action (**78:65**).

The Lord defeated his enemies (**78:66**) and rejected the large northern tribes of Joseph and Ephraim in favour of the smaller southern tribe of Judah (**78:67-68**). The temple in Shiloh was destroyed and the place where God was worshipped moved to Mount Zion, where Solomon's great temple was built (78:68-69).

Here too we see God's judgment and his mercy. God had been a shepherd to his people in the past, leading them, seeking them, and bringing them back when they went astray as he *guided them safely* out of Egypt, through the wilderness, to the land of Canaan (78:53). But God also wants human leaders who will shepherd his people. Thus he chose David to be king. David knew what it was to be a shepherd caring for a flock of sheep. God called him to the much greater task of being a shepherd of Israel, and he *took care of them with unselfish devotion and led them with skill* (**78:70-72**, GNB).

The OT often speaks of prophets, priests and kings as shepherds, and the NT calls the leaders of the church shepherds (1 Pet 5:1-4). All who aspire to, or find themselves in, positions of leadership, especially in the church, should strive to follow David's example. They should guide, protect and provide for those whom they lead; they should never harass, terrorize or intimidate or marginalize their flock or shun any sections of it. Our ultimate example must be Jesus, the Good Shepherd (Luke 15:1-7; John 10:1-30).

Psalm 79: 'Where Is Their God?'

Several parts of this psalm are similar to passages in other psalms or in the prophets, showing that the psalmist was echoing prayers and prophecies that he and his people were familiar with. This psalm is a cry to God from the midst of great trouble and distress. It is not, however, the cry of an individual but of everyone in the nation. We see the people's plight vividly described, we hear their prayer, and then the psalm finishes with a promise.

79:1-4 Their Plight

The time was probably 586 BC, when the Babylonians conquered Jerusalem. The city was left in ruins (**79:1**). So many people died that their bodies were left unburied – a terrible thing for the Hebrew people as for people of many other cultures (**79:2-3**; see also Jer 19:7). The nations around them – such as Edom, Ammon and Moab – laughed at them and rejoiced at their defeat (**79:4**, see 44:13; Ezek 25:3, 6, 8; Obad 11-14).

The Israelites were not distressed just because of their personal sorrows and their loss of independence as a nation. The worst thing, as this psalm puts it, was the challenge to their faith in Yahweh, their God. They believed that the Lord would never leave them or forsake them, but people of other nations were saying, *Where is their God?* suggesting that he was powerless to help them (79:10; see also 42:3; 115:2;

Joel 2:17). It was God's *holy temple* that was defiled, God's *inheritance* that had been invaded (79:1).

79:5-12 Their Prayer

Realizing what defeat had meant to them in terms of their personal distress, their pride as a nation, and above all in terms of their faith, they prayed. They realized, as prophets like Jeremiah had warned them (see Jer 16:16-18; 19:7-8; Mic 3:9-12), that their defeat was the result of their unfaithfulness to their God and their neglect of his law. Their God was a jealous God (**79:5**; Exod 20:5), although his jealousy is not like human jealousy, which is self-centred and seeks evil for others. Rather, his jealousy flows from his holiness and his dignity as the Creator and Lord of all. The people knew that they had to ask God to forgive their sins and the sins of earlier generations that had led to all their troubles (**79:8-9**). They deserved God's righteous anger, but they could only ask, *How long, O Lord?* (79:5, see 6:1-4, 13:1-2). How long must they suffer for their sins? Weren't the sins of the nations who did not serve God at all much worse? (**79:6-7**; Jer 10:25). Shouldn't those nations be the ones to suffer most under God's righteous anger? Those nations laughed at the true and living God, as if he were not able to do anything. Under the circumstances, the argument that the other nations should have suffered God's righteous anger seemed fair.

But the truth is that God shows no partiality, and from those to whom he has committed much, he expects much. Israel had been blessed with the knowledge of God's law, and they should lead others in obedience to God. They had no right to regard themselves as superior to other nations in God's sight. In fact, none of us have any right to receive blessings from God. As Christians, we ask God's mercy on the basis of what God has done for us in Jesus Christ. So the nation prayed for mercy from a holy and righteous God, asking that he would hear *the groans of the prisoners* and the cries of those *condemned to die* (**79:11**). God had acted in justice, and now they begged, *may your mercy come quickly to meet us, for we are in desperate need* (79:8). God owes us nothing. We owe him everything. So it is presumptuous to chide God for disappointing us when we do not get the expected answer to our prayers. We need to remember that God's ultimate purpose in whatever he allows to happen to us is vastly superior to the pain we may experience in the meantime (John 13:7; Rom 8:28; 2 Cor 4:18). Whatever happens, it is God's mercy we must plead for and his unfailing love is our reason for hope.

We who know the way of Jesus must not pray a prayer like that of **79:12** for sevenfold vengeance and the utter destruction of our enemies. Instead, we must seek the salvation of those who have not known the reality of the true God (see Matt 28:18-20; Acts 1:8). However, the prayer for God to avenge the slaughter of human lives *before our eyes* should not be understood in terms of a desire for personal revenge, but as an expression of the desire that God's justice be recognized and seen to be done *among the nations* (**79:10**).

At the same time, we should notice that the people's concern here was not just for themselves, but for God's name and God's honour and glory (79:9). They urge God to take action in response to *the reproach they have hurled at you* (79:12; see also 89:50-51). Their concern has changed from self-pity to the desire to see God's name hallowed and glorified. This should be the spirit of our prayers if they are to be pleasing to God, for Jesus taught us to pray, 'Hallowed be your name; your kingdom come' (Matt 6:9-10).

79:13 Their Promise

In spite of all the trouble Israel experienced and deserved to experience, the psalmist knew that prayer to God would never be in vain. When Israel turned to God, they knew that they could always say, we are *your people, the sheep of your pasture* (**79:13**, see also 95:7; 100:3). So they promised that they would give thanks to God for ever. They wanted the generations yet unborn to know the mighty works of God and to honour him. The psalm that began with complaint ends with a promise of praise, as the prayers of those who truly know God should always do. This praise was not an attempt to bribe or persuade God to answer their prayer. They sincerely wanted God's name to be glorified, which should also be our motive in prayer, especially when we make vows or promises when we are in difficult situations.

Psalm 80: The Song of the Vine

The reference in the heading to *The Lilies of the Covenant* probably indicates the tune to which this psalm was to be sung. It may be the same tune used for Psalm 45, where it is simply referred to as 'Lilies'. The word 'covenant' may be included in the title here because the disaster that had struck the northern tribes may have caused those assigning the heading to reflect on what it meant for Israel to be the covenant people of God.

The history of Israel recorded in the OT often involves the unfaithfulness of the people, and the constancy of God's saving love and help. Psalm 78 recalled many parts of that story. This psalm tells another part. After the death of Solomon, the kingdom of Israel was divided (as we read in 1 Kgs 11–12). The northern tribes, which included Ephraim, Benjamin and Manasseh (80:2), were no longer ruled by the descendants of David, and under kings like Ahab they turned away from God. They became weaker and weaker until they finally fell to the Assyrians in 721 BC. This psalm may have been written at about that time. At the very least, we can say that it was written at a time when the people had turned from God, and it seemed that God had also turned away from them.

This psalm describes three ways in which God relates to Israel.

80:1-2 God as the Shepherd King

Earlier in the Psalms God has been spoken of as a shepherd (23:1), and Israel has been called God's flock. In Psalm 77:20, the psalmist said, 'you led your people like a flock by the hand of Moses and Aaron' (see also 78:52). The people could feel grateful that God led them, provided for them and brought them back when they strayed, as a shepherd would do for his sheep. So this psalm begins with a prayer to the *Shepherd of Israel* (**80:1a**).

But God is more than just a shepherd, for he is also *enthroned between the cherubim* (**80:1b**). The winged cherubim were carved creatures on top of the ark of the covenant, who upheld the unseen throne of God in the Holy of Holies, first in the Tabernacle or Tent of Meeting and later in the temple that Solomon built (Exod 25:17-22; 1 Kgs 8:6-7). It was there that God's presence was especially felt. That presence was like light, like the shining of God's face as described in the priestly blessing, 'The Lord make his face shine upon you, and be gracious to you' (Num 6:25).

God is especially asked to shine upon *Ephraim, Benjamin and Manasseh* (**80:2a**). In the OT the tribe of Benjamin is sometimes linked with the southern tribe of Judah, sometimes with the northern tribes. Here it is mentioned together with Ephraim and Manasseh because these three tribes were grouped together when the Israelites camped in the wilderness (Num 2:18-24). Now all three northern tribes are in trouble (see the introduction) and the people pray to the Lord for rescue (**80:2b**).

80:3-7 God as Angry

The people felt that God's face was no longer shining upon them. Instead he was angry with their prayers (**80:4**). They were suffering because they had turned from his ways. They felt that tears were their food and drink (**80:5**), and their enemies had been allowed to overpower them and despise them (**80:6**). So they had one prayer above all others, *Restore us, O God; make your face shine upon us, that we may be saved* (**80:3**), a refrain that sums up the psalm and is repeated at 80:7 and 80:19.

80:8-19 God as the Gardener

The Lord is next described as a gardener or vineyardkeeper responsible for the people, who are compared to a vine. Israel was like a vine that God had brought out of Egypt. Land was prepared for them, and they were planted in it (**80:8**). Like a vine, they put down roots and grew to fill the land (**80:9-10**). They spread from *the Sea* (the Mediterranean) to *the River* (the Euphrates) (**80:11**).

In parts of the world where grapes are not grown and there are no fruiting vines, it can be difficult to understand the full force of this image. A grapevine has deep roots and spreads widely. If it is a good vine, it produces fruit that is both good to eat and valued for making wine. Because vines were so important in Israelite culture, the vine was often used as a symbol for Israel in the Bible (Isa 5:1-7; Mark 12:1-12).

But it seems to the psalmist that the walls of the vineyard have been broken down (**80:12**) and the vineyard has been left defenceless, so that anyone can now pluck its fruit and *boars from the forest* root it up (**80:13**). These images give a vivid picture of what foreign invaders did to Israel's land. So the people prayed, *Return to us, O God Almighty! Look down from heaven and see! Watch over this vine, the root your right hand has planted, the son [or branch] you have raised up for yourself!* (**80:14-15**).

This 'son' is also referred to as *the son of man you have raised up for yourself* and *the man at your right hand* (**80:17**). The psalmist may be referring to Israel as the people who have a special relationship with God, just as believers do today (see Isa 43:21). Or he may be referring to the king as the Lord's anointed (see 2:7). It is also possible that it refers to Benjamin, for the name Benjamin means 'son of my right hand' (Gen 35:18). If this last interpretation is correct, this would give the whole psalm a special connection with what happened to the tribe of Benjamin.

The psalm ends with the refrain: *Restore us, O Lord God Almighty; make your face shine upon us, that we may be saved* (**80:19**; see also 80:3, 7). This time it is preceded by an urgent prayer – *revive us* – and a promise – *then we will never turn back from you* (**80:18**, NRSV), a promise that is easier to make than to keep. God's word is always constant, and he says: 'Return to me ... and I will return to you' (Zech 1:3) and 'Come near to God and he will come near to you' (Jas 4:8). Yet even today, as when this psalm was written, it is hard for people to remain constant in their relationship with God, although God himself does not change.

Psalm 81: The Worship and the Word of God

The heading of this psalm includes the words *According to Gittith,* which may refer to the tune to which the psalm was sung (see also Psalm 8). The psalm is clearly both a call to the people of Israel to worship the Lord and a challenge to them to hear his word.

81:1-5 The Worship of God

The call to worship, with its exhortation to praise God with songs, shouts of joy and musical instruments (**81:1-2**), was made at the time of one of the special festivals that were prescribed in the law (**81:4**). The beginning of each month, the *New Moon* (**81:3a**), was like the Sabbath in that it was regarded as a special time to praise God (see 2 Kgs 4:23; Isa 1:13; Hos 2:11; Amos 8:5). But this psalm also refers to

a feast that was held *when the moon is full* (**81:3b**). This was probably the Feast of Tabernacles, which was held on the fifteenth day of the seventh month (Lev 23:23-43; Num 29). It commemorated God's provision for the people during their forty years in the wilderness after they left Egypt. Every seven years the law was read clearly and publicly at that feast in such a way that everyone present could understand it (Deut 31:9-13). The Feast of Tabernacles was thus a time when the people were challenged to renew their covenant loyalty to God. It was therefore appropriate that they should hear God's word through a priest or prophet, and that is what we have in 81:6-16.

The psalm speaks of God's law as a *statute for Joseph* (**81:5a**). Here the name 'Joseph' is used for all the covenant people, in the same way as 'Jacob' is used elsewhere (see 79:7). This name may be chosen because in 81:6 God speaks of what he did for the people in Egypt, the country to which Joseph had taken them and in which *we heard a language we did not understand* (**81:5b**), namely the Egyptian language.

81:6-16 The Word of God

God's word, as so often is the case in the OT, is first of all a reminder of what he had done for his people. In Egypt they were slaves and were made to carry great burdens, heavy baskets of building materials for construction projects (**81:6**; Exod 1:11-14). They cried out to the Lord in their distress (**81:7a**; see Exod 2:23-25), and he answered them. He came to them in the *thundercloud* on Mount Sinai and gave them his law (**81:7b**; Exod 19). At Meribah, where the people complained about the lack of water (Exod 17:1-7; Num 20:11-13), the people put God to the test (see 95:8-10), but God was also testing them (**81:7c**; see Deut 8:2-5; Jas 1:2-4, 12).

After this list of what the Lord has done for them in the past, the psalmist inserts *Selah,* allowing a pause for reflection, before conveying God's message for them in the present, a message that can be summed up in the words, *Hear ... listen ....*

Hear, O my people (**81:8**) is how the summing up of the law began in Deuteronomy 6:4. The Jewish people have always called that passage the *Shema,* which is the Hebrew word for 'hear'. It means more than just 'listen'; it means being attentive and willing to obey. If only the people would listen to the Lord, then they would remember that it was he alone who brought them out of their slavery in Egypt and made them his people. They would realize that they must have no other god but the Lord alone, as the first two commandments stated (**81:9**; Exod 20:2-6; Deut 5:6-10).

The words at the end of **81:10**, *Open wide your mouth and I will fill it,* are usually taken to mean that if God's people turn to him in repentance, obedience and prayer, they will receive abundant blessings. This is certainly what is said in **81:16**. It is possible, however, that the opening of the mouth at this point in the psalm is to receive God's word (compare what Jer 1:9 says about the prophet receiving God's word in his mouth). This verse should not be taken as presenting a prosperity gospel for individual Christians today and suggesting that if we serve God we will enjoy material riches and plenty. Many have had to suffer hardship and have been deprived of their earthly possessions for Christ's sake. This psalm is speaking of the blessing of the nation when it remains faithful to the Lord.

The sad story of Israel's history, however, was that they *would not listen* (**81:11**) and were not willing to serve God whole-heartedly. They might have been deeply religious, but their hearts were far from God (see 2 Tim 3:5). *I gave them over to their stubborn hearts* (**81:12**) describes the worst thing that can happen to anyone. If people refuse to follow God's way and to say, 'Your will be done' (Matt 6:10), the Lord lets them go their own way and have their own will. The same point is made in other parts of the Bible, where people who have *stubborn hearts* are left to *their own devices* and must suffer the consequences (see especially Rom 1:18-32). Self-chosen ways can never be good compared with God's wise and loving purpose for our lives. When people reject God's will, they always get less than the best.

Yet God gives his people another opportunity, though they have rebelled against him. He says, *If my people would but listen to me, if Israel would follow my ways* (**81:13**). What would happen then? They would prove God's victory over all the forces of evil that oppose them, and he would provide for all their needs in their land, a land that was often said to be 'flowing with milk and honey' (Num 13:27; Deut 31:20).

The words of this psalm are as meaningful for Christians today as they were for the Jewish people in OT times, for the worship of God and the word of God still belong together. God intends us to come together regularly for worship (see Heb 10:25). In particular, we come together for our special feast, the Lord's Supper (Holy Communion) when we remember what Jesus Christ has done for us by his sacrificial death on the cross (1 Cor 11:23-26). It is right that at such a time of worship there should also be preaching of God's word, so that we are reminded of what God has done and are called afresh to hear him speak to us, challenging us to serve only him in our daily lives. Christians should always pray for those who have the responsibility of preaching God's word and leading others in worship.

Psalm 82: Gods and Judges

When we read this psalm, we naturally ask, 'Who are the gods that are spoken of here'? and 'What is the great assembly (or divine council)'? These are important questions, but there is a message in this psalm that is even more important than answers to those questions. That message

is God's demand for justice. We will, however, try to study both the questions and the message as we consider the psalm.

82:1, 6-7 The Divine Council

The people of Israel were constantly reminded that there was one God whom they should worship. The law was summed up in the words: 'The Lord our God, the Lord is one. Love the Lord your God with all your heart and with all your soul and with all your strength' (Deut 6:4-5). Christians too believe that there is only one God, the Father, Lord and Creator of all, who is supremely made known to us in his Son, Jesus Christ, through his Holy Spirit (Heb 1:1-3). But throughout history, many people have thought that there are lesser gods as well as the one supreme God. So they have also thought of there being a council of gods. The Apostle Paul is speaking in these terms when he says that 'there are many "gods" and many "lords"' (1 Cor 8:5), although he makes it clear that the many gods people worship are only 'so-called gods'. But is this really what is meant by *the great assembly* (**82:1**)?

In the passages where the OT speaks of a heavenly council (1 Kgs 22:19-22; Job 1:6; 2:1-6; Deut 33:2-3; Ps 89:5), it seems to be speaking of spiritual beings such as angels standing in the presence of God and serving him. The word *elohim*, normally used for God, can be used for such beings, and the book of Daniel speaks of heavenly representatives of earthly rulers (Dan 10:13, 20-21) This is the way that some would understand 82:1. But the problem with this interpretation is that **82:6-7** would then be saying that those heavenly beings are condemned to die.

It is also possible that the word *elohim* means judges or rulers (see Exod 21:6; 22:28; commentary on Ps 58:1). It seems that Jesus interpreted it in this way in his response to the Jews' attempt to stone him because of the special way in which he spoke of God as his Father. He said that if people like judges could be spoken of in the OT using the term 'gods', how could it be wrong for 'the one whom the Father set apart as his very own and sent into the world' to be called God's Son (John 10:34-36). If we take this interpretation, then 82:6-7 is saying that though these judges are very important and are treated in a special sense as *sons of the Most High* (82:6), they will die like any other human being.

82:2-5, 8 Justice for All

God demands that all people, and especially those in positions of leadership, act justly. Judges have to be fair to all and must not *show partiality to the wicked* (**82:2**). The payment and acceptance of bribes undermines this impartiality, for 'a bribe corrupts the heart' (Eccl 7:7) and 'blinds the eyes of the wise and twists the words of the righteous' (Deut 16:19). Judges have a special responsibility to uphold the rights of the weak and poor and to make sure that widows and orphans are not oppressed (**82:3**). Christians too should always be ready to help those in their own communities who are *weak and needy* (**82:4**) and in danger of being neglected or taken advantage of by those who are richer or stronger than they are.

To act unjustly is to act with *neither knowledge nor understanding* (**82:5**, NRSV). There is *darkness* and not light in the life of a nation or organization where there is injustice, and where there are no secure foundations on which the society can base its values.

When we are faced with injustice, we should pray the prayer in **82:8**, asking God to *rise up* and judge every nation. But we should also make sure that we ourselves always act justly in our relationships with other people, no matter how much or how little power we have. As the prophet Micah reminds us: 'And what does the Lord require of you? To act justly and to love mercy and to walk humbly with your God' (Mic 6:8).

Psalm 83: Lord, May All Nations Seek You

This is the last of the psalms of Asaph (see note at the beginning of Book 3). It is an urgent prayer, not just for an individual in need, but for the nation. As is so often seen in such prayers in the Psalms, the present situation is brought to God, there is a recalling of what God has done in the past and there is a desire for the future.

83:1-8 The Present Situation

The people were so threatened by enemies that if God was silent and did not speak and act to defend them, they would be destroyed so completely that no one would even remember them (**83:4-5**). Their situation explains the cry of the first verse; *O God, do not keep silent; be not quiet, O God, be not still* (**83:1**).

The people pleaded with God, saying in effect, 'they are not just our enemies, they are *your enemies*, plotting *against your people* (**83:2-3**). God's name and God's purposes were threatened. This conviction may have helped the people to avoid despair (83:18). It may also help us to exercise self-restraint. In the face of injustice and persecution, it is easy to lash out to vindicate ourselves. But when we think of unjust and oppressive people as God's enemies, we learn not to avenge ourselves but to 'leave room for God's wrath' (see Rom 12:17-21).

Israel was surrounded by enemies. *Edom* and the *Ishmaelites* or Midianites were to the south, and *Moab* to the south-east (**83:6**). Both Edom and Moab were descendants of Lot (**83:8b**). The Hagrites (perhaps descended from Hagar, who bore Ishmael to Abraham – Gen 16) are only mentioned elsewhere in the OT in 1 Chronicles 5:19-20, where it is clear that they lived east of the Jordan river.

Gebal (if it is the same place mentioned in Joshua 13:5) was in the north (in the area of Biblos in Phoenicia). Ammon and Amalek often threatened Israel, raiding it from the east and south, as did the Philistines from the south-west, while Tyre was powerful in the north (**83:7**). Assyria was the great power in the time of Isaiah and Hezekiah and overwhelmed the northern kingdom of Israel in 721 BC (**83:8a**).

There were alliances of various peoples against Judah in the time of Jehoshaphat (2 Chr 20:1-4) and of Uzziah (2 Chr 26:6-8), and later in the time of Nehemiah. But in none of these cases, as far as we know, were all these peoples linked together. The psalm may list them together because at various times Israel faced the opposition of all these nations.

83:9-12 The Past Remembered

When they prayed, the people remembered the past. A number of the psalms recall how God brought them to freedom from slavery in Egypt and led them to possess their land. Here they are reminded of the victories in the days of the judges. Under Gideon, the Midianites were conquered with their captains Oreb and Zeeb and their princes Zebah and Zalmunna (**83:9a, 11**; see Judg 6–8). Under Deborah and Barak, Sisera and Jabin were defeated *at the river Kishon* and at *Endor* (**83:9b-10**; see also Judg 4–5). The people believed that God had protected the nation then and helped it to conquer their enemies. 'Do it again,' was their prayer.

Many enemies (Pharisees, Sadducees and Herodians) united in their opposition to Jesus, and over the past two thousand years, enemies have often united in their opposition to Christians. We can learn how to face opposition and persecution from what the apostle Paul says in Philippians 1:27-30 and from the prayer in Acts 4:23-31. And like the psalmist, we do well to keep a record of God's special interventions in our lives. When we find ourselves in difficult situations, faith is strengthened when we remember how God has helped us in the past.

83:13-18 Hopes for the Future

The people hoped that their enemies – God's enemies – would have no more power than dust that is swept away before the wind (**83:13**). They wanted those enemies to be terrified by the power of the Lord, as people are by a raging forest fire or by a frightening storm (**83:14-15**). They wanted them to be ashamed of their aggression and to *perish in disgrace* (**83:17**). We have read many prayers like this in the Psalms, and have realized that, as men and women who have experienced God's grace and forgiveness in Christ, we must pray for the conversion of those who oppose the purposes of God and the people of God, and not for their destruction. We want to pray, like Jesus, that 'they may know you, the only true God, and Jesus Christ, whom you have sent' (John 17:3). This prayer is actually the same as the highest prayer in this psalm, that God's actions would cause the nations to seek the Lord (**83:16**) and know that he is *the Most High over all the earth* (**83:18**). That is a prayer that we can and should always pray for others.

Psalm 84: The Joy of the Worship of God

For information on the instruction *According to Gittith* in the heading of this psalm, see the comments on Psalm 81. The *sons of Korah* (see also Pss 85; 87; 88) were descended from Levi (Exod 6:21-24) and were linked with the Levites in the worship of the temple (1 Chr 9:19; 26:1-19).

As we have seen in other psalms, the temple had a special place in the lives and the affections of devout Hebrew people in OT days. For those who lived outside Jerusalem, pilgrimage was very important. But more important than the place or the pilgrimage was trust in the living God who was worshipped in the temple. This psalm thus adds to our understanding of what true blessing is (see also 1:1; 32:1-2; 41:1; 94:12; 128:1).

84:1-4, 10 The Temple

The temple was *lovely* in the eyes of the psalmist and greatly loved by him (**84:1**). He lived far from it, but with all his being he longed to be there (**84:2**). He thought of how even the birds were able to nest there safely, and felt that he was always welcome and secure when he went there. Yet he went there not just to be secure but to worship the one whom he addressed as *my King and my God* (**84:3**). The temple was indeed the place to worship and praise God (**84:4**), and the place where God's presence was especially real to those who sincerely sought him. So he could say that one day spent there was *better than a thousand elsewhere* (**84:10a**).

The psalmist knew that it was better to have the humblest place at the gate of the temple than to live with those who did not serve God or seek to obey him (**84:10b**). His attitude is a challenge to us all. Evil people with power or political authority often try to buy the support of good people or to silence prophetic voices raised against them by offering money, favours or high positions in government. Too often, discerning Christians find it hard to know how to pray or speak in opposition to dictators in their own countries or elsewhere because some church leaders and others who would describe themselves as Christians are seen to be working to support these dictators. Those who love the Lord are challenged to reject evil in all its forms and to realize that the love of money is at the root of all kinds of evil (97:10; 1 Tim 6:10). True worship and faithfulness to God are priorities for all who claim to be Christians. We should be like the psalmist, able to say, *With my whole being I sing with joy to the living God* (84:2, GNB).

84:5-7 Pilgrimage to the Temple

The three great annual festivals (Passover, Weeks and Tabernacles) were celebrated in Jerusalem by all who could possibly go there (Deut 16:16). We read in the NT (Luke 2:41) that Mary and Joseph were in the habit of going to Jerusalem for the Passover. The psalmist had no doubt that blessing could come from such a pilgrimage (84:5-6).

The Hebrew in **84:5** says literally 'in their hearts are highways'. It does not mention Zion, but the thought is probably of pilgrimage there, and it speaks of those who are eager to make the pilgrimage. Even though it may not be possible for them to go to Jerusalem, they make the pilgrimage in their hearts.

In the course of their pilgrimage, they have to pass through *the Valley of Baca* (**84:6**), which was probably a dry valley. But God supplies refreshment to his people as they travel. However, the word *baca* may mean 'weeping', in which case the psalmist is speaking of God's gift of joy even in the midst of sorrow. Whichever interpretation is correct, it is clear that the reality of faith is shown in perseverance and triumph through pain. The journey may be difficult, through barren country, but the sense of God's presence on the journey is like the blessing of abundant rain watering the dry ground. Realizing that, people seem to increase in strength as they go on. Instead of being worn out by the difficult journey, the faithful *go from strength to strength* (**84:7**; compare Isa 40:29-31). The thought of their eventual arrival at the temple, where they believe God to be especially present and ready to answer prayer, is an additional source of inspiration for the faithful pilgrim.

For the Christian there is a different source of inspiration. It is not in a building, but in the abiding presence of God. Jesus said 'where two or three come together in my name, there am I with them' (Matt 18:20). His promise frees us from those who depend on external things or who try to use religion as a way of making money or controlling others. The promise of God's presence is for those who 'worship in spirit and in truth' wherever they are (John 4:24).

84:8-12 The God Worshipped in the Temple

The temple was just a building, albeit a sacred one. It was God, whose temple it was, that really mattered. Church buildings and religious houses, however great and ornate, are still temporary structures. We must never venerate a building or any object rather than God. The names by which God is addressed in this psalm help us to realize this. He is the *Lord Almighty* (84:1, 3, 12), *the living God* (84:2), *my King and my God* (84:3), and the *God of Jacob* (84:8).

The images used to describe God also add to our understanding of him. He is like the *sun* bringing light and warmth to his people, and like a *shield* protecting them (**84:11a**). The Bible speaks of God being our protection in many different ways (see Exod 13:21-22; Pss 23:4; 46:1-2; 125:1-3; Matt 28:20; John 10:27-30; Col 3:3).

But leaders – both political and religious – should also be a *shield* to their people (**84:9**; see Acts 20:28; 1 Tim 5:17; 6:20). God gives strength to those who trust him (**84:5**) and answers their prayers (**84:8**). These prayers are also for their king as God's anointed, the person who is intended to be their protector and defender (**84:9**). Christians too are urged to pray for those in authority (1 Tim 2:1-4; Rom 13:1-7). We are also to exercise a prophetic ministry of speaking and living in ways that will promote obedience to God, and so work to bring about a just and humane society.

People often seek favour and honours from the world, but the truest favour and honour comes to those who serve God. God keeps back nothing that is good from those who rely on him (**84:11b**). Whether they are in the temple or far away, whether they can make a pilgrimage to Jerusalem or not, *blessed is the man who trusts in you* (**84:12**). This is the central message of this psalm. Trust in the Lord is what matters most of all.

What about Christian people today? What does this psalm mean to us? We have no temple as the Jewish people had. We have no command to make pilgrimages to Jerusalem or other holy places as a means of salvation, as Muslims do. For Christians, the meaning of the temple was fulfilled in Jesus. He was 'tabernacle' and 'temple' (see John 2:19-22) and 'God with us' (Matt 1:23) in the most perfect way. And now the Holy Spirit makes our lives and the fellowship of Christians his temple (see 1 Cor 6:19-20; 2 Cor 6:16).

Our greatest desire – like the psalmist's – should be to worship the Lord in our daily lives. Through prayer and meditation on the Scriptures, we can draw strength and courage to live each day in joyful obedience to God and, in the power of the Holy Spirit, to have a loving and caring attitude towards others (see Eph 5:18-20). And we should also rejoice in the fellowship of God's people, meeting together to worship and encourage one another in his service, to hear God's word, and to draw spiritual strength (and even physical healing) as we renew our faith through communion (Acts 2:42; Heb 10:24-25). The experience of God's people in both Testaments encourages us to expect God's presence, through his Holy Spirit, to be particularly real at such gatherings. When his people dwell in unity, honesty and love, they can confidently call on him with pure and sincere hearts (2 Chr 7:1-3; Ps 133; Acts 4:27-31).

Psalm 85: Righteousness and Peace

This is another psalm attributed to the *sons of Korah* (see Ps 84). Like many others, this one recalls the goodness of God in the past, forgiving and restoring his people after they had suffered great loss through turning away from him (85:1-3). It then describes the troubles being faced in the present. The people have again turned aside from the Lord and are suffering under God's righteous anger and chastening, so that they pray for his mercy and saving power (85:4-7).

85:1-3 Looking Back

We can always look back and see God's blessings on us in the past. Israel could say how good God had been to them (**85:1**). They knew that they had not deserved his favour, yet he had forgiven them (**85:2**), and all his righteous anger, which they deserved because of their rejection of his laws, had been turned away (**85:3**). The psalmist may have been thinking of the way God had forgiven them and brought them back to their land after their sin and unfaithfulness had led to the fall of Jerusalem and the destruction of the temple (Isa 40:1-11; Jer 33:7-9).

85:4-7 Looking Round

But difficult times had followed, as described in the books of Ezra and Nehemiah. Haggai 1:1-11 shows how the people failed to put God first and therefore once more lost his blessing. So they again prayed for a renewal of God's work among them, asking him to *restore us* or 'bring us back' in the GNB (**85:4**). We depend on God's help to restore us to a right relationship with him when we stray from him. Our own experience confirms this, for we know that our New Year's resolutions come to nothing, and that mystic guides to the perfect life are frustrating at best in dealing with the sin factor in human life (see Col 2:20-23). Both God's part and our part are expressed in the words of Lamentations 5:21: 'Restore us to yourself, O Lord, that we may return; renew our days as of old'.

The people had sinned, and their sin and rebellion stood between them and God. God seemed far away. They were wondering whether their failure would separate them from God's blessing for ever (**85:5**; see also 74:1; 79:5; 80:4). *Will you not revive us again?* they asked (**85:6**). It was nothing less than new life that they needed, like the dry bones coming to life in Ezekiel's vision (Ezek 37:1-14). Then they would be restored to the joy of God's salvation (**85:7**; see also 51:12).

85:8-13 Looking Forward

Often God's word comes in answer to his people's prayers. Those who ask for guidance and help should take the attitude of the psalmist, saying, *I will listen to what God the Lord will say* (**85:8a**). God's word to them is *peace*, providing they do *not return to folly* or unfaithfulness (**85:8b**; see also 1 Cor 10:12). The Hebrew word *shalom* means more than the English word 'peace'. It has come into many African and Asian languages as 'salaam' or something similar, with the meaning of 'perfect wholeness' or 'total well-being'. It speaks of true welfare and so involves God's *salvation* of those who fear him, and a sense of the *glory* of his presence (**85:9**). This promise of peace gives hope to God's people (85:8-9). It makes them think of the blessing of knowing the steadfast love and faithfulness of God in a new way as they respond by living righteous lives and so find God's blessing on their land (85:10-13).

If people experience the *love* and *faithfulness* and *righteousness* of God (**85:10**), what more could they want or need? True righteousness and real peace belong together, as God's gifts, in the lives of individuals or nations. One cannot exist without the other. The life that results is what the Igbo of Nigeria describe as *Ezi-ndu,* a life that involves total well-being as well as the fullness of justice and moral uprightness. When God's righteousness (from heaven) and human faithfulness (from earth) meet in the life of a nation, there will truly be blessing in the land (**85:11-12**).

When God's love, faithfulness and righteousness are evident in the life of an individual, peace and joy result. This is beautifully illustrated in Luke's version of the announcement of the birth of Christ to the shepherds. The blessings spoken of in this psalm are realized most of all in Jesus Christ, in his life, and in what he has done for us by his death and resurrection. When people submit themselves to God to give him glory, the result is peace, *shalom,* on earth to 'men on whom his favour rests' (Luke 2:14). When an individual responds with submission to the person and message of Jesus Christ, the outcome is a changed and enriched life. 'Today, salvation [*shalom, Ezi-ndu*] has come to this home (see Luke 19:9-10).

The last verse of the psalm reminds us that the paths that God sets for us to follow are always paths of righteousness (**85:13**). That is also the message of the Shepherd Psalm, 'He guides me in paths of righteousness for his name's sake' (23:3). It is when we order our lives along these 'paths of righteousness' under the guidance of the word of God that we can enjoy 'blessings' or lasting success, God's *shalom* (Josh 1:8). Jesus makes the same promise when he says, 'Blessed are those who hunger and thirst for righteousness, for they will be filled' (Matt 5:6). We are to 'seek first his kingdom and his righteousness' and leave everything else in God's hands (Matt 6:33).

Because God's name or honour is at stake when his people go astray, spiritually or morally, God takes time to guide and guard the ways of those who trust him and desire to please him. As Jude reminds us, this God is not only the judge of the wicked, he is also the Saviour of those who trust him. He is the one 'who is able to keep you from falling' (Jude 1:24).

Psalm 86: Prayer in a Time of Need

The psalms teach a lot about how to pray. They model how to tell God sincerely of our needs. This is what the psalmist does here. We can also learn from the particular requests that are made in this psalm, and from the words that are used in expressing them. Often we just want to pray in our own words. That is good. But there are times when it is helpful to us and to those who pray with us to use words from the prayers of others that may inform our minds and express our needs better than we could do ourselves. This is especially true of expressions of the praise of God that are found in various parts of the Bible. The writer of this psalm often used words that are found in other psalms and in other parts of the Bible – compare 86:1 with 40:17; 86:4 with 25:1; 86:8 with Exod 15:11; 86:14 with 54:3; and 86:15 with Exodus 34:6.

The prayer that Jesus taught was given to teach us not only to pray but how to pray and what we should ask for (Luke 11:1-4). Many of us memorized the Lord's Prayer in our childhood, but it is well worth our while to memorize some of the other great prayers in the Psalms – like this one – and in the NT (for example, Eph 3:14-21; Phil 1:9-11; Col 1:9-12; Heb 13:20-21).

86:1-4, 14 The Greatness of Human Needs

Because we cannot live as we ought without God's help, we need to learn to come to God with a humble attitude and confess that we are *poor and needy* (**86:1**). The psalmist appeals to God to *guard my life* because he is under attack from ruthless enemies who gave God no place in their lives (**86:14**). But he claims God's protection, because, in his words, *I am devoted to you* (**86:2**). He is not boasting of special godliness, but expressing something similar to *your servant who trusts in you* in the second part of the verse. He knows that he needs the help of the Lord *all day* and every day (**86:3**), as well as in special days of *trouble* when the need is urgent (86:7).

The needs expressed in this psalm are ones we often share. In danger, whether of body or soul, we need to ask for God's protection and salvation (86:2). We need to ask him for gladness and joy when we are discouraged (**86:4**), as well as for grace and forgiveness when we realize our failures and sins (86:5).

86:5-10,12-13, 15 God's Greatness and Goodness

The psalmist knew that he could say of the one to whom he prayed *You alone are God* (**86:10**). He knew God as *forgiving and good, ... abounding in love to all who call to you* (**86:5**), *a compassionate and gracious God, slow to anger* (**86:15**). There is no other like him because he is Creator and Lord of all. There are no works like his (**86:8**). Consequently, all nations will ultimately come to know and worship him (**86:9**; see also 66:1-4; Isa 2:2-4; Zech 8:21-23; Mal 1:11; Matt 28:18-20; Acts 1:8; Rom 10:14).

In addition to doing great and *marvellous deeds* for the world in general (86:10), the Lord had also provided for the needs of the psalmist himself, so that he could say that the Lord *delivered me from the depths of the grave* (**86:13**), perhaps referring to a time when he came very close to death, or when the evil forces that opposed him were at their strongest. So he had every reason to say, *I will praise you, O Lord my God, with all my heart; I will glorify your name for ever* (**86:12**).

When we realize how much we have to thank God for, and when we stop to think of his goodness, greatness and love, we are helped to pray on in trust and confidence.

86:11, 16-17 Great Requests

Perhaps the most important of all the prayers in this psalm is the prayer that God will teach us his way so that we may walk in it faithfully and that we may do so with *an undivided heart* (**86:11**; see also Jer 32:39; Phil 3:13-14). The psalmist has no desire to be like those who 'utter lies to each other; with flattering lips and a double heart' (12:2, NRSV). As James 1:7-8 reminds us, such 'double-minded' people cannot expect to receive the Lord's blessing. Verse 86:11 should be the sincere prayer of all Christians every day.

In any kind of trouble, we can ask God to be near and support us, to turn to us and give us strength to face our trouble (**86:16**; 46:1-3). When we ask him for a sign, as in **86:17**, we need not be asking for some miraculous sign, but simply for some action that shows that he has heard and is answering our prayer. We should want that support not just for our own sakes, but so that the world may see that God helps and comforts those who trust in him, and so be drawn to him (see also 86:9).

Psalm 87: The City for All Nations

The heading of this psalm links it with *the sons of Korah* (see the comments on Ps 84). It is a short psalm, but not an easy one to understand when we first read it. Like Psalm 84 (and 46, 48, 76) it speaks of the glory of Jerusalem and of the temple built there on Mount Zion. It makes two main points: that Zion is the city of God, and that the city of God is for all nations.

87:1-4 The Glory of Zion as the City of God

The gate of an ancient city was the social heart of the city. That was where meetings took place, where justice was administered, and where many important transactions were carried out. Thus when the psalmist speaks of *the gates of Zion* (**87:2**), he means Zion itself. This place is not more favoured *than all the dwellings of Jacob* because it is more deserving of the Lord's love. Deuteronomy 7:6-8 and 10:15 rule out that possibility. Rather, it is favoured because God has a special purpose for Zion. That was where the temple was located. *Glorious things* could be said of the *city of God* (**87:3**) because of God's presence there, because of the

worship of God there, and because of God's past blessing of, and future purpose, for the city.

87:5-7 The City of God for All Nations

Many peoples have thought that their country is the most important one in the world, and that their city is the centre of the world, even the centre of the universe. Many of us have thought ourselves superior to other nations and peoples and have looked down on others. The OT prophets and psalmists did not allow Israel to think like that. Whatever privilege they thought they had through their knowledge of God – the God of the whole earth – it was theirs to share with others. So although the people of Israel could say that they belonged to the city of God by birth, God wanted people of other nations to share that privilege. *Rahab, Babylon, Philistia, Tyre* and *Cush* would be brought to know the Lord (**87:4**). Rahab, the name of a monster in ancient Near Eastern mythology, stood for Egypt (see Isa 30:7), the nation that had held Israel captive for generations. Babylon was the powerful enemy who had conquered Jerusalem and destroyed the temple. The Philistines had tried to take land from Israel for many years. Tyre had a dominant commercial empire in OT days. Cush was the ancient land of Ethiopia, to Israel a strange and distant land on the African continent. Yet God wanted people of all these nations to be like freeborn citizens of Zion (**87:5**) and recorded in his book (**87:6**). And it is not simply the psalmist who said this. The prophets also spoke about God's international purpose for Israel and for Jerusalem (see Isa 2:2-4; 19:23-25; 44:5; 56:6-7; 60:1-3; Zech 8:20-23).

The psalmist's words remind us of the responsibility that goes with the privilege of knowing God as revealed in Christ. The vision of the universal reign of Christ at the end of time should challenge us to take the gospel to all the world and to all peoples. After all, we ourselves have already benefited from this universality, and so are 'no longer foreigners and aliens, but fellow citizens with God's people and members of God's household, built on the foundation of the apostles and prophets, with Christ Jesus himself as the chief cornerstone' (Eph 2:19-20).

Another point to note is that God's coming kingdom will include even those who have previously opposed his rule and persecuted his people. 'The vilest offender who truly believes, that moment from Jesus, a pardon receives. Praise the Lord!' So as the people of Israel sing and dance, people of other nations should sing and dance with them! (**87:7**). The presence of God in his city and among those who know him is like an unending spring. It is not a summons to an exclusive ghetto, the club of the faithful, but a signal to 'let the earth hear his voice'.

The thought of the last verse is like that of 46:4, 'There is a river whose streams make glad the city of God'. It is like the vision in Ezekiel 47 of the stream that flowed down from the temple in Jerusalem and became a river that brought life and fruitfulness in all the dry places to which it went.

How does this apply to Christian people? We have been made members of a new Zion, the spiritual Jerusalem, the Christian church that the apostle Paul speaks of as 'our mother' (Gal 4:26). By the new birth of which John 3 speaks, we are members of God's people and belong with those of every tribe and nation. The barriers between tribes and nations, cultures and races have been broken down in Jesus Christ (Eph 2:11-22). We belong together in the city of God. We are challenged to express that in every way we can. It will be realized perfectly in our heavenly home, when we will stand with our fellow believers from different tribes and nations and worship the Lamb (Rev 7:9-17; ch. 21).

Psalm 88: All Is Dark

Like Psalms 84 and 87, this psalm is associated with the *sons of Korah,* who were involved in the temple worship in Jerusalem. *Mahalath leannoth* may be the name of the tune to which it was to be sung, but the words may mean 'the suffering of affliction', which would link with the theme of the psalm. Heman the Ezrahite and Ethan the Ezrahite, who is mentioned in the heading of the next psalm, are among the temple musicians named in 1 Chronicles 15:17.

The book of Psalms gives us the prayers – and the praises – of people in all kinds of different situations and experiences of life: joys and sorrows, blessings and deep problems. This particular psalm has been called the saddest in the book. Other psalms speak of great troubles, but have a note of hope at the end. This psalm begins and ends with woes. Two things make the psalm so desperately sad: the psalmist seems to face trouble in every possible way, and he has no hope of anything beyond death and the grave.

88:1-9, 13-18 Trouble Upon Trouble

For some people, life seems to be full of troubles. Think of all those who face injustice or natural disasters, famine and hunger, with no one to help. Think of refugees, leaving their homes and countries with nothing more than the clothes they are wearing. Think of those who face continuing illness and whose prayers for healing seem unanswered. Such people may well say with Job, 'man is born to trouble as surely as sparks fly upward' (Job 5:7). We cannot deny the immense troubles that some people have to face, and there is often no easy answer to the question 'Why?'

This was the situation in which the psalmist found himself. *My soul is full of trouble,* he said (**88:3a**). He seems to have been brought near to death by an illness that may have afflicted him since his youth (**88:3b-5, 15**). It may have been a disease like leprosy (or like HIV/AIDS nowadays). Either because of his disease or for some other reason, his friends and neighbours forsook him and regarded him as *repulsive* (**88:8, 18a**).

Worst of all, he felt that God was angry with him because of his sin and had cast him off (**88:6-7, 14**). He blames God for all his troubles. Notice how many times 'you' and 'your' are used in 88:6-8 and 14-18 as he speaks of what God has done. He did not see even a glimmer of hope, so that *the darkness is my closest friend* (**88:18b**).

Yet in spite of the lack of answers, the psalmist still turned to God. He prayed *day and night* (**88:1**), *every day* (**88:9**), and every *morning* (**88:13**). He still believed in the steadfast love, faithfulness and saving help of God (88:11-12), and did not doubt or deny them. *O Lord, the God who saves me* he prayed (**88:1**). That is a lesson to all of us.

88:10-12 What Hope Beyond Death?

In 88:10-12 the psalmist asks six questions, all anticipating the answer 'No'. He was sure that the dead can no longer know God's steadfast love and faithfulness, experience his saving help and praise him. God could work wonders for the living, he felt, but not for the dead (see also 30:8-9; Isa 38:18). He speaks of the grave as *Sheol* and as *the Pit* (88:3, 5, 11 – KJV) and of death as Destruction (**88:11**; *Abaddon* – KJV). He also speaks of 'the dead' and 'the slain' (88:5).

A few of the psalms speak of some hope of life after death (16:11; 23:6; 49:15; 73:24; 139:7-12), but this hope only became certain through the resurrection of Jesus Christ, who 'destroyed death and has brought life and immortality to light through the gospel' (2 Tim 1:10). Because of that hope, our prayers need never be as woeful as the prayers of this psalm. With the Apostle Paul we can say, 'I consider that our present sufferings are not worth comparing with the glory that will be revealed in us' (Rom 8:18).

We need to pray every day for those whom we know or know about who face great trouble or suffering. We should pray that they may know the presence of God now and have in Jesus Christ a firm hope for the future.

Psalm 89: He Will Not Abandon Forever

For the reference to *Ethan the Ezrahite* in the heading of the psalm, see the comments at the beginning of Psalm 88. This psalm, like Psalm 78, is a long one. It divides easily into three parts. The first part is like a hymn about the goodness and greatness of God (89:1-18). The second part celebrates God's purpose for David and his descendants to be kings of Israel (89:19-37). The third part is a prayer uttered when it seemed that the purposes of God had failed (89:38-51).

89:1-18 The Goodness and Greatness of God

We need to consider what the first part of the psalm says about the love of God, the power of God and how good it is to be the people of God.

89:1-8 *The love of God*

The Psalms often speak about God's steadfast love and his faithfulness. In this psalm, the words *your faithfulness* are used time after time (**89:1, 2, 5a, 8**). God is always to be trusted and is unchanging in his purpose. Part of that purpose was the choice of David to be king and for his descendants to reign after him (**89:3-4**; 2 Sam 7:12-13; see also comments on 89:19-37).

The next few verses describe God, not just in relation to people on earth, but in relation to heavenly beings (**89:5b-7a**). All acknowledge that God is *more awesome than all who surround him* (**89:7b**). There is none like him, for he alone is Lord and God over all, worthy of the praise of heaven and earth alike.

89:9-13 *The power of God*

Sometimes it seems that God's creation is unruly, like the wild waves of the sea. But ultimately, God is in control. The reference to the sea in **89:9** makes us think of Jesus stilling the storms on Lake Galilee, so that the disciples marvelled, and said, 'even the wind and the waves obey him!' (Mark 4:35-41). Rahab (**89:10**) is sometimes used as a name for Egypt (as in Isa 30:7), but in ancient Near Eastern mythology Rahab was a monster who was conquered when the world was made (see Isa 51:9). God has power over all who oppose him.

If we look to the north and the south, all that we can see – and far more – was created by God. Hermon was a mighty mountain in Lebanon to the north-west, and Tabor, though not nearly as high, stood out from the plain to the west of Galilee. Both mountains made people think of the power of the Creator (see Jer 46:18). As we look on God's creation round about us, we should contemplate God as creator and allow these thoughts to influence our lives.

89:14-18 *The people of God*

Blessed are those who have learned to acclaim you says **89:15a**. Happy are the people who join in the praise of God. The word here translated 'acclaim' is used in the OT for a war cry, a shout of victory over enemies, a shout of welcome for a king, but it could also express people's single-minded enthusiasm in their worship, proclaiming God as Lord and King over their lives. Those who acclaim God have learned to live in the light of his presence (**89:15b**; see also Num 6:24-26; Pss 31:16; 67:1; 80:3, 7, 19). Such people know God's *love and faithfulness* leading them as they seek to walk in his ways, and they know that *righteousness and justice* are found wherever he rules (**89:14**).

Psalm 75:10 spoke of 'the horns of the wicked' and 'the horns of the righteous', and we noted that a 'horn' was a symbol of strength, just as the horn of a wild animal expresses its strength. This psalm speaks in the same way

of *our horn* (**89:17**). The GNB translates this verse as *You give us great victories; in your love you make us triumphant.*

The idea of the king being given to the people recurs in **89:18**, where he is described as a *shield* to protect them. 'Princes' are spoken of in the same way in 47:9. In fact, the word translated 'shield' could also be translated 'sovereign'. As long as the king truly belongs to the Lord, he is the shield and defender of his people, and they can thank God for him. This verse could, however, also be translated as the NEB renders it, 'The Lord, he is our shield; the Holy One of Israel, he is our king.'

89:19-37 A King for God's People

The first part of the psalm speaks of the goodness and greatness of God, but it also speaks (89:3-4) of God's purpose for David and his descendants. This second part of the psalm tells the story of God's choice and blessing of David, and the purpose to be fulfilled in him and his descendants after him.

89:19-20 *God's choice of David*

The first two verses summarize the history given in 1 Samuel 16. God sent Samuel to Jesse in Bethlehem to tell him that one of his sons was to become king in Israel. One by one, the sons of Jesse were brought before Samuel, and all were rejected because 'the Lord does not look at the things man looks at. Man looks at the outward appearance, but the Lord looks at the heart' (1 Sam 16:7). Eventually, David, the youngest son, came before Samuel, who recognized that this was the *young man* chosen by God, or *found* by God, as this psalm puts it (**89:20a**). Samuel anointed him with holy oil, the outward sign of the gift of God's power to do the work involved in being a king (**89:20b**), and the 'Spirit of the Lord came upon David in power' (1 Sam 16:13).

89:21-27 *God's blessing of David*

This psalm has already spoken of the power of God and of victory over enemies (89:1-18). Now it is said that God promised to strengthen David with that power (**89:21**). His enemies will not be able to overpower him (**89:22-23**). Whereas 89:17 spoke of God exalting our horn, **89:24b** says that the horn of David *will be exalted*. Similarly, the earlier part of the psalm spoke of the steadfast love and faithfulness of the Lord; now assurance is given that David would experience that steadfast love and faithfulness (**89:24a**).

If **89:25** is linked with 89:9, it can be interpreted as saying that God who rules 'over the surging sea' (89:9) gives the one he has anointed power over seas and rivers. But the verse may also be intended as a reminder that passages like 1 Kings 4:21 describe the kingdom of Israel as reaching from the sea (the Mediterranean) to the great river (the Euphrates).

David would be able to turn to the Lord as his Father, his God and the Rock of his salvation (**89:26**), and would be treated as God's *firstborn, the most exalted of the kings of the earth* (**89:27**).

89:28-37 God's purpose for David's descendants

Through the prophet Nathan, God informed David that his son and his son's son, and their descendants after them would rule on the throne of Israel (2 Sam 7:12-14). This message is repeated in **89:28-29**. However, the experience of the full blessing of God always depends on the obedience of those who are called to serve him. Again, closely following 2 Samuel 7:14, the warning is given that if David's descendants are unfaithful to God, they will suffer for their sin (**89:30-32**). Yet in the end the purpose of God could not fail. God's word, God's covenant, God's promises can never ultimately fail (**89:33-35**; 2 Tim 2:12-13). The sun and moon and all nature show the faithfulness of God (**89:36-37**). God's word and his purpose are as dependable as his creation.

What happened to the descendants of David? Did God *establish his line forever* (89:29, 36)? David's son, Solomon, ruled after David. Then the foolishness of Solomon's son, Rehoboam (1 Kgs 12), caused the kingdom of Israel to break into two parts. David's descendants continued to rule in the south for about 400 years. There were some godly kings among them, including Hezekiah (2 Kgs 18–20) and Josiah (2 Kgs 22–23). But many failed to be just and wise and were not God-fearing kings. They forsook God's law, did not follow his statutes, violated his decrees and failed to keep his commandments (89:30-32). In their times, prophets were inspired to give a message of hope that one day in the future there would be a king who would rule 'with justice and righteousness' (Isa 9:7). One would come to 'reign wisely and do what is just and right in the land' (Jer 23:5). There were many such prophecies, and the NT reveals that they found their fulfilment in the coming of Jesus. Thus Mary was told that her son 'will be great and will be called the Son of the Most High. The Lord God will give him the throne of his father David, and he will reign over the house of Jacob forever; his kingdom will never end' (Luke 1:32-33).

89:38-52 The Wrath and Mercy of God

This psalm began with a celebration of the steadfast love and faithfulness of God (89:1-18). Then the emphasis shifted to the promise of that same steadfast love and faithfulness to David and his descendants (89:19-37). But, as this third part shows, at the time this psalm was written, it seemed, that God's steadfast love and faithfulness had been removed because of the sins of the people.

89:38-45 The King's Situation

Great promises had been made to David for his descendants. But now instead of giving favour, God seemed to be *very angry* with the king (**89:38**). The covenant that was never supposed to fail (89:28) had been *renounced*. The king's crown was *in the dust* (**89:39**), and it seemed that God had *cast his throne to the ground* (**89:44**). The people had been conquered and the Davidic king disgraced.

The reference to the cutting short of *the days of his youth* (**89:45**) suggests that this psalm may have been written at the time the Babylonians conquered Judah, when the eighteen-year-old Jehoiachin, who had been king for only three months, was made a prisoner in Babylon (2 Kgs 24:8-12). It was a tragic time that is described for us in the book of Lamentations. The psalmist asked what had happened to the steadfast love and faithfulness of God. Instead of the victory over his enemies that the king had been promised, his enemies had defeated him, and all the surrounding nations had taken advantage of his weakness (**89:40-43**).

89:46-48 The People's Situation

The psalmist's thoughts now turned from the situation faced by the king to that faced by his people and by all people: life is short, and death brings it to an end all too soon. Are we just created for *futility,* to finish up in the grave? (**89:47-48**; see also Ecclesiastes). God has reason to show his wrath, his righteous anger against us because of our sins. Isaiah has rightly said: 'Your iniquities have separated you from your God: your sins have hidden his face from you' (Isa 59:2). But must that wrath of God go on burning like fire, and must God hide himself forever? (**89:46**).

89:49-52 Why? Why? Why?

The question, *Lord, where is your former great love?* (**89:49a**) takes us back to 89:1-18. God's love and goodness had been shown in the past, so why not now? And what has become of God's promise of faithfulness to David in 89:28-37? (**89:49b**). So the psalmist pleads with God: it is *your servant* who has been mocked (**89:50**), it is *your enemies* who have the upper hand (**89:51a**), it is *every step of your anointed one* that they mock (**89:51b**).

God gives no answer to these questions, but the psalmist continues to turn to him in earnest prayer. Sometimes Christians too feel that there is no answer to their prayers and that God is far away. In such circumstances, we should remember that God is not angry with us for ever. If we turn to him in repentance and faith, we can be completely sure of his forgiveness. Because Jesus went through the darkness of death for us and was raised to life, death is conquered, and through Christ we have the hope of eternal life. Because of what God has done for us and for others, we can be sure that, however dark and troubled our way may seem, God's love and faithfulness will never fail us. In short, no matter how dark and difficult our path, we must not lose sight of the mercy of God. We need to learn to take George Matheson's advice in his hymn, to 'trace the rainbow through the rain, and know the promise is not vain, that morn shall tearless be'.

The last verse (**89:52**) probably did not originally belong to this psalm, but was the conclusion of Book 3 of the Psalms. There are similar brief expressions of praise at the end of Book 1 (41:13), Book 2 (72:18-19), and Book 4 (106:48). All our thoughts about God should lead us to think: *Praise be to the Lord for ever! Amen and Amen* (May it be so!)

BOOK FOUR: PSALMS 90-106

Psalm 90: The Eternal God, Our Home

The heading of Psalm 90 links it with Moses. The psalms contain many things that remind us of the books of the Law. For example, it refers to God's creation of humans from dust in Genesis 1–3. Moses is here referred to as *the man of God* (see also Deut 33:1; Josh 14:6; Ezra 3:2). It is good to consider who else in the Bible is called a 'man of God' and what it means for a person to be called a man or woman of God (see 1 Kgs 17:18, 24; 2 Kgs 4:8-9; 2 Chr 8:14; 1 Tim 6:11; 2 Tim 3:16-17).

The psalm sharply contrasts God's eternity and the shortness of our human lives, God's holiness and our sinfulness. Yet it leaves us aware not only of our weakness and failure but also of the compassion and steadfast love God offers us.

90:1-6 God's Eternity and Our Short Lives

God is unchanging – eternal in the past and the future. The earth itself is very old – a fact about which we today know even more than our ancestors did – and the *mountains* do not seem to change with the passing generations (**90:1-2**). But before the mountains were brought into being, God was there. He was their Creator. A thousand years is a very long time to us – but to God things that happened a thousand years ago are like the things that happened yesterday to us (**90:4**). This same theme of the unfathomable greatness of the Lord is presented in Isaiah 40.

In **90:3**, the psalmist echoes the words of God's judgment on Adam and Eve in Genesis 3:19, 'for dust you are and to dust you will return' (see also Eccl 12:7). He then goes on in **90:5-6** to give three pictures that illustrate how brief our life is in comparison with that of God. It is like a light object swept away by a flood of water. It is like a short sleep or a dream, soon forgotten. It is like grass that is fresh and green in the morning but withered in the evening after a day's scorching wind (compare 103:15-16).

No wonder we feel the need to pray with the hymn writer, 'Change and decay in all around I see, O thou who changes not, abide with me.'

90:7-12 God's Holiness and Our Sinfulness

But the shortness of our life is not our only problem. A far greater problem is our sinfulness, which places us under God's wrath (**90:7, 9**). Sometimes we may take our sins lightly, but this psalm reminds us of two important things. First, God knows every wrong thing that we do. What is secret from others is not secret to God (**90:8**; compare Jer 16:17; Luke 12:2; Heb 4:12-13). Second, we need to be aware of the reality and power of God's anger. God, who is utterly good and holy and true, hates sin – for what it does to others, for what it does to us and because it is rebellion against his wise and loving purposes for us. We are right to fear him and his wrath (**90:11**).

Compared with God's eternity, the longest human lives stretch to a mere seventy or eighty years. As the years go by and our strength and our faculties begin to fail us, we experience weakness and illness, *trouble and sorrow* (**90:10**). When we combine an awareness of how short and uncertain our lives are with an awareness of the awesomeness of God and of his wrath, we will sincerely pray the prayer of **90:12**: *Teach us to number our days aright, that we may gain a heart of wisdom.* The NT too stresses that we need to learn to live wisely and use the opportunities we are given (Eph 5:15-17; Col 4:5; Jas 4:13-16; 1 John 2:15-17).

90:13-17 God's Compassion and Steadfast Love

The shortness of our life and the seriousness of our sin might come to us as bad news. But the psalm also has good news. We know enough of what God is like to pray for his *compassion* and *unfailing love* to be shown to us (**90:13-14**). We can pray that he will forgive our sins, restore us and give us a deep inner joy in the days and years of life that we have (**90:15**; compare 51:10-12). We can pray for God's pardon and redemption to be seen in our lives and for his *splendour* to come to us in our weakness (**90:16**). Then we can also ask him to bless and prosper the work that he has given us to do with our hands (**90:17**).

As God's people we can look back and say, *Lord, you have been our dwelling place throughout all generations* (90:1). We can also look forward and say, 'Lord, you will always be our home, present with us while our life on earth lasts, and then you will take us to our eternal home.'

Psalm 91: Under the Shelter of the Almighty

Psalm 91 begins by speaking of the confidence that people who sincerely trust in the Lord can have – he will be their shade in the heat, their shelter in the storm, their refuge and fortress in the face of enemy attacks (91:1-2). It ends with God's promises of deliverance, protection, rescue and salvation (91:14-16). In the middle, it gives the assurance that, weak and helpless as we are, we can find our secure home, our *dwelling,* in the presence of God (91:9).

91:1-8 Protection from Trouble

We face many dangers in life. The psalm mentions some that the psalmist faced: fowlers, pestilence, arrows, lions and snakes. A *fowler* (91:3) was someone who caught birds in snares. Psalms like 124:7 often compare the plots of evil-doers against God-fearing people with the snares used by fowlers. Faced with these dangers, people relied on *shields* (91:4) to protect themselves in battle and on strong *fortresses* (91:2) with *ramparts* (91:4) to protect their homes and families. We too face many dangers, some of which are different from those the psalmist faced. We face danger from diseases such as malaria, cancer and AIDS and from violent people as well as danger in times of civil unrest and everyday danger like traffic accidents. We also face spiritual dangers – attacks by evil powers or evil people and subtle temptations that try to lead us away from God and from a healthy way of life.

Christians all through the years and all over the world have been able to tell how they have been kept safe in times of great danger, physical or spiritual. All of us have been protected by God in countless ways, even from our earliest years (see Matt 18:10), and even when we have not realized it. Those who reject God's protection and salvation may fall (91:7-8), but those who trust in the Lord find that his loving faithfulness guards them from evil. As a mother bird protects her young under her strong wings, so God protects his own (91:4; see also Deut 32:11; Matt 23:37).

91:11-12 The Wrong Kind of Trust

Satan used 91:11-12 to tempt Jesus. Because the devil can use Scripture for his own purposes, we must be aware of that danger. Jesus was taken to the pinnacle of the temple in Jerusalem and invited by Satan to throw himself down. That would make people take notice of him and, as the devil said, 'You will come to no harm, "He will command his angels concerning you and they will lift you up in their hands, so that you will not strike your foot against a stone" ' (Matt 4:6). Jesus rejected this use of the psalm. He knew that God's promise of protection is not intended to cover every foolish thing that a person may choose to do. We must understand that our lives are in God's hands, but we cannot 'control' him by using the cross or the Bible as a good luck charm. Spiritual protection, freedom from fear, the security of God's presence – these are assured to those who truly trust God. We need not fear the demonic, the spiritual powers of evil, for there are spiritual powers of good, the angels, to protect us (91:11) and the power of God is always far greater than any power that can be used against us.

91:9-10; 13-16 Protection in Trouble

The Lord promises: *Since he loves me … I will rescue him, I will protect him, for he acknowledges my name* (91:14). Does this psalm mean that those who trust in God are safe from all dangers and sicknesses and accidents? No, for God-fearing people sometimes suffer in road accidents or at the hands of violent people. Sometimes they live in countries that suffer from famines, civil wars or corrupt political leaders who enrich themselves at others' expense. The word of the Lord is not 'I will save them from all trouble', but *I will be with him in trouble* (91:15). The promise that *no harm will befall you* (91:10) means that nothing that is outside God's control can happen to us (see also 2 Cor 12:7-10 and Rom 8:35-39, which is a NT parallel to this psalm).

Sometimes people have been literally delivered from lions and snakes (91:13), but these images may also stand for powerful and subtle enemies who attack those who seek to serve God (see Luke 10:19). When the apostle Paul was facing almost certain death for his faith, he could still say, 'The Lord will rescue me from every evil attack and will bring me safely to his heavenly kingdom' (2 Tim 4:6-8, 18). Though *the terror of the night* and the dangers of the day may be very real, those who trust the Lord can be assured, *you will not fear* (91:5).

Verse 91:16 should not be taken to mean that every godly person will live a long life. Long life is a blessing from God when the quality of that life is good. It meant much to people in OT days who had little knowledge or hope of life after death. The Christian rejoices in the assurance of eternal life whether life in this world is long or short.

Psalm 92: Praise of God's Love and Justice

The heading of Psalm 92 speaks of it as a song *for the Sabbath Day.* The Greek translation of the Psalms gave headings to this and other psalms prescribing their use for different days of the week. This psalm could be seen as especially appropriate for when people met together to praise God for his mighty creation and his works of salvation.

92:1-3 Praise the Lord

The psalm begins with the assertion, *It is good to praise the Lord and make music to your name, O Most High* (92:1). It is good because praise is due to the Lord for all he is and for all that he has done. Our lives are turned in the right direction when they are turned to God in praise. The psalm then goes on to speak of the 'why', 'when' and 'how' of praise.

Why should we praise God? Because of his *name* (92:1), that is, all that God is in his very nature, and especially because of his *love* and *faithfulness* (92:2).

When should we praise God? Both *in the morning* and *at night* (92:2). This may be the same as saying that any time is the right time to praise God, or it may indicate how good

it is to have a time both at the beginning and at the end of
the day when we turn to God in prayer and praise (see also
Deut 6:7; Ps 5:3; 42:8; 55:17; 63:6; 119:147-148). Christians should try to make their whole life express praise of
God and yet should also have special times for praise and
prayer.

How should we praise God? With the *music of the ten-
stringed lyre and the melody of the harp* (**92:3**). The lyre and
harp were traditional Hebrew musical instruments (more
are mentioned in Ps 150). It is good to use our traditional
music to lift our hearts and voices in God's praise.

92:4-7 God's Ways and God's Works

Fools fail to understand and those who are dull in spiritual
wisdom fail to know the truth (**92:6**). On the other hand,
those who are open to hear God's word appreciate the
truth expressed in Isaiah 55:8-9, '"For my thoughts are not
your thoughts, neither are your ways my ways," declares
the Lord. "As the heavens are higher than the earth, so
are my ways higher than your ways and my thoughts than
your thoughts".' As the psalmist puts it, *how profound your
thoughts!* (**92:5**). When we see the working out of his purposes in what he does, we are glad and *sing for joy* (**92:4**).
Sometimes it seems – even for a long time – that *evildoers flourish* (**92:7**), wielding great power, and there is much
injustice in the world. At such times, we should remember
and be glad that God is just and that their prosperity will
not endure.

92:8-11 The Oppressors Are Brought Down

Salvation and judgment must go together. If the oppressed
are to be delivered, then the oppressors must come under
God's judgment. The psalmist (perhaps he was a king of
Israel) had to face many enemies who by their wickedness
were indeed God's enemies. Yet he could say that God had
wonderfully given him strength, even as a wild ox was strong
because of its powerful horns (**92:10a**). If the psalmist was
indeed king, **92:10b** may refer to his anointing or otherwise it could speak of God's blessing and encouragement
as 23:5 does: 'you anoint my head with oil; my cup overflows'.

*Though the wicked spring up like grass and all evildoers
flourish* (92:7), they will not continue in power for ever. They
cannot withstand God's judgment (**92:9**). Their downfall is
sure (**92:11**). We should not read this psalm as expressing a desire for personal revenge, but for the victory of God
and of God's purposes, and that those who oppose God's
purposes and persecute the powerless would be brought
down from their positions of power. It is the Lord alone who
is *exalted for ever* (**92:8**) and 'the salvation of the righteous
comes from the Lord; he is their stronghold in time of trouble' (Ps 37:39).

92:12-15 The Oppressed Lifted Up

In contrast with 92:7, which says that evildoers flourish
briefly like grass, **92:12** says *the righteous will flourish like
the palm tree, they will grow like a cedar of Lebanon*. The date
palm produced valuable food and the cedars of Lebanon
were famous for their strength and beauty. These trees are
described as *planted* in *the house of the Lord* (**92:13**), meaning that the righteous live in fellowship with God and draw
strength from him. The righteous also have the secret of
endurance. Even in their old age their lives are still beautiful and fruitful (**92:14**). God renews their inner strength
even when their physical health and strength fail (compare
2 Cor 4:16-18). They know that they enjoy these blessings
not because they are especially holy and good, but because
God is good to those who trust in him and renews their
strength to endure day by day. Consequently, they will proclaim his praise and declare that he is a Rock to those who
rely on him. He is the utterly faithful one (**92:15**).

Psalm 93: The Lord Reigns

Isaiah 52:7 describes what good news it is for all who trust
God to hear *'Your God reigns!'* But what does it mean when
we say, *The Lord is king* (93:1 NRSV), or *The Lord reigns* (NIV)?
According to this psalm, it certainly means three things.

93:1a He Is Great and Majestic

When a king or queen, a president or a paramount chief
appears on a great national occasion, clad in splendid robes,
their appearance is often majestic. But the mighty God, our
Creator, is infinitely more majestic. The Bible gives us many
visions of God, which help us to appreciate this. For example, when the prophet Isaiah had a vision of God, he said
that just 'the train of his robe filled the temple' and the
heavenly beings in his service cried, 'Holy, holy, holy is the
Lord of hosts; the whole earth is full of his glory' (Isa 6:1-8;
see also Ezek 1; Rev 1:12-20). Here the psalmist says that
he is robed in majesty and *he is armed with strength*. In majesty and strength he is great beyond all others (**93:1a**).

93:1b-4 His Rule Knows No Limits

God created the world, indeed the whole universe. What
he has created he also upholds so that *it cannot be moved*
(**93:1b**). This is true not only of our world, but also of all
the stars of heaven. The laws of nature hold, because they
are God's laws by which he has created all things and sustains them. In the universe, things do not happen by chance.
The movement of stars does not control or affect our human
lives. Both their movements and our lives are under the
control of God.

God's throne was *established long ago,* and God himself
is *from all eternity* (**93:2**). Psalm 90:2 has expressed this:
'from everlasting to everlasting you are God'. He is eternal

in the past and in the future. The book of Revelation in the NT speaks of him as the one 'who is and who was and who is to come, the Almighty' (Rev 1:8).

Revelation also says that at the end of time there will be 'a great multitude, like the roar of rushing waters and like loud peals of thunder, shouting: "Hallelujah! For our Lord God Almighty reigns"' (Rev 19:6). For us and for our future there is complete security in him and nowhere else, because he has power over all other powers. Human beings have always been awed by the power of water in a great waterfall or in the waves of a stormy sea. But the Lord our Creator is *mightier than the thunders of the great waters, mightier than the breakers of the sea* (**93:4**). This statement was particularly significant for the psalmist, because in his day people thought of the waters of the great deep as the place of chaos, 'formless and empty', to which God brought order and life (Gen 1:2). The Bible also treats the seas as a symbol for the power of unruly and oppressive nations. Thus 65:7 says God 'stilled the roaring of the seas, the roaring of their waves, and the turmoil of the nations' (see also 89:9-10; Isa 8:7-8; 17:12-13; Jer 46:7-8). Though such nations may *lift up their voice* (**93:3**), the Lord can bring their power to nothing. As 46:6 puts it, 'Nations are in uproar, kingdoms fall; he lifts his voice, the earth melts'.

93:5 His Laws Cannot Be Bent

Just as Psalm 19 moves from speaking of the greatness of God's creation to the blessing of his word, so this psalm turns from God's power over creation to speak of his *statutes* (**93:5a**). They are the laws of his kingdom; the principles by which we should live.

Holiness adorns the temple, which is God's house (**93:5b**). Consequently, those who worship God there are also called to be holy, that is, set apart to obey and serve him. Christians are referred to as the house of God, the temple of God and the family of God, and we should take care to live up to this description (1 Thess 4:7; Heb 12:14; 1 Pet 1:14-16).

Psalm 94: God's Justice Will Surely Triumph

There are still oppressive rulers in the world, just as there were in the time of the psalmist. The message of Psalm 94 is that God does not allow proud, persecuting rulers to remain in power for ever. He stands for justice and defends the poor and the oppressed. It is the way of the fool to think that God will never bring the oppressor to judgment. It is the way of the wise to trust God's care and concern for those who turn to him. As Abraham said: 'Will not the Judge of all the earth do right?' (Gen 18:25).

94:1-2 The Judge of the Earth

This psalm begins by addressing God as *the God who avenges* (**94:1**). Should we think of our God as a 'God of vengeance'

(NRSV)? The word 'vengeance' brings to our mind people determined to settle scores with those whom they see as their enemies. This is not what the psalm is saying about God. It speaks rather of God as the *Judge of the earth* (**94:2**), who is perfectly just in all his ways.

94:3-11 The Way of the Fool

The psalmist prays, *O Lord, how long will the wicked be jubilant?* (**94:3**). He grieves over their *arrogant words* (**94:4**) and the way that they crush God's people, God's *inheritance* (**94:5**) who belong to him. They do great harm to those for whom God has a special concern, namely the widows and orphans and those who are strangers in the land. God makes it clear that rulers (and ordinary believers) have a duty to help people who live in poverty and have special needs (see Exod 22:21-24; Deut 26:12; 27:19; Isa 1:17; Jer 7:5-7; 22:3; Zech 7:8-10; Mal 3:5).

It is utter folly for the wicked to think God does not see what they are doing (**94:7**). They are *senseless* and the most foolish of mortals to think that God who created the eye and the ear is not able himself to see and hear (**94:8-9**). The God who *is in charge of the nations ... the teacher of all* (**94:10** GNB) knows what they are up to and he will call them to account. Compared with God's wisdom, human thoughts and plans are *futile* (**94:11**).

94:12-14 The Way of the Wise

There are many scriptural passages that begin with the words *Blessed is* and then proceed to indicate the source of true happiness and blessing (see 1:1-3; 32:1-2; 112:1-9; 119:1-2; 128:1-2; Prov 3:13-17; 16:20; 29:18). According to this psalm, the way of wisdom and true happiness is to be taught God's law. God in his love and care disciplines those who are his children (**94:12**; see also Prov 3:11-12; Heb 12:5-6). There may be *days of trouble* (**94:13a**), but God will help those who serve him through such times. They can know that the wicked will themselves fall into the pit that they have dug for others (**94:13b**; see also 7:16; 57:6). God's people may be crushed by cruel oppressors, but the Lord will not forsake *his people* and will not abandon *his inheritance* (**94:14**; see also 94:5).

94:15-23 The Triumph of Justice

The psalmist is confident that *judgment will again be founded on righteousness* (**94:15**). In his problems he asks, *Who will rise up for me against the wicked? Who will take a stand for me against evildoers?* (**94:16**). But he already knows the answer to his question. God had been his help in the past. He had sometimes thought that he was slipping and was in great danger, but God's steadfast love had held him up (**94:18**). When he thought he was approaching *the silence of death,* God had come to help him (**94:17**). When his cares and anxieties threatened to overwhelm him, God had given him inner peace and had consoled him (94:19).

Could wicked rulers have God on their side? Does God support those who bring in unjust laws that do harm rather than good to their people (94:20)? Certainly not. There is no way that God can support unjust oppressors. They may *band together against the righteous and condemn the innocent to death* (94:21), but the last word is with God. The Lord will repay them (94:23). Those who trust in the Lord and seek to serve him will always be able to say, *The Lord has become my fortress, and my God the rock in whom I take refuge* (94:22).

Psalm 95: Worship and Warning

Psalm 95 may have been written for some special occasion of worship and thanksgiving to God, or it may have been written simply to prepare people's minds and hearts for the true worship of God. It has certainly been used in this way in services in the church for centuries. But what is especially striking about the psalm is that while the first part is a call to worship, the second part is a challenge to hear God's word and heed a solemn warning against hardness of heart.

95:1-2, 6 The Call to Worship

In 95:1-2 and again in 95:6a we are called: *Come, let us … What are we called to do?* We are called to sing joyfully to the Lord, praising him from our hearts and with our voices, thanking him for what he has done (95:1). We are also called to come humbly to God, remembering that he is our Maker (95:6b). By God's grace we can come freely to him, but we should still realize his greatness and holiness and our smallness and sinfulness. Only with this humble attitude will we offer true worship.

The people may have sung 95:1-5 as they were going up to the temple and then 95:6-7 as they entered the temple gates and prepared to *bow down* and *kneel* in the worship of the Lord. (95:6). This is why the call to worship is repeated.

95:3-5, 7 Reasons for Worship

The two calls to worship are followed by the reasons why we should worship. The first is that the Lord alone is God, a mighty God and a great King (95:3). People may make themselves gods to worship, but the Lord alone is the true God and ruler over all. The whole earth, indeed the whole universe, is under his control (95:4). Sea and dry land alike are his (95:5). In fact the more we learn about God's creation, of sea and land, of earth and sky, of trees and flowers, of birds and animals and of our own human bodies, the more we realize the wonder and wisdom of God as Creator.

After the second call to worship, we are told that we should worship because *he is our God* (95:7a). We belong to him as sheep to a shepherd. Just as the shepherd leads and provides for his flock, so the Lord guides and sustains us (95:7b; see also John 10:1-18).

95:7c-11 Worship in Life

It is possible for people to participate enthusiastically in a worship service and yet not obey and serve God in their daily living. That is the challenge and warning of the latter part of the psalm. *Today, if you hear his voice, do not …* (95:7c). The warning is strengthened by a reminder from the early history of Israel. God had brought the people out of slavery in Egypt, guided them to safety and provided for them in the wilderness. Yet the people grieved the Lord and he was *angry* with them (95:10), because when they were short of water, instead of asking the Lord's help, they 'quarrelled and tested the Lord, saying, "Is the Lord among us or not?"'. This incident occurred at places called *Meribah* and *Massah,* names that mean 'quarrelling' and 'testing' (95:8; see Exod 17:1-7; Num 20:1-13). Incidents like this made God solemnly swear 'not one of the men who saw my glory and the miraculous signs I performed in Egypt and in the desert but who disobeyed me and tested me ten times – not one of them will ever see the land I promised on oath to their forefathers. No one who has treated me with contempt will ever see it' (Num 14:20-23). The psalmist summarizes this judgment with the words, *They shall never enter my rest* (95:11).

Hebrews 3:7-4:16 takes up the words of the latter part of the psalm and applies them to us as Christians. Our *today* is now, our time of opportunity to hear God's word as it comes to us in Jesus Christ (95:7c). God offers us *rest* – peace with God and peace in our hearts now, and in the end eternal rest in heaven. But to enter into this rest we must make sure that we truly believe, obey and never turn back from the Son of God who has come to bring us salvation.

Psalm 96: 'Sing to the Lord a New Song'

Psalm 96 is a song of celebration that was sung at the time when David brought the ark of God into Jerusalem. It is quoted at length in 1 Chronicles 16:23-33.

96:1-3, 7-9 Ways to Worship

People are often called to *sing to the Lord a new song* (96:1; 33:3; 40:3; 98:1; Rev 5:9; 14:3). We can sing a new song because we can find new reasons to praise God every day. This psalm mentions five ways to worship that we can practise today, just like those for whom it was first written.

- Give glory to the Lord. We are to think of him as he has made himself known to us – which is what is meant by *his name* in **96:2a** and **96:8a** – and give him the honour that is due to him.

- Tell others what he has done. We know many of *his marvellous deeds* (**96:3**). As Israel in OT days knew the *salvation* (**96:2b**) of the Lord when they were set free from Egypt and later from Babylon, so we know the power of Christ saving us from sin and evil. All nations of the world should hear of that salvation, and we all have our part to play in sharing the good news.
- Bring an offering. We should bring ourselves to God as an offering (**96:8b**; see Rom 12:1-2) and bring what we are able of our possessions to honour him and to support the work of his kingdom.
- Sing his praise wherever we are. The instruction to come into his courts (96:8b) means that we are to come together in the place where God's people meet for worship (see Heb 10:25). There we are to 'Sing psalms and hymns and spiritual songs among yourselves, singing and making melody to the Lord in your hearts, giving thanks to God the Father at all times and for everything in the name of our Lord Jesus Christ' (Eph 5:19-20, NRSV).
- Tremble before him. We are to revere God (**96:9**). We must respect the beauty of God's holiness and realize that holiness in us is what is beautiful before God. We are called to live in that holiness, hating all evil and loving all that is good and true (see 1 Pet 1:13-21).

96:4-6, 10-13 Why We Should Worship

It is easy to say *great is the Lord* and to add that therefore he is *most worthy of praise* (**96:4**), but we should think about what that statement means. People have other gods in their lives. We are all tempted in different ways to give something, or even someone else, the place in our lives that only God should have. All other gods of any kind are idols (Isa 46:1-4). We have to carry those other gods, while God is the one who carries and supports us. He has done so from our birth and will do so till our old age. He is the one who made the heavens (**96:5**) and the earth – the whole universe. We should meditate on his *splendour* and *majesty,* his *strength* and *glory* (**96:6**).

We know many of the things that God has done in the past. We know his character. This knowledge assures us that the future is in his hands. The world is safe in his hands (**96:10b**) even if we sometimes think it is full of trouble and under the control of godless people. The nations can be told *The Lord reigns* (**96:10a**). Because he is king, injustice and oppression will not triumph in the end. God is working out his judgments in our human history. Because we have the promise of Jesus Christ, we can say with even more assurance than the psalmist that the Lord comes to *judge the world in righteousness and the peoples in his truth* (**96:13**). Much in the world has been spoiled by human sinfulness, but we look forward to the day when the *heavens*

rejoice and all creation joins in worship and praise because God reigns (**96:11-12**; see also Rom 8:21). Thank God for that vision of the future.

Psalm 97: God Rules – Let the Earth Rejoice

Psalm 97 is another psalm that celebrates God's rule over the world – over the whole universe. It begins and ends with a command to rejoice.

97:1-6 God Rules over Nature

Like Psalms 93 and 99, this psalm begins, *The Lord reigns!* This statement is then followed by a summons, *let the earth be glad!* (**97:1**).

All creation shows the power of God as Creator and Lord. We can see it in the dark storm clouds and powerful winds (**97:2a**), in the lightning that *lights up the world,* in earthquakes that make the ground *tremble* (**97:4**) and volcanoes that make *mountains melt* (**97:5**). These manifestations of his power remind us of how God spoke to his people on Mount Sinai (see Exod 19:16-18). There he revealed his power and holiness through the 'thunder and lightning', a 'thick cloud', 'fire' and the mountain shaking violently. Many other OT passages describe God's revelations of himself to his people in a similar way (see Judg 5:4-5; Ps 18:7-15; Isa 64:1-3; Hab 3:3-15).

The brilliance of the sun and of lightning also shows the power of God and is used as a metaphor to describe him. Thus we are told that 'God is light and in him there is no darkness at all' (1 John 1:5). Just as we cannot physically look directly at the sun that he created, so we cannot spiritually gaze on the brightness of his holiness. That may be the reason why he is described as surrounded by *clouds and thick darkness.* What we can know is that *righteousness and justice are the foundation of his throne* (**97:2b**), or in other words, he rules the world in a way that upholds right, truth and justice.

97:7-9 What God's Rule Means for the Wicked

The wicked should take warning from the realization that God is king. Those who oppose God and oppress other people will not be able to do so for ever. They will be called to account and will come under God's judgment. Those who put other gods such as money or power before the one true God will be put to shame (**97:7a**)

Like many other passages of the Bible, this psalm speaks of these gods as worthless idols. But it also seems to call on them to worship God when it says, *worship him, all you gods!* (**97:7b**) and *you are exalted far above all gods* (**97:9**). In these contexts, the word 'gods' must refer to spiritual beings such as angels.

97:10-12 What God's Rule Means for the Godly

Those who seek to serve God may often face difficulty and seem to be in *the hand of the wicked*, that is, under their control (**97:10**). But they can rejoice knowing that God is ultimately in control. Although the world may sometimes seem a very dark place, *light is shed upon the righteous* (**97:11a**). Although it may seem a very sad place, there will be joy for *the upright in heart* (**97:11b**). As the CEV puts it: 'If you obey and do right, a light will show you the way and fill you with happiness'. Even if believers have to die for their faith, they can be confident of their salvation. When the apostle Paul was facing death as a martyr, he could still say, 'The Lord will rescue me from every evil attack and bring me safely to his heavenly kingdom' (2 Tim 4:18).

The message of this psalm and of **97:12** is well put in Charles Wesley's hymn: 'Rejoice the Lord is King, Your Lord and King adore; Mortals, give thanks and sing, And triumph evermore; Lift up your heads, lift up your voice, Rejoice, again I say rejoice!'

Psalm 98: Lord of Past, Present and Future

Psalm 98 is another psalm that calls us to think of the work of God in the past, present and future. We know what he has done in the past. Because of who he is, we should praise him in the present. And we can trust him for what he will do in the future.

98:1-3 What God Has Done in the Past

Like Psalm 96, this psalm begins *Sing to the Lord a new song*. It is always right to thank God in new ways because he is always doing new and *marvellous things* (**98:1a**). When the psalmist speaks of *his right hand and his holy arm* (**98:1b**), we are reminded of the power God displayed when he saved Israel from slavery in Egypt (see Exod 15:6; Deut 5:15). God is also spoken of as acting in *love and faithfulness* (**98:3a**). These words are always true with regard to God's actions. In love and compassion he saves the oppressed and righteously judges the oppressors and wins victory over them. This work of God is for *all the ends of the earth* (**98:3b**) to see. This is how God has acted in history, as the OT record bears witness time after time.

98:4-6 Worthy of all Praise in the Present

Because of what God has done and because he is *the Lord, the King* (**98:6b**), the same in the present as he has been in the past, so *all the earth* should *shout for joy* and *burst into jubilant song* (**98:4**). If we are on the Lord's side, we can always rejoice at his victories in the lives of people and in his saving power. The psalmist wanted stringed instruments like the *harp* (**98:5**) and wind instruments like *trumpets* and *horn* (**98:6a**) to lead music in God's praise. May all the best

music today in every culture and in every land help our praise of God!

98:7-9 Worship for His Acts in the Future

Birds and beasts, seas and mountains cannot praise God as can humans, who are made in his image. But their existence tells of the greatness of God as their Creator. The roaring of the sea, the flowing of rivers, the beauty of mountains, all tell of God. Their music is like a vast orchestra of creation telling of the presence of the Lord, like crowds of people clapping their hands in acclamation (**98:7-8**). Through them and through God's work in human history, people in any part of the world should be able to know certain things about him (Rom 1:20).

But this psalm gives us another reason for calling on all of these things to praise the Lord, a reason that relates to the future: *for he comes to judge the earth* (**98:9a**; see Ps 96:13). There is much injustice and suffering in the world, but we can be sure that God will not allow it to go on for ever. He has promised that evil will be overthrown, since *he will judge the world in righteousness and the peoples with equity* (**98:9b**). Then, more than ever before, all creation will rejoice and praise God.

Our hope for the future and for the triumph of the goodness and truth of God is made more sure for us through Jesus Christ (see Matt 13:36-43; Rom 8:18-25; Rev 21–22). We can join with Paul in saying, 'Thanks be to God, who gives us the victory through our Lord Jesus Christ' (1 Cor 15:57).

Psalm 99: Our God Is Holy

Different countries and cultures have different ideas about what is holy. Holiness is sometimes attached to things that are not to be touched except under special arrangements and to people who have special religious duties. But this psalm deals with the holiness of God, which Isaiah glimpsed when he was called to be a prophet (see Isa 6:1-8). The word 'holy' is repeated three times in the declaration, *He is holy!* (99:3, 5, 9).

This psalm says three things about God's holiness.

99:1-3 God Is Great Above All Others

The Bible often speaks of the temple as holy and the hill of Zion on which it was built as God's *holy mountain* (99:2, 9). Israel is the Holy Land, and the people are God's holy people. They are things and people set apart for God. That is what 'holy' means. When we say that God is holy, we are saying that he is apart from all others because he is the Creator and Judge of all.

This psalm, like several others, begins, *The Lord reigns* (**99:1a**), *Great is the Lord in Zion* (**99:2a**). He rules over his people and, more than that, *he is exalted over all the nations*

(**99:2b**). His *name* – that is, what he is really like – is so *great and awesome* (**99:3**) that the nations should tremble and *the earth shake* (99:1). As other psalms encourage us, we can worship the Lord with joy, but we should also have a deep sense of reverence before him.

When God is spoken of as *enthroned upon the cherubim* (**99:1b**), the psalmist may be thinking of his throne as being between the golden cherubim that bowed over the ark in the Most Holy Place in the temple (see Exod 25:22). But he may also be thinking of God as riding on the back of the cherubim, as he is described in Psalm 18:10: 'he mounted the cherubim and flew; he soared on the wings of the wind'. Whichever image he had in mind, he was clearly presenting God as the Lord over all things and creatures on earth and in heaven. After all, the temple (1 Chr 28:2; Ps 132:7) and even the whole earth (Isa 66:1) can be pictured as no more than *his footstool* (99:5). We are reminded of Isaiah's vision where just 'the train of his robe filled the temple' (Isa 6:1). All of these are vivid ways of speaking of the greatness of God over everything in the universe.

99:4-5 God Is Supremely Righteous and Just

God's holiness means that he hates all evil. Our *King is mighty* and *loves justice* (**99:4a**). He has *established equity* (**99:4b**). In other words, his laws stand for what is fair in human life. Because of this, we should *exalt the Lord our God* (**99:5**). In the Bible and in particular in the history of the people of Israel, we see that justice and righteousness are upheld in all that God does. And he requires his people – and most of all their rulers – to act in justice and righteousness. 'What does the Lord require of you,' the prophet Micah (6:8) asks, 'but to act justly and to love mercy and to walk humbly with your God?' Or, as Amos (5:24) says, 'let justice roll on like a river, righteousness like a never-failing stream!'

99:6-9 God Is Supremely Good

In 99:4b the psalmist spoke of what God has done for Jacob, that is, for the whole nation, and now he goes into more detail about this. He speaks especially of Moses, Aaron and Samuel, whom God called to act as priests and prophets to bring his people back to himself. They *called on his name;* that is, they *called on the Lord* (**99:6**) on behalf of their people and God was pleased to answer them (Exod 32:7-14, 30-34; 34:6-7; Num 14:11-25; 1 Sam 7:3-9; 8:4-9; 12:6-25).

When the people came out of slavery in Egypt, journeyed to Mount Sinai and then travelled through the wilderness, God *spoke to them in the pillar of cloud* (**99:7a**; see Exod 13:21-22; 33:7-11; Num 14:14). In love and mercy God spoke to his people, leading them to keep *his decrees and the statutes that he gave them* (**99:7b**).

It is against this background that we can understand how 99:8 can describe God both as *a forgiving God* and as one who *punished their misdeeds* (**99:8**). There is no contradiction here. God is the only one who can forgive our wrongdoings, and he wants to forgive all who turn from their sins and ask his forgiveness. But because he is a righteous God, those who refuse to turn from their wrongdoings must realize that he is their judge.

Because God is righteous and just above all others, we must realize his holiness and have a sense of reverence before him. But because he is good above all others, welcoming us when we turn to him in prayer and asking forgiveness, we can say he is *our God*. These words are used three times in 99:8-9: *O Lord our God* answers us, so let us *exalt the Lord our God ... for the Lord our God is holy.*

Psalm 100: Call to Joyful Worship

Like Psalms 66, 81, 95 and 96, Psalm 100 is a call to worship the Lord. Its heading, *For giving thanks,* may link it with the thank offerings that the people brought to God (see Lev 7:11-18; 2 Chron 29:31-32; 33:16 for the kind of occasions on which these offerings were made). We can study it best if we ask who should worship, how they should worship and why they should worship.

100:1 Who Should Worship

All who reckon themselves as God's people should make worship a priority in their lives. In fact, *all the earth* should worship the Lord (**100:1**). No one in the world should fail to acknowledge God, for he is the Creator and Giver of all that we have. The lifestyle of Christian believers should lead people in every part of the world to worship.

100:2, 4 How We Should Worship

We should worship God *with gladness* and *with joyful songs* (**100:2**). This may seem very different from Psalm 99, which called us to worship God with reverence and awe. But there is no contradiction here. As we realize the greatness and holiness of God, we will indeed worship him with reverence and awe. But as we realize all that God has done for us, there will be gladness and joy in our worship. We *praise his name* (**100:4b**) when we think of all that God is and speak well of him, leading others to honour him as well.

In OT days, the temple was the most important place for worship and it was intended that all Israel should go there. Those who were far away were expected to go there at the times of the great annual festivals. When the people came through the gates and into the courts of the temple (**100:4a**), they felt that they came into God's presence (100:2) in a special way.

We do not have one central place of worship as Israel had. We have churches and many different kinds of meeting places in different parts of the world. But what matters is that all of us who are Christians do worship, not only in our individual lives, but coming together as God's people to worship him (see Heb 10:24-25).

It is also worth noting that the word used for 'worship' in 100:2 literally means 'serve'. We should both worship and serve the Lord, and do both *with gladness* (see also Rom 12:1-2).

100:3, 5 Why We Should Worship

Psalm 100:2 calls us to worship God, and **100:3** gives the reasons. The *Lord is God,* that is, he alone is ruler over all, the one true and living God in all the universe. *He made us;* he is our great Creator and the Creator of all that exists in the universe. *We are his people;* he has lovingly made himself our God and calls us to be his people, related to him as children to a parent. We are *the sheep of his pasture;* he cares for us, leads us and provides for us as a shepherd cares for, leads and provides for his sheep (see also Pss 23:1-2; 28:9; 80:1; 95:7).

Psalm 100:4 is another call to worship God, and **100:5** gives the reasons. *The Lord is good.* Many reasons why God is called good are given in Psalms (see Ps 25:8; 34:8; 119:68). *His love endures for ever.* Psalm 103:10-13 reminds us that his love is especially expressed in his forgiveness and compassion for us. *His faithfulness continues through all generations.* From one generation to another he is the same and can always be relied on. Many psalms, such as Psalm 89, say a great deal about the steadfast love and faithfulness of God. These and other similar words are found in many places in the OT (106:1; 107:1; 118:1; 136; 2 Chr 5:13; 7:3; Ezra 3:10-11; Jer 33:10-11).

Psalm 101: A Guide for Governors

Psalm 101 is a statement of what a godly king, whether David or one of his successors, wanted for his rule and his kingdom. He wanted to live in God's way himself, and he wanted the same for his family, his court and the whole nation.

The ideals for leadership expressed in this psalm apply to the leaders of our own nations and to those who lead in the life of the church (see also 1 Tim 3:1-13; 2 Tim 2:14-24; Titus 1:6-9). We need to pray for all such leaders and for judges, magistrates and the police, that they may uphold the ideals of truth and justice expressed in the psalm.

101:1-2 The Way for the Life of the King

The psalm begins with praise of God's rule *I will sing of your love and justice* (**101:1**). The Bible states again and again that the Lord rules the world in perfect justice. All that he does is fair to all people. The word translated 'love' by the NIV is often translated 'steadfast love', 'mercy' or 'loving kindness'. It speaks of God's loving faithfulness in the covenant that he has made with his people.

Singing of these qualities of God's rule makes us want them for our own lives. Thus the king expresses his determination that in his personal life, as well as in his home and family and as an example to his household, he will live *a blameless life ... with a blameless heart* (**101:2a**). He wants to follow the way of integrity and truth.

It is difficult to be sure of the exact meaning of the question *When will you come to me?* (**101:2b**). It may express the psalmist's great desire to know the nearness of God's presence as he seeks to live by the rule of which he writes.

101:3-4 The Way the King Avoids

The king knows the path he does not want to follow. He does not want to keep any *vile thing* before his eyes. A 'vile thing' is literally 'a thing of Belial', that is, something or someone who is worthless and corrupt (see the KJV translation of Deut 13:13; 1 Sam 2:12). The king does not want to allow such things to influence his thoughts, words or actions (**101:3a**). We too should be careful about what kind of influences we allow before our eyes through what we read, see and hear through the media and in advertising (see Phil 4:8).

Faithless men like to associate themselves with the powerful. Their lack of faithfulness means that they are also perfectly willing to abandon God's ways and to serve other gods (see Ps 40:4; Deut 29:18). But the king says here that he will not let their influence cling to him and shape what he says and does (**101:3b**). He wants to have nothing to do with *men of perverse heart* (crooked dealers) and to give no place to *evil* in his life (**101:4**).

101:5-8 The Way for the Life of the Nation

The king wants *faithful* people, people of integrity, to have responsible positions in the land (**101:6**). He says quite clearly the kind of people whom he does not want to have any influence. He does not want anyone *who slanders his neighbour in secret* (**101:5a**), anyone with neither standards of truth nor care for others. Secondly, he does not want those who are *haughty* and *proud* (**101:5b**), for they neither desire to serve God nor seek the best for others. Thirdly, there are those *who practice deceit* and who *speak falsely* (**101:7**). The king wants his people to truly be God's people and his city to be *the city of the Lord* (**101:8b**).

In the courts and in the nation's laws, the king wanted to uphold the same standards of truth and integrity, of faithfulness and justice as he had for his personal life and for his family. Thus *every morning,* which was the time when cases were heard in the courts, he would *put to silence all the wicked* (**101:8a**). Other translations say the wicked would be 'destroyed'. But we are not to think of the king spending every morning chopping off the heads of evildoers! Rather, he would be dispensing a justice that could not be questioned.

Psalm 102: Distress – Personal and National

The heading of Psalm 102 says that it is *a prayer of an afflicted man, when he is faint and pours out his lament before the Lord*. He faced both deep personal distress and distress in the life of his country. Some have thought that this psalm may have begun as a personal prayer and then come to be used also in relation to the life of the nation in its distress.

102:1-11 Personal Distress

The psalmist plunged straight in with his cry to God: *Hear my prayer ... let my cry of help come to you* (**102:1-2**). Then he went on to describe the many troubles he was facing, which made him feel that his days were vanishing *like smoke* (**102:3a**). They included physical illness: a fever made his bones seem to *burn like glowing embers* (**102:3b**). He felt too weak to eat (**102:4**) and had become so thin that his bones were clinging to his skin (**102:5**). He felt desperately alone, like the solitary owls in the wilderness or like a lonely bird, deprived of its mate and lamenting on a housetop (**102:6-7**). He had personal enemies who laughed at him in his misfortunes and even used his name as a means of bringing a curse on others (**102:8**).

He was so depressed that his *tears* became his *drink* and his daily bread was *ashes* (the sign of mourning) (**102:9**). His strength was broken in the midst of his life, and it seemed as if God was shortening his days (102:23-24). He could think of his days only as an evening shadow that grows longer and longer and then vanishes in the night, or like grass that grows up, lasts a little while and is then either cut down or dried up by the sun (**102:11**). Similar images of the shortness of life recur often in the Scriptures (see 37:20; 90:5-6; 109:23; 144:4; Job 8:9; Isa 40:6-8; Jas 1:9-11; 4:14).

Worst of all, it seemed that God had discarded him, lifting him up and throwing him aside. He could only think that this must be a judgment he deserved in God's *great wrath* (**102:10**). Yet in spite of all these things, the psalmist believed that he could turn to God, and so he began by begging that the Lord would hear his prayer and not hide his face from him in the day of his distress (102:1).

102:12-17 His People's Distress

Not only was the psalmist feeling destitute himself, but his people were also destitute (**102:17**). He was probably writing after Jerusalem had been taken by the Babylonians. The city was now choked with dust and rubble. But the *stones* broken down from its walls and buildings and even its *dust* were precious to the people (**102:14**).

The city and the land had come under God's judgment because of the people's unfaithfulness. But Jeremiah had said that after seventy years God would again have mercy on his people if they turned to him with sincere hearts (Jer 29:4-14). So the psalmist prays that God will *arise and*

have compassion on Zion, for it is time to show favour to her; the appointed time has come (**102:13**). It was the time, as the prophets had also said, for God to act in such a way that the nations around would see God's glory in what he was doing and come to fear his name (**102:15**; see also 22:27; 67:7; Isa 45:14-23; 59:18-19; 60:1-3). Then *the name of the Lord would be declared in Zion and his praise in Jerusalem,* and peoples would gather to worship him (102:21-22).

102:18-28 Confidence in the Lord

The psalmist could have confidence in the Lord because he knew that he could speak of God's *compassion* and that it was his very nature to *respond to the prayer of the destitute* (102:17). He could echo the prayer of Psalm 79:11, asking God *to hear the groans of the prisoners and release those condemned to death* (**102:20**), because that is what he had done long before when the people were slaves in Egypt (see Exod 2:23-25).

When we who are frail and sinful turn to God, feeling that our lives are short, and perhaps also distressed about the state of our country, we can realize that God is the great and mighty Creator, unchanging with the passing years (**102:25-27**). Therefore, although we may not know the future, we can rely on God and find our true security in him. His presence will always uphold us. As Christians, we can be even surer of this because we know our Lord Jesus Christ. The words of 102:25-27 can be applied directly to him because he is one with the Father in his nature as the Son of God and as God's agent in the creation of the universe (Heb 1:10-12).

God's goodness and love for us in all our needs is so great that it is worth telling all people and all the generations to come, so *that a people not yet created may praise the Lord* (**102:18**).

Psalm 103: Blessings – Personal and National

The writer of Psalm 102 brought the things that distressed him to God. He spoke of his personal needs and of his concerns for his country. Psalm 103 is a counterpoint to that one, as the writer speaks of the blessings of God on the psalmist personally and on the entire nation. The writer starts by calling on himself to *Praise the Lord* (**103:1**) and ends by inviting heaven and earth to join in the praise of a mighty and loving God.

103:1-5 Personal Blessings

It is as if the psalmist is saying to himself, remember all the ways that God has blessed you (**103:2**). Remember how often you have sinned and God has forgiven you (**103:3a**). Remember how often you have been sick and God has healed you (**103:3b**). Remember the times when you have been near to death and *the pit* and God has restored you to life and health (**103:4a**). Think of the way that God's love and mercy have been like a *crown* on your head (**103:4b**), how God has brought satisfaction and joy to your life (**103:5a**). As you grow old, you are still renewed, just as the eagle though old still soars up into the sky with its strong wings (**103:5b**; see also Isa 40:31). No wonder it is important not to forget *all his benefits* (103:2; see also Deut 4:9-14, 23; 6:12; 8:11-20).

103:6-10 Blessings on God's People

Not only individuals but the whole nation had reason to 'bless the Lord' (103:1-2, 20-22). God had shown himself to be a God of justice who delivered them when they were oppressed (**103:6**). The people had known this from the time of Moses when they had been set free from slavery and oppression in Egypt (**103:7**). They, and we like them, did not deserve God's goodness and salvation. If God dealt with us and punished us as our wrongdoings deserve, we would be in a very sorry state. But when we turn to him, sorry for our sins and wanting to turn from them, we find that *he does not treat us as our sins deserve, or repay us according to our iniquities* (**103:10**). Instead of his righteous anger we find his pardon and love.

103:11-18 Understanding of Human Weakness

As humans we can be very proud and feel that we are strong and important. But in fact we are weak morally and our physical bodies are frail. God knows this perfectly well (**103:14**). He meets us in our sinfulness and if we give him the place in our lives that we need to give him, he takes our sins away from us even *as far as the east is from the west* (**103:12**). We have to realize that his love is greater than we could even describe, even *as the heavens are high above the earth* (**103:11**). Or, if we put it in a very human way, God is like the wisest and most loving parent that we could imagine. His compassion for us is like that of a father for *his children* (**103:13**; compare Hos 11:1-4; Matt 7:7-11).

We are reminded that we are made from the dust (Gen 2:7; 3:19). We have life that God has breathed into us (Gen 2:7), but it is frail and limited, like that of the grass or flowers in a field (**103:15-16**). But the wonderful thing is that frail life can be linked to *the Lord's love* (**103:17**), which is unchanging and everlasting in the past and in the future. The NT reveals fully what this means: nothing less than the gift of eternal life through our Lord and Saviour Jesus Christ.

Many of God's blessings, the 'benefits' that he offers us, have been listed in the words of praise in this psalm. But there are conditions for our full enjoyment of those blessings. Three times it is said that these blessings are for *those who fear him* (103:11, 13, 17). In other words, our part is to revere the Lord as our mighty and holy God and to seek to serve him, to *keep his covenant* (**103:18a**). God's side of the covenant is the promise of blessing; our side is obedience in doing his will. We are to *forget not all his benefits* (103:2) and are to *remember to obey his precepts* (**103:18b**).

103:19-22 Praise the Lord, All Creation

Each of us should personally want to praise the Lord because of all his blessings to us. This psalm begins and ends with the same words, *Praise the Lord, O my soul* (**103:22b**). At the same time the writer of the psalm wants all creation to join in God's praise. He is the Lord of all and *rules over all* (**103:19**). Angels are also summoned to praise him (**103:20-21**). Angels are regularly spoken of in the Bible as doing God's will, and Jesus taught us to pray for God's will to be done on earth as it is done in heaven (that is, by the angels). May all God's works in creation and in all of the universe praise him (**103:22a**)! Because 'you are worthy, our Lord and God, to receive glory and honour and power, for you created all things, and by your will they existed and were created' (Rev 4:11).

Psalm 104: 'How Many Are Your Works, O Lord!'

Psalm 104 is a great hymn of praise to God as Creator. It makes us think of the different parts of God's creation the way the first chapter of the Bible presents them. In fact Psalm 104 has been described as Genesis 1 in poetry. It calls us to look around at the world in which we live and, thinking of all God's creatures, to say, *I will sing to the Lord all my life; I will sing praise to my God* (104:33).

104:1-4 The Forces of Nature

God's first words in Genesis 1:3 are 'Let there be light', and this is also where the psalmist begins his praise of God's creation (**104:2a**). Without light, there would be no life. Without it, we would see nothing. Light is broken up into the colours of the rainbow, and so we have the beauty of colour all around us.

God's creation of light is followed by his creation of what the KJV calls 'the firmament' and the NIV calls 'an expanse' (Gen 1:4). The psalmist presents this poetically as God creating a tent for himself and setting up his palace within his new creation (**104:2b-4**). It is clear that the basic elements – heaven, earth, wind and fire – all come from the hand of our Creator.

As translated in the NIV, 104:4 means that God uses the winds and fire to carry out his purposes in the world. Although that is probably the meaning intended, the verse could also be translated, *he makes his angels winds, his servants flames of fire*, and this is the way Hebrews 1:7 speaks of angels.

104:5-9 Land and Sea

Although the earth moves ceaselessly around the sun, the land is solid under our feet as if set on a foundation (**104:5**). The whole earth had originally been covered with water (**104:6**; Gen 1:2), but God restricted the mighty ocean to part of the earth's surface (**104:7-9**; Gen 1:9, Job 38:8-11). The boundary of sea and land is marked by rocky coasts or lovely beaches.

104:10-13 Birds and Animals

As the water from the oceans evaporates, it forms clouds, from which the rain falls on the earth again and then flows down to the sea in rivers and streams (**104:10**). This water nourishes the great variety of birds and animals around us (**104:11-12**). God has created them and he provides for them. The waters of streams and lakes and rivers are given to quench their thirst as well as ours. What a blessing it is that God waters mountains and plains! (**104:13**). That is why we need to pray to him for the rain our land needs and acknowledge it as God's gift for which we should be truly thankful.

104:14-18 Plants and Trees

On the third day of creation, God made vegetation (Gen 1:11-13), and this is the topic on which the psalmist now meditates. Our crops, our fruit and vegetables are able to grow in the fertile ground and are God's gift to us and to all living creatures (**104:14**). The psalmist celebrates three particular examples of things we can obtain from crops: wine, oil (such as olive oil) and bread. His celebration of these things reminds us that all God's gifts are good as long as they are used properly. Although food nourishes us, we should neither eat too much nor eat any unhealthy foods and so misuse our bodies. While drink *gladdens the heart of man* (**104:15**), we are not to lose control of our bodies and bring shame to ourselves and suffering to others by drinking too much.

The vegetation God has created is not only for our benefit. Humans may use the tall cedars of Lebanon to build temples and palaces, but God has given them to the birds for their nests (**104:16-17**; 1 Kgs 5:6). He has also provided for those animals that live on rocky mountainsides (**104:18**).

104:19-23 Moon and Sun

On the fourth day of creation, God gave us the sun and moon (Gen 1:14-19). The moon measures the months and so marks the seasons and the special times of the year that we celebrate (**104:19**). As the earth turns round, we also enjoy the blessing of day and night. We have the day to work in (though in some occupations people have to work during the night hours) and the night to rest, for we could not endure twenty-four hours of daylight all year round (**104:22-23**).

Some creatures are creatures of the night, and God provides for them too – even for the lions! (**104:20-21**).

104:24-26 The Sea and Its Creatures

On the fifth day, God created the many creatures that fill the sea (Gen 1:20-23). Those who live far from the sea may not realize the mighty power of the ocean, nor the countless variety of sea creatures (**104:25**). While we can travel by air to almost any part of the world within twenty-four hours, people in Bible times thought travel by sea on ships was very special. They thought of the greatest sea creature, the *leviathan* (**104:26**), with awe, as we think of the huge whales that are many tons in weight.

How many are your works, O Lord (**104:24**) is the key verse in this psalm and sums up what has gone before.

104:27-30 Life and Death in God's Hands

We need to realize for ourselves and all creatures that God is the one who both gives and sustains life (**104:27-28**). We are all dependent on his favour, on whether he hides his face (**104:29a**; Deut 31:16-18; Ps 30:7) or turns it towards us so that it shines on us (Num 6:24-26). And all of us alike must die, including the most powerful rulers and dictators in the world. Genesis 3:19 says, 'You are dust, and to dust you shall return' and this is repeated in **104:29b**. But God keeps on giving and renewing life on the earth (**104:30**). Through Jesus Christ we know the truth that there is life beyond death for those who believe in the Saviour who came to us, died and rose again for us (John 3:16).

104:31-35 All Praise to God

God's wisdom and care are seen in all his work in creation (**104:31**). Mostly, we see this in the gentleness of nature, but earthquakes and volcanic eruptions make us realize the power of those forces and think of the almighty power of the Creator (**104:32**).

Sin and wickedness spoil the beautiful world that God has made. That is why the psalmist prays, *May sinners vanish from the earth and the wicked be no more* (**104:35**). His desire is not that wicked people be punished, but rather that evil may be no more so that only the glory of God is seen in his works. For our part we should want to bless the Lord with our lips and turn away from everything that soils and destroys God's handiwork.

Psalm 105: Remember God's Wonderful Acts

Psalm 105 is a hymn of praise – like 78 and 106 – for what God had done in the life of Israel. But unlike those psalms, it says nothing of the weaknesses and failures of Israel. It speaks only of what God had done in power and lovingkindness towards his people, as revealed in the *wonderful acts* recorded in the OT.

105:1-6 Call to Praise God

This call to praise was among the songs sung when David brought the ark of God into Jerusalem (1 Chr 16:8-13). We should take note of each of the things that God's chosen people are called to do. They are to give thanks for what he has done and to call on his name (**105:1a**), which means relying on him as their God and Lord (105:1a). They are also to make his deeds known among people far and near (**105:1b**). They are to *sing praise to him* (**105:2a**). They are to *tell of all his wonderful acts* (**105:2b**). They are to *glory in his holy name* (**105:3**), that is, to take pride in him because of who he is. They are to seek his presence continually, wanting always to realize that he is near and that he is their strength (**105:4**).

We read this psalm today as Christian people, NT people, that is, people under the new covenant. Spiritually, we are the *descendants of Abraham* and *sons of Jacob* (**105:6**; see Gal 3:6-9; 6:16). As we look back on what God has done for us in Jesus Christ, we should praise him in all the ways mentioned here.

105:7-11 God's Covenant Promises

We refer to God's *covenant* (**105:8**) more often than we think, because the word 'testament' means 'covenant'. Thus when we speak of the Old Testament, we are really speaking of the covenant (or the covenants) that God made. God wants to have the special relationship that a covenant expresses with his people. Genesis 9:8-17 speaks of a covenant with all humanity, made after the flood. Then there was the covenant with Abraham (Gen 12:1-3; 15:1-6, 18-21; 17:1-8), with Isaac (Gen 26:1-5) and with Jacob (Gen 28:10-17) and then with Israel as a nation (Exod 19:5-6), giving them their land and above all calling them to a special role in working out God's purpose for the whole world (**105:9-11**).

105:12-22 From Abraham to Joseph

God's covenant with Abraham meant that he was watching over his descendants when they were *few in number* (**105:12**) and were still waiting to possess the land that was promised to them. He protected Abraham and Sarah (Gen 12:10-20; 20:1-18), treating them as his representatives (like *anointed ones* and *prophets* – **105:15**). When there was famine in the land, God had provided in advance for the help that Abraham's descendants would need. Joseph had been sold by his brothers as a slave and taken down into Egypt (**105:16-18**; Gen 37:12-36). There he was unjustly put into prison (Gen 39:1-23). Different English versions have different translations of 105:18. It may speak of his 'neck' being put *in irons,* as in a collar, or of his 'soul' suffering such a painful experience.

Then what Joseph had said, of his own dreams and the dreams of others, came true (**105:19**; Gen 37:5-11; 40:1-23). He was able to interpret Pharaoh's dream about famine and

was made prime minister of Egypt over all the rest of Pharaoh's officials (**105:21-22**; Gen 41), helping to provide corn for Egypt's needs; and for his own father and brothers – the descendants of Abraham.

105:23-38 Egypt and the Exodus

Jacob came down into Egypt (also called *the land of Ham* – **105:23**, 27) in the time of famine, and his family was provided for there. From a family they became a nation. But then they came to be hated and oppressed and treated as slaves by the Egyptians (**105:24-25**; Exod 1). As the people turned to God in their need, Moses and Aaron were chosen and called (Exod 3–4). *Miraculous signs* and *wonders* were shown in Egypt (**105:26-27**).

A nation or a powerful ruler may oppress others for years, even for generations, but in God's purpose the power of the oppressor will finally be broken. So it was with the Egyptians. They suffered under the plagues described in Exodus. Eight of the ten plagues are mentioned in **105:28-36**: *darkness* over the land (Exod 10:21-23), the water turned *into blood* (Exod 7:14-25), *frogs* (Exod 8:1-15), *flies* (Exod 8:20-29), *gnats* or mosquitoes (Exod 8:16-19), *hail with lightning* (Exod 9:13-35), *locusts* (Exod 10:13-15) and finally the death of the *firstborn* sons of Egypt (Exod 12:29-30). So in the end the Egyptians were glad when the people of Israel left their land, taking with them *silver and gold,* a kind of payment for their years of slavery (**105:37-38**; Exod 12:35-36)

105:39-45 The Journey to Canaan

The story of the journey from Egypt to the promised land is told briefly. God provided a pillar of *cloud* and *fire* that protected them and guided them (**105:39**; Exod 14:19-20; 13:21-22) and provided manna, here described as *the bread of heaven* (see also John 6:30) and *quails* for their food (**105:40**; Exod 16). So at last they were brought into the land promised long before in the days of the covenant with Abraham (**105:42**).

But the psalm ends with the reminder that there are two sides to a covenant. God's purpose was not just to save Israel from oppression and give them land. They were to live as his people, following his laws (**105:45**).

Psalm 106: Failure and the Lord's Goodness

Psalm 105 spoke only of the great things that God did for his people. Psalm 106 now adds the story of Israel's failures to the record of God's goodness. Normally, we are unwilling to speak of past failures, whether personal or those of our people. When we come to God, however, we should admit our failures in a spirit of sincere repentance.

This psalm can be compared with other OT passages where people confess the sins of the past and seek God's grace and forgiveness (see 1 Kgs 8:22-53; Ezra 9:5-15; Neh 9:6-37; Dan 9:3-19).

106:1-6 Prayer

The psalm begins with the call to praise God for his *mighty acts* (**106:1-2**) and with the reminder that true praise involves not just words but doing *what is right* (**106:3**). Though most of the psalm recalls the story of the whole nation, **106:4-5** is a personal prayer. This reminds us that when we think of our nation, we should remember the part that we personally have to play in it. Similarly, when we pray for ourselves, we should remember our nation. When we pray personally, we also have to remember that we belong together with our *fathers* in our sinfulness. We are no better, and no worse, than they. We and they alike *have sinned … have done wrong and acted wickedly* (**106:6**).

106:7-12 Unbelief

The story of the Exodus from Egypt, recalled by the Hebrew people every year at Passover time, is a story of the *mighty acts of the Lord* (106:2). The Lord made his power known to them in the miraculous plagues in Egypt (**106:7a**) and when he led them across the *Red Sea* (or the Sea of Reeds) and gave them complete victory over the Egyptian army that pursued them (**106:8-11**; Exod 14–15). The sad part of the story is the unbelief of the people in spite of all that they had been shown of God's concern for them and his power to help them. When they saw the Egyptians behind them and the sea in front of them, they blamed Moses and said that they would have been better off remaining as slaves to the Egyptians (**106:7b**; Exod 14:11-12). Thankfully, however, they eventually learned their lesson and *believed his promises and sang his praise* (**106:12**).

106:13-15 Impatience

After leaving Egypt, the people sometimes faced difficulties, as we all do. On one occasion they found only bitter water, and they came to Moses and asked 'What shall we drink?' (Exod 15:22-27). Then they complained about food and said that it would have been better for them to have died in Egypt (Exod 16). Another time they camped in a place where there seemed to be no water, and the people complained again (Exod 17:1-7). In each case *they soon forgot* (**106:13**) what God had done for them already and were unwilling to wait for him to help them again. They *put God to the test* (**106:14**), questioning whether he could and would provide for them. He did provide food and water each time, but they suffered because of their foolish unbelief and impatience (**106:15**; see also Num 11:18-20, 33).

106:16-18 Jealousy

God had chosen Moses and Aaron as the leaders of the people, but Korah, Dathan and Abiram challenged their leadership and wanted to have their positions for themselves (Num 16). Israel was taught by the calamities of earthquake and fire that it is a serious thing for people to try to exalt themselves in the service of God and to be jealous of others in higher positions (**106:17-18**). It was jealousy that led the religious leaders of Israel to reject Jesus and to have Pilate condemn him to death (Matt 27:18). Jealousy can still do great harm in the life of the Christian church.

106:19-23 Idolatry

While Moses was communing with God on Mount Sinai, the people persuaded Aaron to make an image of a *calf* (such as other peoples around them had) for them to worship (**106:19**; see Exod 32). It was a terrible mistake for two reasons. It made the centre of their worship *an image of a bull, which eats grass* instead of the one who is Creator of all (**106:20**). And it meant that they had forgotten the living God and all that he had done for them in bringing them out of Egypt (**106:21-22**). We may be amazed at their foolishness, but as human beings we are often tempted to put created things at the centre of our lives rather than our Creator, our loving God and Redeemer.

Moses' qualities as a leader, which have been demonstrated in the different incidents already referred to in this psalm, emerge most clearly here where he *stood in the breach* (**106:23**) to intercede for the people (Exod 32:30-34).

106:24-27 Rejection of God's Promise

From the time of Abraham the people had been promised a land that would be their own. When they finally came near it, they sent 'spies' to see the land. These men reported that it was a fertile and *pleasant land* (**106:24**), but that they would never be able to overcome the people there and to occupy it. They refused to trust God and to believe that he was able to fulfil his promise. They suggested that they would be better to go back to Egypt, to slavery there. As a result that generation remained in the wilderness and it was only the next generation that occupied Canaan (Num 13–14; Deut 1:19-33).

106:28-31 Pagan Practices

The worship of the *Baal of Peor* (**106:28a**; Num 25) was one of the worst kinds of worship that Israel could follow. It involved prostitution and *sacrifices offered to the dead* (**106:28b** – NRSV). This provoked the Lord to whom alone they should have offered worship and whose commandments they should have obeyed. Moses had interceded for the people when they turned aside to idols before (106:23), but now it was *Phinehas* who intervened (**106:30**). Such a person's example should be remembered *for endless generations to come* (**106:31**).

106:32-33 Unbelief Again

At *Meribah* the people failed to trust God to provide the water they needed. This time their unbelief exhausted Moses' patience and *trouble came to Moses because of them* (**106:32**). He spoke *rash words* and 'struck the rock' instead of speaking quietly and himself trusting God (**106:33**; Num 20:2-13; Pss 81:7; 95:8).

106:34-39 Human Sacrifice

The OT speaks of 'holy war'. We can appreciate the understanding given to the people in those times, that they were to destroy the pagan peoples of Canaan so that Israel would not be tempted to follow terribly corrupt ways and worship (**106:34**). In Islam there is the principle of *Jihad*, or 'holy war' for the faith. For us in Christ, physical violence is not the way. The NT makes clear that our warfare is a spiritual one against the forces of evil. Our battles are to be fought by prayer and by using 'the armour of God' (see 2 Cor 10:1-6; Eph 6:10-20).

The people did indeed yield to the temptations offered by heathen ways, particularly in regard to something that was always forbidden to Israel – the offering of human sacrifices. Their own *sons and daughters* were offered, and it could not be said that they offered them to the Lord, but rather to *demons* (**106:37**).

106:40-48 Repeated Unfaithfulness

The book of Judges tells of what happened again and again, 'The Israelites did what was evil in the sight of the Lord and worshipped the Baals' (see especially Judg 2:11-23). Deprived of the help they could have had in the Lord, they were conquered by their enemies. As this psalm puts it, *their enemies oppressed them* (**106:42**), but then God in his mercy *many times delivered them* (**106:43**) and *he took note of their distress when he heard their cry* (**106:44**). The psalm recalls these things not only to tell the story of human failure, but also of God's mercy and goodness. As the NT puts it, 'These things happened to them as examples and were written down as warnings for us' (1 Cor 10:11).

106:47-48 Prayer and Praise

The psalm ends with a prayer that may well have been the prayer of the people when, because of their unfaithfulness and failure to rely on God, they had gone into exile. It was a prayer for salvation, asking that God would gather them from among the nations and lead them back to serve him more faithfully (**106:47**). But more than salvation from guilt and the results of sin, they wanted the freedom and power to give thanks to God and to glory in praising him.

Finally, in **106:48** there is a great doxology that ends Book 4 of the Psalter with praise, just as praise ended the earlier books (41:13; 72:18-19; 89:52).

BOOK FIVE: PSALMS 107–150

Psalm 107: Thanksgiving Service

Psalm 107 reads like the description of a great service of thanksgiving after the people's return from exile in Babylon. Commentators argue about whether it speaks of four different groups of people or whether each of the subsections describes the plight of all the people in exile in a different way. Both of these interpretations of the psalm make good sense and give us the same application today. We have all experienced situations in life that feel like being lost in the desert, shut up in prison, dying of some sickness, or facing storms at sea. In such situations, the word of the Lord to us is always, 'Call on me in the day of trouble; I will deliver you, and you shall glorify me' (Ps 50:15).

107:1-3 A Call to Thanksgiving

The psalm begins with the person leading the service calling on everyone to unite in giving thanks to the Lord, for one reason: *he is good; his love endures for ever* (**107:1**). The particular situation was that the people had come back from exile. They had been scattered and under the power of their enemies, but now they were free and gathered again in their own land (**107:2-3**). All the people knew that when they had *cried to the Lord in their trouble … he delivered them from their distress* (107:6, 13, 19, 28). So they should *give thanks to the Lord for his unfailing love and his wonderful deeds for men* (107:8, 15, 21, 31).

107:4-9 Desert Travellers Brought Safely Home

Those of us who have roads leading to every town and village find it hard to imagine what it is like to travel in the desert where there are no marked roads. Often in biblical times, people knew what it was to be lost in the desert without food or water (**107:4-5**). Then there was, certainly, reason to thank God when their prayer was answered and they were brought safely *to a city where they could settle* (**107:6-7**). We may not have had that experience, but many people know what it has been to wander without purpose in life, to be lost, and then to know the blessing of coming back to the Lord and to his way.

107:10-16 Captives Rejoicing in Their Freedom

Others have had the experience of being captives or prisoners through their own fault, because they *rebelled against the words of God and despised [his] counsel* (**107:11**). Individuals have faced the humbling experience of being in prison, or have felt bound to forces of evil too great for them. The people of Israel had suffered the loss of their freedom and were taken into exile in Babylon. Yet God looks in mercy on all those who turn to him, and he is able and willing to bring them *out of darkness and the deepest gloom* (**107:14**) and set them free. It did not matter to him that the great city of Babylon was described as having a hundred bronze gates in its great walls, for God *breaks down gates of bronze and cuts through bars of iron* (**107:16**; see Isa 45:2).

107:17-22 Finding Healing

Not all sickness is the direct result of people's wrongdoing (**107:17**), as the NT clearly shows (see John 9:1-5). But often people do suffer because of wrong habits in life – the abuse of alcohol or drugs, loose sexual living, making a god of food or pleasure or power. Yet many have experienced healing and deliverance by turning to the Lord, and realize that they indeed have great cause to thank God and *tell of his works with songs of joy* (**107:22**).

In **107:20** God's *word* is described as his personal messenger, doing his will in the world and healing his people. God is so powerful that he has only to speak and his will is done – including the creation and sustaining of the universe and ourselves (Gen 1:3, 6, 9, 11, 14, 20, 24, 26; see also Ps 147:15, 18; Isa 55:11). We should respond to God's word on our behalf with our own words, telling of his deeds with songs of joy (**107:22**), and praising him in the congregation of the people (**107:32**).

107:23-32 Escaping the Dangers of the Sea

With the development of air travel not as many people travel by sea as they did in the past. But cargo ships are still important for trade between one country and another, and so there are still *merchants on the mighty waters* (**107:23**). In facing storms at sea, they know only too well the experience described in **107:26-27**. Often in little boats, and even in great ships, people cry to the Lord for help, and they have reason to thank him when he brings them safely to port (**107:28-32**). The same is true of us when we turn to God and find help in the storms of life.

107:33-43 Thanksgiving

The final verses of the psalm are a song of thanksgiving for everyone to join in. If we study what God has done in people's lives and down through history, we realize both his blessings and his judgments. He answers the prayers of those who turn to him, and gives rain to parched land and blesses crops, vineyards and cattle (**107:33-38**; see Isa 41:18; 42:15; 50:2). The Lord also brings down proud oppressors (**107:40**) and raises the oppressed (**107:41**). So the final advice the psalmist gives is *Whoever is wise, let him heed these things and consider the great love of the Lord* (**107:43**).

Psalm 108: Singing the Old Songs Again

Psalm 108 is almost exactly the same as parts of two other psalms: **108:1-5** is the same as 57:7-11, and **108:6-13**

is the same as 60:5-12. What did those two psalms have to say, and why have they been drawn together to make another psalm?

108:1-5 God's Glory (see 57:7-10)

Psalm 57 is clearly a psalm that was written from a situation of great danger and difficulty. In the earlier part of the psalm, the writer began by crying to God as he faced those who trampled on him. He spoke of them as being like lions, and their tongues being like sharp swords. He said that he knew he must take refuge in God 'until the disaster has passed' (57:1). But it is not the early part of the psalm that is used here but the latter part, which expresses confidence in the *love* and *faithfulness* of God (**108:4**). Because he knows the goodness of God, the writer says that he is determined to keep his heart steadfast, trusting God, praising him, and praying that his glory might *be over all the earth* (**108:5**). These verses from Psalm 57 are certainly a good beginning for any praise and prayer to God.

108:6-13 A Prayer of Hope (see 60:5-12)

Psalm 60 begins in a mood of great discouragement. The people felt rejected by God and thought that, in his judgment of them, he had caused them to be defeated by their enemies. But that part of the psalm is not used in this prayer for victory. The part of the psalm that is used speaks first of God's promise and gift of the land to the east and the west of the Jordan. Jacob came to Succoth and Shechem when he had been far away from the land promised to him (Gen 33:17-18). *Ephraim,* one of the largest tribes, was strong like a helmet, while *Judah* was the one with the sceptre, symbol of the Davidic kingship (**108:8**). Then the psalm spoke of the surrounding nations – *Moab, Edom, Philistia* – as being like servants of the Lord (**108:9-10**).

When Psalm 60 was written, Edom was a bitter enemy. Even though Israel and Edom were descended from the brothers Jacob and Esau, there had been enmity between them for generations (Amos 1:11). When Jerusalem fell to the Babylonians, the Edomites rejoiced (see Obad 10-14).

When Psalm 108 was formed, Edom may have again been threatening the Israelites. Or the threat may have been from new enemies, represented symbolically by the old enemies of Moab, Edom and Philistia. Certainly, it must have been another time of great need, a crisis in the nation's life. It helped the people to turn to God with the confidence expressed by Psalm 57 and to remember the promises and assurances in Psalm 60. They realized that they needed more help than mere humans could give (**108:12**). They would make the song of earlier generations their prayer in their new situation. The psalmist could also end with the same confidence: *With God we will gain the victory, and he will trample down our enemies* (**108:13**). These words can also ring true in our lives (Heb 13:6).

It can be a valuable exercise to follow the psalmist's lead here and combine passages of Scripture in a way that throws fresh light on both of them. For example, we could pair Mark 10:42-45 and 1 Peter 5: 2-6, or John 13:34-35 and 1 John 2:7.

Psalm 109: 'They May Curse, But You Will Bless'

Psalm 109 is another that addresses the situation of those in the world today who face continued injustice, oppression and persecution. It causes us to think about how we should pray for them, and how we should encourage the oppressed to pray for themselves.

Some of the prayers given here are ones that we, as Christians, should not pray, prayers for the downfall of our enemies: 'May my persecutors be defeated, and may I, your servant, be glad. May my enemies be covered with disgrace; may they wear their shame like a robe' (109:28-29 GNB). Some translations try to get around this difficulty by adding the words, 'They say' at the beginning of 109:6, suggesting that the curses in 109:6-19 (or at least 109:6-15) are not the prayer of the psalmist, but the prayer of his enemies. The argument in favour of this position is that the psalmist speaks of enemies as 'they' and 'them' in 109:3-5, whereas 109:6-19 seems to be directed at just one person, referred to as 'he'. While this argument is attractive, the words 'they say' are not in the original Hebrew manuscripts of 109:6. Moreover, it is hard to think of some of the things said in 109:16-18 being said about a godly man. We can understand many false accusations being brought, but an evil person would hardly say, *for he never thought of doing a kindness, but hounded to death the poor ... He loved to pronounce a curse* (109:16-17).

Whichever way we read it, there can be no disputing that this psalm contains two kinds of prayers: prayers that seek evil to fall on ungodly men, and prayers that seek God's justice in the world.

109:1-20: Prayers That Seek Evil

The psalmist was certainly in real trouble, and turned to God to ask him to speak and not to *remain silent* (109:1), and to act strongly on his behalf. He had enemies who spoke lies against him and accused him falsely. They attacked him *without cause* (109:2-3). They cursed him and wanted evil to fall on him. Sadly, there are plenty of powerful people in the world who oppress others. There are plenty of people who use words with the intention of bringing trouble on others and causing them to live in fear. When facing such trouble we, like the psalmist, can only bring our situation and our fears to God.

We are taught by Jesus to love our enemies and to pray for those who persecute us (Matt 5:44; Luke 6:27-31; Rom 12:14-21), and so we cannot make petitions like some of

those in this psalm. Yet we should see that they are not prayers that seek evil like those of the psalmist's enemies, but rather prayers that seek justice. If people deal in curses as naturally as they wear clothes, then it is only just if curses return on their heads (**109:17-19**). The law even specified that if a person brought false witness against another, it should be done to him 'as the false witness had meant to do to the other' (Deut 19:16-20). Acts 1:20 also quotes **109:8** in relation to Judas Iscariot.

109:21-31 Prayers for Justice

The psalmist prayed for right to triumph over wrong. The basis of that prayer was the honour of God's name: *Deal well with me for your name's sake; out of the goodness of your love, deliver me* (**109:21**). But the prayer also sprang from the terrible suffering of *the poor and needy,* the weak, the distressed and the despised (**109:22-25**), and the utter injustice of those who oppressed them. The assurance that God is good means that justice must triumph over evil. The psalm, though it brings a desperately difficult situation to God, begins and ends with praise (109:1, 30-31).

The psalmist felt that an accuser stood at his right hand to have him condemned (109:6). But in the end he feels that God indeed *stands at the right hand of the needy one, to save his life from those who condemn him* (**109:31**). People may curse, but God's blessing is stronger than any human curse (**109:28**). We can have that same assurance when people use their words to try to harm us. God's word is more powerful than any human words, and God's spiritual protection of those who rely on him is stronger than all the forces of evil (see 1 John 4:4).

Psalm 110: Celebration of the Priest-King

Psalm 110 is another of the royal or kingly psalms (see also Pss 2; 45; 72). It is related to the life and rule of a king of Israel, and may have been used when David and the Davidic kings who ruled after him were crowned in Jerusalem. But it is also quoted in the NT more often than any other psalm, and so is related to our Lord Jesus Christ as King and Priest. Because he has this rank, we can 'approach the throne of grace with confidence, so that we may receive mercy and find grace to help us in our time of need' (Heb 4:14, 16).

110:1-3 The King

The word of the Lord, probably through a prophet, is spoken to the king in 110:1 and again in 110:4. The king is addressed as *my Lord* (110:1). Jewish scholars recognized that no king ever truly attained the high honour presented in this psalm, and thus they believed that David had been inspired by the Holy Spirit to give a prophecy about the promised Messiah. Jesus was referring to this belief when he challenged the Pharisees to recognize that the Messiah would be more than David's son; he would be David's Lord (see Matt 22:41-45).

In the first prophetic statement the king is regarded as the anointed of the Lord, set at God's *right hand* (**110:1a**). This can only be a symbolic exultation for the king, but it is uniquely true of Jesus, the Son of God, who after his death was raised by the Father and exalted to his right hand, meaning that he was raised to the position of greatest authority (see Matt 26:64; Acts 2:32-35; 5:31; Rom 8:34; Eph 1:20-21; Heb 1:13; 1 Pet 3:22).

God promises the king victory over all his enemies. They are set under his feet, like a mere *footstool* (**110:1b**). The *mighty sceptre* (**110:2**) that is extended is the staff or rod that was the sign of the king's power and authority. Young people will come willingly to serve under their king (**110:3a**). They will be like those described as 'the willing volunteers' in battle under Deborah and Barak (Judg 5:9).

In a number of places in this psalm the meaning of the Hebrew text is not quite clear, as is shown in the differences between English translations. The NIV speaks of the forces of the king as *arrayed in holy majesty* (**110:3b**), which is probably the correct translation. However, other translations like the NRSV speak of the king leading his forces 'on the holy mountains', which would mean the mountains of the 'holy land' that God had given to the people.

There is also disagreement as to whether it is the young people who are fresh like the dew of the morning, or whether the king is pictured as going out strongly at the dawn of the day (*from the womb of the dawn* – **110:3c**).

110:4 The Priest

In the second prophetic statement, the king is told, *You are a priest for ever in the order of Melchizedek* (**110:4**). Genesis 14:16-20 is the only other place in the OT where we read of this Melchizedek. He was king of Salem (that is Jerusalem) and 'priest of God Most High'. When David became king, he was, as it were, a successor of Melchizedek. He was king in Jerusalem, and although he was not like the Aaronic or Levitical priests, he had a priest's task of leading his people in the ways of God.

Jesus is not only our King but also our Priest, having offered himself as a sacrifice for our sins to bring us to God. In the NT, Hebrews especially speaks of the work of Christ as our High Priest. Hebrews 5:7-10, 6:19-20 and 7:1-28 demonstrate how Jesus can be described as *a priest for ever in the order of Melchizedek* (110:4).

110:5-7 The Warrior

The first verse spoke of the king being at the right hand of God. It can also be said that God is at *your right hand* (**110:5**). God will help him and enable him to overthrow his enemies, refreshing and strengthening him constantly.

If 110:3 is interpreted as referring to the king setting out at dawn, then **110:7** may picture the king refreshing himself in the heat of the day by drinking from a stream as he pauses in pursuing his enemies. Or the picture may be of God-given refreshment, the 'river whose streams make glad the city of God' (46:4).

There is a difference between the situation of the OT king and the NT understanding of Christ our King. The king in the OT was a warrior-king, given strength by God to overcome his enemies, who were regarded as enemies of God and under God's judgment (**110:6**). But Christ is the Prince of Peace. The enemies he fights are, above all, spiritual enemies, the forces of evil that challenge his rule of blessing. He seeks those who will come to the Father through him as their great High Priest, and then offer themselves willingly to serve him and bring others to acknowledge him as Lord.

Psalm 111: 'The Beginning of Wisdom'

Psalm 111 and the next one (as well as others like Pss 9, 10, 25, 34) are acrostics. That means that the lines are arranged on the basis of the Hebrew alphabet. In the NIV, the first words, 'Praise the Lord', represent the title of the psalm: 'Hallelujah'. The second line, *I will extol* is a translation of a Hebrew line that begins with the first letter of the alphabet, and the next line, in *the council* begins with the second letter in the Hebrew alphabet, and so on until all twenty-two letters have been used. This pattern made it easier to remember what was said about the works of the Lord, the character of the Lord, and the fear of the Lord.

111:1-9a The Works and Character of the Lord

This psalm, like the two that follow, begins with a resounding *praise the Lord* (111:1) followed by the psalmist's statement that he will give thanks to the Lord with *all my heart* (**111:1**). There are many things that we should do with 'all our hearts', and giving praise is one of them (see Deut 4:29; 6:5; 10:12; 11:13). Then the psalmist goes on to speak of the *works* and *wonders* and *deeds* of the Lord and to celebrate the mighty things that God has done.

He begins with creation. We have reason to delight in God's work in creation, and the more we study that work, the more we are filled with wonder at the wisdom and power of God. Science is really the study of God's work, 'thinking God's thoughts after him', as one great scientist said. That is why the words of 111:2 are engraved over the entrance of the Cavendish Laboratory in Cambridge, England, where many great modern scientific discoveries have been made.

The psalmist also reminds us of how God provides for the needs of *those who fear him* (**111:5a**). He may be thinking of God's special provision for the Israelites when they wandered in the wilderness. But people everywhere have reason to be thankful as God provides for their daily needs.

It is also possible that the psalmist was thinking of the *covenant* that God made with Noah (Gen 8:22) in which he promised that 'as long as the earth endures, seedtime and harvest, cold and heat, summer and winter, day and night, will never cease'.

The people of Israel were especially aware that the Lord had *shown his people the power of his works* in giving them their land (**111:6**). We all can be thankful for the land in which we live and for its resources and its beauty. God has also *provided redemption for his people* (**111:9a**). The psalmist would have been thinking of their release from Egypt, or possibly later of their release from their exile in Babylon. As Christians, we think of a far more wonderful redemption, our release from sin and death through the death and resurrection of our Lord Jesus Christ.

All of the works of God we have mentioned are among the wonders that he *has caused ... to be remembered* (**111:4a**). He did this by instituting three annual festivals: Passover, Weeks and Tabernacles (Exod 12:14; Deut 16:1-17). As Christians, we too have been given a way of remembering what Christ has done (1 Cor 11:23-26). And it is not only we who are to remember these things, for in the very next we are told that God too *remembers his covenant* (**111:5b**).

God's works cannot be separated from his character. God has done all of the things listed above because of the kind of God that he is. First of all, he is *great* and *glorious* and *majestic* beyond anything that we could ever think or imagine (**111:2-3**). He is also righteous, just and upright. All that God does is right, and he always upholds what is true and just (**111:7-8**). Because of this, he hates all that is evil. Yet because he is also *gracious and compassionate* (**111:4b**), he is patient with us, seeking to turn us from what is wrong to what is right, and willing to forgive us when we do turn back to him.

Some people worship gods of whom they are deeply afraid because they never know how the gods will act, whether in kindness or hostility. The one God of whom we learn in the Bible, and whom we know in Jesus Christ, is not like that. He is *faithful and just* (111:7). He does not change and can always be relied on to act according to his character of truth and love.

111:9b-10 The Fear of the Lord

The description of all that God has done and of all that he is makes us realize our smallness and God's greatness and power and justice. This is what Isaiah realized when he had a vision of God as he worshipped in the temple (Isa 6:1-7). With the psalmist, we have to declare, *Holy and awesome is his name* (**111:9b**).

The word *awesome* in 111:9 literally means 'to be feared'. The next verse gives us a better idea of what such fear means when it says, *The fear of the Lord is the beginning of wisdom* (**111:10**). Often in the Bible we read of the 'fear'

of God. It does not mean being afraid of God. Hundreds of times we read of the Lord, or his messengers, saying, 'Do not be afraid' (see Gen 15:1; 21:7; 26:24). The 'fear of the Lord' that we are encouraged to have is reverence for him. That reverence means that we recognize his greatness and our smallness. It means that we put him in the centre of our lives, and desire to serve him and to walk in his ways. To have that fear and reverence is to be truly wise. As the GNB puts it, 'The way to become wise is to honour the Lord; he gives sound judgment to all who obey his commands. He is to be praised for ever!' (111:10).

Psalm 112: 'Happy Are Those Who Fear the Lord'

Psalm 112 is an acrostic (see the explanation at Psalm 111). Its theme is the blessing that comes to people who fear the Lord. It closely parallels Psalm 111.

112:1-5 The Character of the Godly

The last verse of Psalm 111 said that 'the fear of the Lord is the beginning of wisdom'. This psalm starts off by saying *Blessed is the man who fears the Lord* (**112:1**). Those who fear the Lord put him first in their lives and see his commandments not as a burden but as a *great delight*. They realize that God's plan for our lives is drawn up in perfect wisdom and love.

Psalm 111:3 says of God that 'his righteousness endures for ever', and amazingly, **112:3** says the same thing about the righteousness of godly people. The words remind us that both the OT and the NT stress that there should be a likeness in character between God and those who are godly. After all, we were originally created 'in the image of God' (Gen 1:26), and so are able to have fellowship with him, despite the effects of the fall.

One of the characteristics for which God was praised in 111:4 is that he is 'gracious and compassionate'. God's people should show the same qualities (**112:4b**). Similarly, where 111:5 speaks of the generous giving of God, **112:5** stresses the generosity of those who serve God. The godly will be able to see God's light themselves and share it with others who face times of darkness and distress (**112:4a;** Matt 5:14-16; Phil 2:14-15). Justice will be the mark of all their dealings with others, and they will be generous to those in need (112:5, 9).

The call to show the character of God in our lives becomes clearer still in the NT, which has much to say about the privilege of being accepted as children of God. Jesus called his disciples to be 'merciful' and to be 'perfect' as they knew their heavenly Father to be 'merciful' and 'perfect' (Matt 5:48; Luke 6:36). The Apostle Paul says, 'put on the new self, created to be like God in true righteousness and holiness' (Eph 4:24). He adds that we must forgive one another 'as in Christ God forgave [us]', and 'be imitators of

God, as dearly loved children, and live a life of love, just as Christ loved us' (see Eph 4:32-5:2).

112:6-10 The Blessings of Godliness

The psalm promises great blessings to the godly, but also raises some hard questions as we read it. Are godly families always blessed with *wealth and riches,* and do they always become *mighty in the land* (112:2-3)? We have to say, 'Not always'. And the psalm itself hints at that. It speaks of the *bad news* that may come to them (112:7), and of the fact that there are foes (112:8) that they have to face in life. We cannot teach that those who commit their lives to God will be assured of material prosperity but our hearts should be *steadfast* and *secure* (112:7-8), and if we are righteous, we *will never be shaken* (112:6; see also 15:5; 16:8; 46:5).

Jesus made very clear to his disciples that they must be prepared to face hardship and suffering in his service. Yet in the end it is true that 'righteousness exalts a nation' (Prov 14:34). A family that honours the Lord is blessed with security and strength and, for the person who loves God, ultimately 'all things work together for good' (Rom 8:28). In the end also those who reject God's ways will find themselves powerless, unsatisfied and angry (112:10). The NT sums it up: 'A man reaps what he sows' (Gal 6:7).

Psalm 113: God's Greatness Shown in Grace

Psalms 113-118 are known as the psalms of the Egyptian *Hallel* (the word *hallel* means 'praise') because they were used to celebrate Israel's deliverance from Egypt. Psalms 113 and 114 were sung immediately before the eating of the Passover meal, and Psalms 115 to 118 were sung after the meal. So these were the last psalms Jesus sang as he celebrated the Last Supper with his disciples. Reading these psalms with this in mind adds to our understanding of the Jewishness of Jesus, and simultaneously gives us insight into his suffering, death and resurrection.

113:1-3 Praise God

Psalm 113 begins and ends with praise. It calls on all who serve the Lord to *praise the name of the Lord* (113:1), that is to praise him for who he is. He is to be praised every day and throughout the day, from sunrise to sunset (113:2-3). This may mean that God is to be praised every hour of the day, or it may mean that he is to be praised in all the world, from furthest east to furthest west (compare Mal 1:11). There is a hymn that expresses both thoughts:

As o'er each continent and island, the dawn leads on another day,
The voice of prayer is never silent, nor dies the strain of praise away. (John Ellerton)

113:4-6 The Greatness of God

The greatness of God and the grace of God are all-embracing reasons why we should praise him. The greatness of God is great beyond all others. *Who is like the Lord our God?* (113:5) His glory is *above the heavens,* and on the earth he is high *over all the nations* (113:4). Isaiah 40:15-17 puts it like this: 'Surely the nations are like a drop in a bucket; they are regarded as dust on the scales; he weighs the islands as though they were fine dust … Before him all the nations are as nothing; they are regarded by him as worthless and less than nothing.'

But how different is God in his greatness from people who think themselves great and important! Such people often despise the poor but God looks down and is concerned for those in need (113:6). This is the grace of God, and it does not contradict his greatness. Rather it shows what true greatness is. 'For this is what the high and lofty one says – he who lives for ever, whose name is holy: I live in a high and holy place, but also with him who is contrite and lowly in spirit, to revive the spirit of the lowly, and to revive the heart of the contrite' (Isa 57:15).

It is no wonder that the question 'Who is like the Lord our God?' (113:5) is one that arises repeatedly (see Exod 15:11; Deut 4:33-35; Ps 35:10; Isa 40:18-26; 46:5).

113:7-9 The Grace of God

Psalm 138:6 says, 'though the Lord is on high, he looks upon the lowly', and that is what this psalm is saying. He sees the poor and is concerned to help them. He sees the *needy* on *the ash heap,* that is, the rubbish dump, and rescues them (113:7). They are as important to him as princes (113:8). He sees childless women and is concerned for them (113:9a). The OT is full of examples of childless women who, in answer to prayer, were blessed with children: Sarah (Gen 18:1-15), Rebekah (Gen 25:21), Rachel (Gen 30:22-23), and Hannah the mother of Samuel (1 Sam 1).

The OT is also full of examples of men and women who turned to God in great need and of the Lord answering their prayers. The supreme demonstration of the greatness of God is seen in his looking on us in grace in the coming of the Lord Jesus Christ. In Jesus, God not only looked down on us in love, but came down to us. As the Apostle Paul reminds us, 'though he was rich, yet for your sakes he became poor, so that you through his poverty might become rich' (2 Cor 8:9; see also Phil 2:5-11; John 13:1-20). We may be very unimportant and poor by the world's standards, but we are more than princes because we are sons and daughters of God through faith in our Lord Jesus Christ. What great reasons we have for echoing the beginning and end of the psalm, *Praise the Lord* (113:9b)!

Psalm 114: God of the Past and the Present

The people of Israel again and again looked back on what
God had done for them in the past. The festivals they kept
each year reminded them of it. So did the records in their
sacred books. So did the songs that they knew by heart and
sang, like this one. But as they thought of the past, they
were intended to realize that the same, unchanging God
was still with them as he had been with their ancestors.
This realization should also come to us, as Christian people,
as we reflect on the great things God has done for us.

114:1-6 God of the Past

Psalm 114 is full of brief allusions to important events in
Israel's past: They had been slaves in Egypt, among *a people
of foreign tongue,* and God had set them free (**114:1**). Moses
had been their human leader, but they always thought of
their freedom as the work of God (see Exod 15:1-21). God
had made them his own people with a special relationship
to him. He ruled over them as King, and they were his
dominion. He was present with them and among them, and
so they were *God's sanctuary* (**114:2**; see Exod 19:5-6). In a
similar way, Christian people are spoken of as God's temple
(see 1 Cor 3:6-16; 2 Cor 6:16-18; Eph 2:19-22; 1 Pet 2:4-5).

When they came out of Egypt, and it seemed that they
were trapped between the waters of the Red Sea and
the Egyptian army, God led them safely through the sea
(**114:3a, 5a**; see Exod 14). When they travelled on through
the desert, God provided for them, giving them water when
there seemed none to quench their thirst (114:8; see Exod
17:1-7; Num 20:1-13). At Mount Sinai God made his presence known to them in power, in thunder and storm and
volcanic activity on the mountain, and gave them his law
(**114:4, 6**; see Exod 19-20). Then when they were to go into
the land that they were promised and the river Jordan was
in front of them, God made it possible for them to cross the
Jordan and occupy the land (**114:3b, 5b**; see Josh 3).

114:7-8 God of the Present

The people of Israel did not just celebrate these things as
something God had done in the past; they thought of God
in the present, the same unchanging God. Sometimes they
may even have acted out the past events in a kind of drama,
with the sea and the river Jordan and the mountains being
like actors in the drama. These witnesses of the past events
still surrounded them. The earth should still *tremble ... at
the presence of the God of Jacob* (**114:7**). He is still the great
and mighty God who still gives pools and springs of water
to satisfy his people's needs. As people in a dry and arid
land know even better than those who live in a land with
plentiful rainfall, unless God gives water, plants and trees,
animals and human beings die. We are all utterly dependent
on God for our physical life and for our spiritual life. We

should thus rejoice that we can pray, 'This is God, our God
for ever and ever. He will be our guide for ever' (48:14).

Psalm 115: Glory Be to God

Psalm 115 begins by expressing the right attitude for all
who serve the Lord. We deserve no praise. All praise is due
to God, the Giver of every good gift that we have. If we have
this attitude, three things will follow.

115:1-8 We Will Know that Our God is Different

God's name – that is, God's character – is *love and faithfulness.*
So we should say, *Not to us, O Lord, not to us, but to your
name be the glory* (**115:1**).

The nations around Israel might sometimes question
God's faithfulness, saying, *Where is their God?* (**115:2**; see
also 42:3, 10; 79:10). They may have said this because the
Lord's disciplining of Israel meant that the nation did not
always seem to have his support. Or they may have said
it because Israel had no god that could be seen. The other
nations had idols of wood and stone, but where was the
image of Israel's God?

The answer to this challenge was simple: *Our God is in
heaven* (**115:3**). This statement does not mean that he is far
away, but that he rules over all. The people who had gods
that could be seen had powerless gods. Their idols might
be made of gold and silver or of wood and stone covered
with gold and silver, but of what use were they? (**115:4**).
What could they do with their mouths, their eyes, their
ears, their noses, their hands, their feet? (**115:5-7**; see also
Isa 44:8-20; Jer 10:2-10). What were they in comparison
with Yahweh, the living God, who heard the prayers of his
people, spoke his word to them, and acted in power and
goodness?

The Bible's words about idols are sometimes criticized
by those who say that the worshippers of idols do not really
regard them as their gods, but only as representations of
their gods. Whatever the case, the true and living God, our
Creator, cannot truly be represented by anything we make
with our hands. Any image we make would simply be a copy
of something he has created. But the most wonderful truth
is that God has made himself known to us by his Son Jesus
Christ becoming human. He is the image of God, and so
shows us what God is really like (John 1:14-18).

What we worship shapes who we are. All through history, people have made gods of the kind that they would
like to have. And as they serve these gods, they become like
them. This is what the psalmist meant when he said, *Those
who make them will be like them* (**115:8**). This warning is one
that we should remember. We may not worship a physical
idol anymore, but too often we worship money and material
possessions.

This warning is also an encouragement to us to become more like the God we serve. Psalms 111 and 112 spoke about the character of God and the character of those who serve him. Christians are repeatedly exhorted to become more like Jesus whom they worship as their Lord, and are promised that they will be restored to the 'image of God' in which they were made (Rom 8:29; 2 Cor 3:18; Col 3:9-10).

115:9-15 We Will Rely on Him Alone

If we believe that there is only one God who rules over all, *the Maker of heaven and earth* (**115:15**), we know that he alone is the source of all the strength and wisdom we need. So we should trust him. The psalm calls on the people of Israel generally, the priests, or *the house of Aaron*, and everyone who knows that it is right to *trust in the Lord* (**115:9-11**). They will find him to be *their help and their shield*, that is, their protection, as the large shield protected men in battle in those days (115:9-11). In the past God had always remembered his people with whom he had entered into a covenant, and he remembers them in the present (**115:12**). So they can continue to trust him in their daily living, regardless of whether they are *small* or *great* in the world's eyes (**115:13**). God makes no distinctions between persons as the world does.

115:16-18 We Will Praise Him Here and Now

Heaven and earth alike are the Lord's, but he has entrusted the earth to us as our home, and given it to us to care for (**115:16**). Thus we are to praise him while on Earth. The statement that *it is not the dead who praise the Lord* (**115:17**) in part reflects the lack of a clear hope of life after death in OT days. Now we have the hope of life in heaven through the resurrection of Jesus Christ and his conquest of death, and know that we will be able to praise him for ever. But for now we have special opportunities to serve and glorify him on earth, by our lives and by our witness to him, and we should take those opportunities as long as our life here lasts (**115:18**). As 113:2-3 has put it, the Lord should be praised from furthest east to furthest west, and 'both now and for evermore'.

Isaac Watts expresses the same idea in his great hymn:

I'll praise my Maker while I've breath,
And when my voice is lost in death,
Praise shall employ my nobler powers;
My days of praise shall ne'er be past,
While life and thought and being last,
Or immortality endures.

Psalm 116: How Can I Thank God Enough?

Psalm 116 is the thanksgiving of one who has been in great trouble.

116:1-7 Reasons to Be Thankful

The psalm begins *I love the Lord* (**116:1**). The psalmist's love springs from gratitude. He was so sick that he thought that *death* and the *grave* were near (**116:3**). In his sickness, he was probably very aware of his own failure and sinfulness. So when he experienced God's blessing in response to his prayer, he realized again that *the Lord is gracious and righteous; our God is full of compassion* (**116:5**). Like so many others, he could testify to the fact that God cares for *the simple-hearted*, for those who are poor and *in great need* in the circumstances of their lives (**116:6**). The word here translated 'the simple-hearted' is often used in the Book of Proverbs. The GNB translates it as 'the helpless'. It speaks of those who would not know the right way or have the experience to choose rightly apart from the help of God.

Secure in the care of God, the psalmist could say, *Be at rest once more, O my soul* (**116:7**; see also 37:7).

116:8-16 A Thankful Life

Many have been able to echo the grateful words that the psalmist addresses to God, *For You, O Lord, have delivered my soul from death, my eyes from tears, my feet from stumbling* (**116:8**). He had experienced great weakness and need. His life had been threatened by illness. His faith was sorely tested, and yet he could say, *I kept my faith, even when I said, 'I am greatly afflicted'* (**116:10** NRSV). The NIV translation of this verse, which has 'therefore' rather than 'even when', reflects the ancient Greek translation of this verse, which is the one the Apostle Paul quotes in 2 Corinthians 4:13. Certainly it is true that our words, even our words of complaint, stem from what we believe in our hearts.

Human help had proved to be of no use in his time of special need, and realizing this, the psalmist said, *All men are liars* (**116:11**). The contrast between God, who is always true, and human beings, who often cannot be trusted, again arouses his gratitude and prompts him to ask, *How can I repay the Lord for all his goodness to me?* (**116:12**). But he realizes that there is no way he can repay his debt to God. All he can do is gratefully take up *the cup of salvation* (**116:13a**). This may have been an actual cup lifted up and drunk at a thanksgiving feast. But the image also indicates that he can do nothing to deserve God's blessings or repay him for them. All we can do is gladly accept the salvation he has given us and continue to *call on the name of the Lord* and rely on him (**116:13b**). In 116:2 the psalmist expressed the same idea when he said, *I will call on him as long as I live*. His gratitude is also expressed in his recognition of the reason for which he was healed: *that I may walk before the Lord* (**116:9**), that is, live in a way that consistently honours him (see Gen 17:1; 24:40; 48:15).

God's love for his people is strikingly expressed in the GNB translation of **116:15**: 'How painful it is to the Lord when one of his people dies!' We are reminded that God values our lives. His care for us is also expressed in the words, *you have freed me from my chains* (**116:16**). Shown such love, it is no wonder that the psalmist says, *truly I am your servant,* and expresses the desire to continue to serve God with his life.

116:17-19 A Thankful Witness

Not just silently in his heart, nor just privately in his life, but publicly in the presence of all God's people, the psalmist wanted to offer praise (**116:18**; see 116:14). We have seen in other psalms how people in those days often made a vow when they prayed. It was a promise to serve and praise God in a particular way after their prayer was answered, and so they came to *the courts of the house of the Lord* and paid their vows (**116:19**). It was a little like what happens in churches in many places today, when there is opportunity in a public service of worship for people to bring their personal thanksgiving and share with the congregation. It can encourage the faith of others when we humbly tell what God has done for us, especially when there have been times of great difficulty when we have prayed.

Psalm 117: 'O for a Thousand Tongues to Sing'

Psalm 117 is the shortest of all the psalms, but it is like many other hymns of praise in the way that it calls on people to praise the Lord and gives the reasons for doing so.

117:1 All Nations to Praise God

There are many psalms that call on people to praise God, but not many that call all *nations* and *peoples* to praise him (see also Pss 67, 96). Yet those who believe that there is only one God know that he must be the Lord of all the earth, the God whom all nations should praise. From the call of Abraham (Gen 12:3), it is clear that those who came to know him as the one God were to take the blessing of that knowledge to others. Israel was to be a 'light to the nations' (Isa 42:6; 49:6). If they shared their knowledge of God, then the nations would be able to praise him. This verse is quoted by the apostle Paul in Romans 15:11, along with other OT passages which show that God's purpose is for all nations to know and serve him.

Charles Wesley captures the spirit of this verse in his hymn:

O for a thousand tongues to sing,
My great Redeemer's praise,
The glories of my God and King,
The triumphs of his grace.
My gracious Master and my God,
Assist me to proclaim,
To spread through all the earth abroad,
The honours of thy name.

117:2 The Reason for Praising God

The reason for praising God is given using the words that the psalms often use: God's great steadfast *love* and God's enduring *faithfulness.* These characteristics of God are spoken of often in the OT (see also Exod 34:6-7) and are shown in what God did for his people then. Today, we see his love and faithfulness even more fully through the coming of Jesus Christ (see John 1:14).

Psalm 118: Celebration of Thanksgiving

Psalm 118 is like a great service of thanksgiving and celebration. It would be sung as the people moved in procession towards the temple, entered through its gates, and worshipped God there. Like all the psalms from 113 to 118, it was sung at Passover, when many people approached the temple 'in the name of the Lord' (118:26) to worship and to offer sacrifices. But it took on new meaning in the NT. We see how it was fulfilled in the way that Jesus came into Jerusalem (Mark 11:1-11; Luke 19:29-40) and in his rejection, death, resurrection and ascension (Mark 12:1-12; Acts 4:5-12; Eph 2:19-20; 1 Pet 2:1-7).

118:1-18 Approaching the Temple

The procession to the temple begins with words often used as a summons: *Give thanks to the Lord, for he is good; his love endures for ever* (**118:1**). That great reality of the goodness of God was to be declared by the people (**118:2**), the priests (*the house of Aaron* – **118:3**), and all who honour the Lord (**118:4**; compare Psalm 115:9-10).

This shout of praise from the whole nation is followed by an expression of individual thanksgiving by one person who had called to the Lord in distress and found help (118:5-7). His words are echoed in Romans 8:31 and Hebrews 13:6. The speaker may have been the king or some other special representative of the people, because he speaks of being opposed not just by individuals but by *all the nations* (118:10). There were many against him, numerous and fierce as a swarm of *bees* (**118:12a**). The second half of this verse can be translated in different ways. It may mean that the attack of the enemy was like a blazing fire, or it may mean that their attack flared up and then died out *as quickly as burning thorns* (**118:12b**). In the end, the help of the Lord gave victory and there were songs of praise in the camp of God's people (**118:15**).

The one who brings this praise to God, either for himself or for the nation, admits that he deserved punishment from the Lord because of his sin, but as he turned to God he found forgiveness and help, and was not allowed to die (**118:17-18**).

As the psalms often do, this psalm emphasizes what is important by repeating it. So twice the singer says *The Lord is with me* (**118:6, 7**). Twice he says, *It is better to take refuge* *in the Lord* (**118:8, 9**). The enemy surrounded him, but three times he says, *in the name of the Lord I cut them off* (**118:10, 11,** 12). God's power in action is also stressed by the triple repetition of *the Lord's right hand* in 118:15, 16.

118:19-24 At the Temple Gates

The procession of worshippers, led by the one who brought his special thanksgiving, reaches the temple gates in **18:19** and asks to enter. The response welcoming the righteous is given in **118:20**, and the song of thanksgiving for God's salvation is taken up again in **118:21**: *I will give you thanks, for you answered me.* The nation had been like a stone that was rejected as of no use in the building of the temple, but then it was placed in the most important and most honoured position (**118:22**). What God had done was truly *marvellous* (**118:23**). It was a time to *rejoice and be glad* (**118:24**), and to pray for God's continued blessing (118:25).

118:25-29 Blessing and Response

The arriving worshippers are probably greeted by the priests in the temple, who pronounced God's blessing on those who came *in the name of the Lord* (**118:26**). These words took on a new meaning in the NT when Jesus, in a way beyond all others, came 'in the name of the Lord' (Matt 21:9), and offered himself as a sacrifice there in Jerusalem. At his triumphal entry into the city, the people took up the cry, 'Hosanna', which means *save us* (**118:25**). But they failed to continue to look to him for salvation, and the nation as a whole was unwilling to accept him as the one who came 'in the name of the Lord' (see Matt 23:39). He, beyond all others, became like 'the stone the builders rejected' who then became 'the capstone' (118:23).

The people are invited to join the procession up to the altar (**118:27**). Some older translations understood this verse to mean that a sacrificial animal was bound to the *horns of the altar,* that is, to its corners. But that was not a normal practice with sacrifices as described in the OT, and the Hebrew speaks of a *festal procession* rather than a sacrifice. The NIV interpretation, which refers to the worshippers at the Feast of Tabernacles carrying bundles of branches, seems likely to be more accurate. The JB translates this section of the verse as, 'With branches in your hands draw up in procession as far as the horns of the altar'. At the altar, the worshippers confess their faith in the Lord (**118:28**) and repeat the words of praise that began the psalm (**118:29**).

Psalm 119: The Gift of God's Law

Psalm 119 is by far the longest of all the psalms and, like a few other psalms, it is arranged as an acrostic. This means that its 176 verses are arranged in twenty-two sections of eight verses each, the first eight verses all beginning with the first letter of the Hebrew alphabet, the next eight with

the second letter, and so on through the twenty-two letters of the Hebrew alphabet. This explains why the NIV has a different Hebrew letter with its name before each section.

The acrostic form was probably intended to help people to remember the psalm. It is also as if the psalmist is saying that it took all the letters of the alphabet and all these 176 verses to fully express the importance and richness of God's law, which is the theme of this psalm. There can be no doubt about the theme, for almost every one of the 176 verses uses one of eight different names for the law of God. It is referred to as God's law, his decrees, his judgments (or laws), his commandments, his ways, his statutes, his precepts, and his word. Each of the key terms represents a different Hebrew word. While they are almost synonymous, each looks at the expressed will of God from a different perspective. For example, 'law' refers to it collectively, while 'laws' looks at each regulation separately. In the final analysis, however, the terms can be used interchangeably.

The psalmist expresses what God's word means to him and what he believes he should do with it. Many of the things the psalmist says of the law, many of the things he says he will do with the law, many of the prayers that he may live by God's law occur time and time again in the different sections of the psalm.

As we read the psalm, we realize that the writer is not just sitting quietly and reflecting on how wonderful it is that God has given his word to his people. He is facing real life with its many challenges and difficulties, and the questions and criticisms of those who do not share his desire to serve God. This means that the psalm speaks to us in our situations as we face the challenges, problems and perplexities of life today.

119:1-32 God's Law Instructs Us

Psalm 119 begins with the words, *Blessed are they ... who walk according to the law of the Lord* (**119:1**), taking us step-by-step in the journey through life as God intends. The Hebrew word for 'walk' is *halak,* and the Hebrew people took that word and used it when they spoke of *halakah* as the life that was lived walking in God's ways, or 'according to the law of the Lord'.

The word here translated 'law' is used twenty-five times in this psalm. It is the Hebrew word *Torah,* which to the Jewish people came to mean the law of Moses, that is, the first five books of the Bible, which include many laws. We may get the impression that God requires us to obey a great number of commandments and regulations. This belief brings with it the danger of legalism, in which there is a greater concern for the letter of the law than for its spirit and purpose. This attitude was often criticized by Jesus (Matt 23:23).

The original meaning of *Torah,* however, was 'instruction' or 'teaching'. This is how the word is translated in

Psalm 78:1, 'O my people, hear my teaching; listen to the words of my mouth', and Proverbs 1:8, 'Listen, my son, to your father's instruction and do not forsake your mother's teaching.' So what the psalm speaks of is the fact that God has given us teaching. He has instructed us by his word, so we have guidelines for our lives. We have the way of true blessedness (119:1-2), the way to keep our lives *pure* (**119:9**), so that we will *not be put to shame* (**119:6**).

Because God has given this instruction, the psalmist repeatedly expressed his determination to learn from what God has given. *I will praise you with an upright heart, as I learn your righteous laws* (**119:7**). 'Heart' is another word that recurs frequently in this psalm (see, for example, **119:2, 10, 11, 30**). The authors of the Bible thought of the heart as the central place that directed one's emotions, thoughts and actions (see Prov 4:23; Matt 12:34). That was why it was so important that God's word should have a central place in one's heart (119:11). Jesus provided a clear example of how knowing God's word and having it in our hearts can help us to avoid sinning when we face temptations (Matt 4:1-11).

But our hearts are easily distracted, so the psalmist prays, *Turn my heart toward your statutes, and not toward selfish gain* (119:36). If we are to truly benefit from God's instructions that will guide our lives and be a light on our path, we need to ask God to teach them to us. This prayer is repeated many times in the psalm. In this part of the psalm, we have *teach me your decrees* (**119:12, 26**), *graciously teach me your law* (**119:29** NRSV), *let me understand the teaching of your precepts* (**119:27**), and the prayer that countless people have used in reading the Scriptures, *Open my eyes, that I may see wonderful things in your law* (**119:18**). That last prayer makes us realize that we need to have a sincere desire to understand God's ways and that we need to depend on him in order to understand his word. The desire to understand and the desire to obey God must go together (see especially 119:100).

The image of turning our hearts (119:36) also reminds us that God's law is described as his *ways* (**119:3**), that is, the path we are to follow and that we must pray not to stray from it (119:10). His way is a *way of truth* (119:30) and a way of *life* (119:37) and we are to walk, and even run, in it with enthusiasm (**119:32**, 35). We should follow the example given in 119:59, *I have considered my ways and have turned my steps to your statutes.*

The NT also has much to say about 'walking' in the ways of God (Rom 6:4; 8:4; 2 Cor 5:7; Eph 4:1; 5:2, 8; Col 1:10; 2:6; 4:5). In all of these passages a word meaning 'walk' is used, although sometimes it is translated in different ways that also express the meaning that this is how one lives one's life. The NT also gives us guidance about how we should be 'running' the race of life (1 Cor 9:24-26; Heb 12:1-2).

119:33-72 God's Decrees Are Precious

In this psalm, God's law and teaching are also often described as his *decrees* (see, for example, **119:33**). The Hebrew word translated in this way is closely related to words that mean 'witness' or 'testimony'. The Ten Commandments, which were the human side of God's covenant or agreement with Israel, were written on two stone tablets called the 'tablets of Testimony'.

The reference to the Ten Commandments reminds us that God's law is also referred to twenty-two times as his 'commands'. A command is an order from God, but because God is loving and wise, always wanting the best for his people, his commands are never hard or unreasonable, keeping from us what is good and enjoyable. The psalmist knew that God's way is the way of freedom. In **119:45** he says, *I will walk about in freedom, for I have sought out your precepts.* James makes the same point when he speaks of 'the law that gives freedom' (Jas 1:25; 2:12).

Another word that is used for God's expressed will is translated in the NIV as his 'laws' and in the NRSV as his 'ordinances' (see, for example, 119:43). The focus of this is 'law as judgments'. The laws are seen as representing the decisions of the just Judge. So what they give us are statements of truth and justice.

Because the psalmist sees the decrees, commands and judgments of the Lord as true and just, he values them highly. He speaks of seeking them (119:45) and of treasuring them (119:72). *How I long for your precepts,* he says (**119:40**), *my heart aches with longing; I want to know your judgment at all times* (119:20 GNB). Given his love for them, it is not surprising that *your decrees are the theme of my song* (**119:54**). The psalmist knew that God's word mattered more than anything else for the future as well as for the present, and so he spoke of his hope being placed in God's law (**119:43, 48**; see also 119:147). He even interprets the ancient priestly blessing of Numbers 6:24-26 in terms of God's decrees when he asks, *Make your face shine upon your servant and teach me your decrees* (119:135).

This certainty of the value of God's decrees helps us to speak boldly about God's statutes (**119:46**). The Bible contains many examples of people who were not ashamed to bear witness to the truth before rulers, even though they risked their lives in doing so (Dan 3; 6; Acts 4; 24; 26). It is the Holy Spirit who gives us the courage we need to witness to Christ by words and by deeds (Acts 1:8).

This psalm also contains many prayers for God's grace, a concept that we associate more with the NT, but which OT writers were very aware of too. Praying for grace means that we come to God as needy people, not deserving to receive anything from him, but confessing our need of help and strength to live in God's ways, obeying his word. Thus we find the plea, *I have sought your face with all my heart; be gracious to me according to your promise* (**119:58**; see also

119:124). In 119:97, the prayer is *Let your compassion come to me, that I may live* because our life itself depends on the loving care of God. That is why God's law is better than all the money in the world (**119:72**; see also Luke 12:13-34; 1 Tim 6:6-10, 17-19).

119:73-104 God's Precepts Guide Us

In this section of the psalm, the writer mentions many difficulties that he is facing, and how he is facing them. In these circumstances, he often turns to God's *precepts* (**119:78**). This word is used twenty-one times in the psalm. It refers to the idea of something that is appointed or laid down to guide a person's life. What God directs in his word is what is best for us, individually, in our families, and in our society. God is concerned that all the details of our lives should please him, and thus also be for our greatest good.

This thought leads to prayer for determination and faithfulness in obeying God. In this part of the psalm, we have prayers such as **119:80**, *May my heart be blameless toward your decrees, that I may not be put to shame.* The psalmist has to face the opposition of proud and arrogant people persecuting him (**119:84-87**; see also 119:121-122), and he prays that the Lord will spare his life (**119:88**). But, whatever the opposition or discouragement he faces, he is determined to keep seeking to follow God's *precepts* (**119:94**) and to *obey* them (**119:100b**).

The psalmist wants to be an example, a person to whom others can turn and be encouraged to go on in the ways of God (**119:79**). He can do this across the generations, for the principles of God's law stand unchanging, able to be applied to one generation after another, and to every race and culture. The psalmist can say, *Your word, O Lord, is eternal. Your faithfulness continues through all generations* (**119:89-90**). *All your words are true; all your righteous laws are eternal* (119:160). *Your statutes are for ever right* (119:144). The GNB brings out the meaning of **119:96** clearly, *I have learned that everything has limits; but your commandment is perfect.*

The psalmist realizes that there is greater wisdom to be found in God's instruction than in the wisest men and women who might be his teachers (**119:98-100**). *I gain understanding from your precepts* (**119:104**) he says; *your word is a lamp to my feet and a light to my path* (119:105). This means that step-by-step as we travel through life, we can have the guidance of God's word.

It is not that the psalmist has confidence in himself. In fact, he describes himself as being *like a wineskin in the smoke* (**119:83**). Skins of animals were used for holding wine. An old skin would be dry and shrivelled up, and blackened by the smoke in a house. The simile paints a picture of what trial and opposition may outwardly do to a person, but in spite of this the psalmist said that he would not forget God's law.

119:105-144 God's Statutes Endure

Twenty-three times in this psalm, God's law is referred to as his 'statutes'. The word translated 'statutes' originally related to something that was engraved or inscribed in stone, so it has the idea of something unchangeable. God himself is unchanging and so his purpose for us does not change. Again this does not speak of something harsh. Keeping within God's good plan for our lives should not be seen as a burden to bear but as a comfort and joy (119:52). Thus the CEV translated **119:111** as saying that God's statutes *will always be my most prized possession and my source of joy.* The psalmist can simply say, *I love your statutes* (**119:119**). The strength of this love is also apparent in 119:31, where he says *I hold fast* [or cling] *to your statutes, O Lord.* In saying this, he is obeying the command in Deuteronomy 13:4, where the people were told, 'It is the Lord your God you must follow, and him you must revere. Keep his commands and obey him; serve him and hold fast to him.'

Two different Hebrew words are used in the psalm for 'keeping' God's law. The one is translated 'keep' (as in 119:2), and the other as 'obey' (as in 119:8) or 'live according to' (as in 119:9). Together, these two words are used more than thirty times. When the OT speaks of the law of God being given through Moses, the people are told repeatedly to 'keep it' or 'observe it'. 'Observe the commands of the Lord your God, walking in his ways and revering him' is what Deuteronomy 8:6 says, and this was the psalmist's determination. In **119:112** he puts it as, *My heart is set on keeping your decrees to the very end.*

He was also determined that he would not 'forget' or 'neglect' God's word (**119:109, 141**; see also 119:16, 55, 61, 83, 93, 153, 176). When we read what is said in this psalm about 'remembering' and not 'forgetting' God's word, we need to realize that the words mean more than just keeping it in mind (see, for example, Deut 6:12; 8:11, 18; Eccl 12:1).

With such a determination to keep God's commandments and cling to his way, we can understand that the psalmist often felt the need to pray for God's help and strength to do as he had resolved. *Sustain me according to your promise, Uphold me, and I shall be delivered; I shall always have regard for your decrees* he asks (**119:116-117**). *Direct my footsteps ... let no sin rule over me* (**119:133**). *Strengthen me according to your word* (119:28).

119:145-176 God's Word Speaks to Us

The simplest and the most important way of all to think of God's law and commandments is that it is God's *word* (**119:169, 172**). This is how Jesus referred to it when resisting temptation (Matt 4:4, quoting Deut 8:3). Sometimes this psalm uses the word 'word' but at other times it speaks of statutes and laws as coming from 'your mouth'

THE BIBLE

The Bible, the best-selling book in the world, derives its name from the Greek *biblion*, which denotes any kind of written document, but originally one written on papyrus. The invention of writing made it possible for the word of God to be passed on accurately. It could be written on clay or stone tablets, on parchment, which is made from animal skins, as well as on papyrus, which is made from reeds. The earliest Christian use of *ta biblia* ('the books') with reference to the holy books of the Christian church dates to about AD 150. However, Daniel, writing during the sixth century BC, used the same term to refer to the OT prophetic writings (Dan 9:2).

Book of Books

The Bible comprises sixty-six books, divided between the Old Testament and the New Testament.

The thirty-nine books of the OT are arranged in four groups: 1) the Pentateuch (Genesis to Deuteronomy); 2) the Historical Books (Joshua to Esther); 3) the Wisdom Literature and Poetry Books (Job to Song of Songs); and 4) the Major and Minor Prophets (Isaiah to Malachi). This arrangement does not reflect the order in which the books were written, for Job is probably the oldest book and Malachi the most recent one. The Hebrew (Jewish) Bible includes the same books but arranges them slightly differently as the Law (or Torah), the Prophets, and the Writings.

The twenty-seven books of the NT are divided into 1) the Gospels, 2) the Acts of the Apostles, 3) the Letters or Epistles and 4) the book of Revelation. Paul's letters were probably the first of these books to be written (from about AD 48) and the last was the book of Revelation, written in about AD 100. The entire NT deals with God's revelation in his Son, Jesus Christ.

The OT records God's covenant with Israel, by which he became their God and took them as his people. The Israelites repeatedly failed to keep this covenant and so a new covenant was promised (Jer 31:31-34). Jesus instituted this new covenant, which completes and supersedes the old one (Matt 26:26-29; Mark 14:22-25; Luke 22:14-20; I Cor 11:23-26; Heb 7–10). Christians included the OT in their Bible because it was used by Jesus Christ and his apostles and because it records God's revelation to the people of Israel through his acts and the prophecies that point towards Jesus Christ. In speaking of the unity of the Bible, it is commonly said that the OT is the NT concealed, while the NT is the OT revealed.

The overall purpose of the Bible is to bring people to salvation through the knowledge of God and of his Son, Jesus Christ (John 20:30-31). It is a unique book in that it was written over a period of sixteen hundred years (from 1500 BC to AD 100), written by both God and humans (2 Pet 1:21), written on three different continents (Asia, Africa and Europe), and by people with very different professions – Paul and Moses were philosophers, Peter was a fisherman, Amos a farmer, and David a shepherd. Amazingly, despite all this diversity in its origins, the Bible contains no contradictions.

Authoritative Book

People sometimes ask how these particular books were chosen for inclusion in the Bible. It is difficult to tell precisely how the OT canon was formed. The first five books of the OT were the first to be recognized as having divine authority, and these were the only books recognized by the Samaritans. Most of the books referred to as the Writings (that is, the Historical and Wisdom books) were recognized as authoritative before the exile to Babylon. Large portions of the Prophetic books were written during and after the Babylonian captivity. Some scholars have suggested that Ezra, the priest who returned from exile about 458 BC, compiled the first Hebrew canon. By 280 BC, when the OT was first translated into Greek, the Hebrew canon had already been fixed.

Many other books were produced between the time that the OT canon was closed and the beginning of the NT. Some of these books came to be known as the Apocrypha. They were never included in the OT canon.

In the NT era, different church groups initially had different lists of authoritative books. In particular, there was disagreement about the status of the OT books of the Song of Solomon, Ecclesiastes, Esther, Ezekiel and Proverbs and about the NT books of Hebrews, James, 2 and 3 John, Jude and Revelation. The first criterion for determining whether a book was authoritative was authorship: the book had to have been written by a true prophet of God, or by one of the apostles or their immediate disciples. It was also important that the book was accepted by the majority of churches and that the church fathers, the first followers of the apostles, had shown that they approved of it by quoting it. And it was important that the teaching of the book did not contradict that of other books that were already recognized as authoritative, and that the book inspired, convicted and edified churches and individuals. Using these criteria, the Third Council of Carthage in North Africa recognized the twenty-seven books of the NT as canonical in AD 397.

The OT was written mainly in Hebrew. However, with the Babylonian exile, Aramaic became the dominant language and certain passages in Ezra, Jeremiah and Daniel were written in this language. The entire NT was written in Greek, which was the universal language of the Roman Empire, as English and French are universal languages in much of Africa. Over the centuries, it became necessary to translate the Bible into other languages so that different peoples could understand it. The first translation that we know of is the Septuagint, a translation of the Hebrew OT into Greek by seventy Jewish scholars in Alexandria, Egypt in 280 BC. In the fourth century AD, the Bible was translated into Latin and into the African languages of Coptic and Geez. Since then, the Bible has also been translated into English and into more than eight hundred and fifty African languages. The work of translation continues.

Life-Changing Book

The Bible makes the following claims for itself: God's word is permanent and eternal (Isa 40:8; Matt 24:35); it is inspired by God himself for our training and equipping (2 Tim 3:16-17; Heb 5:13-14; 1 Pet 1:22-23); it is truth (Ps 119:151, 160; John 17:17; Eph 1:13; 2 Tim 2:15; Jas 1:18); it is a powerful spiritual force (Jer 23:29; Matt 4:4-10; Eph 6:11-17; Heb 4:12); it cleanses our ways (Ps 119:9; John 15:3; John 17:17; 1 Pet 1:22); it is a source of grace that builds up (Acts 20:32; Rom 15:4); it is a testimony to its own sufficiency (Deut 4:2; 1 Cor 1:18; 10:6, 11; Gal 1:8, 9; 2 Pet 1:3-4); it always accomplishes God's purpose (Isa 55:11; Rom 10:17; 1 Thess 2:13); it is the standard for judgment (John 5:24; 8:47, 51; 12:48; Heb 4:12); it dwells within us (Ps 1:2; 37:31; 119:11, 15, 23, 48, 97; Col 3:16); it is to be obeyed and not merely heard (Matt 7:24-27; Luke 11:28; John 13:17; Jas 1:22, 24); it is as vital to our health as food (Deut 8:3; Ps 19:10; Matt 4:; 1 Pet 2:2); and it is a light to guide our way (Pss 19:7; 119:9, 99, 104, 105, 130, 165; Prov 6:23; 2 Pet 1:19).

When reading the Bible, it is important to remember that it is not a merely human book but is God's revelation of himself through the record of what he has said and done. He supervised its growth, development and completion, and thus the Bible is authoritative, reliable and truthful. The human authors' choice of words, objects, dates, names, places, images, materials, documents, and so on was guided by the Holy Spirit (2 Tim 3:16). This means that the words of the Bible are actually God's own words and the final written document is inspired in its entirety. As the authoritative word of God, the Bible is to be the sole authority for what we believe and how we act, governing how we live and the way we respond to events around us. The majority of African Christians agree with this statement and regard the Bible as the word of God.

Yusufu Turaki

(119:72, 88). Or it speaks of God's 'promise' (see, for example, **119:148, 154, 170**). These expressions that refer to God speaking are used more than forty times in the psalm. This is important because they indicate that God in his love and concern for us speaks to us, and he gives us the ability, if we are willing, to hear his word. God's word, as we have it in Psalms and in all Scripture, tells us what God has done in the past. It gives us the assurance of his presence with us now. It also gives us a guarantee about the future, and so it is often spoken of as his promises.

To the person who believes that the living God, our Creator, has spoken to us, nothing in all the world could be more wonderful or more precious than his word. The psalmist was such a person. He said *Oh, how I love your law! I meditate on it all day long* (119:97). Ten times in the psalm he speaks of that 'love' (see **119:159, 163, 165** and **167** in just this last part of the psalm). Six times he speaks of 'meditating' on God's word. Whether it was night or day, he wanted God's law to be in his thoughts and so to direct his life (see also Ps 1:1-3; Josh 1:6-9). He speaks of his great joy in it, *I rejoice in your promise like one who finds great spoil* (**119:162**; compare 119:14, 111). *Your law is my delight* he says (**119:174**).

At the same time, the psalmist was aware that what was heard was the word of a holy God, calling for his people to live in truth and justice, so he spoke of an attitude of reverence, expressed in words like *my heart trembles at your word* (**119:161**).

This reverence is due to God because he is the giver of life. Many of the prayers in this psalm ask for wisdom, help, strength and determination to walk in God's ways. But there are also many petitions where the psalmist looks to God as the source and giver of life itself. God alone can sustain his life in the face of all the forces of evil that are against him.

Hear my voice in accordance with your love he says, *preserve my life, O Lord, according to your laws* (**119:149**). He wants to continue living so that he can praise God (**119:175**). But he realizes that true life is not just physical life, but life rightly related to God, continuing in his ways. So the psalmist prays, *preserve my life according to your word* (119:37), *Preserve my life in your righteousness* (119:40), and *let your compassion come to me that I may live* (119:77).

As we have been reading this psalm, we may have found ourselves thinking that the psalmist is boasting that he has always kept God's law faithfully. However, we should read **119:153**, *I have not forgotten your law,* and **119:157**, *I have not turned from your statutes* as expressions of his desire and determination rather than of what he actually achieved. This is shown by the way that he says *Before I was afflicted I went astray* (119:67), and *It was good for me to be afflicted, so that I might learn your decrees* (119:71). The last verse puts these two aspects together as the psalmist confesses, *I have strayed like a lost sheep; seek your servant.* Then he speaks of his sincere resolve, *For I have not forgotten your commands* (**119:176**).

Psalm 120: Seeking Peace and Finding Strife

Psalm 120, like all the psalms from 120 to 134, has the heading, *A song of ascents.* Of all the possible explanations of this heading, the most likely one is that these psalms came to be sung as the people 'went up' to Jerusalem for the great annual festivals. This 'going up' or 'ascent' to Jerusalem (which stood high above sea level) is referred to in such passages as Matthew 20:17 (see also Pss 24:3; 122:4). A Hebrew word, *aliyah*, which is similar to the Hebrew for 'ascents', is used today for Jewish people returning to the land of Israel.

Not all of these songs of ascent were originally to be sung in these circumstances. In Psalm 120, as in many others, we hear the cry of a person who was in great distress because of what people were doing to him. It is one of the hardest experiences in life to want to live in peace, indeed to be a 'peacemaker', and to find nothing but hostility and opposition from other people. This was supremely true of our Lord Jesus Christ himself, and it is the situation that many Christians have faced and are facing today.

120:1-3 Hostile Words

In his distress, the psalmist prays, *Save me, O Lord, from lying lips and from deceitful tongues* (**120:1-2**). He is well aware of the harm that can be done by words. Psalms (see 57:4; 64:2-4), like the book of Proverbs (see Prov 25:18; 26:18) often refers to words as being like 'spears', 'swords' or 'arrows', the weapons that were most feared in those days. Words can utter curses, and the power of a curse was greatly feared, as it often still is. Words can also be 'deceitful', as when politicians mislead the people or when advertisers or other people tempt us to adopt a non-Christian lifestyle. Words are also often used to utter unkind and unjust criticisms.

The expression in **120:3**, *What will he* [that is, God] *do to you? And what more besides?* is derived from the common expression in OT days, 'May God deal with you, be it ever so severely' (see 1 Sam 3:17; 2 Sam 3:9). The psalmist is praying that God will bring a just judgment on those who were hostile to him.

120:4 The Saving Justice of God

The psalmist is sure of God's judgment. Those whose words have been like arrows injuring other people will find God's *sharp arrows* (**120:4a**) reaching them. Those whose attacks on peaceful people have been like throwing coals of fire on them will find that God's judgment is like the *burning coals of the broom tree* (**120:4b**; compare Pss 7:12-13; 140:10). He specifies the type of tree because the *broom tree* or juniper was used to produce charcoal that burns with a very strong heat.

As we have often found in Psalms, there is an emphasis on the fact that God is just and those who oppress others will come under his judgment. Yet knowing the way of Christ, we today must not pray for God's judgment, but rather that oppressors will turn from their evil ways.

120:5-7 Hostile Actions

The psalmist faced hostile actions as well as hostile words. His reference to *Meshech* and *Kedar* indicates that he felt like an alien in his own land (**120:5**). The people of Meshech lived in an area south-west of what today is Russia, and they had a reputation for hostility and slave-trading (see Ezek 27:13; 32:26). The people of Kedar were an Arab

tribe living to the south of Israel who were also noted as warriors (Isa 21:16-17). The GNB translation captures the meaning well: *living among you is as bad as living in Meshech or among the people of Kedar*.

The psalmist was confronting people who brought strife to him when all he wanted was peace (**120:6-7**). We may often be in a situation like that of the psalmist. We are called by Christ to be 'peacemakers' (Matt 5:9) and are told, 'If it is possible, as far as it depends on you, live at peace with everyone' (Rom 12:18). Yet we often face hostility. Though we know in Christ the way of peace, peace with God and inner peace, we may face strife in the world, perhaps even opposition to our Christian faith from family or close friends (see Matt 10:34-39). Jesus said, 'Peace I leave with you; my peace I give to you.' But he added, 'I do not give to you as the world gives' (John 14:27).

Psalm 121: 'The Lord Watches over You'

This is another *song of ascents* (see Ps 120). We have no knowledge of who wrote this psalm or how it was first used. In ancient times it was probably used by pilgrims going to Jerusalem for the great festivals or recited by people as they went on dangerous journeys. We can imagine a father saying these words to his son as he went away from home, or a mother saying them to her daughter as she was married and left to establish a new home. People still use it on such occasions. David Livingstone used these words as he said goodbye to his father and set out for Africa. James Hannington, Uganda's martyr bishop, used these words every day as he travelled. There is great comfort in the assurance, offered five times in this psalm, that God *watches over* those who rely on him.

121:1-2 In Every Place

What do the opening words of the psalm mean, *I lift up my eyes to the hills* (**121:1a**)? Sometimes in the OT the hills were seen as the place of the idolatrous worship of the Baals, and those who served the Lord knew that no help came from there (see Jer 3:23). Other people looked at the hills, especially the much-loved hills of Jerusalem, and thought of the God who made them. Still others must have looked at the hills and thought of the dangerous journey that lay ahead. But if there were many different responses to looking at the hills, there was only one possible answer to the question, *where does my help come from?* (**121:1b**). Help comes from the one who is the Creator of heaven and earth and of everything in them (**121:2**). He is present in every place to which we could ever go. As 139:9-10 puts it, 'If I rise on the wings of the dawn, if I settle on the far side of the sea, even there your hand will guide me, your right hand will hold me fast.'

121:3-6 At Every Time

There is no time, day or night, when God fails to watch over us. The living God whom we worship never slumbers (**121:3-4**). The nature gods, like the Baals, might be thought to be asleep till the right season came for their activity (see 1 Kgs 18:27). Sometimes people, praying wrongly, thought that the Lord was asleep and had to be roused to answer their prayers (see 7:6; 35:22-25; 44:23-26). We may not always understand God's ways, and why he does not intervene when we think he should, but we can be quite sure that he never goes to sleep. The Lord is always at our *right hand* (see also 16:8; 109:31). He provides *shade* that will protect us both by day and by night (**121:5-6**; see also 36:7; 91:1; Lam 4:20). Travellers in Palestine faced physical danger from the sun on the hottest days, and many feared that the moon was a source of evil influences at night. English is not the only language in which the word for madness (lunacy) is linked with the word for 'moon' (Latin – *luna*).

121:7-8 In All Circumstances

God is able to protect us from all dangers, whether real or imagined. This does not mean that we will be kept from all trial and difficulty and suffering. But we will be kept *from all harm* (**121:7**) in the sense that if we trust in the Lord we will not be overcome by the forces of evil or by the most difficult circumstances. Whatever we face, in all our comings and goings in life, we can trust God to guard and protect us. We who through Jesus Christ know victory over death and the hope of heaven can say with deeper meaning than the psalmist that God will keep us *both now and for evermore* (**121:8**; see also Jude 24-25). As 2 Timothy 4:18 puts it, 'the Lord will rescue me from every evil attack and will bring me safely to his heavenly Kingdom'.

If we want to see how this works out in practice, we can look at OT characters like Jacob (especially the record of his life in Genesis 28–33). Or we can look at a NT character like Paul (see especially Acts 19–28) and consider how in the midst of trial and danger they knew the presence and keeping power of God.

Psalm 122: The Peace of Jerusalem

Psalm 122 is another *song of ascents* (see Ps 120) and is associated with *David*. It expresses the feelings of pilgrims going up to Jerusalem. Just as Muslims today go to Mecca, so the tribes of Israel had to go up to Jerusalem for the three great annual festivals (see Exod 23:14-17; 16:16-17). The psalm shows us why it meant so much to the people.

Although we as Christians are not called to make such pilgrimages, we too are commanded to make worship a priority in our lives, for there are commands about worship addressed to us (1 Cor 11:23-26; Heb 10:24-25).

122: 1-5 Rejoice in Jerusalem

We can appreciate the joy felt by those who loved the Lord when the time came to *go to the house of the Lord* (**122:1**), and then the excitement of reaching their destination and saying, *Our feet are standing in your gates, O Jerusalem* (**122:2**).

Four things made Jerusalem very special to all Jewish people. First, it was a beautiful city. The psalmist describes it as *closely compacted together* (**122:3**), meaning either that its fine walls and buildings were very different from the villages and small towns the pilgrims came from, or that it was the place *where people come together in unity* (122:4 – NEB). Second, it was the greatest place of worship for the people of the nation. They referred to it as *the house of the Lord* (122:1, 9), the place where they came, above all, to meet with their Lord, and *to praise the name of the Lord* (**122:4**). Third, it was the place where justice was to be upheld; where *the thrones for judgment stand* (**122:5a**). The political leadership in Israel was responsible for upholding justice in the land (2 Sam 8:15; 1 Kgs 3:28, Ps 72:1-4, 12-14; Isa 16:5; Jer 21:11-12). Finally, it was the place of *the thrones of the house of David* (**122:5b**). There David had reigned and God's promises were made to those who followed him as king (2 Sam 7:12-16).

122:6-9 Pray for Jerusalem

Because Jerusalem meant all these things to the people, it was right that they should pray for the peace and true welfare of the city and of the land of which it was the capital (**122:6-7**). The psalmist said that he would make this prayer for the sake of his *brothers and friends* (all his people), and *for the sake of the house of the Lord* (**122:8-9**).

Jerusalem is still a great city, important to Jews, Muslims and Christians alike. We should pray for the peace of Jerusalem as it affects all the countries of the Middle East and beyond.

When we read this psalm, we think first of the situation for which it was originally written. However, we can also apply it to our situations and pray for our own 'Jerusalems'. We should pray for our own countries and for their capital cities. If we are far from our own home country, we should pray for the country in which we are living (see Jer 29:7). We can thank God for all that is good in the life of our own country and its cities, and pray that true worship of God may flourish there. We should also pray for wise leadership given by men and women of integrity, who will rule in justice and peace.

When we read psalms that celebrate the city and temple of Jerusalem, we can also think of the way that the Christian church is like the temple of God and the city of God (see 2 Cor 6:16-18; Eph 2:19-22). So we should pray that we, as God's people, will offer him true worship, have good leadership that upholds truth and justice, and so will show the world the way of peace, unity and loving fellowship.

Let this psalm lead you to pray for Jerusalem today, and for the countries of the Middle East, for your own country, and for the whole Christian church.

Psalm 123: Eyes Turned to God

Psalm 123 is another *song of ascents* (see Ps 120).

There are times when people who seek to love and serve God find themselves surrounded by those who look on them with *contempt*. That word is used twice in this psalm (123:3, 4). It is the attitude of the *arrogant* that makes people feel that they are not worth even considering as human beings. The Jewish people in OT days often felt that they were being treated with contempt (Isa 36–37, Lam 3; Neh 2:17-20; 4:1-23). Christians too have often felt like that, and still do in many situations.

There is only one thing to do when others despise us, and that is to turn to God with the prayer, *Have mercy on us, O Lord* (123:3). So the psalm begins with prayer to God as the only one who can help. *I lift up my eyes to you* (123:1a), says the psalmist to the Lord. God surely can help because his *throne is in heaven* (123:1b), and so he is Lord over all creation.

The psalmist describes the way that we look to God as being similar to the way a servant, or slave, looks up to his or her master or mistress (123:2). What does this image mean? We hate the thought of slavery, and thank God that it has been abolished from most countries of the world. So why should our attitude to God be like that of a slave?

The Bible often describes our relationship with God in terms of human relationships – parent to child, husband to wife, master to servant. But we know that all these pictures are imperfect. When we speak of God as our Father, as the husband of his church, as the Master of us all, we know that he is infinitely greater than any human father or husband or master. He is supreme and perfect in goodness and love, wisdom and power and holiness. Because of this, we can confidently *look to the Lord our God, till he shows us his mercy* (123:2).

We are not like slaves serving a sinful master, with no freedom and no opportunity to change our position and our lot in life. Our attitude to God is not one of subservience but of reverence as we realize his greatness and holiness. We look to God as the One who is able to help us, the One who loves and cares for us as his own, as those who belong to him (see also 141:8). The Apostle Paul was fully aware of this, for he spoke of himself as the 'servant' (literally the 'slave') of Jesus Christ (Rom 1:1), yet he preached and experienced true freedom in Christ (see Gal 5:1, 13; Rom 6:15-23).

Psalm 124: If Not for God – Disaster

Psalm 124 is another *song of ascents* (see Ps 120), and another psalm that is associated with *David*. Its words speak to all who have trusted God in times of difficulty and danger when there seems no human hope of escape from overwhelming troubles. This psalm is written from a national perspective, but the thoughts can also be applied to our individual lives (see also 94:16-22).

124:1-5 Through Many Dangers

The psalm starts by contemplating the disasters that would have happened, *if the Lord had not been on our side* (124:1a, 2). It repeats this phrase twice to emphasize the reality of the danger the nation faced. *Let Israel say* (124:1b) calls on the people to join the psalmist in acknowledging what God has done for them.

We can see part of his deliverance of the Israelites in their history, as recorded in the OT. For example, there was a time when Jacob (Israel) the great ancestor of the people, used very similar words: 'If the God of my father, the God of Abraham and the Fear of Isaac, had not been with me' (Gen 31:42). If God had not been with him to help him, he would have been in great trouble. So it was for all Israel, because they – but for God's help – would have been kept as slaves in Egypt. They would have been conquered by the Canaanites when they came into the land of Palestine and by the Philistines in the time of David, and would have been wiped out as a nation by the Assyrians and the Babylonians. Because of the Lord's help, though they had not deserved it, they had continued to survive.

The psalm uses vivid images to describe the dangers that threatened the people. The anger of their enemies is described as having *flared* (124:3) like a fire that consumes everything. They were in danger of being *swallowed ... alive* as by an earthquake (Num 16:31-34) or a great monster. Proverbs 1:11-12 speaks of people being overwhelmed by the wicked just as death swallows people up. Their danger was also like that faced when one is in a valley that is dry because there was no rain, but which suddenly fills with a *torrent* of rushing water (124:4; see Judg 5:21; Matt 7:24-27). The same image was used in 69:1, when the psalmist prayed, 'Save me, O God, for the waters have come up to my neck'.

In our place and times we might use other pictures to describe the pressure upon us, but the dangers and threatened disasters that the psalm describes are clear.

124:6-8 Sing God's Praise

In all the dangers faced, the psalmist could say that the Lord had been at hand to help. He cries out, *Praise be to the Lord, who has not let us be torn by their teeth* (124:6). The image this time is of being attacked and eaten by wild animals (see also 7:2 and 22:13). He changes the image yet again, and refers to the people as having been as helpless as a bird caught in a snare or net set by a fowler, but thanks God that the snare was broken and they escaped (**124:7**).

The Lord was able to deliver his people because he is none other than *the Maker of heaven and earth* (**124:8**), and thus Lord over all. So the words of Psalm 121:2 are echoed, 'My help comes from the Lord, the Maker of heaven and earth'. We as NT believers can enjoy the even greater assurance of God's protection given in the words of Romans 8:31-39: 'If God is for us, who can be against us? He who did not spare his own Son, but gave him up for us all – how will he not also, along with him, graciously give us all things?'

Psalm 125: The Source of Security

Psalm 125, another *song of ascents* (see Ps 120), begins with a statement of the security and confidence of those who trust in the Lord, continues with a promise of God's keeping power, and ends with a prayer for God's justice to be shown. It can be read in conjunction with Psalms 16:8; 37:5-7; 46:1-3; 63:6-8 and 112:6-8 which also speak of our finding security through trust in God.

125:1-2 Security

Some of us live near mountains, and perhaps we think of them as solid and unchanging. If we live by the sea we may think of the ocean as powerful and unchanging. The people of Jerusalem, and those who went there on pilgrimage, thought like that of the city and especially the hill of the temple, Mount Zion. Because they saw it as strong and unchanging, and because the temple was the place where they felt the presence of God as they went to worship there, they could say, *those who trust in the Lord are like Mount Zion, which cannot be shaken but endures for ever* (**125:1**; see also 1 Cor 15:58). Jerusalem was surrounded by even higher hills, and so they said, *As the mountains surround Jerusalem, so the Lord surrounds his people* (**125:2**). Trust in God gives a security that nothing else can, whatever storms and difficulties life brings.

125:3 Promise

The people of Israel certainly knew God's presence and help in the many ups and downs of their history. They had been slaves in Egypt, and God had set them free and *allotted* them the land of Palestine (**125:3b**). Sometimes they turned away from God and without his help they were defeated by their enemies. Yet they believed that if they turned back to him they would find protection. They were *the righteous* (**125:3c**) in the way that they were called to live, and if they sought to live righteously they could count on God's protection, and their land would not be taken by enemies.

The sceptre of the wicked (**125:3a**) probably means the rule of foreigners over them (the 'sceptre' is the symbol of rule and kingship). God kept unjust and ungodly rulers from ruling his people because *if they did, the righteous themselves might do evil* (125:3c GNB). God would not allow his people to be tempted beyond their strength to resist. These words remind us of the promise of 1 Corinthians 10:13, 'God is faithful; he will not let you be tempted beyond what you can bear. But when you are tempted, he will also provide a way out so that you can stand up under it.'

125:4-5 Prayer

God's people can have the confidence that if they seek to be *good* and *upright in heart* (**125:4**), then they will prove the goodness of God in their lives. They can pray also that God in his own time and way will bring evil to an end and frustrate *those who turn to crooked ways* (**125:5**). The prayer for peace upon Israel (125:5) is a prayer that justice and righteousness will flourish in Israel, so people will live in right relationships one with another. That brings true wellbeing to a nation. This is the real meaning of the Hebrew word *shalom* translated as 'peace'. We should bear in mind this meaning of the word 'peace' when we read the prayers for peace in Romans 1:7, Galatians 6:16 and 2 Peter 1:2.

Psalm 126: Restore Us Again

Psalm 126 is another *song of ascents* (see Ps 120), and like a number of other psalms, begins with thanksgiving for past blessings, and goes on to prayer – and to promise.

126:1-3 Thanksgiving

The people could look back and see what great things God had done for them. Perhaps they thought especially of how they had been rescued from exile in Babylon, *when the Lord brought back the captives to Zion* (**126:1a**). Their hope was almost gone, but then God had wonderfully made it possible for them to go free and return to their own land. We can imagine the feelings that are expressed in the words, *We were like men who dreamed. Our mouths were filled with laughter, our tongues with songs of joy* (**126:1b-2a**). Even the other nations, who had despised their God as powerless to help them, said, *The Lord has done great things for them,* (**126:2b**) and they echoed it, *The Lord has done great things for us* (**126:3**). What great joy that was!

We find other descriptions of the joy of people at being set free from Babylon in Isaiah 44:23; 48:20; 49:13; 51:11 and 55:12. Christians should experience a similar joy when reflecting on the blessing of God's salvation (1 Pet 1:8).

126:4 Prayer

Years had passed since that great deliverance from exile. Times were hard again. Perhaps it was the time of Nehemiah (see Neh 1–6). So the people asked God to act again as he had acted in the past, *Restore our fortunes, O Lord* (**126:4a**). They knew what they wanted – they wanted God's blessings to be *like the streams in the Negev* (**126:4b**). The Negev is the area to the south of Jerusalem, Bethlehem and Hebron. In the dry season, the valleys or watercourses have little or no water in them. Then the rain comes and the water pours down, plants grow, the land becomes green and productive again, and there can be crops to meet the people's needs.

126:5-6 Promise

These verses are a promise from God given by a priest or prophet in God's name. Sowing is always a hard time for farmers. They have to break up the ground, prepare it carefully, and then sow the seed. But harvest follows, and those who have worked patiently on the land *return with songs of joy,* bringing in the crops (**126:6**). That is how it is with farming. That also is how it is in many areas of our lives, such as in our work, bringing up children, preaching the gospel, encouraging fellow-Christians, or whatever our work is for the kingdom of God. First there is a time like that of sowing in tears (**126:5**). But, ultimately, God will bless our labours, although we may not see the results ourselves. Even if it is only in our eternal home, God's people *will return with songs of joy* (126:6) and with praise to God on their lips. Then they will truly understand Jesus' words, 'Blessed are those who mourn, for they will be comforted' (Matt 5:4).

This psalm is not the only place in the Bible where work and witness, including the preaching and teaching of God's word, are compared to sowing and reaping. A similar picture is used in Isaiah 55:10-11, Matthew 13:1-43, John 12:24, 2 Corinthians 9:6-8 and Galatians 6:7-10.

Psalm 127: Without the Lord – 'in Vain'

This is another *song of ascents* (see Ps 120). This one is associated with Solomon. Four of the main human activities are spoken of in this psalm: building, providing security, daily work and family life. All of them depend on God's blessing if they are to be meaningful and successful. Without the Lord, all human effort will in the end be *in vain … in vain … in vain* (127:1-3).

127:1-2 Buildings and Security

We all need homes to live in, and that involves building. Those who are rich spend much time and money building and improving their homes. In our cities there are attempts to erect bigger and better buildings all the time. All over the world, building work goes on, but at the deepest level it is true that *unless the Lord builds the house, its builders labour in vain* (**127:1a**). For our building projects – home and church and nation – let us sincerely ask God's guidance in the use

of our resources and his blessing on the work. Otherwise, as Leviticus 26:20 warns us, 'Your strength shall be spent in vain'.

We are also all concerned about security. In many African countries, violent crime is increasing. But as Psalm 121 reminds us, our truest security is in God. Many nations in the world spend vast amounts on weapons to defend their countries. How much better it would be to use the money to feed the hungry and care for those in need, and to look to God for security, for *unless the Lord watches over the city, the watchmen stand guard in vain* (**127:1b**).

The words about the vanity of working hard in **127:2a** should not be understood as encouraging us to be idle or lazy. We should all do our daily work, and do it as well as we can. What this verse speaks against is anxious toil, or making work our idol. It is possible for a person to *rise early and stay up late* (127:2) in order to do more and more work, whether in business or any other way – and yet to miss God's purpose in living. In God's wisdom and love and goodness, we are given time for work and time to rest and sleep and to find relaxation (see also Matt 6:25-34; 1 Peter 5:7).

It is also possible to translate **127:2b** in the way shown in the footnote in the NIV, *for while they sleep he provides for those he loves.* When we are tempted to be anxious and think that everything depends on what we do, it is good to remind ourselves that God is giving good gifts to us even while we sleep (see, for example, Mark 4:26-28).

127:3-5 Family Life

In family life especially we should seek the blessing of God. Children are indeed a blessing from God. Some couples, especially in Western societies, are saying that they want the joy and companionship of marriage but do not want children. They may find themselves lonely in old age, and they may be very selfish in wanting to avoid the responsibility of a family. (These words should not be taken as a criticism of single people and couples whom God has not blessed with children. The Bible has much to say to such people as well, and promises them other blessings.)

Children are not only a blessing, they are also a responsibility. Those of us who are parents can rejoice in our children when they do well, and, having cared for them as they grew up, we can look forward to their support in our old age. But our greatest desire should be that we faithfully bring them up in the ways of God, so that they will serve the Lord whatever else they do in life. This should be our daily prayer for our families, and for the families of our country. We should also exert ourselves to discover the principles that should guide Christian people in their family life, and as they care for and train their children.

Some people reading **127:3a** may point out that it says *sons are a heritage,* and may deduce that sons are more important than daughters. But the word here translated 'sons' is sometimes used for both sons and daughters, as in the frequently used expression 'the children of Israel' or 'the people of Israel'. And the word *children* in **127:3b** certainly includes both daughters and sons. Both male and female are equally 'in the image of God' (Gen 1:27). Both are equal in their life in Christ (Gal 3:28). We should never think of sons as worth more than daughters nor of daughters as worth more than sons.

In biblical times, men held great power in society. Evil and powerful men might have positions *in the gate,* that is, in the place where justice was administered (**127:5**). Such men might take advantage of an old person. Then it would be a great advantage to have *sons born in one's youth* (**127:4**), now grown up and able to defend a parent in difficulties.

A warrior was well prepared for battle when he had his *quiver* full of good *arrows.* Similarly, parents are well-prepared for the future when they have many children (127:4-5). But should these verses be interpreted to mean that we should have as many children as possible? We need to remember that in the psalmist's times as in Africa today, many children died in early childhood from the ravages of disease, as well as from the effects of war. It was a blessing indeed if parents were able to have a large family. Now many of our countries fear overpopulation, and we also have to think about how many children we can care for, educate and prepare for life. In this we need to ask for the guidance of God. There can be wise 'family planning' when, above all else, we ask the blessing and direction that comes from God himself.

Psalm 128: The Ways of God

This is another of the *song of ascents* (Ps 120). The three parts of this psalm focus in turn on the individual, the family and the nation.

128:1-2 For the Individual

The psalm begins by stating, *Blessed are all who fear the Lord* (**128:1a**). This 'fear' means reverence for God as Lord and Creator of all, holy and just and good. We express that reverence as we *walk in his ways* (**128:1b**), that is, as we move step by step through life following the guidelines of God's word. The godly person will not labour in vain, but will find satisfaction and joy in life. As the psalmist says, *prosperity will be yours* or 'it will go well with you' (**128:2**, NASB).

128:3-4 For the Family

Next we are led to think of the family, the God-given unit of society: husband, wife, children. Vines and olives are often used as symbols of fruitfulness and blessing (see 52:8; 80:8-11). Sitting under vines and fig trees was a picture of peace and plenty (see 1 Kgs 4:25; Mic 4:4; Zech 3:10). The wife is likened to *a fruitful vine* within the house (**128:3**).

She may indeed also have a part to play in public life outside the home, in church and community, but neither wife nor husband should neglect the part that they have in their home, with children growing up and enjoying the fellowship around the table.

The thought of the first verse is repeated in **128:4**. Other passages of Scripture teach that this blessing does not mean freedom from suffering and trial (see, for example, Matt 5:3-10). And some godly men and women may live a single life or not be able to have children. The prosperity of ungodly people and the suffering of those who serve the Lord are often perplexing (but see Pss 37 and 73). Yet at the deepest level there is great blessing in serving the Lord. The apostle Paul had to face great suffering (see 2 Cor 11:23-28), but he would never have wanted to change that life he lived in the service of his Lord. And he proved God's promise, 'My grace is sufficient for you' (2 Cor 12:9), and could say to others, 'my God will meet all your needs according to his glorious riches in Christ Jesus' (Phil 4:19).

128:5-6 For the Nation

Jewish people in OT days were taught not to be only concerned with their individual lives and their families walking in the ways of God. They were also to be concerned for the *prosperity of Jerusalem* (**128:5**), for the worship of the temple there, and the life of their capital city. They were to be concerned that *peace be upon Israel* (**128:6**), and for the life of the generations to come, their children's children. We should think in this way too, and realize how the welfare of individuals, of families and of the state belong together. The strength of any country depends on the strength of its family life and the godly living and concern of its people. Thus we should pray for God's blessing on the family life of our communities and nations.

Psalm 129: 'Afflicted – but Not Crushed'

Psalm 129, another *song of ascents* (see Ps 120), has two parts: first, what God had done for Israel in the past, and then, what God could be expected to do for them in the future.

129:1-4 The Past

All of us can look back to our younger days, and when we do, even if we faced difficulties then, we should think of what God had done for us, helping and protecting us and blessing us with many gifts. Here the thought is of the younger days of the nation of Israel. The prophets spoke of that time as the days when the nation had been a child and a young bride (Hos 2:15; 11:1; Jer 2:2). But life had not been easy for them, as the whole nation could acknowledge (**129:1**). They had been attacked. They had known battles with Egyptians, Amorites, Philistines, Syrians, and later with the powerful empires of Assyria and Babylon. Sometimes they had been like a person flattened to the ground and having a plough drawn over his back, making deep furrows there (**129:3**). It was as if their enemies had said, 'Fall prostrate that we may walk over you, and you made your back like the ground, like a street to be walked over' (Isa 51:23). This picture of the suffering of God's people reminds us of the sufferings the Servant of the Lord endured for the sins of others (Isa 50:5-7; 53:4-5).

Yet in the end Israel's attackers had not prevailed (**129:2**). God's people survived all the attacks, because their faithful God had protected and defended them, as he always will (Matt 16:18; 2 Cor 4:8-10). Israel could remember and acknowledge his goodness, saying, *the Lord is righteous; he has cut me free from the cords of the wicked* (**129:4**).

129:5-8 The Future

This latter part of the psalm can be read as a prayer, and if so it needs to be understood in the same way as other prayers in the psalms for the just judgment of God. Alternatively, it can be understood as a kind of prophetic assurance for the future. The enemies of God's people will not be able to prevail. Zion was the temple hill where Yahweh the Lord God of Israel was worshipped, and those who hated Zion hated the worship and service of the Lord and those involved in it (**129:5a**).

These verses present a vivid picture of what must happen in the end to the wicked. They will not win and be allowed to continue to oppress others, but will *be turned back in shame* (**129:5b**; compare 40:14). They will be like grass growing on the roofs of houses (**129:6**). At that time, houses in Palestine had flat roofs made with wooden beams covered with rushes or branches and then with earth. So grass might grow on the housetop, but there was no depth of soil, and so it would only grow for a short time, and then it would wither in the hot sun and only a few stalks might survive. There would not be enough for a reaper to have a handful to cut or a person to gather as much as a sheaf in her arms (**129:7**; see also 37:1-2; 103:15; Isa 40:6-8; Matt 13:5-6; Jas 1:9-11). What a contrast with the abundant harvest that is promised when a seed falls into good soil and produces much fruit (Matt 13:8, 23).

In the end, no one will greet the wicked with a blessing, or give them the greeting of peace. 'Everyone praises good people, but evil hides behind the words of the wicked. Good people are remembered long after they are gone, but the wicked are soon forgotten' (Prov 10:6-7 – CEV).

Psalm 130: A Cry from the Depths

This is another of the *songs of ascents* (see Ps 120). It is also one of a group of seven psalms (6, 32, 38, 51, 102,

130 and 143) that have been called the church's 'penitential psalms'.

It has been suggested that some psalms originally began as deeply personal prayers, and that endings were added which made them into prayers in which the whole community could join. This may be the case with this psalm. But it may also be true, as we have suggested, that the psalmist, knowing first what it meant to find God's grace and forgiveness for himself, wanted to encourage all his people to experience the same joy. Christian people have always felt that this psalm beautifully expresses how we should turn to God in repentance, trust him to forgive, and then know the peace and joy of sins pardoned.

130:1-3 The Need for God's Forgiveness

Many a man or woman has cried to God *out of the depths* (**130:1**), from the feeling of being overwhelmed as by deep waters (see also 69:1-2, 15). They may have been in the depths of sorrow, of despair, of discouragement or depression. They may have been in the depths of great weakness, of feeling the demands of life to be greater than can be borne. They may feel like the psalmist did here, as he reflected, 'I am a person in great need. I urgently need the help of God. But how can I claim help from God? I have so often done what is wrong in God's sight. If a record was kept of all my sins and held against me, how could I possibly stand before God?' (**130:2-3**).

The idea of our appearing or standing before God as our king and our judge is a common one in the Scriptures. Many passages speak about who can and who cannot stand before God (see, for example, Pss 1:5; 15:1; 24:3; 143:2; Rom 5:1-2; 1 Cor 15:1-2; Col 4:12)

130:4 The Assurance of God's Forgiveness

The psalmist realized his sinfulness before God, but he also knew that God was willing to forgive those who sincerely turn to him in penitence. He could say to God *with you there is forgiveness* (**130:4a**). The OT often bears witness to the forgiving love of God (see, for example, 103:10-14). We see this love even more clearly in the NT, especially in light of the death of Christ on the cross for our sins. The NT expresses it clearly, 'If we claim to be without sin, we deceive ourselves, and the truth is not in us. If we confess our sins, he is faithful and just and will forgive us our sins and purify us from all unrighteousness' (1 John 1:8-9).

Our knowledge of God's forgiveness should not lead us to take it for granted or presume on it, but should lead us to exclaim with the psalmist, *therefore you are feared* (**130:4b**; see also Rom 2:4). Here the word *fear* has the meaning of 'revered'.

130:5-6 Waiting on God

The psalmist knew that however overwhelmed he felt, he could trust the Lord to come to his help. Because he knew God's promise, he could say, *in his word I put my hope* (**130:5b**). Because he knew God's forgiving love, he could say, *I wait for the Lord, my soul waits* (**130:5a**). The picture that describes his attitude is that of a watchman, perhaps in a military camp, or perhaps in the temple, waiting for the signs of dawn that meant that temple worship would begin (**130:6**). Like such watchmen, the psalmist sat in darkness but longed for the dawn, confident that it would eventually come.

130:7-8 Sharing His Confidence

The psalmist's hope was not misplaced. Like Jeremiah, he could say,' I called on your name, O Lord, from the depths of the pit; you heard my plea ... You came near when I called on you, and you said, "Do not fear!" ' (Lam 3:55-57). When people find that they have not turned to God in vain, and realize that he has lifted them from the depths of guilt and despair and weakness, they can encourage others and share their confidence. This is what the psalmist does. To all Israel, his own people, he says, *put your hope in the Lord* (**130:7a**). Realize his *unfailing love* and that *with him is full redemption* (**130:7b**). Those who turn to him he can set free from all their iniquities that would drag them down, and from all the power of evil that is against them (**130:8**).

Psalm 131: Resting in the Love of God

In the three verses of this short psalm, another of the *songs of ascents* (see Ps 120) associated with *David,* the way of pride is rejected, the way of trusting love is accepted, and others are encouraged to follow the way of trust and hope in the Lord.

131:1 The Way Rejected

The psalmist rejects a way that seemed right to many people. *My heart is not proud* (**131:1a**) speaks against pride and feelings of self-importance. *My eyes are not haughty* (**131:1b**) speaks against looking down on others. Pride can also involve striving to achieve selfish ambitions, trying to reach beyond God's wise plans for one's life. Pride is always displeasing to God, and it also robs us of contentment, which is the way to have inner peace. For more about what the Scriptures teach about pride, ambition and humility, see 2 Chronicles 26:16-18, Proverbs 6:16-17, 16:5, Isaiah 2:11-22, Jeremiah 45:5, Micah 6:8, Philippians 2:3-11, James 4:7, 10 and 1 Peter 5:5-6.

131:2 The Way Accepted

The way that the psalmist wants to follow is pictured in the simple illustration of a child resting in its mother's arms (**131:2**). Before weaning, a little one demands to be fed regularly at its mother's breast. But after weaning, the child is glad just to be with its mother, resting trustfully in her love. The Bible often pictures God's care for us as a mother, or a father's love (see Deut 1:31; Isa 46:3; 49:15; Hos 11:3-4).

131:3 The Way Encouraged

As with many of the psalms that describe an individual's experience of God, this psalm ends by applying its lessons to people generally (see also Ps 130). The psalmist wants all Israel to learn the lesson, *put your hope in the Lord*, and he wants them to keep this attitude of hope and trust *both now and for evermore* (**131:3**). The attitude he wants to encourage is that shown by Paul in Philippians 3:12-14.

Psalm 132: Ark, Temple and Promise

Psalm 132 is another *song of ascents* (see Ps 120) celebrating three things that mattered greatly in the faith and worship of Israel: the ark of the covenant, the temple in Jerusalem, and the promises given to David. All three are linked together and celebrated in this psalm.

Because of what this psalm says about the ark and the temple, some people have thought that it may have been written for the dedication of Solomon's temple, or that it was used in an annual commemoration of that dedication. It may also have been used in the enthronement of a king of the house of David, or in a ceremony in which year by year the people of Israel renewed their covenant with God and their commitment to worship him, and to uphold the king as the Lord's anointed.

132:1-10 The Ark and the Temple in Jerusalem

The psalm starts with a call to the people to look back on the way that David had endured hardships and difficulties to bring the ark to Jerusalem, which he had wanted to make his political capital and the national centre of worship, and where he was preparing to build the temple (**132:1**). The depth of David's desire to do these things is expressed here in terms of unresting determination (**132:2-5**; see also 2 Sam 6-7:1-3). His determination to do what he believed God wanted him to do should be a model for us.

The first thing he did was to bring *the ark of your might* to Jerusalem (**132:8b**). The ark was a sacred box that had been an outward sign and reminder of the presence of God with the people since the time of Moses. Inside it were the stone tablets on which the Ten Commandments were written (Deut 10:1-5). The ark was kept in the tabernacle or Tent of Meeting, and whenever the people went out to battle, the ark was carried before them and there was the prayer 'Rise up, O Lord! May your enemies be scattered' (Num 10:35). We hear an echo of this prayer in **132:8a**.

The ark had been taken into the promised land in the days of Joshua and kept in the shrine at Shiloh (1 Sam 1–3). To Israel's great distress it was captured by the Philistines, but was later returned to Israel and housed in Kiriath Jearim (called *Jaar* in this psalm – **132:6**; 1 Sam 4:1-7:2). The town of *Ephrathah* is also mentioned in that verse. This name is sometimes linked in the OT with Bethlehem, the town from which David came, and so the psalmist may be saying that David heard about the ark in Bethlehem. But it is also possible that there was another place called Ephrathah near *Kiriath Jearim* or that Ephrathah is a variant spelling of Ephraim. For Shiloh, where the ark had previously been kept, was in the territory of Ephraim (1 Sam 1:3).

But it was not enough just to have the ark in Jerusalem. David also wanted to build *a dwelling* or house for God in Jerusalem (132:5; see 2 Sam 7:1-3). He wanted it to be a *resting place* for the Lord, where his presence would always be known, and his *footstool* (**132:7, 8a**; see also 99:5). The reference to it as a footstool makes it clear that no matter how magnificent the temple would be, it would not even come close to the glory of the Lord it honoured.

David was not permitted to build the temple. That was done by Solomon, his son, but it did become a special place of worship where the people of Israel could meet with the Lord. The dedication of the temple is described in 1 Kings 8 and in 2 Chronicles 6, where the words of 132:8-10 are quoted (2 Chr 6:41-42). Over the years, as the people looked back on the history of the ark, on what David had endured, and on the dedication of the temple, they prayed that true worship would be offered there, that the priests would be upright, and that faithful people would praise God with enthusiasm (**132:9**). They also prayed that the promise to David would be fulfilled and that God would look favourably on the anointed king (**132:10**).

132:11-18 The Promise to David

The prophet Nathan had to tell David that God did not want him to build the temple for him in Jerusalem, but God responded to David's oath and vow (132:2) by making his own oath or promise to David. God would establish his descendants after him, and they would reign as kings in Israel (**132:11**) as long as they remained faithful in keeping God's covenant and obeying God's laws (**132:12**). Those promises that came to David through the prophet Nathan (2 Sam 7:8-16) are also referred to in Solomon's prayer (1 Kgs 8:23-26) and in Psalm 89:3-4. The fulfilment of the promise to David was tied both to the obedience of David's descendants (**132:12**) and the plan the Lord had for Zion. He had chosen it for himself and for his people (**132:13-16**).

God's purpose was to have a king over his people, who would be strong as a *horn* (**132:17a**). A horn is often used

as a symbol of strength, and in Daniel 7:7-8, 24 and 8:5 it is the symbol for a king. The kings of the house of David are spoken of as being like a horn that will *sprout up* (NRSV). The word 'sprout' or 'shoot' or 'branch' is also used of a Davidic king to come (Jer 23:5-6; 33:15; Zech 3:8; 6:12).

The king is also described as being like *a lamp* shining for the truth, not conquered by his enemies but continuing to rule well in Israel (**132:17b-18**; see 2 Sam 21:17; 1 Kgs 11:36; 15:4; 2 Chr 21:7). Israel was also meant to be a 'light to the nations' (Isa 42:6; 49:6).

God's purposes were fulfilled in part in OT days. The ark and temple meant much to the faith and worship of the people, and there were some good kings among the descendants of David. But many of the kings failed to fulfil the condition of 132:12, and thus the hope expressed in 132:17-18 was never fully realized. The prophets were inspired to explain that God had promised the one whom we speak of as the Messiah, the one who would come from the family of David and bring justice, peace and salvation (see Isa 9:6-7; 11:1-9; Ezek 34:23-24; Mic 5:2-4).

We, as Christians, believe that God 'has raised up a horn of salvation for us in the house of his servant David' (Luke 1:69) – Jesus, God's Son, our Lord. We also know that though sacred objects and sacred places may help our faith and be reminders of the presence and promises of God, just as the ark and temple were in Israel, yet now, in every place and need, we can know God's Holy Spirit is with us. Because of the coming of Jesus into our world, his death and resurrection and the coming of the Holy Spirit at Pentecost, our lives are now God's temple, indwelt by his Spirit.

Psalm 133: Family Fellowship

Psalm 133, a very short psalm, is another *song of ascents* (see Ps 120), associated with David. Its theme is the blessing of fellowship and unity, and it can be applied to the human family, the extended family, a community of God's people, or to the unity of Christians: *How wonderful it is, how pleasant, for God's people to live together like brothers* (**133:1** GNB). There are two pictures of the blessing of that harmony.

133:1-2 the Anointing Oil

The first picture, of oil running down from Aaron's head and beard to the collar of his robes (**133:2**), might not immediately appeal to some of us. Some things might help us to appreciate this picture. First, in a hot dry climate, oil is very soothing to the body. Psalm 23:5 says that one of the blessings the heavenly Host offers to a guest is 'to anoint my head with oil'. Second, the anointing of Aaron and the other priests was something very special, and a symbol of God's blessing on them for the work they were called to do (Exod 29:7; Lev 8:10-12). Third, this anointing oil had a lovely fragrance (see Exod 30:22-31). Thus when we read this image, we should think of the anointing of Jesus with such fragrantly perfumed ointment that 'the house was filled with the fragrance' (John 12:1-3). Such is the loveliness of family fellowship, whether in our homes or in the life of the Christian church.

132:3 The Dew of Hermon

The second picture is of the dew. Again we must think of the land of Palestine. Like many areas of Africa, it is dry and without rain for many months of the year. The dew that falls at night refreshes it. Dew like that which fell on high Mount Hermon would have refreshed *Mount Zion* in Jerusalem (**133:3**). Such is the loveliness of family fellowship, whether in our homes or in the life of the Christian church. Moreover, God's blessing is granted when people live and work together in unity. The full blessing of God is hindered when there is division and disunity in our families or among Christians.

Christians should pray that the Lord will give us the grace and the desire to 'keep the unity of the Spirit through the bond of peace' (Eph 4:3) to the glory of his name and the blessing of us all. We can also praise him for expressions of unity like this commentary, written by African scholars from across Africa and from many different denominations.

To encourage us in our pursuit of peace, we should read Jesus' words about reconciliation (Matt 5:23-24) and his prayer for the unity of his followers (John 17:11; 20-23). We should also note Paul's frequent encouragement of Christians to live in fellowship (2 Cor 13:11; Eph 4:1-6; Phil 2:2-8; Col 3:14-15).

Psalm 134: Praising and Being Blessed by God

The words 'praise' and 'bless' are the key words in Psalm 134, the last of the *songs of ascents* (see Ps 120). There are references to either praise or blessing in each of its three verses. We are reminded that our relationship with God is a two-way process: we praise God and God blesses us.

134:1-2 'Praise the Lord'

When this psalm was written, the *servants of the Lord* were the priests and the *house of the Lord* was the temple in Jerusalem (134:1). They lifted up their hands as they lifted up their hearts and their voices to God (**134:2**). It may be that there were regular times in the night as well as in the day when some of the priests met and praised God (1 Chr 9:33; Luke 2:37), or this may only have happened during the great annual festivals like Passover and the Feast of Tabernacles (Isa 30:29).

As Christians, we are all servants of God, and God's temple is our own bodies (1 Cor 6:19) and the fellowship of Christian people together (2 Cor 6:16). So we may truly say that by day and by night, individually and together, we should *praise the Lord* for who he is and for all that he has done (**134:1**; see also Eph 1:3-14; 1 Pet 1:3-7). Our awareness of what he has done should prompt us to cry out with all the saints, 'Praise and glory and wisdom and thanks and honour and power and strength be to our God for ever and ever!' (Rev 7:12)

134:3 'The Lord Bless You'

As we turn to God to thank him and praise him, we can also ask for his blessing. In OT times the priests spoke of God's blessing on the people (as in Num 6:24-26). Now that Jesus is our great High Priest, we know the fullness of God's blessing on us through him. As we turn to him we 'receive mercy and find grace to help us in our time of need' (see Heb 4:14-16). We should always remember too that the God who blesses us is no other than the *Maker of heaven and earth* (**134:3**).

Psalm 135: 'The Lord Is Good'

The beginning and end of Psalm 135 call on all who serve the Lord to praise him. In between, it speaks of different ways in which God's goodness and greatness are shown. Just as we do today in our songs and hymns, the psalmist draws on other people's praise and the language of Scriptures. So we can compare 135:1-3 with Psalms 113:1, 134:1 and 147:1; 135:4 with Deuteronomy 7:6; 135:6 and 135:15-20 with Psalm 115:3-13; 135:7 with Jeremiah 10:13; 135:10-12 with Psalm 136:17-22; and 135:14 with Deuteronomy 32:36. Having the words of Psalms or other parts of Scripture in our minds can help us to praise God and to trust him in all the situations in our lives.

135:1-5, 19-21 A Call to Praise

The calls to praise at the beginning and end of this psalm parallel each other. Both are addressed to the priests (the *house of Aaron* – **135:19b**) and Levites (the *house of Levi* – **135:20a**) who *minister in the house of the Lord* (**135:2**). But any suspicion that these are the only people addressed is put to rest in **135:19a** and **135:20b**, which call all those who call themselves God's people, all who fear the Lord, to join them in praise. The reasons for praise can be summed up by saying, *the Lord is good* (**135:3**) and *the Lord is great* (**135:5**). But the psalmist goes on to expand on exactly what these statements mean in the rest of the psalm.

135:6-7 The Great God of Creation

Scientists study nature, the seas and their tides, the winds and the weather, the sun and the rain, all the things that the psalmist mentions in **135:6b-7**. Through science we learn more and more wonderful things about the world in which we live, and about the universe beyond our world. Yet those who discover things about our universe are only 'thinking God's thoughts after him', as one wise scientist put it. For God as Creator and architect of all has ordered all things, and from the beginning he has done in heaven and on earth *whatever pleases Him* (**135:6a**).

135:8-14 The Great God of History

The people of Israel believed that God had chosen them (135:4) and that he had shown his care for them in their history. Pharaoh of Egypt had held the people of Israel as slaves, making them work hard under cruel taskmasters, but in the end the Lord had brought judgment on the Egyptians with the *signs and wonders* described in Exodus 7–12 (**135:8-9**). He also controlled history as the Israelites travelled towards the promised land, enabling them to defeat Sihon, Og and other kings of Canaan, so that they could inherit their land (**135:10-12**; see, for example, Deut 2:24-3:11). God had shown compassion to Israel (**135:14**), and they could always say, *Your name O Lord endures for ever, your renown, O Lord, through all generations* (**135:13**).

God had a special purpose in history when he took the Israelites as his own people and *his treasured possession* (135:14; Exod 19:4-6). God was preparing them for the day when he would send his own Son into the world. But if they had a special privilege, they also had a special responsibility. God had his purpose for other nations as well (Gen 12:3). This is a guide to the way that we should still think, individually, in our different nations, and in the life of the Christian church. We can have confidence that God has a great purpose for us if only we allow him to work it out by being obedient to him. But our confidence must not be selfish or self-centred, for God also has a special purpose for other people and other nations. He wants to work all things together for the good 'of those who love him, who have been called according to his purpose' (Rom 8:28).

135:15-18 The Only Living God

The words of 115:4-8 are repeated almost exactly in **135:15-18**. The Bible often speaks of God's 'mouth', not because he is like a human being in form (see John 4:24), but because he speaks to us. The Bible speaks of his 'eyes' and 'ears' because he sees us and hears our prayers. Other gods are idols without life or power to help.

As we read these words about idols, whether our idols are *silver and gold* (135:15), or whether they are our possessions, our work, our pleasure, or anything else, we should realize the foolishness of giving the place in our lives that should be given only to the living God. We are called to serve him with all our heart, soul, mind and strength. No wonder the psalm ends with a summons to praise!

Psalm 136: God's Love Endures for Ever

Psalm 136 was probably intended to be used as a responsive reading in public worship. It may seem rather much to repeat *his love endures for ever* twenty-six times, but the truth enshrined in these words is the explanation for everything else that can be said about the work of God. No one who has used this psalm can ever forget those words – and we too should remember them. They are used in other psalms (like 107:1) and in other places in the OT which tell of the worship of God's people (see 1 Chr 16:34; 2 Chr 7:3, 6; 20:21). God acts in love, mercy and faithfulness, and all of these ideas are included in the word that our translation renders as 'love'. In creation, in history, and in all God's care for us, we see the same steadfast love.

136:1-9 God Has Acted in Creation

The psalm begins and ends with the call to *give thanks to the Lord* (**136:1**, 26). God is good. God is great. God is wise. Whatever or whoever people may speak of as their gods or lords, there is one God and Lord over all (**136:2-3**).

The heavens are among the *great wonders* that reveal God's wisdom, love and understanding (**136:4-5**). Think of such details as the distance between the earth and the sun. If the two were much closer together, we would burn up in the heat of the sun. If they were further apart, we would freeze to death. Think of the sea and land, and how we are blessed with both. Think of the water under the ground that provides for our needs in areas where there are no rivers or lakes (**136:6**). Think of the blessing of the day with the light and warmth of the sun, and of the night with the gentler light of moon and stars for the time when we need rest (**136:7**). If you need more encouragement to think of the wisdom of God in creation, read Job 9:8-10, Proverbs 3:19, 8:22-31, Isaiah 40:12-14 and Jeremiah 10:12.

136:10-22 God Has Acted in History

The events of their history convinced the people of Israel of the Lord's love and mercy. Many of these events were mentioned in Psalm 135. God released them from their slavery in Egypt, overcoming Pharaoh when he tried to stop their journey to freedom (**136:10-12**). God enabled them to cross the Red Sea to safety (**136:13-15**). He led them through the wilderness and gave them the land of Canaan as their *inheritance*, overcoming kings like Sihon and Og who opposed them (**136:16-22**; see Num 21:21-35). God's *mighty hand and outstretched arm* (136:12) – his power to help and his willingness to reach out in power on behalf of his people – are spoken of with gratitude in many other passages in the OT (for example, Deut 26:3-9).

136:23-26 God Helps and Provides

We all have many reasons to thank God for creation and for what he has done for us and for our people in history. He is the one who *gives food to every creature* (**136:25**) – all people, and all birds and animals and living creatures of every kind (see 104:27-28; 147:9). We may feel our *low estate* (**136:23**), that is, that we are very weak and unimportant, and perhaps discouraged as well, but we can be sure that the Lord remembers us (1 Cor 1:26-31). He rescues us from our spiritual enemies as we turn to him, and he provides for our needs. He is *the God of heaven,* yet he cares for us on earth. No wonder we should *give thanks* to him and declare over and over again that *his love endures for ever* (**136:26**)

Psalm 137: Weeping for Zion

In 587 BC, as the prophet Jeremiah had warned, the Babylonians conquered Jerusalem, destroyed much of the city including the temple on Mount Zion, and took many of the people into exile in Babylon. The exile was a time of grief and distress, when the people were moved to pray earnestly for God's judgment on their enemies.

137:1-4 Deep Grief

The opening verses of Psalm 137 describe their grief in terms of their weeping beside *the rivers,* or irrigation canals, of Babylon (**137:1**). It was no time for singing the happy songs of their homeland (**137:4**). Rather than playing their harps, they hung them on the branches of the poplar trees (**137:2**). The Babylonians around them, tormenting them, asked them to sing one of their songs. But the *songs of Zion* (**137:3**) were not just Jewish folk songs. They were *the songs of the Lord* (137:4). They were songs like Psalms 46, 48, 84 and 122, songs about rejoicing in the presence of God and about the blessing of worshipping the Lord in the temple on Mount Zion. It was as if Christians in prison camps were asked to sing Christian songs and hymns so that their captors could laugh at the faith.

We need to remember that while songs can be a source of deep grief, they can also bring comfort. Many Africans who were carried away as slaves to America and the Caribbean islands became Christians. They composed songs and lyrics about their new faith in their African dialects, using African metaphors. Many of these songs have significant messages and are in use in African churches today. One example is the song, *Kosoba bire kosi, Oba toseru domo, kosoba bire* ['There is no other king like you, King who transforms a slave into a son, there is no king like you'].

137:5-6 Great Distress

The people's grief was about more than being far away from homes and homeland, it was also about their faith being laughed at. Their enemies made it seem as if their God was unable to help them. Thus Jerusalem and the temple were much in their thoughts (137:5-6). They felt that they would not be true to their deepest faith and convictions if they failed to think of Zion. The GNB translates **137:5-6** like this: *May I never be able to play the harp again if I forget you, Jerusalem! May I never be able to sing again if I do not remember you, if I do not think of you as my greatest joy!*

137:7-9 A Terrible Prayer

The great grief and distress that the people in exile would have felt led to a terrible prayer. They thought of the Edomites, the descendants of Esau the brother of Jacob. Two hundred years earlier Amos had said that the Edomites were filled with anger and hatred for Israel (1:11). When Jerusalem fell to the Babylonians, the Edomites rejoiced and took advantage of the defeat of Israel (Lam 4:21-22; Ezek 25:12-14; 35:1-9; Obad 8-21). So the Jewish exiles prayed that God would *remember ... what the Edomites did* (**137:7**) and bring judgment on them.

Then they thought of the *daughter of Babylon,* using a common way of referring to nations in the OT (**137:8**). The Babylonians had treated them and their little children with great cruelty. So they prayed that God would allow others to treat the Babylonians and their children with equal cruelty and pay them back for what they had done. Like many such prayers in Psalms, these prayers were for God's justice to prevail.

Perhaps it is only people who have been oppressed and persecuted for their faith who can really understand what the Jews in exile felt. Yet Christians know a higher and better way. Bishop Festo Kivengere in Uganda knew what it meant to suffer under the rule of the dictator Idi Amin, and he longed for Amin to be overthrown. Yet one Good Friday he realized that Christ had died for everyone in the world, including Idi Amin, and that he should be praying for the cruel dictator's conversion rather than for his judgment. So he wrote his little book *I Love Idi Amin.* This is the way that Jesus taught, 'Love your enemies and pray for those who persecute you' (Matt 5:44), and what Jesus himself did as, dying on the cross for the salvation of sinners, he prayed, 'Father, forgive them' (Luke 23:34). We need to pray that whatever sorrow or trouble we face, we will turn to the God of all love and power and find grace to help in our time of need.

Psalm 138: The Greatness of God

God is truly great in the ways that he has revealed himself to us. Psalm 138, which deals with three aspects of his greatness, can be compared with Mary's song in Luke 1:46-55. The incarnation of the Son of God is also a perfect illustration of what the psalm says about the greatness of God.

138:1-3 His Name and His Word

Some people serve other gods, and we may be tempted to do the same. But as we, with the psalmist, know God's steadfast love and faithfulness, we will surely also say, *I will praise you, O Lord, with all my heart* (**138:1**). The Jewish author of this psalm expressed his dedication to God by turning towards the temple in Jerusalem as he prayed, just as Muslims turn toward Mecca (138:2a; see also 1 Kgs 8:48; Ps 5:7; 28:2; Dan 6:10). Christians do not need to do this, for we know that the Lord is God of the whole world, and cannot be contained in any one place. That is why we have many churches and can pray to God wherever we are and facing in any direction.

The psalmist praises God's *name* (**138:2a**). As we have often seen in Psalms, God's name means God's nature, what he is really like. As this verse goes on to remind us, God's nature is characterized by *love* and *faithfulness*. The psalmist says, *you have exalted above all things your name and your word* (**138:2b**). However, a more exact translation of what the Hebrew says is 'you have exalted your word above your name', which may mean, as the NJB puts it, 'your promises surpass even your fame'. God's 'word' also refers to the way in which he shows us his way and his will, and nothing in life can be more important than that.

Because of God's faithfulness, we can always rely on him, and, if we sincerely turn to him, we will find his love. We will find that when we call to him, he answers us, and for our weakness gives us inner strength in our souls (**138:3**; compare Eph 3:16).

138:4-6 His Care for the Lowly

The psalmist prays that when great and powerful rulers see the ways of God in the world, they will acknowledge and praise him, *for the glory of the Lord is great* (**138:4-5**). But God's ways are very different from the ways that such people naturally follow. They think that greatness is shown in having authority and power over many people, and see the poor and weak as of no importance. God sees people very differently. God's greatness and wonderful love are in fact seen in his care for the *lowly* (**138:6a**). The same point is made by Isaiah: 'This is what the high and lofty One says – he who lives for ever, whose name is holy: "I live in a high and holy place, but also with him who is contrite and lowly in spirit, to revive the spirit of the lowly, and to revive the heart of the contrite"' (Isa 57:15). That is why Christians should follow Jesus' example and the command given by Peter to 'clothe yourselves with humility toward one another' (1 Pet 5:5).

In that same verse, Peter says that 'God opposes the proud'. The psalmist also recognizes that the proud and haughty fail to experience the nearness of the Lord. Rather he seems far away from them (**138:6b**). This part of the verse may be translated as saying that God knows the proud from afar, or that he humbles the proud from afar, or that the proud cannot hide in the distance from God. But whichever translation we take, it is clear that there is a difference between the way that the Lord looks on the proud and the way he looks on the humble.

138:7-8 His Loving Purpose

Those who trust in the Lord can know that, even though powerful enemies bring them trouble (**138:7**), God has a purpose for them, and he will *fulfil his purpose* (**138:8**) The good work that he has begun in us and for us he intends to complete (see Phil 1:6). The greatness of God is the greatness of his loving concern even for the details of our lives. Indeed we have reason to say again, *I will praise you, O Lord, with all my heart* (138:1).

Psalm 139: My God, How Wonderful

Psalm 139 is deeply personal. The writer is overwhelmed by the thought of the greatness of God, yet not as a great God far away, but as the God who is concerned with every detail of his life. He says three things about his understanding of God, and then three things about the effect that this understanding has on him.

139:1-6 God's Perfect Knowledge

It is one thing to say that 'Nothing in all creation is hidden from God's sight' and to acknowledge that God knows everything in his vast universe. It is quite a different thing to grasp that because of this 'everything is uncovered and laid bare before the eyes of him to whom we must give account' (Heb 4:13). But the psalmist had grasped this truth, and that is why he bursts out: *O Lord, you ... know me. You know when I sit and when I rise; you perceive my thoughts from afar* (**139:1-2**), *Before a word is on my tongue you know it completely, O Lord* (**139:4**; see also 44:20-21; Jer 12:3; 17:10).

The realization that God knows everything about us can be comforting or frightening. Those who are opposing God will be terrified when they have to say, *You have laid your hand on me* (**139:5**). But if we seek God and want to do his will, his hand will be laid on us in blessing, and we need not fear.

139:7-12 God's Presence Everywhere

Again it is one thing to say that God is present everywhere. It is another thing to say to God, *Where can I flee from your presence?* (**139:7**). Many people do try to avoid God. Jonah (Jonah 1:3) and Adam and Eve (Gen 3:8) tried to hide from him. Today, people still try to do this. Some seek to build their own heaven of success or pleasure. Others seek to hide *in the depths* (**139:8**), the dark underworld of drugs or playing with the demonic. Or they may try to hide from God by travelling or endless activity (**139:9**). Many people feel that the darkness will hide what they do (**139:11**). But while it may hide them from other people, it will never hide them from God, to whom *the night will shine like the day* (**139:12**). As the Yoruba of Western Nigeria say: *Afokun jale, bi oba aiye kori o ti orun nwo o,* meaning: 'he who steals in darkness, unseen by an earthly king, is being observed by the heavenly king.'

It is frightening to those who oppose God to realize that God knows what they are doing wherever they are. Yet they should also be brought to realize that God does not use this knowledge merely to judge them. In the Gospels, Jesus presents himself as the Good Shepherd, who comes to seek the lost sheep (Luke 15:3-7).

The psalmist, however, had no desire to escape God's presence. Like all who seek to love and serve God, he found it a tremendous comfort to be able to say, *your hand will guide me, your right hand will hold me fast* (**139:10**).

139:13-16 God's Amazing Power Seen in Creation

God's knowledge of us goes back to our conception. Indeed it is by God that we are *fearfully and wonderfully made* (**139:14**), our bodies formed so intricately in our mothers' wombs, hidden from human sight, as if *in the depths of the earth* (**139:15**). God sees and knows the whole process. He also has a plan for each human life. So we can say, *You saw me before I was born. The days allotted to me had all been recorded in your book, before any of them ever began* (**139:16** GNB).

139:17-24 The Fruit of Knowing Such a God

Three things follow from the psalmist's awareness of this all-seeing, all-present Creator God.

The first is a sense of awe and wonder. *How precious to me are your thoughts, O God! How vast is the sum of them* (**139:17**) is similar to what the Lord says to us in Isaiah 55:9, 'For as the heavens are higher than the earth, so are my ways higher than your ways and my thoughts than your thoughts.' To come to the end of all our thinking and understanding, and to be able to say, *I am still with you* (**139:18**) is a privilege and blessing beyond what words can tell.

Understanding the wisdom and goodness of God's creation should also increase our awareness of how terrible it is that people rebel against God and hate God. Although **139:19-20** is not a Christian prayer, and we are not to respond to people with the hatred expressed in **139:21-22**, we can understand the emotions that gave rise to these words. If only all rebels were judged and God's perfect plans for human life carried through! And that will indeed happen when Christ returns and judges his enemies.

But while the psalmist condemns those who oppose God, he knows that he himself is not perfect. So he prays that God will search his heart, show him where he has been

wrong, and lead him *in the way everlasting* (**139:24**; see also 19:12, 14).

Psalm 140: The Defender of the Oppressed

There are powerful oppressive people in many parts of the world today. Those who try to live godly lives when surrounded by such people need the kind of faith that the psalmist had.

The word *Selah*, which was last used in Psalm 89, is used frequently here in Psalm 140. It probably indicates a pause, allowing people to think about the meaning of the words of the psalm, possibly while musical instruments played.

140:1-5 The Oppressors

Those who are oppressing the psalmist have no moral standards, but are *evil men* (**140:1**), who *devise evil plans and stir up war every day* (**140:2**). Three times in this psalm they are described as *men of violence* (140:1, 4, 11). It is not only their actions that are violent. They also use words as weapons, using their tongues just as a snake uses its bite to poison its victim. They may seem to speak pleasantly, but *the poison of vipers is on their lips* (**140:3**, quoted in the NT in Rom 3:13). The Scriptures place much stress on how important words can be and the damage they can do (see Eph 4:29; 5:4; Jas 3:1-12).

The oppressors are also described as *proud men*, arrogantly thinking only of themselves, and the position and power they have over others, while they lay traps for the powerless (**140:5**). Their power seems almost overwhelming, but the psalmist believed that the power of God was far greater than that of the oppressors. The power of God would endure and these oppressors would not remain powerful for ever. So he knew that he could ask God to *keep* and *protect* him (**140:4**).

140:6-13 The Psalmist's Faith

The psalmist could say to the Lord, *You are my God* (**140:6**). The Lord had answered his prayers in the past and protected him in conflict and the psalmist believed that he could do so again. But in his perception of the divide between people like himself, to whom God is a friend, and his enemies (140:5) to whom God is also an enemy, he prays that God will bring trouble on them (**140:9**). This perception is one that Jesus corrected when he taught us to love our enemies (Matt 5:43-47).

The psalmist's reference to God protecting his head in **140:7** is echoed in the NT (Eph 6:17; 1 Thess 5:8). He also believed that God was concerned to secure *justice for the poor* and to uphold *the cause of the needy* (**140:12**). God could be trusted to uphold justice in the end. He has done so in one nation after another throughout history.

The word translated *slanderers* in **140:11a** literally means 'men of tongue', and again a reference to verbal violence is paired with the phrase *men of violence* (**140:11b**).

Oppressors have often been overthrown by the violence of others, or they have come to the end of their days and their powerlessness has been shown in death. The way for those who would live righteously is to praise God's *name*, or in other words, give thanks for God's love, compassion and justice. After all, we have the assurance that *the upright will live before you* (**140:13**). God will never leave us nor forsake us, and in the end, by his grace, we will see his face and worship and serve him for ever (Rev 22:3-4). Given this confidence, we can have courage to stand for justice and truth in our troubled world, and to care for all who are poor and distressed.

Psalm 141: Deliver Us from Evil

This is another psalm that is an urgent cry for help. The psalmist had two great needs: victory over temptations that came to him, and deliverance from the traps set for him by ungodly people. We express the same needs in the last two petitions in the Lord's Prayer: 'lead us not into temptation, but deliver us from the evil one' (Matt 5:13).

141:1-2 The Nature of Prayer

The psalmist's prayer is urgent, *O Lord, come quickly to me* (**141:1**). Yet he does not want it to be seen merely as a cry for help, but also as an expression of worship. That is why he compares his prayer to *incense*, the sweet-smelling substance that was burned to express worship to God (**141:2a**). This image is also used in the NT, where the prayers of all God's people are likened to incense (Rev 5:8).

He also compares his prayer to *the evening sacrifice* (**141:2b**). In OT days the offering of sacrifices expressed a desire for forgiveness, cleansing from sin and the restoration of fellowship with God. The psalmist wanted the lifting up of his hands in prayer to be like the offering of a sacrifice. He is not alone in this, for worship of the heart and obedience of life are often related to the bringing of sacrifices and offerings in Psalms (see, for example, 40:6-8, 50:5-15; 51:170).

141:3-5a Lead Us Not into Temptation

We are all often tempted to speak unwisely, unkindly, even dishonestly. It is important to pray, *Set a guard over my mouth, O Lord; keep watch over the door of my lips* (**141:3**; see also 34:13; 39:1; Prov 13:3; 21:23; Matt 12:34-37; Jas 3:1-12). Because our thoughts come before our words, even when we speak without thinking much, it is also necessary to pray that our hearts will be kept from evil. But our thoughts lead not just to words but also to actions, and so we also need to pray that we will not *take part in wicked deeds* (**141:4a**).

What makes temptation very powerful and dangerous is that often it seems that the way of life of ungodly people is attractive. So the psalmist prayed that he might not want to live *with men who are evildoers* or be enticed by their *delicacies* (**141:4b**). Real friends will correct us when we go wrong, hence the prayer of **141:5a**, and the wisdom of Proverbs 27:6, 'Wounds from a friend can be trusted'. He compares such wounds to *oil on my head.* In the dry and dusty conditions of Palestine, a host would anoint guests with oil (see 23:5; Luke 7:46). It is better to enjoy such hospitality of friends than to take pleasure in the hospitality of 'evildoers'.

141:5b-10 Deliver Us from Evil

There are not a great number of places in the Bible where the meaning of the original Hebrew is quite uncertain, but this is the case in regard to **141:5b-6**. Thus there are many different translations of these verses. The NIV translates **141:6** as *their rulers will be thrown down from the cliffs.* But the NJB understands the word translated 'cliffs' (a regular word for 'rock') as a reference to God and translates the verse, 'They are delivered into the power of the rock, their judge'. Similarly, in **141:7** it is difficult to know whether the *bones* are those of godly people who have suffered tragedies or those of ungodly people who have been judged. But despite the confusion about the exact meaning of these verses, the main message and teaching of the psalm is abundantly clear.

The psalmist knew not only the pressure of the temptation to follow the ways of ungodly and evil people, but also the way such people would attempt to trap and trouble him. Those who attack godly men and women have often been described as being like hunters trying to trap animals or ensnare birds (**141:9**). Those who face such attacks can be sure of two things. In the end ungodly people will be caught in the traps that they try to make for others (**141:10**). More importantly, the Lord is always a *refuge* for those who turn to him, and they are not given *over to death* (**141:8**). We can be confident that 'God is faithful; he will not let you be tempted beyond what you can bear. But when you are tempted, he will also provide a way out so that you can stand up under it' (1 Cor 10:13).

Psalm 142: 'No One Cares for Me'

Psalm 142 is described as a *maskil* (see comments on Ps 32). The heading links it with the experience of David *in the cave.* This may have been the cave of Adullam (1 Sam 22:1-5) or the one in En Gedi where David was when he was escaping from Saul (1 Sam 24). But, whatever the case, the psalm relates to many experiences of loneliness and trouble. We can compare it with other experiences of human loneliness described in Scripture (Elijah – 1 Kings 19; Paul – 2 Timothy 4:16-18).

142:1-4 Loneliness

Life in this world is lonely for many people. It is lonely for those who have been bereaved of a wife or husband or parent, for those who are refugees, for those who have to stand alone for their faith. This psalm is another urgent cry to the Lord by one who is in great trouble, discouraged and downcast. *My spirit grows faint,* he says (**142:3**), *I am in desperate need* (142:6).

The psalmist stood alone. His many enemies persecuted him, and he had no strength to resist them (142:6). They watched out for him and tried to trap him, as a hunter would try to catch an animal (142:3). The OT often speaks of one who helps another as being at his or her 'right hand', but the psalmist can only say, *Look to my right and see; no one is concerned for me* (**142:4**). Life was just like being in prison (142:7), or as we might say, in solitary confinement.

142:5-7 The Cure for Loneliness

Though there was no human being to whom the writer of this psalm could turn, he knew that he could still turn to God. He knows three things about God. The first is that *you know my way* (142:3). When the word 'know' is used of God, it means more than just that he knows the facts. He cares and is ready to help (see 1:6). 'You are watching over my path' is the way that the NJB translates the words of 142:3 (see also Matt 6:25-34; 10:28-31).

The second thing the psalmist knows about God is that *you are my refuge* (**142:5**), that is, the one who protects in time of trouble. This word is often used of God. Psalm 46:1 says, 'God is our refuge and strength, an ever-present help in trouble', and Psalm 61:3 says, 'You have been my refuge, a strong tower against the foe'.

Finally, the psalmist knew that *you are ... my portion* (142:5). The word *portion* is used for the land that was allotted to the tribes and families in Israel. But the Levites, the priestly tribe, had no tribal area assigned to them, and it was said that the Lord was their portion (Num 18:20). When the psalmist said that the Lord was his portion *in the land of the living,* he was saying that though he might have no human help and no worldly possessions in this life, to know God – God's presence and love – was the greatest possession of all.

Because the psalmist could pray to God in his loneliness and trouble, he knew that in the end God would 'deal bountifully' with him (**142:7** NRSV), and he would be able to praise God in the midst of his fellow-believers. His desire to be released from loneliness was not so that he could do whatever he wanted to do, but so *that I may praise your name.*

Psalm 143: 'Teach Me to Do Your Will'

In Psalm 143 three human needs are brought to God, needs that we all have in different ways: the need for pardon, for protection, and for guidance.

143:1-2 Pardon

The psalmist was going to pray for help against his enemies, but he first acknowledged that he himself was a sinner in God's sight. He could pray with confidence because he knew God's *faithfulness* and *righteousness* (**143:1**) and thus knew that God could be trusted. But he also knew that *no one living is righteous* before God (**143:2b**). The Apostle Paul constantly emphasized that everyone needs God's grace and forgiveness because all are sinful (Rom 3:19-20; Gal 2:15-16). Like the psalmist, we must always ask God, *Do not bring your servant into judgment* (**143:2a**) and pray that he will show mercy and forgive us.

143:3-7 Protection

Then the psalmist presented his great need: *the enemy pursues me, he crushes me to the ground* (**143:3a**). He was so discouraged and depressed that he felt he counted in the world no more than those who had died long before and were forgotten (**143:3b-4**).

He remembered that God had been good to him and his people in the past (**143:5**; see also Ps 77), but now, he says, *My soul thirsts for you like a parched land* (**143:6**). Those of us who live in places where there are months without rain can understand this image. We know how the dry land soaks up the first showers and suddenly there is green growth again. But do we also know the same depth of desire for God that the psalmist expresses here? (see also 42:1-2). Do we also remember what God has done for us and for others in the past, and allow the remembrance to strengthen our faith as we pray?

If God continued to hide his face, that is, if he showed him no favour, the psalmist would be *like those who go down to the pit,* that is, the grave (**143:7**). *Rescue me, from my enemies, O Lord,* he pleaded (143:9).

143:8-12 Guidance

Faced with the darkness of the grave, the psalmist prayed that God's steadfast love would come to him as light in the morning (**143:8a**). He desperately wanted the light of God's guidance that would *show me the way I should go* (**143:8b**). Then he repeats this request: *Teach me to do your will* (**143:10a**). He does not just want to 'see' or 'know' God's will, but also to 'do' it. His prayer, *may your good Spirit lead me on level ground* (**143:10b**), may be a request to be kept from stumbling in the way, or it may express his desire to be kept in ways that are righteous and morally straight.

The psalmist knew that God was *righteous* and thus he begs him to act *for your name's sake* (**143:11**) – that is, because such action would be in accordance with God's character. And, because he felt that his cause was just, he prayed, *In your unfailing love, silence my enemies* (**143:12**).

Psalm 144: God's Blessings on His People

Psalm 144 has two parts, the first a prayer for deliverance and victory in war for the ruler of the land, and the second a prayer for God's blessing of the people with peace. Many of the verses in it are similar to those in other psalms (see Pss 18:2, 9, 14, 16, 34, 46-50; 33:2-3, 12; 104:32). This reminds us of the value of having the words of Scripture in our memory so that we can use them in praise and prayer.

144:1-11 Prayer for Deliverance and Victory

We may be startled when someone speaks of God as the one *who trains my hands for war, my fingers for battle* (**144:1**). We tend not to think in those terms, for as Christians we are called to be peacemakers (Matt 5:9) and to try to 'live at peace with everyone' (Rom 12:18). But we do have spiritual enemies, and we need to know how to fight spiritual battles (2 Cor 10:4-5) and to use the spiritual armour that God offers us (Eph 6:10-18). When we think in these terms, it is easier to identify with what the psalmist is saying.

It is a great thing when a leader, especially a country's ruler, confesses that God is his or her *Rock* and *fortress, deliverer* and *shield* (**144:1-2**) – in other words that there is no one else to turn to but the living God. It is also a wise ruler, and a wise man or woman in any situation in life, who realizes human weaknesses and limitations and knows that our life is like a *breath* or a *fleeting shadow* (**144:3-4**; see also 39:5-6; 62:9; 102:11). Yet despite our insignificance before God, he still thinks of us. What a privilege! (see also 8:3-8; Matt 6:25-32; Acts 17:26-28; Heb 2:6-18).

The psalmist turned to God for help because he knew how God had helped his people in the past. His call for God to come down with storm lightning and volcanic activity looks back to God's self-revelation at Mount Sinai (**144:5-6**; see Exod 19).

The psalmist's enemies were strong and threatened to overpower him like *mighty waters* (**144:7**). Those enemies were deceitful. Even when they made promises on oath by raising the right hand they could not be trusted (**144:8, 11**; see also 106:26). But with God as his help, he knew he could be delivered from them and be given victory, just as God had given victory to David and his successors in the past (**144:10**).

144:12-15 Prayer for the Blessings of Peace

The psalmist then thinks of what a peaceful nation would look like. He thinks first of all the young people. Instead of dying in battle or growing up stunted because of hardship, the young men will grow up like healthy plants or trees. The young women will be as beautiful as the columns that support the roof of a palace or give beauty to its rooms (**144:12**). They will be strong and straight, not bent with troubles, and will proudly contribute to the well-being of the whole nation.

He then goes on to think of the nation's economic prosperity. They will be blessed with abundant supplies and livestock (**144:13**). The NIV understands **144:14** to mean that they will also suffer no national defeat or disaster. However, the words may continue the thought of the blessing of God on sheep and cattle, so the GNB translates this verse as *May our cattle reproduce plentifully, without miscarriage or loss.*

When we read such promises of blessing in the OT, we need to remember that they are speaking of the nation rather than of individuals. If a nation is free from bribery and corruption, if justice is upheld, if rulers are concerned to help the poor, then there will be the blessings of peace and righteousness. How greatly people suffer in many of our countries, because there is injustice and rulers misuse their power and take wealth for themselves instead of sharing it with those in need! We should pray for godly leaders who will truly care for their people.

We should not take these verses out of context and use them to preach what has been called a prosperity gospel, suggesting that if people turn to God and serve him well, they will be strong and healthy, they will prosper in their work or business, and everything will go well with them. Jesus did not promise his disciples any such thing. He warned them that the way might be very hard, and they might have to suffer for their faith, though they could be sure that he would never leave them.

Whatever circumstances we face, as individuals, or in the life of our nation, we can rely on the truth that this psalm expresses and is summed up in its final words, *Blessed are the people whose God is the Lord* (**144:15**).

Psalm 145: The Greatness and Goodness of God

Psalm 145, like Psalm 119 and several others, is an acrostic in which each verse begins with the next letter of the Hebrew alphabet. For a long time, the verse for one of these letters was missing, but with the discovery of a text of Psalms among the Dead Sea Scrolls, we have been able to recover that lost line. It reads, *The Lord is faithful to all his promises and loving toward all he has made* (145:13).

145:1-6 The Greatness of God

This psalm begins (**145:1**) – and ends (145:21) – with the determination to praise God every day in the present and in the future. This call to oneself or to others to worship God is followed by reasons for such praise.

The first reason that God is *most worthy of praise* (**145:2**) is because he is great beyond anything that we can possibly express or even imagine (**145:3**). Together and alone we need to stop to think, or 'meditate', on what God has done. There are his *wonderful works* in creation, the power of wind and storm, thunder and lightning. There are his *mighty acts* of redemption, mercy and judgment (**145:4-5**). When we think of these things, we realize how much we have to *proclaim* (**145:6**).

145:7-10 The Goodness of God

God's almighty power is certainly awesome, but we can also *celebrate* his *abundant goodness* (**145:7**). The description of God in **145:8-9** is similar to the one Moses was given when he asked to see God's glory. He was told that the Lord is 'a gracious God, slow to anger, abounding in love and faithfulness' (Exod 34:6-7). These characteristics of God are so important that they are repeated many times in the OT (see Exod 34:6-7; Num 14:18; 2 Chr 30:9; Neh 9:17, 31-32; Pss 86:15; 103:8; Joel 2:13; Jonah 4:2). How wonderful it is that we can say that God *has compassion on all he has made* (**145:9**). God's *saints*, his faithful people should certainly bless his name (**145:10**).

145:11-13 The Greatness of God's Rule

When the Bible speaks of God's kingdom, we are not to think in terms of a nation with a fixed territory and borders. God's kingdom is his rule over all. When **145:11** speaks of the glory and power of God's kingdom, it is speaking of God's rule over our world – over the whole universe. If we have eyes to see, we can realize God's *mighty acts* and *the glorious splendour* (**145:12**) of his rule.

But people often resist his rule. Those in authority in the nations of the world often try to work against God. But their authority will not last long, while God's kingdom is *an everlasting kingdom* (**145:13**). These words are quoted in the book of Daniel (4:3, 34). At that time the Babylonians had conquered the Jewish people and taken them into exile. The kings of Babylon seemed to have unlimited power. But it was not so. Those powerful kings died and the Babylonian empire was conquered by others. And the work of God's kingdom went on.

145:14-20 The Goodness of God's Rule

Powerful people often try to show their power by forcing their will on others. God's power is shown in love. The powerless and oppressed can take heart. God seeks to lift up the fallen (**145:14-16**). Those who truly turn to him can take comfort in knowing that he is near (**145:18**; see also Phil 4:4-7; Jas 4:8). He answers the prayers of those who turn to him and will fulfil their desires (**145:19**; see also 34:17-18; 37:3-4). The wicked who reject God and despise what he offers them cannot live for ever, but God's unfailing care is shown towards those who seek to serve him (**145:20**).

The goodness of God's rule is summed up in **145:17**: *The Lord is righteous in all his ways and loving toward all he has made.*

Psalm 146: I'll Praise My Maker

The last five psalms in the book of Psalms all begin and end with the words, *Praise the Lord*. These words are a translation of the Hebrew words *Hallelu Yah*, which have become familiar in many languages throughout the world in words like 'Alleluia' or 'Hallelujah'.

This psalm begins with the psalmist's determination to keep praising God as long as he lives. God is worthy of praise – and always to be trusted. As we think of ourselves and as we think of God, we constantly need to appreciate human powerlessness and the power of God. This psalm eloquently reminds us of both.

146:1-4 Human Powerlessness

We have all been helped by others: family, friends and people who care for us. But we need to realize the limits of human help. Even if our friends are powerful and influential, they will still die *when their spirit departs* (**146:4**; see also Gen 3:19; Isa 2:22). A person may have great plans for helping others, but when they die *their plans come to nothing*. Others may have great plans for harming others, but when they die *their plans come to nothing*. There is only one who does not die and whose plans and purposes never fail (see 118:8-9).

146:5-6 The Power of God

The formula *blessed is* (or 'blessed are') occurs twenty-five times in the book of Psalms (see, for example, 1:1; 32:1-2; 40:4; 94:12; 112:1). In Jeremiah 17:5, we find the opposite formula: 'cursed is the one who trusts in man'. God is the only one we should trust, and thus the psalmist says, *Blessed is he whose help is the God of Jacob* (**146:5**). Jacob did not deserve God's help, but he and his people after him received it. 'The God of Jacob' always helps those who turn to him (see Pss 20:1; 46:7, 11). He is none other than *the Maker of heaven and earth, the sea and everything in them* (**146:6**). He is the completely reliable and unchanging God. He is concerned to bring justice to those who are oppressed by others. He is concerned that all people should have their daily needs met by his provision for them.

146:7-10 The Compassion of God

Many people have special needs, whether through their own fault or the faults of others, or through the difficult circumstances of their lives. We can think of prisoners, the blind, the discouraged, strangers and foreigners, orphans and widows (**146:7-9a**). The Bible often speaks of God's special care for such people, and of how those who serve the Lord should also care for them. God cares for those whom the world rejects and treats as outcasts.

But he honours those who seek to live *righteous* lives before him, while those who deliberately continue to follow *wicked* ways cannot expect to enjoy the saving grace that they have rejected (**146:9b**). There are no limits to the power of God. There are no limits to the compassion of God on all who turn to him. There is no end to his rule.

The psalm ends with the assurance, *The Lord reigns for ever.* Zion, God's people, and the church of Jesus Christ today, can be sure that he reigns *for all generations.* So *praise the Lord* (**146:10**). One way we can do this is by singing one of the greatest hymns in the English language that was based on this psalm:

I'll praise my Maker while I've breath;
And when my voice is lost in death,
Praise shall employ my nobler powers;
My days of praise shall ne'er be past,
While life, and thought, and being last, or
immortality endures (Isaac Watts).

Psalm 147: God's Word and God's Work

Psalm 147 is another psalm of pure praise, with no requests, but only thanks to God. Three times there is the call to praise God (147:1, 7, 12), followed by reasons for praise. This psalm has close links with other psalms and other parts of Scripture, suggesting that the psalmist had them in his mind as he wrote.

147:1-6 Healing Hurts

The statement that the Lord *builds up Jerusalem* and *gathers the exiles* suggests that this psalm was written after the people's exile in Babylon (**147:2**; see also Isa 56:8). The Lord brought them back to their land, restored them to Jerusalem, and healed their hurts (**147:3**; see also Isa 61:1). It is encouraging to know that God is always concerned for the broken-hearted and *sustains the humble,* and that he will judge those who have caused helpless people to be downtrodden and oppressed (**147:6**). It is an even greater encouragement to realize that the one who helps, heals and restores us is the one who created the vast number of the stars in the skies and gave to each its place (**147:4**; see also Isa 40:25-31). Our God is *great* indeed, *mighty in power,* and *his understanding has no limit* (**147:5**).

147:7-14 Providing for Needs

God has created our world so that clouds are formed, rain falls on the earth, grass and crops grow, and there is food for birds and animals as well as for people (**147:7-9**; see also Job 38:41). God wants us to trust him to supply these needs and for security in the face of enemies. In those days, people were tempted to depend on strong warriors and horses and chariots (**147:10**; see also 33:16-17), just as today nations depend on building up armies and equipping them to fight on land or sea or in the air. True strength and real security are found in God (20:6-9), for *the Lord delights in those who fear him,* that is, in those who recognize his

greatness and truth and justice and *who put their hope in his unfailing love* (**147:11**).

God knew that his people needed security, and he made it possible for them to rebuild the walls of Jerusalem and have strong bars on its gates again (**147:13**; see also 102:16; Neh 3). More important still was his blessing on the people, giving them peace and providing them with what they needed (**147:14**). The Lord seeks to bless our countries and nations today, but we must seek to live in his ways and to rely on him to meet our needs.

147:15-20 Sending His Word

The closing verses of the psalm speak of God sending his word. God's word is powerful. It is like a messenger running to do God's will (**147:15**). So it was at the beginning of creation: 'God said, "Let there be light"; and there was light' (Gen 1:3). So it is with every part of his creation. *Snow* and *frost* and *ice* are unknown in tropical countries and were also rare in Palestine. That was why the psalmist mentions them as a particular work of God. God's word sends the warm winds that melt the ice so that that the rivers flow (**147:16-18**).

An even more important aspect of God's word was that it revealed God's *laws and decrees* to Israel (**147:19**). Other nations also had laws, just as every nation does today. But the reason it could be said, *he has done this for no other nation* (**147:20**; see Deut 4:8) is that Israel's laws were part of God's covenant with them. When the Israelites kept the laws, they were expressing their obedience to God and showing that they wanted to live in a covenant relationship with him. That covenant was the great privilege of Israel, just as the new covenant is the great privilege of Christians today.

The Israelites were to share the privilege of knowing God and his word with people of all nations (see Isa 42:6; 49:6). Christian people today have an even greater responsibility to do this (1 Pet 2:9). After all, we have an even greater revelation of God's living Word, his Son Jesus Christ (John 1:1-18).

Psalm 148: Praise from Earth and Heaven

Like the last five psalms, Psalm 148 begins and ends with the words *Praise the Lord.* It is a call to everything in heaven and earth to join in praising the great, wise and loving God who made them and who is responsible for their continuing existence.

148:1-6 Praise from Heaven

When the Hebrews thought of heaven, they thought of the angels who serve in the presence of God, that is, the whole host of spiritual beings that God has made (**148:1-2**). Secondly, they thought of the sun, moon and stars. They did not think of these as gods, as some nations did, but as things made by God and known perfectly to him (**148:3**; see also 147:4). Then they thought of the sky and the water in the clouds that falls as rain upon the earth (**148:4**). God spoke, and all these were created (**148:5**). God is responsible for the existence of everything in the universe. The dependability of creation, its continuing order, also testifies to his greatness and the trust we can have in him (**148:6**; see also Gen 8:22; Jer 31:35-37; 33:25-26).

148:7-10 Praise from Earth

Think of the great and powerful ocean and the living creatures in it, some very small, some *great sea creatures* like whales and sharks (**148:7**). Think of the power of a storm, of thunder and lightning, of the snow and ice so rare in Palestine (**148:8**; see 147:16-17). Think of mountains and valleys, of trees, both the mighty trees of the forest and those whose fruit we enjoy (**148:9**). Think of animal life, including wild animals and domestic animals like sheep, goats and cattle. Think of the endless varieties of birds and creeping creatures and insects (**148:10**). The Lord God made them all, and intended them to belong together and to depend on one another. They declare the wisdom of the Lord. Consequently, we, whom God has entrusted with the care of creation (Gen 1:26), have a responsibility to see that the balance of nature is maintained and that God's good gifts are not destroyed by war, chemicals or their misuse or overuse.

148:11-14 Praise from God's People

As far as we know, none of the other creatures on earth have the same understanding of God as do humans, who are made 'in the image of God' (Gen 1:26). All other creatures praise God by fulfilling the purpose for which he made them. They thus show his power and wisdom and care, and their beauty tells us much about the *name* and character of God (19:1). But we humans are made to know God and to live in fellowship with him. So we, above all, should praise him. The greatest ones of the earth – *kings ... princes ... rulers* (**148:11**) are very small before their Creator. So they should praise God like everyone else, men and women, young and old. We praise God for his creation, but even more we praise him for what he has done for us (Isa 43:21). He has restored us and given us strength (the meaning of *raised up for his people a horn,* **148:14a**).

Whereas 145:18 spoke of the nearness of God to all who call on him, this psalm speaks of God's people being brought to live *close to his heart* (**148:14b**; see also Lev 10:3; Pss 65:4; 73:28). Ephesians 2:13-18 reminds us that the way we are brought near to God is by the redeeming work of Christ in dying for us. No wonder we should *Praise the Lord.*

Psalm 149: Praise of God and Battle for God

Psalm 149 is in two parts, joined by 149:6. The two parts are so different that we need to look hard to understand how they belong together. Praising the Lord is the subject of the first part; battle with *a double-edged sword* the topic of the second part.

149:1-5 Praise of God

Again we have a psalm that begins and ends with *Praise the Lord [Hallelu Yah].* A *new song* (**149:1**) is to be sung as God has done new things for his people (compare 33:3; 96:1; 98:1). God's people are to *be glad* and *rejoice* and praise the Lord with singing and dancing and musical instruments (**149:2-3**). They are to worship the Lord as their *Maker* and their *King.* It is the most wonderful thing that ordinary *humble* people can rejoice that *the Lord takes delight in his people* (**149:4a**). They can never deserve this, but as they look to him for salvation (**149:4b**), they prove his love and his power.

The instruction to *sing for joy on their beds* (**149:5**) may mean that God's victory has given the people security so that they can rest in their beds at night in peace and thankfulness. Or the psalmist may have been thinking of a feast of celebration and victory in which people would recline on couches and thank God. It is also possible that the word translated 'beds' would be better translated as 'places of prostration', like the prayer mats used in some religions. The NJB translation interprets it this way, and says that the people *shout for joy as they worship him.*

149:6-9 Serious Battle

How can people praise God and rejoice in the Lord, and at the same time have *a double-edged sword in their hands* (**149:6**)? Some have suggested that the psalmist is referring to a victory dance in which the dancers held swords. This dance would have represented Israel's battles against the nations, in which they wanted to take kings and nobles captive and put them in chains (**149:7-8**). The words also remind us of the situation in Nehemiah's day, when the people faced attack from enemies who were trying to stop them from rebuilding the walls of Jerusalem. They prayed to God for help against their enemies, and then worked with one hand and held a weapon with the other; or had their swords at their side as they built (Neh 4:17-18).

Christians have sometimes wrongly used this psalm to encourage people to fight for the Lord with swords and other weapons. (This is not to say that no Christian can ever join the army.) But Jesus did not intend his followers to fight for him. He said 'all who draw the sword will die by the sword' (Matt 26:52). Violence leads to more violence. Our battle is a spiritual battle, which we must fight by spiritual means, 'for our struggle is not against flesh and blood, but against the rulers, against the authorities, against the powers of this dark world and against the spiritual forces of evil in the heavenly realms' (Eph 6:12; see also 2 Cor 10:3-5; Eph 6:10-18; Heb 4:12). In that spiritual battle, we can fight with God's strength and in God's way and at the same time praise him. Then we will be able *to carry out the sentence* (literally, the written judgment) against those who oppose God's will (**149:9**). Similar words of judgment are written in many places in the Scriptures.

Psalm 150: The Climax of Praise

The psalms have expressed all the feelings that we experience in life: sorrow and joy, discouragement and thanksgiving, perplexities and worries, fears of enemies and of death, deep needs for healing, forgiveness and rescue from danger and oppressed peoples' cries for justice. Freely and frankly, the psalmists have brought those feelings to God, and told of their experiences of blessing and of woe. This last psalm, Psalm 150, is pure praise from beginning to end. Thirteen times it calls on us and all living creatures to praise the Lord.

150:1 Where?

We are to *praise God in his sanctuary* and *in his mighty heavens* (**150:1**), that is, on earth and in heaven alike (see also 148:1, 7).

150:2 Why?

Two things sum up why we should praise God. We should praise him *for his acts of power* (**150:2a**) – for all that he has done in creation, in providing for all our needs and for redeeming and forgiving us. The deeds that he has done show *his surpassing greatness* (**150:2b**), for which we should also praise him. He is great in wisdom, in power, in justice and holiness, in love and mercy. He is greater than we could ever express or think.

150:3-5 How?

All over the world, people find that music helps them to lift their hearts above their worries and troubles to worship God. Different nations and cultures use different instruments of music. Many peoples also express their joy and praise in the movement of dancing. An increasing volume

of sound made by the Hebrew musical instruments is described in **150:3-5**. First there was the *trumpet* that was blown to call people together on occasions of danger or to a celebration. It was joined by stringed instruments, like the *harp* and *lyre*. Then came the hand drums or *tambourines*, which were often played as people danced. Other instruments joined in, like *strings* and *flute*. Finally, there were the loud sounds as the metal of the different kinds of *cymbals* clanged and crashed together. What music! All to assist the praise of the One who is worthy to be worshipped with all that we have and are.

We too can use music and dancing and other activities to help us to worship God, provided these things do actually help our worship and are not given the kind of prominence that hinders sincere worship of God.

150:6 Who?

Let everything that has breath praise the Lord (**150:6**). All people, of all cultures, in all lands, should worship God. God intends every knee to bow before him and every tongue to acknowledge him (Isa 45:23; Phil 2:10-11). The book of Revelation, giving us hope and inspiring our praise now, pictures for us the worship of heaven, with myriads of angels joining with God's human creation to sing with full voice, 'Worthy is the Lamb' and 'To Him who sits on the throne and to the Lamb be praise and honour and glory and power, for ever and ever!' (Rev 5:11-13). What a scene! And what a responsibility it lays on us. If we truly want all people in all the world to be able to join in the worship of God, we are responsible to share our knowledge of God, and especially of Jesus Christ, with others.

'Praise God from whom all blessings flow;
Praise him all creatures here below,
Praise him above ye heavenly host;
Praise Father, Son, and Holy Ghost.'

Cyril Okorocha

Further Reading

Eaton, J.H. *The Psalms*. TBC. London: S.C.M, 1967.

Kidner, D. *Psalms*. TOT. Leicester: Inter-Varsity Press, 1981.

White, R.E.O. *A Christian Handbook to the Psalms*, Exeter: Paternoster/Grand Rapids: Eerdmans, 1984.

PROVERBS

We feel at home and yet distant when we read the book of Proverbs: at home because proverbs are a universal phenomenon in various cultures and societies – and particularly in traditional societies; distant, because we live in completely different times and cultures. Yet as Africans we can make a contribution to an enhanced understanding of the message of the book of Proverbs, for we still maintain a semblance of traditional community and there is much proverbial lore in our own languages.

Affirming that proverbs are a universal human phenomenon does not mean that there is no difference between biblical proverbs and the proverbs that are the product of the common grace given to humanity at large. Although the thrust of the message of all proverbial lore is to live wisely in the context in which we find ourselves, biblical proverbs are given in the context of the Scriptures and, therefore, in the context of the special revelation that God has given to humankind. Biblical wisdom cannot be properly understood unless we relate it to the covenant relationship between God and his people. This statement applies equally to the so-called 'absolute statements' made in Proverbs, to Job's struggle with God's seeming injustice and to Solomon's struggle in Ecclesiastes with the many injustices and contradictions he observes in human life. All these seemingly intractable problems have to be related to the sovereign Creator and Lord of the universe and his mysterious ways of dealing with his creation and with his covenant people.

Background

Reading the book of Proverbs, and especially chapters 10 to 29, we tend to find ourselves lost in 'the thicket of individual sayings' (*TOT*). We understand the frustration of David Atkinson when he says, 'The more I have explored this part of the wisdom literature of the Hebrew Bible, the more I have been impressed by the continuing topicality of its teaching, and frustrated by trying to bring its apparently disorganized mass of material into some sort of accessible form' (*BST*). This frustration is one reason why the book of Proverbs tends to be neglected in the worship and teaching of God's people.

Another reason the book has fallen out of favour is the moralistic tone of many of the proverbs. 'They seem to stress how we ought to behave more than what God has done for us' (*CC*). But to say this is to miss the point that 'what God has done for us' should result in transformed lives, and the proverbs give us guidance on how we ought to behave as we live these lives.

The accusation that Proverbs lacks order is also not entirely warranted. The book does, in fact, have a distinct structure, which can be traced in the headings found in 1:1, 10:1, 22:17, 24:23, 25:1, 30:1 and 31:1. These subsections form the starting point for the structure of this commentary. As will be shown in the commentary, there are also common threads that tie together groups of proverbs that may appear at first glance to be a random mix.

Individual proverbs show a distinct structure based on the standard form of Hebrew poetry. They are presented as grouped couplets or paired lines in what is referred to as parallelism. Such parallelism is especially clear in chapters 10 to 29 of the book. When the parallelism expresses the same idea in slightly different ways, this is referred to as synonymous parallelism (see, for example, 18:18). We also find antithetical parallelism, where the second part of the couplet contrasts with the first part (see, for example, 10:9); synthetic parallelism, where the second line develops the thought of the first (see, for example, 10:10); and comparative parallelism, in which one thing is compared to another.

Outline of Contents

COMMENTARY

1:1-7 Introduction

The opening verses of Proverbs serve as an introduction to the first major division of the book (chs. 1–9) as well as to the entire book.

1:1 Title and Author

The book introduces itself as *The proverbs of Solomon son of David, king of Israel* (**1:1**), and thus acquires its title. However, the question that immediately arises is, what does the word 'proverb' mean? In Africa today a 'proverb' is understood to be a short wise saying. But as we read the book of Proverbs it becomes clear that this word had a far wider meaning for the ancient Israelites. The Hebrew word used originally simply meant 'a comparison' as, for example, in 11:22 and 12:4. Gradually, however, its meaning broadened to encompass maxims or observations of the type we find in chapters 10 to 22, sermons such as the one in chapter 5, wisecracks like the one in Ezekiel 18:2 and even doctrinal revelations (Ps 49:4).

Solomon is said to be the author of the book, but it is clear from the headings of the various sections that he was not the sole source of its contents. Some proverbs are attributed to 'the wise', to Agur and to others. Only 10:1-22:16 and chapters 25 to 29 are specifically said to have been written by Solomon. Thus some scholars argue that the mention of his name in 1:1 is either a later addition or a carryover from those sections. But there is no reason to doubt, as maintained in the Jewish and Christian traditions, that Solomon was a wise man par excellence (1 Kgs 3:4-15, 16-28; 4:29-34) and that he played an important role in shaping the book of Proverbs as we have it.

1:2-6 Purpose

After naming the book, the author sets out its purpose, using a string of infinitives (which are translated as such in the NASB, but which the NIV translates as 'for'). The benefits to be gained by the study of this book are the attainment of *wisdom and discipline*, the understanding of *words of insight* (**1:2**), the acquisition of *a disciplined and prudent life* in which one does *what is right and just and fair* (**1:3**), and the garnering of *prudence* and *knowledge and discretion* by the young and simple (**1:4**). The string of verbs giving reasons for studying this book is interrupted in **1:5** by an aside pointing out that it is not merely the young who will benefit from studying it. Then in **1:6** the author returns to the list and speaks of the need to understand *proverbs and parables, the sayings and riddles of the wise,* or in other words the literary forms teachers use when imparting wisdom.

Commenting on these verses, Hubbard states, 'The regnant word ... is wisdom' and the eight or so additional nouns used to elaborate this basic concept 'are calculated to show wisdom's well-stocked larder' (*CC*). Kidner makes much the same point when he says that 'the book of Proverbs opens by breaking up the plain daylight of wisdom ... into its rainbow of constituent colours' (*TOT*).

All classes of people are invited to receive the teaching of wisdom. Among the beneficiaries are *the wise* (1:5), who are exhorted to hear and increase their learning. Indeed, the wise are more inclined to receive more wisdom and become wiser than the scoffers and the wicked (9:7-9). Even kings and princes are among those who are later invited to avail themselves of what wisdom is offering (8:15-16). However, the main targets of the teaching of wisdom in this introduction and in the early chapters of Proverbs are *the simple* (or inexperienced) and *the young* (1:4). They are the ones with the greatest need in the light of the temptations they encounter as they make character-forming decisions.

1:7 Motto

Having named the book and told readers why they should study it, the author now presents a motto that is actually the theme statement for the entire book. The NIV is correct to set this off as a separate paragraph between the preceding verses and the beginning of the first major division of the book, for this is its position in the Hebrew text. To emphasize its importance, this theme statement is later repeated, in slightly different forms, at the end of the 'Reflection on Wisdom' (9:10) and at the end of the book itself (31:30).

The motto verse summarizes the characteristics of the two categories of people depicted in this book: the wise and fools. The wise are referred to in the first half of the couplet in its statement of what constitutes *the beginning of knowledge,* while in the second half, fools are described as those who *despise wisdom and discipline* (other English versions translate the second word as *instruction*). This saying is also repeated, with slight variations, in Job 28:28 and Psalm 111:10.

The phrase *the fear of the Lord* recurs frequently throughout Proverbs (for example, in 10:27; 14:26, 27; 15:16, 33; 16:6; 19:23; 23:17, and in a modified form in 8:13; 14:2; 24:21). It is clear that here 'fear' does not mean the dread of the unknown or mysterious, or the terror related to the wrath of God. Rather, it means reverent and humble submission to the revealed will of Yahweh, which is accompanied by worshipful adoration of him. 'Although it includes worship, it does not end there. It radiates out from our adoration and devotion to our everyday conduct that sees each moment as the Lord's time, each relationship as the Lord's opportunity, each duty as the Lord's command, and each blessing as the Lord's gift' (*CC*).

The meaning of the phrase *the beginning of wisdom* is also debated. Some interpret it as referring to the first step in wisdom, the point of departure for gaining more wisdom. But it seems more likely that what is meant is that the fear of God is the fundamental component, the principal part, of wisdom.

1:8-9:18 Reflections on Wisdom

These reflections on wisdom constitute the first major division of the book of Proverbs and set the tone for the teaching of the whole book. What we have here are longer discourses, whereas much of the rest of the book contains short, self-contained sayings. Understanding the long discourses will help readers to orient themselves and make sense of the flurry of individual sayings in 10:1-22:16.

The text of 1:8-9:18 can be broken up into ten separate lectures or discourses (*TOT*): a warning against evil companions (1:8-19), Wisdom's impassioned appeal (1:20-33), the fruits of wisdom (2:1-22), the blessings of obedience and devotion (3:1-35), a lifetime commitment (4:1-27), a warning against adultery and a commendation of marriage (5:1-23), pitfalls for the unwary (6:1-35), an object lesson of the dangers of adultery (7:1-27), Wisdom's excellence and her role in creation (8:1-36), and rival feasts (9:1-18).

All of these lessons are directed to *my son* (a term that is used some fifteen times – 1:8, 10, 15; 2:1; 3:1, 11, 21; 4:10, 20; 5:1, 20; 6:1, 3, 20; 7:1; see also 4:3), and to *my sons* (used four times – 4:1; 5:7; 7:24; 8:32; see also 8:4). The greatest concentration of 'my son' or 'my sons' in the entire book of Proverbs is found in this section. It is the concern for the young and the simple that we saw in the introduction to the commentary that motivates 'the vivid details, the fatherly earnestness, and the insistence that the final outcome should be faced' (*TOT*).

However, who is the teacher? At times, it seems that the son is being admonished by his actual parents (for example, in 1:8). At other times, it is a teacher of wisdom who is giving the instruction. In three of the discourses, we are clearly told that the speaker is personified wisdom (1:20-33; 8:1-36; 9:1-12). But a question arises: 'Is the father/son relationship restricted to the human level only?' We are given the impression that the real source of the instructions is beyond the human sphere. Proverbs 3:11 seems to indicate that the source of instruction is not simply human parents or sages, or even personified wisdom, but Yahweh himself.

1:8-19 Warning Against Evil Companions

The first discourse opens with real parents exhorting their son: *Listen ... to your father's instruction and do not forsake your mother's teaching* (**1:8**). The word 'instruction' is the same one that was translated as 'discipline' in the purpose statement (see 1:2). It is associated with the father, while the word 'teaching', which is a translation of the Hebrew word for 'law' is associated with the mother. The mention of both parents here (and again in 6:20) is a tribute to the significant role played by mothers in the Hebrew family, a role that was unusual in the cultures of the ancient Near East.

The reason why the son should listen is given in **1:9**: these teachings *will be a garland to grace your head and a chain to adorn your neck.* He is reminded of the beauty and delightfulness of a life lived in obedience to parents in his immediate context and to the Lord in the long run. Such teaching is almost unknown today, when each generation feels obliged to repudiate the beliefs of its parents.

The parents are well aware that theirs are not the only voices their son will be hearing, and so they launch into a specific warning that contrasts sharply with what preceded it (1:10-19). The social setting seems to be a town or city, and the other voices are those of a criminal gang. They entice the young man to join them (**1:10**), to get on the bandwagon (**1:11, 14a**) and to share their loot (**1:13, 14b**), which they will get by waylaying *some harmless soul* (1:11) and swallowing *them alive, like the grave, and whole, like those who go down to the pit* (**1:12**). This type of peer-group pressure justifies the comment that 'folly is not just an individual matter but a social one as well' (*CC*).

As exciting as the thrice-mentioned 'let's' of this peer group and as enticing as their promises are, the consequence of accompanying them is nothing short of death. Not content with merely prohibiting friendship with this group (*do not give in to them* – 1:10; *do not go along with them, do not set foot on their paths* – **1:15**), the parents explain in no uncertain terms the final destiny of such *sinners.* They are so consumed by greed that they stop at nothing (**1:16**). They are either as stupid as birds that will allow themselves to be caught by a net that they saw being set up, or even more stupid, for an intelligent bird will shun that snare (**1:17**). 'These men are so blinded by evil that they fail to recognize the trap' (*EBC*). What is the trap? The fact that though their intention was to *lie in wait for someone's blood* (1:11), they actually *lie in wait for their own blood* (**1:18**). Though they said *let's waylay some harmless soul* (1:11), *they waylay only themselves* (1:18). Proverbs 26:27 makes the same point: 'If a man digs a pit, he will fall into it'. The parent's warning ends, *such is the end of all who go after ill-gotten gain; it takes away the lives of those who get it* (**1:19**).

1:20-33 Wisdom's Impassioned Appeal

Whereas in the previous passage it was the parents who were speaking, here the speaker is personified wisdom. She is introduced as she *calls aloud* and *raises her voice in the street* and *in the public squares* (**1:20**); *at the head of the noisy streets she cries out, in the gateways of the city she makes her speech* (**1:21**). Whereas the parents were imparting wisdom in the confines and privacy of the home, wisdom utters her clarion call in a public place. The writer is emphasizing that wisdom has strategically positioned herself where her message can be heard by as many as possible as clearly as possible. The image reminds us of African street evangelists, broadcasting their message from strategic locations in the city.

It is interesting to note that the word translated *wisdom* in 1:20 is plural in the Hebrew. Most scholars agree that this is a plural of intensity, pointing to 'her majesty many-sidedness' (*CC*), the same diversity that was depicted by

the cluster of words used to describe wisdom in the purpose statement (1:2-6).

The content of wisdom's message is given in 1:22-33. She starts with the words *How long* repeated twice in **1:22**, suggesting that she has been waiting for some time for a response from her audience. That this is the case is clearly stated in **1:23**, where she speaks of what would have happened *if you had responded to my rebuke.* A response would have produced a good outcome: *I would have poured out my heart to you and made my thoughts known to you.* What the NIV translates as 'heart' and 'thoughts' are 'spirit' and 'words' respectively in the Hebrew. This translation has been retained by the NASB as well as by the translation in Tigrigna, the official language of Eritrea.

The people addressed are described as *simple ones* and *mockers* and *fools* (1:22) – a group of words used in the book of Proverbs to depict 'the fools' who stand at the opposite pole to 'the wise'.

Although wisdom is exhorting them to listen to her 'rebuke', the answer to the question 'How long?' seems to be a foregone conclusion. The simpletons', scoffers', and fools' rejection of wisdom's reproofs and counsel has invited retribution in kind: *Since you ignored all my advice and would not accept my rebuke, I in turn will laugh at your disaster; I will mock when calamity overtakes you – when calamity overtakes you like a storm, when disaster sweeps over you like a whirlwind, when distress and trouble overwhelm you* (**1:24-27**). Wisdom elaborates on her rejection of them by saying, *they will call to me but I will not answer; they will look for me but will not find me* (**1:28**). There is a limit to wisdom's patience and her offer of instruction, and a consequence for exceeding that limit. This consequence is spelled out again: *Since they would not accept my advice and spurned my rebuke; they will eat the fruit of their ways and be filled with the fruit of their schemes* (**1:30-31**). Her words contain an echo of the theme verse when she describes their misguided lifestyle: *they hated knowledge and did not choose to fear the Lord* (**1:29**; see 1:7).

The discourse concludes with a summary statement of the destinies that result from accepting or rejecting wisdom: *For the waywardness of the simple will kill them, and the complacency of fools will destroy them; but whoever listens to me will live in safety and be at ease, without fear of harm* (**1:32-33**; see also 2:21-22; 3:33-35; 4:18-19; 8:35-36).

2:1-22 The Fruits of Wisdom

Chapter 2 is the most organized unit in the whole of the book of Proverbs. It forms a single long poem. In the original Hebrew, it can even be described as a single sentence!

This poetic lecture begins with the same words as 1:10: *My son, if …* (2:1). But what follows is very different. Whereas the advice up to this point has been negative, now it is positive. Whereas the emphasis in the earlier passage was on the danger of being enticed into evil, here it is on the benefits that flow from acquiring wisdom. The teacher speaks of the successful search for wisdom (2:1-8), the results of finding it (2:9-11), gives two examples to illustrate his point (2:12-15 and 16-19), and wraps up with a conclusion (2:20-22).

2:1-8 The search for and acquisition of wisdom

Whereas in the previous passage it was wisdom who cried out (1:20), in the present one it is the seeker of wisdom who is admonished to *call out* and to *cry aloud* (2:3). The first four verses explain the intensity of this search. The preliminary address, *My son*, is followed by three 'if' statements: *If you accept my words and store up my commands within you, turning your ear to wisdom and applying your heart to understanding* (**2:1-2**), *and if you call out for insight and cry aloud for understanding* (**2:3**), and lastly *and if you look for it as for silver and search for it as for hidden treasure* (**2:4**). In typical Hebrew fashion, the writer uses a chain of verbs to emphasize the intensity required: 'accept', 'store up', 'turn', 'apply', 'call out', 'cry aloud', 'look for', 'search'. But the order in which these verbs are given also implies something about the structure of the search. It does not involve free speculation, but takes its starting-point in revelation, comprising specific information (*words*) and practical instruction (*commandments*) (*TOT*). The searcher treasures and explores received teachings in an attempt to understand the underlying principles, and the goal of the search is not academic but spiritual. The outcome of such earnest seeking on the basis of what God has already revealed is assured: *then you will understand the fear of the Lord and find the knowledge of God* (**2:5**).

The fact that 'the fear of the Lord' and 'the knowledge of God' are presented as parallel phrases confirms our earlier interpretation of this phrase (see comments on 1:7). Here 'the fear of the Lord' is the reward for the search for wisdom. Yet it is not solely the outcome of the human search, for the writer stresses that *the Lord gives wisdom, and from his mouth come knowledge and understanding* (**2:6**). Those who seek find, not necessarily because of their search but because God gives wisdom and knowledge. An Umbundu proverb from Angola underscores this: *Uloño wosi wo manu lu kulihiso vitunda tunda ku Suku* ['All wisdom is from God. Also, all things rest with God'].

Not only does God give wisdom to those who trust him, but he also provides protection: *He holds victory in store for the upright, he is a shield to those whose walk is blameless* (**2:7**). How does God hold 'victory in store'? How does he play the role of a shield? The answer comes in **2:8**: *he guards the course of the just and protects the way of his faithful ones.*

2:9-11 The results of finding wisdom

God offers protection to those who seek wisdom, and the wisdom itself becomes a source of protection. In 2:5 the 'then' indicated that the person searching for wisdom would find it; in 2:9, the 'then' refers to the results that possessing wisdom will produce: *then you will understand what is right and just and fair – every good path* (**2:9**). These benefits of wisdom are precisely the ones promised in the purpose statement in 1:3. The explanation of the benefits of wisdom continues with the *for* of 2:10, which spills over into 2:11. The fact is stated first: wisdom and knowledge have taken residence in the life of the disciple (**2:10**). As a result of this, *Discretion will protect you, and understanding will guard you* (**2:11**).

2:12-19 Examples of wisdom's protection

The first illustration of the protection that wisdom offers relates to protection *from the ways of wicked men* (2:12). A vivid description of these men follows. They are *men whose words are perverse, who leave the straight paths to walk in dark ways, who delight in doing wrong and rejoice in the perverseness of evil, whose paths are crooked and who are devious in their ways* (**2:12-15**). In the first discourse, the son was warned against associating with people like this. In the second discourse, he is given assurance that both God and wisdom will protect him from them.

The second illustration of protection relates to evil women (2:16-19). The specific woman referred to is described as *the adulteress* and *the wayward wife ... who has left the partner of her youth and ignored the covenant she made before God* (**2:16-17**). Some translations, such as the NASB, follow the Hebrew in translating the last part of 2:17 as 'the covenant of her God', which should not be interpreted as suggesting that she is a foreigner and not an Israelite. The only way in which she is foreign is in her behaviour, which is inappropriate for one of the covenant people of God. Some scholars think that the author is referring to both this national covenant and the marriage covenant here. Others take the verse as referring only to her breaking of the marriage covenant (see also Mal 2:14), a breaking which also involves both God and her partner. Not content with having broken that vow, she is now trying to entice the young man with *seductive words* (2:16). But consorting with her is the gateway to death: *for her house leads down to death and her paths to the spirits of the dead. None who go to her return or attain the paths of life* (**2:18-19**). This is a theme that will be repeated over and over again in these discourses (5:3-6, 20; 6:23-35; 7:1-27; 9:13-18).

2:20-22 Conclusion

By gaining wisdom and avoiding the snares of evil men and evil women, the young man will preserve his life: *thus you will walk in the ways of good men and keep to the paths of the righteous* (**2:20**). The final reward of the righteous and the judgment of the wicked are clearly depicted. Whereas *the upright will live in the land* (**2:21**) that God has given to those who obey him, *the wicked will be cut off* (**2:22**) and uprooted from it. In the context of the covenant people, the land in question can be taken to mean the promised land. However, for Christians it can be taken to mean the earth. Whichever version of land is being referred to, there can be no doubt of the contrasting destinies – a contrast that will be returned to repeatedly in these discourses.

3:1-35 Blessings of Obedience and Devotion

This is a relatively long discourse, which can be divided into five subsections.

3:1-12 Actions and consequences

Here we hear admonitions from the wisdom teacher to the one who is being instructed. The teacher presents the world as a rational place in which specific actions can be expected to produce specific consequences. He presents six pairs of actions and the corresponding consequences.

The first of these pairs is introduced immediately: *My son, do not forget my teaching, but keep my commands in your heart* (**3:1**). The results or consequences of obeying follow: *for they will prolong your life many years and bring you prosperity* (**3:2**). The benefits of obeying the teaching of the sages are years of life and prosperity. Thus the student is told: *Let love and faithfulness never leave you; bind them around your neck, write them on the tablet of your heart* (**3:3**). The terms used here remind us of the covenant loyalty that exists between the Lord and his people. The reference to binding these virtues around one's neck recalls the garland and necklace of 1:9 and, even further back, the instructions in Deuteronomy 6:4-9. If the student does this, *Then,* says the teacher, *you will win favour and a good name in the sight of God and man* (**3:4**).

The subject of the next double pair (3:5-8) is trust in the Lord. Trusting in the Lord and not relying on one's own understanding (**3:5**) will result in experiencing God's guidance: *he will make your paths straight* (**3:6**). Similar advice is given in **3:7**: *Do not be wise in your own eyes; fear the Lord and shun evil.* What will be the outcome of this? *This will bring health to your body and nourishment to your bones* (**3:8**). Wisdom is sometimes described as the art of steering a course through life, but that description may give the impression that it is our human ability to think our way through the complexities of this world that will crown us with the blessings of a meaningful and successful life. These verses say it once and for all: it is not a person's trust in his or her ability

and resources but trust in the Lord that will bring wholeness and fulfilment of life.

The final set of pairs is an interesting juxtaposition. First, the young man is directed to *honour the Lord with your wealth, with the firstfruits of all your crops* (**3:9**). The result follows: *then your barns will be filled to overflowing, and your vats will brim over with new wine* (**3:10**). This verse would seem to endorse a prosperity gospel, but Kidner reminds us: 'The generalization that piety brings plenty chimes in with much of Scripture … and of experience. [However,] if it were more than a generalization (as Job's comforters held), God would be not so much honoured, as invested in, by our gifts' (*TOT*). And thus, there is the balancing effect of the next pair: *My son, do not despise the Lord's discipline and do not resent his rebuke* (**3:11**). The reason for this instruction follows: *because the Lord disciplines those he loves, as a father the son he delights in* (**3:12**). The writer of Hebrews quotes this passage to encourage believers whose faith was being severely tested (Heb 12:4-6).

3:13-20 The delights of wisdom

The next group of verses is a cluster on the topic of wisdom. *Blessed,* indeed, *is the man who finds wisdom, the man who gains understanding* (**3:13**). The author beautifully elaborates the reason for this blessedness. First of all, *she is more profitable than silver and yields better returns than gold* (**3:14**). Wisdom is even *more precious than rubies; as a matter of fact nothing you desire can compare with her* (**3:15**). The reason wisdom is incomparable is because her gifts to those who seek her are worth more than all the precious gems mentioned in the preceding verses. Her gifts are then described: *Long life is in her right hand; in her left hand are riches and honour* (**3:16**). Not only that, but *her ways are pleasant ways, and all her paths are peace* (**3:17**). Moreover, *she is a tree of life to those who embrace her; those who lay hold of her will be blessed* (**3:18**). This image of a tree reminds us of the description of one who is blessed as being 'like a tree planted by streams of water' (Ps 1:3). In passing, it is worth noting that this and many other references to the book of Proverbs refute those who say the wisdom books have nothing to do with other parts of the Bible.

This section ends with a statement that adds a theological dimension to what the preceding verses have said about the benefits of wisdom. The writer praises the value of wisdom by linking it to God's work in creation (**3:19-20**). What is mentioned here only briefly will be explained at length in 8:22-31.

3:21-26 The practical benefits of wisdom

The next set of admonitions again begin with 'my son' and return to the cause and consequence pattern of the earlier admonitions: *My son, preserve sound judgment and discernment, do not let them out of your sight* (**3:21**). The outcome is explained more extensively in 3:22-24: *they will be life for you, an ornament to grace your neck* (**3:22**). Life in all its bounty has already been mentioned in relation to wisdom, and the idea that it is an ornament has been mentioned in 1:9. *Then you will go on your way in safety, and your foot will not stumble* (**3:23**). There is no stumbling when one is walking in the paths made straight by the Lord (see 3:6). But the safety is not only when one is moving, for the idea is expanded as follows: *when you lie down, you will not be afraid; when you lie down, your sleep will be sweet* (**3:24**). After these positive assurances, the disciple is again admonished to *have no fear of sudden disaster or of the ruin that overtakes the wicked* (**3:25**), for if the advice given here has been heeded, then *the Lord will be your confidence and will keep your foot from being snared* (**3:26**).

3:27-32 Generosity and good neighbourliness

The next set of admonitions has to do with generosity and good neighbourliness. They are given as prohibitions: 'do not'. *Do not withhold good from those who deserve it, when it is in your power to act. Do not say to your neighbour, 'Come back later; I'll give it tomorrow' – when you now have it with you* (**3:27-28**). In the original Hebrew, the phrase translated 'from those who deserve it' literally means 'from the ones whose it is'. It may sound strange to our ears, but God is saying that the needy have a right to our assistance if we have the ability to give it. Thus procrastination is not merely callous, it is also unjust! A similar idea is expressed in the Latin proverb 'He gives twice who gives promptly'.

The next set of admonitions (**3:29-32**) deal with maintaining peace in the neighbourhood. Where there is plotting rather than trust, accusations rather than friendship, violence rather than peacemaking, there can be no community. No wonder the Lord *detests a perverse man* but honours a righteous one, whom he *takes ... into his confidence* (3:32).

3:33-35 Concluding summary

The contrast between two lifestyles in 3:32 is brought sharply into focus in the antithetical lines of the concluding verses, where the second line of each couplet presents the opposite of what is described in the first line. The one lifestyle is cursed by the Lord, while the other receives his blessing (**3:33**); one is mocked by him, the other given his grace (**3:34**); and finally, *The wise inherit honour, but fools he holds up to shame* (**3:35**). This contrast in the destinies of the wise and the fools will be repeatedly underscored throughout the book of Proverbs.

4:1-27 A Lifetime Commitment

4:1-4 A family affair

This passage is one of the few in Proverbs where the plural *sons* or 'children' (in some versions) is used for the

addressees (4:1). In the first section (4:1-9) of our present discourse the teacher is reminiscing about what he himself was taught by his parents. By this linking of three generations he underscores that he is passing on what he himself has received. Atkinson comments: 'This rich little paragraph revolves around the central point that in the education process, we learn most of all from those around us, especially those in our families. This father (4:1) learned from his father and mother (4:3), and is passing the wisdom on to his sons (4:1)' (BST). The passage is also a vivid demonstration of an Israelite family carrying out the injunction given in Deuteronomy 6:7.

This ideal way of passing wisdom to the younger generation chimes well with the African context, especially where the extended family system is intact. But with the onslaught of modernity and the emergence of the nuclear family, African Christian families must do some soul searching. Are we meeting the challenge of training our young ones in godliness or are we delegating this tremendous responsibility to the churches or even to our educational institutions?

In the passage, this wise parent admonishes his children: *Listen ... to a father's instruction ... and gain understanding* (**4:1**). Since he has received and appropriated this instruction in his own life, he is speaking with authority and confidence: *I give you sound learning, so do not forsake my teaching* (**4:2**). The generations and the teachings appear to overlap here. He starts out speaking to *my sons* (4:1), but, as he proceeds, he changes to the singular *my son* in 4:10 and 4:20. It is possible that he is focusing his attention on his eldest son. Just as there is no indication of where the audience changes from several sons to one son, so there is no indication of where his father's teaching ends and his own teaching begins. What is important is that he is passing on the tradition – what he has received – and is not concocting his own innovative teaching. Thus the education that is reflected in these chapters is to be primarily understood in its Israelite setting – both in its format and in its content.

4:5-9 Seek wisdom

The first part of the father's teaching is an instruction to seek wisdom. He tells his children to *Get wisdom, get understanding; do not forget my words or swerve from them* (**4:5**). Once they have received wisdom, they should not forsake it for it will protect them; they should love her and *she will watch over you* (**4:6**). As indicated in earlier passages, the only safe haven in life is in the unrelenting pursuit of wisdom. The verses that follow develop this point further: *Wisdom is supreme; therefore get wisdom. Though it cost all you have, get understanding* (**4:7**). This is because, as we saw in the preceding discourse, wisdom is priceless (3:13-18). *Esteem her, and she will exalt you; embrace her, and she will honour you* (**4:8**). In fact, as already indicated in 1:9, *She will set a garland of grace on your head and present you with a* *crown of splendour* (**4:9**). One who is in possession of divine wisdom is recognized as dignified and honourable even by secular society. The Ovimbundu of Angola, whose proverb was quoted earlier, not only believe that God is the source of all wisdom but also affirm that wisdom is priceless. They prize wisdom above all beauty and strength and regard it as a great possession.

4:10-19 Choose wisdom

The renewed admonition *Listen, my son* is followed by the presentation of two ways of living: the way of righteousness and the way of wickedness – The learner can mature safely by choosing the one and rejecting the other. Making the right choice will mean that *the years of your life will be many* (**4:10**). First, the teacher presents the life-giving option: *I guide you in the way of wisdom and lead you along straight paths* (**4:11**). The disciple is promised that *when you walk, your steps will not be hampered; when you run, you will not stumble* (**4:12**). There are no hidden traps or obstacles here, as there are on the other path, for the disciple will be led 'along straight paths'. Hence the additional exhortation, before the father goes on to describe the path of the wicked: *Hold on to instruction, do not let it go; guard it well, for it is your life* (**4:13**).

The learner is warned against taking the other way: *Do not set foot on the path of the wicked or walk in the way of evil men* (**4:14**). He should not even contemplate their path, let alone set foot on it: *Avoid it, do not travel on it; turn from it and go on your way* (**4:15**). The teacher then elaborates on the lifestyle of a world turned on its head: *For they cannot sleep till they do evil; they are robbed of slumber till they make someone fall* (**4:16**). What depravity! The warning continues: *They eat the bread of wickedness and drink the wine of violence* (**4:17**). This may mean either that 'wickedness' and 'violence' are their daily menu – their bread and drink – or that they make a living by these. Once again, we are reminded of the ever-increasing gang violence in our urban centres. What in the world has gone wrong with our societies? Our chance of living a decent, secure life – not only here in Africa, but even in the richest and militarily best-equipped nations – is becoming more and more remote because humanity has turned its back on God's blueprint. What a challenge for the church!

The father concludes with a summary contrasting the outcome of the two ways, a summary that could be taken as applying to the entire discourse: *The path of the righteous is like the first gleam of dawn, shining ever brighter till the full light of day. But the way of the wicked is like deep darkness; they do not know what makes them stumble* (**4:18-19**). There is a contrast here 'between danger and constant bewilderment on the one hand, and safety and growing certainty on the other' (*TOT*).

4:20-27 Concentrate on wisdom

The final section contains another set of exhortations and promises. After another reminder to heed his instructions and of the benefits of obedience to them (**4:20-22**), the teacher says, *Above all else, guard your heart, for it is the wellspring of life* (**4:23**). In the preceding verses, the teacher has already indicated how to guard the heart. It is by keeping the words of the wise *within your heart* (4:21). He is in agreement with the psalmist: 'How can a young man keep his way pure? By living according to your word' (Ps 119:9), and 'I have hidden your word in my heart that I might not sin against you' (Ps 119:11). So *put away perversity from your mouth; keep corrupt talk far from your lips* (**4:24**), says the teacher. He admonishes us to concentrate on the path instead: *Let your eyes look straight ahead, fix your gaze directly before you* (**4:25**). The secret is a single-minded focus on the path that leads to eternal life. Although the promise to lead the disciple along straight paths has already been given (4:11), the disciple must cooperate: *Make level paths for your feet and take only ways that are firm* (**4:26**). Furthermore, the disciples' eyes must be fixed firmly heavenward. The motto is 'Do not be distracted or sidetracked'! (**4:27**). The same point is made in a Kaonde (Zambian) proverb, advising that a leader should stay focused: 'One who enters a thicket should not worry about the things rustling around in there'. In other words, one should not allow the complaints or criticism of others to hinder one's work.

5:1-23 Warning Against Adultery

In 2:16-19 there was a brief warning against the adulteress and wayward wife. Here the warning is elaborated. It is a point to which the teacher returns again and again (6:20-35; 7:1-27; 9:13-18).

5:1-6 A description of the adulteress

As before, the sage exhorts his hearers to pay attention to his wisdom and to incline their ears to his understanding (**5:1**). He gives his reason in **5:2**: *that you may maintain discretion and your lips may preserve knowledge.* The reason for the stress on lips here becomes apparent as he moves into his description of a character the NIV calls *an adulteress* (5:3-6). She is a seductive speaker with lips that *drip honey* and speech that *is smoother than oil* (**5:3**). The sweetness and smoothness of her words may fool those whose lips are not protected by knowledge. *But in the end she is bitter as gall, sharp as a double-edged sword* (**5:4**). The sting is in the phrase 'in the end'. For those who have not equipped themselves with wisdom, the realization comes too late. Not only do her words mutilate with the sharpness of a sword that cuts both ways, but her feet, too, *go down to death* and *her steps lead straight to the grave* (**5:5**). 'Death' and 'grave' can be taken as synonyms, for both end in destruction. Since her feet lead to death, it comes as no surprise that *she gives no thought to the way of life* (**5:6**). Had she done so, she would have mended her ways. Although *her paths are crooked* – 'unstable' would be a better translation – she does not realize this.

5:7-14 Consequences of adultery

After the usual preliminaries (**5:7**) the teacher says, *Keep to a path far from her, do not go near the door of her house* (**5:8**). It is only logical to instruct youngsters to keep to a path as far away as possible from that of the adulteress, which leads to death.

The essence of the warning is given in the clauses beginning with *lest* and in the words attributed to the remorseful disciple. The first consequence of not heeding the warning is the wasteful loss of *your best strength* (**5:9**), no doubt referring to youthful vigour. These are the same *years* in which one would build up one's reputation and one's career (to put it in modern terms), or whatever it was to which one devoted the prime of one's life. The result of wasting these years will be that *strangers feast on your wealth* and that *your toil* will *enrich another man's house* (**5:10**). Ross comments: 'The price of infidelity may be high; for everything one works for – position, power, prosperity – could be lost either through the avaricious demands of the woman or the outcry for restitution by the community' (*EBC*).

The words of the remorseful disciple are introduced by the following statement: *At the end of your life you will groan, when your flesh and body are spent* (**5:11**). 'Bereft of all that sustains life – self-esteem and material goods – he is left with nothing to do but mourn, literally "groan" or "growl" like a beast mortally wounded, flesh and body consumed' (*CC*). The remorseful words of the student follow: *How I hated discipline! How my heart spurned correction! I would not obey my teachers or listen to my instructors. I have come to the brink of utter ruin in the midst of the whole assembly* (**5:12-14**). Hubbard comments: 'The teacher's technique here is powerful: he places a litany of grey regrets on his student's lips that were earlier commissioned to guard wisdom (5:2). Guard it they do, but too late' (*CC*). This is a very powerful way of impressing upon the hearts and minds of learners the importance of listening now to avoid public humiliation 'in the midst of the whole assembly'.

The NIV's translation 'the whole assembly' actually hides the fact that the original Hebrew uses two synonyms here. Thus the NKJV and NASB's translation 'assembly and congregation' is to be preferred. But what do these two words mean? Both words are generally used in connection with Israel as the people of God (Exod 12:3; Deut 31:30). This connection is strengthened when we remember the way adultery was addressed in the law of Moses: 'If a man is found sleeping with another man's wife, both the man who slept with her and the woman must die. You must purge the

evil from Israel' (Deut 22:22). The remorseful man recognizes that he has been an evil element among his people.

5:15-20 Commendation of marriage

The teacher follows the extended warning about the danger of falling victim to the enticements of the adulteress with a vibrant commendation of marriage. Rather than indulging in promiscuous relationships, the young men should satisfy their sexual desires within the context of marriage. He tells them to *drink water from your own cistern, running water from your own well* (**5:15**). Where the adulteress was a source of honey that turned bitter when tasted, the wife is represented by a cistern and a well that is a continual source of fresh, flowing water. Then the water imagery shifts to the man: *Should your springs overflow in the streets, your streams of water in the public squares?* (**5:16**). The rhetorical question implies that the man's sexual vigour and potency should not be wasted in promiscuous relationships. Rather, *let them be yours alone, never to be shared with strangers* (**5:17**).

The teacher now utters a prayer expressing the type of marriage relationship he wishes for his son: *May your fountain be blessed, and may you rejoice in the wife of your youth* (**5:18**). He describes the wife as *a loving doe* and *a graceful deer* before abandoning imagery to describe the real person: *may her breasts satisfy you always, may you ever be captivated by her love* (**5:19**). What is being described here with poetic eroticism is the beauty and blessing of lovemaking in the context of marriage. No wonder the teacher asks his 'son', why squander your sexual vigour – 'which should be reserved for the woman he is pledged to and the children she is to bear' (*CC*) – with a loose woman, who is a stranger in the sense of being *another man's wife* (**5:20**)?

5:21-23 Consequences of adultery

The discourse ends with the sad destiny of the wicked man. Whatever a man does – even in what he thinks is the most secret of places – his *ways are in full view of the Lord, and he examines all his paths* (**5:21**). Hence, the judgment: *The evil deeds of a wicked man ensnare him; the cords of his sin hold him fast. He will die for lack of discipline, led astray by his own great folly* (**5:22-23**). The outcome of being 'captivated' by an adulteress (5:20) instead of being 'captivated' by the love of one's spouse (5:19) is, to use Hubbard's word, 'lethal' (*CC*).

6:1-35 Pitfalls for the Unwary

This section does not begin with the usual exhortation to listen to the instructions of the teacher. That comes later, towards the middle of the discourse (6:20). It is possible that this is a literary device to emphasize the urgency of action to avoid the dangers described here.

6:1-5 Beware of standing surety

Standing surety for someone else is exceedingly dangerous. This is brought out by the way this admonition is given. It starts as a conditional statement in which the 'ifs' are piled one on top of another before we come to the 'then': *If you have put up security for your neighbour, if you have struck hands in pledge for another, if you have been trapped by what you said, ensnared by the words of your mouth* (**6:1-2**). The statements are basically saying the same thing, but the tempo seems to be increasing with each repetition to signal the precarious situation the person has landed himself in. The person on whose behalf the surety is given (the debtor) is described as 'another', but the sense of the original Hebrew word is 'a stranger'. It appears that the surety was given hastily out of a desire to help, but without thinking through the possible consequences.

Thus the addressee is advised to humble himself before the creditor ('your neighbour') and extricate himself from the situation as quickly as possible: *Then do this, my son, to free yourself, since you have fallen into your neighbour's hands: Go and humble yourself; press your plea with your neighbour!* (**6:3**). No time should be wasted! *Allow no sleep to your eyes, no slumber to your eyelids* (**6:4**). The imagery used to press the point home is dramatic. *Free yourself, like a gazelle from the hands of the hunter, like a bird from the snare of the fowler* (**6:5**). We have here very practical, down-to-earth advice.

6:6-11 Beware of laziness

Where the student has previously been addressed repeatedly as 'my son' (6:1, 3), in this passage he is repeatedly addressed as *you sluggard* (**6:6, 9**). And this is not the only humiliation that the teacher uses to make his point about diligence and indolence. The sluggard is sarcastically advised to go and learn from ants. 'A person with gifts of speech, with a brain the size of a whole anthill, is told to bend over, peer down, and learn from the lowly ant' (*CC*).

The lesson is that although ants do not have a leader – a fact underscored by the use of three synonyms for the position of leadership – their industriousness is evident in the way they store up provisions at the right time (**6:7-8**). This is followed by the exhortation *How long will you lie there, you sluggard? When will you get up from your sleep?* (6:9). The sluggard is warned that poverty will come to him as *a bandit* (NIV) or 'a vagabond' (NASB) if he does not learn his lesson and mend his ways (**6:10-11**).

6:12-19 Beware of mischief-makers

This warning against mischief-makers who cause dissension in the community is given in two forms. In 6:12-15, a mischievous person is described and in 6:16-19 similar information is repeated in a numerical saying. The way this saying is introduced, *there are six things the Lord hates, seven that are detestable to him* (**6:16**), shows that this list is not

meant to be exhaustive. Such lists of sayings are structured in a way that throws the emphasis on the final item in the list, and suggests that it captures the essence of the preceding six items.

Several things mentioned in the first descriptive passage are repeated in the second. Verse **6:14b** is repeated in verse **6:19** in a slightly different form. Moreover, two synonymous Hebrew words, both translated *heart* in English, appear in **6:14a** and **6:18a**, and the same Hebrew word is used in **6:12** and 6:18a (translated as *corrupt* and *wicked* by the NIV, where the NASB correctly uses 'wicked' in both places). Other parallels include *his eye* (**6:13**) and *haughty eyes* (**6:17**); *with his feet* (6:13) and *feet* (**6:18b**); *evil* (6:14) and *into evil* (6:18). The fate of the mischief-maker is clearly spelled out in terms of the suddenness with which his judgment is meted out: *Therefore disaster will overtake him in an instant; he will suddenly be destroyed – without remedy* (**6:15**).

6:20-35 Beware of immoral women

In the second half of the chapter, the teacher returns to the familiar warning against immoral women. The warning is preceded by the usual exhortation to obey the parents' commands (**6:20-21**; see also 1:8-9). Yet there is something unusual here too. In **6:22-23** the commands and teaching of the wise are described as a *lamp* and a *light*, respectively. This suggests that they have the same authority as the divinely revealed law (see Ps 119:105).

The purpose of the commandment, the law and the corrections of discipline, says the wise teacher, is to keep *you from the immoral woman, from the smooth tongue of the wayward wife* (**6:24**). The admonitions to stay away from her begin with *do not lust in your heart after her beauty or let her captivate you with her eyes* (**6:25**; 'eyelashes' is a better translation). Lust is not merely the first step to sin; Jesus taught that it is itself sin (Matt 5:27-28).

The reasons for avoiding her are then given. *For the prostitute reduces you to a loaf of bread, and the adulteress preys upon your very life* (**6:26**). This is not saying that consorting with a prostitute is a lesser and less costly evil than consorting with an adulteress. There is no contrast or comparison here; rather, this is an example of synonymous parallelism where the second line reinforces what has been said in the first line.

Next the wisdom teacher uses rhetorical questions and analogy to drive home the folly of committing adultery (**6:27-28**). The obvious answers to the questions are 'yes, his clothes will be burned', and 'yes, his feet will be scorched'. *So is he who sleeps with another man's wife; no one who touches her will go unpunished* (**6:29**). The message is powerfully delivered! 'It does not need AIDS and other sexually transmitted diseases to remind us of the destructiveness of promiscuity' (*BST*).

A comparison – maybe 'contrast' would be the better word – is drawn between a thief who steals to satisfy his hunger (**6:30-31**) and an adulterer (**6:32-33**). There is no condoning of the sin of theft here. The Ten Commandments condemn it (see Exod 20:15; Deut 5:19), and the *sevenfold* reparation mentioned here, which goes beyond the legal provision for restitution (Exod 22:1), appears to be a hyperbole intended to make that very point. The point of contrast is the folly of the adulterer in committing this sin, and the shame, stigma, ignominy and insecurity it brings.

After presenting the case of the robber, the teacher says: *But a man who commits adultery lacks judgment; whoever does so destroys himself* (6:32). Not only does he lack judgment and commits an act that destroys his life, and by inference his life after this, but *blows and disgrace are his lot, and his shame will never be wiped away* (6:33). The reason given for this fate is that *jealousy arouses a husband's fury, and he will show no mercy when he takes revenge. He will not accept any compensation; he will refuse the bribe, however great it is* (**6:34-35**). We are warned that an adulterer lives on the verge of death, for an offended husband will not rest until he has dealt with him.

7:1-27 An Illustrated Warning Against Adultery

Here we have, for the first time, an entire chapter devoted to teaching against adultery. It is basically an extended object lesson, presented 'not in generalizations but dramatically' (*TOT*).

But first, there are the introductory exhortations of the teacher, which are more copious here (7:1-5) than elsewhere. In addition to the usual *keep my words and store up my commands, keep my commands* and *guard my teachings* (**7:1-2**), there is the command *bind them on your fingers; write them on the tablet of your heart* (**7:3**), which has a familiar ring (see also 3:3). The sage is saying that these instructions are to be treated in the same way as the Mosaic law (see Deut 6:8).

In **7:4** the disciple is told, *Say to wisdom 'You are my sister', and call understanding your kinsman.* The student is to have an intimate association with wisdom, an association that will keep him from associating with strange women: *They will keep you from the adulteress, from the wayward wife with her seductive words* (**7:5**). (The word the NIV translates as 'wayward wife' should actually be 'strange woman'.)

After these introductory remarks, we come to the object lesson proper (7:6-23). The wise are keen observers of human interactions. So the author of our text begins by describing what he has seen: *At the window of my house I looked out through the lattice. I saw among the simple, I noticed among the young men, a youth who lacked judgment* (**7:6-7**). The description of the young men here is neutral. They are described as simple, naive, inexperienced. The one among them who provided the sage with his object lesson is described as lacking judgment. The reason for this characterization will be made plain before too long. Note the steps he is taking. First, separating from the group, he goes *down the street near her corner, walking along in the direction of her house* (**7:8**). Secondly, it was the time of the *twilight, as the day was fading, as the dark of the night set in* (**7:9**). Kidner rightly comments, 'He wanders into temptation, where place (7:8) and time (7:9) can join forces against him; and if *he* is aimless, his temptress is not' (*TOT*).

The next verses describe the adulteress. *Then out came a woman to meet him, dressed like a prostitute and with crafty intent* (**7:10**). It is an unequal contest when the one who lacks judgment (literally, 'lacking of heart') meets one 'with crafty intent' (literally, 'cunning in heart'). It is the former who loses. After describing her waywardness and reckless behaviour (**7:11-12**), the text says *she took hold of him and kissed him* (**7:13a**). The steps that the seductress takes are carefully calculated to trap the inexperienced young man. And then the words spoken *with a brazen face* (**7:13b**): *I have fellowship offerings at home; today I fulfilled my vows. So I came out to meet you; I looked for you and have found you!* (**7:14-15**). Commentators who take the adulteress to be an Israelite associate the 'fellowship offerings' with the offerings referred to in Leviticus 7:16-18 and see in her words a 'bland secularization of her religion' (*TOT*). Those who think she is a foreigner relate the offerings and vows to her pagan religious obligations and specifically to the prostitution that took place in Canaanite fertility cults. Seductively, she promises luxury: *I have covered my bed with coloured linens from Egypt. I have perfumed my bed with myrrh, aloes and cinnamon* (**7:16-17**). Finally, she goes in for the kill (**7:18**), with the reassurance that *my husband is not at home; he has gone on a long journey* and *will not be home till full moon* (**7:19-20**). Interestingly enough, the Hebrew says 'the man' where the NIV has 'my husband'. A Luganda (Ugandan) saying illustrates this aspect of human nature well. A suspicious husband, asked when he intends to come back, answers, 'One who travels sees (what will happen)', that is to say, 'I can't tell you now'. He does not want to specify when he will return because he wants to keep his wife in a state of uncertainty. She will not be able to say, like the woman in our passage, he 'will not be home till full moon'. A pithy Amharic (Ethiopian) proverb reinforces this point: *yalteretere temenetere* ['one who is not suspicious is destroyed'].

The woman moved in for the kill and was successful, for we are told *All at once he followed her* (7:22). The description of him as being *like an ox going to the slaughter, like a deer stepping into a noose till an arrow pierces his liver, like a bird darting into a snare* (**7:22-23**) all give dramatic effect to the kill. Note the last clause of 7:23: *little knowing it will cost him his life.* For what this means in the context of Proverbs, we just need to remember 6:34-35. In the OT, adultery was punishable by death (Deut 22:22).

The wisdom teacher concludes with the exhortation he gave before, that is, the hearers should under no circumstances turn aside or stray into the path of the adulterous woman, for *her house is a highway to the grave* (7:27). This passage (7:24-27) emphasizes that the choice to obey is not merely a question of following one's own whims. It is a matter of life and death. The young man in this object lesson clearly lacked understanding.

8:1-36 Wisdom's Excellence and her Role in Creation

One breathes a deep sigh of relief as one moves from chapter seven's depiction of the deadly attacks of a foolish woman to the present chapter, where wisdom's life-fulfilling excellence and credentials are the focus. Because of the theological significance of this discourse, especially verses 8:22-31, it will be dealt with more extensively than the other discourses.

8:1-5 Introduction

The first three verses of this chapter are similar to 1:20-21, except that the present chapter opens with a rhetorical question. Moreover, wisdom not only *calls out* but also *raises her voice* (8:1). She is determined to be heard above the clamour of greedy gangsters (1:10-19), lying crooks (2:12-15), smooth talkers (2:16-19), corrupt men (4:14-17) and mischief-makers (6:12-15). 'The battle is joined, and a shaky trumpet will not summon the troops. Wisdom leaves no doubt about the importance and meaning of her call' (CC).

Note the places from where wisdom shouts her summons: *On the heights, along the way, where the paths meet, beside the gates, at the entrances* (8:2-3). She uses every available venue where people gather. 'A chapter which is to soar beyond time and space, opens at street-level, to make it clear that the wisdom of God is as relevant to the shopping centre (8:2, 3) as to heaven itself (8:22)' (TOT). Wisdom's call is both personal and public. Although it begins with the individual, 'it is wisdom in the public domain, shaping the entire life of the community' (CC).

The circle of the people to whom wisdom is calling is also expanding. In fact, she is issuing a universal call: *To you, O men, I call out; I raise my voice to all mankind. You who are simple, gain prudence; you who are foolish, gain understanding* (8:4-5). The invitation is not only to the simple and foolish, 'but to all of us who carry the constant potential of foolish conduct' (CC).

8:6-21 Wisdom's excellence

In his elaboration of wisdom's excellence, the writer focuses on the superiority of her moral instruction and her priceless value. By way of motivating her audience to listen, wisdom says *for I have worthy things to say; I open my lips to speak what is right* (8:6). The 'worthy' of NIV is translated 'excellent' by some versions. What is more, *my mouth speaks what is true, for my lips detest wickedness. All the words of my mouth are just; none of them is crooked or perverse* (8:7-8). Those who are *discerning* and *who have knowledge* can prove this for themselves (8:9). After exhorting the listeners to choose *my instruction instead of silver, knowledge rather than choice gold* (8:10), she proceeds to affirm to them that wisdom herself *is more precious than rubies, and nothing you desire can compare with her* (8:11) – a thought we have come across before (see also Job 28).

Then wisdom starts to list her assets: *I, wisdom, dwell together with prudence; I possess knowledge and discretion. To fear the Lord is to hate evil; I hate pride and arrogance, evil behaviour and perverse speech* (8:12-13). Kidner comments: 'These two verses are necessary partners. True wisdom is canny and resourceful ... yet being rooted in the fear of the Lord ... it is free of the faults of worldly wisdom' (TOT). After stating that *counsel and sound judgment* and *understanding and power* are hers (8:14), wisdom lists the high and powerful of society among her beneficiaries (8:15-16).

Wisdom cares for her followers, saying *I love those who love me, and those who seek me find me* (8:17). The second half of this verse sounds like the Lord's words in Jeremiah 29:13 and like Jesus' promise in Matthew 7:7-8 that whoever asks receives, whoever seeks finds and whoever knocks on the door will find it opened for him (see also James 1:5). Not only does wisdom love her followers, but, as mentioned earlier, she also bestows herself and her wealth on them (8:18-21).

8:22-31 Wisdom's role in creation

The second part of wisdom's discourse addresses the question of why we should believe what wisdom tells us when we are told to reject so much of what others tell us. 'Like the classical prophets who tell their sceptical listeners how they were called to the prophetic task, Wisdom tells her audience about her origin. In effect she says, "I trace my beginnings and my authority back to the Lord".' (ITC).

The passage that follows has been much debated over the years. The problem is that Paul seems to be applying this personification to Christ when he speaks of him as 'the wisdom of God' (1 Cor 1:24) and 'the firstborn over all creation' (Col 1:15). Christ's role in creation also seems to parallel the role given to wisdom here. But what do we make of the fact that this passage describes wisdom as 'the first of his works' (8:22)? Does this imply that Christ was a created being, rather than God himself, as some would claim?

Any answer to this question involves careful study of the exact meaning of the verbs used in connection with wisdom in 8:22-25. Wisdom says, *the Lord brought me forth as the first of his works, before his deeds of old* (8:22). 'Brought me forth' is one word in the original, and its overall meaning is 'to get, to acquire'. When used in relation to God, it can mean either 'originating, creating' or 'victoriously redeeming his people'. The NKJV and NASB'S rendering 'possessed me' seems to be close to the word's meaning in this passage (*TOT*). T. T. Perowne has some wise words on the debate as to the word's exact meaning: 'it is impossible to understand the word … as indicating that Wisdom ever had a beginning, or was ever properly speaking created. Wisdom is inseparable from any worthy conception of him who is "the only wise God" (1 Tim 1:17), and therefore is like him "from everlasting to everlasting" (Ps 90:2)' (*CBSC*).

8:23 reads *I was appointed from eternity, from the beginning, before the world began.* The Hebrew word represented by 'I was appointed' can have three different meanings: the first is 'to pour out, to pour a libation or to cast metal images'; the second meaning is 'to weave'; and the third is 'to set, to appoint or to install'. The last meaning is the one that applies here in Proverbs (see also Ps 2:6), which is why the NIV translates it as 'appointed', the NASB and NKJV as 'established' and the KJV as 'set up'.

In **8:24** we read, *when there were no oceans, I was given birth, when there were no springs abounding with water.* The Hebrew word translated 'I was given birth' comes from a root that can mean 'to dance' or 'to twist or writhe in pain (either in childbirth or severe anguish), in contrition, or in anxious longing' or 'to whirl or whirl about'. The meaning is 'be made to writhe' or 'be brought forth'. This form of the verb occurs only in Psalm 51:5, Job 15:7 and here in Proverbs 8:24-25. Where NIV has 'I was given birth', NASB has 'I was brought forth' (in the text) and 'I was born' (in the margin).

Kidner ties all three verbs used in relation to wisdom in 8:22 to 8:25 together when he says, 'While 8:22 has stolen the limelight, the adjacent verbs state the matter in terms of wisdom's installation in office (8:23a) and its birth (8:24, 25). The latter verb, indeed, by its repetition, is the predominant one; and the passage as a whole may be meant to bring to mind a *royal birth*' (*TOT*). All three verbs underscore the relationship of wisdom with Yahweh. Yahweh possessed it, installed it and brought it forth.

But this still leaves the question of what it means to say that wisdom was *the first of his works* (8:22). There are two words in this Hebrew phrase: the first can mean either what is first in importance or what is first in sequence; the second is the word for 'way' or 'path' with the marker for third person, masculine singular. The NIV's translation 'works' is, therefore, wrong. The translation 'at the beginning of his way' in the NASB is closer to the original. Kidner is right on target when he warns that 'the "works" of verse 22b should not be confused with "his ways" in verse 22a' (*TOT*), which is exactly what the NIV has done. Wisdom as Yahweh's 'way'

of doing things and 'his works' as the outcome of that 'way' should be distinguished.

The time-markers used in this passage are also very important indications of wisdom's relationship with Yahweh and his creation. After affirming that Yahweh possessed her at the beginning of his way (8:22a), wisdom further asserts that Yahweh's possessing of her took place *before his deeds of old* (*works,* NASB) (8:22b). A variety of Hebrew markers are used to emphasize that wisdom was there before even one particle of the created universe came into existence. The works of Yahweh are listed: the *world* (earth, NASB), the *oceans* (depths, NASB), the *springs,* the *mountains,* the *hills,* the *fields,* the *dust,* the *heavens,* the *horizon,* the *clouds* (the skies, NASB), *the fountains of the* deep (the springs of the deep, NASB), *the sea, the foundations of the earth* (8:23-29). Wisdom – possessed, installed and brought forth by Yahweh – existed before any and all of his works. Before they came into being, wisdom says *I was there* (**8:27**). She was there, not in the sense of being part of the creation, but in the sense of being already there before any of God's creative works came into existence.

Nor was wisdom merely a passive observer of God's creative work. She 'was there' as God's means or instrument in bringing creation into existence (see 3:19-20). Kidner emphasises that 'not a speck of matter (**8:26**), not a trace of order (**8:29**), came into existence but by wisdom' (*TOT*). To appreciate where this interpretation comes from, we need to grasp the meaning of the words *I was the craftsman at his side* (**8:30**).

The exact meaning of the Hebrew word translated 'craftsman' is the subject of much debate. As many as five different meanings have been proposed. The majority of scholars are agreed that it can have two main meanings. It may be referring to wisdom as an architect or master-workman, through whose agency Yahweh executed his creative activity. Alternatively, it may be depicting wisdom as a nursling, a young child who delights and plays in the presence of God (**8:31**).

The final two verses of this section on wisdom's role in creation (8:30-31) are arranged chiastically around the words *delighting* and *rejoicing.* This arrangement means that both words occur in each verse, but the order in which they appear is reversed in the second one. This playing with words helps to emphasize the intense joy and the playfulness of wisdom in its dual relationship – with Yahweh and humankind. 'The thought is that Wisdom, who found glad exercise in every part and stage of creation as it advanced, had her consummated joy in the adaptation of the completed whole to be the dwelling place of man, and in the "sons of men" for love of whom she had created it' (*CBSC*).

8:32-36 Conclusion

Wisdom's appeal in 8:32-36 gains depth and intensity against the backdrop of her role in creation, which has just been discussed, and particularly in light of her joy in humankind. Whereas her opening words were addressed to the 'simple', the 'foolish', 'men' and 'mankind' (8:4-5), here in the conclusion she addresses them all as *my sons* (8:32). This is the first time that personified wisdom speaks to her hearers in this way. She pleads with them to obey so that they may be blessed (**8:32-33**): *Blessed is the man who listens to me, watching daily at my doors, waiting at my doorway* (**8:34**). The appeal closes with the ultimate reward of life for those who find wisdom and the ultimate threat of death to those who sin against her and hate her (**8:35-36**).

9:1-18 Rival Feasts

This, the last of the ten discourses in this section of Proverbs, brings the issue of choosing wisdom or folly, life or death into a sharp focus by juxtaposing two rival feasts. The first six verses describe the feast prepared by wisdom, and the last six verses the feast prepared by folly.

9:1-6 Wisdom's invitation

The thoroughness and generosity with which wisdom prepares her feast are clear: *Wisdom has built her house; she has hewn out its seven pillars. She has prepared her meat and mixed her wine; she has also set her table* (**9:1-2**). Having participated in the work of creation on the cosmic level, wisdom here prepares her house among humans. The 'seven pillars' of this house may be pointing to her industriousness and the perfection of her abode. Once the *table* is set and the preparation completed, she sends out her maids to invite her guests. But wisdom realizes that such an invitation is not sufficiently urgent, and ignoring her maids she herself calls out *from the highest point of the city* (**9:3**). Her message is *Let all who are simple come in here! ... Come eat my food and drink the wine I have mixed* (**9:4-5**). *Leave your simple ways,* pleads wisdom, *and you will live; walk in the way of understanding* (**9:6**).

9:7-12 Possible guests

The connection of this middle section with the invitation of wisdom that has gone before and the invitation of folly that follows is not immediately clear. Perhaps the best way to deal with it may be that taken by Hubbard, who describes the chapter as 'an envelope: it begins and ends with calls to eat, one issued by wisdom, the other by folly. In the heart of the envelope ... are the descriptions and commands about dealing with the scoffer and the wise, who mark the two ways in which the calls can be answered' (*CC*). Kidner agrees that this middle section is giving us 'character sketches of the typical products of these opposing camps:

the scoffer, with his closed mind, and the wise man, ever teachable and ever progressing' (*TOT*).

The mocker ('scoffer', in some versions) and the wicked are familiar characters we have met before. All that is added here is a warning that it is inadvisable to correct a mocker or rebuke a wicked person because his only response will be to insult and abuse you (**9:7-8a**). A wise man reacts differently: *Rebuke a wise man and he will love you. Instruct a wise man and he will be wiser still; teach a righteous man and he will add to his learning* (**9:8b-9**).

The theme of the whole book, *the fear of the Lord*, is repeated right at the centre of this chapter (**9:10**; see 1:7). It is followed by wisdom's encouragement to those who listen to her: *For through me your days will be many, and years will be added to your life* (**9:11**). Then, as in many of these discourses, the consequences of wisdom and folly are reiterated: *If you are wise, your wisdom will reward you; if you are a mocker, you alone will suffer* (**9:12**).

9:13-18 Folly's Invitation

Just as wisdom summoned people to her feast, so does folly. Not only that, but folly's words are almost identical to those of wisdom (compare 9:4 and **9:16**). But while folly may attempt to mimic wisdom, she does not imitate wisdom's careful preparation or share her urgency. Instead folly is described as a rowdy and undisciplined woman who lacks knowledge (**9:13**; compare this with the description of the adulteress in 7:11). She simply *sits at the door of her house* (**9:14**), a house that does not seem to compare with wisdom's splendid seven-pillared structure (see 9:1).

Folly's invitation promises that *stolen water is sweet; food eaten in secret is delicious* (**9:17**). From the way it is put here and from the symbolism in earlier chapters (for example, 5:15-20), there is no doubt that the invitation of the foolish woman invites one to enjoy sensual pleasure. Further evidence of her connection with the adulteress of previous chapters is found in the final destiny of those who respond to her invitation (compare **9:18** with 2:18-19 and 7:26-27).

10:1-22:16 Various Proverbs of Solomon

The title of this section, *Proverbs of Solomon* (10:1), is shorter than the title given in 1:1. So are the instructions given in this section of the book. Whereas Proverbs 1–9 contained ten lengthy discourses, now we come to a section of the book filled with some 375 typical proverbial sayings, most of them a mere two lines long. 'Here at last are the sayings that we recognize as proverbs: short, self-contained, poured out apparently at random' (*TOT*).

But how are we to make sense of what seems like a random mix? Scholars have offered different approaches. Some believe that the sequence of verses is completely random, and therefore feel free to arrange them by topic in order to get their message. Others, however, believe that the order we have is intentional and prefer to interpret these sayings in the order they have come to us in the Scriptures.

A scholar who takes the former approach is Hubbard, whose 'basic approach is to deal with two or three topics in each chapter using its relevant verses and also applicable sayings from other chapters'. He admits that 'the task of organizing them is a judgment call' and that many of the proverbs 'would fit more than one of the thirty or so subject categories which I have identified' (*CC*).

Farmer takes the other approach. Although she admits that 'sense units seldom consist of more than one verse', she asserts that 'there are, however, some identifiable collectional features' (*ITC*). She then elaborates on this point: 'Although a connected train of thought cannot be traced through the whole of any chapter, there are occasions when it is possible to discern intentionality on the part of those who collected, arranged, or recorded these sayings in their present order' (*ITC*). She illustrates this intentionality by citing 10:2-5 and 10:18-21, which contain clusters of proverbs dealing with one subject – the former with wealth and poverty and the latter with speech – and drives her argument home with her analysis of 18:11 (see commentary). Further evidence of intentionality is the type of parallelism we find in these proverbs – for example, in chapters 10 to 15, where the second line states the opposite of the first line.

It is also true that what we have just read in chapters 1 to 9 provides an interpretative context for this section of the book of Proverbs, enabling 'the reader ... to orientate himself in the thicket of individual sayings which he enters in Section II (10:1-22:16), and to see in each cool, objective aphorism a miniature and particular outworking of the wisdom and folly whose whole course he has seen spread out before him in Section I' (*TOT*).

There is no reason why we should not benefit from using a mix of the approaches outlined above. We can begin by emphasizing intentionality, but also feel free to arrange the proverbs topically to extract their message and theology.

10:1-32

The fact that the first proverb in this collection (**10:1**) has such strong links to what precedes it cannot be accidental. Its reference to a *father* and *mother* clearly evokes the parental instructions we heard in 1:8; 4:3; and 6:20. A still stronger link is provided by the contrasting of wisdom and folly, particularly when subsequent verses contrast righteousness and wickedness. The compilers seem to be emphasizing that chapters 1 to 9 and 10 to 22 are related, and that righteousness and wickedness are alternative terms for the two paths – the path of wisdom and the path of folly – that were clearly depicted in the introductory section of the book.

The next few verses (10:2-5) appear to form a cluster dealing with wealth and poverty. Before approaching them, it is worth noting that in the context of Proverbs 'wealth ... may not mean exorbitant riches, but only enough on which to be self-sufficient and to be able to help others' (*CC*). In the final analysis, wealth acquired by unrighteous means 'has no value', whereas righteousness is of greater value because the Lord provides in times of famine and delivers his own from death (**10:2-3**; see also 14:32). Diligence, under God's guidance, is the secret of acquiring wealth; whereas a lazy person is not only a disgrace to those who are around him but is heading for a life of poverty (**10:4-5**). An Ewe proverb from Ghana makes a similar point when it says, 'The lazy cat eats dead mice'. An industrious cat will have fresh meat to eat. The meaning is that hard work brings rewards, and that people must learn to work hard in order to avoid the consequences of laziness.

In 10:6-7 the lives of the righteous and the wicked are contrasted. *Blessings crown the head of the righteous* – their reward is quite manifest (**10:6a**). Even *the memory of the righteous* is a blessing (**10:7a**). On the other hand, *violence overwhelms the mouth of the wicked* (**10:6b**; see also 10:11) and their *name will rot* (**10:7b**). We may be surprised that the blessing in 10:6 is not contrasted with a curse in the second half of that verse. 'But the point is rather that behind the speech of the wicked is aggressive "violence" ... as he cannot be trusted' (*EBC*). Kidner explains the contrast as being between the crown on the head of the righteous and 'the man's evil, written ... all over his face' (*TOT*).

The contrast in **10:8** is between a person who is *wise* and one who is a *fool*. One who is wise (the word is singular in Hebrew, although the NIV translates it as plural) is obedient to the orders of superiors, whereas a fool is so busy talking that he pays no attention to what he is being told to do.

In the following verse, the contrast is between *the man of integrity* and *he who takes crooked paths*. One *walks securely*, whereas the other is *found out* – that is to say, his crooked lifestyle will be exposed (**10:9**; see also 28:18, which Kidner describes as 'the brother to this verse' – *TOT*).

Whereas all the proverbs so far have been antithetical, that is, contrasting two different lifestyles, **10:10** is an example of synthetic parallelism, where the second line develops the thought of the first. In repeating the second line of 10:8, it puts the person *who winks maliciously* and the *chattering fool* side by side – both of them in the opposite camp from wisdom. The one *causes grief* and the other *comes to ruin*.

The next cluster is found in 10:11-14 and focuses on the subject of speech. This topic is of the same importance today as it was in ancient times. Although the two lifestyles are variously represented by *the righteous* and *the wicked* (**10:11**), *hatred* and *love* (**10:12**), *wisdom* and one *who lacks judgment* (**10:13**), *wise men* and *a fool* (**10:14**), the subject matter is the same. The word 'mouth' is found three times (10:11, 14) along with related words like 'dissension' (10:12) and 'lips' (10:13). The proverbs state that *the mouth of the righteous is a fountain of life* (10:11), *love covers all wrongs* (10:12), *Wisdom is found on the lips of the discerning* (10:13) and *wise men store up knowledge* (to which Ross adds, 'rather than foolishly talking prematurely' – *EBC*) (10:14). In sharp contrast to these are *the mouth of the wicked* which is overwhelmed by violence (10:11), hatred which *stirs up dissension* (10:12), the rod falling on the back *of him who lacks judgment* (or as Kidner phrases it: 'Man – God's mouthpiece or God's mule' – *TOT*) (10:13) and *the mouth of a fool* which *invites ruin* (10:14).

Moving on to the topic of wealth, we read: *The wealth of the rich is their fortified city, but poverty is the ruin of the poor* (**10:15**). The first half of this verse is repeated in 18:11, but there the parallelism is synthetic (see also 14:20; 18:23; 19:7 and 22:7, where the rich and poor are also mentioned). In this verse, the point being made is that just as a fortified city protects its inhabitants, so wealth protects its owners. But this is not all there is to be said on the subject, as will be seen when we look at 18:11. Yet, as Kidner reminds us, we should not despise wealth or romanticize poverty (*TOT*). It all depends on how the wealth is acquired, as the following verse shows: *The wages of the righteous bring them life; but the income of the wicked brings them punishment* (**10:16**). This point is underscored in **10:17,** which speaks about the blessing of obedience and the negative consequences of disobedience. Note, however, that the wicked person does not only bring harm to himself (implied), but also *leads others astray.*

WEALTH AND POVERTY

Our attitude to money, wealth and poverty reveals our eternal values, as well as our character and relationship to both God and others. It can be a root cause of all kinds of evil (1 Tim 6:10), leading us to break the first and last commandments (Exod 20:3-17). Examples of those who have been consumed by love of money and wealth include Achan (Josh 7), Gehazi (2 Kgs 5:20-27); Ananias and his wife Sapphira (Acts 5:1-11), Simon the sorcerer (Acts 8:18-23), the rich fool (Luke 12:13-21) and the rich ruler (Luke 18:18-30). Yet money can be a source of blessing, and the Scriptures also include examples of rich and holy men (Abraham, Isaac, Jacob, Job and King Solomon).

Poverty is a recurring theme in the Bible. It is also the experience of many Africans, for half of those in sub-Saharan Africa live on less than US $1.00 a day. Many are poor because we live in a world where injustice and a skewed economic order mean they lack access to education, land and other means of improving their material conditions (Jas 5:1-6). Nowhere do the Scriptures equate material poverty and piety, and Christians must work to remove the barriers that prevent people from escaping from poverty (Lev 25:38-55; Luke 3:10-14; 18:22; Col 4:1).

The Bible does, however, speak harshly to those who are poor because they have not used their God-given mind, strength and resources. Laziness or slothfulness are condemned (Prov 6:6-11; 10:4-5; 14:23; 20:4, 13; 2 Thess 3:10). Those who work hard, learn a trade, improve their knowledge and skills, are entrepreneurial, learn to save and invest small amounts, and who are faithful to God are often able to improve their material conditions (Prov 21:5).

The Bible's guidance on wealth may be summarized as follows:

• Our life is to be God-centred not thing-centred (Matt 6:25-34).

• The basis of all wealth is God's bounty. Everything belongs to him (Ps 24:1) and he gives the ability to produce wealth (Deut 8:10-18). We are stewards (or managers) of the talents and possessions God gives us and are accountable to him for how we use them (Luke 16:1-15; 19:11-27).

• We should keep an eternal perspective. We are to build treasures in heaven 'for where your treasure is, there your heart will be also' (Matt 6:19-21).

• There are biblically approved ways to earn money and create wealth. Gambling, stealing, exploiting our workers and the poor, as well as all dishonest business deals are condemned by God (Lev 19:11-13, 35; Prov 1:11-19; 10:2; 11:18; 13:11; 15:27; 21:5; 22:22-23; 28:8). Money is to be acquired through diligent work (Prov 14:23), inheritance (Prov 13:22), wise, non-speculative savings (Prov 6:6-11; 20:21) and investment (Luke 19:11-27).

• The way we spend our money is important. We are not to be like the prodigal son (Luke 15:11-32) and spend our wealth on wild living and drunkenness. Instead we are to use it to meet the needs of our family and to leave a reasonable inheritance to our children (1 Tim 5:8; Prov 13:22). We are also to use it to honour and worship God (Lev 22:18-23; Lev 27:30; Prov 3:9), and to do so consistently, generously and joyfully (2 Cor 8, 9). Those who are rich are commanded 'to be generous and willing to share' (1 Tim 6:17-19). We are also to pay legitimate taxes to the state (Rom 13:6-7).

In sum, wealth in the hands of the righteous is a powerful tool to serve God and others. Money as a purpose for living is not worth it even if one gains the whole world, for this is done at the cost of one's eternal soul (Matt 16:26).

Stephen Adei

In 10:18-21 we encounter another cluster of proverbs that also seem to deal with the topic of speech. The two lines of **10:18** are synonymous, putting someone *who conceals his hatred* and *whoever spreads slander* side by side. Then **10:19** makes the point that too much talk is likely to entail sin, and that it is wise to be economical with one's words. The next contrast is between *the tongue of the righteous* and *the heart of the wicked*, with the former described as *choice silver* and the latter as *of little value* (**10:20**). Whereas we are told that *the lips of the righteous nourish many, fools* appear to be standing in place of their words in this contrast and to be judged by them – they *die for lack of judgment* (**10:21**). This emphasis on nourishment provided by the words of the righteous serves as a counterbalance to the earlier reminder that many words may issue in sin (10:19).

Wealth that is from the Lord is an unadulterated blessing and is not accompanied by troubles (**10:22**; see also Ps 127:1-3).

The contrast in **10:23** is between *a fool* and *a man of understanding*. Whereas the former *finds pleasure in evil conduct*, the latter *delights in wisdom*. 'One's character is revealed in what one enjoys' (*EBC*).

The next two verses (10:24-25) go together and present dramatically contrasting outcomes. What wicked people dread will happen to them, whereas the righteous will be given what they desire (**10:24**). Although the point is not stated explicitly, it is clear that this outcome must be directed by the Lord. In fact, Kidner is of the opinion that in the final analysis what the wicked dread and the righteous desire is God, and that this proverb will be fulfilled when both groups stand before him (*TOT*). When trouble comes, represented by *the storm, the wicked are gone, but the righteous stand firm for ever* (**10:25**).

10:26 sets up a comparison. Vinegar sets one's teeth on edge, and smoke irritates one's eyes. Just as irritating and unpleasant to those who send him is a lazy person sent on an errand or mission.

The theme of the book, *the fear of the Lord*, appears to represent the righteous in **10:27**, since 'the wicked' are mentioned in the second half of the proverb. Righteousness *adds length to life*, whereas its lack cuts short the years of the wicked. In a similar contrast of the two classes of people, **10:28** says *joy* is in store for the righteous, whereas *the hopes of the wicked come to nothing* (see also 11:7). One and the same thing – *the way of the Lord* – is a refuge for the righteous and *the ruin of those who do evil* (**10:29**). This is due to the different responses to it: the righteous obey and walk in it, but the wicked rebel against it. *The righteous will never be uprooted* – because they are planted in the Lord – *but the wicked will not remain in the land* (**10:30**; see also 10:25). For the connotations of 'land', both then and now, see comment on 2:21-22.

10:31-32 again forms a unit on the subject of speech. *The mouth of the righteous brings forth wisdom* (**10:31a**) and their *lips know what is fitting* (**10:32a**) – they know what is appropriate to say. By contrast, everything about the wicked is *perverse*, including the words they speak (**10:31b, 32b**). As a punishment, their tongues will be cut out.

11:1-31

The first proverb in this chapter takes us to the world of business. It contrasts what the Lord hates and delights in. Hubbard says, 'The words are strong ones and bring a distinct religious tone to the marketplace' (*CC*). It is clear that the law (Lev 19:35-36; Deut 25:13-16), the prophets (Ezek 45:9-12; Amos 8:4-6) and wisdom all speak with the same voice as regards *dishonest scales* and *accurate weights* (**11:1**; see also 20:10, 23).

According to **11:2**, with *pride* comes *disgrace* but humility's fruit is *wisdom*. Next the integrity of the upright and the duplicity of the unfaithful are contrasted. The outcome is that the integrity of the former *guides them*, whereas the latter *are destroyed by their duplicity* (**11:3**). Wealth, which earlier was described as the *fortified city* of its owners (10:15), is now said to be *worthless in the day of wrath*, whereas *righteousness delivers from death* (**11:4**). 'Righteousness, therefore, which is pleasing to God, is more valuable than riches when anticipating divine justice' (*EBC*).

The next two verses can be taken together. *The righteousness of the blameless makes a straight way for them* (**11:5a**); likewise *the righteousness of the upright delivers them* (**11:6a**). However *the wicked are brought down by their own wickedness* (**11:5b**) and also *the unfaithful are trapped by evil desires* (**11:6b**).

11:7 is another example of synthetic parallelism. It seems to augment the second half of the antithetical parallelism in 10:28. The difference is that in the earlier verse the perishing of hope seems to happen while the person is still alive, whereas here it comes with death.

The use of the conjunction *and* by the NIV in **11:8** is confusing. It should have consistently used 'but' (which is present in the Hebrew, and is used in the NASB translation) to indicate the contrast, so that the verse should read: *The righteous man is rescued from trouble, but it comes on the wicked instead.*

The contrast in **11:9** is that whereas *the godless* man *destroys his neighbour* with his mouth, *the righteous escape* from such destruction *through knowledge*. Verses 10 and 11 can be taken together, although the former is synthetic or continuous (where the idea of rejoicing is resumed) and the latter antithetical. Basically, **11:10** seems to say that when justice prevails – for that is what the prosperity of the righteous and the perishing of the wicked implies – *the city rejoices* or *there are shouts of joy* (although some understand the 'shouts' here as not 'of joy' but as those of the perishing wicked). By way of augmenting this idea, **11:11** portrays how the destiny of a city is affected by the *blessing of the upright* and *the mouth of the wicked*. As a result of the former, *a city is exalted*, but due to the latter *it is destroyed*.

The contrast in **11:12** is between *a man who lacks judgment* and *a man of understanding*. The former *derides his neighbour*, whereas the latter *holds his tongue* (see also 10:19). **11:13** is also on the subject of speech. *A gossip* is a person who *betrays a confidence* (see also 20:19), *but a trustworthy man keeps a secret*.

The next proverb deals with matters affecting a nation, but the principle applies equally to church, business and personal decisions. A contrast is drawn between a situation where there is a *lack of guidance* and one where there are *many advisers*. The former leads to the fall of a nation, whereas the latter *make victory sure* (**11:14**). Kidner summarizes this proverb as 'Get all the advice you can' (*TOT*), although he adds a warning: 'one can take too many opinions' (*TOT*). One also needs to make sure that one's advisors are well chosen, otherwise one may end up in the type of situation Nelson Mandela referred to in his famous remark about US President Bush's policy in relation to Iraq: 'He is a good man but those around him are dinosaurs'. For **11:15** see comments on 6:1-5 (see also 17:18; 20:16 and 27:13).

Then we come to a rare contrast between the genders: *A kind-hearted woman gains respect, but ruthless men gain only wealth* (**11:16**). Some interpret this as meaning that the main goal for a woman should be to gain 'the honor and respect that cause her and her household to carry weight and win regard in the community' (*CC*), while that of a man should be to gain financial security, 'enabling him to care for his family, share his goods with his neighbors … and praise God from whom all blessings flow' (*CC*). However, when this verse is taken together with the following one – *A kind man benefits himself, but a cruel man brings trouble on himself* (**11:17**) – it seems more likely that the contrast is between 'kind-hearted' and 'ruthless' rather than between 'women' and 'men'. Kidner appears to endorse this view when he says, 'Ruthlessness is not the only way to the top' (*TOT*). Moreover, the use of the word 'only' before 'wealth' in 11:16 indicates that 'respect' and 'wealth' are also being contrasted. 'The idea seems to be that one can seize wealth by any means, but honour is the natural reward for the gracious person' (*EBC*).

A similar thought is found in the next proverb, *the wicked man earns deceptive wages* (**11:18**; see also 10:16), *but he who sows righteousness reaps a sure reward*. Still comparing the two classes of people, **11:19** says *the truly righteous man attains life, but he who pursues evil goes to his death*. But since the Hebrew verse begins with the word meaning 'as', it seems likely that this should be understood as a comparative proverb ('As the righteous man attains life, so he who pursues evil goes to his death') rather than as the antithetical

proverb it is in the NIV. However, the change makes little difference to the meaning.

It is possible that verses 20 and 21 are meant to be taken together: *The Lord detests men of perverse heart* (**11:20a**) and hence they *will not go unpunished* (**11:21a**). *But he delights in those whose ways are blameless* (**11:20b**) and thus *the righteous will go free* (**11:21b**). The *be sure of this* in 11:21 is literally 'hand to hand' in the Hebrew, evoking the image of two people shaking hands to signify that a contract has been concluded. The expression emphasizes the certainty of retribution.

11:22 is another comparative proverb among the predominantly antithetical proverbs in these chapters. Who would be so stupid as to put expensive jewellery on a pig's nose, particularly in the context of Israelite society, where pigs were despised as unclean animals? The jewellery would be worthless, just as beauty is wasted on *a beautiful woman who shows no discretion*. A Tigrigna saying from Eritrea '*seeli ab geli* [literally, 'a picture on a potsherd'] makes the same point. A potsherd is a fragment of a broken pot, something that is discarded as useless. Painting a beautiful picture on one is a waste of effort and resources. A beautiful woman without skill, tact or wisdom is equally useless, in exactly the biblical sense. Nothing can compare with wisdom, as we saw in chapters 1 to 9. 'Without it, no amount of physical beauty will provide adequate compensation. In fact the disjunction between loveliness in face and form and churlishness in speech and behavior is as jarring as the waste of "a ring of gold" mounted in the pierced "snout" of a pig' (*CC*).

The desire of the righteous ends only in good, but the hope of the wicked only in wrath (**11:23**). This proverb shows how retributive justice is worked out in the lives of the two categories of people.

Next, we come to another cluster of proverbs, this time on the topic of generosity (11:24-26). **11:24** appears to be paradoxical – how can giving away wealth increase wealth? – but the paradox is resolved if we remember that the Lord is the source of wealth and the one administering justice (see Matt 16:25; Luke 6:38). **11:25** is a synthetic proverb, developing further in the second line, the idea mentioned in the first line. What is being commended in these verses is sharing one's resources with others. Hoarding and selfishness are condemned. **11:26** brings this into a sharp focus: *People curse the man who hoards grain, but blessing crowns him who is willing to sell*. The word 'sell' suggests that what is going on here is speculation at the expense of others. Hubbard says, 'The saying assumes that normal business practices were being suspended for some devious purpose of the seller' (*CC*). While **11:27** does not specifically mention generosity, similar principles apply in this verse. As Kidner says, 'What you seek for others, you will get yourself' (*TOT*).

Once again riches are mentioned in **11:28**: *Whoever trusts in his riches* – implied is 'instead of in the Lord' – *will fall, but the righteous will thrive like a green leaf* (see Ps 1:3). The natural image of a green leaf is replaced by another natural phenomenon, wind, in the next verse: *He who brings trouble on his family will inherit only wind, and the fool will be servant to the wise* (**11:29**). Here 'wind' refers to nothingness, something as insubstantial as the wind. This is the fruit produced by 'an avaricious man who deprives his family of livelihood and brings them to nothing but distress' (*EBC*). By contrast *the fruit of the righteous is a tree of life* (**11:30a**).

The meaning of **11:30b** is puzzling: what does it mean to say that *he who wins souls is wise?* Kidner interprets this as meaning that 'a righteous man has a life-giving influence, and a wise man wins others to wisdom' (*TOT*; see also Dan 12:3).

The final proverb in this chapter is given in the 'if … then' format of a conditional statement: *If the righteous receive their due on earth, how much more the ungodly and the sinner!* (**11:31**). This proverb will be either reassuring or threatening depending on whether one is among the righteous or the ungodly. It implies that retribution is evident even here on earth.

12:1-28

The message of **12:1** is one we heard clearly in chapters 1 to 9, the first major division of Proverbs. Then the instruction continues with the contrasting of *a good man* and *a crafty man* in **12:2**. The former *obtains favour from the Lord*, but the latter, *the Lord condemns*. The repetition of the negative statements in **12:3** is another way of saying that the righteous are established, whereas the wicked will be uprooted (see also 10:25).

The next proverb gives a brief sketch of the wife whose portrait will be drawn in 31:10-31: *A wife of noble character is her husband's crown* (**12:4**). By contrast *a disgraceful wife* (whether the disgrace is of the type described in 11:22 or of the extreme type presented in ch. 7) *is like decay in his bones*. What a contrast! 'Her husband's morale is affected right to his bones (which in Hebrew can stand for his whole inner self, not just his skeletal frame), which turn weak as though hollowed by rottenness (see 14:30 for the noun, 10:7 for the verb)' (*CC*). The psalmist also spoke of suffering affecting his very bones (Ps 32:3).

The justness of *the plans of the righteous* and the deceitfulness of *the advice of the wicked* are contrasted in **12:5** without mentioning their consequences. But in **12:6**, *the words of the wicked lie in wait for blood*, whereas *the speech of the upright rescues them*. As a result of this rescue, *the wicked men are overthrown* while *the house of the righteous stands firm* (**12:7**).

The next two proverbs refer to how one is evaluated. The first states that *a man is praised according to his wisdom*

(**12:8**) – that is, in proportion to his intelligence, for that is the literal meaning of the word here translated 'wisdom' (see 1 Sam 25:3), referring 'to the capacity to think straight' (*EBC*). *Men with warped minds*, however, *are despised*. The second, a comparative proverb, brings out the hollowness of pretending to be other than you are. Where the NIV translates it as *better to be a nobody and yet have a servant* (**12:9**), the RSV translation is preferable: 'Better is a man of humble standing who works for himself than one who plays the great man but lacks bread.' The reason for the different readings is that the original Hebrew was written using only consonants, and the interpretation of the words here depends on which vowels one thinks should accompany these consonants.

Animal rights groups will be happy to hear that the kindness of a righteous man extends even to his care of animals (**12:10a**). But that should come as no surprise, for the righteous man is only being a good witness of the care God has for his creation (see Job 38:39-39:30; Ps 104). By contrast, even *the kindest acts* of the wicked are cruel (**12:10b**).

The contrast between the man *who works his land* and the man *who chases fantasies* is a contrast between plenty and hunger (**12:11**). We are reminded of the fate of the sluggard (6:6-11; 24:30-34). We have no indication of what these fantasies are, although the next verse may give us a clue when it says *the wicked desire the plunder of evil men* (**12:12**), suggesting that the previous proverb refers to those who are chasing get-rich-quick schemes.

The following few proverbs (12:13-23) are all, in one way or another, related to speech. *An evil man is trapped by his sinful talk, but a righteous man escapes trouble* (**12:13**). There may be several reasons for the escape of the righteous, but they will probably include the fact that he knows what to say and when to say it: 'he holds his tongue' (11:12); when he talks his 'mouth brings forth wisdom' (10:31); and he 'knows what is fitting' (10:32). In fact, his words will produce rewards just as surely as his physical labour does, for *from the fruit of his lips a man is filled with good things as surely as the work of his hands rewards him* (**12:14**).

Where a fool is opinionated, and listens only to his own ideas, a *wise man listens to advice* (**12:15**). The volatile nature of the one and the patience of the other are contrasted in **12:16**: *A fool shows his annoyance at once, but a prudent man overlooks an insult* (see also 14:29; 16:32; 25:28; 29:11).

12:17 contrasts *a truthful witness* and *a false witness*. The former gives *honest testimony*, whereas the latter *tells lies*. The reckless words – we can add 'of the fool' in line with the parallelism – are like the deep thrust of a sword, wounding the person they are directed to. The tongue of a wise person, however, *brings healing* (**12:18**). Yet while the words of a fool may pierce deeply, they will not endure like truthful words, for *a lying tongue lasts only a moment*

(**12:19**). The word used for 'a moment' is literally translated 'while I would twinkle', 'referring to the brief instant when the light hits the iris just right and the eye flashes' (*CC*). Not only that, those deceitful men *who plot evil* will not know the joy of those *who promote peace* (**12:20**). The unexpected use of *joy* as a parallel to *deceit* in this verse serves to emphasize the sorrow that will come to evil men. Thus what follows is an appropriate sequel: *No harm befalls the righteous, but the wicked have their fill of trouble* (**12:21**). The reason for this is that *the Lord detests lying lips, but he delights in men who are truthful* (**12:22**; see also 11:20).

When the proverb says *The prudent man keeps his knowledge* (**12:23**), it 'does not mean that he never speaks; rather it means he uses discretion' (*EBC*). As a contrast *the heart of fools blurts out folly* and, consequently, 'the fool gives himself away, as well as his secret' (*TOT*).

We have already been told that diligence will result in 'abundant food' (12:11), but here we learn still more: *Diligent hands will rule* (**12:24**). *Laziness,* however, *ends in slave labour,* 'like the men conscripted by Solomon to break their backs on his massive constructive projects' (1 Kings 4:6; 5:13-17; 9:15) (*CC*). The lazy person may have landed 'in slave labour' as the result of the poverty that was predicted for him earlier in Proverbs (6:9-11).

Anxiety indeed weighs down the heart; but what an encouragement *a kind word* is (**12:25**)! And who better to bring the word that cheers someone up than a friend who is righteous! That is why **12:26** advises one to walk circumspectly and be careful in one's choice of friends. A wicked person throws caution to the wind.

Returning to the contrast between the lazy and the diligent, the next proverb reads: *The lazy man does not roast his game, but the diligent man prizes his possessions* (**12:27**). The Hebrew word here translated 'roast' is ambiguous, for it may mean either 'roast' or 'catch'. That is why the English versions vacillate between the two meanings (NASB has 'roast' in the text and 'or catch' in the margin). And the second half of the verse is little clearer, for the NIV's translation *but the diligent man prizes his possessions* is challenged by the NASB's alternative 'but the precious possession of a man is diligence'. Is the lazy man being criticized because he failed to roast the game he has hunted or because he failed to catch the game in the first place? Whichever the case, 'whether as non-finisher or non-starter, the indolent man throws away his chances' (*TOT*).

The message of the last verse of this chapter (**12:28**) underscores the incomparable benefits of righteousness, mentioned several times in what we have covered so far.

13:1-25

In the first verse, we are again reminded of the parental instruction we encountered repeatedly in the opening chapters of this book (**13:1**). The next two verses also return to a familiar theme, that of verbal communication. *A man* in line one is contrasted with *the unfaithful* in line two (**13:2**). In the context of chapters 10 to 22, the man must be wise or righteous for he *enjoys good things* as *the fruit of his lips;* whereas *the unfaithful have a craving for violence* – that is, 'violence will be his menu' (*CC*). The contrast continues in **13:3**: *He who guards his lips guards his life, but he who speaks rashly will come to ruin.*

In **13:4** the sluggard and the diligent are again contrasted: the one *craves and gets nothing; the desires* of the other *are fully satisfied.* True to their character, *the righteous hate what is false;* the wicked, however, *bring shame and disgrace* upon themselves (**13:5**). The last line can be vividly translated as 'causes to stink and makes ashamed'.

In 13:3 we were told how the righteous man must 'guard his lips' in order to guard his life. Now in **13:6** we have the converse: *Righteousness guards the man of integrity.* There is reciprocity or mutual cooperation here: the righteous man holds on to righteousness and righteousness guards him. This guarding or protection 'may work through divine intervention or natural causes' (*EBC*). Wickedness does the opposite to the sinner: it *overthrows* him.

Returning to the topic of wealth, it appears that **13:7** has much the same message as 12:9, although it differs by speaking of *great wealth* and using a different type of parallelism. The wealth of the rich, which was described as 'their fortified city' in 10:15, is now used to defend them by paying a ransom (13:8), a situation which reminds us of the kidnappings and hostage-taking we read of in the newspapers. The poor man, on the other hand, has no such worries, he *hears no threat* (**13:8**). Yet we should remember that earlier his poverty was said to be his ruin (10:15).

The two categories of people, the righteous and the evil, are now contrasted in terms of light (**13:9**). The former is a *light* that *shines brightly* and keeps on shining, while the *lamp* of the other is *snuffed out.*

The contrast in **13:10** is between pride and wisdom. The quarrels are probably the result of the competitive and uncompromising posture of pride. But *those who take advice* are spared such unpleasantness.

The first half of **13:11** is summarized in the English saying 'easy come, easy go', which is often applied to the winnings of gamblers. On the other hand, *he who gathers money little by little makes it grow.* The 'little by little' is literally 'by hand' in Hebrew, referring to honest labour. Money earned from honest labour or honest investment may be slow in coming, but it will certainly grow. The idea of patient waiting may be the connection between **13:12** and the previous proverb. When that waiting is eventually rewarded, it is *a tree of life.*

In **13:13** the words *instruction* and *command* may be implicit references to Scripture, which may account for the punishment meted out to those who scorn it and the reward for those who obey it. The value of teaching is again emphasized in the next proverb, **13:14**, where the same point is made through a different literary form. Whereas the previous proverb was antithetical, this one is synthetic and thus the second line elaborates the benefits to be obtained from the teaching of the wise, rather than focusing on the fate of those who reject such wisdom.

Listening to instruction will create *good understanding*, which in turn *wins favour* both from people and from God, *but the way of the unfaithful is hard* (**13:15**). The exact meaning of the Hebrew word translated by 'hard' is not clear, but it is generally agreed that it means 'not lasting' – in the sense of perishing, which is a point made in earlier verses. People's characters are shown in the wisdom or folly of their actions (**13:16**; see also 12:23; 15:2). These actions may include acting as a messenger. Where a messenger is wicked, trouble follows, but one who is trustworthy *brings healing* (**13:17**).

The key words in **13:18** are *discipline* and *correction*, which are related both to each other and to wisdom. Heeding them or ignoring them makes the difference between enjoying honour and enduring *poverty and shame*.

For the first line of **13:19**, see comment on 13:12. But what exactly is the point of the contrast? It could be that the failure of fools to forsake evil means that they will not enjoy the sweetness of a good desire fulfilled. Another consequence of a fool's reluctance to abandon his ways and his friends is given in the next proverb: *He who walks with the wise grows wise, but a companion of fools suffers harm* (**13:20**). The company we keep tells who we are. Kidner calls this 'education by friendship' (*TOT*).

Misfortune for the sinner, but prosperity for the righteous (**13:21**) is an emphatic restatement of the law of retribution (though we need to be cautious in applying this to specific situations – see the commentary on Job). The same principle is restated in **13:22** in terms of what becomes of a good man's and a bad man's inheritance. Ross reminds us that 'divine justice determines the final disposition of one's inheritance' (*EBC*). Yet this justice is not always evident, as can be seen in the next example, where injustice deprives a poor man of the crop he has managed to cultivate (**13:23**). But what is the injustice referred to here? It may be enemy action, as in Gideon's day (Judg 6:3-5) or it may be the injustice of a landlord, extorting an excessive share of the crop from the poor man to whom he rents the land.

Many of those who would applaud the accuracy of the previous proverb would be much more ambivalent in their approval of the next proverb, which contrasts two fathers, one of whom loves his son while the other hates him. The father who loves his son *is careful to discipline him*, but the one who hates his son *spares the rod* – that is, he fails to discipline him (**13:24**). In Kenya, the caning of students has been banned in schools because it can be cruel, but the role of physical punishment is again being debated because indiscipline is manifesting itself in arson. Although caning may have been irresponsible in the context of schools, parental love is displayed in disciplining a child responsibly (see Eph 6:4; Heb 12:5-11).

Another contrast between the righteous and the wicked is given in the final verse of this chapter. The former *eat to their hearts' content*, whereas the latter go hungry (**13:25**).

14:1-35

The chapter opens with a contrast between *the wise woman* and *the foolish one* (**14:1**) (although the original Hebrew reads 'wise women', using the plural). The former *builds her house* – like the wise woman *par excellence* in chapter 31 – but the latter *tears hers down*, and that *with her own hands*. We are reminded of the words in 9:1: 'Wisdom has built her house'.

14:2 contrasts a man *whose walk is upright* and *he whose ways are devious* in terms of their attitude towards the Lord: one *fears* him, the other *despises him*.

14:3 states that *a fool's talk brings a rod to his back but the lips of the wise protect them*. In the Hebrew, the phrase translated 'a rod to his back' is actually 'a rod of pride'. Some vernacular versions reflect this Hebrew original. The meaning may be that the proud talk of a fool brings punishment on him.

The message of **14:4** is also not immediately clear. The absence of oxen and the empty manger of the first line may indicate a farmer who does not have to take the trouble to feed or care for animals. But the second line reminds him that *from the strength of an ox comes an abundant harvest*. The message to the farmer is that it is worth taking the trouble to maintain animals if they are to maintain him and his family.

The next group of proverbs all refer to knowledge in some way. The contrast of true and false witnesses in **14:5** echoes 12:17. One who is only interested in mocking *seeks wisdom and finds none*, but those who exercise discernment will find that *knowledge comes easily* (**14:6**). Readers are advised to *stay away from a foolish man for you will not find knowledge on his lips* (**14:7**) in a synthetic proverb, which interrupts the string of antithetical proverbs by giving a reason for the advice in the first line. The theme of knowledge and discernment also underlies the contrast in **14:8**. Whereas *the wisdom of the prudent* enables them to reflect seriously on *their ways* – that is, on their conduct or behaviour – *the folly of fools is deception*, 'not merely falling short of the truth but side-stepping it' (*TOT*). The next verse develops this idea: *Fools mock at making amends for sin, but goodwill is found among the upright* (**14:9**). Not only are fools incorrigible, they even mock at the very thought of acknowledging that they were wrong, whereas the upright are always open to correction.

Ross cogently articulates the message of **14:10**: 'There are joys and sorrows that cannot be shared' (*EBC*). Only those who experience the deep emotions of *bitterness* or *joy* can truly understand those feelings.

The message regarding the destruction of the house of the wicked and the flourishing of that of the upright (**14:11**) is repeated again and again in this section of the book. So is the message of **14:12**, which is often quoted and preached on (see also 16:25). It puts the folly of man's rebellion in the strongest possible terms: *There is a way that seems right to a man, but in the end it leads to death.*

Kidner explains the 'bitter-sweet gaiety' of **14:13** as follows: 'One of two meanings seems likely: a) there is tragedy in life, from which gaiety offers no full or final escape (compare Luke 6:21, 25; John 16:20-22); b) our moods are seldom untinged with their opposites, and are none of them permanent' (*TOT*). Hubbard, however, seems closer to the wording of the original when he says, 'The teachers knew that emotions may be mixed, that … feelings swirl within us in complex patterns. Laughter and sorrow can be present at the same time in the same heart. And what begins as unsullied joy ("mirth" – NKJV) may at the end be exposed as grief' (*CC*).

It is not clear whether **14:14** is a synonymous or antithetical proverb. It simply states that *the faithless* and *the good man* will be rewarded for their ways, without specifying the rewards.

The next few verses contrast *a simple man* and *a prudent man*, underscoring things we have already noticed. Whereas the former *believes anything*, the other *gives thought to his steps* (**14:15**; see also 14:8). The prudent *wise man* who *fears the Lord* and *a fool* are contrasted in **14:16**. The former *shuns evil* (see also 1:7 and Job 1:1; 28:28) but the latter is *hotheaded and reckless*. The description of this hothead continues: *A quick-tempered man does foolish things* (**14:17**; see also 14:29; 15:18; 29:22). It is a synonymous proverb, both halves of which describe someone who is acting badly. The second half refers to *a crafty man*, who may not display his emotions as quickly, but who also *is hated* for his actions. As in 14:15, the simple and the prudent are again mentioned together: the former inheriting *folly*, while the latter are *crowned with knowledge* (**14:18**).

Another synonymous saying dealing with people on the wrong path is **14:19**: *Evil men will bow down in the presence of the good, and the wicked at the gates of the righteous.* Kidner comments: 'The Old Testament in its own terms, and the New Testament in fuller detail, promise complete vindication' (*TOT*) of the good and righteous.

In the next verses, we revisit the poor and the rich. While the former *are shunned even by their neighbours*, the latter *have many friends* (**14:20**; see also 19:4 and 19:7). The intensity of this avoidance is caught in the NKJV translation, in which the poor man is 'hated'. Hubbard comments as follows: 'Wealth encourages friendships, not so much because of the rich person's largess but because the rich make no material demands on their friends. The opposite is true of the poor' (*CC*). Other possible explanations for avoiding the poor may be that the better off are disturbed by their appearance and manners, or that being among them makes those who have more feel guilty about their wealth. It is important to remember that, as Hubbard adds, 'these verses should be read as descriptions of how we human beings do behave, not as prescriptions of how we should behave' (*CC*). The next verse emphatically makes this point, for sin is ascribed to the one *who despises his neighbour*, whereas the one *who is kind to the needy* is described as *blessed* (**14:21**).

If there is anything new about the following contrasting lines (**14:22**), it is that the first line is a rhetorical question, the answer to which is 'yes'. If *those who plan what is good find love and faithfulness*, then in the spirit of antithetical parallelism something terrible must be in store for those who plot evil and go astray.

The next proverb makes a very authentic contrast: *All hard work brings a profit, but mere talk leads only to poverty* (**14:23**). Indeed, it is hard work and not idle talk that produces results and 'brings a profit'. Although no characters were mentioned in the previous verse, the mention of 'the wise' and the 'fools' in the next one chimes with this proverb, for we are told, *The wealth of the wise is their crown, but the folly of fools yields folly* (**14:24**). The first line makes the same point as 8:18, while the second line 'emphasizes by its very tautology the barrenness of folly, which is its own reproach and its own harvest' (*TOT*).

The next verse contrasts a witness who speaks the truth and one who does not: *A truthful witness saves lives, but a false witness is deceitful* (**14:25**; see 12:6, 17; 14:5; 21:28). But what does it mean to say that the one saves lives? The answer may be that in situations where deception abounds, the lives of innocent people may be at risk. A truthful witness may, indeed, save lives by telling the truth.

Verses **14:26** and **27** both speak about the benefits of fear of the Lord. The former speaks about the refuge and security that a man gets, for both himself and his family, as the result of it. The latter says that *the fear of the Lord is a fountain of life* and that it delivers a man *from the snares of death*.

14:28 contrasts *a king* with *a large population* and *a prince* who is *without subjects*. The former's subjects are his *glory*, whereas the latter is headed for ruin without them.

With regard to **14:29** see comments on 14:17. The impatience of the quick-tempered man contrasts with the *heart at peace* in the next verse (**14:30**). The Hebrews recognized that emotional health and physical health are closely linked. Thus a peaceful heart and health go together, while envy *rots the bones* (see comment on 12:4).

Returning to the theme of the poor, two individuals (or categories of people, for that matter) are contrasted in **14:31**, based on their attitudes or actions towards the poor. *He who oppresses the poor shows contempt for their Maker, but whoever is kind to the needy honours God.* 'How people treat the poor displays their faith in the Creator. Here is the doctrine of creation in its practical outworking' (*EBC*). Both the wealthy and the poor were created in God's image (Gen 1:27; Job 31:15). Thus *whoever is kind to the needy honours God.* What a contrast between this attitude to the poor and the attitude displayed in 14:20!

Next is a contrast of the fate of the wicked and the righteous in the context of calamities. *The wicked are brought down,* but the righteous *have refuge* even when they are face-to-face with what is humanly speaking, the ultimate calamity – death (**14:32**; see comments on 15:24).

The synthetic proverb in **14:33** is an interesting one, especially the second half: *Wisdom reposes in the heart of the discerning and even among fools she lets herself be known.* There is a debate among scholars about the meaning of the second line. Some even add the word 'not', changing the proverb into an antithetical one (*CC*). But in light of the Hebrew text, it seems that a better interpretation of the meaning is 'While wisdom's true abode is with the wise, even among fools it is not wholly unrecognized' (*TOT*).

Another popular text in the pulpit is *Righteousness exalts a nation, but sin is a disgrace to any people* (**14:34**; see also 16:12). Some interpret this in political terms. Kidner, for example, thinks this 'is the most searching test of policies and achievements' (*TOT*). Hubbard, however, argues that ' "people" describes the populace of an area more than its political system' (*CC*). The exaltation mentioned 'is not material but a moral term here, as its converse shows' (*TOT*). The reference to national affairs is followed by a proverb contrasting two servants of a king: *a wise servant* in whom *the king delights* and *a shameful servant* who *incurs his wrath* (**14:35**; see also 16:14; 19:12; 20:2).

15:1-33

The chapter begins with two proverbs on speech. **15:1** teaches that the way we answer in a tense situation either contributes to peace or adds fuel to the fire. The contrast in **15:2** is that whereas *the tongue of the wise commends knowledge* to others, *the mouth of the fool gushes folly.* Changing from speech to vision, we are told that the ever-present eyes of the Lord keep *watch on the wicked and the good* (**15:3**; see 2 Chr 16:9; Ps 33:13-15), indicating that he will be right when he judges. Then, returning to speech in **15:4**, we are first told of *the tongue that brings healing,* symbolized here as *a tree of life.* The *deceitful tongue,* on the other hand, *crushes the spirit,* suggesting 'the effect of words on morale' (*TOT*). The lesson of **15:5** is by now quite familiar.

Next *the house of the righteous* and *the income of the wicked* are put side by side (**15:6**). The former *contains great treasure,* whereas the latter is depicted as a source of *trouble.* The question for us is, what are we storing up? What goes out from these two types of people also differs: *The lips of the wise spread knowledge; not so the hearts of fools* (**15:7**). The wise do not hoard the knowledge they commended in 15:2, but share it with others.

In **15:8,** we find a rare mention of prayer in Proverbs (we will meet it again in 15:29) in the context of contrasting what is hateful and pleasing to the Lord. Issues concerning worship – the temple, sacrifices, prayer – are hardly mentioned in Proverbs. Maybe as Kidner has eloquently stated it, the book's 'function in Scripture is to put godliness into working clothes' (*TOT*).

The Lord's detesting of evil is the link to the next verse. Whereas in 15:8 he is said to detest *the sacrifice of the wicked,* here he *detests the way of the wicked* (**15:9a**). Sacrifice is useless – even hypocritical – when the whole life is in rebellion against the Lord. By contrast, just as God delighted in the prayer of the upright in 15:8, in **15:9b** we are told *he loves those who pursue righteousness.*

The idea of mortal danger links the next two proverbs. **15:10** is synthetic in nature, developing the idea that it is those who are in such danger who need *stern discipline.* The message of the *how much more* comparison in **15:11** is similar to that of 15:3. God knows all there is to know about the evil and the good.

The synthetic parallelism of **15:12** comes as no surprise. Since the mocker resents correction, it is no wonder that he does not ask the wise for advice.

The next few proverbs deal with the attitudes of the heart. Both *a happy heart* and one oppressed with *heartache* appear to have physical manifestations: the former *makes the face cheerful* and the latter *crushes the spirit* and thus (implicitly) makes the face sad (**15:13**). The contrast of *the discerning heart* and *the mouth of a fool* (**15:14**) reminds us of 14:24, especially with its play on folly. *The cheerful heart* in **15:15** is nearly identical in meaning with the 'cheerful face' in 15:13. Kidner brings these two verses together: 'If verse 13 shows that our prevailing attitude colours our whole personality, this saying makes it also colour our whole experience' (*TOT*).

Two proverbs with a *better ... than* comparison follow. They show the superiority of spiritual values over material gain or benefit. The fear of the Lord is better than wealth, even when the latter is without the *turmoil* mentioned here (**15:16**). *Love* and *hatred* are contrasted in **15:17**. Love with *a meal of vegetables* is better *than a fattened calf with hatred.* These two proverbs show us what our priorities should be.

For **15:18** see comments on 14:17 and 15:1. The Akan of Ghana are also aware of the dangers of being hot-tempered, for they have a proverb that says 'a bad heart [one given to excessive fits of anger] kills its owner'. In the next proverb, the obstacle is in the attitude (the mind) of the sluggard. Because he is not willing to move, he imagines his way is *blocked with thorns* (**15:19**). Since the upright person is prepared to move with the Lord, his path *is a highway* with no obstacles.

The next few proverbs deal with wisdom and folly. For **15:20,** see the note on 10:1. Delighting in folly reveals nothing but a lack of judgment (**15:21**), whereas *a man of understanding keeps a straight course,* just as the upright have no difficulty in following a highway in 15:19. With regard to **15:22**, see comments on 11:14. The wise counsel of the previous verse leads naturally on to the *apt reply* celebrated with *how good is a timely word!* (**15:23**). In **15:24** the *path of life* for *the wise* is said to lead *upwards,* with the implication being that only fools will be on the path of death, which leads *down to the grave.* This proverb seems to hint at the possibility of life after death, although this doctrine will only be elaborated later in the Scriptures.

The Lord's reaction to evil is the theme of the next few proverbs. He gives the proud man the punishment he deserves, while protecting the defenceless widow (**15:25**). His reaction to the wicked in **15:26** should be read in conjunction with 15:8 and 15:9.

In **15:27**, the trouble that *the greedy man* brings to his house must be the result of taking bribes, for the second line tells us, *he who hates bribes will live.*

The discretion of the righteous is a now maxim (**15:28**); as for the mouth of the wicked, it *gushes evil* (see also 15:2). This evil is what determines the Lord's response to the prayers of a wicked man. The statement *The Lord is far from the wicked* (**15:29**) has nothing to do with physical distance – such distance does not matter to God. The Lord is far from the wicked, because their prayers, if they pray at all, are not heard by the Lord in the same way as he hears *the prayer of the righteous.* The sacrifices and way of life of the wicked are also detestable to the Lord, as we saw in 15:8 and 15:9.

Whereas 15:13 was antithetical, and began by stating that a happy heart produces a cheerful face, **15:30** is synonymous and expands the relationship: *a cheerful look* from someone else can give *joy to the heart,* just as *good news* gives energy to the body.

The next two verses must be taken together. *He who listens to a life-giving rebuke will be at home among the wise* (**15:31**), because the latter have also been prepared to listen to rebuke (see 9:8). In fact, this is the basis of their wisdom. One who ignores discipline is not showing self-respect or a 'good self-image', rather he is despising himself (**15:32**). By contrast, one who heeds correction – like the wise of 15:31 – will gain understanding. This is the type of humility that will precede honour (**15:33**).

The chapter closes with a reminder of the theme of the entire book.

16:1-33

The dominance of antithetical proverbs now comes to an end. From this chapter on, the format of the proverbs will be a mixture of synonymous, synthetic, comparative and antithetical proverbs.

The name of God appears frequently in this chapter, either in the covenantal form given to Moses (Exod 3:13-15) and represented here by 'Lord', or in its more general form, translated as 'God'. In fact, the first eleven verses (with the exception of 16:8 and 16:10) all mention the covenant name (the Lord). Hubbard points out that up to this point the focus has been on the wisdom that the sages have accumulated about how to live in the Lord's creation. 'But much of the time until chapter 16, the divine presence has been implicit, except in those places that call on the hearers to do their living in fear of Him. The necessity and the meaning of that fear become clearer here than ever before' (*CC*).

The chapter opens with the saying, *To man belong the plans of the heart, but from the Lord comes the reply of the tongue* (**16:1**). There is no doubt that 'the plans of the heart', that is, thoughts about what to say, are human. But despite all this planning, what is actually said, 'the reply of the tongue', comes in the final analysis from the Lord (see Matt 10:19). A Tigrigna proverb (from Eritrea) makes the same point: *Seb amami Ezghi fetsami* ['Man begins; God completes'] and so does the English saying, 'Man proposes, God disposes'. Ross says, 'This verse can be taken in one of two ways: a) the thoughts and the speech are the same or b) the speech differs from what the person had intended to say. The second view fits the contrast better' (*EBC*). What this and the following proverbs are teaching us is utter dependence on the Lord and not on our innate abilities to steer through life

16:2 says, *All a man's ways seem innocent to him, but motives are weighed by the Lord* (see also 21:2). The problem is that even the way of a fool seems right to him (12:15). The truth of the matter is that the all-knowing Lord is the true and final judge. In the light of the message of the preceding verses, the wise decision is to *commit to the Lord whatever you do, and your plans will succeed* (**16:3**). After all, everything – even the wicked and their destiny – will, in the end, accomplish the Lord's plan or purpose, even though he is not the author of evil (**16:4**). The Lord's detestation of the proud who prefer to go their own way is such that it is absolutely certain *they will not go unpunished* (**16:5**; see also 15:8, 9, 26; 16:18).

We should not understand **16:6** as contrasting 'atonement for sin' and 'avoidance of sin' in the sense that one is the work of God and the other the work of man. As a synonymous proverb, it is speaking about human responsibility in both lines. *Love and faithfulness* are attributes of the covenant Lord, but they should also be human attributes (see 3:3-7). Just as someone's fear of the Lord leads him or her to avoid sin, so also people's faithfulness to the God of the covenant will result in their sin being atoned for (see also Ross, *EBC*).

Kidner sees **16:7** as 'an encouragement to fearlessness' (*TOT*). Certainly it is a great encouragement and promise for God's people who work in very hostile conditions.

The point of the proverb in **16:8** is not to deny that it is possible for wealth to coexist with justice. But it does say that it is better to be poor and righteous than to accumulate wealth through injustice (see also 15:16, 17).

The point made in **16:9** is similar to that in 16:1.

Next come a cluster of proverbs about kings. The first, in **16:10** is not easy to interpret. It seems that the meaning is along the lines that since a king in his official capacity metes out judgment on behalf of God, *his mouth should not betray justice* (see also 31:1-9). For **16:11**, see comments on 11:1. The righteousness mentioned earlier in the context of the nation (14:34) is now associated with the king and his rule (**16:12**; 20:28; 25:5; 29:14). After stating that the only sure foundation for a throne is righteousness, Hubbard continues: 'Both the divine order in creation and the divine vigilance over history are geared, sooner or later, to topple unrighteous kings from their royal seat. Enforcing justice is virtually an act of regal self-preservation' (*CC*). **16:13** brings the righteousness that should characterize the rule of kings to the individual level. Officials and citizens should also be honest.

Wrath or anger from any person may be fatal, but the danger is even more acute when a powerful king is angry. *A wise man,* however, *will appease it* (**16:14**). By contrast, when the king is pleased, and his *face brightens,* life, rather than death, is the result. The second line of the verse develops this idea: *his favour is like a rain cloud in spring* (**16:15**).

Gold and silver cannot compare with wisdom – the latter is much more precious (**16:16**). Another expression of the value of right living is found in the synonymous proverb in **16:17**. One who follows the path or *highway of the upright* avoids evil and thus *guards his life.*

Just as 'humility comes before honour' (15:33), so *pride goes before destruction* (**16:18**; see also 18:12). The same idea is repeated in the second parallel line: *a haughty spirit before a fall.* Kidner comments: 'The special evil of pride is that it opposes the first principle of wisdom (the fear of the Lord) and the two great commandments. The proud man is therefore at odds with himself (8:36), his neighbour (13:10) and the Lord (16:5). *Destruction* may appropriately come from any quarter' (*TOT*). **16:19** gives a better alternative, though it may be sacrificial.

The blessing of heeding *instruction* and trusting *in the Lord* is again underscored in **16:20**. In **16:22**, which is an antithetical proverb, *understanding* and *folly* are contrasted. The former *is a fountain of life;* the latter *brings punishment.* One source of understanding is the wise, and thus there follow a small cluster of proverbs which deal with what the wise say and how it is said. Both **16:21** and **16:23** speak 'of the impression which true wisdom cannot fail to make' (*TOT*) and **16:24** explains the delightful and healing effect of *pleasant words.* They are compared to a *honeycomb* in that they are *sweet to the soul and healing to the bones.*

16:25 is a repetition of 14:12, and is followed by a down-to-earth proverb (**16:26**) that identifies one of the motives that enables a person to continue with the drudgery of labour – hunger! (This and other motives for work are also discussed in Eph 4:28; 6:7-8 and 2 Thess 3:10-13).

The issue of speech surfaces again, now on the lips of the *scoundrel* and the *perverse man* (**16:27** and **16:28**). Their objective is to plot evil, cause dissension and drive a wedge between close friends. The machinations of evil people are also presented in the verses that follow: *A violent man entices his neighbour and leads him down a path that is not good* (**16:29**). The synonymous lines of **16:30** speak of one *who winks with his eye* and another *who purses his lips.* They are plotting evil without speaking a word.

It is not old age in itself that is commended in **16:31**. Rather, the focus is on what the grey hair symbolizes, a life lived in righteousness.

In **16:32** *a patient man* is a parallel to *a man who controls his temper* and a *warrior* parallels *one who takes a city.* The point of the comparison is that the first group is better than the second group (see also 25:28). The true heroes, as far as the teachers of wisdom are concerned, are not the military strategists and generals who conquer cities and nations but those who control their spirits.

16:33 speaks about casting lots, that is, a way of making decisions by throwing dice or something similar (see also 18:18). The message of this proverb is not that we should use lots for guidance. Rather, it is asserting that even in such an apparently random act as casting a lot, the Lord is in control, for *its every decision is from the Lord.* Ross encapsulates this and the entire chapter when he comments, 'so the chapter ends as it began, with a word about God's sovereignty' (*EBC*).

17:1-28

Although there may be a slight change of vocabulary, what is being compared in **17:1** is no different from what we have seen before (see also 15:16, 17; 16:8). **17:2** points to the reversal of privileges that may flow from wisdom or folly. The *wise servant* rules over a *disgraceful son* and inherits as if he were a brother, whereas the disgraceful son is disregarded and disinherited.

Fire tests the purity of metals – here silver and gold – but it is the Lord who *tests the heart* (**17:3**). The testing is constructive, not destructive. But while the Lord is concerned for purity and truth, this is not true of *a wicked man*, who can be described in much the same terms as *a liar* (**17:4**). Besides using their tongues to lie, the wicked also *mock the poor* (**17:5**). The first line of this proverb is similar to 14:31. In the second line, the gloating may be another manifestation of the mocking, if we take the *disaster* as referring to the poverty of the poor. Someone who does this *will not go unpunished*.

It is not only grey hair (16:31) that is *a crown to the aged*, so are grandchildren (**17:6**).

The next proverb is difficult to interpret in the NIV, but makes more sense given the NASB translation, which translates the first word as 'excellent' rather than as *arrogant*. The meaning of **17:7** is then that it is even more inappropriate for a ruler to lie than for a fool to speak of lofty things. The corruption of power is also the message of **17:8,** where a bribe is described as a magic wand for the one who gives it: *wherever he turns, he succeeds.* But this is not all that the wise have to say about bribery – these words should be compared to 17:15 and 23; 15:27.

17:9 is antithetical, explaining how love and friendship can be nurtured or destroyed. The person in the first line *promotes love* by covering over *an offence;* the other *separates close friends* by talking about *the matter,* that is, the 'offence' mentioned in the first line (see also 16:28).

The next few verses stress the incorrigibility of fools. Whereas *a man of discernment* is sensitive to a mere *rebuke, a fool* can ignore even *a hundred lashes,* that is, a severe beating (**17:10**). However, justice will finally catch up with the evil man (**17:11**). The danger represented by a foolish man is presented in a vivid image. One would think that nothing could be more dangerous than meeting a wild animal that has been separated from its young, but the teachers say that it is safer to meet *a bear robbed of her cubs than a fool in his folly* (**17:12**).

The proverbs then move on to discuss specific evil actions that people reap what they sow is the message of **17:13,** referring to those who are ungrateful. Do not open the floodgates of dissension is the advice of **17:14**. The perversion of justice is another thing that *the Lord detests* (**17:15**).

17:16 is a rhetorical question. The proverb is not implying that wisdom can be bought with money. Even if it could be, the fool would not bother to buy it because he does not recognize its worth!

17:17 is a synonymous proverb, making the point that the love of a true friend is constant and family ties become more meaningful in times of difficulties. For **17:18**, see comments on 6:1-5.

The meaning of the first line of **17:19** is clear, but what does the second line mean? It is possible that the building of *a high gate*, which seems to be contrary to social norms, reflects the quarrelsome person's problems with his neighbours. Treating it under the caption 'Asking for trouble', Kidner says 'arrogance, Godward and manward, must be paid for' (*TOT*).

17:20 is about *a man of perverse heart* and one *whose tongue is deceitful*. As the one *does not prosper,* likewise the other *falls into trouble.* These consequences of folly explain the grief or lack of joy that is the lot of the father of a fool (**17:21**). This grief contrasts with the *cheerful heart* in **17:22** (see 15:13, 15, 30).

The next few proverbs repeat ideas we have already encountered. We again see bribery leading to miscarriage of justice (**17:23**). An antithetical proverb contrasts the fixed gaze of the wise man and the wandering eyes of a fool (**17:24**). Then **17:25** repeats the idea of 17:21, although this time the sorrow of the mother is also mentioned.

Another manifestation of injustice is addressed in **17:26**. A particle in the Hebrew, which can be translated as 'also' or 'even' is dropped by the NIV here, but is included in the NASB translation, which thus reads: *It is also not good to fine the innocent, nor to flog officials for their integrity.*

The chapter wraps up with two proverbs about speech. **17:27** is a synonymous proverb, treating *a man of knowledge* as equivalent to *a man of understanding.* One *uses words with restraint* just as the other *is even-tempered.* If a fool can imitate these virtues, others may even mistakenly conclude that he is wise (**17:28**).

18:1-24

The chapter opens with a proverb describing a person who is harmful to the community. Not only does he *pursue selfish ends* or his own desire, he doggedly *defies all sound judgment* (**18:1**). The same lack of judgment is shown by the foolish person described in **18:2** who negatively *finds no pleasure in understanding* and positively *delights in airing his own opinions.*

The next verse describes what Kidner calls 'sin's travelling companions' (*TOT*): *When wickedness comes, so does contempt, and with shame comes disgrace* (**18:3**).

The interpretation of **18:4** depends on whether we read the two lines as synonymous or antithetical. Kidner takes it as antithetical, because he interprets the *deep waters* of the first line as hiding something (see 20:5) and concludes that 'the proverb is contrasting our human reluctance, or inability, to give ourselves away, with the refreshing candour and clarity of the true wisdom' (*TOT*).

The justice system referred to in **18:5** appears to be rigged for *the wicked* and against *the innocent.* That is why *it is not good.*

The next three proverbs again deal with speech. **18:6** and **18:7** both speak about the *lips* and *mouth* of the fool (although the order is reversed in 18:7) and point out that his words precipitate *strife, beating* and *his undoing* and are *a snare to his soul.* Gossip, too, can be a snare, and **18:8** articulates its diabolic attractiveness: *The words of a gossip are like choice morsels; they go down to a man's inmost parts* (see also 26:22). The phrase 'choice morsels' (or 'titbits') comes from a root that means 'to swallow greedily'. Ross comments: 'When such tasty bits are taken into the innermost being, they stimulate the desire for more' (*EBC*).

18:9 describes a person who leaves a job unfinished as equivalent to someone who *destroys* things. This verse is of great relevance to our continent, which is littered with the remains of projects begun but never properly completed or maintained. What a waste of scarce resources! The verse also applies to someone who is not properly doing a job that needs to be done.

18:10 says that *the name of the Lord is a strong tower; the righteous run to it and are safe.* Giving strong support to Farmer's argument that the sequence of the proverbs in these chapters is not completely random, the very next verse describes the wealth of the rich as *their fortified city* (**18:11**). But the contrast with what has gone before means that this proverb cannot be taken at face value, and there is a distinctly sarcastic flavour when the second line says that *they imagine* their wealth is an unclimbable wall. Kidner summarizes these verses as contrasting a strong tower and a castle in the air and says: 'The world thinks that the unseen is the unreal. But it is not the man of God (18:10) but the man of property, who must draw on his imagination to feel secure' (*TOT*).

For **18:12**, see comments on pride in 16:18. One of the features of pride, which we all often share, is the habit of assuming that we know the answers, so that we jump to conclusions or answer before listening to what is being said. This response is here described as *folly* and *shame* (**18:13**; see also 18:2, 17).

18:14 underscores the priority of the spiritual over the physical in times of crisis. Inner spiritual vitality can sustain a person during physical sickness, *but a crushed spirit who can bear?* Despair and depression destroy all ability to cope.

18:15 is a synthetic saying about the wise: *The heart of the discerning* acquiring *knowledge* and *the ears of the wise* seeking *it out.*

There is some disagreement about the interpretation of **18:16**: *A gift opens the way for the giver and ushers him into the presence of the great.* The issue is whether the word translated 'a gift' here is actually different in meaning from the word translated as 'bribe' in 17:8. The latter can also mean 'a present', although Kidner is emphatic that it is 'never used of a disinterested gift' (*TOT*). Hubbard argues

that the gift referred to is 'money, handcrafts, spices, or perfumes like the gifts of the Magi which Matthew records' and is intended merely to give the giver access to important people. It is 'not bribery, whose purpose is not to encourage favor or friendship but to influence judicial or administrative decisions (Exod 23:8; Amos 5:12). Such gifts were undoubtedly subject to abuse. But that is not the teachers' point here' (*CC*).

But it appears that the distinction between these two Hebrew words was not as watertight as suggested by these two commentators. In 21:14 both words are used: *A gift given in secret soothes anger, and a bribe concealed in the cloak pacifies great wrath.* Not only are the two words used together, the two lines of the proverb are synonymous – they have the same meaning. And elsewhere the plural form of the same word, which is here translated as gifts, is translated as bribes. For example, *A greedy man brings trouble to his family, but he who hates bribes will live* (15:27). Not only can the same word be translated as gift and bribe, but the proverb is antithetical – that is, the second line is in contrast to what is stated in the first line. Thus the greedy man of line one is contrasted with the man who hates bribes, implying that the first man's greed has led him to accept bribes. Thus our conclusion is that while Proverbs realistically recognises that gifts can achieve results, it does not approve of the giving of bribes in order to sway things in one's favour.

The next proverb seems to hark back to the instruction in 18:13 to listen before speaking. **18:17** reminds us to hear both sides of a case before we come to a conclusion, irrespective of who speaks first or last. The second line, *till another comes forward and questions him,* may be referring to a court setting where witnesses must be heard and cross-examined before a case is decided.

For **18:18**, see comments on 16:33. The next proverb is a serious warning that we should carefully guard and nurture our relationships. The phrases, *more unyielding than a fortified city* and *like the barred gates of a citadel* (**18:19**) make the point that 'the invisible walls of estrangement' are 'so easy to erect, so hard to demolish' (*TOT*).

Both **18:20** and **18:21** deal with speech in terms of fruit. They make the point that we need to watch our words as they affect the quality of our lives. The tongue can spread destruction, but it can also give life and healing.

The final three proverbs in this chapter all deal with relationships. There is no doubt that *a wife* is a gift from the Lord and, indeed, the man who has been blessed with one has already received *favour* from him (**18:22**). The next relationship is less happy, as *a rich man* dismisses a poor man's pleas (**18:23**). Jesus spoke of a similar situation in the parable of the unjust judge and the widow (Luke 18:1-8). Although this proverb may depict the realities of this world, we need to balance it against the other sayings about how the rich should treat the poor (for example, 14:21, 31). Finally, there is the contrast between many friends and one true *friend* (**18:24**). Having many friends does not guarantee success, especially if those friends have ulterior motives. They may even lead one to destruction. But a gem may be discovered among them: *one who sticks closer than a brother* (see also 17:17).

19:1-29

The chapter begins with a 'better … than' comparison of the poor and the fool (**19:1**). The first line of this proverb is repeated in 28:6, but there the 'better … than' comparison is between the poor and the rich. Taking the message of the two proverbs together, *a poor man whose walk is blameless* is better than both *a fool* and *a rich man* whose *lips* and *ways*, respectively, *are perverse.*

Zeal without knowledge is not good; it is equivalent to being in too much of a hurry and missing the turn-off (**19:2**). Zeal or haste without direction is wasted effort, and all too common. We run into difficulties because of our own folly, and then blame God for our problems (**19:3**).

The next few proverbs deal with friendship and truthfulness. **19:4** should be understood in the light of what has already been said about the poor and the rich and the immediate context (see 19:6-7; also 18:23-24). **19:5** is reproduced almost verbatim in 19:9. The punishments that befall a false witness and a liar are reiterated again and again in the book of Proverbs. Many lies may be told in an attempt to *curry favour* with someone whom the NIV translation describes as *a ruler* and the NASB as 'a generous man' (**19:6**). He certainly hands out gifts, a topic that is discussed at some length under 18:16. But there is a marked contrast in the attitude to one who is poor: he is *shunned by all his relatives* and has no friends (**19:7**). His situation is similar to the one described in 19:4. For further comments, see 14:20. Note that this proverb is unusual in being longer than two lines.

19:8 is a synonymous proverb. *He who gets wisdom* corresponds to *he who cherishes understanding* and *loves his own soul* parallels *prospers*. For **19:9**, see comment on 19:5.

We have another 'how much worse' comparison in **19:10**. *It is not fitting for a fool to live in luxury.* Why? Because he does not deserve it. But the verse goes on to say *how much worse for a slave to rule over princes!* This is another instance of what Kidner calls 'jarring absurdities' (*TOT*). Looking at the verse as a whole, Ross says, 'In these reversals the fool would only make worse his bad qualities – boorishness, insensitivity, and lack of discipline – and the slave would become arrogant and cruel' (*EBC*). Similar ideas are expressed in 11:22, 17:7, 26:1 and 30:21-23.

We may find it odd that a virtue like patience is described in terms of *glory* in **19:11**. Kidner comments that this proverb 'brings out here the glowing colours of a virtue which in practice may look drably unassertive' (*TOT*). The opposite of virtue is rage, and this is the topic of **19:12**, which seems to be a brief restatement of the idea in 16:14-15.

19:13 parallels *a foolish son* and *a quarrelsome wife*. The former is *his father's ruin* and the latter is as annoying as a steady drip (see also 27:15). What a contrast to the *prudent wife* mentioned in **19:14**. She is indeed a blessing *from the Lord,* as was stated in 18:22.

Laziness brings not only a little sleep (6:10) but a *deep sleep* (**19:15**), which means things go from bad to worse. The outcome, of course, is hunger.

Obedience and disobedience are a matter of life and death, as pointed out by many of these proverbs (**19:16**). One of the areas where obedience is called for is in being kind to the poor. One who does this not only honours God (14:31) but in fact *lends* to him (**19:17**) and the Lord *will reward him for what he has done* (Matt 25:31-40). While *there is hope* in disciplining a son, failing to do so is tantamount to being *a willing party to his death* (**19:18**). At times this discipline may take the form of standing back and letting someone suffer the consequences of his or her own actions. This is what is being referred to in **19:19**, in its warning against trying to sort things out for a person who cannot control his temper. That temper will be bound to flare again soon, so that *if you rescue him, you will have to do it again.* If you let him suffer the consequences of his actions, he may learn a lesson and amend his ways. But it is better to avoid the need for such desperate measures, and that is why the next proverb stresses the need to pay heed to instruction and the benefits that will be gained by doing so (**19:20**).

19:21 is summarized in the saying 'Man proposes, God disposes' (see also 16:1, 9). The next verse speaks of the value of loyal love, which the NIV translates as *unfailing love* and the NASB as 'kindness' or 'loyalty' (in the margin) (**19:22**). It is better to be poor and enjoy this kind of truthful love than to make false protestations of love and be surrounded by those one cannot trust. The word here translated 'unfailing love' is the same one that is used elsewhere to describe the covenant faithfulness of the Lord to his people. The same faithfulness and honesty should characterize the relationships among people (see also 19:1).

By way of expanding on the blessing of *life* that results from fear of the Lord, the second line of **19:23** describes it as a state in which *one rests content, untouched by trouble.* However, there is a difference between such contentment and a sluggard's inertia, which is described in a humorous proverb depicting someone at a meal who is too lazy even to take the trouble to put the food into his mouth (**19:24**).

Although **19:25** appears to be antithetical it may not be – especially if we concentrate on the results of the two lines rather than on the apparent contrast of *flog a mocker* and *rebuke a discerning man.* The flogging of the mocker is not for his own benefit but to teach others to beware of doing the same stupid actions that led to the flogging. Likewise, rebuking *a discerning man* has a positive result: *he will gain knowledge* (see also 21:11).

What is happening in **19:26** is contrary not only to the teaching of the sages, but also to the fifth of the Ten Commandments (Exod 20:12; Deut 5:16). It is thus not surprising that **19:27** is addressed to *my son* – except for the fact that while this form of address was frequently used in chapters 1 to 9, it is almost absent in chapters 10 to 22. This proverb also differs from the usual one in that instead of starting with an exhortation to 'listen', it begins with *stop listening to instruction*. Having got the young man's attention by this unexpected twist, it carries on to make the same point as before: the result of not listening to instruction will be straying *from the words of knowledge*.

19:28 is a synonymous proverb: *a corrupt witness* parallels *the mouth of the wicked* and *mocks at justice* parallels *gulps down evil*. **19:29** mentions the consequences of such mocking behaviour: *Penalties are prepared for mockers, and beatings for the backs of fools*.

20:1-30

A proverb on the evil of drinking opens this chapter. In **20:1** the intoxicants, *wine* and *beer*, are personified and given labels that characterize fools: *a mocker* (see 19:29) and *a brawler* (see 15:18). No wonder it says *whoever is led astray by them is not wise* (see also 23:20-21, 29-35; 31:4-7)!

The king's anger is as frightening as *the roar of a lion* (**20:2**). Its fatal consequences have been mentioned in 16:14. But kings are not the only ones who become angry, and the next antithetical proverb contrasts the cool-headedness of a wise man and the quarrelsome nature of a fool (**20:3**).

In 19:24, a sluggard had food but was too lazy to eat it. He was fortunate to have food at all, for **20:4** reminds us that a sluggard who has been too lazy to plough in the spring will go hungry when he has no harvest to reap.

The purposes of a man's heart are deep waters (**20:5**). A similar description of a man's words is seen in 18:4. In both cases, this seems to mean that they are not easy to interpret, which is why it takes the insight of *a man of understanding* to draw them out. A similar point about the disparity between what people say about themselves and their true character is made in **20:6**. Profession and practice are not the same thing. While the second half of this proverb seems to despair of the chance of ever finding a faithful man, this pessimism must be balanced by the description of the true friend in 18:24.

The blessings of a righteousness man pass on to his offspring (**20:7**; see also 14:26).

The next two verses seem to go together. The first refers to the role of a king in judgment: *When a king sits on his throne to judge, he winnows out all evil with his eyes* (**20:8**; see also 20:26). The second, however, refers to a fear of

judgment by an even higher court: *Who can say, 'I have kept my heart pure; I am clean and without sin?'* (**20:9**). Kidner says, 'The practised eye of a true ruler sifts the chaff from the wheat; still surer is the Spirit of the Lord' (*TOT*).

God's detestation of crooked business dealings, expressed in **20:10**, has already been dealt with under 11:1 (see also 16:11; 20:23). The *even* of **20:11** appears to connect it with what has gone before, implying that even a child would know that such cheating is wrong. **20:12** not only affirms God is the Creator of *ears* and *eyes*, but also reminds us that we have them as part of his creative gift for a purpose. The hearing and seeing we do with them may extend beyond merely physical use of our senses to the spiritual dimension of hearing and seeing (Isa 6:10; Matt 13:11-17). Next, **20:13** returns to the theme of the sluggard and the consequences of indulging in too much rest (see also 20:4).

We are all familiar with the haggling technique described in **20:14**, where the buyer denigrates the thing he wants to purchase in order to drive down the price: *'It's no good, it's no good!' says the buyer; then off he goes and boasts about his purchase*. He may well have obtained a bargain, but it is as nothing compared to the *rare jewel* of **20:15**, which is wisdom, the value of which is greater than even gold and rubies (see 8:10-11), and which is found on *lips that speak knowledge*.

The saying in **20:16** is repeated in 27:13. This proverb appears to contradict the law of Moses, which specified that 'If you take your neighbour's cloak as a pledge, return it to him by sunset, because his cloak is the only covering he has for his body' (Exod 22:26-27). But here the proverb says that the pledge should not be returned: *take the garment, hold it in pledge*. This action is recommended only if the person offering the pledge has put up *security for a stranger*, or, in the parallel second line, *if he does it for a wayward woman*. Hubbard discusses the contradiction at length, and interprets the action as justifiable because the person's actions are so reckless that they represent a security risk affecting not only the lender but the whole community (*CC*). Another possibility is that refusing to return the pledged garment at night is a punishment for the foolish person who was prepared to stand security for 'a stranger' or go with 'a wayward woman' – two things that were specifically condemned in 6:1-5.

In an amusing proverb, we are reminded that while stolen food may *taste sweet* to begin with, the person *ends up with a mouth full of gravel* (**20:17**). A similar point was made about the loose woman in 5:3-4 and 9:17.

The advice of **20:18** is most likely directed to the king. However, not everyone is a wise choice as an advisor. Thus one is advised to avoid a gossip if one does not want confidential information betrayed. It is interesting that very similar points about seeking advice are made in 11:13-14 – see comments there.

The next two proverbs revert to relations between the generations. This time the *lamp* of the disgraceful *son will be snuffed out in pitch darkness* (**20:20**; see also 19:26). Should a foolish or disgraceful son inherit wealth from his parents, he will not benefit from it, as is well illustrated by the case of the prodigal son (Luke 15:11-24). Like the dishonest money in 13:11, the inheritance will disappear in no time (**20:21**; see also 21:6).

Cursing and threatening those who we think have wronged us is never the right action. We should not revenge ourselves, but should wait for the Lord's deliverance (**20:22**; see also 17:13; 24:29). Paul makes the same point in Romans 12:19 when he quotes the Lord's words in Deuteronomy 32:35, 'Vengeance is mine' (KJV; 'it is mine to avenge' in the NIV). For **20:23**, see comments on 20:10.

Just as the Lord can be trusted to work things out so that justice is done, so *a man's steps are directed by the* Lord (**20:24**; see also 16:9). But if this is the case, we may be directed into paths we do not understand; hence the question *How then can anyone understand his own way?* The answer is that we do not need to understand everything; rather, we should commit our ways to the Lord (Prov 3:5-6; Ps 37:5, 23-24). But the fact that God's ways may be mysterious does not absolve us of the need for caution. Earlier we were advised not to rush into speech (18:13). If hastiness in relation to human affairs is foolish, it is even more so when it comes to matters divine (**20:25**; see also Eccl 5:1-7). For **20:26**, see comments on 20:8. **20:27** is a great saying that challenges us to approach God in prayer, asking him to use his lamp to search our spirits (Ps 139:23-24).

Earlier it was said that the throne of a king *is established through righteousness* (16:12), and in **20:28** the point is made that it is kept secure through *love and faithfulness.*

Every stage in life has qualities that can be celebrated. Thus, while young men can be proud of their strength, older men can be proud of their grey hair, particularly in light of 16:31 (**20:29**).

The final saying in this chapter seems strange. One is tempted to ask: How can *blows and wounds cleanse away evil* and *beatings purge the inmost being?* (**20:30**). The answer seems to be that what is being referred to here is physical discipline of a child, a topic to which Proverbs returns frequently (see 13:24; 22:15; 23:13-14; 29:15). Kidner comments that 'where conscience is sluggish it may need such a spur' (*TOT*).

21:1-31

The first four verses of this chapter are all related in some way to human hearts. The first heart mentioned is that of the king (**21:1**). Under the caption 'King of kings', Kidner lists a number of heathen kings who 'are all examples of autocrats who, in pursuing their chosen courses, flooded or fertilized God's field as He chose' (*TOT*). For **21:2**, see comments

on 16:2. The Lord's insight into the heart explains **21:3**, on which 1 Samuel 15:20-23 is a good commentary. And *the haughty eyes and a proud heart* of the wicked are the *lamp* by which they are guided – but not in right paths, for as the last two words of **21:4** tell us, they *are sin.*

The next few proverbs refer to different ways of earning money and living. In **21:5** the careful planning of those who are *diligent* is compared to the hastiness with which others rush in. Planning will *lead to profit as surely as* undue *haste leads to poverty* (see Luke 14:28-32). While the hasty are not prepared to do the planning required, others are not prepared to do the honest work needed, and try to earn money by *a lying tongue.* But a fortune acquired by dishonest means is both *a fleeting vapour* – here one moment and gone the next – *and a deadly snare* (**21:6**). Perpetrators of evil are destroyed by their own machinations (**21:7**). The next verse is antithetical. *The way of the guilty* is being contrasted with *the conduct of the innocent;* the former is *devious*, whereas the latter is *upright* (**21:8**).

While a wife is a gift from the Lord (18:22), the difficulty of living with a quarrelsome wife is emphasized by the *better … than* comparison in **21:9** (repeated in 25:24; see also 21:19; 19:13; 27:15-16). In **21:10**, we are told of a frightening aspect of the wicked person. He not only does evil, but *craves* it. As a consequence *his neighbour gets no mercy from him.* For **21:11**, see comments on 19:25.

The next few proverbs deal with justice, both divine and human. God's retributive justice against the wicked is presented in **21:12**. Another form of retributive justice for the mistreatment of the poor is described in **21:13** (see Matt 18:21-35). For **21:14**, see comments on 18:16. **21:15** beautifully sets out the two reactions to the manifestation of justice: *it brings joy to the righteous* – most likely, because they are vindicated – *but terror to evildoers*, because they are condemned.

It comes as no surprise that *a man who strays from the path of understanding* ends up *in the company of the dead* (**21:16**; see also 14:12). Pleasure that can tempt one to stray, and hence the warning in **21:17**. But it is not pleasure as such that is being condemned, for the word used here is the same one that is translated 'joy' in 21:15. Rather, it is the love of pleasure that is the problem, the pursuit of it as the goal of life (see also 21:20-21).

21:18 is a synonymous proverb making a statement about *the wicked* or *the unfaithful* and *the righteous* or *the upright.* The former become *a ransom* for the latter. The meaning of this may be explained by 11:8, as illustrated by the case of Haman and Mordecai in the book of Esther.

21:19, like 21:9, speaks about a quarrelsome wife. **21:20b** may also be referring back to an earlier proverb. The *foolish man* who *devours all he has* seems to be equivalent to the pleasure-seeker of 21:17. On the other hand, although the houses of the wise are stocked with such pleasant things as *choice food and oil* (**21:20a**) and they *find life, prosperity and honour* (**21:21**), these are not their main objectives in life. What they pursue is righteousness. All the other things come as additional blessings (see also Matt 6:33).

With regard to **21:22**, Kidner says, 'The truth that wisdom may succeed where brute force fails (see also 24:5-6) has many applications, not least to spiritual warfare. But in this [the spiritual] realm, earthly wisdom avails nothing (2 Cor 10:4)' (*TOT*).

21:23 once again underlines the point that the wise are careful when they speak. But in contrast, *The proud and arrogant man … behaves with overweening pride* (**21:24**). Such a man loves to scoff at others, and so we are told that his name is *Mocker*. Note how the adjectives are piled up to depict this unattractive personality: *proud, arrogant, mocker, overweening*.

In **21:25** we again encounter the sluggard. He has a need – in fact, a craving – but he will not work to satisfy it. What can he expect but death, unless someone comes to his rescue. And who are the rescuers likely to be but the righteous, who do not crave things for themselves, but *give without sparing* (**21:26**).

The next few proverbs all speak of people who are more interested in appearances than in truth. The first part of **21:27** has been said a number of times; but what makes this sacrifice here even more odious is the *evil intent* with which it is brought. A false witness, too, perverts the truth with an evil intent, but both he and the one who listens to him will perish together (**21:28**). Kidner distils a maxim for life out of **21:29** when he says 'a bold face is no substitute for sound principles'.

Hubbard follows the line of thought of the text when he says that **21:30** means that 'no human intellectual skill can guarantee the success of a venture when the Lord is set against it. To be wise and to oppose God is a contradiction in terms' (*CC*). Ross, on the other hand, puts the message in a positive way: 'Human 'wisdom' … 'insight' … and 'counsel' … must be in conformity to the will of God to be successful' (*EBC*). Kidner establishes a strong link between this verse and the one that follows: 'If 21:30 warns us not to fight against the Lord, **21:31** warns us not to fight without Him. It condemns, not earthly resources, but reliance on them' (*TOT*).

22:1-16

A good name – like wisdom – *is more desirable than great riches; to be esteemed is better than silver or gold* (**22:1**). Hubbard points to the underlying theme of wisdom when he says, 'The esteem of the community – *a good name* … is one of wisdom's highest prizes' (*CC*). This chimes well with African world view, for acceptance by the community is

important in order to be able to have a positive impact on others.

Rich and poor have this in common: The Lord is the Maker of them all (**22:2**). It is only through the focus on that commonality that the one will be kept from pride and the other from desperation.

The next three proverbs discuss how one should live. The first virtue to be recommended is prudence. **22:3** makes the point that 'blind optimism is not faith, but folly' (*TOT*). The verse is repeated in 27:12. The virtues recommended in **22:4** and the rewards they bring are emphasized in numerous proverbs. The antithetical proverb in **22:5** reminds us that *the paths of the wicked* are strewn with *thorns and snares,* but the prudent and righteous man *who guards his soul stays far from them.*

The promise in **22:6** is a popular topic in the pulpit. The promise is implicit in the structure of the saying: If you *train a child in the way he should go,* then *when he is old he will not turn from it.* Some have interpreted 'the way he should go' as referring to a child's unique character and gifts, so that one should respect each child's individuality when training them. While this principle is true, it is probably not the point here. 'In the Book of Proverbs there are only two "ways" a child can go, the way of the wise and the righteous or the way of the fool and the wicked' (*EBC*). As Kidner reminds us, we are to have respect for each child's individuality but not for their self-will.

22:7 is merely realistically presenting the economic leverage one set of people have over others when it states: *The rich rule over the poor, and the borrower is servant to the lender.*

22:8 has both warning and encouragement: warning to the one who *sows wickedness* and encouragement to those who suffer. The wicked person will reap *trouble* and *the rod of his fury,* which brought suffering to others, *will be destroyed.* Encouragement is also given to the righteous in **22:9** (see comments on 11:25).

22:10 is a synonymous proverb. When the first pair, *Mocker* and *quarrels,* are driven out, the second pair, *strife* and *insults,* will also come to an end. There is a striking contrast between this instruction to drive out someone whose speech causes problems and the description of someone who is welcomed into the company of royalty (**22:11**; see also 16:13). What attracted the king to this person was that he was someone *who loves a pure heart and whose speech is gracious.*

The next three proverbs all deal with words in some form. First, we are told in **22:12** that, in keeping with his just superintendence of his creatures, *The eyes of the Lord keep watch over knowledge, but he frustrates the words of the unfaithful.* Then we are given the words of the sluggard, finding any excuse, no matter how implausible, to avoid having to do something (**22:13**). Finally, there is the mouth of an adulteress, whose words and kisses are a deep pit of which we have been warned before (**22:14**; see also ch. 7).

22:15 is well summarized in the truism 'spare the rod, and spoil the child' (see also 13:24).

Why do both the characters mentioned in **22:16** *come to poverty*? The answer is that although the one oppressing the poor may increase his wealth, he will finally be judged by God. Meanwhile the one who gives gifts to the rich is only wasting his money. When all is said and done, both of these will come to poverty.

22:17-24:34 Various Sayings of the Wise

We now come to another collection of proverbs, this time subdivided into 'sayings of the Wise' and 'Further Sayings of the Wise'.

22:17-24:22 Sayings of the Wise

The topics of this section are almost as varied as those of chapters 10 to 22 and 25 to 29. However, there are more clusters of proverbs here than in the previous section, although these clusters are not nearly as large as in chapters 1 to 9.

After starting with the familiar personal exhortations to listen and the reasons for doing so (**22:17-19**), the author refers to this group of proverbs as *thirty sayings* (**22:20**). Scholars say that if the translation 'thirty sayings' is correct, there must be a relationship between this section of the book of Proverbs and the Egyptian instruction manual *Amenemope*, which has thirty chapters. Such a relationship is possible, for God has also given other nations practical wisdom like that contained here. But the Israelite context of these sayings is clear from the instruction to trust in the Lord in 22:19.

But there is a problem when working out how to count the thirty sayings. Kidner says 'the section can be divided into this round number of paragraphs' (*TOT*), whereas Ross isolates thirty sayings by sometimes taking the proverbs separately and at other times lumping two or three of them together (*EBC*). The difficulty in identifying the thirty sayings may mean that there is a translation problem here. A very slight change in a Hebrew vowel would give the meaning, 'Have I not written to you excellent things' (NASB and NIV margin).

Once students have imbibed the wisdom that is embedded in these *sayings of counsel and knowledge* and *true and reliable words*, they will be able to *give sound answers to him who sent you* (**22:21**) .

The sayings begin with exhortations to social justice: *do not exploit the poor* and *crush the needy* (**22:22**). This is a concern we saw again and again in the previous sections. If they do, then *the Lord will take up the case* of the needy (**22:23**). We also meet the hot-tempered person again

(**22:24**), with the additional warning that the one who associates with him may gradually become like him (**22:25**). The warning against striking hands to make a pledge is also repeated (**22:26-27**; see also 6:1-5), with the reminder that by doing this one is risking losing one's bed. This danger may be an echo of the 'What else will he sleep in?' in the passage in Exodus that addresses the issue of pledges (Exod 22:26-27).

Land in Israel was an inalienable gift from God (**22:28**; 23:10-11). Hence removing landmarks was gross violence not only against an individual but also against his family's rights.

The wise remind us that, then as now, a skilled man is highly sought after (**22:29**; see also 22:11).

In chapter 23, the wise move on to the subject of greed. First, they discuss its manifestation when eating with a ruler (**23:1-3**). Greed can also manifest itself in the inordinate desire to get rich (**23:4-5**). Wisdom knows that wealth is unstable – it can take wings like a bird and disappear. Greed to hold on to possessions can also lead to extreme stinginess, and hence the reminder to keep one's appetite under control when eating with *a stingy man,* as well as when eating with a king (**23:6-8**). One wonders why such a miser invited anyone to eat with him in the first place!

23:9 gives good advice which is repeated in Jesus' instruction: Do not throw your pearls to pigs (Matt 7:6).

23:10-11 has been cited in relation to 22:28. One thing that needs emphasis is the advocacy of the Lord. As in 22:22-23, so here, the Defender *of the fatherless* is strong and *he will take up their case against you.*

Then we return to another set of verses that focus on the importance of gaining wisdom. They start with an instruction to concentrate and listen (**23:12**). For **23:13-14,** see comments on 13:24 and 19:18. Once again, as in chapters 1 to 9, the teacher adresses the learner as *my son* (23:15; also see 23:19, 26; 24:13). Note the zest with which the encouragement to apply the teaching is given (**23:15-16**). The disciple is admonished not to *envy sinners* but rather to *always be zealous for the fear of the Lord* (**23:17**), for *there is surely a future hope for you* (**23:18**). After a further exhortation to listen (**23:19**), the learner is told there is nothing to envy in the life of sinners (**23:20-21**).

The next proverb deals with the learner's relationship with his real parents (**23:22**, 25; see also 1:8; 6:20). *Buy the truth and do not sell it, get wisdom* are counsels we have heard before (**23:23**; see also 4:7). A son who listens to these exhortations is indeed a son to be proud of (**23:24-25**).

The teacher then moves on to warn the young man against two temptations a young man will face: prostitutes and alcohol. Prefaced by the admonition *My son, give me your heart and let your eyes keep to my ways* (**23:26**), the prostitute we have met before, especially in chapters 1 to 9, is mentioned once again (**23:27-28**). The subject of drink-

DEBT

Being in debt has become common. In advanced economies one is even expected to build a credit history by incurring debt to show one's creditworthiness. The Bible, however, does not speak favourably of financial indebtedness. We are told, 'Let no debt remain outstanding, except the continuing debt to love one another' (Rom 13:8). While Christians disagree about whether this verse prohibits incurring debt altogether, what is clear from all of Scripture is that God does not want his people to be saddled with the curse of debt (Deut 28:44-45).

The scriptural teaching on debt is as follows:

- Borrowing leads to enslavement (2 Kgs 4:1; Prov 22:7).

- Debt is associated with great need, such as that experienced by widows and during famines (2 Kgs 4:1-7; Neh 5:2-12).

- People are to avoid actions that are likely to lead to poverty and debt. Such actions include laziness (Prov 6:6-11; 14:23; 20:4,13) and pledging security for strangers (Prov 6:1-5; 11:15; 22:26-27).

- People are to avoid debt if at all possible and make every effort to repay it (Matt 5:25-26; Rom 13:8). Failure to repay debt when one has the ability to do so is condemned as wickedness (Ps 37:21).

- Those who are better off materially are not to exploit the poor by things such as charging high interest rates and taking a debtor's livelihood in lieu of money owed (Deut 24:6; Ps 15:5; Job 24). In rural Africa, moneylenders tend to charge very high interest rates, sometimes over 100% per annum. That is usury and the Bible condemns it.

- Debt was to be totally forgiven every seventh year by the ancient Israelites (Lev 25; Deut 15:1-18). The principle is that after a certain time, a debtor must be given an opportunity to make a new beginning.

- We are to pray, 'Forgive us our debts, as we also have forgiven our debtors', a request that applies to both moral and financial debts (Matt 6:12).

In Africa, traditional customs have been amplified by today's generation and people now get into debt because of elaborate celebrations of births, weddings and funerals and excessive bride prices. The church has a responsibility to teach biblical values and transform these cultural practices (Mark 7:8; Rom 12:2).

Believers need to know that the cost of debt is not simply financial, but is also emotional and psychological. Thus even in cases where one may have to borrow part of the initial outlay, such as when buying a house or a vehicle, the tendency to overcommit oneself for decades must be avoided. One should also not accumulate consumer debt by using credit cards.

While the Bible does not say that being in debt is sinful, the reasons why one is in debt may be so, for debt is often the result of greed, living beyond one's means, bad management of God-given resources, presuming that there will be enough income to pay the debt in future, and a lack of faith in God as provider. These things should not characterize Christians.

Debt can often by avoided by working hard and not trying to match the lifestyle of others. If you are already in debt, commit yourself to getting out of debt and to living debt free. Start the process with the following practical steps:

- Cease adding to your debt.

- Increase the rate at which you repay the debt by selling some unneeded possessions, working hard to increase your income and denying yourself things you are currently buying.

- Start saving and investing your money so that you have a safety net to guard against future indebtedness.

What has been said about personal debt also applies to national debt. National leaders should not mortgage the future of their young people by borrowing money that can never be repaid.

Stephen Adei

---

ing was touched on earlier (23:20-21) but now the teacher expands on what was said there (23:29-35). He starts in **23:29** with a series of questions, a type of riddle. The answer to the riddle is given in **23:30**. Then a clear instruction is given in **23:31**, and the consequences of failing to obey this instruction are presented in **23:32**. There is a vivid depiction of someone who is drunk in **23:33-34**, and then finally we hear the drunkard's own words in **23:35**. Ross summarizes this passage as follows: 'The sage gives a vivid picture of the one who drinks too much: he raves on and on, picks quarrels and fights, poisons his system with alcohol, gets bloodshot eyes, loses control, is confused, is

unable to speak clearly, imagines things, and is insensitive to pain' (*EBC*.).

The following section returns to the starting point, with a repeated warning not to envy sinners or associate with them (**24:1-2**; see also 23:9-20; 24:17-21).

Having dealt with the ways of evil persons, the wise move on to a celebration of wisdom. In a beautiful passage, a house is described as built, established and well stocked through wisdom (**24:3-4**; see also 9:1-2; 14:1). Wisdom is strength and sound advice is the secret to victory (**24:5-6**; see also 11:14; 20:18; 21:22). There is no way a fool can attain to wisdom while his life is contradicting it (**24:7**).

Consequently, he will have *nothing* worthwhile *to say in the assembly at the gate,* that is, in the place where the wise and respected of the community meet to discuss legal and business matters and make decisions.

The schemer and the mocker are universally detested (**24:8-9**).

Verses **24:10-12** are a strong statement of our responsibility to others. Kidner comments: 'Exceptional strain (24:10) and avoidable responsibility (24:11-12) are fair tests, not unfair, of a man's mettle. It is the hireling, not the true shepherd, who will plead bad conditions (24:10), hopeless tasks (24:11) and pardonable ignorance (24:12); love is not so lightly quieted – nor is the God of love' (*TOT*).

The warning of the need to show courage is followed by a more welcome recommendation to eat honey and a reminder that its sweetness is similar to the sweetness of wisdom (**24:13-14**). The future that is acquired through wisdom *will not be cut off* (24:14; see also 23:18). The resilience of the righteous is then mentioned as a warning to those who plot evil against him and as an encouragement for the righteous (**24:15-16**).

The next four verses should be read as a unit. Whereas **24:17-18** exhort the righteous not to gloat when God judges the wicked, **24:19-20** emphasize that judgment of the evil man is inevitable: he *has no future hope* and his lamp *will be snuffed out.*

Although the fear of the Lord is the theme of the book, the fear of the king is explicitly mentioned here for the first time (**24:21-22**). Godliness incorporates godly citizenship. There is a warning of the *sudden destruction* that *those two* – the King of kings and the king – will send on the rebellious (see also Rom 13:1-7; 1 Pet 2:17).

24:23-34 Further Sayings of the Wise

Another section is introduced with the announcement, *These also are sayings of the wise* (24:23). The second half of **24:23** begins a theme which is continued up to 24:25: partiality in judgment is not good (see also 17:15, 26; 18:5). Righteous judgment convicts the guilty rather than telling them *you are innocent.* Consequently, one who perverts justice will be cursed by people and denounced by nations – the parallelism emphasizes the punishment. *It will go well,* however, *with those who convict the guilty and rich blessings will come upon them* (**24:25**). Connecting **24:26** with the preceding verses, Kidner says, 'The right word spoken seals all, like a kiss on the lips' (*TOT*). According to Herodotus, Persians regarded such a kiss as a sign of true friendship – the type of friendship characterized by truth (*EBC*).

24:27 gives advice to prioritize activities when it comes to building a homestead (see also 24:3-4). The next set of verses speak against the desire for revenge (**24:28-29**; see also on 20:22). Then we return to the fields that were mentioned in 24:27, but this time the field belongs to a sluggard (24:30-34;

see also 6:6-11). The sage first describes what he saw in the neglected field of the sluggard (**24:30-31**), then he summarizes the lesson he learned (**24:32**) and shares his conclusion with his students: *A little sleep, a little slumber, a little folding of the hands to rest – and poverty will come on you like a bandit and scarcity like an armed man* (**24:33-34**).

25:1–29:27 Proverbs Copied by Hezekiah's Men

Here we have another set of Solomon's proverbs, *copied by the men of Hezekiah king of Judah* (**25:1**). Chapters 25 to 27 contain miscellaneous proverbs much like 10:1-22:16, although the sayings are generally longer. However, the proverbs in chapters 28 to 29 tend to be short and are, therefore, more like those in 10:1-22:16 in content and form.

25:1-28

This chapter begins with proverbs about kings (25:2-7). Although the usual 'but' is not there, **25:2** is antithetical, contrasting *the glory of God* and *the glory of kings: to conceal a matter* and *to search out a matter* (see also 20:8), respectively. Atkinson comments: 'It is part of the king's role to search out the detail of a matter so that wise judgments and decisions can be made, even though this takes place before the mystery of the ways of God' (25:2) (*BST*). Though it is the glory of kings to search out matters, *the hearts of kings are unsearchable* (**25:3**). **25:4-5** uses the example of purifying a metal to symbolize an instruction to *remove the wicked from the king's presence* so that his throne can *be established through righteousness* (see also 16:12; 29:14). The advice that follows is directed to the courtiers of the king (**25:6-7**; see also Luke 14:7-10).

Although an eyewitness is required to testify in court, one must not be too hasty to do so in case *your neighbour puts you to shame* (**25:8**). Nor should *another man's confidence* be betrayed in the heat of an argument, for that would give one a bad reputation for life (**25:9-10**). By contrast, *a word aptly spoken* is like a beautiful ornament, appropriate in its context (**25:11-12**). Carrying on with the theme of speech, **25:13** speaks about the refreshing effects of *a trustworthy messenger* (contrast 10:26; 13:17). On the other hand, a man *who boasts of gifts he does not give* is *like clouds and wind without rain* (**25:14**). *Patience* and *a gentle tongue* can change what appear to be insurmountable obstacles (**25:15**; see also 15:1; 16:14).

Honey symbolized wisdom in 24:13, but in **25:16-17** it is used to make a different point (see also 25:27). Too much of anything, even honey, can be unpalatable. A Tigrigna proverb captures this: *Me'ar entebezhes yimerir* ['If there is too much honey, it becomes bitter'].

The next two verses both contain proverbs of comparison. **25:18** shows how dangerous someone is who gives *false testimony,* and should possibly be read in conjunction with 25:9-11. The next proverb points out that *reliance on the unfaithful in times of trouble* is as useless as *a bad tooth* and *a lame foot* (**25:19**). They do not serve the purpose they were intended for when the need arises.

The person described in **25:20** is supremely insensitive as he or she *sings songs to a heavy heart*. An Oromo (Ethiopian) proverb points to this when it says *Of argaan/nama hinargu* ['The one who looks at himself, doesn't see others']. The meaning is that a self-centred person does not care for others. There is a great contrast with the kindness of the person in the next proverb, who returns good for evil (**25:21-22**; see also Rom 12:19-20).

25:23 is another proverb of comparison, indicating how surely *a sly tongue* will bring *angry looks*. For **25:24**, see comments on 21:9.

There are more proverbs of comparison in the rest of the chapter, using the examples of water and food. The first says – how truly – that *good news from a distant land* is like *cold water to a weary soul* (**25:25**). There is a great contrast between this refreshing drink and the polluted water that symbolizes believers who do not practice what they profess (**25:26**). The next proverb, which again refers to honey, is more puzzling. It seems to be saying that while honour, like honey, is a good thing, too much honey is unpleasant, and so is excessive seeking of honour for oneself (**25:27**). A person who lacks self-control is vulnerable (**25:28**).

26:1-28

The first twelve verses of this chapter, with the possible exception of 26:2, all deal with fools. The chapter starts with the assertion that *honour is not fitting for a fool*, for it is as inappropriate as *snow in summer or rain in harvest* (**26:1**). **26:2** speaks about another unfitting thing: *an undeserved curse does not come to rest*. **26:3** is a short rhyme about the way beasts of burden, including fools, are controlled. (Earlier, commenting on 10:13, Kidner spoke of a fool as 'God's mule'.)

Put side by side, **26:4** and **26:5** appear to be contradicting each other and have been a source of perplexity to many. 'The rabbis … solved it by saying that v. 4 referred to secular things but v. 5 to religious controversies … In negligible issues one should just ignore the stupid person; but in issues that matter, he must be dealt with lest credence be given to what he says' (*EBC*).

Whereas 25:13 spoke of the blessings of having a reliable messenger, **26:6** says that *sending a message by the hand of a fool* is *like cutting off one's feet or drinking violence*. Imagine amputating one's limb or 'drinking violence' as a consequence of the wrong delivery of one's message! Even a proverb suffers in the mouth of a fool (**26:7**).

Verse 26:1 said that *honour is not fitting for a fool*, and **26:8** appears to give the reason why – it is thrown away like *a stone in a sling*. Likewise **26:9** may be giving a reason for the comment in 26:7 – the fool flails around with the

proverb, hurting others, rather than conveying wisdom. Again, *he who hires a fool or any passer-by* is *like an archer who wounds at random* (**26:10**).

The Hebrews despised dogs, and a fool is as disgusting and as impossible to teach as a dog that keeps returning to eating its own vomit (**26:11**). Yet there is one person worse than a fool! This is the person who is so convinced that he has all the answers that he will not learn from anyone else (**26:12**). There is a similarity between this person and the infamous sluggard with all his excuses (**26:13**) and laziness (**26:14-15**) and his false self-image (**26:16**). He mistakenly thinks that he is wiser than anyone else.

We have already heard descriptions of a foolish action involving hiring a passer-by in 26:10, and in **26:17** we hear of more stupid actions by a *passer-by* who interferes in other people's quarrels. Then we read about a person who misleads his neighbour and says *I was only joking* (**26:18-19**). He is likened to *a madman* who shoots *firebrands or deadly arrows*.

The remaining verses of the chapter deal with malicious utterances. Gossips and quarrelsome people *kindle strife* (**26:20-21**). For **26:22**, see 18:8. A man with *fervent lips* and *an evil heart* is deceptive. He may appear charming, *but his wickedness will be exposed in the assembly* (**26:23-26**). The evil that a man hatches will finally trap him (**26:27**). Kidner interprets **26:28** as follows: 'The heart of the matter (26:20-28) is exposed in 26:28, with the fact that deceit, whether it hurts or soothes, is practical hatred, since truth is vital, and pride fatal, to right decisions' (*TOT*; see also 27:6).

27:1-27

We have to live a day at a time (**27:1**). Our Lord also spoke on the same subject, though he replaced *do not boast* with 'do not worry' and *what a day may bring forth* with references to 'trouble' and 'worry' (Matt 6:34).

The next few verses all speak of emotions. First comes pride and self-adoration, which are out of place for those who walk in the fear of the Lord (**27:2**). Then there is a reference to the heavy burden imposed by the need to respond correctly to the *provocation by a fool* (**27:3**). Finally, jealousy is presented as even more destructive than open anger (**27:4**; see also 6:34-35). Keeping to this theme of openness, **27:5-6** teaches that the *open rebuke* of a friend is preferable to the *hidden love* or *multiple kisses* of an enemy. An enemy may conceal his real intentions with a show of affection (as when Judas betrayed Jesus – Matt 26:47-49). A true friend will not keep silent but will utter a rebuke or point out a fault if it becomes necessary to do so.

For a satiated person, even the sweetest thing is loathsome; for the hungry, however, *even what is bitter tastes sweet* (**27:7**).

27:8 compares *a man who strays from his home* with *a bird that strays from its nest*. Ross interprets this as 'asserting that those who wander lack the security of their home and can no longer contribute to their community life' (*EBC*), a point which is poignant given the tide of refugees in our continent, for the bulk of the world's refugees come from Africa!

27:9-10 speaks about the beauty, joy and reliability of true friendship. One should, therefore, be careful to nurture it. A wise son is, indeed, a joy and pride to his father (**27:11**; see also 10:1; 15:20; 17:21; 19:13; 23:22-25; 29:3).

For **27:12**, see comment on 22:3, and for **27:13** see comment on 20:16.

Why is it interpreted as a curse *if a man loudly blesses his neighbour early in the morning* (**27:14**)? Kidner says, 'It matters not only *what* we say, but *how, when* and *why* we say it' (*TOT*). Ross agrees, but adds that the blessing and curse may also 'refer to the loud adulation of a hypocrite, the person who goes to great length to create the impression of piety and friendship but is considered a curse by the one who hears him' (*EBC*).

We have already heard much about the quarrelsome wife described in **27:15-16** (for example, at 21:9). The point of **27:17** is that constructive criticism among friends develops character. **27:18** underscores the rewards for honest work and good service. **27:19** teaches that water, acting like a mirror, shows only one's external appearance, but a person's true self is what lies within.

We know by experience that human desires are never satisfied (**27:20**; see also 30:15-16). One of our insatiable desires is for praise, and the way we handle praise is a test of our character (**27:21**; see also 17:3). A good example of how this works is seen in 1 Samuel 18:7, where 'the proportions of praise meted out to Saul and David … threw both men into the crucible' (*TOT*). Yet while a crucible can separate contaminants from pure gold and silver, there is no way to separate a fool and his folly. They have so interpenetrated each other that it is impossible to separate them no matter how hard one tries (**27:22**). As was already indicated in relation to the fig tree (27:18), a person who looks after his flock will greatly benefit from them (**27:23-27**). The owner who diligently provides them with fodder will later enjoy the security of being able to sell them to provide for himself and his family (27:26).

28:1-28

As was mentioned in the introduction to this section, chapters 28 and 29 resemble chapters 10 to 22 in that they consist of individual proverbs that are often characterized by antithetical parallelism.

The trust of the righteous in the Lord makes them *as bold as a lion,* whereas *the wicked man flees* though no one is pursuing him (**28:1**).

The next verses refer to nations and their rulers. **28:2** contrasts a righteous nation where order and stability are maintained through the *understanding and knowledge* of one

man and a *rebellious* one, which is subjected to the rapacity of several warlords. Somalia, which has had no central government for the last thirteen years due to the selfishness of competing warlords, is a good illustration of the disastrous effects of having numerous rulers.

A merciless ruler who oppresses the ruled is the subject of **28:3**. Such merciless rulers, and those who support them and other wicked men, are reversing the standards the Lord gave his people in the Law (**28:4**). The antithetical proverb that follows seems to give the reason for this: *Evil men do not understand justice, but those who seek the Lord understand it fully* (**28:5**).

The next few verses all refer in some way to wealth. For **28:6**, see comment on 19:1. Then **28:7** contrasts *a discerning son* and one who is *a companion* of *gluttons,* that is, of those who overindulge in food (and probably in other things too). The former *keeps the law,* but the latter *disgraces his father.* Wealth gained through unrighteous means, such as charging *exorbitant interest* on a loan, will end up in the possession of *another, who will be kind to the poor* (**28:8**).

Without obedience, sacrifices and prayers are detestable to the Lord (**28:9**; see also 15:8). And we are again reminded that attempts to harm the righteous will fail. *He who leads the upright along an evil path will fall into his own trap* (see 26:27), *but the blameless will receive a good inheritance* (**28:10**).

The discernment of the rich and the poor are again contrasted in **28:11**. Kidner points out that 'a) wisdom is no respecter of rank; b) complacency is no symptom of wisdom; c) a man's peers are not always his best judges' (*TOT*).

For **28:12**, see comments on 11:10-11 (see also 29:2).

The next two proverbs refer to differing responses to God. In **28:13** one man refuses to admit his sins – leading to a situation where 'sin buried' becomes 'sin kept' (*TOT*). But repentance and the renunciation of sin bring the forgiveness and mercy of God (see 1 John 1:8-9). **28:14** is another antithetical proverb that contrasts the blessing of *the man who always fears the Lord* and the falling *into trouble* of the one who refuses to listen to God, and *hardens his heart.*

The type of ruler who was described as *like a driving rain that leaves no crops* in 28:3 is now *like a roaring lion or a charging bear* (**28:15**). Still on the same topic, **28:16** contrasts *a tyrannical ruler* who *lacks judgment* and one *who hates ill-gotten gain.* The latter *will enjoy a long life.*

A murderer is a fugitive till death – his guilt pursues him (**28:17**; see also 28:1). Is this not the testimony of Cain, the first murderer and fugitive, when he says 'I will be a restless wanderer on the earth, and whoever finds me will kill me' (Gen 4:14)? The sage warns *let no one support him.* What a contrast between this hunted life and the security of one *whose walk is blameless!* One whose walk is not blameless, but *whose ways are perverse,* will come to a tragic end (**28:18**; see also 10:9).

The one *who works his land* and the dreamer are contrasted in the next verse. The former gets *abundant food*, while the latter has *his fill of poverty* (**28:19** see also 12:11). Faithfulness *will be richly blessed*, whereas undue eagerness *to get rich will not go unpunished* (**28:20**). We have seen the first part of the synthetic proverb in **28:21** before (see 18:5). Injustice may be perpetrated for a very cheap price. Continuing with the warning against being eager to be rich, we are warned against one manifestation of the desire for wealth – stinginess (**28:22**; see also 23:6). The stingy person does not realize that *poverty awaits him* – a poverty that may be material or spiritual.

For **28:23**, see 27:5-6, 14. Stealing is stealing, whether it is from the parents or others (**28:24**).

The remaining verses of the chapter are all in antithetical parallelism. The reason the greedy man *stirs up dissension* could be in order to get something from competitors or from its rightful owners. By contrast, one who is prepared to trust that God will supply his needs *will prosper* (**28:25**). The concept of trust is picked up in the first line of the next proverb, which contrasts a fool who *trusts in himself* with one who enjoys security because he *walks in wisdom* (**28:26**). Then, returning to the idea of trusting God to supply our needs rather than being stingy, we are told that *he who gives to the poor will lack nothing.* By contrast, one who refuses to help the poor will certainly enjoy a wealth of one thing – curses (**28:27**; see also 22:9). Those who refuse to help the poor are among *the wicked*, hence the antithesis in **28:28** must be between their *rise to power* and people going *into hiding*, and their perishing and the thriving of the righteous (see also 28:12; 29:2).

29:1-27

The chapter opens with a straightforward statement about the sudden destruction of the *stiff-necked* man. The phrase *without remedy* underscores the finality of it all (**29:1**). For an extended exposition of what this destruction means, see 1:24-33 (see also Jer 19:10-11). For **29:2**, see comments on 11:10-11 (see also 28:12, 28). For **29:3**, see 27:11.

A just king and a greedy one are contrasted in **29:4**. The former gives *a country stability;* the latter *tears it down* (see also 29:14). The greed expressed by a desire for bribes has a similar effect at the family level (15:27). Bribes are one tool to manipulate people, flattery is another. We have met the flatterer several times already, most recently in 28:23. But the second line of **29:5** is ambiguous. Is the flatterer *spreading a net* for his own feet or for the feet of the one being flattered? We know that the flatterer himself is in danger from our encounters with him before (see, for example, 28:23). But here the flatterer may be preparing a trap for the flattered by encouraging inflated self-esteem. Continuing the image of a net, **29:6** contrasts *an evil man* who is *snared by his own sin* (see 26:27) and *a righteous one* who is free to *sing and be glad.*

The next few proverbs relate to social concerns. It is second nature for the righteous to make sure that the poor are treated justly, but *the wicked have no such concern* (**29:7**). Mockers love to cause trouble, but wise men seek to reduce anger rather than rouse it (**29:8**; see also 11:11). The conditional statement in **29:9** raises the ambivalence one experiences in dealing with a fool: is it worth the trouble to take them to court? (see comment on 26:4-5).

Bloodthirsty men hate and seek to kill *a man of integrity* and *the upright* (**29:10**) because their lifestyles are at loggerheads. For **29:11**, see comment on 12:16.

A leader attracts people to him who are like him (**29:12**). The next proverb is a synthetic one that brings the oppressor and the poor together: *the Lord gives sight to the eyes of both* (**29:13**; see also 22:2). But what is the significance of the common gift? Hubbard sees it this way: 'Conscience or consciousness is the result of this illumination: the poor man, who is the victim, has light to see that he belongs to God despite the evil treatment; the oppressor, who is the culprit, has light to see that he has violated God's will and God's creature by his extortions' (*CC*). The consequences of fair treatment of the poor are spelled out in **29:14** (see also 16:12; 29:4).

For **29:15** see comment on 13:24. The aim of the discipline is to prevent the child from the bad influence of the wicked who encourage sin (**29:16**). They are not to be emulated, for *the righteous will see their downfall* and a child who grows to be one of the righteous will bring peace and delight to his parents (**29:17**). But parental discipline alone is not enough. We are reminded that revelation is also needed (**29:18**). It is interesting that here we have a proverb (part of the wisdom literature) that refers to the prophets (who received *revelation*) and to keeping God's *law*. This verse thus touches on all aspects of God's revelation that the Jews identified in the OT, namely the Law, the Prophets and the Writings or Wisdom literature (see Jer 18:18).

A stubborn and pampered servant who *brings grief in the end* is the subject of **29:19** and **29:21**. As for **29:20**, see 26:12 and 19:2. For **29: 22**, see comment on 14:17. Coming to **29:23**, we learn that there will be many reversals when God's just scales are applied.

The saying in **29:24** clearly refers to someone who is a friend or *accomplice of a thief* and who is called into court to testify in a trial. He takes an oath to tell the truth, an oath which takes the form of a curse (see KJV) on anyone who witholds or perverts the truth. 'He then refuses to reveal what he knows and thus is guilty of false witness. His fate is the "curse" pronounced in Leviticus 5:1. His silence is ample proof that he "hates his own life" which is sorely threatened by the curse which God Himself will enforce' (*CC*). The reason for his silence may be fear of what will happen to him if he tells the truth, but **29:25** stresses the folly of this in its contrast between the fear of man and the fear of the Lord (implied in *trusts*). The former is *a snare,* whereas the one who practices the latter *is kept safe* (see also 16:7; Jer 17:5-8).

Next comes another antithetical proverb: the reason *many seek an audience with a ruler* is – by inference from the second line of the proverb – to get justice; *but it is from the Lord that man gets justice* (**29:26**; see also 16:1, 9, 33; 19:6).

This collection of proverbs ends by strongly contrasting two groups of people who are diametrically opposed to each other and, in fact, detest each other: *The righteous detest the dishonest; the wicked detest the upright* (**29:27**). The strength of the wickeds' hatred is spelled out in 29:10.

30:1-33 The Words of Agur, Son of Jakeh

After the introductory verse, which names the author and his audience, this chapter can conveniently be divided into two sections: Agur's reflection on the knowledge of God, his word and his grace and providence (30:2-9) and his reflection on God's creation (30:10-33).

30:1-9 Reflection on the Knowledge of God

In **30:1** the author's name is given as Agur, son of Jakeh, and what he says is described as an *oracle* (see also 31:1). However, there is considerable debate about the meaning of this word. As can be seen from the notes in the margin of the NIV, it can also be translated as *Massa*. If this second translation is correct, then the word may be a place name or the name of the tribe to which Agur (and King Lemuel in 31:1) belonged. There were Ishmaelite people with this name in northern Arabia (Gen 25:13-14; 1 Chr 1:30). Farmer states that 'since Ishmael was Abraham's firstborn son, the sages of Israel may have recognized that they had a family relationship (of sorts) with the people of Massa' (*ITC*). They were thus prepared to include the words of two people who were probably not Israelites, namely Agur and Lemuel, in the book of Proverbs. Ithiel and Ucal also appear to be people's names.

In **30:2-3**, Agur starts by humbly admitting his ignorance, especially when it comes to the knowledge of God, to Ithiel and Ucal. Kidner comments that he 'is refreshingly conscious of his unfitness to speculate about God' (*TOT*). Agur then goes on to affirm that it is impossible to know God without revelation (**30:4-6**). *Who has gone up to heaven and come down? Who has gathered up the wind in the hollow of his hands? Who has wrapped up the waters in his cloak? Who has established all the ends of the earth? What is his name and the name of his son? Tell me if you know* (30:4). The last statement, 'Tell me if you know', is a sarcastic way of deflating human claims to knowledge, especially knowledge of God. The reference to 'his name and the name of his son' is intriguing. The son referred to is Israel in the immediate context (see Exod 4:22; Hos 11:1), but in the light of revelation, which is the focus of this passage, the son referred

to is ultimately Jesus Christ (Matt 2:14-15; see also Ps 2). Thus what we have here is 'a subtle anticipation of the full revelation in the New Testament' (*EBC*).

After this series of questions, Agur continues: *Every word of God is flawless; he is a shield to those who take refuge in him. Do not add to his words, or he will rebuke you and prove you a liar* (30:5-6). He concludes this part of the chapter with a prayer in which he confesses his utter dependence on God's grace and providence. He begins with *Two things I ask of you, O Lord* (**30:7**), an opening which prepares us for the numerical sayings that follow in the rest of the chapter. The request that follows in **30:8-9** is typical of the balance that is portrayed in the teaching of the sages in its recognition of the particular temptations of both wealth and poverty.

30:10-33 Reflection on God's Creation

In the remainder of the chapter, we have a number of groups of sayings each of which lists four things: 30:11-14, 15-16, 18-19, 21-23, 24-28 and 29-31. The first set, 30:11-14, differs from the others in not specifically mentioning numbers, but all of the others begin with *three things ... four*, except for the last set, 30:24-28, which starts immediately with *four*. (A similar pattern was used in 6:16-19.) These self-contained numerical sayings are interspersed with short sayings (30:10, 17, 20, 32-33).

The short saying in **30:10** is not completely unrelated to the saying about arrogance that follows in **30:11-14**. Kidner explains the connection in these terms: 'This stands appropriately enough between the prayer of 30:7-9 and the portraits of 30:11-14, for arrogance (30:11) breeds oppression (30:14), while the fear of God (30:7-9) engenders respect for the weak. If the servant is innocent, his curse will count (see also 26:2), for there is a Judge' (*TOT*).

The numerical saying in (**30:15b-16**) is prefaced by a short proverb referring to *the leech* whose two daughters cry *Give! Give!* (**30:15a**). What connects the leech and her twins to the numerical saying is, perhaps, the idea of insatiable craving.

The severe warning of verse **30:17** mentions both father and mother and may be related to the cruel and arrogant people mentioned in 30:11-14.

30:18-19 deal with four things that leave the wisdom teacher amazed and wondering how do they do it. If, as appeared to be the case in 6:16-19, the lesson of a numerical saying is clinched in the item listed last, then what Agur finds most amazing is *the way of a man with a maiden*. But if a man can manipulate a woman, it comes as no surprise that a woman can do the same to a man. Thus this saying is followed by a brief comment on the adulteress, who calmly denies that she has done anything wrong (**30:20**).

The four things under which *the earth trembles and cannot bear up* are *a servant who becomes king, a fool who is full of food, an unloved woman who is married and a maidservant who displaces her mistress* (**30:21-23**). The reason why these situations are so bad is that they are 'unfitting' (19:10) because these people will certainly abuse their new role.

The next four things *are small, yet they are extremely wise* – and therefore can teach us humans if we are humble enough to be prepared to learn from them (**30:24-28**). The tiny ants can teach us about the need to work to lay in provisions when supply is abundant so that we have a supply to fall back on when troubles come (30:25; see also 6:6-8). The conies, or hyraxes, recognize that they are weak, and so find themselves a strong and secure place to live (30:26). Locusts individually are weak, yet when they band together in massive numbers like an army, their swarms can devastate vast regions 30:27). A lizard does not let its smallness deter it from boldly entering the homes of the powerful (30:28).

The last set of four things that are *stately in their stride* or that *move with stately bearing* is given in **30:29-31**. There may, however, be a gentle reminder here 'of the thin line between the stately and the strutting, in the choice of at least one of the king's fellow striders' (*TOT*). This same awareness continues in **30:32**, with its stress that exalting oneself is synonymous with foolishness. Clapping one's

---

DEMOCRACY

Africa has seen many political ideologies, including Senghor's negritude, Nkrumah's African personality, Nyerere's *ujaama*, Kenyatta's *uhuru*, Kaunda's African humanism, and Mobutu's cultural revolution. None of these political ideologies has significantly bettered the lot of Africans, for we are still faced with many social, political, religious, economic and cultural crises. Some now argue that democracy is the solution to Africa's problems. Others regard it with suspicion and consider it a tool to further a Western political agenda. How should we respond to this debate as Christians?

Democracy has been defined as government of the people, by the people, for the people and is associated with civilian government, elections, free speech and human rights. It is said that such a system of government promotes social justice. However, the economic policies espoused by some of those who are the most ardent supporters of democratic values seem to contradict the focus on the people and on human rights by transferring power to corporations and global institutions.

It is important that Christians recognize that democracy is a human political creation, just like all other political systems. At the heart of all such systems is the question of the correct way to exercise political authority.

In traditional African society, authority is community based and derived from the community and its ancestors. Its chief purpose is to preserve the group, and hence the rights of individuals or of those who are not considered part of the group are often ignored. Political authority imposed from the outside lacks legitimacy and is usually resisted. During the colonial era and since then, political authorities have made selective use of aspects of the traditional system to advance their own causes, often by benefiting one group at the expense of another.

In contrast, modern societies expect political authorities to use their power to safeguard and protect the rights of individuals rather than groups. Individual rights rank far higher than group rights.

As historical development has forced Africa to move from the one model to the other, there has been much confusion and gross misuse of political authority. This misuse of authority has produced dictatorships, militarism, racism, ethnicity, tribalism, corruption and moral and spiritual decadence.

Africa needs to be reminded that all political authority ultimately derives from God and must be exercised in accountability to him. One of the major flaws in Western democracy is the fact that its concept of authority is rooted in human laws made without any reference to divine authority. God's supreme authority and power are left out of the scheme of things. But the Bible clearly calls God the Creator, the Maker of heaven and earth (Gen 1–3). As such, he is sovereign and is the ultimate source of all principles of authority and good governance.

In the OT, God used the nation of Israel to show how people should live with him as their supreme ruler and authority. The function of the laws laid down by the political authority was to preserve God's divine laws, protect his creation, maintain humanity and kindness to others and introduce the concept of redemption. When the rulers forgot this, the prophets spoke out to stress the importance of upholding God's justice, righteousness, humility and kindness (Jer 9:23; Hos 10:12-13; Amos 5:24; Mic 4:8). Democratic systems that do not incorporate these universal biblical norms and principles will in the end be unjust.

The Bible also makes it clear that all human authority and power, even that of unbelieving authorities, is delegated from God (Dan 2:21; 5:26; Matt 28:18; John 19:11; Rom 13:1-7; 1 Pet 2:13-14). For this reason, all human institutions of authority, laws, decrees, constitutions, and statutes, etc., must be in conformity with God's universal laws and order.

God's creation of human beings also implies another principle that must never be forgotten. He created all of us in his own image (Gen 1:26). While this image may have been damaged in the fall, it nevertheless gives every man and woman a universal stature, dignity and value that exceeds the value of the state, the tribe, the race and all human institutions. God created people as moral beings and gave them the gift of dignity, right, equality and freedom (Acts 17:26-31; Rom 2:6-11; Gal 3:28). These are universal norms that transcend humanity and its institutions. While these norms are not democratic values, they have been incorporated in the definition of democracy.

Yusufu Turaki

hand over one's mouth may indicate either forcing oneself to keep silent or shame at what one has already said or done. If the folly that manifests itself in self-exaltation is not checked or repented of, it will produce strife (**30:33**).

Kidner, commenting on this chapter as a whole, says that it could well serve as an example to an artist or a journalist: 'It not only encourages a lively interest in our fellow beings of all shapes and sizes, but combines this insatiable curiosity with, on the one hand, a deep humility in face of mystery, and on the other hand, a clear insistence on the values that have been revealed to us' (*TOT*).

31:1-31 Royal Instruction and Wifely Excellence

This chapter can be conveniently divided into two sections, 31:1-9 and 31:10-31.

31:1-9 Instructions to King Lemuel from his Mother

The words in this section are not the words of King Lemuel of Massa but of his mother (**31:1**). They contain the first instructions in this book that are addressed directly to a leader, in the style of the instruction manuals of Egypt and Mesopotamia. The passage is a direct address in the imperative mood and is phrased in very personal terms (**31:2**). Thus, while earlier exhortations in Proverbs have pointed out the universal perils of loose living (for example, ch. 5 deals with promiscuous sex and 23:29-35 with drunkenness) and the universal duty of compassion (see 24:11-12), here these things are put in the unique context of power and the heightened obligations it brings. Lemuel is told *do not spend your strength on women, your vigour on those who ruin kings*' (**31:3**). Moreover, *It is not for kings ... to drink wine, not for rulers to crave beer* (**31:4**). The reason is provided: *lest they drink and forget what the law decrees, and deprive all the oppressed of their rights* (**31:5**).

The people referred to in **31:6 and 31:7** are trying to drown their problems in the drink (see also 23:29-35). But the king should not do this, for as Kidner says, 'an administrator has better things to do than anaesthetize himself.'

After dealing with the negatives, Lemuel's mother instructs him in what he should do instead: *Speak up for those who cannot speak for themselves, for the rights of all who are destitute. Speak up and judge fairly; defend the rights of the poor and needy* (**31:8-9**). These verses contradict the idea, which is too prevalent on our continent, that leadership involves grabbing things for oneself. Rather, the leader should be the epitome of compassion and justice.

31:10-31 Poem in Praise of a Virtuous Wife

This poem is interesting in several respects and rewards detailed study. Here we can only scratch the surface. It is an acrostic poem, in that each verse begins with a different letter of the Hebrew alphabet, in sequence. In 18:22 a blessing was pronounced upon one who finds a wife. The extent of that blessing is beautifully articulated in **31:10-12**. Moreover, the responsibilities that this woman discharges are indicative of the important role of the woman in ancient Israelite society: she provided both clothing and food for her family and servants (**31:13-15, 19, 21-22**), managed the estate (**31:16-18, 27**), cared for the poor (**31:20**), sold her own handwork (**31:24**), and engaged in teaching (**31:26**).

No wonder the husband of such a wife *is respected at the city gate, where he takes his seat among the elders of the land* (**31:23**)! The repetition of *at the city gate* in **31:31** shows that the public honour with which she has crowned her husband is also rightfully hers. It comes as no surprise that *her children arise and call her blessed* and that her husband joins in the chorus (**31:28**). In fact he even goes further and adds, *Many women do noble things, but you surpass them all* (**31:29**). Words fail to exhaust the accolade of such a woman, who in addition to all that has been said, works hard to secure the future of her family (**31:25**). In short, as Kidner puts it, the 'A to Z of wifely virtues' (*TOT*) are given to us here. In addition, this woman embodies most of the qualities of wisdom described in Proverbs and most of all, the religious criterion or motto which we met at the beginning of the book, for **31:30** reminds us that *a woman who fears the Lord is to be praised.* What we have here is 'the picture of godliness that is severely practical, of values that are sound and humane, and of a success that has been most diligently earned' (*TOT*).

Conclusion

Proverbs shows that there are only two paths that human beings can pursue in this life. One is the way of wisdom and righteousness, which is rewarded with abundant life in the presence of God. The other is the way of folly and wickedness, the outcome of which is destruction and eternal doom. Whether we realize it or not, we are walking in one or the other of these paths.

Tewoldemedhin Habtu

Further Reading

Farmer, Kathleen A. *Who Knows What is Good? A Commentary on the Books of Proverbs and Ecclesiastes.* ITC. Grand Rapids: Eerdmans, 1991.

Habtu, Tewoldemedhin. *A Taxonomy of Approaches of Five Representative Scholars to the Nature of Wisdom in the Old Testament in the Light of Proverbs 1–9.* Ph.D. dissertation, Trinity International University, 1993.

Kidner, Derek. *Proverbs.* TOT. Reprint. Leicester: Inter-Varsity Press, 1988.

Ross, Allen P. *Proverbs.* EBC. Grand Rapids: Zondervan, 1991.

ECCLESIASTES

Ecclesiastes is the most difficult book of the Bible to understand in terms of both its structure and its theology. The apparently unorthodox and pessimistic statements in the book have earned it the label 'the black sheep of the Bible'. Its inclusion in the canon of Holy Scriptures has been treated with great suspicion.

The interpretation of the book has also been controversial. Many commentators consider the book to be the work of two, three or even nine writers or editors. For example, some say that certain sections were written by Qohelet, others by a Pious Man, and still others by a Wise Man. They argue that Qohelet (Hebrew) or the Preacher or Teacher in English versions, was the original writer responsible for the rebellious or pessimistic overtones in the book. The Pious Man added his orthodox interpolations to counteract Qohelet's unorthodox views. Finally, true to his tradition, the Wise Man sprinkled in the maxims and proverbs we find in the book.

Other scholars believe that there was only one author. This commentary begins from the presupposition that, in spite of appearances, the book comes from the hand of Qohelet and is, therefore, a unified composition. Qohelet is identified with Solomon, who is said to be the author of the book (1:1, 12). Yet, even among scholars who hold this position, there are a variety of opinions regarding the theme of the book or the main thrust of its message. Many of these divergences arise as the result of focusing on certain passages rather than looking at the book as a whole.

Michael A. Eaton has said that 'a search for a convincing account of the purpose or theme of Ecclesiastes must begin by accepting the textual integrity of the book as we have it' (TOT). This process should be as natural as picking up any book and attempting to find out what it is that the writer wants to get across to his or her readers. Where do we look for clues to this message? A preface, where the author lays out what he or she plans to do in the rest of the book, is always helpful. In a well-organized book, the conclusion usually summarizes what the writer has been trying to communicate to his readers. And as one reads through the book, something that occurs repeatedly – like a refrain in a song – is also certain to be helpful in identifying the message. Applying these investigative techniques to the book of Ecclesiastes, we discover several clues that help us unlock the purpose the writer had in composing it. In the preface to the book, immediately after the title verse (1:1), the Teacher makes the startling announcement: 'Meaningless! Meaningless … Utterly meaningless! Everything is meaningless' (1:2). These words are repeated in 12:8 at the end of the book. These two verses thus form what literary scholars call an *inclusio,* meaning that the section of the book bracketed by these two passages – that is, the entire book with the exception of the title verse and the conclusion (12:9-14) – is to be understood in the light of this refrain.

References to the meaninglessness of life on this side of eternity occur close to forty times in this book. However, it is not the only refrain that is repeated. Other recurring phrases are 'under the sun' (along with the similar but less frequent 'under heaven'), 'chasing after the wind', statements that have to do with toil or labour, statements referring to the experience and observation of the writer ('I saw/have seen', 'I said', 'I know', 'I thought', 'I reflected', 'I tested', 'I realized'), 'eat and drink', 'grievous evil', questions like 'what does a man gain/benefit?' or 'who knows?', statements relating to 'time and chance' and the fear of God. Then we have the conclusion which we mentioned earlier – although some would prefer to speak of a double conclusion or two conclusions (12:9-12 and 12:13-14) rather than one.

For the purpose of this commentary, I will adopt a fivefold division similar to that which has been used by many others. This division respects the integrity of the text and appears to follow the literary clues mentioned in the preceding paragraphs.

Outline of Contents

1:1-2:26 What's the Point?
3:1-5:20 A Look Behind the Scenes
6:1-8:15 Is God Fair?
8:16-12:8 Closing Counsel
12:9-14 Conclusion

COMMENTARY

1:1-2:26 What's the Point?

We have already noted that the main message of this book is the meaninglessness of earthly life. The Hebrew word *hebel* (1:2) is variously translated as 'meaningless', 'empty', 'vanity', 'futility', 'useless', 'nothing' and so on. Of the seventy-three uses of this word in the OT, thirty-eight, or more than half, are found in Ecclesiastes. The constant repetition of this word drives home the theme of the book.

In 1:2 and 12:8, the form of the word in the original is actually a superlative, so that the NIV's *Meaningless! Meaningless!* does not capture the full impact of the word. The NASB and KJV come closer with their translation 'Vanity of vanities', where the phrase has the same superlative meaning as in the title 'Song of Songs' meaning 'the best song' (Song 1:1). The writer is speaking of the nadir of meaninglessness. Yet the translation 'vanity' also has its problems, as the word has acquired new meanings in English. Consequently, a word like 'breath-like' or a reference to a puff of air might better capture the transitoriness of all aspects of earthly life – whether its toil, possessions, pleasure, joy – that is being depicted here.

The writer opens the first division of the book with the question *What does man gain from all his labour at which he toils under the sun?* (**1:3**). This is the only book in the OT in which the phrase 'under the sun' occurs, and it occurs some thirty times. Along with the similar phrases 'under heaven' (1:13; 2:3; 3:1) and 'on earth' (5:2; 8:14, 16; 11:2 [translated in 11:2 as 'upon the land' by the NIV]), it speaks of life focused on this world only.

By way of answering his own question, the Teacher speaks of the impermanent but unending cycle of nature and history (1:4-11). *Generations come and generations go, but the earth remains forever* (**1:4**). The Teacher is contrasting the brevity of human life and the permanence of the earth. A Tigrigna proverb from Eritrea captures this truth: *meriet ndahrai, qadra nbe'al b'eray* ['the land for the one who comes after; the fallow ground for the one with an ox'. The first half means that while generations come and go, the land remains forever.] The Teacher then moves on to focus on specific aspects of the visible material creation. *The sun rises and the sun sets, and hurries back to where it rises* (**1:5**). He is not concerned here with scientific accuracy, but with getting his point across to the common person. Everyone – whether a scientist or not – has observed the rising and setting of the sun. Similarly, they will have observed that *the wind blows to the south and turns to the north; round and round it goes, ever returning on its course* (**1:6**). Likewise, *all streams flow into the sea, yet the sea is never full. To the place the streams come from, there they return again* (**1:7**). There is constant movement, but none of it is getting anywhere. In Eaton's words, 'the repetitious cycles of the sun, like a runner on a circular track; the wind blowing round its circuits to no apparent purpose; the waters gushing into the seas without ever finding their task accomplished' (*TOT*) underscore the meaninglessness of life. Only the earth itself 'remains forever' (1:4). As far as the Teacher is concerned, *all things are wearisome* (**1:8**). Not only does no one find fulfilment or get anything accomplished, but there is nothing new as far as the writer is concerned (**1:9-11**).

He illustrates the 'wearisome' nature of life 'under the sun' from his personal experience. He begins by speaking

in general terms of how he scanned the human scene intellectually (1:12-18) and then gives more specific information about his attempts to find fulfilment in pleasure and creative works (2:1-11).

He tells us that he devoted himself *to study and to explore by wisdom all that is done under heaven.* His summary of what he has learned: *What a heavy burden God has laid on men!* (**1:13**). When it comes to the things people do, *all of them are meaningless, a chasing after the wind* (**1:14**). This is true even with regard to the study of wisdom (**1:17-18**).

Turning to examples from his own personal experience, the Teacher says, *I thought in my heart, 'Come now, I will test you with pleasure to find out what is good'* (**2:1a**). He tried wine, great projects, many servants, herds and flocks, wealth (silver and gold), singers and a harem – in fact, all *the delights of the heart of man* (**2:3-8, 10a**). He was the best positioned and endowed to do all this for himself (**2:9**; see also 1 Kgs 3:10-14). Even this *proved to be meaningless* (**2:1b-2**). In his own words: *when I surveyed all that my hands had done and what I had toiled to achieve, everything was meaningless, a chasing after the wind; nothing was gained under the sun* (**2:11**).

In 2:12-23, Solomon once again reflects on wisdom and folly and evaluates the outcome of all that he has toiled for (see 1:12-18). He bewails the fact that the same fate awaits both the wise and fools (**2:12-16**). Not only are the things he has achieved unsatisfactory in themselves, but he can only possess them for a short while before they either disappear or his earthly life ends. And the person who inherits them may not be worthy to take over all that he has laboured for (**2:17-21**).

Many African proverbs also stress that death is the fate of all human beings – whether wise or foolish, rich or poor. Thus we find sayings like 'Death does not know a chief' or 'Death has no friends'. Death comes to all equally, and grants no favours. This truth is illustrated by the death in exile in Morocco of ex-President Mobutu of the Democratic Republic of Congo (then Zaire), who was at one time said to be the fourth richest person in the world.

The writer of the book of Ecclesiastes continues, *so I hated life, because the work that is done under the sun was grievous to me. All of it is meaningless, a chasing after the wind* (2:17-18). He comes full circle, asking the same question he started with: *What does a man get for all the toil and anxious striving with which he labours under the sun?* (**2:22**). The answer has already been given but, just in case his readers have missed it, he reiterates it: *This too is meaningless* (**2:23**).

The section concludes with the first positive recommendation in the book (2:24-26) – although it may have been hinted at in **2:10b**. This refrain, urging one to *eat and drink* and enjoy one's labour, recurs throughout the book (3:12-13, 22; 5:18-20; 8:15; 9:7-9; 11:8, 9a). This concluding statement affirms that life is to be enjoyed, that it is a gift of

God and that the gifts of *wisdom, knowledge and happiness* are for *the one who pleases God* (**2:26a**). Although we may produce and accumulate the things that we think will give happiness, the ability to actually enjoy them is not within our power – it comes from God.

Here the Teacher presents an alternative to the gloomy picture that he has been painting. No longer is everything happening 'under the sun' meaningless; God is seen to be at work: *but to the sinner he gives the task of gathering and storing up wealth to hand it over to the one who pleases God* (**2:26b**). The contrast here is between the outcomes of two lifestyles – that of 'the sinner' and that of 'the one who pleases God'. The meaninglessness of life 'under the sun' is the lot of the sinner who has no understanding of the life beyond death. For such a person, everything is *meaningless, a chasing after the wind* (**2:26c**). This final statement must relate to what has been said about the sinner and not to the entire concluding statement.

3:1-5:20 A Look Behind the Scenes

The Teacher continues to pile up evidence to advance his argument. He starts this section by affirming that *there is a time for everything, and a season for every activity under heaven* (**3:1**). The fourteen poetic lines in **3:2-8** encompass twenty-eight events spanning the range of human activities, both personal and corporate. He mentions the opposing pairs of birth and death, planting and uprooting, killing and healing, tearing down and building, weeping and laughing, mourning and dancing, scattering stones and gathering them, embracing and refraining from embracing, searching and giving up the search, keeping and throwing away, tearing and mending, being silent and speaking, loving and hating, going to war and making peace. Some would argue that these times are predetermined by God in a way that stifles human freedom, but that is not how the Teacher sees it. Rather he is presenting a beautiful depiction of God's absolute control of events 'under heaven'.

In spite of the beautiful plan of God that has just been described, the writer returns to the familiar question, *What does the worker gain from his toil?* (**3:9**; see 1:3; 2:22). He sees toil and frustration at work without progress as *the burden God has laid on men* (**3:10**; see also 1:13). Even more frustrating is the fact *that everything appears beautiful in its time* (**3:11a**), yet that time is limited. Human beings long for eternity, yet they cannot find out *what God has done from beginning to end* (**3:11c**), because they are finite.

We may be puzzled at how each event that God allows to take place at its own appointed time and place can be said to be 'beautiful' (3:11a) – how can war, mourning, death (and all the other unpleasant things mentioned in 3:2-8) be sources of delight? We may not understand it, but is this

not what the apostle Peter is thinking of when he advises believers to rejoice in their suffering (see 1 Pet 4:12-16)?

We may also be puzzled by the exact meaning of the phrase, *God has also set eternity in the hearts of men* (**3:11b**). Eaton suggests that the 'eternity' here should be seen in conjunction with the *for ever* in 3:14, and goes on to say, 'the eternity of God's dealings with mankind corresponds to something inside us: we have a capacity for eternal things, are concerned about the future, want to understand things "from the beginning to the end", and have a sense of something which transcends our immediate situation' (*TOT*). Wright comments that this sense of transcendence explains the entire human search for knowledge, and all science, philosophy and theology (*EBC*).

This sense of eternity in our hearts may also have given rise to the concept of the living dead in most African traditions. But the truth of the matter is that the only possible way to know eternity is through a personal relationship with the eternal God.

Finally, there is the 'yet' statement, which says that humans 'cannot fathom what God has done from beginning to end' (3:11c). That is part of the frustration that only human beings confined to life 'under the sun' experience. According to Eaton, 'This is the nearest [the Teacher] comes to Augustine's maxim: "You have made us for yourself, and our hearts are restless until they can find peace in you"' (*TOT*). Those who have submitted themselves to God are able to go through life a day at a time and enjoy it (**3:12**), even though they may not know God's plan 'from beginning to end'.

The Teacher's solution to the burden borne by autonomous humanity is to turn to God and receive the fulfilment of life as a gift from him (3:12-13; 3:22; 5:18-20). Nothing can be added to or taken away from what God has done (**3:14-15**); and God's purpose in what he has done is *so that men will revere him* (**3:14**). The reverence or fear of God resurfaces at crucial stages in the development of the Teacher's theme (see 5:7; 7:18; 8:12-13; 12:13).

In 3:16-4:16, the writer cites various incidents that appear to contradict the idea that God has an all-embracing and admirable plan. There is what appears to be an outrageous reversal of God's way of doing things – wickedness sitting *in the place of judgment* and *justice* (**3:16**). A Tigrigna proverb from Eritrea vividly depicts this reversal when it says *zeben grimbitosh mai n'aqeb* ['during the time of reversal, water flows uphill', that is, during a time of trouble when true justice is perverted, everything is turned upside down]. But in due time this wrong will be redressed by God's judgment (**3:17**). As things now stand, God is telling human beings that as long as we tyrannize one another, death will clearly demonstrate that we are no better than animals who perish in the dust (3:18-21). That is the logical outcome of a life lived solely 'under the sun'.

Debates rage around the exact point the Teacher is making in this passage. He is not saying that this is how God created humans or, for that matter, that this is God's eternal purpose for humanity. We were created in the image of God (Gen 1:26-27). The uniqueness of humanity is clear from the statement that 'the Lord God formed the man from the dust of the ground and breathed into his nostrils the breath of life, and the man became a living being' (Gen 2:7), which forever establishes a distinction between humans and animals. Ecclesiastes agrees with the creation account when it says that God's eternal purpose for humankind is unique: 'and the dust returns to the ground it came from, and the spirit returns to God who gave it' (12:7). Humans are *like the animals* (**3:18**): they share the same fate as animals for *all have the same breath; and man has no advantage over the animal* (**3:19**) only because they have become earthbound – forgetful of God's ownership and control of their lives and his design for them. The utterances in verses 20-21 do not spring from belief but from unbelief, which is the outcome of a life lived without God. For those who believe, the answer to the query *Who knows?* (**3:21**) is that those who believe God's revelation in the Scriptures know. For those who fear God, although they are similar to animals in the sense that their bodies return to dust, their final destination is with God (see 12:7; also John 14:2-3).

The injustice mentioned earlier is described more starkly in **4:1-3**. Then the frustration of toil 'under the sun' is elaborated further in the rest of the chapter. The motive for the toil is envy. While the laziness of the fool who *folds his hands* is not commended, the Teacher recognizes that enough *with tranquillity* is better than much obtained *with toil* (**4:5-6**). Unless the fruit of our toil is put to good use for ourselves and for others, our toil is in vain and we will prove the truth of the Tigrigna proverb from Eritrea, *Habti, nlebam megelgeli'u n'asha meseyteni'u* ['wealth is a servant for the wise, but bedevils fools'].

Yet while toil may be meaningless, laziness is unacceptable to the Teacher and in any culture. The Ewe of Ghana emphasize its negative reward when they say, 'A lazy man's farm is a breeding ground for snakes.'

Toil is also meaningless for a person who lives alone (**4:7-8**). Two are better than one in all respects (**4:9-11**). Three are even better, for *a cord of three strands is not quickly broken* (**4:12**). These verses contrast the security and blessing of companionship with the hazards and pain of loneliness. The African world view is based on community life. This is reflected in the various versions of the adage, 'I am because we are, and since we are, therefore I am.' The Akan of Ghana, for example, underscore the need for cooperation by saying, 'One person alone cannot build a town.'

A further illustration of what is 'meaningless' and 'a chasing after the wind' is the case of the wise youth who succeeded a foolish old king, but whose succession was opposed by those who came later (**4:13-16**).

The first seven verses of chapter 5 are quite different from the verses that precede and follow them, which focus on meaninglessness. Some commentators see these seven verses as a warning against neglecting religious duties in response to the type of situations that the Teacher has been describing. Others see them as contrasting the loneliness and human friendship mentioned in 4:7-12 with the incomparable companionship of God. Whatever the case, the Teacher is teaching his readers more about a life that is acceptable and pleasing to God. He has already indicated that it is God who gives the ability to enjoy the fruit of one's hard work (3:13). But how is God to be approached? The answer is, 'with caution'. Those who want to establish a close relationship with God are warned: *Guard your steps when you go to the house of God. Go near to listen rather than to offer the sacrifices of fools, who do not know that they do wrong. Do not be quick with your mouth, do not be hasty in your heart to utter anything before God* (**5:1-2a**). Here the Teacher reminds us of the speech patterns characteristic of the wise and the fool that are spelled out in the book of Proverbs. Fools are quick to speak and have a lot to say, whereas the wise think about what they should say and when and how to say it to people – let alone to God. Thus the appropriateness of the reminder that *God is in heaven and you are on earth, so let your words be few* (**5:2b**). Just as dreams disturb our sleep when we have many worries, so the babbling of many words indicates that we are fools (**5:3**). The admonitions to *draw near to listen* and *let your words be few* should be especially remembered *when you make a vow to God* (**5:4-7**). We must mean what we say and do it, or else keep our mouths shut. The point is that we should think before we speak – whether in making a vow or otherwise. A Luganda (Uganda) saying encapsulates this wisdom: 'One who talks, thinks; but one who keeps silent, thinks more.'

The Teacher reminds his readers that injustice should not come as a surprise. There is a hierarchy of authorities from whom redress should be sought (**5:8-9**; see also 3:16-17; 4:1-3). High above all human systems of justice is the tribunal of God – our final and efficacious court of appeal (see 3:17).

Toil and the accumulation of wealth cannot satisfy the deepest needs of humanity 5:10-17. The lives of the wealthy who are not connected with God are summarized for us here (compare Matt 16:26). First, their wealth is used by others (**5:11**; see 2:26). Their wealth causes them to have sleepless nights (**5:12**). Although the cause of the sleeplessness is not specified, one of the reasons may be the fear that it will *be lost through some misfortune* (**5:13-14**). Even if they manage to retain their wealth, it is left behind when they die (**5:15-16**). And finally, though they may spend it on themselves, the spending is done *in*

SECULARISM AND MATERIALISM

The African approach to all of life is deeply religious. This attitude is now threatened by the Western philosophy of secularism, which promotes a way of life and thought that is concerned only with this world and is opposed to thinking in terms of what is sacred or spiritual.

Secularism originated in Europe, in part as a reaction against the control of all areas of life by a church that was riddled with economic and political corruption. There was a growing desire to remove religion from the public place and make it a private affair. People wanted to have a secular society in which the state does not impose a religion on people who do not accept it. Christians can agree with this, for we know that God does not force people into his kingdom, and so we should not seek to impose religion by law. In this respect, Christianity differs from Islam, which cannot tolerate secularism in any form.

However, Christians are opposed to the aspect of secularism that leads people to stop seeing God in all of life and to be interested solely in human reason, science, technology, history and philosophy. This type of secularism questions the existence of God, the supernatural, miracles, spiritual beings and revelation, and asserts that humans are independent and that there is no Creator God. This approach to life and knowledge leads to a glorifying of human wisdom and achievements and a rejection of God (Rom 1:21-23).

A form of secularism known as materialism has infected even those who do not explicitly reject religion. It has affected Christians in the West and its influence is spreading to Africa, leaving many Christians lukewarm or indifferent to their faith. People's lives are dominated by their desire for worldly pleasures and bodily comforts, and revolve around money, possessions and the things of the world rather than spiritual values. This is an inevitable consequence of the failure to love God above all else. Jesus warned us: 'What good is it for a man to gain the whole world, and yet lose or forfeit his very self?' (Luke 9:25; see also 1 John 2:15-17).

People who rely only on possessions and on human philosophical, scientific or material interpretations of things have made human reason their god. Such reliance can lead only to ruin and damnation (Ps 14:1). The Bible dismisses worldly wisdom and its corollary, materialism, as meaningless and futile (Eccl 1:12-18; 2:1-11, 17-26; 1 Cor 2:6-8; Jas 3:13-18).

Some Africans have responded to secularism by rejecting Western education. While it is true that some aspects of Western education contain values that are contrary to the teachings of the Bible, we need to remember that these negative values are not the facts of education, but are only ways of seeing, interpreting and applying knowledge. A true Christian who loves the Lord and believes in the teachings of the Bible sees no contradiction between the truths of philosophy and science and those of the Bible. All truth is God's truth (John 1:3-9, 14; 8:32; 14:6; 1 John 1:5-6). God is the source of knowledge and wisdom, and so true knowledge and wisdom lead to him and his Word.

Our society contains believers and nonbelievers, and we all need to live together. Religion provides ethical and social values that affect people in their private and public lives and makes for responsible living. Christians who live in secular and materialistic societies are to exhibit their Christian light and salt (Matt 5:13-16). They are to let their good deeds shine before others. Practical and effective Christianity is demonstrated in our way of life. This must not be secular or materialistic but must demonstrate our love of both God and our neighbour (Matt 22:37-40).

Yusufu Turaki

---

darkness, with great frustration, affliction and anger (5:17). These unenviable options of the wicked rich are in themselves a manifestation of the operation of God's justice here and now, when contrasted with God's gift of enjoyment of the fruits of their labour to those who please him.

The chapter ends with a repeat of the injunction to *eat and drink* (5:18). Turning from the bitter and miserable life of the rich, the Teacher presents another model: 'There is another life, equally outward, real, observable. ... It is enjoyable *in toil,* not in its absence' (*TOT*). It is clear that the Teacher is not condemning wealth in itself, for it, too, is a gift from God (5:19). But what is important for a contented life is an 'acceptance of the style of life God apportions, and awareness of the God-given nature of all wealth ... a man must be in control of his attitude to wealth rather than his attitude to wealth in control of him' (*TOT*).

6:1-8:15 Is God Fair?

In the first two sections of the book, the Teacher has clearly shown that accumulated wealth does not, in and of itself, give joy for that is a gift of God. Now he proceeds to tackle the problem posed by the inequalities of divine providence.

The Teacher begins by saying *I have seen another evil under the sun, and it weighs heavily on men* (6:1). Though he concluded chapter 5 by saying that enjoyment is a gift of God (5:19-20), here he makes the point that wealth, honour and family do not necessarily bring joy (6:2-3). In fact *a stillborn child* is better off than a person who has all these things and whose perspective on life is limited to what takes place 'under the sun' (6:4-6). Someone who is poor but wise and who is satisfied with what his eyes can see is better than someone whose *appetite is never satisfied* (6:7-9). Humans cannot change or dispute what God has ordained (6:10-11).

Two questions are posed in **6:12**, asking who knows what is good for them and what will happen on earth after they are gone. The answer is clearly 'no one' – thus affirming our ignorance. All that we do know is that those who know God are at peace in his presence (Luke 16:19-31).

If prosperity is not necessarily good for someone, what about adversity? (7:1-14). Using proverbial sayings in the form 'x is better than y', the Teacher contrasts death and birth, mourning and feasting, sorrow and laughter, rebuke and song, and endings and beginnings of a matter (**7:1-8**). Each time, what is mentioned first is said to be better than what comes second. The 'x is better than y' format of these proverbial sayings is similar to that used in Tigrigna proverbs from Eritrea, such as *kab hamimka hkmna, tekhena-khinka t'ena* ['from being sick, medication; from taking care, health', meaning it is better to take care of oneself and enjoy health than to be sick and seek medical help. Or in other words, 'Prevention is better than cure.']

However, when we look at the message of the proverbial sayings in 7:1-8, it may be difficult for us to recognize that the things mentioned first are actually better in human terms. But we are told not to ask questions about why our lives are worse now than they were in the past, *for it is not wise to ask such questions* (**7:10**). Wisdom enables one to see that there can be benefits in unpleasant events (7:11-14). In fact, *wisdom is a shelter as money is a shelter, but the advantage of knowledge is this: that wisdom preserves the life of its possessor* (**7:12**). In **7:13-14**, the Teacher goes on to make the point that God gives both the good times and the times of affliction, and that it is impossible to change what God has ordained. We should not try to anticipate the future, but should live 'in a state of constant dependence and trust in God for whatever lies beyond the present; which would not be so much the case if there were some evident rules for the distribution of good and evil' (Zuck; see also 1:15). The reason that God does not give us more information is not because he has 'a petty need to keep humans under control by denying them insight into the future; rather it is the concept of grace which undergirds Qohelet's argument' (*ITC*). This grace enables God's people to accept their lot – be it prosperity or adversity – without the need to explain how things will finally work out in the future.

In reflecting on God's providence, one should not only consider people's outward fortunes but also their characters (7:15-29). Again referring to his own observation of reality 'under the sun', the Teacher reports that he has witnessed *a righteous man perishing in his righteousness, and a wicked man living long in his wickedness* (**7:15**). A biblical example of this is found in the conflict between Naboth and Jezebel (1 Kgs 21; see also 1 Kgs 18–19). However, it is not easy to understand the advice he gives to the reader here (7:16-18). While it is easy to understand that being overly wicked may lead to premature death (**7:17**; see also 1 Tim 5:24),

how is it possible to overdo righteousness or *be overwise* (**7:16**)? This verse has been interpreted in several ways, but in view of the preceding discussion of God's providence, what he may be referring to is an overzealous attempt to impress God with our righteousness in order to receive his blessings and avoid his punishments. The danger of doing this is clearly shown by the legalism of the Pharisees in NT times. By contrast, *the man who fears God will avoid all extremes* (**7:18**).

The need for wisdom that is clear from 7:18 is elaborated on in 7:19-22: it makes one *more powerful than ten rulers in a city* (**7:19**); it helps one to be conscious of one's limitations and fallenness and, therefore, cautious (**7:20-22**).

Verses 23-25 show that true wisdom is not easily accessible. The Teacher may appear to be contradicting himself when he simultaneously states that *All this I tested by wisdom* (**7:23**) and admits that *this was beyond me* and that *whatever wisdom may be it is far off and most profound – who can discover it?* (**7:24**). The point is that true wisdom is at the same time the outcome of man's search and God's gift (see also Prov 2:1-6).

Having mentioned *the woman who is a snare* and who is *more bitter than death* (**7:26**; see also the references to the adulteress in Prov 2:16-19; 5:1-14; 6:20-35; 7:1-27; 9:13-18), the Teacher adds that in spite of the fact that humankind was created upright, only one in a thousand is *truly virtuous and good*. A righteous person is a rare find (**7:27-29**; see also 7:20).

The comments on women in **7:28** have 'generated considerable modern anxiety, and some creative interpretations' (*NICOT*). Eaton summarizes the Teacher's meaning as being that wisdom is rare in men, but rarer in women (*TOT*). Some commentators insist that this verse proves that Solomon was a misogynist, while others deny the accusation. In weighing our response, we have to look at everything that Scripture has to say on this subject before we can come to any conclusion. In context, however, it is probably best to read this verse in the light of the statement that *God made mankind upright* (**7:29a**). In the original 'scheme of things' (**7:25, 27**), wisdom would have been abundantly manifest in both men and women. But humanity has abandoned God's original design and *gone in search of many schemes* (**7:29b**). Fallen humanity is responsible for its own predicament.

The apparent inequities of God's providence will, in due time, be redressed by government – both human and divine (8:1-14; see also 5:8-14 and the comments given there). The Teacher's reflection on wisdom continues right into **8:1**, helping him to make a smooth transition to the next point. After endorsing obedience to human governments (**8:2-4**), he asserts that these will address problems in due time: *Whoever obeys his [the king's] command will come to no harm, and the wise heart will know the proper time and procedure. For there is a proper time and procedure for every matter, though* *a man's misery weighs heavily upon him* (**8:5-6**; see 3:1-8). Despite the 'misery' and ignorance – whether of God's eternal plan or of the future – vindication will eventually come at 'a proper time and procedure' for those who wait patiently. What will come, will come – including death. No human being has the power to prevent or to avoid what is coming (**8:7-8**).

One may even come to realize that human government, which in the preceding verses is portrayed as correcting injustice, may itself turn out to be repressive and unjust (**8:9-10**). Those who lorded *it over others* and *who used to come and go from the holy place and receive praise in the city* were those who were in positions of leadership.

Delayed justice may encourage wicked people to continue to pursue their rebellious lifestyles (**8:11**). This is well illustrated by the general breakdown of respect for the law in South Africa under the apartheid system. However, the Teacher confidently affirms, *Although a wicked man commits a hundred crimes and still lives a long time, I know that it will go better with God-fearing men, who are reverent before God* (**8:12**). On the other hand, *it will not go well* with those who do not fear God. Though on the superficial level it appeared the wicked man *lives a long time,* in actual fact, says the Teacher, *their days will not lengthen like a shadow* (**8:13**).

The human justice system may fail (**8:14**), but such glaring reversals of justice will be a thing of the past in the realm beyond. Those who fear God wait for his intervention or for the manifestation of his kingdom, where the injustices of this life will be redressed. Again, the section concludes with the recommendation to those who know God's gift and who have faith to receive and enjoy it that they should *eat and drink and be glad* (**8:15a**). This gladness is not merely a momentary froth. The godly person is promised a joy that *will accompany him in his work all the days of the life God has given him under the sun.* (**8:15b**).

8:16-12:8 Closing Counsel

The fourth division of the book does not necessarily launch into new territory. Rather it pulls together ideas we have seen in the sections that went before – especially in the immediately preceding one – and brings them to their logical conclusion. The Teacher spends the first part of this section (8:16-9:9) admonishing his readers that the lack of a comprehensive knowledge of God's eternal plan should not deter them from enjoying his gifts. So instead of leaving the injunction to 'eat and drink' till his concluding remarks, as he does in the previous three sections, here he places it close to the beginning (9:7-9).

All the sage's reflection on his own experience and his observation of *man's labour on earth* (**8:16**) lead him to assert that *no one can comprehend what goes on under the sun. Despite all his efforts to search it out, man cannot discover its*

meaning. Even if a wise man claims he knows, he cannot really comprehend it (**8:17**). The repeated 'it', of course, must be referring back to *all that God has done,* mentioned at the beginning of the verse. No matter what some may boast, we are trapped in invincible ignorance. Kaiser comments: 'Human insight, understanding, and reason, like water, cannot rise higher than their source or own level. Therefore, to the degree that God reveals his plan to believers, to that degree only are they able to apprehend that much of the plan of God ... Only God knows entirely.'

While we can be encouraged that *the righteous and the wise and what they do are in God's hands,* yet we remain ignorant of what lies in the future, whether love or hate, prosperity or adversity (**9:1**; see 9:6). Only one thing is certain, so certain that the Teacher says it twice: *All share a common destiny* (**9:2**) and *the same destiny overtakes all* (**9:3**). There is no distinction between *the righteous and the wicked, the good and the bad, the clean and the unclean, those who offer sacrifices and those who do not* – all are overtaken by this 'common destiny'. The Teacher characterizes this fate as *the evil in everything that happens under the sun*' (9:3), and identifies it as death. Just as God 'causes his sun to rise on the evil and the good, and sends rain on the righteous and the unrighteous' (Matt 5:45), so he makes all submit to this destiny.

From a purely earthly perspective, death is the worst thing that can happen to a person (9:4-6). Those who hold a traditional African world view would agree that this is so. But they would be shocked by the statement in 9:5-6. Rather than joining the ancestors ('the living dead') at death and continuing to be part of the community, the dead no longer have any participation in the life they have left – *even the memory of them is forgotten* (**9:5**). Moreover, *their love, their hate and their jealousy have long since vanished; never again will they have a part in anything that happens under the sun* (**9:6**). It is important to note that the Teacher is not denying that there is life after death; rather he is asserting that death ends all relationship with the present world.

Even with this dark prospect of death hovering over them, those who please God are encouraged to go and eat their food *with gladness* and drink their wine *with a joyful heart, for it is now that God favours what you do* (**9:7-9**). The Teacher tells them to *enjoy life with your wife, whom you love, all the days of this meaningless life that God has given you under the sun – all your meaningless days* (**9:9**). The earthly life of both the wicked and the righteous is 'a mist that appears for a little while and then vanishes' (Jas 4:14). The reason they should enjoy life is that *this is your lot in life and in your toilsome labour under the sun.* As Zuck has put it, the most perplexing mysteries of death 'should prevent no one from enjoying life with a constant sense of the divine favor.'

Not only does the Teacher counsel his disciples to enjoy God's gift in the midst of life's perplexities, but he also encourages them to be engaged in their earthly occupation with the utmost zeal and concentration (**9:10**; 11:6). Against the backdrop of the inevitability of death, he says to them, *Whatever your hand finds to do, do it with all your might* (9:10). There may be frustrations and disappointments, for that is the way things sometimes turn out in this life 'under the sun'. *The race* may not necessarily be *to the swift* or *the battle to the strong* (**9:11a**). *Nor does food come to the wise or wealth to the brilliant or favour to the learned* (**9:11b**). Instead, as the sage puts it, *time and chance happens to them all* (see 3:1-8). Preoccupied with the evil that awaits all, he adds: *As fish are caught in a cruel net, or birds are taken in a snare, so men are trapped by evil times that fall unexpectedly upon them* (**9:12**). These can be natural or man-made catastrophes – for example, the hostage-taking of our days and the loss of life that ensues. Yet even the prospect of lurking imminent death should not be able to break one's concentration on fulfilling one's vocation.

The advantage of wisdom over folly is illustrated by the example of a poor wise man who delivered *a small city* from the attack of *a powerful king* (**9:13-16**). Yet once again, the dark side of life 'under the sun' triumphs, for in spite of what he has done *the poor man's wisdom is despised, and his words are no longer heeded* (9:16).

The proverbial sayings that follow in 9:17-10:20 expand on the theme of the benefit of wisdom and the destructiveness of folly. Here the family traits that link the books of Proverbs and Ecclesiastes emerge clearly, even as regards content (compare **10:8-9** and Prov 26:27).

The contrast between the blessings of wisdom and the curse of folly stands out clearly at the level of national leadership: *Woe to you, O land whose king was a servant and whose princes feast in the morning. Blessed are you, O land whose king is of noble birth and whose princes eat at a proper time – for strength and not for drunkenness* (**10:16-17**). The land whose leaders 'feast in the morning' instead of putting their hearts, hands and minds to the challenges of the day can expect nothing but destruction. The Lugbara of northeastern Congo (DR) and north-western Uganda say, 'Without a leader, the ants are confused' – meaning, without a leader a community disintegrates. The Kikuyu of Kenya agree with this wise saying when they say, 'Goats with a lame leader do not arrive at the grass' – meaning that a community is helpless without a leader. On the other hand, the land is blessed whose leaders eat at the proper time – and that not for debauchery but for the restoration of the strength expended in the discharge of their duties.

The composure that wisdom brings is illustrated by the reactions of the wise to the behaviour of national leaders. In **10:4** a wise person is urged to remain calm and hold on to his post even when a ruler is angry. Similar advice is presented in the Tigrigna proverb, from Eritrea, *aqli waga beqli* ['patience, the cost of a mule': acquiring a mule is very costly, and therefore patience is a precious trait, bearing good fruit at the end]. The Ewe of Ghana add to this when they say, 'If you are patient enough you can cook a stone and it will become soft.'

In **10:20** a wise person is warned not to rebuke or curse national leaders *even in your thoughts*. As the Fante of Ghana say, 'The chief has ears like those of an elephant' – meaning he hears whatever is said about him.

As we move to the concluding chapters of the book, it is obvious that the Teacher is emphasizing the practical out working of wise behaviour in the light of all that has been said. In 11:1-6, generosity and hard work are once again recommended. We are reminded that 'lack of complete knowledge is no excuse for inactivity' (*TOT*).

Several of the exhortations here take the form of proverbial sayings, as, for example, **11:1**: *Cast your bread upon the waters, for after many days you will find it again.* What exactly does this mean? Although commentators agree that an element of faith or venture is involved, there is no agreement on exactly what this means. Some say that the saying refers to philanthropy or good deeds; others think that it refers to a business venture. If we take this saying as recommending generosity, the 'waters' represent the beneficiaries. The 'many days' remind us of the need to wait patiently for God's reward.

The same idea is repeated in **11:2**, where we read *Give portions to seven, yes to eight, for you do not know what disaster may come upon the land.* The Hebrew translated 'upon the land' can also be translated 'on the earth'. It is clear that giving is equivalent to investing in God, who is the best security for the future. The clouds *full of water* and pouring *rain upon the earth* (**11:3**) also symbolize the generosity mentioned in 11:1-2. The Kaonde of Zambia have crystallized this idea in their proverb, 'That which you have given away returns' – meaning, if you are generous, other people will be generous to you in their turn.

The next three verses (11:4-6) should be interpreted together as they all relate to hard work. Repeating his earlier admonition not to wait for complete knowledge or favourable circumstance, the Teacher warns, *whoever watches the wind will not plant; whoever looks at the clouds will not reap* (**11:4**). Although the farmer *cannot understand the work of God* (**11:5**), he should undertake his activities, trusting in *the Maker of all things.* So we are to make use of the time we have: *sow your seed in the morning, and at evening let not your hands be idle* (**11:6**). Why? *For you do not know which will succeed, whether this or that, or whether both will do equally well.* There is always a need to step out by faith.

The concluding passage of this section of the book (11:7-12:8) again includes the recommendation to enjoy life

(11:7-10), but with the reminder that we are also to *remember your Creator* (12:1). Although the Teacher appears to be focusing on the young (11:9-10; 12:1), others are not excluded (11:8). The description of light as sweet and the pleasure of seeing the sun (**11:7**) reminds us of the earlier references to 'under the sun', that is, to life on earth. But this enjoyment is tempered by the knowledge that many *days of darkness* will follow (**11:8**; see also 12:1-8). Still, the encouragement to be joyful reverberates: *Be happy, young man, while you are young, and let your heart give you joy in the days of your youth* (**11:9a**).

It is not completely clear what the Teacher is trying to say in **11:10,** with *so then banish anxiety from your heart and cast off the troubles of your body.* The 'anxiety' and 'troubles of your body' may refer to the general frustrations and perplexities of life on earth that have been referred to throughout the book. On the other hand, he may be referring to the particular concerns of the young. After all, this follows the advice to *follow the ways of your heart and whatever your eyes see,* which is paired with the reminder *that for all these things God will bring you to judgment* (**11:9b** – a hint foreshadowing the conclusion of the entire book). Whatever the specific troubles, they are obstacles to the happiness that the Teacher has commended earlier and thus they are to be banished.

This advice is followed by a sobering and difficult passage (12:1-8). After exhorting the young to *remember your Creator in the days of your youth* (**12:1**; see also 11:8; 12:6), the Teacher proceeds to give a detailed poetic description of the old age and death that await them. The repetition of 'before' (12:1, 2, 6) in the NIV translation captures the sense of impending doom in the injunction to 'remember'.

This passage abounds in images and metaphors, some of which can be clearly identified while others simply contribute to the cumulative impact of the whole. *Before the sun and the light and the moon and the stars grow dark, and the clouds return after the rain* (**12:2**) refers to the gloom, dimness and loss of joy that begin to enshroud the ageing person and contrast with the earlier enjoyment of the light (11:7). *When the keepers of the house tremble* refers to arms and *the strong men* that *stoop* (**12:3**) to the legs. The *grinders* that cease to function *because they are few* are teeth, and *those looking through the windows* which grow dim are the eyes. Interpreters differ in their interpretation of the metaphors in verse four. Some take *the doors to the street* (**12:4**) literally, as referring to the doors of the home, while others take them to mean the mouth and ears. Depending on the meaning given to these 'doors', *the sound of grinding* that fades is either associated with 'the grinders' of 12:3 or with the actual sound of women grinding within the homestead or in the neighbourhood. The *sound of birds* may refer either to the old rising early or to the sleep of an old person being easily disturbed. There is also no more enjoyment of song

either. Being *afraid of heights and of dangers in the streets* (**12:5a**) can be taken as a literal characterization of old age. The white blossom of the almond tree is associated with the white hair of old age, the grasshopper dragging itself along with the difficulty in walking experienced by the aged, and the absence of desire with the loss of appetite of all sorts.

As the gradual deterioration of old age reaches its inevitable conclusion, *man goes to his eternal home and mourners go about the streets* (**12:5b**). Death has come. But the Teacher uses additional metaphors to drive home the importance of what is happening. *Remember him,* he adds, *before the silver cord is severed, or the golden bowl is broken; before the pitcher is shattered at the spring, or the wheel broken at the well* (**12:6**). The moment of death is depicted as a golden bowl being severed from a silver cord and shattered, and as a wheel at a well snapping and as allowing a clay pitcher to fall into the well and shatter. Then the metaphorical language ends and the language of Genesis resurfaces: *and the dust returns to the ground it came from, and the spirit returns to God who gave it* (**12:7**; see also Gen 2:7; 3:19).

The segment concludes with the refrain that brackets the message of the entire book: *'Meaningless! Meaningless!' says the Teacher. 'Everything is meaningless!'* (**12:8**). Death is coming, and the time to remember one's Creator is 'in the days of your youth'– while one still has vigour and zest!

12:9-14 Conclusion

In some of the verses in this section, the Teacher is referred to in the third person. This does not necessarily mean that he did not write these words. Moreover, it would be quite unusual to ascribe the concluding statement – *Now all has been heard; here is the conclusion of the matter* (**12:13**) – to someone else. We can, therefore, accept that these verses are the concluding remarks of the Teacher himself.

He starts by speaking about himself – who he is and the contributions he has made: *Not only was the Teacher wise, but also he imparted knowledge to the people* (**12:9**). He refers to his searching, observation and pondering and the setting out of what he has learned in proverbs and underscores his use of appropriate words and the truthfulness of all he has written (**12:10**). Associating himself with other sages, he says, *The words of the wise are like goads, their collected sayings like firmly embedded nails* (**12:11**) – both prodding the disciples in the way of obedience and gripping their hearts and minds with the power of accumulated wisdom. The mention of *one Shepherd* – which is to be understood as referring to God – indicates that the words of the Teacher are of divine origin. Thus the injunction *Be warned, my son, of anything in addition to them* (**12:12**). What follows in this verse appears to be similar to what the wise man has already said in 1:18.

The message of the book is then finally summed up: 'Now all has been heard; here is the conclusion of the matter' (12:13). What needs to be said has been said, and the Teacher has reached his conclusion. And what is that conclusion? *Fear God and keep his commandments for this is the whole duty of man*. Although the fear of God has been mentioned several times throughout the book, this is the first mention of the commandments of God. We are told that keeping these 'is the whole duty of man'. The reason we should keep them is that *God will bring every deed into judgment, including every hidden thing, whether it is good or evil* **(12:14)**. Everything done 'under the sun', whether done secretly or in the open, will be scrutinized and rewarded or punished.

The Teacher has shown us the perplexities and frustrations of living life with a purely earthly perspective. Such a life can only be described as meaningless. Those who experience joy in the labour of their hands are those who accept their life as a gift from God. But each and every one of us, and each and every deed, will be judged by God when he wraps up earthly life and ushers in eternity.

Testoldemedhin Habtu

Further Reading

Eaton, Michael A. *Ecclesiastes*. TOT. Leicester: Inter-Varsity Press, 1983.

Farmer, Kathleen A. *Who Knows What Is Good? A Commentary of the Books of Proverbs and Ecclesiastes*. ITC. Grand Rapids: Eerdmans, 1991.

Zuck, Roy B. *Reflecting with Solomon*. Eugene, Ore.: Wipf & Stock, 2003.

SONG OF SONGS

One of the consequences of the fall, as far as we humans are concerned, is that we find it difficult to find our bearings and maintain our equilibrium. Be it individually or corporately, when it comes to issues that concern us we have a tendency to swing like a pendulum from one extreme to the other. This tendency stands out particularly clearly in our attitude to and practice of our God-given sexuality. On the one hand, we are told by society – at least in its traditional or conservative manifestations – that it is taboo to talk about sex. On the other hand, we are bombarded with the glamour of sex in the electronic and print media. The advent of information technology has simply stepped up the rate of this bombardment and widened its range.

We live in an age when the institution of marriage and marital fidelity are being attacked from all sides and sexual promiscuity – whether pre- or extramarital – is being put on a pedestal. Various sexual perversions are now being promoted as nothing more than inherent biological propensities. In the face of the HIV/AIDS pandemic, which is decimating our continent and much of the world, the best solution offered is often the use of condoms for what is called 'safe sex'.

In the midst of the mess that we find ourselves in, the Song of Songs comes as a reminder to return to the basics as regards the understanding and expression of human sexuality. True, the book has been misunderstood and misinterpreted, even by the very faith communities to whom it was given by God. But an unbiased and natural reading of the book brings out the message that sexual desire is God-given and beautiful when practised in the context of a heterosexual, committed and loving relationship.

History of Interpretation

The first question that comes to mind when one reads this book is, 'Why is a poem describing the love between a man and a woman in highly erotic language included in the Bible?' That question has baffled interpreters of the book throughout the centuries, and still puzzles some readers today.

Some Jewish and Christian scholars solved the problem by deciding that the book should be interpreted allegorically. That is, to the Jews it spoke of the love relationship that God had established between himself and his covenant people, Israel. To Christians it symbolized the love relationship between Christ, the bridegroom, and his church, the bride – or for that matter, with individual believers. Although scholars debate whether Jews or Christians first started the allegorical interpretation, there can

be no doubt that one of the earliest Christian allegorists was Hippolytus, who died in AD 235. However it was Origen, in the third century AD, who gave this interpretation its classical formulation and influenced the church's understanding of the book for generations to come.

Over the centuries, individuals who have advocated a literal interpretation of the Song have sometimes paid a high price for their views. The church insisted on an allegorical interpretation until the Reformation in the sixteenth century. Among the Reformers, Calvin adopted an allegorical interpretation whereas Luther tried to follow the literal sense, though not consistently. It is only since the end of the eighteenth century that a literal interpretation has predominated.

The current consensus among biblical scholars is that we must take what the text is saying seriously and try to understand it literally first – for there is nothing wrong with sexual attraction or with the expression and practice of sexual love in the context of a permanent commitment to one another. After all, sexual desire is God's creation and he declared it very good when he created them male and female (Gen 1:27 and 31). In fact, the garden motif that frequently surfaces in the romantic exchanges between the two lovers reminds us of the Garden of Eden where Adam and Eve were placed. But although the literal sense is the main thrust of the Song, that is not all there is to it. As Murphy says: 'we should be open to the possibility that our predecessors, despite their foibles, may have caught a glimpse of theological reality that is not exhausted by the literal sense of the Song's poetry.'

Interpreting the book in its biblical context, there is no question that it communicates deep and rich lessons to its readers. After all, there are many passages in both the OT and the NT where the relationships of God and Israel and of Christ and the church are compared to that of a husband and wife.

Authorship

I am working from the assumption that the book was written by Solomon and that he is also the male protagonist. This, of course, gives rise to the problem of how a man who practised polygamy and had seven hundred wives and three hundred concubines (1 Kgs 11:3) could write such a book.

The answer may lie in a consideration of the stage of his life in which he wrote it. Tradition has it that Solomon wrote the Song of Songs in his youth, Proverbs in his mature years, and Ecclesiastes in his old age. If this is true, then it was probably written in the years before he became king, in what may have been the most innocent stage of his life. It certainly offers no support to those who advocate a polygamous lifestyle. On the contrary, the reference to the lover wearing his beloved 'like a seal over your heart, like a seal on your arm' (8:6) and the exclusive claims of jealousy in the same verse indicate that true marital joy can only be found where two individuals are exclusively and permanently bonded to each other in love.

The church in Africa has long been struggling with issues of polygamy and needs to uphold the biblical teaching on the exclusiveness of marriage among its membership if it is to be vibrant. Our Lord knew that the ᴏᴛ refers to many polygamous individuals, even among God's covenant people, but He still upheld God's creation ordinance of 'the two becoming one flesh' (Matt 19:4-6).

Outline of Contents

It is difficult to assign titles to the sections of this poem. Thus they will simply be identified by uppercase roman numerals.

1:1-2:7 Section I
2:8-3:5 Section II
3:6-5:1 Section III
5:2-8:4 Section IV
8:5-14 Section V

COMMENTARY

1:1-2:7 Section I

The book is introduced as *Solomon's Song of Songs* (**1:1**), immediately associating the Song with the wisest and one of the greatest kings of Israel. The Hebrew form 'Song of Songs' is a superlative, indicating that this is the best or the greatest song.

In this beautiful love poem, it is the girl who speaks first (**1:2-4**). Of the 117 verses of the Song, half are spoken by her (55 verses are definitely spoken by her, and in another 19 she is probably the speaker). To African ears, a girl initiating a love relationship sounds unrealistic and unacceptable. Yet the Song clearly puts the female on what is at least an equal footing with the male when it comes to the expression of their love. 'It is more her love story than it is his, though there is no failure on his part to declare his love and admiration for her' (*EBC*). In this respect the Song of Songs complements the Genesis account, where we hear the male saying, *This is now bone of my bones and flesh of my flesh* (Gen 2:23).

In the opening verses the girl is yearning for her lover to physically express his love to her. Hence we hear her saying, *for your love is more delightful than wine* (**1:2**). The change between speaking of her lover as 'him', to addressing him as 'you', and then moving on to 'us', all within three verses, may be confusing to some, but such variations are not unusual in Hebrew poetry. The reference to the lover's *name* (**1:3**) shows that he is a person with a good reputation. Indeed in elaborating her intense desire to be with him in *his chambers*, the beloved tells us that her lover is a king (**1:4a**; see also 1:12; 3:9, 11; 7:5).

The *daughters of Jerusalem* mentioned in **1:5** start to speak as *we* in **1:4b** and express their admiration for the girl's lover (the word 'you' is masculine here). This group is referred to again in 2:7; 3:5, 10; 5:8, 16; and 8:4, and in **1:11** they are called the *daughters of Zion*. They may be the girl's friends or a specific group of girls from the city of Jerusalem.

Rather than responding to the young women directly, she turns to her lover and says *How right they are to adore you* (**1:4c**). She appears both apologetic and confident as she talks about herself to them. She mentions Solomon in the context of describing her complexion as *dark like the tents of Kedar, like the tent curtains of Solomon* (**1:5**)

With her attention fixed on her lover, she asks where he grazes his flock (**1:7a**). The shift from king to shepherd has led some scholars to think that the girl is torn between two competing lovers, a shepherd and the king. However, in the period in which this book was probably written, kings were often referred to as shepherds. Even the King of kings is known as a 'shepherd' in Psalm 23. The woman's point is that she wants to be where her lover is rather than to *be like a veiled woman* (**1:7b**) next to the flocks of the other shepherds. A 'veiled woman' may be a prostitute (see Gen 38:14-15) and this woman does not want to be suspected of such behaviour. She is committed to her lover and wishes only to be with him.

She gets a reply first from the daughters of Jerusalem (**1:8**). This group regularly uses the phrase *most beautiful of women* when speaking to her (see. 5:9 and 6:1). Then her lover speaks (**1:9-11**). He, too, praises her physical beauty, addressing her as *my darling* (**1:9**; also see 1:15; 2:2, 10, 13; 4:1, 7; 5:2; 6:4) and promises her jewellery to augment her beauty.

The girl responds with her own admiration of her lover (1:12-14). As she thinks about their relationship, the pastoral scene quickly changes to one of a royal banquet, where the girl muses, *my perfume spread its fragrance* (**1:12**). And then, *My lover is to me a sachet of myrrh resting between my breasts. My lover is to me a cluster of henna blossoms from the vineyards of En Gedi* (**1:13-14**). Her awareness of him is as real, delightful and pervasive as the scent rising from a sachet of perfume.

WEDDINGS AND LOBOLA

Lobola is a South African word for 'bride wealth' or gifts that a man's family gives to the family of the woman he wishes to marry. This ancient custom of giving bride gifts was also practised in biblical times (Gen 24:53). While the type of gifts, the amount given and the process to be followed differ from one African culture to another, the basic meaning of the practice is the same. It binds the two families together and legitimizes the marriage. It transfers the woman from her family to the home of her prospective husband and gives the husband legal ownership of children from the union.

Some matrilineal African cultures do not practise lobola. In these cultures, small gifts are exchanged as symbols of the bond that has been entered into by the two families, but these gifts do not involve the transfer of ownership of children to the husband's family or the transfer of the wife to her husband's home.

Where lobola is practised, it is believed to have a stabilizing effect on marriage, for if a woman decides to end the marriage and go back to her family, she is expected to return either all or some portion of the bride wealth. (This presents problems for those who claim that lobola is a gift and not a bride price, for why should a gift be returned?)

Traditionally, the process of negotiating bride wealth also had spiritual aspects because it involved rituals to inform the ancestors of both families about the marriage relationship and seek their protection. This practice continues, even in some Christian families. Church and civil weddings are performed only after the traditional negotiations have been completed and all or some of the gifts have been given

Churches have taken various positions with regard to this custom. Some refuse to marry a couple if lobola has not been paid. Others have banned the practice because of its links to African traditional religion and because the parents of prospective brides have abused the system by asking for large gifts. Some families rate the value of a girl in terms of her education and achievements in the secular world. The more educated the girl, the higher the bride price. This has resulted in church weddings being postponed and even in church members cohabiting before marriage in cases where men could not afford the prohibitive bride wealth. In cases where men borrow money from relatives to pay the lobola, the woman is sometimes treated as a chattel by those who feel free to abuse her because they contributed to her bride price.

Some women have also complained that they are unable to negotiate safe sex with an unfaithful husband because he has paid lobola for them. They are thus in danger of contracting HIV/AIDS.

However, payment of lobola is not the only reason Christian couples postpone church weddings. The commercialization of weddings means there is undue emphasis on having a large bridal party, expensive clothes and a large reception. Churches should encourage their members to focus on the meaning of Christian marriage and have less expensive weddings.

Isabel Apawo Phiri

In **1:15–2:3** the lovers exchange words of endearment. *How beautiful you are, my darling*, says the man (**1:15**). *How handsome you are, my lover*, responds the woman (**1:16**). *Like a lily among thorns is my darling among the maidens*, says the lover (**2:2**). *Like an apple tree among the trees of the forest is my lover among the young men*, replies the beloved (**2:3**).

The girl concludes this section with further yearning to be in the presence of her lover and to bask in the physical expression of his love (**2:4-7**). In her stark transparency, she says *I am faint with love* (**2:5**; see also 5:8). She has earlier wished that he would kiss her 'with the kisses of his mouth' (1:2), now she longs for him to embrace her (**2:6**). The NIV translation of this verse implies that he is already holding her, but the sense of the original is closer to the NASB, *Let his left hand be under my head and his right hand embrace me*, or to the RSV, *O that his left hand were under my head, and that his right hand embraced me*, and expresses a sense of yearning.

It is difficult to tell whether it is the girl or the lover who is speaking in **2:7**. The NIV's translation, *Do not arouse or awaken love until it so desires*, appears to make the girl the speaker, whereas the NASB, by translating it *That you will not arouse or awaken my love until she pleases* makes the lover

the speaker. The commentaries are equally divided, but in the end many assume that in light of the similar exhortation to the 'daughters of Jerusalem' in 5:8 and 5:16, the girl is the one speaking here. She adjures the daughters of Jerusalem 'not to encourage love beyond its right and proper place'. She is calling for restraint rather than unbridled expression of their love (*EBC*).

2:8-3:5 Section II

The injunction not to awaken love seems to mark a temporary pause in the exchanges of love. Suddenly the scene changes and the girl is back in her parents' house (**2:9b**). All of a sudden she sees her lover *leaping across the mountains* and *the hills* (**2:8**), running towards her, and finally standing next to the wall of the house *gazing through the window* and *peering through the lattice* that covered them (**2:9c**). We are not sure whether this is happening literally or whether the girl is remembering a past meeting. Be that as it may, she recites for us what her lover said to her (**2:10**). The verses that follow express the lover's yearning for her (**2:10-13**). He invites her, *Arise my darling, my beautiful one, and come with me* (**2:10**). Encouraging her to come out, he describes the romantic beauty of nature that he wishes to share with her (**2:11-13**). *See!* he tells her, *the winter is past; the rains are over and gone. Flowers appear on the earth; the season of singing has come* (**2:11-12a**). He goes on to mention *the cooing of doves* and the fig tree forming its early fruit while *the blossoming vines spread their fragrance* (**2:12b-13**). Kinlaw, quoting Gordis, says this may be the most beautiful expression of love in the spring to be found anywhere in literature (*EBC*). The lover presses his invitation (**2:13**).

The girl must have made a precautionary withdrawal as suggested by her words in 2:7 (see also 3:5 and 8:4). Otherwise, why would her lover refer to her as *My dove in the clefts of the rock, in the hiding places on the mountainside* (**2:14a**). She is clearly not available to him, for the lover pleads with her to show him her face and to let him hear her voice. *For,* he says, *your voice is sweet, and your face is lovely* (**2:14b**). In **2:15** the two jointly request those who have their good at heart to remove the obstacles to the relationship that is developing between them.

In the rest of Scripture, the social conventions associated with marriage tend to overshadow the expression of the romantic love that is here given free rein. But these lovers are not engaging in 'free love', as some would like us to believe. In spite of their free, reciprocal and passionate expressions of love, they are not isolated and thinking only of themselves. They are observed by the 'daughters of Jerusalem' (2:7; 3:5; 8:4) and they encounter the 'watchmen' (3:3; 5:7). 'Twice the young woman refers to constraints her elder brothers try to impose on her activities (1:6; 8:8-9). And she acknowledges that it would be indiscreet to greet her lover in public with a kiss (8:1)' (Murphy). Given these constraints, the lovers are clearly not thinking in terms of 'free love'.

It is clear that the social context provided in traditional African societies has many positive elements in discouraging free love. But the lack of balance mentioned in the introduction to this commentary as a result of the fall still manifests itself in other ways. The societal control in traditional African cultures can be so strong that the kind of equal and mutual love we see in the Song of Songs, which is the basis for a strong and permanent marital relationship, does not have the right environment in which to blossom.

One element of African tradition that may work against the establishment of strong and fulfilling marriage relationships is the practice of relatives of the partners arranging their marriage. Such marriages can be entered into for a number of reasons – for wealth, as payment for debts, for political reasons, or to secure other types of alliances. The most important questions of whether the man and woman love each other or consent to the union are put aside. With the encroachment of modernity, this practice may change. But the question is, will it change for the better? And the answer is, not unless the church shoulders the tremendous responsibility of preparing the young to be the committed and loving life-partners celebrated in this beautiful song.

In **2:16**, the woman again speaks and affirms that their relationship is as strong as ever: *My lover is mine and I am his* (**2:16**). She likens her lover to *a gazelle or a young stag* (**2:17**; see also 2:9) – a reference to the energy and passion with which she wants him to seek her.

The hide-and-seek, or as some would put it 'lost and found' or 'presence and absence', motif in the ongoing relationship of the lovers continues in **3:1-5**. Most commentators think that what the girl is relating here must have happened in a dream – indicating that her lover is in her thoughts day and night. Although fast asleep in her room, she continues to search for her lover: *All night long*, she says, *I looked for the one my heart loves* (**3:1a**). The Hebrew plural translated 'all night long' and the repetition *I looked for him* (**3:1b**) underscore the intensity of the search. But she *did not find him*. She, therefore, resolves to look for him around the city, *through its streets and squares*. Her determination is expressed in her words – *I will get up now, I will search* – and her action – *So I looked for him* (**3:2**). But the outcome is no different from the search around the bed: she *did not find him*.

Refusing to give up her relentless search, she encounters the watchmen doing their nightly rounds in the city. It may appear foolish to us, but she asks them, *Have you seen the one my heart loves?* (**3:3**). One commentator remarks: 'It does not occur to her that the local constables would have no idea who it was she was seeking – she knows her lover, and therefore the whole world does too!' (*TOT*). But hear her surprise and action when she finds her lover: *Scarcely had I passed them when I found the one my heart loves* (**3:4a**). She continues, *I held him and would not let him go* (**3:4b**). Having found him after such an arduous search, she is both relieved and determined not to let him out of her sight. She 'clutched him and refused to slacken her embrace' (*TOT*) *till I had brought him to my mother's house, to the room of the one who conceived me* (**3:4c**). In taking him to her mother's room she makes it clear that she is not taking him to her own bed. So does the repetition of the passage urging restraint in **3:5** (see also 2:7). Kinlaw comments, 'She is not looking for an illicit consummation of their love. Consummation she wants, but even in her dream she wants that consummation to be right. Where in human literature does one find a text so erotic and yet so moral as this?' (*EBC*).

3:6-5:1 Section III

This section is the heart of the book. Everything that has gone before leads to it and everything that follows radiates from it.

In **3:6-11** we have what the commentators call Solomon's wedding song or the bridal procession. Whoever it is who asks the question about who is coming (**3:6**), they seem to answer it themselves in the next verse with the shout of recognition, *Look!* (**3:7**). What they are seeing advancing is the procession as the bridegroom and his companions, who are *sixty warriors* (**3:7**), escort the bride from her home to his city for the wedding. The approaching company is described as *coming up from the desert* (though other translations prefer 'wilderness') *like a column of smoke perfumed with myrrh and incense made from all the spices of the merchant* (**3:6**) This description appears to focus on the perfumed bride as the centre of attraction – as in any wedding. However, it is also possible that the reference to a column of smoke refers to an elaborate ceremonial burning of frankincense as they advance. The Hebrew word translated *this* in verse six is feminine singular and therefore can refer either to the girl or to *Solomon's carriage* (NASB has *of Solomon*).

It seems that Solomon himself has had personal oversight over the elaborate construction of his *carriage* or *travelling couch* (NASB – 3:9-10). The daughters of Jerusalem also have a part to play, in that they are the ones who upholstered the seat of the carriage *with purple* and *lovingly inlaid* its interior (**3:10b**). Under their other name, *daughters of Zion*, they are invited to *Come out … and look at King Solomon wearing the crown, the crown with which his mother crowned him* (**3:11a**). This crown should not be confused with his royal crown (see 2 Kgs 11:12), which is put on the king by the high priest as God's representative. Here it is the crown of the bridegroom, which in Israelite tradition has been given to him by his mother. This feature of culture is not unique to Israel, for even in Africa a bride and bridegroom may be addressed as queen and king for the duration of their honeymoon.

It is instructive that the text parallels *the day of his wedding* and *the day his heart rejoiced* (**3:11b**). Clearly this marriage is being entered into freely and joyously.

In **4:1-15**, we hear the bridegroom admiring the beauty of his bride in the most extravagant and erotic language we have witnessed so far. Beginning with the words *How beautiful you are, my darling! Oh, how beautiful!* (**4:1**; see 1:15; 2:13; 6:4), he admires her eyes, hair, teeth, lips, mouth, temples (some versions have 'cheeks'), neck and breasts (**4:2-5**). When he says that he *will go to the mountain … and to the hill of incense* (**4:6**), he is not referring to any journey but to his bride. He is eager to make this flawless woman his own without any restraints (**4:7**).

In the remaining verses of this passage (4:8-15) he invites her to join him with the repeated, *Come with me from Lebanon* (**4:8**; note the repetition of 'Lebanon' in 4:15). Furthermore, he invites her to descend from Amana, Senir and Hermon – different peaks in the mountains north of Israel. In her virginity, his bride has been as distant and unattainable as those peaks, but now is the time for her to come *with me*. He tells her she has stolen his heart and addresses her as *my sister, my bride* for the first time (**4:9**). He repeats these words of endearment four times (**4:9, 10, 12; 5:1**) and again refers to her as 'my bride' in 4:11. In the Ancient Near East 'sister' was an expression of love. It is clear that the consummation of the marriage is imminent. Up to this moment, the beloved has been *a garden locked up … a spring enclosed, a sealed fountain* (**4:12**). But before long she will completely open herself to her bridegroom.

Even the literary structure of the Song confirms that **4:16-17**, which celebrates the consummation of their love, is the pivotal passage. These verses are in the exact middle of the Hebrew text, with 111 lines preceding them and 111 lines following them. As Carr puts it: 'Everything thus far has been moving towards this consummation. From this point on, everything moves towards the consolidation and confirmation of what has been pledged here. The sister/bride now becomes the "consummated one" (see on 6:13-7:5), as lover and beloved extend to each other the fullness of themselves' (*TOT*).

In response to the bridegroom's praise and his invitation to come down and join him, the bride commands the *north wind* and the *south wind* to come and *blow on my garden* and waft *its fragrance* abroad (**4:16**). In metaphorical language she is opening herself to passion and inviting her lover to come to her, as he has invited her to come with him. Continuing the metaphor of a garden that was introduced in 4:12, she invites her lover *come into his garden and taste its choice fruits.* The lover replies, *I have come into my garden, my sister, my bride; I have gathered my myrrh with my spice. I have eaten my honeycomb and my honey; I have drunk my wine and my milk* (**5:1a**). This imagery of delightful eating and drinking proclaims the consummation of their marriage in beautiful language that 'fits the holiest of all human relationships' (*EBC*). Such delights are celebrated by the wise authors of Proverbs 5:15, 18-19 and contrasted with the tawdry charms of illicit sex (Prov 7:18; 9:17).

Some commentators have been baffled as to who is speaking and who is spoken to in the invitation *Eat, O friends, and drink; drink your fill, O lovers* (**5:1b**). After all, if the drinking and eating refers to the consummation of love between the bride and the bridegroom, this cannot be shared with anybody else – it is theirs and theirs alone! The NIV is quite correct in identifying the speakers as the friends who have come to witness and participate in their wedding. They are addressing the bride and the bridegroom. The friends are encouraging them to enjoy the physical consummation of their love. In fact the Hebrew words translated 'drink your fill, O lovers' could easily be translated 'be intoxicated with love-making'.

5:2-8:4 Section IV

What follows is the working out of the 'life of love' celebrated in the wedding ceremony and sealed by the sexual consummation. As so often happens in real life, moments of joy and unity are followed by misunderstandings that need to be resolved. In **5:2-8** we witness a low ebb in the relationship and repetition of the hide-and-seek episode recounted in 3:1-4. Most commentators, once again, understand this to be a dream sequence. Half asleep, half awake, the beloved hears her lover knocking and saying, *Open to me, my sister, my darling, my dove, my flawless one* (**5:2**). Sleepy and reluctant to get out of bed, despite the chain of endearing words spoken by the lover, she makes excuses and delays opening the door (**5:3**). The man tries to open the door for himself (**5:4**), and the woman is suddenly wide awake. Filled with desire, she rises to open the door (**5:5**), but it is too late, her lover has given up and gone (**5:6a**). She calls his name but hears no response, and again sets out to search for him (**5:6b**). Once again she meets the night watchmen, but this time they beat and bruise her and steal her cloak (**5:7**). Once again she turns to her friends: *O daughters of Jerusalem, I charge you* – but this time the charge is different from what it was on the other occasions when she used this formula (2:7; 3:5; 8:4) and urged them not to arouse love. This time she asks, *if you find my lover, what will you tell him?* and answers her own question, *Tell him I am faint with love* (**5:8**).

The 'daughters of Jerusalem' respond with their own set of questions, basically asking what makes her lover so special that they should act as her messengers (**5:9**). In response she launches into a celebration of the physical beauty of her lover (**5:10-16**) that parallels his description of her in 4:1-7. After the introductory *My lover is radiant and ruddy, outstanding among ten thousand* (**5:10**), she speaks about his head and hair, eyes, cheeks, lips, arms, body, legs, appearance and mouth (**5:11-15**). She concludes – as she began – with praise of his stature, comparing him to the beautiful cedars of Lebanon. Then she simply adds: *This is my lover, this my friend, O daughters of Jerusalem* (**5:16**).

This description of the young man has aroused the interest of the others and now they offer to help in the search for him (**6:1**). But the woman seems to be suspicious of their sudden interest and answers ambiguously. Earlier she described herself as his garden (4:16) and she returns to that image in **6:2**. When she tells them that *I am my lover's and my lover is mine* (**6:3**), she is reminding them that 'his interest is in me and me alone'.

Suddenly the lover appears on the scene and, in his turn, praises his wife's beauty (**6:4-9**). He compares her to Tirzah, a beautiful and important city situated at the end of a fertile valley in northern Israel, and to Jerusalem, which is also famed for its beauty (**6:4-9**). Her beauty is as awesome as a parade of *troops with banners* (**6:4**; see also 6:10)

– a sight which the Greek poet Sappho, writing in the 6th century BC, described as something some people considered 'the fairest thing seen on the black earth'. His gaze lingers on her eyes, hair, teeth and temples (**6:5-7**) and he affirms that his beloved is incomparable – in a class by herself (**6:9**). The mention of *sixty queens … eighty concubines, and virgins beyond number* (**6:8**) need not be a reference to Solomon's harem. It can be taken as a general statement meaning that all women, regardless of their number and status, cannot compare with the beloved. Rather, they would all have admired her *and called her blessed* (**6:9**).

The bystanders – most likely the daughters of Jerusalem – pick up the theme of the beauty of the beloved and ask: *Who is this that appears like the dawn, fair as the moon, bright as the sun, majestic as the stars in procession?* (**6:10**).

In a number of instances in this book, it is difficult to tell who is speaking. Is it the man or the woman who speaks in 6:11-12? The NIV caption tells us the lover is the speaker. But if we take these verses in conjunction with the question of the daughters of Jerusalem in 6:10, and their appeal to the woman to return after the reference to chariots in 6:13, it makes more sense if the woman is the speaker here. She goes to the *grove* or garden to check *the new growth* and the budding (**6:11**). This may be a metaphorical reference to the renewal of the love relationship after it has gone through a cold spell. Suddenly she is caught up again in the position of honour and privilege that has come with her marriage, and tells the maidens *Before I realized it, my desire set me among the royal chariots of my people* (**6:12**; see also 3:6-11).

The daughters of Jerusalem beg her to return so that *we may gaze on you* (**6:13a**) and admire her beauty. This verse is the only one in which the word *Shulammite* appears in the entire Bible. There is some dispute as to exactly what it means, but one possible interpretation is that it is a feminine form of Solomon, indicating that she is 'Solomon's lady'. The lover, who is presumably with her in the royal chariots (6:12), responds to their pleas with, *Why would you gaze on the Shulammite as on the dance of Mahanaim?* (**6:13b**). He may be referring to the name of some wedding dance. The reference to dancing may be what again turns his attention to the physical beauty of his wife (**7:1-9a**). Beginning with the *sandalled feet* that danced, he lets his eyes move up her body, admiring her legs, navel, waist, breasts, neck, eyes, nose, head and hair (compare his description of her in 4:1-5). He ends with *How beautiful you are and how pleasing, O love, with your delights!* (**7:6**). Enraptured, he seeks to embrace her and kiss her, saying, *your mouth is like the best wine* (**7:8-9a**). It is clear that love has, indeed, been restored and is blossoming again.

The beloved responds to him in **7:9b-8:4**. He has spoken of her kisses as wine, and she responds with *May the wine go straight to my lover, flowing gently over lips and teeth*

(**7:9b**) and again affirms their mutual commitment: *I belong to my lover, and his desire is for me* (**7:10**). She offers her lover what Carr describes as 'Consummation – again'. *Come, my lover,* she says and invites him to the open countryside – to *the villages* and to *the vineyards* (**7:11-12**). In the most explicit language so far, she promises *there I will give you my love* (**7:12**).

Among the fruits she mentions in **7:12-13** are *mandrakes*. These are also known as 'love apples' and are the fruit of the mandrake plant, which has long been known in the Middle East as an aphrodisiac. Carr comments: 'not that these lovers needed any additional stimulation, but the use of such items has long been a part of the lore of love-making' (*TOT*).

The beloved elaborates on her offer of love: *at our door is every delicacy, both new and old, that I have stored up for you, my lover* (**7:13**). In fact, she would embrace and kiss him out in the open were it not for the restraints of convention (**8:1**). Moreover, she speaks of bringing him into her *mother's house* and giving him *spiced wine to drink, the nectar of my pomegranates* (**8:2**). She again pictures herself in the embrace of her lover (**8:3**) and ends with the usual refrain (**8:4**) – but it is clear that the time for restraint is now over, and the time for arousing love has come. By repeating the refrain, she reminds us of the long period of waiting and rounds off the literary structure of the Song.

8:5-14 Section V

It is not easy to make sense of this last section of the book. Various groupings of the verses have been suggested. All that is clear is that the many links to what has gone before indicate that this section is part of the main text. Kinlaw is probably right when he links it with what has immediately preceded it, saying, 'The drama is now almost over. The couple have followed her desire and now return from the trip into the fields and the villages' (*EBC*). The daughters of Jerusalem see the couple returning and ask, *Who is this coming up from the desert leaning on her lover?* (**8:5a**; compare 3:6).

The woman ignores the question as she speaks to her lover in **8:5b-7**. It seems that they have been to the place where the lover himself was conceived, continuing the cycle of life and love. She requests her lover to place her *like a seal over your heart* and *on your arm* (**8:6a**). Both then and now, a seal indicates ownership. Thus having a 'seal' that represents the bride *over your heart* and *on your arm* is an indication that each belongs to the other. Next she launches into one of the greatest passages on the commitment and consuming nature of true love, pointing out that it *is as strong as death* (**8:6b**). This truth is reflected in the marriage vows that bind a couple together 'until death do us part' – pointing to their lifetime commitment to one another. She

also insists that love's jealousy is as *unyielding as the grave* (**8:6c**). This jealousy is not to be interpreted as the negative emotion that can destroy relationships because partners do not trust each other. Rather, it is a jealousy similar to that of God, who describes himself as 'a jealous God', that is, one who asserts his rightful claim to ownership. This link is strengthened by the fact that the phrase translated *like a mighty flame* (**8:6d**) ends with *yah* in the Hebrew. Some commentators interpret this as the first mention of God's name in the Song, and the NASB supports this argument by translating the phrase as 'the very flame of the Lord'.

The strength of love and its powers of endurance are summed up in **8:7**: *Many waters cannot quench love; rivers cannot wash it away. If one were to give all the wealth of his house for love, it would be utterly scorned.*

We know from 1:6 that the woman has brothers, and it seems to be they who are speaking in **8:8-9**. The brothers protected their sister during her youth. Now that she has matured and is actually in the embrace of a loving husband, she expresses her appreciation for their having been like guard towers on a city wall in the days when *her breasts are not yet grown* (**8:8**). Now, she insists, *I am a wall, and my breasts are like towers* (**8:10**). Rather than being the one the others have to look after, she now has something to offer her lover: *Thus I have become in his eyes like one bringing contentment* – a wonderful affirmation of the fulfilment the couple are enjoying in their marriage.

The image in **8:11-12** is also difficult to interpret. Earlier, the imagery of vineyards and gardens was symbolic of sensual interaction between the lovers, but that does not seem to be the way it is being used here. Rather, what the bride appears to be saying is that what is important and of abiding value is not wealth (Solomon's vineyard) but the mutual self-giving and commitment expressed in her words *But my own vineyard is mine to give* (**8:12**; compare 1:6).

The book concludes with the couple exchanging love – both in words and action – as we have seen it happening over and over again throughout the book (**8:13-14**). The lover begs his beloved, *let me hear your voice!* (**8:13**). She replies, *Come away, my lover, and be like a gazelle or like a young stag on the spice-laden mountains* (**8:14**). By now we are at home with this metaphorical language and understand what she is inviting her lover to do: 'She urges him to make haste and resume the delights of love' (*EBC*).

Conclusion

As we conclude the study of this superlative song, we need to remind ourselves that human sexuality is God-given and beautiful when practised within the parameters God has ordained – that is, within the context of a committed and loving relationship between husband and wife. The Song does not endorse sexual promiscuity, but affirms the pure joy of divinely instituted marital love.

We also need to remember the broader theological significance of marital love that was mentioned in the introduction to this commentary. There are numerous passages in the OT that represent God's relationship with his covenant people in terms of the relationship of a husband and wife (for example, Isa 54:5-8; Jer 3:1-10; Ezek 16; 23; Hos 1-3). The NT refers to Christ as the bridegroom and the church as the bride (2 Cor 11:2-3; Rev 19:7-9). Murphy puts it well when he says, 'Within biblical traditions themselves, knowledge and experiences of God that nurture faith are always interrelated. Among the manifold ways this interrelationship comes to scriptural expression is the recognition that human love and divine love mirror each other' (HC).

The knowledge that the love within our marriages can mirror God's love is extremely meaningful and heart-warming, especially as we look forward to the consummation of all things. The Apostle John writes, 'Blessed are those who are invited to the wedding supper of the Lamb!' (Rev 19:9). The yearning that we witnessed in the love relationship of the lovers of the Song of Songs should be burning within us in a purer and deeper sense, driving us to cry out with the writer of Revelation, 'Come, Lord Jesus.'

Tewoldemedhin Habtu

Further Reading

Carr, G. Lloyd. *The Song of Songs*. TOT. Leicester: Inter-Varsity Press, 1984.

Kinlaw, Dennis F. *Song of Songs*. EBC. Grand Rapids: Zondervan, 1991.

Murphy, Roland E. *The Song of Songs*. HC. Minneapolis: Augsburg Fortress Press, 1990.

INTRODUCTION TO THE PROPHETS

The sixteen prophetic books in the OT comprise a large portion of God's Word. Isaiah, Jeremiah, Ezekiel and Daniel are known as the Major Prophets, whereas Hosea, Joel, Amos, Obadiah, Jonah, Micah, Nahum, Habakkuk, Zephaniah, Haggai, Zechariah and Malachi are known as the twelve Minor Prophets. The division into major and minor prophets is based on the length of their books and should not be taken as indicating that some are more important than others.

The books are not arranged in the Bible in chronological order. Some were probably written before the fall of the northern kingdom (Isaiah, Hosea, Joel, Amos, Jonah and Micah). Others were probably written around the time of the fall of the southern kingdom and the exile (Jeremiah, Ezekiel, Nahum, Habakkuk, Zephaniah and Obadiah). Still others were written after the exile (Haggai, Zechariah and probably Malachi).

They are not addressed only to the covenant people (Israel and Judah) but also to foreign nations. Obadiah is addressed to Edom, and Nahum to Nineveh, the capital of Assyria. Long sections of Isaiah, Jeremiah, Ezekiel and Zephaniah are also addressed to other nations.

When we think of OT prophets, it is important to remember that it is not only the authors of these sixteen books who count as prophets. In fact, in the Jewish tradition, the books from Isaiah to Malachi are known as the 'Latter Prophets' and the books from Joshua to 2 Kings are the 'Former Prophets'. This is because these history books contain stories of important prophets like Samuel, Nathan, Elijah and Elisha.

The Prophetic Books are often considered the most difficult books in God's Word to interpret and understand. Yet, if we understand the prophets, their purpose and message, we will learn to greatly appreciate them and their messages to us today.

Who Were the Prophets?

God chose a variety of people to act as his prophets. He used both men and women (for examples of female prophets, see Exod 15:20; Judg 4:14, 2 Kgs 22:14, Isa 8:3; Luke 2:36). They were drawn from every walk of life; for example, Elijah seems to have been from an unimportant social class, while Isaiah was probably a high court official in Judah. What they did have in common was that they were all chosen by God, and did not presume to be prophets on their own initiative (Exod 3:1-6; Isa 6:1-7; Jer 1:4-5; Ezek 1:3; Hos 1:1-2; Amos 7:14-15; Jonah 1:1).

The prophets did their work and prophesied by means of the Holy Spirit (Ezek 11:5; Mic 3:8; Zech 7:12). Their books often begin: 'The word of the Lord came to …' (Hos 1:1; Joel 1:1; Micah 1:1). Similarly, their prophecies often begin: 'This is what the Lord said to me …' (Jer 27: 2, 4, 11; Amos 1:3). They did not act or speak on their own authority.

The prophets received their divine messages by various means. Some heard an audible voice (Exod 3:4), others saw visions and dreams (Amos 7:1-9; Zech 1:8; 2:1) or received words personally written by God (Exod 24:12; Dan 5:22-28). In many instances, the prophets were simply compelled to speak (Amos 3:7-8).

The prophetic messages were originally spoken to the people, often at religious sites during the religious festivals (Amos 7:13). Afterwards the messages were written down, sometimes by the prophet himself, sometimes by a scribe (Jer 36:4).

What Was Their Message?

The prophets were God's mouthpiece to a generation (2 Kgs 17:13). As divinely authorized messengers, they spoke the very words of God. To disbelieve their words was to disbelieve God; to disobey their words was to disobey God.

We tend to think of the prophets as foretellers, predicting events that would occur in the future. But they were also 'forthtellers', who called the people to repentance and obedience to God's word. Time and again they cried out against what was happening in their own times: idolatry, greed, injustice, oppression of the poor by the rich, corruption in the courts and growing immorality. They stressed that God would punish sin. Yet in summoning the people to repentance, they also spoke of God's undying love for his people, his compassion and his forgiving spirit (see Isa 54:7).

Their messages included predictions of events that would happen very soon (see, for example, Exod 7:1-5; 2 Sam 24:11; 1 Kings 11:29-32). Other predictions concerned events that would come in the near future, such as the miseries of exile and destruction (Amos 3:11; Mic 1:6-7). Still other prophecies spoke of events that would occur in the distant future, including the return of the Jews to their homeland (Jer 25:12-14; 30:1-3).

A prophecy has a single meaning, but it can have near and distant fulfilment. For example, there are near and distant fulfilments of Malachi's prophecy that Elijah the prophet will return before the day of the Lord (Mal 4:5-6). In the NT, Jesus taught that Elijah has already come in the person of John the Baptist (Matt 11:14; Mark 9:11-13). Yet Elijah the prophet will also return at the end of time (Rev 11:3-6). We should not assume that the prophet foresaw only one of these fulfilments. Rather, we should see each prophecy as a generic whole, in which a series of events are so connected that they constitute one vision.

How Did They Present Their Message?

The prophets presented their message from God in many different forms, each of which contributed to getting people to heed what God had to say to them. Sometimes they presented it as if they were watching a lawsuit in which God was the judge and his people were the defendants. When the prophets use this form, their prophecy often contains a summons, a charge, evidence and a verdict (Isa 3:13-26).

At other times, the message was presented in a clear oracle of woe. Such oracles are characterized by an announcement of distress, a statement of the reason for the distress and a prediction of doom (Mic 2:1-5; Hab 2:6-8; Zeph 2:5-7).

At still other times, the message from God came in the form of a promise of future blessings (Jer 31:1-9; Hos 2:16-20; Amos 9:11-15). These blessings were usually connected with the covenant categories of life, health, safety and agricultural abundance.

Some of the prophets made their messages memorable by acting them out. We see this particularly in Ezekiel (for example, in Ezek 4 and 5).

The prophet's messages were often presented in the form of poetry, which would have made them easier for their audience to remember. This does, however, sometimes mean that they can be difficult to understand if we do not recognize the Hebrew poetic form in which they are expressed.

One other barrier to understanding the prophets is the fact that they are rooted in the religious, historical and cultural life of their own times, which were often characterized by political, military, economic and social unrest and religious unfaithfulness. To understand them properly, we cannot simply read them casually, but need to have some understanding of the background against which the prophets spoke. That is why it is important to turn to books like the *Africa Bible Commentary*, other more detailed commentaries, and Bible dictionaries and handbooks in order to understand their message.

What Is Their Relevance Today?

God spoke to his people through the prophets, condemning idolatrous practices, promising judgment on those who disobeyed him, and consolation to those who returned to him. The Prophetic Books bring the same message to us today. God still condemns us for putting our modern idols before him, promises to bring judgment on those who disobey him, and brings consolation to those who return to him with their whole hearts. The prophets' words can be trusted, for whatever God promises, he will definitely do.

The Prophetic Books help us rediscover the values that God calls his people in every age to live by and are a constant reminder that God is in control of history.

Yoilah Yilpet

PROPHETS TO ISRAEL AND JUDAH

God provided his people with kings as political administrators and also with prophets as their spiritual advisors. The prophets served as God's spokespersons to the kings on issues to do with justice and righteousness, while at the same time having a message for all the people. The chart below is an attempt, within the limits of the data available to us, to relate the kings of Israel and Judah to the prophet or prophets who ministered during each king's reign.

Prophets to Israel	Kings of Israel	Dates BC	Prophets to Judah	Kings of Judah	Dates BC
Ahijah (1 Kgs 11:29, 30; 12:15; 14:4-6)	Jeroboam (1 Kgs 14:20)	933-912	Shemaiah (1 Kgs 12:22)	Rehoboam (1 Kgs 14:21)	933-917
				Abijah (Abijam) (1 Kgs 15:2)	917-915
	Nadab (1 Kgs 15:25-26)	912-911	Azariah (2 Chr 15:1)	Asa (1 Kgs 15:9, 10)	914-874
Jehu son of Hanani (1 Kgs 16:1, 7, 12)	Baasha (1 Kgs 15:33, 34)	911-888			
	Elah (1 Kgs 16:8)	888-887			
	Zimri (1 Kgs 16:15)	887			
	Tibni (1 Kgs 16:21)				
	Omri (1 Kgs 16:23)	887-876			
Elijah (1 Kgs 17-19)	Ahab (1 Kgs 16:29-33)	876-854		Jehoshaphat (1 Kgs 22:42)	874-850
	Ahaziah (1 Kgs 22:51-53)	854-853			
Elisha (1 Kgs 19:19-21; 2 Kgs 3:13-15)	Joram (Jehoram) (2 Kgs 3:1, 2)	853-842		Jehoram (2 Kgs 8:16, 17)	850-843
Elisha (2 Kgs 9:1)	Jehu (2 Kgs 10:36)	843-816	Joel	Ahaziah (2 Kgs 8:26)	843-842
				Athaliah (2 Kgs 11:3)	842-837
Elisha, Jonah	Jehoahaz (2 Kgs 13:1)	816-800		Joash (2 Kgs 12:1)	837-798
Elisha (2 Kgs 13:14)	Jehoash (2 Kgs 13:10)	800-785		Amaziah (2 Kgs 14:2)	798-770
Amos	Jeroboam II (2 Kgs 14:23)	785-745	Isaiah	Azariah (Uzziah) (2 Kgs 15:1, 2)	792-740

Prophets to Israel	Kings of Israel	Dates BC	Prophets to Judah	Kings of Judah	Dates BC
Hosea	Zechariah (2 Kgs 15:8)	744	Isaiah Micah	Jotham (2 Kgs 15:33)	740-735
	Shallum (2 Kgs 15:13)	744			
	Menahem (2 Kgs 15:17)	743-735			
	Pekahiah (2 Kgs 15:23)	735-734		Ahaz (2 Kgs 16:2)	735-720
	Pekah (2 Kgs 15:27)	734-730			
	Hoshea (2 Kgs 17:1)	730-722		Hezekiah (2 Kgs 18:2)	720-692
				Manasseh (2 Kgs 21:1)	692-638
			Nahum Zephaniah	Amon (2 Kgs 21:19)	638
			Jeremiah Zephaniah Prophetess Huldah (2 Kgs 22:14)	Josiah (2 Kgs 22:1)	638-608
			Jeremiah	Jehoahaz (2 Kgs 23:31)	608
			Jeremiah Habbakuk Zephaniah	Jehoiakim (Eliahim) (2 Kgs 23:36)	608-597
				Jehoiachin (2 Kgs 24:8)	597
			Ezekiel	Zedekiah (Mattaniah) (2 Kgs 24:18)	597-586

ISAIAH

We know very little about the prophet Isaiah, except that he lived during the reigns of Uzziah, Jotham, Ahaz and Hezekiah, who were the kings of Judah between roughly 767 BC and 687 BC (1:1). His ability to write (8:1), his knowledge of other books of the OT, his interest in the politics of his country (chs. 30–31) and his access to kings (7:3; 38:5) suggest that he was a well-educated and influential person living in Jerusalem, the capital of Judah. His message is directed primarily to the people of this city. He seems to be a man sincerely devoted to the Lord and deeply concerned about the fate of his contemporaries (1:15; 6:5, 8; 64:7-11).

Isaiah lived in troubled times. For some 150 years, the nation had been divided into two kingdoms: Israel in the north and Judah in the south (1 Kgs 12:1-24). These kingdoms were often in conflict (7:1). Moreover, Assyria, the dominant power of the time, had imposed a ruinous tribute on them. Both nations were tempted to revolt and form coalitions with Syria or Egypt. During Hezekiah's reign, the northern kingdom was completely destroyed by the Assyrians, who then invaded Judah. Jerusalem itself narrowly escaped capture (2 Kgs 18–19).

The religious situation was also confused. Influenced by the political and religious currents of the time, the nation had turned to the gods of surrounding nations (2 Chr 28:22-24). The Lord was often thought of as just one god among many.

It was in this context that Isaiah denounced the moral and religious corruption of the people and announced God's judgment on the nations. But he also proclaimed salvation for those who remained faithful to the Lord and for those who repented, as well as the future restoration of Jerusalem.

The theme of God's chosen one, the Messiah who will bring salvation, is central to the book, which contains the most openly messianic prophecies in the whole OT. Perhaps the most famous of Isaiah's messianic messages are the four passages known as the Servant Songs (42:1-9; 49:1-6; 50:4-9; 52:13-53:12). Some of these songs may originally have referred to Hezekiah, the king of Judah, or to Cyrus, the king of Persia, the people of Israel or even Isaiah himself, but it became clear that they were messianic, pointing to Jesus Christ. Isaiah's focus on Christ means that he is sometimes known as the Fifth Evangelist. His importance was recognized by the authors of the NT, with the result that there are almost as many references to the prophecies of Isaiah in the NT as there are to all the other OT prophets put together.

The book may be divided into three parts. The first part (chs. 1–39) consists primarily of short-term prophecies concerning the period in which the prophet lived, that is, from about 767 to 687 BC. The second part (chs. 40–55) contains medium-term prophecies concerning the end of the Babylonian exile in about 539 BC. The third part (chs. 56–66) deals with the long term, announcing a salvation that will be available to all nations and a permanent reign of peace in Jerusalem.

The events spoken of in this book thus take place over a much longer period than any human lifespan. Yet in some places the text is remarkably specific. For example, in 45:1 Cyrus is named as the king of Persia, even though he lived about two hundred years after the prophet. Details like this have convinced many commentators that the book is a collection of texts written by at least two authors in different periods. Thus the three sections into which the book falls are sometimes known as First, Second and Third Isaiah. However, at the heart of this book is an understanding of God as a being outside of time. He is perfectly capable of announcing events that will happen far in the future (44:6-7; 46:9-10). African readers will have no trouble accepting that this is so, for in our culture past, present and future are intimately linked.

Indeed, there are numerous similarities between African culture and that of Isaiah's time, as well as many similarities between the economic, political and religious circumstances of Judah in his time and those now prevailing on our continent. The prophet's concern for his people should mirror ours for the African church.

Outline of Contents

COMMENTARY

1:1 Introduction

Like many of the other Prophetic Books, the book of Isaiah conveys a lot of information in the introductory verse. To start with, it indicates the way God speaks to his prophet, namely, through a *vision* (**1:1a**).

We are then given some brief biographical information about the prophet. He is the son of a certain *Amoz*, but his mother's name is not mentioned. As regards the place and time of his ministry, we are told that it concerned *Judah and Jerusalem* – in other words, the southern kingdom that had remained faithful to the Davidic dynasty (1 Kgs 12:1-20). The names of the kings who reigned during Isaiah's ministry are listed (**1:1b**): *Uzziah* (also called Azaraiah – 2 Kgs 15:1-7; 2 Chr 26:1-23), *Jotham* (2 Kgs 15:32-38; 2 Chr 27:1-9), *Ahaz* (2 Kgs 16:1-20; 2 Chr 28:1-27) *and Hezekiah* (2 Kgs 18:1-20:21; 2 Chr 29:1-32:33). These details help readers to understand the religious and political context of Isaiah's ministry.

1:2-39:8 Part 1: Prophecies for Isaiah's Time

The first part of the book of Isaiah consists primarily of short-term prophecies, addressed to Isaiah's contemporaries.

1:2-31 Introductory Oracle: Judgment of Judah

The opening vision introduces the themes that the prophet will develop later. The vision is presented in the form of a court case at which God hands down his judgment before two witnesses, the *heavens* and the *earth* (**1:2**; see also Deut 30:19). God identifies himself using the personal pronoun 'I' and speaks as a wounded person with a heart full of grief (1:2-3). He reproaches his people for their ingratitude and their crimes (**1:4**).

For God, this is not a new situation. His words show that as a good father and master he has repeatedly tried to correct the behaviour of his people. But they have not responded to his correction (**1:5-6**). Eventually, his patience has run out. He has used foreign forces to judge his people and has allowed the cities of Judah to be *burned with fire* and their fields to be *stripped* (**1:7**; see 2 Kgs 15:37; 16:5; 18:13, 17). Only the city of Jerusalem, *the Daughter of Zion,* has been spared (**1:8**).

God's speech is suddenly interrupted by human voices in **1:9**. The few who have survived acknowledge that *the Lord Almighty* has played a protective role. Their mention of *Sodom* and *Gomorrah* indicates that they are aware that God could have totally destroyed them, just as he destroyed those two cities (Gen 18:20-19:29).

When God speaks again, it is to make it clear that there are similarities between them and Sodom and Gomorrah. He destroyed those cities because of their sin, and Jerusalem is just as sinful – he even refers to it as *Sodom* and as *Gomorrah* (**1:10**). The only remedy for the situation of Jerusalem is a genuine return to the Lord, which will involve far more than just religious rituals (**1:11-15**). Such rituals can fool others into thinking we are in a right relationship with God, but God can see through hypocrisy. What he requires is not rituals but a sanctified life, manifested in love for one's neighbour. This love must be shown in our economic and political behaviour, as well as in our religious behaviour (1:11-17).

God's words, *Come now,* invite the people to a real meeting with him, the only one who can forgive their sins. They are invited to meet him in order to *reason together* (**1:18**). It seems that this reasoning involves their weighing up the benefits of obedience, which will bring blessing (**1:19**), against the results that will follow if they continue in their rebellion (**1:20**).

God exclaims over the change in attitude that has taken place in Jerusalem. Where once the city was faithful to him, now it has become like a prostitute, adopting any god who takes its fancy (**1:21a**; see Ezek 16:15-43; 23:22-49; Hos 2:4-8). *Righteousness* and *justice* have been replaced by murder, corruption and indifference to wrong (**1:21b-23**).

A similar type of change has taken place in Africa with the rise of dictators like the late Mobutu Sese Seko in the Democratic Republic of Congo (DRC) and the late Idi Amin Dada of Uganda. We too often see unconditional veneration of those in power and of power itself, which justifies any means used to gain or maintain power, including corruption, sex and violence. A cloak of false patriotism and a veneer of Christianity have enabled similar attitudes to infiltrate

many religious and political circles in Africa. This sort of thinking lies behind much of the misery and chaos in Africa today, and constitutes a serious threat to the church on this continent. We are in a similar situation to the ruined people of Jerusalem.

God does not remain inactive in the face of such circumstances. No longer does he speak as a wounded father (1:2-4); now he declares himself to be *the Lord Almighty, the Mighty One of Israel,* ready to take on his enemies (**1:24**). But his aim in taking action against them is not to destroy Jerusalem but to restore it (**1:25-26**). Once again, God says that those who repent may count on his forgiveness, but he warns those who persist in their rebellion that they face humiliation and death (**1:27-31**).

2:1-6:13 Prophecies During Jotham's Reign

The prophecies in this section were probably uttered during the reign of Jotham, Uzziah's son (2 Kgs 15:32-38). However, it is possible that some of them were uttered during the years when Uzziah was stricken with leprosy and Jotham acted as his regent and was largely responsible for running the country (2 Kgs 15:5). The section begins with another series of visions (2:1) and ends with the account of Isaiah's call 'in the year that King Uzziah died' (6:1).

2:1-4 The restoration of Jerusalem

Isaiah's vision concerns the ideal situation that Jerusalem will experience *in the last days* (2:1-2). It is expressed in words that remind us of the days of Solomon, when representatives of foreign nations flocked to Jerusalem to hear his wisdom (**2:3**; 1 Kgs 4:29-34). There will be peace in the last days, as there was during Solomon's reign (**2:4**; 1 Kgs 5:4-5). Yet the situation will be even better, because God himself will replace King Solomon, teaching his law and officiating as judge.

2:5-22 Confidence in God alone

With such a prospect, the author invites the people to think seriously about whom they are going to trust. He calls on them to *walk in the light of the Lord* (**2:5**). But instead of choosing this path, Jerusalem arrogantly prefers to place its trust in the accumulation of idols, money and military power (**2:6-8**). Whereas the people were earlier described as sinning against their neighbours (1:17), now they are described as proudly sinning against God. They will pay a heavy price for their attitude, for they will be humiliated and left destitute, stripped of all they trusted in (**2:9-21**).

This section can be summed up in the final words: *Stop trusting in man, who has but breath in his nostrils. Of what account is he?* (**2:22**). Jeremiah would later make the same point, saying 'Cursed is the one who trusts in man' (Jer 17:5).

3:1-15 Religious and political chaos

What can Jerusalem hope for without the help of God? The text is clear: nothing. Jerusalem will be without *supply and support* (**3:1**). There will be no wise leaders, for the city will lose its military, political and religious leaders, as well as all its skilled craftsmen (**3:2-3**; see 2 Kgs 24:14). The leaders who remain will be either inexperienced or ruthless (**3:4-5**). The situation presented in Isaiah is one we are all too familiar with in Africa. Too often, ignorant, inexperienced upstarts and opportunists decide the fate of their betters.

Desperate for leadership, the people will not choose their religious and political leaders for their competence or charisma. Instead, they will be chosen because of their tribal or ethnic connections and because they have at least managed to hang onto a few meagre possessions (**3:6**).

But the one offered authority over the *heap of ruins* that is all that will remain of Jerusalem will not accept it. He will know that he can do nothing for the starving people (**3:7**). If only African leaders were like this man in being reluctant to take over the religious and political ruin that has been made of our continent. Too often, we are led by those who seek only to lead despite having nothing to offer.

The reason that Jerusalem will come to this state is their sin *against the Lord* (**3:8**). And the people are not even ashamed of what they do, but *parade their sin* in public. In this, they are following the example of the people of *Sodom,* with predictably disastrous results (**3:9-11**; Gen 19:4-11).

Isaiah now returns to the lack of leadership he mentioned in 3:1-7. Those who are currently leaders are leading the nation astray and allowing unqualified youths and women to control affairs (**3:12**). This verse must not be used to refuse women any positions of leadership, for the Bible contains examples of godly women leaders (Judg 4–5). What Isaiah was complaining of was the fact that those who should have been the leaders of Jerusalem were failing to carry out their responsibilities.

God also reproaches the *leaders of his people* for their oppression of the poorest among them (**3:14-15**). He does not object to their occupying positions of political leadership, but he strongly condemns what they have done with their leadership and their use of it to exploit others. These verses should rouse the African church to action. The gospel planted in Africa pays almost no attention to oppression and social misery. Yet God lays great stress on social issues, and his church should do likewise.

3:16-4:1 Scandalous women

After reproving the men for their lack of commitment to leading the city, the prophet turns to the women of Jerusalem. They are reproached for their pride (**3:16**) and their excessive love of *finery* (**3:18-23**). They are only interested in flirtation and seduction. Here the prophet touches on a theme that is addressed in the book of Proverbs (Prov 6:20-7:27;

31:3). It is not that God dismisses any attempt to look attractive – the Song of Songs gives the lie to that idea. But a woman's aim should be to create or maintain faithful love that feeds into reverence for the Lord and the development of virtue (Prov 11:22-23; 31:30; Matt 19:3-6). She should not seek to be worshipped in place of the Creator.

Unfortunately, in Africa today women are often seen solely as objects for adoration and desire. They are encouraged to cultivate a casual attitude towards morality and to dress expensively. Many wear excessive amounts of expensive jewellery featuring ivory and diamonds, paint their nails and wear wigs, but pay no attention to their inner values. Such behaviour is an assault on traditional African culture in which women contribute to the moral foundations of the community.

The women of Jerusalem are proud, but God will humiliate them. They will be reduced to poverty and *baldness* (**3:17, 24**). For a woman to be bald was often a sign of disgrace, but wearing *sackcloth* and having one's head shaved were also signs of mourning (see Gen 37:34; Amos 8:10). Soon these proud women will be mourning their sons and husbands (**3:25-26**; 13:11-12).

Their situation will be so desperate that they will do anything to find a husband rather than endure the shame of being single. They will willingly submit to polygamy as groups of them latch onto the only available man (**4:1**). This verse parallels 3:6-7, where the men were so desperate that they would regard even possession of a cloak as a qualification for leadership and would seize on the first available person to fulfil their need for a saviour.

4:2-6 The glory of the redeemed

The next section starts with the important words, *in that day* (**4:2a**). This phrase is repeated about thirty times in Isaiah. The biblical poets and prophets used it to proclaim their hope of divine intervention. While 'that day' will bring disaster for the wicked, it will bring comfort and renewal to the upright and the oppressed (2:17; 11:10; Jer 30:8; Ezek 20:6; Joel 3:18). In difficult times, we Christians should cling to this hope and should not succumb to fatalism.

Again the prophet speaks in the voice of a minority who recognize God as their saviour (**4:2b**; see 1:9). He again announces that the Lord will intervene for this remnant. He will make them like a beautiful fruit tree, which will be the envy of everyone around (see also Ps 1). He will give them a natural *pride* and *glory* that is of far more worth than the trinkets and haughtiness that characterized the idolatrous nobility (3:16-23).

The rest of the passage is a beautiful description of God's return to a people and an individual. It starts with his gift of a new identity and of sanctification (**4:3-4**; 2 Cor 5:17-19). Then comes an assurance of God's presence with those who come to him (**4:5**; Matt 18:20). The *cloud of* smoke and *the flaming fire* that symbolize the presence of the Lord would remind the people of the exodus from Egypt and the consecration of Solomon's temple (Exod 13:21; 24:16-17; 2 Chr 5:13). Finally, God guarantees peace and comfort despite external threats (**4:6**).

This last consequence of the Lord's intervention is truly both a dream and a necessity for Africa. In our search for prosperity, we must not forget that the way to prosperity is through purification and seeking God's presence. We should first seek the kingdom of heaven and then all these things will be given to us as well (Matt 6:33).

5:1-7 The song of the vineyard

The prophet then sings for God, who is here referred to as the *one I love* and as *my loved one* (**5:1**). As in the preceding section and 1:9, the Lord is recognized as someone who longs for the good of his people (see Jas 1:16-17). But he has been deeply hurt. God does not want to express himself directly, so the prophet takes it upon himself to speak for God.

The song describes the relationship between God and his people as being like that of the owner of a vineyard and his vines. The grower has devoted himself to the vineyard, and has done everything that he can to promote good growth and to protect the vines. Yet his vineyard produces only *bad fruit* (**5:2, 4b**). The good fruit that he expected was *justice* and *righteousness,* but all that has been produced is *bloodshed* and *distress* (**5:7**).

Later, Jesus uses this same image of God as the owner of a vineyard to emphasize the unfaithfulness of the nation (Matt 21:33-41). He presents himself as the good vine to which his followers must be attached if they are to produce good fruit (John 15:1-8).

God asks the *dwellers in Jerusalem and men of Judah,* to whom the song is directed, to be the judges of their own behaviour (**5:3-4a**). He does not treat them as traitors but simply lays out his case. We can picture him standing respectfully before the elders in the city gate, the place of justice, just as Boaz did (Ruth 4:1-12). God's justice is not incomprehensible to human beings. We can grasp its principles and express it ourselves (2 Sam 12:1-7; Matt 7:2; 21:40-41). Thus we have no excuse for accepting that corruption is inevitable and justice an unattainable ideal. Honesty and justice are realities that we need to support and live by.

The Lord's judgment is proportional. The people had rejected him, and so he would stop protecting and blessing them (**5:5-6**). But the consequence of this mutual abandonment was that the people would now find themselves at the mercy of threats from all around.

5:8-30 Judgment on the careless

In the same vein as the song of the vineyard, the prophet reproaches the people for not seeing the *deeds* or *works* that the Lord has done for them (**5:12b, 19**). They will be punished for their *lack of understanding* (**5:13a**).

The prophet lists the sinful attitudes that hinder people from seeing the works of the Lord. They include greedy accumulation of property (**5:8-9**), drunkenness (**5:11, 22**; Prov 31:4-5; Amos 2:11-12), manipulation and lying (**5:18, 20**), the pretence of wisdom (**5:21**; 1 Cor 1:18-31) and the perversion of justice (**5:23**). The source of all these attitudes is their rejection of *the law* and *the word of the Holy One of Israel* (**5:24**).

The Yombe (DRC) have an expression *kambu lumbu,* which means that people can do anything they want, but that one day they will be trapped by what they have done. That is what is happening here. The people party as if they have nothing to worry about (**5:12a**), but God's judgement will catch up with them (Matt 24:36-44). Those who have accumulated land and houses will reap almost no crops and their homes will be ruined (**5:10, 17**; see also Amos 3:15), those who have partied wildly will die of hunger and thirst (**5:13b**). Instead of eating, they will be eaten by death (**5:14**). All their pride will come to nothing (**5:15**; 25-30).

This time, the punishment is not simply abandonment (5:5-6). Instead, God himself *strikes them down* (**5:25**). More than that, he summons a foreign nation to come and attack his people (**5:26**). This nation is described as having divine attributes, for it will not grow tired or sleep (**5:27**; see Ps 121:3-4). It also enjoys divine blessings, for all its equipment is in perfect condition (**5:28**). Its troops are as fierce as lions and as irresistible as the sea (**5:29-30**).

6:1-13 An appearance by God

Chapter 6 contains an account of Isaiah's call to ministry. We have similar accounts for the calls of Jeremiah and Ezekiel (Jer 1:1-10; Ezek 1:1-3:3). They too caught a glimpse of the heavenly court and felt themselves to be physically in the presence of the Lord. The dialogue between the Lord and his prophets in these scenes has a greater intimacy than in other parts of their books. But whereas the calls of Jeremiah and Ezekiel are placed where we would expect them, at the start of the book, Isaiah's call is only introduced six chapters into the book. The reason may be that the death of Uzziah, who had been on the throne for fifty-two years, marked the end of an era and was accompanied by increased urgency in the international situation, and hence a corresponding change in Isaiah's responsibilities.

In the context of the wicked behaviour and judgment outlined in chapter 5 and the lack of faithfulness in the second part of Uzziah's reign (2 Chr 26:16-23), the death of *King Uzziah* assumed great significance (**6:1a**). As we know from our experience with African dictatorships, after the death of a leader things may carry on just as they were before, or there may be a radical change for the better or for the worse.

It is thus at an important time in the life of the nation that God appears to the prophet. Although King Uzziah has gone, there is not a power vacuum. The Lord, who has previously manifested himself as a father (1:2) and a farmer (5:1), now appears as the only true king, *seated on a throne, high and exalted* (**6:1b**). He commands cosmic forces. Angelic creatures recognize his holiness and his glory (**6:2**; 40:25-26). He expects equal adoration from his people.

The angels' cry of *holy, holy, holy* is interpreted by some as a veiled allusion to the Trinity (**6:3a**). However, it is more likely that this repetition is simply the Hebrew way of affirming that something is very important. God's holiness is central to his character. Meditating on it, as the angels are doing, leads to adoration.

The phrase *the whole earth is full of his glory* (**6:3b**) clearly refers to the whole of creation, the beauty of which should lead us to praise God. But one part of his creation does not praise him – humankind (1:2).

The angel's adoration is accompanied by a demonstration of power. Their voices shake *the doorposts and thresholds,* and *smoke* fills the building (**6:4**). These phenomena are associated with the intervention and presence of God (4:5; see also Josh 6:1-20; 1 Kgs 8:10).

The prophet knows that a sinful man cannot survive in the presence of God. He is deeply disturbed, just as Moses and Gideon were in similar circumstances (**6:5**; Exod 3:6; 33:20; Judg 6:22). However, his sins are forgiven through the symbolic act of touching him with the *live coal* taken from the altar. This coal may have come from a sacrifice of repentance or adoration that Isaiah has just offered (**6:6-7**).

God then speaks, calling Isaiah to ministry. It is worth noting that this call is not issued at random. Isaiah was already someone who went to the temple in a time of crisis. He was listening to hear what God had to say and was concerned for his people. Thus when he hears God speak of a need, his immediate response is *Here am I. Send me* (**6:8**).

The message that God asks the prophet to take to his people is an example of the double role of the word of God: it both saves and destroys (Heb 4:12). It is intended to be something that the majority reject or refuse to understand (**6:9-10**). There is no way that God will now revoke the judgment he has previously announced (**6:11-12**). But this word also proclaims salvation for a minority (**6:13**). God will be faithful to his promises and will preserve a faithful remnant (4:2).

Jesus quoted 6:9-10 to explain his use of parables (Mark 4:12).

7:1-10:4 Prophecies during Ahaz's Reign

The first set of prophecies seems to have been spoken during the reign of Jotham, Uzziah's successor. But by the time of the events of chapter 7, Jotham too has died and has been replaced by Ahaz, his son.

7:1-25 Challenge to the king

Ahaz's reign was marked by instability, for he had to face an invasion by a coalition of Syria and Israel (**7:1**). According to the books of Kings and Chronicles, this invasion was a punishment for the unfaithfulness of the king and the people (2 Kgs 16:2-5; 2 Chr 28:1-5).

The invasion presents a very real threat, and Ahaz and his people are terrified (**7:2**). Anticipating a siege, Ahaz sets out to inspect the city's water supply, *the aqueduct of the Upper Pool.* While he is doing this, the Lord sends Isaiah to him with a message that he should *keep calm and don't be afraid* (**7:3-4a**). He need not fear being deposed and replaced by Tabeel (**7:5-6**). The kings of Syria and Israel who are threatening him are only men and they only have authority over their own small kingdoms (**7:8-9**). That is why the Lord of the whole earth can dismiss them as no more than *two smouldering stubs of firewood* (**7:4b**). Evil consumes them just as fire consumes a block of wood, and they will disappear.

The prophet invites Ahaz to return to firm faith in God: *If you do not stand firm in your faith, you will not stand at all* (7:9). He knows that Ahaz has no need to take the dangerous course of sending to Assyria for help (2 Kgs 16:7). The history of the kingdom of Judah has repeatedly shown that faith in God is more important than the size of the nation's army or arsenal (2 Chr 13:2-18). But Ahaz has forgotten that truth, or dares not trust it. As the Yombe (DRC) say, *Uzola vanda tuama tsembo* ['without courage, the fetish will not be effective'; in other words, a fetish will only produce the expected result if the fetishist believes in its power]. Feelings of inferiority, fear (Judg 7:3; 2 Kgs 6:15-16; Jer 1:7-8; Luke 12:32) and doubt (Judg 6:36-40; 2 Kgs 7:1-2, 18-20; Luke 1:18-20) are the three main enemies of the servants of the Lord because they all reflect a lack of trust that prevents us from acting boldly for God. That is why these emotions are sometimes treated as synonymous with sin.

Isaiah tells the king to choose the sign he would like to see to confirm that his message comes from the Lord (**7:10-11**). But Ahaz, even though he was unfaithful to God, replies by quoting the law of Moses: *I will not put the Lord to the test* (**7:12**; Exod 17:2, 7; Deut 6:16). Asking for a sign from God is often evidence of a lack of faith (Matt 12:38-42; Heb 11:1-2). The king's reply proves his faith in the prophet's message.

Faced with Ahaz's refusal to ask for a sign, *the Lord himself* gives him a sign to confirm his word: the birth of a child (**7:14**). In some African cultures, the birth of a child is always regarded as conveying a message. Here the message is about the end of Judah's enemies (**7:16**). This child will have enough food to eat, and before he is even old enough to know the difference between right and wrong, the two kings Ahaz fears *will be laid waste* (7:15-16). In the historical context of this confrontation between Isaiah and Ahab, this child may have been one of Ahaz's sons, possibly Hezekiah, his successor, who was one of the most faithful kings (see 2 Kgs 23:25). If so, then this prophecy guarantees the continuity of the Davidic line (1 Kgs 2:4).

In the long term, however, this prophecy refers to Jesus Christ. Both Matthew and Luke record that Jesus was born of a virgin, Mary (Matt 1:18; Luke 1:26-35), and Matthew even calls him 'Immanuel' (Matt 1:23).

The instruments that God is going to use against Judah's enemies are *Assyria* and *Egypt* (**7:17-20**). They will deport the inhabitants of the kingdom of Israel during the reign of Hezekiah (2 Kgs 18:9-12). The devastation they wreak will give way to desolation as agriculture is replaced with animal husbandry and previously large flocks are reduced to no more than one cow and two goats (**7:23-25**).

8:1-22 Various forms of divine revelation

Under divine inspiration, the prophet goes on to warn Ahaz in various ways that Assyria will nevertheless make incursions into the kingdom during his reign and that of his successor, Hezekiah (2 Kgs 18:13-19:37).

The first thing Isaiah is told to do is to take a large scroll and write the words *Maher-Shalal-Hash-Baz* on it (**8:1**). These words mean 'quick to the plunder, swift to the spoil' and are a warning of a coming judgment. Then he calls in two *reliable witnesses* to certify that he has written this message at this time (**8:2**). This was the standard way in which legal documents were handled in those days (Deut 19:15-17; Jer 32:10-12).

Isaiah and his wife, referred to as *the prophetess,* then conceive a son, whom they name *Maher-Shalal-Hash-Baz,* using the same words written on the scroll (**8:3**; see also Hos 1:4-8). His brother, Shear-Jashub (7:3) also has a name with a symbolic meaning, namely 'a remnant will return'. The names of these two boys summarize the prophet's message up to now: devastation is coming, but a few will survive. Immanuel will still be a child when Rezin and Pekah are defeated (7:16), and Maher-Shalal-Hash-Baz will still be very young when their countries are plundered (**8:4**).

Isaiah then uses the imagery of water to explain what will happen to Judah. Rather than trusting in God and being content with the quiet *waters of Shiloah* that flowed near Jerusalem (**8:6a**), Ahaz and the people had sought help from the king of Assyria to repel the invasion by Israel and Syria. It was as if they had summoned the Euphrates River into the land (**8:7**). They had rejoiced when Assyria attacked Syria and Israel (**8:6b**), but had failed to recognize that this

powerful nation would sweep on like a flood into their own territory. They will not drown, but the water will come up to their necks (**8:8a**).

The image of the flood ends with the statement *its outspread wings will cover the breadth of your land, O Immanuel* (**8:8b**). Immanuel was the son born as a sign of the offer of God's grace to Ahaz (7:14). His name means *God is with us,* and Isaiah uses it to offer reassurance that Assyria's *plan* will not *stand* (**8:9-10**). The land belongs to Immanuel, not to Assyria! The promise of God's presence is part of the covenant between the people of Israel and the Lord (Gen 28:15, 19-20; Exod 3:12; Josh 1:5, 9; Jer 1:8). Jesus' words about his presence with his followers in Matthew 28:20 are thus an affirmation of his divine status and of his introduction of a new covenant.

God's presence has practical consequences. Although the prophet lives among the people and feels concern for them (6:5), he must not *follow the way of this people* (**8:11**; John 17:15-17). God tells him and his contemporaries not to become caught up in the media agitation of their time. They must not pursue *conspiracy* theories and *fear what they fear* (**8:12**). First and foremost, they must fear the one who is holy (**8:13**). He is the one who offers them *sanctuary* (**8:14a**). However, if his offer of sanctuary is despised, he will be *a stone* that constitutes a danger because people will *stumble* over him (**8:14b**). This same image is taken up in Psalms 118:22, which Jesus quotes when speaking of his own ministry (Matt 21:42-44; Luke 20:17-18).

Recognizing that God's judgment is coming, and that the people will *fall and be broken* (**8:15**), Isaiah takes a firm stand on what he does know: the law of the Lord, written in the *testimony* and the *law* (**8:16, 20a**). He has heard God's voice in relation to his own mission and the naming of his children, and he and they are prepared to serve as *signs and symbols in Israel* to make sure that the word of the Lord is not forgotten (**8:18**). He contrasts their devotion to the Lord with those who explicitly disobey God's law by turning to the dead for advice (**8:19**).

The question of our relationship to our deceased ancestors is a delicate one on our continent. While remembering and showing respect for ancestors is very important in building faith (Exod 20:12; Deut 32:7), we must be honest and admit that the Bible condemns consulting the dead about the future or asking them to avert calamities (Deut 18:10-13). The Bible does at times show the dead interacting with the living, but this happens only when God permits them to act as his servants, and not when humans seek them out (1 Sam 28; 2 Kgs 13:20-21; Matt 27:51-53; Mark 9:2-9; Luke 16:27). Rather than seeking a word from the dead (8:19), the living should turn to the word God has given them (**8:20b**; Luke 16:19-31; Heb 1:1-4) and call on the living God alone (Jer 33:3).

Those who do not seek the light of his word will be condemned to wander in darkness (**8:21-22**).

9:1-7 The coming of the light

But God is capable of changing the people's circumstances (**9:1**). *Galilee of the Gentiles,* the border area that would be the first to be invaded by Assyria, will enjoy honour in the future as the *shadow of death* gives way to the *light* (**9:2**). This light will be the source of fruitfulness, of joy and abundance (**9:3**). The oppressors will be defeated as easily as Gideon defeated *Midian* (**9:4**; Judg 7:9-22). Bloody battles will be no more as even the clothes worn by soldiers are discarded and burned (**9:5**).

This turnaround in the situation is due to the birth of a *child* who is called to reign (**9:6**). He is the 'Immanuel' announced in 7:14 and addressed in 8:8. While this child may be the young Hezekiah, his human attributes of wisdom, peace, uprightness and justice are combined with divine qualities that only God possesses when he is hailed as the *Mighty God, Everlasting Father* (9:6-7). No wonder this passage is seen as referring to the Messiah, who will be the only one who can fully deserve to be spoken of in these terms (Matt 1:23; 4:14-16).

9:8-10:4 The disappearance of Ephraim

The house of David will endure (**9:7**), but not the northern kingdom of Israel (see 7:4-8, 17-20), here addressed as *Jacob* and as *Ephraim* (**9:8-9**). This kingdom ignores the Lord and is supremely confident in its own strength (**9:10**). But it will discover the stupidity of such boasting as it is overwhelmed by its enemies, who will attack from the east and from the west (**9:11-12a**). The people who believed themselves safe will be taken in a pincer grip.

But this punishment will not be enough. The Lord remains angry: *Yet for all this, his anger is not turned away, his hand is still upraised* (**9:12b**). This refrain will be repeated several times in this section (**9:17b, 21b; 10:4b**). Although God is by nature compassionate and gracious (Ps 86:15), he will not ignore Israel's stubbornness and refusal to repent (9:13).

God's punishment will fall on the political and religious leaders of the kingdom who have led the people astray (**9:14-16**). He will judge them all, from the most important leader (the *head* and the *palm branch*) to the least important (the *tail* and the *reed*). The Lord says that he will cut them off, which he does by having them deported by Assyria. Because of the impiety and wickedness of both the leaders and the led, God will go against his own nature. He will no longer show his usual compassion for the young, the orphaned and the widowed (**9:17a**; Ps 68:5; Hos 14:3).

The prophet uses fire as a metaphor to illustrate the kingdom's condition. On the one hand, the fire represents the wickedness of the people, which spreads and destroys all around it (**9:18**). But the fire also represents God's

blazing anger at their sin (**9:19**). Fire devours what it burns and constantly seeks more to burn. In the same way, the wickedness of the people will lead them to turn on each other. In a vicious cycle of greed and despair, crime and tribalism will fuel civil wars and wars with their neighbours (**9:20a-21a**).

Yet even this is not the end of the punishment they will endure (9:20b). In times of instability, those holding power seek to retain their dominant position by increasing social injustice for their own profit. Such people *deprive the poor of their rights … making widows their prey and robbing the fatherless* (**10:1-2**). The Lord has noted their behaviour and will ensure that they are punished for their treatment of the helpless.

Unfortunately, the situation Isaiah has described sounds similar to what we see under many authoritarian regimes in Africa. The community spirit that is so dear to our continent is trampled by some leaders, their followers and their lying prophets (9:15) They are only interested in promoting their own interests in times of crisis. It takes great courage to resist their violence and to speak out as a prophet for the oppressed. Some who have done so have paid for it with their lives or are rotting in prison. No, politics does not necessarily go hand-in-hand with high moral values. No wonder Paul tells us to pray for our leaders and politicians (1 Tim 2:1-2).

Through the prophet, God warns the wicked leaders that one day they will be called to account for their behaviour. The intoxication of power often blinds those who oppress their people. They believe that they have set up laws that will protect them, but all their machinations will be useless *on the day of reckoning.* Having destroyed their community, they will find themselves alone and without *help* (**10:3**). We are reminded of the futility of human glory.

The oppressor will be presented with two humiliating options: either *to cringe among the captives or fall among the slain* (**10:4a**). King David knew how to repent and avoid these consequences (2 Sam 24:14). Others such as Saul and Ahab remained stubborn or tried to outwit God and avoid them. But they did not escape his judgment (1 Sam 31:1-10; 1 Kgs 22:1-39).

10:5-39:8 Prophecies During Hezekiah's Reign

Isaiah's prophecy was fulfilled. The kingdom of Israel was invaded by the Assyrians and its population deported during the early years of Hezekiah's reign (2 Kgs 18:9-12). Then Assyria turned its attention to the kingdom of Judah (10:11).

10:5-34 The pride of Assyria

In the preceding prophecy, Isaiah proclaimed 'Woe' to the nation of Israel, and particularly to its leaders (10:1). He takes up the same theme in **10:5a**, but this time the *Woe* is

WIDOWS AND ORPHANS

God's special compassion for widows and orphans is clear throughout the OT. There are strict warnings against abusing them (Exod 22:22). God declares that he is their defender (Deut 10:18) who cares for and protects them (Pss 68:5; 146:9). Malachi states that those who oppress widows do not fear Almighty God (Mal 3:5). God declares that a widow and her children can depend on him to sustain them (Jer 49:11). God's curse comes upon those who mistreat widows and orphans (Deut 27:19), but those who care for them are promised God's blessing (Jer 7:5-7).

In the NT, we find that the early church appointed deacons to see that the needs of widows were met equitably and adequately (Acts 6:1). Widows with no family to support them were to be put on a list for church assistance, subject to certain conditions regarding their age and lifestyle (1 Tim 5:3-14). Those who were on the list pledged to remain unmarried and chaste for the rest of their lives.

Widows were widely used in the ministry of the early church. They visited homes, brought food to the hungry, cared for the sick, comforted the bereaved, fasted and prayed, and assisted in teaching. Timothy even arranged for needy widows to receive compensation for their labours in the church (1 Tim 5:9-10). The Apostle Paul considered widowhood an ideal opportunity to attend to God's work without distraction (1 Cor 7:32, 34-35). He advised widows to forgo remarriage (1 Cor 7:8, 17-24), yet he encouraged remarriage in the case of younger widows in order to avoid the dangers of immorality (1 Cor 7:9; 1 Tim 5:11-14).

Widows still have much to share, especially lessons learned through their bereavement and the social, financial, legal, emotional and spiritual challenges in its aftermath. A widow's experience is a resource that she can draw on. When fortified by studying and appropriating God's word, experience becomes a basis for reaching out to other people who are in need.

The Hebrew word for 'widow' derives from a root word meaning 'unable to speak' and reveals the legal status of the widow in the ancient world: she had no one to speak for her. The Greek word for 'widow' comes from an Indo-European root that means 'left empty'. A woman who is left without a husband is potentially 'left empty'. In many parts of the world, widows are likely to suffer loss of status, financial support, property, health and even their own identities after their husband's death. This is now almost uniformly the case on the African continent. However, in the past African widows did not experience the isolation and loneliness they do today. When a man died, his family cared for the widow, including her sexual and procreative needs. She remained a valued and respected member of the community. With the coming of Christianity, some aspects of African culture were abandoned. Now it is up to the churches to go back to their African roots and recover what was good, such as the earlier loving care for widows and protection of orphans by the community.

Mae Alice Reggy-Mamo

---

directed not at Israel but at those who have overthrown it, the Assyrians.

The Assyrians are guilty of thinking themselves greater than God. In those days, battles were not thought of as just being between nations, but as also being between the gods of these nations. God has given the king of Assyria victory over Samaria (**10:6**), but the king now thinks that he is entitled to attack whomever he pleases (**10:7**). He boasts of his military ability and of the territories he has conquered (**10:8-9, 14**). He assumes that he is stronger than the gods of Jerusalem and that they will not be able to resist him (**10:10-11**). He boasts of his own strength, wisdom and understanding (**10:13**). In speaking of himself as being *like a mighty one* he sets himself up as almost equal to God. Nebuchnezzar, the king of Babylon, was guilty of the same inordinate pride (Dan 4:25-30).

The prophet speaks to remind us that God is the master of history (Dan 2:21-23). Once the Assyrians have served their purpose as his tool, he will take action (**10:5b, 15**). Their *wilful pride* will only be tolerated until *he has finished all his work against Mount Zion and Jerusalem* (**10:12**).

The Yombe (DRC) say, *Mvuala mfumfu i mfumu* ['The king's messenger is the king']. But this proverb only holds true when the messenger is humble and faithful in carrying out his master's commands. Abraham's servant could negotiate as his representative (Gen 24:32-50) and Paul could speak as Christ's ambassador (2 Cor 5:20). These men did not boast of their authority but humbly served the one who sent them.

The wise taught that pride precedes a fall (Prov 16:18-19; 17:19), and Isaiah proclaims that the Lord will humiliate the proud Assyrian army. The army will be destroyed as completely as when illness destroys a human body, or fire destroys the countryside, or an axe fells a forest (**10:15-19, 33-34**). Daniel spoke similarly of God's ability to overthrow a mighty tree (Dan 4:17-22). God emphasizes the miraculous aspect of the humiliation they will face: this great army will be defeated *in a single day* (10:17).

However, the prophet warns his fellow Israelites that the Assyrians will arrive at the gates of Jerusalem, after taking several Judean cities on the way (10:28-32). The Lord is using them as his instrument to achieve his goal. He is carrying out his righteous judgment on the sins of Judah (10:23; see 3:1-26). But he is also using this invasion to bring the population of Jerusalem, the *survivors* of the invasion, back to himself (**10:20a**). They had called on Assyria for aid, but the one who was supposed to help them had turned against them (**10:20b**). But God promises that a *remnant will return* (**10:21-22**) – in Hebrew, 'shear jas-hub', which is also the name given to one of Isaiah's sons (7:3). This renewed confidence in the Lord means that they will *no longer rely on him who struck them down* (10:20b; 2 Kgs 18:13-19:19).

These words should strike a chord with us in Africa. Despite the fight for independence, we remain strangely fascinated by those who formerly enslaved us. We have not yet broken free of our emotional and financial ties to the old colonial powers. It is now time for the African continent to take the initiative and work for its own development.

When the remnant have returned to the Lord, he will intervene. The Assyrians who have wielded a *rod* and *club* (**10:24**) will suddenly find themselves suffering under God's *whip* and *staff* (**10:26**). God will defeat them as easily and completely as he did when he gave Gideon victory over the Midianites at *the rock of Oreb* (see also 9:4; Judg 6:25). He will show his power against them just as he did when he miraculously rescued the Israelites from the *club* of their Egyptian oppressors (Exod 14). Isaiah announces a time of abundance when the people will be *fat* and will no longer be enslaved by others (**10:27**).

11:1-12:6 Renewal of David's line

The Lord's intervention has been described as being like an axe that will lay low the great trees of the forest (10:33-34). The trees he will fell include Assyria and Samaria. Judah, too, will suffer destruction, but *the stump of Jesse* (David's father – Ruth 4:22; 1 Sam 16:1), that is, all that remains of the tree of Judah, will not be dead. It will send out a new *shoot* that will grow strongly and produce a legitimate leader worthy of the Davidic line (**11:1**). In its historical context, this 'shoot' is King Hezekiah, who demonstrates trust in God during the Assyrian invasion (37:1-20; 2 Kgs 19:1-19).

But the description of the perfect reign of this proph-esied king makes it clear that he is no human king. This shoot must be the promised messiah. For Christians, it is highly significant that the word translated 'shoot' is *netzer* in Hebrew, the same word from which we get the adjective 'Nazarene' (Matt 2:23).

This king receives *the Spirit of the Lord*, a sign that he has been specially chosen by God (**11:2**; see also 1 Sam 10:6; Luke 3:21-22). This passage lists three characteristics of a person filled with this Spirit: *wisdom and understanding* (Gen 41:39; Exod 31:2-3; 1 Kgs 3:12; Eccl 2:26), abundant *counsel* and *power* (Judg 15:14; Dan 5:14), and *knowledge* and *the fear of the Lord* (Ps 111:10).

The presence of the Spirit and especially *the fear of the Lord* and faithfulness to God will produce *righteousness* and a commitment to *justice* (**11:3-5**). This king will not be guilty of the failures of justice that undermine political regimes. He will not be distracted by appearances and rumours, nor will he be *indifferent to the poor*.

The prophet Hosea vividly describes a world where the Lord is not known (Hos 4:1-6). But in the reign of the messiah, the presence of the Spirit and, in particu-lar, *the knowledge of the Lord* will bring peace (**11:9**). The 'knowledge' referred to here is presented as being as deep and all-pervading as the water of the sea, an image that expresses the great intimacy of the relationship with God.

Isaiah uses other striking pictures to illustrate the peace of this reign. He shows us carnivorous animals like wolves, leopards, lions and bears living peacefully alongside the lambs, goats and calves that would normally be their prey. A child can safely move and play among these ferocious animals and deadly snakes (**11:6-8**). This situation is so idyllic that most commentators see it as also symbolizing the reconciliation brought about by Christ and the paradise to come (Mark 1:13; Luke 2:14; John 20:19; Rev 21:1-4).

In that day (see comments on 4:2), Israel, through *the Root of Jesse*, will again become a refuge and a testimony to the nations. Once again, we are reminded of the period of King Solomon when people travelled long distances to come to Jerusalem to seek his wisdom (see comments on 2:1-4). The king is a rallying point (**11:11-12**) and a mediator (**11:13**). He will attract people from foreign nations and put an end to the fierce rivalry between the tribes of Ephraim and Judah (**11:14**; Hos 1:10-11). If the prophecy is under-stood as being interpretable on more than one level, it can be argued that this prophecy is fulfilled in the church, in which there should be no distinction between races, nations and tribes (Gal 3:28).

The Yombe (DRC) say, *tukula kumbusa mvilasananga* ['unity makes for power' or 'two are worth more than one'] (Eccl 4:9-12). Re-establishing unity makes for secure bor-ders. The traditional enemies of Israel will be overcome (11:14). Faithfulness to God was generally recognized as the source of security for the kingdoms of Israel and Judah (2 Sam 7:18-8:18; 2 Chr 17:3-11).

Memories play a very important role in constructing a community. Thus Isaiah compares the provision God will make to allow his dispersed people to return with the way he intervened to enable them to cross the Red Sea at the exodus (**11:15-16**; Exod 14:21-31). Just as Moses rejoiced with a song after that miracle (Exod 15:1-18), so the peo-ple will break into song about what the Lord has done for them (**12:1**). This tradition of song was deeply rooted in the hearts of the people of Israel (Judg 5:1-31; 2 Sam 6:14-15; Luke 1:46-55, 67-79). It is also common in African culture, which often expresses itself through singing and dancing.

The song of thanksgiving serves two purposes. First, it expresses faith in God as the source of salvation (John 4:14; 1 Cor 10:4; Rev 7:17). Isaiah had previously used his sons' names to convey a message (7:3; 8:3; 10:21), but now he plays on the significance of his own name, 'Isaiah', which means *God is my salvation* (**12:2**).

In the second place, the song of thanksgiving is a testimony. In an arid land, the discovery of a source of water is very good news (**12:3**). It should not be selfishly hidden. Thus by their song, the people make the God of salvation known *among the nations* and *to all the world* (**12:4-6**). The mission of God's people is to be a witness to the nations. Instituting a new covenant and a new people, Jesus encouraged his disciples to go to the nations (Matt 28:19-20; Acts 1:8; 9:15) just as he had come from heaven to live among them (John 1:10-12; Phil 2:5-8).

After this song, the prophet does indeed turn to address the nations.

13:1-14:23 Prophecy against Babylon

The start of a new section of the book is indicated by the repetition of the information given in 1:1 – except that this time the oracle no longer focuses solely on the fate of Judah and Ephraim but instead turns to the fate of the then-known world. The formal introduction of the section underscores the seriousness of its contents.

Isaiah's contemporaries may have been surprised that he gave an *oracle concerning Babylon* (**13:1**). In Isaiah's day, it was Assyria and not Babylon that represented a direct threat to Israel (39:1-9; 2 Kgs 20:12-19). However, the prophet received the revelation that Babylon would rise to become a great power, as arrogant as the Assyrians had been (**13:11b**). He also foresaw that Israel would be taken into captivity and that the Lord would have compassion on them and bring them back to *their own land* (14:1-2).

God is massing an invading army at the gates of Babylon (**13:2**). He has summoned them from *faraway lands* (**13:5**) and calls them *my holy ones* (**13:3**). By this he does not mean that the soldiers are necessarily righteous people, but rather that this is an army he has set aside to be the instrument to implement his holy will. Later, he identifies the Medes as the ones who will bring about the downfall of the Babylonian Empire (13:17; Dan 5:25-31).

The Lord positions himself as the general of the army that will *carry out my wrath* (13:3-4). The sound of the army mustering ... *for war* is *like that of a great multitude ... an uproar ... like nations massing together* (13:3-4). Babylon's population is overcome with *terror* even before the hostilities begin (**13:6b-8**).

Unfortunately Africans are all too familiar with this type of fear as rebels and dictators direct their militias against civilian targets. But, unlike such armies, God is not seeking to oppress the weak in order to consolidate or seize power. Rather, he is out to render justice, punishing the arrogant and the wicked (**13:11a**). He is taking the role of the avenger of blood (Gen 9:5; Num 35:16-19).

Once again, Isaiah speaks of *the day of the Lord* (see comments on 4:2). Once again, this is a terrible day for the guilty (**13:6a**, **9**, **13**) and a day of rejoicing for God's people (**14:1**).

The disappearance from view of the heavenly bodies is a direct attack on the political, religious and scientific pride of Babylon, which was known for its study and worship of the stars (Dan 2:27-28; 4:3-6). The point that the Lord is making is that he is master of his creation, the one who controls it and who can destroy it if he so chooses (13:10-11)

The Babylonians are warned to expect the calamities that accompany all war. First, the prophet repeats the point he made in 4:1: war always destroys more men than it does women and children. Men become scarce and precious – like *gold* (**13:12**). Other calamities linked to war are the scattering of the population, murder and sexual abuse (**13:14-15**, **16b**).

The Medes who conquer the Babylonians *do not care for silver* or *gold* (**13:17**). Consequently they cannot be corrupted or persuaded by bribery to stop their conquest. What a contrast with the way Babylon coveted the riches of the palaces and temple of Jerusalem (39:1-6; 2 Kgs 20:13; 25:13-17; Dan 5:1-4). Nor do the Medes understand pity – not even for small children (**13:16a**, **18**).

The city of Babylon could be called *the jewel of the nations* because of its magnificent architecture, which included one of the seven wonders of the ancient world – the hanging gardens (**13:19**; Dan 4:28). But its beauty will not influence the Lord. He will treat it the same way that he treated Sodom and Gomorrah, cities not noted for refinement (1:9-10; Gen 19:1-29). Like Jericho of old (Josh 6:26), Babylon will be abandoned and no one will live there (**13:20-22**).

The reason for the fall of Babylon will be God's *compassion* on Israel. He will be touched by the repentant attitude of the generation in exile (Ps 103:13-14; Lam 3:22-23). The statement *once again he will choose Israel* (**14:1a**) refers back to the first covenant between God and his people (Deut 7:7-8). It also introduces the idea of a new covenant that will be proclaimed by Jeremiah and will be fully realized in Jesus Christ (Jer 31:31-34; Matt 26:27-28; John 4:22-24; Heb 8:8-13). This new covenant will include foreigners who will *unite with the house of Jacob* (**14:1b**). Their former oppressors will become the servants of Israel (**14:2**).

For reasons of ethnic survival, the Jews who returned from exile did not welcome foreigners but excluded them (Ezra 10:10-12; Neh 13:23-31). Yet foreigners would ultimately come to share in the covenant through the work of Jesus Christ (Rom 1:14-17; 3:21-31; Eph 2:11-18).

Remembering what God has done for them is of the utmost importance for his people. The best time for remembering is often during a time of rest – which is one reason why God instituted the Sabbath (Deut 5:15). When the people do enter God's rest after their deliverance from Babylon, they will need to remember that he has delivered them from a tyrant. That is why they will *take up this taunt against the king of Babylon* (**14:3-4a**).

The end of *suffering* and *cruel bondage* is marked by an exclamation of surprise and delight: *How the oppressor has come to an end!* (**14:4b**, 12). Often this expression is used to signal grief (2 Sam 1:25, 27; Lam 1:1), but no one grieves the fall of one who has oppressed *all the lands* (**14:7**). The oppressor, swollen with power and success, may have never imagined that such an end was possible, but the Lord can break the one who *subdued nations* (**14:5-6**). Only the kingdom of God is to last for ever (35:10). His kingdom manifests itself on earth through the church (Matt 16:17-19; John 18:33-37). It will be characterized by *relief from suffering* (14:3), 'quietness' (30:15) and 'joy' (12:1-6), which are all signs of the intervention and presence of God. The African church should embody these three benefits in our often-troubled countries.

To describe the end of the tyrant, Isaiah returns to the image of the *woodsman* and the forest, which he used in 10:33 and which is also used in Daniel 4:4-27. Now the *pine trees and the cedars* (**14:8**) symbolize the kings of the nations who had previously been subjected to the Babylonian axe. Once again, God's tool, having served its purpose, is laid low (10:15).

Remembering our ancestors is an important part of our spiritual life (see comments on 8:19-21; Heb 11:4-12:1). But this is not the case for tyrants who have survived by killing all those who could oppose them. Death may be a gain for a Christian (Phil 1:21), but it is not so for a tyrant. When he enters the place of the dead, his victims rejoice at his fall. They greet him and judge him in the same way an African village would judge someone who had thought himself too important to associate with them (**14:9-10**). The tyrant is mortal, just like everyone else (**14:11**). That is why we should neither trust nor fear tyrants (2:22; 7:4-5; Ps 103:13-16; Matt 10:28).

Some commentators think that at this point Isaiah ceases to speak about the overthrow of the earthly Babylon. They argue that 14:12-15 describes the fall of Satan. In support of this, they link the reference to him as the *morning star* (in Latin, 'Lucifer'– **14:12**) with Paul's comment that Satan can disguise himself as 'an angel of light' (2 Cor 11:14) and with Jesus' words about having seen Satan fall from heaven (Luke 10:18). But against them we have to point out that a 'star' is not necessarily a symbol of the devil. The same image is used when speaking of the Jewish Messiah (Num 24:17), Jewish believers (Dan 12:3) and Christ (Luke 1:78-79; 2 Pet 1:19). Not only that, but Christians are called to shed light (Matt 5:14-16; Phil 2:15).

It seems more likely that Isaiah is still speaking about Babylon here. The Babylonians worshipped the heavenly bodies (see 13:10) and placed great faith in astrologers (Dan 4:3-7). Thus in exalting himself *above the stars of God*, this man seems to have been thinking that he was one of his pantheon of gods, and possibly even superior to them. He claimed, *I will sit enthroned … on the utmost heights of the sacred mountain* (**14:13**). But no one can be *like the Most High* (**14:14**). To think that one can be like him is a supreme example of pride and idolatrous folly.

To drive home the stupidity of such thinking, Isaiah again shows us the dead inspecting the new arrival who had taken himself for God and who had once seemed invincible (**14:16-17**; see 14: 9-10). Had they known them, they might have sung the words of the Congolese musician Luambo Makiadi Franco: *Ba botoli ye tonga* ['the needle of power was snatched from him'].

This king will not even have a tomb worthy of his station (**14:18-20a**). This was the fate of unfaithful kings (see, for example, 2 Chr 28:27). His wickedness had led to the destruction of his country and the loss of his people, who might have mourned him. The prophet would have agreed with the Malian writer Moussa Konate: 'Since you are in power, nothing works any longer. You have deceived us with sweet words … you have brought the night.' Leaders who serve their own interests and harm those for whom they are responsible will come to a bad end.

The sins of the Babylonians are visited on their children. This may seem a contradiction of the principle of individual responsibility for sin announced by Jeremiah and Ezekiel (Jer 31:29-30; Ezek 18:1-3). Here, however, the Lord has a precise goal: to put an end once and for all to the spirit of conquest of the Babylonians (**14:20b-22**). Children inherit both the good and evil consequences of their parents' behaviour. Thus the wise teach that 'righteousness exalts a nation, but sin is a disgrace to any people' (Prov 14:34).

God will decide to make a final end of Babylon, sweeping *her with the broom of destruction* (**14:23**; see also 13:20-22). The official and irrevocable nature of this sentence is underscored by the repetition that these are the words of *the Lord Almighty* (14:22, 23).

14:24-27 Prophecy against Assyria

The prophecy against Assyria is much shorter than the one against Babylon, possibly because Isaiah has already dealt with the fall of Assyria (**14:24**; 10:5-34). Once again, he uses the image of a broken *yoke* to symbolize deliverance from oppression (**14:25**; 10:27). This prophecy was fulfilled during Hezekiah's reign (37:36-38).

The specific emphasis of the present passage comes from its insistence on the firmness of God's purpose. What he says concerns *the whole world* and *all nations* (**14:26**). No one can thwart his plans (**14:27**). His decisions are final (Prov 16:1-2). Because of this, and because we can trust him to stand by his word, we can have confidence in his covenant with us. God's faithfulness means that his word will never pass away (see Matt 5:17-18).

14:28-32 Prophecy against the Philistines

King Ahaz had been at war with the Philistines, who had made some successful incursions into Judah (2 Chr 28:18). They would have rejoiced to hear of the death of their enemy (**14:28**). But the prophet warns them that the next king will be even stronger. Hezekiah, the 'shoot' from the 'stump' (11:1) is going to completely dominate the Philistines (2 Kgs 18:8). It may seem strange that Isaiah uses the image of a *viper* to represent Judah's line (**14:29**). Indeed in the Christian culture, snakes represent evil because of the story of the fall (Gen 3:1-16). However, in the Bible, snakes also represent a saviour (Num 21:6-8; John 3:14-15).

We must beware of turning an image or an animal into an idol. Hezekiah was aware of this danger when he destroyed the serpent that Moses had made because it had become an object of worship (2 Kgs 18:4). African tradition sometimes contributes to this when it allows people to take certain animals as totems and to seek to assume their characteristics with a view to controlling others. Thus Jonas Savimbi in Angola was known as *o galo que voa* ['the rooster that flies'] and President Mobutu of Zaire (now DRC) as *nkoyi mobali* ['the leopard-man'].

The *poorest of the poor* (literally, 'the firstborn of the poor') and the *needy* are the people of Judah. Once peace is restored, their young men will no longer have to serve in the army and will be able to devote themselves to raising herds in safety (**14:30a**). But the Philistines, by contrast, will experience famine and death (**14:30b**). No one will escape, whether the leaders who would have assembled at the *gate* in times of peace (Gen 19:1; Ruth 4:1-2; Job 29:7-25) or the people of the *city*. The Assyrians will advance *from the north* and will overrun their region (**14:31**).

Isaiah thus encourages Judah not to enter into any alliance with the Philistines when the Assyrians invade. The Philistine *envoys* must be told that Judah is safer trusting in God than in any alliance with a pagan nation (**14:32**).

15:1-16:14 Prophecy against Moab

Two parallel sentences indicate that the two main cities of Moab will both suffer the same fate: rapid destruction (**15:1**). The Moabite people will be left humiliated and mourning, as shown by their wailing and their physical appearance (**15:2-4a**; Gen 37:33-34). The sudden misfortune will terrify the army and the people will flee (**15:4b, 5b**).

The drying up of the streams and withering of the grass may echo the Psalms' description of the end of the wicked (**15:6-7**) and the futility of human life (Pss 37:2; 103:15). But they may also be a literal description of an environmental disaster that accompanies the invasion.

The waters of *Nimrim* have failed and those of *Dimon* are *full of blood* (**15:9a**). The blood flows from a massacre, but the words would also have reminded the Israelites of God's divine intervention in Exodus 7:17. It is possible that

Dimon is the same place as the *Dibon* referred to in 15:2. The prophet may have chosen to use a different spelling to pun on the similarity between the name and *dam*, the Hebrew word for blood.

The last misfortune to strike Moab is a *lion*, which probably represents Judah (**15:9b**; Gen 49:9). This would explain the tribute in lambs, food of lions, paid to *the Daughter of Zion* (**16:1**). But the offering of lambs also symbolizes the need for salvation (53:6-7; see Lev 9:3; John 1:29).

Whereas the 'Daughter of Zion' seems confident, *the women of Moab* who, like African mothers, are symbols of life, identity, stability and tenderness, have become like helpless young birds *pushed from the nest* (**16:2**; see also Prov 27:8). They are at the mercy of any man.

Through Isaiah, the Lord expresses his compassion for the misfortune of the Moabites. His *heart cries out* and *laments* her fate (**15:5a**; 16:11). He asks the king of Judah to welcome the refugees from Moab (16:3-4). By speaking of the king as *one from the house of David,* he may be reminding him that King David's grandfather was the son of a Moabite refugee (Ruth 1:16; 4:13, 17). This call to hospitality reminds us that the Jewish people saw hospitality as a sacred duty (Gen 18:1-5; Exod 22:21-23; 23:9; Matt 11:28; Luke 24:28-29). African Christians, too, should welcome strangers, both because it is part of our tradition and because the Apostle Paul urges Christians to practise hospitality (Heb 13:1-3).

The Lord identifies even with the Moabites, whom he describes as *my refugees* (**16:4a**, HCSB). Whatever the state of a person's spirit, God remains a compassionate father (Ps 68:6; Luke 15:11-32). God tells the king that he has no reason to be afraid to do good to the Moabites, because the one who has devastated their land is no more (**16:4b**). He is probably referring to the Assyrians, who will be stopped at the gates of Jerusalem (10:5-34).

The king should show evidence of kindness. He should not follow the example of Lamech (Gen 4:23-24), and seek revenge against this traditional adversary. God exhorts him to follow moral principles rather than the Machiavellian principle of shedding the blood of his enemies so as to solidify his throne in the eyes of the people. It is in this way that he will be blessed. He will *be established,* and will be like Solomon in being *one who in judging seeks justice* (**16:5**).

But Moab cannot hope to be established. There is a lesson to be learned from the fact that her *overweening pride* had led to her fall and lamentation (**16:6-7**). The king of Judah should take note of why the judgement is coming on the Moabites and be warned. Pride leads to a fall (Dan 4; 1 Pet 5:5-6) and has done so for many leaders, particularly in Africa, where leaders easily slide into megalomania.

But despite Moab's sins, the Lord does not dismiss the nation. It is possible that he remembers how Abraham had prayed for his nephew Lot (Gen 18:20-33), who became the ancestor of the Moabites (19:15-38). He may also have remembered that Ruth, a Moabite, was David's great-grand-mother (Ruth 4:13-17). Whatever the case, these people, like the people of Judah, have the right to a song like the song of the vineyard (**16:8-10**; see 5:1-7). Once again we see the tears of the vineyard owner over his fruitful vine that turns bad. Yet because Moab has chosen idolatry, all the tears and prayers are in vain (**16:12**).

Despite his attachment to these people and his sorrow at their suffering, the Lord has decided to punish the Moabites. But as another indication of his concern for them, he gives them a precise date for when this prophecy will be fulfilled. Those in Moab who listen to God's prophet will have time to escape the coming disaster. The fact that the *three years* are described as counted the way *a servant bound by contract would count them* gives these years a legal reality, indicating that they are not approximate or symbolic but are to be measured in the normal human way (**16:14a**).

There will be survivors from Moab, but they will be *very few and feeble* (**16:14b**). By contrast, the remnant of Israel will become stronger (14:1-2, 30; 15:9). Their different fates are due to the logic of growth in the Bible, where those who are faithful to God experience his blessing and grow stronger (Gen 1:28; 17:1-2; Acts 2:47).

17:1-14 Prophecy against Damascus and Ephraim

The prophet returns to the shameful alliance between the northern kingdom (*Ephraim*), and Syria (*Damascus*), and their coming destruction by Assyria (see comments on 7:1-25). They will both suffer the same fate (**17:1-3**).

However, the prophet then concentrates on the future of Ephraim. Even if the northern kingdom has become like the idolatrous foreign nations, it too is descended from Jacob (**17:4**). But the use of that name reminds us of the ambivalent character of Israel's ancestor. He stole his brother Esau's birthright (Gen 25:29-34) and blessing (Gen 27:1-40) and tricked his father-in-law Laban (Gen 30:25-43). But he received divine grace in spite of everything (see also Hos 12:3-8, 13-14).

We need to see our own ancestors with similar honesty. We need to recognize the intellectual, spiritual and perhaps even moral weaknesses of our ancestors while at the same time retaining a deep respect for them.

As with Moab (16:14), only a small remnant of Ephraim will survive. The prophet describes what he means by introducing three agricultural images, each introduced by *as when* (**17:5-6**). He knows how to speak to his contemporaries using pictures from their daily life, just as Jesus did with his parables (see Matt 20:1-16).

In their crisis, the Moabites turned to their idols (16:12). However, when disaster strikes the remnant of Israel, the Israelites will leave their idols and turn toward *their Maker – the Holy One of Israel* who does not put up with impurity

(**17:7-8**; Exod 33:20; 2 Sam 6:6-7; Rev 4:8). Suffering can teach lessons that can turn individuals and even whole nations back to the right path.

The *strong cities* that were the pride of the North (9:9-10) are now abandoned (**17:9**). These useless fortresses were set up without any regard for the true source of protection: *God your Saviour ... the Rock, your fortress* (**17:10a**). The Law and the Psalms clearly teach that those who forget the Lord (51:13; Deut 8:11; 32:15; Ezek 22:12) and do not put their trust in him (26:1-4; Ps 18:3, 32) are headed for disaster. Christians, too, must take care not to discard God when making plans, for as the English proverb says, 'Man proposes, God disposes' (see also Prov 16:9; Jas 4:13-16).

Once again, Isaiah turns to the world of agriculture. He uses the image of *imported vines* to show Israel the uselessness of placing its confidence in pagan nations and their gods (**17:10b-11**). Israel had not known enough to protect itself against weeds, and it would not reap the harvest it had hoped for (Matt 13:24-30). The other nations may *rage* and create an *uproar*, but the Israelites should not fear them because God can defeat these nations easily and rapidly, blowing them away like straw or chaff in the wind (**17:12-14**; see also Ps 1:4).

18:1-7 Prophecy against Ethiopia

Ethiopia, or *Cush*, which the prophet addresses next, was not the same as modern Ethiopia. It covered a much larger area, reaching from the Congo basin to Egypt, which was sometimes ruled by Cush. It can therefore be said without exaggeration that the prophet is here speaking to black Africa. He pays it great attention, and prophesies that its future will resemble that of God's people.

First, the prophet draws an impressive picture of Ethiopia, twice describing the natural environment, the physical characteristics of the people and their economic and military power (**18:1-3**, 7; see also 2 Chr 14:9). What a contrast between such power and riches and Africa's situation today! Yet while we often have good reason to feel sorry for ourselves because of the havoc wrought by imperialism, we need to remember that it is not only the whites who have practised oppression. Isaiah's words shows that tall and muscular blacks were also oppressors many hundreds of years ago. We need to work to make Africa rise to what it was in the past – but not by using the same tactics.

As for the Lord, he is not impressed by human power. He remains unmoved, unperturbed (**18:4**). In his own time, he will *cut down* the Ethiopian empire as easily as a farmer prunes a grapevine (**18:5**). The Ethiopians will lose their sovereignty and will be oppressed and exploited by other powers, just as still happens today in Africa (**18:6**).

But Ethiopia is not forgotten, and the second reference to it is still more important than the first one. Like the Israelites (17:7), Africa will turn to God in its misery (see comments on 4:2) and its former glory will be restored (**18:7**). What a message of hope for our continent!

19:1-25 Prophecy against Egypt

The Lord returns to Egypt as he left it. Then he had been in the cloud that guided and protected the people of Israel; now he returns, riding a *swift cloud* (**19:1**; Exod 13:21-22). Reminded of their bad memories of those days, the Egyptians' hearts will *melt within them*. Their idols are still as powerless as they were in the confrontation between Moses and Pharaoh's magicians (Exod 8:16-19), and thus they *tremble* before the true God. The difference between the previous encounter and this one is that then God had spoken through Moses and Aaron; this time he uses no intermediary.

The first step in God's battle strategy is to destroy the unity of Egypt (see Mark 3:24). The country will be plunged into a bitter civil war (**19:2**). It will find itself weakened and losing confidence in its own wisdom as God brings *their plans to nothing* (**19:3**). But rather than turning to the Lord, the people will turn to occult practices. The sensible African from Madagascar, Congo or Cote d'Ivoire knows full well that such practices are powerless and can do nothing to calm a civil war. God is the only one who is capable of bringing Africans together (18:7).

Weak and divided, the Egyptians can do nothing when the Assyrian generals and their king, these instruments of divine anger, invade the country (**19:4**; 10:5-6; 20:1-4).

The Lord then strikes at the heart of Egypt, the Nile. The kingdom's whole economy depended on that river, and it was worshipped as a god. But the river dries up (**19:5-6**). The producers of Egypt's wealth, the farmers (**19:7**), fishermen (**19:8**) and weavers (**19:9**), are hard hit. The economic crisis leaves both the salaried overseers and the workers without income (**19:10**).

God reproaches Pharaoh's advisors for not discerning that he is behind this crisis (**19:11-12**). He uses terms similar to those directed at Ephraim's leaders as he accuses them of leading the people astray (**19:13**, **15**; see 9:13-15). But this time, the Lord pushes them on in their waywardness, making them drunk with folly (**19:14**). God intervenes in the deepest part of the human personality in order to guide wisely (Gen 28:10-22) or to induce those who harden their hearts against him into further wrong (Exod 4:21; 1 Kgs 12:15-16; 22:15-23).

But this judgment is not the end of the story. Isaiah moves on from preaching about the geopolitical situation of his day to speak of *that day*, a future time when God will show grace to Egypt (19:16, 18, 19, 23, 24; see comments on 4:2).

The statement *the Egyptians will be like women. They will shudder...* is not a further description of judgment, as we might think at first glance (**19:16**). Rather, it is the first step on the road to restoration, for 'the fear of the Lord is

the beginning of knowledge' (Prov 1:7). We must admit that women are often wiser than men in this regard.

This new fear of the Lord develops into fear of and submission to Judah, the symbol of God's presence (**19:17**). To show the extent of the change, Isaiah uses images of conquest. The conquered people adopt the language of their conquerors, and the victors erect a monument to commemorate the victory (**19:18-19**). But this will not be an oppressive conquest, for the Lord will *send them a saviour and defender* (**19:20**).

The use of the word 'know' in the statement *the Lord shall be known to Egypt, and the Egyptians shall know the Lord* (**19:21a**, KJV) is significant, for the verb 'to know' was sometimes used to refer to the relations between a man and a woman (Gen 4:1, KJV). Isaiah may thus be suggesting that the Egyptians are married to God. Paul later uses this same image to describe the relationship between Jesus Christ and the church (2 Cor 11:2). Becoming a couple implies an element of reciprocity, with each person bringing something to the relationship. In this case, Egypt brings sacrifices and genuine vows (**19:21b**), while God brings healing (**19:22**).

Vertical reconciliation with God leads to horizontal reconciliation between warring nations (**19:23-24**). The Lord confirms this prophecy by publicly announcing that in the future he will adopt Egypt, speaking of it as *my people*, the same form of address as he uses for Israel (Hos 11:1-3). He will no longer regard Assyria as simply a tool (10:5-6), but as *my handiwork* (**19:25**).

20:1-6 The fall of Ethiopia and Egypt

After prophesying the return to God and the restoration of Ethiopia (18:7), the grace shown to Egypt and the reconciliation with Assyria (19:21-25), Isaiah returns to the realities of his own time. He uses the Assyrian attack on Ashdod, a Philistine city that was closely allied with Egypt (**20:1**), as an opportunity to announce the imminent defeat of Egypt and Ethiopia by Assyria and the deportation that will follow (**20:4**).

At God's command, Isaiah communicates his message by word and action, stripping off most of his clothes and going barefoot, as if he himself were prisoner (**20:2**; compare 8:1-4). He identifies with those who will be deported and suffers their humiliation (20:2-3). He was not like some in Africa who claim to be prophets and use their prestigious status to accumulate wealth with minimum effort. The reality of a prophet's life is very different. God asked his *servant* Isaiah to take on the suffering of his contemporaries (**20:3**) and he called on Hosea and Ezekiel to experience the suffering of God (Hos 1:2-3; Ezek 24:16-24). The supreme example of the cost of serving God by identifying with his people is Christ himself (John 1:29).

Those who witness this humiliation will be reminded that there is no point in trusting in foreign alliances for safety (**20:5-6**).

21:1-10 The fall of Babylon

Assyria was located in northern Mesopotamia, while Babylon was in the south. Thus even though the city itself was far from the sea (that is, the Persian Gulf) the whole area could be called *The Desert by the Sea* (**21:1a**). Isaiah has already proclaimed the future destruction of this city (13:1-14:23). Here he briefly repeats the crimes of which it stands accused: cruelty and idolatry (**21:2a, 9b**). He again announces the unavoidable advance of the Medes and Persians, who are well armed, well ordered and as uncontrollable as a *whirlwind* (**21:1b, 2b, 7, 9a**).

Like the preceding section (20:1-6), this one throws light on the task of the prophet. Isaiah shows the sensitivity to suffering of God's representative (**21:3-4**). He does not enjoy foreseeing such violence, but simply obeys a clear call from the Lord. Indeed, the command *Go* addressed to the prophet (**21:6a**) reminds us of his call in 6:9, where he was told to proclaim God's message of salvation and of judgment. God addressed the same command, 'go', to Abraham (Gen 12:1), to Balaam (Num 22:20), to Hosea (Hos 1:2) and to Jonah (Jonah 1:2; 3:2). That command had to be obeyed, even when in God's sovereignty it brought suffering, for the consequences of disobedience would be even more terrible.

In this section, the role of a prophet is said to be like that of a *lookout* or 'watchman' (**21:6b**; Ezek 3:17). Serving in this position is very tiring because it requires constant vigilance to observe the signs of the time (**21:8**; see also 20:1-6). As God's representative, Isaiah focused on only two things: the words God had spoken to him and the words that God was recorded to have said in the past (**21:10**; 8:20; Deut 27–28), and how the events and behaviour of the time related to these messages from God. His focus on God surprised listeners (Mark 6:2-6; Luke 5:15, 26; John 7:45-46) and resulted in the prophet either being loved by the oppressed (Mark 6:30-34) or detested by the oppressors (1 Kgs 18:1-19:18; Mark 6:14-29).

21:11-17 Prophecy against Edom and Arabia

After this aside on the role of the prophet, Isaiah returns to his tour of the nations. This prophecy is introduced as an *oracle concerning Dumah* (**21:11a**). There is uncertainty about where Dumah was, or whether this is simply a word play on the similarity between the word for 'silence' and the word for 'Edom'. However, *Seir* is easily identifiable and indicates that this prophecy concerns the Edomites, the descendants of Esau (Gen 32:3). This nation is also addressed in the book of the prophet Obadiah.

The Edomites ask the prophet, who is God's watchman (21:6), when the misfortune, *the night*, will arrive (**21:11b**).

The anticipated disaster may be the Assyrian invasion of the area (8:1-10:34). The prophet replies that *morning* is coming as well as *night*. However, to experience the day, the Edomites need to *come back* or *return* (kjv) to God; that is, they need to be converted (**21:12**; 37:15-38). There is no other way to escape *the night* (see 38:16).

The prophecy directed against Edom is followed by one directed against Arabia (21:13-17). The *Dedanites, Tema* and *Kedar* clearly refer to tribes who lived in this region (Gen 25:3, 13, 15). The message to them is similar to the prophecy against Moab (**21:16-17**; 15:1-16:14). Once again, there is a reference to years as counted by *a servant bound by contract,* implying technical precision in the timeline of divine punishment, but allowing the careful reader to prepare for what is coming. The Arabians are also given the assurance of a small group of survivors, a sign of decline but also of God's mercy (see 16:13-14).

22:1-25 Prophecy against Jerusalem

Judah is placed on the same plane as all the other nations against which Isaiah has prophesied. But in this prophecy against Jerusalem, he refers to it as *the Valley of Vision* (**22:1a**). This is confusing, because Jerusalem is in fact situated on a hill, and has been repeatedly described as being on a mountain (for example, in 2:3). It may be that in his condemnation of the city, the prophet is saying that it is not sitting on a mountain from which it can clearly see what is approaching. Rather, it is in a valley, where the 'vision' on which it prides itself is reduced so that it does not see its own danger. Alternatively, Isaiah may be thinking of the various valleys that lay around the hill on which the city was situated.

Other nations are facing misfortune, but the people of Jerusalem are at ease and rejoicing. God questions them ironically about their behaviour, knowing that their confidence will be turned to shame (**22:1b-2a**). When their city comes under siege, their officers will flee the battle, as did indeed happen during the siege of Jerusalem by the Babylonians (**22:2b-3**; 2 Kgs 25:4).

The celebrations of the people are contrasted with God's sadness. He is already in mourning for *the daughter of my people* (**22:4b**, kjv). The book of Jeremiah has a similar lament for the city (Jer 8:19-23). God considers the inhabitants of Judah his 'children' (1:2) and has a special place in his affection for this city, which he speaks of as his little daughter.

God's sadness is so great that he prefers to isolate himself in order to mourn (**22:4a**). Such an attitude is striking, for in both the Jewish culture of that day and in Africa today, the loss of a loved one is mourned in company with the whole community.

Despite his affection and his sadness, the Lord must act against the sin of the people (**22:5, 14**). Only when the walls of Jerusalem are flattened (2 Kgs 25:10) will the people turn to him. The people's *crying out to the mountains* reminds us of Psalm 121, with its insistence that God is our only source of protection. But the people have forgotten this. Instead, faced with the invasion from Mesopotamia, referred to here as *Elam* (**22:6-8a**), the people prefer to trust their own strength (**22:8b**). They look to the *Palace of the Forest,* that is, to the king's palace where the weapons were stored (1 Kgs 7:2; 10:16-17). They have forgotten that they cannot win by 'might nor by power' (Zech 4:6).

The people trust not only in their weapons but also in their walls and their reserves of water (**22:9-11a**). They are prepared to tear down people's houses in order to maintain these. But God dismisses all these human arrangements for security; his sovereign plan of destruction was laid down *long ago* (**22:11b**). He had watched similar vain activity by the people of the city of Samaria (9:8-10).

God had been alone in mourning the coming destruction of the city, but now he calls the people to do so too, and to repent of their sin (**22:12**). But the inhabitants of Jerusalem remain unconcerned and continue their celebrations (**22:13**; see 22:2). Without repentance there can be no forgiveness, and so the Lord pursues his plan against Jerusalem (**22:14**).

Two high officials in the service of King Hezekiah (36:11, 22) provide ideal examples of the attitudes Isaiah has been denouncing and of the attitudes that God favours. The first is *Shebna,* who is only looking out for his own interests. He signals his power and prestige by building himself a magnificent tomb and piling up riches, including *splendid chariots* (**22:15-16**, **18b**). (In this he is similar to those today who flaunt the cars they own.) Shebna clearly has no concern for the well-being of the people. God will punish him for this and will throw him out of office, leaving him destitute (**22:18a, 19**).

Eliakim is a very different sort of leader (**22:20**). He is described in terms that show his concern for the people of God. He is described as *my servant,* just as Isaiah is (22:20; 20:3). He wears a *robe* and *sash* of office, like those worn by Aaron, the priest (Lev 8:7; Isa 11:5). Like God, he will be like a father to the people, (**22:21**; 1:2). The *key* that he carries is the symbol of ruling power (**22:22**; see Matt 16:19). His almost messianic stature is completed by the description of him as the solid *peg* on which many other things can depend (**22:23-24**).

But even such an honourable man as Eliakim will not be able to turn back God's punishment for the people's sin. They may hang on him and depend on him, but because he is human and not God, he too must fail (**22:25**).

23:1-18 The fall of Tyre and Sidon

The cities of Tyre and Sidon were built by the descendants of the Canaanites and were situated in the area today known as Lebanon. Their inhabitants were famed seafarers, who controlled the sea trade and thus the commerce of the countries along the Mediterranean coast (**23:1-2**, 8). Even Solomon had negotiated with them for supplies for building his temple (2 Chr 2:2-16). They were closely associated with Egypt, which grew the agricultural products that the inhabitants of Tyre and Sidon bought and sold (**23:3**, **5**, **10**).

It seems that the inhabitants of these cities worshipped the sea that brought them their revenues. But the Lord had created the sea, and here he speaks as if it is the sea speaking to Tyre and Sidon, denying the powers they ascribe to it (**23:4**). Isaiah has similarly spoken out against the Babylonian worship of the stars (see 13:10).

As the bankers and financiers of the day, the inhabitants of Tyre and Sidon were often decision-makers, or at least had a powerful voice in geopolitical matters. But God belittles the financial power of these cities and of their *princes* (**23:8a**). His plan is to remind them of who he is by humbling *all who are renowned on the earth* (**23:8b-9**, **11-12**). The means chosen by God to bring the inhabitants of Tyre and Sidon low are the Assyrians, who had recently defeated the Babylonians (23:12-14). (Many years later, the Babylonians would again rise to power and would also destroy Tyre – Ezek 26–28). Instead of being a place of palaces and princes, Tyre would soon be of *no account* (**23:13**).

The prophet Ezekiel also wrote a dirge about the fall of Tyre and Sidon, seeing their downfall as the consequence of their arrogance (Ezek 27–28; see Prov 16:18). His words and those of Isaiah remind us of the futility of the pride that flows from material wealth (see also Luke 12:13-21).

Africans often express their ideas and feelings in a rhythmic way and to musical accompaniment. African history was also recorded in this way. Acting like an African griot, the prophet sets the fate of Tyre to music (**23:16**). It seems that in many ways its fate seems to resemble that of Jerusalem. It, too, is labelled a prostitute (1:21; Hos 1-3). And just like Jerusalem, it will be shown mercy at the end of seventy years (23:15, 17; Jer 25:11; Dan 9:1-2). Despite the immensity and persistence of the sin, God always continues to show himself as the merciful God. It is possible that this time when the city is described as a prostitute, the term is not focusing on a sinful lifestyle but on her trade with a large number of other cities. That is why the Lord is happy to foresee the wealth of this city being used for his glory (**23:18**).

24:1-27:13 Prophecies concerning the end time

After dealing with the fate of Judah and its neighbours in the near future and showing how God will use other nations to accomplish his purpose, Isaiah speaks now of a more distant time when the Lord himself will act directly.

The four chapters that follow have certain similarities with what is known as apocalyptic literature. This type of literature uses vivid and disturbing imagery to reveal truths about the future and the divine plan. It foresees times of great trouble before the final vindication of the righteous. The major biblical apocalyptic books are Daniel and Revelation, and there are also apocalyptic chapters in the Gospels: Matthew 24, Mark 13 and Luke 21. The particular chapters of Isaiah discussed in this section are sometimes referred to as 'the little apocalypse'.

24:1-23 THE DESTRUCTION OF THE EARTH The concept of an end time or final judgment often does not figure prominently in the thinking of religious or political leaders. But God announces the coming end of almost all human life and of the earth itself (**24:1-4**). This end is the consequence of humanity's failure to obey God's laws (**24:5, 20b**).

Sin has led to the *curse* that *consumes the earth* (**24:6a**). This curse was spelled out in Deuteronomy 28:15-68, and here we see earth tormented by its effects. But God is merciful, and a *very few* will survive (**24:6b**). This is the central message of Isaiah (1:9; 4:2; 11:11, 16; 16:14; 21:17).

The cities are in ruins, the supplies of wine and beer, symbols of prosperity and celebration, have dried up and there is no sign of the joy that flows from drink (**24:7-13**). But surprisingly there is another flowering of joy, a more important joy, among the small remnant who have survived (**24:14-16a**). True joy is a gift of God and is used to praise him (Gal 5:22).

But the prophet does not join in this rejoicing. Instead he cries, *Woe to me!* He sees the horror, treachery and suffering that will precede this day of praise (**24:16b-20a**).

In destroying the earth, the Lord shows the hollowness of all the elements of human power. None of them are beyond his reach. He punishes the religious powers (*the powers in the heavens above* – see comments on 13:19; 34:4; Ps 36:9; Matt 24:29). The political powers (*the kings of the earth*) will have to account for their management of human history (**24:21-22**). *The moon* and *the sun* will pale before the glory of *the Lord Almighty* (**24:23**). While reading these words, we need to remember that all these powers have now been given to Christ (Phil 2:9-11).

25:1-26:21 THE SONG OF THE REDEEMED The account of the just judgment of sinners and the preservation of a small number of faithful believers is followed by a song of gratitude from the believers. The song begins with a statement of faith, acknowledging *O Lord you are my God* (**25:1a**). These words echo Exodus 20:2-3: 'I am the Lord your God … You shall have no other gods before me.' The prophet is affirming his commitment to God. This commitment leads him to praise God's *name*, that is, the character of God, who is the only one to be exalted.

Two things in particular justify this praise: the marvels God has done and his faithfulness in bringing about what he had said he would do (**25:1b**). This faithfulness gives believers confidence in their salvation and in carrying out the ministries to which God has called them (Jer 1:2-10; see Rom 8:28-30).

Then the Lord is praised because his actions are unique. He sets himself apart from other powers and confounds them (**25:2-3**). Unlike many powerful people in this world, he does not protect only those close to him while sacrificing the interests of others. Instead, he provides a shelter for the *poor* and *needy* (**25:4-5**). Welcome and assistance for the most underprivileged is a characteristic of God, as is most clearly demonstrated in the incarnation of Christ (Deut 10:17-19; Ps 68:6; Matt 8:2-3; 19:14; 2 Cor 1:3).

God's judgment of oppressors and the song of praise by the redeemed are followed by a celebration – a feast at which the redeemed express their joy in the Lord's victory (24:14). Wine, a sign of life and of prosperity, is abundant (**25:6-7**; contrast 24:11). Jesus, too, spoke of wine and feasting in his kingdom (Matt 22:1-4; Luke 22:18; John 2:1-11).

Not only is there joyous feasting, but the fear of death is also removed as the Lord *destroys the shroud* and wipes away *the tears from all faces* (**25:8**). These words hint at belief in the victory of life over death and the possibility of resurrection for the just. The Israelite faith tended to assume that there was no life after death (38:18-19; Ps 6:5). But the prophets (see Hos 13:14; 1 Cor 15:54-57), the Pharisees (see Acts 23:6-8) and finally Jesus and those who bore witness to his resurrection worked hard to change this outlook (see Matt 28; Mark 16:1-8; Luke 24; John 11:21-26).

Returning to the earlier proclamation of his faith (25:1), the prophet now gives a further reason for praising God: God's victory over death means that we can praise him for our salvation (**25:9**). Not only that, but all opposition to the people of God is defeated, a victory that is presented symbolically in terms of the fate of Moab (**25:10-12**; see also Num 22–25).

While Moab's walls have been destroyed, Judah is in possession of *a strong city* with *walls* and *ramparts* (**26:1**). This statement should not be interpreted as evidence of nationalistic pride. As we have said, Moab is here seen more as a symbol than as a nation. Moreover, we need to interpret these words in terms of the thinking of Isaiah's contemporaries. They did not see war as simply a conflict between two human armies. Each army carried its gods with it, and when battle was engaged, these gods were seen as engaged in the battle through the men who fought for them. Victory or defeat was dependent on the respective power of each god. The Israelites, too, thought in these terms, for they took the ark of the Lord with them when they went into battle (1 Sam 4:1-11). Thus when Isaiah celebrates Judah's glory, he is seeing it as representing God's victory over all other deities. That is why he does not describe the walls as being made of brick or stone, but as being made of the *salvation* offered by God (26:1).

The feast initiated in 25:6 is celebrated with a triumphal march into the city of the righteous whom the Lord has kept safe (**26:2**; contrast 24:12). The characteristic of this *righteous nation* is that it *keeps faith*. In other words, it has *steadfast* confidence in God despite any trials (**26:3**; 7:9; Jer 1:17-19; Matt 26:36-44; Acts 20:22-24). This steadfastness is evidence that they are indeed living as those made in the image of God, who is worthy of confidence and who keeps his promises (**26:4**; 25:1).

The victory celebrated is first of all a moral one, which has overturned a corrupt value system, raising the oppressed above *those who dwell on high* (**26:5-6**). The prophet rejoices in this because he recognizes the need for justice and knows that the only one who can bring it is God (**26:7-11**; 33:22; Ps 63:2).

Whatever humankind does that is good comes from God (**26:12-15**). Despite efforts as intense as those demanded by childbirth, humans cannot create a just society or save the world (**26:17-18**). Nor have they been able to conquer death – but the Lord can do that (**26:19**). With these words, the prophet returns to the theme of resurrection (see 25:8).

African healers, witch doctors and fearsome sorcerers try to convince their clients and their victims that they hold the power of life and death. But we need to learn from Isaiah's insistence that only the Lord has the power to bring death to sinners and to restore life to the dead. He is the master of history, the true saviour of the innocent (Job 19:25). The prophet reminds his audience of this by giving an instruction that recalls the Passover, when God sheltered his people while punishing the Egyptians (**26:20-21**; see Exod 12:21:30).

27:1-13 THE LORD AGAINST HOSTILE FORCES Isaiah continues his account of the end of time and speaks of the punishment inflicted by the Lord on *Leviathan* (**27:1**). Leviathan is the great *monster of the sea* that is mentioned in the mythology of a number of countries in the ancient Near East. It seems that here Isaiah is using it as an image that his readers would know to represent God's victory over the forces of evil that oppose him (see also Gen 3:1-6; Rev 12:7-9). On the other hand, it is also possible that the name Leviathan had come to be identified with an ordinary animal (as in Job 41, where it seems to refer to a crocodile). In that case, what the prophet is speaking of here is God's destruction of a hostile fleet of ships coming to attack Judah. The sea serpent then symbolizes ships, just as in our days a railway line might be called an 'iron snake'.

Whatever the explanation of 27:1, it is clear that the tone suddenly changes, so that God is now not acting as a judge but as a protector, whose role is celebrated in the second song of the vineyard (27:2-6). In the first song (5:1-7), the vine that symbolized Judah was only a source of frustration for its owner, the Lord. He decided therefore to abandon it to briers and thorns and ordered that no rain should fall on it. But in this second song, God is pictured as a faithful guardian who waters it and fights an ongoing battle with the weeds that seek to take over the garden (**27:2-4**). This gardener is even prepared to show mercy to the *briers and thorns* if they *make peace* with him. The sincerity of this pledge is shown by the fact that it is stated twice (**27:4**). This peace with God is obtained by faith in Jesus Christ (Rom 5:1).

Judah and the 'briers and thorns' will benefit from the work of this gardener. But so will *Israel,* here representing the northern kingdom (**27:6**). During the reign of King Hezekiah of Judah, Samaria fell and the people of the northern kingdom were deported (2 Kgs 17:5-6). This event no doubt gave God the reputation of being a hard master, as evidenced by the questions the prophet repeats (**27:7**).

The reply to this question in **27:8** is also a difficult verse to translate. The NIV takes it as a statement of the form taken by God's judgment on Israel. However, it can also be translated as *in measure, by sending it away, you contended with it* (NKJV). If this translation is correct, Isaiah is saying that God's judgment was carefully controlled. He did not destroy Israel, but simply dispersed her (27:8). This reasonable treatment corresponds to the saying 'One who loves well disciplines well.' The purpose of this firm treatment is to separate Israel from idolatry and make forgiveness possible (**27:9-10**).

God's compassion seems to be linked to humankind's *understanding* (**27:11**). In this context, 'understanding' means knowledge of God and doing what is right (Job 28:28; Jer 9:23-24). Disobedience to God's commandments atrophies our ability to respond to God's message.

Isaiah has already announced that Judah will be re-established, but he has made no similar promise to Israel, although he did say that some of those in the northern kingdom would survive (17:3-14; see 14:1). Here, he announces that God will bring them back *one by one* (**27:12**). God is concerned for each one of his children. That is why Christ can describe himself as a mother hen, wanting to gather her chicks safely under her wing (Luke 13:34).

When the redeemed Israelites return, they will come to worship in Jerusalem, a promise which implies a religious reunification of the two kingdoms (**27:13**; 10:20-23).

28:1-35:10 Prophecies about Israel and Judah

After this vision of the redeemed and of the future reunification of Judah and Israel (24:1-27:13), the prophet returns to the realities of his time and the present situation of the two kingdoms.

28:1-29 PROPHECY AGAINST EPHRAIM The first part of this prophecy (28:1-8) uses strongly contrasting images to show the difference between the northern kingdom and the Lord.

The first images concern symbols of power. Wreaths and flowers would have been worn by the wealthy and powerful as they partied, and the city of Samaria itself is described as being like a floral wreath crowning the hill on which it stood (**28:1**). But severe weather blows the beautiful wreath off the head of the one who is wearing it, leaving it to be *trampled underfoot* (**28:2-3**). Its flowers will wilt and fade, and can be easily picked by anyone who comes by (**28:4**).

By contrast, God is said to be like a *glorious crown* set with unfading precious stones (**28:5**). He will be like a *beautiful wreath*, or a *diadem of beauty* (KJV), for *the remnant of his people*, who are here probably the people of Judah. Christians, who are called to be like God, should be like his crown in terms of visibility and endurance (Matt 5:15-16; 13:20-23).

The second set of images concerns the competence of the rulers. The political and religious leaders of Ephraim are drunk, possibly because of the orgies associated with the worship of Baal or other idols. The *vomit* and *filth* noticed by the prophet fit both with excessive drinking and with Isaiah's attitude to these idols (**28:8**). He provides a long list of words that characterize their incompetent leadership of the country: they *stagger, reel*, are *befuddled* and *stumble when rendering decisions* (**28:7**; see Prov 31:4-5). But God does not stagger; he is upright and provides support (**28:6**). He responds to the drunkenness and filth of Ephraim by sending a messenger who is like cleansing *rain and a flooding downpour* (**28:2**).

We next hear the words of Israel's leaders. They are indignant that God is trying to correct their behaviour, claiming that he is treating them like little children (**28:9**). They claim to know what they are doing and to be in control, but their behaviour and attitude to the Lord show that the Lord was right when he said that they were ignorant and 'without understanding' (27:11). The Hebrew of **28:10** is difficult to translate. The rulers may be complaining about the *rule on rule*, that is, the many principles that God is trying to teach them through his prophet. On the other hand, the Hebrew *sav lasav kav lakav kav lakav* (NIV footnote) may simply be meant to be a mocking imitation of a child's jabbering.

God will respond to the leaders as they have responded to him. They accuse his prophet of meaningless jabber. So they will be forced to listen to the incomprehensible jabber of the foreign language spoken by the nation that he will send to rule over them (**28:11**). Paul quotes this verse when writing to the Corinthians on the topic of speaking in tongues to make the point that God normally first communicates his messages to people through intelligible speech (1 Cor 14:21).

The prophet does not back down in the face of this teasing about being a teacher of children. He still insists that they should trust in God and *rest* on him (**28:12**). If they do not listen to *the word of the Lord*, they will stumble and fall (**28:13**). God expects believers to listen attentively to his

word and to be willing to make the effort to understand it (Deut 6:4-6; Mark 4:9).

The prophet addresses those to whom he is speaking as those *who rule this people in Jerusalem* (**28:14**), which may seem odd, as this prophecy has been addressed to the southern kingdom, with its capital in Samaria. But the comment makes sense when we realize that the kingdom of Israel had an enormous influence on Judah right up until the fall of Samaria during the sixth year of Hezekiah's reign (7:1-9; 2 Kgs 18:10). Their influence makes it particularly important that they too hear the word of the Lord.

The leaders of Israel claim to be protected from the *scourge*, the invasion that Isaiah has announced. This protection must have come from some sort of *covenant* with occult forces, linked no doubt to idolatry (**28:15**). Africans are familiar with this idea of seeking the protection of the spirit world. Political leaders like Mobutu and even some church leaders have turned to the spirits to achieve or maintain power. But all such occult practices are condemned by God (Lev 19:31). Moreover, the sense of immortality and invulnerability that such protection provides does not promote mercy and compassion towards others. We should rather seek to be like Paul, who preferred to rejoice in his weakness and his concern for others (2 Cor 11:29-30).

The king of Babylon also considered himself invulnerable, but Isaiah had already foretold his fall (14:11-17). Charms may appear to be effective for a time, but the truth is that we will all one day die. Only God has power over death and can enable humans to escape it (see 26:19).

The leaders of Israel have put their trust in an illusionary covenant. God, however, is building Jerusalem with materials that inspire confidence (**28:16-17a**). The Apostle Peter quotes this reference to a *cornerstone* and applies it to Christ in whom we can have absolute confidence (1 Pet 2:6).

Isaiah clearly indicates the futility of the position taken by the leaders of Israel by returning to the image of destruction that he used at the start of this prophecy when he spoke of 'a flooding downpour' (**28:17b**; see 28:2). The scourge cannot be avoided no matter how much they mock his prophecy (**28:18-22**).

The key verse in this chapter is **28:23**, in which the prophet solemnly asks four times to be heard. His appeal here is far more intense than it was in 28:14. The survival of Ephraim is at stake! The people must learn from the two illustrations that the prophet is about to give them.

First, Isaiah shows that a farmer must respect a very precise order if he wishes to have a harvest (**28:24-25**). This natural order of things comes to him from God and cannot be ignored (**28:26**). Isaiah used a similar image when he spoke about the ox and the donkey knowing who their master is (1:3). The lesson here is that the leaders of Israel are failing to recognize or abide by the divine order of all things.

The second illustration uses the example of grinding different types of grain and seeds. Each must be ground in the appropriate way if it is to nourish human beings (**28:27-28**). The leaders should not deceive themselves about God. He creates life, but he may also use suffering and death to accomplish his purpose (45:7-8).

This mystery of suffering and death is at the heart of Christianity. Jesus explained his death and his role as saviour using a similar illustration of a seed that dies in the ground to produce life (John 12:23-33). Like Christ, Christians will endure times of suffering with the aim of glory (Rom 8:18-39; 1 Pet 4). But suffering should not be sought for its own sake. To do so is to fall into the trap of asceticism (1 Tim 4:1-8).

The prophet knows that God is the one who has set the laws that the farmers and threshers obey, but he does not presume to know why God operates in the way he does. He is content to admire the Lord's *counsel* and *wisdom* (**28:29**).

29:1-24 PROPHECY REGARDING JERUSALEM After having condemned Israel, the prophet turns toward Judah and more particularly Jerusalem, its capital, which is here called *Ariel*, a name that probably means 'lion of God' (29:1). The lion was the symbol of Judah and of God's favour to that tribe (Gen 49:8-10). God had enabled Judah to capture Jerusalem and it had been *the city where David settled* (**29:1**; 2 Sam 5:6-10). It was thus a city that had enjoyed God's favour. But that situation would not continue. Rather than the city being the lion, God would come against it like a lion (see Jer 25:30; Amos 1:2). The city would become a place of burning, like an altar hearth (**29:2**). (Here Isaiah is playing on two meanings of the words 'ariel'.) God would come in judgment and besiege the very city he had helped David capture (**29:3**).

The city is reminded of the supremacy of the Creator over his creation. By his word God created human beings from the dust of the earth (Gen 2:7). Human voices fall silent before the voice of God, and Jerusalem's proud claims to enjoy God's favour will be no more than smothered mumbles in the dust (**29:4**; Gen 3:19).

But while Judah will be brought down to the ground, her attackers *will become like fine dust* or *chaff* that the Lord will blow away (**29:5**). The noise that accompanies God's arrival at the city in **29:6** contrasts strongly with the helpless whisperings of the city in 29:4. We are reminded of the way he manifested his presence at Mount Sinai (see Exod 19:16-18). The attackers who seemed to be so powerful will vanish like a dream vanishes when one awakens (**29:7-8**; see 2 Kgs 19:35).

But while the enemy may be dreaming, Jerusalem cannot pride itself on being awake. It is in a state of spiritual blindness and drunkenness (**29:9**). Sin blinds and God sometimes increases this blindness as part of his judgment. He has allowed their *prophets* and *seers* to be as blind as everyone else (**29:10**; Exod 7:13; 9:12).

Because they are blind, they cannot understand the message God is sending them. They see it only as *words sealed in a scroll* (**29:11a**). Even those who might be interested in hearing the words do not receive them. They are prevented from doing so by a physical obstacle to reading the words (the seal) or by their own lack of knowledge: *I don't know how to read* (**29:11b-12**).

To its credit, Africa is spiritually thirsty. Unfortunately, however, the lack of demand for theological training materials and illiteracy in the church leave the door wide open to the commercialized preaching of charlatans, with disastrous religious, social and economic results. Success does not come from personal experience or visions but from meditation on the Scriptures (Josh 1:7-8).

The general lack of emphasis on the written word in Africa is due in part to the fact that African culture still favours strong emotions and oral traditions. While we must continue to respect Africa's oral tradition as a source of knowledge, it is high time that we valued great writers as much as we value great orators. As Isaiah shows, true prophets are born of a combination of the teaching of Scripture and the inspiration of the Spirit. The church should therefore strongly encourage literacy and should insist that its leaders have thorough theological training, on this continent or abroad.

Isaiah links knowledge of God with sincerity of heart. The person who does not seriously seek the Lord in his word will ultimately fall into religious superficiality (**29:13**).

The Lord is not impressed by those who believe themselves to be wise and intelligent (**29:14**; 1 Cor 1:20-25). The wisdom and intelligence that comes through knowledge of God is what makes people stand out (Prov 8). We see this in the examples of Joseph (Gen 41:39-40), the midwives of Egypt (Exod 1:15-20), Bezalel (Exod 31:2-5), Abigail (1 Sam 25:18-25), Solomon (1 Kgs 3:9, 28), Daniel (Dan 2:46-49) and Ezra (Ezra 7:10, 25). The statement that God will *astound these people* reminds us of the people's reaction to the wisdom of Jesus Christ (Mark 6:2; Luke 2:46-47; 7:34-35).

God pronounced his first 'Woe!' against Jerusalem because of its lack of knowledge of him (29:1). The second *Woe!* is directed against those who try to hide their plans from God (**29:15**). Nothing can really be hidden from him, for his wisdom searches everything (1 Kgs 3:9; Prov 7–8). The Creator's omniscience is emphasized by the image of a clay pot stupidly thinking that it is cleverer than the potter who made it (**29:16**). Both Jeremiah and Paul use the same image when speaking of the relationship between God and those he has created (Jer 18:1-6; Rom 9:20-21).

The foolishness of the clay is underscored by the stress on God's omnipotence in **29:17** (see also Luke 1:37). He can do anything – even the unimaginable, like changing the state of matter so that water becomes wine (John 2:1-11).

The high mountains of Lebanon were famed for their forests (2 Chr 2:7-8), but God can turn this area into flat plain for a farmer to plough, and vice versa. Once again we are reminded God has the power to raise up as well as to put down (see 29:4).

With the messianic expression *In that day,* the prophet leaves his own time and looks to the far future (see comments on 4:2). In that day, God will show mercy to those who are incapable of seeing and hearing *the words of the scroll,* and thus cannot meet its standard (**29:18**; see 29:11-12). He will heal the spiritual diseases that prevent them from knowing him. Verses like this led to the expectation that the time of the Messiah would also be associated with the healing of physical diseases (see 32:3-4; 35:5-6). This is why Jesus refers to this type of passage when he replies to John the Baptist's question about whether he really was the Messiah (Luke 7:18-23).

At this time, *the humble will rejoice in the Lord* (**29:19**). The people of the world have a tendency to exalt the arrogant, some of whom even think that they can make a covenant with death (see 28:15). But in both the OT and the NT, the kingdom of God is the inheritance of the humble (Job 22:29; Ps 147:6; Mic 6:8; Matt 5:3; 1 Pet 5:5). Anyone who intends to walk long with God needs to acquire humility. But it is not something that comes cheaply. To be humble is to be flexible, self-denying, and prepared to ignore one's own interests. Christ is the supreme example of humility (Matt 11:29; Phil 2:1-8), moving Mahatma Gandhi to say that only a humble man could pray, 'Father, forgive them' and be answered (Luke 23:34). Christ proves to Africa and to the world that a humble spirit can overcome a belligerent one.

Oppressors and all those who serve their causes *will be cut down* (**29:20-21**). They will lose the techniques they use to maintain power: false accusations and perversions of justice. We should take God's word to heart here, for in Africa we often see this fulfilled on a smaller scale. Each time a dictator falls, his followers share his fate, whether that be exile or death. It is useless to claim that one was simply following orders.

The rehabilitation of the Jewish people is spoken of as coming from *the Lord who redeemed Abraham* (**29:22**). Three important points flow from this allusion to Abraham. First, the prophet is reminding his audience of God's power to transform someone into an instrument of salvation (Gen 12:2-3; Josh 24:2-3). Second, he is reminding them of the Lord's faithfulness in fulfilling his promises to the patriarch. The reference to Jacob shows that God's promise of blessing has continued down the generations (Gen 32:10). Third, the prophet may be hinting at the possibility that God, who made a covenant with Abraham (Gen 17:1-11), will make a new covenant with his people.

In **29:23-24** we see the nation experiencing a sort of Pentecost (Acts 2:1-4). There is a spiritual awakening, and

worship and knowledge of God are restored. Interestingly, the prophet here regards their former complaints against God as arising from ignorance.

30:1-31:9 DENUNCIATION OF ANY ALLIANCE WITH EGYPT After the brief aside about the times of the messiah (29:17-24), the author returns to the condemnation of Judah, uttering his third *Woe!* (**30:1a**; 29:1, 15). Once again, he denounces taking action without taking God into account. He again describes the relationship between the people and the Lord as one in which *obstinate children* rebel against their father (see 1:2). Such rebellion heaps *sin upon sin* (**30:1b**). The situation could be summed up as 'Near the Father, far from sin; far from the Father, near to sin.' This theme will be central to the teaching of Jesus, who will speak of repentance and reconciliation with the Father (Luke 15:11-32).

The specific action denounced here is Judah's entering into an alliance with Egypt (**30:2**). Assyria had invaded the kingdom of Israel and was now threatening the kingdom of Judah. Some counsellors must have urged the king to seek the protection of Egypt and must have gone to Egypt to negotiate the terms of the alliance (2 Kgs 18:9-21). They were seeking a place of refuge in Egypt's *shade.*

But the only one who offers true shade and real protection is the Lord, 'the Rock eternal' (26:4). While the Egyptian government may look strong with its officials and envoys in cities spread out across the Nile Delta, this strength is illusory (**30:4**). Instead of protection, all that Egypt will bring is *disgrace* and *shame* (**30:3, 5b**). The Israelites will have to face dangers from wild animals as they transport the tribute that Egypt will demand in return for her protection (**30:6**), but her help is *useless* (**30:5a, 7a**). The Israelites are hoping that Egypt will rise like the mythical monster known as Rahab and put the Assryrians to flight. But God derisively calls the monster *Rahab the Do-Nothing* (**30:7b**). There will be no help from Egypt (49:4).

As Africans, we too have to learn to trust God as our father, and not to turn to Europe or America as soon as we face political or religious crises. Such behaviour is evidence of immaturity. Our Father God calls us to take responsibility for our own countries, to seek his solutions to our problems, and to move forward counting on him.

God now speaks as the true king, commanding Isaiah to write down his words. This was the way in which the kings of the time recorded their judgments, and what was written had the force of an irrevocable law (Exod 31:18; Esth 8:7-8; Dan 6:9; Matt 5:18). 'Speech flies but writing stays', says a French proverb. The written word is what endures (**30:8**; see comments on 29:11-12).

The prophet now returns to the theme of rebellious sons (**30:9a**; see 30:1). He mentions three specific features of their rebellion. First, he says that the Israelites refuse to listen to the Lord's instructions (**30:9b**; Deut 28:1, 15). Listening is central to the life of the believer.

Second, they want to have a religion that imposes no obligations, puts no restrictions on them. They want God's blessing, but aren't prepared to make any effort to live holy lives (**30:10-11**). This attitude is one that continued. The Apostle Paul had to denounce a similar wilful misunderstanding of God's grace (Gal 5:13-26).

The third component of the rebellion is the way Judah reacts when danger threatens. Faced with the Assyrian threat, the kingdom did not turn to God but instead chose *oppression* and *deceit* (**30:12**). By turning to Egypt, Judah accepted the logic of war and power. But this desire for confrontation and power will not produce the expected results. The wall the kingdom erects for protection may look strong, but it is cracked and bulging, and can easily crash down in ruin (**30:13-14**). Faced with a threat, the solution is not to attack or to flee, but to trust in God. Trust is the key to peace (5:15; 7:9; 26:4; Matt 11:28; Mark 5:36; Heb 4:3-6).

But the people's response to Isaiah's message is that they prefer fleeing rather than remaining calm in front of the menace. God will take them at their word. If they prefer to run, they will have to run. In fact, they will run away even when there is no need to do so (**30:16-17a**). Judah will collapse and only Jerusalem will survive, like a *banner on a hill* (**30:17b**; see 1:7-8; 2 Kgs 18:13; 19:15-20, 35).

But the God who is punishing the nation *longs to be gracious* if the people will place their trust in him. Those who reach this point are called *blessed* (**30:18**). The only reason that people can be described in this way is because of God's compassion (Ps 1:1).

Many similarities exist between the description of the 'blessed' here and in the Beatitudes in Matthew 5:1-11. Both passages speak to the particular needs of Africa. Thus both **30:19** and Matthew 5:4 call for drying of tears (see also Isa 25:8; Rev 21:4). Both **30:20a** and Matthew 5:6 deal with hunger and thirst, which Matthew sees in the context of social justice. And **30:20b-21** and Matthew 5:8 both speak of the fellowship developed with God by those who seek purity. This purity and fellowship with God inevitably go hand in hand with a distancing from all that relates to foreign worship (**30:22**). Syncretism of the kind we know in Africa has never had God's approval. He has always insisted on a clear distinction between himself and all other gods (Exod 20:1-3).

Jesus' use of these themes from Isaiah in his Beatitudes, the idyllic situation described in **30:23-25**, and the cosmic upheaval described in **30:26** all suggest that these verses do not refer so much to the deliverance of Jerusalem under Hezekiah as to the future and perfect deliverance at the Lord's return (Rev 21:1-4, 23).

But the prophet turns from this vision of the future to God's intervention against Assyria – once Hezekiah had turned to God rather than to Egypt (2 Kgs 19:19, 35).

The way in which the prophet introduces the Lord in action speaks powerfully to African readers. It does this in the statement that *the Name of the Lord comes from afar* (**30:27a**). In Africa, names carry a message. They often refer to someone's ancestral origins, for ancestors are revered. Isaiah shows God as the supreme ancestor.

Africans are also struck by the fact that God shows his power by his very *breath*. His mere word brings devastation (**30:27b-28**). Most African cultures attribute similar authority to the words of their elders. Indeed we seldom fear someone because of what they know or possess (as Westerners do); instead, we fear the effects of their words. This is why sorcerers and fetishists, who are often among the poorest in the community, are nevertheless the most feared, for it is widely believed that they hold the power of life and death. But God's words in Isaiah indicate that he is the one who truly has this power.

The Lord invites the people to rejoice when he intervenes against Assyria on their behalf (**30:29, 32**). While it is true that the Scriptures teach us to love our enemies and not to rejoice over their loss (Obad 12; Matt 5:43-45), we are permitted to be glad when God intervenes to save us.

God's action proves to the people of Jerusalem that he is the true Rock on which they must lean (26:4). Jeremiah later denounces those who rely on the flesh rather than on the Rock (Jer 17:5).

The images used to describe the punishment of the Assyrians in **30:30-31** remind us of God's actions in the past. The *cloudburst* reminds us of the flood (Gen 6–9) and *hail* was one of the ten plagues of Egypt (Exod 9:13-35). Isaiah uses these images to vividly bring these events back to people's minds.

God is presented as having the last word regarding evil. When we see suffering, we may doubt and exclaim, 'How long?' as Habakkuk did (Hab 1:2). But the Lord tells us that he has been preparing his judgment for a long time. The final and inevitable destination of the king of Assyria is a *fire pit … deep and wide* (**30:33**). We are reminded of the 'lake of fire' where those who oppose God will be thrown at the last judgment (Rev 20:10, 14; 21:8). Here too, the fire is associated with sulphur.

The cry of *Woe!* in **31:1a** signals a return to the topic of those who do not *seek help from the Lord,* but prefer to make an alliance with Egypt (29:15). Isaiah speaks of the Egyptians' *horses* and *chariots* – subtly reminding his audience of what had happened to the Egyptian horses and chariots when they attempted to cross the Red Sea during the Exodus (Exod 14:28; 15:1, 19). The whole history of the kingdom of Judah should drive home the point that military power is worthless when compared with trust in the Lord (**31:1b**; 1 Sam 17:45-47; 2 Chr 13:3-18; 20:1-24).

The prophet contrasts the human wisdom that seeks the support of a strong ally with God's wisdom that focuses on seeking justice (**31:2a**). Isaiah reminds us of the account of creation when he insists that the Egyptians and their horses are made of flesh, and are nothing without the 'spirit', the breath given by the Creator (**31:3**; Gen 2:7). This opposition of 'flesh' and 'Spirit' will be further developed by the Apostle Paul (Gal 5:16-28). The prophet, like the apostle, denounces all compromise with sin. The person who allies himself with the wicked exposes himself to the risk of sharing their fate (**31:2b**).

A *whole band* of people who make their *shouts* and *clamour* heard above others may impress us (**31:4**). We often assume that the presence of large numbers or a great public presence is a sign of a success. But God is not impressed by numbers or noise. He is so powerful that he has no fear of those who oppose him (Exod 4:10-12; 1 Sam 16:7).

But God does not only describe himself as being like a powerful *lion* in the preceding verse; he is also like the *birds* that take care of their little ones and protect them (**31:5**; Deut 32:11; Matt 23:37). It is striking to see God presenting himself in successive verses as being like a father and a mother. The contrasting verbs *shield* and *deliver* in parallel to *pass over* and *rescue* underscore this mix of qualities that are traditionally male and female. The blend of these qualities in God is implicit in the statement that both men and women are made in the image of God (Gen 1:27).

If they are to benefit from God, the warrior and protector, the people must *return to him* (**31:6**). In other words, they must turn away from evil ways (Ps 7:12). In this case, the people must turn from idolatry. It is not that the objects made with such materials as *silver* and *gold* are evil in themselves (Exod 31:1-6). We do not have to throw all African art that our *hands have made* out of our churches. But we must take care not to worship anything we have made (**31:7**).

Isaiah follows his call to repentance with another promise of miraculous intervention by the Lord (**31:8-9**; 37:36-38). **32:1-20 THE RETURN OF JUSTICE** Whenever the people of God entered into an alliance with any superpower such as Assyria or Egypt, the moral and spiritual life of Judah was corrupted. That was why the prophets regularly warned the nation against such alliances (1:21-23; 31:2-3). But their return to God will bring a return to righteousness and justice (**32:1**). The social contract between leaders and people that had become frayed in 1:23 will be re-established. These God-fearing people can now be described in terms that are usually used only for God (**32:2**; see 4:6; 26:4; Ps 1:3).

The return of justice will bring a complete change in all aspects of life. Human senses will be renewed (**32:3-4**; see 29:18; 35:3-6) and they will see clearly at last. This transformation is a sign of the messianic age. It is partly accomplished by the removal of the veil over our hearts and faces when we turn to Christ, and become increasingly like him (2 Cor 3:15-18).

One of the first consequences of this return of justice experienced by humankind is that people will be known for who they really are, and each will have his rightful place in society (**32:5**; see 3:1-7; 5:20). Corrupt scoundrels are condemned for the evil that they do to the weakest in society (**32:6-8**). In Africa, we too often allow tribalism and other forms of discrimination to distort the way we choose the leaders of our countries. Family relationships and self-interests are given precedence over knowledge and integrity. The church should take a strong stand in favour of justice in this regard too. Not only is this a biblical value, but it is also true to our African tradition, which used to favour the wise and experienced.

There are many similarities between this chapter on the re-establishment of justice and 3:1-4:6. Once again, after having denounced the way the people are governed (3:1-15), the prophet turns to the *complacent* attitude of the female citizens who think that all is well in the land (**32:9**; 3:16). It must be noted that it is not women in general who are reproved, but only some of them. The prophet's concern to address these women also suggests that they had the capacity to influence the rest of the city.

The complacency of these women is replaced by humiliation and mourning (**32:11-12**; 3:17-4:1). The high parts of the city (**32:14, 19b**) and the forest (**32:19a**; see also 10:12, 17-19) – symbols of pride – are abased. But this humiliation prepares for the coming of the Spirit. The people had not been bothering to consult God's Spirit (30:1), but when he is poured out, it will be like a cleansing breath infusing a new creation (see 4:4; Gen 2:7; Ezek 37:1-14; Acts 2:1-4; 2 Cor 5:5, 17). By a domino effect, the environment will be transformed, with deserts becoming fields, and fields becoming forests (**32:15**). The fruit of the Spirit's reign will be *justice, peace, quietness and confidence* (**32:16-19**; Gal 5:22-23).

This section began with the cry of 'Woe!' addressed to those who sought to solve their problems by allying with Egypt (31:1). It ends with a picture of the blessing that will be enjoyed by those who show confidence in God (**32:20**). **33:1-24 JERUSALEM PROTECTED** Once again, the prophet marks the start of a new section with a cry of desperation: *Woe!* (**33:1**; see 29:1, 15; 30:1). He speaks out against a *destroyer* and *traitor* (**33:1a**). The Babylonians have already been described in these terms (21:2). However, the reference to deliverance in 31:3 suggests that here he is speaking of the Assyrians (2 Kgs 18:17; 19:35). They were described as traitors because they could not be trusted to keep any agreements they entered into with others (33:8). Moreover, they were going beyond the task God had assigned them, that of subjugating Israel (10:5-15). By rejoicing in carnage and taking all the glory for their conquests, the Assyrians were exposing themselves to being *destroyed* and *betrayed* (**33:1b**). Without the grace of God, evil always recoils on the one who perpetrated it (Gal 6:7).

The inhabitants of Judah are called to pray to God, asking God to show them grace (**33:2**). In their prayer, they acknowledge God's sovereignty as the one *exalted* over the nations (**33:3-5**; Matt 6:9-10). His protection goes hand in hand with *wisdom, knowledge* and *fear of the Lord.* These qualities often go together in the Bible (Ps 111:10; Prov 1:7). Wisdom comes from God and is given to the one who fears him and asks him for it (Eccl 2:26; Jas 1:5). These qualities, which are sources of blessing (Exod 1:20-21; Job 1:1-3) and of salvation, are more precious than riches, for riches cannot buy them (**33:6**).

The need for salvation is acutely felt because the invaders have devastated the land (**33:7-9**). They have reduced even strong men to tears (although the word here translated as *brave men* is difficult to interpret, and might also refer to Ariel, the city of Jerusalem – see 29:1).

It is in this context that the Lord decides to intervene (**33:10**). He is going to show the uselessness of human actions, which are no more weighty than *chaff or dry straw* (**33:11**; Ps 1:4). Then he is going to demonstrate his sovereign power, a force pictured as *fire* that will easily consume the chaff and *thornbushes* (**33:12-13**).

Isaiah knows how to draw on the memory and culture of his contemporaries. Thus his description of the Lord as a fire would have reminded his listeners of events like those described in Judges 6:20-22 and of Elijah's encounter with the prophets of Baal on Mount Carmel (1 Kgs 18:36-39; 2 Kgs 1:10). It was certainly an image that was familiar to the Jews, for it recurs in Luke 9:54.

The inhabitants of Jerusalem are terrified by this fire, and ask who can survive in the face of God's anger (**33:14**). The answer demands an extraordinary moral commitment. All of a person's actions must be on the right path if he or she is to survive (**33:15-16**; 32:3-5; see Ps 15:2-5). The natural reaction would be to say that this is an unattainable ideal. However, it is a realistic goal for believers, through the grace of God expressed in Jesus Christ, who helps us to achieve it (33:2; Dan 3:8-30; Matt 19:25-26; Rom 6:1-14).

The stress on avoiding corruption is worth noting (33:15). The plague of corruption is eating away at our continent, destroying society. Our religious and political leaders need to listen to the voice of the prophet. After all, God's law strictly laid down that leaders must refuse bribes in order to maintain their integrity (Exod 23:8; Deut 10:17). We must not be interested in money, as Judas Iscariot was (Matt 26:14-16). Rather, despite our economic and social difficulties, we should follow the example of Joseph, who could not be corrupted (Gen 39:7-12), and of the principled Daniel (Dan 5:17). If we do this, we will experience future glory (Phil 3:17-4:1).

Those who survive the fire of God's wrath are given the grace and privilege of seeing the rebirth of the nation. As in David's time, the king will be a symbol of unity and the object of great attention and admiration (**33:17**; 2 Sam 5:1-3). They will look back on the time when they feared their foreign oppressors and were forced to pay tribute to them. They will contrast the state of their city then with what it looks like now, when it can be described as *the city of our festivals* (**33:18-20**). Where the people were once like nomadic wanderers during the exodus and the exile, they now have a place from which they need never move on. All this is the Lord's doing, for he is the *Mighty One* who protects the city from all attack (**33:21**).

To communicate a global idea of what the Lord does for Israel, Isaiah shows how God combines in himself judicial power (*our judge*), legislative power (*our lawgiver*) and executive power (*our king ... who will save us*) (**33:22**). He is the equal of the absolute monarchs of the time. But he can do even more than they can, for he is also the healer of his people. He provides both physical healing (**33:23-24a**) and spiritual healing, including the forgiveness of sins (**33:24b**). In this he is greater than any king of Israel or Judah. None of them could provide such healing (2 Kgs 5:7-8; 2 Chr 7:14). But Jesus could, and as shown in the gospels, he fulfilled this role. He is the one who forgives sin and heals (Mark 2:9-12; 3:7-10; John 1:29; 8:1-11). (While on this subject, we must take care not to automatically link sickness and sin, as our culture traditionally does and as many sorcerers, fetishists and charlatans encourage us to do – John 9:1-3.)

34:1-17 THE PUNISHMENT OF EDOM After presenting himself in the preceding chapter as a God who shows mercy, the Lord now presents himself in a terrifying way in his judgment of Edom. This nation is the object of very severe treatment. The book of Obadiah will be completely devoted to its condemnation. The descendants of Esau are accused of having betrayed their brothers, the descendants of Jacob, by participating in the plundering of Jerusalem (**34:8**; Ezek 35:5; Obad 10-11). They probably did this during the capture of Jerusalem by the Babylonians (2 Kgs 25:1-21).

The Lord starts by affirming his sovereignty. He is not a local god. He is the God who speaks to *the world* as a whole, to all the *nations* and *peoples* (**34:1**). He is master of *the heavens* and can use their power (**34:4-5a**).

God *will totally destroy* the people of Edom (**34:2**; Josh 6:17, 21), which means that he will kill all the human and animal inhabitants of the land (34:3, 5b-7). This description of a terrible massacre shocks our Christian conscience and our vision of God as a God of love. This sort of text reminds us of the gravity of sin and that its consequence is death (Rom 6:23). It leads us also to Christ who spares us from this divine anger by suffering our punishment as a substitute (John 1:29). It is now our responsibility to preach this grace (Matt 28:19-20). We should never use a passage like this to justify any ethnic cleansing.

When a city was devoted to destruction, people were never again supposed to live there (**34:9-10**; **12-13**). This was the fate of Jericho in its time (Josh 6:24, 26), and would be the fate of Edom. The Lord gives this land to the animals, as a reserve where they may live and reproduce in peace (**34:11, 14-15**). This decision is stamped with an official seal: the different animals are counted and recorded in a book and their territorial limits are precisely laid out (**34:16-17**). The prophet's audience is called on to verify the fulfilment of the prophecy (*look ... read*) so as to recognize that God is faithful to his decisions (25:1).

35:1-10 THE MESSIANIC PERIOD After the desolation of Edom in the preceding chapter, the tone suddenly changes. The prophet no longer speaks of an area being transformed into a desert (34:9-10) but rather of a desert flowering anew (**35:1-2a**). The places in Israel and Lebanon that were laid waste in 33:9 again find their *splendour* (**35:2b**).

The tone of the prophetic message changes as well. It no longer announces misery (29:1, 15; 30:1; 31:1; 33:1) but instead it encourages and affirms God's people (**35:3**). In fact the writer of Hebrews used this verse to encourage Christians to persevere in the way of sanctification and grace (Heb 12:12-15).

The prophet's message announces salvation and God's coming in person (**35:4**; John 1:1-18). His coming will be accompanied by healing (**35:5-6a**). At that time, healing was God's prerogative and therefore a sign of his presence (see 29:18; 33:23-24).

Nature, which Paul tells us has also suffered from the fall (Rom 8:20, 22), will start to revive (**35:6b-7**). Nature, humans and God will be reconciled (see 11:6-9). Indeed, we will be present at a cosmic restoration. A *highway* called *the Way of Holiness* will allow those people who are *redeemed* by God to enter an ideal Zion (**35:8-10**; Rev 21:2-4). The early Christians may have picked up on this verse when they referred to those who believed in Jesus Christ as followers of 'the Way' (John 14:6; Acts 9:2; 22:4; 24:22).

36:1-39:8 Reign of Hezekiah

Chapters 36–39 are very similar to 2 Kings 18:13-20:19. They conclude Isaiah's prophecies for his own time and are intended to validate the prophet's view of God and show the truth of his predictions. In particular, these chapters show Assyria's failure to capture Jerusalem and suggest the looming threat of Babylon.

36:1-22 THE ASSYRIAN THREAT In Isaiah's day, Assyria was the greatest power in the region. Its army had a fearsome reputation for cruelty. As predicted by Isaiah (8:7-8; 10:24), the Assyrians invaded Judah and advanced on Jerusalem. Sennacherib, the king of Assyria, sent his representatives to demand that the city surrender (**36:1-2**). In reporting this, Isaiah does not mention the tribute Hezekiah had paid to the king of Assyria, nor does he mention the group of high officials sent to Judah's capital (2 Kgs 18:14-17). He is only interested in the theological elements in the speech of the field commander (or *Rabshakeh* – a title that means 'chief cupbearer').

Among the high officials who went out to meet the Assyrian envoys were Eliakim and Shebna, two men whom Isaiah saw as examples of good and bad governance (**36:3**; see also 22:15-25).

The *field commander* begins the exchange with a question to Hezekiah: *On what are you basing this confidence of yours?* (**36:4-5**). He then outlines the things that Jerusalem might be trusting in, and sets out to refute them. Some parts of his speech are similar to Isaiah's thinking. However, there are important differences between his pagan understanding of God's role and that presented by the prophet.

The field commander denounces the alliance between Judah and Egypt as useless (**36:6**). In this he is in complete agreement with Isaiah (30:1-31:9). Egypt had not responded when Assyria attacked its ally.

The field commander then says that the king of Judah cannot hope for help from the Lord, because he must have angered him by removing all objects of pagan worship from the temple, destroying the high places in Judah and insisting that the only place to offer sacrifices was the temple at Jerusalem (**36:7**; 2 Kgs 18:4; 2 Chr 29; 31:1-2). As a pagan, the Assyrian would have believed that the more places there were for offerings and the more rituals that were performed, the greater the chance of winning divine favour. But Isaiah has declared that what God actually considers important is holiness, justice, and doing what is right (1:11-17).

The Assyrian field commander then makes ironic comments about the weakness of Judah's army. Even if he were to give them horses to defend themselves, they would not have enough men able to ride them (**36:8-9**). Isaiah, too, had condemned any idea that the people could trust in force and numbers to protect them (see 31:1; 1 Sam 17:45-47; 2 Chr 13:3-18; 20:1-24).

The field commander also states that it is the Lord who is sending the Assyrians against Judah (**36:10**). Isaiah had certainly seen the judgment of God behind the Assyrian invasion, but he denounced the bloodthirsty and proud conduct of these people who were going beyond their assigned task (10:5-15). God's envoy may not go beyond God's commands (Matt 5:17-20).

Finally, the field commander ignores the official envoys and speaks directly to the people (**36:11-13**). He seeks to discredit King Hezekiah, who has been encouraging the people to trust only in the Lord (**36:14-15**). He uses two arguments to persuade them to rebel against their king.

First, he promises the people an ideal situation if they surrender. His description of the land to which they will be deported is a sort of parody of God's promised land (**36:16-17**; Exod 3:17). Here we hear echoes of the desire to return to

Egypt rather than trusting in God (Exod 16:3). Our continent is familiar with politicians who make promises like this, deceiving the people by promising them an earthly paradise. The reality is far different, to the point that some people even long for a return of the colonial era. The church should faithfully play its prophetic role and should help African believers look for our true hope – the promised land or the new Jerusalem (Matt 6:24-33).

The field commander's second argument is that the Lord, whom Hezekiah has chosen to follow, is too weak to protect them (**36:18-20**). The gods of Syria and Israel were not able to deliver their countries from the Assyrians. Why then should the God of Judah be able to do so? Isaiah had fought against this misunderstanding of the Lord as a regional god limited to Judah. He had insisted that the Lord is the Creator of all things and sovereign over all nations (see 34:1).

Hezekiah had ordered the people to remain silent despite the provocation of this Assyrian officer (**36:21**). It is a sign of spiritual maturity. 'Speech is silver; silence is golden' says the proverb. When confronted by such arrogance, silence is a sign of wisdom and trust in God (Exod 14:13-14; Prov 17:28; Matt 7:6).

Despite putting on a brave face while facing the Assyrian envoy, the representatives of the king of Judah were discouraged by his words. They tore their clothes as a sign of mourning before reporting his message to their king (**36:22**).

37:1-38 HEZEKIAH'S REACTION The king of Judah is as disheartened as his envoys. Not only does he tear his clothes, but he also puts on *sackcloth*. But despite his dejection, he shows courage and clear thinking. He does not give up his faith in the Lord, even though the situation seems hopeless. His immediate reaction is to go to the temple, no doubt to pray (**37:1**).

He also sends representatives to consult a true man of God, Isaiah. Most likely he now recognizes that the warnings of the prophet about the Assyrian invasion and the futility of an alliance with Egypt were from God (30:1-31:9). Sending leaders like *Shebna*, one of Isaiah's adversaries (22:15-19), and the religious authorities to fetch him underscores his recognition of Isaiah as a true prophet. Hezekiah trusts in the one who had announced God's intervention against the invaders and asks him to pray *for the remnant that still survives* (**37:3-5**). His reference to a 'remnant' suggests that the king remembers what Isaiah has said in the past (1:9; 30:27-33).

The prophet tells the messengers God's initial response to his prayers. God will use a *certain report* to send Sennacherib back to his home, and there he will die (**37:6-7**). This 'report' took the form of a rumour announcing that a *Cushite* army was advancing on the Assyrians (**37:8-9a**). The Cushites were black Africans who lived to the south of

Egypt. Clearly African armies were feared in antiquity (see comment on 18:1-7).

But the king of Assyria will not abandon his plan to attack Jerusalem, and sends Hezekiah a letter in which he repeats his threats against Jerusalem and again treats the Lord as no different from the gods of the peoples he has conquered (**37:9b-13**).

Faced with this repeated threat, Hezekiah perseveres in his faith and returns to the temple with the letter that Sennacherib had sent him (**37:14**). Once again, he prays (**37:15**), and this time we are given the words of his prayer. It is rich in theological content and shows a king whose mind is saturated with the Pentateuch. He acknowledges that God is the Creator of all things and is therefore sovereign (**37:16**; Gen 1:1). More than that, he affirms that the Lord is the only God (Exod 20:1-3). Other deities do not exist, they are merely human inventions (**37:19**). But the Lord is living, he can see and hear (**37:17**). It seems that the king is asking for deliverance for Jerusalem not so much to save his own life but so that God's glory may be recognized by others (**37:20**).

Isaiah brings God's second response. The solemn character of this response is marked by the recording of the messenger's full title, *Isaiah son of Amoz* (**37:21**). The Lord reaffirms his sovereignty (**37:22-24a**). He is the one who created the splendours of nature that the king of Assyria claims to have mastered (**37:24b-25**). He is the one who planned history, and gave Sennacherib his victories (**37:26-27**). Sennacherib is recalled to reality: he is only a creature among others. God can lead him where he wishes like an ox or a donkey (**37:28-29**).

The prophet announces to Hezekiah that the king of Assyria will not take Jerusalem and that the survivors in the city will slowly resume their normal life (37:30-34). God will intervene not only for the glory of his own name as Hezekiah prayed (37:20), but also because Hezekiah has shown himself to be a worthy successor of David, and God remembers his promise to David (**37:35**; 1 Kgs 2:2-4).

God had promised that the Assyrians would not even *shoot an arrow at the city* (37:33). This promise is kept when a terrible plague strikes the Assyrian army. The mention of *the angel of the Lord* reminds us of the plague that struck Israel under the reign of David (2 Sam 24:15-17). Sennacherib abandons his plan to besiege Jerusalem and returns to his own country where he dies, just as Isaiah has foretold (**37:36-38**). This divine intervention must have impressed the survivors of Jerusalem and given much credibility to Isaiah's later prophecies.

38:1-21 HEZEKIAH'S ILLNESS AND HEALING The king of Assyria could not avoid his fate (37:7, 38), but what about the king of Judah? In the episode which follows, Hezekiah suffers from an illness that Isaiah informs him will be fatal (**38:1**). The king's first reaction is still to pray to God (**38:2**; 37:1,

15). In his previous prayer, he had put the glory of God first rather than his own situation to obtain deliverance (37:20). Here, however, he puts his own faithfulness and *devotion* and his good behaviour first (**38:3**). He considers himself a worthy successor of David, and an inheritor of the promise made to him (see 37:35).

In the OT, we do sometimes find people claiming to be faithful or upright before God (1 Kgs 19:14; 1 Chr 29:17-18; Neh 13:14). We need to remember that the OT regarded someone as righteous if his deeds and behaviour were pleasing to God. But this was not the same as saying that the person was sinless. Only Christ is sinless. Only he could issue the challenge, 'Can any of you prove me guilty of sin?' (John 8:46). Only he in his sinlessness could overcome death (Rom 5:18-19).

The Lord answered Hezekiah's prayer and granted him an extension of his life (**38:4-5**). These extra years are guaranteed to be years of peace despite the nation that was menacing Jerusalem (**38:6**). Friendship with God does not guarantee this sort of answer to prayer, but verses like this encourage us to live in sincere intimacy with the Lord.

In the book of Kings, the announcement of a reprieve is followed by the outline of the means of healing and the request by Hezekiah for a sign (2 Kgs 20:7-8). In Isaiah, these verses describing the means of healing are placed at the end of the chapter (38:21-22).

The king's healing is brought about by the application of a *poultice of figs* at Isaiah's instruction (**38:21**). At a time when medical science was little developed, only someone close to the Creator could know the cure for some illnesses. Religion and medicine were closely connected (see 29:18; 2 Kgs 5:7-8) as they often still are in the towns and villages on our continent.

To confirm the healing announced by God, Hezekiah asks for a sign (**38:22**) and receives it (**38:7-8**). This sign is similar to that given to Joshua (Josh 10:12-14). In the Bible, requests for signs are seldom granted, and then only to confirm that a message and a mission are really from the Lord (Exod 4:1-5; Judg 6:36-40). Signs confirm an already existing faith and do not precede it (Matt 12:38-39).

Conforming to his culture, and also to African culture, the king of Judah composed a song of praise following his healing (38:9-20; see also 12:1-6). However, the comparison to the African culture ends there. In traditional African culture, death is only a passage to another world. Life continues after death in another form, and communication is possible between the worlds of the living and the dead. But Hezekiah regarded death as the end of all life and of all connection with *the land of the living* (**38:10-11**, **18**). But there is an underlying messianic element: God can save from death by pardoning our sins (**38:15-17**; see also 25:8; 26:19).

39:1-8 THE BABYLONIAN ENVOYS The account of Hezekiah's life ends on a more sombre note. This king, who knew enough

to turn away from the alliance with Egypt, trusted in God at the siege of Jerusalem and experienced divine healing, falls into the trap of an alliance with a pagan nation.

The Babylonians, who like Judah were enemies of Assyria, were gradually growing in power. Under the pretext of a courtesy visit after Hezekiah's illness, they took an inventory of the king's wealth. Hezekiah himself gave them a conducted tour of his palace from top to bottom (**39:1-2**). It seems that he was naïve about the motives of the Babylonians and too easily flattered by their visit. While it is true that we are to trust God and be calm in the face of adversity (30:15), this does not excuse us from our responsibility to be watchful and to avoid compromising our position. We need to give thought to whom we open our hearts and our homes to (Judg 16:17-21). Discretion is a key to good management, both of our homes, and of our countries.

The prophet responds swiftly to what Hezekiah has done. He informs the king of the future invasion by Babylon and that all his wealth and some of his descendants will be carried off to Babylon (**39:3-7**; 2 Kgs 24:8-25:21).

Hezekiah's response to his news is ambiguous. On the one hand, he seems to continue to be concerned for the immediate security of his people (37:1, 17-20) since he rejoices that this invasion will not take place during his lifetime (**39:8**). On the other hand, he does not seem adequately concerned about the fate of the generation to come. But a good spiritual leader will take pains to leave things in good condition for those who come after. This was what David did for Solomon (1 Chr 28:9-10), and it is what the Apostle Paul does in his letters to Timothy.

40:1-55:13 Part 2: The Time of Consolation

Apart from a few messianic asides such as 35:1-10, the prophet Isaiah has so far been interested in Israel and Judah over the short term. He has dealt with the Assyrian invasion, the end of the kingdom of Israel and Jerusalem's deliverance under Hezekiah (between 722 and 704 BC). Now he turns to more long-term prophecies, which will be fulfilled after his death. He will now supplement what was said in 13:1-14:2 and 21:1-10 about the capture of Babylon by the Persians (539 BC) and the return from exile of God's people.

The theme of God's servant, the messiah, is central to this part of the book of Isaiah. The messiah is here interpreted primarily as Cyrus, the king of Persia, Israel's liberator. However, the prophet sees much farther and envisages another servant of God who will initiate a new and eternal covenant between God and humankind (55:3).

40:1-31 God Brings Deliverance

The prophet addresses the population of Jerusalem, and is no doubt speaking about the return of those who had been exiled (40:9). God announces a message of comfort to the city and to his people (**40:1**). As Christians who have received forgiveness of our sins through Christ, we are also called to a mission of comforting others (2 Cor 1:3-5).

The word *comfort* is repeated twice in 40:1, possibly to balance the assertion that the nation has received *double* punishment for her sins. God has made an example of the nation that was supposed to be his representative (Deut 4:5-8, 23-24), but he also reveals himself as one who shows mercy (**40:2**). In exile, the Jewish people will recognize that their situation is due to their sin and will cry out for the grace proclaimed by the prophet (Ezra 9:6-8; Neh 1:5-10; Dan 9).

The exiles hear a herald's voice, ordering that a highway be built *in the desert* (**40:3**). The desert often symbolized divine punishment and desolation (34:8-15; Num 32:13), but paradoxically it has also been the place of discovering God or returning to God (Exod 3:1-2; Hos 2:14). Africans, who are often literally or metaphorically on the edge of the desert, have an incredible opportunity to develop intimacy with and profound dependence on God.

The herald seems to be preparing this highway in the desert for a second exodus as the exiles return from Babylon to Jerusalem (40:3; Exod 16:10). It will be a smooth road, with no obstructions (**40:4**). But the image of this ideal road also has messianic implications (see 35:8-10). Thus the gospel writers saw that this announcement also applied to the role of John the Baptist, preparing the way for the coming of Christ (Mark 1:3; Luke 3:4; John 1:23). The deliverance of the people of God (or the coming of God among his people) reveals God's glory (**40:5**).

The prophet again affirms that God's plans will be carried out. His plans are not like those made by human beings, who are as short-lived as *grass* or *flowers* (**40:6-7**; see also Ps 103:15). They live and die as the breath of the Lord blows on them (Gen 2:7). By contrast, *the word of our God* is utterly reliable (**40:8**; see 25:1). It has eternal value.

Because of God's reliability, his message of salvation can be proclaimed fearlessly from the high hills (**40:9**). From the beginning, God had entrusted to the Jews a mission of salvation for the world (Gen 28:14; John 4:22). This mission was fully accomplished with the coming of Christ among his people. It is now up to the church to proclaim these *good tidings* (see Mark 16:15).

The divine deliverer whose coming is proclaimed to Jerusalem is represented both as a strong man with muscular arms (**40:10**; Exod 6:6; Ps 79:11) and as the tender good shepherd (**40:11**; Ps 23; John 10:11). His immense power and wisdom are celebrated in a great poem (40:12-17; Job 38–39). The poem reminds us of the wonders of God's creation by asking questions about God that open the way to a faith that is mature and thoughtful. The faith in our churches is still often childish and unwilling to study. God pushes us to use our intellectual capacities to the fullest

extent and calls us to reflect on the wonders he has made (Prov 1:1-7).

Compared to the greatness of God, human nations are utterly insignificant (**40:15, 17**). They have nothing to offer him. All the mighty cedars of Lebanon are not enough to burn an offering of the size God truly deserves (**40:16**). People have no reason to be proud of their nations and their leaders (**40:21-24**; see 40:6-8). Twice the hearers are asked *To whom, then, will you compare God?* and *What image will you compare him to?* (**40:18, 25**). Both times, the answers underline humanity's inability to totally comprehend God. Human efforts at artistic representations of the deity are ridiculous (**40:19-20**). The one who makes the idol has to take care that it *will not topple,* but the one it is supposed to represent is the one who can balance *the heavens like a canopy* (40:21-22). Rather than building foolish idols or trusting in princes, we should contemplate and meditate on God's handiwork in creation (**40:26**; Rom 1:20).

Faced with these reminders of the scope of God's power, we may sometimes be tempted to think that we are too small to attract his interest (**40:27**). But believers should not think that we are forgotten by God in difficult times (such as during the exile) and become discouraged (40:27). God reminds us that his knowledge is infinite and that he does not grow weary (**40:28**). If we persevere and place our hope in the Lord, we will share in his characteristics and have the strength to endure (**40:29-31**; see 2 Cor 3:17-18).

41:1-29 Confidence in God

Verse **41:1** is similar to 1:2 and 34:1 in that God is again summoning all the *nations* to hear what is said. The *islands* are those countries that are farthest away. All need to give God their full attention in light of his impending judgment. That judgment will be carried out by someone whom God has raised up *from the east* to carry out his purposes (**41:2-3**). This person must be Cyrus the king of Persia (45:1). He will not be acting as an independent agent, but will be under God's control, as all others have been since the beginning of time and will be till the end of time (**41:4**; see also Rev 22:13). The eternal Creator is the only enduring link across the generations.

Yet even when they face God's imminent judgment, the nations prefer to take refuge in idolatry, even though their idols are made with their own hands and are so powerless that they need to be nailed down to prevent them from toppling over (**41:5-7**). *Israel,* however, is called to behave differently. As the Lord addresses them, he recalls their ancestors. *Jacob* was God's servant and the one he had chosen in preference to his brother Esau. *Abraham* was God's *friend* (**41:8**). Africans remember their ancestors and their wise conduct, and see them as models for later generations and as examples of how to behave in times of crisis. The

Lord does the same, and does not forget his covenant with past generations (**41:9**; see Gen 17:7).

The people of God are repeatedly urged not to be afraid (**41:10a**, 13-14). This insistence is important. God knows that we are naturally fearful. It is a defence mechanism when we are faced with danger or an adversary who seems stronger than we are. We need to learn to trust in God's help (**41:10b**). He will transform situations, so that those who tried to make us feel ashamed will themselves be ashamed (**41:11**). We will even find ourselves looking to see where our enemies who loomed so large have vanished to (**41:12**). Over the ages, many of God's servants have needed to be reminded not to fear (**41:13**; Josh 1:7-9; Jer 1:17-19; Luke 12:32). God is pleased to use *little Israel*, a mere *worm* for his glory (**41:14**). Jeremiah and the Apostle Paul are examples of people who were acutely aware of this (Jer 1:6-10; 2 Cor 12:7-10). With God's help, this little 'worm', will become a force that destroys even mountains (**41:15-16a**).

Not only should the people not fear in the face of adversity, they should also find reasons to *rejoice in the Lord* (**41:16b**). While it cannot be said to be a specific command, Christians are strongly urged to practise the discipline of seeking reasons to rejoice before God (Phil 4:4). And God provides many reasons to rejoice, for the desert where the people were before is replaced by a lush landscape with abundant water and luxurious vegetation (**41:17-20**; see 35:1-2; 40:3).

Continuing to reassure his people, the Lord, through his prophet, openly defies the gods in whom other nations trust (**41:21**; see also 41:6-8). Two tests are suggested to see if these gods are real. The first is their capacity to interpret the past or foretell the future with certainty (**41:22**; see Deut 18:22). The other is their ability to intervene in the physical world (**41:23**). We are reminded of Elijah's challenge to the priests of Baal (1 Kgs 18:21-39). But, as with Elijah, the results of Isaiah's challenge prove that the idols are useless. Isaiah dismisses them as *less than nothing* and *worthless* (**41:24**). By contrast, the Lord himself is quite prepared to make a prediction and to take the action needed to fulfil it. He announces that in the future he will raise up *one from the north*, that is, the king of Persia, who will bring good news to Jerusalem (**41:25-27**).

None of the gods worshipped as idols could do anything like this. Isaiah dismisses them as *false*, mere *wind and confusion* (**41:28-29**). The book of Isaiah does not accept that there is any being, even any spiritual being, present in the idols or fetishes that frighten so many of our compatriots.

42:1-25 God's Servant

In this first of the great Servant Songs in Isaiah (42:1-9; the others are at 49:1-6; 50:4-9; 52:13-53:12), the servant and his mission are introduced. In its immediate, historical application, this servant is Cyrus, the king of Persia who ended the exile of the Jews. If we compare **42:6** and 45:13,

there is a clear link between the servant's mission and that entrusted to Cyrus (see also 41:2-3, 25).

However, the servant is also someone greater than Cyrus, and Matthew 12:18-21 explicitly applies 42:1-9 to Christ. The messianic characteristics of the servant include the fact that he did not proclaim himself to be sent by God but was clearly *chosen* by God (**42:1a**). A Yombe proverb from the DRC says, *Kimfumu bieka kibiekuanga* ['No serious person makes himself the leader of others']. Christ was not exempt from this rule (Mark 1:9-11).

This servant of God also has a universal vocation. He brings *justice to the nations* (**42:1b**), and to the most distant countries, the *islands* (**42:4b**). He is *a light for the Gentiles* (**42:6b-7**). Christ's work of salvation has this universal scope (Matt 28:19; Acts 10:28).

The servant does not seek to force his message on people by raising his voice or using his eloquence, as do so many of our so-called prophets who fail to give proof of wisdom (Prov 17:28). What he will do, however, is *bring forth justice* (**42:2-3**).

Finally, the chosen one of God is faithful in his ministry, just as Christ was in offering himself in sacrifice (see 53:7) and he *will not falter* (**42:4a**).

God then twice identifies himself in ways that enhance the servant's authority as his representative. First, he identifies himself as the Creator, using language similar to that found in Genesis 1:1 and 2:7, and specifies that it is he who directs his servant (**42:5-6a**). Second, God reminds us of the name Yahweh by which he revealed himself (Exod 3:14-15) to indicate that he gives his glory only to this person (**42:8-9**). Jesus will claim to be the only true representative of God (John 14:6-7).

In response to the universal mission of justice of God's servant, there is a universal concert of praise (**42:10-12**). The Lord is about to act (**42:13**). After a time of silence, such as during the exile, the Lord will again intervene on behalf of his people (**42:14-15**). God announces that he will heal the blindness and deafness of his people, characteristics of their idolatry (**42:16-20**; 29:18).

In 42:21-25, the prophet speaks for his people. He recognizes that Israel's desolation and exile come from the hand of the Lord because of their sin against him. Their sufferings were intended to serve as a lesson for the future, teaching them to *pay close attention* when God speaks (**42:23**). They need to hear the message of redemption that will be proclaimed in the next section.

43:1-28 The Redemption of Israel

In the preceding chapter, God reminded us that he is the Creator of heaven and earth (see 42:5). Here, he uses the same verbs as in Genesis 1:1 and 2:7, *created* and *formed*, but applies them to Israel. The existence of this nation is no accident but is entirely the work of God.

The exhortation *fear not,* already used in chapter 41 (see comments on 41:1-29), returns here twice (**43:1b, 5a**). This absence of fear is strongly linked to the growth of a sense of belonging to God (**43:1a**).

God's promise to be with them when they *pass through the waters* (**43:2a**) would have reminded the people of what he had done for them at the Red Sea and at the Jordan (Exod 14:21-22; Josh 3:4-17). The promised protection when they *walk through the fire* would encourage them to show the same faithfulness as Daniel's friends when faced with the threat of the furnace (**43:2b**; Dan 3:1-30).

God's words in **43:3a** echo the great statement of faith that introduces the Ten Commandments (Exod 20:2). But here their deliverance is presented in broader terms than at the first exodus. Egypt was not the only rich and powerful nation to be sacrificed for the redemption of Israel (**43:3**).

Those who belong to God will return to Israel from the four corners of the earth (**43:5b-7b**). The book of Ezra reports on Cyrus' announcement which permits the Jews everywhere to return, in partial fulfilment of this prophecy (Ezra 1:3, 5). But the redeemed who will ultimately flock to Israel will include far more than just the physical descendants of Abraham. They will include *everyone who is called by my name* (**43:7a**). Like the Jewish nation described in 43:1, they too have been *created* and *formed* by God.

In 43:8-13, Isaiah returns to the themes of chapters 41–42. Israel's deliverance is compared to the healing of a blind and deaf nation, whose disabilities are the result of their idolatry and are thus more spiritual than physical (**43:8**; see 42:16-20).

Once again, the Lord confronts foreign nations and their gods. He again applies the test set out in 41:21-23, and triumphantly demonstrates that he alone can predict an event and cause it to happen (**43:9**). There can be no doubt that he alone is the true God, the first and eternal and all-powerful being (**43:10-13**; see 41:4, 24-29).

God now gives more precise details, than he did in 42:1, of the event that he predicts and will bring to pass. He is speaking of the fall of Babylon (**43:14**). Despite the Babylonians' pride in their fleet of *ships,* which no doubt brought them great wealth and power, the richest and the most powerful nation of that era would be brought low by God.

The Lord again reminds his people that this will not be the first time he has humiliated a great nation. He did the same when he drowned the powerful forces of the Egyptian army in the Red Sea during the first exodus (**43:15-17**; see 43:2-3; Exod 14:21-31). But they must not focus on what he has done in the past (**43:18**). Instead, they need to look up in the present and see that God is doing *a new thing,* preparing the road for a new exodus (**43:19**). In the past, he had made *a way through the sea* (**43:16**), but now he is making a well-watered *way in the desert* (**43:20**; see also 35:1-10; 40:3-4; 41:17-19). The animals are grateful for this supply,

but its purpose is to supply the needs of his people so that they may praise him (**43:21**; see also 42:10-12).

Just as in chapter 42, praise of God is immediately followed by the memory of the people's sin against God. They have neither served him nor honoured him. He has laid few obligations on them, but their only response has been to accumulate sins against him (**43:22-24**; see 42:21-25). Yet despite the people's failure to obey and to offer sin offerings, God himself has decided to pardon them! This amazing truth is stressed by the emphatic *I, even I, am he* (**43:25**). We will later see Jesus showing this same ability to forgive sins (Matt 9:1-8; John 1:29).

God makes it clear that the people have no right to expect this forgiveness (**43:26**). He reminds them of the sins of their *first father,* Jacob, who certainly was not a model of virtue. He also reminds them of the sins of their leaders, the *spokesmen* of the people (**43:27**). These sins had resulted in Israel's disgrace (**43:28**).

Africans should take note of these words about the failures of the Jews' ancestors. We tend to be so careful to venerate our ancestors and to show respect for our leaders, that we tend to overlook their shortcomings. While retaining our respect for our ancestors and our leaders (Exod 20:12; Heb 13:17), we must be careful not to slip into blind admiration (Acts 5:29).

44:1-28 The Lord is the True God

The first eight verses of this chapter restate the themes in chapter 40. Thus Israel is again reminded that it was chosen and created by God (**44:1-2**; see 41:8-9; 43:1). Here Israel is referred to as *Jeshurun,* 'the upright one', a rare name for Israel that is also used in Deuteronomy 32:15. The name reminds us of the calling of the people of God.

We also find the theme of a desert replanted and watered for those who belong to the Lord (**44:3-5**; see 41:17-20; 43:19-20). The new element here is God's promise to *pour out my Spirit* (see also Joel 2:28). The coming messianic period will coincide with the coming of the Spirit. Jesus made the Spirit a theme of his preaching (John 3:5; 7:37-39). It is vital that the Spirit be present in the hearts of a people and of individuals. The Apostle Paul will urge readers not to 'put out the Spirit's fire' (1 Thess 5:19) and lists the fruit of the Spirit in Galatians 5:22.

Once again, God challenges all others who claim to be gods and insists that he is the only God because he alone, as the first and the last, can foresee what is to come (**44:6-8**; see 41:21-29; 43:9-13). Because of who he is, believers have no need to fear (44:2, 8; see comments on 41:1-29; 43:1).

While still dealing with the theme of the Lord being the only true God, the author now moves on to new ground as he speaks at length about the uselessness of making idols. This topic has been touched on briefly earlier in the book (see 40:18-20; 41:6-7).

The author starts by pointing out the stupidity of thinking that a person who is not God and who depends on things created by God for life can create a god with his hands (**44:9-12**). He goes on to point out the irony that the same material used to make the idol is also used to keep the idol-maker alive by providing warmth and cooking his food (**44:13-17, 19**). How can one piece of a block of wood be worshipped while another piece is burned? Because we end up resembling what we worship, the person who bows down before such idols becomes like them: *they know nothing, they understand nothing* (44:9, 18-20).

God, by contrast, is fully alive. He does not forget his people and they are called to *remember* him (**44:21**). He alone has the power to forgive *offences* (**44:22**; see also 43:25) and he alone controls creation (**44:23-24**). He confuses *false prophets* (2 Chr 18:19-22) and confirms the word of *his servants* (no doubt including Isaiah) who announce the rebuilding of Jerusalem (**44:25-27**).

IDOLATRY

Idolatry takes many forms in the different cultures of Africa, but at its heart is anything that supplants God in people's lives. It is specifically prohibited in the Ten Commandments (Exod 20:1-6), where it is described as serving, worshipping or following any image, spirit, god or idol apart from the true and living God.

Despite this command, Aaron made a golden calf for the people to worship (Exod 32; Ps 106:19-20). Later, they would also worship other deities including the sun, moon and stars (Jer 8:1-2). Analysis of their behaviour reveals that turning away from the glory of the Lord to idolatry corrupts value systems, thought processes and regard for human life, and results in a corrupt society. When people worship and serve idols, they are entering into an alliance with the spirits that those gods represent (Ps 106:28). They are ensnared by the powers of darkness, just as an animal caught in a snare is immobilized, in pain, in bondage and at the mercy of predators (Ps 106:36).

God also warned the children of Israel to avoid various aspects of idolatry: 'Let no one be found among you who sacrifices his son or daughter in the fire, who practises divination or sorcery, interprets omens, engages in witchcraft or casts spells, or who is a medium or spiritist or who consults the dead' (Deut 18:10-11). It is disturbing to note that many of the practices listed here are woven into our culture. So is the worship of a variety of creatures, some of which have become totems. For proof that this continues we need only think of the extent to which witchcraft, divination and sorcery are common among politicians and football players.

God describes himself as a jealous God (Exod 20:6), who will not tolerate the evils represented by rival gods. Accordingly he responds to idolatry with anger and distances himself from people who practise it (Rom 1:21-24). He punished the Israelites for their ongoing idolatry by allowing them to be conquered by Gentile nations (Ps 106:40-43).

In the NT Paul categorically condemns idolatry and urges believers to flee from it (1 Cor 10:14). He describes Gentile sacrifices as sacrifices to demons and not to God, and concludes that 'you cannot drink the cup of the Lord and the cup of demons too; you cannot have a part in both the Lord's table and the table of demons' (1 Cor 10:21). This is a call for total separation.

The eating of the things that are sacrificed during idolatrous feasts and festivals also defiles people (Ps 106:28).

Unlike Paul, some African theologians have called for accommodation of African traditional religions, claiming that the High God worshipped in those religions is the same as the God of the Judeo-Christian religion. Some even refer to Jesus as 'a paramount ancestor'. By doing this, they validate traditional religious beliefs and worship that the Bible condemns (Exod 20:3-4; Matt 4:10).

There are also more subtle forms of idolatry in our day. For instance, an inordinate obsession with money and material things is tantamount to idolatry and is condemned by Jesus in no uncertain terms (Luke 16:13). Many, especially the younger generation, venerate modern technology, mass media and the cyber highway, forgetting that any human-made god is an idol (Isa 40:19-20).

Our response to idolatry must be to intercede for our people as Moses did (Exod 32:11-13). We need to repent of our own wickedness, disobedience and rebellion and that of our ancestors (Ezra 9:5-15; Neh 1:5-11; Dan 9:4-19). Idolatrous practices must be renounced (Ezra 10:11-12; Acts 19:8-9). The covenants involved in trafficking with idols and spirits need to be verbally broken because the ancestors or people who instituted them spoke words that established the relationship.

The land itself will also need to be redeemed because the blood shed during human sacrifices, the building of altars, and the dedication of certain portions of land to spirits brings the devil onto the land legally. We must properly terminate the leasehold of the enemy and invoke the reconciliation that God has provided through the blood of Jesus Christ (Col: 19-20).

Idolatry not only dishonours God, it also dishonours humanity. In worshipping created things, people are abandoning the authority over creation that was given to them by God (Gen 1:26). The steps outlined above help restore this authority after peace has been made with God through repentance.

Emeka Nwankpa

Anticipating the next chapter, the author announces that this rebuilding will be made possible by Cyrus, king of Persia (Ezra 1:1-4). Cyrus is called a *shepherd* because he will gather the people to Jerusalem (**44:28**; 40:11; 43:5-7).

45:1-25 Cyrus, the Lord's Messiah

The king of Persia is described as the Lord's *anointed,* or in other words, as his messiah (**45:1**). He becomes God's servant, like Saul and David were (1 Sam 10:1; 16:13). It is not unusual for God to use foreign kings to accomplish his purposes (see 2 Kgs 8:7-15). After all, he is not just a regional deity but the God who created all things (**45:6-8**; Dan 4:34-37).

God does not require that people know him or acknowledge him before they can serve him (**45:4-5**). Every creature is subject to him. Cyrus will discover the hand of the Lord behind his easy victories (**45:2-3**). And neither he nor the Israelites have any right to complain about what God is doing. A pot cannot rebel against the potter who made it, and little children cannot challenge their parents, and so humans have no right to challenge the plans of the Creator of the universe (**45:9-12**). God had earlier used the Assyrians to punish Israel and Judah (10:5), and now he will put the king of Persia where he wants him. He will see to it that Cyrus allows the people of Israel to leave without even demanding compensation (**45:13**; Ezra 1:4, 6-11).

As announced in 43:3, God delivers Ethiopia (*Cush*) and the kingdom of *Sheba* (which may have been in Arabia or in Africa) to the king of Persia in exchange for the liberation of his people (**45:14**). Those nations are confused by the ineffectiveness of their idols (**45:16**) – even if God's name is not yet clearly acknowledged because he *hides himself* (**45:15**). But Israel will know who has delivered them. They may not see his face, but they can know his creation and his word of justice and uprightness (**45:17-19**).

Not only does God save his people but he wants to be the God of *the fugitives from the nations,* of those from the *ends of the earth* (**45:20**, **22**). Once again, he confronts their idols and presents himself as the only God and therefore the only possible saviour (**45:21**; see 41:21-24; 44:7-8). He announces that a time is coming when he will be worshipped, recognized not only as the God of Israel but as the God of all people of all languages (**45:23-25**). The Apostle Paul quotes 45:23 to show the universal scope of salvation in Jesus Christ, who fulfils this prophecy (Phil 2:10-11).

46:1-13 Humiliation of Babylon's Gods

The author returns to the theme of 'every knee will bow' (45:13) and applies it to *Bel* and *Nebo,* two of the gods worshipped by the Babylonians. The images of these gods are proudly paraded around the city on the backs of beasts, but with the invasion by Persia these images will soon be thrown down and carried far away (**46:1-2**; 21:9). Babylon

will suffer the same fate that it inflicted on the temple in Jerusalem. Apart from the grace of God, 'all who draw the sword will die by the sword' (Matt 26:52; see Gal 6:7-8).

Following this prophecy, the Lord tells his people to listen to him (**46:3a**). Believers must be willing to listen to God and other people (Jas 1:19). Listening is fundamental to the relationship between the Lord and his people (Deut 6:4). From the very beginning, those who refuse to listen to God's counsel pay dearly for it (Gen 3:1-4:15). Listening is the opposite of hardening one's heart (46:12; Exod 7:3-4). The African church should take this quality to heart and teach it to people of all ages, for we belong to a culture that values speaking more than listening.

No doubt, some of the Jews in exile in Babylonia had started to think of the Lord as being just another God among the Babylonian gods. God voices his strong objection to being considered comparable to their lifeless, inactive idols (**46:5-7**; see also 40:18-20, 25-26). Unlike an idol, God is actively present with believers from *birth* to *old age* (**46:3b-4**; Ps 139:1-18).

The command to listen is followed by the command to *remember* (**46:8**). They are to remember what God has done for them in the past, even though they rebelled against him (**46:9a**). But above all, they are to remember the point that is drummed in again and again in this section of Isaiah: the Lord is the only true God (**46:9b**). They are again reminded that he alone can predict the future and bring it about (**46:10**). And once again they are told that they will see this come true in the future liberation of Israel by the king of Persia (**46:12-13**; see 41:21-29; 43:9-13; 44:6-8).

47:1-15 Humiliation of Babylon

Babylon is told to *sit in the dust,* a characteristic feature of mourning in those days (**47:1a**; see Esth 4:1-3; Job 2:8). Whereas Jerusalem was described as a 'harlot' (1:21), Babylon is said to be a *virgin.* By this the author probably means that the city has never been subject to another nation. But this has given her a false sense of importance, and she now assumes that she is entitled to be *the eternal queen* (**47:5**).

The city is compared to a pampered noblewoman, *tender* and *delicate* and living in luxury off the work of others (**47:1b**). She arrogantly exploited those whom God had given into her power, showing Israel *no mercy* (**47:6**). Like Assyria before her (10:5-7), she went beyond the limits God had assigned her.

God will punish her for these sins. He will not show mercy either and will *spare no-one* (**47:3b**). The pampered virgin will be put to work grinding corn and working in the fields like a peasant. Where previously she was draped in veils, her nakedness will be exposed like that of a harlot (**47:2-3a**).

Besides being punished for her cruelty, Babylon is also accused of the same sins mentioned in the earlier prophecy on the fall of this city (13:1-22). They include complacency and love of luxury (**47:8a**; 13:17, 19) and the extreme self-ishness and pride revealed in statements like *there is none besides me!* (**47:8b**, **10**; 13:11).

The author now also expands on the theme that was touched on lightly in 13:10. The Lord condemns the Baby-lonians' astrology, worship of the stars and their dabbling in magic (**47:9-13**). These words speak to Africa, where we have traditionally attempted to protect ourselves from misfortune by wearing amulets or engaging in magic rites (see comments on 28:15). The Lord strongly condemns all such practices, whether used for protection or to foretell the future. Not only do they draw his wrath, but they are useless. They will not protect the Babylonians from God's judgment (**47:14-15**).

48:1-22 The Lord, the Only Master

Following the denunciation of Babylon, the Lord again asks his people to listen (see comments on 46:3a). They too need to change their attitudes. The Lord refuses to accept hypo-critical worship (see 1:11-17). Religiosity without *truth or righteousness* is useless (**48:1-2**; see 1 Sam 15:22). It is not enough for the people just to claim their traditional culture, calling themselves *citizens of the holy city* and invoking *the God of Israel.* They really need to pay attention to God.

God reminds them that he told them what he was plan-ning to do long before it happened (**48:3**). He had two reasons for doing this. First, he knows that human beings are stubborn and set in their evil ways. They had been described as a stiff-necked people at the time of the exodus (Exod 32:9; Deut 9:6). Nothing had changed. It was as if the *sinews of your neck were iron* (**48:4**). The people were still refusing to submit to God's law.

God's second reason for describing his plan in advance was that the people had never been exclusively faithful to the Lord. They had often treated him as if he was just another god alongside their other idols (17:7-8; 31:7; 40:18-20; 44:9-20; 46:5-7). The advance warning he had given them should have proven he was the only true God (**48:5-6**).

But the people may have been thinking only about God's prophecies of judgment against Jerusalem in the past, and may have shrugged off his words with *Yes, I knew of them* (**48:7**). So God explicitly teaches them something *new.* They cannot make the excuse that they are bored: any refusal to listen this time is because of their presumption and rebel-lious attitude (**48:8**).

God would be right to be angered by such an attitude, but he keeps his anger under control and undertakes a course of action that will bring these people to glorify him (**48:9, 11**). He has punished them in order to refine them and make them better, not to destroy them (**48:10**).

If Africa is indeed the cradle of humanity, our very first culture was in direct communication with the Creator (Gen 2–4). Yet like the Israelites, we often allow fetish practices to take a place alongside God in our worship. We need to become aware of God's anger at such practices, and of his efforts and patience on our behalf. We should commit our-selves unreservedly to him.

The Creator reminds his people of who he is. He is the one who controls the natural elements that these foolish people both fear and worship (see 13:10-11). He alone can predict the future, and specifically the fall of Babylon at the hands of the king of Persia. None of the idols can do this (**48:12-15**; see 39:21-29; 43:9-13; 44:6-8; 46:10-13).

Verses **48:16-17** strongly resemble the poem in which wisdom speaks in Proverbs 8:22-36. Wisdom was estab-lished by God *from the first announcement* and was the means by which he taught humankind. The author is pointing out that wisdom can be obtained only from the Lord (Jas 1:5; 3:13-18).

If the people had been faithful to God, they would have enjoyed all the blessings of the covenant made with Abra-ham (**48:18-19**; Gen 22:17). But what they can look forward to now is a new exodus, similar to the first, in which God will provide for their needs and tyranny will be overthrown (**48:20-22**; see Exod 17:6).

49:1-26 The Light for the Gentiles

Chapter 49 deals with God's choice of Israel, its failure and its redemption through God's chosen one. It starts with the second of the Servant Songs, in which the servant speaks of his commission (49:1-6; see 42:1-9; 50:4-9; 52:13-53:12).

The opening verses of this Servant Song are similar to the start of the first song in 44:1-2. God designates *Israel* as his *servant* from birth (**49:1**; see also 41:8-9; 43:1). This election goes along with a well-defined mission: *to display my splendour* (**49:3**). The servant will do this by spread-ing the word of God, his law, which is symbolized by the *sharpened sword* placed in the mouth of the servant (**49:2**; Heb 4:12; Rev 1:16; 19:15). It seems that Paul also draws on this description when he describes his own mission to the Gentiles (Gal 1:15).

The prophet then replies to God in the voice of Israel. The people recognize that they have failed in the mission entrusted to them. Rather than representing God, they have *laboured … in vain and for nothing* (**49:4a**). Now the people have a repentant attitude. In contrast to their attitude in 40:27, they now recognize that despite this, God has not abandoned them, even in exile, and that *what is due to me is in the Lord's hand* (**49:4b**).

After this repentance on the part of the people, the Lord speaks. He raises up another *servant* to save Israel and *gather* them from exile (**49:5**). This is the mission entrusted to Cyrus in 44:28 and 45:13.

This servant acknowledges that he has been honoured by God, and receives a still greater honour. He is given the mission of being *a light for the Gentiles,* and taking them God's *salvation* (**49:6**). This saving light was also mentioned in the first Servant Song (42:6). In discussing that song, it was pointed out that the prophecy was capable of a dual fulfilment. The same is true here. Cyrus did indeed free all the nations under Babylonian rule. However, the description of that salvation as extending *to the ends of the earth* makes us think of the still greater salvation accomplished through the universal work of Christ (49:6; John 1:9, 29; Acts 13:47).

The work of God's messenger is followed by the second exodus of the people, rich in imagery drawn from the first exodus. The one who was a *servant* and those who were *captives* will be freed from the yoke of the tyrant, who must bow before God (**49:7, 9a**; Exod 12:31, 35-36). A new *covenant* will be made between the Lord and the people (**49:8**; Exod 24:3-8). The Jews who returned from exile did indeed make a new agreement before God (Neh 9:38-10:39). Remembering the hardships of the first exodus, God assures his people that they will find abundant food and drink on their journey (**49:9b-10**; Exod 16:4; 17:6). Isaiah also repeats his favourite images of the end of the exile: the creation of a level highway and the gathering of God's people from the four corners of the earth (**49:11-13**; see 40:3-4; 43:6-7).

The author then turns to Jerusalem and its restoration. God's love for this city is said to be greater than a mother's love (**49:14-15**). God is beyond gender and he demonstrates this by his willingness to use both masculine and feminine images to describe himself (see comments on 31:5; see also Luke 13:34). Both men and women are created in the image of God (Gen 1:27).

Many of the themes mentioned in relation to the restoration of Jerusalem (49:16-26) are also found in the books of Ezra and Nehemiah. So we observe concern about the ruined state of the city (**49:17, 19**; Ezra 3:12; Neh 1:3-4), separation from the foreign oppressor (49:17; Ezra 10:2-3; Neh 13:23-31), concern for repopulation (49:18-21; Ezra 2:1-70; Neh 11:1-12:26) and the participation of kings in the re-establishment of the city (**49:22-23**; Ezra 1:1-11; 7:12-26; Neh 2:4-8).

The people express their incredulity at these promises (**49:24**), but God assures them that he will indeed fulfil them all. Those who had formerly oppressed them will be overthrown, and *all mankind will know that I, the Lord, am your Saviour* (**49:25-26**). God will indeed have displayed his splendour in his people (49:3).

50:1-11 The Lord's Faithfulness

In the book of Isaiah, the people swing back and forth between gratitude for God's intervention and a feeling of abandonment (1:9; 40:27; 49:4, 14). Here, the Lord assures them of his faithfulness.

When God asks the question, *Where is your mother's certificate of divorce?* (**50:1a**), he seems to be thinking of the type of situation presented by the prophet Hosea. He compares the relationship between God and his people to that of a man searching for his wife even though she is a prostitute and unfaithful (Hos 1–2). God's second question is, *to which of my creditors did I sell you?* This question calls to mind the situation of the woman whom Elisha helped when her sons were in danger of being sold to settle a debt (2 Kgs 4:1-7).

These questions are purely rhetorical. God never divorced his people; he never sold them (48:8-11; 49:15). It is because of their own sins that the people find themselves in exile (**50:1b**). God is the one who pursues them and helps them (**50:2-3**).

The author then presents the third of the Servant Songs (50:4-9; see 42:1-9; 49:1-6; 52:13-53:12). In this song the servant again speaks, this time describing how he is being instructed, disciplined and strengthened for his mission. As a disciple with *an instructed tongue,* he is available to those whom he teaches and comforts, while all the time listening to God (**50:4**; see comments on 46:3a). He is a model disciple, a humble person who is willing to be taught and who does not insist on being the teacher (John 13:12-17).

This disciple is also a model because he does not react to adversity, violence or complaints: *I have not been rebellious* (**50:5**; see Matt 5:39). Nor does he show cowardice: *I have not drawn back* (**50:6**). He has endured these tests while waiting for the Lord's help (**50:7**).

In Africa, it is often assumed that one who serves God will enjoy prestige and success. But the true disciple, following Christ's example, is willing to suffer (see comment on 20:2-3; see also John 15:20).

Who is this *servant* referred to in **50:10a**? His mission of teaching and listening to God does not correspond to that of the servant Cyrus (45:1-4). In 49:3, the servant was the nation of Israel, but here the text clearly refers to an individual, and not a nation. The individual might be Isaiah himself, but the servant's claim of innocence (**50:8-9**) and his power to condemn (**50:11**) also make him a foreshadowing of Christ (see John 5:22, 27; 8:26). This foreshadowing will continue in the fourth Servant Song (52:13-53:12).

This passage closes with a powerful image. Those who trust the Lord may sometimes feel that their lives are *dark,* and that they see *no light.* In such circumstances, they must continue to *trust in the name of the Lord* and walk in the light shed by his word which shows them the path they should follow (**50:10b**; Ps 11:105). They should not be anxious to seek out other sources of light, for these are merely flaming torches that will be extinguished soon, but not before they have burned those who hold them (50:11).

51:1-23 Liberation of the Children of Abraham

Israel as a nation had failed to fulfil God's purpose (see 49:4). However, some of the people remained faithful to the mission of God and of his servant (50:4-6). These people actively *pursue righteousness* (**51:1a**). Jesus will declare such people 'blessed' (Matt 5:6).

The Lord now speaks to encourage these people. He invites them to remember Abraham, the father of their faith, and his wife Sarah (**51:1b-2a**). As Christians, we too should look to Abraham as a model, for he is described as a precursor of faith in Christ (Rom 4:3; Heb 11:8-19; 12:1-2). Just as God blessed this man and made him fruitful, so he will bless Jerusalem and make her fruitful (**51:2b-3**). Once again we find the picture of the desert transformed so that it is *like Eden … like the garden of the Lord* (51:3; see 35:1-10; 41:17-20; 43:19b-20; 44:3-5).

We are given a clear indication of why the man who seeks the Lord's righteousness is said to be 'blessed'. God promises justice, righteousness and salvation, and these are things that will endure. The heavens and the earth will decay, and humans will die *like flies*. But God's salvation *will last for ever* and his righteousness *will never fail* (**51:4-6**). Those who invest in God's righteousness, invest in eternity (Matt 6:19-21). What wonderful encouragement for those of us who live surrounded by corruption!

Like the servant (50:4-9), those who are faithful to God should not fear what others say about them because of their righteousness (**51:7**). Their persecutors, who seem so strong and confident, will soon be as useless and fragile as moth-eaten cloth (**51:8**; see also 50:9; 51:6) while God's righteousness will endure (Matt 10:28).

The same theme is picked up in 51:12-16. There God's people are reminded that the humans who persecute them are merely *grass,* whereas the God they serve is the one who created the world itself (**51:12-13**). The believers may cower before their oppressors who imprison them, but those oppressors themselves will cower before the one who has all the strength of the sea at his command (**51:14-15**). God's people can take comfort that God will give them the words to say and will shelter them with his hand (**51:16**; see also Luke 2:12-19). More than that, the Creator of the universe will call them *my people.*

The words of encouragement are accompanied by two separate trumpet calls: *Awake! Awake!* The first summons is directed to *the arm of the Lord,* which symbolizes his action on the earth (**51:9**; Deut 5:15). Isaiah stirs the memory of what happened in the *generations of old.* Then, God overthrew Rahab, the primeval monster that Isaiah has used as a symbol of Egypt (see comment on 30:7). The Lord made a road out of Egypt for his enslaved people (**51:10**). In the same way, he will bring the people back from exile.

We have already seen the importance of memory to faith (see 46:8-9). In our culture, which is still the culture of the

storyteller, of the griot, we owe it to ourselves to maintain the memory of God's blessings on his church and his people in Africa.

The second set of trumpet calls summons Jerusalem to awake (**51:17a**). The city was still in ruins, abandoned after the Babylonian conquest (Neh 1:3). It had drunk to the full from the cup of God's wrath, or in other words, it had endured his judgment on the wicked (**51:17b-20**; see also Ps 75:8). Once again the prophet reminds us of the link between a nation's abandoning God's law and its inability to find a good leader (51:18; see comments on 3:1-7). But the Lord now announces a time of grace and the recovery of Jerusalem (**51:21-22**). God's wrath will turn on those who tormented them (**51:23**).

52:1-12 The Purification of Jerusalem

Once again the restored Jerusalem is called on to *Awake* (see 51:17). This time, however, she is told to take the same action as God does in 51:9: *clothe yourself with strength* (**52:1a**). The city is to put on *garments of splendour.* These garments, which would be equivalent to our Sunday clothes, symbolize respect for God and his holiness (**52:1b**; see Zech 3:1-5; Matt 22:11-14). Of course, we need to remember that what God is actually speaking about here is an attitude of heart, not specific uniforms or costumes such as are worn in some African churches (see also Joel 2:13).

Jerusalem can also lift its head because it will not have to scrape together the money for a tribute that will pay for its freedom. The Lord will give it liberty and will not charge for its salvation (**52:2-3**; see 45:13; 55:1-2; Rom 3:24). Their oppressors, nations such as Egypt and Assyria, had not paid for the privilege of conquering God's people, so why should Jerusalem have to pay to be delivered from them (**52:4-5**)?

In response to the city's deliverance, the people again take up the mission entrusted to them by God: to be his messenger (see 49:1-4). They will become messengers bringing *good tidings* (**52:6-10**; see 40:9). These 'good tidings' include three things: *peace, salvation,* and the news that *God reigns.* It is no coincidence that the very word 'gospel' means 'good news' (Matt 4:23; Mark 1:14-15; Luke 16:16) and that the gospel brings peace (John 14:27), salvation (Luke 7:76-77) and the news that 'the kingdom of God has come' (Matt 12:28). While the African church preaches salvation in Jesus Christ loudly and clearly, it is often silent on the other two themes that affect our societies: peace between different social or ethnic groups, and the principles, such as justice, that are the foundation of the kingdom of God. Only when we make the effort to preach the full contents of the 'good tidings' will we truly be salt and light for our continent (Matt 5:13-16).

The purification of Jerusalem is accompanied by the purification of the people who are returning from exile and bringing back the holy articles that had been stolen from the temple (**52:11**; see Ezra 6:5). As at the time of the exodus, God guarantees them protection on their journey by providing a vanguard and a rearguard (**52:12**; Exod 13:21; 14:13-14, 19-20).

52:13-53:12 The Suffering Servant

The purification of Jerusalem is then extended to the nations through a servant who foreshadows Jesus the Messiah (see 50:8-11). This is the fourth Servant Song (see also 42:1-9; 49:1-6; 50:4-9).

Like Israel in exile, this servant will be humiliated before being exalted for the salvation of the nations who have not heard of him (**52:13-15**; Rom 15:21; Phil 2:6-11). It is in this way that salvation is offered to Africa. In fact, it was an explanation of this section of Isaiah that would lead to the salvation of one of the first African converts to Christianity (Acts 8:26-39).

The author next explains why this humiliation of God's servant was necessary. The first reason is that God does not play to appearances in order to win. Because someone's appearance is one of the first things people look at, they will not immediately approve of this servant (**53:1-2**). Thus the Gospels tell us nothing at all about what Jesus looked like – but they do tell us that he considered a right attitude of the heart far more important than any ostentatious display (Mark 12:38-44).

The servant is also said to be *a man of sorrows, and familiar with suffering* (**53:3**). The book of Isaiah has made it abundantly clear that anyone who is faithful to God must know how to face persecution for the sake of righteousness (see 20:2-3; 50:5-6; 51:7). However, God's servant here is suffering not only for righteousness, but also for the sins that all of us have committed (**53:4-6**). Because of these sins, the sufferer, though innocent himself, is put to death (**53:7-9**). The concept of something without sin dying to atone for the sins of someone who is guilty was embedded in the regulations for the *guilt offering* in Leviticus 5:15 (**53:10a**). The sacrifice of this servant will bring peace and will justify many people (**53:5, 11, 12**).

For this work, the servant is repaid by God. He who was in the tomb will see his days prolonged, just as Hezekiah's were in Isaiah's time (**53:10b**; see 38:1-20). This is not the first time that the prophet foresees the possibility of resurrection (see 25:8; 26:19). Besides being given back his life, the servant also receives great power from God.

The many similarities between this passage and the ministry, death and resurrection of Christ led his disciples to recognise this passage as a prophecy that was being fulfilled in their time (Matt 8:17; Luke 22:37; John 12:38; Acts 3:26; Rom 15:21; 1 Pet 2:22-25).

54:1-17 A Covenant of Peace with Israel

This chapter is full of idealized pictures of life under the covenant, all drawn from the OT. Did this idyllic situation actually exist in post-exilic Israel? In its historical context, this needs to be interpreted as literary symbolism, an evocation of a situation rather than a detailed description. However, if we take into account the fact that this prophecy is placed after the account of the work of Christ in 53:1-12, we are justified in reading it as a symbolic description of a heavenly reality (Gal 4:21-27).

In his covenant with Abraham, God promised him many descendants (see comments on 51:1-3; Gen 17:15-19). That promise is remembered in **54:1**, in the joy of the barren woman who now has many children.

In his covenant with the people of Israel, God promised them land (Exod 3:8; 34:10-11). Now, his gift is no longer just the area of the promised land, but whole nations (**54:2-3**).

The prophet next reminds the people of yet another covenant, that between a husband and a wife (**54:4-8**). He has already depicted the relationship between God and his people in these terms (50:1-2). This image no doubt refers back to the prophet Hosea, Isaiah's contemporary, who depicted the strains and the reconciliation in this marriage (Hos 3:1).

The fourth picture, which is more explicit, recalls God's covenant with Noah, in which God promised never again to destroy the earth (Gen 9:8-17). This commitment is now transformed into a promise that God will never again destroy Israel (**54:9-10**).

This promised peace brings about three consequences. The first is prosperity, symbolized by the precious stones that are used to build Jerusalem (**54:11-12**). This picture will be taken up in the description of the heavenly Jerusalem in Revelation 21:18-21. The second consequence is a serene faithfulness to the Lord (**54:13-14**). The third consequence is absolute security because God will provide his people with impregnable defences (**54:15-17**).

55:1-13 Salvation Offered to All

The Lord invites all those who are hungry and thirsty to a banquet. This image is associated with the promise of eternal life (25:6-8). What is new here is the announcement that access to this banquet is free. Our invitation is purely a result of God's grace (**55:1-2**).

Does the statement that all are freely invited mean that this verse can be used to teach that all are saved? No, for later in the same passage the prophet speaks of the need for repentance (55:7). In his similar parable about a banquet, Jesus also speaks of a wide invitation, but adds a warning against assuming that no conditions whatsoever apply (Matt 22:1-14).

The use of a feast to illustrate salvation has great appeal in Africa, where community spirit is still strong and hospitality is a core value (see 16:3; Heb 13:1-3). We should use this image to present the grace of God to our contemporaries.

The Lord also promises to enter into a covenant that will be a continuation of the one made with David (**55:3**; 1 Chr 17:14). Christians will see in this a foreshadowing of the ministry of David's son, Jesus Christ (Matt 1:17; Acts 13:34). They will also see this in **55:4-5**, where the one described has the attributes of the Messiah (see 52:15; 53:10b, 12a).

Participation in this covenant requires an act of repentance and the abandoning of evil ways. It also seems that there is a time limit on this offer (**55:6**). The day will come when we will no longer have the option of turning to our Creator in repentance and receiving his help and forgiveness. As Ecclesiastes says, we must remember God before the end of our life (Eccl 12:1-7).

But if wicked people turn to God, they will be welcomed. The Lord will *freely pardon* them. In this, he goes far beyond what we ourselves are capable of doing (**55:7-9**). Jesus, too, will preach a message of forgiveness (Matt 18:21-35).

The second part of the book of Isaiah ends with the assurance that the word of God is far more than mere words (**55:10-11**). It produces fruit, and is effective in accomplishing his purposes. Isaiah's hearers can rest assured that the promise of salvation and celebration will be fulfilled (**55:12-13**).

56:1-66:24 Part 3: Reproach and Promises

In part 2 of the book of Isaiah, the author focused mainly on the end of the exile and the role of Cyrus, although every now and again he alluded to the coming messianic era. But from chapter 56 on, the prophet ceases to deal with the era of exile and turns his full attention to the new ideal era, in which there will be salvation for all nations and exceptional glory for Jerusalem. He constantly contrasts the future blessings promised by God with the distressing attitude of the people in the present.

56:1-12 A United People

The author had previously proclaimed salvation for those who seek God and his righteousness (see 51:1, 5). Here he again speaks of righteousness and salvation, but this time he makes it even clearer for whom this salvation is destined. Whereas 51:2 could leave us thinking that only the historical descendants of Abraham would be saved, here redemption is offered to every human being (literally, 'son of Adam'), who respects the Lord's commands (**56:1-2**). This wider scope of salvation agrees with the universal mission of God's Messiah, Jesus Christ (see 49:6; 50:4-9; 52:15).

It may be because of this wider scope that Isaiah here places such stress on keeping the Sabbath in this chapter (56:2, 4, 6; 58:13). The Sabbath was first established at creation (Gen 2:2; Exod 20:8-11) and thus applies to all of

humanity, whereas other provisions of the law were given only at a later date. When all human beings turn to God, all will keep his Sabbaths as an expression of their faith in the God of Israel.

The word *blessed* in 56:2 reminds us of Psalm 1:1 and the beatitudes of Matthew 5:3-12. Now that blessing is extended to the *foreigner*, that is, to someone who was not an Israelite by birth, and to the *eunuch*. This clarification is revolutionary because it is these two categories of people that had previously been excluded from worshipping with the people of God (Exod 12:43; Deut 23:1-8).

Eunuchs, depending on the extent of their handicap, might not be circumcised and, of course, could not have children, which is why a eunuch might describe himself as *a dry tree* (**56:3**). Not only was he excluded from the assembly, but he also could not hope for the many descendants that were one of the concrete manifestations of the covenant between God and Abraham (Gen 17:6-11). He would have no heirs and his name would be forgotten. But God now promises him *an everlasting name* that is preserved *within my temple* (**56:4-5**).

Foreigners who love God and keep his law will also now be fully integrated into the people of God (**56:6-7**). It was verses like this that led the Apostle Paul to recognize the spiritual dimension of God's covenant with Abraham. Thus Paul emphasizes the saving faith of the patriarch and circumcision of the heart, rather than physical circumcision (see Rom 2:29; Gal 3:6-14).

Many Africans feel themselves excluded from the modern world. Rapid urbanization and globalization have overturned the dependable values of their former villages, and have replaced them with rampant individualism. In response to this, the African church must become more than simply a place where we meet on Sundays. It must become a place where a spirit of community is reborn through extending a warm welcome to all who come. It must become a place where people can see righteousness lived out at the local level. The church should be the 'village' for the lost.

Jesus must have meditated on these verses, for we find him quoting 56:7 when he cleanses the temple (Mark 11:17). He saw both the opening of the temple to all nations, and the fact that it should be a place of prayer.

The Lord is seen as the God who *gathers* Israel and all of the peoples (**56:8**). It is in this that we see the picture of the good shepherd applied to God and to his Messiah, the one who will safely lead his people and save them (see 40:11; 44:28; Ps 28:9; John 10:11-18).

The author contrasts this image of the true leader with the failings of those who claim to be the shepherds of the people in his time (**56:11**), but who leave their people exposed to external dangers (**56:9**). These leaders are described as *blind* and *mute* (**56:10a**), the same terms used elsewhere to describe those who serve idols and are unfaithful to God (see 42:16-20; 43:8). These men are like the objects that they worship (see 44:9, 18).

The prophet accuses the religious leaders, who should be watchmen, of deceiving themselves and losing the people. Dreaming and drinking are their main occupations (**56:10b, 12**; see also 29:8-10). They have no commitment to maintaining justice and doing what is right, as commanded at the beginning of this passage. Such interests would involve a concern for others and for God, but all these leaders prefer to *turn to their own way* (56:11). Their attitude is an echo of the disastrous situation of the people in 53:6.

57:1-21 God, the Righteous and Idolaters

With the greedy and self-centred political and religious leaders described in the preceding chapter (56:9-12), it is not surprising that the righteous are sacrificed on the altar of ambition and in the struggle for power. What is especially criticized here is indifference to the situation (**57:1a**). In many of our countries, life has become cheap due to misery or war. Many of us have become hardened by repeated deaths. The African church should proclaim the importance and value of every human being in the eyes of God.

However, thanks be to God, the death of the righteous is not in vain. They move on to a better life, serene and free from *evil* (**57:1b-2**). The Apostle Paul was aware of this when he said that we need not fear death because it can only benefit Christians (Phil 1:21-24).

The prophet contrasts the peace and restfulness acquired by the righteous with the evil agitation of idolaters. These people do one horrible or useless thing after another: they practise human sacrifice (**57:5**), make offerings to gods of stone (**57:6**), patronize prostitutes (**57:7-8**) and embark on fruitless pilgrimages (**57:9**). As has already been shown, seeking the support of a foreign power is a sign of spiritual immaturity (see 30:2-7). This is something that our continent needs to learn,

The rest enjoyed by the righteous is contrasted with the weariness of those who persist in consulting idols (**57:10**). Yet their *collection of idols* will not help them to escape judgment (**57:13a**). It would be far better to fear the Lord (**57:11**) and to be recognized as righteous by him (**57:12**; see comments on 56:1-12).

Whereas the idols are useless, God is a welcoming God who can actually provide salvation (**57:13b**). The command to build a road in **57:14** reminds us of the similar command in 40:1-4, where it accompanied the announcement of the end of the exile.

Paradoxically, God, who is absolutely holy and inaccessible, is also present among those who are humble and oppressed (**57:15**). This amazing truth is shown particularly clearly in his incarnation in Jesus Christ (see Heb 7:26). We see God's response when Jesus responds to the cry of the blind Bartimaeus: 'Jesus, Son of David, have mercy on me'

(Mark 10:46-52). Not knowing the full truth about Jesus, Bartimaeus hailed him by the name of King David, another friend of the oppressed and the weak (1 Sam 30:11-12; 2 Sam 6:18-19; 9:6-13).

The Lord recognizes that to totally punish sin, as he did at the time of the flood, would mean the death of all humankind (**57:16-17**; Gen 8:21). None would escape his wrath, for all have sinned (Rom 3:22-23). Thus God chooses to show mercy to *the mourners* among his people, and even to those beyond his people. These 'mourners' are those who have a repentant attitude (**57:18-19**). But he will show no mercy to the wicked who behave stubbornly (57:5-10). They will find *no peace* (**57:20-21**). These words were last said when God condemned the cruelty of Babylon (48:22).

58:1-14 The True Fast

Since 'there is no peace ... for the wicked' (57:21) but God does show mercy to the one who turns from his evil ways (55:7), the prophet of the Lord has the duty to warn the people (**58:1**). The prophet Ezekiel also stresses this responsibility of warning the wicked of their sad fate (Ezek 3:17-21). Christians, too, have a duty to rescue their brothers and sisters who are stumbling (Matt 18:15).

In the previous chapter, the prophet spoke to idolaters (57:3-13); now he turns his attention to those who offer false worship to the Lord. Some people seem to think that they can win favour with God by fasting and humbling themselves. They are surprised that their privations are not producing results (**58:2-3a**).

The prophet informs them that fasting is useless if it is not accompanied by abstaining from evil. These people fast 'on that day' which is possibly Yom Kippur, the Day of Atonement, which the Lord had appointed as a special day of fasting to atone for sins (Lev 16:29-34). It was a day on which people were required to humble themselves and deny themselves. But the people were hypocritically fasting once a year to obtain pardon for their sins while continuing to behave badly on that very day (**58:3b-5**).

Humbling oneself is useless if it is merely a matter of appearing humble. It is not enough simply to dress as if one is in mourning for one's sins, without any real sorrow for them (58:5; see also 15:3; 35:35-36). Jesus made the same point when he insisted that those who want to fast and deny themselves before God should not do it in any ostentatious way if they want to avoid falling into hypocrisy (Matt 6:5-6, 16-18). God should be worshipped 'in spirit and in truth' (John 4:24).

The good behaviour that the Lord wants to see in place of vain religious practices is still appropriate for Africa today: opposing slavery (**58:6, 9b**) and misery (58:7, 10). The exhortation to welcome the hungry, the homeless and the destitute (**58:7**) should again encourage the church to emphasize the strong African traditions of hospitality (see commentary on 16:3; 55:1-2). **58:10** can be translated as saying that we should give ourselves *on behalf of the needy,* or that we should give our own bread to them. This instruction reminds us of the Yombe (DRC) proverb, *Dia lobula,* which means that we should give our neighbour the bread that we already have in our mouth. We should not give the poor only those things that we do not want ourselves. As Jesus emphasizes, we should treat others as we ourselves would like to be treated (Matt 7:12).

Those who are involved in such activities and who also seek the Lord sincerely will be blessed by God (**58:8**, **11**, **13-14**) and will contribute to the reconstruction of their country (**58:12**). This text must have inspired Nehemiah to fight against the misery and the enslavement of others during the rebuilding of Jerusalem (Neh 5:1-19). It should also be an encouragement to us to take an active part in the reconstruction of our countries and not simply rely on foreign organizations to do it for us.

59:1-21 The Crimes of the People

In their misery, the people of Israel think that the Lord has abandoned them (40:27; 49:14). But the prophet confirms that God is ready to save. His *arm,* ready to reach out, recalls miraculous interventions of the past (Deut 4:34; 5:15). His *ear,* ready to hear, reminds us of his promise to hear the prayer of his people when they obey him (**59:1**; 2 Chr 7:14-15).

It is not God who is the problem; it is the sin of the people (**59:2**). A person's hand cannot find the hand of God when it is covered with blood and is busy weaving traps as a *spider* does (**59:3a**, **5-6**). God's holy ear cannot endure the crooked and deceptive words that humans speak (**59:3b-4**). The statement that humans *hatch the eggs of vipers* reminds us of the truly treacherous speech of the serpent in the garden of Eden (**59:5**; see Gen 3:1-5).

The thought of **59:7a** is also recorded in Proverbs 1:16. These *feet* that *rush into sin* contrast strongly with the feet of 'those who bring good news'. The first bring ruin and the absence of peace (**59:7b-8**) whereas the second announce reconstruction and peace (52:7).

The people are aware of the gravity of their sin, but at the same time recognize their inability to free themselves from it (59:9-15a). There is a difference between what they long for and what they achieve (**59:9**, **11**). We are reminded of the words of the Apostle Paul: 'For what I do is not the good I want to do; no, the evil I do not want to do – this I keep on doing' (Rom 7:19). Paul found that deliverance comes only from Jesus Christ (Rom 7:24-25).

Because the Lord finds *no justice,* he intervenes on earth (**59:15b-16**). He comes to punish those who remain his enemies (**59:17b-19**), and to save those of his people who *repent* (**59:17a**, **20-21**). This same power to condemn or save characterizes the Messiah (see comments on 50:8-11).

The military imagery used in 57:17 will be taken up by Paul when he encourages Christians to fight against evil (Eph 6:13-17).

60:1-22 New Glory for Jerusalem

After having announced God's decision to show mercy to the repentant (59:17a, 20-21), the prophet turns his attention to the restoration of Jerusalem. The arrangement of the chapters here is the same as that in chapters 51 and 52, where the first chapter announces the deliverance of the people and the second the renewal of Jerusalem.

This chapter repeats what has been said about the renewal of the city, but here the images are even more intense. Jerusalem is utterly transformed, and the light of the city and the glory of the Lord blend to form a sort of sun that banishes the shadows of the world (**60:1-3**, 19-20; Ps 36:9).

Themes that were touched on briefly in 49:22-23 are here developed at length. First there is the announcement of the return of the people (**60:4**), then the announcement that foreign kings will meet the needs of the city (**60:5b-9**). These kings are even described as nursing mothers (**60:16**; see 49:23). Once again, we hear of the kings bowing down before God's city (**60:14-15**). The concept of the participation of so many foreign rulers in the reconstruction of Jerusalem is an expansion of the model provided by Cyrus (**60:10**; see 44:28; 45:13; Ezra 1:4; 6:3-5).

The rebuilt, repopulated and restocked city will no longer experience the misery caused by an invasion (**60:18**; 54:14-17). Only people faithful to the Lord will live in Jerusalem, and they will prosper (**60:21-22**; see also 54:13).

The reconstructed Jerusalem after the return from exile in Babylon could never match the city described in this chapter. The only comparable city is the heavenly Jerusalem described in the book of Revelation, as we can see if we compare 60:3-5a, 11, 19 with Revelation 21:23-27 (see also comments on 54:1-17).

61:1-11 The Messenger of Salvation

Chapters 61–62 repeat the pattern in chapters 51–52 and 59–60: first the salvation of Israel and the nations and then the new glory for Jerusalem are addressed.

The theme of chapter 61 is thus the salvation that will be accomplished by a messiah, that is, by someone *anointed* by God, which is what the word 'messiah' means (see 45:1). One can accomplish a mission carried out in God's name only if one has received his *Spirit,* for when the Spirit rests upon a person, God is present in that person (**61:1a**; Prov 1:23; Matt 3:16-17; Acts 4:8-13).

The deliverance proclaimed here is described as *the year of the Lord's favour* (61:2). This seems to be a reference to the Jubilee Year proclaimed in Leviticus 25. Each fiftieth year, the Israelites were to allow all the land to lie fallow (that is, uncultivated) and were to free all those who were enslaved (**61:1b-2a**). God undertook to guarantee security and food for his people in those years. It seems that the Jubilee Years were never observed in Israel, but God is here proclaiming that such a year has begun.

Jesus turned to this passage when he described his ministry (Luke 4:18-19). His action underscores the link between the description of the servant in the book of Isaiah and the work of Christ (see comments on 49:1-6; 50:1-11; 52:13-53:12).

Yet once again, God's intervention brings both deliverance and judgment (see 59:17-21). It will be a day of liberation, but it will also be a *day of vengeance* on behalf of *all who mourn* (**61:2b**; 34:8). Here the author picks up the theme of 'the day of the Lord' that is dealt with in many of the prophets (see comments on 4:2). Jesus, and later his disciples, also preach about the day when God will judge humankind and avenge the oppressed (Matt 12:36; Luke 21:22; Rom 2:5; 2 Pet 2:9). On that day, the judge will be Jesus (see 50:11; John 5:25-30).

In 49:1-4, the messiah could be interpreted as the people of Israel, but the way he is represented in these opening verses of chapter 61 shows that he must be a person who acts on behalf of others. He gives them *oil of gladness,* which symbolizes a reward for having sought justice (**61:3a**; Pss 45:7; Heb 1:9). The *garment* that he gives them symbolizes an internal change, a purification, which finds expression in *praise* (**61:3b**; see Zech 3:1-5; Matt 22:11-13).

Then we again find the themes of reconstruction and of the people of Jerusalem being served by the nations (61:4-7; 49:22-23; 60:3-11). Here the purpose of this service by strangers is clarified; it allows the people to be free to serve God (**61:6**). The Lord insists, it seems, that the work be paid for; he does not like people to be robbed of the fruit of their labour (**61:8a**). Hence in the church, the pastor should be properly paid by the congregation (1 Tim 5:18), although this requirement should not be abused.

God's blessing on his people will be evident to those around (**61:7, 9**; Gen 26:12-31; 41:37-41). He confirms his everlasting covenant with all those who serve him (**61:8b**).

The author then transcribes a song of praise to be sung by the messiah. Whereas in 59:17 God put on armour for spiritual battle (see also Eph 6:10-17), here he gives his follower festive clothes that celebrate his salvation and righteousness (**61:10**). These garments are suited to the new order that God is introducing (61:10). The image of a seed that produces fruit seems to foresee the ministry of Jesus who will die as a seed in the ground in order to provide salvation (**61:11**; John 12:23-24).

62:1-12 Jerusalem, the Lord's Bride

The announcement of salvation in chapter 61 is followed in chapter 62 by the announcement of the restoration of Jeru-

salem (see the discussion of this pattern in the commentary on 60:1).

The introductory verses start by recalling the focus on light in the preceding section devoted to Jerusalem (**62:1-2a**; 60:1-3, 19-20). But then the prophet changes the image, and begins to describe the city as a bride.

First, the Lord promises Jerusalem a *new name* (**62:2b**). In Africa, certain initiation rites may be accompanied by a change in someone's name. In both African and biblical culture, such a change of name signifies a new character and a new destiny (Gen 17:5, 15; 35:10-11; Matt 16:17-19). This is what awaits Jerusalem as the Lord makes her one of his precious ornaments (**62:3**).

The city's old names were *Deserted* and *Desolate,* and served to remind Jerusalem that she had been an abandoned and barren woman in an age when such circumstances were a cause of deep shame (54:1, 7). But God has already said that he does not reject his bride, but instead seeks her when she wanders away (see comments on 50:1-2; Hos 1–2). So the new names that will be given to Jerusalem are *Hephzibah,* which means 'my delight is in her', and *Beulah,* which means 'married' (**62:4**). The idea of the city being married is explained in terms of her people returning from exile and settling in the land (**62:5, 10**; 60:4). The city will have other news names too: *Sought After* and *City No Longer Deserted* (**62:12**).

God sets watchmen around the city whose task is to engage in constant prayer that God will re-establish and glorify his city (**62:6-7**). Christians, too, must pray without ceasing, like these watchmen who take *no rest* (Eph 6:18; 1 Thess 5:17).

As a protective husband, the Lord will protect the city from all attack. His *mighty arm,* which has been used to protect the people in the past (see 51:9-10; 59:1), will ensure that the city is never again raided and its stores plundered. The people will enjoy the fruits of their labour (**62:8-9**).

63:1-64:12 The Day of Vengeance and Redemption

It may seem strange that Isaiah now moves abruptly from rejoicing in the healing of Jerusalem and its future glory to a scene of devastation, which is followed by a desperate prayer. One explanation for the lack of a strict chronological sequence in this section of the book may be that here we have a collection of prophecies that Isaiah uttered at various times. They were not necessarily uttered one after another, as they appear to be when we see them on the page. Another point to remember is that Isaiah is a prophet, not a historian. He does not have to follow a strict chronological sequence when presenting the messages he has received from the Lord.

63:1-6 The day of vengeance

Chapter 34 had horrifying images of the slaughter of Edom, taken as representative of all who oppressed God's people. Now the prophet returns to these in his vision of the *day of vengeance* (**63:1-6**; see also 61:2). The same God who saves the repentant righteous is the uncompromising judge of the stubborn wicked. Christians are shocked to read such words, for we tend not to think about this side of God's character. But these words remind us of how deeply God hates sin, and of how grateful we should be for his salvation.

63:7-64:12 Prayer for redemption

The violence of God's judgment deeply disturbs the people, who express their concerns in a long prayer of intercession and repentance (63:7-64:12). This prayer seems to have made a profound impression on learned Jews, for the prayer offered in Nehemiah 9:5-37 follows the same pattern. It begins by reminding God of how he delivered them in the past (63:7-14; Neh 9:6-15). It then stresses God's *might* as well as his *tenderness and compassion* (63:15-64:4; Neh 9:16-31) and finishes with an expression of the people's repentance for their sins (64:5-11; Neh 9:32-37).

63:7-14 RECOLLECTION OF THE PAST The *Holy Spirit* plays a major role in the section on past deliverances. Misfortune comes when our actions *grieve* him (**63:10**). The Apostle Paul will pick up this expression in Ephesians 4:30 when he is exhorting Christians to lead a holy life. To make a covenant with God is to welcome his Spirit among us (**63:11**). He is our guide, who will lead us to a place of *rest* (**63:14**).

63:15-64:7 AN APPEAL TO GOD The people recognize that it is only God's grace that prompts him to take an interest in them. They cannot make any claims on the basis of their human ancestry. But they appeal to God's 'tenderness' and twice call out to him as *our Father* (**63:16**). He is the only ancestor worthy of being invoked and capable of saving (see 30:27a; 43:27).

Yet God seems to have hidden his face from them (**64:7**) and seems to be ignoring Israel's fate. It is as if he turned his back on them because of their sins.

64:8-12 REPENTANCE The image of *clay* and the *potter* was used in 29:15-16 to denounce the political intrigues with Egypt that some thought they were carrying out behind the Lord's back. Here, however, the focus is on the clay's helplessness in the hands of the potter. It is totally dependent on what he chooses to do with it. This may be why the people could complain in 63:17 that God had hardened their hearts so that they wandered away from him.

Once again, God is referred to as the Father (**64:8**). Jesus himself will also speak of God as the Father who sees what takes place in secret (Matt 6:3, 6).

The people cry out to God not to remain *silent* any longer while his people suffer (**64:11**). They feel that their punishment is more than they can endure and cry out to God not to punish them *beyond measure* (**64:9, 12**).

65:1-25 The Lord's Promises

The people's accusation that God has neglected them prompts him to respond. He is not hidden from everyone. He has reached out to foreign nations who were not even seeking him (**65:1**). He has held out his hands to welcome his people, but they have not bothered to respond, because they have been too busy *pursuing their own imaginations* (**65:2**). The Apostle Paul will quote these same verses in Romans 10:20-21.

The people have deliberately chosen to *walk in ways not good*, including practising idolatry (**65:3**), and probably also some sort of occult cult of the dead, which is why they *sit among the graves* and have *secret* ceremonies (**65:4a**). They ignore or are ignorant of the dietary laws laid down by Moses, and eat foods that are forbidden as 'unclean' (**65:4b**; Lev 11:7). Yet despite ignoring God's law, they hypocritically consider themselves too holy to be approached (**65:5a**).

People who do these things are a constant irritant to God, like annoying smoke from a fire (**63:5b**). Consequently he has decided to punish the sins of the people as well as those of their fathers (**6:6-7**). These words may mean that children will suffer the consequences of their parents' sins (Exod 20:5), or God may be speaking of his final judgment at which those of all generations will appear before him (Matt 12:41-42). Many African Christians assume that the first of these explanations applies, and feel that they are cursed because of the occult practices of their ancestors. Such a belief hinders their fellowship with God.

We need to remind Christians who hold this belief that the Lord does not curse his *servants*. They will escape judgment (**65:8**; Exod 20:6; Jer 31:29-30; Ezek 18:1-3). Isaiah illustrates this with another example drawn from a vineyard (see 5:1-7). The owner may be about to throw away a bunch of rotten grapes, when someone points out that some of the grapes are not yet mouldy. The owner will keep the good grapes.

The different fates of the faithful and of idolaters are shown in 65:9-14. The faithful will have descendants and will live in a fruitful land. Even the Valley of Achor (literally, Valley of Trouble), which had been the place of God's wrath in Joshua 7:26, will become a peaceful place of rest (**65:9-10**). But things will be very different for those who worship false gods like *Fortune* and *Destiny* (**65:11**). They will meet their 'destiny' – and it will be destruction and slaughter because they refused to listen to God (**65:12**).

God then gives a series of swift contrasts between those who enjoy his blessing and those who do not (**65:13-14**). This list culminates in the assertion that the name of these people will end up being used as a curse word (as the name 'Judas' is today), while the servant of God will receive a name that is worthy of great honour (**65:15**). In this new era of peace, their past troubles will be *forgotten* (**65:16b**).

These people cursed by God try in their turn to curse the elect (**65:15a**). This is also something that many Africans fear: a curse put on them by an enemy. But here again, the Christian should give evidence of confidence, because these curses are useless against the one who is walking with God in *truth* and faithfulness (**65:15b-16a**; Matt 28:20).

For his chosen ones, the Lord creates *new heavens and a new earth* (**65:17**; 2 Pet 3:13; Rev 21:1). This prophecy should be read in conjunction with chapter 24, where God announced the destruction of the earth and the darkening of the heavenly bodies. It seems that this new creation is highly symbolic. The destruction of the earth and the hiding of the heavenly bodies represent the end of evil and of all

objects of idolatry (for the sun and moon were worshipped in those times). The new creation will be a world of *delight*, one where misery is unknown (**65:18-19**). Christians are called to live in this new reality right now (Phil 4:4-5).

The statement that anyone in that world who dies at the age of one hundred will be thought to have died young is a hint of the coming victory over death (**65:20**; see also 25:8; 26:17-19; 38:15-17).

Verses **65:21-23** are a development of 62:8-9, signifying that the people will no longer experience invasion and pillaging. They will be secure.

The climax of the new creation is reached in 65:24-25. Fellowship between God and people is restored (**65:24**). So is fellowship between hunters and prey, wild animals and domestic animals, signalling reconciliation between human-

REWARD AND RETRIBUTION

In the African world vew, the notion of reward and punishment plays an important role in understanding nature and its equilibrium. The Ovimbundu people of Angola, for example, experience God as a compassionate and kind being who is involved in the daily life of the people by providing them with sun and rain. Like other Africans, they see God (*Suku*) as good and as a supreme king who rewards or punishes people for what they do to themselves and to nature. Sinful behaviour that does not manifest *ubuntu*, that is, love for one's neighbour, is destructive of community life and will always be punished.

While we tend to focus on God's retribution (divine punishment), there are many places in the Bible where the writers are equally concerned to show that pleasing God through obedience to the law brings rewards. Retribution theology refers to the conviction that reward and punishment are not deferred, but rather follow immediately on the heels of the precipitating events. Deuteronomy, for example, stresses that disobedience to the law of Yahweh will bring judgment and disaster, but also stresses that obedience and righteousness will yield the fruit of peace and prosperity (Deut 4:1-2; 28:1-68).

The narratives of Genesis 1-11 are of immense theological importance. They present scenes from the story of humankind's original aberration and God's punishment for it. On the basis of these stories, one can say that the Bible is a record of the relationship between God, humankind and the universe. The stories also make it clear that human sin does not lead to final condemnation. The same point is made in the book of Chronicles, where the writer gives repeated examples of how God's retribution can be tempered by repentance and God's grace. The fundamental tenet is that God, the creator of the universe, has established a covenant with Israel. This covenant defines both the privileges and the obligations of the covenant people and sets out the eternal law in whose

light the actions of human beings are judged. The Bible clarifies the nature and consequences of humankind's sin or guilt, as well as the role and purpose of the punishment, and the conditions necessary for forgiveness.

The central message of the Bible is, however, that forgiveness and reconciliation are more important to God than punishment. God's forgiveness transcends all human limitations and persists in spite of human beings' rebellion against God.

One might ask why the Old Testament has more demands for repentance than promises of reward. The striking imbalance between the frequency of warnings about punishment and demands for repentance and the infrequency of promises of reward was caused by the crisis affecting the relationship between God and the covenant people. While God is infinitely holy and absolutely good, humankind is radically sinful. His true purpose in punishing people is to warn them of the consequences of their actions and to prepare them to receive his reward. Retribution is thus a mark of God's grace.

All the biblical writers adhered to a theology of retribution that shaped their record of the history of Israel. However, they did not insist that suffering is always proof of punishment. Job is an example of someone who suffered even though he was righteous.

Biblical writers also acknowledged that unbelievers sometimes seem better off than those who believe (Ps 73). However, the Bible makes it clear that the success of the ungodly is only temporary. Even though they may escape retribution in this world, they will be thrown into the hell prepared for all those who do not accept the good news brought by the only begotten Son of God, Jesus Christ our Lord. Believers, by contrast, will be rewarded and will rejoice in the presence of the God and his court in heaven (1 Pet 4-5).

Luciano C. Chianeque

kind and nature (**65:25**; see 11:6-9). The statement that nothing will *harm nor destroy* also implies that humans are reconciled with each other (65:25).

66:1-24 True Worship

While it would be going too far to say that the last chapter of Isaiah is a summary of the book, it does touch on most of the major themes: denunciation of hypocritical worship of the Lord, the restoration of Jerusalem, God's intervention as both judge and saviour, and salvation for Israel and the nations.

The chapter begins with a theme that has been present from the very beginning of the book: the call to sincere worship of God (66:1-6; 1:10-20). At the dedication of the temple, Solomon had made it clear that he understood that God cannot be confined to one specific location (**66:1**; see 1 Kgs 8:27). Consequently humans cannot expect to obtain God's favour simply by going to a consecrated place. And in speaking to Solomon after the dedication of the temple, God had stressed that people must humble themselves before him (**66:2**; 2 Chr 7:14). Jesus illustrated this same truth when he told the parable of the Pharisee and the tax collector (Luke 18:9-14).

The sacrifices referred to in **66:3-4** were no doubt offered in Solomon's temple. Unfortunately, those who offered them were often hypocrites, pretending a reverence they did not feel. So the prophet speaks of these sacrifices in the same breath as other actions condemned by the law of Moses (Exod 20:13; Lev 11:1-7). It is possible that the people were actually committing murder and making these unclean offerings to idols, but it is also possible that the prophet is speaking symbolically, saying that hypocritical offerings are as unacceptable as these other offerings would be.

The words in 66:1-4 will inevitably lead to the end of ritual worship. Jesus will make this explicit when he states that worship does not need to be associated with the temple, but that what is required is adoration of God 'in Spirit and in truth' (John 4:21-24).

The people of Isaiah's time were like those of Jesus' time. They mocked those who truly worshipped God and asked for a sign to prove that they were genuine (**66:5**). But the sign they will get is not the type of sign they were seeking (**66:6**; see comments on 38:7-8; Matt 12:38-42).

The prophet then returns to the theme of a new glory for Jerusalem. Earlier he spoke of her as a bride (62:4-5, 12), but now he speaks of her as a pregnant woman. God's intervention will mean that she will not experience long labour pains before the nation is born (**66:7-9**). The Jews will suddenly be allowed to return to Jerusalem, an event that will mark the end of misery and the beginning of rejoicing and prosperity (**66:10-13**; see 62:5, 10; 65:18-19).

But once again Isaiah reminds us that while God brings salvation and blessing to his servants, he also brings judgment on the wicked (**66:14**). We are repeatedly told that he will come with *fire* (**66:15-16**). While fire can be used to symbolize the purification and sanctification of believers (Prov 17:3; Matt 3:11), here it is a symbol of the destruction of God's enemies (Matt 3:12; Mark 9:47-48).

The Lord will judge *all men* (**66:16**), but he will deliver his faithful ones, who will not just be Jews but will include people of *all nations and tongues* (**66:18**). More than that, God will send out the survivors to proclaim his glory to far away nations. The nations mentioned in **66:19** are scattered across the then-known world, from Tarshish in Spain, at the western end of the Mediterranean, to Libya in North Africa, to Lydia in Turkey and to Tubal, which lay somewhere to the north, and to Greece and to the 'distant islands', which would embrace the rest of the world. God's people will travel to all these places to proclaim him – as the disciples did in Jesus' day, and as believers still do today when they set out to proclaim the good news of Jesus Christ.

Faithful Jews (*your brothers*) will stream back to Jerusalem (**66:20**). But it seems that here the 'brothers' may also include all those others to whom God has extended his salvation (see 49:6; 52:15; 56:2).

Not only will people of all nations come to Jerusalem, but some of them will even be appointed as *priests and Levites*, to serve God in the temple (**66:21**). In 61:6, such service to God seemed to be reserved for the Jews alone, but God's ultimate plan is broader than this (66:21-23).

Given God's plan to welcome the nations into his kingdom, the church in Africa should also set out to show the world what his kingdom will look like by being itself a multiracial and multiethnic community (see comments on 3:6; 16:3; 52:6-10).

In the new heavens and the new earth that God will establish, his Sabbaths and religious festivals will be celebrated joyously by all the true people of God.

Isaiah has concluded his great prophecy with a vision of the new heavens and the new earth that are being prepared for the redeemed (66:22-23; see Rev 22:12-21). But, as is typical in prophecies relating to the end times, he does not neglect to sound a warning about hell (**66:24**; see also Matt 13:24-30). His aim is to encourage people to choose heaven by shunning hell.

Edouard Kitoko Nsiku

Further Reading

Oswalt, John N. *The Book of Isaiah, Chapters 1-39*. NICOT. Grand Rapids: Eerdmans, 1986.

Oswalt, John N. *The Book of Isaiah, Chapters 40-66*. NICOT. Grand Rapids: Eerdmans, 1998.

Webb, Barry G. *The Message of Isaiah*. BST. Downers Grove: InterVarsity Press, 1996.

JEREMIAH

Jeremiah was born about 645 BC. He came from a priestly family who lived in the village of Anathoth (1:1), a little settlement about four miles (six km) north of Jerusalem in the territory of the tribe of Benjamin. It was the place where King Solomon had exiled Abiathar the priest whom he 'removed from the priesthood', thus fulfilling the prophecy against the descendants of Eli at Shiloh (1 Sam 2:27-36; 1 Kgs 2:26-27).

Jeremiah received his commission in about 627 BC, when he would only have been about eighteen years old (1:2). He continued his prophetic ministry until the destruction of Jerusalem in 587 BC. Following that traumatic event, he spent some time in Egypt (43:1-7). He was a contemporary of the prophets Zephaniah (Zeph 1:1), Habakkuk (Hab 1:6) and Ezekiel (Ezek 1:2), the last of whom preached a similar message among the Judean exiles in Babylon.

The first part of Jeremiah's ministry took place during the reign of Josiah, who ascended the throne after the assassination of his father, King Amon, in 640 BC. When the scroll of Deuteronomy was discovered in the temple in 622 BC (2 Kgs 22:8-20), Josiah undertook religious reforms to lead the people back to obedience to the law. Jeremiah may well have played an active role in these reforms. However, in 609 BC Josiah was killed at Megiddo while fighting Pharaoh Neco. Jehoahaz, one of his sons, reigned in his place, but within a few months he was deposed by the Egyptians and replaced by Jehoiakim, a king of their choosing (2 Kgs 23:31-34).

During the reign of Jehoiakim, the second part of Jeremiah's ministry began, along with his sufferings. Jeremiah favoured submission to Babylon, announced that the temple would not save Judah and denounced the pro-Egyptian policies and injustices of the king (22:13-19). His message did not please either the palace or the prophets attached to the royal court.

In 605 BC the Egyptian and Babylonian armies met at Carchemish. The Babylonian king, Nabopolassar, died and was replaced by his son Nebuchadnezzar, who won a stunning victory over the Egyptians. The Babylonians besieged Jerusalem and forced Jehoiakim to surrender. They carried off the king and an initial group of captives, most of whom were young aristocrats. This group included Daniel and his three friends (Dan 1:1).

The captive king was replaced by his son Jehoiachin, whose reign was very short. Jeremiah's prophecies were fulfilled and Jerusalem was taken in 597 BC. Nebuchadnezzar appointed Mattaniah as king in place of Jehoiachin, changing his name to Zedekiah. This new weak king

allowed himself to be influenced by pro-Egyptian loyalists who encouraged him to revolt against Babylon. Once again Jerusalem was besieged, defeated, plundered and left in ruins. Many of its inhabitants were killed and others were taken into captivity. The temple itself was burned (2 Kgs 25; 2 Chr 36:11-21). Following these dramatic events, Jeremiah received messages of comfort and restoration. This was the third part of his ministry.

Nebuchadnezzar named Gedaliah as the governor of Judah. Gedaliah shared Jeremiah's political convictions. However, he was assassinated. The frightened Judeans asked Jeremiah what they should do, but did not listen to what he said. Against his advice, they decided to flee to Egypt and forced Jeremiah and Baruch, his secretary, to accompany them (chs. 40–44).

The fourth and final part of Jeremiah's ministry took place in Egypt. There he proclaimed his oracles, denounced the idolatry of his fellow Judeans and announced the invasion of Egypt by Babylonian troops. Tradition tells us that he died in Egypt, stoned by his compatriots who refused to accept his message.

The Structure of the Book

Unlike the other prophetic books, Jeremiah does not follow the chronological order of the prophet's life or of the events reported. Instead, it is a collection of various oracles, interspersed with biographical anecdotes and conversations that the prophet has with the Lord. These dialogues between Jeremiah and the Lord have been called 'complaints'.

Several prophecies are given in two different locations in the book. As a result, the Hebrew version of the book (the Masoretic text), which includes these repetitions, is much longer than the text in the ancient Greek version of the OT, known as the Septuagint.

Length is not the only difference between these two versions. The order of some of the passages is also different. For example, in the Greek version the oracles about the nations (chs. 46–51) come immediately after 25:13 and do not follow the same order as in the Masoretic text.

These differences have led theologians to think that there must have been two different Hebrew texts of Jeremiah's prophecies: a longer version represented by the Masoretic text and a shorter one, whose translation resulted in the Septuagint.

However, we must point out that the differences between the two texts change nothing as regards the value or the quality of the book's teaching. The text is therefore absolutely dependable despite the difficulties related to its transmission.

The Message of the Book

Jeremiah's message is, above all, one of renewal, rebuilding and restoration. But this renewal must of necessity be preceded by a radical removal of what already existed. This is why the account of his call involves three pairs of verbs, the first two negative and the third positive: he is to uproot and tear down, to destroy and overthrow, to build and to plant (1:10).

The mission 'to uproot and tear down' has an important place in Jeremiah's ministry and message. He denounces the deep and irreversible corruption of God's people that is expressed in sin. Sin soils, and the guilt it generates requires judgment and punishment (2:3). But sin is also an incurable disease that takes root in the human heart. It makes people incapable of any relationship with God. It guarantees the failure of any human effort to return to God (13:23).

Faced with this complete failure on the human side, the Lord announces a new order. He is going to establish a new covenant with his people (31:31-40), which will be characterized by the Law being written on their hearts, and no longer only on tablets of stone. The new order will also be marked by the knowledge people will have of the Lord and, finally, by the forgiveness he will extend to all.

Outline of Contents

COMMENTARY

1:1-19 Introduction and Calling

1:1-3 Introduction

Jeremiah, whose name in Hebrew means 'The Lord is exalted', was a priest who came from the village of *Anathoth*, which is today known as Anata (**1:1**). This was one of the cities in the territory of the tribe of *Benjamin* that was given to the descendants of Aaron (Josh 21:18). The prophet's calling is clearly dated to *the thirteenth year of the reign of Josiah*, that is, 627 BC (**2:2**). As stated in the general introduction, Jeremiah was only eighteen years old at the time, which makes him very young to be called to such a public ministry. He would carry out his ministry in Judea for about forty years under various kings until the fall of Jerusalem in 587 BC (**1:3**).

1:4-19 Jeremiah's Call

The account of Jeremiah's call begins with the statement, *The word of the Lord came to me* (**1:4**). These exact words, or some equivalent expression, recur throughout the book of Jeremiah (for example, in 7:1; 11:1; 14:1; 16:1; 18:1).

God's opening words to Jeremiah reveal that it was solely on the Lord's initiative that he was chosen to be a prophet. He was predestined for this role. God formed him in his mother's womb and, after his birth, consecrated or set him apart for this specific task (**1:5**; see also Gal 1:15). He is to be *a prophet to the nations,* that is, primarily to Israel and to Judah, but also to Israel's neighbours. Jeremiah addressed a number of prophecies to these other nations (chs 46–51).

Jeremiah's reaction shows he was not a volunteer! His attempt to avoid God's call reminds us of Moses (Exod 4:10-13). But whereas Moses raised the problem of his difficulty in speaking, Jeremiah points to his age, saying *I am only a child* (**1:6**). By this he does not mean that he was what we would call a child. He was probably indicating that he was not yet thirty years old, which was the age at which the Levites could begin to carry out their official duties (Num 4:46-47; see also Judg 6:14-16; 1 Kgs 3:7; Luke 3:23).

God's response involves both a promise of help and a sign. He promises to be with his servant to deliver him, which implies that he will face difficulties and opposition in the exercise of his ministry (**1:7-8**; see also Exod 3:12). Then God gives him a sign by touching his mouth to enable Jeremiah to speak *the word of the Lord* (**1:9**; see also 11a; Isa 6:6-7; Ezek 2:8-3:3; Dan 10:16).

Jeremiah's ministry will have a double nature. Using images from agriculture and construction, the text shows that destruction (four verbs: *uproot and tear down … destroy and overthrow*) is going to occupy a more important place than construction (two verbs: *to build and to plant*) (**1:10**). The catastrophic spiritual condition of Judah demands that destruction precede rebuilding. But Jeremiah's work will extend even to foreign nations and kingdoms (see 1:5).

Jeremiah is then shown two inaugural visions. The first is of a *branch of an almond tree* (**1:11**). In Hebrew, the word for 'almond' (*shaqéd*) and the verb 'to watch' (*shoqéd*) sound similar. The Lord thus explains that the meaning of this first vision is that he is watching to make sure that all the words that he will ask Jeremiah to speak in his name are accomplished (**1:12**). The second vision is of a *boiling pot tilting away from the north,* so that its contents would spill out towards the south (**1:13**). This vision points to the coming Babylonian invasion from the north (20:4). This was the direction from which other invaders such as the Syrians and Assyrians had also come. The purpose of these invasions is to punish Judah's idolatry (**1:14-16**).

It is important to notice here how the Lord makes the young prophet participate in the elaboration of his message. He does not give him the whole message at once. Jeremiah himself is expected to look, see and understand. He must use all his faculties in the Lord's service. These visions are sometimes regarded as part of God's training of him before he embarks on his full ministry.

Then the Lord urges Jeremiah to prepare himself for battle. He is to be faithful in announcing the oracles of God and is not to fear anyone (**1:17**). His word will affect people of all social classes in Judah, from the political and religious leaders to the ordinary people. All will oppose him, but God promises he will be with him and will protect him (**1:18-19**; see also 1:8).

2:1-29:32 Prophecies Regarding Judah and Jerusalem

This section of the book includes some of the earliest prophecies given by Jeremiah. Those in chapters 2 to 6 may have been given during the reign of Josiah (3:6). Chronological order is quite closely followed until chapter 20.

2:1-4:4 Judah's Infidelity

2:1-37 The people's prostitution

In his first address to the people, Jeremiah recalls the time when Judah was completely devoted to the Lord (**2:1-2**). The nation belonged solely to God and anyone who harmed it faced punishment (**2:3**; Ps 105:14-15). But now the people have strayed far from the Lord their God (**2:4-5**). They have forgotten that he delivered them from slavery in *Egypt* (**2:6**) and gave them the *fertile land* of Canaan (**2:7**). God's servants, *the priests, the leaders* and *the prophets,* have become rebellious and idolatrous (**2:8**). They have willingly forgotten the marvellous works of the Lord. Such an attitude calls for divine judgment (**2:9**).

Israel has done something that no other nation has done, not even *Kittim* (Cyprus, to the north-west) and *Kedar* (in the south-east), which are cited as representative of all the surrounding pagan peoples who do not know the Lord (**2:10**). Not one of these other nations has ever abandoned its gods, even though these gods are only idols (**2:11**). The seriousness of Judah's sin must horrify and cause the heavens to *be appalled* and *shudder* (**2:12**). The people have in fact committed a double crime: not only have they denied their God, the source of *living water,* but they have trusted *broken cisterns that cannot hold water* and have no power to save (**2:13**).

The consequence of this sin is that Israel, the covenant people, has been handed over to the nations (**2:14-15**). Sin always has a dramatic effect on the identity of those who embrace it. Israel has ceased to be a legitimate son, and has become a slave.

The nation has been judged by what it has endured at the hands of *the men of Memphis* and *Tahpanhes,* two prominent Egyptian cities (**2:16**). Jeremiah may here be referring to the battle of Megiddo in 609 BC, in which Josiah was killed by the Egyptians (2 Kgs 23:29).

The nation has abandoned the living water that God supplies and instead it is turning to the 'broken cisterns' of *Egypt* and *Assyria,* seeking *to drink water from the Shihor,* which was a branch of the Nile, and from *the River,* the Euphrates (**2:18**).

Abandoning the Lord is a sin that always has bitter consequences (**2:19**). The Bible treats such turning from the living God to worship idols and carry out pagan celebrations as equivalent to religious and spiritual prostitution (**2:20a**; Isa 57:3-13; Ezek 16). Baal has been worshipped *under every* *spreading tree* (**2:20b**). The stain of this sin has marked the skin of those practising it, and not even *soda* (that is, lye or potash used as soap) can remove it (**2:21-22**). Though they may try to deny their sin (**2:23a**), proofs are everywhere. Not only have they sinned and practised idolatry *on every high hill* (2:20b), but they have also sinned *in the valley* (**2:23b**), which some commentators identify with the Valley of Ben Hinnom (7:31). Idolatry may be attractive to the people, but it ends in disgrace (**2:24-26**).

To say *my father* to *wood* and *you gave me birth* to *stone* is the supreme rejection of the Creator God (**2:27**). Yet despite their abundance, wood and stone cannot save in the hour of need (**2:28**).

The people, however, proclaim their innocence and do not admit that they have turned from the Lord (**2:29**). Even when he disciplines them, his children do not turn back to him (**2:30**). They persist in denying that they have done anything wrong (**2:31-33**). But the marks of evil are still present on their clothes (**2:34**; Lam 1:9). They go so far as to think of the Lord's correction as arbitrary (**2:35**).

God warns them that in the end, their allies will be of no help since the Lord has rejected them. Israel will go out into captivity humiliated, with their hands on their heads (**2:37**).

3:1-5 The impossibility of return

The beautiful time described in 2:1-3 is long past. Now, Israel is like a divorced woman (**3:1a**). She has given herself to innumerable lovers everywhere in the country (**3:1b-2**). Her prostitution had unfortunate effects on the seasons: the skies no longer give rain (**3:3**). Yet, she insists on calling God *my Father,* though her attitude is false and any change of heart superficial (**3:4-5**).

On a number of occasions the book of Jeremiah points to a causal link between sin and the disruption of the seasons. The earth itself is affected by human sin. The same point is made in many African cultures. We need to pay careful attention to how we behave, for no action is insignificant. Every blameworthy action will have consequences for the one who does it, as well as for his or her neighbours and for the environment.

3:6-4:4 Call to return to the Lord

Israel's adulteries and prostitution had led to that nation being taken into exile, but Judah did not learn from her sister's mistakes, and the people's behaviour did not change (**3:6-10**). In this, she was worse than Israel (**3:11**). So Jeremiah is to deliver a message that is apparently directed to the exiled people of the northern kingdom (3:12).But those who are intended to hear it are the people of the southern kingdom of Judah. The Lord is indirectly inviting Judah to repent and return to him (**3:12-13**). The idea that the covenant people are one, rather than a divided kingdom,

may also be present. The people must understand that they have no other God but the Lord and that all of them belong to the same covenant people (**3:14**). If Judah returns, the Lord will give her *shepherds* after his own heart, *with knowledge and understanding* (**3:15**); Jerusalem will be known as the *Throne of the Lord* and no longer simply as the location of the ark of the covenant (**3:16-17**). The Lord will also accomplish the reunification of Israel and Judah (**3:18**; Isa 11:12; Ezek 37:15-28).

Like the inhabitants of Judah, we often fail, both as individuals and as states, to learn from the experiences of others. We always think that things will be different for us. Yet, as the Apostle Paul told the Christians in Corinth, it is important to learn from the experiences of those who have preceded us (1 Cor 10:6).

The Lord always wants the best for his people, *a desirable land … a beautiful inheritance* and a stable relationship (**3:19**). But Israel was unfaithful to her God (**3:20**). Then there are tears of repentance, and God promised restoration and healing (**3:21-22**). The people recognize that idolatry has brought no blessings. On the contrary, the shameful worship of Baal has brought them to ruin (**3:23-25**; Deut 8:33).

Like Israel, many people today still invest huge sums of money in seeking protection, security and peace, without ever finding them. Unfortunately, such people are even found in churches. They are always asking whether the protection that the Lord Jesus promises is really effective against all dangers. Then they run hither and thither in a frantic search for stronger protection, and fail to recognize that all that they are doing is enriching charlatans of all kinds.

Returning to the Lord involves resolutely turning our backs on sin (**4:1**), confessing that there is no other God but the Lord (Deut 6:13-15), and embracing truth, uprightness and justice (**4:2**). If Israel returns to the Lord in this way, they will fulfil their true calling and all nations will be blessed because of them, as God had promised Abraham (Gen 12:2-3; 22:18).

The call to return to the Lord ends with a double recommendation and a warning. They are to *break up* their unploughed ground (**4:3**; Hos 10:12) and to *circumcise* their hearts, both of which are signs of sincere and genuine repentance (**4:4**; Deut 10:16). Circumcision had long been the sign of the covenant (Gen 17:10). It involved cutting off the foreskin of boys at eight days old. Jeremiah points out that what is really needed is not just external circumcision of the foreskin, but rather an internal circumcision of the heart as a sign that the heart is willing to obey God. If the nation does not adopt this attitude, it will have to face God's judgment.

4:5-6:30 Disaster from the North

4:5-31 Sound the alarm

The invaders described in this section are probably the Babylonians. The trumpet was sounded to warn the population to flee the impending disaster (**4:5-6**). The invader is compared to *a lion* whose attack spreads desolation and mourning (**4:7-8**). Everyone is affected, especially the false prophets who had proclaimed peace to the people (**4:9**). According to some Greek manuscripts, it is these same prophets who are speaking in **4:10**. They have deceived the people and now want to blame the Lord (see 6:14; 8:11; 14:13; 23:17). How dare they!

The description of coming judgment continues in **4:11-12**, and the invader with his instruments of war is described in **4:13**. The only way of salvation is for the people to purify their hearts and minds (**4:14**).

We know that *Dan* is situated in the extreme north of Israel and that *the hills of Ephraim* are north of Judah (**4:15**)and so closer to Jerusalem than Dan is. We can thus follow rumour that the *besieging army* from a *distant land* is coming to attack Jerusalem (**4:16-17**). All of the hardship reported is the result of Judah's *conduct* (**4:18**).

While listening to the trumpet call that signals war, the prophet is filled with *anguish* (**4:19**). The stupidity of the people has brought this great disaster on them (**4:20-22**). The destruction caused by the enemy returns the earth to its original state – *formless and empty* (**4:23-24**; see Gen 1:2). All life disappears (**4:25**) and the orchards and vineyards become a desert (**4:26**). Yet, the Lord announces that the destruction will not be complete – something will remain (**4:27**).

Everything that the Lord has determined will take place (**4:28-29**). But how will Judah react to these events? Will she go into mourning? Will she seek the Lord her God? Or will she persist in her superficial reactions (**4:30-31**)?

5:1-19 Not one righteous person

The accent is now on the deep corruption that prevails in Jerusalem. It is impossible to find even *one person who deals honestly and seeks the truth* (**5:1**). Reading these verses, we cannot avoid thinking of Abraham's pleading with God to spare the cities of Sodom and Gomorrah if there were even ten righteous men there (Gen 18). Every word spoken by the inhabitants of Jerusalem is a lie, even when they swear that they are telling the truth (**5:2**; 4:2).

The trials that we face are often intended to lead us back to the Lord (**5:3-5**). But when we refuse teaching, when we return evil for the good that the Lord does for us (**5:6-7**), when we are eager to commit adultery (**5:8**), punishment can no longer be delayed (**5:9**).

For a second time, the Lord declares that he will *not destroy them completely* (**5:10**; 4:27). Judah's many infideli-

ties force him to punish his people (**5:11-17**; see Lam 3:33), but he will still preserve a remnant (**5:18**), hoping that their trials, and especially the exile, will produce sincere repentance and a genuine turning back to him (**5:19**).

5:20-31 Israel has a rebellious heart

Perverted by evil, the eyes and ears of Israel no longer function. The people have become like their idols *who have eyes but do not see, … ears but do not hear* (**5:21**; see Ps 115:1-8).

Faced with the grandeur of God's creation (*the sea*) and the generosity of his gifts (*rains in season* and the *harvest*), the people should have had a deep respect for God (**5:22-24**). Instead, they rebelled and their sins have upset God's beautiful creation (**5:25-26**).

The secret of the Israelites' riches is revealed: their houses are full of corruption and injustice (**5:27-28**). They think that they can hide their crimes behind the walls of their houses, but the Lord sees them. This is why he will avenge all the evil done by the prophets and priests with the approval of the population (**5:29-31**).

6:1-21 Jerusalem will be besieged

The impending siege of Jerusalem is announced once again. This time, the prophecy is addressed to members of one of the two major tribes in the southern kingdom, the tribe of *Benjamin.* Jerusalem provides no security, so they must flee (**6:1**). The city will be destroyed (**6:2**). Earlier the prophet had warned that the assailants would surround the holy city (4:17). Here in **6:3** he compares these invaders to *flocks* (the soldiers) led by their *shepherds* (the officers of the Babylonian army). They encourage each other to attack the city (**6:4-5**) and the Lord tells them how to take it (**6:6**).

As before, the reason for the punishment is stated: the people have sinned against God. However, again the Lord announces that although the city is sick and wounded, her condition need not be fatal (**6:7**). Israel can still avoid its punishment if it decides to open her ears to hear and understand God's word, and so abandons the evil way that it has taken (**6:8-10**). If it does not do this, God's anger will be poured out on her and will spare no one (**6:11**). Others will forcefully take what the people consider most precious: their *houses, fields* and *wives* (**6:12**; see 8:10). This horrible thing takes place because the *prophets* and the *priests*, the equivalents of pastors and church leaders today, are full of greed (**6:13**; see 1 Pet 5:1-3). They take little care of the people entrusted to them (**6:14**; 8:11) and are incapable of feeling any shame for the evil that they themselves commit (**6:15**).

Still, the Lord continues to invite his people to follow *the good way* (**6:16**) and to pay attention to the *watchmen* he has appointed (**6:17**). However, since the response to his pleading is always negative, the Lord will bring the threatened disaster (**6:18-19**). The religious practices of the people, even those that involve burning valuable incense imported from as far away as *Sheba* in southern Arabia and offering sacrifices, are meaningless as far as the Lord is concerned (**6:20**). As long as the people's hearts remain rebellious, they are headed for disaster (**6:21**).

6:22-30 The destroyer is here

We are again reminded that invaders are coming from the north, and that they are cruel and warlike (**6:22-23**; 1:13-14). The announcement of their arrival fills the people with terror (**6:24**). They try to avoid the places where they might encounter him and there is *terror on every side* (**6:25**). This phrase is often found in Jeremiah's writings (see 20:4, 10; 46:5; 49:29). But the people do not flee, as Jeremiah advised (6:1); instead they go into mourning (**6:26**).

In the midst of this distress, the Lord speaks to Jeremiah (**6:27**). God had called him to *test* his fellow-countrymen as one tests metals. The Judeans have hardened their hearts so as not to hear the voice of God (**6:28**; 5:3). They have undergone a process like that used to purify silver, but they cannot be purified (**6:29**). This image underscores the seriousness of their situation, for the Lord has *rejected them* as a refiner would reject useless material (**6:30**).

7:1-10:25 The Incurable Wound

7:1-11 Threats at the door of the temple

The prophecy presented in 7:1-11 is also recorded in chapter 26. It isoften referred to as the Temple Sermon, because the prophet gave it right at the gate of the temple in Jerusalem in about 609 BC (**7:2**; 26:1). This is the appropriate place to denounce the idolatry in the temple. Jeremiah warns that if the people do not radically change their attitude toward the Lord, the temple will be of no use to them. It will only be one more idol on which they call with incantations (**7:3-4**). If, on the other hand, there is a real conversion and the people obey the Lord's commands wholeheartedly, they will live not only in the land promised to their ancestors but in the presence of God (**7:5-7**).

However, the people are incorrigible and repeatedly commit sin, all the while believing that the fact that the Lord's house is among them will save them (**7:8-11**; see Matt 21:12-13).

7:12-8:3 The valley of slaughter

God's sanctuary had been located at Shiloh for many years, from the time when Joshua conquered the land to the days of Eli (Josh 18:1; 1 Sam 1:3; 3:21; 4:3). But by Jeremiah's day, Shiloh, that great centre of Israelite worship, no longer existed. It had been destroyed, probably by the victorious Philistines after the defeat recorded in 1 Samuel 4:10-22. Now the Lord clarifies that the destruction of *Shiloh* was his doing and that it was done because of the wickedness

of Israel (**7:12**; 1 Sam 2:12-17, 22-25). The same cause will produce the same result in Jerusalem, and the temple will suffer the same fate as the sanctuary at Shiloh (**7:13-14**). The destruction of the temple is equivalent to a rejection of the people of Judah (**7:15**; Lam 2:7). God will treat them just as he treated *Ephraim*, that is, the entire northern kingdom of Israel that had been deported to Assyria about a century before Jeremiah's time.

The Lord forbids the prophet to even intercede for the people (**7:16**). The same refusal to hear any intercession is also found in 11:14, 14:11, and 15:1 (see also Exod 32:10; Lam 3:8, 44). God no longer listens to prayer because all the people, from the children to the parents, have become idolaters (**7:17-18**). They prepare special *cakes of bread* and offer them to *the Queen of Heaven*, who was the Mesopotamian goddess of fertility called Ishtar (also known as Astarte or Ashtoreth – 44:17-19; 1 Sam 7:3). She was associated with the planet Venus. In some manuscripts, such as the ancient Greek translation known as the Septuagint, this verse is taken as referring to the 'the Army of Heaven' rather than to the 'Queen of Heaven' (see 8:2).

The people are not harming God by worshipping these idols, but they are bringing harm on themselves by sinning against the Lord. They will be the ones who will suffer *shame* (**7:19**). As for the Lord, he will pour out his anger, destroying *this place* (see 7:3), *man and beast*, *trees of the field* and the *fruit of the ground* (**7:20**). Nothing will escape the fury of his anger.

In some translations, the words in **7:22** may seem to suggest that the Lord did not prescribe any sacrifices in the OT, for the verse can be translated, *For I did not speak to your fathers, or command them in the day that I brought them out of the land of Egypt, concerning burnt offerings and sacrifices* (NASB). But there can be no doubt that he did speak on these topics, for in **7:21** he sarcastically directs them to disobey his instructions when he tells them to *eat the meat* of their burnt offerings. In Leviticus 1:6-9, he had stressed that none of the meat from such an offering was to be eaten (although the meat from guilt offerings and fellowship offerings could be eaten – Lev 7).

The NIV translation captures the spirit of 7:22 when it adds the word 'just', so that the verse reads, 'I did not just give them commands'. The Lord takes more pleasure in obedience to his word than in sacrifices (**7:23**; 1 Sam 15:22). Yes, obedience to God is more valuable to him than many sacrifices. We could spend time offering many things to the Lord, to the church or to God's servants, all the while living a life contrary to the word of God (**7:24**). Such sacrifices have no importance to the Lord. They serve only to provide the givers with the illusion that they are pleasing God, and often nurture pride in those who come to believe that they are important members of their community. We need to hear the teaching of 7:21-28 every bit as much as the people in Jeremiah's day.

However, the Lord did not tire of sending men and women to tell his people what he expected of them (**7:25**). The words *day after day, again and again* emphasize the regularity with which he sent prophets. Despite all of this, the people did not listen. On the contrary, they behaved even more badly than their ancestors (**7:26**), so that no further good could be expected of them (**7:27**). The conclusion is that these people distinguish themselves by their refusal to obey their God (**7:28**).

In a number of African cultures, a shaved head, particularly on a woman, is a sign of mourning or of dishonour. The same was true in the OT (Job 1:20; Isa 15:2). In fact, people who had consecrated their life to God by taking the Nazirite vow were forbidden to cut their hair (Num 6:5; Judg 16:17). Thus the command to *cut off your hair and throw it away* was telling the people to publicly acknowledge their shame, a foreshadowing of their coming rejection by God (**7:29**).

The temple had been defiled by *detestable idols*, specifically by the Asherah pole that Manasseh had set up there (**7:30**; 2 Kgs 21:7). King Josiah, in whose reign Jeremiah began his ministry, had removed it along with other objects of pagan worship (2 Kgs 23:4-7).

Idolatry was also practised at *Topheth in the Valley of Ben Hinnom*, situated to the south-west of Jerusalem (see 19:2). Here horrible child sacrifices were carried out (**7:31**). Because this place was a symbol of the very worst abominations, the Lord promises to turn it into the *Valley of Slaughter*, filled to overflowing with the bodies of slain Judeans (**7:32-33**; 16:4). The bodies would become food for the birds and wild beasts because there would be no one to bury them. In Judean society, as in most societies worldwide, to lie unburied is a terrible curse. Someone who has no funeral has no family, no friends, and does not count as a person.

Those few who escape the carnage will no longer know the joy of celebrations such as weddings. *The land will become desolate* (**7:34**).

Another shocking happening will be the removal of the bones of the dead from their graves (**8:1-2**). The reason for their disgrace is that these people had been idol worshippers, and thus do not deserve honoured burial. Their bones will be left exposed to the sun and moon that they had worshipped, which will be powerless to spare them this indignity. God's judgment will be so unbearable that the living, no matter where they may be scattered, will prefer death to life (**8:3**).

8:4-17 A refusal to return

If someone falls when walking, we expect them to get up again. We cannot even imagine them being content to lie where they fell (**8:4**). Yet that seems to be the attitude of the people of Judah. They are rebellious people who insist on walking into trouble (**8:5**). The Lord may wait and hope that they will change, but no one living in Jerusalem speaks of repentance (**8:6**). Even animals are more intelligent that God's people, for at least they know enough to obey the rules that control their lives (**8:7**).

Rather than returning to the Lord to be saved, the people flatter themselves that they are wise because they possess God's law (**8:8**; Deut 4:5-8). Their attitude to the law seems to be similar to their attitude towards the temple (7:4). But the people do not realize that the scribes have given them an incorrect interpretation of the law. The result is that those who think themselves wise are in fact confused and frightened (**8:9**). Because they have not wanted to obey God's word and have been far more interested in the search for wealth, the Lord will give their wives and their fields to their enemies (**8:10a**; 6:12). The rest of **8:10b-14** is a repetition of 6:14-15.

The false prophets have deceived the people (**8:11**) and the peace that they announced has not come (**8:15**). The noise of the *enemy's horses* can already be heard as an attack is launched from *Dan* in the north (**8:16**). The Lord declares that it is he who is sending this enemy against his people, using words that would have reminded Jeremiah's hearers of the time when God had used *venomous snakes* to punish their rebellious ancestors (**8:17**; Num 21:5-9).

8:18-9:6 The prophet's complaint

Jeremiah is deeply disturbed by the judgment that is coming on his people. He can already hear the cries of his countrymen who are taken far away into exile (**8:18-19**). Their deportation makes them realize God's absence. Through the prophet, the Lord asks why his people gave themselves over to such idolatry.

The seasons come and go, and yet there is no sign of salvation. The exiles are in despair (**8:20**). Suffering along with his people, the prophet is *crushed* (**8:21**). Jeremiah is a true prophet and does not rejoice at seeing that his prophecies are proving true. He does not gloat that events have proved him right. The opposite is true. He suffers because he sees that in their stubbornness, the people were not able to avoid catastrophe.

The region of *Gilead* was known for its perfumes and especially for its *balm*, which was used to heal wounds (**8:22**; 46:11; Gen 37:25; Ezek 27:17). But the prophet seems to have understood that the sickness of his people was incurable, and he wept for the many dead among his countrymen (**9:1**).

Jeremiah longs to distance himself from his fellow-Judeans (**9:2**). Their sin is closely linked to the way they use their tongues (5:2; 8:2; Prov 10:14; 13:3; 18:7; Jas 3:2). They are no longer trustworthy; they lie to each other and deceive one another (**9:3-6**).

YAHWEH AND OTHER GODS

The God of the Bible introduces himself as Yahweh, which means 'I am who I am' (Exod 3:14). This declaration of being goes hand in hand with a denial of all other divinities. The first of the Ten Commandments prohibits God's people from serving other gods at the same time as Yahweh. The second commandment reinforces this point by prohibiting the making and worshipping of idols (Exod 20:3-5). Thus, like Abraham and Jacob, and Dionysius and Damaris in the NT, we must decide to abandon our gods in order to be able to draw near to God (Gen 35:1-4; Josh 24:2-3; Acts 17:16-34).

Other Gods in the Bible

But who are the 'other gods' of which the Bible speaks? They are the gods of the geographic regions in which the biblical revelation was given, namely Mesopotamia, Canaan and Egypt. The Israelites were surrounded by cultures that were saturated in polytheism, and too often they yielded to the temptation to abandon Yahweh and follow these gods (see, for example, Judg 2:10-12).

Abraham initially had to separate himself from the Mesopotamian deities, who were often manifestations of cosmic powers. The sun, the moon and the stars were deified and worshipped. Then when he and his descendants settled in Canaan, they encountered the worship of agricultural gods, including Baal, the god of thunder, and Astarte, the goddess of fertility (Judg 2:13). The Israelites also spent much time in Egypt, where the gods were often portrayed in animal form. The decision to make a golden calf probably reflected the worship of the god Apis in the form of a bull at Memphis (Exod 32:1-4).

The NT writers lived within the context of the many Greco-Roman deities, as can be seen from a crowd's mistaking Paul and Barnabas for gods (Acts 14:11-15) and the introduction to Paul's sermon in Athens (Acts 17:22-23)

Other Gods in Africa

There are many similarities between these ancient beliefs and traditional African systems of belief, where many gods and spirits are invoked. But Africans would also recognize the God to whom Paul pointed the Athenians, the god who 'made the world and everything in it' (Acts 17:24). Many African peoples have a concept of a Supreme Being who has created all things, including humankind and who sustains the universe. This God is known by different names, but his identity never changes. The name he used when he made himself known to Moses and the Israelites was Yahweh (Exod 3:13-14), but the biblical authors also spoke of him using the name of the Canaanites' supreme God, El, a name that can be translated as the 'Most High' (Gen 14:18; Deut 32:8). On the basis of their example, we can use the name of the Supreme Being of African peoples to refer to God. But we need to remember that the key point here is not what the Creator God is called, but how he is represented and how his relationship with his creation is understood.

In regard to how God is represented, we need to remind people that he cannot be represented by something made by human hands. This point is strongly made in the second of the Ten Commandments (Exod 20:4) and by the prophets (Isa 44:9-20).

When it came to God's relationship with his creation, the ancients, and African traditional religions, came to feel that the Creator God was so exalted that he was beyond the reach of human beings. Thus they created a whole pantheon of gods to take care of different human needs. In Africa, spirits or physical objects were eventually given so much prominence that the worship of the Most High was lost sight of in the day-to-day business of life. Instead, spirits were invoked, either for their own powers or to act as intermediaries between the Most High and his creation. But God has revealed to us that the only mediator that we need to approach is Christ, who himself stated, 'No one comes to the Father [the Most High] except through me' (John 14:6; see also 1 Tim 2:5).

The Only God

Some might ask, why should we worship only Yahweh, the Creator God, and not all the other gods? The answer is that he is the only living God. All other things perceived to be gods are dead things, often made by human hands (Isa 44:6-8). Yahweh is the creator of all the elements of the natural world that the other gods represent (Gen 1:1-31). He is a living spirit who gives life (John 4:24; Acts 17:24-28). The other gods are only the product of the imagination and creativity of human beings (Jer 10:1-16; Acts 17:29).

Like the other gods, Yahweh inspires fear (Gen 28:16-17; Exod 3:6), but this is not because he subjects human beings to his arbitrary whims. Our fear of God can be accompanied by confidence (Ps 40:4; Prov 14:26), for God respects the covenants he establishes with his people (Deut 7:9; 2 Tim 2:13). His favour, unlike that of other gods, is not dependent on receiving sacrifices and offerings. What he desires is conduct that honours him (Ps 40:7-9). While he may be like other gods in administering retribution (Deut 7:10), he differs from them in that his nature is to offer pardon and salvation to those who trust him (2 Chr 30:9).

Abel Ndjerareou

9:7-22 The Lord threatens

The Lord wants to purge his people of the deception and falsehood filling the land (**9:7**). Again, we read of the misdeeds of the tongue (**9:8**; see 9:3-6). The ruin of Jerusalem and the nation is described in **9:10-11**. The city will be transformed into a ruin where only jackals will live and the nation will be left desolate.

In 8:8 the people boasted of their wisdom, but **9:12** says that real wisdom consists of understanding the reasons for what is happening to them. Such understanding requires more than just an intellectual grasp of the facts; it also involves the ability to learn from what they are experiencing (Hos 14:9).

Once again the causes of the misfortune are presented: the people have hardened their hearts against the Lord, as their ancestors had done (**9:13-14**). Hence the Lord announces that he is going to curse their water and food (**9:15**; Lam 3:15) and send them as captives among foreign peoples (**9:16**).

In the meantime, the people must prepare for mourning by sending for professional mourners (**9:17-18**). They will be amazed at the extent of the coming devastation (**9:19**). The women are to teach their daughters to weep because death will be everywhere (**9:20-21**). As in the Valley of Slaughter (7:32-33), human corpses will lie scattered with no one to take care of them (**9:22**).

9:23-26 True and false circumcision

It is pure folly to depend on possessions, wisdom, strength or riches, for the deep meaning of life is not to be found in such things, but rather in knowing God (**9:23-24**). The Lord is the only security for humankind. To know the Lord is also to experience that he alone is gracious, upright and just. The apostle Paul quotes this passage in his letters to the Corinthians (1 Cor 1:31; 2 Cor 10:17).

The time is coming when the Lord will judge all those who live for appearances (**9:25**). They may have received circumcision, the sign of the covenant with God in their bodies (Gen 17:10), but they have no intimate knowledge of God (Gal 6:13). Such circumcision is false and has no value before God (Phil 3:2-3). The people of Judah may be circumcised, but they are acting as if they have no knowledge of God, and so they are listed along with all the pagan nations that also practised circumcision: *Egypt ... Edom, Ammon, Moab* (**9:26a**). Some translations, like the NASB, also include a reference to clipping 'the hair on their temples' in 9:26. This practice was associated with idolatry and was thus strictly forbidden to Israel (Lev 19:27; 21:5).

The chapter ends with a statement of a theme that will be developed at length in the book of Jeremiah: circumcision of the heart (**9:26b**; see also 4:4).

10:1-16 No one compares to the Lord

Having spoken of true and false wisdom and of true and false circumcision, the prophet now contrasts the true God and idols. First, he tells the people of Israel to avoid behaving like pagans. Many pagan nations, the Babylonians in particular, were devoted to magic, astrology and superstition. They regarded heavenly bodies like the sun and moon as divine beings and often experienced fear when they observed what they thought of as *signs in the sky* (**10:1-2**). Such practices are still common today, even among Christians. We must not imitate either the behaviour or the practices of those who do not know God, who confuse the creature and the Creator.

Jeremiah shows the absurdity of trusting in idols and other fetishes. They are made completely by human hands. An idol is fashioned from *a tree out of the forest* by a *craftsman* and then covered with *silver* or *gold* (**10:3-4**). Jeremiah emphasizes the point that these idols have to be fastened down with *nails* so that they will not *totter*. The idols are absolutely useless: they can neither *walk* nor *speak*, do neither *good* nor *harm* (**10:5**). There is therefore no reason to fear them.

In contrast to idols, the Lord, the God of Israel, is great and powerful (**10:6**). He is the one who should be feared because no one is like him (**10:7**). All others are *senseless and foolish* (**10:8**). Idolaters may seem to be intelligent people but they trust in inert wood! And wood is all that an idol is, even if it is covered with expensive materials brought from such far away places as *Tarshish*, which was a Phoenician commercial city probably situated on the Atlantic coast of Spain (**10:9**; Isa 23:6; Ezek 27:12; Jonah 1:3). We do not know where *Uphaz* was located, but some ancient manuscripts give this name as Ophir, which was a city famous for its gold (see 1 Kgs 9:28; 10:11). Blue and purple fabrics were also extremely expensive in Jeremiah's day.

Unlike idols that are dead by nature, the Lord is *the living God*. It is before him and not before his creatures that human beings should tremble (**10:10**; see 10:2). Idols that never created anything do not deserve to occupy any place under the sun (**10:11**). The Lord created everything (**10:12**) and all of his creation obeys him (**10:13**).

The beginning of **10:14** is difficult to understand. It may read, 'from lack of knowledge everyone is senseless', but if we link it to the preceding verses, it can be translated, *everyone is senseless and without knowledge.* Everyone who makes an idol will end up ashamed because there is no life in it. Idols cannot survive their judgment (**10:15**). But the Lord Almighty, the God of Israel, is very different! Nothing and no one is like him. He created all things and he has nothing in common with idols (**10:16**).

10:17-25 Desolation in Jerusalem

The exile is unavoidable (**10:17**). The inhabitants of Judea will be hurled out of their own country like stones from a sling (**10:18**). To heighten the effect, the prophet grieves on behalf of his people – their evil cannot be borne, their wound is incurable (**10:19**; see also 15:18; 30:12, 15). Their dwelling places will be completely devastated with no one to rebuild them (**10:20**; 4:20; Lam 2:4).

The shepherds are not reproached for having led the flock badly but rather because they *do not inquire of the Lord* (**10:21**). If they had had the Lord himself as their shepherd, they would have known how to accomplish their mission well. To seek the Lord first is the secret of all successful ministry.

Desolation comes to Judah from the north and the country will soon be transformed into a desert, inhabited only by *jackals* (**10:22**). Such a prospect leads the prophet to confess that human beings cannot control their own destiny (**10:23**; Pss 31:15; 37:24; Prov 16:9; 20:24). Recognizing that what is happening to the people is the just result of their sins, he asks that the punishment not result in total destruction, from which the nation will never recover (**10:24**; 4:27). But he does call for total judgment on the pagan nations the Lord has used to discipline Israel (**10:25**).

11:1-12:17 Jeremiah's Conflict and Suffering

11:1-17 A broken covenant

Jeremiah now begins a new discourse. Some commentators think that the prophecies in this section of the book were made after the discovery of the Book of the Law during Josiah's time (2 Kgs 22: 8-10). Others place it during the reign of Jehoiakim when the people were being unfaithful to the law.

The *covenant* of which Jeremiah speaks in **11:2** is the one made between the Lord and his people at Sinai (Exod 19:1-8). King Josiah had renewed his loyalty to this covenant (2 Kgs 22:8-23:25). The prophet is commissioned to announce to Judah and the inhabitants of Jerusalem that everyone who refuses to obey the terms of the covenant is *cursed* (**11:3**). The penalties associated with breaking the covenant are clearly set out in Deuteronomy 27:15-26, where each verse begins: 'Cursed is the man'.

The people are reminded of the terrible suffering of their ancestors when they had been slaves in the *iron-smelting furnace* that was Egypt (**11:4**; Deut 4:20). The Lord had brought Israel out of Egypt and into a covenant with himself, because he wanted to make them into a special nation, whose God he would be. It is because of this covenant that the Lord had promised Israel's forefathers to give them the special land in which the people were now living (**11:5**).

The prophet is commanded to remind Judah of *the terms of this covenant* and to encourage them to *follow them* (**11:6**). This message was an old one, for the Lord had never ceased

to remind Israel of the importance of obeying him (**11:7**; Exod 15:26; 2 Chr 36:15). But the people hardened their hearts and refused to obey, obliging the Lord to impose *the curses of the covenant* on them (**11:8**; Lev 26:14-43).

The people of Jerusalem have joined with the rest of the country in returning to the pagan practices and idolatry of their ancestors, and thus they had *broken the covenant* that bound them to the Lord (**11:9-10**). Consequently the Lord will punish them and will close his ear to their prayers (**11:11**). No matter how much they pray to their numerous idols, they will find no help (**11:12-13**; 2:28).

Once again the Lord forbids the prophet to intercede for his people (**11:14**; see also 7:16; Exod 32:10). The people's inconsistency is shown by the fact that they still go to the temple, but also practise idolatry (**11:15**). One cannot serve two masters (Matt 6:24).

Israel is often compared to a vine (2:21; Isa 5:3-7), but here in **11:16** it is compared to an *olive tree* (Rom 11:17-18). But the Lord is setting this tree on fire to destroy it (**11:17**; see also Joel 1:6-7). The idolatry of Israel and Judah was an evil they committed against themselves, just as all the sins that we commit primarily affect ourselves (1 Cor 6:18).

11:18-23 'A prophet without honour'

We now come to the section that theologians have called 'Jeremiah's complaints', that is, passages in which the prophet expresses his suffering and the difficulties he faced in his ministry (11:18-12:6; 15:10-21; 17:14-18; 18:18-23; 20:7-18). Sometimes these complaints take the form of dialogue between him and the Lord.

Just as our Lord was rejected by the people from his own home town (Mark 6:4), so the prophet Jeremiah faced a plot against him by the people of his own village of Anathoth. If the Lord himself had not warned the prophet about this plot, it might have been successful (**11:18**). Jeremiah would have been *like a gentle lamb led to the slaughter* (**11:19**). These words remind us of the suffering of the Servant of the Lord in Isaiah 53:4-7. It is possible that John the Baptist had passages like these in mind when he spoke of Jesus as 'the lamb of God, who takes away the sin of the world' (John 1:29).

The discussion among themselves by the people of Anathoth about Jeremiah recalls Psalm 83:5. The prophet's countrymen wanted to silence him so that he would no longer prophesy *in the Lord's name* (**11:20-21**). If he refused to stop prophesying, they would simply eliminate him.

The attitude of the people of Anathoth can be understood in the light of their history. As we noted in the introduction, the inhabitants of Anathoth were probably descendants of Abiathar, the high priest who had been dismissed from his office by King Solomon and sent back to Anathoth (1 Kgs 2:26-27). Thus all the priests from that area felt that they were under a cloud. They were looked down on and barely tolerated by the priests at Jerusalem, and so did not want to attract attention. They felt that when one of them, in the person of Jeremiah, stood in front of the temple in Jerusalem and made a speech like the one in chapter 7, he was endangering not only his own family but also all his relatives. They might be suspected of trying to regain power in the temple. Thus the people of Anathoth were not specifically rejecting the word of the Lord when they told Jeremiah not to prophesy. Rather, they were expressing their fear that his message would anger the people in power in Jerusalem and lead to reprisals against them. They were afraid that history will repeat itself.

What the people of Anathoth seem not to have noticed is that Jeremiah is not speaking of his own accord. He is the Lord's spokesman (1:4-19). That is why the Lord himself takes the prophet's situation into his hand (**11:22**). He promises to do to the people of Anathoth exactly what they wanted to do to Jeremiah. Whereas the Lord had always said that he would leave a remnant in Israel and Judah, there will be no survivors from Anathoth (**11:23**).

This incident in Jeremiah's life teaches us that we must avoid attacking God's servant simply because we are annoyed by the message he or she gives. If God's word makes us uncomfortable, we must not seek to change the message but to change ourselves. Silencing a minister of the word will not eliminate God's demand that we heed his word and change our ways.

12:1-6 Why do the wicked succeed?

The 'complaint' begun in 11:18 continues here. Jeremiah asks the old questions that are always relevant: 'Why do the wicked prosper?' 'Why does injustice seem to trump justice?' 'Why are those who publicly flout the law so little concerned about doing so?' 'Why does everything seem to go well for those who have no fear of God?' The scandalous prosperity of the wicked has often troubled the thoughts of the faithful (Job 21:7-15; Ps 73; Mal 3:14-15).

Before asking the questions, Jeremiah reminds himself that the Lord is righteous (**12:1**). He is not trying to find fault with God when he questions him. He does so simply because he cannot understand the relationship he is seeing between injustice and prosperity. What bothers him even more is that the people of whom he is speaking often use God's name, but have no place for him in their hearts (**12:2**).

Jeremiah asks that his enemies may suffer the same fate they had planned for him (**12:3**). His attitude is similar to that which we find in those psalms that are called 'imprecatory psalms' (Pss 5:10; 28:4; 31:17-18; 35:8; 40:14-15; 137:8).

Creation suffers the consequences of human sin, yet the people still insist that the Lord does not see them (**12:4**). Jeremiah asks how long this state of affairs can continue.

God does not reply directly to the prophet's question (**12:5**). He simply asks him to take courage because in future he will face trials that will be more difficult than those he is complaining about now. In fact, it is not only his neighbours he must fear, but also his own family (**12:6**). In times of crisis, betrayals become more common.

12:7-13 The Lord abandons his house

Terrible words are now spoken: The Lord is going to abandon his house (the temple) and give his people over into the hands of their enemies (**12:7**). These are terrible words for the Lord to utter, for at that time the defeat of a nation was considered to be the defeat of their god, and he knows that his name will be dishonoured. But more than that, the Lord loves his people deeply, and even refers to the nation as *the one I love* (see also 11:16). It is with deep grief that he tells his prophet to pronounce these words.

These words are also terrible for those who hear them, for they expose the people's ingratitude for God's love and the guilt of their rejection of him. Their hostility to God is blasphemous (**12:8**). As a punishment for this, they will be handed over to the fierce onslaught of a pagan nation (**12:9**).

The Lord's vineyard will be completely destroyed, leaving it desolate (**12:10-11**). But we must never forget that it is the Lord himself who is bringing this judgment on his people (**12:12**). He will use pagan nations to do it, but he will also express his anger through the natural world, as the people find that the earth no longer produces the expected harvests (**12:13**).

12:14-17 Judah's neighbours

The final four verses of this chapter concern Judah's neighbours. They will suffer the same fate as Judah: deportation to Babylon (**12:14**). But once they have been taken into captivity, the Lord will have *compassion* on them and will cause them to return to their lands (**12:15**). For these nations, there will be a possibility of conversion and integration among the Lord's people. But they will have to learn to live according to the principles of the Lord's word (**12:16**). That will be the only way of salvation. If they do not take it, they will be destroyed (**12:17**).

13:1-14 The Sign of the Linen Belt

The Lord asks Jeremiah to perform a symbolic act that will provide a lesson for the people of Judah. Commentators have called this an acted prophecy (see also 27:2; 32:25; 43:9; 51:63-64). He is to buy a *linen belt,* wear it around his *waist,* then remove it and hide it in a *crevice in the rocks* near *Perath,* and finally recover it (**13:1-6**). When the prophet withdraws it from the crevice, it is obviously useless (**13:7**).

The lesson is clear: everyone knows that a rotten belt is of no further use. It cannot serve its purpose on anyone's clothing. In this way, the Lord will make the people of Judah useless (**13:9**), because they were a proud people that had not learned to humble themselves by turning from their idolatry (**13:10**). However, the people of Israel and Judah were formerly like a belt around the Lord's waist (**13:11**). He was proud of them, but they did not know how to maintain their position. They disobeyed and now they are of no further use.

The fact that the belt was buried near Perath may also be an indication that the people would be carried off to Babylon on the Euphrates River, for in Hebrew the spelling of the two names is very similar.

In the OT in general and in Jeremiah in particular, wine is often used to represent the Lord's anger (see 25:15-16; 48:26; 49:12; 51:39, 57; see also Ps 60:3; Isa 51:17, 22). The prophet announces that the Lord's anger is inflamed against the whole of Judean society, from the Davidic kings to the priests and prophets to the ordinary people (**13:12-14**).

13:15-27 Warnings and Punishments

The Lord then gives a final warning to his people calling them to renounce their pride and confess their sins (**13:15**). The call to *give glory to the Lord your God* (**13:16**) means to agree to live in a way that honours God. His judgment is looming closer, for the words *darkness* and *darkening* indicate the fading of hope. Elsewhere, the OT speaks of the 'day of the Lord' which is presented as a day of darkness, weeping and terror (see Lam 2:22; Ezek 22:24; Amos 5:18-20; 8:9; Zeph 1:14-15).

The prophet's tears express the Lord's profound suffering at the disastrous state of his people (**13:17**). This nation seems blind, unable to see that they will soon be taken into exile.

The next command is directed to the two principal figures at the royal court, the *king* and the *queen mother*, or possibly 'the queen' (**13:18**). Jeremiah may here be speaking of King Jehoiachin and his mother Nehushta, whose departure for exile in Babylon is recorded in 2 Kings 24:8, 15. These two are commanded to *come down* from their thrones. The translation in the KJV is 'sit down', which brings out the point that they will no longer sit on their thrones but on the ground. Sitting there would be a sign of their mourning and shame. They will also no longer wear the *glorious crowns* that are symbols of their royal status. They will be destitute like everyone else, and will be deported along with all the other people of Judah (**13:19**).

Jerusalem is told to *lift up your eyes and see those who are coming from the north*, that is, her enemies (**13:20**). Judah was accustomed to bowing to the spiritual authority of foreign nations and following their gods. Now it is going to suffer a hard political and religious domination (**13:21**).

It will be as surprised as a woman who suddenly goes into labour.

The female captives in particular will endure at least two types of shameful treatment. The first is that their clothes, and specifically their *skirts,* will be torn off (**13:22**). This punishment is mentioned several times in the OT (Isa 47:3; Nah 3:5). The second, which the NIV translates as *your body ill-treated,* literally says that their 'heels will suffer violence'. Some think that this refers to the prisoners being forced to walk barefoot. Others, however, think that Jeremiah is speaking of the captives being raped.

Jeremiah expresses the impossibility of any change in Judah's behaviour in the form of a traditional proverb. An *Ethiopian* cannot possibly change the colour of his *skin,* and a *leopard* cannot get rid of his *spots.* These are characteristics that cannot be changed. Similarly, Judah is characterized by the fact that it is always *doing evil* against the Lord (**13:23**). There is no way that the nation can change and start *to do good.* This saying expresses a particularly pessimistic view of the people's situation. There is no further hope for this nation: their disease is incurable (see 10:19).

Hence, exile is unavoidable (**13:24**). It will be the experience of those people who have abandoned the Lord and trusted in idols instead (**13:25**). They will have to endure the humiliation common to captives (**13:26**; see 13:22).

The Hebrew of the last part of **13:27** is difficult to understand. The prophet may be asking, *How long will you be unclean?* or he may be saying, 'Will you still not be made clean?' (NKJV).

14:1-22 Drought and Total Disaster

This chapter is entirely devoted to a description of a devastating drought that Judah experienced, probably during the reign of Jehoiakim. Drought was among the curses that followed disobedience to the covenant with the Lord (3:3; Lev 26:14-20; Deut 28:22-24; Amos 4:7-8). There are many similarities between the reality described in this text and the experience of many countries in Africa.

The first thing that the prophet notes in relation to this drought is that it has thrown Jerusalem and Judah into deep distress. He hears the sound of mourning and wailing (**14:2**). People who still have some authority send those who depend on them to find water, but there is none to be found (**14:3**). They return with empty jars and with their heads or faces covered as sign of their dismay and mourning (see 2 Sam 15:30; 19:4; Ezek 24:17).

Those who have never suffered thirst to the point of fearing that they may die cannot really understand what the Judeans experienced during this drought. People who have not walked long distances under a burning sun, looking for water, only to find a dried-up waterhole, cannot understand the sense of dismay among the people of Jerusalem.

Farmers, whose livelihood is dependent on good rainfall, are in despair (**14:4**). Their crops fail and their animals grow weak. Wild animals suffer as much as the humans and even change their habits because of the lack of food and water (**14:5-6**).

The description of this disaster is followed by the lamentation of the people (14:7-9) and the Lord's response. Speaking through the prophet, the people recognize that their terrible suffering is the consequence of their sin. They ask the Lord to act on their behalf, not because of any righteousness on their part, but for the sake of his name (**14:7**). How many times has he acted solely because of his name, whether to prosper his plans for Israel despite their failures or to avoid allowing pagan nations to misunderstand certain circumstances in the life of his people (Ps 25:11; Isa 48:9-11; Ezek 20:9; 36:22-23; Dan 9:19)! He has often done the same in our individual lives as well as in the life of the churches and our countries!

The Lord is the *Hope of Israel,* the one who has saved them in times of distress. The people cannot understand why he remains indifferent to their present plight (**14:8**). It seems that he is acting like foreigners and travellers, who come for only a short time and do not usually notice and understand what their hosts are experiencing. That is why there is a saying, which is attributed to the Baoule of Cote d'Ivoire, that the foreigner has big eyes that do not see.

The people ask why the Lord is acting *like a warrior powerless to save* (**14:9**). Many passages in the OT present the Lord as the victorious hero of his people (20:11; Isa 42:13; Zeph 3:17) and so the people cannot understand how the Lord can be among them and not deliver them. They remind him, *we bear your name,* meaning that they belong to him. How can he then abandon them?

The Lord's only response is that he is committed to punishing the sins of Judah (**14:10**). The people have wandered here and there, serving first this god and then that god, and have not been faithful to him.

The prophet pleads in favour of the people, but even that does not change the Lord's response. In fact the Lord forbids him to *pray for the well-being of this people* (**14:11**; 7:16). Even if the people *fast* and *offer burnt offerings and grain offerings,* the Lord will not pay any attention (**14:12**). *Sword, famine and plague* will be his only response to all the religious practices of his people. Even confession of sins and Jeremiah's intercession are unable to change the situation.

Jeremiah now speaks, pointing out that the message he has just received from the Lord is the exact opposite of the one that all the other prophets of the time were proclaiming. They were insisting that the people would *not see the sword or suffer famine* (**14:13**). How can these prophets, supposedly the Lord's messengers, proclaim peace and all sorts of good things to the people while their message is being contradicted by the facts of the situation?

The Lord's reply is quite clear. The prophets have lied. Moreover, he had not sent them. They are speaking on their own accord and have invented their message (**14:14**).

What audacity! How dare someone use the Lord's name to say things that do not make sense? How dare someone say, 'The Lord told me' when he has never heard anything from the Lord? And yet, as in Judah at that time, our cities and villages, and even our churches, are today full of such people. All day long they invent stories, each one more bizarre than the next. They rush to make pronouncements on topics about which they themselves know little. Their aim is to be the first one to speak. Should anyone be experiencing difficulty or should there be any perplexing problems in the life of a person, a family or a country, these prophets have already heard what the Lord had to say about it! Unfortunately, they are often lying to people, deceiving believers and closing the door of faith to those truly seeking the Lord.

The self-appointed prophets who have proclaimed peace and plenty will be the first to suffer the torments of war and famine (**14:15**). Those who believed their lying messages will share the same fate. Their bodies will be scattered everywhere in the city of Jerusalem without burial (**14:16**).

As for Jeremiah, he must continue to weep so that the people may see in him God's suffering because of what is happening to Judah (**14:17**). The Lord is not a heartless tyrant who takes pleasure in making his people suffer. He does not rejoice at the calamities that befall this world, causing indescribable suffering. No, God suffers with his suffering people.

What follows is a description of horrible scenes that are all too familiar wherever there is war and famine (**14:18**). Hundreds, or thousands, of men have fallen in battle, but no one has either the time or the means to bury them. Their bodies are left lying in the fields. Meanwhile the cities are full of men, women and children who are still alive, but whom famine is about to destroy.

This unbearable sight forces the prophet to speak again to the Lord. Has God rejected his people? Why does the suffering never end? Why has misery replaced peace (**14:19**)? The people have admitted their wickedness and their sin. They have even confessed the sins of their ancestors (**14:20**). He now asks the Lord to act for the sake of his own name. He claims the covenant by which the Lord pledged to be Israel's God (**14:21**). He confesses that the Lord alone is God, and that he alone is the benefactor of human beings and of Israel in particular (**14:22**).

15:1-9 It Is Useless to Plead!

Despite Jeremiah's pleas, the Lord does not change his mind. For the fourth time, he tells Jeremiah that he should not pray for Judah (7:16; 11:14; 14:11). This time, however, as if to show that his decision is made and nothing will change it, he recalls the memory of two important people in Israel's history, *Moses* and *Samuel*, pointing out that even their intervention would not change the situation (**15:1**; see also Ezek 14:14, 20). We know that these two men had an effective prayer life and that their prayers brought about change on many occasions in Israel's history.

A number of passages in the OT describe Moses as a great intercessor (Pss 99:6; 106:23). He prayed at the time of the plagues in Egypt (Exod 5:22-23; 8:12-13; 9:28; 10:17); on behalf of his sister Miriam (Num 12:13); and for all the people during their wandering in the desert (Exod 32:11-14, 30-32; Num 11:2; 14:13-19; 16:22; 21:7; Deut 9:25-29).

Samuel, too, is listed among the three great intercessors mentioned in Psalm 99:6-8. We are specifically told that he prayed at the gathering at Mizpah that preceded the victory over the Philistines (1 Sam 7:5-9) and before his farewell speech (1 Sam 12:18-19); and that he promised to continue to intercede for his people (1 Sam 12:23).

If even the prayers of such great men cannot make a difference, then all hope for the people is gone. They may ask Jeremiah's advice, saying *Where shall we go?* But the only options he can give in reply are *death,* the *sword, starvation* or *captivity* (**15:2**). They will endure all the calamities described in the curses laid down as punishment for disobedience to their covenant with the Lord (**15:3**; see Deut 28:25-26). And all this is taking place because of the sins of *Manasseh, son of Hezekiah* (**15:4**). This man came to the throne very young, at twelve years of age, and reigned in Jerusalem for fifty-five long years (2 Chr 33:1). His father, Hezekiah, and his grandson, Josiah, were godly kings, but Manasseh was one of Judah's worst kings. He was especially idolatrous (2 Kgs 21:1-18; 23:26-27; 24:3-4; 2 Chr 33:1-20). The city of Jerusalem is experiencing the consequences of the abominations that Manasseh had perpetrated within it.

No one will have pity on the city (**15:5**). The people will have to endure God's judgment because they have not known enough to return to the Lord by changing their behaviour (**15:6-7**).

The next verse could be read with the Lord's promise to Abraham in mind. The Lord had promised him 'descendants as numerous as the stars in the sky and as the sand on the seashore' (Gen 22:17). But here, the promise is reversed. It is widows who will be *more numerous than the sand of the sea* (**15:8**). The young men have been killed in great numbers and their mothers are gripped with terror.

In Hannah's song, we read of the barren woman giving birth to seven children (1 Sam 2:5). Seven sons was probably regarded as symbolic of the greatest blessing a woman could enjoy (Ruth 4:15). For a woman who has experienced this greatest of blessings to die in misery and shame is the ultimate misfortune. The fact that everything around her is in shadow although it is midday shows that the day of the Lord has arrived (**15:9**; Amos 8:9). She will die, and all her surviving children will be killed by their enemies.

15:10-21 Jeremiah's Complaints

A new 'complaint' is introduced with Jeremiah regretting his very existence (**15:10**). As the complaint proceeds, it becomes apparent that it is a particular part of his life, his role as a prophet, that prompts his misery. Everyone is against him because of the messages from the Lord that he has been proclaiming.

The Lord's reply is a reminder to his servant of what he has done for him in the past: 'Surely I have intervened in your life for good, surely I have imposed enemies on you in a time of trouble and in a time of distress' (**15:11**, NRSV). However, the Hebrew text is difficult to interpret, and thus the NIV translates this as referring to the future: *Surely I will deliver you for a good purpose; surely I will make your enemies plead with you in times of disaster and times of distress.* But regardless of whether the Lord's words are a reminder of past deliverances or a promise for the future, what is clear is that the Lord is reassuring his prophet.

The prophet cannot remain quiet because he faces opposition. The message must be announced because the Lord will bring it about. Thus we again have a reference to *the north,* which always reminds us of the Babylonian invaders (**15:12**). Jeremiah's message, which had made him so many enemies, is reaffirmed (**15:13-14**).

The prophet again appeals to the Lord: *remember me and care for me* (**15:15**). Here 'remember me' is a request for God to watch over him (see Pss 25:6; 106:4). Jeremiah's attitude shows that he has decided to obey God by continuing to announce his word despite the opposition he faces. He entrusts himself to God.

When Jeremiah was called, the Lord said, 'I have put my words in your mouth' (1:9). Now the prophet says he has indeed received and eaten those words (**15:16a**). His heart was filled with joy as he did so. Ezekiel, Jeremiah's contemporary, also speaks of eating the word of God (Ezek 2:8-3:3).

Jeremiah had belonged to the Lord since before his birth, when God had set him apart for his service (1:5). Because of this special calling, he can say, *I bear your name* (**15:16b**). But the prophet knows that his calling has affected his life. He has had to be careful of the company he keeps (**15:17**; Ps 1:1). Every calling involves a certain degree of loneliness and it will not be long before Jeremiah speaks of this at length (16:1-5). This loneliness may result in suffering. Jeremiah has had bitter experiences and he becomes angry with God for having given him such a calling. He even asks God, *Will you be to me like a deceptive brook?* (**15:18**; see also Job 6:15). He seems to be wondering whether he can actually trust God.

Jeremiah's sufferings may have prompted him to say too much (15:10, 17-18), and the Lord now calls on him to change his attitude and to be restored to his God (**15:19**). He is reminded that the people are supposed to listen to Jeremiah; he is not supposed to listen to them. He must never be concerned about pleasing the people but must rather seek with all his might to please the Lord.

After these words, the Lord renews Jeremiah's prophetic calling, repeating some of the words that were said at the time of his first call (**15:20**; 1:18-19). It is important to note that renewal of Jeremiah's call involves the promise of the Lord's help. The servant is never left on his own; his master is always by his side. This knowledge should greatly encourage all those men and women who are serving God but who for some reason feel alone, abandoned by their people. The Lord will always deliver his servants from *the hands of the wicked* and *the grasp of the cruel* (**15:21**).

16:1-15 Deep Prophetic Loneliness

Jeremiah's single state is to be an integral part of his message (**16:1-2**). As a sign to Judah, he is to take no wife and thus he will father no children. He will never have an opportunity to enjoy family life. The reason he is not to have these joys is because of the dark future that awaits all wives and children in his day. They can anticipate only sickness, sword and famine. They cannot even hope to be mourned or given decent burial, for their bodies will be food for wild beasts and fertilizer (translated as 'refuse' in the NIV) for the soil (**16:3-4**; see also 7:33; 15:2-3).

As if the loneliness of living without a wife and children were not enough, the Lord asks Jeremiah to distance himself from all major social functions. He is to stay away from funerals (**16:5**). He must not *show sympathy* to those who are suffering because the Lord himself will no longer show kindness or compassion to the people of Judah. Moreover, his refusal to attend funerals will be a reminder of his prophecy that soon there will be so many dead that no funerals will be held. Nor will people any longer carry out any of the traditional practices associated with mourning, such as ritual cutting of their bodies and shaving of their heads (**16:6**). Although these pagan customs were specifically forbidden by the Law (Lev 19:28; 21:5; Deut 14:1), they were practised by the people of Israel (see also 41:5).

As is still the custom in many areas of Africa today, food was served to the relatives and neighbours who came to console the family in their mourning (Ezek 24:17, 22; Hos 9:4). But in the near future, this practice too will disappear along with everything else associated with funerals (**16:7**).

Jeremiah is also forbidden to attend all feasts and celebrations (**16:8**). He is not to share in the joys of his people. Soon there will be no more joy, because the Lord will bring it to an end (**16:9**; 7:34). There will be no more celebrations, no more marriages.

The people will respond to this message with blank incomprehension. They will ask him to explain what spe-cific failure or sin they have committed to deserve such a judgment (**16:10**). He is to reply by reminding them of the idolatry of their ancestors (**16:11**). They rejected the law of the Lord in favour of worshipping idols. But that is not the only reason for the coming distress.

Besides the sins of their ancestors, there are the failures of the Judeans themselves (**16:12**). Their situation is even more serious because they have failed to learn from the experience of those who went before them. It is as if the practices of their ancestors had inscribed a sort of law in the lives of their descendants, a natural inclination to do what their forebears had done. But this passage insists on the personal responsibility of the Judeans of Jeremiah's day because the cycle of guilt could have been broken. Unfortunately the prophet's compatriots have not done so. That is why the Lord will be sending them into exile (**16:13**). He speaks ironically when he tells them that they will have even greater freedom to worship idols in the foreign land to which they are going.

However, there is some good news! The prophecy of exile is accompanied by a prediction of the people's return from exile (**16:14-15**). After that return, the exodus from Egypt will no longer be the ultimate point of reference when people speak of the great things God has done for his people Israel. Rather, it will be the second exodus, the return from exile, that will be cited to demonstrate the greatness of the Lord's power.

As the wise say, 'However long the night, the day always comes'. The Lord will cause a new day to begin for Judah.

16:16-17:27 Warnings and Punishments

This long passage includes several warnings, a description of Judah's sin, thoughts on the stupidity of those who trust in human beings, and a call to respect the Sabbath.

16:16-21 God, Judah and other nations

There is no place to hide from the eyes of the Lord (**16:17**; 32:19; Ps 139), and no human action can be hidden from him (Job 34:21-22). The Lord can call for *many fishermen* and *many hunters* (**16:16**). The image of fisherman is also employed by the prophet Habakkuk to describe the Babylonians (Hab 1:15). The Lord's hunters and fishermen will find the people hiding in their places of refuge, the *crevices of the rocks*. In Isaiah 2:10, people are said to hide there in an effort to escape the 'dread of the Lord and the splendour of his majesty'.

The NIV translation of **16:18** leaves out the word 'first', which is present in the original, so that the text should read, *I will first doubly repay their iniquity* (NASB). This 'first' is assumed to indicate that the punishment spoken of here will precede the deliverance spoken of in 16:15.

This verse also teaches that the practice of idolatry profanes a country and defiles the land. This warning must be taken seriously, for many people do not seem to have understood that the many misfortunes that have saddened our countries are the result of our rejection of God and our widespread occult practices. No occult practice is without consequences. All affect those who practise them, and also their families and their environment.

The recognition by the nations that idolatry is *false* and *worthless* begins with a confession of faith that is familiar from the Psalms (**16:19**; see Pss 18:3; 46:1-2). The nations will abandon their *own gods*, which *are not gods* and will turn to the Lord (**16:20**). Jeremiah had already announced the salvation of pagan nations (3:17; 12:15-16). With a demonstration of his *power and might*, the Lord will show all the nations that he alone is God (**16:21**). The word here translated 'power' is literally 'hand' (as in the KJV). The OT often refers to God's 'arm' or his 'hand' (see Exod 6:6; Num 11:23; Deut 4:34; 5.15; 1 Kgs 8:42).

17:1-11 Judah's sin

The gravity of Judah's sin is expressed by the terms *engraved* and *inscribed* (**17:1a**) which remind us that the law of the Lord was engraved on tablets of stone (Exod 32:15-16). Here it is the sin of the people that is engraved, not on stone, but on their hearts. The use of *an iron tool* and *a flint point* to do the engraving shows how hard their hearts are! Later, Jeremiah will speak of something else being inscribed on their hearts – the law of the Lord (31:33-34).

The *horns* of the *altars* were where the blood of animals that were sacrificed as sin offerings was sprinkled (**17:1b**; Exod 30:10; Lev 16:18). They were also what people grasped in order to claim sanctuary (1 Kgs 1:49-53; 2:28). However, in this verse and the next, the word *altars* does not seem to refer to those in the sanctuaries where people worshipped the Lord They were associated with *Asherah poles* confirms (**17:2a**; Exod 34:13; 1 Kgs 14:15; 2 Kgs 23:6). Jeremiah is speaking of the altars on which the people of Judah had offered sacrifices to idols under *spreading trees* and on *high hills* (**17:2b**; Deut 12:2-3; 2 Kgs 17:9-10). He is again denouncing the people's idolatry.

Verses **17:3-4** are very similar to 15:13-14. The people's inheritance will go to others and Judah will become the slave of her enemies in a foreign land. The Lord's anger is compared to a fire that Judah has lit by her evil behaviour, a fire that *will burn for ever* (17:4).

Psalm 1 is brought to mind by 17:5-8, which underlines the consequences of faithfulness or unfaithfulness in relation to the Lord. Not only is it stupid to trust in human support, but it brings a curse because it is a sign that the person has turned away from the Lord (**17:5**). Such a person will never know happiness, but will live a life comparable to that of a plant struggling to survive in an arid wasteland (**17:6**).

On the other hand, the person who puts their trust solely in the Lord is blessed (**17:7**: Ps 125). As Psalm 1 puts it, such a person is like a tree that does not lack water and does not experience drought. No season causes it concern and it *never fails to bear fruit* (**17:8a, c**).

The word translated 'fear' in the clause, *it does not fear when heat comes* (**17:8b**), is literally 'see', as in the KJV, 'shall not see when heat cometh'. This translation enables us to see the parallel that is being drawn between the person who is cursed and does not see prosperity and the person who is blessed and does not see heat coming. This does not mean that the person who is cursed does not notice when prosperity comes, or that the one who is blessed does not notice the heat. No! The meaning is that the cursed will never experience prosperity and that the heat will never disturb one who is blessed.

Now Jeremiah returns to the gravity of the human condition (**17:9**). The human *heart is deceitful*; it cannot be relied on (see 9:3-5). Deceit is part of its very nature. No human being can sound the depths of his or her neighbour's heart. Only the Lord is capable of reading the human *heart* as an open book (11:20; Job 34:21-22; Heb 4:12-13). Since nothing is hidden from his eyes, he alone can repay to each one what their behaviour deserves (25:14; 32:19; Rev 2:23). The words *heart* and *mind* are often found together in the Bible (**17:10**; 20:12; Pss 7:9; 26:2) and indicate the depths of the human person, the most intimate core of their being.

Jeremiah next quotes what must have been a well-known proverb that makes the point that 'ill-gotten treasures are of no value' (Prov 10:2). Their owner may lose them as quickly as they were obtained and it is then that he will realize how pointless his actions were (**17:11**).

17:12-18 Jeremiah's prayer

The next verses are a prayer or a complaint by Jeremiah. The *glorious throne, exalted from the beginning* is the throne of the Lord (**17:12**; 14:21; Isa 6:1). In calling it *the place of our sanctuary*, the prophet is probably thinking of Mount Zion (8:19; 31:6; 50:5).

Some translations of **17:13** include both the voice of the prophet and that of the Lord. Jeremiah begins, O *Lord, the hope of Israel, all who forsake you shall be ashamed,* and the Lord responds by affirming that *those who depart from me shall be written in the earth, because they have forsaken the Lord* (NKJV). But whether we follow the NIV or the KJV translation, it is clear that all those who distance themselves from him will experience shame and death (17:13; see 2:13; 14:8). They will be abandoning the one who is the *spring of living water* (see 2:13; see also John 7:37-38).

Jeremiah resumes his prayer in **17:14** and again asks for healing and salvation (see also Ps 103:2-3; 147:2-3). He knows that there is no salvation apart from the Lord. The end of the verse reminds us of 9:23-24, where all who wish to glorify themselves are invited to find their glory in having the intelligence to recognize that the Lord is the God of 'kindness, justice and righteousness on earth'.

We again hear the voices of Jeremiah's enemies in **17:15**. They accuse him of being a false prophet because he has announced things that have not happened (17:15; see Isa 5:19; 2 Pet 3:4). In response, Jeremiah simply affirms his faithfulness to the calling God has given him (**17:16**). He has no desire to see the disasters he has been prophesying, but he has to pass on what the Lord has told him to say (1:1). He has been obedient, and so in **17:17** he asks the Lord not to fulfil the threat he made to Jeremiah at the time of his call: 'Do not be terrified by them, or I will terrify you before them' (1:17).

Jeremiah's prayer ends like an imprecatory psalm as he calls for the Lord's judgment on his *persecutors* (**17:18**; 15:15; Pss 35:4; 40:15). He asks that they be doubly punished, as if to emphasize the intensity of the disaster that he wishes to happen to them.

17:19-27 A call to respect the Sabbath

The message about the Sabbath is to be given in a precise place, which was possibly the door connecting the temple and the palace. It is then to be repeated at other gates of the city (**17:19**). Everyone must have an opportunity to hear it (**17:20**).

Jeremiah calls for a scrupulous observance of the Sabbath as a sign of the covenant between the people and the Lord (Exod 20:8-11; Isa 58:13-14). The word 'Sabbath' derives from a root that means 'to stop' or 'to be inactive' (Exod 16:29-30; 34:21). It was a day of rest that was to be observed once a week as a day devoted to the Lord, who himself rested on the seventh day of creation (Gen 2:2-3). Such texts as Exodus 23:12 and Deuteronomy 5:14 show that as well the purely religious aspect of being a day devoted to God, the Sabbath also had a social function. It allowed everyone (sons and daughters, male and female servants and foreigners) to rest from the week's work. The memory of their slavery in Egypt should prompt the Israelites to avoid forcing their employees, as well as their own children, to a rhythm of work that would devour their lives (Deut 5:15).

Jeremiah uses carrying a load *through the gates of Jerusalem*, where he is standing, as an example of Sabbath-breaking (**17:21-22**). But it is possible that he is not focusing so much on the mere carrying of a load as on the commercial transaction that is taking place on the Sabbath. Nehemiah 13:15-21 describes a scene similar to the one the prophet is denouncing here.

To sanctify the Sabbath day means to set it apart, to consecrate it to God. While it is true that Christians need not celebrate the Sabbath as the Jews did with their very strict rules and rituals, it is nevertheless important that believers observe the principle that was established by the Lord. We need to stop being busy with all the other matters that preoccupy us and to acknowledge that the Lord is God and that we owe him everything. The whole purpose of public worship derives from the community's weekly turning of their attention toward God and recognizing that he is their Lord.

The Sabbath is also meant to be a day of rest. Unfortunately, for many Christians Sunday is the longest and most tiring of the week. The worship services may be long and exhausting, and if there are additional afternoon and evening gatherings, there may be no opportunity at all for rest! The Lord wants us both to celebrate him and to rest ourselves on that day. He does not suggest this as an option we might consider, but as a rule of life. If we do not respect it, we bear the consequences, which often manifest themselves in a weariness that can degenerate into various kinds of illnesses. But while we should observe the principle of the Sabbath, we should take care not to fall into the legalism for which Jesus rebuked his contemporaries (Matt 12:1-8; Luke 13:10-16; 14:1-6).

Israel's ancestors, to whom the Sabbath had been given by the Lord, did not respect it (**17:23**). Now the Lord reminds them of it and promises them many blessings if the people obey his word (**17:24**). The first blessing will be political stability (**17:25a**). If there are *kings who sit on David's throne,* it will mean that the royal family has survived and that the succession to the throne is proceeding smoothly. We in Africa have a particular appreciation of this blessing since we know from experience that national crises often erupt around the issue of a change in leadership.

The second blessing, which will flow from the first, is social peace. Jerusalem will be inhabited and its inhabitants will be governed by Judean leaders, not by strangers (**17:25b**).

The third blessing is religious and spiritual (**17:26**). Peace will allow people from all over the country to travel to Jerusalem to offer sacrifices to the Lord. This resumption of their worship means that their relationship with the Lord is restored.

However, if the people decide to disobey the Lord and continue to ignore the Sabbath, the results will be catastrophic. The Lord *will kindle an unquenchable fire* that will destroy everything in the city of Jerusalem (**17:27**; 4:4; 15:14; 17:4; 21:12).

18:1-20:18 The Sign of the Potter

18:1-17 Jeremiah at the potter's house

Several elements in this section remind us of the account of Jeremiah's call in chapter 1. First, there is the invitation to the prophet to turn his attention to some scene for the purpose of drawing a message from it (1:11-15). Then there is the use of the three negative verbs that characterize

Jeremiah's mission ('uproot', 'tear down' and 'destroy'). Finally, there is the use of two positive verbs ('build' and 'plant') that also characterize Jeremiah's prophetic ministry (1:10).

The scene that the Lord asks Jeremiah to go and see is completely ordinary. It is a potter working in his shop (**18:1-3**). As usual, he is making pots. It is not the fact that he is doing this that is important, but the meaning that Jeremiah will attach to what he does once his attention has been drawn to it.

Jeremiah notices that one of the pots the potter is working on is not a success. It is not coming out the way he intended it to. So the potter squashes the soft clay back into a single lump and begins to use that lump to make another pot (**18:4**).

Jeremiah suddenly recognizes that there is an analogy between what the potter is doing and the Lord's relationship to Israel. There is no need to answer the rhetorical question in **18:6**, for the answer is obvious. The Lord is the potter and Israel is the clay. Just as the potter can make anything he chooses out of a lump of clay, so the Lord is absolutely free to shape the people of Israel into what he wants. His purpose is to have the nation conform to his design.

The lesson taught in 18:7-10 was an important one for Judah at that time and is still important for us today. The Lord is ready to turn away his anger from everyone who repents of his evil ways and returns to God, recognizing him as the only true God. As we said earlier, the verbs *uprooted, torn down* and *destroyed* were used to describe Jeremiah's prophetic activity (**18:7**; 1:10). This message, addressed especially to Judah, means that the threatened exile of the people can be avoided on one condition. If they repent, God will relent (18:8). In the KJV, God is said to 'repent', a translation that has caused confusion. God does not repent as we humans do. What he does is 'relent', that is he no longer does what he had intended to do.

This promise means that no nation is inevitably condemned. There is always a way of salvation. For us individually, this means that as long as we live, God is always offering us the possibility of changing our attitude and so escaping the judgment that awaits those who turn away from the Lord to trust in idols.

However, no nation is inevitably blessed either. Disobedience and idolatry can result in a nation losing all the blessings that the Lord has promised them (**18:9-10**). God does not repent as we humans do. What he does is that he 'relents', giving up what he had intended to do (26:3, 13, 19; 42:10; Ezek 18:21-23; Joel 2:13).

The Lord warns Judah, *I am preparing a disaster for you* (**18:11**). In Hebrew, the word 'preparing' or 'making' comes from the same root as the word translated 'potter', showing that this warning is closely related to the incident that Jeremiah has just seen. It is not that the Lord is devising evil plans against his own people. The disaster that is coming is the unfortunate consequence of their disobedience to God's word. The Lord urges the Judeans to change their behaviour. But the people have deliberately chosen not to do so (**18:12**).

Such a blatant refusal to listen to the Lord and abandoning of him is almost unimaginable (**18:13**). It is as unnatural as it would be if there were no snow on the high summit of Mount Lebanon or if the water ceased to flow in the rivers (**18:14**). However, this verse is difficult to translate, and so it can also be interpreted in another way. It may be making the point that the Lord is like a rock or a spring of cool water (see 2:13), but that Judah has turned away from him to worship idols (**18:15**). The consequence of this idolatry that Jeremiah repeatedly condemns will be the devastation of the country and the nation being scorned by others (**18:16**; 48:27; Ps 22:7; Job 16:4).

The people have turned their backs on the Lord, and he will respond by turning his back on them (**18:17**; 2:27; 2 Chr 29:6; Prov 1:24-32). When the Lord shows his face, it is a sign of his grace and goodness (Num 6:24-26; Pss 21:7; 31:17; 67:2). But when he hides his face, disaster follows (Pss 13:2; 27:9; 30:7).

18:18-23 Jeremiah threatened again

We now hear of a second plot hatched against Jeremiah (for the first one, see 11:18-23). To drum up support, his opponents refer to what appears to be a popular saying about the three main forms of ministry known in OT times (**18:18**). It mentions *the priests,* who were responsible for *teaching* and explaining *the law* (see Neh 8:13); *the wise,* who gave *counsel* regarding how to achieve harmonious social and political life (see also Eccl 12:11), and *the prophets,* who made God's messages, his *word,* known to the people (Amos 3:7). Jeremiah has repeatedly said that all these groups will be judged (see, for example, 13:13; 14:18), but his enemies deny that any judgment is coming. They attack him with their *tongues,* that is, with their words, and reject all his prophecies (9:3; see also 1 Cor 4:13).

The Apostle James compares the tongue to a fire (Jas 3:5, 6, 8) because of the enormous damage it can do. It can be used to slander, give false witness and report rumours that the speaker has not taken the trouble to verify. Such speech destroys the confidence and cohesion of Christian communities.

In the prayer that follows, the prophet begins by asking the Lord's help against his adversaries. He is surprised that they repay the good he has done with evil. Jeremiah had prayed fervently for the people of Judah (14:7-9), but in return, they want him dead (**18:20, 22**). His statement that *they have dug a pit to capture me* means that his enemies have tried to trap him (see Ps 57:6).

Jeremiah responds to this plot by asking that all his accusers (men, women and children) be struck down with various plagues (famine, the sword, sterility, and so on) and that God will not pardon the sin of the people (**18:21, 23**). We may find Jeremiah's words here very harsh. They certainly reveal the depth of the prophet's suffering at the hands of his fellow Israelites.

19:1-13 The Valley of Ben Hinnom

This chapter begins in a similar way to the preceding one as the Lord instructs the prophet to go to a certain place (**19:1**; see **18:1-2**). When he gets there, he is to do specific things, as he did previously in the acted prophecy involving a linen belt (**13:1-14**).

In this case, Jeremiah is told to buy a *clay jar* and to take *some of the elders of the people and of the priests* to the *Valley of Ben Hinnom*, by the *Potsherd Gate* (**19:1-2**; see **7:31**). This gate is not mentioned elsewhere in Scripture. Some commentators think that it may be the same as the Dung Gate (Neh 2:13).

The oracle from the *Lord Almighty*, which can also be translated as 'the Lord of Hosts' (see **11:17; Isa 1:9**), is addressed to *kings of Judah and people of Jerusalem* (**19:3**). It announces a disaster so staggering that those who hear about it will have trouble believing their ears.

This disaster will come because the Lord's people have abandoned him and have profaned the city of Jerusalem with their idolatries and crimes. They have shed the *blood of the innocent* in the child sacrifices that took place in the Valley of Ben Hinnom, where Jeremiah is now standing (**19:4; 7:31; 32:35**). Such sacrifices were strongly condemned by the law (**19:5; Lev 18:21**).

Verse **19:6** is almost identical with **7:32**. The change in the name of the valley announces what will take place there. The Lord will ruin all the plans of Judah and Jerusalem, will cause their inhabitants to die and will abandon their corpses to the birds and wild beasts (**19:7; 7:33**).

Verse **19:8** seems to repeat what was said in **18:16**, about the fate of the city. But this time cannibalism is foretold – an atrocity that is associated with times of great crisis, such as occur when a city is under siege or during civil wars (**19:9**). The book of Lamentations also speaks of cannibalism at the time of the fall of Jerusalem (Lam 2:20). There are scandalous testimonies of such practices in most African countries that have experienced civil wars in recent years. But in these cases, the perpetrators have not eaten human flesh because they are hungry but as part of an occult rite to acquire a power that will make them invincible in battle. Jeremiah presents cannibalism as the result of the Lord's curse on his people.

After Jeremiah has proclaimed his message, he is to break the clay jar that he had bought (**19:10**). This act signifies that Judah and Jerusalem will be broken without any hope of salvation (**19:11-12**). The message is driven home by the fact that the Hebrew word for 'jar' is very similar to the Hebrew word for 'ruin'.

Topheth will be made impure by the presence of unburied corpses, and the same fate awaits the houses in Jerusalem and even the palace of the kings of Judah. All these places have been contaminated by the idolatry that has been practised in them (**19:13**). The *starry hosts* are the same false gods who were denounced in **8:2**.

19:14-20:6 Pashhur has the prophet beaten

Until now, the prophet Jeremiah has spoken of his enemies as a group. Even the people of Anathoth were referred to as a group (**11:21**). Here for the first time, the text reveals the identity of a particular enemy. For the first time also, Jeremiah suffers physical violence because of his message. The scene takes place while Jeremiah is prophesying in the temple courts after has returned from *Topheth* (**19:14**). He is telling the people that all the miseries that he has prophesied against Jerusalem will definitely take place (**19:15**).

Jeremiah's enemy is *the priest Pashhur son of Immer* (**20:1**). He may have been a descendant of the Immer mentioned in 1 Chronicles 24:14. As the *chief officer in the temple,* Pashhur was in charge of the 'police' responsible for maintaining order in the temple courts (**29:26**).

Pashhur ordered that Jeremiah be beaten (**20:2a**). This is the first record we have of him experiencing physical violence, but he will encounter more of it later in his ministry (**26:7-11; 36:26; 37:11-16; 38:4-6**). After the beating, Jeremiah is put *in the stocks*.

The Hebrew word that is translated as 'stocks' suggests that this was some device that forced the victim to sit or stand hunched over or in a bent position. Jeremiah is forced to do this in a very public place, the *Upper Gate of Benjamin at the Lord's temple* (**20:2b**). This was not the same as the Benjamin Gate in the city wall (see **37:13; 38:7**).

The next day, as soon as he is freed from the stocks, Jeremiah sends a message to his torturer (**20:3**). He announces a change in the man's name. He should no longer be called Pashhur but rather *Magor-Missabib*, meaning 'terror on every side', an expression frequently used in the book of Jeremiah (**20:4a, 10; 46:5; 49:29**). Pashhur's new name foreshadows his personal destiny and that of Judah. He and his friends will become the victims of their enemies; Judah will be delivered to *Babylon* and taken into captivity (**20:4b**). This is the first time the name of Judah's enemy from the north is plainly stated in this book (see also **25:9**).

All of Jerusalem's wealth and all the wealth of Judah's kings will be handed over to the Babylonians (**20:5**). Meanwhile Pashhur and his entire household will go into exile in Babylon. That is where Pashhur will die and be buried, along with all those who have listened to him (**20:6**).

Jeremiah's behaviour at this time teaches us a great lesson. The text does not mention any reaction on his part when Pashhur beat him for proclaiming the Lord's message. It seems that he did not try to defend himself. He seems to have trusted his fate to the one who had sent him and in whose name he spoke. As a servant of God, he was no longer living for himself. His only concern was to do what the Lord asked of him. He entrusted his life and his physical safety to God. And God passed judgment in his favour. By acting in this way, Jeremiah is a forerunner of the suffering Christ (Isa 53:3-7; Mark 14:34-36; Acts 8:32).

20:7-18 Jeremiah's complaint

This complaint is one of the most intimate that Jeremiah has left on record for us. It expresses his profound loneliness and suffering. He begins by complaining that the Lord gave him no choice about his prophetic vocation (**20:7**). He goes so far as to say that he has been *deceived*. He could not resist God's call and has to speak what God puts in his mouth, but instead of insisting that his messenger be honoured, God is allowing him to be ridiculed. *Everyone mocks* him because of the content of his messages (15:17; Lam 3:14).

Jeremiah would love to announce something other than exile and destruction (**20:8**). The message he has to proclaim isolates him from society. No one is interested in hearing what he has to say. He is constantly swimming against the tide of Judean society.

He has even reached the point where he no longer wants to speak for the Lord (**20:9**). He has tried to resign his commission, but he cannot. All his efforts not to speak the word of God were doomed to failure. God's word was like a burning fire with him, and it was better to deliver the message than to be consumed by it. Paul says much the same thing when he insists that he is compelled to preach the gospel (1 Cor 9:16; see also Amos 7:14-16).

Jeremiah's listeners laugh at him. They quote his words, *Terror on every side*, but only to deride him (**20:10**). Even those with whom he has had a friendly relationship are now looking for an opportunity to trip him up.

But in the depths of his suffering, Jeremiah knows that the most important thing for anyone, and particularly for a servant of God, is that the Lord is with him. He expresses his confidence in God, comparing the Lord to *a mighty warrior* (**20:11**; 32:18: Exod 15:3; Isa 42:13). He believes that the Lord will protect him and will frustrate his enemies and throw them into confusion. After all, he is the *Lord Almighty*, or as the KJV puts it, the 'Lord of hosts' (**20:12**; see also 19:3; Isa 1:9). And he has the ability to search the human *heart and mind* (see also 17:10).

The prophet's confidence in the Lord leads him to invite everyone to celebrate the Lord (**20:13**). He knows that the only one to whom he can turn for deliverance from those

who wish him harm is the Lord (Ps 59:10). The Lord will deliver him; he will save him (Pss 18:20; 31:8; 118:5).

Yet his confidence in the Lord's help is not enough to remove all traces of despair, and Jeremiah returns to the theme of his weariness and suffering. He regrets having been born (**20:14**). He had already said much the same thing in 15:10, but here he expresses the idea even more strongly, cursing the day of his birth. He even curses the person who informed his father that he had been born (**20:15-16**). If only he had died while still in the womb! (**20:17**).

Jeremiah's despair arose from his ministry and from his certainty that the exile and all the other disasters he prophesied would come about (**20:18**). He was not an uncaring prophet who cheerfully announced misfortune without feeling any pity for those whose unbelief meant that they were headed for disaster. He suffered for the people he loved and whose salvation he longed for.

21:1-23:8 Oracles to The Kings of Judah

We now come to six oracles regarding the kings of Judah. These messages are addressed to Zedekiah (597-587 BC), to all David's heirs, to Jehoahaz (609 BC), to Jehoiakim (609-598 BC), and to Jehoiachin (598-597 BC), and conclude with the promise of a righteous ruler.

21:1-10 Oracle to Zedekiah

The first oracle is the Lord's response through Jeremiah to a request by Zedekiah (**21:1**). This request was delivered by two people who should not be confused with others with the same names. *Pashhur son of Malkijah,* should not be confused with 'Pashhur, son of Immer' (20:1; 1 Chr 24:14), and *the priest Zephaniah son of Maaseiah* should not be confused with Zephaniah the prophet, who was the son of Cushi (Zeph 1:1).

The idea of consulting the Lord was a familiar one for OT believers. In Exodus 33:7-11, we are told that Moses erected a tent, which he called the Tent of Meeting, where any one who wished could come to consult the Lord, with Moses acting as an intermediary. However, the practice of consulting the Lord was far older than Moses' time. Genesis tells us that Rebekah, Isaac's wife, consulted the Lord regarding the children in her womb (Gen 25:22).

People consulted the Lord for various reasons, ranging from purely personal and private matters, as in Rebekah's case (see also Saul in 1 Sam 9:6), to situations related to the entire nation (Judg 20:18; 2 Kgs 22:13). There is thus nothing surprising about Zedekiah asking Jeremiah a question (see also 37:3).

Zedekiah wishes to know whether the Lord will act in favour of Judah against the Babylonian attackers. This is the first time that the name of *Nebuchadnezzar,* king of Babylon, appears in the book of Jeremiah (**21:2**). In making his request, Zedekiah recalls the Lord's deliverances of the past (see Ps 44:1-8). We are reminded that we should never forget the goodness of the Lord, but should nourish our faith with testimonies of his great deeds (Pss 77:12; 103:2;145).

Jeremiah receives the Lord's answer (**21:3**). It is devastating and not at all what the king was hoping for. The answer is given in three parts.

In the first part of the response, the Lord states that he will put an end to any attempt to fight the Babylonians outside the city, and that the Judean defenders of Jerusalem will all be penned up inside the city (**21:4**). The Lord will fight against his own people as if he were siding with Babylon (**21:5**; see also Isa 63:10). The expression *with an outstretched hand and a mighty arm* refers to the strength exercised by the Lord. The same expression is often used in Deuteronomy with reference to the powerful way in which the Lord delivered his people from slavery in Egypt (Deut 4:34; 5:15; 7:19; 26:8). But now that same strength will be turned against his people, for their unfaithfulness has roused the Lord's *anger and fury and great wrath*. Sin is never unimportant or without consequences. It is always serious because it dishonours the Lord and prompts his anger. *Men and animals* will fall before God's judgment, which will not only come through the hostile army but also through *a terrible plague* of the kind that he so often used to punish nations (**21:6**; see for example, Exod 5:3; Lev 26:25; Num 14:12; Deut 28:21; 2 Sam 24:15). Jeremiah often speaks of God's use of plague (see 14:12; 21:6-9; 24:10; 27:8, 13; 29:17-18).

The second part of the Lord's response concerns Zedekiah personally and those who escape the plague. They will fall into the hands of Nebuchadnezzar, who will kill them (**21:7**). This prophecy will be repeated to Zedekiah (37:17) and its fulfilment will be described in 39:5-7.

The third and final part of God's response is directed to the people. It is an expression of God's mercy even in circumstances in which he could have completely destroyed them. They are offered a choice between *the way of life* and the *way of death* (**21:8**; see Deut 30:15). As when the people were presented with a choice by Joshua (Josh 24:15), they have to decide either to believe in the Lord or to dismiss what he says and put their faith in idols.

But the choice is not an easy one. If they are to save their lives, the people must surrender to their enemy, the Babylonians (**21:9**). Willingly submitting to the enemy must have seemed inconceivable to most Judeans – but often the way of salvation does seem incomprehensible, even ridiculous. The Apostle Paul was well aware of this when he told the Corinthians that 'the message of the cross is foolishness to those who are perishing' (1 Cor 1:18, 23). Yet it is always better to listen to the Lord than to trust in purely human reasoning, no matter how wise it may appear (17:5, 7).

The message to Zedekiah ends with a restatement of what was said in 21:5 about the Lord's determination to

judge his people. The words, *I have set my face against this city for harm and not for good* (**21:10**, NASB) present a frightening prospect (Pss 13:1; 27:9; 30:7).

21:11-22:9 Oracle to David's line

The oracle to Zedekiah is followed by one addressed to all the kings of David's line, that is, to all the kings who were direct descendants of King David. These kings are referred to variously as *the royal house of Judah* (**21:11;** see also 22:2) and the *house of David* (**21:12a,** see also 22:4).

The Lord demands that the Davidic kings be active in creating and maintaining a society where justice reigns. Their political, economic and social policies should aim to promote the well-being of all the people they govern. This is their particular responsibility (1 Kgs 3:9, 28). The Lord's threat to punish them if they fail to do this indicates his concern for the well-being of the ordinary people and the weak of society (**21:12b**). These words should be taken very seriously by all governments. They should make a deep impression on those in power in Africa today, who often seem to be working for the benefit of specific groups rather than for all those they govern.

The word 'Jerusalem' is not in the Hebrew text of **22:13a**, which simply speaks of the *inhabitant of the valley and rock of the plain* (NKJV). Many commentators agree with the NIV, however, in seeing this as a reference to Jerusalem that is situated on a hill overlooking a valley. Others, however, think that the prophet is referring specifically to the royal palace that was built on Mount Zion, the highest point in the city. It is clear that the leaders of the city boast of their strong position and claim to be safe from all danger (**21:13b**). But pride is something that the Lord hates (Amos 6:8). It is listed as the first among the 'six things the Lord hates, seven that are detestable to him' (Prov 6:16). The reason he hates pride is that pride sees itself as the standard in everything and trusts in its own abilities and possessions. Consequently it is arrogant and haughty and looks down on all others. But pride can vanish in an instant. That is why the book of Proverbs says that 'pride goes before destruction, a haughty spirit before a fall' (Prov 16:18). Recalling Proverbs 3:34, the Apostle James writes that 'God opposes the proud' (Jas 4:6).

The Lord will punish the kings of Judah for their misconduct and injustice (**21:14**). Once again he speaks of *fire* as the instrument he will use to discipline his people (see 21:10; 52:13; 2 Chr 36:19). Fire is often used in this way in the OT (Gen 19:24; Lev 10:2; Num 11:1; 16:35; 2 Kgs 1:10) and in the NT (2 Thess 1:7; 2 Pet 3:10).

Jeremiah has been speaking to the kings of Judah (21:11), but now he is told to go to *the palace of the king of Judah* to deliver a prophetic message to the king, the officials and all the people (**22:1-2**). In this message, he amplifies and clarifies the points made in 21:12b. Whereas he had previously

TRUTH, JUSTICE, RECONCILIATION AND PEACE

In 1995, South Africa set up a Truth and Reconciliation Commission to investigate human rights abuses under apartheid. Those who confessed their crimes were granted forgiveness, and those they abused were given compensation. Confronting the truth about what had happened has resulted in progress towards community healing, reconciliation and peace. Nigeria, Ghana and other African countries have followed suit, setting up their own human rights commissions.

Rwanda, by contrast, took the path of litigation after the 1994 genocide. After ten years of court cases, which have accomplished little, it too is seeking to follow the South African approach where people can admit to their crimes.

The Concepts

Clearly, issues of truth, justice, reconciliation and peace are high on the political and ethical agenda in Africa today. It is important that Christians think biblically about them.

Truth is not merely an abstract concept but an attribute of a person. God's character is the standard of truth. Human beings are to be as dependable, truthful and upright as God is. This is particularly important in the case of rulers and leaders, who are God's representatives on earth. When they fail to manifest God's character, their failure becomes evident in bad governance and bad leadership.

Justice and judgment are used interchangeably in the Bible, and the adjective 'just' is treated as equivalent to the word 'righteous'. Justice can thus be interpreted as bringing about the reign of God in human society or, in other words, revealing the character of God and his will in human society. In the OT, the law and the prophets have a lot to say about God's reign and his demand for justice. His justice necessitates that we be punished for the particular sins we have committed, which are in themselves evidence of the fact that our basic nature is sinful. But Christ paid the full penalty for us on the cross (Isa 53:3-6; 2 Cor 5:21). In human terms, it is as if a loving judge had to sentence his son to jail, but then served the jail term himself so that the son could go free. Every sinner who approaches God through Christ will be forgiven and justified (Rom 5:9, 18-19).

Reconciliation refers to doing away with enmity and bringing together parties who were formerly hostile to each other. As a result of the fall (Gen 3), we live in a world where there is an urgent need for reconciliation between God and humanity (Rom 5:8-11; 2 Cor 5:18,19; Col 1:19-22) and between human beings (Eph 2:11-22). There is also a need for cosmic reconciliation, that is, the redemption of fallen creation (Rom 8:18-22; Col 1:19-22; 2 Cor 5:19). Our hope of reconciliation is rooted in the work of Christ on the cross, which set aside God's wrath and his judgment upon humanity. Consequently human beings now have access to God and can enjoy his peace and forgiveness when they repent and believe in Jesus Christ (Rom 5:1,2; 5:8-11; 8:1). The cross of Christ also promotes horizontal reconciliation with our fellow human beings. It breaks down boundaries and reconciles groups who were once enemies by making them one in Christ (Eph 2:11-22). This unity eliminates all the barriers created by human selfishness, greed, ethnicity, tribalism, racism and nationalism. It leaves no room for enmity, hatred, prejudice, stereotyping, discrimination, bias or anything else that seeks to exclude others (Gal 3:28).

Peace has to be understood in the context of reconciliation, for peace springs from reconciliation and reconciling is making peace. The Hebrew word *shalom,* translated 'peace', refers to the complete well-being of an individual, a city or a country, including its material prosperity and physical safety. Paul constantly greets and prays for believers with the words 'Grace and peace'. He relates God's peace to Christ's 'making peace through his blood, shed on the cross' (Col 1:20) and emphasizes that peace is grounded in Christ's redemptive work (Rom 5:8-11; 2 Cor 5:18-21; Eph 2:14-15; Col 1:19-22).

The Church's Task

Christ's church is mandated to live out and proclaim the mission and message of Jesus the Messiah to the whole world. He has entrusted it with a ministry of reconciliation (2 Cor 5:18-21), and thus the church must be ultimately concerned about matters of justice and peace. These virtues must first of all be apparent within the Christian community, which should be characterized by love, fellowship, affection, mercy, like-mindedness, agreement, selflessness and humility (Phil 2:1-8).

But the church must always remember that God's truth, peace and justice as revealed by the cross of Christ are intended not only for the church and believers, but also for the entire world. We are called not merely to believe in peace and justice but to work to achieve them for everyone without any distinction or discrimination. Peacemaking is thus an important Christian virtue.

Like its Lord, the church must do works of love and mercy and seek justice for everyone, whatever the cost (Isa 11:1-5; 61:1-3; Luke 4:18,19). It must be compassionate in order to see and hear the cry of the oppressed and the downtrodden and must identify with just and righteous causes. The greed and selfishness of individuals and groups need to be exposed and condemned in light of biblical teachings.

Yusufu Turaki

spoken of the oppressed in general terms, now he specifically mentions *the alien* (that is, immigrants or foreigners living in Israel), *the fatherless* and *the widow* (**22:3a**). These three groups were the weakest and most vulnerable in Israelite society. The alien had no means of support, the widow no husband and the orphan no father. The Lord insists on a number of occasions that no one is to take advantage of such people and deny them their rights (Exod 22:21; Deut 14:29; 24:17, 19; 26:12; Prov 23:10; Isa 1:17).

The Lord not only demands that the rights of the alien, the widow and the orphan be respected, but also sets an example by acting to defend such people (Deut 10:18). The NT says that religion that is pure and faultless looks 'after orphans and widows in their distress' (Jas 1:27). Society in general, and the African church in particular, would benefit from taking another look at our attitudes towards these groups. In many countries today, foreigners, simply because they are foreign, have become popular scapegoats. They are blamed for any rise in crime and any misfortunes that befall the host nation. They are easy targets for abuse. But the word of God invites us to reconsider our attitude towards them.

As we will see later, the Bible also asks foreigners to seek the peace of their host country because their fates are linked (29:7). It is sad and surprising to see people who have lived in a country for many years, who owe everything to that country, becoming that country's worst enemies. As soon as there is any trouble in the country, these people suddenly remember that it is not their homeland and that they are from elsewhere. Such an attitude is irresponsible and ungrateful.

The command not to shed innocent blood (**22:3b**; 7:6) reminds us of the death of Abel, killed by his brother Cain (Gen 4:8), and of the many similar commands issued elsewhere in the OT (Deut 19:10, 13; 21:8, 9; 1 Sam 19:5). Above all, it reminds us of the death of Jesus of Nazareth, whose blood was both innocent and cleansing (Matt 27:4, 31-35; Heb 12:24).

Those who receive the prophetic message and put its advice into practice are promised political stability (**22:4**). This same promise has been made to those who will observe the Sabbath correctly (17:24-25). However, political chaos will follow disobedience to the word of the Lord (**22:5**).

The royal palace is described as being *like Gilead,* which was a fertile mountainous region, similar to the mountains of *Lebanon* (**22:6**). The comparison suggests that the palace was as exalted and stable as these mountains. However, the Lord says that if those who occupy the palace do not listen to his voice, this stability will count for nothing. The palace will cease to be like a fertile mountain and will instead resemble an uninhabited *desert*.

Moreover, the Lord is already preparing those who who carry out his judgment on the king's house. The NASB translation of **22:7** is closer to the Hebrew when it says *I will set apart destroyers against you.* It is as if the Lord is setting them apart for a ministry. These men *will cut down your choicest cedars* (NASB). The mention of 'cedars' here reminds us of the reference to Lebanon in the previous verse, for Lebanon was famed for its cedar trees, which still appear on the country's flag (1 Kgs 5:13; 2 Kgs 14:9; 2 Chr 2:8; Pss 29:5; 92:12; Hos 14:6). Jeremiah is saying that the best cedar trees in Judah will be cut down and burned (again, he is using the image of fire). The NIV translation takes the reference to cedars more literally, and sees God as saying that the *fine cedar beams* of the palace will be cut up. We know that there was such wood in the palace, for the palace that Solomon built was called 'the Palace of the Forest of Lebanon' (1 Kgs 7:2; see also Jer 22:14-15, 23).

The ruin of Jerusalem will be so great that everyone will wonder why the Lord inflicted such a great disaster on it (**22:8**). The answer is simple; the city is desolate because of the infidelity and idolatry of its kings and its inhabitants (**22:9**). They broke their covenant with the Lord in order to worship idols.

22:10-12 Oracle to Jehoahaz

The oracle to Jehoahaz is both brief and clear, which serves to accentuate the severity of the judgment. The *dead king* who is not to be mourned is King Josiah, who had been killed in the battle at Megiddo in 609 BC (**22:10a**; 2 Kgs 23:29-30; 2 Chr 35:20-25).

The king who is to be mourned is the one who has been taken captive to a foreign country (**22:10b**). This king is Jehoahaz, who is here referred to by his other name of Shallum (**22:11**; 2 Kgs 23:30, 34; 2 Chr 36:1). He has left the country of his birth for good and will die in a foreign land. The land in question was Egypt (2 Kgs 23:34), where Jehoahaz did in fact die after being carried off by Pharaoh Neco.

22:13-19 Oracle to Jehoiakim

The name of King Jehoiakim appears only at the end of the oracle, but there is no doubt that he is the one to whom this oracle applies. He is described as having no concern for justice. We are given one example of this in relation to his building projects.

Even though he had first had to pay tribute to Egypt and then to Babylon (1 Kgs 23:35-24:1), and could not have been as wealthy as his predecessors, King Jehoiakim refused to give up his dreams of grandeur (**22:14**). He could not understand that times had changed. He insisted on building himself a luxurious home but had no money to pay the workers. So he forced them to *work for nothing*, without pay, contrary to the clear instructions that no one should withhold a labourer's salary even until the next day (**22:13**; Lev 19:13; Deut 24:15).

Like him, many of those who are in power in our day do not understand the times and hence do things that put their people at great risk of unspeakable suffering.

In **22:15**, God addresses Jehoiakim directly. The king may think that he is establishing his kingdom by outdoing his predecessors in regard to the magnificence of his palace. But his father, Josiah, had been a king who understood that what was important was not the luxury of his living quarters but the extent to which he was faithful to the Lord (2 Kgs 22:1-23:28). The last half of 22:15 summarizes his life: *He did what was right and just.*

For Josiah, doing what was right and just had involved defending *the cause of the poor and needy,* exactly as 22:3 expected of the kings descended from David (**22:16a**). He had acted as a true king, and his actions had proved that he knew the Lord (**22:16b**). This praise of King Josiah strongly suggests that Jeremiah had deeply appreciated the reforms that Josiah initiated in 605 BC.

Be that as it may, this verse teaches us about the true meaning of knowing God. To know God is to take his word seriously by putting it into practice (Hos 6:6; Mic 6:8; Titus 1:16). As the Apostle James says centuries later, claiming to know God counts for nothing without the works that prove it (Jas 2:14, 17). Our countries, cities and churches are full of people who insist that they know and love God. Yet for all that, we do not see changes in society. So what real influence do these people have on their society? Why do we not see the results of their faith in their communities and workplaces? Recently, someone drew my attention to the fact that he knows of a large hospital where almost all the administrative and medical staff frequently listen to Christian radio broadcasts. But these same people sell black-market drugs to the families of patients. Obviously, something is seriously wrong. Countless people have died because of such practices, for the theft by the medical and administrative staff results in shortages of medications.

Because Josiah did what was right and just, *all went well with him* (22:15, 16).

Jehoiakim is very different. He is proud and violent, a king who thinks only of himself and who is prepared to trample the innocent in order to get what he wants (**22:17**). His heart is *set only on ... oppression and extortion.* These two words underscore his cruelty (26:20-23). Unfortunately, we still see the same characteristics in many modern heads of state.

Jehoiakim's name is first mentioned in **22:18a**. It is as if the prophet wants to leave no doubt in anyone's mind that this is the man whose fate he is prophesying. The main consequence of Jehoikim's evil practices will be that no one will give him a proper burial. Rather, his body will be thrown away outside the city, just like that of a common animal (**22:18b-19**; see 36:30). If such a fate is a curse for ordinary people, it is even more so for a king.

Some readers may be puzzled by the fact that 2 Kings 24:6 seems to suggest that Jehoiakim had a normal burial, for he is said to have 'rested with his fathers'. But it is likely that these words are simply the standard phrase that is used in Kings to indicate the end of a king's reign (see, for example, 1 Kgs 2:10; 11:43; 14:20; 2 Kgs 8:24; 10:35; 15:22; 21:18). Thus they do not contradict the prophecy in 22:19 or 36:30.

22:20-30 Oracle to Jehoiachin

The first words of this oracle are addressed to the city of Jerusalem, but the oracle itself is meant for Jehoiachin, the son and successor of Jehoiakim. He reigned for only three months, and during that whole period Judah was besieged by the Babylonians (2 Kgs 24:8).

Lebanon in the north and *Bashan* and *Abarim,* east of the Jordan, were mountainous regions from which the whole of Israel was visible (**22:20a**). The Abarim range included Mount Nebo from which Moses saw Canaan, the country that the Lord had promised to give to his people Israel (Num 27:12; Deut 32:49). This is also the land from which the Lord will now be removing them. Judah cannot hope for help from any of her *allies,* that is, the nations with whom she had made alliances against the Babylonians. These allies, Egypt, Assyria, Edom, Ammon and Phoenicia, will all be defeated and subjugated by Babylon (**22:20**; 27:1-7; 28:14).

Judah's fate is not simply the consequence of its recent behaviour. Its roots lie far in the past, for the nation first refused to listen to the Lord in its youth, at the time of its exodus from Egypt (**22:21**). Ever since then, the nation has been insubordinate and rebellious (Deut 31:27). The Lord has long been patient with them, but now his patience is at an end. We should note that it is wise to interpret God's patience as giving us an opportunity to return to him, rather than assuming that it a sign of God's weakness in accomplishing his purpose (2 Pet 3:9).

God will blow away the *shepherds* of the nation, a term that often refers to all those who lead the nation, including its kings, priests and prophets (**22:22**; 2:8, 26; 5:31; 23:1). Here, however, it seems to refer particularly to the kings. They will be like the chaff carried away by the wind. Judah's allies will suffer the same fate. Without anyone left to turn to, Judah will be confused and ashamed. These are emotions that the Bible often describes as overtaking the wicked (17:13; Pss 25:3; 119:78; Isa 26:11; 45:16, 24; Ezek 16:61; 43:10; Hos 4:19; 10:6). They feel shame as their consciences are stricken about the foolishness of their attempt to rebel against the Lord.

Jeremiah now addresses the king as *you who live in Lebanon ... in cedar buildings* (**22:23**). We must not make the mistake of thinking that he is addressing the king of Lebanon. He is speaking to the Judean king, whose palace has been as stable as the mountains of Lebanon (22:6) and is full of expensive cedar wood (see 22:6, 14). But none of this guarantees the safety of the king. On the contrary, he will be seized with sudden *pain like that of a woman in labour,* a common biblical analogy for sudden, severe pain (4:31; 13:21; 49:24; Isa 13:8; 26:17; Hos 13:13; Matt 24:8; Mark 13:8; 1 Thess 5:3; Rev 12:2).

The oath, *as surely as I live* (**22:24a**), reminds us of the well-known 'I am who I am', the divine response to Moses when he wanted to know the name of the one who was sending him to deliver the children of Israel (Exod 3:13-14). This phrase is often used in the prophetic books to introduce oracles (Isa 49:18; Ezek 5:11; 14:16, 18, 20; 16:48; 17:16; 18:3; 20:3, 31, 33; 33:11, 27). It serves to guarantee the truth of the oracle by attesting that what is said is sure to occur because the oracle comes from the living God.

The name of the one to whom the oracle is addressed is also given in 22:24. It is Jehoiachin, son of Jehoiakim, king of Judah, whose name means 'the Lord will uphold'. His name is also given as Coniah (KJV) and Jeconiah (Matt 1:11).

The Lord makes it clear that even if Jehoiachin were as precious a possession as a *signet ring,* he would be completely rejected (**22:24b**). A 'signet ring' was a ring that carried a person's seal, which was used to authenticate official documents (1 Kgs 21:8; Esth 8:8) and to identify the person (Gen 38:25). Someone's personal seal would be hung on a cord or chain around his neck (Gen 38:18) or, as here, worn on his finger. No one would lightly part with a signet ring! Thus it is an extraordinary thing for the Lord to speak of getting rid of his signet ring (compare Hag 2:23).

The punishment of king Jehoiachin will involve his being handed over to his enemies, who are described in four ways: *those who seek your life, those you fear, Nebuchadnezzar king of Babylon* and *the Babylonians* (**22:25**). He will be deported along with his mother Nehushta. the daughter of Elnathan of Jerusalem (**22:26**; 2 Kgs 24:8). This oracle was fulfilled to the letter (2 Kgs 24:12, 15). Jehoiachin surrendered to Nebuchadnezzar, who deported him to Babylon. Despite his heart's desire, he would never have the opportunity to return from exile in Babylon, neither he, nor his fellow captives (**22:27**).

The two questions asked in **22:28** cast light on the Lord's rejection of Jehoiachin by reminding us of related passages in the OT. The reference to him as a *despised, broken pot* reminds us of God's command to Jeremiah to break a jar before witnesses. This acted prophecy declared that the people of Judah would be similarly broken and that no one would be able to do anything to change the situation (19:10-11). Next the king is referred to as an *object no one wants,* which reminds us of Hosea 8:8: 'Israel is swallowed up; now she is among the nations like a worthless thing'. The further statement that *he and his children* are *cast into*

a land they do not know is a clear reference to the exile that awaits him.

The land or the country is now summoned to hear what the Lord has to say (**22:29**). It is as if the Lord is calling the earth itself to be a witness in his case against his people (Deut 4:26; 30:19; Ps 50:4). Similar words are used in Deuteronomy 32:1 and Isaiah 1:2. Now the earth is to hear his judgment on Jehoiachin: He will have no children, and will be a failure, for none of his descendants will ever succeed him on the throne (**22:30**).

A superficial reading of these verses may give the impression that there is a contradiction between what God says here and the record in 1 Chronicles 3:17-18, where Jehoiachin is said to have had at least seven sons, whose names are given. But the point that is made in 22:30 is well captured in the NIV translation: *record this man* as *if childless.* It is not that he will have no children, but none of them will ever be king in Jerusalem. This is exactly what happened. Jehoiachin was succeeded by Mattaniah (also known as Zedekiah) who was not his son, but his uncle (2 Kgs 24:17).

For OT royal families, as in most ancient and even some modern cultures, it was assumed that the natural order of succession was from father to son (2 Sam 7:12-13, 16; 2 Kgs 10:30). David was even promised that this would be the case if his sons were righteous before the Lord (1 Kgs 2:3-4). A break in the line of succession was seen as a curse on a royal house (2 Sam 3:9-10). And those who found themselves excluded from power would do almost anything to regain the position they believed they were entitled to (see 41:1-3). Many rebellions have been hatched by the frustration, valid or otherwise, of people who have felt themselves unjustly excluded from the management of their country's affairs, as Jeremiah 40–41 demonstrates.

23:1-8 Promise of a righteous Branch

The sixth and final oracle regarding the kings of Judah contrasts two types of shepherds. On the one hand, there are the evil ones who will be rejected by the Lord. On the other hand, there is the good shepherd whom God will raise up.

The oracle begins by announcing disaster to the shepherds who neglect the flock. They destroy and scatter the sheep rather than gathering and caring for them (**23:1-2**). The Lord rejects these shepherds and, for the time being, will care for his people himself. He goes on to announce what steps he will take to *gather the remnant* of his flock (**23:3**). This gathering contrasts with the scattering that was done by the evil shepherds. He promises a return from exile (Deut 30:1-3; Isa 11:11; Zeph 3:20: Zech 10:10) and that his people will enjoy favourable conditions, described in terms of fruitfulness and an increase in numbers. The idea that a remnant will return is also presented in many of the other prophetic books in the OT (see 31:8-9; Isa 10:20-21; Mic 2:12; Zeph 2:7).

After gathering the remnant of his people, the Lord will give them very different shepherds (**23:4**). One of the first actions of these shepherds will be to give the people confidence so that *they will no longer be afraid or terrified.* Moreover, none of the sheep will be lost (John 6:39; 10:28).

The ultimate shepherd whom the Lord will raise up for his people is called a *righteous Branch,* a term used in the OT as a Messianic title (**23:5**; 33:15; Isa 4:2; 11:1; Zech 3:8; 6:12). The association of this Branch with David is very important, for it indicates that, despite all the unfaithfulness of the kings and people of Judah, the Lord is going to fulfil the promise he made to David: 'Your house and your kingdom shall endure for ever before me; your throne shall be established for ever' (2 Sam 7:16).

The 'righteous Branch' will fulfil all the requirements for a true king. He will reign with wisdom and justice (Isa 9:6-7; 11:1-5; 32:1; 42:1-7). Under his reign, Judah will be delivered and Israel will again *live in safety.* We are also told that besides being called the 'righteous Branch', this future shepherd will be called *the Lord Our Righteousness* (**23:6**). This name is similar to that of Jehoiachin's successor, Zedekiah, whose name means 'the Lord is my righteousness'. But this passage is clearly not referring to King Zedekiah, for his life did not match up to that of the king described here (see 2 Kgs 24:18-19). It is quite possible, however, that the prophet Jeremiah deliberately used this similarity to emphasize the great difference between the Zedekiah whom he and his contemporaries knew and the coming righteous king.

The return from exile is again described as a new exodus in **23:7-8**, which repeats the words used in 16:14-15.

The oracles about the kings of Judah thus end with the announcement of the coming of the Messiah. The one referred to is clearly Jesus Christ, whom the Lord God will send to deliver, save and offer salvation to Israel and the entire world.

23:9-40 False Prophets

We now come to a very long indictment of Judah's false prophets, against whom Jeremiah has spoken in the past (see 2:8; 4:9-10; 5:30-31; 6:13-15; 14:13-15; 26:8, 11, 16). It can be divided into five smaller subsections.

23:9-12 Godless prophets

As the first part begins, we hear Jeremiah's voice, expressing his great distress at what the Lord has revealed to him about Judah's prophets (**23:9**). The country is described as full of *adulterers* (**23:10**). While it is true that this word is often used to describe Israel's spiritual infidelity, here it seems to have its standard meaning of illicit sexual relationships, which are clearly and strongly condemned by the

word of God (Exod 20:14, 17; Deut 5:18). The *curse* mentioned here was probably imposed because of the sinful acts committed in the country where everyone is behaving badly and enjoying wickedness (8:5-6).

The sin of the religious leaders, the prophets and the priests, is denounced in **23:11**. Their sin is all the more serious because they are the ones entrusted with the word of the Lord. They should be teaching it, not trampling on it! The NT speaks very strongly about the hypocrisy of those who pretend to know God's word, who even teach it, but who deliberately disobey it every day (Rom 2:18-23).

A *slippery* path awaits these negligent servants (**23:12**; see Pss 35:6; 73:18; Prov 11:5; 29:1). It will not be a pleasant path to walk and will end in *darkness,* a characteristic that is associated with the Day of the Lord, which is a day of judgment (Joel 2:2; Amos 5:18, 20; Zeph 1:15; 2 Pet 2:4).

23:13-15 Two sets of prophets

Jeremiah goes on to compare the prophets of Judah to the prophets of Samaria, the capital of the northern kingdom, which was known as Israel. The prophets in Samaria had practised idolatrous worship along with all kinds of abominations (1 Kgs 16:32; 2 Kgs 13:6; Amos 8:14; Mic 1:5-7). But their worst crime was that they had abandoned the Lord to prophesy for Baal (**23:13**). These prophets had been swept away in the Assyrian invasion of the northern kingdom in 721 BC.

Unfortunately, the prophets of Jerusalem have learned nothing from the fate of their predecessors, and are behaving even worse than the prophets of Samaria. They are adulterers who practise and encourage lying (**23:14**). Their attitude is an encouragement to others to continue to live in sin. They do nothing to lead their fellow countrymen to turn from sin. They are compared to the people of *Sodom* and *Gomorrah,* who were held to have been the greatest of sinners (Gen 18:20-21; see Isa 3:9; Lam 4:6; Ezek 16:46-49). The names of these cities had become synonymous with the worst misfortune and the most terrible judgment (49:18; 50:40; see Gen 19:24-25; Deut 29:22; Isa 1:9; 13:19; Amos 4:11; Zeph 2:9).

The result of the sins of the prophets and priests is that the Lord is going to give them *bitter food* to eat and *poisoned water* to drink (**23:15**; see 8:14; 9:15).

23:16-22 False visions

Jeremiah now turns to the false visions of the false prophets (**23:16**). *The Lord Almighty* tells the Judeans not to listen to these prophets because their message does not come from him. They themselves have made them up (14:14). The proof is that these prophets are claiming that the Lord is announcing *peace* to people who are openly living in defiance of his word (**23:17**). They even promise that *no harm will come* to these who are hardening their hearts so as not to hear or obey God. These prophets are leading the people astray, perhaps to better hide their own shortcomings.

But these prophets have no access to the depths of God's thinking, for they have never *stood in the council of the Lord* (**23:18**), that is, in the place where God makes decisions and lays out his plans, the centre of divine deliberations. The Lord's thinking is too deep for humans to fathom (see Isa 40:28; 1 Cor 2:16). Those who claim to speak for him but do not listen to him can only utter lies and deceit.

A partial reply to the question asked in 23:18 is found in 23:20. The prophets who claim to speak in the name of the Lord have not been sent by him (14:14-15; 23:32). This leads us to understand that the true prophet is someone who is sent by the Lord and to whom the Lord God has spoken; someone in whose mouth the Lord has placed his words (1:9; Ezek 2:8-3:3). However, this message is heard only in the divine counsel; that is, in the intimacy of genuine communion with the Lord. If these prophets had really stood in God's presence, they would have announced the word of the Lord. Their preaching would have reinforced Jeremiah's message, and the people would have repented and changed their way of life (**23:22**). These words remind us that the word of God transforms people. Neither preachers nor the methods they use can do this on their own. If the word proclaimed is truly to transform people, it must come from the Lord.

The Lord's judgment on these faithless prophets is pronounced in **23:19-20**, which are repeated in 30:23-24. He makes it clear that nothing will thwart his anger, which will run its course (Isa 14:27). In *days to come* the people will recognize that the false prophets' message of peace is not fulfilled. These 'days to come' are not necessarily the last days at the end of the world (23:20). They are the days that will soon come when Jeremiah's prophecies are fulfilled and when the people will finally grasp what he has been saying.

23:23-32 Dreams versus God's word

The fourth part of this section contrasts the dreams of the false prophets with the true words of the Lord. It is introduced by the question in **23:23**. This question can be interpreted in various ways. Some think that the Lord is saying that he is not a local deity who can be manipulated at will, but rather the God of the whole universe, who decides to whom he wants to reveal himself. Others claim that the Lord is pointing out that he is present everywhere and so can see all that happens, both near and far. Still others read the verses as if the focus is on the time, so that the Lord is saying that he is both the God of the immediate moment and the God of eternity (Deut 32:17).

The Lord's omnipresence is affirmed in **23:24**. No one can hide from the Lord (see Pss 11:4; 14:2; 139:7-12). His presence fills the earth and sky, the universe that he himself has made (Exod 31:17; Josh 2:11; 1 Chr 16:30; Ps 33:6, 13; Hab 3:3). This omnipresent God has heard what the prophets who are falsifying his word have said (**23:25**).

In Numbers 12:6, the Lord had said that he would reveal himself and speak to his prophets in a vision or a dream. The false prophets probably have promises like this in mind when they claim to have had a dream, but their dreams have not come from the Lord. That is why the Lord asks how long the *lies* and *delusions* of the false prophets will continue. Their lies arise from their own *hearts* and *minds* (**23:26**). These corrupt hearts cannot produce anything but corrupt ideas (Matt 12:34; Jas 3:11).

These prophets perpetuate an attitude they have inherited from their predecessors (**23:27**). Just as the prophets of Samaria had turned the people away from the Lord and led them to serve the Baals, so these Judean prophets want to lead the people away from the Lord.

The Lord uses a metaphor to bring out the difference between the lying words of the false prophets and the words of a true prophet (**23:28**). The former is like *straw* – light and without value (13:24; Job 21:18; Mal 3:18); the latter is like *grain* – the most important part of the ear of corn (Luke 3:17).

Two similes are used to describe the word of the Lord (**23:29**). First, it is said to be *like fire* (see 5:14; 20:9). Fire is used to reveal the true nature of things (1 Cor 3:12-13) and for purification (Zech 13:9). The word of the Lord is also said to be *like a hammer that breaks a rock*, underlining its power and effectiveness. From the very start of Jeremiah's prophetic ministry, the Lord had told him that he would watch over his word to make sure that it was fulfilled (1:12). This fulfilment is proof that what a prophet speaks is indeed a true prophetic word (Deut 18:21-22). Long after Jeremiah, the author of the Letter to the Hebrews would say that the word of God is 'living and active'. It judges human intentions and their deepest secrets (Heb 4:12; see also John 12:48; 1 Thess 2:13).

In **23:30-31** the Lord repeats his strong opposition to false prophets who make a travesty of his word. This same opposition was expressed in 14:15. The wording of his condemnation of them, with its repeated combination of the words *I am* with the phrase *declares the Lord*, shows that what is said here is of the greatest importance. We find the same construction in **23:32**, which concludes this part of the text and which repeats what was said in 23:25-26. It hammers home the point that the false prophets have not been sent by the Lord. Consequently all that they say is false and can only lead the people who listen to them astray. Such prophets cause great harm to the people of God.

23:33-40 The Lord's threat

The last part of this section is built around a play on words in Hebrew. The word *massa* means both 'burden' and 'oracle'. It is used with the sense 'oracle' in many biblical passages (Isa 13:1; 14:28; 15:1; 17:1; 19:1; 23:1; Zech 12:1; Mal 1:1).

Jeremiah is told that when someone (whether a prophet or a priest or one of the ordinary people) asks him, *What is the oracle of the Lord?* he is to reply that the Lord's 'burden' is that he will reject them, or as the NRSV translates it, *You are the burden, and I will cast you off* (**23:33**). There have been so many lying announcements by false prophets that the Lord no longer wants anyone to say *this is the oracle of the Lord*. In fact, anyone who says these words and pretends to announce an oracle from the Lord will be punished with all of his family (**23:34**). What the people really need to do is to seek to understand what the Lord had actually said (**23:35**). For this they need to turn to the true prophet (33:3; 42:4) and not to pretend to be prophets themselves when they have clearly not been sent by God.

Those who take the risk of saying 'the oracle of the Lord' will find that their so-called oracle becomes a burden, for false prophets have never stopped twisting the meaning of the Lord's word (**23:36**; Acts 13:10; 2 Pet 3:16). They do not understand anything that the Lord has said, but all the same they want to make their voices heard.

The point made in 23:35-36 is repeated in **23:37-38**. There is a formal prohibition: no one is ever again to say 'the oracle of the Lord'. Anyone who stubbornly insists on speaking in the Lord's name even though he was not given a message from him will be forgotten and cast out (**23:39**). Not only will the false prophets be rejected, but so will the inheritance that the Lord has given them.

This section on false prophets concludes with a terrible message: The Lord will bring *everlasting disgrace* and *everlasting shame* on those who continue to announce false oracles (**23:40**). What makes the judgment terrifying is its duration; it will be everlasting. Shame and humiliation will be the lot of the wicked and godless, particularly those who turn away from the Lord to offer worship to idols (6:15; 20:11; 48:13; Isa 42:17; 44:9, 11).

24:1-10 Vision of Two Baskets of Figs

The historical context of the vision of the baskets of figs is the first deportation of the people of Judah in 597 BC (see 2 Kgs 24:10-17). The city of Jerusalem had been besieged by the Babylonians and Nebuchadnezzar came in person to attack it. Jehoiachin, the son and successor of Jehoiakim, gave himself up to the attackers and was deported to Babylon, along with his mother, his officials and the dignitaries of his kingdom. Nebuchadnezzar also carried away a large number of the artisans and men capable of fighting.

Sometime after this event, Jeremiah received a vision (**24:1**). This incident is similar to the first two visions that Jeremiah saw immediately after his call to be a prophet (1:11, 13). What we have here are not oracles (messages addressed to the prophet) but rather images shown to him. The message flows from what the prophet sees.

In this case, he sees *two baskets of figs.* But the quality of the figs in each basket is very different. One basket contains good, healthy figs, but the figs in the other basket are spoiled and inedible (**24:2**; 29:17). Figs are the fruit of the fig tree of which the Bible often speaks. The book of Proverbs says that the one who cares for a fig tree eats its fruit (Prov 27:18). Matthew and Mark tell of the fig tree that the Lord cursed (Matt 21:19-20; Mark 11:13-14). Luke tells the parable of the fig tree (Luke 21:29-30). John tells us that Nathanael was sitting under a fig tree when Philip called him (John 1:48).

The Lord's question to Jeremiah in **24:3** is exactly the same as the one in Jeremiah 1:11 and 13. We should note the importance of observation to this prophet. Prophetic ministry is not simply a matter, as some think today, of repeating words. It involves all the prophet's faculties. It means deliberately looking in order to see. It was not for nothing that early prophets were called 'seers' (1 Sam 9:9). The prophet needs to see in order to understand. He has to grasp something with his intelligence in order to communicate it.

What Jeremiah sees in this vision is very clear. The good figs are very good and the spoiled ones are very bad. It is after he has seen this that he receives the message that explains what he has been shown (**24:4**).

The good figs represent the Judeans who had been deported to Babylon (**24:5**). The Lord announces that he will look on these exiles with favour, just as someone takes pleasure in seeing good figs (**24:6**). This favourable attention to the exiles is going to lead to specific action, namely that the Lord is going to bring the exiles back to their ancestral homeland. Again we are reminded of the verbs that characterize Jeremiah's ministry (1:10). Four of those verbs are repeated here, and the emphasis is on the positive aspects, on building and planting, and not on tearing down and uprooting. The nation will again be built and planted.

The words in **24:7** are all associated with one of the major themes in the book of Jeremiah, as well as in the book of Ezekiel: the new covenant. Central to this new covenant is the gift of a heart that is open to knowing the Lord (see also 31:31-32; Ezek 11:19; 36:26). It is in the heart that the knowledge of God is either found or not found (see Deut 5:29). It is with the heart that we seek the Lord or refuse to do so (2 Chr 11:16). This nation will be the people of the Lord and the Lord will be their God, a statement that is characteristic of the covenant between the Lord and his people (30:22; 31:33; 32:38; Ezek 11:20).

However, it is important to note that this promise also requires that the people *return to me with all their heart* (24:7). The God of Israel does not want his people to love him half-heartedly or with a divided heart (1 Chr 28:9; 29:9;

Hos 10:2; 1 Cor 7:35). We must belong to God wholehearted-edly. If a heart is not entirely his, it is not devoted to him at all.

As for the spoiled figs, they represent Zedekiah, the uncle and successor of Jehoiachin, those who work with him, the population that remains in Judea and all those who had thought it wise to seek refuge in Egypt (**24:8**; 42:13-17; 44:12-14). They will not only be cursed, but they will also be a source of curses for other people and other nations (**24:9-10**). They will be insulted and will be the object of mockery among other nations. Moreover, they will experi-ence war (Lev 26:25, 33; Ezek 32:11), famine and plague (14:12; 15:2; 27:8; Ezek 5:17; 28:23). These disasters will carry them away and none of them will remain in the land that the Lord had given them.

25:1-14 Seventy Years of Captivity

Some theologians consider that 25:1-14 contains the con-tents of the scroll that Jeremiah dictated to Baruch, his secretary, in 605 BC (25:1; see 36:1-4). The fact that these words are dated to the fourth year of Jehoiakim's reign suggests this, for it was in that same year that this scroll was read to the king, who burned it (36:1-26; it was later rewritten – see 36:27-32). However, since the contents of that scroll comprised everything that the Lord had said to Jeremiah over his twenty-three years of ministry (36:2), this section may represent only part of the scroll.

The section starts with a summary of Jeremiah's min-istry from the time of his call to the prophetic office to the twenty-third year of his ministry (**25:1-3**). Throughout this long period, Jeremiah had not ceased to proclaim the word of the Lord to Judah. What an example of faithfulness and perseverance! Twenty-three years of preaching the same message, to an audience that refused to listen! Few mis-sionaries or preachers today could match this. Instead, after a year or two of apparently unfruitful ministry, many of them begin to question their calling and everything else. In our world where statistics are all important, Jeremiah teaches us that true success in ministry is not measured by visible results, but rather by the faithfulness with which the servant of the Lord accomplishes the task entrusted to him or her.

Despite the fact that Jeremiah persevered in consist-ently proclaiming his message, the people did not listen – in other words, they did not obey it. Jeremiah was not the first prophet that the Lord had sent to speak to his people (**25:4**; see 2 Chr 36:16; Isa 48:16). In fact he had sent prophets to them *again and again* (see also 25:3), words which translate a Hebrew idiom that literally means 'getting up early and doing something'. Not only does the idiom imply that the message was repeated, it also testifies to the importance of the message. When one gets up early in the morning to do something, one is making that thing one's top priority. That

is why in many African cultures, the most important busi-ness or family matters are discussed early in the morning.

The fact that the word of the Lord had been proclaimed regularly emphasizes the guilt of the people who never both-ered to listen to it. They were stubborn, closing their ears to the word of God. This attitude is often described in the OT as 'stiff-necked' (Exod 32:9; 33:3, 5; 34:9; 2 Kgs 17:14). The Bible includes numerous warnings against such stubborn-ness (see Ps 32:9; 78:8; Isa 46:12, 48:4).

The message of the prophets who came before Jeremiah's time is summarized in **25:5**. They had called on the people to radically change their behaviour and to abandon the prac-tices the Lord condemns (Isa 1:10-20). This is what the Bible means when it calls for repentance (Ezek 33:11; Joel 2:12; Matt 3:2; Acts 3:19; 8:22; 17:30). The call to return to the Lord was accompanied by a promise. The men and women who committed themselves to love and serve the Lord alone would live safely in the land that he had given them (Exod 20:3-5).

Those who are committed to the only true God must dem-onstrate their commitment in a practical way by refusing to practise idolatry (**25:6**; 1 Thess 1:9; 1 John 5:21). Making idols and worshipping any deity other than the Lord pro-vokes him to anger (8:19; Isa 42:8). This anger should not be interpreted as no more than the frustrated response of someone who has been abandoned. No, the Lord is angered by idolatry because he knows that idols are useless and can do nothing to help those who depend on them (10:14; see also Isa 42:17; 44:9; 45:16, 20; Acts 14:15). As with the previous verse, this one too ends with a promise: The Lord will be gracious to those who turn from idolatry.

Despite this appeal to the people, they have not listened to the voice of the Lord (**25:7**). Instead, they have behaved in a way that provokes God's anger (Num 14:11; Deut 9:7; 31:20; Ezra 5:12). The people have thus contributed to their own misfortune (44:8). What these misfortunes will be is spelled out in the long list of troubles that follows **25:8**.

The instruments of God's judgment will be *the peoples of the north* and *Nebuchadnezzar,* the king of Babylon. It is worth noting that this enemy of God's people is also referred to as God's *servant* (**25:9a**; 27:6). The Assyrians were described in similar terms in Isaiah 10:5, and Cyrus, too, will be spo-ken of as serving the Lord (Isa 41:2; 45:1).

The Babylonians will attack not only Judah, but also all of the neighbouring countries (**25:9b**). This message is probably intended to make the Judeans aware that they can-not expect to receive any help from their allies (22:20, 22).

The word translated 'destroy' in **25:9c** is the same word that is used when something is consecrated to the Lord (Lev 27:28). It can be used of human beings (Deut 7:1-2), animals or cities (Deut 2:34). Any human being who was declared to be consecrated to the Lord was to be put to death (Lev 27:29; Deut 13:15-16). The only exception was first-born sons, who were to be redeemed by a sacrifice (Exod 13:2, 12-15). The announcement that Judah and her neighbours will be consecrated to the Lord in this way shows the extent of the disaster about to strike them. The country and its environs will be left desolate and will be the subject of universal scorn (18:16).

All *joy and gladness* will disappear from Judah (**25:10**). No longer will there be ordinary, happy events such as feasts, engagements and weddings (see also Lam 5:15). No longer will there be the everyday routine of grinding grain to feed a family and lighting lamps. The light that symbolizes life will be put out.

This time of hardship will last for *seventy years* (**25:11**). This is often thought to be a round figure, for the Babylonian domination, and the exile may have lasted only sixty-seven years if we count from the first deportation of Judeans in 605 BC to the capture of Babylon by the Medes and Persians in 539 BC. However, if we date it to the time when the first of the exiles returned to Jerusalem, it comes to seventy years (536 BC).

Daniel was well aware of this prophecy that the exile would last seventy years. He specifies that he knew about this because he had read Jeremiah's prophecy (Dan 9:2). His example reminds us that the prophets did not work in isolation but exercised their ministries in the light of the ministries of their predecessors. Like Daniel, they took time to read the writings of those who had gone before them, when they had access to them. Their approach testifies to their wisdom and humility. There is wisdom in seeking to understand how the Lord has used those who have gone before us and how and why they succeeded or did not succeed in their ministry. There is humility in the firm conviction that we do not know everything and that we need to learn from others. Many young servants of God, especially those who are well equipped in terms of the intellectual training they have received, would benefit by learning this lesson. The degrees we have earned from theological seminaries or the fruit that God has given us in the early months of our ministry do not excuse us from listening to those who have served before us.

Once the seventy years are completed, the Lord himself will bring the Babylonian domination and the exile to an end (**25:12**). He will punish Babylon as he punished Judah. The sin of the Babylonians was that, like the Assyrians before them, they did not recognize that they were carrying out the Lord's judgment on his own people (Isa 10:6-7). They went beyond what was asked of them in order to satisfy their own selfish interests (Zech 1:12-15). Their country, too, will be laid waste.

In **25:13** God confirms all the prophecies that had been given against Babylon in the book of Jeremiah. The prophecies in **25:14** were accomplished to the letter in 538 BC, when the Medes and Persians destroyed the Babylonian

empire. The next year, Cyrus decreed that the Judeans could return to their own land (29:10; 2 Chr 36:22-23; Ezra 1:1; Dan 9:2).

25:15-38 Prophecies Against the Nations

One of the major differences between the ancient Greek text of Jeremiah found in the Septuagint and the traditional Hebrew text occurs at this point. In the Septuagint, 25:13 is followed by the prophecies against foreign nations that are found in chapters 46–51 of our Bibles. This commentary will follow the Hebrew text, which here has a section that announces the prophecies against pagan nations that will be made later (chs. 46–51). We are reminded of the international extent of Jeremiah's prophetic ministry, which had been predicted at the time of his call (1:5, 10).

The one addressing Jeremiah is the God of Israel (**25:15**), who is here also frequently referred to as the *Lord Almighty*, which in this context might be better translated as the KJV and NASB do, as the *Lord of hosts* (25:27, 28, 29, 32; see also 2:19; 5:14; 6:6; 7:3, 21; 8:3).

The Lord gives Jeremiah the cup of his wrath, which is an image of judgment. This cup is mentioned not only in the book of Jeremiah, but also in Isaiah 51:17, Lamentations 4:21, Ezekiel 23:32-34 and Habbakuk 2:16. Jeremiah is to offer this cup to all the nations to which he is sent so that they may drink it and experience its consequences (**25:16**). The prophet obeys the Lord's command (**25:17**).

Judgment begins with the Lord's own city, Jerusalem, and the other cities of Judah (**25:18**). The kings and officials are implicated and the judgment is described in the same terms as before (25:9). The mention of *as they are today*, may indicate that this prophecy had begun to be fulfilled while Jeremiah was writing these words. However, some commentators suggest that these words may have been added by a scribe after the prophecy had been fulfilled.

The cup of judgment is next offered to Egypt and to Pharaoh, its king, as well as all its population (**25:19**; 46:2-28; see also Isa 19–20; Ezek 29–32). Judgment will also fall on the many *foreign people* living in Egypt in order to benefit from its riches, especially its agricultural riches (**25:20a**).

Many other places are also mentioned in **25:20b**. *Uz* was situated east of the Jordan (Job 1:1; Lam 4:21). *Ashkelon, Gaza, Ekron* and *Ashdod* were four cities that belonged to the *Philistines* (see Josh 13:3; Amos 1:8). For some reason, the fifth Philistine city, Gath, is omitted from the list. Historians tell us that the city of Ashdod was defeated and destroyed by Pharaoh Psammetichus I, the father of Pharaoh Neco, after a siege lasting nearly thirty years.

Edom, Moab and *Ammon* (see also 48:1-49:22) as well as *the kings of Tyre and Sidon* are mentioned in **25:21-22**. In Jeremiah 27, the prophet will address an oracle to the ambassadors of these nations who had come to see Zedekiah in Jerusalem. The message may be summarized as saying that although these nations oppose Babylon, they will be defeated. Some think that *the coastlands across the sea* may be the island of Cyprus.

In **25:23-24**, God's judgment falls on the kings of the desert region in the north of the Arabian Peninsula: *Dedan* (Gen 10:7), *Tema* (Gen 25:15) and *Buz* (Gen 22:21). Some versions, like the NASB, include an additional phrase here, applying the judgment to *all who cut the corners of their hair.* In the NIV, this phrase is only mentioned in a footnote (see also 9:26). The cutting mentioned here is probably related to the marginal note on 9:26, where it was explained that this is probably a reference to a practice related to idolatry.

The location of *Zimri* is unknown (**25:25**). *Elam* (Ezek 32:24) and *Media* were situated to the north-east of Babylon. Elamites were among the nations who were present in Jerusalem on the day of Pentecost (Acts. 2:9).

Finally, *all the kings of the north* are mentioned (**25:26a**; see also 25:9; 50:9) – and then, the message is summarized as being to *all the kingdoms on the face of the earth.* The last person to drink the cup of the Lord's wrath will be *the king of Sheshach,* another name for Babylon (**25:26b**; 51:41).

After mentioning all those who are to receive this prophetic message, the text now gives the contents of the message itself. They are to drink the cup of the wrath of the Lord, which will leave them drunk so that they vomit and fall, unable to rise again (**25:27**). The nations have no choice whether to drink from this cup or not. They will all be obliged to do so (**25:28**).

As we have already seen, judgment begins with Jerusalem, the city of the Lord (**25:29**, 18). Peter makes the same point in 1 Peter 4:17. Beginning the judgment among his own people proves the justice of the Lord. He begins by calling to account those who claim to be his, before moving on to deal with those who have not paid him any attention, and who cannot be held innocent (Exod 20:7; Num 14:18).

We are reminded of the prophecies of Joel and Amos in the way in which the Lord is described as roaring like a lion in **25:30** (see Joel 3:16; Amos 1:2). This roar is directed against his own people. But the sound of the Lord's voice also resounds *to the ends of the earth* (**25:31**), which is appropriate because the Lord intends to bring a charge against all the nations of the earth (Joel 3:2). He announces that a *disaster is spreading from nation to nation* and that *a mighty storm is rising from the ends of the earth* (**25:32**; 2 Chr 15:6; Isa 34:1-2). The hurricane with its rising winds symbolizes the coming wrath and judgment of the Lord (30:23; Isa 17:13; 29:6; 41:16; 66:15).

Once again, the absence of funerals for the victims of the catastrophe coming adds to the horror (**25:33**). Those killed at this time will be neither mourned nor buried. Instead, their bodies will remain *lying on the ground,* where they will decompose and become *like refuse,* after decomposition (see 16:4, 6; 22:18; 34:20). Today, those countries in Africa and

elsewhere that are enduring wars see this on a daily basis. Rotting bodies are seen everywhere because no one has either the time or the will to bury them.

Because of the awful disaster that is coming, the leaders of the people are urged to go into mourning (**25:34a**; 6:26). In the OT, and still today in many areas of Africa, people will *weep, wail* and *roll in the dust* at funerals. But it is rarely the chiefs who mourn in this way. If the leaders are doing this, things must be in a very bad state indeed.

The leaders of the people are to weep for themselves, because they are about to be *slaughtered* and scattered. Moreover, if they do not mourn for themselves, no one else will mourn for them (25:33). Their fall is compared to that of *fine pottery* which falls and breaks into so many pieces that no one can repair it (**25:34b**).

The leaders of the people will have no chance to escape their punishment. They will find no hiding place, no one to protect them (**25:35**). All they can do is weep bitterly because their country, *their pasture,* is destroyed by the Lord (**25:36**). Nothing living remains in the once lush pastures because the fierce anger of the Lord has wiped everything out (**25:37**). He has abandoned his land and destroyed it completely. His wrath has left nothing intact; all is desolation and ruin (4:7; Hos 5:14).

26:1-24 Oracle about the Temple

The oracle (26:1-24) about the temple dates from the beginning of the reign of Jehoiakim, who ruled in Jerusalem from 609 to 598 BC (2 Kgs 24:1-7; 2 Chr 36:5-8).

This relatively long section may be divided into four smaller parts: the sermon about the temple (26:1-6), the arrest of Jeremiah (26:7-16), the defence made by the elders of the city (26:17-19) and the execution of the prophet Uriah (26:20-23). It is possible that 26:24 should follow immediately after 26:19, which is why the NIV puts the passage on Uriah between parentheses.

26:1-6 The sermon about the temple

The Lord asks the prophet to stand in the temple *courtyard* to proclaim the message entrusted to him to everyone passing by, whether they come from Jerusalem or from any of the other cities of Judah (**26:1-2**). Jeremiah had received a similar commission in the past, but then he had been asked to stand at the gate of the temple (7:2). This time, Jeremiah is not going to be speaking to passers-by, but to those coming to worship the Lord. The prophet is to faithfully announce the whole message given to him, leaving nothing out.

The Lord longs to see his people take his word to heart so as to turn from their sin (**26:3**). We are reminded that the Lord takes no pleasure in punishing his children (Lam 3:33). When he speaks about judgment, it is always with the hope that they will understand the gravity of their sins and will renounce all evil and return to him. If they repent, the

Lord will withhold his judgment. God shows great love and patience as he appeals to his people (Gen 18:32; Neh 9:30; Acts 17:30; Rom 2:4).

The message that must be passed on to the people is a touching plea to listen to the words that the Lord had entrusted to his *servants the prophets* (**26:5a**). The people had never been ignorant of the Lord's will. He had made it know to them through those he sent to them, and specifically through the law he had given them (**26:4**; 11:8; Exod 20; 1 Kgs 9:6). The prophets had been sent to Judah *again and again* (**26:5b**; 7:13, 25; 11:7; 25:3-4), but the people have not listened to them. If the people continue to refuse to obey the word of the Lord, he will destroy the temple just as he had overthrown the sanctuary at *Shiloh,* the home of the ark of the covenant (**26:6**; see also 7:12, 14; 1 Sam 4:10-11). It is said that the catastrophe at Shiloh was so tremendous, and the grief that it caused so great, that the people of Judah avoided even speaking of it. The fact that Psalm 78:60 and the book of Jeremiah are the only places where it is mentioned seems to support this idea.

26:7-16 The arrest of Jeremiah

Jeremiah's words are heard by the religious leaders (*the priests* and *the prophets*) and those who had come to worship at the temple in Jerusalem (*all the people*). All of them *heard Jeremiah speak these words* (**26:7**). The presence of prophets in his audience confirms that Jeremiah is not the only one exercising a prophetic ministry at that time. Their presence in the temple probably also indicates that some of them were closely associated with this centre of worship.

As soon as Jeremiah ends his sermon, he is seized by his hearers, who demand that he be put to death (**26:8**; 11:19; Amos 5:10; Matt 27:20). They accuse him of being hostile to the temple and the city of Jerusalem (**26:9**). This accusation suggests that they have heard only the threatening part of the message. They do not seem to have understood that the Lord was giving them an opportunity to escape the fate that Shiloh had suffered. They were concentrating on what could happen to the temple (the consequences) without taking time to think about and understand why this was happening (the cause), which was really the most important point. They needed to understand why they were in danger and identify what they needed to do to avoid the threat being carried out.

People today are not very different from those of Jeremiah's day. We rush to find a solution to a problem, without taking time to analyse it and discover its cause. We need to learn to look for causes both in our personal lives and in the affairs of the state.

News of the uproar in the temple eventually reaches the political leaders (**26:10a**). They immediately leave the palace and come to the temple to investigate what is going on. Taking their seats at the gate of the temple called the *New Gate* (**26:10b**; 36:10), which is probably the same as the Upper Gate mentioned in 2 Kings 15:35, they ask what has happened. These political leaders are adopting a wiser and more restrained attitude than the religious leaders and the crowd of worshippers. They wanted to listen and understand things before reaching any decision.

The different attitudes displayed by the religious people and the politicians remind us of what happened in Jesus' time. A large crowd of religious people and their leaders called for his death, while Pilate, a political leader, took the time to question him in order to find out whether the accusations against him were really valid. Pilate found that Jesus was not guilty of any crime (Matt 27:22-25; Luke 23:4).

As soon as they have finished giving their version of events, the priests and prophets again demand the death penalty for Jeremiah because he has prophesied against the city of Jerusalem. (**26:11**; 38:4; see also Matt 26:66). Interestingly, they no longer mention any threat to the temple but only to the city. Were they possibly trying to shift the focus to the political aspect alone, in an attempt to persuade the political leaders to agree with them and execute Jeremiah? It is very possible. Once again, we see the same pattern at Jesus' trial, where his accusers try to persuade the Roman authorities that Jesus' claim to be king of the Jews shows that he is a dangerous agitator and a rebel who must be executed in order to maintain social peace (Matt 27:11).

Until now, Jeremiah has not responded to his accusers, Now he speaks, but not to plead for his life in the face of those who seek his death. He simply states that the Lord sent him to deliver the message he has given (**26:12**). He asks that his listeners change their way of life by acting honestly and with justice (**26:13**). If they listen to the voice of the Lord and obey him, the Lord will abandon his plan to destroy the temple, the city and its inhabitants.

Jeremiah shows little concern for his own life (**26:14**). All that he wants to do is to fully and faithfully announce the message entrusted to him. The people can treat him anyway they like. However, he does remind the political and religious leaders and the people in the temple that if they decide to take his life, they will be guilty of spilling innocent blood and will have to face judgment themselves (**26:15**; 7:6; 22:3; 2 Kgs 24:3-4).

Jeremiah shows real courage in this passage and proves himself to be a true prophet of the Lord, one who no longer clings to his own life but seeks to serve the Lord God, whatever the cost. He exemplifies what Jesus later identifies as one of the criteria of a true disciple: the willingness to lose one's life and die to self in order to be able to follow the Lord (Matt 10:38-39; 16:24-26). Jeremiah's attitude also reminds us of that of Stephen in the NT, who prays for his persecutors at the very time that they were stoning him to death (Acts 7:59-60).

Jeremiah's example challenges those of us who serve the Lord today to examine our motives for serving God. Are we willing to proclaim completely and faithfully the message he entrusts to us on the basis of the specific call he has given us? Or do we try to adapt our message to the attitudes of our audience, accommodating some, sparing others? Are we so afraid for our lives and our reputations that we no longer preach the whole message entrusted to us?

After hearing the report of the religious leaders and the summary that Jeremiah himself gave of his message, *the officials and all the people* come to the deep conviction that Jeremiah is speaking the truth and that the Lord is really speaking through him (**26:16**). So the politicians and the crowd distance themselves from the priests and prophets and refuse to allow Jeremiah to be executed. Their role is similar to that of Gamaliel, a member of the Sanhedrin in the time of the apostles. When the furious crowd wanted to kill Peter and the apostles, this man was wise enough to ask the people to wait until the passage of time revealed the true nature of the apostles' action (Acts 5:17-42).

26:17-19 The elders defend Jeremiah

Besides the political leaders, some other men, elders of the land, rose to plead in support of Jeremiah, or rather of his prophetic message (**26:17**). These men base their case on what had happened to *Micah*, who had prophesied about a century before Jeremiah (Mic 1:1) during the reign of *Hezekiah king of Judah* (**26:18**). We are told that Micah had proclaimed an identical message to the one that Jeremiah had just given regarding the temple and the city of Jerusalem (Mic 3:12). Such agreement between prophecies from different eras is a sign that they can be trusted (Deut 13:2-5).

Micah had also prophesied doom, but he had not been put to death by King Hezekiah or by the people (**26:19**). On the contrary, Hezekiah and his people had recognized and accepted the word of the Lord. They repented of their sins and the Lord did not punish them. The elders of the people had learned from this previous experience that a prophet should not be killed because he calls for repentance. Instead, the prophecies should be listened to carefully to see whether they come from the Lord. If they do, they should be obeyed (1 Thess 5:20-21).

26:20-23 The execution of Uriah the prophet

The account of the death of the prophet *Uriah,* who *prophesied in the name of the Lord,* leaves us in no doubt that Jeremiah was in real danger (**26:20**). Uriah was originally from *Kiriath Jearim,* a town near Jerusalem (Josh 15:60; 18:14; 1 Sam 6:21). This prophet is not mentioned elsewhere in the OT. He is said to have preached a message identical to that of Jeremiah. When Jehoiakim and those at his court heard the words of Uriah, they sought to silence him by killing him (**26:21**). Frightened, the prophet sought

refuge in *Egypt,* but he did not count on the murderous determination of Jehoiakim who sent people to bring him back (**26:22**). The king then put him to death. His body was thrown in what was likely a mass grave. In any case, we are given to understand that he had a shameful burial (**26:23**).

26:24 Ahikam's protection of Jeremiah

As for Jeremiah, he benefited from the protection of *Ahikam son of Shaphan,* the king's secretary (**26:24**; 2 Kgs 22:3, 9, 10). He had been part of the delegation that King Josiah had sent to consult the Lord regarding the contents of the book that had been discovered in the temple (2 Kgs 22:8-20). In 39:14 another member of this same family will come to the aid of Jeremiah.

27:1-22 A Yoke on the Neck

There is a textual difficulty in **27:1**, where the traditional Hebrew text gives the name of the king as Jehoiakim. But some other Hebrew manuscripts and the ancient Syriac version give the king's name as *Zedekiah.* In all the manuscripts, the name Zedekiah is used in the text that follows (27:3, 12; 28:1). The NIV is thus correct to interpret 27:1 as referring to Zedekiah.

The Lord again tells Jeremiah to act out a prophecy, or, in other words, to do something that illustrates the message he is to convey (see also 13:1-14; 32:25; 43:9; 51:63-64). Here, he is to build something that looks like the yoke that is placed over the necks of oxen to control them for work in the fields or for other tasks (**27:2**). Jeremiah is to place the yoke he has made on his own neck.

This acted prophecy is directed at *the kings of Edom, Moab, Ammon, Tyre and Sidon* whose ambassadors were in Jerusalem (**27:3**). These foreign diplomats may have been hoping to persuade Zedekiah to agree to join them in a revolt against Babylonian domination. The prophet is to respond with a message from the Lord Almighty, the God of Israel (**27:4**; 25:8; Isa 1:9).

Jeremiah's message begins with an affirmation of the sovereignty of the Lord (**27:5**). It is a reminder that all creation – earth, people, animals – are his (Neh 9:6; Pss 8:3; 33:6-9). It is through the Lord's power that everything came into being; everything belongs to him completely and he gives whatever he wants to anyone he pleases.

Confident in his ownership of everything, the Lord tells the kings' representatives that he has subjected their countries to *Nebuchadnezzar king of Babylon* whom the Lord again describes as *my servant* (**27:6**; see also 25:9; 43:10). Everything is delivered into Nebuchadnezzar's power, including the animals.

All these nations will have to serve first Nebuchadnezzar, then his son Evil-Merodach and finally his grandson Belshazzar (**27:7**; 2 Chr 36:20; Dan 5:22). This detail is an accurate indication of the length of the Babylonian domination. It also specifies that the Lord himself will use *many nations and great kings* to end it. These words are a clear reference to Cyrus and his allies (25:14).

The nations are warned not to try and escape from Babylonian rule, which is symbolized by the yoke that the prophet wears (**27:8**). Anyone who refuses to submit will be struck by three disasters, *the sword, famine and plague* (21:7; 24:10), until they are completely wiped out.

The recipients of the prophetic message are exhorted not to listen to their many prophets, diviners, interpreters of dreams, sorcerers and the like (**27:9**). These cruel, lying charlatans are telling them that they do not need to submit to Babylon. But rather than really being able to discern the future, these people are only saying what their listeners want to hear. We see the same thing today among the many diviners who ensnare the poor people of our countries. Sadly, such diviners are not only found in the traditional places where they have long been consulted. They are even found in our churches! Anyone who rushes to announce things that he has not received from the Lord is equivalent to a witchdoctor, a diviner and a liar.

The lies the charlatans in Jeremiah's day were telling would expose the people to the very thing they were trying to avoid (**27:10**). By encouraging the people not to submit to Babylon, they are creating a situation where the submission will be even more brutal and one in which all the people will be taken into captivity. If, however, they submit to Babylon, they will be allowed to remain in their country and cultivate their land (**27:11**).

The message delivered to the ambassadors of Judah's allies also applies to Judah and its king, Zedekiah (**27:12**). He, too, must submit to the political authority of Nebuchadnezzar and must serve Babylon. This is the price for saving his own life and those of his people. If he refuses to submit, the people will have to endure *the sword, famine and plague* and they will be destroyed (**27:13**).

The Judeans, too, are told not to listen to the false prophets who say that they will not go into exile (**27:14**). Their message is false and deceiving. None of them have been sent by the Lord (**27:15**; 23:21; 29:9). They are wrong to use his name and, without knowing it, they are contributing to the ruin of their people.

In the first deportation in 597 BC, the Babylonians had also carried off objects used in worship in the temple (2 Kgs 24:13). The false prophets were specifically telling the priests – who were particularly affected by the removal of these objects – and the people that these articles would soon return to Jerusalem (**27:16**). On behalf of the Lord, Jeremiah denounces such messages as lies. The people should not listen to them but should serve the king of Babylon if they hope to escape with their lives (**27:17**).

True prophets intercede for their people (**27:18**). So the prophets to whom Jeremiah is speaking are invited to take a test. If they claim to be sent by the Lord, let them pray that the few remaining articles used in worship remain in the temple, and that the goods of the royal palace and the belongings of the rest of the Judeans are not carried away to Babylon. If the Lord answers their prayer, they are true prophets; but if these goods are carried off, they are shown to be false. This test is somewhat like the test between Elijah and the prophets of Baal (1 Kgs 18:16-39). On that occasion, the prophets were to pray either to Baal or to the Lord, and the God who sent fire would be recognized as the true God and his servant as the true prophet.

Jeremiah's words in **27:19-22** are both a revelation of what awaits the Judeans who are still in their homeland and a reply to the false prophets. A second deportation is coming in which everything that remains in the temple, the palace and their houses will be carried off to Babylon. All these goods will remain in Babylon with the things that were taken earlier until the Lord himself decides that it is time to return them to the land of Judah.

28:1-17 Jeremiah and Hananiah

The description of the confrontation between Jeremiah and Hananiah indicates that it takes place in the same year as the message in chapter 27 (**28:1**). These two chapters are therefore in chronological sequence.

Hananiah son of Azzur, was a prophet from *Gibeon,* one of the cities given to the Levites (Josh 21:17), situated about seven miles (ten kilometres) north of Jerusalem (Josh 9:3). It was here that Joshua had asked the Lord that the sun should stand still (Josh 10:12-14) and it was also here that the Lord had appeared to Solomon in a dream, inviting him to ask for whatever he wished (1 Kgs 3:5). Some think that the sanctuary at Gibeon had replaced the one at Shiloh, which had been destroyed by the Philistines (1 Kgs 3:4-15; 1 Chr 16:39; 21:29; 2 Chr 1:3).

The exchange between Hananiah and Jeremiah probably took place in the temple courtyard, where it was witnessed by priests and people. Hananiah presents his message as a word from the Lord. There is nothing about its presentation that distinguishes it from the prophecies that Jeremiah himself made. He even uses the same expressions as Jeremiah does when he says that he speaks on behalf of *the Lord Almighty* and *the God of Israel* (**28:2**).

But the content of the message is the exact opposite of the content of Jeremiah's message in chapter 27. Hananiah insists that the Lord will break the Babylonian yoke. He specifically predicts that *within two years* the Lord will bring back to Jerusalem all the items from the temple that were carried off by Nebuchadnezzar (**28:3**). In the same breath, he predicts the return of *Jehoiachin* and all those deported from Judah with him (**28:4**).

His words pose a serious problem. How can two prophets, each claiming to speak in the name of the same God and on his behalf, understand the same event so differently? Does God contradict himself? Did one prophet misunderstand what was told to him? Or did one prophet simply invent his message? What follows will provide the answer.

Everyone present must have waited with great interest for Jeremiah's response to Hananiah's challenge (**28:5**). It is very simple. He starts with *Amen!* Which means 'so be it!' He seems to be agreeing with Hananiah (**28:6**). He will be delighted if this prophecy comes true. However, he invites Hananiah to listen to what he has to say (**28:7**). His message will be addressed not only to the prophet from Gibeon, but also to all the people of Judah and, more particularly, to those present that day at the temple.

Jeremiah speaks as if Hananiah were an authentic prophet like himself. He speaks of *you and me,* referring to himself and Hananiah, as having a place in the succession of prophets who have spoken to Israel (**28:8**). He reminds him that all the prophets who have gone before have prophesied *war, disaster* and *plague.* Jeremiah seems to be saying that his own message is not an unusual one.

But Hananiah is proclaiming *peace.* If he is to be considered a true prophet of the Lord, the word he claims to give on behalf of God must be fulfilled (**28:9**; Deut 18:22). It is the fulfilment of a prophecy that reveals whether the one who speaks is truly sent by God.

Following this statement by Jeremiah, Hananiah, who no doubt wants to show that he firmly believes that his prophecy will soon be fulfilled, *took the yoke off* Jeremiah's neck *and broke it* (**28:10**). This act was intended to symbolize the breaking of the Babylonian domination symbolized by the yoke Jeremiah was wearing. Hananiah explains this symbolism in **28:11a**, where he again insists the Lord who is announcing that in two years he will bring an end to all of Babylon's power and will free all the nations that have been oppressed by it.

When Hananiah broke the yoke and spoke for the second time, *Jeremiah went on his way* (**28:11b**). His response is instructive. Facing a situation in which one word from the Lord appears to contradict another word from the Lord, he decides not to get into a fight with Hananiah. He may be perplexed by the situation, but he prefers to hold his peace. Jeremiah seems to have understood that it is not his personal honour that is at stake, and so he does not seek to justify his position at any price. His silence indicates that he had full confidence in the Lord. He knows that the Lord is sufficiently powerful to reveal which message he had really given. Jeremiah is therefore quiet until the Lord speaks to him again, thus showing himself to be both a humble man and an obedient servant who speaks only what he hears from his Master.

Jeremiah's attitude teaches us that some silences are worth much more than long speeches in which someone tries in vain to show that the word of God is true. Very often in such cases, the one trying so hard to be convincing is showing that he is not really sure of God's word and believes that he will lose face if he does not succeed in proving it is true.

Sometime later, the Lord again spoke to Jeremiah and told him what to say to Hananiah (**28:12**). Hananiah had been able to break the wooden yoke that Jeremiah was wearing, but he cannot hope to break the iron yoke that the Lord will place on the necks of all the nations mentioned in chapter 27 (**28:13**). Their subjugation to *Nebuchadnezzar king of Babylon* will be so complete that it will extend even to *the wild animals* (**28:14**; 27:6).

After refuting Hananiah's prophecy, the Lord has a message for Hananiah himself. First, he declares him to be a false prophet (**28:15**). Like all other false prophets, Hananiah has not been sent by the Lord and, like the others, he has told lies and aroused false hopes in those who heard him. The style of his prophetic discourse is not enough to prove its authenticity.

Then the Lord's message announces Hananiah's imminent death. He will be removed *from the face of the earth* (**28:16**). This is his punishment not only for having lied, but also for opposing a true prophetic word. Such opposition is equivalent to launching a revolt against the Lord.

Within two months of the initial confrontation, Hananiah was dead, just as the Lord had predicted (**28:17**; see 28:1). This sad story is a warning to the many people who claim to be prophets today. We hear many prophecies these days, all put out by people who claim to be speaking for the Lord. The story of Hananiah shows that those who take the name of the Lord in vain will suffer the consequences. It is better to remain silent if we have not received anything from God than to lie and bring the Lord's judgment on ourselves.

29:1-32 A Letter to the Exiles

29:1-3 Delivering the letter

Chapter 29 contains the letter that Jeremiah wrote to the Judean exiles in Babylon, who had been taken there in 597 BC (**29:1**). They included Jehoiachin (referred to in the Hebrew by his alternative name of Jeconiah), his mother, the high officials of the royal court of Judah, as well as numerous artisans (**29:2**).

Jeremiah takes advantage of a diplomatic mission from King Zedekiah to Nebuchadnezzar to send his letter. He entrusts it to two of Zedekiah's envoys (**29:3**). The first is *Elasah son of Shaphan,* the brother of Ahikam who had supported Jeremiah after his sermon about the temple (26:24). The second is *Gemariah,* who was also among those who supported Jeremiah (36:25). Jeremiah clearly had powerful friends in Judah. Though they provided valuable help, none of these friendships hindered the prophet from faithfully carrying out his ministry. Jeremiah did not compromise in any way.

29:4-9 Life in Babylon

The letter that Jeremiah had written was a prophecy that the Lord told him to proclaim to the exiles. It begins in exactly the same way as all the other messages Jeremiah had given orally to the people of Judah: *This is what the Lord Almighty, the God of Israel says* (**29:4**; 24:5). It then goes on to stress that it was the Lord who had deported the recipients of the letter to Babylon. They should thus pay particular attention to what will be said, for the God who is speaking to them is the same God who directs the history of the world and, specifically, that of Judah.

The exiles may have been surprised by the first set of instructions in the letter, for they were very different from what they were being told by the other prophets among them. The Lord tells these exiles to *build houses* in which to live in Babylon and to *plant gardens* and vineyards so as to be able to *eat what they produce* (**29:5**). This instruction contains two of the verbs ('build' and 'plant') that were used in Jeremiah's call in 1:10, but here they have a literal and not a figurative meaning.

The exiles are also instructed to establish a normal lifestyle, to *marry*, have children and arrange marriages for those children (**29:6**). The number of Jews in Babylon must *increase and not decrease*. This command to multiply reminds us of the Lord's command to all the creatures he had created and to the first human couple (Gen 1:22, 28), as well as to Noah and his sons after the flood (Gen 9:1).

The first two instructions in Jeremiah's letter to the exiles indicate very clearly that the Lord is calling them to settle in Babylon for a long time. When we are not sure whether we will be staying in one place for any length of time, we do not build a house there, but instead try to live with friends or family for a while or rent a house. Building, planting, marrying and giving in marriage are also signs that a normal community has been established.

The words of the next verse are even more startling than those of the previous two. The exiles are told to *seek the peace and prosperity of the city to which I have carried you* (**29:7**). They are even asked to pray for the country. The Lord is telling the exiled Judeans in Babylon to change their way of looking at things. They are no longer to think of the Babylonians as their worst enemies. The reason for this advice is given at the end of the verse: If Babylon enjoys peace, *you too will prosper.*

29:10-14 True hope for the future

Like the inhabitants of Judah, the exiles also have to deal with lying prophets. They too are being told that the end of the exile is imminent. But Jeremiah's letter denounces these false prophets and diviners (**29:8**). They have not been sent by the Lord, and thus their prophecies are lies (**29:9**).

The Lord confirms that it will be a full *seventy years* before he will change the course of history for both Babylon and Judah. Only after that long period, will he fulfil his promise to the people of Judah by bringing them back to their land (**29:10**; 25:11-12; 2 Chr 36:21; Ezra 1:1).

The Lord's words in **29:11** demonstrate his perfect control of Judah's history. He knows what he is doing and that his plans for Judah will bring peace, not misfortune. He is preparing a future full of hope for his people. While it is true that those enduring exile would not consider the experience a blessing, the Lord seems to be saying that this suffering is not their ultimate fate. Through it, God is preparing something fundamentally different and pleasant for Judah, his people.

In this future time of hope, Judah will again be able to have a normal relationship with God (**29:12**). They will be able to pray to the Lord and he will answer them. Such answered prayer is a sign of a good relationship between God and the people; it means that God is again listening to them and that they are again pleasing him (Ps 6:9; 1 Kgs 9:3). We may almost forget the times when the Lord forbade Jeremiah to intercede for the people (7:16; 11:14; 14:11; 15:1).

The people will find the Lord because they will seek him with all their heart (**29:13**). He will let himself be found by his people when they seek him in this way (**29:14**, a contrast with Isa 65:1). These two verses show that there will have been a radical change of attitude among the people. The exile will have transformed their hearts. Once this change has taken place, the Lord will fulfil his promise to bring the exiles back to Judah. He will bring them back *from all the nations and places* where he has scattered them. The fact that he can do this shows that the Lord knows all about his people. He watches over each Judean; he knows where each one is and he is able to seek them and bring them back into the land of Judah. He is like the good shepherd who goes out to look for his lost sheep (Matt 18:12).

29:15-19a A blow to false hopes

Despite the Lord's wonderful promises and his assurance that he will accomplish them, the captives may reply that they prefer to listen to the prophets among them in Babylon (**29:15**). They are convinced that these prophets have been sent by the Lord, although that is not the case (29:21, 24).

So the prophet tells the exiles what will become of their fellow-citizens who had not been taken into captivity, and specifically to the king and the people (**29:16**). The Lord says that they will have to endure *the sword, famine* and *plague:* these three terrible curses that nearly always go together (see 24:10; 38:2). The situation of the people will be like that of rotten figs that no one can eat (**29:17**; see 24:3-8). Consequently they will be *abhorrent* and *an object of cursing and horror, of scorn and reproach* (**29:18**; 15:4; 24:9; 26:6).

All this terrible misfortune will come upon them because the people have not listened to the messages that the Lord has sent through his servants the prophets (**29:19a**). Once more, it is stressed that God had sent prophets *again and again*, with the regularity of their sending accentuating the guilt of the people who have stubbornly refused to listen.

29:19b-23 The fate of the false prophets

The prophet now returns to the situation of the exiles, introducing the change with the words, *And you exiles* (**29:19b**). They have refused to listen in the past, but now they are to act differently from their compatriots who remain in Judah. They are to listen to the word the Lord sends them through Jeremiah (**29:20**).

False prophets are taking control among the exiles in Babylon. These men include *Ahab son of Kolaiah and Zedekiah son of Maaseiah*. These prophets, who are mentioned nowhere else in the OT, are telling the people that the Lord is about to deliver them. But it is rather the false prophets who will be delivered to Nebuchadnezzar, who will put them to death *before your very eyes* (**29:21**).

The names of these two men will henceforth be used as a sort of curse. When someone wants to curse another person, he will use the names of these two men and recall their fate (**29:22**; Isa 65:15). The use of *fire* to kill these two false prophets, reminds us of the experience of Daniel's three friends who were thrown into the furnace (Dan 3:6, 21). However, the comparison goes no farther, for the reasons for their being consigned to the flames and the outcomes were completely different.

Ahab and Zedekiah were condemned for two serious wrongs they had committed. The first was that their way of life contradicted their claim to be prophets. They had *committed adultery with their neighbours' wives* (**29:23a**). Such behaviour is condemned as *outrageous* (see also Josh 7:15). In other words, their behaviour was dishonourable and shameful.

The men may have taken advantage of the respect that people had for them as 'prophets' in order to accomplish these reprehensible acts. Unfortunately some church leaders and Christian workers today yield to the same temptation to use their position in order to do what is wrong, or to have it done for them. The wrong may not be as blatant as adultery, but it may involve any of the areas in which people are not free to act in any way they choose. The apostle Peter severely condemns leaders who are guilty of unethical behaviour (2 Pet 2:12-14). There should be absolute consistency between the message that the servant of God preaches and his or her lifestyle.

The second thing for which these people are condemned is that they used the name of the Lord when telling lies. These are false prophets, whom the Lord did not send. They may have been able to hide their duplicity from the people, but the Lord had seen everything. None of their actions was hidden from him (**29:23b**).

29:24-32 Shemaiah and Jeremiah

After he became aware of the letter that Jeremiah had written to the exiles, Shemaiah, one of the false prophets among them, wrote a letter in response. This man is said to have come from *Nehelam*, a place that is not known today (**29:24**). He sent letters from Babylon *to Zephaniah, the son of Maaseiah the priest and to all the other priests* (**29:25**). From the contents of his letter, we can tell that Zephaniah had succeeded Pashhur (20:1) and Jehoiada as head of the temple police in Jerusalem. His job was to maintain order in the temple, especially by controlling anyone who claimed to be a prophet (**29:26**). The reference to a *madman* indicates that at times an ecstatic trance was closely associated with prophetic ministry (1 Sam 10:10-11; 2 Kgs 9:11; Hos 9:7; John 10:20).

The purpose of Shemaiah's letter was to demand an explanation of why Zephaniah had not arrested Jeremiah, but had allowed him to proclaim his oracle at Jerusalem (**29:27**). As part of his complaint, Shemaiah quotes from Jeremiah's letter to the Judean exiles in Babylon (**29:28**; 29:5).

When Zephaniah receives Shemaiah's letter, he shows it to Jeremiah (**29:29**). Once again, the Lord tells Jeremiah how to respond (**29:30**).

The Lord asks Jeremiah to pass on a message about Shemaiah to all the exiles in Babylon (**29:31**). The message is similar to the one regarding Hananiah, another false prophet (28:15). It is clearly stated that Shemaiah has not been sent by the Lord and is inspiring false hope in the people. Thus the Lord will take action against him, and this man and his family will no longer be counted among the people of Judah. As for Shemaiah himself, because he has not believed, he will not see the fulfilment of the Lord's promises to his people (**29:32**). As in the case of Hananiah, Shemaiah's words are considered as a revolt against the Lord.

The condemnation of Shemaiah's unbelief reminds us of an incident in the time of Elisha, when Ben-Hadad, king of Syria, was besieging the city of Samaria (2 Kgs 7). Elisha had proclaimed the end of the famine that accompanied the siege, but one of the servants of the king of Israel refused to believe him. Worse still, he mocked the prophet. Elisha replied that what he had said would really happen and that the man would see it with his eyes but would not benefit from it. This prophecy was fulfilled when the siege was unexpectedly lifted and the king's unbelieving servant was crushed to death in the scramble for food that followed.

30:1-33:26 The Book of Restoration

The first major division of the book of Jeremiah dealt with his call (ch. 1). Then came the long section from chapter 2 to 29 that contained prophecies addressed to Jeremiah's contemporaries in their current situation. Now, in the third section of his book, the focus shifts to prophecies dealing with the restoration of the people of Judah.

Chapters 30 to 33 of the book of Jeremiah consist of a number of texts with a common theme, that of the restoration or the consolation. Hence, theologians have given this part of the book the title 'The Book of Restoration' or 'The Book of the Consolation of Israel'.

According to the information in 32:1, chapters 32 and 33 were written during the final months of Zedekiah's reign, only a few months before the fall of the city of Jerusalem. We can therefore date them to 587 BC (see 39:1; 52:4, 12-13). Chapters 30 and 31 are not dated, but they were probably written in the same period as chapters 32 and 33. Although there is no need for this – since Israel and Judah are often used interchangeably – the use of the name 'Israel' in chapters 30 and 31 had led some commentators to think that these prophesies were initially given with reference to Israel, the northern kingdom, and that they were later reworked to apply to Judah, the southern kingdom.

Chapter 31 is considered by most commentators as the heart or the high point of the prophecy of the man from Anathoth. Besides its profound message regarding the return of the captives, it contains the prophecy regarding the new covenant that the Lord will make with his people. This prophecy will be repeated and enlarged in various passages of the NT that apply it to the Lord Jesus Christ.

30:1-24 The Return from Captivity

30:1-11 Anguish replaced by salvation

The Lord begins by asking Jeremiah to write down all the words that he has spoken to him (**30:1-2**; 36:2). This command reminds us of Moses, another servant of the Lord, at another very important time in Israel's history (Exod 17:14). Writing down the Lord's words was vitally important for Jeremiah, not only because of the value of the messages, but also to preserve them until the distant day when they would be fulfilled. God wants us to preserve the memory of what he has done in the past (Isa 46:9), but he also wants us to remember all the promises he has made that are still to be fulfilled when the appointed time comes (Hab 2:3).

In the distant future, the Lord will bring home the captive people of both *Israel and Judah* (**30:3**; 29:14). They will return to the land that the Lord had given to their ancestors, the land of Canaan. They will take possession of it just as their ancestors had done long ago (Gen 15:7; 17:8; 48:3-4).

The sounds of *fear* rather than *peace* in **30:5** may remind us of 'the great commotion' that is foretold in 10:22, which speaks of what the Babylonians will do to the land of Judah. But it may equally remind us of 8:15, in which the people express their disappointment that they are experiencing the opposite of what they had hoped for and expected (4:10).

The picture of *a strong man with his hands on his stomach like a woman in labour* (**30:6**) reveals the intensity of the suffering experienced by the people (4:31). So does the fact that their faces have turned pale. The day on which this great suffering will come is the day of judgment (**30:7**; 13:16; Joel 1:1-2). But it is important to know that judgment will precede deliverance just as night precedes and announces day. The Lord announces that *Jacob ... will be saved out of it.* Here the nation of Israel is referred to by the other name of its famous ancestor (Gen 32:28).

The day of anguish will be followed by the day of salvation. On that joyous day, the Lord will *break the yoke off their necks,* meaning that he will end the Babylonian domination of his people (**30:8**; see also 25:12-14; 27:22). The *foreigners* who have enslaved them are the Babylonians. Freed from their domination, the people of Israel and Judah *will serve the Lord their God and David their king* (**30:9**; Isa 55:3). The 'David' referred to here cannot be the historical character that we know from biblical texts, for he had died many years before Jeremiah's time. The way this passage speaks of him, and specifically the statement that the Lord will raise him up, makes us think that this must be the 'Righteous Branch' of whom the same thing was said in 23:5. This 'David' is therefore the Messiah, who bears the name of David to shows that he is a descendant of the famous dynasty that ruled over God's people (Ezek 34:23). Similarly, all the kings of Egypt are referred to as 'Pharaoh'.

Israel is again referred to using the name of Jacob, their ancestor, in **30:10**. The nation is told not to fear or be dismayed because the Lord is coming to save them (Isa 41:10-14). Once the Lord has brought his people back from captivity, he will guarantee their security in the land and will guard them from all other invaders. Of course, as their history shows, the fulfilment of this promise was conditional on their obedience to God.

The announcement of the Lord's presence among his people is the guarantee of their salvation. When God says *I am with you* it is the same as saying *I will save you* (**30:11a**). He will save his people and *completely destroy* their enemies.

While God's people can be confident that they will not be completely destroyed, they cannot expect to completely escape punishment for the sins they have committed (**30:11b**; 10:24). But the discipline they will receive will be like that of a child or a friend whom one loves and hopes will prosper (Job 5:17; Ps 141:5; Heb 12:6-7; Rev 3:19). In such cases, correction is a blessing in that it teaches the one who endures the punishment how to behave from then on (Deut 8:5; Prov 29:17). The Apostle Paul had this type of discipline in mind when he told the Corinthian believers that the Lord corrects us by his judgments 'so that we will not be condemned with the world' (1 Cor 11:32).

Before leaving 30:11, it is important to notice how many of the words and expressions used in it are also used elsewhere in this book. Thus 'I am with you and will save you' is also found in 1:8 and 15:20; *I will not completely destroy you* is also found in 4:27; 5:10, 18; 46:28; *the nations among which I scatter you* is also found in 9:16, and *I will discipline you but only with justice* is also stated in 10:24.

30:12-24 Healing of an incurable wound

The greatness of the comfort to be extended to the people is brought out by the description of their current plight. They are reminded that their *wound is incurable* and their *injury beyond healing* (**30:12**). Similar imagery has been used on several occasions (8:21-22; 10:19; 14:17). The wound or injury symbolized the judgment with which the Lord strikes a nation or an individual because of their sin (see Exod 11:1; Num 11:33). The same idea is also found in prophets such as Nahum (Nah 3:19) and Zechariah (Zech 14:12, 18).

To make matters worse, no one else has the slightest interest in what is happening to Israel (**30:13**). No one seeks to care for the wounded nation. But even if there was someone who cared, it would make no difference, for there is no medicine for a wound this severe (46:11).

The nation of Judah had once had many *allies* or *lovers* as the NKJV translates it (**30:14**; see 3:1; 22:20, 22). But the whole world seems to have recognized that there is no point in any further alliance with Israel, and all her allies have abandoned her. The situation is similar to what happens to many countries today that can no longer attract allies because of their insignificance. Judah was no longer considered of strategic importance by any of the great powers of the day.

Everyone has abandoned Israel because the Lord has struck her. The judgment was severe, but was also appropriate given her many serious sins. And because the punishment was deserved, the people should not complain (**30:15**; Lam 3:39).

However, as shown in the previous section, judgment will be followed by comfort; the wound and the injury will be followed by healing and restoration (**30:16**). The enemies of Jerusalem will themselves suffer exactly what they have meted out to the Lord's people. There will be a just reversal of fortune. Those who devoured will become the ones devoured; those who took others captive will themselves go into exile; those who have plundered will themselves be plundered.

The Lord will create a new life for his people and he will heal their incurable wound (**30:17**). The first part of the verse can be literally translated as saying that the Lord will put new flesh on Zion. The image reminds us of the dry bones on which tendons and flesh grew at the word of Ezekiel (Ezek 37).

The return of the captives is again announced in **30:18**, but this time the stress falls on the compassion that the Lord shows to Israel and Jerusalem. New structures will be erected on the ruins of the destroyed city. (The Hebrew word for *ruins* has given the us the word 'tel' that archaeologists use to indicate a hill formed by the repeated destruction and rebuilding of a city on the same site.)

To appreciate how much the situation of the people will change, we need to remember that earlier the Lord had predicted that he would cause cries of joy and gladness to disappear from Judah, as well as the songs of brides and bridegrooms (7:24; 16:9; 25:10). But now we read that the people of Judah will raise voices in *thanksgiving* and *rejoicing* (**30:19a**). The thanksgiving will be addressed to the Lord in recognition of the great deliverance that he has given his people. The rejoicing will be a sign that life has returned to normal and that the population feels secure again (see 23:6; 31:13; 32:37).

In the letter Jeremiah had sent to the exiles in Babylon he had told them to marry and give their children in marriage in order to become a large nation (29:6). Here he repeats this idea, saying that God will multiply his people (**31:19b**; see 33:22; Gen 15:5; 22:17). In other words, the nation will continually grow. The Lord will take away their shame and no one will despise them. The Israelite community will re-establish its life as it had been before the exile (**30:20**). Some theologians see the reference to the *days of old* as an allusion to the time of David and Solomon, when Israel was one united nation, before the division between the northern and southern kingdoms.

The promise made in 30:21 offers something that is valued by all the nations in the world: political independence. When the person chosen to lead a nation comes from that nation and is chosen by a process that is free and fair, a nation can truly be said to be politically independent. No nation in the world can rejoice if their leaders are imposed on them from outside. Whenever that seems to be the case, the population shows its discontent in various ways – many of which are violent.

Many in African countries are frustrated by the perception, which may be right or wrong, that they have no voice in the choice of their leaders, who are always imposed by others. Elections rarely express the true will of the people. Thus the statement that *their ruler will arise from among them* is a powerful statement that Israel will again enjoy political independence (**30:21a**).

The statement that the leader *will come close to* the Lord can be understood as implying that this leader has a priestly function (**30:21b**). However, the meaning could be the one given in the NRSV translation: *I will bring him near, and he shall approach me, for who would otherwise dare to approach me*. No one should risk approaching the living and all-powerful God unless the Lord himself invites him to do so (Exod 33:20; Judg 6:22-23; 13:22; Isa 6:5).

The words *you will be my people and I will be your God* are a formulaic utterance that signals the conclusion of a covenant between the Lord and his people. This is the purpose of everything that the Lord has done. He has always wanted his people to truly belong to him and to serve no other god but him (**30:22**; 24:7; see Exod 20:2-3).

The final two verses of this chapter (**30:23-24**) are a word for word repetition of 23:19-20 (see commentary on those verses).

31:1-30 Re-establishment of Israel and Judah

31:1-2 Finding favour in the desert

The key formula of the covenant, which was used in 30:22, is repeated in the introduction to chapter 31. The only difference here is that this time the Lord specifies that *all the clans of Israel* are his people (**31:1**). Jeremiah is preparing his listeners (and readers, too) to understand that all that follows concerns Israel and Judah, not Judah alone.

The reference to the *desert* in **31:2** recalls the exodus and the Israelites' deliverance from the hand of Pharaoh, whose troops were drowned in the Red Sea (Exod 14:5-23). At that time, Israel did not serve other gods, but followed the Lord faithfully as they journeyed to the promised land (Hos 2:16-17). It was also a time when Israel and Moses, their leader, experienced the *favour* of the Lord. In the passage relating Moses' intercession on behalf of the people after the incident of the golden calf, the expression 'found favour' is used five times (Exod 33:12-17 – NASB). The desert image was also used extensively by the prophet Hosea (Hos 2:16; 13:5, 15). The time in the desert was seen as an ideal period in the relations between the Lord and his people (Hos 12:9).

But, as in the present context, the desert may also symbolize the Babylonian exile. Through this terrible experience, the Lord is going to demonstrate his great love for his people, exactly as he had for forty years in the desert under Moses' leadership. Israel will walk through this Babylonian desert towards the place where they will find rest.

31:3-14 Love and rejoicing

There is a minor difference between the Hebrew and Greek texts in regard to **31:3**. The Hebrew says, 'appeared to me' and the Greek has, 'appeared to him'. The NIV adopts a compromise solution with its translation, *appeared to us*. But what is really important is the fact that *the Lord appeared* and declared his *everlasting love* for his people. This love is constant and is not affected even by terrible experiences such as the exile. On the contrary, the Lord says that *I have drawn you with loving-kindness.*

The consequence of such love is that the Lord will radically transform his people's situation. He will rebuild them without anyone being able to raise any objection (**31:4a**). The way that this is put in the original Hebrew text indicates that this rebuilding will last.

Here at last is the positive side of Jeremiah's ministry. For many years, he has proclaimed a message of uprooting and destruction, but now his mouth is full of words of restoration, and he speaks of rebuilding in 31:4 and planting in 31:5 (see 1:10).

Life will return to normal and there will be joyous occasions for the people. The people of Israel, compared here to a young woman, will again play their *tambourines,* musical instruments that were brought out at feasts and on other joyous occasions in Israel's life (**31:4b**; Exod 15:20; Judg 11:34; 1 Sam 18:6; Ps 68:25). Israel will again be found among those who celebrate.

The Israelites will also return to live in Samaria, the capital of the northern kingdom of Israel, which had been conquered by Assyria between 722 and 721 BC (2 Kgs 17:6, 24). The prophet proclaims that the Israelites will again *plant vineyards* there and *enjoy their fruit* (**31:5**).

Jeroboam I, the first king of Israel after the division between the northern and southern kingdoms (1 Kgs 11:29-32), had decided that it was too politically risky to allow his subjects to continue to worship God in Jerusalem. So he had encouraged them to go to the sanctuaries he set up at Bethel and Dan (1 Kgs 12:26-33). Going to Jerusalem, the capital of the southern kingdom, could be interpreted as an act of defiance against the king, even if one's sole purpose in going there was to worship the Lord. Thus the announcement in *Ephraim* (in the northern kingdom) that it is time to undertake one of the annual pilgrimages to Jerusalem to worship the Lord is highly significant (**31:6**). It is an indication that the two kingdoms, Israel and Judah, have been reunited (see also 23:6).

A call to celebrate the Lord because he has saved his people Israel follows (**31:7**). This celebration is the response of God's people to the divine actions in 31:2-6.

The Lord promises that he will bring his people back from *the land of the north,* which in this book has always been Babylon (**31:8a**; 1:13-15; 3:12; 4:6; 6:1, 22; 10:22). The return is all the more startling and miraculous because it will include even those who are normally considered unfit for such a long journey: *the blind and the lame, expectant mothers and women in labour* (**31:8b**).

The crowd of former exiles will return weeping, according to the Hebrew text of **31:9a**. These will be tears of joy flowing from the powerful emotions associated with their return to their land. The Greek text, however, reads that the captives were weeping as they left for exile. Tears undoubtedly flowed on both occasions.

The rest of the verse uses fatherly language. The Lord is a father to Israel, which is also referred to by the name Ephraim. It is this fatherly love that leads God to bring his people *beside streams of water* so that they can be refreshed and *on a level path* so that they *will not stumble* (**31:9b**).

All the nations are invited to listen in order to give testimony, in distant countries, to the unbelievable work that the Lord is doing (**31:10**). The one who had scattered his people is bringing them back, taking care of them like a good shepherd.

The deliverance granted to the people of Israel resembles a redemption. It is as if the Lord has paid the ransom for the liberation of his people (**31:11**). But this is clearly only a picture here, for the Lord did not give anything to the Babylonians in order to persuade them to free Israel. On the contrary, he punishes nations like Babylon and Assyria that had held Israel captive (25:12; 50:1-3).

The *bounty* that is described in **31:12a** corresponds to what the Lord promises his people if they keep the covenant that binds them to him (Deut 7:12-13; 11:13-15). The comparison of the soul to a *well-watered garden* is an image of profound beauty and depth, expressing peace and quietness (**31:12b**). It evokes complete satisfaction and fullness. Hence, we can understand the assurance of the absence of all sorrow in the last part of the verse. In such living conditions, all those who make up the nation cannot help but give themselves over to joy (**31:13**). Gladness will have replaced mourning; and rejoicing, sorrow. The people will be comforted with the perfect comfort that comes from the Lord.

Sacrifices will be reinstated, and the priests will be able to receive the part of the sacrifice that was their due (**31:14**; see Lev 7:33-35; 10:13). Although the NIV translation of this verse says that they will enjoy *abundance*, the Hebrew originally used the word for animal fat. In those days, unlike today, the fat of an animal was considered the best part of the meat (Lev 3:3).

31:15-20 Comfort for Rachel

Cries are heard from *Ramah* a few kilometres north of Jerusalem. Since the route to Babylon led northwards, Ramah would have been the first stop for the captives being led into exile (40:1). Ramah was also in the area allocated to the tribe of Benjamin, among whom Jeremiah had grown up (1:1). It was in this vicinity that *Rachel*, the mother of Benjamin and Joseph, had died, and now her voice is heard weeping for her lost children (**31:15**; Gen 35:19; also see Matt 2:17-18). These children include her grandsons Manasseh (Gen 41:51) and Ephraim (Gen 46:20), who were born to Joseph. The people of the tribes of Manasseh, Ephraim and Benjamin have all been taken away as captives.

The Lord addresses Rachel and tells her to stop weeping because her children will return from exile (**31:16**). Their return from exile will be like a reward for all the work she has put into raising them. She did not bear children for nothing. They will again be useful. This return from exile is so certain that the Lord repeats it (**31:17**). Secure in this hope, Rachel can end her lamenting.

The Lord says he has heard Ephraim asking to be brought back from exile (**31:18**). Ephraim recognizes that the exile was the result of his sin (**31:19**) and he seems to have understood that true returning to God can only take place as God himself acts. Indeed, only the Spirit of God can work in someone's heart to lead that person to turn to the Lord (John 6:44). Ephraim has admitted his sin and confessed his wanderings. He regrets it (indicated by the statement *I beat my breast*) and returns to the Lord, his God. His experience reminds us of that of the prodigal son in the parable told by Jesus (Luke 15:11-24).

We can sense the greatness and the depth of the love of God for his people (**31:20**; see also Hos 11:8; Mic 7:18-20). The NT provides the same testimony when the Apostle Paul writes that nothing can separate us from the love of God (Rom 8:38-39). The heart (or 'bowels' – KJV) is considered the source of feelings (see 4:19; Isa 16:11; 63:15). It is there that we feel all the great emotions of both joy and pain.

31:21-30 Days of blessing

After speaking of Ephraim, the text returns to Israel, addressed as *O Virgin Israel,* who is told to take note of the route they will follow on their return journey (**31:21**). Isaiah frequently uses this image of a highway for God's people (see Isa 35:8; 40:3-5; 42:16; 43:1-7; 49:9-13). The people are not called to go into a vague and uncertain future. No, they are returning to take possession of the cities that were theirs before.

It is time for their years of wandering to come to an end; their rebellion must stop. To do this, the Lord will *create a new thing on the earth – a woman will surround a man* (**31:22**). This statement has been interpreted in various ways, but the simplest and most straightforward interpretation is to see this as a picture of a marriage relationship, in which the Lord is the husband and Israel is his wife. For a long time, the wife had turned away from her husband. But now God is going to make a profound change in Israel's heart, so that she (the woman) will start to seek for her Lord (the man). If this seems new and surprising, it is because normally it is the man who seeks out the woman.

When the Lord has brought back the exiles, the land of Judah will again be blessed. The Lord says that Judah will again be his *righteous dwelling* and that the *sacred mountain* will be there, referring specifically to the temple that will be rebuilt (**31:23**; Ps 2:6; Isa 2:2-3). Just as the Israelites had returned to reclaim their possessions (31:21), so the Judeans will also come to resettle in their territory (**31:24**).

The images in **31:25** recall 31:12b and show how profound the Lord's work will be on behalf of his people. The KJV gives a more literal translation when it says, *For I have satiated the weary soul, and I have replenished every sorrowful soul.* The word 'soul' refers to the whole person – one's emotional, physical and intellectual self – and the promise indicates that the Lord will put an end to weariness and despair. The people will experience total satisfaction and will live in perfect peace.

Now Jeremiah awakens from his *sleep* (**31:26**). The visions he has seen during this sleep were more than simply dreams. The Lord had used them to reveal the future that he is preparing for his people. Once awake, Jeremiah can still hear the word of the Lord, who confirms the message sent in the dream by repeating it.

The metaphor of sowing seeds is introduced in **31:27**, where God says, I *will sow the house of Israel and the house of Judah with the seed of man and the seed of beast* (NKJV). The exile had considerably diminished Judah's population, and the domestic animals had either been taken by the captors or had been killed and eaten by the starving population who remained in the land. The Lord announces that he is going to remedy the situation. He will plant both people (see Hos 2:23) and animals, and will multiply them.

31:28 is very important. It is the only verse that reminds us of Jeremiah's prophetic call by using all six of the verbs used to describe his ministry in 1:10. It states that the time of destruction and demolition has passed. Now is the time of building and planting. But there is one important point to be noted. Both of these periods of time are directed by the Lord himself. It is he who decides when it is time to act. As he had told Jeremiah during the early days of his ministry, he is watching to see that his word is fulfilled (1:12).

This section ends with the announcement of a new state of affairs. The coming restoration will not merely affect aspects of physical life but will involve a deeper change in the relationship between God and his people (31:29-30). The parallel text in Ezekiel 18:2 shows that the proverb being quoted in **31:29** expresses a complaint that was being made by Jeremiah's contemporaries. They thought they were enduring punishment because of what their forefathers (see Lam 5:7). But God tells them they should take individual responsibility for the sins that precipitated God's judgment. Children will no longer be able complain that they are paying the price for their parents' sin (**31:30**; Ezek 18:20).

When we read such passages, we must be careful to distinguish between responsibility for a sin and the consequences of a sin. The focus here is on individual responsibility. But while a child will no longer be held responsible for his parents' sins, it remains true that parents' behaviour has long-term consequences that do affect their children. Thus while the children are not punished for their parents' sin, they may have to endure the suffering that is the consequence of sinful acts or of spiritual practices that are contrary to the word of God.

31:31-40 A New Covenant

It seems that the expressions 'in those days' (31:29) and *the time is coming* refer to the same period. The new order of which 31:29-30 spoke is now going to be described in more detail as *a new covenant* that the Lord is going to conclude with all his people, that is, with both Israel and Judah (**31:31**).

The word 'covenant' refers to the establishing of a particular relationship between God and people. It was not a new concept, for in the past the Lord had made covenants with several people and groups of people. These included Noah and his sons (Gen 6:18; 9:9), Abraham (Gen 15:18; 17:2, 4, 19), Moses and all the people of Israel at Mount Sinai (Exod 19), Phinehas (Num 25:10-13) and David (2 Sam 7:5-16). However, this is the first and only time that the OT specifically speaks of 'a new covenant', although the reality of such a covenant is implied in many OT passages (see Isa 42:6; 55:3; 59:21; Ezek 34:25; 36:24-28; 37:26; Hos 2:18-22).

The NT will also take up this theme of the new covenant and will use it. Thus at the Last Supper, when the Lord Jesus Christ passes the cup to his disciples, he describes it as 'the new covenant in my blood'. Speaking about the celebration of communion, the Apostle Paul, inspired by the tradition of the gospels, reminds the Corinthians about these words (1 Cor 11:25). Paul even describes himself as someone whom God has made a minister of the new covenant (2 Cor 3:6). Finally, the author of the letter to the Hebrews quotes Jeremiah's prophecy (Heb 8:8-12; 10:16). He writes that Jesus Christ is 'the mediator of a new covenant' (Heb 9:15; 12:24).

This new covenant will be radically different from the one the Lord concluded with his people when he delivered them from slavery in Egypt (**31:32a**). Some translations have 'in the day' here, instead of 'when'. But the translation 'when' is more accurate, for the Hebrew is not trying to say that the covenant was made on the very day of the people's deliverance from Egypt. The time frame is not specific and simply emphasizes that this covenant was made shortly after the departure from Egypt.

God's saying that he had taken Israel *by the hand* to lead them out of Egypt emphasizes both his personal initiative and his very great care for the nation. But in spite of this, Israel broke the covenant. They did not even consider the fact that the Lord was a *husband to them* (**31:32b**).

The Lord has said that the new covenant will be different from the Sinai covenant, and now he shows in what way it will be different. He says, first, that he will put his *law in their minds and write it on their hearts* (**31:33a**). The focus is on the way the law is written. In the time of Moses, the Lord had written his commandments on tablets of stone (Exod 34:1). The law had thus been something external to the people. But now the Lord is saying that he himself will write this law on their hearts. So we move from an external system to an internal system. In 2 Corinthians 3, the Apostle Paul makes exactly the same contrast between the old covenant that was inscribed on tablets of stone (that is, the

Ten Commandments) and the new covenant that writes the law in the heart.

Once the law of the Lord is written in the heart of the people, they will have a different relationship to God. But before speaking of that, the Lord again uses the covenant formula: Israel is his people and he is their God (**31:33b**; see also 30:22; 31:1).

The description of the new covenant continues in **31:34a**. In this new era, everyone will know God (Isa 11:9; 54:13). This was not the case in the OT, when people needed to encourage one another to learn to know the Lord. That is what the prophets devoted themselves to doing (Isa 55:6; Amos 5:4, 6; Zeph 2:3). But in the new order, all will know the Lord (1 John 2:27). God himself will have made this knowledge possible by removing the major obstacle – sin (**31:34b**; see also 33:8).

This new covenant will endure. The Lord is the one who controls both the great celestial objects like the sun and moon and the great terrestrial forces like the sea (**31:35**). He set unchanging laws that govern all of his creation (Ps 148:6). His choice of Israel is every bit as sure and stable as these laws that govern the cosmic order (**31:36**; Isa 54:10). Thus, though the new covenant will bring profound changes, it will never annul the promises the Lord has made to his people in the past. There will be continuity between the past and the future. The Lord will never reject his people (**31:37**).

The new covenant requires a new Jerusalem, and so the next few verses deal with the reconstruction of specific parts of the city of Jerusalem. The Lord says that it *will be rebuilt for me*, a way of saying that the city will again live up to its calling as a city consecrated to the Lord (**31:38**). The various names that are mentioned refer to parts of the city that would have been well known to Jeremiah's hearers. The use of a *measuring line* indicates that the city is going to grow larger and will need new buildings (**31:39**). Even such contaminated places as the *valley where dead bodies and ashes are thrown* (the valley of Ben Hinnom – see 7:31-32; 19:2, 6; 32:35) will be restored and dedicated to the Lord, who will reign there in absolute security (**31:40**).

32:1-44 Jeremiah Buys a Field

32:1-15 The command to buy the field

After the wonderful vision of the future, Jeremiah returns to the present. It is 587 BC (**32:1**) and Jerusalem is besieged by the Babylonian army. It is clear that it will soon fall (see 32:24). Meanwhile, Jeremiah has been arrested and thrown into prison in *the courtyard of the guard in the royal palace* (**32:2**; see also 33:1). King Zedekiah had been disturbed and outraged by Jeremiah's prophecies of the approaching fall of the city and of the king's arrest and exile in Babylon. He had arrested Jeremiah in order to silence him (**32:3-5**).

While Jeremiah was in prison, the Lord revealed to him that his cousin *Hanamel* would come to find him in order to suggest that Jeremiah buy his field back in their village (**32:6-7**). Hanamel tells Jeremiah that *it is your right and duty to buy it*. He is referring to the laws that governed the sale of land. When the land of Israel had been divided up among the twelve tribes, no property had been assigned to the Levites or the priests. However, they had been assigned the fields around the towns that had been allocated to them, one of which was Anathoth (Num 35:4; Josh 21:18). They had no right to sell these properties to anyone other than a near relative (Lev 25:32-34). The purpose of this restriction was to prevent a family losing all its land and finding itself reduced to poverty because it lacked any property (Lev 25:26-34). Ownership of land also meant that the land could be improved to enhance its value and that its crops could be harvested.

The Lord's words to Jeremiah are soon fulfilled. His cousin does come to visit him in the prison to suggest that he purchase his field (**32:8**). Recognizing the Lord's hand in this transaction, Jeremiah agrees to buy it for a price of *seventeen shekels of silver* (**32:9**). 'Seventeen shekels' was not equivalent to seventeen coins or a certain number of bank notes, such as we use today. A shekel was a unit of weight, equivalent to about half an ounce (12 grams). Jeremiah thus had to hand over about seven ounces (200 g) of silver. This is why the text says that he *weighed out the silver on the scales* (32:10). Jeremiah also carries out all the necessary steps to satisfy the legal demands of the time and to make sure that this transaction was handled properly. Thus he first signs a legal *deed of purchase and* then has it signed by witnesses who can also testify that the sale price is paid in full. The legal documents are then handed to Baruch, Jeremiah's secretary, for safe keeping (**32:10-12a**).

Jeremiah's behaviour here sets an important example for us. We must remember that this whole transaction is taking place in prison, in a city under siege. These are not normal circumstances. But despite that, the prophet complies with all the required legal procedures. He does not argue that because of the special circumstances, he does not need to adhere to the law. On the contrary, he submits to the law and applies it rigorously. If all of God's servants and all Christians in the various countries of Africa were to decide to act this way, corruption would almost disappear from our countries. The economy would be in better shape and those who spread the gospel would be more credible.

Jeremiah now gives Baruch, his secretary, instructions to store the documents in a secure place, so that they will be safe for a long time (**32:13-14**). Then he reveals the meaning of what he has done. It may seem pointless to buy property when the entire population is about to be killed or deported, but his action signifies that life will one day return to normal. Then *houses, fields and vineyards will again* *be bought in this land* (**32:15**). Jeremiah's purchase of the field is yet another of the prophetic mimes that he has been asked to act out (see 13:1-7; 27:2).

His action may also have had personal political implications. The tone of Jeremiah's preaching may have led some people to think that he favoured the Babylonians. His calls for the people to submit to the king of Babylon may have led to his being labelled as someone who collaborated with Judah's enemies. Buying a field at this time proved Jeremiah's attachment to his native land. It may have been for this reason that the prophet had insisted that the deed of sale be signed in the presence of as many witnesses as possible (**32:12b**).

32:16-25 Jeremiah's prayer and question

After the prophet returned the contract to Baruch to guard in a safe place, he turns to the Lord in prayer (**32:16**). The question that he wants to ask the Lord is very specific and very short (32:25), but it is preceded by a long and very instructive prayer.

The prayer begins by recalling what God has done (**32:17**). He has demonstrated his great power in his creation of the heavens and the earth (Gen 1:1). His *outstretched arm* is a symbol of his power (Exod 6:6; 15:16). The entire creation testifies that there is nothing too difficult for the Lord.

Jeremiah then goes on to speak of the Lord's character. He shows love and compassion to *thousands*, which shows the extent of his mercy (**32:18**). But this merciful God is also a just God, who punishes sin.

Next, Jeremiah mentions God's sovereignty and omniscience (**32:19**). The Lord sees everything that happens everywhere in the entire world. Nothing is hidden from his eyes. He knows all that human beings do and will treat everyone as their actions deserve.

Then Jeremiah recalls the greatest work that the Lord had accomplished for Israel: their deliverance from Egypt. This was accompanied by *miraculous signs and wonders* in the form of the plagues that struck the Egyptians (**32:20**; Exod 7–11). Further miracles marked the long forty-year journey in the desert (Num 14:11, 22) and the Lord has shown other signs since those days. All these actions have added to the Lord's reputation.

Finally Jeremiah refers to the Lord's fulfilment of his promise to their ancestors when he gave them the land of Canaan (**32:22-23**). The people had left Egypt in order to take possession of this land.

However, despite all that the Lord had done for them and the mercy he had shown them, the Israelites did not obey him. Instead, they became rebellious and rejected his law. The result is the misery that the people are now experiencing. The city of Jerusalem is besieged and its inhabitants will soon go into captivity. All the signs of defeat are present: the *siege ramps* have been built, and enemies armed with *swords* will soon stream in over the wall. Meanwhile *famine and plague* are doing their work within the city. The Lord's word is being fulfilled (**32:24**).

Yet while all this is going on, the Lord tells his prophet to buy a field (**32:25**). Jeremiah seems to be thinking of several questions at once: 'Why ask a prisoner to buy a field?' 'Why buy a field in a country under foreign occupation?' 'Why buy a field when there is no guarantee that one will ever be able to get anything out of it?' 'Why?'

Once again, Jeremiah is teaching some important lessons. He demonstrates that obedience to God should always precede our questions, no matter how legitimate the questions. Jeremiah carried out God's instruction to buy the field before asking the Lord why he was to perform such a senseless act. Moreover, he was careful to observe all the legal rules relating to the transaction, despite wanting to ask God why he was to do this.

Jeremiah also teaches us that no one can claim to be a messenger of the Lord unless the message transforms the way he or she lives. Jeremiah could simply have continued to proclaim that the Lord would bring the captives back and that normal life would begin again in the land. People would have heard his words. But they might not have listened to them. However, when someone sees a man buying a field in a country whose ruin is imminent, what he says seems more believable.

Finally, Jeremiah teaches us that the Lord is master of time, a point that will become clearer from the Lord's response to his questions. God does everything at the right time, for his own purposes. The timing of some of his actions may seem wrong to us, but it is better to obey God than to rely on our own intelligence.

32:26-44 The Lord's reply

The Lord's reply is addressed to Jeremiah, but does not directly answer his multifaceted question (**32:26**). Just as Jeremiah had prefaced his question with a long introduction, so the Lord also gives his reply only after a long explanation. He starts by simply telling his prophet that he is the Lord who reigns over all and that there is nothing that he cannot do (**32:27**, 17; Matt 19:26). The rest of the reply is in two parts. There is confirmation of the judgment that Jeremiah had proclaimed and then confirmation of the deliverance that he had also proclaimed.

The city will indeed be delivered into the hands of *Nebuchadnezzar king of Babylon* (**32:28**). The Babylonians will enter the city and burn the houses. This fire will be punishment for the acts of idolatry that have been committed in the city, all of which have provoked the Lord to anger (**32:29**). Israel is accused of having done the opposite to what the Lord wanted since their *youth*, that is, ever since they left Egypt (**32:30**). The long practice of idolatry in the city of Jerusalem has ultimately transformed the city into an abomination in God's eyes, an object of his wrath (**32:31**). That is why he will destroy it.

The entire population has been involved in the disgusting activities that have led to the city's judgment. Kings, princes, priests, prophets and people – all are guilty (**32:32**). The politicians and religious leaders have not been good guides, but have led the people astray, just as they themselves went astray. How can someone who is blind be a good guide to others who are blind (Matt 15:14; Luke 6:39)?

The people have been determined to turn away from the Lord. His repeated lessons to them accomplished nothing (**32:33**). *Again and again* (see 7:25, 25:3) is repeated here as a reminder of how often the Lord had spoken to his people.

The rebellion had led the people *to set up their abominable idols* in the temple itself (**32:34**), a situation that the prophet had already denounced (7:30). Manasseh had put an Asherah pole in the temple (2 Kgs 21:7) and Jehoiakim had done the same thing. At about the same time, the prophet Ezekiel was preaching against the presence of idols in the court of the temple (Ezek 8:3, 5-6).

The most heinous form of idolatry was that the Israelites had actually allowed themselves to be drawn into offering human sacrifice in the *Valley of Ben Hinnom* near Jerusalem (**32:35**). There they offered their children to foreign deities. It seems that the word *Molech* is of Phoenician origin and originally referred to a type of sacrifice in which human beings were burned. Later, the name for this type of sacrifice may have come to be used as if it were the name of a god (Lev 18:21; 2 Kgs 23:10; Acts 7:43).

The sheer number of the sins and abominations presented in the preceding verses has led to the impending capture of Jerusalem and the exile of its population (**32:36**). So the Lord confirms the judgment that he had charged Jeremiah to announce to his people.

But the message of judgment is followed by a message of deliverance. The promises of chapters 30–31 are repeated in **32:37**. The great indignation that the many sins of Israel had stirred in the Lord led him to scatter his people, but he commits himself to bringing them back and promises that he will *let them live in safety* in their land. He will make a covenant with them, as the formula in **32:38** indicates (see also 24:7; 30:22; 31:1, 33).

Mention of this covenant formula leads on to something that recalls one of the characteristic features of the new covenant: the renewal of the heart (31:33). The Lord had already said that he would give his people a heart that would enable them to know him (24:7). Here, he says that he will give them *singleness of heart and action* (**32:39**). An undivided heart has no duplicity and guides its possessor to behave honestly. With their hearts renewed in this way, the people will fear the Lord and they and their children will be better off for it.

The Lord's covenant with his people is called *an everlasting covenant* (**32:40**). The durability of this covenant was also mentioned in 31:35-37 (see also Isa 24:5; 55:3; Ezek 16:60). Within the framework of this covenant, the Lord will show favour to his people. He will place fear of himself in their hearts – a fear that enables them to please him as obedient children and which keeps them from wandering away from him.

It is worth noting the special emphasis on the *good* that the Lord wants to do for his people in 32:39-41. We can see that the Lord is delighted to be doing them good. After having uprooted them and sent them into exile, he will once again plant them and restore them completely.

It is only in **32:42** that the Lord begins to address the question Jeremiah had asked him. Just as he has brought *calamity*, so he will bring *prosperity*. The Lord has foretold both and will see that his prophecy is fulfilled (31:28). The true significance of the purchase of the field is then outlined. The country may now be desolate, stripped of both people and animals, but the day is coming when normal life will return (**32:43-44a**; see also 32:15). Every single legal step that Jeremiah had followed in his purchase of the field will be repeated over and over as such transactions again become commonplace. One day, things will again be normal in the country.

It is not just Jerusalem that will be restored. The *territory of Benjamin*, where Anathoth and the field that Jeremiah has purchased are located, is mentioned. So are various other places in the land of Judah, from the area immediately around Jerusalem to distant cities (**32:44b**). Earlier, the Lord had proclaimed that people would come from all these areas to worship him in the temple at Jerusalem (17:26).

33:1-26 Rebuilding Judah's Cities and Houses

This chapter relates the second revelation that Jeremiah received in *the courtyard of the guard* where king Zedekiah had imprisoned him (**33:1**). The first revelation was given in chapter 32.

The Hebrew text of **33:2** refers to *the Lord who made it* (NKJV), without specifying what the 'it' is. The Greek text, however, speaks of *the Lord who made the earth* (NASB). This identification of the 'it' is probably correct, for the verse is very similar to 32:17, which speaks of the creation of the heaven and the earth.

The Lord invites Jeremiah to call on him, as he is ready to reveal wonderful things that the prophet cannot find out in any other way (**33:3**). The words that follow indicate that these wonderful things relate to God's judgment of his people (33:4-5) and his plans to comfort and restore them (33:6-26).

Once again, God insists that Jerusalem will be taken by the Babylonians and that it is pointless to try to resist them (**33:4-5**). All the houses in Jerusalem will be full of the bodies of those the Babylonians have killed. This disaster will take place because the Lord has turned his back on the city.

But the story does not end in slaughter and death. God will ultimately bring *health and healing* to his people and this city (**33:6-7**). As in 30:17, there is a suggestion that this healing involves the creation of new flesh for his people. And the *peace and security* they will enjoy can be characterized as *abundant* (see 31:12). The time of restoration will also be characterized by purification and pardon for sins (**33:8**). These words remind us of 31:34 where God speaks of the new relationship that he will establish with his people.

The city of Jerusalem, which had been transformed into an abomination by Judah's idolatrous practices (24:9), will become a cause for joy to the Lord (**33:9**). The other nations will struggle to believe what the Lord has done for his city, so great will be the transformation (Isa 60). The city will truly enjoy *prosperity* and *peace.*

The Babylonians may leave the city a pile of ruins, but one day all kinds of songs of *joy and gladness* will be heard there again (**33:10-11**). There will be weddings again, celebrations of the Lord at the temple, sacrifices to him. All of these will take place once the Lord has brought his captive people home.

The restoration will also affect the animals. Flocks and sheepfolds will again be seen in all areas of Judah (**33:12**; see 17:26). Shepherds will again have the joy of counting their herds (**33:13**; Lev 27:32).

The *gracious promise* (or *good word* – NASB) that the Lord says he will fulfil in **33:14** is the prophecy made in 23:5 concerning *the righteous Branch* that would *sprout from David's line* (**33:15**). The reign of this righteous Branch is described in the same way as in 23:5, and the next verse is identical to 23:6, with one difference. In that reference, it is the righteous Branch that is called 'the Lord our Righteousness'; here, that name is given to the city of Jerusalem (**33:16**).

The mention of David leads the prophet to recall another ancient promise made to that great king of Israel: the promise that he *will never fail to have a man to sit on the throne of the house of Israel* (**33:17**; 2 Sam 7:16; 1 Kgs 2:4). Now follows a promise of the same sort. This one applies to a group that is far larger than the descendants of David: *the priests, who are Levites* (**33:18**). Their permanent presence means that there will be no further interruption in the worship offered to the Lord. This prophecy will be perfectly fulfilled in Jesus Christ, the perfect priest (Ps 110:4; Heb 5:6-10; 6:19-20; 7:11-25).

The laws that control the sun and moon are presented as clauses in a covenant that the Lord had concluded with these great celestial bodies – a covenant that will never be broken (**33:20-21**; see also 31:35-37). The Lord's covenants with David and with the Levites are as stable as the covenants that govern the natural world. The descendants of David and the Levites will be as numerous as those promised to Abraham, Isaac and Jacob (**33:22**; see Gen 13:16; 15:5; 22:17; 26:4; 32:12).

The *two kingdoms* (or, more accurately, 'families' as in the marginal note) in question could be either the nations of Israel and Judah, or those of David and Levi that are spoken of in the preceding verses (**33:23-24**). What is clear is that some people are speaking scornfully about the Lord's people, claiming that the Lord has rejected them and that they are no longer a nation. The prophet repeats the words of 33:20 to indicate that the Lord has not rejected his people (**33:25**).

The Book of Restoration ends with two references to the Lord's people in **33:26**. First, it refers to them in terms of the divided kingdom when it speaks of the descendants of Jacob (the nation of Israel) and the descendants of David (Judah). But then it goes back even further in time and identifies both groups in terms of their common ancestors, Abraham, Isaac and Jacob. Thus Jeremiah stresses that the ultimate restoration of the Lord's people will also see their reunification.

34:1-35:19 Various Messages

34:1-7 The Fate of Zedekiah

Nebuchadnezzar and the Babylonians were not acting alone when they besieged Jerusalem, but enjoyed the help of their allies from *all the kingdoms and people in the empire he ruled.* Nor was Jerusalem the only city being attacked. Its *surrounding towns* were also besieged by the enemies (**34:1**). These towns including *Lachish,* fourteen miles (twenty kilometres) and *Azekah,* twenty miles (thirty kilometres) to the south-west (**34:7**; see also Neh 11:30; 2 Chr 11:9). The city of Lachish is particularly well known because of its courageous resistance to Sennacherib, king of Assyria (2 Chr 32:9).

At some time during the siege of Jerusalem, probably near its beginning, the Lord sends Jeremiah to tell *Zedekiah king of Judah* what is going to happen to the city and to him (**34:2a**). The city will be handed over to Nebuchadnezzar who will *burn it down* (**34:2b**; see also 21:10; 32:3, 29). Zedekiah will be taken captive, will meet Nebuchadnezzar *face to face,* and he will be taken into exile in Babylon (**34:3**, see also 32:4-5). However, he will not die violently but will die a natural death and will be given a funeral similar to that of his predecessors, the kings of Israel (**34:4-5**; 2 Chr 16:14).

Jeremiah faithfully passed on all these words to the king despite the risk entailed in announcing to a king not only his political defeat but his exile and death (**34:6**). As we have already seen, Jeremiah's obedience to the Lord's commands cost him his liberty, for after hearing Jeremiah's message, Zedekiah threw him into prison.

34:8-22 Slaves Freed and Re-enslaved

The law of Moses laid down that Hebrew men and women could be enslaved for only six years. In the seventh year, they were to be set free (Exod 21:2-6). Apparently, King Zedekiah and all the people had made a covenant committing themselves to obeying this particular law (34:8-10). The text does not say why the king suddenly decided to apply this rule, nor why the people were willing to go along with him. It seems unlikely that they were motivated solely by a concern to obey the Lord. So various other possibilities have been suggested. Some think that Zedekiah was trying to do something to make himself acceptable to the Lord and to gain God's favour in his country's critical situation. It is not uncommon for people to submit to the word of God in hopes of receiving some benefit or deliverance from trouble in return. It may also be that the king wanted

to free these slaves so that they would be available to help defend the city against the Babylonians. The army would be larger if the slaves joined it. Some have also suggested that the slaves were freed because many of them could no longer do their usual work, particularly those whose work would have involved going outside the city gates. By freeing these slaves, their masters could escape the responsibility of feeding and caring for them. This option would have been particularly attractive because the siege meant that supplies of food were running low.

Whatever the reason, everyone freed their Hebrew slaves. But they did not do this on the basis of any deep conviction or firm determination to obey the word of the Lord. Consequently they soon changed their minds and *took back the slaves … and enslaved them again* (34:11).

SYNCRETISM

The word 'syncretism' is derived from a Greek word that means 'to mix together, to unite one thing to another' and does not always have a negative meaning. It is used by Paul to describe how God put together different parts of the human body to function as a whole (1 Cor 12:24). It also appears in Hebrews 4:2 where it is said that most of the OT saints did not enjoy the promised rest in the land of Canaan because, although they heard the word spoken to them, their hearing was not mixed with faith and trust in God.

Today, syncretism is defined as the mixing of different religious beliefs and systems. Many religious movements in Africa have been called syncretistic folk religions, since their adherents integrate traditional elements with more recent alien faiths such as Islam and Christianity.

Historically, Western writers and church leaders have been hostile to syncretism and have used the word pejoratively to describe some of the innovations and initiatives of African indigenous churches. These churches have been accused of distorting or watering down the essentials of the Christian faith. But careful examination of some of the motives behind the integration of African traditional themes and elements with the Christian faith reveals that it is misleading to label every indigenous movement as syncretistic, although some undoubtedly are.

The question that arises is whether faithfulness to orthodox Christian beliefs forbids one from adapting any traditional elements that make one's faith more culturally relevant. Christians sometimes forget that traditions and customs have shaped the Christian message over the centuries. The church has either consciously or unconsciously accepted some form of cultural syncretism ever since its beginning in Jerusalem and in the wider Greco-Roman world. Examples of this include the pagan roots of Christian festivals such as Easter and Christmas, the design of our church buildings and the

forms of our funeral and marriage rites. Most of the hymns quoted in the New Testament are clearly Jewish or Hellenistic in form although their content is strongly Christian (see the hymns in Philippians 2:6-11 and Colossians 1:15-20 and the Logos poem in John 1:1-16.)

The early church leadership was certainly mindful of the culture of Gentile Christians when it met to finalize the church's missionary policies in regard to the thorny issue of the extent to which Gentile believers should be required to adopt Jewish customs such as circumcision (Acts 15:1-35).

Since then, the presentation of the Christian message has been shaped not only by Scripture but also by church councils and creeds, the events of church history, and the writings and lives of saints and theologians.

All these influences have led theologians like Wolfhart Pannenberg to argue that rather than there being a sharp divide between God's special revelation in Scripture and his general revelation in culture, God is at work in both areas, so that they influence each other.

The creative diversity expressed in the Christian faith should help us to realize that the church needs to relate to a world that is increasingly religiously and culturally pluralistic. The church in Africa can learn from Islam and African Traditional Religions in regard to making our faith grounded and relevant within our cultures. Evangelicals must not allow their fear of syncretism to prevent them from contextualizing their faith to allow for meaningful local expression of it. However, such contextualization must be accompanied by a firm stand for the absolutes or cores of the gospel message. We need to be rigorous in guarding against any form of Christo-paganism, but there is nothing wrong theologically and missiologically with integrating culture and the gospel as long as the finality and supremacy of Jesus Christ alone as our Lord and Saviour is not sacrificed at the altar of multicultural and religious relativism.

Lawrence Lasisi

Responding to what such behaviour revealed about the character of the inhabitants of Judah, the Lord sends them a message through Jeremiah (**34:12**). He reminds them of the context in which he had first given this law regarding the freeing of slaves and points out that their ancestors had not obeyed it (**34:13-14**). He had been pleased when Jeremiah's contemporaries had decided to observe it (**34:15**). But by going back on their decision, they had seriously offended the Lord (**34:16**). They had promised before him that they would free their slaves. It was as if they had called him as a witness to their desire to obey this law. And now, suddenly, they have broken their promise. This is a sinful betrayal. Consequently the Lord is punishing his people with *the sword, plague and famine* (**34:17**). This judgment is aimed especially at those who had committed themselves to the covenant by carrying out the custom of cutting an animal in half and walking between the two parts (**34:18-19**).

The people will experience defeat and will be ruled by their enemies. Those who will be killed will have no burial. The birds and wild animals will feed on their dead bodies. The Lord will cause the Babylonians, who had started to lift the siege of Jerusalem, to return. They will eventually take the city and burn it (**34:20-21**; 32:29).

35:1-19 The Recabites' Example

The incident described in chapter 35 took place during the time of Jehoiakim, one of Zedekiah's predecessors (**35:1**). It involves a group of people, the Recabites (see 2 Kgs 10:15-23; 1 Chr 2:55), who had taken refuge in Jerusalem because of the invasion of the land by the Babylonians and their allies (**35:11**).

The Lord asks Jeremiah to invite the Recabites to a meeting in one of the rooms of the temple. There he is to offer them wine to drink (**35:2**). The prophet obeys the Lord's instructions and delivers the invitation to *Jaazaniah son of Jeremiah* and his family (**35:3**). The Jeremiah who is Jaazaniah's father is not the same person as the prophet Jeremiah.

The Recabites duly assemble at the designated location and Jeremiah presents them with wine and encourages them to drink some of it, exactly as he had been asked to do (**35:4-5**). Note that he is not content to merely ask them whether they would like some wine to drink, but actually serves it to them, following the Lord's command to the letter.

The Recabites refuse to drink the wine because their ancestor, *Jonadab, son of Recab* had ordered them not to drink wine (**35:6**). He had also given them other rules to live by. They were not to build houses but were to *live in tents*. They were also not to plant crops or vineyards, nor even to own cultivated fields and vineyards (**35:7**).

The Recabites were thus people who followed a strictly traditional lifestyle (**35:8-10**). They had renounced sedentary life and resolutely opted for a nomadic life. Their traditions set them apart from all other people, but that did not hinder them from having relationships with other people, as is shown by their decision to seek refuge in Jerusalem (**35:11**). Their customs did not make these people either superior or inferior to others; they were simply unique to them and part of their identity. It is sad to see how often people today seek to lose their identity and become something they really are not.

The strength of the Recabites' commitment to their traditional life provides Jeremiah with a powerful illustration for his message to the inhabitants of Judah (**35:12-13**). The Recabites remain true to their ancestor's instructions and continue to do exactly as he commanded them. But the Lord's children, the Judeans, had not given him the same kind of obedience (**35:14**). And yet, the Lord had not tired of sending prophets to them. He had given precise commands (repent, change your way of life, do not practise idolatry), but the people had paid no attention (**35:15**). The Recabites had a lot to teach the Judeans. They knew how to obey the teachings of the father, not just for a short time but for many long years. They had developed their own identity by following their ancestor's rules. But Judah had done nothing of the kind (**35:16**). Their refusal to obey the Lord will bring them misfortune, the capture of their city and the exile of its inhabitants (**35:17**).

As for the Recabites who have so faithfully obeyed all the commands of their ancestor, the Lord, the God of Israel, promises that their descendants will serve in the temple of the Lord (**35:19**; see also 33:18).

36:1-45:5 Jeremiah's Trials and Suffering

The next ten chapters in the book of Jeremiah deal with the painful events of the prophet's life during the siege of the city of Jerusalem and after its capture. Some of the events reported after the capture of the city take place in Judah, others in Egypt.

36:1-32 Destruction of the Scroll

The story starts during the reign of Jehoiakim, king of Judah (**36:1**). The Lord tells Jeremiah to *take a scroll* and write down all the messages that God had given him since the beginning of his ministry (**36:2**; 30:2). In Jeremiah's time, writing was often done on specially prepared animal skins. After it had been written on, the skin was rolled up, hence these books are called scrolls.

The Lord's purpose in asking the prophet to record the messages he had given was to make it possible for others to hear them being read, become aware of their sin and change their attitude. The Lord was seeking a way to lead his people to repentance so that he could pardon their sins (**36:3**).

Baruch, Jeremiah's secretary, writes all his master's words down on a scroll (**36:4**). Jeremiah then tells Baruch to go to the temple to read the scroll that he has written, as Jeremiah himself is *restricted* (**36:5**). Even if the word translated 'restricted' is the same one used in verse 33:1, it is not necessary to assume that Jeremiah was in prison at this time. In fact, 36:19 and 36:26 clearly show that the prophet was still free.

Baruch is to read publicly from the scroll that he had written at Jeremiah's dictation (see also Exod 24:7; Neh 8:8). He is to read it during a time of fasting, when people from different parts of the country gathered in Jerusalem to pray to the Lord (**36:9**; see Lev 16:29-31; 23:27-32; Num 29:7). The aim of the reading is to bring the people to repentance (**36:7**).

Baruch obeys Jeremiah as carefully as the prophet obeys the Lord (**36:8**). On the day of fasting, he reads the scroll aloud while standing in the room of *Gemariah*, the brother of Ahikam (26:24), in the upper court at the *New Gate*. The New Gate was where the officials had sat to hear the case against Jeremiah after he had proclaimed his earlier prophecy in the temple (**36:10**; 26:10).

Like his master, Baruch shows considerable courage. He knows the contents of the scroll, and he also knows that there will be those who will not approve of the message he is delivering. Moreover, it seems likely that the reason the people were fasting on that day was because they were seeking deliverance from their enemies. To appear on such an occasion and proclaim the exact opposite of what the people were hoping to hear exposed him to very real danger.

One of Baruch's audience, *Micaiah*, the son of Gemariah, in whose room Baruch was reading, and grandson of Shaphan, ran to the royal palace as soon as Baruch has finished reading (**36:11**). He went to the council chamber (**36:12**) and told *everything he had heard* (**36:13**).

The officials send for Baruch (**36:14**) and ask him to read them the scroll that he has read before the people in the temple. Baruch does so (**36:15**). On hearing the contents of the scroll with their own ears, the officials are seized with fear. They now realize the great danger that threatens their city and its people. Their reaction is to immediately inform the king, no doubt hoping that he will do something to avoid the coming tragedy (**36:16**).

But before going to find the king, the officials want to know more about how the scroll had been written. They learn that the author of the scroll was Jeremiah, and they want to know how Baruch came to write down the words the prophet spoke (**36:17**). Baruch informs them innocently that Jeremiah had dictated the words and that he had written them on the scroll with ink (**36:18**).

The officials are well aware of the danger to which Baruch and his master have exposed themselves by giving a public reading of a scroll containing such a message. It seems that these men are not totally opposed to Jeremiah and his secretary. But they seem to have been nervous about something

– probably the king's reaction to the message in the scroll. So they recommend that Baruch and Jeremiah go into hiding (**36:19**). In similar circumstances, Elijah had to go into hiding near a stream east of the Jordan after he had delivered a terrible message from the Lord to King Ahab (1 Kgs 17:3).

After warning Baruch and Jeremiah to hide, the officials went to the king, but they took care to leave the scroll in the room of *Elishama*, another of the king's secretaries (**36:20**). Then they themselves reveal the contents of the scroll to the king.

The king sends someone named *Jehudi* to get the scroll that the officials had taken care to leave in Elishama's room (**36:21**). This Jehudi is the same person whom the officials sent to look for Baruch when they learned that he had read the scroll publicly in the temple courtyard (36:14). Jehudi returns with the scroll and reads it before the king and his officials.

Verse **36:22** specifically notes that all of this is taking place in winter, the coldest season of the year. The king is therefore in his winter palace, where he spends this season (see Amos 3:15) and he sits beside a fire to keep warm.

As Jehudi reads from the scroll, King Jehoiakim tears off the columns already read and throws them into the fire (**36:23**). He arrogantly despises the word of the Lord. His attitude is completely different to that of his father, King Josiah, when Shaphan, the secretary (whose son and grandson are now supporting Jeremiah – 36:10-11), had read him the book of the law found in the temple. King Josiah had torn his clothes as a sign of mourning and repentance (2 Kgs 22:10-13). Jehoiakim does nothing of the kind. Instead, he treats the word of the Lord with contempt. His attitude spreads to his attendants (Ps 64:5-6). They were afraid when Baruch read to them from the scroll, but now they follow Jehoiakim's example. They should tear their clothes in mourning, but **36:24** makes it clear that they do not.

But not all of the king's officials share his indifference to and scorn of the word of the Lord. A few, *Elnathan, Delaiah* and *Gemariah*, try to persuade the king not to burn the scroll (**36:25**). But their protests are ignored. Not content with burning Jeremiah's prophecy, Jehoiakim also orders some of his attendants to go and arrest Baruch and Jeremiah. However, they do not find them because the Lord has taken care to hide them (**36:26**).

After these events, the Lord speaks to Jeremiah and tells him to take another scroll and rewrite everything that had been in the one Jehoiakim had destroyed (**36:27-28**). He is also to deliver a new message to the king who had criticized him for having prophesied the destruction of the land of Judah and the exile of its population (**36:29**; see 26:9). The message informs Jehoiakim that because of his pride and unbelief, none of his descendants will reign on the throne of Judah. He himself will be killed and his body will be left exposed to the elements. He will have neither tomb nor funeral, the worst possible disgrace for a king (**36:30**). The Lord will also act ruthlessly against Jehoiakim's descendants and attendants. He will punish their sins by carrying out all the threats that they had heard read from the scroll (**36:31**).

Some might argue that the prophecy in 36:30 is not fulfilled. Jehoiakim's son, Jehoiachin, does succeed him on the throne. But Jehoiachin's reign lasted barely three months (2 Kgs 24:8) and scarcely qualified as a real reign in OT terms. Jehoiachin was then taken captive to Babylon, where he died (2 Kgs 24:15; 25:27-30).

Jeremiah takes another scroll, gives it to Baruch and together they produce a new collection of Jeremiah's prophecies. This second scroll of Jeremiah's oracles includes texts that were not included in the first one (**36:32**).

37:1-39:18 The Siege of Jerusalem

37:1-10 Zedekiah consults Jeremiah

The focus now shifts to the reign of Zedekiah, whom Nebuchadnezzar had installed on the throne of Judah after the brief reign of Jehoiachin (**37:1**; 2 Kgs 24:17-18). His reign is summed up in the words of **37:2**: *Neither he nor his attendants nor the people of the land paid any attention to the words the Lord had spoken through Jeremiah the prophet.*

However, when the city is besieged by the Babylonians, Zedekiah sends men to consult Jeremiah. He wants the prophet to pray on Judah's behalf (**37:3**). *The priest Zephaniah son of Maaseiah,* who has already been mentioned, was among Zedekiah's envoys (see 21:1-2; 29:25-29). This visit takes place before Jeremiah is arrested and put in prison (**37:4**).

Zedekiah seems to have been requesting prayer for the success of a manoeuvre that he was launching with Pharaoh Hophra of Egypt (44:30). Egypt was an ally of Judah and, at Zedekiah's request, the Egyptian army had set out to come to the aid of the Judeans. When the Babylonians learn that the Egyptian army is on the move, they lift their siege and leave Jerusalem (**37:5**; 34:21-22).

Zedekiah must have been hoping that the Egyptians would defeat the Babylonians and drive them out of the land, but the Lord's reply to Zedekiah shows that things will not turn out the way he anticipates, or at least hopes (**37:6-7**). The Lord informs him that the Egyptian army that has set out to help Judah will turn round and go home. Any hope that the news of their approach has generated will evaporate. Judah will find itself in exactly the same situation as before. The Babylonians will return and take up the positions that they had abandoned (**37:8**). They will take the city and will burn it, exactly as Jeremiah has proclaimed on the Lord's behalf (34:22).

Therefore the Lord tells the king and the people of Judah not to deceive themselves by celebrating victory too soon. There is no point in nurturing the illusion that their troubles are coming to an end. The Babylonians will not go away (**37:9**).

The Lord also warns Zedekiah about the futility of this war with the Babylonians. He can choose to sally forth to attack the Babylonian troops who have just lifted the siege of Jerusalem. But even if he were to win a battle and only wounded survivors remained, he would not save Jerusalem. Whether they are wounded or not, Nebuchadnezzar's soldiers will destroy the city (**37:10**).

The message is clear for anyone who is prepared to listen. There is nothing more that can be done. Judah's fate is sealed. The city will be taken and burned, and its inhabitants will be led away from their land as captives. Those who remain in the country will suffer famine and shame. The Lord has spoken.

37:11-21 Jeremiah arrested and imprisoned

The news of the approach of the Egyptian army and the departure of the Babylonians creates an uneasy calm among the people, who consider resuming the activities that they have been unable to do during the siege (**37:11**). Jeremiah decides to go to his birthplace in *the territory of Benjamin* to take care of personal and family matters (**37:12**). It is not clear exactly what he is intending to do there. It may have been something to do with land that he owned. It may even have been to discuss the purchase of the field that he would later buy from his cousin, at the Lord's command (32:6-15 – the arrangement of the book of Jeremiah is not chronological). Whatever his purpose, it is clear that Jeremiah intends to leave Jerusalem for a period, although he probably also intends to settle matters quickly and return to the capital.

But as he prepares to go through the gate and leave the city, he is arrested by *the captain of the guard* who was on duty at the gate (**37:13**). This man, *Irijah,* accuses him of wanting to go over to the enemy. We can understand why he is suspicious. Jeremiah has been telling the people of Judah to surrender to Nebuchadnezzar, king of Babylon. He has proclaimed that Nebuchadnezzar will take the city and burn it. And now he seeks to leave the city, just as the Egyptian forces march to their aid and the Babylonians begin to withdraw. These events seem to contradict Jeremiah's prophecies. Has he sensed that the wind is changing? Is he trying to leave the city to go over to the Babylonians whom he seems to support? It seems like this to Irijah.

Jeremiah's insistence that he is loyal to Judah is ignored. Irijah does not believe him. He arrests the prophet and takes him to Zedekiah's officials (**37:14**). These men interpret the situation in the same way as Irijah does. Angered by what they assume to be Jeremiah's motives, they have him beaten and then imprison him in *the house of Jonathan,* the king's secretary (**37:15**). This is how Jeremiah ends up in prison, where he remains for *a long time* (**37:16**).

King Zedekiah takes advantage of Jeremiah's being in prison to send for him secretly for an interview. The king wants to know whether the prophet has had any further revelations. Jeremiah replies that the only word that the Lord has for Zedekiah is that he will be delivered into the hands of the king of Babylon (**37:17**). Jeremiah does not change his tune because he is being interrogated privately in the palace. He is not influenced by the riches of the palace or by the privilege of being in the king's presence. He does not try to say something politically correct. He will only proclaim what the Lord has revealed to him. Nothing more!

But the prophet does ask the king why he is being imprisoned. Nothing that he has done merits the treatment he is being given (**37:18**). In fact, the people should now be listening to him because events had shown that he was right, and that the prophets who had proclaimed that the Babylonians would never attack Jerusalem were wrong (**37:19**; 23:16-17). The Babylonians have just been besieging the city. If events have confirmed Jeremiah's message, why is the king refusing to listen to him? Why is he being treated like a common criminal?

Jeremiah pleads to be set free (**37:20**). He is not asking a favour, even if his request is described as a *petition.* He is simply asking for justice and the restoration of his rights, for nothing he has done justifies his being held in the terrible conditions of his prison. He will die if he is kept there much longer.

King Zedekiah does not comply with Jeremiah's request, but he does arrange for the conditions of his detention to be improved. He is moved from the dungeon to the courtyard, and orders are given that he is to be given bread every day until there is no more bread available in the city (**37:21**). These measures prove that King Zedekiah has respect for Jeremiah. It is possible that his reason for not giving him his freedom is that he fears the reaction of his supporters to such a step (38:5). Jeremiah, for his part, does not complain against the Lord. He does not regret having obeyed the Lord and proclaimed his word. For the time being, the king's intervention seems to have brought him enough relief.

38:1-13 Jeremiah thrown into a cistern

Despite being in prison, Jeremiah continues to deliver his message (**38:1**). He seems to recognize that the reason he is in this prison is so that he can proclaim the word of the Lord to the other prisoners and to the prison officials (see Acts 16:23-32; Phil 1:12-14). The Lord often places us in situations that we may not understand. But Jeremiah's experience proves that the Lord always has a purpose in the various circumstances of our life (see Rom 8:28).

The prophet's message is summarized in **38:2**: *whoever stays in the city will die ... but whoever goes over to the Babylonians will live.* The city will definitely fall to the Babylonians (**38:3**). Jeremiah changes absolutely nothing in his message, even if his words can be taken as evidence that supports the case of those who accuse him of being a traitor who sides with the enemy.

Putting Jeremiah in prison does not seem to have silenced him, and so Zedekiah's officials plot a more radical solution. They suggest putting him to death (**38:4**). Their justification for doing this is that Jeremiah is dangerous because he is demoralizing the troops and the people. He is prophesying destruction, rather than peace and prosperity. Thus he is guilty of high treason and must be executed.

The king's reply reveals the character of this man. He has no real authority. Like many political leaders today, he is hostage to the wishes of his officials and his advisors. He simply allows his officials to treat Jeremiah in whatever way they wish. There is no greater evidence of a lack of authority than this (**38:5**).

The officials then have Jeremiah thrown into a cistern that belongs to *Malkijah,* one of the king's sons (**38:6**). A cistern is an underground tank for storing rainwater, and this one is so deep that they have to use ropes to lower Jeremiah into it. While there was no water in it, Jeremiah sank deep into the mud at the bottom. The description of this pit reminds us of the words in the book of Lamentations: 'They tried to end my life in a pit and threw stones at me; the waters closed over my head, and I thought I was about to be cut off' (Lam 3:53-54).

The prophet's enemies assume that this is the end of Jeremiah. There will be no more talk about him and his prophecies, and they will at last be able to encourage the people to put up a courageous defence against the Babylonian attackers.

But there is one man in Jerusalem who will not stand for this. We do not know his name, because he is simply referred to as *Ebed-Melech,* which means 'servant of the king'. All that we know about him is that he was an African, specifically, an Ethiopian, who served King Zedekiah (**38:7**). We also know that he saw what was done to Jeremiah. He could not voice any protest or do anything about it, because those involved were powerful men. Who would have listened to him? Would any of them even have deigned to speak to him? After all, those who are anonymous are expected to keep silent, as if mute. It is better for all concerned if they stay that way. At least, that is what the know-it-alls often think.

Ebed-Melech, however, does not remain silent. He goes to speak to the king who is sitting at the *Benjamin Gate,* exactly where Irijah had seized Jeremiah when he wanted to visit his hometown (**38:8**; 37:13). He does not do it to make a name for himself. All he wants is to be a voice speaking on behalf of the one who is now silenced in the depth of the muddy cistern (Ps 82:4; Prov 14:25; 31:8-9).

The Ethiopian does not plead at length on Jeremiah's behalf. He simply states that the other servants of the king *have acted wickedly* with regard to Jeremiah. It was wrong to have him thrown into the cistern. And now, the king must intervene and show who is really in charge. He should arrange for Jeremiah to be pulled out of the cistern before he starves to death (**38:9**).

The king must have known what had happened to Jeremiah. He had allowed it to happen because he was weak. It takes an anonymous man to remind him, indirectly but forcefully, that he, too, has acted badly towards Jeremiah. Zedekiah knows that Jeremiah is upright and honest and that he speaks on the Lord's behalf. And yet, he has neither protected him nor given him justice. It takes this nameless African to remind the king of the injustice that has been perpetrated and to ask him to correct it.

By acting in this way, the nameless man became a spokesman and an intercessor. The rest of the story shows that he succeeded in his mission. It was not necessary that he be recognized by any particular name. What was necessary was that he act. Anonymity is not bad in itself. It is inaction that is shameful. That is what kills. Action saves lives. It provides a name. So, over the centuries, thousands and thousands of Bible readers have known the name of this Ethiopian who had no name! In the same way, many generations of readers and hearers of the gospel will hear of the anonymous woman who poured very expensive perfume on Jesus' head (Matt 26:6-13).

The king responds to the Ethiopian's intervention and intercession by giving him an assignment (**38:10**). He is to *take thirty men* and free Jeremiah. The Ethiopian makes all the necessary arrangements and carries out his mission well (**38:11**). Then, with his mission accomplished, he disappears and we hear nothing more of him until the fall of the city. But the Lord remembers him then, and sends him a message of salvation through the prophet Jeremiah (39:16-18). In the same way, the Lord saved the prostitute Rahab who had helped his people (Josh 6:25).

38:14-28 Final interview with Zedekiah

As before (37:17), King Zedekiah secretly summons Jeremiah *to the third entrance to the temple* – which may have been an entrance connected to the royal palace. As before, he asks the prophet to give him the Lord's message (**38:14**). But Jeremiah refuses to answer him because he is not convinced that the king sincerely wants to hear the message (**38:15**). Will he have him killed if the message is unfavourable? Will he take the message seriously if the prophet gives it to him?

When Zedekiah responds with an oath that guarantees that he will not harm Jeremiah, the prophet agrees to reveal the word of the Lord to him (**38:16**).

This time, the Lord offers Zedekiah an opportunity to escape judgment. He can still avoid the worst for his family, the city and all the people. But doing so will involve surrendering himself to the Babylonians (**38:17**; 38:2). If,

on the other hand, he insists on staying in Jerusalem and refuses to surrender to the Babylonians, they will take the city, burn it and capture him (**38:18**; 27:8; 37:8).

King Zedekiah seems to be ready to do what the prophet advises, except for one obstacle. He is afraid of the attitude of the Jews who had already *gone over to the Babylonians*. He fears that the Babylonians will turn him over to them and that they will enjoy his humiliation and will mock him and *mistreat* him (**38:19**). It is surprising that in his life-and-death situation, Zedekiah still clings to what he considers to be his honour. Yet Jeremiah offers him reassurance from the Lord. If he surrenders, nothing bad will happen to him, either at the hands of the Babylonians or of the Jews (**38:20**). But, if he does not listen to the Lord's word, there is something else that awaits (**38:21**).

In antiquity, when a king lost a war, all the women of his palace passed to the conqueror (**38:22**; see 2 Sam 16:21-22). So if Zedekiah does not surrender to the Babylonians, all the women of the palace will be taken to the Babylonian camp to become the property of Nebuchadnezzar's officials. Worse still, these women will say sarcastic things to Zedekiah. If the king fears being insulted by the Jews who had joined the Babylonians, how will he feel when insulted by the women of his own house?

The threat is repeated in **38:23**, which indicates that if the king does not surrender, not only will he be handed over to the Babylonians, but so will his wives and his children. The city will be set on fire.

When Zedekiah hears these words, he tries to strike a deal with the prophet (**38:24**). He asks Jeremiah not to say anything to anyone about this interview. He knows that his officials will learn that they have met and will interrogate Jeremiah about what was said (**38:25**). He suggests that if anyone asks Jeremiah what he said to the king, Jeremiah is to say that he was begging the king not to send him back to the prison he had been kept in at first (**38:26**). This excuse would have been plausible, for although Jeremiah was still being held in the courtyard (38:12-13), the incident involving the cistern could have led him to fear that he might be sent to a worse prison. If Jeremiah agrees to say nothing, the king will save his life. As the NASB puts it, *Let no man know about these words and you will not die*.

The king's officials do indeed come to interrogate Jeremiah, and he reports the version of the conversation that the king wants known (**38:27**). He may have done this in order to save his own life, or it may have been because he hoped that, given time, Zedekiah would decide to surrender to the Babylonians, if he were not prevented from doing so by his officials. Whatever the reason, he does not reveal what he and the king had actually discussed. This is not the first time in the OT that someone decides not to reveal the truth about something about which they are specifically asked (Josh 2:5; 1 Sam 20:6).

After this interview, Jeremiah remains confined in the prison courtyard until the fall of the city (**38:28**). Zedekiah has had his final interview with the prophet. Did the king know this? Did he realize that he had now had his final opportunity to save his kingdom, his family and his own life?

39:1-18 Jerusalem taken

The beginning of this chapter provides very precise dates for this siege of Jerusalem. The siege began in the *ninth year* of Zedekiah's reign on the tenth day of *the tenth month* (**39:1**; 2 Kgs 25:1; Ezek 24:1-2). This would have been equivalent to January/February 588 BC. The city falls *on the ninth day of the fourth month of Zedekiah's eleventh year,* which would have been in July 587 BC (**39:2**). The siege of the city thus lasted about eighteen months.

As soon as *the city wall was broken through,* Nebuchadnezzar's officials took positions in the city, specifically at the *Middle Gate.* Though we know little about this gate, the statement that they *took seats* indicates that they are now the authorities in the city and are sitting where the judges sat to hear cases (**39:3**). We are also given a list of the Babylonian leaders.

Zedekiah and his remaining soldiers try to flee the city. Under cover of night, they leave the city by a path through the king's garden towards the south of the city, on the side of the valley of Hinnom (**39:4**). Unfortunately for them, their flight is cut short because they are overtaken by some of the Babylonians who have pursued them (**39:5**). Zedekiah is captured in the plain of Jericho and taken to the king of Babylon, who had set up his camp at *Riblah* (see 2 Kgs 23:33; 25:6) in the land of *Hamath,* which is present-day Syria. There Nebuchadnezzar pronounced judgment on Zedekiah. He slaughtered all Zedekiah's sons before his eyes (2 Kgs 25:7) and executed the *nobles* of Zedekiah's court (**39:6**). As for the king himself, Nebuchadnezzar put out his eyes (2 Kgs 25:7) and put him in chains, preparatory to deporting him to Babylon (**39:7**). In this way, all of Jeremiah's predictions regarding Zedekiah and his family were fulfilled (34:3-5; 37:17; 38:18, 23).

The Babylonians set fire to the royal palace and to all the houses in Jerusalem and broke down the city's walls (**39:8**). *Nebuzaradan,* the captain of Nebuchadnezzar's guard, deports all the people that remain in the city (**39:9**). Only the weak and the poor are allowed to remain in Judah, where they are allocated fields and vineyards that they can cultivate in order to live (**39:10**).

We now learn that the new masters of the city know about Jeremiah, who had not fled the city. Nebuchadnezzar had given Nebuzaradan precise instructions regarding the prophet (**39:11**). No harm was to be done to him; he was to be well treated. But they are to keep a close watch over him (**39:12**). This makes us think that the Babylonians were also suspicious of Jeremiah.

The most senior Babylonian authorities in the city of Jerusalem send for Jeremiah, who is still in the prison courtyard (**39:13-14**). They entrust him to Gedaliah, son of Ahikam, son of Shaphan, who is to care for him. Thus Jeremiah was not among those deported.

While he was in the courtyard prison, the word of the Lord came to Jeremiah again (**39:15**). This time, it did not contain any revelation about the situation of the country of Judah or the royal house. Rather, the Lord had remembered the nameless Ethiopian who had helped Jeremiah when the officials of Zedekiah had thrown him into the cistern (38:10-13). The Lord warned the Ethiopian of the imminent judgment that he was about to bring on the city of Jerusalem (**39:16**). At the same time, he told Ebed-Melech that he need not fear the attacking Babylonians (**39:17**). The Lord himself will rescue the Ethiopian so that he will not be killed by any Babylonian sword. His life will be saved because he believed Jeremiah's word from the Lord. His fate is similar to that of Rahab, the prostitute, who welcomed the spies that Joshua had sent to explore the country (Josh 2:1; 6:17, 23-25).

40:1-43:7 After the Siege: In Judea

Chapters 40 to 44 contain the last part of the chronological record of events recorded in the book of Jeremiah. All the prophecies recorded from chapter 45 on in our Bibles were given before the events recorded in chapter 40, except for the final words of chapter 52 (52:31-34).

40:1-6 Jeremiah freed

There must have been some breakdown in the chain of command, for despite Nebuchadnezzar's orders (39:11-14), Jeremiah is caught up in the crowd of Judeans who are being deported from Jerusalem. He is already on the road towards exile in Babylon when Nebuzaradan releases him at Ramah (**40:1**). He reminds Jeremiah that the Lord foretold the disaster that has now overtaken his people (**40:2**). What has happened to them is a judgment for sinning against their God (**40:3**).

Nebuzaradan frees the prophet from his chains and offers him a choice: He can either come to Babylon, where he will be well treated, or he can remain in Judah, wherever he wants to live (**40:4**). His words, *the whole country lies before you,* remind us of what Abraham said to Lot, his nephew, when he was suggesting to him that they part company because their shepherds were not getting along (Gen 13:9).

Even before Jeremiah had time to reply, Nebuzaradan suggests that he return to Gedaliah, the grandson of Shaphan, whom the king of Babylon had just *appointed over the towns of Judah,* although he is free to go anywhere else if he wishes to do so. He is then given the provisions he will need and allowed to go free (**40:5**).

Jeremiah chooses to go to Gedaliah at *Mizpah,* which was eight miles (thirteen kilometres) from Jerusalem. It had once been the nation's sanctuary (Judg 20:1; 1 Sam 7:5). There he lived among the people of Judah who had remained in the land (**40:6**).

40:7-16 Gedaliah governs Judah

The news that Gedaliah has been appointed as the new governor of Judah spreads (**40:7**). The survivors of the Judean army, those men who had not been in Jerusalem when it fell, gather around him at Mizpah and declare their loyalty to him (**40:8**). He reassures them and gives them a message that is very similar to the one Jeremiah had been preaching before the capture of the city: If they remain in the country and serve the king of Babylon, they will have nothing to fear (**40:9**).

There is no doubt about what Gedaliah's position is. He is to remain at Mizpah, available to Nebuchadnezzar, king of Babylon. He knows that the land is no longer independent and understands that it is best to collaborate with the occupying Babylonians (**40:10**). This is the price that the people who have remained in the country will pay for peace. If they submit, they will be able to enjoy the fruit of their land. He asks all the soldiers who have gathered before him to return to the cities they had occupied and resume normal life.

News that Gedaliah has been appointed as governor of the country also reaches the Jews who had fled to the neighbouring countries of Moab, Ammon and Edom (**40:11**). Reassured by the latest news from their country, they decide to return home. They, too, gather around Gedaliah (**40:12**). That summer, they harvested an excellent crop from their fields and vineyards.

But the Judean army officers who had returned to Gedaliah at Mizpah, with their leader *Johanan,* now bring him a warning that a plot is being hatched against him (**40:13-14**). They insist that one of the Judeans who has returned from the country of the Ammonites, named *Ishmael, son of Nethaniah,* has evil motives for returning. He is in the pay of *Baalis king of the Ammonites* who wants him to kill Gedaliah. The governor did not take this warning seriously. He dismisses it and refuses to believe the officers.

However, Johanan persists in voicing his suspicions. He begs Gedaliah not to take unnecessary risks for himself or for those who have gathered around him, by leaving Ishmael alive. He suggests that the governor allow him to secretly kill Ishmael. Gedaliah denies his request. He does not believe Johanan when he says that there are traitors around him.

41:1-18 The assassination of Gedaliah

Gedaliah is wrong not to listen to Johanan. In the seventh month, that is, in September/October 587 BC, *Ishmael son of Nethaniah,* of the royal line, comes to Gedaliah at Mizpah

(2 Kgs 25:25), accompanied by ten men (**41:1**). The KJV translation implies that these men were all *princes of the king,* but other translations take these words as applying only to Ishmael. The king in question is not named, nor is there any indication of how closely Ishmael is related to the royal family. His associates are probably people who supported Zedekiah and who have now rallied around another member of the royal family.

Gedaliah, the governor of Judah, receives his guests graciously and, as is the custom, offers them food (Gen 18:6-8). But during the meal, Ishmael and his men assassinate Gedaliah (**41:2**). Although we are not given any explanation of the reason for this assassination, it is possible to make an informed guess. It was not simply that Baalis the king of the Ammonites had corrupted Ishmael, as Johanan had feared (40:13-14). Rather, Baalis may have played on Ishmael's belief that because he *was of royal blood* (41:1), he should have been the one to succeed Zedekiah. Gedaliah came from a noble family, but he was not of royal blood, and so Ishmael may have considered him a usurper. Moreover, Ishmael may have regarded Gedaliah as a traitor because he was prepared to work with the enemies of Judah. The assassination was thus a political crime, rooted in jealousy, and encouraged by the king of the Ammonites.

In his murderous fury, Ishmael also kills a large number of the Jews who have returned to the country after the appointment of Gedaliah. He and his men even kill some *Babylonian soldiers* (**41:3**). However, they manage to prevent news of their crimes from leaking out (**41:4**). Consequently, the next day a group of eighty people approach Mizpah, not knowing what has happened the day before (**41:5**). The people in the group have come from important cities in Israel: Shechem (Gen 33:18; 37:13), Shiloh (Josh 18:1) and Samaria (1 Kgs 16:24). These people have heard of the disasters that have struck the city of Jerusalem and particularly the temple, and they are coming to mourn for the city and the house of the Lord, as is shown by their shaved beards and torn clothes. They have also *cut themselves* as a sign of mourning. Although this practice was banned by the law (Lev 19:27-28; Deut 14:1), many Israelites did it anyway (16:6; Isa 3:24). They have also come to make offerings and to burn incense.

Ishmael again shows his hypocrisy and deceit. He implies that Gedaliah is still alive and offers to take them to meet him (**41:6**). But his intention is simply to gain their confidence so that he can slaughter them, which is what he and his men do once they have brought them into the city. Seventy are killed outright. Ten, however, survive by assuring the murderers that they can supply them with provisions that they have *hidden in a field* (**41:7-8**).

The bodies of the dead are tossed into a cistern that had been dug by *Asa,* a king of Judah, in his defence against *Baasha,* king of Israel (**41:9**; 1 Kgs 15:17-22; 2 Chr 16:6).

Ishmael takes captive all those in Mizpah whom he has not killed and sets out with them on the road towards the country of the Ammonites, from which he had come to commit his many crimes (**41:10**). But Johanan and the other army officers who are scattered in various parts of the country learn of what Ishmael has done and launch a counter-attack. (**41:11-12**). They find him and his captives at *Gibeon,* only a few kilometres north of Jerusalem. Ishmael has not travelled far, possibly because of the speed with which Johanan and his men have responded.

The people Ishmael has taken captive welcome their rescuers, but Ishmael and eight of his men manage to escape. They return to the country of the Ammonites, from where they had seen sent to sow trouble in Judah (**41:15**).

Johanan and his men are left to deal with the aftermath of the death of Gedaliah. They are faced with a serious political problem. Killing a representative of the Babylonian administration is tantamount to declaring war against the power that had installed him in office. While Johanan and his men have had nothing to do with the assassination, they fear the retaliation that will inevitably come from the Babylonians. They are eager to escape to Egypt to avoid the coming trouble (**41:16-18**).

42:1-43:7 The people consult Jeremiah

Before carrying out their plan to take refuge in Egypt, Johanan and the other army officers have the wise idea of consulting the Lord through the prophet Jeremiah (42:1-2).

Chapter 42 reintroduces Jeremiah into the story. He is not mentioned anywhere in chapter 41, which dealt with Gedaliah's assassination and its aftermath. Thus we do not know Jeremiah's attitude to what had gone on, but it is safe to assume that he was deeply distressed by it. Jeremiah knew Gedaliah well (39:14; 40:6). He had known first his grandfather, Shaphan (26:24), then his father, Ahikam, as well as other members of the family, such as Elasah (29:3; 40:5). Jeremiah had also chosen to remain with Gedaliah in Mizpah rather than go with Nebuzaradan to Babylon (40:6). All this shows that Jeremiah was fond of Gedaliah.

The army officers led by Johanan who have played the major role from 40:7 to 41:18 as well as *all the people* now come before Jeremiah and present him with their *petition* (**42:1-2**). This word is used several times in the book of Jeremiah (see also 36:7; 37:20; 42:9). It refers to an urgent request that is offered with a submissive spirit. These people all want to know whether the Lord approves of their plan to go to Egypt (**42:3**). It is commendable that they are seeking to identify the Lord's will. This is what King Zedekiah also did in 21:2. But it is not enough just to know the will of God; one must also be willing to submit to it. The people seem to understand this, and so even before Jeremiah receives an answer to the request he has presented to the Lord (**42:4**), they commit themselves to obey whatever the Lord will tell them through his prophet (**42:5**).

By calling on the Lord to witness their oath, the people are inviting him to bear witness against them, and they are laying themselves open to a curse should they fail to keep their oath of obedience, whatever answer the Lord gives (**42:6**; see Gen 31:50; Judg 11:10; Mal 3:5). We get the feeling that the people were talking too much and too soon. They do not seem to realize that it can be dangerous to make hasty commitments before the Lord (Eccl 5:2), especially when, as is shown clearly in 41:17-18, they already have a clear idea of what they want to do. The proverb is right when it says that when one eats at the king's table, one should not speak for fear of saying (or promising) something stupid.

Jeremiah takes their request to the Lord, and awaits his response. This wait is an important reminder to believers in general and servants of God in particular that we cannot set the schedule for when God will speak to us. The Lord is not an idol that can be manipulated to produce a revelation. He is the Lord of heaven and earth, and it is he who decides how and when to speak.

In his earlier altercation with the false prophet Hananiah, Jeremiah showed that he could be silent when the Lord had said nothing to him (28:11-12). He does exactly the same here, waiting to receive a word from the Lord before he speaks. This time, the wait lasts ten days (**42:7**). During this time of waiting, Johanan and his men may have come several times to ask the prophet if he had received a reply to their question. The people probably became impatient, and all of this would have put pressure on Jeremiah. However, he waits for the Lord to speak.

When the word of the Lord finally comes, Jeremiah summons all those who have asked for it *from the least to the greatest,* that is, everyone who is involved, and not just the leaders (**42:8**; see also 42:1). He then gives them the Lord's answer (**42:9**). It is that they are to remain in the land of Judah. This message is identical to the one that the prophet has been proclaiming for many years. The people's interest is best served if they submit to the Babylonians (27:11). The message is filled with the same verbs that have characterized Jeremiah's ministry from its beginning: *build, tear down, plant* and *uproot* (**42:10**; see also 1:10; 24:6; 31:28). The Lord says that if the people remain in Judah, he will build them up and plant them.

The Lord puts his finger on the main reason why the Judeans want to go to Egypt: they are afraid of how the Babylonians are going to react to the assassination of Gedaliah. But they are told not to fear the Babylonians (**42:11**). The Lord's presence will be with them and will guarantee their safety. The Babylonians will do them no harm. The Lord himself will have compassion on his people (**42:12**; Hos 11:8; Mal 3:17; Jas 5:11) and he will prompt the Babylonian king to show compassion as well.

If the people decide not to obey the word of the Lord (**42:13**), if they decide despite everything to go to Egypt

(**42:14**), they will face the very situations that they are trying to escape (**42:15-16**). It seems that the Judeans want to flee not only for fear of reprisals by the Babylonians, but also because they fear famine. Famine leads people to do stupid things. It can drive men and women to leave their villages, their cities and their countries of origin to search for a better life elsewhere. As the proverb says, 'the neighbour's vegetable garden is always better watered'. Yet when we see the incredible risks that some Africans today will take in order to reach Europe or America by illegal means, we wonder if it is really worth the trouble. Salvation may be found in the very place where we are. Maybe we simply need to look at things differently.

The Lord clearly asks his people to stay in Judah because what awaits them in Egypt is the *sword, famine* and death (**42:16**). There will be no survivors of the disasters that will strike the people in Egypt (**42:17**). They will have to endure the same judgment that has already struck *Jerusalem* (**42:18**; 24:9). This is the first time since the capture and destruction of Jerusalem that the Lord warns his people at such length and in such detail.

Jeremiah issues a clear and solemn warning in **42:19**. Its solemnity is enhanced by the formal construction used, with its clear identification of those addressed and of the one issuing the warning. But the warning on its own is a solemn one: *Do not go to Egypt* (see also Isa 30:1-7).

The people are told that their hypocrisy will recoil on them. They are fooling themselves if they believe that they can manipulate the Lord. Since they have sought the Lord's will and it has been revealed to them, they must submit to it. If they do not, they face disaster! It is no light matter to ask to know the Lord's will and to commit to obey it, as they have done (**42:20**; 20:5), and then to deliberately choose to turn away as if it does not matter (**42:21**). Such disobedience is costly. The remnant of the people of Judah will find that the wages of sin will be the sword, famine or plague, just when they counted on finding peace, abundant food and a better life (**42:22**).

The people's reaction to the Lord's response to their request is surprising. They promptly accuse Jeremiah of lying (**43:1-2**). Azariah takes the lead, but Johanan and all the others go along with him in rejecting the message that Jeremiah had delivered to them. However, to make it appear that they are not directly resisting the Lord and his prophet, they accuse Baruch of wishing them evil and of having influenced Jeremiah's response (**43:3**). But it makes no difference: opposing the Lord's servant is tantamount to rejecting the Lord himself.

It appears that the army officers and the people had already decided what they wanted to do before they came to consult the Lord. How else can we interpret their immediate refusal to obey the Lord's message, even though they had publicly and solemnly committed themselves to respect it?

(**43:4-5**). They had been determined to go to Egypt all along (41:17-18). They had consulted the Lord simply so that they could put a spiritual gloss on a decision they had already made. But before we are too shocked at such hypocrisy, we need to look at ourselves. How many times have we had a definite idea of what we want at the very time we are asking the Lord to accomplish his will in a specific situation?

Johanan is again mentioned first in 43:4 and 43:5, driving home the point that he is the leader who plays a key role at this moment in Judah's history. Unfortunately, he is not the type of leader who guides his people in obedience to the Lord (**43:4-5**). Those he leads into Egypt include *men, women and children and the king's daughters* (**43:6**). These 'daughters' are also mentioned in 41:10. It seems likely that these were women who had belonged to King Zedekiah's court. Jeremiah and his secretary, Baruch, are forced to accompany them.

The stress in **43:7** that this move is undertaken *in disobedience to the Lord* (see also 43:4) drives home the point that this is an act of flagrant disobedience, which will be punished.

43:8-44:30 After the Siege: In Egypt

43:8-13 Prophecy at Tahpanhes

Jeremiah and Baruch did not willingly go to *Tahpanhes*, in Egypt. They had been forced to go there by the remaining people of Judah and, in particular, by the army leaders. Yet even beyond the borders of Judah, the Lord continues to speak to Jeremiah (**43:8**). God's servants can still serve him wherever they are, even though they may have the impression that they are where they are because of some horrible mistake.

Once again, Jeremiah is called to act out a prophecy, this time by burying some stones in front of *Pharaoh's palace* (see 27:2; 32:25). This was probably not the main palace of the king of Egypt but his residence in the city of Tahpanhes (**43:9**). Jeremiah is to bury these stones in full view of the people of Judah who have taken refuge in Egypt. Then he is to explain the meaning of what he has done.

Jeremiah is to inform the people that Nebuchadnezzar, king of Babylon, is the Lord's *servant* in the sense that he accomplishes the Lord's purposes (**43:10**; see 25:9; 27:6). God will bring him to attack Egypt just as he attacked Jerusalem. He will be victorious and his throne will be set up at the entrance to Pharaoh's palace, exactly where Jeremiah has buried the stones. Putting his throne there will be a sign that he has replaced Pharaoh as the political authority in Egypt.

Nebuchadnezzar's action in Egypt is described in terms similar to those used to describe the catastrophe that befell the inhabitants of Judah (**43:11**; 15:2). As in Jerusalem, the Babylonians will burn down the places of worship (**43:12-13**).

This action is intended to show that the attackers' gods have defeated the gods of the nation they have overcome. The same idea is present in the statement that Nebuchadnezzar will *take their gods captive.* Having conquered the people, he will take their gods back to his home.

But God sees what happens as more than simply the defeat of one nation's gods by another nation's gods. Rather, he is passing judgment on the nations and condemning idolatry wherever it is practised. Whether it takes place in Judah or outside its borders, idolatry is an abomination in the eyes of the Lord, and he is ready to act severely against those who practise it wherever they may be found. This will not be the first time that God carries out a judgment against the gods of Egypt. He did the same on the night of the Passover, the night that preceded the exodus of the people of Israel from Egypt (Exod 12:12).

The metaphorical statement that Nebuchadnezzar will *wrap Egypt around himself* points to his coming invasion of the land of Egypt (44:12), in which he will even reach the great city of Heliopolis, the site of the *temple of the sun.*

44:1-30 Speech to the Jews in Egypt

The Judeans who had moved to Egypt were living in different cities in the country. Some were in *Migdol,* east of the Nile delta and close to the Egyptian border (Exod 14:2). Others were at *Tahpanhes* and *Memphis* in the Nile delta (2:16), while others lived in *Upper Egypt,* that is, in the region south of Memphis (**44:1**).

There follows a reminder of all that has happened to the people of Judah. The Lord recalls the facts, but takes special care to explain the causes of the disaster that he has brought on his people. The Judean refugees in Egypt had witnessed the ruin of Jerusalem (**44:2**). This ruin was the consequence of their idolatry (**44:3**). They had disobeyed, not out of ignorance, but in spite of the fact that the Lord had regularly sent prophets to reveal his will to them (**44:4**). Despite all the efforts made by the Lord to turn his people away from false gods, they had persisted in their idolatrous practices (**44:5**). Consequently the Lord's anger had burned against the people so that everything was destroyed, leaving only ruins as the Judeans could now see with their own eyes (**44:6**).

All disobedience to the Lord, all the sins that we commit, only bring us misery (see Prov 8:36; 11:3, 19; Isa 3:9). This point becomes particularly clear when we compare different translations of **44:7**. The NIV says, *Why bring such great disaster on yourselves?* whereas the NKJV says, *Why do you commit this great evil against yourselves?* The fact that the same word can be translated as both 'evil' and 'disaster' is a reminder that sin is a disaster for those who commit it.

It seems that the Judean refugees have not learned from what has happened to their land and to the population of Jerusalem. They have not grasped that it was the idolatry practised in Jerusalem that led to its destruction by the Babylonians (**44:8**). Because they have not taken time to reflect on events, they have forgotten all the evil that their parents and their kings had done. It appears that the women had also played a leading role in the pagan cults that had been celebrated in Jerusalem. So as soon as they arrive in Egypt, they again commit the same sins that brought such terrible judgment on Judah (**44:9**).

The absence of reflection on past events, the unbelief, the pride and the hardness of their hearts will destroy the people, for they call down a new judgment from the Lord. His words, *I am determined to bring disaster,* echo the obstinate attitude of the Judeans who were 'determined to go to Egypt', regardless of the Lord's will (**44:10-11**; 42:15).

Consequently, as the Lord had warned in 42:16, *They will all perish in Egypt* (**44:12a**). Many things emphasized the seriousness of this judgment. First, there is the insistence that all the people will die, *from the least to the greatest.* Second, there is the emphasis on the *sword* and *famine* in **44:12b**, which is immediately repeated in **44:13** as the *sword, famine* and *plague.* These were the same instruments of judgment that the Lord had used before (11:22; 14:12; 15:2; 21:7). Finally, there is the accumulation of words describing how others will see them. They will *become an object of cursing and horror, of condemnation and reproach* (18:16; 24:9).

The Lord will treat the Judeans in Egypt in exactly the same way that he treated the population of Judah (**44:13**). The completeness of the judgment that was stressed in 44:12 is reiterated in **44:14a**, with its insistence that no one will escape and no one will be able to return to the land of Judah. Yet at the end of **44:14b**, we do find mention of a *few fugitives* who will return. The idea that the Lord always preserves a small remnant of his people is a very important one, and will return in 44:28.

The people' response to Jeremiah's prophecy is both surprising and incomprehensible. The first surprise is the extent of the idolatry and the number of people practising it – *a large assembly* of men and women (**44:15**). The major role of women in these pagan cults is again emphasized (see also 44:9). However, these women were not practising this idolatry without their husbands' knowledge. The men knew about and must have approved of their wives' behaviour. Both spouses were involved in doing evil (see Rom 1:32).

The people make it very clear that they do not intend to obey the word of the Lord (**44:16**; see Zech 7:11-12). They explicitly reject his commands and declare that they will continue to practise idolatry (**44:17**). The goddess they will worship is *the Queen of Heaven,* that is, the Mesopotamian goddess of fertility known as Ishtar or Astarte (see also 7:18; 1 Sam 7:3). This goddess was associated with the planet Venus. The people will burn incense to this goddess and offer her drink offerings. Aaron and his sons had been instructed to offer incense to the Lord (Exod 30:1-11;

Lev 2:1-2). Drink offerings, usually wine (Lev 23:13; Num 28:14; Deut 32:38) were also associated with sacrifices offered to the Lord (Num 29:6, 11, 19). But now these practices will be associated with idolatrous worship.

The Judeans and their ancestors, kings and princes had practised idolatry everywhere in the land of Judah. And they attribute their riches and their various blessings (in food and good fortune) to the goddess Ishtar whom they worshipped. Now they attribute the disasters that have struck them to their ceasing to worship her (**44:18**). Their attitude is similar to that of the Israelites who left Egypt under Moses' leadership. As soon as they faced any difficulty, they recalled all the good things that they had had in Egypt (Num 11:4-6). They even began to forget that they had been slaves in Egypt. Now their descendants who have returned to Egypt are behaving in exactly the same way. They regret having abandoned their idolatrous practices. They think that it was these idols that provided for their needs.

The women again claim that they have acted with the complicity of their husbands (**44:19**). They have not only burned incense to the goddess and offered her drink offerings, but they have also made *cakes like her image,* that is, cakes that represented the naked goddess Ishtar and that were offered in idolatrous worship.

Jeremiah responds that it is not their abandonment of idolatry that has caused their misfortune (**44:20**). Quite the opposite! It is because they have practised idolatry that the Lord's judgment had come on them in the first place (**44:21**). He had become so tired of their many idolatries that he had destroyed the land, transformed it into a ruin and emptied it of all its people (**44:22**; 22:6; 25:11). The people's situation is thus the consequence of their idolatry, their disobedience and their disdain for the law of the Lord (**44:23**).

Jeremiah continues to address the people and, in particular, the women. He encourages them to listen to the Lord's word (**44:24**). He acknowledges their determination to persist in idolatry (**44:25**; 16-17). But he also reports that the Lord swears by himself, by his own *great name,* saying that he will no longer allow any Judean settled in Egypt to *invoke* his name (**44:26**). His words indicate that these people are still calling on the Lord while offering worship to the goddess Ishtar. They will no longer be allowed to use the ancient formula, *as surely as the sovereign Lord lives,* that they were accustomed to invoke when making vows (22:24; 38:16).

If the people had obeyed the Lord and stayed in Judah, the Lord would have been with them and would have protected them (42:11-12). But their disobedience means that the Lord is now *watching over them for harm, not for good* (**44:27**; see also 1:12; 31:28). Once again, he speaks of the sword and famine as the means of exterminating his people. However, their destruction will not be total. The Lord will leave a remnant. A small number of people will return to Judah. All the rest will die in Egypt. Everyone will then know that the word of the Lord is true and will always be fulfilled (**44:28**).

The Lord concludes by promising to send them a sign that will prove that what he says will be fulfilled (**44:29**). The sign is that *Pharaoh Hophra* will be handed over to his enemies (**44:30**; see 46:25-26). This sign must have been unnerving to Judean refugees in Egypt because he was the one who had come to the aid of Judah when the Babylonians laid siege to Jerusalem (37:5). His approaching defeat is compared to the fall of King Zedekiah, whom the Lord gave into the hands of Nebuchadnezzar king of Babylon (39:5).

This prophecy was fulfilled in 569 BC when Hophra (or Apries in Egyptian sources) was assassinated.

45:1-5 Jeremiah Encourages Baruch

It is clear from **45:1a** that this chapter should be located after 36:8, where the Lord commanded Jeremiah to write down all the words that he had spoken to him. The prophet had then dictated his prophecies to Baruch.

For most of the book of Jeremiah, we have been listening to messages the Lord has sent to the people and the political and religious leaders of Judah through Jeremiah, his prophet. Here, however, the Lord gives Jeremiah a message that is directed specifically to Baruch, his secretary (**45:1b-2**). Baruch has shared Jeremiah's suffering in the exercise of his ministry, and it seems that he is tired and discouraged. *I am worn out with groaning* (**45:3**). So the Lord speaks to him in words that will remind him of what he knows of Jeremiah's call, for the Lord again speaks of his destructive actions of overthrowing and uprooting (**45:4**; 1:10). Baruch may have other plans for his life, but the present circumstances will not permit him to accomplish them (**45:5a**). The Lord asks him to recognize this and give up these plans. The only thing that Baruch can save is his life. The Lord will keep it safe for him despite anything and everything (39:16-18). The Lord says, *Wherever you go, I will let you escape with your life* (**45:5b**).

The Lord's words to Baruch remind us of Jesus' warning that we will lose our lives if we try to save them. It is only by being willing to lose our lives in God's service that we will indeed save them. Like Baruch, we are to put God first (Mark 8:35).

46:1-51:64 Prophecies Against Pagan Nations

46:1 Introduction

We now come to a section of the book of Jeremiah that is entirely devoted to prophecies against nine pagan nations (**46:1**). The list begins with Egypt and ends with Babylon. Between the prophecies addressed to these two great powers are prophecies addressed to Philistia to the west; Moab, Ammon and Edom to the east; and Syria, Persia and nomadic groups to the north-east.

In the Septuagint, the ancient Greek translation of the OT, these prophecies are placed after 25:13 and are presented in a different order to the one seen here.

46:2-28 Against Egypt

The first section has a very simple title: *Concerning Egypt* (**46:2a**). Two oracles are delivered against this nation. The first relates to the great historical battle of Carchemish, where Egypt and Assyria were defeated by the Babylonians under Nebuchadnezzar, and the second deals with Nebuchadnezzar's later invasion of Egypt.

A substantial part of these oracles is in poetic form.

46:2b-12 Oracle concerning Carchemish

The historical context of this oracle against Egypt at the time of the Battle of Carchemish is set out in 2 Kings 23:29-24:1 and 2 Chronicles 35:20-36:4. The battle took place in *the fourth year of Jehoiakim, king of Judah* (**46:2b**).

The oracle begins with a description of the Egyptian army preparing for battle (**46:3-4**; see also Joel 3:9; Nah 2:1). We hear the voices of the Egyptian army officers issuing orders to their troops. But suddenly there is a change that takes the speaker by surprise, so that he asks, *Why have I seen this?* (**46:5** – HCSB). He is seeing the same soldiers who were boldly preparing for war being seized with fear. They tremble and run. Even the best of them, *the warriors*, are taking to flight. *There is terror on every side,* an expression that recurs many times in the book of Jeremiah (6:25; 20:4, 10; 49:29). It indicates both the scope of the threat and the depth of the panic that seizes the people. The fact that the soldiers fall *by the River Euphrates* reminds us that this battle was fought far to the north of Judah and Israel (**46:6**; see also 46:2).

Egypt had been making bold claims before this battle. It had thought that its invading army would be as irresistible as the Nile floods, destroying both cities and their inhabitants (**46:7-8**). It had also recruited foreign mercenaries to fight alongside the Egyptian troops (**46:9**). These mercenaries came from places like Ethiopia (*Cush* in Hebrew), *Put,* a region south of the Red Sea, and *Lydia* (Ezek 27:10; 30:5). Commentators are divided as to the location of Lydia. Some understand it to be the city of Lydia in Asia Minor (Isa 66:19), while others believe that the name refers to North Africa (Gen 10:13). Still others suggest reading 'Lybians' for Lydians, on the basis of Nahum 3:9 where a coalition is formed by Ethiopia (Cush), Egypt, Put and Lybia.

The day of the battle is described as the day of the Lord's vengeance (**46:10a**), but the motive for this vengeance is not stated. It could have been vengeance for the death of King Josiah, who had been killed by the Egyptian army as they slowly advanced towards Carchemish. But what is clear is that the Lord takes vengeance on his enemies, the

Egyptians. The blood that is spilled is said to be a sacrifice offered to him (**46:10b**; see Isa 34:6).

The recommendation that the Egyptians go to Gilead, a place famous for its healing balm, to find a remedy for the nation's wound proves that Egypt has been seriously injured (**46:11**). Here she is called the *Virgin Daughter of Egypt,* in contrast to Virgin Israel (see 18:13; 31:4, 21). But nothing is gained by going to Gilead because Egypt's wound is incurable (see 15:18; 30:12, 15).

Egypt's defeat is shameful, dishonourable and humiliating (**46:12**). The shame is all the greater since its soldiers, rather than facing the enemy, stumble and fall on top of each other (see Isa 19:2).

46:13-27 Nebuchadnezzar's attack on Egypt

The battle of Carchemish had been fought in the far north on the Euphrates (46:2), but now Jeremiah looks at what will happen when Nebuchadnezzar king of Babylon marches south and attacks Egypt directly (**46:13**; see also 42:10-11).

The cities that are told to prepare for the worst are exactly the same cities where the Judeans had gone to find refuge (**46:14**; see 44:1). The Lord himself will fight against the Egyptian soldiers (**46:15**). He will sow fear among them, until they lose all stomach for the fight and are interested only in returning home and escaping the war (**46:16**).

A cry of *Pharaoh king of Egypt* (**46:17**) might once have hailed Hophra's arrival and celebrated his power and glory. But Pharaoh has failed to show any power. He has not seized the opportunity to show what he can do. All the noise with which he had been greeted was no indication of his power. It was mere noise and human vanity (see also Exod 15:9-10).

Unlike Pharaoh Hophra, *the Lord Almighty* or *the Lord of Hosts* (KJV) is the true *King* (**46:18**). He is hailed as 'King' in many passages in the book of Jeremiah (see 8:19; 10:7, 10; 48:15; 51:57). He will send a conqueror to Egypt who will tower over the land just as the mountains of *Tabor* and *Carmel* tower over Galilee. *Egypt* is to prepare for exile (see Isa 20:4). The great city of *Memphis* will be left in ruins (**46:19**).

Egypt is compared to a *beautiful heifer.* Some commentators think that this is an allusion to the worship of a bull-god in Egypt. But a *gadfly,* a small biting insect, *from the north* will bite the heifer and put her to flight (**46:20**). Elsewhere in the Bible insects are also used as symbols of an enemy attack (see, for example, Exod 23:28).

The mercenaries hired by Egypt may be as pampered and admired as *fattened calves,* but they are destined for slaughter and will flee before the Babylonian enemy (**46:21**). The *day of disaster* and *the time for them to be punished* make us think of the Lord's 'day of vengeance' (46:10).

The crown of Egypt incorporated a snake, a cobra, so the snake was closely associated with that land. But the hissing sound that will be heard is not that of a snake poised to strike, but rather that of *a fleeing serpent* (**46:22**). The snake will be fleeing from those who are coming against it like woodcutters, coming *with axes* to *chop down her forest* (**46:23**). This forest may seem dense, but trees are incapable of resisting and the number of attackers will be so great that the country will be laid low. Again changing the metaphor, the attackers are described as being as being *more numerous than locusts* (see Judg 6:3-5). Egypt will be defeated by the Babylonians and totally *put to shame* (**46:24**).

Amon, the chief god of the Egyptian pantheon, was worshipped at *Thebes* in Upper Egyp, the town that was referred to as No in the KJV (**46:25**). The Lord announces that he is going to bring an end to the idolatry there and will judge Pharaoh, his country and all his gods, as well as all those who have put their trust in Pharaoh. They will all be delivered to their common enemy, the Babylon king Nebuchadnezzar (**46:26**). However, the Lord reassures Egypt that its history will not end with its defeat by Babylon. He Lord promises that after all its torments, Egypt will again be inhabited. This promise is further evidence that the destiny of all the nations of the world is in the hands of the Lord. It is he who controls the history of all the peoples on earth.

The oracle concerning Egypt ends with reassuring words addressed to Israel. As in 30:10-11, the people (here referred to as *Jacob*) are told not to *fear* or *be dismayed* because the Lord will enable them to return to live in security in their own land (**46:27**). Here he is announcing the return of the exiles from Babylon.

The reason the exiles need not fear is that the Lord is present with them (**46:28**). He will destroy the nations that have taken his people captive. Israel will endure the punishment it deserves, but the nation can be confident that it will not be wiped out.

47:1-7 Against the Philistines

The oracle against the Philistines was given to Jeremiah before the attack on *Gaza* by *Pharaoh* (**47:1**). We do not know exactly which Pharaoh is referred to in this verse. It may have been Pharaoh Neco, who fought at Carchemish and is mentioned in the oracle against Egypt (46:2), or it may have been Pharaoh Hophra (44:30; 46:17). The city of Gaza that he attacked is one of the five Philistines cities. The others are Ashdod, Ashkelon, Gath and Ekron (see Josh 13:3).

Although the vision is dated with reference to an attack from Egypt in the south, the vision that Jeremiah sees is of an invasion from the north, the direction the Babylonians came from (**47:2**; see 1:14; Isa 14:31). The sounds of war are vividly described, including the clatter of *galloping* horses and the *rumble* of chariot wheels (**47:3a**; 8:16). In their terror, people will not even try to save their own family members. Paralyzed with fear, *their hands will hang limp* (**47:3b**).

It seems that the Philistines were allies of the Phoenicians who lived in *Tyre* and *Sidon* (**47:4**). They may have provided mercenaries to support them. But neither things nor people can stand up against the Lord. He will destroy *the remnant from the coasts of Caphtor,* probably a reminder that the Philistines had originally come to Canaan from the island of Crete (Gen 10:14). The Philistines will be completely destroyed.

Philistia will be left in deepest mourning, as can be seen from the traditional signs of mourning: a shaven head (Gaza), silence (Ashkelon) and people cutting themselves (**47:5**).

The Lord, the God who reigns over all the nations of the earth, is carrying out this judgment against Philistia. The *sword of the Lord* takes no rest (Ezek 21:9; Rev 19:15). It will continue until its work is finished (**47:6-7**).

48:1-47 Against the Moabites

48:1-17 The destruction of Moab

The Moabites were the offspring of the incestuous relationship between the older daughter of Lot and her father (Gen 19:37). Along with Edom, Ammon, Tyre and Sidon, Moab was a nation to whose king Jeremiah passed on a message from the Lord: submit to the political authority of Nebuchadnezzar, king of Babylon (27:1-11).

This text has a number of similarities to Isaiah 15-16, which also forms part of a section of a book that is devoted to prophecies against foreign nations. We shall look at some of these similarities as we examine this prophecy.

The oracles against Egypt and Philistia were introduced as 'the word of the Lord that came to Jeremiah the prophet concerning …' (46:1; 47:1). Here, however, the Lord speaks directly to Moab, and Jeremiah is not mentioned (**48:1a**). This does not mean that the text was written by someone other than Jeremiah himself.

The Lord announces the destruction of Moab by giving a list of the places that will be destroyed:

- *Nebo* was the name of a town in the territory of Reuben (Num 32:3, 38), but it seems more likely that the reference in **48:1b** refers to the mountain of that name situated to the north-east of the Dead Sea. It was where Moses had died (Deut 32:49).

- *Kiriathaim* was a city (Josh 13:19; Ezek 25:9). It was possibly the same place as the name translated as Misgab in the KJV, which the NIV translates as *the stronghold* (**48:1c**). The exact location of this city is unknown.

- *Heshbon,* the capital of Sihon king of the Ammorites (Num 21:26), had been given by Moses to the tribe of Gad (Josh 13:24-27). The name 'Heshbon' sounds like the Hebrew word for 'plot', and hence the prophet puns: Her name is Plot and in her *men will plot her [Moab's] downfall* (**48:2a**).

- *Madmen* is another city whose location is unknown. Here, too, there is a play on words. 'Madmen' sounds like the Hebrew for 'be silenced', and Jeremiah puns: Be silenced will *be silenced* (**48:2b**). Everything that Moab values will be wiped out by *the sword.*

- *Horonaim* is another place mentioned several times in this chapter (**48:3**, 5, 34). Great cries will accompany the devastation of this city. **48:4** specifies that these cries come from the *little ones.* Here there is a difference between the Hebrew and Greek texts. The Greek text reads like Isaiah 15:5, and says 'announce it in Zoar'.

- *Luhith* is also a city whose location is unknown, but it was probably not far from Horonaim (**48:5**). The description of what awaits it is almost identical to that given in Isaiah 15:5. The population of Moab will be *weeping bitterly* because of what has happened to their country.

Suddenly, the scene of the weeping refugees straggling along the road is transformed into a scene of panic. The people are encouraged to flee into the desert to save their lives (**48:6**). They are to be like *a bush,* or as the NASB translates it, like the small *juniper* bush that grows in the desert. Our understanding of what this means is enhanced if we remember that the same word is used in 17:6, where someone who does not trust in God is said to be 'like a bush in the wastelands; he will not see prosperity when it comes'. An alternative translation might be, 'be like a wild ass in the desert' (NRSV), which also creates an image of something struggling to survive in a harsh environment.

Moab had placed its confidence in its *deeds* and its *riches* (**48:7**; 17:5; 49:4). But the Lord states that these things will be of no help because the people will be *taken captive.* The proof of their complete defeat will be the fact that *Chemosh,* the god of Moab, will be taken into exile along with *his priests and officials.*

Once again, the extent of Moab's defeat is stressed by speaking of the destruction of all the cities in the country: *every town* will be destroyed (**48:8**). The reference to *the valley* and *the plateau* clearly describe the geography of Moab, with the valley probably being that of the Arnon and the plateau representing the rest of Moab (see Josh 13:9). Everything will be destroyed at the Lord's word.

The Hebrew text of **48:9** is difficult to understand and is translated in various ways by the different versions of the Bible. Possible translations include *give wings to Moab* (KJV) and *put salt on Moab,* as in the NIV. Whatever reading is chosen, the idea seems to be that the destruction of Moab is imminent. *The destroyer* who was spoken of in 48:8 is to conscientiously carry out the full judgment against Moab and is to strike without restraint (see 46:10).

So far, Moab has never had to face the suffering associated with exile (**48:11**). It had been a prosperous nation with rich vineyards (Isa 16:8). Jeremiah speaks of the taste and aroma of the wine produced there. But its peaceful existence will end. If the whole country can be compared to good wine, then its end can be compared to the spilling of that wine and the smashing of the jars in which it was stored (**48:12**). The pouring out of the nation may also refer to the people being taken into exile. Their god, *Chemosh,* will not be able to do anything to save them. His people will be ashamed that they ever put their trust in him (**48:13**). Their reaction will be like that of the Israelites, who were brought to see their folly in practising idolatry at Bethel (1 Kgs 12:32; 13:1-3; 2 Kgs 10:29; 23:15; Hos 6:10).

Moab's inhabitants may boast that their warriors are *men valiant in battle* (**48:14**). But even her *finest young men* cannot save her. Their country will be destroyed, its towns invaded and its young people killed (**48:15**). There is a bitter wordplay in this verse that is captured in the NRSV translation: *The destroyer of Moab ... has come up, and the ... young men have gone down.*

Once again, the Lord is spoken of as *the King* (8:19; 10:7, 10; 51:57). He announces that the destruction of Moab is *at hand* (**48:16**) and orders Moab's neighbours to mourn her disaster (**48:17**). The opening word of their mourning, *How ... ,* is the same word that is used to introduce the book of Lamentations. The *mighty sceptre* and the *glorious staff* that Moab used to wield are now *broken.* The contrast between what Moab had been before the Lord's judgment and its present situation astounds those who are watching.

48:18-47 Mourning for Moab

Before the arrival of the destroyer, the Lord tells Moab to abandon its pride (or *glory*) and come down and sit in the dust on the *parched ground.* A similar invitation was extended to Babylon in Isaiah 47:1. There Babylon was called the 'Daughter of Babylon', just as Moab is here called the *Daughter of Dibon* (**48:18**). This town is also mentioned in 48:22 (see also Num 21:30; Isa 15:2).

Moab is next referred to by the collective name of *you who live in Aroer,* referring to one of the cities situated in central Moab (**48:19**; Deut 2:36; 4:48). The nation is to take up a position as a sentinel and *stand by the road and watch.* The survivors of the catastrophe are to be interrogated about has happened to their country.

The idea of *disgrace* returns in **48:20** (see 48:1). This disgrace seems to be linked to the fact that Moab is *shattered.* Once she had held a 'mighty sceptre' and a 'glorious staff' (48:17), but they are both broken. The news of Moab's fall is to be announced by the *Arnon,* a swift river that ran through Moab (Num 21:13), so that the news will spread rapidly.

Once again, we are given the names of places in Moab on which God's judgment has fallen (**48:21-24**). These towns are mentioned as representative of the whole country. They are *Holon* (Josh 15:51; 21:15), *Jahzah* (1 Chr 6:78), *Mephaath* (Josh 13:18; 21:37), *Dibon* (48:18; Num 21:30), *Nebo* (48:1),

Beth Diblathaim (Num 33:46-47), *Kiriathaim* (48:1; Josh 13:19), *Beth Gamul* (which some commentators locate in the vicinity of Dibon), *Beth Meon* (Josh 13:17), *Kerioth* (Amos 2:2) and *Bozrah* (Amos 1:12).

The prophet announces that Moab's *horn is cut off* (**48:25**). In the OT, a 'horn' is a sign of strength and often also of pride (1 Sam 2:1, 10; Ps 75:5, 10). An *arm*, too, is a symbol of strength (Exod 15:16; Deut 7:19; 33:27). When someone's arm is broken, he or she is totally defeated.

Moab will drink the cup of the Lord's anger (**48:26**; 25:15-16, 27). It will make her drunk, so that she *wallows in her vomit* and is an *object of ridicule* to others. Could there be a clearer image of degradation and humiliation? Her situation will be like that of Israel, at whose behaviour Moab shook her head in scorn, expressing her astonishment and disgust (18:16; Ps 22:7). But now the one who mocked others will herself be mocked (**48:27**; 2:26).

The rapidly approaching judgment means that the cities are no longer safe (**48:28**) and so the Moabites are encouraged to leave them to find refuge in *the rocks*, like *a dove* who *makes its nest in the mouth of a cave* (see Num 24:21; Job 39:28; Obad 4).

Moab's pride has already been hinted at several times in this chapter (48:14, 18, 26), but now it is explicitly condemned as the prophet speaks of her *pride*, her *overweening pride and conceit*, her *arrogance*, her *haughtiness* and her *insolence* (**48:29-30a**). The Lord knows of Moab's boasting, but he also knows that such *boasts accomplish nothing* (**48:30b**).

The prophet puts himself in the place of the victims of the Lord's judgment and weeps for the country (**48:31**). He mourns for *Kir Haresheth*, elsewhere called Kir Moab, which was the capital of the country (Isa 15:1; 16:7, 11). His use of the word translated *moan* suggests that his grief and pain are such that he cannot even speak aloud of the terrible fate of its inhabitants.

The prophet uses yet another name to refer to Moab. This time he speaks of it as embodied in the *vines of Sibmah* (**48:32**; see Josh 13:19; Isa 16:8-9). Sibmah was located between Heshbon and Nebo, and was probably in the same area as Jazer. The verse reminds readers of the flourishing Moabite vineyards. But all of them will be destroyed. The destroyer's work will be the opposite to that of the vinedresser. Thus joy and happiness will depart and wine will no longer flow. The cries that will be heard will no longer be cries of joy (**48:33**). In fact, cries of desolation will resound from one end of the land to the other (**48:34**; Isa 15:4-6).

Not only will the destruction eliminate Moab's material riches (the vineyards), but it will also affect what the Moabites would have considered their spiritual riches, for all idolaters and idolatry will also be swept away (**48:35**).

The prophet had begun to lament in 48:31, and now his heart begins to vibrate *like a flute*, an instrument whose sound was traditionally associated with mourning (**48:36**;

Isa 16:11). He laments for the inhabitants of Kir Hareseth, who have lost everything.

Four other signs of mourning are also evident (**48:37-38**): shaved heads (7:29), the beards that have been cut off, the cuts that people have made in their hands (41:5) and the sackcloth they are wearing (4:8; 49:3). There are funerals everywhere in the land because the Lord has struck Moab. Its situation is compared to that of a broken jar that no one can salvage (19:10).

The wailing in **48:39** is a reminder of the command to wail in 49:20. It seems to evoke astonishment at what has happened to Moab, who is now ridiculed by all her neighbours. She dare not even look them in the face, but turns her *back in shame*.

The enormous eagle that swoops down over Moab is Nebuchadnezzar, king of Babylon (**48:40**). He is the one who will bring the destruction throughout Moab (and also throughout Edom – see 49:22). Kerith, which was mentioned in 48:24, and all the other important cities will fall into the hands of the Babylonian invader. The Moabite warriors will be thrown into disarray. They will be as overwhelmed and incapable of fighting as a woman in labour (**48:41**; see also 49:22; Isa 13:8; 21:3).

The pride and presumption of Moab are again presented as the reason for the Lord's judgment, which will destroy Moab and scatter its population (**48:42**). No one will escape. All that awaits them is *terror and pit and snare* (**48:43**). In the original Hebrew, this threat is underscored by the repetition, for all three of the Hebrew words used begin with the same letter. Thus the people are told that the fate that awaits them is *pahad, pahat* and *pat*.

The meaning of this threat is explained in **48:44**. They cannot escape danger. They are like the man described by the prophet Amos, who flees from a lion and meets a bear. When he takes refuge in a house, he leans gratefully against the wall – and is promptly bitten by a snake (Amos 5:19).

The words of **48:45-46** are almost identical to Numbers 21:28-29. It was an ancient song that celebrated the victory of Sihon king of the Amorites over Moab (Num 21:26) at a time when Heshbon was the capital of Moab, before Israel took over the region. The references to fire and flame emphasize the dreadfulness of this judgment on Moab, here called *the people of Chemosh* (48:46).

Yet the passage does not end with judgment. The Lord announces that he will bring the people of Moab back to their land (**48:47**). The exile will not be the end of the Moabites. The same thing is said of Egypt (46:26), of the Ammonites (49:6) and of the Elamites (49:39).

49:1-6 Against the Ammonites

The Ammonites were the descendants of the incestuous relationship between Lot's younger daughter and her father

(Gen 19:38). Their territory was situated to the east of the Jordan, north of Moab (Deut 2:19).

After the conquest of Israel by the Assyrians and the deportation of its population in about 722 BC (2 Kgs 17), the Ammonites had taken over the territory of Gad (**49:1**; Josh 13:24-28). The NIV has the prophet asking, *Why then has Molech taken possession of Gad?* Molech was the god worshipped by the Ammonites. However, the word here translated by 'Molech' is actually *Malcam* in Hebrew, which may also mean 'their king' (KJV).

Rabbah was the capital of Ammon (**49:2**; 2 Sam 12:26), situated in present-day Jordan and now known as Amman. The Lord announces that he will fight against this capital and its *surrounding villages* (*her daughters* – KJV). He will restore to Israel the property that Ammon had taken.

Heshbon is also mentioned in the judgment on Moab (48:2). It may be that this city had also come under Ammonite control by the time of the events reported in this prophecy (**49:3**, 48:34; Judg 11:26; Isa 15:4-5). Heshbon is to lament the destruction of *Ai*, an Ammonite town that should not be confused with the Canaanite town with the same name (Josh 7:2; 8:1).

The towns dependent on the capital of the Ammonites are told to go into mourning, because their king has been taken captive (for *Molech*, see comment on 49:1). Though the Bible does not mention this destruction of Ammon, the Jewish historian Flavius Josephus maintains that Nebuchadnezzar destroyed Ammon during the twenty-third year of his reign (582 BC). The king of Ammon is here presented as going into exile with his priests and his officials.

We do not know exactly why Ammon was so proud of its valleys (**49:4**). We may, however, guess. First, the reference to their fruitfulness and the fact that they are associated with *riches* suggests that these valleys played an important role in Ammon's economy. The crops grown there must have brought much wealth to the country. The fact that the question *Who will attack me?* is asked in the same context may also indicate that these valleys played an important role in the nation's military strategy.

Despite all of Ammon's confidence in its economic and military resources, the Lord says that he will send *terror* on it from all sides. It will be destroyed and its population will flee (**49:5**).

However, the Lord promises Ammon that he will restore it (**49:6**). An identical promise has been made to Egypt (46:26) and to Moab (48:47). This promise testifies to both the goodness of the Lord towards the nations of the earth and his sovereignty over all the nations.

49:7-22 Against Edom

The oracle against Edom is very similar to that given in the short book of Obadiah. Biblical tradition presents a very negative image of Edom. At the time of the fall of Jerusalem

in 587 BC, the Edomites, though they were related to the Israelites and the Judeans, were on the side of the enemies of Judah and pillaged it. Their behaviour led all the prophets and other biblical writers after this event to denounce Edom (Lam 4:21-22; Ps 137:7; Ezek 25:12; 35:15).

The region of *Teman* in Edom enjoyed a reputation for the wisdom of its people (**49:7**). One of Job's friends is described as a Temanite (Job 2:11). Thus the mere question of whether there *is no longer wisdom in Teman,* or whether they now lack counsel, is an indication that disaster has befallen the country of Edom.

Dedan seems to have been the name of a person before it became the name of an Edomite city (**49:8**; 25:23). Because of the coming disaster, its inhabitants are told to flee and seek refuge in caves (see Isa 2:19). The disaster will fall on *Esau,* the ancestor of Edom (Gen 25:30; 36:1, 8).

The metaphor in **49:9** indicates that nothing will remain after the judgment on Edom. These verses are almost identical to Obadiah 5-6.

Although the people of Edom will try to hide, their attempts will fail because the Lord will *uncover* their *hiding places* (**49:10**). Like their neighbours, they *will perish*. The reference to their orphans and widows having to turn to God for protection is an indirect assertion that all the men will have been killed (**49:11**).

The image of the cup of the Lord's anger occurs again in **49:12** (see 25:15-29; 48:26). How can Edom hope to escape the judgment when even Judah, the Lord's own people, are not spared? (There is an element of ambivalence here for it is well known that Judah deserved the punishment it received.)

The capital of Edom was *Bozrah* (Isa 34:6; a different city with the same name is mentioned in relation to Moab – 48:24). Like all the other cities of Edom, Bozrah will be reduced to ruins (**49:13**; see also Amos 1:12).

Edom's strong geographic location among the *rocks* and on the *heights of the hill* had made it proud. But the Lord announces that no matter how high and secure Edom thinks it is, he will bring it down (**49:14-16**; see also Job 39:27; Isa 14:13-15). These verses are identical to Obadiah 1-4.

Edom's degradation and humiliation will be so great that *all who pass by will be appalled* (**49:17**; 18:16). Its fate will be the same as that of *Sodom and Gomorrah,* which were uninhabitable after God's judgment had come on them (**49:18**). This is the second time that the prophet uses the names of these two cities that had known a frightful destruction (23:14), and he will speak of them again (50:40).

Verses 49:19-20 are almost identical to 50:44-46. The Lord will come like a lion, chase Edom from its land and install someone else to rule it. He asks three questions, the answers to all of which show his supreme position (**49:19**). His supremacy entitles him to make decisions about Edom, and now he announces what he has decided: Edom will be dominated and its territory destroyed (**49:20**). Its fall will arouse cries that will be heard far and wide, even as far as the Red Sea (**49:21**).

The first part of **49:22** is identical to 48:40, except that here it is evidently against Edom that the invader is *spreading its wings*. The image of the woman in labour expresses the profound pain that accompanies it and the anguish associated with the risks of giving birth (see 48:41). The warriors of Edom will have no more heart for war.

49:23-27 Against Damascus

The oracle against Damascus is the shortest of Jeremiah's oracles against pagan nations. No mention is made of the cause or causes of the judgment that will strike the city, but a comparison with the prophet Amos (Amos 1:3, 5) gives us some idea of the city's guilt.

Damascus, which is today the capital of Syria, was the capital of the land of the Arameans (2 Sam 8:5; 1 Chr 18:6). The city is also mentioned in the NT, particularly in relation to events surrounding the conversion and call of the Apostle Paul (Acts 9; 22:5-11; 26:12-20; Gal 1:17).

The oracle begins by announcing that *Hamath* and *Arpad* have received *bad news* (**49:23**). Hamath was a city situated to the north of Damascus and is sometimes spoken of as a country (39:5; 2 Chr 8:4). Arpad was also a city and may have been situated north of Aleppo (2 Kgs 19:13). What happens to these cities is compared to a turbulent sea whose waves are never calm.

Damascus is in the same situation as the two cities mentioned in the preceding verse (**49:24**). It tries to flee, but is paralysed by fear and anguish. It is seized with the same type of pains as the warriors of Edom in the preceding oracle (49:22; 6:24; Isa 13:8).

The comment in **49:25** seems to be made by an inhabitant of the country, or perhaps even by the king of Damascus. He is surprised at the calamity that has struck the city that, in earlier times, was his pride and joy.

The *streets* of Damascus will be littered with the bodies of its young men. As for the warriors, those who should protect and, if need be, free the city, they are reduced to silence, proof of their total lack of power (**49:26**).

The oracle ends with an announcement of the burning of the city of Damascus and of the fortresses of the king of Syria (**49:27**; Amos 1:4). The name *Ben-Hadad* does not refer to any particular person; it was the title used to refer to any king of Syria (1 Kgs 20:1-2; 2 Kgs 6:24).

49:28-33 Against Kedar and Hazor

The next oracle is addressed to both *Kedar* and *the kingdoms of Hazor*. Kedar was the name of one of Ishmael's sons, a grandson of Abraham and Hagar (Gen 25:13). In this oracle, however, the name refers to a nomadic Arab tribe that lived in

the Syrian desert (2:10). They are often mentioned in the OT (Ps 120:5; Song 1:5; Isa 21:16-17; 42:11; 60:7; Ezek 27:21).

Hazor should not be confused with the city by the same name situated to the north of the Sea of Galilee (Josh 11:1; 1 Kgs 9:15; 2 Kgs 15:29; Neh 11:33). Here, Hazor refers to a group of semi-nomadic Arab tribes, including Dedan, Tema and Buz (25:23-24).

This group of tribes had been defeated by Nebuchadnezzar (**49:28a**). According to Babylonian records, this defeat of Arab tribes took place in 599-598 BC.

The oracle begins with an explicit instruction from the Lord to go and destroy Kedar, who are also referred to as the *people of the East* (**49:28b**). This expression (or the equivalent phrase, 'eastern peoples') is quite frequent in the OT (Gen 29:1; Judg 6:3, 33; 7:12; 8:10; Job 1:3; Isa 11:14; Ezek 25:10). It refers to the tribes living in the desert to the east of the Jordan. These people are often mentioned in conjunction with the Midianites and Amalekites (Judg 6:3).

The Babylonians will take everything that the people of Kedar own. The list includes *tents ... flocks ... shelters ... goods* and *camels*, indicating that these people are semi-nomadic shepherds (**49:29a**).

Once again we hear the shout of *terror on every side* (**49:29b**; see 20:4, 10; 46:5). The terror experienced by the people of Kedar is linked to the plots that Nebuchadnezzar is making against the inhabitants of Hazor. This is why the people of Hazor are told to flee and find hiding places (**49:30a**; 48:6; 49:8).

Whereas in 49:20 it was the Lord who developed a plan against Edom, here in **49:30b** it is the king of Babylon who does so against Hazor. But all he will be doing is carrying out the judgment of the Lord (49:28).

The Babylonians are to attack a nation that has enjoyed considerable security. As those who have lived in tents in the desert, their homes have had neither doors nor bars (**49:31**). Their wealth was in their *large herds* of camels and other livestock, but these will all be driven off by their conquerors (**49:32**). The Lord's action against them is compared to that of a farmer winnowing his grain to separate it from the chaff (see Matt 3:12). In the context of this verse, the idea of their being scattered in all directions by the wind suggests that they too will be exiled. They will experience *disaster ... from every side,* an expression that reminds us of the 'terror on every side' spoken of in 49:29. Hazor will be left desolate, a place that is inhabited only by jackals (**49:33**; 9:11; 10:22; 51:37).

49:34-39 Against Elam

Unlike the last four oracles against Moab, Ammon, Edom and Kedar, the oracle against Elam is dated. The Lord addressed it to Jeremiah at the beginning of the reign of Zedekiah, king of Judah (**49:34**). We can thus date it to about 597 BC.

Elam was situated to the east of Babylon (25:25; Isa 21:2). Its capital was Susa (Ezra 4:9; Dan 8:2). Elamites were among the crowd gathered at Jerusalem on the day of Pentecost (Acts 2:9).

The first thing said of Elam is that Lord will break the nation's *bow*, which was a symbol of its power (**49:35**). To fully appreciate this threat, we have to know that the bowmen of Elam were famous in the ancient Near East (Isa 22:6). To break the bow of such a nation is not only to destroy its military power but also to seriously damage its pride.

Elam will be assaulted by *the four winds* from the *four quarters of the heavens*, an image used often in the ot (**49:36**; Ezek 37:9; Dan 8:8; Zech 6:1-8). The nation will be scattered and dispersed among all the surrounding countries. The entire nation of Elam will be wiped out by the effects of the Lord's *fierce anger* (**49:37**).

49:38 eloquently expresses Elam's defeat. Another throne will be set up there, incontrovertible evidence that it is being forced to submit to the domination of a foreign power (1:15; 43:8-13). The nation's own king and princes will all be killed.

However, the Lord promises that he will allow the Elamite exiles to return (**49:39**). The same promise was made to Egypt (46:26), Moab (48:47) and Ammon (49:6).

50:1-51:64 Against Babylon

The oracle against Babylon closes the series of oracles against pagan nations. This prophecy is the longest of all, occupying two entire chapters of the book of Jeremiah. This shows both the importance accorded to Babylon in Jeremiah's time and the great guilt of this nation, which has sinned against the Lord. Two themes predominate: the fall of Babylon and the return of the exiles from Israel and Judah.

50:1-51:58 The oracle

After the title verse that indicates that the oracle concerns Babylon (**50:1**), there is a long invitation to make public the news concerning Babylon's fall (**50:2a**). There are no less than five verbs by which the Lord asks that this be published: *announce, proclaim, lift up a banner, keep nothing back* and *say*. The event is so important, and also perhaps so surprising, that the whole world must know it. Babylon has fallen into the hands of those who are stronger than her.

The Babylonian god, who was known both as *Bel* and as *Marduk*, and all the secondary divinities will be thrown into confusion, shame and terror by the defeat of Babylon (**50:2b**; 51:44; Isa 46:1). The prophet's contempt for these gods is clear from the fact that the word translated *idols* literally means 'rubbish'.

The reason the images are *put to shame* is that a nation coming from the north will sow destruction in Babylon (**50:3**). The country will be transformed into a desert such that humans and animals will no longer know where to go.

This nation coming from the north is not identified, but disasters often come from the north in the book of Jeremiah (1:14; 4:6; 6:1; 15:12; 46:20; 47:2).

While Babylon will experience utter confusion, the Israelites and Judeans will live out their gratitude (**50:4**). This will primarily be a spiritual rebirth. The two nations walking together will shed tears of repentance and will seek the Lord their God. They will seek the road to *Zion* and will *turn their faces towards it* (**50:5**). They will encourage each other to enter into an eternal covenant with the Lord (31:31; 32:40; Isa 55:3; 61:8; Ezek 37:26).

Before the Lord's intervention that is described in this oracle, the shepherds (that is, the political and religious leaders) had failed to carry out their responsibility to guide the people in accordance with the Lord's instructions (2:8; 5:31). Instead, they had led them on the path of idolatry, which had taken them far from the knowledge of God (32:32). Consequently, the people had been handed over to their enemies, who overcame them (**50:6-7**). But now, in anticipation of the destruction that is going to happen to Babylon and the salvation that will come to Judah, the Lord encourages his people to leave the land of Babylonia (**50:8**; 51:6). After the first deportation, Jeremiah had told the exiles to settle in Babylon and to live normal lives there (29:5-7). But the time for that it is over. It is now time to leave.

The *alliance of great nations* that is going to come against Babylon *from the north* is sent by the Lord (**50:9**). They are, in fact, a coalition of Medes and Persians and their allies (51:27-28). These nations will take Babylon by force and will seize all the wealth that it has accumulated (**50:10**).

Judah's adversaries had rejoiced over the bad treatment that they had meted out to the Lord's people (**50:11**). They had plundered the Lord's *inheritance*, that is, the land of Israel, the people of God. This land was God's property (10:16; 16:18). But although they now rejoice and *frolic* and *neigh like stallions*, the day is coming when their own mother will suffer disgrace. This *mother* is Babylon (**50:12**). She is the mother of all the enemies of Judah, and so she will be reduced to be being *the least of the nations* of the earth. She has roused *the Lord's anger*, and thus will be left uninhabited, uninhabitable and the object of scorn (**50:13**). In fact, she will be left in exactly the same state to which she formerly reduced other cities (34:22; 44:6). Her state will shock all those who pass near her (see also 49:17).

Those who are to attack Babylon are told not to hold back. They are to *spare no arrows* (**50:14**). The city will surrender, although the expression translated *surrenders* could more literally be translated 'has given her hand' (NKJV), as if appealing for help (see Lam 5:6, NKJV – *We have given our hand to the Egyptians and the Assyrians, to be satisfied with bread*). But all appeals for help will be useless. The city's foundations will be undermined and its *towers* and *walls* will collapse in rubble (**50:15**). There will probably be a famine, for crops will neither be sown nor reaped (**50:16**). Faced with the double threat of famine and *sword,* all those whom Babylon has captured and taken into exile will take flight and try to return to their countries of origin.

In case we should forget why Babylon is suffering this fate, we are reminded of the sufferings of Israel, here thought of as comprised of all God's chosen people. The nation is compared to a *scattered flock* and those who persecute her to *lions* (**50:17**). The first 'lion' that devoured part of the flock was *the king of Assyria.* This king was Tiglath-Pileser, who in 722 BC overthrew King Pekah of Israel, captured his capital Samaria and deported the inhabitants of the northern kingdom to his country (2 Kgs 15:29; 17:1-6). The last 'lion' to have fed on Israel was Babylon and Nebuchadnezzar (2 Kgs 24:1). The reference to the crushing of their bones alludes to the fall of Jerusalem, the capital of Judah, in 587 BC.

The Lord Almighty, the God of Israel, declares that he will intervene to avenge his people (**50:18**). Indeed, he has already avenged Israel against the Assyrians. Nineveh, the capital of Assyria, fell in 612 BC (Nah 3:1-7; Zeph 2:13-15). Like Assyria, Babylon will be punished and will also fall. In these two cases, the king represents the whole of the population of his country. It is therefore not the king alone who is the target of the Lord's judgment, but the entire country.

The enemies of the Lord's people will be punished, but Israel will be restored (**50:19**). The neglected, scattered and preyed-on flock (50:6-8; 17) will again return to its *own pasture.* The first two places mentioned in this verse, *Carmel* and *Bashan,* were fertile regions, which were good for raising livestock (see Isa 35:2; Mic 7:14). *Ephraim* and *Gilead* were also areas that belonged to Israel. Israel's return to those regions will be proof that the exile is over and that the people have regained their political independence.

This time of political restoration will also be a time of spiritual renewal as the Lord forgives *Israel's guilt* and *the sins of Judah* (**50:20**; 31:34; 33:8; 36:3). The picture of someone searching for guilt but being unable to find it is a beautiful illustration of what the Lord's pardon means. His forgiveness is complete. He never again remembers what he has pardoned (Ps 103:12; Mic 7:18-20).

The text returns to the theme of judgment against Babylon with another message addressed to her enemies. They are told to attack *the land of Meratham* (**50:21a**). The word 'Merathaim' means 'double rebellion'. The prophet may possibly have been playing on words by combining the idea of rebellion against God with the name of a region to the south of Babylon. There may be further wordplay in the reference to *Pekod,* a word that means 'punishment' and resembles 'Puqudu', the name of a nation living near the Tigris River. Again the attackers are told not to hold back, but to *pursue, kill and completely destroy them* (**50:21b**). There will be *great destruction* (**50:22**).

We hear exclamations of surprise at Babylon's fall (**50:23**). The Babylonians had been like a *hammer,* a powerful implement used as a weapon of war by the Lord to punish his people Israel, as well as other nations (51:20-23; Isa 10:5; 14:5-6).

Babylon has fallen into the trap the Lord set for it (**50:24**). This image seems to indicate the suddenness of its capture by the Medes and Persians (51:8; Isa 47:11). It seems that the Babylonians had not understood that they were acting on God's behalf when they attacked Judah. They had carried out their assigned task with pride and cruelty, and in so doing had exceeded their mission and had ended up attacking the Lord himself. The Lord now needs to deal with those who had formerly been his instruments, and so he calls people from the ends of the earth to come and complete the ruin of Babylon (**50:25-26**). As in 50:21, the attackers are told to *completely destroy* her (see comment on 25:9c).

The *young bulls* who are to be slaughtered probably represent the princes of Babylon or the best warriors in the land (**50:27**). Their fate is similar to that of the young men of Moab (48:15). Their day may have come, but it is not a day of achievement – rather, a day of slaughter and punishment.

Fugitives from Babylon will bring news of its fall all the way to Jerusalem. Hearing them, the Judeans will understand that the Lord has avenged all the disasters that the Babylonians inflicted on them (**50:28**). In particular, he has avenged the pillaging and burning of his temple by Nebuchadnezzar's troops when they captured Jerusalem (2 Kgs 25:13-17; 2 Chr 36:18-19).

Babylon's arrogance and pride are the causes of the judgment that *the Lord, the Holy One of Israel* (**50:29**; see Isa 1:4) has brought on Nebuchadnezzar's country. His people will suffer what he had made other nations suffer (Rev 18:6). God's judgment will be total and no one will escape, not even the *young men* or the *soldiers.* The bodies of the former will litter the *streets* while the latter will be *silenced,* absolutely terrified by what is happening to them (**50:30**). They will share the experience of the inhabitants of Damascus (49:26).

The Lord clearly declares his opposition to the people of Babylon because of their pride (**50:31**). Consequently, Babylon is going to fall so hard that she will never rise again. No one will come to *help her up.* Her cities will be burned just as she burned the cities of others (**50:32**).

We now return to the situation in Israel and Judah. As the prophet speaks, they are still oppressed and held prisoner (**50:33**). Their captors will not release them or allow them to return home (Isa 14:17). In this respect, their situation is similar to that of their distant ancestors, whom Pharaoh had refused to allow to leave Egypt (Exod 7:14, 22; 8:28; 9:2, 7; 10:20). But the Israelites had been delivered from Egypt, and the one who had brought about that deliverance is now working on behalf of the exiled Israelites and Judeans. He is called their *Redeemer*, the one who will save them and be kind to them (**50:34**). He is *strong*, which means that he is capable of forcing the oppressors to free his people. His name is the *Lord Almighty*. He will appear as their advocate, defending them in the court of justice, and he will win the case. He will free his people from exile just as he saved them long ago from slavery in Egypt (32:21) and he will throw the Babylonians who had held the Israelites as prisoners into confusion.

The next section, 50:35-38, consists of short intense sentences, almost all of which contain the word *sword*. The only exception is **50:38**, where the word 'sword' is replaced with the word *drought* (which has the same consonants as 'sword' in Hebrew). The destructive sword is first directed at the inhabitants of Babylon, *her officials and wise men* (**50:35**). It then attacks Babylon's *false prophets* (Isa 47:12-13), who will *become fools*. The sword will also strike the *warriors*, who *will be filled with terror* (**50:36**). The weapons of war, *horses and chariots*, will not be spared as the sword strikes them, as well. It will also strike all the foreigners in Babylon, who will become like women, who do not ordinarily take part in battle (51:30; Isa 19:16; Nah 3:13). The sword will carry off all of Babylon's riches (**50:37**). As if to complete the devastation, drought will grip the land (**50:39**). The streams of water will dry up, making agriculture and raising animals impossible. The numerous idols that filled the land of Babylon will be able to do nothing to save the Babylonians. Their utter weakness will mean that people *will go mad with terror*.

Babylon's destruction will be so great that no human being will live there any longer. Only wild animals will be found there (50:39). The comparison with *Sodom, Gomorrah* and *their neighbouring towns* gives an even clearer idea of the greatness of the catastrophe that will befall Babylon (**50:40**). This is the third time that the prophet has compared a situation with that of Sodom and Gomorrah, but the reasons for the comparison are not the same in all three cases. In 23:14, the comparison was between the enormity of the sin of Judah's prophets and the sin of the people of those two cities. But in 49:18 and here, it is the level of devastation of the cities and the consequences of the devastation that are compared.

What was said in 6:22-24 is repeated in **50:41-43a**, but this time the invaders are coming to attack Babylon, not Zion. They are described as *a great nation* with powerful kings and as coming *from the north*. The whole description points to the coalition of the Medes and Persians and their allies (see 50:9; 51:27-28). They are skilled in the use of weapons of war such as *bows* and *spears*, (6:23; Job 39:23; Neh 4:11, 17). They show no *mercy* and the sound of their approach is like the noise of the waves of the sea. Mounted on horseback and in strict *battle formation*, they are advancing on Babylon.

When the king of Babylon learns that they are approaching and recognizes what will become of him and his country, his strength fails him and a terrible anguish and *pain like that of a woman in labour* takes hold of him (**50:43b**).

The prophecies made against Edom in 49:19-21 are now repeated in **50:44-46**, But whereas the fall of Edom provoked a cry that was heard as far away as the Red Sea, the fall of Babylon will create an even greater cry that will be heard in all the nations. We can speculate that in Israel and Judah this cry will be heard as the announcement that they will soon be delivered by the Lord (50:28).

The Babylonians are again referred to using a code word, *Leb Kamai*, which means 'the heart of my enemies' in Hebrew. The Lord will direct a destroying wind against them (**51:1**). The picture of winnowing speaks of judgment (**51:2**; 15:7), which will be implemented by foreigners who will come from all sides to destroy Babylon.

The beginning of **51:3** has been translated differently in various versions, which shows that the text involves some difficulties. The idea seems to be brought out in the NIV, namely, that there will be no resistance by the Babylonians. Yet despite this, the enemies are asked to show no mercy to the young soldiers and are to exterminate the entire army (see also 50:21). The Babylonian warriors will be killed and their bodies will litter the streets of the city (**51:4**).

The prophet returns to the situation of Israel and Judah. Despite their guilt in the Lord's eyes, these two nations have not been abandoned by their God (see also Isa 54:4-8). However, it is also possible that the *land* in **51:5** may refer to the land of the Babylonians. In that case, this verse involves a comparison of the situation of Babylon, guilty and judged, with that of Israel and Judah, which are upheld and delivered by the Lord.

The prophet urges the Israelites to leave Babylon quickly so that they are not caught up in the judgment that the Lord is sending on the Babylonians (Rev 18:4). This same call to flee from Babylon was also given in 50:8. This is a time for *the Lord's vengeance*. Israel should not take the risk of staying there and sharing Babylon's fate (**51:6**).

The image of a cup is again used to represent the Lord's anger (**51:7**; 25:15; 49:12). Babylon was *a gold cup in the Lord's hands*, which he forced the nations to drink from. Judah and Jerusalem in particular had to drink from that cup (13:12-13; 49:12-13). But after having been used as the instrument of the Lord's judgment, Babylon will be judged in her turn. She too will drink the cup of the Lord's anger and will unexpectedly *fall and be broken* (**51:8**). The call to wail over her and to try desperately to heal her wound indicates that Babylon's situation is truly serious.

The identity of those who act and speak in **51:9** is not clear. It may be the Israelites who wanted to heal Babylon, but found it impossible. Her case is hopeless: *her judgment reaches to the skies*. The only thing left to do is to abandon her and return to their own countries.

In **51:10**, however, the voices are clearly those of Judeans who have returned from exile in Babylon. By judging their former enemies, the Lord has brought justice to his people (see 50:28; Ps 37:6). He has avenged them and has given them reason for gratitude. The people are invited to *tell in Zion* what *God has done* (**51:10**; Ps 105:1-3).

Then the scene returns to the attack against Babylon (**51:11**). The Lord is determined to destroy Babylon. This destruction will be his vengeance for the temple that the Babylonians had destroyed (see 50:28). To accomplish this task, he has chosen and prepared *the kings of the Medes*. The use of the plural here does not means that the Medes had several kings at once, or that the action was carried out by several successive Median kings. It is simply a reference to the fact that a number of kings were allied with the Medes (see 50:41). The most prominent among these at the time of Babylon's fall was the king of Persia. It is possible that the Persians are not mentioned here because in Jeremiah's time they were not a powerful force.

We can watch the preparation for the final assault on Babylon (**51:12**). The *guard* is reinforced to be sure that the action is successful. *Watchmen* are to be on the alert so that they can observe any movement by the people in the city. An *ambush* will be set to catch any who try to flee.

Babylon is described as being near *many waters* (**51:13**). These waters are the Euphrates River and the numerous irrigation canals that had been dug around the city (Ps 137:1). Babylon was also *rich in treasures*. Some of this wealth was its own, but much of it had been obtained by pillaging other nations. We see this particularly in relation to Judah and Jerusalem (52:12-13, 17-23; 2 Kgs 24:13; 25:13-17; Dan 5:2-4). But now, the city's life of luxury and its legendary greed are all coming to an end. It will be invaded by those who are as numerous and as destructive as *a swarm of locusts* (**51:14**; see also Nah 3:15). They will take the city and will yell in triumph within it. There can be no doubt that this is coming, for the Lord has sworn it by his own name (see also 49:13).

We now encounter another example of similar texts in different places in the book of Jeremiah, for **51:15-19** repeats 10:12-16 (see comments on those verses).

Babylon was earlier compared to a 'hammer' (50:23) and now the nation is described as the Lord's *war club* (**51:20a**). Precise information is then given on the various things that the Lord has shattered with his 'club' or 'hammer': there were *nations, kingdoms, horses* and *riders, chariots* and *drivers* (**51:20b-21**; see Isa 41:15-16). There were also *men* and *women, old* and *young,* all victims of Babylonian barbarity (**51:22**; see 2 Chr 36:17). The *shepherd* and his *flock,* the *farmer* and his *oxen, governors* and *officials* were all equally

struck by the Babylonian club (**51:23**, 57). No one escaped the terrible treatment inflicted by the Babylonians, no matter what their age, sex or social class. But all these details serve to underline the guilt of the 'club' itself. That is why the Lord will repay Babylon and its inhabitants for what they have made Zion suffer (**51:24**).

Babylon is now compared to a *destroying mountain* (**51:25**; see Zech 4:7). The idea is the same as that found in 51:20-23. This nation had crushed many other nations on earth, but now it faces destruction. The 'destroying mountain' will itself be burned. The Lord will set fire to it and it will burn so completely that nothing can be salvaged, not even a rock that one could use for the cornerstone or foundation of a house (**51:26**).

The summons to war against Babylon is again issued (**51:27**). It is addressed to a number of nations and kingdoms. *Ararat* was a kingdom to the north of Mesopotamia, to the east of present-day Turkey. Some identify it with Armenia (Gen 8:4). *Minni* was in the north-west of Iran, and *Ashkenaz*, the kingdom of the Scythians, lay to the north and east of the Black Sea (Gen 10:3). All of these nations will unite against Babylon. Officers will be hired to be responsible for recruiting warriors for the battle against the Babylonians. The list of Babylon's adversaries concludes with the *Medes* and all their allies (**51:28** see 51:11).

As the Lord's plan against Babylon become apparent, the very earth shakes. It *trembles and writhes* (**51:29**; see 10:10). Babylon will soon be transformed into an immense desolation where no one can live. Meanwhile, its warriors have lost heart and have withdrawn into their fortresses (**51:30**). They are behaving like women, who had no role to play in fighting (see 50:37). Behind them, the abandoned city is burning. We see messengers coming in from all directions to inform the king of Babylon that his city has fallen (**51:31**; 50:2). They also tell him that *the river crossings* have been seized, the protecting *marshes set on fire* and that all his soldiers are *terrified* (**51:32**).

In **51:33** the scene shifts from these vivid images of war to two metaphors that describe what is happening. The city of Babylon is being threshed (see also 51:2) and harvested (Joel 3:13; Mic 4:12-13; Mark 4:29; Rev 14:15-16).

The inhabitants of Zion now speak to remind us of the evil that the king of Babylon did to Jerusalem when he captured the city and deported all who lived there (**51:34**; see 50:17). It is as if those taken to Babylon were swallowed by a monster. The Judeans ask that the Babylonians be punished for the evil done to them (**51:35**), evil that is expressed as *violence done to our flesh* and *our blood*.

In reply to Zion's request, the Lord promises that he will avenge his people and judge Babylon by sending it drought (**51:36**). Babylon's *sea* is the great Euphrates River, whose springs will dry up. Because of this, the country will be transformed into a desert, *a haunt of jackals*, without human beings. Observers will be both surprised and scornful (**51:37**; 25:9).

The Babylonians are compared to lion cubs who *roar* and *growl* from hunger (**51:38**; 2:15). But the Lord is preparing a feast for them. However, what he will give them to eat, or rather to drink, is the cup of his anger. They will drink it, will become drunk and will sleep their final sleep (**51:39**). They will never awaken. The Lord will bring them down to the abattoir to be killed as *lambs, rams* and *goats* are killed (**51:40**; 48:15; 49:27).

Once again, the prophet stresses the surprise that the fall of Babylon will provoke (**51:41**). Here the city is again referred to by the code name *Sheshach,* which was also used in 25:26. Babylon considered itself to be the centre of the universe, the glory of the whole earth, a fact that is expressed by its pride and haughtiness (49:25). But it has fallen, completely destroyed. Two apparently opposite images express its condition: on the one hand, it is a victim of the waters, swallowed by the waves of the sea (**51:42**; 46:7; 47:2; Isa 8:7); on the other hand, it has become a desert (**51:43**). What both these images have in common is that they both represent places *where no one lives.* Both the flood and the desert evoke devastation and death.

Bel is another name for the Babylonian god Marduk (**51:44**; 50:2), who had swallowed the people that Babylon held captive, including Judah (see also **51:34**). He will be forced to give up both the people he has taken and the riches that he carried off from the temple at Jerusalem (2 Chr 36:18-19).

The Lord's people are urged to leave Babylon so as to avoid the coming judgment (**51:45**; see 50:8; 51:6). Apparently the fall of Babylon will drag the country into a long period of political instability. Rumours will fly, violence will spread and there will be fierce power struggles (**51:46**).

Babylon's judgment will also be a judgment of the idolatry practised there (**51:47**). The defeat of its idols will bring shame on the entire country as the warriors who could not resist the invader lie dead in the middle of the city. This defeat by troops from the north will bring cosmic rejoicing (**51:48**). *Heaven and earth and all that is in them* will rejoice at Babylon's fall, as if all the evil that she has done had affected them as well.

The Lord speaks to Judah's exiles in Babylon and tells them that the city that has caused so many deaths in Israel will fall, just as it has made other nations fall and has caused so many deaths *in all the earth* (**51:49**). Then he urges those who have survived the wars to flee Babylon and not to hang around in its vicinity. However, once they have put a safe distance between themselves and Babylon, they are to *remember the Lord* and *Jerusalem* (**51:50**).

The exiles' response to the Lord reveals something of their suffering as slaves in Babylon. They feel themselves *disgraced* and have insults thrown at them. But their deepest shame is that memory of the capture and destruction of the temple in Jerusalem by pagans (**51:51**).

The Lord responds by again announcing the judgment he will bring on Babylon (**51:52**). It is as if he wants to attest that there is absolutely no doubt that what he has said will take place. While it will be a judgment on Babylon's idols, there will also be many human victims. And it will be unavoidable, no matter what precautions Babylon may take to try to avoid it. It will make no difference if it attempts to raise itself to the skies (see Gen 11:4-9). Nor will it help to try to make the city impregnable by greatly increasing the height of its walls and towers. Destroyers who are sent by the Lord cannot be stopped (**51:53**).

We now come to the final description in this book of the catastrophe that awaits Babylon (51:54-58). It starts with *a cry,* probably a cry for help, followed by the *sound of great destruction* (**51:54**). The destroyers have arrived and are at work. The noise they make is like the roar of the waves of the sea (**51:55**; see 51:42). The elite soldiers of the Babylonian army are captured and their bows are broken. They will be of no further use. The Lord is doing to them what they have done to others (**51:56**).

It is not only the soldiers who suffer. God makes all the authority figures of Babylon also drink the cup of his anger. They become drunk and sleep the sleep of death (**51:57**; 51:39). They no longer have the right to speak. The only one who can still speak is *the King, whose name is the Lord Almighty,* who announces that the *walls* of Babylon will be destroyed and that its impressive *gates* will be burned, reducing to nothing all the effort put in by the builders of the city (**51:58**).

51:59-64 Delivering the oracle to Babylon

In the fourth year of the reign of Zedekiah (594 BC), he was summoned to Babylon by Nebuchadnezzar, possibly because there were questions about his loyalty, given his later rebellion against Babylon (**51:59**; see 27:3-12). One of those who was to accompany him to Babylon was a man called *Seraiah son of Neriah, the son of Mahseiah.* Before he set out on the journey, Jeremiah took him aside and gave him a scroll on which he had written his prophecies against Babylon (**51:60**). Seraiah was told to read this scroll aloud when he arrived in Babylon (**51:61-62**). After reading it, he is to carry out an acted prophecy similar to those that Jeremiah had used during his ministry in Jerusalem (27:2; 32:25; 43:9). Seraiah was to *tie a stone* to the scroll and to *throw it into the Euphrates* so that it would sink into the water (**51:63**). The meaning of this act is very clear. It is a message for Babylon. Just as the weight of the stone drags the scroll to the bottom of the river, so Babylon will be swallowed up and will never be able to recover from its fall (**51:64**).

It is impressive that the prophet Jeremiah wrote and made public such an announcement about fifty years before the fulfilment of his prophecy about the fall of Babylon.

52:1-34 Appendices

This final chapter of the book of Jeremiah is largely a repetition of 2 Kings 24:18-20, 25:1-21 and 25-30. It tells of the siege and capture of Jerusalem, the arrest of king Zedekiah and the rehabilitation of Jehoiachin. Many commentators think that this chapter was added to the book to show that Jeremiah's prophecies were actually fulfilled. Jerusalem was indeed taken and burned as Jeremiah had announced. King Zedekiah was arrested and his sons killed, just as Jeremiah had prophesied. And the rehabilitation of Jehoiachin can be seen as foreshadowing the restoration of Israel and Judah that the prophet had also predicted.

52:1-11 Zedekiah's fate

Zedekiah had been installed on the throne of Judah by Nebuchadnezzar to replace Jehoiachin whom he was deporting (2 Kgs 24:17). His mother's name was Hamutal (2 Kings 23:31). His maternal grandfather had the same name as Jeremiah (**52:1**).

His reign is given a negative evaluation by the author, who asserts that his actions resembled those of Jehoiakim (**52:2**). This type of positive or negative evaluation of a king's reign is common in the books of Kings and Chronicles (1 Kgs 15:11, 26, 34; 16:25, 30; 22:53; 2 Kgs 3:2; 8:18, 27; 24:19; 2 Chr 14:2; 22:4; 24:2; 25:2; 36:12-13).

The many sins of the people of Judah and Jerusalem aroused the Lord's anger (**52:3**) and brought disaster on them. The act that precipitated this disaster was Zedekiah's rebellion against the king of Babylon (see also 2 Kgs 24:20; 2 Chr 36:13). It seems that he was expecting Pharaoh of Egypt to side with him and help him to break free from Babylonian rule (37:5-8).

We are given very precise details (year, month and day) of the beginning of the Babylonian siege of Jerusalem and of its duration (**52:4-5**; 2 Kgs 25:1). The tactics employed by the Babylonian army are identical to those mentioned in 32:24.

On the *ninth day of the fourth month* of the eleventh year of Zedekiah's reign, Babylonian soldiers managed to break through the wall of Jerusalem and entered a city that had been severely weakened by famine (**52:6-7**; 39:4-10). Knowing that the city was now lost, the king, his sons, his close advisors and his army attempted to flee from the city under cover of night, hoping to escape the watchful eyes of the Babylonian sentries. Unfortunately, they were spotted and the king was captured and his soldiers scattered before they reached Jericho (**52:8**).

The king of Babylon had set up his camp at *Riblah*, south of *Hamath*, where Zedekiah was brought to him to hear what the penalty would be for having attempted to free himself from Babylonian rule (**52:9**; 27:3-8). Zedekiah was forced to watch as all his sons and all his officials were executed (**52:10**). Nebuchadnezzar also acted to make sure that these terrible sights would be the last things Zedekiah would ever see, for he then put out his eyes and had him chained and deported to Babylon. There he was thrown into prison (**52:11**).

52:12-30 Jerusalem's fate

Jerusalem is now left in the hands of *Nebuzaradan,* the commander of the imperial guard. The account of his actions that is given here covers the time from the nineteenth year of Nebuchadnezzar's reign (586 BC) to his twenty-third year (582 BC).

Nebuzaradan entered Jerusalem in July 586 BC and began the demolition of the city by burning all the buildings (**52:12**; 2 Kgs 25:8-21). He started with the *temple of the Lord* (see Ps 74:7; Isa 64:11; Mic 3:12). Then he burned the *royal palace* and, finally, all the houses and buildings in Jerusalem that were of any importance (**52:13**). Meanwhile the rest of his troops set about demolishing the walls that surrounded the city (**52:14**; 39:8; Neh 1:3).

When these tasks were completed, Nebuzaradan rounded up most of the people who were still in the area and carried them into exile (**52:15**; 39:9; 2 Kgs 25:11). He left only a few of the poorest people whom he *authorized to work the vineyards and fields* (**52:16**).

It was not only the people who were carried away; Nebuzaradan also took with him many things that had been removed from the temple of the Lord. These included the two great *bronze pillars* that stood before the temple, the *moveable stands* and the great *bronze* basin (used for ritual washing) that was known as the *Sea* and the bronze oxen on which it rested (**52:17, 20a**; 1 Kgs 7:15-24). They also carried off all the utensils of *gold, silver* and *bronze* (**52:18-19**; 1 Kgs 7:49-50). King Solomon had gone to great trouble and expense to have these made, even importing a particularly skilled craftsman from Tyre to do the bronze work (1 Kgs 7:13-51). Their loss would have been deeply felt by the people of Judah. But beyond the value of the articles carried away, what caused the deepest suffering of the people was the sight of unbelievers destroying the house of the Lord (51:51).

No one had any idea of how much bronze had been used in making the utensils for the temple (**52:20b**). The king had never done any calculations; he had simply set out to provide the best possible house for the Lord. But the quantity must have been enormous. For example, each of the two hollow columns in front of the temple was about twenty-seven feet (eight metres) high and had a circumference of roughly eighteen feet (five and a half metres). The bronze of which they were made was about three inches (eight centimetres) thick (**52:21**). Each of the columns was surmounted by a capital, also made of bronze, that was over seven feet (two metres) high. The capitals were decorated with a network of pomegranates, with ninety-six pomegranates on each (**52:22-23**).

We are given some information about the more important people who were rounded up. These included *Seraiah*, the *chief priest*, and *Zephaniah*, his assistant. Also mentioned, but without naming them, are the three priests who were *doorkeepers* (**52:24**). Nebuzaradan also took away *the officer in charge of the fighting men*, seven royal advisers, the *secretary* in charge of conscription for the Judean army *and sixty of his men* found in the city of Jerusalem (**52:25**). The Babylonian commander took this group to Nebuchadnezzar at Riblah (**52:26**). The king had them all killed (**52:27**, 10).

We are then told how many people were removed from Judah during the various deportations during Nebuchadnezzar's reign (**52:28**). In the seventh year of his reign (598 BC), 3023 Jews were deported. This number is smaller than that given in 2 Kings 24:14 and 24:16. It is possible that the number here represents only the men, while that in 2 Kings includes their families. In the eighteenth year (587 BC), 832 people were taken away (**52:29**) and in the twenty-third year (582 BC), 745 people (**52:30**).

52:31-34 Jehoiakim is Pardoned

The final section of the book of Jeremiah describes events during the reign of *Evil-Merodach*, the son and successor of Nebuchadnezzar, who reigned for a mere two years (561-559 BC). Jehoiachin's exile in Babylon had been foretold by the prophet Jeremiah in 22:24-30, and the fulfilment of that prophecy is recorded in 1 Kings 24:12-15.

The restoration of Jehoiachin to his royal privileges (even though he remained in exile) took place during the first year of Evil-Merodach's reign (**52:31**). It may have been one of the types of favours that kings often extended on their accession to the throne. What is striking is that Jehoiachin is still called *the king of Judah*, even though it is almost forty years since he had been removed from his throne in Jerusalem.

The new Babylonian sovereign treats Jehoiachin in a particularly kind way. Not only does he free him from prison, but he gives him a higher position than other kings taken

captive to Babylon and invites him to sit at his own table. This favourable treatment continued to the end of Jehoiachin's life. Since we know that Nebuchadnezzar's successor was king for only two years, this means that his successor must have had the same kind attitude towards the former king of Judah (**52:32-33**). The allowance that was given to Jehoiachin must have been sufficient to meet his personal needs and provide for the upkeep of any family members or servants who were with him in Babylon. His household was kept at the expense of the Babylonian court (**52:34**).

Jehoiachin's end must be seen as a foretaste of the rebirth of the entire nation of Israel and Judah. The people had suffered all the judgments that their numerous sins against the Lord their God had brought on them. Their country had been subjected to foreign powers, their cities taken, the temple at Jerusalem pillaged and burned down. The kings and people had been taken captive. All these disasters corresponded to the first aspect of Jeremiah's ministry, which was to tear down, destroy and overthrow (1:10).

Once all that has been done, Jeremiah's ministry could turn to building and planting. He then proclaimed the restoration of the nation and the new covenant that the Lord would one day conclude with his people (chs. 30–33). The restoration of Jehoiachin serves to confirm these promises to his people. It makes a statement that is even more strongly expressed in the book of Lamentations. First, the Lord is not rejecting his people forever and never willingly humiliates and afflicts them (Lam 3:31, 33). Second, the goodness of the Lord never ends, nor does his compassion ever completely fail (Lam 3:22). Finally, just as he afflicts his people because of their sin, so he shows them his great goodness and his mercy (Lam 3:32).

Issiaka Coulibaly

Further Reading

Craigie, Peter C., Page H. Kelley and Joel F. Drinkard, Jr. *Jeremiah 1–25*. WBC. Dallas: Word, 1991.

Guest, John. *Jeremiah, Lamentations*. CC. Waco, Tex: Word, 1988.

Keown, Gerald L., Pamela J. Scalise and Thomas G. Smothers. *Jeremiah 26–52*. WBC. Dallas: Word, 1995.

Thompson, John A. *The Book of Jeremiah*. NICOT. Grand Rapids: Eerdmans, 1980.

LAMENTATIONS

In most of our Bibles, Lamentations is located among the prophetic books, right after Jeremiah. However, in the Hebrew Bible this book was located in the third part of the canon, called the Writings. It was one of the five books that were read in the synagogue during the annual feasts. Ruth was read at the Feast of Ingathering (also known as the Feast of Weeks), the Song of Solomon was read at Passover, Ecclesiastes at the Feast of Tabernacles, Lamentations at the anniversary of the destruction of the temple in 587 BC and Esther at the Feast of Purim.

Circumstances and Date

The contents of the five poems that make up Lamentations reveal the circumstances in which they were written. After the death of King Josiah, the kingdom of Judah entered a period of increasing instability. An initial revolt against its Babylonian overlords in 597 BC led to the first siege of Jerusalem. The city fell and its elite were deported to Babylon. A second revolt in 589 BC provoked a second siege and the pillaging and destruction of the holy city. Many of its inhabitants were killed and most of the survivors were taken into captivity. Worst of all, the temple was burned (2 Kgs 25; 2 Chr 36:11-21).

Lamentations was probably composed very soon after 587 BC. The tone suggests that the author still has vivid memories of the atrocities he witnessed.

Literary Form: Lamentation or Complaint?

In the Hebrew Bible this book, like the books of the Pentateuch, derives its title from its first word, 'eyka', which means 'how' or 'oh!' It is a cry that combines astonishment and suffering. The English name 'Lamentations' was given to it because it is written in the style of a Hebrew lament or elegy. These laments were usually composed on the occasion of the death of an important person (see, for example, 2 Chr 35:25), although the Bible also contains traces of funeral laments for personified communities, cities and even countries. The problem with this name is that 'lamentation' is not an English literary style. Instead, the word is often associated with the self-pitying tears and moaning of someone who has given in to despair. However, the five poems that make up this book are far from despairing. On the contrary, in these pages suffering and misfortune are acknowledged, their cause is sought and found, and a happy future is foreseen after repentance and a return to God.

Lamentations consists of five poems, four of which are acrostics or alphabetical poems: that is, each verse begins with a letter of the Hebrew alphabet (which has 22 letters), used in order. Consequently chapters 1, 2 and 4 each have 22 verses. Chapter 5 also has 22 verses, but unlike the others, it is not alphabetical. The construction of the alphabetical poem reaches a higher level in chapter 3 where three consecutive verses each begin with the same letter, which means there are 66 verses (3 x 22) in that chapter.

Alphabetic poems are also found in places such as Psalms 9, 10, 25, 34, 37, 111, 112 and 119, and in Proverbs 30:10-31.

Authorship

A very old tradition preserved in the Greek (the Septuagint) and Latin (the Vulgate) translations of the Bible attributes the book to Jeremiah. Today a number of important theologians do not think that Jeremiah was the author, although they do admit that he had a great influence on the book. But they argue that he would not have written a call for vengeance like that in 3:59-66 or have looked to Egypt for help, as in 4:17, for he recommended submission to Babylon.

Others, however, cite the similarities between the contents of the books of Lamentations and Jeremiah. They cite the similarities between the contents of the books of Jeremiah and Lamentations. These similarities involve ideas, style and expression: for example, the references to the oppressed virgin (Lam 1:15; Jer 8:21), the eyes overflowing with tears (1:16; 2:11; Jer 9:1, 18), those who formerly loved the city now forgetting her (1:2; Jer 30:14), the theme of mocking and shaking of heads (2:15; Jer 18:16), the author's suffering as the laughingstock of the people (3:14, 63; Jer 20:7) and the cup of divine judgment (4:21; Jer 49:12). These theologians also argue that there is nothing in 3:59-66 that goes against what Jeremiah says elsewhere. He sometimes saw the Babylonians as God's instruments to punish his people and sometimes as cruel enemies. In relation to 4:17, these theologians point out that the text speaks only of 'a nation', and does not explicitly mention Egypt.

Even if there is no conclusive proof that Jeremiah is the author of Lamentations, there is little reason for refusing to ascribe it to him.

The Message of Lamentations

Lamentations contains more than just laments. The author realizes the importance of reflecting on his own suffering and that of his people. He seeks, and finds, the reasons for suffering and misfortune. The book thus models meditation on and during suffering so as to understand its place in the scheme of things, adopting the right attitude towards suffering and recognizing that suffering is not the end of everything. As he does this, the author of Lamentations deals with two important questions.

The first question relates to suffering, whether individual or collective. The question is not so much about the origin of suffering but about how to face it when it comes. Lamentations teaches us to express our sufferings, putting our distress into words that we address to God in prayer.

The second question is about the purpose of suffering. Even in the depths of suffering, it is possible to see a glimpse of light at the end of the tunnel. Suffering may be the path by which God leads us back to himself. There is thus a future for which to hope. This hope should be seized by an act of faith and stubborn will (3:21). We need to change the way we are thinking, to make a firm decision about what we are going to focus on. Despite appearances to the contrary, the author knows that the mercies of God have not failed. 'They are new every morning' (3:23). However, we need to lock onto them, centre our attention on them, and see everything that is happening around us through the prism of this truth.

Outline of Contents

COMMENTARY

1:1-22 Lament I: Jerusalem in Enemy Hands

This chapter introduces the book by presenting the setting and the situation. Disaster had befallen the kingdom of Judah in 587 BC. No one in the kingdom had imagined that such a thing could happen. It posed a critical question: Did the destruction of the temple and the taking of the nation into exile mean the end of the covenant between the Lord and his people? Were they no longer God's chosen people?

The chapter may be divided into two parts (1:1-11, 12-22). In the first part, the author describes the situation of the personified city. In the second, it is the city itself that speaks to express its pain and make its confession.

1:1-11 Jerusalem: The Widow in Mourning

The very first word of Lamentations expresses surprise and sorrow. *Eyka!*, it says in Hebrew (**1:1a**), which our English version translates as 'How!' This astonishment and mourning is a response to the current situation of Jerusalem. The city is like a widow who has lost both her husband (the Lord) and her children (its inhabitants). Yet no one goes into mourning with her. She has been abandoned in her solitude and misfortune.

There is a striking contrast between her present situation and the past. Yesterday the city was populated and renowned; she had *lovers* (**1:2**). This term refers to the nations with whom Judah made alliances in its struggle against Babylonian domination, rather than turning to the Lord, her husband. These nations included Egypt, Assyria, Edom, Moab and Ammon (Jer 2:36; 22:20; 27:3). But nothing is left of the past. She is now no more than a slave, seeking peace and rest without finding them (**1:1b, 3**; Deut 28:65).

None of the religious feasts are celebrated, because the Babylonians have destroyed the temple (**1:4**; 2 Kgs 25:13-17; Jer 52:13, 17). This event had traumatized the Judean community, for they had believed that the temple was indestructible. In fact, they had even regarded it as their insurance against all risks (Jer 7:4). It was inconceivable that foreigners would ever set foot in this holy place (**1:10**; Jer 51:51).

Then comes the first statement of a revelation that will be clarified later in the story: the affliction of the city is the work of the Lord himself and is because of Zion's sin (**1:5**). In other words, the Babylonians are nothing more than God's instruments (Hab 1:6).

A West African proverb says that 'Happiness is only appreciated when it is lost!' The truth of this saying is illustrated in **1:6-7**. It seems that only after the capture of the city that its inhabitants realized that treasures were now lost forever. Jerusalem remembered, but it was too late. The hand of the enemy had carried everything away. It is even possible, as the sad history of several countries in Africa and elsewhere teaches us, that the sons and daughters of Judah had collaborated with the enemy in pillaging and ruining their own homeland.

The author returns again to the reason for the misfortune: *Jerusalem has sinned greatly* (**1:8**). Because of that, it had become *unclean*. This term is also used for the menstrual impurity of a woman. In this condition, all women in Israel were ostracized from conjugal, social and cultural life. (Lev 12:2, 5; 15:19-30). There could be no better picture of the isolation of the city. Jerusalem hid herself but it was a lost cause because her uncleanness remained obvious: *her filthiness clung to her skirts* (**1:9a**).

The loneliness and pain of the abandoned city are emphasized by the words *there was none to comfort her* (**1:9b**). This theme will be repeated later. For the moment, Zion turns toward the Lord and begs him to look at her (**1:9c, 11b**). Unfortunately, the spectacle is not beautiful, even for God himself, because sacrilege is involved. The uncircumcised, those who are called 'blakoro' in the Djoula language of West Africa, are in the sanctuary (**1:10**). The spectacle is not beautiful for the city either: the inhabitants have been reduced to bartering their treasures for bread (**1:11a**). The author is alluding to the famine that gripped Zion (Jer 52:6). When it came to a choice between dignity (even when stripped of all else) – a dignity that would come with holding firmly to social, cultural and religious values – and survival at any price, the choice was quickly made. Dignity cannot be eaten!

1:12-22 No One Comforts Me!

The city, which has already interrupted the narrator twice (1:9, 11), now speaks for herself. She reproaches those who walk by without even bothering to stop and sympathize with her deep suffering (**1:12a**). She speaks out against indifference and the indifferent.

The city again acknowledges that her misfortune comes from God himself (see 1:5). Her reference to *the day of his fierce anger* (**1:12b**) reminds us of the frequent references to *the day of the Lord* in the prophetic literature in the OT (Isa 13:6, 9; Jer 46:10; Ezek 30:1-26). That day is a day of judgment.

Verses 1:13-15 describe how God's 'fierce anger' was shown against Jerusalem. Three phrases describe the severity of the Lord's judgment: *he sent fire, sent it down into my bones* (**1:13**); he placed a heavy yoke on the neck of his victim (**1:14**); he crushed the Judeans *in his winepress* (**1:15**).

The refrain *No one is near to comfort me* is repeated several times in this chapter (1:2, 16, 17, 21). It was not that the city was not seeking comforters, for *Zion stretches out her hands* (**1:17**). But now she has no friends, no allies, no comforters. The misery and repugnance of the city seems to have driven everyone away. The reference to being *an*

unclean thing in 1:17 uses the same word that we met in 1:8, which refers to the menstrual impurity of a woman.

Coupled with the city's indignation at the attitude of the indifferent is a double confession of faith and of sins: *The Lord is righteous, yet I rebelled against his command* (**1:18**). God is just in the sense that his actions are in perfect conformity with who he is. It is not because of any evil action by God that the city is in its present state. On the contrary, it is the city that rebelled against the commands of the Lord. Jerusalem tried to settle her own problems by crooked means. She tried to sort things out by herself. But her allies, her friends of the past, and her former lovers betrayed her (**1:19**). The result of her crime was that her young people, the future of the nation, went into exile (1:18) and the priests and elders died in their search for food (1:19)!

This first lament ends with the city calling on God again, inviting him to consider her distress (**1:20**). The confession of her sins has not relieved her misery. Externally as well as internally, she is affected by the evil. Those who are not being killed by the sword of the enemy are being struck down by famine (and likely plague).

As if tired of pleading, the city subsides into sighs and groans (**1:21-22**). In a final effort, she asks God for justice on the *day you have announced*, that is, the day of judgment on the nations. She seems to have understood that the instrument that God uses against her today will not escape his judgment tomorrow (Jer 51:24, 35-37).

2:1-22 Lament II: The Lord Is Angry

Like the previous chapter, this one is divided in two (2:1-12, 13-22). It too starts with the word 'Eyka'! This repetition makes it clear that the author has not yet recovered from the shock of the destruction of the city and of the temple, and that the suffering and tears have not yet ended.

2:1-12 The Lord: An Enemy?

The first lament suggested that the Lord was behind the attack by the Babylonians (1:12). The second lament is more explicit: The Lord's attitude to his people is that of an enemy. This section describes God's hostile and destructive actions against Zion. The words used include many OT expressions that generally refer to God's judgment, including *the day of his anger* (2:1), *fierce anger* and *fire* (2:3).

The divine anger has spared nothing. It covered with *cloud*, meaning shadow, the formerly much loved city (**2:1a**). Even the temple, the pride of Israel, was affected. Mount Zion, the part of the city of Jerusalem where the temple had stood (1 Kgs 8:1; Pss 20:2; 74:3), had been devastated, and the Lord's *footstool* (the ark of the covenant – 1 Chr 28:2; Ps 132:7) had been destroyed. Nothing had escaped his anger.

The Lord began a process of separating himself from his people. His decision not to remember them (**2:1b**) meant that he abandoned them, and thus spread death. The same idea is expressed by the verb *swallowed up* (**2:2, 5**). The breach between them expressed itself most clearly in his destruction of the *place of meeting*, the temple (**2:6**). By this act the Lord put an end to all cultural life: there would be no more feasts, no more Sabbaths. The king and the priests who were responsible for directing and maintaining the spiritual life of Israel were all wiped out.

But the author makes one important point clear: God is the owner of all he decides to destroy – the meeting place, the *altar* and the *sanctuary* are all *his* (**2:7**). It is as if the greatest priest of some ancestral religion had himself set fire to the sanctuary of the god and thus put an immediate end to all religious guardianship.

The final act of the rupture is a non-action. It is silence. The Lord does not speak, or rather, his prophets receive no further *visions* (**2:9**). The silence is that of desolation and mourning (**2:10**). Yet the city continues to weep. Even the innocents, little children and nursing babies, are suffering the pangs of hunger (**2:11**). Only their questions break the silence, and break their mothers' hearts. (Where were their fathers – all dead or taken away into exile?)

We may be surprised that even the children ask for wine: *Where is bread and wine?* (**2:12**). In the ot, wine is a symbol of joy (Isa 24:11; 25:6; Jer 48:33). However, in this case, what the children are asking for is simply basic everyday food. In African terms, the children are asking for fish and attiéké (a dish made with grated cassava), or bread and cheese. These are foods that belong together. 'Bread and wine' is the last dream of these small victims of adult politics; and with that dream, they die.

2:13-22 I Am Completely Broken!

In misfortune, we sometimes seek comfort in thinking of someone whose situation is worse than ours. It seems the author is doing so in **2:13**. He is looking for someone to comfort Zion, but can find no one because the disaster that has overtaken the city is so great. The reference to the sea accentuates the immensity of the catastrophe.

The tragedy is that Jerusalem's prophets had not fulfilled their roles as watchmen. Rather than revealing sin, they had preferred to say what people wanted to hear (Jer 23:14, 17). The situation was exactly like the one Paul would warn the young Timothy about many years later (2 Tim 4:3-4).

The *visions* of these prophets are described as *false and worthless*. Their *oracles* were *false and misleading* – a repetition that drives home their failure (**2:14**). Unfortunately, the same situation arises in many African countries ravaged by civil wars and natural calamities. Numerous 'prophets' arise and hold forth night and day. But when we listen to them carefully, we recognize on the one hand that their 'prophecies' are often contradictory (which is proof that some of them lie), and on the other hand, many of the prophets are simply seeking fame so that they can eat! This dramatic

situation highlights the church's failure to be the lighthouse that the entire nation seeks.

In **2:15**, we find a hint of a sad reality that few dare face. The misfortune of important people reassures ordinary people: 'We thought that such things happened only to the poor!' When important people are brought low, they are reduced to mere human beings. Thus, *the perfection of beauty* can become merely good looks, and the disappearance of *the joy of the whole earth* enhances the value of other joys. That is why the passersby find reason to laugh.

But the rejoicing of Jerusalem's enemies reveals a serious misunderstanding on their part. They regard the disastrous situation in which the city finds itself as their personal victory. They act as if they are responsible for Zion's defeat: *We have swallowed her up! This is the day we have waited for; we have lived to see it* (**2:16**). But 2:2 and 2:5 make it clear that it is the Lord who has done the swallowing. The author corrects this mistake, saying 'No, it is not you, but God': *The Lord has done what he planned* (**2:17**; 2:8; Jer 18:11). The reference to *his word, which he decreed long ago* refers to earlier warnings against disobedience to his divine commands (Deut 28:15-45).

By doing what he had said he would do and demolishing everything without mercy, the Lord had delighted his people's enemies. But that had not been what he set out to do; as will be clarified later, he had not willingly afflicted and humiliated his children (3:33). Despite appearances, the Lord is not on the side of the enemy, but is with his people. He is always Emmanuel. The apparent victory of the enemy over the people of God is temporary; it will not last.

The city and its inhabitants are now called to prayer. They should not let themselves be defeated by their suffering but should rise and pray. Prayer is not the easy way out, as we sometimes think. On the contrary, it is a battle – a battle on God's side and not against him. Thus they should pray every day, without rest (**2:18**). The call to pray in *the watches of the night* (**2:19a**) reminds us that the Israelites divided the night into three watches: the first watch ended at midnight; the second continued until three o'clock in the morning; the third, until six o'clock. (By nt times, there were four watches in the night: the first, from six to nine o'clock in the evening; the second, from nine until midnight; the third, from midnight until three in the morning; and the fourth, from three until six.)

The inhabitants of Zion were asked to pray *as the watches of the night begin*, meaning during each watch, which means all night (see also 2:18). So there is not, as some now teach, any specific hour of the night that is more favourable for prayer than another. The command here is to pray without ceasing, all day and all night. They are to exercise the vigilance of a watchman.

In Israel, prayers were commonly offered with the worshipper's hands lifted up (**2:19b**; Exod 9:29; Pss 28:2; 63:4;

141:2; Ezra 9:5). Those who pray in this position are committing themselves completely to God. The same gesture is used in many areas of Africa, with different meanings. Hands can be raised to heaven as an expression of one's helplessness, as they are when we weep and mourn at a funeral. But we also raise our hands to heaven to express our joy and thanksgiving to God for his answers to our longings and prayers. The NT exhorts us to *lift up holy hands in prayer* (1 Tim 2:8).

In **2:20a**, the prayer becomes a questioning of God. Zion now speaks, *Look, O Lord* (see also 1:9, 11). She calls God to witness and deplores the dreadful things that the famine has brought: mothers eating their own children (2 Kgs 6:28-29; Jer 19:9); the massacre of the priests and prophets in God's sanctuary; the slaughter of children and of young men and women (**2:20b-21**). God was permitting genocide! (**2:23**). The city seems to be asking God: 'Has your anger become so unreasonable that you have forgotten that those whom you are treating like this are your chosen people?'

3:1-66 Lament III: Hope for the Future

With this third lament, we are in the heart of the book, reaching the most intimate depths of the man who has seen the suffering. The author writes personally, using the pronouns 'I', 'me' and 'we'. We watch him move from a description of the depths of his pain to an expression of his great hope in the Lord and to a call to return to God with confession of sin and thankfulness for life spared. Finally, the Lord is invited not just to look at Jerusalem but also to look at the enemy and to destroy them forever.

3:1-18 I Have Seen Suffering

This lament does not begin with the characteristic cry of 'Eyka' that began chapters 1 and 2. In this poem, we meet *the man* who speaks of the suffering he himself has endured, who speaks of his personal experiences, not those of others (**3:1**). Who is this man? Is he the narrator speaking on behalf of the city and its inhabitants? Is he the high priest Seriah of whom the book of Jeremiah speaks (Jer 52:24)? Is he the prophet Jeremiah himself? There do seem to be marked similarities between what is said here and the suffering Jeremiah endured. In fact, this similarity is an argument in favour of the claim that Jeremiah is the author of Lamentations.

Whoever the man is, he provides us with many details of all that he has suffered. But at first he identifies the one responsible for this violence only by a pronoun, *he*. Is he hesitant to utter a name? Perhaps because the actions he describes do not fit with that person's image? It is only in 3:18 that the identity of the one who is torturing him is revealed: he is the Lord.

We are presented with a contrast that is both surprising and frightening. On the one hand, there is the powerful presence of the Lord, who is mentioned more than twenty times as 'he' and once as 'you'. On the other hand, we get the impression that his presence serves only to emphasize his refusal of all contact with the sufferer. He obliges his victims to *walk in darkness* (**3:2, 6**), he builds walls as if to better isolate them (**3:5, 7**), he does not listen to prayer (**3:8**), he closes all escape routes (**3:9**) and so on. We are amazed that God's presence is so negative. He is present, yet absent. He has turned his back on his people and his presence terrifies rather than comforts.

The poor victim has to endure being mocked by all (**3:14**; Jer 20:7). His only food is bitter herbs and gall (**3:15**; Job 9:18; Jer 9:14), making life unbearable. He has no peace and has long ago *forgotten what prosperity is* (**3:17**). Utterly exhausted, all the man can say is *my splendour is gone and all that I had hoped from the Lord* (**3:18**). But does this dramatic view really represent the end of everything?

3:19-39 Your Goodness Every Morning!

Plunged into the depths of despair, the man mourns: *I remember my afflictions* (**3:19-20**). But that is not all that he remembers. He also remembers *the Lord* (**3:21-22**). The first set of memories trap him in distress and defeat; the second set have the power to change him. He suddenly realizes that he must not give up the fight. He cannot. He refuses to believe that everything is lost.

Nothing is heavier than one's head when one is struggling; raising one's eyes requires great effort. Yet such effort is exactly what is called for here. The man takes himself in hand. He makes a decision, voluntarily affirming his faith, and acts with resolution and determination. Lifting up his eyes, he looks beyond the current situation and focuses his thought on God, whose goodness and compassion have not failed (3:22). More than that, *they are new every morning* (**3:23**). Circumstances have changed, but God has not! The more the author thinks about it, the more he recognizes that the Lord is his real treasure, more precious than the riches of the temple and the city that he loves. He decides, *I will wait for him* (**3:24**), and reminds himself *It is good to wait quietly for the salvation of the Lord* (3:26).

Confidence in the Lord helps us to accept whatever comes. This attitude is not fatalism, but faith. We do not keep silent because there is nothing to say, but because we know that God will deliver us in his own time and in his own way (**3:26, 28**). Yes, there is reason for hope! In fact, God takes no pleasure in suffering (**3:33**); his judgments are carried out with compassion (**3:31-32**). He sees all the evil that is done under the sun, including what Babylon has done (**3:34-36**). He will bring justice because he is the true ruler (**3:37-38**). Thus it is time to stop complaining. Can it be right to complain when one's life has been spared despite one's many sins (**3:39**)?

3:40-47 We Have Been Rebellious

The rediscovery of the goodness of God results in an exhortation to the whole city to do two closely related things: turn to God and confess their sins. The author includes himself with those he is appealing to, using the pronouns 'we' and 'us' as he speaks of the need to do an about-face and *return to the Lord* (**3:40**). When we do this, we must come with not just *our hands* raised to him but also *our hearts* (**3:41**). His compatriots must be sincere as they admit that their present situation is the result of the nation's unfaithfulness and rebellion (**3:42**). Recognizing the nation's guilt, the narrator also recites God's judgment on it, mentioning God's anger (**3:43**), his refusal to listen to prayer (**3:44**) and the destruction of the people (**3:45-47**).

3:48-56 You Have Heard Me

The trial is so great that the mere memory of it brings on *streams of tears* (**3:48-49**). The situation described in **3:52-56** is certainly similar to the experience of the prophet Jeremiah (Jer 38:1-13). His opponents threw him into a cistern (an underground water tank) without any food. He sank in the mud and almost died, but was saved by the intervention of an Ethiopian servant of the king. The past tense in 3:56 gives us reason to think that the author is recalling a past experience to illustrate his current request for deliverance.

3:57-66 You Will Destroy Them, Won't You?

After having started with numerous references to *he*, meaning God, the lament ends with an appeal to *you*. The change in pronoun is evidence that the situation between God and the man has eased. It is as if intimacy has been restored. God had responded to the man's prayer by coming near to him and reassuring him (**3:57**). The Lord becomes the advocate, the saviour (**3:58-59**) and the confidant of the one who had been without hope (**3:61-63**). Confident in God's support, the man calls on him to curse his enemies as a vindictive response to what they have done (**3:64-66**).

4:1-22 Lament IV: The Unbelievable Has Happened!

The fourth lament is similar to the first two in that it has 22 verses and begins with the expression *Eyka!* The focus is no longer on the invader entering the city but on the consequences of the invasion for those who live in the city. They had hoped for human help that had not materialized. But they are promised that the Lord, the true liberator, *will not prolong your exile* (4:22).

4:1-11 The Fine Gold and the Clay Pot

To express his amazement and sorrow at the unbelievable things that are taking place, the author uses 'Eyka!' twice (4:1, 2). Unfading gold is fading! Some commentators think that *the sacred gems* (or precious stones) represent the trea-sures of the temple that were carried off by the conqueror. But **4:2** invites us to see these stones as symbolizing the people of Zion. In fact, in Hebrew the same adjective, *precious*, is used before the word for *gold* and the word for *sons of Zion*. The comparison is between yesterday's situation, when they were *fine gold,* and today's, when they are *pots of clay.* Mention of the clay pot and the potter remind us of Jeremiah 18:1-10, which teaches that God (the potter) can do with Israel (the clay) what he wishes.

The author returns to the suffering of the infants who are no longer nursed by their mothers. Jackals have something to teach the mothers of Zion who are crazed with hunger. They have become like ostriches that are known for their cruelty (**4:3-4**; Job 39:13-17).

The rich have not been spared disaster (**4:5**). The rubbish heaps have become their beds; the street corner, their cemetery. The contrast between *purple* and *ash heaps* mark extraordinary change that has taken place. Yesterday's luxury has given place to misery. The princes are also hungry. Those who yesterday ranked as the 'beautiful people' are no longer recognizable because they are disfigured by dirt and famine and deepest misery. They are reduced to skin and bones – and that skin is *shrivelled,* – ... *dry as a stick* (**4:7-8**). (Note that some translations read 'Nazirites' instead of 'princes'. The Nazirites were people who had taken a vow of total consecration to God – Num 6:1-21; Jer 35).

In **4:6**, the author says either that the people had committed a sin greater than that of Sodom or that their *punishment* was *greater than that of Sodom*. At least the residents of Sodom had died quickly. As **4:9** reminds us, a quick death by the sword is preferable to a slow and painful wasting away from famine, watching one's own moral and physical decline. All the refugee camps that have arisen across the African continent (such as those in the Democratic Republic of Congo or Liberia or Sudan) could tell terrible tales of the ravages of hunger. Famine can even transform *compassionate* mothers who love their children into cannibals (**4:10**; 2:20). These women were seen to grab their children, cook them and eat them! The unthinkable has happened!

For the first time in this fourth lament, the name of the Lord is mentioned (**4:11**). It is he, in his *fierce anger*, who started the fire that has burned right down to the foundations of society when mothers eat their own children. They can fall no further.

4:12-16 The Enemy Within Jerusalem

In 1:10 the city lamented having seen the enemy in the sanctuary. Now we learn that no one had ever believed that *enemies and foes could enter the gates of Jerusalem* (**4:12**). The expressions *kings of the earth* and *the world's people* indicate that this was universally unthinkable. It was thought impossible both because the Lord himself watched over the city and because the site of Jerusalem was a natural fortress that had been strengthened by the building of additional fortification walls (2 Sam 5:6; 2 Chron 26:9; 27:3).

Once again, the narrator specifies that the presence of attackers within the holy city is the result of the sin of the prophets and priests (**4:13**). He specifically emphasizes the responsibility of the spiritual leaders of the people. Today pastors, evangelists and Bible teachers are in exactly the same position. They carry a heavier responsibility than others because of the extent of their knowledge and the importance of the ministries they exercise (Luke 11:46, 52; Rom 2:17-24; Jas 3:1).

The reference to Sodom in 4:6 may suggest that the sin of the people was similar to that of Sodom, presumably in that they had committed spiritual adultery against the Lord, their husband. Here, a second sin is mentioned: the prophets and priests *shed ... the blood of the righteous* (4:13). We do not know exactly whose blood was shed, but we do know that in the ot the term 'righteous' could also be translated as 'believing'. What is clear in the text is that the Lord himself defends the innocent. He has punished the city for both these sins.

The 'they' referred to in 4:14-16 are the unfaithful prophets and priests, not the righteous. These verses describe the miseries of these so-called men of God. They had 'shed the blood of the righteous', and now they themselves are *defiled with blood* (**4:14**; see Num 35:33). They should have enjoyed respect as those who are pure and consecrated to God, but now they are driven away like lepers (**4:15-16**; Lev 13:45-46). The unthinkable has happened!

4:17-22 Help Has Not Arrived

Now the author returns to 'we' in order to speak of the vanity of their hope of help. The alliance has failed! Their ally, a nation they had expected would help them if they faced outside aggression, has disappointed them (**4:17**). Those who believe that the ally referred to here is Egypt argue that this verse is evidence that Jeremiah is not the author of Lamentations because he had steadfastly opposed any alliance with Egypt (see Jer 37:7). However, the text does not say that Egypt is the nation referred to here.

Abandoned by its ally, the city fell. The enemy occupied it, *the end has come* (**4:18**). The people have nowhere to go and are harassed, worn down, defeated (**4:19; 5:4-5**).

This lament has spoken of the fate of the ordinary citizens, of the Judean aristocracy, and of the prophets and priests, and now it speaks of the fate of the king, referred to as *the Lord's anointed* (**4:20**). Because he was anointed by God, the king was perceived as having God's special protection (1 Sam 2:10). That was why the people trusted him.

The king is also described as *our very life breath* (4:20), the one who gives life. This way of referring to a king was probably borrowed from another culture, for it treats the king as a sort of god. The author is making the point that

the people had placed too much confidence in the king. But the king has been captured by the invader and was unable to save either his people or himself. This reference to the king in conjunction with the mention of pursuit in 4:19 seems to correspond to the fate of King Zedekiah, who was captured by the Babylonians as he was trying to flee from the besieged city (2 Kgs 25:1-7; Jer 39:4-7; 52:6-11).

The end of the lament consists of two messages, one addressed to Edom and the other to Zion (4:21-22). Edom is the name of the descendants of Esau, while Zion stands for the descendants of Jacob (Israel). The descendants of these brothers had long been enemies. The fall of Jerusalem elicited mocking laughter from the Edomites. They had even taken part in the pillaging of the city (Obad 12-14). The narrator reminds them that 'he who laughs last laughs longest'. He announces that Edom too will be punished (Isa 21:11-12; Ezek 25:12-14; Amos 1:11-12). She will be handed *the cup* of the wrath and judgment of the Lord (**4:21**).

Zion is promised that her suffering and exile will end (**4:22**). All political and human alliances have failed; the king cannot save. The Lord is now presented as the true liberator of his people. Only he can put an end to disaster and suffering.

5:1-22 Lament V: Bring Us Back

Is this fifth and final chapter really a lament? It is not alphabetical like the others, even though it has 22 verses. It seems more like a prayer in which the author speaks using the pronoun *we*. He calls on the Lord, reminds him of the misery of the people, and asks him to intervene to create something new. But for all that, he does not forget to confess the sins of the people. His final questions are more than ever an expression of his faith and of his deep hope.

5:1 Do Not Forget!

Calls to *look* and *see* have been on the lips of the people many times in these laments (1:9, 11, 12, 18, 20; 2:20; 3:63). Here, this call is accompanied by another request, *remember* (**5:1**). These are not commands addressed to the Lord. Far from it! They are the prayers of people who have decided to commit themselves entirely to the One whose eyes run to and fro through the whole earth and who sees everything (Ps 139). This prayer is addressed to the only One who really knows what is worth retaining of our individual histories and of our national history.

We ask God to *remember* because, despite today's shadows and misery, we will continue on our way tomorrow, along with all those around us. Today's murderer may end up not far from us. He may live next door. We need to know how to live with the memory of what we have just suffered.

Should we forget? Can we forget?

Lord, help us, thanks to your righteous judgment, to live with the memory of what neither you nor we can ever forget.

5:2-18 A Slave Rules Over Us

These verses again reveal the suffering and misery of the people who remained in the country after the deportation. But this time the emphasis is on the frustrations of life under the occupation.

The inheritance referred to in **5:2** is not only the property of the Judeans, but also of the city and the country as a whole that the Lord had given to his people (Deut 1:25; Jer 3:18). These possessions had been *turned over* (literally 'poured out') to the people referred to as *aliens* and *foreigners* – people who are not Judeans. We are not told who it was who turned the property over to foreigners. The author may have been thinking of the Lord, but he may also have been thinking of the Babylonian occupiers who seized land.

The *orphans* and *widows* (**5:3**) are those left behind after the death or exile of most of the able-bodied men. But the author may also have been thinking of the city as a widow (see 1:1-2) and of its inhabitants as orphans. He may even have been thinking of the nation as having been left orphaned by the deportation of the king, the father of the nation (4:20).

Because they no longer own their land, the Judeans are now obliged to pay for everything, including such basic necessities as water and wood (**5:4**). In their own country, they have become slaves who work under duress (**5:5**).

In their trouble, they remember that they had once voluntarily submitted to others when the nation entered into alliances with Egypt and Assyria (**5:6**). The Lord had condemned these alliances (Jer 2:17-18, 36-37), which is why **5:7** speaks of them as sinful. They are acknowledging the principle of collective responsibility, of solidarity in error. This principle is found in the book of Jeremiah (Jer 31:29; see also Ezek 18:2), although Jeremiah also announces that that principle will soon no longer apply (Jer 31:30).

To be ruled by slaves (**5:8**), by the most insignificant members of the army of occupation, is the greatest possible humiliation.

Driven by hunger and poverty, the people have to take risks (5:9). If they venture into the fields to find firewood or to grow crops, they may be attacked by the *sword in the desert* (**5:9**), probably groups of bandits who profited from the situation by attacking the helpless people who remain in the city. The situation was similar to that in areas of Africa such as Angola, Mozambique and the Darfur region of Western Sudan that have experienced war. Conflict leads to the proliferation of armed bands who raid, rape and kill. Today men, women and children also risk death and dismemberment from the antipersonnel mines scattered in areas they must enter in a desperate search for food.

Many atrocities are perpetrated: women and young girls are raped (**5:11**), princes are hung by their hands (**5:12**), perhaps as a warning against any attempts to regain power. The old are shown no respect (their assailants obey no rules of social conduct); young men are reduced to slavery (**5:13**); all the official activities of the government are stopped, for these were all conducted at the gate of the city (**5:14**). It seems that life has ground to a halt (**5:15**).

The survivors acknowledge the reason for all this misfortune: *we have sinned* (**5:16**). The expression *our hearts are faint* reveals their deep emotional pain, as does the statement that their eyes no longer see the light (**5:17**). Beyond their immediate suffering, the reason for their despair is that *Mount Zion,* and more precisely the temple situated there, has been left *desolate* (**5:18**). With the temple destroyed, they have no place to worship God. He seems very far away!

5:19-22 Lead Us Back

The tone suddenly changes in the last part of this lament, which is also the conclusion of the book. The author suddenly remembers that the mere fact that the temple is destroyed does not mean that the Lord has ceased to reign! On the contrary, his throne and his reign are without end (**5:19**). They are not connected to any one particular place.

The questions in **5:20** stress that the God of whom this whole book speaks cannot forget or abandon his people for ever. If he were to do this, it would mean that his choice of the nation had collapsed. That is why the author can say, *restore us to yourself* (**5:21**; Jer 31:18). This verse makes it clear that any movement to return to God cannot be solely a human decision. Such a return can only be commanded and accomplished by the Lord. In this sense, any return to God is the result of pure grace. It is God's gift.

The conditional clauses in **5:22** anticipate a negative response. They reinforce the idea expressed in 5:21 – so much so that when this book was read in synagogues, the reader would repeat 5:21 after reading 5:22. The book does not end on a note of doubt, but with an assurance rooted in the words in 3:22-23: 'Because of the Lord's great love we are not consumed, for his compassions never fail. They are new every morning. Great is your faithfulness.'

Issiaka Coulibaly

Recommended Reading

Ellison, H.L. 'Lamentations' in *Isaiah, Jeremiah, Lamentations, Ezekiel*. EBC. ed. Frank E. Gaebelein. Grand Rapids: Zondervan, 1986.

Guest, John. *Jeremiah, Lamentations*. CC. Waco, Texas: Word Book Publishers, 1988.

EZEKIEL

Prophets and prophecy are not unique to the Bible. From time immemorial human societies have recognized prophets as one type of religious authority. Prophecy was prevalent in the ancient Near East, in African societies and in traditional African religions. Prophets were and still are among the most creative and dynamic religious leaders in Africa. Many names could be mentioned from all over Africa. For example, in the Sudan there were Ngundeng and his son, Gwek of the Nuer and Arianhdit of the Dinka; in Uganda there was Rembe of the Lugbara; in Kenya there was Mugo wa Kibiru of the Kikuyu; and in the Democratic Republic of Congo there was Simon Kimbangu. The African Instituted Churches and certain charismatic groups even use the title 'prophet' for their founding fathers or current leaders.

When we look at prophets or prophecy, we need to address some very important questions. Who is the source of the message? How did the so-called prophet receive his or her message? What is the content of the message? For whom and for what purpose was the message given? How does one establish the authenticity and truth of the message? Rather than trying to answer these questions in the abstract, we will look at the life and work of Ezekiel, a prophet of the living and eternal God. Careful study of his message will help us to formulate better answers to these questions.

Author and Date

Ezekiel came from a priestly family (1:3). Hence, he would most likely have joined the temple priesthood if his circumstances had been different. His name means 'may God strengthen' or 'God strengthens'. In the light of his prophetic message and the audience he had to confront, he undoubtedly needed such strengthening! He was a messenger who was so controlled by the Spirit that it is sometimes difficult to distinguish the man from his message.

Ezekiel was born and called to the prophetic ministry of God in a time of political and social turbulence. The Assyrians had long been the dominant power in the ancient Near East, and they had invaded the northern kingdom (Israel) and deported the people in 721 BC (see 2 Kgs 17:1-6). However, the Babylonians under Nebuchadnezzar managed to defeat a combined force of Assyrians and Egyptians at Carchemish in 605 BC (see Jer 46:2). This victory led to the destruction of the Assyrian Empire. Their Egyptian allies were forced to retreat, hotly pursued by the Babylonians. In the process of asserting their authority over the whole region, the Babylonians deported hostages from Judah, including the young Daniel (Dan 1:1-5).

The southern kingdom (Judah) later rebelled against these Babylonian overlords, with the result that it was again attacked and conquered by the Babylonians. In 597 BC King Jehoiachin and many others, including Ezekiel, were deported to Babylon (1:2). (A final deportation took place ten years later, in 587 BC.) Ezekiel was thus an exile when God called him to the prophetic ministry.

As an exile, Ezekiel prophesied mainly to his fellow exiles in Babylon. Yet his ministry may not have been confined solely to them, but may have extended to the other two areas where Jews were located – Judah and Egypt (2 Kgs 25:25-26). We cannot, however, be certain that his message reached Egypt.

Ezekiel's ministry lasted for twenty-two years, from 593 to 571 BC (1:2; 29:17). We can be certain of this because the book contains fourteen dated references (1:1, 2; 3:15-16; 20:1; 24:1; 26:1; 29:1, 17; 30:20; 31:1; 32:1, 17; 33:21; 40:1). These dates are generally given with reference to the deportation of King Jehoiachin in 597 BC.

Since most of the reporting in the book, with the exception of one or two incidents, is given in the first person ('I'), we have to accept that the book was put together by Ezekiel himself. His message encountered much opposition from the people and from false prophets, and it is likely that he wrote down his oracles in order to keep them intact so that posterity would recognize that they had come from a divine source.

The Message

The book of Ezekiel is often considered strange and complicated. One writer even claims that it 'has bewildered many and has discouraged them from continuing their study of this prophecy' (*EBC*). Many of us must confess to similar sentiments when we first read this book. But the book itself is not disorganized. It consists of a series of visions given to the prophet and his proclamation of the truths revealed to him. Three of these visions dominate the book: the vision that marked his initial call (chs. 1–3), the vision of the departure of the glory of God from the temple (chs. 8–11) and the vision of the restored land and temple (chs. 40–48). There is also a section of the book that consists of oracles against the surrounding nations (chs. 25–32).

The message of the book of Ezekiel is essentially one of judgment and restoration based on the covenant relationship between God and his people. Judgment came because of a double tragedy: the people's rebellion against the revealed will of God and their false belief that they enjoyed eternal security. Ezekiel's contemporaries felt sure that even if they failed to keep the terms of the covenant, God was obliged to rescue them because of his covenant with Israel, and more specifically with the house of David, and because of his ownership of the land and his choice of Jerusalem and the temple as his permanent dwelling.

False prophets encouraged this false hope, but judgment could not be averted. The land was overrun by the armies of Nebuchadnezzar. Jerusalem and the temple were destroyed, and a substantial number of the people and their leaders went into exile. God upheld his word and vindicated the message he had sent by his prophets.

God's covenant people needed to learn that they had to keep their covenant obligations if they were to continue to enjoy God's blessing. But Ezekiel also made it clear that Yahweh would judge the nations that had rejoiced at and contributed to the demise of Israel. Yahweh is not only the covenant God of Israel, but also the Sovereign Lord of the universe.

The book of Ezekiel thus deals with the nature of God; the purpose and nature of the judgments of God; individual responsibility; the ethical, religious and moral history of Israel; and the nature of Israel's restoration and worship in the new temple.

Outline of Contents

COMMENTARY

1:1-3:27 Ezekiel's First Vision and His Call

1:1-28 The Vision of God's Glory

The first of the three visions that dominate the book of Ezekiel can be labelled the 'call vision'. The fact that Ezekiel's commissioning for prophetic ministry is preceded by this awe-inspiring manifestation of the glory of God indicates that Ezekiel will speak and act on God's initiative. This truth will be confirmed beyond any doubt in the rest of the book.

1:1-3 Introduction

The opening words of the book introduce not only the first vision, but also the entire book. Two dates are mentioned. The first is *in the thirtieth year* (**1:1a**). The thirtieth year of what? Many scholars settle for the answer that was first suggested by the African church father Origen, namely that it was the thirtieth year of the prophet's life. This was the year in which he would have become a full-fledged priest in the temple had he stayed in Jerusalem. In this year Ezekiel, whose status was now no more than one *among the exiles,* had an amazing encounter with the Holy One in which *the heavens were opened* and he saw *visions of God* (see also 8:3; 40:2).

The second date is *the fifth year of the exile of King Jehoiachin* (**1:2**). This is the first of many dates in the book to be correlated with the exile of King Jehoiachin. It locates the prophet historically.

Then the introduction tells us more about this young man to whom *the word of the Lord came* (**1:3a**). He is located socially, as we are told his name, family name and vocation (**1:3b**). Geographically, he is said to be living *by the Kebar River* (**1:1b**), *in the land of the Babylonians* (1:3). The Kebar River was probably one of the many canals in the Tigris-Euphrates river basin. These canals irrigated the land around the ancient city of Nippur, not far from present-day Baghdad. The exact place where the exiles were settled is later given as Tel Abib (3:15). Ezekiel, however, was beside the canal at that time of receiving the vision. It was *there* (a word that is emphasized by its place in the original Hebrew) that God spoke to him. It must have been tremendously significant that the God of Israel suddenly manifested himself in a foreign and polytheistic environment. Ezekiel and his fellow Jews may have been in despair at being so far from God's temple, but to their joy they found that God was still 'there', even in Babylon! However despairing we feel, we need to remember that there is no place or situation in which God cannot manifest himself.

The statement that *the hand of the Lord was upon him* (1:3b; see also 3:14, 22; 8:1; 33:22; 37:1; 40:1) is the third assertion in these three verses that Ezekiel has received a special revelation (the other two being the reference to his vision in 1:1 and to the 'word of the Lord' in 1:3a). These words strongly assert that the prophet is under the total control of God in what he does and says.

1:4-28 The vision

Like Isaiah (Isa 6), Ezekiel received his call to ministry after receiving an awe-inspiring vision of the Lord. Isaiah does not give us many details about his vision of God and his attendant angels. Where Ezekiel does give details, they are not easy to understand. The very obscurity of the details of vision is part of the paradox of God's disclosure of himself to us – he reveals and veils himself at the same time. What is clear is that the God who is prepared to reveal himself to human being is not someone to be taken for granted or approached with too much familiarity: 'The God who, with incredible grace, chooses to live in friendship with the humble, is the transcendent occupant of the throne of the

universe' (*BST*). The idea of God's incomprehensibility portrayed in this vision is also suggested by the Akan proverb in Ghana *Onyame bo pow a, odasani ntumi nsan* ['When God ties a knot, a human being cannot untie it', meaning that God's wisdom and power so much surpass our own that no one can untie a knot he has made].

1:4-14 THE LIVING CREATURES We are not told whether Ezekiel was alone beside the river or with someone else when he saw this vision. Nor are we told what he was doing at the time – though he may have been praying. What he experienced was not a trance, a dream, or a hallucination (as some would like us to believe). Ezekiel was wide awake when he saw this vision, for he says, *I looked and I saw a windstorm coming out of the north* (**1:4a**). At first, this looked like a natural phenomenon. But as it came closer, it was revealed to be *an immense cloud with flashing lightning and surrounded by brilliant light* (**1:4b**). Moreover, *the centre of the fire looked like glowing metal* (**1:4c**). At this point, Ezekiel's description of what he was experiencing appears to gradually make a transition from the familiar and natural to the awesome and supernatural.

As the object of the vision came closer, the prophet saw that *in the fire was what looked like four living creatures* (**1:5**; see also Rev 4:6-8). Although the dominant form seemed to be human (1:5), these creatures were not human, for each had *four wings* (**1:6, 8**). Two of their wings were raised so that they touched the wings of the adjacent creature, while the other two wings were used to cover the body (**1:9a, 11**). Yet under these wings, these creatures had human hands (1:8). But the most startling aspect of these creatures was that each had *four faces,* namely, the face of a man, a lion, an ox and an eagle (1:6, **10**). We see these same creatures around God's throne in the vision in Revelation 4:7. Their faces may be chosen to represent the mightiest living things in God's creation, for the rabbis held that the eagle was the mightiest of birds, the ox the mightiest of domestic animals, the lion the mightiest among wild animals, and man was the mightiest of all.

The four living creatures could move in any direction without turning (**1:9b, 12a**). It appears that their movement was energized and led by *the spirit* (**1:12b**). The Hebrew word here translated 'spirit' can have a range of meanings: wind, breath and the Spirit of God. It seems probable that the movement going on here was directed and empowered by the Spirit of God.

The living creatures are described as fiery beings, their appearance being *like burning coals of fire or like torches. Fire moved back and forth among* them and *it was bright, and lightning flashed out of it* (**1:13**). Their very movement *sped back and forth like flashes of lightning* (**1:14**).

What and who are these creatures? Ezekiel later refers to them as 'cherubim' (10:1, 6-8). This identification associates them with the figures that were placed above the ark in the Tent of Meeting. God told Moses, 'above the cover between the two cherubim that are over the ark of the Testimony, I will meet with you and give you all my commands for the Israelites' (Exod 25:18-22). In the Psalms, God is often described as 'enthroned between the cherubim' (Ps 80:1; 99:1). These are thus appropriate creatures to herald Ezekiel's vision of the Lord.

Another clue to the identity of these creatures lies in the repetition of the number four. There are four creatures, with four faces and four wings each, and they face in four different directions. This number reminds us of 'the four quarters of the earth' (Isa 11:12) and suggests that they must thus also represent all of creation. Their function may be to point to God's sovereign authority over his creation, a point that will emerge even more strongly as the chapter continues.

1:15-21 THE WHEELS Ezekiel has already noted the speed and mobility of the living creatures (1:9, 12, 14), and now he notes another element that enhances this impression as he sees the *wheel on the ground beside each creature* (**1:15**). There was thus a wheel on each of the four sides of the square formed by the cherubim with their touching wings. The wheels were identical in appearance and each of them *sparkled like chrysolite,* that is, like a yellow gemstone (**1:16**). This gem-like appearance, combined with the height of the wheels and the fact that their rims were *full of eyes all around* (**1:18**), made these wheels very impressive, or *awesome* as Ezekiel describes them. The 'eyes' may be intended to symbolize the all-seeing nature of God, or they may simply indicate that the wheels were inset with eye-shaped chrysolite gems (1:16).

The movement of the wheels is clearly synchronized with the movement of the four living creatures (**1:17,** 19-21). The description of the wheels as being *on the ground* (1:15) and as having *a wheel intersecting a wheel* (1:16; see also 10:10-11) may give the impression that these wheels helped the living creatures move in all four directions. But the passage does not support this interpretation. Instead, the wheels are presented as following the living creatures wherever they go, and as standing still when they stand still (**1:19, 21a**). Moreover, wheels would be no use once they leave the ground, for we are told *when the living creatures rose from the ground, the wheels also rose* (**1:21b**). Rather than being a mechanical means of propulsion, the wheels, like the living creatures (1:12), are energized by the spirit. We are told that *wherever the spirit would go, they would go … because the spirit of the living creatures was in the wheels* (1:20-21). 'The spirit of the living creatures' could also be translated as 'the Spirit of life', which would fit in well with the reference to the 'seven spirits of God' in Revelation 4:5, where the living creatures are also mentioned.

1:22-28 THE THRONE Continuing to describe what he saw, Ezekiel speaks of *what looked like an expanse, sparkling like ice, and awesome* that was *spread out above the heads of the living creatures* (**1:22**). The word translated 'expanse' is translated as 'firmament' in the KJV, suggesting that Ezekiel is speaking of the great curve of the heavens, as in Genesis 1:6. But this does not seem to be what Ezekiel is describing here. Rather, he seems to be speaking of some kind of platform above the living creatures, something that resembles the 'pavement made of sapphire' under the feet of God in Exodus 24:10 or the area that looked 'like a sea of glass, clear as crystal' before the throne of God in Revelation 4:6.

The fact that the outstretched wings of the four living creatures are underneath the platform does not mean that they are supporting it. It is likely that they are not, for Ezekiel speaks of *the sound of their wings* (**1:24a**), which implies that their wings are moving and not simply supporting a structure. Moreover, he says that *they lowered their wings* (**1:24c**), which would leave the platform without support if it rested on the wings.

The sound produced by the beating wings of the creatures is described using three similes: It was *like the roar of rushing waters, like the voice of the Almighty, like the tumult of an army* (**1:24b**). But this awesome torrent of sound is stilled at the sound of another voice that speaks from *the expanse over their heads* (**1:25**). Clearly this speaker is even more awesome than the cherubim, who serve him.

Trying to locate the source of the voice, Ezekiel saw that *above the expanse over their heads was what looked like a throne of sapphire* (**1:26**). The Hebrew word translated as 'sapphire' may mean lapis lazuli, which was one of the most precious gems of the ancient Near East. Ezekiel has to use the most beautiful things he can think of to explain the magnificence of what is being revealed in his vision.

As the prophet moves to the climax of the vision, he says, *and high above on the throne was a figure like that of a man* (1:26). Figurative language piles up as he attempts to describe what he saw: *I saw that from what appeared to be his waist up he looked like glowing metal, as if full of fire, and that from there down he looked like fire; and brilliant light surrounded him* (**1:27**). The radiance that surrounded him was *like the appearance of a rainbow in the clouds on a rainy day* (**1:28a**).

Ezekiel is strikingly cautious in his description of his vision. He uses figurative language and constantly stresses that what he sees is 'like', but not identical with, what he describes. He uses versions of 'looked like' in 1:4, 5, 7, 10, 13, 16, 22, 24, 26 and 27 and stresses the word 'appeared' or 'appearance' in 1:5, 13, 16 and 27. He even combines these two when he speaks of 'like the appearance of' in 1:28a. The reason for his caution is that what he is describing is *the appearance of the likeness of the glory of the Lord* (**1:28b**). Ezekiel is acutely aware of the impossibility of describing God in human form, even in metaphorical language, and his attempt to do so 'was incredibly bold, for was not Yahweh invisible and therefore indescribable?' (*TOT*).

Overpowered by what he saw, Ezekiel *fell face down* before the one he saw in the vision (**1:28c**). This should be our position as human beings before our glorious Creator and Redeemer. But God does not leave us prostrate. He has granted Ezekiel this awe-inspiring revelation in order to prepare him for ministry, and thus the next thing that Ezekiel becomes aware of is *the voice of one speaking* (**1:28d**). But whatever else happened to Ezekiel, he would never lose his consciousness of that first awesome vision (see 3:13, 23; 8:4; 10:1-22; 11:22-23; 43:3).

2:1-3:27 The Call to Prophetic Ministry

Ezekiel's experience of the glory of the Lord is followed by his call to serve the heavenly king, who revealed himself in the vision in chapter 1. Whereas chapter 1 was full of visual images, the focus now shifts to what Ezekiel heard, that is, to the words of God to the prophet. We are now told what the voice that spoke in 1:28 actually said in a message directed specifically to Ezekiel.

2:1-5 Ezekiel's audience

Ezekiel is flat on his face before the Lord (1:28). As if to drive home the appropriateness of this posture, the Lord addresses Ezekiel as *son of man* (**2:1**). He is not thinking of the exalted 'son of man' whom Daniel sees (Dan 7:13-14) but is making the point that Ezekiel is merely a human being, regardless of the visions he receives or the high calling he will be given. This reminder will be repeated throughout the book, for Ezekiel is consistently referred to in this way.

But God does not want Ezekiel simply to remain prostrate in worship. He has a job for him to do, and so Ezekiel is told to stand up in order to receive his commission. But it is only with the help of God's Spirit that he can stand: *The Spirit came into me and raised me to my feet* (**2:2**).

It is only after this preparation and empowerment that God speaks to Ezekiel, telling him, *I am sending you* (**2:3a**). These words indicate one of the critical distinctions between a true and a false prophet: a true prophet is sent by God, a false one speaks of his own accord. Ezekiel and his older contemporary Jeremiah often had to contend with false prophets as they carried out their missions (Ezek 13; Jer 23:9-32; 28:1-17; 29:20-32).

The description of the audience to whom God is sending Ezekiel must have made him think that he was being given an impossible task. However, as we all know and as will be demonstrated through the ministry of Ezekiel, what is impossible for human beings is possible for God.

The Lord is sending Ezekiel *to the Israelites,* who are described as *a rebellious nation that has rebelled against me.* The story of the covenant people is not simply a story of God's redemptive grace; it is also a story of rebellion and disobedience. This has been the case throughout the nation's history, so that God can say that both they *and their*

fathers have been in revolt against me to this very day (**2:3b**). The people are said to be *obstinate and stubborn* (**2:4a**), or as the KJV translates this, *impudent ... and stiffhearted*. The latter adjective is clearly similar in meaning to the frequent description of the people as 'stiff-necked' (see Exod 32:9).

Ezekiel's task is to tell this people: *This is what the Sovereign Lord says* (**2:4b**). God is frequently referred to as the 'Sovereign Lord' in Ezekiel. It is a title that establishes his great authority over all other rulers and the importance of any message coming from him. The rest of the book of Ezekiel deals with the details of God's message and the people's response to it.

God gives Ezekiel no assurance that the people will listen to his message, but simply says he is to speak *whether they listen or fail to listen* (**2:5**). In fact, a negative response appears to be a foregone conclusion, for the Lord again describes them as *a rebellious house.* But they will have no excuse when God's judgment that is looming on the horizon comes on them, for *they will know that a prophet has been among them.*

2:6-7 The Lord's encouragement

After presenting Ezekiel with the prospect of a hostile and unresponsive audience, in **2:6** the Lord equips his servant for the coming spiritual confrontation by three times encouraging and exhorting him, *do not be afraid.* He is to fear neither these people nor what they will say about him. He will have reason to fear, for the hostile environment in which he will carry out his ministry will make him feel as if he is surrounded by *briers and thorns* and living *among scorpions.* He will face all the opposition that a spokesman for the true God can expect from those who are *rebellious,* an adjective that is repeated three times in these three verses.

Ezekiel's call to serve the Lord would undoubtedly bring loneliness. 'From this point on he was set apart from the rest of his people ... a terribly painful thing in a culture where personal identity is predominantly shaped by community belonging' (*BST*). While any disciple of Jesus Christ may experience such loneliness, it is likely to be felt more strongly by African disciples than it would be in the West, for the pull of community is strong in Africa. Here we constantly hear variants on the saying 'I am because we are, and since we are, therefore I am'. The Akan of Ghana, for example, say, 'One person alone cannot build a town', underscoring the need for cooperation. They would even insist that it is only in community that a person can realize himself or herself. While there are many positive aspects to such a sense of community, it can also exert a negative influence. Ezekiels ministering in an African context need to fight the temptation to ignore God's calling or dilute God's message in favour of identifying with the community. We need to put on 'the whole armour of God' (Eph 6:11) and hear God's voice saying 'Do not be afraid', if we are to remain faithful to the Lord and his message.

2:8-3:3 Ezekiel's ministry

God also warns his servant that he needs to watch out lest the same virus of rebellion that has infected the people infect him: *Do not rebel like that rebellious house* (**2:8b**). He is to *listen to what I say to you* (**2:8a**). The mark of a true servant of God is not success with an audience but faithful obedience to what God has revealed.

The first test of Ezekiel's obedience comes immediately, as God says, *open your mouth and eat what I give you* (**2:8c**). Ezekiel is not given any opportunity to make excuses or to claim to be the wrong man for this mission, as Moses and other prophets did (Exod 3:11-4:17; Jer 1:6). The only glimpse we are given of Ezekiel's own feelings is in 3:14.

Ezekiel now sees an outstretched hand holding a scroll (**2:9**). This hand was undoubtedly the hand of Yahweh, who is presented as the one speaking in these verses (3:3). As Ezekiel watches, the scroll is unrolled before him and he sees that it is written on both sides. He can read the writing and sees that it consists of *words of lament and mourning and woe* (**2:10**). The scroll contains the message that he must preach, and it will not be one of comfort to his people. The prophet of God chooses neither the audience nor the message, but must simply obey God and proclaim the message God gives.

Twice more Ezekiel is told to *eat the scroll* (**3:1, 3a**). In fact, he is told to *fill your stomach with it* (**3:3b**). The scroll is full of God's words, and the prophet, too, must be so full of them that he has no room for words of his own.

Obeying God's command, even if it sounded strange, Ezekiel says, *So I ate it, and it tasted as sweet as honey in my mouth* (**3:3c**). The words on the scroll were of bitter sorrow, but when we take God's divine word into ourselves in obedience, it is always sweet (see Ps 19:10; Jer 15:16).

3:4-11 The charge repeated

God repeats his charge to Ezekiel: *Son of man, go now to the house of Israel and speak my words to them* (**3:4**). Why this repetition, when he had already been given his commission in 2:3-4 and 3:2? It may be that this was a second commissioning after the vision of the scroll, or it may be that God recognized that Ezekiel needed additional encouragement given the rebellious audience he would be facing.

God is certainly preparing him for conflict as he again describes the hard-heartedness of the people. He reminds Ezekiel that the people will not refuse his message because they do not understand what he is saying (**3:5-6**). Rather, they will refuse it out of sheer defiance. As the saying goes, 'there are none so deaf as those that will not hear' (see also 12:2). The Tigrigna of Eritrea say much the same thing – *felitu zedeqese, harmaz neynqnqo* ['An elephant cannot waken someone who is deliberately sleeping', meaning that people can refuse to wake up to what is happening around them]. 'Israel's unnatural unresponsiveness would not result from

a lack of understanding but from a spiritual barrier, a deliberate refusal' (*WBC*). Thus God reassures Ezekiel, *the house of Israel is not willing to listen to you because they are not willing to listen to me* (**3:7**).

God's second step in preparing Ezekiel is the promise, *I will make you as unyielding and hardened as they are* (**3:8**). Ezekiel will live up to the name his parents gave him, which means 'God strengthens' or 'God hardens'. He will be resolute, for God says, *I will make your forehead like the hardest stone, harder than flint* (**3:9**). Ezekiel will not be susceptible to browbeating!

Finally, in **3:10-11**, God admonishes Ezekiel to listen carefully to what he will continue to reveal to him and directs him to his specific audience: *Go now to your countrymen in exile and speak to them.*

3:12-15 Ezekiel's reaction

As his call and commissioning draw to a close, Ezekiel is not only made to stand on his feet (2:2), but the same Spirit of God also raises him up and transports him to his place of ministry (**3:12a, 14a**; see also 8:3; 11:1, 24; 37:1; 43:5). But as he leaves this place of vision, he is reminded of the glory he had seen: *I heard behind me a loud rumbling sound – May the glory of the Lord be praised in his dwelling-place* (**3:12b**). This cry of adoration is related to his inaugural vision, for he hears *the sound of the wings of the living creatures brushing against each other and the sound of the wheels beside them, a loud rumbling sound* (**3:13**).

The prophet is said to have left with an emotion of *bitterness and in the anger of my spirit* (**3:14b**). The meaning of the words is clear, but why is the prophet bitter and angry? The most probable explanation is that he was 'caught up into the righteous anger of God against His people' (*TOT*). However, some commentators argue that he was 'infuriated by the divine imposition on his life and the implication of Yahweh's commission for him' (*NICOT*). Jonah had tried to avoid his ministry to Nineveh (Jonah 1:3), and Ezekiel, with different motives, may have disliked being called to pronounce judgment on his own people, and to do it in the knowledge that they would not respond (2:8). Yet it seems unlikely that Ezekiel was really forced into the ministry against his own will and was thus bitter and angry. There is certainly no sign that God called on him to repent, as he did the recalcitrant Jonah.

It is possible that the motive for Ezekiel's anger was some mixture of these reasons. Certainly, he was deeply shaken by his encounter with the living Lord and by receiving his commission to prophesy in such a hostile environment. Back among his fellow exiles in Tel Abib, Ezekiel took a week to digest the implications of his call (**3:15**).

3:16-21 'A watchman for the house of Israel'

After the seven days of reflection were over, the word of God comes to Ezekiel again (**3:16**). It seems that God wishes to give Ezekiel more details about his specific prophetic role. This role is introduced here, but is elaborated in still more detail in chapters 18 and 33:1-20.

Ezekiel is told that he is to be *a watchman for the house of Israel* (**3:17a**). A watchman was appointed as a guard, to keep those in a house informed about what was happening outside and to alert them to any danger that threatened so that they could take action to save their lives (see 2 Sam 18:24-27; 2 Kgs 9:17-20; Isa 56:10-12). As a watchman, Ezekiel will not be warning 'the house of Israel' about the usual human dangers, but will instead be passing on the warning that comes from God. He is to *hear the word I speak and give them warning from me* (**3:17b**; see also Jer 6:17-21; Hos 9:8; Hab 2:1). He is to warn sinners about the consequences of their actions. Some will choose to ignore this warning and will die – but that is their own fault. The watchman will not be blamed for not having warned them (**3:18-19**).

Even those who appear to be living righteous lives need such warnings, for there is always the possibility that they will fall into sin, which leads to death. They may fall when God puts *a stumbling block* in their way (**3:20a**; see also Isa 8:14; Jer 6:21). God is not saying that he is responsible for human sin, but is saying that he does not hinder people from exercising their will. Yet even those who fall can be saved if they listen to the watchman's warning about the danger they are in and repent and return to God (**3:20b-21**).

We can draw evangelistic and pastoral lessons from this passage – evangelistic in warning sinners about judgment and pointing them to Christ, pastoral in warning believers about the dangers of backsliding.

3:22-27 Bound and mute

Ezekiel was now asked to *go out to the plain*. Although the ever-present *hand of the Lord was upon* him (**3:22**), he was not carried by the Spirit this time, for he says, *So I got up and went out to the plain* (**3:23a**). Once there, his devotion was recharged by a brief encounter with the same vision of the glory of the Lord that he had earlier seen *by the Kebar River* (**3:23b**). The change of venue may have been God's reminder to Ezekiel that he was not confined to one place. God could be met by the rivers of Babylon and on its plains, as well as in Jerusalem. Again, Ezekiel fell *face down*. And again, *the Spirit came into me and raised me to my feet* (**3:24a**; see 2:2, 12-14).

After all this preparation for his prophetic ministry, Ezekiel is finally assigned his first prophetic task – but what a surprise it is! He is told to *shut yourself inside your house* (**3:24b**). Not only that, but God says, *they will tie you with ropes; and you will be bound so that you cannot go out*

among the people (**3:25**). Still more surprisingly, God adds, *I will make your tongue stick to the roof of your mouth so that you will be silent and unable to rebuke them, though they are a rebellious house* (**3:26**).

The prophet is to be confined, immobile and mute! 'Why?' we are inclined to ask. Though God has promised that Ezekiel will speak for him (**3:16**) and promises to open Ezekiel's mouth, it will be seven and a half long years before that happens (**3:27**; see also 29:21; 33:21-22). The one demanding that he be confined is God, but the binding – although God may also be involved in it (**4:8**) – is basically done by the people. The muteness is the work of God. It does not, however, appear to have been total, for we find passages where Ezekiel is talking to people (11:25; 14:1-5; 20:1-3; 24:18-24). It seems that he is mute in the sense that he speaks only when the Lord wants him to speak – he will only be a mouthpiece of God.

The book also contains hints that the prophet's muteness is a sign for the people (4:1-3; 12:3-6; 24:21-24, 27). God is using Ezekiel as a warning that he himself will stop speaking to the people. The silence of God is an indication that judgment is coming. Ezekiel's confinement and immobility may also be portents of the siege that will be imposed upon Jerusalem by the Babylonians.

4:1-24:27 Prophecies Against Israel and Judah

Ezekiel now proceeds to deliver prophecies of judgment against the Jewish nation. The judgment focuses on the city of Jerusalem because that was the political, religious and social hub of the nation. However, he also pronounces judgments on the temple, land and people.

As a watchman, Ezekiel had to issue warnings to the nation (3:16-21) and he now begins to carry out this ministry as he vividly acts out parables to warn his fellow exiles about the coming siege of Jerusalem (chs. 4–5) and the future desolation of the land (chs. 6–7).

4:1-5:17 Acted Prophecies Against Jerusalem

By God's orders, Ezekiel was silent and confined to his house (3:24-26). Yet the Lord still had a message that Ezekiel was to convey to the people by acting out the siege of Jerusalem. He engages in four symbolic activities in 4:1-5:4. These activities are then interpreted more fully in 5:5-17.

4:1-3 Besieging a clay tablet

The first symbolic act involves an image of Jerusalem. God tells Ezekiel to *take a clay tablet, put it in front of you and draw the city of Jerusalem on it* (**4:1**). He may have done this by taking soft clay and pressing an outline of the city into it, or he may have used a sharp object to scratch a drawing of the city on a hard clay tablet.

Ezekiel is then told to *lay siege to* the city. He does this through four activities that were standard procedure in the siege warfare of his day (**4:2**). First, he erected *siege works* or siege walls around it. These walls would offer protection against any counter-attack by the defenders of the city and would also prevent them from escaping. Next he built *a ramp* that would enable the attackers to come closer to the tops of the walls and would provide an approach for the siege engines. Then he *set up camps* around the city, representing the tents of the enemy soldiers strategically positioned around it. Finally, he installed *battering rams around it.* These siege engines would assault and break through the walls that surrounded ancient cities. We are not told whether Ezekiel drew pictures of these things in the sand around the clay tablet with the map of the city on it or whether he made models from soft clay and put them around it.

Then comes the most disturbing part of this acted prophecy. Ezekiel is to *take an iron pan, place it as an iron wall between you and the city and turn your face towards it* (**4:3a**). Placing an impenetrable iron wall between the prophet (God's representative) and the city symbolizes Yahweh separating himself from his city. In fact, the phrase 'turn your face towards it' suggests that Yahweh has become the enemy. Setting his seal on Ezekiel's symbolic act, God says, *It will be under siege, and you shall besiege it,* explaining that both the prophet and his action *will be a sign to the house of Israel* (**4:3b**).

4:4-8 Lying on his side

For his second symbolic act, Ezekiel is instructed to *lie on your left side and put the sin of the house of Israel upon yourself* (**4:4a**). He is to lie like this for 390 days (**4:5**). Thereafter, he is to *lie down again, this time on your right side, and bear the sin of the house of Judah* (**4:6**). He is to lie like this for 40 days (4:6). It seems that he lay like this from shortly after the seven days in which he digested his call until about the time of his next vision (8:1). This is approximately fourteen months, which is close to 430 days.

What is the meaning of this sign? We are also told that the days represent *the years of their sin* (4:5), but which years are these? Do they represent Israel's and Judah's past years of rebellion when they existed as the northern and southern kingdoms, or do they represent the future period during which Israel and Judah will endure punishment for their rebellion against their covenant God? Scholars also argue about whether the 40 days are to run concurrently with the last part of the 390 days, or whether Ezekiel is actually to lie on his left side for 390 days followed by 40 days on his right side, making a total of 430 days.

We do not have space to explore the different arguments, and so I will simply present my understanding of this passage. That is that the days (representing years) do not refer to the covenant people's past years of sin but to the future in which they will endure the punishment for their sin. When the prophet is told *you are to bear their sin* (**4:4b**) what is meant is that he is to endure the punishment beginning with their captivity. Because I see the days as consecutive, I interpret his sign as meaning that this punishment will continue for 430 years. Thus it would endure from 597 BC when the Davidic monarchy ended with the deportation of Jehoiachin to 167 BC, when the Maccabees at last re-established an independent Jewish kingdom. (In the intervening years, the Jews had returned from exile, but Israel had been subject to foreign rulers like the Persians and the Macedonians.)

The significance of Ezekiel's symbolic siege of Jerusalem (4:1-3) is heightened as Ezekiel is told to *prophesy against the city* (**4:7**). He does this both by his actions and by the words that follow in 5:5-27.

Once again God speaks of the binding of the prophet (**4:8**). In 3:25, this binding was done by the people, but here it is done by God in order to make sure that the symbolic act described here is followed to the letter, and that Ezekiel does not accidentally roll over in his sleep.

4:9-17 Rationing unclean food

Some commentators see two symbolic acts here rather than one. According to them, 4:9-11 deals with the rationing of food in the besieged city, whereas 4:12-19 deals with unclean or defiled food. I will deal with the passage as a single symbolic act, depicting conditions during both the siege and the exile.

The prophet is told to *take wheat and barley, beans and lentils, millet and spelt* (**4:9**) and make bread from them to be eaten throughout the time of the siege. While the mix of ingredients was nutritious, it was an unusual recipe for bread and signalled that the people under siege would be so desperate for food that they would combine anything they could find to make bread. This point is underscored by the careful weighing of the small amounts of food and water to be consumed each day (**4:10-11**). Ezekiel was to eat just eight ounces (225 grams) of bread and drink just two cups of water a day.

Ezekiel was told to bake his bread *in the sight of the people, using human excrement for fuel* (**4:12**) as a sign that *the people of Israel will eat defiled food among the nations.* Scholars disagree about whether this food is regarded as defiled because it involves a mix of different kinds of grains and legumes (see Lev 19:19; Deut 22:9) or because of the way it is baked. The people of Israel would be eating 'defiled food' because it would be difficult for them to observe the dietary laws laid down in Leviticus when they were under siege or subject to foreign domination.

Ezekiel, as a devout Jew and a priest, recoils with horror at the order to cook his food over human excrement (**4:14**) and explains that he has always been scrupulously careful to observe the dietary laws. The Lord understands Ezekiel's feelings and allows him to use an acceptable substitute, cow manure, a fuel that is still often used in arid regions of the world (**4:15**). God has already communicated his important message of judgment to the prophet.

God concludes by explaining that the symbolic food rationing symbolizes his coming judgment, when he *will cut off the supply of food in Jerusalem* (**4:16-17**).

5:1-4 Shaving and destroying his hair

Ezekiel's fourth symbolic act, performed at God's command, is to *take a sharp sword and use it as a barber's razor* to shave his head and his beard (**5:1a**). In spite of the sharpness of the sword, this must have been an odd and excruciating experience for the prophet! He then weighs the hair he has removed and divides it into three small piles (**5:1b**).

When the days of his siege, that is, the days for which he is lying on one side, come to an end, he is instructed to burn one of these piles of hair inside the city, to strike the other with his sword so that it is scattered around the city, and to scatter the third pile to the wind (**5:2**). He is to make it clear that this is what God will do to the inhabitants of Jerusalem.

Finally, he is to retrieve a few of the scattered *strands of hair and tuck them away in the folds of your garment* (**5:3**). These hairs represent the remnant who make up the exiled community. But this symbolism should not lure them into complacency. They still face God's judgment, for he tells Ezekiel to take out a few of the hairs he had retrieved *and throw them into the fire and burn them up* (**5:4**). The fate of these members of the remnant may also affect the entire covenant people, for God warns about the *fire that will spread from there to the whole house of Israel.*

5:5-17 The significance of the symbolic acts

Ezekiel's acts should not be thought of as some form of sympathetic magic, in which something done to a model or representation of someone or something will have a similar effect on the person or thing represented. Sympathetic magic was common in the ancient Near East and is still practised in traditional African religions today under the guise of witchcraft, divination and sorcery. But Ezekiel made no claim that what he did to his model of Jerusalem or to his hair would cause the coming suffering of Jerusalem. All that he was doing was creating a vivid picture of what God was intending to do to that city. This point is made even clearer by the interpretation of the symbolic acts that follows in 5:5-17. The people are left in no doubt that Ezekiel is not speaking for himself, but that *this is what the Sovereign Lord says* (**5:5a, 7a, 8**).

The Lord had intended Jerusalem to be the showcase of his greatness and wisdom when he set it *in the centre of the nations, with countries around her* (**5:5b**; Deut 4:5-8). But the

city had become wicked and rebellious, a place where God's covenant *laws* and *decrees* were trampled under foot (**5:6**). It had been found lacking even when measured by *the standards of the nations around* it (**5:7b**).

God thus pronounces judgment on the city. Instead of the covenant promise 'I will be with you', he says, *I myself am against you* (**5:8a**). God's holy name had been treated with contempt in full view of the surrounding nations, so the punishment would be inflicted *in the sight of the nations* (**5:8b**). The gravity and unprecedented nature of this punishment is underscored by God's solemn words, *I will do to you what I have never done before and will never do again* (**5:9**).

God's description in **5:10-12** of how the drama acted out by Ezekiel mirrors what will happen in the siege of Jerusalem is so horrible that we are tempted to think that God's judgment is unreasonable. But we need to remember that in our preaching of God's grace, we may have forgotten to 'reckon with the darkness of his fury. The danger that we should perceive God from only one side is always present and can lead to a romantic view of one's relationship with him. But God will not condone infidelity, rebellion, wickedness, abominations' (*NICOT*).

The punishment of Israel will be such that both Israel and the nations *will know that I the Lord have spoken in my zeal* (**5:13**). Instead of being a showcase for God's wisdom, the nation will be a showcase for his wrath; instead of being admired, they *will be a reproach and a taunt, a warning and an object of horror to the nations around* (**5:15**).

The judgment of the city concludes with a list of the horrors God will use to implement his judgment: *famine … wild beasts … plague and bloodshed* (**5:16-17**).

6:1-7:27 Judgment on the Whole Land

Chapters 4 and 5 have focused on the city of Jerusalem, but in chapters 6 and 7 the focus shifts to the whole land. Chapter 6 speaks of judgment on the mountains of Israel, while chapter 7 announces that the terrifying judgment is near.

6:1-7 Judgment on idolatrous sites

Once again *the word of the Lord* came to Ezekiel (**6:1**; see also 7:1). Just as he had earlier prophesied against Jerusalem, so now Ezekiel is commanded to prophesy *to the mountains and hills, to the ravines and valleys* of Israel (**6:2-3a**; compare 4:7). They are targeted for judgment because they were the places where the people conducted their idolatrous worship and had set up their *high places* (**6:3b**). These 'high places' were local centres of worship, some of which had been dedicated to the worship of Yahweh (1 Sam 9:14). But with the building of the temple, the high places became centres of idol worship. The prophets denounced them, and godly kings like Hezekiah and Josiah tried to bring about a revival of religion by removing them. But the high places had a deep grip on the hearts of the rebellious people, and they refused to give them up. So God pronounces a fearsome judgment on them. As God's people, we also need to be careful to examine ourselves and see whether there is any sin that we are clinging to that prevents God from blessing us. When we identify such a sin, we must humble ourselves and remove it from our midst.

Both the high places and all the paraphernalia of idolatrous worship will be destroyed. The people who have worshipped there will be killed and their bodies and bones scattered around the sites where they had worshipped (**6:4-6**; see Lev 26:30). The presence of human bones on these sites would defile them and make them unsuitable as places of worship in future (see 2 Kgs 23:14, 19).

As they see this judgment coming upon them, the people will indeed *know that I am the Lord* (**6:7**).

6:8-10 Judgment tempered by mercy

God is not only a God of judgment, but also a God of mercy. That is why we now find the word *But*. From the previous verses it appeared that there might be no survivors of his wrath, but now he promises, *I will spare some* (**6:8**). These exiles will see the sins that led to their suffering and captivity in a new light, and *will loathe themselves for the evil they have done and for all their detestable practices* (**6:9b**). They will remember God (**6:9a**) and will *know that I am the Lord* (**6:10a**). They will know that God's warnings are not vain but must be heeded. They will also know that God's chastisement was not *in vain* because it has brought them back to himself in repentance (**6:10b**).

6:11-14 Outcome of the judgment

The prospect of mercy is merely glimpsed, for the immediate judgment involves devastation of the land and of the population by *sword, famine and plague* (**6:11b**). No one will be able to escape God's wrath (**6:12**). No wonder the prophet is commanded to pronounce these terrible things with a clap of his hands, a stamp of his feet, and a shout of *Alas!* (**6:11a**).

The land will be laid waste because of the people's idolatry. But this is not the sole outcome of his judgment. Another outcome that is mentioned repeatedly indicates God's ultimate purpose in this judgment: He wants his people to *know* who he is (**6:13-14**).

7:1-14 Nearness of the judgment

Ezekiel was not the only prophet to warn that judgment was imminent. Amos had proclaimed the same message before the fall of the northern kingdom (Amos 8:2). But now the urgency and frequency of the watchman's call is alarming: *The end! The end has come upon the four corners of the land. The end is now upon you* (**7:2-3a**). The Lord says *I will unleash my anger against you,* as someone might turn loose

a hunting dog (**7:3b**). The reason for the judgment is given again as *your conduct and your detestable practices,* a phrase that is repeated again and again (**7:3c, 4, 8, 9a**). The effect of the judgment will be to make them acknowledge the Lord (**7:4, 9**).

Another salvo of warnings of imminent judgment are fired off in **7:5-7a**: *Disaster! An unheard-of disaster is coming. The end has come! The end has come! It has roused itself against you. It has come! Doom has come upon you ... The time has come, the day is near.* Joy is replaced by panic upon the mountains (**7:7b**, see also 6:2). The Lord's patience is exhausted and he is about to pour out his wrath without sparing anyone or showing any pity. They will know, beyond any doubt, that it is *the Lord* – not the Babylonians – *who strikes the blow* (**7:9b**).

The frantic trumpet blasts sounded by the watchman ring out again: *The day is here! It has come! Doom has burst forth, the rod has budded, arrogance has blossomed* (**7:10**). What is 'the rod' mentioned here? It does not seem likely that this is Aaron's rod that blossomed as a confirmation of his priestly office (Num 17:10). The clue lies in the next sentence: *Violence has grown into a rod to punish wickedness* (**7:11**). The rod that has budded and blossomed is Nebuchadnezzar of Babylon, whom the Lord will use as a rod to punish his people.

With judgment at the door, there is no point in buying or selling property – the Babylonians will destroy both property and lives, so that there will be no winners, only losers (**7:12-13**).

The watchman's warning and the trumpet summoning the people to battle will, however, be in vain, for paralyzing fear will prevent anyone from answering the summons (**7:14**; see also 7:17).

7:15-22 Further outcome of the judgment

The comprehensive and devastating nature of the judgment is again stressed, as it was in 6:11-14. No one will escape (**7:15**). Even those who appear to have escaped the sword by fleeing to the mountains will be incapable of doing more than uttering helpless moans, like the plaintive calls of doves, because of the disaster brought on them by their sins (**7:16**). They will be terrified and covered with shame, and any wealth they have accumulated will be of no use in such terrible circumstances (**7:17-19**) – in fact, they will find it repulsive because it will remind them that they used their wealth to honour idols (**7:20**). God will give all their wealth as plunder to the victors (**7:21**). Not only will the Israelites lose their own treasure, but the foreign invaders will also invade and pillage God's *treasured place* – his temple (**7:22**).

7:23-27 Summary

Defeat and captivity are so certain that the people might as well start preparing their chains in advance (**7:23**). *The most wicked of the nations* are poised to overrun the land (**7:24**). There will be no point in even trying to *seek peace*, for it will be too late (**7:25-26**).

When Jeremiah predicted a similar catastrophe, the rebellious people rejected his words and said, 'the teaching of the law by the priest will not be lost, nor will counsel from the wise, nor the word from the prophets' (Jer 18:18). But Ezekiel makes it clear that prophets and priest and elders will have no wisdom to offer in the face of the impending catastrophe (7:26). The political leadership will collapse in the face of the threat, for they themselves will have no hope of escape (**7:27**).

8:1-11:25 Judgment on City and Temple

Fourteen months after his first vision (8:1; see 1:3), Ezekiel was still confined to his house. He may still have been spending much of his time lying on his side. But the restraints on his movements were not restraints on his ministry, for the *elders of Judah* had come to visit him, maybe to seek a word from the Lord (20:1; see also 14:1-3). The vision that, humanly speaking, may have been triggered by this visit also shows that while his body was confined, God could still take him wherever he wanted him.

We do not know how long Ezekiel and the elders sitting before him had to wait before this vision came. What this tells us is that, 'a true prophet like Ezekiel would never give an answer on the spur of the moment, as some less worthy prophets were' – and still are – 'inclined to do, but would await a word from God' (*TOT*).

8:1-18 Reasons for judgment

In his vision Ezekiel sees the progressive withdrawal of the glory of the Lord, which has already been hinted in 5:11, against the backdrop of a detailed description of unspeakable abominations within the temple itself.

8:1-6 'T_HE IDOL THAT PROVOKES TO JEALOUSY_' As at other times, *the hand of the Sovereign Lord came upon me there* (**8:1**) – that is, in Ezekiel's house, as the elders of Judah were seated before him. The *figure* he sees is so similar to the one seated on the throne in his first vision that it is safe to assume that it is Yahweh himself – not an interpreting angel – who lifts him up by his hair, takes him to Jerusalem, and takes him on a tour of the temple premises (**8:2-3a**; compare 1:27).

In Jerusalem the Spirit drops him at *the entrance to the north gate of the inner court* of the temple (**8:3b**), which is identical with *the gate of the altar* referred to in **8:5a**. At this gate, there stood *the idol that provokes to jealousy* (**8:3c, 5b**; see 2 Kgs 21:5; 23:12). Sandwiched between these references to the idol in 8:3 and 8:4, is Ezekiel's report that he again saw a vision of *the glory of the God of Israel,* as he had seen it before (**8:4**; see 1:25-28; 3:23). The juxtaposition

of this glory with the idol brings the incongruity of what is happening in the temple into sharp focus. God describes the situation as *utterly detestable* and refers to what is happening as *things that will drive me far from my sanctuary* (**8:6a**). But Ezekiel is still standing only in the entrance to the temple. God informs him that there is even worse to come (**8:6b**, see also 8:13, 15).

8:7-13 I_DOLATRY OF THE ELDERS_ In his vision, Ezekiel moves through the gate and enters the inner court, where he sees *a hole in the wall* (**8:7**). Following God's instructions, he either widens this hole, or digs another next to it, and finds *a doorway*, which he is told to enter (**8:8-9**).

On entering a room, he sees the *wicked and detestable things* of which God had warned him. What he sees is a room filled with paintings of *all kinds of crawling things and detestable animals and all the idols of the house of Israel* (**8:10**). In front of these images stand *seventy elders of the house of Israel* (**8:11a**). The number 'seventy' remind us of the seventy men who were chosen to help Moses lead the people (Exod 24:1, 9) and thus indicates that these are the leaders of the community. They are engaged in idolatrous worship as each of them offers incense to the animals and idols depicted on the walls (**8:11c**). They are offering these images the worship due to the only true God (Exod 20:3-4). *Standing among them* – perhaps even leading them in this worship – was a man Ezekiel recognized: *Jaazaniah son of Shaphan* (**8:11b**; see 2 Kgs 22:3).

Ezekiel is told that this is what the leaders are *doing in the darkness* (**8:12a**), possibly in the vain hope that the all-seeing God does not see in the dark – a hope that shows how darkened their own minds have become. But their words *the Lord does not see us* may need to be interpreted in light of the next phrase, *the Lord has forsaken the land* (**8:12b**, see 9:9). They are claiming that the Lord no longer cares about them, and so they are now seeking help from idols. But their own idolatry is what caused God to withdraw from them. They have not recognized their own sin and its consequences.

Shocking as this image is, God assures Ezekiel, *You will see them doing things that are even more detestable* (**8:13**), and brings the prophet to the next scene.

8:14-15 I_DOLATRY OF THE WOMEN_ It was not only the men who were involved in idolatry. The women too had been corrupted, as is evident from the group of women Ezekiel sees sitting *at the north gate of the house of the Lord* (**8:14a**). They were *mourning for Tammuz* (**8:14b**), a vegetation and fertility god, whose banishment to the underworld for six months of every year was mourned by his wife, his mother and his sister, and by women who worshipped him. His worship was similar to the worship of Baal – and it was being carried out in public view at the entrance to the temple!

Bad as this is, Ezekiel is warned that there is still more to come (**8:15**).

8:16-18 IDOLATRY OF SUN WORSHIP The blatant idolatry in the temple encroaches on the very heart of the temple as Ezekiel is brought into *the inner court of the house of the Lord* (**8:16a**). *There at the entrance to the temple, between the portico and the altar, were about twenty-five men* (**8:16b**). And what were these twenty-five men doing? The text says it all: *With their backs toward the temple of the Lord and their faces toward the east, they were bowing down to the sun in the east* (**8:16c**).

Not only are these men worshipping the sun, in violation of God's clear instructions (Deut 4:19), but they have also turned their backs on the temple. Their very posture is an insult to the covenant Lord. 'In bowing down to the sun, these men were literally lifting their backsides to God … The insult is blatant and breathtaking' (*BST*).

God's anger at these men was directed at more than just their idolatry, for he adds, *they also fill the land with violence* (**8:17**). He also describes them as *putting the branch to their nose.* The meaning of this phrase is obscure, but it may represent some obscene gesture.

Faced with this fourfold provocation, there is no way that the Lord will not punish these people. He tells the prophet: *Therefore I will deal with them in anger. I will not look on them with pity or spare them. Although they shout in my ears, I will not listen to them* (**8:18**).

At this point, it would be wise to pause and ask ourselves how often we provoke our almighty Creator and Redeemer with our substitute gods or alternative solutions to our problems. Too often, African Christians revert to traditional practices such as consulting witchdoctors in times of crisis, as if our God were not sufficient for all times and circumstances. We need to affirm and reaffirm that he is omnipotent, omniscient and omnipresent.

9:1-10:8 The punishment of Jerusalem

Having witnessed the abominable idolatry that has drawn God's judgment on Jerusalem and his people in 8:5-18, Ezekiel now observes the working out of that judgment in the form of the punishment of Jerusalem. Its unrepentant inhabitants are killed by the Lord's guards and fire is scattered on the city (10:1-8). An even worse judgment will follow, as the glory of God progressively withdraws from the city.

9:1-11 THE GUARDS OF THE CITY Now God commands, *Bring the guards of the city here* (**9:1**). The word translated 'guards' in the NIV and 'executioners' in the NASB could more literally be translated 'official visitors'. When God visits his people, he can do so either to bless or to punish. In the case of Jerusalem, the official visitors are here to execute his judgment.

There are seven guards. Six of them carry deadly weapons in their hands, while the seventh is *clothed with linen* and carries a scribe's *writing kit* (**9:2a**). They approach them *from the direction of the upper gate, which faces north* – the

same gate at which Ezekiel entered the temple, that is, the northern entrance to the inner court of the temple. The fact that *they came in and stood beside the bronze altar* (**9:2b**) is instructive, for that was where the leaders of the people were conducting their idolatrous worship (see 8:16) and where the judgment would to begin (see 9:6b).

As these men stand before the altar, *the glory of the God of Israel went up from above the cherubim* (**9:3**). These *cherubim* were the carved figures that sheltered the ark of the covenant in the holy of holies. God's glory thus leaves the holy of holies and moves *to the threshold of the temple.* The city's punishment and the withdrawal of the glory of God begin at the same time.

God now issues his instructions to his guards. First, he addresses the man clothed in linen. He is to *go throughout the city of Jerusalem and put a mark on the foreheads of those who grieve and lament over the detestable things that are done in it* (**9:4**; see also Rev 7:3; 9:4; 14:1). This mark identified those who not only remained faithful to the Lord but who were also deeply grieved by the types of sins that would bring God's judgment on the city. All of those who bear this mark will be delivered from the imminent judgment.

The other six guards are to follow this man as he moves around the city and *kill, without showing pity and compassion* all those who have not received his mark, regardless of their sex or age (**9:5-6a**). The marking and the slaughter are to *begin at my sanctuary,* that is, at the temple itself (**9:6b**; see 1 Pet 4:17). After all, that is where the leaders were taking part in abominable ceremonies. The result of this slaughter will be that even the dwelling place of the holy God will be defiled by human corpses (**9:7**; see 6:4-5, 13).

Left alone in a sea of slaughtered humanity, Ezekiel cannot not stand it any more. Though his forehead has been made 'harder than flint' (3:9), his heart has not. It is still tender, and so he pleads with the Lord: *Ah, Sovereign Lord! Are you going to destroy the entire remnant of Israel in this outpouring of your wrath on Jerusalem?* (**9:8**). The inhabitants of the northern kingdom had been deported by the Assyrians in 721 BC. The same fate had befallen the southern kingdom in 605 BC and 597 BC, when many had been deported to Babylon. A remnant had remained in Jerusalem, and now it seemed that this remnant was being wiped out!

But God will not relent – at least not yet (see 11:16-20). He reminds Ezekiel that *the sin of the house of Israel and Judah is exceedingly great* (**9:9a**). They are guilty of the abominations in the temple, bloodshed in the land and injustice in the city. They had abandoned God, and had then claimed, *The Lord has forsaken the land; the Lord does not see* (**9:9b**; see 8:12). In response, the Lord had indeed forsaken them, and will have no pity for them (**9:10**).

It is at this stage that the man in linen returns to report that *I have done as you commanded* (**9:11**). This report in itself may represent an answer to Ezekiel's prayer. This man has marked God's faithful servants so that they will be delivered from the slaughter. A remnant will indeed survive. Israel will not be completely destroyed.

10:1-8 COALS OF FIRE SCATTERED OVER THE CITY Once again, Ezekiel catches a glimpse of what he had seen in his inaugural vision (**10:1**; 1:22, 26) and receives a reminder of God's withdrawal from the city in the repetition of 9:3 in **10:4**. But this time he is not focusing on these details but on the continuing judgment of the city, as the Lord commands the man clothed in linen (see 9:2, 3, 11) to *go in among the wheels beneath the cherubim. Fill your hands with burning coals from among the cherubim and scatter them over the city* (**10:2**). After the death of its inhabitants, the city will be burned to the ground. This fire will not be lit by foreign invaders, but is sent from beneath God's throne, as an indication that this too is part of his judgment.

The mysterious man is handed the burning coals by one of the cherubim and then goes out to perform the task he has been assigned (**10:6-8**). For some unexplained reason, we do not actually see him carrying it out.

10:9-11:25 The departure of God's glory

The final element in God's judgment on this city is his gradual withdrawal from it. This departure had been hinted in 9:3 and 10:3-5, but now it becomes a reality. The detailed description of the cherubim who surround God's throne underscores the glory that is now being lost as God withdraws from his temple,

10:9-21 THE CHERUBIM The description of the cherubim and of the living creatures in this chapter is very similar to Ezekiel's description of his inaugural vision in 1:6-21. This section will focus on the new details that emerge.

The most striking is that whereas Ezekiel had previously identified the beings he saw only as 'living creatures', now he identifies them as *cherubim* (**10:9**; compare 1:15). He makes this identification explicit: *These were the living creatures I had seen beneath the God of Israel by the Kebar River, and I realized that they were cherubim* (**10:20**). It is possible that his vision of the temple has reminded him of the cherubim above the ark of the covenant, so that he now recognizes these creatures.

Another difference between the two visions is that the wheels beside the cherubim are referred to as *the whirling wheels* (**10:13**). We are also told that one of the four faces of each cherub is no longer the face of an ox but is now the face of a *cherub* (**10:14**; compare 1:10).

But the most significant difference between this chapter and the earlier one is that whereas in chapter 1 Ezekiel had seen the vision approaching and the cherubim were associated with the manifestation of God's glory, now they are associated with the withdrawal of that glory from the temple and the city as God imposes his judgment (**10:18-19**).

11:1-12 JUDGMENT ON THE LEADERS OF THE CITY Chapter 10 ends with the cherubim standing at the eastern gate of the temple, poised to depart (10:19). Ezekiel's account leaves them standing there while he includes further information that is also an important part of the story of the departure of the glory of the Lord. This information relates first to the people in Jerusalem (11:1-13a) and second to the exiles (11:13b-21).

Ezekiel was brought *to the gate of the house of the Lord that faces east* (**11:1**), the same point at which the cherubim had paused. There he sees a different group of *twenty-five men* from the one he had seen before in 8:16. This new group was composed of *leaders of the people*. Two of them – *Jaazaniah son of Azzur and Pelatiah son of Benaiah* – are people Ezekiel recognized from his pre-exilic days (see 8:11).

The Lord tells Ezekiel that these men *are plotting evil and giving wicked advice in the city* (**11:2**). He mentions two examples of the things they are saying. The first is *Will it not soon be time to build houses?* (**11:3a**). This question implies that they are completely ignoring God's warning of impending judgment and are intending to carry on living as before.

The second example of their wickedness is their saying, *This city is a cooking pot, and we are the meat* (**11:3b**). This statement is hard to interpret, because it seems from the context that the leaders are encouraging a false sense of security. But how can one find security in 'a cooking pot'? Some commentators suggest that the type of pot referred to here is actually a storage pot rather than a cooking pot. But it may simply be that the men are claiming that they are the choice meat, the best in society, and that they are as secure as meat in a tightly closed pot. Despite the warnings of God's servants, they may be thinking that Jerusalem is impregnable and that it will never fall.

God instructs Ezekiel, *Prophesy against them; prophesy, son of man* (**11:4**). The repetition of *prophesy* may reflect the intensity of the provocation and the urgency of the message. God gives Ezekiel his message, which begins with a refutation of what these people are saying: *That is what you are saying … but … you fear the sword, and a sword is what I will bring against you* (**11:5, 8**). *This city will not be a pot for you, nor will you be the meat in it* (**11:11**).

This contradiction of their false sense of security is followed by an exposure of their sins. The basic sin is their failure to meet their covenant obligations: *You have not followed my decrees or kept my laws but have conformed to the standards of the nations around you* (**11:12**). Touching on specific sins, the Lord says, *You have killed many people in this city and filled its streets with the dead* (**11:6**). Using the same image that these leaders had used, God says, *The bodies you have thrown there are the meat and this city is the pot* (**11:7**). The leaders have risen to the top over the corpses of others, and hence they should await the certain judgment of God. They may think they are secure in the city, but God says, *I will drive you out of the city ... I will execute judgment on you at the borders of Israel* (**11:9-10**).

11:13-21 ENCOURAGEMENT TO THE EXILES Ezekiel is still prophesying when, to his horror, he sees Pelatiah, one of the leaders whom he knows, fall down dead (**11:13a**). This death authenticates the divine source of the prophecy, but deeply disturbs Ezekiel, who cries out *in a loud voice* his second intercessory prayer (**11:13b**; see 9:8): *Ah, Sovereign Lord! Will you completely destroy the remnant of Israel?* In 9:9, the Lord refused Ezekiel's request, but this time the answer is positive. There will indeed be a remnant left.

The people of Jerusalem – represented by the leaders described in the preceding section – had dismissed the exiles, including Ezekiel, as *far away from the Lord* and had claimed the land for themselves, saying, *this land was given to us as our possession* (**11:14-15**). They had said that they were the choice meat, whereas the exiles were the bad meat that had been thrown away.

Not so, says the Lord. Speaking about the exiles, he says, *I have been a sanctuary for them in the countries where they have gone* (**11:16**). Nowhere else in the OT is the word 'sanctuary' used of any place other than the Tent of Meeting in the desert or the temple in Jerusalem. Thus the statement, that the Lord is 'a sanctuary' for his people in exile must have been of great comfort to the exiles.

God's promise of restoration rings out like a gospel message. Rather than having abandoned the exiles, the Lord promises, *I will gather you from the nations and bring you back from the countries, and I will you give you back the land of Israel again* (**11:17**). He will not only restore them to their land, but will restore them to himself: *I will give them an undivided heart and put a new spirit in them; I will remove from them their heart of stone and give them a heart of flesh* (**11:19**; see 36:26). As a result *they will follow my decrees and be careful to keep my laws* (**11:20a**). That is why, after returning to the land, they will *remove all its vile images and detestable idols* (**11:18**) which had led to their captivity in the first place.

Although the word 'covenant' is not mentioned anywhere in this passage, what we have here is a great covenant-renewal statement: *They will be my people, and I will be their God* (**11:20b**). But *those whose hearts are devoted to their vile images and detestable idols* will be destroyed (**11:21**).

11:22-25 FINAL DEPARTURE OF GOD'S GLORY Once Ezekiel has delivered his message of judgment and received his message of comfort, God's glory withdraws completely from the temple and from the city. However, it withdraws only as far as *the mountain east of it* (**11:22-23**), which must be none other than the Mount of Olives.

The vision is ending, and the same *Spirit of God* that had taken Ezekiel to Jerusalem in 8:3 now returns him to his home in Babylon (**11:24**). The prophet indicates the end of the vision when he says. *the vision I had seen went up from me.* He then faithfully reported to *the exiles everything the Lord had shown* him (**11:25**).

12:1-19:14 Prophecies and Objections

No date is given for the prophetic actions and oracles recorded in chapters 12 to 19. However, since they come immediately after the vision given in chapters 8 to 11, one can assume that they happened shortly after the prophet's report on that vision.

12:1-28 Prophecies of exile

The exiles may have been reluctant to hear God's message of judgment. So just as in chapters 4 and 5 Ezekiel acted out the siege of Jerusalem, now he is instructed to act out the exile and its implications.

12:1-16 DEPORTATION The Lord once again reminds Ezekiel that he is *living among a rebellious people* (**12:2a**). The adjective 'rebellious' is repeated a number of times in this chapter (12:3, 9, 25). The people are characterized as those who *have eyes to see but do not see and ears to hear but do not hear* (**12:2b**; see also Isa 6:9-10; Jer 5:21). No wonder God asked Ezekiel to dramatize his message! Jesus adopted a similar technique when he used parables to communicate with the Jews of his time, and could say that 'though seeing, they do not see; though hearing, they do not hear or understand' (Matt 13:10-17).

In an attempt to get the message to sink in, Ezekiel is commanded to act as if he is someone who is going into exile. During the day he is to pack what he can of his belongings into a knapsack and carry it on his back, as he would if he were being forced to leave his home. At night he is to act as if he is trying to flee something by tunnelling *through the wall* of his house, rather than using the door (**12:3-5**). Moreover, he is to cover his *face so that you cannot see the land* (**12:6a**). He is to do all this as *a sign to the house of Israel* (**12:6b**). Ezekiel reports his response: *So I did as I was commanded* (**12:7**).

Not surprisingly, people who saw this behaviour would have asked Ezekiel, *What are you doing?* (**12:8-9**), and the next day the Lord provides the answer: *This oracle concerns the prince in Jerusalem and the whole house of Israel who are there* (**12:10**). They will suffer the fate that Ezekiel has acted out and *will go into exile as captives* (**12:11**).

The 'prince' referred to here is Zedekiah, who was still ruling in Jerusalem at this time. The prophecy, which is given in more detail in **12:12-14**, was fulfilled when Zedekiah later tried to flee from the besieged city by a back way, but was captured, blinded and taken into exile (see 2 Kgs 25:4-7; Jer 39:2-7; 52:7-11).

When they see this prophecy come true, those who heard it *will know that I am the Lord* (**12:15**). Yet again, God remembers mercy in the midst of judgment, for a remnant will survive to acknowledge the sovereignty of the Lord (**12:16**).

12:17-20 FEAR The fear that will come upon the land is acted out by the prophet as he trembles while eating food and shudders while drinking water (**12:17-18**; see 4:16). Eating and drinking are normal acts – what is abnormal is for them to be accompanied by fear. But this is what the inhabitants of Israel will be reduced to (**12:19**). The reason they will suffer like this is *the violence of all who live there.* Those who have perpetrated oppression and violence will now have a chance to know what it feels like to suffer under it!

Sadly, one wonders why people have to go through calamities before they will acknowledge *that I am the Lord* (**12:20**).

12:21-28 DENIAL Two sayings seem to have been doing the rounds among the people. The first was a rejection of prophecy in general, as the people said: *The days go by and every vision comes to nothing* (**12:22**). These words sound very much like the scoffing of those who reject the truth of the Lord's return (2 Pet 3:3-4). God's pithy response says that exactly the opposite is true: *The days are near when every vision will be fulfilled* (**12:23**). Other prophets may have delivered *false visions or flattering divinations* (**12:24**), but Ezekiel's words will come true within the lifetime of those who have dismissed him (**12:25**).

The second saying seems to refer specifically to Ezekiel. People were saying, *The vision he sees is for many years from now, and he prophesies about the distant future* (**12:26-27**). The Lord responds by reiterating that whatever he says will be fulfilled without delay (**12:28**).

People can invent many excuses for not listening to the word of God, but what he says will come to pass at the appropriate time. We need to remind our hearers of this as we speak of the day of Christ's return and God's judgment.

13:1–14:11 False prophets

The proverbs cited in the previous section and the reference to 'false vision' in 12:24 naturally lead into the issue of true and false prophecy, a theme that continues until 14:11. God had given directions on how to distinguish true and false prophets (Deut 13:1-5; 18:20-22), but the people seemed to lack the capacity to do so (see, for example. 1 Kgs 22:1-28). Jeremiah and Ezekiel seem to have been the two prophets who faced the greatest challenge from false prophets, possibly because they spoke at particularly crucial times in the history of God's people. Thus chapters 13 and 14 are basically concerned with God's response to the false prophets who opposed Ezekiel. He starts by condemning two groups of pretenders: male prophets in 13:1-16 and female prophets or prophetesses in 13:17-23.

13:1-16 FALSE PROPHETS CONDEMNED The accusation against the male prophets is set out in 13:1-7. They are accused of prophesying *out of their own imagination*, and yet proclaiming *Hear the word of the Lord* as if God had sent them (**13:2**).

Instead of being led by God's Spirit, they *follow their own spirit.* Where Ezekiel has seen visions, they *have seen nothing* (**13:3**).

God describes these men as being *like jackals among the ruins,* fending for themselves, with no concern for the people (**13:4**). Had they truly cared for those they spoke to, they would have worked to fix what was wrong, not ignored it (**13:5**; see 22:30). Instead, *their visions are false and their divinations a lie* (**13:6a**; see Jer 23:16).

Since these false prophets proclaim *'The Lord declares',* when the Lord has not sent them (**13:6b**), the Lord will face them as an enemy: *I am against you* (**13:8**). Notice the triple judgment that will come upon the false prophets: *They will not belong to the council of my people* (that is, they will no longer be respected as leaders), they will not *be listed in the records of the house of Israel* (that is, they will no longer be regarded as belonging to the covenant people) and they will not *enter the land of Israel* at the time of the restoration (**13:9a**). What a terrible prospect! Then, God says, *you will know that I am the Sovereign Lord,* not someone whose name can be carelessly bandied about (**13:9b**).

One way the false prophets misled the people was by *saying, Peace, when there is no peace* (**13:10a**). Whereas God's true servant, Ezekiel, prophesies that judgment is coming in order to lead the people to repentance, these pretenders give them a false promise of security that will lead only to complacency.

Another metaphor elaborates this destructive activity of the false prophets: *When a flimsy wall is built, they cover it with whitewash* (**13:10b**). Their pronouncements gave the impression that Jerusalem was secure within its walls, and that no judgment was coming (**13:16**). Rather than exposing the rebelliousness of the people, as Ezekiel was doing, they whitewashed things to give the people a false sense of security. But the Lord will expose their work for what it is (**13:11-15**).

Teachers and preachers must proclaim the word of truth faithfully, regardless of what their hearers want to hear. They will at times have to say unpopular things.

13:17-23 FALSE PROPHETESSES CONDEMNED The OT sometimes speaks of the existence of women prophets among God's covenant people (Exod 15:20-21; Judg 4:4; 2 Kgs 22:14; Isa 8:3; see also Neh 6:14). However, because women prophets are seldom mentioned, the condemnation of the false prophetesses in this passage comes as a great surprise.

Like the false male prophets discussed in the preceding section, these female prophets, referred to as *the daughters of your people* in **13:17**, *prophesy out of their own imagination.* The accusations against them, introduced with *Woe,* are that they *sew magic charms on all their wrists and make veils of various lengths for their heads in order to ensnare people* (**13:18**). Although these women are said to 'prophesy', the description of their activities suggests that they were engaged in witchcraft and sorcery. Although it is not clear what was done with their charms and veils, what is clear is that they were used 'to ensnare people'.

Such magic is not harmless. Rather, it is a matter of life and death for those who believe in it: *You have killed those who should not have died and have spared those who should not live.* All this to earn no more than *a few handfuls of barley and scraps of bread* (**13:19**).

As in the case of the false prophets, God says, *I am against your magical charms.* He will deliver his people by tearing off the charms and veils with which they have been ensnared (**13:20-21**). He reminds the female prophets of why they are being judged: *Because you disheartened the righteous with your lies, when I had brought them no grief; and because you encouraged the wicked not to turn from their evil ways and so save their lives* (**13:22**). They will be forced to stop their evil practices and to recognize the sovereignty of the Lord (**13:23**).

14:1-11 The effect on the leaders The elders of Israel had come to Ezekiel to seek a word from the Lord before (8:1), and they will come again (20:1). Their appearance at this time (**14:1**) seems to say to the prophet 'You are denouncing these people (the false prophets and prophetesses), but what alternative do you offer?'

God, who searches the inner recesses of human hearts, recognizes that despite their external behaviour, these elders and the people they represent are idolaters at heart (**14:2-3**). He addresses them as such through his servant: *When any Israelite sets up idols in his heart and puts a wicked stumbling-block before his face and then goes to a prophet, I the Lord will answer him myself in keeping with his idolatry* (**14:4**). That person will get the answer he deserves! The Lord will respond with denunciation or punishment because he wants to recapture the hearts of his people (**14:5**). Hence the clarion call: *Repent! Turn from your idols* (**14:6**). God then repeats his words in 14:4, and issues a warning that if anyone guilty of idolatry does not repent, *I will set my face against that man and make him an example and a byword. I will cut him off from my people* (**14:7-8**).

False prophets and prophetesses may be persuaded to issue a prophecy that does not come from God. While such a prophecy is false and the individual uttering it responsible for what he or she says, there is also a sense in which God can say that he himself *enticed him* to utter it (**14:9**). This does not mean that God has led the prophet into sin, but rather that he has permitted circumstances in which the prophet could choose to act in a way that honoured God or in a way that was false to him. The choice made by the false prophets reveals that their hearts are not set on serving God. They and the person who sought the prophecy will be punished (**14:10**).

After the punishment has been meted out, there will come a time of great restoration and covenant renewal, when the surviving Israelites *will be my people and I will be their God* (**14:11**).

The rebuke to the elders reminds us that if we are seeking God's guidance or a time of refreshment and renewal, we must not approach him with a double mind or a divided heart, but with complete submission of our entire being to him and to his will (Jas 1:6-8).

14:12-23 Personal righteousness

In light of the impending judgment on Jerusalem, the exiles may have asked, 'Cannot God forgive the city for the sake of the few righteous persons that are in it? Abraham, our father, did pray for sinful Sodom along the same lines. And even righteous Daniel is among us, serving in the court of the Babylonian king!' (see Dan 1:3-6).

Then comes the prophetic word. God responds to the unfounded hope of the people by painting a hypothetical scenario: *if a country sins …* (**14:13a**). He then lists the four standard punishments he unleashes in judgment on sin: *famine* (**14:13b**), *wild beasts* (**14:15**), the *sword* (**14:17**), and *plague* (**14:19**).

God comes to the crux of the matter when he raises the issue of what would happen if the sinning city or country were prayed for by three of the most righteous people in Jewish history: *Noah, Daniel and Job* (**14:14**, see also **14:16**, **18, 20**). He insists that even these men *could save only themselves by their righteousness.* There is no hope for the city. The firmness of God's decision is underscored by the triple repetition of the oath formula, *as surely as I live.*

Turning from the hypothetical example to the real case of Jerusalem, the Lord says, *How much worse will it be when I send against Jerusalem my four dreadful judgments – sword and famine and wild beasts and plague* (**14:21**). His judgment is inevitable, and no amount of prayer will avert it.

We, like Ezekiel's audience, are probably surprised by God's statement: *Yet there will be some survivors.* These survivors are not the same as the righteous remnant who will return to the land after the captivity. The survivors mentioned here are those who somehow escape the calamities that fall on Jerusalem and are brought to join the exiles in Babylonia (14:22). The main reason that God allows them to survive is so that when the exiles see *their conduct and their actions* they *will be consoled* that the Lord was right in his judgment of the city: *You will know that I have done nothing in it without cause* (**14:22-23**). These words suggest that when the exiles meet the new arrivals, they will be shocked by their godless lives.

When we witness natural disasters and injustice in society, we have a tendency to blame God. We need to remember that although we cannot fathom why he allows things to happen, he is just in all that he does and that in some way or other his purposes will be accomplished.

15:1-16:63 Depictions of Jerusalem

Chapters 15 and 16 focus on Jerusalem, not just as the capital city but as the city that represents the whole nation.

15:1-8 A USELESS VINE Israel had been described as a vine before Ezekiel's time (see Gen 49:22; Ps 80:8-16; Isa 5:1-7). However, generally the focus had been on the fruit associated with the vine. Ezekiel does not even mention fruit here. Instead the passage focuses solely on the wood in the stem, which is only useful for burning – a reference to the judgment that is coming on the city.

The Lord asks a series of rhetorical questions about this vine. The answers to the questions are all in the negative and stress the uselessness of the vine. *How is the wood of a vine better than that of a branch on any of the trees in the forest?* (**15:2**). Answer: It is no better. *Is wood ever taken from it to make anything useful?* (**15:3**). Answer: No. *Do they make pegs from it to hang things on?* Answer: No. *And after it is thrown on the fire as fuel and the fire burns both ends and chars the middle, is it then used for anything?* (**15:4**). Answer: No.

This last question does raise the issue of why anyone would throw vine wood into the fire and remove it after it has been charred. As God says, *If it was not useful for anything when it was whole, how much less can it be made into something useful when the fire has burned it and it is charred?* (**15:5**). But this situation is mentioned because of what actually happened to Jerusalem. The city was charred (partially burned) by the fire of the Babylonians in 597 BC, but survived. The coming fire of judgment in 587 BC will completely consume it (15:7).

The interpretation of this parable is given in 15:6-8. *As I have given the wood of the vine among the trees of the forest as fuel for the fire, so will I treat the people living in Jerusalem* (**15:6**). Twice God says, *I will set my face against them* (**15:7**). The Lord makes explicit what the verbal picture of the burning of the worthless vine suggested: *I will make the land desolate* (**15:8**). Once again, the outcome will be that *you will know that I am the Lord* (15:7).

16:1-63 A FAITHLESS WOMAN This long, allegorical chapter, with its explicit sexual imagery presents many difficulties to translators and commentators. Scripture often refers to idolatry as spiritual adultery, but in this chapter adultery and idolatry are virtually fused into one. This fusion is less surprising once we learn that the Canaanite fertility religions to which Israel succumbed often involved cultic prostitution. Yahweh presents himself as a faithful husband whose love has been trampled under foot by his whoring wife (Israel). He describes her behaviour 'in the most graphic terms, so that when the judgment falls, all who witness it will recognize the justice of God' (*NICOT*).

At the outset, Ezekiel is commanded to *confront Jerusalem with her detestable practices* (**16:1-2**). Doing this involves telling her story, beginning with her origins.

Given the role of the patriarchs as Israel's ancestors (see Deut 26:5), it is strange to hear Ezekiel speak of the nation's Canaanite ancestry with an *Amorite* father and a *Hittite* mother (**16:3**). It is possible that here Ezekiel is focusing on Jerusalem's Canaanite origins as a Jebusite city (Josh 15:8, 63). The city is described as having been an unwanted child, one who was abandoned to the elements at birth so that she could die of exposure (**16:4-5**).

That was the condition in which God found Jerusalem/Israel. Her relationship with God started when God *passed by and saw you kicking about in your blood, and as you lay there in your blood I said to you, 'Live!'* (**16:6**). It was the timely arrival of the divine rescuer and his command, 'Live!', that reversed the death sentence on this infant and started her on life's journey. Not only that, he provided all that she needed to grow and in health and beauty, so that she became like *the most beautiful of jewels* (**16:7**).

When the girl had matured to marriageable age, the Lord made her his own by spreading *the corner of my garment over you* (**16:8a**; see Ruth 3:9), effectively taking her as his wife. The marriage was confirmed by a *solemn oath* at which time he *entered into a covenant with you ... and you became mine* (**16:8b**). Historically, this event is associated with the establishment of the covenant on Mount Sinai.

After making this abandoned infant his own, God continued to shower her with tokens of his love, to the extent that she was elevated to the enviable status of a *queen* (**16:9-13**). *And your fame spread among the nations on account of your beauty, because the splendour I had given you made your beauty perfect* (**16:14**). As Hannah testified, God is indeed one who 'raises the poor from the dust and lifts the needy from the ash heap; he seats them with princes and has them inherit a throne of honour' (1 Sam 2:8; see Luke 1:52-53).

It is an indication of spiritual maturity to remember where God brought us from and always be grateful to him for his redemptive grace.

The word *But* at the start of 16:15 indicates that things have taken a turn for the worse. And what a turn! Jerusalem/Israel uses the very things that God has showered upon her against him: *You trusted in your beauty and used your fame to become a prostitute* (**16:15-19**). 'The temptation to make the gifts of God the object of trust instead of trusting in the giver is one that has never failed to snare God's people through history, and is still a deadly trap for many of us today' (*BST*). Such idolatry will take us down the drain and back to the gutter if we are not careful.

Following the gods of the nations also led to child sacrifice (**16:20-21**). This is all the result of forgetting – forgetting where God brought her from: *In all your detestable practices and your prostitution you did not remember the days of your youth* (**16:22**).

Introducing the elaboration of Israel's prostitution with a double *Woe!* (**16:23**), God accuses her of practising her trade in *every public square* and with all the nations, *offering your body with increasing promiscuity to anyone who passed by* (**16:24-26**). She is repeatedly described as *insatiable* and *not satisfied* (**16:28-29**). God is here speaking of Israel's entry into political alliances with other nations, which involved relying on them rather than on the covenant Lord and worshipping their gods as a gesture of subservience. Hence the judgment: *So I stretched out my hand against you and reduced your territory* (**16:27**).

The perversity of this prostitute is evident not only in her preferring *strangers to your own husband* (**16:32**) but also in the fact that she is not attractive to others. Other prostitutes are paid for their services, but this woman has to pay others to come to her (**16:33-34**).

Although God's judgment was already touched on in 16:27, here we have the sentence delivered in full. It is introduced with the solemn words *Therefore, you prostitute, hear the word of the Lord* (**16:35**). After restating her crimes (**16:36**), God declares that he will punish his wife in the same way that all adulterers and murderers are punished (**16:38**). Her former lovers will carry out his sentence. They will demolish her shrines, take her wealth, burn her houses, strip her naked, and hack her to pieces, thus putting an end to her prostitution (**16:39-41**). This terrible fate will come upon her because she did not remember what the Lord has done for her (**16:43**; see 16:22).

After exacting his just retribution, God says, *my jealous anger will turn away from you; I will be calm and no longer angry* (**16:42**).

God now mentions the proverb, *Like mother, like daughter* (**16:44**). Jerusalem's conduct is similar to that of her mother and sisters, who also *despised their husbands and their children* (**16:45**; see also 16:3). Israel had despised her husband (Yahweh) and her children (that is, the people), an attitude that is demonstrated by her offering her children as sacrifices in idolatrous worship (see 16:20).

Jerusalem's sisters are named as Samaria to the north and Sodom to the south (**16:46**; see also 23:1-49). The Hebrew words for 'north' and 'south' are identical to the words for 'left' and 'right', suggesting that these three sisters are walking side by side, doing the same things. The other two cities had already experienced God's judgment and were despised by the Jews (see 2 Kgs 17; Gen 19), but in God's eyes Jerusalem was even *more depraved than they* (**16:47-48**). The sins of the two sister cities are described in **16:49-51**, but God insists that their sins pale by comparison with those of Jerusalem (**16:52**; see Matt 11:23-24).

God will, however, restore the fortunes of these three sisters – but each time he promises this, Jerusalem's restoration is mentioned last in the list (**16:53, 55**). The others will be restored first, *So that you may bear your disgrace and be ashamed of all you have done in giving them comfort*

(**16:54**). Self-righteous Jerusalem would not even mention Sodom *in the day of your pride, before your wickedness was uncovered* (**16:56**). But now Jerusalem's own wickedness has become public knowledge, and she too is despised by the surrounding nations (**16:57-58**). What a reversal!

After a reminder of what Israel deserves because she has broken her covenant with God (**16:59**), we are suddenly confronted with the word *Yet,* which introduces the promise of a glorious future reversal when God *will establish an everlasting covenant* with his people (**16:60**; see also Jer 31:31-34). In this new covenant, those who were earlier referred to as Israel's sisters will be given to her *as daughters* (**16:61b**). This will be a gift of grace, not something to which they are entitled on the basis of a covenant.

God declares that after his restoration you *will remember your ways and be ashamed* (**16:61a, 63**). Does this mean that God acts grudgingly when he restores his people, and that his people can never really enjoy their redemption because they are always aware of their shame? No, for our shame will simply drive us to 'the realization that God's judgment is just and that his salvation is entirely a matter of his incredible grace, not our merits' (*BST*).

17:1-24 The parable of two eagles and a vine

The story of the two eagles and a vine has been described as a riddle, a parable, an allegory or a fable (**17:1-2**). But whatever label we use, it is clear that God intends this passage to be read in the light of specific events in the nation's past, present and future history.

17:1-10 THE PARABLE The story starts with a description of a great eagle who lands on the top of a cedar tree in *Lebanon* (here to be understood as the land of Canaan or Judah – see Josh 1:4; 2 Kgs 14:9). The eagle broke off the *topmost shoot* of the cedar *and carried it away to a land of merchants* (Babylonia – see 16:29) *where he planted it in a city of traders* (Babylon – **17:3-4**). The eagle also took seed from the land and planted *it in fertile soil* and *abundant water, and it sprouted and became a low, spreading vine* (**17:5-6a**). Moreover, *its branches turned toward him, but its roots remained under it* (**17:6b**).

Then another eagle appeared, one that was not as glorious as the first one. Ignoring the fact that it had been planted in a perfect place, where it had everything it needed for splendid growth, *the vine now sent out its roots toward him from the plot where it was planted and stretched out its branches to him for water* (**17:7-8**). This decision to treat the second eagle as its source of nourishment had terrible consequences, for the vine will be *uprooted and stripped of its fruit so that it withers* (**17:9a**). The vine will no longer thrive, no matter what care is lavished on it, and will soon die (**17:9b-10**).

17:11-21 THE INTERPRETATION The Lord instructs Ezekiel to interpret this parable to the *rebellious* people (**17:11**) for it deals with the issue of rebellion, and specifically with Zedekiah's rebellion against the king of Babylon (2 Kgs 24:20; Jer 37–39). Rumours of this may have triggered a false hope of imminent return among the exiles.

Ezekiel explains that the first eagle is Nebuchadnezzar of Babylon, who deported 'the topmost shoot', that is, King Jehoiachin of Judah and his nobles, to Babylon in 597 BC (**17:12**; see 2 Kgs 24:8-17). Nebuchadnezzar then put Mattaniah (Jehoiachin's uncle) on the throne of Judah, after changing his name to Zedekiah (2 Kgs 24:17-20). Zedekiah was the seed planted in fertile soil that grew into fruitful vine (17:5).

When Nebuchadnezzar made Zedekiah ruler of Judah, he made a treaty with him *under oath*. The intention was to keep Zedekiah and Judah subservient to Babylon, *so that the kingdom would be brought low, unable to rise again, surviving only by keeping his treaty* (**17:13-14**). However, Zedekiah was attracted by the second eagle, representing Egypt, and broke the treaty *by sending his envoys to Egypt to get horses and a large army* (**17:15**). The results of this rebellion were disastrous. For some reason, the Egyptian army did not arrive to help Zedekiah when he needed it (**17:17**). Just as the Lord predicted, Zedekiah's rebellion failed and he died *in Babylon, in the land of the king who put him on the throne, whose oath he despised and whose treaty he broke* (**17:16**, **20-21**; Jer 52:3-11).

What really surprises us about this message is the fact that God held Zedekiah responsible for breaking his treaty with the king of Babylon (see **17:18**; see 17:15, 16). It appears that the Sovereign Lord of creation and redemption expects individuals, families, communities and nations to keep their promises (Num 30:2; Deut 23:21-23; Eccl 5:4-7). Psalm 15:4 praises the person 'who keeps his oath, even when it hurts him'.

God even goes so far as to speak of Zedekiah as having despised *my oath* and broken *my covenant* (**17:19**). But what was broken was a treaty between Nebuchadnezzar and Zedekiah! Yet Zedekiah had made this oath 'in God's name' (2 Chr 36:13), and thus God takes it as a promise made to him.

17:22-24 A GLORIOUS FUTURE Earthly imperial powers (the two eagles) have attempted to exercise kingly rule over God's people. God says 'no' to that. Returning to the parable, he says, *I myself* (note the emphasis) *will take a shoot from the very top of a cedar and plant it ... on a high and lofty mountain* (**17:22**). These *mountain heights of Israel* (**17:23a**) may be Mount Zion, which the prophets identify as the hub of the messianic kingdom (20:40; see also Ps 2:6; Mic 4:1).

The cedar that God plants will flourish and will provide shelter for *birds of every kind* (**17:23b**). It will be clear that this is God's work, for he will introduce a reversal in which the *tall tree* falls while *the low tree* grows tall (see 17:14), and *the green tree* dries up while the *dry tree* flourishes

(**17:24**). The tall tree and the green tree may be the political powers that have tried to subjugate God's people. When God brings these down and exalts his people, *all the trees of the field* will know that he is indeed the Lord. This great passage of hope and restoration concludes with *I the Lord have spoken, and I will do it.*

18:1-32 Individual responsibility

Biblical scholars have long debated the relationship of corporate and individual responsibility in the life of God's covenant people. This chapter, which is often invoked in that debate, does not present individual responsibility as being in contradiction to the corporate responsibility of the nation before God. Rather, it shows that Israelites are both corporately and individually responsible to the covenant Lord.

18:1-4 GOD'S RESPONSE TO A PROVERB The opening words of this chapter make it clear that a dispute is raging between God and his people in exile: *What do you people mean by quoting the proverb about the land of Israel: 'The fathers eat sour grapes, and the children's teeth are set on edge'?* (**18:1-2**). The fact that Jeremiah 31:29 also mentions this saying shows that it was on the minds of the exiles at this time. The people quoting this proverb were saying that they were suffering the consequences of the sins of their forefathers. As they put it in Lamentations 5:7: 'Our fathers sinned and are no more, and we bear their punishment.' These words imply that that God is being unjust in allowing things to happen in this way.

God's answer through his messenger is simple: *As surely as I live, declares the Sovereign Lord, you will no longer quote this proverb in Israel* (**18:3**). God then states two fundamental truths that support his royal pronouncement. The first is that *every living soul belongs to me.* He created us all, and so we all belong to him. The heredity issue does not apply, for *the father as well as the son – both alike belong to me* – individually (**18:4**). The second fundamental truth is that *the soul who sins is the one who will die.* We are individually responsible to God for our actions and how we conduct ourselves. We cannot hide behind any excuse, or blame our ancestors or our parents, our upbringing, poverty, ignorance, our environment or anything else for our predicament.

18:5-18 GOD'S PRINCIPLE The destinies of Ezekiel's audience are in their own hands (as are our destinies). The choice of life or death is theirs. To drive this point home, God presents the cases of three hypothetical individuals: a father, a son and a grandson.

First, the case of a righteous father. God starts by saying, *Suppose there is a righteous man* who reveals his righteousness in what he does (**18:5**). His actions are listed in what may be a standard catalogue of virtues. These virtues relate to religious and sexual practices (**18:6**) and economic, financial and legal relationships (**18:7-8**). They are stated both positively and negatively – that is, they include things the righteous person does and does not do. This man's way of life is summed up in **18:9a**: *He follows my decrees and faithfully keeps my laws.* God's verdict on such a man is *that man is righteous; he will surely live* (**18:9b**).

This righteous father has a son who is not at all like him. He is *a violent son, who sheds blood* (**18:10-11a**). The list of things the son does and does not do in **18:11b-13a** is very similar to the list of virtues in 18:6-8 – except that the son does the exact opposite of what his father does. The fact that the lists are so similar reminds us that God, 'the Judge of all the earth' (Gen 18:25), does not use one set of standards for one person and another set of standards for another. The bedrock principles of his justice are the decrees and laws mentioned in 18:9.

Just as God gave an assurance that the righteous father will live (18:9), so he makes it equally clear that the unrighteous son will not live (**18:13b**). This son cannot blame anyone for his situation: *His blood will be on his own head.*

Finally, we come to the grandson of this hypothetical family, *who sees all the sins his father commits and though he sees them, he does not do such things* (**18:14**). The son does not blindly follow his father's bad example. He exercises his God-given power of choice and 'does not do such things'. The full catalogue of virtues is not repeated in **18:15-17a**, although much of the list is given. God's verdict on this grandson is that *he keeps my laws and follows my decrees* (**18:17b**; compare 18:9). The outcome of his life is stated positively and negatively: *He will not die for his father's sin* (his father's sour grapes will not set this son's teeth on edge)*; he will surely live.*

As if to put the wages of the two ways side by side, God reminds us, *But his father will die for his own sin, because he practised extortion, robbed his brother and did what was wrong among his people* (**18:18**).

18:19-32 FURTHER EXPLANATION OF THE PRINCIPLE But the people are curious, asking *Why does the son not share the guilt of his father?* (**18:19a**). After all, they are assuming that they are suffering for the sins of their fathers (18:2). So why does God allow this son to escape their fate?

God answers their query by summarizing what has gone before and by restating the principle as follows: *Since the son has done what is just and right and has been careful to keep all my decrees, he will surely live. The soul who sins is the one who will die. The son will not share the guilt of the father, nor will the father share the guilt of the son. The righteousness of the righteous man will be credited to him, and the wickedness of the wicked will be charged against him* (**18:19b-20**).

God then elaborates on this principle from a slightly different angle, dealing not with punishment for parent's sins but with punishment for one's own sins. He presents the hypothetical case of a man who has been wicked but who

truly repents of his sins, is reconciled with God and seeks to obey him. God announces that such a man will also live (**18:21**). Not only will this man escape death, but also God says, *None of the offences he has committed will be remembered against him. Because of the righteous things he has done* (that is, after he has been reconciled with God), *he will live* (**18:22**).

God explains his verdict in terms of a fundamental truth about his nature: *Do I take any pleasure in the death of the wicked? ... Rather, am I not pleased when they turn from their ways and live?* (**18:23**; see 33:11). God cannot allow sin to go unrepented and unpunished, but he does not enjoy doling out punishment. 'What pleases him is that moment of repentance and genuine turning on the part of the sinner which liberates God to exercise his unique and greatest divine capacity in the granting of life. *Life* is God's gift. Life is his creation. Life is his desire. Life is his pleasure' (*BST*).

God then describes the opposite scenario, in which *a righteous man* backslides into sin, and asks the question: *Will he live?* The answer is that *he will die* (**18:24**).

Ezekiel's audience react by saying, *The way of the Lord is not just* (**18:25**). God responds by saying that he is acting in perfect justice, and that it is the *ways of the house of Israel* that are unjust. He then restates the cases of the backsliding *righteous* person and repentant *wicked* person (**18:26-28**), before repeating the Israelites' accusation and his response to it (**18:29**).

God's final impassioned appeal to the Israelites to repent is addressed to the *house of Israel* corporately, but also stresses individual responsibility in that he promises to judge *each one according to his ways* (**18:30a**). He passionately pleads with his covenant people to repent: *Turn away from all your offences ... Rid yourselves of all the offences you have committed ... Why will you die, O house of Israel ... Repent and live!* (**18:30b-32**). Whereas in 36:26 it is God who gives them 'a new heart' and puts in them 'a new spirit' (see 11:19), here the people are told to *get a new heart and a new spirit* (18:31) as if it were within their power to do so. This only underscores the need for personal choice that God is hammering home in this chapter. The contrast between 18:31 and 36:26 reminds us of 'the mysterious interaction between what humans are required to do, and what God alone can do for them' (*BST*).

19:1-14 A lament for Israel's leaders

This poem is clearly labelled as *a lament* (19:1, 14). Both form and content work together to get the message across. Ezekiel may not have shed many tears over the wicked last kings of Judah – least of all Zedekiah – but he could not have witnessed the demise of the Davidic dynasty without profound sorrow.

The lament neatly divides into two parts, with the break marked by the change of imagery from a lioness and lions (19:1-9) to a vine (19:10-14).

The use of a lion to represent individuals, nations or royalty was familiar to Israelites (see Gen 49:8-10; Num 23:24; Mic 5:8). In this passage, the lioness represents the nation as a whole, rather than an individual mother. She *brought up one of her cubs and he became a strong lion* (**19:1-3**). When he *learned to tear the prey* and started to devour *men, the nations heard about him, and he was trapped in their pit. They led him with hooks to the land of Egypt* (**19:4**). This lion must represent Jehoahaz of Judah, who was seized by Pharaoh Neco in 609 BC and taken to Egypt, where he died (see 2 Kgs 23:31-35).

When the lioness realized that there was no hope of the first strong lion returning, *she took another of her cubs and made him a strong lion* (**19:5**). This lion appears to be even stronger than his predecessor, for in addition to tearing *the prey* and devouring *men,* he also *prowled among the lions* (**19:6**). *He broke down their strongholds and devastated their towns,* to such an extent that *the land and all who were in it were terrified by his roaring* (**19:7**). Hence, *the nations* and *those from the regions round about him* came and *spread their net for him, and he was trapped in their pit … They pulled him into a cage and brought him to the king of Babylon* (**19:8-9**).

Scholars are divided as to who this second lion was. Some say it represents Jehoiachin, who was deported to Babylon in 597 BC. Others say it represents Zedekiah, the last king of Judah, who was blinded and taken to Babylon after the fall of Jerusalem in 587 BC (see 2 Kgs 25:1-7).

The vine is also a well-known symbol of Israel (15:1-6; 17:1-10; see also Ps 80:8-16; Isa 5:1-7; 27:2-6). Thus the mother, representing the nation, is said to be like *a vine … planted by the water … fruitful and full of branches* (**19:10**). These branches are said to be *strong, fit for a ruler's sceptre* (**19:11**), bringing in the idea of royalty. However, a vine is not usually a towering plant, so the description of it as being *conspicuous for its height* may suggest that pride was an element in its downfall. Whatever the case, *it was uprooted in fury and thrown to the ground* (**19:12a**).

The mention of *the east wind* (**19:12b**) and of the vine being replanted *in the desert, in a dry and thirsty land* (**19:13**) are understood to be pointers to Babylon, which withered the strong branches and consumed them with fire (**19:12c**). It is striking that one of the vine's own branches contributed to its demise: *Fire spread from one of its main branches and consumed its fruit* (**19:14**). This is understood to be a reference to Zedekiah, the last king of Judah, whose rebellion precipitated the Babylonian captivity. Now the prophet laments that *no strong branch is left on it fit for a ruler's sceptre.*

Many human institutions self-destruct in this way. Even the church needs to be on guard against self-destructive elements that may arise from within its own ranks.

20:1-23:49 Like Leaders, Like People

The elders of Israel came and sat down before Ezekiel seeking to hear a word from the Lord (20:1; see 8:1; 14:1). We are not told exactly what their concerns were. The Lord's response to their queries is given in chapters 20–23.

20:1-44 A history of rebellion

20:1-4 PROLOGUE TO THE HISTORY In the introductory verses of chapter 20, God responds to the presence of the elders of Israel, *who came to inquire of the Lord* (**20:1**). His response sets the tone for what follows: They do not have any right to ask anything from the Lord because of their rebellion (**20:2-3**).

God sternly charges his prophet: *Will you judge them? Will you judge them, son of man? Then confront them with the detestable practices of their fathers* (**20:4**). Ezekiel then goes on to review the bleak history of the people, as he has already done in chapter 16 and will do again in chapter 23. His aim is to help the exiles to reflect on their situation and return to God. 'Ezekiel's intention is to force the exiles to look again at the history they thought they knew, the history which was giving them such a misplaced sense of confidence (while Jerusalem was still standing) and of grievance (when it finally fell)' (*BST*). This history is presented in metaphors and allegories in chapters 16 and 23, but here in chapter 20 it is told as straightforward history. It is presented in terms of four periods: in Egypt (20:1-9), in the wilderness (20:10-26), in the promised land (20:27-29) and in Ezekiel's day (20:30-44). A clear pattern can be observed in the first three periods – God's grace, the people's rebellion, his threat of judgment and his relenting for the sake of his name.

Some scholars mistakenly describe Ezekiel's presentation of the history of the people of Israel as 'revisionist' or 'distorted'. Such labels ignore the fact that it is perfectly reasonable to interpret history so that it speaks to the audience to whom the history is being presented. Moreover, responsibility for any 'revisionism' here must be laid at God's door, not Ezekiel's – the prophet is merely saying what God tells him to say.

20:5-9 REBELLION IN EGYPT Reminding them of the grace he has showered on them, God says: *On the day I chose Israel, … I swore to them that I would bring them out of the land of Egypt into a land I had searched out for them, a land flowing with milk and honey, the most beautiful of all lands* (**20:5-6**). It comes as a surprise to us to hear God's speak as if his choice of Israel was first made when they were in Egypt rather than with the patriarchs. We are also surprised that the first rebellion is said to be simultaneous with the exodus, before the incident with the golden calf at Sinai. The people are said to have disobeyed his command to *get rid of the vile images you have set your eyes on, and do not defile yourselves with the idols of Egypt, I am the Lord your God* (**20:7**). Maybe God is trying to drive home the point that they were a rebellious people right from the outset.

But the people did not respond to God's gracious gesture. They rebelled against him, refused to listen to him and did not *forsake the idols of Egypt*. What could God do in the face of such rebellion? *I said I would pour out my wrath on them and spend my anger against them in Egypt* (**20:8**) – at the time of the exodus! But God did not follow through on this threat, and he tells us the reason why: *But for the sake of my name I did what would keep it from being profaned in the eyes of the nations they lived among and in whose sight I had revealed myself to the Israelites by bringing them out of Egypt* (**20:9**).

20:10-26 REBELLION IN THE DESERT The pattern we saw in the preceding section – the manifestation of God's grace, the rebellion of the people, the threat of God's judgment and his relenting for the sake of his name – is repeated here with regard to both the first (20:10-17) and the second generation (20:18-26).

Not because the exodus generation deserved it, but because of his everlasting mercy, God *led them out of Egypt and brought them into the desert* (**20:10**). Having brought them into the desert, the next great thing he did for them was that he *gave them my decrees and made known to them my laws, for the man who obeys them will live by them* (**20:11**). Moreover, *I gave them my Sabbaths as a sign between us, so they would know that I the Lord made them holy* (**20:12**). The Sabbath – whether in its weekly (Exod 20:8-11; Deut 5:12-15) or annual forms (Exod 23:10-11; Lev 25; Deut 15:1-18) – has significance beyond what we can realize because it is deeply entrenched in the covenant of the creator and redeemer God.

And what was the people's response to this gracious God of creation and redemption? They *rebelled against me in the desert* (**20:13**). Not only did they reject God's law, but they also *utterly desecrated my Sabbaths*. Hence, God wanted to *pour out my wrath on them and destroy them in the desert*. But again, for the sake of his name, he relented (**20:14**). Nevertheless, *with an uplifted hand* – a customary way of taking an oath in those days – God swore that the first wilderness generation would not enter the promised land (**20:15**). This measured response is highlighted by the twin statements: *For their hearts were devoted to their idols* (**20:16**), and *yet I looked on them with pity and did not destroy them and put an end to them in the desert* (**20:17**).

Coming to the second wilderness generation, God instructed them, *Do not follow the statutes of your fathers or keep their laws or defile yourselves with their idols* (**20:18**). The first generation had rejected God's laws and substituted

their own statutes and laws! Reinforcing his counsel to the children of that rebellious generation, God says, *I am the Lord your God; follow my decrees and be careful to keep my laws* (**20:19**). He also repeats his instruction about *my Sabbaths* and ends with the statement, *then you will know that I am the Lord your God* (**20:20**).

Unfortunately, the account continues *But the children rebelled ... They did not follow my decrees, they were not careful to keep my laws* (**20:21a**). And thus another *So* (**20:21b**). And yet again, *But I withheld* (**20:22**). How long-suffering is the covenant Lord! God's measured response to the sin of the second generation was that although they would be preserved and be able to enter the promised land, he would later *disperse them among the nations and scatter them through the countries* (**20:23**).

God then returns to the issue of their disobedience and adds more details of it and of his judgment. *Their eyes lusted after their fathers' idols* (**20:24**), and so God *gave them over to statutes that were not good and laws they could not live by* (**20:25**), and allowed them to *become defiled through ... the sacrifice of every firstborn* (**20:26**).

We may react to the last two statements by asking: 'How can God give them over to statutes that were not good and laws they could not live by'? And: 'How can he let them become defiled by the sacrifice of their firstborn?'

The answer to the first question is found when we remember that 20:18 declared that the first wilderness generation had set up their own statutes and laws. We should not be surprised if the second generation, whose 'eyes lusted after their fathers' idols', also followed their fathers' statutes and laws. Therefore 'the laws they could not live by' are of their own making, not God's.

Coming to the second question, the Canaanite practice of child sacrifice is explicitly condemned by God (Lev 20:2-5). Therefore we cannot think that God encouraged this. What the text says is that God *let them* (20:26) – in the same sense as he 'gave them over' (20:25). This carries the same meaning as Paul's words in Romans 1:24, 26, 28, where he says, 'Therefore God gave them over'. God did not encourage or condone such practices, but he did not step in to prevent the people from experiencing the human consequences of their rebellion.

20:27-29 REBELLION IN THE PROMISED LAND The people's rebellion continued even after they had inherited the land. The pattern we observed in the description of earlier rebellions is not to be seen here nor in the section that follows – which may be an indication that judgment is imminent. Though brief, it is a telling description. Not only have the fathers of the exilic community *blasphemed me by forsaking me* (**20:27**), says God, but *when I brought them into the land I had sworn to give them and they saw any high hill or any leafy tree, there they offered their sacrifices, made offerings that* *provoked me to anger, presented their fragrant incense and poured out their drink offerings* (**20:28**).

This is exactly what God had warned them not to do. Before they even entered the land, he had told them to completely destroy the high places (Deut 12:2-4, 29-31). God contemptuously asked why they continued to go to this *Bamah*, or high place, which survived despite the condemnation of all such places by prophets and attempts at reformation by godly kings (**20:29**; 1 Kgs 3:2-3; 12:31-32; 22:43; 2 Kgs 18:1-4). The people's persistence in worshipping there was one of the factors that precipitated the judgment of the captivity.

20:30-44 Rebellion in ezekiel's day Turning to the elders gathered in Ezekiel's house, God reminds them of how their sins are the same as those of their ancestors: *You defile yourselves the way your fathers did and lust after their vile images* (**20:30**). They even appear to be practising child-sacrifice at the same time as they come to seek to hear from the Lord! So God returns to the point he made at the start of their gathering, *Am I to let you inquire of me, O house of Israel? ... I will not let you inquire of me* (**20:31**; see 20:3). They cannot expect to hear from him while they *want to be like the nations, like the peoples of the world, who serve wood and stone* (**20:32a**; see also 1 Sam 8:4-5).

But God will not allow them to be 'like the nations'. He has a higher plan for them, and he persists with it until it overwhelms their persistent rebellion. In his great grace, he will not give up, as we would be tempted to do. Instead he says, *I will rule over you with a mighty hand and an outstretched arm and with outpoured wrath* (**20:32b-33**). We may not welcome 'outpoured wrath', and we may not think that it looks like grace – until we remember that God is a loving father. His judgment is not intended to punish and destroy but to discipline his people and bring them back to him: *I will bring you from the nations and gather you from the countries where you have been scattered* (**20:34**). God brings them into *the desert of the nations,* that is, into exile in the Babylonian desert, where they will be forced to meet with him *face to face* in judgment, without any of their usual props to hide behind (**20:35**).

Yet even this promise of judgment is softened by the words *As I judged your fathers in the desert of the land of Egypt, so I will judge you* (**20:36**). God remembers mercy in judgment, and here he appears to be holding out the hope of another exodus as well as another judgment! This hope grows brighter as the next verse says: *I will take note of you as you pass under my rod and I will bring you into the bond of the covenant* (**20:37**). But this will happen only after God purges them: *I will purge you of those who revolt and rebel against me* (**20:38**). It seems that just as those in the first wilderness generation who rebelled against God died in the desert, so those who persist in rebellion in 'the desert of the nations' will die there. They will not re-enter the land with

the 'purified who acknowledge Yahweh and with whom he can start anew' (*NICOT*).

God tells the still rebellious *house of Israel* gathered before him to *Go and serve your idols, every one of you* (**20:39**). And yet his *But afterwards* introduces a wonderful promise of restoration: *You will surely listen to me and no longer profane my name.* God confirms that one day *the entire house of Israel* will serve him *on my holy mountain, the high mountain of Israel* – the very mountain that was the site of the detestable abominations of the people (**20:40**; see 6:1-3). The returnees are described as *fragrant incense* as he brings them from among the nations. Not only will they *know that I am the Lord,* but his holiness will also be vindicated (**20:41-42**). What is said about the returnees in **20:43-44** may be unpalatable to human pride, but 'the good news of the gospel is not that "there *must* be something truly wonderful about us if God can love us and accept us so readily," but that there must be something truly wonderful about God!' (*NICOT*).

20:45-21:32 Judgment on Ezekiel's contemporaries

This passage is all one chapter in the Hebrew. It falls into four sections: three introduced with the prophetic formula *The word of the Lord came to me* (**20:45**; **21:8, 18**), and one with *And you, son of man, prophesy and say* (**21:28a**). All of them are united by the theme of the sword as an instrument of God's judgment. Even though the prophecy of 20:45-49 speaks of fire, it is explained in 21:1-7 in terms of the sword.

20:45-21:7 The burning of the southern forest Having surveyed the rebellious history of the covenant people, God now signals that judgment is imminent by commanding his messenger to prophesy towards the southern part of Judah, where Jerusalem is located (20:46). He is to prophesy that a great fire will consume all the trees in that area (20:47). This fire will clearly come from the Lord (20:48).

Then for a moment we hear Ezekiel speak, with the exclamation, *Ah, Sovereign Lord!* His exclamation may be one of surprise, but given what follows it is more likely to be one of frustration about the reaction of the people to his word: *They are saying of me, 'Isn't he just telling parables?'* (**20:49**). The people may be dismissing his prophecy with contempt, or they may simply be failing to understand it. But God makes sure that it's meaning is clear, for he gives an interpretation of the parable of the forest fire in 21:1-7.

Although the section opens with *The word of the Lord came to me* and, therefore, may appear to be the beginning of completely different oracle (**21:1**), we are not treating it as such because it has so many similarities to the oracle against the southern forest. There Ezekiel was told *set your face towards the south* (**20:46a**), here he is told *set your face against Jerusalem* (**21:2a**). There he was told to *preach against the south* (**20:46b**); here he is told to *preach against* *the sanctuary* (**21:2b**). There he was told *to prophesy against the forest of the southland* (**20:46c**). Here he is told to *prophesy against the land of Israel* (**21:2c**).

There it was said that the fire would consume *both green and dry* (**20:47a**); here God says, *I will draw my sword from its scabbard and cut off the righteous and the wicked* (**21:3**). There it was said *every face from south to north will be scorched* by the fire (**20:47b**); here God says, *my sword will be unsheathed against everyone from south to north* (**21:4**). There God says, *everyone will see that I the Lord have kindled it; it will not be quenched* (**20:48**); here God says, *then all people will know that I the Lord have drawn my sword from its scabbard; it will not return again* (**21:5**). Could there be any doubt that 21:1-7 is the interpretation of 20:45-49? The only difference is that the judgment is by fire in the previous section whereas it is by the sword in the present section.

The judgment leaves us uneasy because it indiscriminately consumes green and dry, the righteous and the wicked (20:47; 21:3). This is what happens when the whole land – *everyone from south to north* – is engulfed in judgment. As the Tigrigna proverb from Eritrea reminds us, *besenki nequts yinedid rhus* ['because of the dry wood, the green wood is burned']. The judgment that comes for the wicked also affects the righteous.

The prophet is then asked to dramatize the terrible judgment that will come upon the people. God commands him to *groan before them with broken heart and bitter grief* (**21:6**). When the people come and ask him why he is groaning, he is told to respond: *Because of the news that is coming*. This news will be so terrible that *every heart will melt and every hand go limp; every spirit will become faint and every knee become as weak as water!* (**21:7**). And there is no doubt that it is coming, for the Lord declares, *It will surely take place*.

21:8-17 THE SONG OF THE SWORD This prophecy is in the form of a poem or song, with a couple of prose comments (21:10b, 13). Some commentators think the prophet may even have brandished a real sword while saying these words.

The song opens with a double announcement of the coming of the sword: *A sword, a sword, sharpened and polished – sharpened for the slaughter, polished to flash like lightning!* (**21:9-10a**; see also **21:11**, **15b**). The sword is ready for use and is being brandished to drive the people to repentance before it is put to use. God says that he has *stationed the sword for slaughter at all their gates* (**21:15a**).

The one holding the sword (who is later identified as the king of Babylon – 21:18, 21) is instructed to *let the sword strike twice, even three times*, multiplying the slaughter it wreaks (**21:14b**). The sword itself is even personified and given instructions by God: *O sword, slash to the right, then to the left, wherever your blade is turned* (**21:16**).

Both the prophet and God strike their hands together in a physical affirmation that God is acting in judgment (**21:14a**, **17**). However, neither of them rejoices in what

is happening. In fact the prophet is to *cry and wail* and *beat your breast* – a physical sign of sorrow and heartbreak (**21:12**).

The two prose interruptions of the song in **21:10b** and **21:13** are extremely difficult to interpret, which is why there are so many different versions of them in different translations of the Bible. The NIV tries to solve the problem by adding the word *Judah*, which is not present in the Hebrew as the two marks around the word in the NIV show. It then treats these verses as if they both show the sword despising the sceptre. It justifies this interpretation by referring back to the messianic prophecy about Judah and the sceptre in Genesis 49:9.

The NASB stays closer to the Hebrew in that it does not add any words, but says 'or shall we rejoice, the rod of My son despising every tree? (21:10b) and 'For there is a testing; and what if even the rod which despises will be no more?' (21:13). But while these may more accurately reflect the original, the meaning is still very obscure.

It seems, however, that these words imply that, despite the imminent judgment, the Jews are still holding on to the belief that God's covenant with David in 2 Samuel 7 means that Jerusalem will be saved and that a Davidic king will rule there. They may have taken the words, 'the sceptre (or rod) of my son' as their slogan. God sarcastically asks them what will happen if it *does not continue?* (21:13).

21:18-27 A ROAD MAP FOR THE BABYLONIANS In this oracle it looks as if God is instructing the prophet to draw a road map for the king of Babylon so that he can come and besiege Jerusalem: *Son of man, mark out two roads for the sword of the king of Babylon to take, both starting from the same country* (**21:19**). The king will probably approach from the north. Shortly after the road going south leaves Damascus in Syria, it branches. At this point Ezekiel is to *mark a signpost* indicating which fork leads to Jerusalem and which to *Rabbah of the Ammonites* (**21:20**).

It seems that the king of Babylon has not yet decided which city to attack. So he seeks divine guidance as to which to attack first (**21:21**). Throwing *arrows*, consulting *idols* and examining the *liver* of a sacrificed animal were all standard ways of divination in the ancient Near East. God says that he will make sure that the outcome of this divination identifies Jerusalem as the target (**21:22**). History records that Nebuchadnezzar did indeed take the actions recorded in 21:22.

The Jerusalemites under the leadership of Zedekiah will be full of false confidence. They have failed to listen to God and will dismiss the omen that Nebuchadnezzar receives as false (**21:23**). They will despise it in the same way they had earlier despised the treaty by which they swore allegiance to the king of Babylon and turned to Egypt (see 17:16). Humanly speaking it was that action that has led to this siege (**21:24**).

Zedekiah the king is sent a personal message, addressed to him as the *profane and wicked prince of Israel, whose day has come* (**21:25**). He is told to *take off the turban* and *remove the crown* – both of which signalled his status (**21:26**).

We hear a trumpet blast ring out in judgment: *A ruin! A ruin! I will make it a ruin!* (**21:27**). But, amazingly, this trumpet also signals hope. The crown will be restored when *he comes to whom it rightfully belongs*, that is, the Messiah (see Gen 49:10) who will usher in the eternal kingdom of God.

21:28-32 POSTPONEMENT OF JUDGMENT ON AMMON The Ammonites who lived in Rabbah had also been involved in the revolt against the king of Babylon (Jer 27:1-3) and could easily have been the target towards which Nebuchadnezzar advanced (21:20). Relieved that Jerusalem will bear the brunt of that judgment, they turn against their ally and hurl insults at Jerusalem. But once again the song of the sword is sung (**21:28b**; see 21:8-17), indicating that they too will face judgment. Their *false visions* and *lying divinations* will not prevent it (**21:29**). Like Jerusalem, the Ammonites will find that sword laid against their necks.

But the time for their judgment has not yet come, and therefore God commands, *Return the sword to its scabbard* (**21:30a**; see also 21:5). The Babylonians – God's instrument of judgment on these nations – are not to strike the Ammonites now. They must focus on their assignment with Jerusalem. However, though they are spared for now, he will judge the Ammonites in due time for their eagerness to turn against his covenant people and heap insults on them (**21:30b-32**; see also 25:1-7). We are reminded of the saying, 'If a man digs a pit, he will fall into it; if a man rolls a stone, it will roll back on him' (Prov 26:27).

22:1-31 Jerusalem's idolatrous leadership

This chapter returns to the theme that judgment is coming on Jerusalem, where the leadership of the nation is concentrated. The chapter is divided into three parts by the prophetic formula *the word of the Lord came to me* (22:1, 17, 23).

22:1-16 DISOBEDIENCE TO THE MOSAIC LAW The indictment starts with a call to Ezekiel to *judge this city of bloodshed* (**22:1-2**). The theme of bloodshed returns repeatedly in this section (22:3-4, 6, 9, 12-13). But it is only one of the city's *detestable practices* (22:2; see also 20:4). It is also guilty of idolatry (**22:3-4**). The city has hastened the coming of its day of judgment and shortened its life by these violations of God's law. When God's judgment falls on her, all the nations – *those who are near and those who are far away* – will mock her (**22:5**).

The sins listed in **22:6-12** are all violations of the law of Moses as regards respect for parents, care for strangers and the poor, ritual purity and respect for God's Sabbaths, truthfulness, sexual purity, covetousness and usury. All these things are taking place *in you* (22:6-7, 9-12), so the whole city is implicated in the sins of its inhabitants.

God indicates that the judgment of the city is inevitable when he says, *I will surely strike my hands together* (**22:13**) and challenges her to stand up to his wrath (**22:14**). His judgment will take the form of dispersing the people *among the nations* (**22:15**). Jerusalem will not only be the *laughing-stock* of the nations (22:4), it will also be *defiled* in their eyes (**22:16**). Then the humiliated inhabitants of the city will remember *that I am the Lord*.

22:17-22 THE PURIFYING EFFECT OF THE JUDGMENT God uses the language of metalworking – specifically the process of smelting ore – in these verses to illustrate the sin of his people and the method he will use to purify them. He exposes the rebellious nature of the people when he says, *the house of Israel has become dross to me; all of them are the copper, tin, iron and lead left inside a furnace* (**22:17-18**). Even after the smelting process that the nation has endured in God's previous judgments, all that remains is *dross* and not pure metal. So God says, *I will gather you into Jerusalem. As men gather silver, copper, iron, lead and tin into a furnace to melt it with a fiery blast, so I will gather you in my anger and my wrath and put you inside the city and melt you* (**22:19-20**). When the people take refuge in the fortified city for security, they will simply be moving into God's smelting furnace, where they will soon recognize that God is pouring out his wrath on them (**22:22**).

22:23-31 THE WICKEDNESS OF THE LEADERS After an indictment of the land as a whole (**22:23-24**), the rest of the chapter (except for 22:29) deals with the leaders who have failed God and the people. First the Lord accuses their *princes* of being *like a roaring lion tearing its prey; they devour people* (**22:25**). They take the *treasures and precious things* from the people. The fact that they *make many widows* within the city points to the bloodshed associated with their activities.

The *priests*, too, have neglected their duty. God accuses them of doing *violence to my law* (**22:26**). In profaning the *holy things* of God, in failing to *distinguish between the holy and the common*, in teaching the people *that there is no difference between the unclean and the clean* they have failed to fulfil a responsibility that was explicitly given to them (Lev 10:10-11). In shutting *their eyes to the keeping of the Sabbaths*, they also do violence to God's law. Instead of sanctifying his name among the people, they permit it to be *profaned among them*.

The 'princes' mentioned in 22:25 may have been members of the royal family. The *officials* mentioned in **22:27** were probably administrative officers. But there is little difference between them as regards their actions. The princes are like lions (22:25) and the officials are like *wolves* – either way, the people are devoured. The bloodshed, hinted at in 22:25, is explicitly mentioned here: *They shed blood and kill people to make unjust gain.*

The *prophets*, like the false prophets of chapter 13, are involved in whitewashing evil actions and offer *false visions and lying divinations* (**22:28**).

'Like leaders, like people' goes the saying. The *people of the land*, following in the footsteps of their leaders, *practise extortion and commit robbery* (**22:29**). What their leaders do to them, they do to those who are below them in the social hierarchy: *They oppress the poor and needy and mistreat the alien, denying them justice.* They have forgotten that 'he who oppresses the poor shows contempt for their Maker' (Prov 14:31).

God says, *I looked for a man among them who would … stand before me in the gap on behalf of the land so I would not have to destroy it* (**22:30**). This was what Moses had done on two occasions (Exod 32:11-14; Num 14:11-19; see also Ps 106:23). But in an environment of universal apostasy, God cannot find one such man.

We may ask, 'But wasn't righteous Jeremiah still in Jerusalem?' Yes, he was, but no one was willing to listen to him or to accept his leadership. Hence they will experience God's judgment (**22:31**). 'Any nation which lacks godly leadership, as Israel did at that time, must surely be on the way out' (*TOT*).

23:1-49 Two adulterous sisters

The history of Israel has already been reviewed twice (16:1-63; 20:4-44), but God repeats it here for the third time. When judgment strikes, the people will have no basis to accuse him of not having warned them. Like chapter 16, the present chapter is an allegory and focuses on the adultery of Jerusalem.

23:1-4 OHOLAH AND OHOLIBAH Whereas we read of three sisters in 16:44-48, here we have two sisters. Whereas the history began in Canaan in chapter 16, here, as in chapter 20, the history begins in Egypt. The *prostitution* of the two sisters started *in Egypt … from their youth* (**23:2-3**). Their names are given as *Oholah* (the older – Samaria) and *Oholibah* (the younger – Jerusalem) (**23:4**). Although their names mean 'her tent' and 'my tent in her' respectively, the names appears to have no other significance than their use in the allegory. God says, *They were mine and gave birth to sons and daughters* (that is, to the inhabitants of the two cities).

23:5-10 SAMARIA'S PROSTITUTION Focusing on Oholah/Samaria, God accuses her of lusting after her lovers, the Assyrians, while she was still his (**23:5**). Not only did she engage in prostitution with the handsome young men of Assyria, she also *defiled herself with all the idols of everyone she lusted after* – a continuation of what she began in Egypt (**23:6-8**). Consequently, God used the very people she lusted after to punish her and made her *a byword among women* (**23:9-10**). As in chapter 16, the prostitution here symbolizes Samaria's worship of other gods, but the emphasis falls more on her political prostitution, that is, on her 'seeking security in the strength of other nations rather than in God's omnipotent protection' (*EBC*).

23:11-34 JERUSALEM'S PROSTITUTION While both Samaria and Jerusalem are condemned, the greater attention paid to Jerusalem shows where the spotlight falls. Although Jerusalem knew of the judgment God meted out to Samaria through the Assyrians in 721 BC, she did not learn the lesson. We humans hardly ever learn our lessons – if we did, it would not be necessary for history to repeat itself. In fact *in her lust and prostitution she was more depraved that her sister* (**23:11**). She lusted after the same *Assyrians* her sister lusted after (**23:12-13**) and also after the *Chaldeans* (Babylonians – **23:14-17a**). Yet *after she had been defiled by [the Babylonians] she turned away from them in disgust* (**23:17b**) – a statement that 'reflects the pendulum-like swing from a pro-Babylonian policy to an anti-Babylonian policy that marked Judah's political history during the last hundred years before the exile' (*TOT*). Besides all this, Jerusalem had been in a disgustingly promiscuous relationship with the Egyptians (**23:19-21**).

Having said *I turned away from her in disgust, just as I had turned away from her sister* (**23:18**), God elaborates on Jerusalem's judgment. She will suffer the same fate as her older sister. God will turn her lovers, the Babylonians and the Assyrians, as well as hordes of other peoples, against her (**23:22-24**). The cutting off of *noses* and *ears* (**23:25**) was a punishment for adultery and was also inflicted on prisoners of war by the Assyrians and Babylonians. God's action *will put a stop to the lewdness and prostitution you began in Egypt* (**23:27**).

God continues his threat to hand Jerusalem over to *those you turned away from in disgust* (**23:28-31**; see 23:17). Moreover, he will cause her to drink her *sister's cup*, meaning that she will suffer the same punishment as her sister (**23:32**). She will have to drink everything in the cup, no matter how bitter, right down to the last drop (**23:33-34**).

23:35-49 GOD'S JUDGMENT This passage speaks about the sisters together. Through his messenger, God reminds them once again: *Since you have forgotten me and thrust me behind your back, you must bear the consequences of your lewdness and prostitution* (**23:35**). The indictment the prophet is commanded to bring against them moves from the bloodshed related to the *adultery* they committed *with their idols* – even to the extent of sacrificing *their children* – to defiling *my sanctuary* and desecrating *my Sabbaths* (**23:37-38**). We sense God's shock in what follows: *On the very day they sacrificed their children to their idols, they entered my sanctuary and desecrated it. This is what they did in my house* (**23:39**).

In revisiting the lewdness and promiscuity of the sisters, the focus appears to be on Jerusalem. Thus the verbs in **23:40-41** are feminine singular in the Hebrew and **23:42-44** refers to *the woman* and *her sister*.

The *righteous men* God uses to judge the two sisters must be the Assyrians and Babylonians (**23:45**). They are not 'righteous' in the sense of being in a covenant relationship with the Lord, but are righteous in that they do the Lord's will. After the judgment of these 'righteous men' is carried out – through the instrumentality of a mob – Jerusalem and Samaria will know that *I am the Sovereign Lord* and *all women will take warning and not imitate you* (**23:46-49**).

As we come to the conclusion of this chapter we may ask – if we have not done so already – why it is filled with such nauseating sexual language. The answer is that this is how Ezekiel and God wanted to get their message across. 'The feeling of nausea which a chapter like this arouses must be blamed not on the writer of the chapter nor even on its contents, but on the conduct which had to be described in such revolting terms' (*TOT*).

24:1-27 Judgment Carried Out

The verbal and nonverbal messages of judgment come to a fitting climax in this chapter. In addition, since it contains prediction and fulfilment within itself (24:12-18), this chapter vindicates God and his servant Ezekiel.

24:1-14 The parable of the cooking pot

God appears to attach great significance to the date given here. For, over and above Ezekiel's note of the year, the month and the day that *the word of the Lord came* to him (**24:1**), the Lord himself specifically commands him to *record this date, this very date*. The reason this date is so important is *because the king of Babylon has laid siege to Jerusalem this very day* (**24:2**). The Lord then instructs the prophet to communicate what is going to happen to *this rebellious house* through the parable of the cooking pot (24:3). After describing a daily chore, he then applies it to the city in two stages, each beginning with *Woe to the city of bloodshed* (**24:6a, 9a**).

In a perfectly ordinary setting, Ezekiel is told to take a *cooking pot*, add *water, pieces of meat* and *bones*, and *pile wood beneath it* as if cooking a meal (**24:3-5**). We may be hearing ominous echoes of 11:3, 7-11 in the use of the cooking pot and in the pieces of meat that go into it – especially *all the choice pieces, the best of these bones* and *the pick of the flock* (24:4-5).

The first application follows immediately after the mention of the 'city of bloodshed', which must be Jerusalem. The pot is said to be *encrusted*, with *deposits* or *rust* (NRSV) that *will not go away* (**24:6b**).

The command to *empty* the pot *piece by piece* (**24:6c**) refers to the dispersion of the inhabitants of the city, and the statement that this must be done *without casting lots for them* (**24:6d**) implies that it will take place without any discrimination. The blood guilt of the city is underscored in **24:7**, which speaks of blood *poured on the bare rock*, revealing the brazenness with which sin was committed. This provocation added to God's anger (**24:8**).

Once again the 'woe' formula is used, and then God says, *I, too, will pile the wood high* (**24:9b**). Whereas Ezekiel had initially been instructed to pile the wood in the acted parable, here it is God who does this. It seems that the meat and bones are now being roasted in the open fire rather than boiling in the pot (**24:10**). This would explain why the bones are *charred*. The empty pot is then *set on the coals till it becomes hot and its copper glows so its impurities may be melted and its deposit* [or rust] *burned away* (**24:11**; see 24:6). But all these attempts to purify the metal of the pot are unsuccessful (**24:12**).

God then explicitly links the cooking pot and Jerusalem, saying that just as the pot could not be cleansed, neither can the city, not even by the fire of his judgment that they have already experienced (**24:13**). The Lord concludes this section by declaring that *the time has come for me to act, I will not hold back, I will not have pity nor will I relent* (**24:14**). 'The oracle concludes with the most emphatic affirmation of divine resolve in the book' (*NICOT*).

24:15-27 The two signs

The Lord gives two signs in support of his message about the demise of the city of Jerusalem: the sudden death of Ezekiel's wife (24:15-24) and the end of Ezekiel's muteness (24:25-27).

The *word of the Lord* about his wife must have struck Ezekiel like a thunderbolt: *With one blow, I am about to take away from you the delight of your eyes* (**24:15-16a**). Speculation as to whether Ezekiel's wife was sick or not matters little – God's announcement 'with one blow!' says it all. As if the extraordinary hardship he has gone through in his four and a half years of ministry are not enough, God removes his only human source of consolation.

He is specifically commanded not to go through the customary mourning rites of the day. He is not to *lament or weep or shed any tears*, he should *not mourn for the dead*, but is told to *keep your turban fastened and your sandals on your feet*. He is not permitted to *cover the lower part of your face or eat the customary food of mourners* (**24:16b-17**). He is told only to *groan quietly*. And sure enough, as Ezekiel puts it, *I spoke to the people in the morning, and in the evening my wife died* (**24:18**). Totally committed as he is to the will of God, *the next morning I did as I had been commanded*.

As usual, the people were curious about Ezekiel's strange behaviour. His wife whom he clearly loved (she was 'the delight of your eyes') has suddenly been snatched away from him and he does not mourn! From past experience, they suspect that there may be a message for them in this. Therefore they ask Ezekiel, *Won't you tell us what these things have to do with us?* (**24:19**).

The prophet tells them exactly what the Lord wanted said: *I am about to desecrate my sanctuary – the stronghold in which you take pride, the delight of your eyes, the object of your affection* (**24:20-21a**). Not only that, but *the sons and daughters you left behind will fall by the sword* (**24:21b**). And since the prophet has been given as *a sign to them* (**24:24, 27**; see 4:3; 12:6, 11), they will behave as he does and *will not mourn or weep* (**24:23**). But while the prophet was told to 'groan quietly', the people are told, *you will waste away because of your sins and groan among yourselves* (24:23). Then they *will know that I am the Sovereign Lord* (24:24).

The second sign has to do with the removal of Ezekiel's muteness. This will happen *on the day* the messenger brings news that the first sign has been fulfilled (**24:25-26**). Not only will the predictions of the prophet be vindicated, but the man who has been dumb during most of the time the oracles of judgment were being proclaimed – verbally and non-verbally – will at last be free to speak (**24:27**; see 3:26). *So you will be a sign to them*, with the outcome that *they will know that I am the Sovereign Lord* (24:27).

From now on, Ezekiel will be proclaiming messages of hope and restoration, not of doom – with the exception of the oracles to the foreign nations who rejoiced at Israel's demise. 'Ezekiel's mouth would be opened; and he would have the freedom to move among his people and proclaim continually the message of hope for the future' (*EBC*).

25:1-32:32 Prophecies Against the Nations

Ezekiel was not the only prophet to utter oracles of judgment against the nations (see Isa 13–23; Jer 46–51; Amos 1–2; Zeph 2). But why are these oracles placed between the prophecy of the coming of a messenger with the news that Jerusalem has fallen (24:26) and the fulfilment of that prophecy with the arrival of the messenger in 33:21?

The answer may be that placing them here heightens the dramatic tension. We would like to move on immediately to the arrival of the messenger 'and the reaction to the news itself. But instead, like the exiles themselves, we must sit and wait' (*BST*). Moreover, these prophecies against the foreign nations are 'negative messages of hope' for the despairing exiles (*NICOT*). The fact that God is judging these enemies of Judah for the way they have treated her at the time of her greatest need says there is light at the end of the tunnel for the exilic community.

These oracles are carefully arranged. The first is directed to Ammon in the north-east, and then the writer moves clockwise to Moab and Edom in the south, after which he turns north to Philistia, Tyre and Sidon, before reversing direction and ending with the huge nation to the south – Egypt. Ninety-seven verses deal with Egypt, and ninety-seven with the other nations. These two blocks of text are balanced on either side of 28:24-26, which some commentators

describe as a fulcrum or as the 'key that unlocks the entire unit' (*NICOT*).

25:1-7 Judgment Against Ammon

Chapter 25 contains short oracles against the four close neighbours of Judah. In fact they are so close that 'all four countries could be seen by the naked eye on a clear day from a vantage point in Jerusalem itself' (*BST*). It comes as no surprise to us – and maybe to the exiles – that the Ammonites, whose judgment was postponed in chapter 21, come first in this roster of judgment oracles. The pattern in these oracles is introduction, accusation, verdict.

Ezekiel brings two charges against the *Ammonites*. The first flows from their words: *Because you said 'Aha!'* (**25:3**), and the second flows from their actions: *Because you have clapped your hands and stamped your feet* (**25:6**; see also 6:11; 21:14, 17). In both cases, they are gloating over the destruction of Jerusalem and the deporting of the covenant people.

As punishment for their sinful words, God will *give you to the people of the East as a possession* (**25:4-5**). These 'people of the East' may be the Babylonians or they may be nomadic groups from the Arabian desert. 'It is worth noting that not long after this both Ammon and Moab were overrun by Nabatean tribesmen and ceased to have any independent existence as nations' (*TOT*). As punishment for their sinful actions, God will devastate their land and *exterminate you from the countries* (**25:7**).

The outcome of this judgment is stated twice: *You will know that I am the Lord* (25:5, 7). But how can they acknowledge God after they have been 'exterminated'? Does that mean 'that a knowledge of the Lord will be experienced only in the calamity of final destruction'? (*TOT*). On a more positive note, some commentators suggest that what we have hints at the future salvation of these very nations that are being judged (see Isa 19:23-25; Jer 12:14-17; 48:47; 49:6).

What is certainly true is that 'the earth is the Lord's, and everything in it, the world, and all who live in it' (Ps 24:1). Everything that takes place on the international stage is under the sovereign will of God and extends the knowledge of him. 'All that really mattered for Ezekiel was that both in Israel and in the world of nations, the glory of God would be revealed, the honour of God's name would be restored, and the truth of God's identity would be known' (*BST*).

25:8-11 Judgment Against Moab

The oracle against Moab is short (compare Jer 48:1-47). This nation is said to have agreed with *Seir* (another name for Edom) that *the house of Judah has become like all the other nations* (**25:8**). Not only is this a denial of Judah's special status among the nations, but it is also a direct assault on Yahweh himself, because it is he who granted this status to his people. In response, God *will expose the flank of Moab*, that is, its impregnable mountainous terrain, to attack

(25:9). The three frontier towns mentioned were strongly fortified cities on a north–south alignment. Their importance is evident from the description of them as *the glory of the land*. As in the case of the Ammonites, the instruments of God's judgment are *the people of the East* (25:10). In addition to the judgment already announced, the Ammonites *will not be remembered among the nations* and God *will inflict punishment on Moab* (25:11).

25:12-14 Judgment Against Edom

The Ammonites and the Moabites were related to the covenant people through Abraham. Lot, their ancestor, was Abraham's nephew (see Gen 12:4-5). The relationship of Edom and Judah is even closer, because their ancestor Esau was the twin brother of Jacob (see Gen 25:23-26). However, the conflict that began with these brothers persisted throughout the history of these nations, despite Moses' positive instructions concerning them as the Israelites travelled to the promised land (see Deut 2:2-6; 23:7).

Edom receives a guilty verdict because it *took revenge on the house of Judah* (25:12). Hence God says he *will stretch out my hand against Edom and kill its men and their animals* (25:13a). He *will lay it waste … from Teman to Dedan* (25:13b). This phrase is the Edomite equivalent of 'from Dan to Beersheba'. It represents the whole land. The instrument of God's judgment on Edom will be his own people (25:14). This prophecy was fulfilled many years later in the time of the Maccabees.

25:15-17 Judgment Against Philistia

Although *the daughters of the Philistines* are mentioned in 16:27 and 57, this is the first time the Philistines are mentioned as a nation in Ezekiel. Their origins are not definitely known, but they are classified among the Sea Peoples who appeared in the eastern Mediterranean in the thirteenth century BC. According to Amos 9:7, the Philistines arrived from Caphtor, which is identified as the island of Crete. When the covenant people entered the land under the leadership of Joshua, the Philistines were concentrated in the five coastal towns of Gaza, Ashdod, Ashkelon, Gath and Ekron (Josh 13:2-3). David dealt a devastating blow to them (see 2 Sam 5:17-25), but it appears that they remained a constant threat to Israel.

The Philistines, like the Edomites, *took revenge*. They did it *with malice in their hearts, and with ancient hostility sought to destroy Judah* (25:15). God's judgment on them is similar to his judgment on the Edomites: *I will cut off the Kerethites and destroy those remaining along the coast* (25:16-17). The name 'Kerethites' indicates a relationship with the Cretans and seems to be a reference to some group within the Philistine nation. The Kerethites and Pelethites, who were both Philistines, were among David's security guards (2 Sam 8:18; 20:23).

26:1-28:19 Judgment Against Tyre

Tyre was a famous city on the coast of what is now Lebanon. We know from both biblical and extra-biblical accounts that the Phoenicians who lived there were great seafarers. Tyre's maritime trade extended as far away as Tarshish, thousands of miles away in Spain. Consequently its fame and wealth were legendary. In terms of modern East Africa, it could be compared to Dubai in terms of its wealth and influence.

The prophecies against Tyre consist of a judgment prophecy against Tyre (26:1-21), a lament for Tyre (27:1-36), a judgment prophecy against the king of Tyre (28:1-10), and a lament for the king of Tyre (28:11-19).

26:1-21 Prophecy against Tyre

This prophecy can be divided into four parts, separated by the words, *This is what the Sovereign Lord says* (26:7, 15, 19). The first part (26:1-6) is similar to the judgment oracles against the four nations we have just covered. It follows the same pattern of accusation and then judgment, and the *Aha!* in 26:2a reminds us of the *Aha!* of the Ammonites (25:3). The Lord accuses Tyre of rejoicing over the fall of Jerusalem. This glee was purely selfish: *The gate to the nations is broken, and its doors have swung open to me; now that she lies in ruins I will prosper* (26:2b). Tyre was rejoicing over the downfall of a trade competitor, because Jerusalem was strategically located on the international trade routes.

God says, *I am against you, O Tyre, and I will bring many nations against you,* and he says it in language a seafaring nation would understand when he says that these nations will come *like the sea casting up its waves* (26:3). The attacking nations *will destroy the walls of Tyre and pull down her towers*. To emphasize that he is the main actor, God adds, *I will scrape away her rubble and make her a bare rock* (26:4). There appears to be a wordplay here, for the name of the city is related to a Hebrew word meaning 'rock'.

There were two parts to the city of Tyre – the main part was built on a rocky island in the Mediterranean and the other part was on the mainland. That is why God can say that after the judgment, the city *will become a place to spread fishnets* (26:5). Tyre will become *plunder for the nations* God will use to punish her, and *her settlements on the mainland will be ravaged by the sword* (26:6).

God will use many nations to punish Tyre, but the first of these will be the Babylonians. *Nebuchadnezzar king of Babylon* will come with his war-machine: *horses and chariots, horsemen and a great army* and *siege works* (26:7-8). God says, *He will direct the blows of his battering-rams against your walls and demolish your towers with his weapons* (26:9). The description of his horses, wagons and chariots in 26:10-11 is meant to instil terror. They will spread devastation and loot the rich city (26:12). Tyre and its merriment will be no more! (26:13). This part of the prophecy concludes with repetition of the statement that Tyre will be reduced to a *bare rock* (**26:14**; see 26:4-5), 'with no buildings and no soil for any cultivation' (*TOT*).

The downfall of Tyre will have international impact. Although Ezekiel records a longer lament in the next section (27:1-36), here he briefly records the coastlands' reaction to the shocking news. The *coastlands* were probably the satellite cities and villages that were part of Tyre's extensive trade network (**26:15**). These dependent cities and their princes will tremble with terror at the crushing fall of Tyre (**26:16**). 'If this is what has befallen Tyre', they will say, 'then what will become of us?' They express this fear in a lament for the city (**26:17-18**).

Although God uses human agents of judgment, he is the one directing their actions. Repeating the imagery of *the sea casting up its waves* (**26:19**; see 26:3), God tells Tyre, *I will bring you down with those who go down to the pit, to the people of long ago* – in other words, the inhabitants of Tyre will join those have already died (**26:20**). The statement that follows underscores this point: *You will not return or take your place in the land of the living.* The end has come for Tyre and that end is irrevocable (**26:21**). What a dreadful end for such a *city of renown!* (26:17).

27:1-36 Lament for Tyre

The Lord next directs Ezekiel to *take up a lament concerning Tyre* (**27:1-2**). A lament is usually a dirge for someone who has died. Traditionally, it begins with some account of the kind of life they have lived and then speaks of the circumstances of their death. The form is also sometimes used for cities and nations, and that is how the prophet is told to use it here.

God describes Tyre as *situated at the gateway to the sea* (**27:3a**). Tyre had similarly described its competitor Jerusalem as the 'gate to the nations' (26:2). God also speaks of it as the *merchant of peoples on many coasts.* Ezekiel picks up this theme in his lament, which falls into three parts: the magnificence of the ship that is Tyre (27:3-11), the vast international trade links of the city (27:12-25) and the sinking of the ship with its crew and cargo (27:26-36).

Ezekiel begins with the self-glorification of Tyre: *I am perfect in beauty* (**27:3b**) and then goes on to show why Tyre might think this to be true. He does it by describing the city as being like a trading ship. He describes a magnificent ship, giving a detailed account of the carefully chosen materials from a range of sources that the shipbuilders used to bring its *beauty to perfection* (**27:4**). The body of the ship was of timber obtained from the *pine trees from Senir,* another name for Mount Hermon. The mast was one of the famous cedars from Lebanon, and the oars were made of *oaks from Bashan.* The deck was made of *cypress wood* of *Cyprus,* and was inlaid with ivory set into the wood. The ship's sails were of *fine embroidered linen from Egypt* and served as a

banner to identify the ship. The *awnings* that provided shade for the crew were *of blue and purple* and came *from the coasts of Elishah,* which was in Cyprus or Syria (**27:5-7**). Such a ship would have been very valuable and very beautiful.

The crew, too, was carefully selected for their skills. The *oarsmen* and *seamen* came from the nearby city of *Sidon* and from *Arvad,* a small island a hundred miles to the north. They were commanded by skilled mariners from *Tyre* itself. While voyaging, the ship would be kept in good working condition by *veteran craftsmen* from *Gebal,* that is, from the city of Byblos, not far from Tyre (**27:8-9a**).

When such a fine ship manned by fine sailors came in sight, it was no wonder that *all the ships of the sea and other sailors came alongside to trade for your wares* (**27:9b**).

The lines between city and ship blur as Ezekiel describes the soldiers who guard the ship and the city. They come from *Persia* to the east (modern Iran), *Lydia* to the north (in modern Turkey) and *Put* in the south (either Libya or Somalia). The walls of the city were manned by soldiers from *Arvad, Helech* (which may have been in Cilicia in modern Turkey or in Syria) and from *Gammad* in Phoenicia (**27:10-11**). The shields and armour of these men added to both the strength and beauty of the city, bringing her *splendour* and *beauty to perfection.*

The materials that went into the construction of the ship of Tyre were international, and so were its builders and defenders. So, too, were its trading partners and the goods traded. The trading partners mentioned here are *Tarshish* (in Spain), *Greece, Tubal and Meshech* (in Asia Minor), *men of Beth Togarmah* (in Armenia), *men of Rhodes, Aram, Judah and Israel, Damascus, Danites and Greeks from Uzal* (in Yemen or Asia Minor), *Dedan, Arabia and all the princes of Kedar* (in Arabia), *the merchants of Sheba and Raamah* (in Yemen), *Haran, Canneh, Eden, Asshur and Kilmad* (all in Mesopotamia) (**27:12-24**).

The goods traded were also very diverse. They included metals and gems, *slaves, articles of bronze,* animals (*horses, mules,* sheep, *goats*), *ivory tusks, ebony, turquoise,* fabrics and rugs, agricultural products (*wheat, oil, honey, wine*) and spices and perfumes (27:12-24). Some of these goods were carried in Tyrian ships, others were brought to the market place in Tyre and traded there. Trade goods were also distributed to and from Tyre by *ships of Tarshish* (**27:25a**).

It is, however, the ship/Tyre itself that is *filled with heavy cargo* of the types just listed and is in *the heart of the sea* (**27:25b**). And it is here that disaster strikes: *Your oarsmen take you out to the high seas. But the east wind will break you to pieces* (**27:26**). The ship and everything in it – human beings, animals and cargo – *will sink into the heart of the sea on the day of your shipwreck* (**27:27**).

Commentators argue about whether 'the east wind' in 27:26 is just a natural storm – for there is no indication of God's direct intervention – or whether it is a pointer to God's instrument of punishment: the Babylonians, who came from the east. God has already indicated that he will use Nebuchadnezzar of Babylon to punish Tyre (26:7). Whichever the case, the God of nature and history clearly has sovereign authority over the affairs of nations.

It is not clear whether the disaster strikes as the ship leaves or arrives in port. The commotion in *the shorelands* (**27:28-31**) suggests that the ship may just have set out and been within sight of the port when it sank. Alternatively, other ships saw it sinking and brought news of its fate to the mainland. News of the sinking of the ship of Tyre sends shock waves through the region and through the international trading community. Everything comes to a standstill as people mourn the loss of the ship, crew and cargo.

What follows is a lament within a lament. After expressing their grief in the customary way of the time (27:30-31), *the mariners and all the seamen* (27:29) *take up a lament concerning* Tyre, asking *Who was ever silenced like Tyre, surrounded by the sea?* (**27:32-34**). The sailors are not saying they have never seen a ship sink. But they are amazed that this can happen to a ship as strong and wealthy as the ship of Tyre – and with such speed. They are joined in their grief and horror by *kings,* and by *all who live in the coastlands* and by *the merchants among the nations* (**27:35**). The hissing referred to in **27:36a** is not an expression of derision, for the people are lamenting Tyre's fall. It is involuntary expression of shock.

There are two lessons to be learned from this chapter. The first is that pride carries the seed of destruction within itself (Prov 16:18). The city that boasted, *I am perfect in beauty* (27:3) was destroyed *and will be no more* (**27:36b**). The second is that the fate of the nations is in God's hand. 'In her apparent invincibility, Tyre represented the glory of human achievement. Because her successes were driven by avarice and pursued in defiance of God, however, she could not stand. The Lord of history always has the last word' (*NICOT*).

28:1-10 Prophecy against the ruler of Tyre

The first part of the chapter is a judgment oracle against *the ruler of Tyre,* who may have been Ethbaal II. As usual the accusation is given first. Reflecting *the pride* of the city over which he rules, this man says, *I am a god; I sit on the throne of a god in the heart of the seas* (**28:2a**). God affirms that the man does have *wisdom and understanding,* and that his *great skill in trading* has helped him to amass *great wealth –* including *gold and silver* (**28:4-5a**). However, God's reaction to his claim to deity is, *you are a man not a god, though you think you are as wise as a god* (**28:2b**). And although he is wise, he is not nearly as wise as God's servant Daniel, who was serving in the court of the Babylonian king at the time – let alone as wise as God (**28:3**). The only reason he could make this foolish claim was that *because of your wealth your*

heart has grown proud (**28:5b**). Human pride is the reason that Tyre is judged.

God, therefore, proceeds to announce the verdict on *the ruler of Tyre.* He may claim to be a god, but the Lord is the one who is in control of world affairs, and he says, *I am going to bring foreigners, against you, the most ruthless of nations* (**28:7a**). The instrument of God's judgment will be the Babylonians (26:7). Their *swords* will be directed *against your beauty and wisdom* and they will *pierce your shining splendour,* that is, all those qualities that had deceived a human being into thinking of himself as a god (**28:7b**).

In contrast to the ruler's claim to 'sit on the throne … in the heart of the seas' (28:2a), God says, *You will die a violent death in the heart of the seas* (**28:8**). Rather than ruling there, he will die there. God sarcastically asks, *Will you then say, 'I am a god,' in the presence of those who kill you?* (**28:9a**). Hammering home the message in 28:2b, God answers his own question: *You will be but a man, not a god, in the hands of those who slay you* (**28:9b**).

The Phoenicians practised circumcision, whereas the Babylonians did not. Thus to *die the death of the uncircumcised at the hands of foreigners* – and uncircumcised foreigners at that – would be a double tragedy (**28:10**). It would be a disgraceful death, 'a barbarian's death', even by Phoenician standards (*EBC*).

28:11-19 Lament for the king of Tyre

This section 'is one of Ezekiel's most intriguing artistic creations and one of the most difficult texts in the whole book' (*NICOT*). There are sharp differences between how the church has traditionally interpreted it and how modern biblical scholarship understands it. The question is whether the text refers only to the historical king of Tyre, or whether there is also another level of meaning.

Two linguistic factors that contribute to seeing a shift in the topic here are the change from speaking of 'the ruler of Tyre' in the previous section to speaking of 'the king of Tyre' here, and the fact that all the verbs in this passage are in the past tense, whereas in the previous section God's judgment was proclaimed using the future tense.

Once again, *the word of the Lord came* to Ezekiel, telling him to *take up a lament concerning the king of Tyre* (**28:11-12a**). Once again, this lament describes the king's life and his ultimate fate (see comment on 27:1-2). The life of this 'king' can be described as perfect, until we come to the watershed verse: *You were blameless in your ways from the day you were created till wickedness was found in you* (**28:15**). The 'till' of this verse marks the 'before' and the 'after' of his life and career. The 'before' is given in 28:12b-15 and the 'after' is given in 28:15-19.

The ruler of Tyre had earlier been said to have 'wisdom' and 'beauty' (see 28:7), but here Ezekiel uses superlatives: He was *full of wisdom and perfect in beauty.* For the first part of his life, this person was *the model of perfection* (**28:12b**). The Hebrew word translated 'model' is better translated as 'seal', as in the NASB: 'You had the seal of perfection.' The idea is that this person was as perfect as it was possible to be.

Ezekiel then introduces OT references to reinforce this image of perfection. He speaks of *Eden, the garden of God* and of *the day you were created* (**28:13**; see Gen 2–3). Thus some commentators think that Ezekiel is here speaking about Adam before the fall. But the allusions do not stop there. He is also described as having been adorned with *every precious stone* – which seems to allude to the precious stones on the breastpiece of the High Priest's garment (28:13; see Exod 28:15-20).

The person was also given great responsibility, for he is described as *anointed* and *ordained* by God. He was intended to be *a guardian cherub* (**28:14**; see comment 1:4–14). Not only was he in Eden, he was also *on the holy mount of God*, that is, in the place where God dwells – whether in heaven or on earth (Ps 15:1; 24:3). *The fiery stones* among which he is said to walk may be a reference to the precious stones that shone on his robes (28:13), but they also remind us that the cherubim who are the guardians of God's throne are associated with fire (1:13). As the culmination of his glory, this person is described as *blameless in your ways from the day you were created* (**28:15a**).

It is possible that the historical king of Tyre could have enjoyed such exaggerated praise from his contemporaries, but it is difficult to see how God could describe a pagan king in such glowing terms.

Then, with the solemn words *till wickedness was found in you* (**28:15b**), the tone of the poem changes. Whereas previously it was a song of praise, now it changes not into a lament but into an oracle of judgment. The reference to *your widespread trade* (**28:16a**) suggests that this 'king of Tyre' is indeed the same as the 'ruler of Tyre' of 28:1-10. His greed led him to his being *filled with violence* and he *sinned*.

Contrasting his state 'before' and 'after' his sin, God says, *So I drove you in disgrace from the mount of God, and I expelled you, O guardian cherub* (**28:16b**, see also 28:14). While this may refer to the fall of the historical king of Tyre, it also seems to refer to the fall of someone greater than he was. Some commentators thus argue that this passage refers to the expulsion of Adam from the garden of Eden. But given the description of this being in 28:12b-15, and his role as 'guardian cherub', it would seem that someone even greater than Adam must be meant. Traditionally, this person is interpreted as Satan.

The root cause of his disgrace (and of most human disgrace) is pride (**28:17a**). Instead of being grateful for the *beauty, wisdom* and *splendour* that God had given him (see also (28:7), he became swollen-headed, or as the Hebrew would put it, his *heart became proud*. God punished his pride by throwing him *to the earth; and I made a spectacle of you before the kings* (**28:17b**).

If we ask from where God throws him 'to the earth', the answer may be found in a passage in Isaiah that is often associated with the present passage: 'How you have fallen from heaven, O morning star, son of the dawn! You have been cast down to the earth' (Isa 14:12). This same passage in Isaiah also ascribes this downfall to pride: 'You said in your heart, "I will ascend to heaven; I will raise my throne above the stars of God; I will sit enthroned on the mount of assembly, on the utmost heights of the sacred mountain. I will ascend above the tops of the clouds; I will make myself like the Most High"' (Isa 14:13-14). This passage in Isaiah may be taken as describing the fate of the historical king of Babylon, just as the present passage is about the king of Tyre. However, if we are looking for a referent beyond Ethbaal II of Tyre or Nebuchadnezzar of Babylon, we can turn to Revelation 12:9, which speaks of ' that ancient serpent called the devil, or Satan, who … was hurled to the earth'.

The *sanctuaries* in **28:18** may be places of worship in Tyre or Satan's dwelling place in heaven. The *fire* that consumed him came from within, and may be the fire of rebellion in the form of his self-destructive wickedness (28:15) or pride (28:17). The conclusion is, *you have come to a horrible end and will be no more* (**28:19**; see 27:36).

28:20-26 Judgment Against Sidon

Like Tyre, Sidon was a rich, Phoenician seafaring city. Given that the last three verses of this section deal with God's people, we are left with only three verses that actually speak about Sidon (28:21). No wonder the oracle does not deal with the reasons for the judgment but goes straight to the punishment.

The Lord commands the prophet, *Set your face against Sidon; prophesy against her* (**28:21**). Ezekiel's message is that God is *against you and … will gain glory within you* (**28:22**). God will gain this glory when he *inflicts punishment on her* and shows himself *holy within her*. The form the punishment will take is *a plague* and bloodshed *in her streets* (**28:23**). The purpose of this punishment is underscored by the repetition of the formula *they will know that I am the Lord* in 28:22, 23. God's purpose is to bring people to know him as the sovereign Lord of creation and redemption.

The remaining verses, directed to the covenant people, are like an oasis in this desert of judgment. God promises his people that their *malicious neighbours* – the nations being judged – will no longer be a thorn in the flesh for them (**28:24**). He will gather them in the promised land from *where they have been scattered* and they will live there peacefully, building *houses* and planting *vineyards* (**28:25-26a**). He will do this *in the sight of the nations* and both his people and these nations *will know that I am the Lord* (**28:26b**).

29:1-32:32 Judgment Against Egypt

Egypt, the seventh nation to be addressed by Ezekiel, was a major international player at the time and had a strong involvement in Judean affairs. This may explain why four of the eight chapters devoted to judgments against the nations deal with Egypt. Seven separate oracles are addressed to that country.

29:1-16 Introductory oracle

The introductory oracle was given almost a year after the second siege of Jerusalem (**29:1-2**; see 24:1-2). It focuses on Hophra, who was then *Pharaoh king of Egypt* (29:3-6a), and on *all Egypt,* that is, on the country as a whole (29:6b-16).

Pharaoh is compared to a great crocodile lying in the River Nile (**29:3**). He confidently claims, *the Nile is mine* and we cannot disagree, for he was indeed its ruler. We could, however, fault him for his failure to acknowledge the Sovereign Lord of history who gave him his position (Rom 13:1). But it is in the second half of this assertion that human pride rears its ugly head: *I made it for myself.* Pharaoh is claiming the divine prerogative of creation. The Lord does not tolerate this, and specifically mentions this as one of the reasons for his judgment (see 29:9).

'Pride goes before destruction' (Prov 16:18), even in the case of Hophra, king of Egypt (**29:4-5**). 'For all his arrogant pretensions, the glorious lord of the Nile is no match for Yahweh, who toys with him as a fisherman plays with his catch, then throws him away as carrion, unfit for human consumption' (*NICOT*).

Once again, the outcome of God's judgment is that *all who live in Egypt will know that I am the Lord* (**29:6a**).

But God's judgment does not end with the judgment of the leader. The saying 'Like leader, like people' holds true. Egypt – collectively as a nation and as represented by its ruler – must have been involved in the sin that invited God's judgment. Moreover, both the leaders and the people of Egypt were found to be unreliable when it came to helping *the house of Israel.* Ezekiel uses what must have been a popular metaphor when he speaks of Egypt as a *staff of reed* (**29:6b**; 2 Kgs 18:21; Isa 36:6). A dry papyrus reed was useless: *When they grasped you with their hands, you splintered and you tore open their shoulders; when they leaned on you, you broke and their backs were wrenched* (**29:7**). This assessment of Egypt is borne out by the historical context. Pharaoh Hophra appears to have mobilized his army to help King Zedekiah during the siege of Jerusalem by the Babylonians, but does not seem to have accomplished anything (Jer 37:4-8).

God's judgment on Egypt is summed up in the twin statements: *I will bring a sword against you* (**29:8**) and *I will make the land of Egypt a ruin and a desolate waste* (29:10). As the result of the first, men and animals will be killed and *Egypt will become a desolate wasteland* (**29:9**). As the result of the second, the land will be desolate from one extreme (*Migdol*)

to the other (*Aswan, as far as the border of Cush*) and the people will be scattered among the nations for forty years (**29:10-12**). The scattering of the Egyptians brings to mind the scattering of the Israelites, although the duration of the dispersal fits better with the time of the wilderness journey than with the seventy years of Babylonian captivity. What makes the comparison more interesting is the hope of restoration given in 29:13-16. In language that echoes the promise of restoration given to the covenant people, God says, *At the end of forty years I will gather the Egyptians from the nations where they were scattered* (**29:13**). He continues, *'I will bring them back from captivity and return them to Upper Egypt, the land of their ancestry'* (**29:14a**). Although it is not specificied, this promise of restoration may even include coming to a saving knowledge of the Lord (see Isa 19:19-25).

Egypt will not, however, be restored to imperial power. It will be a lowly kingdom (**29:14b**). As the result of this humbling work of God, Egypt will never again exalt itself above the other nations and will no longer be a source of confidence for the people of Israel (**29:15-16a**). Both the Egyptians and the Israelites *will know that I am the Sovereign Lord* (**29:16b**).

29:17-21 Compensation for a costly siege

This prophecy about Nebuchadnezzar is one of the shortest of Ezekiel's oracles. It is out of sequence as far as the dates are concerned. This may have been intentional in order to keep it close to the oracles against Tyre, to which it is related. Despite its brevity, it has generated a lot of discussion among commentators because it seems to imply that the prophecy that the Babylonians would destroy Tyre and plunder its wealth was not fulfilled (26:7-14). In assessing this, we need to remember that it is in the nature of prophecy that it is not completely fulfilled in one incident. The final destruction of Tyre took place during the campaign of Alexander the Great in the fourth century BC, and he did indeed throw the city into the sea.

Nebuchadnezzar's siege of Tyre was undoubtedly costly and exhausting. It lasted thirteen long years, so it is no surprise to find Ezekiel saying that it was *a hard campaign,* during which *every head was rubbed bare* by the chafing of helmets *and every shoulder made raw* by the carrying of the material used to build the siege works and the ramps leading up to the walls (**29:18**; 26:8). Tyre did eventually surrender and become a vassal of Babylon, but the wealth obtained was nowhere near enough to cover the cost of such a hard and prolonged siege. Because God was using Babylon as his instrument to punish both his covenant people and the surrounding nations, he decides to allow *Nebuchadnezzar king of Babylon* to capture Egypt: *He will loot and plunder the land as pay for his army. I have given him Egypt as a reward for his efforts because he and his army did it for me* (**29:19-20**). The Lord was punishing the pharaoh of Egypt

WAR

Can war ever be justified? This question poses a great challenge to the Christian conscience. The challenge is even more intense given that the Bible describes God as a warrior who casts Pharaoh's chariots and his army into the sea and drowns them (Exod 15:3-5). God is also praised for training the hands of his people for war and battle. He gives his people the strategies and plans that enable them to defeat his enemies (Ps 144:1; I Chr 14:8-17). On the other hand, in the NT Jesus tells his followers not to resist evil but to turn the other cheek when an enemy strikes them (Matt 5:39; 26:52).

War in the Old Testament

The Bible accepts that warfare, spiritual and physical, is an inevitable aspect of our human existence. Violence was first introduced into the human community shortly after Adam and Eve disobeyed God's command in Eden, when jealousy led Cain to kill his brother Abel. The first recorded account of a full-scale war is found in Genesis 14, where four kings led by Kedorlaomer came together as allies to fight a coalition of five kings led by Bera, king of Sodom. The five kings were rebelling after having been forced to serve Kedorlaomer for twelve years (Gen 14:4). When the rebellion was crushed, Abraham's nephew, Lot, was captured, and Abraham had to launch a rescue mission. He defeated Kedorlaomer and his allies and 'brought back all the goods, and also brought back his brother Lot and his goods, as well as the women and the people' (Gen 14:16). Then Melchizedek king of Salem met Abraham, blessed him, and attributed the victory over his enemies to God Most High (Gen 14:20).

This war had some of the major characteristics of war in the rest of the OT, where we often find that victory is attributed to God. Not only that, but in some cases God is the one who sanctions a war and commands his people to go to war, and he establishes the kingdoms that are won through wars fought at his command (Exod 14–15; 17:8-16; Num 21:34-35; 31:1-18; Josh 5:13; 6:1-27; 12:1-24; Judg 4:1-24; 6:11-24; 7:1-25; 1 Sam 15:1-3; 17:1-58; 2 Sam 5:17-21; 2 Chr 17:1-19; 20:1-30). In such wars, the enemies of Israel are God's enemies too (Ps 139:19-22).

The reasons given for waging war in the OT include a response to unjust laws and oppressive decrees or policies that deprive the poor of their rights and deny them justice. God himself declares war on nations, including Israel, that adopt such policies (Isa 10:1-14; Amos 5:1-4). God also declares war on nations that indulge in idol worship and other pagan practices. His reason for declaring war on them is his unremitting hatred of sin. Here, too, God does not discriminate between Israel and other nations. When Israel or Judah is the offender, God may send Israel's enemies, such as the Assyrians or Babylonians, against his own people, hoping that they will repent and return to him (Deut 4:23-31; Isa 10:5-6; Jer 21:5-7; Hab 1:5-11).

In some circumstances, a war could be declared a 'holy war' in which God placed a ban on the goods and property of the defeated nation or people. These goods were then set apart for God and no one had the right to take any of them for their personal use. Failure to comply with such bans resulted in severe punishment, such as that administered to Achan and to King Saul (Josh 71-26; I Sam 15:1-1-35).

God's involvement in the struggles of his people went beyond merely giving them strategies and the strength to use physical weapons. He also required them to pray and to be spiritually in tune with him (Exod 17:8-13). The battles in which they were engaged were sometimes reflections of larger battles on the spiritual level (Dan 10:10-21).

Although the OT sanctions war, there are some passages in the prophetic writings that clearly look forward to the day when war will be totally eradicated from human existence and peace will be fully established by the Davidic king and enjoyed by all peoples on earth (Isa 9:2-7; 11:1-9; Mic 4:1-3).

War in the New Testament

In the NT, the use of brute force, violence and war to bring in God's kingdom is not encouraged. When Jesus was arrested and Simon Peter drew his sword and struck the high priest's servant, Jesus told Peter to put his sword away (John 18:11). When Pilate questioned Jesus about his kingship, he was told, 'My kingdom is not of this world. If it were, my servants would fight to prevent my arrest by the Jews' (John 18:36). These words point to non-violence as the Christian option, and thus condemn medieval crusades and any other wars fought to promote the kingdom of God.

However, Christians are called to engage in spiritual warfare. Jesus himself constantly engaged in it and gave his disciples the power and authority to destroy the strongholds of Satan. The Apostle Paul tells us that through Christ's death on the cross God has 'rescued us from the dominion of darkness and brought us into the kingdom of the Son he loves' (Col 1:13). We are encouraged to use 'the full armour of God' as we wage spiritual warfare for the sake of the kingdom of God (Eph 6:10-18; see also Luke 10:1-23).

The main issue that confronts Christians is whether Jesus' words to Peter and Pilate mean that pacifism should be the only option under all circumstances. We cannot avoid this issue, for Christians, like other citizens, live in states that are 'ordained by God' and do not 'bear the sword for nothing' (Rom 13:4). These words imply that the state may sometimes legitimately use force or wage war in order to protect its citizens and maintain peace.

It is often argued that the OT endorsement of war was necessary because Israel had to embark on war of conquest in order to fulfil God's promise to Abraham to give him a land and make him into a nation. After the conquest, Israel had to engage in wars of defence in order to maintain the land acquired by force and by promise. However, in the NT and in today's world, Christians are scattered among the nations, and thus they should neither go to war nor engage in any form of violence. This argument is not without difficulties. For instance, how does one reconcile this position with Jesus' statement about buying a sword in Luke 22:36? Should Christians be prohibited from taking up military careers as a means of defending their country or as peacemakers? It should be noted that when soldiers went to John the Baptist, they were not asked to leave their career, but were admonished to do their work honestly and be content with their wages (Luke 3:14). Jesus himself commended a military officer highly for his faith (Matt 8:10-12). In Acts, another military officer's faith and good works were acknowledged and he received the Holy Spirit just as the apostles had (Acts 10:1-48). None of these soldiers was asked to leave military service.

However, the acceptance of military careers should not lead us to conclude that Jesus would endorse the wars that soldiers fight. War is a necessary evil that has come into human existence because of the reality of individual, corporate and structural sins (see Jas 4:1-3). Because freedom is preferable to bondage, people may sometimes have to wage war if they are being deprived of freedom and peace. Some soldiers may have to lay down their lives so that other soldiers and civilians can live in peace. This was the position taken by the many Christians who fought alongside other freedom fighters to liberate Africa from colonial oppression.

Jesus Christ himself, the 'Great Shepherd of the sheep', had to wage the ultimate war against sin on Calvary in order that we might live. As Christians we look forward to the day when our Lord comes riding 'a white horse' to judge with justice, to make war on sin and death, and to usher us into the new heaven and the new earth (Rev 19:11-16; 21:1-4).

Robert Aboagye-Mensah

and compensating the Babylonians at the same time.

The covenant people have persistently sought Egypt's help, but instead the Lord says, *I will make a horn grow for the house of Israel* (**29:21a**). This will happen on the day the Egyptians are punished by the Babylonians. Help will come to the covenant people, not through their own machinations, but in God's way and in God's timing. Even the servant of God, who may have been despondent from the seeming non-fulfilment of his prophecy against Tyre, will be given new utterance, for the Lord promises, *I will open your mouth among them.*

Once again the ultimate purpose of God in all these events is reiterated: *Then they will know that I am the Lord* (**29:21b**).

30:1-19 Egypt invaded by Nebuchadnezzar

This prophecy is not dated. We may, therefore, assume it is a continuation of the prophecy about Egypt given in 29:1-16, which was interrupted by the brief prophecy referring to Tyre (29:17-21).

The prophet is commanded to *prophesy and say: 'This is what the Sovereign Lord says'* (**30:2a**). He does not mention Egypt immediately, but instead prophesies that *the day is near, the day of the Lord is near* (**30:2b-3a**). He may possibly be speaking about the day of the Lord at the end of human history, when he comes in judgment. But we need to remember that any day can be a day of the Lord if he is doing a specific work on that day. Here the context seems to indicate that this day of the Lord 'relates specifically to God's judgment on Egypt through the instrumentality of Babylonia' (*EBC*). Thus this day is also referred to as *the day of Egypt's doom* (**30:9**) and *the day at Tahpanhes* (**30:18**).

Like the eschatological day of the Lord, this day will be dark and *a day of clouds* (30:3b, 18). It will be a day of judgment

not only for Egypt but also for all her satellite nations – including the Jews, here referred to as *the people of the covenant land* (**30:3b-5**). When Egypt is defeated and looted, *anguish will come upon Cush,* that is, the area which now comprises Eritrea, Ethiopia and Sudan (30:4). (*Cush* is also mentioned in 30:5 and 30:9.) Other nations that are mentioned include Put (possibly Libya), Lydia in modern Turkey, and *all Arabia* (30:5). These *allies of Egypt,* who probably stood with Egypt against the Babylonians, *will fall* (**30:6**). They will be slaughtered from one end of the country to the other, or as Ezekiel puts it, *from Migdol* in the northern Nile delta *to Aswan* at the southern boundary with Sudan. On the same note, he adds, *they will be desolate among desolate lands, and their cities will lie among ruined cities* (**30:7**). Cush had thought it was safe with a powerful neighbour between her and the Babylonians, but the news brought by ships travelling up the Nile will frighten Cush *out of her complacency* and bring anguish *on the day of Egypt's doom* (**30:9**).

Once again, the effect of the Lord's judgment will be that those judged *will know that I am the Lord* (**30:8**).

Our attention is now directed to the agent of this judgment. This is none other than the ruthless *Nebuchadnezzar king of Babylon* (**30:10-11**; see also 28:7; 31:12). As the satellite nations will be made desolate and their cities turned to ruins, so will Egypt be laid waste and its cities destroyed. Though Nebuchadnezzar is his instrument, in the final analysis it is God himself who does the judging. He says, for instance, *I will dry up the streams of the Nile* (**30:12a**) – an image that is all the more striking because in 29:3 Pharaoh claimed to be the one who had created the Nile.

The emphatic statement *I the Lord have spoken* indicates the power of God's mere word (**30:12b**). What he has spoken will take place!

Next the impact of the day of the Lord on various areas of Egypt is described. The Lord begins by saying, *I will destroy the idols and put an end to the images in Memphis* (**30:13a**). Possibly, Ezekiel starts his survey of the devastation of the land with Memphis because it 'was the centre of the cult of Ptah, one of the two principal deities of Egypt' (*NICOT;* see also Exod 12:12). The close link between the Egyptian gods and the pharaoh is highlighted by the words that follow: *No longer will there be a prince in Egypt, and I will spread fear throughout the land* (**30:13b**). Ezekiel mentions the destruction of *Upper Egypt* or Pathros (KJV), the fire that consumes *Zoan* or Tanis, and the punishment of *Thebes* or No (**30:14**). The next target of God's punishment is *Pelusium* (also known as Sin or Sais) on the Mediterranean coast, near Port Said. It is described as *the stronghold of Egypt,* but when the Lord pours out his wrath on it, it will *writhe in agony* (**30:15-16**). *Heliopolis* (On or Aven) was one of the oldest cities of Egypt and a centre of the worship of the sun god. Jeremiah calls this city Bethshemesh (Jer 43:13, KJV). The city of *Bubastis* is the same as modern Basta, north-east of Cairo. God says that *the young men* of both cities *will fall by the sword, and the cities themselves will go into captivity* (**30:17**). The last city to be mentioned is *Tahpanhes.* There God will *break the yoke of Egypt* and *her proud strength will come to an end* (**30:18**). The Lord ends this section by saying, *So I will inflict judgment on Egypt,* before concluding with the usual statement that his judgment will force Egypt to acknowledge him (**30:19**).

30:20-26 Pharaoh's broken arms

This oracle is once again dated, this time to a year after the fall of Jerusalem (**30:20**). God dramatically announces, *I have broken the arm of Pharaoh king of Egypt* (**30:21**). He seems to be referring to Hophra's failed attempt to relieve Jerusalem from Nebuchadnezzar's siege in the previous year. Not only is Pharaoh's arm broken, but it is broken never to be healed; for God says, *It has not been bound up for healing or put in a splint to become strong enough to hold a sword.* Nor is it a question of one arm only, for God stresses that he *will break both his arms, the good arm as well as the broken one,* and thus *make the sword fall from his hand* (**30:22**). These words are particularly significant, for the pharaoh was often depicted with his arm flexed, ready to wield a sword. It was a common symbol of his strength (*EBC*). The Egyptian king will be incapacitated, but his enemy the king of Babylon will be strengthened as God puts *my sword in his hand* (30:24). Hophra was indeed killed in a civil war before Nebuchadnezzar invaded Egypt after the siege of Tyre.

As a consequence of God's dual action in weakening Egypt and strengthening Babylon (**30:24-25**), the Egyptians will be dispersed among the nations (**30:23, 26**). Again, the outcome of this will be acknowledgment of the

covenant Lord as the only Sovereign Ruler of creation and history (30:25-26).

31:1-18 The fates of Assyria and Egypt

The downfall of the king of Egypt and the country he rules over is retold here using the metaphor of a great tree. This prophecy was given two months after the preceding oracle (**31:1**).

31:2-9 THE MAGNIFICENCE OF THE TREE The description of the majesty of Pharaoh begins with a rhetorical question: *Who can be compared with you in majesty?* (**31:2**). God then suggests one subject for comparison: *Consider Assyria,* which he describes as being like *a cedar in Lebanon* (**31:3a**). These cedars were the tallest and most magnificent of the trees known at that time, and the one that represents Assyria had *beautiful branches overshadowing the forest* (**31:3b, 7, 9a**). It was *nourished* by *the waters* and *deep springs made it grow tall* (**31:4**). The abundant and unceasing supply of water is elaborated further: *Their streams flowed all around its base and sent their channels to all the trees of the field.* The Tigris and the Euphrates rivers may be in mind, but things are being described in Edenic terms.

It comes as no surprise that *the trees of Eden* and *the garden of God* are mentioned in this context (**31:8, 9b, 18**). As a result of its abundant nourishment, this tree *towered higher than all the trees of the field; its boughs increased and its branches grew long* (**31:5**). Because it was such a great tree *all the birds of the air nested in its boughs, all the beasts of the field gave birth under its branches; all the great nations lived in its shade* (**31:6**). The reference to the 'nations' betrays the fact that what is being spoken of is more than a mere tree. It was so majestic and beautiful that no other tree could rival it (31:8). God relishes his creative genius when he says, *I made it beautiful with abundant branches, the envy of all the trees of Eden in the garden of God* (31:9). Such was (notice the *once* of 31:3) Assyria, the greatest empire of its time, before its fall in 612 BC.

The clear admiration for this majestic tree leads to the observation that 'power and empire are not intrinsically evil; they fall legitimately within the sovereign permission of the Lord of history' (*BST*).

31:10-18 THE FALL OF THE TREE But the beautiful tree was corrupted by its own beauty and stature and God took action against it: *Because it towered on high, lifting its top above the thick foliage, and because it was proud of its height, I handed it over to the ruler of the nations, for him to deal with according to its wickedness* (**31:10-11**). God handed Assyria over to the Babylonians, who then became the dominant world power.

The Babylonians cut down the tree and left it (**31:12**). The magnificent tree lay fallen, spread out across the mountains and valleys. *The nations of the earth,* which had once lived in its shade, deserted it (31:12). A Tigrigna (Eritrea) proverb captures the fate of this tree: *Zwedeqe gereb msar* *yibezho* ['A fallen tree is chopped by many axes']. When the fortunes of the powerful, rich or famous change for the worse, people turn against them or despise them.

The birds and the beasts, on the other hand, settled on the fallen tree and remained among its branches (**31:13**). 'The fall of the cedar also means the end of its beneficent protective role ... Instead of building their nests in its branches and bearing their young under its boughs, the birds and the animals sit exposed on its fallen remains' (*NICOT*). The birds and animals could also be thought of as feasting on carcasses, if we remember that this fallen tree also represents a human empire (see 32:4).

God wants others trees (or nations) to learn from the fate of the great tree (Assyria). In particular, he wants Egypt to note what has happened to it. God is happy for a nation to grow and prosper, but he does not want any one of them to *tower proudly on high* nor to ever *reach such a height*. They should remain conscious that death is their end. The point that death is the final destiny of all humanity is repeated over and over again: *They are all destined for death, for the earth below, among mortal men, with those who go down to the pit* (**31:14**).

Once the great tree is *brought down to the grave*, the life-giving nutrients cease: *I covered the deep springs with mourning for it; I held back its streams; and its abundant waters were restrained* (**31:15**). The entire forest (all the nations) mourned the demise of this great tree. The tremendous thud of its fall and its descent to the grave reverberated throughout the then-known world (**31:16a**).

We are told that *all the trees ... were consoled in the earth below* (**31:16b**). But what consolation is there in going *down to the pit*? The next verse helps to explain this: *Those who lived in its shade, its allies among the nations, had also gone down to the grave with it* (**31:17**). The consolation was in the very fact that they were in the same place with this nation that had terrified and subjugated all of them. Death is, indeed, the great leveller.

Would Egypt turn over a new leaf? Would it learn a lesson from Assyria's fate? As the Lord started this oracle with a question (31:2) so he concludes it, asking Egypt: *Which of the trees of Eden can be compared with you in splendour and majesty?* (**31:18a**). He reminds her that her destiny will be the same as that of Assyria and the other nations which were brought down *to the earth below*.

The Egyptians are known for their elaborate preparations for the afterlife. The pyramids are standing witnesses to this. Therefore, to be dismissed to the grave along with *the uncircumcised*, without a decent burial, would be unthinkable for the rank and file Egyptian – let alone Pharaoh. But this exactly is the judgment that is being meted out to *Pharaoh and all his hordes* (**31:18b**).

32:1-16 A lament for Pharaoh and Egypt

The command to *take up a lament concerning Pharaoh king of Egypt* (**32:2a**) comes exactly a year and nine months after the oracle of judgment in chapter 31 (**32:1**) and about two months after the prophet and his audience got the news of the fall of Jerusalem (33:21). The actual fall of the city took place close to five months before the news reached them.

In Ezekiel, a lament often follows a judgment oracle. The NIV begins this lament by saying: *You are like a lion ... you are like a monster* (**32:2b**), making these two parallel images with regard to Pharaoh. But the NASB translation is preferable. It contrasts what Pharaoh thinks of himself and what the Lord says he is: 'You compared yourself to a young lion of the nations, Yet you are like the monster of the seas' (see also 29:3).

God will capture this sea monster in a net, drag it up onto dry land, and *throw you on the land and hurl you on the open field* (**32:3-4**). There, Pharaoh and his hordes will be devoured by *the birds of the air* and *the beasts of the earth* (**32:4**). There are many similarities between what is said about the fate of the fallen tree in 31:12-13 and the fate of Pharaoh in **32:4-6**. When God brings this judgment upon Pharaoh, there will be signs in the heavens similar to the signs associated with the eschatological day of the Lord (**32:7-8**; see Isa 13:10: Joel 2:31; 3:15; Amos 8:9; Matt 24:29). The judgment against Pharaoh will send a shock wave through the nations (**32:9**). Not only will they be *appalled at* what has happened to Pharaoh, but *each of them will tremble every moment for his life* (**32:10**).

Beginning with 32:11, the lament shifts from Pharaoh to Egypt. The lament is now also one that will be chanted by *the daughters of the nations* (**32:16**). God again says that he is sending *the most ruthless of all nations*, the Babylonians, against Egypt (**32:11-12**). They will be God's instrument for executing his judgment on the Egyptians as *they shatter the pride of Egypt*. As the result of God's judgment, the *waters* will no longer *be stirred* nor *muddied* by the monster (**32:13**; see also 32:2); rather, God will make them *flow like oil* (**32:14**). When all this happens, *then they will know that I am the Lord* (**32:15**).

32:17-32 The demise of Egypt and the other nations

The date given for this prophecy mentions only the year and day (**32:17**). The month may be the same as in 32:1, in which case this oracle was given two weeks after the one recorded in the first half of the chapter. The section opens with a continuation of the lament for *the hordes of Egypt* (**32:18**).

Although Egypt may have cherished a high regard of itself and may have despised the other nations, God commands: *Go down and be laid among the uncircumcised* (**32:19**). Thus *the mighty leaders will say of Egypt and her allies, 'They have come down and they lie with the uncircumcised, with those* *killed by the sword'* (**32:21**). 'As happened with Tyre (see 28:8-9), the much-vaunted grandeur of Egypt will appear as nothing when she stands at the entrance to the underworld and is drawn to lie with the uncircumcised' (*TOT*).

Ezekiel then lists the nations with whom Egypt lies in the earth below: *Assyria* (**32:22-23**), *Elam* – to the southeast of Assyria (**32:24-25**), *Meshech and Tubal* – in eastern Anatolia (present-day Turkey) (**32:26-27**), *Edom* (**32:29**), *all the princes of the north and all the Sidonians* (**32:30**). As if to underscore the shameful death of Pharaoh, he is listed among these nations: *You too, O Pharaoh, will be broken and will lie among the uncircumcised, with those killed by the sword* (**32:28**). All these are nations who at one time or another *spread terror in the land of the living* (32:23, 25, 27, 32). Now, however, *they lie uncircumcised with those killed by the sword and bear their shame with those who go down to the pit* (32:30). The only consolation Pharaoh will get in his descent to the underworld is that he is not alone (32:31-32).

The prophecies against the nations in chapters 25–32 teach three important truths. The first is the sovereignty of the Lord in international affairs. The second is 'the transience of all human power and glory, whether political, military or economic'. The third is that 'the goal of all God's action is that the nations will know him to be God' (*BST*). These are truths that we as biblical Christians need to affirm again and again in our contemporary world.

33:1-48:35 Restoration after Judgment

In terms of subject matter, we now enter into a completely different world. Whereas judgment has been the dominant theme in the book up till now, the motif from here on is the restoration or hope that was mentioned only in passing in earlier chapters.

33:1-39:29 Restoration to the promised land

The people who have been broken and expelled from their land are promised healing, restoration and return to their ancestral land.

33:1-33 A transition to a new world

This chapter serves as a transition from the current state of affairs to God's message of hope in the chapters that follow. It is strongly linked to what has gone before. Ezekiel was made a watchman for his people at the time of his call (3:16-21); in 33:1-9 he is reminded of that responsibility. He had warned the people of their personal responsibility as regards wickedness and righteousness (18:21-29); in 33:10-20 he is asked to do the same. But the most crucial passage in terms of Ezekiel's recommissioning for the task ahead is 33:21-22. These verses mark a pivotal point in Ezekiel's ministry.

The duties outlined for a watchman in 33:2-6 were the standard ones in time of war. The watchman would take up his position in the tower of a walled city and would scan the horizon for any sign of an approaching enemy. At the first sight of the enemy, he would blow *the trumpet to warn the people* (**33:2-3**). The people out in the fields would then rush to the safety of the city, and those in the city would prepare to defend it. If someone ignored the warning and was killed by the enemy, this death was his or her own fault, not the result of any negligence on the part of the watchman (**33:4-5**).

However, if the watchman failed to sound the warning and consequently someone was killed, the watchman would be held responsible *for his blood* (**33:6**). The words *that man will be taken away because of his sin* indicate that here the Lord is speaking of more than simply physical security from attack and prepares us for what follows.

The reiteration of the charge to Ezekiel to be a watchman for his people is a reminder of what has gone before, for he had prophesied about the destruction of Jerusalem (**33:7-9**; see comments on 3:16-21). But it is also an affirmation that his ministry will continue.

But Ezekiel's ministry will, from now on, change to a positive message of restoration. We see the first signs of this in **33:10**, which is also the first clue that Ezekiel's faithful and persistent ministry may be bearing fruit. We hear the people saying, *Our offences and sins weigh us down, and we are wasting away because of them. How then can we live?* This confession is very different from their earlier quotation of the proverb: 'The fathers eat sour grapes, and the children's teeth are set on edge', implying that they were suffering because of the sin of their fathers (see comments on 18:2). The Lord seizes the opportunity to remind them that he is merciful and takes *no pleasure in the death of the wicked*. Instead, he urges them, *Turn! Turn from your evil ways! Why will you die, O house of Israel?* (**33:11**; see also 18:32). Then in **33:12-20** he repeats the teaching on repentance and obedience that was given in 18:19-32.

This teaching is followed by two pivotal verses that signal a change in Ezekiel's life and ministry (**33:21-22**). He had been mute since the time of his call (see 3:24-27). But he had been promised that on the day a fugitive arrives to tell the exiles of the fall of Jerusalem, 'your mouth will be opened, you will speak with him and will no longer be silent' (24:26-27). This prophecy is finally fulfilled *in the twelfth year of our exile, in the tenth month on the fifth day* when *a man who had escaped from Jerusalem came to me and said, 'The city has fallen!'* (33:21). The Lord had clearly informed Ezekiel that the man's arrival was imminent, for *the evening before the man arrived, the hand of the Lord was upon me, and he opened my mouth ... and I was no longer silent* (33:22).

But his message is not yet totally positive as regards those few people still remaining in Judah. After the exile of King Jehoiachin and his group (which included Ezekiel) those who had been left in the land had taken over their land for themselves, saying: 'They are far away from the Lord; this land was given to us as our possession' (11:15). God reports that the same thing is happening now, after the destruction of the city: *The people living in those ruins in the land of Israel are saying, 'Abraham was only one man, yet he possessed the land. But we are many; surely the land has been given to us as our possession'* (**33:24**). Whether the reference to Abraham is intended to justify their actions by referring to their covenant claim to the land, or is merely focused on the number of survivors, what is clear is that their only concern is to grab the land and possessions of those who have been deported. Unfortunately, such behaviour was common then and is often present today.

God's answer to these callous and selfish people is swift and uncompromising. He has not given them the land because they are still violating his laws. In **33:25-26** he gives examples of particular laws that are being broken: the law against eating *meat with the blood still in it* (Lev 17:10-14), the law against idolatry (Exod 20:3), the law against murder (Exod 20:13) and the law against adultery (Exod 20:14). It was precisely because of this type of disobedience that the Lord handed the land over to the Babylonians and sent most of the nation into exile (see 22:6-12). The disobedient people who remain in the land will not possess it but will, instead, be destroyed (**33:27-28**).

As always, when God's judgment falls, *they will know that I am the Lord, when I have made the land a desolate waste because of all the detestable things they have done* (**33:29**).

The hope of restoration lies with the exiles, not with the remnant in the land (11:18-20). God is speaking about these exiles when he tells Ezekiel *your countrymen are talking together about you by the walls and at the doors of the houses* (**33:30a**). Having heard that his prediction of the fall of Jerusalem in 24:25-27 has been fulfilled (see 33:21-22), they are now *saying to each other, 'Come and hear the message that has come from the Lord'* (**33:30b**). They are now recognizing that Ezekiel is a true prophet of God.

If Ezekiel were like some of our modern evangelists who glorify themselves rather than glorifying God, this recognition might have gone to his head and made him brag about his success. But Ezekiel is realistic about his audience's response to his message. He knows they are hearers and not doers (**33:31**; Jas 1:22-25). In fact, they are guilty of deception and greed: *With their mouths they express devotion, but their hearts are greedy for unjust gain.* We do not know what they were greedily seeking, but it seems that 'as with Simon Magus (Acts 8:18), their receptivity to the word of God was distorted by the inner feeling of "what is there in this for me?"' (*TOT*).

Ezekiel has become little more than a source of entertainment for these people: *To them you are nothing more than one who sings love songs with a beautiful voice and plays an instrument well, for they hear words but do not put them into practice* (**33:32**). But there will come a day when they will realize *a prophet has been among them* (**33:33**).

34:1-31 The shepherds of Israel

In the ancient Near East, it was not uncommon for rulers or kings to be referred to as shepherds. Hammurabi and his Assyrian and Babylonian 'successors defined their role with a series of pastoral titles, and a Babylonian proverb had it that "A people without a king (is like) sheep without a shepherd"' (*NICOT*). A Luganda (Uganda) proverb captures the message of Zechariah 13:7, 'Strike the shepherd, and the sheep will be scattered', by saying 'when death strikes the cock, it leaves the hens in confusion'.

Turning to the Bible, not only are the leaders of God's people spoken of as shepherds (see also Jer 23:1-6), but some of the most outstanding leaders, men like Moses and David, had also worked as shepherds. God himself is referred to as a shepherd (Ps 23) and our Lord presents himself as 'the good shepherd' (John 10:1-18).

In the present chapter, God condemns the negligent shepherds of Israel, promises to gather his scattered sheep and look after them himself, and speaks of a time of peace under a Davidic ruler.

Ezekiel is told to *prophesy against the shepherds of Israel* (**34:2**). God had used these same words when he confronted Jerusalem and its inhabitants (5:8; 15:7) and the foreign nations (chs. 25–32). Now he is about to confront *the shepherds of Israel.* The reason God has become their enemy is that they *take care of themselves,* instead of looking after the sheep they are supposed to be caring for.

These shepherds were only too happy to benefit from the sheep. They ate *the curds* of the sheep's milk, clothed themselves *with the wool* and slaughtered *the choice animals* for meat. But they did nothing to care for the flock (**34:3**). They did not worry about sheep that were not thriving, or that were ill or injured. They made no attempt to retrieve sheep that strayed away from the flock or became lost. Instead of caring for the animals, they *ruled them harshly and brutally* (**34:4**). As the result of their selfish and irresponsible behaviour, the sheep were *scattered* and were easy prey *for all the wild animals* (**34:5**). The sheep they were treating so badly were not even their own, for God speaks of them as *my sheep,* making it clear that he is the actual owner of these neglected and scattered sheep (**34:6**).

Unfortunately, this description of negligent shepherds applies not only to the behaviour of the later kings of Israel and Judah, but can also be applied to the Christian church. 'Those who have been entrusted with leading the people of God have always been exposed to the temptation of "fleecing the flock" for their own advantage in terms of money or status, rather than the genuine and costly work of caring for the lost, the sick, the wounded and the strays' (*BST*).

The verdict follows the indictment. Having summoned the *shepherds* to hear *the word of the Lord* (**34:7, 9**), God again outlines their failures in **34:8** and announces that he will hold them responsible for the damage done to his flock. More than that, he will no longer employ them as shepherds, so that they cannot continue to *feed themselves* at the expense of his flock (**34:10**).

What is encouraging is that God will himself take the place of the unfaithful shepherds. He promises to *search for my sheep and look after them* (**34:11**). He will be a true and compassionate shepherd who will care for his sheep and *rescue them from all the places where they were scattered on a day of clouds and darkness* (**34:12**).

Clearly referring to the covenant people and the restoration from Babylonian captivity, the Lord promises to *gather them from the countries, and … bring them to their own land* (**34:13**). He describes the care he will give his restored sheep in language reminiscent of Psalm 23 (**34:14-15**). As the good shepherd, he will do the opposite of the negligent shepherds: *I will search for the lost and bring back the strays. I will bind up the injured and strengthen the weak* (**34:16a**; compare 34:4).

However, God will not be as gentle with *the sleek and the strong,* but will destroy them (**34:16b**). His reason for doing this is to uphold *justice.* It is not just the official leaders who abuse the sheep, but some of the sheep abuse each other. Thus God says, *I will judge between one sheep and another sheep and between rams and goats* (**34:17**). The series of rhetorical questions in **34:18-19** makes it clear that some of the sheep are selfishly ignoring the needs of others and trying to keep the best food and water for themselves. God condemns such selfish and callous behaviour (**34:20-21**) and promises: *I will save my flock, and they will no longer be plundered* (**34:22**).

God will save his flock by bringing in a reign of peace and harmony under a Davidic shepherd: *I will place over them … my servant David, and he will tend them* (**34:23**). This ruler who God *will place over them* is none other than the Messiah.

The statement *I the Lord will be their God* (**34:24**) brings the covenant relationship between God and his people into focus (see also 34:30-31). The essence of the covenant is then explained. It is called *a covenant of peace* (**34:25**). The people will live in peace and safety because God will rid the land of all dangers, whether from *wild beasts* (34:25) or other nations (**34:27b-28**). There will also be no fear of hunger, for God will send *showers of blessing,* resulting in abundant harvests (**34:26-27a**). In a land that will be *renowned for its crops,* the people *will no longer be victims of famine* (**34:29**).

The ultimate blessing is that the people will truly grasp the meaning of the covenant relationship mentioned earlier: *They will know that I, the Lord their God, am with them and that they, the house of Israel, are my people* (**34:30-31**). The source of security and all the blessings associated with the covenant relationship is God himself.

35:1-36:38 The restoration of land and people

Not only will God allow his people to return to their ancestral land, but he will also transform their hearts so that they can willingly put into practice the requirements of the covenant. But before he does this God provides 'pastoral reassurance, as damaged self-respect is built up with recourse to faith in a powerful covenant God' (*BST*).

35:1-36:15 Restoration of the land Given the positive and gentle prophecy in chapter 34, it comes as a shock when the very next chapter is another prophecy against Edom (*Mount Seir* is another name for the land of Edom – **35:2**). After all, the Edomites have already been mentioned, though briefly, in the oracles against the nations (25:12-14). Why devote an entire chapter to them at this stage in the book? The answer comes in two parts. The first is that the Israelites would have been acutely aware of the way the Edomites had treated the refugees from Jerusalem after its recent collapse. The second is that, given the promise that the restored Israel would be a place of peace, with the removal of all that threatened her (34:25), her hostile neighbours would have to be dealt with before this could happen.

The Lord announces that he will turn Edom into *a desolate waste* (**35:3-4**) and then gives the reasons for this judgment. The first reason is that the Edomites *harboured an ancient hostility* (or 'everlasting enmity' – NASB) *and delivered the Israelites over to the sword at the time of their calamity* (**35:5**). It seems that 'Edom, perhaps more than any other nation, had continually detested and resented Israel' (*EBC*). This hostility had been shown at *the time their punishment reached its climax,* that is, at the fall of Jerusalem in 586 BC (see Obad 10-14).

The Lord swears that *as surely as I live* judgment is coming, and it will fit the crime (see Exod 21:24-25). They *did not hate bloodshed* and, consequently, *bloodshed will pursue* them (**35:6**). In 6:3 a sword was directed against 'the mountains and hills … the ravines and valleys of Israel'; now the same sword is directed at Edom: *I will fill your mountains with the slain; those killed by the sword will fall on your hills and in your valleys and in all your ravines* (**35:8**). The Edomite towns will be left uninhabited. The outcome of this judgment will be that they will know that he is *the Lord* (**35:9**, see also 35:4, 15).

The second reason for God's judgment is that the Edomites had said that Israel and Judah *will be ours and we will take possession of them* (**35:10**). Greedy to extend their borders at the expense of these two nations, they did not even recognize that the Lord, the true and living God, was there with his people. 'It is interesting to note that, even in the hour of Judah's judgment, God is still regarded as being there in the land and is shown to identify himself with his people' (*TOT*). Again the Lord appears to make the punishment fit the crime (**35:11**). Because he was there, he has heard *all the contemptible things you have said against the mountains of Israel* (**35:12**). These 'contemptible things' include comments like, *They have been laid waste and have been given over to us to devour.* The Lord has also heard the Edomites as they have *boasted against me and spoke against me without restraint* (**35:13**).

The Lord repeats what he said in 35:9 about leaving Edom *desolate,* but this time adds that it will be in this state while the rest of the *earth rejoices* (**35:14**). This contrasting emotion also fits the crime. The Edomites will weep while others rejoice *because you rejoiced when the inheritance of the house of Israel became desolate* (**35:15**).

God's words here are a warning to us to watch ourselves to make sure that we do not rejoice at the calamities of others, even of our enemies. If we do, God may speak the same words to us that he spoke to Edom.

With Israel's hostile neighbours – represented by Edom – removed, it is now time to speak of the restoration of the land itself. Yet, although the prophecy is directed *to the mountains of Israel* (**36:1**), the first part of this oracle returns to the enemies who have ravaged the land and slandered the people. 'The prophecy of encouragement interestingly took the form of a judgment speech. The accusation provided the basis on which God would encourage the "land" of Israel' (*EBC*).

Having invited the mountains *to hear the word of the Lord* (36:1), God repeats the gloating words of the enemy about Israel (**36:2**; see also 35:10). He knows that the other nations have *ravaged and hounded* Israel, seized her land, and engaged in *malicious talk and slander* about her. These actions have been carried out with *glee and with malice* in a spirit of greed as they seek to *plunder its pastureland* (**36:3-4, 5b**). The special mention of *Edom* underscores the fact that this nation led the scramble for possession of 'the mountains of Israel'.

God responds to such scornful behaviour with *burning zeal* (**36:5a**) and *jealous wrath* (**36:6**). He proceeds to make a solemn oath *with uplifted hand,* a gesture that symbolizes his strength and commitment. In 20:5 this same gesture was used with respect to his promise to rescue the nation from Egypt at the time of the exodus. God swears that the enemy nations, represented by Edom, will be paid back in kind for what they have done. They will *suffer scorn* (**35:7**).

The mountains can, however, ignore any threat from Edom and will be transformed into places of abundant fruitfulness as they await the return of the people of Israel, who *will soon come home* (**36:8**). God's rejuvenating mercy comes to the surface when he says, *I am concerned for you and will look on you with favour; you will be ploughed and sown* (**36:9**).

Not only will the produce of the land be multiplied, but the people will also multiply and ruined towns will be rebuilt to accommodate *the whole house of Israel* (**36:10**). In fact, the area will be even more prosperous than it was before (**36:11**). This time, it is in the context of blessing that the land will acknowledge that *I am the Lord.*

It is puzzling to hear the Lord tell the land that it will never again deprive *my people Israel ... of their children* (**36:12**). But the idea is repeated in **36:13-14**, with the promise *you will no longer devour men or make your nation childless.* Ezekiel seems to be referring back to the fears that the spies had expressed about entering the promised land (Num 13:32). But this time, the Israelites will have nothing to fear, and the land will no longer *hear the taunts of the nations* nor *suffer the scorn of the peoples* (**36:15**).

36:16-38 RESTORATION OF THE PEOPLE We cannot draw a clear line between the prophecies about restoration of the land (36:1-15) and those about restoration of the people (36:16-38), for the people are mentioned in the previous section (36:10-11) and the land in the present section (36:30, 34-36). This may be due to the fact that land and people are inseparable when it comes to Israel. Nevertheless, in this section the focus falls on the restoration of the people to their ancestral land. In order to refresh their memory and underscore God's mercy in the restoration, the exiles are reminded why they were dispersed in the first place (36:16-21). This explanation is followed by the beautiful account of the restoration itself (36:22-32) and of the future happy state of the people and the land (36:33-38).

God starts by reminding the people of the sin that led to the Babylonian captivity. Addressing the prophet, the Lord says, *when the people of Israel were living in their own land, they defiled it by their conduct and their actions* (**36:17a**). In fact *their conduct was like a woman's monthly uncleanness in my sight* (**36:17b**). In other words, they left the land ceremonially unclean, as a woman was during her menstrual period (Lev 15:19-30). It was not that a menstruating woman was sinful, just as the land itself was not sinful, but what was happening in the land was making it unclean. By their behaviour, the people of Israel were endangering their relationship with the covenant Lord and inviting his wrath *because they had shed blood in the land and defiled it with their idols* (**36:18**). To punish them for these sins, God dispersed them among the nations (**36:19**).

Yet, although the dispersal was God's just punishment for their sins, it had a negative effect on God's reputation. It was not only the Israelites who were taunted by their captors and enemies (35:11-13; 36:3-7) but the God of the covenant people as well. Because God, people and land were so intertwined in the thought of the ancient Near East, it was assumed that Yahweh had been too weak to keep his people in their land (**36:20**). Consequently God's holy name was profaned. The repeated references to such profanation in this section (see 36:20, 21, 22, 23) indicate how seriously God takes it. Wright (*BST*) gives an example of such profanation in his imaginary reconstruction of a possible conversation between two Babylonians witnessing the arrival of the captives in Babylon:

'Who are these people?'

'Israelites from the land of Judah. Nebuchadnezzar has captured their city and deported the survivors.'

'What's the name of their god, then?'

'Yahweh, or so I've heard.'

'So, they are Yahweh's people but they've been expelled from Yahweh's land! Yahweh is not much of a god, then, is he? No better than the gods of all the other nations our great king has conquered. Glory be to Marduk!'

The Assyrian field commander had used very similar words when addressing King Hezekiah and the people of Jerusalem over a century earlier (2 Kgs 18:33-35; see also Isa 36:18-20). No wonder God was angered and jealous for his reputation when he heard the Babylonian god Marduk praised and his own name disparaged.

These words remind us that our own words and actions will also be seen as representing the Lord we serve in our communities. We need to ask ourselves, Is the witness of the church among the nations of Africa bringing glory to the name of the Lord or taking it down into the gutter? Is the global church speaking and conducting herself in such a way that the earth may be 'filled with the knowledge of the glory of the Lord' (Hab 2:14)? Are we truly living for God's glory?

God will bring restoration to Israel. But he says, in no uncertain terms, that he is not doing this because Israel deserves it, but for the sake of his own name (**36:22**). He is determined to *show the holiness of my great name*, so that *the nations will know that I am the Lord* (**36:23**). He will do this through the restoration of his people in the sight of the nations.

The scope of the restoration is detailed in 36:24-30. After bringing them back into their *own land* from among the nations (**36:24**), God will *sprinkle clear water* on them so that they may *be clean* from their *impurities* and *idols* (**36:25**). In NT-like language (see Col 3:10), God promises: *I will give you a new heart and put a new spirit in you* (**36:26**). They will no longer be hard-hearted when it comes to God, but will have *a heart of flesh*. The obedience that was not possible with a *heart of stone* will be made possible with the help of God's indwelling *Spirit* (**36:27**; see also 37:24; Jer 31:31-34). The covenant relationship between God and the people will be renewed: *You will be my people, and I will*

be your God (**36:28**). This renewed relationship will bring blessing to their very fields and crops, so that *famine* will be a thing of the past (**36:29-30**).

This celebration of God's favour and restoration is, however, suddenly jolted by the people's remembering of their *evil ways* and their self-loathing for their past *sins and detestable practices* (**36:31**). God again reminds them that they are right to be ashamed of themselves, and have no right to expect the blessings they are receiving (**36:32**). What is clear is that the blessings the people receive in 36:28-30 should not lead 'to fresh displays of complacency and a return to pre-exilic forgetfulness and rebellion, [but] should instead produce a salutary sense of shame that such blessings can be enjoyed in spite of such a disgraceful past' (*BST*). We are all reminded that we should never forget that we are sinners saved by grace and that we should never cease to marvel at the amazing and undeserved favour that God has showered upon us.

The remaining verses of the chapter elaborate on the subject of restoration. Towns that were in ruins will be rebuilt, and land lying idle and desolate *will be cultivated* (**36:33-34**). The restoration will be like a return to Eden, and admiring observers will state: *This land that was laid waste has become like the garden of Eden* (**36:35**). These observers are most likely the same who had earlier rejoiced at the calamity that had befallen the covenant people and their land (36:5). After witnessing the marvellous transformation the Lord will bring in his land and among his people, they will know that *the Lord* has indeed been at work (**36:36**).

To match the rejuvenated land and rebuilt cities, God will multiply the people (**36:37**). He will make them as *numerous as sheep, as numerous as the flocks for offerings at Jerusalem during the appointed feasts* (**36:38**). One wonders whether Ezekiel 'thought beyond the mere numerical similarity to the picture of a people who were ready to be offered, like the sheep, as living sacrifices in the service of God' (*TOT*). With the renewed acknowledgment of the Lord among the nations and the covenant people, that is not impossible.

37:1-28 Restoration continues

The theme of the restoration of the covenant people continues in this well-known chapter with its dramatic imagery. We need to take care that the very familiarity of this chapter does not result in us missing its real meaning. We also need to pay careful attention to the full context of the vision, both historically and within this book.

37:1-14 THE VALLEY OF DRY BONES Ezekiel opens the chapter with the now familiar statement *the hand of the Lord was upon me* (**37:1**). God brought him out by the power of *the Spirit* and set him *in the middle of a valley*. Since *valley* and *plain* are the same word in Hebrew, this may be the same place where Ezekiel received his call (see 3:22). The valley *was full of bones.* Having been led *back and forth among them,* the prophet says *I saw a great many bones on the floor of the valley, bones that were very dry* (**37:2**). This must have been a shocking experience for Ezekiel – not only because of the sheer number of human bones, but also because he was a priest, and contact with dead bodies would make him ceremonially unclean (Lev 21:1-4; 22:4).

The Lord asks him, *Son of man, can these bones live?* (**37:3a**). Ezekiel may have been aware of the resuscitation of a number of dead persons – the son of the widow of Zarephath (1 Kgs 17:17-24), the son of the Shunammite (2 Kgs 4:18-37), the man who was thrown into Elisha's tomb (2 Kgs 13:20-21). But the idea of dry bones filling a whole plain – and 'very dry' bones at that – coming to life again is mind-boggling. How is Ezekiel to answer the Lord's question? To answer 'yes' would be presumptuous. To answer 'no' would be limiting God's ability. Ezekiel says, *O Sovereign Lord, you alone know* (**37:3b**).

Ezekiel's humble response leads to God's next command: *Prophesy to these bones and say to them 'Dry bones, hear the word of the Lord!'* (**37:4**). Ezekiel is to contribute to the revival of these bones. He is to proclaim to them what God has told him: *I will make breath enter you … I will attach tendons to you and make flesh come upon you and cover you with skin; I will put breath in you, and you will come to life* (**37:5-6**). This passage highlights the cooperation of the divine and the human. God commands and the prophet obeys, even though he does not understand what is going on: *So I prophesied as I was commanded* (**37:7a, 10**).

The outcome of this cooperation is amazing: *And as I was prophesying, there was a noise, a rattling sound, and the bones came together, bone to bone* (**37:7b**). Not only that, but Ezekiel says, *I looked, and tendons and flesh appeared on them and skin covered them* (**37:8a**) – exactly as he had prophesied (37:6). 'That's all. He just spoke aloud with ordinary words. No magic. No secret incantations. No conjuring tricks with bones. Just the living power of the word of the living God invading the valley of the shadow of death' (*BST*).

The bodies of the dead had re-formed, but *there was no breath in them* (**37:8b**). So Ezekiel was commanded to prophesy again: *Prophesy to the breath … and say to it … Come from the four winds, O breath, and breathe into these slain, that they may live* (**37:9**; see also 37:5). The same Hebrew word can be translated *Spirit* (as in 37:1, 14), *breath* (as in 37:5, 6, 8, 9, 10) and *winds* (as in 37:9). The variety of possible translations points to the rich significance of the word. The basic meaning is air in motion, which leads to the idea of wind or breath. 'It comes to mean both man's spirit, or disposition, and also emotional qualities like vigour, courage, impatience and ecstasy. It covers not only man's vital breath, given to him at birth and leaving his body in his dying gasp, but also the Spirit of God who imparts that breath' (*TOT*). The single most important effect of the

activities of the Spirit in this passage in Ezekiel 'is life, life out of utter deadness' (*BST*). Again, the efficacy of the prophetic word is revealed: *and breath entered them; they came to life and stood up on their feet – a vast army* (**37:10**).

Questions have also been asked about the significance of the two-stage revival of the dry bones, and numerous answers have been given. But one thing that is clear is that what is being re-enacted here is the creation of humanity in Genesis 2:7. Ezekiel is witnessing the recreation of Israel (and humanity) from its deadness!

God explains this vision to Ezekiel (37:11-14). He is told, *Son of man, these bones are the whole house of Israel* (**37:11a**). The exiles felt themselves to be as useless, as hopeless and as lifeless as dried bones (**37:11b**). Just as Ezekiel prophesied to the bones in the vision, so he is to prophesy to his people. They should not think themselves as good as dead and buried, for the Lord says, *O my people, I am going to open your graves and bring you up from them; I will bring you back to the land of Israel* (**37:12-13**). The same Spirit that had given Ezekiel this vision and set him *in the middle of the valley* (37:1) *will settle* the covenant people in their *own land* (**37:14**).

The familiar formula *then you will know that I am the Lord* is repeated twice in the space of two verses to emphasize the miraculous nature of their revival (37:13-14).

37:15-28 A RENEWED AND UNITED NATION What the covenant Lord has in mind for his people is not only revival but unity as well. 'If death can be reversed, so can division' (*BST*). That is why Ezekiel is asked to perform his last symbolic act. God tells him to *take a stick of wood and write on it, 'Belonging to Judah and the Israelites associated with him'* (**37:16a**). He is then told to *take another stick of wood, and write on it, 'Ephraim's stick, belonging to Joseph and all the house of Israel associated with him'* (**37:16b**). Finally, he is commanded to: *Join them together into one stick so that they will become one in your hand* (**37:17**). The Hebrew word translated *a stick of wood* simply means 'wood', and thus some scholars believe that what Ezekiel wrote on was a flat writing tablet rather than a stick. It would certainly be easier to glue two writing tablets together than two sticks. But whatever it was that he wrote on, what is important is the message that this visual aid communicated: the unity of God's renewed people.

The names *Judah* and *Ephraim* or *Joseph* that were written on the two sticks were reminders of the divided kingdom that had existed before the exile. But each name is also accompanied by a reference to *the Israelites associated with him.* These words highlight the fact that both groups were composed of Israelites, and thus point to the unity of the nation after the restoration. The object lesson is saying that they will become one. And that is the message that Ezekiel gives when asked about the significance of his lesson (**37:18-19**). The people's return to the land (**37:21**), their unity under one ruler (**37:22**) and their cleansing from sin (**37:23a**) are all dealt with in these verses, which culminate in a renewed covenant: *They will be my people, and I will be their God* (**37:23b**).

Some limited unity was achieved with the return of the exiles after the edict of Cyrus in 538 BC. But it is obvious that what Ezekiel is pointing to here will be fulfilled only in some future time, long after the return from exile under Zerubbabel, Ezra and Nehemiah (and even long after the establishment of the state of Israel in 1948).

God clarifies that he is pointing to the messianic kingdom with the words, *my servant David will be king over them, and they will all have one shepherd* (**37:24a**). Reminding us of what he said earlier (36:27) and of the new covenant of Jeremiah 31:31-34, God says, *they will follow my laws and be careful to keep my decrees* (**37:24b**). When David becomes *their prince forever,* God *will make a covenant of peace with them; it will be an everlasting covenant* (**37:25-26**). Ezekiel's point 'is not so much ethnic and geographical, but theological … He is determined to insist that the future of God's people is a future for *one* people. One God, one people, one covenant' (*BST*). In order for that oneness of God's people to materialize, the Jews will have to embrace the new covenant which has been effected once for all through the sacrifice of God's incarnate Son, Jesus Christ (see Rom 11:25-27). Only then will they see God's promise fulfilled: *My dwelling place will be with them; I will be their God, and they will be my people* (**37:27**). At that time, *the nations will know that I the Lord make Israel holy, when my sanctuary is among them forever* (**37:28**; see Rev 7:15; 21:22-27).

38:1-39:29 Seven oracles against Gog

We may be puzzled as to why chapters 38 and 39 suddenly interrupt the flow of thought, which we might have expected would have carried straight on into chapters 40 to 48. What these chapters describe is a threat that will come from a seemingly unbeatable enemy after God has restored his people and had given them peace and tranquillity in their land. Of course 'a huge eschatological battle between the forces of evil … and the faithful people of God' should not be new to the students of Scripture (*TOT*).

38:1-2 INTRODUCTION TO THE SEVEN ORACLES When we look at their structure, it is obvious that these two chapters form a unit, made up of seven oracles. After having given Ezekiel the command to prophesy against the one identified as the object of the prophecy (**38:1-2**), each new oracle is introduced by the statement, *This is what the Sovereign Lord says* (38:3, 10, 14, 17; 39:1, 17, 25). As we study these seven oracles in the sequence in which they are given, we will come to understand the message of this prophecy. The content of these oracles should be 'thoroughly integrated' in our hearts and minds so as 'to create a sequence of events

whose total impact is much greater than the sum' of the parts (*NICOT*).

First, however, we need to identify who *Gog* is (38:2). The only other references to the name Gog in the entire Bible are in Chronicles, Ezekiel and Revelation. Chronicles identifies him as a descendant of Reuben, the firstborn of Jacob (1 Chr 5:4).

Our present passage also identifies him as a person, and adds that he is from *the land of Magog.* In Genesis 10:2 and Chronicles 1:5, Magog is said to be one of the sons of Japheth. In this passage from Ezekiel, it is obviously the name of the area where one would find the places called *Meshech* and *Tubal.* These last two places are generally understood to have been in the area east of modern Turkey, south-east of Russia and north-west of Iran (see also 27:13; 32:26). (The NASB translates the word 'Rosh' as another place name, whereas the NIV interprets it as meaning 'chief', used as an adjective to modify 'prince'. The NASB's interpretation suffers from the problem that it has proved difficult to identity a place named Rosh in the Bible or in the ancient Near East.)

In Revelation 20:8, both Gog and Magog are presented as the nations that Satan deceives and musters to surround 'the camp of God's people and the city he loves' after the millennium.

Various other ancient sources have also been used by commentators anxious to identify who Gog is. But when we read any speculation about this, we need to remember that 'the origin of the name is less significant than what it symbolizes, namely the personified head of the forces for evil which are intent on destroying the people of God' (*TOT*).

38:3-9 FIRST ORACLE In this first oracle there is an alliance of nations from the north and the south, from the east and the west (**38:5-6**) under the leadership of *Gog, chief prince of Meshech and Tubal* (**38:3**) against the people of God. Both human will and God's sovereignty are involved in this mustering of armies. Whereas Gog and *all his hordes* are said to be *ready* and *prepared* (**38:7**) and *brandishing their swords* (**38:4b**), it is actually God himself who is bringing them to the land where his restored people are living in peace and tranquillity (**38:8**). In fact, the Lord tells Gog, *I will turn you around, put hooks in your jaws and bring you out with your whole army* (**38:4a**). The magnitude of the invasion is *like a storm; you will be like a cloud covering the land* (**38:9**). Although the historical context of this attack is the time after the restoration from the Babylonian captivity, the phrases *after many days* and *in future years* (38:8, 16) point to an indefinite time in the future. The words 'after many days' in particular are sometimes used 'to reach as far as the end times' (*EBC*). Thus what we have here is 'an eschatological vision, not a tight historical prediction, except in the sense that it is definitely envisaged as taking place long

after the return from exile and the resettlement of the land'
(*BST*).

38:10-13 Second oracle The second oracle speaks about the
evil scheme of Gog (**38:10**). The *safety* of God's people (38:8,
14) is clear from Gog's description of them as living in *a
land of unwalled villages ... a peaceful and unsuspecting people
– all of them living without walls and without gates and bars*
(**38:11**). 'Israel has never enjoyed such idyllic tranquillity
... which suggests that Ezekiel here has in view the future
golden age' (*EBC*). The statement that these people are
living at the centre of the land reminds us of the centrality of
Jerusalem in Jewish thought (**38:12**; see 5:5). Rabbinic writings even referred to it as 'the navel of the earth' (*TOT*).

It is not clear what *Sheba and Dedan and the merchants of
Tarshish and all her villages* have in mind when they ask Gog,
*Have you come to plunder? Have you gathered your hordes to
loot, to carry off silver and gold, to take away livestock and
goods and to seize much plunder?* (**38:13**). It is likely that
these rhetorical questions spring from a selfish motive.
'Gog's enterprise has roused the greed of other nations to
join in the plunder, or to traffic in the stolen goods. They are
typical of those who will not initiate wrong-doing, but are
eager to cash in on the proceeds of it' (*TOT*). Our crooked
human nature still tries to take advantage of the vulnerability of others, as evidenced by the looting that followed
the tsunami in the Indian Ocean and Hurricane Katrina in
the USA. Looting and theft are also common in our African
societies whenever there are riots or traffic accidents.

38:14-16 Third oracle The next oracle develops a point
mentioned in relation to the first oracle – the involvement
of both human beings and God in Gog's enterprise. The Lord
says, *You will come from your place in the far north* (**38:15**).
This statement applies only to the leader of the alliance,
for the participating nations come from the four points of
the compass. Yet while *Gog will advance,* in the final analysis the initiative is God's: *I will bring you against my land*
(**38:16**). For what purpose? *So that the nations may know
me when I show them myself holy through you before their eyes.*
'What Gog imagines to be a victory for himself, the Lord
turns into an opportunity for His glory' (*TOT*).

38:17-23 Fourth oracle The fourth oracle proclaims God's
judgment of *Gog* and his hordes. They will meet 'more
than their match' in God (*BST*). At that time, the Lord will
ask him: *Are you not the one I spoke of in former days by my
servants the prophets of Israel?* (**38:17**). We are once again
reminded that not only is God in control of events, but that
he knew about them long before they happened. His prophets had long predicted Gog's attack. Although Gog is not
mentioned by name, the Scriptures do contain many prophecies about the final destruction of the enemies of God's
people (Deut 30:7; Isa 26:20-21; 34:2-4; Jer 30:18-24; compare Rev 16:13-16; 19:17-19; 20:7-10).

Gog's attack on the covenant people will provoke God's
anger and precipitate his judgment on him and his hordes
(**38:18**). This judgment will manifest itself on land, sea and
air and *all the people on the face of the earth will tremble at
my presence* (**38:19-20**). To protect his defenceless people
against Gog's callous attack, God will turn *every man's sword
... against his brother* (**38:21**). He will also use disease and
the forces of nature to punish Gog and *the many nations with
him* (**38:22**). Through this judgment, God says *I will show
my greatness and my holiness* and the nations *will know that I
am the Lord* (**38:23**; see also 38:16).

39:1-16 Fifth oracle The commentary *NICOT* titles chapters 38 and 39 'The Defeat of Gog' and 'The Disposal of
Gog' respectively. The similarity of these headings makes
it clear that we can expect the second chapter to repeat
some of what is said in the previous chapter (compare, for
example, **39:1-2** and 38:1-4, 15).

This oracle also deals with the utter destruction of the
invading armies of *Gog.* First of all, he will be disarmed: *I
will strike your bow from your left hand and make your arrows
drop from your right hand* (**39:3**). The people of Israel will be
able to use these discarded weapons as firewood *for seven
long years* (**39:9-10a**).

Gog and his hordes will be given as food to the birds
of the air and the beasts of the field *on the mountains of
Israel* (**39:4-5**). His homeland, *Magog,* will be set on fire
so that they may know *that I am the Lord* (**39:6**). The honour of God's *holy name* is again stressed in **39:7-8** (see also
38:23). He will reverse the circumstances of those who
thought they could plunder Israel (**39:10b**).

Not only are Gog and his hordes destroyed on the mountains of Israel; they are also disposed of in the land of
Israel. The bodies of the whole army will be buried *in the
valley of those who travel east towards the Sea* (**39:11**), which
will thereafter be known as *the Valley of Hamon Gog* (the
hordes of Gog). This is probably located 'east of the Dead
Sea' (*TOT*).

It will take the Israelites *seven months* to bury them and
thus *cleanse the land* (**39:12**). What *a memorable day* it will
be when the people see the Lord glorifying himself in this
manner and removing the enemy forever! After all the visible bodies have been buried, *men will be regularly employed
to cleanse the land* (**39:14**). Their task will be to search the
land to locate any remaining human bones. When they find
any, they will mark the spot and send *gravediggers* to collect
and bury these bones with the others *in the Valley of Hamon
Gog* (**39:15**). In fact a town called *Hamonah* (or Horde) will
be built close to the burial site (**39:16**).

This meticulous cleansing of the land is necessary
because 'if God is to dwell again in full harmony with his
people, then his dwelling-place must be clean and holy. No
trace of the pollution of his enemies will remain' (*BST*).

39:17-24 Sɪxᴛʜ ᴏʀᴀᴄʟᴇ In 39:4 God said that the dead bodies of Gog and his hordes would be food for birds and wild animals. Now he elaborates on that theme. He instructs Ezekiel to call *every kind of bird and all the wild animals* to a great sacrificial feast (**39:17**). But instead of animal sacrifices, they will eat human beings *as if they were rams and lambs, goats and bulls – all of them fattened animals from Bashan* (**39:18**). There will be so many bodies to eat that the animals will be *glutted* (**39:19**). And if they are bored with one type of meat, God promises that *at my table you will eat your fill of horses and riders, mighty men and soldiers of every kind* (**39:20**).

Although the idea of the dead being a great sacrifice is present in other prophetic texts (Isa 34:6-7; Jer 46:10; Zeph 1:7-9), nowhere else in the Bible is there anything like this event except in Revelation 19:17-21. It can be strongly argued that John's message of restoration and the messianic kingdom matches that of Ezekiel. Thus the invasion of Gog and his hordes points to Satan's mustering of the armies of 'Gog and Magog' against 'the saints and the beloved city' at the end of the millennium (Rev 20:7-10).

In the remaining verses of this oracle God affirms, first, that he will display his *glory among the nations,* enabling them to *see the punishment* he inflicted upon them (**39:21**). As they witness this punishment, God's covenant people, too, *will know that I am the Lord their God* (**39:22**). The nations will also *know that the people of Israel went into exile for their sin* (**39:23-24**) and not because the Lord was powerless to deliver them from their enemies. The scandal that the exile had brought to his *holy name* will be forgotten (see 39:7; 36:20-21).

39:25-29 Sᴇᴠᴇɴᴛʜ ᴏʀᴀᴄʟᴇ The last oracle is a beautiful reversal of the shame of Israel and the profanation of God's holy name by the sin of his people, which had landed them in exile among the nations. It seems that this oracle represents 'a deliberate attempt to round off the Gog oracles and to relate their message to the immediate needs of the post-587 ʙᴄ generation of exiles' (*TOT*). Concerned both for his people and his name, the Lord says, *I will now bring Jacob back from captivity and will have compassion on all the people of Israel, and I will be zealous for my holy name* (**39:25**). When God accomplishes the restoration of his people (**39:27-28**), *they will forget their shame and all the unfaithfulness they showed* (**39:26**). Not only will they know that he, indeed, is *the Lord their God* (39:28), but they will also experience his countenance afresh, for he says *I will no longer hide my face from them* (**39:29**; contrast 39:24; see also 36:25-27). Moreover, God promises to *pour out my Spirit on the house of Israel.* What a marvellous restoration it will be!

40:1-48:35 The Return of God's Glory

The extremely careful dating in 40:1 indicates that we are starting a new section of the book – indeed, the final section.

Here we witness the Lord returning to his temple and dwelling permanently in his city among his covenant people. This part of the book of Ezekiel must have enabled the prophet's exiled community to take a deep breath of relief and look forward to a glorious future of peace and tranquillity.

However, as we read this vision of the temple, we may be left puzzled about what it means for us as Christians. We know that the temple Ezekiel sees is not the temple that was rebuilt by the exiles (Ezra 6:14-15), for the words of post-exilic prophets like Malachi prove that the promise that 'Israel will never again defile my holy name' (43:7) has not yet been fulfilled (Mal 1:6-13).

Nor is the temple in the vision equivalent to Herod's temple, from which Jesus drove the moneylenders (Matt 21:12-13; Mark 11:15-17; Luke 19:45-46; John 2:13-22). Jesus' action is often referred to as 'the cleansing of the temple', but it was not so much an act of purification as a prophetic sign that pointed to 'the coming destruction of the temple itself and the end of all that it stood for in contemporary Jewish theology and politics' (*BST*). But this sign is not solely negative, for it also points to the positive message that Jesus himself is the messianic embodiment of the temple (John 2:18-22). The words of Hebrews 10:19, 12:22 and 13:10 indicate that 'in Jesus we have all that the temple signified for Israel, and indeed all that Ezekiel's vision of restoration implied' (*BST*). Moreover, the temple imagery is applied not only to Jesus but also to the people who are in him, both individually (1 Cor 6:19-20) and corporately (Eph 2:19-22; 1 Pet 2:4-5). In John's great vision of the new Jerusalem there is no temple, 'because the Lord God Almighty and the Lamb are its temple' (Rev. 21:22). Yet there 'God will at last dwell with his redeemed humanity' (*BST*).

As we read Ezekiel's vision of the temple in 40:1-42:20, we should think about what the building reveals of the holiness of God. And as we hear God's promise to be with his people (43:1-12), we should give thanks that this promise has been and will be fulfilled in Christ and should commit ourselves to living holy lives.

40:1-4 Introduction

The date notices given here (*in the twenty-fifth year of our exile ... in the fourteenth year after the fall of the city* – **40:1a**) indicate that this is the last oracle but one (see 29:17) given to Ezekiel. There is a gap of more than ten years between the restoration oracles given in chapters 33 to 37 (see 33:21) and the glorious culmination of the fortunes of God's people given in this section.

On that very day (that is, *on the tenth of the* first month) says Ezekiel, *the hand of the Lord was upon me and he took me there* (**40:1b**). Since the city is mentioned in connection with the second date notice, the *there* must be Jerusalem. God must, therefore, have whisked Ezekiel from Babylon to Jerusalem for a second time (see 8:1-4).

Ezekiel elaborates: *In visions of God he took me to the land of Israel and set me on a very high mountain, on whose south side were some buildings that looked like a city* (**40:2**). The mention of a 'very high mountain' and the buildings on the south side of it 'that looked like a city' may suggest that these visions refer to the situation that will prevail in the end times.

Ezekiel *saw a man whose appearance was like bronze* standing at *the gateway with a linen cord and a measuring rod in his hand* (**40:3**). This angel will be his guide and interpreter during this vision. In fact, 'the whole unit is held together' by the mention of the city at the beginning and at the end (40:2 and 48:35) and 'by the guide who escorts the prophet around the temple complex' (*NICOT*).

The angel instructs the prophet to *look with your eyes and hear with your ears and pay attention to everything I am going to show you, for that is why you have been brought here* (**40:4**). Moreover, he is commanded, *tell the house of Israel everything you see.* The message was to be received and then shared with God's people.

40:5-42:20 The new temple

Ezekiel is then taken on a tour of a new temple complex.

40:5 THE TEMPLE WALL The tour starts with a panoramic view of the temple area: *I saw a wall completely surrounding the temple area,* separating 'the sacred area from the secular world outside'. This wall was as thick as it was high – that is, *one measuring rod thick and one rod high* (**40:5**). According to the information given in the text, the *measuring rod* would be close to ten and a half feet. The separation of this holy area is impressed upon us more and more as we accompany Ezekiel on his tour.

40:6-47 THE TEMPLE COURTS The temple has two courts, an outer court and an inner court. The tour begins at the east gate of the outer court (**40:6**). The angel leading Ezekiel proceeds to climb the *steps* of *the gate facing east.* We are not told how many steps there were, but from the description of the north and south gates we can deduce that there were *seven steps* (40:22, 26). 'This indicates that the temple area is thought of as a huge raised area, built up above the level of the surrounding land' (*TOT*). This too is a reminder that here is a sacred space.

As he leads Ezekiel along, the angel takes the measurements of the various structures of the temple complex that they pass. Among the things measured are *the threshold … the alcoves … the portico … the jambs … the entrance to the gateway … the parapet openings* (**40:7-16**).

Focusing on the outer court itself, Ezekiel says: *I saw some rooms and a pavement that had been constructed all around the court* (**40:17**). After specifying that *there were thirty rooms,* Ezekiel explains that they were built *along the pavement.* The pavement is called *the lower pavement* because it is lower than the level of the inner court (see 40:31, 34,

37), although it is *seven steps* higher than the area outside the temple premises.

The angel *then … measured the distance from the inside of the lower gateway* (compare the just-mentioned 'lower pavement') *to the outside of the inner court.* This distance was recorded as being *one hundred cubits* (**40:19**). The long cubit, which is the measurement used here, was about 20½ inches (50 centimetres), so that the distance was about 50 yards (45 metres). Still within the confines of the outer court, the angel leads Ezekiel to the north (**40:20-23**) and the south gates (**40:24-27**). The measurements are the same as those of the east gate (40:21-22, 24). Additional things mentioned here are the *palm tree decorations* (40:23, 26) and the *seven steps* referred to earlier.

Though *the inner court* is mentioned in 40:19, 23, 27, we are given a detailed description of it only in 40:28-47. Here Ezekiel describes the inner gates (40:28-37), the rooms and tables used for sacrifices (40:38-43) and the rooms allocated to the priests (40:44-47).

Ezekiel was led into the outer court via the east gate, but he enters the inner court via the south gate (**40:28**). All three inner gates are mentioned and their measurements given.

'Although it does not say so, we must suppose that another wall surrounded the inner court' (*TOT*). Add to this the *eight steps* that lead from *the lower pavement* to the three inner gates (**40:31, 34, 37**) and one is left with the impression that the holiness of this space is being underscored. The higher one goes and the farther towards the centre one moves the holier the place becomes.

A room used for washing *the burnt offerings* appears to be located *by the portico* (that is, facing the outer court) *in each of the inner gates* (**40:38**). Moreover, *two tables* are placed *on each side* of the portico *on which the burnt offerings, sin offerings and guilt offerings were slaughtered* (**40:39**). Two other tables were placed *by the outside wall of the portico of the gateway, near the north gateway, on either side of the steps* (**40:40**). By way of summary, the text says: *So there were four tables on one side of the gateway and four on the other – eight tables in all – on which the sacrifices were slaughtered* (**40:41**). It is not clear whether the eight tables were at each of the three inner gates, or only at *the north gateway* (40:40; see 46:19-20), or only at the east gate (see 46:2) or on both the east and north gates. If the room for washing the burnt offerings was located *in each of the inner gates* (40:38), then one would also expect the tables to be placed at all three gates. 'It is not impossible that each of the three gates had this sacrificial equipment, and that worshippers could approach by any of the three entrances' (*TOT*).

There were also four tables of dressed stone for the burnt offerings (**40:42**). The use of these additional stone tables is explained: *On these were placed the utensils for slaughtering the burnt offerings and the other sacrifices.* The section concludes by repeating that: *The tables were for the flesh of the offerings* (**40:43**).

Two rooms were designated for priestly use, *one at the side of the north gate and facing south, and another at the side of the south gate and facing north* (**40:44**). Each of the two rooms is assigned to a specific category of priests (**40:45**). All of these priests were from among *the sons of Zadok, who are the only Levites who may draw near to the Lord to minister before him* (**40:46**; see 44:10-16). *The court* (**40:47**) is the inner court, at the centre of which, just *in front of the temple, the altar* of sacrifice is located.

40:48-41:26 THE SANCTUARY AND ITS ATTACHMENTS Eventually the prophet is *brought* to the entrance *of the temple* itself. After giving the dimensions of the various parts of *the portico*, Ezekiel mentions that the temple *was reached by a flight of stairs* (**40:48-49**). Some commentators suggest that there were probably ten steps, and that the general design of the temple was similar to that of the temples of Solomon, Zerubbabel and Herod. The exact number of steps is less important than the point that the heart of the temple is situated on still higher ground than both the outer court and the inner court, symbolizing that it is even more sacred than they are.

Ezekiel is *brought … to the outer sanctuary* (**41:1**) or what is generally referred to as the Holy Place. As a priest, he was allowed to enter this area, but only the guiding angel *went into the inner sanctuary* (**41:3**) or what is generally referred to as *the Most Holy Place* (**41:4**). Only the high priest was allowed to enter it, and that only once a year (Lev 16). Whereas the Holy Place was *forty cubits long* (20 yards/18 metres) *and twenty cubits wide* (10 yards/9 metres) (**41:2**), the Most Holy Place was *twenty cubits* square (41:4). As Ezekiel has moved deeper into the temple complex, the entrances have become progressively narrower – from *fourteen cubits* (7 yards/6.5 metres) for the portico (40:48) to *ten cubits* (5 yards/4.5 metres) for the outer sanctuary (41:1) to *six cubits* (3 yards/2.7 metres) for the inner sanctuary (41:3). This narrowing of the entrances is also symbolic of increasing holiness.

Side rooms had been built around the temple *on three levels, one above another, thirty on each level, to give* a total of ninety rooms (**41:6**). The three levels were connected by *a stairway* that *went up from the lowest floor to the top floor through the middle floor* (**41:7**). Although *the side rooms* surrounded the temple on three sides, there was no direct access to them from the temple. *There were entrances to the side rooms from the open area, one on the north and another on the south* (**41:11**). We are not exactly told what these rooms were used for, but they may have been 'store-rooms for temple equipment and furnishings, and for the tithes and offerings that were paid to the temple servants (see Mal 3:10)' (*TOT*). They can be compared with the *side rooms* of Solomon's temple (1 Kgs 6:5-10).

Another building, 90 by 70 cubits (45 by 35 yards/41 by 32 metres) stood *facing the temple courtyard on the west side* (**41:12**). The temple and its courtyard, including the walls, was 100 cubits square (50 yards/45 metres) (**41:13-15a**). The temple area and *the portico facing the court, as well as the threshold* were all *covered with wood.* This wood covered *the floor, the wall up to the windows, and the windows* (**41:15b-16**). *At regular intervals*, the inner and outer sanctuaries were decorated with *carved cherubim and palm trees* (**41:17-18a**). Ezekiel tells us that *each cherub had two faces, the face of a man toward the palm tree on one side and the face of a lion toward the palm tree on the other. They were carved all around the whole temple* (**41:18b-20**). Both *the outer* and *the inner sanctuary* had *rectangular* doorframes as well as *double doors*, with *cherubim and palm trees* carved on them (**41:21-25**).

The description of the doors is interrupted by the description of *a wooden altar* that Ezekiel's angel guide tells him is *the table that is before the Lord* (41:22). The twelve loaves of bread placed on this table every Sabbath (Exod 25:23-30; Lev 24:5-9) were both an offering to God and also a reminder that God is the one who provides all that is needed to sustain life. We do not know why this is the only item of furniture in the temple that Ezekiel mentions. The carvings *on the sidewalls of the portico* represented only *palm trees* (**41:26**), with none of the cherubim that decorated temple proper.

42:1-14 THE PRIESTS' ROOMS The angel next led Ezekiel out of the inner court and *northward into the outer court and brought me to the rooms opposite the temple courtyard and opposite the outer wall on the north side* (**42:1**). Here the priests had two sets of rooms located on the north side (42:1-9) and on the south side (42:10-12) of the temple courtyard, facing the outer court. Ezekiel gives the measurements of the building on the north side where these rooms were located (**42:2-3**) and describes the passageways and the doors (42:4). These rooms were on three levels (**42:5-6**), like the side rooms we saw earlier (41:5-11). Since the rooms were built in a rectangular arrangement, there was a row of rooms on the side next to the outer court and another row on the side nearest the sanctuary (**42:7-8**). It appears that these rooms could be approached both from the north and the east (**42:4, 9**).

Turning to the building on the south side and the rooms located there (**42:10**), Ezekiel underscores the similarity of the two sets of rooms: *These were like the rooms on the north; they had the same length and width, with similar exits and dimensions* (**42:11-12**). The angel who was guiding him told him that these rooms were for the *priests who approach the Lord* (see 40:46). He is told that in these rooms, *they will eat the most holy offerings. There they will put … the grain offerings, the sin offerings and the guilt offerings* – all three of which are described as *the most holy offerings* (**42:13**). These rooms must also be where the priests change their clothes, for *once the priests enter the holy precincts, they are* *not to go into the outer court until they leave behind the garments in which they minister, for these are holy* (**42:14**). In other words, the priests are not to wear their temple dress when they go anywhere near the places that are open to the people. Changing their clothes is an outward ritual that reminds both priests and people of the difference between the holy and the profane. As the following chapters show, the failure by the people in general and the priests in particular to distinguish between the holy and the profane (or the common) was one of the factors that precipitated the captivity. However, in the future the priests will teach this distinction and will model it to the people (44:5-23).

42:15-20 Measurements of the entire complex When the angel *had finished measuring what was inside the temple area*, he took Ezekiel *out by the east gate and measured the area all around* (**42:15**). So Ezekiel started and completed his tour of the temple complex at *the east gate* (see 40:6). The angel guide measured the wall that surrounded the temple area (40:5) *on all four sides* (east, north, south and west – **42:16-20**). It was *five hundred cubits long and five cubits wide*. There is uncertainty about the exact unit of measurement in these verses. The NIV has *cubits*, but the NASB has 'reeds', and speaks of 'the measuring reed' rather than the measuring rod (NIV). Since this reed or rod *was six long cubits* in length (40:5), the NASB takes the temple complex as being 3,000 (500 by 6) cubits square, while the NIV takes it as 500 cubits square. The NASB translation is closer to the original Hebrew, because different Hebrew words are used for 'cubit' and 'reeds' and the phrase 'measuring reed' is repeated four times in the original. The best solution is probably to understand the 'reed' as 'an instrument rather than' as 'a unit of measurement', and to translate the four-times-repeated statement as 'it was five hundred cubits – in rods, using the measuring rod' (*NICOT*).

We are again reminded that the purpose of the wall that enclosed the temple complex was *to separate the holy from the common* (**42:20**).

43:1-12 The return of God's glory to the temple

Ezekiel had seen – with a heart sorrowing to breaking point – the glory of the Lord leaving the temple (10:4-5, 18-19; 11:22-23). And now, nineteen years later (compare 8:1 and 40:1), the prophet sees the return of the Lord 'to occupy and to consecrate this new building to be His holy sanctuary' (*TOT*). It is as if 'all the preceding process of inspection and measurement was like a guided tour of an empty palace before the grand arrival of the king himself' (*BST*).

Ezekiel witnesses the Lord's glorious return from *the gate facing east* (**43:1**). The prophet has told us, in the preceding passage, that the angelic guide led him *out by the east gate* (42:15). Thus the repetition of *the gate facing east* in our present passage must be to underscore the fact that Ezekiel was strategically positioned to witness the great

spectacle of the return of *the glory of the God of Israel* to the temple. The Lord of heaven and earth does not simply sneak into the temple he left years before. He is boisterous: His voice and his radiant glory proclaim his return (**43:2**; see also 1:4, 24; 3:12).

There is a connection between this vision and Ezekiel's vision at the time of his call (**43:3**; chs. 1–3). There is also a link between it and his vision of the departure of the Lord from the temple due to the abominations that were taking place there (chs. 8–11). Once again, Ezekiel's reaction to this manifestation of God's glory is to fall on his face, for 'neither years of reflection nor decades of divine service have dulled his sense of awe and terror at the sight of the glory of God' (*NICOT*).

God does not want Ezekiel to stay flat on his face and miss what is happening, and so once again *the Spirit lifted* him up (**43:5a**; see also 1:28; 2:1-2) and gives 'him an aerial view from *the inner court* as the *glory of the Lord* proceeds majestically in a dead straight line through the east gate of the outer wall, then the east gate of the inner court, then the great east door of the temple itself … finally into the Most Holy Place itself' (*BST*). As had happened at the time of the consecration of the Tent of Meeting erected by Moses (Exod 40:34-35) and of the temple built by Solomon (1 Kgs 8:10-11; 2 Chr 7:1-3), *the glory of the Lord filled the temple* (**43:5b**).

It is interesting to note that Ezekiel *heard someone speaking to me from inside the temple*, while the angelic guide was still *standing beside* him (**43:6**). How did Ezekiel know that the Lord was speaking to him and not to *the man who was standing beside* him? The answer is that it was because he was addressed as *Son of man*, a phrase which both the prophet and we the readers are very familiar with by now (**43:7a**).

Having occupied his rightful place in the temple, the Sovereign Lord of the universe starts to speak reassuring words to his faithful servant from what he describes as *the place of my throne and the place for the soles of my feet* (**43:7b**). We are reminded of the words spoken at the dedication of Solomon's temple: 'Will God really dwell on earth? The heavens, even the highest heaven, cannot contain you. How much less this temple I have built' (1 Kgs 8:27), and of God's words to Isaiah: 'Heaven is my throne, and the earth is my footstool. Where is the house you will build for me? Where will my resting place be?' (Isa 66:1). A 'mere house on earth, however symmetrical and beautiful, could not contain the throne of the sovereign of all the universe' (*BST*). Yet God graciously promises, *This is where I will live among the Israelites for ever* (**43:7c**). It is God who comes to us, not we who build a house for him.

God's presence among his people has always been what has set them apart. Moses was acutely aware of this: 'How will anyone know that you are pleased with me and with your people unless you go with us? What else will distinguish me and your people from all the other people on the face of the earth?' (Exod 33:16).

There is a startling similarity between the proclamation to Ezekiel here and the triumphant announcement in the final chapters of Revelation: 'And I heard a loud voice from the throne saying, "Now the dwelling of God is with men, and he will live with them. They will be his people, and God himself will be with them and be their God"' (Rev 21:3). God's presence in the midst of his people 'remains the ultimate visions of the new creation' (BST).

The 'for ever' of God's presence is balanced by the 'never' in his next words: *The house of Israel will never again defile my holy name* (**43:7d**). This defilement was produced by their *prostitution,* that is, their spiritual adultery and the practice of sacred prostitution, which were described in chapters 8 to 11.

Here the addition of the words *neither they nor their kings* suggests that the kings have committed some special sin. This sin is twice referred to as *the lifeless idols of their kings* (43:7, 9), or, as the NASB translates this, 'the corpses of their kings'. We know from the books of Kings that a number of the kings of Judah had been buried in the City of David, which was the area of Jerusalem right alongside the temple (see, for example, 2 Kgs 8:24; 15:7). Yet the law had laid down that contact with a dead body caused ceremonial uncleanness (Num 19:11-16). Thus God pointed out that by burying their kings where *their threshold* was *next to my threshold and their doorposts beside my doorposts, with only a wall between me and them* (**43:8**), they had failed to make 'any clear line of demarcation between what was sacred ... and what was profane' (TOT).

After again stressing that his presence will be permanently with his people, God instructs Ezekiel to remind the people of their responsibilities. The prophet is commanded to *describe the temple to the people of Israel* (**43:10a**; see also 40:4). But why is this description meant to arouse shame (**43:10b-11a**)? The answer may be that the vision of this new temple would arouse shameful memories of the old one and of how they had polluted it.

The command to instruct the people is reiterated. Ezekiel is told to *write these down before them so that they may be faithful to its design and follow all its regulations* (**43:11b**). Then the status of what he has been told is reinforced: *This is the law of the temple ... Such is the law of the temple* (**43:12**). Repetition is an effective pedagogical tool, as a pithy Tigrigna (Eritrea) proverb reminds us: *temhertn 'awdn degagimka* ['both learning and threshing involve repetition']. Oxen threshing grain have to go round and round the threshing floor many times before the grain and chaff are fully separated, and in the same way a teacher has to cover the same material again and again before it is remembered.

43:13-46:24 *Ordinances of the new temple*

God has returned to his earthly dwelling place and his glory has once again filled the temple. But how is he to be worshipped in this temple? What type of worship will be acceptable and pleasing to him? The section that follows answers this kind of question by dealing first with the role of the priests (43:13-44:31), and then with the role of the prince in the restored land (45:1-46:24).

43:13-44:31 PRIESTLY SERVICES The altar in the new temple was located 'in front of the temple' (40:47b). Its shape was similar to that of a Babylonian ziggurat in that it consisted of three square blocks of decreasing size, one on top of another. Each block was two cubits shorter than the block beneath it. The base seems to have been surrounded by a space bordered by what is called *a rim.* The uppermost level of the altar was called *the altar hearth* and had *four horns,* or in other words, it had a raised point at each corner (**43:13-17a**).

The height of this three-stage altar was comparable to the height of the altar in Solomon's temple (2 Chr 4:1). The original altar in the Tent of Meeting was much smaller (Exod 27:1-2), possibly because it had to be easy to carry around during the journey through the desert. Although Exodus 20:24-26 had specifically prohibited the use of steps leading up to the altar, the sheer size of this new altar meant that steps were needed. These steps faced east (**43:17b**).

Once the altar itself has been dealt with, Ezekiel is given instructions concerning *the regulations for sacrificing burnt offerings and sprinkling blood upon the altar when it is built* (**43:18**). However, the bulk of this passage speaks about the dedication of the altar itself. Once again there is great stress on the idea of purifying *the altar* (43:20, 22, 26). First *a young bull* is to be sacrificed *as a sin offering* (**43:19-21**). Then *a male goat without defect* is to be given *for a sin offering* (**43:22**). The same offerings were to be repeated *for seven days ... to make atonement for the altar and cleanse it; thus they will dedicate it* (**43:25-26**). We are reminded of the dedication of the altar Moses erected (Exod 29:36-37), of the tabernacle (Exod 40) and of Solomon's temple (1 Kgs 8).

We may wonder why the altar in particular had to be cleansed so thoroughly. Some commentators argue that this is because 'everything associated with man partook of sin and therefore needed to be cleansed, especially if it was to be used in the worship of the Lord' (EBC). Others go even further and argue that it was not just ordinary human sin that was involved, but that 'the memories of the defilement of the previous altar by all the detestable practices that had gone on in the temple needed to be cleansed away' (BST).

It is only after the altar has been cleansed for a week that the people can bring *burnt offerings and fellowship offerings* (**43:27b**). Then they will hear God's wonderful words of reconciliation: *I will accept you.* God's declaration here 'is the language of love, of welcome, of warmth and invitation'

(*BST*). The same acceptance is offered to all believers through the cross of Christ.

A quick reading of the text might leave the impression that *the priests, who are Levites, of the family of Zadok* are the ones leading in the sacrificial offerings (43:19, 26; see also 40:46; 44:15-16). This is certainly the case *from the eighth day on* (**43:27a**). But during the seven days in which the altar is being purified, it seems that Ezekiel, the prophet-priest, also has a role to play. He is instructed *to give a young bull as a sin offering to the priests* who will offer it to the Lord (43:19), but that was not his only role. He is also instructed to take some of the blood of the young bull *and put it on the four horns of the altar and on the four corners of the upper ledge and all around the rim, and so purify the altar and make atonement for it* (43:20). He is also to *offer a male goat without defect for a sin offering, and the altar is to be purified as it was purified with the bull* (43:22). It appears that in **43:23-24** he is doing this alongside the Zadokite priests. It seems that Ezekiel is assuming 'the role of a second Moses, inaugurating a fresh start for the worship of Israel, as Moses had done in the purification and consecration of the original altar in Exodus 29:36ff.' (*BST*). This vision must have been especially meaningful to Ezekiel, because he had been taken into exile as a young man and thus had never had an opportunity to serve as a priest in the temple in Jerusalem. When the temple was destroyed by the Babylonians, he must have lost all hope of every offering sacrifices to God. But God had graciously allowed him to do this in a vision.

After the dedication of the altar, Ezekiel's angelic guide took him *back to the outer gate of the sanctuary, the one facing east* (**44:1**). This was the gate by which Ezekiel had entered the temple in 40:6, but now he sees that the gate is shut, so that no one can enter. He is told that it is to *remain shut because the Lord, the God of Israel, has entered through it* (**44:2**; see 43:4). No human being can use a gate that has become holy by being used by God. The closed gate may also indicate that God is within his temple and will not be leaving it again (43:7, 9).

The only exception allowing someone to come anywhere near this gate is made to *the prince,* and even he may not come through the gate. The most that is allowed him is that he may enter the area of the gate from the west side and sit in the portico of the gate *to eat in the presence of the Lord* (**44:3**). This meal would be a sacrificial meal of the type described in the law of Moses (for example, Deut 12:5-7).

The guide then returned Ezekiel *by way of the north gate to the front of the temple* (**44:4**). Ezekiel, too, could no longer use the gate he had used before. The prophet again *looked and saw the glory of the Lord filling the temple* and again *fell face down.*

Then, in words similar to those uttered by the angelic guide in 40:4, the Lord gives Ezekiel further instructions

concerning all the regulations regarding the temple of the Lord (**44:5**). The first concerns the *detestable practices* of *the rebellious house of Israel* (**44:6**), specifically that they *brought foreigners uncircumcised in heart and flesh into my sanctuary* – thereby *desecrating my temple* and breaking *my covenant* (**44:7-8**). It seems that the Israelites had used 'foreign captives as temple servants to aid the priests' (*EBC*). The Bible records that this happened with the Gibeonites during the time of Joshua (Josh 9:23, 27) and it is possible that the Carites mentioned in 2 Kings 11:4 and the temple servants mentioned in Ezra 8:20 may also have been foreigners. These verses state that this practice is unacceptable and must not continue in the new temple: *No foreigner uncircumcised in heart and flesh is to enter my sanctuary, not even foreigners who live among the Israelites* (**44:9**). The outcome of this kind of instruction is visible in the notice posted in Herod's temple that warned Gentiles that if they went further into the temple than the outer court, they would be put to death. However, this instruction does not mean that foreigners would not be accepted among the Israelites in the new temple era (see 47:22-23).

The Levites were to be the ones who worked as temple servants. *The consequences of their sin* include being assigned menial tasks (**44:10-12**) and being told *they are not to come near to serve me as priests* (**44:13**). The *Levites* are to *stand before the people* (**44:11**), but *the priests* are to *stand before* the Lord (**44:15b**). While the tasks they were assigned were mundane ones, we should not look down on these Levites, for they had the honour of having been given specific tasks by God (**44:14**). Ordinary people were not even permitted to do these tasks. In the same way, there are many in our churches today who perform humble but valuable service and regard it as 'a privilege to be attending on the people of God in the more mundane details of their religion' (*TOT*).

The rest of chapter 44 deals with the responsibilities of the priests. The priests chosen for this holy assignment must be *Levites and descendants of Zadok* (44:15-16; see 40:46; 43:19). The Levites were rebuked for their unfaithfulness (44:10-14), but the Zadokite priests are commended for having *faithfully* carried *out the duties of my sanctuary when the Israelites went astray from me* (**44:15a**; 48:11). The line of Eli had been disqualified from the priesthood in the days of Samuel (1 Sam 2:30-36). His place had been taken by Abiathar and Zadok during David's time (2 Sam 8:17; 15:24-29), but when Solomon became king he 'removed Abiathar from the priesthood of the Lord' and replaced him with Zadok (1 Kgs 2:26-27, 35). The Lord specified that only the Zadokite priests *are to enter my sanctuary; they alone are to come near my table to minister before me and perform my service* (**44:16**).

The priests are given specific instructions about the kind of clothes they are to wear when serving in the inner court or within the temple itself. Their clothes must be made of *linen*. They are forbidden to wear *woollen* clothes, which might cause them to perspire and thus defile the holy place (**44:17-18**). Before going off duty, they are to remove these clothes, *leave them in the sacred rooms, and put on other clothes* (**44:19**; see 42:14). The reason for this command is *so that they do not consecrate the people by means of their garments*. Those who came in contact with something holy would absorb some of its holiness. Thus 'wearing sacred vestments out among the people would violate the holiness of the temple by distributing its sanctity' (*NICOT*). The idea that holiness was contagious was common at that time

Several other regulations governing the behaviour of the priests are outlined in 44:20-27. *They must not shave their heads or let their hair grow long* (**44:20**; Lev 21:5), they should not *drink wine* when they go into *the inner court* (**44:21**; see Lev 10:8-11), they are to *marry virgins of Israelite descent or widows of priests* (**44:22**; see Lev 21:7-15), they have to teach the people *the difference between the holy and the common and show them how to distinguish between the unclean and the clean* (**44:23**; see Lev 10:10-11). They *are to serve as judges* in any dispute (see Deut 17:9) and are to keep the *appointed feasts* (**44:24**). No priest is to *defile himself by going near a dead person* except in the case of *his father or mother, son or daughter, brother or unmarried sister* (**44:25**; see Lev 21:1-4). If he is defiled by any of these exceptional cases, he should be *cleansed* and bring *a sin offering* before he enters *the inner court of the sanctuary to minister* (**44:26-27**). The purpose of all these regulations was to enable the priests to teach the people, by word and deed, the difference between the holy and the common. Spiritual leaders are expected to model the life of holiness to the people by what they say and do, and by all aspects of their lifestyle. Moreover, they are to depend entirely on the Lord for their livelihood. God is to be *the only inheritance the priests have* (**44:28-31**; Num 18:23-24). They will be supported by the *sin and guilt offerings, the best of the firstfruits, special gifts,* and in fact *everything in Israel devoted to the Lord.*

45:1-46:24 ROLE OF THE PRINCE IN THE RESTORED LAND Chapter 45 begins by delineating *a sacred district* that is set aside for *the Lord* (45:1-8 see also 48:8-22). This district will occupy only the central portion of the land and will not replace the tribal divisions of the land that will be dealt with in chapters 47 and 48.

From north to south the sacred district consisted of an area of 25,000 cubits by 10,000 cubits (7 miles by 3 miles/ 11 kilometres by 5 kilometres) allotted to the Levites (**45:5**); another area of the same size set aside for the sanctuary and for houses for the priests (**45:3-4**); and an area measuring 25,000 cubits by 5,000 cubits (7 miles by 1.5 miles/ 11 kilometres by 2.5 kilometres), for the city (**45:6**).

Commentators disagree about whether the sacred district is a large square measuring 25,000 cubits on each side

or a rectangle *25,000 cubits long and 20,000 cubits wide,* as specified in 45:1. It is a square if we include the area for the city in this district; a rectangle if we exclude the area for the city and focus only on the area assigned to the temple personnel. The sanctuary itself occupied an area that was *500 cubits square* (250 yards/228 metres) in the portion assigned for the priests (**45:2**; see 42:15-20). It was to be surrounded by *50 cubits* (28 yards/22 metres) of *open land* 'which would serve as a buffer protecting the absolute holiness of the sanctuary itself' (*NICOT*).

The land bordering each side of the area formed by the sacred district and the property of the city – extending westward and eastward from the sacred district which is in the centre – is allotted to the prince (**45:7-8a**). This same prince was mentioned in relation to the east gate (44:3) and will be mentioned frequently in the remaining chapters of the book. But who is he? He is definitely not the Messiah, for he receives an inheritance among the people and he has a family of his own (46:16-18). The mention of other princes in 45:8 indicates that he is just the first among equals (see Deut 17:14-20). The Lord promises that these princes *will no longer oppress my people but will allow the house of Israel to possess the land according to their tribes* (**45:8b**; see 46:18).

God then exhorts the princes to *give up your violence and oppression and do what is just and right* (**45:9**), which includes using accurate weights and measures (**45:10-12**).

It appears that in Ezekiel's temple *the prince* is responsible for providing the offerings *to make atonement for the house of Israel* that are offered at all the *appointed feasts of the house of Israel* (**45:15**, **17-18**). These include *grain offerings, burnt offerings and fellowship offerings.* To help him do this, the people are to bring him a *special gift* (**45:13**, **16**).

Ezekiel then provides a description of the special festivals and the offerings associated with them. He specifically mentions New Year (**45:18-20**), Passover (**45:21-24**), and the Feast of Tabernacles, although he does not mention its name (**45:25**). Surprisingly, he does not mention the Feast of Weeks, even though this was one of the three main festivals according to the Mosaic legislation (Deut 16:9-12).

The east gate of the outer court was permanently closed (44:2); but *the east gate of the inner court* is to be shut *on the six working days,* but is to stand open *on the Sabbath day and on the day of the New Moon* (**46:1**). The prince will enter *from the outside through the portico of the gateway and stand by the gatepost* (**46:2a**). He may not enter the inner court, but standing in the doorway he can watch the ceremony as *the priests sacrifice* the offerings he has brought on his own behalf and on behalf of the people (**46:4-7**). The people, too, will *worship in the presence of the Lord at the entrance to that gateway* (**46:3**). Once the prince has worshipped and partaken of the offerings (44:3), *he is to come out* in the manner he came in – that is, *through the portico of the gateway*

(**46:8**). In the evening, after the prince and the people have completed their worship, the gate will be shut (**46:2b**).

Directions are given about how the people are to move through the temple complex, especially at the time of *the appointed feasts* (**46:9**). People entering *by the north gate* are to leave the temple area through *the south gate,* and people who enter *by the south gate* are *to go out* through *the north gate.* We are not told the reason that *no one is to return through the gate by which he entered,* but it is likely that this was intended to be a crowd-control measure at the feasts. 'By entering one gate and leaving through its opposite, the flow of the festive crowd was regulated and confusion eliminated' (*EBC*). This regulation can even be described as 'the first known one-way system' (*BST*).

The statement that *the prince is to be among them, going in when they go in and going out when they go out* (**46:10**) indicates either that he must go to the temple at the same time as the people, or that 'on all non-festival days the prince will be regarded as one of the people and will come in and go out in the same way as they do' (*TOT*). Certainly on the days of *the appointed feasts* the prince *is to come out the same way* he came in – that is, *through the portico of the gateway* (45:8).

Next we are given regulations regarding *the grain offering at the festivals and the appointed feasts* (**46:11**), a *freewill offering* made by the prince (**46:12**) and the daily *burnt offering* (**46:13-15**). As indicated in 44:3, the prince has privileged access to *the gate facing east* when he *provides a freewill offering to the Lord.* Although the inner gate is usually shut on weekdays (46:1), it will *be opened for him* when he comes to make this *offering* and *will be shut* after he has finished and *has gone out.*

It is strange that the daily *burnt offering* is offered only once a day – *morning by morning* (repeated three times in 46:13-15). The Mosaic law stated that it was to be offered twice a day, in the morning and evening (Exod 29:38-41). No explanation is given for the change. This offering is described as *a lasting ordinance* – 'a daily reminder' of the commitment of the people to their covenant Lord (46:14).

The issue of land, which was discussed in 45:1-8, now comes up again. The prince can make a gift of land to *one of his sons,* who would be entitled to inherit it (**46:16**). But he cannot make a permanent gift of land to *one of his servants.* Because his land is part of his sons' inheritance, it will revert back to them in *the year of freedom* (**46:17**). This year of freedom was probably the Jubilee year specified in Leviticus 25, in which all debts were cancelled and all land reverted to its original owners. The prince is also not entitled to give anyone else's land to his sons or to other people: *none of my people will be separated from his property* (**46:18**; compare 45:9).

Ezekiel's guided tour of the temple now resumes. He is taken to the *sacred rooms facing north,* and at the *western end* of these rooms he is shown *the kitchens* used by the priests to *cook the guilt offering and the sin offering and bake the grain offering, to avoid bringing them into the outer court and consecrating the people* (**46:19-20**; see 44:19). The guide next shows him four *enclosed courts* opening off *the four corners of the outer court* (**46:21-22**). These are equipped with *a ledge of stone, with places for fire built all around under the ledge* and function as *kitchens where those who minister at the temple will cook the sacrifices of the people* (**46:23-24**). The presence of these kitchens is a reminder that the temple was not just a place of prayer, but was also a place where communal meals were cooked and eaten. There was thus a fusion of spiritual and social activities in Ezekiel's temple. 'The Christian church has been the poorer when it has drawn a firm-dividing line between spiritual life and social activities' (*TOT*).

47:1-48:35 Division of land among the twelve tribes

The final section of this book deals with the division of the land among the twelve tribes. This is not altogether surprising, given Ezekiel's stress that God will restore the land to his people (ch. 36), and the fact that 'the land has played a significant role in the history of God's people' (*EBC*). Yet the other two components of Ezekiel's vision – the temple and the city – are also in view.

47:1-12 THE RIVER OF THE NEW TEMPLE Ezekiel prefaces his words about the division of the land with a vision of a river that flows out of the temple and through the land. This river brings healing and cleansing to a land that had seen such evil that 'it could bear its defilement no more and "vomited" the people out into exile' (*BST*).

The angelic guide brings Ezekiel *back to the entrance of the temple,* where he sees *water coming out from under the threshold of the temple toward the east* (**47:1**). More specifically, *the water was coming down from under the south side of the temple, south of the altar* (**47:2**). The source of the water was thus the temple – the very presence of God.

From the temple, the river flows east and then south, through the Judean desert and into the Dead Sea. The surprising thing is that, although no tributaries are mentioned, the river keeps increasing in volume and depth. Ezekiel is aware of this because his guide repeatedly measures off 500 yards (457 metres) and then leads him *through the water* so that he can experience its depth for himself (**47:3-5**). The river *was ankle-deep* the first time, *knee-deep* the second time, *up to the waist* the third time and *a river that no one could cross* the fourth time. The angelic guide's question, *Son of man, do you see this?* (**47:6a**) may be intended to check that the prophet was understanding what he was experiencing.

Ezekiel's guide next leads him *back to the bank of the river* (**47:6b**) and Ezekiel witnesses the cleansing, healing and life-giving power of the river in the *great number of trees* on each side of the river (**47:7**). His guide explains that this river flows down into the Dead Sea (**47:8**). This sea has been given this name because its water is so salty that it is undrinkable and only a very few forms of life can survive in it. But when the river empties *into the Sea, the water there becomes fresh.* The Dead Sea will become a live sea, full of fish and other kinds of living creatures (**47:9b**). Fish will be so plentiful that there will be a thriving fishing industry: *Fishermen will stand along the shore; from En Gedi to En Eglaim there will be places for spreading nets* (**47:10**). En Gedi is located 'mid-way down the west coast of the Dead Sea' (*TOT*). The exact location of En Eglaim has not been identified, but it probably lay somewhere to the north of En Gedi. The fish harvested from the Dead Sea *will be of many kinds – like the fish of the Great Sea* (the Mediterranean Sea).

The life-giving effects of the water will be evident in the *swarms of living creatures* that will inhabit the previously desert region where this river now flows (**47:9a**). However, there is one area that will not change: *the swamps and marshes* around the Dead Sea *will not become fresh* (**47:11**). The reason that they will not change is not that God lacks the power to change them, but the practical one that they are a valuable source of salt. God will ensure 'that these rich mineral deposits can still be exploited, presumably for both domestic and liturgical use (43:24)' (*TOT*).

Returning to the topic of the trees that Ezekiel had seen lining the river banks (47:7), we are told that they are not only of *a great number* but also *of all kinds,* and that they bear fruit *every month* without fail (**47:12**). Moreover, *their leaves will not wither. Their fruit will serve for food and their leaves for healing.* The trees will be so fruitful *because the water from the sanctuary flows to them* (47:1). The idea of a river and life-sustaining and healing trees reminds one both of the garden of Eden (Gen 2:8-10) and of the river that flows through the new Jerusalem (Rev 22:1-2). The only difference between the river in Ezekiel's vision and that in Revelation is that the one in Revelation originates 'from the throne of God and of the Lamb' rather than the temple, since there will be no temple in the eternal city 'for the Lord God, the Almighty, and the Lamb, are its temple' (Rev 21:22).

47:13-48:29 ALLOTMENT OF LAND In this last portion of the book, Ezekiel returns to the issue of the land. He begins by giving general directives for dividing the land (47:13-14, 21-23) and a description of the boundary of the land (47:15-20).

The land is to be divided *equally among* the twelve tribes (**47:14**), the only exception being that *two portions* will go to Joseph (**47:13**). This arrangement means that the tribes descended from the two sons of Joseph, Manasseh and Ephraim, will each receive a full a portion as individual tribes in their own right (see 48:4-5). The distribution is similar to that provided for in the Mosaic law and

implemented by Joshua. Clearly God favours a 'broad and equitable distribution of the land' (*BST*).

There is, however, a unique feature in Ezekiel's plan for distribution, namely the inclusion of *aliens* in this equitable distribution of land (**47:21-23**). Although the Israelites were instructed to love the aliens as themselves and treat them 'as one of your native-born' (Lev 19:33-34), the law had not specified whether they were to be allocated land. Ezekiel's position can be described as 'an interesting example of broad-mindedness' (*TOT*). 'The resident alien is to share inheritance rights in Israel's most prized possession – the land. Their citizenship is assured' (*BST*).

The boundaries of the land that is to be distributed are next set out. Not all of the places mentioned can be clearly identified. The description begins in the north and moves clockwise to end in the west. The northern boundary begins at a point on *the Great Sea* (the Mediterranean Sea) and ends at *Hazar Enan* (which may have been in the area of the town known as Caesarea Philippi in NT times – *TOT*) (**47:15-17**). The eastern boundary runs from *Hauran and Damascus* in the north to *the eastern sea* (that is, the Dead Sea) (**47:18**). The southern boundary begins with *Tamar* at the south-western tip of the Dead Sea and ends at the Mediterranean Sea (**47:19**). And lastly, the Mediterranean Sea itself forms the western boundary of the land (**47:20**). (These boundaries can be compared with those given in Numbers 34:3-12, although the description there begins with the southern boundary.)

This general description of the boundaries of the land is followed by information about the actual allotment of the land among the twelve tribes. They are divided into two groups – seven tribes in the north (48:1-7) and five tribes in the south (48:23-29) – with *the special portion* offered *to the Lord* (48:8-22) sandwiched between them.

Dan is assigned the first portion of the northern allotment, land in the extreme north (**48:1**). Then Asher (**48:2**), followed by Naphtali (**48:3**), Manasseh (**48:4**), Ephraim (**48:5**), Reuben (**48:6**) and Judah (**48:7**) are assigned portions in that order.

The allocation of the land to the tribes is then interrupted by a long section dealing with *the portion you are to present as a special gift* (**48:8**). The information given here expands on what was said in 45:1-8. This sacred portion is a square area with each side measuring 25,000 cubits (7 miles/ 11 kilometres) (**48:20**). It is subdivided into three parts, the last of which is slightly narrower than the others:

- an area *for the Zadokite priests* (**48:9-12**). The *sanctuary of the Lord* was to be located at the centre of this area (48:10; see also 45:2).
- an area of the same size for *the Levites* (**48:13-14**). The Levites are specifically instructed that *they must not sell or exchange any of it … it is holy to the Lord.*

- a slightly smaller area *for the common use of the city, for houses and for pastureland* (**48:15-19**). *The city will be in the centre of* this portion (48:15). The 'pastureland' will be farmed by *workers … from all the tribes of Israel* who will produce *food for the workers of the city* (48:18-19). The population of the city will thus be a microcosm of the nation. Thus, *The entire portion will be a square* (25,000 cubits by 25,000 cubits – **48:20**).

The centrality of the special portion offered to the Lord is underscored in a variety of ways. First of all, it lies between the land allotted to the seven northern tribes and that allotted to the five southern tribes. The land on either side of this portion to the west and east *will belong to the prince* (**48:21**; see 45:7-8). Once again we are reminded that *the sacred portion with the temple sanctuary will be in the centre of them* (that is, in the centre of the prince's land). This point is again stressed in **48:22**: *So the property of the Levites and the property of the city will lie in the centre of the area that belongs to the prince.* In other words, not only is the sacred portion sandwiched between the allotments of the tribes in the north and the south, but it is also sandwiched between the two allotments of the prince in the east and the west. Add to this the fact that *the sanctuary* is at *the centre* of the portion assigned to the priests (48:10) and the city proper is at *the centre* of the land allotted *for common use* (48:15), and the stress on centrality becomes quite obvious – and so does its message. 'The God who had been marginalized by his people and who had finally abandoned his land in destructive judgment had now returned to the centre – the centre of the land, which, as Ezekiel has earlier pointed out, was also "the centre of the nations" (5:5)' (*BST*).

Ezekiel next deals with the second batch of tribal allotments. The first portion south of the special gift went to Benjamin (**48:23**), followed by portions for Simeon (**48:24**), Issachar (**48:25**), Zebulun (**48:26**) and Gad (**48:27-28**) in that order. It has already been indicated that the land is to be divided *equally among* the tribes (47:14).

It is clear that the allocation of the land is here done by slicing across the land, without any regard to the territories historically occupied by different tribes. The only exception is that Judah and Benjamin are allocated the land closest to Jerusalem, which reflects their historical ties to that city. The sons of Israel by his two wives (Leah and Rachel) are settled nearest to the sacred portion (four on each side), whereas the tribes descended from the maidservants of his wives are settled in the extreme north and south.

The division of the land concludes with an affirmation from *the Sovereign Lord: This is the land you are to allot as an inheritance to the tribes of Israel, and these will be their portions* (**48:29**).

48:30-35 THE NEW JERUSALEM AND ITS GATES The last six verses of the book draw our attention to the city again, and specifically to *the gates* (48:31) or *exits of the city* (48:30). There are twelve gates in total – three on each of the four sides of the city. The gates are *named after the tribes of Israel*. The gates *on the north side* are named after Reuben, Judah and Levi (**48:31**); those *on the east side*, after Joseph, Benjamin and Dan (**48:32**); those *on the south side*, after Simeon, Issachar and Zebulun (**48:33**); and those *on the west side*, after Gad, Asher and Naphtali (**48:34**).

In the NT, John describes the Holy City, the heavenly Jerusalem, as also having twelve gates with 'the names of the twelve tribes of Israel' written on them (Rev 21:12-13). But this city has an additional feature: 'the names of the twelve apostles of the Lamb' are written on the 'twelve foundations' of the city (Rev 21:14). By doing this John reminds us that there are two covenants but one people of God.

The city about which Ezekiel is speaking is clearly Jerusalem, but here it acquires a new name – *And the name of the city from that time on will be: THE LORD IS THERE* (**48:35**). This new name underscores the point that has already been made by the emphasis on the centrality of the sacred portion, the temple and the city. Ezekiel's closing words are 'a grand finale to his book and to his ministry. In his twenty-five years of exile and in the forty-eight chapters of his book, Ezekiel had seen the Lord withdraw from His temple because of the sins that were committed there … Now at last the Lord would be there, with His people, for ever' (*TOT*).

We as believers look forward to entering that same city (Rev 21:3), and being for ever with the Lord.

Tewoldemedhin Habtu

Further Reading

Alexander, Ralph H. *Ezekiel*. EBC. Grand Rapids: Zondervan, 1986.

Block, Daniel I. *The Book of Ezekiel*. NICOT. Grand Rapids: Eerdmans, 1997.

Taylor, John B. *Ezekiel*. Reprint. TOT. Leicester: Inter-Varsity Press, 2003.

Wright, Christopher J.H. *The Message of Ezekiel: A New Heart and a New Spirit*. BST. Leicester: Inter-Varsity Press, 2001.

DANIEL

The book of Daniel ties together the history of the Jews and of the Gentiles from the seventh century before Christ until the end of all human history and governments – when 'the kingdom of this world has become the kingdom of our Lord and of his Christ' (Rev 11:15). Its detailed prophecies concerning God's programme give us a preview of how the Messiah's kingdom will end the world powers (7:17-18, 21-22) and help us to interpret the book of Revelation.

Throughout the book, it is demonstrated both implicitly and explicitly 'that the Most High rules in the kingdoms of men and gives them to anyone he wishes' (4:17; see also 2:28, 4:25, 5:26 and 7:26). No matter how terrible some of the despotic regimes that Africa has endured, God has not relinquished his ultimate rule over human affairs.

Additionally, the book powerfully demonstrates that believers can serve with distinction under ungodly regimes without compromising their convictions. Daniel offers the church in Africa a model of servant leadership that is desperately needed today.

Authorship and Date

The accuracy of the predictions regarding the reign of Alexander the Great some two hundred years later has led some to doubt that this book was written in the sixth century BC. These sceptics claim that the second half of the book, at least, must have been written in the second century BC by a historian pretending to be Daniel. But to refuse to accept predictive elements in Scripture is not only to deny the Bible but also to question the existence of an all-knowing personal God who has power both to predict and reveal minute details of future events. According to the Yoruba of Nigeria, the priests of their gods can foretell the future and reveal secrets. It is, therefore, not incredible that the Most High God could reveal past, present and future secrets to his servants as he did to Daniel.

Daniel personally claims authorship of this book in 7:1, 28; 8:2; 9:2; 10:1-2 and 12:4 and the autobiographical first person is used from 7:2 onward. Jesus Christ also names Daniel as the author (Matt 24:15). The testimony of Josephus, a secular Jewish historian, also supports Daniel's authorship.

The chronology of the book is as follows:

605 BC – Nebuchadnezzar subdues Jerusalem. Daniel, along with thousands of others, is deported to Babylon (Dan 1:1).

597 BC – Second batch of deportees, including the prophet Ezekiel, are taken to Babylon (Ezek 1:1).

586 BC – Judah falls and Jerusalem is destroyed. Third batch of Jews deported (Jer 52). End of Jeremiah's forty-one-year ministry.

539 BC – Babylon overthrown by a coalition of Medes and Persians (Dan 5:25-30). Daniel thrown into lions' den (Dan 6).

538 BC – First exiles permitted to return to Judah by a decree of Cyrus, king of Persia (Ezra 1:1; Isa 44:24-45:7). By this time Daniel was about eighty four, and probably too old to travel.

536 BC – End of Daniel's seventy years of prophetic ministry (Dan 10:1; 12:4,13).

535 BC – Writing of the book of Daniel.

Literary Style

The book was originally written in two languages. Chapters 1:1-2:4a and chapters 8-12 were written in Hebrew, the language of God's covenant people, Israel. The message here is largely apocalyptic showing God's future plan for his people. Chapters 2:4b-7:28 were written in Aramaic, the lingua franca of the Gentile world in Daniel's day. The message of these chapters (barring chapter 7) is largely historical, showing God's dealing with the Gentile empires.

Despite the change in language, the book is still a unity. The great human image of chapter 2 (Hebrew) closely parallels the vision of the four beasts of chapter 7 (Aramaic). The contrast between God's kingdom and the kingdoms of this world runs through the whole book. His kingdom is said to be eternal four times in the first half (2:44; 4:3, 34; 6:26) and three times in the second half (7:14, 18, 27). But the most powerful unifying factor is Daniel himself: he is the interpreter of dreams in the first half and the dreamer in the second.

Outline of the Book

1:1-21 Tough Times Don't Last, Tough People Do
- **1:1-7** Captivity
- **1:8-10** Separation of Daniel and Friends
- **1:11-16** Sacrifice That Pays Back
- **1:17-21** Spiritual Endowment of Daniel and Friends

2:1-49 God's Reign in a Crisis
- **2:1-13** The Crisis of a Concealed Dream
- **2:14-23** Counsel of Daniel
- **2:24-45** Divine Construction of World Empires
- **2:46-49** Honour for Daniel

COMMENTARY

1:1-21 Tough Times Don't Last, Tough People Do

Africa has been variously described as 'a retarded continent' by Ali Mazrui; 'a lost continent' by the World Bank; 'a hopeless continent' by *Time* magazine; and 'a bleeding continent' by President Moi of Kenya. Africans of the twentieth century had to fight to regain their human dignity and reassert their identity after ruthless deportation, an inhuman global slave trade, cultural dislocation, and forceful occupation by foreign colonial powers. It was a tough century.

The twenty-first century does not look promising either. Africa's problems include the HIV/AIDS pandemic, regular famines and droughts, disputes over land tenure, corruption, and modern slavery in southern Sudan. Over fifty per cent of the world's 15 million refugees are Africans. Many of them are Christians. It is no wonder that the story of Daniel and his three friends, who as teenagers knew what it was to be exiles subjected to forced removals, speaks to us as an example of how to triumph in trials and endure through hard times.

1:1-7 Captivity

Daniel begins with history: the capture of Judah's capital city, Jerusalem, by the superpower of his day, the Babylonian Empire under the leadership of its king, Nebuchadnezzar (1:1-2). This took place *in the third year of the reign of Jehoiakim king of Judah* in approximately 605 BC (see also 2 Kgs 24:1-2 and 2 Chr 36:5-7).

The moral apostasy and idolatry of the ten tribes of the northern kingdom of Israel had already led to their fall to the Assyrians in 722 BC (1 Kgs 11:5; 12:28; 16:31; 18:19; 2 Kgs 21:3-5; 2 Chr 28:2-3). The Lord had warned Judah, the southern kingdom, that it faced a similar fate. Jeremiah lamented: 'The sin of Judah is written with a pen of iron … Their children remember their wooden images … I will cause you to serve your enemies' (Jer 17:1-4). Later,

Jeremiah named Nebuchadnezzar as the enemy into whose hand the Lord would deliver his people, saying they would be captives for seventy years (Jer 25:8-11). Daniel had no doubt that the fall of Judah represented divine judgemnt: *And the Lord delivered Jehoiakim king of Judah into his hand, along with some of the articles from the temple of God* (**1:2**).

Jehoiakim himself remained in Jerusalem as a vassal (or slave) king to Nebuchadnezzar (2 Kgs 24:1), but some 3023 of the Jewish nobility (Jer 52:28) were deported to Babylon. Eight years later, a further 832 Jews were deported, including King Jehoiachin, the son of Jehoiakim, and the prophet Ezekiel (2 Kgs 24:8-15; Jer 52:29; Ezek 1:1). The third and final deportation, together with the destruction of Jerusalem itself, took place in 586 BC during the reign of King Zedekiah (2 Kgs 25:1-12; 2 Chr 36:20).

When the deportees arrived in Babylon, the best of the Jewish exiles were selected for training to serve in the king's palace. The standard was high: Their parents must be either royal or members of the nobility; physically, they must be young and without any blemishes; politically they must be well informed, diplomatic and wise; and publicly they must be handsome, teachable and persuasive. They were to study *the language and literature of the Babylonians* for three rigorous years, while living at the king's court and eating his food (**1:4-5**). Moses went through a similar programme in the court of Pharaoh (Acts 7:22).

We are not immediately told why the four Hebrew lads, Daniel, Hananiah, Mishael and Azariah, are specifically mentioned (**1:6b**). But what we are told is that their captors immediately began a process of depersonalization, starting by changing their names. To Semitic people, names are not merely labels. Just as African names connect Africans with their ancestors, their tribal values and collective destiny, so do those of Hebrews. *Daniel* means 'God is my judge'. *Hananiah* means 'whom Jehovah has favoured'. *Mishael* is a question: 'Who is what God is?', and *Azariah* means 'Yahweh has helped'. These young men must have been raised in godly Judean homes. Daniel may even have been a descendant of King Hezekiah, a God-fearing king (see 2 Kgs 20:17-19; Isa 39:6-7).

In order to disconnect them from their ancestors, their covenant relationship with Jehovah, and their collective destiny as a people, Ashpenaz gave them names derived from Babylonian deities. *Belteshazzar* means 'Bel's prince', after Bel, the patron god of Babylon (Isa 46:1; Jer 51:44). *Shadrach* means 'inspired by the sun-god, Aku'. *Meshach* means 'who can be compared to Shak?' the name under which the Babylonians worshipped the goddess Venus. *Abed-nego* means 'servant of the shining fire', an allusion to the fire-god or a corruption of the name Nebo.

Africans, too, have had their names changed. Some have been given names or have taken names from their colonial masters. Others have been forced to drop their African names upon their conversion to Christianity (or Islam) and replace them with so-called 'Christian' names, which are nothing more than European names. However, recently, some Christians whose family names have a connection with traditional deities have been replacing them with titles like 'Oluwa', which means 'Lord' or simply 'Jesus'. Daniel and his friends had no choice about their names, and both sets of names are used interchangeably in the book. However, where they had a choice, and where it mattered most, they chose for Jehovah.

1:8-10 Separation of Daniel and Friends

But Daniel purposed in his heart that he would not defile himself (**1:8** NKJV). In the Bible, the heart is the point of connection with God, where the mortal meets the immortal. It is what determines our belief system, dictates our morals and values, and directs our actions. Whenever God is looking for a woman or man to use, he checks the heart (1 Sam 16:7; 1 Chr 28:9). Our Lord identified the heart as the manufacturing centre for evil thoughts, attitudes and behaviour (Mark 7:20-23).

Daniel resolved to discipline his heart and his body (**1:8**). Such self-control is terribly lacking among the spiritual leaders of our day. The problem he faced was that both the Babylonian food and the way it was prepared did not conform to the Mosaic law (Lev 7:11; Deut 14:3-21), and that the food and the wine would have been offered to the Babylonian gods. Partaking of them would result in religious defilement. He therefore refused to conform. The New Testament's call for believer's separation from the world is similarly a call to nonconformity (Rom 12:1-2; 2 Cor 6:14-18; 1 John 2:15-17).

Leadership is the ability to influence others. Though only Daniel is specifically mentioned as having decided not to compromise on his diet, the official response to his request is directed to him and to his three friends (**1:10**). It is worth noting that this response is shaped by God working behind the scenes (**1:9**). The principle still holds that 'those who honour God, God honours' (1 Sam 2:30).

1:11-16 Sacrifice That Pays Back

It seems that the chief official transferred oversight of Daniel and his friends to a junior officer with the title *melzar*, which is best translated as 'warden' or 'steward'. Daniel very politely requested that he and his friends be allowed a ten-day test on a vegetarian diet with only water to drink (**1:12-13**). The boys did not boycott the king's food, for they still accepted vegetables and water. Nor did they demand special treatment, but requested it politely. (Note that this incident cannot be used to argue for vegetarianism. Daniel was not concerned about eating meat as such but about avoiding religious contamination. The four boys were making a sacrifice, which was why the officials were hesitant to grant their request.)

The steward consented to Daniel's request (**1:14**), undoubtedly due to God's favour, though this is not explicitly stated. At the end of the ten days, Daniel and his friends *looked healthier and better nourished* than their peers (**1:15**). For such an effect to be that noticeable in just ten days must have involved divine intervention.

1:17-21 Spiritual Endowment of Daniel and Friends

God had blessed their outward appearance and he also poured out his invisible spiritual gifts of wisdom, knowledge, understanding and skill upon Daniel and his friends who had chosen to honour him by not compromising (**1:17**). This is God's way of honouring them in return and is consistent with God's character and manner of doing things. Whenever he calls someone to any task, he equips them with the appropriate tools in form of talents, training and the spiritual gifts needed to get the work done (see Exod 31:1-6; Luke 4:18-19; Acts 10:38).

The fact that God gives spiritual gifts does not eliminate the need for rigorous human training. Daniel and his friends did not drop out of college, but studied hard and completed the three-year programme assigned by the king (**1:18**; 1:5). Although all four of them were blessed with an intelligent understanding of Chaldean literature (as required by their curriculum – 1:4) and were able to distinguish the true from the false, only Daniel had understanding of visions and dreams. God was equipping him for the role he would play in later years.

Godly servant leaders for church and society are desperately needed across Africa today. Daniel has modelled for us where to begin – with a personal faith in Christ – and how to continue – with an uncompromising commitment to Christ and diligent service.

King Nebuchadnezzar was not only intelligent enough to be able to interview his scholarly citizens, but also to hold them accountable. The state under his leadership had invested heavily in these students. At the end of their education and training he examined them thoroughly (1:19-20). Contrast this with the attitude of many African heads of state who at best sideline intellectuals, or at worst eliminate them. Nebuchadnezzar did not invest in them in order to be entertained but so that they could assist him in solving the tough problems of governing a nation. The best assets for any nation are people who are well trained, well endowed and well behaved.

At the end of the gruelling examination, the king found Daniel, Hananiah, Mishael and Azariah to be *ten times better than all the magicians and astrologers in his whole kingdom* (**1:20**). What this means is that the king was astonished at how smart and forthcoming the Hebrew lads were in response to every question he asked. It was clearly a sign of God's blessing upon their lives. Concrete evidence of their wisdom will be seen in chapter 2.

Some have argued that **1:21** does not belong in chapter 1. That is possible. It is clear that the book is not in strict chronological order, for if it were chapters 7 and 8 would precede 5 and 6. However, such details do not affect the accuracy of Daniel's record.

2:1-49 God's Reign in a Crisis

Mortals have long believed that behind the visible lies the invisible, behind the tangible lies the intangible, and behind the natural lies the supernatural. The power and knowledge available in the invisible world are believed to be far greater than is available in the visible world. Consequently rulers have surrounded themselves with consultants, advisers and wise men who are believed to possess esoteric knowledge that can be used to solve life's enigmas. Moses' Pharaoh had his wise men, sorcerers and magicians, and so did Daniel's Nebuchadnezzar. Just as king Saul consulted the medium at Endor in his days of trouble (1 Sam 28:7-19), so many African political leaders today turn to mediums and witchcraft, especially when elections loom.

2:1-13 The Crisis of a Concealed Dream

King Nebuchadnezzar had the dream recorded here during *the second year of his reign* (**2:1**), yet it seems that Daniel had already finished a three-year training programme. The explanation for the mismatch in the dates is that for one year Nebuchadnezzar reigned jointly with his father, Nabopolassar, who died in September 605 BC. In the Chaldean system of reckoning, that first year was not credited to Nebuchadnezzar's reign. Thus his second year coincided with the third and final year of Daniel's training.

Visions, dreams and prophecies are means of communication between the spirit world and the material world and can reveal present and future realities (see, for example, Gen. 37:41). Nebuchadnezzar was thus disturbed when he had a number of dreams (2:1-2), including one in particular that troubled him (2:3). So he summoned his certified spiritual experts – magicians, astrologers, sorcerers and the distinguished priestly caste called 'Chaldeans' in the original text (**2:2**) and asked them to explain his dream.

Speaking on behalf of all the consultants, the Chaldeans ('astrologers' in the NIV) responded to the king *in Aramaic* (**2:4**). Hebrew and Aramaic were sister languages. The Jews spoke primarily Hebrew, while the Babylonians and Persians spoke primarily Aramaic, which was the diplomatic and commercial language of the empire. Daniel was fluent in both. From 2:4 to 7:28 he wrote in Aramaic, partly because the heterogeneous population of Babylon used it freely.

DREAMS

More than a third of our lives is passed in sleeping, and in that sleep we have many dreams, most of which we will not remember. These dreams have many functions. Some, such as anxiety dreams, merely reflect our state of mind. Others may reveal or conceal secrets. Victims of war often relive their traumatic experiences in nightmares.

Across Africa, it is also believed that serious dreams are a means of communication between this world and the spirit world of the ancestors, divinities and the High God. The living communicate with their ancestors through sacrifices and divination, and the latter respond through dreams and visions, and sometimes through mediums.

Dreams can have national and global effects. In the late nineteenth century, King Mswati I of Swaziland dreamed of a foreign guest arriving, holding a scroll and a round metal disc. The scroll was interpreted as a Bible and the disc as a coin. On waking, the king advised his subjects to welcome the guest and accept the book, which would bring peace and prosperity to the nation. But they should reject the coin, which would bring misery and greed. Soon after this, white missionaries from South Africa came to Swaziland to plant churches. Today, more than 83 per cent of Swaziland's population claim to be Christians.

Christians will not be surprised by this story, for the Bible recognizes that God can use dreams as a means of communication. Dreams may reveal God's plans or the future as they did in the case of Joseph (Gen 37:5-10; 41:1-7). With Abimelech king of Gerar, God used a dream to restrain evil by warning him that Sarah was married (Gen 20:1-7). God revealed his covenant to Jacob in the dream of the stairway to heaven (Gen 28:10-22). He revealed his redemptive plan for the establishment of his kingdom on Earth to Daniel (Dan 2:4, 7). Through dreams, God gave instructions to Joseph

(Matt 1:20; 2:12, 13, 19, 22) and issued a warning to Pilate (Matt 27:13, 19).

It seems that dreams, like visions, communicate two major attributes of God, namely his presence and his power. They are frequently used when God or his kingdom breaks into the Gentile world. With the coming of the Holy Spirit to take up permanent residence in believers, less use is made of dreams as a means of revelation. Thus while books like Genesis and Daniel have seventy eight references to dreams (that is, some 65 per cent of all the references to dreaming in the Bible), there are only nine references to dreams in the NT: six in Matthew, two in Acts and one in Jude. However, as prophesied by Joel, the Holy Spirit still uses dreams to communicate with believers and to direct their ministries (Joel 2:28).

Dreams may be auditory (Job 33:15-17) and are often symbolic (Gen 41:8; Dan 2:2). The symbolism means that they are not always easy to interpret. Like Nebuchadnezzar, dreamers become anxious in the absence of interpretations (Dan 2:1-12). Both Joseph and Daniel proved that interpretation belongs to God (Gen 41; Dan 2:24-45).

Like any other gift, dreams can be counterfeited and abused. Consequently God has provided two tests for dreams: the word and the Spirit. Any dream that contradicts the Scriptures is not of God (Deut 13:1-5). A Spirit-filled believer can use the gift of discernment to differentiate between real and counterfeit dreams (see Jer 23:25-32; 29:8-11; 1 Thess 5:21).

Many African indigenous churches originated in the dreams of their founders. Some claim that bizarre doctrines, liturgies and practices were revealed in dreams. Regardless of how successful such groups are (Deut. 13:1-2), their practices must be judged by whether they are consistent with or contradict the Bible.

Tokunboh Adeyemo

The Chaldeans were expecting things to be easy: *'Tell your servants the dream, and we will interpret it'* (2:4). But the king would have none of it. He wanted them to tell him his dream and its interpretation. They would die if they failed, but would be handsomely rewarded if successful (**2:5-6**).

Was the king deliberately withholding the dream in order to test the claims of his wise men, or had he actually forgotten it? He may not have been able to recall all the details, but it seems that he could remember enough of it to be able to tell if they lied to him (**2:9**).

The counsellors were dumbfounded, and the king was horrified by their failure. He demanded an answer on the spot, reminding them of his threat to kill them and destroy their houses (2:5, 8-9). Still they refused to take the risk of guessing wrong. In desperation they declared: *There is not a man on earth who can do what the king asks! ... No one can reveal it to the king except the gods, and they don't live*

among men (**2:10-11**). Their answer fitted with the belief that there are things which the gods know but humans do not. Nevertheless, the king angrily rejected it because these men were supposed to be representatives of the gods and had been trained to reveal secret things. Furious, he ordered the summary *execution of all the wise men of Babylon* (**2:12**). The severity of the sentence was probably attributable to the fact that their comments in 2:10-11 had not been very tactfully phrased.

Daniel and his companions had not been among those summoned to the king, but his edict applied to them as well. The executioners sent to kill the wise men went to find Daniel and his friends (**2:13**).

2:14-23 Counsel of Daniel

It didn't take long for Arioch, the captain of the king's guard, to locate Daniel. Making polite use of his God-given wisdom, Daniel was able to gain information about what was going on, secure an audience with the king, and obtain a stay of execution (**2:14-16**). The text does not say how much time he was given, but it cannot have been very long given the king's desperation and anger. While it is possible that Daniel's request was granted partly because the king's anger had subsided, it cannot be denied that God's hand was upon him. 'When a man's way pleases the Lord, he makes even his enemies to be at peace with him' (Prov 16:7).

Daniel immediately engaged his colleagues in fervent prayer (2:17-18). Proverbs says 'It is the glory of God to conceal a matter, but the glory of kings is to search out a matter' (Prov 25:2). Knowing this, and trusting in God's invitation 'Call to me and I will answer you and tell you great and unsearchable things you do not know' (Jer 33:3), Daniel and his companions turned to prayer. Their prayers were addressed to *the God of heaven* (**2:18, 19**), a way of referring to God found in only three other books of the Bible: Ezekiel, Nehemiah and Revelation. The young men's prayers were direct, specific and desperate. They knew that failure to get an answer meant death. It has been said that God doesn't answer just any prayer; rather, he answers desperate prayer made in accordance with his will.

True to his promise, God revealed the king's dream to Daniel *in a vision* (2:19). In dreams, which usually come at night, the dreamer is passive and only the subconscious mind is involved. By contrast, a vision can occur at any time of the day or night and it is usually interactive and participatory. When Saul of Tarsus had a vision of the Lord on the road to Damascus, he talked to Jesus. Similarly there was interaction between the Lord and Ananias when he received a vision instructing him to go and pray for Saul (Acts 9:10-17).

Daniel's response to receiving the vision was to worship and praise the revealer (**2:20-23**). Daniel's concept of God embraced his almighty wisdom, his omniscience and his omnipotence. God has power to readjust times and seasons, to raise up rulers and remove them, to reveal deep and secret things, and, of course, to redeem his people from death and destruction by making known to Daniel what the gods of the Chaldeans could not reveal (2:23). We have no record of his prayer, but his praise remains indelible. That's the way it should be for all believers: more praises than petitions!

2:24-45 Divine Construction of World Empires

Confident that the Lord had answered his prayers, Daniel immediately requested an end to the execution of the wise men (**2:24**). Arioch quickly took him to the king, announcing *I have found a man among the exiles from Judah* (**2:25**). He gives the impression that Daniel had not been allowed to see the king before (but see 2:16). Yet the way the king addressed Daniel, probably using his Babylonian name,

Belteshazzar, shows that he saw through Arioch's self-serving introduction (**2:26**).

Daniel's humility as he addressed the king also stands in sharp contrast to Arioch's arrogance. He started by stating clearly that no one in Babylon or anywhere in the world could disclose the king's secret dream, *but there is a God in heaven who reveals mysteries* (**2:27-28**). This is a powerful public testimony to the greatness of our God. Remember that at this time Daniel must have been about twenty years old, fresh from college. He was defending his Babylonian colleagues by underscoring their (and his own – **2:30**) human limitations, and thereby gave all the glory to God.

He then proceeded to describe what Nebuchadnezzar had seen in his dream (**2:31-35**). The king must have been awestruck as Daniel described each detail of the statue. It was made of metal, with its head of gold, its breast and arms of silver, its abdomen and thighs of bronze, its legs of iron and its feet a mixture of iron and clay. There was thus a clear deterioration in quality from the golden top to the clay feet. There was a corresponding decrease in weight but an increase in hardness from top to bottom (except for the feet of clay).

Daniel then went on to reveal how a stone which was cut out without human hands struck the image at its weakest point and crushed it to powder that was carried away by the wind, leaving no trace of the great statue. Instead the stone became a great mountain and filled the whole earth (2:35).

Daniel did not ask the king whether his description of the dream was correct (**2:36**). The source of his revelation cannot lie (Titus 1:2). So he went straight on to the interpretation of the dream (2:36-45) in terms of five different empires:

- **The head of gold** represented Nebuchadnezzar's Babylonian kingdom. He himself is described as *a king of kings*, a title that indicates dominion and supremacy. But Daniel immediately reminds him that he has not achieved this position by his military might but by divine appointment of *the God of heaven*, the Supreme King who reigns in heaven and on earth. For now, he reigns on earth by delegation: *He has given you a kingdom, power, strength, and glory* (**2:37**).

- **The chest and arms of silver** represent a kingdom that Daniel does not name but describes as *inferior to yours* (**2:39**). That kingdom is later identified as that of the Medes and Persians, which conquered Babylon in 539 BC (5:26-31). The dual origins of that kingdom was reflected in there being two arms.

- **The belly and thighs of bronze** represent a kingdom that is also not identified until a later revelation (8:20-21), where it is named 'the kingdom of Greece'. Alexander the Great led the Greek army in a series of military advances that began in 334 BC and overran the Medes and Persians.

- **The legs of iron and feet partly of iron and partly of clay** represent a fourth world empire that is one kingdom in form but diverse in composition (iron and clay) and in substance (ten toes). Of the four metals, iron is the strongest, and *as iron breaks things to pieces, so it will crush and break all the others* (**2:40**). This should not be interpreted as meaning that the fourth kingdom will find the three previous kingdoms still existing, for according to the text the first was destroyed by the second, and the second by the third. Rather, the materials of the first two kingdoms were incorporated in the third and are destroyed with it. Yet this iron kingdom that ruthlessly crushes everything in its path is characterized by division and incoherence. This is clear from the fact that iron and clay do not mix well, as well as from the presence of two feet and numerous toes (**2:41-42**). The inner discord is further complicated by the fact that *the people will be a mixture* (**2:43**). This expression can be literally translated as 'they shall mingle themselves with the seed of men' and has been given a number of interpretations. Some take it as referring to the marriage politics of the rulers, while others think it describes a democratic form of government as opposed to a dictatorship, or an attempt to mix the rule of law with rule by violence. Whatever the case, the fourth kingdom will not achieve real unity.
- **The stone kingdom** is the one that will destroy all the other kingdoms, including the iron kingdom (**2:44-45**). The great human statue will be shattered by a stone not cut out by human hands that will became a great mountain and fill the whole earth. Daniel identified that fifth kingdom as established by *the God of heaven,* who will never leave it *to another people,* and as being indestructible and eternal. Later, in Daniel's own vision, this fifth kingdom is given to the saints of the Most High (7:18).

The terminal points of the first three kingdoms are clear from the prophecy itself and from history. The Babylonian Empire succumbed to the Medo-Persian Empire in 539 BC, and it fell to the Greeks between 334 and 331 BC. The Greek Empire crumbled under the Roman invasion in 146 BC. The date of the end of the fourth kingdom is less clear. In the dream it ends with the sudden catastrophic impact of the stone followed by the establishment of the kingdom of God. Since this has not yet happened in history, 'the times of the Gentiles' have not yet ended and world governance is still operating under the aegis of the fourth kingdom with all of its strengths, diversity and weaknesses. The fifth kingdom is yet to come (compare 2:28).

2:46-49 Honour for Daniel

Overwhelmed by Daniel's ability to reveal and interpret his dream, Nebuchadnezzar fell down in worship before Daniel (**2:46**), but he exalted and praised Daniel's God (not Daniel) as the most supreme ruler and revealer of secrets (**2:47**).

Before this most powerful king at the time, Daniel, by prayerful and constructive engagement had proved that his God reigned. In the face of the crises confronting Africa today, it will take more than roadside signboards to convince the world that Christ is the answer. We need Josephs and Daniels who are able to reveal secrets, interpret dreams and solve enigmas.

Daniel not only brought glory to God but was himself promoted to the position of governor over the whole province of Babylon as well as chief executive officer over all the wise men (**2:48**). Unlike Joseph, who was given an Egyptian wife (Gen 41:45), Daniel's gifts did not include a wife. Fittingly, he remembered his three prayer partners. His request that they also be given positions of power and influence in the province was granted by the king. Many who gain power forget those who helped them get there. Daniel did not.

3:1-30 Faith Under Fire

Nebuchadnezzar may have constructed the golden image towards the middle of his forty-one year reign, when he was at the zenith of his power. Or, more likely, he may have been inspired by Daniel's interpretation of the dream, in which case it would have taken place earlier.

3:1-7 Command to Worship an Idol

Nebuchadnezzar celebrated the news that the God of heaven had given him a kingdom, power, strength and glory (2:37-38) by erecting an imposing golden image as an object of worship. The image stood 90 feet (27 metres) high, as tall as a 9-storey office block, and was 9 feet (2.7 metres) wide. It cannot have been of solid gold, for the weight and cost would have been prohibitive, but it had a dazzling coating of gold. It stood on the plain of Dura, about 9 miles (15 kilometres from Babylon, the capital city (**3:1**).

There has been much speculation about why Nebuchadnezzar erected the statue. It seems likely he was trying to impose a new state religion. As a despot, he regarded failure to accept this religion as treason, punishable by death (**3:6**). Among the Akan of Ghana and the Yoruba of Nigeria, the supreme traditional king is also regarded as an immortal and all-powerful deity, who is said to be second-in-command to the gods. When he dies, he is worshipped as one of the ancestors. However, these kings differ from Nebuchadnezzar in that they do not force their subjects to worship them.

3:8-12 Charge against Daniel's Friends

The Chaldeans, whose lives Daniel and his friends had saved (2:24), resented the promotion of Shadrach, Meshach and Abed-Nego. So they accused them of disrespect to the king (they *pay no attention to you, O king*), disloyalty (they don't *serve your gods*), and disobedience (they don't *worship the image of gold*) (**3:12**).

The first accusation was clearly untrue, for they had obeyed the order to attend the dedication ceremony (3:2-3). The other two charges were partly true, in that they did refuse to violate the First Commandment (Exod 20:3). But in all other respects they were loyal to the land and served the king faithfully.

Why was Daniel not charged too? He may have been away on official business, or he may have been left out because of his special relationship with the king. More likely, he was left out because the jealousy focused only on those responsible for the province of Babylon (3:12).

3:13-18 Courage of Daniel's Companions

Courage has been described as fear that has said its last prayer. The three lads must have been terrified as they were threatened by the furious king (**3:13-15**) but they refused to compromise and demonstrated a robust faith in God. They were neither superstitious nor fanatical (**3:17-18**), but they had a confident faith in God and submitted humbly to his will. They had no doubt about God's ability to deliver them. They were also convinced that he would (3:17b), since Nebuchadnezzar had openly challenged him (3:15c). But they were aware that the battle was not theirs but the Lord's (2 Chr 20:15). Should the Lord choose not to deliver them through death, so be it (3:18). They would rather burn than bow to idols! Their heroic example has inspired the church throughout history (Heb 11:34). It strengthened the ninety-nine Ugandan martyrs tortured to death because they refused to renounce Jesus as Lord. We are faced with the same demand: absolute Lordship demands absolute surrender.

3:19-25 Conflagration Made Seven Times Hotter

The lads' polite yet bold response only fuelled the king's anger. Consequently he commanded that the furnace be even hotter than usual. Believers sometimes face extreme trials, especially in the Islamic world. Recently, in northern Nigeria church buildings have been destroyed and believers who were formerly Muslim have been killed for their faith.

Nebuchadnezzar's furnace was so hot that the fire blasted the soldiers who threw the youths into the furnace. This was an act of God's judgment before the king's eyes. But there was more. He had thrown three bound men into the fire, but could now see four men walking around in the fire, unbound and unharmed, and the fourth looked like *a son of the gods* (**3:25**). Nebuchadnezzar could not recognize the pre-incarnate Son of God, and so he described him as an angel or a divine being (3:28).

The Lord here fulfilled his promise: 'When you walk through the fire, you will not be burned; the flames will not set you ablaze. For I am the Lord, your God, the Holy One of Israel, your Saviour' (Isa 43:1-3).

3:26-30 Commendation of Daniel's Friends

Nebuchadnezzar was awestruck as he called out to Shadrach, Meshach and Abed-Nego, addressing them as *servants of the Most High God* (**3:26**). He had encountered this God as a 'revealer of mysteries' before (2:47), but now he encountered him as a deliverer (**3:28-29**). Unfortunately Nebuchadnezzar did not embrace this God for himself. He merely declared that this God was unique in being able to save his servants and forbade any insults to him on pain of death.

The three Hebrew lads had earned the king's respect and he promoted them (**3:30**). Interestingly, after the miracle they neither reprimanded the king nor bragged about their faith, as many would do today. It was the Lord's battle to start with, and the Lord's opponent, Nebuchadnezzar, had admitted defeat. What more could be said? We hear nothing more of these men in the rest of the book.

4:1-37 Humiliation of King Nebuchadnezzar

The stories about Nebuchadnezzar in the book of Daniel span the forty-three years of his reign, from his rise to power through his fall due to pride to his eventual repentance, followed by his salvation and restoration. His case speaks of the long-suffering mercy of God who desires all people to be saved (1 Tim 2:1-7). It also speaks of the faith and tenacity of Daniel, who refused to compromise his principles but did not cease to serve the king. The events described in this chapter come towards the end of Nebuchadnezzar's life.

4:1-18 Nebuchadnezzar's Declaration and Dream

King Nebuchadnezzar records a testimony of his conversion and gives an account of the dream God used to reach him. Daniel may have been the king's scribe, for he had been the evangelist who proclaimed to him the way of salvation: *Renounce your sins by doing what is right, and your wickedness by being kind to the oppressed. It may be that then your prosperity will continue* (4:27). We desperately need bold prophetic witness like this in Africa today. Though it took the king some eight years to come to grips with this call to repentance, he eventually did so, and humbly made public his story by way of the decree recorded here.

The first three verses are the formal introduction to the decree. They give the sender's name, *King Nebuchadnezzar* (**4:1a**), making it clear who the 'I' is who writes. Next, they state to whom the decree is sent, namely to his own subjects and to others outside his realm (**4:1b**). The formal greeting that the NIV translates as *May you prosper greatly* (**4:1c**) was actually *Shalom,* a common expression of good wishes in Semitic languages (see also 6:25). The king then sets out the purpose for which he is writing, namely to share the amazing signs and wonders wrought in his life by the Most High God (**4:2-3**).

Nebuchadnezzar describes his kingdom as enjoying peace and prosperity (**4:4**). By this time he had subdued Syria, Phoenicia, Judea, Egypt and Arabia, and had accumulated enough wealth to make Babylon one of the most fabulous cities of the ancient world. (Similarly, the mineral resources of Africa were looted by colonizing powers and used to develop the great capital cities of London, Paris and Lisbon.) His affluence was a source of pride (4:30).

At this point in his career he had another dream, which he remembered. But once again his Babylonian experts could not interpret it for him (**4:5-7**; see also chapter 2). It is also possible that they were afraid to interpret it, fearing the king's reaction when he learned what this dream meant.

Daniel was finally called in. Nebuchadnezzar addressed him by his Babylonian name but acknowledged that he had a different spirit within him (**4:8**). Though the king was still a polytheist at this stage (hence his reference to 'gods', he nevertheless distinguished the spirit that was the source of Daniel's wisdom as 'holy' (**4:8, 9, 18**). In 2:47 he had spoken of Daniel's God (singular), so it is possible that he may here have used a plural form as a way of showing respect.

Nebuchadnezzar's remark that *no mystery is too difficult for you* (**4:9**, 18) sets a goal for true servants of God. They should be problem solvers, not sources of problems. God assigned this role to the prophets in both the Old and New Testaments. They were messengers of hope in every grim situation (Deut 13; 1 Kgs 17-18; Luke 4:18-19; Acts 10:38).

Nebuchadnezzar had dreamed of an enormous tree that provided food and shelter for all (**4:10-12**). In his dream, he saw a divine messenger issuing a command for the tree to be cut down, its branches trimmed, its leaves stripped and its fruit scattered. Its stump and roots were left in the ground, albeit bound with iron and bronze (**4:13-15a**). Then, in a dramatic twist, the image changed from a tree to a man drenched with dew and left to live among animals in the field (**4:15b**). Worse than that, the man was given the mind of an animal for a period of seven years (**4:16**). Still in the dream, the king was told why this was being done: that *the living may know that the Most High is sovereign over the kingdoms of men and gives them to anyone he wishes and sets over them the lowliest of men* (**4:17**).

Few dispute that God reigns supreme over human affairs in general. What many find hard to understand is why a good God has allowed notoriously wicked leaders to hold power over many African nations. Nor do Africans perceive their chiefs, kings and presidents as 'the lowliest of men'.

4:19-27 Daniel's Decoding of the Dream

This time, the spirit of the holy God gave Daniel instant understanding of the dream. But he was troubled because of what it foretold for the king he had been serving for over thirty years and for whose salvation he must have been praying. Diplomatically, he began his presentation by wishing that the dream were for the king's enemies (**4:19**). Then without mincing words he decoded the dream: *You, O king, are that tree!* (**4:22**). The tree represented Nebuchadnezzar at the height of his glory. The Most High had issued a decree that Nebuchadnezzar would be insane for seven years until he acknowledged God as the sovereign Lord (**4:24-25**). When he repented and did this, his kingdom would be restored to him (**4:26**).

Daniel concluded his interpretation with an invitation: *renounce your sins by doing what is right* (**4:27**). This is consistent with prophetic indictments throughout the ages: Nathan before King David (2 Sam 12:7); Elijah before Ahab (1 Kgs 18:18); and John the Baptist before Herod (Luke 3:19-20). The church in Africa needs such a prophetic voice today. In the struggle against apartheid in South Africa, Archbishop Desmond Tutu was such a voice. In the days of Idi Amin in Uganda, the late Archbishop Janani Luwum provided such a voice.

4:28-33 Nebuchadnezzar's Derangement

Judgment did not happen immediately, and so Nebuchadnezzar ignored his dream. Twelve months later he stood on the flat roof of his palace, admiring his achievements. It is reported that the outer wall of his palace was six miles long. There were two other battlemented walls within and a great tower and three gates of bronze. Nebuchadnezzar credited all he had achieved to his own power and saw it all as contributing to his own glory, with no acknowledgment of God. Like Lucifer's, his pride led to his downfall (Isa 14:12-15). Suddenly the verdict fell from heaven, *your royal authority has been taken from you* (**4:31**). There could be no doubt as to the connection between the crime and the punishment.

Immediately Nebuchadnezzar became insane, was driven away from people and ate grass like cattle. He paid no attention to personal hygiene and his hair became wild like eagles' feathers and his nails like birds' claws (**4:33**). It seems that although he was relieved of his royal duties, he was protected, kept in the palace gardens away from abuse by common people.

This disease in which a person thinks he is an animal is known as insania zoanthropica, or boanthropy when the person thinks he is an ox. A case similar to Nebuchadnezzar's is said to have been observed in a British mental institution in 1946. Similar cases exist today, but treatment is now available for sufferers.

During Nebuchadnezzar's period of insanity, his son, Evil-Merodach, is said to have reigned as his regent (Jer 52:31). Daniel continued to serve as head of the wise men and must have worked to ensure kind treatment of the king in the light of his interpretation of the dream and the hope of Nebuchadnezzar's restoration.

4:34-37 Nebuchadnezzar's Decision and Restoration

Salvation involves personal conviction and repentance, even for Nebuchadnezzar. After seven years of humiliation, God brought him to a point where he no longer raised his heart in pride, but rather raised his eyes to heaven in humble surrender (**4:34**). God responded in mercy and restored his sanity. Consequently the king burst out in praise and worship, not of Daniel as he had done some thirty-seven years ago (2:46), but of God whom he described as the Most High, a name he must have picked up from the divine messengers in his dream (4:17, 25). It has been said that nothing is more insane than human pride, and nothing is more sober than praising God. That this once arrogant king bows down and humbly worships *him who lives forever* (4:34) is evidence of an inner transformation.

Nebuchadnezzar's royal honour and splendour were returned to him, his advisors and nobles (including Daniel) sought him out and he was restored to his throne in even greater glory (**4:36**).

Nebuchadnezzar concluded his testimony with one of the most powerful statements of faith in God recorded in the Scriptures: *I, Nebuchadnezzar, praise and exalt and glorify the King of heaven* (**4:37**). His words reflect the fruit of Daniel's influence and prayer for him. Prayer is never in vain!

5:1-31 God Removes a Blasphemous King

Daniel was not a historian and did not pretend to be writing a history of the empire. He was a prophet and a statesman. His reason for including this chapter is to show that the prophecy regarding the fall of Babylon (2:32, 39) was fulfilled in October 539 BC. The resulting change in government would affect his own people.

5:1-4 Blasphemy of King Belshazzar

Belshazzar is introduced as the king of Babylon (**5:1**) and a son of Nebuchadnezzar (**5:2**). Critics have used these two statements to challenge the historical accuracy of the book of Daniel, alleging that no king by the name of Belshazzar ever reigned in Babylon, let alone was a son of Nebuchadnezzar. However, the discovery of the Nabonidus Cylinder and extrabiblical writings by Berosus and Herodotus, Babylonian and Greek historians, have provided archaeological support for the biblical record.

Nebuchadnezzar died in 562 BC and was succeeded by his son, Amel-Marduk (562–559 BC), also known as Evil-Merodach (2 Kgs 25:27-30; Jer 52:31-34). He was assassinated by his brother-in-law, Neriglissar (559–555 BC). Neriglissar's son, Labashi-Marduk (555 BC), reigned for only nine months before being assassinated and replaced by Nabonidus (555–539 BC), who was married to either a daughter or a widow of Nebuchadnezzar by the name of Nitocris. Belshazzar was their eldest son. Though Nabonidus did not come from the royal line of Nebuchadnezzar, Belshazzar was descended from him through his mother. Just as David is called the father – meaning ancestor – of Jesus in Luke 1:32, so Nebuchadnezzar could be called Belshazzar's father.

Nabonidus reigned for seventeen years. For thirteen of those years, he ruled jointly with his son Belshazzar, whom he stationed in Babylon while he himself lived at Teima in Arabia. This co-regency explains the way Daniel refers to Belshazzar and also explains why the reward offered in 5:7 is to be made third ruler – there were already two rulers.

According to Herodotus, the events described in this chapter took place on one of the great festival days of the Babylonians. Cyrus the Persian had already been besieging the city for about three months and hope was fading. Nabonidus had tried to relieve the city, but had been beaten back by the Persian army. As often happens in a time of crisis, the king turned to a combination of religion and license to try to boost morale. He invited a thousand of his nobles and his wives and concubines to a great banquet. Then, probably to assert their faith in their Babylonian gods who, supposedly, had granted them victory in the past against the Jews, the king ordered that the gold and silver goblets that his grandfather had captured seventy years earlier in Jerusalem be brought out and used (5:2). So the guests drank from the vessels from God's sacred temple while they praised their *gods of gold and silver ... and stone* (**5:4**). Belshazzar was challenging the holy God of Israel.

Like Belshazzar, we in contemporary Africa often turn to wine, women and witchcraft when a crisis comes. These offer no solutions.

5:5-9 Writing on the Wall

God did not let Belshazzar's challenge go unanswered. Suddenly, a supernatural hand appeared, writing a verdict on the wall where the king could see it. Though the king was able to feign no fear of the war outside the city, he could not hide his horror at this apparition. He turned pale and his wine-bolstered courage deserted him to the point *that his knees knocked together and his legs gave way* (**5:6**).

He called loudly for his experts (**5:7**), who hurried in. They had failed his grandfather Nebuchadnezzar in his hours of crisis (chs. 2 and 4), and they failed Belshazzar too, intensifying the king's perplexity and fear (**5:8-9**).

5:10-17 Reward Rejected

Hearing the uproar, the king's mother came in (**5:10**). (She is referred to as *the queen*, but must have been the queen mother as Belshazzar's wife was already present at the party – 5:2-3). She spoke calmly and reminded her son about Daniel's incredible feat in the days of Nebuchadnezzar (**5:11-12**). The king listened to her and immediately summoned Daniel, asking him to interpret the writing on the wall (**5:13-15**). If Daniel was successful, he was promised money, fame and a position next in rank to the king himself (**5:16**; see comments on 5:1-2).

Many ministers of the gospel in nation after nation in Africa have sold their birthrights and compromised the truth for luxury or position. But Daniel rejected the king's offer in no uncertain terms (**5:17**). Nevertheless, he was prepared to read and interpret the writing.

5:18-24 Like Father, Like Son

Before interpreting the inscription, Daniel reminded his terrified audience of how Nebuchadnezzar had been deposed and disgraced for seven years – a fact known by every member of the royal family – until he bowed down to the Most High God (**5:18-21**). He then went to the heart of the problem, saying: *But you his son, O Belshazzar, have not humbled yourself, though you knew all this* (**5:22**). He denounced Belshazzar's blasphemy and folly. *You have set yourself up against the Lord of heaven* (**5:23**), meaning that the king was on a collision course with the Lord God who held his life in his hand.

A popular song in Nigeria has a similar theme. It sings of a recent head of state who arbitrarily abused power and defied every constituted authority at home and internationally. But when God said 'Enough!' his military might could not avert his death.

5:25-31 Message of Judgment

God's memo to Belshazzar read: *MENE, MENE, TEKEL, PARSIN. Mene*, repeated twice for emphasis, means 'numbered'. God was telling Belshazzar: 'Your time is up!' The word *tekel* means 'weighed', and has a secondary meaning of 'found too light'. God has found Belshazzar to be too light morally and spiritually (**5:27**). The word *parsin* means 'broken' or 'divided', and has a plural ending to indicate the plural nature of the conquering power: *Your kingdom is divided and given to the Medes and Persians* (**5:28**).

Some have asked: 'Why Medes and Persians' when the Persians were the stronger in this coalition? The answer may lie in Daniel's knowledge of the prophecies of Isaiah and Jeremiah many years before (Isa 13:17-22; 21:1-10; Jer 51:33-58). Daniel would have remembered his interpretation of Nebuchadnezzar's dream, where the golden head was succeeded by the chest and arms of silver (2:32, 39).

Belshazzar carried out his promise of honouring and rewarding Daniel and proclaimed him the third highest ruler in the kingdom. Apparently he was not expecting an immediate fulfilment of the message. Many people in our day make the same mistake. But *that very night Belshazzar … was slain, and Darius the Mede took over the kingdom, at the age of sixty-two* (**5:30-31**).

6:1-28 Persecution of Righteous Daniel

'All who desire to live godly in Christ Jesus will suffer persecution' (2 Tim 3:12) and Daniel was no exception. 'No servant is greater than his master,' says Jesus, 'If they persecuted me, they will persecute you also' (John 15:20). Unfortunately we are bombarded by an unbiblical painless (or pay-less) theology that wants a crown without a cross. Yet the importance of persecution is attested by the amount of space given to it in both the Old and the New Testaments and in this book of Daniel.

6:1-3 Daniel's Position Under a New Regime

Darius the Mede took over from the slain Belshazzar. Yet the problem is that there is no record of any king of Babylon with this name, and there seems to be confusion in Daniel's record between Darius and Cyrus (1:21; 6:28). Evangelical scholars offer three possible solutions: a) Darius is another name for Cyrus the Persian; b) Darius was actually Cambyses, the son of Cyrus; and c) Darius is another name for Gubaru, the governor Cyrus appointed over Babylon immediately after the fall of the city.

The last explanation enjoys the most support. The language of 5:31 and 9:1 supports the interpretation that Darius was a sub-king under Cyrus. He is described as 'ruler over the Babylonian kingdom' (that is, of Babylonia – 9:1), whereas Cyrus is referred to as *king of Persia* (that is, of the empire – 10:1). Just as Belshazzar was co-regent with Nabonidus, his father, so Darius the Mede was co-regent with Cyrus the Persian, the senior partner in the coalition.

Darius had vast administrative ability. He rejected the despotic rule of the Babylonians and introduced a system based on power sharing. His reason for doing this was primarily economic: *so that the king might not suffer loss* (**6:2**). He appointed 120 district assistants under three provincial governors, one of whom was Daniel. By this time Daniel was over eighty-four years of age, with over sixty years of public service behind him. His knowledge of Babylon and his record of integrity meant that it did not take long for Darius to notice him. As a result he *planned to set him over the whole kingdom* (**6:3**). 'Do you see a man skilled in his work? He will serve before kings; he will not serve before obscure men' (Prov 22:29).

Daniel was a statesman who served three different regimes with integrity. We should seek to emulate his qualities as we strive to be salt and light in our generation. Someone has said: 'Christians should be so "Daniel-good" that they cannot be ignored'.

6:4-9 Plot Against Daniel

Daniel's favour with the king aroused the jealousy of his fellow officials, men who were probably much younger and anxious to get ahead. What started as jealousy turned into envy; envy turned into racial hatred (see the label in 6:13); and hatred turned into a plot.

Daniel could not be credibly accused of corruption (**6:4**). But his virtue made him vulnerable, for it meant that his enemies could predict how he would react in certain circumstances. So they decided to use *the law of his God* to entrap him (**6:5**). They must have been thinking of the second commandment (Exod 20:4). Daniel had not been a secret disciple of Yahweh. His enemies knew that he would not bow down to anyone other than his God.

Drawing on the prevailing notion of the divinity of kings, the conspirators asked the unsuspecting king to sign an edict declaring that he was to be the sole being to be prayed to (**6:6-8**). The king might have asked, 'Why limit the decree to the next thirty days?' But he did not. The decree flattered his vanity. It was another case of a man wanting to be a god.

6:10-11 Daniel's Prayer

Despite the administrators' claim that this was a unanimous decision (6:7), Daniel had obviously not been present when the conspiracy was planned or when the decree was presented to the king. As soon as he learned of it, he must have known what was going on. He now faced not a choice but a challenge to his faith. If it had been merely a choice, he could have resolved it by choosing not to pray at all. Since the decree did not command anyone to pray, not praying would not have constituted an offence.

What did it mean to pray to the king? He may have been expected to have an image representing Darius or to call out the name of Darius (see also 1 Kgs 18:26-29). More likely, to judge by Daniel's behaviour, he may have been meant to face towards the king's palace when praying (as Muslims must face Mecca). Daniel's response is clear. He prays three times daily with his windows opened towards Jerusalem (**6:10**). The practice of praying towards Jerusalem had been adopted by David, the man after God's own heart (Pss 5:7; 28:2), and his son, Solomon, had institutionalized it (1 Kgs 8:33, 35, 38, 44, 48; 2 Chr 6:34-39). The prophet Jeremiah had encouraged the exiles to seek the Lord (Jer 29:1, 12). Centralized temple worship had become so vital to the Jews that many years later they would totally miss the point when Jesus said, 'destroy this temple, and I will raise it again in three days' (John 2:19-21; see also John 4:21-24).

Daniel faced the challenge as courageously as his companions had done in chapter 3. He openly prayed to Yahweh, as he had always done. His consistency and faithfulness are a challenge to all believers, and particularly to busy Christian professionals of the dot-com generation. The secret of Daniel's strength was his prayer in his room!

6:12-13, 15 Prosecution of Daniel

Daniel's enemies lost no time in reporting his behaviour. Cleverly, they did not immediately mention his name. Instead, they asked the king to confirm that he meant what he had said (**6:12**). Once they had an affirmative answer to this question, they proceeded to disclose that Daniel was not obeying the law. The king was very distressed when he heard this and did his best to protect Daniel (6:14). So the conspirators came to him a third time to remind him that his decree could not be changed (**6:15**). Darius' inability to reverse the decree has been used by some to support the argument that he was a subordinate king to Cyrus.

6:14, 16-17 Predicament of King Darius

When the king learned that he had been tricked, he was not angry with Daniel but with himself. Having tried all he could do within the law to rescue Daniel and failed, he reluctantly gave the order for Daniel to be thrown into the lions' den (**6:16**). (Unlike the Babylonians, the Persians were Zoroastrians by religion. Because they regarded fire as sacred they would not use it to execute offenders.)

Saying farewell to Daniel, the king prayed, 'May your God, whom you serve continually, rescue you!' (6:16). Was this merely a wish by a frustrated pagan king? Given Daniel's influence on the king (shown by his behaviour – 6:18), it seems likely that it was a genuine prayer. Daniel had made a deep impact on the arrogant Nebuchadnezzar, and also, it appears, on Darius.

Then Daniel was lowered into the den, which was probably a deep pit with a cover over it. Once the cover was in place, the king sealed it with his signet ring and those of his nobles to ensure that it was not opened (**6:17**).

6:18-23 Protection of Daniel

That night the king fasted: he had no food, no music, no entertainment, and no sleep (**6:18**). He may well have prayed all night, for what else explains his rush to the den early in the morning to see whether Daniel was still alive (**6:19**).

At the den he calls out to Daniel, addressing him as a *servant of the living God* (**6:20**). He recognizes that Daniel continually serves his God, and that God is 'living' as opposed to 'dead' idols. It is also clear that he had at least some expectation that Daniel would be delivered (6:20). He was overjoyed when Daniel responded (**6:23**).

Daniel had no doubt that it was the Lord who had protected him (**6:22**). His heroic faith is commended in the NT (Heb 11:33).

6:24 Punishment of Daniel's Detractors

Daniel had taught Nebuchadnezzar that his God is a God of justice (4:27). Darius learned the same lesson. He thus punished those who had conspired against Daniel, ordering that they and their wives and children be thrown into the lions' den (**6:24a**). As the proverb says *Eniti o ba da eru, ni eru nto* [Yoruba – Nigeria: 'Ashes follow the one who throws them into the air']. The text does not say how many people were executed. Given their immediate destruction (**6:24b**), it is likely that it was just the ringleaders rather than all 120 assistants plus the other two governors and their wives and children. Their deaths show that Daniel did not survive merely because the lions were not hungry, but because of God's miraculous intervention.

6:25-28 Prosperity of Daniel

Greatly impressed, Darius issued a decree that people everywhere in his kingdom *must fear and reverence the God of Daniel* (**6:26**). This was tantamount to legalizing the worship of Yahweh. He described Daniel's God in terms almost identical to those used by Nebuchadnezzar after his deliverance (4:34-37). The similarity of the two decrees has led to suggestions that Daniel may have drafted both.

Daniel did not merely triumph over persecution, he prospered. Not only did he enjoy material success, but he must have rejoiced at seeing the fear of God take root in the hearts of pagan kings. In a foreign land, Daniel made his God known, feared and worshipped. Yahweh became known as *the God of Daniel* (6:26). We Christians face a similar challenge in Africa. We need to show that there is a difference between our God (Jesus Christ) and all other gods.

Daniel's other cause for joy is hinted at in the closing words of the chapter, with its reference to *the reign of Cyrus*

CHRISTIANS AND POLITICS

Many Christians will not participate in politics, claiming that 'drinking and driving don't mix, and neither do religion and politics'. They regard politics as a dirty game that Christians should avoid. This attitude is rooted in our colonial history and in a failure to distinguish between party politics and political participation. Political participation includes exercising one's rights to vote and be voted for, speaking out against any wrongdoing by those in power and holding leaders accountable for their actions. Such behaviour has deep roots in the communal orientation of traditional African society, where decision making was based on democratic principles that formed the basis for community relations. That tradition fits well with current Western democratic values.

While Christians tend to avoid political participation, Muslims understand its importance. Consequently they control political power in many African states, even those where they are a minority. Unlike Christians, they do not believe in the separation of church and state because it encourages secularism.

Jesus, too, did not separate religion and politics. In his mission statement in Luke 4:18-19 he declared that his ministry was to those suffering various forms of bondage and oppression, including economic oppresssion (poverty), physical oppression (diseases and disabilities), political oppression (injustice and oppressive rule) and demonic oppression (various forms of occult practices). These same evils plague Africa today.

Other biblical examples of political participation include Joseph in Egypt, who saved many from hunger and starvation (Gen 41); Amos, who warned the political leaders of his time against injustice (Amos 4, 7) and Daniel and his three friends, who changed the political equation in Persia (Dan 3, 5, 6).

Nehemiah, too, made a personal sacrifice in order to serve his people (Neh 1–2, 5). In the NT, Paul refused to give up his rights as a citizen when the political authorities put him in prison and flogged him without giving him a proper trial (Acts 16:37-38; 22:25)

Throughout history, the common people have turned to the church in times of need. It has followed Christ in recognizing their suffering and giving them a voice to speak out against injustice and oppression. Moral bankruptcy, corruption, poverty, disease and ignorance: all clearly call for Christian participation in politics. Some African Christian leaders have responded to the call. Sir Francis Akanu Ibiam of Nigeria led protests to Queen Elizabeth II of England during the Nigerian Civil War. President Matthew Kereku of Benin convened a reconciliation conference to apologize to African Americans for the role of African leaders in the nineteenth-century slave trade. Archbishop Desmond Tutu played a strong role in liberating South Africa from the apartheid regime and continues to work for reconciliation.

Other Christian leaders such as former president Frederick Chiluba of Zambia and President Olusegun Obasanjo of Nigeria have, however, disappointed their fellow Christians by their actions or lack of action regarding corruption in high places. One reason for their failure may be that they lacked support from fellow Christians and were thus exposed to the corrupting influence of non-Christians.

African Christians need to understand that the destinies of their nations rest on their political participation. As the Bible says, 'When the righteous thrive, the people rejoice; when the wicked rule, the people groan' (Prov 29:2). Good people can enjoy life when the righteous are in authority, but people will always suffer under wicked regimes.

James B. Kantiok

the Persian (**6:28**). After praying for that day for some seventy years, Daniel must have witnessed the emancipation of his people from captivity by the decree of Cyrus in 538 BC (Ezra 1:1-4; Dan 1:21).

7:1-28 Kingdoms in Conflict: The Four Beasts

So far, the book of Daniel has been mainly historical and written in the third person; from here on, it is written in the first person and is mainly prophetic. Whereas Daniel has been interpreting others' dreams, from now on an angel is interpreting his visions. The focus also shifts from Gentile world powers to Israel and how it will be affected by world history.

Altogether Daniel was given four visions (chs. 7, 8, 9, and 10–12) over a period of about sixteen years in his old age (552–536 BC). The first two were given during the reign of Belshazzar (7:1 and 8:1) while the last two came after the fall of Babylon (9:1 and 10:1). Chronologically, chapters 7 and 8 should thus come before chapter 5. All the visions portray the ultimate triumph of God's kingdom on earth against the background of seemingly hopeless struggles.

When he interpreted Nebuchadnezzar's first dream (ch. 2), Daniel was about 21 years old. He was in his early seventies when he received the vision described in this chapter. Yet despite the fifty-year gap, these two dream-visions communicate essentially the same message. Both describe four great world empires between the sixth century BC and the climax of world history when Jesus Christ returns and God's eternal kingdom is inaugurated on earth.

7:1-8 Sequence of World Empires

Daniel received this vision *in the first year of Belshazzar king of Babylon* (**7:1**). This was a worrying period for the citizens of Babylon and their foreign captives. The Babylonian Empire had declined steeply, and Nabonidus, though a competent leader, did not live in Babylon (see comments on 5:1-2). God saw fit to reassure his people that he was still in charge and that they had not been forgotten, even though Daniel himself found his visions deeply disturbing (7:15, 28).

In his vision, Daniel saw *the four winds of heaven,* representing the four cardinal points of the compass, and thus the whole world, stirring up the Mediterranean Sea, which here symbolizes the sea of humanity (Isa 17:12, 13; 21:1; 57:20; Rev 17:15). The stress on 'of heaven' implies that supernatural forces are using natural means to stir up turmoil among nations.

Then four great beasts appear in succession, each different from the others in appearance and behaviour. The first beast was like a lion with eagle's wings (**7:4**). Elsewhere, Nebuchadnezzar is likened to a lion in strength (Jer 4:7; 5:6) and an eagle in swiftness and agility (Jer 48:40; 49:22;

Ezek 17). Daniel had identified him as the head of gold representing the Babylonian kingdom (2:38), and here the lion-like beast also represents Babylon. The changes that this beast undergoes symbolize the king's humiliating insanity and his eventual salvation – when he was given *the heart of a man* (**7:4**). In the African context, when a ruler misbehaves he is called a beast *'eranko'*, but when he does right, they call him an angel *'malaika'*.

The second beast was like a bear, a beast second only to the lion in its strength and fierceness, as was the Medo-Persian Empire that succeeded the Babylonian Empire in history (Isa 13:17-18). The two sides of this bear were clearly different, with one stronger than the other, just as the Persians under Cyrus were the stronger party in the coalition with the Medes. (These two parties are also represented by the two arms on the statue in chapter 2 and the two horns of the ram in chapter 8). The three ribs in the bear's mouth and the message to *get up and eat your fill of flesh* (**7:5**) reflect the Medo-Persian conquest of an empire extending from the Indus River in the east to Egypt and the Aegean sea in the west.

The third beast was like a leopard with four bird-like wings and four heads (**7:6**). Leopards are characterized by agility, speed and an appetite for blood, and the fact that this one has wings means that it can act exceptionally fast. This third beast has been identified as the Grecian Empire that succeeded the Medo-Persian one. Under Alexander the Great, the borders of Greece were rapidly enlarged. The four heads symbolize the four generals who divided Alexander's realm after his death.

The fourth beast is given more extensive coverage than all the other beasts combined (7:7-8, 11, 19-25). It is not compared to any animal but is said to be *terrifying and frightening and very powerful* (**7:7**). With its iron teeth, it *crushed and devoured its victims and trampled underfoot whatever was left.* Amazingly, *it had ten horns.* Suddenly an eleventh horn sprang up among the ten, and though it was smaller than they were, it uprooted three of them. It had eyes like a man and *a mouth that spoke boastfully* (**7:8**). Everything about this beast inspired fear.

Daniel was so disturbed by the entire vision, and especially by the fourth beast, that he asked for help in interpreting it (7:15-16; 19-20).

Since the fourth beast emerged after the third, and since the Grecian Empire was conquered by the Romans, this fourth beast must symbolize the Roman Empire, which was ruthless in its destruction of previous civilizations and peoples. It killed thousands and sold many more into slavery. Rome had little interest in raising those it conquered to any higher level of development, just as the fourth beast trampled its victims underfoot (7:7). Sadly, within living memory, some colonial powers have treated their colonies similarly.

The ten horns represent ten kings reigning as contemporaries during the Roman Empire. History has no record of ten such kings, nor has it recorded the rise of something equivalent to the little horn (7:7, 8, 20-25). Furthermore, since no other animal rose from the sea after the fourth beast, its dominion seems to be open-ended (extending to and including contemporary history) until the beast is slain and destroyed by the Ancient of Days (7:11, 22, 26). Thus the final act of the drama involving the fourth beast lies in the future, a position that is scripturally corroborated by the end-time prophecies of the NT (Rev 13; 17; Matt 24; 2 Thess 2).

7:9-14 Sovereignty of the Ancient of Days

Suddenly the scene changes from beasts to a superhuman being, from warlords to a judging monarch, and from a terrestrial to a celestial plane. The central players are God the Father and his Son, referred to respectively as *the Ancient of Days* (**7:9**) and the *Son of Man* (7:13). The title 'Ancient of Days' refers to someone who is very old. It is used only in this chapter (7:9, 13, 22), and can refer to none other than 'the high and lofty One … who lives forever' (Isa 57:15). Where his age speaks of his eternal existence, his garment and his hair speak of his purity. Though there are many thrones, probably occupied by angels, only the Ancient of Days is the judge. His judgment is swift, righteous and just, and is compared to a river of fire as it pours out upon the wicked, especially here upon the fourth beast and the little horn, the antichrist (**10, 11**). Though books were opened, the judgment here was not based on the books, as will be the case later (Rev 20:12).

Immediately after the judgment, Daniel saw someone 'like a son of man'. In the Gospels, Jesus frequently uses this term to refer to himself (Matt 8:20; 9:6; 10:23; 11:19). This son of man was given a kingdom that will not pass away (**7:13-14**). It will be universal, encompassing *all people, nations, and languages* (KJV), everlasting in that it *will not pass away*, and unconquerable, in that it *will never be destroyed* (see also Ps 2:6-9; Isa 11).

7:15-20, 23-24 Struggle Against the Saints

Troubled by the vision, Daniel asked one of the angelic host (probably the angel Gabriel – 8:16; 9:21) for an explanation of what was going on. The angel identified the four great beasts as four world empires that would rise and fall, but the fifth kingdom, which would not wane, would be the kingdom of *the saints of the Most High* (**7:18**). These saints are those brought into the fifth kingdom of the Son of Man to serve him (7:14). They are referred to six times between 7:18 and 7:25, each time in the context of struggle and then success.

Scripture reveals that people can only be made holy by faith in Jesus Christ and his atoning work on the cross

(Acts 4:12; Rom 5:1-2; Eph 2:8-10; 1 Pet 1:18-19). The cross of Christ is the non-negotiable means of salvation and sanctification. Since Christ is the lamb that was 'slain from the creation of the world' (Rev 13:8) and the 'Lamb of God who takes away the sin of the whole world' (John 1:29), it does not matter at what period in history one is made holy – whether before or after Christ's crucifixion. What matters is the fact of it, and its monopoly. Christ states: 'I am the way and the truth and the life. No one comes to the Father except through me' (John 14:6).

This claim is contested by the beast who demands worship even from the saints, and punishes non-compliance with death (Rev 13:3-9).

7:21-22, 25-28 Setbacks and Triumph of the Saints

Preachers sometimes imply that Christians always triumph, but the vision shows that God allows his saints (like his Son) to be defeated by the beast's little horn, who waged war against them and prevailed until God himself intervened (**7:22**). Though the period of the enemy's success is left indefinite in 7:22, it is later defined as 3.5 years (*a time, times and half a time* – **7:25**). This same period is mentioned three times in chapter 12 (12:7, 11, 12), where the Arch angel Michael describes it as a time of intense persecution, unprecedented in world history (12:1).

The warfare against God and his people will take such forms as blasphemy, political injustice, social harassment, economic deprivation, and physical ridicule and torture (Zech 13-14; Rev 13:1-18). Some or all of these tactics are used in persecution of believers today, especially in the Muslim world.

When the persecution becomes unbearable, the sovereign Lord will step in to deliver his people at his own appointed time (1 Cor 10:13). The court will be convened and the power of the antichrist will be taken away and completely destroyed by the Ancient of Days (7:22, 26). *The sovereignty, power and greatness of the kingdoms under the whole heaven will be handed over to the saints, the people of the Most High* (**7:27**). This presentation of the kingdoms is the same as the one that was made to the Son of Man earlier in the vision (7:14). Daniel is not seeing two kingdoms, and the saints do not reign as kings. What he is seeing is one kingdom, the kingdom of God on earth, where Jesus reigns as king and the saints are his subjects. This will be an everlasting kingdom (7:27, see also 7:14).

8:1-8:27 Empires at War; Battle for Holy Land

Two years after his first vision, Daniel was given a second vision (**8:1**) which gave more details about the second and third kingdoms he had seen. This time, instead of a bear and a leopard, he saw a ram and a he-goat. He also saw another little horn that was very similar to the little horn on the fourth beast in chapter 7, except that this horn grew on the head of the beast representing the third kingdom. The behaviour of this horn foreshadows the activities of the other horn. Commentators agree that the little horn of chapter 8 represents the antichrist of the OT and therefore of history, while that of chapter 7 is the antichrist of the NT and therefore of eschatology. One prefigures the other, although when the vision was given to Daniel both of them were still in the future.

8:1-4, 20 Conquest by the Ram

The setting for this second vision was Susa (**8:2**), a town about 250 miles east of Babylon and 120 miles north of the Persian Gulf. It was little known at the time of Daniel, yet in his vision he saw it as a fortified palace. The vision was prophetic, for Cyrus was to make Susa one of the royal cities. It was the home of Queen Esther and Nehemiah, and it was there that archaeologists found the famous Code of Hammurabi in 1901.

What was unusual about the ram with two horns, which symbolized the Medo-Persian coalition (**8:20**), was that the horn which developed later grew longer than the other (**8:3**). Persia was a minor power and Media a major one in 612 BC when Media helped Babylonia defeat Assyria. But by 550 BC Cyrus, a Persian, had gained control over Media. His conquests extended the Medo-Persian Empire to the west (Babylonia, Syria, Asia Minor), to the north (Armenia and the Caspian Sea region), and to the south (Egypt and Ethiopia). A century and a half earlier, the prophet Isaiah had predicted Cyrus' victories (see Isa 45:1-3) and the relative ease with which they would be accomplished. Daniel's vision confirmed that this was the case (**8:4**).

8:5-8, 21 Challenge from the He-Goat

At the height of the Medo-Persian Empire, a he-goat representing the kingdom of Greece (**8:21**) swept across from the west so fast that it seemed to be *crossing the whole earth without touching the ground* (**8:5**). It attacked the ram and broke both its horns. The prominent horn on the goat represents Alexander the Great, a great military strategist whose armies advanced swiftly. He defeated the Persians, and swept on towards India. While returning to Babylon from the east, he took ill and died in June 323 BC at the age of thirty-two. Thus the prominent horn was broken (8:22).

In its place *four prominent horns grew up toward the four winds of heaven* (**8:8**). After a lengthy power struggle, Alexander's great empire was divided among four of his generals. Cassander received Macedonia and Greece to the west; Lysimachus, Thrace and much of Asia Minor to the north; Seleucus, Syria and vast regions to the east; and Ptolemy, Egypt to the south.

8:9-14 Rise of the Little Horn

The Holy Spirit now gives Daniel additional information about one of the four fragments of Alexander's empire and about the end times. The little horn grew from one of the four horns that succeeded Alexander and grew very large, expanding toward the south, the east, and towards Israel, which is described as *the Beautiful Land* (**8:9**). It oppressed and persecuted the people of God, referred to as *the host of the heavens* (**8:10**), and in its arrogance it blasphemed God, who is *the Prince of the host* (**8:11**). It desecrated the sanctuary (8:11); and instituted a travesty of Mosaic law and the true religion (**8:12**). Daniel was told that the oppression of his people would last for 2300 days, after which the sanctuary would be cleansed and restored (**8:14**).

8:15-19, 22-27 Interpretation of the Vision

Once again, Gabriel interpreted what Daniel had seen (**8:15-16**). He started by stressing that the vision concerned *the time of the end* (**8:17**), *the appointed time* (**8:19**), *the distant future* (**8:26**). Some commentators interpret this as referring to the time when Antiochus IV Epiphanes tyrannized the Holy Land and fulfilled the prophecies regarding the little horn, resulting in the Maccabean revolt of the second century BC. The problem with this view is that Antiochus' oppression did not mark the end of Jewish suffering. Nor did the first coming of Christ and his crucifixion, which is another interpretation of the phrase. It seems better to see Antiochus' oppression as a partial fulfilment of the vision in history, while its complete fulfilment awaits a future antichrist (Rev 11:2-3; 13:3-9; 17:7-14) who will attack Israel as a nation, its prince, the Lord Jesus Christ, and its temple in the end time.

Gabriel explained the symbolism of the ram and the he-goat (8:20-22). He then devoted four verses (8:23-26) to describing the little horn, which is both the Antiochus IV Epiphanes of history and also the antichrist of the future.

Antiochus (175–164 BC) was the eighth ruler in the Syrian dynasty that descended from Seleucus, one of Alexander's generals. He thus fulfilled the prophecy that he would come to power *in the latter part* of the reign of the four kingdoms (**8:23a**). There is no doubt that he was a cruel and cunning *master of intrigue* (**8:23b**). On the death of his brother, Seleucus Philopator, Antiochus used flattery and bribery to attain the throne (**8:24a**; 11:21) despite not being the rightful heir. Once crowned, he gave himself the name Epiphanes, meaning 'illustrious', and set out to destroy Judaism and substitute the worship of Zeus Olympius for that of Jehovah in Jerusalem. He identified himself with Jupiter and wished to be worshipped too. So mad was he in this regard that he was called Epimanes, meaning 'madman'. These characteristics are predicted in 8:24-25 (see also 11:36).

None of the Jews' previous conquerors (Nebuchadnezzar – 4:31-34; Darius – 6:27-28; Cyrus – Ezra 1:2-4; or Artaxerxes Longimanus – Ezra 1:11) had systematically opposed the Jewish religion. Thus the Jews needed to be warned of what was coming to prepare them for the struggle against Antiochus. The Maccabean revolt, sparked by Antiochus' desecration of the temple in 171 BC, was a fruit of Daniel's prophecy (1 Macc 2:59). Under Judas Maccabeus the temple was cleansed and restored on December 25, 165 BC (see the 2300 days of 8:14).

Daniel predicted that *he will be destroyed, but not by human power* (**8:25**). Antiochus is said to have died of grief and remorse in Babylon (1 Macc 6:8-16). The future antichrist will also be destroyed without human intervention (Rev 19:20-21).

Daniel was so overwhelmed by this vision that he was ill for days before recovering and resuming his work (**8:27**).

9:1-9:27 Searching the Scriptures, Seeking God

Babylon had fallen. Nebuchadnezzar was long dead. But Judah was still in captivity. Daniel must have wondered, 'What's next on God's agenda?' As a prayerful man, Daniel knew that it was time to search the Scriptures and seek the Lord.

9:1-2 Daniel's Panting for Truth

The first year of Darius the Mede (538 BC) was a time of transition (**9:1**). The Babylonian Empire had ended and the Medo-Persian one begun. Cyrus the Persian ruled from his headquarters at Ecbatana, and appointed Darius ruler over Babylon. Darius appointed Daniel to his cabinet (6:1-2). But Daniel had interests outside Babylonia, and was concerned about the fate of his people. So he started searching the Scriptures. He studied and prayed over Jeremiah's prophecy that God would punish the Babylonians after the seventy years of captivity were over (**9:2**; see also Jer 25:11-12 and 29:10).

Daniel demonstrates what it means to pray in accordance with God's will. Such prayer involves knowing God's word and offering it back to him by citing his covenant promises in prayer. Unfortunately, to many believers in Africa, the Bible is largely a closed book. Someone has said, 'if you want to hide a thing from an African, put it in a book.' The church in Africa must put an end to such an adage! It must teach and preach the Bible, and our prayers must be informed by the word.

9:3-19 Daniel's Prayer for God's Mercy

Daniel allowed what he had heard in God's word to burden him as he turned to seek God in passionate prayer and fasting (**9:3**). He did not see the issue as something affecting the nation and not himself, but he took it personally, despite the fact that he must have been almost eighty-three years old. He had been in Babylon for nearly seventy years, but he had not forgotten Jerusalem nor the law of his God. He knew that Judah was in captivity because of its sin (9:5-15). He also knew that Jehovah was loving, compassionate, kind and full of mercy (**9:4, 9, 18**). He understood God's covenant that 'if my people ... will humble themselves and pray and seek my face and turn from their wicked ways, then I ... will hear from heaven and will forgive their sin and will heal their land' (2 Chr 7:14). It was not emotionalism that drove Daniel to prayer, it was his knowledge of the word of God. One can almost hear Daniel say: 'Give me Judah or I die!'

How many African Christians carry this type of burden for their nations? We tend to blame others, especially leaders, and excuse ourselves. But Daniel does not say 'they have sinned' but *we have sinned* (**9:5, 6, 7, 8, 15**). His approach is a truly African one that recognizes that 'I am because we are!' He recognizes that 'God resists the proud but gives grace to the humble' (Prov 3:34; 1 Pet 5:5). His agenda is God-centred: *O Lord, listen! O Lord, forgive! O Lord, hear and act! For your sake, O my God, do not delay, because your city and your people bear your Name* (**9:19**).

When a prayer is about nothing but God's own interest, it cannot go unanswered.

9:20-23 Gabriel's Courier Service

Daniel was undoubtedly a man of prayer. Four of the twelve chapters record him praying. Some 125 of the 356 verses in the book deal with Daniel's prayer. In chapter 2 he prayed until God revealed the king's dream. In chapter 6 he prayed and the angel shut the lions' mouths. It is no surprise that his prayer was used against him by his enemies in chapter 6, or that he was *highly esteemed* in heaven's throne room (**9:23**; 10:11, 18). For Daniel, prayer was work! It should be so for us too. He prayed until there was a breakthrough. He never gave up!

Here he continued to pray until an angel, Gabriel, brought him an answer in the form of a third vision, the scope of which gives us a glimpse of Daniel's heart for God. Interestingly, Daniel was given insight to understand the vision before it was even revealed (9:22-23).

9:24-27 God's Prophetic Programme in Seventy Weeks

This portion of Daniel's vision speaks of *seventy 'sevens'* (**9:24a**), which are interpreted as weeks, with one week also equalling seven years. In the Bible, the number seven represents completion and perfection. It is the number for deity, while six is the number for humanity. This number reminds us that in God's economy, things don't just happen: they happen at God's perfect time. 'When the time had fully come' Jesus Christ came into the world (Gal 4:4). 'When the full number of the Gentiles has come in', Israel will turn to

God for salvation (Rom 11:26). Being all-knowing, God can be exact in predicting future events.

All of Daniel's earlier dreams and visions had been highly symbolic, but in this one the meaning is more straightforward. The source, content and beneficiary of the message are unambiguous (9:23). Gabriel made it clear that what was being revealed was a divine decree, meaning that there was no way it could be changed, and that it applied specifically to Daniel's people and his holy city of Jerusalem (**9:24b**). God has six goals in mind, which can be subdivided into two categories. The first three goals (*to finish transgression, to put an end to sin, to atone for wickedness*) all deal with the taking away of sin, and thus with the negative side of deliverance. The remaining three (*to bring in everlasting righteousness, to seal up vision and prophecy and to anoint the most holy*) deal with the establishment of righteousness, and thus with the positive side of deliverance.

The first three goals were fulfilled in principle at Christ's first coming. Their fulfilment in terms of Israel as a nation will take place at his second coming when the nation will truly turn to God and the last three items will also be fulfilled.

Gabriel refers to a decree for the restoration and rebuilding of Jerusalem (**9:25**). This may be Cyrus' decree issued in 538–537 BC (Ezra 1:1-4; 6:3-5), or the one that Artaxerxes issued to Ezra in 458 BC (Ezra 7:11-26), or the one that the same Artaxerxes issued to Nehemiah in 445–444 BC (Neh 2:5-8, 17-18). Given the date of this vision (the first year of Darius' reign), the urgency of Daniel's prayer, and God's promise to return his people to their land after seventy years, Cyrus' decree is probably the one referred to.

There are two gaps of an unspecified number of years within the framework of seventy weeks laid out here. The first gap is between the seven weeks and the sixty-two weeks (9:25), and the second is between the sixty-nine weeks and the seventieth week (**9:26-27**). The first gap shrouds the exact date of Christ's first coming, and the second gap that of his second coming. Accordingly it is safe to recognize the broad timeline that Scripture sets out, but we need to remain silent where Scripture is silent.

Using the broad timeline, the prophetic agenda that Daniel sees is as follows. First, there will be a decree to rebuild Jerusalem (9:25a – see also Ezra 1:1-4; Isa 44:28-45:7). Next, the Messiah, *the ruler,* will come (9:25b). The date referred to could be the angelic announcement of Christ's birth, or his Father's authentication of him at his baptism, or his first public reading at Nazareth (Luke 4:14-21), or his triumphant entry to Jerusalem. After the sixty-two weeks, the Messiah is crucified (9:26a). His death is followed by yet another destruction of Jerusalem and the temple (9:26b). Evangelical scholars generally consider that this prophecy was fulfilled in AD 70 when the Roman legions destroyed Jerusalem. Finally, during the seventieth week, the antichrist

will arise (9:27). Key features of the regime of the antichrist will be a week-long covenant (that is, one that lasts seven years), the breaking of this covenant in the middle of the week, the stopping of temple worship, the setting up of an abomination of desolation (see Matt 24:15) and the defeat and destruction of the antichrist. This scenario matches the activities of the little horn described in chapter 7 and in 11:36-45.

10:1-11:1 Spiritual Warfare in the Unseen World

Paul identifies the true nature of believers' conflicts: 'Our struggle is not against flesh and blood, but against the rulers, against the authorities, against the powers of this dark world and against the spiritual forces of evil in the heavenly realms' (Eph 6:12). These evil forces employ human agents, just as God empowers believers to do his will. So Daniel devotes the last three chapters of his book to a series of spiritual conflicts between superhuman intelligences – good and bad – that are striving to control the affairs of nations and shape human destinies.

10:1-9 A Vision of the Pre-incarnate Christ

It was during the third year of Cyrus King of Persia (536 BC) that Daniel was given his fourth and final vision, which occupies chapters 10, 11 and 12 of his book (**10:1**). The restoration and rebuilding of the temple had begun (Ezra 1–3), but enemies had forced it to stop (Ezra 4:4-5). News of this must have broken Daniel's heart and forced him to seek God's face afresh. He fasted and mourned, eating no tasty food, meat or wine and using no lotions for three weeks (**10:2-3**). What a consistent man Daniel was! The discipline of fasting, searching the Scriptures, and seeking God that he had engaged in as a teenager (see chs. 1–2) had remained with him into his old age. By this time he was probably about eighty-five years old, but rather than settling into spiritual retirement and waiting to die, Daniel proved that old age can be a time of intense spiritual activity and accomplishment (see also Luke 2:36-37). God rewarded him by giving him a glimpse into the spiritual dynamics of the great conflict that was going on in the unseen heavenly realms for the control of his nation and people, a conflict that would continue to the end of human history.

First, he was shown who was and still is in charge: *a man dressed in linen* (**10:5**). This was not the angel Gabriel, with whom Daniel had spoken twice before. It seems likely that this man was the pre-incarnate Christ, for the language is similar to that used in 7:13, Ezekiel 1:26 and in John's vision of Christ (Rev 1:12-20). He stands 'above the waters', set apart, where even angels dare not stand, and the angels appeal to him as having superior knowledge (12:6; see also Heb 1:2-8). The effects of the vision upon Daniel and his colleagues also support this identification. Even though those who were with Daniel did not see the vision, they knew something was happening. They fled in terror, as did Paul's companions on the Damascus road (**10:7**; Acts 9:6-7). Daniel himself was overcome with awe and left without strength (**10:8**). The Lord recognized his pain and panic and soothed him into a deep sleep (**10:9**).

How awesome and majestic is the Lord's presence! He reigns supreme in heaven and on earth.

10:10-13 Battle of the Angels

A hand touched Daniel, who was lying on the ground completely exhausted, and set him on his hands and knees, trembling (**10:10**). The breathtaking vision had sapped his strength. Then he heard a voice he recognized, addressing him with a title he had heard before, *O Daniel, you who are highly esteemed* (**10:11**; see also 9:23). Encouraged and comforted, Daniel was able to rise shakily to his feet

The one who had touched him disclosed that a war had been going on in the spirit world for the past twenty-one days – ever since Daniel began to pray (**10:12**). All the time Daniel had been wrestling with God in prayer, the angelic messenger sent to deliver an answer had been delayed by someone referred to as *the prince of the Persian kingdom* (**10:13**). Since Michael is referred to as *Daniel's prince* (10:21), and another angel is referred to as *the prince of Greece* (10:20), the prince of Persia must be an angel specially assigned to Persia. Since he resisted God's messenger, he must be a messenger of Satan, a fallen angel, a demon. Satan appoints special emissaries to influence governments against the people of God.

Around the world, church buildings have been set on fire and Christians killed for no known crime except faith in Jesus. Such behaviour defies logic. It is satanic, demonic. Should Christians respond in kind? No, for to do so would violate Christ's gospel of love and of non-retaliation (Matt 5:38-48). When believers leave revenge to God, he will send reinforcements if the situation demands it, as he did in the case of Daniel. The one sent to help here was the Archangel Michael, who is mentioned only three times in the OT (10:13, 21; 12:1) and twice in the NT (Jude 9; Rev 12:7). He is identified as *one of the chief princes,* indicating his high rank. He was the one assigned to be the prince of Israel, God's chosen people (12:1).

Daniel's experience does not justify praying to and seeking help from angels, as some African churches do. Daniel prayed to God, and God was the one who responded by sending his angels with a message to Daniel. This is appropriate, for angels are 'ministering spirits sent forth to serve those who will inherit salvation' (Heb 1:14).

In the battle of the angels, God's holy angels always win (Rev 12:7-12). God has never lost a battle to Satan.

10:14-21; 11:1 Bewildered by the Vision

Daniel was told that this vision, like all the others, *concerns a time yet to come* (**10:14**). All his visions teach that ultimately the saints of the Most High shall inherit the kingdom after a lifelong, bitter war.

Daniel was speechless. However, following a touch on his lips, he gathered enough strength to say how he felt: *I am overcome with anguish because of the vision … my strength is gone and I can hardly breathe* (**10:16-17**).

The angel touched him a third time (**10:18**), giving him strength. He was also encouraged by being addessed yet again as *highly esteemed* and by being told *Do not be afraid …. Peace! Be strong now* (**10:19**). Time and time again God has spoken peace to his servants when they are perplexed or troubled (see also Matt 14:27; John 20:19, 20, 21).

Strengthened by these words, Daniel was ready to receive two more disclosures. The first was that more angelic battles lay ahead, including one against the prince of Greece, the kingdom that would succeed the Medo-Persian Empire (**10:20**). The second disclosure is mistakenly marked as the first verse of the next chapter, but is actually part of the conclusion of this chapter. Gabriel tells Daniel that he and Michael help each other. Here Michael assisted Gabriel (10:13), but in the past, during the first year of Darius, their roles had been reversed (**11:1**). It seems that Gabriel is referring to events at the time of the Jews' return to Judah under Sheshbazzar (see Ezra 1:1-11).

11:2-11:45 Prophecies of a Dark Future

Daniel had been praying and fasting regarding the future of the newly emancipated people (10:2-3). In response, Gabriel had been dispatched to tell Daniel what is written in the Book of Truth (10:21; 11:2). The message is both sour (chapter 11) and sweet (chapter 12). Part of it deals with historical events shortly after Daniel's time, a major portion deals with future events, and a small part with the end of the world.

Chapter 11 of Daniel has been attacked by many critics over the centuries. They claim that it shows that the book of Daniel is historical fiction written about 165 BC to motivate the Jews to resist Antiochus IV Epiphanes. The reason they make this claim is that the first 35 verses of these chapter contain at least 135 prophesies that have been fulfilled literally in history. But as Walvoord says, 'the issue is a clear-cut question as to whether God is omniscient about the future. If He is, revelation may be just as detailed as God elects to make it, and detailed prophecy becomes no more difficult or incredible than broad predictions.'

11:2 Persia in Decline

Daniel was told that four more kings would reign in Persia after Cyrus before the empire fell to the Greeks (**11:2a**).

History has proved these kings to be Cambyses, Pseudo-Smerdis, Darius Hystaspes and Xerxes I (apparently the Ahasuerus of Esther). The focus here is on the fourth king, who is said to *be far richer than all the others* (**11:2b**). Xerxes I (486–465 BC – Ezra 4:6) led an army of 2 641 000 men against Greece. It took him over four years to build such a huge army, and it could only be sustained at the expense of other national interests. His ambition proved counter-productive, and it was the very size of his army that defeated him. At the battle of Salamis in 480 BC, Xerxes I was defeated by the Greeks and driven back to Asia.

The history of Africa since independence in the 1960s is littered with ambitious leaders like Xerxes I, who have ravaged their nations, plundered national resources, and plunged their people into nonsensical wars. Oh that we would learn from history 'that all who draw the sword will die by the sword' (Matt 26:52). While Xerxes represented the acme of Persian power, he also represented the start of its dissolution.

11:3-4 Rise and Fragmentation of the Greek Empire

Gabriel goes on to announce the rise of *a mighty king* (**11:3a**) who will rule with great power. The account matches the career of Alexander the Great (356–323 BC), known for his amazing strength and military brilliance. As described in Daniel 8:5-8, he conquered all of Persia in one continuous campaign.

The prophecy said that the king will *do as he pleases* (**11:3b**). Alexander imposed his will on his army and on the people he conquered. He succeeded in keeping his army intact for thousands of miles of travel and campaigning, and his empire stretched from Greece in the west to India in the east. However, when he died prematurely in 323 BC at the zenith of his power (8:8), the prophecy came true: *his empire will be broken up and parcelled out towards the four winds of heaven* (**11:4**). Alexander's two sons were killed, and his great empire was divided among four of his generals. Daniel had prophesied all this in 539 BC.

11:5-20 Power Struggle Between South and North

Of the four divisions of Alexander's empire, Gabriel spoke of only two, which lie to the south and north of Palestine. The kingdom of the South is clearly Egypt (11:8) and the kingdom of the North is Syria. Syria was not as well known as Egypt, and that is why it is described in terms of its location. For about 150 years after Alexander's death these two kingdoms were at war, and Palestine was their battleground.

The king of the South (**11:5a**) is clearly Ptolemy I Soter, one of Alexander's generals, who became the satrap of Egypt in 323 BC and proclaimed himself king in 304 BC. He continued to reign until 283 BC. His commander who *will become even stronger than he and will rule his own kingdom with great power* (**11:5b**) has been identified as Seleucus I Nicator, a lesser general under Alexander. He was sent as satrap to Babylonia in 321 BC, but was forced to flee to Egypt by another general, Antigonus. With the help of Ptolemy, Seleucus fought back and defeated Antigonus. He not only regained control of Babylonia but also became stronger than Ptolemy. He rapidly expanded his kingdom to include Syria and Media, and assumed the title of king in the same year as Ptolemy.

The descendants of these two kings tried to cement their friendship through a political marriage (**11:6**). Ptolemy II Philadelphus gave his daughter Berenice to Antiochus II Theos, forcing him to divorce his Syrian wife, Laodice. Within a few years of the marriage, Ptolemy II died. Antiochus II then took back his first wife, who took revenge for her earlier humiliation by murdering her husband, his Egyptian wife, and their infant son.

A number of African freedom fighters, including Kwame Nkrumah, Kamuzu Banda, Daniel Arap Moi and Nelson Mandela, also entered into political marriages and divorces to strengthen them in the fight for national independence. The church was silent on the topic, rather than confronting these leaders as Nathan did David.

In 246 BC Berenice's brother, Ptolemy III, succeeded their father Ptolemy II (**11:7**). He invaded Syria to avenge his sister's murder, and carried off booty that included 40 000 talents of silver and 2500 images of idols previously taken out of Egypt to Persia by Cambyses (**11:8**). The young Syrian ruler, Seleucus II Callinicus, survived this invasion by staying in a remote part of Asia Minor. After Ptolemy had returned to Egypt, Seleucus recovered much of the lost territory and was also able to rebuild and strengthen his army, prior to launching the counter-attack prophesied in **11:9**. However, he was forced to *retreat to his own country*.

Seleucus Callinicus had two sons (**11:10**). The older became Seleucus III Ceraunus, but died four years later, to be succeeded by his younger brother, Antiochus III the Great. The sons continued their father's war with Egypt, and eventually Antiochus' army of 70 000 soldiers regained control of Palestine.

The king of the South at this time was the easy-going Ptolemy IV Philopator (221–204 BC). His army had a surprise victory over Antiochus at the battle of Raphia on the southern Palestinian border, capturing a large Syrian army (**11:11**). But success made Ptolemy proud and lethargic. He did not follow up his victory with more attacks, thus fulfilling the prophesy that *he will not remain triumphant* (**11:12**). In this, he was like many contemporary Christians who celebrate their past victories over the devil while forgetting that the devil leaves only to regroup (Luke 4:13).

Some years later, allied with Philip V of Macedonia, Antiochus the Great returned with a larger army to wage war against the son of Ptolemy IV Philopator, who had died in 203 BC (**11:13**). The new king of Egypt, Ptolemy V Epiphanes, was not only young but also inexperienced in warfare. As prophesied, his forces were *powerless to resist* Antiochus the Great (11:13-16). The Jews aided the Syrians in driving the Egyptians out of the Holy Land (**11:14**). Little did they realize what the Syrians would later do to them under the demonic reign of Antiochus IV Epiphanes (**11:16**).

Another diplomatic marriage was arranged between the two warring dynasties. Hoping to gain absolute control over Egypt, Antiochus the Great gave his daughter Cleopatra to be the wife of Ptolemy V in 192 BC (**11:17**). The ploy failed, for instead of backing her father's plans, Cleopatra remained loyal to her husband. Disappointed but not discouraged, Antiochus turned his campaigns to coastlands of the Aegean Sea (**11:18**). He captured a number of the islands and would have occupied Greece had he not been stopped by the rising power of Rome under Scipio (11:18), who routed Antiochus' army at Magnesia in 190 BC. Returning in disgrace to his own land, Antiochus III was killed while plundering a temple in Elam (**11:19**).

He was succeeded by his son Seleucus IV Philopator, who inherited a great debt to Rome. In order to meet the enormous annual payments, he sent tax collectors throughout his kingdom (**11:20**). His prime minister, Heliodorus, was sent to plunder the temple treasury in Jerusalem, but was foiled by divine intervention (2 Macc 3). Seleucus reigned for eleven years and died mysteriously, possibly assassinated by Heliodorus.

Africans are all too familiar with the problems caused by national debt. Excessive borrowing from the West, especially from former colonial masters, has meant that the yoke of imperial colonialism has not been completely broken. Many African thinkers agree with the late Nkrumah that political freedom without economic emancipation is a makeshift.

11:21-35 Persecution of the Jews

A terrible period followed for the Jews. Fifteen verses are devoted to the reign of Antiochus IV Epiphanes (175–164 BC), the son of Antiochus III and brother of Seleucus IV. He is introduced as *a contemptible person* (**11:21**), one who cannot be trusted, a schemer and a deceiver. He is the 'little horn' of Daniel 8:9-27 (see the commentary there). He is called the antichrist of the OT and is seen as prefiguring the antichrist of the end time. Here the stories of the two antichrists are put back to back, not merely for emphasis but because they both involve open hatred of God and persecution of the Jewish people.

Antiochus' rise to power met with internal resistance from forces loyal to Heliodorus (**11:22**), but he countered this with foreign assistance and intrigues. He murdered the high priest in Jerusalem, Onias III, who is referred to in the prophecy as a *prince of the covenant* (11:22). (In 11:28, 30 and 32 the word 'covenant' is used to refer to the Jewish state, which was a theocracy at that time with the high priest as its head.)

Antiochus' foreign policy towards Egypt began positively (**11:23-24**). His sister Cleopatra had been in the powerful position of queen mother since the death of her husband in 181 BC. Thus it was easy for Antiochus and his nephew Ptolemy Philometor to reach a gentleman's agreement (11:23). But Antiochus always had an ulterior motive for his actions, for he believed that the end justifies the means. By making and breaking alliances and through bribery, he extended his power throughout Syria, Palestine, Edom, Ammon and Moab (11:24).

His friendship with Egypt soon frayed. Antiochus attacked his nephew and defeated him at the border of Egypt in 170 BC, aided by a mutiny within Ptolemy's own army (**11:25-26**). The two kings agreed to a truce, but while the they were talking peace, their hearts were *bent on evil* (**11:27**). Africa has frequently witnessed such hypocritical peace negotiations. We have seen them repeatedly in the long and destructive war between the government in Khartoum in the north of Sudan and the Sudan People's Liberation Army in the south. While millions die, leaders from both sides meet and sign ceasefire agreements in neighbouring capitals like Nairobi and Kampala. Similarly, warring parties from Liberia met in Accra, Ghana to discuss peace, while at the same time battles were launched around Monrovia, the capital. If Antiochus' behaviour is typical of the antichrist, then Scripture is right when it says that there are many antichrists in the world already (1 John 2:18).

On his return from Egypt, Antiochus ransacked the temple in Jerusalem and put down a small insurrection there. As predicted, he returned to Syria with lots of loot (**11:28**).

It comes as no surprise that Antiochus attacked Egypt again two years later, in 168 BC (**11:29-30**). This time, however, his attack was repulsed because the Egyptians had succeeded in getting support from the Romans (11:30). Humiliated and frustrated, he turned his anger against the Jews on his way home, in the actions recorded in 1 and 2 Maccabees. Conniving with apostate Jews (*those who forsake the holy covenant* – 11:30), Antiochus polluted the holy altar by offering a pig on it, forbade the daily sacrifices, erected an image of the Greek god Zeus Olympius, and declared the Mosaic ceremonies illegal. These actions were described as setting up *the abomination that causes desolation* (**11:31**). The parallel prophecy in Daniel 8:23-25 covers the same story, and Christ refers to it in Matthew 24:15.

This was a time of great trials for the Jews. Antiochus' actions precipitated the Maccabean revolt, which was cruelly suppressed with tens of thousands of Jews perishing (**11:33-34**). Knowing that the Jews would not fight on the Sabbath, the Syrian soldiers deliberately attacked on that day. They slaughtered, burned and captured many and plundered their possessions. Mattathias Maccabeus and his five sons, together with a large number of others who truly knew Jehovah, stood firm even at the expense of their lives (11:32). Like the three Hebrew teenagers in Daniel 3, they refused to compromise their faith or to worship an idol.

This entire story prefigures the rise of a future antichrist during the Great Tribulation. Yet the call to follow Jesus Christ at any time implies cross-bearing and may bring Christians into serious persecution, as many Muslims have found when they turn to Christ. Amazingly, persecution such as that described here has a purifying and refining effect, making those who survive it better Christians in terms of moral uprightness, spiritual commitment, effectiveness in witness and steadfastness (11:35).

11:36-45 Wilful King of the End Time

The prophecy moves quickly on to the even more horrendous story of a man who will make himself a god, worship himself and demand worship from his subjects, wage war and conquer many nations, but will eventually come to his end. Described as the *king who will do what he pleases* (11:36a), he is the antichrist of Daniel 7:24-27; 8:23-25; 9:26-27 and Revelation 13, 17.

Nothing is said about where this wilful king will come from (11:36). He is clearly neither from the south nor the north, for the two traditional rivals unite to oppose the newcomer (11:40). Although he is similar to Antiochus IV Epiphanes in some respects, he is a distinct character. Like Lucifer of Isaiah 14:13-14, he will claim supremacy above every god and will blaspheme the true God (11:36b; see also 2 Thess 2:4; Rev 13:6). Though he acts independently and prospers in what he does, the text makes it clear that his power is not infinite. His success and freedom will last for only seven years (9:27).

Because of the statement that *he will show no regard for the gods of his fathers* (11:37) some African theologians have argued that the antichrist cannot be African. Africans venerate their ancestors and love to worship traditional deities. The *one desired of woman* (11:37) is the Messiah, whom every Jewish woman longed to bear. The main point of this verse, however, is that the antichrist will come from a religious background but will turn his back on it. He will be irreligious, unsentimental, and utterly full of himself. His lavish spending on military hardware will seem like religious offerings. His ideas will be strange to his forebears (11:38).

The time at which the antichrist will operate is described as *the appointed time* (11:35), *the time of wrath* (11:36) and *the time of the end* (11:40). Commentators agree that it will mark the end of world history as we know it. There will be two types of war: one human (11:40-45), the other angelic (12:1). On the human front it will be 'the mother of all wars'

with the two archenemies, the king of the South and the king of the North, fighting in coalition against the antichrist. He will be fought on land and sea (and, in modern times, in the air) (11:40), in something reminiscent of the Gulf Wars against Saddam Hussein of Iraq. Yet despite their military might and the sophistication of their weaponry, the coalition forces will not succeed. The antichrist will gain widespread success in many nations including the Holy Land, Egypt, Libya and Ethiopia, but he will not gain absolute control of the whole world (11:41-43). Edom, Moab and Ammon, all lying to the south-east of Palestine (in modern Jordan) are among the nations not delivered to him (11:41).

While he is occupied in looting Africa, he will receive reports of a new coalition forming against him in the east and the north (possibly a coalition of the Chinese and the Russians). He will react quickly, counterattacking with devastating force (11:44). Then he will establish his headquarters *between the seas at the beautiful holy mountain* (11:45), probably at Jerusalem, which is situated between the Mediterranean Sea and the Dead Sea. Yet in spite of his military victories, this last world ruler *shall come to his end, and no one will help him* (11:45). This is startling! How can such a great warrior come to a lonely, quiet end without a spectacular final battle? The answer has already been given: 'Yet he will be destroyed, but not by human power' (8:25). Chapter 12 goes on to describe the divine intervention.

12:1-13 Prophecies of a Glorious End

A lion once wanted to prove his supremacy. So he went to various groups of animals, asking: 'Who is the king of the animals?' Trembling, all acknowledged, 'You, of course'. But when he approached an elephant with the same question, it did not reply. So the lion repeated his question a second time, and a third. At that the elephant wrapped his trunk around the lion, lifted him up in the air and smashed him to the ground. Humiliated, the lion shambled off, mumbling, 'You don't have to be angry just because you don't know the answer.'

This story is a metaphor for the humiliation that awaits Satan in his battle against the Lord and humanity at large.

12:1 Rise and Role of the Archangel Michael

The chapter opens with repeated references to *At that time* (12:1 – three times in 12:1 alone, and again in 12:4, 7, 9 and 11). It seems that Michael does not just appear at one specific moment, but that there is a period of time in which he will be active, a period that will coincide with the time of the antichrist (11:45). Michael will arise either when the antichrist starts his career (11:36), or, more probably, in the middle of the antichrist's career when he turns his attention to the Beautiful Land (11:41). Several prophecies refer to the time of the antichrist as a period of distress, darkness and gloom (9:27; see also Deut 4:30; Jer 30:7; Joel 2:2). It will last for seven years, Daniel's week of years. During the first half of these years, the antichrist will be friendly to Israel, but then he will break his covenant (9:27) and turn on Israel. Jeremiah describes this as 'a time of trouble for Jacob' (Jer 30:7). The services of Michael will be needed!

Michael had aided Gabriel when he was being prevented from delivering his message (10:13, 21). Here he is referred to as a guardian angel charged with the protection of Daniel's people, the nation of Israel. He is ready to fight, for it is a critical time for Israel. Satan's agent, the antichrist, is about to unleash the most horrendous genocide ever seen in human history.

Details of what Michael will do are revealed in Revelation 12:1-9. The battle will be final and decisive. It seems, however, that this victory will precipitate the antichrist's wrath, popularly referred to as the Great Tribulation (see Matt 24:21-22). This time of trouble will last for three and a half years (12:7, 11; Rev 12:12-14). Unfortunately not every Israelite will enjoy protection and deliverance, but only those whose names are found in the book. The immediate text does not tell us the criterion for inclusion in that book, but from an earlier revelation (7:13-14), we know that it is acknowledging Jesus Christ as the Messiah.

A rabbi once commented to a Protestant clergyman: 'You Christians are expecting the second coming of your Saviour, but we Jews are looking for the first coming of our Messiah.' The clergyman asked: 'How will you recognize him?' While the rabbi pondered, the clergyman quoted the prophet Zechariah, 'And they shall look on me, the one they have pierced' (Zech 12:10). There is only one way of salvation for all peoples and all times: the cross of Jesus Christ.

12:2-4 Resurrection of the Righteous and the Wicked

Thousands, both righteous and wicked, will die during the Tribulation. Many millions (including Daniel – 12:13) will die before it starts. But there is life beyond the grave (**12:2a**), a life either of blessing or of eternal contempt (**12:2b**). Those Jews and Gentiles whose names are in the book will end up sharing life eternal with Christ their Saviour and Lord. Those whose names are missing from the book will end up far from Christ, enduring everlasting shame.

Revelation 20:4-6 states that those saints who die during the tribulation because of their testimony for Jesus and because of the word of God 'shall come to life and reign with Christ a thousand years' but 'the rest of the dead did not come to life until the thousand years were ended'. Gabriel was content to tell Daniel about the fact of resurrection, without going into details of its timing.

Those who have invested in sharing the Gospel with others will reign with Christ. They will be rewarded for having led *many to righteousness* (**12:3**) and are described as wise, with wisdom here defined as soul-winning (Prov 11:30).

They will shine with the brightness of a starry heaven, thus manifesting the glory of the Lord (Ps 19:1). A great African Christian puts it this way: 'You are not yet a disciple of Christ until you have discipled another disciple.'

Daniel was now told to close up the words securely and to preserve what he had written for generations to come (**12:4**). It would be relevant at all times, but particularly during the Great Tribulation. A similar instruction had been given to him at the time of his second vision (8:26).

'All Scripture is God-breathed and is useful for teaching, rebuking, correcting and training in righteousness, so that the man of God may be thoroughly equipped for every good work' (2 Tim 3:16-17). The revelation given to Daniel increases our understanding of the events of the end time. The creation of the State of Israel in 1948 has led to a revival of interest in prophecy, with numerous conferences being held and thousands of books published. Some have been too quick to give dates or to label prominent leaders like Anwar Sadat as the antichrist. Events in the Middle East, wars in the Gulf, the introduction of a common currency for the European Union, the transformation of the OAU into the African Union, global terrorism, and other global events have increased people's anxiety about the future and about the proximity of the end times. Even Daniel was nervous at the prospect of what lay ahead!

12:5-12 Duration of the Great Tribulation

As Gabriel finished speaking, Daniel looked from his position on the bank of the Tigris River (10:4) and saw two other angels and *the man clothed in linen* (**12:5-6**). This man was definitely the pre-incarnate Christ of 10:6. One of the angels inquired how long the Great Tribulation would last (12:6). The Lord solemnly swore that it would last *a time, times and half a time* (**12:7**). This answer, which means three and a half years, has been consistent throughout the book (see also 7:25; 12:11; Rev 12:14).

As if anticipating Daniel's next question (12:8), the Lord also explained that *when the power of the holy people has been finally broken, all these things will be completed* (12:7). In other words, the Lord will allow the persecution of his people to last as long as is necessary to break their self-sufficiency and make them rely on Christ as their rightful king. It is not the antichrist but the Lord who is setting the schedule.

Like Habakkuk, who could not understand why the Lord would use a wicked nation to punish his people (Hab 1:12-2:1), Daniel was bewildered. So he asked: *My Lord, what will the outcome of all this be?* (**12:8**). The Lord responded by assuring Daniel that what he had said would undoubtedly happen (12:9). Daniel need not worry about the details. Then the Lord expands on the purpose he has already mentioned in 12:7, and says that the purpose of the suffering is to make his people ready to meet him (**12:10**). In all Christian suffering, two invisible forces are at work: the devil and the Lord. The devil uses trials to try to break and destroy believers (Job 1), but the Lord uses them to refine, reform and revive us spiritually (Ps 119:67, 71). So the Lord unequivocally states that the wise will understand what he is doing (see also Rom 8:28).

The Lord then repeats the information about the Great Tribulation that had already been given in 8:11; 9:27 and 11:31. The number of days is similar to that mentioned in 7:25, where three and a half years is equivalent to 1260 days (using the Jewish calendar, which had 30 days in each month). The text here speaks of 1290 (**12:11**) days, which means that an additional 30 days are added to the time in 7:25, as well as an additional 75 days to reach the 1335 days mentioned in **12:12**. These extra days may be required for logistic and administrative reasons in mopping up after the war and setting up Christ's millennial kingdom.

12:13 Rest, Resurrection and Reward

The book ends with a glorious assertion of the Lord's sovereignty and of Daniel's final destiny. Daniel, and all who trust in the Lord, face not death and destruction but abundant life. Daniel is told, *As for you, go your way till the end* (**12:13**). In other words, he is not to be afraid but is to live life to the fullest! As in 12:9, where the same expression

occurs, the Lord is telling Daniel to stop worrying about these confusing visions of future events. The Lord is in control.

The Lord then assures Daniel that he will rest in death, and in due time rise again with the company of the righteous mentioned in 12:2. We inscribe R.I.P. on tombstones, but not every dead person lies resting in peace. The story of the rich man and Lazarus (Luke 16:19-31) and other parables clearly demonstrate that the wicked do not rest, nor are they in peace.

Daniel will not only enjoy peaceful rest but also an inheritance in the Lord's millennial kingdom. Just as Daniel faithfully served Nebuchadnezzar, Belshazzar, Darius and Cyrus, so he will serve Jesus Christ, the King of kings (see Rev 5:10). Daniel confronts us with a challenge: It is not how well we start a race that matters, but how well we finish it! Make sure you finish well.

Tokunboh Adeyemo

Further Reading

Luck, G. Coleman. *Daniel.* EvBC. Chicago: Moody, 1958.

Walvoord, John F. *Daniel: The Key to Prophetic Revelation.* Chicago: Moody, 1971.

Wood, Leon. *A Commentary on Daniel.* Grand Rapids, Zondervan, 1973.

HOSEA

Hosea is the first of the twelve Minor Prophets. They are not called 'minor' because they are less important than the Major Prophets (Isaiah, Jeremiah, Ezekiel and Daniel) but because their books are much shorter.

Hosea wrote just before the fall of the northern kingdom to the Assyrians in 721 BC. So, like Amos, Micah and Isaiah, Hosea prophesied almost eight hundred years before the birth of Christ.

While Micah and Isaiah prophesied to the southern kingdom (Judah), Hosea and Amos prophesied to the northern kingdom (Israel). Hosea, however, was a native of the northern kingdom, while Amos was a 'foreign' prophet, having come from the south (Amos 7:10-15). Hosea uses the term 'Ephraim' to refer to the northern kingdom (4:17; see also Isa 7:8-9, 17), while he refers to the southern kingdom as Judah (6:4).

The Prophet

Hosea, whose name means 'Yahweh saves', was a passionate man. Deep emotions are seen in the passages on his troubled marriage and in his abundant use of some quite extraordinary imagery to describe his relationship with his God, with his wife and children and with Israel, as well as Israel's relationship with God. Apart from the parallels between Hosea's marriage and Yahweh's relationship with Israel, Israel is compared to a stubborn heifer (4:16; 10:11), a flat cake (7:8), a dove (7:11), a wild donkey (8:9), grapes and a fig-tree (9:10), a spreading vine (10:1; 14:7), and a lily and a cedar (14:5). God compares himself to a moth (5:12), a lion (5:14; 11:10; 13:7), a leopard and a bear (13:7), and a green pine tree (14:8).

Hosea's Times

Hosea lived in troubled and chaotic times. The forty-year reign of Jeroboam II as king of Israel was followed by great political and social instability. We could compare the situation to the one too often seen in Africa today, where long periods of dictatorial rule are followed by political and social unrest. At one point in the civil war in the Republic of Liberia, the country had three heads of state – each one in control of his own segment of the small capital city. Similarly, in the Israel of Hosea's day, several coups and counter-coups took place within a very short time (2 Kings 14–15). Hosea 4:1-3 gives a sense of the deterioration of social, political and community life.

The religious situation was equally bad. From the very start of the book, Hosea accuses Israel of turning away from the Lord and going after false gods (1:2). The people had forgotten God's law as well as God's faithfulness, pro-

vision and protection since he brought them out of Egypt. Worst of all, they had forgotten God himself!

Hosea found the entire leadership of Israel and the people guilty of this apostasy and spiritual degeneration. They had corrupted their worship of God, mixing it with elements of Baal worship. The priests had failed to teach the law (4:6). The kings did not trust the Lord to protect Israel, and instead looked to Assyria and Egypt for help (7:8).

Hosea's Message

Hosea identifies Israel's basic problem as its sin in turning away from the Lord. The two most frequently used words in the book are 'return' and 'know'. These words summarize Hosea's message: 'return to the Lord' and 'know the Lord'. This return must be genuine, for God is not interested in superficial, ceremonial repentance (6:1-6). He desires repentance that leads to a life characterized by integrity of heart, mind and action.

Knowledge of the Lord is first and foremost relational. It means having an active, vital, healthy and wholesome spiritual relationship with God, knowing God with one's heart. But knowledge of God is not simply an emotional relationship. It also has a mental or cognitive dimension, for it involves studying and remembering God's law, as well as remembering the stories and traditions that tell of God's faithfulness in the past. Finally, knowledge of God also results in integrity in one's actions and leads to healthy relationships between people. There is a social and ethical component to knowing God.

Hosea is concerned that Israel's sin has so trapped it that it cannot escape. But God does not abandon Israel. Instead, like the hound of heaven in Francis Thompson's poem of that name, he pursues the nation that flees from him. Hosea expresses the terror of this pursuit by a God of justice, while also insisting that God's justice is both retributive and restorative. God pursues his people in love, longing for them to turn to him so that he can welcome them home, just as the father welcomed the prodigal son (Luke 15:11-32). Hosea recognizes that God's gracious forgiveness and compassion are the only means by which his people can ultimately be restored to him.

Structure

The book of Hosea divides into two parts. Chapters 1–3 present Hosea's marriage and children as an allegory of Israel's relationship with the Lord. Chapters 4–14 consist of a series of prophecies delivered by Hosea at various times. It is not easy to identify when all these prophecies were delivered, or even if they were delivered in the order they are recorded. Nevertheless, they make sense as they are, and they contain eternal truths about the relationship between the people of God and the Lord.

Outline of Contents

COMMENTARY

1:1 Introductory Formula

The book of Hosea opens with the traditional prophetic formula that indicates that the prophet's message is inspired and does not come from him but from the Lord (**1:1**). Hosea is then identified as the *son of Beeri* and by the historical era in which he ministered. The reigns of the kings mentioned are dealt with in 2 Kings (Jeroboam – 2 Kgs 14:23-28; Uzziah (Azariah) – 2 Kgs 15:1-7; Jotham – 2 Kgs 15:32-38; Ahaz – 2 Kgs 16:1-19; Hezekiah – 2 Kgs 18:1-20:21).

1:2-3:5 Hosea's Family

1:2-2:1 God's Command and Hosea's Response

This first chapter introduces the main themes that will be developed in the rest of the book: Israel's turning away from the Lord, the resulting judgment, restoration, and the grace and mercy of a God who is faithful, even when his people are not.

Commentators disagree on the details of Hosea's marriage. Some are so shocked at the idea of a prophet marrying a prostitute that they insist that he is merely presenting an allegory. Others argue that Gomer cannot have been a prostitute at the time Hosea married her. The position taken in this commentary is that she was probably already a prostitute at the time of their marriage.

1:2-3 Marriage to Gomer

The opening clause, *When the Lord began to speak through Hosea* (**1:2a**), reminds us that the message we are about to hear comes from the Lord, and that Hosea is only God's spokesman. It also reminds us that all the prophet does is in obedient response to the word of the Lord. His example challenges us to listen and be obedient to the Lord's message.

The first command Hosea receives from the Lord is shocking: *Go, take to yourself an adulterous wife.* The reason given for this command is that Israel has departed from the Lord and is *guilty of the vilest adultery* (**1:2b**). Thus Hosea's personal life and marriage are linked to the larger story of Israel. His situation provides a succinct introduction to the rest of the book: Israel has abandoned the Lord, but the Lord appeals to the nation to return to him and know him.

Hosea's response is unquestioning: *so he married Gomer* (**1:3**). In traditional African contexts, where kinship regulates marriage, marriage to a woman like Gomer would bring great shame and dishonour to the entire family. The situation would have been the same in Hosea's day, which makes his obedience even more striking.

Gomer is a symbol of Israel's grave sin. More significantly, Hosea's marrying her is a picture of God's love that will not let Israel go. God pursues his unfaithful and rebellious people to bring them back to himself.

1:4-9 Naming Gomer's children

When Gomer bears a son, God again speaks to Hosea, this time regarding the naming of the child (see also Matt 1:21; Luke 1:13, 31). Although there are different systems of child naming among African peoples, the act of naming itself is significant across the continent. The father will almost always have a say in the child's name.

To appreciate the weight of the name *Jezreel* (**1:4a**), one need only imagine a Rwandan mother naming her son Genocide, or a Kenyan named Mau Mau, or a Sierra Leonean boy named RUF (Revolutionary United Front), or a South African named Sharpeville! Jezreel had become synonymous with bloodshed and massacre. Just as *Jehu* killed Joram and so ended the house of Omri (**1:4b**; see 1 Kgs 21; 2 Kgs 9), God will now destroy the house and lineage of Jehu, and the rest of Israel along with it.

The reference to *breaking Israel's bow* is an ominous warning that the Lord, instead of fighting on Israel's behalf, has now become Israel's enemy (**1:5** see 5:14; 13:7-8).

Following the birth of Jezreel, Gomer gives birth to a girl and then a boy. Hosea may or may not have been the father of these two children (see 2:5). As with the first child, the Lord provides the names of the two children: *Lo-Ruhamah,* meaning 'not loved' (**1:6a**), and *Lo-Ammi,* meaning 'not my people' (**1:9a**).

Taken together, the names of the three children portray an increasingly severe judgment. The Lord will destroy both king and nation. He will show no love to Israel (**1:6b**) and will ultimately reject and disown them as his people (**1:9b**). Complete severing of family relationships and kinship ties is the ultimate judgment.

Judah will be saved from the imminent judgment, perhaps because it has not sinned to the extent that its northern relatives in Israel have (**1:7**).

1:10-2:1 God's promise

After the stark announcements of judgment in the preceding verses, God's final word is one of salvation. He promises a reversal of judgment and restoration of the nation. In reversing the judgment, the Lord goes all the way back to the promise given to Abraham (**1:10**; Gen 22:17). The promise that the people of Judah and the people of Israel will be united under one head points to a future ideal (**1:11**; see Ezek 37:15-22). He will restore the nation, and they will again be *my people* (**2:1**). Paul applies this promise to the inclusion of Gentiles in the people of God (Rom 9:25-26).

God's promise here is also evidence of the truth that 'where sin increased, grace increased all the more' (Rom 5:20). As the Krio saying from Sierra Leone goes, *Famble tik go ben bot ee nor go broke* ['Family ties may come under great strain, but they will never be severed'].

2:2-23 The Lord's Relationship with Israel

The relationship between Hosea and Gomer forms the background to the powerful poem, which describes the relationship between a man and his wife. At the start of the chapter, their relationship is badly broken; by the end of the chapter, it has been restored. The wife's prostitution stands in stark contrast to her husband's efforts to produce a restored and harmonious marriage. Their relationship symbolizes the relationship between Israel and God.

The thrust of the argument in this chapter is that Israel is guilty of breaking its covenant relationship with God. Despite this, he does not reject the nation but instead pursues it. His disciplinary actions focus on its relationship with its lovers (other gods) and on the emotional, religious, and ethical aspects of its conduct, as well as its misconceptions about reality. He combines both sternness and tenderness as he draws the nation back into faithful and loving union with him.

2:2-5 A broken marriage

Some commentators interpret this section as the plaintiff's evidence in a court in which he is seeking to divorce his wife. However, it seems more likely that what we have here is a poetic description of a marriage gone sour. For all practical purposes, the marriage is dead. The divine husband is speaking to his family, not to a court of law. That is why it is the children of the marriage who are told to *rebuke your mother* (**2:2a**). They need to realize that her behaviour threatens the unity of the whole family and invites discipline.

The rebuke is prompted by the wife's adultery (**2:2b**). Her unfaithfulness, and not any wrongdoing on the part of the husband, has destroyed this marriage. But the fact that the husband thinks it worth his while to issue a rebuke suggests that there may yet be room for hope.

The rebuke is intended to bring about a change in the wife's behaviour and is accompanied by a threat of punishment that will fall not only on the mother but also on her children (**2:3-4**). The children's fate is wrapped up with their mother's, which gives them an added incentive to confront her.

The husband then moves from a general charge to two specific accusations. First, his wife has been promiscuous. Her sexual behaviour has been both sinful and destructive of their relationship. The statement that her children were conceived *in disgrace* may well imply that her children are not her husband's (**2:5a**; see comment on 1:6-8). She has brought dishonour and shame to her husband, her family and her community. In ancient Israel, as in many parts of Africa today, such disgrace would be deeply felt.

The second accusation is that the wife's reasoning is faulty. She has credited her lovers, rather than the Lord, with providing her with all that she needs for a comfortable life (**2:5b**). This accusation takes on particular force when we remember that the Canaanite god, Baal, was a fertility god. The Israelites were thanking Baal for their harvests of grain and wine, and for the growth of their flocks and herds. But in reality it is God who gives or withholds prosperity.

2:6-13 An angry husband

The Lord now gives details of how he will respond to the behaviour described in the preceding verses. The first part of his response will be negative: he will punish her for what she has done. This punishment also takes two forms, each presented in a section beginning with the word *therefore* (2:6, 9; see also 14).

In the first phase of God's punishment, he deals with his wife's immorality and contempt for their relationship. He does this by putting obstacles in her way, frustrating her and demonstrating that she is mistaken in thinking that her lovers were providing for her (**2:6-7a**). He hopes that her frustration will bring her back to her first love. However, this plan is only a partial success. The wayward wife does return, but only because all her desperate efforts to pursue her lovers and their supposed gifts have proven futile (**2:7b**). She still does not recognize the real gift-giver and uses God's gifts to worship Baal (**2:8**).

To correct her thinking, the Lord announces that he will go one step further. Not only will he hinder and frustrate her, but he will also remove the very gifts that she attributes to Baal and is using to worship Baal (see comment on 3:5). He will take back those things that give her a comfortable life and cover her *nakedness* (**2:9**; see 2:5). Not only will Israel be exposed, but she will be exposed in the presence of *her lovers* (**2:10**; see 2:2). Her celebrations, which had now become empty religious rituals, will cease

(**2:11**). The gifts the wife valued included *vines* and *fig trees* (**2:12**), but these too will be taken away from her. She will be deprived of both her lovers and of the gifts she thought they had given.

The accusations against the wife culminate in **2:13**. Not only has she taken other lovers and wilfully deceived herself about who provided the gifts she enjoys, but most seriously of all, she has completely forgotten her true husband and benefactor, who is here identified as the Lord himself.

2:14-23 A renewed relationship

Despite her punishment, Israel's response is only half-hearted at best and selfish at worst. It appears that, left to her own devices, Israel not only will not but cannot respond positively to the Lord. But God is under no such constraint. *Therefore* he changes his tactics. He has used disincentives; now he offers the incentive of a fresh love. He woos Israel, speaking *tenderly* to her and seeking to re-establish a covenant relationship with her. His first covenant with the nation had been made in the desert at the time of the exodus, and that is why he leads the nation there again (**2:14**; Exod 24:1-8). He will care for her and re-establish the loving relationship that existed when the nation *came up out of Egypt* (**2:15**). He reverses the actions he took before, giving Israel back the vineyards he had taken from her (2:15; 2:12). The *Valley of Achor*, which had previously been a place of God's wrath and of his judgment on sin (Josh 7:25-27), will become *a door of hope*.

The restored relationship will mean that the woman will no longer call her husband *my master*, which in Hebrew is my 'Baal', the title used for foreign gods (**2:16**, **17**). Instead she will lovingly refer to him as *my husband*.

The climax of this section is the complete renewal of the covenant relationship as the Lord affirms: *I will betroth you in faithfulness, and you will acknowledge the Lord* (**2:20**). In Hosea's day, a betrothal ceremony was far more binding than a mere engagement is today. It was the first step in marriage. Thus God is not simply taking back an errant wife, he is starting the marriage all over again. His betrothal gifts to his beloved include *righteousness, justice, love, compassion* and *faithfulness* (2:19-20). These characteristics will define their new relationship. They are the characteristics of God himself, and they are also the characteristics that he will instil in and expect from his people.

The promised restoration will be holistic and complete, involving even the animals and the environment (**2:18, 21-23**). In this way Hosea indicates that the ideal is for God's people to live in right relationship with God, with each other, and with the environment.

As with ancient Israel, our relationship with the Lord is restored not because of us, but first and foremost because of the grace of God

3:1-5 Love Again

After the poetry of chapter 2, chapter 3 goes back to Hosea's account of the life of his own family. Unlike chapter 1, this chapter is Hosea's own account of his marriage. But both chapters describe the same reality: Hosea's difficult marriage to an unfaithful wife.

The great Jewish theologian Abraham Heschel commented that 'to be a prophet was both a distinction and an affliction'. This was certainly true for Hosea. His message and ministry were woven into his personal and family life, as can be seen in his taking back and loving his unfaithful wife again, just as the Lord did for Israel (3:1). The relationship between Hosea and Gomer is a concrete demonstration of the relationship between the Lord and Israel.

The description of Gomer as *an adulteress* who is *loved by another* (3:1a) suggests that, since we last saw her at the end of chapter 1, Gomer has not only had an extramarital affair, but had also moved out of their home and is now living with another man. This may explain why Hosea has to buy her back (3:2).

Hosea's purchase of Gomer and his restoration of her to himself are symbolic of God's redemption and restoration of unfaithful Israel, who has worshipped other gods and participated in pagan feasts (3:1b). Both God's love and Hosea's love involve discipline, which is not administered in a spirit of revenge or to end the marriage, but in order to restore it. Gomer is subjected to restorative discipline and is instructed to cease all her adulterous activities and be faithful to Hosea, who is now not only her rightful husband but also her redeemer (3:3).

This same restorative discipline is applied to the nation. Israel, like Gomer, will be disciplined for a while. The nation will go into exile (3:4) and will lose its political, religious, and national symbols and institutions. However, the exile will not end God's covenant with his people. He will be faithful to the covenant he made with David and will restore his people (3:5). In the end, the people will come *trembling* to admit that it is 'because of the Lord's great love we are not consumed, for his compassions never fail. They are new every morning; great is your faithfulness' (Lam 3:22-23).

As in 1:11, this promise is made to the people, rather than to the nation. So, while the nation of Israel did not return from the Assyrian exile, some of the people would have integrated with the people of Judah during the period of the exile, and these people would then have returned.

4:1-14:9 Israel's Unfaithfulness

Whereas chapters 1–3 focus on Hosea's marriage, chapters 4–14 focus on Israel and its relationship, or lack of it, with God. The difficulties of Hosea's personal relationships now give way to the difficulties in the public relationship between God and Israel. In these prophecies, Hosea often refers to events in Israel's history, especially the story of Jacob (12:2-4, 12) and the story of the nation's deliverance from Egypt and their years of wandering in the desert (9:5-17; 11:1-4; 12:9-10, 13; 13:4-6).

4:1-19 The Lord's Charge Against Israel

Hosea knows that knowledge of God is not simply the source of morality, it is morality itself. Israel's spurning of the knowledge of God led to its spurning the ethical conduct that goes with such knowledge. Its interest in false revelation resulted in sexual promiscuity and injustice.

Christian growth and maturity require growth in understanding, growth in moral conduct and growth in commitment of the heart. Failure to grow in any one of these areas leads to impoverished discipleship, as the experience of the Israelites shows.

4:1-9 Failure to gain knowledge

The opening words are an announcement of the legal case that the Lord is launching against Israel. His accusation is that the virtues of *faithfulness, love,* and *acknowledgment of God* are missing from Israel's national and social life (4:1; see 2:19-20). Instead, the society is characterized by vices such as *cursing, lying and murder, stealing and adultery* (4:2). The result is chaos, anarchy and the complete breakdown of society: *the land mourns and all who live in it waste away* (4:3). This breakdown is not limited to human society but extends to all of creation. *The beasts of the field and the birds of the air, and the fish of the sea* are presented as dying in the reverse order to their creation (4:3; see Gen 1:20-24). Similar vices and a similar disintegration of community and national life and of the environment are all too familiar in contemporary Africa. Here, too, the result is political and social turmoil.

The fundamental reason that such vices exist in the community is a *lack of knowledge* of God (4:6a). The *priests,* whose primary duty was to teach the law of God to the people, had failed to do so (4:6b-7) with the result that priests, people and nation alike stumble and perish (4:4-5). For Hosea, as for the other prophets, this law went beyond the strict legal code and embraced all divine revelation and all the instructions given to guide the Israelites in their relationships with God and with each other. Similarly, knowledge of God meant more than simply a mental understanding of God's word. It involved a deep-seated spiritual relationship with the Lord, involving commitment of the heart as well as of the mind. The Christian church and individual Christians are called to similar knowledge of their Lord.

Not understanding God's word and not submitting to his authority produced tragic consequences. The religious leaders neglected their responsibilities, abused their positions, were more concerned about personal gain than about faithful discharge of their high calling, and brought shame and dishonour rather than glory and honour to the Lord. The end result was that the Lord rejected both priests and people, reminding Israel, and us, that the final word belongs to the Lord (**4:9**).

4:10-15 Moral failure

Covenant morality apart from devotion to the covenant Lord is only a figment of the imagination, for there is a relationship between knowledge and moral behaviour. Israel may have deluded itself into believing that it could indulge in idolatry and still maintain wholesome personal and social relationships. But Hosea knows better. The moral lapses of those who are ignorant of God cloud the mind and have a deadening effect on moral judgment (**4:11**). The people now indulge in alcohol and prostitution. In an illegitimate and futile quest for revelation, they have turned to idols and divination (**4:12-13a**). Such worship of false gods is prompted by *a spirit of prostitution* because it leads them to be unfaithful to their true Lord. Given the stress on fertility and sexuality in Baal worship, it is not surprising that promiscuity now abounds and their *daughters turn to prostitution* (**4:13b**).

God's response to this immorality is surprising. Much to everyone's surprise, he announces that he will not mete out specific punishment to the promiscuous women. Why not? Because the men are behaving no better, and have set a precedent by their sinful promiscuous conduct! All of them will come to ruin because they are *a people without understanding* (**4:14**). There is nothing new about having a double standard for what is expected of men and of women, but the Lord judges both impartially. Nor is there anything new about trying to give reasons that explain and excuse our moral failures, but such justifications do not stand the Lord's judgment.

The Lord is concerned that Israel's idolatry should not spread to Judah: *let not Judah become guilty* (**4:15a**), although other passages suggest that this may be inevitable (see 5:12, 14; 6:4, 11). The places that Judah is urged not to visit were the sites of idolatrous shrines, which might be a source of temptation (see also Amos 4:4). *Beth Aven* (**4:15b**), 'house of wickedness', is a mocking name for 'Bethel', which means 'house of God'. It reveals the true nature of the worship that went on there (1 Kgs 12:28-33).

4:16-19 Emotional failure

Israel shows no signs of repenting of its behaviour. Instead it persists in promiscuity, intoxication and idolatry (**4:18-19**). The people have no knowledge of God and are unwilling to learn anything about him. They can only be characterized as *stubborn* (**4:16**) and their company is best avoided (**4:17**).

5:1-15 God's Judgment

5:1-4 Judgment of deeds

This section opens with a threefold divine summons, *Hear this … Pay attention … Listen …* (**5:1a**), reflecting the rightful authority of the one making the summons. Those summoned are the leaders (the *priests* and the *royal house*) and the people (the *Israelites*). They are being summoned to *judgment*. Two reasons are given for the judgment. The first is the people's idolatry at the shrines in *Mizpah* and *Tabor*. The words used, *snare* and *a net spread out,* suggest a hunter's trap (**5:1b**). The second reason for the judgment is the people's rebellion (**5:2**). However, this verse could also be translated as in the NRSV: *you have been … a pit dug deep in Shittim,* which would point to another idolatrous shrine (5:2; see also Num 25:1-9).

The people may not know God (4:6), but God as their creator and Lord knows all about them (**5:3a**). His accusation of them is true, for he has all the evidence. They cannot make any excuses. He knows all about the promiscuity and corruption that have affected Israel's moral and religious life (**5:3b**; 4:11-19).

Israel's corruption and evil deeds now have such a hold on the people that they have lost the ability and desire to return to their Lord. These verses paint a picture of a cycle of bondage. Apostasy allows and encourages the *spirit of prostitution* (**5:4**). The spirit of prostitution promotes wicked deeds, which then inhibit a fitting response to the promptings of the Spirit. Thus this section ends with the damning indictment: *they do not acknowledge the Lord.* Like chapter 4, this section warns believers against the mistaken notion that spiritual life and worship have no relationship to moral health.

5:5-7 Judgment of attitudes

Attention now turns to *Israel's arrogance* (**5:5a**). The people *seek the Lord,* that is, to perform religious rituals, in a spirit of pride and self-assurance, convinced that all is well (**5:6**).

There are at least two things, however, that Israel had failed to recognize. The first is that rottenness and decay have already set in. So *the Israelites stumble in their sin* (**5:5b**). The second is that judgment had already begun: the Lord *has withdrawn himself from them* (**5:6**; see 5:13-15).

5:8-12 Judgment of injustice

Earlier there was a threefold command to listen (5:1), and now there is a threefold command to sound the trumpet – either as a fanfare announcing the king's arrival or as an alarm warning of imminent danger (**5:8**; see also 8:1). The prophet is announcing that the king is coming, and that he is coming in judgment! Specifically, he warns of an invasion of the territory of Benjamin by Judah.

The towns mentioned in 5:8, *Gibeah* and *Ramah* and *Beth Aven*, were all in the territory of the tribe of *Benjamin*. They lay close to the border between Israel and Judah, and thus there was constant fighting as Judah attempted to gain control of them. Because of this persistent strife, the Lord will judge and punish both Israel and Judah.

These attempts by the leaders of Judah to extend their northern border by forcefully annexing the territory of Benjamin were equivalent to moving *boundary stones* (**5:10**). These stones marked the extent of a family's land, and moving them amounted to theft of land, which would deprive people of the ability to support themselves. That is why the practice is so strongly condemned in Deuteronomy 19:14 and 27:17, and again draws God's wrath here.

Israel (Ephraim) will suffer because it is *intent on pursuing idols*, which the NRSV translates as *determined to go after vanity* (**5:11**). These words may refer to the futile alliance Israel made with Syria against Judah, which resulted in the nation being *trampled* by the invading Assyrian army, which conquered and oppressed it (2 Kgs 16:5-9).

The Lord has raised a battle cry (5:8-9), but his judgment is already at work before the dramatic devastation of Israel and Judah and the events of the Syro-Ephraimite war and its aftermath. In the days and years leading up to those events, God himself will be the agent of destruction. He will be like *a moth* or *rot*, *bringing about internal decay*, destroying the fabric of society and weakening the nation (**5:12**).

5:13-15 God's withdrawal

Israel's leaders recognized the weakness of the nation. They also recognized that this was the first sign of God's judgment, but instead of turning to the Lord in repentance, they sought political help from Assyria (**5:13**; see 2 Kgs 16:7). This act of political expediency turned out to be futile. The Lord's response will be to *tear them to pieces ... to carry them off*, as indeed happened when both Israel and Judah were carried off into exile (**5:14**; 2 Kgs 17:6; 25:11).

The Lord will withdraw his presence and leave the people in exile *until they admit their guilt* and actively seek him (**5:15**). These words show that his judgment has a restorative purpose. He wants the people to truly return to him, and only then will he restore them to their land.

6:1-11a The Problem of Shallow Repentance

The people respond to the Lord's threat to withdraw (5:6, 15) and his condemnation of their alliance with Assyria (5:13) by again seeking the Lord and trying to ally themselves with him (6:1-3). But they fail to realize that turning to the Lord involves more than mere words. Hence the Lord's response to their repentance (6:4-11a).

6:1-3 Call to repentance

God has said that he would hide himself until the people seek him (5:15), and so the people summon each other *to return to the Lord* (**6:1a**). They recognize that God is carrying out the judgment he threatened in 5:11-14. But they also recognize that although the Lord has attacked them 'like a great lion', he is also a caring shepherd who will faithfully care for his wounded flock (**6:1b-2**).

The call to return to God is repeated: *Let us acknowledge the Lord* (**6:3**). The Israelites' failure to acknowledge him had been condemned in 4:1, and so they seek to set this right. They are certain that if they do this, the Lord will respond by revealing himself and blessing them. They are as confident of this as they are confident that the sun will rise tomorrow. Like the regular *winter* and *spring rains*, he will reveal himself to those who desire him and will renew and refresh them. His behaviour is as predictable as the seasons.

Like the wayward wife in 2:9, Israel has recognized the futility of its ways. Like the wife, the people have been forced to recognize the real source of blessing and of trouble, and they know that their former partner still cares for them. But in both cases, the motive for return is selfish. Neither the wife nor Israel shows any love for the one they are returning to. They admit no guilt, and are only interested in what they can get out of the relationship.

6:4-11a The Lord's response

The Lord sighs as he responds to the people's call: *What can I do with you, Ephraim? What can I do with you, Judah?* (**6:4a**). He is seeking to establish a faithful, loving relationship, like that celebrated in a betrothal (1:19). All that the people are offering is manipulation of his character.

The people have claimed that the Lord is faithful (6:1-3), but the Lord knows that they are fickle. He may come to them like the seasonal rains (6:3), but their coming to him will last no longer than the *morning mist* and *early dew* (**6:4b**). He thus rejects their request, dashing their certainty, because he knows that they are insincere and have made no deep and lasting commitment to knowing him (**6:5**). He is not impressed that they have resumed praying to him and making sacrifices to him (6:6). He is not like the gods worshipped in the Baal cult, who are satisfied if their mere existence is acknowledged by sacrifices but who do not require a personal relationship or moral conduct in those who worship them. What God is looking for, and cannot see in Israel, is *mercy* and *acknowledgement of God* (**6:6**). By this he means not merely verbal acknowledgement of him but the type of conduct that is to be expected of those who know him. He insists that ethical conduct takes precedence over mere religious rituals (see also Matt 9:13; 12:7).

God again invokes the metaphors of covenant and marriage to describe the problem. Israel has *broken the covenant* and has been *unfaithful to me* (**6:7**). The specifics of the charge of covenant breaking are laid out. Gilead is described as *a city of wicked men, stained with footprints of blood* (**6:8**; see also 12:11). Men from this town had been involved in the assassination of King Pekahiah (2 Kgs 15:25). Even the *priests* were behaving like marauding bandits, lying in wait for their prey and committing murder (**6:9**). Moreover, promiscuity was still rampant (**6:10**). Hosea's time was characterized by great political instability, which contributed to the violence he describes. No wonder he laments the absence of the covenant virtues of true mercy and knowledge of God.

Despite what Israel says in 6:3, the nation is still guilty of the charges made in 2:10-13 and 4:1. The people neither 'know the Lord' nor understand what it means to know him. The Lord will only return to them when they truly repent of their sin. Such repentance will lead to true worship, founded on a real experience of the Lord, and to a life lived in obedience to God's word.

6:11b-7:16 The Paralysis of Sin

Hosea moves on to a devastating indictment of Israel, giving details of the wrongs and injustices perpetrated by the nation's leaders. It makes sad reading.

6:11b-7:7 Deceit and intrigues

The Lord longs to help Israel, but he recognizes that the nation has become incapable of repentance and change: *Whenever I would restore the fortunes of my people ... the sins of Ephraim are exposed* (**6:11-7:1a**). Nothing can be done for a nation that will not admit its sin.

The people in general are engaged in deceit, theft and banditry (**7:1b**). They think that they can get away with it, but they are mistaken, for the Lord remembers *all their evil deeds* and will judge them (**7:2**). God's memory is not a vague recollection of past events; it is vivid and a spur to action, for *their sins ... are always before me.*

The people, however, are simply following the example their leaders set at the royal court, which is a hotbed of wickedness, lies and adultery (**7:3-4a**). The emphasis is not simply on what these leaders are doing, but on the intrigues, scheming, plotting and planning that takes place night and day (**7:4b-6**). Leaders like this are not passionate about justice but about injustice. Their unbridled and wicked ambition is captured in the image of a burning oven (7:6).

7:8-16 Futile political alliances

Israel is condemned because it *mixes with the nations* (**7:8a**), becoming like them and so compromising its witness to them and ceasing to be a channel of blessing to them (see Gen 12:1-3). We are reminded of Jesus' prayer that his followers may be in the world but not of the world (John 17:11-16). Because of Israel's compromises and lack of

discernment, it is like *a flat cake not turned over* – burnt on one side and raw on the other and thus useless, with all its potential for good wasted (**7:8b**).

While on the surface everything seems well, in reality the rot has already set in, life is ebbing away, and the nation does not know it. To the casual observer, a tree rotting from the inside may still seem healthy. The trained eye, however, can spot signs of decay (**7:9**). The prophet already sees the signs of degeneration and death in Ephraim, although the nation arrogantly denies it (**7:10**).

The political alliances that drained the nation's strength and resources are the reason for its judgment (**7:13**; see 8:7-10). Caught between the two great political powers of its day, *Egypt* in the south and *Assyria* in the north, Israel was constantly shifting its political allegiance. But while its leaders may have thought that they were playing the game of political survival well, God sees that they have no more sense than *a dove* that is *easily deceived* (**7:11**).

All Israel's political manoeuvring could not save it. The hoped-for saviours would turn out to be its captors, and the nation would be *ridiculed* by those it had courted as allies (**7:16b**). There have been many similar situations on the African continent, where those who have been hailed as political saviours have proved to be dictators and murderers of the worst kind.

Israel's captivity would not be an unfortunate accident but would be God's judgment on it (**7:12**). What would make this captivity especially tragic was the fact that it did not have to happen. The Lord longed to redeem Israel (7:13). But instead of turning to the Lord, the nation alternated between complaining and over-indulging in food and drink (**7:14**). They refused to turn back to the Lord, who was the one who had first established them (**7:15-16a**).

The nation and its leaders are paralysed by sin in two ways. First, their addiction to wrong and evil leaves them incapable of doing what is good and right. Second, and even more seriously, their sinful ways make them unable to return to the Lord.

8:1-14 The Certainty of Judgment

8:1-3 Israel's rebellion

Another *trumpet* sounds, announcing imminent judgment (**8:1a**; see 5:8). An *eagle,* representing the Assyrians, hovers over the nation, ready to seize it in its talons (8:1a). The judgment announced in the previous chapter is not far away.

The reasons given for the judgment are the breaking of the *covenant* and rebellion against the *law* (**8:1b**). The covenant and law were at the heart of the relationship between God and Israel. They set out the requirements for maintaining that relationship which, like every relationship, had its privileges, responsibilities and binding commitments.

Israel is again accused of facile and insincere claims of loyalty (see 6:1-3). While it glibly claims *to acknowledge* the Lord, in reality it continues to reject *what is good*, that is, the covenant and the law (**8:2-3**).

Israel may have been relying on its history and traditions when it claimed to acknowledge the Lord. Jeremiah 7:3-8 records a similar folly on the part of the people of Judah, who apparently believed that the presence of the temple would save them from destruction. Like them, we are treading on dangerous ground when we allow tradition to take the place of an ongoing relationship with the living God.

8:4-6 Corruption of kingship and worship

Once more, Hosea moves from the general to the specific, criticizing the political and religious systems. His criticism of the kingship is most likely related to the frequent replacement of kings during his time (**8:4**). In coups and counter-coups, new leaders were appointed without consulting the Lord.

The separation of church and state in modern democracies is relatively recent. In many traditional societies, where life is more holistic, the religious and political institutions support each other. The danger in such societies is that politics and religion can both become corrupt and dictatorial. This certainly seems to have been the case in Israel (see also Amos 7:10-17). The fact that both kingship and worship are mentioned in 8:4 may suggest that these forces were at work.

The idol in **8:5-6** is probably the one erected at Bethel by King Jeroboam I (1 Kgs 12:28-30), for this would have been the one closest to the capital of Samaria. When Hosea calls it *the calf of Samaria*, he is not stating where exactly it was erected, but that it was worshipped by the people of Samaria. It is likely that Israel incorporated worship of this idol into its worship of God, as happened at Sinai (Exod 32). Hosea is thus appealing to the people of Israel to do away with the idol that has corrupted their worship.

Syncretism is an ever-present danger, and the church must constantly be alert for its pernicious influence.

8:7-10 Dangerous political alliances

The folly of Israel's shifting political alliances was dealt with in 7:8-16. Now the prophet returns to this with vivid metaphors that express the futility of Israel's policies. Entering into an alliance with Assyria is equivalent to sowing wind. The wind will grow and yield a great harvest – a devastating whirlwind (**8:7a**). Assyria will respond to Israel's overtures by destroying the land.

To change the metaphor, the crop they have planted will not produce any grain for *the stalk has no head* (**8:7b**). The Assyrian alliance will yield no benefits. Even if it did, the benefits would not be for Israel to enjoy, but would be swallowed up by *foreigners* (**8:7c**). In fact, Israel herself will be swallowed up by foreigners and will be a subject for ridicule (**8:8**; see also 7:16).

In moving towards Assyria, Israel was *like a wild donkey wandering alone* (**8:9**), separated from the herd and acting without intelligence to guide her. If she had any sense, she would have turned to the Lord, but instead she will suffer under the oppressive boot of the *great king* of the Assyrians, in whom she had placed her hope (**8:10**; see 5:13). Pragmatic politics end in political disaster. Hosea leaves no doubt that this is God's judgment on Israel.

8:11-14 The perversion of religion

The chapter ends with another look at the theme of corrupt worship. Hosea sees a great separation between religious activity and true worship. The number of places of worship has multiplied, but their purpose has been twisted. Rather than being places for worship, they have become places for sin (**8:11**). The precise nature of the sinful religious practices is not clear. But it is clear that they are not based on any understanding of God's law, for the law appears *alien* to the people (**8:12**). It is also clear that God does not accept their sacrifices (**8:13a**) and that the nation has forgotten who God really is (**8:14**). He is described as *Israel's Maker* because he is the one who created the nation by bringing them out of Egypt at the time of the exodus. But they have forgotten this, and him, and so they will return to the captivity and bondage they knew in Egypt years before (**8:13b**).

Religious fervour does not necessarily mean spiritual vitality. 'It seems to be an occupational disease of worshippers to think more of the mechanics than the meaning of what we do; more of getting it right than of getting ourselves right' (*BST*). Paul warns against having a form of godliness but denying its power (2 Tim 3:5).

9:1-17 The Terror of Judgment

In this, the darkest chapter of the entire book, pictures of judgment pile up. Israel will be deprived of everything that makes it a people, a community, a society, a nation. The nation will lose its key political, religious, kinship and economic institutions. It will be driven from God's presence and disinherited, and will suffer shame, rejection and separation (9:17).

9:1-4 The threat of exile

Wild parties and orgies were often associated with the harvests, which were times of rejoicing for all nations, and particularly for those that worshipped Baal. But Israel is commanded not to rejoice (**9:1**). It may desire to be *like the other nations*, but this is not its calling (see also 7:8). It has been called to be a holy nation, different from all other nations, and to thank God for his gifts. But instead of doing this, it has been eager to commit spiritual adultery by following other gods.

The consequences of the nation's adulterous behaviour follow thick and fast. The crops will fail, ruining the economy (**9:2**). The ultimate judgment will be exile and captivity in Assyria. There, Israel will be stripped of everything familiar and everything that formed its identity. It will be separated from land, temple, food and worship (**9:3-4**).

9:5-17 Three lessons from history

The deprivations mentioned above mean that Israel's festive days will be times of mourning rather than times of rejoicing (**9:5**). With this, Hosea moves beyond merely announcing judgment and announces its inevitability: even those who might escape it will perish in foreign lands (**9:6**). In addition to the certainty of judgment, he announces its imminence; the days of judgment are not simply *coming,* they *are at hand* (**9:7a**). The reason for the judgment is the sin and hostility of the people. This hostility is not only directed at God but also at his *prophet,* who is *considered a fool* (**9:7b**). Slandering the messenger is a time-honoured technique when a message is unpalatable. Being called to be a prophet was a call to both honour and affliction – as it still is today. We should, however, make sure that when others treat us with disrespect or dismiss our words, the cause is the offence of the gospel message itself, and not our insensitive or careless presentation of it or any wrong action on our part.

The depth of Israel's sin is shown by references to three historical events, which occurred at Gibeah, Baal Peor and Gilgal. The people are said to be as corrupt *as in the days of Gibeah* (**9:9**). Gibeah was the site of the disgusting rape and murder of the Levite's concubine (Judg 19).

When God founded Israel, he loved it and took absolute delight in the nation, but that delight turned to revulsion at *Baal Peor,* where the men of Israel indulged in sexual immorality with Moabite women and the people sacrificed to and worshipped Moabite gods (**9:10**; Num 25:1-18). Israel's current behaviour is as bad as its ancestors' behaviour at Baal Peor. But an even more devastating point is being made. Israel has spurned and turned its back on divine love. By turning to the worship of false gods, it has rejected divine grace. By associating with *shameful idols,* Israel itself has become shameful.

Hosea uses the community values of honour and shame to describe Israel's actions and the consequences. The people's actions have brought shame and dishonour upon Israel and on its God. Consequently, God will shame Israel and take away *Ephraim's glory,* that is, the people (**9:11**). The punishment meted out to the nation will be the loss of its people, graphically portrayed as *wombs that miscarry and breasts that are dry* (**9:12-14**). This terrible judgment amounts to a reversal of the promise and blessing of Genesis 12:1-3.

The third and final historical reference is to *Gilgal* (**9:15**; see 1 Sam 15). The sin associated with Gilgal is not specified in this text, but Gilgal has already been mentioned in the context of immorality in 4:15. So it is likely that immorality practised at centres of worship is what is meant here (see also Amos 4:4; 5:5). Yahweh's response to this wickedness is clear and is expressed in the stark opposition of 'hate' and 'love': *I hated them* and *I will no longer love them* (**9:15**). The action that flows from these emotions is expulsion from *my house,* the house of the Lord. Their families will fail to thrive (**9:16**). In effect Israel is disinherited, the kinship relation is broken, and the privileges of being a member of the family are lost.

Hosea uses these three historical references to highlight Israel's tradition of sinning and turning away from the Lord. Yet at the same time, his reference to God's love for them in the desert (9:10) reminds them of the Lord's grace, his love and his choice of Israel.

10:1-15 Agricultural Images for Israel

10:1-8 A vine and weeds

A vine was a commonly used image for Israel (see, for example, Isa 5:1-7). Hosea uses the example of a luxuriant vine to describe Israel's material prosperity (**10:1**). With this prosperity came a greater display of religious zeal, shown in the multiplying of altars. But this was simply a way for people to show off their wealth and their confidence in their strength and abilities. The altars were not proof that they were giving credit to the Lord for their prosperity. In fact, most of these altars were probably dedicated to Baal.

Religious zeal and fervour are not the same as true and sincere worship of the living God, and so Hosea points out that *their heart is deceitful* (**10:2**). Consequently, the Lord will *demolish their altars.*

Israel's pride and idolatry will eventually result in the northern kingdom being overthrown, as happened near the end of Hosea's ministry. The people's words at that time, *We have no king* (**10:3**; see 7, 15) will reflect the reality of their situation. They will correctly identify the reason for their plight as their false worship. They will also be disillusioned with human rulers, asking what a king could do for them. We sense the disappointment and depression of people enduring severe political distress and their resignation to their fate. But that lies in the future.

In the present, the people's worship is insincere, and so is their speech. Their *promises,* their *oaths* and *agreements* are false, and thus *lawsuits* have multiplied *like poisonous weeds in a ploughed field* (**10:4**). The lack of honesty in business and social life breaks the bonds that hold a community together, with the result that injustice and chaos are the order of the day.

The *calf-idol* is the ultimate symbol of empty worship and empty words (**10:5**; see 8:5-6). The Lord will have both the people and the object of their syncretistic worship taken into exile in far away *Assyria* (**10:6**). Their very places of worship – *the high places* – will be ruined (**10:8a**). Far from being a rooted vine, the king and nation will be *like a twig floating away on the current* (**10:7**). The nation will lose both its religious and political institutions.

In despair, the people will cry to the *mountains* and *hills: 'Fall on us!'* (**10:8b**). They will have nowhere to flee to and no one to turn to. This is what happens when the Lord strips us of everything that we cling to, exposing our folly in putting our trust in people and things rather than in him.

10:9-15 A trained heifer

Hosea returns to Israel's sin at *Gibeah* (**10:9**; see 9:9). He reminds the people of what happened there (Judg 19) and accuses them of acting in the same spirit. Just as God punished the people of Gibeah by drawing together a coalition of tribes that nearly wiped out the community (Judg 20) so *the nations will be gathered against* Israel to punish it (**10:10**).

Hosea describes the nation as being like a *heifer that loves to thresh* (**10:11**). This type of threshing, trampling the harvested wheat to separate the grain from the stalks, was easy work and did not demand much effort from the heifer. But God wants to direct this heifer's potential to productive and positive outcomes. Consequently, the Lord will put a yoke on her and guide her ploughing with a disciplined hand so that she can *sow … righteousness, reap the fruit of unfailing love,* and *seek the Lord* (**10:12**). Clearly, seeking the Lord must be accompanied by justice and unfailing love. The similar terms, 'acknowledgement of God' and 'mercy', are used in 6:6 to indicate the kind of just conduct that the Lord desires and expects of those who claim to know and love him. Hosea's contemporary Micah makes the same point: 'What does the Lord require of you? To act justly and to love mercy and to walk humbly with your God' (Mic 6:8).

But the only crop Israel has planted is *wickedness* and what has been reaped is *evil* (**10:13a**; see also 8:7). The fruit seen in Israel is unrighteousness and injustice (10:14). The contrast between what the Lord expects and what happens in Israel is similarly described in Isaiah 5:1-7. As in 6:1-6, Israel falls short of what the Lord expects. The initial pleasures of sin soon give way to its dangerous stranglehold that weakens resolve and the capacity for good and justice.

Hosea will return to Israel's habitual failure to repent and turn to the Lord in the rest of the book. For now, he closes the chapter with the announcement of judgment on Israel (**10:15**). The strength and military might on which Israel prided itself will be the very means that the Lord will use in judgment and destruction (**10:13b-14a**). We do not know exactly who *Shalman* was, but it is clear that the town of *Beth Arbel* suffered a terrible fate at his hands (**10:14b**). Israel can expect no better. Its men will be defeated in battle and its women and children taken captive.

11:1-11 A God Who Will Not Let Go

In the first three chapters of his book, Hosea used the marriage metaphor to describe Israel's relationship with God. Now he changes to another image drawn from everyday family life to give a portrait of a God who will not be unfaithful to his covenant promises and who will not let go of his people.

11:1-4 A God of gracious love

Two distinct images are used to paint a picture of God's love. The first image is of the relationship between a parent and a child. God became Israel's parent when he called the nation *out of Egypt* (**11:1**). As a parent, he taught and guided his child: I *taught Ephraim to walk* (**11:3a**). The second image of God's love is based on the relationship between a good farmer and his animals: *I led them with cords of human kindness, with ties of love; I lifted the yoke from their neck and bent down to feed them* (**11:4**).

The fact that God is the one who calls his child to him (11:1) and teaches him all that he knows is a reminder that God's call and election arise solely out of his love. God does not call us and save us because of anything we have done. He is always the one who takes the initiative. As Paul reminds us, our salvation depends entirely on God's grace (see Eph 2:4-9; Rom 5:6-10).

God's gracious love shines out even more clearly against the background of Israel's response. The people deliberately and consciously rejected God's love. Notice God's lament: *The more I called … the further they went from me. They sacrificed to the Baals … burnt incense to images* (**11:2**). *They did not realize it was I who healed them* (**11:3b**). Not only did Israel turn away from the living God, it turned to false gods. In the words of the General Confession in the Anglican prayer book, they 'left undone what [they] ought to have done, and did what [they] ought not to have done'. We identify with Israel when we say: 'there is no health in us'.

C. S. Lewis noted that loving deeply brings with it the possibility of being deeply hurt. This is God's experience. There is a stark contrast between God's gracious love and Israel's stubborn response. To the question 'What kind of God is your god?' Hosea's response is 'a gracious, loving God, rejected by his own'.

11:5-7 A God of justice

God is not only a God of love, he is also a God of justice. His judgment on Israel is imminent and certain. Israel will be sent into captivity and bondage (**11:5**) and its cities will be destroyed (**11:6**).

These days, it is not fashionable to speak of sin and judgment. But to be faithful to Scripture, we must wrestle with Scripture's teaching on these subjects. We are called to remind the world of the paradox that human beings are created in God's image but are also fallen and prone to unspeakable evil. We are to proclaim that God abhors wrong and injustice.

11:8-11 A God of redemptive justice

But how is the God of love related to the God of justice? In the final section of this chapter, Hosea shows the tension between these two fundamental aspects of God's nature. Once again, God speaks as a parent as he cries out, *How can I give you up … all my compassion is aroused* (**11:8**). We feel that tension of love and discipline familiar to every parent. For God, the tension is far more than an academic issue. And we ourselves should not treat it as an academic issue. It is of vital importance to our worship as well as to our study; to our family life as well as to our professional life. With Hosea, we should recognize that the answer does not lie in making a choice between the love and the justice of God. It is not a question of either/or, but both/and. God is just and God is love.

Israel undoubtedly deserved judgment and God was committed to seeing that justice was done. We need to proclaim the truth that he does judge and will judge sin. But there is the further truth that his love led him to pay the penalty for our sins. The cross of Christ is the place where justice and forgiveness meet. We dare not proclaim a cheap grace.

God's love means that he is irrevocably and passionately committed to his people. This commitment is founded in his divine nature: *For I am God, and not man – the Holy One among you* (**11:9**). Because he is the 'Holy One', he will bring restoration after devastation. He will be like a lion in judgment (5:14), but the lion's roar will also signal restoration and summon his people to him (**11:10**). After the exile, God will form a new community that will follow him and he will *settle them in their homes*. This promise is echoed in Jesus' declaration, 'on this rock I will build my church, and the gates of Hades will not overcome it' (Matt 16:18).

Hosea's understanding of God embraces justice rooted in love. Hosea's God is not capricious and vengeful, enjoying the dispensing of judgment. His judgment is certain, but it is tempered by the 'love that will not let go'. So in all that we think and speak and do, we are called to live out the tension of God's love and justice.

11:12-12:14 Return to the Lord

After disclosing the very heart of God, Hosea returns to the everyday routine of human disobedience and the present reality of Israel's estrangement from God. Many aspects of the condemnation of Israel in this chapter parallel what has been said in chapters 7 to 9.

11:12-12:6 In Jacob's footsteps

Israel is full of deceit, lies, and violence and can be said to be *unruly against God, even against the faithful Holy One* (**11:12**). Once again, Hosea speaks of the futile political

intrigues and constantly shifting alliances with Assyria and Egypt (**12:1**; 7:11).

What does one do with such a partner? Hosea says that God has a charge, that is, an accusation, to make against Israel and he will punish *Jacob according to his deeds* (**12:2**). Those to whom Israel pledged allegiance will turn out to be its oppressors. In seeking freedom from God, it ends up in bondage. This was true for Adam and Eve in the garden; it is true for us today. Sin results in separation and a broken relationship.

Hosea looks beyond punishment, and holds out the option of restoration. He uses three events in Jacob's life as the basis for his appeal to Israel to return to the Lord. The first is his birth. Jacob was born grasping Esau's heel (**12:3**; Gen 25:26). There was an unpleasant side to the character of the young Jacob. He was a supplanter, a deceiver, a schemer, taking what did not belong to him. Hosea appears to be saying to Israel, 'You are just like your father Jacob was!'

But Jacob also wrestled with the angel of God at the ford of the Jabbok (**12:4a**; Gen 32:22-32). This second event marked a turning point. At Jabbok, Jacob met his match, turned to God and was never the same again.

The third event is Jacob's encounter with the Lord at Bethel (**12:4b**; Gen 28:10-22; 35:15). There he met with no less a person than the *Lord God Almighty* (**12:5**).

These three events span Jacob's life. Hosea is pleading, 'Look at your ancestor Jacob. He began badly, but encountered God, turned from his evil ways, and ended well.' Follow his example, turn from your wicked ways, *maintain love and justice, and wait for your God always* (**12:6**).

12:7-14 Injustice, pride, and destruction

How does Israel respond to Hosea's plea? Will it once again respond with shallow and insincere repentance (see 6:1-6)? It seems that it no longer even does that. Instead the nation remains dishonest, boastful and unrepentant. Like a dishonest trader who likes to cheat and extort, Israel practises social injustice and takes pride in doing so (**12:7-8**). The appeal to *maintain love and justice* (12:6) has clearly fallen on deaf ears as the wealthy and powerful gloat over their unjustly acquired wealth and oppress the weak and helpless.

Israel appears to have forgotten the God of the exodus (**12:9**; Exod 20:2). God had commanded the people to live in shelters like tents during the Feast of Tabernacles in order to remember how he had led them through the desert (Lev 23:40-43). They were still doing this, but had forgotten the reason for doing it, just as they had forgotten their maker (8:14). So will make them live as refugees in tents again until they do remember him.

God had used the prophets as his messengers to speak to his people (**12:10**). But Israel has consistently failed to heed the prophets' appeal to return to the Lord and know him. The people of *Gilead* and *Gilgal* are again given as examples of where such behaviour leads (**12:11a**; 6:8; 9:15). The result will be that Gilead will be reduced to nothing and the multitude of altars of false worship will be reduced to scattered heaps of stones (**12:11b**).

Just as Jacob had to work hard to gain his wife, so the Lord has worked hard to gain Israel. But where Jacob handed over sheep for his wife, the Lord has handed over his prophets, men like Moses and Samuel (**12:12-13**). But Israel has not listened to them and persists in disobedience (**12:14**). So the Lord of Israel will cease to be its ally and will become its enemy, as will be shown in the next chapter.

13:1-16 The Folly of Ingratitude

In his final indictment of Israel, Hosea delves back to the beginnings of Israel's history to remind them of the Lord's mighty acts of deliverance and to contrast God's faithfulness with the people's sin.

13:1-8 The Lord – a lion, leopard and bear

Ephraim's ingratitude in turning away from its maker and towards false gods is a familiar theme. The folly of the people's idolatry is accentuated by their increased propensity to sin and their worship of idols they have made with their own hands (**13:2**). They have turned from the worship of the living God to the worship of empty nothing! No wonder that their fearsome reputation (*men trembled* when they spoke) and exalted status have evaporated (**13:1**). They will become as transient as *the morning mist,* ... *early dew,* ... *swirling chaff,* and rising *smoke* (**13:3**). Their very existence will be as transient as their love for God (6:4).

Israel's foolishness and ingratitude stand in vivid contrast to the love and faithfulness of God. As in 11:1-3 and 12:9, Hosea again returns to the exodus and Israel's time in the wilderness. The historical reference highlights God's initiative, deliverance, sustenance and love (**13:4-6**). It was the Lord, not Baal, who delivered Israel from bondage in Egypt (Exod 20:2). It was the Lord, not Baal, who provided for Israel in the wilderness for forty years. It was the Lord, not Baal, who repeatedly delivered Israel from every kind of peril and danger. Israel owes everything to God, who is its Maker and deliverer.

Yet, instead of showing gratitude and faithfulness, Israel responds with pride, ingratitude and immorality. The sequence *satisfied ... proud ... forgot me* (13:6) reminds us of the unfaithful wife in chapter 2. She wrongly attributed her blessings to the generosity of Baal, forgetting the Lord, the true source of her deliverance and blessings.

The tragedy of Israel sprang from a prosperity that was allowed to breed pride and ingratitude, in combination with foolishness that resulted in lost opportunity. Proverbs 16:18 comes to mind: 'Pride goes before destruction, a haughty spirit before a fall.' Self-exaltation means that we are focusing on ourselves rather than on the Lord. Paul, too, comments on this type of pride: 'What do you have that you did not receive? And if you did receive it, why do you boast as though you did not?' (1 Cor 4:7).

God's anger and his utter destruction of Israel are expressed in a fourfold reference to ferocious beasts of prey in **13:7**: *a lion ... a leopard ... a bear ... a lion* (or lioness, as in the NASB). These images are vivid reminders of the terror of God's judgment and of its finality. We are reminded of the terrifying description of the day of the Lord by Hosea's contemporary Amos: 'It will be as though a man fled from a lion only to meet a bear, as though he entered his house and rested his hand on the wall only to have a snake bite him' (Amos 5:19).

13:9-16 A final announcement of judgment

You are destroyed, O Israel (**13:9**) is a difficult verse, and may be translated, *It is your destruction, O Israel* (13:9 – NASB), with 'it' referring to Israel's rebellion against God. This translation emphasizes that in rebelling against its only deliverer, Israel has invited God's judgment on itself.

Israel had once clamoured for a king (1 Sam 8:6), but its kings were unable to save it (**13:10-11**). The danger of putting ultimate trust in things and people – especially so-called political saviours – rather than in the living God is not limited to Israel. We do well to remember the wisdom of Psalm 20:7: 'Some trust in chariots and some in horses, but we trust in the name of the Lord our God.'

Israel's guilt and sin are undeniable; the evidence is well preserved and on record for all to see (**13:12**). The metaphor of a potentially fatal childbirth combines the promise of new life with a tragedy that need not have happened (**13:13**). In its foolishness, the nation refuses the very possibility of deliverance and restoration that the Lord offers.

There is only one reason why Israel will not be left to perish in its own foolishness: the Lord will bring restoration and life because of his grace and promise (**13:14**). Paul applies the promise of this verse to the resurrection (1 Cor 15:55). As the following chapter will make clear, the Lord will ultimately restore his people for his own name's sake.

Before restoration occurs, however, judgment will take its course. The analogy is taken from nature: a scorching *east wind* will bring drought and the failure of the harvest (**13:15**). Flourishing Ephraim will be plundered and deprived of its wealth and prosperity. This prophecy was probably fulfilled when the Assyrian army invaded from the east in 721 BC, spreading death and destruction and bringing the northern kingdom to an end. The tragic fate of Samaria, the once proud capital, is shown in **13:16** (see also 9:14-17; 2 Kgs 17:5). It is a stern reminder of how much the Lord loathes sin.

14:1-9 Israel Will Be a Garden

Hosea's God is the God of second chances. Thus his final words to the people are words of hope, rather than words of judgment.

14:1-3 The final exhortation

The radical change of mood from 13:16 to 14:1 focuses attention on the surprise exhortation to repentance. Throughout the book, Hosea has made repeated pleas for Israel to return and be restored. Indeed, 'return' is the word most frequently used in Hosea. It captures both the problem of Israel and the solution to the problem.

The problem, seen in the very first verses of chapter 1, is that Israel has turned away from the God who formed, called and redeemed it to follow false gods. The solution to the problem is for Israel to *return ... to the Lord* (**14:1a**). This means more than just to turn back. What is required has become increasingly evident as we have moved through the book. It means acknowledging the Lord with all their heart (2:20). It means knowing the Lord with all their mind (4:6). It means living like people who know the Lord (6:6). It means following the example set by Jacob (12:3-6). It means acknowledging the Lord as the only God. The exhortation is both demanding and exclusive. This time around, no half measures will do.

The reason for the exhortation is simple: *Your sins have been your downfall* (**14:1b**). The Hebrew tense used suggests that this has become Israel's permanent state. The nation is reminded of its past conduct and its failure to repent sincerely (see 5:4; 7:10; 11:5). Given Israel's intransigence in the face of the calls to repent in 6:1 and 12:7, we have to doubt whether the response this time will be any different.

The words of confession that Hosea urges contain many echoes of chapters 1–3. The plea that the Lord should forgive all their sins is a reminder of the Lord's commitment to forgive and show compassion (**14:2**). He is asked to make the promise in 2:1 a reality, and reverse the threat symbolized by the name 'Lo-Ruhamah', which means 'not loved' (1:6-7). This confession also involves a renunciation of the sins of inappropriate political alliances, dependence on military prowess, and idolatry (**14:3**). The appeal to the Lord's forgiveness is rooted in his compassion.

14:4-8 The Lord will be 'like the dew'

The dramatic shift in **14:4** is similar to the shift between 2:13 and 2:15. The Lord responds to the words of confession

with the gracious proclamation, *I will heal their waywardness, and love them freely, for my anger has turned away from them.* The statement reverses the previous harsh declaration, *Because of their sinful deeds, I will drive them out of my house. I will no longer love them* (9:15). It reaffirms the gracious declaration of 11:8-9.

We should note that the people had done nothing that entitled them to God's forgiveness. It was given 'freely'. Their final restoration depends entirely on the Lord. Israel has no part to play, and is, in fact, unable to play any part.

The Lord's pardon brings total restoration to the people of God. He promises to be like *dew to Israel,* bringing blessing and fertility (**14:5a**). The picture is that of a luxuriant garden. The restored people of God, like a well-watered tree, will be fresh, fruitful, stable and vigorous (**14:5b-8**; see also Ps 1:1). They will dwell in safety, and the fame of the nation will be restored (14:7). The rich imagery in these verses echoes the promise of restoration in the Lord's love song (2:14-23). The Lord of Israel is the reason and basis for this restored state. He will answer his people, care for them and make them fruitful (14:8).

14:9 Conclusion

The book concludes with a final exhortation. This time, the appeal is directed not only to Israel but also to all who, through the ages, will read these words and desire to follow the Lord. The contemporary hearer and reader are summoned to heed the continuing challenge of the past.

The exhortation unites the intellectual and the practical by insisting that to understand the prophetic message is not simply to be intellectually stimulated but to live out the message through wise and appropriate conduct. Our knowledge of God is to be reflected in obedience to and practise of God's ways.

The basis of the appeal is the justice of God, whose *ways are right.* All those who truly return to and know the Lord will experience this for themselves.

Douglas Carew

Further Reading

Kidner, Derek. *The Message of Hosea.* BST. Leicester: Inter-Varsity Press, 1981.

McComiskey, Thomas E. ed. 'Hosea', in *Hosea, Joel, Amos.* Vol 1 of *The Minor Prophets: An Exegetical and Expository Commentary.* Grand Rapids: Baker, 1992.

JOEL

The name 'Joel', which means 'Yahweh is God', seems to have been a common one, for the OT mentions thirteen individuals with this name. The Joel who wrote this book was a prophet from the southern kingdom of Judah who probably lived in Jerusalem and was the son of a man called Pethuel (1:1).

The absence of any mention of a specific king of Judah or Israel suggests that the book was written in a period when no king held political power. This was the case in the ninth century BC, when Joash was a child and real power was in the hands of Jehoiada, the high priest and husband of the king's aunt (2 Kgs 11-12; 2 Chr 22:10-24:16). If the book was written this early, then Joel is the first prophet to speak of the 'day of the Lord' and the remnant (translated 'survivors' in 2:32).

Other scholars believe that Joel was written in the fourth century BC, long after the exile, when there was no king. If this date is correct, then Joel is quoting Amos and Isaiah, rather than Amos and Isaiah quoting Joel.

I find the evidence for the early date more convincing. Fortunately the timeless teaching of the book is unaffected by the uncertainty about its date.

Occasion and Purpose

The book was written shortly after a locust plague and drought had ruined all the crops and affected all areas of life. Joel predicts that this disaster will be remembered for generations to come. He is convinced that God was punishing his people for taking him and his blessings for granted. He warns that the locust plague was merely a warning of a greater judgment to come and urges the people to return to God. As bad as the locust plague was, the coming day of the Lord will be far worse (2:1-11).

Rather than mentioning the exact sins of which the people are to repent, Joel stresses that on the day of the Lord, God himself will come at the head of his army in a holy war against evil. God's holiness is the driving force behind his ultimate judgment of sin. But God is also merciful and will deliver those who turn to him in repentance and faith.

Unity of the Book

Some scholars have argued that the book has more than one author. They claim that most of 1:1-2:27 was written by a pre-exilic prophet after a locust plague and that a later post-exilic prophet supplemented his work with the sections about the day of the Lord (2:28-3:21). More recent scholars, however, regard the book as the work of a single author.

Outline of Contents

COMMENTARY

1:1-2:27 Present Judgment and Blessings

1:1-20 Forerunners of the Day of the Lord

1:1-4 The past locust invasion

Joel starts by identifying himself and the source of his message (1:1). His message came from *the Lord* (Yahweh), and should thus be heeded. So he summons everyone (both the elders and the people) to listen.

The elders must take the lead in facing up to the meaning of the recent locust invasion. Joel's question in (1:2) reminds them that this plague is the worst thing that has ever happened in the land of Judah. It will be remembered for generations to come as a warning not to disobey God and suffer the same fate (1:3; see also Exod 10:2, 6, 14).

The four words used for the locusts in **1:4** may refer to the successive stages in the insect's life cycle, or, more probably, to four varieties of locust. Each swarm of locusts eats whatever has been left by the locusts in the earlier swarm. They gather in vast swarms that cover and eat everything in their path. What once looked green and beautiful rapidly becomes a scene of devastation.

We in Africa can certainly understand the desolation and desperation that would accompany a locust plague. Their destruction of a harvest results in hunger and starvation.

1:5-12 The results of the devastation of the land

The locust invasion affected everyone in the land, from the leaders (priests and elders) to the lowest (farmers and drunkards), but Joel addresses his message to some specific groups. First he turns to the drunkards (**1:5a**). The destruction of the vineyards means that there is no wine for them (**1:5b**). Instead of being the last to realize what is happening around them, they will quickly awaken from their drunken sleep to mourn the lack of alcohol (see also Prov 23:35). The swarm is a wake-up call, summoning them to mourn and repent.

The locusts have been like a powerful invading army (**1:6a**; see also Prov 30:27). Their teeth are as destructive as those of a lion (**1:6b**). Not only have they destroyed the vines by stripping their leaves, they have also chewed the bark off the fig trees, leaving them bare and white (**1:7**). Figs were one of the mainstays of the economy of Israel, and thus their destruction signals economic calamity. African countries devastated by locusts suffer serious economic consequences. Food becomes too expensive for average people to afford and foreign currency has to be spent on importing food rather than on developing the country.

The locust plague also affected worship in the temple, and thus the second group the prophet addresses are the priests (1:8-10). The crops provided food for them (see Exod 29:27-28; Lev 1–2; Num 28:5-8) and for the offerings that honoured God – but no crops will be reaped. The destruction of the land is so great that the prophet calls on the citizens to mourn like a young woman (a virgin) whose betrothed (that is, her intended husband) dies before the marriage is consummated. Instead of joyously adorning herself for her wedding, she sadly dons black sackcloth (**1:8**). Similarly, the usual joy of the harvest is now replaced by sackcloth, mourning and sorrow.

The lack of grain, wine and oil, used to represent all agricultural products, affects the worship services in the temple (1:9-10). The very ability to worship God is compromised by the inability to provide the offerings commanded in Leviticus 6:14-18 and 7:11-18. How can the people anticipate blessing if they cannot offer the formal sacrifices prescribed by the Law?

Farmers and vine growers are the last group addressed (**1:11**). They were often tenant farmers or landless agricultural workers and were among the poorest people in the land (2 Kgs 25:12; Isa 61:5; Jer 40:7-10; 52:16). These farmers were suffering the effects of a drought, for everything is parched (**1:10, 12a**). Not only had they lost their crops, but they would also be unable to pay the rent that was due. African readers can identify with their despair and understand Joel's statement that the joy of the people has dried up with their crops (**1:12b**).

1:13-14 A call for prayer and fasting

The locust plague was an indication of divine displeasure (see also Hos 4:1, 3) and thus everyone in the land must cry out to the Lord for his help. Only by turning from sin in repentance could Israel begin to experience the blessing of God again. The priests are summoned to lead the whole nation in mourning (**1:13**). They are told to replace their richly embroidered robes (Exod 28:39-43) with rough, scratchy clothing that would symbolize the depth of their grief and repentance (see also Amos 8:10). They are to pray all night, declare a holy fast and organize a sacred assembly at the temple for mourning (**1:14**). In the OT, people often fast during times of calamity (see, for example, Judg 20:26; 1 Kgs 21:27; Ezra 8:21). In other words, they deny themselves food in order to focus their attention on God as they approach him with humility and sorrow for their sin and with urgent requests.

Many churches in Africa practise prayer and fasting on a regular basis. This practice is important for the spiritual revival of individuals, local churches and nations (see 2 Chr 7:13-14; Jonah 3:7).

1:15-18 A further description of the devastation

Joel briefly mentions the topic of *the day of the lord* (**1:15**), which he will develop in more detail in chapter 2. The locust plague is only a forerunner of an even more devastating judgment to come. Then he returns to describing the plight of the nation.

People are starving because of the locusts and the drought (**1:16**). No offerings are being brought to the temple, and hence there is no joy and gladness there. The seeds lie shrivelled beneath their hoes (**1:17a**) and the food storage facilities are in a state of disrepair – the barns are desolate and the granaries trampled down (**1:17b**). The locusts have been as destructive as foreign invaders (Judg 6:3-6). The cattle and sheep, too, have been left without pasture and moan in their distress (**1:18**). The land that was once flowing with milk and honey is now barren.

1:19-20 A Call to the Lord for help

Instead of sinking into despair, Joel sets an example by calling to the Lord for help (**1:19a**). Identifying with those to whom he is called to minister, Joel breaks into a lament, telling God what the disaster has done to the land. Pastures and trees are gone, and the water supply has dried up. Even the wild animals are crying out to God, for the whole of creation shares in the suffering brought about by sin (**1:19b-20**; see also Gen 3:17-18; Jer 12:4; Zeph 1:2-3; Rom 8:20-22).

Like Joel, Christians need to model the response that our Lord wants from all his people. An example of this comes from a small village in Nigeria. The rains were late, crops could not be planted, and drought and starvation threatened. The people gathered in the church to cry out to the Lord for rain. Yet only the chief had sufficient faith to bring his umbrella. When God answered the fervent prayers immediately, the chief was the only one who got home without getting wet.

2:1-17 The Coming of the Day of the Lord

2:1-11 The future invasion

The destruction the locusts have caused will be as nothing compared to God's final judgment, which will come sometime in the near future (**2:1**; see also Rev 9:3-11). The blowing of the trumpet warns the people to prepare for this dreadful *day of darkness and gloom* (**2:2**) about which Joel and other prophets often spoke (2:11; 3:14; see also Isa 13:6-10; Ezek 30:2-3; Amos 5:18-20; Obad 15, Zeph 1:14-17; Zech 14:1-3). It often seems that they are referring both to the day of judgment that would come in the near future with the capture of Jerusalem and the destruction of the temple by the Babylonians, and also to the far distant future when there would be a day of judgment at the end of time. Similarly, Christ's prediction of the events of the end combines events associated with the destruction of Jerusalem by the Romans in AD 70 and events that will happen at the end of the world (Matt 24).

Joel now develops the analogy between an invading army and the locust swarm. The land may be *like the garden of Eden*, but the invaders will leave it a desolate wilderness (**2:3**). Like locusts, they will swarm over the whole land. They will advance as rapidly as galloping horses (**2:4**) and the sound of their advance will be like the rumbling of chariots – the most feared form of combat at the time when Joel was writing (**2:5**). Their onslaught will terrify their opponents (**2:6**). The locusts will easily climb obstacles like city walls and overwhelm the defenders (**2:7-8**). Then they will run along the wide tops of the city walls and, ignoring doors, will burst in through the windows of houses (**2:9**).

This army will be unlike any human army, for cosmic signs will accompany it (**2:10**). The earth and heavens will shake and the sun, moon and stars will be darkened (see also Isa 13:10, 13; Matt 24:29-31; Mark 13:24-25; Luke 21:25-26). More than that, God himself will be at the head of his terrible army (**2:11**; see also Zech 14:3). He will be its commander, and thus its victory is certain.

The rhetorical question *Who can endure it?* (2:11) clearly expects the answer 'no one' (see also Mal 3:2). No one will be able to resist the Lord when he comes in judgment on all evil and disobedience. The African church needs to warn and prepare its people for the Lord's coming so that they will be on his side in this final battle.

2:12-17 A plea for heartfelt repentance

The far greater disaster that lies ahead is an even greater reason for the people to repent than is the locust plague (see 1:13-14).The Lord appeals to them, using the phrase *even now* to indicate that it is not yet too late to appeal to him for forgiveness (**2:12**). Joel, too, calls them to repentance.

Deep remorse was often shown by tearing one's clothes. But God does not want a merely outward display of penitence, and so he says, *rend your heart and not your garments* (**2:13a**; see also 1 Sam 16:7; Matt 23:1-36; 1 John 3:18).

Repentance is possible because God *is gracious and compassionate* (**2:13b**). One of the great themes of the OT is that the holy God who judges sin is also a God of compassion and mercy (see also Exod 34:6-7; Num 14:18; Pss 103:8; 145:8; Jonah 4:2; Nah 1:3, 7). So Joel reminds the people that God is *slow to anger*. He has compassion on all who turn to him in repentance and may delay his judgment and avert the prophesied calamity (see Zech 1:3; Mal 3:6-7). If he does this, the fertility of the land will be restored and the sacrifices of grain and drink offerings will be resumed (**2:14**).

We, too, will come under God's judgment unless we turn around and confess our sin. But we can be confident that broken hearts and changed lives will result in spiritual revival (see also 2 Chr 7:14).

The trumpet that had earlier sounded the alarm in the face of an impending attack (2:1) now summons the people to repentance, prayer and fasting (**2:15**; see also 1:13-14). The urgency of the call is shown by the fact that no one is exempted from this solemn assembly and holy fast, not even infants, nursing mothers or newlyweds, who would normally be excused from such duties (**2:16**; Deut 20:7; 24:5). The bride and groom must even delay the consummation of their marriage.

The priests, as spiritual leaders, are called upon to set an example by leading the way in repentance. They are to lead the people in liturgical worship of Yahweh and implore the God of all grace to have mercy on the people and to spare them, not only for the good of the people but also for his own honour. They are to beg Yahweh not to allow his people to become an object of mockery (**2:17**; see also Ps 44:14; Deut 28:37). The nations should not be able to suggest that he is no longer able to save his people.

In the OT, the Lord's judgment of his people is often described as making them an object of scorn or horror (2 Chr 7:20; 29:8; Ps 79:4; Jer 18:16; 19:8; Ezek 5:14-15). We, too, need to remember that sin will bring shame to ourselves and to the name of the Lord whom we are supposed to represent before the world. Only by turning from our sins in repentance, prayer and fasting can we begin to experience the blessings of God and healing for our land.

2:18-27 God's Response to Repentance

Suddenly Joel changes to the narrative past tense to indicate that the people had responded to his pleas. In the Hebrew text, he uses four past tenses, 'become jealous', 'took pity', 'replied', and 'said', to ... (**2:18-19a**). (Some translations, such as the NIV, have tried to simplify this passage by treating these verbs as being in the future tense, but Hebrew grammar does not support this.) These four verbs indicate that the people did repent and heed Joel's call for a spiritual response to the events of the day.

The words, *then the Lord was jealous* indicate God's fierce commitment to his people (2:18). God cares intensely about us and about how we live. As a result he punishes us when we sin and interrupts our fellowship with him, but he also blesses us when we repent and respond to him. This blessing produces both immediate material results (2:19-27) and spiritual results that will come in the distant future (2:28-32).

God's first response is to restore the material blessings that had been destroyed by the locusts (**2:19b**). The land's productivity will be restored, and the fields, orchards and pastures will again produce crops of grain, new wine and oil. No longer will his people suffer hunger; instead they will be fully satisfied (see also Deut 6:10-11; 8:7-10; 11: 13-15). But not all God's blessings find full fulfilment in the present. His promise that they will never again be scorned by the nations awaits the second coming of Christ (see comments on 2:1).

God also promises security and protection as he drives back the *northern army* (**2:20**), which was earlier described in terms of locusts. This may be the army of Israel's historical enemies, such as the Babylonians and Assyrians, or it may be the army from the north in history's final battle (see also Ezek 38–39, esp. 39:2). God will drive these enemies into a dry and desolate land where they will be destroyed. Some of them will be destroyed in the eastern sea (the Dead Sea) and others in the western sea (the Mediterranean).

The land, animals and people are called to rejoice in God's intervention. Where joy and gladness had once disappeared, they are now restored (**2:21**; compare 1:16). The beasts of the field will soon have an abundance of pasture (**2:22a**; compare 1:18-20). The fig tree and the vine will bear their fruits (**2:22b**; compare 1:7, 12). The people of the covenant are to join in celebrating with the animal and plant kingdoms because the Lord is able to restore the land (**2:23a**).

In the midst of this rejoicing over the immediate effects of God's response to his people's repentance, we suddenly encounter the startling prediction that not only will the Lord give them material prosperity, but he will also provide *the teacher for righteousness* (**2:23b**, NIV footnote). In

NIV, this verse is translated as *the autumn rains,* but righteousness is not normally a quality associated with rain, and the Hebrew contains a definite article, indicating that a specific person is meant. The prophet is playing on the similarities between the word for 'rain' (*yôreh*) and the word for 'teacher' (*môreh*), and using rain as a metaphor to describe the coming of divine righteousness on the land (see also Ps 72:5-7). The coming of God's teacher will be accompanied at first by the coming of the autumn and spring rains (**2:23c**), and 'afterwards' by a downpour of the Holy Spirit (2:28-29). Once again, the land will produce an abundant harvest and what had been eaten by the locusts will be restored (**2:24-25**). This coming teacher must be the Messiah, who will personify and teach righteousness so that the people can experience inner transformation and live holy lives.

God promises his people that they will never again experience a disaster like the locust plague (2:26-27). This promise is similar to the one in 2:19, which is to be fulfilled on the day of the Lord. But from elsewhere in Scripture, it is clear that this promise will only hold if God's people remain truly repentant and consistently follow him and his ways (Deut 28:15-48). It will only be after the final day of judgment that God's people will never again experience this kind of disaster (Zech 14:9-11; Rev 21:4).

God's goodness and deliverance of his people from disaster should lead them to praise and worship him (**2:26**). They will realize that he is present with them (see also Jer 31:33-34) and that he is God, and that *there is no other* (**2:27**; see also Deut 4:35; Isa 45:5, 6, 18, 22; 46:9; Ezek 36:11). There should be no room for idolatry among God's people. Our response to his compassion and mercy in sending Christ to save us should be to give him our exclusive loyalty and worship. Like the people of Israel, we should testify of God's goodness and wonders to those around us.

2:28-3:21 Future Blessings and Judgment

2:28-32 Spiritual Blessings in the Distant Future

Joel 2:19-27 deals with God's first act of blessings in response to his people's repentance. But in 2:28-3:21, we learn of the blessings that will come *afterward* (**2:28a**), that is, in the distant future. Joel starts by speaking of three promises God makes for the future.

2:28-29 Promise of the Holy Spirit

The showers that come with the teacher of righteousness will be followed by an even more abundant outpouring, when the Holy Spirit will be poured out on *all people* (**2:28b**), including even Gentile slaves in Jewish households (**2:29**). It will be given to daughters as well as sons, to women as well as men, indicating that both men and women have a role in Christian ministry. The Holy Spirit can enable every believer, regardless of age, sex or social status, to prophesy, dream dreams and see visions (see also Num 12:6).

In both the OT and the NT, believers were filled and empowered by the Holy Spirit to help them do God's work (Exod 31:2-3; Num 11:29, 1 Sam 19:20-23; Ps 51:11). The importance of the Holy Spirit in the life of a believer and in the church cannot be overemphasized. He regenerates us, lives within us, and makes us part of the one body of Christ (1 Cor 12:13). He gives us the power to live a holy life and to fulfil God's plan for our lives.

Peter recognized that the outpouring of the Spirit prophesied by Joel occurred on the day of Pentecost (Acts 2:16-21). He interprets the 'afterward' as equivalent to 'in the last days' (Acts 2:17; see also 1 Pet 1:5, 20) and sees God pouring out his Spirit in a measure far more abundant than the promised rain (see 2:22-26). Yet this was only a partial and preliminary fulfilment of Joel's prediction. Its total and ultimate fulfilment awaits the second coming of Christ (see Isa 32:15).

2:30-31 Promise of wonders on the day of the Lord

Joel also predicts that frightening signs will mark the day of the Lord (**2:30-31**). God's supernatural power will cause extraordinary changes in nature, reminding us of the terrible plagues of Egypt, and will ultimately destroy both the earth and the sky.

The Spirit was poured out on the day of Pentecost, but these cosmic events are still to come at the end of history, as the book of Revelation makes clear (Rev 6:12-13, 17; 8:8-9; 14:14-20; 15:8; 16:4-9; 19:1-18). Yet Peter quoted 2:30-31 in his speech on the day of Pentecost (Acts 2:19-20), not to imply that the prophecy has been fulfilled, but to warn his hearers and us to fear God and turn to him in repentance (Acts 2:40). The day of the Lord is described as *great and dreadful* for God's enemies, for it will be a day of judgment on which they will have to face the divine wrath.

2:32 Promise of salvation for the remnant

In the midst of judgment and catastrophes, God promises salvation to *everyone who calls on the name of the Lord* (**2:32a**). The 'everyone' means that both Jews and Gentiles can partake in the blessings of redemption (see also Rom 10:12-13). That is why the church in Africa today is made up of believers from every tribe on the continent.

To 'call on the name of the Lord' is to call on him in believing faith (Pss 99:6; 145:18; Rom 10:13). We must trust God and accept his salvation or we will perish with the unrepentant. In the NT, Peter leaves no doubt that 'calling on the name of the Lord' means calling on the name of Jesus, the only name 'by which we must be saved' (Acts 4:9-12; see also Acts 9:14, 21; 22:16; 1 Cor 1:2; 2 Tim 2:22).

The repentant people who call on the Lord are also described as *the survivors whom the Lord calls* (**2:32b**). God's people are divinely chosen by him, but have a choice

of whether to accept or reject his offer of salvation. Those who call on him will become the renewed and transformed people of God in the future.

3:1-17 Future Judgment of the Nations

3:1-8 The basis of the judgment

The phrase *in those days and at that time* refers to the future day of the Lord, when God will *restore the fortunes of Judah and Jerusalem* (**3:1**; see also Jer 30:18; 31:23; 33:15-18). Their prosperity will be renewed and Jerusalem will be rebuilt and protected. This change in their fortunes is directly related to the change in their hearts reported in 2:12-13, and 2:32.

God will also call to account the evil nations who have oppressed his people (3:2-8; see also Isa 13:9; 26:20-21; Zeph 1:15-18). He will gather them together (see also Isa 66:18a; Zeph 3:8) and judge them in the *Valley of Jehoshaphat* (**3:2a**). This valley may be a physical place (see 2 Chr 20) or it may simply be the place where 'Jehovah judges', since this is what the name 'Jehoshaphat' means. In 3:14, this valley is also referred to as 'the valley of decision'.

The nations will be judged for mistreating God's people. Their crimes are that they had dispersed God's people among the nations (**3:2b**; see also Zech 1:18-21), divided up God's land for themselves (**3:2c**), and sold God's people into slavery and valued them so cheaply that they cast lots for them (**3:3**). The depth of the nations' crimes is shown by their treatment of the children. There is a sense in which any society can be judged by how it treats children.

Tyre, Sidon and Philistia had long been enemies of God's people (**3:4**; see also Ezek 25:15-17), but here they represent all of God's enemies throughout history. Yahweh speaks of *my land* and *my people* (3:2), making it clear that the crimes committed against his people were also committed against him (see also Matt 25:31-46). When they took the silver and gold of God's people, it was God's silver and gold (**3:5**). They had also sold his people to Greek slave traders, so that they were taken far from their homeland (**3:6**).

God will repay the nations in kind for oppressing his people (**3:7-8a**; see also Isa 24:14-23; 2 Thess 1:6-8). The children of the slave traders will be sold to the children of God's people, who will sell them to others who will take them far from their homes. The principle that emerges is that we should treat others in the way we would want to be treated.

The concluding clause, *The Lord has spoken*, asserts the authority and certainty of Joel's prophecy (**3:8b**).

3:9-13 The nations prepare for war

The nations are challenged to prepare for the final war against God and his people in the Valley of Jehoshaphat (**3:9-12a**; see also Ps 2:1-2; Isa 13:3; Jer 6:4; 46:3; 51:27-28). The nations believe they are being called to do battle, but in reality they are being called together for judgment. No one can hope to fight God successfully. The idea of a great final struggle is found in many of the prophets (see also Isa 17:12; Mic 4:11-13; Zech 12:2-3; Rev 16:14-16).

All segments of society are to prepare for this war. The mighty men of battle are called up for duty. Basic agricultural tools are reshaped into instruments of war (3:10). This contrasts with God's promise elsewhere of a future golden era of peace in which he will abolish war and when 'they will beat their swords into ploughshares and their spears into pruning hooks' (Isa 2:4; Mic 4:3).

The armies of heaven are summoned to execute God's judgment on the nations (3:11). As the armies of the nations assemble for battle in the valley, they have actually gathered themselves into the winepress of God (3:12b-13). The image is of God trampling out the grapes of his wrath in the winepress of judgment (see also Isa 63:3; Rev 14:14-20). The nations are ripe for judgment; their wickedness is so great that it overflows the vats.

3:14-17 Cosmic signs at the time of judgment

Joel describes multitudes like a swarm of locusts waiting in the *valley of decision* (3:14), also known as the 'Valley of Jehoshaphat' (3:2, 12). They think that they have come there to fight and defeat God, but God has planned to use this occasion to render his judicial decision against rebellious humanity.

We need to remember that the day of the Lord is imminent. Now is the time to repent and prepare for this coming day of judgment. If we understand its severity, we will take this warning seriously and warn others to accept God's offer of salvation.

The cosmic signs accompanying this final battle are signs of the end times: the sun and moon are darkened and the stars will not shine (3:15; see 2:10); the Lord will come out of Zion like a lion roaring for its prey (3:16a; see also Isa 29:6-8; 30:30-31; Zech 14:3-7; Amos 1:2; Rev 16:16-18); the earth and sky will shake and tremble (3:16b; Isa 13:13). But, in the midst of this, *the Lord will be a refuge to his people* (3:16c; see also Nah 1:7) and they will be delivered from the punishment of the wicked. God's people, both Jews and Gentiles, will experience God's eternal compassion as he delivers them and they enjoy his abiding presence with them (3:17; see also Isa 60:16; Ezek 34:30).

3:18-21 Blessings of the Day of the Lord

While the day of the Lord will be terrible for God's enemies, it will bring blessings for God's people. The land will be restored and transformed (3:18a). Where there had been

drought and famine, the vegetation will flourish and the mountains and hills will flow with wine and milk (see also Amos 9:13). The abundant water and rich harvests are symbols of the blessedness of the future age.

The image of water continues, with the restored land being described in terms that remind us of the garden of Eden with a river flowing from it (3:18b; see also Gen 2:10). This river flowing from the Lord's house represents the blessings that come from God (see also Ezek 47:1-12; Zech 13:1; 14:3-8). Revelation 22:1-2 also speaks of a life-giving river in a place where there will be only fruitfulness and no drought or death. God's people will never lack anything, but will be fully satisfied and fulfilled forever.

But while the land of God's people will become a paradise restored, the land of its enemies, such as Egypt and Edom, will become *desolate* as Judah had been after the invasion of the locusts (3:19). Nations that have shed innocent blood will find no refuge when God avenges and totally vindicates his people (see also Deut 32:35; Rom 12:19; Rev 6:10).

However, the land of God's people will be *inhabited forever* (3:20). There is full assurance of victory and peace for those who belong to God.

The final blessing on the day of the Lord is that the Lord will dwell with his people in Zion (3:21b). But first he has to pardon their sins (3:21a), for he is holy and nothing sinful can live with him. The Lord himself will abide in the midst of his people in all his glory forever (see also 3:17; Ezek 48:35; Zech 8:3-8).

God's people can take comfort in the fact that they will be vindicated on the day of the Lord. God will never abandon his promise that repentance brings forgiveness. Joel's message to us is that there is still time to call on the Lord's name and be forgiven and saved (see 2:12-14, 32). Those who turn to God will receive his pardon and enjoy the blessings described in Joel's prophecy, including the enjoyment of God's presence forever (see Rev 21:2-3), but those who refuse face punishment and destruction.

Yoilah Yilpet

Further Reading

Allen, Leslie C. *The Books of Joel, Obadiah, Jonah and Micah.* NICOT. Grand Rapids: Eerdmans, 1976.

Dillard, Raymond. 'Joel' in *The Minor Prophets: An Exegetical & Expository Commentary.* EC. Edited by Thomas Edward McComiskey. Grand Rapids: Baker, 1993.

Patterson, Richard D. 'Joel' in *Daniel and the Minor Prophets.* EBC. Edited by Frank E. Gaebelein. Grand Rapids: Zondervan, 1985.

AMOS

Amos came from the southern kingdom of Judah, and specifically from Tekoa (1:1a), a town that was in the hill country about twelve miles (nineteen kilometres) south of Jerusalem. However, his prophecies were addressed primarily to the northern kingdom of Israel. He insisted that he was not born into a prophet's family, but was called by God to be a prophet. Before becoming a prophet, he had been a rancher and a farmer, breeding sheep and caring for sycamore figs (7:14-15). Sycamore-fig trees, which produce fruit once every three months, do not grow in the highlands around Tekoa, and so Amos must also have worked in the warmer lowlands and fertile oases in the Jordan Valley as it approaches the Dead Sea.

Amos dates his prophecy to 'two years before the earthquake' (1:1b). That earthquake must have been a terrible one, for Zechariah, writing two and a half centuries later, refers to it as something that was still remembered when he says, 'You will flee as you fled from the earthquake in the days of Uzziah king of Judah' (Zech 14:5). Archaeologists have found evidence of earthquakes in Israel that date back to the time of Amos. This event must have had additional significance to Amos because it was a confirmation of what he had prophesied (8:8; 9:1).

Zechariah's reference to Uzziah ties in with the other dates given in 1:1c; 'when Uzziah was king of Judah' (that is, between 790 and 739 BC), and Jeroboam II was king of Israel (that is, from 793 to 753 BC). At that time, Assyria in the north and Egypt in the south were weak, and thus these kings of Israel and Judah enjoyed long reigns that were characterized by stability and economic prosperity. They also enjoyed military successes that led to territorial expansion. Jeroboam II's expansion to the north, especially into Aram (2 Kgs 14:23-29), gave Israel control of trade routes that brought wealth and prosperity to the northern kingdom, which was then at the height of its power.

In Uzziah's later years, he was afflicted with leprosy, but this disease struck long after Jeroboam's death and thus long after the earthquake.

Outline of Contents

COMMENTARY

1:1-2 Introduction

Amos is introduced in terms of one of his lay jobs as *one of the shepherds of Tekoa* (**1:1**). The Hebrew word translated 'shepherd' was one that was used for a sheep breeder, who probably owned large herds of sheep and goats and was in charge of other shepherds. The same word is used to refer to the king of Moab in 2 Kings 3:4. Tekoa was a town in the hill country of Judea.

The opening words of Amos present the Lord as being like a lion that *roars from Zion* (**1:2**). Zion, or Jerusalem, was the place from which God ruled as king. The roaring is a sign of his anger. Most of the people over whom he ruled were farmers, who would have become aware of God's wrath as they saw the pastures wither and the drought affect even the mountain tops like Mount Carmel. Amos' listeners would have grasped the seriousness of the message that he had to deliver.

1:3-2:16 The Judgment of God

Amos moves into a series of denunciations of various nations. All the denunciations follow the same pattern. First there is a statement of the certainty of God's judgment, then a statement of the particular offence that has led God to intervene and finally God reveals the particular punishment for each offending nation.

Each of the denunciations begins with the words, *For three sins of ... even for four, I will not turn back my wrath* (1:6, 9, 11, 13; 2:1, 4, 6). This use of numbers was common in OT times (Job 5:19). Three and four add up to seven, which was the number that symbolized completeness. Thus the formula is a poetic way of stating that the nations could do nothing to avert God's judgment as pronounced through the prophet. His judgment was certain.

1:3-2:5 Judgment Against Other Nations

The prophet Joel foretold God's judgment on Tyre and Sidon (treated as one nation), Philistia (Gaza) and Edom for the wrongs they had done to Judah. He also foretold that God would leave Egypt desolate (Joel 3:1-8, 19). Amos pronounces judgment on the same nations (except for Egypt) and adds Damascus, Ammon, Moab and Judah for a total of seven nations. He may have chosen seven as the number of completeness to indicate that all nations come under God's judgment, or he may simply be focusing on the nations that were special enemies of God's people. The surprise is his inclusion of Judah in this list. Although Judah was supposed to be composed of the people of God, it too was alienated from him and, like the other nations, was in rebellion against him.

As we read the list of atrocities in this chapter, we are reminded that similar things happen in Africa in our day. Women are raped, children are seized and forced to become fighters, whole communities are slaughtered or forced into refugee camps, hundreds die of hunger because civil wars and landmines disrupt agriculture and food supplies. God's wrath blazed against those who did such things.

In presenting his message of judgment, Amos refers to the nations mentioned in the historical books of Kings and Chronicles. He spells out the reason for the condemnation of each nation:

- The Syrians, with their headquarters in *Damascus*, were condemned for their cruelty. When they defeated their enemies, they would run studded threshing-sledges over their bodies (**1:3-5**). Syrian cruelty is also referred to in 2 Kings 8:7-15 and 13:3-4. God's prophecy of destruction and exile in Kir was fulfilled through the Assyrian king Tiglath-Pileser (2 Kgs 16:9).

- The Philistines, with their headquarters in *Gaza, Ashdod* and *Ekron* (**1:6-8**), were condemned for being ruthless slave traders. God hates the slave trade, for he hates anything that treats a human being as no more than something to be used to make a profit for someone else. The prophecies against the Philistines were fulfilled when these cities fell to the Assyrians: Gaza fell to Tiglath-Pileser in 734 BC, Ashdod to Sargon in 711 BC, and Ekron to Sennacherib in 701 BC.

- *Tyre* was guilty of the same sin as the Philistines: it participated in the slave trade. The sin of Tyre was aggravated by the fact that this was a violation of a previous covenant, based on friendship. Many years earlier, David and Solomon had enjoyed a close relationship with Hiram, king of Tyre. Hiram had provided David and Solomon with supplies and workmen to help in the construction of the royal palaces and the temple (2 Sam 5:11-12; 1 Kgs 5:1-7). He also seems to have recognized God's hand in the exaltation of David and Solomon to the throne of Israel, and in his letter to Solo-

mon he wrote, 'Praise be to the Lord today, for he has given David a wise son to rule over this great nation' (1 Kgs 5:7). Solomon and Hiram also signed a treaty (1 Kgs 5:12). Signing a treaty involved far more than just putting two signatures on a piece of paper. The treaty would have involved a covenant, solemnized with religious rites and accompanied by sacrifices. In ignoring this covenant, the Tyrians were also sinning against the light they had received. They ignored this *treaty of brotherhood* when they delivered up *whole communities of captives,* selling all the Jews who came into their hands. The covetousness of Tyre fed the cruelty of Edom. God vowed to punish them, a vow that was fulfilled when the city fell to Nebuchadnezzar after a very long siege, and still later, in 332 BC, when it was destroyed by Alexander the Great.

- *Edom* could be described as a *brother* to Israel because Jacob, the father of the Israelites, and Esau, the father of the Edomites, were the twin sons of Isaac (Gen 25:24-30). Despite this close relationship, the Edomites hated the Israelites (**1:11**) and were happy to buy Israelites as slaves from the Philistines (1:6) and the Tyrians (**1:9**). God would punish them for their lack of love and compassion by destroying their headquarters at Bozrah.

- *Ammon*, too, was a blood relation of the Israelites through Lot, Abraham's nephew (Gen 12:5; 19:30-38). In a war with the Israelites in Gilead that was prompted by greed for land, the Ammonites committed atrocities (**1:13**). God noted what they did, and would punish them for it (**1:14-15**). This message should be a warning to all those who try to seize land that belongs to others.

- *Moab* violated an almost universal unwritten law of ancient times when it desecrated a corpse (**2:1**). God noted this action, and would punish Moab for it (**2:2-3**).

- *Judah* is the last nation (with the exception of Israel) to hear judgment. The people are condemned for rejecting the laws of God and returning to idolatry (**2:4-5**).

2:6-16 Judgment Against Israel

The Israelites probably smiled as they heard the condemnation of their old enemies such as Syria and the Philistines. They may, however, have begun to shift uneasily when they heard the denunciations of their former ally Tyre and their blood relatives Edom and Ammon for breaking the laws of kinship. But they would have become very disturbed when the series of condemnations reached Judah. There is a Hausa (Nigeria) saying, 'when you see your brother's beard on fire, you put water on yours'. Clearly, Israel would be next.

In fact, Israel was the main target of Amos' preaching. His job was to warn the Israelites that they too were under God's judgment. The other nations had sold people into slavery, and the Israelites were just as hard and callous: *they sell the righteous for silver, and the needy for a pair of sandals* (**2:6**). These expressions can be interpreted as referring to bribes that persuade judges to rule against the righteous, or as referring to a community or society that is so greedy that it will sell a poor person into slavery for a debt no greater than the price of a pair of sandals (see 8:6). There was clearly rampant social injustice as the poor were oppressed and injustice prevailed (**2:7a**).

There was also serious social and moral decline. Temple prostitutes were made use of by young and old, with a father and a son using the same girl in total contravention of God's laws (**2:7b-8**; Lev 18). The very existence of temple prostitutes shows that the people have turned away from the worship of the God of their ancestors to the worship of idols. And in their sexual immorality they also violated God's laws of compassion, for they lay down on *garments taken in pledge,* despite the law's requirement that such garments must be returned to their owner before nightfall (Exod 22:26-27). Their contempt for justice and for true religion is also shown by their partying in the temples drinking *wines taken as fines.*

In the case of the seven other nations, their punishment was mentioned immediately after the accusation. But in the case of the Israelites, the intensity of their guilt is revealed by placing their actions in the context of what God had done for them in the past (2:9-16). He had protected and sustained them for four decades as they wandered in the wilderness (**2:10**). Then he had helped them uproot and destroy the powerful tribes that they met in Canaan, against whom they would have been helpless if God had not been on their side (**2:9**). The spies made this abundantly clear when they reported that the Israelites were 'like grasshoppers' before the inhabitants of the land they were going to possess (Num 13:28, 33). God also raised up good leaders for them in the form of prophets and Nazirites, who were totally dedicated to God (**2:11**; see Num 6:1-21).

Not only had the Israelites forgotten God's faithfulness and broken his laws, but they had also gagged God's messengers, forbidding the prophets to speak and forcing the Nazirites to break their vow by drinking wine (**2:12**).

God's judgment will come because of these offences. They were enjoying a time of prosperity, but the cart loaded with grain will crush them to death, an image that shows the intensity of the judgment (**2:13**). The statement that not even the strongest, swiftest and bravest warrior will escape, even if mounted on a horse, shows that no one can hope to escape it (**2:14-16**).

When God's judgment is delayed, let us not assume that it is not coming. It is foolish to assume that because God is loving and longsuffering, he will not punish sin. The only way of escape is true repentance.

3:1-6:14 The Reasons for God's Judgment

3:1-15 Israel's Sin

God had chosen the Israelites from among all other nations, watched over them, cared for them in a unique way, and specially revealed himself to them and blessed them. They should have responded with loyalty, love and obedience. But they had not, and had repeatedly broken their covenant agreement with God. Now they were to discover the truth of the saying, 'From everyone who has been given much, much will be demanded; and from the one who has been entrusted with much, much more will be asked' (Luke 12:47-48). God would punish them both because of their oppression of others and because of their violation of his covenant (**3:2**).

In 3:1-8, Amos uses seven examples taken from everyday life to illustrate the cause-and-effect relationship that will result in their judgment. Each time he starts by looking at the effect, and then looks for the cause. For example, when we see two people walking together along a road, we can deduce that they must have met and agreed to travel together (**3:3**). Similarly, if we hear a lion roaring and growling we know that it is protecting the prey it has caught (**3:4**). If we see a bird caught in a trap, we know that someone must have set it, and the action of the trap shows that something must have triggered it (**3:5**). The level of violence in the examples has been increasing, and rises still further in Amos' two final examples: a trumpet call signals a military emergency and a disaster is evidence that the Lord has judged a city (**3:6**). The loving and patient God becomes the one who brings calamity on Israel.

This disaster should not be unexpected, for the Lord has never done anything major among his people without first revealing it to his servants, the prophets (**3:7**). The revelation may be about something that will happen shortly or many centuries in the future, but there can be no doubt that it will come to pass. As the Hausa people of Nigeria say, 'no matter how high you throw a stone, it will come down', and 'no matter how long the night seems, the day will break'.

Because Amos was the prophet through whom the *Sovereign Lord* was prophesying, his hearers should listen with fear (**3:8**).

Amos next summons nations who are experts in injustice: the Philistines from Ashdod and the Egyptians. They are to gather near Samaria to witness the injustices committed by Israel (**3:9**). These ancient enemies of Israel will be surprised to see that oppression and violence against both people and property have become so common that they are now part of the Israelite character. The Israelites no longer know how to do what is just, honest and right (**3:10**).

The Israelites had confidence in the fortresses that they had built and could not imagine that anyone could capture them. But God will do so (**3:11**). The lion that has roared in

3:9 will devour the nation, and only a few useless fragments will remain (**3:12**).

Not only will their fortresses be destroyed, but also their luxurious houses (**3:15**) and their religious centre at Bethel. This altar had been set up as an alternative to the temple in Jerusalem and had become a place of idolatrous worship (**3:14**; see comment on 5:5 and compare 1 Kgs 12:25-33). Its destruction was also predicted by a prophet earlier than Amos in 1 Kings 13:2. That prophecy was fulfilled long after Amos' time by King Josiah of Judah (2 Kgs 23:15).

But Amos' warnings about God's impending judgment fell on deaf ears. The Israelites felt secure and believed that the Lord would come to their rescue whenever they were threatened. They forgot that he would only do so if they walked in his ways.

4:1-13 The Sin of the Whole Society

The luxury-loving women of Samaria had made themselves fat at the expense of the poor (**4:1**). They were like the well-fed cows of fertile Bashan, and they would eventually be treated like cattle, led away as captives with hooks through their lips or noses (**4:2-3**). This was the way the Assyrians often treated those they captured.

God hated the Israelites' hypocrisy because they kept up a religious façade. As someone has said, the hypocrite and the hippopotamus in a river have one thing in common: they show only their faces, not their real selves. The Israelites boasted about their obedience to the ritual requirements of the law as they brought sacrifices, tithes, thank-offerings and freewill offerings to the sanctuaries at Bethel and Gilgal (**4:4-5**). But at the same time they carelessly crushed the helpless, ignoring the fact that in the law God had ordered that such people receive special care and protection (Deut 26:12; 27:19).

A good father chastises his children out of love in order to correct them (Heb 12:4-11). God had warned the people that he would do the same when he made a covenant with them in Leviticus 26 and Deuteronomy 28. Like any ancient covenant, it spelled out clearly what curses and punishments would follow if the covenant were broken. Disobedient or disloyal subjects would find themselves enduring drought, famine, plagues, defeat at the hands of their enemies and burning devastation. All of these disasters had indeed come upon Israel (**4:6-11**). The account of each disaster ends with the words, *yet you have not returned to me.* God had hoped that the Israelites would respond by turning around and repenting, but they persisted in their sinful ways.

God had exhausted all his efforts to persuade them. Now he will come himself in judgment, and Israel must prepare for a terrifying encounter with the creator, *the Lord God Almighty* (**4:12-13**). The only possible preparation is repentance – or a willingness to accept destruction. What a terrible state to be in!

5:1-27 An Appeal for Repentance

Amos has no desire to see the nation of Israel destroyed, and that is why he raises a lamentation over the fate that will befall them (**5:1-2**). He reminds the Israelites that the Lord has said that they will be decimated (**5:3**). But the Lord himself does not want to destroy them, and so he appeals through Amos to the people of Israel to repent and thus save their lives (**5:4**).

Why does God tell the people not to go to Bethel, Gilgal and Beersheba? (**5:5a**). One reason is that these cities were in strategic locations, which meant that they would be prime targets in the event of any attack on Israel and Judah (**5:5b**). But there was also another reason. Bethel was the location of one of the golden calves that Jeroboam I had set up (1 Kgs 12:28) and the site of a royal sanctuary belonging to the northern kingdom (7:13). The god worshipped there was not the Lord. There was a fundamental incompatibility between seeking the Lord and seeking the god worshipped at Bethel. Those who sought God there would not find him. Making a play on words, Amos tells them that if they go to Bethel, a name that means 'the house of God', all that they will find is Bethaven, 'the house of idolatry' (or worthlessness, vanity and nothingness). The NIV hides this pun with its translation, *Bethel will be reduced to nothing.*

Beersheba was the place where Abraham 'called upon the name of the lord, the Eternal God' (Gen 21:33) and where God revealed himself to Isaac and Jacob (Gen 26:23-24; 46:1). It had, however, also become a place of idolatry (see 8:14; 2 Kgs 23:8). There was a certain irony in the people of Israel setting out to seek God in Beersheba. Jeroboam I had installed the golden calf at Bethel on the pretext that the journey to Jerusalem was too long. Yet the distance from Samaria to Beersheba was four times as long as the distance from Samaria to Jerusalem!

Amos was not simply calling on the people to stop worshipping at the false sanctuaries at Bethel or Beersheba and instead to worship at Jerusalem. What God wanted was for the people to repent and actively seek him. This was their only hope of survival. This message is repeated three times in this chapter (5:4, 6, 14-15). Even though God was judging the nation, individuals could still repent and live.

Seeking the Lord will involve a total transformation of their worship and of their private and public lives. Once again, God speaks out against their perversion of justice, which leaves a foul taste in one's mouth, their discarding of righteousness, their contempt for those who tell the truth, their oppression of the poor, and their willingness to take and give bribes (**5:7, 10-11a, 12b-13**). Because the courts failed to deliver proper justice, the poor, the weak and those who did not have wealth or influence enjoyed no protection from their oppressors.

The oppressors may feel free to throw out God's standards, but God reminds them of who he is. His power is so great that he controls the seasons (symbolized by the stars in the constellations of Orion and the Pleiades) and the coming of day and night (**5:8a**). More than that, he controls the destructive forces such as floods and fire that can easily demolish the strongholds and cities in which those who ignore him put their trust (**5:8b-9**). He knows their sinfulness, and they should not expect that he will allow them to enjoy the beautiful homes they have built and the crops they have grown (**5:11b-12a**).

The fact that **5:14** (*seek good, not evil, that you may live*) is so similar in form to 5:6 (*seek the Lord and live*) underscores the connection between right worship and right living. Like the Lord, we are to *hate evil* and *love good* and uphold justice (**5:15**).

The Lord promises wailing, anguish and mourning when he comes in judgment (**5:16-17**). Some of the people were looking forward to a coming *day of the Lord* when he would judge their enemies and exalt the nation of Israel (**5:18a**). But Amos insists that, contrary to their expectations, this will not be a day of rejoicing and deliverance but a day when the sinful nation of Israel will be punished for its wickedness (**5:18b, 20**). He illustrates what it will be like by using images that express the same meaning as the proverb 'out of the frying pan into the fire' (**5:19**).

God was fed up with their religious hypocrisy and refused to accept their worship. The repeated negatives in (**5:21-23**), *hate ... despise ... cannot stand ... will not accept ... will have no regard ... will not listen* emphasize the intensity of his feelings. He will not accept the worship of those who have no interest in justice and righteousness (**5:24**). The Israelites have forgotten the God they worshipped in the desert and instead what they worship are idols they have made for themselves (**5:25-26**). In punishment for their idolatry and hypocrisy, God will send them *into exile beyond Damascus* (**5:27**).

6:1-14 Judgment on Blind Pride

Human beings generally fall prey to a sense of false security when they become wealthy and live comfortably. Their way of life insulates them from the real issues of life. The Lord detested the arrogant self-confidence, complacency, materialistic indulgence and pride of Israel (Mount Samaria) and of Judah (Mount Zion) (**6:1**). The leaders of Israel regarded their cities as superior to other cities such as *Calneh* and *Hamath* (both possibly in Syria to the north) and the Philistine city of *Gath* to the west (**6:2**). But they had no grounds for satisfaction, for in their focus on material luxury they were looking at the wrong things. What they should have been looking out for was the coming *evil day* and the *reign of terror* that their own evil actions would bring (**6:3**). Instead, the wealthy inhabitants of Samaria completely ignored all the warnings of God's impending judgment and focused on enjoying the good things of life: elegant homes, fine meals, music, fine perfumes and skin creams, and an abundance of wine (**6:4-6**). Their complete lack of concern for the welfare

of the nation leads God to assure them that they will be among the first to suffer when the end comes (**6:7**).

The *pride of Jacob* leads *the Sovereign Lord* to declare their doom with a solemn oath. They have now passed the point of no return (**6:8**). They can forget about trusting in the human security provided by fortresses and cities. They will face a judgment that will wipe out whole households. Whether caused by a siege, a famine or a plague, the situation will be so bad that any survivor who uses expressions like 'for God's sake' or 'God willing' will be told not even to *mention the name of the Lord*, for fear of attracting further judgment (**6:9-10**). No one would escape, and even their buildings, from the greatest to the smallest, would be completely destroyed (**6:11**).

The nation had turned the natural order of things upside down. It is as if a horse were to try to run on the rocks like a mountain goat, or oxen were used to plough rocks. Justice should be healing, but they have made it like poison; *the fruit of righteousness* should be prosperity and peace, but they have made it yield only *bitterness* (**6:12**).

The nation rejoiced in its military conquest of places like *Lo Debar* and *Karnaim* on the east side of the Jordan (**6:13**), but these victories were hollow, as is shown by the very name of the town Lo Debar, which means 'nothing'. Karnaim means 'horn', a symbol of strength. Israel claims to have conquered this 'strength' *by our own strength*. But God's strength is far mightier than this. He is raising up a whole nation against them (**6:14a**). Throughout history, God has raised up different people to do his will. These include judges, prophets, Nazirites, priests and kings who have willingly served him. But it also includes others like Pharaoh (Exod 9:16) and the nation referred to here by Amos, who think they are acting independently but who are actually being used by God to punish his people and ultimately bring them to repentance.

Israel has oppressed others, and now it will be oppressed *all the way from Lebo Hamath to the valley of the Arabah* (**6:14b**). *Hamath* was a strong town to the north that Jeroboam II had recaptured for Israel (2 Kgs 14:25, 28). *The valley of the Arabah* was the location of the Dead Sea far to the south. These two points marked the boundaries of the land of Israel and Judah. God is saying that both nations will suffer. The land that had been the scene of their triumphs will now be filled with affliction and woe.

This prophecy was fulfilled some forty-five years later when Tiglath-Pileser invaded the land. When we refuse to listen to the Lord's plea to repent and turn to him, his judgment is inevitable, even if it does not come immediately.

7:1-9 Visions of Locusts, Fire and a Plumb-line

Amos is now shown two visions of utter doom for the Israelites. The first is a vision of locusts that will destroy the crops that remain for food after a large portion of the harvest has been paid to the king as a levy (**7:1**). The nation will be utterly wiped out by the resulting famine. And so Amos begs God to spare his people, and God relents (**7:2-3**). Next, God shows Amos a vision of a fire so intense that it dries up the sea and consumes all the land (**7:4**). Once again, Amos stands in the gap and prays for his people (**7:5**; see Ezek 22:30). We should be like him in praying for our nations.

Once again, God hears the prayer of Amos and relents (**7:6**). When the Lord 'relents' or 'repents', it means that he mercifully changes his mind, on the basis of the prayer of his servant, and spares his wayward people.

With the next vision, the Lord speaks to Amos by name, asking *What do you see, Amos?* (**7:8**). This personal address, as if to a friend, reminds us of how well the Lord knows us. He told Moses, 'I know you by name' (Exod 33:17) and Paul tells us that 'The Lord knows those who are his' (2 Tim 2:19). He is the same 'yesterday and today and for ever' and does not change (Heb 13:8). Thus we should not be upset when people on Earth forget our name, despite having been told it many times. No matter how many names and nicknames we have, God knows exactly who we are.

Amos' intercession had twice persuaded God to relent. But God has to judge sin, and so he shows Amos another vision, whose meaning is not immediately apparent. What Amos saw was the Lord holding a plumb-line against a wall (**7:7**). A plumb-line is a long cord with a lead weight at one end. It is used by builders to ensure that a wall is properly vertical. If the plumb-line does not hang straight down next to the wall, the wall is tilted and will have to be torn down and rebuilt. God's plumb-line would show that the nation of Israel was not upright. The foundation of the wall had been well laid and the people had once obeyed him, but as the walls had risen over time, they had started to lean at an angle. As a builder, God had no option but to tear them down, destroying both the political and the economic structures of the nation. This is the judgment God pronounces in 7:7-8. Amos is given no opportunity to appeal against this verdict.

God uses a similar image of the nation as a building in the book of Isaiah, when he says, 'I will make justice the measuring line and righteousness the plumb-line' (Isa 28:17). The Israel that Amos has described was certainly defective as regards both righteousness and justice.

In this judgment, as at the last day, God makes it clear that his condemnation is not arbitrary, but deserved. He sets the plumb-line *among my people* to show that he will make trial of every nation, and judges each one in proportion to its own guilt.

7:10-17 Opposition to Amos

Amaziah, the priest of Bethel, was probably the high priest, in imitation of the high priest of the order of Aaron who served in Jerusalem and who was appointed by God. The altar at Bethel was intended to be an imitation of the one at Jerusalem, and thus would have had similar officials. Amaziah may have been concerned that instructions such as *do not seek Bethel* (5:5) would affect his position of power and influence (as was the case with Demetrius the silversmith – Acts 19:23-27). But that was not the case he put to Jeroboam. He presented Amos as a political threat alleging that *Amos is raising a conspiracy against you* (**7:10-11**). The same tactic was used by Jesus' opponents, who told Pilate, 'If you let this man go, you are no friend of Caesar. Anyone who claims to be a king opposes Caesar' (John 19:12). It was also used against Paul (Acts 16:20-21; see also 17:6-7).

Amaziah's opposition suggests that Amos' message was a powerful one that was attracting attention. So does his use of the word 'conspiracy', which suggests that Amos was not acting alone. This word, combined with Amaziah's instruction to Amos to go back where he came from, that is, to Tekoa in Judah (**7:12a**; see 1:1) suggests that he suspected that Amos was in the pay of the king of Judah and was speaking in the interests of Judah. While this allegation was not true, the fact that it could be made suggests that some Israelites had listened to Amos' message, reformed their lives, and were worshipping God with him.

Besides falsifying Amos' message by suggesting that it was part of a conspiracy, Amaziah also suppressed part of the message. He reported only the judgment Amos had pronounced, and did not say anything about the reasons Amos gave for this judgment – the injustice that prevailed in Israel. He omitted to mention the hope of escape implicit in the call to repentance, and the statement that if they sought the Lord, they would live (5:4). He also did not mention Amos' intercession for his people. Such selective presentation of the truth is no different from a direct lie.

Jeroboam apparently did not act on Amaziah's report. He may have been restrained by his respect for the memory of the prophet Elisha, who had prophesied about his father's success (see 2 Kgs 13:14-25). So Amaziah himself confronted Amos. Like many worldly people, he assumed that someone who was doing the Lord's work was just in it for the money. So he told Amos to go and prophesy for a living somewhere else (**7:12b**).

Amos had no hesitation in replying. He insisted that he had not set out to be a prophet, but had been a shepherd and someone who tended sycamore fig trees (**7:14**; see introduction to this commentary and 1:1). He would still have been doing those jobs if the Lord had not told him to come and prophesy to Israel (**7:15**). That was why he always introduced his prophecies with words like 'This is what the Lord says' (see, for example, 1:3, 6; 2:1; 3:1). Since he had authority from God to communicate the message, he would not be silent, and opposition to his message would be punished. Amaziah himself would die in exile, and the invading army would abuse his wife, kill his children and seize his land (**7:16-17**).

8:1-14 Visions of Fruit and Famine

The final vision that Amos is shown is *a basket of ripe fruit* (**8:1**). Fruit that is perfectly ripe will soon start to rot, and thus this image of fruit reveals that Israel is ripe for destruction and ruin (**8:2-3**). Once again, Amos is given no chance to intercede for them. The judgment has come!

The poor are of special concern to God. So his anger is especially directed at those who abuse the poor (**8:4**). These people were so focused on making money that they considered all the religious festivals that God had given them to be nuisances because they interfered with their business. In particular, they complained about the New Moon and the Sabbath festivals. The celebration of the New Moon was a reminder that God had created an orderly world. It took place on the first day of every month, and was accompanied by special offerings (Num 28:11-15). Selling and other forms of work were forbidden on this day, as well as on the Sabbath, which the Lord had declared to be a day of rest (Exod 20:8-11; Deut 5:12-15).

Amos denounced those who saw these festivals as meaningless rituals. Although they observed them, the people were bored and impatient for the days to pass (**8:5a**). They saw them as interruptions and hindrances to their aggressive, covetous and corrupt business deals. No wonder the Lord complains, 'These people come to me with their mouths and honour me with their lips, but their hearts are far from me' (Isa 29:13).

Prayer went up to God on the Sabbath, and fraud against the poor went up to God in every transaction on the other six days. When the merchants sold their wares, they cheated by not properly filling their measures, charging high prices, and using *dishonest scales* (**8:5b**). God had expressly forbidden all such dealings when he said, 'Do not have two differing weights in your bag – one heavy, one light. Do not have two differing measures in your house – one large, one small. You must have accurate and honest weights and measures, so that you may live long in the land the Lord your God is giving you' (Deut 25:13-15).

When the oppression by the rich had left the poor destitute, stripped even of what land they may have possessed, they were sold in violation of God's command against enslaving fellow-Israelites (Lev 25:39-42). They are said to have been bought and sold for the price of *a pair of sandals* (**8:6a; 2:6**). What a contemptuous valuation of those who are made in the image of God! It is possible that these words refer not so much to the price of the sandals as to the way the person became enslaved. For example, a poor man may have bought a pair of sandals on credit. When he could not make the payment on time, the seller would sell him or members of his family as slaves to cover this trivial debt (see 2 Kgs 4:1). The abuse here is similar to that of some unscrupulous companies who encourage people to buy things they cannot afford and then demand exorbitant payments that result in a poor buyer paying far more than the product is worth.

Not only did those selling grain cheat by selling less than they promised at inflated prices, but they also sold an inferior product – grain mixed with *the sweepings of the wheat* (**8:6b**). These were the unfilled grains of wheat that had no kernel. They should have been discarded or fed to animals, but instead they were mixed into the grain and sold.

These business practices are not confined to Amos' time. Some local traders still knock the bottoms of their measures upward to cheat unsuspecting customers. They adjust their scales so that they do not show true weights. When potatoes, oranges, tomatoes and other fruits and foodstuffs are sold in heaps or in bags, some traders place defective ones or very small pieces at the bottom of the bag, while claiming that everything in the bag is the same size and quality as the ones on top. Oils may be mixed with poorer quality or cheaper products. Some of these ways of cheating not only steal customers' money but also hurt their health. Amos' condemnation of these practices still resonates today. We need to take this prophecy to heart.

In the end, the poor are always the worst hit by these evil practices. The merchants despise them, and consider them too unimportant to matter. But that is not how God sees things. He does not consider cheating at a market stall or anywhere else a minor sin which he will ignore. God sees and knows everything (Ps 139:7-12). There is nothing we can hide from him and he promises *I will never forget anything they have done* (**8:7**).

Part of God's judgment will be a terrible earthquake that makes the whole land *mourn* (**8:8**). We are reminded that Amos' prophecy is dated *two years before the earthquake* in 1:1. Another sign of judgment is that the Lord *will make the sun go down at noon, and darken the earth in broad daylight* (**8:9**). There does not seem to have been any earlier eclipse of the sun that would have suggested this image to the prophet's mind. It was a revelation given specially by the Lord. But the prophecy was fulfilled by an eclipse that took place in 784 BC, a few years after this prophecy, in the year of the death of Jeroboam II. This particular eclipse was said to have reached its height in Jerusalem just before midday. There was also a second eclipse several years after this first one.

Sceptics may wonder how a regular natural phenomenon, such as an eclipse of the sun, can be regarded as having any connection with the moral government of God. The answer is that God can use such events when they come in association with a prophet's prediction, as was the case with Amos. Moreover, we need to remember that in Amos' time there were many people who worshipped the sun as a god. The seeming defeat of the sun would have been interpreted in religious terms.

Not only would there be darkness around them, but this would also be a time of the darkness of grief, with mourning and weeping in every home. Religious feasts will be replaced by a terrible fast: *a famine of hearing the word of the Lord* (**8:10-11**). If they do not listen to God when he speaks to them through his prophets such as Amos, he will eventually stop speaking. They will look for his word all over, from the Dead Sea in the south to the Mediterranean Sea in the west, in the *north* and to the *east*, covering all points of the compass, but they will no longer hear from God (**8:12**).

Even the young people will faint and die from exhaustion – and tragically they will still be calling on the false gods as they die (**8:14**). Their elders are to blame for the loss of these *lovely young women and strong young men*, for they never heeded the words of the Lord in the past, and now it is too late. And if even the young die, what hope is there for the old?

9:1-15 The Destruction of Israel

It is a terrible thing when God stands in the presence of his people to destroy instead of to bless. When his people do well, they should expect him to bless them (5:14). But when his people decide to sin instead, they should expect to be punished. When you insist on cutting your vein with a sharp knife, you should expect blood to gush out.

Our African elders say, 'If you refuse to hear, you will not refuse to see'. When God's anger is kindled to the point where he has to rise up against his people (**9:1**), there is no escape (**9:2-3**). Even those who are taken to foreign lands, herded away like cattle, will find that no foreign king or god can protect them from the God who had fixed his eyes on them *for evil and not for good* (**9:4**). They should not be surprised at the reach of his power, for he is *the Lord Almighty*, who controls the earth and the heavens, the sea and the dry land (**9:5-6**).

The prophecy of Amos began with condemnation of the nations surrounding Israel (1:3-2:5). He returns to that point now, and points out that as regards his justice, God judges Israel just as he does the other nations. They should not think that they are more valuable to him than the *Cushites* from North Africa. It is true that he had originally brought them up out of Egypt, but they were not unique in being led to a new place: he had brought the Philistines from a place called Caphtor (which may have been the island of Crete or of Cyprus) and the Arameans from Kir (the place to which they would be returning under his judgment – 1:5) (**9:7**). Israel can be certain that *the eyes of the Sovereign Lord are on the sinful kingdom* and that he will destroy it because of its sins (**9:8a**).

9:11-15 The Restoration of Israel

But although God will judge Israel as he does other nations, it is also true that the nation is in a special relationship to him as his chosen people, and so he *will not totally destroy the house of Jacob* (**9:8b**). In 5:14-15, we were given an indication that in the midst of God's justice, his mercy would be extended to those who feared him. So when God shakes the nation *as grain is shaken in a sieve*, the good grain will fall through into the pile of wheat, but all the *pebbles*, that is, *the sinners among my people* who have refused to repent, will be destroyed (**9:9-10**).

All previous references to *that day* in Amos (2:16; 3:14; 8:3) have spoken of it as a day of darkness and destruction. But now the tone changes and the day is seen as a day of renewal for God's people (**9:11**). The nation is now referred to as *David's fallen tent* that will be rebuilt *as it used to be*. This mention of David is an indication that God has not forgotten his promise to establish David's kingdom forever (2 Sam 7:10-16). It also indicates that once again Israel and Judah will be united in one kingdom. The restored Israel will then go on to fulfil God's promise to Abraham (Gen 12:3), that 'all peoples on earth' will be blessed through him and his descendants.

The promise that the restored Israel will possess *the remnant of Edom* harks back to the threatened destruction of Edom in 1:12. There will be a *remnant of Edom* just as there will be a remnant of Israel. But rather than being an implacably hostile nation, it will be incorporated into Israel (**9:12**), along with all the other nations *that bear my name* – that is, the Gentiles who will be saved by calling upon the name of the Lord in the end times.

Where previously the land had been cursed with drought and blight (4:6-9) and the people with illness, exile and an inability to enjoy the fruit of their work (4:10; 5:11), these curses will be removed and replaced with covenant blessings. The land will yield wonderful harvests – so much so that the person heading out to plant a new crop will find that the previous crop was so large that it is still being harvested (**9:13**). The people will live safe and productive lives, enjoying the fruit of their labour (**9:14**). This is a promise of abundance and peace.

The book concludes with God's solemn promise that after the storm of his judgment he will personally plant Israel in the land that he has given them, never to be moved or uprooted again (**9:15**).

Daniel Bitrus

Further Reading

Cripps, Richard S. ed. *A Critical & Exegetical Commentary on the Book of Amos.* London: SPCK, 1969.

McComiskey, Thomas Edwards. ed. *Hosea, Joel, Amos.* Vol.1 of *The Minor Prophets: An Exegetical and Expository Commentary.* Grand Rapids: Baker, 1992.

OBADIAH

All we know about the author of Obadiah is his name, which means 'one who serves God'. This name may be significant, for, like African names, Hebrew names were more than merely identifying labels. A name could express a prayer, honour a deity, or refer to event.

In reporting his vision, Obadiah seems to have drawn on elements from other sources (compare 1-9 and Jer 49:7-22). As with oral tradition in Africa, messages conveyed through visions become communal property, with the focus on the message rather than on the particular person who conveys it.

The allusion to the capture of Jerusalem in verses 10-14 helps to date the book, for the Babylonians captured Jerusalem in about 587 BC. Other records clearly show that the Edomites played a role at that time (Ps 137:7; Lam 4:21-22; Ezek 25:12-14; 35:1-15).

Like Nahum and Habakkuk, Obadiah emphasizes God's universal rule by pronouncing his judgment against a nation, here Edom. Edom must not escape scot-free after what it had done to Israel. The intensity of the desire for revenge on Israel's enemies is matched by only a few psalms (for example, Ps 139:19-22). There is no condemnation of Israel's sin that led to the fall of Jerusalem.

Yahweh's response was reassuring, but it also lifted the issue to a higher plane than mere revenge. Obadiah's God is the sovereign Lord of history, working out his purposes through past, present and future events. His message of justice is intended for both Edom and the Israelites.

Outline of Contents

COMMENTARY

1 Introduction

The book describes itself as a *vision* (**1a**), a term used here to refer to a revelation from God about something that will happen in the future. The one receiving the vision sees beyond surface appearances, grasping the meaning behind the facts.

The source of Obadiah's revelation was *the Sovereign Lord* (**1b**). The 'Lord' is God's personal name (Yahweh) and he is sovereign, that is, an owner who has unfettered authority to rule. Thus at the outset we are reminded that we are dealing with a God of history and that this vision fits in with God's purposes for the whole world.

In Africa, visionaries, seers or diviners are very influential. Yet many of them do not know the God who was speaking to Obadiah and who is far more powerful than they are. Africans need to be brought to know this God, the God of history and the judge of the world, in order to be set free from the influence of other diviners or seers.

The vision that Obadiah received was *about Edom* (**1b**). In the OT, Edom is sometimes an alternative personal name for Esau (Gen 25:30; 36:1, 19 – the NIV has these references in parentheses indicating that they may be later editorial additions). At other times, it refers to a tribe (Num 20:18, 20, 21; Amos 1:6, 11; 9:12; Mal 1:4). It can also refer to the land inhabited by that tribe (Gen 32:3; 36:31; Num 24:18), which stretched for about 160 km from the Wadi Zered, its boundary with Moab in the north, to the Gulf of Aqaba in the south, where Midianite territory began. The area is rugged and, while not very fertile, it can sustain some agricultural activity. The varied meanings of 'Edom' reflect the Hebrew understanding of personhood, in which an individual shares in the corporate personality of the tribe and is identified with a particular piece of land.

Most OT references to Edom refer to the tribe and country, but the historical relationship between Esau and Jacob, the two sons of Isaac, was not forgotten by the Israelites (Deut 23:7-8) and is important background to the book of Obadiah.

Deuteronomy encouraged a tolerant attitude to Edom (Deut 23:8). Some of Job's comforters may have been Edomites. Nevertheless, there was constant hostility between Israel and Edom (2 Sam 8:13-14; 1 Kgs 11:15-16; 2 Kgs 14:7; 2 Chr 25:11-12). Many Israelite prophets regarded the Edomites as a people who had never known God and who were subject to divine judgment (Isa 11:14; 34:5-17; Jer 49:7-22; Ezek 35). Amos repeatedly refers to their buying of slaves (Amos 1:6, 9) and denounced their ferocity in the war (Amos 1:11-12).

At this point the flow of the vision is interrupted by an interlude that seems to involve intelligence gathering and reporting. The source of the intelligence is clear: *We have heard a message from the Lord* (**1c**). But who are the 'we'? They may be a prophetic guild or school that God informs about some envoy who is fomenting a conspiracy. The message was heard by many, not just by Obadiah.

Human communities thrive on information in the form of news, gossip, reports and speeches. Reports of war in particular arouse concern and create a need for collective protection. When such a report comes from God, it must be taken very seriously.

The alliance that is being formed involves a number of nations that will launch an attack on Edom. The message that the envoy carries is *Rise, and let us go against her for battle* (**1d**).

2-9 The Destruction of Edom

God next describes what he will do to Edom: *See, I will make you small among the nations* (**2**). Edom will be humiliated, reduced to no significance, trimmed in size and stripped of honour. The point is repeated for emphasis: *You will utterly be despised.* Nations, like human beings, have a sense of their own value, feelings of self-worth and importance. This sense of dignity depends on such things as military power, trade, knowledge, cultural unity and cohesiveness, the economy, and the size of the country and its population. All these things create pride and ambition, especially among the ruling class, and can lead to national conflicts. It is important to understand the various features of a nation's character so as to deal with those that tend to undermine its true greatness.

Edom's sense of self-worth led to *pride of the heart* (**3**). The heart is considered the seat of our personalities and thoughts; it follows that national pride has its origins in human hearts, the very centre of both our personal and national being. Pride leads to self-deception, distorting our estimate of ourselves as individuals and groups, and encouraging exaggerated ambitions. Edom had territorial and economic ambitions and wanted to expand its fortunes at the expense of other nations. It was thus a threat to other nations' peace and security.

Edom considered itself invincible because of its strong natural defences. Hence the mention of *the clefts of the rocks.* Birds and animals would find refuge in those clefts from hunters and predators. We, too, have things we rely on for our security, including charms, military power, ethnic identity, witchcraft, cultural ideologies of male power and domination, and political power. We need to ask ourselves why we seek refuge in something other than God.

The rhetorical question *Who can bring me down to the ground?* anticipates the answer 'No one', an answer that underlines Edom's defiant pride, self-confidence and security. There is no power that can prevent it from doing whatever it wants. But power can be deceptive, giving a false sense of confidence. Edom has either defied or forgotten to take into account the God of history. He emphatically contradicts Edom: *Though you soar like an eagle and make your nest among the stars, from there I will bring you down,*

declares the Lord (**4**). An eagle is a symbol of pride as it soars aloft, scanning the earth with its keen vision. Edom may have power, but it lacks vision. It fails to see that the God who is called Yahweh, who is sovereign in the cosmos and not merely a tribal god, will defeat its soaring pride.

The theme of the vision changes from pride to ruthlessness (**5**). Thieves or robbers cannot carry everything away; they have to select some things and leave the rest. Similarly, people harvesting grapes cannot pick every single grape, and may even deliberately leave some for the poor to glean, as required by the Mosaic law (Deut 24:21). But nothing will be left behind for Edom: *Esau will be ransacked* (**6a**). All their possessions will be taken or destroyed and the place left in ruins. Even their *hidden treasures* will be *pillaged* (**6b**). Edom was located on an important trade route and it mined copper and iron. The Edomites had thus amassed some wealth, which the ancient Greek historian Diodorus Siculus reports they stored in vaults in the rocks. But it will not be safe even in these hiding places.

The interjection *Oh, what a disaster awaits you* (**5b**) emphasizes the gravity of the disaster that awaits the unwitting Edom (see also Jer 49:8).

Despite its pride and wealth, Edom was not a powerful military nation. It relied on its strong natural defences and political and military alliances to stave off attacks and ensure relative peace. But Obadiah warns that Edom will be betrayed by its allies, friends and *those who eat your bread* (**7**). Not only will its allies fail to help it; they are actively conspiring against it while it lives in ignorance of their plots. All of us, too, are involved in various alliances such as friendships, marriage, and economic and political alliances. Betraying an alliance is considered a serious crime. But how much do we and our African leaders take God into account when making alliances? And are we faithful to those alliances we have made?

The vision moves on from the destruction of property to the destruction of Edom's people. The phrase *in that day* that is used to introduce this section is common in prophetic oracles concerning events in the indefinite future. When the time comes, the sovereign Lord says, he will *destroy the wise men of Edom* (**8**). The intellectuals are always a very important segment of any society. They offer leadership and provide a sense of direction to a civilization and culture. A nation robbed of its intellectual leadership is reduced to cultural, spiritual, economic, social and political poverty. But all of Edom's wisdom will not help it to understand the signs of the times.

Teman was one of the major towns in Edom, but the warriors there will be terrified and slaughtered, along with all the others (**9**). Soldiers protect a nation and its political leaders. Without an army to defend itself against external aggression, no nation can prosper. The future prospects of Edom after God's visitation will be bleak indeed.

VIOLENCE

Violence is the use of force to injure or wrong someone else. The violence may be perpetrated by individuals, groups or institutions, and is not necessarily physical. People are subjected to violence whenever they are treated in a way that denies them justice, equality, freedom and human dignity. Such violence often springs from tribalism, colonialism, sexism and religious bigotry. It can also spring from greed (Jer 22:17). While individual violence comes from the evil in individual hearts, institutional violence is the result of structural evil, that is, evil that has permeated a system, institution or society.

The Bible makes it clear that God abhors violence (Gen 6:11, 13; Mal 2:16). He instructs us to avoid it and to turn from it: 'Give up your violence and oppression and do what is just and right (Ezek 45:9; see also Jer 22:3). Jesus pronounced a specific blessing on those who bring an end to violence, saying 'Blessed are the peacemakers' (Matt 5:9).

Human beings tend to meet violence with violence, sword with sword, and evil with evil. But violence cannot be addressed on its own terms. Violent revolutionaries only succeed in setting up regimes more oppressive than those they have overthrown. The Bible recognizes this when it speaks of someone's violence coming 'down upon his own head' (Ps 7:16) and states that 'all who draw the sword, will die by the sword' (Matt 26:52).

By contrast, Jesus calls on us to meet violence with peace (Rom 12:17-21), the sword with forgiveness, evil with good (Luke 6:27-31), and wrath with love. Jesus and the apostles modelled non-violence by not retaliating when they suffered violence (1 Pet 2:20-24).

Jesus' approach to violence was based on his knowledge of the nature of God, as the sovereign judge and ruler, and on the nature of his mission. He did not fail to retaliate because he was weak but because he deliberately chose to demonstrate God's power over human circumstances. He also dealt with the root cause of human violence, which is evil and sin. Thus he patiently endured the violence of the Jewish Sanhedrin and the Roman government until he overthrew both by his resurrection from the dead. The way of the cross brings eternal liberation and the eradication of evil.

Christians are called to imitate Jesus. Following his model in regard to violence calls for deep spiritual discipline. Our patience and perseverance must be based upon a firm belief in the sovereignty of God, his coming kingdom and what he can do in people. Through our Lord Jesus Christ's redemptive work, we can draw on the power of grace and of the Holy Spirit to enable us to go beyond the requirements of human justice. Doing this will unleash tremendous spiritual and moral power.

But does following Jesus mean that Christians can never use force? Saint Augustine wrestled with this problem. He argues that while we may not use force to redress violence or wrongs against ourselves, we may make limited use of it to challenge or stop an aggressor and to defend or liberate the oppressed. This teaching applies in regard to both physical and institutional violence.

The effectiveness of Jesus' model is seen in its lasting influence. Modern non-violent resistance movements, like those of Gandhi and Dr Martin Luther King Jr, drew on Christian teaching about meekness, peace, love, patience, grace, justice and human dignity. Liberation movements such as liberation theology in Latin America, black theology in the USA, feminist theology and cultural theology have drawn on the Bible as well as other sources, including Marxian theories of society. Nelson Mandela and his party, the African National Congress, did not adopt non-violent methods, for they took up arms against apartheid. But after his release from prison, Mandela used unconditional forgiveness and the power of love to disarm those who supported apartheid.

Yusufu Turaki

10-14 The Reasons for Edom's Destruction

Finally, a reason is given for all this destruction. It is because of Edom's *violence against your brother Jacob* (**10**). The Bible often refers to a nation as if it were a person, so here Jacob is used to refer to Judah (Israel), just as Esau is used in 6, 8 and 9 as another name for Edom. Both nations participate in the life of their progenitors. The relationship of the brothers foreshadows the historical relationship of their descendants: 'Two nations are in your womb, and two peoples from within you will be separated; one people will be stronger than the other, and the older will serve the younger' (Gen 25:23; see also Gen 27:39-40).

Edom had at times been subject to Israel, but in its search for independence it was guilty of excessive violence. What follows is a summary of the prosecution's evidence against Edom for what would today be termed crimes against humanity. Edom failed to intervene on behalf of Jacob when Jerusalem was being ransacked by strangers and parcelled out among them (**11**). Edom despised Judah and gloated over the misfortunes of Jerusalem. It boasted about its own survival while rejoicing in the destruction of its neighbour (**12**). Edom took part in the looting following the fall of Jerusalem (**13**). Edom killed those fleeing from Judah and even handed some fugitives back to their enemies (**14**). Edom showed no mercy to Judah; rather, it added to their sufferings.

Pride and a desire for revenge governed Edom's behaviour, just as today they affect wars in Africa. Ethnic pride and solidarity have led to ethnic conflicts and cleansing that pose a real threat to peace and stability on the continent. There is a lack of concern for the plight of the many refugees and displaced persons. We need to seek the welfare of others and to encourage our leaders to do so, while also repenting and asking God's forgiveness for our own pride.

The continuing hostility between Edom and Israel contrasts strikingly with the reconciliation between Esau and Jacob (Gen 33:10-11). They were prepared to set aside the hurt and bitterness of the past. Their story reminds us that our destiny is not fixed; curses can be broken and better relationships established. Some people in both Edom and Israel probably harped on the negative aspects of the history between the brothers, with disastrous consequences for both nations. Africa needs to be wary of people who perpetuate historical roots of bitterness.

15-16 The Terrible Day of God

Obadiah now makes it clear that God's judgment on *the day of the Lord* (**15**) applies to all nations, including Edom. The principle of 'an eye for an eye' will prevail. Edom will get its just desserts and will suffer the same fate it has inflicted on others. It will be *as if they had never been* (**16**). The annihilation will be as total as the destruction of straw by fire (**18**).

The phrase *The Lord has spoken* makes it clear that this is an irrevocable pronouncement. Edom must prepare to meet its God.

17-21 The Restoration of Israel

Edom would be destroyed, but Israel would survive (**17-18**). The land of Edom would be reoccupied by other peoples, some of whom would be remnants of the scattered Israelites. Since Edom was part of an alliance, the land of the Philistines would also be occupied. The people of the Negev would move into Edom, while those from the hills west of Hebron would move into Philistine land (**19**). Returning exiles from both the northern kingdom (*Israel*) and southern kingdom (*Jerusalem*) would settle in a swath from the Negev in the south to as far north as Zarephath in Sidonian territory (**20**). Edom will be governed from Jerusalem (**21**). The rulers are called *deliverers* and they will be acting on behalf of Yahweh since it will be his kingdom. When nations fail to act justly, God removes them in order to establish his rule (see Ezek 34:11-16; 36:1-7).

Augustine Musopole

Further Reading

Allen, Leslie. *Joel, Obadiah, Jonah and Micah*. NICOT. Grand Rapids: Eerdmans, 1976.

Eaton, J. H. *Obadiah, Nahum, Habakkuk and Zephaniah*. TBC. London, SCM, 1961.

Watts, John D. W. *Joel, Obadiah, Jonah, Nahum, Habakkuk and Zephaniah*. CBC. Cambridge: Cambridge University Press, 1975.

JONAH

The book of Jonah tells the story of a man identified as 'Jonah son of Amittai' (1:1). He seems to be the same person as the prophet by that name who prophesied during the reign of Jeroboam II (about 793–753 BC) and foretold economic prosperity and political success (2 Kgs 14:25). He was a contemporary of Amos and Hosea, who were also active during the reign of Jeroboam II. He came from the Galilean village of Gath-Hepher, which belonged to the tribe of Zebulun. His name means 'dove'.

It is not known whether Jonah himself wrote the book that bears his name. Some scholars argue that it was written by an anonymous author after the exile. They base this argument on the fact that the text shows God including Gentiles in his plan of salvation and on the use of the past tense in 3:3. They claim that this shows that Nineveh is only a memory at the time of writing and that one or two centuries must have elapsed since the destruction of the city in 612 BC.

Others argue convincingly that the book was written by Jonah himself well before the exile and close to the time of the events described. They point out that the idea of God including the Gentiles in his plan of salvation is also found elsewhere in the OT (Gen 9:17; 12:3; 26:4; Lev 19:33-34; 1 Sam 2:10; Isa 2:2-3; Joel 3:1-5). Moreover, 3:3 by itself does not support the idea of a later date. Nor does the description of the vast size of the city, so large that a literal translation of the verse says it took three days to walk across it, suggest it was remembered only in legend. According to Diodorus of Sicily, a first-century historian, the name Nineveh referred to the whole region that we today call the Assyrian triangle and included the cities of Kalakh (now known as Nimrud) in the south, Nineveh (now known as Kouyunjik) in the west, and Dur Sharrukin (now known as Khorsabad in the north).

The theme of the book is the universal divine mercy revealed without favouritism to Jews and Gentiles. Jonah is the tool that God uses to proclaim his message to all the nations.

Outline of Contents

COMMENTARY

1:1-17 Jonah's Flight Reveals God to Sailors

The book starts with God assigning Jonah a mission: he was to go to Nineveh to warn the city of coming disaster, though we are not given the details of his message (1:1-2). This is the only case in which an OT prophet is sent directly to Gentiles.

Jonah left home as if he were going to obey God, but instead of heading east to Nineveh he set out westward for Tarshish, which was probably a Phoenician colony on the south-west coast of Spain. (1:3). He was hoping to escape from God, but forgot that as the African proverb says 'there is nowhere on earth where the wind does not blow' (see also Ps 139:7-10). One reason for his disobedience may have been a belief that the Jews, the chosen people, were the only ones entitled to receive God's mercy.

Jonah's disobedience resulted in God sending a great storm (1:4) and in the Gentile sailors discovering that they, too, could benefit from God's grace. The crew are the real heroes in the second part of this chapter. The statement that *each cried out to his own god* (1:5) suggests that they were from different countries and worshipped different gods. Their prayers indicate they were convinced that the order of the universe was disrupted because some sin had been committed that angered the gods. Their gods did not answer their prayers, and so they turned to the one person who was not praying to his god – Jonah, who was sound asleep (1:6).

The crew resorted to a common practice of the time and drew lots to identify the person responsible for bringing the divine curse on them (1:7; Josh 7:14-19; Prov 16:33). Despite being cast by Gentiles, the lots were effective in exposing a guilty servant of God. God was using their beliefs and practices to force his wayward servant to confess his sin and tell them about his God (1:8). The fact that the lots provided the correct answer also argues in favour of the sovereignty of God, who is unrestricted in what instruments he can use to accomplish his purpose. He can make use of a donkey (Num 22:28-30), a fish (Matt 17:27), or lots as part of his plan to show his mercy to the Gentiles.

The prophet's message to Gentiles revealed that the God who created heaven and earth was the one at work (1:9). His power is greater than that of all the gods to whom the sailors had prayed, none of whom were able to save their lives. Learning of the existence of this great God terrified them and led to their next question, *What have you done?*

(1:10). How could the prophet possibly think that he could escape such a great God!

The prophet told the sailors what would have to be done to allay God's anger, but they were very hesitant to carry out his instructions (1:11-13). However, as the danger increased even more, they turned to the Lord rather than to their gods, carefully using the same holy name that Jonah had used for God (1:14a). They recognized that either Jonah would have to throw himself into the sea, or they would have to carry out the sentence themselves. They thus prayed for their own lives to be saved and also for the life of the prophet, so that they would not be held guilty of his death. Their words, *you, O Lord, have done as you pleased* (1:14b) show that the sailors were entrusting themselves to the sovereignty of God, the only one who could save his prophet.

God immediately granted their first request and the storm calmed (1:15). They offered sacrifices as an indication of their awe at what God has done and promised to become his servants and to trust him from then on (1:16).

Jonah's only hope lay in divine intervention. God's sovereignty, which the sailors had just confessed, showed itself in the arrival of a great fish, possibly a whale or a shark, that swallowed Jonah (1:17). Since the Jews reckoned part of a day as a whole day, the statement that *Jonah was inside the fish three days and three nights* does not require that he was there for a full seventy-two hours. He may have been there for only one twenty-four-hour day plus parts of two other days.

In Matthew 12:40, our Lord compared the length of his impending burial to Jonah's stay in the belly of the fish, thus confirming the historicity of Jonah's story.

Jonah's being swallowed by a fish and his miraculous survival have caused much debate among commentators. Some are sceptical and treat the incident as simply a fable intended to convey a message to the Jews. Others accept every detail as true history and cite historical precedents. There is no point in giving a detailed account of the different positions, for all spring from a mindset and an approach to literature that is at odds with the African oral tradition that gives precedence to the spiritual significance of events and sees the Creator revealing himself through the relationship between humans and nature. Thus Africans have no problem with the intervention of an animal (as also in Num 22:28-30; 1 Kgs 17:3-6) and are far more interested in Jonah's reaction to his experience, as expressed in his prayer.

2:1-10 Jonah's Repentance and God's Response

The fact that Jonah could even pray *from inside the fish* (2:1) underscores the point that God is present everywhere, and we can call on him from anywhere (see Ps 139:7-12). We have no need to run to a particular prayer mountain in a time of crisis. Nor do we need to take our troubles to diviners and magicians, as many Africans do. Nor should we assume that our troubles are so overwhelming that there is no point in prayer. Jesus taught that we ought to pray at all times, without giving up (Luke 18:1).

So deep was Jonah's distress that he felt he was in the depths of the grave. Nevertheless, like the disciples in the storm-tossed boat (Matt 8:23-27), Jonah *called to the Lord* (2:2). God heard his cry, for God rarely says no to a prayer of desperation.

In 2:3, 5-6, Jonah graphically described his experience before being swallowed by the fish. He saw his experience as a punishment from the Lord, and mourned, *I have been banished from your sight* (2:4a). He had wilfully run away from God's presence (1:2) and God had granted his desire by expelling him, as it were, from his presence. This is one of the bitter consequences of sin for a believer (see also Ps 51:11). Yet, like David, Jonah hoped to look again towards God's *holy temple* in Jerusalem (2:4b; see Pss 5:7; 42:1-5). He knew that God is merciful and will welcome us back if we turn to him in true repentance (Luke 15:11-24; 1 John 1:9; 2:1-2). Jonah did just that. He did not react indignantly to being punished, but penitently said, *I remembered you, Lord, and my prayer rose to you, to your holy temple* (2:7). The 'temple' here refers to God's heavenly sanctuary, while the reference in 2:4 refers to his sanctuary in Jerusalem. Jonah prayed in hope and anticipation. Unlike unbelievers who forfeit the grace of knowing the only true God and cling to worthless idols (2:8), Jonah covenanted to bring his thank offering to God's house with a song (2:9a; Ps 56:12-13).

The climax of Jonah's prayer of confession, hope and faith was the great affirmation: *Salvation comes from the Lord* (2:9b). This statement is sometimes referred to as Jonah's second confessional statement (the first was in 1:9). Salvation here is best taken as deliverance from death.

The storm revealed divine mercy to the sailors, and the great fish did the same for Jonah. The fish did not bring death, but salvation (2:4,7). Just as the sailors had done (1:16), Jonah offered to make a sacrifice in renewal of his fellowship and commitment to God (2:9).

In response to Jonah's prayer of repentance God commanded the fish, and it vomited Jonah onto dry land, presumably on the coast of Palestine (2:10). Every creature obeys the Creator except human beings, who often turn their backs on him (see Isa 1:2-3).

3:1-10 Jonah's Preaching and Nineveh's Repentance

God's command will be carried out whatever happens, as is clear from 3:1-3, for 'okra cannot grow bigger than the one who plants it: either it ends up in a stew or it is dried for next year's sowing.' Jonah is like God's dried okra, sown in Nineveh to produce the fruit of repentance.

When we turn from our sins, God is always ready to start again with us. Thus **3:2** repeats 1:2: *Go to the great city of Nineveh and preach against it.* The message remained the same to underline God's unchanging character and the transformation in Jonah. But whereas in 1:3 Jonah refused to obey, this time, having experienced the omniscience and mercy of God, he *obeyed the word of the Lord* and set out for Nineveh (**3:3a**).

Ninevah is said to have been a very large city (**3:3b**). (For comments on its size, see the introduction to this commentary.) Jonah's message to the Ninevites was not simply that punishment was coming because of their sinfulness, but also that a forty-day period of grace would give them time to repent (**3:4**).

The result was immediate. Led by the king, all the people decided to turn from their sin and ask God's forgiveness. They demonstrated the sincerity of their faith by ceasing all normal activities and fasting and praying to God. They dressed in sackcloth, as if they were mourners (**3:5-8**). The king uttered the moving words, *Who knows? God may yet relent and with compassion turn from his fierce anger so that we will not perish* (**3:9**). These words were an indirect plea for

POWER AND ACCOUNTABILITY

Power can be defined as the ability to exercise influence and authority in the physical, mental or spiritual sphere. Synonyms for it include strength, vigour, force, capacity, wealth, means, substance, might, dominion, energy, authority and majesty. Authority is the right to use power or to act (Mark 3:15; Acts 4:33).

The Bible is very explicit about the source of power: 'Yours, O Lord, is the greatness and the power and the glory and the majesty and the splendour, for everything in heaven and earth is yours' (1 Chr 29:11). Jesus Christ stresses this in the Lord's Prayer (Matt 6:13). Believers need to remember this truth in these days when many others claim power.

People tend to see power, like energy, as a finite resource and thus the object of fierce competition – something to be clung to and not shared. But Jesus clearly demonstrates that power can be shared without the sharer losing authority (Luke 10:1-22; Mark 16:15-18). Paul, too, demonstrates this attitude in his relationships with his colleagues like Timothy, Silas, Titus and Apollos (see, for example, 1 Thess 1:1).

God's power is manifested to motivate people to worship him (1 Chr 29). It gives meaning and life to worship. God is not satisfied with a form without power, and believers are instructed to turn away from those who have only the form of godliness but deny its power (2 Tim 3:5).

In Africa and elsewhere, God's power has also healed people of various diseases. However, our preaching should not focus on his power but on his love, greatness and holiness, and on his work in human lives (Matt 10:1; Rom 15:18-19).

God's power enables God's people to be his witnesses to the nations (Acts 1:8). It is transformational, enabling Christians to make a difference at local and national levels as well as in their callings or professions. It is also transforming dormant congregations in all parts of Africa, creating vibrant missionary movements.

But power can be abused, even in the church, and the greater the extent and intensity of the power exercised by the leadership of a congregation or a mission agency, the greater the need for accountability. Accountability is rooted in the acknowledgement that God is the source of power and that he controls life and human resources (Ps 24:1; Ezek 18: 4). Good stewardship requires that we account for how we use the power with which each of us has been endowed.

Like everyone else, Christian leaders are personally accountable to God (Rom 14:12; 2 Sam 12:1-24) and are not to use their power to promote their own selfish interests or the selfish interests of believers. Awareness of their vertical accountability differentiates casual leadership from durable leadership. Those who lack this sense of accountability are basically followers.

Those who follow leaders are also responsible for the decision to accept them as leaders. The fortunes of the nation of Israel fluctuated in accordance with who was leading them (see, for example, Jer 29:15-23).

Accountability is owed both to God and to others (2 Cor 8:20-21). The NT pattern of empowering people and releasing them for mission and ministry is accompanied by a reciprocal obligation of accountability, for empowerment without corresponding accountability breeds irresponsibility.

It is important to note that accountability means more than being subject to control. It is also more than merely accounting: accounting is something one *does*, while accountability involves both what one *does* and what one *is*.

The biblical pattern of accountability involves using the right people (Ezra 8:24, 30) who follow the right procedures (Ezra 8:24-34). In doing this, they should be guided by right and standard documentation (Ezra 8:34). Some organizational structures that have been adopted to promote biblical accountability are apostolic networks and functional governing boards.

Adherence to the biblical pattern of accountability by Christian leaders will restore and enhance public trust and interest in matters concerning the gospel of our Lord Jesus Christ. As the Christian church uses its God-given power for its God-given purpose, it will have a transforming impact on those around it.

Remi Lawanson

divine mercy, expressed very simply and humbly. God cannot refuse such an appeal and he granted them a reprieve, turning aside from the misfortune that he had planned for them (3:10).

This act of mercy raises the question, can God change his mind? Some argue that God is not 'a son of man that he should change his mind' (Num 23:19). Others argue that God's contractual dealings with individuals or nations include a mercy clause as well as a justice clause (see Ezek 33:13-16). God's apparent change of mind was not based on second thoughts, but was part of his original intention when his terms are met.

It is surprising that the Ninevites believed Jonah, an unknown man speaking on behalf of an unknown God. What was it that roused their faith? It is possible that they had heard of Jonah before he arrived. The sailors might have returned to Jaffa and told of the prophet's fate. The news might have spread as far as Ninevah. The sudden reappearance of Jonah would then have caused consternation among the inhabitants of the city and would have added weight to his message. Another more likely possibility derives from the multicultural nature of the Gentile world with its deep religious superstition. In such a setting, the sudden appearance of a stranger claiming to have been sent by God to warn the people of impending destruction might have had a profound effect on the consciences of both people and leaders. Moreover, because superstitious people have a high regard for the art of divination, they would have respected a newly arrived prophet who revealed their wickedness. But beside these human reasons, there was also the reason that God must have been at work in their hearts, anxious to draw them to himself because he takes 'no pleasure in the death of the wicked' but would rather that 'they turn from their ways and live' (Ezek 33:11).

4:1-11 Jonah's Discontent and God's Response

Jonah was angry that his prediction was not fulfilled, for he believed that the Jews should experience divine mercy while the Gentiles should experience divine judgment and punishment (4:1). So strong was his conviction that he preferred to die rather than remain alive and see mercy extended to the cruel Gentiles of Nineveh (4:2-3).

This attitude is still common today in some African Christian groups. It may underlie the abuse and curses heaped on sorcerers and notorious criminals. Christians with this attitude find it difficult to believe that such apparent enemies are also among God's creatures. However, these believers differ from Jonah in that they would rejoice to see the sorcerer or criminal converted.

God responded to Jonah first with a word and then with an act. First, he asked him a question, inviting him to think about God's love and discover its real mystery (4:4). Persevering in his pouting, Jonah accused God of having changed his mind and of failing to carry out his threats. Taking a seat on a hill east of the city (4:5) from which he could watch what took place in the valley may even have been an attempt to blackmail God into taking action.

God then chose to teach Jonah using an object lesson, a common technique in African stories. He caused a plant to grow rapidly during the night (4:6) and then allowed it to die while Jonah suffered the effects of the heat and of a hot wind blowing from the east (4:7). The sudden death of the plant was intended to teach Jonah that just as he felt pity for the plant, so God felt pity on the Ninevites. However, Jonah felt pity for the plant only because he was feeling self-pity. The plant had brought him happiness and restored his desire to live. But with the plant destroyed, his life was also destroyed since he identified so closely with it (4:8-9).

Jonah and the plant provide a picture of God and humankind. When people prosper, God is happy; when they die, God suffers. Because God is full of compassion and love, he is loath to punish us (4:10-11).

In this book, Jonah is forced out of the comfort zone of easy faith. Did he understand the lesson? The story ends without providing further details. The reader is left with the task of following through. To those who do not know the Lord, this book issues a call to repentance to escape the final judgment of the Lord. Nineveh was granted a brief reprieve, but when the people's repentance proved shallow, God sent Nahum to prophecy their doom, and the city was destroyed in 612 BC. We, too, will not escape if we reject God's call to repent.

But the book also challenges those of us who are God's servants to accept the tasks he assigns us and to love those to whom he sends us. We are not to be grumbling servants who have to be forced to obey his orders on who fail to obey Christ's command to love even our enemies. At the end of our race, when we appear before Christ may we each receive his commendation: 'Well done, good and faithful servant' (Matt 25:21).

Cossi Augustin Ahoga

Further Reading

Alexander, T. Desmond, David W. Baker and Bruce Waltke. *Obadiah, Jonah, Micah* (TOT). Downers Grove: InterVarsity Press, 1988.

Ellison H.L. 'Jonah' in *Expositors Bible Commentary*, vol 7. Edited by Frank E. Gaebelein. Grand Rapids: Zondervan, 1985.

Stuart, Douglas. *Hosea–Jonah*. WBC. Waco: Word, 1987.

MICAH

The name Micah was a common one, and the author of this book should not be confused with Micaiah son of Imlah (1 Kgs 22:6-28; 2 Chr 18:3-27), who prophesied to the northern kingdom during the reign of Ahab a century earlier.

Micah lived from about 735 BC to 690 BC and prophesied primarily to the southern kingdom. Moresheth, his home town, was about twenty miles south-west of Jerusalem near the Philistine city of Gath. Isaiah came from the same area. Micah's identification by his town rather than by his father's name may indicate that he was of humble origins. Certainly he is a prophet who speaks for the exploited poor.

Micah ministered to Judah, the southern kingdom during the reigns of three kings (1:1) and also ministered to Samaria, the northern kingdom, before it fell to the forces of Assyria in 722 BC (1:6).

Occasion and Purpose

Micah lived in a time when wealth and power were concentrated in the hands of a few, and this brought social injustice. Greed and corruption were rampant and false prophets flourished. Yet the people still felt entitled to God's blessings and protection. Like Isaiah, Hosea and Amos, Micah insists that genuine faith produces social justice and practical holiness. He warned of coming judgment and called the people to repentance. Like his contemporary Isaiah, Micah also held out the hope of future restoration with the coming of the divine Messiah. The book falls into three sections, each beginning with an imperative 'hear' or 'listen' (1:2; 3:1; 6:1), which is followed first by a message of judgment and then by one of hope and salvation. These themes are reflected in Micah's name, which means 'Who is like Yahweh?', a phrase that is echoed in 7:18: *Who is a God like you, who pardons sin and forgives the transgression of the remnant of his inheritance?* (7:18).

Micah prophesied the fall of Samaria, the capital of the northern kingdom, which took place in 722 BC during Micah's lifetime (1:6-7; 2 Kgs 17:1-6), and the invasion of Judah by Sennacherib (1:9-16). Hezekiah's repentance postponed the fall of Jerusalem until 586 BC (3:12; 7:13). Micah also foretold the Babylonian exile (4:10), the return from captivity, and the future peace and supremacy of the remnant people of God (4:1-8, 13; 7:11, 14-17). Supremely, he foretold the birth of the messianic king in Bethlehem (5:2) who will be a merciful ruler who will gather the people into one nation and establish his kingdom (2:13; 7:18-20).

Micah makes frequent use of dramatic interruptions of arguments and answers (2:5, 12; 3:1-3; 6:6-8; 7:14-15), of the image of a shepherd (2:12; 4:6; 5:4-5; 7:14) and of historical references (1:13, 15; 5:5; 6:4-5, 16; 7:20). There is also an abundance of figures of speech, such as similes (1:8, 16; 2:12-13; 4:9) and wordplays (1:10-15).

Outline Of Contents

1:1 Superscription

1:2-2:13 First Sermon
   1:2-16 Denunciation of Samaria and Jerusalem
      1:2-7 The coming judgment on Samaria
      1:8-16 Lament over the coming judgment on Judah

   2:1-11 Reasons for the Judgment
      2:1-5 Covetousness
      2:6-11 False prophets

   2:12-13 A Message of Hope

3:1-5:15 Second Sermon
   3:1-12 Denunciation of the People's Sinfulness
      3:1-4 Indictment of the leaders
      3:5-8 Indictment of the false prophets
      3:9-12 Destruction of Jerusalem

   4:1-13 Promise of Restoration
      4:1-8 The mountain of the Lord
      4:9-13 The remnant will be saved

   5:1-15 A New King and a New Kingdom
      5:1-4 The Messiah
      5:5-6 His reign of peace
      5:7-9 The remnant will rule with the Messiah
      5:10-15 Cleansing the kingdom of idolatry

6:1-7:20 Third Sermon
   6:1-16 God's Complaint Against His People
      6:1-8 God's anger
      6:9-16 Reasons for God's judgment

   7:1-20 Lamentation and Promise
      7:1-6 The prophet's lament
      7:7-10 The promise of salvation
      7:11-20 God's glorious grace

COMMENTARY

1:1 Superscription

The statement that this book contains *the word of the Lord* (**1:1a**) gives it an authority and power that contrast with the words of the false prophets who only pretend to deliver a message from God in order to deceive the people (2:11; 3:5, 8).

Micah is identified as the author of this book. The date at which he prophesied is identified with reference to three kings of Judah (**1:1b**). *Jotham* (750-732 BC), though mostly a good king, did not remove the idolatrous high places (2 Kgs 15:32-38). *Ahaz* (732-716 BC) was a wicked king who adopted a pro-Assyrian foreign policy. He set up pagan idols in the temple and finally nailed the temple doors shut. During his reign the northern kingdom fell to the Assyrians (2 Kgs 16). *Hezekiah* (715-686 BC) was one of Judah's best kings. He was anti-Assyrian and God miraculously delivered him from Sennacherib in 701 BC (2 Kgs 18–19).

Micah's *vision* (**1:1c**) comprises the whole of the book. It concerns Samaria, the capital of the northern kingdom, and Jerusalem, the capital of the southern kingdom, for the leaders of the nations were responsible for much of the idolatry and social and economic injustice.

1:2-2:13 First Sermon

1:2-16 Denunciation of Samaria and Jerusalem

Micah summons all the people of the world, not just Israel and Judah, to listen as God appears as a prosecutor with a case against his people (**1:2**; see also Deut 31:28; 32:1).

1:2-7 The coming judgment on Samaria

The sermon opens dramatically as God descends from his dwelling-place in heaven (**1:3a**; see also 1 Kgs 8:30; Ps 11:4). He is so awesome that even *the high places* cannot stand before him (**1:3b**). These 'high places' were the sites of altars dedicated to idols (see 2 Kgs 9–11), but they are also the mountains that will *melt* with the fiery wrath of God against sin (**1:4**; see Exod 20:18-21). When God manifests himself in power, all creation acknowledges his presence (see also Judg 5:4-5; Pss 18:7-15; 65:9-13; 68:8; 97:5; 114:3-8; Isa 64:1-3).

God is angry because of the sin of Israel and Judah. Samaria will be the first to suffer his judgment. This was the capital for the ten northern tribes of Israel, here called *Jacob* (**1:5a**). Judah, too, will not escape judgment because of the idolatry in Jerusalem (**1:5b**; see also 2 Kgs 12:3; 14:4).

Samaria's punishment is related to its specific sins. The prosperous city on the hill is turned into a field with vines planted among the ruins (**1:6**; see Hos 12:11). The idols that were worshipped there and the offerings given to them will all be smashed (**1:7a**). God will judge all idolaters in the same way.

Samaria had copied its neighbours and permitted prostitutes to be employed in the service of a pagan deity (**1:7b**; see also Exod 34:15; Judg 2:17; Isa 23:17; Ezek 23:30; Hos 9:1). God had forbidden this (Deut 23:17-18). The *gifts* within the temple were payments for prostitutes. God's punishment was that the people would turn to prostitution not because of their religion but because of their poverty.

Idols are attractive because they make no moral demands. Thus the Israelites willingly exchanged the worship of the true God for the revelry of religious prostitution. We, too, may be allowing other things to seduce us away from God. We need to remember that judgment will begin with the people of God (1 Pet 4:17).

The worship of idols and false gods still prevails in some parts of Africa. We must pray that God will end this through the preaching of the gospel so that these people can escape his judgment.

1:8-16 Lament over the coming judgment on Judah

The same devastation is in store for Judah, if she refuses to repent, and so Micah mourns the coming captivity of his people. As a sign of his distress, he goes about barefoot and naked (**1:8a**; see also 2 Sam 15:30; Isa 32:11; Ezek 24:17, 23; Amos 5:16). His cries evoke fear and loneliness, like the cries of jackals or of owls, which are symbols of cruelty and uncleanness (**1:8b**). It is appropriate to grieve, even for those who deserve their punishment.

Samaria's end was inevitable, because her sin was like an incurable wound (**1:9a**; see also Jer 8:22). Jerusalem had also been infected, and judgment would come to its very gates (**1:9b**). Micah is probably referring to the invasion of Sennacherib, King of Assyria, who in 701 BC captured many towns in Judah, but was stopped just short of taking Jerusalem (2 Kgs 18, 19; Isa 36:1-37:37).

Micah's words, *tell it not in Gath* (**1:10a**), may be warning not to weep lest the Philistines learn of what is coming, or they may be a proverbial expression for disaster, as in David's lament for Saul (2 Sam 1:20). Micah then lists a string of towns that would be on Sennacherib's route as he moved towards Jerusalem. All were near Micah's birthplace, Moresheth-gath. The prophet puns on the Hebrew names of these towns.

- *Beth Ophrah* means 'house of dust', and the inhabitants are to *roll in the dust* (**1:10b**) in mourning and grief, and also in abject, humiliating defeat (Gen 3:14; Josh 7:6; 1 Sam 4:12; Job 16:15; Jer 6:26; 25:34; Ezek 27:30).
- *Shaphir* means 'beautiful' or 'pleasant', but its people will suffer the unpleasantness of *nakedness and shame* (**1:11a**; see also Deut 28:48; Isa 47:3; Lam 4:21). They

will be led into captivity with all their wickedness exposed (see Ezek 16:37; Hos 2:10).

- *Zaanan* means 'to come out', but the inhabitants will not dare to move out because of their fear of the invaders (**1:11b**; see also Jer 6:25).
- *Beth Ezel* means 'the house of taking away' (**1:11c**), and because its *protection is taken away,* its citizens will be taken away by Sennacherib.
- *Maroth* means 'bitterness' (**1:12**). The inhabitants will suffer the bitter fate of waiting for a rescuing army from Jerusalem that will never come because the Assyrian army will march right up *to the gate of Jerusalem.*
- *Lachish* was a fortress city protecting southern Judea, but the people there should prepare their chariots not for battle but for flight (**1:13**). Sennacherib conquered this city and made it his headquarters (2 Kgs 18:14, 17; Jer 34:7). Micah singles out Lachish as *the beginning of sin* to Zion, implying that the people there were the first in Judah to follow the sinful practices of the northern kingdom and had influenced many to follow their evil example.
- *Moresheth-gath* sounds similar to the Hebrew word for 'betrothed' (**1:14a**). A father gave parting gifts to his daughter as she left for the home of her new husband. But this city, Micah's home town, will be given as a bride to Assyrians who will deport the inhabitants.
- *Aczib* means 'deception' or 'disappointment'. This city might have been able to help *the kings of Israel* (**1:14b**), but it will be unable to do so.
- *Mareshah* sounds like the Hebrew word for 'conqueror', but ironically it will be conquered (**1:15a**; see also Jer 8:10).
- *Adullam* was known for its caves, where David had once hidden from Saul (1 Sam 22:1; 2 Sam 23:13). Soon *the glory of Israel,* that is, the people and their princes (Hos 9:11-13) will be forced to hide there (**1:15b**).

The prophet ends by calling on all the people of Judah to cut their hair as a sign of a mourning as deep as that of a young mother for her children (**1:16**; see also Ezra 9:3; Job 1:20). Their children will soon go *into exile.* The northern kingdom suffered this fate in 722 BC, and in 701 BC Sennacherib carried away 200 150 people from the southern kingdom.

Judgment, destruction, sorrow and humiliation are the consequences of disobeying God.

2:1-11 Reasons for the Judgment

2:1-5 Covetousness

In 1:5-7, Micah denounced the sins of rebellion and idolatry. Now he turns to social sins, beginning with the corrupt practices of wealthy landowners who seize other people's land and property. They stay awake at night plotting how

to defraud the poor and then rise early to carry out their wicked plans (**2:1**). Evil thoughts lead to evil deeds.

These people acted without any concern for morality (see also 7:3). When they coveted fields, lands and houses, they seized them even if this involved defrauding others (**2:2**; see also 1 Kgs 21; 2 Kgs 9:21-37). The loss of land would condemn people to poverty, since agriculture was the source of their livelihood.

Such coveting was prohibited in the Ten Commandments (see Exod 20:17; Deut 5:21; Rom 7:7-8). Taking other people's land or property was also specifically forbidden by the law (Lev 6:2-5; 19:13; Deut 27:17). God is the real owner of the land, and he intends each family to have some of it (Lev 25:14-34.).

While the wicked were plotting evil, God was planning a disaster that they could not escape (**2:3**). They had been arrogant, but they will be mocked and humiliated (**2:4**). Their land will be taken away and given to others. What had once belonged to Israel will become the property of its enemies.

God can assign land to whomever he wants (**2:5**; see also Dan 4:34-35). Those who have been oppressing others will have no say in later decisions about dividing the land. Jesus says that only the meek will ultimately inherit the earth (see also Ps 16:6; Matt 5:5).

2:6-11 False prophets

False prophets, who were proclaiming messages that served the interests of those who paid them, opposed Micah's message of judgment, and forbade him to prophesy (**2:6a**; see also 3:5, 11). They assumed that God was unconditionally on their side (**2:6b**). Even today, there are false teachers who do not preach the whole counsel of God but proclaim only his love and never his judgment.

The false prophets claimed to be of the *house of Jacob* (**2:7a**). They thought that God could not curse Jacob because of his covenant promises to his people, and so they asked, *Is the Spirit of the Lord angry? Does he do such things?* (**2:7b**). They forgot that the true covenant is spiritual, based on faith and obedience (Rom 9:6) and assumed that it was not in God's character to punish his people. A false view of God's character will lead to a false view of his actions.

Micah responds that God's words only benefit those who believe and obey them (**2:7c**). Those who have rejected God and his covenant have lost their privileged position and become God's enemies (**2:8a**) – and also the enemies of the poor. Like hostile soldiers, they attack defenceless travellers and steal their clothing (**2:8b**). They rob women and children, who are the object of God's special protection (**2:9a**; see Exod 22:21-24), of their homes and deprive them of God's blessing. The children suffer the indignity of being sold as slaves (**2:9b**; see also Amos 1:6, 9). Those who participate in this corruption are judged and are commanded to leave the promised land, which they have polluted (**2:10**; see also Lev 18:24-28; Ps 95:11).

The people prefer the teaching that tells them only what they want to hear (**2:11**; see also Jer 5:31). So the false prophets prophesy wealth and prosperity, represented by plenty of wine and beer (Isa 28:7; Amos 2:12).

Some preachers today preach a similar message of health, wealth, financial gain and happiness regardless of whether those listening to them are living according to God's standards. Such half-truths lead people to destruction and death. We must be prepared to speak the unpopular truth, proclaiming God's judgment on those whose lives are dominated by materialism and who oppress the poor for financial gain.

2:12-13 A Message of Hope

Micah concludes his message with a promise of salvation. Although God must punish his disobedient and unrepentant people, he will *surely gather* and *surely bring [them] together* – phrases that emphasize the certainty that this promise will be fulfilled. Micah uses the familiar image of God's people as sheep and God or the Messiah as the Good Shepherd who gathers his scattered flock (**2:12**).

When the time comes for this flock to be released from the pen, it will not be leaderless, for leadership is promised three times in 2:13. Just as God rescued his people from captivity in Egypt and led them through the wilderness, so he will go before them to guide and deliver them (see Exod 13:21; Deut 1:30, 33; Isa 52:12).

The one who will lead them out is described as *One who breaks open the way* (**2:13a**). The Hebrew parallelism indicates that the *One* and *their king* are the same person (**2:13b**) – Yahweh (**2:13c**). This one who smashes through the gate to set the people free is the Messiah, our Lord Jesus Christ. He goes ahead to remove obstacles in the path and to clear the way for the people.

If we repent, we too can be part of the Messiah's flock when our Lord Jesus Christ returns. That prospect should give us hope and motivate us to turn from sin.

3:1-5:15 Second Sermon

3:1-12 Denunciation of the People's Sinfulness

3:1-4 Indictment of the leaders

Micah's second sermon begins with a denunciation of the leaders for neglecting their duty. They are not enforcing justice (**3:1**; see 3:9). Unlike the shepherd-king of 2:12-13, they hate good and love evil (**3:2a**; see also Amos 5:14-15). Micah describes them as being like cannibals, tearing the flesh from their victims and cooking them for food (**3:2b-3**). They are like wolves preying on the people, not shepherds

tending God's flock. The corrupt officials take what belongs to ordinary people and use it for their own benefit (see also Ps 14:4; Prov 30:14). They have no compassion or respect for those they are supposed to serve.

When the day comes that these wicked leaders need God's help, they should not expect to receive it (**3:4**). They did not listen when those they were mistreating cried out for mercy (see also Prov 21:13; Matt 6:14-15; Gal 6:7). How can they expect God to hear their cry? His face will not 'shine upon them' (Num 6:25), but will be hidden.

Many African countries also suffer under corrupt, selfish and tyrannical leaders. Officials have been corrupted by the love of money, and a bribe is required before any service is rendered. Employers do not pay their workers their wages on time. Injustice reigns in our law courts, where accepting bribes is the order of the day. Even some Christian ministers and priests are more interested in monetary gain than in serving God and the people.

We need prophets and ministers like Micah to teach and preach the truth of God's word. All office holders must be warned to fear God and realize that they are ultimately accountable to him. If they do not repent of their injustice, they face condemnation, suffering and eternal death.

3:5-8 Indictment of the false prophets

The false prophets mislead people and turn them away from the Lord. They are motivated solely by greed. If you give them plenty to eat, they predict peace and a bright future for you (**3:5**; see also Jer 6:14; 2 Tim 4:3). But if you are poor and cannot satisfy their greed, they turn on you with angry abuse. They do not merely accept bribes; they demand them. They use a divine gift for personal profit.

God's judgment is that the gift of prophecy will be taken from these false prophets (**3:6**). They will no longer see visions and revelations, but only darkness. They will be disgraced because what they predict will not come to pass (**3:7a**; see also Prov 29:18). Consequently, they will be regarded as unclean (Lam 4:13-15) and will be reduced to silence as they cover their faces in shame and mourning (**3:7b**; see also Lev 13:45; Ezek 24:17, 22). God will not answer their prayers.

Unlike the silenced false prophets, Micah, a true prophet, is full of *the Spirit of the Lord* (**3:8**). He does not take personal credit for his ministry; it is God's Spirit who empowers him to truly proclaim God's message. He does not lie to the people about their spiritual condition, but speaks out powerfully for justice (see also Isa 11:2-5; 61:1) and warns them about the consequences of their sin. He boldly and impartially declares God's holy judgment in the hope that people will repent.

Power and moral courage are signs of the Spirit's presence in the life of a true prophet (see also Acts 4:13; 2 Tim 1:7). God expects his servants to say what he wants them to say and do what he sends them to do. When religious leaders turn a blind eye to corruption and evil, they become partly responsible for it.

Those who proclaim God's Word for personal profit or who proclaim a prosperity gospel are false prophets. They lack any sense of what is right because the Holy Spirit is not present in their ministry.

3:9-12 Destruction of Jerusalem

Micah calls on the nation's corrupt leaders, rulers, priests and prophets to listen to God's verdict on them. They have detested justice and perverted all that is upright (**3:9**; see also Lev 19:13, 15; Deut 16:19; Amos 5:10; 6:12). The commandment says, 'you shall not murder', but they shed innocent blood (**3:10;** see Gen 9:6; Exod 20:13; Deut 19:13; 21:9; 1 Kgs 21; 2 Kgs 9:7). The abuse of justice frequently results in the death of innocent victims (2 Sam 3:31-34; 4:11; 2 Chr 19:10; Hab 2:12).

These men have all taken bribes (**3:11**). The rulers, who act as judges, base their decisions on bribes, which are explicitly prohibited (Exod 23:8; Deut 16:19; Prov 17:23; Isa 33:15). The priests, who should teach the people God's law, demand a fee for doing so. The prophets will provide a favourable message if paid an acceptable fee. These people are using their positions for their personal profit rather than to serve God and others. Yet they still claim God's presence is with them! They trust that God will protect his chosen people regardless of how they behave.

But God demands obedience, and when that is not present he himself will destroy the city of Jerusalem (**3:12**). It will become a heap of rubble, and even the temple, the visible sign of God's presence, will be demolished. The hill on which it stood will be overgrown with weeds. Micah's audience must have been shocked to hear that they would experience the same fate as Samaria.

The people under King Hezekiah listened to Micah and repented. Consequently, this judgment only came one hundred years later, in 586 BC (2 Kgs 25; see also Jer 26:18-19; 18:8-10). At that time, Jeremiah lamented 'for Mount Zion, which lies desolate, with jackals prowling over it' (Lam 5:18; Neh 2:17; 4:2).

4:1-13 Promise of Restoration

4:1-8 The mountain of the Lord

Abruptly, Micah shifts from a message of judgment to one of hope. Beyond the gloom of the immediate future he sees a glorious vision of *the last days* (4:1), the time when the Lord, the Messiah, will come (see also Dan 10:14; Hos 3:5). In those days, Mount Zion, where the temple stood, will become the centre of all religious and political activities on earth. It will be above all other mountains, not because of its physical features but because God has chosen it as his earthly dwelling (**4:1a**; see also Isa 2:2-4).

Zion will become like a magnet drawing all peoples of the earth to the Lord (**4:1b-2a**). There will be a constant flow of people to Jerusalem to learn God's law. The converted Gentile nations will encourage one another to make a pilgrimage to the temple of God to learn how to live according to his law (**4:2b**; see also Ps 122:1, 4). The word of God *will go out from Zion*, for they will carry it with them as they return to their lands to put it into effect. All nations will have become part of the true Israel that enjoys the blessings of the new covenant through its mediator Jesus Christ (Gal 3:26-29; see also Jer 31:31-34; Ezek 36:24-31; Heb 8:6). This prophecy has been partially fulfilled in the church, which consists of believers from all over the world.

When the nations follow God's law, they will experience the blessing of peace. The Messiah will be the arbitrator who will settle all disputes among them on the basis of what is right (**4:3**; see also Isa 11:3-4; Hab 1:12). With no wars, there will be no need for weapons. *Swords* and *spears,* the major weapons of the time (see 1 Sam 17:47), will be turned into agricultural implements like *ploughshares* and *pruning hooks.* There will no longer be any need to train soldiers.

The peace of the messianic kingdom contrasts with Joel's challenge to the nations to beat their ploughshares into swords to fight against God and his people (Joel 3:10). If one rejects God and his Messiah, then the only option is to fight against him and be woefully defeated.

The peace of this era is also described using farming imagery. Individuals will live out their lives in prosperity, sitting comfortably in their homes under their own vines and fig trees (**4:4a**; see 2 Kgs 18:31; Isa 36:16; Joel 2:22; Zech 3:10). They will live without fear (see 1 Kgs 4:25; Isa 65:20-25; Hos 2:18).

Obeying God's word will affect every area of society, including our educational and political systems and our economies. It will bring peace in our lives and communities. Africa has known too much of wars, bloodshed and a lack of peace and security, and we look forward to the establishment of the Messiah's kingdom of peace and security.

This peaceful future is guaranteed by the sovereign Lord (**4:4b**). However, it will only come when the kingdom of God comes in its fullness (Rev 21–22). In the meantime, even though all others may still be following their own false gods, the faithful remnant must reaffirm their commitment to *walk in the name of the Lord our God* (**4:5**). They must take the nature and character of God as the standard of what is right. We, too, are to trust and obey the Lord, even though others around us are not following him. Secure in the knowledge that our worship of God will continue, *for ever and ever,* we are to be faithful to the end (2 Pet 3:11-13; 1 John 3:3).

The phrase *in that day* (**4:6a**) refers back to 'the last days' of 4:1, reminding us that Micah is still focusing on the future. He also refers back to the shepherd-king of 2:12-13, who is again described as bringing together the scattered and injured remnant of the people after God has punished them (**4:6b-7a**). God will transform this remnant into *a strong nation* (**4:7b**) and will establish his kingdom and *rule over them in Mount Zion* (**4:7c**). The kingdom restored by Jesus Christ will last for ever (see Isa 9:6-7; Dan 7:14, 27; Rev 11:15). Those who enter it will never perish.

Micah refers to two symbolic places when describing this kingdom. One of them is a tower near Bethlehem, David's birthplace, from which a shepherd could look out over his flock and protect it from wild animals and thieves (**4:8a**). The tower symbolizes the future kingdom of the Messiah, who will come from the royal house of David and who will be the Good Shepherd who will watch, protect, and secure the remnant for ever.

The second place is the *stronghold of the daughter of Zion* (**4:8b**). This was a fortified section of the old city of Jerusalem (2 Kgs 5:24; 2 Chr 27:3; 33:14), which is used to represent the whole city. The *daughter of Zion* refers to the inhabitants of the city. Micah is saying that in the last days Bethlehem and Jerusalem will be restored to the prominence they enjoyed in the days of David and Solomon.

4:9-13 The remnant will be saved

Before God's kingdom is established, God's people must first experience deep humiliation. They will cry out in distress as judgment comes as unavoidably as the pangs of a woman in childbirth. The nation of Israel will go through pain before she gives birth to the messianic king and the new era (**4:9**; 5:2-3). Her king and his counsellors will be killed or carried away to Babylon (4:9). The people will be forced into exile until God delivers a remnant from Babylon (the 'there' is repeated twice for emphasis) and helps them return to their land (**4:10**; see also 2 Chr 36:9-23; Ezra 1–2).

God will make those he saves strong enough to defeat their many enemies. These enemies are not the Assyrians or the Babylonians, but those who gather to attack Jerusalem before the second coming of Christ (see Ezek 38–39; Joel 3; Zech 12, 14). These nations intend to defile the holy city and take malicious pleasure in its distress and shame (**4:11**). But they are unaware that their gathering against God's people is part of his plan. God is in control, and he is gathering them *like sheaves to the threshing-floor* (**4:12**; see also Isa 21:10; 41:15-16; Jer 51:33; Hos 13:3). God will make his people so powerful that they will completely crush these nations under their feet, just as threshers trample sheaves until the grain is separated from the chaff (**4:13a**; see also Isa 41:15: Hab 3:12).

All the wealth of defeated nations is to be devoted to the Lord, meaning that it is to be utterly destroyed

(Josh 6:17; 2 Sam 22:43; 2 Kgs 23:6, 15). All this will be done by the *Lord of all the earth* (**4:13b**).

5:1-15 A New King and a New Kingdom

5:1-4 The Messiah

Micah now returns briefly to the coming siege by Sennacherib, a threat so real that Micah speaks as if it were already happening. The people must gather in troops to face it. Hezekiah was spared the humiliation of being struck on the *cheek with a rod* (**5:1**; see also 1 Kgs 22:24; Job 16:10; Ps 3:7) because he repented. A century later in 586 BC King Zedekiah, the last Davidic king, was publicly humiliated after the city fell to Nebuchadnezzar (2 Kgs 25:1-21).

But Micah announces that a new ruler in David's line will arrive from *Bethlehem Ephrathah* in Judah (**5:2a**). 'Ephrathah' was the ancient name of Bethlehem, and also the name of the district (see Gen 35:16, 19; 48:7; Ruth 4:11). Bethlehem was a minor town, not one held by a large and powerful clan, but it was the birthplace of King David (1 Sam 16:1; 17:12) and will also be the birthplace of the Messiah, Jesus Christ (Matt 2:3-6; Luke 2:4-7). Micah is the only prophet to identify Christ's birthplace.

While the town may be humble, the ruler who comes from it will be unique, for he will come forth *for me*, that is, on my behalf, says the Lord (**5:2b**). He will serve God, not himself. Not only that, but he will be someone *whose origins are from of old, from ancient times* (**5:2c**). Human beings begin to exist at birth, but not so the Messiah. Here, we have a reference to Jesus' incarnation and deity, indicating that he is both human and God (see also Pss 2:7; 45:7; 110:3; Isa 9:6; John 1:1-3).

The Messiah will not bring immediate deliverance; that will have to wait until the one *in labour gives birth* (**5:3a**), that is, until the time of suffering reaches its destined end. Until that time, God will abandon his people to their enemies. The Messiah's birth will only mark the beginning of the end of the days of suffering (see also Hos 1:9; 3:4-5). When he comes a second time, however, the deliverer from Bethlehem will establish his glorious kingdom and will lead *the rest of his brothers* back to God (**5:3b**; see also Rom 11:26-27). The Messiah will bring unity to his people as he stands and rules in their midst.

At his second coming, the Messiah will begin his reign. He will be a shepherd, who will lead, guide and protect God's people with strength that comes from God. He will bear *the name of the Lord his God* and his rule will endure for ever, extending to the ends of the earth (**5:4**; see also Ps 72:8; Isa 9:6; 10:21; Mic 4:1-4). His people will enjoy great security.

God specializes in choosing the small and the weak of the world to accomplish his mighty purposes (1 Cor 1:26-31). Africa may once have been called the dark continent, but

God has chosen many of its people to bring light to others through preaching the gospel of Jesus Christ. All this is done by God's power. Yet many problems remain with bad leadership and corruption, and we need to turn to the Messiah, Jesus Christ, as our shepherd, guide and protector.

5:5-6 His reign of peace

When the Messiah returns, he will establish a kingdom of peace, for he will be his people's peace (**5:5a**; see also John 14:27; Eph 2:14). Isaiah calls him 'the Prince of Peace' (Isa 9:6). At his second coming, all wars will cease and all weapons will be destroyed (4:3-5).

Micah predicts future attacks on Israel by *the Assyrians* (**5:5b**), and by *the land of Nimrod* (Babylonia – Gen 10:8-12; 1 Chr 1:10) (**5:6a**). These attacks are forerunners of the final attack on God's people that is to come at the end of time (Isa 13; 14:1-23; Jer 50, 51).

The prophets often refer to events that have both near and distant fulfilments. It is as if they are looking down a long tunnel of time, and see present and future events that are so intimately related that their outlines overlap and the prophets cannot tell the distance between them.

The Messiah's troops will have more than enough leaders to defend his kingdom if they can raise *seven shepherds, even eight leaders* (**5:5c**). The enemy forces will be destroyed and driven out (**5:6b**).

Christ has not yet established worldwide peace, but he has already given us peace with God and peace within our hearts despite the turmoil that surrounds us. He has also given us the living and active sword of God's word (Eph 6:17; Heb 4:12) and has promised that even the gates of hell will not overcome those who confess him as the Son of God (Matt 16:16-18).

5:7-9 The remnant will rule with the Messiah

The faithful followers of God who await the appearance of the Messiah are referred to as *the remnant of Jacob* (**5:7a**, **8a**). This remnant consists of faithful Israel and all true believers in Christ. They will be instruments both of God's blessings and his judgment in the end times, in the same way as Christ is both the 'Lamb of God' (John 1:29) and the 'Lion of the tribe of Judah' (Rev 5:5).

Micah first compares the remnant to dew in the heat of summer and showers on dry land (**5:7b**). Just as rain gives life and blessing, so the remnant will bring refreshment and renewal to those who thirst for God and will draw the nations to Jerusalem to receive salvation (4:1-4). They will not do this in their own strength, for the dew is described as coming *from the Lord*. Humans cannot manipulate God's gracious and faithful blessings, for they *do not wait for man* (**5:7c**).

The remnant are also like *a lion* (**5:8b**), an animal that surpasses all others in pride, prowess and ferocity, and retreats before none (Prov 30:30). Those who reject the

Messiah will find the remnant as dangerous as a lion that captures its prey, *and no one can rescue* (**5:8c**; see also Zech 8:13). They will be a strong nation in the midst of mighty nations, *like a lion among the beasts of the forest.* What a contrast with the weak people whom the Messiah had to rescue from their enemies (5:5b). Now no nation will be able to withstand them. Yahweh's hand will be lifted up as a sign of victory (**5:9a**; see also Exod 15:6; Ps 89:13; Isa 26:11). It is God who fights the battle (see also Exod 13:9; 14:8, 13-14) and it is all his foes who *will be destroyed* (**5:9b**).

Only God can refresh us and use us to bring blessing and salvation to others. We may suffer now, but ultimately Christ will rule over the whole of his creation.

5:10-15 Cleansing the kingdom of idolatry

In that day, when the Messiah establishes his kingdom (**5:10a**; see 4:1, 6), he will destroy everything that his people might rely on: their military weapons and might, such as *horses* and *chariots* (**5:10b**; see also Deut 17:16; Isa 2:7; Zech 9:10); their defence systems, such as fortified *cities* and *strongholds* (**5:11**; see also Deut 29:23; Isa 6:11; Lam 2:2; Hos 10:14; Amos 5:9); their witchcraft, that is, the practice of consulting sorcerers or soothsayers (**5:12**; see also Exod 22:18; Mal 3:5; Rev 21:8; 22:15); and finally, their pagan idols, such as the *carved images* and *sacred stones* and wooden images of Asherah (**5:13-14**; see also Exod 20:4; 34:13; Deut 5:8; 7:25; 16:21-22). God's people tended to put more trust in these things than in God, and that had led to their downfall (2 Kgs 13:6; 23:6).

Some members of African churches ignore what Scripture says and seek help from witchdoctors, sorcerers and diviners (Lev 19:26; Deut 18:9-14). God wants us to trust in him, not our traditional religions. We must prepare for God's kingdom by living cleansed and holy lives (Eph 5:26-27).

Once God has purified his own people, he will use them to punish those who do not submit to his rule (**5:15**; see also Isa 65:12). Micah speaks of God's *vengeance.* Human vengeance is a vindictive mix of envy and jealousy, but God's vengeance is his action to uphold the honour of his name against those who refuse his lordship and profane his holiness (see also Ezek 20:41; 28:22; 36:21-24).

6:1-7:20 Third Sermon

6:1-16 God's Complaint Against His People

6:1-8 God's anger

Now Micah speaks as if he is attending a court case where God is the plaintiff, the prosecutor and the judge, and Israel is the defendant. The ancient hills and mountains are called to serve as witnesses as God brings his *charge against Israel* (**6:1-2**; see also Hos 4:1; 12:2). These mountains were present when the Lord and Israel entered into a binding covenant at Sinai (Deut 4:26; 30:19; 31:28; see also Gen 31:43-50; Josh 22:21-28), and they were silent witnesses when the covenant was ratified (see also Deut 32:1; Ps 50:4; Isa 1:2). The charge is that the people had promised to obey God's law (see also Exod 24:7), but have repeatedly broken their promise.

God starts the lawsuit by asking the people why they have turned against him and whether he has wearied them by making too many demands (**6:3**). They cannot answer these questions because God has been good to his people and has not burdened them. They have forgotten what he has done for them, and so God reminds them of it. They would still be slaves in Egypt were it not for God's miraculous deliverance (**6:4**; see also Amos 2:10). He had given them godly leaders for forty years in the wilderness: Moses, the lawgiver who taught them the law (Exod 18:20); Aaron, the high priest, who brought reconciliation to the people (see also Exod 28:1-3; Num 17, 18); and Miriam, the prophetess, who led them in songs of praise to God (Exod 15:20-21). Moreover, God had turned the curse that Balak wanted the prophet Balaam to utter into a blessing on Israel (**6:5a**; see also Num 22–24). God had also miraculously dried up the Jordan River so that the people could walk across on dry land from Shittim in Moab on the east of the river to Gilgal in the promised land, on the west side of the river (**6:5b**; see also Josh 2:1; 4:19).

God was outraged because his people had forgotten him and broken the covenant, but his rage does not end his love, for he still addresses them tenderly as *My people* (6:3, 5; see also Isa 1:2; Hos 11). He wants them to return to him.

The people recognize that they have displeased God, but claim that they do not know what God really wants from them. Their question indicates that they do not understand that God is more interested in their hearts than in their sacrifices (**6:6**). They think that they can make up for their sins by offering even bigger sacrifices (**6:7**; see also Isa 1:11). They are even prepared to sacrifice their firstborn children – an offer that betrays their ignorance of the covenant. Only pagan gods required such a cruel sacrifice (2 Kgs 3:27; 16:3; 21:6; Jer 32:35; Ezek 16:20-21). Yahweh had explicitly forbidden it (Lev 18:21).

Micah pointed out that there was no need for more sacrifices (see also Amos 5:21-22). What the people needed to do was repent of their unbelief and injustice and obey the covenant laws. God has already told them what he desires (**6:8a**; see also Deut 10:12). What he requires of them *is good*. What he forbids is evil. God himself, and he alone, is good (Pss 100:5; 136:1; Mark 10:18) and he wants his followers to act in accordance with his own character and to exercise justice, mercy and humility (**6:8b**; see also Isa 1:17; Hos 6:6; Matt 23:23). There is no point in carefully following the law's requirements for sacrifice (Lev 1–7),

while ignoring its demand for righteous living (Lev 19:18; Deut 11:1, 13, 22).

When we feel guilty because of some sin, it is useless to try to earn God's forgiveness by doing good works, participating in church activities or carrying out traditional rituals. Such attempts are as pointless as Micah's contemporaries' offer to sacrifice their children. God requires that our lives show the Christian qualities of righteousness, love and humility. Humility includes admitting that Jesus Christ has made the final and complete sacrifice acceptable to God, and that only by trusting him can our sins be forgiven and our guilt removed.

6:9-16 Reasons for God's judgment

Micah summons the attention of the people of Jerusalem: *Listen!* (**6:9a**). He advises them to show wisdom by fearing God (**6:9**). Treating God casually is foolish and dangerous, for he holds *the rod* of discipline (**6:9b**).

The prophet forcefully informs the people that they may have forgotten God, but he has not forgotten what they have done. How can they expect him to forget his own standards? He condemns the wealth acquired through dishonest business practices such as defrauding customers by using false measures (**6:10**). A *short ephah* is a container that claims to hold one ephah of wheat or some other product but actually holds less. The use of such measures will bring God's judgment. So will the use of false weights to cheat buyers and sellers (**6:11**; see also Lev 19:35-36; Deut 25:13-16; Ezek 45:10; Hos 12:7). Those who have become rich through violence and corrupt commercial practices are full of violence and speak lies (**6:12**).

God cannot overlook commercial crimes and sins, and his judgment on these people fits what they have done (**6:13**; see Gal 6:7). They will lose the very things that motivated them to do evil. They will eat but will not be satisfied (**6:14a**; see also Deut 28:30-31; Hos 4:10). They will have no savings, for they will lose everything in war (**6:14b**; see also Lev 26:16; Deut 28:40, 51). The productivity of the land will be affected. Seed will be sown, but there will be little or no harvest. And where there is a harvest of olives or grapes, the oil and wine will be taken by others. (**6:15**; see also Deut 28:38-40). No matter how hard they work, they will not achieve material prosperity. The Lord will execute the covenant curses on his disobedient people (see also Lev 26:26; Deut 28:15, 18).

The people had also followed the pagan religious practices of Omri (1 Kgs 16:21-26) and Ahab, his son, Israel's most wicked king (**6:16a**; see also 1 Kgs 16:29-33). These kings were known for their support of Baal worship in the northern kingdom. Ahab had also illegally taken someone else's land (1 Kgs 21). Because the people of Judah have followed the same evil practices, they will be destroyed like Samaria. God will hand them over to ruin and *derision* (see Deut 28:15) and they will be scorned by other nations (**6:16b**).

Because of the poor economies in many African countries, some people claim that they have to use any means available to achieve material wealth. They are prepared to cheat, lie and even use violence to achieve success. But no society characterized by evil practices will prosper. Nor will individuals who regard their businesses as more important than their personal relationship with God.

7:1-20 Lamentation and Promise

7:1-6 The prophet's lament

Micah loves his people (see 1:8) and laments their sinfulness and the punishment awaiting them. He is like someone with a craving for fruit, bitterly disappointed that there is no fruit to be found (**7:1**; see also Isa 24:13; Hos 9:10). He has a similar craving to find some godly people, but he cannot find even one (**7:2a**; see also Jer 5:1; Ezek 22:30). There is no one who desires to follow and obey God (see Isa 57:1).

The prophet describes his society as one in which there is no concern for human life, for all the people are like hunters looking for prey (**7:2b**; see also Gen 4:9). They indulge in evil with *both hands,* showing their eagerness for it. They have become experts in doing evil. Bribery and corruption are the norm for the rulers and judges (**7:3**; see also Isa 1:23; Hos 4:18). Powerful officials need only to say what they want and it will be done. They cooperate in perverting justice for money. Even those who appear not quite as bad as the others are like a *brier* and *thorn hedge,* plants that will rip anyone passing too close to them (**7:4a**).

The prophets, who are the watchmen, have warned that punishment from God is at hand (**7:4b**; see also Isa 10:3; Jer 6:17; Ezek 3:17; Hos 9:7). God's judgment will strike suddenly, because the people have totally disregarded these warnings and the requirements of the covenant.

The society is so corrupt that it is unwise to trust friends or neighbours, or even those closest to one, like one's wife (**7:5**). Even she may use information against her husband. Leaders cannot be trusted, and everyone is suspicious of everyone else. Instead of honouring their parents (Exod 20:12; Lev 19:3), children treat them with scorn. Family members are hostile to one another, so that one's enemies are one's own household (**7:6**; see also Jer 9:4-5). When the family, society's foundational unit, is weakened through a lack of authority and discipline, the society itself becomes unstable (see also Exod 21:15, 17; Lev 20:9).

Disobedience to God's word and neglect of ethical values plunges communities into chaos and anarchy. Dishonesty and deceit flourish and soon it becomes impossible to trust anyone. The African church needs to realize that this moral decay is already taking place. Do we feel the same sadness as Micah did at his people's spiritual defeat? Do we really care about the moral and spiritual climate of our societies? Do we fear the coming judgment of God if we do not repent and mend our ways?

7:7-10 The promise of salvation

Micah does not succumb to utter despair. He knows the character of his Saviour and thus is confident that God will answer his prayer (**7:7**). His statement of faith is followed by a confession of sin by the repentant remnant. Because they look beyond God's judgment to a time of restoration, they can confidently tell their enemies not to rejoice at their suffering, because they will rise again (**7:8a**). They may now *sit in darkness,* a phrase that expresses their distress as they suffer God's wrath (**7:9a**), but since the Lord himself is their light, their darkness will not last for ever (**7:8b**; see also Ps 27:1). So they acknowledge their sin and recognize the justice of God's punishment. They know that eventually God will plead their case and decide in their favour (**7:9b**). Then he will act on their behalf and they will see his righteous salvation.

God will reverse the positions of the remnant and of their enemies. Those who had mocked God's people will be covered with shame. Those who said *Where is the Lord your God?* will see God vindicating his people (**7:10**; see also Joel 2:17). Those who said that God is powerless will be crushed underfoot like mud (see also Isa 10:6; Zech 10:5).

God will judge the sins of individuals and of nations who reject him, but he will also grant salvation to those who repent. Through Christ, we can have a relationship with God that will give us a confidence, like Micah's, that God is with us even as we go through difficult times and that we shall ultimately be victorious over all our enemies.

7:11-20 God's glorious grace

A glorious future awaits the remnant. Three times Micah refers to the coming *day* (**7:11-12a**), emphasizing the certainty of God's future restoration of his people. The rebuilding of walls and the extending of boundaries (7:11) is not simply the rebuilding that took place under Nehemiah but symbolizes God's restoration of the remnant in Zion (Pss 51:18; 69:35; 102:16; 147:2; Isa 60:10; Jer 31:38-40) comprising both Jews and Gentiles.

The influx of people from the Gentile nations to the new Jerusalem indicates that Micah is speaking of the Messiah's second coming to set up his great kingdom, when the Gentiles will be part of the righteous remnant (**7:12b**; see also 4:1-4; Zech 14:16; Rom 4:16-17; 9:30; Gal 3:6-9). Those who will come include Israel's ancient enemies, Assyria and Egypt, symbols of all the Gentile nations who will join God's people in that final day (see also Isa 19:23-25; 60:3; Amos 9:11-12; Zech 10:11). People will come from the farthest reaches of the world.

The salvation of the righteous will be accompanied by judgment upon the whole earth. The kingdom of the Messiah will replace our present world, which will become desolate because of its sin (**7:13**; see also Isa 24:1, 3; 34–35; 1 Thess 5:1-11; 2 Pet 3:10-13).

The prophet prays that God will shepherd his people, a prayer that recalls the prophecy of the messianic shepherd-king (**7:14a**; 5:4). The Lord himself is the Good Shepherd who rules, guides, leads, feeds and protects his people (Pss 23; 95:7; 100:3; John 10:1-16). With his staff, God will restore the righteous remnant who are *the flock of your inheritance* and defeat their enemies (**7:14b**; see also Pss 28:9; 74:1; 80:1). As God's people, they will live separate from the pagan nations that surround them (see Deut 33:28; Num 23:9; Jer 49:31). Micah prays that the flock may be brought into the rich pasturelands of Bashan and Gilead (**7:14c**; see also Num 32:1, 26; Deut 32:14; Jer 50:19). He wants to see them restored to the prosperity and blessings they enjoyed *long ago*.

Responding to Micah's prayer, God promises salvation and the performance of wonders, such as delivering his people from slavery in Egypt by bringing plagues on Egypt, opening the Red Sea and leading the people through the wilderness (**7:15**; see also Exod 12:50-51; 13:3, 9, 14, 16). The fact that these miracles can be repeated reveals the magnitude of God's power (Hos 11:11; 12:9; Zech 10:10). He will demonstrate the same power on behalf of the righteous remnant in the end-time (see also 1 Cor 10:1-4).

Hostile nations will find that their power will be as nothing compared to God's power (7:16). All they can do is *lay their hands on their mouths* in a gesture of awe and reverence (**7:16a**; see also Job 29:9-10; Isa 52:15). They will no longer blaspheme Yahweh and mock his people or listen to the vain boasts by others (**7:16b**). Instead, they will be so humiliated that they will *lick dust like a snake* (**7:17a**; see also Isa 65:25), which is a symbol of defeat (see 1:10; Isa 49:23). We are reminded of the curse on the serpent in the garden of Eden (Gen 3:14), a curse that will be fulfilled when God crushes him under the church's feet (Rom 16:20).

The defeated nations *will come trembling* from their hiding places to appear before God (**7:17b**; see also 2 Sam 22:46; Ps 18:45; Isa 19:16; 33:14). Confronted with God's power, they will become afraid of God's people (**7:17c**).

Micah concludes his prophecy with the remnant's triumphant song of praise to God. Their question *Who is a God like you?* plays on the prophet's name, Micah, which means, 'Who is like the Lord?' (**7:18a**; see also Exod 15:11). It is a reminder of the uniqueness and incomparable character of God (see also Isa 40:9-31).

God forgives the sin of those who confess their guilt and ask for his forgiveness (**7:18b**: see also Exod 34:6-7; 1 Tim 1:15-17). Those who have done this are called the *remnant of his inheritance,* implying that God has inherited them. They are his special possession. God does not *stay angry for ever* because he is a God who delights in mercy (see also 6:8; Ps 103:9-10; Jer 9:24). Though his people are unfaithful, he remains faithful (see also 2 Tim 2:13).

When God's people confess their sins, he will have compassion on them even though they do not deserve it. He will get rid of their sins, throwing them under his feet (**7:19**). Just as God hurled Pharaoh's chariots into the Red Sea, so he will *hurl all our iniquities into the depths of the sea* (see also Exod 15:4-5). All our sins have been removed and buried by God's grace through the cross of Jesus Christ (see Col 2:13-15).

Micah and the remnant's hope of salvation rests on God's grace and faithfulness to his covenant with Abraham and Jacob (**7:20**; see also Gen 12:1-3; 22:15-18; Deut 30:1-10; Ps 105:8-11). They can be confident because God keeps his promises, for he cannot lie (see also Heb 6:18).

Only the kingdom of the Messiah will last for ever, and only those who receive the Messiah and live holy and godly lives will share in that kingdom. We may sometimes fail, but if we turn to God, obey his word and live according to his will for our lives, we will experience his grace and mercy (Deut 30:1-3; Luke 1:72-73; 1 Thess 5:24).

Those who continue to reject the Messiah need to know that they will suffer the same fate as the enemy nations. But Jesus Christ can pardon, forgive and forget our sins. If we accept and trust in him, God will delight to show us the same mercy, faithfulness and compassion that he offers to all who come to him (Gal 3:26-29; Eph 2:18-19).

Believers in some African countries face enemies and opposition to the gospel. If they remain faithful, God will ultimately vindicate them and they will triumph over their enemies. God has promised to lead all his people (including Africans) out of the darkness of sin and into his light. Victory belongs to believers in Christ!

Yoilah Yilpet

Further Reading

Allen, Leslie C. *The Books of Joel, Obadiah, Jonah and Micah.* NICOT. Grand Rapids: Eerdmans, 1990.

Smith, Ralph L. *Micah-Malachi.* WBC. Waco, Tex.: Word, 1984.

Waltke, Bruce K. 'Micah' in *The Minor Prophets: An Exegetical & Expository Commentary.* Edited by Thomas Edward McComiskey. Grand Rapids: Baker Book House, 1993.

NAHUM

We know very little about the Nahum who wrote this book. All that the text tells us is that he came from Elkosh (1:1), a town that may possibly be in Galilee. The name Nahum is certainly known in that area, for the town of Capernaum that is mentioned in the gospels is actually Kaphar-Nahum in Hebrew, which means 'the village of Nahum'. A man by the name of Nahum is also mentioned in Jesus' genealogy in Luke 3:25, but he may not be the same person as the prophet.

The name 'Nahum' derives from a verb that means to regret, console, comfort, appease, satisfy or revenge. The nation of Judah, to whom the book is addressed, stood in need of all these things. Nahum, the 'comforter', comforted it and those who trusted in the Lord. But he also proclaims God's anger at injustice.

Date

Nahum must have been written after the destruction of Thebes (or No Amon) in Egypt by Ashurbanipal, king of Assyria in 663 BC (3:8-10). It is also clearly written before the destruction of Nineveh by the Babylonians and the Medes in 612 BC. Thus it must date from some time between 663 and 612 BC.

Theme

Nahum announces the impending fall of Nineveh, the capital of Assyria and the largest city of the time. It was the capital of an empire that was renowned for the ruthlessness and cruelty of its conquests.

Jonah had warned the people of Nineveh of Yahweh's wrath, and they had learned that God is 'slow to anger' (Jonah 4:2). They had repented at his preaching, but the change had only lasted for a generation or two. Soon they resumed their evil and arrogant ways. Now they will learn, through Nahum, that the God who restrained his anger in Jonah's time will let it loose if they return to evil. He is a 'jealous and avenging God' who 'does not leave the guilty unpunished' (Exod 34:7) and who has pity on his suffering people. He will not spare Nineveh this time. This message would comfort Judah, which had seen its neighbours from Israel deported by the Assyrians (2 Kgs 17:3-6) and had itself been attacked by them (2 Kgs 17:13-19).

Nahum's prophecy regarding Nineveh shows God's anger at those great powers that oppress the weak. As the proverb says, 'God chases away the flies for the hyrax that has no tail.' God controls events and governments and brings down those who destroy. He brings hope to the hopeless.

Outline of Contents

COMMENTARY

1:1 Introduction

The first verse of this book introduces its author and describes the book's contents as a *vision*. A vision is not the same as a dream. Dreams usually come at night and the dreamer is often passive. By contrast, a vision can occur at any time and the one seeing the vision is often caught up in what is happening. The vision Nahum saw concerned the fate of the great city of Nineveh.

1:2-15 The Majesty of God in Judgment and Mercy

1:2-8 God's Wrath

In the Hebrew original, **1:2-8** is a psalm or poem describing the majesty of God when he appears to act on earth. The psalm has three stanzas.

In the first stanza (**1:2-3a**) Nahum writes as if he is replying to the question, 'Who is Yahweh?' His reply stresses two inseparable aspects of God's character, namely that he is both fearsome and good. He gives four reasons why God is to be feared: he is a jealous God, he takes revenge, he is full of wrath, and he does not forget his anger at his enemies (1:2). God's reaction to evil is similar to that of a betrayed husband, who is elsewhere described as reacting to his betrayal with jealousy, fury and revenge (Prov 6:34).

God's jealousy needs to be understood in terms of his rights. He created everyone and thus is entitled to have authority over everyone, and in particular over his chosen people. He reacts strongly to any violation of his authority. He is *jealous* in the sense that he does not put up with insults (see Exod 20:5). But his vengeance should not be confused with a merely vindictive emotional response. God is an *avenging God* because he does not back away from his obligation to defend what is right and because he upholds the interests of his people. He is the one who is insulted, and he will be the one to take revenge (see Rom 12:19). God's *wrath* is a 'holy anger' in that it is a reaction to injustice and the violation of rights.

God's anger does not blaze out immediately, for he is slow to anger (1:3). There is a relation between power and patience: the stronger a person is, the more that person is able to show kindness and patience. However, the fact that God's enemies are currently enjoying peace should not reassure them about the future because they have tested God's patience to the limit. The storm is gathering and is about to break.

The second stanza (**1:3b-6**) describes a theophany, that is, God's appearing in this world. Here the effects of his wrath are described in general terms. The application to Nineveh will come later. The images used are familiar ones in the OT, associating God with the awesome power of storms and whirlwinds (1:3b; see also 2 Kgs 2:1; Job 9:17; 38:1; Pss 18:6-15; 29:3-10; Isa 39:6; Hos 13:15; Amos 1:14). As humans travel, they stir up dust clouds, but as God moves, he stirs up the clouds that cover the sky (Ps 68:4). The storm that accompanies his coming is so violent that the natural world is thrown into turmoil: the sea dries up, the hills melt like water and the earth quakes (**1:4-5**). There is no escape from God's wrath which is spreading like a volcanic river of fire (**1:6**; see also Deut 4:24).

The geographic place names that appear here (Bashan, Carmel and Lebanon) indicate that Nahum knows Palestine well. Bashan was a fertile plain east of the Jordan, and Carmel and Lebanon were mountains famed for their rich vegetation, but all plant life withers in the face of God's wrath.

The third stanza (**1:7-8**) presents Yahweh as one who protects his own and destroys criminals. This abrupt interruption of the description of the wrath of God reveals that this anger is not a blind force that strikes without distinction. The Lord knows those who are his, and is himself a refuge for his people (1:7). As many hymns of praise and prayers remind us, he is the only refuge in the midst of the terrors of judgment. But his enemies will be annihilated (1:8). His judgment on them will not be a temporary trial followed by a time of respite but will involve their utter ruin.

1:9-15 Application to Nineveh

The attitude to Nineveh in these verses is well expressed in the Senegalese proverb, 'The crab in the water thinks it is king. But the crocodile is right behind it'. Nineveh may think itself powerful and weave its plots *against the Lord* (**1:9a, 11**), but its destruction is certain. All resistance is pointless. *Trouble will not come a second time*, for the Lord

will destroy it so completely that there will be nothing left to restore (**1:9b**). The Ninevites will be as vulnerable to the fire of the Lord's wrath as dry straw (**1:10**).

Nineveh's army has attacked the nation of Judah and enslaved many of its people (**1:12-13**; see 2 Kgs 17:13-19). But despite the strength of their oppressor, the chosen people can be certain that what has been predicted will take place and that army will be destroyed. Judah will be freed from the *shackles* that bound it. Moreover *the Lord has given a command* about what will happen (**1:14**). In the NIV this command appears to be against the nation of Nineveh, but many commentators agree that it is directed against the *one who plots evil* in **1:11**, who may be Ashurbanipal, the Assyrian king. This man is cursed: no offspring will perpetuate his name, his gods will be destroyed and God himself will dig his grave.

Jerusalem is located in hill country, and that is why the people of Judah are told to look to the mountains to see messengers bringing the good news of the fall of Nineveh (**1:15a**; see also Isa 52:7). This will be a time of celebration, and a time to keep the promises that were made to God when the people prayed for deliverance (**1:15b**).

2:1-13 The Capture and Destruction of Nineveh

The Lord has raised a coalition of Medes and Babylonians to wipe out the oppressor of his people. The prophet sarcastically warns the city of the imminent attack and gives it some advice on how to prepare itself for what is coming (**2:1**). But the city will not be able to mount an effective resistance against an assailant sent by God. There will never be one eternally powerful human state to which all others will for ever be subject. This is a warning to all human powers: their present positions are only temporary. As the proverb says, 'The big new *daba* (hoe) that turns the soil to make the furrows will become the little hoe that weeds between the furrows'.

The reference to Jacob and Israel in **2:2** is intended to remind us that in 722 BC the Assyrians had wiped out the nation of Israel (the Northern Kingdom), seizing its treasures, damaging its vineyards and deporting its people. The impending destruction of Assyria is simple justice in exchange for the restoration of Israel and the freeing of Jerusalem. However, the prophet does not foresee the physical restoration of the nation of Israel, but rather the glorification of Judah (see 1:15), which implies the glorification of Jacob/Israel as well. The man originally known as Jacob or Israel (Gen 35:10) had been the common ancestor of both Israel and Judah. Thus the message of restoration is one that simultaneously announces pardon for Israel and comfort and hope for Judah, which had not yet fallen.

Nahum describes the fall of Nineveh in poetic language, focusing on specific details of colour and light and flaming torches to create a vivid picture of a battle in progress (**2:3-4**). The reader is transported to a scene of frantic activity that underscores the end to the threat posed by Nineveh.

The meaning of **2:5** is not clear. The prophet may be describing the arrival of Babylonian infantrymen before the gates of the city, with orders to set up war machines. But the messages to them stop because the outcome is certain and they are the first to recognize it. Alternatively, it may be the Assyrian troops who run to defend the wall, but do not achieve their aim.

The reference to *the river gates* being thrown open (**2:6**) may refer to the opening of the city gates which face towards the Tigris and Khoser rivers, or to the flooding of the city by dams that some suggest were on these rivers and had been captured by the attackers. However, many commentators see the open gates as a figurative reference to the opening of the doors of chaos, that is, the doors of the forces of death.

Without detailing the actual battle, the prophet leads us into the destroyed city of Nineveh where only captive women remain, grief-stricken and confused (**2:7**). The city is now *like a pool* that is emptying. Trying to prevent the loss of its inhabitants and riches is as difficult as trying to stop water flowing from a broken water tank (**2:8-9**). No wonder *hearts melt, knees give way, bodies tremble, every face grows pale* (**2:10**).

Nahum next presents the destruction of Nineveh in terms of what archaeology has shown to be a favourite activity of the Assyrian kings: a lion hunt. Assyria had been as cruel and invincible as a lion (**2:11-12**) but the situation was about to change. Now God is the hunter, who declares, *I am against you* (**2:13**). These terrible words are followed by a description of what will happen to Assyria: the nation known for its pitiless conquests will be totally destroyed. Its formidable army will be brought to nothing.

The destruction of the city of Nineveh can be seen as a guarantee that God will one day destroy the strongholds of his other enemies, Satan and the Antichrist. He also has the power to destroy Satan's strongholds in our own hearts.

3:1-19 The Reason for the Fall of Nineveh

Nahum summarizes the causes for Nineveh's punishment: it was bloodthirsty, greedy and pitiless (**3:1**). He describes its bloody conquests in an agitated poem that captures the noises and confusion as Nineveh captured a city. The images are like a series of snapshots of a battle in progress with chariots, swords, spears and scenes of carnage, with hundreds of bodies filling the city (**3:2-3**).

All this carnage takes place at the whim of a city that God compares to a prostitute whose splendour and magnificence dazzle neighbouring nations (**3:4**). Her power to do so may even derive from witchcraft. But while this prostitute

may have been *alluring,* that is, very attractive, she was also very cruel. Not only did she encourage the bloodshed described in 3:3-4, she also enslaved those she conquered.

Once again, the Lord declares, *I am against you.* This prostitute will be seized and forced to stand in a place where she will endure public humiliation and scorn (**3:5**). She will be mocked by passers-by and will have *filth* thrown at her (**3:6**). No one will want anything to do with the pitiable spectacle she presents (**3:7**).

Nineveh deserved such punishment because of its unjust domination of others and especially because of its enslavement of them. Its fate is a message to powerful nations, who abuse human rights and fail to recognize that the ranking of nations may change. If God is the one who controls history, what happened to Nineveh could be repeated. This message gives hope to the weak and downtrodden.

Nineveh will share the same fate as Thebes (or No Amon, 'the city of the god Amon', in some translations) (**3:8**; see also Ezek 30:14). In 663 BC, that great city, the capital of Upper Egypt, had been pillaged by the Assyrian armies of Ashurbanipal. It had fallen despite being protected by the Egyptian navy and surrounded by the Nile and its canals. Its king was a Nubian, who commanded the combined forces of Egypt and Cush (modern-day Sudan), and it had strong allies in Libya and Put (probably located in modern Eritrea and Somalia), but its strength had not saved it (**3:9**). The fate of Thebes is described in detail. The people were taken into exile, the children were murdered, and the aristocracy sold as slaves (**3:10**).

The prophet recalls the fate of Thebes to make the point that Nineveh is without excuse. The Ninevites should have recognized that the ungodly will suffer judgment. God has no favourites: he cannot be seen to be partial and at the same time remain faithful to his holiness. If God did not spare Thebes, he will certainly not spare cruel Nineveh. The disaster will be so great that people will reel and stagger as if they were drunk. (**3:11**; see also Isa 51:15, 21-23; Jer 25:15-28; Lam 4:21; Ezek 23:33-34; Obad 16; Hab 2:16).

Bitter humour flavours the depiction of Nineveh's forts as being *like fig-trees* that will drop their fruit as soon as they are shaken (**3:12**). Scorn colours the description of Nineveh's warriors as *women* (**3:13a**). When the defences are this weak, the enemies will have no difficulty in taking the city. The *gates of the land,* that is, the approaches to the city, are open to the enemy, and there is no hope of closing them for *fire has consumed their bars* (**3:13b**). This fire will spread to consume the city.

Because this attack is God's judgment on the city, no defence will be of any use. Thus there is irony in Nahum's recommendation that the people of Nineveh prepare to resist the enemy. They will need a good supply of water, and must work feverishly to make mud bricks to strengthen and repair the city walls (**3:14**). But no matter how hard they work or how many of them help, fire and sword will bring down the great city (**3:15a**).

Nineveh had been a flourishing trade centre, with as many merchants as there are *stars of the sky*. But the merchants will vanish, and all that they have accumulated will be carried off by the enemy, who will strip the city like locusts. Nineveh will not enjoy any of the benefits of their trade (**3:15b-16**). This reference to trade should not be interpreted as meaning that Nineveh will simply collapse because it has been weakened by luxuries and decadence; its end will be at the hands of its enemies.

Locust invasions wreak havoc in Africa today, just as they did in Assyria in ancient times. We can recognize the image Nahum uses here as he compares the city's guards, governors and officials to locusts resting on a wall. They may seem like a vast horde, but they will take flight and vanish like a cloud of insects in the scramble to escape the ruin of Nineveh (**3:17**).

The prophecy ends with a final satirical poem that describes the rulers of the city as asleep, the people as scattered and leaderless, and the nation as dying from an incurable wound (**3:18a**). The city declines into inactivity and paralysis as disaster looms. Nothing can be done to save it. This news will be a cause for rejoicing among all those who have suffered under Nineveh's domination (**3:19**). They will applaud its punishment.

Conclusion

The book of Nahum, whose main message is the destruction of godless Nineveh, ends with the sad recognition that inhabitants of the city are *scattered on the mountains with no one to gather them together* (**3:18b**). We are reminded of Jesus' description of the people of Israel as 'harassed and helpless, like sheep without a shepherd' (Matt 9:36). Nahum does not prophesy the coming of the Messiah, but he shows the need for him.

The news that the eternal God has not forgotten his people but will re-establish them (1:13, 15) is still good news in Africa today, where we need to remember that God is concerned for those who suffer under all kinds of oppression. This message of hope for the oppressed is also a warning to the oppressors. God will judge them.

The message of comfort in the book of Nahum can have a powerful impact on the life of the new Christians of Africa. God takes our case seriously and the salvation of our continent is certain. The God who ruled in Jerusalem is the same God who governs all of Africa, and one day all his children will confess that he is God.

Cossi Augustin Ahoga

Further Reading

Baker, D. *Nahum, Habakkuk, Zephaniah.* TOT. Downers Grove, Ill.: Inter-Varsity Press, 1988.

Feinberg, Charles L. *The Minor Prophets.* Chicago: Moody Press, 1990.

Robertson, O. Palmer. *The Books of Nahum, Habakkuk, and Zephaniah.* NICOT. Grand Rapids: Eerdmans, 1990.

HABAKKUK

We know very little about the prophet Habakkuk, whose name appears twice in this book (1:1; 3:1). He is not mentioned in any other book of the Bible. *Bel and the Dragon,* an apocryphal book, states that he was a contemporary of the prophet Daniel, while a rabbinical tradition suggests that he was the boy whom Elisha raised to life in 2 Kings 4:32-36. But we have no evidence to support either of these beliefs.

All that we can deduce about him is that he was a prophet who spoke to Judah and that he may have been one of the temple singers (3:19), in which case he would have been a member of the tribe of Levi. We also know that his name, Habakkuk, comes from a Hebrew root that means 'embrace'. In his prophecy, Habakkuk was true to his name in that he embraced a strong faith in Yahweh (3:17-19).

The principal event in the book of Habakkuk is the Babylonian invasion of Israel in 605 BC. The text makes numerous references to the Psalms and the book of Isaiah. There is also a great similarity of thought with the book of Jeremiah. All of these factors suggest that Habakkuk was probably written in the seventh or sixth century BC.

The book is written in the form of a dialogue between the prophet and his God and deals with one of the great mysteries that continues to trouble us all – the apparent triumph of evil in a world created and ruled by a good, loving and sovereign God. Can good triumph in a situation that seems hopeless, one where evil reigns? Does God really intervene?

Habakkuk was a prophet of social justice who wrestled with God in questioning and courageous prayer, yet who also had unshakeable faith and hope in God. Such a courageous servant of God is desperately needed in Africa today.

Outline of Contents

COMMENTARY

1:1-4 Habakkuk's Questions: How long? Why?

The book of Habakkuk begins by announcing that it records a revelation given to *Habakkuk the prophet* (**1:1**), a title that places him in the company of the other biblical prophets. The revelation is described as an *oracle*, using a Hebrew word that literally means a 'burden' or 'load' (as in Exod 23:5). It is often used of prophetic proclamations of judgment in the OT (see Isa 13:1; 15:1; 17:1; Nah 1:1). The word translated *received* is literally 'saw' (as in Isa 1:1). The combination of 'burden' and 'saw' in this prophecy suggests that there was a visual dimension to God's communication with this prophet.

Habakkuk complains that the wicked are imposing injustice and suffering in his country while God remains silent and inactive. The question *How long ... ?* indicates that this has been going on for a long time and is still continuing (**1:2a**; Pss 6:3; 13:1-2; 94:3). His cry of *Violence* (**1:2b**) well describes the social, political and religious situation in the seventh and sixth centuries BC. It was a period of great instability (see 2 Kgs 23:31-25:7). The prophets Jeremiah and Ezekiel warned their contemporaries that divine judgment was coming because of this violence (Jer 6:6-7; Ezek 7:23).

The parallelism in 1:2 aligns the verbs *listen* and *save*. A good listener, whether human or divine, is someone who pays attention to another's needs and brings salvation. Men and women of God should demonstrate this quality (Exod 2:23-25; 1 Sam 25:24, 33).

Habakkuk's words suggest that he has been given special awareness of the situation in his country, causing him to ask, 'Why do you make me look at injustice?' (3:3). He sees the oppression and the perversion of justice clearly and cannot ignore it. The wicked paralyze the law, so that it cannot work to produce justice. In this respect, the world of Habakkuk is very similar to ours. The wicked of our day make unjust laws and ignore those good laws that are intended to promote justice. Our world needs men and women who love justice and are ready to suffer and die for it so that it can prevail.

Habakkuk is on the same wavelength as the prophet Jeremiah. He suffers for justice because his views go against those of the society he lives in, but he is not prepared to renounce his faith in God and his belief that God will intervene (Jer 20:7-10).

Even today, the spiritual, social and political life of many countries is characterized by violence, injustice, corruption, hate and immorality. These are the tools used to gain and maintain power. Do we have the eyes to see and the moral authority to denounce this tyranny of evil? The prophet invites us to healthy indignation and fervent pleas to God who alone can save.

1:5-11 The Lord's Reply

God's reply to Habakkuk and to those who share his grief and anger is that he is preparing an unprecedented judgment. Violence may reign supreme, but it will be punished with even greater violence (**1:9**). The rulers who claim that 'might makes right' will have to deal with truly ruthless men *whose own strength is their god* (**1:11**).

The Lord's reply to Habakkuk comes in a series of imperative verbs: *Look … watch – and be utterly amazed* (**1:5a**). These imperatives are in the present tense, implying that God is already doing something. God is doing a work in Habakkuk's days that Habakkuk and his people *would not believe if told* (1:5b, RSV). Elsewhere in the Bible, God reproaches people for failing to discern what he is doing (Isa 5:12; Matt 16:2-3). Paul quotes this same verse from Habakkuk in his sermon in Acts 13:41, to warn his listeners of the danger of ignoring what God is doing in their midst through Jesus Christ.

Habakkuk complains about God's silence and his inactivity in the face of evil, but God's answer reminds him that the sovereign God of the universe, the holy and just God, does not wait to be informed or supplicated by his prophet before acting. He already had a plan of action well before the prophet voiced his complaint. When God seems far away, absent from the scene, the text suggests that we pray: 'Oh Lord, open my eyes that I may see the work that you are doing in my time' (see also 2 Kgs 6:17).

God says that what he is doing is *a work* (**1:5b**, RSV), a term that is used to refer to a powerful act of God (Pss 44:2; 46:9). God introduces his more detailed description of this work with the words, *I am raising up the Babylonians* (**1:6**). Similar words are found in other biblical prophecies referring to God's using a foreign nation to act for him (see also Jer 5:15; Amos 3:11; 6:14). God announces to Habakkuk that he will raise up the Babylonians to punish the evil of which the prophet is complaining.

God does not ignore the true nature of those whom he uses as his agents of judgment, as can be seen from the portrait of the Babylonians in 1:7-11. They are described as *feared* and *dreaded*, a people who are agile, swift, arrogant and as greedy as vultures. They are compared to the top predators in the animal world (**1:8**). They arrogantly refuse to recognize any laws other than those that they make on the basis of their own desires (**1:7**). Their power is the only god they trust (**1:11**). Habakkuk cannot understand how God can be prepared to use such people.

This ugly portrait of the Babylonians brings out an important lesson: in spite of their power, pride and impiety, the Babylonians are still subject to the power of the Almighty God. He can use even the ungodly to accomplish his purposes. In times of trouble, we need to fix our eyes on the God of Habakkuk, a God who is all powerful, holy and just, rather than on the tyranny of sin and injustice or on spiritual powers and ungodly human beings. All of these forces that oppose God are still subject to him, and 'if God is for us, who can be against us?' (Rom 8:31-39).

1:12-2:1 Habakkuk's Question: Why Them?

As predicted (1:5), Habakkuk was astonished at the Lord's reply. How can a holy and just God use such ungodly people as the Babylonians to punish people who are *more righteous* than they are (**1:13**)? After all, this enemy is like an insatiable fisherman whose power, strategies and means of destruction are his *hooks, net* and *drag-net* (**1:15**). These are instruments that catch prey at random, pulling in any fish that are in the area. In the same way, an attack by the Babylonians will harm everyone in the region, whether they are righteous or unrighteous. Moreover, instead of recognizing that it is the Lord who is giving them victory, the Babylonians will take credit for themselves, or praise gods that they themselves have set up and consider worthy of sacrifices (**1:16**).

Yet, despite his consternation at God's methods, Habakkuk remains humble and wants to trust in God. He acknowledges that God is *from everlasting*, and so has the last word. He is also sure of the ultimate salvation of God's people: *We will not die!* (**1:12**). The meaning is synonymous with Jacob's confident 'we will live' in Genesis 42:2 and 43:8, expressing an assurance that would continue throughout the history of Israel. Habakkuk is even prepared to recognize that the enemy is on a divine mission, yet he still wonders why God is using such a terrible enemy. So he decides to think of himself as being like a lookout posted on a city wall, watching to see how God will reply to his doubts (**2:1**). This image may have come to his mind because of the passage in which Isaiah referred to a lookout when he prophesied the future fall of Babylon (Isa 21:6-9).

Habakkuk's response is a model for Christians. He demonstrates both faith and hope, two fundamentals of the Christian life (Rom 5:1-2). He is also willing to honestly express his doubts. His is not a blind and unreasoning faith (see also Acts 17:10-12).

2:2-20 The Lord's Reply

God's new response to Habakkuk again begins with commands: *Write … and make it plain* (**2:2**). The Lord wants his words to be helpful to others as well. The second half of this verse is more difficult to translate. The NIV translates it as *so that a herald may run with it,* the NKJV has 'that he may run who reads it' and the HCSB has 'so one may easily read it'. The original Hebrew uses two verbs: 'read' and 'run', and it seems that the meaning is closer to the NKJV translation above. The vision must be written down so clearly on clay or wooden tablets that those who read it will recognize that they need to run for their lives. The prophet-lookout has been given this instruction in order to save their lives, for God's inevitable judgment is coming soon (**2:3**).

The Lord next replies to the prophet's two questions: why the just share in the punishment, and why an ungodly nation will carry out the judgment (see also comments on 1:15-16). First, he contrasts someone who is wicked, whose soul is swollen with pride, with someone who is *righteous.* Judgment is inescapable for the former, but *the righteous will live by his faith* (**2:4a**). God is endorsing Habakkuk's positive words in 1:12, but is also indicating who exactly the 'we' are who will not die. The 'we' is not all the prophet's people, but rather those who are righteous. God confirms that he will not make the righteous die with the wicked (see also Gen 18:20-33).

The key verse in this book is *the righteous will live by his faith* (**2:4b**). It is quoted three times in the NT (Rom 1:17; Gal 3:11; Heb 10:38). To understand what it means, we need to examine each of the main words in their context.

First, who are 'the righteous'? In the OT, the word 'righteous' is used as a synonym for 'innocent' and 'right' and as the opposite of 'wicked' (Gen 18:23; Ps 37:21). Someone who is wicked is associated with violence, injustice, wrong, strife and conflict, paralysis and perversion of the law, oppression, destruction, pride and idolatry (1:1-4, 13-17; 2:4a, 5, 6-18). This contrast between the righteous and the wicked permits us to conclude that the 'righteous' person referred to here is anyone who lives in conformity with the will of God expressed in the Mosaic law.

In the book of Habakkuk, the term 'the righteous' is once used to refer to all the people of Judah in comparison with the Chaldeans whom God will use as executors of his judgment (1:13). However, in 1:4 and 2:4b, the term is restricted only to the faithful, loyal remnant among Judah who still obeyed God's law. These righteous will live 'by faith', which here means 'by faithfulness', that is, with an attitude of unshakeable trust in the God of the Bible. The word 'live' conveys a hope of salvation for the righteous in the context of threatened destruction. It suggests deliverance from the present Chaldean invasion and from evils to come, as well as enjoyment of the blessings of the promised land.

What Habakkuk is saying in 2:4b can thus be interpreted in two ways:

- If we stress the link between the concepts of faith and righteousness, the verse is saying that those who are righteous because of their faith will live. With this inter-pretation, the verse is teaching justification by faith. But reading the verse in this way may be reading a Christian meaning back into it. Habakkuk's message to his original readers dealt with the issue of surviving a very specific event, and not with quiet reflection on salvation in the Christian sense.

- If we stress the link between the concepts of faith and living, the verse is saying that those who are righteous will continue to live by their faith. This interpretation fits the grammar and the context, which does not contrast legal righteousness and the righteousness that comes by faith. Habakkuk is not dealing with the issue of how one is justified, but of how believers should live during dark and evil days. They must persevere in God and continue to be faithful in spite of adversity.

The Apostle Paul twice quotes 2:4b. In Romans 1:17, he quotes it to emphasize the power of the gospel for the salvation of everyone who believes. In Galatians 3:11-12, he cites it to contrast two modes of justification and to argue for the impossibility of being justified by the law. He could use the same verse in two different contexts because faith or faithfulness is the condition that makes righteousness possible, and thus makes salvation possible. Paul sees this verse as applying to the work of Christ, the one who alone will enable full justification by faith (Gal 3:11-14) and who achieved this by being perfect right to the end of his race (Heb 12:1-2).

In 2:5-20, the Lord replies to the prophet's second question: Why use a wicked people as his agents? The answer takes the form of five woes that make it clear that the Babylonians will also be punished. This passage provides a good illustration of the principle of double intent. The same event may achieve two separate purposes: the purpose of God and the quite different purpose of his agent. God was using the Babylonians as a judgment on the wickedness of his people, but the Babylonians were pursuing their own ends. The motives with which the Babylonians were acting would be the ones for which God would call them to account.

The Babylonians' wrong motives are set out in the first four woes (**2:5-17**). They are hungry for domination, glory, grandeur and wickedness. These same motives still explain the numerous murderous encounters between Africans and their fellow citizens. But a warning is issued: wicked plans will eventually recoil on those who made them (**2:8, 16**). Thus God tells the Babylonians, *In plotting the ruin of many peoples you forfeited your life* (**2:10**). We are reminded of Jesus' question: 'What good will it be for a man if he gains the whole world, yet forfeits his soul?' (Matt 16:26).

The final woe relates to the idolatry of the Babylonians (**2:18-19**). They are guilty of wilful self-delusion when it comes to their gods, trusting them even though they know that these images *are lifeless stone* and are incapable of giving them any guidance (see also Pss 115:4-8; 135:15-18).

What a contrast between these dumb idols and the sovereignty and transcendence of the true God! He can indeed speak, and it is all creation that is reduced to silence before him (2:20).

3:1-19 Habakkuk's Prayer

The tone of the book now changes. Habakkuk asks no more questions. Instead, chapter 3 is entitled 'Habakkuk's Prayer' (3:1). He has been satisfied by the divine promise of hope and justice in 2:2-20, and now utters a prayer of praise.

He begins his prayer by saying *I stand in awe, O Lord, of your work* (3:2a, NRSV). The word 'work' reminds us of what God is doing in the days of Habakkuk, the prophet, the work of using the Babylonians to bring judgment (see 1:5-6). So Habakkuk also asks the Lord to *remember mercy* (3:2b) or, in other words, to preserve the righteous as he has promised (see 2:4).

Habakkuk goes on to exalt his God as an invincible warrior. Not only the Babylonians but also all natural elements and all nations are submissive to him (3:3-15). The prayer is a psalm filled with echoes from other psalms and earlier prophetic proclamations. It proclaims God as the defender of the people of Israel (Exod 15:1-18; Deut 33:1-29; Pss 18; 68; 77).

In spite of his fear of the impending invasion (3:16-17), the book of Habakkuk ends on a very positive note: *I will rejoice* (3:18). The prophet places his entire confidence in the Lord and draws his strength from him. He recognizes that God is the source of salvation (3:18-19). What an encouragement for us in Africa! In the midst of wars, famine and social injustice, we can still rejoice on the basis of our trust in the sovereign God. God is doing great works in our continent. He is looking for men and women who will build up the wall and stand before him in the gap on behalf of the continent so that he will not have to destroy it (Ezek 22:30).

Youssouf Dembele

Further Reading

Baker, D. *Nahum, Habakkuk, Zephaniah.* TOT. Downers Grove, Ill.: Inter-Varsity Press, 1988.

Feinberg, Charles L. *The Minor Prophets.* Chicago: Moody, 1990.

Robertson, O. Palmer. *The Books of Nahum, Habakkuk, and Zephaniah.* NICOT. Grand Rapids: Eerdmans, 1990.

ZEPHANIAH

Zephaniah was a fourth-generation descendant of King Hezekiah, and was also probably of African descent (1:1a). He was born in the days of Manasseh (695-642 BC), the most evil king in Judah's history and may have been given the name *Zephaniah*, which means 'the Lord has hidden or protected', as a statement of God's power to protect his faithful servants from persecution (2 Kgs 21:16). However, the name was a common one.

Manasseh and his son Amon (642-640 BC) encouraged idolatry and tolerated child sacrifice, witchcraft, temple prostitution and violence (2 Kgs 21; 2 Chr 33). There was a general disregard for God and his word. They were succeeded by Josiah (640-609 BC), the most righteous of all the kings of Judah (2 Kgs 21:26-23:30; 2 Chr 33:25-35:27). Josiah was eight when he came to the throne. Zephaniah was probably prophesying in about 630 BC, when the king was a teenager. Zephaniah's denunciation of moral and religious depravity and his repeated urging of the people to 'seek the Lord' in repentance may have laid the foundations for the great revival that took place later in Josiah's reign as he sought the Lord with all his heart and soul. Like his contemporary, Nahum, Zephaniah also proclaimed that the Assyrian empire would be destroyed.

Unfortunately, after King Josiah's death the leaders and many of the people reverted to their old ways, as can be seen in the prophecies of Habakkuk and Jeremiah.

The book of Zephaniah falls into two sections, the first dealing with the imminent coming of the Day of the Lord (1:1-18) and the second being an exhortation to repent and seek God's salvation (2:1-3:20).

Outline of Contents

COMMENTARY

1:1 Superscription

Zephaniah's genealogy is given to the fourth generation, possibly to establish his link to King *Hezekiah*, and possibly because his father, *Cushi*, was not a Jew, but an African, for 'Cushi' means 'Ethiopian'. Cushi may have entered Israel from Egypt, which the Ethiopians ruled from 712 BC to 663 BC. Zephaniah needed to establish the pure Jewish ancestry of his mother to four generations if both he and his father were to be fully accepted into the community of the Lord (Deut 23:7-8).

1:2-18 The Coming Day of the Lord

1:2-3 Universal Judgment

Zephaniah proclaims God's coming judgment not only of Judah but also of the whole world. God will once again act as he did in the days of Noah, and will *sweep away* all his creation (**1:2**; see Gen 6:7). Everything will be destroyed, including animals, birds, sea creatures and all humanity (**1:3a**). The totality of the destruction demonstrates God's great anger at the sin and evil in the world. It also reveals that all creation suffers because of human sin (see Rom 1:18-20; 8:20-22).

When God's anger sweeps everything from the earth, Africa will not be spared. Thus as part of the gospel message we must warn others of God's judgment and urge them to repent in order to escape this fate. This message is not something of our own making, but comes from the Lord himself (**1:3b**).

1:4-6 Judgment on Judah and Jerusalem

The prophet then narrows his focus from the whole world to just the people of Judah and Jerusalem (**1:4a**), who have stopped *following the Lord*, and no longer seek him (**1:6**). God expects a higher standard of behaviour from them, for they are his covenant people and have received a special revelation of him. So his judgment begins 'with the family of God' (1 Pet 4:17).

The Israelites had not obeyed God and had not destroyed all the pagan inhabitants of Canaan as they were commanded to do (Deut 7). Instead they had started worshipping the Canaanite gods, the chief of whom was Baal (**1:4b**; see also Jer 9:13-14; 32:29). Some people were prostrating themselves on their rooftops, worshipping the sun, moon and stars (**1:5a**; see also Deut 4:19; 2 Kgs 23:5, 11; Jer 8:2; Ezek 8:16). They were worshipping created objects instead of the Creator (see Gen 1:14-17; Rom 1:25).

The people were also mixing religious systems, combining the worship of the Lord with the worship of idols, and specifically of Molech (**1:5b**; see also Lev 18:21; Jer 5:7). Molech was an Ammonite god to whom children were offered in human sacrifice (1 Kgs 11:5, 33; 2 Kgs 23:10, 13; Jer 32:35). Scripture explicitly forbade any worship of him (Exod 20:3; Lev 20:2-5; Deut 12:31; Josh 23:7; Jer 2:11).

Unfortunately, some Africans still mix traditional African religious beliefs with Christian beliefs. Some are even prepared to kill members of their families in order to fulfil religious rituals or become rich. Others who claim to be Christians and attend church regularly, also belong to secret societies that call upon powers other than the true and living God for help. But God demands our absolute loyalty. He condemns all hypocrisy and the mixing of our faith with other beliefs and practices.

The African church should strongly teach that we are to seek the Lord only and put our faith and trust in him alone. While we should tolerate other people's religions in our countries, we must strongly reject the practice of mixing Christian faith with other religious systems.

1:7-13 Description of the Judgment of Jerusalem

Because of the awfulness of the coming destruction, the prophet calls for silence in the presence of the *Sovereign Lord* (**1:7a**; see also Amos 8:3; Hab 2:20; Zech 2:13). Everyone must listen and prepare, for the day of God's judgment is fast approaching (**1:7b**; see also Isa 13:6; Ezek 7:7; 30:3; Joel 1:15; 2:1; 3:14; Obad 15). The people of Judah have been prepared as a sacrifice, and God will use the Babylonians, whom he has consecrated for this purpose, to slay this sacrifice (**1:7c**; see also Isa 13:3; Jer 46:10; Ezek 39:17). They will be God's instruments of judgment, invading the land and killing the people. This judgment is a preview of the more dreadful final judgment day of the Lord (Matt 24:6, 36-39).

The leaders of Judah, including the nobility, the king's sons, and members of the royal court will be punished (**1:8a**). Their wearing of *foreign clothes* was a symbol of the way they had led the people in adopting the pagan way of life and idolatrous practices. (**1:8b**; see also Num 15:38-39).

People also demonstrated their idolatry by avoiding stepping on the threshold of a house (that is, on the paving in a doorway) in order not to provoke the pagan gods who supposedly guarded the house (**1:9a**; see also 1 Sam 5:1-5). This action shows that they do not trust God to protect them. The temples of the pagan gods are also filled *with violence and deceit* (**1:9b**), for many of the offerings made there were obtained by oppressing the poor. The worship of pagan gods is false and violent; it seeks to deceive and oppress rather than reveal the truth and liberate.

As the Babylonians invade, there will be wailing from various sections of the city. The enemy will come from the north, and thus the wailing will begin at *the Fish Gate* in the north wall (**1:10a**; see also 2 Chr 33:14; Neh 3:3; 12:39). Next to the Fish Gate was the *New Quarter* (also known as the Second District), which was an extension of the residential area beyond the old walls (**1:10b**; see also 2 Kgs 22:14; Neh 11:9). This was where the rich lived, but their riches and luxurious homes will not save them. Cries of terror will also come from the *market district* (also called the Mortar) as all the merchants and traders there are wiped out (**1:11**).

Zephaniah even pictures God as going up and down the streets of Jerusalem *with lamps*, searching out the wicked and sinners to punish them (**1:12a**; see also Jer 5:1). Those who are complacent and indifferent will all be punished (see also Isa 32:9; Jer 48:11; Ezek 30:9; Amos 6:1). These people thought that it did not matter how they acted, because they assumed that God would do nothing (**1:12b**).

The rich will lose all their wealth, their homes and their vineyards as God brings upon them the curses of the covenant (**1:13**; see also Lev 26:32-33; Deut 28:30, 39; Amos 5:11). Their goods will be seized and their houses plundered. There will be no place to hide from God's judgment.

We, too, should repent of our evil ways, if we are to enjoy God's blessings. No social class can hope to be spared; all will be judged.

1:14-18 A Great and Terrible Day

Zephaniah's description of the *day of the Lord* that is quickly approaching is similar to that in Amos 5:18-20 and Joel 2:11. It is not something to anticipate with joy and to long for, but rather a day of bitter weeping and of violent shouts as the Lord himself comes as a warrior against mankind (**1:14**; see also Jer 20:11; Ezek 30:4-5). His *trumpet and battle cry* will be heard as he attacks the nations of the world like enemy forces storming a city (**1:16**; see also Num 10:9; Jer 4:19; Joel 2:1; Zech 14:3).

God is long-suffering and patient, beyond human comprehension. But he cannot ignore sin, because he is holy, just and upright. His anger against it will be expressed on this *day of wrath* (**1:15a**; see also 1:18; 2:2-3; Jer 4:8; 12:13; Ezek 7:3-19; Hos 5:10). People will experience emotional *distress and anguish* (**1:15b**) and physical *trouble and ruin* (**1:15c**; see also Jer 16:19; Obad 12, 14; Hab 3:16). Physically and psychologically, it will be *a day of darkness* *and gloom* (**1:15d**), with the cosmic darkness and clouds adding to the psychological trauma (**1:15e**; see also Isa 13:10; Ezek 34:12; Joel 2:2, 10, 31; Amos 8:9).

All in all, the horrors of this day of the Lord are too awful to comprehend. Even grown men will cry in fear. People will experience such distress that they *will walk like blind men,* staggering and stumbling in the darkness of their own disobedience (**1:17a**; see also Deut 28:29; Isa 59:10). This terrible judgment comes *because they have sinned* against God and his holiness (**1:17b**). Because God is holy, he cannot clear the guilty.

Human *blood will be poured out* as if it were merely dust to be trampled upon (**1:17c**; see also Lev 17:11; 2 Kgs 13:7). Human corpses and their entrails will be scattered about like refuse on the ground (**1:17d**; see also Ps 83:10; Isa 5:25; Jer 8:2; 9:22; 16:4; 25:33).

The wealthy must not think that their money will enable them to escape God's judgment (**1:18a**; see also Job 20:20; Prov 11:4; Ezek 7:19). They may in the past have been able to buy security and power with money, but God does not take bribes.

The whole world will be consumed by *the fire of his jealousy* and there will be no escape (**1:18b**; see also 1:2-3; Deut 4:24; 2 Pet 3:10-12). This universal destruction will be total and quick, and will come without warning (**1:18c**; see also Jer 46:28; Ezek 11:13).

We should not think that with the Babylonian conquest of Judah, this day of judgment is now in the past. There is still a coming judgment when the Lord returns at the end of history. The prophets often combine similar events in one prophecy, and thus, the day of the Lord has already come for Judah but is still to come for us. We will endure the same fate as the people of Judah, and no wealth will save us when Christ comes in judgment (2 Thess 2:1-2; Rev 20:12-15).

Although our money or power will not save us, one thing that can – Christ's death on the cross on our behalf (1 Thess 1:10; 2 Tim 1:12). If we know him, the day of the Lord will be transformed into a bright day of salvation as Christ comes for his people (Matt 16:27; John 6:39-40, 54; 1 John 4:17; Rev 22:12).

2:1-3:20 Repent and Seek God's Salvation!

2:1-3:8 Exhortation to Repent

2:1-3 An exhortation to seek God

The nation is described as *shameful* because of its behaviour. The people are called upon to *gather together* before the day of judgment blows in as rapidly as chaff that is being blown before the wind and the people themselves are blown like chaff before it. (**2:1-2**). The word 'before' is repeated three times to urge them to act immediately, 'before' the decree is issued, 'before' God's fierce anger comes, and 'before' the day of God's wrath.

The next verse is the key to the whole book of Zephaniah: The people are urged to use the little time that remains to *seek the Lord* (**2:3a**; see also 2 Chr 7:14; Amos 5:4-6, 14). They have not been seeking him (1:6), but now they should repent, seek him and *do what he commands.* Anyone who truly seeks God will be willing to obey him.

They also need to seek two qualities: *righteousness* and *humility* (**2:3b**). Those who seek righteousness will be committed to doing what is right themselves and to establishing just societies. They will conform to God's standards in their conduct and will take his word seriously (see also Deut 30:16, 20). The humility they are to seek is a dependence on God, so that they rely on him and are not complacent and proud (see also 1:12; Prov 15:33). The humble are willing to admit that God alone must be obeyed and worshipped. This attitude pleases God (Ps 51:17; Isa 57:15; 66:2; Matt 5:5; 1 Pet 5:6).

If the people repent of their self-confidence and evil practices, God, who is always merciful and compassionate, may possibly relent in his judgment (**2:3c**; see also Jonah 3:9).

Zephaniah's instruction to actively search for God, righteousness, and humility implies that the search involves serious commitment. Jesus said that it should take precedence over all other concerns in our lives (Matt 6:33). We need to search for them in Jesus Christ, who will shelter us from God's anger. But the shelter he offers is not characterized by 'cheap grace' (see Rom 6:1-2). Some who claim to be Christians treat their cultures, customs, traditional medicine man, money and businesses as equal to or even greater than God. This is a form of idolatry. God alone must be the centre of our desires, and we must live in total dependence on him and be committed to obeying his commands.

2:4-15 God's judgment on the nations

Zephaniah delivers God's message of judgment to foreign nations located at the four points of the compass. They are Philistia to the west (2:4-7), Moab and Ammon to the east (2:8-11), Cush (Ethiopia) to the south (2:12), and Assyria to the north (2:13-15). These four nations had long been enemies of Judah and Israel, but they are also symbolic of all nations that oppose God and his rule.

Zephaniah first proclaims the doom of the great city-states of Philistia. He warns four of them, Gaza, Ashkelon, Ashdod and Ekron, of their impending destruction (**2:4**). He does not mention the fifth Philistine city, Gath, because it has probably already been destroyed (2 Chr 26:6). The Philistines had been enemies of Israel since the days of Joshua. They inhabited the Mediterranean coast (south-west of Judah) and were also known as Kerethites (**2:5-6a**; see also 1 Sam 30:14; 2 Sam 8:18; Ezek 25:16). God's judgment will mean that the place where the Philistine cities had stood will become grazing land (**2:6b**). With their enemies destroyed, the remnant of the people of Judah will pasture their animals there and enjoy rest, provision and God's protection (**2:7**).

Moab and Ammon, Judah's eastern neighbours, had been in conflict with Judah since the time of Moses (Num 22-24). They shared a common ancestor with the people of Judah since they were descendants of Abraham's nephew, Lot (Gen 19:30-38), but they hated, ridiculed and attacked them (**2:8**; Deut 23:3-6; Judg 3:12-30; 1 Sam 11; 2 Sam 8:2; 10:1-19; 2 Kgs 3:5-27; 13:20-21). God will keep his promise to Abraham, 'whoever curses you I will curse' (Gen 12:3). He will also punish their pride (**2:10**; see also Isa 16:6; Jer 48:29-30).

Moab and Ammon will be destroyed like Sodom and Gomorrah (**2:9b**), which were made a wasteland because of their deeds (see Gen 19:24-26; Deut 29:23; Isa 1:9-10; 13:19; Jer 23:14; 49:18; 50:40; Amos 4:11). Their destruction will be so complete that no useful vegetation will grow there. They will be sterile and barren, *a place of weeds and salt pits* (2:9c). The certainty of this punishment is guaranteed by God's solemn oath, an oath that he swears by himself to underscore its reliability (**2:9a**; Isa 15-16; Jer 48:1-49:6; Ezek 25:1-11; Amos 1:13-15; 2:1-3).

The righteous remnant will inherit the land of the Moabites and Ammonites (**2:9c**; see also 2:7). When the Lord rises to help his people, he will be awesome and terrifying to their enemies (**2:11a**). The gods of the nations will be reduced to nothing (**2:11b**). God alone has the real power, and he is to be worshipped. The prophet looks forward to the time when paganism, false religions and idolatry will be replaced by universal worship of the one true God (**2:11c**; see also Mal 1:11; John 4:23).

Zephaniah next predicts God's judgment on Cush in the south (**2:12**). Cush means 'Ethiopia' or 'black', but it denotes more than just the present Ethiopia. It refers to Egypt as well, since the Cushites ruled Egypt for many years. The area of Cush includes Nubia, the upper Nile region, and parts of Arabia bordering the Red Sea. God will bring them to an end just as he will Moab and Ammon. The sword will be the instrument of God's judgment (see also Isa 34:5-6). This judgment may possibly be identified with the Babylonian defeat of Egypt in 605 BC (see Ezek 30:24-25). But the much greater slaughter of unbelievers on the African continent awaits the final day of judgment (see Isa 18; Ezek 30).

Finally, the prophet turns northward to Assyria and declares God's judgment on it. Assyria had been the dominant power for three centuries and Judah's most implacable foe. By Zephaniah's time, Assyrian power was declining, but it was still the strongest military power of the day. Yet God *will stretch out his hand* against Assyria and destroy it. Its capital city, Nineveh, with its famous irrigation system and

impregnable walls will be left *utterly desolate and dry as the desert* (**2:13**). Only animals and birds will inhabit the rubble and debris that was once a great city (**2:14**; see also Isa 34:9-15; Ps 102:6).

Nineveh will fall because of its pride. It boasted *I am, and there is none besides me* (**2:15a**; see also Isa 36:4-10, 13-20; 47:8). Only Yahweh can make this claim (see Isa 43:10-11; 44:6; 45:5-6, 18, 21-22; 46:9). God will respond to the city's arrogance by leaving it a ruin, a den for wild beasts, and an object of contempt for every passer-by (**2:15b**; see also Jer 19:8).

Nahum, too, predicted the destruction of Nineveh, which took place in 612 BC, about ten years after Zephaniah had predicted it. The city was captured by the Babylonians.

These messages of judgment tell us that God cares for his people and will fight on their behalf, destroying their enemies so they are free to serve and worship him alone. This knowledge should be a source of hope and comfort to the African church. It may be enduring persecution and insults in places like the *sharia* states of Nigeria, but God sees it all and at the right time he will act on its behalf.

The destruction of the other states is also a warning not to imagine that we are self-sufficient and do not need God (Rev 3:17). We must reject our tribal gods, which have no real existence apart from the devotion of those who serve them (see 1 Cor 8:4-6), and must acknowledge and worship the only true God, revealed to us by our Lord Jesus Christ.

3:1-8 God's judgment of Judah

Having dealt with the surrounding nations, the prophet turns to Judah and its capital, Jerusalem. He cries out that grief is coming to the city because she has become a *city of oppressors* who disregard the rights of the poor, orphans, and widows (**3:1a**). It is rebellious, polluted by bloodshed, and defiled, and she refuses to submit to God's will (**3:1b**; see also Isa 59:3; Jer 4:17; Lam 4:14; Mal 1:7, 12).

Zephaniah lists some specific charges against the people: First, they have not obeyed God's voice through his prophets (**3:2a**; Isa 30:8-12). Second, they do not receive correction or learn when God disciplines them (**3:2b**; see also Jer 5:3). Third, they do not trust in their promise-keeping Lord (**3:2c**). Fourth, they do not draw near to him (**3:2d**); instead they put their confidence in pagan gods and alliances with foreign nations.

Judah's political, social and religious leaders are specifically rebuked. The *officials* or 'princes', the royal leaders, should serve their people, but instead they act like tyrants, or *roaring lions,* that devour the people by taking whatever they have that is precious (**3:3a**; see also Ezek 22:25). In their greed for personal gain, the *rulers* or 'judges' pervert justice. They are like *evening wolves* that roam about under cover of darkness, devouring their victims and leaving nothing for the morning (**3:3b**; see also Ezek 22:27). The *prophets* are described as *arrogant* and charged with treachery (**3:4a**). They may claim to be prophets of God, but they are impostors who do not represent him. There is no truth in anything they say, for they tell the people what they want to hear (see also Jer 23:28, 32; Ezek 22:28). Finally, the *priests* do not distinguish between what is holy and what is not, or between the clean and the unclean (see also Ezek 22:26). By leading the people in profane worship that dishonours God, they pollute the temple (**3:4b**; see also Ezek 8:5-18; Mal 1:6-14). They do *violence to the law* by distorting it so that it serves their own interests (**3:4c**; see also Ezek 22:26). Instead of teaching obedience to God's word, they ignore it or twist it to say what they want it to say.

Even today, there are ministers of the gospel who do things that discredit the gospel message and do not apply God's Word to themselves and to the people they serve. They too will face God's judgment for failing to reflect his character and represent him to the world. For unlike the wicked leaders, God is holy, just and faithful (**3:5a**; see also Lev 19:2). He is not involved in any wrongdoing (**3:5b**). The 'wolves' leave nothing in the morning (3:3), but every morning God demonstrates his unfailing justice (**3:5c**). God's moral standards are visible for everyone to see and measure themselves by. Yet the wicked are so hardened that they feel no shame of guilt for what they do (**3:5d**).

The people of Judah should learn from what has happened to other nations that were corrupt and that neglected the living God and his word (**3:6**). They have already seen the effects of God's judgment in the Northern Kingdom (Israel) that had gone into captivity in 722 BC. But the people do not fear God and refuse to turn to him (**3:7a**). They reject God's mercy, which would suspend the coming disaster (**3:7b**). In fact, they are *still eager to act corruptly* and disobey God (**3:7c**). Since the people will not accept correction, God has no choice but to punish them (see also Deut 28:15-26).

God will gather all the nations of the earth to attend the terrible day of the Lord (**3:8a**), when human depravity will be met with God's fierce and holy anger. God will be the prosecutor, witness and judge of all the peoples of the world (**3:8b**; see also Jer 29:23; Joel 3:2; Mic 1:2; Zech 12:3; 14:3). He will execute the sentence by consuming the whole world with fire (**3:8c**; 1:2-3; see also Deut 4:24; Ps 97:3; Isa 33:14; Heb 12:29). Justice will prevail and evildoers will be punished (see also 2 Thess 1:5-10).

We are wise if we take this warning of coming punishment of sinners seriously. God will judge everyone according to what he or she has done (see Rev 20:12). When we refuse to repent, his only option is to punish us 'with everlasting destruction' and to have us 'shut out from the presence of the Lord' (2 Thess 1:9).

3:9-20 God's Promise of Salvation to Jews and Gentiles

3:9-10 The nations will turn to God

Terrible as the judgment of the world will be, it will also usher in the era of full restoration. Starting from 3:9, the prophet enumerates some promises and blessings in this period when all Jews and Gentiles will be believers. One of these is that God will purify their lips so that the words they speak are pure in that they come from a pure heart of love for God (see also Isa 6:5-7). The unified world will *call on the name of the Lord* (**3:9a**) and worship and serve him *shoulder to shoulder* or 'with one accord' (**3:9b**; see also Jer 32:39).

The previously scattered believers will gather from as far away as the rivers beyond Cush (or Ethiopia), which was then considered the end of the earth (**3:10a**; see also Isa 2:1-4). They will come to worship God together and to present offerings in gratitude for their salvation (**3:10b**; see also Ps 72:10).

Believers should look forward to this era of unity when the church will become truly one. There will be no denominations. We will all serve the one Lord and call upon him in unison (Zech 14:9). Some would even argue that we will all speak the same language as we worship him. However, on the basis of the events at Pentecost (Acts 2:4-12), it can also be argued that we will retain our own languages, but that these will cease to be barriers that separate us. Instead we will all be united in love and service to God.

3:11-13 Salvation and transformation of the remnant

On that day, the day of the Lord, God will remove all wrongdoing and all cause for shame from the remnant. He will also remove all proud and haughty people from the city, as well as all sinful people. No such people will live in God's paradise (**3:11**). Instead Zion, the holy city, will be inhabited by humble people who fear God and are faithful to him (**3:12**; see also Isa 66:2). Thus the meek will inherit the earth (Matt 5:5).

God will also produce a radical transformation in the characters of the new people of God, whom Zephaniah refers to as the righteous *remnant*. They are called the 'remnant' because they are the small group who remain after all others have been swept away. Their old sinful natures will be done away with. They will do no wrong, and deception and unrighteousness will not be found in them (**3:13a**). They will live in perfect peace, tranquillity and security, for *no one will make them afraid* in Zion (**3:13b**; see also Mic 4:4). *They will eat and lie down* in the restoration of the Garden of Eden.

Many can attest that God is already in the business of changing the lives of those who receive Jesus, the Messiah and are willing to let God work in them. But the transformation will never be complete in this world, for we still possess a sinful nature. That sinful nature makes us think that meekness and humility are signs of weakness, and leads us to admire those who are self-reliant and arrogant. But God is opposed to the proud and haughty, and seeks those who fear him and live in humility and dependence on him alone. He also calls on us to avoid lying and deception and to be faithful in all that we say and do.

3:14-17 The joyful response of the remnant

Now God gives Zephaniah a vision of the far distant future, when the remnant will be blessed. Zephaniah's response to this vision is to speak to the faithful remnant of what he had once called the 'shameful nation' and the 'city of oppressors'. Now, however, he calls them the *'Daughter of Zion'*, *'Israel'* and the *'daughter of Jerusalem'* (**3:14**) and repeatedly urges them to rejoice, using four imperatives: *'sing'*, *'shout aloud'*, *'be glad'*, and *'rejoice'* (**3:14**). The era of salvation and restoration has begun and their punishment is over.

Reasons for their rejoicing are spelled out in 3:15-16. First, the judgments against them have been removed (**3:15a**). They no longer have to fear being punished, for their punishment is over. Second, their enemies are *turned back,* that is, they have been defeated and cast out (**3:15b**), suffering the fates described in chapter 2. Third, the Lord God, their true king has come to live with them (**3:15c**). He has been on the throne all along, but his people did not acknowledge this. Now, however, Yahweh will function as his people's protector and shield them from all danger (**3:15d**).

In **3:16a** the positive side of the coming *day* of Yahweh (or the Messiah) is emphasized. When that day comes, his people will have no more reason to fear anyone or anything. They are not to let their *hands hang limp* (**3:16b**) in a gesture of paralyzing fear and numbing despair (see also Neh 6:9; Isa 13:7; Jer 6:24; Heb 12:12). God's enemies will experience those emotions, but his people are assured, *The Lord your God is with you* (**3:17a**; see also 3:15b). What a contrast between the relationship expressed in the words 'your God' and the earlier denunciation of the unrepentant people (1:4-13).

Once again, the Lord is presented as a *mighty* warrior (**3:17b**). But where this warrior had fought against Judah in the past (1:14), now he fights on behalf of his remnant people and establishes a new relationship with them as their deliverer. After his victory, Yahweh claims his people as his bride to show them divine love (**3:17c**; see also Isa 49:18; 61:10; 62:5). He will rejoice over his people as a bridegroom rejoices over his bride. God will overwhelm us with the demonstration of his love. He will quiet us with his love as we fellowship with him. There will be mutual joy as God and his children have fellowship with each other. Amazingly, God himself is presented as finding so much pleasure in

fellowship with us that he will break out into shouts of joy over his people (**3:17d**).

God's deep love for us and his promise of salvation are ours both now and in the future. He is a victorious warrior, who will ultimately annihilate our enemies and give us victory. He will make his power and love available to us, enabling us to respond joyfully to trials and confess our hope in the midst of them. But only those who have received his salvation here will enjoy the unending fellowship with him in the wonderful messianic era.

3:18-20 The vindication and restoration of the remnant

The people who had been scattered in judgment were in sorrow as they yearned for the old religious assemblies at the appointed feasts (**3:18**), but now they will be able to approach and worship the Lord, who will remove their sorrows and reproach from them. Part of the cause of their sorrow has been their oppressors, but God will deal with them (**3:19a**; see also Isa 59:17-21; 66:15-16).

The remnant had been in poor condition, and could be described as *lame* and *scattered* (**3:19b**; see also Mic 4:7). But God will gather them together. Instead of being an insignificant minority, they will be praised and honoured in the various countries where they had been humiliated (**3:19c**).

The promise of restoration is repeated in 3:20. The pronoun *I* is repeated four times in this verse to emphasize that God is committing himself to doing this. On the day of Yahweh, God will bring those who have been scattered *home* (**3:20a**). Not only that, but he will also give them *honour and praise among all the peoples of the earth* (**3:20b**). They will be totally vindicated, and their fortunes fully restored (**3:20c**). The remnant will experience that their God is truly great and able to save.

The promise of ultimate vindication and restoration should give hope and encouragement to God's people. He will work on their behalf and they will be delighted. But the unspeakable joy of being with God in paradise is only for those who accept God's work of salvation now. For those who refuse the Messiah, Jesus Christ, the great 'day of the Lord' will be a day of despair, and not one of glorious hope.

Yoilah Yilpet

Further Reading

Barber, Cyril. *Habakkuk and Zephaniah*. EvBC. Chicago: Moody, 1985.

Robertson, O. P. *The Books of Nahum, Habakkuk and Zephaniah.* NICOT. Grand Rapids: Eerdmans, 1990.

Walker, Larry Lee. 'Zephaniah', in *Daniel and the Minor Prophets*. Edited by Frank E. Gaebelein. EBC. Grand Rapids: Zondervan, 1985.

HAGGAI

Haggai's name, which means 'festival', suggests that he was born on the day of a Jewish feast, possibly before Solomon's temple was destroyed (2:3). If so, he must have been a very old man in 520 BC when he delivered the prophecies recorded in this book. In Ezra 5:1-2 and 6:14, his ministry is mentioned along with that of Zechariah.

BOTH ZECHARIAH AND HAGGAI WERE DEEPLY CONCERNED THAT FOR SOME EIGHTEEN YEARS, NO PROGRESS HAD BEEN MADE ON THE RECONSTRUCTION OF THE TEMPLE (FOR THE BACKGROUND TO THE DELAY, SEE EZRA 3–4). HAGGAI'S MESSAGE IS THAT GOD'S PEOPLE MUST HAVE GOD AT THE CENTRE OF THEIR LIVES AND THAT THE TEMPLE IS A SYMBOL OF THIS COMMITMENT. AS A RESULT OF THIS MESSAGE, THE TEMPLE WAS REBUILT BY 516 BC (1:14-15; SEE ALSO EZRA 6:14-16).

NOTE THAT IN THIS COMMENTARY THE SPECIFIC DATES MENTIONED ARE ADAPTED TO THE MODERN CALENDAR, WHEREAS HAGGAI USED THE JEWISH CALENDAR.

Outline of Contents

COMMENTARY

1:1-15 A Call to Rebuild God's House

1:1-6 Wrong Priorities

Haggai's first message was delivered on 29 August 520 BC, which was the day of the New Moon festival when great numbers of worshippers would gather in Jerusalem (Num 10:10; 28:11; Ps 81:3; Isa 1:13-14; Hos 2:11; Amos 8:5). The message was urgent and authoritative because it came from the Lord through Haggai, who is identified as *the prophet* (**1:1, 3**; 2:1, 10) and *the Lord's messenger* (1:13). It was addressed to Zerubbabel, the governor of Judah, and Joshua, the high priest (Ezra 5:2).

Shortly after the exiles had returned to Israel in 537 BC, they had rebuilt the altar for burnt offerings and laid the foundations for a new temple (Ezra 3:1-3, 8, 10). However, the project had been abandoned for sixteen years. God was so displeased about this that he speaks of *these people* instead of 'my people' (**1:2a**). He did not accept their excuse that *the time has not yet come* (**1:2b**). The time is never just right to do God's work, for it is always opposed.

The people's wrong priorities are exposed by the rhetorical question in **1:4**. They were more concerned with building themselves comfortable houses with wood laid over the stone or clay walls than with building God's house (compare David's attitude in 2 Sam 7:2; 1 Chr 17:1-2; Ps 132:1-5). God does not need a house, but the temple was the place where he had said he would meet with his people (Num 14:10; 16:19; 1 Kgs 8:10-13). By neglecting it, the people showed that they did not care whether the Lord was among them or not.

Haggai repeatedly urged the people to stop and think about how they were living (**1:5**; 1:7; 2:15; 2:18; see also Lam 3:40). Because of their wrong priorities, they were experiencing the calamities God had threatened in Deuteronomy 28:38-45 (see also Amos 4:6-10). Their hard work was producing only a small harvest (**1:6a**; see also Mic 6:15). They never had enough to eat and drink (**1:6b**; compare Hos 4:10). Their clothes did not keep them warm (**1:6c**). They were always short of money – their wages disappeared as though they had holes in their pockets (**1:6d**).

We should carefully examine our own lives to make sure that we are doing God's will. God does not accept our excuses for delaying to do his work and living in spiritual indifference or complacency. We should not give material things or our own interests priority over God and his work. When we do put him first, he will provide for all our physical, spiritual and material needs (Matt 6:33) and will give the harvests that are so desperately needed if Africa is to avoid hunger and starvation.

1:7-11 Admonition to Build God's House

Haggai calls on the people to demonstrate their repentance by resuming work on the neglected temple, an act that will please and glorify God (**1:7-8**). These should always be the chief goals of God's people.

God explains that he has used economic calamities to capture his people's attention. They have experienced agricultural disaster, with even the little harvest they were able to bring home being dispersed (**1:9**). God's judgment is expressed in the form of a pun. The temple lies in ruin (*chareb*) and so he has called for a drought (*choreb*) (**1:10-11**; see also Deut 28:22-24). The people's three major crops (grain, grapes and olives) have all failed and all their work has been for nothing.

Our sins and actions affect the productivity of our lands and our economy (see also Gen 3; Rom 8:20-22). We need to maintain a right relationship with God in order to enjoy his blessings.

1:12-15 Response of Obedience

The people accepted and obeyed the Lord's message (**1:12**). They *feared the Lord*, not in the sense of being terrified of him, but by obediently turning from evil and serving him (Ps 2:11; Prov 8:13; 9:10). Their repentance was shown not by their words but by their actions. The changed attitudes of the leaders and people led them to resume rebuilding the Lord's house on 21 September 520 BC, twenty-three days after Haggai's first message (**1:14-15**). If only God's people today would respond with equal alacrity to his message! We need to pray that his Holy Spirit will stir up our spirits (Zech 4:6) so that we, too, will serve God with a common vision and enthusiasm.

God was pleased and sent a message of comfort and encouragement. He promised his divine presence: *I am with you* (**1:13b**). He has promised to be with believers no matter what problems and opposition we face (Matt 28:20), and with him all things are possible (Matt 19:26).

2:1-9 The Future Glory of the New House

2:1-5 Encouragement

Haggai's second major message was delivered on 17 October 520 BC, on the last day of the Feast of Tabernacles (**2:1-2**; see Lev 23:39-44). This was a harvest festival, but that year the harvest was scanty (1:6, 11).

The people had been working on the temple for almost a month, but were becoming discouraged because the new building was so inferior to Solomon's magnificent temple (see 1 Kgs 6; Ezra 3:8-13). So Haggai asks: *Who of you is left who saw this house in its former glory?* (**2:3a**). The temple had been in ruins for sixty-six years, so only those who were over seventy years old would have even faint memories of its predecessor. These older people thought of the new temple as small and worthless, *like nothing* (**2:3b**) by comparison with the old one.

This negative attitude would discourage the younger people who were doing the building. So Haggai encourages them, exhorting the leaders and all the people to *be strong* (**2:4a**; see also Deut 31:7, 23; Josh 1:6-9, 18; 1 Chr 22:13; 28:10, 20). Three times he reminds them that the Lord says they are not to lose heart and that he is with them (see also 1:13). God will support and protect them and give them the energy they need to complete the work (see also 2 Cor 12:9; Heb 13:21).

This promise of God's presence is linked to the covenant that he made with his people on Mount Sinai (**2:5a**; see Exod 19:5-6; 29:45-46; 33:14). God was committed to their ancestors, and he was committed to them. God's Spirit will also remain with them (**2:5b**; see also Ps 51:11; Isa 63:11; Zech 4:6), so the people have nothing to fear (**2:5c**).

Across Africa, there are numerous abandoned building projects. We should not let this happen in God's work. He will give us the strength and resources we need to complete the work he has given us. He also recognizes that we sometimes become discouraged, and that is why he has given us the Holy Spirit. Without his presence and help, we are bound to fail.

2:6-9 Future Glory

God tells the people that he will act powerfully *in a little while,* a phrase that emphasizes that he is the one who determines when things happen in history. When he acts, he will *shake the heavens and the earth* and *all nations* (**2:6-7a**; see also Exod 19:16-19; Judg 5:4-5; Ps 68:7-8; 114:1-7; Hab 3:6). He is speaking of the end of the world, when Christ will come again (Matt 24:7, 29, 31; 1 Cor 7:31; 2 Pet 3:10; Rev 16:20; 20:11) and all the nations will be judged (Heb 12:26). Knowing this, we ought to be committed to living holy lives and serving God with reverence (Heb 12:28; 2 Pet 3:11). The only things that are of enduring value are God's kingdom and human souls (Dan 2:44; Heb 12:28-29).

God promises that *the desire of all nations will come* (**2:7b**, KJV), meaning either the Messiah, Jesus Christ, or the treasures that the nations will bring to the temple as offerings. The messianic reading seems preferable. Jesus Christ is the only one who can satisfy the longing of all nations for a Saviour.

The new temple is part of God's plan to establish his presence on the earth for the benefit of all nations. He will fill it with his glory, just as he filled the first temple (**2:7c**; 1 Kgs 8:11; 2 Chr 5:14). This glory is the real presence of the Lord, which will be revealed at Christ's second coming (Mal 3:1).

The people do not need to worry that their temple is a poor one, for if God wanted a temple like that of Solomon, he could easily arrange for it to be built because he owns all the wealth of the world (**2:8**; see also Job 41:11; Ps 24:1; 50:12). We should not use our poverty as an excuse not to do God's work. Our churches are poorer than Western churches, but as long as we are willing to do the work God gives us, he will provide the resources.

God promises that the new temple will be even more glorious than the former one because of the presence of the Messiah (**2:9a**; see also 2 Cor 4:6; Heb 1, 2). Moreover, it will be a place of peace (**2:9b**; see also Ps 85:8, 10; Isa 9:6-7). The Messiah is the prince of peace, and Jesus has made peace through his shed blood on the cross (see also Rom 5:1; 2 Cor 5:18-19; Col 1:20).

2:10-19 Blessing on the People

2:10-14 Past Defilement

Both the third and the fourth messages were given on 18 December 520 BC (**2:10**, 20) when the people would have been hoping for the early rains. It was almost three months since they had begun to rebuild the temple.

The Lord has another lesson to teach about being and remaining holy. He does this by asking some questions of the priests, who are the experts on the details of the law (**2:11**; Lev 10:10-11; Deut 33:10; Ezek 44:23; Mal 2:7). The first question concerns someone carrying a piece of *consecrated meat* in the fold of his robe. If that fold comes into contact with some food, will it automatically consecrate the thing it touches? (**2:12**) The answer is *No*, for while the consecrated meat will consecrate the robe that is in direct contact with it, the robe will not transfer that consecration to other things (Lev 6:27). Holiness is communicated only by direct contact (see also Exod 29:37; Ezek 44:19; Matt 23:19). So contact with someone who is in contact with God will not make one holy. Only God can do that.

Haggai's second question is whether someone who has been defiled by touching a corpse can transfer that defilement to other things (**2:13**). The answer is *Yes* (Lev 22:4-6; Num 19:11-22). Uncleanness is contagious. Holiness or cleanness cannot be transferred, but sin is contagious and corrosive.

To use another example, one piece of good fruit will have no effect on a box of rotten fruit. But one piece of rotten fruit can easily spoil a whole box of good fruit. Similarly, a sick person does not become well through contact with a healthy person, but the healthy person can be infected by their disease.

God's point is that the people's disobedience and wrong priorities meant that everything they did, including their sacrifices, was unclean in God's eyes (**2:14**; see also Heb 12:15). They did not deserve to be called God's people, and so God refers to them as *this people*.

We Africans sometimes treat religious activities or 'holy' objects as good luck charms. Thus some keep their Bible under their pillow, thinking that God's word will automatically protect them or make them more spiritual. Some think that they can inherit the benefits of their parents' or grandparents' holy lives. But goodness is not contagious.

Everyone has to live their own holy life in Christ Jesus, and must show true repentance and obedience from the heart (1 Sam 15:22; Ps 66:18; Jer 7:21-23).

2:15-19 Future Blessings

Again, Haggai calls on the people to think carefully and to compare their situation before they responded to Haggai's first message with their situation *from this day on* (**2:15** see also 2:18; 1 Sam 16:13; 30:25). While they neglected the temple, their barns and wine vats were only half full (**2:16**). God sent catastrophes like blight, mildew and hail that caused crop failures (**2:17a**; see also Exod 9:25; Deut 28:15-26; 1 Kgs 8:37). But the people had refused to turn back to God (**2:17b**; see also Jer 3:6-10; Amos 4:9) until they were moved by Haggai's preaching.

Refusing to repent is the worst sin of all, for it eliminates all hope of forgiveness and salvation. But what a difference repentance makes! When we put God first, he provides for all our physical, spiritual and material needs (Matt 6:33). The people would soon see this as God blesses them with an abundant harvest from their vines, fig trees and olive trees (**2:18-19**).

God wants to bless us, but our sin and disobedience get in the way. So sometimes he has to cause us pain to remind us that he must be first in our lives.

2:20-23 The Messianic Kingdom

2:20-22 The Kingdoms of the World Overthrown

Haggai's final message was delivered the same day as the third one (**2:20**; see also 2:10). In it, he describes events that will occur 'on that day' (2:23a), that is, on the day of the Lord when Christ returns.

This message is specifically for Zerubbabel, Judah's governor. God again says that he will cause universal upheaval before he establishes his kingdom (**2:21**; see also 2:6-7). He will *overturn* the thrones of the world's kingdoms, and destroy their power (**2:22a**). The Hebrew word translated 'overturn' is often used to describe the overthrow of Sodom and Gomorrah (Deut 29:23; Isa 13:19; Jer 20:16; Amos 4:11). God is saying that the destruction will be as sudden and final as that of those cities.

The overthrowing of *chariots and their drivers; horses and their riders* (**2:22b**) recalls the destruction of Pharaoh's army (Exod 15:1, 4-5). The terror and confusion will be so great that God's enemies will turn on each other, just as the Midianites did when Gideon attacked (**2:22c**; see also Judg 7:22; 2 Chr 20:23-24). Their behaviour illustrates the self-destructiveness of sin: those who oppose God end up destroying themselves. Only those who have trusted in and obeyed Christ will escape this final judgment and inherit the Messiah's enduring kingdom (Dan 2:44).

2:23 God's Unshakeable Kingdom

In his prophecy to Zerubbabel, Haggai uses highly symbolic language. Zerubbabel is seen as representing the coming Messiah who will rule over God's future kingdom *on that day* and who will also be a descendant of David (see Matt 1:12-13; Luke 3:27). God's words, *I will take you* indicate that he has been specially chosen (see also Exod 6:7; Josh 24:3; 2 Sam 7:8), just as Jesus Christ was chosen for this task before the world began (1 Pet 1:20). The description of Zerubbabel as *my servant* also echoes one of the most frequently used titles for the Messiah (Isa 41:8; 42:1; 49:5-6; 50:10; 52:13; 53:11; Ezek 34:23; 37:24).

Zerubbabel is described as the *son of Shealtiel* (**2:23a**), his legal father, probably because of a levirate marriage (Deut 25:5-10). However, his actual father was Pedaiah, a descendant of King David's son Nathan (1 Chr 3:19). Yet although Zerubbabel was in David's royal line, he was not a king. The exile had ended the Davidic kingship. But God would keep his promises to David (2 Sam 7:8-11).

God promises that his Messiah will be like the ring that was engraved with the seal that was the symbol of the king's authority (**2:23b**; see also 1 Kgs 21:8; Esth 8:8; Dan 6:17). King Jehoiachin (Jeconiah) was rejected as God's signet ring (Jer 22:24), but that honour is restored to Zerubbabel. It is a sign of the authority and honour of the Messiah as God's personal representative, a position that Jesus occupied (Matt 28:18; John 5:22-23).

This prophecy to Zerubbabel is similar to the one made to David. He planned to build the Lord a house (2 Sam 7:1-3), but was instead told that the Lord would build him a house (2 Sam 7:8-11). Zerubbabel is building the Lord's house (1:1-4, 8) when God repeats his commitment to building David's house. The messianic hope of Israel is guaranteed and awaits its fulfilment in Jesus Christ, who will return to exercise God's authority on earth, shattering the power of enemy nations and setting up his unshakeable kingdom (see also Ps 2).

Believers in Christ have every reason to be encouraged. Jesus Christ will ultimately reign as King of kings and Lord of lords over all who trust in him. Our task is to persevere in the work he has called us to do.

Yoilah Yilpet

Further Reading

Alden, R. L. 'Haggai', in *Daniel and the Minor Prophets*. EBC. Edited by Frank E. Gaebelein. Grand Rapids: Zondervan, 1985.

Baldwin, Joyce G. *Haggai, Zechariah, Malachi*. TOT. Downers Grove , Ill.: Inter-Varsity Press, 1981.

Motyer, J. A. 'Haggai', in *The Minor Prophets*. Edited by T. McComiskey. Grand Rapids: Baker Book House, 1998.

ZECHARIAH

The book of Zechariah is the longest and most messianic of the twelve Minor Prophets. It is often quoted in the NT. Like the book of Revelation, on which it had a great influence, it is written in the apocalyptic genre and thus makes much use of symbols, significant numbers and vivid pictures. The prophecies are given in the form of direct prophetic speech, accounts of visions and symbolic acts.

Historical Context, Occasion and Purpose

In 538 BC, the Babylonian Empire was overthrown by Cyrus king of Persia (538-530 BC; see Isa 45:1), who then issued an edict allowing exiles to return to their homelands (see 2 Chr 36:22-23; Ezra 1:1-4). For the Jews, this meant the end of seventy years of Babylonian exile. Many of them returned to Jerusalem under the leadership of Zerubbabel.

The returned exiles found Judah ravaged and Jerusalem in ruins, but they had high hopes of resettling and rebuilding. Soon after their return they laid the foundations of the temple (Ezra 3:8-10). But they met with various obstacles, which weakened their enthusiasm, and the work stalled for about sixteen years (Ezra 4:1-5).

It was in this context that the prophets Haggai and Zechariah confronted the people and encouraged them to complete their task. Zechariah was a prophet of hope and encouragement in difficult times. The temple was finally completed and dedicated in 516 BC, signifying God's return to dwell with his people (1:17; 2:10, 12; 8:8). Zechariah called on the people to return to God and not to follow the ways of their forefathers. He reminded them of God's faithfulness and assured them that the kingdom would come in its fullness after God's enemies had been completely destroyed. The people were challenged to live lives characterized by justice and righteousness.

Date

Zechariah received his visions in stages. In chapters 1 to 8 his messages are dated. His first revelation came in 'the eighth month of the second year of Darius' (1:1), which is equivalent to November 520 BC. He thus began his prophetic ministry three months after Haggai delivered his first message (Hag 1:1). The messages in these chapters encourage the returning exiles to put away sin in their lives and to continue rebuilding the temple.

It is difficult to ascertain exactly when the prophecies contained in chapters 9–14 were delivered, although they obviously date from many years later, after the completion and dedication of the temple (see Ezra 6:15-18). The theme of these later prophecies is the judgment and salvation to be brought by the Messiah.

Zechariah's prophetic ministry may have lasted for a total of fifty years until 470 BC, much longer than Haggai's.

Unity and Themes

Some scholars maintain that Zechariah 9–14 was written by a different author or authors than chapters 1–8. However, ancient Jewish and Christian tradition supports the unity of the book, and all the existing Hebrew manuscripts treat the book as a unified whole.

Outline of Contents

COMMENTARY

1:1 Superscription

The book begins with a traditional prophetic formula, giving first the date and then the prophet's name. The date was eighteen years after Cyrus of Persia had issued his decree (538 BC) allowing the Jews to return to Jerusalem to rebuild the temple. The prophet's name, *Zechariah*, means 'Yahweh remembers' (**1:1**; see 1:7; 7:1, 8). There are thirty-one people with this name in the OT. This Zechariah was *the son of Berechiah* and grandson of *Iddo,* one of the heads of the priestly families that returned from Babylon with Zerubbabel and Jeshua (Neh 12:4,16). Thus, Zechariah was from the tribe of Levi, and like Jeremiah and Ezekiel he was both a priest and a prophet (Jer 1:1; Ezek 1:3). His father Berechiah may have died young, for Zechariah succeeded his grandfather Iddo as head of his priestly family (Neh 12:16). Zechariah was himself young when he began his ministry (2:4).

The word of the Lord is a technical phrase, meaning the subject of the whole prophecy, and it shows the divine origin of the prophet's message. The oracles are spoken and given by God. The verb *came* should not be taken as implying that the prophet was no more than a passive recipient of God's word. The prophet is reporting what he actively heard. The verb shows the vitality of the divine word, which not only 'comes', but is also fulfilled (see Isa 55:8-11).

1:2-6 A Call to Repentance

The book begins with a strong statement about God's divine wrath and his mercy. Zechariah speaks of the reason for the exile and God's future plan to restore his people. He also issues a strong call to repentance. These verses are a solemn reminder that enjoyment of God's blessing depends on one's relationship with him.

1:2-3 The Need to Repent

Zechariah opens with a statement that God was *very angry* with the people's *forefathers* (**1:2**). Wrath is part of God's holy character. Because he is holy and just, he is angered by sin and rebellion (Exod 34:6-7; Deut 7:7-11; John 3:36). His anger at sin is in fact a mark of his love.

The word *therefore* (**1:3a**) calls for reflection on the sins of their forefathers that led to the exile and destruction of the temple. It also calls for reflection on the fact that God is merciful and will put aside his wrath if the rebellious repent. He calls on the present generation of his people to *return* to him. 'Returning' implies a repentance that involves more than merely being sorry about what has happened. It involves a turning around from one's chosen direction to follow God's chosen direction with one's whole heart.

God promises that if the people repent, he will return to them (**1:3b**). There is thus reason for hope in the present and future (see Isa 55:6-7; Joel 2:12-13; Matt 3:2; 4:17; Acts 2:38; 3:19; 20:21).

We, too, need to repent in order to enjoy fellowship with God. We cannot experience the joy of walking with God without confessing and repenting of our sin (1 John 1:6).

1:4 The Lessons of History

Most of those to whom Zechariah speaks had been born in Babylon and were accustomed to a foreign culture. They had never experienced life in pre-exilic Israel, where their forefathers had refused to listen to God's *prophets* and turn from their *evil ways* and *evil practices* (**1:4b**). 'Evil ways' denotes a mindset or tendency to choose the evil option, while 'evil practices' denotes actually doing evil. Zechariah commands his generation to learn from history: *Do not be like your forefathers* (**1:4a**). These forefathers had rejected God's prophets, which is equivalent to rejecting God and invites judgment. Unlike them, the new generation should heed the call to turn to God.

We can reap the benefit of the present only if we learn from the mistakes of the past.

1:5-6 The Unavoidability of God's Word

Two rhetorical questions remind Zechariah's listeners of human limitations and of mortality (**1:5**). Neither the *forefathers* nor the *prophets* lived for ever. They were all dead. *But*, in sharp contrast, God's *words* and *decrees* are immutable and eternal (**1:6a**; Isa 40:6-8; 1 Pet 1:25). Though the prophets are gone, God's word endures to be fulfilled. It stands for ever. God's 'decrees' are the specific requirements of the law, including the penalties for breaking his law, which will always *overtake* wrongdoers (**1:6b**; see Deut 28:15, 45; Jer 23:29). The exile was proof of the eternal effectiveness of God's word.

Zechariah's generation took God's word seriously, for *they repented* (**1:6c**). They learned their lesson from history. Their example should motivate us to repent and obey God, knowing that his promises will certainly come to pass and that no one can frustrate his will.

1:7-6:15 Eight Night Visions

In February 519 BC, some three and a half months after his first prophecy and exactly five months after the rebuilding of the temple had resumed (Hag 1:14-15; 2:10, 18, 20) Zechariah receives a series of eight visions in one night (**1:7-8**). These visions should be interpreted as a whole, because each one contributes to the total picture of the role of God's people in the new era to come. They make it clear that the scope of God's activity is not restricted to the land of Judah alone. It is cosmic, for he is sovereign over the whole world (see Ezek 40–48). These visions disclose God's gracious purposes for the people and give them hope and encouragement to finish rebuilding the temple.

1:7-17 A Man Riding a Red Horse

The man riding a red horse (**1:8a**) is also referred to as *the angel of the Lord* (**1:11a**), a being who is identified in the OT as the second person of the Trinity (see Exod 23:20-21). Those accompanying him and the one to whom Zechariah speaks are merely angels (**1:8b-10**). These angels report to the angel of the Lord, Jesus Christ, that the nations that have oppressed God's people are *at rest and in peace* (**1:11b**). God's righteousness is offended that those who have practised injustice and who have exploited and oppressed God's people are at peace. It is clear that although wicked nations may prosper, their prosperity will not endure. God will bring upon them the punishment they deserve.

God is particularly angry with the nations he has used as a rod to punish his people because they have gone beyond what he intended and have *added to the calamity* that has befallen his people (**1:15**). These nations now have little reason to *feel secure*, for even though God's people had disobeyed and rebelled against him, God declares that he is still *very jealous* for them (**1:14**). God's jealousy is different

from human jealousy, and shows the intensity of his love for his people. He says, *I will return to Jerusalem with mercy* (**1:16a**), and will restore the fortunes of the nation. His covenant with his people will be upheld and their enemies will be judged. The glory of his people's land will be re-established as *my house will be rebuilt* and *my towns will again overflow with prosperity* (**1:16b-17**).

Today we can be equally certain that the church will triumph over every obstacle and defeat all its enemies. At its darkest hour and the enemies' highest moment, God will intervene to judge the enemies and show his mercy to his church.

1:18-21 Four Horns and Four Craftsmen

The vision of *four horns* and *four craftsmen* supplements the first vision, reinforcing God's comforting words of vindication and vengeance on behalf of his people. In the OT, horns symbolize power and authority (see Ps 75:4-5; Dan 8). The four horns seen here represent the kingdoms that scattered Judah, Israel and Jerusalem (**1:18-19**). The fact that there are four of them may indicate that these enemies came from all directions.

But God has a plan to deal with the kingdoms that have oppressed his people. He has appointed craftsmen to overcome them (**1:20-21**). We are reminded that God provides a response to every enemy we face. Though enemies surround God's church, they will not prevail. Instead, God's enemies will be destroyed and replaced by his own kingdom.

2:1-13 A Man with a Measuring Line

The next vision about the future prosperity of Jerusalem amplifies God's word of comfort in 1:14-16. In this third vision, Zechariah sees *a man with a measuring line in his hand*, about to measure the length and breadth of Jerusalem (**2:1-2**; see Ezek 40:2-3). Then another angel comes to inform him that there is no need to do this, for the rebuilt city will be *without walls*, because its population will be so great (**2:3-4**). In the ancient world, cities had walls for defence and the lack of a strong wall was a sign of disgrace, as Zechariah's contemporaries knew from their own experience (Neh 1:3). But in God's future kingdom, the lack of a wall will not be a sign of weakness but a sign of God's blessing on the city. God himself *will be a wall of fire around it* (**2:5**). He promises to be the city's *glory within*, guaranteeing it his protection, guidance and presence.

Zechariah admonishes those of God's people who are still in Babylon to return quickly to rebuild Jerusalem, for Babylon will soon be destroyed (**2:6-7**). God cares for his people and describes them as *the apple of his eye* (**2:8**; see Deut 32:10; Ps 103:13; Matt 25:34-46). In other words, they are like the pupil in one's eye, that one instinctively protects. God will raise his hand to punish all nations that have plundered and oppressed God's people (**2:9**). The

Messiah, as well as their own servants, will be the agents of their destruction.

God promises the people of Jerusalem, *I will live among you* (**2:10**; see John 1:14; Rev 21:3), and says that many nations will come to know him (**2:11**). This will fulfil the promise that God made to Abraham (Gen 12:3) and calls for great rejoicing. Since the coming of Jesus Christ, people from all nations have come to know God through him (see Isa 2:2-4; 60:3). They will become God's inheritance, and participate in the glories of the new earth. Jerusalem will be the centre of God's presence on earth (**2:12**; see Mic 4:1-3). It will be like a magnet for other nations.

This vision closes with a reference to the universal judgment that will take place at the Messiah's second coming. *All mankind* is to *be still before the Lord,* for his judgment is about to begin (**2:13**; see Hab 2:20; Zeph 1:7).

3:1-10 The High Priest's Clothes

The first three visions dealt with God's work on behalf of his people. In this vision and the fifth one, the focus is on God's ministry within the people themselves. The prophet sees *Joshua, the high priest,* who returned to Jerusalem with the remnant and began to rebuild the walls (see Hag 1:1, 12; 2:4). Joshua is *standing before the angel of the Lord,* with *Satan* at his *right side* accusing him (**3:1**). Satan means 'adversary' or 'accuser' (see Job 1:6-10; 2:1-7; Rev 12:10). He is the chief enemy of God and his people, and seeks every opportunity to oppose them. Joshua, the high priest, represents God's people. The people's sins, symbolized by Joshua's *filthy garments* (**3:3**), give Satan the grounds to accuse them.

Satan's accusations are rejected by God. The Lord rebukes him twice and defends his people (**3:2**). Satan is reminded that God has chosen Jerusalem and the people (see Lev 26:42-45; Jer 32:38-40; Rom 11:1-5). Joshua and the people are snatched as a *burning stick* from *the fire.* The 'fire' refers to the Babylonian captivity. God punished his people through the fire of captivity but he delivered a remnant to carry out his future plans. This image of being snatched from the fire also looks back to the redemption from Egypt (Deut 4:20; Jer 11:4) and forward to the deliverance in the coming tribulation (Jer 30:7; Rev 12:13-17). When God's people are accused by Satan, it is God who responds (Isa 50:8-9; Rom 8:33-34). Satan's attempts to devour God's people cannot succeed against God's faithful purposes and power.

Joshua's filthy clothes are exchanged for clean, *rich garments.* The command to *take off his filthy clothes* shows that the power to justify lies in God's hand (**3:4**). These clothes polluted by sin are replaced with the pure garments of God's righteousness and salvation (Isa 61:10; Rev 7:9, 14; 22:14). This vision reminds us that we cannot do anything ourselves to obtain cleansing except confess our sins to

God and receive his mercy and forgiveness (Ezek 36:25-32; 1 John 1:9). Christ has taken away our sins and replaced them with God's righteousness (2 Cor 5:21; Eph 4:24; 1 John 2:1-2). This vision shows that our personal faults are no grounds for distrusting God's mercy. God's mercy is received not by personal righteousness, but by imputed righteousness. The robes of righteousness are acquired by faith.

The *clean turban* that is given to Joshua is a mark of authority and direct access to God (**3:5**; see Exod 28:36-38; Job 29:14). It gives public testimony to the forgiven person's new state of righteousness before God.

During the exile, the priesthood could not function and it had to be reinstated when the people returned to the land. In this vision God himself installs Joshua as the high priest (3:5; see also Hag 1:1, 12, 14; 2:2). Joshua is to be the mediator between God and the people. The angel of the Lord gives a threefold promise to Joshua and the people. If they obey God's commands, then they will be his representatives on earth and will a) rule over his house, that is, over God's people (**3:6-7a**; Num 12:7; Heb 3:2, 6; 1 Pet 2:9; Rev 5:10); b) exercise authority over the temple and its courts to protect it from pollution and idolatry (**3:7b**); and c) have the privilege of serving before God in heaven and working with the angels, with unhindered access to God (**3:7c**; see Heb 4:14-16).

Joshua and his *associates* are *symbolic of things to come,* that is, of the future high priest called *my servant, the Branch* (**3:8**). These are two well-known ot titles for the Messiah (6:12-13; see Isa 4:2; 11:1; 42:1; 49:6; 50:10; 52:13; Jer 23:5; 33:15). Thus Joshua and his associates foreshadow the coming of Jesus, the Messiah, the high priest who will truly cleanse his people (see Heb 4:14-16; 10:8-22).

The *stone* (**3:9a**) is another title for the Messiah (see Ps 118:22-23; Isa 8:13-15; 28:16; Dan 2:35, 44-45; Matt 21:42; Eph 2:19-22; 1 Pet 2:6-8). This stone has *seven eyes.* Seven is the number that represents completeness, and thus these seven eyes represent the eyes of God that watch everything that happens on earth through his seven spirits (**3:9b**; see 4:10; Rev 5:6).

There is an inscription engraved on the stone: *I will remove the sin of this land in a single day* (**3:9c**). This task was first accomplished by Jesus Christ on Calvary in a single day at his first coming (Heb 7:27; 9:12; 10:10; 1 Pet 3:18), but the spiritual cleansing and forgiveness will be finally realized at his second coming (12:10; see Rom 11:26-27).

This vision closes with a statement of the peace, contentment and rest that God's people will enjoy on *that day,* when everyone will be able to sit under his own *vine* and *fig-tree* (**3:10**; see 1 Kgs 4:25; Mic 4:4), since their sins have been forgiven and the Messiah rules supreme in his kingdom.

This chapter shows that peace and prosperity must be preceded by moral cleansing; spiritual cleansing comes before spiritual blessings. God will not pour out his blessings on those who are unclean. If we repent now and accept the Messiah, our sins will be forgiven and we shall have a place in his kingdom.

4:1-14 The Golden Lampstand

In interpreting Zechariah's fifth vision, we need to examine other passages of Scripture. Each passage helps in interpreting the other, but none contradicts the other.

The first object that he sees is a *solid gold lampstand* with a bowl on its top in which *seven lights* are burning. The lamp burns continually because it has an unlimited reservoir of oil (**4:1-2**). Standing on either side of the lampstand are two olive trees (**4:3**). Zechariah is puzzled by the vision, and asks, *What are these, my lord?* (**4:4**).

The Lord's answer to Zechariah's question, *not by might nor by power, but by my Spirit* is the central message of this vision (**4:6b**). Zechariah's contemporaries would have recognized a connection between the lampstand seen here and those that used to be in Solomon's temple, where they symbolized God's presence (2 Chr 4:7). There is also a parallel between this lampstand and the one John sees in Revelation 1:12, which represents the abundance of God's power reflected in the light provided by the Holy Spirit. The *two gold pipes* that pour out *golden oil* thus represent the Spirit's abundant power flowing to God's servants (4:12). This vision shows that God will supply the necessary power and divine resources for his work to be done. It is intended to encourage *Zerubbabel*, the governor of Jerusalem, who had started to rebuild the temple (**4:6a**; Ezra 3:2; Hag 1:1; 2:23). This task may seem like a *mighty mountain*, that cannot be moved with merely human strength or resources, but Zerubbabel can be assured that no mountain is so great that God cannot level it (**4:7a**). With the help of God's Spirit, the task will be accomplished, despite all the difficulties and opposition he has encountered (Ezra 4:4-24). He will hear the great shouts of rejoicing and praise as the last stone, *the capstone* is set in place to hold the building together (**4:7b**). The cries, *God bless it! God bless it!*, are an acknowledgment that God's favour is behind the successful completion of the building (**4:7c**). This prophecy did indeed come true, for the temple was completed in 516 BC during Zerubbabel's lifetime (Ezra 6:14-18). This is evidence that the Lord truly spoke through Zechariah (**4:8-9**).

God's message to Zerubbabel also reminds us that human effort without the Holy Spirit will burn itself out. The Holy Spirit alone provides power for the church. It is futile to attempt to do Christian ministry without the Holy Spirit. Moreover, the image of a lampstand reminds us that we are called to be light-bearers as we witness for God in our world (Matt 5:16; Rev 1:20; 2:5).

In comparison with Solomon's magnificent edifice, the new temple was relatively insignificant (Ezra 3:12; Hag 2:3).

Thus some people were discouraged and had a negative attitude toward Zerubbabel's temple. But God's response to such attitudes is to ask a question: *Who despises the day of small things?* (**4:10**). Though something may look small and pitiful, if God is involved it will become great and successful. We should not despise small beginnings if what we are doing is in accordance with God's will.

Zechariah then asks the angel about the oil flowing from the olive trees through the olive branches to the gold pipes and into the lampstand, supplying fuel for the lights (**4:11-13**). The angel replies that these two olive branches are *the two who are anointed to serve the Lord of all the earth* (**4:14**). At the time of the vision, these two anointed ones were Joshua and Zerubbabel, who served as high priest and governor in the kingly line. Later, under Jesus Christ, these two offices would be combined in the Messiah who is both priest and king (6:13; Ps 110:4; Heb 7).

In Revelation 11:3-4, the two olive trees are also associated with the two witnesses who will come to prophesy to the nations in the end times.

5:1-4 The Flying Scroll

Zechariah next sees an enormous *flying scroll*, which is *thirty feet long and fifteen feet wide* (**5:1-2**) The significance of these dimensions is not given, except that the scroll was large and unrolled so that everyone could read its words. The flying scroll is God's *curse that is going out over the whole land* (**5:3a**; see Ezek 2:9-10). This scroll represents God's law and covenant with his people and makes plain his condemnation of sin. On the scroll are written two example sins, one on each side: theft and swearing falsely. These two sins represent the whole of God's law, for theft is a sin against one's neighbour (see Exod 20:12-17; Deut 5:16-21), and swearing falsely is a sin against God's holiness (see Exod 20:3-11; Deut 5:6-15). The punishment for all such sins is banishment from God's people (**5:3b**).

All who break God's law are objects of this curse. It will enter their houses and will destroy them (**5:4**). The completeness of the destruction indicates the severity of God's judgment on unrepentant sinners.

Each of us is responsible for our own deeds and will be judged for them. We will all receive God's punishment. The only way we can escape God's curse is by repenting and accepting Jesus Christ.

5:5-11 A Woman in a Basket

In the previous vision, unrepentant sinners were removed. In this seventh vision, it is the very principle of evil or sin that corrupts people that is banished.

Zechariah sees a vision of a woman in a basket. The basket and the woman represent the wickedness of the *people* of *the land* (**5:6-8**; see also Prov 9:13-18; Rev 17:3-5). The fact that she is in a *measuring basket* signifies that the measure of evil is full and ready for judgment. The woman is banished to *Babylonia* (or 'Shinar', NASB), which represents the centre of idolatry and wickedness (**5:10-11a**; see Gen 11:1-9; Rev 14:8; 16:19; 17:5). Babylon was also the place of exile. The woman tried to escape, but was overpowered and pushed back into the basket (5:8). This shows that God has total control over sin and evil.

The *two women* with wings are divinely chosen agents who carry away the people's iniquity (**5:9**). They are said to have *the wind in their wings*. The word 'wind' can also be translated 'Spirit'. Thus, these two women are being helped by God's Spirit, which shows that he is the one who removes sin. Wickedness and sin will be removed from God's people, and indeed from the entire earth, when Christ returns.

Babylon symbolizes the place of those who have rejected the worship of the true God. It will be the permanent home of wickedness, and a temple will be built there for the basket and its contents (**5:11b**). But Babylon with all its wickedness will eventually be completely destroyed, for victory belongs to God. He will purge the human heart of sin, to make way for the true worship of God. Meanwhile, let us purify ourselves from all forms of idolatry to serve God alone.

6:1-8 Four Chariots

The eighth and final vision is of chariots and horses that correspond to the horses and riders of the first vision (1:7-17). In the first vision, the horses had gone out to patrol the earth and bring back their report. In this eighth vision, the horses are pulling war chariots that will go out to execute divine judgment.

The *four chariots* and *horses* of different colours (see Rev 6:1-8; 19:11, 14) emerge from between *two mountains of bronze* (**6:1-3**). They are very *powerful*, and will subdue the nations that have troubled God's people. They are identified as *the four spirits* (or winds) *of heaven* (**6:5a**; see Jer 49:36; Rev 7:1), which are God's messengers (see 2:6; Ps 104:4). They are angelic beings, agents of divine justice, employed by God to execute his will and purposes. These angelic beings come from the very *presence* of God, *the Lord of the whole world* (**6:5b**), to go and destroy this world's kingdoms. Judgment will come upon those who oppress God's people.

The horses and their chariots are sent in different directions. Attention is focused on *the black horses* with their chariot that are sent *north* (**6:6, 8a**). The north is singled out because it was the direction from which most of the enemies of God's people came. The angel of the Lord says that this chariot has *given my Spirit rest in the land of the north* (**6:8b**). God's Spirit is satisfied and at rest because the work of the war chariots in the north has been accomplished. God's righteous wrath has finally been expressed. We may assume that the same result has been achieved by the others, patrolling the world to execute judgment. The

nations have been judged. Victory in the north is the last battle against entrenched evil. It achieves the triumph of the Lord.

6:9-15 The Crowning of the High Priest

When the evil kingdoms of this world are destroyed, God will enthrone his Messiah on the throne in his glorious kingdom. The section containing eight night visions closes with a remarkable coronation of Joshua, which is symbolic of the crowning of the king-priest, the Messiah himself. What is described here is not a vision, but an actual historical act.

Zechariah is asked to go to the house of *Josiah son of Zephaniah* and collect *silver and gold* from some returned exiles, who came *from Babylon* (**6:9-10**). With these gifts Zechariah is *to make a crown, and set it on the head of the high priest, Joshua son of Jehozadak* (**6:11**). The Hebrew word here translated 'crown' is actually the plural, 'crowns' (see Rev 19:12). The plural emphasizes the magnificence of the crown and points to the double office of priest and king that the person wearing this crown will occupy. The crowning of Joshua unites the priestly and kingly offices in one person, who will be both priest and king.

Joshua is seen as foreshadowing the messianic Branch, the Davidic king, who will reign in God's new kingdom (**6:12a**; see 3:8; Isa 4:2; Jer 23:3-6; 33:14-26). This Branch will *branch out from his place*, that is, from his humble and obscure origins (Isa 53:2; Mic 5:2), and God will exalt him (compare 2 Sam 23:1; Ps 89:19-20). *He will build … the temple of the Lord* (**6:12b-13a**); the pronoun 'he' is emphatic, and could be translated 'He himself'. This temple is not the same one that Zerubbabel is rebuilding, but is a new temple to be built by the Messiah in the messianic age (see Isa 2:2-4; Mic 4:1-5; Hag 2:7-9).

The Messiah *will be clothed with majesty*, a word that is normally used to describe God's majesty as king (**6:13b**; Ps 96:6). He will have splendour, glory, royal authority and honour. He *will sit and rule on his throne*. The once-despised Messiah will one day be universally acknowledged as the everlasting king. He will rule for ever and ever.

The Branch *will be a priest on his throne* (**6:13c**), making it very clear that the coming Messiah will be both a king and a priest (see Ps 110:4; Heb 5; 7). The *harmony* that will exist between these two offices might have seemed an unlikely combination in Zechariah's day. The Messiah will produce peace because as king he rules in righteousness and as priest he cleanses his people of sin (3:8-9). He brings them into fellowship with God and one another. This is a time that God's people look forward to, but for the present the crown is to be kept in the temple as a reminder of the coming union of the two offices in one person (**6:14**). It will keep the messianic hope alive.

When the royal priest rules, *those who are far off* [Gentiles] *will come and help to build the temple of the Lord* (**6:15a**;

see 2:1; 18:22; Isa 2:2-4; 56:6-7; Mic 4:1-4; Acts 2:39; Eph 2:13). This prophecy finds partial fulfilment in the NT with Jesus establishing his church as a living community of all peoples.

To partake in the Messiah's coming kingdom, we must be committed to obeying the Lord our God (**6:15b**). Unless we are committed to obedience, we cannot share in this blessing (Deut 28:1). If we obey, then we shall surely be included in God's kingdom.

7:1-8:23 Fasting and Morality

This section expands on the previous one, addressing the problem of fasting and morality. The people are told that their fasting and feasting have become mere rituals devoid of any spiritual content. They are just following in the footsteps of their forefathers, who rejected the messages of the earlier prophets. Zechariah seeks to bring about spiritual renewal and moral reformation among God's people. But the section ends by giving hope to God's people with the promise that the Lord of Hosts will again dwell in Jerusalem, which will become the centre of worship for all nations.

7:1-3 A Question about Fasting

About two years after receiving his first oracle, Zechariah received a message *in the fourth year of King Darius … on the fourth day of the ninth month, the month of Kislev* (**7:1**). This corresponds to December 518 BC. A delegation from *Bethel,* in what used to be the northern kingdom of Israel, came to Jerusalem *to entreat the Lord* (**7:2**). They asked the priests and prophets whether they should continue to *mourn and fast in the fifth month* since the temple was almost finished (**7:3**). God had commanded only one fast: on the Day of Atonement (Lev 16:29-31; 23:27-32). But after the destruction of Jerusalem and the temple, the people had instituted fasts to commemorate these events. The delegation's question suggests that the fast had become wearisome to them, with no spiritual meaning. For the past seventy years they have been observing this fast in August, but did they really need to continue to do this given that the new temple was almost completed?

7:4-7 Fasting Without Obedience

The prophet responded by issuing a rebuke to *all the people of the land and the priests* (**7:4**). They were fasting because of the destruction of the temple in the fifth month (2 Kgs 25:8-9) and the murder of Gedaliah in the seventh month (**7:5a**; 2 Kgs 25:25; Jer 41:1-3). But these fasts were simply commemorating past disasters and had nothing to do with any desire to be obedient to God and his word. God asks, *Was it really for me that you fasted?* (**7:5b**). The answer is 'No', just as they were not celebrating God's goodness at their feasts (**7:6**).

The earlier prophets had condemned the futility of ritual fasts and worship that did not spring from any genuine desire for inward change (**7:7**; Isa 58:1-7). At that time, their land had still been *prosperous,* but the people had ignored the prophets and so had been taken into exile.

7:8-14 True Obedience

If we want to please God rather than ourselves we must choose to do things God's way, identifying with his purposes, desires and concerns (1 Sam 15:22-23; Mic 6:6-8). God's concern is not with abstaining from food but with abstaining from evil. He lists the actions he considers important: *Administer true justice, show mercy and compassion to one another. Do not oppress the widow or the fatherless, the alien or the poor. In your hearts do not think evil of each other* (**7:9-10**; see 8:16; Exod 22:21-22; Deut 22:1; Isa 1:17, 23; Jer 22:3; Hos 12:6; Mic 6:8; Jas 1:27). Widows, orphans, foreigners and the poor are the most common victims of oppression and the most disadvantaged people in any society. God cares for such people and wants his people to do the same, rather than focusing their attention on the question of whether a memorial fast should or should not be observed.

The people's ancestors had *refused to pay attention* to the prophets and had *made their hearts as hard as flint* (**7:11-12**; see Deut 9:13; Neh 9:29; Jer 17:23; Ezek 3:7-9; Acts 28:27). Their disobedience and rebellion aroused God's anger. Since they refused to pay attention to him, he refused to listen to their prayers (**7:13**; see Isa 1:15; Jer 14:12; Mic 3:4), and *scattered them with a whirlwind among all the nations* (see Ps 44:11; Deut 4:27), and made their *pleasant land desolate* (**7:14**; see Deut 28:41-42; Jer 44:6).

God's requirements are the same today as they were then. He does not want us to focus on performing religious acts rather than on doing what is right. Others should be able to experience God's love through our demonstrations of mercy and compassion. If we do not listen to God and do not show compassion, he may bring a similar judgment on us today. That is why it is important that we learn from the mistakes made in the past and pay attention to God's word.

8:1-13 The New Jerusalem

Even though Jerusalem had been destroyed and left desolate, God is concerned to restore its fortunes. His desire to bring about its spiritual and physical restoration is no less intense than his judgment on the city (**8:1-2**). He assures Zechariah that one day he will come and dwell personally in the new Jerusalem (**8:3a**; see 1:16; 2:10; Isa 52:8; Rev 21:1-3). The dwelling of God with his people is the supreme blessing that will come with the messianic reign of Christ in his kingdom on earth. Because of God's presence in Jerusalem, society will be righteous. The city and its inhabitants will be characterized by truth, faithfulness, righteousness and holiness (14:20-21), and the absence of fear, abuse, insecurity and unrest. The city will be called *City of Truth* and the *Holy Mountain* (**8:3b**; see also Isa 1:26; Jer 33:16).

In the new Jerusalem *men and women of ripe old age* and *boys and girls*, the two groups who are most vulnerable in wartime, will live in complete peace, prosperity and security (**8:4-5**; see also Isa 65:20). No one will be harassed, victimized or despised in this new society. This may seem impossible to the people in Zechariah's day because of their recent experiences, but nothing is too difficult for God (**8:6**; see Gen 18:14; Jer 32:17; Matt 19:26). It may seem impossible to us because of our experiences, but with God it is quite possible.

God promises to gather his people from all over the world. They will come to Jerusalem and be filled with his presence, which will restore them physically and spiritually. This promise of forgiveness and restoration is for all God's people wherever they are (see Isa 11:11-12; 43:5-7; Jer 31:7-8). He says, *they will be my people, and I will be faithful and righteous to them as their God* (**8:8**; see Gen 17:7-8; Exod 6:6-7; Deut 7:6; Jer 31:33). God is seen here as loving, saving, forgiving, and restoring those who trust in him to the end (see Hos 2:19-20).

The people had heard God's encouraging words spoken through the *prophets* when *the foundation was laid* for the new temple (**8:9a**; see Ezra 5:1-2). Now they are encouraged to finish the work they had begun a few years earlier: *Let your hands be strong* (**8:9b**; see Hag 2:4). Let us commit ourselves to the Lord, and he will make us strong through the Holy Spirit to do his work to the end.

The people's present conditions are compared with their previous ones. *Before that time*, that is, before 520 BC when they had not yet obeyed God's word to rebuild the temple (**8:10**; see Hag 1:6-11; 2:15-19), there was no stability, security or prosperity for either humans or animals. *But now* there has been a change (**8:11**). It points to a better economic future with peace and safety for the people. This is shown in the remarkable fertility and productivity of the land and the favourable weather conditions (**8:12a**).

This change will be the result of the people's repentance and obedience (see Lev 26:3-10; Deut 28:11-12). God will give all this prosperity as an *inheritance to the remnant* (**8:12b**). This 'remnant' are those who have genuinely turned to God and whose hearts are with him. They are a redeemed people.

The prosperity will be experienced in God's presence in the future when God's people will no more be *an object of cursing among the nations* (**8:13a**; see Deut 28:15-19). The reference to both *Judah and Israel* shows that all of God's people will be saved and reunited in the end, and they will be *a blessing* to others (**8:13b**). In light of this future promise, the people are commanded not to be *afraid*, but to be

encouraged and remain steadfast in their obedience to God (**8:13c**).

8:14-17 The Past and the Future

Just as God was firm in his determination *to bring disaster upon* his people because of their disobedience (**8:14**), so now he is equally *determined to do good* to them (**8:15a**). God keeps his word, and he will certainly fulfil his purpose and promises (see Num 23:19). As his people, we have no reason to fear that he might fail us (**8:15b**). God wants us to obey his word, so that we can be blessed and renewed spiritually. Since we are going to be citizens of the new Jerusalem, we should conduct ourselves honestly and righteously now.

Zechariah gives two positive injunctions: *speak the truth to each other, and render true and sound judgment in your courts* (**8:16**; see 7:9; Amos 5:15; Eph 4:25), and two negative injunctions: *do not plot evil against your neighbour, and do not love to swear falsely* (**8:17**; see 5:3-4; 7:10; Prov 3:29). As God's children, our attitudes and actions should reflect God's character. Since he is truth, lying is unacceptable and we are to be honest in our dealings with one another. We are to hate the corruption and injustice in our courts that destroy society. We are to keep our hearts pure (see Gal 5:19-21).

8:18-23 Universal Longing for God

With God dwelling among them, the remnant need no longer practise fasting. The fasts will be replaced by joyous festivals (**8:19a**). These fasts commemorated past misfortunes: the breaching of the city wall in the *fourth* month (2 Kgs 25:3-4), the temple's destruction in the *fifth* month (2 Kgs 25:8-9), the murder of Gedaliah in the *seventh* month (2 Kgs 25:25) and the siege of Jerusalem in the *tenth* month (2 Kgs 25:1-2). Because of God's blessings, his people will no longer need to commemorate past misfortunes. Rather, they will rejoice in the benefits of his grace. The people are urged to love *truth and peace* (**8:19b**) so that their present behaviour will reflect their future realities

The prediction that *many nations* will *seek the Lord Almighty* concludes the first part (chs 1–8) of the prophecy of Zechariah (**8:20-22**; see 2:11; Isa 2:1-5; Mic 4:1-5). There will come a time when the longing for God will be universal, and Jerusalem will be the centre and rallying point. Non-Christians will finally realize the truth of God's word and that God's people have a special relationship with him. A number of people will hold the *hem* of the *robe* of *one Jew* to accompany him to Jerusalem because they know that God is with the Jews (**8:23**; see Isa 45:14). God will vindicate his holiness.

The Christian's godly life can attract non-Christians to seek a new way of life and to be included in God's great blessings. As God blesses his people, they in turn reach out to bless others. The Lord is in the new Jerusalem and all peoples gather there to seek him.

9:1-14:21 The Universal Rule of the Messiah

In Zechariah 1–8 the king is described as priest, and in Zechariah 9–14 he is described as shepherd. The second part of the book contains two main oracles, or messages from God. The first coming of the Messiah is described in chapters 9 to 11, and his second coming in chapters 12 to 14. He will come to establish God's kingdom. He will conquer all his enemies and reign over all creation for ever. But before he does this, he will come to die and to rescue us from sin.

9:1-11:17 The Messiah's First Coming and Rejection

Although this section of the book of Zechariah deals primarily with the first coming of the Messiah, some of the events described here have yet to be fulfilled. Events have occurred that are similar to some of these prophecies, but the prophecies have not yet been completely fulfilled on a worldwide scale.

9:1-8 Victory over the nations

The prophet opens with God's people surrounded by their enemies, the unbelieving nations. God will defend his people and destroy the attacking nations: Aram, Phoenicia and Philistia. The key cities in these nations are mentioned as representatives of our world's pagan and idolatrous nations. They are opposed to God and his people. Judgment will begin in the north in the *land of Hadrach,* with *Damascus,* the capital of Aram (modern Syria) and *Hamath* (**9:1-2a**). It will then proceed southward to *Tyre* and *Sidon,* the great Phoenician cities on the Mediterranean coast (**9:2b**; compare Ezek 28:1-24). Although they were maritime powers with great wealth, they will not escape God's judgment. They will be completely destroyed (**9:3-4**).

The Lord marches further south against the four key Philistine cities: *Ashkelon, Gaza, Ekron,* and *Ashdod* (**9:5-6**; see Amos 1:6-8). They were the traditional enemies of God's people. These cities are afraid after the fall of Tyre and Sidon, for they too will be destroyed. Gaza's king will be killed, and Ashdod will be inhabited by foreigners (**9:5-6**). The 'I' in the middle of **9:6** still refers to the Lord who explains what he will do to the stubborn, proud Philistines. They were involved in various idolatrous practices and unclean customs that God had forbidden (**9:7a**; see Lev 3:17; Isa 65:4; 66:3, 17). Those who survived would be adopted as part of God's people, like the Jebusites, who were not wiped out when David conquered Jerusalem (**9:7b**; see 2 Sam 24:16; 1 Chr 21:18-19). Some of the remaining Philistines will even become leaders of God's people. This

shows their total acceptance by God, and is an example of the conversion of unbelievers in the OT.

While these other cities will be destroyed and lie in ruins, God promises to defend his people and Jerusalem (**9:8**). His *never again* anticipates the fulfilment of this promise during the Messiah's second coming. In this future day, God's people will never again have to worry about invading enemies, for God will have his watchful eyes on the city and his people to protect them (9:8; see also 4:10; 12:4; Isa 26:1; 54:14; Joel 3:17). The Lord will certainly have victory over the enemy nations, and God's people will be preserved and delivered to worship the universal King who is coming (see 14:16-19).

9:9-10 The king on a donkey

The prophecy of the arrival of the king was made against the background of Jacob's blessing of the tribe of Judah, in which he spoke of a coming ruler from that tribe who would wield a sceptre, but who would also 'tether his donkey to a vine' (Gen 49:10-11). This person would be the Messiah.

God's people are to *rejoice greatly* at the arrival of this long-awaited king (**9:9a**; see 2:10; Zeph 3:14-15). *Daughter of Zion* and *Daughter of Jerusalem* are expressions that refer to God's people as a whole, who are all to rejoice because *your king comes to you* (**9:9b**; see Ps 24:7). Unlike the wicked kings of the past, this king is *righteous* (see 2 Sam 23:3-4; Ps 72:1-3; Isa 9:7). He brings *salvation* because he comes to deliver his people (see Zeph 3:17). He is also *gentle,* without the pomp and arrogance usually associated with kings (see Isa 53:2-7; Matt 11:29).

The Messiah King will come to his people *riding on a donkey, on a colt, the foal of a donkey* (**9:9c**). In the ancient Middle East, the donkey was the preferred means of transport (see Judg 5:10; 10:4; 12:14). The Messiah does not come riding a horse, which is associated with warfare (see Deut 17:16; 20:1; Ezek 26:10). He does not come as a conqueror but as God's humble and peaceful servant.

This prophecy was fulfilled in Christ's first coming when he entered Jerusalem 'riding on a donkey' (9:9c; see Matt 21:15; Mark 11:1-10; Luke 19:28-38; John 12:12-15). At his first coming, he showed all the characteristics of the ideal king described by Zechariah. He died to give salvation from sin and to give righteousness to all who will trust in him.

Given that the details of Christ's arrival in Jerusalem were accurately predicted more than five hundred years before it occurred, we can trust God to keep his word regarding Christ's second coming. At that time he will come as a divine warrior, to reign in righteousness and deliver his people from their enemies (see Jer 23:5-6). He will destroy all the weapons of war, both the ancient ones like *chariots, war-horses* and the *battle-bow* and modern ones (see Isa 2:4; Hos 2:18; Mic 4:3). *He will proclaim peace to the nations,* not just to the land of Israel (**9:10**; see Isa 9:5-7). The extent of his reign will be universal, *from sea to sea and from the River* [the Euphrates] *to the ends of the earth* (Ps 72:8-11). This world will have lasting peace only when the Messiah, the Prince of Peace, comes to establish his universal, peaceful kingdom. Then there will be no more wars or conflicts.

9:11-10:1 Deliverance and blessing

But before the Lord gives peace to his people in the last days, he will have to conquer all their enemies (see Ps 110:5-7). Only then can his reign of peace be realized.

9:11-13 AN INVITATION TO RETURN God issues an invitation to his people to return to him both spiritually and physically. They had been exiled to Babylon because of their sins, but can now return to the *fortress* of Zion (**9:12a**). We have already come to Zion in Christ (Heb 12:22; see Rev 21:2), who is the only source of real peace and security. The basis of this deliverance is the *blood of* the *covenant* (**9:11a**). In the OT, the covenant was confirmed by blood sacrifices (Gen 15:9-11; Exod 24:3-8; 29:38-46), but these sacrifices all point to Christ's blood shed on the cross that sealed the new covenant for the saved (Mark 14:24; Heb 13:20). Through his blood, the *prisoners of hope,* who have trusted in the Lord and his promises, are united with him (**9:12a**).

When the Messiah returns, those who are prisoners will all be saved physically and spiritually from *the waterless pit:* the prisons of this world (**9:11b**; see Jer 38:6-13). God promises to restore his people completely and to shower full blessings on those he has redeemed (**9:12b**). God will use them to defeat his enemies (**9:13**). The reference to *Greece* as one of these enemies may be a prophecy of the eventual defeat of Antiochus Epiphanes by the Maccabeans some two hundred years later. The oppressed will eventually be victorious.

9:14-10:1 YAHWEH'S DELIVERANCE AND BLESSING The Lord is now described as coming like a warrior to deliver his people (**9:14-15a**; 2 Sam 22:8-18; Ps 18:7-15). He will defend and protect them while they fight their enemies. With the Lord on their side, God's people will certainly be victorious.

Then comes the time to celebrate the victory. The people will celebrate God's victory at a great feast, at which there will be abundant food and drink (**9:15b**). The redeemed people will rejoice without restraint in God's mighty salvation.

On this future day, they will be his flock and he will be their shepherd (**9:16a**; see Ps 100:3). No wonder they will experience complete safety. They can also be described as *jewels in a crown* (**9:16b**). God will care for them as precious treasures (see Exod 19:5-6; Isa 61:6). They will shine with joy and glory as they live with God. There will be no more poverty and humiliation, but only an abundance of grain and wine (**9:17**). These crops will be guaranteed because God will be in control and everything will work as it should. Even the rain will come at the right time (**10:1**). There is indeed a blessed future hope for God's people. If we seek

and trust him, then he will save and prosper us. We should turn to him, and not to fertility gods when seeking productivity for the soil and praying for rain during the farming seasons.

10:2-3 Punishment of the evil shepherds

Zechariah has used the metaphor of the good shepherd to refer to God as the leader of his people (9:16). But the people's leaders have been bad shepherds. God will judge selfish, corrupt, and unreliable leaders, and he will care for his people and completely restore them.

The evil shepherds fail to obey God's word, and they put their trust in *idols* and lying *diviners.* But idols cannot send rain (see Jer 14:22), and the diviners *see visions that lie* (**10:2a**). Their visions deceive the people, and the *dreams* they report are the products of their own imagination rather than messages from God (10:2a; see Jer 23:30-32; 27:9-10; 29:21-23). The diviners also give empty *comfort* when they make false promises of good things to come and of peace (see Jer 6:14; 8:11; 14:22; 23:25-26; Ezek 13:6-12).

The use of diviners to find out what course of action one should take is prohibited in God's word (Deut 18:9-14; Josh 13:22; 1 Sam 15:23). God has provided true prophets to inform and guide his people according to his will. They have no need to consult diviners (see John 6:14).

In some of our traditional African religions, divination is used to discover the future. The church must preach strongly against this. We should teach church members to trust only God and his promises in the Bible for their future. We must also teach them that the modern idols of money, power, fame, pleasure or achievement will never satisfy us or give us peace and security.

The results of bad leadership cause God's people to wander around *like sheep oppressed for lack of a shepherd* (**10:2b**; see Mark 6:34). The leaders have led God's people astray, because of their lack of proper spiritual direction. Thus God declares, *I will punish the leaders.* The Lord takes care of his flock, and will turn them into his *proud horse in battle* (**10:3**). God will provide for all the physical and spiritual needs of his people, and all the bad leaders in the church and in the nations will not go unpunished.

10:4-12 Victory of God's people

10:4-5 THE VICTORIOUS PEOPLE WITH THEIR MESSIAH The prophet announces the coming of a new, good leader for God's people. This leadership will come 'from him', from the Lord who cares for his flock, and not *from Judah* as the NIV translates it. As a leader, this Messiah will be the 'cornerstone', the 'tent peg' and the 'battle-bow'.

The *cornerstone* (**10:4a**) is the most important stone in any building, the one that holds it together either at the foundation or at the top of an arch. It is thus also a symbol of stability and dependability in a leader. The description of the Messiah as the cornerstone shows that he is the foundation and head of God's kingdom. Jesus describes himself as the stone that was initially rejected but eventually became the cornerstone or capstone (Matt 21:42; see also Ps 118:22; Isa 28:16).

A *tent peg* (**10:4b**) holds the whole tent up and can also be used to keep the door flaps open or closed. It symbolizes the authority of the Messiah, on whose shoulders God has put the affairs of the kingdom (see Isa 22:22-24; Rev 3:7).

The *battle-bow* (**10:4c**) is the weapon of a warrior and protector (see Ps 45:5). When the Messiah comes the second time, he will destroy all his enemies (Ps 2:9; Isa 63:1-6; Rev 6:2; 19:11-21). All peoples will be subjected and obedient to him.

All these metaphors show that the coming Messiah will be strong, stable, compassionate, victorious and trustworthy. *From him* will come every faithful and compassionate ruler in the future (**10:4d**). They will face and overcome their foes *because the Lord is with them* (**10:5**).

10:6-12 A NEW EXODUS The Messiah's victory will result in a new exodus as he brings his people home. He promises to *have compassion* on *the house of Judah* and *the house of Joseph*, who represent all of God's people in that future day of the Lord (**10:6**). This compassion will lead him to *restore them* so that they will feel as though he had never *rejected them* (10:6). God's people will be strengthened. They will become *like mighty men* and will be filled with joy (**10:7**). When we are in close fellowship with the Lord, he promises to strengthen us to do his will, and to fill us with joy through his Spirit.

Only God can gather all his people and unite them as one. He *will signal for them and gather them in* and they will be strong and *numerous,* in fact, *there will not be room enough for them* (**10:8, 10**; see Isa 35:10; 49:19-21). Even though God's people have been scattered widely due to exile and persecution, they will still remember God and worship him in distant lands (**10:9**).

Egypt and Assyria will be subdued (**10:11b**; see Ezek 29:15-16; Zeph 2:13). These nations represent all the past enemies of God's people. These enemies may have enslaved God's people and taken them into exile, but God will orchestrate a new exodus that will bring all his people back to his land (10:11; see Isa 11:11; 27:13; Ezek 39:27-29; Hos 11:11). He will remove all the barriers to make their journey easy and smooth. They will pass through *the sea of trouble,* for it will be dried up so that the people can pass in safety, just as happened with the Red Sea at the start of the first exodus and the Jordan at its end (**10:11a**; see Exod 14:21-31; Josh 3:14-17; Isa 11:15; 51:10).

This section ends with a repetition of God's promise to strengthen his people in their journey (**10:12**; see 10:6). With this promise let us also abide in the Lord to enjoy his blessings and have his power available to us. For the Lord himself is the source of our strength. He will protect us by his miraculous power as he has done in the past. Let us continue to walk in the Lord by obeying his word (10:12; see Mic 4:5). With God on our side, we will enjoy victory over our enemies as we join in the host streaming away from the lands of sin and oppression and set out for the new Jerusalem.

11:1-17 Rejection of the Shepherd-King

Zechariah predicts that when the Messiah first comes, he will be rejected by his own people. He will suffer and die to save those who receive him. But those who reject him will suffer terrible consequences.

11:1-3 THE FATE OF FALSE SHEPHERDS The account of the rejection of the Messiah starts with a brief poem about the coming judgment on the false leaders (10:2-3). Because of them, the land will be destroyed by fire. The leaders are compared to the trees consumed by the blaze. All of them will come down, from the mighty cedars of *Lebanon* (**11:1**) to the lowly *thicket of the Jordan* (**11:3**). The false shepherds who have failed their sheep will *wail* (11:3; see Jer 25:34-38) and those who terrified the land as *lions* will find that they are left exposed, their habitat destroyed.

11:4-14 REJECTION OF THE TRUE SHEPHERD The prophet then portrays the rise and rejection of the good shepherd whom God chose to care for his flock. This flock is *marked for slaughter,* for God will soon punish them for their evildoing. But God gives his people one last chance by instructing Zechariah to be their shepherd (**11:4**). Although God, as the owner of the flock, is the only one who may command their slaughter, he knows that bad shepherds have already been selling his sheep to be slaughtered by others. These shepherds are only interested in using the sheep for their own personal profit (**11:5**; Jer 50:6-7; Ezek 34:2-3). Such abuse of people, which can take the form of human trafficking or slave trading, is condemned by God (see Amos 1:6).

Zechariah, representing the Messiah, uses two staffs as he cares for *the flock marked for slaughter.* The one staff is called *Favour* and the other *Union* (**11:7**). He wants the people to experience divine favour and to have harmony and unity among themselves. We look forward to the day when all the divisions within the Christian church will be done away with and all of God's people will live in unity and harmony.

The Lord's shepherd removes the bad shepherds *in one month* (**11:8a**). We do not know the identity of the *three shepherds* he dismisses, but they might represent the three offices of prophet, priest and king, now combined and united in the one perfect leader, the Messiah himself. He alone is the true shepherd of the flock, and he will not share his office with any other. He can replace the bad leadership of any church or nation. We pray that he will give us good leaders in our African churches and countries.

One would expect the oppressed people to welcome such a shepherd and be grateful for all he is doing for them, but this is not what happens. The flock detest him, for they too are interested only in their own greed and evil desires (**11:8b**). A pastor cannot do his work without the cooperation of the people he is trying to lead and serve, and so this shepherd *grew weary of them* (**11:8c**; see Isa 1:13-14) and decides to leave them to their own ways, knowing that they will destroy one another (**11:9**). When God no longer has *pity on the people of the land* and withdraws his presence and care, people will attack one another (**11:6**; see also 14:13; Deut 28:54-57). There will be spiritual and political confusion and oppression, for rebellion against God and his word always leads to judgment.

The Lord's shepherd breaks the staff called 'Favour' and terminates the covenant he *had made with all the nations* to restrain them from destroying God's people (**11:10**; Ezek 34:25; Hos 2:18). The nation was actually destroyed in AD 70, when the Romans laid siege to Jerusalem after the Jewish rejection of Jesus Christ (Matt 27:19-26). Only *the afflicted of the flock* understand that the coming judgment is the consequence of the people's rejection of the Messiah (**11:11**). They are the faithful remnant who recognize and understand God's word, and see that it is being fulfilled.

The prophet asks to be paid for his work as the true shepherd. The people decide to pay him *thirty pieces of silver*, which is the same price that the law laid down for a slave killed by a bull (**11:12**; see Exod 21:32). For the Lord's shepherd to be valued at this price is an insult. He is dismissed with shame. This was also the price paid to Judas for betraying Jesus (Matt 26:15; 27:9). The Messiah was valued at the price of a slave!

Zechariah is told to cast the thirty pieces of silver *to the potter* (**11:13a**). Potters were part of the lowest social class in the society of the time. The reference to the sum as a *handsome price* is full of irony and sarcasm, for the payment is far too small. The prophet obeys and throws the money *into the house of the Lord to the potter* (**11:13b**; see Jer 18:1-6).

This prophetic act was fulfilled by Judas when he threw the money for betraying Jesus into the Lord's house (Matt 27:5). However, because this was blood money, it was tainted, and could not be kept in the temple treasury (see Deut 23:18). Thus, the priests used it to buy a potter's field as a burial place for strangers (Matt 27:6-10). It is quite striking to see how every detail of this prophecy has been fulfilled. Zechariah accurately foresaw the sad events connected with the betrayal of Jesus five hundred years before they occurred.

The prophet also breaks the *second staff called Union* to show that there will be no unity and harmony among God's people, who at that time were the nations of *Judah and Israel* (**11:14**). Because the people have rejected their true shepherd, God will also reject them. But a time will come in the future when God will unite all of his people (Ezek 37:16-28). Already all of God's people are one in Christ in the church. However, there will be a much greater unity, harmony and oneness to be realized when the Messiah returns to reign in this kingdom. While we wait for his return, we should work towards peace and unity within the church in our present world.

11:15-17 THE TRUE SHEPHERD'S REPLACEMENT With the good shepherd rejected, a *foolish shepherd* comes to replace him. In the Bible, someone who is described as 'foolish' is someone who is morally deficient (**11:15**; see Prov 1:7). This shepherd does *not care for the lost, or seek the young, or heal the injured, or feed the healthy* (**11:16**; see Ezek 34:3-4; John 10:12-13). He will brutally oppress them in the cruelest manner. The people will suffer incredible hardship and maltreatment under his leadership.

Chapter 11 began with a poem of lament (11:1-13) and it ends with another poem pronouncing woe on this *worthless shepherd* (**11:17**; see also Jer 23:1; John 10:12). Not only is he selfish, corrupt and greedy, but he *deserts the flock*. In punishment, God will *strike his arm and his right eye* with the sword. He will lose all his ability to fight in battle, for his arm will *be completely withered* and *his right eye totally blinded* (11:17). He will suffer the same torments he inflicted on others.

This worthless and evil leader foreshadows the antichrist, who will oppress God's people and exercise terrible power in the end times (Dan 7:25-27; 11:36-45; Rev 13:1-10).

We need to remember that if we reject the Lord's shepherd, Jesus Christ, we reject God's help and salvation. We cannot then expect to receive his blessings, but will suffer the consequences of living without the benefit of his presence in our lives.

The description of the foolish shepherd should also remind us that there are many foolish and worthless pastors who are shepherds in the church today. They do not care for the people under their charge, but take advantage of them for their personal benefit. They do not take the responsibility of their pastoral ministry seriously. For example, they have no concern for those who are lost spiritually. They do not seek out the young to help strengthen and correct them, or help care for the sick and injured. They do not provide spiritual nourishment for the people. God will hold such pastors accountable for the spiritual condition of his people and will remove them from their posts (Ezek 34:10).

As pastors, we are to follow the example of the good shepherd, Jesus Christ. The African church needs good, true pastors to tend the flock for God's glory.

12:1-14:21 The Messiah's Second Coming in Glory

Zechariah's second great prophecy concerns the glorious coming of the Messiah-King 'in that day'. He describes the final battle in which the enemies of God's people are defeated and destroyed, after which the Messiah can finally establish his everlasting kingdom.

12:1-9 Zion's victory

12:1-3 THE SIEGE OF JERUSALEM In the last days, there will be a vicious war against God's people, unlike any other in their history. Jerusalem will be the object of worldwide hostility. But the Lord, *who forms the spirit of man within him* (**12:1**), promises to intervene directly on its behalf. God, who has absolute power and ability as creator and giver of life, will neutralize every attack against his city. He will make the nations drink the *cup* of his wrath (**12:2**). *On that day,* the day of the final great battle, he will personally intervene to protect his people and win a decisive victory. He will make *Jerusalem an immovable rock for all the nations;* those who try to move this rock will only hurt themselves, for the rock will crush them (**12:3**; see Luke 20:18).

God will accomplish his purposes for his people in the end, for there is no power either in heaven or on earth that can stop him. The nations are incapable of winning the war against Jerusalem and God's people.

12:4-9 DIVINE DELIVERANCE AND PROTECTION Zechariah describes the great victory won by God's powerful intervention. *On that day* God will strike his people's enemies with *panic, madness* and blindness (see Deut 28:28), and *will keep a watchful eye* to guard and protect his righteous people (**12:4**). Then the leaders of God's people will realize that the Lord is with them, and that they are *strong, because the Lord Almighty is their God* (**12:5**).

With the Lord on their side, the righteous will be like a fire, burning wood or sheaves of grain; they will consume all their enemies (**12:6**; see Isa 10:17-18; Obad 18). By saving the outlying areas (*Judah*) before the capital and the seat of power (*Jerusalem*), God shows that all the credit for the victory goes to him alone so that no one can boast (**12:7**; see Jer 9:23-24; 1 Cor 1:29-30; 2 Cor 10:17). The Lord will be their shield, and he will give his people supernatural strength so that the weakest individual will be *like David* (Isa 60:22), and the leaders will be *like God, like the angel of the Lord* (**12:8**). The angel of the Lord, who is God himself, will lead them in this final battle (see Exod 14:19). *On that day,* the Lord intends to judge and destroy all the nations that gather to attack his people (**12:9**; Isa 29:7-8; Mic 4:11-12). At the end of history, God will destroy all evil persons and abolish pain and oppression for ever. But he will save all those who trust in him.

12:10-13:9 Cleansing of sin

12:10-14 THE CRUCIFIED MESSIAH After describing the physical salvation of God's people, Zechariah then describes their spiritual salvation, which comes by way of true repentance. The Messiah, the true shepherd, was rejected by the people, and this rejection had terrible consequences (11:1-17). Here the Lord promises to *pour out … a spirit of grace and supplication* on his people (**12:10a**). This is the Holy Spirit, who gives grace to sinful and rebellious hearts to enable them to repent and cry out in supplication for forgiveness and pardon. The Lord is gracious and compassionate, forgiving sin when there is true repentance. But it is the Holy Spirit who first convicts us of sin, and shows us God's standard of righteousness and judgment (see Isa 44:3; 59:21; Ezek 36:26-27; 39:29; Joel 2:28-29; Acts 2). It is the Spirit that fills us and helps us to pray (see Rom 8:26).

The use of pronouns in 12:10 is quite striking. Yahweh (*I*) is the speaker, but he says *that they will look on me … and will mourn for* him. The 'me' and the 'him' are the same person, the Messiah. This means that Yahweh and the Messiah are here identified as one and the same. Thus, this passage supports Jesus' claims to deity.

God's Spirit will cause the people to see that the Lord Jesus, *the one they have pierced* and killed is indeed their Messiah (**12:10b**). John points out the startling fulfilment of this verse when he tells how Jesus' side was pierced with a spear (John 19:34-37; see also Isa 53:5). This verse also clearly shows that two comings of the Messiah are taught in the OT. At his first coming, he will be pierced and put to death; at the second coming, the people will recognize what they have done.

When the Messiah is finally recognized and appreciated, the people will *grieve bitterly for him as one grieves for a firstborn son* (**12:10c**). Their deep grief indicates the genuineness of their conversion. The enormity of the people's sense of loss when they realize what they have done will lead to mourning that can be compared to the *weeping of Hadad Rimmon in the plain of Megiddo* (**12:11**). Here Zechariah is probably referring to the mourning for the tragic death of King Josiah in battle with Pharaoh Neco at Megiddo (2 Kgs 23:29; 2 Chr 35:22-24). Josiah's death was a terrible national loss and he was greatly mourned by his people.

Each clan will mourn *by itself* and *their wives by themselves.* This will not just be a formal national ritual, but one that involves each family and each individual in deep repentance. It will affect all of God's people, from the royal house of David down to the ordinary people (**12:12-14**). What we see here is both universal and individual loss and grief.

13:1 A FOUNTAIN OF CLEANSING WATER Following the people's mourning, God promises a work of purification and restoration. The Lord, who is gracious and compassionate to forgive even the sin of piercing and killing the Messiah, will respond to his people's repentance. He says, *On that day a fountain will be opened* (**13:1**). The image of a fountain symbolizes the never-ending abundance of God's forgiveness made available to his people (see 3:4, 9; 14:8; Ezek 36:25-28; 47:1-2). This fountain will *cleanse them from sin and impurity.* 'Sin' refers to every way in which we fall short of God's will and requirements, and 'impurity' refers to the ceremonial and sexual impurities that under the Mosaic law barred a person from coming into God's presence.

The church today drinks from that fountain and experiences God's forgiveness and cleansing through Christ's atoning death (see Matt 26:28; Luke 22:20; John 4:13-14; 7:37-39; 1 Cor 11:25-26). However, these blessings are still to be experienced by the Jewish people, who will repent at the second coming of Jesus Christ (Rom 11:25-32).

13:2-6 REMOVAL OF FALSE PROPHETS AND IDOLATRY In the last days, there will be a great interest in idolatry, false prophets, demon worship and the antichrist. All these interests and idolatrous practices are inspired by Satan (Matt 24:4-5, 15, 23-26; 1 Tim 4:1; Rev 9:20; 13:4-15). But when Christ comes, he will utterly destroy them all, for he alone will be exalted and rule in his kingdom. That is why there will be no place in the new earth for false prophets. They and the *spirit of impurity* behind them will be removed from the new earth (**13:2**; see Isa 2:18-20; Jer 23:30-32).

In this future day, the opposition to false worship will be so strong that even a false prophet's own parents will oppose him for telling *lies in the Lord's name* and will put him to death (**13:3**; see Deut 13:1-11; 18:20; Jer 23:34; Ezek 14:9). The Hebrew word here translated *stab* is the same as the one translated 'pierced' in 12:10. There it was the Messiah who was pierced; now that will be the fate of false prophets.

Those who have been false prophets *will be ashamed of* their *prophetic vision* (see Jer 6:15) and will be reluctant to identify themselves. They will not wear the prophet's uniform *in order to deceive* (**13:4**; see 2 Kgs 1:8; Matt 3:4). Rather than identifying themselves as prophets, they will claim to be farmers (**13:5**). They will try to explain away the wounds they received in ecstatic, prophetic and idolatrous rituals by claiming that they were *given at the house of my friends* (**13:6**; see Lev 19:28; 1 Kgs 18:25-28).

These prophets lied about what they were doing. As Bible teachers or Christians involved in disciplining others, we must be careful that we do not do the same. We must not be like the false prophets, who distort God's word, or twist it or even lie about it. Spiritual issues in the lives of those we are working with concern their eternal life.

13:7-9 THE SHEPHERD STRUCK AND THE FLOCK SCATTERED Zechariah returns to the theme of the smitten and rejected shepherd of chapter 11 and closes this chapter with a poem. In the last days, a shepherd belonging to and dear to the Lord will be struck at his command. He is the same person pierced by the people in 12:10. The sheep had rejected this shepherd and were marked for slaughter (11:4, 7). They had thus come under the control and rule of the foolish worthless shepherd, whom Yahweh and his Messiah have struck down (11:15-17).

But now Yahweh again calls for a sword to be used, not against a worthless shepherd but against *my shepherd* and

the man who is close to me (**13:7a**). This shepherd is the Messiah, who is both human ('the man') and divine (for God says, he is 'close to me'). He is Jesus Christ, the equal of the Lord (see John 1:1-2; 10:30; 14:9-14).

Yahweh calls for this good shepherd to be struck (**13:7b**; see Isa 53:4-10). His death will not be a mistake or an accident, but is part of God's plan (see Acts 2:23). It will be a means of salvation for all people.

When the shepherd is struck, *the sheep will be scattered* (**13:7c**). *The little ones* are the 'afflicted of the flock', who are part of the remnant (11:11). Jesus quoted this verse just before his arrest to show its fulfilment in himself and his disciples (Matt 26:31-32, 56; Mark 14:27, 49-50). He knew beforehand that his disciples would desert him when he was arrested, for the Scriptures must be fulfilled. The death of the shepherd did indeed scatter the flock (see John 10:11). Of all the OT passages about sheep and shepherds this one seems to have influenced Jesus the most.

The shepherd's death will result not only in the scattering of his followers but also in the suffering, pain and death of many in the land. Yet a remnant will be preserved: *In the whole land … two-thirds will be struck down and perish; yet one-third will be left in it* (**13:8**; see Ezek 5:2-4, 12). It seems that here there is a shift from the time of Christ's death to the end time, when the third that will survive is the righteous remnant. They will be under divine care, but they will also be refined and purified like *silver* and *gold* in the crucible of suffering (**13:9a**; see Ps 66:10; Isa 1:25; Ezek 22:20-22; Dan 11:35; 1 Pet 1:6-7). Through this process, they will be prepared to welcome the Messiah. They will enjoy the fellowship with the Lord, the Messiah. They will call on his name, and he will answer their prayers. He *will say,' They are my people', and they will say, 'The Lord is our God'* (**13:9b**; see 8:8; 10:6; Lev 26:12; Ps 50:15; Isa 30:19; Jer 30:22; Hos 2:23).

Let us be sure that we will be part of the remnant people at the end time. Let us resolve to obey and follow the Lord no matter what difficulties, trials or troubles we may face at times. These things should only help to strengthen and confirm our faith in Christ. Let us remain spiritually pure and run the race with endurance to the end.

14:1-21 The Messiah returns to Zion

14:1-5 THE MESSIAH'S VICTORY This chapter describes the second coming of Jesus, the Messiah, who will come as mighty warrior to put an end to all God's enemies (see Rev 19–20). Here, we have more prophecies about a coming *day of the Lord* (**14:1**; see also Isa 13:6). That day is still in the future and is known only to Yahweh (14:7; see Matt 24:36).

On that day, the Lord *will gather all the nations to Jerusalem to fight against it* (**14:2a**; see 12:3; Ezek 5:8; Rev 16:13-21). The coalition of 'all the nations' suggests that there will be one world political system at that time.

The enemy nations will at first have victory. They will capture the city, ransack the houses and rape the women. Half of the city's population *will go into exile,* but the rest will be preserved (**14:2b**). This will be a day of darkness for the inhabitants of Jerusalem. However, God is in absolute control; he uses the human evil to achieve his own purposes. It seems that this is when two-thirds of the people will be destroyed (13:8).

The battle being described here is the same one that Joel speaks of as taking place in the Valley of Jehoshaphat (Joel 3:2, 12, 14), and that John foresees as happening at a place called Armageddon (Rev 16:16). It is God's means of bringing the nations to judgment, the final war on earth to end human history.

After the initial success of the nations, the Lord himself will come to fight against them to save the righteous remnant (**14:3**; see 9:14-15; 12:9). He will appear as a divine warrior, just as he has done in the past (see Josh 10:14).

The Messiah will physically stand on *the Mount of Olives* (**14:4a**). This is the very place to which God's glory departed before the temple was destroyed in 587 BC (Ezek 10:18-19; 11:22-24), the place where Jesus spoke with his disciples concerning the end times (Matt 24), and the place from which he ascended into heaven (Acts 1:12). It will also be the place to which he returns. When he again stands on the Mount of Olives, it *will be split in two from east to west, forming a great valley* (**14:4b**). This will provide an escape route along which his people can flee from their enemies, just as their ancestors fled the earthquake in King Uzziah's time (see Amos 1:1; Rev 16:18-19).

The Lord himself will then come with his *holy ones,* that is, his saints and angels, to destroy his enemies (**14:5**; Isa 66:15-16; Matt 16:27; 24:30-31; 25:31).

14:6-9 THE NEW CREATION The coming of Christ will indeed be glorious and wonderful for those who have accepted and trusted him as their Lord and Saviour, for they will share in the new age that his coming introduces. In the new age, the heavenly bodies will no longer be needed to shine their light (**14:6**). On this *unique day,* the presence of God's glory will give light to the whole universe, and there will no longer be any difference between day and night (**14:7**; see Rev 21:23-25).

In the new creation, *living water will flow out from Jerusalem* (**14:8a**; see also 13:1; Jer 2:13; Ezek 47:1-12; John 4:10-14; 7:37-38; Rev 22:1-2). This living water will satisfy and refresh God's redeemed people both physically and spiritually. As Jesus said, anyone who drinks of this living water 'will never thirst again' (John 4:14). It will well up in them to eternal life. The constant supply of living waters will flow out of the new Jerusalem in a river to *the eastern sea* (the Dead Sea) and *the western sea* (the Mediterranean), in the dry *summer* season as well as in the wet *winter* season (**14:8b**).

In that day, *the Lord will be king over the whole earth,* and *his name the only name* (**14:9**; see 9:9; Ps 47:7-8; Obad 21; Eph 4:5-6; Rev 17:14). We are reminded of the words of the Jewish *Shema:* 'The Lord our God, the Lord is one' (Deut 6:4). On that day, our Lord Jesus alone will be Lord without any rivals. All forms of idolatry and polytheism will be done away with.

14:10-15 ENEMIES DESTROYED The Lord will establish his universal kingship following the last battle described here. There will be war on the earth, but first, as a result of the great earthquake (14:4), the landscape will be altered from *Geba,* six miles to the north of Jerusalem to *Rimmon,* thirty-five miles to the *south of Jerusalem,* and will *become like the Arabah,* the great plain of the Jordan Valley (**14:10a**). Thus, the land around Jerusalem will be altered into a great plain, while *Jerusalem will be raised up, and remain in its place* (**14:10b**; see 12:6; Isa 2:2). Jerusalem will be exalted and honoured as the capital of the new world and as the city of God. It will be the centre of the worship of God for all peoples. It will be inhabited and *secure* (**14:11**; see 2:4; Ps 48:8; Jer 23:6; Rev 22:3).

Christ will judge the enemy forces that attacked Jerusalem. He will strike them with a devastating plague: *their flesh … their eyes …* and *their tongues will rot* (**14:12**). He will also strike them with *great panic* (see Gen 35:5). Just as in the day of Gideon, the enemy forces will attack and destroy one another in their panic and confusion (**14:13**; see Judg 7:22; 1 Sam 14:15-20; 2 Chr 20:22-23). *On that day, the Lord will distinguish between believers and unbelievers,* just as he did in Egypt when the plagues affected only the Egyptians (see Exod 9:7). God's people will be involved in fighting enemy armies in the final battle to defend Jerusalem (**14:14a**; see also 12:2). They will utterly defeat the attacking armies and gather the spoils of battle. They will collect and share all the wealth of the enemy nations – their *great quantities of gold and silver and clothing* (**14:14b**; see Isa 23:18). Whereas previously Jerusalem had been plundered by enemy forces (14:1-2), now it will be enriched by their wealth.

The animals and everything that accompanies the enemies will also be struck by the plague (**14:15**).

14:16-21 UNIVERSAL WORSHIP OF THE KING Despite the fierce war, there will be *survivors from all the nations* (**14:16a**). These will repent and turn to God, submitting themselves to the millennial kingdom of the Messiah. The Messiah will take his throne in Jerusalem, and all believers will go up there annually to worship him at the Feast of Tabernacles (**14:16b**; see 8:21-22; 14:9; Isa 60:3, 6-9). It will be a time of great joy and celebration.

The Feast of Tabernacles, like all the major feasts celebrated in Israel, was rooted in the exodus, when the Lord brought the Israelites out of Egypt (Lev 23:33-44). It was a joyous time in which the people had to live in fragile shelters to remind them of how their ancestors had lived during their wanderings in the desert and of the need to live in dependence on God's care (Deut 16:13-15). Because this feast coincided with the time when the harvest was gathered, it was also a harvest celebration (Lev 23:34, 39). As such, it anticipated the time when the Lord's world harvest will be gathered and all believers from all the nations will come into God's kingdom. Those who are in Christ look forward to this event when all families of the earth will go to Jerusalem to celebrate together.

We need to remember that Zechariah's vision of Jerusalem was not restricted to the geographical city of Jerusalem. He has already described it as a 'city without walls' (2:4) and composed of 'many nations ... joined with the Lord' (2:11). He is using Jerusalem as a symbol of the truth about God's kingdom, which, as Jesus says, is 'not of this world' (John 18:36). In Christ, we have already come to the city of Zion, the new Jerusalem (Heb 12:22), which will descend from heaven in the end time (Rev 21:2). This is the city that Zechariah is referring to.

During the millennial reign of Christ, those who refuse to acknowledge and worship him *will have no rain,* and there will be nothing they can do about it (**14:17**). Egypt is mentioned here as an example of a nation that may stubbornly refuse to come. But if they do not come to the feast, they will suffer from drought and will experience once again the plague which the Lord will inflict on all those who refuse to obey and submit to him (**14:18**; see 14:12, 15). Egypt had been humbled by God in the past at the time of the exodus, and God can do this again to Egypt or to any nation that tries to be disobedient and stubborn in the end time, for 'every knee should bow' and 'every tongue must confess' that he is Lord (Phil 2:10-11).

Believers must take the worship of Christ seriously in our present generation. Unfortunately, there is negligence in our present worship of our Lord. We must change and become serious and consistent for God's glory. We are to acknowledge him as our Lord and Saviour daily wherever we find ourselves. For he alone is worthy of praise and worship as the King of kings and Lord of lords.

God's holiness is the supreme attribute of his being and is the foundation of his eternal existence. Everything God does bears the imprint of his holiness, which never diminishes. Since he is holy, God is completely set apart from sin. In the coming kingdom everything will be characterized by the Lord's holiness. In our present order, no one can look upon God's glory and live. But in that day, even common, ordinary objects such as *the bells of the horses and the cooking pots* will have HOLY TO THE LORD inscribed on them, just as it was on the turban of the high priest (**14:20**; see Exod 28:36-37). Both cooking pots and the sacred bowls used in the temple *will be holy to the Lord Almighty,* and every person that goes to worship the Lord will be completely holy and pure (**14:21a**). No one will be able to distinguish between the sacred and secular any more.

The new Jerusalem stands in contrast to the old one, for there will be no need for any *Canaanite,* a word that can also mean 'trader' or 'merchant', and probably refers to those who sold holy objects to pilgrims who came to worship in the temple at Jerusalem (**14:21b**). The city, its people and every object in it will be totally holy and pure. Thus, Zechariah concludes his great prophecy with a picture of God's holiness triumphant in his kingdom over all sin and evil.

The prophet has given us assurance that God knows and controls the future and has revealed it to Zechariah, his prophet. His words encourage us to put away sin in our lives and to do God's work for his glory. We need to live holy lives now if we are to enjoy God's blessing in the present, and holy living will also characterize our lives in God's future kingdom. We are given hope that Christ will come again to establish his eternal kingdom, and to reign as King of kings and Lord of lords over the whole world (Rev 11:15; see also 19:16). Our response now must be to praise and worship him daily for who he is. Come let us worship and bow down to Christ, our present and future King.

Yoilah Yilpet

Further Reading

Baker, Kenneth L. *Zechariah.* EBC.Grand Rapids: Zondervan, 1985.

Baldwin, Joy G. *Haggai, Zechariah and Malachi.* TOT. Leicester: Inter-Varsity Press, 1972.

Kaiser Jr, Walter C. *Micah–Malachi.* CC. Dallas: Word, 1992.

MALACHI

Malachi, the last of the OT prophets, prophesied after Haggai and Zechariah. He may have spoken around 516 BC, shortly after the reconstruction of the temple, or in about 444 BC, in the time of Ezra and Nehemiah.

The people and priests of Malachi's day had become disobedient, unfaithful and arrogant. Malachi, whose name means 'my messenger' or 'my angel', warned them of judgment and called on them to repent.

The book falls into six sections. Each begins with a statement, followed by an objection in the form of a question introduced by 'you ask', and then by a refutation of the objection. The first three sections focus on the broken covenant between God and his people. The last three sections focus on God's intervention to restore the covenant.

Outline of Contents

COMMENTARY

1:1 Introduction

Malachi's message to *Israel*, that is, to the whole Jewish community after their return from exile, is described as *an oracle*, using a Hebrew word often used for prophecies of judgment (**1:1**; see also Zech 9:1; 12:1). Because it is an authoritative *word of the Lord*, it is reliable.

1:2-2:16 The Broken Covenant

The Israelites are heirs to all the covenant promises, but their failure to meet their covenant obligations gives Malachi's message its sense of compulsion, urgency and even dread.

1:2-5 How Has God Loved Us?

1:2a-2b Doubting God's love

God starts by affirming his love: *I have loved you* (**1:2a**). That was why he had chosen Israel to be his people and blessed them greatly (Deut 7:7-8; 10:15; 33:3). And that love continues. It is not based on their greatness or righteousness, but on his promise of blessing, guaranteed by his oath to Abraham, Isaac and Jacob (Deut 9:4-6). It is demonstrated even when they rebel against him (Amos 3:2).

Instead of responding to God's love with trust and obedience, his people grumble, *How have you loved us?* (**1:2b**). They have forgotten what he has done for them and their forefathers. They have wandered far from God, and now accuse God of being far from them. Many people today make the same mistake.

1:2c-4 Evidence of God's love

God responds to the people's scepticism by presenting them with two evidences of his love: he had specifically chosen Jacob and he had punished their enemies.

Jacob and Esau were brothers, yet God says, *I have loved Jacob* (**1:2c**). Human reasoning cannot explain God's choice. It had nothing to do with birth order or anything Jacob had done, for Jacob was the younger brother and was chosen before he was born (Gen 25:23). It was an example of God's undeserved love and favour (see Rom 9:11-16).

When God says but *Esau I have hated* (**1:3a**), he is not expressing a personal dislike, but merely stating that he had chosen Jacob's descendants (the Israelites) rather than Esau's descendants (the Edomites – Gen 36) for the special task of bringing blessing to all nations. The Edomites became Israel's enemies, rejoicing and actively helping the Babylonians when they invaded the land in 587 BC. The Edomites even harassed the fleeing Israelites (Ps 137:7; Ezek 35:15; Obad 8-16).

God also punishes his people's enemies. He had promised to wipe out the Edomites and give their territory to Israel (see Jer 49:7-22; Ezek 25:12-14; Joel 3:19; Amos 1:11; Obad 8-10, 18-19, 21). This promise had not yet been fulfilled, but Malachi affirms that Edom will not escape God's righteous judgment, and its end will be irreversible (**1:3b**). The land will be laid waste and emptied of its people. The survivors will not be able to rebuild (**1:4**). The Lord fulfilled his promise, and Edom no longer exists as a nation.

1:5 Accepting God's love

The effects of this love will be felt far *beyond the borders of Israel* (**1:5**). The Lord wants his people to tell the whole world about his goodness and greatness. The offer of salvation that came through the descendants of Jacob is intended for all. Rather than doubting God's love for us, we should accept it so that we can bear witness to it and bring glory to God in our communities, tribes and nations.

1:6-2:9 How Have We Failed as Priests?

Instead of honouring God as a father and respecting him as their master (Exod 20:12; Luke 6:46), they have showed him no reverence (**1:6**). The priests protested against God's assertion, saying *How have we despised your name?* and *How have we defiled you?* (**1:7**).

1:6-10 By offering unacceptable sacrifices

The priests were God's servants and the spiritual leaders of the people.

The answer is that they have shown disrespect by offering unacceptable sacrifices (**1:8**). The Mosaic law specifically forbade the offering of blind, lame and sick animals and insisted that any animal offered to cover anyone's sins and guilt must be without any defect (Exod 12:5; Lev 22:17-25; Deut 17:1). Yet these priests offered the Lord animals that it would be an insult to give to any human ruler! Their actions show that they neither respect nor fear God. No wonder he is *not pleased* with them (**1:10b**). He prefers no worship to irreverent, hypocritical worship. So he suggests that the priests *shut the temple doors* and no longer *light useless fires* on his altar (**1:10a**; see also Isa 1:11-15; 29:13).

As Africans we honour and respect our parents and elders. God deserves even more honour and respect. But some churches have become nothing more than meeting places where the worship is meaningless (Rev 3:15-16). Those who attend such churches must repent and return to worshipping God in spirit and in truth.

1:11-14 By denying God's glory

The priests may insult the Lord's great name, but God can and will raise up true worshippers elsewhere. The Gentiles worldwide will come to exalt God's name (**1:11**; see also Isa 66:19, 20; Zeph 2:11; 3:9; Acts 10:34-35). They will offer him *incense,* which symbolizes believers' prayers rising to God (see Ps 141:2; Rev 8:3). *Pure offerings* will be offered *in every place,* and no longer just in Jerusalem (see Deut 12:11; John 4:20-24; Eph 2:11-22). The Lord's kingdom will extend from east to west (see also Ps 113:3; Isa 45:6; 59:19).

The priests also show contempt for the Lord by despising his altar, saying that it is *defiled* and its food *contemptible* – despite their insistence that they had not defiled it (**1:12; 1:7**). They are bored with their vocation and consider their work burdensome (**1:13**).

God rejects their unacceptable sacrifices and pronounces an additional curse on cheats who make a vow to him and deliberately fail to fulfil it (**1:14**). Such vows were voluntary, so the deceit was inexcusable.

2:1-9 By neglecting priestly duties

If the priests do not repent, the Lord will turn their blessings into a curse (**2:2**). They have insulted God, and so they will suffer insults. They will have the bowel contents of the animals they have sacrificed thrown in their faces and will be expelled from God's presence (**2:3b**). When this happens they will remember that God foretold it (**2:4a;** see also Ezek 15:7).

God's curse will extend to their offspring (**2:3a**). The priests occupied their position because the zealous service offered by Phinehas, Aaron's grandson, had led God to make a *covenant of life and peace* with his descendants (**2:4b-5a;** Num 1:47-54; 25:11-13). But they would not keep this position if they were unfaithful to God and his laws (Deut 4:40; Hos 4:6). In addition to offering sacrifices, they also had to guard and teach God's law, reminding the people of God's promises and his curses (Deut 31:9-13). They could not do this if they did not live by that truth themselves. Like their ancestors, they must fear (that is, deeply respect) the Lord, and no one else (**2:5b;** see also Ps 2:11; Prov 9:10; Luke 12:4-5).

A true priest teaches God's truth without twisting it to make it more popular (**2:6a;** see also Lev 19:15; Deut 33:9-10; Prov 8:7; Hos 4:6; Mic 3:11). Those who do this walk with God *in peace and uprightness* (**2:6b**). They live according to his will and the Scriptures. Their example shows others how to walk in the same close fellowship with God. The goal of all faithful teaching and proclamation of God's word is to turn others from the error of their ways (**2:6c;** see also Jer 23:22; Ezek 18:21, 23; 33:8-11; Jas 5:19-20).

The *knowledge* that the priests *preserve* is not a secret known only to them. It is the knowledge of God that leads to the desire to do the will of God and obey his commandments

(2:7a). Because every priest is a *messenger of the Lord Almighty* (2:7b), the people have a right to expect sound *instruction* from them. They are the interpreters and teachers of God's will. In fact, they were God's ambassadors, just as believers are today (2 Cor 5:20). As such, we must take care that our lives demonstrate what it means to obey God and bring honour to his name.

But instead of turning the people from sin, the priests in Malachi's day led them into sin. They broke the covenant, and led the people to do the same (2:8; see also Neh 13:29). Not only that, but they were guilty of favouritism (2:9b), even though they were commanded not to take bribes and not to discriminate between rich and poor, young and old, powerful or powerless (Deut 10:17; 16:18-29; 17:8-13).

God's punishment for the priests who neglect their duties fits their crime. Since they have despised and dishonoured his name, they will lose all the respect they enjoy and will be disqualified from serving him (2:9a).

2:10-16 How Have We Failed as God's People?

The people, too, are rebuked for their unfaithfulness. The priests' failure to teach the truth has led to a devastating collapse of marriage and family life.

2:10-12 By practising idolatry

This time it is Malachi who asks the question, *Did not one God create us?* (2:10a). Here he is not speaking of God as the creator of all humanity, but as the father of Israel, the covenant people (2:10b; see also 1:6; Isa 43:1; 60:21). God created them to be his special people, set apart from the rest of the world (Exod 19:5-6; Lev 20:24, 26). Because they are his family, they should not act treacherously towards each other – but this is what they have done (2:10c).

The people had promised on several occasions to obey God's command and not marry unbelievers (for example, in Neh 10:30). But they had broken that promise (2:11). God is not opposed to interracial or intertribal marriages, but to marriages between believers and unbelievers. Such marriages brought idolatry into the heart of Israel as people accepted their spouses' gods (Ezra 9:1-2, 14; Neh 10:30; 13:23-30). God had foreseen this danger and that is why he had forbidden such marriages (Exod 34:11-16; Lev 21:6-8, 14-15). He wants his people to remain distinct (2:11). One of the reasons Israel had been sent into exile was because they had accepted the gods of other nations. Now, the community that had returned from exile was committing the same sins!

God takes this sin so seriously that he insists that the offender must be excommunicated (2:12). It would be hypocritical to make an offering while one is flagrantly disobeying God.

Christians too are forbidden to marry unbelievers (2 Cor 6:14-16). Those who do should be rebuked for their disloyalty to God and to their fellow believers. Failing to distinguish between Christians and unbelievers is equivalent to denying the difference between Christ and pagan deities.

2:13-16 By marital unfaithfulness

Divorce is just as abominable to God as mixed-faith marriages. Divorce seems to have been rampant in Malachi's time, so that the Lord's altar must have been flooded with the tears shed by the forsaken wives. Consequently, God refuses to acknowledge the sacrifices made by the husbands who divorce them. He has forsaken them, and will not respond to their tears or prayers and bless them (2:13).

When the husbands ask *why* God rejects their offerings (2:14), Malachi reminds them that they have broken a covenant. Marriage involves a solemn vow that is witnessed by God (see Ezek 16:8). Loyalty to one's spouse is required, and God punishes unfaithfulness. One cannot simply discard one's first wife in favour of another woman.

Malachi 2:15 is a strong argument against divorce, but it is also one of the most difficult verses in the OT. Several different translations have been offered, but the one that seems most likely, and that is adopted in the NIV, takes the word 'he' as referring to God, and the 'one' as referring to the 'one flesh' of Genesis 2:24. In the marriage relationship, God makes two people (that is, the man and the woman) become one, just as he had made each individual out of two parts, flesh and spirit (see Matt 19:4-6; Mark 10:7-9). Two people in marriage become as one person.

Why did God want men to have only one wife? Because he wanted families to raise godly children (2:15). Polygamy and divorce are not conducive to nurturing children in the fear of God. The prophet warns the people not to *break faith* with their wives, but to guard their spirits.

God's intense hatred for divorce does not contradict the teaching of Deuteronomy 24:1-4. Divorce was permitted because of the hardness of human hearts, but that does not mean that God approves of it (Matt 19:3-8). Moreover, the main issue discussed in that passage in Deuteronomy is someone remarrying his first wife after he had divorced her and either he or she had remarried in the meantime.

God hates not only divorce but also *a man's covering himself with violence as well as with his garment* (2:16). Spreading one's garment over a woman was a way of claiming her as a wife (see Ruth 3:9; Ezek 16:8). A man who 'covered himself with violence' was someone who did not spread his garment over his wife to protect her, but instead treated her violently.

The prophet concludes this section by repeating the warning given in 2:15 and 2:16: remain faithful to your marriage partners.

2:17-4:6 God's Restoration of the Covenant

2:17-3:6 Is God Just?

The people had earlier questioned God's love. Now, they question his justice.

2:17 A distorted idea of God's justice

The people *have wearied the Lord* with their hypocrisy and sin. They claim that God does not differentiate between evil and good and even favours those who do evil (**2:17a**; see also Isa 1:14; 5:20; 43:24).

These charges are a direct attack on God's character. The Bible makes it clear that God hates those who do evil (Exod 23:6-7; Ps 94:21-23; Prov 17:15) but delights in those who keep his law and practise mercy and justice (Isa 56:1-8; Hos 6:6; Mic 6:8). Yet these people question this truth, asking *Where is the God of justice?* (**2:17b**). They have disobeyed God, and so have not received his blessing, and yet they regard his failure to intervene to solve their problems as indicating that he is not just!

3:1-4 The coming messenger of justice

God responds by saying that, as the God of justice, he will send them two messengers. The first will prepare the way of the Messiah (**3:1a**; see also Isa 40:3-5). This messenger is later identified as John the Baptist, who came in the spirit and power of Elijah and whose work was to call the people to repent and prepare them morally and spiritually for the coming Messiah (Matt 3:1-3; 11:11-14; Mark 1:2-3).

The second messenger will be *the Lord* himself (**3:1b**). The word 'Lord' is singular and is preceded by the definite article, making it clear that the one referred to is the divine Lord (see Isa 1:24; 3:1). He will come to *his temple,* of which he is the legitimate owner (**3:1c**; see also Ezek 43:1-5; Hag 2:9). But 'the Lord' is also one of the titles of the hoped-for Messiah (see Ps 110:1) who will be *the messenger of the covenant* (**3:1d**), just as the angel was in Exodus 23:20-23. He comes to bring in the new covenant which will take the place of the old covenant the people have broken or violated (Heb 8:8-13; 12:24). The God of justice is on his way!

When he comes, he will come in judgment (Amos 5:18-20), causing Malachi to wonder, *Who can endure the day of his coming?* That day is also known as 'the day of the Lord' (**3:2a**; see Joel 2:11; Zeph 1:15). Malachi's second question, *Who can stand when he appears?* underlines the point that few are morally and spiritually ready to face the Messiah's judgment (4:5; Rev 6:16-17).

Rather than approving of those who are evil (2:17), the Messiah will purify God's people. A smith purifies silver by heating it until it melts so that any impurities can be skimmed off. When the impurities are gone, the refiner can see his own reflection in the smooth surface of the metal. In the same way, we will be purified by God until his reflection shines in us (**3:2b-3a**; see Rom 8:29). The purification process is also compared to the way a launderer scrubs clothes with soap to remove any dirt (**3:2b**). Both images make it clear that the process will not be pleasant (Isa 48:10; Ezek 22:18-22; 1 Pet 1:7).

Yet God wants us to be open to his purification process and allow the fire of his holiness to destroy the sin in our lives (see Heb 12:7-11; 1 Pet 4:17-18). Purified people and priests will carry out their work in the right spirit and God will accept their offerings (**3:3b-4**). Malachi is here describing the true worship of God using the language and terms of his own day (see also Hos 14:2; Rom 12:1-2; Heb 13:15). For those who truly trust and obey God, the Messiah's coming will bring salvation and joy.

3:5 The judgment of evil

When the Messiah comes in judgment, he will be a witness who testifies against and punishes those who do evil (**3:5a**; see also Pss 10:14-15; 73:17-20; 94:23). The list of evildoers includes *sorcerers, adulterers, perjurers* (that is, those who swear falsely), those who cheat their workers by defrauding them of the wages they are owed, those who oppress widows and orphans and those who deny justice to aliens. All these sins stem from the people's lack of fear of God (**3:5b**). Such fear is 'the beginning of knowledge' (Prov 1:7).

3:6 God's nature does not change

The Lord's nature, attributes, moral character and determination to punish evil and reward good do not change (**3:6a**; see also Num 23:19; Ps 102:26-27; Jas 1:17). He had promised that he would never violate his covenant with Abraham, Jacob and David (Gen 28:12-15; 35:9-13; Ps 89:34) and he keeps his promise despite the fact that the people of Israel have not kept theirs (2:10) and have wearied him (2:17). They deserve to be destroyed, but he has preserved them because he does not change (**3:6b**). What a comfort to all believers!

3:7-12 What Does Repentance Mean?

3:7 A call to repentance

Throughout their history, the people of Israel disobeyed God, rebelled against his commandments, and failed to learn from the judgments he inflicted on them (**3:7a**). But God remains faithful to his promise to receive those who seek him with all their heart (**3:7b**; see also Jer 29:13; Zech 1:3-4). He has always been willing to accept those who repent and to pour out his blessings upon them.

But the people's response to this call amounts to a denial that they have done anything wrong: *How are we to return?* (**3:7c**). They have clearly not been listening to Malachi and recognizing what needs to change in their society.

3:8-9 Stop stealing from God

God responds by focusing on one example of their disobedience: they were negligent in giving their *tithes and offerings*. These offerings were required from time immemorial (Gen 14:20) and are specified in the law (Lev 27:30-33; Num 18:24-28). They provided practical support that enabled the priests and Levites to concentrate on serving God, and supplied food for those in need, such as orphans, widows, and aliens (Exod 29:27-28; Num 5:9; Deut 14:22-29). Spiritually, they represented an acknowledgement that all we possess belongs to God. Withholding tithes is equivalent to robbing him because we are refusing to give him what is rightly his (**3:8**; see also Neh 10:32-39; 13:10-13; Acts 5:1-11)

Failure to obey God's word always brings a curse that affects the whole land (**3:9**; see also Hag 1:5-11; Zech 5:1-4). So in robbing God, we poison ourselves (Prov 11:24).

3:10-12 Obey and enjoy blessings

To teach his people that their obedience does make a difference, God challenges them to *test* his generosity (**3:10**). If they obey him and *bring the whole tithe* to the place where the tithes are stored, he will flood them with blessings (Deut 28:12; 2 Chr 31:10; Prov 3:9-10). Their land, which had evidently been suffering from drought, will be revitalized (**3:11**). Pestilences and crop failures will cease (see also Amos 4:9; Hag 2:19; Zech 8:12). He will make their work fruitful and keep away the locusts. Furthermore, everywhere they will be called *blessed* (**3:12a**; Isa 61:9). Their land will be a delight to all who see it (**3:12b**; see also Isa 62:4; Dan 8:9).

Note that any challenge to test the Lord must be related to a call for repentance that demonstrates our faith and dependence on him. God promises an overabundance of his blessings if he is obeyed.

3:13-4:6 What's the Point of Serving God?

3:13-15 Serving God with cynicism

The question in **3:14** reveals that these people were only interested in obeying God if there was some immediate gain. They thought that all that was needed was an outward show of repentance, and tried wearing sackcloth and ashes and pretending to grieve for their sins. God would not bless such superficial repentance, and so they claimed that God has failed the test (see 3:10) and asserted that *the arrogant are blessed, ... evildoers prosper, and even those who challenge God escape* (**3:15**; see also Pss 73:12; 95:9). They represented God as unfair and obeying his word as useless.

It is a mistake to think that serving God must bring wealth and happiness and that outward service is all that is required. Those who preach a prosperity gospel are making the same mistake. God is not interested in self-seeking service rooted in a desire for profit. He inspects the heart.

3:16-18; 4:2 The destiny of the godly

Not everyone was cynical. Some *feared the Lord ... and honoured his name* (**3:16**), and were also described as *the righteous* and *those who serve God* (**3:18**). These believers repented of their sin, loved and obeyed the Lord and worshipped him with pure hearts (see Rom 11:4). Just as the Lord heard the cynical blasphemies of the sceptics, so he listened to the faithful conversation of believers.

The godly have resolved to trust God regardless of their circumstances (see Ps 73). God knows them and keeps a written record of what they have done (3:16; see also Exod 32:32-33; Ps 56:8; Dan 12:1; 2 Tim 2:19; Rev 20:12). The knowledge that they will be his *treasured possession* gives great encouragement and comfort (**3:17a**; see also Exod 19:4-5; Titus 2:14; 1 Pet 2:9). They are set apart to be members of a royal priesthood and to share God's special blessing, both now and in the glorious future that he has prepared for his own (see Isa 62:2-3).

When God executes his final judgment, he will show compassion to those who faithfully serve him and will care for them like a proud father (**3:17b**; see Ps 103:13). On that day, everyone will be able to see the difference *between the righteous and the wicked* and all will recognize that God does judge justly and distinguishes *between those who serve God and those who do not* (3:18; Ps 58:11; Dan 12:2).

The night of evil will end when *the sun of righteousness* rises (**4:2a**). This 'sun' is the Messiah, Jesus Christ (see Isa 9:2; 49:6; Luke 1:76-79). The 'righteousness' he brings is much more than just the forgiveness of sins; it is also the victory, vindication and glory of those who fear the name of God (see also Isa 51:6-7; 62:1-2). This sun will not burn but will bring physical and spiritual healing for the righteous (see Ps 107:20) as they walk in the blessed light of eternity (see also Isa 50:10; 60:20; Rev 21:23-24). Their joy will be like that of calves when they are set free from their confining stalls (**4:2b**; see also Mic 2:12-13).

In our present sufferings, we can wait with anticipation for God to bring light and healing. The rising of the 'sun of righteousness' will mark the start of a whole new day for God's people.

4:1, 3 The destiny of the ungodly

As *surely* as the righteous can expect to rejoice, so the ungodly can expect to experience the day of the Lord as a terrible day of judgment (**4:1a**). This day is repeatedly foretold in the OT (see Isa 13:6; 30:27; Jer 21:14; 46:10; Ezek 30:3; Zeph 1:7-18; 3:8). It will be a day when *all the arrogant and every evildoer* will be burned up like *stubble* or chaff in the *furnace* or oven of God's wrath (**4:1b**; see also Ps 21:9; Isa 5:24; Obad 15, 18; Rom 2:5; 2 Pet 3:7, 10; Rev 16:14). The phrase *not a root or a branch will be left* indicates that the destruction will be complete (**4:1c**; see also Amos 2:9; 2 Thess 1:6-9).

The ungodly who prospered in Malachi's day will not be envied on that day of judgment. Then they will be helpless and will be trampled underfoot like ashes (**4:3**; see also 2 Sam 22:43; Isa 63:1-6; Mic 7:10; Rom 16:20; 1 Cor 6:2).

Which group are you in – the group that God has marked as his treasured possession, or the group he has marked for destruction?

4:4-6 The law and prophets as guides

The only way to avoid the coming judgment is to take God's law and his messages through the prophets as guides. The law was given to Moses at Mount Horeb (another name for Mount Sinai) (**4:4**) and reflects God's moral character. It applies to all generations, for Jesus made it clear that every word of the law is important and will be fulfilled (Matt 5:17-18; Rom 3:31). If God's people do not obey God's law, then they will suffer judgment.

Malachi closes his book with a prediction that Elijah will come and prepare God's people for the *great and dreadful day of the Lord* (**4:5b**). Elijah was one of the greatest prophets in the OT and here he represents all the other prophets and their teachings, just as he does on the Mount of Transfiguration (Matt 17:3). Just as God promised to send his messenger as the forerunner of the Messiah (3:1), so here he promises to send Elijah before the coming of the Messiah (**4:5a**). John the Baptist came 'in the spirit and power of Elijah' (Luke 1:17; see also Matt 17:10-11; Mark 9:11-12) as a forerunner of Jesus Christ and courageously and uncompromisingly denounced sin and urged people to repent. There also appears to be an intimation that Elijah will return before the day of the Lord to restore all things. He can be identified as one of two witnesses described in Revelation 11:3-12 because one of the miracles described in Revelation 11:6 is identical to Elijah's miracle (see also 1 Kgs 17:1; Jas 5:17). The other of the two witnesses may well be Moses.

Elijah's ministry will prepare God's people for the coming judgment and turn the hearts of fathers and of their children first to the Lord and then to one another (**4:6a**). People need to be reconciled to God before they are reconciled to one another. Elijah's mission will bring peace and unity within families. This was also a part of the ministry of John the Baptist (Luke 1:16-17).

If the people refuse to turn to God, he will *strike the land with a curse* (**4:6b**). The word translated 'curse' refers to the practice of devoting certain things or people to the Lord, often by means of total destruction (as in Josh 6:21). It implies that at the second coming of Christ, God will completely destroy those who reject him, but he will shower his blessings on those who repent and accept Christ (see also John 1:11-13).

We are prone to the same sins as the people in Malachi's day. But God's unchanging love still calls us to repentance and offers us salvation. The central theme of both the OT and the NT is redemption. Those who love God and are committed to him will be ushered into God's presence in eternity on the day of the Lord. But those who refuse to turn from their sins and to God will be destroyed.

Yoilah Yilpet

Further Reading

Baldwin, Joyce G. *Haggai, Zechariah and Malachi*. TOT. Downers Grove, Ill.: Inter-Varsity Press, 1981.

Feinberg, Charles. *The Minor Prophets*. Repr. Chicago: Moody, 1990.

Kaiser, Walter C. Jr. *Micah, Nahum, Habakkuk, Zephaniah, Haggai, Zechariah, Malachi*. PC. Nashville: Nelson Reference, 2002.

THE INTERTESTAMENTAL PERIOD

The intertestamental period covers some 450 years between the writing of the last book of the Old Testament (Malachi in 435 BC) and the writing of the earliest book of the New Testament in about AD 45. (Some would argue that the period ends with the appearance of John the Baptist in about AD 30, or with the birth of Christ.)

Among the religious groups to emerge during this period were the Pharisees, whose key characteristic was strict adherence to the law. They awaited the Messiah whose coming would usher in the resurrection of the dead and the kingdom of God. By contrast, the Sadducees enjoyed their status as priests in the temple and were not particularly interested in the Messiah. Their political power at times led them to compromise in regard to the law. They did not believe in the resurrection of the dead (Matt 22:23). The Essenes seem to have practised asceticism and monasticism. John the Baptist's lifestyle (Mark 1:4-6) may indicate that he was associated with this group. The Qumran community (who may also have been Essenes) saw themselves as the defenders of Yahweh's cause in the last days. The Zealots were a group whose zeal for the law ultimately led them into a war against anything associated with Rome that resulted in the destruction of Jerusalem in AD 70.

During the intertestamental period the Jews were subject to the Persian, Greek and Roman empires. The Greeks under Alexander the Great spread Greek culture through most of the then known world. One of Alexander's successors, Antiochus Epiphanes, severely persecuted the Jews. His desecration of the temple in 167 BC roused the Jews to fight against the enemies of Jehovah. Though they were divided into different religious parties, they rallied under the Maccabees to fight a common enemy. Their behaviour contrasts with that in Africa, where ideological or political party divisions are allowed to stand in the way of efforts to address such challenges as HIV/AIDS, poverty, wars and famines.

The Jews' refusal to despair despite threats and severe persecution is also a model for African believers. They saw their troubles as a passing cloud, beyond which lay the coming of the Messiah who would gather them together and lead them to victory against all their enemies.

During this period seventy scholars translated the OT into Greek. Although some sections were very freely translated, this Septuagint translation (*septuaginta* means 'seventy' in Latin) is still a valuable tool for reconstructing and interpreting difficult or damaged sections of the OT text.

This period also saw the production of the fourteen books of the Apocrypha, a name derived from the Greek word meaning 'hidden' or 'spurious' and referring to the doubt about whether these books are truly part of Scripture. These books throw light on events at the time of the Maccabees and on the religious beliefs of the time. A number of other books known as pseudepigrapha (meaning 'false titles') were also produced. It is claimed that these books have been written by famous characters in the Bible but they were actually written between 250 BC and AD 200.

The Dead Sea Scrolls, which are the remains of the library of the Qumran community, date from roughly 250 BC to AD 68. The some 870 scrolls have made an important contribution to the study of the OT text and of the background of the NT. They show that the Gospel of John is not a Greek book written more than a century after Jesus died, as some scholars have suggested, but fits in with Jewish thought. The scrolls have also helped with the dating of the Pastoral Epistles by showing that as early as AD 68 Qumran had an organizational structure in which an overseer ruled over elders.

The writings of the period show that the name of God was highly honoured. Anyone speaking his name aloud in Qumran was expelled from the community, and the writer of 1 Maccabees makes a deliberate effort not to mention God's name.

The Jews at the time also believed in a hierarchy of evil in the spirit world, headed by a prince of evil called by various names including Masteba, Belial (2 Cor 6:15) and Sammael. These names (along with Beelzebub – Matt 10:25; 12:24, 27) are interchangeable with the term Satan. This evil system was opposed by angels with names such as Uriel, Raphael, Michael and Gabriel, who took an active role in people's lives.

The profound belief that obedience to the Law, and specifically to the regulations concerning the Sabbath, was the way to find favour with God meant that the study of the Law enjoyed the highest priority in this period.

Samuel Ngewa

THE NEW TESTAMENT

THE NEW TESTAMENT

PRINCIPLES OF INTERPRETATION

For communication to be effective, the speaker must not only express his or her thoughts well, but the hearer must also interpret what is said correctly. This is particularly important when reading the Bible. God uses the Bible to communicate his thoughts to us, and we need to take care that we interpret his words correctly. Over the years, believers have developed certain guidelines that can help us to do this.

The first thing we need to remember is that although the Bible comes from God and therefore contains no errors (2 Tim 3:16; 2 Pet 1:21), God used human beings as his scribes. These people had different writing styles and temperaments. Each writer remained himself even as the Holy Spirit watched over what he wrote. And the writers used the everyday language that was spoken around them, not a 'holy language' that was specially given by God. Like them, we will all preach God's word in different ways, but we must also all work to communicate it in the everyday language of the people around us so that they can clearly understand God's message.

Questions of Culture

God directed his words to particular people in particular historical and cultural situations. We see this in the historical books, but also in Paul's instructions that we should lift up our hands in prayer (1 Tim 2:8) and that women should cover their heads (1 Cor 11:5-6). In the culture to which Paul was writing, these actions had specific meanings and communicated specific messages. If we insist on behaviour that was appropriate in ancient Greece when preaching on these passages in Africa, we may not be communicating the correct message.

Another way of putting this is to say that we must be sensitive to the difference between absolute instructions and those that are culturally dictated. While there is disagreement about how to interpret such passages as 2 Timothy 2:12, 'I do not permit a woman to teach or have authority over a man; she is to be silent', there is no doubt that the instruction was given in the context of Ephesian culture. Being sensitive to such matters will make one both effective and wise in applying such verses to today's situations.

Because the Bible was written to particular people in particular situations, we need to know as much about these situations as possible if we are to understand the message that the author of a specific passage intended to communicate to his original readers. This is not easy to do because thousands of years separate us from those original readers. So it is important to try to find out as much as possible from faithful people who have studied the past and written books to help us understand it.

Styles of Writing

Not only did the authors of the Bible write at different times, but they also produced different types of writing. Some wrote histories, others taught doctrine, and still others wrote poetry. Those who wrote of the last things, like the authors of Daniel 7-12 and Revelation, often wrote in a special, highly symbolic style that is known as apocalyptic style.

We need to remember that while some things in the Bible are meant to be taken literally, others are meant to be symbolic. We need to read each passage in the Scriptures in the way the author intended it to be read. For example, with a story about historical events, it is probably right to read a long passage and look for a single moral lesson. But when we are reading one of Paul's letters, we may need to pay attention to the theological meaning of individual words and phrases. Similarly, if we are reading a historical section, we will think of Babylon as the capital of the ancient Babylonian empire, but in the book of Revelation, Babylon may represent an enemy of God or of his people.

While thinking of what type of passage we are reading, we also need to remember what we will not find in the Bible. The Bible is not a scientific textbook, or a textbook on geography, astronomy, politics or any of the other subjects that interest us. It is a revelation of God's way of redemption, how that was achieved, and what we need to do about it. Everything else is secondary to this main focus. Thus when the Bible speaks of the sun setting and rising, it is not claiming to make a scientific statement. Rather, it is speaking in terms that its original readers will understand so that they are not distracted by other things but can focus on the central teaching on the subject of salvation.

Direction or Description

We also need to remember that sometimes the Bible commands things and sometimes it merely describes them. We are not expected to imitate all the behaviour described in the Bible. Some of the behaviour is clearly wrong, but the Bible simply reports what happened. We are not even expected to do everything that the men and women of God in the Bible did. When events are described, we are often expected merely to learn a principle, not to imitate the action. For example, the account of Elisha restoring life to the Shunammite's son by lying on him (2 Kgs 4:34) is not an instruction manual on how to restore the dead to life. It is teaching the principle that our God is able to do great things through his servants.

Although the Bible is a unit, it is divided into two sections, the Old Testament and the New Testament. God never changes, but the way he interacts with human beings varies depending on how much they know about him at the time.

The way people behave is also influenced by how much they know about God. Thus in the OT we find passages like Psalm 3:7, which asks God to 'strike all my enemies on the jaw; break the teeth of the wicked'. With Christ's coming, God taught us more about grace and forgiveness, and those attitudes should now govern our behaviour. Similarly, Christ's resurrection and the victory over death that he offers to believers gives a new perspective on miracles. Pastors may not be expected to raise the dead today, but they must proclaim the message that death has been overcome once and for all.

The previous paragraph stressed that we must interpret passages depending on their context, that is, whether they were in the OT or the NT. But this principle has an even broader application. We need to read every passage in the Bible both it terms of its immediate context (the words surrounding it) and in terms of the teaching of the entire Bible. If we do this, we will avoid making mistakes such as assuming that the words 'ask and it will be given to you' (Matt 7:7) are an open-ended promise.

One way of keeping our focus on the context of what we are reading is to ask questions such as Who said it? To whom? In what circumstances? What conditions are given or implied? Where possible, we should prefer the simple and obvious meaning of a word, rather than attempting to find some obscure meaning in order to give the impression that we are learned and original.

Impact of Information

Pride is dangerous when interpreting the Bible. We need to be willing to listen to other peoples' interpretations. Just as iron sharpens iron, so hearing what others have to say about a passage will help to sharpen our own thinking. It is encouraging when others agree with what we think. When they disagree, we are challenged to look carefully at what we believe, and can then either reaffirm or modify our views.

We need to listen carefully to the interpretations of our friends and pastors, but they are not our only source of help. The interpretation of the Bible is as old as the Bible itself. Even as the NT writers wrote, they interpreted the OT. There are dozens of commentaries on every single book in the Bible. While such commentaries can be wrong, they, too, are tools to sharpen our understanding.

Finally, it is vitally important to remember that the information in the Bible is not intended merely to feed the mind but also to transform the heart. While we need to try to understand the meaning the author intended to communicate to the original readers, our ultimate goal is to see how a passage applies today. Every passage of Scripture must therefore be applied correctly (in terms of meaning) and relevantly (in terms of the needs of today's hearers).

Study of the Bible should not produce believers who are excited but ignorant, nor believers who are knowledgeable but whose hearts are cold. It should produce believers who have been fed a nourishing and well-balanced spiritual diet and who are thus fit spiritually, intellectually and emotionally. Such believers can carry God's word to others.

Samuel Ngewa

MATTHEW

The four gospels tell the story of Jesus' life on earth. Early Christians had to create a new kind of literature to tell this story. This kind of literature is called a gospel. The first three gospels are very similar and contain a lot of common material. They are therefore known as the Synoptic Gospels, as they can be seen together (synoptically). The differences between the four gospels reflect the different perspectives of the four evangelists and their different readerships. Matthew is concerned with Jesus' teaching and his Jewish background. Mark presents Jesus as the servant of God. Luke concentrates on the human side of Jesus and John gives us a picture of the divine Jesus. Together these four writers present us with a fuller picture of who Jesus is than any single writer could.

All four spend a large part of their books on the events in the last week of Jesus' life. His death, burial, resurrection and ascension were obviously the most important part of his mission on earth.

Date and Authorship

Matthew's Gospel was probably written before the destruction of the temple in AD 70. Matthew was an eyewitness of many of the events he records. He was a tax collector before he was called by Jesus and had scribal skills and knowledge of Judaism. He wrote for a Jewish-Christian readership and wanted to emphasize Jesus' Jewish heritage and to demonstrate how Jesus fulfils the OT prophecies of the Messiah.

Structure of the Gospel of Matthew

Matthew's Gospel is a teaching gospel, containing five great blocks of teaching divided by narratives about Jesus' ministry activities. Some scholars attach significance to the fact that there are five books of Moses and here we have five blocks of teaching. The blocks are the Sermon on the Mount (5:1-7:29), the mission of the Twelve (9:35-10:42), the parables of the kingdom (13:1-52), the community of the kingdom (18:1-35), and finally the woes of legalistic religion and the signs of the end (23:1-26:25).

Lessons for Africa from Matthew's Gospel

Matthew's Gospel has many lessons to teach Africa today:
- **Leadership:** Matthew presents Jesus as the perfect teacher and leader. Those who seek to follow him must place the needs of those they lead before their own. In the church, leadership must be characterized by service.

- **Mission:** Matthew stresses the importance of the Christian mission that Jesus began. Jesus calls the African church to reach out with his love to the peoples of Africa and all the peoples of the world. African churches must learn to be more active in mission and cease to be merely passive receivers of the gospel.
- **Living in community:** Matthew shows us how we should live with one another. Jesus' followers are all equal before him, and Africans must learn to abandon their concern for titles and status. The poor, the disabled, the downtrodden, refugees and those with HIV/AIDS are all our brothers and sisters in Christ. Humility is the basis of proper relations within the church.
- **Christian values:** If the African church is going to successfully challenge corruption, fatalism, laziness, tribalism, disunity and ungodly cultural and religious practices, then it must show a radical commitment to the truth of Jesus reflected in patterns of thought, work and lifestyle that are clearly different from what we are accustomed to.
- **Cost of discipleship:** Matthew teaches that following Jesus can sometimes lead to suffering. The so-called prosperity gospel has captured the imagination of many people in the African church over the last two decades. However, any preaching of the gospel that denies that Jesus' disciples will suffer is deficient.

Outline of Contents

COMMENTARY

1:1-4:11 The Beginning

1:1-17 Jesus' Ancestors

The Gospel of Matthew begins with *a record of the genealogy of Jesus Christ* (**1:1**). A genealogy is a list of a person's ancestors or descendants. The importance of such a record is clear if we consider the role genealogies have come to play in the politics of Africa. For example, since 1991 all Zambian presidential candidates have had to be able to trace their genealogy back through at least two generations living in Zambia. This rule was originally introduced to bar the autocratic Kenneth Kaunda, the first president of Zambia (1964–1991), from ever holding that office again, because his parents had emigrated to north-eastern Zambia from Malawi. Although originally aimed at one man and his political aspirations, this provision now affects perhaps a third of the present generation of Zambians, and may yet rise to haunt the nation in some civil unrest. This is because Zambia was created by bringing previously distinct groups together in a nation-state during the nineteenth-century scramble for Africa.

Genealogies were also exceedingly important for locating a person within Jewish society. Thus people in the Bible are often introduced with a formula such as that used for Samuel's father: 'Elkanah son of Jeroham, the son of Elihu, the son of Tohu, the son of Zuph, an Ephraimite' (1 Sam 1:1). Such formulas were particularly important in establishing a claim to membership in Israel, or to the right to perform one of the special functions carried out by the people of God. For example, in the sixth century BC, the children of Hobaiah,

Hakkoz and Barzillai 'were excluded from the priesthood as unclean' because they could not prove the purity of their pedigree from family records (Ezra 2:61-62). Herod the Great also resented the fact that, although he was king, his name was not included in the official genealogies of Israel because he was half-Jewish and half-Edomite. He ordered the destruction of the records, so that no one could claim a purer lineage than his own or dispute his claim to the throne of Judah.

Whereas other long genealogies in the Bible consist of a list of the person's descendants (see Gen 5:1-32; 10:1-7, 13-18, 21-26, 32), in Matthew's Gospel we have a list of Jesus' ancestors. Matthew is making the point that the history of Israel and the lives of individuals like Abraham and David make sense only in the light of Jesus and his life. That is why Matthew's list begins with Abraham (**1:2**), and not with Adam, as Luke's genealogy of Jesus does (Luke 3:23-38). Jesus is the heir to God's promises to Abraham to bring blessings to all the peoples of the world (Gen 12:1-3). Matthew wants to make it clear from the very beginning that Jesus' vocation is related to God's intervention in the affairs of all human beings. The blessings of God, the provisions he makes for the flourishing of humanity, were promised through Abraham. The people of Israel, the descendants of Abraham, had sought to fulfil this mandate. Jesus Christ, the son of Abraham, comes to bring to completion that which his illustrious ancestor had begun.

The other differences between Matthew's genealogy of Jesus and that of Luke can also be explained in light of the particular intentions that each writer had when selecting which material to include in his gospel.

Matthew organizes his list into three groups of fourteen (note that the last group is actually only thirteen names – indicating that Matthew did not create new material in order to fulfil his desire for symmetry). He did, however, drop names or telescope the lists in order to achieve the desired number of generations, fourteen. Thus his list is not chronologically perfect. For instance, in the five centuries between Zerubbabel and Joseph, Matthew has nine names compared to Luke's eighteen.

Matthew's focus on the number fourteen obviously helps the memory, but that is not his sole purpose for dividing the genealogy like this. He is probably also making use of *gematria*, that is, the practice of giving a numerical value to Hebrew names and words and then deriving significance from this number. Since Hebrew did not have a separate set of numerals, each letter of the Hebrew alphabet also stood for a number. In English this would be A = 1, B = 2 and so on. In Hebrew, adding the numbers associated with the letters in the name 'David' gives a total of fourteen. Seven is the number of perfection, and two sevens signify total perfection. This obviously helps the memory, but more than that it indicates that Matthew saw in Jesus the Messiah,

the perfect one, the royal son of David, the rightful heir to the throne of Israel and the king of the Jews (27:11, 37; 1 Chr 17:11-2). In Jesus, the time of preparation has found its intended goal as indicated by the artificial unifying of all of Israel's history in this three-fold division.

Matthew's inclusion of five women is interesting. For a start, women were not usually included in genealogies, as they had no independent legal status. Moreover, Matthew has chosen to include some unexpected names. *Tamar* (**1:3**) was a woman who had to prostitute herself in order to force Judah, her father-in-law, to fulfil his legal obligation to arrange her marriage to his son Shelah (Gen 38:11-30). *Rahab* (**1:5a**) was a prostitute from the besieged Canaanite city of Jericho who helped the Israelite spies (Josh 2:1, 4-9). *Ruth* (**1:5b**) was also a Gentile from Moab (Ruth 1:4). *Uriah's wife* (**1:6**) was Bathsheba. She was most probably a Jewish woman, the daughter of Ammiel (1 Chr 3:5), but her husband Uriah was a Gentile, thus making her a Gentile at the time she committed adultery with King David before marrying him (2 Sam 11:3).

Matthew deliberately ignored other important ot women such as Sarah, Rebecca, Leah, Rachel, Deborah and Hannah. He did so in order to point to the universal application of the gospel even in the history of the people of Israel. The ancestry of none other than the perfect one of God included marginalized and despised Gentiles. In Jesus the normal human barriers are down: prostitutes and Gentiles are welcome, despised women are received with respect, both sinners and saints are drawn to him. The gospel that Matthew announces is truly wonderful!

1:18-25 The Birth of Jesus

The relationships in this passage may prove difficult to understand without some knowledge of the traditions surrounding the conduct of marriages in societies like Israel's 2000 years ago. They were similar to the traditions in many African societies today.

Traditionally in some African communities, a young man wishing to get married will initially approach his parents and signal his intention. He may already have identified a young woman, or he may ask his parents to choose a suitable life companion for him. The parents will then appoint a trusted friend or relative to act as a 'go-between'. This person will visit the parents of the chosen young woman to inform them of the young man's intentions. The news may or may not come as a surprise to the girl's parents. They will then seek to find out whether the young woman is willing to accept the proposal, and will investigate the history of the young man's family. If all parties are satisfied, they will give their consent to the marriage.

The go-between will offer a small amount of money, which, if accepted, will signal the goodwill of the young woman's family. The act of accepting the money is in itself the official engagement. This may or may not be followed by a Western-style engagement party, complete with rings. From then on, the young woman's family is not at liberty to entertain any other suitors unless they break the engagement by returning the money they have accepted. The go-between will be informed of the dowry, which the young man must pay. This must be paid in full before wedding arrangements can proceed. However, at the discretion of the young woman's family, permission may be granted to proceed with wedding arrangements after a certain amount has been paid.

In Israel, there were three stages to getting married. There was the engagement, often arranged while the couple concerned were still children. This was followed by the betrothal, a confirmation of the engagement. During the twelve-month period of betrothal, the couple enjoyed the status of marriage without the rights of marriage. They might or might not be allowed any periods alone together. Breaking a betrothal was a serious business and was considered a divorce. The Bemba say *Nkobekela: te cupo* ['an engagement is not a marriage'], but the Israelites would have insisted that *Nkobekela: cupo* ['betrothal is marriage'].

At the wedding, full rights of marriage were conferred upon the couple, and from then on they would be free to consummate their marriage in sexual intercourse. If a young betrothed woman was found to be pregnant and her suitor was not responsible, as was the case with Mary (1:18), she would be publicly shamed and executed by stoning (Deut 22: 23-24). But in Joseph's time, execution was the prerogative of the Romans and would, therefore, not be an easy option.

We know very little about Joseph, and he drops out of the gospel narratives very quickly. We can assume that he was a young man between the ages of 18 and 20. If, as many assume, he came from Galilee, custom there, unlike in Judea, frowned on betrothed men and women spending any time together in private. Joseph's knowledge of Mary would therefore have been based almost solely on the testimony of their families and Mary's own reputation. He lived in a male-dominated, honour-centred culture where wounded honour had to be avenged in a public way.

What does Matthew mean when he describes Joseph as *a righteous man* (1:19)? 'Righteous' can have at least two meanings. There is the strictly Christian sense, in which it is used of a person who by faith in Jesus has found acceptance with God and been declared righteous (Rom 1:17; 3:22). This is obviously not the sense in which it is applied here. The word can also be used with an ethical and moral dimension, in which case it means 'just, honest, good, and conforming to the laws of God and man'. What evidence do we see of Joseph's righteousness in this passage?

First, we see that Joseph exercised uncommon self-restraint in sexual matters. He did not have intercourse with Mary before they were engaged, during their twelve-month period of betrothal, or up to and after the birth of the baby Jesus (1:25). His self-discipline compares with that of another young man called Joseph in the house of Potiphar in Egypt (Gen 39:7-10). Matthew's words about Joseph's behaviour also emphasize the agency of the Holy Spirit in creating a body for the Messiah. There was no human agency in his conception (1:18, 20).

Joseph's righteousness is also evidenced by his decision to divorce his wife quietly or secretly. He would not derive any pleasure in seeing the woman he loved publicly disgraced. Under these difficult circumstances, a divorce was a relatively easy way out, and would be sanctioned by both Roman and Jewish law. A decision to divorce would be more difficult and unpleasant because the husband, quite apart from personal hurt, would be putting his reputation at stake. He could be accused of violating the law, indiscipline, exploiting his wife as a prostitute, bringing reproach on his family, or impotence. However, if he divorced her quietly he would also suffer economic loss, for he would not be able to demand the dowry back. Negotiations for the return of the dowry would inevitably involve the help of village elders, thus making the matter public.

A divorce routinely involved a simple document, called a 'bill of divorce', and two witnesses. It could therefore be carried out with minimum publicity. Joseph was prepared to lose his honour, reputation and some economic benefit, in order to minimize the suffering of another person, even if that person had hurt him through sexual betrayal. In his mind, justice and mercy went together.

Joseph's righteousness is also demonstrated in his taking God at his word (1:24). An *angel of the Lord* appeared to him in a dream telling him, *'take Mary home as your wife'* (1:20). Dreams were recognized as a channel of revelation in the OT (Gen 37:5-11; Dan 1:17; 2:19-45). Even today, dreams can have a powerful influence upon people in certain cultures. Many a Zambian child's name is determined by the repeated appearance of a particular ancestor in dreams during the latter stages of pregnancy. Many African Christians come to know Christ through dreams. Undoubtedly, in our day, the influence of dreams must not be set above the word of God for revelation and conduct. Even in Joseph's dream this connection between word and dream was very clear in that the angel of the Lord made direct reference to a text of Scripture (1:23; see also Isa 7:14).

So Joseph married Mary and became the legal adoptive father of Jesus. Since Joseph was a descendant of David, Jesus legally became a descendant of Israel's greatest king. God's will and the obedience of his people have great power in changing the course of individual lives and indeed the history of the world.

Joseph was truly a righteous young man. In his character we see a perfect combination of a sense of right and wrong, self-discipline and restraint, justice tempered with mercy, and obedience to the word of God. What a remarkable challenge to any young person in their late teens! It is a pity that our general understanding of faith in the first century is heavily coloured by Jesus' quarrels with the Pharisees. We do not see enough of the simple but principled and devout ordinary men and women of Israel.

In this chapter, Matthew uses three titles to spell out Jesus' vocation: *Jesus, Christ* and *Immanuel* (1:18, 23).

- *Jesus* is the Greek rendering of a common Jewish name, Joshua. It means 'God is salvation' and Jesus' work would be to save *his people from their sins* (**1:21**). The heart of the message of Christianity is God's provision for dealing with human sin. Sin is not just individual acts of deceit, immorality and so on, nor is it the sum total of all such acts. Sin also includes a natural tendency to rebel against the will of God. This rebellion separates humans from God (Isa 59:2; Rom 3:23; 6:23; Eph 2:1-3) and lies at the heart of all social misconduct and conflict. Jesus came into the world to liberate humans from sin and from the consequent wrath of God, whose very nature is opposed to sin in every form (see Hab 1:13).
- *Christ* is the Greek rendering of the Hebrew word *messiah,* meaning 'someone who has been anointed for a specific task'. Matthew uses this title four times in the first eighteen verses of this gospel (1:1, 16, 17, 18), which suggests that it is the title he has chosen to designate Jesus and his mission. Jesus embodies the fulfilment of Jewish expectations of the coming of one appointed by God to deliver his people from their enemies and to extend God's blessings to the Gentiles.
- *Immanuel* is a Hebrew word meaning *God with us* (**1:23**; see also Isa 7:14). It does not seem to have been used of Jesus as a name, but Matthew uses it to indicate that Jesus is no less than God himself. God does not assign the ministry of saving his people from sin to someone else, but carries it out himself.

In this first chapter of Matthew, Jesus Christ is thus introduced as belonging to the people of God, the Jews, by virtue of his genealogy and link to Abraham. He belongs to the royal lineage of David, and is therefore the royal Messiah, and he is God in person dealing with the most difficult human problem, the question of sin. His birth was supernatural in origin, although like all God's miracles it was not a curiosity but conformed to nature. He is the Messiah for all humanity, because even in his Jewishness, some of his ancestors were Gentiles. The gospel has universal appeal.

2:1-11 The Arrival of the Magi

Matthew next presents three types of people and their reactions to the news of the birth of Jesus, who is described as the king of the Jews. There is King Herod, the current ruler of the Jews (2:3, 7-8); there are the chief priests and teachers of the law (2:4-6); and there are the group of foreign visitors normally called the Magi, or wise men (2:1, 7, 9-12). Evidently, and perhaps surprisingly, we are meant to identify with the Magi, a group of foreigners, rather than with the mainly Jewish establishment of King Herod and the religious leaders. This is all the more surprising, considering that Matthew was a Jew and his original readers were mostly Jewish.

2:1-2 Jesus Christ, the King of the Jews

Wise men, or Magi, were an important part of most imperial administrations in the ancient Near East (**2:1**). In Persia, where this particular group most likely came from, they were a priestly class, with expertise in astrology, magic and divination (see Dan 2:2), and sometimes their predictions were correct. Many Jews, although officially opposed to astrology and magic, recognized that these forces were very influential, as indeed they still are in our own world.

These wise men are here presented in a good light and we are encouraged to identify with them. This may seem odd to us, for the Bible is very clear in its condemnation of the practice of magic and divination (Deut 4:19; 18:9-14; Isa 47:11-14). It also stresses the religious impotence of such activities in the face of the fullness of the revelation of Christ (Col 2:16-19). But Matthew is not condoning horoscopes as a normal way of seeking God's guidance. Rather, what this passage shows is that God will reveal himself wherever people are looking for him. Many Muslims have become Christians because they had a dream, often while at prayer, in which they were directed by Allah to seek out Christians so they could be led to Christ and his word. Moreover, the Magi needed to have their revelations confirmed by the revealed word of God, which only the Jews had. We may infer that any extra revelations in the form of words, pictures, dreams, visions and prophecies are only partial and must all conform to the revealed word of God as contained in the OT and the NT. So what this passage is saying is that God reserves the right to reveal himself wherever he chooses. People may find him as they search for him in the Koran, in horoscopes, in ancestral worship and so on, but their initial revelation of him must find confirmation in the true revelation of the written word of God and his Living Word—Jesus Christ, the Saviour.

The arrival of a party of what are traditionally said to be three Magi, accompanied no doubt by their attendants and a caravan of animals, would have been impressive and would likely have caused a stir in Jerusalem.

It was not unusual for Magi to visit foreign lands, especially at the birth or crowning of a king, and it was natural for them to assume that if a king had been born, he would be found in the king's palace. So they went to Herod and asked to see *the king of the Jews* (**2:2**). This title appears only in the Gospels, and it applies only to Jesus. It is not a political title, for Jesus neither sought nor accepted political office within the Jewish establishment of his day. He did not challenge Herod or Caesar in their political careers. 'King of the Jews' in relation to Jesus has strictly messianic connotations. It goes back to a covenant God made with David (2 Sam 7:10-16). At that time God promised that he would raise up a king who would occupy David's throne in an eternal kingdom. This passage was given a messianic interpretation from early on (Heb 1:5). Eventually the title would find its climax in Revelation 19:16, where Jesus is hailed as 'KING OF KINGS AND LORD OF LORDS'.

When Herod and the chief priests learned that 'the king of the Jews' had been born, they knew that this was *the Christ,* the one promised by the prophets to be God's Messiah (**2:4-5**). He would sit on the throne of his father David, and the sleepy little town of Bethlehem would be raised to great heights of glory, as the prophet Micah had said (**2:6**; Mic 5:2). How then do people respond to this king of the Jews who will one day be acknowledged as the King of Kings and Lord of Lords?

2:3, 7-8 The hatred of Herod

Herod was not a Jew; he was a native of Idumea (formerly known as Edom). He was a shrewd politician who had managed to convince the Romans to make him king over Galilee in 47 BC. Seven years later, he had added Judea to his realm. To make himself and especially his descendants more acceptable to the Jewish people, he married the daughter of a Jewish high priest and built the Jerusalem temple as a gift to the nation.

Herod is said to have been *disturbed* by the arrival of the Magi and their news (**2:3**), which was confirmed by the prophetic word (2:6). He immediately began to prepare to eliminate such unwanted competition. So he discreetly gathered information from the Magi that would help him to estimate the age of the child (**2:7**). For all his smooth words, his hope was that they would help him identify the child so he could eliminate him (**2:8**).

2:4-6 The indifference of the religious leaders

The chief priests were the custodians of the word of God. They were the trained theologians of the day. They knew exactly what Scripture said about every subject. Their training was indeed thorough. Starting as early as five years old, they followed the most learned rabbis, until they were about thirty years old, when they would be recognized as rabbis in their own right and were qualified to train disciples. Although these experts knew what Scripture said and were able to guide the Magi to Bethlehem (2:5-6), they themselves did not bother to follow them to worship Jesus. That is why John said, 'He came to that which was his own, but his own did not receive him' (John 1:11).

The successors of these experts would be at odds with the adult Jesus, and in the end they would conspire to put him to death. The most knowledgeable church people often include those who take Jesus for granted. It is a dangerous situation to be in. It is no less a sin than the outright hatred of Herod, for in the end it leads to the same destiny (where Herod failed to kill the baby Jesus, the chief priests succeeded). Our pride in our knowledge of Christ, the Bible and the church may turn out to be a snare in the end.

2:9-11 The worship of the Magi

The worship of the Magi when they found the baby Jesus was characterized by three features: first, joy (**2:10**), such as we see in the OT when kings ascended to their thrones (Solomon – 1 Kgs 1:40; Joash – 2 Kgs 11:20); second, humility as they bowed down before the baby, aware that he was a great king (**2:11a**); and third, presentation of some of the costliest gifts of the day: *gold, incense* and *myrrh* (**2:11b**; see also Rev 18:13). Worship is the only fitting response to God's revelation, and it should be characterized by joy and lavish gifts to him.

This passage makes it clear that the worship that Jesus would later receive from the Gentiles was anticipated and approved of. The nations will bring their offerings to him.

Essentially there are only two possible attitudes to Jesus. You can respond to him either with love and devotion or with contempt, hatred and rejection. The latter response leads to attempts to destroy him. No one can be indifferent or sit on the fence. All those who appear to sit on the fence will some day fall into one camp or another. All those who, unlike the Magi, reject the Messiah instead of worshipping him will ultimately seek his death and the deaths of those who follow him. Herod is not alone in rejecting the Christ child and seeking his death. The Sanhedrin, too, rejected Jesus and sought his death. Events in Ethiopia in the 1970s clearly showed that when Mengistu's communist regime rejected the Lord, they persecuted his followers.

2:12-23 Escape to Egypt and Return to Nazareth

The OT records several attempts to thwart the plans of God for harmonious co-existence between himself and the people he has made.

- In Eden, Satan tried to bring enmity between God and his creatures Adam and Eve by deceiving them into disobeying the expressed will of God (Gen 3:1-7). Their act of disobedience led to their expulsion from the Garden of Eden. Fellowship with God was broken and their capacity to freely interact with him was impaired. Sin entered human experience and human nature through that one act of rebellion (see Rom 5:18-19).
- In Egypt, the Egyptians attempted to wipe out the nation of Israel, by killing all the male children born to Israelites (Exod 1:22). If this policy has been allowed to

continue for thirty years or so, there would have been no men to continue the nation of Israel, and therefore God's chosen path for the coming of the Messiah into the world would have been cut off. But God intervened by miraculously saving Moses (and many others).

- In the book of Esther, we learn how Haman sought to destroy all the Jews in the world because Mordecai refused to bow down to him. If he had succeeded, the path of the coming Messiah would have been cut off. But God intervened and overthrew Haman's plans.

Now, in the NT, Satan tries again to thwart God's plan, using Herod as his tool. But his scheme is thwarted when the Magi listen to God's warning and do not reveal the whereabouts of the Messiah to Herod (**2:12**). Satan would try again later when he sought to persuade Jesus not to go to the cross (4:8). He thought that if Jesus avoided the cross not only would he be obeying Satan in much the same way as Adam and Eve had done, but also that human beings would remain under his command. Jesus went to the cross to destroy sin and free human beings from the tyranny of the world, sin and Satan.

2:13-15 A new exodus and a new salvation

The exodus from Egypt was a great act of salvation, and had a strong place in the memory of the Jewish nation. So Matthew introduces Jesus as the new Moses who comes to inaugurate a new era of God's salvation: the age of the Messiah. Matthew probably intends us to see parallels between Moses and Jesus. Both came from Egypt as great deliverers of their people, and both fled murderous rulers. God's people had been led down to Egypt by one Joseph; now another Joseph was to take God's son down to Egypt (**2:13-14**).

God's command to Joseph to take Jesus to Egypt is not surprising, for at that time Egypt had a large Jewish population, especially in Alexandria where the first Greek translation of the OT had been made two hundred years earlier. Moreover Egypt had always been a place of economic and political refuge for Israelites, including Abraham (Gen 12:10), Jacob (Gen 46:6), Jeroboam (1 Kgs 11:40), the remnant after the assassination of Gedaliah (2 Kgs 25:25-26) and the prophet Uriah (Jer 26:21).

Matthew quotes the prophet Hosea, *Out of Egypt have I called my son* (**2:15**; see also Hos 11:1). This verse is not prophetic in the sense that it predicted the future, but rather as an explanation of the origins of Israel. Just as Israel was God's son, so too is Jesus. Indeed, Jesus has come to fulfil in his person and vocation the calling of the whole nation. He is the true Israel who through the new exodus brings the new messianic age. He will save his people from the greater bondage to sin and Satan.

The fact that Jesus was a refugee on African soil should teach us many lessons. God was not ashamed to let his son become a refugee. By sharing the plight of stateless refugees,

Jesus honoured all those who suffer homelessness on account of war, famine, persecution or some other disaster. There are millions of refugees on the African continent and many of them have a terrible life. In Zambia there are three generations of Angolan refugees living in the Meheba Resettlement Scheme. Neither the Zambian nor the Angolan government is prepared to recognize them as citizens. The result is that these people are stateless and are condemned to live out their years as virtual prisoners on a piece of land in north-western Zambia.

The sad thing is that far too many Christians are either unconcerned or believe the lie that every refugee is a troublemaker. Yet the Bible is full of men and women who knew what it meant to be refugees: Abraham, Moses and Jacob, as well as the whole nation of Israel in Egypt and Babylonia. God not only identifies with those who are suffering this particular plight, but he also uses people from among the landless and stateless. We must not despise refugees or other marginalized people. The signs are already clear that Europe will most likely be saved from the logical fulfilment of humanistic secularism by the masses of downtrodden migrants from the developing world. In big cities like London, the majority of churchgoers are recent immigrants from the southern hemisphere. God defends the fatherless, the widow and the alien. Where are the people of God who demonstrate his compassion?

2:16-18 Another massacre

Just as Pharaoh had attempted to kill Moses along with all the other Israelite boys, so Herod attempted to kill Jesus along with all the young boys in Bethlehem when he realized that the Magi had not returned to give him information identifying the Christ child (**2:16**). Rulers, and this includes church leaders, are frightened by the prospect of opposition. They often use the power of their office to inflict cruel punishments on the opposition and on innocent people.

Although Herod was here acting as a tool of Satan, who sought to destroy the boy Jesus and thus put a stop to God's plans for the salvation of humanity, he was not a helpless tool. He was already a mass murderer. The first-century Jewish historian Josephus records that Herod had his own wife strangled, and executed at least three of his own sons, as well as several large groups of suspected conspirators. On his deathbed, he ordered the deaths of many nobles to ensure that people would weep at his funeral (the nobles were released, thus leading to a celebration instead of weeping). The murder of thirty to forty children is only one of many outrages in his murderous reign.

Matthew links the lamentation of the grieving mothers in Bethlehem to *Ramah* (**2:18a**), a place approximately six miles north of Jerusalem. After the fall of Jerusalem to the Babylonians, the captives had been held at Ramah before they were sent off on the 400-mile (600-km) journey into exile (Jer 40:1). Jeremiah says that Rachel, the mother of Joseph and Benjamin, wept as her descendants were led away from their land (Jer 31:15). Rachel was even more closely associated with Bethlehem, for she was buried there (Gen 35:19). It is no wonder that Matthew is reminded of *Rachel weeping for her children* (**2:18b**).

Yet the quotation from Jeremiah also offers hope following injustice and sorrow. The deportations to Babylon (Jer 31:15-17) would be followed by a new exodus and a new hope as the people returned to the Promised Land under Ezra and Nehemiah. Similarly, this suffering and the forced departure of Joseph, Mary and Jesus to Egypt would result in the safety of Jesus, the source of salvation and rejoicing for all who come to him.

2:19-23 Return to Nazareth

Jesus was born in 6 BC and Herod died about two years later in 4 BC (**2:19**). It was now safe for the exiles to return to Israel (**2:20**). However, the character of Herod's successor, *Archelaus*, was little better than that of his father. So Jesus' family did not return to Bethlehem, but to *Nazareth* (**2:21-23a**), where Joseph and Mary had lived before they went to Bethlehem to register under the census ordered by Caesar Augustus (see Luke 2:1-4).

The description of Jesus as *a Nazarene* (**2:23b**) may be a word play, referring to the Nazirites, a group of people dedicated to God (see Num 6:1-21). It may also be intended to show that Jesus came from an insignificant town full of Gentiles (see comment on 4:15). He was, therefore, not the royal Messiah many people expected, but a suffering one (see Isa 53; Ps 22).

Throughout this chapter, we have seen God actively involved in initiating the action. He directed the Magi and Joseph through dreams and visions (2:12, 13, 20, 22). The events that unfolded in response to these dreams and visions are consistent with Scripture, so there is continuity between the events Matthew records and the history of the people of God. The birth of Jesus and his whole life were ordered by God. The Gentile church must not forget that Israel of old is still part of the ultimate purpose of God.

We have also seen that God is not afraid to take risks. He trusted teenagers with his son. He did not shield his son from the ravages of political life. But in all these things his will was fulfilled. God may well be working out his purposes even in the seemingly insignificant acts of our lives.

3:1-12 John the Baptist: The Forerunner of Jesus

Matthew ignores thirty years of Jesus' life and focuses on the three critical years of his public ministry, which included teaching, healing, disciple-making and his death on the cross. The account of these years begins with Jesus' baptism by John.

All four gospels mention John and his ministry, and all four stress that his ministry is subordinate to that of Jesus (Mark 1:2-8; Luke 3:1-20; John 1:19-28). The fact that Matthew refers to him as *John the Baptist* (**3:1a**) may lead some to forget that his ministry involved more than baptizing. He came to call the nation of Israel to repentance in preparation for the coming of the Messiah and the age to come. He should really be called John, Jesus' forerunner, the preacher of the baptism of repentance for Israel!

This section of Matthew is full of allusions to the OT. One of these is the fact that John appeared in the *Desert of Judea* (**3:1b**). The nation of Israel had been formed in the desert under the leadership of Moses. Thus the exodus from Egypt and its association with the desert was so deeply ingrained in the national memory that subsequent renewal movements, both genuine and false, were associated with the desert (see Isa 40:3; Hos 2:14-15; Acts 21:38).

The quotation of Isaiah 40:3 in **3:3** refers to one such renewal movement when the nation was returning from exile to be reconstituted under the leadership of people like Zerubbabel, Ezra and Nehemiah. Matthew was convinced that these words from Isaiah could also be applied to John in his role as the forerunner of Jesus, the Messiah. A new and infinitely greater renewal movement is about to take place. This renewal will not be an escape from Egypt, a return from exile in Babylon, or even a deliverance from Roman political domination. It will be a release from even greater bondage: the bondage to sin and Satan of all the peoples of the world.

Whereas in Isaiah 40:3 the renewal was described as the work of the Lord, Yahweh, Matthew applies these words to Jesus. He is making a quiet statement that Jesus is equal to the Father.

John's message was almost identical to that of Jesus. Both preached repentance *for the kingdom of heaven is near* (**3:2**; see 4:17; 10:7). At the heart of the message of repentance is the call to turn one's mind back to God. In Israel the prophets called the people from worshipping foreign idols to return to a life of covenant obedience (see Jer 3:7, 10, 14; 4:1-2). Repentance is not just saying sorry publicly to save face after being caught doing something wrong; it is a real change in one's thinking. True repentance is an inward reorientation affecting the whole of one's thoughts, but it expresses itself in outward acts. In repentance one turns away from idolatry, sin, evil, wrongdoing and any other way of life that is contrary to God's word, preferring instead to treat the word of God as a 'lamp to my feet and a light for my path' (Ps 119:105). Repentance is a prerequisite for entering the kingdom of heaven. In this message John and Jesus were united. They were not rivals; they complemented each other. Jesus built on the foundation that John laid.

John appeared in the desert of Judea wearing clothes and eating food reminiscent of another great prophet, Elijah

(3:4; see also 1 Kgs 17:2-6; 2 Kgs 1:8). His appearance and lifestyle challenged the people of power in his day. During the days of godly kings, prophets could and did operate in the palaces (for example Nathan in David's court, 2 Sam 12:1-25). But in days of evil kings, most prophets, like Elijah, retreated to the wilderness. Just as Elijah clashed with the king of his day, Ahab, and his wife, Jezebel (1 Kgs 17:1; 18:17; 19:1-3), so John would in time clash with Herod, which lead to his death (14:1-12). The examples of these two great prophets, and many others in Israel, indicate that the Christian church's ministry should always be prophetic and should challenge the powers that be and the norms of the times. Its message should be countercultural. John showed the way this should be done both by what he said and especially by the way he lived. We, too, need to make sure that our lifestyles match our words.

John's chief activity in the wilderness of Judea was preaching and baptizing. It is clear that his ministry was very significant and affected many people for quite a long time (3:5-6; see also Acts 19:3-4). His preaching was not a novelty, except that it had been a long four hundred years since the voice of a prophet had last been heard. Similarly his baptism was not strange, except that normally Jews did not undergo baptism (except for those joining the Qumran community – a separatist renewal movement that cut itself off from normal society and lived in the wilderness of Judea to avoid contamination). Baptism was reserved for Gentiles who converted to Judaism. It was a once-for-all ritual indicating a radical shift in allegiance from their old national gods to the God of Israel. In calling Jews to be similarly baptized, John was treating them as spiritual Gentiles. They, too, needed to enter the approaching kingdom of heaven by repentance and baptism.

John threw a number of challenges at the nation of Israel. It simply would not do for the people to hide under the spiritual covering that membership of the elect nation was assumed to provide. They were indeed the children of Abraham, the rock from which all people of faith have been hewn (Isa 51:1-2). But they could not take this for granted because God was able to *raise up children for Abraham* from any other source (3:9). This challenge must have been particularly irksome for the Pharisees and Sadducees who had turned up, maybe from a genuine desire to hear John's message, or more likely to check out the authenticity of what was going on. John made a stinging attack on them, calling them *a brood of vipers* (3:7). John's message of repentance called for a personal response.

In fact the whole nation was in danger of judgment as the tree image indicates (3:8, 10). Judgment would start with the household of faith. John's audience needed to hear this message. We also need to hear it. John's message is a necessary correction for people who use status in the church or society as a badge of recognition or importance.

Paul makes this same point strongly when writing to the Corinthians (1 Cor 1:26-31). Human status counts for nothing before God. I fear that the popularity and multiplicity of titles like pastor, reverend, or even bishop by those in the African church who do not have an established episcopal structure (as do groups like the Episcopalians, Methodists and Lutherans). It does not augur well for the church in a continent already blighted by status consciousness.

John describes Jesus as one who will come *after me* (3:11a). 'Coming after someone' at times implied being someone's disciple, because literally and figuratively most disciples would walk behind their masters. Here, however, it simply means that Jesus' public ministry would follow John's. John knew that Jesus was mightier than he was. Disciples would regularly serve as servants or virtual slaves of their masters. However, the task of removing and carrying the master's sandals was regarded as too menial even for them. That was slave's work. So in 3:11b John is saying that he is not fit even to be Jesus' slave.

John goes even further, saying that even his baptism, which was an outward symbol, would soon give way to Jesus' baptism *with the Holy Spirit and with fire,* both of which would indicate a real cleansing as the prophets had anticipated (3:12; see also Ezek 36:26-27; Joel 2:28-29). The day of Pentecost would fulfil both the reality and the imagery.

3:13-17 Jesus is Baptized

John's renewal movement caused a great stir. People went to him from far and near, confessing both personal and national sins, and they were baptized in the river Jordan (3:5). Onto this stage came Jesus, to start his public ministry. His first act was *to be baptized by John* (3:13). John protested, saying something to the effect that it was he who needed Jesus' baptism and not the other way around (3:14). Jesus answered that his baptism was necessary to *fulfil all righteousness* (3:15).

This statement means several things. Jesus wanted to fully identify with and endorse the message of John, and thus to identify with the faithful remnant of Israel. He may even have wanted to show that, unlike faithless Israel, the true Israelite fulfils all righteous requirements. By this act, Jesus was not just submitting himself to John, but was also committing himself to total consecration in life and holiness of character in obedience to the demands of the law. Jesus' submission to John, the superior submitting to the inferior, is an example we should all follow. Pride and arrogance are not qualities of a life given to God.

At his baptism, the Holy Sprit descended upon Jesus *like a dove* (3:16). The symbolism is reminiscent of Noah's dove, yet another sign of the start of a new era in God's plan (Gen 8:6-12). But Matthew has made it clear that Jesus was conceived by the Holy Spirit (1:18). Presumably this meant that he already lived in the power of the Spirit. So why this public show in the form of a dove?

The answer is that receiving the Spirit meant several things to Jesus. It was an assurance of the rightness of the mission he was embarking on. It was the outward sign of the inner filling of the Spirit. It marked the arrival of the messianic age predicted by the prophets (Joel 2:28-29). It was also evidence of the involvement of the Trinity in the work of Jesus on earth. So on the occasion of his baptism, he is filled with the Spirit and also hears the Father speak words that confirm his calling: *This is my Son, whom I love; with him I am well pleased* (**3:17**; see also Ps 2:7; Isa 42:1). Jesus is the King, the Son of God. He is the rightful heir to the throne of David who will establish righteousness and justice on earth. But he is also the servant of God whose calling is to lay down his life in suffering on behalf of the world.

For us today, baptism symbolizes our repentance, God's forgiveness of our sins and our willingness to obey him. It is a public declaration of our status as children of God.

4:1-11 Jesus Tempted in the Desert

Immediately after his baptism, Jesus was *led by the Spirit into the desert to be tempted* (**4:1**). It may seem strange that the first port of call after being anointed for ministry should be the wilderness. However, the experience of many Christians would suggest that it is not uncommon for believers to undergo temptations immediately after experiencing a rich and exhilarating spiritual high. A genuine work of God will always attract the unwholesome attentions of Satan, the enemy of God. But at the same time spiritual mountain-top experiences need to be tested in order to strip them of purely euphoric froth and expose the bedrock reality beneath the experience.

Jesus' temptations have been interpreted in at least three ways. Some suggest that they show Jesus as the true Israelite who succeeded where Israel had failed (see Deut 6:16; 8:1-20). Others argue that the temptations reveal what kind of Messiah Jesus was, and specifically that he was neither an economic miracle worker nor a political revolutionary. Still others regard this passage as providing an example of how Jesus' followers should handle temptations. It is not necessary to choose between these three interpretations; they all have valid and appropriate lessons to teach.

Jesus spent *forty days* in the wilderness (**4:2a**). This period immediately brings to mind Israel's forty years of wanderings in the wilderness of Sinai before entering the Promised Land (Deut 8:2). Jesus' time in the wilderness comes before he paves the way for humanity to enter the messianic age. But the forty days also remind us of Moses' time on Mount Sinai (Exod 34:28) where he fasted and received the Ten Commandments from the Lord. Jesus is cast as a new Moses who brings to fulfilment the law of God that Moses and the prophets had given (5:17-20).

Three temptations are described in this passage:

- **Satan tempted Jesus to use spiritual power to meet his personal needs** (4:3-4). After forty days alone in the desert with either very little or no food, Jesus *was hungry* (**4:2b**). He had real human needs. He also had the power to make bread miraculously (**4:3b**). He used that power on two occasions to meet the needs of others (14:15-21; 15:32-38). But to use the power for his own personal needs at the suggestion of Satan would be at best a dangerous distraction and at worst a selfish, undisciplined demonstration of magical powers. Jesus knew that to focus his powers on meeting his own material needs would be a dangerous diversion from his path of obedience to God's word.

  We should not be misled by the conditional *if* in **4:3a**. Satan knows that Jesus is the Son of God (3:17). We should understand the 'if' not as an expression of doubt but as a challenge saying 'As you really are the Son of God, you can turn these rocks into bread.' But for Jesus, some things are more important than food: *Man does not live on bread alone* (**4:4**).

- **Satan tempted Jesus to put on a sensational display of power.** Satan reminds him that God would not let his son be hurt (**4:6**; Ps 91:11-12). Instead he would command his angels to ensure his safety. God is committed to the protection of those who trust him. Indeed, Jesus himself would later affirm that he could command thousands of angels to come to his aid at any moment (26:53). But Satan was seeking to create an artificial crisis, and calling on Jesus to put on a public display of power in a self-gratifying manner. But such behaviour would amount to putting *God to the test* (**4:7**; see also Deut 6:16). We can trust God for safety as we serve him obediently, but sometimes his purposes are best fulfilled by allowing his servants to undergo suffering. Jesus' own commitment to the cross is a prime example, and many of his followers since have honoured him in suffering and even death.

- **Satan tempted Jesus to use political power to achieve his ends.** Satan knew that Jesus came to earth to establish the kingdom of God, that is, to have power over all the kingdoms of the world. So he took Jesus to a *very high mountain,* either in reality or in his imagination, and showed him *all the kingdoms of the world* (**4:8**). Satan promised to deliver these kingdoms to Jesus if he would *bow down and worship* him (**4:9**). Jesus would ultimately achieve his purpose, but by way of the cross. This would involve much suffering for him and for his disciples. But in the end, the whole world will acknowledge that he is Lord (Phil 2:10-11; Rev 20:11-21:4). Satan sought to make the process easier by cutting out the cross and the necessity for suffering. Jesus would get political power without having to go through the painful process of trial, humiliation and death at the hands of those he had created.

Satan may not have been lying when he said he had the power to deliver the kingdoms of the world to Jesus, for there are some passages of Scripture that suggest he has real power in the political realm – though only by God's permission and only for a limited time (Luke 4:6; John 12:31; 2 Cor 4:4). By doing what Satan suggested, Jesus would be accepting idolatry and setting Satan on a tier of universal leadership just below God (**4:10**). Moreover, the victory that Jesus would gain would be a hollow one and would not deal with the basic human problem of sin. Only the cross of Jesus was adequate to deal with that.

When the temptation had passed, angels came to minister to Jesus. They provided for his physical needs (see 1 Kgs 19:5-9) and affirmed that he had done the right thing.

Compromise with Satan for temporal gains, however attractive, is not the way to fulfil God's calling. The passage also suggests that it may be dangerous to seek to use political power to accomplish God's will. The spectacular fall from grace of such leaders as Frederick Chiluba, and the subsequent demise of his ill-fated Christian nation experiment in Zambia, is a warning regarding all the dangers of seeking to wed contemporary political systems and the establishment of the kingdom of God. God's will must be fulfilled by appropriate means.

Temptations are a fact of life. We cannot and should not seek to avoid them. But we must follow Jesus' example and stand up under them. One of the most effective weapons against temptation is the 'sword of the Spirit', the word of God (Eph 6:17). Jesus responded to each temptation with Scripture: *It is written* … (4:4, 7, 10). Paul adds that 'No temptation has seized you except what is common to man. And God is faithful; he will not let you be tempted beyond what you can bear. But when you are tempted, he will provide a way out so that you can stand up under it' (1 Cor 10:13). Jesus' knowledge of Scripture, his absolute commitment to doing the will of God and God's faithful help for those who are tempted won the day. That is why we need to be able to say with the psalmist, 'I have hidden your word in my heart that I might not sin against you' (Ps 119:11). At every turn temptations need to be fought with Scripture, prayer and determination.

Although this is the only passage in which Jesus is specifically said to have been tempted, temptations followed him all through his ministry (16:23; 26:36-46). Thus although Satan left Jesus (**4:11**), it was just for a time. He would return again and again to try to tempt him to disobey the will of the Father.

4:12-25 The Beginning of Jesus' Public Ministry

4:12-17 Jesus' Preaching Begins

John's arrest by Herod brought his ministry to an end (**4:12a**). He would never leave prison, and would eventually be executed there (14:1-12). His arrest appears to have been the signal for Jesus to set out on his own public ministry in Galilee (**4:12b**), where he commanded a very large following. In fact it is true that most of Jesus' success was in Galilee, and that almost all his official adversaries and trials came from Jerusalem, where he would eventually die (2:12, 14, 22; 12:15; 14:13; 15:21).

We know from John 3:22 that Jesus had been baptizing (through his disciples – John 4:2) in Judea near the area where John was doing his work. But now he moved from the banks of the Jordan River to Galilee and switched from a ministry focused on baptism to one of preaching and healing. In spite of the break from John's style of ministry, the message Jesus preached was exactly the same. He continued to call the nation to repentance in the face of the coming of the *kingdom of heaven* (**4:17**).

Jesus did not base his work in Nazareth, where he had been brought up, but in the nearby town of *Capernaum* (**4:13**). It is described as *in the area of Zebulun and Naphtali* because it had been given to those two tribes by Joshua (Josh 19:10-16, 32-39). The Jewish population of the area had been deported by the Assyrians and replaced by people from other parts of their empire (2 Kgs 17:23-24). This is why Isaiah referred to it as *Galilee of the Gentiles* (**4:15**; Isa 9:1). But many Jews had settled in Galilee after the exile in Babylon, and in the second century BC the Hasmonean kings had attempted and largely succeeded in repopulating the area with Jews. In general, Galilee was despised by the Jerusalem hierarchy (John 7:52), but Isaiah had seen prophetically that a great light would appear in Galilee, and Jesus was the fulfilment of that prophecy (**4:16**; see also Isa 9:1-7).

A Bemba proverb from Zambia warns against despising people, saying *Ako usulile: e kopa noko* ['the person you despise might well marry your mother']. For all you know, the person you despise might become someone you have to acknowledge and respect. The long-awaited Messiah of the Jewish people appeared not in the palaces or temple of Jerusalem but in Galilee, a despised backwater of the nation. This situation may be similar to that today in which the economically insignificant and much marginalized sub-Saharan Africa is fast becoming the anvil on which world Christianity in the twenty-first century will be forged!

4:18-22 The First Disciples Are Called

All four gospels record the call of the first disciples quite early in Jesus' ministry and show that they remained at his side to the end of his days on earth. These men were being trained to succeed him and carry on the work he had started. A rabbi with a group of disciples was a common feature in Palestine in Jesus' day. But there were some real differences between Jesus and all other rabbis; indeed it is debatable whether Jesus should be called a rabbi. Unlike the other rabbis, he took the initiative to call his disciples; he did not point them to an authority higher than himself, he displaced the Torah as the basic textbook and there would be no graduating from his school.

The first disciples, two sets of brothers, were Galilean fishermen (**4:18, 21**). The simple command, *Come, follow me … I will make you fishers of men* (**4:19**), created a crisis in their lives. All of them abandoned their means of livelihood and set out to follow Jesus (**4:20, 22**).

There are similarities between this call to become disciples and the call of Abraham (Gen 12:1-4). In both cases, God (Jesus) took the initiative and the response of obedience was immediate. In both cases, there is a promise to turn those called into a force they had not been before. Abraham was to become a great nation, and through him and his descendants all the families of the world would be blessed. The disciples were similarly going to be turned into a force bringing human beings into the kingdom of God. The result is the same. Abraham was to engage in mission, and so too were the disciples. The Christian faith has always been and will always be a missionary faith. It exists to send followers out into the world to draw people to the good news that God's appointed Saviour of the world is Jesus, and that he died so that we may have life eternally.

4:23-25 Jesus' Other Followers

Although Jesus was followed by the close-knit group of disciples, there were many others who heard his teaching and experienced or witnessed his healing and followed him (4:25). His ministry would develop and be characterized by teaching and healing (**4:23**). These two components of his ministry should be parts of our work as well.

The closing verses of chapter 4 are the first of Matthew's many summary statements about how Jesus' fame spreads throughout a region (8:16; 12:15; 14:25-36; 15:30-31; 19:1-2). The region in which he was preaching was located on a major trade route that linked Damascus to the north with Egypt in the south. All the villages and towns were reasonably densely populated, as were the bordering territories of *the Decapolis* and Perea, to which his fame spread (**4:24-25**). Even the non-Jewish residents of the area heard of him (see 15:21-28).

The chapter began with Jesus alone in the wilderness fasting and being tempted by Satan. It ends with him surrounded by his disciples in the midst of a large crowd of followers who heard his teaching about the coming kingdom of heaven and who witnessed or benefited from his healing ministry.

5:1-7:29 Teaching I: The Sermon on the Mount

The Sermon on the Mount is the first of Matthew's five major teaching blocks (see the introduction to this commentary). Here Jesus shows what life should be like in 'the kingdom of heaven', which is Matthew's term for the kingdom of God. The kingdom of God is all-embracing: nothing in the whole universe falls outside his authority. But God's reign has been affected by the rebellion that sin introduced into the world. The people of God recognized that some day in the future, God's kingdom, heralded by the Messiah, would break into history to put a stop to the rebellion and to introduce the age to come. That is what Jesus does as he announces that the kingdom of heaven has come. Yet this kingdom has not yet fully come. It is still restricted to the lives of those who have accepted Christ as the Messiah and have become his disciples. These disciples have the responsibility of living their lives in terms of the values that prevail in the kingdom of heaven. They must demonstrate that the Christian life is truly countercultural, regardless of the culture from which they come.

5:1-12 The Beatitudes

In the true Jewish teaching style of his day, Jesus sat down to expound his material. His listeners sat at his feet (**5:1-2**). The beatitudes which follow are introduced in formulaic fashion by the expression *Blessed are …* .

Many Africans use the expression 'to bless' to refer to what a superior, usually a parent or grandparent, does to show their goodwill to a child or grandchild. Such blessings are most commonly given just before an aging parent dies or when young people are setting off on a long and perhaps dangerous journey. The Bemba word *ukupala* [to bless] describes the action of softly spraying spittle on the person to be blessed. The one doing the blessing invokes the greatest spiritual powers he or she knows to come alongside the person being blessed to give them protection, guidance, safety, and help in time of need. The resulting state of blessedness leads to *umutende* [well-being], or what the Jews called *shalom* – a rich concept embracing inner peace and outward harmony with both the material and the spiritual worlds.

But the Beatitudes are not talking about this kind of blessedness! Jesus is not teaching a passive reception of God's approval. The Beatitudes are congratulatory exclamations, more like 'O the blessedness of the poor in spirit!' They teach that blessedness results from the cultivation of certain attributes that are approved of by God. Those who have entered the kingdom must go on to develop these attributes in the present. They are what every disciple should aspire to and achieve, even if they will only fully blossom in the age to come. The blessing and joy that they bring are deeply rooted and are not affected by the unpredictable ups and downs of life.

5:3 The poor in spirit

The term *poor in spirit* has its roots in material poverty (**5:3a**). Someone who is poor has no influence, power or prestige. Then, as now, they were often taken advantage of and exploited. This state of helplessness and destitution can and does lead to a deep dependence upon God (Luke 6:20). In many African cities today people use the expression 'by the grace of God' to explain how it is they survive when they live on far less than the one dollar a day designated by the United Nations as the absolute minimum for survival.

Those who are 'poor in spirit' are thus those who have realized their own utter helplessness on account of sin in their life, and who acknowledge their complete dependence upon God not just for spiritual needs but also for material needs. Such a person develops a certain detachment from material things and an attachment to God. The Westerner needs to learn detachment from material things, but most Africans need to learn detachment from spirits in order to develop a healthy trust and attachment to the one true spirit, the Holy Spirit! Those who have this attribute are God's people: *theirs is the kingdom of heaven* (**5:3b**). Or the verse may be saying that such people are to be found in the kingdom of heaven. In that kingdom, there can be no competing interests. Those who belong to it have learned the secret of utter dependence on God leading to complete obedience to his will.

5:4 Those who mourn

The term *mourn* (**5:4a**) is commonly associated with the pain and grief caused by bereavement. But mourning can also be caused by recognition of wrongdoing and its consequences. That is why mourning is commonly associated with repentance. Mourning proceeds from a true recognition of one's own or society's sin. Such recognition can be triggered by right teaching, a good example, tragic consequences resulting from one's lifestyle or a brush with the purity and holiness of God. Isaiah saw the Lord and cried out in grief, 'Woe to me … I am ruined … I am a man of unclean lips, and I live among a people of unclean lips' (Isa 6:5).

Personal and social experience combine to remind us of the gravity of sin. There is sin in our lives, in our cultures, in our economic structures, indeed in everything that we put our hands to. Global warming has tragic consequences for human survival. So does ethnic cleansing, which has devastating consequences for countries. Personal choices and actions demonstrate a catalogue of human activities that must make us weep with deep grief. Isaiah shuddered with grief when he saw the purity of the Lord. We will shudder with the same grief when we look at the purity of Jesus and the challenge of his cross. The Lord sees such grief and responds with comfort. God forgives personal sin and wipes the slate clean with the blood of his son Jesus. But God also

inspires and strengthens his 'mourners' to work to remove the offences that too often lead to personal and structural sin. The very word 'comfort' implies this, for it comes from a Latin root that means 'to strengthen' (**5:4b**).

5:5 The meek

We tend to confuse meekness and weakness. Weakness is characterized by indecision, a lack of moral or physical strength, fearfulness and low self-esteem. But these are not the characteristics Jesus praises. What he is speaking of is meekness (**5:5a**), a word that was used to describe both Moses (Num 12:3) and Jesus (Matt 12:15-21). No one could accuse either of them of being weak and indecisive! Meekness is the ability to control one's power and use it only for the benefit of others. It is the opposite of arrogant, selfish assertiveness and uncontrolled emotions. The meek do get angry, but at the right time, and not because of wounded pride. They humbly place all their abilities and emotions under God's complete control and do not allow their personal circumstances, however adverse, to disturb their peace.

The reward for meekness is to *inherit the earth* (**5:5b**). God can trust such people with the earth, that is, his new future earth (Rev 21:1). He knows they will not spoil it for their own selfish appetites (see Ps 37:9-11), since they already possess everything in Christ (2 Cor 6:10). This beatitude will be fulfilled literally in the fullness of time.

5:6 Those who hunger for righteousness

Hunger and thirst are warning signals that we need more food or liquid. If we do not respond to these warnings, we will starve or become dehydrated. Both conditions are life-threatening, but can easily be corrected with the right amount of food or drink. However, natural appetites can grow and become ends in themselves. People can become infatuated with eating or drinking, not because they need to eat and drink more but for sheer love of eating and drinking. Appetites of this kind grow and grow. They are deceitful desires, for they promise much, but deliver little (Eph 4:22).

Hungering and thirsting for righteousness is a safe appetite, for God will always fill those with this hunger and thirst (**5:6**). The beatitude challenges us to eagerly seek righteousness, to seek God and his righteous instruction in much the same way that the very hungry or thirsty seek something to eat or drink (Pss 42:1; 119:40). Such seeking will not deceive or disappoint.

5:7 The merciful

A biblical commentary on this beatitude is found in one of Jesus' parables (18:21-35). Those who show mercy will receive mercy (**5:7**, 6:12-15; see also Jas 2:13). Mercy is a loving response to an offender who may or may not realize their offence. In mercy, God withholds the just desserts of sinners, while in grace he extends love to the undeserving. Mercy implies the ability to enter into another's world with all its misery, to feel for that person and to act to alleviate their misery. It is an intense understanding of another and their problems. The Samaritan showed mercy when he cared for a man left for dead by robbers, without regard to his own safety or convenience (Luke 10:37).

Mercy calls us to exercise forgiveness more often. We must not live aloof and detached from others and their problems. God in Christ did not remain aloof and detached. He felt our pain and entered into our world with a solution that we could not even have dreamed of. When we exercise mercy, others will treat us similarly, and God himself, who has already shown us mercy in Christ, will show us even greater mercy.

5:8 The pure in heart

A pure metal is one in which there are no impurities. A pure heart is one that is wholeheartedly devoted to God (Deut 6:5). Those who are pure do not have mixed motives. We see the effects of such purity when two people suffer the same natural disaster and lose all but their lives. One may curse God, while the other praises him. Those whose hearts are pure *will see God* at work in the present, and will see him with their own eyes in the age to come (**5:8**).

5:9 The peacemakers

Sudan, and especially the Darfur region, is just the latest part of Africa desperately needing peacemakers. In the recent past, we have seen conflicts in Congo, Uganda, Angola, Ethiopia, Sierra Leone, Liberia, Côte d'Ivoire, Western Sahara, Rwanda and Burundi. Africa is a bleeding continent. Conflicts have ravaged the landscape and continue to do so at an alarming rate. Oh that God would raise up an army of peacemakers! But who are these peacemakers and why will they be called sons of God? (**5:9**)

'Peace be with you' is a common greeting in many cultures (in Bemba, for example, we would say *Mutendepo mukwai* when greeting a stranger). When Jesus appeared to his disciples after his resurrection, he used the traditional Hebrew greeting to wish them peace (John 20:19). But his greeting was different in that he is the Prince of Peace, the greatest of peacemakers who brought peace between God and human beings (Eph 2:14-18). Whenever his disciples preach the gospel so that people are reconciled to God, they are working as peacemakers and acting as the sons and daughters of God they truly are. But peacemaking is more than just bringing about spiritual reconciliation between God and human beings. It involves actively working for reconciliation between hostile factions. Africa desperately needs men and women of peace, sons and daughters of God who make peacemaking a priority so that the continent may live in peace. The peacemakers are rightly called the *sons*

of God because they demonstrate in reality not just their relationship with God but their participation in his most characteristic work. In so doing they establish realms where the kingdom of heaven is indeed effective.

5:10-12 The persecuted

Over the past fifteen years, in Africa as elsewhere, there has been a phenomenal rise in the popularity of Pentecostal and charismatic churches, especially those which adhere to what has become known as the 'health and prosperity' gospel. According to this gospel, all children of God can and should claim health and prosperity as a matter of right. In spite of its popularity, this gospel is inadequate because it lacks a theology of suffering. Suffering is not a virtue in itself, yet many, if not most, of the OT prophets suffered. Some even lost their lives in the process of bringing God's word to the nation of Israel. Jerusalem gained a reputation as 'the slayer of the prophets' (23:37-38). Jesus himself died in Jerusalem at the hands of those who persecuted him. On a number of occasions Jesus told his disciples to be ready even to die for his name's sake (Mark 8:34-35).

This beatitude does not say that all suffering leads to blessing. There are sufferings that we bring upon ourselves for reasons that have nothing to do with righteousness. But those who suffer in the course of following Jesus are blessed and the kingdom of heaven belongs to them (**5:10**).

Matthew's first readers had a lot of experience in suffering. Christianity was a new religion and was subject to persecution from family, work and especially the state. Roman emperors regarded themselves as divine. Every citizen was required once a year to burn a pinch of incense to a statue of the emperor and declare, 'Caesar is Lord.' Christians insisted that 'Jesus is Lord'. Many died because of their refusal to acknowledge Caesar. Such suffering is meritorious and is comparable to the sufferings of the prophets of old (Ps 44:22).

Persecution is inevitable for those who live righteous lives (2 Tim 3:12), for the simple reason that righteous living challenges wickedness in individuals and societies and unsettles their consciences. They retaliate by attempting to silence the source of the troublesome conscience, and so persecute Christians. Persecution is an integral part of what it means to be the church. But God will reward in his own way those who suffer for the cause of Christ (**5:11–12**).

5:13-16 Salt and Light

Disciples who display the qualities spelled out in 5:1-12 play an important role in society. They are like salt, which purifies, preserves and enhances the flavour of food. They will influence society and make the earth a better and more wholesome place.

Salt that has ceased to be salty has lost these qualities and is as useful as refuse (**5:13**). Ordinarily sodium chloride –

common salt – does not lose its saltiness. But the salt used in first-century Palestine could. It was similar to the Cibwa salt produced in the villages in the Mpika District of Zambia. This salt was made by burning a special kind of grass that grew in the Lwitikila salt pans, filtering water through the ashes and then leaving the compound in the sun to evaporate. If the resulting ball of salt was exposed to rain, the salt could be leached out and the ball would lose its saltiness and become worthless. The same is true of disciples who refuse to live lives that are true to their calling. They will have no influence and will become unserviceable, worse than useless.

Jesus' disciples are also to be like light (**5:14a**). They would have been familiar with this image, for both Israel the nation and Jerusalem its capital were considered 'a light for the Gentiles' (Isa 42:6). Jesus, however, declared himself to be the 'light of the world' (John 9:5). The light that will come from his disciples is not their own, but shines through them on account of their remaining in the true light, Jesus their Lord. They need to be connected with him in the same way as a light bulb needs to be connected to a generating plant if it is to give light.

It is the nature of light to illumine, to give guidance in darkness. In the same way, the disciple has to be visible. Secret discipleship is not biblical (**5:14b-16a**).

If Christians are called to be salt and light, then it follows that the world into which they are sent needs these qualities. It is a place of insipid morality, decay and darkness. The disciple brings illumination to the world through witnessing that points to and attracts people to the origin of the light: *your Father in heaven* (**5:16b**).

5:17-20 Jesus and the Law

In Judaism 'the Law' was primarily the Pentateuch, that is, the five books from Genesis through to Deuteronomy. But the term also included 'the Prophets' and the Writings, so the whole OT was the law. The Jewish leaders studied the OT with great care, but too often they focused solely on rules and missed the main point. Jesus broke their rules, but does that mean that he dismissed the law? No, he strongly affirmed it, saying that he had not come *to abolish the Law or the Prophets but to fulfil them* (**5:17**; see also Luke 16:16-17). There is no division between the two halves of the Bible. Jesus fulfils the teaching of the OT. He did things as laid down in Scripture, and his life and teaching brought out the full meaning of Scripture (**5:18-19**).

Jesus' instruction that his followers were to be more righteous than *the Pharisees and the teachers of the law* was a daunting one (**5:20**). The Pharisees were the experts on the law. They spent their lives studying every detail of it and perfecting rules for keeping it. They were admired as pillars of society. But Jesus taught that we are saved and made righteous by God's grace, rather than by obedience to a set

of rules. This was a lesson that Paul, a former Pharisee, understood clearly (see Phil 3:3-9).

5:21-48 Application of the Law

After stating that he has come to uphold the law, Jesus takes six passages from the law and reveals the truth behind them. In each example, he quotes a Scripture and then, using a common teaching method, goes on to explain the meaning more fully. As he does this, he calls for greater righteousness than the Pharisees did, and also establishes his authority not only over the Pharisees and the scribes but also over the OT as well. He goes beyond a legalistic or literal understanding of the texts and deals with the spirit or motivation behind them. He can go further than the teachers of the law would have done because his authority is higher. So when he says, *but I tell you,* he is not contradicting Scripture, but a wrong interpretation of it (**5:22**).

5:21-26 Murder, litigation and judgments

Jesus begins with the sixth commandment (**5:21**; see also Exod 20:13) and points out that it is not just the taking of another's life that is a sin, but the anger that leads to the destructive action. This same anger may express itself in insults like *Raca* (meaning 'stupid' in Aramaic) and *fool*. These Jewish insults are similar to the African 'son of a dog'. While the Jews considered some insults so serious that those uttering them could be brought before the Sanhedrin (the Jewish council), Jesus' point is that all insults hurled at a brother or sister carry the penalty of *the fire of hell* (**5:22**). It is wrong to hurl insults at others, and God will judge those who do.

The Greek word translated 'hell' comes from the name of the Valley of Gehinnom – a deep ravine outside Jerusalem. Wicked kings like Ahaz had burnt their sons in sacrifice there (2 Kgs 23:10; Jer 7:31-32), but in Jesus' day it was a rubbish dump, where fires glowed night and day. It was an appropriate symbol of hell.

Jesus goes even further than saying that anger must not lead to murder or insults. Nor is it enough simply to ignore one's anger or control one's temper. He insists that we deal with our anger by seeking complete reconciliation (**5:23-26**). Those with burning anger in their heart cannot offer true worship. The anger will destroy their moral fibre.

5:27-30 Lust and adultery

The seventh commandment, 'you shall not commit adultery' (**5:27**; see also Exod 20:14) prohibited sexual intercourse between unmarried parties. The general understanding in Jewish society was that a woman needed to be chaste before marriage and faithful afterwards. A man, however, was free to have sexual liaisons as long as he was discreet and did not involve a married woman, which would infringe the rights of another man. The people of Jesus' day were very modern in this matter!

Jesus makes no such distinction between men and women, and his teaching goes beyond the physical act of unauthorized sex to the internal lust that may lead to the physical act. The internal desire is just as, if not more, dangerous than the outward physical sin (**5:28**). Therefore one needs to be drastic in dealing with the sources of desire (**5:29-30**). Jesus is not telling us to mutilate our bodies. Instead he is telling us not to use our senses of sight, smell, taste, touch and hearing to stimulate forbidden lust. The Christian must choose carefully what to see, smell, taste, feel and hear.

5:31-32 Divorce and remarriage

In the past, women were not highly regarded and were always at the mercy of either their fathers and brothers or their husbands. Moses had accordingly made a law to protect a woman from a capricious husband, who having divorced her could not later claim her for his wife (**5:31**; 19:8; see also Deut 24:1-4). The bill of divorce protected her right to remarry without interference from her former husband. Jewish scholars used this law as the basis for long arguments about what were legitimate grounds for divorce. Some insisted that the only ground for divorce was sexual unfaithfulness, while others permitted divorce for just about any reason (including a more attractive woman, bad cooking and quarrelsomeness).

Jesus' words reassert the true meaning of marriage commitment and the solemnity of the marriage union (**5:32**) (for his further teaching on divorce, see 19:1-12).

5:33-37 Oaths

Zambians often use oaths to affirm the truth of what they are saying or the certainty of promises they make. The oath implies that God is a witness to what I have said, and if I am lying, let him strike me dead with lightning. The Jews, too, made many vows, some of them to God. Scripture demanded that such vows be fulfilled (**5:33**; see also Num 30:2; Deut 23:21; Ps 50:14). Negatively, Jesus says it is wrong to use an oath to create an impression (possibly false) of commitment. Positively, he commands that all his disciples should be known as people whose word can be trusted (**5:34-37**).

When we find ourselves in a situation where, for example, the need to protect a loved one conflicts with the need to tell the truth, we may decide that being faithful to our loved one takes priority over other values. But such situations are very rare. In almost all cases, Christian discipleship calls us to truthfulness even if it costs us a lot.

5:38-42 Retaliation

Eye for eye and tooth for tooth (**5:38**; see also Exod 21:24) was a great legal advance in its day. It meant justice was not dependent on a person's ability to exact revenge, and the punishment did not exceed the crime. The judge would use this guideline in assessing the damages and therefore the punishment. Often these damages were translated into cash payments. Jesus does not call his disciples to ignore basic principles of justice. He does, however, call for an attitude that abolishes revenge; an attitude that does not assert its rights but puts the needs of others before one's own (**5:39-42**). Christians are called upon to be generous even to those who appear to be their oppressors.

Underlying this argument is the idea that an injured person should not surrender his or her freedom to the oppressor. One must retain the initiative and take action that may surprise the oppressor, making them ashamed of their actions (Rom 12:20).

5:43-48 Enemies

In Leviticus 19:18, the commandment to *love your neighbour* applied where the neighbour was a fellow Israelite (**5:43a**). Attitudes towards outsiders and Israelites who had rejected their faith and their people were quite different (Exod 34:12; Deut 7:2; 23:3-6; Ps 139:21-22). Although *hate your enemy* (**5:43b**) is not commanded in the ot, it can be inferred from the passages quoted above. But Jesus commands his followers to love their enemies (**5:44**). The word translated 'love' is *agape,* which means a strong commitment of goodwill towards another regardless of whether or not they deserve it.

Our attitude towards outsiders, the unlovely and unloving, and even those who persecute us, must not be hatred, rejection or indifference. We must positively seek their good. God has given us the example to follow. His gifts are given freely even to those who do not acknowledge him as Lord (**5:45-47**). Similarly, Jesus' followers must learn to shower all people indiscriminately with love. The African church urgently needs to learn this lesson in order to curb the scourge of tribalism and racism that is ravaging this continent.

To *be perfect* (**5:48**) does not mean to be sinless, but simply to strive to fulfil one's purpose. Jesus calls his disciples to meet the highest possible standard. We are to aim for conformity with the character of God, and not to settle for anything less.

6:1-7:29 Religious Duties

The topic of the sermon now moves away from human relations to religious duties such as almsgiving, prayer and fasting, and a statement about anxiety. This section begins with a warning (**6:1**). The aim of performing *acts of righteousness* is to meet a need, and one should avoid drawing attention to oneself. The person who gives alms, prays or fasts in order to gain a reputation for piety falls into the trap of being a hypocrite.

6:2-4 Almsgiving

The majority of the people in this world are poor. So we need to give generously. In fact, the Jews considered almsgiving a sacred duty, an act of righteousness (Deut 15:7-11; Ps 112:9). The rabbis taught that it was better to give in secret. Rabbi Eleazah (second century AD) is credited with saying that 'he who gives in secret is greater than Moses'. But such advice was not always followed. Gifts for the poor were taken up in synagogue services, and often the donors gave substantially in order to be seen to be giving. They paraded their wealth in a boastful manner to draw attention to themselves. It was equivalent to announcing their giving *with trumpets* (**6:2a**).

Such people are *hypocrites,* or actors (**6:2b**). The feeble accolades and admiration they receive from people is their payment in full. It is better to give secretly so that the beneficiary is not embarrassed and only God, *who sees what is done in secret,* knows (**6:3-4**). The donor's reward is far greater and more significant, for it has eternal consequences. God himself rewards such giving.

6:5-15 Prayer

6:5-8 PRINCIPLES OF PRAYER Prayer was an important part of Jewish religious life. Devout Jews prayed three times a day: at dawn, midday and dusk (Dan 6:10; Acts 3:1). While we have no historical evidence of ostentatious praying in the street, it is not unlikely that certain people organized their day so that the time for prayer found them on a street corner (**6:5**). Jesus questions the motives of those who pray to impress others.

He also condemns prayers that babble on and on (**6:7**). Apparently Greek prayers were often lengthy and included numerous titles for the deity being addressed in order to attract his or her attention. But we do not need to summon God's attention. He knows what we are praying about even before we ask him (**6:8**).

How then should we pray? Jesus does not dictate any particular posture when we pray. Nor does he condemn all public prayer. But when such prayer is called for, it should be directed to God, not others. Most of our praying should be in private, since it is an expression of the relationship between the person praying and God, *who sees what is done in secret* (**6:6**).

6:9-15 THE LORD'S PRAYER Most prayers in the Bible start with an address to God (6:9; see also Dan 9:4; Neh 1:5). Both Daniel and Nehemiah start their prayers with some aspect of God, which becomes the focus of the prayer and from which other issues arise. Jesus does the same in this prayer, in which he addresses God as *Our Father in heaven* (**6:9**).

The fatherhood of God was very dear to Jewish thought (Deut 32:6; Isa 63:16; 64:8). The Jews, however, did not use the term *Abba* [Daddy] that Jesus uses in Mark 14:36.

Christians adopted *Abba,* which expresses an especially close relationship, as the way to address God in prayer (Rom 8:15). We should approach God with the confidence of a small child approaching his or her father. Human parents sometimes neglect their children, but God never does.

In much of Africa, the relationships between children and their parents have traditionally tended to be formal. Similarly, the Jews regarded God reverentially as their father. However, in Africa relationships between alternate generations are more intimate. A grandchild relates to his or her grandparents with complete freedom and informality. This is the kind of intimate relationship Jesus encourages us to cultivate with God.

But intimacy is not the same as disrespect, as is clear from the first three petitions in this prayer. All are concerned with God: his *name,* his *kingdom* and his *will* (6:9-10).

- God's name should always be held in honour and not used casually. In praying *hallowed be your name* (**6:9**), we are asking that we, Jesus' followers, will treat his name as holy, and cause it to be treated like that by others. Using God's name in any other way is wrong. God's name is not a swear word or an exclamation mark. We must use it with awe and reverence, despite the intimacy of our relationship.
- God's *kingdom* is already established in Jesus and wherever his followers are, but we are still to pray for the day when the whole world will acknowledge his rule (**6:10a**).
- The *will* of God is something we will pray to see followed perfectly by all people (**6:10b**).

These concerns for God's 'name', his 'kingdom' and his 'will' form the background for the second set of three petitions, which are about human needs: food, forgiveness and guidance.

- We are encouraged to ask God for *our daily bread,* that is, for material provisions (**6:11**).
- We are prone to fall into sin, which damages our relationship with God, and we constantly need to restore that relationship through forgiveness. The word *debts* reminds us that we owe God far more than just money. The phrase *as we also have forgiven our debtors* (**6:12**) does not apply only to those who owe us money. A debtor is any person who has offended us. Nor does this phrase imply that God is limited by the way we forgive others. It is a reminder that we should forgive others in the same way that we seek forgiveness from God (**6:14-15**). Those who themselves know how to forgive will be more open to forgiveness from God and others.
- We commit our futures to God when we ask for guidance away from *temptation* and the devices of *the evil one* (**6:13**). God does not tempt any one, but Satan tempts us in order to cause the downfall of the followers of Christ.

6:16-18 Fasting

Fasting is not commanded in the OT except on the Day of Atonement (Lev 16:29; 23:26-32), although the practice was commonplace among the Jews in times of sorrow, penitence or judgment (Judg 20:26; 2 Sam 3:35; Neh 1:4-7; Zech 7:5). Individuals (Ps 35:13) and whole nations fasted (Esth 4:16; Jonah 3:4-10). Sometimes fasting was done in preparation for meeting with God (Exod 34:28), as part of intense prayer (Jer 14:11-12), in times of crisis (Joel 1–2), for protection on hazardous journeys (Ezra 8:21-23), and in bereavement (2 Sam 1:12).

In the NT, Jesus is said to have fasted for forty days and nights before the start of his public ministry (4:2). The disciples of John the Baptist and those of the Pharisees fasted regularly (Luke 5:33; 18:12). Jesus seems to suggest that his disciples should not fast while he was with them (9:14-14; Mark 2:19-20).

For many, fasting was simply a means to appear pious, and was devoid of true meaning (6:16). Jesus teaches that fasting, like almsgiving and prayer, must not be ostentatious. It should be undertaken for a concentrated but limited time in order to enjoy close converse with God, *who sees what is done in secret* (6:17-18). The words of Isaiah the prophet are as relevant today as they were in his own time (Isa 58:2-8).

6:19-24 Wealth

Material affluence is associated with materialism. Yet the fact that the majority of Africans are materially poor does not mean that we are free from materialism. Many of us long for the material comforts we see depicted in glossy magazines. One of Africa's problems is the encouragement of Western patterns of consumption without the economic discipline required to achieve them. This longing for material riches fuels the preaching of a prosperity gospel in many parts of Africa.

Jesus warns of the great spiritual danger along this path: *You cannot serve both God and Money* or, literally, 'Mammon', the Carthaginian god of wealth (6:24). A focus on material things can wrest our devotion from God to the god of wealth. Paul rightly warns that 'the love of money is a root of all kinds of evil' (1 Tim 6:10). Christians should always cultivate a healthy detachment from the lure of wealth. Money should be our servant in the service of God, not a god to which we owe allegiance as slaves.

Treasures on earth have a habit of disappointing their owners. They offer no permanent security. Clothes, even the most expensive ones, eventually wear out or get eaten by moths. Rust destroys metals, and there is always the danger of theft (6:19). Even money can deteriorate because of spiralling inflation. In 1986 I took out an endowment policy that at maturity thirty years later would have yielded 45 000 Zambian kwacha, enough to buy a retirement home.

Five years later, the average primary school teacher was earning 110 000 Zambian kwacha a month! My endowment policy was worse than useless!

Money and wealth are useful supports, but we should not put our trust in them. Only treasures stored in heaven are permanently secure. They retain value because they are guarded by God against depreciation or decay (6:20). Such treasures are gained by obedience to God in all areas of life.

The reference to good eyes leading to a sound body and evil eyes leading to a body full of darkness (6:22-23) makes the point that wholehearted devotion to God and a generous attitude to others will lead to spiritual and material health. On the other hand mean-spiritedness and a lack of generousity are a form of blindness will lead to a state of darkness and selfish materialism, which shows no light for the future.

6:25-34 Anxiety and trust

It is important to have the right attitude to material possessions. Jesus' instruction not to *worry about tomorrow* (6:34) does not forbid thrift, thoughtfulness and careful provision for the future; these qualities are good. It does, however, forbid the sort of worry about clothes, food and the future that so consumes the person that there is no joy left in their life. The disciple must combine hard work with quiet confidence in God for the future. The wealthy must not concentrate on their riches, nor the poor on their misery.

The birds of the air work very hard to provide for their offspring. Yet they are not consumed by worry over what they will feed their young. The God who provides for them is the disciple's heavenly father. He will provide for his own just as he provides for the birds (6:26).

Worry does not advance one's cause at all; it cannot (6:27-28). It is absolutely useless. It can take up so much of one's energy that one is paralysed and cannot act. We need to recognize that while the necessities of life, like clothes, are important, they are not to become an all-consuming passion. Solomon's wardrobe fades into insignificance beside the simple beauty of a flower (6:29). A flower has a very short lifespan, but God fills it with beauty in spite of this. How much more will he provide food and clothes for the creatures who bear his image? (6:30-32). He knows our needs, and will provide for them (although he may not necessarily give us all that we want). Instead of worrying, we must learn to focus on serving the Lord wholeheartedly, doing our best and leaving the rest to him (6:33).

7:1-6 Judging others

Jesus is the one who will judge the living and the dead (John 5:22, 29; 2 Tim 4:1) and the secrets of people's hearts (Rom 11:33). He can condemn people to punishment, and eternal damnation (Rom 5:16; Heb 6:2). But only God and his

Christ can do this, not his disciples. His disciples are thus called to leave the role of passing judgment on others to God (**7:1-2**).

Another reason why we ought not to engage in judging others is illustrated by the image of *the speck of sawdust* and *the plank* (**7:3-5**). It is too easy for us to find fault with others, whilst being blind to our own failings. Besides this, we are never really in a position to fully comprehend all the facts, and we are prone to bias and prejudice. Only a faultless being, God, can judge. Disciples who usurp his prerogative will be judged by him.

But while we are not to judge and condemn others, we must still exercise discernment. The point of Jesus' saying about pearls and pigs can be illustrated using a Bemba folk tale about a dangerous leopard that lived in a very tall tree. Many attempts to lure it down from the tree had failed. But one day a man brought a dog and a goat to the tree. He tied them up and offered them food. He set *nshima* [a staple food for humans, which dogs eat but goats do not] before the goat and grass before the dog. Each refused to eat the food it was offered. But the man persisted in trying to get the dog to eat grass and the goat to eat *nshima*.

The watching leopard eventually told the man to give the *nshima* to the dog and the grass to the goat. The man responded with a proverb: '*Kalangilala wa muntu: alapalama*' ['He who would guide a man must draw near']. If the leopard really wanted to help him, then it would have to come down from the tree and show him how to feed the two animals. Then the man went on trying to feed each animal the wrong food. Eventually the leopard could no longer bear such stupidity, and came down from the tree, grabbed the *nshima* and put it in front of the dog and set the grass before the goat. But while it was doing this, the man brought out his axe and killed the leopard.

A key element in this tale is the stupidity of trying to feed good food to an animal that will not eat it. Everyone knows that it is futile to try to do this, and that the only result will be frustration for all concerned. The same idea lies behind Jesus' saying: *Do not give dogs what is sacred; do not throw your pearls to pigs* (**7:6**). Both dogs and pigs eat anything and were considered unclean. It would be perverse to suggest that they should be allowed to eat holy things like sacrificial offerings, or to feed them precious stones. In the same way, disciples were not to offer the gospel to those who would not recognize its value and would only treat it with contempt. The early church interpreted this saying as meaning that unbaptized, and therefore unclean, persons should not be permitted to partake of the Lord's Table (the Eucharist). However, the context seems to suggest that Jesus is advising his disciples to distinguish between those who sincerely honour God's word and those who will only treat it with contempt or use it as a tool to achieve their own ends.

7:7-11 Persistent prayer

Jesus returns to the topic of prayer, which he has already dealt with in 6:5-15. (This may indicate that the material in the Sermon on the Mount was not all preached on one occasion and that Matthew compiled his text using several sources.) *Ask, seek* and *knock* (**7:7**) are metaphors for prayer. The disciples are given confidence to persist in prayer. Because human beings respond positively to repeated appeals, we can be certain that the heavenly Father will answer persistent prayer (**7:8**).

In spite of the human bias to evil, people do not give stones to their children in response to requests for bread, nor do they give them snakes in response to requests for fish (**7:9-10**). Human beings cannot be more generous than God: *How much more* will God give *good gifts to those who ask him!* (**7:11**). The parallel passage in Luke suggests that the most significant of the good gifts that will be given is the Holy Spirit (Luke 11: 9-13).

7:12 The Golden Rule

Jesus' ethical teaching up to this point can be summarized in the words *Do to others what you would have them do to you* (**7:12**; see also Lev 19:18). These words also sum up God's will revealed through *the Law and the Prophets*, that is, the whole of the ot (see 22:37-40). The statement emphasizes the importance of people and relationships. We are not simply to refrain from doing harm to others, although that is very important, but are to go out of our way to help them in time of need. Like the Good Samaritan, we must not rejoice when our enemies suffer harm, but must go out of our way to help them, even if this involves considerable risk and expense (Luke 10:25-37). We are charged with the responsibility of putting other people's needs before our own. Tribalism would not be the blight it is on the African social and political landscape if groups like the Tutsis treated Hutus in this manner, and vice versa. Perhaps it is only the Holy Spirit who can give us the resources to live such a selfless life.

7:13-29 True and false discipleship

Gates, fruit and buildings are all metaphors used in this section to distinguish between true and false discipleship. True disciples enter by the narrow gate, produce good fruit and build their lives on the rock, which is the wisdom derived from the words of Jesus. The numerous false disciples enter by the wide gate, bear bad fruit and build their lives on sand, that is, on worldly wisdom that shuns the words of Jesus.

7:13-14 Two gates Jesus makes it clear that there are only two roads before us, and that choosing wisely is important (Deut 30:19-20; Josh 24:14-15; Ps 1:6; Jer 21:8). The broad road is very spacious and many find it easily. There is no need to stop and think before taking it, for it comes naturally. Its gate is wide, but it leads to destruction (**7:13**).

The narrow road, by contrast, is inconspicuous and leads to a small gate, but this is the way to life (**7:14**). Those who want to follow this road must take care to look for it. It is neither obvious nor the natural way to live. As Jesus has made clear in what he has been saying, the life of a disciple is not easy, but it is immensely rewarding and is ultimately the only way.

7:15-23 GOOD AND BAD FRUIT In 5:11-12 the church, represented by the disciples, was in danger of attack from outside, from those who persecute others for righteousness' sake. In this passage the danger is from within, from among the leadership of the church.

The prophetic ministry of the OT included great prophets like Elijah, Isaiah and Jeremiah. Some of them like Elijah (and John the Baptist) wore the clothes of the poorest people, namely a sheep skin or camel skin turned inside out and worn with the fleece against the body (3:4; see also 1 Kgs 19:19; 2 Kgs 1:8).

In NT times, there were also those who gave up everything and dedicated their lives to wandering about spreading the word of God. But some of those who appeared to be prophets (metaphorically, wearing *sheep's clothing*) were actually false prophets. They were like wolves eager to tear their prey (**7:15**; see also Ezek 22:27; Acts 20:29). Such people proclaimed popular messages that were tailored to suit the tastes of the hearers, but were not the word of God. Jeremiah said they offered peace when there was no peace (Jer 6:14; 8:11).

The false prophets had found an easy way to make a good living. They offered the word of God under the cloak of a respected ministry, and in return received very good hospitality. Still today, it can be said that in poor economies there are two ways to get a good job: become a government minister or a church minister! Too many church ministers are only interested in having an easy life. They are concerned for their own welfare, not that of their congregations. Like their OT counterparts, they preach an easy and attractive gospel, which neglects some of the more difficult demands that the true gospel makes upon Jesus' followers.

False prophets will easily be identified by their fruit (**7:16-18**). 'Fruit' is used in a variety of ways in the Bible. When it is used to mean the fruit of a tree (12:33; 21:19) or to mean people's offspring (Exod 1:7; Mic 6:7), it indicates something that grows naturally. It can also, as here, be used to mean spiritual growth. Sowing the seed of the word naturally produces a harvest of souls for the kingdom of heaven (Mark 4:13-20). Any true work of the Spirit also naturally produces fruit in human character: 'love, joy, peace, patience, kindness, goodness, faithfulness, gentleness and self-control' (Gal 5:22-23).

False prophets may be very gifted people who claim the name of Jesus (**7:21**), and are able to utter prophecies and perform miracles such as driving out demons (**7:22**). We must have discernment and look at the character of such people if we are to avoid being led astray. Do their own lives show the fruit of the Spirit? Thankfully, one day it will become clear which prophets are true and which are false, for all will be exposed by the Lord (**7:19, 23**).

7:24-29 WISE AND FOOLISH BUILDERS We must take care not to be deceived by appearances. Two houses, like two believers, may look very similar on the outside. But the difference between them, and between true and false believers, will be revealed when testing and trials come. A shallow sandy hollow, however attractive, will not provide sufficient strength for the foundation to withstand buffeting by torrents of water (**7:26-27**).

A wise builder must anchor the foundations on solid rock. The solid rock that Jesus is referring to here is his teaching (**7:24-25**) – that is the solid foundation on which true churches and believers must base their lives.

We rejoice that many if not most of our African churches are full to capacity. We are amazed that many primary and secondary schools, hotels, colleges and restaurants host church meetings on Sundays. The growth of the church in Africa is truly phenomenal. But is it all that it appears to be? If people are just hearing Jesus' words but not doing them, the church is built on sand. Knowledge must translate into action, and theology into life.

Jesus was clearly a teacher set apart. *He taught as one who had authority* (**7:29**). His words were the basis of judgment. His authority was not based on reinterpretation of ancient texts, but was the personal authority of an originator. The crowds, who form the background to the ministry of Jesus, recognized this.

8:1-9:34 The Ministry of Jesus: Part I

Throughout chapters 8 and 9, Jesus demonstrates his lordship over different aspects of creation. His actions reveal that the kingdom of God is already present, though not in its fullness.

8:1-4 Healing a Man with Leprosy

Many human beings in all societies have bodily defects that cause them to suffer exclusion, isolation and sometimes worse. In Buddhist cultures and some African cultures, disability of any kind is seen as a punishment for evil deeds or misdemeanours in a previous life and as a reason for rejection. Orphanages are full of disabled children who have been abandoned. The millions of people in Africa who suffer from HIV/AIDS are often treated as outcasts.

In Israel, *leprosy* was grounds for rejection (8:2). It was probably not the disease called leprosy now, but may have included such skin conditions as psoriasis, lupus and ringworm. People with leprosy were officially certified unclean and excluded from society. When approaching healthy people, they were obliged to shout, 'Unclean! Unclean!' so that the others could avoid being contaminated by contact (Lev 13:45-46).

This passage shows that Jesus has the power to deal with apparently incurable diseases and the compassion to restore desperate human beings struggling with social stigma, isolation and loneliness.

The *man with leprosy came* to Jesus boldly and yet humbly (**8:2**). He was not put off by the crowds, although he risked ridicule, and worse. To his mind, the issue was not Jesus' ability to heal, but his willingness to do so. God had been shown in history to be Lord over even incurable diseases (2 Kgs 5:1, 7-15). But the leper does not act rashly in presumption. In humility he kneels before Jesus and asks him to do what only he could. In response Jesus heals the man. He reaches out and touches him, something that no healthy man would do to a leper (**8:3**; see also Lev 5:3)! Jesus also shows his respect for the law by directing the man to go to the priest in order to be restored to his true social status (5:17-20).

The instruction *don't tell anyone* reminds us that Jesus is not concerned about attracting attention to himself, but remains focused on the needs of the desperate man (**8:4**).

8:5-13 Commending a Centurion's Faith

Racism, nepotism, sexism, tribalism and other forms of self-centredness are scandals that have adversely affected the church in Africa. The apartheid system in South Africa was a particularly brutal expression of racism, while the Rwandan genocide showed the evil power of tribalism. In Jesus' day, segregation was based on religion (Jews looked down on Gentiles), power (Romans looked down on those they had conquered) and gender (men looked down on women).

The *centurion* in **8:5** was a Gentile, a Roman officer commanding up to one hundred soldiers (8:9). These Roman troops were hated by most Jews as representatives of the colonizers and worshippers of other gods, including the 'divine' emperor.

The centurion recognized that although he had a high rank, in matters to do with healing Jesus had a still higher rank. So he approached Jesus with respect (**8:6**). The parallel passage in Luke 7:1-10 suggests that he even used intermediaries rather than speaking to Jesus directly. Matthew does not bother to mention these. We need to learn appropriate humility from this centurion. Far too many of us wear our status as if it had permanent value. Such an attitude leads to arrogance, even in pastors and bishops.

Jesus consented to come and heal the centurion's servant (**8:7**). But the centurion objected, saying he did not deserve to have Jesus enter his house (**8:8a**). His words may have been intended to help Jesus avoid the ceremonial uncleanness caused by entering a Gentile's house. Nevertheless, his view of Jesus' authority was astonishing. Using

an idea derived from his own military authority, he argues that Jesus is a man under authority (God's authority), and therefore he can simply command a disease to disappear without having to be in close proximity to the person with the illness (**8:8b-9**).

The centurion used an aspect of the military organization that he was familiar with to demonstrate his faith in Jesus. If his Gentile military culture provided a way of expressing faith in Jesus, then surely African cultures are equally capable of doing so. We do not need to borrow metaphors and categories from other cultures. We must work hard at using our own native thought patterns and processes to make the Christian faith familiar to African eyes.

Another important truth that the centurion recognized is that authority is always derived. There is only one sovereign in the universe, and that is God. All other leaders have is delegated authority, which both authorizes and sets limits on the leader's decisions and actions. A Bemba proverb says, *Umulilo ucingile abakalamba: ta oca* ['a fire protected by the elderly is not dangerous']. Leadership can become dangerous unless it is 'protected', that is, regulated by those with greater authority, such as that enjoyed by the elders in an African community.

The centurion's authority was backed by and regulated by the Roman Empire. Similarly Jesus' authority was backed by and regulated by God. Any pastor, bishop, evangelist or apostle must exercise leadership with the understanding that all of us are under the ultimate authority of our Lord. The church is his, and so are the people. We play a part, a very small part, as leaders entrusted with his work for his glory and joy.

The centurion also showed great insight into the nature of faith. From a human perspective, he recognized that power resides in a person. A command issued by someone with the authority to give it has powerful effects. Jesus' command can make people follow him (9:9), calm rough seas (8:26; see also Mark 4:39), and bring the universe into existence (John 1:3; see Heb 11:3). The centurion's words remind us that faith is belief or trust not in a system but in the person of Jesus Christ the Son of God.

Jesus commended the centurion for his great faith (**8:10**). He then proceeded to clearly signal the unthinkable: some Gentiles will enter the kingdom of God ahead of some Israelites (**8:11-12**). We must not equate faith in God with human distinctions between people. The church must not put up barriers to prevent outsiders from drawing near to Jesus. The exercise of authority and faith must always be focused on Jesus, not on any other person or programme or even the church itself.

8:14-17 Healing Many People

Jesus' healing ministry was not restricted to the official places of worship. He would heal wherever there was need. So when he was in the home of one of his disciples and found that *Peter's mother-in-law* had *a fever* (**8:14**), he immediately healed her with a touch in spite of the normal restrictions on touching people with fevers. The healing was instantaneous, and Peter's mother-in-law immediately served them (**8:15**). This episode suggests a sequence of discipleship. A person who serves Jesus is one in whom Jesus has first done a work of healing, either spiritually or both physically and spiritually.

Peter's mother-in-law was not the only person Jesus healed on that occasion. Many others were brought to him and he healed them all of both physical illnesses and demon possession (**8:16**). Demon possession is the invasion of a human body by evil spirits with the view to controlling what that person does. The spirits may be benign and do no more than simply live in the person, but more often they act through the person. Some demon-possessed people become herbalists or diviners. Others may even become sick and then die. Demon possession can also manifest itself in bizarre ways.

Jesus acknowledged the reality of demon possession and always expelled demons from their hosts. In Africa, there is a great need for such a ministry that clearly demonstrates the power of Jesus over the spirits that have kept many people in bondage. This ministry will also release people whose personalities and characters have been distorted by their bondage to demons.

By his power over both physical and spiritual illnesses Jesus fulfilled the promise of Isaiah that the Servant of the Lord *carried our diseases* (**8:17**; see Isa 53:4).

8:18-22 Counting the Cost of Following Jesus

Very often, passages that deal with discipleship show Jesus on the move. Sometimes he is setting out on a journey or walking by the sea (9:9; see Mark 1:16-19; 2:13-14). Perhaps that is why discipleship is sometimes described as a journey with Jesus.

In this case, Jesus' order *to cross to the other side of the lake* (**8:18**) is followed by a discussion between Jesus and two would-be disciples in which he talks about the cost of being one of his followers.

Jesus tells the first of the would-be followers that his ministry is not going to be a comfortable one in synagogues and temples. Instead it is going to go to where the suffering people are, however uncomfortable that might be. This point is underlined by Jesus' use of his favourite title, *Son of Man* (see Dan 7:13-22). Jesus must suffer before he is glorified (Mark 8:31-33). A disciple must be committed to follow Jesus even if it should lead to suffering or even death (**8:19-20**).

The second would-be disciple is keen to follow Jesus, but has some family commitments to take care of first (**8:21**). Relatives are very important in Africa, as indeed they were

in Israel. In Israel, giving one's parents a good burial was interpreted as part of the honour one was commanded to show them (Exod 20:12). But it seems likely that this man is asking for permission to wait until his father dies before he follows Jesus. He is putting his social and family obligations before his discipleship. Jesus' response makes it clear that following him has priority over all other relationships (**8:22**). His words are a testimony to his equality with God, only God's honour could be placed above honouring one's parent.

8:23-27 Calming the Storm

The key question in this passage is found right at the end: *What kind of man is this? Even the winds and the waves obey him!* (**8:27**). The story itself contains the answer to that question. He is the kind of man who has power over natural forces. A vicious dog that has the power to kill will obey its owner. The winds and the waves recognize their owner in Jesus. He created them, and has power to control them.

The Lake of Galilee is rather like a funnel. To the north are Mount Hermon and the mountains of Lebanon, which stand about 9000 feet (3000 metres) above sea level. The lake itself lies some 600 feet (200 metres) below sea level. Violent winds are drawn down from the mountains and forced into the narrow Jordan Valley. When the winds hit the lake they churn up the waters into fierce squalls that can threaten life itself, as indicated by the cry of these grown men: *Lord, save us! We're going to drown!* (**8:24-25**). The physical danger was very eal and the disciples were frightened.

Jesus by contrast was fast asleep. He may have been so exhausted that nothing could disturb his sleep, or he may simply have been confident that he was secure. When the disciples woke him, he reprimanded them for the lack of faith clearly shown by their fears (**8:26a**). If they had known who it was that was asleep in their boat, they would not have been so afraid. Faith is putting one's trust in Jesus even in the most difficult of situations whether spiritual, physical, emotional or mental.

The second thing Jesus did was even more remarkable. He commanded the winds to die down and the waves to be still (**8:26b**). On inland lakes, waves that have been churned up by violent winds remain unsettled long after the winds have died down. But Matthew records that the wind and the waves both died down instantly. Only the creator of both wind and waves could exercise such control and produce such a great miracle (Job 38:8-11; Ps 65:5-8). Who is this man whom *even the winds and the waves obey* (**8:27**)? He is Jesus the Word of God, the Lord of creation.

8:28-34 Healing Two Demon-Possessed Men

Jesus' ministry was largely confined to the land of Israel (15:24). However, the healing of the two demon-possessed described here (and in Luke 8:26-39) took place outside the boundaries of Israel in *the region of the Gadarenes* (**8:28a**). This region is situated on the east side of the Sea of Galilee, in the territory referred to as the Decapolis. It was Gentile territory; hence the presence of pigs. This incident reminds us that if the church is going to fulfil the Great Commission to tell the whole world the good news, it needs to shed any feelings of racial, tribal or sexual superiority.

Jesus arrived there with his disciples and was confronted by *two demon-possessed men* (**8:28b**). The demons had isolated these men from society, reduced them to a state of inhumanity, given them supernatural strength and made them so violent that *no one could pass that way* (**8:28c**).

Demon possession is very common in Africa today. The influence of centuries of rationalism has left many Europeans and Americans reluctant to accept the possibility of demon possession. They explain it away using modern theories of psychology and psychoanalysis. We in Africa do not have any such difficulties with the idea, and apparently neither did Jesus and his disciples. They recognized that some people were unfortunately slaves to foreign spirits (Acts 16:16). Casting out demons was a major part of the mission of Jesus and his disciples.

The demons had no problems recognizing that Jesus was the king in whom the kingdom of God had come, although not yet in its fullness. So they addressed him as the *Son of God* and as the judge who would put an end to their activities (**8:29**). They knew that *the appointed time* for their torment was the end of time (Rev 14:10; 20:10).

The demons, which up to that point had appeared invincible, were reduced to begging Jesus to let them live another day and asking permission to enter into the pigs (**8:30-31**). Jesus gave them permission, and the whole herd of pigs ran headlong into the sea and drowned (**8:32**). The value of the herd must have been considerable and the loss to the community great. But for Jesus the lives of the two men were infinitely more valuable than the pigs. Grace is extravagant. When Jesus saves, he does not hold back.

By contrast, the people of the community valued their possessions above their relatives and so asked Jesus to leave (**8:33-34**). Similarly, when Paul and Silas delivered a young woman from demon possession, they were arrested, tortured and thrown into prison (Acts 16:16-24).

God values human life above material possessions and his disciples should learn to value people and do whatever it takes to deliver them from any kind of bondage.

9:1-8 Healing a Paralyzed Man

This passage demonstrates Jesus' authority over another aspect of creation, namely sin. The Bible is clear that sin entered into humankind at the fall (Gen 3:6-7). Since then, sin has become part of humanity, and all humans are sinners (Rom 3:23; Ps 51:5) and subject to the wrath of God

(Eph 2:3). There is no more intractable problem in human experience than sin. Sin thrives in every human context. Neither education, nor good upbringing, nor wealth, nor hygiene, nor even religion can eradicate sin.

The healing of the *paralytic* took place in Capernaum, which is here said to be Jesus' *own town* (**9:1-2**; see Mark 2:1). Although Jesus grew up in Nazareth, he moved to Capernaum when he began his public ministry, which was based in Peter's house. Hearing that Jesus had returned, many people came to the house to be healed (Mark 2:1-3). Among them were four people who carried a friend who was paralyzed. They believed that Jesus could heal him. *Jesus saw their faith* and responded by healing their friend (**9:2a**). Jesus responds to faith even when it is exercised on behalf of others. Intercession is a powerful weapon. Through intercession believers can affect other people and systems for good and for God.

The immediate problem was the need for physical healing, but Jesus sought to deal with something else first: the sin that he judged to be at the root of the physical problem. His words, *take heart, son; your sins are forgiven* (**9:2b**), do not imply that all physical illness is the result of sin (John 9:2-3). However, in this particular case, Jesus perceived that the two were connected, or perhaps simply that this man had other problems besides his physical problem.

Many of us carry burdens of guilt that may make us depressed or less responsive to the natural processes of healing. James makes it clear that there can be a link between inner healing and physical healing (Jas 5:14-16). Whatever the case, Jesus judged this man to be in need of healing from sin as well as from physical paralysis.

Ultimately God alone can forgive sin (Jer 31:34), and he will do this at the end of time. But Jesus acted decisively in the present to show that he has authority to forgive sins. His words caused *some of the teachers of the law* to accuse him of blasphemy, that is, of usurping the prerogatives of God (**9:3**; Mark 2:7). After all, only God can forgive sins (although it was true that certain Jewish religious officials could pronounce forgiveness, providing that appropriate atonement had been made). Who was this wandering preacher to assume the role of God, bypassing even the temple mechanism for forgiving sins? This is the first time in the gospel that Jesus differs from the religious establishment. The rift would grow until eventually they would cry out for his blood (27:22-23).

Although their thoughts were unspoken, Jesus perceived clearly what they were thinking about. He has supernatural knowledge (**9:4**; 12:25; 22:18). Jesus is definitely a miracle worker but he is more than that; he is God. So instead of making apologies for his statement, Jesus acted boldly in the physical realm by healing the paralyzed man, thus demonstrating that he does possess power (**9:7**). The *Son of Man* (**9:6**; Dan 7:13) has authority on earth, the authority

God has delegated to him, both to provide physical healing and to forgive sins.

The healing miracle filled the crowd with *awe,* which expressed itself in worship of God (**9:8**). Miracles must never be treated as ends in themselves, or used to impress people. Jesus responded to a need, and in so doing brought glory to God.

9:9-12 Calling Matthew, the Tax Collector

Just as in the other call narratives (4:18-22; 8:18), Jesus is on the move when he calls Matthew (**9:9**). Matthew was a Jew employed by the Roman forces to collect imperial, taxes from his fellow Israelites. His standing in society was therefore similar to that of Africans who, because of their employment in colonial law enforcement units such as the police force and judicial systems, were seen as renegades and collaborators and hence hated and despised.

Not only did Matthew support the colonialists, he and all his colleagues did so in a way that was particularly corrupt, lining their pockets at the expense of their compatriots (Luke 19:8). They were, therefore, the objects of particular hatred. Their morality was so objectionable that their title, *tax collector,* was associated with *sinner* as a byword for everything that was wrong in society (**9:10-11**; Luke 15:1-2). They were regarded as beyond salvation and no prophet would be seen socializing with them. Because they maintained continual physical contact with Gentiles, they were continually ceremonially unclean. 'A friend of tax collectors and sinners' was not a pious designation for Jesus; it was an insult (11:19).

It is thus remarkable that Jesus calls Matthew to be his follower, even though society in general and the nation's leadership in particular would have written anyone like him off as beyond saving! Jesus is interested in people regardless of their backgrounds. In part that is why many tax collectors and sinners followed Jesus. Matthew's calling provided an opportunity for his colleagues to gather around Jesus (9:10).

Jesus responds to the Pharisees' criticism of those he associated with by making the point that good people sometimes find that their very goodness stands in the way of seeing that they too are sinful (**9:12**). Every human being is a sinner and therefore in need of a saviour. The tax collectors were prepared to admit that they were bad people, who were spiritually unhealthy (**9:13**; Luke 18:13). That is why they heard Jesus gladly. Those who recognize their need will find entry into the kingdom more straightforward.

9:13-17 Answering Questions about Fasting

John the Baptist's message was the same as that of Jesus', John's disciples were uncertain about some of the things Jesus and his disciples were doing. They asked, *How is it that ... your disciples do not fast?* (**9:14**). Jesus now supple-

ments his earlier teaching on fasting in 6:16-18, and says that his disciples will fast after he has been *taken from them* (**9:15**). While he is with them, they do not need to go to great lengths to seek his presence!

The two images of the *patch of unshrunk cloth* (**9:16**) and the *new wine* (**9:17**) express Jesus' continuity with the past, but also that he is something radically new and different.

9:18-26 Demonstrating Power over Death

Matthew does not identify the *ruler* (**9:18**), although both Mark and Luke call him 'Jairus, a ruler of the synagogue' (Mark 5:22; Luke 8:4). Death had taken the life of his precious daughter leaving an aching void, but he knew that Jesus could reverse the effects of death. He therefore *knelt before him* in public, probably not so much in worship as in an acknowledgement that only someone with superhuman powers could do such a thing. For a full-grown man and a leader, to kneel before an unrecognized wandering preacher took humility, faith, courage and conviction.

Jesus consented to go and lay hands on the child in order to raise her from death (**9:19**). But their progress is interrupted by the appearance in the crowd of another desperate person: *a woman who had been subject to bleeding for twelve years* (**9:20**). This bleeding would have made the woman and everyone and everything she touched unclean (Lev 15:25-27). She was effectively isolated from society. Marriage was out of the question, and without the normal support of a husband and children, she must have been very needy. She was also burdened with the expense of seeking cures and the regular washing of all her belongings and clothes. Her desperation and need drove her to Jesus, but her fear of being rejected led her to approach him from behind (**9:21**). Her faith seems to have been more in some magical power than in the person of Jesus. Nevertheless, Jesus tells her, *your faith has healed you* (**9:22**). He was not ashamed to be identified with a woman in her condition. Nor should Christ's disciples be ashamed to pay attention to those rejected by society because of disabilities, mentally disturbances and diseases such as leprosy and HIV/AIDS.

Jesus accompanied the grieving father to the funeral house where professional mourners had already begun to grieve in the traditional way (**9:23**). In Zambia, the community gathers at a home where someone has just died and there is loud wailing, especially when new mourners arrive. In Israel, professional mourners were hired. A poor family might have had only a wailing woman and two flute players, but a rich ruler like Jairus could have afforded more.

The mourners derided Jesus when he said that the child was only sleeping (**9:24**). This was a common euphemism for death (1 Thess 4:14), but the euphemism becomes the truth when Jesus is present. He ignored their sneers, and gently took the child's hand in his and raised her from the dead! (**9:25**).

In the late 1990s in Zambia, it was not uncommon for Christians to pray for the resurrection of a deceased brother or sister. While such faith is commendable, Christians should not succumb to a dogged refusal to acknowledge that death is the normal end of all human beings.

9:27-34 Healing the Blind and the Mute

Two blind men followed Jesus, crying out for him to have mercy on them. They called him *Son of David* (**9:27**), a title that Jesus did not use, likely because of its nationalistic and political connotations. However, the Davidic Messiah would also be one who would show mercy (Isa 35:5-6; 61:1), and so Jesus responded to their pleas and healed them. Matthew may set this healing inside a house to stress Jesus' desire not to give his miracles unwanted publicity (**9:28-30**). That did not work, for the people who had been healed went out and *spread the news about him all over that region* (**9:31**).

The casting out of the demon from *a man who … could not talk* also led to great amazement, although his enemies, the Pharisees, attributed Jesus' work to demonic activity (**9:32-34**).

9:35-10:42 Teaching II: The Disciples' Mission

The second of Matthew's five blocks of teaching will begin in chapter 10, where Jesus commissions his disciples and gives them instructions for their mission in Israel. They will eventually be given a universal mandate to take the gospel to all the people in every culture and age (28:18-20). The Gospel of Matthew is itself the result of the mission of the disciples and a missionary document; it came out of mission and is to be used in mission.

Across Africa, countless individuals have gone out on mission, and churches like the Evangelical Church of West Africa have sent out many missionaries. Recently the church in Nigeria has been making great efforts to muster a missionary force to go throughout the whole world to proclaim the gospel. Yet in some areas of the continent, the African church has little missionary strategy or involvement. One of the reasons for this state of affairs is that such churches have become used to the idea of being perpetual recipients of missionaries. But the Gospel writers, and Matthew in particular, do not promote a community of believers that sees itself in terms of receiving all the time. Jesus charged his disciples to be 'fishers of men' (4:19).

Those who follow Jesus must engage in mission to those who have not heard of him and his kingdom. The African church must follow Jesus into mission across many borders to show his love to people who are not related to us by blood. The church of the Senegalese must love the Somalis and Eritreans sufficiently to take them the gospel. Similarly the Zulus and Afrikaners must love the Zandes sufficiently to take them the gospel; the Luos too must love the Yaos.

Across the whole continent and beyond, Jesus calls the African church to reach out with his love to all the peoples of the world. This call is all the more important because, if current trends continue, the leadership of the universal church will pass into African, Latin American and Asian hands over the next fifty years. So we need to pay particular attention to Jesus' teaching here about the immediate mission of the twelve disciples and about the nature of Christian mission in the world.

9:35-38 The Workers Are Few

Before embarking on his teaching about mission, Jesus explained why it is needed. He summoned his disciples to pray to God for more people who could do what he was doing (**9:37-38**). There was then as now, a desperate need for people to follow in the footsteps of Jesus in order to bring much needed relief to others. Jesus had been to *all the towns and villages* (**9:35**), and he knew from personal experience the things that made life difficult for ordinary people. Indeed they appeared as vulnerable as *sheep without a shepherd* (**9:36**).

In this condition, all sorts of people were taking advantage of them. Politically, they bore the burden of heavy taxes, servitude and human rights violations. Their religious leaders were not providing teaching, pastoral care or help with material needs. They endured leprosy, fevers, chronic illnesses, demon possession, blindness, paralysis, and many other troubles. Jesus responded with characteristic *compassion*. He healed their sick and preached the good news to them (Isa 61:1-3).

Mission commitment requires not only assessment of needs, but also a compassionate response in spiritual and material terms. We need an integrated approach that fully meets the needs of harassed people. But this work is spiritual and needs prayer, so that God can send those he chooses *into his harvest field* (9:37).

10:1-15 The First Mission

10:1-4 The first workers

The mission of the Twelve (**10:1**) is a practical response to the desperate need for workers expressed by Jesus. The twelve disciples appear at this point as an established group. Matthew gives no details of their specific call (Mark 3:13-15; Luke 6:13), but he does give us their names (**10:2-4**; see also Mark 3:16-19; Luke 6:14-16; Acts 1:13). Mark's and Matthew's lists of the apostles include someone called Thaddeus, but Luke instead speaks of Judas the son of James. He was probably the same person, known by two different names. In all the lists, Peter is mentioned first, presumably to signify his leadership of the group, and James, John and Judas Iscariot appear prominently.

None of the Gospel writers gives us much biographical information about the men who formed *the twelve,* but it is clear that they were very ordinary people, not distinguished academics or religious leaders. Rather than focusing on their personalities, the Gospels focus on their activities, and specifically on the activities of Peter, James and John. We know hardly anything about the other apostles, except that they were a very mixed bag. Matthew was a tax collector in the pay of the hated occupation forces, while Simon the Zealot was a thoroughgoing nationalist. In Jesus they found oneness and unity.

The fact that there were twelve of them is significant. Jesus was making a conscious claim that his new order would succeed the twelve tribes of Israel, not in a political or geographical sense, but in being the primary vehicle for taking the blessings of God to the whole world. This task had originally been given to Abraham, who is described as the father of those who believe (Gal 3:7). The Twelve will constitute the new Israel.

The twelve disciples are also called *the apostles* (10:2). The word 'apostle' derives from a Greek word meaning 'to send', so an apostle is someone who has been sent on a mission. An apostle's role is similar to that of the 'go-between' who arranges marriages in many African societies. The go-between does not act in his or her own interests. Rather, he or she is an agent (*apostle*) of one family who is sent to another family with a message to make arrangements for a marriage. A go-between does not take liberties with the bride, or as the Bemba put it, *Inkombe: taikata pa cinema* ['a messenger does not place his hand on the lower part of the abdomen']. Similarly, apostles must focus on carrying out the mission or delivering the message someone entrusted to them. In the NT, 'apostle' is not a title designating status but a job description. An apostle does not rank higher than a pastor or bishop, but has a different function in the mission of Christ. Apostles today must be at the forefront of mission, persuading people to follow Christ and enter into his kingdom.

10:5-6 The scope of their mission

The twelve apostles were not sent to the Gentiles or the Samaritans but to *the lost sheep of Israel* (**10:5-6**). This particularism or favouritism can at first appear offensive. But these words must be understood in context. Jesus himself said of his own mission that he was 'sent only to the lost sheep of Israel' (15:24). However, this deliberate limiting of the sphere of operation must be set alongside the vast body of material that shows that God's mission is to all the peoples of the world.

God clearly had a universal goal when he promised that through Abraham all the peoples of the world would be blessed (Gen 12:3). Isaiah had a vision of all the peoples of the world, even the traditional enemies of God's people,

joining with Israel to worship God (Isa 19:23-25). The Gospel of Matthew itself contains evidence of God's universal concern. The centurion is shown to have greater faith than anyone else in Israel (8:5-13), and Jesus asserts that many Gentiles will come from 'the east and the west, and will take their places at the feast with Abraham, Isaac and Jacob in the kingdom of heaven' (8:11). He healed a Canaanite woman's child (15:21-28), fed four thousand outside Israel on the east side of the Sea of Galilee (15:29-38) and made it clear that if the nation of Israel did not embrace his teaching, the kingdom would be taken away from them and given to 'a people who will produce its fruit' (21:43). Before the end of the world the gospel will have been preached to all the nations (24:14), and ultimately all the world will gather before Jesus at the final judgment (25:32).

So the particularism must be understood as strategic and limited to the time of Jesus' own ministry, which was directed to the nation of Israel. The mission of the Twelve and subsequently of the church would embrace the whole world (28:16-20; Acts 1:8). The apparent restrictions must be understood in the Pauline sense of 'first for the Jew, then for the Gentile' (Rom 1:16; 2:9, 10; see Acts 13:46).

10:7-15 Their commission

The disciples were given specific instructions for how they were to conduct themselves on this particular mission.

10:7-8A PREACHING AND HEALING Preaching and healing were inseparable parts of the mission. The message was simple, *The kingdom of heaven is near* (**10:7**). It was the same message that John the Baptist and Jesus preached (3:2; 4:17). Furthermore, they were to *heal the sick, raise the dead, cleanse those who have leprosy, drive out demons* (**10:8a**). Their healing ministry encompassed the same kinds of miracles that Jesus had done in chapters 8–9. This fact, in combination with the restriction to go only to Israel and the message of the nearness of the kingdom, indicates that at this point in time the ministry of the disciples was an extension of Jesus' own ministry. Their own ministry would start only after Pentecost.

10:8B-10 PROVISIONS The disciples were to be careful not to charge for their work, for they had not paid for the ability to perform it. Both the message and the authority to heal had been freely given to them and were to be distributed without charge (**10:8b**). Ministers of the gospel should not be like lawyers who charge for every service or for hours spent in preparation. They must offer prayers, baptisms and sermons free of charge. They are not self-appointed men and women who are in it for the money.

Nor were the disciples to make up for not charging fees by carrying a lot of money with them (**10:9-10a**). The disciples were to travel light so that they could get on with the task and not worry about material provisions. This sense of urgency may have come from Jesus' own sense of the shortness of his time on earth. Yet perhaps all those who engage in mission should have this sense of urgency, for we do not know when the end will come.

The Twelve were not to worry about their material needs, for those who benefited from their ministries were expected to support them by supplying what they needed so that they could concentrate on their work (**10:10b**). This principle still applies today.

10:11-15 HOSPITALITY The disciples were to choose carefully where they lodged. They should stay with someone with a good reputation and should not move from one house to another, perhaps in search of better conditions (**10:11**). Their *greeting,* 'Peace', was a true blessing, the effect of which depended not just on those who spoke but on the worthiness of the recipient (**10:12-13**). Where the message and the messengers were rejected, the disciples were to shake *the dust* of the house, village or town *off their feet* (**10:14**). This gesture would be a sign of the coming judgment on the last day (**10:15**).

10:16-42 Mission in General

Christian mission is dangerous. For the Twelve, the danger would come mainly from the Pharisees whom Jesus describes as *wolves* (**10:16a**). However, all whom Jesus sends into the mission field will face dangers at every turn, and they need to have the right attitudes if they are to survive. They need prudence or wisdom (*shrewd as snakes*) as well as transparency (*innocent as doves*) (**10:16b**). Armed with these qualities, they would avoid unnecessarily antagonizing their opponents and would also not do anything wrong, so that all accusations levelled at them would be false.

The enemies of Christ's followers would include the officials of local *synagogues* (**10:17**) and *governors and kings* (**10:18**). When they faced these formidable enemies, they could draw comfort from the fact that Jesus would be there with them through the Holy Spirit who would provide their defence (**10:19-20**). This promise has often been misinterpreted to mean that preachers need not prepare their sermons or lessons; all they need do is open their mouths and the Spirit will speak through them. We know that the Spirit does indeed work through us, and often in spite of us, but this does not absolve us from the responsibility to prepare. Jesus' promise here is to help his people when they are arrested and forced to defend themselves before hostile courts.

Persecution will also come from close family members, such as brothers and sisters, parents and children (**10:21**). In Africa, this is particularly true when people come to Christ from a Muslim background. Such people often face intense persecution. But believers can anticipate hatred from all who do not believe (**10:22a**).

Such opposition can lead to despair, but Jesus offers the hope that *he who stands firm to the end will be saved* (**10:22b**). They will not be spared persecution but will be saved from God's wrath when he punishes their persecutors. Here Jesus is not saying that we achieve salvation only through endurance. Nor is he saying that someone who does not endure will not be saved. Those theological issues are dealt with in other passages. Here he is simply exhorting believers to endure because there is light at the end of the tunnel.

Given that they can expect persecution, believers' strategy for the present must be to move on to a safer area when persecution becomes intense (**10:23**). There will be enough safe cities in Israel to go to until *the Son of Man comes.* Some have related this final phrase to the destruction of Jerusalem in AD 70, but to do so involves adopting an unusual interpretation of this phrase. Others relate it to the second coming of Christ (see also 24:30; 25:31; 26:64). But in that case, why does Jesus speak only of the *cities of Israel?* The answer may be that Jesus is not here focusing on chronology or geography but on the safety of those who endure persecution because of him. In interpreting this phrase, we should also remember that while Christ will return in clouds of glory at the end of time, it is also true that he comes to each believer within their own experience. The Son of Man's humiliating death and glorious resurrection have broken the power of persecution. Death is no longer a threat to the believer.

When we face persecution, and possibly even death for our faith, we need to remember that Jesus does not ask his disciples to do anything he has not done himself. He endured the scorn of the Pharisees (9:34) and was killed for his work. His disciples should expect the same treatment (**10:24-25**), for death is the logical outcome of their being Jesus' followers. But they should also take courage from the fact that God is in control and will ultimately vindicate his own (**10:26-31**).

Disciples can also rest assured that their devotion, even to the point of death (**10:38**) will not go unrewarded. Jesus will honour his true disciples before the Father (**10:32**). Our devotion to Jesus must exceed our devotion to any other relationships, including those with our nearest and dearest (**10:37**). Jesus' mission separates believers from unbelievers, no matter how close their natural ties (**10:34-36**). In fact, we are to love Jesus more than we love ourselves (**10:39**). This is the stuff of radical discipleship.

All who honour the servants of Christ will be honoured by Christ himself. There are three levels of welcome involved here. To welcome a servant of Christ is to welcome Christ himself, and to welcome Christ is to welcome the Father (**10:40**). These words underscore the importance of showing hospitality to those who are in the service of Christ. In fact, the words about receiving a prophet's or a righteous man's reward in **10:41** indicate that the one providing hospitality will receive the same reward as the servant of Christ whom he or she welcomed.

11:1-12:50 The Ministry of Jesus: Part II

11:1-19 John the Baptist Asks about Jesus

After sending out the Twelve, Jesus carried on visiting towns and villages preaching and teaching (**11:1**). The narrative returns to John the Baptist (see Mark 6:14-29). Jesus has been teaching about persecution, and John's example shows how far persecution can go. John was imprisoned and ultimately executed for his bold statements about the immorality of King Herod (14:1-12). All who speak out in the name of Jesus may reasonably expect to be persecuted (2 Tim 3:12).

John's example also shows that those who introduce Jesus may suffer from doubt. At one stage, John had been very sure that Jesus was the Messiah (3:11-13). But now, possibly because of his imprisonment and reports of rising opposition to Jesus from the Jewish leaders, John sent *his disciples to ask* Jesus to confirm that he was indeed *the one who was to come* (**11:2-3**).

Jesus answered not by confirming in words that he was the Messiah, but by the only true test, his actions (**11:4-5**). He pointed to the miracles he had performed: the blind received their sight (9:27-31), the lame walked (9:1-7), those with leprosy were cured (8:1-4), the deaf heard (although they are not specifically mentioned we can assume that they are included in 8:16-17), the dead were raised (9:18-26) and the good news was preached to the poor (5:3; 9:35; 11:1).

Jesus' attack on the natural and spiritual enemies of human beings mirrors what Isaiah said about the saving activities of God through his servant (Isa 29:18; 35:5-6; 61:1-2). Jesus was encouraging John and his disciples to reread the OT and its prediction of the Messiah's role. Jesus completed his exhortation by proclaiming a blessing on those who accept him and do not fall away on his account (**11:6**). It is not wrong to have doubts, even about Jesus, but when doubts come we need to go back to Jesus' words and the witness of the whole Bible to who he is. We cannot recreate Jesus to fit in with our view of who he should be.

Jesus spoke of John as *a prophet* (**11:9a**). John's place in the tradition of the great prophets of Israel was supported by his wilderness lifestyle and his radical message that fulfilled Isaiah's prophecy (**11:7-8**; 3:3). But John was *more than a prophet* (**11:9b**) in that he was the one who introduced the final exodus from sin conducted by none other than God's Messiah. He was indeed the one about whom Malachi had prophesied (**11:10**; Mal 4:5).

Yet strangely Jesus states that even the 'least' member of the kingdom of heaven is greater than John (**11:11**).

Here Jesus is seeing John the Baptist as marking the transition point between the OT and the NT. The main feature of the OT was the prophetic role recorded in the books of the Prophets and in the Law (**11:13**). These books anticipated the coming of the Messiah, and John's ministry was to prepare the way for this Messiah and thus usher in the kingdom of heaven (3:3). Because of John's powerful ministry (3:5-6), and that of Jesus, the *kingdom of heaven* was *forcefully advancing* (**11:12**). More puzzling are the words translated *forceful men lay hold of it*. From the context, it seems that Jesus is saying that John the Baptist is such a great and bold man that he can even be equated with the prophet Elijah (**11:14**) and that the kingdom he ushered in moves forcefully, capturing even men of power. Yet despite John's greatness, believers are greater than John, for it is as if John stands back, holding open the door so that believers can enter. Given what a privilege it is to be in his kingdom, Jesus exhorts his listeners: *He who has ears, let him hear* (**11:15**). We should not risk missing entry into this kingdom.

We cannot claim to be greater than John because we are more devout than John; the only reason we are greater is because we have a fuller revelation of Christ, and know of the events of the first Easter. See how Christ centred everything is! Christ, and a proper understanding of who he is and what he came to do, are vital for proper development of vibrant Christianity.

Jesus' generation were guilty of refusing to accept the evidence. They had rejected John and were now rejecting Jesus (**11:16-19**). We must be open to the truth, however different it may appear from what we previously believed. This lesson needs to be learned in many ways in Africa today. For one thing, the church in Africa, like the church the world over, is often fragmented along denominational lines. Many of us belong to the churches we do by accident of birth or because of tribal affiliations. But the denominations have become barriers preventing useful interaction between Christians of different persuasions. I count it a great privilege to have worked with the Scripture Union, an interdenominational organization that introduced me to whole groups of Christians outside the confines of my own denominational upbringing. I found incredible riches of grace that God had deposited in the lives of my brothers and sisters.

We impoverish ourselves and our denominations by setting boundaries around what Christ is doing in his church. Mainstream denominations must take an interest in what God is doing in the independent churches, including the African Initiated Churches. We must never limit the power of Christ to our own imperfect understanding of him and his church. The Bemba say, *Amano ya bu weka: tayashingauka ikoshi* ['one person's wisdom cannot prove sufficient for all of life's challenge']. It is only when all the people of

God share their understanding of God that we shall come to have anything approaching a complete knowledge of Christ (Eph 3:10-11).

11:20-24 Woe to the Unrepentant Cities

The prophets of the OT often denounced cities or nations for refusing to accept God's standard. Israel and Judah were not immune to such denunciation (Amos 1–2). Jesus' denunciation of the towns of *Korazin, Bethsaida* (**11:21a**) and *Capernaum* (**11:23**) takes the same familiar form (see Isa 14:12-15). The sins for which these cities are condemned are greater than those of *Tyre and Sidon* (**11:21b-22**; see Isa 23) and of *Sodom,* a byword for sin (**11:24**). What had these towns done that drew such condemnation from Jesus?

In all these places, the people had witnessed God's power in the miracles he performed through Jesus. And yet they would not believe. They rejected the evidence that the Spirit had put before their eyes. We will all be judged for our sins and misdemeanours, but we will also be judged for misrepresenting the evidence of God's power as demonstrated through his work. God's people must not close their hearts to the workings of God lest we share the fate of the cities of Korazin, Bethsaida and Capernaum, for God will judge individuals as well as groups.

11:25-30 Wisdom and Rest

Human wisdom is not sufficient to understand God. Saving knowledge of God comes from God. The *wise and learned* were blinded by their own learning and wisdom, and it was to the *little children* (an analogy for those who are humble and marginalized) that God revealed the truths of Jesus and his mission (**11:25**). The greatest tragedy in this passage is that the wisdom of the learned in Israel was based on the very word of God, the law. Familiarity with matters concerning God is no guarantee to openness to his word.

Matthew points out that the only way to know God is through Jesus (**11:27**). In these days of pluralism, when it is politically incorrect to claim any special status for Christianity, it is important to affirm that it is only through Jesus that true knowledge of God the Father is to be found.

Jesus summons the harassed and helpless (9:36) to come to him, for his burden is easy and in him they will find rest, not exploitation and condemnation. The Pharisees had developed a burdensome religious legalism that weighed the people down; Jesus wanted to free them by substituting his light yoke for their heavy one (**11:28-30**).

12:1-45 Mounting Opposition

Jesus and his mission now face mounting opposition from the Pharisees. They take Jesus to task for what they see as his blatant disregard for the Sabbath and plot to kill him (12:1-14), they falsely attribute his exorcisms to the power of Satan (12:22-37) and they demand a miraculous sign

from him in spite of the many signs they have already seen (12:38-45). Despite the opposition, Jesus' fame continues to grow as people begin to associate his activities with the OT promise of the Servant of the Lord (12:15-21).

12:1-14 Jesus is Lord of the Sabbath

The disciples were doing nothing wrong when they picked a few ears of grain as they walked through a grainfield. The law specified that a hungry person was free to pluck some of the grain and eat it, as long as they did not use a sickle to cut it (Deut 23:25). But the problem was that the disciples were doing this on a Sabbath. During the twenty-four hours of the Sabbath day, the people of the Lord were commanded not to do any work. Their rest honoured the seventh day of creation, when the Lord rested after completing his perfect work (Gen 2:2; see also Exod 20:11; 31:13-15; 35:2; Deut 5:13-15; Ezek 20:20). The Sabbath also made it possible for everyone, including slaves and even domestic animals, to have a whole day of rest from regular work.

If people were not to work, they needed to know what was defined as work. So the Pharisees had identified thirty-nine actions that were forbidden on the Sabbath. These included reaping, threshing and winnowing grain. Under these rules, when the disciples picked and ate *some ears of corn* (**12:1**), they were guilty of reaping (plucking the grain), threshing (rubbing the grain to remove the husk) and winnowing (separating the grain from the chaff). Moreover, the whole process was construed as preparing a meal on the Sabbath, and that too was forbidden (Exod 16:22-30; 35:3). So according to their own rules the Pharisees were justified in condemning the disciples for doing what was *unlawful on the Sabbath* (**12:2**) and Jesus for allowing or encouraging them to do so.

But the Pharisees were in danger of turning law keeping into an end in itself. They had forgotten the original good purpose for which the Sabbath had been instituted and were focusing only on meticulous observance of their rules. These rules were what Jesus took issue with, for they were sometimes extremely burdensome and at odds with the original intention of the law.

Jesus rejected their interpretation of the law and showed that human need and feeding hungry people has priority over the strict observance of the law. He gives the example of David's men, who in an emergency had eaten bread that had been set apart to be eaten only by the priests (**12:3-4**; 1 Sam 21:1-6). He also points out that there was always some work that needed to be done on the Sabbath. For example, every Sabbath day the priests and Levites in the temple would kindle fires, sacrifice animals, clean and do many other things. No blame was ever attached to them and their work (**12:5**). The needs of the temple overrode the provisions of the law. In quoting the prophet Hosea (**12:7**; see Hos 6:6), Jesus emphasizes that human need is more important than rituals. We are called to love the Lord with all our heart and mind and soul, but we are also to love our neighbours (22:37-38).

Jesus is much greater than the Sabbath or the temple, and therefore he can override their rules (**12:6**). Above all, as *Lord of the Sabbath* (**12:8**) he has authority to regulate what is and what is not permitted on the Sabbath. His personal authority is above that of the Pharisaic code.

The Pharisees' inner motives were exposed when they accused Jesus of breaking the Sabbath law when he healed a man with a shrivelled hand (**12:9-14**). He saw through their dangerous childishness as they tried to find a way to accuse him of breaking the law (**12:10**). Instead of debating the law, he met a genuine human need, and demonstrated that it was lawful to do good on the Sabbath (**12:11-13**).

The Pharisees took such offence that he had healed someone on the Sabbath that they immediately started making plans to kill him (12:14). They did not stop to ask whether it is lawful to make plans to assassinate an innocent person on the Sabbath (or any other time)! The irony is glaring, as religious people plot to execute someone for helping a disabled person!

In our reaction to what we perceive to be law breaking, we should take care to ensure that our own thoughts and actions are not out of keeping with the spirit of the law of God. This warning relates to many things, including our reactions to people who work on Sundays and to certain forms of dress and fashion.

12:15-21 Jesus, the Servant of the Lord

On a number of occasions, Jesus tactically withdrew from potentially difficult situations. He even withdrew from a crowd that wanted to force him to be king (John 6:15). Confrontation with the Pharisees at this stage would have undermined his important work of dealing with sin. So here he withdrew from the Pharisees (**12:15**). As a man of peace, he would not use the language or posture of war to confront them, or at least not at this point. As the Bemba say, it is prudent not to approach a barking dog lest the dog bite.

The passage quoted from Isaiah 42:1-4 underscores the peaceful characteristics of the Lord (12:18-21). These words originally referred to the Persian emperor Cyrus. Although he did not know it, he was the servant of the Lord who brought restoration to the nation of Israel and in whom the whole world found help. His colonial policy enabled many conquered peoples to return to their traditional lands and their traditional ways of living, often at some expense to the imperial treasury. But the complete fulfilment of this prophecy pointed beyond Cyrus to Israel and ultimately to Jesus as the true Servant of the Lord. The servant has been chosen by God, and God takes *delight* in him (**12:18a**). The servant is endowed with the Spirit of the Lord and *he will proclaim justice to the nations* (**12:18b**). Rather than brawling with others, he will not *quarrel or cry out* (**12:19**). Instead he will encourage all who are weak and at the point of dying. *In his name the nations will put their hope* (**12:21**).

12:22-37 The kingdom of God and Beelzebub

The undeniable miracle-working power of Jesus was causing the common people to raise the question as to whether he was the promised Messiah, *the Son of David* (**12:23**). Although the Son of David was primarily a conqueror, he was also thought of as a healer (Isa 35:5-6; 61:1-3). The Pharisees could not deny his healings, but attempted to discredit his work by attributing his power to evil and sorcery, claiming that he was in league with *Beelzebub, the prince of demons* (**12:24**). They were saying that Jesus was an instrument of Satan. The demons knew better than this, and never claimed Jesus as one of their own. They knew him to be the holy Son of God (8:29; Mark 1:24).

Jesus counters the Pharisees' accusations with three powerful arguments:

- **Satan cannot fight himself** (**12:25-26**). The Pharisees were right to have a healthy respect for demons. They recognized their power to use human beings and to affect the human condition. Jesus agreed with them that there is a kingdom of Satan, just as there is a kingdom of God. Demons do indeed possess people and accomplish superhuman things through them. Many demon-possessed people are able to see into the future and they become diviners and healers. Where the Pharisees were wrong was in associating Jesus with the power of Satan. If Satan were the source of Jesus' power, that would mean that Satan's agents were at war amongst themselves. Players on the same team in the same game do not work against each other; if they do they make the task of their opponents easier. Surely Satan has more sense than that; otherwise his kingdom *will not stand.*
- **God's Spirit drives out demons** (**12:27-28**). Jesus was not the only one who cast out demons. There were other Jews who also had this ministry (Acts 19:13). They cast out demons by what appeared to be magical rituals and practices, whereas Jesus used *the Spirit of God.* The character of his exorcisms was powerful evidence of the arrival of the kingdom of God to destroy the kingdom of Satan. The many people in sub-Saharan Africa who suffer pain from spiritual sources can find relief and victory in Jesus. The name of Jesus is powerful and his word of command is effective.
- **Jesus is more powerful than Satan** (12:29). Satan claims ownership of the kingdoms of the earth (4:8-9), but Jesus demonstrates he is stronger than Satan. He is like someone who breaks into a *strong man's house* and ties him up so he can carry off his possessions (**12:29**). Jesus came to bind Satan and to release all who are under his evil power and influence.

We must not attribute evidence of God's work to the wrong source, lest we be guilty of opposing God. There is no neutral ground in this war (**12:30**).

The unforgivable sin is deliberate rejection of clear evidence of the work of God (**12:31-32**). The Pharisees seem to have crossed the line from normal scepticism to hardened refusal to accept incontrovertible evidence. We are in danger of committing the unforgivable sin when we deliberately refuse to accept unambiguous evidence of the work of God (Num 15:30-31; Isa 22:14).

Physical and mental abilities can be lost through lack of use. Muscles lose their tone from lack of exercise. A foreign language learned at school is forgotten through lack of practice. The same is true of spiritual abilities. If a person constantly refuses to accept the help of the Holy Spirit in recognizing the truth, and attributes God's truth to Satan, then that person may lose the capacity to repent and any chance of being forgiven. Only God can know when a person has reached this state of irreversible rejection.

As for the Jewish leadership, Jesus says that they have taken a route that ends in this irreversible state. All that they can produce is bad fruit, such as attributing Jesus' deeds to Beelzebub (**12:33, 35**). Their words are so poisonous that he calls them a *brood of vipers* (**12:34**). Their poison will kill those touched by it, unless proper treatment is given. Such leaders are doing a great disservice to the kingdom of heaven, and will be judged for it (**12:36-37**).

12:38-45 The Pharisees ask for a sign

Paul comments that the Jews 'demand miraculous signs' (**12:38**; see also 1 Cor 1:22). These people who were asking for a sign had already been exposed to the many signs that Jesus had given them through his miracles. They were unwilling to accept these, but seemed to have an insatiable appetite for more. Jesus told them that all they would receive was *the sign of the prophet Jonah* (**12:39b**; 16:4). This sign would be his resurrection from the dead (**12:40**). If they accepted it and repented as the men of Nineveh had repented at Jonah's preaching, then they too, like *the men of Nineveh* would be saved (12:41a). But their unfaithfulness has become so great that they could only be described as *a wicked and adulterous generation,* incapable of recognizing the truth (**12:39a**). Jesus is *greater than Jonah* (**12:41b**), just as he is *greater than Solomon* (**12:42b**), and yet his audience refused to recognize him.

The examples Matthew chooses here suggest that even in the OT God's grace had been recognized by non-Israelites such as 'the men of Nineveh' (**12:41a**) and *the Queen of the South* (**12:42a**), even when the Israelites themselves appeared incapable of recognizing it.

Jesus then tells a story that links up with his earlier healing of the demon-possessed man (12:22). It is all very well to drive out one evil spirit (**12:43**), but if those who are listening to him continue in their obstinacy, they will be rejecting the only true God and therefore opening themselves up to a greater and more dangerous involvement with *seven other spirits* (**12:44-45**). His hearers, and not Jesus, were the ones allied with evil.

12:46-50 Who Are Jesus' True Family?

During his public ministry, Jesus' biological family did not believe in him (Mark 3:21; John 7:5). Mark's Gospel reveals that his family were concerned that he was mad, and tried to take him away from the public gaze, perhaps to prevent him from bringing shame on the family. Jesus took the opportunity provided by their visit to affirm that often those who follow him will find least support from among their own blood relatives (**12:46-49**). Even more importantly, he stresses that doing the Lord's will takes priority over all other human relationships (**12:50**). This does not give the Christian freedom to run away from family responsibilities, but one's relationship with the Lord must have pride of place amongst one's relationships.

13:1-52 Teaching III: Parables of the Kingdom

Parables give concrete form to abstract truths. They turn truths into images so that the hearers are able to picture them and remember them clearly. The Middle Eastern mind thought in concrete terms, in images and stories. The African mind is similar and, therefore, parables, both biblical and local, should be a very important part of communicating the truths of the Bible.

Parables take aspects of the hearers' everyday experiences and use them to explain things that may not be immediately obvious. Because of their highly illustrative nature, parables compel listeners to pay close attention and to discover the truth for themselves: *He who has ears, let him hear* (**13:9**). They can have a great impact. A famous example is the parable that Nathan told King David (2 Sam 12:5-6). Parables may conceal the truth from those who are not interested in it. To them they remain simply interesting but meaningless stories (**13:13**).

The parables of Jesus were told in a specific cultural and historical setting, and the correct interpretation must take into account their Palestinian context. The immediate background to this group of parables was the mounting conflict between Jesus and the authorities and resistance to his message. Jesus was no longer welcome in the synagogues and therefore took to the open fields, the lakeside and private houses. He concentrated on teaching his disciples away from the crowds who followed him (**13:1-2**). While the parables were told in the presence of the crowd, the explanations were given only to the disciples (**13:10**, 36).

13:1-23 The Sower

The two key elements in this parable are the sower, the presenter of the message who faces opposition and sees some seed go to waste and the ground, representing those who hear the message and need to respond in ways that lead to fruitful lives as disciples of Jesus.

The parable assumes Palestinian farming practices of the time, when the sowing of seed was imprecise in that it was scattered by hand and ploughed into the ground later. The farm was presumably not virgin land but family land that had been ploughed year after year. During the period between the harvest and the planting, some parts of the field would have been walked over so that a path emerged, and the seed that fell on that path was exposed and therefore easily eaten by birds (**13:3-4**). Other seed fell on a patch of ground where a thin layer of soil over solid rock made it impossible for the roots of the plants to grow (**13:5-6**). Some seed fell on ground where thorny weeds grew, which made it difficult for the seed to flourish (**13:7**). But the seed that fell on good ground in time produced an abundant harvest (**13:8**).

The interpretation is given to the disciples privately (**13:11, 16-17**). The seed is God's word, which is sown by his Son, Jesus, then by the disciples, and subsequently by all who preach the word in every age.

- *The seed sown along the path* represents hearers with closed minds whose lack of understanding, prejudice and perhaps even immorality allows Satan to take away the word so that it does not have a chance to take root (**13:19**). Jesus describes these people using words from Isaiah 6:9-10 (**13:14-16**).
- *The seed that fell on rocky places* represents fair-weather Christians, who enthusiastically receive the word and begin to grow, but owing to shallowness cannot retain and nurture the word, and so their growth does not last. When the true cost of discipleship becomes evident, it proves too high, and the would-be disciple falls away (**13:20-21**).
- *The seed that fell among the thorns* represents those who have all the capacities to be promising disciples, but who get too involved with the usual enticements of this world, and therefore allow their potential spirituality to be crowded out (**13:22**).
- *The seed that fell on good soil* represents those who are open to the word, have the capacity to nurture it in their hearts, keep at it in spite of opposition, lead a disciplined life and keep sensuality at bay. Such hearers of the word will prosper and bear much fruit (**13:23**).

This parable can be retold in terms that would be more familiar in rural Zambia. In Zambian terms, the four types of soil are as follows:

- *Pa lubansa* is the area, immediately surrounding any house, which is swept clean at least once a day. Over time, any topsoil is swept away, exposing very hard earth that is of no use for planting. Any seed that falls on that patch will immediately attract the chickens and other birds. Such seed will have no chance of even beginning to germinate.
- *Ulupili* is the side of a hill, where there is a thin scraping of soil on top of hard rock. The seed can take root there, but it will not continue to grow.
- *Pa chisonso* is the area where rubbish is dumped. This area often contains material that makes very good compost. In the rains all sorts of things grow there, including mango and pumpkin seedlings along with strong weeds. But because no one bothers to weed this area, the good seed often does not survive.
- *Ubukula* is a freshly prepared garden, ready for sowing millet seed. The Bemba would prepare such a garden by lopping branches off trees, gathering them together, and then burning them when they are dry. The ash would then be tilled into the ground before planting the seed. Such gardens are often very fruitful, and their usefulness stretches over two or three planting seasons.

Jesus' parable emphasizes that proclaiming the kingdom of heaven is like farming. The sower should not be discouraged, for despite wasted seeds and some plants that do not thrive, there will ultimately be a very rich harvest. If the harvest is not seen during this lifetime, then it will certainly come at the end of time, for the harvest may be the final ingathering of the people of God when Jesus returns (13:39; see also Jer 51:33; Mic 4:12-13).

Jesus' explanation of the parable focuses on the different types of hearers and the fact that it is the prepared soil that is capable of bearing a rich harvest (13:18-23). Sowers must sow indiscriminately, but hearers must be careful to ensure that they are rich soil, capable of receiving and nurturing the seed, which is the word of God.

13:24-30, 36-43 The Wheat and the Weeds

The three main elements in the parable of the wheat and the weeds are the owner of the field, the good seed that he sowed and the weeds. An enemy attempts to sabotage the owner's harvest by secretly planting seeds of a weed that resembles wheat and which can sometimes be poisonous. The enemy's ploy is only discovered when the crop is established, the shoots have emerged and the difference between the two types of plant has become obvious (**13:24-27**).

At this point, the workers want to weed out the useless and probably dangerous counterfeit crop. But the master counsels caution and patience. Any attempt to separate the two at this stage could easily damage the good crop, because the roots of both crops have become intertwined (**13:28-29**). The separation of the two crops will be done, albeit laboriously, at the harvest, when it will be easier to tell them apart, and then the weeds will be consigned to the fire (**13:30**).

This parable shows the growth of the kingdom of heaven in three stages from the original planting, through its growth, to the final harvest. The enemy's sabotage seems to be effective, but in spite of the competition, the wheat survives and thrives. At the harvest, the final separation takes place as the master destroys the weeds and gathers in the wheat.

Jesus' interpretation of this parable in **13:36-43** spells out its personal and corporate significance. At the personal level, it is important to recognize that we are influenced both by Jesus, who sows good seed, and the evil one, who sows weeds. We need to be wary of the forces of evil. For Africans, the spirit world is alive with all sorts of personal beings with whom we have interacted, and our cultures are based on such interaction. Some of these spirits come from the enemy and have harmful designs upon our lives. So beware!

When we interpret this parable on the corporate level, we need to remember that the kingdom of heaven is not primarily the church, but is God's sovereign rule in the whole universe, including the church. The parable is not about the immediate triumph of believers and the pure church, but about patient waiting until God's purposes are worked out and he brings history to its final conclusion.

In particular, this parable makes it plain that it is pointless to search for the perfect local church or denomination. There will always be weeds in the crop. Moreover, it is sometimes hard to distinguish between those who are of the kingdom and those who are not. We must, therefore, not be quick to judge, as we can easily make mistakes and damage the good seed. We must exercise patience and caution until God, the only judge, finally decides to wind up history and makes the final distinction between those who are his and those who are not. He alone knows those who are called by his name (2 Tim 2:19). Thus church leaders need to be very careful in exercising discipline.

13:31-35 The Mustard Seed and the Yeast

Between the parable of the wheat and weeds (13:24-30) and its interpretation (13:36-43), Matthew inserts the two little parables of the mustard seed (**13:31-32**) and the yeast (**13:33**). Both demonstrate the small beginnings of the kingdom, inaugurated in the relatively inconspicuous coming of Jesus and the initial gathering of his disciples, and its patient but inevitable growth until it reaches its fullest extent. The present obscurity will yield future greatness. In times of discouragement because of the weakness or apparent decline of the church, it is important to emphasize the basic lessons of these two parables: in the end the kingdom of heaven will take pride of place over all other kingdoms.

Similarly, we must recognize that just as great rivers have a very small source, so great movements in history often start in a single moment with an obscure thought, word or action: a young, perhaps even teenage, woman bears her firstborn son in the backwater of a mighty empire and names him Jesus; an unknown German monk, Martin Luther, nails his ninety-five theses to the door of a church building; an almost coincidental sharing of an office between Gaur Radebe and Nelson Mandela introduces the latter to politics in South Africa. Nowhere is this principle of life more fully demonstrated than in the growth and development of the kingdom of heaven.

Although yeast is sometimes used as a metaphor for evil (16:6; Mark 8:15; 1 Cor 5:6, 8; see also Exod 12:15), this parable focuses on yeast's transforming quality. The transforming power of the kingdom can be seen in individuals, who often change dramatically after conversion. Such transformations go on to affect attitudes of the marginalized, including women, children, the sick, the infirm and the downtrodden.

Although Christian missionaries in the colonial period often bore too close a resemblance to the power-hungry, racist, imperial exploiters, it was the missionaries who provided opportunities in education, health and commerce for the downtrodden 'natives'. Until 1945, all education for the native black population in Northern Rhodesia (modern Zambia) was in the hands of the missionaries. The educational opportunities they provided eventually supplied the platform from which many freedoms for Zambians were won. The entire first cabinet (1964) had received their primary education in mission schools. Even to this day, forty-one years after independence, many mission schools still provide good-quality education.

13:44 The Hidden Treasure

The large-scale mining of copper in Zambia's Copperbelt began in 1922. One of the largest of the mines, the Luanshya Mine, is said to have been begun when a prospector shot a roan antelope and then discovered the tell-tale signs of copper ore in the rock next to its body. Frantic efforts must have followed to remove any traditional owners of the land from the area to make way for the construction of the new mine. Because the prospector understood the value of the copper deposits and saw the prospect of great riches, he and his associates went all out to acquire the land and the mineral rights to it.

The parable of the treasure buried in a field is the rural first-century Palestinian version of the story of copper deposits discovered in Zambia. The hidden treasure clearly did not belong to the owner of the land, for if it had, he would never have sold the field. The finder, having discovered the treasure, buried it again and then went away and sold everything he had in order to buy the land knowing that something infinitely more valuable lay buried there (**13:44**).

The kingdom of heaven is infinitely more valuable than any copper or gold. It exists where the will of God is perfectly obeyed. Therefore, when one discovers the will of God, it is imperative that everything else be sacrificed to it. Such obedience may require changing one's ambitions and lifestyle, and even being prepared to lay down one's life (Mark 8:34). But the kingdom of God is worth it! Paul makes this very point when he says that, 'whatever was to my profit I now consider loss for the sake of Christ … I consider everything a loss compared to the surpassing greatness of knowing Christ Jesus my Lord, for whose sake I have lost all things. I consider them rubbish that I may gain Christ' (Phil 3:7-11). In Jesus' day, and less so in our day, the kingdom is hidden. But for those who have eyes to see and ears to hear, it is there to be found.

13:45-46 The Pearl

In Jesus' day, as in our own times, pearls were beautiful fashion accessories. They were very valuable and much sought after (**13:45**). Divers searched the Red Sea and other seas in search of them. The Egyptian princess Cleopatra is said to have worn a necklace containing a pearl worth 25 million denarii (a denarius was a day's wage for a labourer). In the parable, a merchant is said to have spent a lifetime searching for just such a precious jewel. When he found it, he went and joyfully sold all he had in order to acquire it (**13:46**).

As in the preceding parable, the kingdom of heaven is portrayed as something beautiful, valuable and infinitely more enriching than anything else. It is worth sacrificing all for the sake of the kingdom.

Note that the parable does not teach that entry into the kingdom of heaven can be acquired by wealth. The Bible clearly teaches that it is by grace through faith that we enter the kingdom (Eph 2:8-9).

13:47-50 The Net

This parable has much the same message as the parable of the wheat and weeds (13:24-43), but draws its imagery from fishing. A net let down in the Sea of Galilee would have caught both edible and inedible, clean and unclean fish, and the fishermen would have had to sort their catch (**13:47-48**). Similarly, the world in which the 'fishers of men' work will yield nets filled with both bad and good fish. On the day of reckoning, the Lord himself will sort the good from the bad, distinguishing the children of light from the children of darkness. The former will enter into his blessings and the latter into the *fiery furnace* (**13:49-50**).

13:51-52 Teachers of the Kingdom

Matthew emphasizes the continuity between the OT and the words and works of Jesus (13:52). A good teacher must unite them and build the new teaching on what was received from Moses and the prophets. The disciples understand Christ's teaching (**13:51**) because what they learned from him was built on the fine heritage of the OT. What they had before they came to Christ was useful in complementing the new knowledge they were gaining from him.

When people come to Christ, there are often many things they must unlearn, such as speech patterns, habits and sentiments. However, many of their gifts, skills and talents need not be lost, but can be dedicated to Christ and reinterpreted for his benefit and service. For example, I learned to play the guitar at a time when guitar playing was associated with immoral lifestyles. When I became a Christian, I took my guitar to church and used it to joyously play a whole new type of music. God even made my guitar an important part of my ministry among youth.

What is true of individuals is also true of whole cultures. Out of the old will come *treasures* such as one never thought were there (**13:52**).

13:53-17:27 The Ministry of Jesus: Part III

13:53-58 A Prophet Without Honour

'Familiarity breeds contempt' is a famous English saying. It means that when people know someone well, they no longer regard that person as worthy of respect or honour. Many tourists pay a great deal of money to visit the spectacular Victoria Falls on the Zambezi River on the border between Zambia and Zimbabwe. Yet millions of Zambians and Zimbabweans have never taken the trouble to visit one of the seven natural wonders of the world right there on their doorstep.

Jesus was gaining a reputation as an effective itinerant preacher and faith healer, a rabbi with a band of disciples. Crowds followed him and listened to him gladly and expectantly. But when he returned to Nazareth, *his home town* (**13:54**), he got no respect from his former neighbours and friends. They disparagingly referred to him as *the carpenter's son* (**13:55**) and put up a fierce barrier of unbelief causing the message of the kingdom to pass them by.

In a contemporary setting, many sermons are rendered useless not by the fault of the preacher (although no doubt many preachers could improve their preaching), but by the attitudes of the congregation or of family members or contemporaries who know the preacher very well. When listening to the exposition of the word of God, we must listen with expectancy, ignoring the person who at that moment has become God's instrument.

14:1-12 John the Baptist Beheaded

Matthew's record of the death of John the Baptist is significant not only because it tells of the end of the mission of John, but also because it shows how, just as John's mission foreshadowed the mission of Jesus, so his violent death foreshadowed the violent death of Jesus and perhaps even of those who follow him.

Matthew uses the report of Herod Antipas' reaction to Jesus' growing fame to tell the story of the death of John. When Herod the Great died in 4 BC, the Romans divided his territory between his surviving sons, Archelaus (see 2:22), Herod Antipas and Philip. Archelaus was assigned Judea, but he was so cruel that he was soon deposed and his territory governed by a succession of Roman procurators. Herod Antipas received the territories of Samaria (his mother had been a Samaritan), Galilee and Perea. Antipas was never given the title 'king', but was officially referred to as *Herod the tetrarch,* a minor local ruler (14:1).

Herod Antipas had John arrested because the latter had criticized him publicly for immorality (14:13). Herod had contracted a marriage of convenience with a Nabatean princess, but he divorced her in order to marry his half-brother's wife, Herodias. This divorce led the Nabatean king Aretas to wage a successful war against Herod. John, too, opposed this public flouting of morality in the face of clear biblical teaching, saying, *It is not lawful for you to have her* (14:4; 5:31-32; see also Lev 18:16; 20:21). John's opposition was interpreted as sedition, and Herod had him arrested. Herodias nursed a grudge against John and would have liked to see him killed, but Herod was anxious not to provoke the resentment of his subjects, who believed that John was *a prophet* (14:5).

To celebrate his birthday, Herod threw a party to which he invited the great and mighty. Such parties were often characterized by drunkenness and debauchery (Esth 1:11). Salome, *the daughter of Herodias,* danced for the guests and Herod, who may have been drunk, was so pleased by the girl's dance that he promised to grant her any wish (14:6-7). She asked her mother's advice, and then she demanded the head of John the Baptist (14:8). Herod was trapped by his oath (14:9). Having made the pledge publicly before his guests, he could not go back on it, and so he ordered the execution of John although this obviously distressed him (14:9-10).

In killing John without a trial, Herod broke Jewish laws – and also foreshadowed Jesus' death without a fair trial. Beheading, too, was not a punishment approved by Jewish law. It is no wonder that Herod's conscience was unsettled by what he had done, so that he attributed Jesus' miraculous powers to John, whom he thought had come back to life, perhaps to haunt him (14:1-2).

Even in death, John still pointed to Jesus. His disciples, risking their lives, went and took his body for burial and then went to Jesus to report the death (14:12). John's movement found its fulfilment in Jesus. In life and in death, John remained faithful to his calling to make Jesus increase while he decreased (John 3:30).

14:13-21 The Feeding of the Five Thousand

The feeding of the five thousand (in actual fact there were many more, for the number does not include the women and children) stands in contrast to the debauched party at the court of Herod Antipas described in the previous passage. This party in the open was spontaneous and came about on account of Jesus' compassion for the people (14:14a).

Jesus was now too popular to be able to retreat into quietness. Wherever he went, large crowds recognized him and followed him (14:13, 35). Jesus healed the sick (14:14b), but the disciples recognized another need, that is, the need for food.

The area was remote, and could not provide food for the crowds. So the disciples asked Jesus to dismiss the people so that they could attend to their material needs (14:15). Instead, Jesus told the disciples to give them food (14:16). This command challenged the disciples to see who Jesus really was. But their answer revealed their own helplessness to do anything about the material needs of the people, and may possibly also indicate some faith on their part (14:17). The miracle followed: Jesus broke the bread and the fish and had the disciples distribute the food to all (14:18-19). Everyone had enough to eat, and there were twelve basketfuls of leftovers, representing the twelve tribes of Israel (14:20; 15:29-39; 16:5-12). According to John, the people began to say that Jesus might be the 'Prophet who is to come' (John 6:14).

This miracle resembled those in Moses' time, when God supplied manna in the wilderness (Exod 16), and in Elisha's time, when Elisha fed one hundred men with twenty loaves (2 Kgs 4:42-44). If Moses and Elisha could perform such miracles, surely it should have occurred to the disciples that Jesus was capable of doing the same.

If Jesus' actions were also symbolic, then this miracle may not only demonstrate God's compassion, but also anticipates the ultimate gathering of all people at the feast of the kingdom (8:11). Faith recognizes the poverty of human resources, but looks trustingly to the greatness of God.

14:22-36 Jesus Walks on the Water

Jesus sent the disciples off on a boat journey to *the other side* (14:22), to *Gennesaret* (14:34). Matthew says that Jesus compelled the disciples to leave while he dismissed the crowd. This may have become necessary because a dangerous situation had arisen, which Jesus had to deal with alone. John tells us that the people wanted to force Jesus to become a political king because they realized that he must be the prophet whom Moses had promised (John 6:15). Such premature political fervour would prejudice Jesus' mission and confuse his call to go to the cross. Jesus himself retired to the mountain to pray (**14:23**). The Gospels show him to be a person of prayer (Mark 1:35; Luke 3:21).

While they were going across the lake, a storm arose and made progress very difficult for the disciples (**14:24**). *During the fourth watch,* that is, sometime between 3 a.m. and 6 a.m., *Jesus went out to them, walking on the lake* (**14:25**). The disciples mistook him for *a ghost* (**14:26**). They should have known that he who fed the thousands could walk on the water through a storm to rescue them! Once they recognized him, their fear disappeared.

Jesus' identification of himself, *It is I,* was authoritative (**14:27**). This phrase is used at moments of revelation (see Mark 14:62; John 8:58), and may even reflect the divine name: 'I AM WHO I AM' (Exod 3:14).

Peter was always the one who spoke for the other disciples, and this time he asked Jesus if he could go to him walking on water (**14:28**). When Jesus gave his consent, Peter was able to replicate Jesus' miracle. But he soon lost focus and became conscious of his seemingly impossible circumstances. He gave in to fear and began *to sink* (**14:30**). In the midst of the calamity and danger, Peter cried out to the Lord and was saved.

Jesus uses the incident as an object lesson. If Peter had maintained his faith, he would not have sunk (**14:31**). Jesus then helped him, and together they walked to the boat and climbed in. The wind died down and peace returned (**14:32**). The rest of the disciples recognized Jesus as the Lord of nature and worshipped him saying, *Truly you are the Son of God* (**14:33**).

As soon as they landed, the people of the district recognized Jesus and brought *all their sick to him* to him and he healed them (**14:35-36**). His compassion for the people knew no limits. His disciples must show similar compassion for all humanity.

15:1-20 Inward and Outward Cleanness

While Jesus sought to pour out his heart in compassionate ministry to the harassed and helpless, *the Pharisees and teachers of the law* had a totally different set of concerns and priorities. That these members of the religious elite came all the way from Jerusalem to discuss their concerns with Jesus suggests that there was some discomfort in the capital regarding the activities of the strange itinerant preacher from Galilee (**15:1**).

The Jewish leaders were focused on keeping and policing proper Jewish religious etiquette as laid down in *the tradition of the elders* (**15:2**). This tradition went beyond the OT books and included all the additions and elaborations that had been created over the centuries by the elders and that had eventually been codified in the Mishnah. These stipulations often went further than the original provisions

of the law. The Torah prescribed that the priests should cleanse their hands on certain occasions, such as before entering the Tent of Meeting to minister before the Lord (Exod 30:18-21; Deut 21:6). The extensive hand washing that Mark describes (Mark 7:3-4) was a relatively new innovation, and may have developed from a growing hostility to any contact with Gentiles.

Jesus was taken to task yet again for the conduct of his disciples (15:2; 9:14). His opponents implied that if Jesus was a true rabbi, he would have taught his disciples to behave better. Jesus did not reject the accusation; instead he sought to set the priorities right. God's commands take precedence over *your tradition* (**15:3**, **6**). The issues of authority and priority must be settled.

Jesus chose the subject of honouring parents as the battleground. The Torah clearly commanded that children should honour their parents (**15:4-5**; Exod 20:12). The Pharisees themselves laid great stress on obeying and honouring parents, including providing them with financial support. But God's command was being evaded by those who took advantage of the tradition that they could declare on oath that any money or property that might be used to support their parents was *Corban* (see Mark 7:11), that is, dedicated to God, and therefore not available to their parents. However, these goods were still at the disposal of the person who made the oath during his or her lifetime. Here the tradition of the elders clearly undermined the word of God and allowed the unscrupulous to avoid their duty to their parents. Jesus had no time for a tradition that nullified the *word of God* (15:6).

Those who upheld a tradition that permitted such evasion of God's laws might appear to of be God-honouring people, but in fact they were hypocrites whose hearts were far from God (**15:7-9**; see also Isa 29:13). Formal religion that simply adheres to rituals and the formal observance of rules and regulations is far from the spirit of the Torah and the heart of God.

Returning to the original issue of washing hands, Jesus explained that what is eaten enters the digestive system from outside, and therefore does not have the power to make someone unclean. What comes out of someone's mouth, what he or she says, is a clearer indication of the state of a person's godliness (**15:10-11**). The physical environment in which a person lives can have a corrupting influence, but the inner self is an even more powerful source of influence. In saying this, Jesus may have been making an oblique reference to original sin.

Jesus' words undermined the whole elaborate system of ritual observances that characterized Pharisaic Judaism. That is why the Pharisees were shocked and offended by what Jesus said (**15:12**). But Jesus insisted that the Pharisees and scribes were acting as *blind guides:* a danger to themselves and to those who followed them (**15:13-14**).

Jesus' more detailed explanation of his words (**15:15-16**) moves the focus of religion from the outside to the inside, from the external to the internal, from the how to the why. In Jewish thinking, *the heart* was the seat of emotions, motivation and thought (**15:18**). What comes out of the heart by way of what is said reveals the state of the heart and its source of motivation. If the heart reveals *evil thoughts, murder, adultery, sexual immorality, theft, false testimony* and *slander* (**15:19**), then that person is defiled. No amount of washing can change that state (**15:20**). Purity of heart is far above any physical activities we do in the service of God.

15:21-28 The Canaanite Woman's Faith

Matthew describes the woman who sought Jesus' help using the ancient label *Canaanite,* and not the more contemporary label, Syro-Phoenician (15:22; see Mark 7:24-26). This word emphasizes the racial tensions that existed between the Jews and Gentiles like the Phoenicians from *Tyre and Sidon* (**15:21**). The Jews longed for a Messiah who, like Joshua, would rid the land of Gentiles. Many would have regarded the Syro-Phoenicians as similar to the remnant of the seven Canaanite nations that the Israelites had yet to drive out at the time of Joshua's death (Deut 7:1; Josh 13:1-7).

The woman addressed Jesus as *Lord, Son of David* (**15:22**; 1:1), which may indicate a faith in Jesus similar to Rahab's faith when she helped Joshua's spies and saved her own family (Josh 2:8-13). Indeed, as a Canaanite, this woman is a reminder of the other Gentile women in Jesus' genealogy: Rahab, Ruth and Bathsheba (see comment on 1:3, 5, 6).

The woman was initially ignored by Jesus, but would not take 'no' for an answer. She persisted to the annoyance of the disciples who pleaded with Jesus to send her away (**15:23**). Jesus repeated that his mission was limited to the *lost sheep of Israel* (**15:24**; 10:6, 23). He then pointed out that *It is not right to take the children's bread and toss it to their dogs* (**15:26**). 'Dogs' was a Jewish term of abuse for Gentiles. The use of this term on Jesus' lips is surprising, and perhaps it was spoken in humour.

Like Rahab, the Canaanite woman was bold and would not be distracted. Her answer seems to suggest that just as Joshua did not break God's commandment when he saved Rahab, so Jesus could make an exception to the rule without going against the focus of his mission (**15:27**). Perhaps the woman's persistence also indicates that the gospel must go beyond Israel. Jesus the son of Abraham must take the blessings of God to all the peoples of the world.

15:29-39 The Feeding of the Four Thousand

We see further evidence of this extension of Jesus' mission to the whole world in the *great crowds* who *came to him* on the mountainside, where he healed all who were brought to him (**15:29-30**). This crowd must have included many Gentiles, for their reaction to the healings was to *praise the God of Israel* (**15:31**). The crowds remained with Jesus for three days, and in the end he took the initiative to feed them and asked the disciples to supply the needed food (**15:32**). The disciples' reaction to this request, Where could we get enough bread? (**15:33**) may reveal something of the state of their understanding of who Jesus was. In spite of having witnessed the miraculous feeding of the five thousand (14:13-21), they still thought only in terms of normal sources of supply. This would reveal that they still regarded Jesus simply as a human person. But it is also possible that the 'we' in their question was emphatic, in which case their reaction acknowledges their own helplessness and is an appeal to Jesus to do what only he could do. All they could supply was seven loaves and a few small fish (**15:34**). Jesus prayed over the food and asked the disciples to distribute it to the crowd (**15:36**). Everyone ate and was satisfied and they collected seven basketfuls of leftovers, a number that could represent the seven Canaanite nations (**15:37**; 14:13-21; 16:5-12). This miracle, among other things, is a sign of the removal of the barrier of hostility between the people of God and the Gentiles.

16:1-4 The Pharisees and Sadducees Ask for a Sign

In normal circumstances, there was no love lost between the Pharisees and the Sadducees. The Pharisees were a large religious sect, who strictly followed the law and the traditions of the elders. The Sadducees were the small political aristocracy, who rejected the traditions of the elders and actively collaborated with the Romans. However, these two groups came together to deal with a perceived common threat. The Pharisees did not trust Jesus' liberalism, and the Sadducees feared Roman reprisals should popular support for Jesus' leadership assume political significance.

The request for a sign from Jesus was undoubtedly intended as a trap (**16:1**). They knew that he would not agree to provide one. He had refused to give them a sign when they asked the same question earlier (12:38-40).

Jesus responded by reminding them that they were already good at interpreting signs of the weather. If the sunset was red, the next day would probably be sunny. However, a red sky in the morning meant that a storm was brewing (**16:2-3**). They needed to become equally competent at reading spiritual signs. It is strange that the ordinary people were drawing conclusions about Jesus' mission that the leaders either ignored or were totally blind to (15:21-39).

Jesus' life was the sign they were looking for, and the only other sign they would receive was the *sign of Jonah* (**16:4**). Just as Jonah brought a life-changing message to the city of Nineveh, so Jesus brought a life-changing message to the house of Israel. Jesus' three days in the tomb (which parallel Jonah's three days in the belly of a fish) would be the ultimate sign they were looking for. But if they could not believe Jesus and his words and works, then nothing else would convince them to believe.

16:5-12 The Yeast of the Pharisees and Sadducees

Jesus used the opportunity provided by a lack of bread to warn the disciples to beware of the *yeast of the Pharisees and Sadducees* (**16:5-6**). Yeast was fermented dough that was used to make bread rise. A small amount of it could have a powerful effect (see 13:33). It was this literal yeast that the disciples focused on. In their concern about literal bread, they had forgotten that Jesus could easily provide any bread they needed, and that his concerns were spiritual, not physical. They still did not recognize who he was (**16:7-8**).

So Jesus reminded them of the two feedings at which he supplied more than enough food for all (**16:9-10**; 14:13-21; 15:29-39). Jesus was the one who alone had the truth of God. The teaching of the Pharisees was as dangerous as a cancer that destroys the body. It was like yeast in that its evil influence could easily pervade a much larger group.

16:13-20 'You Are the Christ'

Matthew made it clear from the start who Jesus was (1:1). The Father confirmed it at his baptism (3:17) and the demons bore testimony to him (8:29). But the crowds, and even the disciples, were struggling to identify who he was (7:28-29; 9:33; 13:54). The Pharisees' repeated demand for a sign suggests that they, too, were trying to find out who Jesus was (16:1). Jesus himself eventually directly addressed the issue when he was alone with his disciples and outside Israel in *Caesarea Philippi*, near the source of the River Jordan. Jesus asked them, *Who do people say the Son of Man is?*, using his preferred title for himself (**16:13**).

The disciples reported that growing public opinion suggested that he was *John the Baptist* come back from the dead (see 14:2). Other contenders included *Elijah* and *Jeremiah, or one of the prophets* (**16:14**). But Jesus was no ordinary prophet. So who was he? Jesus was asking the disciples what they had made of the parables and his teachings.

The answer came unequivocally through Peter, as always the spokesperson for the group: *You are the Christ, the Son of the Living God* (**16:16**). Jesus confirmed Peter's statement that he was the Son of God, the Messiah of Israel and of the whole world. He made it clear that Peter had not come to this conclusion by human reasoning but had received a direct revelation from God the Father (**16:17**). Every time anyone receives Christ, a direct revelation has taken place in which God has opened the inner eyes of that person to see spiritual truth.

Jesus further declared to Peter that *on this rock I will build my church, and the gates of Hades will not overcome it* (**16:18**). The name Peter means 'rock' in Greek, and the Roman Catholic Church argues that Jesus was saying that he would build his church on Peter, a position that has led to the dominance of the papacy. Evangelical scholars prefer to interpret the rock not as Peter himself, but as the confession he made. While their high regard for Peter's statement is valid, it is also important to acknowledge that Peter himself does have a special place in church history. He was the chief of the apostles in Jerusalem, he was the first to preach at Pentecost, he began the Samaritan mission and he suffered persecution for the Lord. Peter and the other disciples were here given the authority to build the church. The growing church will face strong opposition but will ultimately succeed (**16:18**).

Peter, and by extension the apostles acting on God's behalf and doing his will, were also given the authority to establish rules and regulations for the church. 'Binding' and 'loosing' were technical terms which described the authority of rabbis in determining what conduct was forbidden and what was permitted. Peter received God's delegated authority for that task. His decisions on earth would carry heavenly sanction or rather, given that Jesus uses the future perfect tense (will have been), what Peter authorized or forbade on earth had already been decided in heaven (**16:19**).

After this truly remarkable revelation, Jesus warned the disciples not to tell anyone that he was the Christ. In a politically charged atmosphere, such a statement could easily have been misunderstood (**16:20**).

This passage marks a turning point of the gospel. From now on, Jesus' ministry will focus more on the disciples and will face growing opposition, culminating in his death outside Jerusalem.

16:21-28 Jesus Predicts His Crucifixion

Once the disciples understood that Jesus was the Christ, Jesus began to talk about the cross. He revealed that he was going to be rejected by the authorities and killed and *on the third day be raised to life* (**16:21**; 17:22-23; 20:17-19). To Peter, these ideas seemed contradictory. Surely the Christ could not die! He expected him to be recognized by the Jewish people and given the throne of his father David (**16:22**). Jesus would then subdue the world, beginning with the Romans, and would rule the world on God's behalf from Zion. Peter had no concept of a suffering Messiah, and so he took Jesus aside to rebuke him.

Jesus understood Peter's rebuke as a temptation from Satan, and he gave him the same sort of treatment that he had given to Satan (**16:23**; 4:10). The cross was not optional; it was an integral part of Christ's mission. There could be no glory without it. His attitude contrasts with that of many African leaders who use any appointment to a position of responsibility as a chance for personal gain. But Jesus was prepared even to die in order that the whole world might gain something.

He expects no less of his disciples. A follower of Christ is expected to do three things: *deny himself and take up his cross and follow me* (**16:24**).

- Self-denial means abandoning one's assumed right to self-determination. Only God's will matters for life and for eternity.
- Cross-bearing requires surrendering even one's life in order to fulfil one's calling to discipleship.
- Following is walking in the footsteps of Jesus, doing what he came to do.

It is worth losing everything in life in order to gain Christ's approval (**16:25-26**).

The saying about the future coming of *the Son of Man* is a complex one that encompasses his resurrection, ascension and authoritative position at the right hand of the Father, from where he will come to judge the world (**16:27-28**). The words in 16:28, *Some who are standing here will not taste death before they see the Son of Man coming in his kingdom,* may refer to the Transfiguration, which follows immediately. Alternatively, Jesus may have been speaking of his resurrection or of Pentecost and the spread of the church, as described in Acts. But it is probably best not to see this saying as referring to any single event. It most likely covers the entire manifestation of the glory of the resurrected Christ both in person and in his power shown through his apostles. The final demonstration of this authority will take place at his second coming.

17:1-13 The Transfiguration

Jesus' insistence that he was going to die and that his disciples must also be prepared to die may have shaken the disciples' newly declared faith in him as the Messiah. The transfiguration that followed confirmed to them that he truly was the Son of God. For Jesus himself, the transfiguration confirmed that he was doing the will of the Father.

This transfiguration was witnessed by Peter and the two brothers, James and John (**17:1a**). Jesus asked these same three to stand by him in a later time of distress when he needed to be sure of the will of God (26:36-46). These disciples accompanied Jesus *up a high mountain* (**17:1b**), which was probably in the Hermon range. The scene that followed was reminiscent of Moses' conversation with the Lord on the mountain (Exod 24:15-18). Here, too, there is a mountain, bright cloud, Moses, and the voice of the Lord.

Jesus' face shone *like the sun* (**17:2**). Moses' face had also shone after he was with God (Exod 34:29-35). But Moses' face showed only a reflected glory, whereas Jesus' brightness came from within. Jesus is thus shown to be greater than Moses, for he shares the very nature of God.

The presence of both *Moses and Elijah* was significant (**17:3**). Both men had met God on Mount Sinai (also known as Mount Horeb – Exod 34:27-28; 1 Kgs 19:8-9), both were expected to return in the messianic age (Deut 18:15; Mal 4:5),

and both had mysterious deaths. Elijah did not die, but was taken directly to heaven (2 Kgs 2:11). Moses died, and no one but God knows where he was buried (Deut 34:5-6). Together they represent the Law and the Prophets, meaning the whole of the OT. In their pursuit of the will of God, both had also suffered persecution, as would Jesus within a short time.

Peter, always the first to react, said perhaps the first thing that came into his mind. His suggestion may have been fairly practical, for on top of a mountain, and with such brightness around, shelter would not have been a bad thing. But instead of giving Peter permission to build *three shelters* (**17:4**), God covered them with a *cloud* (**17:5**). This cloud is the same glory that filled the Tent of Meeting (Exod 40:34-35) and the Holy Place in Solomon's temple (1 Kgs 8:10-11).

God spoke out of the cloud, just as he had at Jesus' baptism (3:17), confirming that Jesus was his Son and that the disciples were to listen to him just as Moses had commanded (Deut 18:15). The voice of God terrified the disciples who fell prostrate in fear and worship (**17:6**). Jesus reached out to them, touched them and lifted them up (**17:7**).

The three disciples were told not to tell others about what they had seen (**17:9**), but they had many questions for Jesus. The appearance of Elijah had reminded them of the teaching that Elijah would return before the Messiah would finally inaugurate the kingdom of heaven (**17:10**). Jesus replied that the prophecy had already been fulfilled, for *John the Baptist* was the Elijah who would come before the Messiah to restore all things (**17:11-13**; see Mal 4:5-6), and he himself was the Messiah. John had been martyred, and the Messiah would face a similar fate (**17:12**).

The glory that was natural to Christ must be combined with the humiliation of the cross; the two go together. His disciples too must often face the cross in order to gain glory. Any theology that denies that Jesus' disciples will suffer is deficient and stands in opposition to Jesus' experience, biblical teaching and human experience.

17:14-21 Healing a Demon-Possessed Boy

When Moses returned from the mountain, he found turmoil and failure in the camp (Exod 32:15-17); so too did Jesus. He returned from the Mount of Transfiguration to find a crowd had formed around the rest of the disciples. After the glorious events at the mountain top, he and the disciples were immediately plunged into the sea of human need. They were confronted by demonic activity, as if to remind them that spiritual warfare is a real and constant reality. There may well be a lesson for us all here: the glimpses of glory that God allows us to have from time to time are to confirm our faith as we continue to respond to the various needs of the people around us.

A man from the crowd approached Jesus and asked him to heal his son, who had *seizures* caused by demonic activity (**17:14**; see Mark 9:17-18). This does not mean that all cases of seizures are caused by demons (see 4:24, where demon possession is distinguished from 'having seizures'). The man had brought his child to the disciples for healing, but they failed to cast out the demon (**17:16**). He approached Jesus reverentially and knelt down. In that culture, kneeling before someone symbolised respect and, often, pleading. The gesture has the same significance in many African cultures today. The man prayed, *Lord have mercy on my son* (**17:15**). Jesus accepted the man's faith on behalf of his son. Many other people's faith was similarly honoured (for example, that of the four men in 9:2 and the Canaanite woman in 15:28). Faith on behalf of another undergirds intercessory prayer. God is moved when people pray for others, and he responds to that faith.

With an air of exasperation and impatience, Jesus called his contemporaries an *unbelieving and perverse generation* (**17:17**). His words applied to the crowd generally, but particularly to the disciples, who by this time should have been able to handle this problem successfully, as they had when they went out on their mission (10:8). The reason for their failure was lack of faith (**17:20a**).

Privately, Jesus explained to them that their faith was smaller even than a mustard seed. If it had been *as small as a mustard seed,* they would have been able not only to drive out demons but also to move mountains (**17:20b**). It is not just the amount of faith that matters, but the fact that the faith is grounded in the power of God. He alone can act to accomplish miraculous healings. Faith is not intellectual assent, but practical reliance on God.

17:22-23 Second Prediction of Jesus' Death

Once again using his preferred title, *the Son of Man* (**17:22a**), which implies suffering, Jesus predicts that he must be *betrayed* (**17:22b**) and die, but will rise on *the third day* (**17:23**; see also 16:21-28; 20:17-19).

17:24-27 Jesus and the Temple Tax

The *temple tax* was a half-shekel paid annually by most adult males. The money was used initially for the upkeep of the Tent of Meeting (Exod 30:11-16) and later for the temple (**17:24**). After the destruction of the temple in AD 70, the Romans used this tax to fund a temple of Jupiter in Rome. This incident, therefore, suggests that the Gospel of Matthew was written before the destruction of the temple in AD 70, for after this time the issue of the temple tax would have ceased to be meaningful.

There was no universal agreement among the Jews concerning the validity of the tax. The Sadducees apparently disapproved of it while the Qumran sect paid it only once in a lifetime, which would appear to be more in keeping with the OT. Given the controversy on the subject, what was

Jesus' attitude to the tax? Peter answered that Jesus paid the tax, presumably because he paid it regularly (**17:25**).

In the village where I was brought up, there were two kinds of taxes: the poll tax imposed on every male householder by the British colonial government and the traditional annual tax paid to the local chief's palace, usually in the form of conscripted labour and food donations or tribute. The colonial poll tax was a constant reminder of subjection to a foreign power, while the latter taxes were a matter of customary pride. The traditional taxes were not paid by the chief's sons, but by those who were governed by the chief.

Similarly, Jesus argues that as the Son of God, he does not need to pay the tax, since the temple was the house of God. The temple tax was intended for the maintenance of services to him. However, in order not to unnecessarily offend others, or put a stumbling block before them, he would pay the tax (**17:26-27**). Christians are called to comply with the rules, regulations and obligations of the societies in which they live in order not to give offence. Even when taxes are judged unfair, it is incumbent upon all of us to uphold the concept of government.

18:1-35 Teaching IV: The Kingdom Community

This is the fourth of the five major blocks of teaching in Matthew. It deals with relationships in the community of Jesus' followers, and may rightly be called a Manual for Discipleship. Every community must have core values and clear boundaries that define its character and distinguish it from other communities.

The Christian community is centred on Jesus, who is confessed to be 'the Christ, the Son of the living God' (16:16). He is our teacher and, while his teaching fulfils the OT (5:17), it centres primarily on his own life and words.

18:1-5 Leadership in the Community

Status was exceedingly important in first-century Mediterranean culture. Nothing much has changed over the past twenty centuries! In our world, men and women of status wield power and can get things done. It is not uncommon in many parts of Africa for people who hold power in society or who are connected closely to chiefs or politicians to get into positions of responsibility in Christian churches for which they are ill prepared. The church, too, has been affected: all too often leaders state their office before they give their names. The prevalence of titles such as bishop, archbishop and apostle is another indicator of this malady in Christ's body. The attraction of status is easy to understand, for in many situations it goes hand in hand with respect and opportunities. That was why the disciples argued about who was the greatest (**18:1**; Mark 9:34). But what are the qualities of greatness and leadership within the community of Jesus?

Jesus' answer to this question calls for a re-evaluation of the normal understanding of leadership. Leaders must become like little children (**18:2-5**). Some commentators have suggested that this means that leaders must have such childlike characteristics as innocence, wonder, dependence, trust and the ability to forgive. While these qualities are important, the most significant quality of the child in this story is that he had no status, no importance, except as a responsibility for others to care for. To become like a child is therefore to renounce any notions of self-importance and to embrace insignificance. This is true humility (Phil 2:6-11), the prime characteristic of all who follow Jesus. We have no right to establish hierarchies in the church that separate important people from those who are not so important (see Jas 2:1-4). We must welcome each other in the church as people who all have the same status – that is, no status. Powerlessness is a good quality in the upside-down kingdom of heaven. To be a citizen of heaven means abandoning one's rights and living to serve, not to gain power.

18:6-9 Causing Others to Stumble

We may stumble physically because of something internal, such as a lack of concentration, or something external, such as something placed in our way. And stumbling often leads to falling. What is true physically is also true spiritually. We can all *stumble* (NASB) or *sin* (NIV), and we may cause others to stumble or sin (**18:6**). The person who causes others to sin will suffer severe consequences, worse than having *a large millstone hung around his neck* and being *drowned in the depths of the sea* (**18:6b**). We tend to apply this verse only to how we treat children, but in **18:6a** *little ones* means all disciples, not just literal children (11:25; 25:40).

Jesus affirms that sin and temptations to sin will continue as long as life remains (**18:7**). His disciples, like everyone else, will be vulnerable to external pressure to sin. But the desire to sin can also come from within (**18:8-9**; see 15:11). Our eyes, hands, nose, tongue and ears may become avenues through which temptation enters and leads us to sin. Our eyes may see something that arouses strong passions that mature into sin. This is even more likely now, given the free access to information that has come with books, television and the Internet. Idle hands have always been and will continue to be the devil's tools. We can use our nose to sniff glue or inhale even more potent drugs. The tongue can be as deadly as poison (Jas 3:8-9). We must guard our ears from hearing what does not edify. The body of a Christian must be trained to avoid toying with evil and falling into sin.

Drastic action is needed to deal with any of these sources of temptation (18:8-9). We do not need to take these words literally, but we do need to heed their essential message. We must be discerning in what we see, touch, smell, say or hear. We have to be discerning in what we expose our bodies to, in case such exposure leads to sin. We also need to beware lest our own sin cause someone else to stumble, making us doubly cautious about how we act.

Some have suggested that the drastic actions suggested in 18:8-9 refers to excommunicating people who are sources of stumbling from the body of Christ, the church. However, the focus is primarily on our own lives.

18:10-14 The Parable of the Lost Sheep

Luke groups this parable with the parables of the lost coin and the lost son, as all three speak of God's pastoral heart, his care for his *little ones* (**18:10**; Luke 15). These little ones have direct access to his presence, and if they should be deceived by someone or something and wander away, the Father does not rest until they are safely returned to the fold.

The leaving of the ninety-nine sheep is not to be understood as a reckless act of abandonment (**18:12**). In Jesus' day, shepherds worked in groups, and the diligent shepherd would have left them in the care of others – with the communal herd.

Luke emphasizes the joy that followed the recovery of the lost sheep (Luke 15:1-7), whereas Matthew emphasizes the concern that none of the vulnerable members *should be lost* (**18:14**). Both perspectives are true, for the same concern that leads to the diligent search will express itself in great joy when the search is successful. The Father's pastoral heart not only seeks and restores but also rejoices when straying sheep are safely restored to the fold.

This parable applies, among other things, to parents, who should emulate God's concern for their children. Children are prone to go astray, and may cause hurt to their parents. Nevertheless, the parents should diligently seek to find the child and restore him or her to the family. As the Bemba say, *Umwana kasembe: kakukoma wa bwela wa kobeka* ['a child is like an axe: it cuts you but you still put it back on your shoulder for further use'].

Similarly, pastors and elders (whom Peter calls 'shepherds' – 1 Peter 5:1-2) must seek diligently for members of the church who seem to be in danger of being led astray or deceived into believing something false, or who may be discouraged to the point of losing their commitment. The search must go on until they are found and restored to fellowship. In doing this, the pastors and elders must not be harsh and censorious but gentle and welcoming. The Chief Shepherd, Christ himself, will reward such diligence.

18:15-20 Interpersonal Relationships

A household that is divided against itself will not stand (12:25), for disharmony is a cancer that eats away at the heart of a community. Yet in any community brothers and sisters will sin against each other (18:15). As the Bemba say, *Imiti ipalamene: taibula kushenkana* ['two trees that are close together will rub against each other']. There is no indication of what kinds of sins are involved. It may even be the sin of actively leading others away from the path of discipleship. Whatever the case, sin must not be allowed but must be stopped in its tracks. The community must not tolerate disunity or grudges or hurt feelings because these are injurious to the health and witness of the body.

Jesus outlines three steps to restore harmony, unity and love:

- The first step must be taken by the offended person, who must point out the offence to the offender. The offender may not even have realized that what was said or done was offensive. Doing this privately makes it easier for apologies to be given and the relationship to be restored (**18:15**). Keeping the matter between two people is particularly important in cultures like those in Zambia, where being shamed in public assumes greater significance than the original offence. The privacy preserves people's sense of wholeness before the community and cuts out the damaging gossip that so easily undermines any attempt at sorting out problems.
- If the first attempt at reconciliation is unsuccessful, the offended person should go back with *one or two others* (**18:16**). These independent witnesses should carefully listen to explanations of what has happened, to see whether the parties are earnestly attempting to reconcile or are determined to obstruct the path to harmony.
- The final step involves bringing the matter before the whole assembly (**18:17**). If the offender ignores the verdict of the community, then he or she is to be publicly dissociated from the community. In Judaism this meant the person was to be treated as if they were unclean and, therefore, to be avoided. In his letters, Paul adds to our understanding of this drastic step of full excommunication (see 1 Cor 5:5; 1 Tim 1:20; Titus 3:10-11).

The reference to binding and loosing in **18:18** suggests that the community has the authority, sanctioned by the heavenly court, to pronounce on what is right and what is wrong, on what is sin and what is not sin. Such authority is not to be taken lightly. It was conferred by the Lord Jesus on Peter (16:19), but is now extended to include the whole messianic community. This community is to be one that engages in prayer and enjoys the fellowship of the Lord himself (**18:19**).

18:21-35 The Unmerciful Servant

Hostility between members of a community can result in frustration, paralysis, low morale and a loss of vision. The antidote to such disharmony is forgiveness, which often leads to peace, harmony, unity and acceptance. But forgiveness can be difficult when the same people repeatedly cause disunity through their hurtful actions and words. Is there a limit to how many times one must forgive another before a line is drawn? Peter asked Jesus if the magic number was seven times (**18:21**). The number seven represented perfection, so Peter may have been thinking that after forgiving someone seven times, the offended party had done enough. Jesus' answer makes it abundantly clear that there are no limits to forgiveness. Lamech set no limits to his vengeance, saying he would avenge himself 'seventy-seven times' (Gen 4:24), and Jesus commands no limits to forgiveness (**18:22**).

He illustrated his point with a parable about a king and his servants (a term used to describe high officials in a kingdom). Some of these officials have borrowed money from the king. The king is obviously very wealthy and able to lend vast amounts as well as smaller sums. But he is also committed to collecting his debts. He holds his debtors to account (**18:23-24**).

This is not the place to deal with the whole subject of Africa's crushing debt burden and the need for debt relief, but it is important to make the point that someone who borrows money is obliged to pay it back. A moneylender must call to account all who have borrowed from him or her. While lender nations must do what they can to alleviate the suffering of millions of people on account of Africa's debt, Africa must also face up to its responsibilities, regardless of any action taken by the lender nations.

The first servant owes an incredible 10 000 talents (18:24) – ten times the annual tax revenue for the country in the times of Herod the Great. The figure is probably not to be taken at face value, but is intended to underscore the difference between this sum equal to 100 million denarii and the mere 100 denarii mentioned later on (**18:28**). How could any one official borrow so much money? How could anyone be so foolish as to lend so much money? Such a debt could only have accrued in much the same way that the African debt burden has accrued, that is by charging interest, and then charging interest on the interest, and so on! This man may even have been a tax collector, who had not managed to collect the required money. The king realizes that his servant, despite his promises, will never be able to pay back the debt. So he exercises mercy, cancels the debt and lets the servant go (**18:25-27**).

The recently forgiven debtor then meets someone who owes him 100 denarii. He then calls this debtor to account (18:28). The debtor cannot pay and asks for time (**18:29**). But the moneylender refuses to show mercy; instead he takes the helpless debtor to the courts and has him cast into prison (**18:30**). We are disgusted at how a person who has been treated with excessive grace can fail to show a small amount of grace to another.

Finally, the scene returns to the king's court. Other servants of the king, who have witnessed both the king's exercise of grace and the unmerciful servant's act of gross inhumanity, have reported the matter to the king (**18:31**).

The king summons the unmerciful servant and calls him to account for his actions. The king describes him as wicked and gives the servant the punishment he deserves (**18:32-34**).

This parable reminds us that our moral debt to God is incalculable. Every human thought, word or deed, however lofty, is tainted with sin (Gen 6:5-6; 11-13; Ps 51:5), which means we violate God's moral law even when we are not conscious of doing so. But God in Jesus Christ has provided a way by which all our sins can be forgiven. Whatever debt other human beings owe us, it cannot compare to the debt we owe to God, which he has forgiven. We should follow his example of grace and learn to forgive.

19:1-22:45 The Ministry of Jesus: Part IV

19:1-12 Divorce

About one in two marriages in the United Kingdom and the United States ends in divorce. African statistics are harder to come by. Divorce was also quite common in Jesus' day. But every divorce is one too many. Divorce violates God's original intention for marriage, as Jesus points out in his answer to the Pharisees' question, *Is it lawful for a man to divorce his wife for any and every reason?* (**19:3**).

The background to this question was the debate that raged between two schools of theological thought, both of which took Deuteronomy 24:1-4 as their starting point. Rabbi Shammai taught that a man could only divorce his wife if she was unfaithful, because he interpreted the words 'something indecent' in Deuteronomy as referring to marital unfaithfulness. Rabbi Hillel, on the other hand, interpreted the phrase far more broadly and held that a man could divorce his wife for any reason whatsoever, even for something as trivial as burning his bread. In contemporary terms, we might say that a man might divorce his wife for putting too much salt into his food or (in Zambia) for letting another man use his *akatemba cupo,* the little pot specially set aside to hold boiling water for the husband alone to wash his face in. This theological debate had gained increased prominence because of the recent high-profile case involving Herod Antipas, the tetrarch, who had divorced his Nabatean wife to marry Herodias, who had been the wife of his brother Philip. This marriage had led to the execution of John the Baptist (14:9-11).

The Pharisees were trying to set a trap for Jesus. If Jesus said that divorce was lawful *for any and every reason,* he would be contradicting Moses, who permitted divorce only for indecency (Deut 24:1). But if he said it was unlawful, he would fall foul of the general populace for whom divorce was a common practice.

Jesus saw through their plot, and with prophetic wisdom avoided the superficial scribal debate and infamous politi-

cal machinations by going directly to the original authority. Instead of arguing from Deuteronomy, he pointed to two other biblical passages: Genesis 1:27 and 2:24 (**19:5**). He did not render the Mosaic provision null and void, but set it in the context of God's original intention.

God created human beings 'in his own image' as well as *male and female* (**19:4**; Gen 1:27). Part of what this means is that we have the ability to engage in a marriage relationship characterized by love, confidence, harmony and trust – the same virtues that characterize the relationship within the Trinity. The fact that *the two will become one flesh* (19:5b; see also Gen 2:24) indicates that marriage is an exclusive and ideally indissoluble arrangement (**19:6**). A question then naturally arises: if God intended marriage to be indissoluble and made no allowances for divorce, why did Moses allow it (**19:7**)?

In his answer, Jesus pointed out that Moses' provision for divorce did not nullify God's original intention. Moses allowed divorce because there was so much suffering in marriage on account of sin and the hardness of human hearts (**19:8**). Marriage was intended to allow human beings to experience something of the richness of the relationships that exist between the Father, Son and Holy Spirit. Unfortunately, for many couples, things such as sinfulness, hardness of heart, childlessness and a lack of empathy, sympathy, love, care, trust, respect and commitment mean that their experience of marriage is more hellish than heavenly.

Jesus does allow for divorce, and by implication remarriage, where there is marital unfaithfulness (**19:9**). This concession is an act of harm reduction, as was Moses' ruling. Except in cases of marital unfaithfulness, remarriage while both parties are still alive is adultery (see also 5:32) as it replaces the first marriage sanctioned by God, parents and society with another sexual union (Mal 2:15-16).

We thus have a tension in which the reality of divorce and remarriage falls far short of the original ideal. We must resist the temptation to reduce our principles to the reality, as if that were the standard. Instead, we must strive to fulfil the intention of the Lord as spelled out in Genesis (see Eph 5:31).

Many, including the disciples, felt that being expected to stay in a marriage was very hard, and that the option of divorce and remarriage was a necessary escape clause. So the disciples reacted to Jesus' stricter interpretation by suggesting that it was better to remain single than to marry in the first place (**19:10**). While celibacy is not uncommon in Europe and North America among both men and women, this is not the case in Africa. Here, even where celibacy is imposed from above, as happens in some denominations, many pastors live in flagrant violation of this requirement. The pressure from society to marry, or at any rate have children, is so strong that many Africans, especially men, just

MARRIAGE, DIVORCE AND REMARRIAGE

Marriage has traditionally been a community affair. However, God, who established the institution, made Eve for Adam as a suitable helper to him (singular). The exhortations on marriage in the NT focus on a husband and wife. Therefore, while marriage may be within a community, it is not between the community and the wife. It is between a husband and a wife. The community's role is to help the two succeed in their relationship.

In Genesis we read that, 'For this reason a man will leave his father and mother, and be united to his wife; and they will become one flesh' (Gen 2:24). This position is restated by Jesus when responding to a question on divorce (Matt 19:5; Mark 10:7) and by Paul in his discussion of the roles of husband and wife in marriage (Eph 5:31). The idea was that a man who took a wife agreed to rearrange his priorities, with his wife now taking the most humanly prominent place in his life – a place that his parents had occupied since his childhood. The focus is not on physical leaving, though living separately from one's parents is a good idea, but on the question, 'Who is my best friend?' The correct answer must be 'My wife'. This must not simply be a theoretical affirmation but a Christian husband's practice at all times. This principle applies to both spouses, so that a wife's best friend should be her husband.

Adam understood correctly that Eve was 'bone of my bones' and 'flesh of my flesh'. The result of such recognition is that marriage involves not only leaving one's parents but a meaningful uniting with one's wife, 'becoming one flesh'. This union gives status to the wife such that there is no longer any question of 'his' and 'hers'; what we have is 'ours' because we are one flesh. This is true not only of material goods but also of the blessings and difficulties in life.

Jesus restates the principle of 'leaving' and 'uniting' in Matthew 19:1-12 and Mark 10:1-12. The Pharisees had asked him whether it is 'lawful for a man to divorce his wife for any and every reason' (Matt 19:3). Within the Jewish culture, divorce was a male prerogative. However, within the broader Roman culture, a wife could also divorce her husband, as Jesus' response in Mark 10:11-12 shows.

In replying to the question, Jesus made four key points:

- God created Adam and Eve male and female, showing that his design for marriage involved a man and a woman. By implication, any other design is human and not God's.

- God's will is that a man leave his father and mother and unite with his wife. The leaving is commanded, and the uniting indicates that from the time they are married, the two are glued together by their marriage covenant. The form of the verb 'will become' emphasizes the certainty that this will happen. The certainty is not based on what

they want, but on God's decree that such uniting will take place.

- In marriage, God 'joins together'. By the very act of freely entering into a covenant of marriage, the two are yoked together by God. They must do things as partners if they are to get anywhere, while outsiders must mind their own business or risk fighting God, undoing what he has done.

- No one should attempt to separate two people whom God has joined together. No man or woman can undo what God has done. They can, however, cause confusion in what God has done. This is what happens when marriages break down. It is not that God's work of joining has been undone. Rather, sinful men and women (or Satan, who is always eager to distort the beauty of what God has made) cause confusion so that at times it appears that they have managed to undo God's act of joining together.

The Pharisees correctly understood Jesus to be saying that once a man and woman have contracted a marriage, that contract remains binding at all times and in all situations. This is why they challenged Jesus, asking, 'Why then did Moses command that a man give his wife a certificate of divorce and send her away?' (Matt 19:7). They were thinking of Deuteronomy 24:1-4, which states that if a man is dissatisfied with his wife because he finds 'some indecency ' in her he can divorce her. However, if she thereafter marries someone else, he can never take her back as wife because 'she has been defiled'.

In responding to this question, Jesus made a further three points about divorce:

- Moses' permission was not based on what God intends to happen but on what he permits because of human weakness. God is not compromising but acting in mercy. His normal pattern is not to destroy slow learners but to give them time to learn more about his marvellous ways and eventually grow up to achieve what God desires for them. Jesus' answer agrees with the correct meaning of the passage in Deuteronomy. Moses' point was that a man should think not only twice but thrice before divorcing his wife, because if he later changes his mind, he cannot marry her again if she has already been married to someone else. The Deuteronomy passage thus emphasizes the seriousness of marriage.

- Moses gave the permission because humans can be hard-hearted in their dealings with each other.

- Divorce and remarriage constitute adultery unless the reason for the divorce is prior immorality. The teachers of the law were permitting divorce for trivial reasons. By contrast, Jesus insists that there are no excuses for divorce except immorality. This exception is probably to be interpreted within the context of Deuteronomy 24:4: a wife who has been involved with another man has been defiled, and in that case divorce may be permitted. This exception does not mean that adultery must result in divorce. When we know how much we ourselves owe to God's forgiving grace, we should be prepared to extend forgiveness to a fellow human being.

- The exception clause is also found in Matthew 5:31-32, but not in the parallel passages in Mark 10:11-12 and Luke 16:18. Matthew was writing to people struggling with Jewish regulations, but for others divorce and remarriage are adultery, without any qualification. Combining the accounts of Jesus' words, it seems clear that there is no God-approved basis for divorce. The exception mentioned in Matthew underlines the seriousness of marriage rather than granting permission to divorce.

Paul uses the analogy of marriage to teach about a believer's relationship to the law (Rom 7:1-6). His central point is that only death dissolves a marriage. In 1 Corinthians 7, he speaks of the need to remain together as husband and wife, but adds 'if the unbeliever leaves, let him do so. A believing man or woman is not bound in such circumstances; God has called us to live in peace' (1 Cor 7:15). The key issue here is the meaning of the phrase 'is not bound'. Paul does not tell us what the believer is bound to. Is the person freed from the relationship but required to remain unmarried, or does the freedom include freedom from the marriage vows and therefore allow for remarriage? While acknowledging that Paul's main point is that believers are to nurture their marriages, even marriages with unbelievers, there seems to be

room for the church, under the guidance of the Holy Spirit, to apply this freedom in special cases not only to the relationship but also to the vows and thus allow remarriage. Matthew 18:15-17 lays down the pattern that should be followed in such cases, with the church being a full participant in the process.

One of the most important questions in marriage counselling is identifying the special cases to which the freedom of 1 Corinthians 7:15 applies. It is all too easy to gradually open the door to divorce wider and wider, and to forget that Jesus limited it to cases of adultery and that God wants every couple to keep their marriage vows for life. However, we should not ignore the statement that 'God has called us to live in peace'. Peace is achieved when both partners keep their parts of the vows. But there are cases where husbands actively torture their wives – either by physical beatings, or through financial neglect and absence. When such behaviour proves resistant to counselling, and especially where the wife's life is threatened, she is entitled to claim to be a special case. A wife, too, may be the sinning partner, particularly when she leaves home and chooses to live in a city in a way that denies that she is accountable to her husband in any way. In such cases, and after vigorous attempt to help the erring one to correct his or her ways, the pastor and the church must stand with the hurting party in seeking a way forward. By recognizing these as special cases, the church allows for such options as separation, divorce and remarriage.

Samuel Ngewa

cannot conceive of life without marriage or perhaps more accurately, regular sex.

Jesus acknowledged the difficulty of remaining faithful to marriage vows or remaining in painful unions. He recognized that the demands of Christian marriage can only be met by those who are in a supportive relationship with God (**19:11**). If Christ is the gift that enables his disciples to remain faithful in marriage, then both parties to the marriage must profess faith in him.

Jesus does not, however, regard celibacy as superior to marriage. Heterosexual marriage remains God's ideal for people in general (19:3-9). Celibacy is possible but, like marriage, it is a gift. Eunuchs and people who, like Jesus, have been called to specific ministries that render marriage a practical impossibility are called to live in celibacy (1 Cor 7:7-9, 32-35).

While it is the norm for people to marry and have children, Jesus' teaching makes it clear that these are not necessary for all. We must honour and respect every human being, including those who for some reason have not been able to have children or enjoy a marriage relationship.

19:13-15 Jesus and Little Children

This incident emphasizes the importance of showing respect and honour to those whom society does not respect. Children were not regarded as important (see 18:1-5) and the disciples assumed that a teacher like Jesus was far too busy to waste his time with them (**19:13**). But Jesus took time to show special concern for children and repeated his statement that child-like qualities are important, for *the kingdom of heaven belongs to such as these* (**19:14**). He also showed his concern for other marginalized and despised groups, such as tax collectors, sinners, Gentiles and lepers. There are many people who are similarly dismissed by society in Africa: people with disabilities, those with HIV/AIDS, orphans, unmarried people, childless people, those belonging to despised tribes and so on. As followers of Jesus, we must share his concern for them.

19:16-26 A Rich Young Man Approaches Jesus

The story of the rich young man who asked Jesus *what good thing must I do to get eternal life?* (**19:16**) also occurs in Mark and Luke (Mark 10:17-31; Luke 18:18-30). In those

Gospels, the young man addressed Jesus as 'good teacher'. Such an approach was very respectful and may indicate the high esteem in which many people held Jesus. Matthew, however, attaches the adjective 'good' to the thing the young man must *do to get eternal life*.

Jesus replied that only God is good. 'Goodness' was a quality that Jews associated supremely with God and his commandments. Accordingly Jesus pointed the young man to the good laws of the *One who is good* (**19:17**), and asked him to show due diligence in observing them. The young man had located goodness in a human action, whereas Jesus focused on God's goodness and his good actions. These are what matter when it comes to entry into the kingdom of heaven. The prophet Isaiah likened human righteous action to filthy rags, which would never qualify anyone for eternal life (Isa 64:6).

The specific commandments that Jesus pointed to in **19:18-19** are in the second half of the Ten Commandments and relate to one's dealings with one's neighbours (Exod 20:12-16; Lev 19:18; Deut 5:16-20). The man affirmed that he had kept all these commandments for many years, but there still seemed to be something lacking (**19:20**). Jesus took him at his word, but then pointed to the commandment to love God with one's whole heart, mind and soul (22:37). Had the young man done this? Had he loved God with all his wealth? Jesus tested him by asking him to surrender his wealth and use it to meet the needs of the poor, and to combine that action with following him (**19:21**).

Entering the kingdom of heaven or inheriting eternal life involves more than carrying out certain actions, however good and wonderful. It requires surrendering one's allegiance totally to Jesus: 'If anyone would come after me, he must deny himself and take up his cross and follow me' (16:24; see Mark 8:34). The young man wanted someone to teach him something he could do, but he was not prepared to accept the Lordship of someone who made demands that were sacrificial. So *he went away sad, because he had great wealth* (**19:22**).

Jesus tested this would-be disciple to see whether he was prepared to surrender himself and all he had to him. Poverty in itself is not a virtue, nor is it a qualification for entry into God's kingdom, although poor people have a very special place in God's thoughts (Luke 6:20). Material poverty does, however, predispose one to depend entirely upon the mercy of others. That quality is important for anyone who wants to follow Jesus and enter into the kingdom of God. Jesus is Lord of all, and one must be prepared to give him first place in one's life.

Rich people have greater difficulty surrendering to God than the poor do. Riches give a false sense of security and can make one proud and arrogant. They can absorb a person's energies so that there is no room for God. This lesson is reinforced by an illustration that seems ludicrous. *It is*

easier for a camel [or an elephant or a hippopotamus] *to go through the eye of a needle than for a rich man* [or rather a man who allows riches to come first in his life] *to enter the kingdom of God* (**19:24**). The fact that Africa has an abundance of poor people, along with the characteristic African openness to spiritual matters, means that we have a tremendous window of opportunity to preach the gospel to people who possess fewer barriers to faith than is the case in the Western world today.

The disciples were shocked by Jesus' words, for they, like their contemporaries, assumed that wealth was a sign of God's blessings, and poverty a sign of God's displeasure. So if the rich cannot be saved, *who then can be saved?* (**19:25**). Jesus' response indicates that rich people are not shut out, nor are riches in themselves sinful, although they can be a danger to faith. Jesus' followers included rich people like Nicodemus (John 3:1-8), Zacchaeus (Luke 19:1-9) and Joseph of Arimathea (27:57-61).

19:27-29 Renunciation of Wealth and Rewards

The disciples asked about their own condition, as they had renounced everything, including jobs and family, to follow Jesus (**19:27**). Jesus' answer shows that God is not unmindful of those who sacrifice a lot for him. Family is a big thing to give up. In Africa, we define ourselves by our extended families or clans. To give up one's family is to lose oneself. To be given up by one's family is a terrible tragedy, which often happens when a Muslim becomes a follower of Jesus.

Jesus says we must be prepared to suffer such alienation in following him. Discipleship demands that we be prepared to renounce familiar relationships and to embrace unfamiliar ones if that is what it costs to follow Jesus. But God is no person's debtor. It is impossible to give more than God. He does not ask anyone to do anything he would not be prepared to do himself. Rich rewards in this age and in the age to come await those who are prepared to follow him at whatever cost. The twelve disciples would have the privilege of sitting on *twelve thrones* beside him – a true place of honour (**19:28**). All others will be more than adequately compensated for what they give up for God (**19:29**).

19:30-20:16 The Workers in the Vineyard

The parable of the workers in the vineyard is framed by the teaching that, *many who are first will be last and many who are last will be first* (**19:30**; see 20:16). This frame immediately alerts us to the possibility that God has different standards than we do in regard to how he deals with people.

The parable illustrates a truth about the *kingdom of heaven* (**20:1a**). It is similar in some respects to the parable of the lost son (Luke 15:11-32), which also deals with the issue of jealousy and anger at undeserved generosity. Generosity should be the cause of rejoicing not resentment. This lesson is very important for those who have been Christians for a long time, and who begin to see much younger men and women being richly blessed by God materially, spiritually or in successful ministry. O that we could all be as generous as God, who is totally just to the deserving, but more often outrageously generous to the undeserving!

Using standard imagery, the parable represents God as a *landowner* and Israel as his *vineyard* (**20:1b**; see Isa 5:1-7; Jer 12:10). The landowner went out to hire workers for the day. This practice was typical in the Middle East then and now, and is still common in many parts of the world. In Zambian towns, many young men and women still gather outside the local labour offices early in the morning. Prospective employers come there to recruit casual labourers on a daily basis.

The landowner recruited the first batch of labourers at about 6 a.m. These were probably the only labourers needed for the day, but he returned to recruit more at three-hourly intervals, including one at the *eleventh hour*, that is at 5 p.m., an hour before the end of the working day (**20:2-7**). The later groups were hired not so much because the landowner was desperate for more workers, but because they were standing there looking for work (20:3). It was their need and his generosity that determined their employment.

Labourers like these were at the bottom of the social ladder. Even slaves were better off, because at least their masters provided what they needed. But labourers did not have that security and were completely at the mercy of employers. They could easily be exploited.

When the landowner recruited the first batch, he made sure that they understood that he would be paying them *a denarius*, which was the standard daily wage for a labourer (20:2). When the others were recruited later, he did not specify what they would be paid, but they would probably have assumed that they would be paid less for less work. But when it was time to settle the accounts (this landowner was righteous and did not withhold payment overnight – see Lev 19:13), the landowner instructed the manager of the farm to pay the last first (**20:8**). At a superficial level, the expression the *first will be last,* and the *last will be first* (19:30; see **20:16**) may simply refer to this arrangement. But there is a greater significance.

All the labourers received exactly the same amount. But the workers who had worked longest had seen that those who had worked the least received a denarius for their efforts, and had assumed that they would receive comparatively more (**20:9-10**). They assumed that they deserved more. So when they were paid exactly the same amount as the others, they complained claiming that they had been treated unfairly (**20:11-12**). But as the landowner pointed out they had not been treated unfairly, for they had an agreed contract and they were paid accordingly (**20:13-14**). The wage was a fair one, not generous, but not miserly either.

The Bemba people say *Umupashi wa mubiyo: tawendelwa* ['The luck of your friend should not cause you to set out hoping for similar results']. The fact that your friend was fortunate is no reason for you to expect similar good fortune. This proverb emphasizes the uniqueness of each individual and of the circumstances that affect them. It also makes the point that God's standards are just and generous, not miserly, but that they are not always the same as what we would consider to be fair. God always leans towards the generous side in his dealings with people. We should learn to do likewise, and should certainly not succumb to resentment when we observe God's generosity in action. God saves us by grace. It is all grace and not what we deserve. So the church must learn to celebrate the grace and generosity of God wherever they become evident and should harbour no resentment against God or those upon whom his favour rests.

20:17-19 Jesus Predicts His Death a Third Time

Jesus then made a third prediction of his death (see 16:21-28; 17:22-23). He and his disciples were going to Jerusalem where he would be betrayed to the Jewish authorities, condemned to death, mocked, flogged and finally crucified (**20:17-19**). The form of death is now clearly stated. Jesus did not anticipate an easy death but a horrible, slow, extremely painful and brutal form of execution. However, this tragic death would be followed by a glorious resurrection. The road to glory must go through Calvary. For those who follow Christ, suffering will often precede glory. This is a necessary corrective to the 'prosperity gospel' that is common in some charismatic churches. Suffering was integral to the work of the Messiah; in fact suffering defined what it meant to be the Messiah. Similarly disciples suffering, must not just surrender their rights to Christ but must embrace a willingness to walk the path of death for his sake. That is part of what 'take up his cross and follow me' means (16:24).

20:20-28 James and John and Their Mother

The disciples repeatedly fail to recognize the necessity of the cross. When Jesus first predicted his appointment with death, Peter took him aside and rebuked him (16:22). Death did not feature in the disciples' theological presuppositions about the Messiah's mission. The third prediction is followed by a request which again highlights their misunderstanding of the nature of messiahship, and consequently of the nature of discipleship.

The mother of James and John, who may have been related to Jesus' mother, acted on their behalf to try to secure them key posts in Jesus' kingdom (**20:20-21**). Her reasoning must have been that if Jesus was the Messiah, he would surely take the throne of his father David in Jerusalem. His claim to the throne would be accepted by the custodians of the promises of God, and he would rid Palestine of the Romans. James and John wanted to be in on the action, and sought through their mother to secure themselves positions of authority in the kingdom of heaven.

The other disciples had no better insight into Jesus' messiahship, for when they discovered what James and John had tried to do behind their backs, *they were indignant with the two brothers* (**20:24**). Their minds were focused on the prospect of seniority, authority and perhaps importance and wealth. In fairness to them, they might have been trying to understand when and how they would sit on the twelve thrones alongside Jesus judging the twelve tribes of Israel (19:28)! Their theology might have been right but their timing was wrong.

If the Messiah was to suffer, then it followed that his disciples too would suffer. They would drink from his cup (**20:22-23**), a metaphor for suffering. James and John affirmed that they were ready to share his cup, and when the time came they did indeed drink the cup of suffering. James was executed by King Herod (Acts 12:2) and John was banished to the Island of Patmos, where he had the visions that are described in the pages of the book of Revelation (Rev 1:1).

These later events apart, being first in the kingdom was not the result of personal ambition but of divine grant. God alone would decide who would receive what position.

Jesus used the opportunity to give his disciples another lesson on the qualities of leadership in the kingdom of heaven. In the world, leaders are served and can command people to do their bidding. There, leadership is about power and the exploitation of power (**20:25**). But in Jesus' kingdom, leadership means service to those led (**20:26-27**). It is quite the opposite of what is common in human society. A leader in Jesus' kingdom must be a helper in the biblical sense of the word; that is, a person who comes alongside to enable others to achieve what they need to achieve.

A mother nurturing and leading her children provides a good example of leadership. She is constantly serving them. Yet a good mother is not only one who serves her children, but also one who leads them into maturity. Christian leaders must emulate the good mother, serving their followers well while teaching them the values of the kingdom of God. Jesus does not ask anyone to do anything he was not prepared to do. He came into this world as the Son of God, and yet he did not have the normal attributes and advantages of a leader. In fact he gave *his life as a ransom for many* (**20:28**); he died that we might have a chance to be redeemed. The idea of a ransom derives from the OT provision that a ransom could be paid to set someone like a slave free (Lev 25:47-52; 27:1-8). This substitution of one thing for another is an important part of the vocation of the suffering servant in Isaiah 53.

The exploitation of power has ruined the continent of Africa. Powerful rulers have had little regard for the people over whom they rule, and have lined their own pockets and those of their close relatives at the expense of others. The lifestyles of the ruling elites are vastly different from the lifestyles of those they rule. In most cases, the saying that 'power corrupts' has been more than fulfilled! Leaders should never use their positions to advance themselves. Instead they must put the needs of those they lead uppermost and seek to make the lives of others not just tolerable but pleasurable.

20:29-34 The Healing of Two Blind Men in Jericho

Blindness can easily shut a person up in their own world of shadows and sounds, where they are dependent on other people for physical guidance. Often the only way a blind person can make ends meet is to beg. Blindness robs a person of dignity and the possibility of independence. Unfortunately, in many parts of Africa, blind people are made fun of and not given any respect. With a few exceptions, they are marginalized and denied real prospects. Like children (19:13-15), blind people were not regarded as important in first-century Palestine, certainly not important enough for the Messiah to be concerned with.

The *two blind men* outside Jericho heard a commotion and discovered that Jesus was passing by on his way to Jerusalem (**20:29-30a**). They knew that this man was *the son of David*, the rightful heir to David's throne and the Messiah of the people of God. They had faith; they believed in Jesus. So they sought his favour and mercy to heal their blindness (**20:30b**).

They must have shouted very loudly to be heard over the din of the excited pilgrims on their annual journey to Jerusalem. Those nearest to them sought to quieten them, for they were making a nuisance of themselves and unnecessarily disturbing the Messiah, who had more important things on his mind. There is no doubt that Jesus was to face a momentous week in Jerusalem. His mind was on higher things like the salvation of all humanity, not to mention the sacrifice he was to make! What do the needs of a blind beggar matter in such circumstances? The blind men would not be deterred, and they shouted the more loudly asking Jesus to have mercy on them (**20:31**).

In spite of the weighty matters that lay heavily upon his shoulders, Jesus stopped and turned aside to attend to their need. He placed their need at the centre of his programme at that moment, and he asked them what it was they wanted him to do for them (**20:32**). They answered without hesitation: they wanted their sight (**20:33**). Jesus had compassion on them (see 6:8; 9:36; 14:14; 15:32). He *touched their eyes* and *they received their sight* (**20:34**). Then they followed him, suggesting that as recipients of his mercy they became his disciples.

Marginalized people are close to God's heart. Many of the people who received healing from Jesus were marginal people with no real stake in society. Jesus cares for the poor and the downtrodden. Christian leaders should follow his example and provide care and advocacy for those who are not able to help themselves.

21:1-11 Triumphal Entry into Jerusalem

Passover was the greatest of the annual festivals in Jerusalem. At this time every year, the population of Jerusalem swelled as Jews from all over the world crowded into its streets.

Many Jews from Galilee also made the journey. They would cross the Jordan south of the Sea of Galilee to avoid going through Samaria and then re-enter Israel at Jericho for the final leg of their journey. From Jericho it was a short, but uphill, seventeen miles to Jerusalem. *Bethphage on the Mount of Olives* (**21:1**) was two miles east of the city, where Jerusalem (from which it was separated by the Kidron Valley) first comes into view. The pilgrims would naturally get more and more excited the closer they came to Jerusalem, and the crowds would swell as they approached the city.

Jesus sent two of his disciples to collect a *donkey* and its *colt* (**21:2**). Sending two disciples is important, not only for companionship, but also because each event should be witnessed by at least two people (18:16; see Deut 19:15).

How did Jesus know that these two animals would be there? Was it supernatural knowledge? Some commentators assume that Jesus had made some prior arrangement to use the animals, in which case the words, *the Lord needs them* were a code word, a kind of password (**21:3**). This explanation is unlikely, as the disciples would have been Jesus' agents in setting up any arrangement and would have known about it. Another possibility is that Jesus, as Lord, is demanding the animals for his temporary use. Similarly, when Zambia was still Northern Rhodesia, I saw police officers requisition bicycles from the public in an emergency.

However, the most likely explanation is that Jesus had divine foresight and knew the animals would be there. He had already revealed his supernatural ability to see into the minds of people (9:4) and to see a coin in the mouth of a fish in the sea (17:27). It is therefore not unreasonable to affirm that he would have had supernatural knowledge of the whereabouts of the animals. Similarly he had demonstrated that his word was able to elicit the response he desired from those he called (4:18-22; 9:9-13). Surely the same is true in this case. We do not know whether the owner of the animals was a disciple. Whoever he was and whatever relationship he may have had with Jesus, at the Lord's command he allowed the disciples to borrow his donkey and its colt for the Lord's use.

Matthew explains the triumphal entry by referring to the OT (**21:4**; Isa 62:11; Zech 9:9). Nationalistic hopes for freedom or redemption from occupation ran high at the major festivals in Jerusalem. The arrival of a prophet from Galilee, already linked to messianic claims and deeds like the feeding of the five thousand (14:19-21), would naturally fuel expectations that independence was near. The crowds in Jerusalem would probably have preferred the Messiah to be riding on a warhorse. Jesus, however, while still claiming to be the true king of Israel, entered the city not on a white charger or at the head of an army column but sitting on a donkey, a beast of burden. He was the meek one who came to serve rather than be served (20:28). He entered Jerusalem, his city, as a humble or gentle king on a donkey.

The pilgrims took off their cloaks and laid them on the road in homage to Jesus their king. They took down palm branches and laid them on the road for his donkey to walk on (**21:8**). This use of palm branches may have reminded some of them of the triumphant celebration when Simon Maccabeus entered Jerusalem just under two centuries earlier after defeating Antiochus Epiphanes, cleansed the temple and restored Jewish independence.

The crowds shouted *Hosanna to the Son of David* and sang words from Psalm 118, which celebrated a national deliverance (**21:9**). The word '*Hosanna*', which literally means 'God save us', expressed an oppressed people's cry to their king for help (**2:10**). The celebrating crowds caused a stir upon their arrival in Jerusalem, leading others to ask who was at the centre of this spectacle. The answer was, *This is Jesus, the prophet from Nazareth in Galilee* (**21:11**).

21:12-17 Cleansing of the Temple

Jesus' first act upon entering the city was to tackle head on the authority of the Sadducees and the practices in the temple that compromised the purity of the worship of God, the reason for which the building existed. Every Jew was required to pay a temple tax. During the year, this tax could be paid at specially erected booths in places all over the nation. But nearer to the Passover, the money had to be paid in Jerusalem. So the moneychangers set up shop in the Court of the Gentiles and performed a necessary function, enabling travellers with all kinds of currencies to change the money into the right currency to be able to pay the tax.

Some scholars suggest that the system of money changing was corrupt, and Jesus' action was directed at this abuse. Jesus' reference to *a den of robbers* suggests that the charge of corruption is not unfounded (**21:12-13**). The church in any and every form must not be used for purposes other than to worship and serve God alone. But Jesus' action was also powerfully symbolic. He was showing that the whole sacrificial system was obsolete and had been rejected as the way to worship God.

In the midst of this Jesus carried on a ministry of healing to those who were blind and lame (**21:14**). This incident is significant because in terms of an interpretation of the enigmatic words in 2 Samuel 5:8, the 'blind and the lame' were excluded from the temple. Jesus shows that the old order with its barriers was disappearing at the command of the Son of David.

The children who had heard and had participated in the pilgrims' chanting of 'Hosanna' picked up the chorus again, this time directing their praise to Jesus in the temple, to the obvious chagrin of the religious authorities, who tried to shame Jesus into silencing them (**21:15**). Jesus, however, pointed them to the truth that often children are able to grasp spiritual truth to which adults seem completely oblivious. Their praise was ordained by God and would not be silenced (**21:16**).

After this, Jesus retired to the village of Bethany where his disciples had set up camp for the week of the Passover festival (**21:17**).

21:18-22 Jesus Curses a Fig Tree

The fact that Jesus and his disciples went back to the city *early in the morning* and that *he was hungry* (**21:18**) suggests that their campsite was not set up for preparing meals. They had their meals in the city. On their way back, they walked past *a fig tree*. Jesus sought some fruit from it to satisfy his hunger, but none was found and he cursed the tree (**21:19a**). This action is strange and difficult to understand because it is so contrary to Jesus' normal behaviour. Since his baptism, Jesus had resolutely refused to use his powers to do miracles for his own personal benefit. Satan had encouraged him to turn stones into bread, but he had resisted the temptation (4:1-4; see 26:51-54). The cursing of the fig tree therefore seems to be out of keeping with his character.

The second problem with this story stems from the fact that the fig tree would not have been expected to bear fruit in April, the time of Passover. It might possibly have had some early unpalatable fruit, and the fact that it had *nothing on it except leaves* may suggest that the tree was barren. Still, looking for figs in April was as unreasonable as a Zambian expecting to find ripe mangoes at that time. It would be unreasonable to expect to find ripe mangoes except between November and February, and cursing a mango tree for not bearing fruit out of season is doubly unreasonable. So how do we understand this action of Jesus? Was this simply a fit of bad temper on his part, or was he acting out a parable of the imminent judgment on Jerusalem and Israel?

The fig tree was a symbol of Israel's ease and prosperity (1 Kgs 4:25; Mic 4:4; Zech 3:10). Its destruction was also a symbol of the nation's judgment (Jer 5:17; Hos 2:12; Joel 1:7, 12). The dramatic fashion in which this tree withered emphasizes the imminence of judgment (**21:19b**). Whatever the difficulties with the story as it stands, cursing of the fig

tree was intended to show God's judgment on the temple and on the nation of Israel, both of which refused to recognize the Messiah when he came to look for spiritual fruit from his people. The church and all of us as individual members are in constant danger of becoming so self-absorbed that we lose our intended function under God: to produce fruit of righteousness for the Master and Lord.

In Nature, many trees wither and die, but the process usually takes some time, perhaps even several years. This fig tree withered instantly. Like many of Jesus' miracles, his command compressed a natural process into a single moment. The disciples were amazed at the power of Jesus' word, but they should not have been, for they had seen Jesus do many miracles before (**21:20**). By now they should have known that he was the Lord of the universe and could act with absolute freedom in it.

Jesus then took the opportunity to teach the lesson that faith deals in what is impossible. *I tell you the truth* (**21:21a**) is a formula similar in force to the prophetic 'This is the word of the Lord.' Both introduce direct words from the Lord. The mountain (**21:21b**) must be understood as symbolic, as in Zechariah 4:6-9 where Zerubbabel is confronted with obstacles that are like insurmountable mountains.

Faith is active trust in Jesus and his power to accomplish what at first seems impossible. Humanly speaking, such feats would be impossible, but in Jesus we are not dealing simply with human limitations. His word of power is able to transform even the natural order. Faith is not located in human power of positive thinking but in trust in God. The intercession or supplication, the asking, is important, for it links our weakness to his possibilities (**21:22**). The exercise of faith must be in keeping with the revealed will of the Lord.

21:23-27 Questioning of Jesus' Authority

Within the leadership of the nation, there were different power groups, all of which are mentioned in the series of confrontations during Passover week that ultimately led to Jesus' death. The groups included the chief priests and scribes (21:15), the chief priests and elders (21:23), the chief priests and Pharisees (21:45), the Pharisees and Herodians (22:15-16) and the Sadducees (22:23).

It seems that Jesus and his disciples were spending the night at their campsite on the Mount of Olives near Bethany, while by day they went to the temple where Jesus would teach all who wanted to hear him in the temple courts. There he was confronted by *the chief priests and the elders* (**21:23a**), who were the political and religious leaders of the nation under Roman rule. They had judicial powers, except that they could not impose capital punishment. They kept the peace in Israel and tried to avoid any disruption of the fragile peace with the Roman authorities.

The immediate source of their question *By what authority are you doing these things?* (**21:23b**) is the action Jesus took in cleansing the temple (21:12-17). They wanted to ascertain whether Jesus was a troublemaker who should be dealt with before he came to the attention of the Romans, with adverse consequences for the whole nation. They may also have challenged him because of jealousy and the loss of monetary profit after the cleansing of the temple.

Jesus answered their question with another, *John's baptism – where did it come from? Was it from heaven, or from men?* (**21:24**). If John's baptism was from heaven, which was what the people believed, and John had borne witness to Jesus as the one coming after him who would baptize with the Holy Spirit, then surely Jesus' authority was from heaven. But if the chief priests and elders were to answer Jesus' question by admitting that John's authority was from heaven, they would be compelled to listen to Jesus. This they were obviously not prepared to do. Recognizing that Jesus had outmanoeuvred them, they refused to answer his question (**21:25-27**). The consequences of admitting the truth were too unpalatable. Hypocrisy and expedience forced them to avoid answering Jesus' counter-question. This passage calls us all to acknowledge truth where we see it, however uncomfortable that might be. Ignorance is one thing, but expedient denial of truth is hypocrisy!

21:28-32 The Parable of the Two Sons

After the interlude with the chief priests and elders, Jesus carried on teaching. He told a parable about the nature of true obedience. The parable has three main characters; a father and two sons. The father represents God (**21:28**). The first son, who appears to be disobedient, represents *the tax collectors and the prostitutes*. The lifestyles of this group suggested that they had rejected God's instruction to live righteous lives (**21:29**). But because they had readily embraced the call of John and Jesus to repentance, they would enter heaven ahead of or instead of the group represented by the second son (**21:31-32**).

The second son represents the chief priests and elders. They appeared to have embraced God's instruction, but their behaviour showed that they had rejected his will and were living in a manner contrary to his way of righteousness (**21:30**). Their practice showed them to be in rebellion in spite of appearances.

A vineyard was a common symbol for the nation of Israel as God's nation (see 21:33-46). John the Baptist and Jesus both came to call the nation to repentance. Jesus' actions were meant to call all the people, including the leaders of the nation, but they ignored the evidence and chose to remain expediently in denial. Their obstinate refusal to repent meant that the judgment of God hung over them.

21:33-46 The Parable of the Tenants

The image of a vineyard returns in the next parable, which presents a situation that would have been common in Galilee, where many rich absentee landowners rented their farms to tenants and required part of the harvest as rent. Such masters were often resented by the tenants. When the master in this parable sent his servants to collect the rent, the tenants refused to pay and beat up the servants (**21:34-35**). Subsequent messengers received the same treatment (**21:36**). After a while, the master decided to send his own son whom he thought the tenants would respect (**21:37**). But the tenants, emboldened by their past actions, killed his son (**21:38-39**). Any owner who receives such treatment will come himself to deal with the wicked tenants. Not only will he punish them, but he will give the vineyard to other tenants who will prove more faithful (**21:40-41**).

This parable, like those before and after it, was directed at the intransigence of the Jewish leaders, represented by the first group of tenants. God had entrusted them with his vineyard, the nation of Israel (see Ps 80:8; Jer 2:21; Ezek 19:10). But when God sent the prophets to see that the nation was living according to his righteous will, the leaders had treated them badly. John the Baptist was merely the latest in the long line of abused servants of God. God's patience is clearly shown by the number of times he was prepared to send his servants to them. Eventually God sent his own son, who received the same ill treatment, and who was killed.

The message of the parable is that the time of opportunity was coming to an end. The Jewish leaders were already showing great disrespect for God's son, and soon they would kill him outside the city, just as the son in the vineyard had been killed outside the vineyard. God's patience would run out, and he would bring judgment on those who had rejected him and treated his servants and his son badly. But the disobedience of these tenants would not thwart the purposes of God; he would offer the vineyard to another group of people who would bear fruit in obedience to his will (**21:43**). The new group who would respect the wishes of the owner were not necessarily the Gentiles but included the disciples of Jesus who would become the leaders of the new Israel, which would be an inclusive entity made up of both Jews and Gentiles.

Jesus drives home his point about the fate of the wicked tenants by reminding his hearers of the words of Psalm 118:22-23 (**21:42**). The capstone in a building is the stone on which the whole building depends. Without it, the rest would crumble. It would be a large stone positioned over a door, or used to anchor and align the corner of a wall, or used as the keystone of an arch. In Psalm 118, this stone symbolizes either the king of Israel or Israel as a nation. Although the king or the nation was despised by worldly powers, God used this despised capstone as the focal point for the new order of things in the world. Luke (Luke 20:18, Acts 4:11) and Peter (1 Pet 2:4.7) echo Jesus in using this image to refer to Jesus as the capstone rejected by the nation of Israel who has become the centre of God's new world order. He is vindicated by God through his resurrection. Those who reject him are like pottery that shatters when it is smashed against a rock or when it is crushed by a rock (**21:44**).

The meaning of the parable of the vineyard was not lost on the chief priests and their collaborators. They sought to find a way to get rid of Jesus that would not antagonize the people and risk rousing the wrath of the Roman authorities (**21:45-46**).

22:1-14 The Parable of the Wedding Banquet

This is the third parable in which Jesus points out the logical conclusion of the defiance of the chief priests and the leaders of the nation of Israel. The parable has three groups of characters: the king and his son, the first group of invited guests who spurn the invitation with lame excuses and abuse the servants, and the second group of guests who unexpectedly receive the invitation.

At that time in the Middle East, it was apparently customary to send out two invitations. The initial invitation to dinner would enable the host to determine how many guests to expect, and thus how much food to prepare. If only a few people could come, he would prepare a chicken or two. However, if more than forty guests were coming, he would slaughter a calf. When the meat was nearly ready, the host would send his servants to go and call the guests (**22:1-3**). It was expected that the guests who had said they would come at the first invitation would turn up for the banquet. Turning down an invitation at this point, when one had already made a commitment to attend, would be a great insult to the host.

Similarly in Zambia there is no need to send out written invitations to weddings. Anyone who is a relative or friend is invited by virtue of the relationship. Yet even in this context, older and more distinguished members of the community, whether or not they are relatives, will be sent special invitations. To decline such an invitation with a flimsy excuse is a grave insult.

The host in the parable was amazed when his guests did not arrive, but assumed that there must have been some misunderstanding. So he sent the servants back one more time to ensure that the message had been delivered (**22:4**). This third invitation is met not just with refusal but with contemptuous treatment of the servants. Not only did these guests spurn an invitation to which they were committed, but they added insult to injury by ill-treating the servants and killing them (**22:5-6**).

The message is unmistakable. The guests had done a terrible thing. They had offended the king and provoked him to anger. We know that in Matthew this parable is aimed at the Jewish religious and political hierarchy who, although officially the guardians of the people of God, did not rec-ognize him when he came to them. Their end was terrible, and **22:7** may well be a prophetic allusion to the events of AD 70, when Jerusalem and the temple were burned by the Romans.

Since the banquet was still waiting to be eaten, the king sent his servants out to invite alternate guests (**22:8-10**). Both of the previous two parables had ended with a new and alternate people of God – not necessarily exclusively Gentile but most likely, as is true of the church today, open to both Jews and Gentiles (21:31, 41).

Apparently wedding guests then, as today, usually do their best to dress appropriately. In fact, sometimes the lengths to which many will go to find the right garments are ridiculous. At Zambian weddings, far more money and energy is often spent on clothes for the bride and groom and their attendants than on preparing for a sound marriage. This parable does not endorse such excess.

But it appears that one of the guests at the wedding described in the parable made no attempt to be even clean and well dressed. His clothes were completely inappropriate for a wedding (**22:11-12**). Consequently, he was thrown out of the party. The implication is clear. Although the invitation was free, the individual guests were not free to flout the rules of hospitality. The salvation of God in Christ is offered freely, but once in the kingdom of God, people need to behave appropriately. The same lesson was taught in the previous parable, for the new tenants had to produce fruit to the satisfaction of the landowner. Those who presume on God's grace without truly honouring his Son will be banished *into the darkness, where there will be weeping and gnashing of teeth* (**22:13**; 13:42; 24:51; 25:30).

22:15-46 Incriminating Questions

The rest of the chapter deals with exchanges between Jesus and his opponents in which they try to trap him into either incriminating himself or exposing himself as unpatriotic or irreligious. They hoped that whatever answer he gave, he could not avoid falling into the pitfalls they had dug for him. If he escaped from the frying pan, he would definitely fall into the fire. But Jesus' opponents needed to learn the meaning of the Bemba proverb, *Muteya iciliba cenjela: nga cakufwanta wilila* ['Be careful when you are setting a trap; if it falls on you do not cry' – see also Prov 26:27].

Jesus shows a great ability to take these questions and answer them in such a way that it is his opponents who are left 'amazed' (22:22), 'astonished' (22:33) and with not 'a word in reply ... no one dared to ask him any more questions' (22:46). This it seems is a very clear example of the fulfilment of the promise Jesus made to his disciples that 'when they arrest you, do not worry about what to say or how to say it. At that time you will be given what to say, for it will not be you speaking but the Spirit of your Father speaking through you' (10:19).

22:15-22 Paying taxes

The first of the four questions deals with one's obligations to the state. The Pharisees, their disciples and the Herodians gathered to entrap him. This was a powerful coalition of religious and political heavyweights. The Pharisees were acknowledged religious leaders, and the Herodians were members of the pro-Roman aristocracy who sought the full restoration of the powers of kingship that had once belonged to Herod the Great (**22:15-16a**).

Their question was designed to force him to take sides on a politically controversial matter. The political significance of the question is comparable to the question regarding whether Africans in apartheid South Africa, or indeed in pre-independence Zambia or Zimbabwe, should consent to carry a passbook, which, among other things, was a record of their payment of a hated poll tax. This passbook was seen as an instrument and symbol of black oppression. Political defiance often involved burning passbooks and refusing to pay any poll tax. But those who destroyed their passbooks or encouraged others to do the same incurred the wrath of the governing authorities. Thousands of people were imprisoned for flouting the pass laws, and the Sharpeville Massacre of 1961 near Johannesburg was the direct result of a campaign against the pass laws.

After Jesus' inquisitors had made what were intended to be flattering statements, but were actually the truth (**22:16b**), they asked him to pass judgment on whether it was *right to pay taxes to Caesar* (**22:17**). For religious reasons, every Jew was in principle compelled to reject the idea of paying taxes to Caesar. But doing so could carry dire political consequences. Whatever answer Jesus gave would land him in trouble. Humanly speaking, he was between a rock and a hard place. If Jesus favoured the payment of colonial taxes, he would alienate his followers who hated the imposition of taxes by a foreign occupying army. If he rejected the colonial taxes, he could be charged with sedition and inciting others to dishonour Caesar.

Jesus called his opponents *hypocrites* and for good reason (**22:18**). The Jews were very sensitive about images of emperors. They would not even allow flags or standards bearing imperial images to be carried in Jerusalem. The silverycoin used for paying the poll tax bore an image of the emperor, his name and his title as high priest. However, the Jews did not have to carry this coin, as other coins were readily available for regular commerce. The fact that one of Jesus' interrogators could easily produce a silver coin bearing an image of Caesar meant that while they pretended to hate the Roman coin and what it stood for, they were secretly using it as currency (**22:19-20**). They were hypocrites. If they used Caesar's coins, they had to pay taxes to him. But further, if they were truly made in the image of God, they had to give themselves to God in their entirety (**22:21**).

22:23-33 Marriage after the resurrection

The second question deals with whether marriage is valid in heaven after the resurrection. Like the first question, this one was intended to be a trap for Jesus. The Sadducees did not believe in the doctrine of resurrection (**22:23**; see Luke 20:27; Acts 23:6-8). However, in order to trap Jesus they borrowed a story from Jewish folklore (in the apocryphal book of Tobit 3:8). The background to this story is that in Israel a brother-in-law was duty bound to marry the widow of a deceased brother. Similarly, in some African cultures, there is the practice of widow inheritance (see the article in this commentary). This practice is intended to provide for the widow and also to raise children for the deceased, so as to ensure that the dead man's name is not forgotten (**22:24**;. Gen 38:8-26; Deut 25:5-6).

The hypothetical scenario presented by the Sadducees involved a woman who had been married to seven brothers one after the other, because each of them died. Which one of them, they asked, will be her husband after the resurrection (**22:25-28**)?

Jesus exposed the Sadducees' ignorance of the Bible in general and of the doctrine of the resurrection in particular. He charged them with *error* because they did not know *the Scriptures or the power of God* (**22:29**). These are not two forms of error but one, with the second part being the logical result of the first part. Those who have a superficial knowledge of the Bible will not know the power of God.

There is disagreement among scholars about whether the Sadducees accepted the whole of the OT or regarded only the Pentateuch as authentic. Certainly, in the argument recorded here, Jesus cites only the Pentateuch as he refutes their position. Although the Pentateuch is not as full a revelation as the whole OT, it is still the word of God. A good grasp of its revelation of God and his activities in history should be adequate for acknowledging his power.

Part of the Sadducees' problem may have been that they felt they had the authority to pick and choose what suited them as Scripture. They were the ancient equivalents of modern secularists. The African church may find their views on the resurrection less attractive than its Western counterpart, since African culture does not see a sharp divide between the natural and spiritual realms, and already has a firm belief in the living dead.

What then is the nature of the resurrection? Jesus answers the question using an analogy with angels. Angels do not marry, nor are they given in marriage (**22:30**). They are created immortal and therefore have nothing to do with procreation. Similarly, after the resurrection, humans in heaven will not need to marry and no new children will need to be born.

Regarding the fact of resurrection, Jesus turns to the Pentateuch, where God declares himself to be *the God of Abraham, the God of Isaac and the God of Jacob* (**22:31-32**;

Exod 3:6). These three ancestors were long dead by the time God spoke these words to Moses, yet God spoke as if he was still in a vital and living relationship with them and continued his caring concern for them. His love for them endures forever, as will his love for us! The relationships that God establishes with human beings here on earth do not end with death.

What the Bible teaches and Jesus demonstrates is that those who die in faith in God will continue to have their relationship with God eternally. Those who have rejected faith in God will not have such an opportunity. God would not define himself in terms of a relationship with someone who had ceased to exist. There is life after death.

The important question is, what relationships are important in the afterlife? These decisions are made on this side of death. The doctrine of the resurrection should spur us on to evangelism so that many more people may enjoy the pleasures of a continuing relationship with God, a relationship that is not limited by death.

The logic of Jesus' argument silenced the Sadducees and amazed the crowd (**22:33**).

22:34-40 *The greatest commandment in the law*

The Pharisees must have enjoyed seeing their arch-rivals, the Sadducees, silenced by Jesus with regard to one of the cornerstones of their faith. They came together to see how they could triumph where their rivals had failed (**22:34**; 16:1; 19:3; 22:15-18). The test they came up with was in the form of a question that in itself is completely legitimate: *Which is the greatest commandment in the Law?* (**22:35**). This question seeks to get to the heart of the OT. How would one summarize the OT? What is the essence of OT law? While this may not look like a trap, it was an attempt to involve Jesus in their ongoing theological arguments. They were hoping that his answer would provide grounds for some other attack.

In answering them, Jesus quoted Deuteronomy 6:5 and Leviticus 19:18. Both verses focus on the word 'love' as it relates on the one hand to God and on the other to fellow human beings. The first quotation is from the Shema, Israel's creed, *Love the Lord your God with all your heart, and with all your soul and with all your mind* (**22:37**; see also Deut 6:5). The second is *Love your neighbour as yourself* (**22:39**). Israel's leaders had always held that love was the key to obedience and to ethics. The two commandments do not diminish all the other commandments or reduce them in number, but form the foundation stones on which the rest build.

22:41-46 *Whose son is he?*

Having silenced his enemies, Jesus had a question for the Pharisees, *What do you think about the Christ? Whose son is he?* (**22:42**) Their reply was ready; the Christ is the son of David. This was common knowledge. Matthew has constantly been asserting it, and the people had hailed Jesus as the Son of David (9:27; 12:23; 21:9, 15). But could Jesus be the Christ? If so, how does he relate to David, his ancestor? The point of Jesus' question was not to reaffirm that the Christ is the son of David, but to show that the Christ is greater than David (**22:43**). If David, speaking prophetically, calls the Messiah *my Lord* (**22:44**; see also Ps 110:1), then the Messiah must be greater than David. Jesus is indeed greater than Solomon (12:42), Jonah (12:41), the temple (12:6) and David.

23:1-26:1 Teaching V: Woes and Signs

Chapters 23 to 25 contain the fifth and final block of teaching, which characteristically ends with the words 'When Jesus had finished saying all these things' (26:1; see 7:28; 11:1; 13:53; 19:1).

23:1-39 Jesus' Rejection of Official Judaism

Jesus rejected the official Judaism of his day. The reason for his negative attitude was that Judaism had become little more than a legalistic system that, in spite of its rigour, could not lead anyone to a saving relationship with God. In this chapter Jesus exposes the spiritual bankruptcy of religion (23:1-12), then denounces it with seven fearful woes (23:13-36) and finally issues a damning prophecy against the whole nation (23:37-39).

23:1-12 *Spiritual bankruptcy*

Jesus regarded Judaism as spiritually devoid of any credibility. He held the teachers of the law, the scribes and Pharisees, directly responsible for this sad state of affairs. Jesus' words were directed *to the crowds and to his disciples* (**23:1**) who were in danger of following blindly a religion that in the end would not deliver on its ultimate promise, a saving relationship with God. Jesus' words are intended to win over those among the crowds who were still doubtful about the rightness of Jesus' alternative way.

The teachers of the law (**23:2a**) were highly esteemed, for with the passing of the prophets and the waning of Jewish political power, the law had become particularly prominent in Judaism. These teachers dealt with matters that made the Jews distinctly different from all the other nations of the world.

The Pharisees, a group that arose in the second century BC, were so dedicated to keeping the law that they kept themselves apart from people who did not follow it. But the law they followed was not just the law of Moses; it was also the oral law, which contained thousands upon thousands of rules and regulations attempting to apply the law of Moses to covering every situation in life.

These two groups sat *in Moses' seat* (**23:2b**). As the successors to Moses the lawgiver, they were supposed to expound the law so that their hearers would walk in the ways of the Lord (Deut 10:12-13). Like Moses they were supposed to lead the people into the way of light. They would have taught the people the Ten Commandments, the Pentateuch and the Prophets, but they would also have taught the comprehensive legalism of the oral law. By doing this, they had turned religion into an unbearable burden that offered neither relief nor salvation (**23:4**). Getting caught in their web of legalism was the easiest way to go to hell (23:15). These leaders had ceased to be true shepherds and were now more like wolves in sheep's clothing.

The test of effective Christian leadership and teaching is that people learn to live in a vital relationship with God. Jesus' words to the teachers of the law and the Pharisees are pertinent to all Christian leaders.

Because the religion that was being taught focused on outward observances, Jesus could say that *everything they do is done for men to see* (**23:5**). Moses' instructions to the Jews in Exodus 13:9 had later been interpreted as commanding Jews to tie phylacteries (leather boxes containing scriptural verse onto their arms and forehead). He had also commanded them to wear tassels on their clothing as a reminder that they were God's people. These symbols had, however, become more like fetishes and the charms so many African people carry. The Pharisees made their phylacteries larger than other people did and they wore them more often. The tassels, which were meant to be a simple aid to memory, were made bigger and more clearly visible. They no longer served their original purpose as simple reminders of God's law, but had become a way of drawing attention to the piety of the person who wore them.

The teachers of the law and the Pharisees had also fallen in love with the idea of being honoured. At a banquet they would seek out the seats on either side of the host, and in the synagogue they would take the seats facing the congregation in order to parade their piety (**23:6**).

Many Christian leaders in Zambia today are consumed with symbols of their status: titles such as apostle, bishop, reverend and pastor are much sought after. In Jesus' day, the term of honour was *rabbi* (**23:7**). It signified a person whose wisdom and knowledge of the word of God set him apart as one who could impart good teaching. The Pharisees insisted that they should be addressed thus. Phylacteries and tassels, seats of honour and titles were all used to enhance the social standing of the teachers of the law and the Pharisees.

The follower of Jesus, by contrast, must put God first, and use all his or her intellectual and spiritual resources in the service of others. The principle is God first, others second and self last. Jesus is the one true teacher, the rightful successor to Moses. All his followers are brothers and sis-

ters, of equal standing before him (**23:8-10**). The antidote to the egotism of the teachers of the law and the Pharisees is to be found in the two sayings concerning servanthood and humility (**23:11-12**; see 18:4; 20:26-27).

23:13-34 Seven woes

The seven woes are the converse of the Beatitudes (5:3-12). Whereas the Beatitudes describe the true way to please God, the woes describe the wrong way, and pronounce judgment on those who follow it. One of the central ideas in what follows is the ethical inconsistency in the lives of the teachers of the law and the Pharisees, who are repeatedly described as *hypocrites*, a word that originally meant an actor and came to mean someone who was false (23:13, 15, 23, 25, 27, 29). The other central idea is the failure of legalistic religion to lead to God.

23:13-14 WOE FOR DENYING ENTRY TO THE KINGDOM The Pharisaic system, a human system based on hundreds of laws, effectively shut the door of the kingdom of heaven in people's faces and prevented them from entering the kingdom of God (**23:13**; 5:20; 7:21; 18:3; 19:23-24). It prevented them from doing what God required. This is the basic inadequacy of any human religious system; it cannot establish a saving relationship with God. Only a religion revealed by God is able to do that. Legalism directs people's attention from what is real to what is non-essential. (Note that **23:14** does not appear in the best early manuscripts, and thus the NIV only gives it as a footnote. However, the same words do appear in Mark 12:40.)

23:15 WOE TO THOSE FACILITATING ENTRY INTO HELL The religion of the teachers of the law and the Pharisees did not lead to entry into the kingdom of God but to hell. Unfortunately, this meant that their zealous converts were also going there. Missionaries must always go out in the name of God to lead men and women to God, not to establish Presbyterianism, Anglicanism or any other denomination.

23:16-22 WOE FOR SWEARING FALSE OATHS Oaths were regarded as binding in the OT (Deut 6:13). They originally served as a person's declaration of allegiance to the Lord rather than to idols. God is seen as taking oaths (Gen 22:16), as are many OT characters like Abraham's servant (Gen 24:3-4), Joseph (Gen 47:31) and Joshua's spies (Josh 2:14). But oaths were being abused by those who argued that oaths were not binding if they did not include certain specific phrases. The Pharisees' teaching enabled people to make oaths without any real intention of keeping their word. They could be let off the hook on the technicality that, although they had sworn by the temple or by the altar or by Jerusalem, they had not actually invoked the name of God (**23:16, 18**). This was pure deceitfulness, hidden under a cloak of honesty (**23:17, 19**).

23:23-24 WOE FOR CONFUSING PRIORITIES The teachers of the law and the Pharisees were majoring on the minors. They were meticulous about observing every detail of the oral law, and would go to great lengths to avoid accidentally swallowing a tiny insect in a cup of water, which would make them ritually unclean. But, says Jesus, using hyperbole, they were so busy watching out for the insect that they did not notice that they were swallowing a camel, a very large unclean animal (**23:24**). Similarly, they would obey the OT laws (Lev 27:30; Deut 14:22) and tithe all their crops, right down to cooking herbs like *mint, dill and cummin,* which were grown in very small quantities for household use (**23:23**). But, as Jesus pointed out, the heart of OT religion did not lie in such minor things but in the great issues of *justice, mercy and faithfulness* (see Mic 6:8).

23:25-26 WOE FOR SUPERFICIAL MORALITY The Pharisees were very concerned that all the vessels they used were ceremonially clean. But it did not seem to matter as much what was inside the vessels. Their negligence in matters of greed and indulgence condemned them. Morality is inward before it is outward.

23:27-28 WOE FOR MAINTAINING A FALSE EXTERIOR Jesus compared the Pharisees to *whitewashed tombs, which look beautiful on the outside* but are *full of dead men's bones* (**23:27**). The religion of the Pharisees created very attractive exteriors without touching the interiors. Morality was reduced to the external observance of certain rituals, without regard for the principles behind the rituals. Sinful attitudes and evil thoughts were disguised behind an impeccable religious exterior.

Some aspects of African Christianity appear very similar to what Jesus was criticizing in the Pharisees. Evils such as tribalism, nepotism and corruption lie hidden under a masquerade of vibrant Christianity. Jesus' condemnation is as applicable to our day as it was to his.

23:29-34 WOE FOR KILLING THE PROPHETS From tombs, Jesus turns to the fate of the prophets. The Pharisees claimed to honour the prophets of God who had been killed in Israel (**23:29-30**). The first person to have been killed for his righteousness was *Abel,* who was killed by his brother Cain (23:35a; see Gen 4:8). Many others followed, including *Zechariah* who was killed by King Joash (23:35b; see also 2 Chr 24:20-22). Both Abel and Zechariah were killed because their murderers could not bear to see their own sinfulness exposed. Jesus was to be the next in the long line of righteous servants of God to die in Jerusalem (**23:34**). And down through history, many disciples of the Lord have paid for their faith with their blood.

23:35-39 Prophecy against the nation

The fearful word of judgment in **23:35-36** seems to point to the destruction of Jerusalem in AD 70. Yet Jesus' pastoral heart is clearly seen in his offer of God's love to the rebel city (**23:37**). He patiently waits for the people's response, and does not force them to come to him. However, that

patience will one day run its course, and the time of reckoning will come, with terrible consequences for those who have spurned the offer of love.

24:1-35 The End of the Age: Its Signs

This chapter and its parallels in Mark 13 and Luke 21:5-36 present a panoramic view of the period between the destruction of the temple at the start of the Christian era and Jesus' return. Matthew, like Mark, tells the story in the prophetic style in which two or more events are viewed simultaneously through the same lens. The sphere in which the disciples will live out their discipleship is sandwiched between these events. This sphere is essentially hostile, and the disciples must be prepared for persecution.

Many of the themes in this chapter are drawn from the OT book of Daniel. For example, the destruction of the temple (24:1-3) is mentioned in Daniel 9:26; rumours of wars (24:6) in Daniel 11:44; 'the abomination that causes desolation' (24:15) in Daniel 9:27, 11:31 and 12:11; and the 'Son of Man' (24:30) in Daniel 7:13.

24:1-14 Destruction of the temple

The opening words of this chapter are ominous: *Jesus left the temple and was walking away* (**24:1a**). Jesus would never physically enter the temple again, and within three decades the whole edifice would be razed to the ground. But symbolically and more significantly, Jesus was turning his back on Judaism. He abandoned the whole sacrificial system for which the structure stood. The theme of judgment is central. This marks the start of a new phase of mission in which the disciples of Jesus, and later the Christian church, become the central focus of God's work in the world and the key element in advancing God's mission.

The discourse begins with the disciples' awareness of the beauty and the magnificence of the temple buildings (**24:1b**). The Jewish historian Josephus describes the temple as 'covered all over with plates of gold ... [it] appeared to strangers, when they were at a distance, like a mountain covered with snow; for, as to those parts of it that were not gilt, they were exceeding white'. The foundations of this great building had been laid by Herod the Great in 20 BC, and it would not be completed until AD 64, just six years before the Romans destroyed it. Its great size and beauty may have been because Judaism, unlike other ancient religious systems, had a centralized system of worship, with the temple at its heart. However, the size may also be explained by Herod's pride and political ambitions, for many of his other creations, including the city of Caesarea, were on a similar grand scale.

The Romans destroyed the temple for political reasons, in an attempt to repress a Jewish insurrection that began in AD 66. But there was also a religious reason for its destruction: God's rejection of the worship centred on the Jerusalem temple. Long before, Micah (Mic 3:12) and Jeremiah (Jer 7:12-14) had prophesied the destruction of Solomon's temple, and that had come to pass in 587 BC. Similarly Jesus, the Son of God, who had been rejected by the establishment of his generation just as Jeremiah had been by his contemporaries, prophesied against Herod's temple. The completeness of its destruction is symbolized by the hyperbolic statement that *not one stone ...will be left on another* (**24:2**). This prophecy was fulfilled in AD 70. The worship at Jerusalem had become a stumbling block for the Jews, for it gave them a false security that may have made for insensitivity to sin. If the temple had survived, it might also have tempted the followers of Jesus to rest their faith in what it had stood for and not in Christ. Christ was greater than the temple, and once he had come, it was no longer needed.

The point deserves to be emphasized. Christ fulfilled the religious yearnings of all the peoples of the world. He put an end to all religions created by human beings. No one needs to continue worshipping according to ancient ways. We no longer need to venerate our ancestors as intermediaries between us and God. We may respect, honour and learn from our ancestors, but we should no longer worship them or invest them with divine powers.

In Christ, our cultural roots must not give rise to unique objects of worship but to unique ways of honouring God through Christ. The focus of our devotion must always remain Christ, not our heritage, however godly. Christians must concentrate on building the kingdom of God, not erecting edifices that take the place of the true object of our worship: God himself. Tribal churches, confessional churches, all churches need to ensure that the object of our existence is God and not our history or sense of purpose or mission.

When the disciples asked when this destruction would come (**24:3**), Jesus warned them to be on their guard against religious deception (**24:4-5, 11**) and against false interpretations of natural or human catastrophes as signalling the end of the age (**24:6-8**). The disciples should expect *to be persecuted*, and should also expect the apostasy that so often follows persecution (**24:9-12**; 5:11-12; see 1 Tim 4:1-4; 2 Pet 3:3). But despite this persecution, the gospel will be preached to the ends of the earth (**24:14**). Many of these events, including the gospel reaching Rome – the centre of the then-known world, can be shown to have taken place before the destruction of the temple in AD 70.

Like the disciples, we should not be worried or concerned about rumours of the second coming of the Lord. Instead, all followers of Jesus are called to be actively involved in spreading the gospel to all the people of the world. The African church must take its place as a mission church, sending missionaries to other parts of the world, and must not be content to remain a receiving church.

24:15-31 'Abomination that causes desolation'

This difficult passage on the subject of God's judgment on the city is full of OT imagery. It is, therefore, important that we interpret it both in terms of its OT background, such as Daniel, and in terms of the historical events of the siege of Jerusalem in AD 70. Failure to do so can lead to wild and fanciful interpretations.

The *abomination that causes desolation* originally referred to a pagan statue that Antiochus Epiphanes, a Greek ruler in Syria in the middle of the second century BC, had erected in the temple (see Dan 9:27; 11:31; 12:11). Jesus stated that something similar would desecrate the temple before too long, probably during the war that led to the destruction of Jerusalem and the temple (**24:15**; Mark 13:14). There may also be a reference to the events preceding his second coming (see comment on 24:29).

As Jesus predicted, the siege of Jerusalem was characterized by great ferocity. Those who were wise would have heeded his advice and fled the city before it was sealed off (**24:17-22**). People were to flee to the countryside because survival is more important than comfort – as many refugees know only too well.

The Jews may have hoped that God would protect his city and temple, but when God removes his favour, all protection is gone. Religious symbols cannot protect people against what God has decreed. But thankfully, even during such a trial where godlessness has a hold on life, God takes care of his own and puts in place measures that will lead to their salvation (24:22).

The very difficult time of the siege of Jerusalem will be followed at some later date by the return of Christ (24:36-41). The intervening period will be a time of turmoil and tribulation, in which many religious charlatans will operate. So Jesus warns his followers to be vigilant and not to be led astray by *false Christs and false prophets* (**24:23-26**). When Christ does return, his coming will be so obvious that we will not need to be worried about the possibility of not recognizing it. The signs will be cosmic; no one will need to tune into the BBC World Service or CNN or SKY News to hear about the event. It will be as visible as spectacular lightning cutting its path through a dark rain-soaked sky (**24:27**). It will be as undeniable as it is undeniable that the presence of vultures is a sign of the presence of a carcass (**24:28**).

As presented above, the apocalyptic words in 24:27-29 refer to what will happen at the Lord's return. However, **24:29** echoes Isaiah 13:10 and 34:4, which prophesy the fall of great political powers such as Babylon and Edom. Thus some commentators suggest that what is being spoken of here is the destruction of Jerusalem by the Romans. It is possible that both events may be in view, for in typical prophetic perspective, both 24:15 and 24:29 may be seen from the same vantage point, and may describe events which do not occur at the same time.

The nations will be terrified by Jesus' coming (**24:30**). He will send for *his elect ... from one end of the heavens to the other* and from all over the world (**24:31**). At that time the church will be complete under the visible leadership of the Son of Man.

24:32-35 Sign of the fig tree

Israel has mild winters and thus most trees there do not lose their leaves, as trees do in regions where the winters are very cold. Fig trees, however, do lose their leaves and therefore really stand out in winter. The budding of the fig leaves in late spring is a sure sign that summer is coming (**24:32**). If we take the whole of the chapter as speaking historically, then Jesus is saying that the events of 24:15 will be signs indicating the imminent end of Jerusalem's temple. In this case, there is no problem explaining the reference to 'this generation' in **24:34**. However, if we interpret the chapter as speaking of the second coming of the Lord, then the destruction of Jerusalem is the first sign of the imminent return of the Lord. But in that case the phrase 'this generation' is very difficult to explain.

Jesus asserts that his words are more real than heaven (that is, the skies) and the earth. Nothing will shift them. They will certainly be fulfilled (**24:35**).

24:36-51 No One Knows When Jesus Will Return

The date of the return of the Christ is a closely guarded secret; no one knows it and no one can know it (**24:36**). When the time is right, it will be revealed for all to see. All prophecies that seek to identify the date when Christ will come are exercises in futility. Life will continue in its ordinariness (**24:37-41**), and all the servants of the Lord must be at their stations doing their duty (**24:42-44**). If they are doing this, they will not need to fret or suddenly become more conscientious when their Lord and Master comes. We must live each day as if it was the last day, so that we do not live in injustice and unrighteousness (**24:45-51**).

Herod and the religious people of first-century Palestine knew that the Messiah was coming, but were caught unawares by the coming of Jesus as a baby. We have ample warning not to be like them, but to be engaged in fruitful ministry to the honour of the Lord so that he may be glad when he returns to take his own to be with him for ever.

25:1-13 The Parable of the Ten Bridesmaids

The parable of the bridesmaids continues the theme of the need for Jesus' disciples to be ready for his coming (see 24:42, 43, 46, 50-51). It uses imagery from wedding customs of the day. While some details of this parable stand for higher truths or realities (for example, the bridegroom represents Christ, and the wise and the foolish bridesmaids,

those who are spiritually ready and those who are not), not all the details have symbolic value.

In most cultures, weddings are very significant occasions, but they are also fraught with difficulties. Having been best man at nine weddings before I got married and having conducted many weddings, I can testify that there is always something that goes wrong. On one occasion when I should have been with the wedding party rehearsing for my role as the chief best man on the big day, I was instead at the tailor, frantically trying to get my suit finished on time.

At a Jewish wedding in Jesus' time, the wedding feast took place in the evening, after a day of dancing and other entertainment. At the end of the day, the bridegroom would be taken by his friends to the bride's parent's house, where his arrival would be announced and he and his party would be met by the bridesmaids (**25:1-7**). It was important for all the parties to be ready to play their part at the appointed time, even if that time was unknown. The foolish bridesmaids were not ready, and they missed the opportunity (**25:8-12**).

The parable warns that the return of the Christ is imminent, although the time is unspecified. All the followers of Jesus must be ready for him whenever he returns. For those who ignore the warning, the time will come when it will be too late (**25:13**). Hell is hearing the words 'too late' after the opportunity has passed. In these matters, no one can ultimately depend on the merits of another. Each one of us must be ready individually if we are to enter into the marriage feast of the Lamb and his bride (see Rev 19:7).

25:14-30 The Parable of the Talents

This parable, like the previous one, focuses on the second coming of Christ and the Lord's calling on every one of his disciples to show how well each one has used his or her gifts. It assumes that the time between Christ's ascension and his second coming is a time of opportunity, in which his followers are expected to put to profitable use the 'talents' that the master has given to them. This parable has many similarities with Luke's parable of the ten minas (Luke 19:12-27). However, there are some very clear differences, and it is in these differences that each parable has its particular lessons to teach. Jesus might well have told variants of the same story on different occasions.

In this parable, a 'talent' refers not to a natural ability, such as an aptitude for music or leadership, but to a large sum of money, for a talent was equal to 6000 denarii, and a denarius was a day's wage for a labourer. The master gave different amounts to his servants according to their abilities (**25:14-15**).

After a long absence, the master, intended to be understood as Jesus, returned to settle accounts (**25:19**). He asked each of his servants to account for what they had done with what he had given them. The first two servants had understood that their master intended them to use the money to trade profitably, and had therefore put the talents to good use (**25:16-17**). These profitable servants were rewarded with both commendation and greater responsibilities (**25:20-23**). They were profitable because they were courageous enough to take risks with the investments that the Lord had made.

The third servant had misunderstood the nature of his responsibilities. He would not take any risks; indeed he was scared to do so (**25:18**). He assumed that his role was to do nothing, and thus wasted the opportunity his master had given him. So the Lord took away the one talent and added it to those of the man who had used his investment wisely (**25:24-30**).

God has richly endowed his people with his gifts. These are not to be ignored or treated as ornaments for display. Instead, we as individuals or congregations must see these gifts as investments to be used to gain glory for the master. We must put faith into action by taking risks that will lead to fruitfulness.

God will call us all to account at some time. In cases where God's gifts have been used profitably, more will be added in abundance. Where there has been fruitlessness instead of profitability, the original investment will be completely lost or taken away.

25:31-26:1 The Parable of the Sheep and the Goats

The parable of the sheep and the goats is the climax of Jesus' teaching on the final judgment. The Son of Man, sitting on his throne and surrounded by his holy angels, will carry out the judgment (**25:31**). All people of all nations will be separated into two groups *as a shepherd separates the sheep from the goats* (**25:32-33**). On the one hand will be *the righteous* (**25:37**) and on the other hand will be the *cursed* (**25:41a**). The righteous will receive the inheritance that the Father has prepared for them from the creation of the world (**25:34**). The cursed will be cast into hell pictured as the place of *eternal fire prepared for the devil and his angels* (**25:41b**). When the separation takes place it will be final.

The criterion for judgment is kindness to *these brothers of mine* (**25:35-40**), but there has been much debate as to who exactly these 'brothers' are. Some interpret them as all those who are needy and deprived, for the poor and needy certainly occupy a special place in the heart of God (see Exod 22:22-27; Luke 16:19-25). Others regard the 'brothers' as the special messengers of Christ (12:50; 28:10), and claim that the judgment is based on how the people of the world treat these brothers. Christ has sent them out without food or provisions (10:9-10), and they are exposed to harsh conditions and persecution, including imprisonment. Rejecting one of these brothers is the same as rejecting Christ himself (**25:45**).

Ultimately, we do not need to choose between these approaches, because we are called to respond to all human need, for that is what love does. But this parable must not lead us to assume that demonstration of love for the needy will be enough to bring salvation. Other passages make it clear that belief and trust in Jesus are also significant in the final judgment (10:32-33). People's response to the gospel will be the final determinant of whether they spend eternity among the blessed in the inheritance that God has prepared from the creation of the world (25:34) or in eternal fire (25:41).

The words *when Jesus had finished saying all these things* clearly indicate the end of the fifth and final major discourse (**26:1**; 7:28; 11:1; 13:53; 19:1). But here the words also mark the end of Jesus' public ministry. Matthew may have intended us to remember the similar words shortly before Moses' death (Deut 32:45). When Moses had finished his teaching, he proceeded to his death, and the same would be true for Jesus. Matthew's original readers would also have known that the next verses in Deuteronomy were a reminder that the words of Moses were 'not just idle words for you – they are your life. By them you will live long in the land you are crossing the Jordan to possess' (Deut 32:47). These words are a fitting introduction to the Passion Narratives. Jesus is the one greater than Moses, and his words are much more words of life than the words of Moses.

26:2-46 The End of Jesus' Public Ministry

Two major themes dominate the Passion Narratives. The first is that although Jesus will go to his death, he is not an unwilling victim, but is totally in control of the events that lead to the cross. The second is that the chief priests, the crowds, Pilate and Judas all play their part in the death of Jesus, and are all accountable for their actions. These chapters demonstrate the working out of the divine plan in history. God's work cannot be thwarted by human wickedness, and it is accomplished in spite of human intentions.

26:2-5 The Plot to Kill Jesus

The combined mention of the Passover and Jesus' death in **26:2** is significant. The Passover feast celebrated the original exodus when God intervened on behalf of his people, delivering them from slavery in Egypt, and leading them into the land he had promised to give them. The killing of the Passover lambs in Egypt signalled the start of the exodus, but was also a sign of judgment on all who were not covered by the blood of the lambs. Similarly Jesus' death would open the way for a new exodus, which would bring people from Israel and from all the nations of the world out of their slavery to sin and into the kingdom of heaven. But his death would also bring judgment on those who refused to accept that his blood was shed for them, and would thus also serve to separate the sheep from the goats (25:31-46).

The *chief priests and the elders of the people* gathered to plot how to get rid of Jesus (**26:3-4**). He could easily be arrested because he was in Jerusalem and not far away in Galilee. But at the same time, it would be difficult to arrest him during the feast. It would have to be done in a way that did not alienate them from the crowds who had been listening to his teaching with obvious enjoyment (**26:5**). Judas would provide the welcome answer to that dilemma.

The 'chief priests and the elders of the people' were the official representatives of the nation of Israel. Their involvement in Jesus' death suggests that for Matthew the nation of Israel had turned against the Messiah.

26:6-13 Jesus Anointed with Perfume

Jesus and his disciples were receiving hospitality in the home of a man named *Simon the Leper* in the village of *Bethany* (**26:6**). At meals like these, the host had the responsibility to anoint the heads of the more notable guests with oil, although presumably Simon had not carried out this act of hospitality (see Luke 7:46).

In the middle of the meal, a woman entered and poured some *very expensive perfume* on Jesus' head (**26:7**). The anointing is significant because the word Messiah or Christ refers to someone who is anointed for his mission. Jesus, however, welcomed this action as a premature, but not inappropriate, preparation for his burial (**26:12**).

Matthew may well be comparing the male disciples with their female counterparts. Peter had opposed Jesus' suggestion that the Son of Man must be killed (16:22), but a woman understood the significance of what lay ahead for Jesus and took appropriate action to show her devotion. Jesus commended her for her actions (**26:10, 13**).

All four Gospel writers use this story with variations. Mark 14:3-9 has very similar details to Matthew. Luke 7:36-50 omits Bethany and describes Simon as a Pharisee; the woman is said to be sinful and she anoints Jesus' feet because of her gratitude to him for the forgiveness of her sin. John 12:1-8 locates the story in Bethany in the home of Lazarus where Mary anointed the feet of Jesus for burial. It is difficult to show with any accuracy whether these accounts refer to two different incidents or to one incident that is reported in different ways. But the differences in the details do not take away from the symbolic value of the action. The woman is a model of total devotion to Jesus. Her story is told in her honour wherever the story of the death of Jesus is told (26:13). This privilege is not available to most of the other disciples, whose names do not appear except in the official lists. This woman, like Lydia (Acts 16:14-15), put all her resources at the disposal of the Lord.

Matthew records the disciples' indignation at what they saw as a waste of resources that could have been used to take care of the poor (**26:9**; see also Mark 14:5). Some (excluding Judas Iscariot – John 12:6) may have honestly been concerned about the poor. But their reaction revealed their lack of understanding of who Jesus was and of the significance of the occasion in God's plan of redemption. Jesus' reply did not say that their concern for the poor was misplaced, but rather that their time with him was very short. By contrast, they can give as much as they want to the poor at any time, for there are always those in need of help (**26:11**).

26:14-16 Judas Promises to Betray Jesus

The story of Judas is easily one of the most tragic ever told. His name has become a byword for betrayal. He was a close friend, a compatriot, a companion of three years and the trusted treasurer of the group. That is what makes his betrayal so horrible. The proverb is true that says *Icikupempula: e cikulya* ['that which visits you is the very thing that eats you', meaning that the person who causes you harm is a close friend].

Judas' problem was that he followed Jesus for what he could get out of it. His aim was to make it to the very top of the 'cabinet' of the new regime in the kingdom of God. Similar motives seem to drive many who enter the public service in Africa today, and many who enter the church. For Judas, it proved to be a disastrous policy, for he was exposed for his shallow commitment and unashamed ambition for material gain. For the price of a slave (**26:15**; see also Exod 21:32), he betrayed his master.

Judas' story is a salutary reminder of the foolishness of following Jesus for what can be gained. Jesus warned that whoever saves his life will lose it (16:24-27), and Judas proved this to be the case (27:1-10).

26:17-30 The Passover Meal

The first recorded murder occurred in the context of offering a sacrifice to God and involved betrayal by a close relative (Gen 4:4-8). Similarly, Jesus and his companions sit down to a sacrificial meal, and Jesus is betrayed by a close friend (**26:18-21**). The betrayal results in his death.

It appears that Jesus ate the traditional Passover meal a whole twenty-four hours before the appointed time (without an actual sacrificial lamb, for that could only be ready the following afternoon). He used the age-old ritual to explain the meaning of his death to his disciples, and thus gave them a way to appreciate more fully the purposes of God.

The details of the old story of the first Passover, the bitterness of the bondage, the sacrifice of the Passover lamb and the deliverance from Egypt, all formed the backdrop to Jesus' showing how he himself would be the new Passover Lamb and how his blood would be the new wine of the new exodus (**26:26-28**). The symbolism is powerful and has come down to us in the form of the Communion service (see 1 Cor 11:23-26).

The book of Hebrews shows Jesus as the ultimate mediator between God and human beings (Heb 9:15), and his death as the sacrifice that ends all sacrifices (Heb 9:26). My maternal grandfather had a place of sacrifice on an anthill behind the house of his first wife. Here he would offer beer, flour and the blood of animals to the spirits of the ancestors, who were the mediators between the living and God. Such acts of devotion and the mediation they sought have all been rendered unnecessary by the death of Jesus Christ on the cross. This is the essential message of the Last Supper. Jesus has become the sacrificial lamb and the mediator of a new covenant for all of us, wherever we live.

When Jesus announced that one of the twelve would betray him, the disciples, assuming that the betrayal had not yet taken place, each asked the Lord which one of them would be the traitor (**26:22**). Even Judas entered into the spirit of things and asked the same question (**26:25**). But whereas the others addressed Jesus as *Lord,* Judas used the term *Rabbi.* The distinction between these two titles may well indicate the level of intimacy that Judas felt in his relationship with Jesus at this point.

In the exchange about his betrayal, Jesus clearly states that he will die in fulfilment of the Scriptures, but at the same time insists that Judas must bear his guilt for the betrayal (**26:23-24**). The paradox can be explained because God's plans cannot be thwarted by human evil. He will accomplish his purposes even through the evil acts that humans carry out.

26:31-35 Jesus Predicts the Disciples' Failure

The theme of God's sovereign action in history is continued with Jesus explaining that the disciples *will all fall away,* and that this is the result of God's action. God *will strike the shepherd, and the sheep of the flock will be scattered* (**26:31**; see Zech 13:7). Zechariah saw the striking of the shepherd as a messianic image of how God would refine and restore a remnant. So although initially God's action would have a devastating effect on his people, in time it would lead to the establishment of the community of the people of the Messiah.

Jesus' promise to *go ahead of you into Galilee* (**26:32**) reminds us that in the Gospels, Galilee is presented as the place of new beginnings and successful and fruitful ministry, whereas Jerusalem is the place where Jesus' enemies came from and where he was to die.

The prediction of their failure did not sit comfortably with Peter who immediately remonstrated with Jesus, vowing that he would never fall away (**26:33**). These words prompted Jesus to make a specific prediction of the manner and time when Peter would deny him (**26:34**). Peter continued to argue with Jesus' predictions and the others did the same (**26:35**). Yet in just a few hours, they would all desert him, and Peter would deny three times that he knew Jesus (26:56, 69-75).

26:36-46 The Garden of Gethsemane

Gethsemane, a name that means 'oil-press', may have been an olive orchard on the slopes of the Mount of Olives (**26:36**; see also John 18:2). It served as the campsite for Jesus and his disciples while he was attending the Passover festival. Judas knew the garden well. Jesus could have chosen another place for the night to avoid the coming clash with the authorities, but he was not about to shrink from his destiny.

Nevertheless, Jesus felt a desperate need for companionship in prayer, and so he asked Peter, James and John to support him at this very important time (**26:37-38**). On the Mount of Transfiguration, these three had seen Jesus' glory and had fallen face down before the voice of God (17:1-5; see Luke 9:28-36). But now it was Jesus' turn to fall prostrate on the ground, as his soul was deeply troubled.

As he prayed, Jesus was not pleading with the impersonal forces of the universe; he was speaking to his Father. His horror of the events facing him was so great that he asked whether the Father had another plan that would not involve such suffering. But even as he made his plea, he expressed his submission to the Father's will (**26:39b**). Prayer must always be subject to the Father's will. It is not using an escape clause to prefix one's prayers with 'if it be your will'. Because of Christ's submission, the triumph of Calvary was accomplished in the garden of Gethsemane! Jesus prayed three times asking the same thing: 'Is there a plan B?' (**26:39a, 42, 44**). But the request was always subject to the will of the Father.

The disciples failed to watch and pray (**26:40, 43**), and this failure would prove very costly when their own test of faith came. Jesus prayed, and so passed the test and stayed within the will of the Father even to death. His disciples failed to pray and so when the crisis came they fled, rather than taking up the cross and following him (16:24). In order to be successful in discipleship, it is necessary to discipline the body so as not to give in to its cravings. We also need to be vigilant through prayer.

Having reached the place of peace, having overcome all his doubts and fears and settled to follow the will of the Father, Jesus majestically moved to meet his persecutors while rousing his disciples from their sleep (**26:46**). His example tells us that we must face whatever consequences may come as we fulfil the will of the Father. Suffering should not be allowed to distract us from doing his will. But we need to build up strength to face it through constant agonizing prayer.

26:47-28:15 Jesus' Trial, Death, Resurrection

26:47-68 Jesus Arrested and Put on Trial

Jesus was betrayed by a friend. Times of persecution will present us with the temptation to betray other Christians. It would be salutary to examine the records of the Rwandan genocide for evidence of betrayals; however, such an exercise though instructive would be soul destroying. In this story, it was a disciple who betrayed his master. He did so with a recognized outward sign of devotion and affection: a kiss (**26:48-49**).

One of the disciples rose to the defence of Jesus with a sword, and struck at the ear of *the servant of the high priest* (**26:51**). But Jesus would have none of it (**26:52**)! Even when he was being unfairly arrested, abused and humiliated, he responded to the need of his enemy. Martyrdom without resistance is the way of Jesus for himself and for his followers.

It was not for want of support that Jesus was going to his death, for God could command armies of angels to rescue him (**26:53**), but his death was necessary for a higher reason: the fulfilment of Scripture (**26:54**). However, he had no human support, for *all the disciples deserted him and fled* (**26:56**).

The first of Jesus' trials took place in the house of Caiaphas, the chief priest, before the Sanhedrin, a legal authority composed of the teachers of the law and the elders of the people (**26:57**). It is unlikely that this was a full gathering of the Sanhedrin, although a good representation could be expected because of the threat that Jesus seemed to pose to their political aristocracy. The trial set out to find evidence to fit the verdict of death which had already been determined (**26:59**).

It is clear that although they constituted a court of law, the Sanhedrin did not follow proper legal procedures in Jesus' case. First, they conducted a capital trial at night. Second, they passed a sentence on the same day as the trial. Third, they should have conducted the meeting of the Sanhedrin in the Chamber of Hewn Stone on the Temple Mount and not in the house of the chief priest. Fourth, they broke the law regarding false witnesses (Deut 19:16-21). The trial of Jesus was a mockery of justice. It is ironic that the Son of God, who is just, was denied justice in his world. It is even more ironic that the Sanhedrin, ostensibly the custodians of God's word of truth, should find themselves having to create false evidence (26:59).

Eventually, however, the chief priest charged Jesus on oath to confirm his true identity, *the Christ, the Son of God* (**26:63**). Jesus then affirmed the statement made by the high priest and, to show that his position is truly exalted, he added that he would be seen sitting *at the right hand of the Mighty One* (**26:64**). This addition emphasized that Jesus' power was not earthly and did not threaten the current rulers. They could even have passed off such an apparently ludicrous claim as a joke, except that Jesus did have a great following and could cause difficulties for the authorities. Moreover, his claim was such a great one that it could be taken as a serious offence, if not actual blasphemy. The Sanhedrin certainly declared it blasphemous (**26:65-66**).

26:69-75 Peter's Denial of Jesus

The forlorn figure of Peter is seen following the crowd that had arrested Jesus right into the house of the chief priest (26:58). He was unwillingly thrust into the limelight by a chance identification. A woman who had seen him in the garden of Gethsemane identified him to the crowd (**26:69**). Peter simply denied knowing Jesus (**26:70**). The second time Peter made the denial *with an oath* (**26:71-72**). The third time Peter even called down *curses on himself* (**26:73-74**); perhaps he even cursed Jesus to show that he did not know him and did not care for him. Then the rooster crowed and his memory unleashed a bolt that struck his conscience. He *wept bitterly* (**26:75**). It is hard to imagine what went on in Peter's mind at this time. Whatever it was, it must have been very hard to bear.

27:1-10 The Death of Judas

The full extent of Judas' betrayal became clear to him as he witnessed or heard that Jesus had been condemned to death and was being taken to Pilate to have the death sentence confirmed. (This step was necessary because only the Roman governor could actually pass a death sentence in Judah – **27:1-2**).

It is instructive to compare Peter and Judas at this point. This comparison may well be the reason that Matthew interrupts the flow of the story to report on what became of Judas. Peter 'wept bitterly' (26:75), and Judas was *seized with remorse* (**27:3**). Bitter tears may well lead to repentance and eventual restoration, as happened to Peter. But Judas' remorse led only to recrimination and, in his case, to suicide (**27:4-5**). Peter made no attempt to undo what he had done, but eventually submitted to the authority of Jesus. Judas, on the other hand, tried to undo what he had done, and when he found he could not do so he decided to take his own life.

The disciples knew a lot of failure, exemplified by Peter's denial. And so do we. But failure need not be a permanent condition. However, when we fail, we should not try to work ourselves back into God's favour by what we do. We must recognize that only God can offer forgiveness, and that as the God of grace he has sufficient mercy for all our weakness. Failure may even be useful in showing us that within ourselves we do not have what it takes to remain honourable as disciples. We must at all times and in all cases depend entirely upon God and his mercy.

27:11-26 The Trial Before Pontius Pilate

Pilate was the governor of Palestine. The Sanhedrin could prepare cases and charges, but it was his prerogative to pronounce sentence. He represented the high ideals of the Roman Empire and he, so it seemed, had the power to determine what was right and just. Jesus spoke only once to confirm his identity, although the way in which his answer is phrased suggests he was not satisfied by the way in which this title was being used to identify him (**27:11**). Otherwise, he completely ignored the trial *to the great amazement of the governor* (**27:12-14**). Jesus made no attempt to prove his innocence because the trial was in effect a sideshow. The reason why he was going to die had very little to do with the concerns of the chief priests and the Sanhedrin. He came to give his life as a ransom for many (20:28; see Mark 10:45).

Pilate clearly understood that there was no case against Jesus, let alone a case deserving capital punishment. He perceived that the trumped-up charges were fuelled by envy and jealousy (**27:18**, 23), and his own wife confirmed his suspicions through a dream (**27:19**). There is irony in her testimony, for in her we see a pagan woman hearing the voice of God in a dream, while the people of God were unable to see what was happening before their eyes.

Pilate tried to free Jesus, first by offering the crowd a choice between *Barabbas*, a notorious prisoner, and Jesus (**27:15-17**), then by persuasion (**27:22-23**) and finally by a disavowal of any responsibility for innocent blood (**27:24-25**). However he was too weak to stand up to the demands of the chief priests. So he released Barabbas, who had probably been a real threat to Roman political power and was certainly a social nuisance. Jesus he handed over to be flogged and crucified (**27:26**).This flogging was probably the 'forty lashes minus one' (2 Cor 11:24; see also Deut 25:3), which left a man barely alive.

This episode reveals Jesus' wholehearted commitment to what he understood to be God's will and his refusal to be distracted by irrelevant legal niceties. He took time to heal a servant of the high priest while he was being arrested (26:51), but would not open his mouth in his own defence. Like him, we must defend the rights of others, but be slow to rise to our own defence. God is able to vindicate his own who suffer in his service.

27:27-56 The Crucifixion of Jesus

After the flogging, the Son of God was abused and humiliated by soldiers, paraded in public in a *scarlet robe* and given mock homage with a *crown of thorns* to highlight what they supposed were his comical claims (**27:27-29**). He was given a beam to carry to the place of execution where the soldiers would affix it to the stakes that were left in place for constant use.

Jesus, weakened by the flogging, was unable to carry the beam, and a bystander, Simon of Cyrene (modern Libya), was compelled by the Roman soldiers to carry it for him (**27:32**). The disciples should have been there to perform that last service for their Lord, but here too they failed, leaving that responsibility, or perhaps privilege, to a bystander. Simon's name soon became widely known among Christians for the part he played.

Golgotha was a prominent place outside Jerusalem where criminals were crucified and their bodies left to hang as a warning to others. There Jesus was crucified, with a notice over his head proclaiming the charge against him. This charge read, THIS IS JESUS, THE KING OF THE JEWS (**27:37**). A statement that was no doubt intended to be mockery was actually the truth. God chooses the way his people will bear witness to him, and that way may not be convenient or safe.

Jesus endured the pain to the fullest, refusing to accept the drink he was offered to numb the pain (**27:34**). The crowd who were watching the crucifixion, including *the chief priests, the teachers of the law and the elders,* heaped insults on him, as did the *robbers* who were crucified with him (**27:38-44**). They used majestic titles in derision – so complete was the rejection that Jesus suffered at the hands of all his people including his disciples, who had abandoned him, at least temporarily.

There are many echoes of Scripture in these verses, which suggests that Matthew is interested in the fact that the death of Jesus is the fulfilment of the will and purpose of God as given in the OT. The darkness that covered the earth may well echo Amos 8:9, and shows the displeasure of the Lord (**27:45**). *My God, my God, why have you forsaken me?* is a direct quotation from Psalm 22:1, where a righteous man suffers injustice (**27:46**). The dividing of his clothes by the casting of lots (**27:35**) echoes Psalm 22:18. The offer of wine vinegar reflects the sentiments of Psalm 69:21, where unjust suffering was unrelieved (**27:48**).

Jesus was in control of his life right up to the end when, in a show of strength, he cried out loudly and then *he gave up his spirit* (**27:50**). No one took his life from him; he gave it as a ransom for many. The tearing of the curtain in the temple, which was presumably caused by a local earthquake (**27:51**), had symbolic importance for the Gospel writers. That curtain separated the Holy of Holies from the rest of the temple. Its tearing signalled the opening of the way to God through Jesus, and the rejection of the old system of priests and sacrifices that had dominated the temple and its activities.

It is only Matthew who mentions, after Jesus' death, the *earthquake* and the resurrection, or rather resuscitation, of *many holy people who had died* (**27:52-53**). There is no agreement among commentators about whether he is speaking of something that actually happened, or whether he is making the theological point that Jesus' death and resurrection will lead to the resurrection of holy people. We know from the story of Lazarus in John's Gospel that Jesus was able to bring people who had died back to life. This story makes the same point.

The natural phenomena that accompanied Christ's death led to the climactic affirmation by the soldiers (the same people who had brutally crucified him), *Surely he was the Son of God* (**27:54**). Shortly before, that title had been used in mockery, but now it was restored to its proper use. Many people, including some of his women disciples, witnessed these things. Only three are mentioned by name but it is clear that there were many more and that they had stayed with Jesus right to the end (**27:55-56**).

27:57-66 Jesus is Buried

Joseph of Arimathea obtained permission to bury the body of Jesus so it would not be simply tossed into a common grave, as was the usual practice with the corpses of executed criminals (**27:57-60**). Joseph not only provided his own tomb for Jesus, but was prepared to be ritually unclean during the Sabbath because he had handled a corpse. He wanted to demonstrate his love and respect for his master. The women were still there, watching what was happening (**27:61**).

The chief priests, in their thoroughness, remembered that Jesus had taught that he would rise from the dead after three days (**27:63**). To try to prevent any such 'resurrection', or claims that it had taken place, they asked Pilate to post a guard of his own auxiliary troops outside Jesus' tomb (**27:64-65**).

28:1-15 The Resurrection of Jesus

The witness of women was of little value in Israel; it was certainly not admissible in court. Even the Apostle Paul does not mention women as witnesses to the resurrection (1 Cor 15:5-6). So it is surprising that the Gospels report that the first witnesses to the resurrection were women, *Mary Magdalene and the other Mary* (**28:1**). Matthew would not have made up this detail, because men would not have accepted it. The story is told this way because it is the historical truth.

The appearance of the angelic being and the reaction of the guards to him (**28:2-4**) has many features of what are called theophanies, when God appears to people in human form (see Judg 13:6; 20-22; Dan 7:9-10). This explains the women's fear as they stood in the presence of the angel of the Lord (**28:5**). The angel of the Lord completely ignored the guards and spoke only to the women. He reassured them and told them not to be afraid. He knew they were looking for Jesus, and so he showed them that the tomb was empty (**28:6**).

There were no witnesses to the actual resurrection. Strictly speaking, what the witnesses saw was an empty tomb and the empty shell of the grave clothes that showed the shape of a body (John 20:6-7). Jesus had already risen from the dead in keeping with the promises he had made (16:21; 17:22-23; 20:17-19; 26:32). The angel confirmed that Jesus had risen as he had promised, and would meet them in Galilee, the place of new beginnings and fruitful ministry (26:32). That is where he would give them a new commission to launch their own part in his continuing mission to the world.

As the women were hurrying away, no doubt filled with all sorts of emotions, Jesus appeared to them in person (**28:9**) and greeted them as if nothing had happened. They immediately showed the proper response to the Lord by falling at his feet in worship. Some of the eleven remaining disciples would doubt the reality of Jesus' resurrection (**28:17**), but not so the women. This story is a testimony that lifted these particular women, and womanhood in general, to a position of honour in the eyes of the apostles and therefore before the whole world.

The Lord then repeated the command given by the angel, commanding the women to go and tell the men that he was risen (**28:10**). Their mission did not end with the delivery of this message, nor was it superseded by the Great Commission (28:16-20). Women must continue to tell the world that Jesus has risen from the dead and that he is alive today.

The events of this first Easter morning reverse usual assumption that truth will first come to men, and the men will pass it on to women. It was the women who first saw the risen Lord and told the men about it, and the men only subsequently saw the Lord to confirm the witness of the women. The women who bore testimony to the resurrection are models for discipleship in their devotion, loyalty and obedience. Yet men in general have been very slow to trust women, or to admit them to service within the church. God does not have such problems. He overturns conventions to show his sovereignty and to bestow honour on all of his servants.

On regaining consciousness, the guards rushed to the chief priests to tell them what had happened. The chief priests bribed them with *a large sum of money* to spread the lie that the disciples had stolen the body of Jesus (**28:12-15**). Presumably Pilate might also have needed to be bribed to buy the story (**28:14**). It is difficult to imagine how anyone could believe that a unit of professional guards would possibly sleep through a grave robbery, and not hear a sound. It is even more amazing that the custodians of the truth of God should sink so low as to resort to outright deceit to keep up appearances!

Grave robbery is common enough in history. The Egyptian pyramids have been desecrated by many robbers, some masquerading as scientific historians! In many parts of

Zambia today, it is not uncommon to encase a coffin in concrete to deter would-be grave robbers. Grave robbers are normally interested in what they can steal from the tomb, and not in the body of the deceased (although in parts of Africa, the body might be the main object of a theft). But the empty tomb was not the work of grave robbers. Jesus' resurrection was an act of God, and human efforts to suppress it have never worked and never will.

28:16-20 Go and Make Disciples

The scene in which Jesus issues his Great Commission is strongly influenced by Daniel 7:14, where the Son of Man is given authority by the Ancient of Days, and all the people of the world worship him and there is no end to his kingdom. The Great Commission looks forward to the fulfilment of Daniel's vision in time. Jesus has authority in nature and in the church because he created both (Col 1:15-18). Whatever way one looks at it, Jesus has the highest authority ever in heaven and on earth. Satan had attempted to bribe Jesus with authority over the nations of the world (4:8). But because Jesus was obedient to the Father, he now commands authority not just on earth but in heaven as well (**28:18**). He therefore has the authority to commission his followers to go into the whole world and do his bidding.

The promise to make the disciples 'fishers of men' (4:19) now takes on concrete form, and will lead them to places far away from their boats, nets and fishes (**28:19**). The words of the commission are centred on two active verbs, *go and make*. When Jesus issued an earlier commission (10:1-10), the word 'go' had a prominent place. We can expect that this greater commission will intensify the 'going' that is part of the nature of discipleship. We are to go to the nations and make disciples of all nations.

This is a message that the African church needs to hear loudly and clearly. For too long we have been recipients of the benefits of the gospel, and with few exceptions most of our church communities do not anticipate, let alone participate in, mission. We do not see it as our duty to go and spread the good news to people within our own countries, or to people beyond the borders of our own countries. This is disobedience to the words of the Lord of heaven and earth. We must repent of this sin and take up his call to make disciples of all nations.

Jesus commands us to make *disciples*, not just converts. Discipleship demands a total surrender of one's identity, security and being to the Lordship of Christ. Such surrender demands more than mere outward conformity to a religion; it must affect one's inner being. The task of converting *nations* means that we will have to address all that makes a people a nation, including the deepest elements of their culture.

Baptism is the initiatory step, to be taken at the beginnings of discipleship. But *teaching them to obey everything I have commanded you* (**28:20a**) is a more comprehensive command.

Finally, Jesus gives the assurance of his presence with his apostles (**28:20b**). God's presence with his people in history has always had transformative powers. Moses was changed from a fugitive and a failure into a prophet and a leader; Joshua took over the mantle of Moses and successfully resettled the people of God in the Promised Land. But the presence of the Lord means at least two things: judgment and blessing. God judges sin, and we need to be constantly reminded of our failures and be renewed by his forgiveness of our sinful behaviour. God's presence is a blessing because he empowers and makes resources available to enable us to accomplish his work.

The Great Commission is given by the highest authority in the universe, and it is binding on all disciples for all time. No other task comes with the same authority, the same universal scope or the same eternal consequences. To go into the world and make disciples of all nations is the most exciting, most urgent and most necessary task in the world. As the number of Christians grows in Africa, let the church on the continent be found faithful in advancing the frontiers of mission for the honour and glory of Jesus Christ our Lord.

Joe Kapolyo

Further Reading

Barclay, W. *The Gospel of Matthew*. DSB. Rev. ed. Edinburgh: Saint Andrew Press, 1975.

France, R. T. *Matthew*. TNT. Leicester: Inter-Varsity Press, 1985.

Keener, C. S. *A Commentary on the Gospel of Matthew*. Grand Rapids, Mich.: Eerdmans, 1999.

MARK

This gospel gives no indication of its author's name. However, it has traditionally been attributed to John Mark, the cousin of Barnabas (Col 4:10). John was his Jewish name, while Marcus or Mark was his Roman name. He apparently grew up in Jerusalem and was a young lad during the time of Jesus' public ministry. He may even have been the young man spoken of in Mark 14:51-52. As a young man he accompanied Paul and Barnabas for part of their first missionary journey (Acts 13:13). Later in life he became an associate of Paul (Col. 4:10; 2 Tim 4:11) and Peter (1 Pet 5:13), while they were both in Rome.

The key evidence about the identity of the author is a statement by the early second-century historian Eusebius. He quotes Papias (a Christian bishop who wrote in about AD 110) as saying that Mark was Peter's 'interpreter' (or 'explainer'), who accurately recorded Peter's account of Christ's words and deeds. John Mark's association with Peter must have afforded him the opportunity to hear about the words and deeds of our Lord as Peter preached in Rome. Thus the account that Mark later wrote down comes directly from the apostles.

Audience

The target audience was unmistakably Gentile and specifically Roman. The evidence for this is that Mark supplies interpretations of Aramaic (or Hebrew) words (Mark 5:41) for his apparently non-Aramaic speaking audience and that he took pains to explain Jewish traditions, such as the 'washing of cups, pitchers and kettles' (Mark 7:3-4). Such explanations would not have been relevant to a Jewish audience. Other examples of this can be found in Mark 3:17; 7:11, 34; 14:12; 15:22, 34, 42. The use of Latin words in the original Greek text (Mark 5:9; 12:15, 42; 15:16, 39) also points to a Roman audience.

Purpose

The purpose of this gospel can be deduced from its opening statement. It is to convey the message of the gospel, or good news, about Jesus Christ (1:1). To drive this point home, Mark uses the Greek word for gospel three times in the first chapter (1:1,14, 15). This is the only one of the four gospels that stresses this word right at the beginning. But the other gospel accounts are no less the good news about Jesus Christ. So, why is Mark different?

And there is no doubt that Mark is different. The church has long recognized the difficulty of trying to reconcile the accounts in Mark with those in the other two synoptic gospels (Matthew and Luke). Numerous questions arise: Why is Mark's account shorter than the others? What guided Mark to select these incidents to record? Why is he not as interested in the chronology of events as the authors of the other gospels? Why does his account sometimes differ from the others even when they are dealing with the same materials? All of these questions can be summarized by asking why Mark adopts an uncommon approach to common accounts.

Over the years, Bible students have come to recognize that the arrangement adopted in each gospel is largely dictated by the purpose of the writer. Mark was not setting out to write a chronological account of the words and deeds of Jesus in the correct sequence, nor to give a complete account of his life. Rather he was aiming to give a faithful outline of Peter's preaching and teaching about the good news of the Christ to a Gentile audience in Rome. Thus he used the teaching and preaching materials used by Peter in Rome, in accordance with the needs of Peter's audience.

The fact that the three synoptic gospels give similar accounts of events does not mean that their human authors were dependent on each other's writings, as some scholars argue (see *TOT* for a fuller discussion of this issue). Obviously there was a common apostolic oral tradition behind their accounts. The differences between them can be explained in terms of their different purposes as well as the unique personalities of the human authors. For example, Mark's gospel is distinctively brief and conveys a sense of urgency. This is illustrated in the constant use of 'at once', 'without delay' and 'immediately' when introducing a new segment. Also, Mark often writes in a vivid and graphic manner that appeals to the reader's imagination. Experts in the Greek language who have examined Mark's writing have found underlying evidence of Hebraisms, that is, Hebrew thought forms in his Greek writing. This phenomenon is similar to the way in which Africans sometimes express themselves in colonial languages. A person may be thinking in his or her own mother tongue but speaking in a foreign language. These features of the gospel reflect the personality of the human author.

The vital role of the Holy Spirit in aiding the process of recollecting and writing Scripture must not be overlooked. Jesus promised the apostles that the Holy Spirit would help them to remember his words (John 14:26) and give them a special understanding of his life and ministry (John 16:14). As the Apostle Peter sensed his imminent departure (or death), he reminded believers that he and the other apostles were eyewitness of the words and deeds of

Jesus Christ (2 Pet 1:13-18). John Mark had undoubtedly heard Peter describe these words and deeds over and over again during his time with him in Rome. Peter also spoke of the Holy Spirit's special enabling of the human authors of Scripture. Prophecy or Scripture, Peter said, did not originate with the individual authors but the Holy Spirit enabled them or carried them along (2 Pet 1:20-21). Just as the Holy Spirit reminded Peter of the words and deeds of Jesus as Peter preached the gospel, the same Holy Spirit must have 'carried along' Mark when he later put into writing what he heard from Peter. (See *TOT* on for a fuller discussion of the Synoptic Problem.)

Date

The church in early times held that Matthew's gospel, which was obviously intended for a Jewish audience, was the first one written. In modern times, some scholars have suggested that the first gospel to be written may have been Mark's. Since the gospel itself gives no clues as to when it was written, we are left to conjecture based on extrabiblical evidence.

As discussed above, Mark's accounts must have been based largely on Peter's preaching and teaching. Church tradition says that both Peter and Paul were martyred in Rome between AD 64-67 during Emperor Nero's persecution of Christians, Peter's martyrdom coming around AD 64 and Paul's no later than AD 67. Church tradition also suggests that John Mark died soon after the martyrdom of Peter and Paul. It would appear then that Mark wrote down his record of Peter's teaching soon after the death of the apostle, that is, some time after AD 64. The likely date of writing would be between AD 64 and 67.

Outline of Contents

COMMENTARY

1:1-8 Introduction

The gospels always began at the beginning, and this is exactly what Mark does here. However, he does not define the beginning in terms of Jewish genealogy (as Matthew does), or in terms of the birth stories (like Luke), or even in terms of Jesus' eternal pre-existence (like John). Instead he speaks of *the beginning of the gospel* [or good news] *about Jesus Christ* (**1:1a**).

The name Jesus is the Greek form of the Hebrew 'Joshua' or the Aramaic 'Jeshua', meaning 'Jehovah is salvation'. In many cultures, a name is extremely important; there is even an African saying that can be translated 'a name directs destiny'. The importance of names and naming is clear in the Old Testament (for example, in the comments on Nabal in 1 Sam 25:25). In Mark, it is clear that the Good News, Jesus, is destined to bring Jehovah's salvation to his people (Matt 1:21). The good news is the good tidings of salvation. *Christ* is the title associated with Jesus' office as the one anointed by Jehovah. It means the same as 'Messiah' (in Hebrew).

The good news that Mark unfolds is that this Jesus Christ is *the Son of God* (**1:1b**), that is, he shares God's nature and character, or in other words, he is God. But if he is God, he is eternal, so what does Mark mean when he writes about 'the beginning of the gospel'? He is stating that Jesus introduces a new era to humanity. This underscores the truth that embracing the gospel of Jesus Christ is embracing a new life (2 Cor 5:17). Jesus is the message of the gospel, not any human being, group or association. Thus Mark's use of 'beginning' serves as both the title of his book and as a summary of the contents of the account that follows.

Mark's account begins with the public manifestation of the Christ, who is introduced to the world by the forerunner, John the Baptist. Unlike Matthew, Mark does not often quote the OT, but here he cites it in support of John's role. The promise to send *my messenger* (**1:2**) is from Malachi 3:1 and may even go back to Exodus 23:20, and the description of the messenger as *a voice of one calling in the desert* (**1:3**) comes from Isaiah 40:3. However, Mark writes as if both quotations can be attributed to Isaiah. The reason he does this is probably that Isaiah was the major prophet whom Mark's readers would know best, and so he focuses on him when reporting two complementary prophecies.

The herald's job would be to go ahead of the Lord to *prepare the way for the Lord*. The essence of what he proclaimed is found in **1:3**. The message would point to the Lord who was coming. That is the message that John the Baptist proclaims in the remainder of this introduction to the gospel of Mark.

True to the prophecy, John the Baptist's proclamation took place in the *desert region* of Judea (**1:4**). John himself was similar in many ways to the fiery prophet Elijah of old. Like Elijah, his clothing was of camel's hair, supported by a leather belt or girdle (2 Kgs 1:8), and he ate a simple diet of locusts and wild honey (**1:6**). All of these point to a simple lifestyle, which true prophets of God today should emulate.

The verbs Mark uses make it clear that crowds of people from Jerusalem and the Judean countryside kept on trooping to hear John. As they *confessed* their sins, they were continually being *baptized* in the Jordan River (**1:5**). This baptism is described as *a baptism of repentance for the forgiveness of sins* (1:4). In other words, what John was calling for was a new beginning (see notes on 1:1 above). He was urging a moral and spiritual renewal that would lead to forgiveness of sins. Genuine remorse for and confession of sin was the necessary prelude to water baptism, and so was a willingness to 'produce fruit in keeping with repentance' (Matt 3:8). Those who were baptized by John had identified with John's ministry. They had taken an action that symbolized the dawn of a new life, and so had identified with the dawn of a new era.

It is important to note that John himself did not forgive anyone's sins. Rather, John pointed to the *more powerful* One to come whose mission would be to forgive sins and to save those who genuinely confess their sins (1:7). John diverted attention away from himself to Jesus. He did so by declaring his own unworthiness – not only in his inability to match the mighty acts of Jesus (see John 10:41) and in being less than qualified to stoop down to serve him, but also in terms of the qualitative difference between their ministries of baptism (1:8). Water marked John's baptism, or in other words, water baptism was necessary to be identified with John. But when the more powerful One came, the Holy Spirit would mark those who identified with him. The lesson is clear: in the new era about to be ushered in by Jesus, his true followers are marked by the activities of the Holy Spirit in his fullness and power. That is the distinguishing mark of Jesus (Luke 4:18-19) and of those who truly follow him.

The scene is now set for the introduction of Jesus in his first public appearance preparatory to his ministry.

1:9-13 Baptism and Temptation

Leaving his hometown of Nazareth, Jesus came to John to be introduced publicly to Israel by his baptism. He did not come to confess any personal sin, for he had none. But he humbled himself to identify with John's proclamation of a 'baptism of repentance for the forgiveness of sins' (1:4). We are not told exactly how Jesus was baptized, for all that the text says is that John baptized Jesus (1:9). Some would argue that the reference to Jesus *coming up out of the water* (1:10) implies that he had gone down into the Jordan River. However, Mark is far more concerned about what happened next.

At the moment Jesus came out of the water, he saw heaven beginning to be *torn open* (1:10). Jesus saw the distinguishing mark of his ministry, the Holy Spirit, descending on him *like a dove*, that is, gently. Thus at the dawn of a new beginning, the era of salvation, the Spirit of God hovered over the water of the Jordan just as it had hovered over the waters at the first beginning, at creation (Gen 1:2). We are not told whether Jesus alone saw the heavens opening and the descent of the dove or whether others saw it too. John the Baptist, as least, seems to have seen the dove, as he testifies to this in John 1:32-34. Others may also have witnessed what happened.

The heavenly attestation followed: *You are my Son, whom I love; with you I am well pleased* (1:11). The Father expressed his agreement with what had just taken place and affirmed that Jesus is the Father's beloved son. The 'you are' reminds us of the Eternal 'I AM' and expresses an eternal bond. Jesus did not become the Son of God on this occasion, he exists as the eternal Son of God. Here God was expressing his pleasure at Jesus' willingness to stoop down and identify with sinful human beings in order to bring us salvation. Obedience to the revealed will of God in his Word attracts divine pleasure.

The temptation followed with a sense of divine urgency: *At once the Spirit sent him out* (1:12). For his first assignment, the Holy Spirit thrust him into the desert. Mark does not tell us what took place in the desert, but it is clear that the entire period of forty days witnessed a powerful encounter with Satan (1:13). The mention of *wild animals* implies that Jesus needed protection from them as well as from the machinations of Satan. But the Father was with him and ministering spirits helped him. All who serve the Lord need to remember not to venture out on their own without the Holy Spirit's direction and control. While travelling in this desert world, they will be battling spiritual forces much fiercer than the wild beasts that are visible to human eyes.

Returning triumphantly from this desert experience, Jesus launched straight into his public ministry in Galilee. Mark's extensive account of this ministry in Galilee can be divided into an early and a later Galilean ministry. Each starts with the calling of disciples.

1:14-3:12 The Early Galilean Ministry

1:14-15 The Message of Jesus Christ

John's ministry in Judea ends when he is imprisoned (the word used literally means 'handed over') as Jesus' preaching in Galilee begins (1:14). What became of John is reserved for a later chapter (6:14-29). A vital lesson for us is to realize that there comes a time when our ministry is done.

Jesus preached the coming of a new era or season of God's rule, marked by the nearness of the *kingdom of God*. Jesus' very presence brought the kingdom near. He proclaimed that those who wished to participate in God's kingdom must repent and believe the *good news* that he was spreading (1:15). There was thus continuity between John's message and this new message, for without repentance and faith one cannot embrace the good news of Jesus.

1:16-20 Calling the First Four Disciples

At the start of this early Galilean ministry, Jesus called the first four disciples. By divine appointment Jesus, walking along the shores of the Sea of Galilee, met the Jonas brothers, Simon and Andrew. They were going about their business – fishing (1:16). At his command, *Come, follow* me, and his promise of radical transformation, *I will make you fishers of men*, the pair obediently abandoned their work (**1:17-18**). Going *a little farther*, Jesus met the Zebedee brothers, James and John (**1:19**). The call of command also went to these two *without delay*. They, too, obeyed unconditionally, leaving behind their father and the hired men to follow Jesus (**1:20**). This account shows that the Lord is in the business of calling disciples to himself. When he calls, instant obedience is required. Such obedience requires absolute faith in the living God. The same Lord still calls his own from their everyday concerns into a life of unqualified obedience.

1:21-34 A Busy Day in Capernaum

In this section, Mark presents Jesus in action, teaching with unparalleled authority in the synagogue in Capernaum (**1:21-22**) and wreaking havoc in enemy territory. He evoked amazement among his hearers. Our Lord thus set an example for all who would teach and preach God's good news. The word must go forth with divine authority, otherwise it is robbed of power.

Just then, while he was teaching, he was interrupted by a spiritual confrontation initiated by the enemy. A member of the congregation was possessed by *an evil spirit* (**1:23**), that is, an unclean spirit, in contrast with the Holy Spirit. By possessing a person, an evil spirit takes over control, acting and speaking through that person. The evil spirit claimed that Jesus had overstepped his bounds by coming into the synagogue – *What do you want with us?* (**1:24**). He also claimed Jesus' activities were destructive, obviously to the enemy! The evil spirit claimed to know who Jesus was – *the Holy One of God!* It is sometimes thought that knowledge of someone's name gives one person power over the person. If this was the scheme of the evil spirit, it came to nothing in the face of Jesus' firm *Be quiet!* (**1:25**). Jesus ordered the evil spirit out of the poor soul. The demon left, shrieking (**1:26**).

This episode underscores the fact that satanic forces are present even in the assembly of God's people. The critical issue is whether God's people can recognize the enemy within. Resistance to divine authority, especially when the good news is being proclaimed with power, is a constant reality.

Jesus' teaching was in sharp contrast to any the audience had heard so far: it was *A new teaching – and with authority!* (**1:27**).

The incident in the synagogue was followed by other healings, beginning with that of Peter's mother-in-law, who was instantly healed of a fever and got up and served them (**1:29-31**). By sunset, word had gone round about him and people with all kinds of diseases were brought to his door. Many were healed, including those possessed by demons. But once again, Jesus would not permit the demons to speak or testify to who he was (**1:32-34**).

1:35-39 Setting Priorities in the Use of Time

Two priorities are evident in this account:

- *The priority of prayer:* Before the hustle and bustle of the day began, Jesus took time to commune with the Father (**1:35**). Both the timing and location bear testimony to an uninterrupted time of prayer. Our Lord set a clear example for us, namely that the day's business must never be more urgent than time spent in communion with God.
- *Priorities in ministry:* Although Jesus sought an uninterrupted location and time, his disciples still managed to encroach. Simon spearheaded the group of intruders (**1:36**) with the excuse that *Everyone is looking for you!* (**1:37**). Jesus' ministry on the Sabbath had been so successful that the disciples were apparently happy to respond to the crowd's demand to hear more. Jesus thought otherwise! Wanting many more to hear him and receive the blessings of the good news, Jesus opted to go *somewhere else … so I can preach there also. That is why I have come.* (**1:38**). Consequently he went *throughout Galilee* (**1:39**). The lesson here is that beyond the horizon of the present ministry there often lies much more that God wants to accomplish through his obedient servants.

1:40-45 Healing a Man with Leprosy

'Leprosy' was the term used to describe a variety of skin diseases in Jesus' time. According to the law, a leper was ceremonially unclean. By faith, this leper approached Jesus saying *you can make me clean* (**1:40**). Out of compassion, Jesus responded, *"Be clean!* (**1:41**), and the man was healed immediately (**1:42**). This act of healing was to become *a testimony to them* (**1:44**), that is, to the priests. In other words, the man just healed was to tell nobody about it except the priests and he was to offer the sacrifices prescribed by the law (see Lev 14:1-32). The reason for this may have been to cause the priests to come to an unmistakable conclusion about the person of Jesus Christ. Unfortunately this man disobeyed, and went about literally *to proclaim many things and to spread about the matter* (**1:45**). As a result, Jesus' ministry had to be restricted to the fringes of the main population centres. But even there the crowds still thronged to him.

2:1-3:6 Jesus' Early Ministry in Galilee

This segment concerns a series of controversies with the religious leaders in Galilee.

2:1-12 Controversy over healing a paralytic

The setting was back *home* (**2:1**) in Capernaum. Apparently Jesus had made a second home there, probably with Simon (see 1:29), for Nazareth was his early home (6:1; Luke 2:51). The event apparently happened in a typical Jewish house, which has a flat roof that is often used as a place to dry grains. Four men brought a paralyzed man for Jesus to heal. Since it was impossible to get to him because of the throng of people, the four opted to carry him up the outside stairway and then lower him down through the roof, illustrating the truth that obstacles do not deter faith. Jesus acknowledged their faith and so pronounced the sick man's sins forgiven (**2:5**). This disturbed the teachers (or experts in interpretation) of the law, who were present. They objected in their minds to the possibility of any mere mortal presuming to forgive sins, regarding the claim to be able to do so as blasphemous, since only God can forgive sins (**2:7**). Jesus took them on by bringing to light what they were thinking (**2:8**) and proceeded to demonstrate his authority to forgive sins as the *Son of Man* (**2:10**). The use of the title implies that he is the Messiah – the prophetic figure in Daniel 7:13 who is able to exercise the divine prerogative to forgive human sins. The word of command (**2:9**) brought immediate healing, so that the response of the people was to give praise to God and to acknowledge that nothing like it had ever been witnessed before (**2:12**).

2:13-17 Controversy over the call of Levi

Levi, the son of Alphaeus, was a tax collector. As such, he was one of the most hated people in Israel because tax collectors were regarded as being in league with the Roman oppressors. The attitude to him was not unlike the attitude of many people in African countries to tax collectors during colonial times. Levi was at work (**2:14**) when Jesus called him to discipleship. He responded without a hint of hesitation. Celebrating his new-found freedom after embracing the good news, he held a reception for Jesus to which he invited his friends, who were tax collectors like himself (**2:15**). From the point of view of the experts in the law, in particular those of the Pharisaic sect, no righteous man would be prepared to associate with the likes of tax collectors – sinners and social outcasts that they were! (**2:16**). Responding to their criticism, Jesus spoke to these Pharisees using a form of parable. He (the spiritual doctor) was here to bring (spiritual) healing to 'sinners' such as Levi and his friends. People like the self-righteous Pharisees could not be helped because they presumed that they were in excellent (spiritual) health. He was implying that these Pharisees were cutting themselves off from his ministry of grace.

2:18-22 Controversy about fasting

Immediately after the controversy about feasting with sinners, Mark introduces a related controversy: why was Jesus not fasting with the righteous? In Jesus' day, people demonstrated their piety by engaging in regular weekly fasts. John the Baptist's disciples did this, and so did the Pharisees (**2:18**). The people who came to Jesus to inquire why his disciples did not observe this ritual are not identified, but they could very well have been Pharisees. Jesus' answer was to say that this was not the appropriate time for fasting

(**2:19**), and he illustrated his point with analogies from a wedding, patching clothes and storing wine (2:19, 21-22). However, the appropriate time for fasting would soon come, when the bridegroom (obviously Jesus himself) would be *taken from them* (**2:20**). He was referring to the events related to his passion.

2:23-3:6 Two controversies about the Sabbath

The first of the two controversies presented here concerned gleaning in the grain fields, a practice that was quite lawful (Deut 23:25). However, Jesus' disciples were accused of breaking the law because they were doing this on the Sabbath (**2:23-24**). The Pharisees' objection, based on Exodus 34:21, was that what the disciples were doing was equivalent to working on the Sabbath. Jesus' answer was based on a holistic view of the Scriptures. He accused them of not paying careful attention to the Scriptures, which imply that where human need exists, allowance can be made (**2:25-26**). He reminds them of an incident in *the days of Abiathar the high priest*. This incident actually occurred in the time of Abiathar's father (1 Sam 21:1-6; 22:20), but Jesus refers to Abiathar's era, probably because he became a far more prominent figure than his father. The correct interpretation of the law is that it was put in place primarily for the benefit of humans and not the other way around (**2:27**). Thus to neglect human need so as to keep the Sabbath is to miss the point of Sabbath observance. In addition, Jesus taught that he, as *the Son of Man*, or the Ideal Man, was Lord or owner of the Sabbath, who came to fulfil and not to annul the law.

The second Sabbath controversy took place in a synagogue where a man with a deformed hand was present (3:1-6). Those who were out to catch Jesus violating the Sabbath in **3:2** were probably the same group of Pharisees referred to in 3:6. So Jesus decided to use the man in an object lesson by asking him to *Stand up in front of everyone* (**3:3**). Then he asked his foes whether the law would say that it was better *to do good or to do evil, to save life or to kill?* (**3:4**). This rhetorical question needed no answer. In righteous anger, combined with deep distress at the attitude of these Pharisees, he spoke the word of command and instantly healed the sufferer (**3:5**). It is one thing to argue about words, opinions and interpretations; it is quite another to be face to face with human needs. In the former case, we can be detached, but in the latter we need to be moved to show mercy.

The cumulative effect of this series of controversies is expressed in the final verse of this section. Here we can indeed see the *stubborn hearts* that grieved Jesus because of the spirit with which they left the synagogue that day. They set out to forge an unholy alliance with the secularist Herodians to kill Jesus (**3:6**). What a way to end a worship service!

3:7-12 Close of Jesus' Early Ministry in Galilee

The order of events seems to suggest that Jesus responded to the murder plot (3:6) by withdrawing to the lakeside, away from the population centres. Even then, large crowds followed him (**3:7**). News about him had spread (**3:8**) beyond the region of Galilee to Judea and Jerusalem – the centre of Judaism. People came from as far away as Idumea, the area to the south of Judea that had earlier been known as Edom. (The Herods, who were the rulers of Israel at this time, were Idumean). People also came from Transjordan as well as from the north-western parts of Palestine, in particular the Gentile centres of Tyre and Sidon, which Jesus would later visit (see 7:24, 31). The crowds were so large that to prevent them from crushing him Jesus taught from a little boat pushed slightly out from shore (**3:9-10**).

Throughout Jesus' ministry, there were ongoing encounters with evil spirits. These unclean spirits were in the habit of *falling down before him*, indicating that his power was far greater than theirs, and of acknowledging him as *the Son of God* (**3:11**). Jesus consistently refused to allow them to call him by this name (see also 1:25, 34), not because it was not his true name, but because he did not want honour from unclean spirits who were not confessing his name in the way that believers would. Rather, it seems that these spirits were motivated by the belief that precise identification of a spirit by name enabled one to control it. Even while lying prostrate at Jesus' feet, these unclean spirits refused to submit and were still attempting to gain mastery of him! Satan and his cohorts don't give up, even in defeat. Jesus forbade them to tell who he was (**3:12**), as he would not accept phoney acknowledgement of who he was, and probably also to forestall premature public identification.

3:13-6:13 The Later Galilean Ministry

The later Galilean ministry of our Lord commenced with the appointing of the Twelve, who would continue the ministry he had started.

3:13-19 Appointment of the Twelve

Some, if not all, of the men chosen as apostles were already Jesus' followers by this time (see 1:14-20; 2:13-14). He apparently selected them from a larger pool of followers. He also made the purpose for which they were appointed quite clear (**3:14-15**) by calling them *apostles*, a term that indicated that they would be his emissaries, sent out as heralds proclaiming the good news. As part of their task, they would *be with him*, that is, be his close associates who would learn from him and whom he could then send out to proclaim the good news and to confront satanic forces, armed with his authority.

The names recorded by Mark in **3:16-19** include nicknames, which may suggest that the source of information was an insider, himself one of the apostles. A number of

these nicknames are in Aramaic. *Cephas*, the nickname given to Simon by Jesus himself, means 'the rock'. The Zebedee brothers, James and John, he nicknamed *Boanerges* or *Sons of Thunder* – a reference to their sometimes fiery tempers (see 9:38; Luke 9:54). The other Simon was probably nicknamed *Zealot* to denote a person full of enthusiasm for God (it was probably not a reference to membership of the notorious political party known as the Zealots). *Iscariot*, Judas' nickname, could be a reference to his village of origin or it could be a punning name derived from a word meaning 'assassin'.

Divine providence was undoubtedly at work in Jesus' choice of this group of men. The Lord makes use of the different character traits found among his own as these traits are surrendered into his transforming hands. However, the reasoning behind the choice of Judas remains mysterious to us, although he must clearly have had a chance to be transformed under the tutelage of the Master.

3:20-35 Jesus' Ministry Misconstrued

This segment is put together to demonstrate the extent to which Jesus was rejected. The combination of being misunderstood by family members and subjected to malicious denunciation by his foes underlines his total rejection.

His rejection by his family took place in an unidentified house in Galilee, where a crowd had gathered, so clamouring for his attention that he scarcely had a moment to eat (**3:20**). When news of this reached his family, they misconstrued what was going on. To them, he had gone insane. If he apparently could no longer care for himself, they would go to *take charge of him*, presumably by bringing him home to care for him (**3:21**). But what appears on the surface to be genuine family concern was in fact a ploy to disrupt his mission. The enemy was using his undiscerning family.

Next, Jesus was confronted by his foes – teachers of the law from Jerusalem (**3:22**). These were the same type of people with whom he had already engaged in a series of public controversies (see 2:1-3:6). These experts were sent from Jerusalem to assess Jesus and give a verdict that would settle the controversies once and for all, and so tell the people what to make of him. They concluded maliciously that all his mighty acts had been performed in league with the prince of demons.

In his defence, Jesus pointed out the absurdity of Satan driving out Satan or of a kingdom being divided against itself, or even of a household being divided against itself (**3:23-27**). One does not fight against one's friends. Someone who is disrupting things by entering *a strong man's house* (3:27) must be strong enough to have overpowered the owner. Satan, like the strong man, had obviously been overpowered by Jesus rather than been served by him.

In 3:28-30 Jesus pronounced judgment on these experts of the law as being guilty of an eternal sin. Whereas all categories of sin, including blasphemy, are forgivable (**3:28**),

FAMILY AND COMMUNITY

A community is defined as a social group whose members live together or share common property and interests. Families are always regarded as being at the heart of community life. But one of the most distinctive features of African culture is that the family and the community are totally blended.

The African family is defined in very broad terms and embraces far more than the nuclear family of parents and children. Anyone with whom one shares blood ties, whether close or distant, is regarded as part of one's family. Thus a family includes brothers and sisters, uncles and aunts, cousins and nephews, as far back as anyone can remember. In some cultures on our continent, every adult who associates with my parents is my parent, and everyone in the same generation as myself is a brother or sister.

Our emotional attachment to this extended family remains very strong, despite urbanization and Western influence. It influences many of our choices about such things as work, marriage and religious affiliation. For the African Christian, this cultural understanding of community is a powerful tool for understanding the Scriptures and for integration into the church.

The long genealogies in the Bible remind us that it, too, is a story about family. It begins with a couple created by God who are the ancestors of all the human beings on the earth (Gen 1:27-28; 5:1-32; 10:1-32). Later, God formed a large family, Israel, made up of the descendants of Abraham and intended to be a model for the other families of the earth (Gen 12:2-3). In the NT, this family grows even larger because faith in the work of Christ draws Gentiles to join Jews in the 'family of God' (Acts 13:38-39; Eph 2:19).

The Bible teaches that we are to love, honour and train our own biological family in the faith (Exod 20:12; Deut 6:1-9; Eph 5:25-6:4). But it does not stop there, for from a biblical perspective, the nature and quality of the ties that unite Christians with each other should be stronger than blood ties. What is born of the Spirit is of more value that what is born of the flesh (Matt 10:35-37; 12:46-50; John 3:1-21). Thus when the Bible speaks of the church as a body of which each believer is a member, it is sounding a call to strong community life.

Within the family and community that is the church, we should find plenty of evidence of the moral strengths of African family culture: solidarity, hospitality, joy and the like. When one member suffers, all the members should suffer. Members should care for one another. All should work together, cooperating for the common interest (Rom 12:4-18; 1 Cor 12:12-30).

Of course, we must exercise wisdom when incorporating aspects of our communal culture into the church. For example, while we are right to show great respect for older people and to acknowledge their natural role as leaders, we should not allow our respect for our elders to make it difficult for the younger generation to exercise their gifts. We need to ensure that witness is passed on from generation to generation within the Christian family (1 Tim 4:12-5:3). The solidarity and welcome of the church should also not be reserved for blood relatives, even in the larger sense of all those from our ethnic group. Christians of all nations are equally brothers and sisters in the Christian family (Acts 6:1-7; Gal 3:28).

If we can learn to combine our good family and community spirit with the biblical ideal, the African church will be an example for the world, a model of how to live. We will be saying to the world, *This is the way; walk in it* (Isa 30:21).

Soro Soungalo

---

there is an unforgivable sin – the sin *against the Holy Spirit* (**3:29**). This sin is the malicious attribution of the work of the Holy Spirit to an evil spirit. Such rejection of the work of grace performed by the Holy Spirit amounts to *an eternal sin* (3:29). But the teachers of the law were insistent, for the words that Mark uses can be literally translated *they kept on saying, 'He has an evil spirit.'* As the line of the hymn goes, 'Blind unbelief is sure to err and scan his works in vain'. Wilful unbelief is often accompanied by the irrational and absurd. To continue to discredit God's work leads only to eternal destruction.

The battle line was now clearly drawn. The family members who had left home to come to take control of him (3:21) had now arrived, asking Jesus for a private audience so they could carry out their intention (**3:31-32**). He responds that the true test of whether someone is a relative is not natural but spiritual (**3:33-35**). If one is truly part of God's family and shares in the divine nature, one will, like Jesus, act in conformity to God's will and nature (**3:35**). In many parts of Africa today, having the right connections gains one access in high places. A far more important 'connection' is our connection to God through our Lord Jesus Christ, and our obedience as members of God's family to God's will.

4:1-34 Jesus' Parables

Mark's account of the public rejection of Jesus is followed by a string of parables, a signal that Jesus responded by changing his approach to his public ministry. The change was not that he began teaching large crowds or speaking from a boat (**4:1**) – he had already been doing this in 3:9. What was new was that he made increasing use of parables (**4:2**). The parables are about how the kingdom of God operates. Jesus regularly compared the kingdom to seeds (4:11, 26, 31) and focused on how people *hear* (4:9, 23, 24) its message. Thus the parables were told to test the spiritual sensitivity of those who heard them. They concealed kingdom truths to those *outside* (4:11, 12), while revealing them to the disciples (4:10, 11, 34).

Today, however, we attempt to make the message of the word as plain as is humanly possible, rather than concealing it. Our Lord concealed the message at that point because the time was not ripe for the general populace to receive the truth that he was the Messiah.

4:1-20 Parable of the sower

After hearing the parable of the sower (4:3-8), the disciples had to seek help in interpreting it (4:10). In response, Jesus quoted Isaiah 6:9-10 explaining that the reason he was using parables was to conceal kingdom truth from outsiders, but not from the disciples (4:11-12). Jesus explained that the point of the parable is that differences in the condition of people's hearts result in difference in their receptivity to the message of the kingdom of God (4:14-20). He also emphasizes that God expects that all those who truly hear the message and respond will produce many seeds as a result, even though it can be expected that some will produce more than others.

4:21-23 Parable of the lamp

A lamp is obviously meant to give light in darkness, and thereby reveal what is otherwise hidden. Jesus is the true lamp, whose coming reveals the darkness in human hearts. He is making the point that, despite what was said in 4:11-12, his aim is actually to reveal and not to conceal the truth concerning the kingdom of God. It is the heart condition of humans that prevents *those on the outside* from understanding what he says (4:11). This is why Jesus exhorted, *If anyone has ears to hear, let him hear* (4:23). Spiritual ears (sensitivity) are needed to 'hear' (understand) kingdom truths.

4:24-25 Parable of the measure

Following on the admonition in 4:23, Jesus cautioned his audience to *consider carefully what you hear* (4:24), that is, pay serious attention to what they hear. Then he unexpectedly compares the activity of hearing to measuring something out. It would seem that the kind of 'hearing device' or *the measure you use*, determines the dividends received in one form or another, presumably on the judgment day. In the divine economy, a person who *has* (that is, someone who is spiritually receptive) receives more, while someone who *does not have* (that is, someone who is not receptive) suffers loss. It all depends on the 'measure' one chooses to use (4:25).

4:26-29 Parable of the growing seed

The earlier parable of the sower emphasized different types of soil and the different growth of seeds. This parable emphasizes the different stages in the growth of that seed from the time it is first sown until harvest time. The inner

workings of the message of the kingdom remain a mystery. It operates regardless of any activity by the sower. Thus the seed sprouts, whether the sower wakes up or sleeps, *though he does not know how* (4:27). God is the one who is in control. Human agents sow the seed, but they do not make it grow and so should not become impatient when it does not seem to produce results as soon as they would wish. God's sovereign purpose is still at work.

4:30-32 Parable of the mustard seed

This parable illustrates a vital truth about the kingdom of God – it was not yet fully manifest. Jesus compares it to a mustard seed, a proverbially tiny and insignificant seed, although not necessarily the smallest of all seeds. The kingdom appeared small and insignificant at the time Jesus was speaking. But just as the tiny mustard seed grows into a large shrub, so his kingdom will grow. Its full glory will eventually be revealed.

4:33-34 Concluding remarks

Mark obviously selected these particular parables from many others, because he tells us that Jesus used *many similar parables*, teaching *as much as they could understand* (4:33) on each occasion. He gave fuller explanations of the meaning of the parables when he had time alone with his disciples (4:34).

4:35-5:43 Jesus Demonstrates His Sovereign Authority

Mark follows the parables about the kingdom of God with accounts of a series of incidents that demonstrate Jesus' kingly authority over nature, demons, diseases and death.

4:35-41 Calming the storm

That evening, after what seems to have been a busy day of teaching in parables of the kind just narrated, Jesus suggested that they cross to the other side of the Sea of Galilee (4:35). He knew that an important meeting would take place there (see notes on 5:7). The boat they used was probably the one mentioned in 4:1 as a convenient place from which he could teach (4:36) Some of the disciples piloted the boat, while Jesus rested. Given the day's schedule, it is not surprising that he was soon *sleeping on a cushion*, even though a storm was raging (4:37, 38). The storm was severe enough to be a real threat to Jesus and his disciples. Their rebuke *Teacher, don't you care if we drown?* is the natural reaction of panic-stricken men. In stormy times we tend to overreact and experience fear, panic and even anger. Too often, we turn on the leader as a scapegoat when things turn nasty. We may even charge Jesus with not caring for us! Yet this type of reaction does nothing to calm the storm.

In this crisis, Jesus gets up and speaks to the storm as if it were a person, the first of a series of forces he would engage in this segment of Mark's gospel. He rebuked (a personification) the wind and commanded (another personi-fication) the waves, *Quiet! Be still!* (**4:39**). The wind and the storm immediately obeyed his command! Then, turning to the disciples, he drove home the lesson, *Do you still have no faith?* (**4:40**). His point was clear: fear hinders faith; though dangers are real, when Jesus is with us, we can have perfect tranquillity amidst the storms.

5:1-20 Casting out demons at Gerasa

Gerasa, or Gadara as some translations have it, is a region, not a specific village (**5:1**). The fact that pigs were kept there (see 5:11) indicates that it was inhabited by Gentiles. As soon as they landed, the reason why Jesus had asked to cross the lake that evening became clear. A demon-pos-sessed man met them and gave Jesus a hostile reception when he reached the shore (**5:2**). The poor man was a danger to other people and to himself because of the influ-ence of his masters, the indwelling evil spirits. He had been driven away from among people to live in isolation among the tombs, for he could no longer be restrained – not with chains or any iron shackles, for he broke them all. He had been led down a road of self-destruction, as he cut himself with flint knives and cried out all day (**5:3-5**). He was a maniac whom everyone feared. Such is the work of the devil, who specializes in destruction and killing, and con-tinues to do so today.

The ensuing dialogue must have been between Jesus and a leading spirit among the legion (see **5:9**). The evil spirits indwelling the man challenged Jesus for having come to invade their territory: *What do you want with me?* (**5:7**) Jesus had come to this territory by design, in spite of the hostil-ity of the sea. He knew of the impending power encounter. The demons stubbornly resisted coming out of this man, for Mark tells us that Jesus kept on saying, *Come out of this man, you evil spirit!* (**5:8**). But in the end, the demons succumbed and repeatedly begged Jesus *not to send them out of the area* (**5:10**). Apparently this area was an abode of evil spirits. Rather than leave the area, the evil spirits wanted to inhabit the huge herd of some two thousand pigs that was grazing nearby. These evil spirits seem to have specialized in wreaking havoc, and when Jesus granted their request they succeeded in doing to the pigs what they had nearly done to the man (**5:12-13**). Jesus clearly placed greater value on a human soul than on livestock, although it is unclear why he granted the evil spirits' request.

The man previously possessed was now totally healed and was *dressed and in his right mind* (**5:15**). However, when the Gerasenes heard what had happened (**5:14, 16**), they were clearly more concerned about their economic loss than about the deliverance of this poor man, and so would have nothing more to do with Jesus (**5:17**).

In sharp contrast, the healed man begged to be allowed to accompany Jesus when he was leaving the area (**5:18**). But Jesus charged him to go back to his family and tell them the good news of his deliverance as a result of the Lord's mercy (**5:19**). The man went on to proclaim this good news in the predominantly Gentile region of the Decapolis or the Ten Cities (**5:20**). Spreading the good news begins with tell-ing the story of what the Lord has done in one's life. Until someone has a personal story to tell, he or she has no good news to share.

5:21-43 Exercising authority over diseases and death

Mark is obviously not particularly concerned with the chro-nology of events, so we do not know the time gap between the events at Gerasa and the two incidents recorded here in which Jesus demonstrated his authority over disease and death.

Jesus had disembarked from a boat when a synagogue ruler named Jairus met him and begged him to come and save his twelve-year-old daughter from dying (**5:21-23**). Jesus consented and set out for Jairus' house (**5:24**).

While on the way there, they encountered a woman, whose story is most pitiable. She had been afflicted with an incurable haemorrhage for twelve years. As if that was not bad enough, she had suffered at the hands of *many doctors and had spent all she had* to no avail, instead her condition worsened (**5:25-26**). Unfortunately, even today sufferers battling with chronic conditions of this nature often fall prey to 'many doctors' and traditional healers. Her problem was compounded by the constant state of ceremonial unclean-ness that she had been in for the last twelve years. This would have meant that she could not attend the synagogue and would have been shunned even by members of her own family, who would have become unclean if they had touched anything she sat on or lay on. In faith she sought secret-ly to just *touch his clothes* (**5:28**). Her faith was instantly rewarded (**5:29**). Right there and then (or *at once*) Jesus realized that *power had gone out from him,* that is, divine power to heal. He asked, *Who touched my clothes?* (**5:30**). The disciples found the question strange, because many people surrounded him. But he was conscious of a particu-lar touch! At his insistence, the woman came forward and *told him the whole truth* (**5:33**). Jesus commended her faith and affirmed her healing (**5:34**).

While this woman was receiving hope and reassurance, word reached Jairus that all hope was lost (**5:35**). He may well have interpreted the delay while Jesus attended to the woman with the haemorrhage as a most costly interrup-tion. But Jesus reassured him, telling him to shun fear and embrace faith instead (**5:36**). Fear is the foe of faith. When one turns to God, he gives hope where humans are utterly hopeless and helpless.

Jesus minimized publicity by continuing on to Jairus' house with only three disciples in tow – Peter, James and John (**5:37**). Arriving there, he found that the traditional mourning ritual had begun, most probably with professional mourners. The entire scene was a *commotion* (**5:38**). His declaration that the girl was *not dead but asleep* (**5:39**) was laughed to scorn (**5:40**).

Only the parents and the three disciples were taken to where the dead girl lay. Jesus spoke to the dead in her mother tongue, *Talitha koum!* Mark translated the Aramaic for his readers: *Little girl, I say to you, get up!* (**5:41**). The dead girl obeyed, got up and walked around, to the complete astonishment of the mourners gathered outside (**5:42**). Jesus gave strict orders that they must keep quiet about this, lest there be uncontrollable reactions from the people. It was for that reason that he had excluded them from coming to the house with him (5:37). He then told those in the house to give the girl something to eat to revive her physical strength (**5:43**).

Once again, as in other incidents described in this section, Jesus demonstrated his authority over all the conditions of life that tend to shatter human security. He demonstrated that he is Lord indeed!

6:1-6a Jesus Rejected at Home in Nazareth

In this chapter Jesus has returned to Nazareth, his hometown, with the disciples (**6:1**). On the Sabbath he was given a chance to teach in the synagogue. His teaching there amazed the home audience, making them wonder about the source of his teaching, of his wisdom and of the miracles he was reported to have performed elsewhere (**6:2**). They *took offence at him* because they reasoned that none of what they were seeing could be traced to his human origins (**6:3**). In that they were correct! But they would not go further, and trace their source to God because they still saw Jesus as just *the carpenter*. They had failed to see God at work.

In response, Jesus repeated the proverb that says a prophet receives honour everywhere except in his hometown (**6:4**). Today we might phrase this as 'familiarity breeds contempt'. Except for a few healings, the blessings that Jesus of Nazareth had bestowed on other towns and villages sadly eluded his own – all because of their unbelief. This was a foretaste of Jesus' final rejection as he came to his own and his own received him not (John 1:11). This scenario is all too familiar today, albeit in microcosm, as an individual goes all over the place bringing blessing to others, but is not considered of much significance at home. Jealousy is often the major cause of stumbling in such cases. Jealousy blinds us.

6:6b-13 The Commissioning of the Twelve

It would seem that after this rejection at home, Jesus focused for a time on outlying villages (**6:6b**). He sent the Twelve out in pairs to assist with the work of proclaiming the good news, thus multiplying the effect of his ministry. Jesus gave them his authority, in particular to engage evil spirits (**6:7**).

Their instructions were precise: to go in simplicity, carrying the barest minimum. They were not to move from house to house after settling into a town, for that could breed dissatisfaction. They were not to presume on the hospitality of their hosts. Where they are turned away, they must not force themselves on the reluctant (**6:8-11**). This approach was a necessary training in faith and was also meant to guard their integrity as heralds of the good news. While some of these principles apply at all times, not all do. The enduring principles are the commands such as those to do mission and not to presume on the generosity of their hosts. However, the commands in 6:8-9 should not be construed as principles that apply for all time.

The Twelve went out and preached the kingdom of God, calling people to repentance (**6:12**), driving out many demons, and healing people (**6:13**). The use of the anointing oil for the sick was known among the Jews (see Jas 5:14-15). The oil symbolizes the power of the Holy Spirit. Christians today, however, should beware of misapplying anointing oil by using it as a form of fetish, like pagans.

6:14-9:29 The Withdrawal from Galilee

6:14-16 Jesus' Fame Spreads Far and Wide

Rumours about Jesus spread to Herod Antipas, with conflicting views about his identity. Some said he was John the Baptist who had been resurrected (**6:14**), while others said he must be Elijah, or a prophet like one from long ago (**6:15**). Herod himself was troubled in his conscience, thinking John whom he had killed must have come back to life (**6:16**).

Earlier, Mark had mentioned John's incarceration (1:14) and left it at that. Now, in a flashback, he explains why Herod's conscience was bothering him.

6:17-29 The Arrest and Murder of John the Baptist

Herod had imprisoned John in order to silence him. The fiery prophet had repeatedly spoken against the incestuous relationship between Herod and his brother's wife, Herodias. John stood firmly on the teaching of the law, saying, *It is not lawful for you* (**6:17-18**; see Lev 20:21). God's law is no respecter of persons. It indicts the high and the lowly alike. We are in dire need of fearless modern prophets rather than praise singers who revel in high places, for sycophancy is rife.

Herodias bitterly resented John's preaching and nursed a murderous grudge against him. But Herod protected John from her because he had listened to John's messages and recognized that John was *a righteous and holy man* (**6:20**).

Finally, Herodias saw an *opportune time* (**6:21**). Herod's birthday party would be an occasion for merriment and debauchery in the presence of a who's who in Herod's tetrarchy. She would be able to catch Herod off guard. So when Herod took an ego trip into the land of pride, Herodias struck! He told her daughter to *Ask me for anything* (**6:22-23**), and ask she did, egged on by her mother (**6:24**): *the head of John the Baptist on a platter* (**6:25**). The irony here is that Herod now pretended to be a man of honour – one whose word could be counted on! Herod felt that his oath and the impression he wanted to make on his guests were more sacred than human life, even the life of a 'righteous and holy man' (**6:26**). John was sacrificed on a platter of pride (**6:27-28**). Herodias had done her worst. But as she stared at John's head, she must have known that his soul had gone to rest with his God. His disciples came to pick up the remains and to pay their last respects (**6:29**). Revenge may appear sweet to start with, but it leaves a bitter taste in the mouth.

6:30-44 Solitude and the Feeding of the Five Thousand

Following the parenthetical narrative about John's death, Mark returns to the Twelve and their mission. They gave Jesus a comprehensive report on what they had done (**6:30**). Because so many people were coming and going – demanding his attention – he asked the Twelve to go away with him to find solitude where they could be refreshed (**6:31**). Here Jesus is teaching an important lesson, particularly for those who are very active in ministry. Solitude is a rare commodity for many such people, but our Lord recognized the need for it and recommended it to his followers (see also 1:35; 6:31, 46).

Their attempt to find solitude was, however, frustrated. A crowd was waiting for them on their arrival (**6:32-33**). Jesus responded by extending his compassion to them, for *they were like sheep without a shepherd* (**6:34**). Like Israel of old (Ezek 34), the crowd that sought Jesus were in a pathetic spiritual state. To understand their plight we need only look at the crop of leaders or shepherds they had in the Pharisees and the teachers of the law. The experts from Jerusalem were leading them astray (see 3:22-30). In these circumstances, the Good Shepherd would sacrifice his personal need for rest to tend the sheep.

After he had taught them *many things* (6:34), it started to get dark. The disciples suggested dismissing the crowd so they could go and find food (**6:35-36**). But Jesus, to the disciples' great surprise, had a different idea – *You give them something to eat* (**6:37**). The disciples quickly did some arithmetic and concluded it would take eight months of a labourer's daily wages to feed this lot! They implied it was not desirable to spend so much (6:37).

But still the Master had a different idea – *How many loaves do you have?* (**6:38**). Jesus would use whatever was available, while *looking up to heaven* and giving *thanks* (**6:41**). While the disciples focused on the problem, our Lord taught them to focus on the heavenly Father. A vital lesson here is to learn to look up to heaven not only when one is without resources, but even when one has them. We should learn to give thanks, whether for little or for much. The result was that *all ate and were satisfied* (**6:42**). The lesson in faith continued for the disciples as they collected the

scraps that remained (**6:43**). They had come to find rest in a solitary place, not knowing that the Good Shepherd was going to be preparing a table on the *green grass* (**6:39**) for a crowd of no less than five thousand (**6:44**) who were like sheep without a shepherd.

6:45-52 Withdrawal to Pray and the Walk on the Lake

Mark communicates a sense of urgency in what follows the feeding of the crowd. *Immediately* Jesus compelled both the disciples and the crowd to leave, while he went alone to commune with his Heavenly Father (**6:45-46**). The sense of urgency undoubtedly had to do with his need to speak with the Father.

While Jesus prayed, the disciples were having difficulty during the return journey across the lake. But the Master *saw the disciples straining at the oars* because the wind was blowing against them (**6:47-48a**) This would imply that they were losing control of the boat and were being blown off course. In the dead of the night he went to their rescue, *walking on the lake* (**6:48b**). This was a display of his divine majesty in total authority over the waters (see Job 9:8). But the Master was far from the minds of the terror-stricken disciples. They thought they were seeing *a ghost*! Then came the words of reassurance, *It is I. Don't be afraid* (**6:49-50**). The critical issue here was their slowness of spiritual perception. They missed the Lord's glory and mistook him for a ghost. This despite having watched the feeding of the multitude, which should have reminded them of the way God had fed Israel in the desert. That miracle had been a preparation for this experience on the lake, but they missed both lessons because *their hearts were hardened* (**6:52**).

6:53-56 Withdrawal to Gennesaret

The disciples had set out to go to Bethsaida (**6:45**), but the wind had driven them southwards. Now they landed at Gennesaret (**6:53**). The story was no different here than elsewhere. As soon as he was spotted, Jesus was mobbed – whether in villages, towns, countryside or marketplaces. A great ministry of healing was witnessed. Merely touching his cloak brought healing to many (**6:54-56**).

7:1-23 What Makes a Person Unclean?

We are not told when Jesus encountered this theological commission of inquiry (**7:1**). They may have been part of the earlier group of experts in the law who had come from Jerusalem (see 3:22). Whatever the case, Mark here records another controversy with the religious establishment.

In some parts of Africa, there is a saying akin to the English adage, 'charity begins at home'. It is usually used to link a child's behaviour outside the home to the sort of training he must have been given at home. Here, the religious leaders saw the disciples eating with ceremonially unclean hands (**7:2**) and must have wondered what sort of training they had received from their Master. At this point,

Mark pauses to briefly explain some of what was involved in Jewish ceremonial ablutions, according to the *traditions of the elders* (**7:3-4**). These Pharisees then confronted Jesus directly, blaming him for the 'sins' of his followers. They wanted to know why his followers blatantly disregarded tradition (**7:5**).

Since they had asked for it, so to speak, Jesus gave it to them! He did not mince words. He exposed these religious leaders for what they were – *hypocrites. He* supported his position from Isaiah's prophecy, which he implied was about them. The essence of the hypocrisy is offering 'lip service' rather than practising 'heart service', observing human scruples rather than God's law (**7:6-8**).

How did they practice hypocrisy? Jesus went on to expose them: They had *a fine way of setting aside the commands of God* (**7:9**). The language in Mark's gospel is vivid. These men literally 'loosened' God's commands, in other words, they made them inoperative, while clinging tenaciously to human traditions. Their way of annulling God's command was through technicalities. Jesus illustrated his point by referring to Exodus 20:12 and Deuteronomy 5:16, both of which command respect and care for one's parents (**7:10**). But the elders had developed a vow that enabled something to be declared *Corban*. Mark carefully explains this Aramaic word to his non-Jewish readers: an individual could place under Corban any gift he should have given to his parents, implying it was dedicated to God's use (**7:11-12**). But in practice he was not obliged to deliver that gift to God. So by using a legal trick a person could escape his duty both to God and to his parents (**7:10-13a**). Jesus insisted that this was just one of *many things like that* (**7:13b**).

Then Jesus returns to the original issue of eating with unwashed hands and corrected the wrong impression that these blind guides – the religious leaders – had given the people. What defiles truly *comes out of a man* (**7:14-15**). In the KJV, the importance of this warning is underlined with the words: *If any man have ears to hear, let him hear* (**7:16**). (This verse is omitted from the NIV because ancient manuscripts do not contain it. It may be that it was an exhortation that someone wrote in the margin that later crept into the text.)

Later, in private, the disciples asked Jesus for further explanation of his teaching on clean and unclean things (**7:17**). They thus betrayed their spiritual dullness (**7:18**; see also 6:52). In his explanation, Jesus distinguishes between the *heart* and *stomach*. The elders and the Pharisees were preoccupied with externals – things that enter the digestive system from the outside. These do not morally defile in any way, for they are ingested and then excreted (**7:19**). Mark, at this point, pauses to comment that Jesus was here giving a fuller understanding of the Jewish dietary regulations. By contrast, our Lord focused on the heart. He clarified his earlier point by listing the types of things

that defile, things that are hatched from *inside* an individual (**7:20-23**).

7:24-30 Withdrawal to the Region of Tyre

The next incident Mark records takes place in the Gentile region of Tyre and Sidon – beyond the borders of Israel. This was intended to be a secret journey (**7:24**), but news of Jesus had travelled far. One of those who had heard of him was a Greek woman who had been born in Syrian Phoenicia. Her problem was familiar to Jesus – her *little daughter was possessed by an evil spirit* (**7:25**). She came to Jesus begging him to deliver her child (**7:26**).

As a test of her faith, Jesus put it to her that it was not appropriate to give bread that belongs to children to their dogs! Instead the children should be served first (**7:27**). He was making the point that he was supposed to deal with Israel first. The time of the Gentiles would come later.

This woman's response was incisive. She took the image in her stride and carried it further, arguing that the dogs under the table do eat the crumbs, which are part of the children's bread, after all (**7:28**). By faith, she saw herself, as a Gentile, benefiting from the blessings of Israel.

Jesus always responds to faith. He commended the woman for *such a reply* (**7:29**) and rewarded her faith by granting her request. She returned home to find her daughter delivered (**7:30**).

7:31-8:21 Withdrawal to the Decapolis Region

After this, Jesus moved northwards towards Sidon, and then travelled to the south-east along the Sea of Galilee until he reached the Decapolis, or Ten Cities (**7:31**).

7:32-37 Healing of a deaf and mute man

In the Decapolis, some people brought to him a man who was deaf and partially mute (**7:32**). Jesus took this man aside to heal him in privacy. A peculiarity of this healing act was the use of a physical means (**7:33**). After looking up to heaven, most likely in prayer Jesus uttered the word of command in Aramaic (suggesting that the man was a Jew), *Ephphatha!* Mark again translates this for his readers (**7:34**). The effect was immediate. The man's tongue was loosened so that he now could speak clearly (**7:35**). Try as he might, Jesus could not curtail the spread of this news (**7:36**). Talking about him, people exclaimed, *He has done everything well* (**7:37**), or in other words, he has set straight what is crooked! This miracle attests once more to his divine authority – he straightens what is crooked.

8:1-10 The second feeding of a multitude

This second feeding takes place in a remote region of the Decapolis (**8:4**; see also 7:31). The location is definitely different from that of the earlier feeding (6:35-44) as are some of the other details. Mark emphasizes this point by noting that this was *another large crowd* (**8:1**).

Jesus was motivated by compassion for a crowd that had been with him for three days already. By this time their supply of food would have run out, and some of them, particularly those from far away, might faint from sheer exhaustion on their homeward journey. So Jesus approached the disciples, pointing out the problem (**8:2-3**).

The disciples' helpless response suggests they had not yet grasped the lessons on faith that the Master had been teaching them (**8:4**). We are reminded of his comments on their spiritual dullness (see 6:52; 7:18).

Once again, Jesus asked what provisions they had (**8:5**). He took the seven loaves and a few small fish, gave thanks for them, and ordered that they be distributed to the crowd. The food was multiplied to such an extent that not only were some four thousand men fed, but there were also seven basketfuls of leftovers (**8:6-9**). We can easily identify with the spiritual forgetfulness of the disciples and their inability to draw on their previous experience of the Lord's power and glory. The spiritual victories of yesterday will not suffice for today, for each new experience presents a new challenge to faith.

Following the feeding, Jesus sent the crowd on their way and he and the disciples boarded a boat to go to the region of Dalmanutha (**8:10**).

8:11-13 The Pharisees request a sign from heaven

The context of this encounter with the Pharisees is not specified, although comparison of 8:10 and 8:13 suggests he was still in the same region of Dalmanutha. This time the Pharisees asked Jesus to show them *a sign from heaven* as a means of authenticating himself and his ministry. Given that he had already performed many miracles, it is likely that what they were asking for was some dramatic portent in the skies. But their request was not genuine, for they were in a state of unbelief and were merely trying to test him (**8:11**). Jesus was emphatic in his response: *I tell you the truth, no sign will be given* (**8:12**). He is saying that the sort of 'sign' required by this generation will never be provided! God speaks to humans in plain earthly language that we can understand, not in heavenly language. Unbelief tends to ignore plain language, seeking instead the sensational and bizarre.

8:14-21 Warnings about the Pharisees and Herod

Following the encounter with the Pharisees who demanded a sign, Jesus warned the disciples against *the yeast of the Pharisees and that of Herod* (**8:15**). But they misconstrued his warning because they were preoccupied with the mundane matter of a shortage of bread (**8:14, 16**).

Jesus responded with a barrage of questions, focusing on their spiritual condition: *Do you still not see or understand? Are your hearts hardened? Do you … fail to see and … fail to hear? And don't you remember?* He reminded them that he

had twice fed large crowds and challenged them that they still lacked understanding of who he was (**8:17-21**).

8:22-26 Withdrawal to the district of Gaulanitis

The next miracle took place in the village of Bethsaida, that is, Bethsaida Julias, on the eastern side of the lake. Those who brought the blind man *begged Jesus to touch him*, implying healing (**8:22**).

Jesus sought privacy by leading the blind man to the outskirts of the village. The process of healing once again involved physical means, as with the earlier healing of the deaf and dumb man (**8:23**; see also 7:33). In those days, saliva was thought to have therapeutic effects. Jesus' question to the man about whether he had regained his sight is unusual, and so is the fact that the healing took place in stages rather than instantly. At first the man's vision was blurred, so that people looked like trees, which indicated incomplete healing (**8:24**). After a second touch to his eyes, full sight was restored (**8:25**). It may be that Jesus took these unusual steps to aid the man's faith. The incident also suggests that the Lord does sometimes use physical means in the process of divine healing, even though he can also heal without them. It is also clear that God's work in our lives may be instantaneous or it may take place in stages. What is required of us is basic trust in God.

8:27-9:29 Withdrawal to the Region of Iturea

Jesus next moves further north to the villages around the city of Caesarea Philippi. By this time, he and his disciples were far from Galilee.

8:27-30 The great confession at Caesarea Philippi

Against the background of the ongoing spiritual dullness of the disciples, the opportunity now presents itself for Jesus to confront these men regarding their perception of his true identity. He had revealed his power and deity to them on several occasions, but their response has been a bewildered, 'Who is this?' (4:41). Now, in this remote region where they were alone, Jesus asked them, *"Who do people say I am?* (**8:27**). The disciples responded by repeating the common views of the day *John the Baptist … Elijah … one of the prophets* (**8:28**; see also 6:14-15).

But Jesus wanted to know what these men thought of him, rather than what others said. So he pointedly asked them, *But what about you?* Peter's response was on target – *You are the Christ* (**8:29**) This means the Messiah (in Hebrew) or the Anointed One. Confession that Jesus is the Christ is fundamental to developing the personal relationship that transforms one into a Christian. The lesson here is profound: the popular view of Jesus falls short of the mark. It matters that each individual answers the personal question Jesus put to the disciples, 'But what about you?' Jesus' question lingers today, and is directed pointedly at everyone. But at Caesarea Philippi, the disciples were barred from disclosing his identity, because it was not yet the right time to publicize it (**8:30**).

8:31-33 The first prediction of his passion

We do not know exactly when Jesus started to teach about his death, but it may have followed soon after the confession at Caesarea Philippi. Note the word *teach*. It implies that from this point on Jesus made his mission a subject of systematic teaching. That mission involved suffering, rejection, death and resurrection (**8:31**).

This teaching was done *plainly*, unlike the veiled approach he had employed up to this point, especially when he used parables. He clearly set out that the divine plan for the Messiah's career was that he *must suffer … must be killed*. But this was too much for the impetuous Peter! How could the Messiah have such an ignominious career? Peter's *rebuke* was a vehement rejection of the divine plan (**8:32**). No wonder Jesus attributed Peter's stance to Satan (**8:33**). Peter had played into the enemy's hand, even though he was showing genuine concern for his Lord. Apparently, unknown to Peter, there was an ongoing battle, but not with flesh and blood.

8:34-9:1 The requirements for true discipleship

Some time after his first prediction of his impending suffering, Jesus laid down the requirements for those who wanted to be members of the kingdom as true followers of the Messiah. He may have needed to do this because many were beginning to follow him hoping for material gain. He told a crowd and his disciples that it is necessary to deny one's self, that is, to surrender one's will and life to God's purposes and do what God wants. One must also take up one's cross, that is, be prepared to suffer for the cause of the Messiah (**8:34**; see also Phil 1:29). Self stands in the way of genuine discipleship and prevents identifying with Jesus should suffering become necessary.

Jesus' explanation of these requirements only makes sense in the divine economy. Saving one's life (or refusal to die to self) inevitably results in spiritual death; losing one's life (self-denial or surrender of life and will to God) for the cause of Christ and the gospel inevitably leads to spiritual life (**8:35**). To cradle one's life in one's hand is a sure way to lose it in the long run. Jesus uses a commercial analogy: a merchant hopes to make a gain or profit from an investment rather than forfeiting it, that is, losing what he invested (**8:36**). So if a wise merchant is confronted with an opportunity to exchange two commodities, *the whole world* and *his soul*, he will rapidly decide that this would be a foolish trade (**8:37**). A foolish merchant will forfeit everything!

Cross-bearing or suffering involves shame from a human standpoint. But a true disciple is willing to suffer shame now, *in this adulterous and sinful generation*, because of the eternal consequence when the *Son of Man* returns as judge (**8:38**; see also Dan 7:13-14).

Jesus assured his listeners that the truth of what he was saying would be upheld by some imminent event in which they would have a foretaste of *the kingdom of God come with power* (**9:1**). Mark then immediately proceeds to describe the event to which Jesus was referring.

9:2-13 The transfiguration

The transfiguration must have taken place somewhere in the vicinity of Caesarea Philippi, probably on Mount Hermon. *After six days* refers back to the solemn promise in the previous verse that 'some', who are now revealed to be Peter, James and John, would see the kingdom of God come with power in their lifetime. Those three constituted the inner circle of his followers (**9:2**). While they were watching, he was *transfigured* or metamorphosed. His outward appearance was completely transformed, allowing the trio to catch a glimpse of his inner glory. Even his clothes reflected unsurpassed glory, for they appeared to be of a whiteness or purity unequalled on earth (**9:3**). This was indeed a foretaste of 'the kingdom of God come with power' (9:1). The presence of the glory of God among humans results in a transformation.

The disciples also saw two men, whom they recognized as *Elijah and Moses* representing the Prophets and the Law, speaking with Jesus (**9:4**). It is not clear whether these men were seen in a vision or whether they were briefly resurrected, but what is clear is that in Jesus the Law and the Prophets converge.

Peter, with characteristic impetuousness, suggested that this was a place to linger, obviously not knowing what to say or how to respond (**9:5-6**). But he was not taking into account the fact that the Messiah 'must suffer many things' (8:31). Even members of Jesus' inner circle still failed to understand him and his mission.

In the OT, clouds often reveal or conceal God's glory (see Exod 16:10; 19:9; 24:15-17; 33:10). Here, the cloud that enveloped them served to conceal the glory that had been momentarily revealed. The cloud was accompanied by a heavenly attestation – the second one in this gospel (see 1:11) – in which the Father corroborated Jesus' words and deeds and announced the only appropriate response from humans: *Listen to him!* (**9:7**). Obedience is the only appropriate response when God's voice is heard: 'See to it that you do not refuse him who speaks' (Heb 12:25). After the voice was heard, the glory was promptly veiled once more (**9:8**). The kingdom that some had seen come in power and glory must for now be concealed. The three disciples were indeed a privileged group!

Given that this vision was only for some, Jesus told them to keep it a secret until after his resurrection (**9:9**). But as they descended the mountain, the three kept discussing the subject of *rising from the dead* (**9:10**). They could not reconcile the promise of a future manifestation of the Messiah's glory with the equally promised humiliation.

PRAYER

Prayer is an acknowledgement that there is an invisible superior realm that affects the physical and visible world. Christians believe that God is the sovereign creator and sustainer of the universe. He does not need our prayers to move him to action. So the question is, why pray? The answer depends on an understanding of how God implements his will in the universe.

God delegated dominion over the earth to human beings (Ps 8:4-8). He entrusted them with responsibility and authority, kept in check by lines of accountability (Matt 12:36-37; Rom 2:6). Governance by delegation ensures individual initiative and fosters imagination, creativity and development. Yet in the course of carrying out our God-given responsibilities, we find it necessary to consult God to ensure that we are acting in accordance with his will. St. Paul accurately describes our role as 'working together with God' (1 Cor 3:9). The situation is similar to that in African society, in which elders did not have to make decisions about petty matters but their advice was valued when difficulties were encountered or serious decisions had to be made.

At first, communication with God flowed freely, but the fall introduced another communicator, on whose commands contradicted those of God. God could no longer rely on humans to accomplish his will on earth. The OT contains many examples of people acting presumptuously without consulting God for direction (e.g. 2 Chr 7:14; 14:4; 15:12). Dire consequences usually followed.

In the NT, delegated authority was passed from the first Adam to the second Adam, Jesus Christ, because he completely accomplished God's will on earth (Matt 28:18; John 5:19; 5:30; Eph 1:22-23). Consequently Jesus Christ now provides access to God's blessings (John 14:6; Eph 2:18; 3:12). He guarantees answers to prayers (John 14:13-14). Christians have no other way to communicate with God and to receive his blessings and benefits except through Christ.

Christ provided a model prayer for us in Matthew 6:9-13. It teaches that prayer is rooted in the desire to glorify God, and that to be effective it must be in accordance with his will (Matt 6:10; 1 John 5:14-15). It reminds us that God is our ultimate provider and sustainer, and that relationships, both human and divine, are sustained by forgiveness. It also reminds us that God is our deliverer and that he reigns over all things.

At times of crisis, prayer was often accompanied by fasting (Judg 20:26; 1 Sam 7:6; Ezra 8:21-23). Fasting continued in the NT as a way of making persistent requests regarding important actions (Acts 13:2-3; 14:23; 23:12; 27:9). It expresses humility, sorrow, repentance, earnestness and a desire for God's manifest presence. But God makes it clear that it is not to preoccupy us to the exclusion of a concern for the physical needs of others (Isaiah 58:6-9).

Our communication in prayer is imperfect unless aided by the Holy Spirit (Eph 6:18). Praying in the Spirit is not to be thought of as exercising techniques of mind control in order to receive spiritual experiences. Rather, it involves cultivating a relationship with the Holy Spirit and allowing him to determine how we should pray and what we should pray for (Rom 8:26-27).

Bonifes Adoyo

Nor could they work out where Elijah fitted into the scheme of things. They had been taught that *Elijah must come first* (**9:11**; see Mal 3:1; 4:5-6) to restore things before the Messiah's advent. Elijah had appeared to them, but surely he ought also to appear to Israel? Jesus agreed with the experts that Elijah would come before the Messiah, but he pointed out that scribal teaching had failed to mention the necessity of a suffering Messiah, as well as a suffering Elijah (**9:12**). Isaiah 53 mentions the suffering of the Messiah, and 1 Kings 19:2-10 speaks of the suffering of Elijah. But Elijah (that is John the Baptist) had already come to set straight the crooked (1:3-5), though he had been rejected (**9:13**; see 1:14; 6:14-29). Jesus declared this truth with solemn affirmation of its veracity. Israel was as unready to receive a suffering Elijah as it was to receive a suffering Messiah. Humans must receive the Saviour of God's own design and not a saviour of their own making.

9:14-29 Power encounter

When they arrived at the foot of the mountain, they found argument and confrontation. The argument was between the disciples who had remained behind and the teachers of the law. There was great excitement in the crowd when it was seen that Jesus was returning (**9:14-15**).

Jesus' question may have been directed to his disciples (**9:16**). However, the man in the crowd who responded was the anguished father of a boy who was tormented by an evil spirit that had robbed him of speech (**9:17**) and hearing (**9:25**). The prognosis was terrible. There was evidence of epilepsy (**9:18**), but that was not all that was wrong (see **9:20, 26**). The father had wanted Jesus to heal his son (9:17), but in his absence he had approached the disciples. They were no strangers to casting out evil spirits (see 6:7, 13), but on this occasion *they could not* (**9:18**). This answer to Jesus' question suggests that the disciples' failure was what the argument with the teachers of the law had been about. Were they frauds? Had their Master deserted them? There was much to argue about.

The disciples' failure was in part due to unbelief, although there were other reasons too (see **9:29**). Jesus expressed impatience with the disciples –*O unbelieving generation ... How long ... ?* (**9:19**), solely because time was running out. He had been patient with their spiritual dullness, but he would not be there with them for much longer. For now, however, he stepped in to rescue the situation.

The boy was suffering from no ordinary epilepsy (**9:20**). The father's answer to Jesus' question about the case history (**9:21**) showed that there was a destructive manifestation, as it sought *to kill him* (**9:22**). The father also demonstrated that he was part of the 'unbelieving generation' when he asked Jesus to heal him, *if you can* (9:22). Jesus promptly corrected him, *Everything is possible for him who believes* (**9:23**). The poor man's quick response implies that he would like to have faith, if only Jesus would help him overcome his unbelief (**9:24**). While unbelief sees impossibilities, faith sees possibilities because faith draws on the unlimited resources of heaven. In the ensuing encounter, Jesus gave an authoritative command to the *deaf and mute spirit* to *come out … and never enter him again* (**9:25**). The evil spirit would not leave without a fight. The poor boy suffered from its wrath as it threw him into a violent convulsion that left him as though dead (**9:26**). It is characteristic of Satan to kill and wreak havoc. By contrast, the character of Jesus is to give life. Jesus therefore revived the boy and he was able to stand up (**9:27**).

Of course, the disciples were full of questions: *Why couldn't we … ?* This question was best addressed indoors, in privacy (**9:28**), away from the hearing of the crowd and the teachers of the law with whom the disciples had been arguing (9:14, 16). Jesus' explanation about *this kind* does not suggest that the disciples had not prayed when attempting to cast out the demon. Rather, their hearts had not been prepared. Only time spent alone with God before such an encounter makes victory possible. While fasting should accompany serious sessions of prayer, the textual evidence suggests that the Lord did not link the two on this occasion (**9:29**).

The major lesson here, in addition to the need for prayer, is that in a case like this we need to see beyond the physical. These days, we tend to dismiss any explanations that are not scientific. But the child Jesus healed here was not suffering purely from epilepsy; an evil spirit was also involved. Materialistic thinking is Western in origin. Asian and African cosmology are quite familiar with the age-old challenge of the spirit realm. An awareness of it is even creeping into the West with the rise of New Age ideas.

9:30–10:52 The Journey to Jerusalem

9:30-32 The Second Prediction of his Passion
After this, Jesus and his disciples began to travel southward. They would pass through Galilee, but this time their aim was not to attract attention (**9:30**). Jesus wanted to focus on *teaching his disciples* because he knew that time was short and they were still spiritually dull. We can assume that his teaching, as summarized here by Mark,

focused on his impending betrayal, death and resurrection (**9:31**), although he also addressed other topics.

This is the second recorded prediction of his passion. It is striking that even at this point in his ministry, despite all he had said plainly (see 8:32) and despite the fact that he was heading towards the showdown in Jerusalem, the disciples still *did not understand*. It is no wonder they were afraid to ask for more clarification (**9:32**).

9:33-37 Who Is the Greatest?
When the travellers reached Capernaum in Galilee and entered a house to rest, Jesus confronted his disciples about an incident that occurred along the way. He asked them what they had been arguing, or literally bickering, about (**9:33**). They must have been too ashamed to answer, because they had been fighting about *who was the greatest* (**9:34**). They knew that something important was going to happen in Jerusalem, and their understanding of the kingdom entailed power and prestige.

Jesus then taught them another important lesson as time was running out. *If anyone wants to be first, he must be the very last, and the servant of all* (**9:35**). In other words, they were not to seek honour but to defer to one another. This is a radical tenet of the kingdom of God. Lowliness is the pathway to greatness in the kingdom. To help them understand what he meant, Jesus resorted to an object lesson. He called over a little child to *stand among them*, emphasizing the contrast in status. Then he took the child *in his arms*, illustrating his acceptance of this little one. His true followers must accept the principle he was laying down here. No one can claim to accept the Father and reject Jesus the Son; to welcome one is to welcome the other (**9:37**).

9:38-41 An Exclusive Right to Jesus?
The setting of this incident is not stated, but it forms part of the series of opportunities to teach the disciples how to live together (see the concluding instruction in 9:50). The issue here was about accreditation and not just exorcism. Stopping someone from doing an act in Jesus' name just because *he is not one of us* demonstrates a fundamental misconception (**9:38**). The disciples were acting as if they had exclusive rights to Jesus, much like other students did with their rabbis. What Jesus focused on was the fact that by using Jesus' name this exorcist was acknowledging Jesus' authority, and consequently demonstrating faith in him (**9:39**). What a lesson for us today, who tend to make too much of group affiliations and denominations. All who genuinely fall under the authority of Jesus Christ, regardless of their affiliations, constitute one body in Christ.

Jesus emphatically told his men to stop interfering with this man, for he was a friend and not a foe. He used an adage to buttress his point: *for whoever is not against us is for us* (**9:40**). The point does not just apply to this exorcist;

God will reward *anyone* who does a good deed for Jesus' followers in the authority (name) of Jesus Christ (**9:41**).

9:42-50 Warning Against Being a Stumbling Block

Jesus' warning about causing *little ones who believe in me to sin* (**9:42**) does not apply only to children but to all who are children of the kingdom. Discouraging someone who believes in Christ is a way to make them stumble. The penalty of having *a large millstone tied around his neck* indicates severe consequences in this life, but it not equivalent to eternal damnation.

There are a number of things that can make someone stumble. Jesus here mentions only a few that may pose obstacles within ourselves and makes the point that all potential causes of sin must be done away with. He is not speaking of literal but figurative severance, doing away with anything that would prevent one's entry into the kingdom of God. The *hand* (**9:43**), the *foot* (**9:45**) and the *eye* (**9:47**) are all illustrative. None of these earthly possessions, so to speak, should be allowed to prevent anyone's entry into the kingdom.

The alternative to entering the kingdom is eternal damnation in hell (9:47). Although it is now fashionable to play down the reality of hell, the reader must note the terrible characteristics of this ultimate abode of those who miss the kingdom. Jesus describes it in terms of a quotation from Isaiah 66:24. (In some manuscripts, the words of **9:48** are repeated in **9:44** and **9:46**. The evidence is, however, stronger for having the phrases occur just here in 9:48) The description, *their worm does not die* is a reference to Isaiah's vision (Isa 66:24), where the godless lie slain and their corpses breed worms perpetually. The next line is a picture of incineration, where the fire amidst the rubble in which the wicked lie slain never goes out. This vividly depicts the horror of spiritual ruination. The hearers (and later the readers) are to use all means to avoid sharing the terminal destination of the ungodly.

Jesus then contrasts the unquenchable fire of hell with another kind of fire, which purifies and which is used to test the deeds of the children of the kingdom, who are *salted with fire* (**9:49**). He is probably referring to the trials and tests of the last days, which God uses to purify the children of the kingdom.

The next verse presents quite a different use of salt, namely its use in the home. The children of the kingdom constitute the salt of the earth (see also Matt 5:13). To *have salt in yourselves* (**9:50**) is a charge to the children of the kingdom to live up to their calling and so serve as worthy examples (or 'preservatives') in a sinful world. The squabbling and rivalry among the disciples (9:33-34) threatened this salt-like character, hence Jesus' command that they live at peace with each other. The positive quality of life among believers should serve as a hope or 'salt' for the world. Factions and divisions among believers in Christ have a destructive effect upon their testimony.

10:1-12 Teaching on Divorce

The setting now moves to Judea, following a journey that must have involved a detour around the region of Samaria and a crossing of the Jordan (**10:1**). There Jesus meets some Pharisees, who try to test him by asking *Is it lawful for a man to divorce his wife?*, or in other words, is divorce sanctioned by the law? (**10:2**).

Jesus' initial response was to ask them what they thought Moses had *commanded* in this regard (**10:3**). In reply they said Moses had *permitted* divorce (**10:4**; see Deut 24:1-4). Note the different verb forms used by Jesus and the Pharisees. The Pharisees apparently acknowledged that Mosaic code permitted but did not command divorce.

Jesus then gave a clearer explanation of the Mosaic law on this matter. He taught that this Mosaic code permitted or tolerated divorce because of the hardness of people's hearts (**10:5**). But he went on to cite Genesis, the book of beginnings, to show the Creator's original intention was that marriage should produce 'one flesh', a permanent union in life, in which the couple were *no longer two, but one* (**10:8**; see also Gen 2:24).

The provision in Deuteronomy was clearly meant to minimize the effects of the evil of divorce on the woman. The issuing of a certificate of divorce protected the woman against accusations that she was a prostitute. It was proof that she had been sent away by her husband. If she went on to marry someone else, she was prohibited thereafter from returning to the first husband. Jesus' concluding point says it all: *what God has joined together, let man not separate* (**10:9**). In other words, God joins, he does not separate. Humans are, therefore, prohibited from cutting asunder what God has joined together. In stating this Jesus prohibited divorce. His answer to their question about the legality of divorce was clearly to prohibit it (10:9).

The so-called 'exception clause' in Matthew 5:32 and 19:9 should not be interpreted as contradicting this prohibition. It specifically addresses the toleration for divorce found in the Mosaic code and its interpretation by the Jews. It is no coincidence that that comment is found only in Matthew – the gospel to the Jews – and not in Mark or Luke – both intended for Gentile audiences.

The disciples apparently had difficulty with what Jesus said about divorce, and returned to the topic once they were alone with him (**10:10**). Matthew's account throws some light on what was bothering them. They felt that Jesus' teaching imposed such bondage that marriage became undesirable (Matt 19:10). But God's commandments are not burdensome; rather, it is our sin that makes us think that God is placing us under bondage. God's intention is for marriage to be a lifelong *bond* rather than a miserable *bondage* or trap.

In giving further clarification to the disciples, Jesus condemned both divorce and re-marriage, whether initiated by the man (**10:11**) or by the woman (**10:12**). (Since a Jewish woman could only 'separate' from her husband but not 'divorce' him, Jesus may have been thinking of Gentile women when he made this comment.) Jesus' teaching clearly has men and women on an equal footing. The remarriage of either constitutes *adultery* against the partner, apparently because the paper granting the divorce does not abrogate the union, in God's sight. This explains the Pauline injunction in 1 Cor 7:10-11. In view of the massive assault on the divine institution of marriage today, the children of God need to teach and live by Jesus' words on this matter.

10:13-16 Blessing Little Children

Jewish rabbis customarily blessed children, and so people brought little children to Jesus to be blessed. Once again, the disciples betrayed spiritual insensitivity because they rebuked those who had brought the children (**10:13**). Jesus' response was an indignant rebuke to the disciples, telling them the children should be allowed to come to him (**10:14**). If there is room in the kingdom for little children, certainly there is room for them with the Master. What is more, children are an object lesson in humility to all who wish to enter the kingdom of God (**10:15**). The narrative concludes with vivid and moving image of Jesus cuddling the children, laying his hands on them and blessing them (**10:16**). His example is an important lesson for today, particularly in cultures where children are expected to be seen and not heard. His words also underline the importance of children's ministry.

10:17-31 Materialism and the Kingdom of God

As Jesus set out one day to continue his journey to Jerusalem, he was met by a rich young man who took the initiative in asking Jesus what he must do to inherit eternal life. He addressed Jesus as *Good teacher*, which was an unusual form of address (**10:17**). Jesus responded by asking him why he used the word "good", and pointing out that *No one is good – except God alone* (**10:18**). Here Jesus was not denying that he was 'good'. Rather, he was pressing the man to see the logical implication of addressing him as 'good', namely that he is God! He was telling a self-centred and self-righteous man (**10:19-20**) that only God is truly good.

Then came the acid test. Was he prepared to part with his earthly possessions and follow the Master? Did he love material possessions more than he loved Jesus? He failed the test, and left in sorrow (**10:21-22**).

There tends to be a popular belief that the rich have a greater chance of eternal life because they have the resources to give alms or do good deeds. Jesus challenged that belief with his statement *How hard it is for the rich to enter the kingdom of God!* Riches are actually a potential stumbling block or barrier to salvation (**10:23-25**). The disciples were amazed at this, exclaiming that if even the rich

failed, *who then can be saved* (**10:26**). The answer is that no human being can earn salvation; only God can save people (**10:27**).

At this point Peter spoke up, pointing out that he and the other disciples had done what the rich young man had refused to do, giving up everything to follow Jesus (**10:28**). His unspoken question is, 'What will be our reward?' In response, Jesus acknowledges that the call to discipleship is radical and sometimes entails leaving one's home, brothers, sisters, mother, father, children or fields for him and the kingdom's sake (**10:29**). Nothing should be too costly to renounce, if it prevents one from following Jesus. But the rewards of discipleship include receiving multiple rewards that span both time and eternity (**10:30**).

Jesus concludes with a solemn warning for the overconfident, those who depend on their own efforts or on material possession. These people may be *first* in human eyes. But God values those who are the *last,* that is, people who do not rely on their own efforts or material wealth but on the God with whom all things are possible (**10:31**).

10:32-34 The Third Prediction of His Passion

Jesus' determination to press on to Jerusalem astonished his disciples, while others among his followers were fearful about the coming confrontation (**10:32a**). On the way, he continued to instruct the Twelve privately (**10:32b**; see also 8:31-32; 9:31). This was the third and final prediction of his passion, and the first time he specifically identified Jerusalem as the place where it would happen. As before, he mentioned his betrayal into the hands of the religious establishment, the death sentence, being handed over to Gentiles, who would humiliate and kill him, and his victory over death after three days (**10:33-34**).

10:35-45 The Request of the Zebedee Brothers

The *Then* ... that introduces this incident is significant, for it makes it clear that this new squabble arose immediately after Jesus' prediction of his passion. A similar squabble had followed his previous mention of it (see 9:30-33). This time the Zebedee brothers sparked it, trying privately to upstage the others. They were asking Jesus for a blank cheque, so to speak, when they asked him to grant *whatever we ask* (**10:35**). Specifically, what they wanted was to have the two most important places of honour in the kingdom when he revealed his glory, as he was apparently about to do (**10:36-37**).

In his reply, Jesus plainly told them that their request revealed their ignorance of the true nature of the kingdom on offer at this time. While they concentrated on his glory, they were ignoring what he had said about his passion. There was the cup to drink and the baptism to come – both of which symbolized suffering. But to his question *Can you ...?* (**10:38**), they promptly replied, *We can* (**10:39**). Jesus then predicted that they would indeed share in his cup of suffering (see Acts 12:2; Rev 1:9). But the seats of honour were not his to grant. Besides, God had prepared those positions for someone else (**10:40**). In the kingdom of God, knowing someone who can pull strings is not what determines honour.

Unfortunately, news of the request reached the other ten disciples, who were *indignant* with the two brothers. But their intense anger was borne of equally selfish motives. The earlier instruction that they should practise childlike humility had fallen on deaf ears (**10:41**; see also 9:35-37, 50b). Jesus must have felt anguish that, so close to the end of his ministry, he was still apparently getting nowhere with these men. They continued to be slow to understand spiritual matters. So the Teacher took pains to show them the sharp difference between kingdoms ruled by Gentiles (or unbelievers) and the kingdom of God. Gentiles or pagans practise two leadership principles: they *lord it over* others, that is, throw their weight around, and they *exercise authority*, or literally, play the tyrant (**10:42-44**). By contrast, in the kingdom of God, the one who is first takes the lead in serving others. The Son of Man is the supreme example to follow: his principle of leadership is self-giving service, as he gives his life for a ransom (**10:43-45**).

10:47-52 The Faith of Blind Bartimaeus

The journey to Jerusalem took Jesus and the disciples through the city of Jericho, where a blind beggar named Bartimaeus (Mark translated the Aramaic name for his Roman audience) drew his attention (**10:46**). Although informed that *Jesus of Nazareth* was passing by, Bartimaeus demonstrated faith by using the messianic title *Jesus, Son of David* (**10:47**). Some thought he was a nuisance and tried unsuccessfully to silence him (**10:48**), but his persistence paid off, as Jesus stopped to attend to him (**10:49-51**). Jesus wrong-footed those who thought he couldn't care for a mere beggar. Jesus granted his request for healing, noting that Bartimaeus had exercised faith (**10:52**). Physical blindness is no obstacle to spiritual sight; conversely, physical sight is no guarantee of spiritual sight.

11:1-13:37 The Ministry in Jerusalem

11:1-11 Entry into Jerusalem

The entry into Jerusalem was grand! From Bethphage and Bethany, two villages at the foot of the Mount of Olives, Jesus sent two unidentified disciples on a faith mission to go and bring a particular colt from the village just ahead (**11:1-3a**). They probably were not known in the area, as will be seen in **11:4-5**. While some would argue that this was something that Jesus had organized in advance, it is as likely that this episode attests to his omniscience. He knew where they would find the colt, he knew what questions would be asked, and he knew the outcome. *The Lord needs it*

was a sufficient answer to all the questions. The owner may have been a sympathizer or a disciple, we are not told. But the colt was needed for a temporary mission and Jesus *will send it back here shortly* (**11:3b**).

The mission went exactly as Jesus had predicted (**11:4-6**). They brought the colt to him and prepared it for him to ride on (**11:7**). It is significant that Jesus chose to ride triumphantly into Jerusalem, as a king. From now on he made no attempt to conceal his identity as the Messiah. The crowd responded spontaneously, spreading their clothes and branches along his pathway (**11:8**).

Shouts of *Hosanna!* (Hebrew 'save now') and *Blessed is he who comes in the name of the Lord* (**11:9**) rang in the air. The crowd were quoting from Psalm 118:25-26, which is part of the *Hallel* psalms (Ps 113-118), sung in festive processions and at the Passover meal (see 14:26). The crowd voiced a prayer expressing messianic hope, *Blessed is the coming kingdom of our father David* (**11:10**). They probably did not understand the import of their action, but there was no doubt about the excitement generated. Little did they realize that what they were praying for was in the process of being fulfilled.

After entering Jerusalem, Jesus went straight to the temple, inspected it and then left for Bethany to spend the night there (**11:11**). That would be his base as he entered into the passion week.

11:12-25 Hypocrisy Exposed

11:12-14 Hypocrisy and the fig tree

Early the next morning Jesus and his disciples headed back to Jerusalem, apparently leaving before breakfast (**11:12**). When Jesus saw a fig tree that already had leaves, which are the sign of fruit-bearing, but no coming figs, he took it as an opportunity to teach a fundamental lesson about appearances that don't match reality. He may have chosen a fig tree to make his point because in the OT a fig tree is sometimes a symbol for the nation of Israel (see Mic 7:1; Jer 8:13). The incident that follows underlines his point about the inner decay of Israel.

11:15-19 Hypocrisy of the religious establishment

On entering the temple area, Jesus found that the Court of the Gentiles was bustling with commercial activity. Pilgrims who had brought their own sacrifices from their homes had to have the animals inspected. If they were found unsuitable, as they often were, the pilgrims would have to buy another animal from one of the merchants conducting a thriving business in the temple courts. Other entrepreneurs had set themselves up as money-changers, exchanging foreign currency for coins that could be used in the temple. Still others were using the temple courts as a thoroughfare or shortcut (**11:15-16**).

Jesus was compelled to confront this hypocrisy and the mixing of the sacred and the profane in the name of religion. He justified his action from the Scriptures, as he taught the crowd that God had intended the temple to be *a house of prayer for all nations* (Isa 56:7), but the Court of the Gentiles had been turned into a market, and worse. In calling it *a den of robbers* Jesus was quoting Jeremiah 7:11, where God condemned hypocritical worship which had lost sight of its purpose (**11:17**). Those who had permitted the temple to be used in this way were no better than robbers. Unfortunately, Jesus' lesson is still relevant today. Practices that were originally meant to help worshippers can become corrupted and lose their meaning.

Jesus' actions did not sit well with the religious establishment, who felt that he was disturbing the status quo. It was time to get rid of him before they lost their influence with the masses (**11:18**).

The clearing of the temple and the teaching that followed took up the first of the days of passion week. When evening came, Jesus left the city and returned to Bethany (**11:19**).

11:20-25 Lesson from the withered fig tree

The next morning as they retraced the route back to the city, they noticed the same fig tree they had seen before (**11:20**; see 11:11). Peter remembered what Jesus has said on the previous day. Jesus had pronounced judgment on the seeming hypocrisy of the fig tree, which symbolized the nation's hypocrisy. By judging the tree, he was demonstrating how the nation's hypocrisy would be judged. Peter, however, missed the point about judgment and misinterpreted what Jesus was doing as simply cursing the tree (**11:21**). He was surprised at the rapid result of Jesus' action.

In response, Jesus pointed out that faith in the living God can move mountains (**11:23**). Such faith is a potent condition for effectual prayer (**11:24**). But just as unbelief is a barrier to effectual prayer, so is an unforgiving spirit (**11:25**). Such a spirit will hinder both prayer and faith. This point is repeated in **11:26**, but this verse does not occur in many ancient copies of Mark's gospel, and may be an accidental duplication. It is omitted in the NIV.

11:27-33 Jesus' Authority Questioned

It was probably on the same day, the second full day of the passion week, that Jesus encountered the chief priests, the teachers of the law and the elders (**11:27**). These three groups were represented on the Sanhedrin, the body that governed Jewish religious life and thus represented the Establishment.

This group wanted to know what Jesus' credentials were (that is, where his authority came from) and who had given him authority to act like this. It is likely that *these things* refers to his entire ministry, which had a record of opposition to the religious status quo, while *this* refers specifically to his cleansing of the temple (**11:28b**). Rabbinic argu-

ment allowed for rhetorical questions, and so Jesus turned the tables on them. If they answered his question about the source of John's ministry (*baptism*), he would answer their own question (**11:29-30**). He gave them the only two possible answers: *from heaven, or from men*. Which would they choose? By asking this question, Jesus was implying a direct link between the authority for his ministry and that for John's.

His opponents were boxed into a tight corner, as is clear from their discussion of the options. To admit that John's ministry had been inspired by God would constitute self-condemnation, for they had rejected John, and ultimately God's purpose (**11:31**). But they dared not say that it had been purely a human ministry, for that would incur the people's wrath (**11:32**). The populace believed that John was God's spokesman (*a prophet*). So they hypocritically pleaded ignorance (**11:33**). Since they did not fulfil their end of the bargain, he was not obliged to answer their question. The representatives of the Sanhedrin had been outwitted! Jesus saw no reason to discuss who he was with people who were determined not to believe anything he said.

12:1-12 The Parable of the Defiant Tenants

Instead of answering their question, Jesus launched into a parable about tenants in a vineyard. Those referred to as *them* certainly included the men from the Sanhedrin. They would easily have understood his parable without any further interpretation (**12:1**).

In this parable, God was the *farmer*, Israel the *vineyard*, and the religious leaders the *tenants*. The servants who were sent at harvest time to collect the produce were the prophets who had come in the name of the Lord (**12:1-2**). Some of these the tenants assaulted, others they killed, until the owner had only *one left to send, a son*, clearly a reference to Jesus himself (**12:3-6**). The fate that befell this son was predictive of how they would treat Jesus (**12:7-8**). The parable concluded with a description of God's wrath and judgment of the tenants, and an assurance that after their demise the vineyard would be given to others (**12:9**).

Jesus rooted the outcome of this parable in the testimony of Scripture. He cited the same Hallel psalm the crowd had sang at the triumphal entry: *'The stone the builders rejected has become the capstone'* (**12:10**; see Ps 118:22-23). In other words, in God's good purpose, the one destined for rejection will triumph over all his foes. The result can only be described as of the Lord and *marvellous* (**12:11**).

An African proverb states, 'the one at whom a parable is told clearly knows to whom it is directed!' This was certainly true here, and the Jewish leaders began to plot his arrest for they recognized that he had told the parable *against them*. However, their plans could not be carried out right away because they feared the crowd's reaction (**12:12**).

12:13-17 Pharisees and Herodians Try to Snare Jesus

Later *they*, the leaders, sent other agents to try to ensnare Jesus with his own words. They were attempting to orchestrate the conditions in which he would slip up. The partners in this plot were strange bedfellows. The Herodians were a political grouping who supported Herod; in ordinary circumstances the religious Pharisees would have wanted nothing to do with them (**12:13**).

The smooth flattery with which this group introduced their question smacked of political intrigue. They said he combined *integrity* with principled resolve, so that he was not *swayed by men*. In addition, he was known to teach only the truth. So what were his views on paying tax to Caesar? (**12:14-15a**). If Jesus were to support the paying of taxes, he would lose the support of the people who resented the Roman overlords. However, if he said they should not pay taxes, he could be arrested by the Herodians who, through Herod, were political allies of the Roman emperor.

Jesus was not swayed by their flattery, for he immediately recognized that this was not a sincere question (**12:15b**). His answer caught them off guard: '*Give to Caesar what is Caesar's and to God what is God's.* Anyone who used Caesar's coins implicitly recognized that Caesar had some authority (**12:16**; see also Rom 13:1-7). But God is sovereign over Caesar and over everything else. Thus an obligation to the state is not necessarily incompatible with one's obligations to God. In the end the very people who came hoping to use Jesus' words to trap him were dumbfounded by his words (**12:17**). He could not be assailed for what he had said.

12:18-27 Sadducees Question Jesus

The Pharisees and Herodians had tried and failed to trap Jesus. Now it was the turn of the Sadducees (**12:18**), a group who recognized only the Pentateuch as divinely inspired. They exercised considerable influence in the Sanhedrin and were also represented among the priests. They asked Jesus about a disputed point of theology, specifically in relation to whether there was life after death. They argued that there was not and, in an attempt to ridicule the position of those who argued that there was, they outlined a situation that could arise from an application of the law given in Deuteronomy 25:5-6 (**12:19**). One woman survived seven brothers, each of whom had been married to her in succession: whose wife would she be in the afterlife? (**12:20-23**).

Jesus' first response was to point out their ignorance of the power of God because they did not believe in the world of spirits or angels. They were also ignorant of the Scriptures, as he would demonstrate shortly (**12:24**). Our Lord then clarified his earlier teaching on marriage. He had taught that marriage is indissoluble (10:9), but now he pointed out that marriage is dissolved at death and does

not exist in a future life. After resurrection, humans are like angels who do not marry (**12:25**).

Then he turned to the question of resurrection, which underlay their specific question about marriage. He demonstrated their ignorance of Scripture by quoting evidence of the resurrection in *the book of Moses*, the part of the OT that they accepted (**12:26**). Moses wrote that Jehovah himself had said, *I am the God of Abraham … Isaac, and … Jacob* (Exod 3:6). The patriarchs were long dead when Jehovah spoke these words, but he still maintained that he was their God. If God continued to be the God of these men long dead, they must continue to exist (**12:27**). Jesus uses this verse to argue that if the soul continues to exist after this life, it is not farfetched to hold that it will reunite with the body later on, albeit in some other form of existence. He concluded that the Sadducees' position was badly flawed.

12:28-34 The Greatest Commandment

An unidentified teacher of the law had been listening to the previous debate. He apparently agreed with Jesus' position, and so he asked his own question. He wished to know which is the most important of all the commandments (**12:28**).

Jesus, citing the *Shema*, said that supreme love for God is the weightiest of all the commandments (**12:29-30**; see also Deut 6:4-5). But, he went on, this is inseparably linked to Leviticus 19:18, which commands love for others (**12:31**). The teacher of the law concurred with Jesus that the importance of obeying these two commands surpassed the importance of performing any other religious duties (**12:32-33**).

Jesus rated this pious Jew as *not far from the kingdom of God* (**12:34**). The man had demonstrated keen insight into the true place of religious duties. But he was still outside the kingdom because his understanding was only at the intellectual level. He still needed to surrender his will to the Master.

Mark records that this was the last time his opponents attempted to engage Jesus in debate (**12:34b**).

12:35-37 Jesus Asks a Question

Since Jesus had answered all the questions put to him by his adversaries, he now put his own question to them, to silence the opposition totally. He asked them about the basis for the rabbinic position that identified the Christ as David's son (**12:35**). He quoted Psalm 110:1 in which David, the author of the psalm, speaks of the Messiah. David speaks of *the Lord* (Jehovah) as blessing *my Lord* (Adonai) (**12:36**). How can the Christ be both David's son and his Lord (Adonai)? How did they understand this relationship? (**12:37**). The point he was making was that Holy Spirit had spoken through David to point out that the Christ is no mere son, but is greater even than David. His teaching was a delight to the crowd, even if they did not fully understand it or recognize that the Christ is in fact Lord of all. No answer was forthcoming from his adversaries.

12:38-40 Jesus Warns Against Hypocrisy

Turning from what is taught to those who teach it, Jesus warned the people to beware of the teachers of the law. These men enjoyed being important, wearing impressive clothes, being greeted in public places, and being acknowledged as leaders at the synagogues where they worshipped, and at banquets (**12:38-39**). But in reality they preyed on the innocent and the vulnerable, represented by defenceless widows. Worse still, they tried to mask their evil with pretentious, lengthy public prayers (**12:40**). Jesus warned that people who act like this will be judged harshly. Unfortunately, this warning still rings true in our day. Both the people of God and ministers of the gospel must beware of falling into habits like these that will surely incur God's wrath.

This warning marked the conclusion of Jesus' public ministry in Jerusalem. From here on, he focuses on private instruction of his disciples.

12:41-44 True Giving – The Widow's Mite

As Jesus was sitting in the temple area, probably in the Court of the Women, he noticed a poor widow who was among those giving offerings. Mark deliberately juxtaposed this incident with the preceding warning about the teachers of the law, who preyed upon poor widows. The teachers of the law represented the greedy, who grabbed and devoured everything, using religion as a pretext. By contrast, this poor widow gave everything in true worship to God. In human terms, she was the one who gave the least, *a fraction of a penny*, as compared to the *large amounts* the rich *threw in* (**12:41-42**). But from God's standpoint, she had given the most. The rich gave what they could easily spare, but the poor widow *put in everything* (**12:43-44**). True giving is sacrificial.

13:1-37 The Olivet Discourse

Most probably still on the second full day of the passion week, as he was leaving the temple, the disciples drew Jesus' attention to the *massive stones* of the temple (**13:1**). Josephus, the ancient Jewish historian, confirms that they had reason to be impressed. Herod Antipas (*the Fox*) was still finishing the temple his father, Herod the Great, had begun. It was famous as one of the architectural wonders of the Roman world. Even today visitors to the Temple Mount can see the remains of some of these massive stones. But Jesus was not impressed. He predicted that the stones would *be thrown down* (**13:2**) in judgment. This foretold total destruction.

The scene now moves to the Mount of Olives, from which there is a good view of the city and the temple. The two pairs of brothers – Peter and Andrew, James and John – came to Jesus privately and asked him to elaborate on his comment. They were interested in when the destruction would take place and what signs they should be looking out for (**13:3-4**). Responding to their question, Jesus launched into a great discourse about events that would happen in both the near and distant future.

He starts by describing the beginning signs, which fall into three categories: impostors or deceivers purporting to represent Jesus (**13:5-6**), calamities of human origins such as *wars and rumours of wars* (**13:7-8a**), and natural calamities such as *earthquakes … and famines* (**13:8b**). Jesus told the disciples *not to be alarmed* (13:7) by these events, for they are just *the beginning of birth-pains* (**13:8c**). Although these signs began in the first century, those living in the twenty-first century are no strangers to any of them. Impostors claiming to represent Christ are everywhere, deceiving the gullible. Ethnic clashes, the internal breakdown of law and order, cross-border wars, massive displacements of people as refugees, devastating earthquakes and the like are rife. Alarming as these catastrophes are, children of the kingdom are enjoined 'not to be alarmed' because these events do not signal the end of the age.

Besides these signs, Jesus also predicted intense persecution of the apostles. They would be delivered to Jewish councils and flogged on account of him (see Acts 4:5-7; 5:27-29, 40; 2 Cor 11:24). They would be handed over to Gentile authorities to stand trial on account of him (see Acts 22:30-23:10; 24:1-9; 25:1-12; 23-27). Their persecution would result in the spread of the gospel (see Phil 1:12-14). Note that Jesus' words *the gospel must first be preached to all nations* (**13:10**) seem to be a statement about what will happen rather than a precondition for his return. As they stood trial, they were not to worry beforehand about what to say. The Holy Spirit, the Advocate, would supply the appropriate line of defence.

Jesus also predicted persecution of all others who follow him. Allegiance to Jesus would cause family rifts (**13:12**). His followers would be the objects of intense hatred by unbelievers. But Jesus gave a promise to those who *stand firm to the end* (**13:13**). They would be saved, that is, they would enter into his kingdom. He assures them that ultimately believers will be vindicated.

In all that he has been saying so far, Jesus has been focusing on the question about the signs signalling that the destruction of the temple was imminent.

Next, he moves on to deal with the question of when the destruction of the temple will take place. It will be during a period of *distress* (**13:19**). The period will be signalled by *the abomination that causes desolation standing where it does not belong*. Jesus borrowed this phrase from a prophecy in Daniel 9:27, 11:31 and 12:11. It is a veiled reference to a historical event.

Daniel's prophecy had been partially fulfilled in 168 BC when the Seleucid ruler Antiochus IV Epiphanes desecrated the temple by erecting an altar to Zeus over the Jewish altar of burnt offering and repeatedly offering pigs on his altar. These actions had led to the Maccabean revolt (see 1 Macc 1:45-59; 6:7). Jesus was hinting that more of the prophecy would soon be fulfilled. This did in fact take place when, as Josephus reports, some Jewish Zealots desecrated the temple. This was followed by the sacking of Jerusalem and the destruction of the temple by the Roman general Titus in AD 70. Josephus reports that the temple the disciples had been admiring was flattened.

Jesus warned that when the signal appeared, the faithful who resided in Judea should try to decipher it, *let the reader understand* (**13:14**). This was a coded message to the faithful, warning them that the signal will usher in the judgment predicted here. When they saw it, they should flee to the mountains (13:14). Those who were threshing grain, relaxing on the roofs of their homes, or working in the fields should recognize that survival is more important than material possessions (**13:15-16**). The most vulnerable people would be pregnant and nursing mothers (**13:17**) – a truth that still holds in modern times, as demonstrated by the horrors of war and the fate of displaced people in refugee camps in Africa and around the world. Because the exact time of these events is unknown (see 13:32), the Lord asked the faithful to intercede that it would not come in a season when the weather, too, would be hostile (**13:18**).

Warned by Jesus, Jewish Christians did flee Jerusalem shortly before it was destroyed and took refuge at Pella in the Transjordanian mountains.

In describing the coming events, our Lord used language very similar to that in Daniel 12:1, which refers to 'a time of distress such as has not happened from the beginning of nations until then'. The context of Daniel's words suggests that Jesus did not limit the fulfilment of Daniel's prophecy to the impending destruction of Jerusalem. He also saw it as applying to the great tribulation, for he describes it as an event unequalled in the whole history of the world (**13:19**). Only the mercy of God would relieve the distress, and he would do this for the sake of the elect, those he had chosen as his followers (**13:20**). The period of great distress or tribulation will be marked by religious counterfeits and complicated by confused rumours that Christ has appeared. *False Christs and false prophets will appear* with powerful credentials that could even *deceive the elect, if that were possible* (**13:21-22**).

The reason the elect will not be deceived is that Christ has told them *everything ahead of time* (**13:23**). He has answered the disciples' immediate questions about the destruction of the temple, but now he will go on to tell them what it will be like when he really comes again, not secretly like the counterfeits but in full view of all, including his enemies.

The distress Jesus has just described will be followed by cosmic events associated with his second coming. Jesus quotes from Isaiah 13:10 and 34:4, passages which describe the dissolution of cosmic structures that the prophets associated with the coming Day of the Lord (see also Joel 2:10; 3:15). If phenomena such as the greenhouse effect, acid rain and global warming can attract worldwide attention, imagine how much greater will be the effect of changes in the light of the sun and moon, with stars and planets diverted from their normal courses (**13:24-25**). Every living creature will then listen to what the Lord of the universe has to say! Human history will move to a climactic end as the Lord of history returns *in clouds with great power and glory* (**13:26**). This awesome event is also described in Revelation 1:7 and 1 Thessalonians 4:13-18. The appearance of the Son of Man will usher in the great harvest *from the ends of the earth to the ends of the heavens* (**13:27**) in which the angels will gather together all those who have been saved.

The *lesson from the fig tree* is to encourage them to develop spiritual sensitivity. Just as the budding of the fig tree signals the change in the seasons, so certain events will signal that the things Jesus has spoken of are near (**13:28-29**). The appalling sacrilege in the temple will signal that disaster is about to strike (see 13:14), just as *these things* will signal that his second coming is near.

But what did Jesus mean when he said that *all these things* will occur within *this generation* (**13:30**)? Some commentators limit these events to those Jesus was describing in 13:2-23, excluding the events associated with his second coming in 13:24-27. Others argue that in 13:30 *this generation* would be better translated as 'this race' (see NIV footnote), in which case the Jewish race is in view and not just Jesus' contemporaries. If this translation is correct, 'all these things' refers both to the events leading to the destruction of the temple and to the events of the second coming. Jesus solemnly guaranteed the truth of his words (**13:31**).

Jesus ended the Olivet discourse with a call to constant vigilance because no one, *not even the angels*, knows the exact timing of the events of the second coming. Not even the Son of Man is privy to the exact *day or hour* (**13:32**) when these things will happen. Jesus' ignorance here is a voluntary limitation that he accepted as part of his humanity (Phil 2:8), explained by the *kenosis* doctrine (that is, the doctrine that he emptied himself of some of his divine attributes when becoming human).

He illustrates the need for vigilance by comparing the faithful to servants who must be ready for the owner of a house to return at any time (**13:34-36**). It is clear that the early church believed in Jesus' imminent return. But the call to watchfulness was not just directed to them but *to everyone* (**13:37**), that is, to all of us. We are to *Watch!*

14:1-15:47 The Passion Narrative

14:1-2 The Plot Against Jesus

The Passover lasted from sunset on the 14th Nisan (a month, which roughly approximates our April) until the early hours of the 15th Nisan. It was followed by the Feast of Unleavened Bread, which ran from the 15th to 21st Nisan. Mark now gives the date as being two days before these major festivals. Jesus' archenemies – the chief priests and the teachers of the law – had long wanted to do away with him, but various circumstances had prevented this (see 3:6; 11:18; 12:12). As these feasts approached, they *were looking for some sly way* to get him arrested (**14:1**). But they did not want to do it during the Feast, for fear of a violent protest from the crowd (**14:2**).

14:3-9 The Anointing at Bethany

Jesus was at Bethany, which had been his base since coming to Jerusalem. On this occasion his host was Simon the Leper. We know nothing about this man, but it is possible that he had been healed by Jesus. As was customary, Jesus, his host and the others present were reclining around the table, that is, they were resting on their left elbows while eating. An unidentified woman came in carrying a jar of very expensive, *pure,* meaning undiluted, perfume. To express her deep appreciation of and devotion to Jesus, she poured this perfume over his head (**14:5**). Some of the guests were horrified, because they saw her action as wasteful. After all, the perfume cost more than a labourer would earn in a year, and she had poured it all out at once (14:5). She should have sold it and given the proceeds of the sale to the poor. Some of those responding this way may have objected more because Jesus was being given such honour than because they really cared for the poor. Others, however, may have had a genuine concern, but as Jesus pointed out, they were failing to see the priority of the hour. They could help the poor *any time* they wanted to, but Jesus would not be with them in the flesh much longer (**14:7**). He recognized that *she has done a beautiful thing to me* (**14:6**) and that she had done her best, doing *what she could*, with an action proportional to her ability. She had, in fact, anticipated his burial (**14:8**). While the woman may not have understood it that way, Jesus assigned deep significance to her action. He declared that what she had done would form part of the gospel story that would be told over and over again, and so it has been (**14:9**).

14:10-11 The Betrayal by Judas

In sharp contrast to the 'beautiful thing' done by the unidentified woman is the dastardly thing done by Judas. Mark emphasizes that he was not unknown, but was *one of the Twelve* when he took the initiative and went to the enemies of Jesus (**14:10**). The authorities had previously been unsure about how and when to act (see 14:2), but the arrival of Judas may have given them confidence. Just when they were close to giving up, in walked an informer, and an insider at that. They promised him money and a deal was struck (**14:11**). From that moment on – two days before the feast – Judas was looking for an opportune moment for them to capture Jesus.

14:12-26 The Celebration of the Passover

Judas' opportunity came *on the first day of the Feast of Unleavened Bread.* This may have been the 14th Nisan, when the Passover lamb was killed, or it may have been the day after. Both dates are possible. The disciples asked Jesus about his plans for the Feast. Pilgrims who had come to Jerusalem were expected to observe the Feast within the city, and hence the disciples wanted to know where to make the preparations.

Jesus gave them instructions that were reminiscent of his instructions prior to the triumphal entry (see 11:2-6). Two unnamed disciples were sent into the city and told to look out for a man carrying a jar of water. When they spotted him, they were to follow him. When he entered a house, they were to approach the owner of the house and ask *Where is my guest room, where I may eat the Passover with my disciples?* (**14:13-14**). It is possible that the homeowner may have been a faithful disciple, with whom Jesus had a pre-arrangement. But it is also possible that Jesus was again demonstrating his omniscience. In the house was *a large upper room, furnished and ready* (**14:15**). This would have been an upstairs room equipped with furniture, utensils and all they would need. It was the only shelter accorded him in the city at this time, and it would later serve the disciples in the tense days following his crucifixion (Acts 1:13).

The disciples found everything *just as Jesus had told them* (**14:16**). They then completed the preparations, which would have involved getting the bread, wine, bitter herbs and a sauce made of dried fruit, spices and wine, and roasting the Passover lamb.

In the evening Jesus and his disciples arrived at the upper room (**14:17**). In the course of the Passover meal, *while they were reclining* (see note on 14:3) Jesus announced that one of the Twelve would certainly betray him. His words *one who is eating with me* (14:18) recall Psalm 41:9. A close friend, one who enjoyed fellowship with him, would turn against him! An African proverb says, 'a traitor often hails from one's own household.'

Understandably the disciples were shocked to learn that a traitor was among them, hence the questions that followed, whereby *one by one* they said, *Surely not I?* (**14:19**). But their question smacked of self-confidence. They were actually saying, 'it can't be me, can it?' Jesus is adamant that the betrayer will be one of them: *One of you will betray me … one who is eating with me* (**14:18**); *It is one of the Twelve … one who dips bread into the bowl with me* (**14:20**).

At that very moment the unnamed betrayer was dipping his hand into the same bowl as Jesus at the fellowship meal.

The Son of Man's suffering was a necessity, laid down in the Scriptures. But the betrayer was a free moral agent, whose path to ruin was not a necessity laid down by Scripture. The betrayer courted his own ruin (**14:21**). Jesus must have made this declaration with a sense of deep sorrow for the traitor. The Bible does not deny human free will and personal responsibility and suggest that we resign ourselves to fate. But the exercise of human free will does not negate God's sovereign purpose.

The traditional Passover meal was always celebrated in an atmosphere of worship. After the participants had taken their positions at the table, the head of the family pronounced a blessing on the feast and the wine. Then they drank a first cup of wine, in memory of having been led out of Egypt. After this, the head of the family told the story of the redemption from Egypt, which was followed by a song of praise and the singing of the first part of the Hallel psalms (Ps 113-115). Then they drank a second cup of wine in memory of having been freed from slavery.

Next the head of the family blessed the bread, which was then passed round and eaten with bitter herbs and stewed fruit. This marked the beginning of the meal. The main meal consisted of unleavened bread, symbolizing the bread of affliction in Egypt; bitter herbs, symbolizing the bitterness of slavery; stewed fruit that looked like clay, symbolizing the bricks made during the slavery in Egypt; and roast lamb, reminding them of the 'passing over' of Israel in the plague. At the end of the meal, the head of the family blessed the third cup of wine and it was drunk to celebrate God's mighty act of redemption. This was followed by the singing of the second half of the Hallel psalms (Ps 116-118). The celebration concluded shortly before midnight with the drinking of a fourth cup of wine in honour of the consummation when God will take his people to be with him for ever. The pattern of the four cups of wine was based on Exodus 6:6-7.

As the head of his family of disciples, Jesus led the disciples in the celebration of this Passover. However, he infused new meaning into the whole ritual. After the singing of the first part of the Hallel psalms *Jesus took bread, gave thanks and broke it.* His words, *this is my body* added new significance as he was claiming that he himself is the bread of life (**14:22**;. see also John 6:48, 51). Partaking of him signifies eternal life (John 6:53, 54).

The cup was the third cup, taken at the completion of the meal or 'after supper' (**14:23**; see also 1 Cor 11:25). That cup had been associated with God's procuring of salvation for Israel. Now Jesus gave it new meaning as *my blood of the covenant, which is poured out for many* (**14:24**). Blood was used to seal a covenant. In this case, Jesus' blood, which would soon be shed, would seal a covenant promising eternal salvation to all his followers – the 'many'.

With this new meaning, Jesus pledged his perpetual presence whenever his followers gather to break bread (Luke 22:7; 1 Cor 11:23-26). The communion table around which we gather today thus signifies a fellowship of kindred minds whose faith is in the bread of life. The cup, likewise, was instituted as a perpetual memorial. It is thus clear that only those who have been identified with Jesus in the fellowship of his saving grace may come to this table. It is significant that Jesus firmly declared that he *will not drink again of the fruit of the vine until that day … in the kingdom of God* (**14:25**). Jesus had reinterpreted the third cup as a celebration of the redemption he would procure for many. It seems that he ended the Passover meal with this third cup, and did not go on to take the fourth cup, associated with the gathering to God of his people. This cup would only be drunk at the time of his second coming. The fourth cup is thus postponed. It is for this reason that the celebration of the Lord's Table is a proclamation of his 'death until he comes' (1 Cor 11:26). The last cup will then be drunk *anew in the kingdom of God* at the last great supper (14:25; see also Luke 14:15; Rev 3:20; 19:6-9). It will then be a new or renewed cup. The Lord's Supper must, therefore, be celebrated today as a reminder of two important truths: the *joy* of our salvation that has already been procured and the *hope* of Jesus' second coming and our eternal fellowship with him forever.

The *hymn* (**14:26**) that was sung at the end of the Last Supper would have been from the last half of the Hallel psalms. After singing, they left for the rendezvous at the Mount of Olives.

14:27-31 A Prediction of the Disciples' Denial

We are not told whether the exchange Mark records next took place as they journeyed to the Mount of Olives or in the course of the Passover meal. Jesus announced the certainty that his disciples would deny him and be scattered (**14:27**). This statement was grounded in a prophecy in Zechariah 13:7 that predicted the striking of the shepherd as part of Israel's redemption. This was Jesus' final prediction of his death. However, he offered them the hope of his resurrection and of his being reunited with them later in Galilee (**14:28**).

Peter self-confidently objected to Jesus' words, denying that he would leave him. He even compared himself with the others and felt confident that he would walk tall, even if the others fell, for he would never disown his Master (**14:29, 31**). Jesus emphatically contradicted him and predicted the devastating stumble that Peter would make that very night as he disowned Jesus. His fall will be thorough and complete, so much so that it will happen not once but *three times* (**14:30**). The Lord was warning the disciples, but none of them believed him. They were confident that they would stand firm to the point of death, if need be (**14:31**).

14:32-42 The Agony in Gethsemane

The name *Gethsemane* means 'oil press', so it is possible that the place where Jesus and his disciples now went may have been the site of an olive orchard or an oil press. Jesus told eight of the disciples to stay at the edge of the garden, while he took the other three further on to share with him something of the unimaginable distress of his soul (**14:32-33**). After all, Peter had just said that he was ready to die with Jesus if need be, and James and John had earlier said that they would drink of the same cup of suffering as Jesus (10:38-39).

So deep was Jesus' agony that he described it as sorrow *to the point of death*. He urged the three disciples to *keep watch* that is, to be alert and prayerful (**14:34**). Obviously a spiritual battle was being joined and prayer was the key weaponry Jesus resorted to (14:32, 35). His agony was not because he was facing the agonizing physical death of crucifixion. It had deeper roots in the prospect of the alienation from the Father that would be an inevitable consequence of accepting the punishment for the sins of others (see 15:34 below).

The spiritual battle went three rounds. In the first round (14:35-38), Jesus went alone, away from the three, lay prostrate in surrender to the Father and prayed the Father *if possible* to take *the hour* and *the cup* from him. Here the 'hour' and 'the cup' refer to that mysterious period of suffering when he was separated from the one he referred to as *Abba, Father* (**14:35-36**). The Aramaic 'Abba', translated 'Father' or more colloquially, 'Baba', was the way a Jewish child would address his father at home. A pious Jew would consider it disrespectful to use this word when addressing God. Its use here illustrates the depth of the bond between Jesus and the Father. In the prayer Jesus acknowledged the Father's sovereign ability to do all things, and also his own surrender to the Father's perfect will. Thus the aim of this prayer was not to change the Father's will but to align the Son's will with that of the Father, *not what I will, but what you will* (14:36). In the midst of the battle, Jesus went back to the disciples out of concern for their welfare, and found them all, including Simon the confident, asleep, unable to *watch for one hour* (**14:37**). If they are to avoid falling, they must watch and pray. Jesus conceded that in their spirit they really did want to stand with him, but they were prone to failure because their bodies were weak (**14:38**). The lesson remains: spiritual battles are won or lost on the basis of effective watching and praying beforehand.

In the second round (14:39-40) Mark does not focus on Jesus but on the disciples' failure. Jesus went back to the Father and prayed as he had earlier (**14:39**), but his men, too, were in the same posture as before – asleep rather than watching and praying (**14:40**).

In the third and final round (14:41-42), we can safely assume that Jesus prayed as he had earlier on, while the

disciples were *still sleeping and resting* until Jesus declared it was *Enough!* (**14:41**). It was now too late to watch and pray, for the *hour has come ... here comes my betrayer!* (14:41-42). The men had failed three times. They had clearly demonstrated that they had not learned the lesson of the parable of the servants who were to watch for their master's return (see 13: 34-36). Jesus was now determined to face the hour of trial, saying, *Rise! Let us go!* (**14:42**).

14:43-52 The Betrayal and Arrest

The arresting party would have been made up of the temple guards, drawn from the Levites. The list of those who had sent them leaves no doubt that the Sanhedrin were behind this (**14:43**). At their head stood *Judas, one of the Twelve*, an insider. His services were needed to lead them to a place where Jesus could be arrested quietly, for Judas knew Jesus' movements. Also, at that hour of the night, an insider was needed to clearly identify the one they were looking for.

The depth of Judas' treachery is apparent in the cue he had arranged for signalling whom to arrest (**14:44**). He stepped forward, and hypocritically addressing Jesus as *Rabbi* (meaning 'respected teacher'), he betrayed Jesus with a token act of love, a kiss (**14:45**). Jesus was promptly arrested (**14:46**). A futile attempt to fight back was made by *one of those standing by*, a veiled reference to Peter, who was Mark's source of the account (**14:47**; see John 18:10 and the Introduction).

Jesus pointed out to the guards that their weapons were unnecessary because he had not been *leading a rebellion* (**14:48**). He was not going to resist arrest, for this event and its timing were preordained (**14:49**). On seeing Jesus allowing himself to be arrested, the disciples turned and fled (**14:50**). The abandonment that Jesus had predicted in 14:27, 30 had happened.

The arrest is followed by an incident that is recorded only in Mark's gospel. This has led many to assume that Mark himself must have been the *young man, wearing nothing but a linen garment* (**14:51**). Mark had a home in Jerusalem (Acts 12:12) which tradition suggests was where the Last Supper took place. It would have been quite possible for him to have followed Jesus and the disciples to Gethsemane, or for some of the fleeing disciples to have told him about the arrest so that he rushed to the scene. The linen clothing suggests that he came from a wealthy home, and he might have lingered on while the Eleven escaped. As he followed the arresting crowd, he may have been spotted and identified as a sympathizer, with the result that *they seized him*, causing him to abandon his garment and flee naked into the night (**14:51-52**).

14:53-65 The Trial Before the Sanhedrin

The Sanhedrin hastily convened at the house of the high priest that very night (**14:53**). This was contrary to Jewish tradition, which insisted that such courts be held in the temple precincts or in a market hall. But this trial was so urgent that it could not wait until morning. Clandestine acts often take place in secret, under cover of darkness and with a sense of urgency. While truth will withstand time, error often has compelling urgency and cannot wait.

Peter followed at a distance and ended up in the courtyard of the high priest, where he sat with the guards to warm himself at the fire they had lit (**14:54**). The trial must have taken place in the upper chamber of the house, where Peter may have been able to hear, if not see, the proceedings (see 14:66).

The trial was a travesty of justice for the Sanhedrin was playing the dual role of prosecutor and judge. It did not set out to ascertain the truth; rather, the verdict was known in advance and all that was wanted was evidence to support it. But the evidence they assembled failed to convince even the members of the Sanhedrin (**14:55**). The evidence of the many false witnesses failed to agree (**14:56**). Eventually, someone was found who alleged that Jesus had said that he would destroy *this man-made temple and ... build another, not made by man* (**14:58**). But they were misquoting and misinterpreting his words. He never claimed he would destroy the temple; rather he had challenged the Jews to *destroy this temple* and said that he would then *raise it again in three days* (John 2:19). This last set of witnesses also failed to make a convincing case (**14:59**).

After all these unsuccessful attempts to find sufficient evidence to convict Jesus, the high priest himself, the judge of the court, took over the function of the prosecutor. First he asked Jesus to defend himself against the charges that even the Sanhedrin knew were unconvincing (**14:60**). This was clearly an attempt to have Jesus entrap himself, but he refused to answer the high priest (**14:61a**). Finally, the high priest played his trump card. He asked Jesus, *Are you the Christ, the Son of the Blessed One?* (**14:61b**). The question not only challenged him to claim to be the Messiah, but by implication to state that he was the Son of God. At this Jesus broke his silence and answered, invoking the sacred Name of God – *I am* (**14:62a**; see also Exod 3:14 and John 8:58) His claims would be proved when they saw the Son of Man *sitting at the right hand of the Mighty One and coming on the clouds of heaven* (**14:62b**). He would then be the Exalted One, the judge (see 13:26) who occupies the highest place of honour. That did it! The high priest, confident that he had secured a conviction for blasphemy, symbolically demonstrated his indignation at what Jesus had said by tearing his clothes. He asked the jury to concur with his verdict – *what do you think?* (**14:64a**). Their verdict was cast in legal language: he was *worthy of death.* (**14:64b**). From that point on they turned to humiliating him. He was spat on. Then they blindfolded him and hit him, taunting him to use his powers as a prophet to tell who it was who had hit him (see Luke 22:64). He was also beaten by the guards (**14:65**).

14:66-72 Peter's Denial of Jesus

It is clear that Peter's denial of Jesus was happening concurrently with the trial. Mark's focus shifts from the upper chamber where the trial was being held to the courtyard below (**14:66**). It was here that a servant girl recognized Peter and accused him of having been *with that Nazarene, Jesus* (**14:67**), which is to say that he was a disciple. Peter promptly denied any knowledge of what the girl was talking about and moved away from the fire, where he had been standing (**14:68**). While Jesus was being questioned about his identity as the Son of God, Peter too was facing a form of interrogation about whether he was a disciple. While Jesus owned up to his identity, Peter denied his. That was the first denial.

Peter had moved to the entrance to the courtyard, but there the same servant girl accosted him again, telling those present that Peter was *one of them*, another allegation that he was a disciple (**14:69**). Peter promptly denied this – a second denial (**14:70a**). But those standing around him were not convinced, and after listening to his accent they concluded, *Surely you are one of them, for you are a Galilean* (**14:70b**). This third denial was marked by a complete and thorough disowning of his Lord and Master. Cursing himself and swearing, he maintained *I don't know this man you're talking about* (**14:71**). Then a rooster crowed for the second time, and suddenly Peter remembered Jesus' prediction the previous night (see 14:30), which had now come true (**14:72b**). Peter was immediately struck with deep remorse and broke down in tears. It is the words of the Lord that bring about true conviction and genuine remorse.

15:1-15 The Trial before Pilate

Early the next morning the Sanhedrin regrouped and *reached a decision* (**15:1**). This means they confirmed the previous night's decision by framing charges that might be admissible under Roman law, since the charge of blasphemy would not have held before Pilate.

It is clear from Pilate's question to Jesus that the charge he had been told of was a political one – Jesus was seditious and was claiming to be *king of the Jews.* Jesus did not deny his kingship, but it is clear from the account in John 18:36-37 that his kingship was not to be understood in worldly terms (**15:2**). This was the *good confession* that Paul later alluded to (1 Tim 6:13).

To make the charge stick, the members of the Sanhedrin *accused him of many things* (**15:3**). Something of the nature of these accusations can be gleaned from Luke 23:2, where they are recorded as having charged him with subversion, alleging that he opposed payment of taxes to the Roman emperor and claimed to be 'Christ, a king'. Note how the religious charge was craftily recast as a political one. Evil people are adept at distortion, as illustrated here.

Under Roman law an accused was given a chance to defend himself, but this one *made no reply* (**15:5**), even when Pilate urged him to defend himself (**15:4**). Peter later alluded to this (see 1 Pet 2:23).

There was a custom of granting an imperial amnesty at this festive time, just as today a head of state may release political prisoners on national days. So a crowd of nationalist Jews came to demand that Pilate observe this custom (**15:6, 8**). The prisoner they wanted to see released was an insurrectionist named *Barabbas*, who had committed murder (**15:7**). This Aramaic name may be translated as *bar-Abba* or 'son of the father', a common name at that time. Apparently the supporters of this man came to see Pilate asking for his release just as Pilate was trying Jesus. Pilate knew that Jesus was innocent and had been charged *out of envy* so he proposed a swap as a way out of his dilemma (**15:9-10**). That was a grave miscalculation on his part, for the Sanhedrin outwitted him and prevailed on the crowd to ask for Barabbas instead (**15:11**). In another attempt to manipulate the crowd, Pilate tried shifting responsibility onto them by asking what to do with *the one you call the king of the Jews* (**15:12**). He was not expecting the answer he got, *Crucify him!* (**15:13**). He tried once more to shift responsibility onto the crowd by asking them to decide what Jesus' crime was. But he received the same reply – *Crucify him!* (**15:14**).

Pilate was a morally bankrupt character. He knew very well that Jesus was innocent and what the right action would be, but he failed to act because he wanted to please the crowd, even if it cost an innocent life. The weakness of his character is clearly demonstrated as he had Jesus *flogged* and *handed over* (**15:15**). A Roman flogging was a terrible ordeal, for it was done with leather thongs into which pieces of bone or lead were plaited. The handing over was a legal act signifying a guilty verdict. In this case, the Roman magistrate declared, 'I consign you to the cross.' This was a total miscarriage of justice.

15:16-20 Humiliation by Roman Soldiers

The negotiations just reported took place outside Pilate's palace. When they ended Jesus was led back inside to be humiliated by a *whole company* of Roman soldiers (**15:16-20**).

The soldiers' mockery reflected the charge on which Jesus was convicted. The *purple robe* they put on him signified royalty, and thorns were woven into a crown for his head (**15:17**). The soldiers then mockingly hailed him as a king (**15:18**). A king would have carried a *staff* as a symbol of his authority, so they beat him over the head with one. Where a king would have been greeted with a kiss of honour, they spat on him (**15:19**). When they had had their fill of mockery, they put Jesus' clothes back on him and marched him off to crucifixion (**15:20**).

15:21-32 The Crucifixion and Mocking

Jesus had been so badly beaten that he could not carry his own cross, and so a man who was returning to the city was accosted and forced to carry it for him. The man's name was Simon and he came from Cyrene, a port in Libya in North Africa. He must have been well known to Mark's Roman readers, for the names of his two sons are also mentioned (**15:21**; see also Rom 16:13).

The site of the crucifixion was known as *Golgotha* which in Aramaic means 'skull'. It was probably a hill shaped like a skull, rather than a name for a place of execution (**15:22**). The Latin word for 'skull' is *calvaria*, which is why the name Calvary is often used for this place.

Before they were executed, were usually offered a narcotic potion containing *myrrh* to dull their sensitivity to the excruciating pain of crucifixion (**15:23**; see commentary on 15:44). Jesus refused to drink it, most likely so as to face death with an alert mind. No other details of the crucifixion are given. In keeping with Roman law, and in fulfilment of Psalm 22:18, the soldiers took possession of his clothes and shared them out between them, casting lots to determine who got what (**15:24**). Mark gives the time of the crucifixion as being *the third hour* (**15:25**), which would be about nine o' clock in the morning.

A written notice stating the crime for which someone was being executed was posted at the top of a cross. For Jesus, this notice recorded that he was accused of being the King of the Jews (**15:26**). But he died a rejected king. Those who accompanied him in death were robbers (**15:27**) – a further illustration of how much he had been misrepresented, misjudged and unjustly condemned. His death beside evil men fulfilled the prophecy of Isaiah 53:12. It is not clear whether Mark was the one who pointed this out, or whether **15:28** was a later addition, which is why this text is included only as a footnote in the NIV.

To compound Jesus' humiliation, passers-by (**15:29-30**), his enemies and even those crucified with him (**15:31-32**) derided him and gloated over his circumstances.

15:33-41 The Death of Jesus Christ

Then the sky darkened, and for three hours, from noon (*the sixth hour*) until 3:00 p.m. (*the ninth hour*) darkness enveloped the land (**15:33**) The darkness was a sign from heaven to teach sinful humanity about God's judgment and the horror of what was taking place on the cross. The horror is captured in the desolate cry of the Son as the Father turned away from him because he was taking on himself the full curse of the sins of the whole world (**15:34**; see also Gal 3:13). Utter darkness is appropriate for that dramatic event at Calvary, for what was happening there remains a mystery inscrutable to mere mortals. Jesus was taking our place, enduring the wrath of God that each of us deserves for our personal sins, a wrath that results in eternal separation from God.

It is said that when this gospel story was once told to a remote people group who had never heard it, the village chief interrupted the narrator when he came to the point where Jesus was unjustly hung on the cross to die. The chief exclaimed, 'Take him down! I belong there!' He got the message. Each of us must come to the point where we recognize that Jesus took our place on that cross.

Some of the bystanders misinterpreted Jesus' cry *Eloi, Eloi* in 15:34 as being *Elijah, Elijah* (**15:35**). Apparently one of the soldiers ran to get a sponge, dipped it in wine vinegar and offered it to him on the end of a long stick (**15:36**). The aim may have been to keep him conscious a little longer in order to prolong his suffering, or to see whether Elijah would respond.

Mustering his strength, Jesus uttered another loud cry, as he *breathed his last* (**15:37**). This suggests that Jesus did not die of exhaustion, as was usual with crucifixions. His life was not taken from him (John 10:17-18); instead he gave it up voluntarily when it was the right time to do so. He died as all humans do, yet he died like no human ever will, for he died in the place of all who would recognize that he had hung on the shameful cross in their place.

Jesus' death was accompanied by an amazing spectacle within the temple. The curtain separating the Holy of Holies from the rest of the temple was torn in two (**15:38**), indicating that there was now direct access to God, with no more need for human intermediaries.

The centurion who saw Jesus die acknowledged that what he had seen was most unusual. His statement, *Surely this man was the son of God* (**15:39**) may merely have expressed his pagan belief that some human beings had divine parentage, but Mark records it as a statement that was truer than the speaker may have known.

In a male-dominated society, the Holy Spirit prompted Mark to underscore the prominent role of women, both named and unnamed (**15:40**), as authentic witnesses to the gospel (see 1 Cor 15:3-4). They were eyewitnesses to Jesus' death (15:40-41), to his burial (15:47), and to his resurrection (16:1-8). These women were disciples, for they had *followed him* and taken care of his material needs (**15:41**).

15:42-47 The Burial of Jesus Christ

Jesus died at 3:00 p.m., meaning that only three hours remained before the commencement of the Sabbath at sundown (**15:42**). Jewish law decreed that someone who was executed must be buried before dusk to avoid desecrating the approaching Sabbath (Deut 21:22-23). Consequently Joseph from Arimathea stepped forward and asked Pilate for permission to bury Jesus (**15:43**). This bold move can only be explained by the fact that he was *waiting for the kingdom of God*. Like Nicodemus (John 19:38), he was a secret disciple who finally translated his faith into a bold public act.

Pilate was surprised that Jesus had died so soon (**15:44**), for death by crucifixion was usually a slow process. Victims who were tied to the stake with ropes might live as long as three days before they died from exhaustion as the weight of their own bodies dragged them down and made breathing difficult. Where nails were employed, excruciating pain was experienced while dying. If there was a need to hasten death, this could be done by breaking the victims' legs so that they could not support their weight in any way (John 19:31-33). Pilate first confirmed with the centurion that Jesus was really dead (15:44) before releasing the body to Joseph (**15:45**).

In preparation for burial, the body was tightly wrapped in strips of *linen cloth* (see John 11:44) before it was laid in a tomb *cut out of rock* (**15:46**). Such tombs were not common at the time and belonged only to the rich. The stone rolled against the entrance was probably disc-shaped. It was designed to keep intruders away and would require several people to roll it back (see 16:3).

Mark takes care to record that two women were eyewitnesses to the burial – Mary of Magdala and Mary the mother of Joses. They noted the exact location of the tomb before hurrying off, like everyone else, to be home before the start of the Sabbath.

16:1-8 The Resurrection of Jesus Christ

The Sabbath ended at dusk on the day after the crucifixion, that is, on Saturday. This afforded the women only enough time to prepare spices for embalming the body before darkness fell (**16:1**). They would have had to wait until early the next morning to perform the final rites that they had not been able to do on the day of the crucifixion because of the approaching Sabbath.

Accordingly they set out *very early*, probably sometime between 3:00 a.m. and 6:00 a.m., immediately after sunrise on the *first day of the week*, that is, on Sunday (**16:2**). The question on their minds was how they would get access to the body: *Who will roll the stone away?* (**16:3**).

However, they did not have long to worry about how to remove this *very large* stone barrier, for when they reached the tomb it was already open (**16:4**). The women went straight into the tomb to anoint the body, but to their shock they found *a young man ... in a white robe* sitting inside the tomb (**16:5**). Not only that, but the 'young man' was no ordinary human but a heavenly messenger (see Matt 28:2-3; John 20:12) who told them *He has risen! He is not here. See the place where they laid him* (**16:6**). These words were spoken to calm the fear of these first witnesses of Jesus' resurrection. They confirmed that the body had not been stolen and supported the visual evidence of the empty tomb (see also Matt 28:12-15).

Even though faith is not dependent upon physical evidence, faith and evidence are not mutually exclusive. The angel had shown the women proof of the resurrection by inviting them to *see the place where they laid him* (**16:6**), but they still needed the further proof of actually seeing Jesus alive. So the angel reminded them of Jesus' earlier predictions of his resurrection and his promise that he would precede the disciples to Galilee (**16:7**; see 14:28). This message of joy was for *his disciples and Peter*. Undoubtedly this was a reassurance of restoration after these men, and particularly Peter, had deserted Jesus (see 14:50, 66-72).

The women's fears were not allayed. *Trembling and bewildered … [they] fled … [and] said nothing* (**16:8**). They were still confused. None of the angel's reassuring words had soothed their minds. They fled the scene in silence, saying nothing as they ran, but clearly they subsequently told what they had seen to the others (Matt 28:8; Luke 24:9; John 20:1-2).

At this point, Mark's gospel breaks off abruptly, without any mention of Jesus' post-resurrection appearances, other than the promised meeting in Galilee. We know from the other gospels that the disciples saw the risen Jesus a number of times.

Some would argue that the ending at 16:8 is fitting because the gospel ends on a high triumphant note with the proof of the resurrection supplied by the empty tomb. However, others have found this ending unsatisfactory, and two alternative endings have been supplied, which are known as 'the longer ending' and 'the shorter ending'. The shorter one reads: *But they reported briefly to Peter and those with him all they had been told. And after this Jesus himself sent out by means of them, from east to west, the sacred and imperishable proclamation of eternal salvation.* The language used here is clearly uncharacteristic of Mark. The longer ending, too, contains nothing that is not found elsewhere in the other gospels.

Further evidence that neither of these endings was part of the original gospel is that they are not present in two most reliable early manuscripts of Mark, nor in some of the early Latin and Syriac translations of the gospel. In the first four centuries of the Christian era, church fathers such as Eusebius, Jerome, Clement of Alexandria, and Origen also testified that these endings were not part of the manuscripts known to be accurate copies of Mark. (For further information, consult the *TOT* and *NIBC* commentaries on the Gospel of Mark.)

In this commentary, we will focus on the longer ending.

16:9-20 Appearance, Commissioning, Ascension

The longer ending starts with three accounts of Jesus' appearances, each of which is also reported elsewhere. The accounts seem to follow the pattern of identifying the witnesses to the appearance, reporting what happened, and recording the response of unbelief.

16:9-14 Jesus' Appearances

16:9-11 The appearance to Mary Magdalene

Mary of Magdala was one who loved much, for by the grace of God she had experienced a great deliverance (**16:9**). The encounter recorded here may well be the same as the one in John 20:1-18, although Mark includes few details and does not specifically mention this appearance. Mary Magdalene told *those who had been with him* (**16:10**), that is, the disciples, about her encounter with the risen Lord. However, they responded with disbelief (**16:11**). John's record of Mary's report to the disciples does not mention the disciples' unbelief, but we know of it from Luke 24:11.

16:12-13 The appearance to two disciples

The incident described here seems to match the encounter on the road to Emmaus that is recorded in Luke 24:13-35. The description of Jesus as appearing *in a different form* (**16:12**) is likely because the two disciples did not recognize him at first. The two *returned* to report what they had witnessed. While the account in Mark states that they, too, were greeted with disbelief (**16:13**), the account in Luke indicates that doubt had been dispelled before the two arrived (Luke 24:34).

16:14 The appearance to the Eleven

The final incident described differs from the previous two in that it focuses not on their unbelief as such but on Jesus' rebuke of their unbelief. The difference is justified because whereas the other incidents involved reports brought to the Eleven, here the Eleven themselves encounter the risen Lord. Such collective rebukes of the Eleven are described in John 20:26-29 and Luke 24:36-44. The aim of including this third narrative seems to be to rebuke those whose doubts arise from *lack of faith* and *stubborn refusal to believe*. The lesson is that God supplies evidence to arouse faith in us, but evidence on its own does not automatically generate faith.

16: 15-18 The Commissioning of the Disciples

Jesus' assignment of the Great Commission to his disciples is also recorded in Matthew 28:19 and Luke 24:47-48. The commission is a command to *go* with the *good news* to *all the world* and to *all creation* (**16:15**). It is given to the disciples and to all who believe. The good news is central to the Great Commission, as it was central to Jesus' mission on earth. They are to take the good news to all nations or all creation. While the focus here is on humans, they do not, strictly speaking, comprise all there is in creation. The emphasis on *all* in 'all the world' and 'all creation' implies that there are to be no exceptions.

The good news will have different effects on two classes of people: believers and unbelievers (**16:16**). Believers will be saved from sin, but unbelievers will be condemned because of their sin. Unpalatable as these options are to modern and postmodern people, they are consistent with the testimony of the rest of Scripture (John 3:18; 1 John 5:12; Heb 12:29). The eternal destiny of every individual depends on how that person responds to this good news.

Mark lists signs that will accompany those carrying out the great commission (**16:17-18**). Throughout the ministry of our Lord, there were spiritual encounters with the forces of darkness. Authenticating power (Luke 9:1-6; 10:1-20) and authority (Matt 10:1, 8) to combat the forces of darkness marked the commissioning of the Twelve and of the Seventy. But in no other gospel account of the giving of the Great Commission is the delegation of power and authority described in terms of accompanying signs. In Matthew, the commission was given on the basis of the authority of Jesus (Mat 28:18). In John, Jesus promised those who trust in him will do *greater things* than he had done (John 14:12). Mark's longer ending includes five signs that would be done *in my name*, that is, on Jesus' authority (16:17-18). The first of these is the driving out of demons, which the disciples had done in Mark 6:6-13, and which also occurs in Acts 5:16 and 19:12. The second, speaking in *new tongues* or languages, occurred in Acts 2:4 and 10:46. The third, picking up snakes, occurred only once in Acts (Acts 28:3-5). There is no biblical record of the occurrence of the fourth sign, safe drinking of deadly poison. Clearly the third and fourth signs are not to be claimed presumptuously, whether to put the Lord to the test or to attract attention to one's self, as some do today. The fifth sign, laying hands on the sick in order to heal them, is amply attested in Acts (see Acts 3:1-8; 5:15-16; 19:11-12) and was common throughout Mark's gospel (6:5; 7:33; 8:23).

The most important lesson to note is not the specific signs but the fact that the good news must be proclaimed with the authority (or in the name) of Jesus Christ. The accompanying signs that God may choose to give are not the focus; Christ Jesus is. In the process of authenticating the good news, the messenger must not supplant the message, which is Christ. The accompanying signs point only to the message of the good news; they are not ends in themselves.

16:19-20 The Ascension

Only Luke (24:50-51) – a later gospel – includes an account of the ascension. The early gospels and other records of the early proclamation of the gospel do not mention it (see, for example, 1 Cor 15:3-7). As Mark seems to be an early gospel, the inclusion of the ascension in the longer ending lends weight to the argument that this ending is both uncharacteristic of Mark's style and a later addition.

The obedience of the apostles in going out with the message is reported extensively in the Acts of the Apostles, but nowhere else in the other gospel records except here in the longer ending of Mark (**16:20**). This verse attests to the obedience of the apostles and the fulfilment of the Lord's promise to provide signs that would authenticate the message of the good news.

Victor Babajide Cole

Further Reading

Cole, Alan. *The Gospel According to St. Mark: An Introduction and Commentary.* TOT. Grand Rapids: Eerdmans, 1976.

Hurtado, Larry W. *Mark,* NIBC. Peabody, Mass.: Hendrickson, 1995.

Lane, W. L. *The Gospel of Mark.* NICNT. Grand Rapids: Eerdmans, 1974.

LUKE

Luke's story of Jesus has often been described as one of the most beautiful ever told. It is a story that advances our knowledge about who Jesus is one small step at a time. Luke understood a point that has only recently been rediscovered in academic theology, namely that truth is basically a story, not a concept. In the OT and the Gospels, God's interaction with people is not conveyed by means of abstract or philosophical concepts, but through stories. The Bible is a collection of stories about individuals, families, communities, nations and events, all of which unite to tell the overarching story of God's redemption of humanity. In reading these stories, our concern must be to see how each advances our faith and good works one little step.

While Luke's story advances in small steps, it leaves behind deep footprints regarding what it means to be children of God and *ubuntu,* that is, truly human. It is ultimately a story of joy, the story of the good news.

The Author

The author of this gospel is traditionally said to have been Luke, a medical doctor who is mentioned three times in the NT. Paul refers to him as 'Our dear friend Luke, the doctor' (Col 4:14) and as a colleague (Phlm 24). He was apparently loyal and dependable, not hesitating to run the risk of associating with Paul during his imprisonment (2 Tim 4:11). It can be inferred that he was Greek (Col 4:10-14).

The writer of this gospel does not claim to have been an eyewitness of the life and work of Jesus, but declares that he had access to first-hand sources of information for writing his account. He was in close personal contact with hearers and eyewitnesses and had knowledge of efforts that had already been made to arrange the facts concerning Jesus in narrative form (1:1-2).

Luke tells us that he has carefully investigated the events of Jesus' life and that he is writing his own orderly account so that readers 'may know the truth concerning the things about which you have been instructed'. Out of these traditions, Luke has created a powerful story with many complex themes.

The Purpose

Luke's story deals with the question of the relationship between correct doctrine or faith and correct social action or good works. This is the same issue that touched off the Reformation. Our faith is rooted in the mighty acts of God: the incarnation and humanization, reconciliation,

resurrection, and the presence of Jesus with us in the person of the Holy Spirit. All of these are at the root of our faith. If such root issues are genuine, according to Luke, then they will bear fruits in good works towards the poor, the sick, the oppressed, the outcasts, people with disabilities and sinners. In short, faith will bear fruits of goodness, generosity, compassion, and social and economic justice. To put it differently, if you were planting a garden, would you want all roots or all fruits? The faith versus good works issue is that kind of question. God is engaged in horticulture. We are God's creatures and God wants us to be whole people with strong roots (faith) and healthy fruits (good works).

To put it differently, Luke's story can be approached from two different but complementary angles. The first approach focuses on Jesus' attitude to social issues and is committed to a prophetic concern for the poor, the oppressed, widows, orphans, the ill, senior citizens, children and those with disabilities. This social gospel was an unmistakable feature of Jesus' ministry as is clear from the verses he quotes from Isaiah when he introduces his ministry to his hometown: 'The Spirit of the Lord is on me, because he has anointed me to preach good news to the poor. He has sent me to proclaim freedom for the prisoners and recovery of sight for the blind, to release the oppressed, to proclaim the year of the Lord's favour' (Luke 4:18-19; see also Isa 61:1-2). Luke also shows Jesus affirming the value of several other groups that were denied full acceptance in the society of his day, including women, children, Samaritans, Gentiles, tax collectors and sinners.

The second approach to Luke's Gospel focuses on the expression of the Holy Spirit as power. The Spirit of God is experienced as the compassionate power to heal the sick, to drive out demons, and to transform people so that they are oriented to God. With such spirituality and lively experience of the Spirit come spontaneous expressions of joy in worship in the forms of praise, speaking in tongues, healing ministry, singing and dancing. Even today, testimonies suggest that prayers for the power of the Holy Spirit have liberated people from drugs and alcohol addictions, transformed people who are mean and selfish, and led many to do extraordinary acts of kindness and love.

For Luke these two approaches are one. The same Holy Spirit who transforms people's spiritual lives also seeks to transform societies and nations to social justice. The behaviour associated with these two ways (faith and good works) can be summarized in the following chart:

Lives without faith and good works	Lives of faith and good works
Put human things before God	Put God first
Marked by oppressive inequities	Seek democratic and free societies
Exclude 'sinners'	Include the 'lost'
Accept disparity of wealth and poverty	Share resources equally
Seek honour from people	Honour the humble
Have hard hearts	Repent and are forgiven by God
Love what people love	Love God above all else
Justify their own ways	Are justified by faith alone
Seek their own interests	Empowered by the Spirit of God

Following Jesus' example, the church should at all times speak the truth as it is informed by our faith. We are called to a prophetic ministry that is rooted in local congregations and grass-roots communities struggling with major social issues. Being engaged in such a ministry will result in conflict, mutual reprimands and bitter debate as we seek to resolve differences or to bring inconsistencies to light. The point is that change is sometimes a slow matter, like giving birth. The new life is there, democracy is there, a new spirit of racial coexistence is there, gender awareness and promotion of it are there, but all are being born in much pain. Doing truth, practising our theology, implementing justice, showing loving kindness and walking with God are never simple matters. We are engaged in an on-going struggle.

But we are not alone in the struggle, for the one who washed people's feet is ready to wash our own feet (John 13:4-5). Luke's vision of the gospel is rooted in a profound experience of spirituality, from which emerged a community committed to opposing all forms of injustice in society and seeking to embody God's new world. This community reflects the universality of the gospel by embracing both men and women and people from many races, ethnic groups, walks of life and social classes. Sharing resources with the needy, healings and Eucharistic celebration mark their togetherness, their *ubuntu*.

The concept *ubuntu* is derived from the Xhosa [South Africa] proverb *ubuntu ungamntu ngabanye abantu*, which, translated roughly, means 'each individual's humanity is best expressed in relationship with others' or 'a person depends on other people to be a person.' In short, those with ubuntu care about the deepest needs of others and faithfully observe all their social obligations. Such people

are conscious not only of their own rights but also of their duties to their neighbour. According to Desmond Tutu, ubuntu is closely related to African world view, in which no one is an independent solitary entity. One is human precisely in being enveloped in the community of other human beings, in being caught up in the bundle of life. To be is to participate.

Such human interdependence is built into our very creation by our being created in God's image. Recognizing our identity in each other shows us that we are more than either black or white, with abilities or disabilities, women or men – we are all human (Gal 3:28). People with *ubuntu* will be empowered by the Holy Spirit to carry out courageous acts of good works, especially towards the poor and the oppressed.

Outline of Contents

COMMENTARY

1:1-80 The Birth of Jesus Announced

1:1-4 The Preface

Luke is the only one of the gospel writers who did not know the physical Jesus. He was not present during our Lord's three-year ministry and did not witness Jesus' death and resurrection. His sources for his gospel are eyewitnesses of these events (**1:2**). He visited the people who actually saw the physical Jesus: his family, his disciples and his friends.

Luke acknowledges that he is not the first to try to create a record of Jesus' life (**1:1**). But probably Luke, an educated man, would have started taking notes about what he heard from others soon after he became a Christian. Out of these notes, oral traditions and sources, Luke created his two books, Luke and Acts. Like the other gospel writers, Luke shapes his presentation of the story of Jesus in order to bring out the true meaning of the events he was describing and to create a powerful story with many complex themes.

This gospel was written to a fellow Greek of high rank whom Luke addresses as *most excellent Theophilus* (a name that means 'Friend of God') (**1:3**). Perhaps the secret of the genuineness of Luke's gospel is that it was written to one person, to Theophilus. It is simultaneously the most universal of the four gospels and the most personal. Where

the personal is universal; the general is vague. This truth is illustrated by a preacher I once saw standing in a market, shouting about Jesus to all those passing by. He was ranting about salvation for the world, and nobody listened. Though he was shouting out the Good News, no one stopped and no one heeded him. His message was so general, it was meaningless. In contrast, Luke knows the secret of genuinely effective communication when he says, 'Listen Theophilus, this is not for the world or the crowd, this is just for you.' Given the opportunity to hear a story, the whole world – waiters, taxi drivers, passengers, workers and the business elite – stops. We all enjoy eavesdropping on an intimate story or conversation. By this personal yet universal call, Luke sought to embrace diverse groups – the rich, the poor, children, women, men, the powerful and the powerless, the elite and the marginalized.

1:5-56 Women's Stories

The Gospel of Luke is often called 'the Gospel of the poor' and 'the Gospel of women', for it is clear that Luke is concerned for the marginalized and oppressed. He is the one who provides female readers with female characters as role models in a world of mainly patriarchal characters. It is here that we meet Elizabeth, the mother of John the Baptist, and Mary of Nazareth, the mother of Jesus. But why do these narratives only appear in the Gospel of Luke? One possible reason may be that Luke may have had access to a women's source – a collection of stories and teachings preserved by women and providing insights into women's experience of the Jesus movement. These stories bear traces of women's involvement and leadership. For example, Anna is the only woman in the gospels called a 'prophetess' (Luke 2:36). Anna and Simeon are both described as prophets in the temple in Jerusalem and Elizabeth and Zechariah both belonged to priestly families and *both of them were upright in the sight of God, observing all the Lord's commandments and regulations blamelessly* (Luke 1:5-6). The respect Luke accords these women's stories could well be emulated by the church today, which needs to listen to the prophetic and protest voices of victimized women. In South Africa today, at least one woman is raped every thirty seconds – yet the church is silent about the shaming of women by men.

1:5-25 A woman's story of shame

Elizabeth's story involves a godly woman (**1:6**) who, like Sarah, Rachel and Hannah in the ot, endured the pain and shame of barrenness. In fact, she refers to it as *my disgrace among the people* (**1:25**). Barrenness cancelled what was regarded as a woman's main function in life, the bearing of children to her husband. It denied a woman the highest status and security she could achieve. Barrenness was thought of as the woman's fault (as here in **1:7**), a punishment for sin or a result of God's 'forgetting' the woman (1 Sam 1:11).

A similar situation prevails in many societies where a woman who is barren is denied her personhood. This is also true of African society, where giving birth is regarded as a spiritual experience and women are considered sacred vessels of life. However, when 'too much emphasis is placed on the reproductive abilities of women, it distorts the image of women. The impression given to African women is that they are valued not for what they are but for what they can produce for the society' (Isabel Phiri, 1997). Furthermore, according to some African traditions, the 'most important role of women in African patriarchal society is that of childbearing ... If a sexual union does not result in pregnancy at the expected time, arrangements are made so that the wife has sexual intercourse with one of her husband's brothers. If after having sexual relations with her husband's brother, she does not conceive, then it is concluded that she is to blame' (Dora Mbuwayesango, 1997). A woman who is barren is considered as shamed, and as no better than a girl. In other words, she is denied a place of honour in society and acknowledgement by others as 'honourable'. That is to say, her *ubuntu* or *khoesib* or *menslikheid* is denied.

Jesus teaches a fundamental respect for human nature as a whole. In short, the maxim of a Christian society should never be to shame a woman but to honour her.

1:26-38 A pregnant virgin

Whereas childlessness means shame and pregnancy removes this disgrace, the opposite is true for an unmarried woman. What is more disgraceful than a premature pregnancy in one who ought to preserve her virginity until marriage? Yet this 'disgrace' is what the angel promises to Mary because she has *found favour with God* (**1:30**). For in Mary's case, she has not sacrificed her virginity; rather the power of God was at work in her (**1:35**).

In preparing for the birth of Christ, both Elizabeth's barrenness and advanced age and Mary's virginity are obstacles that God overcomes. Yet the miracle of a virgin giving birth is even greater than that of an elderly married woman doing so. Mary's miraculous pregnancy is intended to surpass Elizabeth's pregnancy, for Jesus is greater than John the Baptist.

It is clear that Luke truly believes in a virginal conception. He regards Jesus as Joseph's 'supposed' son (3:23). We can thus reject theories that deny the virgin birth, arguing that Luke as a Greek failed to understand Jewish marriage customs and did not know that it involved two steps: a formal exchange of consent before witnesses that gave the couple marital status while the wife continued to live at her own family home for about a year, and then the bride's moving to her husband's home.

When the situation is fully explained to her, Mary makes herself available to God (**1:38**), despite being in a situation in which a pregnancy may appear to bring neither happiness nor blessing, and may be seen as a moral and legal offence. For Luke, it is important that Jesus' birth is from God and is accomplished by the Holy Spirit, and that Mary states her willing acceptance. In short, Mary's virginity is seen as a positive condition: instead of being a hindrance and a moral problem, it is an expression of election by grace.

1:39-56 A woman's story of honour

Where Elizabeth is a woman whose human dignity has been despised, Mary of Nazareth, the mother of Jesus, is a woman who understands honour. Honour is the positive value someone has in her or his own eyes, which is accompanied by a positive appreciation of that person by her or his social group and society. It is associated with face ('saving face' and not being 'shamefaced') and respect. At stake is how others see us, and so, how we see ourselves. Mary recognizes her own worth when she says that, although she occupies a humble position in society, God has honoured her and *from now on all generations will call me blessed* (**1:48**). Her understanding of herself is affirmed by her cousin Elizabeth's exclamation: *Blessed are you among women* (**1:42, 45**). Society may not honour Mary, but God and believers do.

Luke's portrayal honours Mary of Nazareth by recording her long poem, the Magnificat (1:46-55) (the title comes from the opening words of this poem in the Latin translation). This is the only section in all the gospels in which women are given an opportunity to make long speeches. We honour people by listening to what they have to say. In African and Jewish cultures, we respect the commandment to 'honour your father and mother', including both our ancestors and those who are still alive. We express this by never addressing people who are older than we are (including our sisters and brothers) or those who are married by their first names. Instead we address them with their proper titles as a sign of respect and honour.

Mary is an independent woman who speaks about such controversial and dangerous topics as God putting down *rulers from their thrones* but lifting up *the humble. He has filled the hungry with good things but has sent the rich away empty* (1:46-56). She makes these revolutionary statements and speaks her mind without being interrupted or corrected.

Karl Marx considered religion the opiate of the people, but it is clear that he had not paid proper attention to Mary's speech, which is not just personal but deals with theology, social ethics, politics and economics. Theological and ethical issues are addressed in **1:50-51**: *His mercy extends to those who fear him ... scattered those who are proud in their inmost thoughts.* Political issues are addressed in the statement that God *has brought down rulers from their thrones* (**1:52**) and economic issues in the statement that *He has filled the hungry with good things* (**1:53**). These are key themes that will be developed in the gospel, especially the proclamation of good news to the poor (4:18-19).

To reiterate, the Magnificat is the great NT song of liberation, a revolutionary document of intense conflict and victory, produced by a woman who proclaims the virtues and values of peace, justice, humanness, compassion and the equality of humankind. It praises God's liberating actions on behalf of women and other exploited people whose rights are daily violated. In the transformed social and economic order, violence is overcome and food is provided for the hungry. In the spiritual realm, the focus is on the might, holiness and mercy of God, who has promised solidarity with those who suffer.

Elizabeth and Mary each had their own theological journey. Elizabeth had to learn to deal with shame, and African women theologians need to address issues that shame women and deny them honour. These include violence in the form of rape, sexual harassment and wife-beating. Such issues are very sensitive, for they touch the core of the male ego. For example, one church leader is even said to have spoken of 'disciplining' his wife and being 'thanked' by her later, while others have wanted to distinguish between violence that resulted in death and 'just hitting' (Musimbi Kanyoro, 1995). African women theologians need to confront this sensitive issue squarely.

Mary drew on her knowledge of the Scriptures (for example, Hannah's song – 1 Sam 2:1-10) in formulating her views in the Magnificat. African theologians, too, need to reread the Holy Scriptures and allow them to shape their thinking. The following story illustrates the value of rereading the biblical text. Nirmala, who had been given the opportunity to serve as a pastor, was rebuked by her devout aunt for going against the word of God, 'since the Bible says that women should keep silent in public.' In response, Nirmala reminded her aunt of the words of the resurrected Lord to Mary, 'Go and tell my brothers that I am risen'. She explained that with these words the mandate to proclaim the message of resurrection was given first to women, and only afterwards to men (Kanyoro 1997:40).

1:57-80 The Birth of John the Baptist

With the birth of John the Baptist we come to the fulfilment of the promises of God that have occupied the first half of this chapter. The similarity between the promises of the births of Jesus and John is continued in the accounts of their actual births and the acclamation that follows. Luke emphasizes the way in which God fulfils his promises and brings joy to his people (**1:64**; see also 1:13-20). Details of the naming of the child again indicate that he is destined for a significant career in the service of God (**1:59-63**; see also 1:13). But at the same time, the narrative points forward to the birth of Jesus and the salvation that God is preparing for his people in the house of David (1:76-79).

The hymn attributed to the Spirit-filled Zechariah in **1:67-79** is a song of praise to God like the song of Mary in 1:46-56. The subject of both songs is the great day for Israel that comes with Jesus. Most of the song focuses on God's redemption of his people, and only 1:76-77 refers to John himself, describing him as *a prophet of the Most High*. Combining the words here with those in 1:14-17, we learn that John will be a prophetic figure *filled with the Holy Spirit, even from birth,* who will work *in the spirit and power of Elijah.* He will go before Jesus *to make ready a people prepared for the Lord.* We see these prophecies fulfilled in the events recorded in 3:1-6 and 7:26-27. It is not surprising that his ministry there is introduced in terms which remind us of the OT prophets: 'the word of God came to John' (3:2).

2:1-52 The Birth and Childhood of Jesus

For Jews, as for Africans, the family is the fundamental unit of the society. But the relationship between Mary and Joseph breaks with the traditional understanding of the pattern of what may be termed a 'natural' family, for Joseph is not the child's father. It is also not clear whether Mary and Joseph were legally married by this time, for she is described as *pledged to be married to him* (**2:5a**). It was a difficult start to a marriage, made even more so by the prospect of undertaking a long and difficult journey with a woman who was heavily pregnant (**2:5b-6**).

2:1-20 The Christmas Story

Do you remember how you felt as a child on Christmas Eve? Most of us simply could not wait for Christmas morning when we would receive new clothes and perhaps new shoes for the first time in the entire year. We would proudly wear our new clothes to the church service, where we would sing the Christmas songs and dramatize the Christmas story. I feel that same sense of excitement and joy when I consider the treasures that God has for us in this chapter on the birth and childhood of Jesus. This is a story that we need to be eager to sit and listen to, and not merely analyze.

The story of the angelic hosts and of the visit of the shepherds to the manger is perhaps the best known of all the nativity stories. But the rich imagery of the entire story appeals to some of the profoundest feelings in the human heart: shepherds caring for their sheep (**2:8**); the mother and father caring for their new baby (**2:7, 16, 19**); the angel choir breaking into the darkness of earth's night to herald the long-awaited sunrise, assuring the humble poor that whatever the mighty governments of the world might be doing, God cares for people, and with a shepherd's heart has chosen that Jesus should be born not in a palace but in a manger (**2:9-14**).

The Christmas story invites all of us to respond like a child as we express our faith not so much in professional terms as in personal ones.

2:21-24 The Circumcision of Jesus

Jesus' parents were obeying the law when they had Jesus circumcised *on the eighth day* (**2:21**; see also Lev 12:3). From an African perspective, the story of the circumcision of Jesus explodes with meaning. In African tradition, someone who has been circumcised is regarded as a full person, ready to shoulder responsibility, exercise authority and guide others. Jesus' circumcision marks him as qualified and authorized to lead. He has been properly initiated into life and can lead us and show us the way of life and command our respect and love. He has sound wisdom and experience.

2:25-40 Jesus' Arrival in the Temple

About a month after Jesus' birth, in obedience to commands about the ritual purification of mothers after childbirth, Mary and Joseph went up to Jerusalem to offer the sacrifice of *a pair of doves or two young pigeons* (**2:22, 24**; Lev 12:1-8). Their offering proves that they were poor people, who could not afford to offer the lamb that was the usual offering (Lev 12:8). At the same time, they also obeyed the command that every firstborn male belonged to the Lord and had to be redeemed (Exod 13:1-2; Num 18:15-16).

When Jesus arrives in the temple, Simeon, too, breaks into a song full of OT allusions which announces that with the coming of Messiah, the old order is to be superseded (**2:25-28**). Simeon makes three striking claims about Jesus. First he declares that in Jesus salvation has come (**2:30**). Then he borrows an expression from one of the Servant passages in Isaiah and calls Jesus *a light ... to the Gentiles ... and glory to your people Israel* (**2:32**; see also Isa 49:6). Finally, Simeon prophesies that a sword will pierce the soul of Mary, the mother of Jesus, referring to the anguish she would suffer on Good Friday (**2:35**).

Jesus' arrival also answers the prayers of the prophetess, Anna. Anna had prayed for the coming of the Messiah as her OT namesake had prayed for the coming of Samuel (1 Sam 1). Just as Hannah had presented Samuel to the Lord, and he 'continued to grow in stature and in favour with the Lord and with men' (1 Sam 2:26), so it was with Jesus (**2:40**). And just as Hannah and Elkanah returned home to Ramah (1 Sam 2:11), so Mary and Joseph returned to Nazareth (**2:39**).

2:41-52 Jesus Discovers His Mission

In the final scene of chapters 1 and 2, Luke brings the reader back to the temple, where the infancy story began with Gabriel speaking to Zechariah over twelve years before. This scene has the same atmosphere of piety that introduced the previous temple scene (**2:41**; see also 2:22-24). Jesus' parents continue their annual practice of going up to Jerusalem for the Feast of Passover; only now Jesus is old enough to join them. The law required every male Jew to attend three annual festivals in Jerusalem each year.

With Jews scattered in many places throughout the Roman Empire, most went only once a year. The women were not required to go, but they often did. The Feast of the Passover, the occasion of this particular trip, is a seven-day event celebrating the deliverance from Egypt. It seems natural that whole families would share this week-long festivity. Despite their poverty (see comment on 2:24), the family stays for the entire seven to eight days. They cut no corners. But Jesus stayed even longer. He was now twelve years old, in the final year before his *Bar Mitzvah* (**2:42**). In a year he would become a full-fledged adult Jewish male, responsible for himself and for all of Israel.

In the second visit to the temple, Jesus takes an active role in an incident that foreshadows his greatness and shows his developing awareness of his special relationship to God and of the obligations which that entails. This incident is linked with the scenes in Luke 3-4, in which through prayer and struggle Jesus arrives at a clear understanding of his mission and accepts it as the task he must fulfil.

Jesus' remaining behind in the Temple when Mary and Joseph set off for home makes for a dramatic reunion after they have searched for him frantically. This reunion, which centres on a confrontation between the parents and the child, contains the first recorded words of Jesus in Luke's Gospel (**2:48-49**). Since Luke has bracketed the scene with reference to Jesus' wisdom (**2:52**; see 2:40), it is not surprising that these first words show Jesus' understanding of his relationship to God as his Father.

What is surprising is that his parents do not understand his words (**2:50**), despite the preceding revelations of Jesus' identity on which Mary has had twelve years to reflect (1:32-35; 2:11, 17, 19). Not only are the parents unaware of Jesus' whereabouts but they do not understand the situation. They took it for granted that he would be with the extended family, with friends and acquaintances. But he, whose extended family would one day stand and watch him from a distance (23:49), stands in a much closer relationship to Another, as he is quick to inform his parents (2:49). To put it differently, his parents must learn to live with the fact that he, their son, is a stranger and guest in their home, for he is under orders from Another. In short, at the age of twelve Jesus discovers, if not the content, at least the larger dimension of his ministry.

This incident in Jerusalem has a revelatory tone. Mary's response is appropriate: she *treasured all these things in her heart* (**2:51**; see also 2:19). First the shepherd's greeting, and now this. In other words, Mary is faced with the same problem that confronts all who hear the word of God. Faith is the single port of entry into the mystery of Jesus' person. Mary is not relieved of that responsibility. Hence Jesus has no special comfort for those, including Mary, who claim a close kinship with him. Now Christians must do like Mary did and ponder the word of God that Jesus brings. A story about another Mary will reinforce this point (10:38-42).

3:1-20 Theological and Ethical Ministry of John

3:1-18 John's Message

The account of the ministry of John the Baptist begins with an impressive list of names, mentioning politicians such as the Emperor Tiberius, Pontius Pilate, Herod, Philip and Lysanius, and the chief priests Annas and Caiaphas (3:1-2a). This list both dates the beginning of John's ministry and helps us to perceive John's stature. While the politicians and religious leaders possessed the highest authority in the political and religious arena, John came with a higher authority. While these political and religious leaders represented the 'establishment', John came out of the desert. But in that desert *the word of God came to John son of Zechariah* – in accordance with the custom of the time, Elizabeth is not mentioned as his mother (3:2b). That word made him a prophet like Hosea, Micah, Jonah, Zephaniah, Haggai, Zechariah, Jeremiah, Isaiah and Ezekiel, who under the direct inspiration of God had counselled, and sometimes rebuked and denounced, political leaders, kings and queens, and religious leaders as well as the nations at large. At the divinely appointed time, God sent first John and then Jesus to the world.

John's message was centred in Jesus Christ, the *one more powerful* (3:16) than any other leader in whom the people may have false confidence. Luke uses an OT prophecy to describe John's ministry and to identify the person whom John announces. In calling on the people to *prepare the way for the Lord* (3:4), Luke is stating in clear theological terms that John's ministry is the fulfilment of Isaiah's prophecy (Isa 40:3-5). John's was the voice that was destined to call on people to prepare the approach road and it follows that the visitor whose approach John announced was the same visitor announced by Isaiah: God in Jesus Christ through the Spirit.

John does not see his own task as being to prepare the nation for the sudden coming in power of a messianic deliverer; rather he prepares the way for God so that God may announce salvation for all flesh (3:6). The salvation that *all mankind will see* is Jesus, in whose person and activity the forgiveness of sins and the display of God's good pleasure become a reality for all humanity.

Since Jesus does not match the vision of the Messiah promoted by the politicians and religious leaders, major revision of national and religious thought is needed if the people are to appreciate God's programme in connection with Jesus. So John sets out to destroy people's false confidence. He speaks to the crowds in uncomplimentary language, calling them a *brood of vipers* (3:7). They are behaving like snakes fleeing before a grass fire; trying to escape the flames but without any intention of having their evil nature changed. They behave as though all they need to do to escape the coming wrath is to submit to the outward ritual of baptism, without giving any practical evidence of repentance. John was not teaching such cheap grace. Nor did he permit them to hide behind the fact that they were physically descended from Abraham, for he warned them that physical descent from Abraham was no substitute for costly grace (3:8). The criterion for salvation is not birth, national identity, religion, class or status.

In destroying false confidence, John was a pattern for Martin Luther. Luther insisted that buying indulgences would not assure one's salvation or guarantee one a place in heaven. His great text was 'The righteous will live by faith' (Gal 3:11), and his words sparked the Reformation. It is not far from what John was saying – that to get right with God, you have to admit you are not right with God. Hence his call for repentance.

So then, Luke has first identified, theologically, the visitor for whom the road had to be made, and then shown us, ethically, what making the road involves.

Various groups of people approached John to ask what repentance would mean in their case. Ordinary citizens were told that their work of repentance would be a willingness to share life's necessities of food and clothing with those in need (3:10-11). Tax collectors were told that for them it would be ceasing to demand more than the appointed amount of tax (3:12-13). Soldiers were told that for them it would be refraining from extorting money or goods by force or by falsely accusing people; they must be content with their army wages and provisions (3:14).

To reiterate, John's message is that we need to rededicate ourselves in the presence and activity of God so that God will spiritually awaken us. Our spirituality needs to be anchored in word and sacrament, including corporate worship, prayer, Bible study and the African understanding of what it is to be human, namely a social being, a being in relation to others. To put it differently, such spirituality is based on love and mutual respect instead of on competition, jealousy and hatred. The outstretched hand of another should not grope in a void but should find prayerful friendship in my outstretched hand. In short, the church needs a spirituality where we find each other, where we respect each other, where we reconcile with each other as sisters, brothers, colleagues, comrades, families and helpmates.

The communal aspects of spiritual life include the ability both to forgive and to receive forgiveness from others, the giving and receiving of encouragement and exhortation, the ability to verbalize and communicate our faith, and the willingness to worship together and not be divided by language, ethnicity and liturgical tradition.

The people of God, according to the Holy Scriptures as interpreted by the church, are called to proclaim and live the gospel of Jesus Christ, the Liberator and Saviour (4:18-19) for all human beings, in all their living conditions. In other words, all Christians have been called and commissioned through baptism, to serve God, one another, and the whole creation (John 13:13-14). Just as the different parts of the body exist to serve each other and give service to the whole, so do the members of the body of Christ. Each part's role is just as vital and essential for the whole body as that of the other parts. It is through the multiplicity that the unity functions. Therefore, the whole people of God, with all their different gifts, are called to administer God's manifold grace.

3:19-20 Prophetic Message and Its Implications

The message of John raised issues with political implications. Luke informs us that the preacher of repentance, the herald of the Messiah, and the prophet of social justice soon ran afoul of the political authorities.

John not only criticized Herod's marriage to Herodias, the wife of his brother, but he also reprimanded him for all other evil things he did (**3:19**). This prophet from the desert did not remove himself from the political arena. Luke leaves no doubt that John the Baptist was an active critic of Herod in his capacity as political leader. Luke's own verdict on John's arrest and imprisonment is that it was one more evil thing that Herod did (**3:20**). Herod was a murderer, a 'fox,' and an adversary of the Messiah (9:7-9; 13:31-32; 23:7-12).

The relationship between John and Herod raises the issue of church and state, that is, the role of religion in public life. In Africa today, we seem to be experiencing confusion as regards the working relationship between the church and the state. For example, when must the church retain its autonomy, its right to make its own decisions without government interference? When must the church maintain its integrity, the necessity for the church to be what it is, the body of Christ, rather than a channel for carrying out government policy? The church must have the freedom to witness, the moral necessity of expressing its inner convictions, even when these run counter to political expediency. Today, we need to debate these issues because there is a high price to pay if the church becomes too politicized or our faith too privatized.

I would argue that relations between the church and the state should always be characterized by institutional separation and functional interaction. By this I mean that churches and governments do have some areas of common interest, usually involving human welfare, in which they can cooperate to achieve objectives. With the growing complexity of modern society, both the church and government have an important stake in solving problems that affect people's lives. But while addressing these social issues and problems, the church should remain the church and the government should remain the government. Put differently, church and government are distinct but not divorced. Rather than building a wall of separation between church and government, there should be institutional separation

and functional interaction, because both the government and the church are part of the society. When the church promotes human rights, it acts within its own rights as an institution that is part of the society. Therefore, it cannot be accused of interfering in government business.

Why are we experiencing an identity crisis as the church when it comes to our mission in this world? The answer may lie in the type of experience the church in Namibia has gone through. During the years of colonialism and oppression, the church essentially refused to cooperate with the colonial regimes. It was very easy to galvanize people into action to fight the evils of political, economic, racial and gender exploitation. The goal was clear. We were opposed to apartheid and colonialism in Africa.

But on 21 March 1990, Namibia gained its independence, and it became time to say both 'No' and 'Yes' to the government. But the churches did not know when to say 'No' and when to say 'Yes'. It was not clear that in the new situation the prophetic 'No' must also include the prophetic 'Yes' to options making for socio-political and economic renewal. The church should loudly and clearly support initiatives that may lead to a new social order. But the task of the church in an independent and democratic state is also to learn when to say 'No' by remaining vigilant about the dangers of political power, specifically its ability to serve its own interests rather than the common good. The prophetic struggle against injustice must continue. Often it requires further conflict, mutual reprimands and bitter debate to resolve differences or to bring inconsistencies to light. The point is that change is sometimes a very slow matter, like a baby being born. The new life is there, but is often only brought into being with much pain.

The church is an institution composed of believing Christians in society. As such, it has the right to make statements explaining its views on issues, and will thus become involved in many kinds of activities. Some of these activities will involve promoting human rights and fundamental freedoms, reconciliation and nation building. The church should jealously defend its right to speak and its voice should be heard publicly and not secretly. In other words, the church is free to support the cause of civil society honestly and calmly.

When the church acts in the society, it should act boldly. God's creation is social and cultural as well as natural and physical. As a consequence, we have to take the secular world and the civil community seriously. The church's social ministry should not be limited to charitable activities that merely bind up the wounds of society's victims. We should be actively engaged in shaping society to prevent such wounds.

Lastly, the church needs to articulate theologically when to prophetically say 'No' or 'Yes' within the context of being distinct from but not divorced from the government.

Without a clear theological standpoint, we all will be confused. If the church cannot sort out this confusion, many will remain without shelter from the rain or without adequate food.

3:21-37 Jesus' Baptism and Genealogy

In Luke, Jesus' baptism is mentioned only as the background to a prayer, a vision and its interpretation. Luke often mentions Jesus' prayer life and clearly considers it of great importance (**3:21**; 5:16; 6:12; 9:18, 28-29; 11:1; 22:32, 39-46; 23:34, 46). In Luke, the prayers of Jesus are often accompanied by visions and voices. For example, while he is praying in 9:28-36, Moses and Elijah appear and a voice is heard saying: 'This is my Son' (see also 22:9-46; Acts 10; 12:5-10). Likewise, in 3:21-22, when Jesus is praying after his baptism, there is a heavenly apparition: *the Holy Spirit descended on him in bodily form like a dove.* The dove symbolizes the loving character of divine life. The Holy Spirit coming to Jesus in the form of a dove actually says that Jesus is beloved of God. The truth of this interpretation is proved by the voice from heaven: *You are my Son, whom I love; with you I am well pleased* (**3:22**). These words are an adaptation of Isaiah 42:1, a passage that is also quoted in Matthew 12:18. The passage speaks about God's servant on whom God has put his Spirit: God's beloved is given God's Holy Spirit.

The words in 3:22 remind us of Jesus' heavenly roots, namely that he is truly God's son. But Luke also reminds us that Jesus was supposedly Joseph's son and gives us his earthly family tree (**3:23-37**). The reference to the 'heavenly genealogy' demonstrates that Jesus Christ is the Son of God, while the reminder of his 'earthly genealogy' stresses his real humanity. It stresses that Jesus was a human being among us humans. In order to save humanity, he became human in the most real sense. Luke stresses this point by linking the humanity of Jesus to Adam and Eve, the founders of the human race.

4:1-22 Jesus' Prophetic Role

4:1-13 Rites of passage

In all religions the most important occasions in the natural progression from birth to death are marked with special ceremonies and celebrations, which sociologists refer to as rites of passage. In Christianity these rites include baptism, confirmation, marriage and funerals. In African traditional religion there are birth and naming ceremonies, initiation and puberty rites, marriage and funeral ceremonies. Many people, even those who claim not to be religious, still make use of churches, synagogues, mosques and temples to mark these rites of passage.

The ceremonies associated with rites of passage from one stage of life to another generally involve the separation of the person from his or her usual surroundings, his or her preparation for a new task or way of life in society, and, finally, his or her reception into this group or community or society. During such rites of passage the person may be exposed to danger in order to test whether he or she is mature enough to face this new life. Once this period of separation is over, it is essential that such a person be initiated into the new group or society with the least possible delay, in order that he or she may once again have a normal place in the community.

Only persons who have passed through all the stresses, strains and problems of human life and no longer fear anything, those who one might almost say are beyond fear, are qualified to officiate at rites of passage. In the case of the encounter between Jesus and the devil, the only one with such experience is God. Therefore the devil tests Jesus before the face of God in order to determine whether Jesus is truly human and truly the Son of God.

It is clear that 3:21-23 describes a period of crisis in Jesus' life and a point of transition. In this sense, it marks a rite of passage. In 2:42 and 2:52, Jesus was a twelve-year-old child, who was increasing in wisdom and in years. In 3:21, when he presents himself for baptism, he is thirty years old but still a private person. But by **4:14**, after completing the rites of passage, a dramatic change has taken place: he has become a public figure, a prophet in Israel, with a new, clearly defined role and status.

Despite the high status accorded Jesus in the infancy stories (1:32-35; 2:11), and his insight into his relationship with God (with God as his Father and himself the Son and Servant of God) and into the divine necessity governing his life's path (2:43, 49), Jesus was still described as a boy (2:43). He must still be initiated into his full adult role. That initiation takes place in a dramatic encounter between two superstars, Jesus and the devil (**4:2**). During this confrontation, Jesus demonstrates that he is worthy to bear the titles of Saviour, Christ and Lord; that is, he is totally loyal to God's affairs and able to function worthily. Therefore, immediately after this rite of passage, Jesus unrolled the scroll, read from Isaiah 61:1-2, and declared, *Today this scripture is fulfilled in your hearing* (4:21).

At various stages of Jesus' life and ministry, Luke shows that he exhibits a profound awareness of the unique role he will play in the history of salvation. At the beginning and end of his ministry, Jesus publicly points to himself as the Messiah (**4:18**) and the Son of God (20:13). However, in this passage, Jesus is put to the test to determine whether he has the qualities he will need to be the Saviour, the Christ and the Lord (2:11). The devil, his arch-adversary, confronts Jesus and attempts to humiliate him before the start of his ministry. His aim is to frustrate God's plan of salvation at the outset by enticing Jesus to break faith with God. His proposal about bread and his quotations from Scripture (**4:3**) both involve things that are normally considered good. Yet under both is hidden the devil's poison. But Jesus, like John the Baptist (3:7-9), can unmask hidden evil and so he rejects these suggestions in order to remain God's Holy One and to speak for God as God's prophet (**4:4, 8, 12**). For all his power, Satan is no match for Jesus.

Then Luke ends this story with a note that will haunt the narrative: *The devil ... left him ... until an opportune time* (**4:13**). Towards the close of the book, we will read that after Jesus has completed his messianic teaching of Israel in the temple, 'Satan entered Judas ... he consented and watched for an opportunity to hand Jesus over' (22:3-6).

4:14-22 The Message of Liberation

At the outset it should be noted that the political language of Luke 4:14-44 is unmistakable. Immediately after undergoing his rites of passage, Jesus announces the five purposes for which God has sent him: *to preach good news to the poor ... to proclaim freedom for the prisoners and recovery of sight for the blind, to release the oppressed, to proclaim the year of the Lord's favour* (**4:18-19**).

This announcement takes place during Jesus' visit to the synagogue of Nazareth where he publicly presents himself to the nation as God's Messiah. Invited by the leader of the synagogue to read from the Scriptures, Jesus stands, is handed a scroll that he unrolls to the intended passage, reads the passage, rolls the scroll up again, hands it back to the attendant, and sits down to speak while all eyes remain fixed on him (**4:16-20**). The interest of those present is intense, and Luke prolongs the silence surrounding the reading to make it clear that the eyes of all in the synagogue are fixed on Jesus' every move.

Jesus' exposition of the text is profound in its brevity: *And he began by saying to them, 'Today this scripture is fulfilled in your hearing'* (**4:21**). Perhaps, this is the shortest and the best sermon ever preached because *all spoke well of him and were amazed at the gracious words that came from his mouth* (**4:22**).

It is clear that from the beginning to end Jesus was oriented to the needs of the poor, both those who were poor within themselves and those who were poor in social, economic and political contexts. His parents were not wealthy (2:24) and lived in a despised village (John 1:46). In his public ministry he lived poorly, mixed with the ordinary folk who were the poor, the 'prisoners', the 'blind' and the 'oppressed' (4:18). Furthermore, he shocked the elite by eating with social outcasts (5:30; 19:7). He acted and spoke in a manner that caused him to be seen as a serious threat by the various establishment groups in his country and by the Roman Empire. Eventually, the religious establishment and the Roman colonial power murdered Jesus.

4:23-5:39 A Ministry of Word and Deed

4:23-44 Ministry Launched

If someone has a message from God to give, the natural place to deliver that message is the place where people come together to worship or to hear the word of God. That is precisely what Jesus did when he began his campaign in a synagogue. He has described the nature of his ministry, saying that its content is preaching 'good news to the poor' and setting at liberty those that are oppressed (4:18-19). Its basis is the anointing of Jesus with the Holy Spirit (4:18). But Jesus is also clear about the results of his ministry (4:23-30). He will be rejected by his own people and he hints that there will be a wider mission to all kinds of people (**4:23-27**). The portrait of Jesus in this section is of someone who is empowered by the Holy Spirit. This empowering divides those Jesus meets into two groups: those who recognize God in Jesus' words and works and those who do not (**4:28-30**).

Luke then moves on to tell the first stories about Jesus' healing ministry. These involve an exorcism in Capernaum (**4:31-35**) and the story of healing of Peter's mother-in-law (**4:38-39**). Such activities brought Jesus a tremendous following (**4:37, 42; 5:1-3**) and led the people of Capernaum to try to keep him in their area (**4:42**). But Jesus responded as he had at Nazareth, indicating that it was necessary that he move on (**4:43**). The word of God cannot be restricted to one single place.

5:1-11 The Calling of Simon Peter

One day Jesus used Simon's boat as a pulpit from which to preach a sermon (**5:3**). Simon sat at Jesus' side right through the sermon but does not seem to have been particularly moved by it. Sensing this, Jesus told Simon to put out into deep water and let down the nets for a catch (**5:4**). Significantly, even in expressing his doubts to Jesus, Simon addresses him as Master (**5:5a**). It is a term that subordinates used to address a superior. Perhaps Simon used this term because of his earlier experience of the miracle Jesus had performed in curing his mother-in-law of a great fever (4:38-39). Perhaps merely to please Jesus and show his gratitude for the healing, but with no hope of catching fish and making a profit, he let the net down (**5:5b**). Suddenly he has so many fish in his net that he has to beckon James and John, his business partners, to bring their boat to help him. In the end, both boats are so full of fish that they are in danger of sinking (**5:6-7**).

The effect upon Simon was understandable. He did not regard the miracle as a lesson in better fishing techniques that might improve his profits. All his attention was focused on the person of Jesus Christ (**5:8a**). His companions and his two business partners were equally astonished (**5:9-10a**).

Focusing his attention on Simon, Jesus tells him that he will now be joining Jesus in his own profession – which someone has translated as 'catching people alive' (**5:10b**). As the first of the disciples to be called, Simon Peter becomes both a spokesperson for the others and typical of them in their faith and weakness. Still, though Jesus focuses on Simon Peter, James and John share in Peter's commissioning. They respond to Jesus' words exactly as Peter does, leaving everything behind and following Jesus (**5:11**). It is remarkable that these men leave their profession and all their equipment to follow Jesus.

Today, we who have long known who Jesus is and what he requires of us in the sphere of our daily secular and sacred work may well have cause to feel even more insecure than Simon Peter when he cried out, *I am a sinful man* (**5:8b**). Our sinfulness as Christians may be seen in the substandard quality of our ministry in the world today, where poverty, gender inequality, a lack of housing, a lack of medical care, and many social ills prevail. We are not called to employment and service in the world for material profit, but primarily in order to please God and be engaged in the ministry of word and deed that 'catches people alive' and makes life liveable, humane and godly.

5:12-26 Believing in Divine Healing

In these episodes Luke gives more details about the healing ministry of Jesus, which was first mentioned in 4:31-41, and tells the story of two separate healings, one of a victim of leprosy and the other of a paralytic. The leper lived to testify to what Jesus had done for him (**5:14**) and the paralytic man went home healed both physically and spiritually – his sins forgiven and in right standing with God (**5:20**). For such individuals, being healed means being restored to one's extended family, friends and community. Health, therefore, implies safe integration into the life of society. Africans have long been aware of this, which is why we greet people by inquiring about their health and the health of their family members, even if the one being greeted is a total stranger. One does not only ask 'How are you?', but also 'How are your people?' Similarly, every farewell, even to a casual acquaintance, involves sending greetings to her or his family.

These human consequences of the healing must not be neglected. Our hearts are moved by the picture of the man falling on his face before Jesus pleading, *If you are willing, you can make me clean* (**5:12, 24**; see also Mark 1:40, Matt 8:2). We are also moved by the desperation of those who carried a paralysed man up onto the roof and let him down through the tiles into the middle of the crowd in front of Jesus (**5:19**). Jesus responds to the desperate faith of the leper and of those carrying the paralysed man and heals them. Such stories invite us to reflect on the church ministry of healing today.

A significant development in Africa is the rise of the African Instituted Churches (AICs). These dynamic and growing churches seek to have a truly African Christianity, not one that is imported from the West, and lay great stress on the theology and ministry of healing. They preach miraculous healing, or healing by the power of the Holy Spirit, and revive the linking of faith with health, healing and medicine that existed in biblical times.

The church as a whole is called to situate its understanding of health and healing within the African world view, which perceives health as more than merely physical well-being. Most Africans have not lost touch in their subconscious self with the world view that sees disease and misfortune as the result of malicious external factors. Fears of witchcraft, sorcery, taboos, curses, bad omens, malicious spirits and a host of other evil forces (often drawn from the interaction of traditional religions with Christianity and Islam with their devil, demons and jinn) are a reality to many Africans, regardless of education, socio-economic status or creed. Thus true health also involves spiritual, mental, physical, social and environmental harmony.

Any healing ministry in Africa that does not take African cosmology seriously is doomed to fail. The AICs have recognized this, and their healing does not aim to supplant medical treatment but to supplement it. Their prayers, visions, dreams, laying on of hands, use of holy water and oil, ashes, drums, staves and other rituals are aimed at dealing with practical problems of life, just as African traditional religion did and still does. In other words, in these churches the African world view is very much complemented by the biblical world view and the healing is done in the name of the Triune God, and particularly of Jesus Christ and the Holy Spirit. We, too, need to take the social context into account as we seek to understand illness and the mediation of healing.

5:27-39 The Difference Jesus Makes

This passage consists of a series of accusations from the Pharisees about the lifestyle of Jesus and his followers and Jesus' answers. The first charge is that they associate with the wrong kind of people (**5:30**). They should not eat and drink with social outcasts. Jesus responds that the sick are the ones who need him, and, therefore, he as host invites sinners to eat with him (**5:31-32**).

The second charge is that the disciples' lifestyle is not serious enough. There is too much eating and drinking and not enough fasting and praying (**5:33**). Jesus says that fasting while proclaiming good news makes no more sense than fasting at a wedding feast. It is unthinkable (**5:34-35**).

Then Jesus tells a double parable. A piece of cloth from a new garment is not used to patch an old one because taking the piece would damage the new garment and the bright colours of the new cloth would not match the faded colours of the old one (**5:36**). New wine is not put into old wineskins, for they are brittle and would burst. Rather, new wine is stored in new wineskins (**5:37-39**). His point is that a new inner religious reality demands a new lifestyle. The marks of Jesus' followers will not be Sabbath observance, fasting and prayers, and avoidance of outcasts, but will be joy like that at a wedding (5:33-35) and an overriding concern for human needs, both spiritual (5:29-32) and physical (6:1-11). Such a way of life has the authority of Jesus behind it. The apostle Paul captured this spirit when he wrote to the Romans: 'The kingdom of God is not a matter of eating and drinking, but of righteousness, peace and joy in the Holy Spirit' (Rom 14:17).

6:1-11 Breaking the Sabbath

It was probably no accident that many of Jesus' 'mighty works' were associated with the Sabbath. It is likely that Jesus deliberately did them on that day. Within Judaism, the Sabbath had come to be regarded as a symbol of the peace, restoration and well-being of Israel, and the peaceful enjoyment of the Sabbath was to be one of the signs that the messianic age had come (Isa 14:3). Jesus' actions indicated to those who were ready to respond that his mission bore the marks of the promised Sabbath of Israel.

In **6:6-11** Jesus' enemies are watching in order to trap him. He publicly heals a man with a withered hand after demanding whether it is right to heal or to harm on the Sabbath. For Jesus, acts of faith and humanitarianism go together.

6:12-16 Choosing the Twelve

The choosing of the twelve disciples marks another turning point in the ministry of Jesus. Once again Luke sets this within the context of prayer; this time, all-night prayer (**6:12**). The choice of a group of twelve suggests that Jesus is consciously making a link between his work and God's work in the OT where he brought the twelve tribes of Israel to the Promised Land. The twelve disciples represent the new Israel. The picture Jesus presents of the kingdom in its final glory has the Twelve sitting on thrones as judges of the twelve tribes of Israel (Luke 22:30). To the eyes of faith, he and the Twelve are signs of the presence of the kingdom.

6:17-49 The Sermon on the Plain

6:17-20a Sermons Today

When the chief priests and the Pharisees sent the temple police to arrest Jesus, they returned empty handed. Asked to explain why, all they could say was 'No one ever spoke the way this man does!' (John 7:40-47). They could not help perceiving the utter difference between Jesus and all other teachers. His words were uniquely original, full of authority, and perplexingly deep in content. When one reads his sermon on the plain, it is almost impossible not to exclaim with those temple police of old: 'No one ever spoke the way this man does!'

But why did Jesus' teaching have such an impact? And what about sermons today – can they also make an impact?

Before focusing on this sermon, let us think about sermons and their place in churches today. Why is it that African Methodist Episcopal churches have only a large pulpit, whereas a Lutheran church building will have both an altar and a pulpit, although the pulpit will be slightly taller than the altar. In a Roman Catholic church, one is immediately struck by the impressiveness, beauty and artistic design of an altar. Why these differences in various Christian denominations?

The answer may be that some denominations stress the need for 'big ears' to hear the Word of God, namely preaching. Other denominations stress the importance of 'big eyes', to see the symbolism that shows us God's mystery and fascination, and still others urge us to have both 'big eyes' and 'big ears', but preferably the latter. Clearly, the importance of preaching in the life of the church is determined by our particular theological doctrines. For some, the sermon is a spiritual starter before the Eucharist, while for others it is the main course of the Sunday service. But the sermon is always important, for Christ was not content merely to perform miracles that blessed and astounded people, he also taught the people, as here.

As regards the content of a sermon, St Augustine pointed out that the ministry of preaching involves three things: teaching, delighting and moving. In other words, a sermon ought to be fresh if it is to teach us; it ought to be delightful in making us feel alive, for without God's grace we are dead in our futile ways and our trespasses and sins; and it ought to move us to turn to God (conversion). If a sermon does not do this, it becomes something to be merely endured!

Preaching is essential in the life of the church because in preaching we attempt to give God's answers to the questions people raise. When a Lutheran pastor, or a Roman Catholic priest, or a Dutch Reformed dominee, or a prophet in an African Initiated Church, or an Anglican bishop steps into the pulpit, the magic moment starts. In the pews sit a university student majoring in Biblical Studies, a banker who has twice contemplated suicide that week, a teacher who has just been informed that he has AIDS, a mother who has lost her firstborn, a young man who has just discovered that he is homosexual, and countless others: all listening as you begin your sermon.

But within the first few minutes, the preacher may have lost her listeners to their own thoughts. Even if much time was spent in preparation, a sermon will not be heard if it is not well delivered. This means you must really say what you intended to say, and not forget important points or confuse them. Your voice must be clear, and varied. Normally, one uses a moderate voice, but there may be times when it is appropriate to reduce one's voice almost to the level of a whisper, while at other times it is appropriate to issue an impassioned appeal. In some ways, the art of preaching is like singing, which needs to include both quiet and loud sections. The preacher also needs to know when to say 'Amen' and stop preaching, before the congregation loses interest and becomes distracted and tired. More of the service will follow the sermon, and it is better to close early when people would still like to learn something more, than too late, when all they want to do is leave.

But presenting a good sermon is not solely a matter of technique. It is also important to pray before starting your sermon, asking God to make you a real witness to your message. When this happens, you will harvest the full joy of teaching and finding listeners, the joy of delighting others and not putting them to sleep, and the joy of moving people to God. As preachers we are blessed by God to be used as his instruments and agents in the ministry of preaching. Therefore, preach so that the Bible comes alive and makes the Christian faith believable. In such a way, the Word of God will become flesh and will live among us (John 1:14).

6:20b-26 A Policy Statement

In the Sermon on the Plain, Jesus issues a major policy statement of the kingdom of God. This address explains more about the 'good news to the poor' which he announced in Nazareth and which he had demonstrated in messianic acts throughout Galilee. Now he speaks, and the message is revolutionary – a series of bombshells. The Beatitudes take our standard notions of what is acceptable and turn them upside down. The people whom Jesus calls 'blessed' the world would call 'wretched'; and the people for whom Jesus prophecies 'woe' are those whom the world professes to admire. This sermon completely overturns the world's values.

These words must have been addressed to the hungry, powerless and socially dispossessed people around Jesus. His announcement of the reign of God, with its concrete promise of a better future, must have stirred up long latent hopes for a time when justice would prevail and their present hardships would be past. They saw their present life and condition as a scandal in the eyes of God. But they looked to the future to change this. The preaching of Jesus revitalized the messianic hope. It was this hope that those around Jesus took to heart, and thus understood themselves as the 'little flock' who were heirs of the coming reign of God (12:32).

The Beatitudes, in Luke's telling, are blunt: *Blessed are you who are poor* (**6:20b**). Throughout his Gospel and in

Acts, Luke relentlessly shows Jesus' focus on the poor and reveals early Christian groups having that same concern. This image both haunts and inspires us today as we consider what it means to be a Christian community in a world plagued by poverty.

When Jesus says that the poor are blessed, he is stating a principle. We are responsible for formulating concrete ethics and principles and policies that will ensure blessedness for the poor today. Theologically speaking, with God's blessings and under the command of the God who co-exists with us, we are invited to take up the task of eradicating poverty while addressing and finding solutions to the challenges facing Africa and the world at large.

The church has a critical role to play in ensuring that the voices of the poor reverberate in the halls of public policy. Perhaps we should even go further and say that the preaching of the gospel will be truly liberating when the poor themselves are the preachers. The location of many churches in the midst of poverty creates strategic opportunity for the faith community to work to eradicate poverty.

6:27-49 Christian Behaviour

Jesus himself is the model who demonstrates the meaning of his teaching regarding the social and ethical behaviour required of his followers. Luke's treatment of Jesus' passion shows how he lived out his own teaching on love in **6:27-38**, praying for those who treated him spitefully (23:34). The Christian who acts in the way laid down here will be pointing to his or her master, Jesus Christ, and will be following in the footsteps of Stephen who prayed for those who were stoning him: 'Lord, do not hold this sin against them' (Acts 7:60).

Jesus states how he sees the relationship between his disciples and himself in **6:39-42**. Discipleship means following someone who knows the way; so that one becomes like a guide. These sayings remind us of John's presentation of Jesus as the way, or the descriptions of Jesus in Hebrews as the 'new and living way' (Heb 10:20). By following Jesus, the disciples are acknowledging that he is no blind guide but knows the way.

The themes of lordship and discipleship are further emphasized in **6:46-49**. Like Jesus, who built his house (the church) on a firm foundation, the 'rock' of Peter's recognition of him as the Messiah, 'the Christ of God' (9:20; see also Matt 16:18), the disciple must build his or her house on the rock which is Jesus himself. Like the author of the Letter of James, Luke is concerned that disciples know what it means to call Jesus 'Lord'. The essence of Christianity is not merely a belief and a confession (*you call me, 'Lord, Lord'*) that can be separated from the way we walk in the world (*and not do what I say*). When the whole self responds totally to the one Lord, the result is an indissoluble union between confession and walk or between faith and good works.

7:1-50 Jesus Deals with Individuals

7:1-10 The Centurion's Servant

The first story in this section introduces the remarkable encounter between the oppressor (a Roman centurion) and the oppressed (Jesus, a Jew). During the first century, an army officer like a centurion would have symbolized all the political and military power of Rome. It is remarkable that such a person cared deeply about one of his slaves at all (**7:2**). The centurion should be commended for affirming the dignity and humanity of one of his fellow creatures.

This encounter also highlights the status of Jesus. A series of representatives are sent by the centurion to request Jesus to come down and heal the worker. The first are some Jewish elders, who describe the Roman centurion as a genuine friend of Israel and appeal to Jesus earnestly, saying, *This man deserves to have you do this, because he loves our nation and has built our synagogue* (**7:3-5**). To put this in political terms, 'we owe him one'. Jesus is willing to help, but as he and the Jewish elders draw near to the centurion's residence, the officer sends a second delegation, composed of his personal friends, with the message, *Say the word, and my servant will be healed* (**7:6-7**). The centurion's argument in **7:8** shows deep respect for Jesus' authority. He is saying that if the orders of the military establishment are obeyed without question, how much more will Jesus' command be obeyed. Even Jesus was impressed and gives a straightforward commendation: *I have not found such great faith even in Israel* (**7:9**). And, of course, the worker was healed (**7:10**).

In summary, Luke here tells a fascinating story of cross-cultural relations, the interaction between the military and religious establishments, and the *ubuntu* of a military officer who fights for the health of a fellow human being, even though that person is one of the oppressed.

7:11-17 The Healing of a Widow's Son

Here we again see Jesus as the compassionate healer (**7:13**). He was deeply moved when he met the funeral procession and saw the mother's grief at the death of her only son (**7:12**). Immediately he healed the young man and *gave him back to his mother* (**7:15**). Witnessing this, one is reminded of the coming resurrection of another Son of a grieving mother.

7:18-35 A Question from John the Baptist

Here John the Baptist is shown for the first time as wondering whether Jesus might be the coming One (that is, the Messiah) (**7:18-19**; see also Isa 35:5-6a; 61:1; Matt 3:11; Mark 1:7; Luke 3:16; John 1:27). In his reply, Jesus refers to

healing and raising of the dead (**7:22**). It is no accident that Luke placed the episodes of the centurion's servant and the widow's son immediately before this section. These healings are signs that ought to indicate who Jesus is.

Jesus' own reply to John is an invitation to go even farther and to see Jesus himself as the Messiah. But on what basis should John believe this? The Baptist is offered the miracles and the proclamation of good news to the poor, both of which are prophesied in Scripture as events of the last days. John is expected to respond to what his disciples had seen and heard (**7:22**; see also 1 John 1:3).

Jesus then invites the crowd around him to think some more about John the Baptist's mission and its relation to himself. His questions remind his hearers about the firmness of John's convictions and message (he was no *reed swayed by the wind* – **7:24**), his life of self-denial (he did not dress in fine clothing – **7:25**) and his prophetic ministry (**7:26**). In fact, Jesus insists that John was even more than a prophet. The prophets had merely foretold that the Messiah would come (see, for example, Deut 18:18; Isa 9:6-7; Mic 5:1-4). John did this, but he was also the forerunner preparing the way for the Messiah's coming, a ministry that makes him the greatest of all *those born of women* – **7:28a**; see also Mal 3:1).

Yet despite John's high status, he is described as being below the one who is *least in the kingdom of God* (**7:28b**), a status that is achieved by letting Jesus rule over our lives while we wait for the full coming of the kingdom in the future. Jesus' message divided his hearers into two categories: those who *acknowledged God's way* as right (**7:29**) and those who *rejected God's purpose for themselves* (**7:30**). Ironically, the first category included *all the people, even the tax collectors,* and the latter, *the Pharisees and experts in the law.* The reason for their different responses lay in the way they had responded to John's message. The tax collectors and ordinary people had accepted John's baptism 'of repentance for the forgiveness of sins' (3:3). They were prepared to admit that they were sinners. Not so the Pharisees and legal experts, who dismissed his message as not for them. Approaching God's word with an attitude that 'I am perfect' means that one misses the greatest of blessings.

The reason for rejecting Jesus and John has nothing to do with the message they brought and everything to do with the wills of those doing the rejecting. Nothing pleased them. They were moved neither by feasting nor mourning (**7:32**). They complained that John fasted too often and ate a restricted diet, and so *has a demon* – a catch-all phrase for someone abnormal (**7:33**). But they equally complained that Jesus (here referred to as the Son of Man – a term Jesus used a lot for himself) did not fast enough, and called him *a glutton and a drunkard, a friend of tax collectors and sinners* (**7:34**). Even today, it is very difficult to bring people like this to Christ. They think they have all the answers.

But, as Jesus points out, they are foolish to refuse to enter the kingdom of God by the path of repentance from sin and acceptance of Jesus.

7:36-50 A Woman Who Was a Sinner

Accounts of a woman anointing Jesus appear in all four gospels (Mark 14:3-9; Matt 26:6-13; John 12:1-8; Luke 7:36-50). No name is given to the woman in Mark and Matthew; in John she is Mary of Bethany. Luke merely calls her *a woman who had lived a sinful life in that town* (**7:37**). However, her exact 'sin' is never disclosed. Attempts to determine what it was may reveal more of the interpreter's biases than the woman's past. Jesus' interpretation of her act is all that matters.

Her action in Luke consists of bringing an alabaster jar of ointment, wetting Jesus' feet with her tears, wiping them with her hair, kissing his feet and anointing them with ointment (**7:38**). The focus on Jesus' feet reminds us of the 'beautiful feet' of 'those who bring good news' of salvation (Isa 52:7). While Luke does not include Jesus' comment that wherever the gospel is preached in the whole world, 'what she has done will also be told in memory of her' (Matt 26:13; Mark 14:9), he does make it clear that this woman is to be honoured for displaying her love for Jesus. There is a marked contrast between her love and the coldness displayed by Simon the Pharisee, the inadequate host (**7:44-46**). Love, in the logic of this story and of the parable that Jesus tells in **7:40-43**, is both the cause and the result or sign of divine forgiveness. The woman embodies that love, and Jesus blesses her with the words, *Your faith has saved you; go in peace* (**7:50**).

8:1-50 Stories of Discipleship

8:1-3 The Women Disciples

Luke associates Jesus with varied groups of disciples, advancing the idea of the priesthood of all believers. There are women disciples (8:2-3), the twelve male disciples (6:14-16), a great crowd of disciples (6:17), the seventy-two (10:1), groups of three disciples (Simon Peter, John and James) or two disciples (Simon Peter and John; James and John) and individual disciples like Levi, who is not one of the Twelve, and Simon Peter, John and Judas. However the main focus falls on the twelve individuals chosen by Jesus in chapter 6.

In Luke 8:1-3 we are introduced to *some women who had been cured of evil spirits and diseases.* We know the names of three of these women: Mary called Magdalene, Joanna and Susanna (**8:2-3**). These and many other women are said to have been *helping to support them out of their own means.* The Greek word used here as well as in Mark 15:41 and Luke 8:3 is *diakoneo,* which means to serve or minister to as a

deacon. There are many different opinions about the type of service the women may have provided. Some theologians insist that in the early Christian community it did not only involve domestic chores but also eucharistic table service and proclamation of the word. Certainly, later references to Priscilla show that a woman could play a role as a teacher (Acts 18:26).

Perhaps because of its predominantly patriarchal structure, the African church has thus far not allowed or encouraged changes in attitudes towards women, especially in regard to ordination. Even in providing education for women, the church has tended to focus on subjects considered appropriate for females. Yet in perpetuating this prejudiced attitude, the church goes against its own teaching that in Christ all things are made new and that the old has passed away (2 Cor 5:17; Gal 3:28). It is clear from the Scriptures that women were among the earliest recipients and carriers of the gospel. They stood by Jesus throughout his life, and were with him when he died on the cross. The women were the only human beings who physically anointed the body of Jesus (7:36-50). Yet the church hesitates to let them consecrate the sacraments that symbolize the same body (Hazel Ongayo Ayanga, 1999).

8:4-15 Whose Fault Is It – The Sower's or the Soil's?

The parable of the sower can be retold in the following terms. One day a farmer went out to plant some seed. As he scattered it across his field, some of the seed fell on a footpath, where donkeys, cars and people stepped on it. Those plants died (**8:5**). Whose fault was that? Was it the fault of the Sower? Why did he scatter valuable seeds on a footpath? Why did he expose seeds to danger? In our text, the Sower is identified with Jesus Christ. Should we blame God?

Is it the fault of the soil? Think of a country like Namibia. It has plenty of sand and stones, bushes and thorn trees, a thinly scattered population, and diamonds, copper, gold and uranium. But it has always suffered from a want of water. On the plains and hills, people are roasted like burned loaves under the scorching rays of a cloudless sky. The big rocks are always a danger to the tiny, vulnerable seeds, and the sharp thorns are scattered, waiting to delay the process of growth of the seed (**8:6-7**). Whose fault is it?

Is it the fault of the Sower (identified as God) or of the soil and unfavourable weather conditions? Or is it the fault of the devil, who *comes and takes away the word from their hearts, so that they may not believe and be saved?* (**8:12**).

Instead, of seeking to assign blame, let us try a different approach. In Genesis 1:28-31 God blessed the human race and gave them seed-bearing plants, animals and birds, and blessed them with the words, 'Be fruitful … and fill the earth and subdue it.' Then God declared the creation good. God created us as good people. He gave us a good creation and a good universe. We as individuals and communities have to take care of this planet. It is our responsibility to prevent anyone from falling into the hands of today's thorns, that is, into the hands of rapists and robbers, and to protect them from the thorn of HIV/AIDS. The beginning point of all this is the obedience to God's word. When we obey it, it creates in us a deep desire to take care of God's creation – exercising righteousness and justice in our relationship with others and care in our relationship to God's good planet.

8:16-25 The Lamp, Jesus' Family and the Storm

In telling the story about the lamp (8:16-18), Jesus wants to make the following point: If God has, in the mission of Jesus, lit a lamp, then one can rest assured that it will succeed in giving its light, even though there may be times during that mission when it looks as if its light has been completely covered. Those who are prepared to forget themselves will find that they have the most insight into the meaning of Jesus. Acting on this insight brings the closest kinship to Jesus.

The episode involving the family of Jesus (8:19-21) deals with two questions: Who is the mother of Jesus? and Who are his brothers and sisters? These questions seem to have intrigued both John (John 7:1-10) and Luke make it clear that the closest kinship to Jesus springs from obedient discipleship. Jesus and his true disciples are together intimately involved in obedience to the Father.

Sudden fierce squalls are common on the Sea of Galilee, and in 8:22-25 one such storm is described. The disciples' boat is in grave danger while Jesus sleeps. Luke (unlike Matthew and Mark) is careful to say that Jesus dropped off to sleep before the storm began (8:23a). When he is awakened by the terrified disciples, he deals directly with the storm. His rebuking of the elements is followed by a calm as sudden as the storm. The disciples respond with fear. Their lack of trust prevented them from recognizing the lordship of Jesus Christ. This lordship will be demonstrated most dramatically in the episode that follows, which shows his dominance over the demonic forces that plague human life.

8:26-39 The Gerasene Demoniac

The story of the Gerasene demoniac is a strange one that we may not always have the right language and frame of mind to understand. It goes like this: An urban man who did not live in a house but in the tombs was possessed by many devils (8:27) and was *chained hand and foot and kept under guard* (8:29). However, at times he would break his chains and be driven by the demon into the wilds. To heal this urban man, Jesus gave the demons permission and they *demons came out of the man and went into the pigs, and the herd rushed down the steep bank into the lake and was drowned*

(8:32-33). After witnessing this incident, the people from *the town and countryside,* that is, both urban and rural people *were overcome with fear* (8:34-37). But the *man from whom the demons had gone out* was *sitting at Jesus' feet, dressed and in his right mind* (8:35).

The story highlights the fact that the only relevance that really matters is relevance to deep human needs. To put it differently, we need to reorient the mission of the church homewards to us as African Christian counsellors, theologians, pastors and laity. It is important to look homewards in our Christian healing ministry. But why?

The great African scholar John Mbiti tells the following anecdote about the return of an African theology graduate to Africa after many years of study in Europe:

> He learned German, Greek, French, Latin and Hebrew, in addition to English, as one part of the requirements for his degree. The other part, the dissertation, he wrote on some obscure theologian of the Middle Ages. Finally, he got what he wanted: A doctorate in Theology ... He was anxious to reach home as soon as possible, so he flew, and he was glad to pay excess baggage, which, after all, consisted only of the Bible in the various languages he had learned, plus Bultmann, Barth, Bonhoeffer, Bruner, Buber, Cone, Kung, Moltmann, Niebuhr and Tillich.
>
> At home, relatives, neighbours, old friends, dancers, musicians, drums, dogs, cats, all gather to welcome him back. People bear with him patiently as he struggles to speak his own language, as occasionally he seeks the help of an interpreter from English.
>
> Suddenly there is a shriek. Someone has fallen to the ground. It is his older sister. He rushes to her. People make room for him, and watch him. 'Let's take her to a hospital,' he calls urgently. They are stunned. He becomes quiet. They all look at him bending over her. Why does not somebody respond to his advice? Finally a schoolboy says: 'Doctor, the nearest hospital is 100 kilometres away, and there are few buses that go there.' Someone else says, 'She is possessed. Hospitals will not cure her!' The chief says to him, 'You have been studying theology overseas for ten years. Now help your sister. She is troubled by the spirit of her aunt.'
>
> He looks around. Slowly he goes to get Bultmann and reads again about spirit possession in the New Testament. Of course he gets his answer: Bultmann has demythologized it (that is, according to Bultmann such things do not exist in reality). He insists that his sister is not possessed. The people shout, 'Help your sister; she is possessed!' He shouts back, 'But Bultmann has demythologized demon possession' (it does not exist).

This story reflects the basic stance of the African Christian church, its priests, pastors and laity, African Christian theology, and African Christian healing and counselling. On a topic such as Christian healing, we have to speak from the inside, speaking to meet real needs in our churches, if we are to be relevant to our own situations.

We need to allow this anecdote to speak to us. If we want to talk about Christian healing and counselling, we have to practise such healing counselling ministries in our own context. We have to know who we are! In the story, our African student has only books by European theologians such as Bultmann, Tillich and Moltmann. Sadly, he does not have a single book by an African theologian and only one by an African-American theologian, James Cone. These books are of no help when an ancestral spirit is believed to have struck down the sister of the African theologian. How can he be of help to her? How can he be an effective pastor to her? How can he carry out his pastoral healing ministry? Bultmann offers no answers. Other Western theologians would advise him to cast out the spirit. But in an African context, where spirits of the dead are believed to visit the living, they are not meant to be cast out; they are meant to be spoken to, reasoned with and bargained with. The theology of Bultmann cannot accommodate this. Bultmann encourages the African theologian to deny the African reality that is staring him in the face. But Jesus spoke with demons, reasoned with them and 'bargained' with them (8:30-32). Yet he did not treat them as equals, but as beings that were subject to him. Like him, we are to exercise authority over them and must not seek their help or consult them, as is done in African traditional religion (Deut 18:9-13; Isa 8:19).

Today, we need a paradigm shift in the healing and counselling ministries of the church. We have to learn the art of hearing the questions being asked 'on the ground'. Only then can we start to answer them and to develop a practical theology that is suitable for Africa.

To give another example: During my theological studies I was taught that proper pastoral counselling takes place in an office, to guarantee privacy and quietness and a suitable atmosphere. We were even advised that the office should contain a table and at least two chairs. But when I started my pastoral duties in Bethanien in the Karas region of Namibia, I found that many people talked to me about their burdens in public places or in the streets, and even requested me to pray with them on the street corner or in the factory where they worked. Mindful of my pastoral counselling education, I was always telling them to come to my office for pastoral counselling. However, the majority of them never came. They wanted to consult me about their problems and burdens wherever we met, whether in an office, on the street, in a soccer stadium or in the church. The point is that the deep needs of the people may come in various forms and we should be prepared to accommodate

them all. But at the same time, we must never forget that our ministry should always be God-centred, for it is only by God's grace that we are able to do such ministries (8:39).

8:40-42, 49-56 Healing of a Twelve-Year-Old Daughter

The episode of the Gerasene demoniac is followed by a narrative about the raising of a twelve-year-old only daughter and the healing of a woman who had been suffering from irregular bleeding for twelve years. The repetition of the number twelve is probably deliberate, especially since the episodes that follow concern the sending out of the twelve disciples and the feeding of the five thousand which resulted in the filling of twelve baskets with scraps (9:17). Number symbolism was important to Jesus and his contemporaries. In most cases, as here, it was used to symbolize the restoration and healing of 'the daughter of Zion' (as Israel was often called in the books of Isaiah and Jeremiah).

The episode of Jairus' daughter dramatically displays the contrast between the absolute trust of Jesus and the lack of trust of the disciples. (For other observations see commentary on Mark 5:21-43.)

8:43-48 Jesus, the Model of Healing

Jesus healed people as whole persons: body, mind and spirit. The woman in this story would have her whole life affected by her chronic bleeding, which had lasted twelve years (8:43). Her physical problems likely included anaemia, weakness and infertility. Her social problems were worse because she was unclean (Lev 15:19-30). Everything and everyone she touched became unclean. She was probably divorced, abandoned by her family and without friends. Grief, depression and anger at society and probably at God filled her mind. Spiritually she was cut off from God because no unclean person could go to the temple to worship or ask for healing.

When she heard about Jesus, she determined to go to him even though her touch would make him unclean. She was taking a risk in doing this, for were she seen doing it, she could be stoned to death. But he was her only hope if she was to be cured and again have a place in society. With great determination she braved the crowd and managed to reach out and touch Jesus (8:44). Immediately she knew she was healed, and turned to flee. But Jesus stopped her (8:45-46). Jesus called this woman to come to him because she herself, as a person, had not yet been healed. Terror filled her heart, for she assumed he would condemn her. With great fear, she told her story and lay waiting for the word of condemnation (8:47). Instead, what she heard totally healed her. She heard Jesus say, *Daughter, your faith has healed you; go in peace* (8:48). With her own ears the woman had heard Jesus call her his daughter! With her heart, she heard him say, 'Come into my family. You are clean and whole.'

Any true ministry of healing involves being touched by human suffering and extending healing in word and deed.

9:1-20 Jesus the Christ

9:1-9 The Twelve and Herod

Jesus now called the Twelve together and gave them power and authority before he sent them to preach and heal (**9:1-2**). His approach foreshadows the experience of the apostles in Acts. At the end of Luke's Gospel, they are instructed to stay in Jerusalem until 'clothed with power from on high' (24:49), which will happen when the Holy Spirit had come upon them (Acts 1:8). Jesus does not assign a task until he has equipped those who are to perform it. We will see this again in the sending of the seventy-two in 10:1-24.

Jesus' operating instructions to the Twelve are simple and explicit. They are to take no walking staff, no food pouch, no bread, no money – not even two undergarments (**9:3**). By adopting such a simple style they will clearly distinguish themselves from those preachers who begged from door to door and may have used their travelling bags to carry what they collected. They would also be more closely identified with the people they were evangelizing, specifically the peasants and artisans living in rural areas. They were to identify with these people to such an extent that they were to share their homes while they were ministering in an area (**9:4**). But while their mission lifestyle was to be simple, they were not to court hardship for its own sake. This is clear from Jesus' instruction: *Whatever house you enter, stay there until you leave that town. If people do not welcome you, shake the dust off your feet when you leave their town as a testimony against them* (**9:4-5**).

The apostles set off on their own for the very first time, and carried out their commission with notable success (**9:6**). But while these twelve representatives of the new people of God are engaged in their brief internship, the narrator turns to Herod. The insertion of the story of Herod and John the Baptist at this point reminds us that Jesus is anticipating an even more dreadful rejection than that suffered by John, and that this is why he is training his followers for their future ministry. John the Baptizer had been Jesus' forerunner in life; now in **9:9** he is presented as his forerunner in death.

9:10-17 Sharing Resources

This story of the feeding of a crowd is recorded in all four gospels (see also Matt 14:13-21; Mark 6:30-44; John 6:1-14). The disciples had returned from their mission and reported what they had accomplished (**9:10**). Jesus then withdrew with them to Bethsaida, but the crowds, finding out where they had gone, followed them. Jesus welcomed the crowd and *spoke to them about the kingdom of God, and healed those who needed healing* (**9:11**).

Late in the afternoon (**9:12**), meaning that it was time for a meal, the disciples are instructed to feed the crowd of more than five thousand. They replied that they didn't have the resources to meet the needs of so many (**9:13**). However, in the opinion of Jesus, there should be resources available. When people come to us with their needs, Jesus suggests, we need to believe that we have the resources to meet those needs – spiritually, emotionally, economically, culturally and politically. To put it differently, in Africa, you do not just walk past people building a hut, you stop and contribute by tying a twig or two. When we are willing to share our resources, God will invariably provide our daily bread. This story answers the questions: 'Can God spread a table in the desert? When he struck the rock, water gushed out and streams flowed abundantly. But can he also give us food? Can he supply meat for his people?' (Ps 78:19-20).

9:18-20 Confessing Jesus Christ

Christology, or the doctrine of Jesus Christ, is the central doctrine of the Christian faith, and, therefore, the position we take about him will have a decisive influence upon our theology and Christian life as a whole. It is thus not surprising that church leaders, theologians and pastors are still trying to analyse the implications of Christianity and belief in Jesus Christ for their particular situations. While all Christians would agree that Jesus Christ is *the Christ of God* (**9:20**), that is, the Messiah, the one anointed by God as the means of redemption, there are differences in regard to who he is today.

We have been presented with many 'images' or 'faces' of Jesus Christ. There is Jesus the healer, Jesus the spiritual leader, Jesus the political activist, Jesus the worker, Jesus the lover of children, Jesus the friend of the sinners, Jesus the exorciser of demons, and so on. To answer the central question of who Jesus Christ is for us today, it is important to take into account the realization among contemporary theologians that Jesus Christ encounters people in various contexts and has been presented and appropriated in a variety of images or 'faces'. The church in Africa has seen several of these faces, but we will discuss only two perceptions of Jesus Christ among some African Christians.

First, there is the unfortunate image of Jesus Christ as the conqueror. Jesus is the warrior, in whose name and banner (the cross) new territories were annexed and subjugated. The aim was to conquer those regarded as 'heathens' and turn them into 'civilized Christians'. People from other religions and faiths were regarded as booty to be looted for Christ. This is the tradition from which come such popular hymns as 'Onward, Christian soldiers, marching as to war, with the cross of Jesus going on before.' This vision of Christ as conqueror is unsuitable for the life and mission of the church. It has dangerous ethical consequences, for it led Christians to make war on others, even killing those whom they regarded as 'heathens' in their urge to bring them salvation. Africa must reject such a dangerous image of Christ.

Second, there is the very popular image of Jesus Christ as the personal saviour, healer, brother and friend of those who believe in him. Rather than percieving Jesus as demanding their subjugation, whether politically, socially, culturally or religiously, many have come to perceive that Jesus Christ accepts them as they are and wants to meet their needs at a very personal level. This vision of Christ is almost always present in our prayer gatherings.

Some church leaders, theologians and pastors reject this view of Jesus, arguing that it is almost like a 'privatization' of the person of Jesus. While this criticism can have some validity, the image of Jesus as a personal friend, a personal healer and a personal saviour has been popular precisely because people need such a personal friend. The face of Jesus Christ who helps them to bear their grief, loneliness and suffering is a welcome one indeed. It was this face of Jesus Christ that sustained African Americans during the cruel days of slavery, so that they could testify to his amazing grace.

Jesus Christ is on the side of the marginalized to give them power and a voice to speak for them. He is actively concerned with the lot of victims of social injustice and with the dismantling of unjust religious, governmental and cultural structures. Christ would, therefore, be expected to be personally on the side of the poor. In summary, by accepting Jesus Christ as a personal friend we will also be able to confess Jesus Christ as our Saviour and liberator.

9:21-10:24 Discipleship, Transformation, Healing

9:21-27 Discipleship

The pattern of the mission of Jesus, as *Son of Man* (**9:22, 26**), is to be the daily model for discipleship. It involves the same path of self-conquest and participation in suffering. The followers of Jesus are summoned to *take up their cross* day after day (**9:23**). As used by Jesus, taking up one's cross daily means that discipleship is a most painful task because it is a self-giving and self-forgetting, like dragging a cross for one's own execution. Taking up the cross means that the Christian life is a dying daily to self, much as Paul does when he says, 'I die every day' (1 Cor 15:31). Later, Luke will present Simon of Cyrene literally fulfilling this summons of his Lord: 'they … put the cross on him, and made him carry it behind Jesus' (23:26).

Many have been puzzled by Jesus' words, *some who are standing here will not taste death before they see the kingdom of God* (**9:27**). Some have even suggested that it means that Jesus was planning to overthrow the Romans and set up a Jewish kingdom, and that his death marked the failure of these dreams. But to say this is to misunderstand him. Others have said that he was talking about his second coming

– but that does not fit with his promise that some of those who were standing with him would see the coming of God's kingdom.

To understand what Jesus means, we have to understand what is meant by the words 'kingdom of God'. Luke uses this expression in the same way as Matthew uses the term 'kingdom of heaven' in his gospel. In both cases, it means the kingdom in which God is the ruler. But this kingdom is spoken of in two ways in the gospels. Sometimes it is spoken of as a physical reality, a realm (Luke 13:28; 22:16). At other times, the kingdom is spoken of as the spiritual sphere where God reigns, that is, where he exercises authority. Jesus is clearly thinking in terms of the second option when he says 'But if I drive out demons by the finger of God, then the kingdom of God has come to you' (11:20) and 'the kingdom of God is within you' (17:21).

So is Jesus focusing on the physical kingdom or on the reign of God when he says the words in 9:27? In the previous verse, he has been talking about his own return *in the glory of the Father and of the holy angels,* so it seems that he may be speaking of the coming of the realm of God. In that case, what he is saying is that in the near future there will be a physical change in which his human nature (which is all many of his hearers were able to see) will be transformed and he will possess the glory of the kingdom of God. This was what happened at His resurrection, which Jesus has just been talking about in 9:22 (see also Matt 16:21). While his resurrection does not mark the full coming of his kingdom, it does signal the start of it and is the first taste of future glory.

But Jesus' death and resurrection would also bring about his reign in believers' hearts – a reign for which he sets the perfect example of obedience and which means that not even the great enemy (death) is a threat to his followers. The church that he founded is thus a fundamental part of the kingdom of God, while it awaits the coming of his full kingdom when Jesus returns. Those who interpret the coming of the kingdom in this way see it as having happened on the day of Pentecost, when the Spirit came in power (Acts 2:1-4).

9:28-36 Transformation

Some scholars have suggested that the transfiguration of Jesus must have taken place after his resurrection. However, Luke clearly records it as having taken place before the resurrection. The details of this appearance are also quite different from those of the post-resurrection appearances. The latter invariably begins with the Lord absent. Then he arrives and speaks, and so reveals himself. But in the account of the transformation in Luke, he is present throughout, and he does not speak to the disciples but only to Moses and Elijah (**9:30-31**). None of his words are recorded. The one who does speak is Peter (**9:33**).

DISCIPLESHIP

Around Easter time, street vendors in Latin America peddle 'cheap crosses'. But in reality there is no such thing as a cheap cross, for though salvation is free, it is not cheap. It cost God the life of his only Son, and it will be costly for us too. This cost has been forgotten in an age that preaches forgiveness without requiring repentance; administers baptism but not church discipline; takes communion without practising confession; and, in general, promotes a Christianity without discipleship.

The importance of discipleship is clear from the fact that variants of this word occur more than 290 times in just the Gospels and Acts. The word itself literally means a learner and refers to someone who follows another person's teaching. Thus in the Gospels we read of the disciples of John (Matt 9:14), of Moses (John 9:28), of the Pharisees (Matt 22:16) and of Jesus (Matt 10:1; John 6:66).

Although the word 'disciple' is found only twice in the OT (Isa 8:16; 19:11), the concept was widely practised. Joshua was Moses' disciple (Exod 24:13; 33:11), Ruth learned from Naomi (Ruth 1:16-18), Samuel led a school of prophets (I Sam 19:20) and Elisha was a disciple of Elijah (2 Kgs 2:1-15).

Growing as a Disciple

Being a disciple involves more than just being a student. It implies a personal attachment to a particular person who shapes the disciple's whole life. It approximates the traditional African practice whereby an apprentice lives with his or her teacher, learning by watching, listening, and participating in everything the master does. The apprenticeship ends only when the apprentice can do what the master does. This passing on of knowledge and experience is essential, for there is no success without a successor. One sure way of preparing one's successors is to disciple them (2 Kings 2:1-14; 2 Tim 1:3-6).

A modern equivalent to an apprenticeship might be the relationship between mentors and protégés. Mentors are trusted counsellors who help their protégés discover, develop and use their abilities. Such relationships also have the benefit of establishing mutual accountability between the mentor and the protégés (Acts 20:17-21).

Besides being *followers* and *learners*, disciples are also *adherents* who stick fast to and continue to support a person or cause (2 Kgs 17:34). The word 'Christian' was first coined by Gentiles to refer to those who followed Christ (Acts 11:26; 26:28; I Pet 4:16).

Disciples are also *imitators*, mimics who try to act like their master. We are commanded to imitate the conduct of missionaries (2 Thess 3:7, 9), the faith of spiritual guides (Heb 13:7) and that which is good (3 John 11). Paul encouraged those he led to the Lord to imitate him (I Cor 4:16; 11:1; Eph 5:1; Heb 6:12).

We can also learn more about discipleship by looking at the relationship between Jesus and his disciples. Their discipleship was a personal response to the call of Jesus (Mark 1:16-17; John 6:60-70) and involved abandoning their own concerns and comforts (Luke 9:57-62). Some found this calling too demanding and turned back (John 6:66-69; 2 Tim 1:15; 4:10).

Jesus spoke clearly about the cost of discipleship (Mark 8:34-38; Luke 14:25-33), stressing that it would involve suffering (John 12:24-26). He called his followers to self-denial, cross bearing, putting him above all other relationships and taking a stand for him.

Living as Disciples

Faithful disciples are characterized by qualities such as abiding in Jesus' word, steadfast faith in him, loyalty to him, love for one another, walking in the light, bearing fruit and humble service to one another (John 8:31-36; 13:34-35). Discipleship also requires obedience to his commands (Luke 6:46), specifically the commands to love God and our neighbours and to make disciples of all nations (Matt 22:37-39; 28:18-20).

Chapters 2, 4, 6 and 11 of the book of Acts describe how a community of Jesus' disciples functioned after his ascension. This fast-growing group was characterized by preaching, repentance, baptism for the forgiveness of sins and filling with the Holy Spirit. They were devoted to Bible study, fellowship, the agape feast and communion, love and sharing, worship and prayer, and evangelism.

Such discipleship brings the benefits of mutual support in prayer and care for one another (Phil 4:18-19; 2 Tim 4:9-12), shared opportunities for ministry (Acts 11:25-26; 1 Thess 3:1-8) and an environment that encourages growth as iron sharpens iron (Prov 27:17).

Discipleship in the NT sense is rare today because of the preaching of cheap grace. Abuse of the concept has given rise to false cults and privatization of faith. The very size of modern churches also works against any sense of community. In order to counteract this, many churches have started house fellowships or cell groups. Organizations such as Navigators, Life Ministry, Scripture Union, Youth For Christ, FOCUS and Emerging Young Leaders (EYL) have also developed specialized tools to encourage true discipleship.

To make an impact on African society today, the church must return to the Bible and rediscover the NT concept and practice of discipleship. Becoming a disciple of Jesus must bring about a transformation of a person's lifestyle and priorities.

Tokunboh Adeyemo

If the Transfiguration does belong to the time of Jesus' earthly ministry, the next question is what was the significance of the event? The answer is that it makes it clear that glory comes through suffering. At the top of the mountain, Jesus is engaged in prayer (**9:28-29**). While he was praying, his face and clothes underwent a transformation that gave the impression of heavenly glory. Moses and Elijah appeared, speaking with Jesus about his impending *departure* in Jerusalem, that is, about his death (**9:31**).

9:37-45 Healing

The next scene is a sad contrast to the glory on the mountain heights. The story of the transformation is followed by the story of the disciples' failure to exorcise an unclean spirit from a boy. The powerlessness of the disciples has dashed the father's expectations. Perhaps his son's condition is hopeless. Even Jesus himself may be unable to exorcize the evil spirit. On the verge of despair he pleads, *Teacher, look at my son* (**9:38**). Jesus responds, *Bring your son here* (**9:41**). But even as the father is bringing his son to Jesus, the boy suffers an epileptic seizure: *the demon threw him to the ground in a convulsion* (**9:42**). The evil spirit demonstrates its awesome power before Jesus in order to display the power it has enjoyed in the boy's life up to that moment. Indeed, it has dominated him from birth, and even jeopardized his life.

The same Jesus who had calmed the storm, defeated a legion of demons, raised the dead, fed the multitudes and walked on the sea has no difficulty in healing the boy who had suffered the epileptic seizure. The source of his abilities has been revealed in his unveiling as God's offspring in the transfiguration (**9:35**).

9:46-48 Who Is the Greatest?

One of the distinctive features of the reign of God is the way in which community leaders, politicians and religious leaders are to function. In Luke the disciples have several persistent failings that bring them into conflict with Jesus. One of these appears in their disputes over who *would be the greatest* (**9:46**). The problem is mentioned here, and it has not been resolved even at the Last Supper, for in 22:24 the same sort of dispute occurs. But for Jesus, being the greatest means being the one who is the most humble, ready to welcome even the insignificant (**9:48**). Such a person will not feel threatened when someone else steps into their role (**9:49-50**). Later, Jesus tells the disciples, 'the greatest among you should be like the youngest, and the one who rules as one who serves', for Jesus himself has taken this servant role (22:26-27). In other words, the servant model is permanently inscribed in his identity, so that when the heavenly Lord returns to his faithful servants, he acts as he did before, assuming the role of servant to his servants (12:37).

9:51-62 The Cost of Discipleship

This section starts with a reminder that there is more to Jesus' current journey than a mere visit to Jerusalem. His going up to Jerusalem is already part of his ascension, for he is soon *to be taken up to heaven* (**9:51**). The word *resolutely* makes it clear that Jesus showed evidence of his conviction that this journey was an essential part of the Father's 'must' for him. However, even on this journey he and his disciples encountered difficulties.

Jesus *sent messengers on ahead* (**9:52**) to a Samaritan village to get everything ready for him as he journeyed. The direct way from Galilee to Jerusalem led through Samaria, but most Jews avoided it. There was a centuries' old quarrel between the Jews and the Samaritans (John 4:9). But Jesus deliberately wanted to take this direct route. He was extending a hand of friendship to a people who were enemies. In this case, not only was hospitality refused but the extended hand of reconciliation and friendship was spurned (**9:53**). James and John responded with indignation, no doubt believing they were doing a most praiseworthy thing when they offered to call in divine aid to blot out the village (**9:54**). But Jesus turned and rebuked them, according to some manuscripts with the words, *You do not know what spirit you are of, for the Son of Man has not come to destroy the lives of human beings but to save them* (**9:55** NRSV).

Having just been refused hospitality by a Samaritan village (**9:53**), Jesus met a man who expressed his willingness to follow Jesus wherever he went (**9:57**). Instead of simply welcoming him, Jesus warned the man of the consequences of following him: Jesus is homeless, and to follow Jesus wherever he goes means sharing the homeless lot of the Son of Man (compare 18:28-30). One needs to ponder the consequences of discipleship when making a commitment.

The same principle applies to the next two incidents. Following Jesus is not a task that can simply be added to a list of other tasks, like *first let me go and bury my father* (**9:59**) or saying farewell to those at home (**9:61-62**; compare 1 Kings 19:19-21). The father whom the person wants to bury was not necessarily dead or even ill. What the man is saying is that he still has family obligations he needs to complete first. Jesus' reply to him amounts to saying that nothing (not even the most important religious duty) should be given higher priority than following him. Discipleship calls for an absolute detachment from property and family and for single-minded devotion to Jesus that perseveres to the end. Christians today are still called to this type of commitment

10:1-24 The Sending of the Seventy-Two

The mission of seventy-two (or seventy – KJV) disciples was something quite new in the methods of Jesus. It was a planned campaign. In the first three years of his ministry, there seems to have been an absence of what we would call organization. Here, however, we have an account of careful, organized work. Jesus *appointed seventy-two others and sent them two by two ahead of him to every town and place where he was about to go* (**10:1**).

It was the last movement in his ministry, and he planned what we should be inclined to call today 'an intensive campaign'. He intended to visit many places, and he had selected the places. They were probably in an area he had not yet visited on the other side of Jordan (Matt 19:1; Mark 10:1). To those selected towns he sent the seventy-two men, two by two, in thirty-six teams that would cover the ground in preparation for his last personal ministry. The specific mission of the disciples was twofold: *Heal the sick ... and tell them, 'The Kingdom of God is near you'* (**10:9**). He thus gave them authority and power to preach and to heal the sick. His other instructions were similar to those he had given his twelve disciples in 9:1-9.

The story of the seventy-two is a wonderful one, involving an intensively planned campaign in a neglected area, the things that happened, the teaching that emerged, the instruction of disciples for their work, and the fact that Jesus empowered them with authority and power before they went out to preach and to heal. The principles underlying it abide for all time, and it has a living message for us.

10:25-42 Altar and Kitchen Connection

10:25-37 Co-travellers

People from countries such as the United States of America, South Africa, Namibia, Rwanda and Burundi and other countries racked by racial and ethnic divisions have a special appreciation of this story of the travellers. It deals with racial harmony and what it means to be human and humane, or to be someone with *ubuntu*, that is, someone who is welcoming, hospitable, warm and generous, with a servant spirit that affirms others and says 'I am because you are; you are because I am'. Such a person recognizes that we are all one another's brothers and sisters and that God has created us to *love the Lord your God with all your heart and with all your soul and with all your strength and with all your mind; and love your neighbour as yourself* (**10:27**). Apparently, such a statement is not self-explanatory, for the question arises: *Who is my neighbour?* (**10:29**).

One might have expected Jesus to make the priest or the Levite the hero of the story, rather than the Samaritan. But Jesus refuses to do this. He deliberately made an unselfish Samaritan the hero in order to show up the failure of the religious authorities and their close associates.

The Samaritans were a racially mixed people, and relations between them and the Jews had deteriorated even more during Jesus' lifetime, after the Samaritans had defiled the temple court one Passover by strewing it with dead men's bones. There was irreconcilable hostility between the two groups. Had the Jew been alive and well instead of being stripped, beaten and left half dead (**10:30**), he would have rejected with indignation even an offer of water from the Samaritan. So it was astonishing that when even the Jewish priest and Levite did not trouble to help their fellow Jew, a Samaritan did. The Samaritan was moved with compassion that overcame religious and racial animosity and he treated the Jew with a sense of *ubuntu*.

The issue of diversity is present time and again in the ministry of Jesus. He was willing to be associated with tax collectors (Matt 11:19). He stated that his message is for the lost sheep of the house of Israel (Matt 15:24), sent his disciples to the 'lost sheep' (Matt 10:6) and told the chief priests and elders of the people that 'tax collectors and the prostitutes are entering the kingdom of God ahead of you' (Matt 21:31).

The Christian accommodation of elements of ethnic diversity was bound to offend ethnic chauvinists and seemed extremely peculiar to others in the first century. Origen quotes Celsus, the learned Roman opponent of Christianity, as describing the Christian approach to ethnic diversity as 'a manifestation that shows that they desire and are able to gain over only the silly, and the mean, and the stupid, with women and children'. However, what Celsus regarded as a ridiculous weakness proved to be the unique strength of Christianity. The rapid spread and eventual victory of Christianity over the many competing religions in the Roman Empire was in part due to of its openness to ethnic diversity. It welcomed all races and classes, men and women, as well as the downtrodden, the outcasts and sinners. It addressed a much larger audience than intellectual elitists and ethnic chauvinists. Jesus' message was directed to groups that other religious and political movements did not take seriously or openly rejected because they considered them racially, intellectually, sexually or socially inferior.

Jesus, the ultimate authority for all Christian proclamation, had always expressed his concern for these outcasts. He is reported as saying that the poor and the sightless would be the guests at the messianic banquet (14:16-24). The hallmark of Christianity is to be open to ethnic diversity and to promote the culture of human dignity and social justice. Such openness shows that the encounter with the living Christ brought into being a new style of life that Christians saw as a real possibility for all human beings: 'For God did not send his Son into the world to condemn the world, but to save the world through him' (John 3:17).

10:38-42 A Sisterly Home

The two sisters, Mary and Martha, are often presented as symbolizing conflict between contemplative life and the active life. The contemplative life is regarded as higher, more spiritual and more essential; the active, practical life is necessary but inferior. But is this what the text says?

Jesus is presented as a guest at the house of Martha, who is *distracted by all the preparations* (**10:40a**). Meanwhile Mary sits at Jesus' feet, *listening to what he said* (**10:39**). Mary never speaks, but Martha bursts in and asks, *Lord, don't you care that my sister has left me to do the work by myself? Tell her to help me* (**10:40b**). Jesus gently chides Martha and leaves things as they are. Martha is silenced. She is the loser, with whom the reader is not supposed to identify. Luther once commented that Jesus was saying: 'Martha, your work must be punished and regarded as worthless … I want no work but that of Mary, which is faith.'

However, not all commentators agree with Luther. They point out that the name Martha is an Aramaic one that means 'sovereign lady', 'ruling lady' or 'lady'. The name helps to emphasize Martha's autonomous, well-off and dominant position. She is the hospitable mother of the house who welcomes a preacher and performs the practical tasks that the visit demands. In fact, her work is repeatedly described as *diakonia,* which would later became a technical term referring to serving at the Lord's table, proclaiming his message and providing leadership in the church. Given that diakonia is presented positively everywhere else in the NT, it is difficult to see that here it should suddenly represent a mistaken choice. Rather, what Jesus disapproves of is the way in which Martha goes about her work, with fuss and agitation. We do not need to separate the gentle, listening, self-surrendering Marys and the pragmatic, busy Marthas. In other words, the Mary in me ought not to repress the Martha, and the Martha in me ought not to repress the Mary. We are called first to listen to the word of God and on that basis we are urged to engage in social services.

11:1-23 Prayer and God's Reign

11:1-4 Lessons on Prayer

The Lord's Prayer is also found in Matthew 6:9-13 as part of the Sermon on the Mount. The words, however, are not exactly the same. In Matthew, Jesus uttered it of his own accord, unasked, while teaching a large number of his disciples how to pray. But in Luke, Jesus gives the prayer under totally different circumstances. It is possible that Luke does not report the prayer in full, meaning that Matthew's longer version may be closer to the original form. The well-known doxology at the end of the prayer, 'for yours is the kingdom and the power and the glory for ever, Amen', which is included in Matthew 6:13 in some manuscripts, is missing from Luke's version.

In response to his disciples' request, *Lord, teach us to pray* (**11:1**), Jesus gave them a prayer that highlighted what is most important and necessary in life, and suggests how we should rank them. Luke's version of the Lord's Prayer contains five requests. First come two requests relating to God's own interests, namely *hallowed be your name* and *your kingdom come* (**11:2**). Then follow three requests relating to our needs, namely *Give us each day our daily bread. Forgive us our sins … and lead us not into temptation* (**11:3-4**). God's interests are put first, followed by ours. That obviously is the true priority in the prayer life of a Christian.

God is addressed as a personal and beloved parent, whose holiness and sovereignty we acknowledge with gratitude and awe when we pray *Father, hallowed be your name* (**11:2b**). We are acknowledging and confessing God's name and that we are in intimate relationship with God.

When we pray *your kingdom come* (**11:2c**), we are stating that our deepest longing is that God's honour be fully vindicated in all creation. We are asking that the reign of God may not merely be a utopian idea to which we cling desperately but a manifest reality.

Turning to our own needs, *Give us each day our daily bread* (**11:3**) is an acknowledgement that life is good and that our physical needs must be met. Our plea is for more than food; it encompasses all the necessities of life. According to Luther, 'when you pray for "daily bread" you pray for everything that is necessary in order to have and enjoy daily bread and, at the same time, pray against everything that interferes with enjoying it. You must therefore enlarge and extend your thoughts to include not only the oven or the flour bin, but also the broad fields and the whole land which produce and provide for us our daily bread and all kinds of sustenance … To put it briefly, this petition includes everything that belongs to our entire life in this world' (*Book of Concord*).

When Jesus tells us to pray *forgive us our sins, for we also forgive* (**11:4**), he is not suggesting that God's forgiveness is dependent on our forgiving. Rather, he is simply assuming that those who seek to learn how to pray from him will indeed forgive their enemies.

The request *lead us not into temptation* can also be translated 'Do not bring us to the time of trial'. We are being warned against any smug assumptions that we are holy or virtuous. Without God's help, we would all fail the trial. As a friend of tax collectors and sinners, Jesus knew well that temptation can simply overcome people. Those driven beyond endurance by poverty, apartheid, colonialism, gender inequality, parental abuse, gang life and drugs are similar to ourselves.

Besides noting the instruction to put God's interests first, and only then to pray for our own, we should also note that of the three things Jesus tells us to ask for ourselves, only one relates to our physical needs. The other two relate to our spiritual and moral needs. The order is significant: we ask first for our physical needs, because meeting these needs is a necessary basis for higher spiritual and moral experiences.

But to the one prayer for our physical needs, we must add two for our spiritual and moral needs. As sinful human beings we need forgiveness each day, just as we need daily bread. At the same time, the spiritual dimension is linked to the moral one. We are to pray that we may not enter into temptation. The best intentions may not be fulfilled, as Peter found out to his sorrow (22:31-32, 46, 61-62).

Finally, Donal Dorr has written the following adaption of the Lord's Prayer that applies to our own context:

Our Father … May your Kingdom come, and may we be active in promoting it – a Kingdom of peace and love, founded on true justice … Give us this day our daily bread, and strengthen us in our efforts to build a world where we all have an opportunity to earn our daily bread through meaningful work, where nobody has to go hungry, and no group lives in luxury while others starve. Forgive us our trespasses – our failure to believe in your Kingdom and your call to us to bring it about, our sinful apathy in the face of injustice, out failure to work together, our dissipation of energy in fruitless resentment rather than courageous challenge. Lead us not into temptation: do not test us beyond our strength by leaving us in our desperate situation. But deliver us from the evil: lead us out of bondage as you led your people in the past out of the slavery and into the Promised Land; raise up leaders for us as you called Moses and Deborah; inspire and strengthen them to lead us into freedom.

11:5-13 The Habit of Asking, Seeking and Knocking

This parable (11:5-8) is found only in Luke. It tells of someone who receives a midnight visitor but has no food to offer him. He goes to a friend's home and shamelessly persists in his requests until the friend gets up and supplies his needs (11:8). The interpretation of this in 11:9-13 points out that if someone who is reluctant to help will eventually do so simply because of his neighbour's shamelessness in persisting, how much more will God, who is eager and willing to answer our prayers. The disciples should pray because God is an answering God. One should make a habit of asking, seeking and knocking because God is certain to answer prayer (11:9-10).

11:14-28 Exorcism, Slander and Commitment

Despite his close relationship with God and his attack on the demonic world in driving out the demon that made someone mute (11:14), Jesus is charged by some in the crowd with being in league with Beelzebub, the ruler of the demons, who is probably to be identified with the Devil. Instead of seeing the *finger of God* (11:20) in Jesus' deliverance of someone from Satan's clutches as a sufficient witness that he was not on Satan's side, they resorted to slander. They declared that his power over the devil was due to the fact that he was in league with Satan. They thus attributed his power not to God but to the devil. Jesus gave them a crushing answer when he said, *Now if I drive out demons by Beelzebul, by whom do your followers drive them out?* (11:19). In contrast to the frustrated attempts by exorcists, who would use much mumbo-jumbo in trying to achieve their goal, Jesus affected his cures with a single command. Hence other exorcists would readily recognize his superior power (11:21-22).

It is not uncommon for people who disagree with someone else to resort to slandering them. It is a measure of desperation, when people have no other good grounds for opposing someone. But the Bible strongly condemns it: 'You shall not give false testimony against your neighbour' (Deut 5:20). Slander is an evil that destroys human relationships. We should prefer to listen to words that praise others, rather than to derogatory words.

Jesus goes on to suggest in 11:21-26 that when he drives out demons there is far more going on than just another astonishing cure of the kind that their own exorcists produced (11:19). When Jesus drives out demons from a person, that person has to make a decision in favour of God. If he or she does not do this, demons will return, and not on their own but accompanied by seven other demons (11:26). Seven was a number that symbolized completeness or perfection, and thus the return of seven demons indicates a combination of every conceivable type of wickedness. A decision to follow God and to believe in the power of God must be held to steadfastly.

The incident in 11:27-28 recalls 8:19-21 in that Jesus makes use of a reference to his relatives to state the truth about relationships with God. How fortunate Mary is to have a son like Jesus! Yes, but still much more fortunate are those who are committed to and obedient to the word of God.

11:29-53 The Lamp and the Pharisees

Despite all that Jesus had done, the crowds keep pressing him to perform more miracles as a *miraculous sign* of his authority. Jesus refuses to do this, and insists that the only sign they will receive is *the sign of Jonah* (11:29-30). He contrasts their obsession with signs with the reactions of Gentiles who were prepared simply to listen to God's word. The Queen of the South came from *the ends of the earth* (11:31 – the farthest point of the then-known world) not to see miraculous signs but to *listen*. She did not ask Solomon for signs as proof that he spoke wisdom (11:31; see also 1 Kgs 10:1-9 – Queen of Sheba). The men of Nineveh also *repented at the preaching of Jonah* without seeing him do any miraculous signs (11:32; Jonah 3:5). Jesus is far greater than Jonah, but the people are not prepared to listen to him! They may look down on the Gentiles and think they are superior to them as God's chosen people, but Gentiles like the Queen of the South and the men of Nineveh will condemn *the men of this generation* (11:31, 32).

There was, however, one miraculous sign associated with Jonah, one that took place long before he arrived in Nineveh. He had spent 'three days and three nights in the belly of a huge fish' (Matt 12:40; see also Jonah 1:17). He had been as good as dead (Jonah 2:2). But God had rescued him and given him back his life (Jonah 2:6). The people of Jesus' generation will see much the same sign as when Jesus dies and is buried for three days before rising again. Jesus' triumph over death will be a clear proof that he is the Messiah, and far greater than Jonah, who had only been close to death.

So it is time to listen to him, and to let his ministry be like a light that illuminates those who enter a house. There is nothing hidden about the light. Any lack of illumination is due to the recipient. If she or he has a healthy eye, light will flood his or her whole being. Luke's point is that Jesus' ministry is a public light to those entering the kingdom of God (**11:33-36**). Failure to respond properly is similar to failing to see properly because of a diseased or blind eye.

Among those who do not see properly are the Pharisees and the experts in the law. Jesus accuses them of both defective interpretation of the Scriptures and a hypocritical lifestyle (**11:37-54**). They like to emphasize their elite position in society by walking about in long robes, enjoying public greetings in the marketplaces, seats of honour in the synagogue and prestigious seats at banquets. But their deeds do not correspond to what they teach or to the honour they insist on as interpreters of God's law to the people. They take property from widows, while at the same time pretending to offer long prayers. Jesus declares that they will receive greater condemnation (**11:50-51**).

12:1-34 Being the Little Flock

It has been said that the theme of this chapter is summed up in Jesus' wondrous assurance: *Do not be afraid, little flock, for it is your Father's good pleasure to give you the kingdom* (12:32). But what are the features of the reign of God? What kind of reign is Jesus establishing? And how should we live in it?

12:1-4 Self-Deception and Hypocrisy

Jesus was dealing with a crowd numbering thousands when he warned them about *the yeast of the Pharisees, which is hypocrisy* (**12:1**). Hypocrisy is living life with a double standard so that there is a discrepancy between what one is and the image one projects to others.

A story about Mahatma Gandhi may show what it means to live a life of integrity, without any tinge of hypocrisy. Before Gandhi was active in India, he lived in South Africa, in a small village populated by people from India. He

was a magistrate, the village father figure to whom people brought a wide range of problems. In this village there was a widow trying hard to raise a teenage son. In the absence of a father's authority, the child would not eat any healthy foods but would consume only sweets.

The widow knew that if Gandhi spoke to the boy he would listen. So she brought him to Gandhi and asked, 'Will you talk to my son and tell him to stop eating sugar?' Gandhi was silent for a moment and then said, 'Would you bring the boy back to me a week from now?'

A week later, she brought the boy before Gandhi and asked again, 'Will you now please tell my son to stop eating sugar?' But Gandhi replied, 'I'm sorry. Would you please bring him back in another week?'

A week passed, and the by now desperate woman came and again asked Gandhi to talk with her son. This time Gandhi carried out the woman's request. He resolved the problem by talking with the boy and telling him that it was imperative to stop eating sugar. When Gandhi was finished, the woman took him aside, thanked him, and then asked, 'When we first came to you, you asked us to come back in a week. Then, when we came back, you asked us to come in another week. Why did you do that?'

Gandhi replied, 'Because I had not realized how difficult it would be for me to give up sugar.'

Gandhi's integrity was such that he would not tell anyone else, even a child, to do something that he himself was not prepared to do. By contrast, we are often all too ready to advise others to do what we ourselves do not do.

Jesus' comments on the Pharisees show that he knows the depths of human weakness and games that 'good' people play. But he is adamant that *there is nothing concealed that will not be disclosed, or nothing secret that that will not be made known … what you have whispered in the ear in the inner rooms will be proclaimed from the roofs* (**12:2-3**). Jesus is not condemning failure as such – for we all fail – but the hypocrisy that makes us pretend to be better than we are. Life in the reign of God means that you are loved and forgiven, and have no need to hide and pretend.

12:4-12 Fearlessness

Before addressing the issue of being afraid or fearful, Jesus calls the disciples *my friends* (**12:4**). With these words he expresses his closeness to and intimacy with his disciples. It is a message of assurance before he moves on to the question of fear.

Jesus distinguishes between the fear that fetters people and the fear that liberates them. We fear demons, but they do not have the power to cast us into hell. It is much more important that we fear the one who, after killing, has the power to cast us into Gehenna (hell) (**12:5**). The only one who has that power is God (Jas 4:12), not the devil. Similarly, we fear persecution by the authorities (**12:11**) and may hesitate to acknowledge what we believe when we are before them. But God is to be feared far more than the authorities (**12:8-10**).

But God is not only someone to be feared, he is also a caring God who watches over his people (**12:6**). God cares even for the birds and even for the hairs on our heads. He is not a terrible God but a loving Father, who will be with us during persecution (**12:12**).

12:13-21 The Peril of Wealth

The wealthy farmer, who thinks that he need not fear shortage of harvests for many years, is a man who wants to live without God and his fellow human beings (**12:19**). But God's comment to him is *you fool* (**12:20**), reminding us that a fool is a person who lives without God (Ps 14:1). He is also a fool because he does not see death looming. Instead of sharing his blessings with God and humanity, he decides to store the crops as security for an early retirement and a life of ease. So he tore down his old barns and built new and bigger ones. The treasure in the barns would be his lifelong security (**12:16-19**). He is completely self-centred, separated from God and others by his love for earthly possessions. He falsely assumes that human life can be measured and secured by wealth, and regards his life and property as his own. In doing this he fails to honour the doctrine that trees, rivers, mountains, forests, birds, night and day, and everything within the creation speaks a godlike language, praises God, and should be used with awe and reverence.

God has created us as human beings who are meant to be interdependent, to live in a fellowship. By his actions, this man denies this principle, which is well illustrated in the following story:

> There was once a man who was a staunch churchgoer and a deeply committed Christian. He supported most of the activities of his local church. And then for no apparent reason he stopped attending church and became just a hanger on. His minister visited him one wintry evening. He found him sitting before a splendid fire with red glowing coals, radiating lovely warmth around the room. The minister sat quietly with his former parishioner gazing into the fire. Then he stooped with the tongs, removed one of those red glowing coals from the fire and put it on the pavement. The inevitable happened. That glowing coal gradually lost its heat, and turned in a while into a grey lump of cold ashes. The minister did not say a word. He got up and walked away. On the following Sunday, the old man turned up in church.

A solitary Christian is a contradiction in terms. As human beings we are meant to live harmoniously with God, with our fellow human beings, and with the rest of God's creation. Artificial barriers that separate human beings on the basis of economic status, gender, race or age are contrary to God's will. Our souls can only relax, eat, drink and be merry together with all other human souls in the presence of God.

12:22-31 Things and Life

In addressing the relationship between 'things' and 'life', Jesus first assures the disciples about God's care (see also 12:4-12). This theme is introduced with words such as *do not worry* (**12:22, 29**), *your Father knows* (**12:30**) and *these things will be given to you as well* (**12:31**).

Jesus warns against the habit of putting the things of this world first while denying others the right to life. Too often we are concerned with ourselves and our narrow self-interest, and thereby we are imprisoning ourselves in the things of this world. This false outlook must go before we can see that God and his purpose are the only things that ultimately matter.

12:32-34 Money and the Reign of God

We have already learned that the kingdom will have a special place for the marginalized and the poor. Jesus brings sinners and tax collectors into his fellowship. The reign of God restores and empowers the poor, releases captives, provides sight to the blind, liberates the oppressed and proclaims the age of peace, justice and reconciliation (4:18-19). A persistent concern for the poor and a persistent call for a radical change in the wealthy and powerful are widely recognized as strong characteristics of Luke. However, what is the perspective of the church on religion and money in the context of poverty and wealth?

One of the areas where the reign of God must be seen is in the economy. Today, we are dominated by a money culture, but there are still areas of human life that resist this culture. One of these pockets of resistance is religion. Yet the Bible does have much to say about the relationship between money and human spirituality. In the OT the Lord says, 'Come, all you who are thirsty, come to the waters; and you who have no money, come buy and eat! Come, buy wine and milk without money and without cost. Why spend money on what is not bread, and your labour on what does not satisfy? Listen, listen to me, and eat what is good, and your soul will delight in the richest of fare' (Isa 55:1-2). In the NT we are reminded, 'For you know that it was not with perishable things such as silver or gold that you were redeemed from the empty way of life handed down to you from your forefathers, but with the precious blood of Christ, a lamb without blemish or defect' (1 Pet 1:18-19).

Jesus spoke more about money than about prayer. His holding up of a coin and asking whose image and inscription was stamped upon it (Mark 12:14-17) can be interpreted in terms of the parallel between coinage and human personality. A human being is like a coin, stamped with the image and inscription of God. But when human life becomes coin-shaped, it is relatively easy for one image and superscription to take the place of the other. Almost without realising it, the image of God is replaced by the image of Caesar and the coin-like character of human life finds increasing expression in literal coinage and the money culture. Jesus advocates adopting a culture of care and self-sacrifice, saying that 'even the Son of Man did not come to be served but to serve, and to give his life as a ransom for many' (Mark 10:45). The values of faith, of grace, of love stand against the corrupting money values. We are offered an image of a new kind of society, in which money will become our servant to enhance our solidarity and our freedom, and no longer our master and our God to turn us into its own image.

The church, however, has had an ambiguous attitude to money. God and money are sometimes seen as almost interchangeable. Rival theologies jostle one another within the spirituality of the money culture. The prosperity gospel assures us that people are rich because God has rewarded them with money, whereas the gospel that emphasizes the bias of God towards the poor and the needy believes that God 'has filled the hungry with good things, but has sent the rich away empty' (1:53). Which theology is correct?

While we create such ambiguities, the message in the Gospel of Luke is clear. Martha is not sinning in having a house in which Jesus was glad to stay, nor is Jesus saying that it is wrong for a Christian to have property or treasures. Quite the reverse. We should aim to enjoy God's creation with its gold, diamonds, copper, fish and cattle. At the same time, I am required to share these resources so that I do not remain rich while my neighbour gets poorer and poorer.

12:35-59 Watchful Waiting

Jesus now turns from dealing with our attitude towards things in the present to talk about our attitude towards the future when he will return.

12:35-40 The Need To Watch

Jesus uses two vivid illustrations to explain the attitude he wants us to have while we wait for his return. The first is that of servants waiting for their master to return from a banquet. The master will not be impressed if he arrives home sometime between 9 p.m. and 3 a.m., knocks on the door and has to wait while his servants stumble around in the dark, trying to throw on their clothes and light a lamp before opening the door for him. He expects them to be *dressed ready for service* and to keep their *lamps burning* until he comes (**12:35-36**). When he finds them like this, he will express his appreciation for what they have done (**12:37-38**).

Jesus reinforces his point with a second illustration: we never know when thieves may strike and so we must constantly be on the alert for them (**12:39**). In the same way, we must be alert for *the Son of Man*, who will *come at an hour when you do not expect him* (**12:40**).

In African terms, we could think of children who expect their father to return from some journey, and know that he always brings them something delicious when he comes. They do not know exactly when he will come, but they keep an eye on the road even while they play. They try to avoid quarrelling or doing anything that might upset their father and spoil the excitement when he hands over the treats he has brought. We should be like this as we watch for Jesus' coming.

12:41-48 Peter's Question and Jesus' Response

Peter has been listening keenly, and he asks Jesus whether this instruction applies only to the disciples or *to everyone?* (**12:41**). Jesus responds by returning to the servant metaphor. A master who is going on a journey will appoint one of his servants to run the household while he is gone (**12:42**). A servant who looks after things well will be rewarded (**12:43-44**). But if the servant exploits his position, getting drunk and beating the other servants, he will be in for a shock when his master returns unexpectedly (**12:45-46a**). The master will *cut him to pieces and assign him a place with the unbelievers* (**12:46b**). It seems that the 'cutting to pieces' is not meant to be taken literally but is simply a metaphor for severe punishment, for the servant is assigned a position 'with the unbelievers' after this. Jesus is not saying that unfaithful Christians will lose their salvation, but rather that they will not enjoy the reward given to faithful servants.

This parable should also be seen as a warning to those African leaders who seek power because of what they can get out of it, rather than as an opportunity to serve their people. The Lord will take note of how they handle their responsibilities.

Jesus then directly addresses Peter's question. The command is addressed to everyone, but God will hold each one responsible in proportion to their knowledge of his will. Everyone who fails will be punished, but those who knew most about what was expected of them but failed to do it will be punished more severely than those who knew less (**12:47-48**). Peter and his fellow disciples will be held to a higher standard of accountability because they have been given greater privileges. This same principle applies to pastors, teachers, leaders and all those in positions of authority. The greater our privileges, the more God expects of us.

12:49-53 Jesus' Mission

Jesus' disciples should not expect to live a life of ease while they wait for him. He bluntly states that his mission will bring *fire on the earth* (**12:49**). It will lead to divisions, even among close relatives (**12:51-53**). He calls for such a radical change from the status quo that his followers will inevitably be persecuted by those who want to keep things the way they are. Yet these changes are so important that those who have identified themselves with his mission should not give up, even if this brings them into conflict with those they love. The end result of their relationship with Jesus is worth all the discomfort they will endure on earth.

12:54-59 Jesus' Rebuke to the People

Jesus now turns from speaking to his disciples to address those who have not responded to his message. He accuses them of showing foresight about the weather but not about the things that really matter in *this present age* (**12:56b**). They know that the rain blows in from the Mediterranean Sea to the west and that a wind from the southern deserts brings heat (**12:54-55**). They need to apply the same intelligence to interpreting spiritual things. If they do not, they are clearly only pretending to be interested in them, and so can justifiably be called *hypocrites* (**12:56a**).

They need to show the same forethought they apply to the weather and to a legal dispute (**12:57-59**) to the coming judgment of God at Christ's return. They should not wait until they hear God's verdict before trying to be reconciled with him. Now is the time to make peace by believing in his son Jesus Christ.

13:1-21 Healing and Growth

13:1-9 Tragedies: Whose Sin?

If there is tragedy in someone's life, who is to blame or whose fault is it? Did someone sin? And if there are no tragedies in someone's life, do they still need to repent? In other words, should the occurrence of a tragedy in a person's life be linked to sin or not? This passage responds to questions like this. It refers to tragedies with human causes (a massacre of Galileans by Pilate – **13:1**) and with natural causes (the fall of the tower of Siloam – **13:4**). Tragedy, says Jesus, is not the measure of one's sinfulness and one's need to repent. Those who are not experiencing tragedies are also in need of repentance.

He then tells a parable about a fig tree that after three years bore no fruit (**13:6-9**). Since a fig tree supposedly reached maturity after three years, the probability was that it would never bear fruit. The owner wanted it cut down and replaced, but the vinedresser asked for one more year to see if it would bear. The point is that the absence of judgment here and now cannot be taken as a sign of one's righteousness. Rather, if judgment does not strike immediately, it is a sign of God's mercy, not his approval.

In sum: tragedy is no sure sign of sinfulness, just as the absence of tragedy is no sure sign of righteousness. All alike – those whose lives are tragic and those whose lives are tranquil – are sinners and all alike must repent before God (see also comments on 8:4-15).

13:10-17 The Compassionate Healer

One day a woman with a disability shuffled her way to the synagogue to hear the Word of God, for it was the Sabbath. Because of her sickness, she would have been isolated in the society of her day. Jesus was the preacher that day (**13:10-11**). When he saw her, he immediately recognized her troubles, *called her forward* and addressed her directly saying, *Woman, you are set free from your infirmity* (**13:12**). Then he touched her. Luke's sense for the human dimension is striking. Whereas the woman with the flow of blood had touched him (8:44-46), here it is Jesus who takes the initiative and touches the woman with compassion so that she will be healed. And immediately, as was characteristic of the healings of Jesus, *she straightened up and praised God* (**13:13**). There was no wondering whether the person was healed when he healed. There was no hysterical delay. People these days may fling their crutches away during an evening healing service and have to pick them up again after a day or two. But when Jesus healed, they never picked them up again.

But not everyone praised God. The Pharisee in charge of the synagogue was indignant and tried to lecture the crowd on the wrong of coming to be healed on the Sabbath (**13:14**). Jesus would have none of this, and interrupted him, exposing his hypocrisy by asking pointedly, *Doesn't each of you on the Sabbath untie his ox or donkey* on the grounds that it was a necessary act of mercy? (**13:15**). Yet the one who had been tied up here was no mere animal but a human being; and not only a human being but *a daughter of Abraham* (**13:16**). For eighteen years Satan had bound her and bent her double so that she could not hold her head high and walk tall or lift her eyes to heaven or look straight into the eyes of others. She was reduced to shuffling along because of her disability. If there is mercy for the donkeys on the Sabbath, shouldn't it be extended to human beings? Wasn't she entitled to healing on the Sabbath? Jesus transformed this woman's life by crossing the boundaries created by cultural and religious traditions of impurity and social sidelining. She was restored to her place in the community of the people of God.

In their understandable concern for religious identity, marked by Sabbath-keeping, the religious leaders lost sight of compassion. Jesus did not. For him, compassion was not something you put a price on. He charged no fee for his healings.

13:18-21 Parables of Growth

The parables on mustard seed and yeast are so closely connected by their content that they must be discussed together. In both cases the beginning is small. The mustard seed is so small that it can be described as 'the smallest seed you plant in the ground' (Mark 4:31). The yeast is only a tiny proportion of the dough that the woman mixed. But both of them grew: the seed developed into a tree in which birds could take refuge (an image that is also used to describe a powerful kingdom that protects its vassals). The yeast worked quietly in the dough which rose and doubled or tripled in size (**13:19, 21**).

Jesus makes it clear that these examples demonstrate how his reign works (**13:18, 20**). His mission has small beginnings, with only a few disciples, many of whom were disreputable characters. But by God's miraculous power this small group would grow and grow until God's people were spread throughout the whole world.

13:22-35 Jesus' Journey to Jerusalem

Jesus is on his way to Jerusalem (**13:22**) and is determined to reach it (**13:33**), even if it means that he will be killed. While making his way to Jerusalem, someone asked him whether all, many or only few are to be saved (**13:23**). The question is not answered directly. Instead it seems as if Jesus replied: 'Do not waste your time debating that question; look to yourself: Are you saved?' In other words, rather than speculating about the fate of others, each person must make sure that she or he will enter the door, however narrow and difficult it is, because at the last day many people will want to enter but will find that they have left the decision until too late (**13:24-30**). For practical purposes, Jesus seems to be saying, it is better to assume that few will be saved, and it is never wise for people to assume the contrary, certainly as far as they themselves are concerned.

The theme of Jesus' journey to Jerusalem comes into sharper focus in 13:31-33. Some Pharisees warn Jesus to flee because Herod wants to kill him (**13:31**). Jesus replied with an expression of contempt for *that fox* (**13:32**), a characterization of Herod that shows Jesus was aware of the political issues of his day. Jesus has a task that must conclude in Jerusalem, and no Herod will be able to divert him from it. He, therefore, has no need to flee. If Herod wants to kill him, he had better go to Jerusalem. Furthermore, Jesus is convinced that in Jerusalem it will be God's plans that come to a head, not Herod's (13:33).

Then Jesus turns his attention to Jerusalem and expresses his love for this city in heartbreaking terms: *O Jerusalem, Jerusalem, you who kill the prophets and stone those sent to you, how often I have longed to gather your children together, as a hen gathers her chicks under her wings, but you were not willing* (**13:34**). In this verse we can hear the heartbreak of God! We cannot read it without seeing God's tears and hearing God's love for this city. The great Mother heart of God is there, especially in the words, 'as a hen gathers her chicks under her wings.'

14:1-24 Stories Around a Dining Table

Chapter 14 appears to be presented as a series of encounters and discourses in the setting of a dinner or banquet

(14:1, 8, 12, 15 and 24). Jesus used the occasion to teach important truths.

14:1-6 A Sinister Plan

The gospels contain several accounts of Jesus healing on the Sabbath. In Luke we have accounts of the healing of Simon Peter's mother-in-law (4:38); of the man with the withered hand (6:6); of a woman who was bent for eighteen years (13:14) and a man who had dropsy (14:2). John tells the story of the healing of the paralytic at the pool of Bethesda (John 5:9) and of the man born blind (John 9:14). Mark includes the healing of a demon-possessed man in the synagogue at Capernaum (Mark 1:21-25). With such a variety of healings on the Sabbath, Jesus' views on the matter must have been well known.

However, his healings aroused opposition. In the eyes of the Pharisees, Jesus was a lawbreaker. Their logic was: Jesus healed on Sabbath; therefore, he worked on the Sabbath; therefore, he broke the law and should be regarded as a criminal. But they were still collecting proof of his behaviour.

On this occasion a Pharisee invited Jesus to a meal on the Sabbath. Just as he arrived, without any explanation, *in front of him was a man suffering from dropsy* (**14:2**). It is unlikely that someone with this condition would have been invited to the meal, for the abnormal accumulation of body fluids associated with this condition causes massive swelling and disfigurement. In the eyes of a Pharisee, such a person was probably under divine judgment. Most likely, the Pharisees had deliberately planted the man with dropsy there to see what Jesus would do, for *he was being carefully watched* (**14:1**). The word translated 'watched' is the word used for spying in an attempt to entrap someone who has a reputation for deviating from the system.

Without being intimidated, Jesus healed the man. At the same time he pointed out that if a person or ox or donkey fell into a well on the Sabbath, any one of them would rescue them at once. Yet here was a man whose body was filling up with water, and they were not prepared to help him! With searing contempt, Jesus demands how, if it is right to help an animal on the Sabbath, it can be wrong to help a person? (**14:5**; see also the comments on 13:10-17).

14:7-14 Seating Arrangements

This story deals with the false notions that some well-to-do people, wealthy landowners and the upper class have concerning their social and economic status. For them a wedding or a funeral is an opportunity to advertize their imagined merit and distinction. They refuse to wait for someone else, such as the host, to confer an unexpected distinction on them or to grant them a place of honour. Instead, they push themselves into the chief seats so that everyone can see how distinguished they are (**14:7**). If they don't have these seats, they do not enjoy the feast at all.

At that time, the most distinguished guests would usually arrive last for a feast. That is why those who picked seats for themselves risked embarrassment by being asked to move when more honoured guests arrived (**14:8-9**). Jesus warned people to avoid such humiliation by not overestimating their status (**14:10-11**). His advice fits with that in Proverbs 25:6-7, 'Do not exalt yourself in the king's presence, and do not claim a place among great men; it is better for him to say to you, "Come up here," than for him to humiliate you before a nobleman.'

Luke's story is about more than social etiquette or politically correct behaviour. Serious economic, political and religious problems can underlie accepted innocent-looking routines. Experience has shown that seeking the chief seats leads to corruption, with exploitation of the poor and oppressed. Instead of seeking such corrupted places we should rather explore alternative seating arrangements.

Today we are living in a world full of inequalities, which create uneven sitting arrangements at today's dining tables. We should be working to ensure, not only that everyone has access to a dining table (**14:12-14**), but also that the table itself is reshaped to accommodate all God's children. We should not merely go and sit at a 'foreign' table but at a table that is authentically ours, in a context suited to African Christianity. Kanyoro suggests that such a table should be a round table, with no sides and no preferred seating position. At such a table, there is no first or last and there is room for all. Such a table is a visual representation of a church in which women and men participate in full equality, carrying out pastoral and healing ministry as part of the priesthood of all believers.

14:15-24 The Great Dinner

Jesus constantly associates God's reign with parties, feasts and banquets, that is, with food and drink. These symbols of the reign of God arouse joy and songs of praise. Unfortunately, there are many Christians today who are denied the right to be joyful because of poverty and lack of food, and this is a scandal that we are called to address. But the reign of God urges Christians to be like people who are forever at a wedding feast.

One way of interpreting the parable of the great dinner is to assume that the host is someone like a tax collector who has become wealthy. He sends out invitations hoping that they will lead to his being fully accepted by the elite. But they all, as if in agreement, reject his invitation. Then in his anger he invites the exploited and oppressed people to his house in order to show the rich that he cares nothing for them and will have nothing more to do with them.

Jesus tells this parable to illustrate both the wrath and mercy of God. The closing verdict expresses the contempt of the host for those who had despised his invitation: *I tell you, none of those who were invited will taste my dinner* (**14:24**). Instead *the poor, the crippled, the lame, the blind* (**14:13**) are

the ones who are blessed and who will *eat at the feast in the kingdom of God* (**14:15**). Jesus says that the future is determined by our present response and the rich have excluded themselves.

14:25-35 Cost of Being a Disciple

For comments, on discipleship as bearing a cross (**14:25-27**), see comments on 9:21-45 above. In 14:28-33 God is inviting all, through the activity of Jesus, to enter the kingdom, but it is an invitation that ought not to be unthinkingly accepted. It requires something like the careful costing of a building project (**14:28-30**) or the preparation for a military operation (**14:31-32**). One should not become Jesus' disciple impulsively, but should make a carefully thought-out commitment, in full awareness of what is involved (**14:33**). Those who make that sort of commitment will be like salt, enabling God to use this new community as seasoning in the world (**14:34-35**).

15:1-32 The Running God

15:1-10 Searching and Finding Solutions

Shepherds and sheep have to walk long distances to find grass and water, particularly in arid regions. The parable of the lost sheep reminded us of such walking. If one sheep is lost, you may not even know where to start searching and a whole day may be spent walking and walking and searching for it (**15:3-4**). We as Africans can identify with such walking, for here most people walk rather than drive or fly. Feet are important here, just as they were in biblical times when Jesus was always walking. Our call to discipleship is a call to put our feet in his footprints.

Walking in his footsteps as he searches for the lost is not easy in a world burdened with lost sheep in the form of refugees and those affected by slavery, colonialism, dictatorship, the debt burden, HIV/AIDS, unemployment, homelessness, sexual abuse and gender inequality. As we walk and search, we must not overlook the realities of Africa.

First, our search is in hostile territory. Africa is a dangerous continent. People are exposed to snakes, wild beasts, devastating droughts and floods, sickness, AIDS, malaria and high infant mortality rates. It is all too easy to succumb to anxiety, fear and superstition. Yet, Africans also have a strong sense of survival and hope and a strong belief in God. In the words of the old hymn, 'Through many dangers, toils and snares; I have already come, 'Tis grace hath brought me safe thus far, And grace will lead me home.'

We should also recognize that our search is for something precious, costly and dear just like the coin the woman has lost (**15:8-10**). She has ten coins and values each of them. She does not argue that the loss of one is not a tragedy, because there are still nine left. It is not the quantity that counts, but the value of each coin as an individual piece. It does not matter whether it was a large or small coin. Big or small, all are her coins!

Likewise, as individuals we are each valued by God. Each of us is a unique being because of the dignity and value that God has conferred upon us. Nobody should regard herself or himself as low, useless, rotten and unproductive. And because each of us is unique, it matters deeply when one of us is lost. The loss of one is as serious as the loss of all! Therefore, we have to stick together. The fact that we belong to each other and are related as brothers and sisters is what makes us human. Because each of us is so precious, we must also constantly be searching for ways to guarantee that no human life will be lost, degraded, exploited, abused or violated.

But what are we to do if this has already happened? If a soul has already been lost or a body violated? What the woman did was make use of what she had to search for the lost coin. She used a lamp to provide light, increasing her chances of seeing it. She used a broom to carefully sweep the whole house. These objects were tools to help her in her quest.

What is the most important, precious, dear and costly thing for us today? Isn't it life? And human lives are being lost to the scourge of HIV/AIDS. As we search for ways to save those who are being lost to it, we need to use the tools we have available, and these include talking openly about sexual matters from biblical, theological and pastoral perspectives.

Many people suggest that condoms are the tool we should be using to fight HIV/AIDS. But we need to make it clear that from biblical, theological and pastoral perspectives, condoms are not the sole solution. We need to be repeatedly stressing, marketing and proclaiming sound Christian, religious and traditional cultural morality that is based on abstinence from sex before marriage and faithfulness within any marriage relationships. Today, promiscuity and drug abuse are key avenues for the spread of HIV/AIDS. Our pastoral ministry has to focus on regaining a sense of the deeper meaning and purpose of sex as the celebration of a mature love in a committed relationship, which provides a 'nest' for the future generation.

HIV/AIDS is no longer a problem that can be ignored by Christians. Sooner or later we shall be confronted with the reality of this virus. In a social environment where up to a third of the population is infected, it is more than likely that some members of our churches are infected as well. Taking Paul's picture of the body seriously, we can say that the body of Christ is HIV positive. Put differently, our church has AIDS. It has become our problem; we have to deal with it; we have to become instruments of God's redeeming love.

To become instruments of God we need to revisit the African concept of *ubuntu* and recognize that the disease does not only affect the physical body, it also affects the

'social body', and thus our whole existence. The first part of the social body to be damaged is family. The sickness and loss of a parent, a spouse, a sibling, a fellow-learner or a student disrupts established family patterns and calls for help and ministry from a caring community.

Besides providing help with the care of the dying and comfort for the survivors, we also need to face the fact that funerals are becoming more expensive by the day. Costly funerals bite deep into poor family budgets. If nothing is done, no families will be able to bury their beloved ones. The situation could become chaotic as corpses may stack up in morgues, to eventually be buried in rows of anonymous graves because people have no money for funerals. The church, with all its members, is called to the ministry of caring. This means promoting the acceptance of people with HIV/AIDS, fighting against discrimination, and developing programmes that address the needs of those living with the disease.

Seeking the lost does not only mean caring for those affected by HIV/AIDS but also preventing its spread. We need to promote faithfulness in marriage and lifelong relationships. But we also have to be realistic and admit we live in a situation where casual sex of every kind is common. Prostitutes are only different in that they admit they do it for cash. Everywhere there is premarital sex, recreational sex, obligatory sex, coercive sex, sex as a gift, sugar-daddy sex, extramarital sex, second families and multiple partners. HIV/AIDS feasts on promiscuity. To fight it, we need to use a range of approaches that are appropriate to the situations of different individuals, a changing morality, rapid urbanization, industrialization, the influence of Western culture, more 'liberal' attitudes towards sex in towns and cities, and the influence of alcohol. This means that we shall also have to talk about condoms, without giving up our preaching of morality. We need to distinguish between the rules, which we would like all to observe, and the reality that many will flout these rules.

In our teaching on ethics, we need to issue a call to all, whether Christian or not, to recognize that we are sexual beings who must express our sexuality with responsibility. We need to encourage a sexual ethic that stresses fidelity, whether in monogamous, polygamous, homosexual or heterosexual relations. We need to teach people who are entering into sexual relations to ask questions such as the following: What do you really want from each other? What is your business with each other? Is there any meaning in it? Is it justified and full of promise because you are honestly and resolutely on the way to achieving a total, lifelong relationship? We need to stress Barth's point that people who, upon entering into sexual relations, are not ready to bear all consequences commit an injustice to each other and, therefore, to society.

Besides teaching ethics for an age of HIV/AIDS, the church needs to embark on a program of education and information so that understanding and compassion can grow. Ignorance, silence, deception, blame and denial – especially on the subject of sex – are extremely dangerous. Despite the concerns of some that encouraging the use of condoms will only promote more promiscuity, the church needs to accept that where sexual discipline has collapsed, teaching about condoms is a lesser evil than allowing people to die because of exposure to HIV/AIDS.

In some circumstances, use of a condom is the best way to obey the commandment 'Thou shalt not kill.' This is most certainly the case in situations where one partner is infected with the virus and the other, who is not yet infected, needs and wants to protect herself or himself.

Even for most spiritual and loyal Christians, HIV/AIDS presents many serious moral dilemmas. After much reflection from biblical, theological and pastoral perspectives, one of the guidelines that has been developed is the ABCD principle:

A is for *abstinence,* that is, abstain altogether from sex before marriage.

B stands for *be faithful* in marriage or any sexual relationship. This is the way that guarantees life. But if you find that you cannot follow this teaching, then choose

C for a *condom,* because the alternative is

D for *death.*

We must not lose sight of the fact that the 'A' (for Abstinence) and the 'B' (for Be faithful in marriage) come first. All Christians are required to follow these rules because they are based on the Holy Scriptures. The church should devote itself to the difficult task of promoting sexual discipline among the unmarried. It should say in no uncertain terms that it will not tolerate promiscuity and the kind of behaviour that endangers human well-being. After having said that, one should be able to stop.

But the reality is that some will fall into temptation, and there is no cure for AIDS. To avoid our teaching leading to death, we may need to state that if you cannot follow the rule, then you must choose option 'C' (a condom).

While teaching this, we also know that a loving God is in control of the situation and is the source of hope in the mists of hopelessness and desperation. If God is God, death and destruction cannot have the last word. That is where Christian hope comes to the picture. We all have to become involved in this struggle for our heritage and our futures.

If we refuse to make use of objects at our disposal then valuable, precious, rare and dear lives will be lost. And these are young lives. Normally, we would expect the old to die first, but today in our own houses we are losing one coin after another, one young person after another.

As religious teachers and leaders, we have a responsibility to be part of the search for those who are being lost. Jesus says, 'go, then, to all peoples everywhere and make them my disciples' (Matt 28:19). Yes, the world out there is waiting for solutions and is begging that nothing should

be lost. According to 9:17, we should gather 'what was left over' just as the disciples filled twelve baskets with the pieces left over from the five barley loaves that the people had eaten. Let us walk together to search for the 'one lost sheep.' Every single thing and every single citizen is costly. Let us also make use of objects at our disposal in our search towards solutions. Light up your lamps and take your brooms and go into the world and search for ways to bring healing to our broken world!

15:11-32 The Waiting, Running, Embracing God

Here is a paraphrase of this well-known parable from an African perspective: A man and his wife had two sons, of whom they were very proud. The older son ploughed, sowed, harvested and took care of the cattle. He worked from morning till night. One day the younger son said to his father: 'Give me my share of the cattle. I want to stand on my own two feet.' The father and mother discussed what to do, and then the mother said: 'Give him his share. He is old enough. We must wait and see what happens.' The father divided the cattle and gave the younger son his share.

The younger son took his cattle, sold them and received much money for them. He went to the city to enjoy life there. At last he was his own master! He had a wonderful time dancing at the discos and spending his money on cars, a television set and women. Soon he did not have a cent left. He went to look for work, but no one would employ him. He became lonely. He had no roof over his head and eventually had to sleep on the street corner, covering himself with newspapers. To alleviate his hunger, he rummaged through garbage cans.

Every day, his father and mother kept a lookout to see when he would return. One day they saw him coming, ragged and scared. They ran together to meet him. Their younger son knelt down and told them he was sorry. The father and mother welcomed him home and let him into the hut. They prepared a wonderful meal and invited the entire village to the feast. There was great joy in the village, and people danced and sang ….

Then the older brother became angry. His father came out of the kraal and asked him to come to the feast. The older son answered: 'You know how I worked for you all these years. I could not even have a party for all my friends. But now my brother has come back, after wasting all our cattle, and you prepare a feast for him.'

The father took him to his mother in the hut and said: 'My son, you were always at home with us. But your brother was dead and has come back to life; *he was lost and is found.*'

This parable can go by many names but is popularly known as 'the prodigal son'. The NIV refers to it as 'the lost son', which makes it clear that this parable is linked to the immediately preceding parables of the lost sheep and the lost coin. When the son is found again, this good news arrives with an invitation to *rejoice with me; I have found my lost sheep* ' (**15:6**). Once again there is *rejoicing in heaven* (**15:7**) and *rejoicing in the presence of the angels of God over one sinner who repents* (**15:10**).

The elder brother in this 'parable of the elder brother' angrily refuses to participate in the rejoicing (**15:28**). For this reason the parable is also known as 'the lost sons.' Both are prodigal, for the elder squanders his joy in his father's and mother's presence and possessions (15:31) and the invitation to the party with the fatted calf (**15:23**). The parable commences with the younger son lost and concludes with the elder son lost.

While the ending is disappointing, the image people are left with at the end of this parable is an image of the waiting, running, embracing, kissing and partying One who has *compassion* for the lost who are *still a long way off* (**15:20**) and for those who have always been near (**15:31**). A banquet of great joy is provided by this waiting One, who is none other than the waiting, running, embracing, partying and kissing God. The parable describes God's goodness, grace, boundless mercy and abundant love.

16:1-31 Faces of Wealth

16:1-9 Make Friends with Your Wealth

Many commentators have said that this story of 'the dishonest manager' is the most difficult of all parables, for incompetence, dishonesty and corruption seem to be rewarded. But the focus of the story is not on dishonesty but on prudence. Let me explain.

The parable of the prodigal son introduced a young man who wasted his wealth in dissolute living. Likewise, the parable of the dishonest manager presents a manager who wasted his employer's goods (**16:1**). The first of the two parables teaches us that if we sinfully waste our lives and then, at the eleventh hour, come back to God in true repentance, we shall meet a waiting, running, embracing, kissing and partying God. The second parable provides the other side of the story: if we waste our lives and the future is bleak (**16:3**), then at the eleventh hour, use our possessions to help others, and we are assured that they will welcome us *into eternal dwellings* (**16:9**).

Some commentators are now challenging the basic assumption that the manager's action in remitting the debts was in itself immoral. They maintain that Jews were forbidden to lend money at interest, but got around this by lending out commodities such as oil and wheat and charging interest on them. Normally, payment was made to the manager, who then paid the owner what he was due but pocketed most of the interest. From this perspective, what happens in this parable, is that the manager, accused of mismanaging his employer's property and finding himself dismissed, shrewdly calls in the debtors one by one and cancels his own share of the interest on the loans, allowing the debtors to return exactly what they borrowed and no more. The wise action praised in the parable is that the manager bought friends who would help him once he was unemployed.

The manager's prompt and shrewd action to meet his imminent crisis is reinterpreted as a prudent example of using one's money to secure one's future. Christian readers are to do the same. They are to use their possessions now to help others, and will receive favour in return. But does the reference to 'eternal dwellings' mean that money can buy someone a place in heaven? The following story may be helpful in answering this question:

> One day a rich tax-gatherer Ma'jan died and was given a splendid funeral; work stopped through out the city, since the whole population wished to escort him to his last resting-place. At the same time a poor scholar died, and no one took any notice of his burial. How could God be so unjust as to allow this? The answer is as follows: although Ma'jan had by no means lived a pious life, yet he had done once a good deed … He had invited the city councillors to dinner, but they did not come. So he gave orders that the poor should come and eat, so that the food should not be wasted. That explains why the poor scholar's funeral was unattended, while Ma'jan was buried with great pomp. However, one of the poor scholar's colleagues was allowed to see in a dream the fate of the two men in the next world: A few days later that scholar saw his colleague in gardens of paradise beauty, watered by flowing streams. He also saw Ma'jan the publican standing on the bank of a stream and trying to reach the water, but unable to do so (Joachim Jeremias).

16:10-17 The Use and Misuse of Wealth

Jesus uses the example of wealth to speak to disciples about social responsibility and stewardship. They are urged to be faithful in the use of their earthly wealth because it is on loan from God. If they cannot be trusted with earthly wealth and possessions, how can they be trusted with the true riches of eternal life? (**16:10-12**). In these verses Jesus applied the idea of stewardship to material possessions. The reason why the use of wealth is tied to eternal life is that *you cannot serve both God and Money* (**16:13**). Discipleship means single-minded devotion to serving God with our earthly possessions, while not neglecting to share our wealth with the community to meet needs (see also Acts 6:1-6; 11:27-30).

16:18 Divorce

Marriage expresses the fundamental movement intended by God at creation: union. What God has yoked together should not be separated by human beings. However, when such a union is broken, the one breaking it commits adultery. The original will of God has precedence over any subsequent concessions made to the weaknesses of human beings as a result of the fall, especially if the reality of God's rule is to be reconstituted. Union was and, now more then ever, is the natural order of things. Separation and divorce are realities that originate from a polluted system that promotes violence and abuse of a partner and children and unfaithfulness.

16:19-31 The Rich Man and Lazarus

The story outlined above of Ma'jan, the rich tax collector, and the poor scholar is a good introduction to the story of the rich man, who, though unnamed, is commonly called Dives (Latin for 'rich man') and the poor man, Lazarus.

Lazarus is someone who has been denied the right to make choices and the opportunity to live a tolerable life. There are millions of Lazaruses in this world today, for whom life is difficult, painful or hazardous. They are deprived of knowledge and communication and robbed of dignity, confidence and self-respect. Poverty means more than a lack of what is necessary for material well-being. It can also mean the denial of the opportunities and choices most basic to human development, that is, the opportunity to lead a long, healthy and creative life and to enjoy a decent standard of living, freedom, dignity, self-esteem and the respect of others.

The point of this parable is not to console those like Lazarus with some pipe dream of heaven. It is not meant to console the poor with the hope of recompense beyond the grave. Rather it aims to incite the rich and the poor to hear and act.

The topic of the relationship between rich and poor Christians is of importance because God is on the side of the disadvantaged and oppressed and expects his followers to stand with him. The mission of the church includes making concrete ethical and political decisions because our belief in God includes rather than excludes human political creativity. Claiming to be on the side of the poor without taking action to address the conditions that give rise to poverty is mere hypocrisy.

At the one extreme in this story is an unidentified rich man, whose clothing, mansion and lifestyle, mark him as one of the rich and famous (**16:19**). The very idea of such lifestyle might have been amazing to some of the original hearers. But deep in the night, when hunger kept them awake, they may have reflected on why some people enjoy life while others have to sweat and scrape just to get by.

At the opposite extreme is a representative of the poverty of the masses, named Lazarus (**16:20-21**). All that he has going for him is the fact that he is the only person in all of Jesus' parables with a name, Lazarus. This name is the Latinized form of Eleazar and means 'God is my help'. Lazarus is a beggar, but he has a name. He is covered with ulcerated sores but he has human dignity. He does not remain nameless.

The sin of the rich man is that he has no heart. He looks at a man with a name, but does not ask him his name. He saw Lazarus' hunger and pain, but did nothing about it. He accepted the poverty of Lazarus as part of the normal order of things and thought it perfectly natural and inevitable that Lazarus should lie in hunger, pain, suffering, sickness and ultimately in death while he wallowed in luxury. There are none so blind as those who will not see.

After death, this man receives the punishment due to one who had not practised *ubuntu* and acknowledged that Lazarus was a fellow human being (**16:23**). He had failed to see Lazarus as a brother and a neighbour. Relishing his wealth and enjoying the envy it aroused in others, he did not realize until it was too late that a life characterized by individualism and a refusal to share one's bread with one's neighbour is detestable in God's sight (16:20-21).

17:1-19 Stories of Healing, Faith and Salvation

17:1-10 Faith before Good Works

In this passage Jesus calls for the renunciation of all self-righteousness. Having been told to rebuke offenders and to forgive repentant sinners (**17:3-4**), the apostles realize that forgiveness is extremely difficult and beg Jesus to *increase our faith* (**17:5**). Jesus replies that faith is not a commodity that can be measured or owned. Rather than wanting 'more faith' or a 'powerful faith', what God needs is a faith that is pure and simple, that is, faith with integrity (**17:6-10**). Our faith does not make us powerful authorities but humble servants of God. It is God who enables *these little ones* (**17:2**) to say to a tree, *be uprooted and planted in the sea* and it will obey them (17:6). Those who do what is commanded cannot boast of their own achievements.

We must also never get it into our heads that we have served God so well that now we have a right to put our needs before God's requirements. Jesus expresses this graphically: *Suppose one of you had a servant* who has just come in from *ploughing or looking after the sheep.* Would you say to him, *'Come along now and sit down to eat?'* Would you not rather say, *'Prepare my supper … and wait on me while I eat and drink; after that you may eat and drink?'* (**17:7-8**).

Jesus' comments here raise the issues of faith and good works. We need to remember that it is in our existence before God that we obtain grace and are justified. In our existence before our fellow humans, we are engaged in great and genuine struggles for freedom and seek to serve others. Faith does not replace works, but the latter follow the former. According to Luther, when 'Christ has been grasped by faith' and when such faith becomes operative, then we do 'good works, love God, give thanks, and practice love towards the neighbour'. It follows that the positive connection between faith and good works should not be concealed but enthusiastically expressed in concrete and revolutionary ways.

17:11-19 A Grateful Samaritan

This story starts with ten men who had to keep *at a distance* and shout in order to get a hearing (**17:12-13a**). People with leprosy were not allowed to enter a village, so they maintained the distance prescribed by Moses (Lev 13:46). It is noticeable that Jesus did not go to them, touch and heal them as he had done with other lepers (5:12-13). Instead, he kept his distance and simply told them to go and show themselves to the priests. Only as they went were they healed (**17:14**). By then, of course, the distance between them and Jesus had increased.

One of the members of this group was a Samaritan (17:16). As explained earlier (see 10:29-37) Jews had no dealings with the Samaritans, and yet in this group a common sickness had broken down the racial and religious barriers. In the common tragedy of their leprosy they had remembered only that they were sick people who were in need. The need for social, cultural, religious and racial segregation was gone. Together they shouted with one voice, *Jesus, Master, have pity on us* (**17:13b**).

It is worth noting the changing distance between Jesus and the Samaritan. As the Samaritan came closer to Jesus and finally *threw himself at Jesus' feet and thanked him* (**17:16**), the physical distance was gone and so was the social, racial and religious separation and every kind of alienation between himself and Jesus and between himself and God. All were removed with the gift, *Rise and go; your faith has made you well* (**17:19**).

The man's grateful recognition of God's power brought him back to Jesus through whom that power had been expressed. Jesus was able to grant him not just physical healing, such as the other nine received, but also a hand of friendship, forgiveness, reconciliation and salvation, removing all the alienation and distance between himself and God. The ingratitude of the other nine appears all the more blameworthy in the face of God's graciousness.

The best thanks we can give to God is to try to express as 'little ones' our thanksgiving: 'Praise the Lord, O my soul, and forget not all his benefits, who forgives all your sins, and heals all your diseases, who redeems your life from the pit, and crowns you with love and compassion, who satisfies your desires with good things so that your youth is renewed like the eagle's' (Ps 103:2-5).

17:20-37 The Second Coming

The Pharisees' question in **17:20** amounts to a request for a sign that they will immediately recognize that the day of the second coming is at hand. But the kingdom of God does not come in a form that anyone can recognize in a superficial effortless way. It is never that kind of indisputable fact.

Instead, if they knew how to look, the signs they are looking for are certainly there. The kingdom is among them – it was in Jesus himself (**17:21**). In short, what is needed is to be vigilant and observant.

Then Jesus gives some OT examples of failure to be vigilant: those living in the world before the flood (**17:26-27**), the citizens of Sodom (**17:28-29**) and Lot's wife (**17:32**). The second coming will come as suddenly as the disasters that befell them and it will be as unwise to look back. Lot's wife was turned into a pillar of salt because she was so attached to her earthly possessions that she could not help looking round to see what was happening to them.

The second coming is pictured in Luke as taking place at night, when people are sleeping (**17:34**), but also, curiously, when women are grinding grain (**17:35**). Some manuscripts add **17:36**: *Two men will be in the field: one will be taken, the other left* (see also Matt 24:40). It seems that it may take place either in the night or in the day.

In **17:37** Jesus repeats the point he made in 17:21-31. The second coming of the Son of Man is not something that can be observed beforehand. The thing to do is to be like vultures who are extraordinarily far-sighted and quick in recognizing the presence of food.

18:1-30 Entrance into the Reign of God

18:1-8 The Revealed God

This parable is found only in Luke. One day, a widow, too poor to influence the judge, approaches him with the only weapon she has – a dogged persistence that will wear the judge down until out of sheer desperation he gives her justice (**18:2-5**). In this parable the widow was a young woman who was denied her inheritance, but she is symbolic of all those who cry out for justice in this world.

Jesus explains the moral of the parable. *And will not God bring about justice for his chosen ones who cry out to him day and night? Will he keep putting them off? I tell you, he will see that they get justice, and quickly* (**18:1, 7-8**). The parable teaches us both the necessity of persistence on our part and the reality of God's mercy, for God is a God of the poor and needy, and of widows and children.

But the parable also raises a question in our minds. Why does God allow people to suffer like this at all? Why does God allow people to despair, be broken-hearted and be denied justice? We have to admit that many things that we experience appear to contradict the idea that God is a loving God. How could such a God permit such evil in his universe? At times he seems more like a hidden, fearsome God.

We may try to avoid the issue by simply attributing all pain to the devil, but we also know that even the devil could not exist without God's upholding power. And often the devil does his work through human instruments, who are also subject to God. Even in the Bible, we see how God acts in ways that we might consider encourage evil when he 'hardens' the heart of Pharaoh or those who are against political liberation and economic justice. Yet we also see how he uses such hardening to achieve justice in the end.

We also see a case of God apparently being hard-hearted in Jesus' treatment of the Canaanite woman (Matt 15:21-28). At first Jesus ignores her pleas for mercy. But still she trusts that Jesus is the Saviour and liberator, even though he seems harsh in not answering. When, at the entreaty of the disciples, Jesus stresses that he is sent only to the house of Israel, she does not give up. When Jesus tells her that bread is not to be taken from children and given to dogs, she does not stop but willingly admits that she is a dog, namely, one of the exploited, oppressed and humiliated. In the extreme circumstances in which she finds herself and from which she needs to be saved and liberated, she insists than even dogs receive the crumbs that fall from the tables of the rich. Then Jesus Christ manifests the humanness of God and declares that she is no longer a dog, but a daughter of God.

The point here is that the way into faith leads through the darkest hours of temptations, which leave no room for self-confidence. Such doubt and temptation teaches us not only to know and understand but also to experience how sweet, how lovely and how comforting God's Word is. God makes us aware of how extreme are the conditions in which people exist and from which they have to be saved and liberated. The cry 'My God, my God, why hast thou forsaken us' is not uttered by the insane but by those who are denied human dignity and economic justice. Hearing the cry of such people, God changes their situation, offering liberation and eternal salvation. This kind of God and this kind of action constitute the core of the gospel.

The other point that we need to remember when pondering the hiddenness of God is that God has reached out to us. He entered human history as the incarnate and human God in Mary's womb so that, as Luther puts it, humans might 'see the love, the goodness and the sweetness of God.'

Consequently, uncertainty and doubt about the possibility of salvation, political liberation, reconciliation and economic justice are clearly camouflaged heresy. Uncertainty can easily become a place of refuge, in which we seek to be protected from the winds of change. But salvation, political freedom and economic justice must be proclaimed decisively. The fact that God became incarnate gives us confidence that he sides with the afflicted, the oppressed and the desperate and plans to exalt them.

18:9-14 Who Are the Unrighteous and the Righteous?

The story of the Pharisee and tax collector raises the question of who is unrighteous and who righteous and which group we identify with. It is only too easy for people to identify themselves exclusively with the tax collector and never to discover something of the Pharisee in themselves.

The Pharisee in this parable has many positive characteristics: he is portrayed as a very religious and spiritual man, and should be commended for his spirituality and commitment to his religious tradition. He fasts twice a week and gives a tenth of all his income to the ministry and work of God (**18:12**). In his prayer he thanks God, admitting that he owes his better self to God, who has made him one of those who take their religious duties seriously. His prayer is similar to that in Psalm 17:4-5, 'As for the deeds of men –by the word of your lips I have kept myself from the ways of the violent. My steps have held to your paths; my feet have not slipped.'

The problem is that instead of being content to give thanks and observe his religious tradition, the Pharisee feeds on his own virtues and makes sinful comparisons. He is typical of those religious people who look upon themselves as more holy and spiritual and exalt themselves above the children of the world. Indeed, the Pharisee does not even hesitate to thank God that he is better than the children of the world, namely *robbers, evildoers, adulterers, or even … this tax collector* (**18:11**). His sin is self-glorification at the expense of someone else. Such self-glorification is reflected in the words attributed to Rabbi Simeon ben Jochai, 'if there are only two righteous men in the world, I and my son are these two; if there is only one, I am he!'

The tax collector, too, stands and addresses God directly. But where the Pharisee offers a prayer of thanksgiving, the other offers a petition for mercy. The tax collector's prayer is similar to that of the author of Psalm 34:8, someone who cries out and is heard by God and saved from every trouble. Standing before God, the tax collector describes himself as *a sinner,* deeply in need of justification and sanctification, begging God to be merciful to him (**18:13**). In his unconditional admission of his sinfulness before God, he *beats his breast.* He has come to true repentance and casts himself with unreserved confession of sin before the feet of God.

Which of these two do we identify with? I suggest that we should see ourselves in both. The good in the character of the Pharisee is his religious commitment; the bad is his self-righteousness. The negative side of the sinner was his sinful exploitation of his neighbours. But he is not content to remain sinful but confesses that he has sinned against God in thought, word and deed, by what he has done and by what he has left undone. He comes to the gate of heaven, which is so low that the only way to enter it is upon one's knees (**18:14**).

18:15-17 Being Touched as Infants and Little Ones

Throughout the Gospel of Luke we encounter stories of Jesus touching or blessing infants and little ones (18:15-17; 17:2; 8:50-56) or stories where Jesus is compassionate towards people living on the margins of society. In these stories the 'little ones' are humble in appearance, timid in their movements, disadvantaged, wounded and damaged

STREET CHILDREN

Jesus loves children. He told his disciples to 'let the little children come to me, and do not hinder them, for the Kingdom of God belongs to such as these' (Mark 10:14). But throughout Africa many children are not coming to Jesus because they are condemned to life on the street. Some of these children are on the streets by day but return home at night, sometimes to parents who demand money from them. Others literally live in the streets, where they experience hardship, fear and insecurity. Drugs and solvents help street children to cope with the scorn, rejection and abuse they receive as they boldly accost adults to demand money. Unscrupulous adults force them into anti-social and illegal activities such as drug pushing and prostitution. As they reach sexual maturity, many become infected with HIV/AIDS and pregnancies are common, resulting in street families.

Many of these children are drawn to the streets by the contrast between urban wealth and the desperate poverty of rural regions. Others are forced there by their parents' death from AIDS, by a lack of food or school fees at home, or by physical and sexual abuse. Peer influences and a desire to escape the discipline imposed by home and school draw others.

It is, however, wrong to assume that poverty alone produces street children. A lack of love from their parents, family members, relatives and communities pushes children onto the streets. Love gives a child a sense of belonging, which builds a sense of self worth and personal identity.

Adults have reacted to the influx of street children in negative ways. Parents in rural areas often lament the movement of their children to cities. Adults in urban communities fear and reject these children. The challenge for the church is to stop children going on the street in the first place and, if they are already there, to rehabilitate them.

In a loving family, parents plan their business and other engagements in a way that will not deny children the opportunity of being with them. They encourage healthy mental, physical, spiritual and social growth. We know that as a child Jesus grew in wisdom and stature, and in favour with God and men' (Luke 2:52).

Loving parents and a loving community help children develop normally in all areas of life. The church needs to build up this love within communities. It also needs to become an advocate for children who are already on the streets, working to 'let justice roll on like a river, righteousness like a never-failing stream' (Amos 5:24). Church members need to become aware of the need to rehabilitate these children. When children cannot see the hand of the Lord, we need to stretch out our hands to them. They need our spiritual guidance, our provision for their basic needs, and access to health services and education. The task is urgent, for the Bible instructs us, 'Train a child in the way he should go, and when he is old he will not turn from it' (Prov 22:6).

Solomon Gacece

in comparison with others in society. They are the people who are constantly in danger of doing something wrong in their job with possibilities of being fired or retrenched. Yet according to Matthew 25:31-46, every one of these little ones is 'a little Christ' to us.

Jesus' attitude to those living on the margins of society, including children, is expressed in his words, *Let the little children come to me, and do not hinder them; for the kingdom of God belongs to such as these'* (**18:16**). Despite this command and Jesus' explicit point that no obstacles should be placed in the way of children coming to him, in most churches the spiritual and educational needs of children are treated far too superficially. All too often, nearly all a church's energy, money and time is devoted to serving adults, while children receive only an insignificant share of the attention, mainly during Sunday school. However, effective services and ministries to children are part of any flourishing congregation. While our cultural tendency is to be stern, tough, severe and disciplinary towards children, we should follow Jesus' example by being tender, compassionate and sympathetic towards them. Jesus was undoubtedly interested in children and fond of them. We see this in his reference to their playing at marriages and funerals in the marketplace (7:32), in his refusal to order them to be silent when they sang

'Hosanna' in his honour in the temple (Matt 21:15) and also in the incident related here. Jesus may be justly acclaimed as the lover of little children.

18:18-30 Sell, Come and Follow

The story of the rich ruler is found in all the Synoptic Gospels (Mark 10:17-31; Matt 19:16-30). Each time, the issue of wealth is highlighted and the call to surrender it for the sake of God's reign is repeated. Luke characteristically stresses the 'all' in his version of Jesus' response: *Sell all that you own and distribute the money to the poor, and you will have treasure in heaven; then come, follow me* (**18:22** NRSV). While the other versions imply the need to leave everything behind, Luke alone specifies that Jesus meant letting it 'all' go. But the ruler was not prepared to do what Jesus told him (**18:23**). His 'Good Teacher' turned out to be merely polite talk (**18:18**).

I think that Jesus was absolutely serious when he answered the question, 'What must I do to inherit eternal life?' The eternal life in question is something that God shares with us. God is good because he is an all-sharing God. In African culture, we say that a good person is one who shares herself or himself and is of use to others. Such a person believes in an all-sharing God. But the rich man described here has no sense of ubuntu.

Our possessions and material goods are to be used to extend hospitality to all. Even today, people in Africa do not hesitate to arrange large parties with relatives, friends and neighbours and to spend money lavishly to keep human contacts as close as possible. My experience as a child illustrates this sense of ubuntu and sharing. My mother always prepared a warm meal for us on Sunday, with assorted meats, rice, mixed vegetables, custard and jelly, and perhaps cake with tea. As children, we always looked forward to such a warm meal in a rainbow of colours. But every week, two or three of the elders would stand talking with my father, who was a pastor, after the services. Time after time, we had to be satisfied with cold food, while the warm meal we had eagerly anticipated was served to the elders of the congregation. The sin of the rich man was that he was not prepared to share what he had.

Another experience that illustrates the need for sharing involved two men who were standing in the rain arguing over a seat in a taxi. Finally the one who had been there first surrendered his place to the other and walked over to where I was standing. 'Why did you give him your seat?' I asked. 'Well, his wife is in hospital,' he replied. As we get new insight into the needs of others, our own agenda needs to be re-examined and revised.

As we have learned in Luke's Gospel, it is the little ones and the children, the needy and poor, the sick and the sinners who enter the reign of God first, and it is the rich and famous who find themselves standing outside the gate. We have to interpret the statement, *What is impossible with men is possible for God* (**18:27**) as implying that it is only through God's miraculous grace that the rich will enter God's reign (see comments on 19:1-9). Those unwilling to share their ubuntu with God and their human fellows already exclude themselves from the circle of God's family in this life. Riches represent such barriers, and are so hard to let go of, that it is indeed a miracle when a rich person lets go and becomes a sister or a brother, and a disciple.

The saying 'it is more blessed to give than to receive' (Acts 20:35) is a fitting conclusion to Luke's presentation of the story of the rich man.

18:31-48 Jesus' Approach to Jerusalem

18:31-34 Jesus Predicts His Death

In this passage the inevitability of Jesus' death and resurrection in Jerusalem is conveyed only to the Twelve. Jesus takes them *aside* before speaking of it, perhaps as an indication to them that he is now going to be talking about a very important and weighty issue. The expectation is that they will transmit this message to others when they are ready

for it, not least by embodying the example Jesus is setting for them.

Jesus describes what he will happen to him in graphic terms. *They (*the Gentiles) will *mock him, insult him, spit on him, flog him and kill him. And on the third day he will rise again* (**18:32-33**). But the twelve disciples appear to have at best a limited grasp of what Jesus has communicated to them (**18:34**). The description of their 'blindness' and inability to see the meaning of Jesus' words is followed by the story of a blind beggar who is given his sight by Jesus because of his faith, and who *followed Jesus, praising God* (**18:43**).

18:35-43 Seizing the Moment of Opportunity

The blind man in this story has something important to teach us all. He was in despair and heard a commotion. He asked what was happening and was told that Jesus of Nazareth was passing by (**18:37**). He saw his moment of opportunity and began to shout, *Jesus, Son of David, have mercy on me!* (**18:38**). It may have been bad manners to shout in public, and those who were at the front of the crowd *rebuked him and told him to be quiet;* but he ignored them (**18:39**). He refused to let this opportunity pass. Jesus heard him, and he asked the man what it was he wanted. *Lord, I want to see* is the reply (**18:40-41**). As in the case of the Samaritan leper (17:19), Jesus declares that the man's faith has 'saved' him or made him well.

The crowd's rebuke of the man shows that they, unlike the blind man, had failed to understand Isaiah 35:5, which says that sight will be restored to the blind in God's time of deliverance. The blind man's request for the removal of his blindness is an invitation to Jesus to validate his credentials as Messiah. Though recording incidents like this, Luke wants readers to see that Jesus has become what he said he would be – a prophet, a teacher and a healer – thus fulfilling the Scriptures that he had read in the synagogue in his home town of Nazareth and then applied to himself. He is bringing 'good news to the poor' and proclaiming 'freedom for the prisoners and recovery of sight for the blind,' 'freedom to the oppressed' and 'the year of the Lord's favour' (4:18-19, quoting Isaiah 61:1-2).

19:1-10 The Rich Man Reformed

Jesus' encounter with the rich ruler (18:18-30) had prompted the question 'Who then can be saved?' (18:26) or more particularly, 'Can the rich be saved?' Can a rich man, really 'sell all' and get through the needle's eye (18:25)?. By emphasizing that Zacchaeus was rich (**19:2**), Luke prepares the reader for a story that will answer these questions.

The name Zacchaeus literally means 'righteous' or 'clean' and is also found in the OT in the form Zaccai (Ezra 2:9; Neh 7:14). Zacchaeus is extraordinarily anxious to see

Jesus (**19:3-4**), and Jesus abruptly asks hospitality from him (**19:5**). Jesus' attitude evokes hostility from the crowd, no doubt because Zacchaeus was a puppet who was working together with the 'enemy'; he participated in and benefited from the Roman rule. From many points of view he was neither 'clean' nor a good Jew (**19:7**). However, he was a man who was willing to take a risk.

It is clear that the question we should be asking is not 'Can the rich be saved?' or 'Can such and such a person be saved?' but 'Who then can be saved?' (18:26). The wealthy or the oppressors are really in no different position than any other sinner, despite the extra difficulties they face.

In the story, Zacchaeus is willing to take up his social responsibility towards his neighbours by declaring, *Here and now I give half of my possessions to the poor, and if I have cheated anybody out of anything, I will pay back four times the amount* (**19:8**). His attitude contrasts with that of the rich ruler, who found it impossible to share his possessions and 'became very sad; for he was a man of great wealth' (18:23).

The presence of Jesus makes possible what is humanly impossible. A wealthy man gets through the needle's eye because he is willing to let go of his wealth. Furthermore, from a political perspective, he is no longer viewed as a puppet of the Roman regime, but as a real brother or *a son of Abraham* (**19:9**). Thus, Zacchaeus now lives up to his name, which means 'clean' or 'righteous,' and becomes a living illustration of a person who is willing to demonstrate *ubuntu* toward the poor.

The story of Zacchaeus may be related to the land issue in countries such as Namibia, South Africa and Zimbabwe, where former oppressors are not willing to share land with the landless majority. Appeals are made to landowners to be more open so that the question of land can be solved peacefully and in accordance with the laws. How wonderful it would be if there were be more landowners like Zacchaeus who would voluntarily declare, 'Look, half of my land I will give to the landless.'

19:11-27 The Parable of the Pounds

While the crowd is still pondering Jesus' statement that salvation is come to Zacchaeus and his house because Jesus has come *to seek and to save what was lost* (19:10), Jesus tells them yet another parable (19:11). This parable answers the questions: What must one do after being justified? What must one do after being assured of salvation?

The parable says that God has given justified sinners the possibility of earning interest or bearing fruit. Each believer needs to recognize that they are now employed as part of the priesthood of all believers and are expected to serve the cause of God in Jesus Christ. Those who faithfully and diligently made the most of the opportunities given by God

to serve God's cause will be richly rewarded (**19:17**). Those who have been faithful and diligent to a lesser degree will also be rewarded, but in a smaller measure (**19:19**). However, a justified sinner who has neglected to do any good works will be rebuked and disgraced (**19:22-24**).

By the grace of God, all believers have received the opportunity to work for God and to be of service to their neighbours through word and deed, in prayer and proclamation, and in many other ways. Those who avail themselves of every opportunity that God gives will become richer and will always have more and better opportunities of working for God and their neighbours, thus laying up treasure in heaven. But those who fail to praise God and serve their neighbours will be disgraced.

19:28-44 Jesus Enters Jerusalem

When, at the end of the long journey, Jesus eventually came to Jerusalem, he made it very clear in what capacity in which he came. Zechariah had prophesied that Zion's king should come to her 'righteous and having salvation, gentle and riding on a donkey, on a colt the foal of an ass' (Zech 9:9). When Jesus reached Bethphage and Bethany, he sent for a donkey (19:29-30). He mounted it and his entry into Jerusalem became a royal procession, with the king surrounded by his disciples and greeted by cheering crowds.

There are three things to note as Jesus enters Jerusalem. First, Jesus sent his disciples to a village where they would find a colt that had never been ridden. They were instructed to untie it and bring it to him (**19:30**). If anyone asked them what they were up to, they should simply say, *the Lord needs it* (**19:31**). The fact that even a small donkey was useful reminds us that we are always regarded as useful in the sight of God. We are of use to God and our usefulness has never expired.

Second, when you are in God's company, you are always expected to do something. In our text, the people threw their clothes on the donkey for Jesus to sit on (**19:35**). They cut branches from the trees and spread them on the road (Matt 21:8). The people shared what they had with Jesus.

Finally, the text ends with joy: *The whole crowd of disciples began joyfully to praise God in loud voices* saying, *Blessed is the king who comes in the name of the Lord! Peace in heaven and glory in the highest!* (**19:37-38**).

Yet not all are joyful, for Jesus weeps over the future fate of the city he loves, which will soon be rejecting him (**19:41-45**; see also 13:34).

19:45-48 Cleansing of the Temple

On entering Jerusalem, the first place Jesus visits is the temple. Such a visit is in line with the words of Malachi 3:1: 'See, I will send my messenger, who will prepare the way before me. Then suddenly the Lord you are seeking will come to his temple; the messenger of the covenant, whom you desire, will come, says the Lord Almighty.' What he finds in the temple is shocking; robbers had infested the very temple of God and there was blatant commercialization of the temple services. Instead of the temple being a place consecrated to God where God could be worshipped, it had become a venue for all kinds of business transactions that degraded the *house of prayer* into *a den of robbers* (**19:45-46**). Taking controversial and perhaps violent action, Jesus makes a whip of cords and chases out all the merchants, sheep and cattle and overturns the tables of the money-changers (John 2:15).

The broad masses of the people probably noted with satisfaction how Jesus had exposed the errors of the religious leaders under whose heavy yoke they had to suffer. Their admiration for his sheer defiance and courage in challenging the entire religious establishment may have led them to listen to him more. They may also all have been talking about his miracles. Many of them could have testified that they themselves had witnessed how he had healed the sick, restored sight to the sightless, healed lepers, fed five thousand and even raised people from the dead. For these reasons, all the people hung on every word he said (**19:48**).

20:1-40 Teaching the People in the Temple

Once Jesus begins his teaching and preaching in Jerusalem (19:47-21:38), the resentment the religious leaders harbour toward him deepens. More intensely than before, the chief priests, scribes and members of the Sanhedrin become hostile and deceitful. Thus, they seek from the outset to destroy him (19:47), engage him in controversy and demand to know on what authority he teaches and preaches in the temple (20:1-8). Following Jesus' narration of the parable of the vineyard, they become so hostile that they want to seize him on the spot and hold back only for fear of the people (20:9-19). They endeavour to snare him by deceit, sending spies to catch him on the question of God and Caesar (20:20-26) and attempting to get the best of him in a controversy concerning resurrection life (20:27-40). However, Jesus answers his various opponents so well that he reduces them all to silence (20:40).

20:1-8 Question and Counter-Question

Whereas the people were spellbound by Jesus' words, the religious leaders were increasingly provoked by his teaching and preaching. So, *one day, as he was teaching the people in the temple courts,* the chief priests, scribes and elders came to Jesus and demanded to know on whose authority he was *doing these things* (**20:1-2**). While 'these things' refers to Jesus' teaching and preaching, it also includes his riding into Jerusalem and his taking the law into his own hands and cleansing the temple. Their question shows that they are thinking in terms of an official authority. They doubtless

thought that if they could force Jesus to admit that he was working for someone else, or that he had no authority at all, it would discredit him with the people, or at least justify them in arresting him.

Jesus responded with a counter question: When baptizing, did John act on divine or merely human, authority? (**20:3-4**). Immediately the religious leaders realized that they have been cornered. Because they had refused to submit to John's baptism (7:30), the only answer they could give Jesus was that John had acted on human authority. However, if they made such a statement, the people might stone them, for they honoured John as a prophet. Fearful of answering Jesus' question, the religious leaders remain silent (**20:5-7**). The whole episode becomes a display of Jesus' ability to refuse to answer a question in a way that would serve his adversaries (**20:8**). Not only did the religious leaders fail to discredit Jesus, but their failure to answer his question represented an indirect answer to it. It would have been clear to the people that Jesus' authority comes from God

20:9-19 Heaven Forbid

After exposing the religious leaders' lack of integrity and refusing to answer their question, Jesus turned to the people (**20:9**) and, in front of their leaders, told them a story designed to state exactly what his authority as the beloved son of God was (**20:13**). His story also warned them that their leaders were about to throw *him out of the vineyard* and kill him (**20:15**). Things would be just as they had been in the past when God had sent prophets to call for repentance, reform and true worship from the people. The religious leaders had often resisted their reforms, suppressed, persecuted and sometimes sidelined the prophets, and as a result had cut people off from God.

In the parable of the vineyard, the leaders are exposed as being about to take even worse action. In the language of the parable, God is the owner of the vineyard, the religious leaders are the contract workers or tenants, and Jesus is the beloved son of the owner. Jesus claimed that the owner had now sent his beloved son, and there can have been no doubt that he was referring to himself. The parable predicted that the contract workers were about to kill the son and that the vineyard, that is, the people, would be given to others. When the crowd heard this, they were shocked and protested, crying out *May this never be!* meaning 'Heaven forbid!' (**20:16**).

Their exclamation indicates that what they had heard was bad news. Profoundly unnerving news was in the making. The hearers assumed that God would be the author of this bad news. The reason they interpreted the parable in this way is that it is closely linked to Isaiah's judgment song of the vineyard (Isa 5:1-7). In both Isaiah 5 and Luke 20, God's judgment rests upon Jerusalem (remember that this parable has been preceded by Jesus' entry into Jerusalem, his weeping over the city and his cleansing of the temple). No wonder the people reacted with horror at the very idea! What would God do if human rebellion led to the murder of his Messiah?

The religious leaders, while they rejected the validity of Jesus' parable, clearly understood that Jesus was saying that God was *against them* (**20:19**). They realized that they were threatened with the wrath of God and that Jesus was the point of decision. Response to him determines one's destiny.

Jesus' rejection by the leaders is, however, not the end. Jesus pointed out, borrowing from Psalm 118:22, that the rejected stone would become the resurrected one. This theme was taken up by the early church (Acts 4:11; 1 Pet 2:7). As the church found out, this stone both crushes and brings to life. 'The Lord has done this' (Ps 118:23), and the rejected stone turns out to be the cornerstone and the instrument of divine justice (**20:17-18**).

20:20-26 God and Caesar

Perhaps these verses should be read in light of Jesus' later warning to beware of people and institutions that seek the *most important seats* and *places of honour* in economic, political, religious and cultural affairs and who *devour* the poor for economic gain (20:46-47). At times in the history of Christianity, and especially where colonialism was being promoted, Jesus' words *Give to Caesar what is Caesar's, and to God what is God's* (**20:25**) have been interpreted as if political and worldly faithfulness to Caesar is on a par with faithfulness to God. But they are not on a par and Jesus' answer about obedience to Caesar is not a blanket endorsement, as is clear from his condemnation of corrupt authorities. When it comes to the absolute choice between them, Caesar cannot win. This is clear from the depiction of Caesar as 'the beast' who demands to be 'worshipped' by those who have been conquered (Rev 13:1-7). In resisting these demands, Christians are right to refuse to be subject 'to the governing authorities … which God has established' and to pay 'taxes, for the authorities are God's servants' (Rom 13:1-7). We see this tension elsewhere in the NT, where the apostles withstood religious and political leaders on the grounds that they were compelled to obey God rather than humans. In situations of tension, corruption, nepotism, oppression, apartheid and colonialism, Christians are urged to 'obey God rather than men' (Acts 4:19; 5:29).

But still the question is whether it is right or wrong to pay taxes to Caesar (**20:22**). The question was designed to trap and destroy Jesus at the political level. If he said it was right to pay the tribute, he would immediately alienate the masses and that would be the end of him. If, on the other hand, he said that it was right to refuse to pay tribute, they could report him to the Roman governor who would have him executed for political subversion (**20:20**). That too would be the end of him.

Jesus responds by asking them to give him a Roman coin. They immediately produce one, thereby tacitly acknowledging that they do make use of Roman currency, and could be expected to pay something for this benefit. They have answered their own question, and have failed to drive a wedge between Jesus and the people. At the end, they had nothing to say and just stood there in silence (**20:26**).

20:27-40 God of the Living

Just when all other religious leaders, including their *spies* (20:20) have been silenced, the Sadducees appear on the scene. They are mentioned only here in the entire Gospel of Luke. The Sadducees did not believe in the resurrection of the body, declaring they could not believe in it because there is no information about it, still less any proof of it, in the books of the law which Moses was held to have written. However, Jesus pointed out that Moses himself had heard God say, *I am the God of your father, the God of Abraham, the God of Isaac and the God of Jacob* (Exod 3:1-6), and that God is not *the God of the dead, but of the living, for to him all are alive* (**20:38**).

Jesus' point is that all of these patriarchs were long dead by the time Exodus was written. But if God says that he is still in a relationship with them, then they must still in some sense be alive, for God is not a God of the dead, but of the living (see also Isa 26:19; Dan 12:2; Ezek 37). To put it differently, God as the eternal God cannot be characterized by something that no longer exists. Resurrection is not a fantasy dreamed up by wishful thinkers; it is a necessary consequence of the character and nature of God.

From an African theological perspective, this discussion naturally raises the issue of ancestors. In the African world view, the origin of life is God, who is related to the people and the entire creation. Life coming from God flows into God's creation, that is, to the ancestors, to the living and then to trees, rivers, mountains, forests, birds, animals and the entire creation. The whole of creation shares togetherness and solidarity.

Communities are held together by their relationship to a common ancestor who founded the community or clan, which is composed of both the living and the dead. While all the dead share in a collective immortality, those ancestors who are still remembered by name are referred to as the 'living dead', and are the immediate object of ancestor cults. These are the ancestors who can still be said to be with us. In fact, the presence and influence of ancestors is so real to most Africans that in many respects they remain part of the community in their capacity of 'spirit elders'.

However, the relationship with the dead does not start after death, but begins as a person is dying. People who are dying are not left alone. Rather, the extended family, friends and acquaintances gather around them to provide assistance and a sense of solidarity in their final hours (see also Matt 26:36-40). Right up to the last moment, a dying person should have the certainty of dying within the community. Our modern society would do well to retain this cultural element within African religion and to give those who are dying a deep sense of belonging.

20:41-47 Teachers of the Law and Widows

In this passage Jesus comments on two cases where the perception differs from reality. The first is in regard to his identity. Some people were expecting the Messiah to be no more than a descendant of David. Jesus challenges this perception by pointing out that in Psalm 110:1, David had called the Messiah his 'Lord'. Jesus, the Messiah must thus be far more than merely the son of David (**20:44**; see also the comments on 3:21-38).

Next he points out the disparity between appearance and reality in the lives of the scribes. In their outer appearances, they are very religious, yet the reality of their lives is that they *devour widow's houses* (that is, they take them as pledges for debts that cannot be paid). The disciples are to be alert to such disparities between outer profession and inner reality (**20:45-46**). The model they are to emulate is found in 21:1-4, which starkly contrasts the piety of the rich and the piety of the poor. (See comments on the Pharisees and the Teachers of the Law in 11:24-53; 10:1-24; 9:1-9.)

21:1-38 Events Before the Last Supper

21:1-4 The Widow's Offering

Here Jesus speaks tenderly about a poor widow's offering. We have seen that time and again Jesus demonstrated his compassion towards persons living on the margins of society. He pronounced blessings on disciples who are poor, hungry, sorrowful and excluded (6:20-23). He had table fellowship with tax collectors and sinners, gracing them with his presence and granting them the forgiveness of sins (5:29-32). He forgave, healed or raised to life the sinful woman (7:36-50), the woman with haemorrhages (8:42-48) and the stooped woman (13:10-17). Jesus overrode the objections of the disciples and received the infants brought to him for touching (18:15-17). And Jesus opened paradise to the repentant criminal who was crucified with him (23:40-43).

The poor widow is one of the 'little people': humble, timid and disadvantaged in comparison to the rich. Not only was she disadvantaged by her poverty but also by her widowhood. In the scene immediately preceding this one, Jesus had condemned the scribes for, among other things, consuming the homes of widows (**20:47**). She was one of those with almost no legal, religious, political or social status.

But Jesus noticed this woman and watched her as she dropped *two very small copper coins* (**21:2**) into the treasury. Then he praised her: *I tell you the truth, this poor widow has put in more than all the others. All these people gave their gifts out of their wealth; but she out of her poverty put in all she had to live on* (**21:3-4**).

The words, 'all she had to live on' imply that she gave away everything she owned. Even though she was one of the poor she held nothing back. Hence her action becomes an example of sacrificial giving, giving that shares unconditionally with the poor. It also serves to highlight the judgment against the rich, who though they may give from their abundance, do not go beyond or even anywhere near the point at which their abundance might be threatened. Only the poor widow grasps the spirit of unlimited love and faith.

21:5-36 Instruction about the Last Things

Signs of times are all around us. We read of floods, earthquakes and hurricanes, of wars and terrorism. There are signs of the earth's upheaval and of nations in chaos. Jesus discussed these signs in Jerusalem twenty-one centuries ago when he spoke of the end of Jerusalem and of the world. In doing this, he used a type of language which is commonly termed 'apocalyptic,' and which traditionally includes reference to catastrophes and cosmic disturbances.

His discourse can be divided into four main sections. The first of these (**21:8-11**) prophesies the coming of false prophets and wars. Jesus says that there will be many false messiahs, who will insist that they know when the end will come. We are not to listen to them. There has been no shortage of false messiahs in every generation. These false messiahs always claim to know more than Jesus did.

Second, before all these things happen, there will be persecution for the disciples, during which they must rely on the help given them by Jesus and persevere faithfully to the end (**21:12-19**). Jesus tells the disciples to *watch and pray* (**21:36**), secure in their insecurity. Their friends may betray them, their spouses may leave them, their children may disappoint them, but, he says, *not a hair of your head will perish* (**21:18**). This phrase sounds proverbial and refers to spiritual safety. The disciples may suffer injury and death, but nothing can really harm their essential being.

Third, the encircling of Jerusalem by troops will be a sign that its prophesied fate is at hand (**21:20-24**). Then, fourth, there will be heavenly and earthly portents, which will be followed by the glorious coming of the exalted Son of Man. These events will signal the coming of the final redemption for the people of God (**21:25-28**). These saying are followed by an assurance that the end will follow the signs of its coming and that Jesus' words will be fulfilled.

The first millennium saw the beginnings of the church in Africa. In the second millennium, African churches celebrated the spread of the gospel in Africa. But now, in this third millennium, we must face up to the challenge of discerning the signs of the times and of looking ahead. Rather than being caught in cheap modern slogans, we need to stand for the truth that never ends.

Being the church today in this world means being a church with prophetic voice that is heard in the homes, villages, towns, cities, parliament, schools, hospitals and any workplace. Being such a voice will often require conflict, mutual reprimands and bitter debate to resolve the differences or to bring the inconsistencies to light. Prophetic ministry is painful and is never complete.

How should we walk together with Jesus in these days with the signs of the times all around us? He gives us some advice in **21:34-36**. We need to find examples of how this is lived out, and get glimpses of hope triumphant over despair. Let me give two examples. First, there is a popular legend that, when he was asked what he would do if he knew the world would end tomorrow, Martin Luther reportedly replied, 'I would plant an apple tree today.' When we face today's crises, we do not despair. We act. Simple acts such as planting trees can send a powerful message to society of our belief in the future and our determination to make it a healthy one. In short, even apart from any thoughts of the 'end of the world' we face the future with a sure and certain promise: 'Remember, I will walk with you always, to the end of the age' (Matt 28:20 – paraphrase).

The second example is from the life of the prophet, Jeremiah. His mission was to announce the judgement of God upon Israel for their disloyalty, and to predict the fall of Jerusalem, the capital of Judah, to Nebuchadnezzer. As a sign that the end was really at hand, Jeremiah was told to abstain from marriage and having children and not even to attend funerals or weddings. His behaviour would signal that the time would soon come when there would be no more opportunity for normal mourning and wedding rites at all. Weddings and funerals are extremely important events in Africa, and they were no less so in Jeremiah's day. His behaviour would have stood out like a sore thumb.

But God's command 'You must not marry and have sons or daughters' (Jer 16:2) was even more shocking. Today, we are accustomed to celibate priests and to ordinary men and women abstaining from marriage, but there was no such notion in Israel during the time of Jeremiah. If one did not marry, one was not considered a 'proper woman' or ' a proper man'. Even today in some African societies a person who is unwilling to marry is considered a freak. Now Jeremiah is told to marry nobody at all as a sign that the people are coming to an end. What a sign!

But is it really the end of life? Will God make us childless, homeless and earthless at the end of the time? Let us take Jeremiah once more. Just before the final fall of Jerusalem in 587 BC we encounter an act of hope. Early in that year, when Jerusalem was already under siege, Jeremiah got word from a cousin in his home village that he was needed to redeem a piece of family property that was in danger of falling to other ownership. He slipped out of Jerusalem and made his way to his home village to purchase the land (Jer 32:1-15). The explanation for this seemingly illogical action, given his circumstances, is God's promise, 'Houses, fields and vineyards will again be bought in this land' (Jer 32:1-15). No matter how endless dark nights of fear and death may be, we know that life will have the last word and that the sun will rise.

22:1-62 Events Surrounding the Passion

22:1-13 The Preparations

Jesus and Judas are each busy with their plans for different reasons. Judas is making arrangements to betray Jesus (**22:3-6**), while Jesus is sending his trusted disciples Peter and John to arrange for the Passover (**22:7-8**). The tension builds between these two kinds of preparations.

In the passion account as in earlier phases of the story, all the disciples (or *apostles* – **22:14**) except Judas continue to serve the purposes of God. They do not break their bond of loyalty to Jesus and forsake him, although their service is limited by their lack of understanding. Out of loyalty to Jesus, Peter and John readily obey him when he dispatches them to prepare for the Passover meal (**22:7-13**).

Luke leaves no doubt that Judas and Satan initiated the events leading up to Jesus' death on the cross. In **22:3**, prior to the account of the Last Supper, Luke reports that *Satan entered Judas*. Thus Judas' betrayal of Jesus to the authorities happened in accordance with Satan's plan. Jesus knows that Satan is temporarily in control, and is therefore, a threat to some of the disciples; hence his prayer that their faith may not fail (**22:31-32**). The Devil's control over the unfolding events of the passion is asserted again when Jesus is arrested, for he declares to those who have come out against him that *this is your hour – when darkness reigns* (**22:53**). The 'power of darkness' refers to the devil. Jesus' assertion implies that the religious leaders are, like Judas, acting as agents of the devil.

For Luke it was 'necessary' that Jesus should suffer and die and on the third day be raised (9:22; 18:31-34; 24:7, 26-27, 44-47). Only by dying and then allowing God to break the bonds of death could Jesus lead the way out of enslavement to Satan. The devil orchestrated Jesus' death, but, ironically, that death spelled the beginning of the end for the devil.

22:14-20 The Last Supper

Luke's account of the actual supper begins with a description of Jesus and the disciples at the table (**22:14**). Jesus expresses how much he wanted to eat this Passover with his disciples before his suffering, since this will be the last occasion he will do so before its fulfilment in the reign of God (**22:15-16**). In the same way, he shares a cup of wine with them with the comment that he will not drink wine again until the reign of God has come (**22:17-18**). Jesus is telling his disciples that this will be their last meal together before his suffering. The next time they share such a meal it will be to celebrate the 'fulfilment' of such meals after the coming of the reign of God.

In addition to celebrating the Passover, Jesus also instituted a completely new ordinance, the Lord's Supper (1 Cor 11:23-26). It was to serve as a set of vivid symbols to remind his disciples of his body and blood given for them and for their deliverance until he came again. It would also be a sign of the new covenant that he was about to inaugurate with his blood (**22:19-20**). At all future celebrations of the Passover – either in accordance with the Jewish ritual or in the forms that evolved in Christian communities – they are to repeat these acts in remembrance of Jesus who gave himself on their behalf.

We ought to pay closer attention to the meaning of the sharing of the bread and wine in remembrance of Jesus Christ. Western countries tend to operate on the principle that writings remain, but spoken words are fleeting. This principle does not hold true in Africa where spoken words do not vanish but remain to guide the community through the centuries. In many African communities, a wise older woman or man will call a child or younger person and give her or him food and drink. While the young person eats and drinks, the older person narrates the entire public wisdom and history of the ethnic group or society. This word, which brings wisdom, must not only be received, but must be swallowed together with the food and drink – actually, it has to be chewed and eaten in the biblical sense (Ps 1:2). It should become part and parcel of the flesh and blood of the listener, so that this person generates and gives birth to life abundantly.

The word, which was heard, 'eaten' and 'drunk' within the community represented by the elders, has to be shared responsibly in a communicative manner within the community so as to bring new life to each and every member. Once again, *he took bread, gave thanks and broke it and gave it to them, saying, 'This is my body given for you; do this in remembrance of me'* (**22:19**).

22:21-30 Betrayal and Strife

The apostles are profoundly distressed when Jesus tells them that he will suffer betrayal by one of his own and wonder which of them will be the traitor (**22:21-23**). But their dismay quickly turns from a questioning of which one of them will be the betrayer to a dispute about who among them deserves the highest rank. One would have expected that at this special moment they would have celebrated their

sense of togetherness. But instead, while eating with Jesus and participating in Holy Communion, they are involved in strife among themselves because of their desire for status (see also 1 Cor 3:1-4; John 13; Matt 23:1-12). The correction for this strife is located in the words of Jesus: *the greatest among you should be like the youngest, and the one who rules like the one who serves* (**22:26**). The basis for this reversal of values is located in the example of Jesus: *I am among you as one who serves* (**22:27**).

22:31-38 Simon and Swords

Jesus predicts a satanic attack on the disciples (the *you* is plural in **22:31**), but assures Simon Peter that because he has prayed for him (the *you* is singular in **22:32**), Satan will not take control of him as he did of Judas (**22:31-32**). Peter must not, however, be overconfident, for he will still deny knowing Jesus (**22:33-34**) but his faith will not ultimately fail. Jesus knows that Peter will repent. Envisaging this, he tells Peter that after he has repented, he is to *strengthen your brothers* (**22:32**).

A new mission is approaching for the disciples, and so in **22:35-38** Jesus states that the conditions he imposed for their first missions (9:1-6 and 10:1-16) no longer apply. Now they need to be ready for hardship, or as stated in 1 Peter 1:6-7, 'In this you greatly rejoice, though now for a little while you may have had to suffer grief in all kinds of trials. These have come so that your faith … may be proved genuine.' Failing to grasp the point, the disciples take Jesus' words literally and produce two swords. Frustrated, Jesus breaks off the conversation: 'That is enough' (**22:38**).

22:39-53 Prayer and Arrest

Jesus had assured his disciples of his prayer for them in their hour of temptation (22:32). Now on the Mount of Olives it is their turn to pray for themselves. Commanding them to pray that they might not fall into temptation (**22:40**), and overcome by profound distress and stunned by the enormity of the prospect confronting him, Jesus withdraws from them because 'My soul is overwhelmed with sorrow to the point of death!' (**22:41-44**; Mark 14:33-34). However, the disciples have no comprehension of what is overwhelming Jesus and fall asleep (**22:45**). Jesus wakes them and repeats the words *Get up and pray that you will not fall into temptation* (**22:46**).

The next moment Judas and a crowd arrive (**22:47**) and Judas identifies Jesus with a betraying kiss. Jesus offers no resistance as he is apprehended and bound for delivery to the Sanhedrin (Mark 14:44). One of the disciples, however, reacts by drawing his sword and cutting off the right ear of a servant of the High Priest. Disapproving of such violence, Jesus echoes his earlier statement 'Enough of this' and touches the man's ear and heals him (**22:51** author's translation; 22:38). While he submits to his illegal arrest, he speaks bluntly to his captors, who have seized him clandestinely under cover of night: *Am I leading a rebellion, that you have come with swords and clubs? Every day I was with you in the temple courts and you did not lay a hand on me. But this is your hour – when darkness reigns* (**22:52-53**).

22:54-71 Two Interrogations

By locating the account of the questioning of Peter between the accounts of the arrest and interrogation of Jesus, Luke suggests that both interrogations were being conducted at the same time. While Jesus was being questioned about his identity by the high priest in the chamber above, Peter, warming himself by the fire in the middle of the courtyard below, faces similar questions begun by *a servant girl* (**22:54-56**).

The high priest's servants had lit a fire in the courtyard of the house and sat around it. Peter sat among them. Presently in the semi-darkness the fire blazed up, the light shone on Peter, and his face gave him away (22:56). When he answered their questions, his Galilean accent gave him away (**22:59**). While Jesus bravely says, *I am* to the high priest's question about his identity as *the Son of God* (**22:70**), Peter says, *Man, I don't know what you are talking about* (**22:57-58, 60**). Peter denies three times that he is a follower of Jesus. Just after he has denied the truth for the third time, and seems to have cut off all connection between himself and Jesus, somewhere out in the darkness of the night a cock crowed. Jesus Christ turned and looked on Peter, *Then Peter remembered the word the Lord had spoken to him, 'Before the cock crows today, you will disown me three times.' And he went outside and wept bitterly* (**22:61-62**). In the case of Peter, he went out and wept bitterly, and repented. In the case of Judas he, too, went out and wept bitterly, and committed suicide (Matt 27:5).

23:1-56 Jesus' Trial and Crucifixion

23:1-25 Trial Before Pilate and Silence Before Herod

The Jews in the time of Jesus had no authority to carry out capital punishment. All death sentences had to come from the Roman governor and be carried out by the Roman authorities. This is why the Jewish council of elders (also called the Sanhedrin), which included the chief priests and scribes (**22:66**), delivered a fellow Jew to Pilate, who was the Roman governor of Judea from 26 to 36 AD.

In the Sanhedrin the charge against Jesus was blasphemy for daring to call himself the Son of God (**22:70-71**). However, before Pilate this particular charge was not mentioned, for he would have dismissed it as merely a religious dispute among various Jewish groups. So the charge was framed in political terms: *We have found this man subverting our nation. He opposes payment of taxes to Caesar and he claims to be Christ, a king* (**23:2**).

Luke does not even bother to point out how baseless these charges were. Instead he introduces a climax in **23:4** where Pilate, after eliciting what seems to be a most incriminating admission, delivers his verdict: 'Not guilty!' He insisted *I find no basis for a charge against this man* (23:4). Then, learning that Jesus is a Galilean and knowing that Herod Antipas is presently in Jerusalem for Passover, Pilate seizes the opportunity to rid himself of a troublesome case and sends Jesus to Herod for trial (**23:6-7**).

Herod was an evil man (3:19) who had jailed and then beheaded John the Baptist (3:19-20; 9:9). He was also the one who, on hearing remarkable reports about Jesus, had wondered who he was (9:7-9). The reason Herod desired to 'see' Jesus was to have him perform some sign or miracle (**23:8**). But Jesus does not perform miracles or signs on demand, for their purpose is to summon people to repentance, and Herod was at that moment not a suitable candidate for repentance.

It seems that Herod regarded Jesus as a curiosity and a source of entertainment. But Jesus was not prepared to play this role. He is the one who takes away the sin of the world. So during his trial before Herod, Jesus is entirely silent. Herod receives no answers to his questions (**23:9**). There was nothing to be said to Herod, and Herod got the message! So he sent Jesus back to Pilate!

With Jesus back in his custody, Pilate assembles both the members of the Sanhedrin and the people and conducts what amounts to the fourth and final phase of Jesus' trial (23:13-25). He firmly reminds them that he has already found Jesus innocent of the political charges brought against him by the Sanhedrin and, he adds, so has Herod (**23:14-15**). He concludes the session by announcing that he will have his soldiers administer a flogging to Jesus and then release him (**23:16**). Pilate declares three times that Jesus is innocent and that he will have him flogged and released (23:4; 15-22). But to no avail. Each time, the religious leaders and the people responded with cries of *crucify him, crucify him* (**23:21, 23**). And so *Pilate decided to grant their demand. He released the man who had been thrown into prison for insurrection and murder, the one they asked for, and surrendered Jesus to their will* (**23:24-25**).

23:26-38 Jesus on the Way to the Skull

Throughout his career, Jesus had concentrated his ministry in the rural countryside. Now at the end of his life, one of the people from the countryside, Simon of Cyrene, carries the cross *behind Jesus* (**23:26**). This action illustrates the nature of discipleship, which involves taking the cross and following Jesus (9:23; 14:27). It also illustrates who Jesus is: one who goes before and opens the way for the others to follow. Jesus has gone before the disciples (19:28); now they are to follow after him in the way he has opened. Simon of Cyrene is a model for disciples who share Jesus' trials.

Luke records the presence of women among the mourners accompanying Jesus (**23:27-31**). Where the disciples had slept during Jesus' anguish in Gethsemane (22:39-46), the women follow Jesus, weeping. They are the only ones who are still with him. The soldiers are absorbed in dividing Jesus' clothing among themselves by throwing dice (**23:34**), the people are looking on, and the rulers are jeering at him: *He saved others, let him save himself* (**23:35**). Abandoned by all except the women, Jesus is alone and desolate.

23:39-49 The Crucifixion

Ironically, the notice indicating the charge against Jesus that is attached to the cross above his head is profoundly true. In death, as well as in life, he is the Messiah. Or, as the executioners have formulated this identity in their distinctively Roman manner, he is *The King of the Jews* (**23:38**).

Only Luke reports a conversation between Jesus and the criminals on the crosses alongside him, culminating in Jesus' declaration to the repentant criminal that *I tell you the truth, today you will be with me in paradise* (**23:43**). Furthermore, only Luke has Jesus cry out, *Father, into your hands I commit my spirit* (**23:46**).

The criminal, who fears God and knows that he deserves to die (**23:40-41**), rebukes the other criminal and entreats Jesus to *remember me when you come to your kingdom* (**23:42**). Jesus replies, *I tell you the truth, I say to you, today you will be with me in paradise'* (**23:43**). Right to the last, Jesus' mission and his reign was extended to the outcasts, to 'publicans and sinners' (7:28).

Jesus' final, dying words from the cross: *Father, into your hands I commit my spirit* also reflect his faithfulness. Immediately after uttering these words *he breathed his last* (**23:46**). Jesus closed his earthly ministry with a peaceful prayer taken from Psalm 31:5: 'Into your hands I commit my spirit; redeem me, O Lord, the God of truth.' In this prayer the speaker declares his or her absolute trust that God will redeem him or her. Luke's version of the crucifixion story makes the point that Jesus trusted and had faith in God to the very end. After praying these words, he died. God never let him out of his sight.

23:50-56 The Burial of Jesus

Jesus, although crucified as a political troublemaker, is not buried as a criminal. As the Sabbath approaches and necessary preparations are made for its observance, his body is removed from the cross in order to avoid the desecration of this sacred time (Deut 21:22-23). Joseph of Arimathea, takes the initiative to give Jesus an honourable burial. He is introduced as a *good, upright man* and *a member of the Council, who had not consented to their decision and action* (**23:50-51**). Whereas the members of the Council had condemned

Jesus to death (Mark 14:64), Joseph undertakes the bold act of claiming Jesus' body from Pilate.

Because there is little time before the Sabbath starts, Joseph is unable to prepare Jesus' body properly for burial. His naked body is simply wrapped in a linen sheet. The witnesses to this event are the women who had followed Jesus from Galilee. After the burial they went back home and prepared spices and perfumes for the body of Jesus.

24:1-43 The Story of the Resurrection

24:1-12 The Role of Women

All four gospels agree on one vital detail about Jesus' arrest, trial, crucifixion and resurrection: women were present. The specifics of their presence may vary from one gospel to another, including, for example, how many women were at the tomb, who greeted them at the tomb, and how they responded to what they saw and heard, but the presence of the women is a constant. These independent, motivated women are both the first witnesses to the resurrection and the first missionaries of the church.

The story of women at the tomb of Jesus started with the question, 'Who will roll away the stone for us from the door of the tomb?' (Mark 16:3). Even today women are still asking that question as they face the many roadblocks placed in their path. But as they recall the resurrection experience, they are reminded that it is faith in Jesus Christ that will roll away the stones that prevent full attainment of humanity and dignity.

The role of women in the story of Jesus' passion, that is, his arrest, trial, crucifixion and resurrection, can be interpreted as reflecting women's willingness to co-operate with God and others. In the words of Oduyoye, 'without women's participation the transformation of human society towards justice, peace and compassion will not happen, because it takes women to insist that hierarchical and periphery/centre paradigms should give way to caring community.'

24:13-35 Walking and Talking as They Go

On the first Easter Sunday, two followers of Jesus were walking and talking as they journeyed home to a village named Emmaus which was not far from Jerusalem. These two followers may have been a man and a woman, for they seem to have shared a home (**24:29**). As they walk, they are joined by a third person, who turns out to be the risen Christ. He is presented as someone who travels with his followers, walking beside them and talking to them in their pain, confusion and fear and bringing healing. He is the one who creates an opportunity for his followers to reframe their perception of the recent events in Jerusalem.

The two disciples fail to recognize Jesus the risen Christ when he joins them. After inquiring why their faces are sad, he proceeds to explain that the tragic and seemingly sense-less end of Jesus was in fact God's plan, attested in the Scriptures (**24:27**). When they invited him to join them at their evening meal, he *took the bread, gave thanks, broke it, and began to give it to them* (**24:30**). This familiar action opens their eyes to the true identity of their visitor. He then vanishes and they see his death in a new light. His crucifixion and resurrection are now seen as the conclusive victory over the sickness and death that stand in contradiction to God's reign. Just as the Messiah must first suffer and only then *enter his glory* (**24:26**), so it will be for his followers.

Excited by this new realization and this new reality of faith in the risen Christ, the two followers rose immediately and set out to hurry back to Jerusalem, where *they found the Eleven and those with them, assembled together* (**24:33**). *The two told what had happened on the way, and how Jesus was recognized by them when he broke the bread* (**24:35**).

24:36-43 The Two Faces of Faith

In this passage we are dealing with two types of faith. First, there is the faith that needs assurance. We need this faith in situations where we are terrified of what is happening around us. On such occasions Jesus stands like a mother beside us to protect us. In our fears, our confusion, our anxiety and our sinfulness, the risen Lord stands with his own and among his own. Like a mother Jesus takes us into his arms to protect us. When Jesus is with us, we know that we are blessed with the peace of his presence. Today our world is cruel and often frightening. We are fearful and prefer to stay behind closed doors. At such moments Jesus Christ comes to us, without being invited, and takes the central place by calming the storms and declaring, *Peace be with you* (**24:36**).

If the first type of faith appeals to our hearts, the second type of faith requires us to share first-hand the experiences of another. The goal is more than empathy or feeling with; it is feeling 'into' the other. In the words of Jesus, *Look at my hands and my feet. It is I myself! Touch me and see* (**24:39**). Jesus insisted on a faith of 'feeling into'. He does not merely want to be heard, but to be seen and touched. Jesus does not want to be confused with false messiahs, false teachers or even ghosts (24:39). He wants to be experienced as the Christ. What others said about Jesus was not good enough; he wanted to be experienced and touched as the Christ. Yes, those who believe without seeing are truly blessed, but sometimes they are also conned into a false religion or immature faith. We would do well if more people demanded a faith of feeling into others. A faith that sometimes strips off the white clothes of religiosity in order to encounter and receive and meet face to face with the risen Lord in

our nakedness. Without our clothing we will be like Adam and Eve after they have sinned and left the Garden of Eden. There God will meet us and touch us and make our faith strong by clothing us with animal skins (Gen 3:21). Such a faith deals with 'the world out there.' It deals with the world from Monday to Saturday. It grapples with existential issues of the day. It prays and actively seeks solutions. It is a faith that has a feeling for God and for people.

To paraphrase St Paul, these two faces of our faith need milk and meat. The faith that they produce is inspired by the resurrection, the message that resulted in the disciples being *continually at the temple, praising God* (**24:53**).

The Gospel according to Saint Luke provides us with life-changing story as we walk and talk and go the way of struggle, conflict, controversies, suffering, oppression, courage, hope, liberation and freedom, reconciliation and steadfastness. This is the 'way' and for Luke this way of existence is blessed (6:20-23). It is precisely by beginning to walk together, to talk together and to go together on this way – the way which faith knows by the name of Jesus Christ – that we, along with our fellow human beings, set out on the path to pray, to witness and to be engaged in the struggle for gender equality, justice and freedom.

24:44-53 Jesus' Ascension

Before Jesus parts from his followers and is taken up into heaven, he provides for their future. He instructs them to stay in Jerusalem until they are *clothed with power from on high* (**24:49**). The Pentecostal gift of the Holy Spirit is Jesus' first provision for his followers who are to carry out his missionary directive. In other words, there is no evangelistic outreach without a prior empowering.

Secondly, Jesus does not leave the disciples until he has put them under the protection of God, namely, until he had blessed them: *While he was blessing them, he left them* (**24:51**). Just as the Gospel of Luke began with the ministry of the priest Zechariah, the last picture of Jesus Christ in this gospel is of the priest giving his blessing, *he lifted up his hands* (**24:50**).

Paul John Isaak

Further Reading

Geldenhuys, Norval. *Commentary on the Gospel of Luke*. NICNT. Grand Rapids: Eerdmans, 1971.

Pilgrim, W. *Good News To The Poor: Wealth and Poverty in Luke-Acts*. Minneapolis: Augsburg, 1981.

Seim, T. R. *The Double Message: Patterns of Gender in Luke-Acts*. Edinburgh: T&T Clark, 1994.

Tiede, D. *Luke*. Minneapolis: Augsburg, 1988.

JOHN

The Gospel of John was written towards the end of the first century AD by someone referred to as 'the beloved disciple' (21:20, 24). It is likely that this person was one of the three disciples who were especially close to Jesus, namely, Peter, James and John (Matt 17:1; Matt 26:37; Mark 5:37;). Since Peter is often described as being with the beloved disciple (13:23-24; 20:2; 21:20-21), he cannot be the author. Nor can the author be James, who was killed by Herod Agrippa I no later than AD 44. John is left as the most likely candidate to be the 'beloved disciple'. He later describes himself as an eyewitness of all that Jesus did (1 John 1:1).

The purpose of the book is spelled out in 20:30-31: 'These [signs] are written that you may believe that Jesus is the Christ, the Son of God, and that by believing you may have life in his name.'

The gospel is organized around seven specific signs which John has chosen out of many other possibilities (20:30; 21:25; see also the miracles recorded in the other gospels). These are the changing of water into wine (2:1-11), the healing of a royal official (4:46-54), the healing of a lame man (5:1-9), the feeding of more than five thousand people (6:1-14), walking on water (6:15-25), the healing of a man who was born blind (9:1-41), and the raising of Lazarus (11:1-46). John sees these events as more than mere miracles; they are signs that force readers to ask, 'Who is this man who can do all these things? How can he be master over quality, distance, time, quantity, natural laws, misfortune, and death?'

John believes that the evidence proves that 'Jesus is the Christ, the Son of God.' The Greek title 'Christ' is equivalent to the Hebrew title, 'Messiah', which means 'one who is anointed'. Anointing sets someone apart for a specific purpose. But whereas others who were anointed for specific tasks fulfilled their task and then died (for example, Aaron and his sons – Exod 28:41), Jesus, God's Son, has been anointed by God to deal with sin for ever (1:29).

Jesus is the Son of God because of his eternal relationship with the Father. The Father identified him as his Son at his baptism (Matt 3:17; John 1:32-34) and at his transfiguration (Matt 17:5, Mark 9:7, Luke 9:35). John does not record these two occasions, but he does include a similar incident in 12:27-28. There Jesus addresses God as Father, implying that he is God's Son, and God acknowledges him with approval.

The relationship of the divine Son and Father is difficult for us to comprehend. We need to remember that God is describing an eternal relationship in a way that we humans can understand. He has chosen to reveal his plan of salvation to us in terms of the Father who sends the Son, the Son who dies on the cross, and the Holy Spirit who applies all this to our lives.

In 20:31, John also speaks of life, which is another great theme in this gospel. Eternal life is available only to those who believe, and they receive it immediately when they believe. Everyone who believes is assured of the possession of this life from that moment on.

Outline of Contents

COMMENTARY

1:1-51 Introduction

1:1-18 In the Beginning Was the Word

The gospel begins by speaking of someone referred to as *the Word* (1:1, 14). In Jewish thought, the Word of God was the way God communicated himself. In Greek thought, the Word was the central idea that holds the universe together. It is clear from 1:17 that the person John is referring to is Jesus.

The first thing that John stresses about the Word is that he is eternal – *in the beginning was the Word* (**1:1a**). The 'was' indicates that the Word already existed at that point in the past labelled 'the beginning'. Some commentators note the similarity between this phrase and Genesis 1:1, and assert that it means the Word was already there when the world was created. While this is true, it is too limiting. John is saying that the Word has existed from eternity.

Next, John stresses the status of the Word in eternity: *the Word was God* (**1:1b**). The past tense 'was' does not indicate that his status has changed since then. Rather, it indicates the contrast between his status in eternity past and his entrance into humanity when *the Word became flesh* (1:14).

Some think that John 1:1b should be translated 'and the Word was a god', arguing that in Greek a noun with an article is definite while a noun without an article is indefinite. But this rule does not always apply. At times an article is omitted in order to stress the quality of something. In this particular case, Jesus' status is that of God, but he does not exhaust what God is. If John had said that Jesus was 'the God' here, he would have been leaving out the Father and the Holy Spirit, who are also persons of the Trinity.

Those who argue for the 'a God' translation deny the full deity of Jesus. But throughout his gospel, John strongly affirms Jesus' deity. In 1:18 he refers to him as *God the One and Only*, and both he and Jesus approve of Thomas' recognition of Jesus as 'my Lord and my God' (20:28). Thus at three key points in Jesus' life – in eternity (1:1), at his incarnation (1:18), and after his resurrection (20:28) – the deity of Christ is asserted.

John also stresses the eternal relationship between the Word and God the Father. The words *with God* (**1:2**) emphasize Jesus' face-to-face relationship with the Father. Throughout this gospel, John repeatedly states that the Father loves the Son and the Son seeks to glorify the Father. Their association, companionship and mutual glorification started in eternity.

The Word, who is eternal, created all things. John states this truth both positively and negatively. Positively, he says, *Through him all things were made* (**1:3**). Negatively, he says, *without him nothing was made* (**1:3**). In the Greek, a strong distinction is drawn between the status of the Word and that of creation. While the Word 'was' in the beginning (1:1), the creation 'came to be' (1:3). The Word existed before the beginning described in Genesis 1:1 and was in fact responsible for all that was made in that beginning.

John does not only present Jesus as the 'Word' but also as the source of life and as light (1:4-5). He provides life to and illuminates the way for those who acknowledge him.

Creation had a beginning, and so did the man named John the Baptist, whose testimony in **1:15** reveals his awareness that Jesus existed before he did – even though Jesus was six months younger than he was (Luke 1:26). John the Baptist recognized the difference in status between himself and Jesus. He was merely *a man who was sent from God* (**1:6**); Jesus was the Word who was 'with God'. Jesus was eternal, while John the Baptist was temporal.

John the Baptist was also very clear about the contrast between Jesus' job and his own. He knew that his place was to be a servant, one sent *only as a witness to the light* (**1:7-8**), while Jesus' place was that of master, for he was himself *the true light* (**1:9a**; see also 3-4). Literally, the text says that he was 'the light, the true one'. Jesus is the primary light. All other lights are secondary and shine only as they reflect his light.

The *coming into the world* (**1:9b**) of this true light brought at least two blessings. First, it brought light for all to share, giving light to every man (and woman). Second, it brought the right of belonging (**1:12-13**). Although many may reject him (1:10-11), his arms are open to all those who want to receive his message. He gives them the power or the authority to belong to God as his sons and daughters. This right to belong to God's family was not based on race (Jewish or non-Jewish descent) or on anything a person has done. It is a gift from God, creating a new nature in those who receive Christ. They are born into the family of God.

Yet, tragically, the very world that he himself had made *did not recognize him* (**1:10**). While 'world' covers all creation in general, the primary focus is on men and women. Human systems and individuals did not respect Jesus. They treated him just like anyone else in Palestine.

But not only was Jesus not honoured, he was also rejected: *His own did not receive him* (**1:11**). 'His own' were the Jewish people. Though Joseph had no part in Jesus' conception and Jesus transcended human existence, he had been born into a Jewish home. His mother Mary and her husband Joseph were Jews. Yet when Jesus came to his own people, many of them wanted nothing to do with him. We should not be surprised by this negative attitude, for we ourselves are guilty of the same thing. He made us all, yet there are many among us who do not acknowledge him as God, the Creator and the God-Man who brings us salvation.

In God's good time (Gal 4:4), *the Word became flesh and made his dwelling among us* (**1:14**). He who is from eternity and who made all things took the status of a creature. The verb 'became' in the phrase 'became flesh' is the same verb used of his making all things in 1:3. This shows that while his status of deity (1:1) has no beginning, his status as human does. We are told about this movement from eternity to time in Matthew 1:18-25 and Luke 1:26-38. The eternal Word was conceived by the mortal Mary through the power of the Holy Spirit. The Word's 'dwelling among us' summarizes his entire earthly life, from his conception till his ascension. It was a temporary dwelling with a purpose, namely, to reveal God (1:18) and to die in the place of humankind (11:50-53).

What Jesus revealed about the Father is his *grace and truth*. This phrase is used twice (1:14 and 1:17), and grace is mentioned on its own in **1:16**. 'Grace' means that something totally undeserved is given freely, with no strings attached. All that the giver wants in response is gratitude. The gift Jesus gives is the right to become a member of the family of God (1:12), and the only response required is to be a grateful member of that family. There can be no question of repaying Jesus for a gift like this!

This belonging ushers one into and keeps one in a new life setting, one where truth prevails. 'Truth' is that which has been tested and found to be right. Here, it means the difference between right and wrong belief and behaviour, as determined by the standard of God.

The blessings of grace and truth are contrasted with the law of Moses (**1:17**). The contrast is not that the former replaces the latter, or even that the law of Moses lacked grace and truth. The point is that the grace and truth Jesus reveals fill up what was lacking in the law. The law was a shadow of the real thing that was to come, even though it was the will of God and was based on the grace of God. The fuller revelation of God through Jesus Christ reveals further grace. That is why John speaks of our receiving *one blessing after another* (1:16). The true thing foreshadowed in the law has now come.

Jesus' revelation of the Father is unique, for *no one has ever seen God, but God the One and Only, who is at the Father's side, has made him known* (**1:18**). Some in the past had seen a faint representation of God, which could be described as his shadow (for example, Moses – Exod 33:11; Num 12:8; Isaiah – Isa 6:5). But no one had seen him directly, for he had warned 'No one may see me and live' (Exod 33:20). But Jesus, who is God, lived among men. Those who saw him, saw not a shadow of God but God himself. He was truly the God-man, in whom one nature did not eliminate the other. He remained fully God while also becoming fully human.

There are many in Africa who deny the message of this passage. They may call themselves Jehovah's Witnesses or representatives of Christ, but unless their message proclaims that Jesus is God, the Creator of all things, and the only basis upon which any man or woman receives blessings from God, they are to be condemned for their blasphemy. They are to be prayed for, but are also to be shunned. False teaching finds ready soil in Africa due to the natural religiosity of African people. It is time, however, that we in Africa became a little more discerning, to distinguish truth from error. We must guard the truths taught in this passage with all our being if we are to be on the same side as God, whose word clearly tells us that Jesus is God.

1:19-28 John the Baptist Prepares the Way

People's speculation about whether John the Baptist was the Christ is implied in John 1:20 but explicitly stated in Luke 3:15. This led the Jews of Jerusalem to send priests and Levites to Bethany where he was baptizing (**1:28**), asking him to confirm or deny this rumour (**1:19**).

1:19-21 The questions of the Jewish leaders

The delegation that came to John the Baptist asked questions that focused on three possible identities for John: was he the Christ, Elijah or the prophet?

In asking whether he was *the Christ* (**1:20**), the Jews were expressing their belief that the Christ, or Messiah, would come at some time. For details about what this term means, see the Introduction. It was expected that the Christ would come either as a supernatural figure sent directly from heaven or that God would raise him up from among the people. John the Baptist emphatically stated that he was not the expected Christ.

In asking whether he was *Elijah* (**1:21a**), the Jews may have been thinking of Malachi's words about a messenger whom God would send to refine the nation in preparation for the coming of the Lord (Mal 3:1-3). The Lord had identified this messenger as the prophet Elijah (Mal 4:5). The Jews interpreted these passages as meaning that Elijah would come before the Messiah, to prepare people for the messianic age. If John the Baptist was not the Christ, then he might possibly be the prophet Elijah, sent to prepare the way for the Christ. But he denied this identity too.

The final question, *Are you the Prophet?* (**1:21b**) was asked with a particular prophet in mind, as is clear from the article 'the'. Moses had said that the Lord had told him, 'I will raise up for them (the Israelites) a prophet like you from among their brothers' (Deut 18:18b). In Acts, both Peter and Stephen identified this prophet as Jesus Christ (Acts 3:22; 7:37). The Jews, however, thought that this prophet would be someone distinct from the Messiah. John the Baptist insisted that he was not this prophet.

1:22-23 John the Baptist's self-identification

The questioners had run out of ideas, so they asked John the Baptist, *Who are you? Give us an answer to take back to those who sent us. What do you say about yourself?* (**1:22**). In light of what John the Baptist was doing and considering the crowds that were thronging to him (Luke 3:1-19), he must have been somebody important. But John chose to identify himself only as a voice: *I am the voice of the one calling*

in the desert, 'Make straight the way for the Lord' (**1:23**, quoting Isa 40:3). John did not see himself as having an independent identity. He was a mere messenger, and his message was far more important than who he was. His message called people to prepare to receive the Lord's teaching and repent of their sins.

1:24-28 John the Baptist contrasts himself with the Christ

John the Baptist's identification of himself as nobody but a messenger (a 'voice') invited the question *Why then do you baptize if you are not the Christ, nor Elijah, nor the Prophet?'* (**1:25**). As far as the Pharisees were concerned, these were the only three who would baptize Jews. Normally, only proselytes who were converting to Judaism were baptized.

Instead of giving a direct answer to their question, John the Baptist pointed out that the issue was deeper than they thought. His words can be paraphrased as follows: *I baptize with water and you notice me and begin to wonder whether I am the Christ, Elijah or the Prophet. Let me tell you, there is the one who is really great. In fact he already stands among you!* (**1:26-27**).

The reference to Jesus as *the one who comes after me* (1:27a) is the same as in 1:15, where it means that historically Jesus comes after John the Baptist. But in the context of John the Baptist's role, the one who comes after John is the one for whom John is preparing the way, that is, the Lord and King. His importance is emphasized when John says, *I am not worthy to untie the thongs of his sandals* (1:27b). Untying sandals was the work of a slave. John the Baptist claimed he was not worthy to offer Jesus even the lowest level of service.

The general attitude in Africa is that when one holds an office, especially a political office, one should grab as much as one can, since the opportunity may never come again. Most of us have not learned to be satisfied with what the Lord has given us. The same attitude is reflected in the search for fame – the desire to be someone important. John the Baptist had an opportunity to be known as an important man, but he was content with the ministry he had been given by the Lord. He was fully satisfied to be less than a servant so that Jesus' glory could be seen.

1:29-36 Jesus, the Lamb and Son of God

In many African societies, any general calamity is traditionally interpreted as being caused by an offence against God, either directly or because something has offended the spirits who protect divine values. Some sacrifice is needed to appease God's anger, and in the past that sacrifice was often a young lamb. John the Baptist was thinking in similar terms when, on two successive days, he drew the attention of his disciples to Jesus and said, *Look, the Lamb of God* (**1:29a, 36**). The source or origin of this Lamb is God. When someone sinned, a lamb had to be sacrificed because God could not just ignore that sin. It had to be atoned for

(Lev 4:20, 26, 31, 35; 5:10, 13). Jesus comes as the Lamb given by God *who takes away the sin of the world* (**1:29b**). The 'sin' here is singular, not plural. It is a collective noun, focusing on the disobedience of Adam and Eve, from which all other sins spring. Jesus' function is to free the world (that is, humankind) from that sin.

John the Baptist was so aware of the contrast between himself and Jesus that he repeated his earlier statement: *He has surpassed me because he was before me* (**1:30**). The Baptist knew that Jesus was eternal while he himself had begun to exist only when he was conceived by his mother, Elizabeth. He stressed that his own ministry of baptism was only a means to an end and not an end in itself: *I came baptizing with water so that he might be revealed to Israel* (**1:31**). Now that this end had been attained (**1:34**), John the Baptist and his baptism were no longer significant.

Besides being the Lamb, Jesus is also the Son of God whose ministry is blessed by the Holy Spirit (**1:32**). He gives that Spirit to others whom he baptizes with the Holy Spirit (**1:33**). This baptism may include many blessings, but the most basic one is that the Holy Spirit puts his stamp on us, giving us the assurance that we belong to God because Jesus has removed the sin in our lives (Eph 1:13).

1:37-42 Jesus Calls the First Disciples

I remember an occasion when a clay pot had been smashed and a curse pronounced: 'May you be broken like this!' Fearful of the effects of the curse, the people sent for someone to cleanse them. When the person arrived, he was an old man, leaning on a stick, with nothing in his hands. He was followed by a young boy, carrying a bag containing everything the old man needed to accomplish the cleansing. The young boy was the old man's disciple, and was there to do whatever his master asked him to do. What a vivid picture of the relationship between a teacher and his disciple!

In this passage in John, we see Jesus starting to build a team of men who would be his disciples and who would learn from him. It seems that he began with the informal contact described here before he issued the formal call recorded in Matthew 4:18-22 and Mark 1:14-20.

Andrew and the unnamed disciple (most likely, John the apostle) had been with John the Baptist for an unspecified period of time and counted themselves among his followers (**1:35, 40**). They would have heard John the Baptist speaking about Jesus (1:15, 26-27, 29, 32-34). So on the second day, when they heard him identify Jesus as the Lamb of God (**1:36**), they interpreted his meaning correctly and left him and *followed Jesus* (**1:37**).

Jesus' question *What do you want?* (**1:38a**) challenged them to evaluate what they were getting into before they even started. If they were only looking for a different teacher, that was not enough. If they were looking for a more comfortable life than they had with John (Matt 3:4), they would not get it. But they were clear about what they wanted. They wanted to know where Jesus was staying (**1:38b**), probably so that they could visit him later. Addressing Jesus as *Rabbi* (teacher) showed that they acknowledged him as someone from whom they could gain knowledge and wisdom.

Jesus' response was *Come ... and you will see* (**1:39a**). There was a sense of urgency. Tomorrow might never come. They needed to visit Jesus that day – in fact, right at that moment. What they would see was more than the house or room he lived in – they would see and feel what it meant to be with Jesus.

The two disciples did as Jesus encouraged them to do. They went and saw where he was staying. More than that, *they spent that day with him* (**1:39b**). Jesus issued his invitation at about the tenth hour, that is, about 4 p.m. (The Jewish method of keeping time was from sunrise at 6 a.m. to sunset at 6 p.m.). By 4 p.m. not much of the day remained, but Jesus and the two disciples abandoned whatever other plans they may have had. Jesus was available to them as host, and they revelled in the experience and stayed as long as the day lasted.

These men acted in a truly African fashion. Their programme was flexible enough to accommodate Jesus' invitation to come now, rather than just making an appointment to see him later. Unfortunately, this is something we are losing rapidly, especially in our cities. A few years ago, I was preaching a series of messages that I was told should be twenty-five minutes long. For the first three Sundays, I managed to keep to this deadline. But the topic for my fourth message needed thirty-five minutes to present it adequately. After the service, I was shocked to be accosted by a lady from the choir: 'Your sermon was far too long! Now I am late, and I have visitors coming!' At first, I was not sure that I was hearing her right, until I remembered that the sons and daughters of Africa have adopted the high-speed life and have allowed some good values to get lost in the process. Having time for one another, and above all for Jesus, is a priority we must strive to keep.

Andrew, having found out how pleasant it was to be with Jesus, wasted no time before sharing his experience with his brother Simon (**1:40**). In fact, John tells us that it was *the first thing [he] did* (**1:41a**). This serves well as our model in the call to 'go into the world and make disciples' (Matt 28:19). Andrew's words, *we have found the Messiah (that is, the Christ)* (**1:41b**), reflected his new personal knowledge of who Jesus was, as well as the message about Jesus that he had heard from John the Baptist (1:29-34). His next act was to bring his brother to Jesus (**1:42a**). He not only knew who Jesus was, but also acted on it. Too many believers in Africa enjoy being with Christ, but view the work of making Jesus known as the pastor's and not theirs. But everyone is called to be like Andrew and to advertise how sweet it is to be with Jesus.

Jesus looked at Andrew's brother and said, *You are Simon son of John. You will be called Cephas* (**1:42b**). Cephas is an

Aramaic name, translated into Greek as Peter, meaning 'a rock'. Like most African names, this was a name with a meaning. Jesus saw in Simon what he would become: someone who would be as firm as a rock in continuing the work of the kingdom once Jesus had departed. Simon is therefore awarded a new name. He will be prepared for the ministry that corresponds to his new name by a master teacher, one who knows the future perfectly, prepares each kingdom worker suitably, and fits each person into positions as he wills.

1:43-51 The Calling of Philip and Nathanael

The day after Andrew, the unnamed disciple, and Simon Peter had met Jesus, Philip, who like Andrew and Peter was from the town of Bethsaida, was also invited to follow him (1:43-44). Like Andrew, he found the discovery too sweet to keep to himself and therefore looked for Nathanael. When he found him, his message (paraphrased here) was, 'We have come into close contact with Jesus of Nazareth, the son of Joseph, and we have identified him as the fulfilment of what Moses and the prophets wrote about' (1:45). As *Jesus of Nazareth, the son of Joseph*, Jesus was like any other man living in Palestine. It is what Philip and others had discovered about him that made him different.

Nathanael was sceptical about this Jesus of Nazareth: He thought the Messiah should come from an important town like Jerusalem (the capital), or Bethlehem (the city of David), or even from his own town of Cana (21:2), not from such an unimportant place as Nazareth. Philip's response to Nathanael's scepticism was, *Come and see* (1:46), that is, 'Don't disagree before you have seen the evidence. Come and meet him yourself first before you decide.'

It took only two statements by Jesus to turn Nathanael from a sceptic into a believer. These statements showed that Jesus is all-knowing (omniscient) and all-seeing (an aspect of omnipresence). His first statement, as Nathanael approached, was *Here is a true Israelite, in whom there is nothing false* (1:47). Nathanael had been honest in expressing his doubts. Admitting that this was an accurate assessment of his character, Nathanael asked Jesus, *How do you know me?* (1:48a). Jesus replied, *I saw you while you were still under the fig tree before Philip called you* (1:48b). Whatever had taken place under the fig tree, it was Jesus' revelation that he knew of it that turned Nathanael's scepticism into faith.

Nathanael then made one of the key declarations about Jesus in the Gospel of John. He said, *Rabbi, you are the Son of God, you are the King of Israel* (1:49). This amounts to saying, 'You are the Messiah. You are the one God has chosen to rule over Israel.' This is exactly what Nathanael had been sceptical about when he heard that Jesus came from Nazareth. But now he has experienced for himself that, in spite of his insignificant home town, Jesus is the greatest of all the men he has known. He has the qualities that only the Messiah could have.

Nathanael became a believer because of Jesus' ability to know what is in people's hearts and minds and to see into hidden places. But Jesus tells him that his belief needs more content. The Son of Man is far more than just a miracle worker; he is also the link between heaven and earth (1:50-51). Jesus presents a vivid picture of this as he speaks of Nathanael and others (the second 'you' in 1:51 is plural) seeing angels, who are God's servants or messengers, carrying messages back and forth between heaven and earth. The 'ladder' that makes this movement possible is the Son of Man. Jesus is hinting at his ministry as the mediator between heaven and earth, between God and man. Nathanael is being challenged to believe in more than just a miracle-performing Jesus. He also needs to believe in Jesus the Saviour.

By using his favourite title, *Son of Man*, Jesus focused on his mission here on earth, involving humble identification with humanity and suffering and death on the cross (Mark 10:45). But the title also relates to his reign as king subsequent to accomplishing his mission as Saviour (Matt 24:30; see also Dan 7:13-14).

Jesus' promise here was fulfilled when he died on the cross and rose from the grave, giving his disciples their central message that the crucified and risen Jesus is the only way of salvation.

Many African men believe that manhood means standing firm in one's convictions. However, there is a manhood that is accompanied by wisdom, and another that is foolishness. The wise man, or woman for that matter, is the one who stands by his or her conviction as long as it still seems right. However, once a conviction has been disapproved by evidence, it is foolish to hang on to it. Nathanael was humble enough to admit that his former scepticism was wrong and to worship Jesus. Sadly, some Africans have totally rejected the gospel of Christ because they want to appear to be tough people. Unfortunately, their toughness is also their foolishness. The evidence is too strong for anyone who is wise to ignore.

2:1-12:50 Jesus' Public Ministry

2:1-11 Jesus Miracle at the Wedding

In parts of Africa, it is not uncommon to see drunken people staggering along the road, despite the risk of being hit by passing vehicles. When told that drinking will ruin them, some quickly reply, 'Jesus made wine in Cana!' They are right, but the lesson Jesus was teaching was not that we should become drunkards. The lessons we should learn are about Mary's initiative in helping to solve someone else's problem and Jesus' ability to help.

Jesus was still in Galilee, where he had met Philip and Nathanael (1:43-45). It was now the third day (2:1) since he had left for Galilee in 1:43. He and his disciples were invited to a wedding in Cana, a wedding that was also attended by Mary, his mother (**2:2**). At that time weddings lasted for seven days or more. The whole period was a time of rejoicing, eating and drinking. The bridegroom and his family were responsible for providing the food and drink, and running out of wine would be a serious embarrassment to them.

Mary became aware of a shortage of wine, and she knew where to go for a solution. She had known who Jesus was before any one else did, for the angel had told her, 'the holy one to be born will be called the Son of God' (Luke 1:35). So she went to Jesus and said to him, *they have no more wine* (**2:3**). Mary was speaking to him as her son. After all, even though she knew that he was special, he had lived with her as a son for thirty years.

In his response, Jesus addressed Mary as *dear woman* (**2:4a**). The word he uses is equivalent to 'lady' or 'madam' in today's English. He did not want to address her as 'mother' because he wanted her to realize that the stage of his life when he lived as her son had ended. It was now time for him to complete his ministry on earth.

His words *Why do you involve me? My time has not yet come* (**2:4b**) gently point out that Mary can no longer give him instructions and tell him when to act. His words are equivalent to 'Leave the matter to me and my timing. At the right time, I will act.' Mary abandoned her attempt to pressure her son into acting as she wanted, but still acknowledged that he could solve the problem if he wished. So she told the servants, *Do whatever he tells you* (**2:5**).

At the time he judged to be right, Jesus turned to the servants and told them to fill six large jars with water. Each of these jars would hold about 20 to 30 gallons (75 to 115 litres) of water to be used for washing hands as part of a Jewish purification ritual (**2:6-7**). Once his instruction had been obeyed, Jesus told the servants to *draw some out and take it to the master of the banquet* (**2:8**). When the master of the banquet tasted this 'water', he called the bridegroom aside and reprimanded him for not doing things in the right order. This wine was so good that it should have been served first (**2:9-10**).

The bride and groom's families must have been filled with gratitude that Jesus had saved them from great embarrassment – and they must also have been amazed both at the miracle and at the quality of the wine Jesus had produced. The picture we have here is not one of people staggering because they have had too much to drink, but of a people rejoicing that Jesus had met their need.

John presents this as Jesus' first miraculous sign. It had two results, according to **2:11**: Jesus *revealed his glory* and his disciples believed. Jesus is not just the son of Mary; he is also the object of faith.

2:12-22 Jesus Clears the Temple Courts

When I was a teenager, I used to catch birds, carefully setting my traps in the bushes. One day, my friends and I were summoned by the village elder and told that we had set our traps in the place the elders used for sacrifice and polluted it. We were reprimanded and warned never to do that again. The place of worship was sacred and was for worship only. Jesus took a similar view of the respect due to the place of worship when he cleansed the temple.

After the wedding in Cana, Jesus, his mother, brothers, and disciples had gone to Capernaum, about twenty miles (thirty-two kilometres) from Cana, for a few days (**2:12**). Then he travelled on to Jerusalem. It was now close to the time for the Jewish Passover (**2:13**), a seven-day mandatory annual feast that focuses on remembering God's deliverance of the Jews from Egypt. It falls roughly in our March or April.

This important feast had come to be treated as an opportunity for trade at the expense of worshippers. Every male over twenty years of age had to pay a half-shekel temple tax (Exod 30:13). The authorities had ruled that payment had to be made with the exact amount, and they charged heavily for changing shekels to half-shekels. Those who only had foreign currency had to pay the equivalent of one penny for every half-shekel given as change. Since there were six pennies in a half-shekel and a labourer was paid only four pennies a day, this was an exceedingly high charge. The requirement that only flawless animals could be sacrificed (Lev 3:6; 4:23, 28, 32; 6:6) was also being used to take advantage of worshippers. The men who inspected the animals had an agreement not to pass animals bought from anyone except the group referred to as the 'sons of Annas' (Annas was the ex–high priest and the father-in-law of Caiaphas, the current high priest). These animals cost five or six times more than animals bought elsewhere. Rather than providing a helpful service to worshippers, the authorities were exploiting the worshippers.

Making money, and not the worship of God, had become the focus of the leadership. So when Jesus *found men selling cattle, sheep and doves and others sitting at tables exchanging money* he took strong action (**2:14-16**). He was driven by his zeal for the house of the Lord (**2:17**, quoting Ps 69:9).

Jesus was promptly challenged by people asking him what authority he had to act like this when the leaders, including the high priest, permitted this trade in the temple. They wanted proof of his authority in the form of a *miraculous sign* (**2:18**). So Jesus promised them a sign: *Destroy this temple, and I will raise it again in three days* (**2:19**). The Jews thought he was speaking of the magnificent temple that Herod had begun to build in 19 BC. Their incredulous response, *It has taken forty-six years to build this temple* (**2:20**), implies that this episode took place around AD 27.

Jesus did not bother to explain that he was speaking about his body (**2:21**), which the Jews would later destroy, and was predicting his resurrection. The Jews were not ready to receive him anyway. However, the disciples did not forget these words, even though they may not have known

how to interpret them until after Jesus' resurrection from
the dead. Then they were amazed that what he had predicted had been fulfilled, and *they believed the Scripture and
the words that Jesus had spoken* (**2:22**). They saw in Jesus
the fulfilment of Scripture and realized again that the death
of their master was not an accident but part of an eternal
plan.

2:23-3:21 Jesus Meets with Nicodemus

The statements made in 2:23-25 provide important background to the meeting between Jesus and Nicodemus. Jesus
is presented as a miracle worker who is the object of faith
(**2:23**) and as one who knows everything about people
(**2:24-25**).

These qualities were probably what attracted Nicodemus' attention. He was *a man of the Pharisees; a member of
the Jewish ruling council,* or Sanhedrin; and an admirer of
Jesus (**3:1-2**). He was also someone who would have understood the saying *'Muulinza si mjinga'* [Swahili – 'one who
asks is not stupid']. The humility to be willing to learn even
simple things is a virtue and not a weakness. Though Nicodemus is often criticized for coming at night and for not
knowing what it means to be born again, a truth which he
should have been able to teach, we should admire his willingness to ask simple questions.

Nicodemus did not stand on his rank but came to visit
Jesus, probably as a courtesy call. But Jesus responded to
Nicodemus' admiring words with a blunt statement about
Nicodemus himself and his need for new birth: *I tell you
the truth, no one can see the Kingdom of God unless he is born
again* (**3:3**). Being 'born again' means acknowledging that
one is a sinner, repenting of sin, and inviting Jesus into
one's heart as Saviour. God responds by declaring that the
one who does this is his child.

Nicodemus takes the words as applying to the physical
realm: *How can a man be born when he is old?* (**3:4a**). His
scepticism finds fuller expression in his second question,
which could be translated, *One cannot enter one's mother's
womb a second time, can one?* (**3:4b**). In response, Jesus
states that this 'new birth' involves being *born of water and
the Spirit* (**3:5-7**). There is some debate about what exactly
this phrase means, but Jesus is probably referring to John
the Baptist's water baptism and his own baptism with the
Holy Spirit. John's baptism was a baptism of repentance. He
called people to leave their old ways of life in preparation
for the coming of Jesus (Luke 3:7-14). Jesus' baptism with
the Holy Spirit (1:33) brings a newness of character and the
energy to move on as a member of the family of God.

The new birth is like the wind (**3:8**). We can hear the
sound the wind makes and see the wind's effects, but we
cannot say where it has come from. In the same way, God
mysteriously brings about the new birth. We do not know
how he does it, but when it has taken place, we can see its
effects.

Nicodemus, beginning to realize that Jesus was not
talking of physical but of spiritual birth, asked the simple
question *How can this be?* (**3:9**). Jesus' response stressed
three essential elements in new birth, namely, the death
of the Son of Man, the love of God the Father, and human
responsibility (3:13-18).

The Son of Man was Jesus' favourite title for himself.
Here he explicitly says that he has come from heaven (**3:13**;
see also 1:1, 14). He also predicts his death: *Just as Moses
lifted up the snake in the desert, so the Son of Man must be
lifted up* (**3:14**). The only way the Israelites who had been
bitten by venomous snakes could escape dying was to look
at the bronze snake Moses had lifted up on a pole (Num
21:4-9). Jesus, too, would be lifted up so that everyone who
believed in him might have eternal life (**3:15**).

The process of the new birth began in heaven, when
God's love for humankind led him to send his only Son,
Jesus Christ, into the world to die for the world (**3:16a**).
Jesus did not come on a mission of condemnation, but on a
mission of salvation (**3:17**). We can enter into the experience of new birth by simply exercising faith (**3:16b**), that is,
by accepting that Jesus has been sent by God to give us the
new birth and asking him to be our Saviour and leader.

Jesus finished his conversation with Nicodemus by pointing out that there are two spheres of existence: the sphere
of light and the sphere of darkness (3:19-21). The sphere of
light centres on Jesus who is the Light that *has come into the
world* (**3:19a**; see also 1:4-5, 9). But in general, people *loved
darkness instead of light because their deeds were evil* (**3:19b**).
Jesus wanted Nicodemus to realize that the only way he
could enter the sphere of light was to believe in the Light
come from heaven.

3:22-36 John the Baptist Testifies about Jesus

I once asked a young African boy, 'What is your name?' He
replied, 'Boy'. I knew that was a nickname, and so asked
him, 'What is your other name?' He replied, 'That's what
Daddy calls me.' So I asked, 'Who is your father?', to which
he replied, 'Daddy'. Trying to get more useful information, I
asked him, 'Who is your mother?' and he told me, 'Mummy'.
I tried again: 'Who does Mummy belong to?', to which he
responded, 'Daddy'. Clearly, he did not yet know his parents' names, and so I tried a different approach. 'Who lives
in the house closest to your house?' The reply: 'Daddy's
friend'. This young man had no identity of his own separate
from his 'Daddy'. John the Baptist was like this. He defined
himself in terms of his relationship to God and Jesus.

Jesus was still in Judea, where he had initially gone for
the Passover (2:13). He had, however, left Jerusalem after
his conversation with Nicodemus and gone into the countryside (**3:22**). Meanwhile, John was baptizing at Aenon
near Salim (**3:23**). The region of Samaria lay between
Judea and Aenon. Jewish travellers often chose to detour
around Samaria by crossing the Jordan River near where

Jesus and his disciples were baptizing and then recrossing it near Aenon (see comments on 4:4). It was probably someone who had followed this route who got into an argument with some of John the Baptist's disciples about the issue of ceremonial washing (**3:25**). During this argument, he seems to have mentioned that Jesus was baptizing lower down the Jordan. John the Baptist's disciples were disturbed by this news because it suggested that John's influence was waning (**3:26**).

When they told John the Baptist about their concern, he pointed out that this was what he had predicted would happen (**3:28**). God had given him his role as the forerunner, and he was quite content to accept what God had given (**3:27**). Then he used another image to explain his role: he was only the friend of the bridegroom (**3:29**). At a Jewish wedding, the friend's role was to serve the bridegroom. When things were going well for the bridegroom, the friend rejoiced because that meant he had done his job well. Jesus is the bridegroom, and thus Jesus' prosperity is John the Baptist's joy. It was appropriate that attention should be focused on the groom, and that was why *he must become greater, and I must become less* (**3:30**).

But Jesus was far more than an ordinary bridegroom. John the Baptist stresses that Jesus comes *from heaven* (**3:31**). As such, Jesus is above all mere mortals and can testify about his first-hand experience of heaven (**3:32a**). John the Baptist, by contrast, can only speak of what he has been told.

Yet despite Jesus' infinitely higher status, *no one accepts his testimony* (**3:32b**). Here 'no one' is not meant to be taken literally. It is a general term, meaning that most people do not accept it. Yet acceptance of Jesus' testimony is crucial, for to refuse it is to deny that it is God's nature to be truthful and to speak the truth (**3:33**). One of the truths that God proclaims is that he will give the blessing of eternal life to those who accept Jesus. This offer is guaranteed by God's truthfulness, as those who possess eternal life can testify.

Jesus has been sent by God and so *speaks the words of God* (**3:34**). To reject his testimony is thus to reject God's word. John the Baptist can testify that the Spirit was given to Jesus in full measure (3:34; see also 1:33). Because *the Father loves the Son* (**3:35a**), he notices who accepts or rejects him. In fact, so great is the Father's love for Jesus that he has placed everything, including everyone's destiny, in his hands (**3:35b**). Jesus has ultimate authority.

Each individual's response to Jesus has consequences. Those who believe in him possess *eternal life* (**3:36a**), that is, a life lived at peace with and in the presence of God both now and in eternity. But those who reject the Son are subject to the wrath of God (**3:36b**), meaning that they will never enjoy peace with or be in the presence of God.

4:1-42 Jesus and the Samaritan Woman

In some African cultures, women are not allowed to eat certain choice cuts of meat that are reserved for men only. The exclusion of women extends to other areas of life too. One begins to suspect that some of these prohibitions have been imposed because they benefit men. Where all women are excluded from certain things, women who carry some kind of stigma fare even worse in terms of social isolation. This was the case of the woman we meet in this passage. Jesus' approach to her speaks loudly about areas of African culture that must change.

Jesus had spent some time in Judea. At Jerusalem he had, among other things (2:23), attended the Passover (2:13), cleansed the temple (2:14-22), and conversed with Nicodemus (3:1-21). In the Judean countryside, he and his disciples had baptized (3:22), although **4:2** stresses that Jesus himself did not baptize. His reason for not performing water baptisms himself, while permitting his disciples to do them, may be that he did not want to distract attention from his basic mission of baptizing people with the Holy Spirit.

Presumably Jesus did not want to attract too much attention at this stage of his ministry, and so when he learned that the Pharisees were taking note of him (**4:1**), he set out for Galilee, travelling by way of Samaria (**4:3-4**).

Many Jews refused to take this route from Judea to Galilee. Instead they took a route that was twice as long, crossing the Jordan somewhere in Judean territory, travelling up the eastern side of the Jordan, and then recrossing the river into Galilee. The hostility between Jews and Samaritans dated back to the time when the Assyrians had settled non-Jews in this area (2 Kgs 17:23-41). Intermarriage between these settlers and local Israelites contributed to the Jews' view that the Samaritans were second-class people who should be avoided for moral reasons. Numerous incidents had kept the ancient enmity fresh over the centuries.

The conversation between Jesus and the woman took place at Jacob's well, about half a mile from the Samaritan town of Sychar on some land that Jacob had bought and given to his son Joseph (4:5-6; Gen 33:18-19). It was about noon (the sixth hour – 4:6) and a tired Jesus was resting at the well when a woman from the town came to draw water. Jesus, who knows people's hearts (2:25), recognized her true need. He used the physical water she had come to draw as a contact point, asking, *Will you give me a drink?* (**4:7**). She refused to do so because he was a Jew and she was a Samaritan (**4:9**).

Jesus responded that she was missing a great opportunity, because he could give her *living water* (**4:10**). Such spiritual water would be far superior to any that came from the well. While the well water was a gift from Jacob (4:12), the living water was the gift of God, available from the one who was speaking to her. Not only that, but the well water would give only temporary relief from thirst (**4:13**), whereas the living water gives eternal life (**4:14**).

The Samaritan woman was thinking in terms of physical water (**4:11-12**), and had only a vague understanding of what Jesus meant. Nevertheless, she said, *Sir, give me this water so that I won't get thirsty and have to keep coming here to draw water* (**4:15**). She was ready to receive the living water, but needed to learn more about it.

Jesus thus turned to the topic of her personal life: *Go, call your husband and come back* (**4:16**). Jesus knew all about her past life and the fact that she had no husband (**4:17-18**), but he wanted to remind her of it. When she responded *I have no husband* (4:17), Jesus commended her for her honesty, but pointed out she was not telling the full truth.

Amazed that Jesus knew about her past, she decided that Jesus must be *a prophet* (**4:19**) and took the opportunity to consult him about an issue that was hotly debated by Jews and Samaritans: Should God be worshipped on Mount Zion in Judea or on Mount Gerizim in Samaria? (**4:20**). Jesus responded by saying that the Jews know more about God than the Samaritans do (**4:22**), but that the question itself is no longer relevant. What is more important than where worship takes place is how it takes place. True worshippers focus on the Father (**4:21**) and worship him *in spirit,* that is, within their own souls, and *in truth,* that is, with sincerity, not formalism (**4:23-24**). The reason for this kind of worship is that the Father is not a person who is located in a particular place, but a spirit who communes with the human spirit.

The Samaritan woman showed growing recognition of who Jesus was. She began by viewing him as just another Jew, and then she thought he was a prophet. Finally, Jesus presented himself to her as the expected Messiah (**4:25-26**). Excited, she left her water jar and ran back to Sychar to tell the people, *Come, see a man who told me everything I ever did. Could this be the Christ?* (**4:28-29**).

Jesus had been alone because his disciples had gone into Sychar to buy food (4:8). When they returned, they found Jesus talking to the woman (**4:27**). Even after she left, he did not seem to be in a hurry to eat, and the disciples wondered whether he had some other source of food (**4:31-33**). Jesus' response was that doing the work of God was his food (**4:34**). Just as his conversation with the Samaritan woman reminds us that there is ordinary water and living water, so his response here reminds us that there is ordinary food and spiritual food. There is deep satisfaction in doing God's work (4:34).

Jesus' response reminds us that just as there is ordinary water and living water, so there is ordinary food and spiritual food. His food is to *do the will of him who sent me,* that is, God.

Jesus saw the Samaritan town as a field ready for harvest, one where the planting and harvesting of the fruit of the good news would happen at the same time (**4:35-36**). As the disciples reaped the fruit of the ministry, however,

they had to remember that others before them (probably John the Baptist and the OT prophets) had prepared the hearers to receive the message (**4:37-38**).

The people of Sychar acted on the woman's invitation to 'come and see' (4:29) and kept on coming to Jesus (**4:30**). Impressed by the woman's testimony, many believed (**4:39**). They asked Jesus to stay longer with them, and he agreed, staying for two days (**4:40**). When the harvest was plentiful, Jesus altered his programme to accommodate the harvesting. The Samaritans were now able to testify that their belief was no longer rooted only in what the woman had told them, but was now based on their own experience (**4:41-42a**). They were convinced that Jesus was truly the Saviour of the world (**4:42b**).

What would have happened had Jesus been like his disciples and thought it inappropriate for a rabbi to talk to a woman in public (**4:27**)? Or if he had asked the opinion of the people of Sychar, who would probably have said, 'Don't talk to that woman; her ways are evil'? Because Jesus treated this stigmatized woman as someone worth talking to, she became a witness to Jesus, and all of Sychar was brought to him. Who knows what potential could be found within the many women Africa dismisses? Maybe they are the instruments Jesus could use to bring all Africa to him. And how many women in our cities and towns have been labelled 'women of evil ways' and dismissed by the church, leaving them at the mercy of the pleasure-seeking men who are their only source of income. Many such women are doomed to die from AIDS. Unless we follow Jesus' example, we are not being good disciples.

4:43-54 Jesus Heals the Son of a Royal Official

We often hear rumours that prominent African people are in some kind of association with Satan, particularly when they are seeking promotions, wealth, election victories and the like. Many, including even some believers, visit witchdoctors and consult the spirits in times of need. But the official in this story knew the right place to turn to for help and he faithfully kept his eyes fixed on it. At the right time, his prayer was answered.

This miracle took place during Jesus' second ministry in Galilee and is described by John as his second sign (**4:54a**). His first sign (the changing of water into wine – John 2; **4:46a**), had taken place during his first ministry there. On both occasions, Jesus had come to Galilee from Judea (**4:54b**), and at the end of each ministry he returned there (1:43; 5:1). The alternating of Judea-Galilee, Galilee-Judea is important for John, although we are not sure why. It is possible that John is making it clear that Jesus paid attention both to 'his own country' and to the capital. Judea, and especially its capital Jerusalem, was the home of Jesus' opponents, yet it was there that the church began. Galilee was Jesus' home territory, but as Jesus himself said, *a prophet has no honour in his own country* (**4:44**). Jesus taught and performed signs both in the place that was hostile to him and in the one that took him for granted. We in Africa need to remember both the cities and the villages. To settle in the city and forget one's village – no matter how backward that village may seem – is to neglect one's foundation and the people who made one what one is today.

After mentioning Jesus' warm reception by the Galileans (**4:45**) John focuses on a certain official who was probably attached to the court of Herod Antipas. The official's son was sick in Capernaum, some twenty miles (thirty-two kilometres) away from Cana where the man met Jesus.

Jesus' initial response to the official's request that he come and heal his son sounds unsympathetic: *Unless you people see signs and wonders you simply will not believe* (**4:47-48**). The 'you' is plural, and Jesus is speaking of the official as a typical representative of the Galileans, and probably of the Jews in general. Jesus' first desire was to bring the official to the point where he would see Jesus as the Saviour of the soul and not simply one who could miraculously heal the body.

But the official stated his need with even greater urgency: *Sir, come down before my child dies* (**4:49**) and Jesus replied, *You may go. Your son will live* (**4:50**).

While the official was on his way home to Capernaum, he met his servants who were on their way to Cana with good news – his son was recovering (**4:51**). When he learned that his son had been healed instantly at 1 p.m. (the exact time when Jesus had spoken the healing words), he and his household believed (**4:52-53**).

5:1-16 A Healing at the Pool at Bethesda

We often see someone standing or sitting at the corner of a building or outside a shop, begging. Some of these people are blind, others lame or deaf, others have been crippled in vehicle accidents, and some may simply be lazy. The sight is so familiar that most of those passing by pay no more attention to the beggars than to a stone on the corner of the street. But the beggars still keep asking, trying to attract the attention of someone who looks prosperous enough to give them something. Most of those seeking help do not enjoy asking for it like this. And sensitive passers-by may also wish that the beggars were not there. Such passers-by are acutely aware that while some of the beggars may not genuinely be in need, there are others who are in desperate need – and we do not have the resources to help them all. The incident described here, which is the third sign John records, reminds us of the importance of helping even one person. We should not let the number of needy people overwhelm us so that we help none.

Jesus had gone to Jerusalem for *a feast of the Jews* (**5:1**). It may have been Passover, Pentecost, the Feast of Weeks, or the Feast of Tabernacles. Whichever it was, it would have meant that many people were in Jerusalem. While there, Jesus went to the pool of Bethesda, which is located *near the Sheep Gate* (**5:2**). Jerusalem was surrounded by a protective wall with gates. The sheep gate was on the northern side of the city and led directly into the temple. Through it the animals were brought for sacrifice.

One of the many who lay in the five colonnades that surrounded the pool of Bethesda, waiting for the water to move, was a man who had been an invalid for thirty-eight years but had not given up hope (**5:3-5**). Jesus approached him and asked, *Do you want to get well?* (**5:6**). The man's response acknowledged that healing was available (the water was stirred from time to time) and that he was anxious to make use of this means of healing (he did try to get into the pool), but he confessed that he could not do it on his own (**5:7**). Jesus met his need, saying, *Get up! Pick up your mat and walk* (**5:8**). And the man did just that! (**5:9**).

The Jewish authorities, who were so accustomed to seeing those needing help that they paid little attention to individuals, suddenly took notice of him. They did not share his rejoicing in being healed after so many years. Instead they accused him of breaking the law by carrying a mat on a Sabbath day (for, as John repeatedly reminds us, the healing had taken place on a Sabbath (**5:10**).

The fact that it was a Sabbath and that he was carrying a mat could not be disputed, so the healed man's defence rested on the authority of the one who had told him to carry his mat, *the man who made me well* (**5:11**). The Jews' attention was thus focused on Jesus (**5:12**). But the healed man did not know that it was Jesus who had healed him, because after the healing Jesus had slipped away (**5:13**).

Later, however, Jesus found the man at the temple and spoke to him, saying: *See, you are well again; stop sinning or something worse may happen to you* (**5:14**). The man then went and told the Jewish leaders that the person who had made him well was Jesus (**5:15**). It is quite possible that they had let the man go free on condition that he find out who it was who had told him to pick up his mat and report him to them. It seems that he was not heeding Jesus' warning in 5:14. He was now sinning again by collaborating with the Jewish authorities. Jesus must have known what the man was going to do, and that he would be an unwilling party to a plot against him. The man's fear drove him to act in a way that was inconsistent with the wonderful mercy he had received.

The Jews now began to persecute Jesus. His crime was that he *was doing these things on the Sabbath* (**5:16**). The Ten Commandments had declared that the Sabbath should be a day of rest (Exod 20:8). To ensure that the day was properly observed, the Jews had expanded on the commandments to specify what actions amounted to 'not resting'. Consequently healing was permitted on the Sabbath only when life was at stake. Someone who had been ill with a debilitating disease for thirty-eight years was in no danger of immediate death, and so healing him was regarded as breaking the law.

5:17-47 The Son Gives Life

I was once asked to settle a friendly argument about 'Which came first, the chicken or the egg?' Pulling out my Bible, I read Genesis 1:20-21, which speaks of God creating birds, not eggs. My answer seemed to satisfy the debaters, but I knew that it presupposed that creation took place in twenty-four-hour days and that other interpretations are possible. If the 'days' represent extended periods of time, there would have been time for an egg to hatch. My answer was satisfactory, but there were still loopholes in it.

We face a similar challenge when trying to define the exact relationship between God the Father and God the Son. No explanation we can offer will ever be complete, with no loopholes. But there are some passages in Scripture, like this one, that can help us understand something about this relationship.

The Jews were persecuting Jesus because he had healed on the Sabbath (5:16). Jesus responded to this persecution with the statement *My father is always at his work to this very day, and I, too, am working* (5:17). Although the Father ended his work of creation on the seventh day, he never takes a break from his work of caring for the world that he has created. Even on the Sabbath, God still supports the world, and Jesus models his behaviour on God's behaviour. The Jewish leaders recognized that Jesus' words were equivalent to claiming to be equal with God, and so they became even more determined to kill him (5:18).

Ignoring their anger, Jesus told them more about himself and his relationship with the Father and with humanity. His relationship with the Father is an equal and intimate partnership (5:19) characterized by love (5:20a), transparency (5:20b), equality in power (5:21), trust in each other's judgment (5:22), and shared honour (5:23). His relationship to humanity determines the destiny of the living and the dead. If the living have faith in him, they will be given eternal life (5:24-25). In due time, the dead will acknowledge him as their judge (5:28, 29). The Son is the source of life (5:26) and the judge of all (5:27).

Jesus then cited several witnesses who could support his claims (5:32), namely, John the Baptist (5:32-35); his own works (5:36); the Father himself (5:37); and the Scriptures (5:39).

The Jews who were listening to him were condemned because they were not willing to come to Jesus to have life (5:40), did not give honour to the Son (5:41), did not have the love of God in them (5:42), and refused the one sent by God but were prepared to receive those who came in their own authority (5:43) and were more interested in being honoured by one another and by the Jewish authorities than in being honoured by God (5:44). They may have had a high regard for the law given through Moses (see 5:16; 9:28), but rather than Moses being on their side in their dispute with Jesus, he is their accuser (5:45). He wrote about Jesus in passages like Deuteronomy 18:18-22, but since they did not believe what Moses wrote, and thus they did not really believe in Moses, no matter what they claimed (5:46-47). The situation was hopeless. If they rejected the words of Moses, a man they honoured, how would they ever believe what Jesus was telling them?

Faced with the claims of Jesus and the witnesses that supported these claims, the Jews reacted with blind stubbornness. They thought they were defending Yahweh's interests, but missed the point that the Son and the Father are so closely related that whatever one does to one of them, one also does to the other.

6:1-15 Jesus Feeds Thousands

Since rainfall in Africa is not always reliable, areas of the continent are frequently struck by famine. Appeals to wealthier nations for aid sometimes provoke dismissive comments such as 'Africans are always starving.' Africans have worked to store water during times of heavy rain, but what can they do when the rains fail and begging for food produces nothing but humiliation? This passage holds one answer to this question. It records Jesus' feeding of many people with very little, a miracle that is the fourth sign John records.

This miracle took place at Bethsaida in Galilee (6:1; see Luke 9:10). People were following Jesus because they were seeing his miraculous signs (6:2). They were more interested in his physical ministry than in the spiritual truths he was teaching. Nevertheless, Jesus took the opportunity to show them who he was by meeting their physical needs.

Jesus also used this as an opportunity to test his disciples and find out how well they were grasping the lessons he was teaching about who he was and the power he commanded. So he asked Philip (who, like Peter and Andrew, was from Bethsaida – 1:44; 12:21), *Where shall we buy bread for these people to eat?* (6:5-6). Jesus already knew how he was going to solve the problem, for he could see the boy with the five loaves and two fish – just as he had seen Nathanael under the fig tree (1:48), knew people's hearts (2:24-25), and knew the history of the Samaritan woman (4:18).

Philip's response shows that he was thinking only in terms of money and the marketplace, for he told Jesus that even if each of the people took only a small piece of bread, it would take more than two hundred denarii to feed them. A denarius was a day's wage for a labourer, and thus the NIV correctly translates the total as *eight months' wages* (6:7). A better answer would have been, 'There are a lot of people, but nothing is difficult for you, Lord.'

Andrew went further than Philip, for he started looking for practical solutions. However, he had little faith in the solution he found. There was no way he could see *five small barley loaves and two small fish* feeding such a large crowd (6:8-9).

Jesus' instruction, *Make the people sit down* (**6:10**), was probably directed to all the disciples. John uses the generic word 'people' here, but he uses the specifically male term when referring to the five thousand men who sat. It seems that each of these men sat down with his family around him. This arrangement would have simplified the distribution of food to the women and children who were also present (Matt 14:21).

Jesus then *took the loaves, gave thanks and distributed to those who were seated ... He did the same with the fish* (**6:11**). Jesus probably did the distribution through the disciples (Matt 14:19), but John focuses on Jesus as the initial distributor because he links this feeding to spiritual feeding in the discourse that follows (6:26-71). In the spiritual realm, each individual eats directly from Christ, the bread of life.

In spite of the large number of people and the limited resources, Jesus fed them all until each was satisfied. Not only that, but the twelve disciples could each fill a basket with food that was left over (**6:12-13**). Jesus was teaching them about who he was and about his power. John, however, focuses on the crowd's reaction to the miracle. They concluded that Jesus was the awaited Prophet and wanted to make him king (**6:14**; see also 1:21). He had given them all they needed without exhausting the resources at his disposal! No wonder they wanted to establish his physical kingdom there and then. What the crowd did not realize, however, was that his kingdom is a spiritual one and that he acts in accordance with the will and timing of his heavenly Father.

The same Jesus watches over the affairs of Africa and the world in general. First, he wants each of us to believe in him as the bread of life. Then, when circumstances are beyond our control, we can expect him to take care of our physical needs, as he sees best. Unlike other nations, he will not turn his back on us in a crisis. We can trust him to provide in some way, for he is the Lord of all possibilities.

6:16-21 Jesus Walks on Stormy Water

It is said that on long journeys my great-grandfather would pull up bushes and find water where the bush had been. Some are impressed by such stories, while others are sceptical. But here we have an eyewitness account of an amazing incident that is the fifth sign that John records.

Jesus thwarted the crowd's plan to make him king by going into the mountains by himself (**6:15**). As darkness approached, the disciples set off towards Capernaum without him (**6:16-17**). It was a windy night *and the water grew rough* (**6:18**).

The disciples had covered about twenty or thirty stadia, which is equivalent to slightly more than three miles (about five kilometres) when they saw a figure approaching the boat (**6:19a**). They did not recognize Jesus, for although they had seen him heal people with a word and multiply food to feed more than five thousand people, they had never

seen him walking on water. Not surprisingly, *they were terrified* (**6:19b**).

Jesus calmed them, saying, *It is I; don't be afraid* (**6:20**). They had no need to fear either the mysterious figure that was approaching the boat or drowning in the stormy sea.

Recognizing Jesus, the disciples were willing to take him into the boat (**6:21**). Jesus, however, had not come to get a ride but to assure his disciples that he was always with them. The boat reached the shore immediately after Jesus had appeared to them.

When the disciples reached the shore, they were no longer frightened. They had confidence in Jesus' presence. Like them, we can trust his words, 'do not be afraid'. He will be with us as we go through the storms of life – whether these storms involve a lack of money, or food, or health, or wars raging around us, or any other calamity.

6:22-59 Jesus the Bread of Life

Traditionally, Africans were very good teachers, whose stories often led smoothly to an appropriate moral. Jesus, the master teacher, uses a similar approach here as he builds on his feeding of five thousand people.

The audience was the same crowd that had followed him to Bethsaida. They had lingered there after he left (6:15), expecting him to return (**6:22**). But Jesus did not return, and his disciples had gone to the other side of the lake. When they recognized that it was unlikely that Jesus would be coming back, they got into some boats from Tiberias (**6:23**) and headed for Capernaum *in search of Jesus* (**6:24**). They found him in the synagogue at Capernaum (6:59).

Jesus' interaction with the crowd falls into at least six sections, each introduced by a question or an action by the crowd. Step by step, he makes the point that he is the bread of life.

6:25-27 The opening question and Jesus' response

The crowd were curious about how Jesus had evaded them, and so their first question was *Rabbi, when did you get here?* (**6:25**). By 'here', they mean Capernaum, where they had found him.

Jesus responded by questioning their motive for looking for him. It was not primarily because they had been impressed by the miracle (not, in itself, a very good motive), but because they had enjoyed the food. Their main concern was with their stomachs (**6:26**).

Jesus wanted them to have higher motives. He told them that they should *not work for food that spoils,* such as the food he had given them at Bethsaida, *but for food that endures to eternal life* (**6:27a**). A far more important type of food was the spiritual food that *the Son of Man will give you* (**6:27b**). The 'giving' is linked to the 'working for'. The Son of Man gives this food to those who work for it.

Jesus' authority to give them this spiritual food is based on the fact that he bore God the Father's *seal of approval*

(6:27c). He is the one authenticated to give the food that leads to eternal life.

The crowd zeroed in on the word 'work', and this prompted their next question.

6:28-29 What works are acceptable to God?

If Jesus wanted the crowd to work for the right things, they wanted a list of what these things were. Hence their question *What must we do to do the works God requires?* (6:28). What works would merit God's favour?

But where the crowd thought of 'works', Jesus talked of only one 'work': *The work of God is this: to believe in the one he has sent* (6:29). He was speaking of a way of life rather than a set of rules to observe. It is a life characterized by the continual exercise of faith in Jesus.

This reply surprised the crowd. It was a new teaching and led them to ask about his authority to make such a claim.

6:30-33 What sign can you give us?

The crowd asked Jesus to prove that what he said was true. Their thinking in 6:30-31 seems to be like this: 'Moses gave us a list of rules to obey in order to please God. Now you say that it's not a matter of lists but simply of believing in the one God sent. We cannot believe you instead of Moses unless you do a miracle to match the one that Moses did. Moses gave manna. What about you; what can you do?'

Jesus immediately corrected the crowd's perception (6:32). It was not Moses who had provided the bread but Jesus' Father (see Exod 16) – the same Father who now gives the true bread from heaven. In other words, there is no competition between Moses and Jesus. Both obtained bread from the same source. But there is a difference between the manna God gave to their ancestors in the wilderness and the bread he offers now. What he gave then served only a temporary purpose; what he is giving now is the true bread. Not only that, but the new bread is a person, *For the bread of God is he who comes down from heaven and gives life to the world* (6:33). This describes Jesus, who constantly refers to himself as 'sent by the Father'. God intends people to eat this bread and live.

6:34-40 Give us this bread

The crowd's request for this bread in 6:34 was based on a partial understanding of what Jesus had said (see also 4:15). They understood that the bread he was speaking of was superior to the manna their fathers ate, but they did not realize that it was not for their stomachs but for their souls.

Aware that the crowd was slow to understand him, Jesus spoke more explicitly: I am *the bread of life* (6:35a). He is the true life-giving bread. Later he describes himself as the living bread – the bread that has life in itself and shares it with others (6:51). This statement is the first of seven key 'I am' sayings in the Gospel of John. (The other six are I

am the light of the world – 8:12; 9:5; I am the gate for the sheep – 10:7, 9; I am the good shepherd – 10:11, 14; I am the resurrection and the life – 11:25; I am the way and the truth and the life – 14:6; I am the true vine – 15:1, 5.)

The condition for receiving the life in this bread is that one must come to Jesus, which is the same as believing in him. If this condition is met, three things will follow:

- Someone who comes to Jesus or believes in him *will never go hungry* and *will never be thirsty* (6:35b). The *never* emphasizes that Jesus offers an unfailing opportunity for a spiritually satisfied life. The talk thus far has been of bread, but the subject of thirst is triggered by the fact that in the wilderness the Israelites were both fed manna and given water to drink (Exod 17:1-7). Everything that the Father miraculously provided for their ancestors in the wilderness, he is now providing in the person of Christ.

- Jesus will never *drive away* anyone who comes to him (6:37b), regardless of race, class or gender. Some may choose to continue in unbelief (6:36) but Jesus is convinced that *all that the Father gives me will come to me* (6:37a). The focus of this statement is not on the individual who is given, but on Jesus himself. Every one of those the Father gives to him will come, and none of them will fail to come. The same point is made again in 6:44, but there Jesus focuses on the individuals who have been drawn by the Father.

- Jesus will *lose none of all that the Father has given* to him (6:39). Whether alive or dead, they are secure in God's plan for them. The basis for this security is that a) Jesus submits to the will of the Father (6:38) and b) what he is promising is the will of the Father (6:40). He makes it clear that failure to believe in him amounts to not being a child of God.

Jesus recognized that the crowd were not convinced: *You have seen me and still do not believe* (6:36). They had been following Jesus for some time and had seen him in action. They had been fed at Bethsaida (6:1-15). But despite all this, they did not believe. Their failure to do so implies that they did not have life. They asked him for the bread of life (6:34), but how could he possibly give it to them if they did not believe?

6:41-51 Grumbling

The crowd now started to grumble about Jesus' claim that he *came down from heaven* (6:33, 38). How could he make such claims when they knew his home and his parents? (6:41-42).

Jesus told them to stop grumbling (6:43) and pointed out that they must be taught (drawn) of God before they could accept his claim to be the bread from heaven (6:44). The word translated 'draw' has the idea of attractive power. It is the same word Jesus uses later in 12:32. As the crowd looked at Jesus, they saw nothing to attract them. He was an ordinary fellow whose parents they knew. However, as God manifested himself through the Son, they would notice more of his glory, and Jesus would attract them more.

The link between being taught and being drawn becomes clear in Jesus' quotation from the prophets: *they will all be taught by God* (**6:45a**; see also Isa 54:13; Jer 31:33, 34). Jesus then adds, *everyone who listens to the Father and learns from him comes to me* (**6:45b**). The Father's interest is in glorifying the Son, through the works the Son does and the words the Son speaks.

Jesus also reminded the crowd that *no one has seen the Father except the one who is from God* (**6:46**). The fact that Jesus is the only one who has ever seen the Father gives his words about the Father and his plan of salvation authority over anyone else's.

He then went on to reiterate some of the key truths he had communicated already:

- The one who believes has everlasting life (**6:47**).
- He (Jesus) is the bread of life (**6:48**).
- The crowd's ancestors appreciated the manna in the wilderness because it was their main food for forty years (see Exod 16). Yet despite the fact that they were eating food that God had supplied, they eventually died (**6:49**). Nevertheless, the supply had been so memorable that it was still remembered as a miracle associated with Moses (6:31).
- The bread that Jesus gives is far better than manna, for anyone who eats the bread from heaven will never die (**6:50**). Refusing the offer of such bread is an illogical thing to do.

Finally, in **6:51** Jesus summarizes all that he has been saying. He stresses that a) he is the living bread come from heaven; b) the one who eats of this bread lives forever; and c) the bread he will give for the life of the world is his flesh. Translated literally, 6:51b reads, *And in fact the bread which I myself will give is the very flesh of mine – for the world's life.* Jesus emphasizes that the bread is his flesh and it is he who will give it. Within a short time, he will voluntarily give his flesh to be crucified on the cross. The purpose of it all will be so that the world (humankind) can obtain life.

6:52-59 An argument among themselves

Earlier the crowd had merely grumbled (6:41), but by now, they were actively arguing with each other about the question *How can this man give us his flesh to eat?* (**6:52**). Probably, some were beginning to understand what Jesus was saying, while others did not.

In his response, Jesus' main goal was to expand on the central idea that the living bread from heaven that gives life is his own flesh. So he stressed that one must eat the flesh of the Son of Man and drink his blood to have life (**6:53**). Those in the crowd still thinking on a physical level must have been even more shocked by what Jesus said here, for God had forbidden the drinking of blood (Deut 12:16).

Those who obey the condition stated in 6:53 have eternal life and Jesus *will raise them up at the last day* (**6:54**). This is the third reference to the resurrection of believers in this discourse (see also 6:40 and 6:44). There can be no doubt that this will happen, for Jesus' flesh is real food and his blood is real drink (**6:55**). The word translated 'real' here focuses on true as opposed to false. There is nothing counterfeit about what he offers.

The word used for 'eating' in 6:54 is repeated again in **6:56, 57,** and **58.** It is a word that usually refers to eating fruit or vegetables with enjoyment. It is also in the present tense, which shows that the spiritual blessing of eternal life is enjoyed by those who have made it their habit to feed on Jesus' flesh with enjoyment and who continually drink his blood. This underscores the point that the one who eats and drinks remains in Jesus and Jesus remains in him (**6:56**). They are bound in an intimate relationship. In fact, they are part of a chain of life that runs from the living Father to the Son to anyone who feeds on the living Son (**6:57**).

Once again, Jesus contrasted what he was offering with the manna their ancestors had eaten. The manna only sustained life for a short time before those who ate it died (**6:58**), but the effect of this living bread (that is, Jesus' flesh) is eternal (**6:58**).

6:60-71 Jesus Deserted by Many Disciples

As Jesus spoke of his flesh being the bread of life, and of the need to eat it and drink his blood, those who heard him included the Twelve (6:67), other disciples (6:60, 61, 66), and a mixed crowd of newcomers (some of whom had joined the crowd as recently as the journey to Bethsaida). The disciples had probably kept quiet while Jesus taught the crowd and the crowd asked questions. Now, however, they spoke up.

This wider circle of Jesus' followers (possibly including the Twelve) said, *This is a hard saying, who can accept it?* (**6:60**). Translated literally, their question is, 'Who is able to hear it with appreciation?' They find it puzzling. How can one eat Jesus' flesh and drink his blood?

Jesus knew that the disciples were grumbling (**6:61**). In this Gospel, we are constantly reminded that Jesus is all-knowing (omniscient). The point is repeated in 6:64. So he responds to their question with a question of his own, that could be paraphrased as 'Since you are offended by my claim to be the bread come from heaven, and my statement that you must eat my flesh, what would happen if you were to see the Son of Man going back to his original state? Would you be able to appreciate that higher glory at all?' (**6:62**). The claim that he is the bread of life is a small one compared to the claims he can make from eternity.

He went on to remind the disciples that his words have a heavenly origin and must be understood in a heavenly context. If they think of eating his flesh and drinking his blood only in earthly terms, they are missing the point. Their type of human logic (*flesh*) counts for nothing; what is important is the spiritual dimension of his words, which are spirit and life (**6:63**). This division between the spirit and the flesh is not new in John, for the same point is made in 3:6.

Jesus was well aware that some of his disciples did not like what he was saying and did not believe his claims (**6:64**). He reminded them that they needed the Father's help to come to him (**6:65**). The 'coming' of which he speaks here is more profound than the 'coming' in 6:45. Here the person comes with expectation, hoping to receive all that Jesus has to offer. Judas and some of the other disciples who did not believe had come to Jesus and were with him physically, but their hearts were elsewhere. Only God could turn those indifferent hearts and bring them to follow Jesus sincerely.

John tells us that *from this time* or *out of this* (the Greek could be translated either way, and both meanings apply) *many of his disciples turned back and no longer followed him* (**6:66**).

So far, the Twelve have not played a prominent role. They have probably been listening and observing quietly while their teacher and master taught very difficult material. They have also watched people they had thought were sincere followers of Jesus stop following him. Then Jesus turned to them, and asked, *You do not want to leave too, do you?* (**6:67**). Clearly, he expected their answer to be 'no'. He knew their hearts, and knew that all of them (except, of course, Judas Iscariot) were sincere. He thus expected more from them than from the outer circle of disciples, and they knew it.

Peter was the spokesman for the Twelve when he gave three reasons why they were determined to stay with Jesus:

- No one compares with Jesus (**6:68a**).
- Jesus has the words of eternal life (**6:68b**). Other teachers could utter learned words to their disciples, but Jesus' words are special. They give eternal life, a life of fellowship with God.
- Jesus is the Holy One of God (6:69). Peter and his eleven classmates had watched and heard, and had drawn the conclusion that Jesus is 'holy', that is, one who has been set apart or consecrated to God.

Jesus' response amounts to saying, 'That is a good answer, but do not forget this also – I myself (note emphasize) chose the twelve of you, but one of you is worse than an unbeliever. He is a devil.' He was speaking of Judas Iscariot (**6:70-71**). The word 'devil' means 'an accuser'. John uses it elsewhere for Satan (8:44; 13:2). While Satan remains the devil proper, those who accomplish his schemes, like Judas Iscariot, are devils because they are imitating or following Satan. As two Akamba (Kenya) proverbs say, *kaswii ka ngo katutasya ngo* ['the leopard's cub takes after its mother'] and *kaswii ka nzoka no nzoka* ['the young of a snake is a snake'].

7:1-13 Jesus Secretly Goes to the Feast of Tabernacles

Jesus continued his work in Galilee and did not go to Jerusalem for the Passover mentioned in 6:4. He was deliberately avoiding Judea, where the Jewish leaders were waiting for him, hoping to kill him (**7:1**). Six months later, however, Jesus' brothers (Matt 13:55; Mark 6:3) challenged him to go to Jerusalem for the Feast of Tabernacles, which was one of the three most important Jewish feasts (**7:2-4**). Their message was, 'You must not miss this great opportunity. There will be huge crowds there to see your miracles.' But there was more to their message than meets the eye. There is a saying, *itho ithuku iyula ngiti* (Akamba, Kenya – 'a dog will always recognize a hostile eye', meaning that wise people can detect hidden ill feelings towards them). John lets us know that *even his own brothers did not believe in him* (**7:5**). Their real motive was to expose Jesus to the scrutiny of the renowned scholars in Jerusalem. He might be able to fool ignorant Galilean peasants, but in Jerusalem he would face a real test.

Jesus responded by contrasting himself and his brothers. He operated in accordance with his Father's timetable, which had a right and a wrong time for doing things. The brothers had no such restriction (**7:6**). Moreover, the brothers did not have to deal with the enmity of *the world* (**7:7**), that is, the system of unbelief that Jesus had constantly been challenging. In Jerusalem, he was hated because he healed on the Sabbath and claimed an intimate relationship with God (5:18). His brothers had not said or done anything that was opposed to the world, and so there was no reason for the world to treat them as enemies.

Jesus concluded by saying, *I am not yet going up to this Feast, because for me the right time has not yet come* (**7:8**). Some ancient Greek manuscripts include the word 'yet' in 7:8 and others do not, which is why there are different translations of this verse. But the bottom line is that Jesus refused to attend when the timing was dictated by his brothers. Similarly, he refused to allow his timing to be dictated by his mother at the wedding in Cana (2:4). His timetable was set by the Father.

Jesus stayed on in Galilee after his brothers had left, but later he did quietly go up to the Feast. Presumably, 'the right time' had then arrived (**7:9-10**). His departure from Galilee was in secret, and so was his stay near Jerusalem until the time came for him to make a public appearance (7:10, 14). But the fact that he was not visible did not mean that he was not talked about. The Jewish authorities were watching for him, wondering whether he would come (**7:11**). They remembered the miraculous healing of the man who had been sick for thirty-eight years and the controversy that had followed.

The ordinary people were also asking the same question and discussing Jesus. Some said, *he is a good man;* others said that he *deceives the people* (**7:12**). They conducted their arguments in whispers *for fear of the Jews* (**7:13**), that is, of the Jewish authorities. No one was sure exactly what the leadership's position was, though it seemed likely that they were hostile, as they had attempted to kill him. One might get into trouble for saying openly that Jesus was a good man. But it was also possible that the leaders would change their minds, and so it was unwise to say too loudly that Jesus was a deceiver. Everyone preferred to wait until the leadership's stand was made public.

7:14-24 Jesus Teaches in Public at the Feast

After resisting his brothers' and the crowd's attempts to give him public exposure, Jesus finally stepped forward in such a way that there was no need for anyone to search for him. In the middle of the Feast, Jesus went up *to the temple courts and began to teach* (**7:14**). His teaching amazed his hearers: *How did this man get such learning without having studied?* (**7:15**). They saw him as a Galilean carpenter who had no formal education in theology. But what he was saying showed that he knew what he was talking about.

Jesus responded by pointing out that his doctrine came from God (**7:16**). Other teachers might cite human authorities as the basis for their opinions, but God himself was the source of Jesus' teaching. So instead of assessing Jesus' teaching in terms of what other traditional authorities had to say on the subject, people should consider how Jesus' teaching related to the will of God. If they really wanted to do God's will, they would be able to come to a correct judgment about what Jesus was teaching (**7:17**).

Jesus also suggested a test they could use to see whether teaching did or did not come from God. The test was whether the teacher was seeking his or her own glory or the glory of God (**7:18**) Jesus had consistently focused on the glory of God, and so his teaching could be judged to be true.

But while Jesus was true, the same could not be said for his opponents. They did not keep the law they claimed to uphold (**7:19**) Their wanting to kill Jesus was not in conformity with the commandment that states, *you shall not murder* (Exod 20:13).

The people responded defensively, denying the accusation and asserting that Jesus was crazy to make it (**7:20**). Jesus reminded them of the reason others were trying to kill him (5:18). He had caused offence by healing a man who had been sick for thirty-eight years on a Sabbath (ch. 5). He then defended his action by comparing it to circumcision. The Jews were quite happy to circumcise a baby boy on the Sabbath (**7:22**). This act focused on only one part of the body, the boy's sexual organ. Jesus, however, had healed a whole man, in numerous parts of his body. If the Jews thought they were justified in attending to one part, then surely there was even more to be said for a still greater healing. So why did the Jews insist that their act was justified but Jesus' act deserved the death penalty? (**7:23**). No

wonder Jesus told them, *stop judging by mere appearances, and make a right judgment* (**7:24**).

7:25-36 How Can the Christ Come from Galilee?

The people had good reason for their confusion about who Jesus was. They knew that the authorities had wanted to kill him (5:18). But why then were they not preventing him from teaching in the temple? Did this mean that the authorities might have concluded that Jesus really was the Christ (**7:25-26**)? But if they had, how could that be reconciled with the widespread belief that *when the Christ comes, no one will know where he is from* (**7:27**). They knew where Jesus came from: he had a home in Nazareth, his parents were Joseph and Mary, and he had brothers and sisters (Matt 13:55-56; Mark 6:3).

Jesus recognized their confusion and cried out that what they knew was true, but there was even more that they did not know (**7:28-29**). They knew his human parents, but they did not know God, who had sent Jesus into the world. Jesus, however, does know God because he is from God. As an ambassador of God who *is true*, he has a valid mission that everyone should listen to.

In spite of the antagonism of some of the people (7:27) and of their leaders' attempts to seize him (**7:30**), many in the crowd put their faith in Jesus (**7:31**). They believed that Jesus had done what the Messiah would do and that there was no way anyone else could *do more miraculous signs than this man*. On this basis, Jesus must be the Messiah.

The rulers' attempt *to seize him* failed because Jesus had a predestined course to follow and no one could interfere with it (7:30). But this did not stop them from launching another attempt, prompted by the people's positive attitude towards Jesus (**7:32**). Jesus responded by announcing that he would only be with them for a little longer and then he would return to the one who sent him (**7:33**). The time was indeed short, for this was said approximately six months before his crucifixion.

Jesus warned them that after his departure, they would look for him and would not be able find him (**7:34a**). They might try to arrest him now, but soon they would not even be able to find him to arrest him because his incarnate state would have ended. He would be in a place they could not reach. It is worth noting Jesus' exact words here. He says, *where I am you cannot come* (**7:34b**). The present tense, 'I am', emphasizes that Jesus is still present with the Father. He has been with him from eternity past, is present with him as he speaks, and will be with him in eternity future.

But while Jesus was speaking of his return to glory, the Jewish leaders thought that he was simply saying that he would go into hiding outside Palestine (**7:35-36**).

7:37-44 Jesus' Final Lesson in the Temple

On the last and greatest day of the feast (7:37), which could be the seventh (Lev 23:34; Deut 16:13, 15) or the eighth day

(Lev 23:36), Jesus made a declaration: *If anyone is thirsty, let him come to me and drink. Whoever believes in me, as the Scripture has said, streams of living water will flow from within him* (**7:37-38**). This statement may have been prompted by the ceremony that celebrated the gift of water from the rock in the wilderness (Exod 17:1-7). The high priest would draw water from the fountain of Gihon, carry it back in a processions to the temple and pour it into a vessel at the altar until it overflowed to the ground Jesus picked up on the physical thirst that their ancestors must have experienced in the wilderness before God miraculously provided water. He offered to meet their spiritual thirst if they would come to him for the water that eternal life.

In the ceremony, the water overflowed its container, and Jesus promised that whoever drank from him (by believing in him) would also be filled to overflowing (7:38) He meant that believers would be filled with the Holy Spirit (**7:39**) and may have been thinking of passages such as Joel 2:28-29) (also quoted in Acts 2:16-21).

Jesus' words split the crowd into at least four groups (**7:43**):

- Those who said he was the Prophet who they thought would prepare the way for the Messiah (**7:40**; see also Deut 18:15).
- Those who said he was the Christ, the Messiah they had been waiting for (7:41; see also 7:31).
- Those who said that he could not be the Christ because he came from Nazareth and not from Bethlehem, the town of David (**7:41-42**). These people did not know the story of his birth.
- Those who said he was a bad man, as implied by the comment that *some wanted to seize him* (**7:44**).

7:45-52 Jewish Leaders Think Jesus Is a Deciever

The guards who had been sent to arrest Jesus (7:32) came back empty-handed, reporting only that *no one ever spoke the way this man does* (**7:45-46**). The Pharisees were not amused and challenged the guards by asking two questions. The first was, *Are you also deceived?* (**7:47**). As temple police officers, the guards were expected to protect the interests of the temple. In speaking well of Jesus, they were behaving just like the crowd. The second question was, *Has any of the rulers or of the Pharisees believed in him?* (**7:48**). The expected answer was, 'No'. That being the case, the guards were wrong – for the rulers and Pharisees were the ones who determined correct belief and practice. This attitude explains their contempt for the ordinary people who acknowledged that Jesus was the Christ (7:41). The Pharisees referred to them dismissively as *this mob that knows nothing of the law.* They regarded those who had not studied the details of the law as misled and thus cursed (**7:49**).

Nicodemus, who had gone to Jesus earlier (3:1-2), now asked his fellow-Pharisees, *Does our law condemn anyone without first hearing him to find out what he is doing?* (**7:50-**51). Once again, the expected answer was 'No'. Nicodemus could cite Scriptures such as Exodus 23:1 and Deuteronomy 1:16 to back up his request for a fair hearing before passing judgment.

Nicodemus' question was meant to prick the consciences of his fellow Pharisees, but they brushed it aside. They had already made up their minds. Rather than dealing with his question, they ridiculed him: *Are you from Galilee too?* (**7:52a**). They knew that Nicodemus was from Judea, but were implying that no Judean could possibly be taken in by Jesus. He was a Galilean and could only deceive Galileans. The Judeans were too bright to believe in him!

Their contempt for the Galileans was also expressed in the statement *Look into it, and you will find that a prophet does not come out of Galilee* (**7:52b**). The Pharisees were probably not denying that any prophet had ever come from Galilee. After all, Jonah came from Gath-hepher, which is only three miles (five kilometres) north of Nazareth. Their point was that the Galileans were not the type of people to produce prophets.

Either Nicodemus was not given an opportunity to respond or he decided to remain silent before his colleagues became suspicious of his continued opposition to their plans.

7:53-8:11 Jesus and the Woman Caught in Adultery

Though there is debate about whether this passage was originally part of John's Gospel, the incident rings true to what we know of Jesus' character. It happened in the temple after the Feast of Tabernacles (**8:1-2**). Bringing this woman to Jesus was part of the strategy of the teachers of the law (scribes) and Pharisees to discredit Jesus (**8:3-6a**). They thought that the only options Jesus had were either to say 'leave her alone' or 'stone her'. The first would suggest that he did not take her sin seriously enough, and the other (although required by the law – Lev 20:10; Deut 22:22) would lead people to doubt whether Jesus lived out his message of love and mercy.

Jesus responded by writing something on the ground (**8:6b**). We are not told what he wrote, but it may have been the sins of her accusers or Scriptures focusing on mercy and kindness. It must have been related in some way to his words *if any one of you is without sin, let him be the first to throw a stone at her* (**8:7**). By saying this, Jesus shifted the focus from himself and the woman to her accusers. He neither denied the validity of the law nor condemned the woman to death. The accusers left one by one, *the older ones first* – probably because of their longer experience of life and temptation (**8:9**). *Undu kikame kiambaa kite kikwatye tiwo kiambaa kyakwatwa* [Akamba, Kenya – 'the bush baby makes a different cry when it is trapped']. When all her accusers were gone, Jesus told the woman, *Neither do I condemn you. Go now and leave your life of sin* (**8:10-11**). Jesus was not in the world to condemn it but to save it (3:17) and those needing to be saved included this woman. He commanded her to begin a new life.

8:12-20 Jesus Defends His Testimony

Jesus then returned to teaching *the people*, that is, the crowd he was teaching when he was interrupted by the teachers of the law and the Pharisees. He declared, *I am the light of the world. Whoever follows me will never walk in darkness, but will have the light of life* (**8:12**). He was speaking just after the Feast of Tabernacles, during which the whole city of Jerusalem had been illuminated by huge candles, and was claiming that he illuminates the whole world, and not just Jerusalem.

The Pharisees mocked his claim: *Here you are, appearing as your own witness; your testimony is not valid* (**8:13**). What one says about oneself is suspect because we tend to present ourselves in a favourable light. As the Akamba (Kenya) say, *mundu avulasya makaa elekelye ngali iyake* ['when people are warming themselves at the fire, each moves the burning charcoal towards himself']. Moreover, the Jewish legal system required two or three witnesses to support any assertion (**8:17**; see also Deut 17:6; 19:15). The Pharisees were saying that Jesus' testimony could not be relied upon in a court of law. Jesus had faced this kind of challenge before, and had responded by listing two or three other witnesses, independent of himself (5:31-47).

On this occasion, however, he did not humbly accept their argument but corrected their assumptions. He is different from other men and his witness is reliable. He can speak with authority because he has come from the Father and is going back to him (**8:14**). He is not just another man talking about himself. He is one with the Father and his testimony is in accordance with the will of the Father.

The Pharisees (and others) were judging by human standards that did not apply to Jesus (**8:15a**; see also 7:24). They thought that he was just the son of Mary and Joseph, whereas he had been with the Father long before his association with them.

When Jesus said that he judges no one (**8:15b**), he was speaking within the context of his mission on earth. He had come to save people, not to judge or condemn them (12:47; see also 3:17). But this did not mean that he would never pass judgment during his time on earth. And at his second coming, he will pass judgment on the basis of what people have done with his offer of salvation (5:27; see also 2 Tim 4:1).

When, out of necessity, Jesus did judge during his first mission, his judgments were right because the Father and the Son are united in judgment (**8:16**). Thus his evaluation of the Pharisees in 8:14 is accurate.

Returning to the original point, Jesus said that if his opponents insisted on having two witnesses, he could give them two – the Father and himself (**8:18**). Jesus had just defended his right to be the first witness, so the Pharisees now tackled him on the subject of the second witness, asking *Where is your Father?* (**8:19a**). They wanted to see Jesus' earthly father because they failed to recognize that Jesus was talking of his heavenly Father.

Jesus ended the debate by again using his prerogative as a judge. He told the Pharisees that a) they did not know him and b) they did not know his Father (**8:19b**). When they looked at Jesus, they saw the man from Nazareth. Their lack of true knowledge about him resulted in their not knowing his Father either. If they had realized that the Father he was speaking of was Yahweh, they would not have needed to ask where he was.

This debate took place in the part of the temple where there were thirteen chests into which people dropped the offerings that supported the various activities of the temple (**8:20**). It was thus an area where there was a constant flow of people.

8:21-30 Jesus, the Way Out of Death

Jesus now returned to a topic he had dealt with earlier: *I am going away, and you will look for me, and you will die in your sins. Where I go, you cannot come* (**8:21**; 7:33). As before, the Jews were puzzled by his words. Earlier, they had thought that he might be going to hide among the Jews living outside Israel (7:33-35). This time, they considered the possibility of suicide (**8:22**). They believed that those who committed suicide went to hell. So if Jesus committed suicide, they would not go where he was going, for they were quite sure that they were going to heaven.

Once again, Jesus had to emphasize the contrast between himself and the Jews. They had come from two different places (**8:23**). Everyone in the crowd had been born and lived on Earth. Jesus, however, had come to earth from somewhere else. As a consequence of their different origins, they were governed by different principles. They operated as people who were part of an evil system; Jesus was not part of that system – he had come to destroy it.

Jesus' response could be paraphrased like this: 'You live completely in this world and have no hope of gaining the world above except through me, because I have come from that world. However, your refusal to accept this fact means that you cannot be helped. You are living in your sins and you will die there' (**8:24**).

The Jewish leaders understood that Jesus was saying that he was quite different from them, and so they asked him directly about his identity (**8:25**). What was his authority? Who was he in God's programme?

Jesus reminded the crowd of what he had been saying before when he was teaching them (8:28). In the discourses recorded in chapters 6 and 7 and in 8:1-24, they had heard him claim to be the bread of life, the light of the world, the one sent from above, and many other things. He then highlighted four things about himself:

- **I am your judge (8:26a)**. He has already stated his judgment that they will die in their sins.
- **I was sent by the one who is reliable (8:26b)**. The theme of Jesus' being sent by the Father comes up again and again (see 4:34; 8:16; 16:5; 17:3; 20:21).
- **I speak the things I have heard from the Father (8:26c)**. What Jesus taught is the truth.
- **I am God's workmate (8:29)**. He and his Father work in total harmony.

Some Jews would only realize the truth of these claims after they had killed Jesus (**8:28**). That evil deed would lead to even greater things that would convince them that Jesus' claims were true.

Although Jesus had predicted they would die in their sins, the way of faith was still open to all. *Even as he spoke,* many chose the path of life and *put their faith in him* (**8:30**).

8:31-38 Jesus, the True Liberator

Many countries in Africa celebrate the day when they ceased to be colonies and became free nations. But not everyone enjoys the fruit of freedom. Many in Africa are still in bondage, suffering evils such as nepotism, corruption, self-centredness, murder and the like. The liberation spoken of in this passage is makes it possible for each resident of a free nation to reap the benefits of political independence.

The passage takes the form of a dialogue between Jesus and Jews who had accepted his message at a mental level only. To them, Jesus says, *If you hold my teaching, you are really my disciples. Then you will know the truth, and the truth will set you free* (**8:31-32**). The 'holding' here involves hearing, accepting and obeying his teaching. It is not enough for them simply to give mental assent to what he says. If they want to be in a real relationship with him, they have to set out to live according to his teaching. As they open their hearts and minds to learn from him, they will experience true freedom.

The Jews, however, felt that they were free already: *we are Abraham's descendants and have never been slaves of anyone* (**8:33**). Some people believed in a tradition that their descent from Abraham gave them royal status, and that although they might be subject to Rome politically, their souls remained free under their only ruler, Yahweh.

Jesus pointed out that the freedom that matters most is moral or spiritual freedom. *Everyone who sins is a slave to sin* (**8:34**). Thus all of them, as sinners, are also slaves. He, however, is not a slave to sin (see 8:46) but the Son in God's family, and as such has the right to free slaves, liberating them from the chains that bind them (**8:35-36**). He does this for those who ask for it in faith. Those who seek to kill him, instead of coming to him for liberation, are clearly enemies of his Father and consequently belong to another father (**8:37-38**).

8:39-47 Jesus, the Basis for Legitimacy in God's Family

The Jews were indignant at Jesus' suggestion that they did not have the same father as his. They insisted that Abraham was their Father (**8:39a**). So Jesus pointed out that sonship to Abraham and a desire to kill Jesus were in contradiction. Abraham, a friend of God who is the Father of Jesus, would not do that. Their actions showed that they could not claim Abraham as their father (**8:39b-41**).

The Jews objected even more strenuously, *We are not illegitimate children.* They were asserting that they were true descendants of Abraham and had only one ultimate Father, *God himself* (8:41). However, as the Akamba say, *mauta ma kwivaka mainoasya* ['oil applied on the body does not make one fat'].

Jesus exposed the falsity of their argument by pointing out that because he had been sent by God, his opponents had only two alternatives: either they accepted his teaching, thus showing that they belonged to God, or they rejected it, showing that they did not belong to him (**8:42, 47**). These Jews had chosen the second option, and thus they must have another father, one who was opposed to God. This father, who had previously been referred to as *your father* (8:38) or *your own father* (8:41) is now identified by name as the devil (8:44). Their plan to kill Jesus, who was not guilty of any crime, and their refusal to believe the truth that he proclaimed were exactly the types of behaviour that would be expected from the devil, for he has always been a murderer and he neither follows nor speaks the truth (**8:43-46**).

One's attitude towards Jesus is what makes the difference between having true descent from Abraham or not – between being a legitimate member of God's family or not a member at all. One's membership in that family is not affected by one's claims (as in 8:41b), but by one's relationship with Jesus.

8:48-59 Jesus Makes Claims About Himself

The group Jesus was speaking to here were earlier referred to as having 'believed him' (8:31). They had accepted some of what he said. However, Jesus' challenge to their false security as Abraham's descendants made them increasingly hostile. After all, Jesus had told them that their conduct did not match Abraham's (8:39, 40), that God was not their Father (8:42), and that their true father was the devil (8:44).

So now they expressed their opinion of Jesus. They no longer referred to him as the son of Joseph and Mary, as they did before (6:42). Now they labelled him *a Samaritan and demon-possessed* (**8:48**). The Samaritans had some Jewish blood but were viewed as impure in their belief and practice. They were looked down on and were not accepted as teachers of the law. And anyone who was 'demon-possessed' could not be teaching the will of God, but only the will of the devil under whose governance demons operate.

Jesus denied the second of these accusations. Rather than being under demonic influence, he sought to honour the Father (**8:49**). The Father, who is the judge in these matters, wants the Jews to honour Jesus (**8:50**). In other words, failure to glorify Jesus is equivalent to disobeying God.

Jesus extended his invitation, saying, *I tell you the truth, if anyone keeps my word, he will never see death* (**8:51**). Jesus was interested in far more than just answering accusations or insults. He wanted to bring his audience to the place where they accepted his word, which gives eternal life.

The Jews, however, thought that Jesus was speaking in terms of physical life, and took this appeal as confirmation that he was mad, or *demon-possessed* (**8:52**). After all, Abraham, their greatest ancestor, had died. So had the prophets, who were God's appointed messengers (8:52). Jesus could be greater than Abraham and he would also die (**8:53**). So how could he dare to say that those who keep his word will not die?

Jesus reminded them again that it is the Father (whom the Jews say is their God) who glorifies him (**8:54**). Thus their insults to Jesus were insults to God. If Jesus were to deny that he knows the Father in a special way, he would be telling a lie (**8:55**). Moreover, Abraham has given total approval to Jesus' ministry. One who gives joy to Abraham cannot be demon possessed (**8:56**).

This claim provoked even more scorn: *You are not yet fifty years old and you have seen Abraham!* (**8:57**). Abraham had lived hundreds of years earlier. Jesus responded by insisting that he was even older than Abraham (**8:58**). The Jews were thinking only in terms of his human existence, which began in Bethlehem in 4 BC, but Jesus was referring to his eternal existence.

The Jews took Jesus' words as an insult to Abraham, their greatest ancestor. Not only did Jesus present himself as equal to Abraham, but he claimed to be older than Abraham! Such an insult should be punished by death (**8:59**). But Jesus slipped away from them, for it was not yet time for him to die.

9:1-41 Jesus Heals a Man Blind from Birth

9:1-12 The healing

Jesus did not go into hiding after the Jews' attempt to stone him (8:59). He went about his business in Jerusalem, and as he *went along* he encountered a man who had been blind since birth (**9:1**).

The Jews believed that every form of suffering was due to sin. So the disciples asked Jesus, *Rabbi, who sinned, this man or his parents, that he was born blind?* (**9:2**). Were his parents being punished for some sin by having a blind son? Or was the man himself being punished for some sin he had committed before he was even born, while still in his mother's womb or maybe in some pre-existent state before his soul joined his body?

Jesus rejected both options: *This happened so that the work of God might be displayed in his life* (**9:3**). After reminding them that he was the light of the world and that there was still work to be done (**9:4-5**; see also 8:12), he proceeded to heal the blind man by spitting on the ground, making some mud with the saliva, putting mud on the man's eyes, and instructing him to go and wash in the pool of Siloam. The man obeyed and received his sight (**9:6-7**). Jesus combined both a miraculous act and a therapeutic touch. The healing required both Jesus' instructions and the man's obedience, for it was not the washing in the pool of Siloam but Jesus who healed the man, yet if he had refused to wash, he would not have been healed.

The man's neighbours and others who knew him were puzzled. Was this really the same man who used to sit and beg? (**9:8**). The change was so great that some doubted his identity. But he *insisted, 'I am the man'* (**9:9**). So they wanted to know, *How then were your eyes opened?* (**9:10**).

The man described what Jesus had said and done. He had only been able to feel what Jesus did, not see it, which is likely why he did not mention the spitting. He had felt Jesus put mud on his eyes. He had heard his voice telling him to go to the pool of Siloam. He had found that he could see after he obeyed Jesus' words. The man simply reported what he had experienced (**9:11**).

Not surprisingly, the neighbours wanted to meet the one responsible for this remarkable healing and asked, *Where is this man?* (**9:12**). But the healed man could not tell them, for after instructing him to go and wash in the pool of Siloam, Jesus did not stand around to wait for him. He went on with his business.

9:13-34 The Pharisees interrogate the healed man

Instead of rejoicing with the healed man, the neighbours focused on the fact that this healing had taken place on a Sabbath (**9:14**). Because they did not have authority to act in regard to this, they took the man to the Pharisees (**9:13**). Although the Pharisees had probably heard the whole story from the man's neighbours, they wanted to hear it for themselves too. They asked him how he had been healed, and he told them (**9:15**).

After hearing his testimony, the Pharisees were divided about how to react. Some focused on the issue of the Sabbath and argued that Jesus could not have come from God because if he had, he would keep the Sabbath. Others focused on the miraculous sign and argued that the healing itself was an indication that he came from God. God would not give a sinner the power to do something like this (**9:16**).

After arguing for some time, they decided to ask the blind man's opinion. Their question to him may have been an honest request for his opinion or it may have been a trap to find out what he thought so that they could deal with him later. The man had no hesitation in declaring, *He is a prophet* (**9:17**), that is, someone who delivers God's message.

In order to eliminate any possibility of mistaken identity, the parents were brought in (**9:18-19**). They were asked to confirm that there had genuinely been a healing and state how it took place. They could confirm that the man was indeed their son and that he had been born blind (**9:20**). As to how he could now see, they simply said, *We don't know* (**9:21**). John tells us that the parents were lying (**9:23**). Their son must have told them that Jesus had healed him, but they were afraid because they knew that Jesus was unpopular with the authorities (**9:22**). They did not want to be put out of the synagogue, the place of worship and the only place, they thought, where one could receive God's blessings.

Seeing that they were getting nowhere with the parents, the Pharisees again asked the man what he had to say about Jesus. The first time they had asked him this question, they had used an open question that gave him the freedom to express his own opinion (9:17). But this time they simply made a statement: *Give God the glory, we know this man is a sinner* (**9:24**). They were implying that the only position that gave God the glory was the one they had taken. Giving Jesus credit for the healing would be equivalent to approving of his breaking of the Sabbath law. Thus the man must be wrong in saying that Jesus was a prophet (9:17).

The man did not know all the theological arguments about the Sabbath and about whether or not it was a sin to heal on the Sabbath. So he replied, *Whether he is a sinner or not, I don't know* (**9:25a**). He would have known that it was a sin to violate a Sabbath regulation for any reason not specifically approved by the Sanhedrin (such as the need to circumcise a boy on the eighth day after his birth, even if this was a Sabbath). But whether God would cooperate with a sinner to bring healing on the Sabbath was an unanswered question. There was, however, one thing that he was sure of, the thing that mattered most to him: *I was blind but now I see* (**9:25b**). He had no doubt whatever about that.

The Pharisees, probably sensing that the man was being evasive and not simply agreeing with them, asked him their last and deciding question: *What did he do to you? How did he open your eyes?* (**9:26**). They probably wanted to extract a list of the exact things Jesus had done that violated the Sabbath law.

The man refused to repeat himself because clearly they were not willing to accept his evidence. He would, however, be prepared to do so if they had a good reason for asking, such as wanting to become Jesus' disciples. But it is clear from the way he phrased his question in **9:27** that he expected their answer to be 'no'.

The man was not only sure of himself but also a threat to the Pharisees' authority. How dared he joke about them becoming disciples of Jesus! They decided to put him firmly in his place. He might be a disciple of *this fellow* (Jesus),

but they were Moses' disciples (**9:28**). They implied that the man was not a proper Jew and was separated from God. This point emerges even more clearly in their next words: *We know that God spoke to Moses, but for this fellow, we don't even know where he comes from* (**9:29**). Moses was the great prophet God had appointed to speak for him. Jesus was an unknown.

The man responded to this attack with a carefully reasoned argument. Jesus had opened his eyes (**9:30**). That was a miracle. No one had ever heard of anything like it. One who could do this could not be a 'nobody'. Then he stated the universal Jewish belief: *We know that God does not listen to sinners. He listens to the godly man who does his will* (**9:31-32**). This demolished their argument that Jesus was a sinner. Finally, the man drew the logical conclusion: *If this man were not from God, he could do nothing* (**9:33**). In other words, since the power to do miracles is derived from God, this man, like Moses, must come from God.

The man's logic could not be faulted, and the Pharisees knew it. But logic would not convince them. Instead they reacted with self-righteous anger: *You were steeped in sin at birth; how dare you lecture us?* (**9:34a**). Like the disciples (see 9:1), the Pharisees believed that either this man's own sin or his parents' sin dated from before his birth, since he had been born blind. The Pharisees had no such physical disabilities. The fact that their eyes and their bodies were healthy was proof, they thought, that God approved of them. So was the fact that they took pains to keep the Sabbath and to obey all the other regulations of the law. How dared this sinner try to teach them anything!

They covered up the weakness of their argument with a show of authority, throwing the man out (**9:34b**). In other words, they excommunicated him from the synagogue and in so doing separated him from God, at least in their own minds. But as the Akamba (Kenya) say, *kiumo kya nguku kiikwataa mbolosya* ['the hen's curse does not affect the hawk']. Their excommunication did not remove this man from God's presence, as the next section shows.

9:35-41 Blindness of the spirit

When Jesus heard what had happened to the man (**9:35a**), he went out of his way to find him. This man not only needed encouragement in the present but also establishment in the faith already at work in his life.

Jesus asked the man, *Do you believe in the Son of Man?* (**9:35b**). He had already confidently asserted that Jesus was from God. He now needed to go beyond believing in the facts to believe in the person, that is, the Son of Man.

The man replied with a question, *Who is he sir? Tell me so that I may believe in him* (**9:36**). He may have heard of Jesus or heard his voice, but he had been blind when they first met and could not recognize him when he saw him. So Jesus identified himself (**9:37**). The man now had no hesitation in answering Jesus' question, saying, *Lord, I believe* (**9:38a**).

In 9:36, he had addressed Jesus as 'Lord', using the title as a term of respect, which is why the NIV translates it as 'sir'. Now he again uses the same Greek word, but this time with a sense of worship. Jesus is not just someone to be respected but someone to be worshipped (**9:38b**). The man had been thrown out of the synagogue, the place of worship, but now he is face to face with the object of worship himself.

Some Pharisees were watching what happened (**9:40a**). They may not have been from the group that interrogated the man, but may have been others who were curious about Jesus. Jesus said in their hearing and for their benefit, *For judgment I have come into this world, so that the blind will see and those who see will become blind* (**9:39**). In saying this, Jesus was relating the physical healing to the spiritual realm. The man who had been physically blind had become a believer, for his spiritual eyes had also been opened. On the other hand, the Pharisees could see physically but were spiritually blind. They could not recognize that Jesus the man was also the unique Saviour, Jesus Christ.

The Pharisees were shocked at Jesus' words. Their question, *What? Are we blind too?* (**9:40b**) anticipated the answer 'no'. They were convinced that they were not blind. They knew the Scriptures. They knew God. They belonged to the chosen nation. How could they be described as blind?

Jesus responded, *If you were blind, you would not be guilty of sin; but since now that you claim you can see, your guilt remains* (**9:41**). They were not blind, or rather, they did not recognize their own blindness. If they had recognized it, they would have seen the need to believe in Jesus, the light of the world (8:12). Believing in him would have rendered them *not guilty of sin*. However, their claim to see kept them from coming to Jesus, and so they were still living in sin.

While the guilt of which Jesus speaks here applies to sin in general, in the case of these Pharisees it applied particularly to their sin of wanting to kill Jesus. They were not following Jesus because they loved him but because he was a threat to their own security. Though divided among themselves, the Pharisees in general were looking for some specific charge that they could use to justify killing him.

10:1-21 Jesus, the Good Shepherd, and His Flock

Here Jesus is still talking to the same group of Pharisees as at the end of chapter nine. Using images from everyday life, he talks about his being the gate for the sheep (10:1-9) and the Good Shepherd (10:10-21)

The use of a gate was what differentiated a shepherd from a thief. If someone was greeted by the watchman at the gate as he went into the sheepfold, people would know that he was the shepherd or owner of some sheep within that fold. But someone trying to avoid being seen by climbing in over the fence would be recognized as a thief (**10:1-3a**).

The behaviour of the sheep at the gate would also make it clear whether they were being cared for by a shepherd or stolen by an enemy. If the sheep came out peacefully following a shepherd, they were his flock and familiar with his voice. But if the sheep were frightened and running away from the person trying to lead them, he was a stranger and probably a thief (**10:3b-5**).

Jesus now utters his second 'I am' statement (**10:7**, 9 – the first was in 6:35). He describes himself as *the gate for the sheep*, protecting the sheep from the thieves and robbers (self-claimed messiahs) who were before him (**10:8**). By describing himself as the gate, he is promising his hearers three things:

- **Salvation.** Anyone entering into God's presence through him *will be saved* (**10:9a**).
- **Safety.** The shepherd would protect the sheep as they grazed and as they returned to the fold (**10:9b**). In the same way, those who enter God's presence through Jesus will come in and go out with God as their protector wherever they are.
- **Satisfaction.** Jesus had earlier told the Samaritan woman of the satisfaction provided by the water he gives (4:14). He had also spoken of the satisfying bread he provides (6:35). Here he promises that those who enter through him will find pasture (10:9b), that is, food that satisfies their every spiritual need.

He asks his hearers to contrast the life he offers with that offered by the thieves and robbers mentioned in 10:8. Their only motive was theft (**10:10**). Robbers may kill an animal so that they can remove it more easily, and willingly leave young ones without their mother.

In speaking of himself as the gate, Jesus has already spoken of himself as having some of the shepherd's responsibilities, and so it is no surprise when he makes his third 'I am' claim, *I am the good shepherd* (**10:11a; 10:14a**). As the shepherd, he contrasts himself not just with robbers but with hired hands.

A hired hand may have slightly more concern for the sheep than a thief does, but his concern comes nowhere near that of a shepherd. Sheep in Palestine were vulnerable to attack by hyenas, jackals, wolves and bears. Of these, the wolf was the most dangerous. Thus when a hired hand sees a wolf coming, he *abandons the sheep and runs away* to preserve his own skin (**10:12**). The sheep are not his, and no matter how much he knows about them, he will not have the same commitment to them that the shepherd (owner) has. He will not suffer personal loss if some sheep are killed.

By contrast, Jesus is 'the good shepherd'. He is not just one good shepherd among a host of others, he is *the* good shepherd. The Greek word here translated 'good' also suggests that he is both effective and gracious. He cares for the sheep with love, and knows them well. He can say, *I know my sheep and my sheep know me* (**10:14**). As the good shepherd he knows the needs and nature of each sheep in his flock. Each sheep, likewise, can recognize that he is its shepherd. Jesus knows the hearts of all men and women and is able to address the needs of each of them, and his sheep recognize him as the one sent from above.

Jesus speaks of two specific actions he will take for his sheep. The first is that as the good shepherd he *lays down his life for the sheep* (**10:11b; 10:15**). Though Jesus' death was still in the future when he said these words, it was so certain that he spoke of it in the present tense. Moreover, his entire life, from his incarnation to his death, was in fact a laying down of his life for others.

Jesus' second action is to bring in the *other sheep* so that *there shall be one flock* (**10:16**). His mission went beyond the Jews to include the Gentiles. This part of his mission was continued by his disciples, who began their ministry in Jerusalem (Acts 2), then went to preach in Samaria (Acts 8; see also John 4), then reached Gentiles in Caesarea (Acts 10) before reaching what, in Jewish terms, was the ends of the earth, Rome (Acts 28). They preached the message of Christ crucified and Christ raised from the dead and achieved Jesus' goal of bringing Jews, Samaritans and Gentiles into one flock under one Shepherd.

Jesus stressed that he is not alone in his mission of being the good shepherd. The Father is involved in it from start to finish. In fact the intimate relationship between Jesus and the Father is the pattern for the relationship between the shepherd and his sheep (10:15). This relationship is characterized by love (**10:17**) and obedience (**10:18b**).

Jesus' mission will end in death, but that does not mean that his opponents will have won. He willingly lays down his life and has the *authority to lay it down and authority to take it up again* (**10:18a**). He knew about Judas Iscariot's scheming. The Jews who shouted 'crucify him' to Pilate were not really in control, nor were the Romans. Jesus allowed himself to endure humiliation in obedience to the Father. He laid down his life in the place of his sheep and took it up again to live for ever as the sheep's good shepherd.

Jesus' words again sparked division (**10:19**). Some were contemptuous, saying Jesus was demon possessed (**10:20**), while others were inclined to believe him because of the healings he had done (**10:21**).

10:22-42 Jesus, a Safe Shelter for the Sheep

Solomon's Colonnade was located in the court of the Gentiles and frequented by many people. John tells us that as Jesus was walking there, the Jews gathered around him saying, *How long will you keep us in suspense? If you are the Christ, tell us plainly* (**10:23-24**).

Jesus responded to this impatient request by insisting that he had already answered their question many times, but that they were not prepared to listen to his answer. They had heard him teach but they remained unbelieving (**10:25**). This proved that they were not among his sheep (**10:26**). These sheep are defined as those who *listen to my voice,* so that Jesus can say, *I know them, and they follow me*

(**10:27**). 'Listening' here includes both hearing with one's ears and responding in obedience from one's heart.

Those who are his sheep benefit by having him as their safe shelter. They experience absolute security, as Jesus gives them *eternal life.* They all experience this eternal life as soon as they believe. It is something they have now, not something they hope for in the future. Thus even though they may go through hard times, and even die, *they shall never perish.* Thieves, hyenas, wolves, jackals and bears may attempt to snatch the sheep Jesus is shepherding, but *no one can snatch them out of my hand* (**10:28**). Trials of all kinds may come, but there is victory when the believer is in Jesus' protection.

Jesus can guarantee this security because *My Father, who has given them to me is greater than all* (**10:29**). To snatch the sheep from Jesus, one would also need to snatch them from the Father, which is impossible because he is above all. More than that, the Father has 'given' the sheep to Jesus (see also 6:37, 44) and he and Jesus *are one* (**10:30**). The Father and Jesus are one in purpose and operation.

The Jews recognized that when Jesus talked of his oneness with the Father, he was claiming equality with him (10:33). Consequently they attempted to stone him (**10:31**), just as they had attempted to do when he claimed seniority to Abraham (8:58-59).

Jesus' question, *I showed you many good works from the Father; for which of them are you stoning me?* (**10:32**), does not show that he failed to understand why they were stoning him. He knows what is in people's hearts (see 2:25). Rather, he was trying to get them to evaluate fairly what he had done and to remember that in Jerusalem itself, where they now were, those he had healed included a man who had been sick for thirty-eight years (ch. 5) and a man who had been blind since birth (ch. 9).

The Jews' response, *We are not stoning you for any of these, but for blasphemy, because you, a mere man, claim to be God* (**10:33**), reveals that they still viewed Jesus as the carpenter's son from Nazareth.

Jesus responded with an argument that we find puzzling. When we read it, we need to remember that these words are part of a particular argument, and are not his final statement about who he is. He pointed out that the Jews were not being fair in their judgment and that his works backed his claims. He also pointed out that in Psalm 82:6, God himself referred to judges as 'gods' because they were supposed to be his representatives to administer justice here on earth (even though the psalm shows that some of them were unjust) (**10:34**). Jesus knew the Jews were not angry with God for calling the judges 'gods' but accepted the statement because it was in Scripture (**10:35**). Jesus, however, is greater than the judges, for he is *the one the Father set apart as his very own and sent into the world* (**10:36**). Should he not be entitled to claim that he is *God's Son?* Accusing Jesus (who is greater than the judges) of blasphemy for claiming to be 'God's Son' when the judges were called 'gods' was unfair.

Jesus wanted the Jews to understand his intimate relationship with the Father and to accept him and be saved. He realized that his words alone might not be enough to convince them, but should because his words were backed up by his miracles (**10:37-38**). His hearers recognized that Jesus' deeds were beyond what a mere human being could do (see 9:16, 32; 10:21) and their questioning of the man born blind (9:15, 17, 24-25) should have convinced them that he was not a fraud.

The Jews did not listen to Jesus' arguments. Again they attempted to seize him, and again he *eluded their grasp* (**10:39**; see also 7:44; 8:59). He then left Jerusalem and went *beyond the Jordan,* returning to the place *where John was first baptizing* (**10:40**), probably the place where he himself was baptized (see 1:28; Matt 3:5-17; Mark 1:9-11). Jesus may have chosen to end his public ministry at the very place he started it. While there, *many came to him* (**10:41**) and *many believed* (**10:42**). It is quite possible that these were people who had wanted to believe all along, but who had been afraid to do so in Jerusalem because of the unbelieving leaders.

11:1-44 Jesus Raises Lazarus From the Dead

While Jesus was across the Jordan, a man called Lazarus who lived about eighteen miles (thirty kilometres) away in Bethany near Jerusalem became sick (**11:1**). Lazarus' sisters, Martha and Mary, sent a message to Jesus: *Lord, the one you love is sick* (**11:3**). This message was a polite request for him to come and heal Lazarus. The sisters must have known about the healings Jesus had done in Jerusalem, which was less than three kilometres from Bethany (**11:18**) and in Galilee. They were confident that he would come, for they knew him well and *Jesus loved Martha and her sister and Lazarus* (**11:5**). Later, Jesus refers to Lazarus as *our friend* (11:11). (The famous incident mentioned in 11:2, however, took place later, and is recorded in 12:3.)

Jesus recognized that this sickness would *not end in death* but would bring glory to God and to his Son (**11:4**). But this glory would only be achieved if Lazarus actually died, not if he was simply another sick man whom Jesus healed. So Jesus stayed where he was for two days after receiving the message (**11:6**). Then he told his disciples that he was returning to Judea (**11:7**).

The disciples thought that this would be too risky, for the Jews there had tried to stone Jesus (**11:8**; see also 10:31). Jesus reminded his disciples that his time for his death had not yet come. It was still daylight, and he could walk safely (**11:9-10**). The timetable of his life was not in the hands of his enemies.

Jesus then told the disciples why they had to go to Judea: *Our friend Lazarus has fallen asleep; but I am going there to wake him up* (**11:11**). Jesus here talks of death as

sleep because resurrection was on the way. The rest of the NT uses the same image for those who die in Christ. Their death is only a sleep (see 1 Cor 15:6, 18; 1 Thess 4:13, 15; 2 Pet 3:4).

The disciples misunderstood Jesus and thought that Lazarus had fallen into a healing, natural sleep and so they argued against the journey (**11:12-13**). So Jesus told them plainly, *Lazarus is dead,* and explained that what was about to happen would teach them more about who Jesus was (**11:14-15**).

One of the disciples arguing with Jesus here was Thomas. Like the others, he expected the worst, but he urged his fellow disciples to stick with Jesus (**11:16**).

By the time they arrived in Bethany, *Lazarus had already been in the tomb for four days* (**11:17**). There was a common belief that the soul remained near the body for three days after death, hoping for an opportunity to return. But after that it left for good, leaving the person irrevocably dead. Lazarus would have been known by all to be truly dead.

On his arrival, Jesus was met by Martha, whose first words were, *Lord, if you had been here, my brother would not have died* (**11:20-21**). These were exactly the same words spoken by Mary later (11:32). The statement probably echoes words the sisters had said to each other again and again, first as they waited for Jesus to come and then as they mourned their brother's death.

Martha's faith had not been shaken, for she also said, *I know that even now God will give you whatever you ask* (**11:22**). The 'whatever' in her statement does not seem to have included the resurrection of Lazarus. She was likely thinking in terms of everyday life, not of a movement from death to life. So when Jesus assured Martha that her brother would rise again (**11:23**), she replied, *I know he will rise again in the resurrection at the last day* (**11:24**).

Jesus then made his fourth 'I am' saying in John (see also 6:35; 10:7;10:11): *I am the resurrection and the life. He who believes in me will live, even though he dies; and whoever lives and believes in me will never die* (**11:25-26**). He then asked Martha, *Do you believe this?* (11:26b), and she replied, *Yes, Lord. I believe that you are the Christ, the Son of God who was to come into the world* (**11:27**). Her answer was a good one, but she did not fully recognize what Jesus had just said. He was not asking Martha who he was, but what she believed about his ability to deal with her situation. He was stating that he had authority over life and over death.

Martha then took a message to Mary, *The Teacher is here and is asking for you* (**11:28**). Mary's interaction with Jesus was similar to Martha, except that this time there were more people present. The people who had been comforting Mary had followed her, thinking she was going to the tomb to mourn (**11:29-31**).

Mary was weeping. So were the Jews who followed her. Seeing their grief, Jesus was *deeply moved in spirit and troubled* (**11:33**) and he, too, wept (11:35). He did not weep because the situation was hopeless, for he knew that he would raise Lazarus from the dead. He did so because he shares the emotions of those he loves.

The mourners accompanying Mary noted Jesus' love for Lazarus (**11:36**). Like the sisters, they also remembered the healing of the man born blind and wondered why Jesus had not healed Lazarus (**11:37**).

Jesus had met the sisters outside the village (11:20, 30) and now he asked to be taken to the tomb (**11:34-35**). Everyone assumed that this was just a gesture of respect for the dead man. But when he came to the tomb, Jesus instructed them, *Take away the stone* (11:39). This was easy to do, since the tomb was simply a cave with a stone rolled across the entrance (**11:38**). However, there was an obstacle, and Martha expressed it: *But, Lord, by this time there is a bad odour, for he has been there four days* (**11:39**).

Jesus gently reminded Martha, *Did I not tell you that if you believed, you would see the glory of God?* (**11:40**). We have no record of his saying these exact words to Martha before, but they do summarize what Jesus had said in 11:25. Believing that Jesus is the resurrection and the life and acting accordingly will lead to actions that bring glory to God. With this reminder, Martha stands aside and allows the grave to be opened (**11:41a**).

Jesus now turned from talking to the sisters and the Jews to talking to the Father. He started by thanking God for hearing his prayer (**11:41b**). Though Lazarus had not yet been raised, his resurrection was so certain that Jesus treated it as already done. He had confidence that his Father would always hear him, because he never asked for anything outside the will of the Father (**11:42a**). Their will was one. Jesus was certain that God wanted him to raise Lazarus. He then stated the purpose for this public prayer: *for the benefit of the people standing here, that they may believe that you sent me* (**11:42b**). Jesus could have raised Lazarus without more ado, but he wanted those watching to realize that he did not operate independently. The Jews were divided over Jesus' origin and his relationship with the Father (see, for example, 9:16; 10:19-21). So he wanted Lazarus' resurrection to show the whole crowd that he was sent from the Father. They had heard Jesus' words; now they needed to be drawn into his sheepfold by believing in him.

After his prayer, Jesus shouted, *Lazarus, come out!* (**11:43**). The shout was not for Lazarus' benefit. He was dead and could hear nothing. Jesus could have raised him with a whisper. But Jesus wanted the living ones standing there to hear the resurrection words and the call to move from the sphere of death into the sphere of life. John, who was there, remembers that *the dead man came out* and Jesus told them to *take off the grave clothes and let him go* (**11:44**). Lazarus was alive and free from the sickness that had killed him. We meet him again in 12:2. Truly, Jesus is the resurrection and the life.

11:45-57 Jesus under Threat of Death

Though many of the Jews who witnessed Lazarus' resurrection put their faith in Jesus (**11:45**), others went to the Pharisees and told them what Jesus had done (**11:46**). This led to the Pharisees calling an urgent meeting of the Sanhedrin at which the main topic of discussion was *What are we accomplishing?* (**11:47**). The NIV translation presents the Pharisees as blaming themselves for allowing Jesus to continue to move about freely. However, the phrase can also be translated as meaning, 'What shall we do because this man is continually doing miraculous signs?' In other words, 'How can we stop him?' This translation emphasizes their perplexity. They knew that they should do something, but they did not know what.

They had already tried to capture Jesus. During the Feast of Tabernacles they had unsuccessfully sent guards to arrest him (7:32). They had tried to trick him with the woman caught in adultery, but he had been too clever for them (7:53-8:11). Their representatives had tried to stone Jesus, but he had slipped away from them (8:59). The same thing had happened when the Jews tried to seize Jesus (10:39).

Jesus' growing popularity with the common people also made it difficult for the Sanhedrin to arrest him (see 7:44; Matt 21:46; Luke 20:19). The more Jesus' popularity grew, the more that of the Jewish leaders declined. Jesus had the potential to have everyone believing in him (**11:48a**). Soon the Romans might start to think that the Sanhedrin had lost control, and then they *will come and take away both our place and our nation* (**11:48b**). By this they meant their position of leadership and the nation (Judea) that they led. At this time, Tiberius (AD 14-37) was emperor and Pontius Pilate (AD 26-36) was the procurator over Judea. So long as order was maintained, the Sanhedrin was allowed to control Jewish domestic affairs. Its function was to examine matters in the light of Jewish religious law. Anxious to avoid any threat to their position, they felt that they needed more vigorous action.

Caiaphas (AD 19-37) was the high priest and chairman of the Sanhedrin, though his father-in-law, Annas, from whom he had taken over the office, was still very powerful (**11:49**). Caiaphas advised the council: *It is better for you that one man die for the people than that our nation perish* (**11:50**). His advice focused on the interests of the council members. If the nation perished, the council would have no one to exercise authority over. But Jesus was only one man. They could handle whatever crisis his death might bring. For the sake of self-interest, the innocence of Jesus and true justice were thrown out the window. Caiaphas' motion was seconded, voted on and passed: *So from that day on they plotted to take his life* (11:53).

Though Caiaphas was speaking only in terms of his own political self-interest, God used him to express one of the central truths about the death of Christ. Jesus would indeed 'die for the people' (11:50), and not only for the Jewish people *but also for the scattered children of God, to bring them together and make them one* (**11:51-53**). Christ died in the place of and for the benefit of sinners. By his death and on the basis of their faith in him, he brought all the scattered and lost sheep into one fold.

Jesus had faced such plots before. Until the right time came, the Sanhedrin's plots would fail. In the past he had strategically slipped away (8:59; 10:39) or stayed away from the region of greatest danger (4:2; 10:40), and he did the same now, *withdrawing to a region near the desert, to a village called Ephraim, where he stayed with his disciples* (**11:54**). If this village is the one mentioned in 2 Chronicles 13:19, it was located in the mountainous country some fourteen miles (twenty-two kilometres) north of Jerusalem. Here it would be more difficult, humanly speaking, for the authorities to seize him and so Jesus remained there with his disciples until his own appointed time (11:54).

The Jewish Passover was approaching (**11:55**) and many people would go from the country to Jerusalem for a week of ceremonial cleansing before the Passover. During this week, many of them were hoping to see Jesus, who had become an important public figure. As they stood around the temple area, they were discussing whether Jesus was likely to attend this feast (**11:56**). On the one hand, they would be happy to see or hear him, and they knew that Jesus loved teaching such crowds. On the other hand, they knew the authorities' attitude to him and that he was a hunted man. Would he be brave enough to come to the feast?

The chief priests and Pharisees were also working on a strategy to arrest Jesus. They knew that he would probably come to Jerusalem for the Passover or would be somewhere in the vicinity. They, therefore, ordered that *if anyone found out where Jesus was, he should report it so that they might arrest him* (**11:57**). This was not merely a request for assistance; it was an order from the supreme court of the day. They hoped that such total mobilization of the people would work. However, it was not their strategy but God's timing that mattered.

12:1-11 Jesus Anointed by Mary

Six days before the Passover, Jesus returned to Bethany where he had raised Lazarus (**12:1**). It was less than two miles (three kilometres) from Jerusalem and so was in the danger zone for Jesus. A dinner was given in Jesus' honour, at which Martha served and Lazarus and others ate with Jesus (**12:2**). It must have been a wonderful time of fellowship. But Mary had a unique contribution to make.

The last time Jesus was at Bethany, Mary had fallen at his feet and cried, *Lord, if you had been here, my brother would not have died* (11:32). Even then she had honoured him as her Lord. Now she expressed her love and gratitude by taking *about a pint* (500 millimetres) *of pure nard* (an expensive

perfume), pouring it on Jesus' feet and wiping his feet with her hair (**12:3**). The oil she used was worth almost *a year's wages*, for Judas valued it at three hundred denarii, and one denarius was a day's wage for a labourer (12:5b). Her use of it showed how precious her Lord was to her. The fact that she poured it on Jesus' feet to clean them showed what humble service she was willing to offer. In Jewish practice, it was slaves, never disciples, who washed guests' feet with water. Finally, her use of her hair to wipe Jesus' feet showed that she did not care what others thought of her so long as she was serving her Lord. Many of those present would have been shocked that a respectable woman would let her hair hang loose in public!

Judas Iscariot objected to her actions, *Why wasn't this perfume sold and the money given to the poor?* (**12:4-5**). John tells us that Judas was not particularly concerned for the poor. He was, however, the treasurer for the disciples and used to help himself to the money given to them. In other words, he was a thief (**12:6**). As the Akamba say, *itho yikatonyeka yambiiaa kuia mana tene* ['an eye that will go blind starts shedding involuntary tears long before']. Judas was already showing his true colours.

Jesus told him to leave Mary alone, and then added, *It was intended that she should save this perfume for the day of my burial* (**12:7**). That day had come. He was heading for Jerusalem and death. Mary's act was, from her perspective, simply a way of telling her Lord how much she appreciated him. From God's perspective, however, her act marked the start of Jesus' passion. This was why Jesus said, *You always have the poor among you, but you will not always have me* (**12:8**). If Mary had not done the service then, she would never have had another opportunity. Jesus was on his way to the cross.

Jesus' presence at Bethany became widely known and many Jews came there (**12:9-10**). They wanted to see and hear Jesus and to see Lazarus whom he had raised from the dead. Someone who could do such a thing must be very important and powerful. Lazarus, too, had become a celebrity because of his resurrection.

The Sanhedrin had already resolved to kill Jesus (11:53), but now the chief priests planned to kill Lazarus as well (12:10). It is interesting to note that only the chief priests are mentioned here. They were from the Sadduccees' party, which did not believe in the resurrection, and the fact that Lazarus was alive contradicted their beliefs. But their primary motive for getting rid of Jesus was that *many of the Jews were going over to Jesus and putting their faith in him* (**12:11**). Lazarus was attracting others to Jesus.

12:12-19 Jesus' Triumphal Entry to Jerusalem

It was now five days before the Passover. Jesus had arrived at Bethany six days before the Passover and this event took place in Jerusalem the next day (**12:12**). It would not have taken long for news of his presence to cover the two miles (three kilometres) to Jerusalem.

As Jesus travelled toward Jerusalem, he was acknowledged by a crowd who greeted him with both deeds and words. The fact that they carried *palm branches* (**12:13a**) as they celebrated his arrival was significant, for there were only two contexts within which the Jews carried palm branches: at the Feast of Tabernacles (Lev 23:40) and at the celebration of the rededication of the temple in 164 BC after its pollution by Antiochus Epiphanes (1 Macc 13:50-51). Ever since that time, the palm seems to have been a symbol of Judea – equivalent to a national flag. Palm branches played no role in the Passover, so it seems likely that the people were thinking of the events in 164 BC, when the Maccabees' victory over the Syrians had been celebrated by waving branches of palm trees. Jesus was being welcomed as another liberator, one who would free them from the Romans. His raising of Lazarus had convinced them that he was powerful enough to lead them to victory against Rome. Thus they greeted him with palms and with shouts of *Hosanna*, which means 'save us, we beseech you' or 'give us salvation now' or 'give us victory now' (**12:13b**).

The crowd also shouted, *Blessed is he who comes in the name of the Lord!* (**12:13c**). They were acknowledging what Jesus had been claiming all along, namely, that he was sent from the Father. They certainly did not understand that he had been sent as a man to die in the place of humankind, but at least they recognized that the authority with which he taught and acted came from God.

Their final cry, *Blessed is the King of Israel* (**12:13d**), underscores their view that Jesus' mission was to rule Israel and that his immediate task was to win victory over the Romans. They were ready to follow him into battle.

The Jesus we have met in John so far does not take orders from other people (not from his mother – John 2:4, his brothers – John 7:6-8, or his friends – John 11:6-15). The Galileans had wanted to make him king (6:15) but he had slipped away from them. Now the people in Jerusalem (including Galileans who had come for the Feast) were again trying to declare him king, but he was not under their orders.

Had Jesus wanted to lead a *coup d'état*, he would have come riding into Jerusalem on a horse, a symbol of war. Instead, he entered Jerusalem riding a young donkey (**12:14**). He had come to die under the Romans, not to conquer them. His mission was mysterious: he showed himself to be a man of great power, but at the same time he submitted to insults, mistreatment and even death at the hands of unbelieving Jews and the representatives of Rome.

Jesus' entrance on a donkey was no accident but a fulfilment of Scripture (**12:15**; see Zech 9:9). After his glorification, the disciples realized that when they helped Jesus get the donkey (see Mark 11:2-7) they were participants in fulfilling Scripture written about 550 years before (**12:16**).

Meanwhile, those who had seen Jesus raise Lazarus continued to talk about it, and those who heard them longed to see Jesus. Hearing that he was coming to Jerusalem, they *went out to meet him* (**12:17-18**). As the news spread, more and more came to meet Jesus and his popularity grew. Clearly, the people were ignoring the order that anyone who found where Jesus was should tell the chief priests and Pharisees so they could arrest him (11:57). Instead, the people were hailing Jesus as their Messiah. No wonder the Pharisees said to one another, *See, this is getting us nowhere.* Their latest plan had failed, and the people were all for Jesus (**12:19**).

It was probably at this point that the Pharisees came up with the idea of using one of Jesus' disciples to help them arrest Jesus, for as the Akamba (Kenya) say, *muthianwa ni mutui ndavitaa* ['one spied on by a neighbour cannot get away']. The Pharisees could not arrest him on their own, for Jesus always slipped away. Relying on the people was not working either, because the people were for Jesus. Their best option might be to bribe one of the twelve men closest to him.

12:20-26 Some Greeks Seek Jesus

The Greeks referred to here were Gentile proselytes, who had come to Jerusalem *to worship at the Feast* (**12:20**). They had seen the welcome Jesus had received, and were interested in seeing this popular figure who was rumoured to have even raised the dead. Meanwhile, Jesus was with a crowd of Jews who had witnessed or heard of Lazarus' resurrection (12:17).

The Greeks approached Philip, who was from Bethsaida in Galilee (12:21). They may have chosen to speak to him because of his Greek name, Philip, which means 'lover of horses'. They said that they *would like to see Jesus* (**12:21**), meaning 'catch sight of him', without necessarily implying anything more than that.

Philip was uncertain about what to do about their request, and so he consulted Andrew, a fellow disciple. In their experience, Jesus had ministered only to Jews or their near relatives, the Samaritans. What would he think of the Greeks? Was their request sufficiently important to justify interrupting his teaching to the Jewish crowd? These were probably the sorts of issues that Philip was unsure about. Andrew seems to have advised Philip that it was best to let Jesus himself decide, and so *Andrew and Philip in turn told Jesus* (**12:22**).

While we are not told exactly how Jesus responded to the Greeks' request, we can assume that the words that follow were prompted by it. Their request gave Jesus an opportunity to teach his disciples, the Jews who were with him (12:17, 34) and probably the listening Greeks as well.

Jesus tells the crowd that his *hour has come* at last (**12:23**). At the beginning of his ministry, Jesus had told his mother, *my hour has not yet come* (2:4), referring to the time to publicly display his power. That hour came a little later, and for about three years Jesus did many miraculous signs. During those years all attempts to hurt or kill him were unsuccessful because his public ministry was not yet complete (see, for example, 8:20; 10:31, 39; 11:53, 57). Now, the hour for his passion has come. The remaining journey is to the cross.

The hour that has come will involve the glorification of the Son of Man (12:23). The Jews thought that this glorification would involve great earthly victories, particularly over the Romans. But Jesus knew that his glorification would come through death. To explain what he meant, he used the illustration of a grain of wheat. No matter how healthy that grain is, its glory lies in its death, for only as it dies will it produces a new plant with many seeds (12:24). If Christ does not die, there will be no Christ-like people. Salvation will only be possible by way of his death.

He goes on to contrast two people. One of them loves his or her life, and the other hates it, at least as far as this world is concerned (12:25). The one who chooses to cling to life inevitably loses it, but the one who hates his or her life gains eternal life. This is the opposite of what we would expect. We would assume that someone who loves life would protect it by having a good security system, eating a balanced diet, exercising regularly and taking other measures in order to stay healthy and secure. On the other hand, we would assume that someone who hates life will be careless about their personal security, what they eat and other dangers. Why do Jesus' words go contrary to common sense? It is because he is the life. Those who love their lives and so refuse to die with him will not see life proper. On the other hand, those who hate their lives and choose to die with Christ (that is, to die to self so that Christ can reign in them) gain eternal life. Even when they sleep in death, they await a resurrection, for their eternal life cannot be interrupted by death.

The ultimate reward for service is for those who follow Jesus and serve him. They will enjoy Jesus' presence and receive honour from the Father (12:26). Jesus makes it clear that the possibility of receiving the reward is open to anyone, including the very Greeks whose request to see Jesus prompted these words. Jews, Samaritans and Greeks are all welcome.

The only condition for receiving the reward is that one must be Jesus' servant, and such servanthood involves following Jesus. Merely seeing Jesus, as the Greeks requested, is not enough. One needs to deny oneself and earthly preoccupations (which is equivalent to hating life – 12:25) and follow Jesus. This 'following' is expressed in the present tense to indicate that it must be a habit. The following cannot be limited to special occasions such as the Feast of the Passover, but must take place all the time.

The two rewards (being with and being honoured by the Father) are expressed in the future tense. This is not because they will only happen in the next world, but because they will only happen after one has obeyed the call to follow and serve Jesus.

Jesus will appear, from a human perspective, to have been rejected, for death on the cross was for someone who had been cursed. Similarly, the one who is Jesus' servant will not receive honour from the world. However, just as the Father will honour the Son by raising him from the dead and giving him a name above all names (Phil 2:9), so also Jesus' servant will enjoy the praise of God. Mockery and even death will be opportunities for the Father to glorify Jesus' servants.

12:27-36 The Son of Man Must Be Lifted Up

Jesus was fully human, and as such he was afraid of the suffering and death that lay ahead in the 'hour' he had now entered. He did not hide this fact, but said, *Now, my heart is troubled* (12:27a) and pondered whether he should pray for salvation from the hour. While such salvation was what he wanted emotionally, he knew that he would be wrong to request it, for *it was for this very reason I came to this hour* (12:27b). Jesus' life had been lived in accordance with a divine timetable. There had been the hour when he became human, the hour when he began his public ministry, and now he faced the hour of his passion.

Surrendering himself to the divine timetable, Jesus prayed, *Father, glorify your name* (11:27c). What mattered most was not how he felt physically but what would glorify the Father's name. Was it death? If so, let it come.

The Father responded by speaking from heaven, *I have glorified it, and will glorify it again* (12:28). The glorifying that had already been done was everything the Son had submissively done since he took upon himself the role of becoming human in order to save men and women. In a sense, the Father is praising the Son for a job well done. The Father will also answer the Son's current prayer in which he has committed himself into the Father's hands. He will direct events in such a way that his name will be glorified yet again.

Jesus had been surrounded by a crowd ever since he left Bethany (12:17). They had given him a triumphal entry into the city as a nationalistic Messiah and they anticipated extraordinary happenings – although all along they failed to grasp Jesus' relationship with God. When the voice came from heaven, some mistook it for thunder and others said that an angel had spoken (12:29). Thunder might have been taken as extraordinary if there were no indications of stormy weather. And an angel speaking would be a mark that Jesus was the Messiah they expected. Whatever the case, the crowd probably took the sound as a sign of God's approval of Jesus leading them against the Romans.

Jesus, however, tells them *This voice was for your benefit, not mine* (12:30). As far as he is concerned this is not possibility of a retreat. The awful death on the cross has to be faced, for this is the eternal plan The crowd, however, has not yet grasped that Jesus is the eternal Son of God, who is sent from above. The Father's words to Jesus should have helped them realize this, but instead they attribute it to thunder or an angel.

Jesus now speaks more about what the hour means and *the kind of death he was going to die* (12:33). The approaching hour (that is, the hour of his death) means judgment on this world, that is, on the system that is opposed to Jesus, and ultimately to the Father who sent him. The judgment means that *the prince of this world will be driven out* (12:31). While Satan's complete removal will only take place in the future (Rev 20:10), his expulsion was begun on the cross where a limit was set to the time of his involvement in history. There Jesus opened the door of escape from the sphere in which Satan rules. What appear to be Satan's victories now (and many examples can be cited on the African continent and elsewhere) are only his struggles to survive. His final destiny is fixed.

The hour will end with Jesus being lifted up from the earth – first on a cross, and then in his resurrection – and then drawing all men to himself as a consequence of his resurrection (12:32).

The crowd welcomed Jesus as the Christ (that is, the Messiah). But now he is confusing them by talking about someone called 'the Son of Man', who it seems will die (12:23-24). He also interchanges the title 'son of Man' and the pronoun 'I'. The crowd has been taught that the Christ will live forever, so if Jesus is the Christ, as they believe, he will not die. Confused, they ask, *Who is the Son of Man?* (12:34).

Jesus does not answer their question. Instead he tells them to act by walking while they still have light and by putting their trust in the light while they have it. He warns them that the light will soon be gone (12:35-36). In only a few days, he will be arrested. It is time for them to respond to his teaching that brings light into their lives.

Jesus then left the crowd and *hid himself from them* (12:36). He did not do this because this crowd wanted to stone him, as earlier crowds had (see 8:59, 10:31) but rather because, like the Galileans in 6:15, they wanted Jesus to become their king and lead them against the Romans. This had been their hope when they flocked to see him at Bethany (12:9) and gave him a triumphal entry into Jerusalem. This crowd had not understood his talk of his death and its implication. So it was time for him to move on and complete his journey to the cross.

12:37-50 Jesus Finishes His Public Ministry

12:37-43 A summary of Jesus' public ministry

Jesus is about to end his public ministry and focus on his final instructions to his twelve disciples. Before he does so, John presents a brief report on the state of Jesus' mission.

The Jews had seen or heard of the many signs that Jesus had done in Judea and Galilee. John has not recorded all of these signs (see 20:30; also 2:23), but he has given details of seven of them: the changing of water into wine, the healing of a royal official's son, the healing of a man who had been sick for thirty-eight years, the feeding of more than five thousand people, the walking on water, the healing of the man who was born blind and the raising of Lazarus. Yet despite all these signs, the Jews as a group in general *still would not believe in him* (12:37). Their leaders and those who followed them rejected Jesus in spite of what they had heard and seen. Even those who admired Jesus and wanted him to be their nationalistic Messiah were not prepared to believe his message of a dying Son of Man.

This unbelief was not due to a lack of evidence but was a fulfilment of Isaiah's prophecy (12:38). John quotes from Isaiah 53:1, *Lord, who has believed our message and to whom has the arm of the Lord been revealed?* The answer to this rhetorical question is clearly meant to be 'no one', or at least very few. The Servant of Isaiah 53 suffered at the hands of men who should have known better, but who chose not to believe and rejected the Servant. Why did they do this? John gives the answer in words from Isaiah 6:10: *He has blinded their eyes and deadened their hearts, so that they can neither see with their eyes, nor understand with their hearts, nor turn – and I would heal them* (12:39-40). But what do these words mean?

Isaiah 6 contains the Lord's commission to Isaiah to 'go and tell this people' (Isa 6:9). The message he was to deliver was 'Be ever hearing, but never understanding; be ever seeing, but never perceiving.' The people to whom he was to speak were God's people, specifically those in the southern kingdom of Judah. They had become untrue to the Lord, and as a result were condemned (see Isa 1:4). God no longer referred to them as 'my people (as he had in Exod 3:7; Lev 26:12; Jer 11:4; 30:2). Instead he called them 'this people (Isa 6:9; see also Isa 9:16; 29:13). The Lord distanced himself from them because of their stubbornness.

The Lord told Isaiah what the result of his ministry would be: 'Make the heart of this people calloused, make their ears dull, and close their eyes.' Why? Lest they 'see with their eyes, hear with their ears, understand with their hearts and turn and be healed' (Isa 6:10). Isaiah's ministry would bring about a further hardening of people's hearts and greater insensitivity to the word of the Lord. John relates this pattern of ministry to what was happening in Jesus' time: *Isaiah said this because he saw Jesus' glory and spoke about him* (12:41).

Like the people of Judah to whom Isaiah ministered, the Jews of Jesus' time were the chosen people of God; they too had heard the Lord's message but had hardened their hearts – deliberately choosing not to believe. Just as Isaiah's ministry was to continue until the Lord brought the deserved judgment for the people's hardness of heart, so it was for Jesus. The Jews had persistently rejected Jesus' claims, ignored the evidence of his miraculous signs and even plotted to kill him. They faced judgment, and were at the stage where the divine ministry they were receiving blinded their eyes and deadened their hearts.

Yet even in the midst of the general unbelief, *many even among the leaders believed in him* (**12:42a**). But they *would not confess their faith for fear they would be put out of the synagogue* by the Pharisees (**12:42b**). To them, such excommunication implied being cut off from fellowship with God and with their fellow Jews. But they were wrong to think so. Believing in Jesus would mean believing in and receiving praise from the one who sent Jesus (that is, God). They were wrong to have preferred to remain in the Pharisees' good books rather than in God's (**12:43**).

12:44-50 Jesus' final plea to the Jews

Jesus' desire that no one should perish (2 Pet 3:9) seems to have led him to return briefly to make a final appeal to the crowd following his departure in 12:36. There he once again stressed that he and the one who sent him are one. Believing in Jesus is also believing in God who sent him (**12:44-45**). Seeing Jesus is the same as seeing the Father. It follows that rejection of Jesus is also rejection of God.

The reason Jesus had come was to be the light of the world (**12:46**; see also 8:12). Those who do not know him as Saviour live in darkness (3:20), separate from God who is himself light (Ps 27:1; 1 John 1:5). Jesus' mission was to provide everyone with a way out of darkness and into light. His prime concern was to save, not to judge (**12:47**). He will be our judge in the future, but the goal of his earthly ministry was to bring salvation, not judgment.

But Jesus' teaching about the salvation he offers in submission to the Father will inevitably be evidence against those who reject it (**12:48**). His words will judge the hearers on the *last day* when God will end human governments and will issue rewards and punishment. At that time no one will be left to do as he or she chooses (as the Jews had chosen to reject Jesus).

Jesus finished his public ministry with a reminder that he faithfully reports what the Father commanded him to say (**12:49-50**). Both his words and his actions were directed by the Father. What Jesus has said is the Father's message, without distortion. Rejection of Jesus' message is rejection of the Father's message. The goal of all his words and deeds has been to offer eternal life. A rejection of his message is thus a rejection of eternal life.

13:1-17:26 Jesus' Final Ministry to the Twelve

Chapters 13 to 16 present Jesus' final words to his twelve disciples before his crucifixion, and chapter 17 contains his prayer to the Father in their hearing. His disciples have been with him since he turned water into wine in Cana (ch.

2). They have seen his miracles and have listened to his teaching, and thus have a very good background for understanding what Jesus will now be saying to them. 'However, they still need to learn more'. But time would be short; Jesus' final ministry to the Twelve, his time of prayer and his subsequent trial, crucifixion, and burial took place within less than twenty-four hours. The events began on Thursday evening and ended during Friday afternoon.

13:1-20 Jesus Washes The Disciples' Feet

John does not tell us where Jesus washed his disciples' feet, but it is likely that it was in the upper room talked about in Mark 14:14-15 and Luke 22:10-12. He does tell us that it takes place *just before the Passover Feast* (**13:1a**). During this Passover, it was not only the Passover lamb that would die but also the eternal Lamb of God. Jesus knew that this was the hour of his death (**13:1b**). Around him were twelve men whom he had loved with special love, one of whom was going to betray him (**13:2**).

In light of his impending death, Jesus wanted to demonstrate *the full extent of his love* for these men (**13:1c**). He did this in a most dramatic way while the evening meal (his last supper) was being served. While fully aware of the greatness of his origins, his power and his destiny (**13:3**) Jesus humbly took on the role of a servant. He got up from the meal (**13:4a**) and took off his outer clothing (**13:4b**). Jewish men usually wore an inner tunic, an outer tunic or robe, and an outer garment or cloak. They normally removed the cloak when indoors, but kept the outer tunic on. What Jesus did was remove his outer tunic and strip down to his inner tunic. Then he wrapped a towel around his waist (**13:4c**). Dressed in this way, Jesus looked exactly like a slave, for this was standard dress for a slave.

Jesus then poured water into a basin (**13:5a**) and began to wash his disciples' feet and dry them with the towel that was wrapped around him (**13:5b**). Not only was he dressed like a slave, but he was doing the work of a slave. Washing feet was such a menial job that no teacher would expect his disciples to do it.

John focuses on what happened when Jesus came to Peter. Characteristically, Simon Peter went from one extreme (*you shall never wash my feet* – **13:8**) to the other (*not just my feet but my hands and my head as well* – **13:9**). At first he was telling Jesus, 'You are my master; I will never allow you to serve me as if you were my slave'. Then his meaning changed to, 'I want to be fully associated with you in every possible way.' Peter meant well, but the lesson Jesus was teaching here only required that he wash everyone's feet.

After Jesus had finished washing the disciples' feet, *he put on his clothes* and asked the disciples, *'Do you understand what I have done for you?* (**13:12**). They were right to call Jesus their Lord and Teacher (**13:13**). But as such, he should have received service from them. Instead, however, he had served them, doing the most humble of tasks.

He then gave a command that we all need to listen to again and again: *You also should wash one another's feet* (**13:14**). Such an act involves acknowledging that one is a slave or servant of the one whose feet are being washed. But no one person is to take the servant's role. They are to wash 'one another', indicating that everyone washes everyone else's feet. Jesus stresses that this is an obligation the disciples owe to each other, and his use of the present tense implies that it is an ongoing obligation, something to be done continually, not just once. And to forestall objections, he points out that he himself has already done this: *I have set you an example that you should do as I have done for you* (**13:15**). No one could logically argue that they would lose status if they washed others' feet if Jesus, their Master and Lord, had done the same (**13:16**). As servants, they were expected to imitate their Master. As disciples of Jesus, each of them would be both master and servant at the same time. Each would receive service and render it.

The concept of service to all, especially to those who are socially beneath one, is foreign to Africa. A chief serving his subjects would be unheard of. Yet that is what Jesus is asking us to do here. If our leaders in Africa would learn this lesson, it would take away more than half of the pain the African continent experiences from day to day.

The command to serve does not come without rewards: *You are blessed if you do these things* (**13:17**). God is the source of blessings. As we receive his blessings, we are happy because we are at peace with God and with ourselves, and this happiness affects our relationships with others.

But not all of those present with Jesus would enjoy this blessing, for one of them would refuse to serve or to acknowledge Jesus as Master and Lord. Jesus was referring to Judas Iscariot, without mentioning his name, when he said, *I am not referring to all of you; I know those I have chosen* (**13:18a**). Judas Iscariot was one of those Jesus had chosen (see Matt 10:1-4; Luke 6:12-16). Jesus knew the heart and motives of each of the twelve men he chose, and he knew that Judas would fulfil the Scripture *He who shares my bread has lifted up his heel against me* (**13:18b**), an expression that describes brutal violence. Jesus was quoting Psalm 41:9, where David spoke of a time when even his intimate friend abandoned him but the Lord delivered him.

Eating with someone, sharing their bread, was a sign of friendship. Judas Iscariot had travelled and eaten with Jesus for three years. He had heard his ministry and shared fellowship with friends such as Mary, Martha and Lazarus. But his heart had not been in it (see, for example, 12:5-6).

Judas was chosen in order to fulfil the Scripture that Jesus would be treated brutally by a group that included his own disciple. We may wonder where God's will ends and Judas' evil begins. In dealing with this issue, the first thing we need to remember is that John's primary point is that

Jesus' death was not an accident. This point is stressed in **13:19**. God's divine plan not only included Jesus' leaving heaven and dying as the God-man here on earth, but also the hour and manner in which he would die. Judas Iscariot was in God's programme. Yet it was not God who directed his actions, but Satan (13:2; see also Luke 22:3).

Judas is held accountable for betraying Jesus (see Matt 26:24; Mark 14:21; Luke 22:22). It seems that it is in the context of God's directive will that Judas was chosen to be a disciple and remained one for three years. However he betrayed Jesus within the context of God's permissive will, which allows evil but does not dictate it. Judas could have acted differently. He could have chosen to remain loyal to Jesus rather than obeying the prompting of the devil.

God knows what is going to happen, from beginning to end. Judas was chosen as one of the team of twelve to do exactly what he did – but not because God made him do it. He acted by his own choice, but God had known what that choice would be from all eternity.

Jesus had washed the disciples' feet, and they in turn will wash 'one another's' feet (13:14) and also the feet of those who will listen to their proclamation of the gospel and accept Jesus. Jesus will send the disciples to the nations. Whoever accepts them and allows them to wash his or her feet will be accepting Jesus who sends them (see 13:8). And whoever accepts Jesus accepts God who sent Jesus (**13:20**). A chain of service is thus set up, from God to Jesus to Jesus' disciples to those who will listen to their message and in turn proclaim it to others. No wonder Jesus told his disciples that they would enjoy God's blessing when they served one another (**13:17**).

13:21-29 Jesus Predicts That Judas Will Betray Him

After he had said this (**13:21**), meaning his warning that one of his disciples was not clean and had not accepted him as his Lord, *Jesus was troubled in spirit*. When he explained the cause of his unhappiness to the disciples, they were shocked (see **13:22**). How could he be betrayed by one who had known his kindness and love for three years?

Trying to resolve the tension between this unimaginable thing and the certainty with which Jesus said it, Peter asked the beloved disciple (believed to be John) to ask Jesus who he was talking about (**13:23-24**). Jesus' replied, *the one to whom I will give this piece of bread when I have dipped it in the dish* (**13:26a**). Even with this clear statement and Jesus' giving Judas the dipped bread (**13:26b**), no one at the table except Jesus and Judas understood all that was happening (**13:28**). When Jesus told Judas *what you are about to do, do quickly*, Judas knew exactly what he meant.

When John says that *as soon as Judas took the bread, Satan entered into him* (**13:27**), he is describing the course of events, not implying that taking the bread caused Satan to enter him. He is simply saying that not much time elapsed between his taking the bread and his coming under the control of Satan.

13:30-38 Jesus Predicts That Peter Will Deny Him

When Judas left (**13:30**) Jesus knew where he was going and what he was going to do. So he spoke of his imminent suffering and death as the glorification of the Son of Man, and through this, the glorification of God (**13:31–32**). Jesus then talked of his departure (**13:33**), the need for the disciples to fill the gap by loving one another in a new way – a way of service, and the witness that such love is to the world (**13:34-35**).

The talk of departure captured Peter's attention and so he asked, *Lord, where are you going*? (**13:36**). Jesus' reply again mentioned the impossibility of the disciples going there now (see also 13:33), but added the important information that *you will follow later*. Peter was not satisfied with waiting till later, and so he committed himself, *I will lay down my life for you* (**13:37**), only to have Jesus tell him *before the rooster crows, you will disown me three times!* (**13:38**). The emphasis here is not on Peter's weakness. In fact, the Lord does not discourage him from laying down his life for him. The focus is on the hardships of the route.

14:1-4 Jesus, the Source of Comfort

Jesus now reassured the disciples that they need not be troubled (**14:1**) – as they clearly already were. Satan would be happy to add to this troubling of the disciples' hearts once Jesus was out of the picture. He would bring doubts that could only be overcome by obedience: *trust in God, trust also in me* (14:1b). Their faith was to be based on what God was ready to do for them and on what Jesus had and was going to promise. Jesus' promise here is most comforting to troubled hearts: *In my Father's house are many rooms; if it were not so, I would have told you. I am going there to prepare a place for you* (**14:2**). Given the reliability of the owner of the house (the Father) and of the one preparing the rooms (Jesus), the disciples could be confident that there would be a place for each of them.

However, it is possible to have a room waiting for one but to fail to reach it because of the dangers on the way. Jesus assures his disciples that they do not need to worry about this, as he will come again and will himself escort them to their destination (**14:3**). To crown it all, Jesus and his disciples will again be together. Their present parting is only a temporary separation.

As Jesus reflects on Peter's question 'Where are you going? (13:36), he tells the disciples, *You know the way to the place where I am going* (**14:4**). Though they have not been there and they will not go there now (see 13:36), the way to the place is familiar.

14:5-14 Jesus the Way, Truth and Life

Thomas, however, was not convinced by Jesus' statement in 14:4 and protested, *Lord, we don't know where you are going, so how can we know the way?* (**14:5**). In reply, Jesus spoke of the destination of the journey and specified how to get there: *No one comes to the Father except through me* (**14:6b**). Here he makes specific what had only been implied in 13:36 and 14:2: the journey is to the Father. That is where Jesus is going, and that is where the disciples will follow later.

Jesus then tells them the way to reach the Father: *I am the way and the truth and the life* (**14:6a**). They will reach the Father by believing in Jesus. This is Jesus' sixth major *I am* saying (the earlier ones are in 6:35 and 6:51; 8:12 and 9:5; 10:7 and 9; 10:11 and 14; and 11:25). Jesus' words here make it very clear that all roads do not lead to Rome, no matter how often we are assured that this is the case. Not all roads lead to possession of eternal life. Jesus is the God-appointed way.

This statement raises the question of the destiny of our African ancestors who died before Christ was presented to them. When pondering this question, we need to remember that there is room in God's judgment plan for judging cases on the basis of people's response to general revelation (Rom 2:12-16). But it is also clear that no cases will be considered outside of Christ. He is God's Anointed and each individual's response to him, whether in the context of special or general revelation, will be central to the judgment. Those who have tried to please God, despite not having heard of Christ, will be accepted, for Jesus has been sent by God, and the one who pleases the Father has already passed the test of obeying the message of the Son.

Yet for most of us, the question of how God will judge those who have never heard the gospel does not arise. The issue for us is, What will we do with the Christ we have heard about? Will we choose life or death? Our decision about Jesus Christ will determine our fate.

Jesus finishes answering Thomas by pointing out that knowledge of Jesus amounts to knowledge of the Father (**14:7**). Philip, reflecting on what Jesus had just told them, asks, *Lord, show us the Father and that will be enough for us* (**14:8**). The word translated 'show' also means 'point out'. Philip wants Jesus to be specific. If he is, the disciples will stop asking questions and will not be troubled anymore.

In answering Philip's question, Jesus makes a key statement: *anyone who has seen me has seen the Father* (14:9). Philip has been with Jesus for three years now, and so Jesus asks him, *Don't you know me, Philip, even after I have been among you for such a long time? How can you say, 'Show us the Father?'* (**14:9**). Since Jesus has been with the disciples for such a long time, they should have no need to ask to be shown the Father. If they believe that Jesus is in the Father and the Father is in Jesus (**14:10**), then their need to see the Father has already been met. Having seen Jesus, they have seen the Father. Jesus' questions are not meant to make Philip feel bad, but to open his eyes to the implications of what he believes.

Jesus goes on to remind Philip and the other disciples of the two witnesses to his relationship with the Father, namely, his words and deeds (**14:11-12**). While it may seem more appropriate to believe in Jesus' words, because this shows faith in Jesus as a person, it is clear that miracles also have their place, especially in initially establishing that faith.

A consequence of Jesus and the Father being one is that whatever is asked of the Father is also asked of Jesus. The Father ultimately owns all things. Jesus, as Son, submits to him, but at the same time, he and the Father act as one. Anything asked from or given by the Father is also asked from or given by Jesus. Jesus thus becomes both the one to be asked for blessing (*ask me*) and the go-between who makes it easier to have requests granted (*in my name*) (**14:13b-14a**).

After Jesus has gone to the Father, those who have faith in him will be able to ask for anything from Jesus and in his name. Not only will believers receive whatever they ask for, they will also be able to do the same or even greater things than Jesus does, so that the Father will be glorified by what believers do. But we should note that our privilege of asking for anything is limited by the twice-repeated qualification, 'in my name' (14:13b, 14a). Asking for something in another person's name assumes that there is a close relationship between the one asking and the one in whose name it is asked. It also assumes that the thing asked for will be used to further the interests of the one whose name is used to get it. Jesus' words *I will do it* (**14:13a, 14b**) are a promise that believers will receive whatever they ask in this way.

Just as Jesus' deeds showed the Father at work (14:10), so the deeds of believers will show Jesus at work. The believers are, however, directly involved in that they must ask. Jesus does not act in a vacuum. He works through believers, those people who are concerned to please him.

Believers will not only be able to do the same things Jesus has been doing but *even greater things than these* (**14:12**). For example, Peter's message on the day of Pentecost (Acts 2:41) led more people to faith than Jesus' preaching did. Jesus had twelve students, but today many Bible teachers teach far bigger classes. The resurrected Jesus will show himself with even greater power than the incarnate Jesus, and he will do this through believers who submit to him.

The purpose for which prayers are answered and power is displayed is the glory of the Father (14:13b). This goal, too, serves to limit what a believer can ask for with confidence that Jesus will grant the prayer. Jesus is telling Philip that the Father will be shown by the works Philip and the other disciples will do as they continue to grow in faith. The

disciples will not just be people who have seen the Father but will be benefactors, showing the Father to others.

14:15-31 Jesus Promises the Holy Spirit

Jesus has been speaking of asking for things, and now he speaks of something that he himself will ask the Father to give to believers, namely, the Holy Spirit (**14:16-17**). Here two titles are used for the Spirit. He is the Spirit of truth, and he is the *parakletos,* a Greek word that means counsellor, advocate or comforter. Jesus has been all these things to the disciples but he is going away. While he will return to them briefly after his resurrection (**14:18**; Acts 1:3) they will need *another Counsellor* to fill their need for divine presence for ever.

The ministry of the Holy Spirit will be to *teach you all things and … remind you of everything I have said to you* (**14:26**). The words, 'all things' and 'everything' both translate the same Greek word, which is used twice. What they will be taught is all-inclusive, excluding nothing, while what they will be reminded of is limited to what Jesus has said in their hearing.

Some people have used this verse as the basis for claiming that the Holy Spirit has taught them all kinds of things. Thus we have to consider whether there are any limitations on what is likely to be taught. The first point to remember is that the Holy Spirit will be sent in Jesus' name (14:26), which means that his will and that of Jesus are one. Thus he will never contradict what Jesus has said. Instead he will continue where Jesus left off. The Trinity are interested in teaching a particular curriculum. Jesus had been the disciples' teacher for three years, and had spoken what the Father gave him to say (see 7:16; 8:26, 40, 47). But three years was too little for the disciples to learn everything they would need to know. There was much more to learn – as is clear from the fact that the disciples have just been asking one question after another about the mystery of salvation (see 13:36; 13:37; 14:5, 8, 22). This is the context in which Jesus promises the teaching of the Holy Spirit. Thus the *all things* must tie in directly with God's plan of salvation and the blessings it brings. Jesus had taught them a good deal about this, and the Holy Spirit will remind them of what he had taught. The rest, he would teach them himself.

Reassured that God has a wonderful plan in place, the disciples can be at peace (**14:27**) and can rejoice that Jesus is being promoted – for his departure is a promotion, as he is returning to the Father (**14:28**). His death may, for a time, appear to represent his defeat by Satan, but it will ultimately teach them that Jesus and the Father are indeed one in purpose (**14:30-31**)

15:1-17 Jesus, the True Vine

Jesus ended his speech to the disciples with *Come now; let us leave* (14:31b), but it seems that he decided to remain in the upper room a little longer in order to help the disciples understand more by giving them the revision lesson found in chapters 15 to 16.

He starts by making the seventh and last of his key 'I am' sayings: *I am the true vine* (**15:1**; the others are in 6:35, 51; 8:12; 10:7, 9; 10:11, 14; 11:25 and 14:6). The word translated 'true' focuses on dependability. Jesus was not saying that he is the true vine and that all others are false, but rather that he is the dependable vine. Others (including African traditional religions) may have much to offer, but they are not dependable. He is God's appointed way of approaching God.

If Jesus is a vine, then the Father is the gardener in the vineyard and the disciples are the branches on the vine (**15:1**, 5). The Father's role is, firstly, to cut *off every branch in me that bears no fruit* (**15:2a**). The 'fruit' referred to here is both holiness in the disciples' own lives and their continuing service of Jesus. One disciple who had not borne fruit was Judas Iscariot, who had ceased to serve Jesus and had left to betray him. The remaining eleven disciples were sincere in their love for Jesus, but they could not afford to become careless. They must continue to *remain in* Jesus (**15:4**). Failure to do so could lead them along the same route as Judas.

Those branches that were not cut off could expect to be pruned to make them *even more fruitful* (**15:2b**). In **15:3** Jesus told his remaining eleven disciples, *You are already clean because of the word I have spoken to you.* He had used the same word earlier, where he had described all but one of them as clean (13:10-11). But despite their cleanness, the disciples could expect that the Father would allow them to go through unpleasant experiences so as to establish them in their faith and Christian ministry (see also 1 Pet 4:14). We know something of the pruning some of the disciples endured. Peter, for example, passed through the 'pruning' of denying Jesus and the restoration that followed (18:17, 25, 27; 21:15-19), mockery (Acts 2:13) and imprisonment (Acts 5:18; 12:1-19). Each pruning experience gave him more energy to move on.

As the true vine, Jesus will enable the branches to bear fruit (15:4-5). He uses the biological fact that a branch not attached to a plant will neither benefit from the sap nor bear any fruit to illustrate a spiritual truth (**15:4**). The exhortation *remain in me* reminds the disciples that they must develop the habit of remembering to draw their energy from Jesus. Abiding in Jesus goes with his abiding in the disciples. The disciples are being exhorted to maintain their side of the arrangement.

It needs to be noted that the focus of this passage is not on a believer losing salvation or being eternally secure, but on those who have believed bearing fruit. The one who was 'cut off ' was Judas Iscariot, who cannot be equated with a believer.

The same thought is repeated in **15:5**: *I am the vine; you are the branches. If a man remains in me and I in him, he will bear much fruit; apart from me you can do nothing.* Without Jesus, there would be no fruit at all (**15:16**); but with him, the disciples would not only bear some fruit, they would bear much fruit. Over the years he was with them, Jesus had prepared them for fruit production. They would be the ones who would establish the church – born on the day of Pentecost on the basis of the apostles' preaching. They would work with other men such as Matthias, who replaced Judas Iscariot (Acts 1:26); Paul, who was dramatically appointed as an apostle by the risen Jesus (Acts 9:1-30; see also Gal 1:11-24) and evangelists like Stephen (Acts 6:5-8:1a) and Philip (Acts 8:4-40). All of these men formed one team, proclaiming the message of Jesus. The reason for their appointment was 'to go and bear much fruit'.

We, too, are called to do this, and if we fail to bear fruit, we fail in our assignment. Not only that, we are to go on from bearing *more* fruit (15:2), to bearing *much* fruit (**15:5**), to bearing *fruit that will last* (15:16). The progression here shows that bearing fruit is a process and that our ability to bear fruit increases as we mature.

In our personal lives, this means that we will not develop just one virtue out of the nine in Galatians 5:22-23 but will work to cultivate all of them. In our evangelism, it means that we will not be content to save just one person, but will work to save an entire village. In terms of our effectiveness, it means that we will not just be a good influence in our local church but throughout the entire nation and the world! Much fruit is the promise. Much fruit should be the goal. Abiding in Jesus and Jesus abiding in us is the key to reaching that goal.

Coupled with the promise of power in bearing fruit is a promise of power in prayer: *If you remain in me and my words remain in you, ask whatever you wish, and it will be given you* (**15:7**; see also 16b). There are no limits so long as the condition of abiding in Jesus is met. Nothing would be denied when it was asked for while they were abiding in Jesus and working for the promotion of the Abiding-in-Jesus Movement!

By bearing fruit, the disciples will both glorify God the Father and prove their discipleship (**15:8**). Jesus' only aim during his three-year ministry had been to glorify the Father. This was also to be the goal of the eleven, in every word they uttered and every deed they performed. Also, because they are connected to Jesus who is the vine, their fruit must be Jesus-like. It cannot be otherwise if they claim to be Jesus' disciples.

As branches (15:2, 4, 5, 6, 16) the disciples have other specific responsibilities besides bearing fruit. They are also to love one another (a point Jesus had already made in 13:34-35). In **15:12**, he tells them to *Love each other* and the same instruction is repeated in **15:17**. While he calls this a *command*, Jesus reminds them that he is exhorting them as his friends, not issuing them commands as slaves (**15:14-15**). Slaves obey because they fear their master; friends obey because they love their friends. Jesus loved his disciples and the disciples were to respond to that love by obeying him (**15:10**). The fact that the disciples had been specifically chosen (**15:16**) should also be an encouragement for them as they face the daunting responsibilities that will soon be theirs.

Love is to be the disciples' way of life. They are to love everyone, at all times. The type of love that Jesus is commanding is the same type of love that the Father has for Jesus (**15:9**), and that Jesus has for his disciples (15:12-13). The Father's relationship with the Son is one of love from eternity, and Jesus, relationship with his disciples is one of love from the time he called them until the time of speaking. Jesus followed the Father's example and loved his disciples as the Father loved him. The disciples were now to follow Jesus' example and love each other in the same way.

The highest level of love is expressed when someone is prepared to die for the sake of a friend (**15:13**). Jesus not only gave his life so that his friends would benefit from his death, but actually took their place (see 2 Cor 5:21; Gal 3:13; 1 Tim 2:6; 1 Pet 3:18). He is telling them to have a love that is not marred by selfish ambitions or ill-will of any kind. Selfish ambition is to be replaced by self-sacrifice and service. They are to wish each other well and work for what is best for one another.

15:18–16:4 Jesus' Disciples Hated by the World

While his disciples are to love each other, they would be hated and treated as enemies by *the world* (**15:18**). The 'world' is that evil system whose head is Satan and whose agents are in opposition to Jesus and his cause.

Three reasons are given for the hostility of the world: the disciples don't belong to the world (15:19), the world hated and persecuted Jesus their master (15:18) and the world lacked knowledge of the Father and of Jesus (15:21).

The disciples had previously belonged to the world, but Jesus had chosen them *out of the world* (**15:19**). The act of choosing gave the disciples a new status. They no longer belonged to the world but to Jesus. Since the world loves only its own, it cannot love the disciples. Instead, it hates them.

The world's hatred of Jesus and rejection of his teaching had been openly expressed in persecution. There had been persistent attempts to kill him (5:18), to seize him (7:30) and to stone him (8:59; 10:31). The world's hatred would soon be crowned by the shouting of 'Crucify! Crucify!' (19:6, 15). Since this was the way the world treated Jesus, it would treat his disciples in the same way (**15:20**).

The world's hostility to the disciples would be entirely due to the fact that they had identified themselves with Jesus. Such persecution shows that those who do it do not know God, no matter how religious they appear (**15:21**).

As if someone had asked Jesus how he could claim that the world was so guilty, he next marshalled his evidence, pointing out that his words (**15:22**), his deeds (**15:24**), the Holy Spirit (15:26) and the disciples (15:27) all combined to show that the world was indeed guilty.

Jesus 'words' were everything he had said to the crowds – including his clear statement of his relationship to the Father and his claims to be the bread of life; the light of the world; the good shepherd; the way, the truth and the life. His deeds backed up his words (15:24; see also 14:11). Yet despite his extraordinary miracles, the Jews remained hard-hearted. However, the world's hatred of Jesus was not unexpected, for it had been predicted in the OT (**15:25** – quoting Ps 35:19; 69:4; 109:3). Hatred of God led naturally to hatred of Jesus and hatred of his disciples.

The Holy Spirit, who speaks nothing but the truth (14:17), will testify for Jesus against those who persecute him (**15:26**). His evidence will support Jesus' claims. Finally, the disciples themselves will support Jesus' claims *And you also must testify, for you have been with me from the beginning* (**15:27**). In this verse, Jesus is not ordering them to testify, he is simply stating what would, in fact, happen. What they had done and what they had become already stood as a witness against the world.

In a Jewish court of law, two or three witnesses were required to establish a case. Here we have four witnesses (Jesus' words, his deeds, the Holy Spirit and the disciples). The world stands convicted. Yes, it may currently enjoy the upper hand as it persecutes both Jesus and his disciples, but it will pay for its sin when God pronounces his verdict.

The world's hatred of Jesus' followers would result in their being put out of the synagogue (**16:2a**). This would mean that they were excluded from the only place in which God communed with his people, the Jews, and would be separated from God's people. However, the persecution of the disciples would go well beyond exclusion from synagogues. Killing them would be seen as honouring God (**16:2b**). Eliminating them would be viewed as removing elements that did not glorify God (as in the incidents recorded in Numbers 25:1–9, Joshua 7 and Judges 19 and 20). This great mistake would happen because of a lack of knowledge of the relationship between the Father and Jesus (**16:3**). Not realizing that Jesus was the One sent by God, people's ignorance would lead them to kill Jesus' servants rather than honouring them and recognizing their link with God.

Jesus twice reminded his disciples that he was not telling them these things in order to increase their fear but for a positive purpose. When persecution came, the disciples' knowledge that this was to be expected would be the first weapon to help them stand firm and not be scattered

(**16:1**). The disciples' faith in Jesus would be strengthened as they related Jesus' words to later events (**16:4**).

Jesus had not told them about the coming danger before because they had not needed to know about it while he was still with them (16:4b). But now that he was departing, they needed to be prepared to handle danger well.

16:5-15 Jesus' Successor, the Holy Spirit

Jesus had already spoken about the Counsellor who would succeed him and would be with the disciples for ever (14:16; 14:26). This Counsellor would come only after Jesus' departure (**16:7a**) and would be sent by Jesus (**16:7b**; see also 14:16). Elsewhere, it is said that the Father will send the Holy Spirit in Jesus' name (14:26). But there are no contradictions here concerning the respective roles of the Father and the Son. What the Father does, Jesus is doing, and whatever Jesus does, the Father is doing. This oneness in purpose is a theme that runs throughout the Gospel of John.

The Counsellor will minister to both the world (16:8-11) and the disciples (16:12-13). He will *convict the world of guilt in regard to sin and righteousness and judgment* (**16:8**). These three represent different targets for conviction. The world would be convicted about sin because by rejecting Jesus it had remained in sin (**16:9**), about righteousness in that it was not on the side of God who is all-righteous (**16:10**) and about judgment because by rejecting Jesus it stood with the devil who is already condemned (**16:11**).

The Holy Spirit's ministry to the disciples would be quite different from his ministry to the world. To the disciples, he would be a reliable guide *into all truth (***16:13a***)*. His guidance can be trusted because he will not speak on his own, but *will speak only what he hears* (**16:13b**). The content of his message centres on the future – *what is yet to come* (**16:13c**). The Holy Spirit's guidance stretches from the very first things that happened after Jesus' departure to include everything that will happen at the end of time. It is primarily concerned with God's programme for his church and only secondarily with God's plan for each individual disciple. Individual disciples are not guided independently of the church, but within the context of the church.

This work of the Holy Spirit is to be viewed in the context of teamwork between the Father, Jesus and the Holy Spirit. The Holy Spirit will speak 'what he hears' from the Father (see 16:13). Jesus, however, describes this in **16:14** as *taking from what is mine and making it known to you*. The Holy Spirit's message is thus both Father-given and Jesus-owned. As Jesus says in **16:15**, *All that belongs to the Father is mine. That is why I said the Spirit will take from what is mine and make it known to you.* The Father's message is Jesus' message, and the Holy Spirit can pass on Jesus' message as his own. Yet because the Holy Spirit succeeds Jesus, his focus is on bringing glory to Jesus (16:14). He does not operate in

a vacuum but builds on the redemptive work of Jesus. His role is to apply that work directly to our lives.

16:16-33 Jesus' Departure

It was only a matter of hours before Judas Iscariot and his crew would arrest Jesus, and so he reminded his disciples, *In a little while you will see me no more, and then after a little while you will see me* (**16:16**). This was not the first time Jesus had spoken of his death and resurrection in these terms (see, for example 13:33). However, in all the earlier references he had highlighted his departure and only implied the resurrection. In the present statement, he gives equal emphasis to both.

The dumbfounded disciples (16:5) at last found words to speak. Some of them asked each other, *What does he mean by saying, 'In a little while you will see me no more, and then after a little while you will see me', and 'Because I am going to the Father'?* (**16:17**). It is clear that they did not know exactly what Jesus meant (**16:18**). Recognizing this, Jesus took time to explain what he was saying (**16:19-20**).

He started by pointing out that they could expect their emotional response to his departure to be quite different before and after his resurrection. He introduced this statement with the Hebrew words *Amen, amen* (translated 'Truly, truly' by the NASB and 'I tell you the truth' in the NIV), emphasizing the certainty of what he was predicting. At the time of his suffering and death, they would weep because their master had been taken away and made to suffer (16:20). But their pain would be like the pain of childbirth (16:21) – intense but soon replaced with joy in the birth of a child. After the resurrection, the disciples would be filled with joy that Jesus had returned to life (**16:21-22**) and with a wonderful sense of satisfaction as the Father met their every need (**16:23-24**).

Jesus' departure would have three specific results for his disciples: two positive (16:25-30) and one negative (16:32). The positive results would be a fuller understanding of God and his ways as things are taught plainly, not figuratively (**16:25**), and direct access to the Father, whereas before they had only had access to Jesus (**16:26-27**). The negative result would be the scattering of the disciples (**16:32**). For Jesus himself, his departure would mean a return to his original home and a celebration of work well done. His statement that *I came from the Father and entered the world; now I am leaving the world and going back to the Father* (**16:28**) summarized his origin, his time on earth and his destination. His past existence was eternal; his stay on earth was temporary; and his future existence with the Father would be eternal.

Finally, Jesus repeated the reason why he was telling them these things: *I have told you these things,* he said, *so that in me you may have peace* (**16:33a**). The purpose of his long discourse was not to create anxiety but to give them

UNITY OF BELIEVERS

Unity may be defined as the condition in which something forms an organic whole. Although different elements are involved, the whole is characterized by agreement and internal coherence. This definition also applies to the unity of believers to the extent that they share a common foundation of faith and practice. While the word 'unity' may be rarely used in the Bible, the idea of unity is often found.

In the OT, the unity of the people of Israel was based on the fear of God and family ties. However, despite having one father, Abraham, Israel was divided into tribes and later into different kingdoms. Even though they had the law of Moses and the warnings of the prophets, the people of Israel were not able to obey God and live as he desired. Consequently they did not achieve real unity.

In the nations and villages of Africa, unity is also strongly dependent on family ties, on the use of a common language, or on the fact of living in the same geographical region. This unity is vulnerable because anyone who comes from another area or who does not speak the same language is perceived as an outsider, or even an enemy. Hence, there is no unity involving all the nations of the region.

In Israel, as in Africa, unity could only be partial, limited to one nation or one close-knit community. But in the NT, there is an unlimited, universal dimension to the unity of believers. This unity knows no geographic, administrative or cultural limits. It is based in Jesus. By his death and resurrection, Jesus opened the way to new alliances for all peoples, who had formerly been without grace and were enemies of God (Eph 2:12-13). Through faith in Jesus, the believer is part of a new nation, reconciled to God and capable of living in genuine fellowship, a visible unity.

This unity is fostered and maintained by the work of the Holy Spirit, the agent of the new birth, the source of life in the believer, and the giver of the gifts and fruit of the Spirit (John 3:5; Eph 4:4). The Holy Spirit transforms believers into brothers and sisters in Christ and also into brothers and sisters to each other. In other words, it is the work of the Holy Spirit that makes believers united in Jesus and among themselves.

This unity should be most evident in the local church. It is because of this unity that the local church is also called the body of Christ or the bride of Christ (1 Cor 6:17; Eph 5:30). Every believer is a living member of this body. In the local church, unity is expressed primarily by collectively listening to the word, by submission to the authority of this word, and by the celebration of baptism and communion.

But the local church is only one link in the unity of the universal church. The unity that God brings extends to all believers of all nations, denominations and times. Tribalism, ethnicity and denominationalism are hindrances to the unity of God's people and must be resisted. Of course, each ethnic group or tribe has its place in the church, but only as links in a long chain. There is no place for ideologies that consider one ethnic group or tribe superior to another. Similarly, individual churches belong to different denominations, but this division must not be allowed to be an obstacle to unity back and be defended on the basis of protecting church doctrine or by arguing that separation from others is the will of God.

Unity was one of the main things that Jesus prayed for in his high priestly prayer. He knew that unity lends credibility to the message of the church and is part of its mission (John 17:21).

Unfortunately, the unity that is presented in God's word has not yet been fully realized. Believers must be disciplined and built up by the word in order to come to maturity and arrive at visible unity. They must also support and maintain this unity through united efforts in such areas as mission and evangelism.

Kuzuli Kossé

---

peace as they trusted in him. Outside of Jesus, there is no peace. That is why he added, *In this world you will have trouble* (**16:33b**). The world was their enemy. It would not treat them well. However, there was hope, for Jesus finished with the words, *But take heart! I have overcome the world* (**16:33b**). They were not expected to take heart on the basis of favourable circumstances, but on the basis of a historical fact, namely, Jesus' victory.

17:1-26 Jesus' Last Prayer Before His Arrest

Jesus ended his discourse in the upper room with a prayer to the Father. It was now time to talk to the Father on behalf of himself, his disciples and all believers before he departed.

17:1-5 Jesus' prayer for himself

Jesus' prayer for himself focused on his glorification. He pleaded with the Father, *Glorify your Son* (**17:1a**). He saw his death and resurrection in terms of promotion and committed them into the hands of the Father so that the Son would emerge highly exalted. He specified that the glory he was asking for was *the glory I had with you before the world began* (**17:5**) and that its purpose was *that your Son may glorify you* (**17:1b**). Jesus would be glorified by being resurrected, and the glorified Jesus would attribute his resurrection to the Father.

The basis on which Jesus made this request was that he had completed the work assigned to him by the Father (**17:4b**). He highlights two aspects of this work – giving eternal life to all those whom the Father had given him (**17:2**) and glorifying the Father (**17:4a**).

17:6-19 Jesus' prayer for his disciples

After praying for himself, Jesus went on to pray at length for his disciples. As though reasoning with the Father, Jesus explains why he is moved to this specific prayer for them. He mentions the fact that the disciples belonged to the Father and had obeyed him (**17:6, 9**), their true knowledge of the Father and of Jesus (**17:7-8**), the fact that their actions had enhanced Jesus' glory (**17:10**) and the fact that they would soon be left alone (**17:12**).

The first thing he requested for his disciples was protection by the Father's power – not so much protection of their physical bodies as of their unity (**17:11**; see also 15:12). The need for Jesus' prayer has been illustrated again and again in Africa. In tribal clashes, believers have betrayed their brothers and sisters in the Lord for fear of being killed by their own tribespeople. Jesus stressed the importance of the unity of believers; however, he did not guarantee that they would be able to maintain this unity without sacrificing their own lives.

Once Jesus was no longer with them as a unifying factor (17:12), the disciples would be exposed to the hatred of the world and to the attacks of Satan, who is referred to as *the evil one* to emphasize his wickedness (**17:14-15**; see 15:18-21).

The second thing Jesus prayed for was the disciples' sanctification (**17:17**). He stresses that this sanctification will be brought about by the truth, that is, by their increasing knowledge and understanding of God's word. The disciples would need such sanctification because they would be living in a world that did not value it but was opposed to God's will (**17:18**). They did, however, have a pattern to follow: Jesus himself, who submitted totally to the will of God (**17:19**).

17:20-25 Jesus' prayer for all believers

Jesus had prayed for unity for his disciples (17:11), and now he prays for it for all believers (**17:20**). Their unity is to be patterned on the unity of the Father and the Son (**17:21a, 22**). But not only is this to be the model for their unity, they are also to share in this relationship (**17:21b, 23a**). Like the Father and the Son, believers are to be united in working towards their goal of bringing the world to believe in the Father and the Son (**17:21c, 23b**).

The second thing he prays for all believers is that they will be reunited with him and able to see Jesus' full glory that he did not show during his earthly ministry (**17:24**). All those whom the Father has given to Jesus will participate in this reunion. Jesus has shared his glory with these believers (**17:22**), but he wants them to share it even more fully.

Jesus concludes his prayer with a restatement of his submission to the Father's will, which will result in the believers being brought into still closer unity with and submission to the Father and to Jesus (**17:25-26**).

18:1-20:9 Jesus' Arrest, Crucifixion and Burial

18:1-27 Jesus' Arrest and Jewish Trial

Upon completion of the priestly prayer, Jesus left the upper room and went to the olive grove where he was arrested (**18:1**). The arresting team was guided to him by Judas Iscariot. They carried torches and lanterns for light and also weapons in case there would be resistance (**18:2-3**). However, they needed no weapons, for Jesus was not hiding in the olive grove. He knew the hour for his arrest had come, and so he went out to meet them and calmly identified himself as Jesus of Nazareth (**18:4-5**). His words *I am he* (18:6) were, however, so powerful that they caused the arresting team to draw back and fall to the ground, not in worship but as if they had been overpowered by Jesus' simple statement (18:6). After getting the arresting team to be very clear about who exactly they were to arrest by having them repeat the name of their target (**18:5, 7**), Jesus told them, *if you are looking for me, then let these men go* (**18:8**). His aim was to protect his disciples from harm.

Peter started to fight for Jesus, and in the process cut off the right ear of Malchus, a servant (**18:10**). But Jesus quickly calmed the situation by healing the ear. He reminded Peter and the rest of the disciples what this was all about: *Shall I not drink the cup the Father has given me?* (**18:11**). He then allowed himself to be arrested, bound and taken for trial.

The main participants in the Jewish trial were Annas, Caiaphas and the Sanhedrin. Annas, the father-in-law of Caiaphas, had been the high priest from AD 6 to 15 and still retained enormous influence. Caiaphas, the high priest from AD 18 to 36, would have had to sign the Sanhedrin's verdict, but Annas' opinion would have weighed heavily on the decision.

While Jesus was being tried by the Jewish authorities, Peter was being tried by the crowd. On three occasions he was identified as possibly one of Jesus' followers (**18:17, 25a-26a**), and on each occasion he strongly denied it. Jesus had predicted that this would happen (13:38), as Peter remembered with shame when he heard the cock's crow.

The Jewish trial focused on Jesus' *disciples and his teaching* (**18:19**). Jesus' responses, however, focused only on his teaching. He pointed out that he had taught in public and those who had heard him could testify about it (**18:20-21**). Jesus was challenging Annas for his refusal to listen to his teaching and also stating a fact. He had taught in the synagogues and in the temple. It should have been easy to find witnesses if there was any crime of which he could legitimately be accused.

Because Jesus' answer was not the one wanted, an official struck him in the face (**18:22**). Annas seems to have ignored this abuse of the prisoner, but Jesus demanded to know what he had done that justified striking him (**18:23**).

Of course, no answer was given. He had done no wrong. On a human level, the officials were simply acting to defend their leadership by removing someone who threatened it.

The Jewish leaders' hostility to Jesus was nothing new. He had first been accused of breaking the Sabbath laws (5:16). To this had been added accusations of blasphemy (5:18; 10:33). But neither charge would have impressed the Roman governor, so when the authorities handed Jesus over to him, they had to produce new charges.

18:28-19:16a Jesus' Roman Trial

Jesus' trial before Pilate and his appearance before Herod Antipas (tetrarch of Galilee from 4 BC to AD 39, who happened to be in Jerusalem at this time) together form the Roman trial of Jesus. His appearance before Herod is recorded only in Luke 23:6–12. It interrupted Jesus' trial by Pilate, who sent him to Herod after learning that Jesus was a Galilean. Jesus did not answer Herod's questions, and Herod and his soldiers simply mocked him and then sent him back to Pilate. Pilate was, therefore, the key player in this trial. He was the governor of Judea from AD 26 to AD 35, appointed to this position by Tiberius, who was the Roman emperor from AD 14 to AD 37.

It seems that the Jewish authorities had difficulty in finding a crime they could accuse Jesus of committing. Annas' interrogation seems to have found nothing, and no convincing witnesses had appeared before Caiaphas and the Sanhedrin. So when Pilate asked about the charge against the prisoner, they replied vaguely that he was *a criminal* who should be executed (**18:29-30**). It is clear that Jesus' accusers were not looking for a fair trial that followed the proper legal process. They wanted the Roman governor to rubber-stamp the sentence that they had already passed.

Recognizing that the lack of charges meant this was not a case he should judge, Pilate told the Jewish leaders to take Jesus and judge him by their own law. They responded that there was no point in doing this. They had already decided that Jesus should be executed, but were powerless to carry out the sentence, since Roman law did not permit them to carry out executions (**18:31**). Further evidence of the lack of interest in a fair trial is the fact that after Jesus' first session with Pilate, the chief priests and their officials did not ask Pilate what his verdict was, but told him what verdict they wanted (19:6a).

Pilate's question to Jesus, *Are you the king of the Jews?* (**18:33**), suggests he had been told that Jesus was the leader of a rebellion against Roman authority, a charge that was important enough to force Pilate to take the case seriously. This charge was supported by twisting Jesus' words and actions. The Jewish leaders probably reminded Pilate of Jesus' triumphal entry into Jerusalem as the Messianic king (see 12:12-15) and emphasized their own loyalty to Caesar (see 19:12). They did not mention the fact that when the people had wanted to make Jesus king (6:15), he had refused and withdrawn from them. Jesus had accepted the people's royal welcome to Jerusalem, but had kept his focus clear. His kingdom was not an earthly one, for his desire was to reign in the hearts of men and women.

It seems that Pilate was not particularly concerned about Jesus being described as a king, provided the qualifier 'of the Jews' was emphasized (see 19:19). The Jews had authority over their own religious affairs, and it did not matter much to Pilate whether they called their leader a king or a high priest, so long as he did not overstep the authority given to him and paid due honour and respect to Caesar and to himself as governor. The tone of his questions suggests that he was not so much looking for evidence of a crime as trying to find out who Jesus actually was. He must have heard about some of the miracles Jesus had performed.

Jesus' response to Pilate's question was, *Is that your own idea, or did others talk to you about me?* (**18:34**). He was encouraging Pilate to reflect on what he had just said. Did Pilate believe that Jesus was the king of the Jews? If he did, he was on the right track. But Pilate waved away the question (**18:35a**). Since he was not a Jew, he was under no obligation to make any decision on the matter of Jesus' kingship. As far as he was concerned, the whole question was merely about a point of Jewish religious belief, in which he was not interested. Thus he distanced himself from what was happening by labelling it a religious matter.

Pilate makes it quite clear that he as governor would have had no objection to Jesus being the king of the Jews. It was the Jewish people (and more specifically the chief priests) who had taken offence at this claim and had handed Jesus over to him for trial (**18:35b**). So Pilate wanted to find out from Jesus what he had done to arouse such hostility. The question *What is it you have done?* (**18:35c**) indicates what a strange trial this was. The accused was supposed to say what he had done, instead of his accusers pressing charges against him! Of course, as we saw from 18:19, 30, his accusers had no clear-cut charges.

In his response, Jesus emphasized that his kingdom was *not of this world. If it were,* he said, *my servants [disciples] would fight to prevent my arrest by the Jews* (**18:36a**). (Peter's cutting off of Malchus' ear does not disprove this statement. It was not done with Jesus' approval.) Rather, his kingdom was *from another place* (**18:36b**). His rule was not over any earthly domain. He was king because he had been appointed such by the Father in heaven.

Pilate wanted to make sure that he had understood what Jesus was saying about his kingship in 18:36 and so asked a further question. The NIV translates 18:37a as a statement, but in the Greek it is in the form of a question and could be literally translated, *You are a king, aren't you?* In replying to Pilate in the rest of **18:37**, Jesus pointed out that Pilate was right to state that Jesus was a king, and that his role as king was *to testify to the truth*. Everyone who was on the side of truth would listen to him.

In Pilate's experience, kingship involved having power over people. Jesus, however, spoke of kingship as being associated with truth, which then drew people to his side. What was all this about? So Pilate asked, *What is truth?* (**18:38a**). Unfortunately for Pilate, he did not wait to hear Jesus' answer to his question. John tells us, *With this he went out again to the Jews*. Pilate missed the opportunity to hear the telling of the good news to its end. His interest was in judicial, not religious, matters.

The reason Pilate went back to the Jewish leaders was to tell them, *I find no basis for a charge against him* (**18:38b**). But the trial was not over yet, and Pilate did not stand by what he knew to be the truth about Jesus.

Having found Jesus innocent, Pilate suggested that he release Jesus, as it was the custom for a prisoner to be released at Passover time (**18:39**). But the Jewish leaders would have none of this, and shouted back, *No, not him! Give us Barabbas!* (**18:40**).

Despite the fact that he thought Jesus was innocent, Pilate ordered him flogged (**19:1**). He was probably hoping that this punishment would be enough to satisfy Jesus' accusers.

At this stage we meet another group who participated in Jesus' trial: the soldiers. They had probably heard his responses to Pilate's question, and mocked his claim to kingship by putting a crown on his head. A crown is usually a sign of power, and is designed to fit comfortably on the head of its powerful wearer. But Jesus' crown was made out of thorns *twisted together* (**19:2a**). It would have been extremely painful, particularly if, as some suggest, it was made out of palm leaves. The long spines at the ends of these leaves can be up to twelve inches long.

They also clothed Jesus in a purple robe (**19:2b**). Purple was the official colour of royalty and a marker of authority and wealth (Exod 28:2, 5, 6; Luke 16:19; Rev 17:4; 18:16). As Jesus was a king, it was the appropriate colour for him to wear. The soldiers, however, were not genuinely acknowledging Jesus' kingship; they were mocking him.

As the soldiers sarcastically honoured him, pretending to salute him and saying, *Hail, king of the Jews!* (**19:3a**), they were addressing him correctly! He was the king of the Jews, and should neither have been wearing a crown of thorns nor standing as a prisoner before Pilate. However, God allowed this to happen (19:11a) so that through Jesus' suffering, those who believed in him would be healed (Isa 53:5).

The soldiers expressed their contempt for Jesus by striking *him in the face* (**19:3c**). Little did they know that the one they had struck was more powerful than Pilate, or even Tiberius Caesar. Soon these soldiers (or others like them) would be surprised when their service as guards at Jesus' tomb turned into a nightmare!

Pilate then presented the bleeding and abused Jesus to the Jewish leaders and made an even more emphatic declaration of Jesus' innocence (**19:4**). But the only response of the chief priests and their officials was to shout, *Crucify! Crucify!* (**19:6a**). Frustrated, he told them to take Jesus and crucify him themselves (**19:6b**). Of course, Pilate knew that the leaders were unable to do this (18:31b), but he was sending them a message that he did not want to be associated with their injustice. Again, he reminded them that he found Jesus innocent (19:6b).

Recognizing that Pilate was wavering and likely to acquit Jesus, the Jewish leaders brought out their number one charge, namely, that Jesus *claimed to be the Son of God* (**19:7**). On hearing this, Pilate became even more reluctant to handle the case, and asked Jesus another question: *Where do you come from?* (**19:9a**). Up to this point, Pilate had been handling the matter in light of Roman law, for the Jewish leaders had refused his offer to allow them to deal with Jesus according to Jewish law (18:31). But now the Jewish leaders had told Pilate that even if Roman law saw no fault in Jesus, their law viewed him as a criminal deserving capital punishment. At this point, Pilate may have wanted to reconcile his conviction that Jesus was innocent with the Jewish leaders' demands by transferring the case to someone else.

Luke tells us that after Pilate had established that Jesus was innocent, he found out that he was from Galilee and sent him to Herod Antipas, who was in Jerusalem at that time (Luke 23:4-7). John, too, makes it clear that Pilate would have been happy to free himself from handling Jesus' case. He wanted to avoid the conflict between what was right in terms of Roman law and the demands of the Jewish leaders.

Jesus did not reply to Pilate's question (**19:9b**). Why? Was he being impolite? No. He was exercising good judgment. He already knew why Pilate wanted to free himself from judging this case, and he also knew that was not going to happen. Jesus had to die on the cross because of human sinfulness and the unchanging holiness of God (Eph 2:16; Col 2:13-14). He also had to die at Passover as the lamb that would redeem people from the Egypt of sin. Passover time had come. A much more immediate reason for his silence, however, was the complexity of any answer to Pilate's question. Pilate would have been happy to hear Jesus say, 'I am from Nazareth', but that answer would have been incorrect because Nazareth was only a stop on his route through this world as he travelled from eternity past to eternity future. If Jesus had given the correct answer, 'I am from heaven', Pilate would not have understood what he meant. If Jesus' divine origin was incomprehensible to the best minds among the Jewish leaders (who knew the Scriptures inside out), how would Pilate, a pagan, understand it? The question could not be answered simply on a purely intellectual level. Only faith in Jesus' claim would make it comprehensible, and Pilate was not following the route of faith. He was merely interested in the legal and political aspects of the matter.

Pilate was annoyed when Jesus did not answer his question about his origin: *Do you refuse to speak to me?* (**19:10a**). In the Greek, the 'me' (referring to Pilate) is placed first for emphasis, contrasting with the less important 'you' (Jesus). The idea behind Pilate's question was 'You do not realize who I am. I am Pilate, the governor, and you are a prisoner at my mercy.' Pilate had interpreted Jesus' silence as rudeness, but that did not bother Jesus. Within a few days, when Pilate would realize who Jesus really was, he would know that it should have been the other way round, with Jesus interrogating him rather than him interrogating Jesus!

Pilate's question about Jesus' silence was immediately followed by a last and more specific question concerning his authority: *Don't you realize that I have power either to free you or to crucify you?* (**19:10b**). In other words, 'Don't you realize that you are totally at my mercy?' Pilate was not exaggerating his power as governor. Tiberius Caesar would not concern himself with what was going on in Jerusalem, so long as there was peace. Which prisoner was freed and which was crucified was of no interest to Rome. The matter was totally in the hands of Pilate, who knew this and asked Jesus if he knew it too.

Jesus' response to Pilate's honest but somewhat proud and mistaken estimate of himself should have kept Pilate pondering for a long time: *You would have no power over me if it were not given to you from above* (**19:11a**). Pilate's power over Jesus was on loan from God, and would last only for as long as and to the degree that the giver determined. Pilate was in no position to boast about his power in his dealings with Jesus. In fact, Pilate was guilty of sin, although *the one who handed me over to you is guilty of a greater sin* (**19:11b**). Pilate's guilt was limited. He was presiding over the unjust trial of an innocent man. However, as an official of the ruling power, he had been forced into this position. Moreover, he himself had not set out to arrest Jesus. Jesus had been brought to him by a person – the singular is used here – meaning either Judas Iscariot or Caiaphas, who had delivered Jesus to Pilate. If Jesus was referring to Judas, he was thinking of the fact that for three years Judas Iscariot had heard Jesus' teaching and experienced his great love, but he had repaid Jesus' goodness by betraying him. If he was referring to Caiaphas, his point was that Caiaphas, as a Jew and the high priest, should have known better than Pilate. The Scriptures of which Caiaphas was the custodian condemned the injustice and untruthfulness that had characterized Jesus' trial.

Pilate became even more anxious to free Jesus, but he was confronted by the Jewish leaders who kept on shouting, reminding Pilate that his loyalty to Tiberius Caesar would be questioned if he released Jesus: *Anyone who claims to be a king opposes Caesar* (**19:12**).

Yielding to the pressure from the Jewish authorities, Pilate finally took up his formal seat as judge and presented the scourged Jesus to the crowd with the assertion *Here is your king* (**19:13-14**). It is not clear what Pilate meant by calling Jesus a 'king' here. He was probably thinking purely in religious terms. But the chief priests responded to Pilate's declaration with *We have no king but Caesar* (**19:15**).

Recognizing the Jewish leaders' implacable hostility to Jesus and the threat to his own position, Pilate abandoned his attempt at a just trial and handed Jesus over to them for crucifixion (**19:16a**).

19:16b-30 Jesus' Crucifixion

With the way now set for the cross, *the soldiers took charge of Jesus* (19:16b). Matthew and Mark tell us that the soldiers first took Jesus into the Praetorium, the palace where Pilate was staying (Matt 27:27; Mark 15:16), and after mocking him they stripped him of the purple robe 'and put his own clothes on him' (Matt 27:31; Mark 15:20). Wearing his own clothes, but still with the crown of thorns on his head, Jesus' journey to the place of crucifixion began.

It was a journey that produced both physical and emotional pain. The physical agony included the weight of the cross he had to carry (**19:17**), the crucifixion itself, and his thirst (**19:28**). There was also the emotional pain of seeing the crowd choose Barabbas for release and not him (18:40), of seeing all his disciples desert him (Matt 26:56), of being crucified between two criminals (**19:18**), of seeing his grieving mother (**19:25**) and of being scorned by one of the criminals at his side (Luke 23:39).

Despite all the suffering and the soldiers and authorities seeming to be the ones in control, the passage makes it clear that everything that was happening was under the control of God. The soldiers did not break Jesus' legs (19:32-33), maintaining his fitness as the Passover Lamb (Exod 12:46; Num 9:12) and fulfilling what had been predicted (Ps 34:19-20). The soldier, though he knew Jesus was dead, pierced Jesus' side, and blood and water flowed out (19:34-37). Blood cleanses from sin (1 John 1:7) and water provides spiritual refreshment (7:38).

In spite of his failure to enforce justice in the handling of Jesus' case and the complaints of the Jews (**19:21**) Pilate's inscription on Jesus' cross was a significant proclamation of who Jesus really was. It was read by many because it was written in the three main languages of the time – Aramaic, Latin and Greek (**19:19-20**).

It is remarkable that, in the midst of all his suffering, Jesus was still concerned about his mother. He committed her to the care of the Apostle John (**19:26-27**) who was with Jesus even at this time.

The outcome of his pain was glorious. When Jesus uttered his sixth word from the cross in **19:30** and said, *it is finished*, he meant that the work of saving humankind was completed. Clearly pain and God's providence are not contradictory. Jesus' suffering, despite his having done no wrong, became the most glorious provision to all humankind – a fitting sacrifice for the sins of all peoples of all generations. Times of pain such as we experience in Africa should not make us give up. Instead we should press forward expecting God to produce some glorious outcome. The innocent sufferer may not see this outcome, but his or her children will.

19:31-42 Jesus' Death and Burial

Jesus' body needed to be buried, and time was of the essence because Jesus was crucified on the *day of Preparation* for a *special Sabbath*, which was due to begin at sunset (**19:31**). Just that morning Jesus had been handed over to the Jews for crucifixion at the 'sixth hour' (6 a.m. – 19:14). Note that John reckoned time the Roman way, counting the day as beginning at midnight. The writers of the Synoptic gospels, however, reported time the Jewish way. Jesus was crucified at 9 a.m. (Mark 15:25: 'third hour' – with Mark designating daytime as beginning at sunrise). The next three hours passed like those of any other day on which a criminal was crucified. But at noon (Mark 15:33: 'sixth hour'– see also, Matt 27:45 and Luke 23:44) something strange happened, as it became dark, a darkness that lasted for three hours (Luke 23:44). Then at 3 p.m. Jesus had spoken his final words, the last of his short utterances on the cross. He had said, 'It is finished,' and then he had bowed his head and given up his spirit (**19:30**).

Meanwhile, in the temple, the Jews had been having their lambs slaughtered for the Passover meal, for at 6 p.m. the Passover week would begin. Jesus was still on the cross, but the Jews did not want him to remain there, as their law said that a dead body should not be left hanging on a tree overnight (**19:31**; see also Deut 21:22-23). Jesus' disciples were nowhere to be found. If no one claimed Jesus' body for burial, it would be thrown into the Valley of Hinnom, where all the garbage of Jerusalem was dumped.

Joseph of Arimathea and Nicodemus undertook to bury Jesus (**19:38-39a**). They were both secret disciples (19:38; see also 3:1-21; 12:42-43) and members of the Sanhedrin (Mark 15:43, John 7:50-52). Because it was the highest Jewish authority recognized by the Romans, those who belonged to it were powerful members of society.

By asking for Jesus' body (Matt 27:58; Mark 15:43; Luke 23:52) these men risked the enmity of their fellow Jewish leaders who had brought about Jesus' death. Unfortunately, today we seldom see a similar attitude of service to Christ in those who have become important, whether as government ministers, members of parliament or civil servants.

What Joseph and Nicodemus were doing was equivalent to members of parliament or judges of the high court taking upon themselves the mundane duty of seeing that a body is properly disposed of. Otherwise it might have been given to the vultures, as the Romans generally had done with the bodies of those crucified.

In our day, we may not have Jesus' body to bury, but we have Jesus' cause to defend. This duty is not imposed only on pastors or bishops, but on every believer in Christ, no matter what his or her position. Joseph and Nicodemus summon us to wake up and defend the cause of Christ. What excuses do we give for not doing this? We may say, 'Our constitution separates the church from the state', or 'I am meant to represent all and not to take a religious stand on issues' – but often these are only excuses. Joseph and Nicodemus risked their political careers to perform a humble service for Jesus. We, too, should do the same if our conviction about who Christ really is goes deep enough. Look around and see what you can do, in your own country, for Christ's cause!

Not only did these two men risk their positions for Jesus' cause, they also gave material goods to it. The spices that Nicodemus brought for use on Jesus' body were not cheap, and the quantity he supplied was far more than would have been needed just for anointing the body (**19:39b**). The tomb in which they buried Jesus was Joseph's own tomb (**19:41**; Matt 27:60). These are men who gave generously.

Why is it that in Africa our theological institutions and Christian projects are so dependent on Western donors that we begin to wonder, 'Isn't there money in Africa?' There is definitely money in Africa. We can see it in the 'palaces' some African presidents have built for themselves, in the chains of rental houses owned by some of our members of parliament, and in the fleets of vehicles owned by the rich. But what is missing is the attitude we see in Joseph and Nicodemus, who gave abundantly and at a cost to themselves. Where are the palaces, the estates, the fleet of vehicles and the rest, for Jesus? These two men who were secret disciples of Jesus, put us to shame – even as we openly claim to be his disciples.

When Joseph and Nicodemus risked their popularity among their peers and gave as they did, they did not see beyond providing an honourable burial for Jesus. If they were prepared to do so much for a dead Jesus, how much more should we, who know him as our risen Saviour, do for him? African believers need to get into action!

20:1-9 Jesus' Resurrection

Jesus stayed in the tomb for all that remained of the day on Friday and then Friday night, all of Saturday, and Saturday night. On the morning of *the first day of the week*, the day on which we now celebrate the resurrection, Mary Magdalene went to the tomb intending to anoint Jesus' body. Approaching the tomb, she *saw that the stone had been removed from the entrance* (**20:1**). Realizing that the tomb was empty, she rushed back to Simon Peter and the disciple Jesus loved (John the Apostle) and said, *They have taken the Lord out of the tomb, and we don't know where they have put him* (**20:2**). Her use of 'we' implies that Mary had not been alone but was speaking as a representative of others (see also Mark 16:1). The 'they' may have referred to the soldiers who crucified Jesus or the Jewish authorities, particularly the Sanhedrin.

John tells us that Peter and the beloved disciple hurried off to the tomb. The *other disciple outran Peter and reached the tomb first* (**20:3-4**). However, he did not go into the tomb. Instead, *he bent over and looked in* from the outside. He could see *strips of linen lying there* (**20:5**). When Peter arrived, he went into the tomb. He *saw the strips of linen lying there, as well as the burial cloth that had been around Jesus' head* (**20:6-7**). Finally, the other disciple followed Peter inside. He *saw and believed* (**20:8**). What he believed was that Jesus' body was no longer there (**20:9**). Soon, they would learn the glorious truth that Jesus had risen, that he had overcome death (20:19).

20:10-21:25 The Risen Lord

20:10-29 Jesus – Alive, Well and Glorious

After telling Peter and the beloved disciple that Jesus' body had been taken from the tomb, Mary Magdalene (and possibly other women) followed the two men as they ran to the garden. Peter and the other disciple, having realized that Jesus' body really was not in the tomb, *went back to their homes* (**20:10**). Here, 'their homes' simply stands for the place where they were staying in Jerusalem. Mary Magdalene, however, *stood outside the tomb crying* (**20:11**). As she wept, she bent over *and saw two angels in white, seated where Jesus' body had been, one at the head and the other at the foot* (**20:12**). The two angels asked Mary why she was crying and she replied, quite honestly from her perspective, *They have taken my Lord away, and I don't know where they have put him* (**20:13**). Having said this, *she turned around and saw Jesus standing there, but she did not realize that it was Jesus* (**20:14**). Jesus asked her the same question the angels had asked, *Woman, why are you crying? Who is it you are looking for?* (**20:15a**). Thinking that she was speaking to the one in charge of the garden, she replied, *Sir, if you have carried him away, tell me where you have put him, and I will get him* (**20:15b**). At this point, Jesus spoke her name, *Mary* (**20:16**). At the sound of his voice, Mary realized that the one she was talking to was not a gardener, but her Lord! Mary turned towards Jesus and cried out in Aramaic, *Rabboni!* (that is, 'My teacher!'). It was now time for worship, not for asking questions. At last she understood clearly

– Jesus was truly alive. She went to the disciples and told them, *I have seen the Lord!* (**20:18**).

Jesus appeared to Mary Magdalene on the morning of the first day of the week, Sunday 16th Nisan. That evening he also appeared to the disciples (20:19a) who were all together (except for Thomas – 20:24). None of them could think that it had been merely a dream, for they all saw him. Nor could his appearance have been wish-fulfilment, for the disciples were not expecting it; indeed, they were afraid (**20:19a**). Jesus was not hindered by locked doors when he *came and stood among them* (**20:19b**). He had not been there before, which is why John uses the word 'came', but there was no denying that he was standing there then.

Jesus' first words to the stunned disciples were *Peace be with you!* (20:19b). *Shalom*, meaning peace, was a common Hebrew greeting and a blessing in the first century. It was appropriate given the disciples' circumstances. They were still recovering from what they had thought was the loss of their teacher.

The world in general, and the continent of Africa in particular, needs to hear Jesus' words 'peace be with you'. Year after year, Africa remains a bleeding continent. If there is not war in the south, it is in the north; if not in the east, it is in the west, and in the central region too. May Jesus send peace to our continent! Yet when Jesus spoke these words to the disciples, he was focusing on peace of mind and heart. May that peace, too, be our experience in Africa as we wait for the peace in the external realm.

We need to grapple with the question What should be my contribution to the peace Africa needs? Much of the self-inflicted lack of peace in Africa has been born of animosity based on differences – whether ideological, ethnic or religious. Jesus' words 'love your neighbour' (Luke 10:27b) and his illustration of what this means (Luke 10:29-37) cut across any boundaries that have been placed by our differences. We are all called to live in peace. Followers of Christ are called upon to promote the ideals of their master – living together in peace and providing comfort to those who lack it. Those who have been widowed and orphaned by war, AIDS, famine or some other cause need to hear the voice of Jesus' followers (the church) echoing our master's words, 'peace be with you'. If the church of Christ lived up to its master's example, people's needs for food, clothing, counselling, encouragement or a sense of belonging would be met.

Just as Jesus sent his disciples (**20:21**) so also he sends us out of our comfort zone to those who need us. We will experience the joy that the disciples experienced upon seeing Jesus as we serve them (**20:20**).

Jesus ended this meeting with the disciples with a reminder about the promise of the Holy Spirit as *he breathed on them and said, 'Receive the Holy Spirit'* (**20:22**). He performed this symbolic gesture to remind his disciples of what he had been teaching about the Counsellor and of what the Holy Spirit would do for them. He had told them that the work of the Holy Spirit would begin after he had gone back to the Father (14:16; 15:26; 16:7). He would then ask the Father to send the Holy Spirit, who would be with them and guide them *into all truth* (16:13), even to the level of discerning how to deal with sin (**20:23**). We, too, need this reminder. We cannot do the task ahead of us on our own. It is only as the Holy Spirit enables us that we can turn Africa around. Combining our availability and the Holy Spirit's unlimited power, Africa can be saved – not just spiritually but also in all other ways.

At his second appearance to his disciples, Jesus focused on Thomas, who had expressed doubts about the reports concerning the first appearance (**20:24-25**). Jesus gently rebuked Thomas (**20:27b**, **29**), but also led him step by step to the confession; *My Lord and my God* (**20:28**). In so doing, he provided a good model for African pastors. Due to our tradition of a chief being a person of power, pastors in Africa tend to issue authoritative rebukes. But when we rebuke others, we must not lose sight of our goal, namely, bringing those we serve to confess Jesus as their Lord and God. Jesus gave Thomas the opportunity to put his fingers into his side and to feel where the piercing had been done (**20:27a**), to help him move from being a doubting Thomas to a believing Thomas. Are we prepared to patiently take others through the lessons to faith – addressing their doubts one by one? Such patience requires a focus on the needs of the sheep and not on the authority of the pastor. We may call ourselves 'apostles' and 'prophets', but our calling is to be shepherds of the flock and to care for our sheep. The Thomases in the African church long for a lowly shepherd to lead them step by step to see Jesus as their living Saviour and Lord.

20:30-31 The Purpose of This Gospel

At this point John reminds us that what he has written is only a small part of what he could have told of the wonders that Jesus did *in the presence of his disciples* (**20:30**). John, like all the other disciples (except Judas Iscariot), became the witnesses to what they 'heard, saw, looked at, and touched' (1 John 1:1). John was not reporting hearsay evidence, but incidents he had himself seen as one of the twelve (Matt 10:1-4; Mark 3:16-19; Luke 6:14-16). His report can be believed because the events described happened in the public eye, and he himself witnessed them.

John is also explicit about his aim in writing: he has chosen to describe the seven particular signs presented in this Gospel (see the introduction to this commentary) so that his readers *may believe that Jesus is the Christ, the Son of God* (**20:31**). The readers are not commanded to believe but are asked to examine the evidence of Jesus' words and deeds and to conclude that Jesus is who he says he is, namely the Christ, the Son of God.

Those who come to this belief will receive the blessing of *life in his name* (20:31). Note that the possession of this life is conditional on believing. A personal decision is required about whether to accept or reject this life that comes with faith. It is entirely accurate to say that this life 'comes with faith', for John uses the present tense for both the word translated 'believing' and the main verb translated 'may have', which in Greek, signals that the two things happen at the same time. Someone who believes is assured of possession of life from that moment on.

The life can be possessed only in Jesus' name. He is the one God has eternally chosen to deal with sin and death and to give life instead (see also comments on 14:6).

21:1-25 Jesus, the Encourager

In chapter 20 Jesus helped Thomas to overcome his doubts, and in chapter 21 he encourages seven of his other disciples and helps Peter recover from his triple denial of Jesus.

Seven of the disciples were together: Simon Peter, Thomas Didymus (a name that means 'the Twin', Nathanael from Cana, Zebedee's sons James and John, and two others – **21:2**). The reference to these 'two others' reminds us that Jesus does not only reach out to well-known disciples. This group decided to spend the night fishing in the Sea of Tiberias, where probably all of them had fished before (**21:3**). However, that night they caught nothing. *Early in the morning, Jesus stood on the shore, but the disciples did not realize that it was Jesus* (**21:4**). Jesus called out to them, *Children, haven't you any fish?* (**21:5**). The NIV has 'friends' instead of 'children', for the original Greek word can also be translated in this way. On hearing that they had caught nothing, Jesus instructed them to *throw your net on the right side of the boat* (**21:6a**). Probably believing that the speaker was a better fisherman than they were, the disciples did as they had been told. The result was that *they were unable to haul the net in because of the large number of fish* (**21:6b**). In 21:11 we are told that there were a 153 large fish.

The beloved disciple was the first to realize that it was not just an experienced fisherman who had told them where to throw the net, but the powerful, all-knowing Jesus. The beloved disciple then told Peter, *It is the Lord!* (**21:7a**). As soon as Peter was told this, *he wrapped his outer garment around him ... and jumped into the water* (**21:7b**). *The other disciples followed in the boat* (**21:8**).

Surprise number one was the great number of fish they had caught. Surprise number two was seeing Jesus. Then followed surprise number three: *When they landed, they saw a fire of burning coals there with fish on it, and some bread* (**21:9**). Where did these come from? From the hand of Jesus! He had miraculously prepared a breakfast for his disciples. Though he could have provided the rest of the meal miraculously too, he chose not to do this, and told them, *Bring some of the fish you have just caught* (**21:10**).

Simon Peter had reached Jesus before the other disciples, and he was the first to climb back on board when the Lord asked the disciples to bring some of the fish. He *dragged the net ashore* (**21:11a**). Surprise number four was that the huge catch had not torn the net (**21:11b**).

Jesus then invited the disciples to have breakfast, an invitation they all accepted. They dared not ask, *Who are you? They knew it was the Lord* (**21:12**) who knew all things (including where to catch fish); who could bring fire, fish and bread out of nothing and who could prevent an overfilled net from tearing.

Jesus was not only their host but also their servant. He *took the bread and gave it to them, and did the same with the fish* (**21:13**). As the disciples ate the fish and the bread that had been miraculously provided, they must have remembered Jesus' feeding of over five thousand men using five small barley loaves and two small fish (6:5-13).

What did Jesus want them to learn on this occasion? The answer must be related to why the disciples went fishing. It was not because they wanted to return to their original occupation. It was because they needed to be fed. Hunger comes to everyone, even a disciple of Jesus! After their unsuccessful efforts to catch fish, Jesus came and provided far more than they needed for a satisfying meal. Jesus wanted to remind them that he would provide for their daily situations and needs. He would take care of all their needs in the future.

Theologians sometimes spend a lot of time debating whether miracles are taking place today or not. This debate has torn apart the church of Christ in Africa, as some assume that if you believe that miracles happen today you are Pentecostal, and if you do not, then you have not known the full power of Jesus. We need to remember that all believers are Jesus' people, and that all other human classifications serve no good purpose. This passage reminds us that Jesus is a Saviour of surprises. What surprises he will do depends totally on him. Today he may supply many fish, tomorrow the fire from nowhere, but he is the same Jesus, yesterday, today and tomorrow. We are not to focus on who we are but on who he is.

As Jesus reaches out to all, including the unnamed disciples (21:2), he still ministers to each at the level of his specific need. Peter had denied Jesus and was still living with that wound. So Jesus took Peter through the process of leaving what lies behind him and becoming the rock that Jesus had predicted he would be when they first met.

After they had finished eating, Jesus said to Simon Peter, *Simon son of John, do you truly love me more than these?* (**21:15a**). Jesus addressed Peter by his ordinary name (see 1:42) and not as Peter or Cephas, the name that he had given to him. Peter's denial had shown that he was not yet 'a rock'. He was still the ordinary Simon. Jesus was not using this name to condemn Peter, but to remind him that he was as feeble as any other man.

The comparison *more than these* (21:15) probably refers to the other disciples, though an ambiguity in the word translated 'these' leads some to interpret it as referring to the fish, which symbolized his life as a fisherman. The question recalls Peter's words in 13:37, where he had told Jesus, 'I will lay down my life for you.' It was only Peter who had made that promise. When the other disciples ran away (Matt 26:56; Mark 14:50) they were breaking no commitment. Peter, however, had indicated that his love would keep him faithful to the point of death. Jesus was asking Peter, 'Does that commitment still stand, Simon?'

After the pattern of questioning, answering and giving of an assignment had been repeated three times (**21:15-17**), Jesus told Peter, *'Follow me'* (**21:19b**). We are not told in what particular ways Peter was to follow Jesus, but it is clear that both his life and his death were similar to those of Jesus. Jesus knew that there were difficult times ahead for Peter, when he would not be in control of events (**21:18-19a**). Some early church fathers tell us that Peter suffered martyrdom under Nero in AD 64 or 65.

Jesus' answer to Peter's question concerning the beloved disciple, *If I want him to remain alive until I return, what is that to you? You must follow me* (**21:21-22**), reminds us that our life plans are in the Lord's hands. What matters is not whether we are martyred for Christ or keep serving Christ into old age. What matters is the Lord's will. As the Akamba say, *tinda na ukome yumanaa na ula uthokewe* ['it is up to the host to decide whether the visitor leaves or stays overnight']. To be like Peter is honourable, and to be like the beloved disciple is desirable, but to be in the Lord's will is profitable.

Those sons and daughters of Africa who, because they are Christians, have met their deaths at the hands of unbelieving 'Idi Amins' of various kinds remain our model to live for Jesus no matter what the circumstances. While our motive should not be to stir up bees, should they be stirred up by the faithful presentation of the word of God, we should faithfully bear their stings. The Lord's plans for our lives (whether they involve life or death for him) are of great profit. He can use us to encourage others in the present, and in the future he will honour our stand. As he gives us life now, let us serve him faithfully so that the Lord will greet us with 'Well done, my faithful servant.'

Samuel M. Ngewa

Further Reading

Carson, Donald A. *The Gospel According to John*. PNTC. Grand Rapids:Eerdmans/Leicester: Inter-Varsity, 1991.

Morris, Leon. *The Gospel According to John*. NICNT. Rev. ed. Grand Rapids: Eerdmans, 1995.

Ngewa, Samuel M. *The Gospel of John: A Commentary for Pastors, Teachers and Preachers*. Nairobi: Evangel Publishing House, 2003.

ACTS OF THE APOSTLES

Acts is the only book in the NT that describes the earliest events in the Christian church. The Gospels focus on the story of Jesus up to his ascension. The Epistles and the Book of Revelation are written to fully fledged churches. Without Acts, it would be difficult to tell where such churches came from. Acts therefore fills the gap between the Gospels and the rest of the books of the NT. Luke associates what Jesus had begun to do, as recorded in the Gospels, during his earthly ministry, with what he continues to do after the ascension, thus indicating that the ministry of Jesus was the beginning of the Christianity that is portrayed in the Epistles.

The narrative of Acts is also unique in its stress on the inclusiveness of the community of the followers of Christ Jesus. Readers of the book should be moved to seek church unity, which is of great importance in the much divided societies of Africa.

Authorship

Traditionally, the authorship of Acts is assigned to Luke, the beloved physician. He was a companion of Paul (Col 4:14; 2 Tim 4:11), a requirement for writing the 'we' passages, where the author includes himself in the narrative (16:10-17; 20:5-28:31). These passages are clearly distinct from the 'them' passages, where the author was not part of the events described.

Whoever wrote Acts was also the author of the Gospel according to Luke, for the prefaces to both books refer to someone named Theophilus (Luke 1:1-4; Acts 1:1). The preface of Acts also refers to an earlier narrative (1:1). These days, scholars regard these two books as comprising a two-part work, and hence they are often referred to as Luke-Acts.

Place and Date of Authorship

It seems that Acts was written in Rome during the two years (AD 59-61) when Paul was a prisoner there. It is generally agreed that the book was composed before the burning of Rome, the first imperial persecution of the church and Paul's second imprisonment in Rome (AD 64-67). It clearly predates the Jewish revolt against Roman rule (AD 66) and the destruction of the temple (AD 70).

Genre and Purpose

Study of the geographical and historical details in Acts that can be checked against other sources has shown that Luke was a careful historian. It thus seems likely that the book of Acts was not written to promote Paul's views (as some scholars argued in the past) but to provide information about what Luke considered to be the most significant events in the early days of the church. His interpretation of what was significant was influenced by his theology, and thus in reading Acts we need to focus on both historical and theological questions.

In terms of its historical context, Acts can be seen as a defence of the Christian faith to the Roman authorities or as an attempt to mediate between Judaism and Christianity, explaining why the Jewish leaders were continuing to reject the gospel message. Acts also has an evangelistic purpose, freeing the gospel from its ties to Judaism and announcing its spread to all of the known world.

In terms of its theology, Acts gives guidance to the church on how to live until Jesus comes again and on how to transmit the gospel to people who had never seen Jesus in the flesh. It explicitly describes the plan of salvation, the proof of prophecy and the fulfilment of God's promises, all of which were implicit in the Gospels. This presentation could not only be used to explain the significance of Christ's death to unbelievers, but would also encourage and strengthen the church by showing them that God was still acting in history.

Luke has sometimes been accused of papering over the divisions in the earliest community because he does not mention the types of problems recorded in Paul's Epistles to churches like those in Corinth and Galatia. However, his aim may not have been to hide problems but rather to model what the community of believers ought to be like when functioning at its best.

Value for the African Church Today

One of the major themes in Acts is inclusiveness. Luke provides strong evidence that the community of believers transcends all racial, regional and social barriers. The church should not be divided on the lines of race, region or social class. Believers are called to reach out to everyone.

The Holy Spirit provided a clear demonstration that the good news was for everybody at Pentecost, where he abolished the differences in languages that had been established at Babel (Gen 11:6-9) and enabled a miraculous hearing of all that the disciples spoke (Acts 2, especially 2:39).

The African continent entered the twenty-first century ravaged by wars both large and small. It knows far too much of hate and disharmony. The church in Africa needs to be challenged by the inclusiveness of the earliest community of believers to provide an alternative model. By spreading the gospel to all, we can counter this torrent of evil.

Outline of Contents

COMMENTARY

1:1-26 The Gospels and the Church

Its connection with Luke's Gospel gives Acts a unique
place among the books of the NT. It tells about the life of
the disciples once their master was no longer physically
present with them. He had promised to send a helper after
his departure, and the book starts by establishing the vital
link between the departure of Jesus and the advent of the
promised Holy Spirit (**1:8**). It thus links the Gospel narrative with the narrative about the church.

1:1-3a Evidence of the Risen Saviour

Both Luke's Gospel and Acts are addressed to a man called
Theophilus (**1:1a**). Luke starts by reminding Theophilus of
the content of his earlier narrative: *all that Jesus began to
do and teach* (**1:1b**). He uses the word 'began' to make it

clear that he has not covered everything that Jesus did and taught. The same point is made in John 20:30.

Then Luke goes on to stress that Jesus Christ is a risen Saviour. Luke records that Jesus *gave them* [the apostles] *many convincing proofs that he was alive* (**1:3a**). The term 'alive' is key to the resurrection account. The disciples had witnessed the suffering and dying of Jesus, and some of them may have doubted whether Jesus had been raised. They needed convincing proof of this extraordinary event (Mark 16:11-12; Luke 24:36-43; John 20:9, 26-29). Luke stresses this point because without a historical resurrection the Christian faith is baseless (1 Cor 15:1-4; 15:12-19). The apostles had to be absolutely convinced that Jesus was alive in order for them to be witnesses to the rest of the world.

The resurrection of Christ was central to the preaching of the apostles (1:22; 2:31; 4:33; 17:18), just as it should be central to our preaching today. The chorus 'Jesus Is Alive Today' expresses our belief that Christ is indeed alive today and does care for us. He deserves to take centre stage in our lives, in our homes, in our churches, in our countries – in everything. As we go about witnessing to the world about our Lord, we need to be reminded that he is alive and is always with us.

1:3b-8 The Final Discourse of the Risen Saviour

A parent's final words to his children are always important. All the family members – and especially the eldest son, who will take over the leadership of the family – listen attentively. Jesus' disciples would have done the same as he spoke to them for the last time. The topic he spoke of was *the kingdom of God* (**1:3b**). We are given no details of what he said. However, we know from Luke that this topic was of central importance in his ministry (see the comments on Acts 8:12; 19:8; 28:23, 31, below).

Jesus gathered the disciples for a final meal, and there he commanded them not to leave Jerusalem after his departure until they received the gift of the Holy Spirit, who had been promised by the Father (**1:4-5**). John the Baptist had stated that the Messiah would baptize with the Holy Spirit and fire (Luke 3:16; see also Matt 3:11; Mark 1:8; John 1:33). Jesus reminded them that he himself had told them that the Father would be sending the Spirit (Luke 24:49; see also John 14:16,26). Now that promise was about to be kept. However, the disciples did not know the specific time when it would happen, nor did they know what else they would need to do before it came. All they needed to do was to trust the words of their Lord and wait to be baptized with the Holy Spirit, an event that would happen a few days later (1:5).

The disciples, however, were more concerned about the actual timetable for setting up the kingdom of God (**1:6**). They did not want to miss the opportunity to establish it then and there, with themselves installed as the ministers of this kingdom. After all, with Jesus alive and the Holy Spirit coming in power, what possible reason could there be for any further delay?

They were right that God would have had no problem in setting up his kingdom at that time. But their perspective on the type of kingdom God wanted to set up was still far too narrow. They were still limiting the kingdom of God to Israel. If Jesus had done what they wanted, there would have been no place for a universal church. Jesus' world view encompasses the whole world.

Jesus responded by reminding the disciples that God is the one who determines the future. He did not reject their question, but reminded them of their role and limitations (**1:7**). God knew his own plans for Israel and did not need encouragement from others. This verse reminds us of question that Peter, James, John and Andrew had raised earlier (Mark 13:3-4; see also Matt 24:3). Then too, Jesus had told them that it was God the Father's sole prerogative to determine the future (Mark 13:32; see also Matt 24:36). The disciples' selfish interests could not influence the future. God will establish his kingdom when it pleases him.

The disciples, however, still had a part to play in the establishment of the kingdom – they were to be witnesses to Jesus in the power of the Holy Spirit (**1:8**). Earlier, Jesus had said that before the end of the world could come, the message of the gospel had to have been preached among all nations (Mark 13:10). This statement is echoed in this verse, where the disciples were to be witnesses of Jesus, who is the content of the gospel, among all the nations. The route to the establishment of the kingdom of God is making Jesus known among all the nations – literally *to the ends of the earth*.

It has been often been pointed out that this verse summarizes the events in the book of Acts: witness to Jerusalem (3:1-7:60), witness to Judea and Samaria (8:1-12:24), and witness to the ends of the earth (12:25-21:26) and the ultimate witness (21:27-28:31). The organization of this commentary follows a similar pattern.

The task facing the disciples is so vast that they will only be able to perform it through the power of the Holy Spirit. He would stay with those who received him and provide power from within (the Greek word used for 'power' is the same one that is at the root of the English words 'dynamo' and 'dynamite'). The rest of Acts recounts the mighty acts performed by the disciples in the power of the Holy Spirit. Some have even argued that the book should be called 'the Acts of the Holy Spirit' rather than 'the Acts of the Apostles'.

1:9-11 The Ascension

The Gospel accounts of Jesus' ascension are very brief (Mark 16:19; Luke 24:51). This section makes it clear that the disciples were present, watching as Jesus was lifted up into heaven and a cloud separated them from their beloved Lord (**1:9**). Probably, they strained their eyes to see him until he disappeared from view (**1:10**).

The sudden appearance of two men standing beside them would have been both frightening and comforting. These men were angels, sent to comfort them, since they were in a state of shock after losing their Master. The reason for there being two angels, both here and at the tomb of Jesus (Luke 24:4), may be that two witnesses were required to establish the authenticity of what was said.

The angels' words were of profound importance to the disciples. They reassured them that they had nothing to worry about, since Jesus was to come back, and they would see him just as they had seen him go into heaven (**1:11**).

1:12-26 Before the Advent of the Holy Spirit

1:12-14 The first apostolic prayer fellowship

The transition from the ascension to this section is abrupt, but it does provide the information that the ascension took place on the Mount of Olives in the vicinity of Bethany (**1:12**; see also Luke 24:50).

The disciples had obeyed Jesus' command not to leave Jerusalem before the coming of the Holy Spirit and had returned to Jerusalem. There they gathered in an upper room, possibly the same room where they had earlier celebrated their final meal with the Lord (**1:13**). The list of the apostles who were there corresponds to the list in the gospels (Matt 10:2-4; Mark 3:16-19; Luke 6:14-16). The only name missing is that of Judas Iscariot, who had died after betraying his Lord (1:18). The statement *along with the women* confirms that both men and women were witnesses of the ascension of Jesus and the coming of the Holy Spirit (2:1-13). Among those present were Mary, the mother of Jesus, and his brothers.

The entire group was united and devoted to prayer as they waited for the gift of the Holy Spirit. The statement that *they all joined together* (**1:14**) underlines their unity in this important period when there might have been a leadership crisis and competition among them. The very word Luke uses emphasizes their special relationship, for the same word which the KJV translates as 'with one accord' is used ten times in Acts, six times to refer to the fellowship of the Christian community. Its only other use in the NT is in Romans 15:6.

1:15-26 The first apostolic election

Peter now assumes the leadership position in this infant church and leads the group in electing a replacement for Judas (**1:15**). Approximately 120 people were present for this election. It is significant that women were counted together with men, although Peter uses the Jewish manner of beginning a speech in **1:16**, when he addresses the whole group as *brothers*. The Greek makes it clear, however, that this was a gender-inclusive community.

Peter paves the way for the replacement of Judas by quoting Scriptures to prove that Judas' behaviour had been in direct fulfilment of the OT (1:16). Judas had been one of the apostles and had participated fully in Jesus' ministry (**1:17**). But his position had not meant that he was above temptation. Those in leadership positions need to remember that no one is safe from the temptation of the evil one. No position guarantees success.

The narrator then inserts a brief comment on what had become of Judas after the betrayal (**1:18**). He had bought land with the money paid to him as a fee for betraying his Lord and had died there. The account of the death of Judas given here differs slightly from that found in Matthew 27:3-10. There we are told that rather than buying a field, Judas returned all the money to the high priests, who used it to buy a field in which strangers could be buried. In the gospel, Judas hanged himself, while in Acts he is described as falling headlong and bursting his stomach.

This seeming contradiction can be resolved if we take Acts as a brief summary of a story that would have been known to some. This summary needs to be interpreted in light of the account in Matthew. In both Matthew and Acts, the field has the same name, meaning that it is the same field. It seems that what happened is that Judas hanged himself in the same field that the chief priests bought with the money paid to him. It is possible that his body was not found immediately and began to decompose, explaining the reference to his body bursting open. The news spread widely in Jerusalem, and hence that field was named Akeldama – Field of Blood (**1:19**).

Judas may even have been tempted to betray Jesus by a desire to get enough money to purchase some land. Such motivation is not uncommon in Africa, where family members, neighbours and nations have fought and shed blood over land. Judas' fate should deter us from valuing land so highly that we are prepared to do anything to obtain it.

The procedure followed in the election of Judas' replacement sheds light on the state of spirituality of the believers after the departure of their Lord. They clearly relied on Scripture to guide their actions. Peter cited Psalms 69:25 and 109:8 in support of finding a replacement for Judas, arguing that these Scriptures directed that his *place of leadership* should be taken by someone else. The disciples were, therefore, acting in direct obedience to the word of God in seeking to replace Judas (**1:20**).

The qualifications for his replacement were carefully outlined to avoid any ambiguity that might cause dissension in the community. First of all, the person had to have been a consistent follower of the Lord Jesus Christ throughout his ministry. To avoid any possible confusion, the time span was specified as from the ministry of John the Baptist to Jesus' ascension (**1:21-22**). Secondly, the suitable person was to become a witness. The obligations given to the apostles in 1:8 would also apply to the one elected. The position offered would not be an easy one to hold.

Two men who met these criteria were chosen by the entire community, as is indicated by the plural pronoun *they* (**1:23**). The community was thus inclusive and democratic (see also 6:1-7). They then prayed for further guidance as to which of the two should be chosen. The content of their prayer clarifies that this early community was willing to depend on God's guidance (**1:24-25**). They begin by acknowledging the omniscience of God and the possibility of deception in human hearts (see also Jer 17:9-10). Then they proclaim their trust in God, who will be the one to choose the right person to fill the place abandoned by Judas.

The final decision was made using a traditional method – casting lots. The lot fell on Matthias (**1:26**). Thereafter he was counted one of the apostles, and thus the size of the group was restored to twelve men, the number Jesus had appointed. No more would be appointed. Thus when James the son of Zebedee was killed, no steps were taken to fill his place, for death could not rob him of his apostleship. Judas, by contrast, had permanently forfeited his place.

2:1-47 The Birth of the Church

2:1-13 The Coming of the Holy Spirit

2:1-4 The Holy Spirit comes to the disciples

There is a clear sequence of events between Jesus' ascension and the advent of the Holy Spirit. The careful listing of the eleven apostles (1:13) and the replacement of Judas by Matthias (1:15-26), all set the scene for the coming of the Holy Spirit. This is not accidental. The purpose of the Holy Spirit's coming was to enable the twelve apostles, representative of the twelve tribes of Israel (see Rev 21:14), to become witnesses to Jesus both to Israel and to the world.

When the day of Pentecost came means, literally, on the day of Pentecost (**2:1**). It is characteristic of Luke to want to locate this event in history, which is why he specified the exact day. Pentecost comes exactly fifty days after the Sabbath of Passover week (Lev 23:15-16). In the OT it is also referred to as the Feast of Weeks (Deut 16:10), the Day of First Fruits (Num 28:26) and the Feast of Harvest (Exod 23:16). The statement that the disciples were *all together* on this day signifies that those present included more than the eleven apostles plus Matthias, the newly elected replacement for Judas. 'They' should be understood to include all the disciples mentioned in 1:13-15.

These disciples were gathered *in one place,* presumably somewhere other than the upper room where the apostles were staying. The most likely place is the temple courts, where the disciples would have gone to pray and join other people in the celebration of Pentecost. If this were the place, it would explain how a large number of people were able to hear Peter preach.

The coming of the Holy Spirit was signified by physical phenomena: a sound like a *violent wind* blowing and *what seemed to be tongues of fire* (**2:2-3**). It is important to note that the Holy Spirit was bestowed indiscriminately on every disciple: *All of them were filled with the Holy Spirit and all began to speak in other tongues as the Spirit enabled them* (**2:4**). There is a play on the word 'tongues' here, with the contrast between 'tongues of fire' and speaking 'in other tongues'. The Holy Spirit came in the physical form of tongues of fire to bring a transformation of the tongues of the disciples so that they would be able to witness to those present who would not have understood the gospel without this miracle.

2:5-13 His coming is seen by many nations of the earth

The miracle of tongues was necessary because there were in Jerusalem *Jews from every nation under heaven* (**2:5**). The crowd had heard the sound, which implies that it was meant to attract people to the disciples. They gathered together to see what was happening and began to hear the disciples speaking in their own languages (or dialects) (**2:6**). Luke describes their *bewilderment* on hearing the disciples declaring the wonders of God in their own languages. The text implies that what the *Parthians, Medes, Elamites; residents of Mesopotamia, Judea, Cappadocia, Pontus, Asia, Egypt and the parts of Libya near Cyrene; visitors from Rome, both Jews and proselytes; and Cretans and Arabs* were hearing was not the Jewish language but the language spoken where they had been born and brought up (**2:7-11**). This experience must have prepared the crowd for Peter's evangelistic sermon.

The hearers were divided in their opinions of what was being said by the disciples. Some were genuinely not sure what all this meant, and hence they asked the question, whether audibly or in their own hearts: *What does this mean?* Others mocked, saying that the disciples were drunk. Even today the gospel elicits similar responses: some people are genuine seekers, while others are arrogant and mocking (**2:12-13**).

Luke's narrative regularly contains questions and answers. The question 'what does this mean?' permeates the entire narrative of Acts, as Luke tells of the beginning and the growth of the early church.

2:14-41 Peter's Powerful Evangelistic Message

2:14-21 The prophecy of Joel

Peter stands up to explain what was going on to all those who had gathered around the disciples. Clearly there were again twelve apostles, for Peter is described as standing with *the Eleven* (referring to the ten other original apostles plus Matthias). He addresses the crowd as *Fellow Jews and all of you who live in Jerusalem* (**2:14**) – indicating that it included both Jews from Judea and others who had come to live there – and pleads for a hearing, for the time had come for him and the Eleven to bear witness to their risen Saviour.

Peter's first words were directed to those who were suggesting that the disciples were drunk: it was too early in the morning for this to be possible (**2:15**). Then he introduces what is actually happening with a powerful *No* – what they are seeing is not a group of drunks but the fulfilment of a prophecy made by Joel (**2:16**). Joel had spoken about a time when God would pour out his Spirit upon *all people* (**2:17**), referring to the indiscriminate manner in which the Holy Spirit had come upon all those present – both men and women – without regard to social distinctions. Both sons and daughters were to prophesy and young men were to see visions, while old men were to dream dreams. God's servants, both men and women, were to receive the promised Holy Spirit and were to prophesy (**2:18**; see also 21:9-12). This verse seems to suggest that both men and women are qualified to be God's ministers and implies a need for caution when considering whether passages such as 1 Timothy 2:11-13 apply at all times and in all circumstances.

Joel predicted that God would show wonders in the skies and signs on the earth. The signs on earth would include blood, fire and billowing smoke, while above the earth the sun will be darkened and the moon will appear blood red. All these were to happen before the great day of the Lord (**2:19-20**). These two verses seem to refer to what will happen at the end of the last days, the period that begins with the coming of the Holy Spirit. The birth of the Christian church was part of the preparation for the end.

2:22-36: Evidence that Jesus is the Christ

Peter again uses a traditional form of address, *Men of Israel* (**2:22a**), which implies that those listening were both Jews and proselytes. He then expounds the work of Christ, declaring that God had proved that Jesus of Nazareth was the Messiah by providing the signs required of a divine agent (**2:22b**). He insists that Jesus' crucifixion was not the consequence of a human plot but a fulfilment of God's eternal purposes (**2:23a**). God's foreknowledge did not make those who crucified Jesus innocent of this evil deed, for they are still referred to as *wicked men* (**2:23b**). But they were not the only ones responsible for Jesus' death. Peter's repeated *you* stresses that his audience must also bear some of the blame (see Matt 27:22; Luke 23:18). Yet although they had killed Jesus, God had restored him to life. It was impossible for death to keep him captive (**2:24**). Peter argues that when King David proclaimed that God would not let his soul stay in Hades, he could not have been

speaking about himself because he was still dead and the crowd knew where he was buried (**2:25-29**). Rather, he was speaking as a prophet, foretelling the resurrection of Christ (**2:29-31**). The disciples were all witnesses to this resurrection (**2:32**).

The sequence of events since the resurrection is made clear: Jesus went to heaven, received the seat of authority and the Holy Spirit from God the Father and had now given the promised Holy Spirit to his followers (**2:33**). Once again Peter cites David: David had not ascended into heaven, but he was able to prophesy about the ministry of the risen Saviour, who now sits at the right hand of God to bring every power under subjection to God (**2:34-35**). Peter concludes with the emphatic assertion that Jesus, whom they had crucified, had now been made *both Lord and Christ* (**2:36**).

2:37-41 The altar call

Devastated by what they had done, the crowd wanted to know what they could do to set it right (**2:37**). Peter instructs them to repent of their actions and to demonstrate their submission to the lordship of Jesus by being baptized in his name (**2:38**). What a humiliation for a crowd that less than two months earlier had cried out for Jesus' crucifixion!

If they followed Peter's instructions, the people would also receive *the gift of the Holy Spirit*. In Joel, God had promise this gift not only to the people of Israel and their children but also to *all who are far off – for all whom the Lord our God will call* (**2:39**). This gift is clearly extended to people outside the Jewish nation.

The rest of Peter's speech is not recorded, but we are told that he urged the people to accept his message and be saved *from this corrupt generation* (**2:40**). Peter lived up to his calling to be a fisher of men on this day, for over three thousand people were added into the community of believers (**2:40-41**).

2:42-47 A Community of Believers Forms in Jerusalem

2:42-43 Living as a community

The success of Peter's preaching meant that the small community of believers had suddenly grown to more than 3120 persons (see 1:15). How would it organize itself? This newly constituted community managed to live together by devoting themselves to four activities: learning from the apostles, doing exploits for Jesus, serving one another and sharing their goods (**2:42**). Their lifestyle was so attractive that it drew others into the faith.

The enthusiasm with which the new community set out to learn all about their faith is captured by the word *devoted*. These new believers were willing learners and the apostles were willing teachers, for Jesus had also commissioned them to teach those who would become his followers (Matt 28:20a). We see this command being fulfilled here.

A faith that is not understood is shaky and has poor foundations, and that is why the new believers had to know what and why they believed. The church in Africa needs to develop the same devotion to teaching. The African church is sometimes described as a mile long and an inch deep, meaning that it has many members but that these members have only a shallow understanding of the word of God. Pastors must be willing to teach, and congregations must be enthusiastic to learn the important tenets of their faith.

The second thing that the narrator tells us about this new community is that they were devoted *to the fellowship,* meaning that the believers were in a friendly partnership. Believers of today, who tend to be individualists, need to be reminded of our need for one another as we seek to serve and worship our Lord.

The third activity to which they were devoted cannot exist without the other two: only a community that has understood its calling and that is characterized by close partnership is able to break the bread of life together. Celebrating the Lord's Supper without close mutual fellowship is a mockery of what was achieved on the cross. The phrase 'breaking bread' is used in the Gospels only in relation to Jesus' actions (Matt 14:19; Luke 24:30, 35). But it also came to be used of the ordinance he instituted to commemorate his death and resurrection (Matt 26:26-29; Mark 14:22-25; Luke 22:14-20; 1 Cor 11:23-25). The church was instructed to continue to celebrate this meal until he returned.

Last, but most certainly not least, the early disciples were devoted to *prayer.* The same verb is used here as for the other three activities: the believers were just as devoted to prayer as they were to the apostles' teaching, to fellowship and to the breaking of bread. In the same way, the church of today must be devoted to prayer. If 'prayer moves mountains', one wonders why so many mountains continue to hinder the development of the African continent and to blight the lives of African believers. Perhaps we need to be as devoted to prayer as the early church was. The prayer of faith will help to bring peace to this beloved continent. But it will not be enough on its own; we also need to be devoted to the other three things: to teaching, to fellowship and to the breaking of bread.

The changed lives and unity of the community of believers were evident to others in their community. The NIV says that *everyone was filled with awe,* but the literal translation is 'fear came upon every person' (**2:43**). Those who had earlier mocked them were now gripped by fear.

There was something extraordinary about this group of Christians, *for many wonders and miraculous signs were done by the apostles*. We are not told exactly what these were, although we can make some deductions from events later in Acts. But what is important to note is that when a community of believers is united, wonders and signs will be associated with them and will have a positive effect on the wider community.

2:44-47 Sharing as a community

This section is not to be interpreted as if the new believers formed some kind of monastic group or commune, isolated from the world, in which no one owned anything and all possessions belonged to the community. What we have is not a community of goods, but a community of believers who were so devoted to one another that they were willing to share everything so that none of them lacked anything (**2:44**).

To understand why some of them may have been in want, we need to return to the circumstances of their conversion. Luke described the crowd listening to Peter as having come from all over the known world (2:5). Many of them would have travelled to Jerusalem for Passover and would have been planning to return home after the Feast of Pentecost. The Ethiopian eunuch may be an example of someone who had this schedule (8:27-28).

These people might also have had a lot in common even before their conversion. They had travelled far to come to Jerusalem, and during their long stay there they would have met others from their own nations with whom they might have shared meals and accommodation. They might already have lived in a sort of community in which they pooled the resources they had bought, which they would have expected to last for about fifty days. Some might have brought goods to sell so that they could buy food or animals for sacrifice in the temple.

Now that they had been saved and added into the community of believers, they probably delayed their plans to return home and it was only natural to continue in the same fellowship. Why should it be strange for them to have *everything in common*?

The original small group of some 120 disciples (1:15) was swamped by the new arrivals. When the group had been small, individual families could cater to it, but this was no longer possible. There was a need to identify those with possessions and goods and to encourage them to sell these and give to the needy in proportion to their particular needs (**2:45**). This type of arrangement recurs repeatedly throughout the book of Acts (4:32-35; 6:1-7; 9:36-41; 11:27-30; 20:34-35; 24:17).

Two other points can be made in support of the position that this was not a community in which everything belonged to everyone. One is that the verbs for 'selling' and 'giving' are both in the imperfect tense, which suggests that the selling and giving took place from time to time, and not on one occasion. Another is the statement that goods were distributed *to anyone as he had need.* If everything had been held in common, there would be no mention of some as owning possessions and goods and others as having needs.

The description of the group as being *together* should not be taken to mean that they were in one place all the time, but rather that they met together for a purpose (**2:46**). They spent much time in the temple because they did not have other things to do, having left their homes to come and worship, and so they may well have met there every day to listen to the apostles. This practice was quite different from that of the Qumran community, who withdrew from contact with all those who were not part of the group and took up residence in the desert.

There is no indication that the apostles encouraged the forming of an exclusive community. Peter's advice to the people to save themselves from this *corrupt generation* (2:40) does not imply a need to form a community away from the world. In fact, the reference to the believers as *enjoying the favour of all the people* (**2:47a**) makes it clear that they were not isolated. What we have here is a new community of believers where all the believers were together and yet remained within the wider society.

The unity and mutual helpfulness of the believers was a living out of what was considered an ideal model of friendship in the Greek world. Luke describes this community in Jerusalem as being *glad and sincere* in their fellowship. The description of them as breaking bread *in their homes* (NIV) or *from house to house* (KJV) may mean that the leaders of the community moved from one house to another to conduct services.

This new community was growing rapidly (**2:47b**). Luke speaks of new converts being added to it. Clearly God is the one doing the adding (2:47; see also 2:41; 5:14; 11:24). The community was also obviously inclusive: once the basic requirements of repentance and baptism had been met, any new believer was automatically accepted. No wonder the number of believers increases rapidly from 120 in chapter 1 (1:15) to more than 3000 in chapter 2 (2:41) to about 5000 by chapter 4 (4:4).

3:1-7:60 Witness to Jerusalem

This section of Acts primarily describes events that took place in Jerusalem and the first major opposition to the witness of the gospel by the religious leaders. The main characters are Peter and John, backed by the Jerusalem church.

3:1-26 Peter and John Bring Healing

The healing of the crippled beggar offered confirmation of the truth of the gospel that the apostles were preaching. It is thus not surprising that it generated opposition from the religious authorities.

3:1-10 The healing of the crippled beggar

Luke has chosen to tell the story of one of the lowest of the have-nots in that society, a man who was unable to work for a living and could only beg for money from people like Peter and John, who were coming to worship at the temple (**3:1-2**). When Peter and John were confronted by this beggar, they had no money to give him, but Peter did give him a unique gift: immediate healing in the name of Jesus (**3:3-7**). As Peter will explain in 4:12, there is no other name that can save. This truth applies equally to beggars and to the respected leaders of the Sanhedrin.

This gift both healed the man and restored his identity, giving him a place in the community of believers. The description of him as *walking and jumping and praising God* (**3:8**) indicates both the completeness of the cure and his unbridled joy in his new-found health, which poured out in praise to God and could not be hidden. It was seen by *all the people* (**3:9**), who were amazed by the change in him (**3:10**). He immediately joined the praising band of the saved and became a powerful testimony for the Christian community (**3:10-11**; 4:14). Someone who had been an insignificant beggar took on a high-profile role in the ministry of the gospel. He did not necessarily preach, for Peter as an apostle did that on this occasion, but his transformed life helped to draw attention to the transforming power of Christ.

3:11-26 Peter's speech to a crowd

As on the day of Pentecost (2:6), so another crowd of astonished people formed on this occasion, attracted by the miracle of the walking cripple (**3:11**). Once again, Peter took advantage of the opportunity to preach the gospel.

3:12-16 JESUS IS THE SAVIOUR Peter immediately deflects the crowd's attention away from himself and John and onto Jesus (**3:12**). But he does not start by saying Jesus' name; instead he starts by talking about what the crowd knew – namely, the *God of Abraham, Isaac and Jacob* and in sum, *the God of our fathers* (**3:13a**). Peter is right to work from the known to the unknown. The God the crowd did know had glorified his servant Jesus – the same Jesus that they had delivered up and disowned before Pilate, even when Pilate had desired to release him (**3:13b**). As in his sermon at Pentecost, Peter accuses the crowd of aiding the killing of Jesus.

The person whom they disowned was holy and righteous, but they had preferred a murderer to him (**3:14**). Rather than punishing the murderer, they had put the Prince of Life to death (see also 5:31; Heb 2:10; 12:2). But God had raised him from the dead, and Peter and John were witnesses to this fact (**3:15**). The now risen Lord had performed this miracle in their presence – and there could be no doubt that it was a miracle, for Peter points out that the crowd knows the man, so that the apostles cannot be accused of faking a healing.

This healing has been made possible by faith in the name of Jesus (**3:16**). The Christian church today needs to have faith in his name if we are to experience miracles in this century that will help the church to point the world to Jesus, the Prince of Life.

3:17-26 THE ALTAR CALL: REPENT NOW Having accused the crowd, Peter carries on to acknowledge that most of them had acted in ignorance when they agreed to call for the crucifying of the Lord. Their leaders, too, had been ignorant of what they were really doing (**3:17**). But acknowledging their ignorance does not mean they are not guilty. Nor does it imply that they do not need forgiveness.

Both the disciples and the crowd were witnessing what God had announced by his prophets (**3:18**). The appropriate response was to repent and return to God in order to have their sins washed away. In his earlier sermon, Peter had promised the gift of the Holy Spirit to those who believed (**2:38**), but now he speaks of *times of refreshing ... from the Lord* (**3:19**). He may be referring simply to the gift of the Holy Spirit, or he may mean that and much more, since the source of the refreshing is the presence of the Lord. The crowd had seen an example of what this refreshing could mean in the healing of the crippled man.

Peter goes on to speak of Jesus in the most wonderful language: he is *the Christ who has been appointed for you*, who is now in heaven *until the time comes for God to restore everything* as God had *promised long ago through the prophets* (**3:20-21**). Jesus is the prophet whose coming Moses had predicted (Deut 18:15,18-19). If people refuse to listen to him, they face condemnation (**3:22-23**). Not only Moses, but all the prophets since Samuel, the first prophet, have predicted the events that are now happening (**3:24**). This statement is not meant to be taken literally, for we have no record of Samuel making any messianic prophecy. Peter's point is that all prophecy is ultimately focused on the coming of Christ.

The hearers are reminded that while they may be guilty, they are also the heirs of the prophets, meaning that they inherit the promises made by them. They are also the heirs of the promise made to Abraham that through them *all peoples on earth* shall receive blessings (**3:25**; see also Gen 22:18). Once again we are reminded of the inclusiveness of the gospel (see also 2:39). But while the blessing will be to all peoples, the Jews have the privilege of hearing it first, and of being given an opportunity to turn from their wicked ways (**3:26**).

4:1-31 The Beginning of the Struggle for the Gospel

Peter's sermon was interrupted by the arrival of *the priests and the captain of the temple guard and the Sadducees* (**4:1**), who promptly arrested Peter and John and put them in jail (**4:2-3**). They were arrested because they were teaching the crowd at the temple in the name of Jesus and were claiming

that he had risen from the dead, which the authorities denied. This arrest marks the start of active persecution of the apostles, but it did not prevent a great harvest being drawn in. A great number believed after hearing Peter's message (**4:4**), demonstrating not only the power of God's word but also that even a beggar is able to attract thousands to faith in Jesus.

4:5-7 Peter and John interrogated before the Sanhedrin

Luke, the historian, records the composition of the Sanhedrin in Jerusalem the next day (**4:5-6**). This body comprised seventy-one elders, and among those present were Annas, the ex–high priest, who had been deposed by the Romans but was still supported by the Jewish people, and Caiaphas, his son-in-law, whom the Romans had now installed as high priest. (This explains why two men are given the title of high priest in Luke 3:2.) We do not know the identity of the *John* and *Alexander* referred to here, but they were undoubtedly powerful men, as were the other relatives of the high priest (**4:6**). Being hauled before such a group could easily have intimidated ex-fishermen like Peter and John.

The interrogation started with a question about the healing of the crippled man, since it could not be denied that this healing had taken place. So the leaders sought to know *by what power* or in what *name* this had been done (**4:7**).

4:8-12 Peter's speech to Sanhedrin

Previously, Peter was speaking to an interested audience (3:12), but now he faces a hostile and contemptuous court. He clearly needs God's help to declare the gospel confidently to this group; hence the mention of his being filled by the Holy Spirit (**4:8a**).

Peter addresses them with appropriate respect as *rulers and elders of the people* (**4:8b**). Then he restates the reason they are on trial, emphasizing that what had been done was *an act of kindness*. The miracle had not been done to attract attention, but since they want to know in whose name it had been done, both they and *all the people of Israel* should know that it had been done in *the name of Jesus Christ of Nazareth* (**4:9-10**). Jesus is referred to in this way a number of times in Acts (2:22; 3:6; 4:10; 6:14; 22:8; 26:9), and the Jewish leaders later refer to the followers of Jesus as 'the Nazarene sect' (24:5). The name shows that Jesus had grown up in Nazareth and was associated with that region.

Saying that something was done in someone's name implies that it was done by his power. Peter boldly asserts the healing power of Jesus, whom the leaders had crucified and God had raised from the dead (4:10). Under the influence of the Holy Spirit, Peter dares to proclaim the truth before the authorities.

He then proclaims a second truth. Not only does Jesus bring healing; he is also the only source of salvation. Peter describes Jesus as the stone rejected by builders that *has become the capstone* (**4:11**). In the ancient world, the capstone, or cornerstone, was the stone that held an entire structure together. The image is first used in the Bible in the book of Job (Job 38:6), where God is said to have laid the cornerstone of the foundations of the world. It is used again in Psalm 118:22, which the Jews interpreted as referring to the young David who was rejected but eventually became king – although this passage also had messianic overtones. Jesus himself used this image in his parable of the vineyard (Mark 12:1-12; see also Matt 21:42). Peter is asserting that Jesus has become the stone upon which the new community of faith is built (see also 1 Cor 3:11; Eph 2:20; 1 Peter 2:4-5).

The primary task of the rulers and elders was to build the community, but they had rejected the stone and chosen a murderer in his place (3:13). For them, the cornerstone had become a 'stone of stumbling' and 'rock of offence' (Isa 8:14; 28:16; Rom 9:33). If the cornerstone is not given its rightful place, it becomes a stone of judgment. Peter makes this point strongly in **4:12**, when he says that *there is no other name under heaven given to men by which we must be saved* (see also 10:43).

4:13-22 The Sanhedrin's response

The rulers and elders were amazed at *the courage of Peter and John* (**4:13**), who were uneducated and should have been intimidated by the powerful, educated men who sat to judge them. Being with Jesus, the master teacher, had changed them and learning from him had compensated for any lack of formal education (Matt 7:28-29; 13:54; 22:33; Mark 1:21-22; John 7:15). Peter and John now spoke like people with education and training. All those in the church of Christ should share this experience, for they too are in contact with Jesus.

Peter and John may also have been emboldened by the presence of the healed man. The reality of the miracle meant that the council could say nothing after Peter's speech, since there was no denying that the beggar standing with them had been healed (**4:14-16**). But instead of listening to Peter's message, they focused on damage control, trying to prevent the new movement from spreading to many more people by ordering the disciples not to speak in the name of Jesus anymore (**4:17-18**).

Peter and John responded that they could not accept this command. They put their dilemma to the council, asking these religious leaders whether it was not more important to obey God than to obey a human court (**4:19**). They knew what they had *seen and heard* (**4:20**), and by keeping silent they would not only be denying it but would also be disobeying a direct command of God (1:8). Their resolve to keep speaking in the name of Jesus regardless of impending danger is an example to those ministering in dangerous areas.

The council were probably confused by this unexpected reaction, and after uttering further threats, they released Peter and John (**4:21a**). Punishment would not have been seen as appropriate when *all the people* were glorifying God for this great miracle (**4:21b**). The man who had been healed was in his forties, a mature man, who would have been known to many and who could himself bear testimony to the miracle (**4:22**).

4:23-31 God answers prayer through Jesus

Peter and John returned to the community of believers and reported what had happened, including the threats that had been uttered (**4:23**). The community's response was united prayer (**4:24**) – reflecting the unity for which Jesus had prayed (see John 17:21). The content of their prayer is striking. Instead of praying for their enemies to be punished, they prayed about accomplishing their mission of proclaiming Jesus to all. They prayed for boldness and left the fate of those who oppose the spread of the gospel to God.

Their prayer can serve as a model for believers. It begins with an acknowledgement of God as the Creator of everything (4:24). Everything and everyone is subject to God's creative power, even the members of the Sanhedrin. Long before, David had expressed the truth that God is greater than any human authorities (**4:25-26**; Ps 2:1-4). However, God's control does not mean that his followers will never suffer. After all, God had permitted the suffering and death of Jesus (**4:27-28**). But given the glorious consequences of his suffering and death, the believers' main request was that they would not be deterred by threats but would continue to boldly proclaim Jesus (**4:29**). They also asked God to continue to perform *signs and wonders through the name of your holy servant Jesus* (**4:30**; 2:22; 43). The primary reason for requesting these miracles was not for their own safety but to confirm the truth that had been prophesied (2:19).

God gave physical confirmation that he had heard and would answer their prayer (**4:31**). The place was shaken and they were filled with the Holy Spirit, confirming Jesus' promise to his followers (1:8). Instead of speaking in tongues as on the day of Pentecost, they *spoke the word of God boldly*. They had prayed for boldness and God had answered their prayer.

4:32-5:11 Witness: A Community Sharing Possessions

The sharing of possessions by the community of believers was already mentioned in 2:44. Some scholars treat 4:32-35 as simply a duplication of what was said there. But if one reads the two passages side by side, it becomes clear that there have been changes in the procedures followed.

4:32-35 Unity in heart and mind

The community of believers was growing rapidly (2:47). In 2:41 there were 3000 believers, and by 4:4 there were

5000. Consequently the burden of meeting their economic needs had grown.

The key statement here is that *all the believers were of one heart and mind* (**4:32**). This oneness of purpose enabled the extraordinary sharing of all that they owned. They were not individualistic and did not claim that their possessions were their own private property. Such sharing is another way of witnessing, since it portrays the oneness that Jesus prayed for in his followers. It demonstrates that Jesus has truly come from the Father (John 17:21). Meanwhile the apostles continued to bear powerful witness to the resurrection of Jesus (**4:33**). God's abundant grace enabled both the witness and the unity of the community.

So generous were the believers that *there were no needy persons among them* (**4:34a**). The use of the word 'needy' instead of 'poor' is interesting. Some of these believers may have been rich in their own right at home, but they were needy now because they were separated from their property. There were no banks to transfer funds, and thus even if they had assets abroad, they were still in need of food once their own supplies had run out.

The reason there were no needy people in the community was not just that *they shared everything* but that *those who owned lands and houses* were willing to sell them and place the proceeds at the apostles' disposal (**4:34b-35**). This was not a community in which people forfeited the right of ownership, but rather one in which owners are willing to part with possessions for the sake of needy fellow believers. When their existing possessions and goods were not sufficient to meet the needs of the growing community, some lands and houses were sold. This statement does not mean that all the believers sold their lands and houses. If they had, they would have had to leave the city and live in the countryside, for they would have had no place to sleep! Moreover, the statement about Saul 'going from house to house' (8:3) would not make sense if all the houses had been sold.

Luke then proceeds to tell us about some specific people who sold their houses and lands.

4:36-37 Joseph/Barnabas: How to share

Joseph was nicknamed Barnabas by the apostles because of his encouraging character (**4:36**). He came from Cyprus, but may have owned some land in Jerusalem as part of his family inheritance. As a Levite, he was a member of a wealthy class, making it even more likely that he might have had land to sell (**4:37**).

Barnabas may be mentioned in particular because many members of the early church would have known him, for he travelled widely on his own and with Paul (11:22; 13:2-3). We should follow his example. There would be no needy believers in our communities either if we were as prepared to share our belongings as Barnabas was.

5:1-11 Ananias and Sapphira: How not to share

One incident related to sharing was very frightening to the community and to everyone else who heard about it (**5:11**). Ananias sold a piece of land, with the consent of his wife Sapphira, and kept some of the money from the sale with his wife's full knowledge (**5:1-2**). But when he brought his donation to Peter, he claimed that he was giving all that he had been paid for the property. His sin was not that he kept some of the money for himself, but that he tried to deceive God (**5:3-4**). Sapphira's sin was not that she failed to prevent her husband from lying, but that she was a willing participant in testing the Spirit of the Lord (**5:8-9**). Her arrival three hours after her husband's death may have been because she was coming to find out what was delaying him.

This story is told for two purposes. First, it emphasizes that the sharing of goods was voluntary (5:4a). Giving should be done freely, as Paul emphasizes in 2 Corinthians 9:7: 'Each man should give what he has decided in his heart to give, not reluctantly under compulsion, for God loves a cheerful giver' (see also Gal 6:9, 10). There is no need to pretend to be giving more than is actually being given. Secondly, there is no benefit in lying; God knows the truth (5:4b). It seems that this couple had allowed Satan, who is a liar by nature (John 8:44), to take the place of the Holy Spirit (5:3, 9).

5:12-42 Witness: Miraculous Signs and Wonders

5:12-16 Many drawn to the Lord

Despite the fear aroused by the deaths of Ananias and Sapphira (5:11), great numbers were being drawn to the Lord. The apostles were enabled to perform many *signs and wonders among the people* (**5:12a**). The unity of the community of believers was also shown by their regular gatherings in Solomon's Colonnade (**5:12b**). They aroused divergent reactions. Outsiders were afraid to associate with them, but did not dare to mock them (**5:13**). But large numbers of people were also converting and joining the community (**5:14**). The fact that both men and women were joining indicates that this was an inclusive community. So impressive were the signs and wonders performed by the apostles that it was believed that even Peter's shadow could heal (**5:15**; see also 19:11-12). Crowds gathered for healing and for release from evil spirits, and *all of them were healed* (**5:16**).

5:17-42 The jealousy of the religious leaders

The high priest and his associates (described here as *members of the party of the Sadducees*) were filled with jealousy (**5:17**), partly because of the success of the apostles' ministry. They were also opposed to the apostles' proclamation of Jesus' resurrection (4:33), for the Sadducees did not believe in the possibility of resurrection (see Matt 22:23;

Mark 12:18; Luke 20:27; Acts 23:8). They therefore led the opposition to the followers of Jesus at this early stage (4:1; 23:6, 7, 8).

The high priest (who seems to have been a Sadducee) and his associates managed to have the apostles thrown into the public jail (**5:18**). Because Peter and John had rejected the earlier warnings of the high priests and the Sanhedrin (4:1-21), the net of persecution had been widened and may now have included all the apostles. And this time their situation was worse, for they were not thrown into the private religious jail (4:3) but into the public jail.

In the face of this heightened persecution, the Lord intervened more directly, using an angel who rescued them and commanded them to go to the temple and proclaim the message (**5:19-20**). They were not to shy away from the danger that this would bring. The apostles duly obeyed their Lord's instructions, and *at daybreak* they went into the temple court *and began to teach the people* (**5:21a**).

When the Sanhedrin assembled and sent for the prisoners, they found that they were not in the jail, although all the doors were still locked and guarded (**5:21b-23**). It is no wonder that the captain of the guard and the chief priests were perplexed (**5:24**).

Their puzzlement as to where the apostles could be was resolved when someone reported that they were teaching openly in the temple courts (**5:25**). The captain and his officers immediately went and summoned them to appear before the council, but they were careful to do it peacefully so as not to arouse the crowd. The people were ready to stone anyone who mistreated the servants of Jesus (**5:26**).

The council accused the apostles of having disobeyed their strict instructions not to teach in the name of Jesus (4:18). Instead they had *filled Jerusalem with your teaching*, suggesting that everyone in Jerusalem had heard the teachings of Jesus. Not only were the apostles still teaching; they were even suggesting that the Sanhedrin was responsible for Jesus' death (**5:27-28**). Since the death and resurrection of Jesus are central to preaching of the gospel, the apostles must have spoken of the role of the Jewish leaders in rejecting Jesus and having him put to death (3:13-17; 4:10).

Peter spoke for the others when he reiterated their determination to *obey God rather than men* (**5:29**). Risking the wrath of the council, Peter insisted that the council had indeed put Jesus to death (**5:30**). But Jesus had been raised by *the God of our fathers*. The apostles were not proclaiming another God, but the same God that the religious leaders claimed to worship. Jesus has now taken up a position at God's right hand, that is, in the position of authority. He now calls everyone to repent so that their sins can be forgiven (**5:31**). Jesus has become both Prince and Saviour in order to grant repentance to Israel. The apostles were unwavering in their witness to these things (**5:32**). Should the leaders doubt their words, the Holy Spirit was also a witness to the truth of what they were proclaiming. However, the Holy Spirit was only available to those who were prepared to obey God (**5:32b**).

A similar speech to the crowd on the day of Pentecost had moved many to repentance (2:37-41). However, this time Peter's speech merely roused such fury in the council members that they wanted to execute the apostles (**5:33**). But this action was prevented by a respected teacher of the law named Gamaliel (**5:34-39**), who advised the council that time would tell whether the teaching was from God or it was human error. He cited two examples of men who had once attracted large followings, but whose influence had petered out. One of these was *Theudas*, who had assembled some four hundred followers, all of whom had scattered after he was put to death, so that his movement came to nothing (**5:36**). Another was *Judas the Galilean*, who had led a revolt at the time of the census (perhaps the census that had taken place in the year of Jesus' birth – Luke 2:2). After he was slain, all of his followers had also scattered (**5:37**). If Jesus was in the same category as these men, the movement he had started would soon die down (**5:38**). If he was not, and the movement had God's blessing, the council would have no hope of stopping it (5:39). It is a dangerous thing to fight against God – as Saul found out on the road to Damascus (9:5).

The council listened to Gamaliel and merely ordered that the apostles be flogged and then released them, with another stern warning against speaking anymore in the name of Jesus (**5:40**).

Public flogging would usually be a cause for shame, but the apostles considered that suffering persecution was part of their duty as servants of Jesus, as is clear from their continuing joy (**5:41**). What a privilege to be considered worthy of facing persecution because of the name of Jesus and by God's design! Ignoring the Sanhedrin's warnings, they continued to teach and to preach both in the temple and from house to house that Jesus was the Christ (**5:42**).

6:1-7 Witness: A United Community

It is wrong to think of the community of believers as fragmented by the discontent regarding the sharing of goods. On the contrary, they were united as they persevered in coping with the increased membership, which must now have risen well above 5000 (**6:1a**; see also 4:4; 5:14).

The increasing number of believers made it more difficult to distribute goods effectively, resulting in some widows being overlooked in the daily distribution of food (**6:1b**). There were complaints that Greek-speaking *Jews* from countries other than Israel were being neglected by Aramaic-speaking *Jews*, who had been born in Israel. Both groups were Jews, so this was not an incident of racial discrimination. Nor had the community of goods failed, although the system of distribution had proved to be flawed.

The apostles alone could no longer cope with the numbers and ensure fair distribution. However, the system did work in that they soon became aware that there was a problem. When a widow went hungry, the community knew of it and took action to ensure that the situation did not continue. This concern for widows was clearly important to Luke.

The apostles had been commanded to proclaim the word of God (5:20), but were finding that they were becoming bogged down in administrative tasks such as serving food (6:2a; see also 4:35b). Moses had faced a similar problem, and God had addressed it by commanding him to appoint seventy assistants (Num 11:16-17). So the apostles requested that seven assistants be appointed to make sure that everyone received what they needed (6:3). The first qualification for these assistants was that they be *known*, that is, that they have a good reputation (see RSV and KJV translations and also 1 Tim 3:2). Those holding such a sensitive position would need to be trusted. Many church leaders have failed the test of being above reproach when given the opportunity to manage church resources, especially money. Churches should consider this principle when electing people to their boards.

The second qualification was being filled with the Holy Spirit. Even an administrative task was a spiritual one, and the filling of the Holy Spirit was as much needed for the distribution of food as it was for the preaching of the word. The unity of the community, which these men had to maintain, was as much a witness to the Lord as was the teaching in the name of Jesus (see also John 17:21).

Finally, to be effective in their task, they needed wisdom to distinguish genuine need from wants. The principle of distribution had been that no one lacked anything, but this also meant that no one received more than others (see also 2 Cor 8:15). The assistants had to be able to judge the exact amount each person needed.

Handing over these tasks to others left the apostles free to focus on preaching and praying (6:2b, 4). The assistants, however, did not restrict their work solely to distributing food, for at least two of them – Stephen and Philip – engaged in evangelistic ministry (6:5; 6:8-7:60; 8:5-40).

It is evidence of the unity of the community that everyone approved of this course of action and was involved in appointing these leaders (6:5). There were no factions. Seven men were chosen: Stephen, described as *a man full of faith and of the Holy Spirit*; Philip; Prochorus; Nicanor; Timon; Parmenas; and Nicolas from Antioch, who is described as a convert to Judaism (6:5). All of these men have Greek names, suggesting that the community chose people who would be close to those they were serving. The Judean believers were prepared to let other believers control the distribution of goods to everyone.

The apostles commissioned these men for their new role by praying for them and laying hands on them (6:6). This

is the first recorded incident where the laying on of hands marks the commissioning of servants of the Lord. It became a tradition that was carried on by the leaders at the church of Antioch (13:3). Later, Paul warns Timothy about laying hands on anyone before they have been subject to adequate scrutiny (1 Tim 5:22).

The quick action by the apostles ensured that the word of God kept spreading and *the number of disciples in Jerusalem increased rapidly* (6:7a). Had the apostles allowed themselves to be sidetracked into administrative work, the spread of the gospel, which was their primary calling, would have been jeopardized. This is an important principle for churches. Pastors are called to be teachers and preachers of the word, and church members must support them and work to ensure that the daily needs of all the members are being met.

By now the community had expanded to include many priests. Its continuing growth proved beyond any reasonable doubt that God was at work (5:36-39) and many former opponents of the gospel became obedient to the faith (6:7b).

6:8-7:60 Witness: The Death of Stephen

Stephen was one of those who had been chosen to administer the community, but that was not his sole task. Like the apostles, he performed great wonders and miracles (signs) (6:8). When he was first mentioned in 6:5, he was described as 'full of faith and of the Holy Spirit', and here too he is described as *full of God's grace and power*. It is no wonder that he was an extraordinary man of God.

Stephen's miracles were performed *among the people*, presumably meaning those who were not believers. He was thus actively involved in evangelizing the Jewish people in Jerusalem, and this aroused the opposition to him.

6:9-15 The opposition to Stephen

Tradition has it that Stephen was a Hellenistic, or Greek-speaking, Jew and that his ministry was among the Hellenistic Jews. This is why his opponents were not the chief priests and the elders of people, who had earlier opposed the apostles (4:1) but other Hellenistic Jews, who are described as belonging to the *Synagogue of the Freedmen*. His opponents included people from Cyrene and Alexandria in Africa, and from Cilicia and the Roman province of Asia, which is now part of Turkey (6:9). They began to argue with Stephen, but were unable to cope with his *wisdom or the Spirit by whom he spoke* (6:10). The Lord instructed Stephen as to what to say, leaving his opponents speechless (see also Luke 12:12).

Unable to refute him verbally, Stephen's opponents hatched a secret plan to have him killed. They encouraged some men to accuse him of blasphemy *against Moses and against God* (6:11) and used these charges to stir up *the people, and the elders and the teachers of the law* (6:12). What had been a debate turned into an ugly confrontation as Stephen was dragged before the council, presumably the Sanhedrin. The accusers then repeated their false accusations that Stephen was constantly speaking out against the temple and the Mosaic law. They insisted that Stephen taught that Jesus of Nazareth would destroy the temple and alter the Mosaic customs (**6:13-14**).

Looking at Stephen to see how he was responding to these charges, the entire group was struck by the change on Stephen's face. His face had become *like the face of an angel* (**6:15**). The startling transformation of the man before them should have made the council listen closely to what he had to say. Maybe this is why he was allowed to speak at such length before his opponents cruelly silenced him (**7:54-58**).

7:1-53 Stephen's outline of history

The high priest asked Stephen, *'Are these charges true?'* (**7:1**). Instead of simply answering 'yes' or 'no', Stephen seized the opportunity to share the story of salvation with a group who would not normally have listened to it. Peter and John had presented the gospel briefly in 4:10-12; 5:29-32, but now Stephen was determined to present it all, starting from the beginning with Abraham.

7:1-8A ABRAHAM Without God's initiative, there would be no holy people, let alone a holy place. God was the one who appeared to *our father Abraham* (**7:2**). (Stephen includes both himself and his hearers in the category of the children of Abraham.) Abraham lived among a people who worshipped other gods in the land of Mesopotamia (specifically in Ur of the Chaldeans), but the God of glory intended to lead him to a new land (**7:3**).

Abraham obeyed God and left his home and his people and moved to Haran. After the death of his father, God led him to move on again to Canaan, the land *in which you are now living* (**7:4**). (Stephen does not include himself in this group, since he was a Greek-speaking Jew and not a resident of Palestine.) Genesis first mentions God appearing to Abraham in Haran, but the story began while Abraham was still in Mesopotamia, when he consented to accompany his father Terah in his migration northward (Gen 11:31). Stephen bases his account on an assumption about what must have happened, and God's appearance in Gen 12:1 should therefore be understood as the second time God spoke to Abraham (**7:4**). The point of telling this story is to emphasize that God appeared to Abraham in another land, and that therefore the temple was not the only place where God could be met. It was important to make this point because Stephen was accused of speaking against the temple (6:13-14).

Abraham himself was not given even a single foot of the promised land, an idiom that means that he was not given any of it. However, long before he became a father, he was told that this land would belong to his offspring (**7:5**). But this would not happen immediately. Before then, God foretold, his offspring would be mistreated aliens in a foreign land – Egypt – for *four hundred years* (**7:6**). The figure represents a rounding off of the actual period of 430 years (see also Exod 12:41). The people would be enslaved, but God would judge the nation that had enslaved them (**7:7**).

God then gave Abraham the rite of circumcision as a sign of his covenant (**7:8a**). This rite was given when Abraham owned no land and there was no possibility of there being a temple. Stephen's opponents spoke of *this holy place* (6:13), but he was making the point that there is no holy place without the presence of the God of glory, who seeks obedience regardless of the place.

7:8b-19 THE PATRIARCHS AND JOSEPH Isaac and Jacob are mentioned in passing as the offspring to whom God had promised to deliver the land (**7:8b**). Abraham became the father of Isaac long after he and Sarah had passed the normal age for having children, again showing God's hand in the story (see Gen 15:1-6; 17:1-7; 18:11; 21:1-5). Abraham passed on the sign of the covenant by circumcising Isaac on the eighth day (Gen 21:4). Isaac then passed the baton to Jacob, who became the father of the *twelve patriarchs*, that is, the men who would give their names to the tribes of Israel.

The sons of Isaac brought the nation of Israel into slavery in Egypt, just as God had foretold. Jealous of their brother Joseph, they sold him as a slave, but *God was with him* (**7:9**). The whole process was managed by God, and while their intentions were evil, God used them to produce a good result (**7:10-14**; see Gen 45:5). Stephen quickly summarizes the life of Jacob and all the patriarchs, who apparently died in Egypt but whose bodies were later buried in the burial ground Abraham had bought in the promised land (**7:15-16**).

After the death of the patriarchs, their descendants remained in Egypt and multiplied. As the time when God's promise was due to be fulfilled drew near, they became enslaved by a king who knew nothing about the story of Joseph (**7:17-18**). He exploited the race of the Hebrews and even murdered their children (**7:19**).

7:20-45 MOSES AS GOD'S DELIVERER The key point in Stephen's telling of the story of Moses is that his own people failed to recognize that God was bringing deliverance to them through him (7:25). Stephen does not mention the midwives and Moses' mother, for they are not as important as God, who had taken notice of Moses and was arranging his life (**7:20**). Moses was adopted by Pharaoh's daughter and thus received the best education in Egypt (**7:21-22**). For forty years he lived in the highest levels of society, but one day he chose to visit (literally, 'it entered his mind to visit') his own people. This decision itself was a big step of faith (**7:23**; see also Heb 11:24-26). However, his own people did not understand his motives and so he had to flee to the land of Midian, where he lived as an alien for another forty years (**7:24-29**).

At the end of the forty years, God sent an angel to Moses in the flame of a burning bush near Mount Sinai (**7:30**). From the bush came the voice of the Lord (**7:31**), who introduced himself as *the God of your fathers, the God of Abraham, Isaac and Jacob* (**7:32**). How could God have appeared to Moses in a burning bush? Where was the temple or the holy land? Stephen reminds his listeners that Moses was standing on holy ground because the presence of God made it holy (**7:33**). God had come to deliver his people from slavery through this Moses who had been rejected (**7:34-35**). He led them out of slavery, performing wonders and miracles in Egypt (Exod 8:1-10:29), at the Red Sea (Exod 14:26-31) and during their forty years in the desert (**7:36**).

Moses had also prophesied that another deliverer like himself would arise from among the Jewish people (**7:37**). Clearly Stephen is here alluding to the coming of Jesus.

The people, however, did not listen to Moses. Instead they turned back to Egypt *in their hearts,* asking Aaron to make them a golden calf – what a stiff-necked people they were (**7:38-41**)! If God had not intervened, the ancestors of the listeners would still be serving idols (**7:42-43**).

Stephen brings his account of Moses' life to a close by speaking about the *tabernacle of the Testimony,* or the ark of the covenant, which was built according to the design given by God to Moses (**7:44**). It was God's idea, not that of Moses or the fathers. This tabernacle was then brought to the promised land by the fathers under the leadership of Joshua (**7:45**). Once again, it is stressed that it was God who drove out the nations that inhabited the land.

7:46-50 The temple for the ark of the covenant David had wanted to build a temple (**7:46**), but it was his son Solomon who was permitted to do so (**7:47**). Stephen points out that God, the Most High, does not need a house – he is the Lord of heaven and cannot fit into an earthly structure (**7:48-50**). Stephen wants to remind the council that the temple was simply built as a place to house the tabernacle of the testimony and was never a dwelling place for the God of glory.

7:51-53 The indictment of the council Suddenly, Stephen turns on the council and concludes his long speech with a stunning indictment. His words are sharper than a two-edged sword and clearly hit home (**7:54**). He accuses them, first, of being stubborn: a *stiff-necked people, with uncircumcised hearts and ears* (**7:51a**). Their hearts cannot be touched by the gospel message because it is as if they are covered by a foreskin. Their ears, too, appear to be covered, meaning that they cannot hear the truth. Consequently they are not willing to turn back to the Lord and will not listen to the voice of the Holy Spirit (**7:51b**). Stephen has been telling them about their ancestors, and now he insists that the council are worthy descendants of their fathers – but not

those fathers who served God. Rather, they are the descendants of those who opposed God's messengers (**7:39**).

Secondly, he accuses them of having betrayed and killed Jesus, whom Stephen refers to as *the Righteous One* (**7:52**). Just as their fathers had persecuted and killed the prophets, now the council members have become betrayers and murderers of Jesus.

Finally, he accuses them of being disobedient to God's law (**7:53**), the law that had been handed down by angels at Sinai (7:38). Stephen's accusation is similar to the one that Jesus had levelled at them (Matt 23:23; Mark 7:9; John 19:7). Stephen had been accused of 'speaking … against the law', but he reverses the charges and accuses the council of failing to obey the law! He may be basing this charge on their murder of the Son of the one who had given the law. Not only that, but they are now continuing to persecute those who preach in Jesus' name.

7:54-60 The martyrdom of Stephen

Stephen's accusations infuriate the council members. Their teeth can be heard grating with their anger (**7:54**). But a deep peace engulfs Stephen. Instead of being frightened, he is full of the Holy Spirit, and gazing intently heavenward he is able to see Jesus standing at the right hand of God (**7:55**). Jesus is in control of the whole situation and is with him, just as he promised he would be (Matt 28:20). This vision of Jesus is very reassuring to Stephen, and is equally so to all who are willing to suffer for the gospel. Stephen excitedly announces what he is seeing – Jesus, the Son of Man, standing in a now-opened heaven (**7:56**).

The council members are not interested in the exalted Son of Man. Stephen has accused them of being deaf to God (7:51) and they underscore the point by covering their ears so that they cannot hear what he is saying as they rush on him (**7:57**). Abandoning their dignity, they resort to mob justice and drag him outside the city where they start stoning him (**7:58a**).

It is at this point that we are introduced to Saul, who will play a major role in the progress of the gospel. The witnesses who are responsible for throwing the stones leave their robes with Saul for safekeeping while they hurl stones at Stephen (**7:58b**).

Stephen calls upon Jesus to receive his soul (**7:59**). To the council, this request, too, would have been an example of blasphemy (Lev 24:14; Deut 17:7), but Stephen prays that God will forgive their ignorance (**7:60**). What a peaceful death for the man of God, who falls *asleep* after uttering a final petition for forgiveness for his killers. Was his prayer answered? Yes, indeed! The very young man at whose feet the witnesses had laid their robes was to become a great preacher of the gospel!

Stephen's death became his greatest witness to the entire world. The same is true of the many missionaries who became witnesses to the African continent through their blood. All Christians must be willing to spread the gospel even if doing so brings death.

8:1-12:24 Witness to Neighbouring Regions

Jesus had told his disciples that they would be witnesses to him in Jerusalem first and then 'in all Judea and Samaria' (1:8). The section of the book of Acts that follows deals with this second stage in the spread of the gospel but reverses the order in that the story begins with a witness to Samaria, rather than Judea. The difference is not important, for the Judeans and Samaritans lived very close together geographically, although they considered themselves distinct ethnic groups.

8:1-25 Witness to All Samaria

Samaria had originally been the capital of the northern kingdom, established by Omri in about 880 BC (1 Kings 16:24), but the whole region was now known as 'Samaria'. Samaritan religion was a mixture of Judaism and paganism, and thus the Jews viewed the Samaritans as outcasts. The early church followed its Saviour's lead (see Luke 10:33; 17:16; John 4:5-40) in its attitude towards the Samaritans (Matt 10:5; Acts 1:8; 8:5-25; 9:31; 15:3). Nevertheless, this would not have been an easy area to witness in, since Jews and Samaritans did not normally mix.

8:1-3 Persecution in Jerusalem

The death of Stephen sparked violent persecution, apparently directed mainly at the evangelists of Hellenistic background (**8:1b**). (This can be deduced from the fact that the apostles do not seem to have been targeted.) Nevertheless, some brave, devout men took the body of Stephen and buried it, not fearing the same fate (**8:2**). Their act may have contributed to unleashing Saul's wrath against the church (8:3). He had been an observer, not an active participant, in the killing of Stephen (**8:1a**), but now he himself *began to destroy the church* in Jerusalem (**8:3**). He went from house to house persecuting all believers indiscriminately – both men and women. He dragged them out, just as the crowd had dragged Stephen out, although Saul did not kill them but merely threw them in prison.

8:4-13 The great dispersion

The severe persecution scattered all the believers from Jerusalem except the apostles (8:1b). Those who scattered seem to have been the teaching leaders of the Jerusalem church and probably the pilgrims who had remained in Jerusalem after accepting the message of the gospel, for the church in Jerusalem continued to exist (see for example, 8:14; 11:1, 18; 12:1, 12-17; 15:6). Those who had been scattered seized

the opportunity to preach the word among the villages as they went on their way (**8:4**).

One of those forced to leave Jerusalem was Philip, who had been chosen along with Stephen to wait on tables (6:5). He went to the city of Samaria and began to preach Christ there (**8:5**). His message was the same one the apostles had preached in Jerusalem, namely that the Messiah has come (5:42). Later, we are also told that he preached *the good news of the Kingdom of God* (8:12), but Luke does not tell us any more about the exact message, just as he did not when Jesus spoke to the disciples about 'the Kingdom of God' (1:3).

Whatever the details of the message, it was certainly good news, and the crowds *paid close attention* to Philip's preaching (**8:6**), particularly as it was confirmed by signs: those who had unclean spirits were being delivered and the paralysed and the lame were being healed (**8:7**). The whole city was rejoicing (**8:8**). Revival had come and the entire population felt relieved of the burden of sin and evil spirits. The kingdom of light was breaking in and dispelling the darkness. This should be the experience of the people of Africa, particularly as we claim to be the continent with the most Christians.

Luke focuses on one of those who had been influenced by the message of Christ, a man known as Simon the sorcerer (**8:9**). He claimed to be *someone great* and had amazed people by his acts of magic. Everyone, from the smallest to the greatest, revered him, calling him *the Great Power* (**8:10**). He may have been the equivalent of a village witchdoctor or diviner. He had enjoyed the people's attention for a long time (**8:11**), but when Philip came preaching the gospel, they stopped following him and followed Jesus Christ with both men and women being baptized (**8:12**). The kingdom of God had come among them.

Simon had no desire to be left out, and so he came forward to be baptized – and became a follower of Philip. It was his turn to be amazed by the display of the real power of God through signs and attesting miracles (**8:13**). It seems likely that Simon had indeed become a believer, although his later misunderstanding indicates that he was not yet a mature believer (8:18). The conversion of Simon the sorcerer should encourage the church to evangelize everyone in their area, including the sorcerers.

8:14-17 The Samaritan believers are included in the church

The church in Jerusalem received the news of the conversion of the Samaritans with keen interest, evidenced by their sending Peter and John to them (**8:14**). They were sent to confirm the news of what had happened and also to serve as a link between the Samaritan church and the Jerusalem community.

When the apostles arrived, they found that these believers had not yet received the Holy Spirit, and so they prayed for them to receive it. Then they laid hands on them, perhaps marking a new partnership between Jews and Samaritans, and *they received the Holy Spirit* (**8:15-17**).

Some have asked why the Holy Spirit had not yet fallen on them, whether such a delay is to be expected with all new believers, and whether the laying on of the apostles' hands is necessary to receive the Spirit. The answer seems to be that there were exceptional circumstances in this case, meaning that it should not be taken as typical. There had been great hostility and bitter rivalry between Jews and Samaritans as each claimed to be worshipping the true God in the most orthodox way (see Jesus' discussion with the Samaritan woman – John 4:7-26). Now the disciples had come to point the Samaritans to the only way by which all people must come to God. The giving of the Holy Spirit set the seal of God's approval on what was happening. It clearly marked the new Samaritan believers as members of the God's family. The sight of Jews and Samaritans worshipping and rejoicing together must have amazed both the apostles and the Samaritans! It is not surprising that Simon was so impressed that he wanted to add the power to distribute the Holy Spirit to his own abilities.

The laying on of hands also seems to be specific to this case, rather than a general principle. In practical terms, it would not have been possible for the apostles to lay hands on each of the thousands of new believers who, we have been told, were coming into the church.

8:18-24 Wrong motives for seeking gifts

While it is easy for us to condemn Simon the magician for trying to buy God's power (**8:18-19**), we sometimes make the same mistake when we think that what we do or give makes us more acceptable to God. Peter's horrified response to Simon's request was *may your money perish with you* (**8:20-21**). Thinking that God's gifts can be bought was enough to bring destruction to both Simon and his money (compare the consequences of Gehazi's sin of requesting and accepting silver from Naaman – 2 Kings 5:20-27). The church must learn from Simon's mistake and stand on the side of Peter, refusing to be compromised by money.

The power of the Holy Spirit enabled Peter to see that Simon's heart was still *full of bitterness and captive to sin* (**8:22-23**). He offered Simon an opportunity to repent, for Simon, unlike Ananias and Sapphira who died instantly (5:5, 10), was quick to ask for prayers so that the curse pronounced by Peter would not take effect (**8:24**).

8:25 The witness to the Samaritan villages

When Peter and John had accomplished their mission they did not simply head straight back to Jerusalem. Instead, they obeyed the command that all areas of Samaria were to be evangelized and used their journey as an opportunity for village-to-village evangelism (**8:25**). All who seek to spread the word of God should follow their example and note that villages are not to be neglected.

8:26-8:40 Witness to All Judea: Beginnings

8:26-39 Witness on the desert road

Why does Luke put the story of the Ethiopian eunuch at this point in Acts, right after the evangelism of Samaria? Some scholars have suggested that the Greek poet Homer and the translators of the Septuagint regarded Ethiopia as the 'end of the earth', and thus this story represents the prophesied spread of the gospel to the 'ends of the earth' (Isa 8:9; 48:20; 49:6; 62:11), fulfilling the command in 1:8.

However, it seems that a better explanation is that Luke wants to show that all parts of Judea were reached, no matter how remote. It was easy for the newly scattered disciples to enter Jewish homes and villages, but they were less likely to have gone to the desert road, although that would have been included in the command to evangelize 'all Judea'. Isaiah 40:3 had included a command to prepare a highway for the Lord in the wilderness, and this command, too, was being fulfilled here.

If we accept this interpretation, then the focus is on the geographical region. Philip is sent throughout Judea as the Holy Spirit moves him. From Samaria, he is directed to go to the desert road (8:26) and after completing his mission there he is caught up by the Holy Spirit and transported to another part of Judea to minister there (8:40). The southern coast of Judea was not neglected.

8:26-27 Divine guidance for Philip Luke now re-introduces Philip, ready for another extra encounter. He receives instructions from the angel of the Lord (also mentioned in 5:19-20) to go south to the desert road that ran from Jerusalem to Gaza (**8:26**). He does not seem to have been told what to expect to find there. Nevertheless, Philip obediently followed the instructions (**8:27a**). His mission was divinely driven. This should still be the case today. Human mission organizations and boards should not take over from the Lord of glory.

8:27b-39 Witness to the Ethiopian eunuch On the road Philip met a traveller, an Ethiopian eunuch who had come to Jerusalem to worship and was now on his way home (**8:27b**). Luke takes time to introduce this man, perhaps to let us know that high-ranking officials were also being reached with the gospel. The Ethiopian eunuch was in charge of all the treasures of Queen Candace and he was a God-fearer, that is, a Gentile with a strong commitment to the Jewish faith, but one who had not been circumcised and become a proselyte. He clearly sought any opportunity to read God's word, and so he was reading a scroll of Isaiah while sitting in his chariot (**8:28**). The angel, who had already sent Philip to this road, now prompted him to go and speak to the man in the chariot (**8:29**). Everything that happened was controlled by God.

Philip obediently ran up to the chariot and asked the Ethiopian whether he understood what he was reading (**8:30**). The man's answer should speak to anyone who despises those who interpret the Bible: 'How could I, unless someone guides me?' (NASB **8:31a**). Guides are needed if the masses are to understand God's word. The eunuch invited Philip to ride with him and help him interpret this portion of Scripture (**8:31b**). Luke quotes the passage being read (Isa 53:7-8) and then records the eunuch's question about who the prophet was speaking about (**8:32-34**).

BIBLE TRANSLATION IN AFRICA

The Bible was originally written in the everyday languages of its first readers. Thus some sections were written in Hebrew, others in Aramaic, and others in Greek. As its message spread, it became necessary to translate it for new audiences. Thus the Hebrew OT was translated into Greek – the lingua franca of the period – sometime around the second century BC. This translation, known as the Septuagint (abbreviated LXX, using the Roman numerals for seventy), was made in the city of Alexandria in Africa. Many of the Gentiles and Jews for whom the Greek NT was written would have been familiar with the Koine Greek in which it was written

In Jesus, God came and spoke to people in a specific culture in a way they could understand. Believers were instructed to follow his example, and thus wherever Christianity spreads, it takes on the cultures and languages of the new believers. After all, as St Augustine of Hippo in North Africa is reputed to have said, God seems nearer to people when he speaks their language.

Some of the first translations of the complete Bible were produced in North Africa. It was translated into the ancient Egyptian dialect known as Sahidic around 300 ad and into the dialect known as Bohairic around the sixth century. The Bohairic version is still the official version of the Coptic Orthodox Church. Nubia and Ethiopia also received the gospel quite early. The Ge'ez translation of the Bible, dating from around 500 ad, is still in use today in the Ethiopian Orthodox Church.

The next wave of African translations came with the nineteenth-century evangelical revival. Christian missionaries used the infrastructure and opportunities provided by European imperial conquest, for colonial expansion and the spread of missions went hand in hand. The missionaries realized that success in communicating the gospel would require mastering African languages and that they would need to translate the Bible into these languages in order to grow churches and disciple Christians. So they set about the task of translation, which involved reducing African languages to writing, preparing grammars and lexicons, translating the Scriptures, and teaching new converts to read their own African languages so that they could engage with the Scriptures.

The successful achievement of these tasks set in motion a complex set of unintended developments. One was that missionaries could no longer claim a monopoly on God's word or control the process they had set in motion. The Bible in the vernacular empowered the African church to evangelize, plant churches and open new frontiers independent of missionary control or of foreign mission centres. There can be no doubt that the phenomenal growth of Christianity in Africa owes an enormous debt to Bible translation.

Among the best known of the early African translation are the Malagasy Bible produced by David Jones and David Griffiths in 1835; the Tswana Bible translated by Robert Moffat in 1857; the Twi Akuapem Bible produced by Johannes Christaller and J.A. Mader in 1871 and the Swahili Bible translated by Johann Krapf and Edward Steere in 1891. While these translations are associated with European translators, African translators were also active. Bishop Samuel Adjai Crowther, the first African bishop in the Anglican church, produced the Yoruba translation of the Bible in 1884, and Duta Kitaakule worked with the missionary George Pilkington to produce the Luganda Bible in 1896.

The work of these pioneers provided a model for current translation work in Africa, which includes revision of missionary translations, the production of vernacular translations for peoples who still lack Bibles in their own languages and for youth and children, culture-sensitive study Bibles in African vernaculars created specifically with African audiences in mind, African Bibles in new audiovisual and electronic media, and translations of liturgy for use in worship. The baton has been passed from the missionary translator to the mother-tongue translator, in most cases with technical support and funding from Bible agencies dedicated to the translation, publication and distribution of the Holy Scriptures.

Some urban Africans, who have grown up with the Bible in English, French, Portuguese or some other colonial language, are tempted to think that the Bible in these languages is all that is needed for theologizing, Christian writing or exegetical work in Africa. But the majority of African peoples depend on the Bible in the vernacular for all these activities. Thus it is vitally important that biblical exegesis be done in the languages in which the majority of believers interact with the word of God – their mother tongues.

The future of African Christianity is inextricably intertwined with the future of the languages and cultures in which the majority of African people think and express themselves. It is in these language that the Holy Scriptures must provide spiritual nurture and support for the life of faith, love and hope.

Aloo Osotsi Mojola

Philip did more than just interpret this portion of Scripture; he preached Jesus to the eunuch (**8:35**). Notice the different emphasis in the content of the preaching – here he preaches Jesus, while to the Samaritans he had preached Christ (the Messiah) (8:5, 12). Philip's preaching here can be compared with the way Jesus himself interpreted events to the disciples on the way to Emmaus (Luke 24:27). In both cases, the preaching was based on Scripture.

After hearing the message of the gospel, the Ethiopian eunuch believed it and could not see why his baptism should be delayed (**8:36**). Philip agreed, as long as the Ethiopian eunuch believed with all his heart. The eunuch gave the classical response, *I believe that Jesus Christ is the Son of God* (**8:37**). (Verse 37 is in a footnote in the NIV because it is not included in all the Greek manuscripts of Luke. However, it faithfully reflects the baptismal practice of the early church.)

Philip's response would have surprised early Jewish believers. They knew that eunuchs were prohibited from coming into the assembly of God's people because they were regarded as ritually impure (Lev 21:20; 22:19-25; Deut 23:1). However, Isaiah had prophesied that one day eunuchs would be allowed into the assembly of God's people (Isa 56:3-5), and that prophecy was fulfilled here in Acts.

As there was water at hand, Philip did not hesitate to baptize the Ethiopian eunuch (**8:38**). The fact that Philip was snatched away by the Spirit of God does not seem to have bothered the now converted Ethiopian eunuch, who went on his way rejoicing (**8:39**). The Lord was pleased to make the gospel known to the continent of Africa at this early stage in the development of the Christian community.

8:40 Witness to the coastal cities

One verse summarizes Philip's witness to the coastal area of Judea (**8:40**). Led by the Spirit, as he had been since his initial witness to the Samaritans, Philip now found himself at Azotus. Just as his counterparts, Peter and John, had done on their way back to Jerusalem from Samaria (8:25), Philip preached the gospel in all the cities up the coast until he reached his hometown of Caesarea, where we meet him again in 21:8.

9:1-30 Called to Witness: Conversion of Saul

Excited by the successful ministry in Samaria and the southern parts of Judea (8:4-40), the reader of Acts may have temporarily forgotten about the murder of Stephen and the severe persecution of the entire church. But a shock of fear is felt as we encounter the description of Saul as *still breathing out murderous threats against the disciples of the Lord* (**9:1**). He was anxious to extend his persecution beyond the city of Jerusalem (**9:2**), and obtained permission to seek out disciples as far away as Damascus and drag them back to Jerusalem. Believers are here referred to as

those who *belonged to the Way*, which seems to have been the term that was used before the name 'Christian' became common. The fact that both men and women were targeted makes it clear that women had a prominent role in the early church.

9:3-9 Saul's encounter with Jesus the Christ

The Lord was not prepared to simply watch this murderous plan unfold. As Saul was about to enter Damascus, a light from heaven shone all around him (**9:3**). Saul could not stand its brightness and fell to the ground, either prostrate or in a position of worship. Then he heard a voice: *Saul, Saul why do you persecute me?* (**9:4**). In other words, 'Why are you continuing to persecute me?' The question seems to have baffled Saul, who had thought he was doing God's will in defending the true religion from the adulterating effect of the followers of Jesus of Nazareth (22:3-4; 26:5; see also Phil 3:6). But he knew that the one speaking to him must be someone great, and therefore he asked, *Who are you, Lord?* The answer must have come as a shock: *I am Jesus, whom you are persecuting* (**9:5**). By persecuting the disciples of Jesus, Saul was persecuting Jesus himself!

Before Saul had time to respond, Jesus told him to enter the city and wait for further instructions (**9:6**). Saul's companions heard the voice speaking, but could not see anyone (**9:7**). When Paul stood up, his sight was gone. He had to be led into the city, where for three days he could neither see nor eat (**9:8-9**).

Saul was so murderous and blinded in his thinking that the only way for him to be evangelized was for the Lord himself to intervene. The Lord Jesus is able to intervene in difficult situations like this for the sake of his church.

9:10-19 Ananias: Linking the church and Saul

The voice that spoke to Paul immediately after his conversion did not tell him his obligations in terms of his future mission to the Gentiles. Paul had been an enemy of the church and still needed to be officially welcomed into it. The church leadership in Damascus had to play a key role in doing this. Yet, as can be deduced from Ananias' conversation with the Lord, a big hurdle had to be crossed before God's message to Paul could be delivered.

The Lord spoke to Ananias in a vision (**9:10**). It is important to note how Ananias responded to the Lord's initial call. His *Yes, lord* (compare 1 Sam 3:4) indicates his readiness to listen to and carry out the Lord's command, despite his reluctance when he learned the details of his mission.

Ananias was instructed to go to a man from Tarsus named Saul (**9:11**). Ananias was familiar with the city of Damascus and must have known Judas and the location of his house on Straight Street (9:11). There may have been several people staying in the house, since there is a need for Saul to be identified by his place of origin, Tarsus. The Lord reassured Ananias that Paul had been praying and would be expecting him because he too had seen a vision (**9:12**). It seems that the Lord gave these details because he knew how much Ananias feared Saul. But the Lord does not give Ananias all the information, for he does not immediately tell him what had happened on the road to Damascus. We can thus understand Ananias' horror at being asked to speak to Saul. He reminds the Lord of what he knows about Saul, how he has persecuted the church in Jerusalem and has come to Damascus to continue this persecution (**9:13-14**). Howard Marshall comments that 'Ananias's comment might have been taken as an expression of disobedience to God; he should have realized that the Lord would know better than he did! But his remarks were entirely natural, and … serve to introduce a further statement by the Lord regarding his choice of Paul to be his servant' (*TNT*). It also introduces a statement about how converted enemies of the gospel were to be included in the community of believers.

The Lord assures Ananias that Paul had now become *a chosen instrument* to carry the Lord's name before Gentiles, kings and the people of Israel (**9:15**). But the task would not be easy, for Saul was going to suffer much (**9:16**).

Ananias obeyed his Lord and went and prayed for Saul (**9:17**), using a ritual that included laying hands on Saul, just as Peter and John had done for the Samaritan believers. This gesture is a reminder that God can use either angelic or human agents to effect deliverance.

Ananias addresses Saul as *Brother Saul,* bestowing the Christian title 'brother' as a sign of fellowship. At this point Luke allows Ananias to mention Paul's encounter with the Lord on the road to Damascus. This same Lord had now sent Ananias to bring a message of relief by restoring Paul's sight and a message of commissioning by announcing the filling of Saul by the Holy Spirit. The mention of the Holy Spirit reminds the reader of the purpose of this filling; that is, Saul was now ready to be a witness (see 1:8). The statement that Paul will witness before Gentiles, kings and the people of Israel is not repeated here, although it is mentioned in a later description of the same event (22:21; 26:17). Saul was healed of his blindness and was baptized in the name of the one he had previously persecuted (**9:18**). He also took food and *regained his strength* (**9:19a**).

Ananias is a hero of inclusiveness, for Saul is now reported to have *spent several days with the disciples in Damascus* (**9:19b**). Ananias was ready to take the Lord at his word and risk his own life by going to a notorious enemy of the Christian community. He models a community where past enemies are able to become friends and call each other brother and is an example to those who find it hard to invite their enemies into the Christian community. With Africa riven by wars and ethnic animosity, African Christians need such an example. How else can believers in countries like Rwanda call each other 'brother' after the 1994 genocide?

Such a change is only possible through the power of the risen Saviour, who has broken down the barriers of enmity.

9:20-25 Saul: A fiery evangelist

Saul began to evangelize in the synagogues (**9:20**). What a contrast: he had come to persecute those who called on the name of Jesus, but ended up proclaiming that Jesus is the Son of God. Paul did not let this amazement of his hearers distract him from his task and continued to argue strongly that *Jesus is the Christ* – and succeeded in proving it to the Jews (**9:21-22**).

His new-found faith did not endear Saul to all the Jews. His partners in persecuting the church were unlikely to have been happy with his change and some people even sought to kill him (**9:23**). We do not know exactly how long this was after his conversion, for Luke only reports that *many days had gone by* (see also Gal 1:17-18).

Saul learned of the plan to kill him (**9:24**) and it became necessary to get him away from Damascus. However, he could not leave by the gates because these were watched by his enemies. So one night his followers lowered him over the city wall in a large basket (**9:25**). The mention of Saul having 'followers' or, literally, 'disciples' has bothered some commentators, but it probably simply refers to the people from Jerusalem who had followed Saul to Damascus (9:7).

9:26-30 Barnabas: Linking the apostles and Saul

Because of the haste in which Paul had to leave Damascus, he did not collect any letters of commendation from the Christian community there. When he reached Jerusalem, hungry for fellowship, the disciples in Jerusalem were afraid of him (**9:26**). Someone was needed to act as a bridge. Barnabas, whose nickname was 'son of encouragement' (4:36-37), was the first to trust Paul (**9:27**). He took him to meet the apostles, where Paul described to them how he had seen the Lord and had become a witness among the Jews in Damascus. There was no need for the apostles to fear him. Barnabas' role parallels that of Peter and John in Samaria, when they welcomed Philip's converts into the wider Christian community (8:14-15). After the introduction by Barnabas, Saul was accepted by the Jerusalem church and *moved about freely*, boldly proclaiming the Lord (**9:28**). His acceptance by the Jerusalem community was very important in establishing Saul's credibility, because in Acts the Jerusalem community is the centre of the Christian mission.

But once again Saul's preaching roused the antagonism of the Grecian Jews, and they too began planning to kill him (**9:29**). This threat led his fellow Christians to send him away to his native city of Tarsus (**9:30**). He was still there when Barnabas went to fetch him to conduct a joint mission at Antioch (11:25-26).

9:31 A Summary of the State of the Church

With the conversion of its bitter enemy, the church enjoyed *a time of peace* (**9:31a**). The use of the singular 'church', rather than the plural 'churches', when speaking of the church in several regions – *Judea, Galilee and Samaria* – depicts the universal church. The church in all these regions enjoyed peace and continued to increase in its unity (being *strengthened*), to grow spiritually (*living in the fear of the Lord*) and to increase in its witness (*encouraged by the Holy Spirit*). But the church did not settle down and relax, for the ends of the earth had not yet been reached, and so it continued to grow in numbers (**9:31b**). The church today has to learn this lesson, for many established churches seem to be content with their state and have stopped trying to grow.

9:32-43 Peter's Witness to Jews in Samaria

We now find Peter travelling through the coastal region of Judea (**9:32**) and visiting two centres where saints (another name for 'believers') lived: Lydda and Joppa. We are given brief summaries of two miracles he performed there, and the reaction to them.

9:32-35 The witness at Lydda

In Lydda Peter met a man named Aeneas who had been paralysed and bedridden for eight years (**9:33**). Peter spoke to him by name, announced that Jesus Christ had healed him and told him to get up and fold up his bed (**9:34**). He did so immediately, leaving no doubt that he had been healed. This healing led many to turn to the Lord (**9:35**).

9:36-43 The witness at Joppa

The healing at Joppa is described in more detail than the one at Lydda. A disciple named Tabitha (or Dorcas in Greek) had died. She *was always doing good and helping the poor* (**9:36**), particularly widows. The believers in Joppa had heard that Peter was in the area, and they seem to have believed that he would be able to raise her from the dead. Consequently they did not bury her immediately (**9:37b**). When Peter arrived, responding to their urgent message (**9:38**), the grieving widows showed him the clothes that Tabitha had made for them (**9:39**). Peter does not seem to have rebuked them for weeping. Believers are allowed to mourn their departed ones.

Peter sent everyone out of the room (compare Matt 9:25), and then knelt down and prayed (**9:40a**). We are not told the content of his prayer, but he must have asked Jesus to restore life to the dead woman. He seems to have been facing away from the body, for after praying he turned and spoke directly to her – calling her by name and commanding her to get up. This was an act of faith on Peter's part, and he must have been delighted to see her open her eyes and sit up (**9:40b**). Peter helped her to stand, and then *excitedly*

called the believers and the widows and presented her to them alive (**9:41**).

As with the healing of Aeneas, many who heard about the raising of Tabitha believed in the Lord (**9:42**).

Peter stayed on in Joppa in the house of Simon the tanner (**9:43**). Luke records this detail to emphasize that Simon's job had no prestige. He worked with his hands at a hard and smelly job processing animal skins, and yet he was host to one of the greatest evangelists and church leaders. He is an encouragement to those who feel that their job has no status in society – nothing is too low to be of use in God's kingdom.

10:1-11:18 Peter's Witness to Gentiles in Samaria

Another dimension of Peter's ministry is associated with a resident of Caesarea named Cornelius, who *was a centurion in what was known as the Italian Regiment* or cohort (**10:1**). This cohort would have comprised about 600 soldiers. The centurion and his family are described as *devout and God-fearing* (**10:2**). He gave alms and *prayed to God regularly*.

10:3-8 The Lord speaks in a vision to Cornelius

Although Cornelius is presented as a pious person who is very close to the kingdom of God, this piety was not enough in God's eyes. Something better had come, and Cornelius needed somebody to link him to it. The Lord thus appeared to him in a vision with special instructions on how to reach the person who would be the link. This vision may have come while Cornelius was deep in prayer, since three o'clock (the ninth hour) was the hour of prayer (**10:3**; 3:1). He was addressed by name, reminding us that God knows each of us by name.

Cornelius responded to the vision with a mixture of inquisitiveness and alarm – staring at the angel (**10:4**). Recognizing that the one he was seeing was his superior, he addressed him as *Lord* and asked the reason for this sudden visitation. Two reasons are given. The first is that his prayers and gifts to the poor had reached heaven. What a privilege to know that God was pleased with his acts of charity and that his prayers had reached the ears of the Almighty! If only all of us could have this sort of assurance from God! Yet in reality we do not need an angel from heaven to announce this to us, for God has already assured us that he will answer our prayers.

The second reason is that he needed to learn more about the way to God, and Simon Peter would be the one to teach him. The angel directed Cornelius to send for Simon Peter (**10:5**), even telling him exactly where Simon Peter was staying (**10:6**). Cornelius promptly called two of his servants and one of his bodyguards (a devout soldier in constant attendance to him) and told them about his vision. Then he dispatched them to fetch Peter (**10:7-8**).

10:9-23a Peter's vision of unclean animals

The next day, while the three men were on their way to fetch him, Peter went up to the flat-roof of the house to pray (**10:9**). It was about noon (the sixth hour), and while Peter was praying he became hungry. He may have smelled the food that was being prepared downstairs or it may simply be that God wanted to speak to him through a vision involving food (**10:10**).

In his vision, Peter saw a sheet that contained animals from the threefold division of the animal world used in Genesis 1:30 (see also Rom 1:23): four-footed animals, reptiles of the earth and birds (**10:11-12**). Some of these animals were ritually unclean and thus forbidden to Jews by the Jewish law. Peter was surprised when ordered to eat them, since he could not see how God could go against his own laws and expect him to eat unclean meat (**10:11-14**). Had he stopped to think about what he was seeing, he might have been struck by the fact that all these animals were being lowered from heaven, suggesting that they were all coming from the hand of God. Since God had declared them clean, he should not have called them unclean (**10:15**).

This vision was repeated three times (**10:16**). Some commentators claim that tradition required a vision to be repeated three times to confirm that it was not from the demonic world. But it is also possible that it was repeated three times because Cornelius had sent three men to fetch Peter, with the vision repeated once for each of the three messengers. But Peter knew nothing about Cornelius and his messengers and was puzzled about what exactly the vision meant (**10:17a**). He would soon learn that it had been sent to prepare him to accept that Gentiles, like Jews, were to be part of the believing community.

While Peter was still puzzling over his vision, the men from Cornelius arrived at the tanner's house and stood at the gate, calling to find out whether one *Simon who was known as Peter was staying there* (**10:17-18**). The Spirit told Peter that three men were looking for him (**10:19**). Now he understood what the vision was about – Gentiles were also to be accepted into the community of believers! The Lord assured him that he had sent the men himself (**10:20**), although he had used Cornelius as his agent (10:5).

Peter went down and met the men, who explained their mission and told how an angel had instructed Cornelius to send for Peter to *hear what you have to say* (**10:21-22**). Peter promptly invited them in *to be his guests* (**10:23a**), something he would never have considered doing before.

10:23b-33 Peter's visit to Cornelius

Peter set out for his first Gentile mission, accompanied by the three messengers and some brothers from Joppa (**10:23b**). Pastors would do well to follow his example and not go alone when visiting church members. Having other

brothers as witnesses to what has happened is important if there is likely to be any controversy (see 11:12).

A large group was waiting for Peter when he arrived, since Cornelius *had called together his relatives and close friends* (**10:24**). Cornelius fell down to pay homage to Peter, but Peter quickly put a stop to this, insisting that he too was just a man (**10:25-26**). Like Peter, we should discourage people from admiring us, directing their attention to God who deserves our worship.

Peter introduced himself to the group, beginning with an explanation of why he was prepared to break the Jewish custom and visit the home of a Gentile. He pointed out that God had shown him *that he should not call any man impure or unclean* (**10:27-28**). Peter who had been exclusive was now inclusive – he would accept people as people (**10:29**).

Cornelius then told Peter about his vision four days earlier and expressed his gratitude for Peter's willingness to come (**10:30-33a**). The most important point in this retelling of the vision is the last statement: *Now then, we are all here present before God to hear all that you have been commanded by the Lord* (**10:33b**). The statement that they were all 'present before God' emphasizes that although Peter was an important link, it was God they had assembled to hear. Church members should have the same attitude whenever they hear their pastor preach. The pastor, in turn, should follow Peter and proclaim 'all' that he has 'been commanded by the Lord'.

10:34-43 Peter's sermon

In his sermon, Peter acknowledged three great truths: First, *God does not show favouritism* (**10:34**). Second, in every nation, whoever fears God and does what is right is welcomed by him (**10:35**). Third, salvation is for all people (10:43). God is not interested in one people or nation, but in all peoples of all nations. He has decided to add the likes of Cornelius and his entire household to the community of believers.

Peter's sermon can be summarized as follows: The heart of the gospel is Jesus Christ, who came preaching peace to the sons of Israel (**10:36**; see also Heb 1:2). Peter's audience was aware of Jesus' ministry that had started in Galilee after the ministry of John the Baptist (**10:37**). They were also aware that Jesus did mighty acts by the power of the Spirit of God, *doing good and healing all who were under the power of the devil* (**10:38a**). Peter pointed out that Jesus could do all these things *because God was with him* (**10:38b**).

In case Cornelius and his friends were sceptical about the stories they had heard about Jesus, Peter affirmed that he and those with him were witnesses of all that Jesus did both in the countryside (*the country of the Jews*) and in Jerusalem (**10:39a**). But despite his good deeds, the people (*they*) crucified him (**10:39b**). Yet that was not the end, for

God had raised him from the dead on the third day and God had granted that he should be seen physically (**10:40**). He was, however, *not seen by all the people*, but instead presented himself alive to his close associates – his followers (including Peter himself), who were able to eat and drink with him after his resurrection (**10:41**).

Peter stressed that they were commanded to preach to the people that Jesus had been *appointed as judge of the living and the dead* (**10:42**) and that the prophets (that is, the books of the Prophets) testified that there is forgiveness for everyone who believes in Jesus by calling on his name (**10:43**).

This sermon makes it clear that Peter and the other disciples were under an obligation to preach the good news (1:8; see also Matt 28:18-20). Salvation through Jesus' name was for everyone who believes in Jesus – that is, who believes that Jesus is the Christ who came doing good and destroying the works of the devil, and who died and rose from the dead on the third day.

10:44-11:1 The conversion of the Gentiles

Peter was still speaking when the Holy Spirit fell upon the whole group who had assembled to hear from God (**10:44**). Peter had no need to make an altar call as he had on the day of Pentecost (2:40). Cornelius' opening words had indicated that they were ready and expectant (10:33) and this was confirmed by the Holy Spirit falling upon them all.

Seeing God's gift poured out upon the Gentiles was a big surprise to *the circumcised believers* (**10:45**). The Jewish believers who had accompanied Peter may have expected that the Gentiles would have to be circumcised, as was the Jewish procedure when welcoming proselytes into the people of God (see Exod 12:48). But clearly God was accepting these people without their being circumcised.

The Jewish believers may have been less disturbed by Cornelius' reception of the Holy Spirit than by its reception by those who were with him. They would have been familiar with God-fearers like Cornelius who attended the synagogues (Acts 14:1; 17:17). But we cannot simply assume that all those present were God-fearing Gentiles. Some of those converted here may have been 'pure' Gentiles. Peter's statement in 10:35 can be interpreted as referring to those who feared God after hearing his sermon, and not those who feared him before the gospel was preached. His statement that 'God does not show favouritism' was meant to encourage those listening to fear God.

The Holy Spirit enabled the listeners to speak in tongues in praise of God (**10:46**). What they said may have been understood by the hearers, although it was in tongues, just as had been the case on the day of Pentecost (2:4, 11).

Peter expected no objection when he asked his question about the water baptism of the now filled believers (**10:47**). He ordered all the now converted Gentiles to be baptized in the name of Jesus Christ (**10:48a**). After their baptism, they asked Peter *to stay with them for a few days*, perhaps in order to teach them more (**10:48b**). It can be assumed that Peter did as the group requested. This may have led to the accusations later hurled at him by Jewish believers (11:2-3).

The news that the Gentiles had received the word of God spread like wildfire throughout Judea (**11:1**). The testimony of revival cannot be hidden and no one should attempt to hinder its spread.

11:2-18 Peter defends the Gentiles' inclusion

Peter faced stiff opposition from circumcised believers because of his dining with the uncircumcised (**11:2-3**). They did not appreciate his amazing ministry, but objected to his having stayed with Gentiles (10:48b). Peter had recognized that this was likely to be a problem when he stated that his visit was a serious breach of the Jewish law (10:28). But the vision he had been sent had convinced him that his accusers were holding on to a tradition that God had abolished, as he patiently explained (**11:4-17**).

Peter told the other believers about the events leading up to his visit to Cornelius' house. He told of his vision of a great sheet lowered from heaven with all kinds of animals – *four-footed animals of the earth, wild beasts, reptiles, and birds of the air* – and how he was commanded by a voice to get up, kill and eat (**11:5-7**). He described how he refused to eat such unclean animals, and how the voice from heaven had declared them clean and warned him against calling unclean that which God had made clean (**11:8-9**). Then, this vision had happened three times and the three men from Caesarea had appeared at that very moment at the house in which he was staying (**11:10-11**). The Spirit had directed him to accompany them without raising any objections (**11:12**).

Peter then pointed to the six men who had accompanied him to Caesarea (**11:12b**) and could confirm the truth of what had happened. He told how God had confirmed that Gentiles were welcome in the kingdom of God through Cornelius' vision and through the fact that the Holy Spirit had filled all who were listening to his message (**11:13-16**). Peter concluded with a question: *If God gave them the same gift [of the Holy Spirit] as he gave us, who believed in the Lord Jesus Christ, who was I to think that I could oppose God?* (11:17). His words echo those of Gamaliel in 5:39. The command to preach to the Gentiles had clearly come from God and had been blessed by him.

Peter's testimony silenced all the objections, and the Jewish believers began to glorify God for considering *'even' the Gentiles* worthy of *repentance unto life* (**11:18**).

The episode of Peter and Cornelius points powerfully to the theme of inclusiveness in the books of Acts as a whole. This story is considered so important that two chapters are devoted to it (10:1-48; 11:1-18) and it is referred to again in 15:7-9, where Peter defends the mission to the Gentiles. This story was at the heart of the inclusion of Gentiles in the community of followers of Jesus.

11:19-30 Witness to the Gentiles in Syria

The narrative now turns to what had become of the scattered disciples after the severe persecution that had ended with the killing of Stephen (8:4). We have already heard about Philip and Peter's ministry in the coastal areas of Lydda, Joppa and Caesarea. The conversion of Cornelius means that salvation could also be preached to Gentiles, and so now Luke goes on to tell more of the mission to Gentiles.

11:19-21 A discriminatory witness ended at Antioch

The scattered evangelists had at first preached the word only to Jewish people, and thus been discriminatory in their witness (**11:19**). Even though they had fled to the Gentile areas of Phoenicia, Cyprus and Antioch, they were not willing to preach the word to the Gentiles there. This selective witness was ended by some evangelists, men from Cyprus and Cyrene, who went to Antioch and began to preach the Lord Jesus to the Greeks (**11:20**). As had been the case with Peter, *the Lord's hand was with them* – that is, the Lord approved of their mission – and a large number of Greeks believed and turned to the Lord (**11:21**). The Lord left no room for doubt about the call to spread the gospel among the Gentiles.

11:22-24 Barnabas: link between Jerusalem and Antioch

News of the conversion of Greeks and the establishment of a church at Antioch reached Jerusalem, and Barnabas was sent to visit the new church (**11:22**). He *saw the evidence of the grace of God* among the believers at Antioch and rejoiced at it. *He encouraged them all to remain true to the Lord with all their hearts* (**11:23**).

At this point, Luke adds a brief note regarding Barnabas, saying *that he was a good man, full of the Holy Spirit and faith* (**11:24a**). That was why he had been nicknamed 'Barnabas' (a son of encouragement) by the apostles (4:36). His work brought many to the Lord (**11:24b**). He should be a model to church leaders who need to be good and full of the Holy Spirit and faith if they are to bring multitudes to the Lord.

11:25-26 Barnabas and Saul at Antioch

Barnabas did not want to continue the ministry at Antioch single-handed. He knew that Saul would enjoy ministering there, and so he went to Tarsus to look for him (**11:25**). Barnabas was not selfish but was willing to link others to his ministry. After finding Saul, he brought him to Antioch, where they both taught for an entire year (**11:26**).

The impact of their ministry was greatly felt in this Gentile city and led to the disciples being called *Christians*. They may have been given this name by Roman officials who wanted to register this new group, or it may have been a mocking name, or one chosen by the disciples themselves. It seems that they were not altogether happy with this name, for it is found only twice in Acts (11:26; 26:28) and once in the rest of the NT (1 Pet 4:16). The believers seem to have preferred to speak of 'the Way' (9:2; 19:9, 24:14; 24:22). Luke mentions the name 'Christian' only in an aside, perhaps in response to a reader's question. One reason for his hesitation may be that being identified with a personal name would make the new community seem like those followers of individuals mentioned by Gamaliel (5:36-39). At this stage, they wanted the movement to be seen as belonging to the God of Abraham and not merely to Jesus Christ; in other words, Jesus had not founded a completely new movement. Another reason may have been that there was a stigma associated with the name Christian, as is clear from Pliny's question (asked at the start of the second century): 'whether it is the mere name of Christian which is punishable, even if innocent of crime, or rather the crimes associated with the name?'. Pliny's question fits with the statement found in 1 Peter 4:16 about being patient when suffering for 'that name'.

11:27-30 The Antioch church helps the Judean church

There were some prophets from Jerusalem at Antioch (**11:27**). One of these, named Agabus (see also 21:10) stood up in the church and prophesied that a great famine would come upon the whole world (**11:28**). Luke tells us this took place during the reign of Claudius (see 18:2).

The way the material is presented here, it seems that the prophecy was spoken and fulfilled in the space of one verse! However, there must have been a time gap between the prophecy and its fulfilment. When the famine did come, the church in Antioch took a collection to help their fellow believers in Judea (**11:29**). It is important to note that the giving was according to each person's means. There was no obligation to give beyond what a person possessed. Moreover the term used indicates that each person gave of their surplus, what was in excess of their needs.

There was also accountability in the giving recorded here, for Barnabas and Saul were put in charge of delivering the money to the elders in Jerusalem (**11:30**). These elders would then make sure that it reached the needy, since the principle of distribution was according to each person's need (2:45; 4:34-35). The church today should demonstrate similar accountability in stewardship without paternalism.

12:1-24 The Persecution by Herod Agrippa I

Previously the church in Jerusalem had been persecuted by the religious authorities, but now the persecution came from another quarter. Herod Agrippa I *arrested some who belonged to the church* (**12:1**). Agrippa, who was born around 10 BC, was a grandson of Herod the Great (Luke 1:5) and the nephew of Herod the Tetrarch (Luke 3:19; 13:31; 23:7-12). After his father, Aristobulus, was executed, he fled to Rome with his mother, Bernice. There he became a friend of a young man, Claudius, who became emperor after the death of Caligula in AD 4. With Claudius' help, Agrippa became king of all of Palestine. He sought to please the Jewish people by attending their festivals and suppressing minority groups that might disturb the *pax Romana* (the peace of Rome). Among such groups was the so-called sect of the Nazarenes (the name given to the followers of Jesus by the Jews – Acts 24:5; 28:22).

12:2 The martyrdom of James

Herod Agrippa's first victim was James the brother of John, who was put to death by the sword (**12:2**). While Luke has only recorded the individual activities of Peter and John and mentioned the other apostles as a group (2:37, 43; 4:33, 36; 5:12, 18, 29, 40; 6:6; 8:1, 14; 9:27; 11:1), it can be deduced that they were actively witnessing to their Lord, for they were all arrested by the religious leaders (5:18). James was beheaded, a method of execution considered more humane than crucifixion, since it did not involve torture (see also Matt 14:10).

12:3-19 The release of Peter from prison

The story of Peter and James comes as a surprise. Why did God allow James to be killed while sparing Peter? God's will is certainly beyond human understanding, and there will always be occasions when we will not be able to comprehend why God allows some things to happen.

Pleased by the murder of James, the Jews encouraged Agrippa to arrest Peter. His aim may have been to keep the Jews happy and to continue to enjoy their support (**12:3a**). Peter was arrested during the celebration of the Feast of Unleavened Bread (**12:3b**), so Agrippa decided to wait until after the Passover before bringing Peter to trial (12:4). Peter, who was regarded as a ringleader, was to be tried in public as a warning to others and to please the Jewish people (**12:11**). Herod Agrippa may have heard about Peter's earlier escape from prison, and not wanting to risk anything similar happening again, he made sure four soldiers guarded him in shifts (**12:4**).

The church prayed fervently for the imprisoned Peter (**12:5**). We are not told the content of their prayer, but it was probably that he would be released and spared from death. James' death would have been fresh in their minds, and the prospect of losing another member of the community, and another apostle, would have been devastating to the entire church.

God heard their prayers and intervened on the night before the trial (12:6-11). Peter was being held under very tight security. He slept between two soldiers, who were chained to him, and there were more guards (probably the other two in the squad) on guard at the prison gate (**12:6**). But despite all this security, an angel of the Lord suddenly entered the cell, filled it with light, and shook Peter from his sleep. As he awoke, the chains fell off Peter's hands (**12:7**). Peter thought he was having a wonderful dream as he followed the angel's directions and got dressed (**12:8-9**). It must have seemed unreal as they walked past one guard and then another, and then saw the city gates opening as if by remote control. They walked on for one street, and then the angel left him (**12:10**). Suddenly Peter realized that this was no dream, but that the Lord had sent an angel to rescue him *from Herod's clutches and from everything the Jewish people were anticipating* (**12:11**).

Peter went straight to the house of prayer, the home of Mary the mother of John Mark (**12:12**). The prayers of the saints had been answered! When he arrived at the door, a servant girl, Rhoda, recognized his voice and ran to announce the answered prayer (**12:13-14**). But the church did not seem to believe in the power of prayer! They told her that she was crazy to think that Peter could have escaped from prison (**12:15**). Peter's insistent knocking eventually brought them to the door, and when they saw him, instead of praising God for the answered prayer, they were simply amazed. Does this not sound familiar? When our prayers are answered and the extraordinary happens, we too are amazed (**12:16**).

The believers seem to have been so loud in their amazement that Peter had to gesture for silence. He told them what had happened and instructed them to pass the news on to James and the brethren (**12:17a**). This James was not the apostle who had been executed (12:1) but another James, who was Jesus' brother.

Peter then *left for another place* (**12:17b**). This statement probably means that he left Jerusalem, and possibly even Judea, to escape being arrested again. The discovery of his escape caused consternation among the soldiers (**12:18**). Herod was so furious that he had the guards executed (**12:19**). His move to Caesarea may have been partly a result of the public humiliation he had suffered.

12:20-24 God's judgment

Luke includes an aside about the fate of Herod. While in Caesarea, he reached a political settlement of some dispute with the people of Tyre and Sidon (**12:20**). He delivered an impressive speech dressed in his full regalia, and they responded by shouting that his voice was that of *a god, not of a man* (**12:21-22**). Herod did not correct them and give God the glory – and his punishment for this blasphemy was death (12:23). Luke says that *an angel of the Lord struck* *him down, and he was eaten by worms,* suggesting that he contracted a severe sickness, clearly sent by God, that eventually killed him (**12:23**). This story is a warning to anyone who is tempted to take God's glory.

But while Herod died, the word of God continued *to increase and spread* (**12:24**). This comment resembles the one made after the conversion of Saul (9:31). The ending of Herod's persecution was a milestone that Luke could not overlook in telling the story of the church, although it was not so much a turning point as a mark of progress.

12:25-21:26 Witness to the Ends of the Earth

The book of Acts now moves on to deal with the final stage of the witness outlined by Jesus: witness to the ends of the earth (1:8). The church had accepted that Gentiles were to be part of their mission, since God had also granted the Gentiles repentance (11:18). Luke goes on to narrate how missionaries were sent out from what was now the headquarters of the mission to the Gentiles – Antioch.

12:25-14:28 First Witness to the Ends of the Earth

12:25-13:3 The commissioning of the first missionaries

Luke now returns to the story of Barnabas and Saul. They returned to Antioch after delivering the gift to Jerusalem (see 11:30), bringing with them a young man called John Mark, at whose mother's house the believers had met to pray (**12:25**; see also 12:12). But they were not the only leaders in the church at Antioch. There were also other prophets and teachers, including *Simeon called Niger* (meaning Black); *Lucius of Cyrene,* a town in North Africa; and *Manaen who had been brought up with Herod the tetrarch* (**13:1**). This was an international church in its own right, and it is no wonder that God chose to send missionaries to the ends of the earth from it.

The call to set Barnabas and Saul apart for the work that God had called them to came in the midst of revival meetings, as the church was busy worshipping the Lord and fasting (**13:2**). Since there were prophets in that church, the Spirit of God was able to communicate with the believers. The church today must be willing to seek the Lord for his direction in the ministry of the word to those who have not yet heard it or made a commitment to follow Christ.

Barnabas and Saul would have been among the prophets and teachers at Antioch, but the church did not use this as an excuse not to send them. A selfish church might have tried to send ordinary members of the church but this church was willing to obey the Lord, and therefore they fasted and prayed some more, to be sure that the Lord had spoken (**13:3**). Convinced that he had, they placed their hands on Barnabas and Saul to commission them for missionary work. This act also emphasized the community's

role in sending out the missionaries. They were going on behalf of the whole community of believers at Antioch (see also 6:6). With prayers and fasting, the missionaries were sent off. This sending may simply mean that the two were released from their teaching positions so that they could take up their new roles as missionaries.

13:4-12 Paphos: The first power encounter in missions

Throughout Acts, Luke stresses that the Holy Spirit controls mission work from start to finish (1:8; see also 13:9; 15:8, 28; 16:6,7; 20:28; 28:25). Since the Holy Spirit had initiated the mission work (13:2), he was also the one to formally send out Barnabas and Saul as missionaries (**13:4**). They needed the power of the Holy Spirit as they went out into the unknown as witnesses of the Lord.

Their first stop was at Cyprus, the Mediterranean island from which Barnabas came (13:4; 4:36). Arriving at Salamis on the east coast, Barnabas and Saul began to share the *word of God in the Jewish synagogues. John was with them as their helper* (**13:5**). From Salamis, the missionaries travelled the island preaching the word of God until they reached Paphos, a town on the west coast that was the seat of the Roman government of the island (13:6).

At Paphos the missionaries were confronted by a sorcerer of Jewish origins named Bar-Jesus (**13:6**). This name means 'son of Jesus' but probably does not refer to Jesus Christ, for 'Jesus' was not an uncommon name at the time. Bar-Jesus is described as a false prophet. He was associated with the Roman ruler of the island, who was called Sergius Paulus. This proconsul is described as *an intelligent man* who *sent for Barnabas and Saul because he wanted to hear the word of God* (**13:7**).

The sorcerer Bar-Jesus is also referred to as Elymas in 13:8. This is not the Greek form of his Hebrew name, but the Semitic form of his Greek title, 'magician'. This name is similar in sound and meaning to the Swahili word *elimu,* which means 'education' or 'wisdom'. This magician sought to prevent Sergius Paulus from hearing the word of God (**13:8**). Paul would have none of this. (Note that from here on in Acts, Saul is referred to by the Greek form of his name, Paul.) He describes Elymas as *a child of the devil ... an enemy of everything that is right ... full of all kinds of deceit and trickery... perverting the right ways of the Lord* (**13:10**). Luke leaves no doubt that the real opposition to the gospel comes from the devil. But whereas Elymas is full of deceit, Paul is described as *filled with the Holy Spirit* (**13:9**). It is in the power of the Spirit that Paul proceeds to pronounce judgment upon Elymas in the name of Jesus. The judgment is that he will be blind for a time (**13:11**).

On witnessing this miracle and hearing the gospel, the proconsul immediately believed (**13:12**). It seems that miracles confirm the truth of the gospel message. They are, however, not enough in themselves, for the missionaries still needed to teach the proconsul, who as an 'intelligent man' needed to learn the content of the faith. The word of God is also for the powerful and highly intelligent.

13:13-52 Pisidian Antioch: A typical sermon in a synagogue

Leaving the island of Cyprus, Paul and Barnabas (from now on Paul is mentioned first, perhaps to show that he is now the leader) sailed on to Perga in Pamphylia. There John Mark, who had accompanied them as their helper (13:5), left them and returned to Jerusalem (**13:13**). The text does not say why he left, but later events show that Paul did not approve of his reasons (15:38).

Saul and Barnabas travelled into the interior, to the Roman town of Pisidian Antioch (different from Syrian Antioch, from which they had come) (**13:14**). As visitors to the synagogue there, they were invited to speak (**13:15**). Luke then gives a detailed account of a typical sermon that Paul would have preached to Jews. A typical sermon to Gentiles is presented in 17:21-31.

13:16-22 A BRIEF HISTORY OF THE PEOPLE OF ISRAEL Paul reminded the Jews that it was God who had chosen them and made them prosper during their stay in Egypt (**13:16-17a**). God's hand was also at work in their deliverance from Egypt (**13:17b**) and his grace had protected them in the wilderness for forty years (**13:18**). Because of his great mercy, God had not destroyed the Israelites when they were disobedient. Instead he had destroyed seven nations to give them a place to live. This whole process of shaping the nation had taken about 450 years (**13:19**).

Once the nation was installed in the promised land, God gave them judges to rule over them until the time of Samuel, when *the people asked for a king*. God duly gave them a king – Saul – who ruled for forty years (**13:20-21**). God then removed Saul and gave the kingdom to David, who was a man after God's heart who would do what God wanted (**13:22**).

13:23-26 SALVATION HAS BEEN GIVEN THROUGH ISRAEL Paul now turns to the salvation that was to come to the people through David's descendant and announces that God has kept his promise and sent the Saviour, Jesus (**13:23**). His coming had been announced by John the Baptist, who was a forerunner who had insisted that he himself was not the Saviour (**13:24-25**). But now the Saviour has come and the message of salvation is being sent out to all who fear God – whether they are Abraham's descendants or God-fearing Gentiles (**13:26**).

13:27-30 THE ROLE OF THE PEOPLE OF JERUSALEM The people who lived in Jerusalem and their leaders had condemned Jesus to the cross (**13:27**), and Pontius Pilate had executed him even though there were no grounds for a death sentence (**13:28**). There could be no doubt that Jesus had died, for he had been buried in a tomb (**13:29**). But, amazingly, God had raised him from the dead (**13:30**).

13:31-37 THE WITNESS IS UNDENIABLE Any who were inclined to be sceptical about the resurrection that Jesus had appeared to his disciples *for many days*. These disciples were people he had travelled with from Galilee to Jerusalem, who had known him well and were now the witnesses to his resurrection (**13:31**). Paul is now bringing the good news to this congregation (**13:32**).

Jesus' resurrection marks God's fulfilment of his promise made long ago to David (**13:33-37**; see also Ps 16:10). Paul argues that the psalmist cannot have been speaking of David himself, since David had died and his body had decayed. It was Jesus, David's son, whose body would not decay.

13:38-41 THE ALTAR CALL If the hearers accepted this Jesus who was being proclaimed to them, they could enjoy forgiveness for all those things which the law of Moses could not cover (**13:38-39**). Faith in Jesus guaranteed a freedom from sin that was not possible by merely trying to keep the law.

Paul concluded by warning the congregation not to let the prophecy of Habakkuk 1:5 apply to them (**13:40-41**). Paul may have been using this prophecy in the same way that the Qumran community did when they warned people to listen to the message concerning the Messiah or to risk missing an eternal opportunity by rejecting the testimony of the new covenant. The missionaries gave the people an opportunity to repent, but also outlined the dire consequences of unbelief. They used Scripture to emphasize the importance of their message (13:41).

13:42-52 THE RESPONSE: REJECTION OF THE GOSPEL Initially the message was well received, and Paul and Barnabas were asked to return and speak again the following week (**13:42**). Many Jews and God-fearing proselytes spoke to them after the synagogue meeting (**13:43**).

The following Sabbath, *almost the whole city* assembled to listen to the missionaries. This response aroused the jealousy of the leaders of the synagogue (**13:44-45a**), who began to express their opposition to the missionaries (**13:45b**).

So Paul and Barnabas turned away from preaching to the Jews and went to the Gentiles (**13:46**). Does this mean that the Jews were not to be evangelized again? Has the witness to the Jews been completed? Does it mean that if some people are not responsive to the gospel, we are to turn away to those who are more receptive? The answer to all these questions is 'no', since we see that in other cities the missionaries also began by witnessing to the Jews before moving on to the Gentiles (see 14:1; 17:1-2).

Paul and Barnabas explained that the gospel message was meant to be preached to the Jews first, and then to the Gentiles (see also Rom 1:16). They proved from the Scriptures that this order was in accordance with God's plan (**13:47**; see also Isa 42:6; 49:6; Luke 2:32). The Gentiles rejoiced that whereas they had previously been excluded by the Jews, they were now being given an opportunity to respond to the gospel (**13:48**).

The mission was so successful throughout the region that the hostile Jews found it necessary to organize mass action against the missionaries, forcing them to leave (**13:49-50**). On leaving, they shook the dust off their feet as a sign of their rejection, probably following Jesus' instruction (**13:51**; see also Matt 10:14; Mark 6:11; Luke 9:5; 10:11; Acts 18:6.)

Paul and Barnabas might be gone, but the believers who remained behind were rejoicing. Despite the opposition, these Jewish and Gentile believers were continually filled with joy and the Holy Spirit (**13:52**).

14:1-7 Iconium: More opposition

Luke's statement that the missionaries entered a synagogue in Iconium clearly indicates that Paul and Barnabas still wanted to witness to Jewish people (13:52). Their preaching at Iconium was very successful, with a large number of both Jews and Gentiles believing the message (**14:1**).

Yet once again, as at Pisidian Antioch, Jews who did not believe stirred up opposition to the missionaries (**14:2**). Nevertheless, the missionaries continued their witness in the power of the Holy Spirit, who enabled them to perform signs and wonders that confirmed the gospel message (**14:3**). The Greek literally says that the signs were done 'by their hands', which may mean that Paul and Barnabas actually laid hands on those they healed, or may simply refer to their entire work of preaching and healing.

The hostile Jews roused the entire city so that the crowd was divided: some being on the side of the missionaries and others siding with the opposition (**14:4**). (Incidentally, this is the first time that Paul and Barnabas are referred to as *apostles*.) Things came to the point where powerful leaders were planning to harm the missionaries (**14:5**). When they learned of this plan, they escaped to the neighbouring region of Lycaonia, and specifically to the cities of Lystra and Derbe and the area around them (**14:6**). There they boldly continued their witness, not deterred by the threats and abuse they had suffered in Pisidian Antioch and Iconium (**14:7**).

14:8-20 Lystra: The healing of a lame man

Earlier, we learned of the healing of a crippled beggar by Peter and John (3:1-10). Now Paul and Barnabas do something similar (**14:8-10**). In both cases, the healing brought a strong reaction from the crowd – the crowd in Jerusalem sought an explanation (3:11) and the crowd in Lystra mistook Paul and Barnabas for visiting Greek gods (**14:11-13**). Whereas the healing by Peter and John led to their being imprisoned, in Lystra Paul ended up being stoned (14:19).

The Lystrians thought that Barnabas must be a human manifestation of Zeus, the king of the Greek gods. Paul, the chief speaker, was thought to be Zeus' son, Hermes, who was the messenger of the gods, as well as the god of roads, commerce, doorways, luck, the conductor of the dead and the patron of shepherds (**14:12,**). The crowd were ready to sacrifice to them (**14:13**). This incident reveals the danger of identifying what is done in the name of Jesus as having been performed by people, and then treating them like gods. The church today needs to be aware of this danger, for personality cults can end up treating those with a remarkable ministry as if they are on the same level as Jesus.

The *apostles'* (the second time this title is used of Paul and Barnabus) reacted swiftly upon learning what the crowd wanted to do. They tore their clothes as a sign of repentance and rushed to explain that they too were mere humans (**14:14-15a**). Their reaction is very different from that of Herod Agrippa I, who was happy to be called a god – and died for it (12:22-23). Peter too had refused to accept worship from Cornelius (10:25-26).

Having insisted that they were not gods, the missionaries used the opportunity to explain the gospel once again, attempting to turn the people away from worthless things and to bring them to the living God, who had created all things. They said that this God had allowed a period of ignorance in all the nations – including the missionaries' nation and the hearers'. But he had not left himself without a witness (see also Rom 1:19-23) through divine provision of rain and fruitful seasons so that people were satisfied and rejoiced at harvest festivals (**14:15b-18**).

The missionaries appealed to God's general revelation of himself in this sermon because of what the hearers had been about to do – sacrifice to Paul and Barnabas because of the healing they had seen. The missionaries wanted them to consider why, if they were so moved by the healing of one lame man, they were not equally moved by what God is and had been doing for them naturally by providing rain and seasons (see also 4:24; 17:24; Ex 20:11; Ps 146:6; Rev 14:7).

The fruit the chief speaker received for his words was a hail of stones (**14:19**). There are both joys and trials in the ministry of the word. The triumphant gospel involves suffering too, and every servant of the Lord must be prepared for both eventualities.

The missionaries moved rapidly from being taken for gods to being condemned as felons due to the attacks of the unbelieving Jews. God's grace was, however, sufficient for Paul, who with the support of the other believers re-entered the city (**14:20**). The next day the missionaries left Lystra for Derbe.

14:21-25 The return journey: Establishing leaders

Despite their trials, the missionaries made many disciples at Derbe (**14:21**). Thereafter they travelled back to Antioch in Syria, passing through Lystra and Iconium on the way. They strengthened and encouraged the new believers there to continue in the faith and to take tribulations positively as the way to God's kingdom (**14:22**). The enemy is not happy with those who follow Christ, and therefore, believers are to expect fierce opposition – yet this is the pathway to the kingdom of God. The church today must be willing to accept tribulations as a necessary part of the Christian walk to the kingdom of God (see 20:19, 23-24).

The missionaries appointed elders in every church, committing them to God with prayers and fasting (**14:23**). There would not be a leadership vacuum when the missionaries left for home – they made sure that the church was in able hands. It is clear that indigenous leadership was also a key point for these early missionaries. However, it is worth noting that many of those converted here seem to have been God-fearers, who would have known much about the Scripture. When they learned about Jesus, the final pieces fell into place. This was not a case of appointing new believers with no background in the faith as leaders.

On their way home, the missionaries continued to share the gospel in the regions they passed through (**14:24, 25**). We are not told whether they actually went back to Pisidian Antioch, or whether they merely travelled through other parts of Pisidia. Certainly, they shared the word in Perga, and in Attalia, which is a seaport.

14:26-28 The mission report at Antioch

From Attalia, the missionaries returned to their home church (to use modern mission terminology) at Syrian Antioch. This church had commissioned them (**14:26**; 13:3) and thus they were accountable to it. Thus the missionaries gave their report to the whole church at Antioch, not just to the leaders (**14:27**).

The missionaries reported all that God had done through them and how he had opened the door for ministry. The mission had been the work of God, since he was the one who *had opened the door of faith to the Gentiles* (**14:27**). Now they were in no hurry to leave again, for they were anxious to enjoy fellowship with the disciples. Luke reports that they spent a long time with the disciples at Antioch (**14:28**).

The first missionary journey was a success because the Lord was the mission director. He directed the missionaries and opened the hearts of those who were being evangelized. Without God's power, our mission to the world is ineffective. The other lesson to be learned from this mission is that the work of the gospel involves both joy and suffering. In other words, 'We must go through many hardships to enter the kingdom of God' (**14:22**).

15:1-35 The Jerusalem Council

The conversion of Cornelius had brought some problems in the Jerusalem church (11:1-3). After Peter's explanation of what had happened (11:4-17), it had been concluded that God had granted repentance to the Gentiles (11:18), and

the matter had been closed. But it seems there were some who were still not satisfied.

15:1-5 The problem: Circumcision

Some men who had come to Antioch from Judea taught that circumcision was necessary for salvation (**15:1, 5**). This group seems to have accepted much of the teaching of the Pharisees and failed to understand that circumcision only made one a Jewish proselyte, and that believing in the name of Jesus was the only requirement for salvation (see also, for example, 4:12; 10:43; 13:39; 16:31). They claimed to speak for the Jerusalem believers, and caused much confusion among the believers at Antioch. The missionaries tried to resolve the dispute, but without success (**15:2**). At issue was not just circumcision, but circumcision according to the custom of Moses (see also 6:14; 21:21; 26:3; 28:17).

Since the problem could not be resolved locally, it was referred to the Jerusalem church, which then acted as the headquarters of Christian mission (**15:3-4**). While travelling there, the missionaries seized the opportunity to visit parts of Phoenicia and Samaria where they told the believers about the conversion of the Gentiles. Their news is reported to have brought much joy to the believers. It seems that the battle for the inclusion of Gentiles in the community of believers had already been won.

At Jerusalem they were received by the church (presumably all the available members of the community of believers in Jerusalem), the apostles and the elders (15:4). Just as the missionaries had appointed elders in the Gentile churches, so the Jerusalem church had elders too.

Paul and Barnabas then presented their report to the whole community of believers in Jerusalem (15:4), telling how God had used them in their mission to Gentiles. However, some of the church members, *who belonged to the party of the Pharisees*, objected to the report, declaring that the Gentile believers *must be circumcised and required to observe the law of Moses* (**15:5**). This was the problem that had to be solved promptly, for these believers would also have rejected the idea of even eating with uncircumcised Gentiles (see also Gal 2:11-13), even though Peter and the other missionaries had been doing this (see also 11:3).

15:6-21 The debate

All the church members heard the missionaries' report, but when it came to making a decision about such an important matter, only the apostles and elders were present (**15:6**). There was free and fair debate, giving each council member ample time to air his views (**15:7a**).

Finally Peter rose to speak. He pointed out that he was the one God had first chosen to preach to the Gentiles (**15:7b**; see also ch. 10). God, *who knows the heart*, had confirmed that their faith was genuine by giving them the gift of the Holy Spirit, just as he had given it to the Jerusalem disciples (**15:8**). Clearly God made no distinction between Jews and Gentiles, but cleansed all their hearts in the same way – by faith (**15:9**; see also Rom 5:1-2.).

Those who were demanding some other grounds for accepting the Gentiles were in essence putting God to the test – implying that God had not done enough (**15:10**). He concluded by reiterating that salvation is only by the grace of the Lord Jesus – and that this applied both to the council members, who were Jews, and to the Gentiles (**15:11**).

The entire council then listened to Paul and Barnabas telling how God had performed signs and wonders through them among the Gentiles (**15:12**). That the missionaries were able to perform these exploits in the name of Jesus was a clear sign that God accepted the inclusion of the Gentiles without demanding circumcision.

James, the Lord's brother and the leader of the Jerusalem church, was convinced that God had chosen to take *from the Gentiles a people for himself* (**15:13-14**). We miss the tremendous significance of this statement if we do not recognize that the Greek term translated here 'People' was one that Jews used to refer to fellow Jews, but never to Gentiles. There is an example of this use in Paul's quotation of Hosea 2:23 and 1:10 in Romans 9:25-26. The term specifically referred to the people of Israel, but James asserts that the OT prophecy in Amos 9:11-12 is being fulfilled as the Gentiles are being called to a special relationship with God (see also Acts 15:15-18).

Amos spoke of a time when God would rebuild the temple for the purpose of making the *remnant of men* seek God. Here the term 'remnant' refers to the Gentiles (**15:16-17a**). The testimony of the missionaries and Peter confirmed that there were *Gentiles who bear my name* (**15:17b-18**). God himself had declared that the Gentiles were to be part of his people.

James, accordingly, saw no need for the church to lay any more burdens on the Gentile believers (**15:19**). He proposed that a letter be sent to the Gentile churches, outlining what was considered essential (15:20). This was that the Gentiles should *abstain from food polluted by idols* (that is, from idol worship); *from sexual immorality*; *from the meat of strangled animals* and *from blood* (**15:20**).

James' comment that *Moses has been preached in every city from the earliest times and is read in the synagogues on every Sabbath* (**15:21**) seems to be intended to assure the council that Gentile believers would be familiar with these requirements. The council's basis for deciding what was right conduct was OT Scripture. Thus their decree may have been influenced by Leviticus 17-18 or by some other part of the OT that was considered relevant.

15:22-29 The consensus

The whole church had been involved in coming to the final decision, and thus the whole church chose their representatives to accompany Paul and Barnabas to deliver the letter to Antioch. Those chosen were Judas (also known as Barsabbas) and Silas, who are described as *leaders among the brothers* (**15:22**).

The senders of the letter were specifically identified as *the apostles and elders, your brothers* and the letter was addressed *to the Gentile believers in Antioch, Syria and Cilicia* (**15:23**). These were the areas where there were churches at the time the letter was written, so there is no implication that the letter did not apply to other areas.

The letter began by stressing that those who had come demanding circumcision had no authority to speak for the church in Jerusalem (**15:24**). The council acknowledged that the matter had disturbed Gentile believers, and said that they wanted to settle the matter through the trusted messengers being sent along with Paul and Barnabas (15:25). These two are described as *dear friends* (**15:25**) and as having risked their lives for the sake of the Gentile believers (**15:26**). Their new companions, Judas and Silas, would *confirm by word of mouth* what the letter said (**15:27**).

The matters addressed in the letter were both divine and human – the Holy Spirit was pleased with the council's decision not to place any greater burden on the Gentiles than was strictly necessary (**15:28**). The guidelines that the council sent to Gentile believers listed certain things that could be termed cultural practices. Thus the Gentiles were to *abstain from food sacrificed to idols;* that is, they were not to eat meat from idol temples (see also 21:25). They were also to abstain from eating *blood,* another practice associated with idol worship in which worshippers are reported to have tasted blood. The instruction to avoid *the meat of strangled animals* may be linked to the fact that they were strangled as part of idol worship. The same reasoning may apply to the instruction to avoid *sexual immorality,* which was also often a part of idol worship (**15:29**).

The exact reasons why these particular items were selected as essential has generated a lot of debate. It is agreed that the reason it was felt necessary to spell these out was that many of those who had been converted had no knowledge of the Jewish religion. So there were people like Simon the sorcerer of Samaria, who had been making money by magical acts and who thought that the Holy Spirit's power would really develop his business (8:13, 18-24). Simon's response to Peter's curse shows that he had acted in ignorance. Others who had been converted after having been involved in magic could fall into the same sort of temptation (19:19). Then there were converts like Demetrius the silversmith (19:24-28), who had been involved in idol worship. It would have been easy for them to continue to eat meat sacrificed to idols, which is why Paul addressed that problem in 1 Corinthians 8.

This background helps us see why James suggested that the council provide minimum requirements for the Gentile believers. These requirements were Jewish in that they stressed avoiding idolatry and immorality, but they did not require Gentiles to adhere to such specific aspects of Jewish law as circumcision, the Sabbath and the dietary laws.

15:30-35 Positive Responses

The believers at Antioch were delighted with the contents of the letter (**15:30-31**). Judas and Silas, who were prophets, encouraged and strengthened the believers at Antioch with a long message – maybe a sermon lasting several hours (**15:32**). Then they returned to Jerusalem (**15:33-34**), although it is possible, according to some manuscripts, that Silas decided to stay on in Antioch, where he later became Paul's companion (15:40).

Meanwhile Paul and Barnabas stayed at Antioch, where they and others taught and preached (**15:35**). It seemed that the major obstacles to the mission to the Gentiles had been overcome. However, the issue would surface again (21:20-28).

15:36-18:22 Second Witness to the Ends of the Earth

15:36-40 Disagreement in the mission team

It seems that Paul, rather than the Holy Spirit, suggested the second missionary visit (**15:36**). He has clearly now assumed a leadership role. Barnabas wanted to take John Mark along with them, but Paul was opposed to this idea (**15:37**). He felt that John Mark had defected from their earlier mission (13:13) and there was no guarantee that he would do better this time (**15:38**). Clearly there was more to John Mark's departure than the narrator wanted to reveal. Whatever the problem had been, Paul was not willing to forgive and forget. This caused a *sharp disagreement* between Paul and Barnabas (**15:39a**). For the first time, we are allowed to witness the near collapse of a missionary endeavour. Even the leading missionaries were clearly human beings, who could disagree.

The sharp disagreement did, however, have a positive result: two mission expeditions were sent out instead of one (although it is also possible that Barnabas and Mark went to Cyprus because it was home rather than to conduct a mission) (**15:39b**). Paul took Silas, who had brought the letter from Jerusalem (15:22), as his new companion (**15:40**). The community of believers at Antioch agreed with Paul's decision and, as before, commissioned the new missionary team and sent them off. The narrator probably does not tell of the commissioning of Barnabas and John Mark because he is interested in telling the story of Paul's mission.

15:41 Summary of the second missionary witness

Although Paul was travelling with Silas, in most of what follows the narrator uses the singular 'he'. Paul travelled through Syria and Cilicia for the purpose of encouraging and strengthening the churches (**15:41**). He was not seeking new mission fields, but visiting the already established churches. He may have felt that there was no need to go further while the already reached churches were weak. Church planters should share his concern for believers.

16:1-3 Timothy: Circumcision for a missionary?

Paul again visited Derbe and Lystra, where he had already established churches (16:1; see also 14:6,7). In Lystra he met a disciple named Timothy, the son of a believing Jewish mother (see 2 Tim 1:5; 3:15) and a Greek father (**16:1**). We do not know whether Timothy had been converted during Paul's first journey or through the witness of the local church. He was a young man with a good reputation both in his own city of Lystra and in the neighbouring city of Iconium (**16:2**). This suggests that Timothy may already have been involved in outreach missions in both places.

Paul wanted to take Timothy with him as they travelled, but he faced the problem that *all knew that his father was a Greek* (**16:3**) and that he had not been circumcised as a Jew. Paul always began his ministry in a new city in the synagogue, and Timothy's status would arouse controversy and become a hindrance to the preaching of the gospel. Accordingly, Paul had to circumcise Timothy. In doing this, he was not contradicting his earlier position. Timothy was already a believer, and the circumcision was solely for reasons of ministry, not for salvation. Timothy himself demonstrates his commitment to mission by his willingness to submit to this ritual in order to reach others (see 1 Cor 9:19-23).

16:4-5 The mission team re-visits the missionary churches

The team now travelled on, presenting the decisions reached at the Council of Jerusalem to each of the churches they visited (**16:4**). The narrator is careful to stress that these decisions did not originate with the missionaries or with their home church but had been *reached by the apostles and elders in Jerusalem*.

The results of this missionary visit are summarized: the churches were strengthened and there was daily growth in numbers (**16:5**). As elsewhere in Acts, the presence of a summary suggests a turning point in the narrative. New areas of mission are about to open up.

16:6-12 The Holy Spirit overrules Paul's mission strategy

Paul now experienced some frustration. The Holy Spirit forbade them to preach on the west coast of Asia Minor, and so they passed through the regions of Phrygia and Galatia (where they may have had some ministry, as evidenced by Paul's letter to the Galatians) (**16:6**) and headed towards

Mysia. But the Spirit of Jesus prevented them from going to Bithynia (16:7), and so they ended up at the Aegean port of Troas (16:8). Where the Holy Spirit had previously been stopping them from preaching, now at last he gave them a clear vision of where they were to go. This guidance came in the form of a vision in which Paul saw a *man of Macedonia* calling him to come to Macedonia and help them (16:9). Obedient to the vision, the missionaries immediately prepared to travel there (16:10). From now on, Luke, the narrator, seems to have been a part of the missionary group, for he starts to use the first person plural 'we' (16:10-18).

We, like these missionaries, need to be attuned to the leading of the Holy Spirit so that we know where God is leading us and where we should be going.

Some commentators have suggested that Paul was not allowed to minister in the Roman province of Asia because Peter and the other apostles were ministering there and had a more legalistic approach than Paul. The Holy Spirit acted to avoid competition and conflict in the spread of the gospel. This explanation seems unlikely as no such conflict is apparent anywhere in the narrative.

It seems more likely that we are simply told these details to show that Paul and his companions did not set out with a rigid plan, but were open to divine guidance. This had been the case right from the start of missionary work, when the Holy Spirit told the church in Antioch to set Paul and Barnabas apart for mission work (13:2). Throughout the book of Acts, the missionary task is divinely directed (see also 4:31; 8:29, 39; 10:44; 13:2, 4).

God's guidance meant that places that might otherwise have been overlooked were not left out. Paul would later preach in the region of Asia when he visited cities like Ephesus (18:19) and spent considerable time establishing the church there (19:1-10).

The missionary party boarded a ship to cross the Aegean Sea to Macedonia, where God had called them. Their first stop was at Philippi, a city nine miles (fifteen kilometres) from the eastern coast of Macedonia on a major Roman highway (16:11-12a). This city was well known for its rich gold mines and water springs, and could thus be described as *the leading city of the district of Macedonia*. It was also *a Roman colony*, which increased its importance (16:12b).

16:13-40 Philippi: A leading city of Macedonia

Philippi did not have a synagogue. Instead the Jews met at the river outside the city gate on the Sabbath. The missionaries accordingly joined them there (16:13). The worshippers appear to have been mainly women, for they *began to speak to the women who had gathered there*. This should be a lesson to those who think that a church cannot be a church without men.

One of those present was a woman named Lydia, who was a trader from Thyatira and is described as *a worshipper of God*. She listened attentively, and *the Lord opened her heart to respond to Paul's message* (6:14). In other words, the Lord enabled her to have saving faith. This is the inside story of conversion – it is the Lord who enables people to have faith in the gospel (see also 10:44). This knowledge should ease the burden of evangelists who worry whether their preaching will lead people to hear the gospel and be converted. God is in control. Our task is to preach the word in the power of the Holy Spirit and leave the results to him.

Lydia was baptized with her entire household, and thereafter she pleaded with the missionaries to stay in her house (16:15). It seems that they were initially reluctant to do this, perhaps because they were men and Lydia was the head of the house. But this reluctance was overcome by the persuasion of this now faithful woman of God.

At Philippi, Paul has his second recorded encounter with satanic power working through an individual. In the earlier case, Paul had declared that Bar-Jesus was a child of the devil (13:10). In this case, an evil spirit of divination was upon a slave girl. Her masters were profiting from her fortune telling (16:16). Traditional healers and fortune tellers are still with us today, and we as Christians can learn from Paul's response in this situation.

The evil spirit in the girl made what seems to be a wonderful revelation to her owners as she followed the missionaries, shouting: *These men are servants of the Most High God, who are telling you the way to be saved* (16:17). She carried on doing this for many days, but there is no record that anyone was converted as a result of her revelation. The evil spirit was not trying to draw people to God, but to cause confusion. Paul became so troubled by this continued shouting that he commanded the evil spirit to come out of her *in the name of Jesus Christ* (16:18a). The exorcism formula seems to follow the same pattern as had been followed by Peter and John in the healing of the crippled beggar at the temple gates (3:6). The name of Jesus is not used as an instrument to get results but to claim the authority of Jesus Christ in driving out the evil spirit (see also Matt 28:18).

The results were immediate – *at that moment the spirit left her* (16:18b). But the consequence of Paul's exorcism was that her masters lost a source of income. Infuriated, they fabricated false accusations against the missionaries, which led to their being beaten in public and imprisoned (16:19-24). Christian ministry inflicts losses on the evil one and he will not give in easily.

Despite the beating and their imprisonment, Paul and Silas used the occasion, and in the quiet of the night we find them *praying and singing hymns to God* (16:25). We are not told what they were praying for, but we can assume that it was something to do with the spread of the gospel. Even though it was close to midnight, their behaviour was not unobserved, for *the other prisoners were listening*. We are challenged to remember that believers' should display joy and thanksgiving despite their circumstances.

The Lord did come to their rescue (16:26), but not as quietly as he had done in the case of Peter (12:5-11). There was an earthquake, all the prisoners' chains fell off and the doors were opened (16:26) – a powerful symbol of how the Lord releases those who have been imprisoned by sin (see also Luke 4:18-19).

The jailer's first reaction was to try to kill himself. Herod had executed Peter's jailers after his escape, and this man may have feared the same fate (16:27). Paul was alert, and intervened to stop the suicide attempt (16:28). Neither he nor the other prisoners had run away. We are not told what became of these other prisoners, for the jailer's story now takes centre stage.

The jailer now addresses Paul and Silas as his superiors (16:29-30). Aware of the higher authority of the God these men serve, he falls face down at their feet to plead for mercy. *What must I do to be saved?* is his desperate cry (16:30). Their response is short and precise – *Believe in the Lord Jesus, and you will be saved – you and your household* (16:31). Salvation came to the jailer and his whole household (16:33-34). The wicked beating of the missionaries resulted in a plentiful harvest, as the jailer and his household were baptized that very night (16:33) and shared a meal with Paul and Silas (16:34).

The next morning, the authorities ordered that Paul and Silas be quietly released. But they would not accept this. Their rights as citizens had been publicly violated, and they demanded a public apology. Paul's statement is telling: *They beat us publicly without a trial, even though we are Roman citizens, and threw us into prison. And now do they want to get rid of us quietly? No! Let them come themselves and escort us out* (16:35-37). The magistrates were obliged to come and make peace with Paul and Silas (16:38-39). Paul and Silas made a leisurely departure from Philippi at their own timing, after having given their usual encouragement to the believers remaining behind (16:40).

Christian workers should not allow their constitutional rights to be violated without complaint because they are Christians. Although our citizenship is in heaven, we are still living in this world and we do have rights. We must endeavour to know what these rights are and to help others respect them.

17:1-9 Thessalonica: Hostile Jews

There was a synagogue at Thessalonica, so Paul went there, as was his custom whenever he visited a new city (17:1-2). He preached at the synagogue on three Sabbath days, trying to prove to them that Jesus was the Christ, the awaited Messiah. He cited evidence from the Scriptures that the Messiah had to suffer and die and rise from the dead (17:3). Some Jews and a large number of the Gentile

God-fearers who attended the synagogue were persuaded to believe in Jesus Christ (17:4). The fact that some of these were prominent women makes it clear that there was no discrimination in the proclamation of Christ; both Jews and Gentiles, men and women were being reached with the gospel (17:4).

Paul's success aroused jealousy in the Jewish leaders, who led strong opposition to the missionaries (17:5-9). In every city they visited, their ministry was opposed by the influence of the evil one. At Philippi, there had been the possessed girl, and here there were *bad characters* who were incited to start a riot (17:5). They targeted the house of Jason because the missionaries were staying with him (17:6-8). The missionaries were accused of being troublemakers who had caused problems elsewhere and were now seeking to cause problems in Thessalonica. Jason was obviously their accomplice, since he had welcomed them to his home. The most serious charge was treason: the missionaries were *defying Caesar's decrees* by claiming that *there is another king, one called Jesus* (17:7). The accusations created an uproar in the city (17:8), but Jason was able to calm the situation and bail out the team (17:9).

17:10-15 Berea: More noble Jews

Paul and Silas had been able to leave other places openly, but the brothers at Thessalonica had to wait for the cover of night before sending them on to Berea (17:10). When they arrived there, presumably in the morning, the missionaries went straight to the Jewish synagogue (17:10). The narrator tells us that the Jews at Berea were *of more noble character than the Thessalonians*, for they not only received the message with eagerness, but also searched the Scriptures to confirm it (17:11). Many of them are said to have believed. The converts also included prominent Greek women and men (17:12). The women may be mentioned first to indicate that the community of believers in Acts was not discriminatory – the gospel is inclusive.

As soon as the Jews in Thessalonica learned where Paul had gone, they followed him to continue their opposition (17:13). But the Berean believers were alert to the danger and escorted Paul to the city of Athens on the coast. Silas and Timothy were left behind, presumably to strengthen the new converts (17:14). Paul, however, gave instructions for them to join him as soon as possible (17:15).

17:16-34 Athens: A typical sermon to Gentiles

Paul was disturbed by the number of idols he saw in Athens (17:16). The artistry with which they were made did not trick him into missing the influence of ungodliness. He had to spend some time there as he waited for Silas and Timothy, and the Spirit of God stirred his spirit to preach the gospel (see also Paul's charge to Timothy to be ready to 'preach the word ... in season and out of season' –

2 Tim 4:1-2). Like Paul, a Christian should seize every opportunity to share the gospel.

Paul's desire to preach the gospel led him to both the synagogue and the marketplace (**17:17**). He reasoned with Jews, God-fearing Greeks, and others whom he met at the marketplace. This mode of ministry was somewhat unusual, since Paul was now reaching three groups at once.

Among those who were interested in what he had to say and were prepared to argue with him were some *Epicurean and Stoic philosophers* (**17:18a**). The Epicureans taught that pleasure is the highest good, and mental pleasure the highest happiness. They understood salvation in terms of being freed from fear of gods and the fear of death. The Stoics, by contrast, taught that knowledge is the highest good and that the material world is the sum of reality. These philosophers were not sure what Paul was speaking about, and referred to him as a babbler (literally, someone who had picked up scraps of knowledge) who was proclaiming strange deities (literally, demons) (**17:18b**). They had never met anyone like him before. So they brought him to the Areopagus, an ancient court that had once governed Athens but now had other duties, one of which was arranging public lectures. It took its name from the Hill of Ares (that is the hill dedicated to the Greek god of war), but by Paul's time it met in the agora, or marketplace. The philosophers sought to hear what Paul had to say, since they had heard strange things from him (**17:19-20**). They all wanted to hear something new (**17:21**), and Paul was ready to tell them some 'all-important' news. In doing so, he provided us with an example of the type of sermon he would have delivered to a Gentile audience.

17:21-22 A COMMENDATION Paul began by commenting on something positive – *I see that …you are very religious* (**17:22**). His basis for saying this was the number of shrines for worship that he had seen, which had even included one dedicated *to an unknown god* (**17:23**). By beginning in this positive way, Paul was able to win the crowd's trust and gain a hearing for the rest of what he had to say.

Like the Athenians, Africans are very religious and have numerous shrines. The concept of the Supreme God in African Traditional Religions (ATR) is also shadowy, not unlike the concept that led to the erection of an altar to the unknown God.

17:23-29 MOVEMENT FROM THE KNOWN TO THE UNKNOWN Paul now moves from the idea of worshipping an unknown God to offering them information about this very God whom they are worshipping in ignorance (**17:23**). Those who practise ATR are still worshipping God in ignorance, since they have not learned that Jesus Christ has provided the correct way to worship him.

Paul identifies the Athenians' unknown God as the Creator who has made all things. As the Lord of heaven and earth, this God is far bigger than any temple the Athenians have built (**17:24**). He does not need their temples or gifts or any human services, since he himself has made people and everything they could possibly offer to him (**17:25**). Having an idol does not make God exist, for he has existed even before creation (see also Gen 1:1-27; John 1:1-3).

Not only has God made everyone, but he has made them all the descendants of *one man* (some later Greek manuscripts read of 'one blood') and has assigned them their places in the world (**17:26**). All people are equal before God, and the differences between language and cultures were part of his plan.

God's chief aim in making these arrangements was to encourage all people to seek him (**17:27**). The altar dedicated to the unknown God is evidence of this desire. And yet, God is not far from us, since *in him we live and move and have our being* (**17:28**). Then Paul quotes Athenian poets, acknowledging their work and using it as a bridge to declare the gospel truth that *we are his offspring*.

If this is true, and we are God's offspring and live surrounded by his works, then it is ludicrous to imagine that he is in any way like an image, no matter how skilfully we craft it. The divine nature is nothing like gold or silver or stone (**17:29**). In other words, human beings cannot create God.

17:30-31 NOW IS THE TIME TO END THEIR IGNORANCE The Athenians, like all other peoples, had acted in ignorance when they made their idols, and God in his mercy has tolerated this. But now Paul has come as a messenger to remove their ignorance and to announce God's command that people everywhere must repent (**17:30**).

Repentance is necessary because God has set a day of judgment. On that day everyone will be judged by the righteousness man whom God has raised from the dead (**17:31**). The death and resurrection of Jesus Christ prove that the way of idols is useless. If the Athenians are willing to repent of their ignorant method of worshipping God and come to Jesus, they will escape judgment, since their debt was paid on the cross.

17:32-34 THE RESPONSE: SOME ATHENIANS BELIEVED The very idea of the resurrection of the dead provoked a strong reaction in the crowd. Some scoffed at the very idea, while others wanted to hear more of what Paul had to say (**17:32**). The preaching of the resurrection to adherents of ATR produces similar results, for the concept of resurrection is foreign to those who believe that a dead person continues to live in another world, the world of the living dead.

At this point, *Paul left the Council* (**17:33**). But a few had been convinced by what he said and came to faith (**17:33-34**). Among those who believed were men, including Dionysus, and one woman who is mentioned by name, Damaris (**17:34**). The reference to *a number of others* may mean that Damaris was not the only woman who believed.

18:1-17 Corinth: An important seaport

Paul moved on from Athens, where he had made few converts, and went to Corinth (**18:1**). There he met Aquila, a native of Pontus, and his wife, Priscilla. They were Jews whom the Emperor Claudius (AD 41-54) had expelled from Rome (**18:2**). Paul joined the couple in a business partnership, since both he and they were tentmakers by trade and all of them needed money to survive in this new environment (**18:3**).

But while Paul now made tents, he did not neglect the ministry of the word. Every Sabbath he preached the gospel to the Jews and the Greeks gathered at the synagogue (**18:4**). Then when Silas and Timothy eventually arrived, Paul stopped his tentmaking and *devoted himself exclusively to preaching* (**18:5**). The content of his preaching was the gospel – *Jesus is the Christ*. When the Jews were not willing to accept that the Messiah had come, Paul shook off the dust from his clothes (rather than his feet) and declared that their blood was upon their heads (see also 2 Sam 1:16; 1 Kgs 2:33; Ezek 18:13; 33:4, 6, 8; Matt 27:25; Acts 20:26). He had done his part to warn them of danger (**18:6**). This act was not intended as a curse on Jewish people in general but addressed a local situation. There were Jews who became believers in Corinth and later in Paul's ministry.

Paul also announced that from now on his ministry would focus on reaching Gentiles. He could no longer preach in the synagogue, so he started preaching in the house next door (**18:7**). The leader of the synagogue, Crispus, was one of those Jews who did believe, along with his entire household (**18:8**). His decision encouraged many other Corinthians to believe in the Lord.

Paul's second missionary journey had been tumultuous, with problems in Philippi, Thessalonica and Berea, and a cool welcome in Athens. Now he was encountering hostility from the Jews in Corinth. Paul may have been in need of encouragement. So the Lord reassured Paul, telling him that he should not be afraid, but should *keep on speaking and do not be silent* (**18:9**). The Lord promised Paul his presence and protection. More than that, he promised that Paul's witness in this city would be fruitful (**18:10**). The Lord of the harvest, who knows human hearts, knew that many more people in Corinth were willing to accept the gospel.

Paul obeyed the Lord's command and spent a year and a half teaching the word of God among the Corinthians (**18:11**). During this time the hostile Jews did attempt to attack him but, as God had promised, no harm came to Paul.

The fact that Paul's opponents took him to court when *Gallio was proconsul of Achaia* (**18:12**) gives us an important clue as to when this was happening. We know that Gallio was appointed proconsul in around AD 51/52 by an edict of Emperor Claudius (who was mentioned in 18:2). Therefore, Paul's ministry at Corinth may have ended some time in AD 51 or 52.

The Jews wanted to have Paul imprisoned on a charge that amounted to blasphemy (**18:13**) and that could have had serious consequences had it been presented before a high priest. But Gallio refused to become involved in religious disputes (**18:14-16**). He was not familiar with Jewish law and refused to judge the case. The Lord was protecting Paul as he had promised (18:16).

The Jews let out their anger by beating up Sosthenes, the leader of the synagogue, but Gallio did not bother to intervene (**18:17**).

God had kept his promise to protect Paul, and will continue to protect us today. Our part, like Paul's, is to trust him and to do the ministry knowing that God has authority even over the schemes of the evil one.

18:18-21 Ephesus: A brief stopover

The opposition did not drive Paul out of Corinth, for he stayed on *for some time*. He was not overly concerned for his personal safety, as missionaries sometimes are today when they are airlifted from supposedly dangerous situations. When he did leave, it was to go to Ephesus in the company of Priscilla and Aquila (**18:18**), who were planning to stay there.

During his brief stopover in Ephesus, Paul was not idle but spent some time reasoning with Jews in the synagogue (**18:19**). Then he left, promising to return later, if it was God's will (**18:20, 21**). God's will was clearly the most important factor guiding Paul's ministry.

18:22 The return journey to Antioch

The return journey to Antioch is presented very briefly. We are told that Paul landed at Caesarea and then went up to visit the church (**18:22a**). This may simply mean that Paul visited the church at Caesarea, which he would visit again later on his way to Jerusalem (21:8). But it is more likely that Paul went up to Jerusalem, since this journey was commonly referred to as 'going up'. Also, the reference to him 'going down' to Antioch would make more sense if he were leaving from Jerusalem than from Caesarea. Thus it seems that Paul paid a brief visit to the church at Jerusalem, before returning to his home base, the church at Antioch (**18:22b**).

18:23-21:26 Third Witness to the Ends of the Earth

Paul's stay in Antioch appears to have been short, and so scholars debate whether this visit marked the end of his second missionary journey or merely a brief break in it. Consequently some commentaries speak of only two missionary journeys, while others speak of three. In this commentary, we shall assume that the second journey came to an end with Paul's return to Antioch (18:22) and will treat the travels that follow as his third journey. While this third journey is the last to be recorded in Acts, Paul's letters clearly indicate that it was not his last journey.

18:23-28 Apollos: An eloquent evangelist

Paul started by travelling through regions where churches were already established in order to encourage the disciples (**18:23**). At the time, a man called Apollos was preaching in the area. He was *a learned man, with a thorough knowledge of the Scriptures* (**18:24**) who came from Alexandria in Egypt. He had arrived in Ephesus some time after Paul's first visit there and his preaching had made several converts (19:1). However, it seems that he only knew about Jesus through the teaching of John the Baptist and had not met the apostles in Jerusalem (**18:25**). Consequently, he seems to have been unaware of the role of the Holy Spirit (**18:26**; see also 19:3). When Priscilla and Aquila heard him preach, they invited him to visit them and in a friendly way taught him more about the faith, probably drawing on what they had learned from Paul. The different evangelists were not in competition with each other, but helped one another in matters of doctrine.

We also see this helpfulness when the time came for Apollos to travel on to Achaia. The community of believers at Ephesus gave him a letter of introduction to the believers there. Priscilla and Aquila would have known these believers, because they themselves had recently come from Corinth, the provincial capital of Achaia. In Achaia Apollos strengthened the disciples (**18:27**) and powerfully debated with the Jews, *proving from Scriptures that Jesus was the Christ* (**18:28**; see also 1 Cor 1:12; 3:4-6, 22; 4:6; 16:12; Titus 3:13). The gospel was firmly grounded in the OT Scriptures. Clearly, Apollos had benefited from his own education and from what he had been taught by Priscilla and Aquila. Education should not be neglected in missions today. It is important to know the truth if one wishes to refute false allegations.

19:1-41 Ephesus: Exploits in the name of Jesus

19:1-7 The Ephesian disciples receive the Holy Spirit Some time after Apollos had left Ephesus for Corinth, Paul arrived there, keeping the promise he had made (**19:1a**; 18:21). He met a group of about twelve disciples (**19:7**) who had probably been converted early in Apollos' ministry, before Aquila and Priscilla had explained the way to him. These disciples knew only of John's baptism (**19:1b-3**).

Paul explained to them that the baptism of John was a preparation for the coming Messiah, the Saviour of the world (**19:4**). That Saviour had come. On hearing this, the disciples were willing to be *baptized into the name of the Lord Jesus* (**19:5**). This may mean that they expressed their belief in Jesus for salvation and were then baptized according to the formula given by Jesus in Matthew 28:19.

After their baptism, *Paul placed his hands on them* and the Holy Spirit came on them, a coming that was confirmed by their ability to speak in tongues and to prophesy (**19:6**). This incident is similar to the one involving the Samaritans (8:14-17). Here, too, the sign of the indwelling of the Holy Spirit was important to show that a new group, in this case the disciples of John, had been fully incorporated into the community of believers.

19:8-22 The hall of Tyrannus In Ephesus, Paul was able to preach in the synagogue for three months (**19:8**), which was far longer than he had managed at many other places (see 13:14, 42; 17:1-2, 10, 17; 18:4, 7). However, after this he found it necessary to move to another venue, possibly because some of those attending the synagogue had *refused to believe* and were publicly speaking evil of *the Way* (**19:9a**) (the term used for the community of believers – see 9:2 and comment on 11:26). Paul could not continue to use a facility that was not neutral. His action here cannot be used to support fragmentation of the church of Christ today, where some are tempted to move out of established churches to form what are called 'independent' churches whenever there is some disagreement.

The venue where Paul continued to preach was a lecture hall belonging to a man named Tyrannus. He may have been a disciple or he may just have been sympathetic to the Christian faith (**19:9b**).

Paul spent two years at Ephesus. His ministry there was very successful, and we are told that everyone *who lived in the province of Asia heard the word of the Lord* (**19:10**). On his earlier journey, the Holy Spirit would not allow him to preach in this province (16:6-7), but the time was now right for him to be there.

Paul's ministry was accompanied by healings and exorcisms (**19:11-12**). There was such power in anything that had come into contact with Paul that people carried them to the sick and they were healed (**19:12**). Not surprisingly, such power attracted attention and imitators among those who were not believers. Among them were the seven sons of Sceva, who seems to have described himself as a Jewish chief priest (**19:13-14**). But evil spirits recognize impostors and can distinguish them from those with real spiritual power, such as Paul and Jesus (**19:15-16**).

This incident had such an impact that many believers who had practised sorcery and magic now brought the tools of the art to be burned (**19:17-19**). Clearly the gospel was reaching all kinds of people, including those who practised witchcraft. In Africa sorcerers and witchdoctors have been very resistant to the gospel, but if African Christianity is to take root, then it must reach everyone, including these people.

The final summary of Paul's ministry in Ephesus is that *in this way the word of the Lord spread widely and grew in power* (**19:20**). Then Luke gives us a summary of Paul's plans for the future. These included a return to Jerusalem, followed by a visit to Rome (**19:21-22**). Little did Paul know that after a trial in Caesarea, he would be sent to Rome as a prisoner (25:10-12).

Paul sent Timothy and Erastus ahead to Macedonia (**19:22**). These two were faithful companions of Paul, for both of them were with him in Rome (Rom 16:21, 23) and when Paul wrote to Timothy he gives him news of Erastus (2 Tim 4:20). After they had left, Paul stayed on in Ephesus a little longer. Paul's ministry was guided by the Holy Spirit, but that did not exempt him from the need to make careful plans. He was also happy to have assistants and relied upon them to finish work that he had not been able to do himself (see Titus 1:5).

19:23-41 The consequences of successful ministry Missionary work may result in persecution when it affects the local economy. This is what happened in Ephesus, where the success of Paul's mission affected the sales of the idol makers. Demetrius, a silversmith who sold shrines of Artemis, met with other silversmiths and convinced them of the harm Paul's teaching of the Way (see 19:9) was causing their business. A riot erupted (**19:23-28**) and the city *was in an uproar* (**19:29a**), perhaps because many had believed Paul's message and sided with him while the rest of the crowd was with the silversmiths. Others were simply caught up in the general excitement (**19:32**)

Two of Paul's companions were seized and hustled into the theatre, where large crowds could gather. Paul bravely wanted to join them and try to speak to the crowd, but was persuaded not to do this by people whom the NIV calls *officials of the province* (**19:29b-31**), but who are called 'Asiarchs' in the Greek. The Asiarchs were wealthy people elected to an office that involved supervising the affairs of a city, particularly in connection to the funds generated by religious festivals and the like. That some of this group are referred to as *friends of Paul* speaks volumes about his status in the city.

At the theatre, the Jews pushed a man called Alexander to the front as their spokesman (**19:32-33**). We do not know what he was planning to say, for as soon as the crowd realized that he was a Jew, and thus a monotheist, they started chanting the praises of their goddess. The chanting went on for some two hours (**19:34**). It is possible that this is the same Alexander, a metalworker, whom Paul warns Timothy against (2 Tim 4:14). The man mentioned in Timothy was in a similar trade to Demetrius the silversmith, although he may not have made idols.

After two hours, the mob must have been tiring, and the city clerk was able to calm them, reminding them that everyone knew that the city of Ephesus had the temple of Artemis and *her image, which fell from heaven* (**19:35**). This image may have been a meteorite that was thought to resemble the goddess. The official pointed out that if there was any legal grievance against the missionaries, Demetrius

should take the matter to the courts, as the Romans did not approve of mob justice (**19:36-41**). This wise leader was able to defuse the situation and prevent great turmoil.

20:1-4 Further travels

After the riot, Paul decided that it was time to move on. But he did not simply abandon his ministry in Ephesus. He stayed until the situation had calmed down and he spent some time encouraging the disciples (**20:1**). This should be a challenge to Christians not to abandon a ministry due to persecution. Paul took time to encourage and comfort the believers and to bid them a formal farewell.

Luke next gives another brief summary of Paul's movements through Macedonia to Greece (**20:2**). He spent three months in Greece, but when a plot to kill him was discovered just as he planned to sail to Syria, he changed his plans and returned through Macedonia (**20:3**). He was accompanied by several people whom we meet later in his letters (**20:4**; see Rom 16:21, 23; Eph 6:21; Col 4:10; 2 Tim 4:20; Phlm 24).

20:5-12 Troas: Eutychus raised from the dead

One of the missionaries' stopping points along the way was the coastal city of Troas (**20:5**). It is interesting to note the resumption of the 'we' passages here, which may imply that Luke rejoined the team at Philippi where he may have been left, since the earlier 'we' passages ended there (**20:6**; see 16:16).

On *the first day of the week* they met with believers at Troas to celebrate the resurrection of the Lord (**20:7**; see also 1 Cor 16:2; Rev 1:10). This day was Sunday, and since then it has become traditional for believers worldwide to meet for worship on the Lord's Day, rather than on the Jewish Sabbath (Saturday).

The believers had come together in the evening *to break bread* and Paul delivered the sermon. He spoke *until midnight* (**20:7**). It was late, and the upstairs room where they were meeting would have been hot and smoky because of the many lamps (**20:8**). A young man called Eutychus fell asleep and fell from the window where he was sitting. The room was on the third floor, and when they rushed down to help him, they found that he was dead (**20:9**).

Paul's approach to reviving the young man was very similar to that used by Elijah (**20:10**; see also 1 Kgs 17:21). After reviving him, he continued to speak until daybreak (**20:11**). Paul made his final journey to Jerusalem after speaking for the whole night and performing a great miracle. It is not surprising that he left the people greatly comforted (**20:12**).

20:13-38 Miletus: A seminar on eldership

Paul's companions set off by sea for Assos. The sea route involved a long journey around a cape, and so Paul chose to take the shorter route and go to Assos on foot (**20:13**).

At Assos, he rejoined his companions on the ship. We are then given a summary of their route, listing the ports at which they stopped (20:14-15). The final port in this list is Miletus, located some thirty miles (forty-eight kilometres) south of Ephesus. Paul had sailed past Ephesus because he was in a hurry to get to Jerusalem before the day of Pentecost (20:16). Nevertheless, he still wanted to speak to the elders of the church in Ephesus, and so he arranged for them to come to him at Miletus (20:17). When they arrived, Paul gave them what amounted to a one-day seminar on eldership.

20:18-27 PAUL'S PERSONAL TESTIMONY Paul started his address to the elders by offering his own lifestyle as an example for them to follow (20:18). He had lived among them for about two years, and his life had been transparent to all. One wonders how many church elders today could make a similar claim with regard to their lifestyle.

Paul's style of ministry was not domineering and bossy. Rather he had served *with great humility and with tears* (20:19a). He had maintained this style despite the provocation offered by those who opposed him (20:19b; see 19:9, 26; 1 Cor 15:30; 2 Cor 1:8-19). He had also not been self-serving, keeping certain knowledge for himself, but had shared everything that would be helpful to the recipients (20:20a). Nor had he restricted himself to public ministry; he had also been happy to teach in private homes (20:20b). He had also not been discriminatory in his ministry, but had preached the gospel to both Jews and Greeks, stressing that everyone needed to respond to the call to repentance and faith (20:21).

In everything he did, Paul was ready to obey the Holy Spirit – even when that obedience meant going to a place where he faced imprisonment (20:22-23). Being in the right place was more important than his own comfort. His main goal was to complete the task God had given him, and to testify *to the gospel of God's grace* (20:24; see also 1 Cor 9:24-27; Phil 3:7-14; 2 Tim 4:7).

Paul somehow knows that he will never meet the Ephesian elders and believers again (20:25). So he solemnly declares that he has done his part by proclaiming *the whole will of God* (20:27), meaning particularly the need to know Christ, to all the people, and that he is innocent of the blood of any among them who have not given their lives to Christ (20:26). He may be thinking of the OT warning that if people died because someone had failed to warn them of impending danger, their blood would be required from that person (Ezek 3:18-19; 33:4-9). Paul's words are a solemn warning to us: Can we be as certain that we are not responsible for the blood of those under our care? Have we taken care to proclaim the 'whole will of God'?

20:28-35 THE CHARGE TO THE EPHESIAN ELDERS Having established his credentials and described his own example, Paul now instructs the Ephesian elders in how to carry out their duties.

His first instruction to them is to *Keep watch* (20:28a). This is not just a casual idiom, as when we say 'Goodbye. Take care of yourself.' It is an instruction to continually be on the alert for danger and error and to respond appropriately. The first people they have to keep watch over are themselves. Church leaders must be above reproach (1 Tim 3:1-7; Titus 1:5-9), for the evil one often attacks believers by slinging mud at their leaders. They must make sure that he has no grounds for accusations.

Second, they are to be like shepherds, watching over the flock of God. They are to watch over *all the flock*, meaning that not one church member is to be overlooked (20:28b). The flock is precious, for God purchased it with his own blood, and the Holy Spirit has placed it in the care of the elders. They are responsible to God.

A shepherd's job is to feed the flock and protect it from the *savage wolves* who will try to ravage the flock after Paul's departure (20:29; see also John 10:12). These 'wolves' will be false teachers, perhaps Judaizers trying to force them to keep the Mosaic law. Some of the false teaching will come from outside, but some will arise from among themselves (20:30; see also 1 Tim 1:20; Rev 2:2). The false teachers will distort the truth in order to gather disciples for themselves (see also Eph 4:14; 5:6; 1 John 2:18-27). It is no wonder that Paul repeats the charge to be alert, reminding them of how he spent three years warning them of approaching danger, often with tears (20:31). They must keep watch, for the danger is real.

Paul prays for the Ephesian elders, committing them *to God* (20:32a). They will need God's presence to face the trials that lie ahead. He also commits them to the *word of [God's] grace*, which will build them up to be strong and will give them an inheritance among the saints, proof that they have persevered in their faith (20:32b; see also Eph 1:11; 2:19-22).

Finally, Paul refutes the slander that he has been enriching himself by his preaching, or using the money collected for the poor believers in Jerusalem for himself (see also 2 Cor 12:17-18). He had not asked the elders for financial support, and categorically denies having *coveted anyone's silver or gold or clothing* (20:33). In order to avoid this kind of allegation, Paul has worked to provide for his own needs and those of his companions (20:34). He was not willing to receive any support that hindered his freedom to proclaim the gospel (see also 1 Cor 9:1-18).

Paul summarizes his approach with the statement that he modelled the correct approach to money *in everything I did* (20:35a). He had left a pattern for others to follow. Just as he had worked hard to provide for the needs of others, so the Ephesian elders are to *help the weak*. Paul backs up this exhortation with a reminder of something Jesus had said.

HOUSE FELLOWSHIP

There is nothing particularly unusual about people with common interests meeting in homes. Such meetings are common in all cultures. For example, in some African cultures, family members, those in the same age groups or others who have close bonds may meet in the home of the head of the family or of any member of the group. Larger group meetings involving a whole village or community are usually held in the marketplace or a common square.

Believers in Christ belong to a common household of faith and share a common purpose, so it is not surprising that they, too, meet in homes. The term 'house fellowship' (or cell group, home cell, home church or even neighbourhood fellowship centre) has come to be used to describe such meetings and to distinguish them from larger gatherings for congregational services.

Our Lord Jesus often met with groups in people's homes. Believers in him met in homes before and after Pentecost (Acts 2:46-47; see also Acts 12:12; 20:20; Rom 16:5; 1 Cor 16:19; Col 4:15; Phlm 2). We know that there were 120 believers in the upper room on the day of Pentecost; other groups may have been smaller or larger. As today, the size of the group was probably limited by the available space in the house.

The purpose for which groups of believers get together is spiritual, rather than merely social. While there are disagreements about the role of house fellowships, there is general agreement that the reason such groups exist is that belonging to a large congregation does not always provide Christians with opportunities to interact effectively and beneficially. Some strongly advocate that house fellowships should replace larger congregations (a few even going so far as to suggest that the existence of larger congregations is a

mark of apostasy). More commonly, house fellowships are regarded as a way of organizing a congregation to promote its relevance and effectiveness.

House fellowships have an inward, upward and outward focus. Inwardly, they nurture members' bonds to each other. True spiritual growth includes developing godly interaction skills for relating with and serving others in Christ. Upwardly, they nurture members' bond to God through Christ. Every Christian needs to grow in intimacy with God. Outwardly, there is the need to reach out to the immediate neighbourhood with a genuine witness to Christ's saving power.

To achieve these goals, groups may use Bible study outlines prepared specially for the purpose. In other cases, they may discuss and analyse the sermon for the week, asking questions to clarify its meaning and apply it to their lives. Social activities such as sharing and caring also take place.

The leadership of house fellowships will vary from place to place, but in general leaders are chosen from among the church members and given training in how to handle small groups. Assignment to fellowship centres is done by the overall leader or a group of leaders. The groups are also encouraged to invite others to attend as a way of reaching out to the unsaved and strengthening the bonds between Christians from different churches.

The church in Africa is growing rapidly, and congregations can number in the hundreds and thousands. House fellowships are necessary to nurture and monitor the spiritual growth, physical welfare and godly interaction of members. This pattern of operation was practised by our Lord Jesus and the early believers. It is biblical and increases efficiency and productivity.

Uzodinma Obed

While the saying quoted here does not appear elsewhere in the NT, its spirit is evident in the Sermon on the Mount (see Luke 6:38). Paul was always anxious to root his practice in the model of the Lord Jesus (see also 1 Cor 7:10, 12, 25; 9:14; 11:24; 1 Tim 5:18; 6:3).

Jesus' saying contrasts giving and receiving. It should not be misinterpreted as meaning that those who are helped are less blessed or that all God's servants must be self-supporting. But they should not be content to simply be takers. Jesus was urging believers not to amass wealth but to give it away. It was in this spirit that the believers in Jerusalem sold their possessions and goods to meet the needs of others (2:42-47; 4:32-37). For the Jerusalem church to be able to continue to share, some believers had to be prepared to work. If they were unable to work, they would have had to sell items to keep up the flow of support. In the same way, the Ephesian church needed to be ready to work so that they would be able to share with those in need.

Giving always means that there is something to be given, and this 'something' is obtained by *hard work* (**20:35b**).

20:36-38 A SAD FAREWELL After concluding his speech, Paul and the elders knelt in prayer (**20:36**; see also Acts 7:60; 9:40; 21:5; for Jesus kneeling in prayer, see Luke 22:41). The prayer probably dedicated both Paul and the elders to the task ahead. There was an outflow of love and emotion as they all wept, embracing him and kissing him farewell (**20:37**). Sadly they escorted him to the ship, grieved that they would never meet again (**20:38**). We need to consider whether our ties with our missionaries and pastors are so close that we would feel similar grief at parting.

21:1-6 Tyre

After this difficult parting, Paul and his companions continued their journey until they reached Tyre (**21:1-3**). There they stayed with some believers for seven days (21:4). These believers also foresaw, through the Spirit, that Paul would encounter suffering in Jerusalem (compare 20:23) and urged him not to travel there (**21:4**), but Paul was determined to carry on. The departure from Tyre is the first time whole families are mentioned in Acts – *All the disciples and their wives and children accompanied us out of the city* (**21:5**). The wives and the children also participated in the prayer before they left.

21:7-14 Ptolemais and Caesarea

The missionaries spent a day with *the brothers* (**21:7**) at the city of Ptolemais. This harbour, the best on the coast of Palestine, is about thirty miles (forty-eight kilometres) from Tyre and is today known as Acre (in Judges 1:31, the city is referred to as Acco).

Travelling south, Paul and his companions pressed on to Caesarea where they visited Philip the evangelist, one of the Seven who had been chosen to serve tables many years before (**21:8**; see 6:5). He is called *the evangelist* to distinguish him from the apostle Philip. This title was clearly known in the early church (Eph 4:11; 2 Tim 4:5).

The mention of Philip's four unmarried daughters who prophesied continues the concept of families being active members of the Christian community (**21:9**; see 21:5). It may also be a reminder of the fulfilment of Joel's prophecy that God would pour his spirit on both men and women (see 2:18). Paul had a high regard for the gift of prophecy, considering it more desirable than speaking in tongues (1 Cor 14:1-33). In the NT, *prophecy* seems to refer to a revelatory ministry that probably included teaching, for Paul says that those who prophesy instruct and encourage the church (1 Cor 14:31). The fact that Philip's daughters were able to prophesy is interesting in view of Paul's instruction that women should remain silent in church (1 Cor 14:33-35). It seems that God enables both women and men to be ministers, and therefore it is not for the church to prejudge any group on the basis of gender.

While they were staying with Philip, Agabus a prophet from Judea, visited them and immediately gave a prophecy concerning Paul's journey to Jerusalem: *The Holy Spirit says, 'In this way the Jews of Jerusalem will bind the owner of this belt and will hand him over to the Gentiles'* (**21:10-11**). This prophecy did not contradict the Spirit's direction that Paul should go to Jerusalem, but confirmed that the Lord was in control of whatever was going to happen (20:22).

The other disciples, however, tried to use the prophecy to dissuade Paul from going to Jerusalem (**21:12**). He was touched by their concern, but remained convinced that it was God's will for him to go there. He would not change his course merely for the sake of his personal safety (**21:13**). For him, it would be an honour to die in Jerusalem for the name of Jesus. Paul was not reckless, and on two previous occasions he had run away from danger (9:23-25; 29-30). But he was prepared to endure suffering if this was God's will (**21:14**).

21:15-26 Jerusalem

Not deterred by the prophecy of suffering, some of the Caesarean disciples escorted Paul and his companions on the last stages of their journey to Jerusalem (**21:15**). Hospitality was arranged for them in *the home of Mnason*, who, like Barnabas, had come from Cyprus. The description of him as *one of the early disciples* may mean that he had been converted on the day of Pentecost (21:14; see 2:9-11).

Immediately after arriving, the missionaries met with the believers in Jerusalem, who received them warmly (**21:17**). They also met the Jerusalem elders, to whom Paul gave a detailed report of *what God had done among the Gentiles through his ministry* (**21:18-19**; see also 15:4). His news brought much joy to the church (**21:20a**).

However, there was a cloud over their celebrations. The elders reported that some church members in Jerusalem were zealous for the law and had been outraged by rumours that Paul was encouraging Jews in the Diaspora to abandon the Mosaic law (**21:20b-21**; see also 16:3; 1 Cor 7:18; 1 Cor 9:19). To avoid trouble, the elders advised Paul to demonstrate his personal commitment to keeping the law. They recommended that he pay the expenses for four devout believers who had taken a vow, enabling them to be released from their vow and to shave their hair (see 18:18). By joining in their purification rites, Paul would show that he still had respect for the law (**21:22-24**; see also Num 6:13-15).

The elders assure Paul that these concerns related only to the Jewish believers in the Gentile world. They still agreed with the earlier decision regarding the inclusion of Gentiles in the community of believers (**21:25**; see 15:19-29) and supported him in his mission to the Gentiles.

The following day, therefore, Paul took their advice and went to the temple (**21:26**).

21:27-28:31 Paul's Ultimate Witness

In this final section of Acts, Paul is captured in Jerusalem, tried and imprisoned in Caesarea, and eventually extradited to Rome, the centre of the Roman Empire. His journey there can be described as his ultimate witness to the ends of the earth (1:8).

21:27-23:22 Trial and Imprisonment in Jerusalem

21:27-36 Paul's arrest

While Paul was in the Temple undergoing ritual purification, he was recognized by *some Jews* who rounded up a mob and seized him (**21:27**; see 20:18-19). The charges brought against him were as false as those brought against Jesus and Stephen. The accusers claimed that Paul had taught *all men everywhere against our people and our law and this place* and had defiled the temple by bringing Greeks into it (**21:28**; see also 21:21). (The narrator clarifies that although Trophimus was with Paul in Jerusalem, he had not entered the temple with him – **21:29**). The Jews who led the outcry came from the Roman province of Asia, probably from the city of Ephesus. They still resented his successful ministry there (19:1-41).

Paul was almost killed in the general uproar, but the commander of the Roman army rescued him by taking him into custody (**21:30-35**). Luke portrayed Pilate as trying to protect Jesus from mob justice (Luke 23:13-23), and here the Roman authorities protect Paul (**21:36**). In both cases, the mob shouted, 'Away with him.'

21:37-22:21 Paul's defence before the angry crowd

Paul politely asked the commanding officer for permission to speak (**21:37**). The commander, who had jumped to the conclusion that Paul was an Egyptian who had earlier led a strike on the city, was surprised that Paul was able to speak Greek (**21:38**). Paul explained that he was in fact *a Jew, from Tarsus in Cilicia, a citizen of no ordinary city* (**21:39**).

Paul's respectful approach to the commanding officer is a model for believers in dealing with the governing authorities. So is his stress on his true identity. He did not hide his citizenship. He was proud to be a Jew from the great city of Tarsus, with its famous university. He was not implying that being mistaken for an Egyptian was an insult; he simply did not want there to be any confusion about his identity.

Paul began his address to the crowd using the same formal words with which Stephen had addressed his accusers: *Brothers and fathers* (**22:1**; 7:2). He uses formal language to show courtesy and respect and terms of relationship because they are fellow Jews. Paul was not arrogant and managed to keep calm despite the assault he had just endured. He wanted to use this opportunity to share his testimony, explaining his life and conduct (see also 25:16; 1 Cor 9:3; 2 Cor 7:11; Phil 1:7, 16; 1 Pet 3:15).

His mode of address and the fact that he was speaking Aramaic got through to the crowd, and *they became very quiet* (**22:2**). Paul had spoken Greek to the commander (21:37), but like any good communicator of the gospel he speaks in the language appropriate to his audience.

Paul begins his defence by speaking about his Pharisaic heritage. In this brief autobiography he explains that he was a Jew born in the city of Tarsus in Cilicia, but had been brought up in Jerusalem. He had undergone rigorous training in the Jewish law under the great scholar Gamaliel (**22:3**). He had been just as concerned about the law as the crowd who had wanted to kill him; in fact, he had actively participated in sending *the followers of this Way to their death, arresting both men and women and throwing them into prison* (**22:4**; see also Phil 3:6). He can even call the high priest to witness that he had been given written permission to go to Damascus and bring any Christians he found there to Jerusalem as prisoners (**22:5**; see also 9:1-2). Paul

carefully refers to the Christian community in neutral terms, as 'this Way'.

Paul was deeply ashamed of his persecution of believers, as is clear from his description of himself in his letter to Timothy (1 Tim 1:13-15). But the story of his conversion makes it clear that God's gift is available to all.

Having established his Jewish credentials, Paul goes on to speak of his conversion on the way to Damascus. An account of this event was given in 9:3-8, but here and in 26:12-18 Paul tells it for himself. There are only minor differences in detail between the three versions of the story.

Here we are told that Paul's party was very near Damascus and that it was *about noon* when he was stopped in his tracks by a flash of *bright light* from heaven that shone around him, making it clear that this was a heavenly visitation (**22:6**; see also 26:13). Paul fell to the ground, possibly as a sign of submission, and in that posture was able to hear a voice that addressed him directly and called his name twice (**22:7**; 9:4; 26:14).

The one speaking is identified as *Jesus of Nazareth* (**22:8**). The *of Nazareth* is not mentioned in 9:5 and 26:15, but is included here because this was the name by which the Jewish audience would have known Jesus (see also 24:5). Jesus declared that persecuting his church is the same as persecuting him. He then directed Paul to go into Damascus ('into the city' in 9:6), where someone would tell him *all that you have been assigned to do* (**22:10**). Paul had to be led into the city by his companions because he had been blinded by the light (**22:11**).

Paul's companions did not understand the voice, but they were able to see the light (**22:9**). However, it had not blinded them as it had Paul. The champion of Judaism now needed human help to perform even the most basic tasks.

The fact that the Lord did not tell Paul all that he had been assigned to do clearly shows that there is a place for human agents in the calling of those whom God intends to use. Paul's later comment that he had not received his apostleship from humans (Gal 1:11-24) does not preclude the part played by Ananias.

Paul describes Ananias as *a devout observer of the law and highly respected by all the Jews living there* (**22:12**). He was also a follower of the Way. Paul is making the point that he had been introduced to Christianity by a devout Jew, and that his being a Christian did not mean that he had broken the law.

Ananias restored Paul's sight (**22:13**). This moment seems to be synonymous with Paul's conversion. He was now ready to receive instructions from the Lord through his servant Ananias: *The God of our fathers has chosen you to know his will and to see the Righteous One and to hear words from his mouth* (**22:14**). These words (which are not in 9:17 and 26:16-18) are meant to show that Christianity was not a blasphemous religion, but was coming from the God of the fathers. God was calling Paul to become a witness to everyone, that is, to an inclusive mission (**22:15**). He was to be a witness of what he had *seen and heard*. This seeing and hearing of the risen Jesus were the grounds for Paul's recognition as an apostle (see also 1 Cor 9:1).

Paul was baptized in the name of Jesus for the cleansing of his sins (**22:16**). This verse should not be taken as teaching salvation by means of baptism (see also 2:38). The focus is on submission to Jesus. As elsewhere in the NT, baptism is an outward symbol of an inward change that has already taken place (Rom 6:4-6; 1 Cor 6:11).

Some time later (the *when* is not specific – see Gal 1:18) God spoke to Paul in a vision as he prayed at the temple in Jerusalem (**22:17**; compare Peter's vision in 10:9-16). The Lord instructed him to leave Jerusalem because not only were the Jews there refusing to accept his message, they were also seeking to kill him (**22:18**; see also 9:29). Paul was surprised at this. Given his history of persecuting believers and supporting those who killed Stephen (**22:19-20**; see also 8:1), his conversion should have impressed the Jews in Jerusalem. If he could be converted, so could others (see also 1 Tim 1:15-17).

The Lord, however, knew better than Paul and sent him off *far away to the Gentiles* (**22:21**). Hearing this, one is reminded that Paul has now returned to place from which God had sent him away. Will the new generation of Jews listen to him?

22:22-29 The advantages of Roman citizenship

The mention of the Gentiles reminded the Jews of what the riot had been about in the first place, and renewed commotion broke out. They were shouting: *'Rid the earth of him! He's not fit to live!'* ... *and throwing off their cloaks and flinging dust into the air* (**22:22-23**; see also 7:57). They were like bullocks, scraping up dust and making threatening noises as they prepare to fight. They were reacting like senseless animals. However, nothing that Paul said insulted them or blasphemed the name of God.

Recognizing that the situation was getting out of hand, the commander ordered Paul to be taken into the barracks, removing him from the mob (**22:24a**). It seems that the commander had not understood what Paul had been saying or why the crowd was so angry, for he ordered that Paul be flogged to find out what was going on (**22:24b**). But Paul pointed out that he was a Roman citizen, and thus was entitled to a proper trial before any flogging could be given (**22:25**; see also 16:37). The commander was nervous and questioned Paul about his citizenship. Whereas the commander had had to pay a hefty price for Roman citizenship, Paul himself was a citizen by birth (**22:26-29**). This cannot simply have been because he was born in Tarsus, for that city was not a Roman colony. Paul's father or grandfather

must either have bought citizenship or been given it as a reward for some service.

Paul knew his rights as a Roman citizen and he did not allow them to be abused (see also Acts 16:35-39). He allowed God to use his high social status to reach those who were high in society (see also 9:15), but did not neglect those who were of lower rank (1 Cor 1:26).

22:30-23:11 Paul's defence before the Sanhedrin

The commander could not keep a Roman citizen in prison unless he had been found guilty of some crime. He therefore released Paul and ordered the Jewish council to assemble the following day so that he could find out exactly what Paul was accused of (**22:30**). This gave Paul an opportunity to defend himself before the Sanhedrin.

Paul's opening words to the council are very different from those he used when addressing the mob the previous day (22:1). He addresses them as *My brothers* (**23:1**), for he had once belonged to this group. Paul asserts that he shares their desire to live according to the will of God, declaring, *I have fulfilled my duty to God in all good conscience to this day* (**23:1**). In other words, he has a clear conscience before God and there is no truth in the accusations brought against him.

Ananias, the high priest, did not wish to hear any more and so he instructed someone to strike Paul across the face (**23:2**; see also John 18:22). Such behaviour was illegal and had no place in this type of council. It was particularly offensive for a Jew in the hands of Jews.

Paul responds by pointing out that this action was illegal. By breaking the law he was supposed to be upholding, Ananias was being a hypocrite (**23:3**). In describing him as a *whitewashed wall*, Paul is using an image similar to the one that Jesus used in Matthew 23:27.

When Paul was told that he had insulted the high priest (**23:4**), he apologized and quoted a law that showed that one should not insult a ruler of the people (**23:5**; see Exod 22:28). He had not intended to show disrespect for the office of the high priest, but he had not known that Ananias now held that office. The last time he had been in contact with the Sanhedrin was shortly before his conversion, when he had probably requested letters of introduction from Caiaphas (4:6; see also Luke 3:2), the previous high priest.

Sensing danger and perceiving that there were different parties in the Sanhedrin, Paul took action, announcing that he was a *Pharisee, the son of a Pharisee* and that he was standing trial *because of my hope in the resurrection of the dead* (**23:6**). This statement was true, for Paul's faith was grounded in the resurrection of Christ. However, Paul also knew that was a controversial issue within the council, for the Sadducees denied any possibility of life after death, while the Pharisees did not (**23:7-8**). When the debate was framed in these terms, the Pharisees argued that Paul had done nothing wrong and that it might even be true that God had spoken to him through *a spirit or an angel* (**23:9**). The debate became so heated that the commander thought it wise to send Paul into the safety of the barracks (**23:10**).

So far, Paul seems to have been alone in his troubles in Jerusalem. But the Lord appeared to him at night and spoke words of encouragement: *Take courage! As you have testified about me in Jerusalem, so you must also testify in Rome* (**23:11**). The Lord had noted Paul's attempts to witness to him in Jerusalem, in the midst of all the confusion and accusations. Now he was letting him know that in some way these events were working to fulfil his long-standing dream of witnessing to the people in Rome (see 19:21).

23:12-22 A plot to kill Paul

Paul needed courage, for Satan was preparing an attack. *The next morning* more than forty Jews took an oath not to eat or drink until they had killed Paul (**23:12**; see also Deut 13:12-15; 20:17). They sought the assistance of the chief priests and the Sanhedrin, asking them to organize another court hearing for Paul. The men would then kill him on his way to the council (**23:13-15**). As Jesus had predicted, these men were convinced that they were doing God's will by plotting to kill one of his servants (John 16:2).

However, God foiled this plot with the aid of *the son of Paul's sister* (**23:16**). Paul's nephew may have come to study in Jerusalem, as Paul himself had done, or he may also have been a follower of the Way. We do not know how he learned of the plot, but as soon as he did so he took the news to Paul in the Roman barracks, who immediately arranged for his nephew to be given audience by the commander (**23:17-18**). The commander believed the young man's account of the plot, and instructed him not to let anyone know that it had been discovered (**23:19-22**). God's protection of Paul was apparent in providing this warning through a family member and in the willingness of the Roman commander to believe him.

23:23-26:32 Trial and Imprisonment in Caesarea

Paul was now transferred to Caesarea, where he would remain in captivity for some time before being transferred to Rome to answer charges before Caesar.

23:23-35 Paul's journey to Caesarea

The commander did not want to have a Roman citizen murdered while under his protection, so he arranged for Paul to be sent to the headquarters in Caesarea, where he would become the responsibility of the governor, Felix. To avoid trouble, Paul was sent off on horseback at nine at night, escorted by at least two centurions, two hundred heavily armed soldiers, seventy horsemen and two hundred spearmen (or lightly armed soldiers) (**23:23-24**).

The commander, whose name was Claudius Lysias (**23:26a**) also wrote a formal letter to the governor (**23:25**). His opening words are the standard forms of address at the time (**23:26b**; see also 1:1; 24:3; 26:25). The rest of the letter summarizes Paul's harassment by the Jews in Jerusalem and includes Lysias' opinion that none of the accusations against him are cause for death or even imprisonment. Lysias hints that he might have released Paul had it not been for a plot to kill him. He has now directed the accusers to present their case before Felix (**23:27-30**).

Paul was duly delivered safely to Caesarea and both he and the letter were handed over to the governor (**23:31-33**). After reading the letter and being told that Paul was from the province of Cilicia, Felix kept him under guard, promising to look into the matter after his accusers had come (**23:34-35**).

24:1-27 Paul's trial before Felix

Five days later, Ananias the high priest and some of the Sanhedrin went down to Caesarea to press charges against Paul (**24:1**). Since they were not familiar with Roman legal procedures, they recruited a Roman lawyer, Tertullus, to speak on their behalf.

Tertullus began his presentation with a conventional expression of gratitude for the peace the country now enjoyed under the wise leadership of Felix (**24:2-4**). History shows that this was flattery rather than truth. Then he asserted that this peace was now under threat because of this troublemaker, Paul, who was causing riots among the Jews, was a ringleader of the Christians and had desecrated the temple (**24:5-6**). Tertullus, and the Jews who were with him, assured Felix that if he examined Paul he would find out that all these accusations were true (**24:8-9**). In some Greek texts, Tertullus speaks at more length, giving details we already know, but because these verses were probably not part of the original, they are not included in the NIV translation.

The governor wisely gave Paul a chance to respond to the accusations (**24:10a**). Paul began his defence by acknowledging that Felix had the experience needed to be able to make a fair judgment in this case (**24:10**). He then denied that he was inciting riots, pointing out that he had only been in Jerusalem for twelve days and had been quietly fulfilling a religious duty. He had not been involved in any public debate in the temple or anywhere else in the city (**24:11-13**).

Paul did, however, admit to being what Tertullus called *a ringleader of the Nazarene sect*, but he explained his belief in somewhat different words: *I admit that I worship the God of our fathers as a follower of the Way, which they call a sect.* But his belief would not lead him to desecrate the temple, for *I believe everything that agrees with the Law and that is written in the Prophets* (**24:14**). Paul was saying that what his accusers called a sect was actually the Way to God (see also 4:12; John 14:6).

Paul and his accusers agreed on some key theological points: *I have the same hope in God as these men, that there will be a resurrection of both the righteous and the wicked* (**24:15**). Christ's resurrection was central to Paul's theology, and while not all Jews believed in the possibility of resurrection (see 23:8), many did. The only differences in their beliefs (apart from whether Jesus had been raised) was that while Jews asserted that the righteous would rise, Christians maintained that the wicked would also rise, but only to face damnation (see also John 5:29; Rev 20:12).

Because of his belief in final judgment, Paul tried *always to keep my conscience clear before God and man* (**24:16**). Even if others do not recognize our faithfulness, God is the ultimate judge who sees all that we do (1 John 3:21). Paul's desire to have a clear conscience before God would also make it unlikely that he would desecrate the temple.

Paul then explained that he had come to Jerusalem *to bring my people gifts for the poor* (**24:17a**; see also 1 Cor 16:1-4; 2 Cor 8-9; Rom 15:25-27) and *to present offerings [worship]* (**24:17b**; see also 18:18; 20:16). If there had been any disturbance around him, he was not the one who had caused it. The Jews from Asia who had started the riot should be the ones to explain what he had done. In fact, the only point on which he could conceivably be accused of starting a riot was the one sentence he had shouted at his hearing before the Sanhedrin (**24:18-21**).

We are not told how Paul's accusers responded to this defence. But Felix, who knew something about Christianity, decided to adjourn the proceedings until he could hear an eyewitness account from the commander, Lysias (**24:22**). Paul was remanded in custody, but was allowed a measure of freedom (**24:23**). His friends were permitted to visit him and take care of his needs. These friends probably included Luke, Aristarchus, Trophimus and Philip the Evangelist (see also 21:8-15).

Felix was married to Drusilla, who was Jewish and the younger daughter of Herod Agrippa. The two of them listened to Paul's witness about Christ (**24:24**). But Felix found Paul's talk of *righteousness, self-control and the judgement to come* difficult to take – perhaps he felt convicted about his own life (**24:25**). He sent Paul away, but summoned him again a number of times. He may simply have enjoyed talking to Paul, but it is also likely that he was hoping for a bribe from Paul or his friends (**24:26**). This stalemate continued for two years. Luke may have used this time while he was forced to remain in Caesarea to research the materials for the Gospel according to Luke.

After two years, Felix was succeeded as governor by Porcius Festus. Because the Jewish authorities were still hostile to Paul, Felix did not release him before leaving, but left him in custody for Festus to deal with (**24:27**).

25:1-12 Paul's trial before Festus

Like Felix, Festus wished to stay on good terms with those he was governing. Consequently one of his first acts as governor was to visit Jerusalem and meet with the Jewish leaders (**25:1-2**). They, in turn, took the opportunity to persuade him to transfer Paul to Jerusalem, arguing that it would be easier for one man to be brought to Jerusalem for trial than for all of them to travel to Caesarea. If their request had been granted, they would have arranged to have Paul ambushed and killed (**25:3**; see also 23:12-32).

Festus refused the request, insisting that some of the leaders accompany him to Caesarea (**25:4-5**). God can use even pagan authorities to protect his people, and we can rest secure in the knowledge that no evil can befall us without God's knowledge (see Ps 23:4).

After spending more than a week in Jerusalem (**25:6**), Festus returned to Caesarea and immediately convened a court hearing for Paul. Luke reports that the Jews brought *many serious charges against him* (**25:6-7**). It is possible that these charges were the same as had been made by Tertullus before Felix (24:5-8). Once again, they could marshall no evidence to support the charges.

Paul's defence is summed up in one sentence: *I have done nothing wrong against the law of the Jews or against the temple or against Caesar* (**25:8**). The words 'against Caesar' suggest he may also have been accused of conspiring against the Emperor Nero, who reigned from AD 54 to AD 68.

Festus faced a dilemma: he had no grounds for finding Paul guilty, yet if he released him, the Jews would be angry (**25:9**). So he tried to compromise, asking Paul whether he would agree to a trial in Jerusalem. This request was absurd: a proper trial had already been conducted. Festus simply wanted to fulfil the earlier request by the Jews to have Paul transferred to Jerusalem (25:3).

Paul knew what would happen if he went to Jerusalem. While he was not afraid to die if he were found guilty after a fair trial, he knew that he would not receive such a trial there. The case should be heard in a Roman court. Festus knew full well that Paul had *not done anything wrong to the Jews* (**25:10**; see also 25:18). Paul knew his legal rights and what protections the Roman law afforded him, and insisted that *no-one has the right to hand me over to them*. Every Roman citizen had the right to appeal to Caesar for a proper trial if accused of a capital offence, and so Paul uttered the fateful words, *I appeal to Caesar* (**25:11**).

After consulting his advisor, Festus granted Paul's appeal and told him he would be sent to Rome (**25:12**). Festus may have thought that the prospect would frighten Paul. Little did he know that for Paul this was a dream come true.

25:13-22 Festus' consultation with King Agrippa

Festus was puzzled about how to formulate the charges against Paul (see also 25:26). So when King Agrippa II (son of Agrippa I – 12:20-23) and his companion Bernice (the sister of Drusilla, Felix's wife) came to pay their respects to Festus, Festus saw this as an opportunity to consult him about Paul's case (**25:13**).

Festus' explanation of the case to Agrippa and Bernice summarizes the story so far. He pointed out that Paul had been left in prison by Felix, thus absolving himself of any involvement in imprisoning Paul (**25:14**). He also explained that Roman law made it impossible for him to comply with the request of the Jewish leaders that Paul be handed over to them (**25:15-16**). This statement sheds light on Paul's bold refusal to be handed over to them (25:11).

Festus had had difficulty in understanding the charges that were levelled against Paul by the Jews. It seemed to him that this was a purely religious dispute concerning doctrine and some dead man, Jesus, whom Paul claimed was alive (**25:17-19**). It is clear that Paul must have preached the resurrection at his trial.

Since these charges had nothing to do with Roman law, Festus had wanted to have the case tried by the religious authorities in Jerusalem. However, Paul had appealed to Caesar and thus had to be kept in custody until he could be sent to Caesar (**25:20-21**).

At this point, King Agrippa tactfully expressed a desire to hear Paul. Festus promised to arrange a hearing the following day (**25:22**).

25:23-27 Paul's trial before King Agrippa

Festus arranged this hearing with great ceremony. It was attended by a who's who of Caesarea and by his chief guests, King Agrippa and Bernice, who arrived *with great pomp* (**25:23**).

In his opening speech, Festus claims that *the whole Jewish community has petitioned me about him in Jerusalem and here in Caesarea* (**25:24**). He is assuming that the chief priests and leaders of people represented the entire Jewish community. However, not everyone in the Jewish community rejected the gospel, for Paul and many other believers were Jewish.

Festus declares that none of the things of which Paul was accused amounted to a capital offence. He would never have sent Paul to Rome had he not appealed to Caesar (**25:25**). So he now faces the problem of how to describe the charges against Paul in his letter to Caesar. He hopes that those who are assembled there and, in particular, his chief guest, King Agrippa, will help him to formulate them (**25:26-27**).

This incident involves gross misconduct by those in positions of authority. They are trying to fabricate charges for political reasons, rather than acquitting someone who is clearly innocent. Leaders who are believers need to beware of this temptation. Even church councils can be seduced into behaving like this in matters of church discipline.

26:1-32 Paul's defence before King Agrippa

Agrippa now takes over from Festus and presides at the hearing. He gives Paul *permission to speak* (**26:1**).

Paul begins his defence by acknowledging that it was a privilege to stand trial before such a knowledgeable man as Agrippa (**26:2**). Compared to Felix and Festus, Agrippa as a Jew had an expert knowledge of the Jewish religion and the controversies associated with it. Paul, therefore, pleads for patience as he presents a fuller defence than he has on previous occasions (**26:3**).

Once again, Paul begins his defence with a brief autobiography. He insists that the Jews have known him since his childhood in Tarsus and in Jerusalem (**26:4**). *If they are willing,* even his accusers could testify that he lived as a strict Pharisee (**26:5**). How many of us could hold our own lives up for public scrutiny, as Paul does here and elsewhere? (see also 1 Cor 4:16; Phil 3:17).

Paul insists that he is on trial because of his belief in God's promise of a Messiah who would suffer and rise from the dead (**26:6-8**; see also 23:6; Rom 9-11; Gal 3). Paul wonders aloud why any of his listeners should *consider it incredible that God raises the dead* (26:8). Such an action is perfectly within God's power.

Having established his innocence as far as his personal life is concerned, Paul moves on to describe how he, too, had once opposed the followers of Jesus of Nazareth. He did *all that was possible* to oppose this movement – but the word 'possible' shows that even in his persecution of the church, Paul followed the law. He sought permission from the appropriate authorities before persecuting the church (**26:9-10**). His zeal even led him to have believers put to death. He carried his campaign against believers from synagogue to synagogue and even *to foreign cities* (**26:11**). Damascus may not have been the only city that Paul went to on his mission of persecution.

Paul then tells of the sign from heaven that disrupted his journey to Damascus. The details given in **26:12-13** are similar to those in 22:6-10, except that Ananias is not mentioned. His role was relevant when he spoke to the Jewish crowd in Jerusalem, but would have been an unnecessary detail before this audience (22:12-16). Jesus is described as speaking directly to Paul while he and his companions lay on the ground (**26:14a**). Jesus quoted a common proverb drawn from ploughing. If an ox objected to being prodded to move forward and kicked back, it would only hurt itself more against the sharp goads (**26:14b**). Working against Jesus has a similar effect – the one who does it is the one who suffers.

Jesus said that he had appeared to Paul to appoint him *as a servant and witness* of what he had seen of Jesus and of what would be revealed to him in the future (**26:16**). Paul's stresses what he had *seen* because this vision made him an eyewitness of the risen Jesus and thus qualified him to be an apostle (see also 1 Cor 4:1; 9:1). Jesus also indicated that Paul's life would not be smooth going, for he would need to be rescued from both the Jews and the Gentiles (**26:17**) – the very groups before whom he was now standing trial.

Paul's ministry would be to both Jews and Gentiles, and it would *open their eyes* (**26:18a**; see also Luke 4:18; Isa 35:5). Sin has blinded people so they do not recognize the blessings of salvation. Opening their eyes is the first step towards conversion (see also Col 1:12-14; 1 John 1:5-7; 2:11).

The conjunction *and* seems to connect the idea of turning people *from darkness to light* with that of turning them *from the power of Satan to God* (**26:18b**). Those whose eyes have been opened cannot continue to submit to the power of Satan. They submit themselves to the power of God. The end result is twofold: forgiveness of sins and a place in God's kingdom with the saints. The only qualification needed to obtain this status is faith in Jesus. No other 'works of the law' are required (**26:18c**; see also 20:21).

Paul had been told to do the work of ministry, and he was and continued to be obedient to this call (**26:19**). He summarizes his work by saying that he preached: *First to those in Damascus, then to those in Jerusalem and in all Judea, and to the Gentiles also* (**26:20a**). His message was that his listeners should *repent and turn to God and prove their repentance by their deeds* (**26:20b**). This clearly shows that Paul's theology of salvation by grace through faith (Eph 2:8-10) does not contradict James' assertion that *faith without deeds is dead* (Jas 2:14-26; see also Gal 3:1-14).

Paul's preaching had made him hated by the Jews and that was why they had attempted to kill him (**26:21**). But God has continued to deliver him *to this very day* and that is why he is able *to stand here and to testify to small and great alike* (**26:22a**) – a statement that affirms to the inclusiveness of the gospel. All of those assembled have an equal opportunity to respond to the message of good news.

Paul insists that everything he says is in agreement with what the prophets and Moses (that is, the five books of Moses) had said: *that the Christ would suffer and, as the first to rise from the dead, would proclaim light to his own people and to the Gentiles* (**26:22b-23**). He sees no contradiction between Judaism and Christianity, and believes that the gospel message can be proved from the Hebrew Scriptures.

Here Festus, probably confused by all the discussion of the ᴏᴛ, of which he would have known almost nothing, interrupts, shouting that Paul is so learned that he has gone insane (**26:24**)! Paul quietly denies this and asserts that Agrippa, who was an expert in Jewish matters (26:3) would understand what he was talking about and would recognize that his argument was *true and reasonable*. Agrippa would have been familiar with the history of Jesus because it was public knowledge (**26:25-26**) .

Paul seizes the opportunity to speak plainly to King Agrippa, of whom he seems to have some knowledge: *King Agrippa, do you believe the prophets? I know you do* (**26:27**). Agrippa's response shows that he recognizes that Paul is asking him to convert: *Do you think that in such a short time you can persuade me to be a Christian?* (**26:28**; see also 11:26; 1 Pet 4:16); Paul replies: *Short time or long – I pray God that not only you but all who are listening to me today may become what I am* and then adds, with a touch of humour, *except for these chains* (**26:29**). He is not bitter about his imprisonment; all he wants is that God will bring some of those assembled to repentance. He models obedience to his own instruction to Timothy about being ready to preach the gospel *in season and out of season* (2 Tim 4:2).

There is no hostility between Paul and the audience, as there had been when he appeared before the Sanhedrin (23:2-5). Although none of them respond to Paul's plea, his presentation of the gospel must have left an indelible mark on their hearts. He had done his part, and now it was for the Holy Spirit to convict them.

Luke reports that the subsequent discussion among the dignitaries was favourable to Paul (**26:30-31**). Agrippa felt that Paul could have been released had he not appealed to Caesar (**26:32**; see also 25:25).

27:1-28:10 Paul's Journey to Rome

27:1-8 A difficult start

At last arrangements were made for Paul and some other prisoners to be sent to Italy in the care of a centurion called Julius. They boarded a small ship that had come from Adramyttium, a city in Mysia in the province of Asia, and which planned to stop in various *ports along the coast of the province of Asia* (**27:2a**).

Paul's companions on this voyage included Luke (the *we* in **27:1** indicates that he was present) and Aristarchus, *a Macedonian from Thessalonica* (**27:2b**). Gaius and Aristarchus were mentioned earlier as Paul's travelling companions (19:29; see also 20:4).

Although Paul was a prisoner, he was treated kindly by the centurion (**27:3**), who allowed him to visit friends who supplied his needs during a stopover at Sidon. There is no record of Paul having visited Sidon before, but there were Christians in Phoenicia (11:19), and that may be why Paul had friends there.

Their route would normally have taken them south of Cyprus, but the need to shelter from very strong winds meant that they sailed north of the island. Cyprus was to their left, and to their right was the coast of Cilicia and Pamphylia (**27:4-5**). They eventually landed at Myra, a busy seaport in the province of Lycia (**27:5**). There the centurion found an Alexandrian ship carrying a cargo of wheat to Italy (**27:6**; 27:38). He duly transferred the prisoners and the soldiers to this ship.

Their progress was slow, for they were in a sailing ship and the winds were against them. They had a hard time trying to sail near the port of Cnidus and eventually abandoned their intended route and headed south, hoping to get out of the winds in the lee of the island of Crete (**27:7**). Moving slowly up the coast of Crete, they passed Salmone and eventually reached *a place called Fair Havens, near the town of Lasea* (**27:8**). Fair Havens is a small bay two miles east of Cape Matala. Because it is open to the east and southeast, it is not a safe harbour in winter.

Paul does not seem to have met with any disciples at Myra or Lasea. There may have been no believers in those areas.

27:9-12 Paul's advice ignored

Luke reports that the sailing had now become dangerous because *it was after the Fast*, that is, after the Jewish Day of Atonement in early October (**27:9a**). From October to March the Mediterranean Sea is swept by fierce storms, which make sailing unsafe. Their slow progress meant that they had failed to reach Rome before these winter storms struck.

Paul warned them: *Men, I can see that our voyage is going to be disastrous and bring much loss to ship and cargo, and to our lives also* (**27:9b-10**). Paul's advice may have been sought, or he may simply have spoken as an experienced traveller. However the confidence of his prediction suggests that he is speaking as a prophet, and that God has revealed the approaching disaster.

It seems that Paul's advice was that they should pass the winter at Fair Havens. However, that harbour was regarded as *unsuitable to winter in* and thus the majority, including the pilot and the owner of the ship, voted to *sail on, hoping to reach Phoenix and winter there* (**27:11-12**). The centurion seems to have had the final say in the matter, because he was of higher rank than the pilot and the owner, and he decided to ignore Paul's advice.

The harbour of Phoenix was fairly close and was also on the island of Crete. But the fact that it faced *both south-west and north-west* means that in reaching it the ship would be exposed to south-westerly and north-westerly winds, making for a dangerous voyage.

Paul's example shows that we should not be afraid to offer advice to the authorities around us, since we all have a role to play and are called to be the light of the world (see also Matt 5:14). Yet even when our advice is sound, it may still be rejected by the majority. When this happens, we should not sulk but should still work with the others, as Paul does for the rest of this voyage.

27:13-26 A storm at sea

A gentle wind encouraged the sailors to pull anchor and start the risky sail along the coast of Crete. Everything was going well, and it looked as if Paul's earlier warning had been misguided. They *thought they had obtained what they wanted* (**27:13**). People today still continue to ignore preachers who warn of dangers ahead because everything seems fine for the present.

Suddenly an extremely violent wind from the mountains on the island swept down on them. Blowing with *hurricane force* from the *north-east* (**27:14**), the wind drove them away from the island and off to the south-west. They had no hope of resisting this wind, and simply had to go where it was taking them (**27:15**). They had a few minutes of respite when they were in the lee of Cauda, a small island south of Crete, which gave them an opportunity to pull the dinghy they had been towing aboard, but even this was a struggle (**27:16**). Luke seems to have been among those who were helping to secure this boat because he says that *we* made the boat secure, but in the next verse he speaks of *the men* passing *ropes under the ship itself to hold it together* (**27:17a**). The ship was in danger of breaking up in the storm.

The crew realized that they were in danger of being driven aground on the Syrtis, sandy beaches off the north coast of Africa. To slow the ship's progress, *they lowered the sea anchor and let the ship be driven along* (**27:17b**). The winds would eventually drive them in a north-west direction, towards Malta, which is 480 sea miles (about 900 km) from Cauda.

By the second day of the storm, the crew decided to lighten the ship by throwing some cargo overboard (**27:18**), thus beginning to suffer the losses that Paul had warned them would come (27:10). The next day the crew in desperation now *threw the ship's tackle overboard with their own hands* (**27:19**). The tackle is the ship's equipment. The storm continued to rage, and was so severe that day and night seemed the same, for it was always dark – *neither sun nor stars appeared for many days and the storm continued raging* (**27:20a**). This meant that they had no idea where in the sea they were. Depression set in as they realized that Paul's prophecy was going to be fulfilled – *we finally gave up all hope of being saved* (**27:20b**) and many gave up eating (**27:21a**).

But believers hope against hope, and Paul had not forgotten that God had assured him that he would reach Rome (23:11). At this dark time, *Paul stood up before them* (**27:21b**). He reminded them that he had warned them of coming disaster before they left Crete, but his speech is more one of encouragement than blame. He assured them that although the ship would be destroyed, God would save their lives (**27:22**). He could say this confidently because he had had a divine revelation the previous night (**27:23**). Paul was careful to specify that the God who sent him this message was the God he served, for the others on board had presumably been praying to their gods, and in particular the god of the sea.

The angel's message shows that Paul too had been tempted to despair, for he was specifically told, *Do not be afraid*. He was reminded that he *must stand trial before Caesar*. But it was not Paul alone who would be saved; the angel told him that: *God has graciously given you the lives of all who sail with you* (**27:24**). It seems that Paul had been praying for the safety of others, as well as for himself.

Paul testified that he trusted God to do what had been promised through the angel (**27:25**) and encouraged his fellow travellers, explaining that they would all survive, although they would soon run aground on some island (**27:26**).

In the midst of a severe storm, Paul was alert to hear from God. As we travel this difficult road to our home in heaven, we too should be sensitive to God's voice even in the midst of storms. Once we discern God's will, we must stand up and declare words of encouragement to a despairing world for whose deliverance we should be praying.

27:27-44 Shipwrecked

It was now fourteen days since they had set sail from Fair Havens and the ship was *still being driven across the Adriatic Sea*. This was not the modern Adriatic Sea, which is between Italy and the Balkans, but the body of water between Italy and Greece.

At about midnight, the sailors sensed that they were approaching land (**27:27**). When they measured the depth of the water, they found it was decreasing rapidly, from *one hundred and twenty feet deep* to *ninety feet deep* (**27:28**). Clearly they were approaching a shore. Fearing that they would run onto rocks in the night, *they dropped four anchors from the stern and prayed for daylight* (**27:29**). They hoped that the anchors would stop the ship from drifting closer to shore, but they also committed the matter to God in prayer. We are not told whether Paul led a prayer meeting for safety, or whether everyone prayed to their own God. This is the first explicit mention of prayer in the entire voyage and may have been influenced by Paul's earlier testimony.

The attempts to stop the ship running ashore do not necessarily show that the sailors did not believe Paul's prophecy that the ship would be destroyed. God's promise of protection did not mean that they were to act recklessly, and they knew that it was advisable to stay on the ship as long as possible.

The ship had been anchored from the stern to stop its forward movement, but now some sailors let down the ship's boat, pretending that they wanted to deploy another anchor from the bow. Their real aim was to get off the ship and try to escape to safety on their own (**27:30**). Paul became aware of what they were doing and warned *the centurion and the soldiers, 'Unless these men stay with the ship, you cannot be saved'* (**27:31**). Although God had promised that nobody would die, the skills of these sailors were to be the channel for deliverance. God uses people to achieve his purposes.

The centurion and the soldiers acted swiftly and *cut the ropes that held the lifeboat and let it fall away* (**27:32**). This time, the centurion was willing to listen to Paul! Even though others may ignore our initial warnings, they will come to accept what we say when what we prophesy actually comes to pass, or when we stand by our prophecy and our lives are consistent with it.

Paul remained level-headed in the midst of a storm, just as we too must attempt to remain calm and vigilant in the midst of the storms of life. He turned his attention to the 276 people on board, many of whom had not eaten for almost fourteen days (**27:33-37**). He urged them to eat, as they would need their strength to cope with the coming shipwreck. They did not need to worry about losing their lives, for Paul assured them, *Not one of you will lose a single hair from his head* (**27:34**; see also Luke 21:18; 1 Sam 14:45; 2 Sam 14:11; 1 Kgs 1:52). This proverb means that no one will die.

Paul led by example: *he took some bread and gave thanks to God in front of them all* (**27:35**). He was acting like the head of a Jewish family, giving thanks for the bread, breaking it, and then beginning to eat. Some have argued that Paul's behaviour followed the pattern of the Lord's Supper, but this should be seen as an ordinary meal (see also 2:42; Luke 24:30). Seeing Paul eating, the others were also encouraged to eat (**27:36**).

Having eaten *as much as they wanted*, the passengers worked to lighten the ship by throwing the cargo of grain overboard (**27:38**).

God answered their prayer for safety until daybreak, and when dawn broke they were able to see a sandy beach ahead (**27:39**). They attempted to steer the ship towards it, but *the ship struck a sand-bar*, that is, a bank of sand surrounded and sometimes covered by water some distance from the shore. The bow stuck fast and the pounding waves began to destroy the ship (**27:40-41**). The people would either have to swim to the shore or drift there on planks (**27:43b-44**).

The soldiers, fearing that the prisoners might escape, planned to kill them (**27:42**). It would have been easier to explain their execution than their escape (remember what had happened to the soldiers who were guarding Peter in Jerusalem after his miraculous escape in 12:18-19). But the centurion forbade this because *he wanted to spare Paul's life* (**27:43a**). Paul had been a great source of encouragement and they all owed their lives to his wise counsel just that night. The centurion had observed that Paul was a valuable asset, and that they were still a long way away from their destination. The other prisoners experienced God's providence through Paul.

The centurion, therefore, *ordered those who could swim to jump overboard first and get to land* (**27:43b**). All who could not swim *were to get there on planks or on pieces of the ship* (**27:44a**). There was a happy ending: *In this way everyone reached land in safety* (**27:44b**). Paul emerges as the hero of the voyage and the shipwreck and a wonderful example of God's providential care (27:24).

28:1-10 Safe on Malta

Once safely ashore, the party discovered that the island on which they had been wrecked was Malta (**28:1**). The inhabitants of this island are referred to as barbarians in the Greek text for the simple reason that the Greeks called all peoples who did not speak Greek barbarians. They were very kind to the new arrivals, even lighting a bonfire for them *because it was raining and cold,* for it was winter (**28:2**). The islanders' hospitality to everyone without any discrimination reminds us of Luke's theme of inclusiveness. In their hospitality to strangers, the inhabitants of Malta were an example to believers.

Paul, still being practical and making himself useful, gathered a bundle of wood to fuel the fire. As he put it in the fire, a snake escaping from the heat *fastened itself on his hand* (**28:3**). The islanders immediately concluded that Paul must be a murderer, because although he had survived the shipwreck, it seemed that justice had still caught up with him (**28:4**). They thought that disaster was proof of guilt and that Paul must be guilty of murder, the only crime that would justify such punishment. Ironically, Paul had been a murderer in the past, for he had agreed with those who murdered the saints (see also 7:57-60; 8:1; 22:20; 26:10), but now he was a different man. The Lord had called him to become a witness to God's power of forgiveness (1 Tim 1:13-17).

As a proof of his innocence, *Paul shook the snake off into the fire and suffered no ill effects* (**28:5**). The islanders had expected him to die within hours, but they waited in vain. Their attitude to Paul changed swiftly – now they thought he was a god! (**28:6**; compare 14:11, 19).

Jesus had promised that one of the signs that would accompany those who believed in him was that they would pick up snakes without being hurt (Mark 16:18). He had also said: *I have given you authority to trample on snakes and scorpions and to overcome all the power of the enemy; nothing will harm you* (Luke 10:19). This promise was fulfilled at Malta. If God is for us, nothing can be against us.

The whole party seems to have been welcomed by Publius, *the chief official of the island* (**28:7a**). Having an *estate,* he could probably accommodate all of them, and he entertained them hospitably for three days (**28:7b**). This generous man had a sick father, who was *suffering from fever and dysentery* (**28:8a**). The mention of these specific diseases supports the tradition that Luke was a physician.

Paul, however, did not provide medication but healing. He came to see the patient, and after a prayer laid hands upon him and *healed him* (**28:8b**). The prayer of faith was rewarded by the healing not only of this patient but also of many more from the island who heard about what had happened and came to Paul (**28:9**).

Paul took every opportunity to do works of ministry. He did not think of himself as a victim of a shipwreck or as a prisoner who was unable to pray for the sick. We should share Paul's dedication to ministry.

The islanders then *honoured us in many ways* (**28:10a**). The Greek here may indicate that they paid Paul and his companions for the services they had received. Paul's acceptance of their honour and gifts demonstrates that it is not wrong to receive payment for services. The islanders' hospitality extended even to giving them travel supplies when the group was eventually ready to sail for Rome (**28:10b**).

28:11-31 The Mission in Rome

28:11-16 Rome at last

After three months, presumably at the end of winter, *they put out to sea in a ship that had wintered in the island* (**28:11a**). Luke tells us that this was another Alexandrian grain ship, which may even have sailed from Alexandria at the same time as the ship that was wrecked. This ship had a *figurehead of the twin gods Castor and Pollux* (**28:11b**). There seems be no significance to the mention of this figurehead.

From Malta they sailed to Syracuse on the coast of Sicily, where they stayed for three days. Then they sailed to Rhegium at the tip of Italy. A favourable south wind enabled them to go northward along the coast of Italy to Puteoli, which was their final port (**28:12-13**). There Paul and his companions found some Christians, who were able to entertain them for a week (**28:14a**). It seems they had not found Christians at any of their other stops since leaving Sidon.

Puteoli was the chief port of the city of Rome, and although there was still an overland journey of some 130 miles (210 km) to Rome itself, Luke happily announces: *And so we came to Rome* (**28:14b**). Paul's dream of visiting Rome had been fulfilled. Shortly before leaving for Jerusalem, he had even written a letter to the church at Rome saying that he hoped to visit them on his way to preach in Spain (Rom 15:22-29).

The Christians in Rome had heard that Paul and his companions were on their way to Rome – the news may have been sent to them during the one-week stay at Puteoli. So they came to meet them, probably in two groups, one travelling as far as the *Forum of Appius* (a marketplace forty miles [sixty-five kilometres] from Rome) and the other as far as *the Three Taverns* (about 30 miles/48 km from Rome) (**28:15**). It is possible that one group was composed of

Jewish believers and the other of Gentile Christians. Both groups walked a long way to meet Paul, whom they had never met before but whose letter they had received by the hand of Phoebe (Rom 16:1). It is no wonder that *at the sight of these men Paul thanked God and was encouraged* (**28:15b**). There were friends waiting for him after his long and dangerous journey, and they would be with him as he awaited trial.

Once in Rome, *Paul was allowed to live by himself, with a soldier to guard him* (**28:16**). Julius may have given a good report of Paul to his superiors, and thus he was given the freedom to live in his own accommodation, with only one soldier as his guard.

28:17-31 Paul's preaching in Rome

After taking three days to settle in and to recover from the 130-miles (210-kilometre) walk from Puteoli to Rome, Paul was ready to meet the Jewish leaders. He wanted to clear up any misinformation they might have received through some of the soldiers who had come with him or through Jews who might have come to Rome after the riots in Jerusalem. So he told them of the events that had led to his coming to Rome (**28:17-18**) and explains, *I was compelled to appeal to Caesar – not that I had any charge to bring against my own people* (**28:19**). In other words, he had had to appeal to higher authority to save his own life, but he was not seeking to make any trouble for Jews. His audience would have been relieved to hear this, for there had been Roman persecution of Jews in the past (18:1).

Paul concluded his speech by pointing out that the message which he preached and which had led to his imprisonment was *the hope of Israel* (**28:20**). He challenged his listeners to start to think about the place of the gospel of Jesus Christ in the history of Israel.

In response, the Jewish leaders said that they had not received any letter from the Sanhedrin incriminating Paul, nor had any of the Jewish brothers who came from Jerusalem mentioned him (**28:21**). They expressed some interest in hearing Paul's views on the Christian movement, which they called a sect, and which they claimed was attracting a lot of negative criticism (**28:22**).

A date was set and a large number of Jews came to hear Paul's views regarding the Nazarenes. The meeting lasted an entire day, as Paul attempted to show his audience, who were familiar with the Hebrew Scriptures, how Jesus had been prophesied in Moses and the Prophets (see 13:16-38; 17:2-3; 24:14-15). He expounded the Scriptures in great detail (see 2 Tim 2:15b) in order to convince them of the truth about Jesus (**28:23**).

Some were convinced by what he said and probably became believers. But as the Akamba people of Kenya say, *wĩngĩnĩvaiyaa mbĩtĩa* ['Where there are many people, some will fall

through']. Some did not believe, and arguments broke out (**28:24-25a**).

The meeting broke up rapidly after Paul's final words, in which he quoted a message from the Holy Spirit to their forefathers (**28:25b**; see also 7:52). Words from Isaiah 6:9-10 present the state of some of the Jewish people after hearing the gospel: *they will be hearing but never understanding.* The Roman Jews had come to *hear what your views are* (28:22), but they do not seem to have understood what they heard. Isaiah had also said, *you will be ever seeing but never perceiving.* They could see Paul and the other Roman Christians, but they could not look below the surface and see the one who had changed their lives, that is Jesus Christ, the long-awaited Messiah (**28:26**). Paul quoted Isaiah's explanation of their deafness and blindness in **28:27**. He had used the same passage when speaking to the Jews at Pisidian Antioch when they rejected the gospel (13:40-41), and Jesus had also quoted it (Matt 13:14-15; Mark 4:12; Luke 8:10).

Paul concluded his speech with the declaration: *Therefore I want you to know that God's salvation has been sent to the Gentiles, and they will listen!* (**28:28**; see also 13:46; 18:6). He did not mean that all Jews were rejected, for he continued to witness to both Jews and Gentiles as he has always done. Romans 11 makes it clear that Paul did not believe that the Jews had fallen beyond redemption, and that he prayed earnestly for their salvation.

In some Greek manuscripts, these verses are followed by verse 29, which repeats verse 25. Presumably someone copying the manuscript felt that the departure of the Jews should be mentioned after Paul's closing words.

This ringing restatement of his mission to the Gentiles is Paul's final utterance in Acts. But we are told that Paul continued to preach the gospel freely from *his own rented house* where he *welcomed all who came to see him* (**28:30**). The last statement makes it clear that he welcomed both Jews and Gentiles, for Luke would have mentioned if only Gentiles had come to see him.

Luke states that Paul stayed in Rome *for two whole years*, during which he *boldly and without hindrance ... preached the kingdom of God and taught about the Lord Jesus Christ* (**28:31**). What better way to end this dramatic narrative and to encourage readers to emulate Paul in continuing to speak boldly about the kingdom of God and teach others about the Lord Jesus Christ.

The gospel of Jesus Christ is always triumphant in spite of the snares of the evil one. The uttermost parts of the earth have now been reached, at least as far as Luke is concerned (1:8). Paul echoes this triumphant note in his letter to the Philippians (Phil 1:12-14), telling them that his imprisonment has encouraged many to speak the message of the gospel boldly and with positive results.

Luke does not tell us what happened to Paul after this imprisonment. Tradition has it that he was released and revisited some of the churches he had founded (see Phil 1:27). He is said to have been arrested again during the reign of Emperor Nero and was probably executed around AD 64 during Nero's persecution of Christians after the fire that destroyed Rome (see 2 Tim 4:6-7,16-18).

Paul Mumo Kisau

Further Reading

Fitzmyer, Joseph A. *The Acts of the Apostles: A New Translation with Introduction and Commentary.* AB. New York: Doubleday, 1998.

Marshall, I. Howard. *Acts: An Introduction and Commentary.* TNT. Leicester: Inter-Varsity Press, 1980.

Stott, John R.W. *The Message of Acts.* BST. Leicester: Inter-Varsity Press, 1990.

INDIGENOUS MISSIONS

There have long been African evangelists all across the continent who have proclaimed the gospel cross-culturally, often in cooperation with Western missions. However, it was only in the late 1940s and early 1950s that these evangelists began to be organized into African missionary agencies. For example, in 1948 the Sudan Interior Mission (now SIM) established the Africa Missionary Society (now known as the Evangelical Missionary Society). That same year the first missionary from this group was sent to Kano, a town in the far north of the Nigeria.

Progress in indigenous missions was slow until the early seventies when revival brought fresh awareness of missions to the minds of many young people, especially university students. Student movements like FOCUS in East Africa and NIFES and GHAFES in West Africa began to make forays into villages as mission teams doing evangelism and church planting. This revival led to the formation of groups like Calvary Ministries (CAPRO) and the Christian Missionary Foundation (CMF) in Nigeria in 1975 and 1982, respectively. The Christian Outreach Fellowship also emerged in Ghana in 1980, and Sheepfold Ministries in Kenya in 1984. These new missionary movements blazed the trail for many indigenous groups.

The indigenous missions were generally led by young university graduates who recruited workers from the universities and other tertiary institutions. They began their own mission training schools and other mission departments. While not all are of the same standard in terms of organization and depth of ministry, all are active in reaching the lost. A number of them have sent African missionaries cross-culturally to other countries. It is good that the missionaries serving with indigenous mission agencies come from many countries in Africa, as this means that international teams work together for the advancement of the gospel.

A further healthy development is that indigenous mission agencies are coming together in different countries to form missions associations. These associations organize training programmes and seminars to improve individual agencies and missionaries. The Nigerian Missions Association (NEMA) was started in 1984 and the Ghana Evangelical Missions Association (GEMA) in 1991. Such associations are helping to strengthen individual mission agencies.

The Evangelism and Missions Commission of the Association of Evangelicals in Africa (AEA) has done much to sharpen the focus of both individual groups and the associations. Its runs COMITA (the Council on Mission Training in Africa) and publishes *Africa Prayer Briefs*, a newsletter, six times a year. Other AEA publications like *Vision* magazine and *MISSIONAFRIC* (a journal of missions practice in Africa) are spurring on indigenous mission agencies. While much remains to be done, it is very gratifying that serious attempts are being made to develop indigenous missions.

Bayo Famonure

ROMANS

The letter to the Romans was written to Christians like us who were facing the problems of their time and context. The world of 'wickedness, evil, greed, depravity, envy, murder, strife, deceit, malice' and other vices (1:29-30) that those Christians had to deal with sounds very like our own. In this letter, Paul explains the real problems with human beings, the reason we do the detestable things we do and how we have completely missed God's plan for humanity. He also explains how God, on his own initiative, has planned and made possible our salvation, how we can appropriate the wonderful gifts and blessings of God and how we can live victorious and transformed lives. Paul makes it clear that those of us who have received God's salvation have obligations toward God and others in this world as we magnify his glory and enjoy the blessings of salvation in his Son, Jesus Christ – blessings that have transformed us already, though their fullness is yet to come.

This commentary shows that Romans speaks to our situation. What the church in Africa needs today is a good understanding of what we believe, the truths or doctrines of the gospel and why we believe what we believe. A strong understanding of the content of our faith will compel us to live as Christians in our societies that so desperately need love and transformation. If we are to respond effectively to the challenges facing our peoples, we must operate from a Christian understanding of what God in his grace has done for us in Christ, and of our obligations in response to his love and grace. In other words, we must live in this world as people of God. Only minds transformed by the power of the gospel can transform nations in need of social and spiritual change.

The Author

The writer identifies himself as Paul, the apostle (1:1). Paul was a Jew from Tarsus, formerly a zealous Pharisee who sought to please God by persecuting the church (Acts 9; Gal 1:13-14). His dramatic conversion on the road to Damascus was also his commissioning to serve the risen Lord in preaching the gospel among the Gentiles: 'This man is my chosen instrument to carry my name before the Gentiles and their kings and before the people of Israel. I will show him how much he must suffer for my name' (Acts 9:15-16).

Romans was probably written in AD 57. After over twenty-five years of successful but challenging ministry in which he had planted many churches in Asia Minor, suffered for the Lord, and written several letters, Paul decided

to go and preach the gospel in Spain. He hoped to break the long journey to Spain by spending some time with the church in Rome, which he had never visited (15:23-24). The richness of the letter to the Romans may be a result of the apostle's many years of reflection on his beliefs and of his spiritual journey, maturity and ministry experience.

The Roman Church

The church in Rome may have been founded by visitors from Rome who had been in Jerusalem at Pentecost and had been converted to Christianity (Acts 2:10). If so, it demonstrates the power of the Holy Spirit to use believers to plant churches. As Jews and God-fearing Gentiles, they would have been grounded in the OT Scriptures and may have had frequent visits from other believers.

The church was a mixed community of Gentiles and Jews. In its early days, the majority of the members were probably Jews and a few God-fearing Gentiles. However, after Emperor Claudius expelled the Jews from Rome in AD 49, Gentile believers became the majority and only a few Jewish Christians remained. The people whom God had prepared to receive Christianity first and from whom the Messiah had come would have found themselves a minority in a church led by Gentiles. We in Africa know only too well that this is a recipe for conflict, divisions, arrogance, boasting, judging, disunity and lack of love. Yet what God has done for believers supersedes all human differences and compels us to live together in unity as the people of God.

The Purpose of the Letter

The letter to the Romans has been referred to as the Christian Manifesto. In it, Paul skilfully presents the gospel of God with the mind of a scholar, a lover of Christ, a passionate pastor and a Jew. Filled with and led by the Spirit of God, the apostle unfolds God's eternal, divine plan for the salvation of human beings, paying particular attention to the relationship between Gentiles and Jews. As he writes, he thinks of possible objections to what he is saying, and sets out to refute them.

Paul wrote to the Romans to inform them of his imminent visit and of his desire to preach the gospel among them (1:11, 15); to prepare them to serve as a base for his future ministry to Spain (15:24, 28); and to address problems in the church in Rome, including reconciling Jewish and Gentile believers and exhorting them to unity (chs. 14 and 15).

Outline of Contents

COMMENTARY

1:1-17 Introduction

1:1-7 Greeting

Like a typical letter of the time, the letter to the Romans begins with the author identifying himself. He is Paul (**1:1**). Because he has never visited the church in Rome, Paul needs to introduce himself to them, and so he starts by setting out the three most important things he wants them to know about himself.

The first, and most important, concerns his relation to his Master. He is *a servant of Christ Jesus*. The word here translated 'servant' means 'slave'. Although the idea of being a slave arouses a feeling of repugnance, this is how Paul wants to be known. He is not alone in this. The same term is used in the OT to refer to Moses (Josh 1:2), David (Ps 89:3, 20) and the prophets (Jer 7:25; Dan 9:6; Amos 3:7). In the NT, the term is even used to refer to Jesus in relation to his Father (Phil 2:7). Like these other servants of God, Paul has committed himself to total subjection, obedience and devotion to Jesus Christ and to serving him as his slave. And like Moses, David, the prophets and Jesus himself, Paul knows that it is an honour to serve God. Elsewhere, Paul uses the same word, 'slave', to refer to Christians in relation to Christ. For him, all believers are slaves of Jesus Christ (1 Cor 7:22-23). They belong to him, owe him total allegiance and submit to his authority.

The second thing they need to know about Paul is his divine calling: he has been *called to be an apostle*. Paul sometimes uses the term 'apostle' to signify a messenger, someone who represents Jesus in the propagation of the gospel (Rom 16:7; Phil 2:25). More often, he uses 'apostle' to refer to those whom Jesus chose and gifted to represent him (1 Cor 12:28; Eph 4:11), those who are seen as the 'foundation' of the church (Eph 2:20). Paul considers himself among the latter. Jesus himself called Paul from his people, his tribe, his religion and his occupation to commit himself to him and to serve him (Acts 9:1-19). Because he was specifically called by the risen Lord, Paul considers himself equal to the other twelve apostles. He recognizes that he does not deserve this calling, for he had persecuted the church (1 Cor 15:9), but he too has seen the Lord and his authority comes from the Lord.

The third thing Paul wants to emphasize is why he was called (Acts 26:9-18): he has been *set apart for the gospel of God*. Jesus called him to proclaim the message of good news. He was 'separated' by God to teach the Gentiles the good news of salvation in Christ. He was ordained by Jesus himself and never lost sight of his mission.

Having established his credentials, Paul immediately shifts attention away from himself to the central theme of his ministry, which he calls *the gospel* (**1:2**). The gospel is not new but is something that God promised long ago in the OT. The concept of a 'promise' is important in the NT. When a father promises, he keeps his promise. In the Messiah, the promise of salvation for human beings has been kept.

The central figure in the gospel is *Jesus Christ our Lord* (**1:3-4**). Jesus, the Son of God, is both human and divine, Messiah ('Christ') and God ('Lord'). His humanity is proven by his descent from Adam (Luke 3:38b), and his descent from David qualified him to be the Messiah. His deity is confirmed by his resurrection and his eternal relationship with the Father.

Paul next gives more details about his own ministry (**1:5-6**). Given his past, the fact that he has been called to proclaim the gospel is evidence of the grace of God, that is, of God's undeserved favour to sinners. But grace is also associated with the power that saves people from sin and that gives them the ability to serve God. By grace, the servants of Jesus are saved, and they need that grace to serve their Master. Paul's task is to call people to respond to the gospel message by committing themselves to Christ in faith. Faith is the desired response to the gospel message. It leads to obedience to Christ.

Paul then says that the Roman believers are included in God's plan of salvation. They are called to belong to Jesus Christ and to be holy (**1:7a**). Paul uses three highly significant words to describe them: they are 'loved', 'called' and 'saints'. The same words are used in the OT in reference to Israel as God's special people, set apart to be holy and to serve God (Deut 33:2-3; Dan 7:22, 27), a description that fits the church. By grace, the church is now loved by God and *called to be saints*. God calls every believer, irrespective of tribe, race or colour, to be a saint. The gospel is universal. Every believer is set apart to belong to Christ and to carry the aroma of Christ in the world.

Christians' participation in the clashes we have witnessed in Rwanda, in the Democratic Republic of Congo and in other places must pain the heart of God. The gospel unites all in Christ and gives a new dimension to differences of race, tribe, class and status. The differences do not cease to exist, but now they become ways to glorify God and to serve our fellow human beings. Those who have stood firm and have saved the lives of everyone they could, no matter what their tribe, 'bless' God's heart and receive blessings from him.

Paul ends the introduction to his letter with a special greeting to his readers – *grace and peace to you* (**1:7b**). His prayer is that the Roman believers will experience what individuals, families, societies and nations are longing for, God's blessings of grace and peace. Lasting peace can only be brought about by divine grace.

Paul had had a remarkable and successful ministry, making it all the more striking that he desires to be known only as a slave of Christ, called and commissioned to proclaim God's message of salvation. The gospel is the central theme of Paul's message, life and ministry. We should be like him in focusing our energy on the proclamation and teaching of the gospel instead of on gaining fame for ourselves. Every message we preach must come from God, be based on Scripture and be focused on Christ.

But this passage also contains an implicit warning: people should never enter the ministry if God has not called them, set them apart and given them the message of the gospel of Jesus Christ.

1:8-15 Thanksgiving and Prayer

1:8-10 Commendation and prayer

After the long introduction to his letter, Paul moves on to express his pastoral attachment to his readers and how much they mean to him. Paul approaches God the Father through the mediation of Jesus Christ to give thanks for the faith of the Roman believers and their good reputation (**1:8**). Paul is an apostle of faith. To him, faith is the basic virtue in the Christian life. Therefore, he commends the Roman believers for their faith, which the whole world has heard about. Finding what is good in others and letting them know that one values it makes for good and lasting relationships and prepares the way for any words of rebuke.

It is, however, not enough to thank God for people. Pastors, like Paul, also need to sustain them by prayer. So Paul speaks of his intercession for the Roman believers. He constantly brings them before God, praying for them and asking that he may be able to visit them, if that is God's will (**1:10**). His concern for them is so genuine that he is not afraid to call on God as his witness to the constancy of his prayers (**1:9**). Paul is an example of the sensitive, loving and caring pastor that churches are eager to hear from.

1:11-15 Paul's obligation

Paul is so eager to meet the Roman believers because he desires to give them *some spiritual gift* (**1:11**). Paul does not specify what exactly this gift is, because he is more concerned with what the gift will do, namely, make them strong. Then he hurriedly corrects the impression that he will be the one doing the giving, and that God's blessings flow only from him to the Romans. Rather, says Paul, he is hoping that they will be mutually encouraged *by each other's faith* (**1:12**). Paul's apostleship did not make him feel superior to others. He himself benefits from sharing with others. No believer, pastor or group of believers is the sole possessor of God's blessings. We need each other.

But, regardless of his desire, Paul's longing to visit the Romans has been repeatedly frustrated (**1:13**). We do not know the cause of this frustration and so we may not want to speculate about it. But we can understand it. We have witnessed situations that have forced pastors and church workers to flee from clashes and live as displaced people without achieving their goals for their ministry. We must encourage them to see their new location as the place God has assigned them for ministry as long as they are there. God not only calls us to Christian ministry, but he also determines the place we will minister. We must preach the gospel wherever we are.

Paul sees himself as under an obligation to preach the gospel to every race and tribe (**1:15**). His world was culturally divided between Jews and Greeks. One would have expected Paul to favour his own group, the Jews. However, as a servant of Jesus Christ, he feels an obligation to both Jews and Greeks (**1:14**). Racism and tribalism are like cancer among believers. They divide the people of God. The servant of God is the primary agent of reconciliation between people and God and between people.

Paul is also under an obligation to those with different levels of education and wisdom. Those who are wise in their own eyes are as much sinners as those who are foolish. They all need salvation.

1:16-17 The Theme: The Gospel and Righteousness

The central theme of Romans is *the gospel* that Paul is eager to preach to the Romans. But one needed courage not to be ashamed of the gospel because it was considered 'a stumbling block to Jews and foolishness to Gentiles' (1 Cor 1:23). But Paul tells us why he is *not ashamed of the gospel* (**1:16a**): the proclamation of the gospel is the proclamation of God's power to transform people's lives. Paul is talking from experience; he was transformed on the road to Damascus (Acts 9:1-22). He knows that the gospel is God's ultimate provision for the spiritual needs of humanity and is powerful. In fact, the Greek word for 'power' that Paul uses is related to the word 'dynamite'.

Paul connects power and salvation. The gospel is *the power of God for the salvation of everyone who believes* (**1:16b**). It is more than just preaching and leading people to conversion; rather, it is the whole Christian message that leads to faith and action. The gospel must be believed and lived out in Christians' daily lives. God uses it to bring about the restoration of the whole person.

Salvation is available to all; the only obstacle is lack of willingness to receive the message. All who do receive it, whether they are Greeks or Jews, benefit equally. At the foot of the cross of Jesus, the ground is level; tribes meet; races embrace; humanity finds unity.

The salvation God has provided satisfies his character, brings humankind into a relationship with him and sets the standard for human behaviour. God's righteousness cannot be attained through observance of law but only *by faith* (**1:17**; Hab 2:4; Gal 3:11). By responding in faith to the

IDEAS OF SALVATION IN OTHER RELIGIONS

For three years Ronald Eyre, a famous BBC television producer, studied the religious quest for meaning. His search took him to all the inhabited continents and resulted in a television series and a book entitled *The Long Search*. At the end, he concluded that all the great religions attack the same problem, though they seem to go about it in a variety of ways, and that all share a desire for wholeness. Ronald Eyre is right!

Theologically, the common problem that all religions confront is sin and its catastrophic consequences for individuals and communities. The desire for wholeness is what theologians call salvation. Hinduism and Buddhism call it *nirvana* and describe it as a state of bliss achieved through extinction of individuality and desires. In African traditional religions (ATR), salvation is portrayed as cosmic equilibrium and community acceptance of individuals. The African theologian Byang Kato states: 'Acceptance is equated with salvation in the language of the Jaba people of Northern Nigeria ... first in the community of the living and then in the city of the dead.'

It is ironic that the Palestinian Jews and Arabs, descendants of a common ancestor, Abraham, have been at war since time immemorial though at the heart of both religions – Judaism and Islam – is *shalom* or *salama*. Derived from the same Semitic root, both words mean peace, wholeness and health in one's relationship with God and one's neighbour.

Different religions offer different prescriptions for achieving salvation:

- *Performing the right rituals:* Salvation is achieved by offering the prescribed sacrifices, participating in festivals and ceremonies, and undertaking pilgrimages to sacred places. The priesthood, which controls access to God or gods, is the central focus of the system. Salvation is by works. Hinduism, ATR, and some popular understandings of Roman Catholicism fall into this category.

- *Losing all desires:* Salvation is achieved by suppressing all desires, thus liberating oneself from *karma* (the law of cause and effect) and arriving at *nirvana* (a state of bliss). The way to suppress desires is to follow the Eightfold Path laid down by Siddhartha Gautama, who was originally a Hindu but later became known as the Buddha, the Enlightened One.

- *Behaving in the right way (moralism):* Salvation is achieved by avoiding harming any person or animal. This concept, which is popular with modern moralists, humanists and vegetarians, is central to Jainism. Like Buddha, Mahavira (great hero), the great teacher of Jainism, reacted against the priesthood, sacrifices and the gods. He considered prayer and worship unnecessary and taught that good is always rewarded and evil punished.

- *Achieving union with the Absolute:* Salvation is defined as union with Absolute Reality, referred to as Brahma (creator). Union with Brahma can be achieved through yoga, that is, through intense concentration, deep meditation in prescribed postures, and controlled breathing. New Age thinkers seek to be one with nature, arguing that there is no god out there; you are in god and god is in you.

- *Pursuing pleasure:* Salvation is sought in good food, dozing in the sun, avoiding politics and family life, and doing good to others. This view, which was held by the Epicureans, is rooted in the belief that the gods have nothing to do with this world.

- *Obeying laws:* Salvation is defined as the blessing and peace flowing from obedience, while disobedience brings curses and death. Both Judaism and Islam have numerous commandments and statutes that regulate personal life and community affairs.

All these approaches differ from Christianity in the way they address the fundamental problem of sin. In all non-Christian religions, sin is regarded as an act. If sin is an act, then people can learn how to avoid doing it. All the paths to salvation outlined above attempt to prescribe how this can be done. However, if sin is actually part of our nature, it cannot be avoided – a saviour offers the only hope. Think of a drowning swimmer in the middle of the ocean. What can he do to save himself? Those who say that sin consists solely of actions argue that he should not have gone swimming in the first place. But that is no help to one who is drowning and cannot help himself.

The critical component in Christianity is the cross, where the sin factor was dealt with. God made Jesus to be sin though he was sinless so that anyone who believes in him can receive God's forgiveness and be saved, 'might become the righteousness of God' (2 Cor 5:21). Salvation in biblical Christianity is a free offer of a new life of joy, peace, love and hope in Christ (John 3:16). 'Salvation means the old has passed away; the new is come!' (2 Cor 5:17). Some accept this offer by faith, others reject it. And Jesus gives those who accept the offer 'the right to become the children of God' (John 1:10-13).

Tokunboh Adeyemo

gospel message, believers will attain eternal life and experience the fullness of life in Christ.

The gospel is good news and must be proclaimed to all people regardless of factors such as their race, tribe or level of education. Like Paul, believers must feel indebted and obliged to proclaim it to all (1:14). They should be ready and eager to preach and teach it (1:15), and never ashamed of it (1:16). The gospel must be preached and salvation embraced if we are to see real changes in people. Those who carry the gospel are like messengers with an unpleasant message. They may face humiliation, intimidation and suffering, but they should never be ashamed or discouraged because the gospel is the only way in which God acts to transform lives.

1:18-4:25 The Gospel's Heart: Justification by Faith

1:18-3:20 The Universal Need for Salvation

The apostle argues that people everywhere are sinners and deserve judgment and death. As God reveals his righteousness (1:16-17), so also he reveals his wrath against all human ungodliness and unrighteousness (1:18-3:20). God is a just judge; he acquits the righteous who live by faith and condemns the wicked. His justice will not leave sin unpunished. His wrath against sin can be understood when we see the level of corruption and perversion in our time, where often wealth is concentrated in the hands of a few, where criminals go free because they pay bribes and where the masses remain poor and unprotected. God is the righteous judge, and the church is here on earth to represent his interests. The church should thus be at the centre of the fight against these evils.

1:18-32 The need of the Gentiles

1:18-23 THE SINFULNESS OF THE GENTILES The wrath of God is his inevitable response to sinfulness, specifically to *the godlessness and wickedness of men* (**1:18a**). Godlessness is vertical – a lack of reverence for God and rebellion against God. Wickedness is horizontal – injustice toward others. When one abandons God, one's relations with other people are also broken.

The truth is that God exists and that he requires people to worship and to obey him, but wickedness leads people to *suppress the truth* whenever it reveals their sinfulness (**1:18b**). Sinfulness, wickedness and suppression of truth are not the result of ignorance but of a deliberate attempt to dishonour God.

Creation is powerful evidence of the existence of a Maker. While natural revelation does not provide the same depth of knowledge of God that special revelation provides through the Scriptures, it still plainly demonstrates God's

eternal power and divine nature (**1:19-20**). This evidence has been available to be seen and understood by all *since the creation of the world*. Those who choose to ignore this evidence have no excuse.

Despite the knowledge of God they could gain from the world God created, Gentiles *neither glorified him as God nor gave thanks to him* (**1:21**). But those who ignore the truth are on a downward path that results in foolish thinking and idolatry (**1:22-23**). They make images out of wood, stone or metal to replace God. Such images do not deserve worship. When the truth about God is suppressed, the truth that human beings are made in the image of God is also suppressed. Then people start to behave wickedly towards one another. Failure to honour God is the root of evil in society, and until we return to honouring God in our relationships, problems will continue to exist in our societies.

1:24-32 THE CONDEMNATION OF THE GENTILES Paul uses the words *therefore* (1:24), *because of* (1:26) and *furthermore, since* (1:28) to introduce the condemnation of the Gentiles. God punishes people because of their sin. When the truth is suppressed and God is not glorified (1:18-23), he intervenes directly and leaves them to follow sinful practices. Paul gives a sample of these practices:

- **Sexual decadence** (**1:24**): Sex outside the bounds of marriage is unclean and dishonouring. Living together as an unmarried couple and all sex before marriage and outside marriage are acts of uncleanness to which God has surrendered sinners.

- **Perversion of the truth** (**1:25**): People swap the truth about God for falsehood by believing that someone or something else besides God can be worshipped.

- **Sexual perversion** (**1:26-27**): Sexual perversion in the form of homosexual activities is shameful, although it is rampant today. It is a sign of godlessness and wickedness. Therefore, all homosexual relations are punishable by God. It is clear statements such as this, which label homosexuality a vice, that have led many African church leaders to resist the moves within the church to have homosexuality accepted.

- **Detestable lifestyles** (**1:28-32**): Failure to acknowledge God makes people wicked, evil, greedy and depraved. Those who ignore God and put themselves at the centre of their lives become insensitive to the presence of God and fail to relate to others as God intended. They become corrupt, greedy and disobedient. They exploit others, kill them in cold blood, become indiscriminate in satisfying their desires, and grossly pervert justice. The actions of such persons are deliberate and they even condone and encourage others to do the same things. Such people deserve to die. But we do not want our fellow Africans to suffer this fate, and thus we need to preach and teach the gospel so every level and aspect of our societies is transformed.

HOMOSEXUALITY

Homosexuality, defined as 'sexual attraction to or sexual relations with members of the same sex' has been around for a very long time in all societies. But whereas in the past homosexual behaviour was widely regarded as sinful and abnormal, today it is presented as an acceptable alternative lifestyle. Many homosexuals insist that they are a minority group and that condemnation of homosexuality represents a denial of human rights. In defence of this position, they argue that homosexuality is a biological condition that has nothing to do with morality or spirituality – it is not a matter of choice, but is genetically determined.

This issue has sparked much controversy in Africa. Some politicians have stated that homosexuals are worse than beasts. On the other hand, Archbishop Tutu has called for tolerance and an acceptance of homosexuality, but his position has been rejected by Anglican churches across the continent. An attempt to address homosexuality in the Kenyan constitution was opposed by both Christian and Muslim delegates.

African tradition has varied in regard to the practice of homosexuality. It is accepted in some communities and rejected in others. Homosexual acts have been seen as the way to gain certain spiritual powers. They are also a way of asserting political and social power, particularly when practised by politicians, soldiers, prisoners and some professions. This quest for power sets aside morality and ethics. Most homosexuals would agree with Christians that such coercive sexual relationships are wrong. But many homosexuals would add that there is nothing wrong with a sexual relationship that is entered into freely by both partners.

Our views on homosexuality should not be derived from human sources but from the Word of God. The Bible clearly defines homosexuality as a sin. We see this in the punishment of Sodom and Gomorrah (Gen 18:16-19:29) and in Paul's words in 1 Corinthians 6:9-10. It is described as a depraved and sinful practice in Romans 1:24-27, where it is seen as a consequence of the idolatry that has led God to give up on humanity. Rejection of God opens up a floodgate of sinful desires and lusts.

God clearly defines a proper sexual relationship as being between a man and his wife who become one flesh (Gen 2:24). The exact working of this 'one flesh' principle is a mystery, but Paul has no doubt that it is a model of the nature of the church as the 'bride' or 'body' of Christ (Eph 5:28-32). We tamper with such a relationship at our peril.

God also instructed the man and his wife to produce offspring (Gen 1:28; 9:7). Clearly, only a male–female sexual relationship can produce children and thus create the type of family God envisages, with a father, a mother and children. All other forms of sexual relationship are abnormal, unnatural and a perversion.

Pastors and counsellors need to recognise that homosexuality has deep roots in our sinful nature. Sin is more than just particular things that we do. Because of the fall, sin has affected all aspects of our inner being. Thus is not surprising that some people show a biological disposition towards homosexuality – sin has warped every aspect of life. It is, therefore, academic to try to make a distinction between a homosexual person and a homosexual act, as if the latter is sinful and the former not. Both are sinful. Believers need to reach out to homosexuals as fellow sinners, tell them of Christ's love for them, bring them to him, and offer them biblical counselling. Only Christ can provide deliverance. Homosexuals, like all believers, must be willing to surrender their sexuality to Christ and to accept the help of fellow believers.

Yusufu Turaki

2:1-3:8 The need of the Jews

Paul warns the Jews not to think that God will be lenient with them because they are a chosen race. God will judge everyone on the basis of the truth of righteousness. His impartial verdict will be that all have sinned.

2:1-16 Principles of God's judgment In terms of ethical standards and moral lifestyle, the Jews considered themselves better than the pagans mentioned in 1:18-32. But the Jews are also condemned because they are doing the same things the pagans do (**2:1**). God's judgment is based on the impartial standard of the truth (**2:2**). Human judgment is based on partial knowledge, on human presuppositions and on racial, tribal and other prejudices. God's judgment is based on facts and knowledge. God knows us fully as individuals, groups, tribes and congregations. He judges us on the basis of what we do, what we think (Matt 5:28) and

what we say (Jas 3:3-12) – and his judgment is right. Paul stresses certain characteristics of God's judgment:

- **It is inescapable** (**2:3**). Jews who pass judgment on the Gentiles and yet commit the same sins will not escape God's judgment.
- **It is patient** (**2:4**). We often wonder why God allows sin and injustice to continue. We think God is indifferent, but Paul says God is patient, and his patience allows room for repentance. Nevertheless, at God's appointed time, all will be judged.
- **It is fair** (**2:5-11**). Paul stresses that *there will be trouble and distress for every human being who does evil*, but *honour and peace* for those who do good. Each person's verdict will be the right one given their actions (2:5-11). God does not tolerate sin nor show any favouritism as far as sin is concerned.

But the Gentiles and Jews are very different in terms of what they know about God, and so how can God judge them fairly? Paul's answer would be that we are judged according to the standards God has given to us (2:12-16). Gentiles will be judged on the basis of the knowledge God has made available to them, and they will be condemned because they sinned despite having that knowledge. Jews will be judged on the basis of God's written laws, which they received but did not obey.

People will not be judged on the basis of what they do not know, but of what they do with what they do know. Those who have never seen a Bible can still know God's revelation of himself in nature and in their consciences. They, too, will be judged. Thus, while the Jews have a moral obligation to obey the law (2:12), the Gentiles have a moral obligation to their consciences. Both those who are self-righteously moral (Jews) and unrighteous (pagans) will be judged for their actions and motives, which are controlled by their consciences (2:13-15).

2:17-29 CONDEMNATION OF THE JEWS Paul now gives examples of the Jews' hypocrisy and inconsistent behaviour. He lists a series of advantages which the Jews brag about and which they believe make them superior to Gentiles. He points out that their lives do not show evidence of these advantages. We Christians, too, must live up to our name, or like the Jews, we will also be condemned (2:16). We must not say, 'Do what I say but do not do what I do.' That is hypocrisy; we must live up to what we believe both in what we say and in what we do.

- **Advantage 1:** 'We are Jews and we have the Law.' The Jews were proud because of their nationality and their covenant with God. Because of this covenant, they had the law, knew God's will, had spiritually superior standards and were instructed in the law (2:17-18). These opportunities made the Jews feel superior, and so they set themselves up as guides for the blind, lights for those in darkness, instructors of the foolish and teachers of infants (2:19, 20). But the Jews themselves had not kept the law (2:21-24). Their behaviour dishonoured God and caused the Gentiles to stumble. As Christians, we claim to have God's revelation and we claim to be God's children and to know the truth, but do these claims translate into actions that bring glory to God? There is often a high level of hypocrisy and inconsistency in the church, which bring shame to God's name among non-Christians. The quality of the African church does not match its quantity. Some countries where the population is more than 50 percent Christian show little evidence of Christian presence in the society. No wonder unbelievers stumble and wonder whether there is any point in being a Christian.

- **Advantage 2:** 'God has given us the sign of circumcision, which shows we are his people.' Paul recognizes the blessing of circumcision, but insists that its value is only symbolic. Outward circumcision is only of value in the context of obedience to the law (2:25). If the law, which is kept in the heart, is transgressed, then outward circumcision counts for nothing (Gal 5:3). The inward circumcision of the heart, which transforms the individual to live a holy life, is the true circumcision. The same point applies in relation to Christian baptism. A child may be given a 'Christian' name like John, Paul or Peter – but many of the criminals of our day were christened with those names. Only God can see inward circumcision and hence he alone can give praise (2:26-29).

3:1-8 JEWISH OBJECTIONS AND GOD'S FAITHFULNESS Paul has touched the most sensitive areas of Jewish life. He has attacked their obedience to the law (2:17-24) and the ritual of circumcision (2:25-29) and has pointed out human wickedness and the righteous judgment of God. We would expect Jewish readers to react to these words. So Paul raises and answers questions that might arise in their minds.

- **Question 1:** What benefit is there in being a Jew or in being circumcised when both Jews and Gentiles will be condemned (3:1-2)? Paul's reply is that the greatest advantage of the Jewish race is that God entrusted them with his very words (Exod 19–20). God has made Israel a worldwide witness of his righteousness. It was through Israel that the Messiah came to the world.

- **Question 2:** If some of the Jews did not have faith in God, will this *lack of faith nullify God's faithfulness* (3:3-4)? This question needs to be understood in terms of a legal contract. If one party fails to keep the terms of the contract, does that mean the other party does not need to be faithful to it? Paul response is 'never, not with God!' Our unfaithfulness will never make God unfaithful. He is always faithful and will continue to be so even though every human being becomes a liar by dishonouring the covenant between Israel and God.

- **Question 3:** Isn't God unjust when our unrighteousness shows his righteousness by contrast, and yet he turns around to punish us (3:5-6)? Paul says such preposterous thinking robs God of his sovereignty and prerogative to judge the world. The fact that our wicked behaviour brings out God's righteousness cannot be used to justify evil behaviour.

- **Question 4:** *If my falsehood enhances God's truthfulness and so increases his glory, why am I still condemned as a sinner (3:7-8)?* Those who make this argument are saying that when we do evil, God's truthfulness shines brighter by contrast. So why should we be punished since our evil benefits God? Paul responds that those who think like this are already condemned. Such thinking is a perversion of the gospel. God remains faithful even when humans are unfaithful. Our sinfulness shows the character of God as he patiently waits for repentance. But his justice will be the standard by which he will eventually judge us all.

3:9-20 Verdict: All human beings are guilty

Having declared the righteousness of God and exposed the unrighteousness of both Gentiles and Jews, Paul gives his verdict: 'No one is righteous before God.' Jews are no better than Gentiles. Both are *under sin* (**3:9**). Paul takes the words of his verdict from several OT passages. The details of the verdict are that no one, whether Jew or Gentile, is right with God (**3:10-12**; Eccl 7:20; Pss 14:2-3; 53:2-3). Human beings are completely depraved in speech and conduct and need a saviour (**3:13-18**; Pss 5:9; 10:2-8; 36:1; 140:3; Isa 59:7-8). The very words we utter are offensive and our actions are evil, leading us to kill and to mock God.

The whole world is guilty before God; no one is righteous (**3:19-20**). The law that the Jews were so proud of has condemned them. It has made them conscious of their sins and inadequacies. What is the remedy for this deplorable state of affairs? Paul will describe it in the following chapters.

3:21-4:25 Justification by Faith, God Provides Salvation

Paul has declared that all human beings are sinners and cannot meet God's standards of righteousness in the natural law or in the Mosaic law. Now the apostle describes God's gracious plan for human salvation. He starts the section with *but now,* thereby introducing a contrast. No one can be made righteous through the law, *but now* God has provided an alternative way of salvation.

3:21-31 Justification by faith in Christ alone

In 1:17, Paul spoke of the righteousness of God being revealed in the gospel, and in **3:21** he returns to this theme. This righteousness is revealed on God's initiative. God has provided an alternative to the law, a means of salvation that has long been part of his plan. That is why it can be described as the fulfilment of OT Scripture. Paul then makes a number of important points about justification.

3:21-23 JUSTIFICATION IS BY FAITH IN CHRIST God's righteousness is available through faith in Jesus Christ (**3:22**). Because of the universal condemnation (1:18-3:20), a universal righteousness is required that can be obtained only by faith in Jesus Christ. All have sinned; all need Christ. Salvation is available to all on an equal basis, regardless of our backgrounds (**3:23**). When we believe in Jesus, he forgives our sins, cleanses us and empowers us to live a new life that is acceptable to God. This truth applies regardless of our race, tribe, gender, social class or any other way we categorize people. Faith in Jesus Christ binds very different people into one people of God, brothers and sisters under the cross of Jesus. It is therefore not in the will of Christ for Christians to fight and kill each other just because the

other Christians are from a different tribe or race. In Christ, we are one.

3:24-26 JUSTIFICATION IS BY FAITH ALONE Justification is a term used in a court of law, where the opposite of justification would be condemnation. Natural law and the Mosaic law condemn us, but God's grace justifies us (**3:24a**). Our salvation in its totality is an act of God's grace, freely given, and received by believing in Christ. To drive this point home, Paul repeats the word *faith* three times in this section (3:22, 25, 26). There is nothing we can do to be justified but believe in Jesus Christ.

The Scriptures emphatically state that it is against God's nature to forgive the guilty (Exod 23:7; Deut 25:1; Prov 17:15; Isa 5:23). So the question arises, how can God suddenly change his nature and justify the wicked (4:5)? The answer is that he can do this because Jesus took the punishment for the sinner.

Paul speaks of *the redemption that came by Christ Jesus* (**3:24b**). In the days of Paul, the word 'redemption' was used to describe the transaction that allowed one to buy a slave and then set him or her free. Christ's blood is the price that set us free from our captivity to sin. He gave his life as a payment for us, and so we now belong to him.

By dying on the cross for us sinners, Christ took upon himself the holy wrath of God, which was to come upon us (**3:25a**). Sending his son as atonement for our sin reveals both the intensity of God's hatred for sin and his immense love for the sinner.

God's divine forbearance might be interpreted as meaning that he is unjust and does not punish sin. But through the cross, God demonstrated his justice and his condemnation of sin, as well as providing a means of atonement so that we sinners can be justified. God justifies sinners to demonstrate his just character (**3:25b-26**).

3:27-31 IMPLICATIONS OF JUSTIFICATION Paul shows that our justification by faith has important implications for our Christian life and our relationships:

- **No more grounds for boasting** (**3:27-28**): The Jews were proud of their nationality, their law and circumcision. Gentiles were insolent, arrogant and boasted about such things as their military strength or their philosophies (1:30). But Christians have no grounds for boasting because the faith through which we are justified is not based on merit. It is available to all.

- **No more racial or tribal divisions** (**3:29-30**): God does not belong only to our tribe or to our denomination since faith has made God accessible to all. There is only one God, the Father of us all. Christians are a family and form a community stronger than any human tribe.

- **No more struggling to meet the requirements of the law** (**3:31**): The Jews believed that the faith Paul was proposing nullified the law. To this Paul says, *Not at all! Rather [faith] upholds the law.* The law is not put aside, but is given its proper place in the justice of God, for Christ has fully satisfied the demands of the law. Justified believers who live by faith are the beneficiaries of Christ's fulfilment of the righteous requirements of the law. As they become more like Christ, they automatically obey the law.

The gospel has the power to set sinners free and to humble those who take pride in human merit. The gospel breaks down barriers and unites believers of all tribes and races in one family. In Africa, family ties are very strong, and we know that family members should not fight and kill one another, but should stand together in trouble, share their resources, and live, play, eat, rejoice and mourn together. We should see the same things happening in the Christian family, which is the greatest family on earth.

The greatest joy in an African family is when the family expands through birth, or when sworn enemies are reconciled and become friends. The gospel we preach has the power to expand the family by bringing sinners to tearful repentance, to make friends out of arch-enemies, to bring peace and unity to our war-torn communities and nations, and to empower Christians to live like 'Christ in us'. If only Christians would live up to their calling, they would change their communities and nations.

4:1-25 Abraham: Illustration of justification by faith

In 1:17 and 3:22, Paul asserted that the gospel is not new but is attested to in the OT. In chapter 4, he presents Abraham as an OT example of someone justified by faith alone. Abraham, who was Israel's first ancestor and father, had a special relationship with God. But what was the basis of that relationship? Was it based on faith or on something Abraham had done to deserve a special relationship? Assuming that his readers know the story of Abraham, Paul quotes Genesis 15:6 and then explains some truths about the justification of Abraham.

4:1-8 JUSTIFICATION BY FAITH, NOT BY WORKS If it had been possible for Abraham to be justified by works, he would really have had something to boast about (4:1-2). But this was not the case. Clearly God did not think that Abraham could secure his own righteousness, for Genesis 15:6 says that *Abraham believed God and it was credited to him as righteousness* (4:3). Paul uses the word *credited* six times in 4:3-8. In a financial transaction, to *credit* someone with something is to put it into his or her account. One's account can be credited with money obtained as wages or as a gift. However, if one has a job, one's wages are not a gift but something one is entitled to. Money credited to someone who has not worked for it is a gift.

Genesis states that Abraham was credited with righteousness because he believed God. He did not do any work to earn this credit, and so was not entitled to be regarded as righteous. He was justified simply because he trusted God. When God credits our faith as righteousness, he is not rewarding our good deeds but displaying his grace. Trying hard to be good does not impress God. All we need to do is to submit to him by faith and allow him to work in and through us.

Paul quotes Psalm 32:1-2 to strengthen his argument that those whose relationship with God is based on faith are blessed. They enjoy being in the presence of God without fear of being cast out, for the Lord has taken the initiative and has forgiven their transgressions, covered their sins, and will never count their sin against them again (4:7-8).

4:9-12 JUSTIFICATION BY FAITH, NOT BY RITE Justification is only by faith, and is not accomplished by any ritual. Abraham was justified because of his faith (Gen 15:6) long before he was circumcised (Gen 17:24). Faith came first, and was followed by circumcision as a seal of the covenant between God and Israel (4:9-11). So Abraham is the father of all those who like him believe in God, whether they are Jews or Gentiles (4:12). No rite will lead to us being declared righteous; we must all respond by faith.

4:13-15 JUSTIFICATION BY FAITH, NOT BY LAW Someone might argue that even if it is true that Abraham was not justified by a ritual like circumcision, he might have been justified because he kept God's law. Paul would respond to this argument by pointing out that Abraham received and believed God's promises long before the law was given (Gen 15; see also Gen 12:2-3). God's promise to Abraham was based on the righteousness that comes by faith, not on Abraham's having kept the law (4:13). The coming of the law cannot annul the promise (4:14). Those who insist that the law is the only way to righteousness are denying the promise and cannot enjoy its benefits, for the promise is based solely on the righteousness of faith (4:13-14). All that the law brings is a sense of sin, guilt and penalty without offering any redemption from one's sinful state (4:15). When God called Abraham, he had not yet given the law, so there was no way that Abraham could either keep or break the law (4:15). Promise was the only factor. To this, Abraham responded in faith and was reckoned righteous.

4:16-25 JUSTIFICATION BY FAITH ALONE Paul's arguments have proved that Abraham was not justified by works, or by a ritual, or by keeping the law, but by faith (4:16a). Such justification by grace through faith is open to all and makes Abraham the father of all who believe. By faith, we who believe are children of Abraham, the father of faith, and so God's promise that Abraham would be the *father of many nations* has come true (4:16b-17a; see also Gen 17:5).

One measure of the reasonability of faith is the credibility and power of the object of faith. The object of Abraham's faith was *God who gives life to the dead and calls things that are not as though they were* (4:17b). His firm conviction of the power of God made Abraham trust in God in spite of the humanly impossible situation he found himself in. If we were to ask Paul, what type of faith did Abraham have? Paul would answer, the confidence that God can do what he promises and that he will keep his word (4:18-25).

There is a lesson here for us. God will credit our accounts with righteousness if we believe in him who offered Jesus for our sins and raised him to life for our justification. No one can impress God; only faith impresses him and that faith is seen in the confidence that God is faithful and will keep his promises.

We make many promises in life, and often we have logical, concrete grounds for believing that others will keep their promises to us. But when God called Abraham to leave his homeland and go to a land that God would give him, Abraham did not have logical grounds for believing the promise. Strangers are not commonly given land in someone else's territory. God's promise of a gift of children was also illogical because of Abraham and Sarah's ages. But Abraham believed God and obeyed. This is the faith that Paul is referring to – the confidence that an illogical promise can be fulfilled. After all, salvation in Christ by faith may seem illogical to some (how can another person's good performance be counted as mine?) but that is the only way that God has provided for salvation.

5:1-8:39 The Assurance and Hope of Salvation

Paul began this letter by setting out the terrible condition of human beings, and he concluded that section by saying that 'there is no one righteous, not even one; there is no one who understands, no one who seeks God' (3:10-11). He then went on to declare God's faithfulness in providing a means of justification: God's gift of salvation by grace through faith in Christ (3:21-4:25). He now proceeds to outline the many benefits of justification. He starts this section with the word 'Therefore', indicating that what follows is the result of what he has said in the previous section.

5:1-5 The Benefits of Salvation

One benefit of salvation is that believers no longer live in a state of hostility with God. Because of the new relationship established through faith in Christ, they now enjoy peace with God (5:1). Human beings crave peace in all areas of their lives, but the ultimate peace is that which believers enjoy with God and which comes through Jesus Christ our Lord. This is a lasting peace that nothing will remove. Those who are justified have obtained personal access to God. We cannot enter into God's presence by our own merit; but through Christ, we have been brought into the presence of God where we stand firmly, with absolute security and confidence (5:2a).

The enjoyment of this peace is grounds for rejoicing. We enjoy blessings related to our past as our sins are forgiven, and to our present as we can now stand in God's presence

because those sins are forgiven and to our future as we anticipate a glorious life to come. No wonder Paul says that *we rejoice in the hope of the glory of God* (5:2b). Through Christ, our future is certain and secure in God's hands.

But how are we to react to our suffering in the present? Paul's answer is that *we also rejoice in our sufferings* (5:3a). Paul and the other apostles understood the meaning of suffering. In Acts 14:22, he told believers that 'we must go through many hardships to enter the kingdom of God.' Believers must develop the ability to face difficulties without giving up their faith. In fact, says Paul, they should rejoice, because suffering has the positive outcome of building endurance, which leads to a tested character, and this character produces hope (5:3b-4).

Believers must continuously put their hope in God who will fulfil his promises regarding their future. They must put their eyes on things to come and hope for a better future when they will share in God's glory. This hope brings a joy that nothing can shake. The presence of the Holy Spirit in our lives makes us aware of the love of God, and this love gives us the unshakeable assurance of things to come (5:5). Therefore, believers must never give up in the face of suffering; God will fulfil his promises. This brings consolation to those of us who are suffering the pains of injustice, war, hunger, HIV/AIDS and many other evils. We can have hope if we believe that we will share in God's glory. Paul had tasted suffering and he was writing out of his own experience. He writes that he is consoled by the knowledge that his future is secure in Christ Jesus.

5:6-11 Demonstration of God's Love

By the death of Jesus Christ (5:6-8), God truly demonstrated his love for us. Christ died for us so that we can come to God and can avoid his wrath. His body was broken for us and his blood shed on our behalf (1 Cor 11:24-26). It is rare for human love to inspire someone to die on behalf of someone else, and when that happens, the person who is loved this much is normally someone who could be described as 'righteous'. But when Jesus died, it was not for 'good' people, but for people who were completely unworthy of his sacrifice (5:6-8). We had no merit in ourselves and were powerless to save ourselves. *At just the right time,* that is, at our highest point of hopelessness, God demonstrated his utmost love by sending his son to die and reconcile us to himself.

God has demonstrated his love by putting us right with himself (5:9-11). The death of Christ has saved us from the future wrath of God. If God showed us such amazing love while we were enemies, imagine what he will do for us now that we have been reconciled to him through the death of his son. Believers will not be forsaken by God; they are secure in him. This is the only firm basis for believers continuing to find joy in the Lord in the midst of the suffering some are enduring on the African continent or when confronted by natural disasters such as earthquakes, tsunamis or volcanic eruptions. No matter what happens, believers are eternally secure in the hand of God. Resurrection and the eternal enjoyment of the presence of God are the end of all things for those who believe.

5:12-21 Universal Applicability of Justification

Paul has spoken of the blessings of believers (5:1-11), but readers may still wonder how the death of one individual could bring such blessing to so many people. Paul therefore uses the examples of Adam and Christ to illustrate the principle of corporate solidarity, in which the actions of one person affect the lives of all their relatives. An African from a community-based society in which 'one is because others are' can easily follow Paul's explanation, for we share the belief of Paul's Jewish community that the actions of one person can affect many others. For example, in Africa a whole clan may need to be cleansed because a senior member of the community has broken a taboo. Those who refuse to participate in the cleansing rituals are believed to be still at risk from the angered spirits. Though many believers choose not to participate in such rites because of their unchristian elements, their refusal is rooted in their security in the forgiveness of God rather than in any denial of the fact that an individual's act affects many others.

Paul contrasts the acts and roles of Adam and Jesus. Adam was the head of the human community, and when he sinned, he brought God's judgment on all humanity. Thus, it can be said that through him all sinned, even before the law was given (5:12-13). We sinned in Adam because he is our representative. The punishment for his sin was death, and that is why death came into the world that God had created (5:14).

In acting as the representative of all humanity, Adam was in a sense a model (or prototype) of Christ. But the actions of the two men were very different (5:15): Adam's act was characterized by disobedience; Christ's act, by self-sacrifice in obedience to the will of God. One man was selfish; the other gave a gift. The results of their actions are also different (5:16). Adam's sin brought condemnation, death and separation from God; the gift of Christ brought justification despite our many sins. Ultimately, Adams' actions led to the reign of death, but Jesus' actions meant that those who receive God's grace will reign in life (5:17).

In 5:18-21 Paul again contrasts the role of Adam and of Christ. Just as Adam's sin brought condemnation and death to human beings, so the sacrificial death of Christ brought justification and life. All became sinners because of the disobedience of Adam. In the same way many will become righteous because of the obedience of Jesus Christ.

Paul then returns to the law, saying that in this pattern of sin, condemnation, grace and justification, the function of the law is to reveal sin. Because it states God's commands

explicitly, the law makes it impossible for us to claim that we did not realize that we were breaking them. In this sense, the law can be said to increase our trespasses. However, God has provided a means of dealing with this, for *where sin increased, grace increased all the more* (5:20b). Through the trespass of one man (Adam's sin), all (everyone) died; but through the righteous act of Jesus (Christ's death) justification is brought to all who believe.

6:1-23 Freedom from Bondage to Sin

Paul next demolishes an argument in favour of sinning: If God declares us righteous and his grace increases 'all the more' when there is more sin, isn't this an encouragement to sin more? (6:1). Paul attacks the seeming logic of this argument, pointing out that someone who wants to go on sinning because God's forgiveness of sin is guaranteed does not understand the meaning of grace or seriousness of sin.

6:1-14 The power of sin is broken

Paul offers a series of overlapping arguments to refute the accusation that God's grace gives us licence to sin:

- **Christians have died in relation to sin (6:2)**. Because Christ died for sin, those who believe in him have died to sin. Christians can be tempted by sin and are capable of sinning. However, Christians have no relationship whatever with sin.
- **Christians are baptized into Christ (6:3)**. Baptism symbolizes death to sin and represents a believer's union with Christ in his death and resurrection. Baptism follows a person's decision to put his or her faith in Christ and shows the person has entered into a relationship with Christ that will not allow him or her to continue in sin.
- **Believers share in Christ's death and resurrection (6:4-5)**. Baptism is a visible demonstration of believers, death, burial and resurrection with Christ. This union with him in his death and resurrection allows them to share the blessing of his resurrection, namely a new life.
- **Believers are crucified with Christ (6:6-7)**. Christians die to sin (their old self) in the body of Christ with whom they have been united in faith and baptism. They have been resurrected with Christ as new people and have started a new and justified life. How can they go back to being their old sinful self, which has died? The old life of sin finished at the death of Christ and the new life of righteousness started with his resurrection.
- **Believers will live with Christ (6:8-10)**. Their present and future lives have been taken care of from the time they believed in Christ. Our death and resurrection in and through Christ give us the power to live with him now and in the life to come. Our union with Christ starts with our death to sin (a one-time act) and continues with a life of perpetual identification with Christ.

- **Believers are dead to sin but alive to God (6:11).** As believers, we must constantly think of ourselves as people who have died and have been made alive again in Christ. Only then will we be able to live as the people of God. We must always remind ourselves that our old self has been crucified with Christ. Our lives must demonstrate our new status in Christ.

The implication of all this is that we must offer ourselves to God. Since we have died to sin and are united with Christ in his death and resurrection, our old self has been crucified with Christ. We should no longer allow sin to reign in our bodies for us to *obey its evil desires* (6:12), nor should we offer our bodies as instruments of sin (6:13a). Rather, we are to offer ourselves to God (6:13b) and the parts of our bodies as *instruments of righteousness* (6:13c). Sin can no longer be the master of the believer because the believer is no longer under the law that condemns but under grace that justifies (6:14).

Africans understand this principle because they understand rites of passage. Once an African has gone through a rite of passage, he or she is expected to live a new life and will face grave consequences if he or she reverts to his or her old self. At a far deeper level, Paul is saying that in Christ the old self is gone, we have emerged as new beings and the implications of what we have done will not allow us to go back to being the old self. If we do, the consequences will be grave.

6:15-23 Believers are slaves to righteousness

Paul states that we are *not under law but under grace* (6:14). This immediately leads to another question: Are we then free to do whatever we want? (6:15). This question is closely related to the one he has just dealt with; but whereas he approached that one in terms of the meaning of baptism, now he uses the example of slavery to make his point.

When we agree to obey someone completely, we become that person's slave (6:16). Our conversion is our agreement to be God's slaves. As slaves, we are under an obligation to obey God (our new master) and never again to follow our own desires (our old master). We can serve only one master (Matt 6:24) and, by our voluntary conversion, that master is God.

Believers have shifted their allegiance. Before our conversion, we had no choice but to be slaves to sin, but with our conversion, our allegiance shifts. The change is total and complete (6:17). We are set free from sin and become *slaves to righteousness* (6:17-18). Slavery to sin leads to increasing wickedness, while slavery to righteousness leads to increasing holiness (6:19-20). This means that although we have been declared righteous because of our faith, we will still need to go through a process of sanctification in which we will gradually be transformed into the likeness of Christ.

The only 'benefit' we obtain from our slavery to sin is death, which is in marked contrast to the benefits of slavery to righteousness, which are holiness and eternal life (6:21-22). We can think of these benefits as wages received for serving a master. And we can choose between two possible masters, sin or God. The wage sin pays for our services is death, *but the gift of God is eternal life in Christ Jesus our Lord* (6:23). When we serve God, what he gives us cannot be called wages, for it is far more than we could ever possibly earn through our service. It is a gift of grace. We are given what we do not deserve and that is eternal life.

It is important to ask ourselves who we are serving. Who are we living for?

7:1-25 Freedom from Bondage to Law

In chapter 6, Paul stressed that those who believe have been set free from sin. When Christ died, they too died to sin. What the law could not do, God did through the death of his Son. But in Judaism, sin and the law are closely related. If we are free from the bondage of sin, then what is the position of the law? Paul has already described the law as that which reveals sin (3:20), condemns the sinner (3:19), makes sin a transgression (4:15; 5:13) and brings wrath (4:15). Because Christians are free from sin, they are no longer under the authority of the law. But it is also true that while believers live in this body, they will still have to deal with their sinful nature and its attempt to dominate their lives. All this forms the background to Paul's discussion of the role of the law in Romans 7.

7:1-6 Limited validity of the law

Paul uses a marriage metaphor to demonstrate that the law is valid only when the people concerned are alive (7:1-3). His argument goes like this. When someone dies, his or her marriage ends and the surviving widow or widower is free to remarry. The law was like a husband to whom one was tied by a set of rules or laws that had to be kept if there was to be any relationship. When Christ died, he fulfilled all the obligations that this legal code imposed on us. And when we died with him, our relationship to that old set of laws also ended (7:4a).

Christ became our new husband (7:4b), but our relationship with him is no longer one in which we obey because we have to. Rather, obedience is our loving response to the will of our new husband. Because Christ's will is actually the same as God's, it truly conforms to the law, which God gave us as an expression of his holy nature (7:12). The problem with the law as a code of regulations was that all it could do was arouse sinful passions without providing any way of escape, with the result that we *bore fruit for death* (7:5). Now, however, the Spirit creates a character like that of Christ in a believer. Christlikeness involves living a life of holiness based on love and not on a code of regulations to be obeyed for fear of a beating (**7:6**).

Paul is making the point that, because the true core of the law was not done away with but was fulfilled (8:3b-4; see also Matt 5:17-19), the law as a set of regulations has ceased to have authority over anyone who has become a believer and identified with Christ by dying with him. Because the believer died to the law before embarking on this new marriage to Christ, the new marriage is perfectly legitimate (**7:2**). Once one partner has died, the other (the law) has no business claiming any role in the believer's life. The only obligation we now have is to bear fruit for God (**7:4c**).

7:7-13 Relationship between law and sin

If we have died both to sin and to the law, the question arises, *Is the law sin?* (**7:7a**). Paul's answer is emphatic: *Certainly not!* The law did not create sin and death. The law is not sin, but it does reveal sin. Where there is no law, we are not aware of the existence and power of sin. For example, we would not have known that it was wrong to want things that belonged to others if the law had not said, *Do not covet* (**7:7b**; see also Exod 20:17).

The law can even provoke us to break a commandment by providing a standard that sin takes advantage of by urging us to do what is forbidden (**7:8**). Without the law, sin would be less active. The problem is not with the law as such, but with sin, which perpetually goes against the will of God.

Paul uses himself as an example to illustrate what he means. At one time, he was simply alive, but did not know the law and had no concept of sin or its implications. But when he grew and gained knowledge of the law, sin was awakened in him and he became spiritually condemned (**7:9**). Speaking from his own experience, the apostle laments that sin deceived him. It took advantage of the law, which was intended to bless, and used it to condemn him to spiritual death (**7:10-11**). The law exposes, stimulates and condemns sin. Nevertheless, the law is not evil. It is *holy, righteous and good* (**7:12**). The law was intended to help humanity, but sin converted the blessings of the law into a curse (**7:13**).

7:14-25 Conflict of the law and sin

In this portion of his letter, Paul gives us a graphic description of the tension between one's spiritual self and one's sinful self. Opinions are divided about whether the picture painted here shows the struggle of an unbeliever, an unspiritual believer or any believer – including Paul himself. But it is clear that he is talking about someone who loves the law, as he did before his conversion (Gal 1:14; Phil 3:5), but lacks the ability to keep it.

7:14-20 THE TENSION BETWEEN THE LAW AND THE FLESH Paul repeats his argument about the tension between the law and the flesh in 7:14-17 and in 7:18-20. In these verses, Paul acknowledges that the law is spiritual, but the flesh, which has been tainted by sin, has become unspiritual. Consequently, there is nothing good in the flesh (**7:18**). The apostle speaks of living with a divided self, a self that wants to do what is good (obey the law), but also what is bad (disobey the law) (**7:15, 19**). Who is responsible for this tension? Paul says it is not the law, for the law is holy and good, nor is it his real and ideal self, because he does not voluntarily disobey the law. Rather, it is indwelling sin that affects him (**7:17, 20**). Although we believe in Christ, we still have a sinful nature that pulls us towards things we do not want to do (**7:21**). But because Christ has saved us from bondage to sin, we are to live for him and not live a life of sin.

7:21-25 GOOD AND EVIL DWELL IN THE BELIEVER Although we are believers, both good and evil dwell in us (**7:22**). The good in the believer, *the law of my mind* (**7:23**) delights in the law of God. But *the law of sin* is in constant opposition to the law of the mind. This conflict creates a tension that holds the believer captive. Paul yearns for a deliverer (**7:24**). No wonder he utters a cry of thanksgiving for the provision of such a deliverer (**7:25a**). Paul concludes that he is a slave to God's law in that he longs to keep it, but that in his sinful nature he is also a slave to the law of sin because he cannot keep the law (**7:25b**). As believers, we must not live in sin but must live in the freedom of the indwelling Spirit, which brings tremendous benefits to the believer.

8:1-39 Blessings and Security of Life in the Spirit

In chapter 7, Paul described the tension between our old and new natures. We have been set free from our bondage to sin, but while we are still in this body, we must continue to deal with our sinful nature and its attempts to control our lives. Yet Paul assures believers that there is power to overcome sin and to live a life of victory and hope. So in chapter 8, he explains the wonderful blessings that believers enjoy: they are not condemned, are indwelt by the Holy Spirit, have been adopted into God's family and are headed for resurrection and divine glory, preserved by God's love and promise. It is through the work of the Holy Spirit that the believer enjoys the blessings and victory of God. Through the Holy Spirit, the believer's new life in Christ is secure.

8:1-8 Ministry of the Spirit

Many blessings are available to those who have been justified by faith:

- **No condemnation (8:1):** As a result of the believer's faith and identification with Christ, nobody can accuse us. Neither Satan nor anyone else can use our past sins and present failures to question our standing in Christ.

Our new position in Christ does not depend on our performance but on what Christ has accomplished on the cross for us and our faith in Christ.

- **Freedom from the law of sin and death (8:2-4)**: What the law could not do, God did by sending his son (8:3) and by giving us the Spirit whose indwelling empowers us to live holy lives. God's action fulfilled *the righteous requirements of the law* (8:4). *The law of the Spirit of life*, proclaimed in the gospel, has liberated the believer into a new life. When we walk in the power of the Holy Spirit, we meet the requirements of the law. The Spirit provides the power to make us holy and to produce fruit.
- **A mind controlled by the Spirit (8:5-8)**: Where *we set our minds* determines how we live. Choosing to set our minds on the desires of our sinful natures leads to sin and hostility with God. Choosing to obey the Spirit leads to obedience and to peace with God. A compromise is not an option. A mind controlled by the Spirit thinks of godly things, while the mind controlled by the flesh is full of the things of the flesh. Our mind sets the agenda for our relationship with and attitudes towards God (8:8). A mind controlled by the Spirit delights in the Lord.

8:9-13 Indwelling of the Spirit

If the Spirit of God dwells in us, he takes control of our lives and counteracts the power of sin (**8:9**; see also 7:17, 20). The Spirit of God is the Spirit of Christ. Having him is the same as belonging to Christ. He lives in our human spirits and makes us alive spiritually. Because the Spirit of God is in us, *God who raised Christ from the dead will also give life to your mortal bodies* (**8:10-11**). Considering what God has done for believers, *we have an obligation* to say no to sinful acts and to live a life pleasing to God (**8:12**). We must resist the desires of our bodies in order to experience Christ and the liberating power of the Holy Spirit (**8:13**).

8:14-17 Goal of justification

If we live under the Spirit's authority and, by so doing, put to death all sinful acts, we demonstrate that we are children of God (**8:14**). This is God's utmost desire, and his Spirit will give us assurance of it. The Spirit will lead us and empower us to live a life pleasing to God.

The Spirit will also replace fear of God with the freedom that children enjoy with their father. Those who are slaves to sin have good reasons to fear God, but as children, we can acquire boldness to approach God as our Father. Because we have received the legal status of sons (**8:15a**), we will be free to address him as *Abba, Father* (**8:15b**). The Spirit testifies with our own spirits that we are indeed children of God (**8:16**).

Finally, the indwelling Spirit will give us the assurance of our eternal inheritance, which we share as co-heirs with Jesus (**8:17**).

8:18-27 The revelation of the glory of God's children

Paul now moves from the ministry of the Holy Spirit in the present life of the believer to discuss the suffering and the glory that lies ahead for believers. Paul has tasted suffering and is convinced that in this world believers will suffer; he is also convinced that the ultimate goal of their suffering is their glorification with Christ in the life to come. Before then, suffering will inevitably be part of our lives.

8:18-22 THE SUFFERING AND GLORIFICATION OF CREATION The price that we pay in suffering when we follow Christ is negligible compared to the glory we will share with him. And we will not be the only ones to be glorified and set free from suffering, for Paul points out that the whole of creation shares our suffering and our hope of glory (**8:18-20**). What he means is that as a result of the sin of Adam, God cursed the ground (Gen 3:17), and so the whole creation is frustrated because it is not as perfect as God originally intended it to be. But the day is coming when creation, too, will be set free from its slavery to sin and death, which inevitably result in decay, and will enter the glorious freedom of the children of God (**8:21**).

In the meantime, creation suffers and groans (**8:22**). Paul compares these groans to the cries of a woman giving birth to a child. There is pain, but there is also the assurance that the pain will eventually produce new life.

8:23-27 SUFFERING AND GLORY OF GOD'S CHILDREN The suffering of creation is similar to that of the children of God. We have *the firstfruits of the Spirit* (**8:23a**). These fruits mark the beginning of the harvest and give assurance of a full harvest to come. Thus, though we have not yet received our full blessing, the witness of the Holy Spirit within us assures us that it is coming. So as we wait for our full adoption and redemption, we have vivid evidence that it will come to pass.

While we await the full blessing, we *groan inwardly* (**8:23b**). The presence of the Spirit in us makes us long for the ultimate blessing of our adoption and redemption. Though we were adopted as children of God when we came to faith and were justified (8:15), we will not fully enjoy that status before our bodies have been saved (or redeemed) from the tendency to sin and decay and have become perfect. The wonderful experience of all that our salvation means is still something that we await with anticipation. We are eager for the day when our frail, mortal and sin-sick bodies will be renewed and transformed and we will enjoy eternal glory.

But we are not to demand that we receive these blessings immediately. In this state of transition, we are to wait *patiently* for the fulfilment of our hope (**8:24-25**). Many things can happen to Christians as they wait. Some may lose patience or sight of what is hoped for, or may even lapse into unbelief. We should not give up but should wait patiently in hope of that which the faithful God has promised.

Our hope is certain because of the love of God, which never waivers. And while we wait, the Spirit continually helps us in our weakness (**8:26-27**). He helps us to pray and intercedes for us with wordless groans. After all, in our suffering we often do not know even how to pray or what to pray for.

8:28-30 The security of the believer

Our present life is characterized by suffering, but we are sustained by the hope of our ultimate good, our glorification. More than that, we can take comfort in the promise that what is happening to us is controlled and directed by God for our good (**8:28**). We will not always understand or enjoy the things we experience, but we can rest assured that we will not experience anything that God does not allow and use for our present and future good. Our sufferings, our groaning, our hope and our joy – all are designed for our ultimate good. God is in control and nothing is beyond his power.

We are told that God *foreknew* us (**8:29**). This foreknowledge of God probably refers to his intimate knowledge of and relationship with believers whom he *predestined* to reach a particular goal: being conformed to the likeness of his Son. Paul uses the term 'predestination' when speaking of God's plan because he wants to make it clear our salvation starts with God's choice, not ours. God has planned for believers to pass through three stages: they are called, they are justified and they are glorified (**8:30**). God's call comes through our response in faith and obedience to the gospel message. Those who believe are justified by faith, and those who are justified will be glorified with Christ.

8:31-39 Conclusion: Believers secure in God

Having revealed God's systematic plan for our glorification, Paul concludes by stating his firm conviction that the believer's eternal salvation is secured. He does this by posing six questions:

- **What then shall we say in response to this?** (**8:31a**). How should we respond in light of God's goodness to us in spite of our sinfulness? Paul answers this question with another one.
- **If God is for us, who can be against us?** (**8:31b**). There are things that oppose us as believers: our sinful nature, suffering, death and the devil himself, but none of these can ever prevail against us because God is on our side. Then Paul expands on this point.
- **He who did not spare his own Son, but gave him up for us all** – *how will he not also, along with him, graciously give us all things?* (**8:32**). If God was prepared to go to the length of giving up his only Son to save us, he will certainly give us everything else we need to achieve his ultimate goal: our sanctification and glorification.
- **Who will bring any charge against those whom God has chosen?** *It is God who justifies.* (**8:33**). Satan and our

consciences still try to accuse us of being unworthy of salvation because we still have sin in our lives. But God has passed his verdict, and that verdict is that we are justified. Once the judge has spoken, the case is closed. All accusations against believers are dismissed.

- **Who is he that condemns?** Christ has been appointed as the one to judge the world (John 5:22). But he is also the one *who died – more than that, who was raised to life* and he is now *at the right hand of God … interceding for us* (**8:34**). So the judge is also the advocate for those who believe in him. He died to save us, and will not condemn those for whom he died. No wonder all accusations against believers are thrown out of court.
- **Who shall separate us from the love of Christ?** (**8:35a**). The answer to this question is the climax of Paul's argument concerning the security of the believer. He mentions seven situations which he himself had experienced that can stand between God and us: trouble, hardship, persecution, famine, nakedness, danger or sword (**8:35b-36**). The love of Christ does not stop us from experiencing these things, but it carries us through them (**8:37**). Having looked at everything in life, Paul knows that nothing whatsoever can separate us from the love of Christ.

We live in a world of uncertainty and suffer frustrations, tragedies and despair. Yet Paul is certain that nothing in this creation (e.g., death, life, angels, the demons that Africans have traditionally feared, the present, the future, powers, height, depth or anything else we can think of) *will be able to separate us from the love of God that is in Christ Jesus our Lord* (**8:38-39**). God has provided for our victory. We can rest assured that his love will never let us down. All we need to do is trust God and be convinced that he can keep his promises no matter how unlikely that may sometimes appear in our circumstances.

9:1-11:36 Israel: God's Justice Not to Blame

Having explained and marvelled at God's abundant grace to the human race (chs.1–8), Paul feels compelled to reflect on the situation of his own people, the Jews (chs. 9–11). Has God abandoned the Jews? They were the people God chose to receive the gospel, but most of them opposed and rejected it. How then can we understand God's choice of Israel and the salvation of the world through them?

These chapters also warn Gentile believers not to boast or look down on the few Jewish believers who are in the church. Whether Jews or Gentiles, believers are all members of one family – the family of God. It does not matter who forms the majority or minority among the people of God. This message is very important for African believers who too often tend to dismiss those who belong to ethnic minorities.

9:1-5 The Unbelief of Israel

Paul identifies himself with his own ethnic group, the Jews, referring to them as 'my brothers' and expressing his deep sorrow over their condition. The sins of our own ethnic groups should drive us to tears before God.

Given the fact that Paul is the great missionary to the Gentiles, some of those listening to him might have questioned his sincerity in saying that he cares for his fellow Jews, so Paul asserts that he is *not lying* (**9:1**). It can be very difficult to preach to others while our own people are not responding well to the good news of Christ (**9:2**). Yet Paul's identification with his fellow Jews is so strong that he says, *I could wish that I myself were cursed and cut off from Christ for the sake of my brothers* (**9:3**). Paul is not saying that he wishes to join his people in their unbelief, but that he would be prepared to take their place if that would mean that they would turn to Christ. Moses uttered a similar prayer in Exodus 32:30-32.

Israel had privileges which identified them as a special people of God (**9:4**): *the adoption as sons* (Exod 4:22), *the divine glory* (Exod 16:10; 24:17; 40:34; 1 Kgs 8:11), *the covenants* (Gen 15:18; 2 Sam 7:12-16; Jer 31–34), *the receiving of the law* (Deut 5:1-22), *the temple worship* and *the promises*. They could also claim *the patriarchs* (primarily Abraham, Isaac and Jacob), who occupied an important place in the history of Israel because through them Israel as a nation had made covenants with God and been given the great promise of a coming Messiah. However, Paul makes it clear that this Messiah belongs to Israel only in terms of his natural descent (*from them is traced the human ancestry of Christ* – **9:5**). From the divine point of view, he is God, the Saviour of those who believe in him.

Just as Paul was weighed down by the spiritual condition of his people, so African pastors and leaders must be weighed down by the spiritual condition of their people. If all African pastors were as concerned as Paul about the spiritual condition of their people, we would definitely see a difference on the continent. Unfortunately, many pastors seem content to see what they do as a job, rather than as a calling. If we are truly concerned about our people's future, we will pray and act in whatever way we can to see more and more Africans come to the Lord.

9:6-13 God's Choice of Particular People

God had ensured that the Jews were more prepared than any other nation to receive Christ. But they did not receive him. Does this mean that God's preparation had failed? No, says Paul, God's word has not failed as some might argue (**9:6a**). There were always some descendants of Abraham who were not among the chosen (**9:6b-7a**). In his sovereignty, God always chose a particular individual or group of individuals to carry on his special blessings. He chose Isaac (the child of the promise) instead of Ishmael (the natural son) to fulfil the promise (**9:7b-9**). In the same way, he chose Jacob (who represents Israel) over Esau (who represents Edom) even before they were born and before they had done anything good or bad (**9:10-13**; Gen 25:23). God is speaking of this choice and its consequences when he says in Malachi 1:2-3 that he 'hated' Esau (**9:13**). Like Paul, we do not know why God made this choice. But God's choice clearly demonstrates that the Jews were wrong to claim to be God's special people simply because they had descended from Abraham. Being the physical children of Abraham does not guarantee God's blessings. People do not become God's children through human descent but only through faith (John 1:11-13). God's election is his invitation for human beings to enter his promises. It requires humans to respond.

9:14-29 God's Sovereignty

9:14-23 God's freedom to do as he wants

Paul knows that what he has said concerning the sovereignty of God in dealing with human beings may raise objections, with people accusing God of being unjust by choosing some and rejecting others (**9:14**). God is not unjust, says Paul. The issue is not about God's injustice, but about his sovereignty when dealing with his creation. God is merciful, but he has the right to choose to whom he wants to show this mercy (**9:15-16, 18**; Exod 33:19). The ultimate purpose of God's sovereign choice, or 'election', is not to elevate some people and destroy others, but to display his power and to make his name known throughout the earth. The hardening of Pharaoh's heart in response to his refusal to let God's people go resulted in God demonstrating his power (**9:17**). Other nations who heard what God did trembled and feared God (Exod 15:1-16; Josh 2:10-11; 1 Sam 4:8).

Some may ask why, if the election depends solely on God, does he blame human beings for not obeying him? How can he hold us responsible for the choice he makes? (**9:19**). This question raises the issue of human responsibility and God's sovereignty. Paul does not even attempt to answer these questions; the best he can do is reaffirm God's freedom in dealing with his creation, illustrating his point with the OT image of a potter using clay (**9:20-21**; see also Isa 29:16; 45:9; Jer 18:6-10). Paul does not say that we can escape responsibility for our actions; he does say we cannot challenge God for what he does.

Paul suggests that God may be dealing with two categories of people: those *prepared for destruction* and those *prepared to receive his mercy* (**9:22-23**). The former are probably the unsaved, those who oppose God and refuse to turn to him (Matt 23:37). They are 'prepared for destruction' not because God has predestined them to destruction but because their sin attracts God's wrath (9:22). Those who are destined for God's mercy are the people who accept

God's grace or the salvation that has been prepared for humanity.

God is absolutely sovereign. We are related to him as his children solely by his grace. But his sovereignty does not exclude human responsibility. We cannot excuse ourselves and blame God. We are guilty whenever we resist God and his calling in our lives.

9:24-29 A new people called from the Jews and the Gentiles

Because God is sovereign in his election, he is free to call both Jews and Gentiles to become his people. Paul supports this argument with quotations from Hosea 2:23 and then Hosea 1:10 to show that those who were not God's people have become his people by his sovereign decision (**9:24-26**). God always selects a group for himself, a remnant out of a great number (**9:27-29**; see also Isa 10:22-23; 1:9). God's words to Israel now apply to both Gentiles and Jews. Under the old covenant, the Gentiles were not accepted as people of God, but now that has changed.

Believers all over the world are among the objects of God's mercy. We are his people, his children, from all the tribes and nations of Africa. God has called us to be a special people belonging to him. God has called us not because of who we are but because of who he is – the sovereign God. We have no right to be proud and arrogant. Our salvation is none of our own doing; it is all by the divine will of God.

9:30-10:21 Christ, the Only Way to Salvation

9:30-10:13 Faith in Christ: Israel's stumbling-stone

Israel tried to obtain righteousness by doing the works demanded by the law (**9:31**). To them, Christ was a stumbling block (**9:32b-33**; Ps 118:22; Isa 8:14; 28:16). The Gentiles, however, accepted the gospel that had been preached to both Jews and Gentiles because they recognized that it is impossible to please God by works (**9:30, 32a**). The only way to please him is to accept that we are not able to satisfy him and then to accept the righteousness that comes through faith in Christ. Jesus did not fulfil the Jews' expectations, so they missed their chance to trust in him.

Why did the Jews miss Christ and salvation? Paul's answer is that the Jews were zealously devoted to God, but their zeal was not based on knowledge (**10:2**; see also Hos 4:6). Having zeal for God is not a bad thing. Jesus (John 2:17) and Paul as a Pharisee (Acts 22:3; Phil 3:6) were zealous. However, Paul's pre-Christian zeal, like that of other Jews, was not based on a correct understanding of the righteousness that God requires. God justifies sinners and accepts them only as they accept his gift of salvation in Christ (**10:3-4**).

We see a similar lack of knowledge among those in Africa who worship idols and things that are not God with the conviction that they are worshipping God. They will perish unless they gain a proper knowledge of God's salvation in Christ and revealed by Christ. As humans, we are always tempted to be misled by our heritage and so be blinded to the will of God. Africans, for example, are so religious that some mistake their religiosity for being acceptable before God. For such people, their religion becomes their idol because it hinders them from coming to a saving knowledge of Jesus. Unless they gain a proper knowledge of God's salvation and accept Christ from the heart, they will perish. Our love for them means that we must not spare any effort to help them to know and understand the will of God in the important matter of salvation.

After his detailed explanation of the kind of righteousness that pleases God (9:30-10:4), Paul goes on to explain how one can achieve this righteousness. He makes three points.

First, God is the one who makes this righteousness possible. The apostle quotes Deuteronomy 30:13-14 to demonstrate that the righteousness of God that comes by faith in Christ as the way of salvation is not difficult and inaccessible, but easy to attain (**10:5**). Christ's coming to earth to provide salvation and his rising from the grave to prove his great saving power are both accomplished facts. No one needs to ascend to heaven to find him or descend to the deep to wake him up (**10:6-7**). All has been done, and all that we have to do is believe. By his incarnation, he has become one of us and by his resurrection he has demonstrated that he is worthy of being the object of our faith. What is now required is to respond in faith to the gospel message by confessing that Jesus is Lord and by believing that God raised him from the dead (**10:8-9**). That is all it takes. It is this belief and this confession that bring salvation (**10:10**; see also Acts 16:31; 1 Cor 12:3; Phil 2:11).

Second, this righteousness is accessible to anyone who believes: *Anyone who trusts in him will never be put to shame* (**10:11**). That is how available the gospel is to both Jews and Gentiles (**10:12-13**). Paul quotes a familiar passage from Joel 2:32, making the point that everyone who calls on the name of the Lord will be saved. While Joel was speaking only to Jews, his words now also apply to Gentiles. Accepting Christ is the factor that unites people of all backgrounds.

Third, to attain this righteousness, one has to hear the gospel. In **10:14-15a**, Paul asks four rhetorical questions, identifying steps that have to be taken for any person to come to faith. The steps are, first, the sending of preachers; second, the preaching of the good news; third, the hearing of the message preached; and fourth, the response to the message, which is believing in Christ and calling on the name of the Lord. These steps show that those who have already confessed Christ and believed in him will be used by God to help others hear the same message. Every believer must be involved in some of the above steps if others are to hear the message of God's salvation. Paul quotes Isaiah 52:7 to indicate that those who bring good news to others are blessed (**10:15b**).

10:14-21 Israel's accountability

But not all the Israelites had *accepted the good news* (**10:16**). In fact, the majority of them had rejected it. Paul is reminded of Isaiah's lament, *Lord, who has believed our message?* (Isa 53:1). Some might argue that the Israelites are not really guilty because they did not adequately hear the message of salvation. But Paul rejects this argument by asking another rhetorical question: Did they not hear? And he answers immediately: Of course, they did (**10:17-18**). He quotes Psalm 19:4 to explain that the Israelites had the same exposure to natural revelation as everyone else. More than that, Moses, the lawgiver, and Isaiah, the prophet, had warned them that they would reject the message of God and that God would extend his grace to the Gentiles (**10:19-20**; see also Deut 32:21; Isa 65:1). *Those who are not a nation* (the Gentiles) will receive and accept the good news of God's salvation and their response will arouse Israel's jealousy and anger. Paul concludes by quoting Isaiah 65:2 to make the point that while the Israelites have been disobedient, God in his grace has not abandoned them. God continues to hold out his hand to them, constantly inviting them to come back to him (**10:21**).

11:1-10 Summary: A Remnant Chosen by Grace

The condemnation of Israel in 9:30-10:21 prompts Paul to come back to the fate of Israel. Has God completely rejected them? (**11:1**). *By no means!* After all, Paul, the apostles and the other early believers were all Jewish. *God did not reject his people, whom he foreknew* (**11:2a**). God had established a special relationship with Israel as the nation through whom the nations of the world would come to know him. Paul reminds his readers of a historical precedent. Elijah long ago had thought that he was the only remaining God-fearing Jew (**11:2b-3**). God informed him that seven thousand others had not *bowed the knee to Baal* (**11:4**; 1 Kgs 19:14, 18). As in the time of Elijah, God has not rejected all Jews but has chosen a faithful remnant with whom he still works. There are Jewish believers (**11:5**). They are not chosen because of human effort (works) but totally on the basis of God's grace (**11:6**).

When we face conflicts, we are sometimes tempted to believe that we are alone in standing for God and become discouraged. We need to remember that God has his people, his remnant, even in difficult situations.

But what about the other Jews, the majority of the Israelites, who had rejected God's grace and been hardened (**11:7**)? Paul uses three OT passages to explain the hardening of their hearts. In **11:8**, he combines Deuteronomy 29:3-4 and Isaiah 29:10 to demonstrate that the hardening

of the heart means deafness, numbness or blindness. The majority of Jews had become insensitive, spiritually drowsy about what God was doing for them and for all of humanity through Christ. In **11:9-10** Paul quotes Psalm 69:22-23 to say that what God intended for Israel's blessing had become a trap to them. Their eyes were darkened so that they could not see what God was doing.

It is a dreadful situation to be the object of God's hardening rather than of his convicting ministry. May that never happen to any of us! It is, however, our own choice. If we hear and obey, we will be among those who receive God's favour.

11:11-32 The Future of Israel

11:11-24 God's purpose in Israel's temporary rejection

The previous section (11:1-10) ended on a negative note. The Israelites' hearts had been hardened and their blessings had become a curse as they refused to accept Christ. Paul asks yet another question, *Did they stumble so as to fall beyond recovery?* Once again, Paul answers with a firm negative, *Not at all!* (**11:11a**). The present state of the majority of the Israelites is a temporary one that is part of God's plan to make it possible for Gentiles to come to salvation and thereby make Israel envious, bringing them back to their God through Christ (**11:11b**). The salvation of the Gentiles is not the end of God's plan for Israel. For if the temporary fall of Israel has become a blessing for the Gentiles, then Israel's restoration will bring an even greater blessing for the world (**11:12**).

In 11:13-15, Paul makes the point to Gentile Christians that his call to preach to the Gentiles should not be interpreted as meaning that God had abandoned the Jews. He makes it clear that his purpose in stressing that he is *the apostle to the Gentiles* is to *somehow arouse* the Jews to jealousy in order to *save some of them* (**11:13-14**). Therefore, Gentile believers should not consider themselves superior to Jewish believers in the church at Rome. For if God's rejection of Israel has brought salvation to the Gentiles, *their acceptance* will bring far greater blessings when Israel is brought from death to life (**11:15**). Paul may here be speaking of a still greater spiritual awakening or of the resurrection of the dead at the last day.

We may not understand all that Paul is trying to say here, but his warning is clear. Gentile believers must welcome Jewish believers and vice versa, for neither is superior to the other in God's sight. Because God has opened the door of salvation to us all, we must learn to accept one another and live as brothers and sisters.

Paul uses two metaphors to illustrate his argument that Israel has a great future. His point is that what happens to one part of something affects the whole. In the first metaphor, taken from the instructions for making an offering in

Numbers 15:17-21, *the part of the dough offered* may refer to the Jewish Christians of Paul's time, and *the whole batch* to Israel. The salvation of the few shows that God still considers the rest holy, set apart for the Lord. In the second illustration of a tree, the *root* of the tree is probably Israel's patriarchs, and the Israelites are the branches. God's promises to the patriarchs continue; Israel is still set apart for God's purpose, and this special relationship gives Paul hope for their future salvation (**11:16**).

Paul now becomes even more explicit in warning the Gentile Christians who were boasting about their salvation and looking down on Jewish Christians (**11:17-22**). He insists that if Jews do not persist in their unbelief, *they will be grafted in, for God is able to graft them in again* (**11:23**). In fact, Paul argues that it is easier for the natural branches (Jews) to be grafted back into the olive tree from which they were cut than it is for Gentiles to be grafted into that tree (**11:24**). All rests with God – whether his kindness in response to the Gentiles' belief or his sternness in response to Israel's unbelief. Gentile believers must keep this in mind. God's kindness must not lead them to conclude that they merited his treatment of them. It is his kindness that has led them to becoming part of his family, and that kindness also calls for continued obedience (10:22). Faith is not a rewarded act but a response to what God has done through Christ.

11:25-32 The salvation of all Israel

The discussion in chapters 9–11 culminates in this section, where Paul discloses what he calls a mystery, that is, something which was hidden and is now revealed through the gospel (16:25; 1 Cor 2:7; Eph 6:19; Col 2:2; 1 Tim 3:16). The mystery he reveals here is that *Israel has experienced a hardening in part until the full number of the Gentiles has come in. And so all Israel will be saved* (**11:25**).

In the end, God will fulfil his plan for the salvation of his people. Israel's hardening is partial and temporary. God has planned that once the full number of the Gentiles have come to salvation, Israel's hardening will end (**11:26-27**). Mark informs us that before this will happen, the gospel must first be preached to all nations (Mark 13:10).

The statement that 'all Israel will be saved' has been understood in various ways. Some view 'Israel' here as referring to the church (Gal 6:16), the spiritual Israel. Others think that 'all Israel' refers only to those Jews God has chosen out of the Jewish people. Still others interpret the phrase as referring to everyone in the nation of Israel. In the ot (for example, in 2 Sam 16:22), 'all Israel' is used to describe some Israelites as representatives of the rest, and this seems to be the way it is used here.

It seems likely that Paul is referring to the salvation of a great number of Jews at the time of the return of Christ. This remnant who believe will join Gentile believers in inheriting the kingdom of God. As far as election is concerned, God has not rejected Israel because of the promise he made to the patriarchs, which he cannot change (**11:28-29**). In fact, Paul concludes, both Gentiles and Jews are disobedient to God and only by God's mercy will any of them be accepted (**11:30-32**).

11:33-36 Conclusion: Praise to God for His Wisdom

Paul bursts into a song of praise to God as he concludes his exposition of God's sovereign, mysterious and gracious plan for the salvation of human beings, and such adoration is the best way to end. God's wisdom and knowledge are far too deep for us to comprehend. They are unsearchable, beyond tracing out. God's plan for his creation is beyond our understanding; nobody can penetrate the depth of the riches of God's wisdom and knowledge (**11:33**). In **11:34-35** Paul quotes from Isaiah 40:13 and Job 41:11 to show that nobody can really know the mind of God, that nobody can be his counsellor.

Whatever God does for us, he does not do because he owes anything to anybody, but solely out of his grace. Because God gives life to everything, sustains everything and determines the purpose of everything (**11:36**), he deserves to be forever glorified. The believers' constant song to such a God must be, 'To God be the glory, great things he has done!'

12:1-15:13 The Transformed Life of Believers

Chapter 11 marks the end of the doctrinal section of the book of Romans. In chapters 12 to 15, Paul moves on to the practical implications of what he has said. What God has done must be translated into action in the lives of those who have experienced his salvation in Christ. But until we are moved by the majesty of God, as Paul has been, we will not be able to understand and live out the consequences of his love for us. That is why Paul follows his song of praise to God with a resounding *Therefore* (12:1).

12:1-2 Appeal for Total Consecration

Because of what God has done for us, or what Paul calls *God's mercy* (described in chapters 1-11), the best we can give to him is our selves, by presenting our *bodies as living sacrifices* (**12:1**). The offering of the living bodies of believers as sacrifices contrasts with the ot offerings of dead animals. Here the word 'body' represents far more than just our belongings or our money. It means the totality of our life, plans and activities. The offering of ourselves is a spiritual act of worship that we can give to God.

Through our bodies we express what we think, what we have and how we live. Thus Paul can also refer to this sacrifice as *the renewing of your mind* (**12:2a**; Eph 4:23; 2 Cor 4:16; Col 3:10; Titus 3:5). This renewing is an internal process, a reorientation of our world view as we seek to live the way Christ lived and to think as he thought. By offering our bodies to God, we are offering him our minds. Nothing is left behind to conform to the pattern of this world.

Once we have made this sacrifice, we are ready for his service. Only when we live this transformed life will we be able to please God and discover and enjoy God's perfect will (**12:2b**). It is, thus, not surprising that 12:1-2 forms the foundation of all that Paul will call believers to be and to do in the chapters that follow.

12:3-8 Humility and Service in the Body of Christ

In 12:3-15:13, Paul deals with living a transformed life in the church and society. As Christians, we live in the community of believers, which is here described as the body of Christ. Believers must learn to live side by side. The first thing they must watch out for is pride (**12:3**). Because we are all equal before God, no group or individual can claim to be better than others. We are all saved by grace through faith. Pride undermines unity in the church. God has given each believer a measure of faith, so that he or she can function as God intended. Believers should act in terms of the measure of faith God has given them, and must take care not to think too highly or too little of themselves.

To explain what he means, Paul compares the church to a human body, which has many different parts. Each part has a different function, and all parts need to work together if the body is to function well (**12:4-5**). Thus, *each member belongs to all the others* (12:5).

Paul lists different gifts that God has given to different believers to enable them to serve the community (12:6-8). This list is not intended to cover every possible gift but to make a point: serve the community with the ability God has given you. Paul encourages Christians to use their gifts to build up the church.

The first gift listed is *prophecy* (**12:6**). In the NT, prophecy is an inspired utterance of truth that guides the church (1 Cor 14:26, 30). It is an outward expression of a conviction (*faith*) that has come to us as we meditate on the word of God and it is in conformity with God's inward voice, that of the indwelling Holy Spirit. While the prophetic word may relate to the future, it often concerns a present situation. It is not necessarily about oneself, but may be about others and church or world events. The focus of a prophecy will not be on what brings glory to the prophet (such as foretelling how long rulers will rule, who will win elections and the like), but on what God is interested in (for example, the effect that a particular decision will have on the state of a local church). God may speak about subjects that appear insignificant to the rest of the world.

Prophecy can easily be abused. The one practising it may try to show off by adding to what God has laid on his or her heart as a message for others. Then, even if God in his grace permits that prophecy to be fulfilled, it will not honour him because it is not born of obedience. Thus, the gift of prophecy is a responsibility to be handled with care, and prophets should speak no more than the specific conviction the Lord has given them.

Unfortunately, it is not uncommon in Africa to hear wild but vague prophetic utterances that those loyal to the prophet can interpret as having been fulfilled. Such careless speech brings prophecy as a whole into disrepute, and then mockery causes some who may have received genuine conviction to shy away from expressing it in public. Paul encourages the Romans to use the gift God has given them.

The second gift is that of *service* to provide for the needs of the community (**12:7a**; see also Acts 6:1-6). The next two gifts, *teaching* and *encouraging* (**12:7b-8a**), are related. Teaching here refers to the transmission of the truth contained in the gospel. Encouragement or exhortation may relate to the activity of encouraging suffering Christians or those who are not living according to God's word. Another gift is that of *contributing to the needs of others* (**12:8b**). This gift relates to helping needy members within or even outside the church community. The one who has this gift should exercise it generously, but without making a show of his or her liberality. Then follows the gift of *leadership* (**12:8c**), referring primarily to leadership in the church as elders (see 1 Thess 5:12; 1 Tim 5:17). Paul instructs leaders to lead diligently. The inclusion of this gift, which is not found in the more extensive listing in 1 Corinthians 12 and 14, is a clear indication that none of the lists is meant to be exhaustive.

Finally, Paul mentions the gift of *showing mercy* (**12:8d**). Those with this gift are sensitive to the needs of other members of the community, particularly those who are suffering in some way.

The gifts must not be used selfishly, as they are given to build up the community. No one can have all the gifts, for such a person would be too self-sufficient. The community of believers must help each other to discover and use their gifts. Often these gifts may be what we most enjoy doing for the Lord or what we are able to do well enough to bless others. We do not need to attend a seminar to discover our gifts; all we need is a community in which we have an opportunity to exercise them. My gift relates more to what my heart is most comfortable doing than to what I have listed on paper even though my heart does not feel like doing it. The Designer who gives these gifts is also the one who has made us the way we are and who has provided us with the opportunities that shape us into what we are. At the same time, we should all realize that no one gift is more important than the others. God created us to relate to one another, and we need one another in the body of Christ.

12:9-21 Love in Social Relationships

This section contains a long list of short instructions to Christians on how to live harmoniously in society. These instructions call for a peaceful attitude and co-existence in the church (12:10, 13, 16) and in society at large (12:14, 17-21). The most important virtue for a harmonious life is love, which must be genuine, not hypocritical (**12:9a**). The remainder of this section is an elaboration on what genuine love is. In other words, 12:9-21 defines true or sincere love.

In **12:9b**, sincere love is defined as hating what is evil and clinging to what is good. This definition rules out our simplistic idea of love as an emotion or sentiment. True love is something we must learn to practise. It demands that we care for one another wholeheartedly and put the interests of others before our own interests (**12:10**).

Paul also encourages Christians not to be lazy in serving the Lord, but to keep their passion for his service; to always rejoice in the living hope; to support each other in prayer and to demonstrate patience and endurance in times of tribulation (**12:11-12**). He concludes this group of instructions by returning to a point he has mentioned in 12:10: Christians have a social responsibility to share their material goods with needy members of the community of faith. The exhortations to *share with God's people who are in need* and to *practise hospitality* (**12:13**) refer to material help. Those who 'have' must share with the 'have-nots'. Christian hospitality focuses on taking care of strangers and guests. Our homes, hearts and pockets must be open to serve them.

In 12:14-16, Paul slightly changes the subject, focusing on how a Christian can demonstrate love by responding to the actions and emotions of others, both Christians and non-Christians. In other words, the question here is, How should we demonstrate love in a hostile world? To do this, Paul urges his fellow believers to bless those who persecute them, stressing that a Christian should bless and not curse (**12:14**). Through such a response Christians will demonstrate to both insiders and outsiders that they possess a genuine love that is different from what the world offers. These words remind us of Jesus' teaching in the Sermon on the Mount (Matt 5:44; Luke 6:27-28), of his response to his persecutors in Luke 23:34 and of Stephen's words in Acts 7:59-60.

In **12:15** Paul recommends that Christians identify with others, both believers and unbelievers, in their joy and in their suffering (1 Cor 12:26). Such identification is a mark of true love, a clear sign that we are not selfish and careless but concerned for others.

In a sense, **12:16** summarizes this section of exhortations. Paul recommends that Christians live in harmony with one another. Living a harmonious life involves exercising both spiritual and social prudence in the way we think of and deal with others. Paul has rightly perceived that the most dangerous enemy of social harmony and genuine love is pride, which is defined as the tendency not to associate with people we consider to be of low status. Pride is also characterized by the tendency to think highly of ourselves. Therefore, Paul urges believers not to be proud but to always be willing to associate with people of low position.

Paul's exhortations in 12:17-21 relate primarily to Christians in their relationship with unbelievers. He urges Christians not to repay evil with evil if someone has caused them harm. By contrast, he calls them *to do what is right in the eyes of everybody* (**12:17**). Going beyond the simple avoidance of vengeance, he tells Christians to live in peace, as far as this depends on them. Here Paul recognizes that it is not always possible to *live at peace with everyone* (**12:18**) because this does not always depend on us. But believers should not be the ones responsible for any lack of peace in their communities or in their relationships with unbelievers.

The apostle appeals to his fellow believers to avoid vengeance because vengeance belongs to God (**12:19**; see also Deut 32:35). Christians should go beyond simply avoiding conflict and should show true love for their enemies through concrete actions such as feeding them when they are hungry and giving them something to drink when they are thirsty. By providing for the needs of our enemies, we will heap burning coals on their heads (**12:20**; see also Prov 25:21-22). Our kindness may make our enemies ashamed of their actions and persuade them to abandon their evil deeds.

We are living in a world dominated by evil. Thus the apostle concludes the chapter by appealing to Christians to remain alert and not to *be overcome by evil* but to overcome evil by doing good or by genuinely loving others (**12:21**).

Paul's advice on how to maintain harmony in the community involves Christians loving unconditionally, showing mercy and being willing to forgive. They must intervene with good motives where harmony has been lost and suffering prevails. The good of the other person must be their focus. Such love involves both a willingness and a conscious decision to constantly work or act for the good of others. It goes beyond an attitude of non-retaliation and seeks to do good even to those who do not love us. Such a demonstration of a different type of life, a Christian life, is badly needed in all corners of our continent, as is shown by the constant conflicts both in churches and in the community at large. If these principles are followed, Africa will be transformed into a community where peace and justice will prevail.

13:1-7 Submission to Civil Authority

Next, Paul writes to the Christians in Rome, the capital of the Roman Empire, about their relationship to the government. This issue is important because we sometimes tend to think that since we are Christians, and therefore belong to the kingdom of God, we have nothing to do with civil authorities. The Christians in Rome may have felt the same way. After all, Christ had been crucified by Roman authorities, and believers were often accused and persecuted by civil authorities.

In spite of this, Paul insists that believers must *submit ... to the governing authorities* (**13:1**), that is, to all those who represent the power of the state, from local authorities to the Roman emperor himself. We need to recognize our subordinate place in a hierarchical system. Certain institutions and people have been placed over us by God, and they have the right to our respect. Anyone who *rebels against the authority* that God has put in place can be said to be *rebelling against what God has instituted* and can expect punishment for such disobedience (**13:2**).

It is important to note that this submission does not mean that we must blindly obey an order from the state that

THE CHURCH AND THE STATE

This article focuses on the relationship between organized bodies of believers and the political state. The relationship between individual believers and the state is dealt with in the article 'Christians and Politics'.

A state is the body that governs the people within a given area. It operates at the local or municipal level, the regional or state level, and the national or federal level. To be able to govern, the state must have the right to rule and the rulers must be accountable to someone. The state must also have laws and the authority to punish those who break these laws. Finally, the government must be relatively stable; that is, it should be able to exist for some time.

The Bible makes it clear that the right to rule is not rooted in the consent of the governed but derives from God (Dan 5:21). Rulers are thus accountable to him, even if they refuse to acknowledge this fact. The state is to protect all its citizens, administer punishment, restrain evil, and promote peace and justice and the general welfare of its citizens (Rom 13:1-5).

Christians disagree on the correct relationship between the church and the state. Some argue for separation. Mission-related Bible churches and traditional evangelical churches tend to view the church and the state as unique institutions with different functions and roles that should not interfere with each other. When taken to an extreme, separation becomes isolation, as with the Jehovah's Witnesses.

Others, particularly in the mainline denominations (Anglicans, Methodists, Presbyterians, Orthodox and Roman Catholics), support transformation. They argue that Christians are called to exert a Christian influence on the state or society and transform it on the basis of biblical values and principles. This attitude can even lead to a situation like that in Zambia, where former president Chiluba declared it a Christian nation.

Finally, supporters of Liberation Theology in Latin America and Black Theology in South Africa and many African-American theologians in the USA argue that the church must work for radical change and promote human rights and the liberation of the oppressed. This approach is difficult to put into practice.

The Bible sees the church as having three functions in relation to the state:

- *A priestly function*: The church must pray for those in authority and for the protection and healing of the nation (1 Tim 2:1-3).

- *A pastoral function*: The church must provide teaching, counselling and direction to the authorities and to those governed (Matt 28:19-29). Thus the church should encourage Christians to be good citizens who obey the authorities and pay their taxes (Rom 13:1,7; 1 Pet 2:13). However, this does not mean that the church can prescribe the details of what authorities must do or of the actions citizens should take, provided their actions are not contrary to God's word.

- *A prophetic function*: The church must rebuke and oppose the state when it turns against God or acts unjustly (2 Sam 12:1-14; Dan 4:20-27; 5:17-28). When it comes to a showdown between Christians and political leaders, our absolute obedience must be to God (Acts 5:29). Such obedience can be costly. The Ugandan church was persecuted for protesting against the tyrannical rule of Idi Amin and in the process Archbishop Luwum was assassinated. Numerous other examples abound across the continent.

Good governance must comply with God's laws that govern his creation and humanity. Thus every state should recognize its moral accountability to God and its citizens and the solidarity and equality of everyone within the state. States should also honour and respect the freedoms that citizens have historically enjoyed and that are necessary for effective political and economic development and participation. Recognizing the reality of their own limitations and the power of sin, states must also be willing to place limits on economic and political power in order to prevent such power being abused.

In many areas such as education, health and development, there is an overlap between the state's responsibility to provide for the welfare of its citizens and the church's desire to serve others. In these areas, the church and the state have often entered into constructive partnerships.

Yusufu Turaki

is evil or goes against Christ's command to love our neighbours. While the citizen is to obey the authorities, those authorities must obey God. Thus, if they stop rewarding good and punishing evil, and, instead, order the opposite, they lose the moral right to expect obedience.

In **13:3** Paul continues to make the point that civil authorities have been set in place to promote stability in society. Therefore, Christians must do what is right if they want to avoid judgment or punishment (**13:4**). But fear of punishment should not be the only reason we submit to civil authorities. We should also do so because of our consciences (**13:5**). In other words, our consciences should tell us that God, who is the ultimate authority, has established a hierarchy and set rulers in place to maintain stability and order, and that to resist them is to resist God's plan for a stable society. Christian responsibility also involves paying taxes to the state (**13:6**), which allows the civil authorities, identified as God's servants, to devote their time to their ministry of leadership.

In his concluding remark (**13:7**), Paul commands believers to give everyone what they owe them. In the context of this entire paragraph, 'everyone' probably means the civil authorities. And what Christians and non-Christians alike owe these authorities are taxes, revenue, respect (or fear, as in the KJV) and honour. These must be paid to our governments.

13:8-10 Love as the Fulfilment of the Law

Paul has been speaking about the need for Christians to pay whatever they owe to civil authorities. He continues with the topic of debt, but enriches it by adding that Christians are not allowed to have any outstanding debt, except for *the continuing debt to love one another* (**13:8**). He is not condemning the idea of paying for something in instalments; rather, he is speaking of the failure to pay others what is rightly theirs. The expression 'one another' may refer to both Christians and non-Christians.

Love fulfils all the other commandments and *does no harm to its neighbour* (**13:9-10**). In other words, if we genuinely love, we will not only obey the explicit commandments of the Mosaic law but will avoid doing anything that may harm others. If all believers practise genuine love, we will lead peaceful but transforming revolutions in our nations.

13:11-14 Living as Children of Light

And do this in **13:11** connects this paragraph with the preceding section (12:1-13:10). It marks the conclusion of the first part of Paul's teaching on Christian living and loving, which he started in 12:1-2.

The consciousness that we are living in the end time and that the return of the Lord Jesus Christ is imminent must stimulate Christians to live a transformed life. The knowledge that our salvation is near, that *the day is almost here,* must be enough to wake us from sleep so we start living as the people of God (13:11-12). The *night* in which the Christians are sleeping is the present evil age, a time of darkness and evil. It contrasts with the coming day, the Day of the Lord, when Christ will intervene to save his people and to judge his enemies. It will be a day of perfect joy for the people of God. Therefore, says Paul, Christians need to prepare themselves by putting *aside the deeds of darkness* and by putting on *the armour of light,* that is, by living as examples in this evil age (**13:12**). Decent living must characterize the children of light (**13:13**). They must avoid behaviour such as orgies, drunkenness, sexual immorality and debauchery, quarrelling and jealousy.

The conclusion in **13:14** strengthens the contrast between the behaviour of Christians living in anticipation of the imminent return of the Lord Jesus Christ and that of non-Christians who are *gratifying the desires of the sinful nature.* We need to consciously and constantly put on Christ, that is, decide to live under his lordship and allow Christ to control all aspects of our lives.

14:1-15:13 Living in Unity

Relationships with fellow believers can sometimes be difficult to maintain. However, our unity as a people of God and in the church is vital if the mission of the church is to succeed. Therefore, Paul addresses some sensitive issues that had the potential to destroy the fellowship among believers. Some were issues of tolerance about things on which they were not agreed, such as eating or not eating meat, observing special holidays and the like.

Given our different backgrounds, there are many potential areas of disagreement. Just as Paul addressed those of his time and context, so we need to address those of our time and context.

14:1-12 Living in unity without judging one another

In the Roman church, the Christians had divided into two groups regarding some issues. Paul refers to one group as the weak in faith, implying that others are strong in faith. Paul is concerned that the strong are not accepting the weak, and urges them to *Accept him whose faith is weak* (**14:1**). Those weak in the faith felt that they must do some things and abstain from others to stay close to God. Because of the role of the law in their past, many Jewish believers probably fell into this group, although they would not have been the only ones in it. One of the areas about which there was disagreement was food, particularly the eating of meat (14:21). The weak were probably those who put some restrictions on their diet by eating only vegetables (**14:2**). Those who were 'strong' would argue that such scruples were unnecessary, and that what one eats or does not eat has nothing to do with one's relationship with God.

In this context, the 'strong' were probably the Gentiles, who were the majority in the Roman church.

The strong Christians despised the weak and the weak condemned the strong (**14:3**). Paul urges both groups to stop passing judgment on one another. The strong must honour the weaks' concern about harming their relationship with God. Weak believers must receive tender care so that their faith is not harmed. The weak, for their part, are cautioned not to judge that those who do not obey the same restrictions as they do are sinning. Instead of judging and criticizing each other, these groups must tolerate and accept one another just as God has accepted them in Christ.

God had accepted all the Roman believers as his servants. And the only person to whom servants have to give an account of their actions is their employer (**14:4**). God is the one to judge whether their service pleases him or not. If a servant's work is not satisfactory, the master will dismiss him from his service, so that *he falls*. However, Paul has just been teaching the believers that God accepts people not because of what they do but on the basis of their relationship with the Lord Jesus Christ. Even the weak believers pass that test of acceptance, and so Paul has no doubt that they will be able to *stand* before God. The only ones who will fall (fail) are those who do not have a saving relationship with Christ.

Paul's reminder that faith cannot be evaluated on the basis of what someone eats or does not eat applies today, though now the argument is often more about what someone drinks or does not drink. All believers agree that alcoholic drinks can be dangerous, but some refuse to drink any alcohol, while others drink in moderation. Those who do not drink have tended to label those who do drink (even if no more than a glass on a special occasion) as not being 'true Christians'. While strict abstinence has undeniable benefits, a believer who drinks is still a brother or sister in the Lord. Saving faith may lead us to abstain from some things, but abstaining is not what determines our standing before God. That is based only on our faith in Christ.

In **14:5-9**, Paul deals with a second issue causing division – considering particular days more sacred than others. The days were probably the Jewish Sabbath and other festivals in the Jewish calendar. What Paul says to the Romans applies directly to the way we treat others in relation to what they do or do not do on Sunday and other such 'holy' days. We are not to judge those who study, open shop or do other such things after the service on Sunday. Paul's appeal for tolerance is based on the fact that both weak Christians (who observe special days and restrict what they eat) and strong believers (who do not observe these restrictions) were trying to please God. In other words, their perception of the issues may have been wrong (see Paul's comments in 14:4, 20), but their desire to please God through observance or non-observance of particular days was quite sincere.

Because no Christian lives for himself or herself, but for Christ who died for each one, and because both the strong and the weak were acting out of love and reverence for their Lord, nobody is allowed to judge someone else by dictating what is right and what is wrong. Only Christ, their Lord and Master, can do this.

14:10-12 concludes this first part of the argument. We will all stand before God's judgment seat. Therefore, judgment should be left to him. Paul quotes Isaiah 45:23 to underline that judgment belongs to God alone. He is Lord and judge over all. We should not usurp his role by judging others on trivial matters like eating or not eating.

14:13-23 Living in unity without offending one another

The question now arises as to what to do when something one Christian thinks is right becomes an obstacle for fellow believers. Paul's response is simple: *make up your mind not to put any stumbling block or obstacle in your brother's way* (**14:13**). Some believers were uncaring; their freedom not only caused offence but also caused other Christians to stumble; that is, it tripped them up and made them fall. Whether we are strong and insensitive to others, or weak and petty about trivial rules, we can become the reason that fellow believers fall into sin. Paul urges us to not cause problems for others (**14:14-16**). On the contrary, we are to serve Christ by maintaining peace among believers. What is important for the kingdom of God is not food and drink but righteousness, peace, harmony and joy in the Holy Spirit (**14:17-18**).

Paul concludes this section with the exhortation to *make every effort to do what leads to peace and to mutual edification* (**14:19**). We must live in a way that promotes peace and builds up the community of believers, which is more important than our freedom. To put it differently, we should not destroy the community of believers, which is the work of God, because of our personal opinions, which often cause disagreement. The problem is not with the cleanness and uncleanness of food but with our causing fellow believers to stumble (**14:20-21**).

Paul concludes **14:22-23** by stating three important principles. First, there are times when we should not voice our opinions if we know that they will offend others. This principle does not mean that we must always keep silent, but that we must wait for an opportunity or a time when we can express our opinions in a way that will build others up, not break them down. For example, there is sometimes controversy about whether we should all speak in tongues. It is wise for a pastor not to belabour the arguments for or against this position when preaching to a general congregation. The place for discussing this controversy might be a Bible study group where everyone is seeking to find out what the Bible teaches.

Paul's second principle is that, whatever we do, we must make sure that we are not acting against our own consciences. His third is that nobody should force fellow believers to act against their consciences.

15:1-13 Unity of the strong and the weak in Christ

15:1-6 PUTTING OTHERS FIRST Believers' relationships with one another, especially in matters of opinion that divided the community, were so important to Paul that he also deals with the issue in chapter 15. These chapters are important for us because unless we know how to deal with different opinions, they will divide us, destroy the community and weaken our testimonies.

In chapter 14, Paul distinguished between strong and weak believers. Now he identifies himself with the strong members of the church (**15:1**), thus placing himself on the side of those who were creating problems in the community and enabling him to speak more freely to them as someone who is in the same position. He appeals to strong Christians *to bear with the failings of the weak* and not to please themselves. They must not merely tolerate the weak; they must patiently and tenderly identify with them as much as possible, sacrificially accommodating the limitations of the weak members of the church (**15:2**). By so doing, the strong will be following the example of Jesus, who gave up his rights and put the interests of others before his own when he suffered and died for us (**15:3**). Paul quotes Psalm 69:9 to support his point, showing that Christ's being willing to suffer for others was an essential part of his mission.

Paul reminds his readers that the record in the Scriptures, whose focus is Christ and the example he has set, is meant to build the virtues of endurance and encouragement in our lives (**15:4**). Maintaining these virtues will help to maintain the unity of believers and to glorify God.

Paul concludes this short paragraph with a prayer that God, the giver of endurance and encouragement, will give the Roman believers *a spirit of unity* as they *follow Christ Jesus* (**15:5**). As a result of such unity, the believers will be able to glorify the Lord together (**15:6**). The prayers and worship of believers united in heart is sweet music in the ears of God. It is a testimony to the world that we belong to Jesus and that the Father is displaying his love in us, as he has done in Jesus. This unity is so important that Jesus specifically prayed for it (17:22-23).

When Jews and Gentiles, strong and weak, and men and women from different races and tribes can unite in Christ and glorify God, unbelievers are amazed and say, 'If such different people can be so united, their God must mean a lot to them.' Believers, let us set aside our differences and proclaim the love of Christ through our unity. Our differences were meant to glorify God and not to tear us apart.

15:7-13 ACCEPTING ONE ANOTHER *Accept one another, then, just as Christ accepted you, in order to bring praise to God* (**15:7**).

This exhortation sums up the teaching on love, acceptance and tolerance in chapters 14 and 15. The command is simple and clear: accept one another. Our model is Christ, who accepted us unconditionally. In dealing with one another in the community of believers, especially when trying to find solutions to issues that divide us, we must take Christ as our example. We have no right to reject others because Christ himself has accepted us as we are, with our weaknesses. Through his servanthood, Christ has presented a model of perfect unity among Jews and Gentiles (**15:8**). Paul argues that the Gentile Christians must not forget that the Jews were accepted first through the promises to the patriarchs. At the same time, the Jewish Christians should remember that through Christ, God has accepted the Gentiles so that they can join the Jews in praising him. Paul offers a series of OT quotations to demonstrate that God has long planned to extend his grace to the Gentiles so that they might be united with the Jews in praise (Ps 18:49 in **15:9**; Deut 32:43 in **15:10**; Ps 117:1 in **15:11**; Isa 11:10 in **15:12**). Paul wants the Roman Christians to transcend their cultural differences and build a united and harmonious church rooted in the values of the gospel.

Paul concludes this paragraph with another prayer in which he asks God to fill the Roman Christians with joy and peace so that they *may overflow with hope by the power of the Holy Spirit* (**15:13**). As they trust in God and seek his help for unity, they will be filled with the Holy Spirit, who will enable them to live in harmony.

15:14-16:27 Conclusion

Paul ends the body of his letter in 15:13 with a prayer for the church in Rome. Unlike his other letters, this letter has a very lengthy conclusion, perhaps because he has never visited the Roman church.

15:14-22 Paul's Ministry

Paul starts the conclusion by telling the Roman Christians that he considers them mature Christians, *full of goodness, complete in knowledge and competent to instruct one another* (**15:14**). In case they wondered why he had written so boldly (sometimes coming close to issuing a rebuke) about basic issues such as unity, he says he was reminding them of what they already knew (**15:15**). However, Paul may simply be being tactful and diplomatic when writing to people he had never visited and or ministered to in person.

Paul then makes a second point: God has given him grace to be a minister of Christ to Gentiles to bring them to God. The apostle thinks of himself as a priest who presents the Gentile Christians before God as an acceptable sacrifice, purified by the Holy Spirit (**15:16**).

The apostle affirms further that he glories in Christ in his service to God (**15:17-19**). He is not boasting of his achievements as a minister of the gospel, but he acknowledges that he has accomplished so much only because Jesus Christ has been working through him and performing signs and miracles. This is why he has been able to courageously proclaim the gospel *from Jerusalem all the way around to Illyricum* (also called Dalmatia; see Acts 20:2; 2 Tim 4:10). His ambition was to preach the gospel where it had never been preached before (**15:20**). God had given Paul a special ministry among the Gentiles, to preach the gospel where people had never heard the good news. He quotes Isaiah 52:15 as a confirmation of the special commission given to him by God: *Those who were not told about him will see; and those who have not heard will understand* (**15:21**).

15:23-33 Paul's Future Plans

Paul has been very busy preaching the gospel in Asia Minor and establishing churches among the Gentiles there. Now he feels that his work in that region is over, probably because churches have been widely planted there (**15:23**). These local churches will be able to expand their ministry. So Paul describes his plans; he is turning his attention to Rome and to Europe in general, and specifically to Spain (**15:24**). On his way to Spain, he will need to stop in Rome to visit and encourage the believers there (and probably to discuss some of the issues he has raised in this letter). He will also need support from the Roman Christians to help him in his ministry in this new field. But before he starts on this journey, he needs to go to Jerusalem. He has to deliver the money that the Gentile churches in Macedonia and Achaia have donated to help the Christians in Jerusalem, who were suffering from poverty (**15:25-27**; 1 Cor 16:1-3; 2 Cor 9:9). The mention of this money sent by Gentile Christians to help Jewish churches also serves to foster unity and fellowship between these two groups by reminding the Gentile Christians (who had contributed) that they owe their spiritual blessings to Jews (4:11-13; 15:7, 9; 16:17). By helping Jewish Christians, the Gentile Christians can acknowledge the blessing they share with them.

The offering that Paul was taking to Jerusalem endorsed his message about unity and mutual support among Christians. We, too, must be willing to pool our resources to help churches in troubled areas on the continent as a way of demonstrating our unity and shared faith.

Paul ends this section with an invitation to Roman Christians to join him in prayer (**15:30-33**). Specifically, they are to pray that he will be delivered from the unbelievers in Judea. These people are Jews who had rejected the good news and had become very hostile to Paul, the apostle to the Gentiles (see Acts 20:23). Second, Paul requests prayer that the gift he is bringing will not be rejected by some ultra-conservative Jewish Christians who might consider it as coming from unclean hands. Only after he has accomplished this mission will he be able to set out joyfully for

Rome. Paul concludes with a prayer that the God of peace will be with the Roman Christians.

We have an account of Paul's time in Jerusalem in Acts 21:27-28:16. Things did not go as well as Paul had hoped, and yet that did not stop him from seeing things from God's perspective. Paul did get to Rome and preached there, although not in the way he had envisioned. Later, writing from prison in Rome, he was able to say that the events the Lord had allowed to happen had advanced the cause of the gospel (Phil 1:12).

Like him, we must learn to see all that happens from God's perspective. At times, it may take a long journey and difficult experiences (for Paul it involved a journey from Jerusalem to Rome as a prisoner) before we can draw God's purpose from it, but God remains good and in control.

16:1-16 Greetings

As a good pastor, Paul has the Romans in his heart and knows by name a number of the believers who are in Rome. This long list of people to be greeted makes the letter very personal and friendly.

He starts by asking them to welcome Phoebe, a woman identified as a sister in the Lord (**16:1**). She was also *a servant of the church at Cenchrea*, an area located not far from Corinth (Acts 18:18). The identification of Phoebe as a sister in the Lord, a servant and someone who has been a great help to many in the church (**16:2**) probably means that she was an influential Christian and held an important position, probably as a deacon. However, some commentators think that Phoebe may even have been the minister or pastor of the church at Cenchrea, for the term *doulos,* translated as 'servant', is one that Paul often uses when speaking of himself. Phoebe was going to Rome and Paul may have asked her to deliver this letter for him. This verse is the basis for the suggestion that Romans was written from Corinth.

In 16:3-16, Paul sends greetings to twenty-six individual members of the Roman church and refers to many others (16:5, 10-11, 13-15). He first conveys his greetings to Priscilla and Aquila (**16:3-4**). Paul first met this couple in Corinth after they had fled from Rome (Acts 18:1-3). He had stayed with them in Corinth and they had ministered together there before they returned to Rome (Acts 18:18, 19, 26; 1 Cor 16:19). Paul adds that Priscilla and Aquila had risked their lives for him. In Acts, there is no specific reference to an occasion when this happened, although Paul may be referring to the riot in Ephesus (Acts 19:23-41). The greetings to Priscilla and Aquila are also extended to the church meeting in their house (**16:5a**). This may indicate that they were reasonably wealthy and owned a house large enough to serve as a place where believers could meet.

Epenetus (**16:5b**) is referred to as a *dear friend* and *the first convert to Christ in the province of Asia.* Paul knew him well – he may even have been converted through the apostle's ministry. The only information we have about Mary (**16:6**) is that Paul commends her for her very hard work for the church in Rome.

Another couple, Andronicus and Junias, are identified as Paul's relatives who had been imprisoned with him for the gospel (**16:7**). They are apostles who became Christians before Paul. The term 'apostle' used for Andronicus and Junias does not mean that they were among the twelve apostles, but that they worked as messengers (as did others, see 2 Cor 8:23; Phil 2:25) or had been commissioned as missionaries.

Paul mentions other Christians who are not known apart from this list. These are Ampliatus (**16:8**), Urbanus and Stachys (**16:9**), Apelles (**16:10**) and Herodion (**16:11a**). In **16:11b** Paul sends greetings to *those in the household of Narcissus who are in the Lord.* It may be that Narcissus himself was not a Christian but that some of his family members and slaves were. The list of Christians who are unknown to us continues in **16:12**. Those greeted include Tryphena, Tryphosa and Persis, all of whom are hard-working women and faithful in the ministry of the church. Rufus is greeted as *chosen in the Lord* (**16:13**). He may be one of the two sons of Simon of Cyrene, who was forced to carry Jesus' cross (Mark 15:21). Rufus's mother is said to have cared about Paul as if she were his own mother. Again, nothing is known about the people who are mentioned in **16:14-15** – Asyncritus, Phlegon, Hermes, Patrobas, Hermas, Philologus, Julia, Nereus and Olympas.

It is important to note that women were among the leading Christians during the time of Paul. In this chapter alone Paul mentions Phoebe (16:1-2), Priscilla (16:3), Mary (16:6), Junias (16:7), Tryphena and Tryphosa (16:12), Persis (16:12), Rufus's mother (16:13) and Julia (16:15). Most of these women are described as involved in significant ministries in the church, and far from disapproving of this, Paul strongly commends them for what they are doing.

Paul finally conveys greetings from all the churches of Christ, probably meaning all the churches he has planted (15:19). Though not all of these churches may have explicitly sent their greetings, Paul is showing that he has them all in his heart as one single body, the Body of Christ.

16:17-27 Final Words and Doxology

Paul opens this last part of the letter with an important warning regarding false teachers. He warns the Roman Christians *to watch out for those who cause divisions and put obstacles in your way that are contrary to the teaching you have learned* (**16:17**). Paul waits until the very end of his letter before he raises this important issue. The people who are causing division and making things difficult for Christians are working for their own interests and not for those of Christ (**16:18**). Their method of persuasion is *smooth talk.*

The reason why these people pose a danger to the Roman Christians is explained in **16:19**. The Roman Chris-

tians are known for their obedience. In other words, they are always ready to welcome the good news and to practise whatever truth they are taught about Christ. But this readiness may also make them easy prey to false teachers. Paul concludes by encouraging the Romans that God *will soon crush Satan* (the one behind the false teachings) *under your feet* (**16:20**).

Earlier in this chapter, Paul greeted the people he knew in the Roman church. He now moves to list others who are sending greetings to that church. These people are close associates who are with him as he is writing this letter. Timothy was the apostle's closest co-worker and friend (**16:21a**). Lucius is mentioned in Acts 13:1, among other prophets and teachers. Lucius may be the Latin equivalent of Luke, the evangelist. If Jason is the same person as the one mentioned in Acts 17:5-9, he is the person who welcomed Paul in Thessalonica and who was dragged before the city officials during the riot. Sosipater may be the same person as the Sopater mentioned in Acts 20:4. Lucius, Jason and Sosipater were all Jews, for they are all referred to as Paul's 'relatives' in **16:21b**.

Tertius (**16:22**) introduces himself as the amanuensis for this letter, that is, the person who wrote it as Paul was dictating to him. Gaius (**16:23**) is also referred to in 1 Corinthians 1:14, where Paul mentions that he and the whole church in Corinth are enjoying Gaius' hospitality. The apostle and some of the other co-workers mentioned in this letter may have been staying in Gaius' home, or a church in Corinth may have met in his house. Erastus, the city director, is also referred to in Acts 19:21-22 and 2 Timothy 4:20. Quartus is not known apart from this list.

Paul concludes the epistle to the Romans by giving praise to God, who is able to establish (or strengthen) the Roman Christians (and all other Christians) in the truth of the gospel. This gospel, the proclamation of Jesus Christ as Lord and Saviour, has long been hidden but is now *revealed through the prophetic writings* (**16:25-26**). Here 'the prophetic writings' refers to the entire OT, which points to Christ and to the revelation of God's righteousness in him. In revealing this mystery, this only wise God wanted all the nations to believe and obey him. This is why both Jews and Gentiles are worshipping together in the church. Paul's response to the greatness and wisdom of God is to glorify him for ever through Jesus, his Son (**16:27**).

David M. Kasali

Further Reading

Bruce, F. F. *The Epistle to the Romans: An Introduction and Commentary.* TNT. Grand Rapids: Eerdmans, 1963.

Cranfield, C.E.B. *A Critical and Exegetical Commentary on the Epistle to the Romans.* 2 vols ICC. Edinburgh: T & T Clark, 1975 (Vol. 1) and 1979 (Vol. 2).

Stott, John R. W. *The Message of Romans.* BST. Leicester: Inter-Varsity Press, 1994.

1 CORINTHIANS

Corinth was a great cosmopolitan city ideally located to thrive as a trading and commercial centre. It stood on a narrow isthmus, only four miles across, with the Saronic Gulf on the west and the Corinthian Gulf on the east. All traffic from north to south and east to west had to pass through it.

The original ancient city on this site was destroyed in 146 BC, but it was rebuilt by Julius Caesar as a Roman colony and the administrative seat of the Roman province of Achaia. Caesar settled his veterans and other freedmen in the city, but it soon became a Greek centre.

Corinth became known as a very depraved city, strongly associated with the worship of Aphrodite, the goddess of sexual love. But Corinth was also the city in which the Apostle Paul stayed for eighteen months, longer than in any of the other cities he visited, except Ephesus. He went there on his second missionary journey (Acts 18:1-17) and had such a successful ministry that a strong church was founded.

We know that Gallio was stationed in Corinth as the proconsul of Achaia during the time Paul was there (Acts 18:12). He is also mentioned in a dated inscription found at Delphi that establishes that he was in Corinth in about AD 52. We know from other sources that he was the proconsul for only one year. Thus it is clear that Paul was in Corinth in about AD 52.

Paul's Correspondence with Corinth

The NT contains only two letters to Corinth, but from Acts and the comments in the letters we have, we can tell that Paul actually wrote four letters to the church there. What happened seems to have been something like this:

- The letter referred to in 1 Corinthians 5:9 was written. Some scholars argue that this letter is now contained in 2 Corinthians 6:14-7:1.
- Chloe's people visited Paul with news of the situation in Corinth, and Stephanas, Fortunatus and Achaicus arrived with a letter from the Corinthian church.
- 1 Corinthians was written in reply to the letter brought by Stephanas and was delivered by Timothy.
- Rather than improving, the situation grew worse, and Paul himself visited Corinth. This visit was a painful failure.
- Paul wrote the 'severe letter', which is thought to be contained in 2 Corinthians 10-13. It was delivered by Titus.
- Paul did not wait for Titus to return with an answer to his letter but set out for Corinth. On his way there, he met

Titus in Macedonia. He learned that all was now well in Corinth and wrote what we know as 2 Corinthians.

Authenticity

Almost no one disputes that Paul wrote this letter. As early as AD 95, Clement of Rome mentions him as the author, and so do other early second-century church fathers such as Ignatius and Polycarp. This letter is the one quoted most often by church fathers like Justin Martyr, Irenaeus and Tertullian. Moreover the historical facts that can be gleaned from the letters match what is known from Acts. The character, style and language of 1 Corinthians are all consistent with what we know of Paul's letters.

Date

Paul wrote this letter from Ephesus (1 Cor 16:8), probably during his long stay there on his third missionary journey. If we allow time for Apollos' ministry, as well as for the writing of the first letter referred to in 1 Cor 5:9, it is likely that Paul wrote this letter towards the end of his three-year ministry in Ephesus, that is, around AD 55.

Outline of Contents

COMMENTARY

1:1-9 Introduction

1:1-3 Greetings

Like a typical letter of the period, this one begins by naming the writer and the addressee and then expressing a greeting. Paul identifies himself as *an apostle of Christ Jesus by the will of God* (**1:1**). He stresses his authority, possibly because that authority will be needed to handle the situation in Corinth. He states that the letter also comes from *Sosthenes*, who is probably the Corinthian Jew mentioned in Acts 18:17, now living in Ephesus.

The letter is not addressed to the Corinthians' church or the church associated with any individual, but to *the church of God in Corinth* (**1:2**). Paul describes the members of this church as *those sanctified in Christ Jesus and called to be holy.* The word translated as 'sanctified' means dedicated and consecrated to God, like an OT sacrifice, while the word translated as 'holy' can also be translated as 'saint'. The root idea is that as Christians they are called to be separate and different for God. His choice of words is remarkable considering the situation in Corinth.

The greeting follows the same pattern we find elsewhere in Paul's letters in that it combines Greek and Hebrew salutations (*grace* and *peace,* respectively) (**1:3**; see also Rom 1:7; 2 Cor 1:2; Gal 1:3; Eph 1:2; Phil 1:2; Col 1:2; 1 Thess 1:1; 2 Thess 1:2; Titus 1:4; Philm 1:3). Paul wishes them all the best that they wished themselves – total well-being.

1:4-9 Giving Thanks

In spite of the divisions and quarrelling, the gross immorality and other vices still rampant in this church, Paul gives thanks for three things:

- *His grace given you in Christ Jesus* (**1:4**).
- *You have been enriched in every way – in all your speaking and in all your knowledge* (**1:5**). Their speech and knowledge is in itself evidence that they have received grace, and this is a reason for thanksgiving. All personal spiritual gifts are gifts of grace (1 Cor 12:4, 9; Eph 4:11; 1 Pet 4:10).
- *Our testimony about Christ was confirmed in you* (**1:6**).

The tense Paul uses when giving thanks indicates that all of these gifts have already been given to the church. Proof of this is the fact that the church possesses all spiritual gifts (**1:7**). If even a church like Corinth can be said to possess all spiritual gifts, the possession of these gifts cannot be dependent on achieving Christian perfection. Paul even looks forward to the church being blameless on the day when our Lord Jesus Christ returns (**1:8**). How can he be so sure about this? The answer lies in the faithfulness of God, who has called them into fellowship with his Son (**1:9**).

1:10-4:21 The Church Divided

1:10-17 Is Christ Divided?

Paul has heard about the divisions in the Corinthian church through visitors from Chloe's household (**1:11**). His initial approach to the problem is to make a passionate appeal to them as though he were Jesus – *in the name of the Lord Jesus Christ* (**1:10a**). He then goes on to speak of the *divisions among you,* using a Greek word that refers to competing political parties, and then calls on them to *agree with one another* (**1:10b**), just as political parties might reach an agreement after resolving their differences. He also uses the medical term for healing broken bones or fixing a dislocated joint when he appeals to them to *be perfectly united in mind and thought* (**1:10c**). Their failure to present a united front is unhealthy and unnatural.

Paul's rebuke is softened by his repeated use of the word 'brother' in 1:10-11. He is not speaking like a schoolteacher, but as a brother, reminding them that it is foolish for a family to be divided.

Paul identifies four parties in this church, each aligned with a different person (**1:12**), although there is no evidence that the leaders supported the parties that claimed their names.

- One group, which may have consisted mainly of Gentiles, followed Paul. He preached a gospel of grace, of Christian freedom and the end of the law. This group may have attempted to use this freedom as a licence to be libertarian, behaving as they liked.
- Another group followed Apollos, an Alexandrian Jew who knew the Scriptures well and was an eloquent and passionate speaker (Acts 18:24-26). Scholars from Alexandria were experts in allegorizing Scripture, and it may have been his ability to do this and his rhetorical skills that attracted followers. Intellectuals in Corinth may have been treating Christianity as just another philosophy.
- Yet another group followed Cephas (the Jewish form of the name Peter). Peter had been Jesus' disciple and was a leader in the Jerusalem church. His supporters were most likely Jews who insisted on the observance of the Jewish law.
- Finally, there were those who self-righteously claimed to follow Christ. This group probably considered themselves the true Christians, as opposed to the other groups that rallied around human leaders. However, all believers belong to Christ.

Some scholars think that in saying *I belong to Christ* Paul is not mentioning the fourth group but is simply stating that he himself does not owe allegiance to any group. He is simply a follower of Christ.

Paul's three questions in **1:13** confront their divisions. He is making the point that Christ is not the property of any small section of the church. It is absurd to think that Paul

was crucified for them. Baptism was in the name of Christ, not Paul. (Note that Acts does not record the use of the trinitarian formula found in Matt 28:19.)

Paul notes that he had baptized a few of the first converts (**1:14-16**): Crispus (see Acts 18:8) Gaius (who is perhaps the Titius Justus of Acts 18:7), and the household of Stephanas, who had been 'the first converts in Achaia' (16:15). Stephanas was one of the three believers who visited Paul just before 1 Corinthians was written and who probably carried the letter back to Corinth (16:17). Paul's point is that his mission was not to perform baptisms but to preach Christ (**1:17**). So on principle, he left the administration of baptism to local leaders.

Likely concerned that his emphasis on his role as a preacher might lead to his being accused of acting like an orator enjoying the sound of his own voice too much, Paul is careful to stress that he is not into rhetoric [literally, 'wisdom of speech']. He is not concerned about preaching elegantly, but wants to allow the cross of Christ to be the source of the power of his message.

1:18-25 The Gospel Confronts False Wisdom

All those who were supporting particular parties in the church were relying on human thinking and ignoring God's desire that the body of Christ be united (John 17:20-23). We still make the same mistake today. In Africa, we frequently witness church divisions based on factors such as age, education and loyalty to the pastor. Such divisions are wrong, for God's way of handling differences maintains unity of the body even as it addresses difficult issues. Thus Paul launches into a discussion of the difference between human and divine wisdom.

People have different reactions to the message of the cross. *To those who are perishing* (including cultured Greeks and pious Jews), it is sheer foolishness, but to those *who are being saved it is the power of God* (**1:18**). 'Those who are being saved' are Christians who are in the process of being saved, with salvation being seen here as a total experience, of which the sanctification mentioned in 1:2 is a part.

Paul then quotes Isaiah 29:14 to show the futility of human wisdom compared to the wisdom of God (**1:19**). He uses rhetorical questions, like those in Isaiah 33:18, to make the point that the champions of human wisdom (*the wise man ... the scholar ...the philosopher of this age*) are utterly foolish before God (**1:20**). 'For all its wisdom the world had never found God and was still blindly and gropingly seeking him', a search 'designed by God to show men their own helplessness' (Barclay).

There were two reasons why the message of the cross was *a stumbling-block to the Jews* (**1:23a**). The first was the belief that 'anyone who is hung on a tree is under God's curse' (Deut 21:23). Thus, in spite of Isaiah 53, Jews could never envisage a suffering Messiah. Second, Jews sought for signs, that is, for spectacular, supernatural events that would prove that the prophet or messenger came with the power of God. To them, a crucified Christ indicated weakness, not power. They looked for a Messiah who would restore the kingdom of David, not one who would die on the cross (**1:22**; see also Matt 16:1-4).

The message of the cross was also foolishness to the Greeks for two reasons (**1:23b**). First, they believed that God was incapable of feeling emotion. It was thus impossible that humans could influence God in any way. God could never suffer and the very idea of the incarnation was revolting. Second, Greeks sought wisdom and so would spend hours looking for intellectual stimulation.

For Paul, the message of the cross is not just God's wisdom, but also God's power demonstrated in the miracles of the incarnation and the resurrection (**1:24**). It shows that God's foolishness *is wiser than man's wisdom* and *the weakness of God is stronger than man's strength* (**1:25**). The Akan of Ghana make the same point in their proverb: 'When God ties a knot, no human can untie it.'

1:26-31 An Illustration: God's Choice

God's choice of the Christians in Corinth illustrates the point Paul has just been making, for most of them were unimportant by human standards (**1:26**). There were a few exceptions. Crispus was the ruler of the synagogue (Acts 18:8), and Erastus was the city's director of public works (Rom 16:23).

The purpose of God's choice was *to shame the wise* and *the strong* (**1:27**) and *to nullify the things that are* (**1:28**), that is, to reduce them to ineffectiveness. His reason for doing this is so that *no one may boast before him* (**1:29**). God is far greater than even the greatest human, and in Jesus, he has become the wisdom of those who have been called. In other words, Jesus is God's wisdom personified – a wisdom that was very different from what the philosophers of the time thought of as wisdom. The three words *righteousness, holiness and redemption* are definitions of what wisdom is or of the qualities that accompany it. Christ embodies all three.

2:1-5 The Proclamation of the Gospel and Power

Three things come to Paul's mind as he remembers the time he took the gospel to Corinth (**2:1a**):
- He did not speak *with eloquence or superior wisdom* (**2:1b**) because he was so convinced that the message of the cross was superior to human wisdom. Shortly before going to Corinth, Paul's preaching had received few positive responses when he had attempted to speak the language of Greek philosophers on Mars' Hill in Athens (Acts 17:22-34). So in Corinth he resolved not to use *wise and persuasive words* (**2:4a**).

- He came speaking *in weakness and fear, and with much trembling* (**2:3**). He was not concerned about his own safety but was in awe of the message that he was proclaiming.
- His preaching was a *demonstration of the Spirit's power* (**2:4b**) and of *God's power* (**2:5**). The Greek word translated 'demonstration' refers to proving a point with absolute certainty. The fact that the Corinthians are now believers is proof of the power of this demonstration.

2:6-10 Wisdom from God

We must take care not to interpret Paul's dismissing of human wisdom as meaning that he disapproved of education or of Christians using their brains. Not at all! What Paul did not like was human wisdom that excluded God and did not recognize Christ as the wisdom of God (1:24). When he came to Corinth, he proclaimed the first level of Christian wisdom, that is, the basic facts of Christianity. Once people had become believers with some degree of maturity, there was a further *message of wisdom* to be taught (**2:6a**). Mature Christians are not perfect Christians; they are believers who have grown to have some understanding of the things of the spirit (see also 14:20; Phil 3:15; Eph 4:13).

The teaching that Paul has for this group is different from *the wisdom of this age or of the rulers of this age* (**2:6b**). In fact, Paul describes it as *God's secret wisdom* (**2:7**). This is not some kind of magical knowledge, but rather something that unbelievers don't understand that is quite clear to believers. Powerful people in this world knew nothing about it, and their ignorance led them to crucify Jesus, whom Paul here refers to as *the Lord of glory*, a title that puts him on a par with God (**2:8**).

Paul concludes this section with a reference to Isaiah 64:4, probably quoting from memory as his version is not word for word the same as that in Isaiah. The quotation emphasizes that knowledge of salvation does not come through human investigation but through God's revelation by his spirit (**2:10**).

2:11-16 Expressing Spiritual Truths

The means by which God gives us this knowledge of *the deep things of God* is the Holy Spirit, who is the only one who fully understands God's mind (**2:11**). (In saying this, Paul is stating that the Holy Spirit is equal to God, just as he earlier put Christ on a par with God.) Paul uses a human analogy – no one *knows the thoughts of a man* except the man himself. Those who have accepted God's way of salvation have received (the Greek tense here indicates at a definite time in the past) *the Spirit of God*, who helps them understand the things God has freely given them concerning this revealed mystery (**2:12**). But those who are mature have a fuller understanding of this mystery.

It is the Spirit who enables Paul to speak as he does, *expressing spiritual truths in spiritual words*, that is, in language that is very different from that favoured by orators (**2:13**, **2:6**). In other words, the Spirit enables Paul, and all those who proclaim the wisdom of God, to communicate truths about God's will in the words that best express that will. (The phrase could also possibly be translated as 'expressing spiritual truths to spiritual people', a translation that finds some support given Paul's mention of spiritual people in 2:13.)

Paul distinguishes between two kinds of people. The first group are those *without the Spirit,* who live as though there was nothing beyond physical life (**2:14**). Their values are all material, and they judge everything from physical and material perspectives. Such people do not, and cannot, understand spiritual things. By contrast, those who are mature or spiritual, whose lives are controlled by the Spirit, enjoy the special privilege of being able to *make judgments about all things,* that is, they can examine them carefully and sift out what is important (**2:15**). Someone who possesses the mind of Christ is able to make the right decisions about issues.

3:1-9 The Foolishness of a Party Spirit

But Paul makes it clear that what he is describing is the ideal situation. His advice to the Corinthians here could be summarized by the Ghanaian proverb, 'You must be mature before you cackle' (as a hen does when it is about to lay an egg). Rather than being the spiritual adults described in 2:15, the Corinthians are still enmeshed in this world and acting, not merely like children, but like infants (**3:1-2**). While there is no shame in being an infant, because we all start out that way, they should be growing up. Their thinking should not still be dominated by the things of this world. Paul emphasizes this by repeating the world *worldly* twice in 3:3 and by twice describing them as *mere men* (**3:3-4**). Their immaturity is clearly shown by the *jealousy and quarrelling* among them.

He stresses how foolish their party spirit is by reminding them that both he and Apollos are merely *servants* (**3:5**). Each had his own task, with Paul planting the seeds of faith and Apollos watering them (**3:6**), but the fact that the seeds had actually grown had nothing to do with them but everything to do with God, who is the only one who actually *makes things grow* (**3:7**).

Rather than being in competition, God's servants are *God's fellow-workers* (**3:9**). They are working together to serve God and to complete the work God wants done.

3:10-23 Building on the Foundation

Paul now changes the metaphor from farming to building. His role in the church in Corinth has been like that of a construction expert who carefully laid the foundations for this particular church during his eighteen-month stay in Corinth (**3:10**). Now the Corinthian Christians have to take personal responsibility for erecting the finished building on this foundation. They cannot change the shape of the foundation itself (the preaching of Jesus Christ – **3:11**), but they can decide whether to build the walls using *gold, silver, costly stones, wood, hay or straw* (**3:12**). Here, Paul is speaking of the value and quality of each person's contribution to the church.

He reminds them that the building will need to survive a test by fire on the day of judgment (**3:13**). If the building materials are strong enough to survive the test, the builders will be rewarded (**3:14**). We reap what we sow, or as the Ghanaians say, 'As you lay your bed, so must you lie on it.' While all believers will be saved, there will be further rewards commensurate with what one has done for God on earth (**3:15**).

Continuing the building metaphor, Paul reminds the believers that they collectively constitute a holy place, like the holy of holies, where God was present in a special way (**3:16**). Damaging God's temple will rouse his anger (**3:17**). They must be careful not to destroy God's church in Corinth through dissension, quarrels and divisions.

Paul concludes by again stressing the folly of worldly wisdom. He does this by quoting freely, in his own words, from Job 5:13 and Psalm 94:11 (**3:18-20**). He tells the Corinthians that their folly has led them to see themselves as lining up behind 'party leaders', when there is no need for them to be subordinate members of factions. The leaders belong to them, and so does everything else (**3:21-22**)! They are masters, possessing all things, but they themselves belong to Christ, who owns them (**3:23**).

4:1-21 Correct Attitude to the Servants of Christ

Here Paul expands on what it means to be a servant, using words that would conjure up specific images for the Corinthians (**4:1**). First he uses a word that the NIV translates as 'servant' but which specifically refers to the man who pulled the oars on the lowest level of the Greek fighting ship known as a trireme. A trireme had three banks of oars, one above the other, and the rowers on the bottom level had the least prestige and took orders from the helmsman and all those above them. Thus Paul does not even see himself and the others as important servants.

The second word Paul uses for 'servant' carries more prestige. He describes himself and the other leaders as stewards, who are responsible for managing a household and making sure it runs smoothly, but who are not the owners or masters (see also Luke 12:42; 16:1). He and the other leaders are stewards of *the secret things of God* (that is, of the mystery of the gospel (2:7; 1 Pet 1:10-12).

Like stewards, Christian leaders ought to be faithful and reliable (**4:2**), and so Paul naturally moves on to assessing reliability. One's reliability can be judged by others or by oneself (**4:3-4**). But by far the most important judgment is the one that the Lord will make when he returns (4:5). So Paul urges the Corinthians not to rush to make judgments but to *judge nothing before the appointed time* (4:5). This instruction does not contradict his earlier statement that 'the spiritual man makes judgments about all things' (2:15). There he was talking about discerning what is true. Here he is talking about passing judgment on other men and women, particularly in cases where there is no clear evidence of what has been done or not done or about their motives. Such things must be left to God's final judgment.

Paul has been speaking about himself and the other leaders, but now he reminds his readers that what he has been saying applies to them too (4:6-7). They, too, have nothing to boast about. Boasting is rooted in the pride that regards one person as better than another, but Paul reminds them that they cannot really boast about gifts God has graciously given them even though they did not deserve them (4:7).

The depth of Paul's dislike of the Corinthians' pride emerges clearly in the scathing, sarcastic verses that follow. Their pride makes them feel self-satisfied and superior. They have become a snobbish clique (4:8). By contrast, the apostles are objects of mockery. Paul uses an image derived from the Roman habit of parading their trophies and prisoners of war in the streets before sending them to die in the arena as a form of public entertainment. The apostles are like these wretched prisoners, while the Corinthians are like the victors who despise them (4:9-10).

Abandoning metaphorical language, Paul lists all that he and the other apostles have had to endure (4:11-13). This includes being *brutally treated*, that is, beaten like slaves, who were regarded not as people but as property. His readers would have been amazed at Paul's response to this treatment, which includes answering kindly when slandered. The Greeks put great store by not being prepared to accept any insult. Christian humility was a virtue that was altogether new to the world of Paul's day.

Suddenly, and characteristically, Paul's tone shifts from strong rebuke to fatherly concern. He reminds the Corinthians that he is not writing these things in order to *shame* them, but to *warn* them, as a father does his *dear children* (4:14). After all, he is in a unique relationship with them. All the other leaders in the Corinthian church are only *guardians*, like the servants who escorted Greek boys to school, but Paul is their spiritual father who first brought them to Christ (4:15). He urges them to be like children who imitate their father (4:16). To help them do this, he will send Timothy, who is also his spiritual son, to remind them of how to live in the Lord Jesus Christ (4:17).

The arrogance of some of the Corinthian believers is destroying their relationship with one another and with God. Paul hopes that he will soon be able to follow Timothy and confront these people (4:18-19). Meanwhile, he hopes they will change and become humble, so that when

he comes he will not have to come as a disciplinarian but *in love and with a gentle spirit* (4:20).

5:1-6:20 Issues of Morality in the Church

5:1-8 Incest

Like much of the modern world, the heathen world of Paul's day focused on pleasure and scarcely knew what chastity was. This was particularly the case in Corinth, which was renowned for its immorality. It is thus all the more shocking that the type of immorality Paul had to confront in the Corinthian church did *not occur even among pagans*. What was happening was that a man was in a sexual relationship with his stepmother, *his father's wife* (5:1). (The father may have died.)

Paul was shocked that the Corinthian church was not ashamed of this behaviour. Instead they were proud (5:2a)! They may have been treating their Christian freedom as a licence to do as they liked. They should *have been filled with grief* (5:2b), as if mourning for someone who has died. They should have responded by handing *this man over to Satan* (5:5a; see also 1 Tim 1:20, the only other place where this expression is used in the NT). Paul is saying that the offender should be excommunicated. He should no longer be considered a member of the church, but should be regarded as living in the world, which was considered the domain of Satan (John 12:31; 16:11; Acts 26:18; Col 1:3). The purpose of the excommunication was not to get rid of him but so that his *sinful nature may be destroyed, and his spirit saved on the day of the Lord,* that is, the day when Jesus returns (5:5b).

Returning to the issue of their boasting (5:6a; 5:2), Paul shows that it is completely out of place. It will affect them in all sorts of ways, just as yeast works its way through a *whole batch of dough* (5:6b). He reminds them that the Jewish Passover required eating bread without yeast (Exod 12:15-20; 13:7) because yeast represented a corrupting influence, and even a tiny piece of it had powerful effects. Similarly, tolerating even one case of immorality will corrupt the whole church. The same point is captured in the Ghanaian proverb, 'The goat thinks it is messing up someone else's compound, without realizing that it is messing up its own tail.'

Because *Christ, our Passover lamb, has been sacrificed* (5:7), Christians cannot afford to celebrate the new Passover with the yeast of immorality and all the sins of the past life. The old life and the new are mutually exclusive. The former is characterized by *malice and wickedness*, while the latter is characterized by *sincerity and truth* (5:8). The word used here for 'sincerity' is one that suggests 'transparent purity of purpose and character' *(IBC)*.

Paul's strong response to immorality teaches a very practical lesson – church discipline must sometimes be administered for the benefit of the church, as well as for the correction of the person concerned. Its aim must always be to cure the one disciplined of the evil and to prevent the evil from spreading. While discipline must never be done in a spirit of hostility, a congregation that ignores immorality will end up with a sick and corrupted church.

5:9-13 The Church and the World

The mention of sincerity in 5:8, and the fact that it suggests a pure and unmixed condition, may have reminded Paul about a misunderstanding that had arisen about something he had said in an earlier letter (see the introduction to this commentary).

Evidently he had told them not to *associate* with *the immoral, or the greedy and swindlers, or idolaters* (**5:9-10a**). These types of sins were as common then as they are now. Lax morality is a sin against ourself, chasing after possessions is a sin against our neighbours and idolatry or superstition is a sin against God. When he repeats this list, Paul adds two other sins, namely, slander and drunkenness (**5:11a**).

The Corinthians had understood him to be saying that they must avoid associating with anyone guilty of any of these sins. But Paul points out that this is impossible as long as they are alive (**5:10b**). All non-believers are guilty of these sins.

What he had meant was that they should not associate with people who claimed to be Christians but who had not left behind their sinful way of life. His directive not even to eat with such people presumably refers to sharing the communion meal with them (**5:11b**).

The church is only responsible for the behaviour of those who claim to be part of it (**5:12**). God is the one who will judge the world (**5:13a**). Paul's advice about how to handle people in the church who still lead sinful lives is very direct: *Expel the wicked man from among you* (**5:13b**; see also Deut 17:7b). Such people are to be excommunicated, rather than being allowed to stay within the church and exercise a corrupting influence. The church would be wise to listen to this counsel today.

6:1-8 Lawsuits and Heathen Courts

The Greeks often had lawsuits against each other, and this habit had been brought into the church. Paul felt very strongly that Christians should not be asking ungodly people to judge their legal disputes (**6:1**). The issue here is not whether or not a just judgment is reached but whether those involved have a relationship with God. Christians should value their common relationship with God in their dealings with one another.

Paul reminds them that during the golden age when the Messiah will reign supreme, the saints will sit in judgment with Christ (**6:2**; Dan 7:22; Matt 19:28; Luke 22:30; Rev 3:21; 20:4). At that time, even the angels will be judged by

the saints. He therefore sees no reason why the saints cannot handle judging trivial temporal issues (**6:3**).

Paul's advice to the Corinthian believers is that they should rather *appoint as judges even men of little account in the church* (**6:4**). The word translated as 'men of little account' is similar to the word translated as 'despised' in 1:28. No matter how insignificant these people may be in the church, it is better to take disputes to them than to unbelievers.

Paul again stresses how shameful it is for Christians to take their cases to unbelievers to judge. Surely they cannot be so stupid that there is no one among them capable of acting as a judge? (**6:5-6**). Moreover, the mere fact that they have a case that they need to take to an ungodly judge signals that they have already lost what is important and have *been completely defeated* (**6:7a**). The issue here is not whether they win or lose the court case, but whether they win or lose as believers.

Paul turns to a principle that the Greek philosopher Plato had laid down and that his readers would be well aware of: it is better to suffer wrong than to do wrong. Christ, too, had taught that Christians should not be overly concerned about their personal 'rights' (Matt 5:40). Rather than trying to take revenge or demand recompense, Christians should accept that they have been wronged (**6:7b**). But instead of having this attitude, Christians were actually doing wrong and cheating their fellow Christians (**6:8**).

6:9-11 A Flashback to What We Were

In 6:8 Paul accused the Corinthian believers of doing wrong, and now in **6:9-10** he deals with the fate of all wrongdoers. They will not inherit *the kingdom of God.* The list of the 'wicked' who will suffer this fate includes the sexually immoral, idolaters, adulterers, male prostitutes, homosexual offenders, thieves, the greedy, drunkards, slanderers and swindlers. Their sins can be boiled down into three groups: sins of idolatry, sins of selfishness and sins of immorality.

The Corinthian Christians had themselves committed many of these sins in the past. But they *were washed* (**6:11**). It seems likely that Paul is speaking of their sins having been washed away rather than merely of the washing of baptism (Eph 5:26; Titus 3:5). He also says that they *were sanctified,* that is, set apart for God and holiness, and *justified,* that is, declared to be a people who are now in right standing with God and no longer under condemnation. The verb tense he uses makes it clear that all these things had happened in the past.

Paul here is not focusing on the order in which these blessings were received. Thus he lists justification last, as the climax of what has been done for them, because he has just been writing about lawsuits and courts and the final judgment of God, when Christ will declare his own to be innocent. All of this has been done *in the name of the Lord Jesus Christ and by the Spirit of our God* (**6:11**). Our salvation and justification are entirely the result of God's initiative.

6:12-20 The Case for Purity: Bought at a Price

Paul now moves on from a discussion of particular examples to a discussion of two great principles that should guide our actions. First, he insists that, though he is free, he will not allow anything to master him. Christian freedom does not make him a slave to his desires and instincts, but their master. He is not 'free to sin' but 'free *not* to sin'. Second, he insists that he is not his own because he has been purchased by Christ.

He begins with a quotation, perhaps one the Corinthians were using, *Everything is permissible for me* (**6:12**). Paul himself may have used these words, but now they are being taken out of context. Alternatively, these words may have been the slogan of the libertarian party (see comments on 1:12). He repeats the maxim twice, each time adding a phrase that comments on it: *but not everything is beneficial, ... but I will not be mastered by anything'*.

The Greeks were inclined to despise the human body. One of their proverbs stated, 'The body is a tomb', and the Stoic philosopher Epictetus said, 'I am a poor soul shackled to a corpse'. This attitude produced two different ways of treating the body. Some Greeks adopted a rigorous asceticism in an attempt to control the body and humiliate its desires and instincts. Others, however, argued that since the body was totally worthless and only the spirit was important, it did not matter what the body did. Clearly, the Corinthians were inclined to the latter view. They felt free to indulge their bodily desires, arguing from the analogy that food is intended for the stomach and the stomach is intended for food.

Paul partially agrees – but points out that God will destroy both food and stomachs. Because the Corinthians were extending the analogy of food to cover immoral indulging of their sexual desires, Paul reminds them *that the body is not meant for sexual immorality, but for the Lord* (**6:13**). He uses a contrast to show the flaw in their argument: God will destroy both food and stomachs, but God does not destroy our bodies – rather, he raises them (**6:14**).

Christians belong to Christ both physically and spiritually. Believers make up Christ's body here on earth, and our physical bodies are as much part of his body as our souls. So when we indulge in sexual immorality, it is as if we are making Christ commit immoral acts (**6:15**)! Paul quotes Genesis 2:24 to remind them that sexual intercourse creates a union, like a glue that binds people together (**6:16**). But Christians are supposed to be glued to the Lord, not to prostitutes (**6:17**).

Paul calls on the Corinthians to *flee from sexual immorality* (**6:18a**). The best way to deal with some temptations is to run away and avoid them. He reminds them of the folly of giving in to sexual temptation by pointing out that this is a sin that affects one's own body (**6:18b**). This point is forcefully made in Ghana in the Ga proverb, 'Nobody sees a pointed stick and runs his eyes against it.' To be sure, other sins like drunkenness, which is mentioned elsewhere in the letter, also affects one's own body, but not to the same extent that sexual sin does.

Finally Paul returns to the point he made in 3:16. He reminds the Christians that each one of them has been given the privilege of being the temple of the Holy Spirit (**6:19**). Immoral behaviour desecrates that temple.

Believers need to remember that they belong to Christ, since he paid for their lives with his blood. That blood redeemed both their bodies and their souls, and now they must glorify and honour God with their bodies (**6:20**).

7:1-11:1 Issues Concerning Social Relationships

7:1-40 Marriage Relationships

7:1-7 General background

Here Paul is not writing a treatise on marriage. Rather, he is replying to specific questions asked by the Corinthians, who had written to ask his advice. That is why he begins, *Now for the matters you wrote about* (**7:1a**). Thus what Paul says here must be interpreted within the context of the circumstances of the day and current attitudes to marriage.

The Corinthians had suggested that *it is good for a man not to marry* (**7:1b**). Paul's response is 'yes ... but' (see also 7:8, 26, 38.) He was realistic and knew that the moral conditions in Corinth would make celibacy very difficult, and thus he strongly recommended marriage. In effect, what he is saying is 'Remember where you are living ... in Corinth where you cannot even walk along the street without temptation rearing its head at you. Remember your own physical constitution and the healthy instincts which nature has given you. You will be far better to marry than to fall into sin' (Barclay). It is clear from the reference to *each man* and *each woman* that the type of marriage he was recommending was monogamous (**7:2**).

Given the Greek belief that the body was essentially evil, the Corinthians also had a question about sexual relations within marriage. In answering this question, Paul stresses that marriage is partnership. Neither the husband nor the wife is independent; each has a responsibility to the other (**7:3-4**). Consequently neither should refuse to have sexual relations with the other. The only exception Paul allows is for brief periods when both partners agree to abstain from sex so that they can devote themselves to prayer. But such periods must not be prolonged, or Satan may use them to sow seeds of temptation (**7:5**).

Does the fact that Paul here seems to speak of marriage only as a protection against immorality mean that he has a low view of marriage? The answer is no. His high view of marriage is clear from such passages as Ephesians 5:22-33, where he uses the metaphor of marriage to describe the relationship between Christ and his church (particularly in 5:31-32) and from Romans 7:1-4, where he uses the same metaphor to show how the believer relates to the law.

Paul does, however, make it clear that he personally favours celibacy, but he recognizes that this is a gift God has given him, just as he has given others the gift of marriage (**7:6-7**). The term used here for 'gift' is *charisma*, exactly the same word that he uses in his discussion of spiritual gifts in chapter 12.

Although Paul was celibate when he wrote this letter, it is almost certain that he had been married at one time. It seems that his marriage had ended either because his wife had died or, possibly, because she had left him when he became a Christian.

7:8-16 Particular situations

Paul next turns to the questions asked about the three specific groups in the church: the unmarried and widows, the married and those in mixed marriages.

7:8-9 THE UNMARRIED Paul restates the advice he has given in 7:1-2. He admits that he would prefer unmarried men and women to *stay unmarried as I am* (**7:8**), but makes it clear that he recognizes this is not to be expected of everyone. For some people, an unmarried life would be an endless and unnecessary struggle against temptation (**7:9**). But Paul himself is firmly committed to living a single life.

Living a single life has long been thought very odd in Africa. But increasingly it has become acceptable – sometimes by choice and sometimes by unavoidable circumstances. In parts of the continent where the proportion of men to women has been greatly reduced by wars, famines and other catastrophes, polygamy is decreasing and so there are no husbands for many women. Paul's example is an encouragement to those who remain single. Clearly singleness did not hinder him from living for God and serving him. Today we need more people like Paul – fully committed to the Lord regardless of whether they are single or married.

7:10-11 THE MARRIED Paul's advice to the married is the same as that of Jesus: he forbids divorce (**7:10-11**; see also Mark 10:9; Luke 16:18). It is surprising that Paul says *a wife must not separate from her husband*. At that time, it was usually the husband who divorced his wife. Probably, Paul was addressing an actual case that had occurred in Corinth, especially as the parenthetical statement added in 7:11 refers only to the woman leaving. Paul insists that in a case like this, remarriage is forbidden.

7:12-16 MIXED MARRIAGES Some of the Corinthian Christians were already married when they came to faith, and now find themselves living with unbelieving partners. Paul cannot cite any specific command of Jesus about this situation, and

has to speak on his own authority as an apostle (**7:12a**). He rules that believing partners should not separate from their unbelieving partners simply because they are unbelievers (**7:12b-13**). He argues that as far as the marriage is concerned, the unbelieving partner becomes sanctified through the believing partner (**7:14**). The type of sanctification he is speaking of here has nothing to do with conversion and salvation. He is addressing the fear of the type of defilement he referred to in 6:15, and may be thinking of the way in which objects were sanctified by being in contact with priests in the OT (Exod 29:27; Lev 6:18). He also sets to rest any fear that the children of such mixed marriages are ceremonially unclean, stressing that they too are *holy*.

On the other hand, the unbelieving partner may decide to end the marriage (**7:15**). In such a case, the believing partner *is not bound*. The reminder that we are called to *live in peace* means that the believing partner is not to cause conflict and turmoil by fighting either to preserve or to end a mixed marriage.

Finally, Paul reminds those in this situation of the possibility that the believing partner may be the means by which the unbelieving partner is saved. Yet he offers no guarantees that this will happen (**7:16**).

7:17-24 Serving God where God has set us

Having dealt with particular cases, Paul turns to the principle that must govern the behaviour of believers: 'Be a Christian where you are' (7:17, 20, 24).

Paul begins by saying that *each one should retain the place in life the Lord assigned to him* (**7:17a**). 'Retain' here means 'continue walking'. Becoming a Christian does not mean a violent break from your past, but rather serving God in the best way possible in your own situation. Paul emphasizes the importance of these words by stating that *this is the rule I lay down in all the churches* (**7:17b**). The *all* in 'all the churches' is emphatic.

One's race, social position, education and so on are not important; what is important is the kind of life that is lived (**7:19**). When Paul says that *keeping God's commands is what counts*, he is referring to God's moral law (see Gal 5:6 and 6:15). Obedience to God is more important than trying to change one's circumstances, or even seeking freedom from slavery (**7:20**). (Although Paul does add, *if you can gain your freedom, do so* – **7:21**.)

One's relationship and standing with God matter far more than one's position. Paul repeats the point he made in 6:20: *You were bought at a price*, and adds, *do not become slaves of men* (**7:23**). He is not referring to physical slavery, but to giving in to social and religious pressures. Christ has bought us and he is our Master. We are responsible only to him (**7:24**).

7:25-38 The advantages of remaining single

The Corinthians' next question was *about virgins* (**7:25**). 'Virgins' were normally young women, although in Revelation 14:4 the word is used for men. In regard to this group, too, Paul did not refer to a specific command from Jesus, but relied on his own apostolic authority as one divinely inspired. He bases his recommendation on the fact that there is currently some crisis facing the church (**7:26**).

What did Paul mean by *the present crisis*? There are three possible interpretations: a) he is referring to the events preceding the second coming (7:29, 31; Luke 21:23), b) he is referring to general opposition to believers, or c) he is referring to some particular circumstances facing Christians in Corinth. He may even have had all three in mind.

Given these circumstances, Paul does not say that marriage is wrong, but he considers it unwise (**7:28**). He points out that those who marry will face many difficulties. As too many Africans know from personal experience, family responsibilities weigh heavily in times of violence and persecution.

Paul also says that *the time is short* (**7:29**). Here he is clearly thinking of Christ's second coming. His advice to the unmarried must be read in the light of this and of the 'present crisis'. He is giving guidance for a time of crisis rather than setting out his full view of marriage. He is sure that *this world in its present form is passing away* (**7:31**), and so counsels them not to be *engrossed* in the things of the world. The present reality is transitory, and so he urges them to maintain only light contact with it.

Paul's purpose in advising against marriage is that he wants the Corinthians to be *free from concern* (**7:32**; 7:28). He wants them, like him, to be concerned only about the Lord's affairs and not about their marriage relationship, which he here calls *the affairs of this world* (**7:33**). He wants them to have a single focus and to be able to be *devoted to the Lord in both body and spirit* (**7:34**) without the distractions that come with marriage. In saying this, his aim is not to impose restrictions on them but to free them to serve God wholeheartedly (**7:35**).

He then moves on to yet another question about the relationship between a young woman and a man. There are three possible interpretations of the words translated *the virgin he is engaged to* (**7:36a**). The relationship may be between a) a father and his unmarried daughter (KJV, RV), in which case the problem concerns whether the father should arrange a marriage for her, b) a couple involved in a 'spiritual marriage' who intend to remain celibate (Moffat and NEB) or c) a young man and his fiancée (NIV, RSV). The first interpretation seems unlikely, and the second one involves a practice that was known in the third century, but probably did not exist at the time when Paul was writing. Thus Paul is probably writing to a man who is engaged to a young woman, but is hesitant about getting married.

Once again Paul stresses that there is nothing wrong with getting married, although he still feels that in the present circumstances it is better to remain single (**7:36b-38**).

7:39-40 Widows

Widows are free to remarry because the marriage bond is binding only as long as the partner lives. The new husband, however, must *belong to the Lord*, that is, he must be a Christian (**7:39**). Paul concludes with a strong assertion that what he says is Spirit-led. His own preference is celibacy, and he considers that a widow will be happier if she remains single (**7:40**).

8:1-13 Food Offered to Idols

The next major area about which the Corinthians had questions concerned food offered to idols. This problem arose because almost all the meat sold in the market at that time came from pagan sacrifices.

Before discussing this issue, Paul, possibly quoting the letter the Corinthians had sent to him, states that we *all possess knowledge* (**8:1**). He reminds them that knowledge tends to give one an inflated opinion of oneself. By contrast, love builds up (see also 10:23; 14:4, 17). Knowledge is hollow; love is solid.

The opening chapters of this letter suggest that the Corinthians were proud of their wisdom. Here, it seems they were proud of their knowledge. Paul challenges this attitude, arguing that true knowledge leads to humility because one recognizes how little one knows and that no one has a monopoly on knowledge (**8:2**). By contrast, someone *who loves God is known by God* (**8:3**). This is the right kind of knowledge. Here, too, a great Christian principle emerges: things should not be judged solely from the point of view of knowledge, but from the point of view of love.

In the next few verses, Paul seems to be confirming statements that the Corinthians have been making. They seem to have been saying, 'An idol is nothing, isn't it? There is only one God, isn't there?' Paul agrees with them that this is what *we know* (**8:4**) (and he has more to say on this topic in 10:14-22). The Greeks believed in many gods, and the Corinthians were right to assert that all these 'gods' and 'lords' were false because there is only *one God* and only *one Lord*. Paul strongly affirms that God the Father is the creator of everything and the one served by those who have been redeemed and that Christ is the one through whom creation took place (**8:5-6**).

But not everyone fully shares this knowledge. For some people, the long-established habit of idol worship can be reawakened if anything associated with those idols comes their way again, bothering their consciences (**8:7**).

While it is true that food does not make us sinful or holy (**8:8**), eating or not eating certain foods is connected with the way individuals are using their Christian freedom.

They need to be concerned about the consciences of their weaker brothers, whose faith may be damaged if they see fellow believers *eating in an idol's temple* at some official function or festival (**8:9-10**).

Paul uses strong metaphors to describe the effect that such eating may have on a brother. It may defile his conscience (8:7), be a stumbling block (8:9), wound him (**8:12**) and eventually destroy (literally, 'ruin') him (**8:11**). Taking responsibility for protecting our fellow believers means that we may have to resolve, *I will never eat meat again, so that I will not cause him to fall* (**8:13**). This example clearly illustrates the contrast between knowledge and love. Knowledge emboldens individuals to eat without concern for their own consciences or those of others (8:10).

Paul is here setting out two great spiritual principles. One is that 'what is safe for one man may be quite unsafe for another', and the other is that 'no man has any right to claim a right, to indulge in a pleasure, or to demand a liberty which may be the ruination of someone else.' Paul also deals with this subject in Romans 14:13-20.

The situation Paul dealt with here still challenges African believers today when, for example, a bridegroom is expected to provide wine for the wedding or to give an animal that will be offered to the spirits. Paul's advice here is that believers should ask God for wisdom to determine what matters and what does not. The key question is, 'What effect will my response have on an unbeliever or a weaker believer?' For example, providing wine would signal approval of drinking alcohol, while giving an animal for sacrifice would communicate that one still has fellowship with spirits. Believers should not provide stimuli to evil but should rather spread the light of the gospel.

9:1-27 Paul's Own Example

9:1-14 Unclaimed privileges

Chapter 9 is not a digression with no relationship to what has gone before. Rather, Paul is illustrating the implications of his teaching in the previous chapter and giving another example of how he has been prepared to give up his freedom and rights as an apostle so as not to *hinder the gospel* (9:12). His attitude contrasts with that of the intellectuals in Corinth, who insisted on their rights and freedoms even if these caused harm to weaker believers.

Paul starts by arguing fiercely that he can claim numerous rights, for he is free and he is an apostle – after all, he has seen the Lord. One of the criteria for being an apostle was that the person had to be a witness of the resurrection (Acts 1:22; 2:32; 3:15; 4:33), and Paul meets this criterion because he saw Jesus on the road to Damascus (Acts 9:4-5). Not only that, but his apostleship is proved by his effective ministry in Corinth. Their very existence as a church was *the seal of his apostleship* (**9:1-2**).

Consequently Paul had every *right* to their support. He and Barnabas (see 9:6) could legitimately have expected the Corinthian believers to provide for their daily needs (**9:4**). He was also entitled to take a believing wife along with him on his missionary tours. Other apostles were doing this, including *the Lord's brothers* (Joseph and Mary's other children – see John 7:5; Acts 1:14; Gal 1:19 – and possibly a wider circle of Jesus' relatives) (**9:5**). There should also have been no need for Paul and Barnabas to engage in secular work to support themselves (**9:6**). None of the other apostles were doing this. This was a real issue in Corinth, because manual labour would have received little respect from those who were Greek (see also 4:12; Acts 18:3; 1 Thess 4:11; 2 Thess 3:8-12). But Paul waived all these rights for the sake of the gospel.

Paul uses a number of human examples to prove that his claims are not unreasonable. Soldiers, farmers and shepherds all get their upkeep from their work (**9:7**). There is no reason why a minister of the gospel like Paul should not get his upkeep from the preaching of the gospel. In fact, his position can be supported from Scripture, as Paul proves by quoting Deuteronomy 25:4 (**9:8-9**). Arguing by analogy from the instruction in Deuteronomy, Paul clearly establishes that he, even more than others, is entitled to assert his rights with regard to the church in Corinth (**9:10-12a**).

But having argued extensively for his right to these privileges, Paul refuses to accept them (**9:12b**; see also 9:15). Instead, he adds, *we put up with anything* rather than allowing our own rights to become roadblocks to the spread of the gospel.

Yet Paul was as entitled to receive support from them as *those who work in the temple* in Jerusalem were entitled to receive their upkeep from the sacrifices and offerings brought there (**9:13**). According to the OT the priests were to be given all the flesh from sin offerings and trespass offerings and almost all the grain from grain offerings. They were also allocated specific cuts from burnt offerings and peace offerings and use of the first-fruits of the harvests of wheat, barley, grapes, figs, pomegranates, olives and honey, and a tithe of the tithes that the Levites gave. They were also supplied with a portion of kneaded bread dough. These supplies would meet all their needs. Paul insists that there should be no difference between this OT practice and what should be taking place in the Christian era. Jesus had made the same point (**9:14**; see also Matt 10:10; Luke 10:7).

9:15-23 The privilege and the task

In case the Corinthians think that Paul is attempting to shame them, he hastens to add that he has not used any of these rights in the past and has no intention of starting to do so now. In fact, he asserts, *I would rather die* than use them (**9:15**). It is the one thing he feels free to boast about. He cannot boast about his preaching the gospel, because he had no choice about that. He says that he feels *compelled to preach* and suffers if he does not preach (**9:16**). He does not say what this suffering is, but it may well be that his conscience bothers him when he does not preach because he feels he is betraying Christ's love for him and will be judged for his failure on the last day. Paul sees his preaching of the gospel as a duty and not as something he volunteered to do (**9:17**). However, he does have a choice about whether to accept any monetary reward for his preaching, and is proud that he refuses to do this and thus presents the gospel *free of charge* (**9:18**). This was clearly his regular practice (1 Thess 2:9; 2 Thess 3:8; Acts 20:33-35; 2 Cor 11:7-15).

Paul's guiding principle was to *win as many as possible* (**9:19**). That is why he did not use his rights and made himself *a slave to everyone*. His self-denying love, which led him to surrender even privileges he was entitled to, contrasts with the Corinthians' knowledge, which they boasted about and clung to even if it might harm others (see 8:1-3).

Paul was flexible, as illustrated by Timothy's circumcision in order to avoid giving needless offence (Acts 16:3; Acts 21:18-26). He *became like those under the law* (the Jews) by observing the law even though he knew that this was not necessary for salvation (**9:20**). Similarly, he became like *those not having the law* (the Gentiles) in order to win them, although he is careful to point out that he was still *under Christ's law* (**9:21**). If believers were weak, Paul was prepared to accommodate their scruples (**9:22a**). In becoming *all things to all men* (**9:22b**) he was not abandoning his principles. Rather, he was demonstrating his willingness to enter other people's lives and share their circumstances. He did everything *for the sake of the gospel* (**9:23**) and from a desire to be a partner in the blessings it brings.

Paul's example shows how we should do evangelism. The recipients of our witnessing must have a sense that we identify with them. This is particularly so when we are seeking to reach groups where we are not known and groups that are likely to be antagonistic to the gospel. In areas of Africa where Muslim influence is strong, a Christian may decide to eat only halal meat, and a Christian woman may decide to wear a veil, even if this is foreign to her own culture.

9:24-27 A real fight

Is following Paul's principle easy? No. That is why he compares the Christian life to a race or a boxing match. Like athletes, Christians need to practise self-discipline. The Isthmian Games, which were similar to the modern Olympic Games, were held in Corinth every two years and attracted athletes from far and wide. The Corinthians would know about the *strict training* these athletes undertook and their need to *run in such a way as to get the prize* (**9:24-25a**; see also 2 Tim 4:7). Those athletes worked extremely hard to win the leafy crown awarded to the victor, a crown that would soon wither. By contrast, Christians are in training to win a crown *that will last forever* (**9:25b**; see also 2 Tim 4:8; Jas 1:12; 1 Pet 5:4; Rev 2:10 and 3:11).

Christians who want to wear that crown must be focused on the goal and have a purpose. They must discipline themselves to run and fight according to the rules, or else be *disqualified* (**9:27**). This disqualification means 'not getting a prize' rather than losing salvation – although some take the latter interpretation. The prize here would be God's 'Well done!' at the end of the race.

Successful African runners and boxers know the need to work hard and be very disciplined if they are to win a medal. Just as the African continent has many sons and daughters who excel internationally in sports, so it needs sons and daughters who will excel in winning a 'well done' from God for living a life of righteous love and exercising justice and mercy.

10:1-13 Lessons from Israel's History

Paul now gives some examples that illustrate the dangers of not practising self-discipline (10:6, 11). What the athlete wins with discipline, the Israelites lost by their indulgence. The word *all* (used four times in these verses) is emphatic. It leaves out none of the Israelites. They *were all under the cloud* (**10:1a**), a reference to the cloud that gave Israel direction, shelter and protection during the wilderness wandering (Exod 13:21-22; 14:19-20; 40:34-38; Num 9:15-23; 14:14; Deut 1:33; Ps 78:14; 105:39). They *all passed through the sea* (**10:1b**), a reference to the crossing of the Red Sea (Exod 14:19-31). With these two experiences they were perfectly united with Moses, their greatest leader and lawgiver, so that Paul says they were *baptized into Moses in the cloud and in the sea* (**10:2**). Not only this, but *they all ate the same spiritual food and drank the same spiritual drink* (**10:3-4a**), a clear reference to manna (Exod 16:11-15) and the water from the rock (Num 20:1-11). The idea of the *rock that accompanied them,* which Paul identifies as *Christ* (**10:4b**), comes from a rabbinic tradition, a legend known to all the Jews, that the rock that Moses had struck followed them right into the Promised Land. (God is often referred to as a 'Rock' in the OT – see Deut 32:4, 15, 18, 30-31, 37; Ps 18:2, 31; Isa 30:29). All of the Israelites experienced these things, yet *most of them* did not find favour with God and died in the desert (**10:5**).

Paul is convinced that *these things occurred as examples* so that Christians will not indulge in the sins that snared the Israelites (**10:6**). They should not *be idolaters* (**10:7**), as the Israelites were in the incident of the golden calf (Exod 32). This is perhaps also a reference to current circumstances, like the Corinthians' misuse of their Christian liberty in attending pagan feasts. They should not *commit sexual immorality* (**10:8**), as in the incident with the Moabites and Midianites (Num 25:1-9) where thousands died. (Paul says twenty-three thousand where Numbers had twenty-four thousand. Presumably the exact number to die was between these two figures, and the author of Numbers rounded up, while Paul rounds down. In any event, Paul's point is not dependent on the exact number involved, and he may thus have felt free to quote the number from memory.)

The Corinthian believers must also be careful not to *test the Lord* (**10:9**), as the Israelites did with their persistent ingratitude (Num 21:5-9). They should not *grumble* (**10:10**), as the Israelites did after the incident with Korah (Num 16:41-50), where Paul says they were *killed by the destroying angel*, God's agent of retribution.

The application of this to the Corinthian believers is that they need to be careful. They were living in the time of *the fulfilment of the ages* (**10:11**), in the brief space between Christ's death and his return at the second coming. They may think themselves wise (3:18), rich (4:8) and full of knowledge, but they must not assume they *are standing firm*. Instead they need to concentrate on not falling (**10:12**). For Paul is sure that temptation will come. He is also sure that the temptations they will face will not be unique, and that there will always be some way of escape (**10:13**). The escape may not be easy, for the word Paul uses refers to a mountain pass. But they will be like an army, apparently surrounded, which suddenly sees a route to safety.

10:14-22 The Lord's Supper and Idol Feasts

The particular temptation the Corinthians are facing in relation to food offered to idols is idolatry. So Paul points out to those he counts his *dear friends* the 'way of escape' (10:13) from this sin: *flee from idolatry* (**10:14**). Flight was also the technique he advised for dealing with immorality (6:18). He is confident that they will recognize that what he is saying here is common sense (**10:15**).

He reminds them that they regularly participate in one feast, the Lord's Supper. There they share in a *cup of thanksgiving* (**10:16**). The term he uses here refers to the third cup of wine that was drunk at the Jewish Passover meal, which was accompanied by a prayer of thanksgiving. When they drink the wine and eat bread together at the Lord's Supper, they are expressing their own association and identification with the sacrificial death of Christ. Not only that: they are also expressing their unity in the body of Christ through the analogy of the *one loaf* (**10:17**). Despite their diversity (see also 12:12-31) they are all one family, sharing the same spiritual food.

The Lord's Supper is not the only feast that expresses the concept of association and identification. When Jews had a feast associated with a sacrifice, all those who ate were regarded as participants in the sacrifice, identifying themselves with what it symbolized (**10:18**). The same applies when one takes part in a pagan sacrificial feast. While Paul agrees with the Corinthians that the idols themselves have neither divine power nor any real existence

(8:4), he also believes that the devil, or demons, encourages idol worship in opposition to the true God. Consequently *sacrifices of pagans are offered to demons, not to God* (**10:19-20**). To participate in a pagan feast is thus to go along with the plans of demons. Consequently Paul has no doubt that *you cannot drink the cup of the Lord and the cup of demons too* (**10:21**). The two feasts are incompatible. Trying to participate in both will only *arouse the Lord's jealousy* (**10:22**). If Paul is here thinking of the warning in Deuteronomy 32:21, it is clear that he identifies Christ with Jehovah. Finally, Paul concludes with the warning, '*Are we stronger than he?*' The Corinthians needed to learn, like the Israelites, that they cannot defy Jehovah.

10:23-11:1 The Limits of Christian Freedom

Idolatrous feasts were not the only context in which believers had to deal with meat offered to idols. So Paul adds some practical advice about what to do in other situations. As he has already stressed, the guiding principle is to do only what is *beneficial* and *constructive* (**10:23**) and to always take into account *the good of others* (**10:24**). Christian freedom should not be used for selfish purposes. We are to live in love, as Christ commanded (Matt 22:39; Luke 10:27-37).

Though it is true that most meat sold in the market had probably been offered to some idol as a sacrifice, Paul advises against being too fussy and causing unnecessary difficulties either in *the meat market* (**10:25**) or in the home of *some unbeliever* (**10:27**). He quotes Psalm 24:1 in support of his position, which is one that agrees with the teaching of Jesus (see Mark 7:14-19; Acts 10:15; 1 Tim 4:4).

However, if someone makes a point of telling you about the source of the meat, and is disturbed by it, then you should not eat it in order to protect the conscience of the person (presumably a weaker believer) who has given you the information. Here, too, Paul is applying the principle stated in 10:24. But he takes pains to stress that it is the conscience of the informant that he is concerned about, not the conscience of the stronger believer who eats anything (**10:29-30**).

Paul concludes his discussion of meat with a strong restatement of the principles he has been stressing throughout this section of the letter. The overriding consideration in all circumstances and in dealing with anyone, regardless of their race or religion (see 9:19-22) must simply be to bring glory to God (**10:31**) and not to *cause anyone to stumble* (**10:32**). This desire *to please everybody* (**10:33**) must not be an attempt to curry favour for ourselves, but must rather be done at our own expense, without regard to our own rights and privileges. We must not seek our own good but that of others, with our ultimate goal being that many *may be saved* (**10:33**). Paul encourages the Corinthians to *follow my example*, just as he himself follows *the example of Christ* (**11:1**).

11:2–14:40 Issues Concerning Public Worship

11:2-16 The Veiling of Women

The Corinthian believers had faithfully kept the instructions Paul had delivered to them, and had written to ask his opinion on certain issues. For this, Paul says *I praise you* (**11:2**). Then he goes on to discuss the issue of head coverings, presenting a missionary's solution to a local situation that had deep implications for Greek women. Within Greek culture, women were often divided into two broad categories: matrons, whose main concern was for their husband and children, and *hetairai* (literally, companions), who were independent and entertained lovers in their homes. Wives were respected, but hetairai were not. The two groups dressed differently, with matrons wearing a veil while hetairai dyed or braided their hair in a way that would attract lovers (see 1 Tim 2:9b).

Throughout his writings, Paul stresses the need for believers to be deeply concerned about the testimony of their behaviour. For the women at Corinth, wearing a veil testified to the decency and dignity that befits a Christian woman. The situation was comparable to that among many Muslim women today.

When we seek to apply Paul's words to Christian women in Africa, we need to remember that he is not giving a rule that is universally binding. But the principle underlying his ruling applies to all cultures and all times. The basic question is, what glorifies God within one's local setting? For Christian women in predominantly Muslim communities, it may be wearing a veil. In other communities, covering one's head may be less important.

It is also important to remember that the type of veil being discussed here is very different from modern hats and from the headgear worn by many African women. It was formed by drawing part of the long outer garment around the head and folding it across the lower part of the face. Paul would undoubtedly have disapproved of the extravagant headgear now worn by some, and might have applied the principles he outlined in 1 Timothy 2:9.

The *head* is the symbol of authority and supremacy, so this problem really concerns issues of partnership and subordination. Paul argues that we are all in a line of subordination: a woman is subordinate to a man, men are subordinate to Christ and Christ is subordinate to God (**11:3**). But Christ is not subordinate to the Father because he is inferior to the Father or fundamentally different from him. Christ is equal with the Father, but he has chosen to submit as a Son in order to accomplish God's purpose (15: 27-28). Thus Paul's statement about the relationships of men and women must not be used to suggest that women are in some way inferior to men.

He also clearly identifies the context in which he is speaking: the repeated references to *prays or prophesies*

(**11:4, 5**) indicate that Paul was talking about the conduct of men and women who were participating in corporate or public worship. This suggests that women took part in public worship in Corinth.

The reason why a woman needed to wear a veil was that because not doing so would be an expression of disrespect for *her head* (that is, her husband) (11:5). In such an immoral city as Corinth, it was very important not to suggest in any way that believers were immoral or disrespectful. In Jewish circles, women who were suspected of adultery had their hair cut, while in Greek circles, lesbian women wore their hair short. Failing to wear a veil would be seen by outsiders as suggesting an equally immoral lifestyle, and so Paul bluntly states that *if a woman does not cover her head, she should have her hair cut off* (**11:6**).

Christian men, by contrast, were to keep their heads uncovered, unlike pagan Roman priests who pulled their togas up over their heads when performing religious rituals and some pagan Greek men who favoured elaborate hairstyles. Christian men were to have their heads bare before God (11:4, 7).

In describing a woman as *the glory of man* (**11:7**) and as created *for man* (**11:8-9**; see also Gen 2:18) Paul is not degrading women but defining their relationship to men. He has more to say on this subject in 11:11-12.

Paul gives two further reasons why a woman should cover her head, but these are difficult to interpret. The first is *because of the angels* (**11:10a**). This can be interpreted in three different ways: a) angels are interested in our salvation and are particularly sensitive to decorum in our worship (see Luke 15:7; Eph 3:10; 1 Tim 5:21), b) women are not to tempt the angels sexually (see Gen 6:1-2) or c) women are to imitate the angels who also veil themselves before God (see Isa 6:1-2).

The second reason Paul gives is that the veil is *a sign of authority over her head* (**11:10b**). The Greek word here translated as 'sign of authority' suggests that the veil is not solely a symbol of subjection to her husband but also a marker of the woman's own authority and dignity.

Paul realizes that he may be giving the impression that women are inferior to men, so he insists that neither sex is independent of the other (**11:11**). Woman is dependent on man because she was made from man, but man in turn is dependent on woman, since she gives birth to him. Both of them, and everything else, come *from God* (**11:12**). The relationship between men and women is one of interdependence. This is a remarkable statement considering the way women were generally regarded at that time.

Paul appeals to their judgment about what behaviour was considered natural, within the limits of the place and period in which he was writing. The Corinthians in general would have found long hair on a man offensive, but would have admired it in a woman (**11:13-15**). This is generally still true in African culture, and so the argument has relevance today.

Increasingly, however, young African men are doing such things as plaiting their hair and wearing earrings. The church should not label such behaviour as signalling whether someone has been saved or not. Rather, Christian young men need to be encouraged to think in terms of whether this, and all other aspects of their behaviour, contributes to building up or breaking down God's kingdom in their own environment and period. They should not adopt practices simply because they have been exposed to them, but should seek to glorify God by using their example to expand his rule in the lives of others. For many, this will mean dressing in a way that will not shock others and turn them away from Christ.

This section ends with a rebuke to those who take delight in argument for its own sake (**11:16**). It is a good thing to take a stand on a point of principle, but there is no place in the *churches of God* for people who merely want to argue.

11:17-34 Proper Celebration of the Lord's Supper

Paul had praised the Corinthian believers in 11:2, but he finds nothing to praise in the way they are celebrating the Lord's Supper. To put it bluntly, their *meetings do more harm than good* (**11:17**). The first reason this is so is because of the *divisions* among them (**11:18**). These divisions, which Paul has already dealt with in the opening chapters of this letter as centring on different personalities, may also have followed the lines of who was rich and who was poor. Paul condemns all such divisions. Just as warring political parties destroy a nation, so also such divisions destroy a church.

Unfortunately, such divisions are common on the African continent. Immaturity in politics makes us unable to handle difference of opinion constructively, and immaturity within the church causes many wounds. All believers are to be on guard and to maintain the unity in Christ that sets no boundaries between believers no matter what their status, or their opinions on church matters or other matters.

The only *differences* in the church that Paul grudgingly approved were those that revealed which believers had understood Christ's words about unity and love and which had not (**11:19**). Will we also agree to disagree and maintain the unity of the body?

The way the Lord's Supper was being celebrated in Corinth made a mockery of the whole thing, so much so that Paul can say *it is not the Lord's Supper you eat* (**11:20**). We need to understand the form that the celebration of the Lord's Supper took at the time. It seems that the believers would meet regularly for a love feast, an *agape* meal, which was rather like a potluck supper. All the believers would bring food, which was then pooled and shared by all. This lovely practice also meant that poor believers had at least one decent meal each week. In Corinth, however, the food was not being shared, with the result that *one remains hungry* while *another gets drunk* (**11:21**). Paul insists that if the Lord's Supper cannot be celebrated with mutual love and sharing, it would be better for everyone to eat at home. He points out that the way they are behaving suggests that they *despise the church of God* (that is, God's people) and are happy to humiliate *those who have nothing* (**11:22**). The contrast with Christ's behaviour is striking.

Paul reminds them of what the Lord's Supper was meant to be by describing how it began, stressing that he is recounting a tradition that has been passed carefully from one person to another. He himself had received it and had passed it on to the Corinthians (**11:23a**). So they had no excuse for their behaviour.

The Lord's Supper began with Jesus taking some bread and offering a prayer of thanksgiving, followed by a declaration, *This is my body, which is for you,* and a command, *do this in remembrance of me*, which implies that the practice will carry on (**11:23b-24**). Then Jesus took the wine and made the remarkable statement that *this cup is the new covenant in my blood* (**11:25**). The bread and wine symbolize the start of a covenant that God is now entering into with human beings, a covenant that is very different from the old one. It is sealed with Jesus' own blood. Jesus makes it clear that the passing of the cup should also be a regular practice, although he does not specify how often it should be done. Paul adds the reminder that the celebration of this meal will continue only until Jesus comes again and there is no longer any need to *proclaim the Lord's death* (**11:26**).

Then Paul moves on to give some warnings and issue some instructions. They must be careful not to eat the Lord's Supper *in an unworthy manner* (**11:27**) through their lack of love, factious spirit, greed and contempt for one another. To do this would be to sin against Christ himself as much as it would be to sin against his church. It is thus important that before taking part in the meal they each check their motives as well as their moral and spiritual condition (**11:28**). Treating the Lord's Supper with casual disrespect represents a failure to recognize *the body of the Lord* (meaning both the Lord's literal sacrifice of himself, which is commemorated in the Lord's Supper, and the church, which is the body of Christ). Paul says that this failure brings judgment. He asserts that this judgment is already evident in that many in the church *are weak and sick, and a number of you have fallen asleep* (**11:30**). God's judgment on the church is intended to cure this evil and prevent the church from getting a bad reputation (**11:31-32**).

Paul's final words on the topic are to tell the Corinthians that if some of them are so hungry that they cannot wait for others to get there, they should eat at home. When they meet as a church to celebrate the Lord's Supper, they should all eat together (**11:33-34**).

12:1-11 Manifestations of the Spirit in Worship

Turning to spiritual gifts, which was another subject probably raised by the Corinthians in their letter, Paul says, '*I do not want you to be ignorant*' (**12:1**), which is his regular way of introducing important subjects in his letters (10:1; Rom 1:13; 11:25; 2 Cor 1:8; 1 Thess 4:13). He reminds them of the days when they were still pagans and were *influenced and led astray* by idols (**12:2**). Now, by contrast, they cannot say '*Jesus be cursed*' if they are *speaking by the Spirit of God*. They will instead say, '*Jesus is Lord*' – which was the standard confession of faith for Christians at that time (**12:3**).

Paul starts by specifying that there are different *kinds of gifts, kinds of service* and *kinds of working*. Emphasizing the unity of function between the different persons of the Trinity, he links the gifts with the *Spirit*, the kinds of service with *the Lord* and the kinds of working with *God* (**12:4-6**).

He then writes about the different ways the Spirit becomes manifest (12:7). As always, he stresses that everyone has a gift that is very useful in the community and that gifts are not given for the benefit of the gifted person, but for the *common good* (**12:7**). Because his focus in this letter is primarily on how the Spirit is manifested in public worship, the list of gifts he gives here is different from the lists found elsewhere in his letters (see Rom 12:4, where the emphasis is on the function of the gifts, and Eph 4:11, where it is on the role of the gifts in ministry).

The specific gifts listed here include the *message of wisdom*, that is, spiritual insight regarding the practical application of Christian principles, and the *message of knowledge*, that is, an intelligent grasp of Christian principles. They also include *faith*, by which is meant not saving faith but mountain-moving faith that defies the impossible (see also 13:2; Matt 17:20; 21:21) and *gifts of healings*, that is, the gifts required to heal various diseases (**12:9**). Other gifts include *miraculous powers*, that is, miracles that were evidently acts of power (see also Acts 5:1-11; 13:11); *prophecy*, which is not so much foretelling the future as declaring God's acts of power, love and grace and *distinguishing between spirits*, that is, having the ability to distinguish between the Spirit of God and evil spirits – an ability that is required of all believers (see 1 Thess 5:20; 1 John 4:1), but is a special gift to some. Finally, there are the gifts of *speaking in different kinds of tongues* and of interpreting tongues, that is, the gifts of speaking and of understanding a language that is not learned, an ecstatic experience given to some (**12:10**). The use of the plural *kinds of tongues* shows that there is considerable variation in the way this gift is manifested.

Once again Paul stresses that all these gifts have a divine source (**12:11**). The Spirit gives them as *he determines* which means that it is foolish to have jealousy and rivalry between believers.

12:12-31 Unity in Diversity

Paul uses the analogy of the human body with its many parts to demonstrate that the body of Christ has many different parts with many different gifts, but is still one body (**12:12**). Regardless of their origins, all Christians are *baptized* (regenerated) *by one Spirit*, that is, by the Holy Spirit and are *given the one Spirit to drink*, that is, are filled with the same one Spirit (**12:13**). All are thus part of Christ's body.

The different parts of the body do not envy each other, and the same should apply to the believers (**12:14-20**). Similarly, there should be no looking down on one another, just as the different parts of the body do not look down on one another (**12:21-26**). Just as God designed the working of the human body, so he has planned the way that different individuals can contribute to his church. The different parts of a body all need each other, just as individual Christians need one another. This point is well made by the African proverb, 'The left hand washes the right and the right hand washes the left'. Even those parts that seem weak are *indispensable* and are *treated with special honour*. God's design requires that the different parts of both the physical body and the church be concerned for one another (12:25), for as the African proverb puts it, 'One hand cannot lift a [heavy] load'. Even pain is not meant to be endured in isolation, for God designed the human body and the church to share in the pain and pleasure of all their components (12:26).

Finally Paul tells the divided Corinthians that, in spite of their many shortcomings, they *are the body of Christ* (**12:27**). The 'you' in this verse is emphatic, and Paul underlines it: *each one of you is part of it*. In his divine sovereignty, God has appointed people with various gifts to serve his church in Corinth and around the world (12:28).

The first gift that Paul mentions is that of *apostles*, a category that includes not just the Twelve but also Barnabas, James the Lord's brother (Gal 1:19) and Paul himself (Rom 16:7; 1 Cor 15:5, 7). It seems that this term has both a technical sense, in which it is limited to those specifically referred to as apostles in Scripture, and a non-technical meaning when it is applied to anyone who is God's messenger. This latter usage only becomes a problem when some people act as if someone called an apostle today has the same power and authority as the biblical apostles. That is certainly not the case.

Others have *the gift of administration*. The word translated as 'administration' is derived from the idea of being able to steer a ship on the correct course. (For a discussion of the other roles mentioned in 12:28, see under 12:8-10.)

Paul uses rhetorical questions to stress the need for diversity in the body of Christ (**12:28-30**). Every gift is needed and is important, but he encourages the Corinthians to *eagerly desire the greater gifts … the most excellent way* (**12:31**). Our holy ambition should be to be controlled by love as Paul makes clear in chapter 13.

13:1-13 The Supremacy of Love

Without love, Paul insists, no quality, however spectacular, whether it is an endowment of spiritual gifts or religious zeal, is of any value (13:1-3). This includes *being able to speak in the tongues of men and of angels.* Unless this spectacular ability to speak in known and unknown languages, earthly and heavenly, is accompanied by selfless, self-sacrificial love, it is worth no more than the boom of a gong or the clang of a cymbal (**13:1**). Gongs and cymbals were used in pagan worship, and so Paul may be saying that without love, tongues are no better than pagan worship. The same applies to *the gift of prophecy* and to understanding *all mysteries, and all knowledge* as well as the gifts of *faith that can move mountains* (a common proverbial phrase used to describe a faith that overcomes great difficulties and accomplishes amazing things) (**13:2**). There is no merit in giving generously to the poor or even in making the ultimate sacrifice of surrendering *my body to the flames* if it is done without love (**13:3**).

A reader might ask what is meant by love, and so in **13:4-7** Paul sets out the characteristics of a truly Christian love. It is *patient* and *kind.* These two together comprise being sweet to all. Love also *does not envy* and *does not boast* and show off its own achievements. Love is *not rude* – it will not indulge in the unmannerly conduct described in 11:5, 6, 21. Nor is it *self-seeking* – a quality that Paul has already dealt with twice in this letter (see 6:1-8; 10:24, 33). Love is also *not easily angered,* or, in other words, it is not quick to take offence. Nor is it like a bookkeeper, keeping a list of what has been done: *it keeps no records of wrongs.* Instead love unites with the truth in rejoicing when wrong is overcome. It *always protects* or shelters others and always has faith in others, even when it may be hurt. Love looks forward to the ultimate triumph of truth and shows a steadfast endurance, the active counterpart of the more passive patience.

Christian love can be described as 'the greater gift' because it is absolutely permanent. It will still be there when all the other spiritual gifts, represented here by the three gifts of prophecy, tongues and knowledge, are gone (**13:8**). Our present life, even at its best, is full of imperfections. We are still in some ways like children, or like people seeing only *poor reflections* in a mirror (remember that at that time there would have been no clear glass mirrors) (**13:9-12a**). But the way of love leads to the day when all these imperfections will have passed away and then we will *see clearly … know fully* and *see face to face* (**13:12b**).

An African proverb addresses the difference that full knowledge makes: 'The words of the elders become sweet the day after.' Our immature state is characterized by a lack of love and imperfect judgment, but once we have achieved maturity, our previous wrong assumptions and incorrect conclusions are overturned.

Finally, Paul reminds the Corinthian believers that love is absolutely supreme. *Hope* and *faith* are good, but without love they are cold and grim virtues. Love is undoubtedly the greatest, for it is like a fire that kindles faith and a light that brightens hope (**13:13**).

14:1-40 Prophecy and Tongues

14:1-25 The superiority of prophecy over tongues

To set the tone for what is to follow, Paul begins by reminding the Corinthians of what he has been saying in chapters 12 and 13 about *the way of love, spiritual gifts,* and *the gift of prophecy* (**14:1**). He urges them to be particularly eager to receive 'the gift of prophecy' (see also 12:31; 14:39). Someone speaking in tongues is using a language *no one understands* and is uttering *mysteries* that are addressed *to God* (**14:2**). But in public worship, which is the focus of this portion of the letter, Paul prefers prophecy (the gift of inspired preaching and inspired utterances that build the congregation) to tongues. The former, which offers *strengthening, encouragement and comfort* to others, is intelligible, while the latter is not. Tongues only edify the individual using them (**14:3-4**). For this reason they should not be used during public worship unless the person speaking or someone else can interpret them (**14:5**). To strengthen his argument, Paul asks them what use he would be to them as a teacher if he spoke in tongues (**14:6**). It was his job to bring them some direct *revelation* from God, some special *knowledge,* some *prophecy* (that is, the proclamation of some truth) and *teaching* (instruction).

Even musical instruments like the flute, harp and bugle (or trumpet) have to make meaningful sounds if people are to respond to a tune or to the message being communicated (**14:7-8**). Similarly, the message conveyed in public worship must be clear and intelligible (**14:9**).

Extending the argument to human language, Paul argues that there are many human languages, all of which are meaningful to the person who speaks them but which will not communicate if the listener does not know the language (**14:10-11**). If their desire is to build up the church, as it should be, then they must aim to communicate their message clearly (**14:12**).

Given this stress on intelligibility, Paul insists that someone who has the gift of tongues must *pray that he may interpret what he says* (**14:13**). There are two reasons for this. One is personal. Tongues benefit only the speaker's spirit, but not the mind, even when used in prayer (**14:14**). Paul thinks it is important to benefit both parts, and so he is happy to pray and praise God with both his spirit and his mind – that is, in an intelligible way as well as in a tongue (**14:15**). Second, because he is dealing with public worship, Paul's paramount concern is for those who do not understand, and particularly for interested outsiders, that is, those who are not yet believers but who are interested in what Christians do when they worship. Everyone should be able to say 'Amen', thus indicating their agreement with what has been prayed for, or given thanks for (**14:16**). No matter how thankful the one speaking in tongues is, someone who does not understand what is being said cannot share in their thanks and is therefore not edified (**14:17**).

Not boasting, but rather forestalling anyone who says he does not know what he is speaking about, Paul reminds the Corinthians that he speaks in tongues *more than all of you* (**14:18**). But he does this in private. In church, *he would rather speak five intelligible words* than thousands of unintelligible ones that benefited no one (**14:19**). He saw no value in parading this gift in public to impress others. In fact, he regarded the desire for such displays as childish and immature. It is true that Christians must be infants *in regard to evil*, but they must think like adults (**14:20**).

Paul next quotes Isaiah 28:11, where God tells the scoffing Israelites that because they have refused to listen to Isaiah's clear message he will have to act in judgment and get his message to them through the Assyrians, who speak a language they find unintelligible (**14:21**). To this extent, tongues are a sign of God's judgment on those who have rejected him. But in public worship of the whole church, the message of God's love is still being proclaimed. Thus the aim must be to avoid a situation in which someone who is interested in the faith or who is still a complete unbeliever enters a group and hears only a babble of unknown tongues, leading them to conclude that *you are out of your mind* (**14:23**). On the other hand, if they enter *while everybody is prophesying*, the result will be very different. They will be *convinced by all* (**14:24**). It is not clear how everyone can be prophesying in a public worship service, but what is probably meant here is that everyone present is declaring their faith and celebrating God's acts of power and mercy in songs of praise. The result is total conversion of the newcomer, who will *fall down and worship God, exclaiming 'God is really among you!'* (**14:25**).

14:26-33a Practical issues

Paul next gives some guidelines for the conduct of public worship. The fundamental principle is that everything that takes place (whether *a hymn, or a word of instruction, a revelation, a tongue or an interpretation*) must contribute to *the strengthening of the church* (**14:26**).

The second principle is that anyone who has a gift must be given the chance to use that gift, but not at the expense of order. Christian liberty does not mean disorder. Thus *two – or at the most three – should speak* in a tongue, and the tongue must be interpreted, and not be merely an ecstatic utterance (**14:27-28**). The same applies to prophesying, and to giving a word of revelation or a word of instruction (**14:29-31**). The speakers must speak one at a time, while the others must use their discernment while reflecting on what is being shared.

For tongues, *if there is no interpreter the speaker should keep quiet* (**14:28**). Some would protest that this is impossible when God takes hold of them, but Paul reminds them that *the spirits of prophets are subject to the control of prophets* (**14:32**), meaning that God does not override human self-control. Each of them can have their turn to speak, which may not even come at one particular meeting. As always, the purpose of speaking must be to instruct and encourage all who are present.

To drive his point home, Paul reminds the Corinthians of God's character: He *is not a God of disorder, but of peace* (**14:33a**). The chaos and commotion that characterized public worship in Corinth were out of keeping with the character of God.

14:33b-36 Women in the church

Paul next insists that the common practice *in all the congregations of the saints* is that women must not talk in church, but *should remain silent* (**14:33b-34**). In light of 11:5, Paul cannot be saying that a woman should never open her mouth in church. So what does he mean here?

The word translated as 'speak' in 4:34 and 14:35 can mean either talking in an ordinary way or asserting with authority. From Paul's reference to *submission*, it seems that some women may have been speaking in a way that went against the virtue of submission. In the Corinthian context, a woman who asserted herself in public in a way that suggested she was not a submissive wife brought disgrace on her husband and her community – in this case the church.

When we relate this prohibition to our times, we need to think about what ways of speaking in public would suggest that a wife is not submissive. Generally, this would involve speaking in a way that humiliates her husband or other men. But it is possible for a woman to express her views, even where she differs with others, without humiliating her husband. Effective African women have demonstrated this. A woman who bullies men with her strong opinions rapidly loses her audience, while a woman who instructs with a humble spirit affects the lives of many.

A similar passage is found in 1 Timothy 2:11-15, and there too submission is at the heart of the discussion. In both places, Paul is not concerned with ability but with the priorities that God has established. As the Timothy passage says, God made Adam first and then Eve and his design is that Eve and her fellow women should submit while Adam and his fellow men should love their wives as Christ loved the church (Eph 5:22, 25).

Paul insists that if women have questions *they should ask their husbands at home* (**14:35**). This may work for married women, but what about unmarried women? Presumably, they should consult members of their families. For Paul, it is *disgraceful* for any woman to ignore the requirements of subordination and submission and disrupt the order of holy worship.

Paul's closing questions in **14:36** clearly show that he seriously disapproves of the disorder and the lack of discipline that have characterized public worship in Corinth (see also ch. 11). He condemns arrogant self-esteem (see also 4:8, 19).

14:37-40 Conclusion

Paul concludes this section with a challenge similar to the one he issued in 11:16, except that here he gives the command of Christ as his source of authority. Even those who regard themselves as prophets or as especially spiritually gifted must bow to this authority or be ignored (**14:37-38**).

He then summarizes the main points he has been making in this section. Prophecy is of paramount importance, but there should be no prohibition on speaking in tongues (**14:39**). Paul does not intend to quench anyone's gift, but the use of these gifts in worship must adhere to the rule of decency and order, with everything in its proper place and sequence as in a well-disciplined army (**14:40**).

15:1-58 Questions about the Resurrection

15:1-11 The Facts of Christ's Resurrection

Paul now turns to a subject he had probably heard the Corinthians had misconceptions about, for there is no indication that they had written to inquire about it. He starts by reminding them of the fundamentals of the gospel he had preached to them in the past and which they had accepted (**15:1**). Now, they have taken their stand on it, and are thus in the process of being saved. However, they need to *hold firmly* to it (that is, to continue to believe in the resurrection and the other basics of the faith) or their faith would have been *in vain* (**15:2**). In saying this, Paul does not mean that they will lose their salvation, for they have met the entrance level of faith (justification). But the entrance level of faith needs to grow into a faith that shows itself in renewal of character so that they become Christlike, that is, sanctified. If a faith that is claimed does not affect our lives, that faith is in vain and the believer will forfeit some rewards in heaven (3:11-15).

Paul stresses that this gospel was not something he dreamed up (see 11:23), but contains facts he had *received* and *passed* on to them about Christ's atoning death (he *died for our sins*) in fulfilment of Scripture (**15:3**). The fact that Christ *was buried* is evidence that he really died. (Interestingly, apart from the Gospel writers, Paul is the only NT writer to refer to Christ's burial – see Acts 13:29; Rom 6:4; Col 2:12.) Another fact that fulfilled Scripture was Christ's resurrection: *he was raised* (or, more accurately, 'he has been raised', for he is still raised (15:12, 13, 14, 16, 17, 20; see also Rom 6:9).

Paul lists the historical witnesses to the resurrection (**15:5-8**). These include *Peter* (see Luke 24:34), *the Twelve* (a general name for the apostles, excluding Judas) and *more than five hundred of the brothers at the same time*. This last appearance is not recorded in the Gospels, but there is no reason to doubt that it happened because the Gospels do not claim to have recorded all of Jesus' appearances. Moreover, the fact that most of these witnesses were still alive at the time when Paul was writing means that people could have checked that what he was saying was the truth. There were also appearances *to James* (Jesus' half-brother) and to *all the apostles* (a term used very broadly – see also 12:28). The final appearance was to Paul, who describes himself as *abnormally born,* by which he probably means that his miraculous, instant conversion on the Damascus road is not the normal way that believers meet the risen Christ.

Paul recognized that his 'birth' was abnormal, and considered himself *the least of the apostles*, not because he lacked apostolic gifts and authority but because in his earlier days he had *persecuted the church of God* (**15:9**). Consequently, he is amazed by the grace God has extended to him and the effects it has had in his life (**15:10**). Because of that grace of God, he has *worked harder than all* the other apostles. But the difference between him and the other apostles does not extend to the gospel. All of them preached the same message, the message that the Corinthians had believed (**15:11**).

15:12-19 Consequences of Denying the Resurrection

Having given the evidence proving that Jesus was resurrected and having pointed out that the resurrection is central to the preaching the Corinthians had heard and accepted, Paul expresses his puzzlement that some of them were denying *the resurrection of the dead* (**15:12**). Their reason for doing this may have been rooted in the Greek belief that while the soul was immortal, the body was worthless (see comments on 6:13-14).

Paul responds by pointing out that if the very idea of bodily resurrection is false, then Jesus, too, cannot have been resurrected (**15:13**). And if Jesus is still dead, there is absolutely no point to his preaching or to their believing (**15:14**). In fact, what was being preached would not only be *useless*, it would also be a pack of lies spread by untruthful witnesses (**15:15-16**). Consequently the Corinthians' faith served no purpose, and their sins would not have been forgiven (**15:17**). Those who had died (*fallen asleep*) would not be with Christ, rather they would have been destroyed (**15:18**). If this were true, Christians should only be pitied, not praised (**15:19**).

15:20-28 Consequences of Christ's Resurrection

Paul follows his sketch of the hopelessness that goes with denial of the resurrection, with vivid images of the glorious results of believing that Christ rose from the dead. The first image he uses is that Christ is *the firstfruits of those who have fallen asleep* (**15:20**). The Mosaic law required that the first grain harvested be brought to the temple (Lev 23:10-11) in grateful recognition that the harvest came from God. The firstfruits thus symbolized the whole harvest to follow. In the same way, the resurrection of Jesus was a sign of the future resurrection of all believers, which would come. It was quite different from the earlier resurrections of people like the widow's son and Lazarus (Luke 7:12-15;.John 11:43-44), for those people would all have died again later.

The second image is that of a new creation. The first man God made was Adam, who sinned and thus brought death into the world. Jesus is a second Adam, who reverses the actions of the first one, destroying death by coming back to life (**15:21**). We have all suffered the effects of Adam's sin and will all know death; but now, we can all enjoy the benefits of life through Christ's resurrection. With Christ, a new power that liberates from sin and death has come into the world, so that just as *all died* then, now *all will be made alive* (**15:22**). Here Paul is obviously focusing on believers and is not addressing the fate of unbelievers.

The process of resurrection will be orderly, like the movements of a disciplined army (see 14:40). The firstfruit (Christ) has to precede the rest of the harvest, who will rise *when he comes* (**15:23**).

History is moving towards a climax – *that God may be all in all* (15:28). This state will only be reached once Christ has handed *over the kingdom to God after he has destroyed all dominion, authority and power* (**15:24**). As history unfolds, Christ will ultimately establish his visible kingdom. All those forces that are opposed to him will then be destroyed and *put under his feet* (**15:25**). Death is included as the *last enemy to be destroyed* (**15:26**), which means that believers will no longer be under the power of death.

While **15:27-28** seem to indicate that Christ is subordinate to God, it needs to be remembered that Paul is using human terms and analogies here to describe eternal truths. Christ is not subject to God as a slave or a servant is subject to a master. Rather he is like a prince who accomplishes a task he has been assigned and returns with the glory of complete obedience as his crown.

15:29-34 Arguments from Christian Activities

Several Christian activities would be meaningless if it were not for the truth of the resurrection. One of these is the Corinthian practice of being *baptized for the dead* (**15:29**). There has been much debate about what this means. Among the possible interpretations are a) being baptized above the graves of the martyrs (but this is unlikely as there were not yet many martyrs when Paul wrote this letter), b) being baptized out of respect and affection for the dead (this is possible, but there is nothing in the text or anywhere in the NT to support it), c) being baptized to fill up vacant

places in the church left by the dead (a lovely thought, but how many of the believers at Corinth had died by the time Paul wrote this letter?) or d) being baptized on behalf of the dead, that is, being baptized on behalf of someone else who had died. Whatever the case, Paul does not necessarily approve of the practice. He is simply citing it for the sake of his argument: if the living have so much concern for the dead as to be baptized for them, then the dead must have an existence beyond death.

Paul's own suffering as a Christian is meaningless if Christ has not been raised. After all, why should he endanger himself to such an extent that he can describe it as dying every day if he has no hope of a future life (**15:30-31**)? Paul assures the Corinthians that he was not exaggerating when he said this – just as he was not exaggerating his pride in them (15:31). He had endured experiences like having to fight with *wild beasts in Ephesus* (**15:32**). There is no reference to such an incident in the book of Acts, so it is possible that Paul is speaking metaphorically, expressing how threatened he was by his fierce struggles with Jews and Gentiles in that city.

Why would Paul put up with these dangers if there were no resurrection? He would be much more sensible to enjoy life in the way advised by a popular saying (15:32; see also Eccl 2:24; 3:21; Isa 22:13).

Paul discourages association with those who deny the resurrection because *bad company corrupts good character* (**15:33**). This is a common Greek proverb that he uses to encourage them to *stop sinning* and not follow the way of those who, shamefully, are *ignorant of God* (**15:34**). As the Akan (Ghana) would say: 'Some types of cassava are not good for cooking.'

15:35-49 The Nature of the Resurrection Body

As a good teacher, Paul next anticipates another question the Corinthians will have: *How are the dead raised? With what kind of body will they come?* (**15:35**). The answer to this question is so easy that he considers the question itself foolish. Then he uses an everyday example to explain the answer.

The seeds that we plant look very different from the plant that grows out of the soil. God mysteriously gives a different body to *each kind of seed* that is sown (**15:37-38**). And it is not just plants that have different types of bodies. So do humans, animals, birds and fish (**15:39**) and even heavenly objects such as the sun, moon and stars (**15:40**). Both heavenly and earthly bodies have splendour, but not the same splendour (**15:41**). Our resurrection bodies will not be identical to our present bodies, but will have the shape God has determined to be appropriate for them.

Paul then outlines the differences between our current bodies and our future heavenly ones. The present body is perishable, treated with disrespect and weak; the resurrection body will be imperishable, honoured and powerful.

While there is a connection between the resurrection body and the natural body, just as there is between a plant and its seed, there will also be differences as great as those between a plant and its seed.

A basic principle of life is that there is a development. *The first man Adam became a living being* (**15:45**; see also Gen 2:7) but *the last Adam* (Christ) became *a life-giving spirit.* The first Adam (natural) came before the second Adam (spiritual). Paul then extends this comparison: the natural man is *from the dust,* while the other is *from heaven*. The man *from the dust* leads the old creation, while the *man from heaven* leads the new creation (**15:46-48**). We are all like the first Adam in that we are human, but in the new creation we will become like Christ (**15:49**). The resurrection enables a transition from the old creation to the new.

15:50-58 The Conquest of Death

Our current bodies cannot be the same as those we will have in the kingdom of God because these bodies are *perishable* (**15:50**) and *mortal* (**15:53-54**). Thus, when the trumpet sounds to announce Christ's return, those who are still alive will *all be changed – in a flash, in the twinkling of an eye* (**15:51b-52**). Paul calls this a *mystery* (**15:51a**) in the sense that it is something that was not known before, and even now is made known only to believers. In an instant our perishable mortal bodies will be changed into something that is imperishable and immortal (15:54), marking Christ's triumph over death. Paul supports what he is saying with a slightly modified quotation from Hosea 13:14. He thinks of death as something venomous, which gets its venom from sin (**15:55-56**). Sin itself becomes powerful because of the law (see Rom 7:4-20). We should be full of gratitude that Christ has given victory over these things in the new creation by rising from the dead (**15:57**).

Paul ends by issuing a practical challenge to the Corinthians. Knowing what they do about the resurrection, they should *stand firm* and *let nothing move* them (**15:58a**). Every Christian should be fully devoted *to the work of the Lord,* for the fact of the resurrection means that no work done in the Lord will ever be *in vain* (**15:58b**).

16:1-24 Conclusion

16:1-4 The Collection for God's People

Using his familiar introduction *Now about* (see also 7:1, 25; 8:1; 12:1; 16:12) Paul moves on to deal with a subject the Corinthians had written to inquire about. It seems that they already knew about *the collection for God's people,* a subject that was close to Paul's heart (**16:1**; see also Rom 15:26; 2 Cor 8:1-15; 9:1-5). By giving, they will be supporting the church in Jerusalem even though they are far away

in Corinth. The Ghanaian proverb will be true for them: 'The antelope says that it never goes to war, but its skin does.'

Paul's advice here is the same as that he gave to the Galatian churches (16:1; see also Gal 6:9-10): every member should give systematically and regularly *in keeping with his income* (**16:2**). The money should be set aside *on the first day of the week.* This is the earliest reference to suggest that Christians met regularly each Sunday (see also John 20:19, 26; Acts 20:7; Rev 1:10). They should save the money given, so that it would be ready when Paul arrived. He would then *give letters of introduction* (**16:3**) to official representatives of the Corinthian believers, who would deliver them to Jerusalem. If he thought it wise, he himself would even accompany these representatives to Jerusalem (**16:4**).

Like most African churches, the church in Corinth was not composed of wealthy people but of poor people. Nevertheless, Paul gave them simple but practical instructions on how the church members should organize their giving and on how those who collected the money should act to make sure that it reached those for whom it was intended.

Christian congregations in Africa have made the occasional collection for missionary work but need to become more sensitive to the needs of others and to take up collections to assist the less privileged. The needs of the displaced, the famine-stricken, victims of AIDS and many others call for our attention.

16:5-18 Personal Plans

Paul intended to travel through Macedonia and then visit Corinth (**16:5**). According to Acts 20:1-2, this did eventually happen, although 2 Corinthians 1:15, 23 suggests that the visit described there may not have been his only visit to Corinth. It is clear that there were several visits, not all of which went smoothly. Paul was hoping that his visit would not be a brief one, but that he would be able to *stay a while* (**16:6-7**). He also hoped that the Corinthian believers would support him as he later continued his journey. However, he would not come immediately because the work in Ephesus was going well, but was also arousing strong opposition (**16:8-9**).

In the interim, he says it is possible that they will receive a visit from Timothy. Paul encourages them to welcome him in such a way that *he has nothing to fear* and then to *send him on his way in peace* (**16:10-11**). Paul's later advice to Timothy (1 Tim 4:12; 2 Tim 1:7) suggests that he may have made these comments because Timothy was both young and timid by temperament.

The *now about* in **16:12** indicates that the Corinthians had written to inquire about when Apollos would be visiting them again. Paul, who obviously did not hold a grudge against Apollos despite there being factions in Corinth (1:12; 3:4-9), said that he had encouraged Apollos to go to Corinth, but that Apollos was not willing to go at that time. It is possible that Apollos was anxious to avoid being associated with the unhealthy party spirit in Corinth. Here both Paul and Apollos are examples of people who did not let the congregations' divisions around them affect their relationship. Leaders should always strive to keep the unity of the body and not try to promote their own parties in opposition to one another. This is something many church leaders in Africa have yet to learn. They need to take pains not to let rivalries interfere with the work of the Lord.

As he moves towards the close of his letter, Paul issues five commands. Four call for militant action and one for love. *Be on your guard* and *stand firm* call for defensive action. The Corinthians are to be alert so that they are not misled, and stable in the Lord so that they are not shaken. *Be men of courage* and *be strong* call on them to take the offensive. They are to act courageously and with strength as they resist the devil (**16:13-14**; see also Eph 3:16). The fifth command, to love, recalls chapter 13 and is a quality that must dominate even in our Christian fight.

In closing, Paul reminds the Corinthians of the sterling work that has been done by the family of Stephanas (who were *the first converts in Achaia*), and by Fortunatus and Achaicus. These people were key figures of the church in Corinth who *devoted themselves to the service of the saints* (**16:15**). Paul says that the church should listen to people like them who put a lot of effort into their service (**16:16**). The three men whose names he mentions seem to have visited Paul in Ephesus, bringing gifts to Paul from the church, and probably the letter he is responding to as well (**16:17**). These men had encouraged Paul, just as they encouraged the church in Corinth. They *deserve recognition* for their work (**16:18**).

16:19-24 Special Salutations and Personal Greetings

Paul concludes his letter with greetings that are being sent to the church in Corinth. They come from the church in Ephesus and the other cities in the Roman province that was known as Asia (**16:19a**), which was not the same as modern Asia. Aquila and Priscilla are mentioned especially because they were intimately associated with Corinth and had offered their home as a base for Paul's mission there

(**16:19b**; see also Acts 18:2-3). In Ephesus, too, the church was meeting in their house, as later the church in Rome would do (Rom 16:3-5).

Paul tells the Corinthians to *greet one another with a holy kiss*, the customary greeting of the day. Their disputes may have driven them apart, so that they no longer greeted each other like this. Paul wants them to return to friendly relationships.

The letter was dictated to a scribe, known as an amanuensis, but Paul notes that he has signed it himself, *in my own hand* (**16:21**). He then calls down a curse on anyone who does not love the Lord. In saying this, Paul is not suggesting that this is how Christians should speak of unbelievers in general. It seems more likely that he is thinking of some specific people within the Corinthian church who opposed his teaching (see, for example, 2 Cor 11:4). Paul has just written fifteen chapters on the meaning and implications of salvation, and is here stating that anyone who listens to the letter being read and then refuses to obey this word of the Lord given through Paul can expect only a curse from the Lord.

He then prays for the return of Christ ('*Come, O Lord*' is a translation of the Aramaic *Marana tha*) (**16:22**). Lamenting what people are turning out to be, Paul asks the Lord to come back before they become worse. An early second-century manual of church order, the *Didache*, also states that this phrase was used in an invocation at the Lord's Supper, that is, in a simple request for Christ's presence with believers at the supper.

Paul ends the letter with a prayer for the *grace of the Lord Jesus* to be with the Corinthian believers (**16:23**) and assures them all of his continuing love for them (**16:24**).

Dachollom Datiri

Further Reading

Barclay, W. *The Letters to the Corinthians*. DSBS. Philadelphia: Westminster Press, 1975.

Fee, G. D. *The First Epistle to the Corinthians*. NICNT. Grand Rapids: Eerdmans, 1987.

Keener, C. S. *Paul, Women & Wives: Marriage and Women's Ministry in the Letters of Paul*. Peabody, Mass.: Hendrickson, 2001.

2 CORINTHIANS

This second letter to the Corinthian church was written by the same author as the first letter and to the same readers. Thus much of the information given in the introduction to 1 Corinthians also applies here. However, it is necessary to comment on when this second letter was written, the situation that prompted it, its characteristics, and the identity of those to whom Paul gives the name 'super-apostles'.

Date and Situation

While Paul was at Ephesus in the course of his third missionary journey (Acts 19), he sent two co-workers, Timothy and Erastus, to Corinth to remind the believers there of the rules of Christian conduct that he had taught (1 Cor 4:17; 16:8-12; Acts 19:22). Timothy returned with bad news. Paul's earlier letter (1 Corinthians) had not corrected the problems. Paul decided to go to Corinth himself, even though such a visit would be painful for him (1:23-2:1). He faced criticism, and one member of the community even set out to offend him (2:5-6; 7:12). Paul then returned to Ephesus and *with many tears* (2:3-4, 9; 7:8, 12) wrote a severe letter (now lost) that he asked Titus to deliver to the Corinthians (2:13; 12:18).

When Paul and Titus met again in Macedonia, Titus gave him good news (2:12-13; 7:5-6). The offender regretted his opposition to the apostle (7:6-7, 13). Unfortunately, however, there was still some opposition to Paul. He was being accused of lacking commitment in carrying out his ministry (1:15-17). His authority was being questioned by newcomers to the community (3:1-2).

Paul considered the gravity of the situation and then in AD 55 wrote the letter that has been preserved for us as 2 Corinthians, which he asked Titus to deliver to Corinth (8:16-17, 23).

One Letter or a Collection of Letters?

The above introduction leaves the impression that 2 Corinthians is one letter from beginning to end. However, not all commentators agree on this point. Some think that 2 Corinthians is composed of several independent letters that may or may not have been written by Paul. They base their case on points such as the following:

- The account of Paul's travels breaks off at 2:13 and resumes at 7:5. It is thus suggested that the passage from 2:14 to 7:4 is a separate letter.
- The collection for the churches is discussed in chapter 8 and again in 9. If this is interpreted as repetition, it suggests that these sections are parts of two different letters.

- There is a marked change in tone between chapters 1 to 9, where the relationship between Paul and the Corinthians seems to be joyous and peaceful, and chapters 10 to 13, where he seems to be angry and deeply concerned for the Corinthians.

While these points need to be borne in mind, they do not justify the conclusion that there are several letters, let alone multiple authors. A long letter such as this one is unlikely to have been written at one sitting. The change in tone may therefore be a result of the time taken to write it. Presumably Paul was also alert to the developing situation in Corinth while he was working on this letter. New information that may have reached him may account for the digressions and for different emphases. The unity of the letter is suggested by the fact that some of the topics first addressed in chapters 10 to 13 are closely related to what is said in chapters 1 to 9.

The Identity of the 'Super-Apostles'

It was probably through Titus that Paul learned that some travelling missionaries had recently arrived in Corinth and had been accepted by the majority of the Christian community there. Though we do not know the details of their teaching, it is clear that they were trying to harm Paul's reputation. The criticisms were clearly serious, for Paul describes his adversaries as Satan's servants disguised as 'servants of righteousness' (11:13-15). Who were these opponents and what did they have against Paul? From the letter, it is possible to make the following deductions:

- They were Jews who pretended to belong to Christ and passed themselves off as his servants (10:7; 11:22-23).
- They had access to several Christian communities, for they carried letters of recommendation (3:1).
- They accused the apostle of being 'weighty and forceful' in his letters, while in person he was unimpressive and lacked eloquence (10:10; 11:6).
- They questioned Paul's apostleship because, unlike the other apostles, he had not accepted support from the Corinthian community (1 Cor 9:12; 11:7). Moreover, the Corinthians felt themselves slighted by Paul's refusal to accept their help (12:13).
- They attached great importance to visions, revelations and miracles, all of which they regarded as proofs of apostleship (12:1, 11-12).
- They accused Paul of living 'by the standards of the world' (10:2); in other words, of not being an apostle.

Paul's letters contain references to several individuals or groups who gave teaching opposed to his. Each group seems to have had its own specific emphasis. For example, Paul's opponents in Galatia insisted that believers must obey the law of Moses by being circumcised (Gal 6:12), but this does not seem to have been an issue in Corinth.

Outline of Contents

COMMENTARY

1:1-2 Address and Greeting

Paul starts his letter by both introducing himself as the author and identifying the recipients. He is *an apostle,* from the Greek *apostolos,* which means 'sent one'. He also specifies by whom he is sent: *Christ Jesus by the will of God* (see 1 Cor 1:1; Eph 1:1). All of this detail is important, since Paul's apostolic authority is being questioned in Corinth.

Timothy is mentioned as the joint sender of the letter (see Acts 16:1-4). But he is merely a *brother,* not an apostle. The letter is addressed *to the church of God in Corinth* and not to the church of Paul or of someone else, and to believers in *Achaia,* a Roman province in the southern half of Greece (**1:1**).

In the greeting, Paul combines the usual Greek greeting, *grace,* and the usual Jewish one, *peace* (**1:2**).

1:3-7 Blessing

Almost all of Paul's letters, except the Letter to the Galatians, begin with thanksgiving. Thus Romans begins, *First, I thank my God* (Rom 1:8), and 1 Corinthians begins, *I always thank God* (1 Cor 1:4). Here, however, what we have is more like a blessing than thanksgiving, as Paul's opening words are *Blessed be the God and Father of our Lord Jesus Christ* (**1:3** NRSV). It is God who is blessed, primarily for his goodness and his capacity to comfort. This comfort is intended to enable believers to comfort others (**1:4**).

The apostle's *troubles* are like an extension of the sufferings of Jesus Christ. The more they increase, the greater the comfort received from Christ (**1.5**). In fact, Paul's suffering will result in the comforting and the good of many others, even those like the Corinthians who have hurt the apostle (**1:6-7**). It will even be for their *salvation,* a word that Paul uses here in its widest sense, which includes their general well-being.

So far, Paul has spoken of suffering and distress without specifying what has caused them. He will do that in the rest of the letter.

1:8-7:16 A Difficult Relationship

1:8-2:4 A Journey

Some commentators think that 1:8 should be read as the follow-up of the blessing. However, it seems better to think of this verse as the beginning of a new section in which Paul tells of the difficulties that he has faced in *Asia,* the Roman province whose capital was Ephesus (1:8-11), and explains why his missionary journey has not gone according to plan (1:15-2:3).

Paul speaks of great *hardships,* but does not state exactly what they were. Yet his words indicate that he had been in a very difficult situation. The apostle and his co-workers (indicated by the pronoun *we*) were burdened with *great pressure, far beyond our ability to endure so that we despaired even of life* (**1:8**). Paul may be referring to the riot that Demetrius led against him and his travelling companions, Gaius and Aristarchus (Acts 19:23-40).

Paul regards his deliverance at Ephesus as being like a resurrection, for he had truly expected to die. This experience therefore reinforces his hope (**1:9-10**). He recognizes that God is delivering him again in response to the prayers of many Christians, including the Corinthians (**1:11**).

Before addressing the accusations that are being levelled at him, Paul states the principles that have characterized his conduct during life's trials in general and in Corinth in particular: *holiness and sincerity* (not manipulation), and *God's grace* (not human wisdom) (**1:12**). What he writes is exactly what he means; there is no need to try to read between the lines (**1:13**).

The Corinthians will be a source of pride for Paul *in the day of the Lord Jesus,* meaning the day of his return, which will be the day of the great unveiling (1 Cor 4:5). In the meantime, the apostle is himself someone of whom the Corinthians can be proud (**1:14**).

Paul had earlier planned to travel from Macedonia to Judea via Corinth (1 Cor 16:5-6). He now refers to a modified version of the same travel plan, stating that he intends to visit Corinth twice, both on his way to Macedonia and then again when he leaves Macedonia for Judea (**1:15-16**). The Corinthians would thus *benefit twice* by seeing him twice.

In the end, this second plan too was abandoned, and the change of plan led to the accusations levelled against Paul in **1:17**. He was accused of doing things *lightly* and of making plans *in a worldly manner.* His word could not be trusted, because he was saying both *yes* and *no* at the same time. The implication that he was not trustworthy leads Paul to set aside the issue of his journey and to focus on the trustworthiness of his teaching, which some people have been disparaging (10:10; 11:6).

Paul calls on God as his witness. God is faithful and worthy of trust, and so is the message Paul has proclaimed. This message is not a case of *yes* and *no* (**1:18**; see also 1 Cor 1:9; 10:13; 1 Thess 5:24; 2 Thess 3:3). Rather, Jesus Christ, who is the subject of Paul's preaching as well as that of Silas and Timothy, is God's 'yes' to all his promises (**1:19-20**). Here Jesus is referred to as *the Son of God,* a title that is used only three times in 1 and 2 Corinthians (1 Cor 1:9; 15:28).

The clear reference to each person of the Trinity in **1:21-22** reinforces the weight that Paul wants to give to the statement that follows: *God* (the Father) has united Paul and the Corinthians *in Christ* (the Son) and has set them apart for himself by his anointing with the Holy Spirit. The association between anointing and the Spirit comes from the ᴏᴛ (Joel 2:28-29). Paul also links the Spirit with the idea of a *seal of ownership* and a *deposit* in Ephesians 1:13-14.

After this brief aside, Paul returns to the question of the postponed journey. Once again he uses a standard form of oath to call God as witness to the truth of his words (**1:23**). It was for the sake of the Corinthians themselves that he changed his plans. He wanted to give them time to straighten out the problems in the community by themselves. He was giving them an opportunity to exercise responsibility, rather than coming in with his apostolic authority (**1:24**).

An earlier visit to the Corinthians had been painful for Paul (**2:1**). That visit had probably followed the report that Timothy had brought after delivering Paul's first letter to them (see the introduction to this commentary). That is why he says that he does not want to *make another painful visit* to Corinth that would *grieve* his hosts (**2:2**). He had written what was clearly a severe letter to them (**2:3-4**). That letter is now lost, although some commentators think that part of it is included in chapters 10 to 13. That letter had been written with distress and tears, as Paul sought to correct the Corinthians while also making them aware of his great love for them.

2:5-11 Forgiving the Offender

In this section, Paul writes about some unnamed person who has offended. Whoever he was, he must have been a member of the church for his sin has affected not only Paul but also a large part of the community (**2:5**).

The community has already disciplined this person in some way, although we are given no details of his *punishment* (**2:6**). Whatever it was, Paul asks that no further punishment be meted out. What is needed now is forgiveness and comforting of this person for fear that *excessive sorrow* will detract from the real purpose of the punishment: his restoration to the fellowship (**2:7**). Paul's statement in **2:8** is an official public statement that annuls all previous statements. Love should replace sanction.

One purpose of Paul's stern letter had been to test the ability of the Corinthians to obey (**2:9**). Would the church submit to his apostolic authority or not? It had done so by condemning the guilty.

In **2:10**, Paul states that he pardons this person because the community has already extended its pardon to him. Paul extends this pardon *in the sight of Christ ... in order that Satan might not outwit us* (**2:11**). Satan would have been the winner if Paul and the Corinthians had refused to forgive their brother, or if their excessive severity had led him to leave the community.

Satan is always scheming to weaken and divide the church and to discourage Christians. In too many Christian communities in Africa, discipline is abused by ethnic groups and individuals. They use it for retaliation, judgment and condemnation, rather than as an opportunity for a member to repent and abandon his or her sin permanently. Rather than removing sin, such discipline unfortunately provides an opportunity for it to grow and sets brothers and sisters against each other.

2:12-13 Troas and Macedonia

Paul has explained why he changed his itinerary and has urged the community at Corinth to forgive the offender. Now he gives a final item of information that proves how deeply concerned he was about the situation at Corinth.

After leaving Ephesus, he had gone to Troas to preach the gospel there (Acts 20:5-12; 2 Tim 4:13). Things were going well, for *the Lord had opened a door* (**2:12**). However, Paul was not at peace because Titus, his co-worker whom he had hoped to meet in Troas, was not there (**2:13**; Gal 2:1, 3). Paul was probably more concerned about the lack of news from Corinth than about Titus himself. He wanted to know how the Corinthians had reacted to the severe letter he had written (7:6-7). So he left Troas and set out for Macedonia himself.

Paul's attitude reminds us that it is better to deal with the problems that exist in our communities than to simply continue establishing new churches whose members will face numerous problems that no one ever takes the time to solve.

2:14-3:18 The Ministry of the New Covenant

Many commentators think that 2:14-17 was clumsily inserted at this point in the letter. These verses seem to interrupt Paul's account of his travels (to which he will return only in 7:5). Other commentators think that these verses should come immediately after 2:11, and that it is thus 2:12-13 that is not in the right place. Still others regard 2:14-17 as a summary of what the apostle is going to say in the following chapters.

Paul begins by giving thanks for two things. The first is that God *always leads us in triumphal procession in Christ* (**2:14a**). He seems to be thinking of the triumphal procession of a Roman general returning victorious from battle at the head of a parade of the victors and the vanquished (see also Col 2:15). Paul applies this idea to the apostles, whom he sees as being led everywhere in God's triumphal procession.

The second matter for thanksgiving is that *through us [God] spreads everywhere the fragrance of the knowledge of him* (**2:14b**). God is using Paul (and the other apostles) to make himself known. They are the good odour of Christ for God (**2:15**). This scent is smelled by all, both those who are already on the way of salvation and those who are on the way of perdition. But these groups do not react to the perfume in the same way. The former welcome it as an odour leading to life; the latter hate it as an odour leading to death (**2:16a**). The response depends on the way someone receives the gospel preached by the apostles.

This thanksgiving ends with a question about the qualifications for the task of spreading the knowledge of God (**2:16b**), and this becomes the theme of the following verses. Paul starts by distinguishing true apostles from mere pedlars, salesmen who try to sell a substandard product at an inflated price (**2:17a**). Such people will alter the gospel by saying only what will please people and win their favour. Paul is not like them, for he sets a very high standard for his ministry (**2:17b**).

The argument begun in 2:17 carries on into the next chapter. Paul had been accused of commending himself, whereas his adversaries parade letters that recommend them to the church (**3:1**; 4:2; 5:12; 10:12, 18). Despite his words here, we know that Paul was not opposed to the principle of sending letters of recommendation. But it seems that he only wrote such letters on behalf of others, such as Phoebe (Rom 16:1-2) and Onesimus (Phlm 10-12).

Paul argues that he has no need of any letter recommending him to the Corinthians (after all, he was the one who founded their church), nor does he need any such letter from them. His letter of recommendation is the Corinthian church itself. Unlike other letters, this one is written on the heart of the apostle himself (**3:2**). It is an open letter that anyone can read.

Paul is clearly comparing his own ministry to that of Moses, the lawgiver of the OT, when he contrasts the letter written on human hearts with the commandments and laws written with *ink* and on *tablets of stone* (**3:3**). The idea of writing on hearts and of the Spirit acting in hearts is borrowed from OT texts that speak of the new covenant (Jer 31:31-34; Ezek 11:19-20; 36:25-27).

Paul next returns to the question asked in 2:16b: 'Who is equal to such a task?' As a human being, he knows he can do nothing. God is the one who enables him to carry out his ministry (**3:5**). God is the source of his *confidence* and the one who makes him *competent* to proclaim the new covenant (**3:4**, 6).

The reference to the new covenant leads Paul to contrast the *letter* of the law, which *kills*, with the *Spirit*, which *gives life* (**3:6**). What follows will illustrate this point by comparing Moses' ministry and that of the apostles.

Moses represents the *ministry that brought death* (**3:7**; see Rom 7:7-13) or that *condemns* (**3:9a**; see Rom 3:19-20). It was characterized by having its text written on stone (Exod 34:27-28), that is, on an object, not on the human heart. While this ministry was glorious (a glory that was reflected in Moses' face – Exod 34:29-35), its glory was short-lived. Paul is not dismissing the law or Moses, but is addressing a misreading of the law that focused solely on mechanical obedience, which easily became hypocritical. Any relationship to the law that does not touch the heart leads to death. That is why Jeremiah proclaimed that the coming covenant would be written on people's hearts, where it would be a source of life (Jer 31:33).

The ministry of the Spirit (**3:8**) or of righteousness (**3:9b**), the one exercised by the apostles, will be so glorious that the ministry of Moses cannot be considered glorious by comparison (**3:10-11**). This ministry fills Paul with great assurance and great boldness (**3:12**). The situation now is not like that of Moses, who covered his face with a veil to prevent the Israelites from seeing the glory shining in his face and the fading of that glory (**3:13**).

The term 'old testament' or *old covenant* is used for the first time in **3:14**, where it is implicitly contrasted with the new testament or 'new covenant' (see 3:6). Reading the OT is the same as reading Moses (**3:15**). Here Paul is undoubtedly referring to the Pentateuch, the first five books of the OT. Paul writes that those who read only the old covenant are hindered because just as a veil covered Moses' face, so a veil obscures their hearts so that they do not clearly discern the meaning of the text.

How are we to understand the statement that the veil disappears only in Christ or when we turn to the Lord (**3:16**)? Some have suggested a translation such as 'the veil was not lifted until this covenant was abolished by Christ.' But it is also possible to understand that only Christ, by his Spirit, makes the human mind capable of understanding the true meaning of the OT. We cannot truly understand Moses without the mediation of the Lord Jesus.

Paul's comparison of the ministries of the old and new covenants wraps up in 3:17-18. The *freedom* referred to in **3:17** is the complete absence of any obstacle to seeing God. There is no longer a veil between us and the Lord. All of us, apostles and believers, can now contemplate the glory of the Lord directly, as Moses did on Mount Sinai. As we do this, we become increasingly like him (**3:18**). This change is produced by the Holy Spirit, who is one with the Lord.

4:1-5:10 Treasure in Clay Jars

Paul's *therefore* indicates that he is now going to draw conclusions from what he has just said regarding the ministry of the new covenant. First, he says that this ministry was entrusted to him *through God's mercy* (**4:1**). He uses a similar expression when speaking of conversion (Rom 11:30) and of his calling and authority as an apostle (1 Cor 7:25; 1 Tim 1:13, 16). God's mercy also gives him courage (see also 4:16). By this he means that it has made him confident, allowing nothing to stop him (5:6-8; 10:1,2).

Paul's words in **4:2** also give some idea of the accusations that have been levelled against him. He finds it necessary to explicitly state that he rejects intrigues, does not behave deceptively and does not *distort the word of God* (2:17). On the contrary, it is by the proclamation of the

truth, which is the *word of God,* that Paul *commends [himself] to every man's conscience.* In **4:3**, he defends himself against the accusation that his gospel is veiled. He insists that it is only veiled to those *who are perishing,* the unbelievers whose thinking is obscured by the god of this age (11:14; see also 1 Cor 2:6; 15:24; Eph 6:12) who hinders them from receiving the clear *light of the gospel ... of Christ, who is the image of God* (**4:4**).

Paul's apostleship is centred on the Christ he preaches. He does not, therefore, push himself forward in his ministry, but rather preaches *Jesus Christ as Lord* (**4:5**). This terminology is a confession of faith expressing the sovereignty of Jesus and calling on everyone to submit to him.

In **4:6**, Paul may be citing Genesis 1:3 or Isaiah 9:1. But whichever verse he has in mind, his point is that the same God whose command produced light in the past has now acted in the hearts of the apostles to give them the light that they must in turn pass on.

But this *treasure* is stored in *jars of clay* (**4:7**). The 'treasure' is the gospel preached by the apostles; the 'jars of clay' are the apostles. Something that is precious and valuable is stored in something that is common and ordinary. Paul uses this image to remind the Corinthians that the incomparable power that the gospel produces is God's, not his. He and his companions are daily beset by all sorts of misfortunes, but these tests cannot beat them down (**4:8-9**).

The point made in 4:8-9 is repeated in other words in **4:10**. Paul regards the sufferings he and others experience in the course of their apostolic ministry as being their experience of the death of Jesus (Phil 3:10). But the death of Jesus is always associated with the life of Jesus (**4:11**). All these trials are endured for the benefit of the Corinthians: Paul is experiencing death so that the believers may enjoy life (**4:12**).

Paul is speaking of himself as an apostle, but it is not only the apostles who should live like this. What he says should be true of all believers, whatever their role in the church.

Paul's behaviour is motivated by faith (**4:13**). In fact, he has the same spirit of faith as the OT writer who wrote, *I believed; therefore I have spoken* (Ps 116:10 in the Septuagint). He makes a clear connection between 'believing' and 'speaking' despite the difficulties.

Paul's faith is based on the assurance of the resurrection. He knows that *the one who raised the Lord Jesus from the dead* (God), will also raise those who believe (in this case, the Corinthians and Paul himself) (**4:14**). This firm conviction is frequently affirmed in Paul's writings (Rom 6:5; 8:11; 1 Cor 6:14; 15:22). Once the resurrection has taken place, believers will be in the presence of Jesus Christ. The verb used here points to access to the presence of God and not to facing him as judge (Eph 5:27; Col 1:22).

All this in **4:15** refers to everything that Paul has said about his ministry and the suffering that it involves. All the things he has spoken of have happened so that God's grace may be extended to many, at Corinth and elsewhere, resulting in praise and gratitude.

In this context, Paul lists a series of contrasts:

- The contrast between the outward and the inward being. As the one steadily deteriorates, the other is steadily renewed (**4:16**).
- The contrast between the present distress and the glory to come. The one is short-lived and superficial (despite 11:24-27!); the other is permanent (**4:17**).
- The contrast between visible realities and invisible things. The one is temporary; the other lasts forever (**4:18**; see also the contrast between faith and sight in 5:7).

In 5:1-10, Paul expands on what he has said in 4:16-18, with the word *now* indicating the link between the two parts (**5:1**). He compares the human body to a *tent* (a temporary dwelling – see Isa 38:12), which can be *destroyed* (by death). This tent is the opposite of a *house* (a solid dwelling). Our house is prepared in heaven by God, and thus is not of human construction. But to say this is not to imply that our 'tent', or earthly body, is of human construction. Paul's point is rather that our present bodies are mortal ('wasting away' – see 4:16), whereas the dwelling prepared for us in heaven is eternal.

As we await our heavenly house, we *groan* with *longing* (**5:2a**). This groaning is not a response to the suffering we endure, but is rather an expression of the hope that fills us. It is possible that Paul had once thought that the Lord would return before he had to endure death, but now, facing the dangers and suffering of his ministry, he seriously considers the likelihood of death (**5:2b-3**). He has no desire to die (*to be unclothed*), but he does have a deep desire (expressed in the words *we groan and are burdened*) to experience the coming of the Lord, at which time he will be clothed with his *heavenly dwelling* or immortality (**5:4**).

This confidence in immortality comes from God (**5:5**). It is he who destined Paul and all believers for this state. And as a guarantee that this state will be reached, God has made a *deposit* in our accounts, by giving us the Holy Spirit.

Paul again expresses his confidence and assurance (**5:6**; 4:16). This attitude is typical of him. After the aside in **5:7** that contrasts faith and sight, Paul again picks up the theme of confidence in **5:8**. He is so confident that he thinks it would be preferable to leave his present body behind and enter the presence of the Lord, awaiting the resurrection (1 Thess 4:15-17).

However, whether still in his body or out of it, Paul claims to have only one preoccupation: pleasing the Lord (**5:9**; see also Rom 12:1; Eph 5:10; Phil 4:18). Paul is not simply passively awaiting what will happen. All that he wants to do is to please the Lord by living and serving in any way that the Lord asks him to. After all, despite his longing to be with the Lord, Paul does not forget that the day is coming when each one of us will have to give an account before *the judgment seat of Christ* regarding what he has done whether good or bad, and for which he will receive his *due* (**5:10**; see also Rom 14:10; 1 Cor 3:12-15).

5:11-6:13 Reconciliation

After speaking of the judgment seat of Christ (**5:10**), Paul introduces this section by saying *we know what it is to fear the Lord* (**5:11a**). But this *fear* should not be understood as terror but as very great respect or very high esteem for the Lord. It leads Paul to persuade people. One cannot have a merely theoretical knowledge of this fear.

Paul states that he has nothing to hide: God knows him perfectly and he hopes that in their inner selves the Corinthians also know him (**5:11b**). In saying this, Paul seems to be returning to the accusations against him referred to earlier, as he also does when he returns to the issue of commendation (**5:12**; 3:1; 4:2). He repeats his earlier point: he has no desire to commend himself. Rather, he seeks to give the Corinthians reasons to be proud of him because, whatever his opponents who pride themselves on appearances may say, he himself is a genuine apostle. In fact, regardless of whether his conduct is seen as extreme or as rational, it is always in keeping with his calling (**5:13**).

The deep motivation of Paul's ministry is *Christ's love* (**5:14**). This love is both the love that comes from Christ (Rom 8:35-39; Gal 2:20) and the love that the apostle and the believers have for Christ. It results from the death of only *one* person (Christ) on behalf of *all* believers. Consequently all must identify themselves with Christ, whether in death (Rom 6:2, 7, 11; Gal 2:19) or in life (**5:15**; Rom 6:11; 14:7).

Before his conversion, Paul had thought of Jesus as merely human. But now that he knows that Christ died on the cross for everyone and that all those who live should live for him, Paul insists that he and all other believers should no longer understand things from a human point of view (**5:16**). Something new has come and what is *old has gone* (**5:17**). In other words, we no longer live as we did before, because we live for Jesus who gives new meaning to our lives. This new order was introduced by God; it is he who has *reconciled us to himself through Christ* (**5:18**). It is also he who has entrusted to the apostles, and to Paul in particular, this specific ministry of reconciliation. This ministry is to announce the pardon that God is offering in Christ (**5:19**).

As an apostle, therefore, Paul finds himself in the position of being a spokesperson or ambassador, responsible for telling people what God expects of them: to *be reconciled to God* (**5:20**). This message is so important and at the same time so urgent that Paul implores his readers to hear it. The importance of the message is found in the fact that to make reconciliation possible, God condemned a just person in the place of sinners (**5:21**).

In **6:1**, Paul concludes this discussion of God's grace by issuing an appeal from himself and his co-workers. Together, they urge the Corinthians to allow the grace of God to be active in their lives. They support their plea with a quotation from Isaiah 49:8 (Septuagint) that indicates that the grace of God must be seized when it is available (**6:2**). The urgency of action is shown by Paul's repeated use of the word 'now'.

In 6:3-10, Paul lays out what commentators have correctly called the paradoxes, or seeming contradictions, of the apostolic ministry. Although Paul takes care not to be a *stumbling block in anyone's path*, giving no reason for anyone to find fault with his ministry (**6:3**), we know that there was much criticism of him in Corinth. He is anxious to show that these criticisms have no real basis and so presents himself as solely a servant of God. As a servant, he shows *great endurance* (**6:4**). Endurance is related to consistency. It is the ability to stand firm in adversity and remain faithful to God. Paul's attitude to the hardships he endures is both an exhortation and an encouragement to all believers, and in particular to those who today live in situations in which their faith is sorely tested. They need to stand firm, knowing that God is faithful and will set a limit to their suffering and will provide a way of escape (see 1 Cor 10:13).

The trials that are mentioned in general terms in 6:4 are described in detail in **6:5**. They have come at the hands of others (*beatings, imprisonments and riots*) and in the form of more common difficulties (*sleepless nights and hunger*).

In **6:6-7**, we have a list of things that characterize Paul's life: *purity* (Ps 24:3-4; 1 Tim 5:22); *understanding* (11:6; Col 1:9); *patience and kindness* (often identified as both divine qualities and the fruit of the Spirit Rom 2:4; Gal 5:22); *the Holy Spirit* (the originator of all apostolic work); *sincere love* (Rom 12:9; 1 Cor 16:24); *truthful speech* (2:17; 4:2); and *the power of God* (Rom 1:16).

These good qualities have not always elicited a good response to Paul's ministry, as **6:8-10** makes clear. He has endured *glory* and *dishonour* (probably when he was present) and *bad report* or *good report* (probably when he was absent). His opponents probably described him as an *impostor, … unknown, … dying* and *beaten*. But Paul knows that these negatives do not tell the full story! Paradoxically, he can equally well be described in opposite terms by those who look beyond what is visible on the surface (his suffering and poverty) and recognize the spiritual realm in which Paul rejoices in unlimited wealth.

In 6:11-13, Paul appeals to the affection of the Corinthians. He says that, in speaking as he has, he has opened his heart to them (**6:11**). All of them have a place in his heart,

and he longs to have an equivalent place in their hearts, in what would be a *fair exchange* of affection (**6:12-13**).

6:14-7:1 Light and Darkness

At first glance, these verses seem to be a sudden departure from what Paul has been speaking of so far. This impression is reinforced by the fact that six verses later, in 7:2, Paul suddenly returns to the point he was making in 6:13. But in reality, this passage follows logically on what precedes it, for Paul is here speaking of what is hindering the Corinthians from opening their hearts to him; namely the roadblocks erected by the false apostles. So Paul emphasizes the need for believers to distance themselves from evil. Whereas previously he spoke of things that seemed to be opposites but were actually both true (for example, that he was poor, yet made many rich – 3:10), here he speaks of some things that are so opposite that they cannot go together. It is impossible to combine *righteousness* and *wickedness, light* and *darkness* (**6:14**), *Christ* and *Belial, believer* and *unbeliever* (**6:15**), *the temple of God* and *idols* (**6:16a**). A choice must be made between these things.

The 'we' of **6:16b** does not refer only to Paul and his collaborators, but to the body of believers as a whole. They all constitute the temple of the living God. To show that this statement is unassailable and that God himself affirms it, Paul cites several Scriptures in **6:16c-18** (see Lev 26:11-12; 2 Sam 7:8, 14; Isa 52:11; Ezek 20:34, 41; 37:27).

Paul regards these Scriptures as promises. Given that they have such promises, the believers must purify themselves *from everything that contaminates* their bodies or their spirits in order to commit themselves to developing the holiness that honours God (**7:1**).

As part of purifying ourselves, we need to be careful not to enter into marriages with unbelievers, and should exercise great care before going into any business partnership with an unbeliever.

7:2-16 The Joy of Reconciliation

Paul now returns to the idea of mutual openness between himself and the Corinthians that he first mentioned in 6:13. He denies having *wronged* anyone or having *corrupted* or *exploited* anyone (**7:2**). His words are ironic, for how could he have corrupted and exploited people from whom he refused to accept any money (12:13)? He wants to make it clear that he condemns no one; on the contrary, he loves the Corinthians with a sincere and steady love, a love that nothing can change (**7:3**).

In both **7:4** and 7:13, Paul says he is encouraged by the Corinthians. He also speaks of his pride in them, and adds that his *joy knows no bounds* despite all his troubles. He then gives the reasons for his experiencing these emotions.

Paul had travelled from Troas to Macedonia looking for Titus who would bring him news of Corinth (see 2:12-13 and the introduction). The troubles that he mentions in **7:5** may have arisen both from opposition to his ministry (*conflicts on the outside*) and from his concern for Titus and the Corinthians (*fears within*).

The *downcast* or literally 'the humble' (**7:6**; the idea, though not the same word, is also found in 11:7; 12:21) are those who are humiliated or afflicted. To these, as to Paul himself, God gives consolation and comfort. He comforted the apostle by bringing Titus to him. But it was not only Titus's arrival that brought comfort, but even more the good news that Titus brought from Corinth (**7:7**). The Corinthians had indeed changed their attitude towards Paul. They had experienced deep sadness at their past opposition to him and had expressed a desire to connect fully with him. Paul was delighted. His letter had produced the desired results. He knew that this letter had originally saddened the Corinthians and had even been tempted to regret writing it (**7:8**). But he no longer has any regrets, for their sorrow, which was *godly sorrow,* had produced the change which Titus had been privileged to witness.

This mention of sorrow leads Paul to reflect on the difference between *godly sorry* and *worldly sorrow* (**7:10**). The one leads to salvation; the other to death. The Corinthians had experienced the former, and its fruits were evident (**7:11**). All this leads Paul to conclude that, in reality, the Corinthians were innocent in this whole affair. This remark has led some commentators to think that the offender may not have been a Corinthian, but rather someone who had come to Corinth from elsewhere.

Verse **7:12** returns to the purpose of the earlier letter (2:4; 7:8): to restore the Corinthians' respect and support for Paul as an apostle. That goal has now been accomplished, and Paul is comforted (**7:13**). His reaction mirrors that of Titus, who had also been comforted and brought to rejoice by his visit to the Corinthians. Paul realizes that he has not been wrong to speak of the Corinthians with pride (**7:14**). The welcome they had given Titus, their respect for him and their obedience had filled Titus with *affection* for them (**7:15**). Paul is happy. He again acknowledges 'his' children in Corinth and his awareness that he *can have complete confidence* in them in every respect (**7:16**).

With this established, he is able to move on to another issue, namely the collection that is being taken for the benefit of their Christian brothers and sisters in Jerusalem.

8:1-9:15 Collecting for the Christians at Jerusalem

8:1-5 The Example Set by the Churches in Macedonia

The collection to help the Jerusalem Christians was not a new project. The principle had been agreed on at the Jerusalem Conference (Gal 2:10) and the collection had already begun (8:6), but the misunderstandings that had arisen

between Paul and the Corinthians had postponed its completion. Paul returns to it now but avoids directly asking the Corinthians to take part. Instead he starts by telling them about the example set by the Macedonian churches (that is, the churches in Philippi, Thessalonica and Berea) that he had founded on his second missionary journey.

By calling the Corinthians *brothers* (**8:1**), Paul immediately indicates what motivates this collection. The family of God are caring for one another. The members of a family must share what they have. The alacrity with which these churches gave confirms that those who are most faithful in the support of God's work are not necessarily those who are rich in the eyes of the world. These communities, which were poor and had experienced severe trials (1 Thess 2:14; 3:3-5; 2 Thess 1:4-10), nevertheless wanted to play a part in supporting the needy Christians in Jerusalem (**8:2**). Their attitude, an astonishing combination of distress and overflowing joy, shows that, in reality, we always have something to give because we are always rich in some area. The Macedonians went *beyond their ability* (**8:3**) asking for the *privilege* of being allowed to share *in this service* (the same Greek word as 'ministry') (**8:4**). It is important to note that the apostle did not insist on receiving anything from the Macedonians. By taking part in such a collection, they exceeded all his expectations.

The secret of the Macedonians' generosity was that *they gave themselves first to the Lord* (**8:5**). They and all their possessions became the Lord's property. Then, acknowledging Paul as an apostle and as a servant representing their Lord, they submitted to his authority as appropriate according to God's will. These words are also a gentle reminder to the Corinthians that their loyalty to false apostles was leading them astray.

8:6-15 Call to Generosity to the Corinthians

After speaking of the example set by the Macedonians, Paul turns to the Corinthians. If the Macedonians who had joined the project later than the Corinthians had taken the collection so strongly to heart, those who had been early supporters should not remain on the sidelines (8:10). Thus Paul encouraged Titus to follow through and complete this *act of grace* on the part of the Corinthians (**8:6**).

The call to generosity starts with a reminder of the various kinds of riches the Corinthians enjoy (**8:7**). Whoever we are and whatever our social or professional status, we always have something to give to God's work.

Paul asks the Corinthians to make this collection another area in which they excel. However, he is not commanding them to give (**8:8**), but rather sees their giving as a proof of their love. It is worth noting that Paul is careful to distinguish between the commands of the Lord (1 Cor 7:10) – words that come with apostolic authority (1 Cor 7:12) – and his own advice (1 Cor. 7:6).

The other example they should follow is that of Jesus (**8:9**). He was wealthy in all the divine privileges (Phil 2:5-8), but he chose to become a poor human being in order to give humans access to the riches of salvation. These riches are not exclusively or even chiefly material riches, as some teach today.

Paul's repeated use of 'you' and 'your' in this verse emphasizes the fact that Christ gave away what belonged to him for the benefit of the Corinthians. They should do the same for others.

Once again, Paul points out that what he is giving is merely *advice* (**8:10**), although the examples set by the Macedonians and Christ indicate that it would be appropriate for the Corinthians to participate fully in the current project. Yet another reason for doing so is the fact that they had already started to collect money based on the instructions Paul had given them (1 Cor 16:1-4). On this point, Paul is firm: *Now finish the work* (**8:11**). Christians and others need to learn the importance of always finishing what we start! The records of many African churches are full of projects that were begun but never completed. This situation discourages Christians and damages the credibility of churches among those outside.

When it comes to giving, our projects should, however, be reasonable, and within our present means (**8:12**). What is being talked about is sharing. We are not being asked to give away all that we possess so that we ourselves are left in dire straits (**8:13**). Paul expects the Corinthians to give what is not absolutely essential for survival to help their Christian brothers in Jerusalem survive. One day, the believers in Jerusalem may be asked to do the same for the Corinthians (**8:14**). This is the equality of which Paul speaks. He concludes by quoting words from Exodus 16:18 which express the same principle (**8:15**).

8:16-9:5 Practical Arrangements Regarding the Offering

Paul introduces this section with thanksgiving that Titus shares his love for and excitement about the Corinthians (**8:16-17a**). Before Paul ever suggested to him that he should return to Corinth to take care of the offering, Titus had already decided to do so (**8:17b**). But he will not go alone. He will be accompanied by another brother, whose name is not given, who has a good reputation because of his involvement in the *service to the gospel* (**8:18**). The local churches had voted to send this brother to help Paul and the others *carry the offering* (**8:19**).

The task of collecting a large amount of money and delivering it to Jerusalem is such an important one that Paul is careful *to avoid any criticism* in this matter (**8:20**). He is conscious of acting *not only in the eyes of the Lord but also in the eyes of men* (**8:21**). He intends his conduct to be blameless in the eyes of all these witnesses. Are we as concerned as he was to avoid any hint of wrongdoing when

we are responsible for any of our congregation's money or property?

There will also be a third person accompanying Titus and the brother already mentioned (**8:22**). His name is not given, but we are told that he is a devout brother who has *great confidence* in the Corinthians. The delegation will therefore consist of Titus, who is Paul's representative, and two others who represent the churches (**8:23**). By their conduct, all three bring *honour to Christ*.

Paul encourages the Corinthian believers to prove their love and to show that he has good reason to be proud of them by warmly welcoming the delegation led by Titus and by contributing to the offering (**8:24**).

Paul does not feel any need to write at length about the offering (**9:1**). He knows that the Corinthians already support it. In fact, he has been so proud of them that he had boasted to the Macedonians that Achaia was already prepared to give a year earlier (**9:2**). This report roused the others to give, but in fact, the Corinthians themselves had not as yet really put their hands in their pockets. They had simply favoured the idea of doing so. Now the brothers are being sent to them to help them to prepare and to *give generously* (**9:3, 5**). It is now time to face up to their responsibility. If they are found unprepared for the offering, both they and Paul will be embarrassed and *ashamed* (**9:4**).

9:6-15 Blessing to the Giver

Having dealt with the practical arrangements for the collection, Paul turns to the question of the way in which to give. He starts with a general truth: *whoever sows generously will also reap generously* (**9:6**). Although these words are not a quotation from the OT, they nevertheless remind us of Proverbs 11:24 or 19:17. They allow the apostle to address each Corinthian individually. Each of them should decide how much to give to the collection on his or her own (**9:7**). In some African churches today, people are pressured and manipulated to give. Such behaviour is wrong. A gift should be given without sadness or compulsion. This way of doing things is desirable because *God loves a cheerful giver* (Prov 22:8-9). In other words, there is no blessing for those who give against their will. But God will give a harvest of blessing to those who give joyfully to his work. In fact, he is able to give them all that they need to face any and every situation (**9:8**). Paul quotes Scripture to support what he is saying (**9:9-10**; see Ps 112:9 and Isa 55:10). He expands on the latter verse to make the point that God will supply and multiply the seed and increase the fruits of righteousness for those who give generously. God gives to us so that we can share what he gives with others, and our harvest of righteousness (**9:10**) is an increasing closeness to God that expresses itself in prayer and fasting, which remind us that he alone is the source of the blessings we enjoy.

Paul continues his reflection on Isaiah 55:10 when he says that the Corinthians *will be made rich in every way so that [they] can be generous on every occasion* (**9:11**). The goal of the collection is thus not only to relieve the needs of the believers in Jerusalem, but also to encourage thanksgiving to God (**9:12**).

In **9:13** the apostle speaks of those who will receive the Corinthians' gifts. They will glorify God when they see the practical outworking of the gospel in the generosity of the Corinthians. The fellowship of believers, expressed concretely here by the joyous sharing of the goods that they themselves had received from God, fills those who benefit with thanksgiving to God and leads to warm prayer for their benefactors (**9:14**).

The section about the collection ends with thanksgiving (**9:15**). Paul looks forward to the completion of the collection and gives thanks to God, not for this specific act alone, but for his *indescribable* and inexhaustible generosity in giving the Lord Jesus to believers and to the world.

10:1-13:14 Paul Defends His Apostleship

The tone of these final chapters is so different from that of the preceding chapters that some commentators have thought they must have been part of a different letter (see the introduction to this commentary). Here Paul expresses his vision of apostolic authority and defends his apostleship.

10:1-18 Paul's Authority

Paul exhorts the Corinthians *by the meekness and gentleness of Christ* (**10:1**). He has lived out these two characteristics of the Lord in relation to the Corinthians, but they have not recognized them for what they are and have taken them as a sign of weakness. Thus they accuse him of being *'timid' when face to face with you but 'bold' when away.*

Paul was also being criticized for living *by the standards of the world* (**10:2**), which means that his opponents thought that his actions were motivated by purely human considerations. Paul admits to being human, but denies living by human principles (**10:3**). The *weapons* he uses in his warfare are not human. On the contrary, they have divine power in God's eyes and are wielded only for God (**10:4**). With these weapons, the apostle demolishes strongholds (Isa 2:11-18), that is, the *arguments and every pretension that sets itself up against the knowledge of God.* He takes *captive every thought to make it obedient to Christ* (**10:5**). The language is military but the apostle does not specify the exact nature of the weapons he uses (contrast Eph 6:11-17). Here he is more concerned with the way the weapons will affect the Corinthians' obedience to Jesus Christ. Once they have acknowledged Jesus as their Lord, Paul will not hesitate

to denounce *every act of disobedience,* whatever its origin (**10:6**).

The verb at the beginning of **10:7** may be translated as, *you are looking* (NIV), but it may also be a question (are you looking?) or a command (look!). The imperative form seems to fit best with what follows. Paul is inviting his readers to think consistently. Anyone who is convinced that he or she belongs to Christ should accept that Paul also belongs to Christ. Some commentators think that Paul's opponents were denying this.

Paul's apostolic authority had been given him by the Lord, and his purpose is to build up, not to tear down (**10:8-9**). He is using words that are associated with the calling of the prophet Jeremiah (Jer 1:10; 12:14-17; 18:7-9). He is not ashamed of being so proud of this authority. But some are claiming that he attempts to intimidate the Corinthians with his letters (10:9). They say that when he is far away from them he writes *weighty and forceful* letters, but that when he is present he is *unimpressive* and no great orator (**10:10**; 11:6). To those who think this way, Paul replies that in reality he is no different when writing his letters than he is in person (**10:11**). The Corinthians have failed to recognize that he was speaking with apostolic humility.

Paul now proceeds to emphasize that he uses different criteria than his adversaries do. First, speaking sarcastically, he says that he does not dare to *compare himself* with the people *who commend themselves* (**10:12**; 3:1-3). He reproaches his opponents for having set up a standard of judgment that is of their own making and that is not the Lord's. In this respect, his battle with the false apostles is similar to the battle that Jeremiah fought against the false prophets who proclaimed so-called messages from God that he had not given them (Jer 23:16-18).

Paul emphasizes that he works within the limits that the Lord had set for him (**10:13**; see also Gal 2:7-10). At Corinth, Paul kept within the framework of the specific call he had received to proclaim the gospel to non-Jews. In **10:14** Paul implies that he and his team *were the first to come all the way to you with the good news of Christ* (NRSV). As the first to arrive, he was the founder of the Corinthian community of believers (1 Cor 9:1-2).

Paul claims no glory for work accomplished by others (**10:15a**; see also Rom 15:20), but he has worked hard there where no one had preached the gospel before him. His goal is to deepen the faith of the Corinthians and their confidence in their apostle, and then to proclaim the gospel in regions beyond Corinth that have not yet received the good news of Christ's death and resurrection (**10:15b-16**). Paul may have been thinking of Rome or Spain (Rom 15:23-24).

Paul's focus on going where no one else had preached the gospel contrasts with what we see today. Missionaries, evangelists and pastors now concentrate in areas that already have a Christian witness. These areas are generally the cities in regions where the living and working conditions are good. Few are prepared to go to areas where the climate is inhospitable, the people poor and many commodities are not available.

This chapter ends with a reminder of the words in Jeremiah 9:23-24 (**10:17**; see also 1 Cor 1:31), as if Paul wants to base everything he has said on that reference. Jeremiah proclaimed that wisdom and strength and riches are no grounds for pride. The only thing worth being proud of is that one has the wisdom to know the Lord, the only one who acts in kindness, uprightness and judgment on the earth. In the long run, it is only the Lord's acceptance and approval that count (**10:18**).

11:1-15 Against False Prophets

Paul has digressed from his defence of his apostleship in 10:12-18, but now he returns to it. He asks the Corinthians to do something for him that they have been willing to do for his opponents: *put up with a little of my foolishness* (**11:1**).

First, he says that what he feels for them is *a godly jealousy* (**11:2**). He speaks as the father of a bride, someone who has given the hand of his daughter (the church he founded – 1 Cor 4:15) to her fiancé (Jesus Christ). The image of a bride is drawn from the OT, which often compares the people of Israel to God's wife (Isa 54:4-8; 62:5; Jer 2; Ezek 16; Hos 1-3). In stressing that he had given the church to only *one husband,* Paul is making the point that the Corinthians are at risk of becoming unfaithful to Christ. He fears that the dangerous teachings of his opponents are leading the Corinthians away from Jesus Christ, just as the words of the serpent led Eve astray in the garden of Eden (**11:3**; Gen 3:1-13).

A number of questions are raised by **11:4**. First, who is the *someone* who *comes?* Some take this to be a specific person, either the apostle Peter or someone sent by the church in Jerusalem. But it is difficult to see how this interpretation fits with what follows. It is more likely that this 'someone' is one of Paul's opponents at Corinth.

The second question is what is meant by *a Jesus other than the Jesus we preached, … a different spirit* and *a different gospel.* We know that the apostle Paul does not believe that there are two gospels (Gal 1:6-9). It is clear that he does not believe in another Jesus either. What he is saying is that there are people who are preaching the gospel in a different way, which completely distorts it.

Paul refers to these people using an ironic title, which can be translated as *super-apostles* (**11:5**). These 'super-apostles' are not the apostles who were based in Jerusalem (the Twelve), but are those referred to in 11:4. They are therefore false apostles. Paul emphatically denies their claim that he is in some way inferior to them.

It seems that these false apostles prided themselves on their speaking skills. Paul admits that they may be better speakers than he is (**11:6**; 1 Cor 2:1), but speaking well is no substitute for the *knowledge* he has (see also Eph 3:4). He reminds the Corinthians that he has clearly demonstrated this knowledge among them (1 Cor 2:6-16).

But the key factor that distinguishes Paul from the false apostles is his unselfishness, which he presents in 11:7-11. He begins this section of his argument by asserting that he lowered himself in order to elevate the Corinthians (**11:7a**). This way of speaking reminds us of what was said of the Lord Jesus in 2 Corinthians 8:9 and Philippians 2:5-11.

In what way did Paul lower himself? It was by proclaiming the gospel *free of charge* (**11:7b**). In Greek society, the value of the philosophy taught by spiritual teachers was judged by whether or not they were paid for their teaching. Paul refused payment, and that was why the Corinthians doubted his apostolic credentials.

Paul was well aware that as the one who had founded the church, he could legitimately claim a salary from them. However, he voluntarily gave that up (1 Cor 9:1-15). In Corinth he met his needs by working as a tent-maker alongside Aquila and Priscilla (Acts 18:1-3). He also accepted financial help from other churches, and particularly from the church in Philippi, so that he could serve the Corinthians without charge (**11:8-9a**; Phil 4:15).

He twice insists that he will continue to refuse to accept financial support from the Corinthians (**11:9b-10**). They should not interpret this as a rejection. God knows that he loves them (**11:11**). But he is determined to show the difference between himself and those who are claiming to be super-apostles (**11:12**). He knows that they are focused on the money that they can make by preaching 'their' gospel, and that they will not willingly give up this source of easy income. In this area, they cannot equal him (11:12b). Their reluctance to preach without receiving any fee reveals their true motives. Unfortunately, their desire for material riches is shared by many who preach in our African cities today.

Only once in the NT are people described as *false apostles* (**11:13**). The term seems to derive from the expression 'false prophets' that is used in the ancient Greek translation of Jeremiah (Jer 6:13; 26:7, 8, 11, 16; 27:9; 28:1; 29:1, 8). Both Jeremiah and Paul were confronted by people who were passing off their own ideas as the words of the Lord (Jer 14:14). In stating that these people are simply *masquerading as apostles of Christ* Paul is stressing how false they are (11:13b). Their deep falseness reveals their real character: they are servants of Satan, who is the deceiver and the liar par excellence (John 8:44; 2 Thess 2:9-10). His servants disguise themselves as he does and pass themselves off as *servants of righteousness,* which they clearly are not (**11:14-15**). For this, they will be judged by God (Rom 3:8; Phil 3:18-19).

11:16-33 Paul's Arguments: Work and Suffering

Paul had denied being inferior to the super-apostles in any way (11:5), and now he sets out to display what it is that identifies him as a genuine apostle. Once again, he asks the Corinthians to allow him to brag and boast as the false apostles do, even though he knows that only fools speak this way (11:16; see also 1:1; 10:8, 13, 15-17). That is why he cannot describe it as *talking as the Lord would* (11:17). He knows that even though he has good grounds for boasting, a boastful attitude is wrong. But since *many* (that is, the false apostles) *are boasting in the way the world does,* Paul will speak up (11:18). The contrast between the Lord's way of speaking and the world's indicates that the latter is focused solely on human advantages.

Paul ironically contrasts himself as a 'fool' with the 'wise' Corinthians (11:19). He is sure that they can put up with him, since they put up with so much else from the adversaries of the true gospel. These people have taken such control of the Corinthians that they have reduced them to a state like that of slavery (Gal 2:4). The false apostles live off the Corinthians (see, for example, Mark 12:40), steal their goods (Gal 5:15) and force them to submit to various kinds of oppression (11:20). The Corinthians accept all this without flinching, just as many African Christians today are forced to do by their fraudulent 'pastors' and 'prophets'.

The Corinthians should be ashamed to submit to such treatment, but instead it is Paul, speaking sarcastically, who says that he is ashamed that he could not bring himself to behave in this way! (11:21a).

Paul then goes on to speak of the specific boasts made by some people. He does not specify who these people are. Thus some have interpreted them to be the apostles in Jerusalem, but it is far more likely that they are the false apostles (11:21b).

Paul's opponents describe themselves using three terms that all refer to the same people group, but have different emphases (11:22). *Hebrews* stresses the racial reality of the Jewish people (Phil 3:5). *Israelites* stresses their social and religious bonds (Rom 9-11). *Abraham's descendants* reminds us that they are the beneficiaries of the promise that Christ fulfilled (Rom 9:6-11; Gal 3:16, 18). Paul can claim each of these labels for himself too.

Then Paul moves beyond the purely Jewish sphere to Christian claims. The false apostles seem to have been particularly fond of referring to themselves as *servants of Christ* (11:23). While Paul has been prepared to admit the truth of their earlier claims, when it comes to this one, he insists that he is a completely different kind of servant of Christ: *I am more* (1 Cor 15:10). He has worked far harder than any of them have. The word here translated as 'worked' is one that Paul often uses when speaking either of the Lord's work in general or of the apostolic task in particular (1 Cor 15:58; 2 Cor 6:5; 10:15; 1 Thess 1:3; 2:9; 3:5).

Because of his work for the Lord, Paul has endured the *forty lashes minus one* (11:24). This beating was a Jewish punishment meted out by synagogues (see Deut 25:2-3). Paul endured it five times, although we do not know exactly where. He also endured Roman punishment when he was illegally *beaten with rods* (11:25). Paul had received this treatment three times, although we have only one account of it (Acts 16:22, 37-38). He had been stoned once (Acts 14:19). And he had been shipwrecked at least three times, but probably more, since the shipwreck recorded in Acts 27:14-44 took place after the writing of this letter. He had also endured *a day and a night in the open sea.*

Paul also lists the dangers he had encountered during his travels on land (11:26). He had forded rivers on foot and the highways were infested with robbers. He had been threatened by his own compatriots, the Jews (Acts 9:23, 29; 13:45; 14:2, 19; 17:5; 18:6, 12), and by *Gentiles* (Acts 16:20-22; 19:23-30). The *false brothers* who had threatened him were his opponents at Corinth as elsewhere (11:13; Gal 2:4; Phil 3:2).

In 11:27, Paul returns to the theme of work (11:23). The nights without sleep were not spent in prayer but were rather sleepless nights because of his pastoral concerns (6:5). The *hunger and thirst* he suffered should not be confused with voluntary fasting. He also endured being *cold and naked.*

In 11:28 Paul speaks as a true pastor. What constantly occupies his mind and his efforts is *the pressure of my concern* for the churches. The plural 'churches' indicates that Paul is thinking not only of those that he had founded but also of all the churches established in the Gentile world of that era (Rom 1:9-13). He is truly the apostle to the Gentiles (Acts 22:21; Gal 1:16; 2:2, 9). Scripture tells us not to be anxious about anything (Phil 4:6), but we need to distinguish between unnecessary anxiety about our own security (Matt 6:25-32) and legitimate concern for God's work (Matt 6:33; Phil 2:12). Paul illustrates this concern. He is weak with those who are weak (1 Cor 9:22; 12:26) and he is so deeply concerned when a believer falls that he feels ill (11:29; see also 1 Cor 8:13).

Paul then sums up these first arguments in support of the authenticity of his apostleship by stressing the way in which he differs from his opponents. They deny his apostolic authority because he is weak and lacks eloquence (10:10). But Paul prefers to boast *of the things that show my weakness* (11:30; 12:9).

Once again, Paul calls God as witness (11:31). This formula using a benediction was widely used in the writings of the rabbis, and is also found elsewhere in Paul's letters (Rom 1:25; 1 Cor. 1:3).

As an afterthought, Paul adds one further example of suffering that he had forgotten to mention earlier (11:32-33). This experience is probably related to Acts 9:23-25.

12:1-10 Paul's Arguments: Visions and Revelations

Paul's apostolic authority is supported not only by his work and suffering but also by his *visions and revelations from the Lord* (**12:1**). As the Baoulé people of the Ivory Coast say, 'It is not because a man has no blood in his stomach that he spits saliva.' Paul has not made an issue of extraordinary revelations until now, but that is not because he had not had any. Driven to it by his opponents and the Corinthians (12:11), he is going to speak of some astonishing experiences the Lord has given him.

But he remains humble. He distinguished the apostle (*a man in Christ*) who had had this experience from Paul, the ordinary man (12:2a, 5). He also recognizes that his account is not complete; only God knows exactly what happened when Paul was *caught up to the third heaven* (**12:2-3**). The word here translated as 'heaven' is the same as the word translated as 'paradise'. But Paul is not speaking of the original paradise of Eden but of the place where the council of God meets (Jer 23:18, 22).

The fact that Paul was 'caught up' shows that the initiative came from God. Paul does not seem to have sought the visions and revelations of which he speaks. His reference to the things that he cannot and dare not utter (**12:4**) also shows that, unlike many believers today, Paul knows how to keep some revelations that he has received secret and personal. He could boast about them, but he chooses not to do so and rather boasts of his weaknesses (**12:5-6;** 11:30). He wants people to remember him for what he says and does, and not for his visions. His attitude teaches us that what is ultimately important is not visions and revelations, but the life that results from the visions and revelations that God gives.

The exact interpretation of **12:7** is not clear. If it links up with 12:6, Paul is saying that he does not want the glory of the revelations he has received to gain him a reputation he does not deserve. However, if 12:7a is more closely associated with the rest of 12:7, he is saying that his extraordinary revelations have resulted in his having *a thorn in my flesh*. This thorn has been interpreted in three main ways:

- as physical suffering, that is, an illness from which Paul suffers;
- as theological suffering because Paul does not succeed in winning the Jews to the gospel;
- as apostolic suffering, in the form of constant opposition to his apostolic authority.

The mention of *a messenger of Satan* has made some think that Paul was possessed by an evil spirit. This is definitely not the case! Rather, behind his painful experience, Paul sees the action of Satan, the permanent opponent of the gospel.

Paul's three prayers remind us of the Lord in the garden of Gethsemane (**12:8;** see also Mark 14:32-42). Despite his persistence, Paul is not delivered. But he did receive a word

from the Lord himself, giving what the tense of the verb suggests is a final answer to his prayer.

The central theme of Christ's answer is *grace* (**12:9a**), which may refer either to the apostolic ministry entrusted to Paul (Rom 1:5; 12:3; 1 Cor 15:10) or to the reproducing in Paul's life of the weakness of Christ (1:5; 4:10; Phil 3:10; Col 1:24). Paul understands that it is in his weakness that the power of Christ is best demonstrated. He is therefore pleased to endure the trials associated with his ministry *for Christ's sake* (**12:9b-10**). We too find that the more we recognize that we are weak and try to depend on God, the more we experience his power.

12:11-21 Paul's Concerns about the Corinthians

By refusing to defend him against the false apostles, the Corinthians have obliged Paul to do so himself (**12:11**). More clearly than in 11:5, he says that, even if he is *nothing* (probably what his opponents were saying), he is nevertheless *not in the least inferior to the 'super-apostles'*.

The things that mark an apostle, that is, the indications that Paul is genuinely an apostle, have been in evidence among the Corinthians. These indications include *signs, wonders and miracles* (**12:12a**). The purpose of every genuine miraculous sign is to point beyond itself to the real author of the sign, who is God. It is only in this way that a sign can authenticate a ministry. But if the sign is the end in itself, and does not force those who see it to go beyond it to see God, it is a temptation to idolatry (12:6-7).

Paul also mentions his *great perseverance* (**12:12b**; 6:3-10; 11:23-33). If perseverance should characterize the life of every Christian (Rom 5:3-4; 8:25; 2 Thess 1:3-4; 1 Tim 6:11; Titus 2:2), it should be shown even more clearly in the life of the apostle and of every pastor and minister of the word.

Paul returns to the point that was discussed in 11:7-11 and, speaking ironically, asks the Corinthians to forgive him for never having been a *burden* to them (**12:13**). He will continue to commit this *wrong* because he is preparing to come to Corinth for the third time, with the same attitude. Once again, he will not live at their expense, for he regards the Corinthians as more important than their possessions (**12:14**). He sees himself as their father (1 Cor 4:15), and as such, it is his responsibility to provide for the material needs of his children. So he will *spend* and *expend* himself for the Corinthians (**12:15**), revealing both his unselfishness and his love for them. But he is not sure that this love will be returned (12:15b).

Some of Paul's opponents were suggesting that Paul had only pretended not to accept support, but had received money indirectly through his co-workers (**12:16-17**). Paul emphatically denies this and reminds them of the behaviour of Titus and the brother whose name is not given (8:18, 22).

Both of them had acted *in the same spirit* as Paul, specifically, with the same moral and financial integrity (**12:18**).

Paul reminds his readers that he is not defending himself in order to win over the Corinthians (**12:19**). Rather, he is speaking *in the sight of God* and *in Christ* (see also 2:17; 5:10; Rom 14:10). His purpose is solely to build up the Corinthians and other believers. This latter point underlines the close tie between the prophetic ministry of Jeremiah and that of the Apostle Paul (13:10; Jer 1:10).

Paul next presents a list of the sins that he hopes not to find in the Corinthian community (**12:20**). The first four are 'acts of the sinful nature' as found in Gal 5:20: *quarrelling, jealousy, outbursts of anger, factions.* Then come *slander* and *gossip,* which are sins of the tongue and relate to spreading rumours about other brothers and sisters in the community (Jas 3:8-10). *Arrogance* is present when we exaggerate our own importance and often expresses itself in pride and insolence. *Disorder* is the failure to abide by the rules that govern the life of the community (1 Cor 14:33).

What Paul fears most is that some of those who have sinned will refuse to repent. He is afraid of being *grieved* (as by a death) by those who could, according to 1 Corinthians 6:9-11, be excluded from the kingdom of God (**12:21**).

13:1-14 Final Words: Warnings and Greetings

Paul repeats that he will make a third visit to Corinth (**13:1**; 12:14). This visit will be different from the one described in Acts 18:1-18, as the quotation of Deuteronomy 19:15 clearly shows. This visit will be disciplinary (Matt 18:16; 1 Tim 5:19).

Paul had already issued a warning during his second visit to Corinth (**13:2**). This warning was to those who had previously sinned without repenting (12:21) and to *others* who should perhaps have intervened to correct the situation. Paul indicates that he will handle no one gently (10:11), so as to show the Corinthians that Christ truly speaks through him (**13:3**; see also 1 Thess 2 13). The apostle may be weak, but Christ will certainly show himself strong among the Corinthians. Paul clearly shows that his apostolic authority is not limited only to doctrinal matters. It is equally valid regarding the ethical and moral values that should be at the heart of the Christian community. The apostle also shows that his life is in the image of that of his Master (**13:4**).

Then he invites the Corinthians to examine themselves. For those who want to know whether Paul is a genuine apostle, it is a matter of asking themselves if they are in the faith and if Christ is living in them; in other words, if they are truly Christians. Some may even *fail the test* (**13:5**). But Paul and his companions will not fail it (**13:6**).

Paul prays that the Corinthians will do *what is right* (**13:7, 9**), that is, that their lives will conform to what they

profess. Living this way, they will give no reason to Paul to be severe when he arrives among them.

The word *truth* in **13:8** is synonymous with 'justice', which means 'what God demands'. In this context, it is equivalent to 'the gospel'. Paul's assertion that he has no power to do anything *against the truth* clearly shows that he has never added anything to the gospel. His concern is always the building up of the Corinthians. Despite the criticism that this practice has brought him in the past, he prefers to be severe in his letters in order to give those to whom he is writing time to reflect and repent, rather than having to be *harsh* with them when he is present (**13:10**; 10:1, 10). The authority the Lord has given him can be used both to build up and to destroy (10:8; see also Jer 1:10), but Paul chooses to use it only for edification.

The word *finally* (**13:11a**) indicates that the letter is ending. It is an expression we often find in Paul's writings (see, for example, Phil 3:1; 1 Thess 4:1). The tone of the letter now changes from severity to greeting and blessing.

Paul's final exhortation includes a number of instructions (**13:11b**):

* *Aim for perfection.* This is what Paul prayed for in 13:9.
* *Listen to my appeal.*
* *Be of one mind.* Encourage one another and exhort one another (1 Thess 4:18; 5:11).
* *Live in peace.* This quality of life is linked to their being of one mind (Rom 12:18; 1 Thess 5:13).

If they live this sort of life, the *God of love and peace will be with you* (**13:11c**). Paul often uses the expression 'the God of peace' (Rom 15:33; 16:20; Phil 4:9; 1 Thess 5:23) and the expression 'the God of love' fits equally well in the framework of Paul's thought (Rom 5:5, 8; 8:39; 1 Cor 13).

The instruction to *greet one another* (**13:12**) can be taken as an addition to the imperatives in 13:11. According to some commentators, a *kiss* was an expression of reconciliation in Judaism. By attaching the adjective *holy* to it, Paul seems to be making it something typically Christian. He gives the same instruction at the close of many of his letters (Rom 16:16; 1 Cor 16:20b; 1 Thess 5:26).

In the blessings at the end of his letters, Paul usually refers to only one member of the Trinity (Gal 6:18; Phil 4:23; Col 4:18; 1 Tim 6:21; Titus 3:15), or to two of them (Rom 16:27; Eph 6:23). But in **13:14** he mentions all three members of the Trinity as if he is seeking to give a final summary of the apostolic gospel to the Corinthians.

Issiaka Coulibaly

Further Reading

Barrett, C. K. *The Second Epistle to the Corinthians.* Reprint. BNTC. Peabody, Mass.: Hendrickson, 1993.

Hughes, Philip E. *The Second Epistle to the Corinthians.* NICNT. Grand Rapids: Eerdmans, 1962.

GALATIANS

Scholars generally agree that this letter was written by the Apostle Paul (1:1), but they are less certain about whom it was addressed to. The most common view (adopted in this commentary) is that 'Galatia' refers to the whole province, in which case the recipients include the southern churches that Paul founded on his first missionary journey when he visited Pisidian Antioch, Iconium, Lystra and Derbe. The letter could then have been written as early as AD 49. But it is also possible that Paul was writing only to the churches in the northern district called Galatia, from which the whole province took its name. If so, it is difficult to identify the churches or know when they were founded, with the earliest possibility being Paul's second missionary journey. This would mean that the letter would have to have been written after the Council at Jerusalem in AD 50 (see Acts 15).

Paul's reason for writing was his concern that the Galatians were listening to false teachers. These Judaizers were telling the Gentiles that they must be circumcised and become like Jews in order to be justified. Paul's response in this letter applies to any group that suggests that believers need to rely on anything other than faith in Christ for salvation.

Outline of Contents

COMMENTARY

1:1-5 Author, Recipients, Greetings

Paul introduces himself as *an apostle*, a word that means 'sent one' (**1:1a**). It appears that some people in Galatia were inclined to dispute his authority, saying that Paul had been made an apostle by Jesus' disciples or by those who commissioned him at Antioch (Acts 13:1-3). So Paul insists that no group or individual made him an apostle (**1:1b**). We are not certain which individual he may have had in mind, but possibilities include Ananias (Acts 9:15-18), Barnabas (Acts 9:27, 12:25), a representative of the original apostles, or someone in the church in Antioch.

Paul is adamant that his apostleship stems directly from *Jesus Christ and God the Father* (**1:1c**; see Acts 9:1-6). The Father is involved because without his resurrection of Jesus *from the dead*, there would not be a gospel to preach nor any apostolic authority for Paul to exercise. But even though he is an apostle, Paul does not act alone and so he acknowledges *all the brothers with me* (**1:2**) as he writes this letter.

Paul wishes the Galatians *grace and peace*. He uses a fairly standard Greek and Hebrew greeting, but he alters it slightly by taking out the common word for greeting and substituting the word 'grace'. He specifies that the grace and peace come from *God our Father and the Lord Jesus Christ* (**1:3**). Thus a general greeting is theologically enriched and also serves as a prayer. Here, as in 1:1 and again in 1:4, Paul speaks of Jesus and the Father in the same breath, leaving no doubt that he sees Jesus as a partner with the Father, at work in his life and in the lives of the Galatians.

In 1:1 Paul described what the Father had done. In **1:4** he describes what the Son has done: he *gave himself*. It is clear that Christ's death was voluntary and that its purpose was *to rescue us*. Because of *our sins* we cannot meet the demands of God's righteousness. By dying for us, Jesus not only restored us to a right standing with God (justification) but also changed our characters so that we can live as God's children. While we may still struggle with the activity of the devil in *the present evil age*, there will be a future age characterized by Jesus' total rule of our lives. Our victory over the devil now, imperfect as it is, is a taste of the age to come.

Paul stresses that Jesus was not acting alone. He was acting *according to the will of our God and Father*. The phrase 'our God and Father' reminds us that the majestic God (who is over all and controls all) is also our loving Father (rescuing us even when we were still his enemies). It is no wonder that Paul burst into praise, *to whom be glory for ever and ever* (**1:5**).

1:6-10 No Other Gospel

Paul now moves from defence of his apostleship to defence of his gospel. It is obvious from what he says and how he says it that some people were attacking his message and having an effect on the Galatians that deeply worried him.

1:6-7 The Galatians and the False Teachers

What disturbed Paul was that the Galatians were *deserting the one who called them by the grace of Christ* (**1:6**). He is implying that they were abandoning God and giving allegiance to false teachers. He was astonished that this was happening at all, and even more so that it was happening *so quickly* (1:6). He may be thinking of the short time that elapsed between the arrival of false teachers and the need for this letter, or of the short time between the Galatians' acceptance of the true gospel and their turning away from it, or of the short time since his last visit to them. Whichever it was, the Galatians were now turning away from the treasure of the true gospel to *a different gospel* – in fact, to something that was *really no gospel at all* (**1:7**). Yet Paul has no doubt that they had possessed the correct gospel. It is the one *we preached to you* (1:8) and the one *you accepted* (1:9). By using 'we' here, Paul includes the members of his team when they founded the churches in Galatia.

The strategy of the false teachers' was to sow confusion, causing the Galatians to desert Christ and accept a different and perverted gospel. They were making progress in turning people away from Christ, and so Paul writes to alert the Galatians to what is actually going on and to express his astonishment that they cannot see the difference between the treasure they had possessed and the falsity with which they are replacing it.

1:7-9 The Unchanging Gospel

Through his choice of Greek words, Paul makes it very clear that there is no other gospel that is even of the same species as the one he had preached and the Galatians had accepted. What his opponents may be calling the 'gospel' is really something totally different. It is not merely an inferior substitute but a counterfeit.

While the false teachers may have had some success in changing the Galatians, they cannot do the same to the gospel itself for *ajagajigi enniti o mi kukute mi 'ra re* [Yoruba, Nigeria – 'he who tries to shake a tree trunk, only shakes himself']. This is due to the nature of the gospel:

- It is distinct. a) It is *of Christ* (1:7) meaning that it belongs to Christ, was proclaimed by Christ, and is about Christ who became flesh, died for us, and rose again in victory over death; b) It involves a calling by God the Father, *the one who called you* (1:6) – what better position is there than one given by the Father? c) The Father's calling is *by the grace of Christ* or *in the grace of Christ* (1:6). (The same word can be translated as 'by' or 'in'.) If we take it as meaning 'in the grace of Christ', Paul is saying that they received their calling within the sphere of grace rather than in the sphere of works. However, it seems more likely that we should translate it as 'by', which means that Paul is emphasizing that God's calling was an act of grace. The Galatians are forgetting the kindness God showed in accepting them as his children.

- It is irreplaceable: Though the false teachers were presenting their teaching as the 'gospel', Paul says that it was *really no gospel at all* (1:7). The true and effective gospel centres on Christ alone as the basis for salvation. It is the same for rich or poor, master or slave, man or woman, president or common man, oppressor or oppressed, wise or foolish, educated or uneducated, Gentile or Jew, Galatian or African. There is only one way for all. No other proposed gospel can save.

- It is bigger than Paul, angels or anyone else. Any other gospel would be wrong no matter what the source. Even if Paul himself or an angel from heaven tried to make some changes, they would be wrong (**1:8a**). What the Galatians had received from Paul was the substance of God's wise plan of redemption and no wisdom from any other source can improve on it.

- Its significance justifies a curse on anyone who distorts it. Twice in this passage, Paul, speaking of those who are preaching a false gospel, says, *let him be eternally condemned* (**1:8b**; **1:9b**). Perverting the gospel is a serious crime in the divine judicial system, and calls for divine punishment. Paul says that this pronouncement is not a new thing, for he has *already said* it (**1:9a**). He may be referring back to his earlier statement in 1:8, but it seems more likely that this is a principle he has mentioned in the past. It is not merely an expression of his feelings towards the Judaizers in Galatia as persons.

1:10 Two Important Questions

Paul finishes this section with two important questions. First, *Am I now trying to win the approval of men, or of God?* (**1:10a**). These are the only two alternatives – seeking human approval or seeking God's approval. Someone who is seeking human approval tends to relax requirements and be less strict so that people will like him. Those who were questioning Paul's authority may have been implying that this was what he was trying to do when he insisted that salvation is by faith alone, while the Judaizers insisted that works were also necessary. So Paul repeats the question: *Am I trying to please men?* (**1:10b**).

Paul emphatically answers his own questions: *If I were still trying to please men, I would not be a servant of Christ* (**1:10c**). Pleasing people may have characterized Paul's life before his conversion, but not now. His only concern is to defend and promote the gospel that God approves, even if this makes him unpopular with some people, including the Galatians and those leading them astray. He has a genuine desire to please God.

1:11-24 Paul's Apostleship and Gospel

Paul now takes time to clearly state the source of the gospel that is so important to him and to the Galatians. To avoid any confusion about what gospel he is talking about, he repeats his description of it as *the gospel I preached* (**1:11**; compare 1:8, 'we preached'). He is contrasting it with any different teaching the Galatians are receiving or may receive in the future. There are two main points he wishes to emphasize: he received it by direct revelation and he did not receive it from a human source.

1:11-16 Direct Revelation from Jesus Christ

Paul's statement that he received the gospel *by revelation from Jesus Christ* (**1:12**) can be literally translated as 'revelation of Jesus Christ'. The revelation was both from and of Jesus. However, at this point, Paul is mainly concerned with the source of his revelation. The Father revealed Jesus to Paul (1:15-16), and Jesus revealed the gospel to Paul

(1:12). Both the Father and the Son have made Paul the person he is and have given him the message he preaches.

Paul strengthens this direct statement by asking his readers to compare what he was like before and after his conversion. Then, his thinking, actions and attitudes had been governed by his Jewish faith. The Galatians knew that he had been far more into Judaism than any of the Judaizers. His life had been characterized by hatred of the church, progress in Judaism, and zealous upholding of the traditions of his ancestors (**1:13-14**). He had not been merely a young and enthusiastic Jew but an advanced scholar. His devotion to Judaism had been expressed in action as he laboured to destroy the church. For such a man now to become a supporter of the church, advocating a salvation that does not depend on the Jewish law, must have involved far more than merely human arguments. Nothing short of divine intervention could have brought about such a change.

Paul describes his conversion as involving two actions by God: he *set me apart from birth* and *called me by his grace* (**1:15**). These two acts acknowledge both God's eternal purpose for Paul's life and its realization within Paul's experience on his way to Damascus (Acts 9:1-19). His stress on grace underlines the point that Paul did not deserve the favour God showed him by revealing himself to him and then commissioning him to be the apostle to the Gentiles (**1:16**; Acts 26:12-18). Paul says this revelation of Jesus by God took place *in me*, suggesting that God took him through the experience of realizing who Jesus actually is in order to change his goal from being an enemy of Jesus to being his passionate supporter.

1:17-24 No Human Source

Paul emphasizes his claim that he received his gospel directly from Christ by stressing that it is *not … from any man* (**1:12, 16**). There seem to have been some who were claiming that Paul had been taught the gospel by Ananias (Acts 9:10-22) or by the original apostles. They implied that Paul was now departing from what he had been taught by leaving out the need for works for salvation.

In order to set the record straight, Paul lists his movements after his conversion (1:17-2:1). He wants to make it clear that he had very limited contact with the other apostles, and that this contact took place some years after he had been converted and begun preaching.

Almost immediately after his conversion he left Damascus and went to Arabia (**1:17**). We do not know whether he preached there or simply reflected on the enormous change that had taken place in his thinking. He was certainly far from Jerusalem and the twelve apostles (Acts 8:1b). He then says that *after three years* he visited Jerusalem. This may have been three years after his conversion or three years after his return to Damascus. His visit to Jerusalem was brief *(fifteen days)* and his reason for going was very specific – he *wanted to get acquainted with Peter* (**1:18**). On this visit he met none of the other apostles except James, the brother of Jesus, who was an apostle, but not one of the Twelve. (**1:19**).

Later he travelled to Syria and Cilicia (**1:21**), again far from Jerusalem. At that time he was not personally known *to the churches of Judea*. He had had no contact with them. All they knew was that a remarkable change had taken place in his life (**1:22-24**). It was only *fourteen years later* (**2:1**) that he paid a second visit to Jerusalem and met with some of the church leaders. This may have been fourteen years after his conversion, or after his earlier visit to Jerusalem, or after he moved to Syria and Cilicia. But the general picture is clear: Paul had no opportunity to learn the gospel from any of the twelve apostles. This is further confirmation of his testimony that it was revealed to him by Christ. Paul feels so strongly about this that he adds, *I assure you before God that what I am writing to you is no lie* (**1:20**). The fact that he was being misrepresented and the gospel distorted caused him pain.

2:1-10 Paul Accepted by the Other Apostles

Although Paul insists that he is not indebted to Jerusalem and the apostles for his gospel, he also wants to make it clear that there is no conflict between him and the leaders in Jerusalem. So he describes his second visit to Jerusalem, focusing on circumcision, an issue that is highly relevant to the Galatians.

2:1 Paul's Companions – Barnabas and Titus

Paul's companions on his second visit to Jerusalem were Barnabas and Titus (**2:1**). Barnabas was a Levite from Cyprus who had become a Christian in Jerusalem (Acts 4:36-37). He was a key figure in helping to bridge the gap between the mission of the gospel to the Jews and the mission to the Gentiles (Acts 9:27; 11:22; 13:1-14:28; 15:2-4, 12, 36-41). This is the first time Paul mentions him in one of his letters. Titus, on the other hand, was Greek and is not mentioned in Acts at all. He seems to have been converted by Paul (Titus 1:4) and became an important associate of his (2 Cor 2:12-13; 7:5-16; 8:6-24; 12:18).

By taking a Jew and a Gentile with him to Jerusalem, Paul may have been demonstrating the peaceful co-existence of the circumcised and the uncircumcised in Christ and his own role in relation to both groups. Or he may have been asking the Jews in Jerusalem (including their leaders) to demonstrate their willingness to accept a Gentile. Whatever his reason had been then, here in this letter he has another important reason for mentioning Titus (see the comments on 2:3).

2:2 Reason for the Visit

Paul says that he went to Jerusalem in response to divine guidance (**2:2a**), implying that he had not been summoned by the leadership or been urged to go by others. It is not clear whether he received this revelation himself or whether it was relayed to him by Agabus (Acts 11:28), but we do know that Paul was familiar with revelation, whether through prophecy (1 Cor 14:6, 26), visions or dreams (Acts 16:9-10; 18:9-10; 23:11; 27:23-24) or God-given conviction (Phil 3:15; Acts 16:6-7; 20:22).

While in Jerusalem, Paul *set before them the gospel that I preach among the Gentiles* (**2:2b**). Later in the same verse, he refers to *those who seemed to be leaders* (**2:2c**). While the NIV translates this as if there was just one meeting, this is not the only way the Greek can be interpreted. It seems likely that there were two. First, there was a public meeting between Paul and his team and members of the Jerusalem church. Later, there was a private meeting with a smaller group of leaders, including James, Peter and John (see 2:9).

At these meetings, Paul presented 'the gospel I preach' (**2:2b**). He uses the present tense here to make the point that he always preaches the same gospel, whether he is in Jerusalem or in Galatia.

Paul refers to his presentation at Jerusalem as setting his gospel before them. The verb translated 'set before' says nothing about the superiority of one party over another. It can be used to refer to communication between friends, or from a superior to a subordinate, or from a subordinate to a superior. In this section of Galatians, it simply means that he told them what he was preaching.

He did this *for fear that I was running or had run my race in vain* (**2:2d**). It is clear from the whole letter that Paul was not doubting the validity of his gospel or his divine mission. Nor was he wanting the approval of the Jerusalem leadership. Rather, he was concerned to maintain the unity of the church in the midst of the diversity introduced by the conversion of Gentiles. Fellowship with Jerusalem would be a blessing on his ministry. His 'running', an athletic image representing his work, would be in vain only if those who failed to understand his message set about undoing his work. He wanted to make sure that the church in Jerusalem understood where he was coming from.

Paul was interested in serving the true gospel and not in competition. However, Judaizers might interpret the visit to Jerusalem as showing that Paul was inferior to the apostles there. So Paul moves on to describe what happened during this visit.

2:3-5 Problems that Arose

The problems on this visit arose from people whose attitude seems to have been similar to that of the Judaizers in Galatia. Paul refers to them as *some false brothers* (**2:4a**), but he does not identify them more specifically nor say whether they caused problems before, during or after this visit. What we do know is that they insisted that circumcision was essential if Gentiles were to be saved. Titus came to symbolize this issue. Yet the issue of whether Titus was or was not circumcised had clearly not bothered the leaders to whom Paul had presented his gospel. While some argue that Paul's statement that *not even Titus … was compelled to be circumcised* (**2:3**) implies that Titus may have voluntarily decided to be circumcised, the important principle is that the Jerusalem church recognized that circumcision was not essential.

The issue of circumcision was dragged up by the false brothers who had *infiltrated our ranks* (**2:4b**) The word 'infiltrated' is used of traitors who pretend to be part of a group so that they can spy on it and weaken it. The 'ranks' Paul mentions may refer to the Christian church in general. The false brothers would be people who had joined the church and probably attached themselves to the mission to the Gentiles, but with evil motives. Some commentators argue that this infiltration may have happened in Antioch, while others argue that these people may have been sent to Jerusalem from some other place where Paul had been preaching in order to disrupt his meeting.

While these people pretended to be genuinely concerned about maintaining the unity of the church as its outreach broadened, their real goal was to insist on the principle that the Gentiles must be circumcised in obedience to the law. Titus was the Gentile at the focus of their argument.

Paul totally rejected their argument, saying that their goal in spying on the freedom of his team was to take it away: *to make us slaves* (**2:4c**). He describes the freedom he enjoys as *the freedom we have in Christ Jesus*. It is a freedom from having to obey the law in order to earn our salvation. This freedom comes by way of Christ and is enjoyed in Christ on the basis that he took care of all the demands of justice and obeyed the law perfectly on our behalf.

Paul summarizes his group's response: *We did not give in to them for a moment, so that the truth of the gospel might remain with you* (**2:5**). The false brothers laid their demands on the table and Paul and his team (particularly Barnabas) refused to budge. They recognized that to give in to this demand would be to endorse the false principle that justification is by works.

Just as the false brothers were wrong then, so the Judaizers in Galatia are wrong now. Their attempt to take away the Galatians' freedom in Christ is to be resisted. It is a matter of principle and the principle does not change no matter what the context.

Paul did have Timothy circumcised (Acts 16:3), but the circumstances were very different. Timothy was the son of a Jewish mother and a Greek father, while Titus was a Gentile proper. Timothy chose to be circumcised in order not to offend weak brothers and to make the missionary team more acceptable to Jews. Thus the goal was solely to make their ministry more effective. But in the case of Titus, circumcision was presented as necessary for salvation. The truth of the gospel was at stake and that could not be compromised.

2:5-6 Outcome of the Visit

The first outcome of this visit that Paul mentions may seem startling. Paul seems dismissive when he says, *those men added nothing to my message* (**2:6d**), but what he means is that they taught him nothing new and did not demand that he add anything to what he was preaching. In particular, they did not demand that Gentiles be circumcised. Paul's point is that if these leaders saw no need to add anything to his message, the Judaizers in Galatia have no right to do so.

Nevertheless, Paul does seem dismissive when he speaks of *those who seemed to be leaders* (2:2); *those who seemed to be important* (**2:6a**); *whatever they were* (**2:6b**); and those *reputed to be pillars* (2:9). The 'pillars' are clearly James, Peter and John, and his earlier references include them but may also embrace a larger group. Why does Paul speak of these men as 'so-called' leaders? He clearly accepts that James, Peter and John had a rightful leadership role in Jerusalem. But the problem was that the false brothers were exaggerating the importance of these men in order to diminish Paul's authority. Consequently Paul is careful not to assert that these three men are the leaders. They were leaders in Jerusalem, but they were not superior to him. He, too, was a leader in the ministry to the Gentiles. Paul totally rejected the Judaizers' view that his message needed to be validated by any of the other apostles.

When Paul says that *whatever they were makes no difference to me,* he seems to be referring to what these people had been in the past. James was Jesus' blood brother, and Peter and John had accompanied Jesus for a number of years. Some people seemed to think that these privileges meant that they were superior to all others in the church. Paul responds by pointing out that *God does not judge by external appearance* (**2:6c**). That is, he does not act on the basis of favouritism or external considerations. Specifically, he does not favour companions or relatives of the historical Jesus over someone like Paul, who received his apostolic commission later. What matters to God, and what matters to Paul, is that he had received his commission from God.

2:7-9 Mutual Acceptance of Each Other's Mission

Paul's statement of the content of the gospel he was preaching, his testimony as to how he had received it, and the results of his proclamation of it, led the leaders in Jerusalem to recognize that Paul had been given the task of preaching the gospel to the Gentiles, just as Peter had been given the task of preaching to the Jews (**2:7**).

The theological basis for this recognition was that *God, who was at work in the ministry of Peter as an apostle to the Jews, was also at work in my ministry as an apostle to the Gentiles* (2:8). God is one. There is not one God of Peter and another of Paul, just as there is not one gospel for the Jews and another for the Gentiles. If the Judaizers recognized the ministry of Peter to the Jews, and they did, they would have no option but to accept the ministry of Paul to the Gentiles.

Because of what they had heard of the grace of God to Paul, James, Peter and John – three men the Judaizers particularly respected – gave Paul and Barnabas *the right hand of fellowship* (2:9a). This was a pledge of friendship and a formal agreement, not simply a private agreement or vague expression of goodwill. It was a historical event that the Judaizers could not deny without denying the authority of the very persons they were using to support their ideas.

The agreement was that *we should go to the Gentiles, and they to the Jews* (2:9b). This was not an attempt to stake out territories, for that had already been done by God who had commissioned both Peter and Paul. It was simply a recognition that this was how they would operate. The division was clearly not based on geography or race. After all, Paul customarily went to the synagogues first (Acts 17:2, 10; 18:4; 19:8) even though his focus was the Gentiles, and both Peter and James had ministries that were not limited to Jews or to Jewish territories (Acts 11:19-21; Jas 1:1; 1 Pet 1:1). Their ministries had both focus and overlap. They were preaching the same gospel with the same goal, but were using two different missionary strategies due to their differences in outlook and background.

2:10 One request from Jerusalem

Paul was not only concerned with asserting his independence of Jerusalem; he also wanted to demonstrate his fellowship with those in the church in Jerusalem. So when they asked him to *continue to remember the poor*, he quickly adds, *the very thing I was eager to do* (2:10).

Paul's visit seems to have taken place sometime around AD 46. At that time there was a famine in Palestine. The Jerusalem church had suffered because of persecution, and may also have been impoverished because members had sold their possessions (Acts 2:45; 4:34). Thus the leaders of both the Gentile and Jewish ministries wanted to share in relieving the poverty there.

2:11-14 Paul Opposes Peter

Mathoka me nthungini imwe mailea ukungulania [Kamba, Kenya – 'axes in one basket will not fail to clang']. It is not surprising that there was sometimes disagreement between Peter and Paul, who were both strong leaders in the young church (2:11). Their clash was not about principles, but about consistency.

2:11-13 Peter's Failure

At some stage Peter had visited Antioch, and had been perfectly happy to eat with the Gentiles there. However, when *certain men came from James* he stopped doing this (2:12a). The 'James' referred to here is the Lord's brother, who was probably the leading administrator in the Jerusalem church until his martyrdom in AD 62. He had not sent these men, and would not have approved of their attitude, but they came from a group in Jerusalem that was associated with him (Acts 15:24).

Paul states that Peter began to withdraw *because he was afraid of those who belonged to the circumcision group* (2:12b). These particular Jews were very proud of having been circumcised and wanted to impose this custom on the Gentiles. While the issue in Antioch was eating together and not circumcision, the incident is relevant to the Galatians' situation. Some people in Antioch were expecting Peter and other Jews in that city to obey the Jewish law in order to be accepted by God.

Peter's behaviour was obviously influential, and other Jews also began to withdraw from association with Gentiles (2:13a). By doing this they were dividing the church. There is a saying, *uko wa mbiti uthuaa undu umwe* [Kamba, Kenya – 'the clan of hyenas limp alike']. Peter led the Jews in limping the 'faith plus works' way. This was contrary to what he, Paul and others had agreed when they had accepted the 'by faith alone' principle of the gospel.

So influential was Peter that even Barnabas, a close associate of Paul, began to imitate him (2:13b). The words used suggest that Barnabas did not take time to think things through but was carried away by the emotions of the time. Nonetheless, his withdrawal and separation from the Gentiles, no matter how short-lived, was like a cancellation of all that he and Paul had preached to them.

2:14 Paul's Response

Peter's behaviour was sending the message that the Judaizers were correct. He was thus both obscuring and violating the fundamental principle that all races interact in Christ. Paul has no hesitation about labelling such behaviour as hypocritical (2:13). Peter and the others were doing the opposite of what they claimed to believe. Consequently Paul accused them of *not acting in line with the truth of the gospel* (2:14). In fact, he *opposed him [Peter] to his face* (2:11) and rebuked him in public. As the Jabo of Liberia say, 'One does not settle a court case by messenger'. The matter was so serious that it could only be settled face-to-face. But the confrontation was not hostile. Peter's act of withdrawal had sent a public message, and so Paul's counter-message had to be equally public.

Paul's public rebuke to Peter was *You are a Jew, yet you live like a Gentile and not like a Jew. How is it then, that you force Gentiles to follow Jewish customs?* (2:14). Ever since his vision (Acts 10), Peter had recognized that the old distinctions between races no longer applied and had been prepared to eat and drink with Gentile converts. But in Antioch he had changed his behaviour, not because his convictions had changed, but from a desire to remain in good standing with some people. What Peter may not have realized (but Paul did) was that this compromised the truth of the gospel. As the Kamba of Kenya say, *makwata nde muunda* – ['the one who holds here and there gains none']. Peter could not have a principle but not live by it and still have an effective ministry.

2:15-4:31 Justification by Faith

There is debate whether 2:15-21 forms part of what Paul said to Peter. There can, however, be no doubt that Paul was still thinking in terms of the incident in Antioch when he wrote these verses. He sets out to show the Galatians how what happened there relates to what is happening in Galatia. He does this by stating some points on which he and Peter agreed, answering someone's objection to the idea of relying only on faith in Christ for salvation and explaining his own position more fully.

2:15-16 Areas of Agreement

Paul and Peter both agreed that there was a difference between the Jews and those they referred to as *Gentile sinners* (**2:15**). Jews were such by birth and enjoyed special privileges, including a covenant with God and his law to govern them. The Gentiles, not having enjoyed this heritage, remained sinners simply because they were outside the covenant and without God's law to guide them.

Paul and Peter also agreed on the means of justification. By the very act of believing in Jesus, Jews who become Christians acknowledge that salvation is by faith. They are admitting that one *is not justified by observing the law* (**2:16**). The central meaning of the word 'justified' is that God, as examiner, declares that one qualifies for salvation. Paul is making the point that one cannot hope to be justified just by keeping the ceremonial and moral rules of the Mosaic law. He repeats this point as a general principle: *by observing the law no one will be justified.* Here he is quoting from the Old Testament (Ps 143:2), which was accepted as authoritative by all Jews (see also Rom 3:20).

While the law could not justify them, they could be justified by *faith in Jesus Christ.* Faith is the means of justification and Christ is the object of that faith. Paul unites himself with the Jewish Christians, saying that *we, too, have put our faith in Christ Jesus that we may be justified by faith in Christ and not by observing the law.* The 'we' includes Paul,

Peter and all the other Jewish believers who were not 'Gentile sinners'. Paul is probably recalling his Damascus road experience and asking the other Jewish Christians to remember their conversion experiences too. It was not because they regarded the law as unimportant that they believed, but because it was unable to justify them.

2:17-21 Answering an Objection

Paul next addresses an objection to justification by faith. The argument was that if believing in Christ results in our abandoning the law, we are then living a life of sin just like the Gentiles. In that case, Christ is encouraging sin, since he takes people away from the law (**2:17**). Paul's horrified response is *Absolutely not.*

He uses two metaphors to explain why this argument is wrong. The first involves demolition and reconstruction, while the second involves life and death. Paul has already demolished the idea that one can be saved by obeying the law (2:16). If one accepts that justification comes by faith in Christ, but then tries to re-establish a set of laws to be obeyed, one is effectively rebuilding a structure that has been knocked down. Logically, this must mean that one is saying that it was wrong to have demolished the old system, and thus one was a sinner (or a *law-breaker*) to have even tried to live outside that system. Alternatively, one is a law-breaker for abandoning what one knows is right and trying to go back to the old system (**2:18**).

Paul called the Gentiles 'sinners', but he uses the term 'law-breakers' for Jews to remind his readers that while a Gentile is involuntarily a sinner, a Christian Jew who goes back to erecting the wall of legalism as the basis for justification consciously deviates from what is right.

He then goes on to give a better picture of what justification by faith in Jesus Christ means by using the metaphor of life and death. He says that *through the law I died to the law so that I might live for God* (**2:19**). The law itself made him aware of his inability to meet its requirements (perfect obedience) and its inability to make him righteous. So he had to look for life elsewhere, an act that must be preceded by death to the law (that is, a turning away from it). The life he found was in God, and the result of his leaving the law is not godlessness but living to please God rather than merely to keep a set of rules.

Not only is he dead to the law, Paul is also dead to himself, for he says *I have been crucified with Christ* (**2:20a**). The Damascus road experience turned a persecutor of Christians into a missionary. Far from justification by faith encouraging believers to live a life focusing on their own pleasures, it leads to a death to self and Christlike life, for *I no longer live, but Christ lives in me* (**2:20b**). There has been a change of masters. Justification by faith does not lead to a life without rules; but to a life in which the rules come from Christ. Every aspect of Paul's physical life is now governed by his *faith in the one who loved me and gave himself for me* (**2:20c**). That one is *the Son of God*, who Paul earlier referred to by his title of *Christ*. That title states that Jesus is God's chosen one, and so faith in him is not a departure from but an affirmation of the will of God.

Finally, Paul points out the unfortunate, but logical, consequences of asserting that one must obey the law in order to be justified. Where justification by faith magnifies the grace of God, taking pride in good deeds as a means of meriting God's favour is equivalent to dismissing God's free provision as unimportant. More than that, if we claim that we can be justified by doing good works, we are saying that there was really no need for Christ to die for us (**2:21**).

3:1-4:31 Arguments in Support of 'Faith Alone'

In 2:15-21, Paul clearly stated the doctrine of justification by faith. Now he gives at least seven more arguments that support his position.

3:1-5 Argument from experience

The idea that the Galatians need to do something in order to be saved contradicts their own experience. They had been so clearly taught about the crucifixion of Jesus Christ that it was almost as if someone had held a placard before their eyes. Crucifixion was the climax of Jesus' obedience as he presented himself as an atoning sacrifice. They had heard his message of free and complete salvation received through faith in Christ, and had accepted it. Paul was so puzzled about why they would want to abandon this belief and adopt a legalistic approach that he suggests they must have been bewitched (**3:1**). This does not necessarily mean that Paul believed in magic. Rather, he was using a cultural idiom to emphasize that the change in their attitudes was so unexpected that some people might attribute it to the influence of demonic powers.

He reminds them that they received the Holy Spirit when they believed, without having to do anything to earn it (**3:2**). Then, drawing on his belief that the Christian life starts, continues and ends in dependence on the Holy Spirit, he points out that the Galatians are doing things the wrong way round. They had started their spiritual journey in the Spirit, so why were they following the illogical course of starting with something of a higher order (the Spirit) and finishing with a lower order (*human effort*) (**3:3**).

In the past, the Galatians had suffered because of their faith in Christ. If they are now deciding that they can be saved by works, there was no need for them to have endured this suffering. If would have been *for nothing* (**3:4**). (Here Paul is not talking about keeping or losing salvation, but about remaining on the right course. To get off that course now and pursue law as the basis for justification is like losing all the ground they had gained.)

Finally, he reminds them of the miracles they have seen. God did not perform these miracles because of something they did but simply because they believed in him (**3:5**).

3:6-9 Argument from Abraham

Turning from the Galatians' own experience to the ot, Paul tells them to *Consider Abraham: He believed God and it was credited to him as righteousness* (**3:6**; see also Gen 15:6; Rom 4:1-6). Paul's opponents may have been citing Moses, the giver of the law, as the authority, or they may have been arguing that Abraham was justified on the basis of meritorious works. They may have cited passages such as Genesis 12 and 17, especially 17:10-14, to support their views. But Paul points out that Abraham, the father of the Jewish race (Gen 12-24; Isa 51:2; Matt 3:9), was accepted by God on the basis that he had faith in what God promised. Those who now believe God's promise of salvation are Abraham's spiritual children (**3:7-9**).

3:10-14 Argument from the only alternatives

There are only two possible ways of being accepted as righteous by God. One is to keep the law perfectly (**3:12**). However, those who try to do this will inevitably fail, and will then be subject to the curse in Deuteronomy 27:26 (**3:10**). The other way to be accepted by God is to exercise faith, as the quotation from Habakkuk 2:4 shows (**3:11**). Those who believe in Christ are justified because he suffers the curse on their behalf (**3:13-14**).

3:15-25 Argument from the relationship of law and promise

Paul next argues that the essence of the Abrahamic covenant was a promise and that Christ was the fulfilment of that promise. He starts with an everyday example: *no one can set aside or add to a human covenant* (**3:15**). Once every signature is in place, a legal agreement is permanent unless the parties who made it agree to change it. God's covenant cannot be less permanent than a human one.

So what was God's covenant? It was a promise made *to Abraham and to his seed*. Grammatically, the singular 'seed' can be a collective noun, but Paul does not interpret it that way theologically. He says that the word is singular and must refer to only one person, Christ (**3:16**), who is the fulfilment of the promise made to Abraham.

Legally, an earlier agreement cannot simply be set aside. God gave the promise to Abraham some 430 years before he gave the law to Moses (**3:17**). (The figure Paul gives does not contradict the reference to 400 years in Genesis 15:13 and Acts 7:6. The numbers are approximate.) If one has to choose between the promise and the law as the source of justification, it is clear that the promise has priority.

This raises the question of why God even bothered to provide the law (**3:19a**). Paul points out that God gave it *because of transgression* (**3:19b**). This may mean that it was

LEGALISM

Some people see rules as an attempt to control them; others see them as guides to how to live. These different perspectives account for many of the conflicts between parents and children. They also account for differences in believers' attitudes towards God. Those who take the control perspective think that strict obedience to God's laws, and particularly to the Ten Commandments, is a way of gaining his acceptance. (It is this sense of legalism that is the focus of this article.) Others argue that God has already accepted us by grace, and that God's law is simply our guide to living. What is the Bible's perspective on this issue?

God's very first words to Adam and Eve included rules (Gen 1:28; 2:17). He issued orders to Noah (Gen 6:14; 7:1-3), to Abraham (Gen 12:1; 13:14; 17:1, 9) and to Moses (Exod 3:5, 15, 16). The Ten Commandments are thus part of a pattern in which God commands obedience from those he has created and chosen (Exod 19:5; 20:1-17). But God's relationship with Adam and Eve, Noah, Abraham and Moses was not just about rules. He also provided for them (Gen 2:16), protected them (Gen 7:23), blessed them (Gen 15:5) and rescued them (Exod 3:7-10). Within a positive relationship, laws are a blessing, but without a good relationship, they are burdensome.

The book of Galatians deals with the place of the law. Paul had preached and the Galatians had accepted that their relationship with Christ was based on faith in him (Gal 1:9b; 3:26-27), but they were being persuaded that their acceptance by God depended on how well they kept the law (Gal 4:9-10). Paul accused them of wanting to return to being young children (Gal 4:1) rather than grown adults (Gal 4:6). A young African boy traditionally hunted grasshoppers and birds. But after he had been circumcised or initiated into adulthood, he was expected to hunt antelope, and even lions if necessary. It would be cause for concern if a young man went back to hunting grasshoppers. But Paul says that this is what a believer in Christ is doing if he tries to keep the law so that God will accept him.

The circumcised young man proudly upholds the rules of his community. He no longer fears being beaten if he disobeys, but keeps the rules because he now identifies himself with the community. In other words, he no longer views the law as a burden to carry but as a life to live. In the same way, believers do not ignore the law but make it part and parcel of their lives as they relate to a holy God. This is what Paul means when he says that while believers are free from the law they now belong to Christ, and are thus his slaves (Gal 5:24; Rom 6:19-22) and tells them to serve each other (Gal 5:13).

We must be clear that God does not accept us because we keep the law. For one thing, we cannot do that perfectly (Gal 3:10-11). But God's Son, Jesus Christ, did obey it perfectly (1 Pet 2:21-22) and paid the penalty for our failure to keep it (Gal 3:13). We also need to recognize that the content of the law is rooted in the holiness of God, and as part of our relationship with him, we will work to be like him. Thus our lives will be immersed in the law, but not governed by it.

Only the law of God, to be understood in the NT in terms of 'the will of God' and 'Christ-likeness', is binding. Thus any attempt to force believers to obey regulations made by men and women must be strongly opposed (see Matt 9:10-11; John 5:8-10). Such regulations result in a focus on human behaviour rather than on God.

Jesus summarized the whole law as undivided loyalty to God and love for others that is as deep as our love for ourselves (Mark 12:29-31; Matt 19:18). These characteristics should define us. If they do, we will not break God's commandments against murder, adultery, greed and lying.

But when I again return to the commandments, am I still saying that we need to keep these laws to be accepted by God? No! Christ has met all the demands of the law for me. Does this mean that the law is not relevant to my situation? No! God's law reveals how he wants us to live if we are to be like him, and we are to seek to imitate our father. Christ declared his obedience to God (John 6:38). How can we do anything less? As we obey the law, we become more Christ-like – and more the type of people for whom Africa longs.

Samuel Ngewa

---

given in order to minimize our transgressions, by letting us know what was wrong so that we could avoid doing it. But this simultaneously has the effect of making us transgressors, because we now have no excuse for not knowing when we are doing wrong. Besides which, there are always those who regard all laws as things to be challenged and broken. The key point for Paul is that the law's function is tied to transgression and not to making anyone righteous.

Moreover, the law only applied for a certain period: *until the Seed to whom the promise referred had come* (**3:19c**). Paul has identified the seed as Christ (3:16) and his point is that the Galatians, who live after the coming of Christ, are wrong to still focus on the law as the basis for acceptance before God. Its function has never been to serve as basis for justification, and it has passed its expiry date.

Finally, Paul argues that the promise is superior to the law because the promise came directly from God to Abraham while the law involved go-betweens or mediators (**3:19d-20**). He may have been thinking of Moses or of the Jewish tradition that angels were present at the giving of the law (based on the Septuagint's translation of Deut 33:2 and Ps 68:18).

Having established the importance of both the promise and the law, Paul needs to describe the relationship between them. Are they antagonists (**3:21a**)? Paul's answer is 'Absolutely not' (**3:21b**). Both were focused on righteousness, but the law had limited ability to produce it (**3:21c**). It was like a doctor who could diagnose an illness but not cure it. The only cure is faith in Jesus Christ (**3:22b**).

Paul even thinks that the law, by making our sin explicit, contributed to our imprisonment in sin (**3:22a**). It acted as a jailer, confining us in case we wandered too far, or as a disciplinarian, preventing us from sinning more. Faith in Christ (the central element of the promise) provides justification and releases us from the law's confinement (**3:24**). Those who have believed in him no longer need a teacher standing behind them all the time, for they have become adults. They have internalized the rules that previously had to be drilled in by their instructor.

3:26-4:11 Argument from comparison of a child and an adult

Paul spells out in detail the blessings that come with being justified by faith in Christ, the most important of which is that the Galatians have been adopted as sons of God (**3:26; 4:7**). Consequently they have become Christlike, *for all of you who were baptized into Christ have clothed yourselves with Christ* (**3:27**). In the early church, baptism signified identification with Christ to such an extent that it was almost as if they were 'wearing' Christ. Their lives were taking on the characteristics, virtues, and intentions of Christ. Because of this change, the differences between them had disappeared, for now they all looked alike as members of Christ's family. Categories like race, status, and gender are no longer important (**3:28**). They have become one, and because they are united to Christ, they share in the promise made to Abraham (**3:29**; see also 3:16). This means that they inherit the promise made to him.

This mention of inheritance leads Paul to contrast the status of an adult heir with that of a child. A child has to do what he or she is told, just like a servant, until the father judges that the son or daughter can handle the inheritance responsibly and decides that guardians and trustees are no longer needed (**4:2**). Those who try to obey the law are still living like children, surrounded by rules, which Paul calls *basic principles* or elementary school material. This category includes things like the Jewish law, the Gentiles' cultic rituals and, in African terms, traditional sacrifices. All of these principles are *of the world* (**4:3**) since their focus is not the law as God intended it to be but as we have misinterpreted and misapplied it.

The elementary-level material is good. It is not useless or unethical. But it is insufficient. It provides no inner energy to move us towards maturity in obedience. But now God has taken action to move us out of primary school so *that we might receive the full rights of sons* (**4:5**). He did this by sending his Son *when the time had fully come* (**4:4a**). In 4:2 Paul said that it is the father who decides when the time

has come for someone who has been the heir all along to advance from being dependent on others to being governor of his or her inheritance. In the same way, God chose the proper time for those who would otherwise still be living under the elementary principles of religion to mature in their knowledge of his redemptive plan. The time was fully prepared in God's program and also in his governance of the world. He had prepared the world for the spread of the gospel in many ways: arousing an expectation of the Messiah among the Jews; using the Romans to provide peace, security and an excellent road network; and establishing a common language, Greek, through the conquests of Alexander the Great.

The one God sent to fulfil his plan was his own Son who was *born of a woman* (and was thus fully human) and *born under law* (and thus subject to all the obligations and demands of the law) (**4:4b**). Jesus fully satisfied the demands of the Mosaic law and also of the law in general, and was thus fit to redeem us. It is faith in him that matters now. Jesus the Son rewards those who believe in him with the status of being sons of the Father, with the Holy Spirit in their hearts (**4:6**). All three persons of the Trinity unite in the believer's interest!

Finally, Paul accuses the Galatians of forgetting that they are now sons and heirs and wanting to return to their inglorious past as they insist on observing *special days and months and seasons and years* (**4:8-10**). Paul fears that all the time he has spent teaching them about the new status that has come with Christ has been wasted (**4:11**).

4:12-20 Argument from the Galatians' relationship to Paul

Paul's fears for the Galatians lead him to make a very strong appeal to them. Normally he simply 'exhorts' believers, but here he 'pleads' with them (the same verb is used in Rom 1:10; 2 Cor 5:20; 8:4; 10:2). He pleads with them to *become like me* (**4:12a**). They can do this by becoming like Paul in realizing that the law is inadequate and trusting solely in Christ for salvation. They will also be like him if they have as warm a regard for him as he has for them. The reason Paul gives for asking them to become like him is that *I became like you* (**4:12b**). He had become like the Jews who had been freed from the demands of the law, and like the Gentiles in that he no longer prized his Jewish heritage as making him superior to them.

Paul adds *You have done me no wrong* (**4:12c**). Just as the Galatians had loved Paul, so Paul loves them, and has no desire to hurt them. But there is a danger that they may hurt him if they start to believe what the Judaizers have been telling them (see also 4:16).

In the past, the Galatians' attitude to Paul had been very warm. Although he was ill when he first preached the gospel to them, they had not treated him with contempt or scorn but *you welcomed me as if I were an angel of God,* as if I were Christ Jesus himself (**4:13**). So deep was their concern that *I can testify that, if you could have done so, you would have torn out your eyes and given them to me* (**4:15**). This comment suggests that Paul may have had serious eye problems while he was in Galatia. The contrast between their attitude then and their present attitude of suspicion and hostility disturbs him deeply (**4:16**). He had only good intentions towards them when he told them the truth, but they are not appreciating this. He blames the change on *those people* (**4:17**), the Judaizers, who are trying to create a rift between the Galatians and Paul, so that the Galatians, too, will become zealous Judaizers. While Paul has no doubt that zeal is a good thing, he makes the point that the Galatians need to make certain that their zeal is being exercised consistently and in a good cause (**4:18**). At the end of this section, Paul sounds like a perplexed parent of unruly teenagers. He feels almost as if he has to start teaching them about their faith all over again from the beginning (**4:19**) and is frustrated that he cannot be there with them in person (**4:20**).

4:21-31 Argument from the relationship of Hagar and Sarah

For his last argument, with those *who want to be under the law* (**4:21**), Paul draws on the story of Abraham, Hagar and Sarah (Gen 16 and 17). He treats it as an allegory, illustrating the differences between the way of grace and the way of the law.

Hagar represents the law (which is why she is equated with Mount Sinai, where the law was given, and with the earthly city of Jerusalem – **4:25**). She was a slave, and thus so was her son, Ishmael. By contrast, Sarah (who is equated with the heavenly Jerusalem – **4:26**) was a free woman, and her son, Isaac, was born as a result of a special promise from God (**4:22-23**). He, and not Ishmael, was the one who inherited from his father Abraham. Paul sees this as an example of a pattern in which promise, freedom and inheritance go together. For the Galatians, who *like Isaac, are children of promise* (**4:28**), this means that they are accepted because they have believed God's promise, and have been set free from the law and become heirs of God (4:7).

There is another parallel, too. There was conflict between Ishmael and Isaac, just as there is conflict between the Judaizers and those who believe in justification by faith. But God left no doubt which side he supported in that conflict (**4:29-31**).

5:1-6:10 Implications of Justification by Faith

5:1-12 Stand Firm and Live Free

The Galatians are to let the truth Paul has been presenting affect the way they live. He wants them to *stand firm* (**5:1**; see also 1 Cor 16:13; Phil 1:27; 4:1; 1 Thess 3:8) and not let themselves *be burdened again by a yoke of slavery because it is*

for freedom that Christ has set us free. In particular they are to resist those who want to insist that they should be circumcised (**5:2**). If they submit, they will be making themselves liable to obey every other detail of the law too (**5:3-4**), and Paul has twice already compared the need to obey rules to being in a state of slavery (4:1, 25). True freedom is found through faith in Christ (4:5-6).

5:13-25 Live by the Spirit

Paul tells the Galatians to *serve one another in love* (**5:13**); *live by the Spirit* (**5:16**); *keep in step with the Spirit* (**5:25**) and *not become conceited* (**5:26**).

He starts by reminding them that though they *were called to be free* they should *not use your freedom to indulge the sinful nature* (5:13). There are two sides to Christian freedom. We have been set free from slavery to the law, but we are called to serve the Spirit and one another. Christian freedom is not a call to irresponsibility or self-indulgence but to a new set of responsibilities. So although we have been set free from whatever enslaved us before (whether the law or paganism or any other '-ism') we are not free to sin and live as we please. If we do, our freedom is not approved by God. The difference is that we no longer do what God wants simply because the law says we must; our God-honouring moral conduct arises from the Spirit of God within us who now governs our actions.

The Spirit teaches us to obey God's most fundamental command, namely that we love one another (**5:14**). This love is not dredged up as an act of will, in obedience to the law. Rather, it flows from within, for it is only God's grace that enables one to love one's neighbour as oneself or to love one's enemy. In an aside, Paul points out that this is not how the Galatians are actually living at present. He compares the arguments disrupting their church to *biting and devouring each other,* and points out that this way of living is destructive for all who take part in it (**5:15**).

The fighting in the Galatian church is an expression of their *sinful nature,* which finds expression in sinful behaviour. Such behaviour indicates that those who practise it have no share in the kingdom of God (**5:19-21**). It is totally at odds with the behaviour the Spirit desires (**5:17, 24**).

Those who truly live by the Spirit may be tempted to indulge in this sinful behaviour (**5:16-17**) but they will resist it just as firmly as they resist being slaves of the law (**5:16, 18**). Their behaviour will demonstrate that the Spirit is within them and is bearing fruit in their actions and attitudes (**5:22-23**). These virtues go far beyond what any mere law could possibly prescribe.

But Paul is aware that when the Spirit starts to grow these virtues in us, we can easily be tempted to boast about how good we are becoming. So he reminds us that there is nothing to boast about (**5:26**) for it is God who is producing these things in us, not our own efforts.

6:1-6 Fulfil Your Christian Responsibilities

Paul next gives the Galatians instructions on what to do when a fellow believer is found to have committed a sin, not as a settled pattern of behaviour but as an isolated act. Paul tells them that such a person should be gently restored (6:1a). He is applying the principle of love. Where the one who has transgressed already feels guilty, there is no need for condemnation. Restoration should be done with sensitivity to the needs of the sinner and the vulnerability of those who are restoring him, for *u wi kivetani nduthekaa ula wi iko* [Kamba, Kenya – 'one in the woodpile does not laugh at one in the fire']. So Paul reminds the restorers to *watch yourself, or you also may be tempted* (6:1b). He is acutely aware of how easily we can slip into sin. We need to constantly remind ourselves that we have nothing to boast of; everything comes by grace. All we can be proud of is what God has enabled us to be or do (6:3-4).

Paul then broadens his call for loving concern, instructing the Galatians to *carry each other's burdens* (6:2). A burden is any hardship, whether physical, emotional, mental, moral or spiritual.

Finally, Paul turns to the needs of those who are teaching the word of God: *Anyone who receives instructions in the word must share all good things with his instructor* (6:6). Instructors must not suffer because of the time they spend teaching. Students must share what goods they have with their instructors to help provide for their needs (6:6).

6:7-10 Sow and Reap

Paul underlines the general principle *A man reaps what he sows* with the warning that *God cannot be mocked* (6:7), meaning that God cannot be fooled, no matter how clever we think we are. It is no use pretending to be very spiritual while living a sinful life. God will judge deliberate disobedience, whether now or later. By contrast, a person who lives a life that pleases the Spirit will receive the reward of eternal life. What we sow will determine what we reap (6:8).

Paul recognizes that crops grow slowly, and so he adds the exhortation, *let us not become weary in doing good, for at the proper time we will reap a harvest if we do not give up* (6:9). He reminds them *as we have opportunity, let us do good to all people, especially to those who belong to the family of believers* (6:10).

6:11-18 Summary and Conclusion

Paul is concerned that after beginning well (3:2-5; 5:7) the Galatians are losing their initial enthusiasm. So he briefly returns to the issue that prompted this letter, and specifically to the contrast between the Judaizers' motives and his own.

The Judaizers' motive is *to make a good impression outwardly* and to avoid suffering by compromising what they believe (6:12). They are hypocritical in demanding that the Galatians keep the law and be circumcised when they themselves do not even succeed in obeying the law (6:13a). Yet they want to boast about how many people they have persuaded to be circumcised (6:13b).

Their attitude horrifies Paul. They are downplaying the importance of the cross of Christ, which he considers the only thing worth boasting about (6:14). Through *the cross of our Lord Jesus Christ,* Paul has been crucified to the world (he has no dealings with it) and *the world has been crucified* to him (it has no effect on him). He is no longer concerned about the impression he makes.

He sums up the whole issue by saying that ultimately whether one is circumcised or not makes no difference. All that matters is the *new creation,* the transforming relationship with Christ (6:15).

Paul ends his letter by wishing *peace and mercy* and *grace* (6:16a, 18) to *all who follow this rule* (that is, who seek salvation in the cross) and who are *brothers*. These people are *the Israel of God* 6:16b). They may not be Jews by birth but they are God's people because of their faith in Jesus Christ. The Judaizers may seek to cause trouble by insisting on a rite that scars the body, but Paul will have none of it. He already bears *the marks of Jesus* (6:17). While he could be referring to a literal tattoo (for example, an X representing Christ) it is more likely that he is referring to the scars of persecution, both physical and emotional. These scars make it clear who own Paul's life. There is no need to add any others.

Samuel Ngewa

Further Reading

Bruce, F. F. *Commentary on Galatians.* NIGTC. Grand Rapids: Eerdmans, 1982.

Longenecker, Richard N. *Galatians.* WBC. Dallas: Word Books, 1990.

EPHESIANS

Most, though not all, scholars recognize Paul as the author of Ephesians, both because of evidence within the letter itself (1:1) and because of the ancient tradition that supports his authorship.

This letter, like Colossians, Philemon and Philippians, was written while Paul was under house arrest (3:1; 4:1; 6:20), probably in Rome, where he was a prisoner between AD 60 and 62. While there, he was surrounded by friends such as Luke, Timothy, Aristarchus, Ephaphras, Onesimus and Tychicus, all of whom he mentions in his letters to the churches. Tychicus delivered Paul's letter to Ephesus (6:21). Even though Paul was a prisoner, his influence was still widely felt because of these faithful friends.

This letter was specifically addressed to Christians living in Ephesus, but it was circulated widely among the Christian churches in what is now known as Turkey. Paul had founded the church in Ephesus during his second missionary journey (Acts 18:18-21). He had then moved on, leaving Priscilla and Aquila to continue the work there. Apollos later joined them in their work (Acts 18:24-26). On a later visit Paul stayed in Ephesus for about three years, and when he left Apollos came to strengthen that missionary work (Acts 18:27,28). His final visit to Ephesus lasted about three months (Acts 19). On his final journey to Jerusalem Paul's ship stopped at Miletus and he invited the elders of the church at Ephesus to meet him there (Acts 20:17-35). Paul had thus put a lot of work into building this church, and we can understand why he wrote this very important letter to Christians whom he had helped to bring up in the Lord. His affinity, passion and love for this church are clearly revealed in this letter.

Purpose of the letter

In the first part of this letter, Paul explains the blessings or riches enjoyed by the believer in Christ (1:1-3:21). In speaking of these blessings, Paul addresses the strategic position of the church in God's universal plan of salvation. It is through the church that God wants to manifest his glory and salvation to the whole world. In the church he is creating a new humanity. In fact, the church has been made the centre of unity for all humanity. Human differences in race, ethnicity, tribe and religion are dissolved or broken down in Christ. In him there is no longer any reason for racial, tribal or religious conflict.

Africa faces the problem of getting people with different tribal, ethnic, cultural and religious backgrounds to live together in peace and harmony in a society that is just, participatory and sustainable. So the message of Ephesians about how different peoples can live together in unity, love and peace is highly relevant.

The second part of the letter deals with the details of how Christians should live in unity (4:1-6:24). Paul addresses what unity means in practice in the church and the family, and how we should use our spiritual gifts and wage spiritual warfare.

Outline Of Contents

COMMENTARY

1:1-2 Greetings

Africans generally regard someone who does not greet others as rude. Such a person will have little spiritual or social impact. Thus we can appreciate the care Paul takes to greet his readers in a way that communicates both his care and love for them.

Paul begins by introducing himself as an apostle of Christ. An *apostle* (**1:1a**) is someone who has been divinely commissioned to represent Christ, especially as a pioneer in establishing new churches or new Christian ministries. The term was not restricted to the original disciples of Jesus, but was also applied to other Christian missionaries and is listed among the gifts of the Holy Spirit (4:11).

Paul stresses that his apostleship is *by the will of God* (see also Gal 1:1). Consequently, his message comes with divine authority. Because of his past (see Acts 26:9-11), Paul is very aware that God's appointment of him as a messenger of the gospel and a witness of Christ is indeed an expression of his grace.

Paul uses two words to describe those to whom he is sending this letter: they are *saints* and *faithful* (**1:1b**). The word 'saint' is not a description of what they are like but of what God has done for them. It indicates that they have been set apart for God and made pure and holy for his service, and thus it applies to both ot and nt believers. We cannot make ourselves *saints*. We are made such by the Lord. By contrast, the word 'faithful' refers to our commitment to maintain a good relationship with the Lord through holding fast to his word and being obedient to him. Just as in Africa we have obligations to the clan to which we belong by virtue of our birth, so now that God has chosen us to be part of the clan of 'saints', we have obligations to one another and to God. Any failure or refusal to live up to these obligations marks us as unfaithful.

The greeting *grace and peace* is a common one in both Hebrew and Greek, but gains rich meaning from its association with *God our Father and the Lord Jesus Christ* (**1:2**). 'Grace' is the act of giving freely when the giver is under no obligation to do so. It is quite different from giving because one has been bribed or persuaded to give. God's grace is shown in his redemption of human beings through Jesus Christ, something that was done purely on God's initiative (1:11-12), as Paul is well aware.

When Paul prays for grace for the believers, he is praying both that God's grace will work in their lives, transforming them, and that this grace will then be apparent in their actions as they themselves show grace to others and gratitude to God.

'Peace' is not a natural state for human beings, for as a result of sin we are more familiar with hostility, conflict,

selfishness and anxiety. But Christ's kingdom is characterized by peace, both between God and believers and between believers. The ongoing wars and violence in Africa indicate a continent that is in deep need of the virtues of grace and peace.

1:3-3:21 The Position of Christians in Christ

1:3-23 Believers' Position: Chosen, Redeemed and Sealed

Originally, 3:3-14 was a Trinitarian hymn sung by the early church in praise of God the Father who chose believers, God the Son who redeemed them, and God the Holy Spirit who sealed them. Such celebrations of all the persons in the Trinity should still play an important part in our worship today.

1:3-6 Chosen by the Father

Paul starts by praising God the Father for who he is and all he has done. Speaking of him as the *Father of our Lord Jesus Christ* (**1:3**) establishes the unique relationship between God the Father and Jesus the Son. But it should not be misunderstood as implying a biological relationship. Rather, it is a theological concept that recognizes that Jesus Christ and God are both equal and eternal.

The God who created the heavens and the earth is the same one who gives us *every spiritual blessing in Christ* (**1:3**). In other words, he gives us the blessings that flow from Christ's redemption of us. These blessings are not material but spiritual. They are what is necessary for salvation and godliness. The *heavenly realms* (1:3) are the unseen world of spiritual realities in which Christians live. Africans are very aware of these spiritual realities, and many live in fear of them. But because of God's blessings, believers in Christ can face them with confidence.

One of the blessings we have received is that God has chosen us *in Christ* (**1:4a**). What an honour, to be specially chosen by God to receive his gift of salvation! This was no impulsive decision, but was made *before the creation of the world* (**1:4b**). God selects believers individually while Jesus Christ does the work of transforming them into a community, the church, his body. The election of believers and the gift of eternal life do not date from the cross of Christ, but are part of God's eternal plan. Jesus Christ was the one who put this plan into effect, making these blessings a reality that all who believe in him may obtain.

The two great purposes for which believers are chosen are firstly to be *holy* and secondly to be *blameless* (**1:4c**). God wants us to reflect his glory by demonstrating his holiness or purity in our lives. Animals for sacrifice had to be *blameless,* that is, without any blemish. We are not called to be physically perfect, but to be morally perfect. If God chose us in Christ so that we can be blameless before him, all of our life should be dedicated to him.

Some people claim that God's choice of believers (1:4) or his predestination of them (1:5) is unfair because it selects some and excludes others. What they fail to see is that the underlying motive for God's choice and predestination is *love* (**1:4d**), which does not exclude anyone (John 3:16). Those excluded in the end are those who refuse God's offer of salvation (John 3:17-19).

Another thing that God has done for us is to adopt us as his sons and daughters (**1:5a**). Adoption is a legal process that makes believers co-heirs with Christ. This special family relationship changes our whole perspective on and relationship to God. He is no longer remote and unapproachable, but becomes a Father who is near and dear to us.

Our adoption is purely an act of God's grace, rooted in his *pleasure and will* (**1:5b**). It is not done out of pity or motivated by selfishness or by what someone has done. Thus we should respond with thankfulness, praise and worship (**1:6**). Africans know how to give praise and honour to national heroes such as Nelson Mandela and Miriam Makeba. Our understanding of what God has freely done for us should evoke even more praise and worship than we give to human leaders.

1:7-12 Redeemed by the Son

Having carefully explained the foundation of God's redemptive plan, Paul moves on to the drama of the cross that put it into effect. Jesus became the sacrificial Lamb for us, whose death freed us from the slavery to sin and the world that had been our fate since our rebellion against God in the Garden of Eden. Christ's death made peace possible between God and us. Whereas previously we had been under God's wrath and judgment, now God could graciously offer *forgiveness of sins* (**1:7a**). The cross of Christ gives forgiveness its legal and righteous basis in dealing with the sin problem. No wonder Paul speaks of *the riches of God's grace* (**1:7b**)! When it comes to matters of redemption and forgiveness, God is never stingy. No matter how much we have sinned, he always has enough grace to redeem us and forgive us.

But while God's grace is given freely, it is not given recklessly. His actions are guided by *wisdom and understanding* (**1:8**). 'Wisdom' is knowledge of the true reality of a situation, rather than of superficial facts. 'Understanding' is the discernment required to distinguish between reality and falsehood. We are always uncertain and doubtful because we have to rely on guesses and assumptions. God knows all things as they really are. We need to pray that he will share his wisdom and understanding with us as we try to follow him and work to build up his church.

God has already given us some insight into his thinking, for he has revealed to us *the mystery of his will* (**1:9a**). This 'mystery' is God's plan of salvation that was revealed through Christ. This plan extends beyond the mere salvation of humanity to embrace all things in heaven and on earth – the entire universe (**1:10**). The entire universe needs salvation because the fall of humanity (Gen 3) produced a universal state of chaos and conflict (Rom 8:19-22). But at the climax of time, God will bring all things into unity and make them all subject to Christ. Jesus Christ will then be the ruler of the entire universe!

There is no way we could know that such a plan exists if God did not reveal it to us. This revelation is also a result of God's grace, here described as *his good pleasure* (**1:9b**). He was under no external obligation to reveal it.

The fact that the will of God is so closely tied to Christ's work of redemption and that he is the one who is to rule has important implications. All others who claim to be intermediaries between God and humanity must be working outside of God's will. God has planned from eternity to make Jesus Christ the only means of obtaining salvation (John 14:6). Thus Christ should not be taken lightly or ignored. The same point is made by Paul's constant use of the phrase *in Christ* in this letter. It was 'in Christ' that God executed his plan of salvation, and it is only 'in Christ' that humanity obtains this salvation.

Paul says that *we were also chosen* (**1:11**). However, these words can also be translated 'we were heirs'. In the OT, Israel was God's chosen people. Now believers in Christ have also been chosen and they have Christ as their inheritance.

The first to believe Jesus was the long-awaited Messiah were Jews like the apostles (**1:12**). Although many Jews rejected Jesus, there were some who believed. The faith of these few Jewish believers brought great honour, glory and praise to God. What a delight to know that our faith in Jesus Christ does the same!

1:13-14 Sealed by the Spirit

In the previous verse, Paul spoke specifically about the first believing Jews, and now he speaks of the believing Gentiles to whom he is writing. Paul assures them that they have been fully incorporated into the community of believers, the body of Christ, and thus are equal to the believing Jews and are also heirs in Christ.

A distinction has to be made between merely hearing the gospel of Christ and the hearing of faith, which brings salvation. The Ephesians had truly *heard* the gospel (**1:13a**), which is here referred to as *the word of truth*. It is no falsehood, but the truth that leads to salvation and liberation from sin and bondage. Anyone who believes this word of truth has salvation and is sealed by the Holy Spirit as a mark of identity or possession (**1:13b-14**). This mark is similar to the chalk mark that an Igbo host in Nigeria puts on the wrist of a visitor. Both the chalk mark and the *seal* indicate that this person is to enjoy the privileges and protection of the entire community.

Jesus Christ sent the Holy Spirit to apply the benefits of redemption in the lives of the believers, that is, to fulfil the promises made by the Father and the Son. Not only does the Holy Spirit mark us as *God's possession*, but he also guarantees that we will indeed receive the full inheritance that God has graciously promised us (1:13b). What the Holy Spirit does brings praise, honour and glory to God.

1:15-23 Thanksgiving and prayer

After this song of praise to the Triune God for his plan and work of salvation (1:3-14), Paul turns to thanksgiving and prayer for the believers at Ephesus. He has heard good news about their faith and responds with joy and thanksgiving (**1:15-16a**). We too should rejoice when we see and hear that God is at work, rather than being envious of the success of others. When we recognize that all that God gives is from his grace, we will respond graciously.

Paul also commits himself to praying for the believers (**1:16b**). He does not indulge in habits that destroy a community of believers, such as not caring for one another, gossiping, being critical and circulating petitions against others. Nor is he the sort of person who will forget old friends and stop praying for them.

The primary thing for which Paul prays is that God will do even more work in the believers. He prays that the truths he has been teaching in 1:3-14 will take root in the inmost hearts of the believers at Ephesus.

His prayer is addressed to the *glorious Father* (**1:17a**). God is 'glorious' because of his exalted nature and his marvellous and gracious deeds. This is the God who planned our salvation from eternity and saw it implemented by Jesus Christ, his dear Son. This God is capable and gracious enough to give the Holy Spirit to help believers apply his spiritual blessings in their lives. The Holy Spirit is the *Spirit of wisdom and revelation* (**1:17b**) because he reveals the mind of God to us. Without him, it would be impossible for ordinary men and women to experience spiritual empowerment and exercise spiritual wisdom, insight and discernment (1 Cor 2:6-16).

The Holy Spirit is very different from the spirits that are worshipped in traditional religion. He is a person, not just an influence or a force. He cannot be manipulated or placated as spirits are in traditional religions. He is also holy and so cannot be associated with anything unholy or demonic. He helps us know God much more deeply (**1:17c**). Without his revelation and wisdom, our knowledge of who God is and what he does for us will be shallow and weak.

The second thing for which Paul prays is that *the eyes of your heart may be enlightened* (**1:18a**). The heart was regarded as the seat of human emotions, the source of our thoughts, judgments and feelings. Sin has blinded it

to the things of God, and only the divine light shed by the Holy Spirit can lighten its darkness and enable it to see clearly. Our natural spiritual blindness means that we are unaware of three things: the hope of our calling, the riches of our glorious inheritance, and the extent of the power of Jesus' resurrection (**1:18b-19**). We may have an intellectual knowledge of these things, but we need to convert this 'head knowledge' into a 'heart knowledge' that excites us and moves us to love and action. The only way that this can be done is through prayer.

The enemies of Jesus thought that they could harness the power of death to silence him, but instead God used his death to demonstrate that his power is even greater than that of death and to glorify and exalt him (**1:20a**; Phil 2:8-11). What a contrast between his power and that of the ancestors, to whom some still pour libations!

Jesus is now seated at the *right hand* of the Father, in a place of honour, power and authority that far exceeds that of all other powers and titles, whether human, demonic or angelic, both present and future (**1:20b-21**). He has become the ruler of the universe!

Africans believe in the existence of many spirit beings and mysterious spiritual forces and powers, and fear them. But they can take courage from the fact that Christ's authority and power are far greater than that of any spirit being. All such beings are subject to him since God has made him their supreme ruler and sovereign Lord (Phil 2:9-11). They are so low compared to him that they can be said to be *under his feet* (**1:22a**).

God has made Christ *head over everything for the church* (**1:22b**). Jesus died to save people and call them into his church, and now God has given him all the power that is needed to build his church. Christ's supreme power was at work in the growth and expansion of the young church in the first century despite the hostility it faced and the opposition of human and spiritual authorities and powers. And it is still at work today to protect his church, empower it and ensure its success.

If Christ is the head, then the church is *his body* (**1:23a**). Individuals who come to faith in Christ join a new community, a new humanity, in which there is fellowship and communion with the Lord and with each other. Christ provides all the resources his body needs to sustain it. He knows how to construct a new humanity out of the one ruined by sin. He quickens that which was dead. He recreates that which was in ruins. He regenerates that which has been deadened by the power of the flesh. He restores that which has been exhausted and impoverished. He nourishes that which has been starved and withered. He pours his life into his church, so that the church becomes *the fullness of him who fills everything in every way* (**1:23b**). The church itself becomes transformed into his image, so that believers become more like Christ and represent him to the world.

But Christ's redemptive work does not manifest itself only in the formation and filling of his body, the church; it also fills the whole creation. His sustaining and preserving power is for both the church and the world.

2:1-10 Believers' Position: Made Alive with Christ

Paul has described Christ's position (1:20-23), and now he describes the position of those who believe in Christ. Whereas believers were once dead to God as a result of a life of sin (2:1-3), their salvation in Christ has made them alive to God (2:4-10).

2:1-3 Old Condition: Dead to God

Before they came to know Christ, the believers in Ephesus could be described as dead in their sins (**2:1**) because their lives were controlled by the power of sin. Their behaviour and attitudes meant that they had as little ability to relate to God as they would have had if they were dead. Their lives were moulded by two forces: *this world* and *the ruler of the kingdom of the air* (**2:2**). The latter expression describes someone who exerts influence in the atmosphere as well as on earth, and who thus influences the whole world. This ruler is Satan, and it is his 'unholy spirit' that makes people disobedient to God. There is a strong spiritual correlation between disobedience to God and slavery and bondage to Satan. His aim is to make a sinful life seem so natural that when their behaviour is challenged, people will simply reply, 'but that is how the world works!'

Paul stresses that it was not just some of them who had been spiritually dead. Every single believer, whether a Jew or a Gentile, had been among those who were disobedient (**2:3a**). For proof of this, we need look no further than our former way of life, which was dominated by our sinful nature. We were once quite happy to do whatever it suggested, regardless of what God thought of our actions. At times, Satan or demons may have exerted a direct influence on us, but most of the time we were simply doing what our own sinful nature suggested. It is our own nature that condemns us. We inherited this nature from Adam, who sinned and brought God's judgment on all humanity (**2:3b**).

2:4-10 New Condition: Alive to God

What a contrast between God's character and ours! While human beings are disobedient and rebellious, God is gracious, merciful and loving (**2:4**). Instead of punishing our rebellion and disobedience with death, God responds with love, making us alive in Christ (**2:5a**). No wonder Paul celebrates the *grace* of God in saving us when we had done nothing to deserve it (**2:5b**)!

God has done three important things for believers: he has made us alive with Christ (2:5a), raised us with him (**2:6a**), and seated us with him (**2:6b**). The resurrection of

Jesus demonstrated God's power to give life to that which was dead, and he has used that power to bring us to life and give us victory over both physical and spiritual death (see also 1:9). Instead of being under the influence of sin and Satan, we are now under the influence of the Holy Spirit.

Believers share not only in Christ's resurrection but also in his authority, power and rule over principalities and powers in the entire universe. We have become co-heirs with Christ! Like Christ, we are victors over sin, Satan, the world systems and death. This fact should give us a profound assurance of security and protection from menacing evil forces.

The reason why God has done these things for believers is to *reveal the incomparable riches of His grace* (**2:7**). Believers have done nothing to deserve exaltation with Christ. But God has saved and exalted them to demonstrate his love, grace, mercy and kindness towards humanity now and in coming ages. Paul hammers this point home in **2:8a**: Our salvation is not the result of any human effort or thought. It was planned by God the Father, implemented by God the Son, and is applied to us by God the Holy Spirit. All that we have to do is to accept it by *faith*.

We cannot even take credit for that faith, for it too is *the gift of God* (**2:8b**). We cannot generate faith on our own. It comes to us through hearing the gospel of salvation or the Word of God and responding to it through the power of the Holy Spirit. We receive grace before we are saved! God does not give us his grace after we have believed; he extends it to us while we are still sinners and in rebellion against him, so that we can believe.

When we achieve something by ourselves, we like to boast about it. Such boasting is a mark of pride, which keeps us from acknowledging our dependence on God. But because God has taken responsibility for all aspects of our salvation, we are left with nothing to boast of (**2:9**). In fact, we should be ashamed of our hopelessly sinful condition before God's grace reached us. Our salvation is a gift, and like all gifts it is to be received with humble gratitude that overflows in praise and worship.

When we are infected by God's grace, we are transformed into what God intended us to be. We are *his workmanship* because he first created us in his own image (Gen 1:26) and then recreated us to bear his image by doing what God has been doing throughout the ages: *good works* (**2:10**; see also 2 Cor 5:17). We do not do such works before we are saved, and they are not a precondition for salvation. Rather, they are the fruits of salvation and show our gratitude for the grace we have been given. The more we receive the work of grace, the more fruit the Holy Spirit enables us to bear in terms of good works. These works will bring God glory, honour and praise.

2:11-22 Believers' Position: United in One Body

An African man from a rural village met an evangelist in the city and became a Christian. Going to church for the first time, he was amazed to see someone there from a tribe that his own people despised. He angrily demanded, 'What is this "dog" doing in the church? Don't you realise that this "pig" has polluted the church? If you knew where he comes from, you would never have admitted him!' His attitude to a fellow believer was similar to that of Jews towards Gentiles, and vice versa. That is why Paul finds it necessary to speak of the position of both Jews and Gentiles in the church and to remind them that although they had once been separated by religion, culture and race, Jesus Christ has now united them in a new community.

Most of the believers in Ephesus were Gentiles and not Jews. Paul reminds them that the Jews had dismissed them as the *uncircumcised* and had proudly called themselves *the circumcision* (**2:11a**). Circumcision was the rite that God had instructed Abraham to perform on every male descendent to secure that child's place in the nation God had chosen. The Jewish pride in being God's chosen nation led them to be contemptuous of others, so that the adjective *uncircumcised* was an insult and not merely a reference to a physical state.

Paul knew the dangers posed by such pride and intolerance, so he reminds the Jews that circumcision is a human operation performed by other humans in contrast with the work that God himself does in believers (**2:11b**). At the same time, he reminds the Gentile believers that before they became believers, they were a) *separate from Christ*, that is, they knew nothing about the promise of the Messiah; b) *excluded from citizenship in Israel*, that is, they had no part in the nation of Israel or in the coming kingdom of God; c) *foreigners to the covenants of the promise*, that is, they had no legal standing in regard to the covenants that God had made with the Jews and his promises to the Jews; and consequently they were d) *without hope and without God* (**2:12**). Paul emphasizes that the Gentiles had nothing to hope for in God as long as they were separated from Christ.

But whereas they had previously been 'separate' and 'foreigners', who were *far away* from God, now they have been brought *near* (**2:13**). They had not gained this new position of privilege by birth or any human ritual, but through the grace of God, expressed in the blood of Christ. His blood had cleansed them of their transgressions and sins and had sealed a new covenant, far superior to the Jewish covenant because it was sealed by God himself, unlike the covenant that was sealed by circumcision done by men.

By bringing together the Jews and the Gentiles, Christ himself has reconciled them to each other, and at the same time has reconciled both of them to God (**2:14**). He has created a new harmony, just as Isaiah prophesied when he called the coming Messiah 'the Prince of Peace' (Isa 9:6).

The *dividing wall* that separated the Jews from the Gentiles was very real. It was a barrier that kept Gentiles from entering the inner parts of the temple in Jerusalem. This was what Jesus Christ destroyed on the cross. In him there is no barrier or dividing wall between the Jews and Gentiles. In fact, in him all human differences, hostility and barriers are resolved. Jesus Christ has a cure for the evils of racism, tribalism and divided humanity.

Just as Jesus Christ abolished the enmity between Jews and Gentiles, so he abolished the Jewish ceremonial law *with its commandments and regulations* that had also been a barrier between them (**2:15a**). The Mosaic law made strict demands that could not possibly be kept perfectly and emphasized the differences between Jews and Gentiles, but Jesus fulfilled it by establishing the new covenant by his death on the cross (see Heb 7–10).

In Christ, both Jews and Gentiles are one. He has made them into *one body* in himself (**2:15b-16**). They have become a new community, the church. What made this possible was the atoning work of Christ on the cross, which destroyed their enmity and brought reconciliation and peace.

Jesus Christ's gospel of peace and reconciliation was preached both to Gentiles *who were far away* and to Jews *who were near* (**2:17**). Both groups needed to hear the message. The Jews were privileged to have had Jesus preach to them directly, while the Gentiles had received his message through his apostles.

Once again, we have all three persons of the Trinity working together to reconcile Jews and Gentiles to each other and to God: the atoning work of Christ made reconciliation possible, and the Holy Spirit now gives us access to the Father (**2:18**).

Paul now returns to his starting point in 2:12, reminding the Gentiles that before they became believers they were *foreigners and aliens* and not full citizens of the kingdom of God. Now in Christ, they have not only full rights of citizenship but also the privilege of being *members of God's household* (**2:19**). They are now brothers and sisters with the older citizens and family members. They can have confidence in this household because it is built on a solid foundation of a) *the prophets* who foretold the coming of the Messiah, b) *the apostles* who proclaimed the gospel of Christ and founded churches, and c) *Christ*, who fulfilled the prophecies and promises of the prophets through his work of redemption and so became the *chief cornerstone* (**2:20**).

In ancient buildings, the 'cornerstone' was highly valued because it tied the whole building together. This is precisely what Jesus Christ does for his church, which Paul describes as a new temple (**2:21**). Jesus Christ is building his church so that it will become *a holy temple*, a dwelling place of God (**2:22**). In the OT, the temple represented the glory and presence of God; now it is the job of the church to do that. The church becomes God's symbol and testimony of salvation to

WHAT IS THE CHURCH?

In the African world view, unity is strength. The larger the unit, the better. This applies not only to the individual family (traditionally polygamous, so as to increase the number of people in the unit) but also to the clan and to the tribe. Each group traces its origins to a particular hero and is united around certain beliefs and practices. The same is true of the church.

The English word 'church' comes to us from the German *kirche* and the Scottish *kirk,* but the word has even older roots in the Aramaic word *kenishta* and the Greek word *kuriakon,* both of which mean 'belonging to the Lord'. The church is thus 'the tribe of Jesus' – called out of all tribes and nations but without renouncing those groups. However, it may at times call for practices and beliefs that override those of one's earthly tribe.

In the OT the term used for such a group was *qahal* ('a people called together by Yahweh') which was translated into Greek as *ekklesia* ('those called out') and used in the NT to refer to the church. The caller is God, the means of unity is faith in his son Jesus Christ, and the governing constitution is the Bible as read and obeyed under the guidance of the Holy Spirit. The members are referred to as believers in Christ.

The church is both an organism and an organization. It is an organism in that it is united around the saving work of Christ and the indwelling of the Holy Spirit no matter where each member is located. It is an organization in that it gathers around a common purpose and doctrine and acknowledges particular officers as leaders. The organism aspect is more important than the organizational one, but the organization is necessary if the church is to accomplish the Great Commission. The organism aspect was, however, the focus when Jesus said, 'I will build my church, and the gates of Hades shall not overcome it' (Matt 16:18).

Metaphors used to describe the nature of church include

- *The body of Christ.* Jesus is the Head (the ultimate leader) who gives the church (as an organism) its life (Eph 1:22–23 and Col 1:18; 2:19).

- *A temple/building/house of God.* The focus of this metaphor is the unity of the church, for in the construction of a building each of the construction materials has a role to play. This metaphor also emphasizes the ownership of the church. It belongs to God, not to people. Jesus is both its foundation (1 Cor 3:9-17) and the chief cornerstone – the stone that controls the design of the whole building (Eph 2:20, 21). The prophets and apostles are also referred to as foundations in the sense that they were the church's first leaders and the people whom God used as the initial transmitters of its doctrine and practice (see 1 Tim 3:15; 1 Pet 2:4-8).

- *The bride of Christ* (Eph 5:31, 32; Rev 19:7; 21:9). Each individual believer is intimately related to Christ from the moment of justification until the marriage ceremony presented in Rev 19:5-9.

- *A flock* (John 10:16, 27). Through his servants (initially the apostles, but now pastors, priests, or any other title used to designate those dispensing his message), Jesus gathers the members together, gives them direction, and looks after the needs of each member.

- *A vine* (John 15). The focus of this metaphor is the believer's need to be 'connected' with Christ if there is to be any nourishment for growth.

Those who belong to the church have been placed on Earth for a mission. Jesus referred to this mission using the terms 'salt' and 'light' (Matt 5:13-16). Just as salt preserves food from rotting, so believers are called upon to stop the world's moral decay. Just as light helps us see our path, so also believers are called to point all people to the true light (John 1:9) who changes lives – creating love where there is hatred, reconciliation where there is hostility, and hope where there is desperation. This is what the church in Africa, and worldwide, is called to do.

Samuel Ngewa

the world. Individual believers, too, have this responsibility, for they are also referred to as the *temple of God,* because the Holy Spirit lives in them (1 Cor 6:19).

3:1-21 Believers' Position: Equal in the Body

Paul begins this chapter by making it clear to the Gentile believers that the reason for his imprisonment was that the Jews misunderstood his message of unity and equality (**3:1**). He had been arrested because he was incorrectly suspected of having brought Trophimus, a Gentile, into the temple in Jerusalem (Acts 21:29).

He also wanted the Gentile believers to know of the particular mission that he had been given as an apostle, namely to present the gospel of Christ to the Gentiles (**3:2**; Acts 9:15). His job was to tell the Gentiles about God's grace and to reveal what had previously been unknown, namely that Gentiles as well as Jews were to make up the church of Christ (**3:6**). Paul reminded them that he had previously sent them a brief written statement about how this mystery, which he here calls *the mystery of Christ,* had been revealed to him, and asks them to read that statement again so that they can understand what he has to reveal (**3:3-4**). He calls the revelation a 'mystery' because it had been kept secret from people of past ages (**3:5**). The Jews had thought they were to remain separate from the Gentiles, which was why Paul's association with Gentiles aroused such opposition.

But God had revealed his true plan to his *holy apostles and prophets* by the Holy Spirit. The word 'holy' emphasizes that the apostles and prophets were set apart for God, and God's specific revelation to them stresses their unique position as pioneers founding the church.

In **3:6** Paul clearly states the secret that has now been revealed: Gentile believers have been included in God's universal plan of salvation with all its privileges and blessings and have been made equal with their Jewish counterparts. He had spoken of this in 2:11-22, and now lists the privileges that Gentiles have received, this time emphasizing the equality of Gentiles and Jews in God's plan by stressing the word 'together'. They are now a) *heirs* together with the Jews, meaning that they share the same inheritance, b) *members* together *of one body,* in an equal relationship, and c) *sharers* together *in the promises of Christ Jesus,* receiving the same promises and blessings.

In case some of his readers think he is arrogant because he claims to have received this special revelation, Paul quickly reminds them that he does not claim that this special knowledge has given him power. Rather, it has made him *a servant of this gospel* (**3:7**). He also acknowledges that he did not deserve the gift of this revelation, but that it was a gift of God's grace, given and received through God's power (**3:7**; see Acts 9:1-15). This rules out any personal ambition or any personal qualification.

Paul does not even consider himself worthy to have been called to be God's servant. He considered himself a nobody whom God had amazingly called to have the privilege of preaching Christ (**3:8a**). God's call, a humble recognition of God's grace, and the blessing of God's power are the prerequisites for getting involved in service for Christ. So is an appreciation of the blessings, wealth and gifts to be obtained in Christ, which are beyond human imagination (**3:8b**), although Paul told us of some of them in the first three chapters of this letter

Paul's calling was not only to preach the gospel of Christ to the Gentiles, but also to explain the mystery of God's plan in such as way that it could be understood (**3:9**). He reminds his readers that this plan had been in God's mind even before the world was created (1:3-4). God kept it hidden for so long because he wanted the church to be the instrument that reveals it. The church may not be highly esteemed by others, but God has chosen it to display the beauty of his wisdom to the rulers of this age (**3:10**). The church, as the centrepiece of God's plan of salvation, reflects the wisdom of God. It came into being through Christ's work of redemption on the cross, as God had planned. This work means that believers, who were formerly fearful strangers (2:12, 19), can now approach God with *freedom and confidence* (**3:12**). They need no longer fear him as a judge or as a king, but can come with a confidence that is not human

self-confidence but is rooted in the knowledge of being in Christ and having faith in him.

Suspecting that his being a prisoner may dampen his readers' spirits, Paul urges them not to be discouraged by his suffering, which is normal for all believers (**3:13**; see also Phil 1:29). His suffering is to be expected because others will refuse to believe the glorious revelation God has given him for them.

His reflection on the amazing mystery of the equality of believing Jews and Gentiles in Christ prompts Paul to burst into prayer that they may have strength and power through the Holy Spirit, that Christ may dwell in their hearts through faith, and that they may be granted the knowledge and fullness of God. His kneeling posture as he prays is a sign of great reverence, submission and adoration, for Jews normally prayed standing (**3:14**). The one before whom he kneels is *the Father,* an expression that indicates Paul's intimate relationship with God is grounded in the confidence he spoke of in 3:12. He is a member of God's family, as also are the Jews and Gentiles who make up the church (2:19). God's *whole family* in heaven and on earth consists of all who name him as their Lord (**3:15**).

Paul begins his request by acknowledging the bounty of God's grace and riches, some of which he had discussed in chapters 1 and 2. There he spoke of the power of God (1:19-20), and now he prays that the believers will be strengthened through the power of the Holy Spirit. He is not thinking of physical strength, but of strength of character and inner strength that comes as the Holy Spirit penetrates into the depth of their hearts, minds and wills (**3:16-17a**), so that it can be said that Christ lives within them. But Christ's residence there is sustained by *faith*. They received Jesus into their hearts by faith when they were saved, and now they must retain his presence in their lives by the same faith, for 'the righteous will live by faith' (Rom 1:17).

Having first prayed that the believers will have power to have Christ governing their lives, Paul next prays that they will have power to know *the love of Christ* (**3:17b-18**). He speaks of love for Christ as being like a tree that has deep roots or like a building with a firm foundation. Such deep *rooted and established* love will empower them to comprehend the love of Christ.

Paul tries to explain the extent of Christ's love by using physical measurements (3:18) but he knows that these examples are inadequate since Christ's love is so wide that it covers the whole world and even beyond. It is so long that it has no limits; it is eternal. It is so high that there is no height that it cannot reach and even exceed. It is so deep that it can reach right down to hell to rescue those held in bondage to Satan. Paul prays that the believers will experience this type of boundless love both as individuals and as a community.

Paul prays that believers will understand this love of Christ even though it is beyond human knowledge (**3:19**), and that this understanding will lead to spiritual growth and maturity in Christ. The aim is not that we are to become gods, but that our character is to become like that of Christ.

The first half of Ephesians concludes with a song of praise to God that acknowledges his sovereignty over the entire universe and the church (**3:20-21**). God has the will and the power to do far more than the believers ask or expect from him, and that power is already at work within the lives of the believers.

Paul has been explaining God's eternal plan of salvation, and here he states the purpose of the plan: to bring glory and honour to God. God's glory is made manifest in the church as those who have experienced salvation live together in unity, serve together in harmony and worship God together without discrimination. He concludes his prayer with an *Amen*, which simply means 'may it be so'.

4:1-6:20 Christlike Living

In the second half of his letter, Paul deals with the practical implications of what he has been teaching in the first half. He exhorts the believers to live in a way that fulfils the purpose for which they were called. They are to make every effort to live in unity, love and peace both in the world and at home. However, they are also to be prepared to face spiritual conflict.

4:1-6 Saved to Walk in Unity

Paul has been speaking of the amazing power of God (3:20) – but he himself is still a prisoner! Instead of demanding his freedom, he uses his status as one who suffers for the Lord to add weight to his call to the Christians in Ephesus to live a life that will glorify the Lord (**4:1**). This is what they were called to do, as was explained in chapters 1-3. What we believe must manifest itself in the way we live.

The characteristics that the believers are to display include humility, not because we are inferior to other people but because we do not regard ourselves as better than others. Christ demonstrated that humility is the basis of service, honour, respect and love for others. We are also to be *gentle*, that is, considerate of others and not seeking to dominate them. This calls for patience to restrain the desire to seek revenge or to escape when others annoy us. Our forbearance is what enables us to put up with the attitudes, manners and faults of others (**4:2**). All of these virtues make for unity and love among believers, as Paul reminds them (**4:3**).

The believers' unity is based on the Trinity. The Holy *Spirit* is the one who has *called* both Jews and Gentiles into the *one body* of Christ, the church, and has given them all

a shared *hope* in Christ (**4:4**; see also 1:13-14). Christ is the Head of the church and its only *Lord* and Master, and the believers are also united by their shared *faith* in him (**4:5**). This faith has led them to identify with his death and resurrection by being baptized as a physical sign that they are part of the one body of Christ. Ultimately, however, our unity and oneness are rooted in the sovereignty of God, who is the only creator of the entire universe and thus has absolute authority over all of creation (**4:6**).

4:7-16 Gifted to Operate in Diversity

Unity does not mean uniformity. Christ gives different spiritual gifts to individuals. Because these are gifts, they cannot be earned (**4:7**). Paul quotes Psalm 68:18, implying that these gifts are like the rewards that a victorious general distributes to his supporters, who may not even have been present at the battle (**4:8**). They are a proof of Christ's victory over his enemies.

Victory implies a battle, and so in an aside Paul stresses that Jesus could not have been victorious over Satan, sin, death and the world if he had not been prepared to endure humiliation, death and the cross (**4:9**). The reference to the *lower, earthly regions* implies that Jesus descended as far as hell (see also 1 Pet 3:19-20, 4:6; Matt 27:52-53). Having descended so low, it is appropriate that he be exalted higher than all others, as the resurrected Lord of the universe (**4:10**; see also 1:20-23).

Paul lists some of the spiritual gifts that have been given for leadership in the church (**4:11**). *Apostles and prophets* were mentioned in 2:20 as laying the foundation for God's church. *Evangelists* travel carrying the message of the gospel of Christ to places it has not reached. *Pastors* and *teachers* work in local churches, where one person is sometimes both a pastor and a teacher. This cluster of five gifts is often referred to as the fivefold ministry of the church. It is basic and fundamental to the planting and growth of the church. All other gifts are supportive.

Spiritual gifts are given to church leaders for the particular purpose of equipping other believers for works of service that will build up the church until it is mature and complete in Christ (**4:12-13**). Thus spiritual gifts are not given for the benefit of the leaders but are intended to be used to help the church to grow physically and spiritually until it reaches maturity.

The path to maturity involves all the believers being united in their faith and having a common *knowledge of the Son of God*. To achieve this, leaders must nurture and protect the church and teach sound doctrine and faith. The ultimate goal is to have all members and the church as a whole become complete in Christ.

Lack of maturity leads to stunted growth, with believers remaining like infants, dependent on others and open to every influence (**4:14**). A lack of sound doctrine and

PROPHETS AND APOSTLES

The word 'prophet' comes from the Greek *prophētēs,* which means 'one who speaks forth' or who 'speaks for' someone. It refers to someone whom God clothes with his authority and his power to communicate his will to people and to teach them (Jer 1:9-10). The word 'apostle' comes from the Greek *apostolos,* meaning 'one who is sent'. An apostle is an ambassador for Christ (2 Cor 5:20). Apostles and prophets are often mentioned together in the NT (Luke 11:49; 2 Pet 3:2; Rev 18:20).

Many Africans have been hailed as prophets or apostles or have claimed these titles for themselves. Among the best known are the nineteenth-century Xhosa prophets Ntsikana and Molageni in South Africa. Another was William Wade Harris, who was born in Liberia and preached in the area around the Gulf of Guinea, especially in Ivory Coast. His message emphasized abandonment of fetishes and idols, and his fame gave concern to French colonial authorities.

At the beginning of the twentieth century, Simon Kimbangu was a prophet in what is now the Democratic Republic of Congo. Despite persecution by the Belgian colonial authorities, the Kimbanguist church developed into a great religious movement in Central Africa. In 1947 Samuel Oschoffa founded the Celestial Church of Christ in Dahomey, now known as the Republic of Benin.

Today, numerous Africans are following such illustrious predecessors and proclaiming themselves prophets or apostles and creating their own religious movements.

The emergence of African prophets and apostles allowed for the proclamation of the equality of blacks and whites in faith and ministry (Gal 3:28; Col 3:11). It also established the principle of the separation of the Christian faith from all colonial political connections. These positive effects justify the reputation these men enjoy.

However, there are also some more negative aspects associated with the emergence of African prophets and apostles. Many of them lack biblical and theological training and rely solely on their own gifts. But the growth of the church depends on the exercise of a variety of complementary gifts. An apostle or prophet cannot go it alone without the help of teachers (Eph 4:11-14). Those who want to preach the word of God must therefore study it seriously or surround themselves with those who have done so.

Despite their claim to be promoting mainstream Christianity, many African prophets and apostles do not take the Bible as the basis for their faith and conduct. Instead their teaching is based on direct revelation that they receive from God for their prophetic and messianic mission. They regard these teachings as additions to the Bible. However, the Bible warns against making the slightest addition to the word (Rev 22:18-19).

Many African prophets and apostles also indulge in a personality cult. They cloak the events of their lives, including the circumstances of their call, in mystery, sometimes citing biblical allusions to the Messiah. They give the impression that they have come down from heaven like Jesus or that they have as much power as he does. Some even claim to be Christ's successors or even another Christ. Such claims make them objects of worship. Sadly, many of them gain almost total control of the minds of their followers. The NT warns us against such people (Matt 24:11, 24; Jude 4-16).

By contrast, the prophets and apostles in the Bible are no different from other human beings. Their family origins are often clearly stated (Isa 1:1; Jer 1:1). They do not hesitate to admit their own weaknesses and they refuse all worship (Jer 1:6; Acts 14:13-15). Those who wish to announce the word of God should not seek titles of honour but should be servants of all (Matt 23:8-12).

While the negative side to the African prophets and apostles is a sad reality, we should not forget to express our gratitude to God for the true prophets and apostles who have exercised and continue to exercise an honourable ministry to the glory of God. This group includes men such as Samuel Ajayi Crowther of Nigeria, who is considered to be truly a father of the African church.

Adama Ouedraogo

---

teaching will result in a fragmented church with a weak faith and inadequate knowledge of Christ. Such a church is vulnerable to the influence of false teachers. Immature Christians accept whatever they are told by teachers who may be motivated by greed or who rely on purely human wisdom. With no stable rock to stand on, weak Christians are tossed around and become unstable.

The mature, however, have grown in their faith and knowledge of Christ and see all things from Christ's perspective. Thus unlike the false teachers they speak *the truth,* and because they are like Christ, they speak it *in love* (**4:15**). The best commentary on what it means to speak 'the truth in love' is found in 1 Corinthians 13:4-8. When we practise and speak the truth, we are in a process of growing up into Christ *who is the Head* of the body (church). Our ultimate goal must be to attain Christlikeness in all things.

As the head of the church, Jesus Christ connects all the parts of the body together, helps the body to grow, helps it to build itself up in love, and enables each part of the body to do its work. He is the one who enables the church to grow into maturity, united in love and service (**4:16**).

4:17-22 Put Off the Old Life

To achieve the goal of becoming united and like Christ, believers have to get rid of the things that belong to their old life. They must abandon the evil practices of their former

Gentile life that was aimless and meaningless (**4:17**). They had been wandering in the dark, separated from the life of God by their ignorance (**4:18**). However, this was not innocent ignorance but was the result of their hardening their hearts against God, which had resulted in their becoming insensitive to God's light, truth and decency. Consequently they had developed an appetite for lust, sensuality and all kinds of immorality (**4:19**; see also Rom 1:24-28).

What a contrast with the holy life of Jesus! (**4: 20-21**). They had come to know Christ as Saviour, and now they needed to learn to live life the way he taught. Believers need to be taught to follow the way of Jesus if they are to be truly his followers or disciples. It is like putting on new clothes. They must *put off* the garment of the old life so that they are ready to *put on* the new garment of Christ (**4:24**). But while clothing affects only our outward appearance, what Paul is calling for is a far deeper transformation of the inner person.

4:23-32 Put On the New Life

Our thoughts, attitudes and deeds are controlled by our minds, and thus it is important that a new *mind* created in Christ Jesus replaces the deceitful *old mind* that corrupted us (**4:23**; see also Rom 12:2). However, we do not achieve this new self simply by trying hard to be different. It is 'a new creation' as a result of the work of Christ on the cross (**4:24**; 2 Cor 5:17). This new self is to be like God in *true righteousness and holiness*. This was our original position before the fall in the Garden of Eden, and is the goal Paul held up in 4:13.

Paul next discusses specific aspects of the old self that must be 'put off' so that a new self can be 'put on' (4:25-31). The first thing to be put off is *falsehood* or lying, which must be replaced by *speaking truthfully* to one's neighbours (see Ps 15:2-3). If the family of believers is truly united, they must be able to trust one another.

Anger is sometimes justified, but brooding on anger and being preoccupied by it is sinful. It can easily provide *a foothold for the devil* to use to promote evil. That is why it should not be allowed to linger overnight (**4:26-27**).

Stealing involves taking away from others to benefit oneself. That is why Paul condemns it and calls instead for gainful labour that shares with others, rather than cheating them (**4:28**). And in the same way as our work should help others, so should our speech. Gossip and slander must be replaced by speech that is *helpful for building others up* (**4:29**).

The Holy Spirit does the work of spiritual transformation or change in us, leading us to put off the thoughts and deeds of the old self and put on those of the new self. When we act in a way that shows we are not willing to put off the old self, the Holy Spirit is grieved and disappointed. Even though the Spirit has sealed us for the day of redemption,

that redemption has still to be consummated (**4:30**). In the intervening period, we are not to do anything that will grieve the Spirit (**4:31**). Consequently we must avoid bitterness, rage, anger and malice that will lead to such things as brawling, slander and other forms of unwholesome talk and behaviour. These vices must be replaced by the virtues of kindness, compassion and forgiveness (**4:32**). Because they have been forgiven by God, believers are to forgive one another.

5:1-7 Imitate God

True Christian fellowship is rooted in this example of Christ, and so we are to take the behaviour of Jesus Christ as our model. Rather than being bitter, he freely forgave us for the wrong things we had done (4:32). His kindness, compassion and love led him to sacrifice himself for others (**5:2**).

We should imitate God's example in the same way that a young child responds to a parent's love by imitating the parent (**5:1**). God has showered his love upon the believers through Christ's love and forgiveness, and we should respond by living a Christlike life of love and sacrifice.

We should imitate God not only in his love, but also in his holiness (1 Pet 1:15-16). Thus believers cannot indulge in *sexual immorality, impurity and greed* (**5:3**). We should also avoid these vices in our talk, and thus should not be guilty of *obscenity, foolish talk or coarse jokes* (**5:4**). The transformation of our hearts and minds should lead us rather to talk of our gratitude to God and to others.

In fact, Paul warns, immorality, impurity and greed are a sign that one is still practising idolatry, giving the first place in one's life to something other than God. Thus people who practise these things do not belong in the kingdom of Christ (**5:5**). He is not speaking of believers who fall into sin and repent of it, but of those who continually practise these vices.

God's standards cannot be replaced by permissive teachings. Those who teach otherwise are deceivers, and both they and those who accept their false teachings will be subject to God's wrath (**5:6-7**).

5:8-14 Walk as Children of Light

Paul had earlier told the believers to imitate God 'like dearly loved children' (5:1) and now he returns to that image, reminding the Gentile believers that they have become *the children of light*. God is holy and God is also light (1 John 1:5). The light of God that is in the believers should show in their *goodness, righteousness and truth*, which contrast with the evil deeds that had once dominated their lives (**5:8-9**). Rather than simply acting impulsively, they should test their behaviour to check that what they are doing *pleases the Lord* (**5:10**). Just as light shows what something really looks like, so the believers who are children of light should *expose deeds of darkness* (**5:11**). Such deeds are *fruitless*, meaning that they serve no purpose.

It is important to note that it is the light of Jesus that exposes sin for what it is, not our conversation or talk about sin. Thus what is shameful and done secretly should not be a topic for discussion and gossip (**5:12**).

Paul repeats that light is what enables people to see things clearly and to recognize evil for what it is (**5:13-14a**). To drive the point home, he cites what may have been an early hymn associated with Easter or baptism (**5:14b**). The hymn calls those who are asleep in death and darkness to wake up. Christ will raise them from the dead and shine his light upon them. This hymn may have been sung when the Ephesian believers were baptized, and if so Paul is reminding them that at their baptism they turned their back on the world with all its darkness, desires and attractions and embraced Christ who now shines on them.

5:15-20 Live Wisely

If we are to live lives of holiness and light, we must think carefully about our conduct and behaviour (**5:15**). The evil in society affords us opportunities to shine as lights for our Lord (**5:16**). We need to learn to recognize these opportunities that God gives us to witness to him and must seek to understand God's will in all situations and circumstances (**5:17**).

Drunkenness does not make for wisdom and discernment. It also often leads to a careless and aimless life dominated by wild living, squandering of money and resources, and an excessive appetite for pleasures. Thus believers should avoid it. Instead of being under the influence of alcohol, believers are to be under the influence of the Holy Spirit (**5:18**).

The filling with the Holy Spirit can even be mistaken for drunkenness at times (see Acts 2:13). But where drunkenness leads to raucous singing and shouting, being filled with the Holy Spirit leads to praise expressed in *psalms, hymns and spiritual songs* (**5:19**). The instruction to *make music* implies that a variety of musical instruments and rhythms can be used. God is not concerned with the type of music but with its content, which is worship, thanksgiving and praise to God and Jesus Christ. The ultimate goal of the Spirit is to bring honour to God and Jesus Christ, and that is why *always giving thanks* is one of the signs that we are filled with the Holy Spirit (**5:20**). Whatever happens to us, we can still give thanks for God's love and mercy that have given us salvation and the gift of the Holy Spirit.

Our songs and thanksgiving are directed to God the Father *in the name of our Lord Jesus Christ* because he is the only one through whom we can come to God (John 14:6; Acts 4:12).

5:21-6:9 Live Responsibly

Submission and obedience to Christ should govern all our relationships and responsibilities at home and at work. A consequence of this is that we are also to submit to one another, that is, to show respect for each other (**5:21**; see also John 13:13-15).

5:22-33 In marriage

The biblical model for marriage presented here applies to marriages across all cultures and ages, including African marriages.

A wife is told to *submit* to her husband because of her reverence for Christ (**5:22**). Her submission signals her acceptance of God's institutional order in the family and the church. God has made the husband the head of a family, just as Jesus Christ is the Head of the church (**5:23**). She is to follow the example set by the church (**5:24**). The church's submission to Christ is total, and wives must imitate this as they submit to their husbands *in everything*.

This divine arrangement does not imply that women are in any way inferior to men or men superior to women. Both wives and husbands have been assigned roles in the home and in the church. In 1 Corinthians 11:12, Paul explains the hierarchy: God is the head of Christ (though both are essentially equal as we saw earlier in 1:3), Christ is the head of the man, and the man is the head of the woman.

If wives are to model their behaviour on the relationship between the church and Christ, then husbands are to model their behaviour on the way Christ loved the church and demonstrated his love by dying for it on the cross (**5:25**). Such divine love goes far beyond sexual love or even friendship love. It sacrifices itself for the one it loves.

The reason why Christ sacrifices himself for the church is so that she can become pure and holy, *without stain, or wrinkle, or any other blemish* (**5:27**) and be fit to be his bride. Coming out of a sinful world, the church needs cleansing by *washing with water through the word* (**5:26**). Baptism alone is not enough, but must be accompanied by the preaching and profession of the gospel of Christ. While a husband cannot be like Christ and save his wife from sin, he can love her sacrificially despite her imperfections, just as Christ did the church, and he can honour and teach the gospel in his home so that the wife becomes more Christlike through her husband's love.

Not only are husbands to love their wives like Christ does, but they are also to love them and treat them with the same care that they would their own bodies (**5:28-29**). Christ feeds and cares for his church because *we are members of his body* (**5:30**), and a husband is to show the same care for his wife.

Wives are neither possessions nor totally separate individuals. Rather, marriage brings about a *union* between a husband and a wife, who leave all other relationships and become *one flesh* (**5:31**; Gen 2:24). The husband and the wife are no longer two, but one. What exactly this means was a mystery until it was explained in the relationship between Christ and the church. Marriage, then, can fully be understood in the light of what Christ does and is to the church and what the church does and is to Christ.

African husbands and wives need to dig deeper into this revealed mystery in Christ and use it as a model for their relationship. Believers should not appeal to traditions or customs as the basis for their relationship and roles in the family and marriage, but to Christ's example. We are to place a higher value on our husbands and wives than we may have in the past as we work towards a complementary relationship characterized by love and respect.

6:1-4 In the family

Like the husband-wife relationship, the parent-child relationship is rooted in love and reverence for Christ. All members of the family must recognize the Lordship of Christ.

Children are commanded to obey their parents, meaning both fathers and mothers (**6:1**). They are also to *honour* them, that is, to show them respect, as instructed in the Ten Commandments (**6:2**; Deut 5:16). Such behaviour comes with a promise that the child will do well and enjoy a long life (**6:3**). There is a reward for a child who obeys and honours his or her parents.

However, parents are not to make unreasonable demands of their children; hence the command not to *exasperate* them (**6:4**). Children who are exasperated by such demands may rebel, and rebellion leads to godlessness. A child who has experienced this is very difficult to win back to the Lord. Thus *fathers*, a term used here as representative of both parents, are to be tenderhearted and considerate in dealing with their children. Their primary task is to train their children in righteousness and to exercise discipline. They must be concerned not just for their children's physical health, but also that they grow into mature people in the home and in the church.

6:5-9 At work

Although Paul's instructions are directed to slaves and their owners, the underlying principles still apply to any relationship in which one person is working for another. He sees all service or work as having a divine meaning and purpose, so that it is possible to say, 'whatever you do, whether in word or deed, do it all in the name of the Lord, giving thanks to God the Father through him' (Col 3:17).

Slaves are commanded to obey their earthly masters and to serve them wholeheartedly. They must do this with *respect and fear, and with sincerity of heart* (**6:5**). They are to respect them just as wives respect their husbands, not necessarily because they deserve it but as a sign of their respect for and obedience to Christ. It is fear of God that must be the spur to obedience, not fear of a human master. If they are *doing the will of God from your heart*, their service will be sincere. They will not be attempting to win favour, or working only when their work will be noticed (**6:6**). They will know that their true master is the Lord and that his eye is always on them, and will serve their human masters wholeheartedly (**6:7**).

The real reward for such service will not come from earthly masters but from their heavenly Lord (**6:8**). All those who do good will receive a rich reward, regardless of their social status. The slaves and the free have equal standing before the Lord.

This equality also has implications for masters (or employers today). Their attitude towards those who work for them must be governed by their own loyalty to Christ. Just as they are masters over the slaves, so the Lord is a master over them (**6:9**). Like their master in heaven, they are to be loving, not threatening and cruel. They must treat their slaves as God has treated them.

God is the judge for both the free and the slave, and he will not favour one group over the other. He will judge each person by how they have obeyed him and how this has been revealed in their attitudes to and treatment of others. Christ gives worth and dignity to every human being, so that 'there is neither Jew nor Greek, slave nor free, male nor female, for you are all one in Christ Jesus' (Gal 3:28). The logical result of adopting such a Christlike attitude is the abolition of slavery.

6:10-20 Into Battle: The Armour of God

Paul concludes his instructions by reminding the believers that they are engaged in a war, and need both power and armour to protect them. The source of their power is the Lord, whose *mighty power* will enable them to resist the enemy (**6:10**; see 1:19-20).

God has also provided *the full armour* the believers need, but before they can use it effectively, they need to put it on. Without it they will not be able to stand firm and oppose *the devil's schemes* (**6:11**). They need this spiritual armour because they are not going into a physical battle but a spiritual one, and because their enemies are many, powerful, evil and everywhere. The enemy is described as *rulers*, or cosmic powers in the universe; *authorities*, or demonic forces that exercise limited authority in opposition to God; *the powers of this dark world*; and *spiritual forces of evil in the heavenly realms* (**6:12**). These enemies are the spiritual forces behind the world systems that oppose God. It is important that believers recognize the spiritual nature of their opponents and thus understand the need to use spiritual weapons to fight them.

Believers will not know when or where the next assault will come, and so they need to have their armour on before the battle starts (**6:13**). Then they will be able *to stand your ground*, alert, fearless and resolute. Because the battle is fierce and may be prolonged, it is important that they persevere and are not swept away or pushed aside.

God has provided both what we need for our protection (armour) and what we need for our attack (a weapon). Paul describes what God has supplied in terms of the equipment of a Roman soldier.

First, he speaks of the things the soldier of Christ is to put on and wear:

- *The belt of truth* (**6:14a**). A belt tied up one's robes, so that they did not get in the way, and was what one tied one's sword to. Wearing a belt thus signals that one is ready for action. Knowledge of the truth (that is, of Jesus Christ, the gospel, and the Bible) prepares us for the battle that lies ahead.
- *The breastplate of righteousness* (**6:14b**). The breastplate protected the heart and the vital organs. Our integrity and character need to be safe from attack by the enemy. But self-righteousness offers no protection. We need the official breastplate that Christ gives when he supplies us with his righteousness.
- *The sandals of the gospel of peace* (**6:15**). With our shoes on, we are ready to move out. We must be prepared to walk long distances in order to spread the good news of the gospel of Christ that brings ultimate peace to the world (Luke 2:14; Rom 10:15).

Next, Paul speaks of the things the soldier of Christ is to take up and carry:

- *The shield of faith* (**6:16**). The shield was used to stop things like *flaming arrows* hurled by the enemy. If our faith is firmly rooted in Christ, there is nothing the enemy can do to us as our strong faith will block all his assaults. Our faith is anchored in the foundational truths of our salvation (Rom 10:9-13).
- *The helmet of salvation* (**6:17a**). The helmet protected a soldier's head. Our salvation means the forgiveness of our sins, reconciliation with God, and the gift of grace and eternal life. This salvation protects us and gives us a sure hope of final deliverance from this body of sin and from this wicked world.
- *The sword of the Spirit* (**6:17b**). The only offensive weapon that a believer carries is the word of God – and that weapon has more than enough power to wound and defeat the enemy.

Finally, as the climax of their preparation, those who are preparing for spiritual warfare must *pray in the Spirit* (**6:18**), not only for their own protection but for *all the saints*, for the battle is one we fight together. Not only that, but the prayers must not be routine mumblings, for the soldier of Christ is to be alert while praying. Soldiers receive their discipline through drills and exercises, but soldiers of Christ derive strength, power and discipline through prayers and supplications.

Praying in the Sprit means far more than praying in tongues. It means praying in communion with the Holy Spirit, that is, in the presence of the Holy Spirit (Rom 8:26-27; 1 Cor 2:6-16). Our wisdom and power come from the Holy Spirit, and to obtain them we must be in constant communion with him, which is why we are told to pray *on all occasions* and all the time (1 Thess 5:17).

Paul requests that the believers pray for him. They might suspect that such a great leader does not need prayer and does not know fear, but Paul knows otherwise and specifically asks them to pray that he may know what to say and will have courage to present the gospel of Christ (**6:19-20**). Paul knows that spiritual battles are won only through prayer. If even the Apostle Paul needed prayer, how much more do our church leaders today!

6:21-24 Conclusion

Tychicus was a true servant of the Lord, whom Paul can refer to as a *dear brother and faithful servant*. It seems that he was entrusted with delivering the letters to the churches in Colosse and Ephesus and giving them all the news about Paul (**6:21**; see also Col 4:7–8). If the churches were worried about Paul's being in prison or other matters, Tychicus would encourage them with his reports on the progress of the gospel.

Paul ends the letter with a blessing that wishes the Ephesians peace, love, faith and grace. These virtues, which have been discussed throughout this letter, should characterize the life of a Christian community.

Yusufu Turaki

Further Reading

Keener, C. S. *The IVP Biblical Background Commentary: New Testament.* Downers Grove: InterVarsity, 1993.

Wood, A.S. *Ephesians*. EBC. Grand Rapids: Zondervan, 1978.

PHILIPPIANS

It is generally agreed that the letter to the Philippians was written by the Apostle Paul. Paul tells us that he is writing it from prison (1:13), and thus the date of the letter depends on which of his imprisonments he is referring to. The book of Acts records that Paul was imprisoned in Philippi (Acts 16:23), in Caesarea (Acts 23:33-35) and in Rome (Acts 28:16, 30). He may also have been in prison in Ephesus, although no long imprisonment there is mentioned in Acts or elsewhere in the New Testament. The circumstances described in the letter have led scholars to deduce that the two most likely places for writing it were Ephesus and Rome, with Rome as the more probable candidate. Paul was in prison in Rome somewhere around AD 61.

The stimulus for writing the letter may have been that Epaphroditus was about to return to his native Philippi and could act as a messenger (2:25). He had brought Paul news from the church in Philippi and had been a help to him during his imprisonment. Paul wanted to respond to the news and to thank the members of the church for their financial generosity. As a pastor, he wanted to encourage them to maintain their Christian unity and love, following the example of humility set by Christ. There was also a need to warn them of the possible danger that could come through false teachers, such as the Judaizers.

The keynote of this epistle is joy. In the form of either a verb or a noun, the word 'joy' is found sixteen times. Other words that recur repeatedly are 'fellowship' and 'the gospel'.

Outline of Contents

COMMENTARY

1:1-2 Greetings

At the very start of the letter, Paul shows that he is a man of fellowship. He could easily have mentioned only his own name, but he includes Timothy in the greeting (1:1), even though elsewhere in the letter (for example, at 1:3) he uses the first person ('I'). Like Paul, ministers should always remember their co-workers and not act as if they are working alone.

Having given their names, Paul proceeds to describe who they are. Both of them are *servants of Christ Jesus* (**1:1**). Jesus Christ is their Lord. The word 'servants' here means bondservants, that is, servants who are committed, loyal and obedient to their master. He has the highest place in their thoughts and life. Paul's identity is defined by his position in relation to the Lord Jesus Christ.

The recipients of the letter are described as *all the saints in Christ Jesus* (**1:2**). The word that is translated 'saints' means 'holy'. It is equivalent to a Hebrew word with the root meaning 'to cut' or 'to separate', and implies that believers are apart from or separated from the evil one. All Christians, wherever and whenever they live, who have faith in Christ Jesus and in his work can be called saints because Christ's blood has accomplished this separation. We can be called 'saints' not because of our own achievements but because Christ died for our sake (1 Cor 15:3-4).

While all believers are saints, Paul recognizes that some of them have a special place and responsibility as active leaders in the local church. He addresses these leaders specifically when he adds *together with the overseers and deacons* (1:2). In African cultures, authorities and community leaders are respected and obeyed. In the church of God it is also important to recognize the special place ministers have. They are responsible for feeding, protecting and administering the flock of God. Such people deserve special honour. However, they are to follow the example of our Lord and the apostles by not using their position as an opportunity to lord it over the church members; instead they are to be examples of Christian service.

When Paul wishes his readers *grace and peace* (1:2) he uses the standard opening for Greek letters in his time. Many standard African greetings are also wishes of peace in general or directly from God, for example, *Tena Yistiligne* [Amharic, Ethiopia – May he (God) give you health (peace)] and *Saro* or *Tuma* [respectively Wolaytta and Hadiyya, South Ethiopia – 'Peace be with you']. In traditional African societies, kindness and peace have been sought from divinities or persons with authority and supernatural powers. Paul makes it clear that he expects the kindness and peace Christians enjoy to come *from God our Father and the Lord Jesus Christ*. By association, the word 'grace' refers specifically to God's kindness, mercy and favour to undeserving, sinful people. Peace is living in calmness, tranquillity, trust and satisfaction as a result of God's reconciliation of sinners with himself through Christ.

Paul uses the phrase 'God our Father' eight times in his epistles, always in his opening greetings (see Rom 1:7; 1 Cor 1:3; 2 Cor 1:2; Gal 1:3; Eph 1:2; Phil 1:2; Col 1:2; Phlm 1:3). In African culture, a father is respected and the entire household looks to him for direction, protection and care in daily matters. Referring to God as our Father shows that he is the protector and head of our homes.

It is striking that in all the places where Paul mentions 'God our Father' he also immediately refers to 'the Lord Jesus Christ'. The fact that he puts Christ side by side with God the Father shows that Paul had no doubt that Jesus is equal to God the Father. He is the source of 'grace and peace' just as the Father is.

1:3-11 Good and Receptive Hearts

Paul had been affected by the attitude of the Christians in Philippi. Their hearts were receptive and they were eager to become partners with him in the cause of the gospel. They stood united with him in mind and purpose. Their active and living testimony filled Paul's heart with joy and moved him to thank God for them (**1:3**). The memory of a loving and active Christian community will always remain with those who have spent some time with them.

Paul's thankfulness was expressed *in all my prayers for all of you* (**1:4**). Paul was a man of prayer. Like Paul, a good minister should be in constant contact with the Lord in prayer, praying not only for himself but also for those whom God has put under his care.

When Paul speaks of their *partnership in the gospel from the first day* (**1:5**) he is probably thinking of the day he first arrived in Philippi, the most important city in Macedonia, after crossing the Aegean Sea on his second missionary journey (Acts 16:11-12). There he had met Lydia, 'a dealer in purple cloth', who had received the gospel of Jesus Christ wholeheartedly. Not only did she believe in the Lord Jesus Christ, but she made her house available for meetings and worship (Acts 16:15, 40). A Philippian jailer and his household had also become Christians (Acts 16:34). In view of the hospitality which Paul and Silas had received, it was appropriate to call the Philippian Christians partners in the gospel. This partnership continued until late in Paul's life. At the time this letter was written, they were supporting him materially by sending gifts (4:18). When the message of the gospel reaches a receptive heart, it bears fruit and

produces action. Similar fruit and actions should be found in our African churches if we have really accepted the gospel: 'the sign of our professed love for the gospel is the measure of sacrifice we are prepared to make in order to help in its progress' (TNT).

The believers' behaviour flows from the work the Lord has been doing in their hearts and lives, for every good work that a Christian does is the result of God's prompting. This makes Paul confident that *he who began a good work in you will carry it on to completion* (**1:6**). Our partnership in the gospel is a lifelong commitment. The seed of the gospel comes from the Lord and continues to grow because he is faithful and will stick with what he has started until the work is completed. The power for Christian perseverance comes from the Lord (Isa 40:30-31).

God's work in the Philippians will continue *until the day of Christ Jesus* (1:6). This day is obviously in the future, for both Paul and the Philippians are expecting it. It will be the day on which one's earthly work, whether good or bad, will end and one will face the verdict of the risen Lord Jesus Christ.

Paul's love and care for the Philippian Christians bursts out again in **1:7**: *I have you in my heart; for ... all of you share in God's grace with me*. This is true whether Paul is free to proclaim the gospel or *whether I am in chains*. This is the first time in this letter that he mentions his imprisonment. An Éwé proverb from Togo says 'It is when you shake hands that you discover who is left-handed', meaning that events reveal people's true nature. The Philippians proved that they were true friends by standing with Paul in the cause of the gospel despite his imprisonment. Because of their sincere love and commitment, Paul longs for them and has *the affection of Christ Jesus* for them (**1:8**). Paul is saying that his love for them is similar to the sacrificial love Christ displayed on the cross. A leader in the church of God should love the believers with that kind of self-giving love.

Paul prays that the Philippians may reach the level of fullness and perfection one can get through Christ. His desire for them is the same as his desire for other believers: he wants them to become mature in Christ (see also Eph 3:14-19). There are three specific things he is praying for here:

- **Abundant love** (**1:9**): This is the kind of love displayed in one's actions and controlled temper. The accompanying references to *knowledge*, *depth of insight*, and *discernment* remind us that Christian love is not blind and irrational. Rather, it is a love that grows and is put into practice consciously and coherently.
- **Discernment** (**1:10**): Christians are not to wander aimlessly. They are to use their critical faculty to *discern what is best*. Christians should walk in constant self-evaluation. Evaluation and discernment should lead them to choose what glorifies the Lord and keeps them

pure and holy, so that they *may be pure and blameless until the day of Christ.*

- **Fruitfulness** (**1:11**): Paul prays that the Philippians may *be filled with the fruit of righteousness.* Righteousness, or behaviour that pleases God, is the opposite of sinful action. Its source is Jesus Christ, as is clear from Paul's description of it as coming *through Jesus Christ.* Those who put their trust in Jesus Christ will be credited with his righteousness (Rom 4:22-25). This righteousness will produce visible ethical characteristics such as those described in Galatians 5:22.

Paul is an excellent model for those of us who have been given the responsibility of caring for the flock of God. He did not want his spiritual children to stray. He wanted them to become mature and live exemplary lives. In the same way, it is our responsibility as ministers and church leaders to pray, counsel and guide so that those we care for will become mature Christians who abound in love and use their faculty of discernment. The daily lives of Christians should show the fruits of righteousness. Such lives will bring glory to God and make people praise his name (1:11).

1:12-30 Being in Christ amidst Suffering

Paul was not imprisoned because he had committed a crime. He was no thief, burglar or arsonist. He was imprisoned solely for preaching the good news of Jesus Christ. While there are a few people, like Lydia, who embrace the gospel message sincerely and joyfully, there are also many who oppose it and are angered when the truth of the gospel, which exposes all sin, is preached to them. Ill-treatment is to be expected from those who refuse to admit their sins and come to repentance. A true messenger of the good news of Jesus Christ should expect it.

Yet despite his imprisonment, Paul saw reason to rejoice (**1:12, 18**). He recognized that Christ can be proclaimed positively by those who believe in him and love his disciples (**1:16**) or negatively by those who reject him and persecute his followers. Both those who loved Paul and those who hated him were preaching the name of Christ, although the latter were doing it indirectly. Both were making the name of Christ known to the public. The palace guards who guarded Paul in prison were hearing about Christ, and so were other people who came into contact with him (**1:13**). The gospel was not confined because he was confined. We often think that only those who have the right motives and love will preach Christ. Paul's understanding, however, is broader. Even those who mention Christ's name for other motives are still making it known!

Like Paul, pioneer evangelists in Africa suffered for their witness to Jesus Christ. Some were beaten, others were imprisoned and ill-treated. However, their suffering was not in vain. They laid the foundation for the growing churches of Africa. The example of the pioneers has encouraged many younger evangelists to become bold and preach the gospel fearlessly. Paul's bold witness and imprisonment encouraged not only the evangelists of his time but also others for many generations (**1:14**).

But it is not only those who are hostile to the gospel who can cause trouble for believers. Wherever there is a true messenger of God, there are those who listen and cooperate with him and others who want to *stir up trouble* (**1:17**). Messengers of God cannot and should not expect everyone to be friendly towards them. Paul found that some people even preached Christ *out of envy and rivalry* (**1:15**). The identity of these people who were preaching in a spirit of *selfish ambition* (**1:17**) is debated. Some think they were Judaizers who wanted Gentile Christians to keep the law of Moses. More commonly, it is thought that they were Christians who wanted to assert their own importance and authority. Ministers of the Lord should not be surprised if they encounter envy, rivalry and partisanship born of self-seeking. Paul certainly experienced these things. But he cheerfully dismisses the fact that he is not being given the respect and honour he deserves as an apostle: '*What does it matter? The important thing is that … Christ is preached* and so *I will continue to rejoice* (**1:18**). His heart can be full of joy regardless of the external situation because the cause of the gospel is advancing.

But Paul does not present himself as a super-Christian. He acknowledges his need for help, which comes to him from two sources. The first is the prayers of his fellow Christians (**1:19**). Paul did not boast of his unique illumination or authority as an apostle. Instead he repeatedly asked his converts to pray for him (Rom 15:30; 2 Cor 1:11; Col 4:3; 1 Thess 5:25). His other source of help is divine, *the Spirit of Jesus Christ* (**1:19**). The Holy Spirit is associated with both the Father and the Son. He is called the Spirit of God (Rom 8:9, 14; 1 Cor 2:10-11, 14) as well as the Spirit of Christ (Acts 16:7; Rom 8:9; Gal 4:6). Paul's experience recalls our Lord's promise that the Spirit will stand with those who are persecuted (Matt 10:19-20).

Paul does not expect that the Spirit's help will automatically result in his release from jail. He is prepared for any eventuality, knowing that *Christ will be exalted in my body, whether by life or by death* (**1:20**). Whatever happens to him, it will be for the sake and glory of Christ. 'There is no purer desire than this, that the whole of our life and Christian service may enhance the glory and esteem of the One who alone is worthy' (TNT). Whatever the alternatives, life or death, suffering or joy, for those who love him and are called according to his will, they lead to the same end: the glory of Christ.

The reason that Paul can have this attitude is simple: *For me to live is Christ, and to die is gain* (**1:21**). Life without Christ is unthinkable to him. It is because of Christ and for his sake that Paul wants to live his earthly life. Elsewhere he states, 'the life I live in the body, I live by faith in the Son of God, who loved me and gave himself for me' (Gal 2:20). The main reason Paul wants to carry on living in the body is so that he can continue his *fruitful labour* (**1:22**) for the Lord Jesus Christ. He is confident that God will give him people who will be obedient to the good news. But he does not expect that this will happen without effort on his part. The word 'labour' reminds us that witnessing requires planned action and hard work.

Yet Paul is not sure of what will happen to him, and it may be that he will be executed. He does not shrink from the prospect, for he can see two benefits in his death. If he dies, he will receive his heavenly reward and the gospel will advance still more if he dies as a martyr. In fact, if Paul had a choice in the matter, he would choose *to depart and be with Christ* because that *is better by far* (**1:23**).

It is clear that Paul cannot think about life apart from Christ, whether in this life or in the life after death. He describes the experience of death as 'departing', as if it is going from one place or reality to another place or reality. He does not see death as either annihilation or a state of unconscious sleep. If Christ is living, then being 'with Christ' involves a real life of fellowship. The lordship and presence of Christ in that reality is assured. Paul had a realistic and optimistic view about life after death.

But Paul recognizes that his desire to be with Christ may be selfish. The believers may still need him to be released from prison so that he can be with them (**1:24-26**). They will then have a chance to learn from him so that they can put down deep roots and grow in their faith. The physical presence of ministers is necessary if communication of the gospel is to have a lasting impact on believers or to win a group of people for the Lord. The Baganda of Uganda have a proverb 'If your mother is not there, your bowels ache while eating', meaning that the presence of one's mother sweetens all food. Paul's bodily presence among the Philippians would give an added dimension to their understanding and practice of the faith. Christ's incarnation is the model for ministry (see Rom 10:14-15).

Regardless of whether he is with them or not, Paul tells the Philippians *conduct yourselves in a manner worthy of the gospel of Christ* (**1:27**). Paul expects them to live lives congruent with the message of the gospel. The gospel of Jesus Christ is not only a matter of words, for as the English proverb says, 'actions speak louder than words'. Among the things Paul wants to see among Christians is a sense of unity, being *in one Spirit* (**1:28**; see also Eph 4:3-6). All of them should stand together *as one man* (1:27). Christians everywhere share the same faith and the same Lord.

It is natural for human beings to be frightened when opposed, but Christians should be bold when others oppose them because of their faith in Christ. The Holy Spirit will give them courage just as he has given it to Paul. Opposition to the gospel is not a tragedy to be lamented, but a sign of destruction to the persecutors and a sign of hope and salvation to those who believe (1:28). It helps believers to find out who is with them and who is against them. Those who walk according to the flesh persecute those who walk according to the Spirit, that is, in faith (Gal 4:29). However, the final outcome of walking according to the flesh is destruction (Gal 6:8). The final outcome of walking by faith in Christ Jesus is victory and salvation.

Suffering for the sake of Christ is part of a Christian's calling (**1:29**). Believers in Christ should stand for their faith despite all the circumstances that try to draw them back from following the Lord. The Philippian Christians are no different. Like Paul, they have to endure opposition and suffering (**1:30**). In fact, 'everyone who wants to live a godly life in Christ Jesus will be persecuted' (2 Tim 3:12). Christ identifies with those who suffer (Acts 9:4-5).

Paul's reference to the *struggle you saw I had, and now hear that I still have* (1:30) undercuts the idea that his joy meant that he did not suffer in prison. Christians should not expect a friendly world. The spirit of the world and the Spirit of Christ are at odds. The world loves its own and persecutes those who belong to Christ. The Philippians, together with Paul, share the suffering that comes as a result of their faith.

2:1-4 The Right Attitude

In 1:27 Paul had called on the Philippians to live an exemplary life. Here he describes this life even more forcefully. The repeated calls to unity and care for one another suggest that there was some division among the Christians in Philippi. This conflict is explicitly addressed in 4:2. Paul is a model counsellor and minister in the way his message relates to the practical issues the Philippians were facing.

Paul begins by referring to the fruits of true fellowship with Christ. In **2:1** he points out that such fellowship has a personal effect on the one who believes, producing encouragement, comfort, and a spirit of fellowship, tenderness and compassion. Following Christ and being united with Christ imprint the character of Christ on the personality of the believer. If a Christian does not reflect the life of Christ in his or her attitude and character, he or she is no Christian!

Being united with Christ has an interpersonal dimension in that it creates unity among the community of faith (**2:2**). Paul wants to see this community being *like-minded*, loving and *one in spirit and purpose*. We are reminded of the words of Christ, 'If a house is divided against itself, that house cannot stand' (Mk 3:25). Unity is a mark of strength. An Amharic proverb from Ethiopia says, 'threads united can tie even a lion'. Paul's call to unity applies 'to divided Christendom, and to every local church in which division and party strife are spoiling the fellowship and marring the witness' (TNT). Unity is the hallmark of the gospel.

The factors that can cause disunity in Christian communities include selfish ambition, vanity, a lack of humility, looking down on others, and focusing on one's own interests (2:3-4). Those who claim to follow Christ should have concern for the community as well as for themselves. True Christians should have a 'body' mindset, the mindset of togetherness. Their attitude should be close to that expressed in Africa as 'I am, because we are', though for Christians this statement should reflect the reality that Christ is in the believer, rather than being merely a cultural philosophy.

The ancient world did not consider humility a virtue. It only came to be regarded as such through the teaching of our Lord. The desire to boast and exaggerate our importance is still deeply rooted in human nature. This excessive concern with ourselves also leads us to be too focused on our own spirituality. So Paul here reminds us to *consider others better than yourselves* (2:3). We are to look for and emulate the good traits in our Christian brothers and sisters. In so doing we will avoid falling into pride and boasting.

2:5-11 Incentive to Unity and Humility

Of course, our greatest model is to emulate our Lord (2:5). To make his point, Paul here quotes a hymn that he may have written himself. (Arguments about who wrote it are based on technical issues of terminology and on the fact that the hymn does not mention some points that Paul stresses elsewhere in his letters.) His point is that the mindset and thought patterns of a Christian should be the same as those of Christ Jesus. A Christian has no liberty to adopt an attitude that differs from or contradicts that of Christ.

What was the character of Christ? The hymn reminds us that Christ was actually *in very nature God* (NIV) or *in the form of God* (KJV) (2:6). The translators Loh and Nida explain that the Greek word used here refers to 'an essential form of something which never alters, a form which corresponds to an underlying reality', or in other words, 'the form which truly and fully expresses the being which underlies it'. Some scholars also link this word with the glory of God. In terms of essence, dignity, honour, glory and power, Christ had the very nature of God. He was truly God in his pre-incarnate state (see also John 17:5; Heb 1:3).

Obviously, we cannot imitate Christ in his divine glory, but we can imitate his remarkable behaviour. Whereas Adam and Eve wanted to seize an opportunity to be like God, Christ did not insist on remaining equal with God. He was prepared to give it all up and become a servant. One who had the very nature of God went to the opposite extreme and took *the very nature of a servant* (2:7). We find it difficult to imagine a slave owner willingly becoming a

slave, but this comes nowhere near the humiliation that Christ accepted.

In 2:7-8 the hymn sets out the details of Christ's incomparable change in status. His humbling of himself was not a one-time act but was spread over his entire life, from his birth in the manger to its climax on the cross. We may be prepared to relinquish some of our privileges. We may even be prepared to go from the highest place to an intermediate place. But Christ went far further than that. Not only did one who was limitless accept the limitations of being human, but he was even willing to accept death, and the worst kind of death, the death that Roman writer Cicero described as 'the most wretched of deaths'. Cicero found crucifixion so revolting that he said: 'Far be the very name of a cross, not only from the body, but even from the thought, the eyes, the ears of Roman citizens.' To the Jews crucifixion implied that the victim was excommunicated and outside the covenant of the people of God, because 'anyone who is hung on a tree is under God's curse' (Deut 21:23). Such a despised death was utterly inconceivable for one who was God! Yet Paul recognized that Christ's dying in this way was the key to our reconciliation with God.

Human beings have no choice about whether to be subject to death, for they cannot escape it. But Christ was different. He became *obedient to death* (2:8). This phrase in itself is enough to hint at his divine origin. As the sinless Son of God, he had no need to die. But he chose to accept death on our behalf to free us from the power of sin and death.

In accepting humiliation, Christ held nothing back: he *made himself nothing* (NIV) or *emptied himself* (NRSV) (2:7). This does not mean that he divested himself of such divine attributes as omniscience, omnipotence and omnipresence, for he could still say 'I and the Father are one' (John 10:30). The 'nothing' focuses on his status rather than his essence. It means that he completely abandoned all the rights and privileges to which he was entitled.

Yet by becoming nothing, Christ gained everything. His reward was exaltation as great as his humiliation had been deep: *Therefore God exalted him to the highest place* (2:9). There is no higher place of honour than the one Christ received after his resurrection. His name, Jesus Christ, is honoured above all other names in the entire universe because he is the only saviour and hope of the world (Acts 4:12). The writer of Proverbs said that 'humility comes before honour' (Prov 18:12) and this proved true on a cosmic scale. One's reward is directly proportional to one's humility.

The all-embracing cosmic authority of our Lord Jesus Christ is shown in the fact that at his name *every knee should bow* (2:10a). In many cultures, bowing shows that one submits to another person. We bow to victors and lords. There can be no doubt that Jesus is a victor given his conquest of

LIFE AND DOCTRINE

Lives consistent with the truth of Scriptures are the most effective witness that believers can bear for Christ. Yet too often we encounter situations where our lives are inconsistent with what we believe. A preacher may curse his opponents and call down God's punishment on them. A woman may sing 'Jesus never fails' in church on Sunday, but on Monday agree to sleep with an employer in order to get a job. Believers from different tribal groups may feud. We even learn that Christians participated in the 1994 Rwandan genocide.

Such inconsistencies show that we have forgotten that God has always wanted his people to be 'a kingdom of priests and a holy nation' (Exod 19:6; 1 Pet 2:9). They are to represent God before other people and to live lives that conform to his holy character. Jesus told his disciples to 'let your light shine before men, that they may see your good deeds and praise your Father in heaven'. This was the only way in which they could be 'the salt of the earth' and 'the light of the world' (Matt 5:13-16).

The apostles usually start their letters by proclaiming theological truths and then applying them to our lives. Thus the first eleven chapters in Romans deal with profound theological truths, and the last four chapters deal with how the Roman Christians should live as God's people. The first chapter of 1 Peter begins by speaking of our wonderful salvation, and then says, 'Therefore prepare your minds for action' (1 Pet 1:13). But this application again leads into a discussion of theology, which feeds back into application, 'Therefore, rid yourselves of all malice and all deceit, hypocrisy, envy, and slander of every kind' (1 Pet 2:1). In the Pastoral Epistles, women are reminded that good deeds are more important than external appearance, and that what they wear should be 'appropriate for women who profess to worship God' (1 Tim 2:9-10). Slaves (equivalent to employees today) are told to serve well, 'so that God's name and our teaching may not be slandered' (1 Tim 6:1) and also 'so that in every way they will make the teaching about God our Saviour attractive' (Titus 2:10). The list could go on and on. But the point is clear. God wants us to live out what we believe.

Here are a few examples of some of the most basic beliefs shared by millions of Christians in Africa and their implications for our conduct:

- God loves people (John 3:16). We should thus extend love and kindness to all, no matter what group they belong to.

- God is a righteous judge (Heb 10:30). Reflecting his justice, we should never demand, accept or give any bribe, even when bribes are part of our culture.

- Jesus Christ is our Saviour (Matt 1:21). He loves us and forgives us for all those sins of which we sincerely repent, even those that may have resulted in us suffering from HIV/AIDS or infecting others with this disease.

- Jesus is our Lord (Phil 2:11) and the Bible is his authoritative word intended to govern our lives (2 Tim 3:16). We should thus obey it every day in every detail of life, not just on Sundays.

- All believers are part of one community led by Christ (Gal 3:26-28). Thus we must refuse to discriminate against or harm other believers who are not of our people group.

- The Holy Spirit is to be our guide (John 16:13), comforter (John 14:16), advocate (1 John 2:1) and enabler (Luke 24:49, Acts 1:8). When a loved one is sick, we must trust in God and the Holy Spirit, rather than asking a witchdoctor to consult other spirits for us.

These are only a few examples of how what we believe should become part of all that we do. Living like this could transform Africa! We need to ask God to give us the will and power to do what we believe.

The desire to live truly godly lives will also change our perspective on ministry. Instead of emphasizing only evangelism when fulfilling the Great Commission (Matt 28:19-20), we will also focus on discipleship, 'teaching them to obey'. We will not pray simply for revival but also for reformation. Revival is temporary, but reformation changes how we live in light of what we believe and lasts a lifetime.

Samuel Ngewa

death, the last enemy of all mortals. The fact that all three domains – *in heaven, and on the earth and under the earth* (**2:10b**) – bow to Jesus shows that he is Lord of the spirit world as well as the physical world. The harvest and allegiance Jesus has won are proportional to the magnitude of his humility and subsequent exaltation. His is the greatest name of power, glory and honour in heaven and on earth. One refuses to admit this at one's peril!

Those who bow to Jesus will also confess *that Jesus Christ is Lord* (**2:11a**). The word translated 'Lord' here is the same one used in the Septuagint to translate the divine

name 'Yahweh', the true God of Israel. The use of the same word for Jesus Christ shows that he is 'installed in the place which properly belongs to God' (TNT). The hymn makes it clear that confessing that this is the case does not reduce the Father's glory but enhances it (**2:11b**).

Jesus' humility has enormous implications on the personal, church and national levels. He makes it clear that humility both precedes and leads to honour and glory. Had all our church leaders followed the way of Christ's humility instead of holding onto their powers and positions, the present decline in our churches could have been avoided.

Had our civil leaders followed the way of humility instead of setting out to grasp power by any means, we would have seen abundant peace and prosperity in our societies. The way to peace, glory and eventual success is the way of humility, setting aside our selfish interests for the sake of communal gain.

2:12-18 An Exhortation to be Blameless

Paul now reverts discussing to the disagreement and competition that seems to have been plaguing the Philippian church (see 2:2-3) and lovingly urges them to listen to what he has said. They should not merely listen to him when he is present, but also when he is absent (**2:12a**). Christian obedience should be genuine and wholehearted. We are hypocrites if our obedience to our Lord depends on whether someone is watching us or not.

He urges them to *continue to work out your salvation* (**2:12b**). We tend to apply this verse to ourselves as individuals, but it seems likely that Paul is thinking of the corporate health of the church. Church members should work hard to maintain their unity, taking Christ as their model and drawing strength from God who enables them.

The words *fear and trembling* (2:12b) indicate that this is not a task to be taken lightly. They should be prepared to work together *without complaining or arguing* (**2:14**). They should be peaceable people, with a positive attitude and the patience to overcome evil with good. If they can learn to live like this, they will *become blameless and pure, children of God without fault* (**2:15a**). Their character as children of God will stand out as clearly as the stars in the night sky (**2:15c**). The accuser will always try to find fault with us, but we should guard against making ourselves easy targets.

Paul contrasts the believers with those around them, whom he refers to as *a crooked and depraved generation* (**2:15b**). The society in which the Philippians lived was far from righteous, honest and loving. In this darkness, the Christians were to stand out, as Christ indicated when he said 'You are the light of the world' (Matt 5:14). The way in which they will do this is by *holding out the word of life* (**2:16**). The psalmist says 'Your word is a lamp to my feet and a light for my path' (Ps 119:105). Those who walk in the light also shine because of the light. Christians shine to the world by living according to the word of God.

While the primary motive for living like this is to glorify God, Paul also introduces a personal note: if his converts walk in the way of holiness, he will be satisfied *on the day of Christ that I did not run or labour for nothing* (2:16). Paul's ultimate joy and reward when Christ returns will be the souls that have been saved through his witness.

Paul's reference to the judgment day is also an indirect encouragement to the Christians to persevere until the end. So is his reference to his own readiness to die as a martyr,

poured out like a drink offering on the sacrifice (**2:17-18**). He anticipates death for the sake of Christ not with bitterness but with joy, and invites the Philippians to share his joy, which is rooted in the ultimate victory of Christ.

2:19-30 Paul's Testimony to his Co-workers

Paul was a team worker and a caring pastor, and his concern for the Philippian believers translated into an eagerness to hear that they are doing well. He was hoping to be able to send Timothy, one of his co-workers, to visit them soon (**2:19**).

Paul praised his teammates highly. Of Timothy he says, *I have no one else like him* (**2:20**). Timothy was an exceptional minister in that he was totally committed to serving the people of God, putting aside even his own interests. It is clear that there are two kinds of ministers in churches. The majority (the *everyone* in **2:21**) look out for their own concerns and well-being. There are only a few like Timothy who place the will and interests of Jesus Christ above their own interests. Timothy had served Paul as if Paul were *his father* (**2:22**), and indeed Timothy was Paul's spiritual son (see 1 Tim 1:2; 2 Tim 1:2).

Because of Timothy's sterling qualities, Paul chose to send him to the Philipians (**2:23**). The gospel is not a private treasure, and so trusted and self-sacrificing ministers are to be chosen to do the work of the Lord and pass it on to others. Timothy would preach the same gospel to the Philippians that Paul himself would when – and if – he was free and able to come to them again (**2:24**). It is important for a minister to recognize, like Paul, that the preaching of the gospel message can be delegated to others.

Another teammate of whom Paul speaks highly is Epaphroditus, whom he describes as *my brother, fellow worker and fellow soldier* (**2:25**). It is clear that Paul respected those who worked with him and treated them as his equals.

The Philippians had sent Epaphroditus to Paul *to take care of my needs* while in prison (2:25). These believers set an example of how a Christian community should take care of its ministers, especially those who serve at great personal cost. But now Epaphroditus was homesick and longing to see his own people, and Paul was sending him back (**2:26**).

Another reason for sending him home was his recent illness. It is interesting to note that he was desperately ill despite being an honoured co-worker with Paul (**2:27**). It is clear that Paul did not hold the view that a good Christian will never be ill, or think he could use his apostolic authority to heal his friends. Instead, he attributes Epaphroditus' recovery to God's mercy to both of them, for Paul would have deeply mourned his death (2:27). The effects of God's goodness extend beyond the immediate beneficiaries.

The Philippian believers were worried about Epaphroditus, and this also contributed to Paul's decision to send him back (**2:28**). This mutual longing and concern of Epaphroditus and those who had sent him models the true care for each other that should exist between a sending body and any messenger who is sent to carry out the Great Commission.

When Epaphroditus eventually reaches home, the Philippians are to *welcome him … and honour men like him* (**2:29**), as we should accept and honour those who give their lives sacrificially for the work of the Lord. The fact that Epaphroditus *almost died for the work of Christ, risking his life* (**2:30**) is also a warning to those who think that working for Christ is all joy and hallelujahs. From his own experience Paul tells us that a minister can even become ill due to the burden of the work he has to do for Christ. But God's mercy is with those who labour for him despite their frailty.

3:1-11 The Only Thing Worth Boasting About

Paul introduces the next section of his letter with *finally* (**3:1**) implying that chapters 1 and 2 contain his main message. In closing he wants to repeat some things he has said earlier and to address some specific things that may cause disunity.

The congregation in Philippi must have included some Jewish Christians, or at least have come under the influence of Judaizers, Jewish Christians who insisted that Gentile Christians should be circumcised and keep the law of Moses. This is why Paul warns them to *watch out for those dogs, those mutilators of the flesh* (**3:2**). He does not even use the word 'circumcision', but refers to it as 'mutilation'. He insists that those who are truly circumcised are those who believe in the Lord Jesus Christ and rely on what he has done on the cross (**3:3**). They can be said to have circumcised their sinful nature when they put their trust in Christ. The life they live now is a life of faith. They are the ones who worship God in the Spirit. Such people do not attach value to their race or social status or anything else that may have been important to them before they became Christians.

To explain what he means, Paul takes himself as an example (**3:4-6**). In the past, he had been extremely proud of his Jewish identity and his adherence to Jewish traditions. He had been circumcised on the eighth day, raised as a Pharisee, and had such zeal for the law that he persecuted the church. But now he has abandoned all his pre-Christian pride in these things (**3:7-8**). He now dismisses the status and dignity given to him by his race, religious rites and traditions as rubbish. Why? Because he has now found a real reason for boasting: *I consider everything a loss compared to the surpassing greatness of knowing Christ Jesus my Lord, for whose sake I have lost all things* (**3:8**). By 'knowing Christ' (3:8, 10) Paul is not referring merely to mental knowledge

about Christ but to an intimate knowledge of him. True fellowship with Christ includes experiencing and appropriating the benefits he offers, especially salvation by faith, without any need for works.

Paul had found an entirely new kind of righteousness (**3:9**). Earlier he had had human righteousness, a *righteousness of my own,* in which he tried to please God by striving to live according to God's law. The new righteousness was not the result of his own actions but of Christ's actions. It was not acquired by human effort but by faith in the completed work of Christ on the cross. Faith is looking at what Christ has done and accepting that it was done for one's self.

The righteousness of God revealed in Christ is relevant to all of us. Without it, none of us can be truly Christian. This righteousness changes us. It gives us a new identity as people of God whatever our past identity and history. Like Paul, we should discard our pride in such things as our race, social status, caste and sex. As new people of God we should boast of our new identity in Christ, and our desire, like Paul's, should be to become like Christ in all respects, including his sufferings, death and resurrection (**3:10-11**).

3:12-21 Keeping the Goal in View

We may think that Paul's desire to share Christ's suffering has been partly realized in his imprisonment for Christ. But Paul is not satisfied. His whole life is governed by his passionate longing to be like Christ. Yet he knows his limitations. Final perfection is not to be achieved on this side of the grave. Until that time comes, there will always be room for progress. He will keep moving forward, persevering in his pursuit of what Christ has for him (**3:12**).

There is a 'not yet' aspect to the Christian life, which Paul acknowledges: *Brothers, I do not consider myself yet to have taken hold of it* (**3:13**). We are not yet complete. We have not yet reached our destination. To claim that we have shows a lack of humility. But we also should not dwell on our past. Paul ignores his past successes and failures as he presses forward expectantly to reach the goal (**3:13-14**). Our Lord, too, does not dwell on our past failures or successes. He wants us to keep moving forward by having faith in him until the day of victory. A mark of a Christian is keeping on towards the goal, trusting in the Lord despite the circumstances. A Christian is like a runner who looks forward to crossing the finishing line.

Paul feels strongly that all Christians who are mature will share his understanding that they should neither expect nor claim to have achieved absolute perfection while still on earth (**3:15**). The perfection one can have here is relative or progressive, but that should be enough to keep us looking expectantly to the future. We should be satisfied with living up to what God has revealed to each of us so far (**3:16**). If there are other things that we need to understand better, God will make these clear to us in his own time.

The idea of living up to what we know leads Paul to offer himself as an example: *Join with others in following my example* (**3:17**; see also 'Imitate me as I imitate Christ' – 1 Cor 11:1). For Christians the model for conduct is not a written code but a life, primarily the life of our Lord and secondarily the life of his followers. Paul had such a commitment to the Lord that he was able to say 'follow my example' and that of others *who live according to the pattern we gave you*. The Greek word translated 'live' in the NIV literally means 'walk'. It refers to practical conduct rather than merely mental activity.

Unfortunately, few live this way. Instead, *many live as enemies of the cross of Christ* (**3:18-19**). There has been no time in which Christians have not been surrounded by people who are opposed to the cross of Christ, which is the source of God's righteousness. The fate and character of these people is obvious. Destruction awaits them. Their ultimate interest is bodily satisfaction and all they think about are earthly things.

By contrast, the Philippian believers have a heavenly citizenship (**3:20**). Because Philippi was a Roman military colony, its residents enjoyed the prestige of being Roman citizens. But Paul reminds them that they have a far more prestigious citizenship in heaven. While those whose *mind is set only on earthly things* (**3:19**) await destruction, Christians await the second coming of the Lord. By his almighty power he will transform my body, which is weak and frail, and make it like his glorious resurrection body (**3:21**). This is our great joy and hope as Christians. Our future is in secure hands.

4:1-9 Affectionate Advice

Paul's excitement at their future hope spills over into an exhortation to *stand firm* (**4:1**) that also expresses his real love for his flock. He refers to them as *my joy and crown*, telling them that they are more precious to him than diamonds, pearls or jewellery. This is the type of love a minister should have for those he serves. It is a love that leads Paul to be willing to give his own life for his flock.

Paul did not have an abstract love for an abstract flock. He knew the church members by name, just as our Lord knows the names of his sheep (John 10:3), and he singled out two women for special mention. Every minister should know his members as well as Paul did. Euodia and Syntyche are advised *to agree with each other in the Lord* (**4:2**). Disagreement weakens the power of the people of God to influence the world around them. These two women had a commendable witness for the Lord in the past, but now they needed help. Someone who had been Paul's *loyal companion* (NRSV) is asked to help them reconcile (**4:3**). Christians, who have themselves been reconciled to God, should also reconcile disagreements among themselves.

Paul refers in passing to Clement, another of his co-workers in Philippi, who is traditionally thought to be the same Clement who later became the bishop of Rome. But regardless of whether Paul explicitly mentions the names of his co-workers, he knows that their *names are in the book of life* (**4:3**), by which he means that they are saved and have their citizenship recorded in heaven.

Instead of arguing, the Philippian believers are to *rejoice in the Lord always* (**4:4**). Paul is reminding them of what he said in 3:1 and in the opening chapter of this letter. Regardless of their circumstances, Christians can rejoice that the Lord has forgiven them and loves them with an eternal love, a love that has triumphed over sin, principalities, death and all forms of evil.

But this rejoicing is not to be with pride or at others' expense. The believers are instructed to let their *gentleness be evident to all* (**4:5**). The word translated 'gentleness' can also be rendered as 'graciousness' or 'fair-mindedness'. There are no hidden or invisible Christian virtues. Our renewed nature as Christians should be clearly displayed.

Rejoicing and gentleness are difficult during times of anxiety, and so Paul counsels the believers that they should be free from any kind of anxiety (**4:6**). How? By being people of prayer and presenting everything to God with thanksgiving for the Lord's mercy and forgiveness. For a Christian, God is an intimate friend and Lord who is able to help in all circumstances. By praying we allow him to share our burdens.

The result of committing our anxieties to God is protection by the peace of God (**4:7**). Our hearts and minds will be relieved of all anxiety. The basis for this peace is the assurance that through Christ Jesus we have been reconciled to God.

Finally, Paul advises Christians to focus on the types of things that please God and express his character (**4:8-9**). He then adds: *Whatever you have learned from me ... put it into practice* (**4:9**). Before accusing Paul of pride, it is worth remembering that before the New Testament books were written and accepted, the only standard for Christian teaching and behaviour was to be found in people who accurately reflected the authority and ethical standards of our Lord.

4:10-20 A Giving and Supporting Congregation

Paul has shown his love for the Philippians, and they had shown their concern for Paul by sending gifts. He rejoices in this visible demonstration of their true love and concern (**4:10**). In thanking them, he also reveals his own attitude to his daily needs. He has *learned to be content whatever the circumstances* (**4:11**). We have much to learn from him. As individuals, we experience gain and loss; communally we experience social upheaval, epidemics, poverty, natural disasters, and both internal and external strife. To live contentedly in the good times as well as the bad times, we need the Lord who always remains the same and continually gives us his strength (4:12-13).

Having discussed the kindness of the Philippian Christians in general terms, Paul goes on to mention specific examples (4:14-16). He assures them that his motive for doing this is not to ask for more help but to praise them (4:17). By supporting the imprisoned apostle, the Philippians demonstrated that they shared in his troubles. By supporting evangelists, missionaries or any workers in the vineyard of the Lord, we are sharing in their ministry, even though we may not be physically present. Good wishes are not enough. As individuals and as churches we should give tangible support to the work of the Lord. Repeated sacrificial giving of the type modelled by the Philippians should be the norm for an active and serving church. Such a gift will be *a fragrant offering, an acceptable sacrifice, pleasing to God* (4:18). God will respond by blessing such an undertaking from *his glorious riches in Christ Jesus* (4:19).

4:21-23 Final Greetings and Blessings

In closing his letter, Paul records an exchange of greetings between believing communities, all of the members of which are saints (4:21; see comments on 1:1). Such an exchange encourages both communities. The Philippian saints may have been especially excited by the reference to *those who belong to Caesar's household* (4:22) as they realized that the gospel has already reached the household of the Roman emperor. The gospel of Jesus Christ would continue to expand across Africa and the world until that day when all will 'confess that Jesus Christ is lord to the glory of God the Father' (2:11).

The closing words are with Paul, and he uses them to wish the Philippians the continual presence of the grace of the Lord Jesus Christ (4:23). The Christian faith begins by grace, exists by grace, and comes to fulfilment by grace.

Eshetu Abate

For Further Reading

Lightfoot, J. B. *Philippians.* Alister McGrath and J. I. Packer., eds. CCC. Wheaton, Ill.: Crossway, 1994.

Loh, I-Jin and Eugene A. Nida. *A Translator's Handbook on Paul's Letters to the Philippians.* New York: United Bible Societies, 1977.

Motyer, J. Alec. *The Message of Philippians.* BST. Downers Grove, Ill.: InterVarsity Press, 1984.

COLOSSIANS

Colossae was a large city in the area known as Phrygia on the River Lycus. Because of its location on the important trade route that ran from Ephesus to the Euphrates, it received many travellers and visitors from the capital of the Roman Empire.

Unlike the church at Ephesus, the one at Colossae had not been founded by the Apostle Paul, but was probably founded by Epaphras, who was one of his closest collaborators. The Christians there were of various origins, but the majority were Phrygians, Greeks or Jews.

There are similarities in style and content between Paul's letter to the Colossians and his letter to the Ephesians. It is thus possible that these two letters were meant to be circulated among the churches in the area, even though each was addressed to a particular church. In fact, Paul specifically recommends that his letter to the Colossians also be read in Laodicea (4:16), a city about twelve miles (twenty kilometres) away. He also refers to the nearby city of Hierapolis. The letter was probably written between 60–62 AD, when Paul was in prison in Rome.

The theme of this letter is often said to be fullness, for it focuses on the fullness of the knowledge of God, or the fullness that the Christians have in Christ. They have everything in him, and consequently need not turn to pagan religions or to the false doctrines propagated by the Judaizers, those who insisted that non-Jews had to be circumcised in order to be accepted by God.

Outline of Contents

COMMENTARY

1:1-14 Greetings

At the start of his letter, Paul specifies his identity. He is *an apostle of Christ Jesus by the will of God* (**1:1**). He is thus making it clear that he did not receive his apostleship from another human being or from some institution. He had not been one of the Twelve who kept company with the Lord during his earthly ministry. Nor had he witnessed his appearances after the resurrection. But his encounter with the resurrected Christ on the road to Damascus had made him an authentic apostle, with no need to defend his status.

Along with Timothy, *our brother* in the faith, Paul greets the Colossians whom he describes as *holy and faithful brothers in Christ* (**1:2**). He does not know them in person because he has never met them. But through the reports he has been given by people such as Epaphras, he has come to know the church and its needs. They are *holy;* that is, set apart for God and his work. They are *faithful brothers* in Christ because they are attached to Christ and his teaching. The fraternal ties between Paul and the Colossians are stronger than blood ties. They transcend ethnicity, race and social status. Paul and Timothy may be different from these brothers in many ways, but in Christ they form one family. And the same holds true for the relationships among the Colossian believers themselves. As 'brothers', their primary identity is in Christ. It is only secondarily that they are of the various origins and the different social classes that are found in any major city.

1:3-8 The Work of the Gospel

Paul is excited about the work the gospel has been doing among the Colossians. Once again he speaks of their *faith in Jesus Christ* (**1:3**), that faith which has made them his *faithful brothers in Christ* (1:2). It is as if he wants to drive home the point that a person cannot have faith in Christ and at the same time be unfaithful to him.

Faith is inseparable from love. The gospel that made the Colossians 'brothers in Christ' produced in them *love … for all the saints* (**1:4**). In 1:2 Paul described the Colossians themselves as 'holy' or as 'saints' (KJV). In using the same word when he speaks of *all the saints*, it seems that he is referring to a still wider circle of believers elsewhere, possibly those whom the Colossians had helped with gifts.

The work of the gospel in Colossians is, therefore, visible: it produces faith and love. This love is based on the *hope* related to the life beyond in the celestial city of God (**1:5a**). So we may say that faith is the foundation of our life here below, love is its fruit in the present, and hope its glimpse into the life hereafter. The celestial city to which we look forward in hope is much better than the abode of the ancestors in African traditional religion, which is in some remote location far from the villages of the living. From there, the ancestors are said to bless the community of the living. But all Christians, whether African or not, have their eyes fixed on the celestial city, living in the hope and expectation of going there some day, as promised in the *word of truth* (**1:5b**).

The *gospel*, which Paul uses as a synonym for 'the word of truth', that has been having such a marked effect on the Colossians, has also borne similar fruit *all over the world* (**1:6**). The Colossians are not unique. They are only another example of the Spirit of God blowing graciously wherever and whenever he pleases (John 3:8). He unites all those who are in Christ in order to make them 'faithful brothers'.

In reading Paul's thanksgiving here, it is worth noting that he does not give thanks for the performance of the Colossians, but for the work of the gospel in the world and, in particular, in Colossae.

The Colossians had received the gospel through the work of men like Epaphras, *our dear fellow-servant* (**1:7**). We know little about this servant of God, but what we do know is that God had used him to teach the Colossians and to inform Paul about their lives, their needs and their concerns (**1:8**). He was thus someone who faithfully communicated information, and deserves to be described as a *faithful minister of Christ*.

1:9-11 Paul's Prayer for the Colossians

Paul and his friends have been constantly praying for the Colossians ever *since the day we heard about you* (**1:9a**). Although Paul praises God for the work the gospel has already accomplished in their hearts, there is still much to be done. Paul accordingly prays for three things:

- For the Colossians to be filled *with the knowledge of his will* (**1:9b**). Paul is praying that knowledge of God may fully occupy the thoughts of the Colossians, and that

they will relate this knowledge to all aspects of their lives, so that they may live in accordance with God's will. If they are filled with this knowledge, there will be no room for other philosophies to gain a foothold. Paul's reference to 'knowledge' here suggests that he may be thinking specifically of gnostic philosophy, with its emphasis on special knowledge and its hostility to the gospel. But knowledge alone is not enough, it needs to be coupled with *spiritual wisdom.* The Colossians must strive to attain and maintain this wisdom, which also leads to *understanding,* or 'discernment' as the Amplified Bible translates this word.

- For the Colossians to *live a life worthy of the Lord* (**1:10a**). Correct knowledge of God is not enough if it remains theoretical, merely a collection of dogmas or truths to be confessed. It needs to bear fruit in the daily lives of believers, fruit that will bring glory to God. In other words, the better the Colossians know God, the better they will live to his glory.

- For the Colossians to *please him in every way* (**1:10b**). Pleasing God should be the primary aim of every Christian.

When we look closely at these three requests, we see that they are all really one request. How can we please God and live in a way worthy of him without knowing him? And how can we know him without exercising wisdom? And this knowledge will produce all kinds of fruit as we live a life pleasing to God and worthy of him. This fruit includes our spiritual growth, which must be characterized by *endurance and patience* (**1:11**). It is thus clear that knowledge of God is the basis of all growth.

1:12-14 An Invitation to Thanksgiving

After having acknowledged the work of the gospel among the Colossians and presenting his prayers for them, Paul invites them to join him in giving thanks to God for three things:

- God has brought them into *the inheritance of the saints* (**1:12**). The term 'inheritance' reminds us of the exodus, when the children of Israel left slavery in Egypt and waited in faith for access to their inheritance in the promised land beyond the Jordan. The Colossian Gentiles were in contact with Christians of Jewish origin, and would have known this history. In the same way, the Colossians will enter into 'the inheritance of the saints', that is, *the kingdom of light,* which is a far better inheritance than Canaan. This kingdom is intended for all the saints, the children of God of all times and all places. In fact, the Colossians already have possession of it, but only in hope; they will fully enter it at the return of Jesus Christ.

- God has rescued *us from the dominion of darkness* (**1:13a**), which is the opposite of the promised 'kingdom of light'.

'Darkness' symbolizes the devil and his army. The Colossians had been under the power of the devil, deprived of their liberty and with their dignity scorned. But God had snatched them from the claws of this fearful enemy and moved them from the darkness into glorious light.

- God has *brought us into the kingdom of the Son he loves* (**1:13b**). The word 'brought' is translated 'transferred' in the NASB. This translation brings out Paul's point that our salvation involves a transfer from one place to another. The Colossians are no longer in this world, under the authority of the devil, but have been transferred to the Kingdom of God. This kingdom is already theirs by faith, but has not yet been fully revealed.

1:15-20 Hymn to Christ

Some commentators think that this passage contains an early Christian hymn that Paul chose to include in his letter. Others say that Paul would not have needed to borrow a hymn, and point out that it is unlikely that a hymn would begin with the words, 'He is the image of the invisible God'. But the pattern of the ideas, sometimes symmetrical and sometimes parallel, and the rhythm that emerges clearly in the original Greek do indeed seem hymn-like.

1:15 Christ, Head over Humanity

In African religions, God the Creator is not only distant, he is also invisible. Hence there is a need for intermediaries between him and human beings. Paul, however, presents Jesus as the very *image of the invisible God* (**1:15a**). Genesis 1:26-27 tells us that human beings were created in the image of God and thus resemble God. But in Genesis 3 humans sinned, and the image of God in them was spoiled. In Jesus, the original perfection of that image is restored, and we can thus see God in him.

Because Jesus represents human beings as they were created to be, he can be described as *the firstborn over all creation* (**1:15b**). But Jesus' status as the firstborn also carries privileges, just as it does in Africa, where the eldest has a special position in the family and can represent the whole family. As the firstborn, Jesus is both the model and the head of humanity.

1:16 Christ, Head over Creation

But calling Jesus the 'firstborn' may lead some to think that Jesus, too, is a created being. So Paul hastily adds that Jesus is not part of the creation but is himself the Creator, *for by him all things were created* (**1:16a**). Yes, creation is generally attributed to the Father, but this hymn affirms that the Son was also involved, not just beside the Father, but with the Father (see also John 1:1-3). The words 'all things' make it clear that nothing is possible and nothing exists without him. It embraces everything that is visible and invisible, physical and spiritual.

Paul specifies that the 'all things' include *thrones or powers or rulers or authorities* (**1:16b**). Some argue about whether he is referring simply to different political powers, or whether he is speaking of the spiritual powers of the devil and his army. But the important point is that all these powers, whether political, administrative or spiritual, are under the authority of Jesus Christ. Consequently, the Colossians should not be afraid of them.

This hymn is particularly reassuring for African Christians, who still often fear the ancestors and spirits who act as intermediaries between the Creator God and the living in traditional African religions. These spiritual powers were traditionally honoured and feared more than God, who was regarded as too remote from the living to be interested in their lives. But the apostle Paul reassures us that as head of creation, Jesus Christ has authority over these beings. He has first place over all others.

Not only is Jesus the creator of the universe, he is also the reason it exists. As Paul puts it, *All things were created ... for him* (**1:16c**). The universe that we now see around us makes no sense without Jesus Christ.

1:18-20 Christ, Head over the New Creation

After having presented Jesus as the head over humanity (1:15) and head over creation (1:16), the hymn next presents him as head over his new creation, the church: *He is head of the body, the church* (**1:18a**). The church is like a new society composed of those who have been reconciled to God by Jesus Christ (1:20).

Jesus Christ is head of the new creation for the following reasons:

- *He is the beginning and the firstborn from among the dead* (**1:18b**). The term 'firstborn' is repeated here. As the firstborn of all creation, Jesus is before and pre-eminent over all creation. As the 'firstborn from among the dead', he precedes by his resurrection all those who are dead in Christ. His supremacy extends over all things, in particular over the church.
- *All God's fullness dwells in him* (**1:19**). He is fully God. This point is made even more explicitly in 2:9, which states that in Christ all the fullness of the Deity lives in bodily form. So Jesus is not only a man and the firstborn of all creation, he is also God, head over the new creation.
- *He reconciles all things to himself* (**1:20**). The word 'all' lends itself to many interpretations. Some think that the word includes all of humanity, and argue that all humans of all times will be reconciled to God by Christ. Others say that the word embraces everything that exists, the whole cosmos. But a better interpretation seems to be that everything that was in rebellion against God will be brought under his power and will submit to him as the head of the new creation.

In just a few lines this beautiful hymn gives an extraordinary summary of the doctrine of the person and work of Christ. His supremacy should reassure Christians. They are delivered from every oppressive and alienating power and have come under the absolute sovereignty of Jesus Christ. Why should they fear the influence of the princes of this world, or of witchcraft or sorcery?

1:21-23 Christ and the Colossians

The hymn describing the person and work of Jesus, and especially his pre-eminence and sovereignty, is followed by an explanation of how the Colossians have benefited from his work. *Once,* they had been strangers, outside of the covenant that God had entered into with the people of Israel. They had no access to God's written law and thus lived as they pleased. They could even have been described as *enemies* of God, for their thoughts were characterized by hostility towards him. Such a thought pattern inevitably results in *evil behaviour* (**1:21**).

But now (**1:22**) they have been reconciled with God through the cross where his Son died. Reconciliation results in justification in the judicial sense, or in other words, in the legal case against them being dismissed. Because of this justification, they are now *holy,* which means set apart for God as a people different from others; *without blemish,* meaning that the devil no longer has any basis for finding fault with them; and *free from accusation,* indicating that no one can find further fault with them.

While the Colossians should rejoice in their total reconciliation with God, they must not grow careless, but must remain *established and firm* (**1:23**). The Christian life is a spiritual battle because the devil, though defeated, is not disarmed. He would love to see them *moved from the hope held out in the gospel.* The Colossians must thus maintain constant vigilance, for there are many ambushes on the road to the celestial city.

1:24-2:5 Christ and the Apostle

The question is sometimes asked whether the reference *to what is still lacking in regard of Christ's afflictions* (**1:24**) means that the sufferings that Jesus endured were not sufficient for the salvation of humanity. Did Paul and other evangelists after him have to suffer as well in order that people might be reconciled to God? A careful reading of the passage in its context shows that there is a great difference between Paul's suffering and the suffering of Jesus. The suffering of Jesus involved his taking our place and redeeming us so that we are reconciled with God. Paul's suffering, and that of other believers, does not save others, but is like that of Jesus in that it springs from a desire to serve God and save other people by proclaiming the gospel not only to

the Colossians but to everyone in the entire world (**1:25a**). If Paul were not in prison (4:3), he would continue the work of evangelism with enthusiasm.

Paul has already spoken about the gospel, and has called it 'the word of truth' (1:5). Now he speaks of it as the *word of God* (**1:25b**) and as a *mystery* (1:26). It can be called a mystery because it is hidden from non-believers, but has been revealed to the saints. This mystery has reached the Gentiles, and here specifically the Colossians, because Christ is now in them. But even they would not have had access to it unless God had commissioned evangelists like Paul to present it to them (1:25a; see also Rom 10:14).

Presenting the gospel involves more than simply proclaiming it once. It also involves *admonishing and teaching everyone* so that they may come to the knowledge of Christ, to adult status and hold firm in the faith (**1:28a**). Paul speaks of this state as being *perfect in Christ* (**1:28b**). This word, 'perfect' is only one of a number of similar expressions that Paul uses in this letter (for example, filled – 1:9; complete – 2:2) to make it clear that the work of God must not be stopped at the halfway point.

Paul's battle involves helping the believers in Colossae, Laodicea and elsewhere to reach the fullness of the knowledge *of the mystery of God* (**2:2**). Christ is at the heart of this mystery (**2:3**). Knowing Christ is therefore vital. Such knowledge requires constant effort, both on the part of Paul as a servant of the Word and on the part of the Colossians, who must put their intelligence to use in order to grasp what they are being taught. Their knowledge of the mystery will protect them from those who advance false knowledge with *fine-sounding arguments* (**2:4**). It is also the key that gives access to the mystery of Christ, and to the riches hidden in him.

2:6-20 What God Has Done

2:6-10 Assurance and Hope

Paul's words, *so then,* indicate that what he is going to say next is based on what he has just said about the supremacy and sovereignty of Christ (1:15-20) and the need to make every effort to know him better (1:28-2:3). The Colossians have been doing well (**2:5**), but they need to remain vigilant and confident. Paul gives them two commands: *continue to live in him* (**2:6**) and *see that no one takes you captive* (**2:8**).

The instruction in 2.6 is translated more literally in the KJV and NASB, where it reads 'walk in him'. In Paul's time, disciples learned from their teacher as they walked and talked together. Teaching often took the form of dialogue. What Paul is saying is that in order to be rooted in the faith, we must walk with Jesus and in his steps. We must follow his teaching.

The instruction to be alert in 2:8 is given because we have many dangerous enemies. Paul specifically warns the Colossians against *deceptive philosophy* (2:8). He is not thinking of philosophy as an academic discipline but as a religious system. Religious practices based on human traditions can be very alluring. Paul is probably alluding to particular heresies that were prevalent at the time and that would be traps for the Colossians.

There is a great contrast between *hollow* philosophy and the *fullness* in Christ. Paul underscores this contrast with the words, *In Christ all the fullness of Deity lives in bodily form* (2:9). In other words, Christ is actually God. In their sometimes difficult walk, the Colossians can be confident because Jesus is *Head over every power and authority* (2:10). Once again, his pre-eminence and sovereignty are affirmed.

2:11-13a Circumcision and Baptism

When faced with Jewish opposition and demands that they be circumcised, the Colossians should rejoice because they have already been circumcised. But the part of them that has been cut off is not merely a piece of skin, as in the Jewish ritual of circumcision, but a whole way of life (2:11). They have received a spiritual circumcision that has delivered them from the lusts of the flesh and all that bound them to their way of life. One part of them has been removed. This circumcision can be said to have been done by Christ because it is related to faith in him.

In an African context, circumcision is a ritual that transforms a young boy into an adult and a full member of the community, ready to assume responsibilities within it. Jewish circumcision was done when boys were infants, and indicated that they shared in the covenant God had made with Abraham, the ancestor of the Jewish people (Gen 17:1-14). The spiritual circumcision accomplished by faith in the work of Jesus on the cross also gives one membership in a community, but in this case the community is the family of God, the church.

Not only has their spiritual circumcision dealt with sin, but so has their baptism. This baptism symbolizes the annihilation of the power of sin, which no longer has power over the believer. It is as if the Colossians had died in the water of baptism and emerged as resurrected to new life (2:12).

Paul seems to be suggesting that the Colossians enjoy a double blessing, which is appropriate for people who were doubly dead! They were dead because they were not physically circumcised and so were not part of God's people, and they were also dead because of their sins (2:13a).

It is interesting to note how Paul's use of pronouns changes in this verse. He starts off by speaking of 'you', separating himself from the Colossians, because he was a Jew and had thus been physically circumcised, whereas they were not. But he changes to 'us' when he says God *forgave us all our sins* (2:13b). He is like the Colossians and

others in the family of God in needing to benefit from the same work of reconciliation.

2:13b-15 God's Actions

Paul goes on to outline a doctrine of Christ that expands on what was said in the hymn he quoted earlier (1:15-20). This doctrine is centred in the cross, the place where pardon was won and where the accuser is reduced to silence. Paul describes what happened there in terms of a legal obligation or debt being annulled. There is a legal document, *the written code, with its regulations,* that indicates that we were hopelessly in the wrong with no possibility of setting things right. It is as if we had accumulated a debt we could never possibly repay. This document is our accuser, and we cannot argue with it. We are clearly in the wrong. But when Christ was nailed to the cross, it was as if God was nailing that document to the cross with Christ. He was cancelling our obligation or debt so that we could go free (2:14).

Paul now changes the metaphor from a courtroom to a victory parade. At that time, when a city surrendered to a victorious general, the conquerors would stage a victory parade at which they would display their conquered enemies and all the goods they had plundered. The authorities and powers, and especially the devil, are the defeated enemies dragged along in Christ's parade (2:15).

2:16-23 Freedom in Christ

Paul now moves from theory to practice. How does what he has said about Christ relate to the philosophies and religious arguments he was talking about earlier (2:4, 8). How does it affect daily life? Those who supported the false teaching demanded asceticism and observing of rules. They forbade the eating of certain foods, and insisted that certain festivals and special days such as Sabbath must be observed (2:16). But all such thinking that focuses on controlling the body is useless. Paul points out that all of these past practices in Judaism were only a foreshadowing of the great reality that is Christ himself (2:17). At most, they pointed to the fact that a Messiah would be coming. But the Colossians now enjoy the reality in Christ, and lack nothing. Why should they allow themselves to be bothered by what are mere shadows?

Other religious practices and false doctrines may come from a pagan background. Such doctrines may include a *false humility* and *worship of angels,* that is, of the hierarchy of gods in pagan religions (2:18). Paul denounces the legalism that may lead to perdition and any personal devotions that are based on asceticism, that is, strict control of our human bodies (2:20-23). The believers in Colossae, whether they came from a Jewish or a Gentile background, needed to get rid of these doctrines and practices and to be filled with the knowledge of Christ.

Many African Christians have inherited the legalism of

ANGELS, DEMONS AND POWERS

The ministry of angels plays a prominent role in the life of the church in Africa, and especially in the African Instituted Churches. This should come as no surprise, for the ministry of angels has been prominent in the life of God's people throughout the history of the church. Their ministry is still needed today. But what does the Bible actually teach about angels?

Angels are created spirit beings (Ps 148:2-5; Col 1:16; Heb 1:14) who represent God's presence, glory and power. They deliver God's messages to humans and promote God's purposes in this world. As created beings, they are not themselves divine or independent, but are subordinate to God and derive their power from him. However, they are of a higher order than human beings (Heb 2:7) and are thus more powerful and not subject to the limitations of human flesh. The angelic ranks include beings known as cherubim (Gen 3:24; Exod 26:31; Ezek 26:1) and seraphim (Isa 6:1-2, 6), who are winged creatures that guard the throne of God.

As messengers (which is what the word 'angel' means), angels act to fulfil God's will in the world and may appear to people in human form (Gen 18:2, 16; Ezek 9:2). Sometimes, but not always, we are told their names (for example, Gabriel (Dan 8:16; Luke 1:19) and Michael (Dan 10:13). We need to be very cautious about accepting the claims of those who say they know the names of specific angels who protect Christians.

Angels engage in ceaseless praise and worship of God and Christ (Isa 6:2-3; Rev 4:8, 11; 5:8-10; 19:1-9). They have also played a prominent role in the life of the community of God's people in both the Old and New Testaments and in the events surrounding the incarnation (Luke 1:11,19, 26), death (Luke 22:43), resurrection (Matt 28:2-5), and ascension of Jesus Christ (Acts 1:10). They will also be involved in the events surrounding Christ's return (Matt 16:27).

Angels also protect, provide for and encourage believers and assist in answering their prayers (Dan 9:20-27), giving directions (Acts 8:26; 10:3, 22), escorting believers to heaven (Luke 16: 22) and executing God's judgment on evil people (Gen 19:12-13; Ezek 9:1-11; Matt 13:39-42; Acts 12:23; Rev 8:2-12, 9:1, 11:15, 14:6-9, 15, 17-18; 16:2-17).

Like all other beings, angels possess free will and knowledge (Mark 13:32). And like humans, some angels have used this free will to rebel against God (2 Pet 2:4; Jude 6). Consequently the Bible distinguishes between good and evil angels, depending on whether they serve and obey God. True angels insist that only God is worthy of worship and refuse any worship from humans.

Demons, too, are created spiritual beings, but the Bible does not give us clear teaching on their origins. Some people think demons are the spirits of deceased people. However, it would be more accurate to say that demons can impersonate deceased people by appearing in a form that resembles them. Many people in Africa claim to have received messages from deceased family members, delivered either physically or in a dream. Many such incidents actually involve impersonation by demons.

Some people suggest that demons are the unnatural offspring of angels and women before the flood, but there is too little information in Genesis 6:2 to support this view. Study of Scripture suggests that the demons were originally angels who followed Lucifer in rebellion against God (Isa 14:12-15; Ezek 28:11-19; Matt 25:41; 2 Pet 2:4; Rev 12:7-9).

Whereas angels are holy, demons are evil or unclean spirits (Matt 8:18; Luke 10:17, 20). They are described as localized (Matt 8:28-34; Acts 16:16), intelligent (Matt 8:29; Mark 1:24) and powerful (Matt 15:22; Mark 5:3-4; 9:22; John 10:21). While good angels serve God, demons work for Satan, the chief of demons, against God's plans for his creation. They oppose God and seek to draw worship away from him to themselves. Thus activities like consulting the dead worshipping and sacrificing to idols and ancestors result in contact with demons (Deut 32:17; Rev 9:20). Such worship may, however, produce results, for demons have the power to perform miracles, to mobilize the kings of the world and to fight against God Almighty (Rev 16:13-14). Demons inspire false doctrine and teachings and give worldly wisdom, which is sensual and demonic (Eph 2:2; I Tim 4:1; Jam 3:15).

Demons try to counter the work of Christ by tempting humans to sin and disobey God. They also harass humanity (Matt 12:22-32; Mark 3:22-30; Luke 11:14-23) and seek to destroy people by afflicting them with diseases such as dumbness (Mark 9:17), deafness and dumbness (Mark 9:25), blindness and deafness (Matt 12:22), convulsions (Mark 1:26; 9:20; Luke 9:39); and paralysis or lameness (Acts 8:7). They oppose the spiritual progress of God's people (Eph 6:12). There also seems to be a relationship between mental illness, sickness and demonic activities (Luke 13:11,16).

However, not all diseases can be directly attributed to demonic possession or activities. As a result of the fall and subsequent curse, everything (including creation and believers) groans awaiting fuller redemption at the time of Christ's return (Rom 8:22-23).

The Bible teaches that demonic activities will increase in the last days (I Tim 4:1; Rev 16:13-14). Believers can, however, take comfort in the fact that affliction by Satan or demons can only come as God permits (Job 1:12; 2:6; 2 Cor 12:7-10). Satan and his demonic team have only limited power.

The Bible also speaks of 'powers'. Paul seems to use this word for several different kinds of powers. Sometimes, he means no more than human authorities (Rom 13:1-3; Tit 3:1).

At other times, however, he is speaking of an angelic hierarchy of thrones, powers, rulers and authorities. These powers are subordinate to God and are not to be worshipped (Col 1:15-16; 1 Pet 3:22). Paul also seems to speak of another group of demonic powers: what he calls principalities, powers, 'rulers of the darkness of this age' and 'spiritual hosts of wickedness in the heavenly places' (Eph. 6:12, NKJV). Unlike the demons who often possess individuals and work against humans in general, these powers wrestle with Christians in their service and prayers to God. However, these powers, too, are subject to the lordship of Jesus Christ because he created them (Eph 1:20-22; Col 2:10; Heb 1:4-14). Thus they are not eternal as God is. They are finite and do not know all things, they are not omnipresent and so cannot be in two places at the same time, and they do not multiply or increase in number.

What are the theological implications for the believer of what has been said? First of all, we need to remember that angels, demons and powers are all created beings (Col 1:15-16). Thus they are not to be worshipped. Only God and the Lord Jesus Christ deserve our worship. Scripture forbids us to worship or put our trust in any other spirituals beings – including ancestral spirits – or the spiritual forces of witchcraft or demonic powers channelled through charms, amulets and the like (Col 2:18-19).

While Satan is active in the world through his agents, African Christians need to remember that witchcraft, sorcery and all forms of demonic activities have been conquered and rendered powerless by Christ through his death and resurrection. Satan and all his demonic forces have been defeated and therefore, they cannot exercise any power over believers and the church of Christ (Col 2:15). Thus believers need not fear them. Nevertheless, because we know of their existence and their desire to harm us, we should not get involved with things and activities that would lay us open to their power. Instead we should oppose them.

How are we to oppose them? Not with human weapons, for they are useless in a spiritual war (2 Cor 10:3-6). We need spiritual weapons and armour if we are to overcome Satan's schemes and tricks (Eph 6:10-18). Protected by this armour, we can defeat demons, witchcraft, charms and all other devices and schemes the devil will use against us. We can wield 'the sword of the Spirit, which is the word of God' and claim the protection of the blood of Christ (Col 2:15; 1 John 3:8; Rev 12:11). Even more, we have at our disposal a myriad of angels to fight for us and to protect us from the wiles and schemes of the evil one. As we confront demonic powers in our Christian pilgrimage, we should face them as victors, for Christ has won the victory over them through his blood.

James Nkansah-Obrempong

the old religions in Africa, which banned many things and imposed numerous restrictions. Tragically, they often still submit to these prohibitions, which have no biblical basis. Such Christians are deprived of the liberty that Jesus gives to those who follow him.

3:1-4:1 Living in Christ

3:1-17 Personal and Communal Holiness

Paul has been speaking of the fullness of Christ, his supremacy and sovereignty, and also on reconciliation and hope and the life Christ offers. He has also issued strong warnings against heresies. But now he turns to deal with the practical matter of how men and women who have been reconciled with God should live.

3:1-4 Focus on the heavenly city

Paul's first recommendation for practical Christian living is to set your hearts on things above (3:1). Other translations bring out what this expression means when they translate it as 'seek' (KJV) and as 'keep seeking' (NASB). It involves making a determined effort to keep one's focus on the things of God and the heavenly realities revealed in Christ rather than on the things that seem important in worldly life (3:2-3). After all, the Christians no longer belong to this world because they have died to it and have been raised with Christ, when they rose from the waters of baptism (see comments on 2:12).

Paul is saying that thinking about the realm of Christ will affect how we live in this present world. But he also speaks of the time to come, when Christ, who is currently seated at the right hand of God (3:1) will reappear, The Colossians should be preparing themselves for the full revelation of Christ's glory, in which they will share (3:4). These realities are not visible because they are spiritual, but they are sure and long lasting. They will last right until we enter the celestial city, which is the object of our Christian hope.

3:5-11 Put your earthly nature to death

The 'therefore' in Paul's second recommendation, Put to death, therefore, whatever belongs to your earthly nature (3:5) indicates the strong connection between this recommendation and what has preceded it. It is as if he is saying, 'Since you have already died and been raised with Christ, it shouldn't be impossible for you to kill off what your earthly nature prompts you to do'. The Colossians are called to make a special effort to once for all rid themselves of what belongs to the world. They are to break free from the tyranny of the flesh and the demands it makes of the body.

To help them identify what types of things belong to the earthly nature, Paul makes two lists, each of five sins. The first list starts off with the most scandalous sexual sins, immorality, impurity, lust, evil desires, but surprises us by ending with and greed, which is idolatry (3:5). Greed is a subtle sin, which we tend to overlook, but Paul emphasizes that the obsessive love of material things, and especially of money, is equivalent to idolatry.

Then as now, many sins are rooted in the desire for sex and money. Such sins, Paul says, are typical of *the life you once lived* (**3:7**) and provoke God's wrath. People who indulge in such sins do not know Christ and are simply going their own way.

The second list of five sins focuses on those that damage human relationships: *anger, rage, malice, slander and filthy language* (**3:8**). These sins all involve the tongue. Intemperate words can destroy what is precious. Verbal assaults on human dignity treat individuals and their neighbours as if they were animals. Paul stresses that all these sins, and lying, which gets a separate mention, are associated with the *old self* (**3:9**). That self should be eliminated as part of their spiritual circumcision (2:11) and they should put on the *new self*, which is shaped by their knowledge of the one who created it (**3:10**).

As they work to rid themselves of their earthly nature, the Colossians will recover the image of the Creator in themselves, as it was when humans were first created (Gen 1:26). That image was stained and distorted by sin, but now it is being restored in Christ. The person in whom this image is restored is capable of overcoming the racial, religious and social barriers that separate Greek from Jew, circumcised from uncircumcised, foreigner from locals, and slave from free (**3:11**). Paul's contemporaries would have considered the Scythians as culturally backward natives. But in Christ, they are all equally members of the Christian community. This text is highly relevant in Africa, where ethnic tensions still persist, even among Christians.

3:12-14 Clothe yourself in virtues

Paul's third word of advice is addressed to the Colossians as *God's chosen people, holy and dearly loved* (**3:12a**). It is as if he is reminding them that they are capable of demonstrating the qualities that characterize the children of God: *compassion, kindness, humility, gentleness and patience* (**3:12b**). By compassion, he means feeling love in our innermost being. What a contrast between this list and the lists of sins he has just given!

In telling them to *clothe themselves* with these virtues, he is using the metaphor of getting dressed. Earlier, he told them that they had *taken off the old self* (3:9) and now they are to put on their new self. In other words, he is saying 'If you don't remove your spiritual clothes that are stained by sin and that identify you as enemies of God and other people, you will not be able to wear the beautiful clothes that characterize Christians.'

These Christian virtues will restore human relationships. But they can only be shown if we are willing to forgive each other when we fail. Such forgiveness may sometimes seem impossible, until we remember our own experience of the Lord's forgiveness (**3:13**). Paul again stresses that God's chosen people need to work at showing love for one another (**3:14**).

3:15-17 Build one another up and be grateful

Paul establishes a close link between forgiveness, love and peace. Forgiveness and love produce peace, and peace leads to good work that pleases God (**3:15a**). Love is expressed by building one another up by the *word of Christ*, that is the gospel (**3:16a**). Paul insists on the importance of the word since no spiritual growth is possible without it. The Colossians, taught and warned by Paul through the word (1:5, 25, 28), must in turn teach and warn one other. It is in this way that they will reach full knowledge (1:9).

Paul also encourages the Colossians to give thanks to God (**3:15b**). It is not the first time that he encourages them to do this because God has done so much for them (see 1:12), but it is the first time that he asks them to do it in song (**3:16b**). He mentions three types of songs: *psalms*, which the Jews had long sung to glorify God; *hymns*, which were songs composed by early Christians and used in their liturgy; and finally, *spiritual songs*. It is not clear what exactly these 'spiritual songs' were. Some think that Paul is speaking of singing in tongues, just as some pray in tongues. Others regard these songs as being like the choruses we sing in church today. What is important is that the grateful singing comes from our hearts. The Christian life should be characterized by gratefulness and thanksgiving expressed through what is done and said (**3:17**).

3:18-4:1 Holiness in the Family

After having dealt with holiness in the family of God, meaning the church, Paul deals with holiness in the Christian family, the household. In the context of this letter, the family is thought of as consisting of a father, mother, children and servants. This structure is similar to that of our families in Africa today. The advice to each group is brief and more concise than that given in Ephesians 5:21-6:9, possibly because, as suggested in the introduction, that letter would also have been shared with the church in Colossae.

Paul begins with the wife because she is the heart of the home. The Colossians would agree with our African belief that a home without a wife is only half a home. In the family structure, she is advised to be submissive because, without the submission of the wife to her husband, family life becomes unbearable. It is no longer clear who is leading, the husband or the wife, the parents or the children. An African proverb correctly states, 'the animal who has no head does not walk.' A family without a head has no life.

Unfortunately, the biblical concept of submission is misunderstood in some societies. Many women have to endure the tyrannical control of their husbands and their dignity as human beings created in the image of God is scorned. The submission of the wife, according to the Bible, is a willingness to recognize the authority of the husband. He is number one in the family. Wives should be reassured that their submission is that of believers *as is fitting in the Lord*

(3:18). They have no need to look to either modern or traditional society for guidance.

To husbands, Paul gives two commands: *love … and do not be harsh* (3:19). In exercising their authority as head of the family, husbands may fail to show love for their wives and this can lead to bitterness and push their wives into passivity or despair.

Children are told to obey their parents (3:20), which in the NT means to listen attentively and put into practice what they teach. This obedience should extend to every area of their lives, as long as they are children. Obedience is a command of the Lord (Exod 20:12) and, in obeying their parents, the children are pleasing the Lord.

Next Paul addresses fathers (3:21). Some versions of the Bible choose to translate this word as 'parents', so that Paul's words are directed to both the father and the mother. However, that translation is not justified because the original Greek specifically refers to fathers. Men, as husbands, have responsibilities towards their wives. As fathers, they also have responsibilities towards their children. Once again, it is a matter of authority. If they exercise their authority badly, fathers may push their children into discouragement. The role of parents, and especially of the father, should be to provide training. When the father corrects his children, his goal should be to train them more than to punish them.

Paul also speaks to servants because they are an integral part of the family. The word he uses is often translated as 'slaves', but in the context of this letter, the word 'servant' fits better. These servants were the men and women who served their masters at home or in the fields. In the pagan world, they had very limited freedom and could own nothing themselves. But Paul's advice to them makes it clear that he does not see them as a lesser type of human being. They are as fully human as all the other members of the family.

The advice given to servants is the longest, possibly because it is a delicate matter. Paul reminds them that they serve two sets of masters: their human masters, whom they serve here on earth for a limited time, and the Lord, whom they will serve through eternity. He advises them to serve their human employers with *reverence for the Lord* rather than just to win their favour (3:22). If servants only think about how they will account for their behaviour to their employers here on earth, they may become hypocritical and serve only when they are being watched. But their attitude will be very different if they are aware that they will have to give account of their behaviour to the Lord. Then their sense of responsibility will lead them to serve with all their heart (3:23). God himself will reward their service. They, too, will share the heavenly inheritance. (3:24). Paul's words make it clear that servants have the same hope as all other believers in Christ, since in him the distinctions between human groups fall away (3:11).

But what about unjust employers who exploit their servants? Such employers, too, will have to face Jesus Christ, their own true master, and he will ensure that justice is done (3:25). Servants will be rewarded for faithful service, but all wrongdoing by both masters and servants will also be paid for. Whatever their social class, all are equal before the justice of God.

Finally, Paul returns again to men. What heavy responsibilities they bear as husbands, fathers and employers. His advice is simple: employers are to exercise authority over their employees in accordance with *what is right and fair;* that is, according to the laws that govern their relationship, provided such laws do not conflict with the law of the Lord (4:1). Christian employers should even go beyond the mere legal requirements because if their eyes are set on things above, they will be aware that they will have to justify how they have treated their employees before the Lord, the master over all masters.

Paul was not a political militant attacking the social structure of his time. Rather, in his advice he was trying to address the social problems that arise because of human weaknesses and manifest themselves in abuse of power, tyranny and dictatorship. By assigning each member of the household a place and reminding them of their responsibilities to each other, Paul was revealing the essential harmony that should characterize a Christian family. This harmony could form the basis for an alternative society.

4:2-18 Conclusion

Paul often closes his letters with snippets of advice. In this letter, he speaks specifically of the importance of prayer and thanksgiving in the life of the Colossians so that the gospel may be proclaimed everywhere (4:2-3). The chains in which he finds himself have done nothing to diminish his great desire to proclaim the *mystery of Christ.* What a paradox! Could imprisonment offer still more opportunities for evangelism?

His encouragement to the Colossians *to be wise in the way you act towards outsiders* is also given with a view to their proclaiming the gospel, both in word and by the way they live (4:5-6).

Finally, Paul talks about his co-workers. His comments reveal that he saw himself as part of a team, and that he knew each one of the members of his team well. Tychicus, like Epaphras, is *a faithful minister and fellow-servant* (4:7). He does the same work as Epaphras, for he too is a messenger (1:7). Paul goes out of his way to mention how deeply Epaphras, whom the Colossians knew well, cares for and works for them and the other believers in their region (4:12-13).

Paul mentions that his co-workers are of different nationalities. Mark, Barnabas and Justus seem to have been the only Jews who were working closely with him at this time.

Aristarchus, Epaphras, Luke and Demas, whom he also mentions, are all Gentiles (4:12, 14). Gradually, Paul will be drawn to working more and more with non-Jews (Gentiles) who have come into the faith. The church is already beginning to assume its universal character.

Paul encourages fellowship between the community of believers in Rome and those in Colossae and the surrounding cities. He does this by passing on news and greetings from those who are in Rome or who are passing through Rome (4:10-14) and by asking news and sending specific greetings to believers in Colossae and Laodicea (**4:16-17**).

Paul's closing words are *Remember my chains* (**4:18b**). He has already mentioned his imprisonment in 4:3. His goal is not to warn them against ending up in the same position, but to remind them that he is in need of their prayers – prayers not for deliverance but for his ability to continue of proclaiming 'the word of God in its fullness' (1:25).

Solomon Andria

Further Reading

Hendriksen, William. *Exposition of Galatians, Ephesians, Philippians, Colossians, and Philemon*. Grand Rapids: Baker Book House, 2002.

O'Brien, Peter T. *Colossians, Philemon*. WBC. Waco, Tex: Word, 1982.

Wright N.T. *The Epistles of Paul to the Colossians and to Philemon*. TNT. Leicester Inter-Varsity Press / Grand Rapids; Eerdmans, 1986.

1 THESSALONIANS

1 Thessalonians seems to be the first of Paul's letters and was probably written from Corinth sometime between 49 and 54 AD. It is addressed to the new believers in the city of Thessalonica. Despite the fact that Paul and his companions had spent less than a month there (Acts 17:1-9), a flourishing church had been born. But these believers were suffering persecution and so he wrote this intimate letter to give them comfort and instruction. He commends them for standing firm and for their testimony, and encourages them to continue, sustained by the hope of Christ's return.

Outline of Contents

COMMENTARY

1:1 Greetings

The letter starts with the names of those sending it: *Paul, Silas and Timothy* (**1:1a**). As a leader, Paul knew how important it is to encourage team spirit. African proverbs remind us that one cannot catch a flea or beat a drum with just one finger. Everyone needs to be involved in the drumming that will proclaim the message of Jesus Christ.

The letter is addressed to *the church of the Thessalonians* (**1:1b**), that is, to the people in the city of Thessalonica who have accepted the offer of salvation from God by believing in Jesus Christ, the Saviour and Lord of the world.

The greeting *grace and peace* (**1:1c**) is a standard formula, much as *shalom* is today. But for Paul these words have additional theological meaning. All human beings are sinners who deserve only death, but God has graciously reached out to us, sending his divine son to take the condemnation we deserve (Rom 5:15-19). Everyone who accepts salvation through Jesus Christ is graciously declared righteous by God. Is it any wonder that Paul wants the Thessalonians to continue to experience that grace?

The grace of God reconciles people to him, and this reconciliation re-establishes peace between God and the person saved by Christ (Rom 5:11). Thus grace and peace belong together.

1:2-20 Prayer and Thanksgiving

Paul thanks God for three Christian virtues that can be seen in the Thessalonians (**1:2**): faith, love and hope (**1:3**; see also Rom 5:2-4). These virtues are proof of their spiritual maturity.

The power of the Spirit should be as obvious in the life of those who have been reborn as it was in the lives of the believers in Thessalonica. They had experienced the authority that the Holy Spirit confers on the spoken word when they came to conversion (**1:4-5**). Their Spirit-given joy in the gospel message enabled them to endure persecution, following the example of Paul and of the Lord Jesus (**1:6**). They had become models to all believers in their country and beyond (**1:7-8**).

The Thessalonian believers had clearly experienced a complete conversion, for they had abandoned their pagan idols and gods, whose worship was a work of the flesh, and had turned to serve *the living and true God* who was powerfully at work among them (**1:9**; see also Gal 5:19-20).

Today, many so-called Christians have not had such a conversion experience. They continue to practise idolatry and to trust in things like fetishes, money, wealth and spirits. They discreetly consult diviners and astrologists. They practise magic. Can such people really be said to be disciples of Jesus Christ? Christians have no need to keep turning to idols. The Jesus whom every believer has received has given every one of us the Spirit of power (2 Tim 1:7).

The conversion of the Thessalonians meant that they were waiting for the return of Jesus, the Resurrected One who delivers us from *the coming wrath* of God. He rescues us by dying on the cross as a reparation or guilt offering, so that we can be justified (**1:10**).

Many of those in our churches need to be encouraged to make a clean break with syncretism in which they mix pagan and Christian beliefs. Too many of them think that being often with Christians is enough to make them children of God. But the West African proverb reminds us, 'A stick in the swamp will never become a crocodile'. A genuine conversion is necessary to make the radical life change that transforms Christians into those who wait with confidence for the glorious return of Jesus Christ.

2:1-12 Paul's Ministry at Thessalonica

Paul reminds the Thessalonians that before he visited them, his party had been persecuted at Philippi (Acts 16:19-40). That experience had not made them too afraid to preach in Thessalonica, even though they were attacked there too (2:2; Acts 17:1-9). They were motivated by their conviction that what they were proclaiming was the truth (2:3). God had given them the task of proclaiming the gospel, and they were working to please him, not other people (2:4, 6). Consequently, he had blessed their preaching with success (2:1). Paul does not dwell on the difficulties they encountered in Thessalonica because such problems were not unusual. The Lord himself had suffered persecution during his earthly ministry and had told his disciples to expect it (John 15:20).

During that visit, Paul and his companions had demonstrated their faith by their behaviour (2:5). They had worked very hard so that they could meet their own needs and be able to help others (2:9; see also Eph 4:28). In our context of poverty and high unemployment, becoming a pastor may be seen as just another way to earn a living. Such thinking is completely wrong and endangers the church. Our motive for preaching should not be financial! We are called to serve God unselfishly and to rely on him to provide for our needs. In some cases, he does this by giving us the ability to work with our own hands. We can then support ourselves while still carrying out the work to which God has called us.

Paul's team were concerned that their own behaviour should not give rise to complaints or be an obstacle to anyone hearing the gospel (2:10). Preachers must be models in word and in conduct (1 Tim 4:12). 'Do what I say, not what I do' has no place in this vocation. We serve a holy and just God, and our lives, and the lives of all Christians, must reflect this fact. God has justified us and is busy sanctifying us through the ongoing work of the Holy Spirit.

But God is not only holy; he is also loving. Our lives must reflect that truth as well. Paul's love for the Thessalonians was as tender as that of a mother for her young children (2:7-8) and as deep as that of father who encourages, comforts and challenges his children (2:11).

Paul comforted the new Christians when they faced trials and challenged them to live lives that conform to the teachings of the word of God (2:12). They can follow the example he and his team have set. The Thessalonians are already participating in God's glory and are already citizens of his kingdom, but God is also calling them to live as citizens of the full kingdom that is coming in the future.

2:13-16 Paul's Testimony Regarding the Church

Paul thanks God that his team's hard work was not in vain, for the Thessalonians had welcomed the message preached as being the word of God (2:12). They were also showing its fruit so well that they were becoming a model to others (1:7). The Bible repeatedly stresses that it is not enough just to hear the word; it has to be accepted by faith (Mark 4:3-20). The word sown in Thessalonica fell on good soil.

Paul moves from thanksgiving to criticism of those who opposed the Gospel. He compares the suffering of the Thessalonians to that of the churches in Judea (2:14). The Jews were persecuting Christians and opposing the preaching of the gospel to the Gentiles. They were thus acting as enemies of God and of his people. Paul accuses them of five specific errors: a) killing Jesus and the prophets (Acts 2:36), b) persecuting Paul and his teammates, c) displeasing God, d) being enemies of the people, and e) hindering evangelism (2:15-16). He puts the crime against Jesus first in this list to emphasize its importance. What these Christian missionaries were enduring was like the treatment endured by Jewish prophets in the past. But persecution did not and does not stop God's work. In fact, the persecution of this young church was proof of the authenticity of their faith. What they were enduring was no different from what the very first Christians in Judea endured.

Many new Christians endure persecution when they abandon ancestral traditional practices. The persecution is particularly strong in Muslim areas. Some have even become martyrs for their faith.

2:17-20 Paul's Desire

Although Paul cannot be with the Thessalonians physically, his thoughts are always with them (2:17). He has been attempting to come to see them again, but Satan has thwarted his plans (2:18). The devil always puts obstacles in the way of the progress of the kingdom of God on earth and tries to hamper the good works of God's servants. Mission work is not always easy. There are constant challenges. But God wants us to share in the task of accomplishing his work, and so we must joyfully persist in it.

Part of Paul's joy is that he knows that he and all other believers are freed from the guilt of their sin and justified in Christ Jesus. So they can look forward to Christ's second coming, when he will reward them for what they have done for him. The reward, or crown, that Paul most looks forward to is seeing those he has led to salvation celebrating the Lord's return with him (2:19). What an incentive to keep working in order to attain the glory that is to come (Phil 3:12-14; 1 Tim 6:12)!

3:1-13 Paul's Pastoral Concern

Unable to visit the Thessalonian believers himself, Paul decided to send Timothy to them to strengthen them (**3:1-2**). The forced departure of the missionaries and the opposition that the young church was facing must have tested their faith, even though they had been warned that such tests would come as part of the Christian life (**3:3-4**).

Paul had, however, feared that the tempter might have been able to take advantage of these adversities to destroy the faith of the Thessalonians (**3:5**). But Timothy's report about the Thessalonian believers has set his heart at rest (**3:6**). The report that their faith is solid and that they are growing in maturity is a great encouragement (**3:7-8**). It moves him to praise God for them and to pray that God will continue to strengthen their faith. *What is lacking* in their faith will be supplied when they meet Paul face to face and are encouraged by his presence and his teaching (**3:9-10**).

Discipling must follow evangelism. It involves teaching new converts about their new life as children of God and training them to live as disciples prepared for the coming of the Lord. As a pastor, Paul is deeply concerned to provide such training, and that is why he attaches such importance to Timothy's visit to Thessalonica. Leaders in the church in Africa should learn from his example. The church here is full of new and recently baptized believers, but too often leaders do not take the time to train them so that they become unwavering disciples of Jesus Christ.

Paul's love for the Thessalonians and his desire to see them is clear from his prayer in **3:11-12**. He also prays that they will continue to grow stronger in the faith, so that they will be blameless at the return of the Lord (**3:13**).

4:1-12 Christian Conduct

Paul next gives some guidelines on how they can develop the blameless lives he has prayed for.

4:1-2 Focus on Pleasing God

Paul emphasizes the importance of what he is about to say by using two verbs, as he both *asks* and *urges* them to live godly lives (**4:1**). The desire to live in a way that pleases God should be the primary driving force in every Christian's life. We should be more concerned about having God's approval than about having other people's approval. Many may have this attitude immediately after conversion, but then it fades. This should not be the case. Our desire to please God should be constant and growing, both as regards the quality and quantity of our service.

Paul reminds them that the instructions he gave them came from the Lord and not from himself (**4:2**).

4:3-8 Live a Holy Life

The Thessalonians' religious background included certain heathen practices that were dishonouring to the body because of the sexual debauchery involved. Paul condemns these heathen practices and stresses that immorality is contrary to the very nature of Christians. God is holy and those who belong to him should be holy too (**4:4**; 1 Pet 1:15). Consequently they should learn to control their bodies so as to be morally pure in the area of sex (**4:5-6**). The unmarried should not seek to have sex, and the married should respect and not abuse their spouse's body. As the temple of the Holy Spirit and members of the body of Christ (1 Cor 6:15, 19), Christians must be holy in spirit and in body (1 Cor 7:34).

Christians should never be guilty of the greed and injustice that leads people to take advantage of others (**4:6**). We are called to be faithful even in small areas, and especially in matters relating to money (Luke 16:9-13). Thus submission to God's will also demands discipline in business matters. God condemns the exploitation of others and will not leave such behaviour unpunished.

Throughout the Bible, the holy God calls on his people to be holy (**4:7**; Exod 19:5-6). That was why he gave the Israelites the law in the ot. If he was to be present among them, they would have to maintain a high degree of holiness and moral purity. This principle of being set apart for God is also stressed in the nt (2 Cor 6:17).

The word *therefore* underscores that **4:8** contains the conclusion of Paul's argument. If God is the one who calls us to be holy, then to reject what Paul has said about holy living is to reject God himself, who has given us his Spirit as the agent of sanctification. The Holy Spirit makes the word of God effective in the life of believers as he teaches and leads them into truth. He is the one who sanctifies them and causes them to bear fruit (2 Thess 2:13; Gal 5:22-23; 1 Pet 1:2).

4:9-12 Love and Care for Your Fellow-Christians

The subject of love for fellow-Christians has already been touched on (1:3; 3:12) and Paul knows that the Thessalonians already show this love to all the believers in Macedonia (**4:9-10**). So all he does is to urge them to love more and more. Love for fellow-Christians should be reciprocal, unconditional and without discrimination. Like all fruit of the Spirit, it should be constantly growing and maturing.

Finally, Paul mentions three other characteristics of a Christian lifestyle: living a peaceful life, avoiding interfering in the lives of others, and taking responsibility for meeting one's own needs. These qualities are linked, for when one's life is peaceful one can more easily take the initiative to achieve independence. No one should be a burden to others.

FUNERAL AND BURIAL RITES

Death is an ever-present reality. Each culture must respond to it in a way that enables the survivors to recover from the trauma of loss and live in hope.

An African funeral is a very social event. A private funeral would be an anomaly. Support comes from neighbours, workmates and church associates, as well as relatives. The funeral of a Christian can often be a reunion of long-separated believers. Christian funeral gatherings also involve much singing of Christian hymns and choruses, often including Psalm 23. Other rituals may include the suspension of ablutions for the close relatives, especially the women, and the shaving of heads to express respect for the deceased.

The modern urban funeral gathering, though emotionally comforting, can nevertheless, be financially burdensome to the bereaved family. They have to feed the mourners and purchase a burial plot and a coffin that sufficiently honours the deceased. Relatives from rural areas may borrow money to travel to the funeral, and the urban relatives will then be expected to finance their return trip and their debt. Consequently funerals are becoming a painful economic burden for many as deaths increase. Fortunately, African solidarity means many people make contributions that lighten this burden, as one is reminded in almost every single graveside speech from a bereaved family.

African funerals are also characterized by overt and communal expressions of emotions. There is no sense of apology for wailing and acting out one's grief. Only the most extreme expressions of grief, which might injure the mourner, would be restrained. Sometimes the less emotional even feel pressure to express more emotion lest their love for the deceased be doubted.

Sometimes misinformed Christians try to forbid other Christians from crying, forgetting that the Bible does not deny the emotions of grief. Joseph, a man of faith, 'threw himself upon his father and wept over him and kissed him' when he died (Gen 50:1). People are often presented as weeping or even wailing aloud (see Mark 5:38; Luke 8:52; Acts 9:39). Nowhere is such wailing condemned. Excesses are certainly frowned upon, but the expression of sorrow is expected.

Unlike unbelievers, Christians mourn with a hope rooted in the resurrection of Jesus Christ (1 Thess 4:13-18). His resurrection assures Christians of a future resurrection of the body to eternal life. Thus while friends and relatives may mourn the person's absence, the dead Christian can rightly be described as sleeping.

Traditionally, burial is taken for granted as the method of disposing of the remains of the dead. Cremations tend to be associated with the Hindu religion, though there are no biblical grounds for asserting that believers should not be cremated. In general, the funeral takes place as soon as the relatives can gather to finalize arrangements, which in rural areas will be on the day of death or the following day. It is important that the relatives participate physically in burying the dead, although often their participation is ritualized.

Some of the rituals associated with burial reflect a fear of the deceased. Thus in Zambia the body must be buried with the head pointing in the right direction to prevent the deceased from returning to haunt the living. The burial may be followed by other rituals designed to protect the living, such as passing through the funeral house and washing in medicated water before dispersing. Many tribes have an inheritance ceremony where the name and status of the deceased are passed on to some chosen relative. Ritual protection of the widow or widower is common, with the widow sometimes being inherited by a relative of the dead husband. The ritual cleansing may even require the surviving spouse to have intercourse with a relative of the deceased in order to protect himself or herself from the spirit of the deceased coming to seek sexual union, which is believed to be both possible and dangerous. The cleansing ritual is also a way of releasing the surviving partner so that he or she may safely enter new sexual relations with the blessing of the family of the dead relative. Because of the spiritual and psychological power of such rituals, Christians should not simply ban them, but should thoughtfully and sensitively replace them with alternative rituals that will meet the spiritual and psychological needs of the fearful widow or widower.

Most of what the Bible says about mourning and burial describes what was done in a particular culture, rather than prescribing what is to be done. In the OT, decent burial was deemed a blessing and its absence a sign of God's judgment. Burial was also the standard way of disposing of the dead. The only exceptions were when the death occurred in a foreign place where burial was preceded by preservation of the body. Thus the bodies of Jacob and Joseph were embalmed and transported to Israel for burial (Gen 49:29-50:14; 50:24-26). The only incidents of burning described can hardly be termed cremations in the way we understand the term. The burning of the bodies of Saul and his three sons (1 Sam 31:11-12) involved the rescue and disposal of mutilated and decomposing bodies in the context of a military conflict.

In the OT, the preferred place for burial was a designated family burial place. Thus we see Abraham making provision for a burial site (Gen 23:4; 24:9-10) and Jacob leaving instructions for his burial (Gen 50:29-33). But this tradition was neither continued nor encouraged in the NT. The Lord Jesus Christ was buried in another man's tomb (Matt 27:57-61). Many of his disciples died at the 'ends of the earth', where they had gone in obedience to his command (Matt 28:19; Acts 1:8). The most that can be asked of Christian believers is that death should be anticipated and preparations should be made in advance.

Joe Simfukwe

Everyone should be involved in productive work, for as a proverb says, 'the one who does not plant peanuts will be holding out his hand at harvest time'.

4:13-18 The Resurrection

The young Thessalonian Christians were concerned about the fate of some of their fellow-believers who had died. So Paul addresses the issue of those *who fall asleep* (**4:13**). He uses this euphemism because the new life in Christ is eternal. Those who believe in him do not truly die (see John 11:11-14). These believers from Gentile backgrounds, like many African Christians today, were puzzled about how the Christian teaching related to their traditional beliefs about life after death.

In many African cultures, those who have died recently are considered the living-dead. They are still part of the family, and watch over its life, fertility, prosperity and security. If they are not reincarnated, they will eventually become supernatural spirits, ancestors who are close to the Supreme Being. Thought of in these terms, physical death is a promotion because it means passing from an inferior to a superior level of life.

In what way is Christian hope different and superior?

Paul reaffirms that the real Christian hope is based on the return of Jesus Christ. Christians already possess salvation, but one day they will enjoy its benefits forever in Jesus' presence. Those who die before this grand finale brings great happiness are sleeping, and they will awaken on resurrection day. African traditional religions offer no such hope of resurrection.

The great confession of faith in **4:14,** *We believe that Christ died and rose again and so we believe that God will bring with Jesus those who have fallen asleep in him,* asserts that the death and resurrection of Jesus Christ are undeniable historical realities. These realities, and what God accomplished in them, guarantee our own future resurrection and the resurrection of those who have died before Christ returns. After his resurrection, Jesus was exalted to heaven, where he sits at the right hand of the Father. But he has promised that he will return (Acts 1:9-11). When the time comes and the trumpet sounds to signal that triumphant return, the dead in Christ will be the first to experience it as they *will rise first* and then those *who are still alive and left will be caught up together with them* to meet the Lord (**4:15-17**). All Christians, living and dead, will share the same destiny as they rejoice in the presence of the Lord.

The certainty that we will one day be with the Lord for ever is the ultimate Christian hope and a source of comfort (**4:18**). When a believer dies, we are sad (1 Cor 12:26), but we are sustained by the hope of the resurrection of the dead and by the knowledge that we will meet with the deceased on the last day.

5:1-11 The Day of the Lord

After what Paul has just said, the new believers will want to know when Jesus will return in glory (**5:1**), so Paul reminds them that *the day of the Lord will come like a thief in the night* (**5:2**; see also Matt 24:43-44). In the OT, 'the day of the Lord' is the day on which God will manifest his power. Paul regards that day as synonymous with the day of Jesus' glorious return. It will be the day on which terrified unbelievers will suddenly confront their final ruin.

It is impossible to know when a thief will strike, and in the same way it is impossible to know exactly when that day will come. It will come as inevitably as labour pains will come to a pregnant woman (**5:3**), but just as she cannot predict when those pains will start, so we cannot tell exactly when the day of God's judgment come.

Evil and thieves appropriately choose to work in the darkness of the night when others are sleeping or drinking (**5:6-7**). However, the children of God are *sons of light and sons of the day* (**5:4-5**), so they should not be found sleeping or drunk when that day comes. Instead they should be in full control of themselves, spiritually vigilant and standing ready dressed in 'the armour of light' (**5:8**; Rom 13:12; see also Eph 6:10-17). The breastplate and helmet they wear are designed to defend vital parts of the human body. Faith and love are like a breastplate in that they guarantee life (John 3:16; Rom 10:9). This armour reassures Christians that they are children of God and guarantees their safety (Rom 8:31-40). Hope protects like a helmet by making them certain of their ultimate salvation when Christ will gather his people and will judge the 'man of lawlessness' (2 Thess 2:3-8). Because they are justified in Christ, believers have no need to fear destruction and the future wrath of God (**5:9-10**). They know they will live in him. Until that day comes, Christians should live with and for God (Col 3:23-24). They should help each other to do this by encouraging one another and building each other up – two verbs that mean much the same thing, but are both used to emphasize how important this support for each other is.

5:12-22 Community Life

As part of building each other up, Christians have responsibilities to their local church. They must support their leaders by acknowledging them, respecting them and loving them (**5:12-13**). Their leaders deserve this support not because of their personal achievements but because of the spiritual function that they exercise in the Lord.

Respect cannot be compelled, just as one cannot force a snail to climb a tree, and that is why Paul asks the Christians to create a climate of goodwill by working together. Such joint work will create a climate of peace.

Paul next gives recommendations about how Christians can work together and help one another (**5:14-15**).

His vision for the church is that it will always be a joyful community, with a life of prayer nourished by thanksgiving (**5:16-17**; see also Phil 3:1; 4:4-5) and by meditation on the word under the direction of the Holy Spirit (**5:19-22**). In **5:16-22** Paul links joy, prayer, the Spirit and prophecy. A holy life is based on prayer and on communion with the Spirit who helps us to pray properly and according to the will of God. Discernment and wisdom will be the fruit of holy life.

Paul's words remind us of the extraordinary privileges we enjoy as believers, which are the source of our joy, but also of our duties and responsibility to avoid evil and put God's word into practice. These words are particularly applicable to the church today, which has been so much influenced by the world that it now harbours all kinds of evil: corruption, immorality, tribalism, division, selfishness, theft. Moreover there is a lack of deep, dynamic prayer. It is time for the church to return to its primary calling to be *the salt of the earth* and *the light of the world* (Matt 5:13-16).

5:23-28 Conclusion

Paul finishes with a prayer reminding us that when the Lord returns, Christians will meet him as complete human beings, with a body (our material nature), soul and spirit (our immaterial nature). He prays that our whole being may be kept holy and blameless for that day (**5:23-24**). Then he requests that the Thessalonians pray for him (**5:25**). Ministers need to be upheld by the prayers of the church because they are the targets of enemy attacks. But prayer is a powerful weapon against the enemy and breaks through barriers.

Prayer is not Paul's sole focus, however. He also strongly encourages fellowship, and that is why he ends his letter with the instruction to greet one another *with a holy kiss* (**5:26**). Believers should welcome each other as close friends, and not as strangers. The exact form the greeting will take will vary from one culture to another. As part of this same fellowship, Christians will happily share the contents of this letter with other believers (**5:27**).

Paul finally takes leave of his correspondents by committing them to the grace of God (**5:28**).

Rosalie Koudougueret

Further Reading

Bruce, F. F. *1 & 2 Thessalonians*. WBC. Waco: Word, 1982.

Morris, Leon, *The First and Second Epistles to the Thessalonians*. rev. ed. NICOT. Grand Rapids: Eerdmans, 1991.

2 THESSALONIANS

Paul wrote this second letter to the Thessalonians shortly after his first letter to them. There are close links between the two letters and the two should be studied together. The apostle reviews his earlier advice about sanctification and offers some further details about the return of Christ, for questions on this subject continue to bother this church. Paul hopes above all that the believers may live in peace.

Outline of Contents

COMMENTARY

1:1-2 Greetings

Paul's greeting to the church at Thessalonica is almost identical to the greeting he used in his first letter to them (1 Thess 1:1). The fact that the same two people are associated with him as the authors of the letter indicates that healthy collaboration has continued between Paul, Silas and Timothy (**1:1**). There is, however, one small difference between the greetings in the two letters. In this letter Paul specifies that *grace* and *peace* come from *God the Father and the Lord Jesus Christ* (**1:2**). This addition may underline his desire to reorient his readers towards what is essential. This letter is, in effect, a fine-tuning of the theology he taught in his previous letter.

1:3-12 Prayer of Thanksgiving

Paul has already been rejoicing because of the *faith* and *love* of the Thessalonians (1 Thess 1:2-3). He had encouraged them to continue growing in these areas (1 Thess 4:1, 9-10) and now he is rejoicing because his advice has been heard (**1:3**). Stagnation is dangerous for a Christian and progress is healthy (Phil 3:12-14).

Paul's satisfaction is all the greater because he had been concerned about how they would cope when faced with persecution (1 Thess 3:3). Once again, the Thessalonians have held firm (**1:4b**).

The apostle then gives them words of encouragement to persevere in what they have been doing. Following his example, the church should embrace and comfort those who are enduring persecution, both physical and especially psychological. Those who turn to Christianity from traditional religion may experience great loneliness. When they refuse to participate in certain rites and customs that are incompatible with their faith, they are often given the cold shoulder by their families.

The first word of encouragement to those who are persecuted concerns an immediate benefit in the here-and-now: a good reputation and influence among other Christians (**1:4a**).

The second word of encouragement concerns the future. Their sufferings are miserable and unsought, but happily they are also a source of blessing (1 Pet 2:20). They make the Christians *worthy of the kingdom of God* (**1:5**). At his return, Christ will give them *relief*, which means deliverance and true fellowship with God (**1:7**; Gen 2:1-3; Exod 20:10-11; Deut 5:15; Ezek 20:12).

Paul has earlier referred to this future life with the Lord and membership in his kingdom as sources of comfort (1 Thess 2:12; 4:17-18). Here he adds a further detail, which is the third encouragement. At his return, the Lord will severely punish those who have persecuted them (**1:6, 8, 9**). These words bring comfort to those who have witnessed genocide or discrimination or who have been the victims of corruption and wanton destruction in our day. As Christians, we know that vengeance belongs to God and that we have no right to treat our oppressors as they have treated us. But we can have the certainty that even if they escape human justice, God will judge them severely.

The apostle's final word of encouragement to the persecuted believers is the assurance that he and his co-workers are consistently praying that the Lord will keep them steadfast to his calling and sincere in fulfilling their purpose (**1:11**). His prayer is a model for our prayers, as he asks that the name of our Lord Jesus may be glorified in every believer, and that every believer may be glorified in him (**1:12**; see also John 17:22-24).

2:1-12 The Day of the Lord

Now Paul comes to the main point of this letter. He returns to his teaching about the moment of Christ's return (**2:1**; 1 Thess 4:16-5:3). Perhaps an incorrect interpretation of his first letter, as well as a false letter said to be from Paul, had led the Thessalonians to believe that *the day of the Lord has already come* (**2:2**). This belief roused deep concern in the church. The apostle urges the Christians not to be easily upset and alarmed by rumours (2:2; Mark 13:7)

He goes on to explain that before Christ returns, there will be a rise in apostasy, that is, of rebellion and abandoning of the faith, and that someone will appear who can be called *the man of lawlessness* (2:3). This 'man' may be either one particular individual, the one referred to elsewhere as the antichrist, or Paul may be speaking of the attitude of people in general (1 John 2:18, 22; 4:3; 2 John 7). The 'man of lawlessness' will actively fight against the Lord and his activity on earth. He will lead a life without God, and will even seek to be exalted above God by claiming divine rights; for example, the right to rule in the hearts of Christians who are *God's temple* (2:4; 1 Cor 3:16). He may also seek to rule in God's physical temple (see Dan 11:36-45; Mark 13:14; Rev 13:1-15). This man will promote his position by all sorts of miraculous seductions and lies that will lead many people astray (2:9-11).

This lawless one has not yet come. Paul assures the Thessalonians: *you know what is holding him back* and *the one who now holds it back will continue to do so till he is taken out of the way* so that apostasy may become evident (2:6-7). This passage does not clearly say who is the one hindering evil from reaching its peak. It may be a powerful angel of God (Rev 20:1-5, 7-10), or it may be the Holy Spirit, or the church, or the Holy Spirit resident in the church. It can be argued that the presence of the church in the world as salt and light represses lawlessness and darkness. But when the church is raptured, the full effects of crime, violence, rage and the like will be felt (see Matt 5:13-16; 1 Thess 4:13-18). Whoever it is, the purpose of this hindering is to provide time for the proclamation of the gospel. The Lord Jesus encouraged the proclamation of the good news of the kingdom to all nations before the end would come (Matt 24:14; Mark 13:10).

In Africa, people are overwhelmed by pandemics, natural disasters, terrorism, moral depravity and the spread of crime. They may be willing to blindly accept the leadership of anyone who claims to be able to save them. But God wants each person to act responsibly. The relationship between each individual and God should result in love for one's neighbours. The gospel of Jesus Christ does not encourage violence and confrontation but rather economic justice, the equality of men and women, the equality of ethnic groups, tolerance and dialogue (Matt 5:1-7:29; Gal 3:28; Col 3:11). It is thus the most effective way to fight against the many evils in our societies.

We must therefore work to proclaim the Good News while it is day. When the right time comes, Christ will destroy the lawless one (2:8) and will judge all those who were willingly led astray by him (2:12). Believers must be discerning and stay loyal to the truth.

2:13-17 Living in the Truth

The apostle presents a balanced view of salvation. *From the beginning,* God has chosen the Thessalonians (2:13a). However, Paul still encourages them to *stand firm* in *belief in the truth* and in *the sanctifying work of the Spirit,* which are the means of salvation (2:13b-14a, 15).

Faith is a person's response to God's offer of salvation. In his sovereignty, he has decided to save sinners, whatever their origins (Rom 10:13). But God, who knows all things, knows in advance that some people will not be willing to accept his salvation. They choose to live in sin (Rom 3:10-18; 8:5-8; 1 Cor 6:9-11). On the other hand, God saves and sanctifies those who believe in Christ (1 Cor 1:30). This salvation means that we will share *in the glory of our Lord Jesus Christ* (2:14b).

While we await the full realization of this glory, God can work in our lives changing, encouraging, helping us to move forward and strengthening us *in every good deed and word* (2:16-17).

3:1-15 Exhortation to Pray and Work

Within the framework of the strengthening mentioned in 2:17, Paul asks the church to pray for fruit in his proclamation of the gospel and for his protection (3:1-2). Even though Paul and his co-workers are strong and mature, they need the spiritual support of other Christians to overcome difficulties. 'No man is an island', as the saying goes, and we all need the help of others. Prayer helps us face the most difficult challenges (Mark 9:29). As 'water is the strength of the crocodile', so prayer is the source of power for a Christian (James 5:16). Without prayer, spiritual life dries up and weakens – hence the popular pun: Seven days without prayer makes one weak. 'As the deer pants for streams of water', so the servant of God should seek, through prayer, continuous refreshment and divine blessing, the source of strength (Ps 42:1; 89:17).

We should note the principle of reciprocity in prayer. Not only is Paul asking the Thessalonians for prayer, but he himself prays for their strengthening and their protection (3:3; see also 1 Thess 3:11-13). Mutual confidence, love and perseverance are the basis of a healthy and effective prayer partnership (3:4-5).

The apostle then returns to the issue of work. Apparently his earlier advice in 1 Thessalonians 2:9 and 4:11 had not been taken seriously. So he makes his point at greater length. He qualifies idleness as living at someone else's expense and meddling in someone else's affairs (3:6-8a, 12). He points out that he and his companions had set them an example by refusing to live in that way (3:8b-10). The rule he gives is similar to the African proverb, 'The hen eats where she scratches the earth and the sleeping hawk catches no fish.'

CULTURAL ISSUES AND THE BIBLICAL MESSAGE

The Bible is now being read in many different parts of the world, in many different languages and cultures. The cultural background of its readers is inevitably very different from that of the authors of the Bible and of some of those who have interpreted it to us. Thus an understanding of the role of culture is of great importance both in understanding what the Bible says and in communicating this message in terms that are meaningful in relation to local culture and issues in Africa.

Defining 'Culture'

It is wise to start by defining what we mean by culture. Culture is a people's way of life, all the different customs, values and traditions that they have learned from their forebears, family and environment, which together unite all the different aspects of their life into a logical whole. It includes such things as the language or languages spoken, the way politics and the economy are organized, the often unspoken rules governing social and religious behaviour, interpretations of the psychological reasons for actions – in fact, all aspects of life have a cultural dimension. Individuals are both shaped by their culture and contribute to shaping it by their own actions and thoughts. Thus culture is not static, but is always developing.

Because our own culture is so much part of our everyday life, we tend to take it for granted and assume that ours is the 'right' way of doing something. We may then be very puzzled or angered when someone from another culture acts in a way that we consider wrong or rude. We may misinterpret their behaviour because of our cultural orientations and assumptions. For example, Western cultures often use eye contact to show that they are listening to a speaker; in most African cultures, it is assumed that people listen with their ears, and thus looking at the speaker is far less important. In fact, eye contact may be thought to signal aggression rather than politeness. The Bible includes examples of body language like the one just given (for example, when Jesus stooped to write in the sand – John 8:6).

Culture and Language

Cultures differ not only in the way they use body language but also in the languages spoken. The way we use language helps to define the way we see the world. Thus people who come from different language backgrounds may have difficulty understanding the world of other people.

African readers of the Bible have to make a huge jump into a world view that was shaped by the Hebrew and Greek background of the original writers. Moreover, while some Africans have access to a Bible that has been translated into their own language, many African Christians still use English translations. Thus they also have to make a transition to interpreting something in what may be their second, third or even fourth language. And when conservative groups prefer to use the King James Version, readers are also being asked to use a form of English that was spoken four hundred years ago. While many educated Africans are very fluent in English, there can be no doubt that the bulk of the populace, especially those who belong to independent churches or fellowship groups, often struggle with the language. This can lead to misinterpretation of the text. What is considered normal behaviour in one language (for example, Jesus addressing his mother as 'Woman' in John 2:4) may be mistakenly interpreted as rude and aggressive.

These differences in language use can even appear when people from different cultures speak the same language, as anyone knows who has had to deal with the differences between American, British and African versions of the English language. So there may be unanticipated problems when a vernacular translation of the Bible is used with people whose own dialect is slightly different from that used in the translation. In interpreting the text of the Bible, African writers and preachers need to work to achieve a complex sensitivity to what it is the writer is saying and how it will be heard by their readers or congregation who come to it from quite a different perspective.

Culture and the Church

Africa is a continent with many countries and a variety of cultures, so it is impossible to list all the ways in which African culture and communication patterns differ from those of Bible times. What is needed are African scholars who are culturally aware and who are thus in a better position to interpret the Bible in a way that is relevant to Africa. Each interpreter of the Bible needs to seek to know his or her own culture and that of the authors of the Bible as well as possible.

One less obvious cultural problem when seeking insight into how to interpret the Bible is that many of the books we turn to for assistance are written by authors from Western cultures for Western cultures. Western cultural assumptions will inevitably affect their interpretation of the text. For example, Western culture tends to be much more individualistic than African culture, where allegiance to the group, clan or family is crucial. Thus some Western interpreters may focus on applying Scripture to people's individual lives, rather than thinking about how to apply it in the community or in the church family as a whole. They may suggest individual solutions to problems, rather than having the whole church work together to solve a problem.

Similarly, Western time-consciousness and intolerance of ambiguity affect patterns of worship, preaching and church goverment. Western worship services tend to be restricted to one hour and to be fairly rigidly structured. African worship is less time-constrained and less structured. This lack of tolerance of ambiguity may also lead Western believers to try to pin down the exact meaning of what the Bible teaches about topics such as predestination and free will, or the exact chronology of the gospels. Africans can happily live with unresolved ambiguity.

Cultural differences may also be present in the way Christians interpret passages relating to authority. In most Western cultures, the leader is accessible and can be challenged, while most African countries have a hierarchical system where the leader is absolutely on top! In their esteem for age and authority, African cultures may find it easier to understand the world of Jewish culture than people from many modern Western cultures where these values have been eroded.

African cultures are also closer to Jewish culture in the value placed on males. Thus there is commonly more jubilation at the birth of a male child than at that of a female child.

If the word of God is to be seen as universal as well as personal, and not as foreign or as a 'white man's religion', it needs to be presented with a full awareness of relevant cultural differences, both as regards the interpretation of the text and the way in which it is communicated to hearers. Biblical stories need to be told in ways that are adapted to local cultures if they are to be easily understood. There is also a need to distinguish between which elements of the Bible are specific to Jewish culture and which have wider implications. A classic example of this is the issue of the wearing of head coverings in 1 Corinthians 11:4-5.

Because culture is not static but is constantly changing, we need to be attuned to the changes that are taking place around us. Many new factors are influencing the lives of young people in Africa today. Not least of these is their exposure to other cultures through TV and videos. We need to understand their culture too, in order to be able to present the gospel in a way that is relevant to this new generation. Christians are challenged to appropriate the message of the gospel of salvation in such a way that they have a positive influence on the society in which they live

Eunice Okorocha

Paul encourages those who are already working to work hard because work allows us to meet our own needs and to contribute to the development of individuals and of the community. To work is to do *what is right* as God asks of us (**3:13**; Col 3:23). Genesis 3:17 must not be misinterpreted: work is not a curse but a task that God has assigned us.

The Thessalonians are encouraged to keep the *teaching* given by Paul (**3:6**). False teaching leads people away from the right path. For example, many Christians think that 'God helps those who help themselves' is a verse from the Bible. Then they use this 'verse' to justify their reliance on charms and magic.

Laziness is such a serious matter that it necessitates disciplinary action on the part of the church (**3:14**). God's people should be disciplined in order to stop them from misbehaving and to help them to change their behaviour. God's servants should therefore be careful to apply discipline in the church. But they must not do so on a subjective basis. And their purpose must not be to punish or to protect the community. Those who wander from the path should be corrected as brothers, not as enemies, in order to win them back to walking with God (**3:15**; Gal 6:1-2). Administering church discipline in Africa is a delicate matter that must be treated biblically (see, for example, Matt 18:15-17).

3:16-18 Conclusion

As in the conclusion of the first letter (1 Thess 4:23-28), here the apostle emphasizes peace. The word is used twice. The *Lord of peace* is Paul's name for the 'Prince of peace' in Isaiah's messianic reference (Isa 9:6). Jesus assumed this role and passed it on to his followers (John 14:27). Here, Paul lays a basis of assurance that he hopes will develop in the Thessalonians *at all times and in every way* (**3:16**). Peace is the divine antidote to all Christian suffering (John 14:27; 16:33) and the primary value that should prevail among Christians in theological debates or in disciplinary action. The church in Africa should be an example so that its peace may spread across a continent that sorely needs it.

To ensure more of this peace, Paul shows the church at Thessalonica how they can distinguish a genuine letter from him from a false one (2:2). Even if a secretary did the writing for him (Rom 16:22), Paul was in the habit of writing the greetings at the end of his letters himself so that people could recognize his handwriting (**3:17**; Gal 6:11).

Rosalie Kougougueret

Further Reading

Bruce, F. F. *1 & 2 Thessalonians*. WBC. Waco: Word, 1982.
Morris, Leon, *The First and Second Epistles to the Thessalonians*. rev. ed. NICOT. Grand Rapids: Eerdmans, 1991.

1 TIMOTHY

Paul's two letters to Timothy and his letter to Titus are known as his Pastoral Epistles because they deal with the life of the church. At the time they were written, the church had been in existence for about thirty years and the apostles were passing away. It was, therefore, necessary to think not only of the changing leadership of the church but also of how the church should be organized. So Paul wrote to give church leaders guidance on how to administer the churches for which they were responsible.

Two of the Pastoral Epistles were written to Timothy, Paul's spiritual son whom he had left at Ephesus to care for the growing Christian community in that great city. Like most of the churches in Asia Minor in the apostolic period, the community of Ephesus was being challenged by false teachings.

Paul's constant stress on the importance of sound teaching should remind us of the critical importance of teaching in our churches today.

Outline of Contents

COMMENTARY

1:1-2 Greetings

As in most of his letters, Paul begins by introducing himself. He is *an apostle of Jesus Christ, by the command of God* (**1:1**). This statement emphasizes his authority. He is an apostle with the same standing as the other apostles, even though he was not among the Twelve. He was specifically chosen to be an apostle by God (Gal 1:1).

Timothy is identified as the recipient of the letter. Paul refers to him as *my true son*, as if he were Timothy's father (**1:2**). Some commentators have suggested that Timothy was in fact Paul's son in human terms, but that was not the case. Rather, Timothy was one of Paul's converts during one of his missionary journeys. Along with many others, he is thus Paul's *son in the faith*. Even before he was converted by Paul, Timothy already had a solid spiritual background, for he had been trained in the Scriptures by his grandmother and his mother (2 Tim 1:5). In describing him as his *true son*, Paul is underlining the close relationship he has with Timothy. In Africa, we have a deep understanding of the bond between a father and son, but spiritual relationships are even more intimate than blood ties.

1:3-20 Personal Encouragement

Paul encourages Timothy to remain at Ephesus to take care of the young church (**1:3a**). Here we see him exercising his authority as a father in relation to his son. He is not overbearing, but urges and persuades with valid important arguments. Given the challenges in the church at Ephesus, Timothy's task will not be an easy one. But Paul had to move on to do important work in Macedonia, and so he had to leave Timothy to carry this burden.

Paul immediately mentions the greatest challenge that Timothy will face in his ministry: *false doctrines* (**1:3b**). These doctrines are not necessarily heresies that have been brought into the church by strangers, but may have been taught by *certain men* within the church. Their teachings do not strengthen faith but revolve around *myths and endless genealogies* (**1:4**). These men were no doubt Jews who were more attached to traditions than to the law, and who enjoyed arguing about the origins of their ancestors and of the patriarchs in particular. Once dragged into this sort of debate, Christians do not easily get free because the whole discussion is pure speculation. So Paul warns the church against empty discussions and *meaningless talk* (**1:6**).

Such debates are especially useless because they are led by people who claim to be experts, learned *teachers of* the law, but who are actually ignorant (**1:7**). Unfortunately there are many such false experts in Africa. Timothy must fight this false teaching not only with healthy teaching, but also by displaying an attitude worthy of God, that is, one that is characterized by love and a *good conscience*.

Then Paul gives a list of those who turn from the law (**1:9-10b**). He lists four categories of sinners: those who contradict the law (*lawbreakers and rebels*), murderers (*those who kill their fathers or mothers*), the sexually immoral (*adulterers and perverts*, that is, homosexuals), and sinners by word (*liars*). The list is not exhaustive. It seems that Paul is implying that there is only a step between false teaching and sins such as the ones he has listed.

Timothy's task will not be an easy one, so Paul offers him encouragement by speaking of his own experience. His ministry is dependent on the mercy of God, who has given him the ability to fulfil this task (**1:12**). We know that Paul had nothing to reproach himself with as regards keeping the law. In relation to ethics, he was blameless (Phil 3:5-6). And yet, he was a sinner because in his ignorance of who Christ was, he persecuted him and his followers (**1:13**). Yet despite this God had mercy on him and granted him the faith that brings real knowledge (**1:4**). More than that, God made him a servant and an example of the benefits of salvation in Jesus Christ. What mercy!

Paul next makes a declaration of faith about what Jesus has done: *Christ Jesus came into the world to save sinners* (**1:15a**). Still thinking of his own history as one who persecuted the church, he describes himself as 'the worst of sinners' (**1:15b-16**). But in saying this he is not implying that his sin was greater than those mentioned in 1:9-10. All sin is very serious in God's eyes. What Paul is doing is setting out the full dimensions of the mercy of God.

Paul's statement of faith is followed in **1:17** by a liturgical text or hymn about the uniqueness of God and his eternal reign. Paul makes a direct link between Christ's being the Saviour of the world and the nature of the eternal God! This link is rooted in his experience of salvation in Jesus Christ and of his calling by the eternal God.

Finally, Paul reminds Timothy that he does not have to rely on Paul's experience alone, for he has also had his own experience relating to his calling. Paul speaks of *prophecies once made* about Timothy (**1:18**), suggesting that his calling was confirmed by the church or by a group of Christian brothers. In carrying out his ministry at Ephesus, Timothy needs to remember that he had not been called to the ministry on the spur of the moment or merely because Paul loved him. God has prepared him and has convinced the church that he should serve.

These prophecies should reassure Timothy and support him so that he can *fight the good fight* (1:18). Paul insists on adding the adjective 'good', because he wants Timothy to be careful about which fights he becomes involved in. He

must not, for example, waste his time by entering into endless arguments (1:4). Such arguments are often more about personal vanity than about truth.

Paul mentions two men, Hymenaeus and Alexander, who have lost the good fight and their good conscience and so, like many others, have *shipwrecked their faith*. Paul has *handed [them] over to Satan,* meaning that he has used his apostolic authority to allow Satan to test these two men (**1:19-20**). His aim is not to exclude them from salvation, but to bring them to repentance so that they decide *not to blaspheme* any more. As a Malgache proverb says, '*Fandio iray siny tsy mahaleo fandoto iray tandroka*' [Madagascar: 'A pot of clean water can't resist a ladle of dirty water']. Even a little dirty water is enough to spoil a container full of clean water. Thus even if there are only a few people whose doctrine will pollute the church, every effort must be made to keep them away from those who hold to pure doctrine.

2:1-7 Prayer as the Basis of Ministry

After having presented the challenge involving the false teaching that leads to serious sins (1:9), Paul recommends prayer that there may be peace, without which nothing good can be accomplished. His words *first of all* stress the priority of prayer (**2:1**). He urges prayer in all its forms, but focuses particularly on intercession and thanksgiving.

We may find it astonishing that Paul advises particular prayer for those in government (**2:2**). After all, the Roman emperor was a dictator who imposed emperor worship and executed all who did not obey him. Yet Paul advises that Christians pray for those in authority, for regardless of whether the government of a country is democratic or dictatorial, those in power play a decisive role in maintaining peace. In much of Africa, we enjoy a religious liberty that was unknown in Paul's day, but the peace we enjoy is sometimes threatened. Hence African Christians should pray that those in authority may be able to maintain peace.

If there is peace, security and dignity, the church can work freely to give everyone an opportunity to hear the Gospel and to turn to God. This is what God wants, for Paul says that God wants *all men to be saved* (**2:3-4**). However, in saying this Paul is not implying that everyone will be saved through the prayer of the church.

The means of salvation is celebrated in **2:5**, which is another liturgical formula or a hymn similar to that in 1:17. Christ is the *mediator* between God and humankind. This verse clearly affirms the humanity of Jesus, which is something that many African Christians struggle to understand. They have difficulty believing that Jesus, though perfect God, was also human. It may help to realize that in some of our African cultures, a mediator has to be one of us, someone similar to us, if he or she is to settle our conflicts. The mediator will understand who we are and know what we expect of him. Jesus, through his human nature, takes the role of mediator for us. He knows us and identifies with us. And it was as a human being that Christ paid the ransom to satisfy the justice of God.

Paul returns to his own task (**2:7**). His apostleship had been given to him so that he could proclaim Christ. His aside, *I am telling the truth, I am not lying*, makes us suspect that the authenticity of Paul's apostleship was still under attack. However, some manuscripts do not include this parenthetical observation. But whether or not those words were in the original letter, there can be no doubt that Paul was proud to be a *herald*, an *apostle* and *a teacher of the true faith* (2:7).

2:8-3:13 The Christian Community

Paul makes it clear that pastoral ministry concerns itself especially with the relationships between the members of the community and the contribution each one makes to the well-being of others.

2:8-13 Men and Women

Paul states that men should adopt a respectful attitude when they pray (**2:8**). In ancient times, hands had to be lifted toward heaven. What is at issue here is more our internal attitudes than our formal religious pose. It is therefore important for us to ask ourselves whether we approach God with the right attitude in our personal worship and in the church.

The words *I also want* indicate that women too should pray with an attitude of respect, just like the men. But women face a particular problem, in that it is easy for them to become preoccupied with their appearance and with looks that take a long time to achieve. But what do such details have to contribute to community life? Decent and honourable behaviour matters far more to God than jewels and expensive clothes (**2:9**). Besides, if Christian *women who profess to worship God* are too concerned about their external appearance, they will forget the essentials and will have neither the time nor the inclination to do good deeds (**2:10**). It is important to emphasize that Paul was not forbidding beautiful jewellery or lovely hairstyles to all Christian women of all time. He was warning against becoming so

---

THE ROLE OF WOMEN IN THE CHURCH

The role of women in the church is a contentious issue, particularly when passages such as 1 Corinthians 13:34 and 1 Timothy 2:11-14 are regarded as laying down absolutes rather than general principles within a particular culture), there can be no denying that women and men are created equal in the image of God. Thus we must not focus on the gender roles that society, church and African cultures have assigned to women. The focus should fall on the biblical call for all human beings to discern what is the will of God in their lives (Romans 12:2). Jesus' radical mission of transformation for liberation (Luke 4:18-27) and fullness of life (John 10:10) means that women and men are equally called and empowered to participate in the same mission in the church. What women and men can do depends on our obedience to the guidance and empowerment of the Holy Spirit.

Because of deeply entrenched patriarchal, hierarchical and sexist attitudes and practices, and the male-dominated leadership in many of the churches in Africa, women have a critical and prophetic role to play in 'stirring the waters' and 'speaking the truth' by asserting their God-given humanity and gifts – not for their own sake but for the sake of the integrity of the gospel. Many women continue to claim their full potential and have taken leading roles. Like the Samaritan woman (John 4:1-42), when women in Africa drink the water offered by Jesus, they go out to witness and spread the word of truth in their homes, villages, communities and churches

with determination, boldness, courage and humility. Some have founded churches, preached, taught Christian theology to people of all ages and translated the Scriptures into African languages.

Where churches have listened to the voice of the Holy Spirit and have accorded women their rightful place in all the ministries of the church, women have been ordained to the ministry of word and sacrament. Other women continue to serve in unordained roles in the local, national, regional and global church. Most, like Tabitha (Acts: 9:36), devote their lives to acts of charity. In this era of HIV/AIDS, most of the caregivers are women. Women have also given generously of their limited economic resources. They are known to be key in raising church funds. Still others, like Lydia (Acts 16:13-15), provide hospitality to strangers and fellow Christians in their homes. As one African-American womanist scholar has put it, in some black churches in the USA: 'If it was not for the women, you wouldn't have a church.' The same is true in many churches in Africa.

Finally, a small but significant number of women are contributing to the search for an authentic Christianity, church and theology in Africa through research and the writing and publishing of scholarly books. Their vital role is to disseminate theological knowledge that is worked out at the grassroots by the majority of people, who are non- or semi-literate, most of whom are women.

Women still face a daunting task in advocating and modelling gender justice in the church and in society.

Nyambura J. Njoroge

attached to clothes and fashions that one forgets the most important thing: pleasing God by doing good deeds.

Then Paul advises women to be quiet during teaching (**2:11**). This advice has raised much debate among Christians in Africa, especially since the rise of feminist theology that asserts, among other things, the right of women to express themselves. Certain versions of the Bible have tried to get around the problem by translating 2:11 in a more acceptable way while still being true to the spirit of the text. Thus *The Message* translates this as 'I don't let women take over and tell the men what to do'. This translation assumes that Paul gave this advice because women were taking a position of authority and even of dominance over men, which was unacceptable in the culture of that day (**2:12**). The requirement for silence in association with teaching may also indicate that the women were talkative during times of teaching or worship.

Paul advises that the women be silent as a sign of their submission to the men and their acknowledgement of men's authority. They will then be obeying the order that God established at creation when *Adam was formed first, then Eve* (**2:13**). The Christian community should be a model for the relationships between men and women.

In applying this instruction in Africa today, we need to think carefully about how women express their submission to the authorities and to men. Or in other words, what is the equivalent of 'silence' in African culture?

A quick reading of **2:14** would suggest that Eve carries more guilt for the fall than Adam, as if sin entered the human race through Eve. However, Adam is actually twice as guilty as Eve. First he listened to his wife's voice – she should have been the one to listen – and then he disobeyed God by eating the forbidden fruit. By listening to Eve, Adam was failing to take up the place of responsibility that had been given to him by virtue of the order of creation (2:13) and was acting as if Eve had authority over him.

There has been much debate about what Paul meant when he said that *women will be saved through childbearing* (**2:15**). Does the 'saved' mean saved from sin, or something like being kept safe in childbirth? The first interpretation appeals to those who like to spiritualize texts, while the latter is particularly appealing in Africa, where many women die in childbirth. Pregnancy can be a time of anguish for a woman and for those around her. But two important truths are clear: a) Women are designed for bearing children, even though this is not their sole calling and not all women become mothers. For the majority of women, especially in Africa, motherhood is a joy. b) Women will not be saved just because they are mothers. To be saved, they must have faith accompanied by love, holiness and modesty (2:15), three virtues that express real faith in daily life.

3:1-7 Pastors

Paul uses the term *episkopos* (meaning 'overseer') to designate those who have been called to care for God's sheep. In English, this word is sometimes translated as 'bishop', but the words 'pastor' or 'shepherd' are also correct.

For the second time in this letter, Paul states *Here is a trustworthy saying* (**3:1**; see also 1:15). This time his confident declaration concerns the noble character of pastoral ministry. Unlike many today, he does not present this ministry in terms of the benefits it offers to the pastor, but in terms of the personal characteristics that fit pastors for their task. These characteristics fall into three categories:

- *In relation to society,* pastors must be blameless (**3:2a**). Their morality must not be open to question. They must also be monogamous (**3:2b**), that is, legally married to only one wife. This standard is important not only in Paul's time but also today in Africa, when common-law marriage is widespread. It would, however, be wrong to assume that Paul's words here mean that only the pastor need be monogamous while other believers can be polygamous. Paul is not here speaking about the relationships of other believers.
- *In relation to themselves,* pastors must be self-controlled (**3:2c-3**). They should not be given to wine or quarrels or an unhealthy love of money. In brief, they must be free from vices that could enslave them and render them unable to freely serve their master.
- *In relation to their homes,* pastors must manage their own families well (**3:4-5**). If a pastor is not respected by his own family, he will not gain the respect of the church for which he is responsible.

The most important requirement for a pastor is maturity (**3:6**). Pride is the worst trap that lies in wait for a new convert given a position of leadership. Once caught in the devil's trap, the pastor and the entire community can no longer give a good testimony for God (**3:7**).

3:8-13 Deacons

Other passages tell us that deacons help pastors in their work and care for the needy in the church, especially widows, the ill and the poor (see, for example, Acts 6:2-4). Deacons must have the same qualities as pastors (**3:8**), for their task is as important as that of pastors (despite the widespread perception that pastors are superior to deacons) and because deacons may also be called on to assume pastoral responsibilities. It is because deacons also take part in teaching and are not solely responsible for social work in the church that they need to have a secure grasp of *the deep truths of the faith* (**3:9**). These deep truths can only be understood by God's children who are enlightened by the Spirit.

There is disagreement about whether the women referred to in **3:11** are deaconesses or the wives of the deacons. In my opinion, it seems likely that Paul is referring to deacons' wives because this section comes between two sections that deal with male deacons. However, others ask why the wives of deacons should be mentioned while those of pastors and elders are not. Whichever interpretation is correct, there can be no doubt that the behaviour of deacons' wives can affect how well their husbands can do their work.

The Christian community must exemplify the cardinal values of marriage: the system set up at creation by God is monogamous. Thus, like pastors, deacons must be strictly monogamous and good leaders in their homes.

3:14-16 Personal Encouragement

As in 1:18-20, Paul follows his advice about community life with words of encouragement to Timothy because of his heavy responsibility in taking care of God's household, which is the church of the living God, *the pillar and foundation of the truth* (**3:15**).

In the ancient world, the pillars that supported great temples often contained inscriptions, poems, and sculptures relating the most important events in the lives of generals, heroes or gods. This information would be lasting and would be read by successive generations as long as the pillars stood. Paul uses this metaphor to make it clear that the church, which is God's house, must proclaim God's deeds and the truths about him.

Inspired by this metaphor, Paul for the third time quotes a liturgical formula or hymn (**3:16**; see 1:17 and 2:5). He presents godliness as a mystery, a truth that the world cannot understand without the intervention of God himself, but which the apostles, pastors and deacons are called to uphold. Like the hymn in 2:5, this hymn speaks of Jesus Christ and concisely summarizes the key points about Christ. *He appeared in a body* refers to the incarnation, a fundamental truth without which salvation is not possible. Jesus was born in Bethlehem, grew up like any other child in Nazareth, and became an adult, a Galilean among Galileans. Jesus *was vindicated by the Spirit* and *seen by angels* at his baptism in the Jordan, an event marking the beginning of his earthly ministry (Mark 1:9-13). The Ephesian believers themselves are evidence that Christ *was preached among the nations, was believed on in the world*. The culmination of the church's proclamation is the truth of Christ's resurrection, whereby he was *taken up in glory*. These truths must be proclaimed and guarded by the church, which is 'the pillar and foundation of the truth'.

4:1-16 Combating False Doctrines

4:1-3 False Doctrines and the End Times

The words with which Paul introduced the next section deserve comment. He claims to have received a revelation from God, so that he can say *the Spirit clearly says* (**4:1a**). Others have latched onto this phrase and used it themselves, arguing in support of their own 'special revelations' from the Spirit, so that we have a profusion of prophecies in the churches in Africa. These prophecies tend to result in a neglect of reading of the Word, which is the means by which God normally reveals himself to us today. We need to remember the difference between the apostles and us. They had been directly entrusted with the faith by Jesus himself, and had later put it in writing (2 Tim 1:14). Paul, as an apostle, had received the mystery of the faith directly from the Lord (1 Cor 11:23; Gal 1:11-12). Here he is claiming that as part of that more general revelation of the way of salvation, he also received a special revelation of truths relating to the end times.

Christians of the apostolic period believed in the imminent return of Jesus Christ, and this belief resulted in much speculation and feverish anticipation of his return. Paul warns them that the end-times will be characterized by much false teaching, which will be inspired by the devil, who is always seeking to undermine the work of the church in every possible way (**4:1b**). This is the fourth reference in this letter to the attacks of Satan and his hosts (see 1:20; 3:6,7). Paul has no doubt that the church is engaged in a spiritual battle.

False teaching always results in sin. In this case, the teaching by *hypocritical liars* (**4:2**) will encourage a false asceticism that leads to the forbidding of marriage, the banning of certain foods (**4:3a**), and *godless myths and old wives' tales* (4:7; see also 1:4).

4:3b-16 Weapons for Combating False Doctrine

Christians are to combat false doctrines by their thankfulness (4:5-6), godliness (4:8-10), teaching (4:11) and example (4:12-16).

- Christians who *know the truth* recognize that everything that God has given us is good, including food and to be accepted with thanksgiving (**4:3b**). We are assured of this by *the Word of God* and our *prayer* (**4:5**):
- As the leader of the church at Ephesus, Timothy is in the forefront of this battle in which godliness, or commitment to God, is the primary weapon (**4:7**). He must make every effort to please God, to resist temptations and to become more and more like Jesus Christ. Godliness is certainly of more value than physical exercise, for it holds *promise for both the present life and the life to come* (**4:8**).

- Once again Paul uses the formula *this is a trustworthy saying* **4:9** (see also 1:15 and 3:1). He insists that the spiritual battle against false teaching and sin requires constant effort that all may be saved (**4:10**). This use of the word 'all' seems to support universalists, who claim that everyone will be saved whatever their religion. They claim that the love of God is great enough to save everyone and that the only advantage Christians have is knowing that they are saved. But while the text affirms that God is *the Saviour of all men,* and that he wants everyone to be saved, it does not say that everyone is actually saved, whether or not they believe. Only believers have access to salvation. Timothy is encouraged to proclaim and teach these truths relating to salvation (**4:11**).
- To teach is one thing, as Paul clearly says, but to exemplify the teaching in one's lifestyle is another matter. In Africa, we have many teachers who possess impressive diplomas, but what we need are models that Christians can imitate. The challenge to Timothy is to be an example of what he teaches (**4:12**).

In the culture of the time, respected leaders were normally over the age of thirty. But Timothy can earn the respect of others by his behaviour and the example he sets, no matter what his age. He can also carry out the three main components of his ministry: the public reading of Scripture, preaching and teaching (**4:13**).

To encourage him, Paul again reminds him of his calling, and of the ceremony where the elders laid hands on him, setting him apart and affirming that he had the gift needed to be a minister of the Word (**4:14**; see also 1:18). He also reminds Timothy that he needs to keep a careful watch on his own life and teaching, not just for his own sake but so that he will be able to care for others (**4:15-16**). He is a believer, just like those he leads. He himself must be sufficiently strong to be able to build others up.

5:1-6:2 Responsibilities of the Community

The section from 2:8-3:13 dealt with the behaviour of believers within the Christian community and with the qualities needed by Christian leaders. Now Paul deals with the responsibilities of the community towards its members.

5:1-2 The Community as a Family

Like a family, the Christian community consists of people of all ages, and, as in African culture, all need to be treated appropriately. A father is not to be treated like a son, nor a sister like a friend. In fact, people within a Christian community should treat one another even better than the people do in the wider society because they are all united in Christ. It will be as difficult for the young Timothy to *rebuke* and *exhort* (**5:1a**) those who are older than he is as it would be

for an African to do so. So he must be careful to address them with all the respect which they are due. They are fathers and mothers. Who would dare speak *harshly* to his parents? In certain African cultures, such a person would be chased from the village!

Timothy must address *younger men as brothers … and younger women as sisters,* with whom he must maintain *absolute purity* (**5:1b-2**). This last requirement is very important, for many leaders have failed in their ministry because they were not careful to maintain purity in their relationships with the opposite sex.

5:3-16 Responsibility for Widows

Paul distinguishes two categories of widows in the church. The first group are those who have children or grandchildren who can care for them (**5:4a**). Those in this group should be supported by their children, who will thus express their gratitude for what their mother or grandmother has done for them while also being useful to the community and behaving as real believers should (**5:4b, 8**). The other group consists of those who have no one else to turn to but rely on God (**5:3, 5**). They should experience God's compassion and the answer to their prayers through the community that comes to their aid.

There may, however, be widows who live *for pleasure,* that is, who are simply interested in looking for a man to satisfy their sexual desires. Paul calls such women spiritually dead. The community should not help them (**5:6**).

Rigorous conditions are laid down regarding which widows the community should take responsibility for (**5:9**). The first requirement is that they must be more than sixty years old. At that age, they can no longer work to support themselves. Sixty is the retirement age in many African countries.

These aged widows should have been married to only one husband and should have given evidence of exemplary behaviour as long as their husband was alive. Paul is not necessarily saying that no woman who has been widowed more than once can be supported, but there would not have been many such women in his day. His focus here is on the issue of whether the woman had been a faithful and exemplary wife (**5:10**).

Paul also makes it clear that these widows must not be parasites on the believing community but must make a useful contribution to it. He lists some, though by no means all, of the tasks they could be given.

The last group Paul speaks of are young widows. They are vulnerable to sexual temptations that will make them want to remarry quickly (**5:11**). When their lack of self-control drives them to marry, they break their *first pledge* (**5:12**). What was this pledge? It may have been the vow the woman made at her first marriage, which has now been ended by the death of her husband. However, it seems more likely that this pledge was some sort of vow taken by a widow to set herself apart to serve the church for the rest of her life. Young widows are also prone to idleness and to all the evils for which bad women are known (**5:13**). Paul advises them to remarry so that as wives and mothers they will be kept busy managing their own homes. He makes it clear that the reason he is giving these instructions is to avoid opportunities for the world to speak badly of Christians (**5:14**).

It goes without saying that widows who have believing family members will not be dependent on the community (**5:16**). They must be cared for by their families, and particularly by believing women.

It is important to emphasize that the community regarded helping the needy as part of its calling. However, the church should not become so focused on doing charitable work that it forgets its central calling.

5:17-25 The Responsibilities of Elders

Paul has already spoken of the roles of a pastor (*episkopos*) and a deacon (*diakonos*). Now he introduces a third term, elder (*presbyteros*). This term generally designated an elderly person, but in this letter it is used to refer to a leader in the community. Commentators agree that *episkopos* and *presbyteros* mean the same thing. The only difference is that the former was used in communities with a Greek background and the latter in those with a Jewish background.

Paul does not discuss the qualities required of elders because he had done this in 2:3-7. Instead he specifies their responsibilities, focusing primarily on their task of *preaching and teaching,* and the related responsibility to *direct the affairs of the church* (**5:17**). When he says that they deserve to be treated with *double honour,* he may be saying that they deserve a double honorarium (meaning a double salary) or double the respect given to others. The quotations from Deuteronomy 25:4 and Matthew 10:10 suggest that he may be thinking in terms of financial support. But whichever interpretation is correct, elders merit both honour and honorariums! They should be regarded as salaried workers (**5:18**).

As public figures and especially as ministers of the Word, elders are vulnerable to all kinds of accusations (**5:19**). Thus Paul recommends application of the scriptural principle that any accusation must be supported by the evidence of *two or three witnesses* (Deut 17:6). It is vital that the church be certain of the facts before it passes judgment. Their cases must be heard *without partiality* or *favouritism* (**5:21**). Elders are not supermen, and they can fall into sin like any other Christian. Timothy must not yield to the temptation to give them special treatment because of their position. This sometimes happens in Africa, where respect for the elderly sometimes results in their faults or failures being overlooked, so that the guilty escape punishment!

Timothy must not overlook sins committed by an elder but must rebuke them publicly, not simply to punish the guilty but to teach others what it means to fear God (**5:20**).

Paul underscores the seriousness of what he is saying with the words, *I charge you, in the sight of God and Christ Jesus and the elect angels* (5:21). The elect angels are those angels who did not fall with Satan. Throughout this letter, Paul has been very aware of the battle that rages between believers and Satan and his fallen angels (1:20; 3:6-7; 4:1).

In **5:22**, Paul returns to the practice of laying on of hands. This act signifies the recognition that someone has been called to a ministry, as had been the case with Timothy (4:14). But laying on hands without discernment may lead to someone who is living in sin being appointed to a ministry. Not only would Timothy then have to deal with this person's sin, but in a sense he would even be an accomplice in the sin. No wonder discernment is needed!

Paul now makes an aside that is worth noting. It reveals that Timothy did not enjoy good health. Paul advises him to take care of himself and recommends that he *use a little wine,* as a medicine (**5:23**). From this verse it is clear that Timothy did not usually drink wine.

Paul then returns to the matter of sin among leaders. Often leaders hide their sins instead of acknowledging them before God and dealing with them. But sooner or later, they will come to light (**5:24**). Similarly, some good deeds will be noticed immediately while others will pass unnoticed (**5:25**). But there is no need to worry about it, for all good deeds will eventually be revealed to the glory of God. Paul seems to be telling leaders that they should not be concerned about their public image. God will take care of that.

6:1-2 The Responsibilities of Slaves

Believing slaves were also part of the Christian community. In the society of that day, there were at least as many slaves as free men. Paul calls on slaves to respect their masters so that their behaviour may be a testimony to true teaching and the glory of God. (**6:1**). Paul does not support slavery – in fact he vigorously condemns the slave trade (1:10) – but he calls on slaves to live out what they believe and express it in respect for others. A slave or domestic servant whose owner or employer is a believer should not assume that because they are brothers in Christ, the employer deserves less respect (**6:2**). Instead they should serve them even better as loyal brothers and sisters.

6:3-10 Causes and Antidotes for False Teaching

For a third time, Paul returns to the issue of *false doctrines* (**6:3**; see also 1:3-11; 4:1-8), which he earlier described as 'things taught by demons' (4:1b). This time, he does not deal with the characteristics of these doctrines, which he dealt with in 4:1-3, but instead focuses on warning against anyone who might attempt to introduce such doctrines into the community.

6:4-5 The Causes: Ignorance and Greed

It is important to discern the type of person who introduces false doctrines. Such people are egocentric, and think only of themselves and their interests (**6:4**). They love useless arguments that lead to quarrels and disputes because such a person is ignorant and *understands nothing.* Their main motivation, however, is greed for they have an unhealthy attachment to money (**6:5**). In our days, such people would probably develop a prosperity gospel because they see religion as source of profit.

6:6-10 The Antidote: Contentment

Ironically, in their greed such people miss out on a great gain (**6:6**). The piety that they exploit because of their insatiable desire for money could have brought them contentment. They fail to rejoice in the fact that they have the necessities of life: food, clothing and, we may add, shelter (**6:8**). In saying this, Paul is not implying that believers should remain poor. Rather, he is pointing out that those who are content with what they have are happier than those who are never satisfied. Those who constantly crave more will fall prey to many sins (**6:9-10**). Even worse, they may wander away from life with God and sink into despair. It is only in the faith that we are able to enjoy peace.

6:11-16 The Antidote: Christian Values

Even though he is the leader of the community at Ephesus, Timothy must not assume that he is safe from the dangers of false doctrines that lead to sin and, in particular, to slavery to money. Constant effort is called for (**6:11**). Once again, he is reminded of the importance of *the good fight of faith* (**6:12**; 1:18).

Timothy is also reminded of an important event in his life – probably the ceremony mentioned in 4:14 where he received the laying on of hands by the elders. At that ceremony, he made a *good confession,* bearing public testimony to his faith (6:12). Reminding him that his *Lord Jesus Christ* also made a *good confession* (**6:13**), Paul exhorts his spiritual son to live a blameless life (**6:14**).

But what confession of faith did Jesus make before the Roman judge? What connection is there between what happened there and Timothy's confession of faith? The link is that Roman justice, represented by Pontius Pilate, found no fault in Jesus and publicly declared his innocence (John 18:38; 19:4, 6). Timothy should take this life *without spot or blame* as the model for his own ministry. It will not be easy, and will require a constant struggle that will end only at *the appearing of our Lord Jesus Christ* (6:14).

Here Paul inserts another liturgical text or hymn about the return of Jesus Christ (**6:15-16**). In the NIV, this hymn is presented as being about God the Father, but other translations treat it as being about Christ. The confusion arises because the Greek only speaks of 'he', without specifying who this 'he' is. I would argue that he is Jesus Christ, because the context deals with the return of Christ. Moreover, in the time of the apostles, the attributes of the Father were often ascribed to Jesus. For example, the title *Lord,* which was used of God in the OT, is regularly used for Jesus in the NT. Here the Lord is presented in his absolute sovereignty, which all will recognize at the end of time.

6:17-21 Assorted Advice

There were certainly rich people in the Christian community at Ephesus. These were not the same people Paul spoke of in the section 6:4-5, where he denounced those who made religion a source of profit or taught a prosperity gospel. These rich people may have acquired their riches honestly. However, that does not mean that they are sheltered from the trap of pride (**6:17**), a sin which Paul never ceases to denounce. Pride encourages the rich to be self-confident, sure that they have enough to provide for themselves until death. But riches cannot guarantee the future.

Rich people who are believers should seek to use their riches to bless others. They should generously share their wealth with those in need in the church (**6:18**), and especially with the widows.

It is important to note that Paul insists that everyone produce good deeds, whether they are poor, widowed, slaves or rich. Good deeds are evidence of authentic faith.

We should not misinterpret **6:19** as if Paul is saying that good deeds are necessary to obtain eternal life. What he is saying is that good deeds and generosity are like an investment in the Kingdom. God will know how to repay those who give generously.

Paul's final words to Timothy in this letter are yet another warning against false doctrine, which is here described as *godless chatter* and *what is falsely called knowledge* (**6:20**). Paul cannot say enough against this pernicious enemy that draws people away from the faith (**6:21**).

Solomon Andria

Further Reading

Kelly, J. N. D. *The Pastoral Epistles.* Reprint. BNTC. Peabody: Hendrickson, 1993.

Guthrie, Donald. *The Pastoral Epistles.* Rev. ed. TNT. Leicester: InterVarsity Press, 1994.

Mounce, William D. *The Pastoral Epistles.* WBC. Nashville: Thomas Nelson, 2000.

2 TIMOTHY

Paul wrote two letters to Timothy, his spiritual son whom he had left at Ephesus to organize and lead the church in that great city of Asia Minor. This second letter was written while Paul was awaiting trial in prison in Rome. He had been accused of propagating an illegal religion at a time when the Roman Empire insisted on emperor worship. Paul knew that he was facing the death penalty.

COMMENTARY

1:1-5 Greetings

Paul does not use his standard greeting in this second letter. Instead of speaking of his authority as an apostle, he speaks of his calling, founded on the promises of God and given for the purpose of proclaiming God's promise of life in Jesus Christ (**1:1**). The greeting also reveals his love for Timothy, whom he calls his *dear son* (**1:2a**; see also 1 Tim 1:2). Paul speaks as if Timothy had been born to him, rather than being a young man with whom Paul had a close relationship based on their shared calling to proclaim Christ.

Paul prays that Timothy may enjoy the blessings of *grace, mercy and peace*, which will come from both *God … and Christ Jesus* (**1:2b**), revealing that Paul sees Jesus as equal with God.

The apostle was following in the steps of his *forefathers*, who had served God in the past (**1:3**). The word 'forefathers' may have reminded him of his own relatives who had taught him the ways of God, and then of Timothy's mother and grandmother who had trained Timothy in God's ways (**1:5**). Given their common background and shared vocation, it is not surprising that the two men worked together as father and son in the cause of the gospel.

A Zulu proverb says, 'When a son is born, a father is born.' So as Timothy took on the responsibility of leading a church, he would have turned to Paul as a father to whom he could look for guidance. The relationship between them was so close that Timothy had wept when he had last said farewell to Paul (**1:4**).

1:6-14 Encouragement

As in the first letter, Paul follows the greetings with encouragement for Timothy, who has taken over from him. He reminds Timothy that his vocation, like his salvation and that of every other believer, was planned by God before *the beginning of time* (**1:9**). This vocation was confirmed when Paul laid his hands on him (**1:6**), possibly as the leader of the elders mentioned in 1 Timothy 4:14. Timothy should thus have no doubts about his calling, or about his competence, or about whether he is old enough to lead a church. Instead he is to cultivate *a spirit of power, of love and of self-discipline:* 'power' to counter any appearance of weakness because he is young, 'love' to counter any undeserved criticism, and 'self-discipline' so that the purity of his life will ultimately silence his critics (**1:7**). God has equipped Timothy for the task to which he has been called, and God's Spirit will continue to equip him. This truth still applies today, and is an encouragement to any African pastors who feel inadequate for the task God has given them.

However, these words of encouragement also bring Timothy face to face with the reality that suffering is an integral part of ministry. Paul suffered as a servant. Timothy, too, will suffer. Paul invites him to follow in his steps in proclaiming the gospel (**1:8**) of which Paul has been *a herald, and an apostle and a teacher* (**1:11**). Paul describes himself as a 'herald' to focus on his role as an announcer of the good news, as an 'apostle' to focus on his authority in doing so (he is 'a sent one'), and as a 'teacher' to focus on his goal of establishing believers in the faith.

Timothy should not be fearful because, like Paul, he is counting on the grace and mercy of God and is doing God's work (1:9). Nor should he be ashamed of being the successor of a man condemned to death (1:8), as other Christians may have been (**1:15**). Timothy's calling is dependent on the work of Jesus, planned before the beginning of time, and manifested in his earthly life, death and resurrection (**1:10**). Paul is convinced that death will usher him into the *life and immortality* that will reach their complete fulfilment on the day when Jesus returns, but which are already the experience of every believer. Paul loves to speak of *that day* (**1:12, 18**) because his hope rests on the glorious return of the Saviour to whom he has entrusted his soul. The Roman authorities cannot destroy that, for it is safe in the hands of God.

Paul has deposited his soul in Jesus' hands (1:12), and in return he, and now Timothy, have been given a *deposit* for which they are responsible (1:14). They have been entrusted with the truth of the gospel, the word that came directly from the Lord Jesus Christ and that must be communicated to the people of God. Elsewhere, Paul speaks of this deposit as *the deep truths of the faith* (1 Tim 3:9). Timothy must make sure that his teaching and conduct guard this deposit and do nothing to detract from it.

Young graduates of theological institutions are often fearful of pastoring people who are older than they are. Paul's words remind them that the God who chose them to serve him will also enable them to perform that service. Others may fear physical danger as they proclaim the Gospel. Paul reminds us that God's protection is eternal – even when the body is destroyed. What a wonderful thing to be called on the basis of God's grace and protected by God's power!

1:15-18 People Who Disappoint and Encourage

As in any personal letter, Paul writes of details of his own life. He has been deeply disappointed by the behaviour of Phygelus and Hermogenes (1:15). He may have wanted them to help meet his needs as a prisoner or to testify on his behalf in the court case. But they had offered no help at all.

Onesiphorus, on the other hand, *often refreshed me* (1:16). He had helped Paul in Ephesus (1:18), and then had gone to seek Paul out in Rome (1:17). Paul's use of the past tense when speaking of Onesiphorus, and the mention of his household without mention of him in 4:19, may imply that he has died. Paul prays for the best from the Lord for his household (1:16) and expresses his heartfelt desire that the Lord will reward him appropriately (1:18).

In difficult times, servants of God may think that their ministry has produced no fruit and that those they thought their friends have abandoned them. As they say in Madagascar, *Ny omby mahia tsy lelafin'ny namany*, ['When the cow is thin, her friends don't lick her']. But God can also provide an Onesiphorus to stand beside his servants. Rather than fretting about the attitude of Phygelus and Hermogenes, Paul praises God for Onesiphorus.

2:1-18 Examples of Servanthood

Timothy has received 'sound teaching' and the 'good deposit' of the faith (1:13-14) from Paul, and he is to pass these on to *reliable men, who will also be qualified to teach others* (2:2b). Timothy must already start preparing those who will succeed him. He will need to exercise discernment in

choosing these men, and would be wise to remember Paul's earlier description of a potential leader (1 Tim 3:1-13).

Timothy received the sound doctrine from Paul *in the presence of many witnesses* (2:2a), or literally 'through many witnesses'. This passage allows for two interpretations: a) Timothy received the gospel through the witness of several people and was not specifically converted by Paul; or b) numerous people witnessed Timothy's commissioning by Paul, possibly at the ceremony of laying on of hands (1 Tim 4:14). The second interpretation seems best because it fits with the encouragement that Paul is providing in this letter and because Paul never stops emphasizing that Timothy is his son, as if he were the instrument of his conversion.

Paul next gives three examples of how Timothy should serve if he is to fulfil his mission. He should be like a soldier who concentrates on pleasing his commanding officer (2:2), an athlete who submits to strict discipline so as to win the prize (2:5), and a farmer who has to work hard if he wants a good harvest (2:6).

While reflecting on these images, Timothy must never forget his Lord, *Jesus Christ* (2:8) – and this thought launches Paul into an aside of the type that often occur in his letters (see Col 1:15-20; Phil 2:5-11). Here he may be quoting some hymn or liturgical formula that focuses on Jesus in his humanity, and particularly on his royal lineage as the son of David. All the kings of Judah were descendants of David, but Jesus' resurrection shows that he is far greater than his ancestor, and is the promised Messiah (or 'Christ'). The gospel that Paul proclaimed and for which he was suffering was that the Messiah had come, had died, and had been raised from the dead. This gospel was opposed by both Jews and Romans, and had led to Paul's imprisonment. But the gospel could not be imprisoned (2:9) and had spread from Paul to Timothy, and would continue to spread from Timothy to reliable men, and from these to others until the message would reach the ends of the earth. Thus Paul endured his suffering not in resignation or fatalism but in hope. He was convinced that despite his imprisonment, more people would come to salvation (2:10).

The mention of salvation prompts Paul to another declaration of faith, similar to those he made in his first letter (2:11; see also 1 Tim 1:15; 3:1). This beautiful hymn about Christ can be summed up in one phrase: Jesus is with us. Since Paul has died with Christ by being baptized into his body and crucified with him (Rom 6:4; Gal 2:20), he will also live as Christ lives. Suffering and death are not the end, for Paul looks beyond his approaching death to the day of glory (2:12a).

There will be some believers who will *disown* Christ, either by their words, by the way they live, or by how they respond to suffering (2:12b). While those who do this may still be saved and go to heaven, Christ will not be proud to present them before the Father (Matt 10:33).

But believers should not be preoccupied with worrying, 'What if I fail?' Those whose hearts are set on pleasing their Lord need not fear. Even if for some reason they fail (*are faithless* – **2:13a**) they will not be cast away. The Lord stands by his word that those who endure suffering will reign with him (2:12a). He has promised this, and it is part of his nature to keep his promises (**2:13b**). He is 'the same yesterday and today and forever' (Heb 13:8).

Paul's final example of service is the worker (**2:15**). Timothy is to show the undivided loyalty of a soldier, the endurance of an athlete, and the patience of a farmer in the work assigned to him at Ephesus. By so doing, he will demonstrate that he is a workman approved by God. As such, he will exhibit certain qualities in his life and ministry – qualities that Paul now proceeds to discuss.

First of all, Timothy must combat false teachings that involve *quarrelling about words* and *godless chatter* (**2:14, 16**; see also 1 Tim 6:20). Such problems continue today in endless debates that make no contribution to the kingdom of God. Thus we discuss where evil comes from, at the expense of teaching what it is and how to shun it. Or we discuss the authorship of the Pastoral Epistles and ignore their message. Or we are so preoccupied with the question of whether our ancestors who never heard of Christ are saved that we fail to tell the present generation the way of salvation. Or we try to establish the day, month, and year when Christ will return at the expense of preparing people to be ready for him whenever he comes. The devil is always anxious to distract us from thinking about what is really important.

'Godless chatter' results in ungodliness and separation from God. Paul compares it to an illness that eats away at the community and destroys whatever it infects (**2:17a**). He then gives one example of the type of false teaching that is to be avoided. Men named Hymenaeus and Philetus have been arguing that *the resurrection has already taken place* (**2:17b-18**; see also 1 Tim 1:20). Consequently some Christians who were waiting for the return of Jesus believed that they had been rejected by God, who had already raised those he favoured. In despair, they abandoned the faith.

Paul mentions the enemies of his ministry two by two: Hymenaeus and Alexander (1 Tim 1:20), Phygelus and Hermogenes (1:15), and Hymenaeus and Philetus (2:17). Jesus sent his disciples out in pairs (Mark 6:7), and it seems that the enemy does the same.

2:19-26 Opponents To Be Confronted

The vicious enemies of the church may be capable of destroying the faith of some (2:18), but God has laid a solid foundation confirmed by two great truths that should reassure Timothy: a) From before the beginning of time, God *knows those who are his* (**2:19**; see Num 16:5). The heretics

and apostates do not belong to the family of God. b) True believers distinguish themselves by their behaviour and their determination to *turn away from wickedness* (2:19).

Paul uses a metaphor to illustrate the difference between true and false believers. True believers work for the glory of God, and are like objects made of gold and silver that a homeowner is proud to use. False believers, however, are like articles of clay that are kept out of sight and used for ignoble purposes (**2:20**). Hymenaeus and Philetus are good examples of ignoble articles that God used, for without their heresy Paul might never have written important parts of the Pastoral Epistles.

Paul says that these articles are *in a large house*, which may be the world or the church, which is called *God's household* (1 Tim 3:15). Whichever the case, true believers are to distance themselves from the stains and wickedness for which their opponents are known and are to be like articles of gold, that their owner will be proud to use (**2:21**).

Paul gives three ways in which Timothy can combat his opponents:

- *Flee the evil desires of youth* (**2:22a**), These desires may be those of the flesh, which are stronger in the young than in the elderly. This view is supported by the warning in this letter against debauchery and various forms of immorality in the fight against false teachings (3:6). But the 'desires' could equally be the passion for *godless chatter* and *stupid arguments* (2:16, **23**), which the young also enjoy. Paul may have both types of desires in mind.

- *Pursue spiritual virtues* (**2:22b**). Paul provides a list of these virtues: *righteousness, faith, love and peace.* Believers should not assume that they have these virtues, just as they should not assume that they will find it easy to live in harmony with their fellow believers. Personality differences, different social and religious backgrounds, combined with the remains of our sinful nature, will mean that human relationships will always present a challenge. Thus Timothy must actively pursue these virtues *along with those who call on the Lord out of a pure heart.* Only true believers call on the Lord in this way (2:19, 22).

- *Teach with gentleness* (2:23-26). Timothy's opponents may enjoy arguments and quarrels (**2:23**) but Timothy should not be drawn into them. Instead he should respond to the verbal attacks of his opponents with gentleness and with quiet instruction. He must pray that God will use his teaching to convict his opponents so that they accept the truth, repent and are freed from the control of the devil (**2:26**). This should be our prayer not only for those with whom we differ on doctrine but also for all those people whom the devil has blinded (2 Cor 4:4). Only the truth will make them free.

CHRISTIAN EDUCATION IN AFRICA

In the 1960s, Christianity in Africa was described as a mile long and an inch deep. Not much has changed since then. Despite the vast number of African Christians, the new churches springing up every day, the all-night prayer meetings, exorcisms and the days of fasting, the continent is still blighted with poor government, bribery, killings, coups, the AIDS epidemic and so on.

This apparent paradox invites us to examine the way in which Christians are nurtured. Is there genuine Christian education in our churches?

We need to recognize that Christian education is far more than just ministry to children. Christian education passes the Christian faith from one generation to the next. It helps believers to make their faith their own and to live it out. Aided by the Holy Spirit who indwells every believer, it gives direction for every stage of life.

One of the reasons many of our churches lack Christian education is ignorance, which is often rooted in the way pastors are trained. Many theological schools provide little more than an introduction to Christian education. More courses are needed to create an awareness of the value of effective Christian education, which will translate into properly organized education in African churches.

The basic educational tools we will need are teachers, materials and methods:

- *Teachers:* The same standard that applies to overseers applies to Christian educators (1 Tim 3:1-6). They should not be inexperienced but must be mature, committed Christians, respected and above reproach. They must be growing in the Lord, so that they can nurture others. Children cannot teach other children. Moreover they must be able to teach, as someone who cannot teach cannot lead a Bible study group.

- *Materials:* Relevant, theologically sound materials that address real-life issues need to be used. Africa must not continue to be a dumping ground for irrelevant materials from elsewhere. It is time for African theologians and educators to arise and write. Their churches are waiting for them.

- *Methods:* The methods we use to teach should be appropriate to the age and ability of the students, because learners of different ages and at different stages in the Christian life require different approaches to the biblical material we are presenting. While we should make use of modern technology when it is available, we should not be dependent on it. Teachers must learn to improvise to make learning fun, inspirational and effective.

Christian education must be practical. Knowledge that is not applied to real-life issues will not transform lives. While memorizing facts is good, it is not enough. Learners need to be challenged to implement what they learn. They will need to be taught skills in analyzing, synthesizing and evaluating if they are to be able to confront the challenges facing our contemporary society.

Christian education is a means of improving, developing and nurturing the church in its authentic walk with Christ so that the applied word of God will have a positive impact on our societies.

Lois Semenye

3:1-17 The Last Times

3:1-9 Godless Behaviour

Paul now turns to the subject of 'the end times' or more precisely *the last days* before the return of our Lord (**3:1**). What days are these? Are they still to come, are we living in them now, or was Paul living in them? From Paul's comments on the wickedness of people in both his letters to Timothy, it appears that he believes the last days have already begun. These days cover the entire period between the giving of the Spirit at Pentecost and the final return of Jesus. Thus Paul was and we are living in 'the last days'.

Paul speaks of the same period as *later times* in 1 Timothy 4:1. There his focus is on the proliferation of false doctrines, but here he emphasizes the wickedness of the people. They are totally self-centred and think only of themselves. They seek to satisfy their own desires with no thought of how others will be affected (**3:3**). They have little interest in religion and are disrespectful of the things of

God, but like to maintain a Christian façade (**3:4-5**). They are passionate about fleshly pleasures (**3:6**) and are interested in new ideas simply because they are new, but are unwilling to *acknowledge the truth* (**3:7**).

The book of Exodus describes a confrontation between Moses and Egyptian magicians (Exod 7–8). Jewish tradition gave the names of two of these magicians as *Jannes and Jambres* (**3:8**). Paul's point is that there have always been people with perverted minds who oppose the truth. But in the last days, these people will become increasingly worse until the day when they face God's judgment for their evil works (**3:9**). Then, like Jannes and Jambres, they will be publicly exposed as deceivers.

There is a link between the proliferation of false doctrines (1 Tim 4:1-7) and the wickedness of the people described in this passage. False doctrine results in sinful behaviour. And those who indulge in sinful behaviour do not welcome sound doctrine and knowledge of the truth (**3:7**).

3:10-17 Timothy's Responsibility

Paul encourages Timothy to stand firm in face of the challenges posed by the last days, following the example of the apostle and holding tightly to the Scriptures.

Timothy had accompanied Paul eagerly on his missionary travels to *Antioch, Iconium and Lystra* (**3:11a**; Acts 14:19-22), but he was not merely to follow in Paul's physical footsteps but also in his spiritual footsteps, imitating Paul's *teaching, way of life, purpose, faith, patience, love, endurance* (**3:10**). Paul knew that he was not only responsible for imparting head knowledge or theories but also had to set an example of how to live by the truths he taught. The same is true for each of us who is in a position where we may influence others – whether as a Bible teacher, pastor, parent, employer or friend.

Timothy had also seen another side of Paul's life: his *persecutions* and *sufferings* at the hands of his fellow Jews and of the Roman authorities, who accused him of propagating an illegal religion (**3:11b**). He also suffered because of the evil of human beings in the last days (3:1-5) and the proliferation of false doctrines among those Paul calls *impostors* (**3:13**). Paul asserts that persecution is part of the normal Christian life (**3:12**). His words are an encouragement to the many African Christians who have suffered for their faith, whether as converts from Muslim families or from families with strong traditional beliefs, or as wives with unbelieving husbands, or for other reasons. Isolation and even physical persecution have been the lot of many believers over the years.

Timothy must follow Paul's example and that of the believers who first instructed him, namely his grandmother and his mother (**3:14**; see 1:5). They had instructed him in the Scriptures, which had worked in his life to make him a child of God through faith in Jesus Christ (**3:15**). Many families in Africa have left all teaching of Bible truths to children to schools and Sunday schools. But there is no better place for children to learn the truths of the gospel than at home, from those who love them. The most valuable thing Timothy inherited from his family was the gospel.

Paul's statement that all Scripture is God-breathed (**3:16a**) is often cited to support the inspiration of Scripture. The Greek, however, can also correctly be translated as saying, All Scripture breathed by God. The problem with the second translation is that it may be taken as suggesting that God has not inspired every passage of Scripture. The first translation is to be preferred because the argument of the whole of Scripture is that all Scripture is inspired (see, for example, 2 Pet 1:20-21). Moreover, nowhere in the NT are we told how to discern which Scriptures are inspired and which are not. All we are told is to proclaim and teach the Scriptures.

But the second translation does emphasize the purpose for which we have been given the Scriptures. Timothy must use them to teach believers, to refute false doctrines, to correct errors and to train believers so that they will be equipped to do good works (**3:16b-17**).

4:1-8 The Centrality of the Word

Paul constantly speaks of the return of Jesus Christ as a glorious day when his reign will be fully manifested (**4:1a**). In light of this coming day, he issues a solemn *charge* to Timothy, that is, a solemn declaration before witnesses as in a legal case where God the Father is the judge and Jesus the lawyer (**4:1b**). Timothy must combat those who surround themselves with false doctrines and false teachers by preaching the Word (**4:2b-3a**). The purpose of his preaching must be to *correct, rebuke and encourage* others. He must be tireless in carrying out his duties (**4:5**) and must preach regardless of whether the circumstances are favourable or not (**4:2a**). Those who wait for 'the right time' risk losing opportunities that will never be repeated. None of us knows how much time we have at our disposal, and as the proverb says, 'remorse is behind us rather than in front of us'. False doctrines are increasing, and are welcomed because they cater to the needs of the flesh. But they are deceptive myths emptied of truth (**4:3b-4**).

Paul knows that he will soon die at the hands of the Romans and uses two metaphors to speak of his approaching death. He sees himself *being poured out like a drink offering* (**4:6a**), that is, like the offering that accompanied the death of a sacrificial animal (Exod 29:40; Lev 23:13; Num 15:5-10; 28:7). He also speaks of his death as a departure to a distant destination (**4:6**). Looking back, he can see that he has *fought the good fight* (**4:7a**), a reference to the challenges and battles that Timothy has watched him surmount, and which still lie before Timothy. Paul sees himself as an athlete who has finished his race (**4:7b**). Satisfied that he has reached his goal, he joyfully anticipates receiving the winner's crown on *that day* (**4:8**). But he does not expect to be the only winner. He will share the podium with *all who have longed for his appearing* (4:8), that is, all those who joyfully await the Lord's return.

Paul's attitude to his departure from active ministry is very different from that of those who seem to hope that their successor will not be too successful and overshadow their ministry. We see this when a pastor retires, but does not smooth the way for the one who follows him. The church is the Lord's and his true servant prays that its glory tomorrow will exceed its glory today.

4:9-22 Various Relationships

What had Paul's friends done to encourage him during his imprisonment? Some, like Demas who *loved this world* (**4:10a**), had abandoned him. Demas may have been an unbeliever or he may have been a believer who could no longer bear the suffering that goes with the gospel. Demas' desertion and the departure of others had left only Luke to attend to Paul, and he urges Timothy to hurry to him (**4:9**).

Paul next turns to more mundane matters, asking Timothy to bring with him some of the baggage he had left behind at Troas while he was travelling in the hot summer months. Now that winter is coming, he needs his coat. He would also like to have his scrolls, especially the parchments (**4:13**). Parchment was more expensive and more durable than papyrus, and thus the parchments would have contained more important writings – possibly Paul's copies of the Septuagint, the Greek version of the OT. The papyrus scrolls may have contained copies of Paul's own letters. Paul may have wanted these documents to help him prepare his defence at his upcoming trial.

Timothy is warned to watch out for someone who has been arrogant and malicious towards Paul (**4:14-15**). The name Alexander was a common one, and that is why Paul identifies him as *Alexander the metalworker*. He is not necessarily the same person mentioned in 1 Timothy 1:20.

Other friends have also proved unreliable, for Paul says that no one supported him *at my first defence* (**4:16a**; see also 1:15), that is when he first appeared before a judge, after which his case was postponed for further investigation. As he writes, Paul is waiting to be called before the judge again to receive what he suspects will be a death penalty. Paul was grieved by his friends' failure to stand by him, but like his Lord (Luke 23:34) and Stephen (Acts 7:60), he was willing to forgive them (**4:16b**).

Has Paul's ministry failed so completely that he is utterly abandoned at the most painful time of his life? Far from it. He still has close friends, but except for Luke, his doctor (**4:11a**; Col 4:14), they are not with him. Crescens has gone to Galatia (**4:10b**) and Titus is working as an evangelist in Dalmatia (**4:10c**). That is why he asks Timothy to bring Mark with him (**4:11b**). Clearly the earlier conflict with Mark has been resolved (Acts 15:36-40). Tychicus, another co-worker, has been sent to Ephesus (**4:12**; Eph 6:21). His friend Carpus (**4:13**) is looking after Paul's belongings in

Troas. Paul is not isolated and is continuing to oversee his work from prison.

Paul admits that it was unpleasant for him to stand alone (4:16a) and as it were in the *lion's mouth* at his first hearing (**4:17b**). But although he may have had no human supporters, the Lord was with him and had delivered him just as Daniel had been delivered from the lion's den (Dan 6:22). Paul had even been able to give a powerful message (**4:17a**).

Paul is confident that the Lord will help him regardless of the outcome of his trial so that the truth will not be twisted (**4:18**). Even if he is not delivered from the human courts, he knows that God will bring him safely to his *heavenly kingdom*.

Paul closes with greetings to more friends (**4:19**), including Priscilla and Aquila (see Acts 18:2, 18, 26) and the household of Onesiphorus (see 1:16-18) and gives news of two others members of his team, Erastus and Trophimus, who are not with him in Rome. Their absence probably adds to Paul's ardent desire to see Timothy again (**4:21**). Some of those who are with Paul in Rome also send greetings. We know nothing about Eubulus, Pudens, Linus and Claudia, although there is a tradition that Linus may later have been bishop of Rome.

Paul's final words to Timothy are, *The Lord be with your spirit* (**4:22**), that is, with you. Paul knew that his death and the problems Timothy would face in his ministry might discourage him, but with his inner being (spirit) strengthened by the Lord, he will be able to carry on. Then Paul adds a greeting to all the believers at Ephesus: *Grace be with you.*

Solomon Andria

Further Reading

Kelly. J. N. D. *The Pastoral Epistles.* Repr. BNTC. Peabody: Hendrickson; 1993.

Guthrie, Donald. *The Pastoral Epistles.* Rev. ed. TNT. Leicester, InterVarsity Press, 1994.

Mounce, William D. *The Pastoral Epistles.* WBC. Nashville: Thomas Nelson Publishers, 2000.

TITUS

Titus, whom Paul describes as his 'partner and fellow-worker' (2 Cor 8:23) was a Gentile convert who accompanied Paul on a number of his journeys and on occasion acted as his representative (see Gal 2:1-3; 2 Cor 7:13-15; 8:16-17). He had accompanied Paul on a mission to Crete and had been left there to consolidate the work (1:5). Paul's letter is intended to give him guidance as he carries out this task.

This letter was probably written some time between the writing of the first and second letters to Timothy. The three letters together are known as the Pastoral Epistles.

Outline of Contents

COMMENTARY

1:1-4 Greetings

Paul's greetings in this letter are far longer than in any of his other letters. He introduces himself as *a servant of God and an apostle of Jesus Christ.* He thus claims the same status as the other apostles in Jerusalem. The purpose for which he is an apostle is to lead *God's elect*, that is, true believers who are the chosen people of God, toward knowledge of the truth (1:1). Such knowledge will enable them to know God and to live in a godly way. For Paul, knowledge of the truth is fundamental. Every child of God must know him as he is and be able to resist the false teachings that were as common in Paul's time as they are in ours.

Paul's being an apostle is part of God's plan to grant human beings *eternal life*, a plan that dates back to *before the beginning of time* (1:2). This plan had been unveiled by God's word, and Paul has now been entrusted with the task of communicating it to others (1:3). Paul's words are a brilliant summary of his ministry – and ours.

Paul calls Titus his son (1:4; see 1 Tim 1:1). But neither Timothy nor Titus was Paul's son in a physical sense. They were his spiritual children, possibly his own converts, and certainly shared the same faith and the same ministry (1:4). Referring to them as his sons shows the close relationship between Paul and these younger men.

1:5-15 Guiding the Church

Paul had left Titus on the island of Crete to complete the work that Paul and he had begun (1:5). In particular, he is to select elders in each town (1:5-9) and to oppose false teachers (1:10-15).

1:5-9 Appointing Elders

Some theologians interpret Paul's instruction to *appoint elders* as meaning that Titus is the bishop of Crete, while the elders are pastors in the towns. Others argue that Paul is not setting up a model for church organization but is focusing on the most efficient way to combat the dangers posed by the false teachers. He uses the terms *episcopos* (translated *overseer* or 'bishop') that Greeks would be familiar with and *presbysteros* (translated *elders*) that Jews would know better without making any distinction between these offices. In fact he uses both for the same group (compare 1:5 and 1:7).

Paul's words here should not be taken as an endorsement of a particular system of church government (whether episcopal or congregational), nor can they legitimately be appealed to in arguments about whether women may be appointed as elders. (However, 1 Timothy 3:11 does suggest that women may serve as deacons.)

The first qualification for an elder is that he must be *blameless* (1:6a; see also 1 Tim 3:2). The word means that he must not be open to having any legal charges levelled against him. There must be no failure or crack in his life that would allow enemies to attack.

An elder must also *be the husband of but one wife* (1:6b). This requirement is stressed because the Cretans of Paul's day were often polygamous. Many had official wives, concubines and girlfriends. Paul's words should not, however, be taken as implying that only elders should be monogamous and that others may be polygamous. Nor does it imply that single men cannot be elders, for if it did, Paul would be disqualified since he clearly states that he is unmarried (1 Cor 7:8). His point is that an elder must respect marriage as God instituted it at creation.

An elder must also manage his family well (**1:6c**; see also 1 Tim 3:4). His family must be a community of believers. Anyone who has unbelieving children leading dissolute lives should first lead them to faith before he is considered eligible to be an elder. If he is incapable of leading this small group, he will not be able to lead a large group of believers.

Paul next lists both the disqualifications and the qualifications for eldership (**1:8**). The two lists reveal that elders must be upright and self-controlled, and not guilty of pride, anger and greed. Their self-control will mean that they will not fall into sexual sin. They must also have the strength of character to cling to *the trustworthy message* (**1:9**; see also 1 Tim 1:15; 3:1) so that they can teach *sound doctrine* and refute error.

Clearly advanced age is not an important criterion when choosing church leaders. Yet in certain African cultures elderly people are automatically given authority, no matter how they live. Paul stresses that it is impossible to separate doctrine from lifestyle and that blameless behaviour gives credibility to the teaching of an elder.

1:10-15 Opposing False Teachers

Elders are in the forefront of the battle against the false teachers who are all talk and are not interested in the truth (**1:10**). What such teachers are really interested in is deceiving people so that they can gain money or status they do not deserve (**1:11b**; see also 1 Tim 6:4-5). They are capable *of ruining whole households* (**1:11a**) who accept their teaching. Paul may be alluding to specific cases, for in 1 Timothy 6:10 he mentions people who have wandered away from the faith to follow false teachings. Such teachers can do great damage to Christian communities.

The false teachers are mainly of Jewish origin (which is why Paul calls them *the circumcision group* –1:10; 1:14), but also include local people. Speaking of these Cretans, Paul quotes Epimenides (600 BC), a Cretan poet who long before had described his countrymen as *liars, evil brutes, lazy gluttons* (**1:12**). This description fits Paul's opponents, whom he has just described as deceivers who are only interested in what they can get for themselves. So Paul calls Epimenides a *prophet*. Here the term 'prophet' is used with a very broad meaning. Epimenides was not a prophet in the sense that he had been called by God to speak for him or on his behalf, but Paul grants him the title because he spoke a truth that still applied hundreds of years later.

Paul tells Titus to rebuke his opponents *so that they may be sound in the faith* (**1:13**). As long as there is life, there is hope that they may return to God. What is impossible with people is possible with God.

Finally, Paul gives some indications about what his opponents were teaching. They were *Jewish myths* (**1:14**), empty of scriptural or historical basis, human teachings invented to turn believers from the truth. The false teaching seems to have forbidden the eating of certain foods that were considered impure (**1:15**). This teaching may have derived from the Jews who still wanted to cling to the dietary laws of the OT that Christ had abolished (Acts 10:10-15). Paul stresses that the false teachers are unable to arrive at the truth because both their intelligence and their consciences are warped.

These opponents may *claim to know God* (**1:16**), in the sense that they say openly and publicly that they are believers. However, their actions give the lie to their words. No matter how good it may look, a bad tree never produces good fruit.

2:1-3:8 Living as Believers

2:1-10 Living as Witnesses

Titus' first responsibility, and that of all elders, is to teach *sound doctrine* (**2:1**). This doctrine must have an effect on the lives of believers, and so Paul gives advice to various groups.

Older men (**2:2**) must set an example of sobriety and self-control. In Africa, 'elders' are respected, and thus they sometimes consider themselves above the law and entitled to do as they please. Paul, however, tells them to live balanced lives. They should be respected not just because they have cultural authority over the young but because their lives inspire respect. They should be known for the *faith*, *love* and *endurance* they demonstrate. Paul has spoken of faith, love and hope as the very basis of the Christian life (1 Cor 13:13), but here he replaces 'hope' with 'endurance', suggesting that the hope that looks forward to the return of Jesus causes believers to persevere in their Christian lives. After all, what good is perseverance if there is nothing to hope for?

Older women should be models for younger women, particularly through their godly lifestyle and their teaching (**2:3**). Too many old people forfeit respect because they are malicious and pass their time in gossip or drinking. Wine was a part of the everyday food of Cretans, as it was in all regions of the Mediterranean, but that was no excuse for drinking too much of it. Older Christian women can show the differences between themselves and others by their self-control.

Younger women (**2:4**) can learn from the older women and can in turn become models for their families. They should love their husbands and their children. Their behaviour will demonstrate the truth of the beliefs they hold. If their actions do not bring honour to God, those watching them may well *malign the word of God* by claiming that what the women believe is merely human teaching. The women need to beware lest their behaviour lead others to commit the serious sin of blasphemy.

The advice for *young men* seems very brief: practise self-control (**2:6**). This same requirement applies to everyone, young and old, in the Christian community. Those who are self-controlled master their tongues, control their moods and practise moderation.

Titus himself is addressed as one of the young men. But as a leader, he also receives additional advice. While the older men must be models for the young men, and the older women models for the young women, Titus must be a model for everyone! (**2:7b**; see also 1 Tim 4:12). Both his teaching and his conduct must be such that nobody can attack them. His teaching should be so well grounded that no one will be able to argue with him, and his conduct must conform to his teaching. His detractors will be left without anything to argue about (**2:8**).

Paul recommends that *slaves* show loyalty and submission (**2:9**). But why does Paul not question the very institution of slavery? The answer may be that although Christians, and especially pastors, must be committed to addressing social problems, Paul is here writing a pastoral letter, not a treatise on social problems. He makes it clear elsewhere that he does not approve of slavery, for he declares that in Christ there is neither 'slave nor free' (Gal 3:28). He invites all to follow Christ, for whom there are no longer any slaves.

Paul is dealing with church life in this letter. If relationships among Christians are brotherly, slaves are simply servants or domestics. A common problem among domestics is talking back to their employers or cheating after they have earned their confidence (**2:9-10**). Such behaviour shows that they scorn authority. Like all other believers, they should prove by their behaviour that their doctrine is sound and so *make the teaching about God our Saviour attractive* (**2:10**).

2:11-15 Grace for Living

Paul realizes that the advice he has just given can easily be transformed into burdensome and constricting laws, and so he turns from a discussion of how we should live to how we can find the ability to live this way. The answer lies in the grace of God that was made evident by the coming of Jesus Christ to bring salvation to all (**2:11**). This saving grace enables us to live a life that glorifies God and strengthens us to resist the temptations of *this present age* and to joyfully live *self-controlled, upright and godly lives* (**2:12**).

If such lives seem difficult, we can take comfort in the fact that we are awaiting a wonderful event – the return of Jesus Christ (**2:13**; see also 2 Tim 4:8). When that day comes, we will see the *glorious appearing of our great God and Saviour, Jesus Christ*. This phrase can be translated in two different ways, depending on whether we take the whole phrase 'our great God and Saviour' as referring to Jesus Christ, or whether we see it as referring to the glory of both 'our great God' and 'our Saviour Jesus Christ'. It seems that the first translation is more likely to be the correct one, for comparison with 2 Timothy 4:8 shows that the 'appearing' of which Paul speaks is the return of Jesus. Moreover **2:14** speaks only of Jesus and of what he did for us when he sacrificed himself for us and died in our place. It can thus be argued that 2:13 is a strong statement of the divinity of Christ.

Returning to his starting point, Paul reminds us that Jesus' sacrifice wiped away our sins and made us his *very own* people, who are eager to follow his example and do good works.

Titus has the heavy responsibility of teaching, exhorting and even rebuking where necessary (**2:15**). He may well attract criticism from his fellow-believers, and especially from the older ones. So Paul encourages him, *Do not let anyone despise you* (see also 1 Tim 4:12). Titus may be young in years, but he is mature enough to lead a church.

3:1-8 Living in Society

Paul now moves on to a topic that he must already have discussed with the Cretan believers, for he tells Titus to *remind* them of the need to *be subject to rulers and authorities* (**3:1**). They are to obey administrative, judicial and political authorities. Doing this could be difficult for Christians in the Roman Empire, where the authorities persecuted Christians and could demand that they worship the emperor. Paul was well aware of this. He had suffered under these authorities and would eventually die a martyr at their hands. Nevertheless, he would not counsel rebellion.

Those of us in Africa who enjoy religious freedom need to remember that, if war comes, we could soon be in a similar position to the Christians under the Roman empire. We should thus pray for our governments and for the preservation of peace so that we may serve God with joy.

Paul also advises believers to maintain good interpersonal relations and a peaceful social life (**3:2**). In this way, they will be different from the quarrelsome false teachers (**3:9-11**; 1:10) and from the people among whom they live – and whom they once resembled (**3:3**; see also 2 Tim 3:2). From the sixteenth century on, European Christians played an enormous role in shaping prosperous and democratic Western societies, even though today the West has become post-Christian. African Christians, too, should work towards building an African society in which life will be pleasant. Such a contribution begins with sound interpersonal relations with unbelievers.

The only reason the believers are now different from their compatriots is because of the work of God their Saviour, who has made them new creatures (3:4-5; see also Eph 2:1-10). This work began with *the kindness and love of*

God our Saviour (**3:4**). God the Father sent Jesus, his Son, and at the end of his earthly ministry Jesus sent the Holy Spirit. Thus all three persons of the Trinity are involved in the work of salvation. This work is described as the *washing of rebirth* and as *renewal by the Holy Spirit* (**3:5**). The 'washing' refers not to baptism but to the cleansing involved in our purification and regeneration. This renewal is the work of the Spirit, who guarantees that we are now *heirs having the hope of eternal life* (**3:7**).

Paul underscores his great statement about the work of God that makes a new person out of a sinner with the words, *This is a trustworthy saying* (**3:8**; see also 1 Tim 1:15; 3:1). The believer who has understood this truth can excel in good works and live a life that glorifies God.

3:9-11 Protecting the Church

Several times in this letter, Paul returns to the danger posed by false doctrines. It seems that the problems in Crete were the same that Timothy faced in Ephesus. In both places, there were those who loved to indulge in speculation about genealogies and pointless arguments about details of the Jewish law (**3:9**; Tim 1:4). If there is anybody in the community who wants to start this type of argument, this *divisive person* (**3:10**) must first be warned of the danger of what he or she is doing. Anyone refusing to heed this warning, and a second one, must be expelled from the community of believers. Paul is adamant about this course of action because such people are a source of division and error.

3:12-15 Final words

In closing, Paul explains that he is hoping to send either Artemas or Tychicus to replace Titus in Crete. We know nothing of Artemas, but Tychicus was one of Paul's regular companions and emissaries (Acts 20:4; Eph 6:21; Col 4:7-8; 2 Tim 4:12). When his replacement arrives, Titus must travel to meet Paul at Nicopolis (**3:10**).

Titus is asked to help two men named Zenas and Apollos, who may have been travelling preachers, and who may even have brought this letter to Titus. All that we know about Zenas is that he was a lawyer, and that his name is Greek. Apollos, on the other hand, was a well-known preacher (Acts 18:24-28; 1 Cor 3:4-6; 16:12). By providing material support for these servants of God, the Cretans would be giving evidence of the good works that Paul has been advocating.

Solomon Andria

Further Reading

Kelly, J. N. D. *The Pastoral Epistles.* Repr. BNTC. Peabody: Hendrickson, 1993.

Guthrie, Donald. *The Pastoral Epistles.* Rev. ed. TNT. Leicester, InterVarsity Press, 1994.

Mounce, William D. *The Pastoral Epistles.* WBC. Nashville: Thomas Nelson Publishers, 2000.

PHILEMON

The Apostle Paul wrote this letter in about AD 62 when he was a prisoner in Rome. It was addressed to Philemon, one of the leaders of the church at Colosse (see Col 4:9, 17, where Onesimus and Archippus are also mentioned). Tactfully and respectfully, Paul deals with an issue that still causes suffering on the African continent, namely slavery. Paul asks his friend to do two difficult things: to pardon Onesimus, his runaway slave, despite the seriousness of his crime, and to accept him from now on as his brother in Christ, his equal.

What the apostle asks Philemon to do is absolutely revolutionary for his time. His request goes far beyond mere legal freeing of a slave, and is in fact a real test of faith.

Outline of Contents

COMMENTARY

1-3 Introduction

Paul starts by introducing himself and *Timothy our brother* as the co-authors of the letter (**1a**). His habit of including his associates in his greetings is a wonderful indication of humility and a reminder that God's work is always a joint effort. His humility is also evident in the way he greets Philemon as a fellow-worker (**1b**) and mentions others to whom the letter is addressed. *Apphia our sister* (**2a**), may be Philemon's wife or some other woman who played an important role in the community. In the church at Colosse, women were respected.

Archippus (**2b**) was probably the senior pastor of this church. By mentioning him, Paul implies that he is to be involved in bringing about the reconciliation between Philemon and Onesimus.

Although the letter to Philemon is the most personal of Paul's letters, he also includes a greeting to *the church that meets in your home* (**2c**). Clearly he does not regard reconciliation as purely a private matter. It affects the whole community and indirectly involves the whole church. The church met in a home because this was common practice until about the third century AD. Doing this enabled Christians to maintain a family spirit.

Paul concludes his introduction with a blessing that is found in most of the apostles' letters. He wishes his readers grace and peace from God the Father and the Lord Jesus Christ (**4**). This greeting is still in frequent use among African Christians – for which we should be grateful. Would our words be worth listening to if they were not accompanied by sincere prayer for God's blessing on the listeners?

4-7 Paul's Prayer

Paul next tells us how he prays for Philemon. His prayer contains thanksgiving and a request. There are three things for which he thanks God: Philemon's faith, the love that he has for the Lord Jesus, and the love that he has for *the saints* (the believers) (**4-5**). There is no real faith in God without love for our brothers and sisters. Philemon's faith is thus consistent. His love has had far-reaching effects, for it has brought Paul *joy* and *encouragement* (**7a**) and has had an impact on other people. Literally, Paul says that 'the entrails (or bowels – KJV) of the saints are rested', but what this expression means is you *have refreshed the hearts of the saints* (**7b**). Yet Paul still prays that God will make Philemon even more effective in sharing his faith. There is always more we can do for God. Philemon is doing well, but he can always do better.

8-21 Plea on Behalf of Onesimus

At the heart of this letter is Paul's plea on behalf of the runaway slave who had become a Christian while fleeing and who is now returning and asking forgiveness. His return is like that of the prodigal son (Luke 15:11-32), except that here Paul acts as a go-between. His plea is in five parts.

8-9 A Request for the Sake of Love

Paul does not want to take advantage of his authority, and so he appeals to Philemon not as an apostle but as an old man (he was then between sixty and seventy years old) and as *a prisoner of Jesus Christ* (**8-9**). In describing himself like this, he is not looking for pity, but is simply seeking to lay aside his authority. Philemon's response must be a willing one, not one that is forced (**14**). Paul, request is made on *the basis of love*. What we have here is a friend appealing to a friend.

10-14 A Description of Onesimus' Worth

Paul describes Onesimus as *my son ... who became my son while I was in chains* (**10**), and as *my very heart* (**12**). He clearly has a loving attachment to the young man whom he had won to the Lord in such unusual circumstances. He is even reluctant to send him back to Philemon (**13**), but has decided that this has to be done in the interests of restoration and reconciliation.

Paul plays on Onesimus' name, which means 'useful'. His words can be paraphrased like this: 'The one whose name means "useful" was formerly useless to you. But now that he has been born again, he will be useful. From now on his behaviour will match his name' (**11**). Only God can make us useful to others, to ourselves and to himself. In Christ, we accomplish what we were made for.

15-17 A Reminder of Onesimus' New Status

Paul invites Philemon to understand what has happened as something that God had planned in order to accomplish something good. There is no such thing as 'luck' in the lives of the children of God. Even as Onesimus ran away, God was watching over him and guiding him to meet Paul in prison. Paul speculates that the main reason he escaped may even have been so that he could be converted (**15**).

The Onesimus who is returning home is no longer the same Onesimus who fled. That is why he is to be received *no longer as a slave, but better than a slave, as a dear brother* (**16**). Paul is telling Philemon that Onesimus has a completely new status, and is indirectly presenting Philemon with a problem. Can a brother be a slave? Philemon will have to answer this question for himself. But later in the letter, Paul expresses his confidence that Philemon *will do even more than I ask* (**21**). He has already asked that Onesimus be accepted as a brother – what 'more' can Philemon do except give him his freedom? This is what Paul is requesting, although he does not say so in so many words.

18-19 An Offer to Take Onesimus' Place

Paul's offer is a beautiful illustration of the doctrine of substitution. He offers to take the place of Onesimus, the runaway who may have stolen his master's goods. The apostle does not try to defend him. He does not try to explain or justify Onesimus' behaviour. Instead he says, *If he has done you any wrong ... charge it to me ... I will pay it back* (**18-19**). And so that there may be no doubt about this, he personally signs the letter to guarantee his commitment. What an example! What love! Anyone wanting to bring about reconciliation must be ready to pay the price, to be personally involved. This is the way in which Christ takes on himself

the debt of our sin. This is how God receives us as his own sons and daughters. What grace!

19-21 An Earnest Appeal

It is only at the end of his letter that Paul makes a strong appeal. In contrast to his attitude at the beginning of the letter, Paul is now almost demanding. He reminds Philemon *that you owe me your very self* (**19**) and wishes to *have some benefit from you in the Lord* (**20**) He concludes by saying that he is *confident of your obedience* (**21**). Does Philemon really have a choice about what he will do with Onesimus?

22-25 Greetings

Looking forward to the possibility of gaining his own freedom and being able to visit Philemon, Paul asks that a guest room be prepared for him. He believes in the power of prayer, and anticipates that Philemon's prayers for him will be answered (**22**).

Paul next sends greetings from a number of his companions (**22-24**). These companions include Mark and Demas, who had formerly deserted Paul but who have returned to work with him. The patience of Barnabas has clearly matured the young Mark (Acts 15:37-39). Demas, who had once abandoned Paul 'because he loved the world' (2 Tim 4:10), has now returned to serve with him.

Conclusion

African readers, aware of the role that slavery has played in our own history, may well be offended that Paul does not insist that Onesimus be freed immediately and that slavery be abolished. But we need to remember that at that time taking a definite stand against slavery would have resulted in immediate conflict between Rome and Christianity. Christianity would have been labelled as harmful to society. So instead of condemning slavery directly, Paul laid out the principles that would undermine slavery.

The letter to Philemon is truly a treatise on the abolition of slavery. It should be a source of hope for Africa that, according to tradition, Onesimus was not only freed but later became a bishop in the church of Jesus Christ.

                                                    Soro Soungalo

Further Reading

Hendriksen, William. *Exposition of Galatians, Ephesians, Philippians, Colossians, and Philemon*. Grand Rapids: Baker Book House, 2002.

O'Brien, Peter T. *Colossians, Philemon*. WBC. Waco, Texas: Word Books, 1982.

Vincent, Marvin R., *A Critical and Exegetical Commentary on the Epistles to the Philippians and to Philemon*. ICC. Edinburgh: T & T Clark, 1987.

HEBREWS

The message of Hebrews was a great encouragement for many believers during the Communist era in Ethiopia (1974-1991). Both the Ethiopian Orthodox Church and the Communist government were deeply suspicious of truly born-again believers. They regarded them as agents of American imperialism and thus as a threat to the nation. They were seen as betraying the traditional national religion by adhering to an imported foreign religion. The Communists, aided by the Orthodox Church, made several fierce attempts to indoctrinate Christians in Marxist philosophy. Trained Communist cadres engaged in a relentless effort to reform the thinking of born-again believers so that they would renounce their faith in Christ. Life became extremely difficult for Christians. Many, including the writer of this commentary, were imprisoned and tortured, and some were even put to death. Others suffered discrimination and were denied jobs, had their property confiscated and their bank accounts frozen. Churches lost assets and were forced to go underground. A new network of small house church groups sprang up throughout the country to contend for the true faith in Christ, in defiance of Communism and religious traditions. However, under intense persecution, some believers went back to the ritualistic national Orthodox religious system. A few members of the house churches also turned out to be spies for the Communist cadres. But the faithful ones stood firm in Christ.

In those dark days, the Ethiopian believers were encouraged by the message of the book of Hebrews, and its message still speaks to all who face the challenges posed by Orthodox religious syncretism, African traditional religion, the day-to-day temptations of worldly passions and, in Muslim countries in Africa, the pressure of extremely difficult situations. The Letter to the Hebrews calls on believers to make a bold commitment to Christ in the face of public abuse, imprisonment and the loss of their property (10:32-34). They should not give in to discouragement and weariness but should continue to contend for the faith (12:1-4).

Date and Authorship

The letter was most likely written before the destruction of the temple in AD 70, probably sometime between AD 64 and AD 68, and was directed to Jewish Christians (the Jews were also known as 'Hebrews'). Both they and the writer of this letter had come to faith in Christ Jesus through the preaching and teaching of those who had heard Jesus (2:3-4; 13:7). They had been believers for some time, possibly even for as long as thirty years (13:7). But their faith in Christ was being undermined by intense persecution.

No one really knows who wrote the Letter to the Hebrews, for no author's name is mentioned in the text. Ancient traditions ascribe it to Paul, Barnabas, Luke or Clement of Rome. All that we know about the author is that he knew the OT very well and was acquainted with Timothy (13:23).

Purpose

The author sets out to encourage the wavering Hebrew Christians by pointing them to Christ Jesus as the fulfilment of the OT covenant. After establishing the overall supremacy of Christ, he goes on to make the case that he is superior to the prophets and even to angels. More than that, he establishes that Jesus Christ outranks Moses and is superior to the entire Jewish priestly system. His point is that faith in Christ is an improvement on Judaism because Christ offers a superior covenant, a superior sanctuary and a sacrifice truly able to cleanse from sin.

In view of Christ's supremacy, the writer exhorts his readers to persevere in the faith in the face of persecutions. He points out the consequences of not doing so and encourages them by reminding them of examples of devoted heroes and heroines of the faith. He ends by explaining the role of discipline and giving them some practical advice for living the Christian life.

The Use of the OT in Hebrews

The author of Hebrews supports his case with at least sixty quotations from the OT. He quotes Psalms twenty-four times, the Pentateuch (especially Genesis and Deuteronomy) twenty-three times, the Wisdom Literature twice, and 1 Samuel once. Most of these quotations are taken word for word from the Septuagint translation, which was the Greek Bible used by most believers in the early church. Yet it was a translation, and sometimes a very free one that paraphrased the original Hebrew. The OT as we have it in our Bibles today is based on the ancient Hebrew texts, not on this Greek translation. Consequently, we will sometimes find differences between a text quoted in Hebrews and the same text in our copy of the OT.

It is also important to remember that the writer of Hebrews is not terribly interested in whether the text in its original context was talking about Christ. His question as he approaches the OT is, 'Can I use this verse to communicate a truth about Christ and his work of redemption?' This was an acceptable practise in the first century.

Given the differences between the Septuagint and our translations and the fact that our approach to exposition is very different from that of the first century, it is not surprising that we are sometimes puzzled by how the writer of Hebrews uses the OT. We may even suspect that he is not quoting it accurately. But that is not the case. The writer is very faithful to the Septuagint text whenever an exact quotation is needed.

Outline of Contents

COMMENTARY

1:1-2:18 Jesus Christ, Supreme over All

The writer of Hebrews recognized the enslaving power of his traditions and the danger Judaism's ritualistic regulations presented to the new faith in Christ. So he skilfully used his knowledge of OT Scriptures to show that Christ is superior to everything that was known to the Jewish people and to their religious system. He began by stressing Christ's exalted position as the Son of God, piling up OT quotations as evidence of Christ's deity and absolute supremacy. By doing this, he is laying a strong foundation for the warnings and encouragements given in the rest of the letter.

We too need to contend for true faith in the deity and humanity of Jesus Christ. We need to defend this truth against those like Jehovah's Witnesses, who deny the deity and supremacy of Jesus, and against those who exalt others to positions which belong only to Christ, as when Roman Catholics and the Coptic Orthodox regard Mary as a mediatrix of grace. In order to do this properly, we need to be like the writer of Hebrews, well acquainted with the religious traditions of our own African cultures and with the Scriptures of both the Old and the New Testaments. God has revealed his redemptive plan in all these Scriptures, and we need to be able to use them to defend the gospel from threats posed by our traditional cultures. It is not enough simply to know the NT for, as the great African theologian Augustine of Hippo (a town in modern Algeria) said: 'The New is in the Old concealed, the Old is in the New revealed.'

1:1-3 Jesus Christ, the Son of God

Hebrews begins with the words, *God spoke to our forefathers through the prophets* (1:1) and the announcement that he has spoken again in Christ. The reference to 'our forefathers' makes it clear that this letter was sent to Jewish believers. God had spoken to their ancestors through the prophets, now he speaks to them through his Son.

This Son is no mere human messenger, for he is the owner and *heir of all things* – all of creation belongs to him. More than that, he created all things (1:2). He is also not merely a pale imitation of his father, as a human ruler's son may be. Rather, he radiates the glory of God and is the *exact representation of his being* (1:3a). The Lord Jesus Christ is the same as God in all respects, so that Paul could say that 'in Christ all the fulness of the Deity lives in bodily form' (Col 2:9). In other words, God's very substance, his divine being, is embodied in Christ. That is why Jesus could say, 'Anyone who has seen me has seen the Father' (John 14:9). He is the word of God who became flesh and lived among human beings. John spoke of him saying, 'We have seen his glory, the glory of the One and Only who came from the Father, full of grace and truth' (John 1:14).

As God, Jesus holds the universe together *by his powerful word*, that word spoken when 'God said' in Genesis 1 and the universe came into being. If he withdrew that word, the world would cease to exist. But he does not withdraw it but upholds and directs the world to its divinely ordained destiny (**1:3b**).

Besides being our creator, Christ is also our priest who *provided purification for sins* (**1:3c**), a point that the author will return to several times in the letter. Now he is sitting as our king, in the place of honour at the right side of the majestic God in heaven because his work is finished (**1:3d**).

This description of Jesus as God, creator, priest and king can leave the readers of this letter in no doubt that he is superior to all prophets. Thus any message coming from him must be superior, that is, more complete and final, than any message God has sent in the past. There is no greater messenger of the word than the Son of God, who is himself the Word of God. African Christians need to remember this truth.

1:4-14 Jesus Christ, Superior to Angels

The Jewish religion had a very high regard for angels. So the writer feels it necessary to stress that Jesus is not just some particularly exalted archangel, but is a different type of being. He does this by using several OT quotations to prove to the Jewish believers that the Christ is superior to angels, who are merely God's messengers and are not his Son and heir (**1:4**).

When the writer says that Jesus *became … superior to the angels* (**1:4**) he is referring to the fact that Christ's voluntary emptying of himself by becoming human (Phil 2:7) meant that for a while his status was lower than that of angels. But with the work of redemption completed, he became superior to them (or, rather, resumed his original superior position). In the same way, though he is the Son from eternity, his obedience to his Father in his incarnate state demonstrated that the title 'Son' is his by right, and cannot be claimed by any angel.

The author lists five ways in which Christ is superior to angels.

- **God calls Jesus 'my son'**. Believers may collectively be called 'the sons of God' (Rom 8:14), but only Jesus Christ is given the title *my Son*. No angel is ever addressed in that way. But that is the title that God uses to express his pleasure in the Messiah, when he says, *You are my Son; today I have become your Father* (**1:5a**; Ps 2:7). The word 'today' is used because Jesus' exaltation marked his entrance into the status of Sonship in a new way. He had been God's Son long before his birth in Bethlehem, as is clear from his prayer, 'glorify me in your presence with the glory I had with you before the world began' (John 17:5). However, his obedient life on earth demonstrated that he truly deserved this status. Jesus'

willingness to become a human being in order to save us led God to exalt him through resurrection to 'the highest place and gave him the name that is above every name' (Phil 2:5-6). Paul makes the same point when he writes: 'Through the Spirit of holiness Christ Jesus was declared with power to be the Son of God by his resurrection from the dead' (Rom 1:4). The writer of Hebrews also quotes God's promise to David: *I will be his Father and he will be my Son* (**1:5b**; 2 Sam 7:14). Although those words initially applied to Solomon, they apply far more to Jesus, particularly when we consider the preceding words in 2 Samuel – "I will establish the throne of his kingdom for ever' (2 Sam 7:13).

- **Angels worship him**. The writer refers to Christ as God's *firstborn* (**1:6a**), an expression that Paul also uses when he calls Christ 'the firstborn over all creation' (Col 1:15). In these contexts, 'firstborn' does not mean that he was literally born first. Rather, it is a title that declares Christ's special position of honour and dignity. It is equivalent to the earlier reference to him as God's 'heir' (1:2). In the culture of the time, a firstborn son was the one who receives the greatest share of the inheritance and a special blessing from his father. The words, *Let all God's angels worship him* (**1:6b**) shows that God commanded his angels to worship his Son as they worship the Father. This quotation, like others in Hebrews, is taken from the Septuagint (see introduction to this commentary). It seems that the writer is quoting Deuteronomy 32:43 (or possibly Psalm 96:7) from memory, because he changes the Septuagint's 'sons of God' into 'angels' – a justifiable change because both expressions refer to the same beings.

- **Angels are messengers, serving Jesus**. The writer quotes a possible translation of Psalm 104:4, which says of God: *He makes his angels winds, his servants flames of fire* (**1:7**). In the NIV translation of Psalm 104:4, the word 'messengers' is used instead of 'angels', but the word 'angel' means 'messenger'. These angels can be referred to as 'winds' because the word 'wind' means 'spirit' in both Hebrew and Greek. The angels are created spirit beings with no physical bodies (although they sometimes assume human form when they appear to human beings). They serve the Father and the Son, who is equal with the Father. Thus they served Jesus when he was on earth and strengthened him in times of trials (Matt 4:11; Luke 22:43). But while the angels serve before God's throne, Jesus sits on that throne, in the place of authority. He has been anointed by God the Father and is enthroned *for ever and ever* (**1:8-9**). In support of this assertion, the writer quotes Psalm 45:6-7, where God the Father addresses the Son.

- **Jesus Christ is the eternal creator of the heavens and the earth**. In support of this assertion, the author quotes the Father addressing his Son in the Septuagint translation of Psalm 102:25-27: *In the beginning, O Lord, you laid the foundation of the earth, and the heavens are the work of your hands* (**1:10-12**). Here God gives his approval to our calling his Son 'Lord', just as he had earlier given his approval to our calling him 'God' (**1:8**). As created beings, angels must also have been created by Jesus Christ, who must therefore be superior to them. The whole creation will change one day when Jesus does away with the old creation and brings in the new creation (Rev 21; see also Isa 66:22), but Jesus Christ himself will never change (**1:11-12**; see also **13:8**).

- **Jesus Christ is the sovereign Lord of all**. God has never invited any angel to sit down in the place of honour at his right side, but that is where Jesus Christ is seated. In support of this, the author quotes Psalm 110:1: *Sit at my right hand until I make your enemies a footstool for your feet* (**1:13-14**). Jesus quoted these same words when he asked a crowd how David, who was speaking by the Spirit, could say that the Christ was his son and also his Lord (Matt 22:43-44; Mark 12:35-37). He also referred to this passage in Matthew 26:64 and Mark 14:62. Peter quoted these verses to describe Jesus' ascension and enthronement at the right hand of God in his great sermon on the day of Pentecost (Acts 2:33-36; see also Mark 16:19). The verse is also often quoted in the NT letters (Rom 8:34; Col 3:1; Heb 1:3, 13; 8:1; 10:12; 12:2; 1 Pet 3:22). Clearly Psalm 110:1 was seen as a strong statement that Jesus the Messiah is now enthroned in glory in heaven.

The author of Hebrews saves one powerful point till last in his description of the status of angels. Not only are they subordinate to Christ and intended to serve him, but they are *sent to serve those who will inherit salvation* (**1:14**). Angels are servants who serve not only the Son but also all believers.

2:1-4 Warning Against Ignoring Christ

My father was a very strict disciplinarian who never allowed any of his children to rebel against him without suffering the consequences. As a young boy, I was very careful to obey him promptly in order not to incur any punishment. If human fathers can require such obedience from their children, how much more should believers be obedient to the message brought by Christ, who spoke to us in the name of his Father! No wonder we are warned not to drift away from the truth of Christ but *to pay more careful attention ... to what we have heard* (**2:1**).

God took strong action when the Israelites neglected the truth they had heard from Moses and rebelled against the message God had sent them by his angels. He made sure that *every violation and disobedience received its just punishment* (**2:2**; see also Judg 2:10-14). Given that Jesus is far greater than Moses or any angel, those who neglect the truth they know about Christ will suffer a far worse fate than those who disobeyed the truth revealed to Moses. The believers would not escape the severe judgment of God if they returned to their former beliefs and ignored *such a great salvation* (**2:3a**).

The writer reminds them of four important witnesses to the divine origin of the message of salvation (**2:3b-4**):

- *The Lord* (Jesus Christ) *first announced* it. This message came to us via God's own Son.
- *Those who heard* the message from the Son were the apostles, whom he commissioned to proclaim his message. These apostles had *confirmed* the truth of the message to the Hebrews.
- *God* (the Father) *testified to it,* confirming the truth of the message by providing *signs, wonders and various miracles,* just as he had done when he established his first covenant with Israel at the time of the exodus.
- *The Holy Spirit* confirmed the message by distributing gifts to believers that were to be used for their encouragement and edification (1 Cor 12:7, 11; Eph 4:11).

All three persons of the Godhead (God the Father, God the Son and God the Holy Spirit) thus contributed to the preaching of this great salvation by their human agents, the apostles. If the Hebrew believers neglected the word that was brought to them by these agents, they would be ignoring the Father, the Son and the Holy Spirit, and would inevitably drift away from the path of truth in Christ.

Unfortunately, many African Christians are neglecting the message of Christ. They neglect it when they fail to read, study and meditate on the word of God and to maintain a private prayer life. Because they do not seek to walk each day in step with the Spirit, their lives do not show evidence of the fruit of the Holy Spirit. Instead they live in disobedience and spiritual lethargy, and suffer from what I call 'spiritual perception disorder'. Not knowing biblical truth, they cannot think in terms of it and so are easily enticed by false teachings. They are Christians only in name and fail to realize that they are suffering from serious spiritual malnutrition.

Like the writer of Hebrews, African church leaders should appeal to local churches to wake up and strengthen their lives with the Lord. Neglectful Christians must be warned to repent and obey the message of salvation.

2:5-18 Christ's Humiliation and Exaltation

The believers to whom this letter was written seem to have been puzzled about the relationship between Christ and angels. They knew that the hierarchy presented in Scripture runs from God, who is spirit, to angels, who are also spiritual beings, to humans, who have physical bodies. They could have quoted Psalm 8:4-5, which says that 'human beings' were created 'a little lower than the angels'. They had been taught that Jesus was fully human with a human body. So wasn't he actually somewhat inferior to the angels? So the writer of Hebrews next set out four good reasons why the fact that Jesus became human does not make him inferior to angels, but superior to them:

- **Christ recovered humanity's lost dominion**. When God first created the world, he created humans beings just *a little lower than the angels* and gave them *glory and honour* and dominion over his creation (**2:6-8a**; Ps 8:4-6; Gen 1:26-31). However, because humans were disobedient, Satan took their authority out of their hands and made himself 'the prince of this world' (John 16:11). Consequently 'the whole world is under the control of the evil one' (1 John 5:19). When he tested Jesus, the devil was telling the truth when he said that humans had given him all 'their authority and splendour' and that he could 'give it to anyone' (Luke 4:5-7). Rather than *everything* being subject to humanity, humans became slaves to sin and the power of darkness. But with Jesus Christ, God changed all that (**2:9**). Jesus became the Son of Man in order to retrieve the glory and honour lost by Adam and Eve. As the last Adam (1 Cor 15:45), he suffered death because of human sin and restored the dominion that was lost because of disobedience. Today, everything is under Christ's feet (Eph 1:20-23) and believers share his kingly dominion (Rev 1:5-6). One day, when he establishes his kingdom, we shall reign with him in glory and honour. Thus in the world to come, human beings will not be inferior to angels (**2:5**).

- **Christ brings many sons and daughters back to glory**. Christ Jesus is *the author of their salvation,* the one who opened the way to the Father (**2:10**). In order to do this, he had to give up his divine glory and become human like us, including suffering like us and for us. He had to identify with humankind, even in our suffering, in order to be the suitable sacrifice for us. He suffered like us, and while he did so led the way in perfect obedience (see also 2:17-18; 5:8-9). Thus he can be said to have been made *perfect through suffering.* Now he is united to us by his humanity, and we are united to God through his salvation. In fact we are now part of God's holy family, which means that we are his brothers and sisters (**2:11**). He has made us holy and enabled us to share his glory (John 17:10, 22-24), so that he *is not ashamed to call* those whom he saved his brothers and sisters. In fact, after his terrible suffering, he will lead us in worshipping the Father like the psalmist did: *I will declare your name to my brothers, in the presence of the congregation I will sing your praises* (**2:12**; Ps 22:22). Changing the metaphor, the author next speaks of believers not as brothers and sisters of Christ, but as Christ's children (**2:13**). He quotes Isaiah 8:17-18, in which the speaker and his children present themselves before God as 'signs and

symbols' of trust in and faithfulness to God the Father in the midst of adversity (see also John 17:1-26).

- **Christ defeated the devil and delivered us from the power of death**. We were all subject to death's power because of the fall, in which every member of the human race died to God and became separated from the life of Christ. Christ knew that in order to save us, he would have to become like us (**2:14a**). It would have been no use for him to take on angelic nature, unless his purpose had been to save angels. But his aim was not to save angels, but to save all those human beings, both Jews and Gentiles, who are Abraham's descendants by faith (**2:16**). So he had to become fully human, taking on flesh and blood so that he could endure human death (John 1:14). Through this death, he acquired victory over death and destroyed Satan who holds the power of death (**2:14b**). The word 'destroy' does not mean that the devil ceased to exist, for he is still alive and working to deceive us (**2:8b**). But he was disarmed, and so can no longer steal, kill and destroy (Col 2:15). Now authority over death is in the hands of our Lord Jesus Christ. Those who trust Christ Jesus have once and for all been delivered from Satan's authority and from the terrible fear of death (**2:15**).

- **Christ became a sympathetic, merciful and faithful high priest**. As pure spirits, the holy angels do not have a corrupt nature like that of human beings and so they cannot identify with human problems. But because Jesus became one of us, he knows the temptations we endure that, even though he himself did not yield to any of them but remained sinless (**2:18**). He knows what it is like to be tired, hungry and thirsty (John 4:6; Matt 4:2). He has experienced rejection and false accusations (Isa 53:3). He suffered on the cross and died a humiliating death. All of this suffering prepared him to be a *merciful* high priest towards humans *and a faithful high priest in service to God* (**2:17**).

In Africa today, some are spreading a false teaching about suffering that results in grumbling and complaining about every painful experience. These people do not see any suffering as coming from God. They teach that all suffering is wrong and blame it either on a generational curse or on Satan. They make no attempt to distinguish between the discipline that comes from God and the suffering that is the result of one's own foolish actions. Such people need to learn that faith in Christ is accompanied by many trials and much suffering, and that this is something that is granted to all who believe in Christ (Phil 1:28-29). We need to take Jesus as our example. He endured temptation and suffering that qualified him to be our example of perfect obedience in the midst of suffering. His example challenges us to allow suffering to produce a godly character in us (Rom 5:3-4). Since Jesus himself suffered when he was tempted, he learned something new for our sake, and now he understands human temptations and is able to help when we are being tempted.

Church leaders must guard the truth of Scripture concerning suffering. If they fail to do so, they will fail to serve God and will be like Eli, the high priest who failed to help his sons to live in the ways of God (1 Sam 2:12-36). But Christ Jesus is not like Eli, who even accused the broken-hearted Hannah of being drunk (1 Sam 1:9-18). Christ knows where we hurt and is a faithful and merciful servant in the household of God.

3:1-4:13 Jesus Christ, Superior to Moses

Confident that he has made his point that Christ is superior to angels, the writer now turns his attention to someone else with whom Jesus might be compared – Moses. The Jews regarded Moses as the greatest man of God the world had ever known because he gave them the law and set up their religious system. However, the writer now seeks to convince the Jewish believers that Jesus Christ is superior even to Moses.

3:1-6 Comparison of Moses and Christ

He begins by assuring the Jewish believers of their status in God, namely that they *share in the heavenly calling* in Christ (**3:1a**). Then he urges them to fix their thoughts on Christ (**3:1b**). This expression means that they were to concentrate on understanding him and recognizing who he is. By concentrating on him, they will avoid the temptation to shift their allegiance to prophets, angels or Moses.

To help them better understand who Jesus is, the author compares him to Moses in terms of the roles they were each assigned. Both had been very *faithful* in carrying out their tasks (**3:2**), but the task given to Jesus was far greater than that given to Moses. Moses had simply been the mediator of the law, the one who brought it to the people. Jesus, by contrast, was God's *apostle* (3:1b). As such, he had been sent from heaven to show humankind what God is like and to teach the truth about God and God's way of salvation through the cross. Christ commissioned his own apostles (Luke 5:13), but he himself received his commission directly from God the Father (John 3:17; 5:36; 6:29; 7:29; 17:3)

Jesus Christ was more than just an apostle. He was also the one and only *high priest* appointed by God. As such, he did not only offer sacrifices, but was himself the sacrifice for sin. Moses could not offer any such sacrifice.

Next, the writer shows that Christ Jesus is worthy of greater honour than Moses because of their different roles in relation to God's house. He illustrates his point by comparing a literal house with God's house, that is, with the people of God. His first point is that the person who builds a house is clearly more important than the house itself (**3:3**).

Moses had been part of God's house (his people) but Christ was the one who had built the house. Or, to change the image slightly, Moses had been a *faithful ... servant in God's house,* that is, among the Israelites (**3:5a**), but Jesus, as the son of the owner, was the one in charge of the house, for the Father's house is his house (**3:6a**). An owner is more important than a servant.

As a faithful servant, Moses testified concerning the coming of Christ (**3:5b**). In particular, he said, 'The Lord your God will raise up for you a prophet like me from among your own brothers. You must listen to him' (Deut 18:15). Christ Jesus is the one who fulfils that prophecy.

The words *we are his house* remind us that believers are God's house, which Moses served, but Christ owned (**3:6b**). But we must not take our membership in his house for granted. Our membership is conditional on faith in Christ. So the writer exhorts the Jewish believers to hold on to the faith and hope in Christ Jesus, which they courageously confess (**3:6c**). We, too, need to *hold on to our courage and hope* if we are to live a practical and victorious Christian life. African believers must hold on to their heavenly calling and keep living for Christ despite the temptations posed by African traditional worship, the culture in which we live, the troubles that come to us, and our own desires.

3:7-4:13 Warning Against Disbelief

The discussion of Moses reminds the writer of the behaviour of those who followed Moses, and he now issues the second of the five warnings in Hebrews. He uses the example of Israel's deliverance from Egypt and their unbelief in the wilderness to show the danger of doubting and disbelieving God's message (Num 14:1-45; Deut 1:26-46).

3:7-19 Don't be like the Israelites

The Jewish believers would have been very familiar with the dreadful history of the Israelites in the wilderness. So the writer does not need to repeat it, but simply quotes Psalm 95:7-11 and applies it to the wavering Jewish Christians, warning them, *Today, if you hear his voice, do not harden your hearts* (**3:7**).

God had delivered the Israelites from Egypt and cared for them, showing his power to do so on numerous occasions. But they still grumbled rather than trusting God during every trial (or *testing* – **3:8-9**). All their experience with God did not enable them to know him better, and they frequently wandered away from the path of obedience to him (**3:10**). Despite what they had suffered in Egypt, they wanted to return there (Num 11:4-6).

Because of their rebellion against God, God decreed that all but two members of the generation who were twenty years of age or older when Moses led them out of Egypt would die before entering his *rest,* that is, the Promised Land he had promised to Abraham and his descendants

(**3:11**; Num 13-14). All the Israelites except Caleb and Joshua forfeited the blessings God had in store for them.

The Jewish Christians can learn an important lesson from the experiences of their own people in the wilderness. God had delivered their ancestors from bondage in Egypt; Christ had delivered the Jewish believers from the dominion of the devil (see Col 1:13). But they must make sure that their resemblance to their ancestors ends there. They must not be like them in rebelling against the one who had delivered them (**3:12**). Thus they must not allow themselves to be enticed away from faith in Christ. In returning to following the traditions of Moses, they would incur the wrath of God. They must take care to avoid being fooled by sin, and must continue to believe in the message of Christ and to *encourage one another daily* (**3:13**). The writer urges them to maintain their steadfast relationship with Christ and to firmly hold to *the confidence* they had in him (**3:14**).

To reinforce his argument, the writer again quotes Psalm 95:7-8 and then asks a series of rhetorical questions to remind his readers of the point he has been making. Even though the Israelites had seen God performing miracles in Egypt, they refused to believe that he would give them victory in Canaan. Their experience of God was of no value to them because they did not trust in him. Therefore, they incurred God's judgment for forty years and their *bodies fell* and were buried in the desert (**3:15-19**). An entire generation was unable to enter the Promised Land, which is God's rest (Num 14:20-35).

Throughout this passage, there is a repeated stress on the word *Today* (**3:7, 15; 4:7**). The psalmist used it when appealing to the people of his day, the writer of Hebrews uses it to appeal to Jewish believers, and the Holy Spirit is still using it to appeal to believers today. We, too, have heard the voice of God in our day proclaiming the gospel of his Son, Jesus Christ. The same Holy Spirit is admonishing us not to miss our opportunity to respond. We must not harden our hearts by refusing to believe in the word of God and preferring to cling to our traditional beliefs. We must hold to the teaching of Christ and cultivate our confidence in him. The word of God should take precedence over every traditional or cultural requirement. If we stand firm in Christ, we will survive victoriously. If we do not, we will live in the wilderness of the flesh, wandering around and around, making no spiritual progress but stuck in the spiritual desert described in Romans 7:7-24 (see also 1 Cor 3:1-4).

4:1-7 Don't fail to enter God's rest

African preachers sometimes mistakenly equate entering Canaan, or the Promised Land, with entering heaven, and ignore the promise that we can also enjoy God's presence and his spiritual blessings in the here and now (Eph 1:3-11; 15-23; 1 Pet 1:3-4). The crossing of the Red Sea and Jordan River do not represent physical death but baptism, which symbolizes spiritual death to our old way of life and resurrection to the new life we enjoy as believers (Rom 6:1-14; Col 2:11-12).

Canaan was the place of God's rest for the Israelites in the sense that it was the goal towards which he was leading them and the place where they could settle down and build homes. But arrival there did not mean the end of all their troubles, as the book of Joshua makes clear (1:8). There were still battles to fight. Thus Canaan illustrates the life of all born-again Christians who live in the battlefield of Romans 6-8.

The Jewish believers to whom Hebrews was written would have understood what the writer meant when he spoke of Canaan, and what he meant when he said that *the promise of entering God's rest still stands* (**4:1a**). They would also have remembered that many Israelites failed to enter the Promised Land and enjoy God's rest (3:18). The writer warns them to take care that none of them *be found to have fallen short* of salvation in Christ (**4:1b**). Just as the promise of rest in Canaan was preached to Israel, so the gospel rest has been preached to the Jewish believers and is available to all who believe in Christ's name (**4:2-3a**). But the Israelites refused to believe the message and thus wasted their opportunity, leading God to declare, *They shall never enter my rest* (**4:3b**).

In case anyone is still confused about what this 'rest' is, the writer explains it in terms of the week of creation. For six days God worked to create the world, but he rested on the seventh day (Gen 2:2). To commemorate this, he declared that the Sabbath day was to be a day of rest for his people (**4:4**; Exod 20:8). Similarly, since Jesus finished his work of salvation and brought in the new creation, he has been resting at the right hand of God the Father (1:13). We are thus offered another opportunity to enter into the rest of God the Father and God the Son, which we should not squander like the Israelites (**4:5-6**). Using the words of Psalm 95:7-8, God announces the new opportunity to enter his rest *Today* (**4:7**; see comment on 3:15). The believers are warned that they should not harden their hearts after hearing the message of salvation rest in Christ. It is only through Christ that they will continue to enjoy salvation rest for their souls (Matt 11:28).

4:8-13 Work hard to enter God's rest

The writer of this letter sees both the Sabbath and the rest Joshua offered as only symbols of the true rest that God was going to provide (**4:8-9**). He stresses that those who enter the *Sabbath-rest* enter *God's rest* and stop doing their *own work,* just as God did (**4:10**). He means that anyone who believes in Christ's finished work of salvation can rest from the effort to earn salvation by keeping God's law. The only work we have to do is to be sure that we remain faithful to God, and avoid the trap of *disobedience.* Disobedience results in believers not enjoying God's rest to the full and in non-believers never entering it (**4:11**).

We cannot hope to cover up our disobedience or our lack of faith so that God will not see it. God has spoken, and his word always produces results. Like God, its source, it is living and has power to penetrate and expose inner thoughts. It is sharp enough to separate our thoughts and our motives, even if they are as closely linked as *soul and spirit, joints and marrow.* It uncovers the hidden secrets of the human heart (**4:12**). His word enables us to see our true nature.

At the end of the day, each of us will have to give an account of his or her life here on earth to God. None of us will be able to stand God's scrutiny, but if we truly walk with him, we will not try to cover up our sins and unbelief (**4:13**). Instead we will humbly acknowledge them and run to Christ to cover our nakedness.

4:14-6:20 Jesus Christ, Superior to Aaron

The writer of this letter has already shown that Christ is superior to angels and to Moses. Now he shows that Jesus' priesthood is superior to that of Aaron, Moses brother. The Hebrew believers were probably tempted to return to the old religious system of their ancestors, which had a visible temple in Jerusalem and a clear set of laws, upheld by the Aaronic priests. They found it easier to walk by sight than by faith.

4:14-16 Christ's Superior Priesthood

The writer encourages the people to whom he is writing to continue holding firm to *the faith they profess* in Christ by reminding them of Christ's pre-eminent status as *a great high priest* (**4:14**). No other high priest, not even Aaron, was ever given the title 'great'. Nor did any other high priest have a similar ministry in heaven. Jesus could have this ministry and this title because he alone is simultaneously the Son of God and the Son of Man. As such, he is superior to everyone else in the whole history of creation.

But despite his superior status, Jesus Christ can still *sympathize with our weaknesses* (**4:15**). He understands the temptations we face because he has been *tempted in every way,* although, unlike us, he did not yield to temptation and sin. His understanding of our situation means that he can carry out his duties with great sympathy, mercy and faithfulness. Ordinary people could never have approached a Jewish high priest for help, but they can approach Jesus. Consequently, the writer encourages those who were tempted to give up their faith and confidence in Christ to confidently approach the throne of grace in heaven so that *we may receive mercy and find grace to help us in our time of need* (**4:16**).

All of us in Africa who believe in Christ can run to this great high priest at any time, in any circumstances and find the help we need. We will find mercy and grace to help us to face the challenges of our traditions and of the world.

5:1-6 Christ's Superior Ordination

The Jewish high priest was selected *from among men.* He was responsible for the earthly tabernacle, where he represented human beings before God as he offered animal sacrifices and other gifts (**5:1**). Because he was merely human, he would understand those who were *ignorant* and *going astray,* for he knew how easily this happened (**5:2**). He was guilty of these same sins, so he did not only offer sacrifices for the sins of others, but also for his own sins (**5:3**). Jesus, too, was human and understood temptation. The major point of difference was that he did not yield to it and thus had no need to offer sacrifice for his own sins (John 8:46).

No one could appoint himself a priest (**5:4**; see 1 Sam 13:9-14; 2 Chr 26:16-21). It was an honour to which God called someone, as he did Aaron. Those who dared to challenge the person God had called were severely punished, as happened to Korah, Dathan, Abiram and two hundred and fifty other men who challenged Moses and Aaron's position (Num 16). Even Jesus did not seize the position of high priest for himself but was given it by God, in accordance with the prophecies quoted from Psalm 2:7 and Psalm 110:4 (**5:5**).

The other point at which Jesus' priesthood was superior is that he was not ordained into the Aaronic priesthood, but to the order of Melchizedek (**5:6**; see comment on 7:1-28).

5:7-10 Christ's Submission and Our Salvation

Whereas all the other high priests had weaknesses that made them fail, Christ never strayed from God. His life was characterized by perfect obedience. But this obedience was not automatic, for Jesus Christ suffered and was tempted to take the easy way out. His prayers were not solely songs of praise but included *loud cries and tears* before *the one who could save him from death* (**5:7**; see Luke 22:39-44).

As the supreme Son of God, Jesus needed to learn nothing; but as the Son of man, he had to learn to submit to God's will no matter what that was. This type of obedience can only be learned through experience. He thus *learned obedience* as he endured temptation, trials, persecution, suffering and death on the cross (**5:8**). It was in this sense that he was *made perfect* (**5:9a**).

Christ's perfect obedience qualified him to be *the source of eternal salvation for all who obey him* (**5:9b**) and to be appointed by God as a high priest in the order of Melchizedek (**5:10**).

5:11-6:20 Warning Against Immaturity

Given the pre-eminence of Christ's priesthood and his superior ministry of salvation, why were the believers to whom this letter was written tempted to go back to Judaism? The answer to that question is suggested by the fact that the writer here interrupts his teaching about Christ's priesthood to address the issue of spiritual laxity and immaturity. Commentators disagree about whether he is here rebuking those he is writing to for their failure to grow spiritually, or whether he is simply using irony to shame the Jewish believers about their slowness to learn. The former seems more likely because the writer seems to be well acquainted with this church.

5:11-14 Signs of Spiritual Immaturity

The writer is addressing believers who may have been in the faith for nearly thirty years, but with no more spiritual maturity than much younger believers. He gives four signs that they are failing to grow as they should:

- **Apathy towards the word of God**. Negligence and unbelief have made them *slow to learn* (**5:11**).
- **Inability to teach and pass on the word of God**. They need to have someone reteach them the basics of the faith, that is, the *milk* of the word (**5:12**). Even if they were not all gifted teachers, after thirty years in the faith they should at least have been able to draw on their life experience in Christ to instruct others.
- **Preference for an infant diet**. Despite their many years in the faith, they were not ready for the *solid food* of the word, which nourishes those who are mature in Christ. Instead, they were living on pre-digested elementary teaching of the truth of the word of God. Thus they were *not acquainted with the teaching about righteousness* (**5:13**) or ready for solid teaching about our Lord's ministry in heaven as the pre-eminent high priest.
- **Lack of spiritual sensitivity and discernment**. As believers, they have failed to regularly study God's word in order to learn how it applies to daily life and to develop the ability to distinguish between what is good and what is evil (**5:14**).

Adults fed on a diet of milk for thirty years would be severely malnourished. These believers are spiritually stunted – yet they must have chosen their own diet! It is tragic to see the people whom God had elected from among all the Jews being anxious to listen to teaching about the prophets, angels, Moses, Aaron and the law, and yet unable to discern the teaching of the Scriptures about the promised Christ. Their failure to perceive the supremacy of Christ was weakening their faith and bringing them close to apostasy.

Astonishingly, many Christians in Africa exhibit the same spiritual immaturity. They may have been in the faith for many years, yet they are not familiar with the Scriptures. They have never developed their spiritual life and exercised godliness by feeding on the truths of the word of God (1 Tim 4:7-8). Wake up, African Christians! Rise from your slumber that Christ may shine on you and through you!

6:1-2 The Call to Spiritual Maturity

God wants every believer to grow in the knowledge of his Son Jesus Christ. So the writer challenges the Hebrew believers to *leave the elementary teachings about Christ and go on to maturity* (**6:1a**). He does not want them to stay on a milk diet, learning only the basics of the faith. He is like the Apostle Paul, who welcomed the ministry of Apollos who built on the foundation that Paul had laid and so led believers on towards maturity (1 Cor 3:5-15).

The writer calls the attention of the Jewish believers to four important things they need to know about spiritual growth.

- **It involves moving on**. It is not enough to remain in the comforting emotional context of childhood. We need to start thinking like adults. For example, when I was a child, I had to learn the Amharic alphabet called the Fidel, with its many phonetic symbols. But once I had learned the consonants and vowels, I was not content to simply keep on reciting the Fidel. I wanted to use it to help me to understand Amharic books and the wealth of Amharic literature. The same is true for spiritual matters. We need to know about such basic things as repentance, faith, baptisms (both with water and with the Holy Spirit), the laying on of hands, the resurrection of the dead and eternal judgment (**6:1b-2**). But we are not to keep going over the same basic teachings over and over again. With God's help, we are to take action to build on the solid foundation that has already been laid down (6:1b-3).
- **It is not inevitable**. If we do not grow towards maturity, we can easily lapse into immaturity and wilful apostasy. We might hope that the writer is merely presenting a hypothetical situation, but Scripture includes examples of people like Saul and Judas who have wilfully turned away from God and reached a dreadful stage from which no return is possible. Though there are differences of opinion about the depth of the spiritual experience of the people the author has in mind (the debate on whether it is possible for a believer to lose salvation still rages) the use of such statements as having *once been enlightened* seem to suggest that they had come to faith in Christ (**6:4**). They had *tasted* and experienced God's heavenly gift fully through sharing in the Holy Spirit's baptism, revelation, illumination of the word, wisdom, knowledge and understanding. Through the power of the word of God, they would also have tasted something of the goodness of the coming age (**6:5**). Those who reject Christ after having experienced all these things will find it very difficult, even impossible, to come back to him through repentance. There is a limit to God's patience with deliberate sinning and apostasy, which is equivalent to *crucifying the Son of God all over again* (**6:6**).

- **It produces visible spiritual fruit**. The writer uses the illustration of agricultural land. Productive land brings blessing to those who farm it and receive *the blessing of God* (**6:7**). Unproductive land will be cursed and burned (**6:8**). Those who persevere in their faith will receive blessings from God and produce spiritual fruit to his honour and glory. But if their lives show only the thorns and thistles of unbelief, they will be in danger of falling under God's judgment. The writer is, however, confident that the Hebrew Christians have not lost their salvation and are bearing some spiritual fruit (**6:9**). In fact, he commends them for the righteousness they demonstrate in their practical love that helps others. He encourages them by reassuring them that God will never forget their work (**6:10**).

- **It requires diligence**. He urges them to continue showing the *same diligence* in helping others to the very end, because it is a sign of practical love for God. This same diligence would make their *hope sure* (**6:11**). Instead of relaxing and becoming lazy, they are to *imitate those who through faith and patience inherit* what God has promised, namely, the Kingdom of God in Christ.

6:13-20 The Certainty of God's Promise

The Jewish believers seem to have been wavering in their faith in God. The writer gives them two reasons for trusting God. First, he reminds them that God's promises are unchangeable. He cites the example of God's promise to give Abraham a son and many descendants (Gen 14:4; 15:5-6). At times, it must have seemed to Abraham that the promise would never be fulfilled, but he maintained his faith in God and waited patiently until he received the promised son (**6:13-15**; see also Rom 4:17-22). Like him, these Jewish believers should continue to wait for God to deliver them in his own time.

The second reason they can trust God is because he not only made a promise but underscored that promise with an unchangeable oath (**6:16-17**). When we make an oath, we swear by someone higher than us who is capable of punishing us if we break it. But there is no one higher than God, and so God swears this oath by himself. This oath and the promise are *the two unchangeable things in which it is impossible for God to lie* (**6:18a**).

With such rock-solid grounds for confidence, the believers should take a firm hold on the hope of salvation that God offers (**6:18b**). This hope can be described as an *anchor for the soul* (**6:19**). The storms of life may threaten to push the ships of our lives onto the rocks, but our anchor is firmly fixed. Though our ships may be storm-tossed, they are not moving from the position they are in. Our anchor of hope is solidly fixed within *the inner sanctuary*, where Jesus is. There he is *a high priest for ever in the order of Melchizedek*

(**6:20**). He is the ultimate firm and solid foundation for our hope of salvation.

7:1-10:39 Christ and the Order of Melchizedek

The warning about immaturity and the need to trust God's promises is preceded and followed by the assertion that Christ is a priest 'in the order of Melchizedek' (5:10; 6:20). But what does this statement mean? In chapters 7-10, the writer explains that this priestly order is superior to the Aaronic priesthood because it offers a superior covenant, a superior tabernacle, and a superior sacrifice. He stresses that the priesthood of Christ is not only ranked higher than the Aaronic priesthood but that it is also unchangeable. Christ's divine priesthood brings to an end the succession of earthly priests, whose service was flawed and limited because of their mortality (see also 5:1-10).

7:1-28 Superior Priesthood

Who is Melchizedek? He is an obscure ot figure who is mentioned very briefly in Genesis 14:17-24. All we are told about him is that he was *king of Salem and priest of God Most High* (**7:1a**). The only other mention of him in the Bible is in Psalm 110:4, a psalm that speaks of the coming Messiah, who will occupy a supreme position as both priest and king. The author now gives a detailed exposition of these two references to him, showing how they can be associated with Jesus.

Melchizedek's name and title were striking in themselves: *His name means 'king of righteousness'* and his title *'king of Salem' means 'king of peace'* (**7:2**). Both of these titles were associated with the Messiah, and specifically with Jesus (Isa 9:6-7; 2 Tim 4:8).

The writer is also struck by what is not said about Melchizedek. In an age when people's family ancestry was regarded as very important, he is presented as a man without *father or mother, without genealogy* (**7:3**). This does not mean that he did not have human parents. He was a real historical person who lived in a real city called Salem, which is most likely present-day Jerusalem. But the lack of information about his genealogical descent and his parents gives him a timeless quality that is enhanced by the fact that we know nothing about how long he was a priest or when he died. He can thus be described as *without beginning of days or end of life*. This timelessness and the fact that he was simultaneously a priest and a king means that he can be seen as a model, or 'type' of Christ, in whom these two offices are united for ever.

Melchizedek's greatness is shown by his relationship to Abraham, the great father of the entire Jewish race. It appears that Abraham acknowledged Melchizedek as his superior, for he gave him a tithe and received his blessing

(**7:1b-2a, 4**). Tithes are always given to superiors, while blessings are given to subordinates (**7:7**).

Abraham's giving of a tithe acquires even greater significance if it is interpreted in terms of the OT law, which laid down that the Israelites were to give the Levites a tithe (a tenth) of everything they acquired (**7:5**). This tithe was the salary for the Levites as they served God on behalf of their fellow descendants of Abraham (Num 18:21). Abraham gave Melchizedek this tithe, even though he was not a Levite (**7:6**). In fact, given that Levi, the father of the Levites, was one of Abraham's descendants, it could even be argued that in Abraham the Levites were paying a tithe to Melchizedek, showing that his priesthood outranked theirs (**7:9-10**).

There is also another difference between Melchizedek and the Levites. The Levites received tithes but were not immortal. They all died. Melchizedek, however, can be said to *living* (**7:8**). The writer is not necessarily arguing that Melchizedek did not actually die. His argument is simply that since the Bible presents him as having no parents and no recorded death, he can be used to show the eternal nature of Christ's priesthood.

Having established that Melchizedek was superior to Abraham and that his priesthood was superior to that of the Levitical priests, the writer next shows that the Levitical priesthood has now come to an end. His rhetorical question makes the point that the ineffectiveness of the Levitical priesthood meant that a new priest was needed (**7:11**). Because the Levitical priesthood was so closely linked to the law of Moses, the start of a new order of priests must mean that the legal basis for the priesthood must have changed (**7:12**). This change is evident in the fact that Jesus did not come from the tribe of Levi, like the OT priests, but from the tribe of Judah (**7:13-14**). Clearly his ancestry was not the basis of Christ's appointment as high priest; it was *the power of an indestructible life* (**7:15-17**; see 7:3).

The entire system of Aaronic priesthood, which was based on the Mosaic law and regulations, was imperfect, for its priests were imperfect (**7:18**). Consequently this system could be described as *weak and useless*. It has now been set aside in favour of a new order of priests that would give people a *better hope* of drawing near to God. This new system enabled the Jewish believers and the writers of the letter to draw close to God (**7:19**). If they returned to their old way of worship, they would move away from Christ Jesus and would lose the enjoyment of life and fellowship with him.

Another sign of the superiority of Christ's priesthood is that God affirms it with an oath in the first half of Psalm 110:4, the same verse that includes the assertion *You are a priest for ever in the order of Melchizedek* (**7:17, 20**; see also 5:6, 10; 6:20). The certainty of any oath and promise from God has already been considered in 6:13-18. No such oath accompanied the appointment of other priests, and this, too, proves that Christ institutes a *better covenant* (**7:22**). Why would the Jewish believers want to return to a system operating under an inferior covenant?

Concluding his scrutiny of Psalm 110:4, the writer focuses on the words 'for ever', and points out that another sign of Jesus' superiority as a priest is the permanence of his office. Death ended a high priest's service in the Aaronic priesthood, and thus over the years a number of men had occupied this office (**7:23**). But Christ lives for ever, and thus he will never cease to be the high priest. Consequently, he can *save completely* because he can always intercede at the throne of mercy and grace for those who trust in God through faith in him (**7:24-25**).

After proving Christ's superiority as a high priest, the writer stresses what this means for believers. *Such a high priest,* who is in the order of Melchizedek, superior to and greater than Aaron, *meets our needs* because he is *holy,* blameless and pure (**7:26**). Because he is not flawed like the Aaronic priests, he could offer himself as a sacrifice *once for all* for the sins of people (**7:17**). God has superseded the law and exalted him high above the heavens, where he will serve as a perfect high priest for ever (7:20-26).

8:1-13 Superior Covenant

In 7:22, while proving that Jesus' priesthood is better than that of other priests, the writer referred in passing to Jesus as the 'guarantee of a better covenant'. Now he expands on that idea and gives three reasons why this new covenant is better as regards its high priest, its sanctuary, and its foundation and promises.

- **A superior high priest**. The high priest of this covenant is not busy offering sacrifices. Instead, Jesus is now sitting in the place of authority, power and honour at *the right hand of the throne* of God (**8:1**). The fact that he is sitting there indicates that he can rest because he has completed the work of establishing the new covenant.

- **A superior heavenly sanctuary**. As high priest, Jesus serves in the heavenly sanctuary, the *true tabernacle set up by the Lord* rather than in one made by humans (**8:2**). The old covenant needed a physical sanctuary because the priests had to sacrifice animals and offer their blood. Jesus, too, had to offer a sacrifice to atone for sin (**8:3**). However, he did this in the heavenly sanctuary, rather than the earthly one, which was only a *copy* or *shadow of what is in heaven* (**8:5**). In fact, he would not even have been allowed to sacrifice in the temple or tabernacle because he was not from the priestly tribe (**8:4**).

- **A superior foundation and promises**. The ministry of Christ is *founded on better promises* (**8:6**). God recognized that the old covenant was not effective. To support this point, the writer quotes Jeremiah 31:31-34, in which God promises to introduce *a new covenant* (**8:7-9**). This new covenant would not only govern people's outward behaviour but would transform their lives by making profound changes in their minds and hearts (**8:10**). This covenant would restore people's relationship with God and help them to know Christ through the mercy and forgiving grace of God (**8:11-12**).

The Jewish believers did not seem to have realized that what God said in Jeremiah meant that the old covenant was *obsolete and ageing* (**8:13**). The coming of the new covenant had been announced at the Last Supper, when Jesus took the cup, saying, 'This is my blood of the covenant' (Matt 26:28), and declared, 'This cup is the new covenant in my blood, which is poured out for you' (Luke 22:20). The blood of Jesus fulfilled the old covenant and established the new covenant with its superior ministry.

9:1-28 Superior Tabernacle

The change in the form of worship was one of the difficult subjects that the writer had been hesitant to tackle because those to whom he was writing were 'slow to learn' (5:11). Now, however, he explains in detail the contrast between worship under the old covenant and worship under the new covenant (9:1-10) and then explains the ministry of Jesus in the new heavenly tabernacle (9:11-28; see also 8:2, 5).

9:1-10 The old tabernacle

Under the old covenant, worship took place in a structure designed in accordance with the instructions Moses had received. This tabernacle had two rooms. The outer room was called the Holy Place. Separated from it by a curtain was an inner room, called the Most Holy Place (**9:1-3**). The writer lists the contents of these rooms, but says that he cannot discuss these items in detail (**9:5b**). However, we can pause to do so, because these objects help us to understand Christ's work of redemption. Like the earthly sanctuary, they had symbolic significance.

The lampstand was a seven-branched golden candlestick that stood in the first room or Holy Place, where its lamps were to be kept burning all night (Exod 25:31-40; 27:20-21). These lamps provided needed light and also represented the light of God. Thus the lampstand was a symbol of Christ, who is 'the true light that gives light to every man' (John 1:9). He is the light of the world and his light shines in the darkness (John 8:12; 12:46; Rev 22:5).

The *holy place* also contained a gold *table* on which stood *consecrated bread*, that is twelve loaves of bread that symbolized the twelve tribes of Israel and the way God had fed them during their forty years in the wilderness (Exod 25:23-30; Lev 24:5-9). This bread was replaced every Sabbath. Only the priests were allowed to eat it. This bread symbolized Christ, the bread of life (John 6:32-33).

Closely associated with the second room or Most Holy Place was a *golden altar of incense* (**9:4a**; Exod 40:5). On this altar, the high priest burnt incense to symbolize prayer ascending to God (Exod 30:1-10; 37:25-29). Nothing else

was offered on this altar, except that once a year, on the Day of Atonement, the high priest sprinkled blood from the sacrifice of atonement on the horns of this altar (that is, on horn-like projections on it). As our high priest, Jesus Christ has entered the Most Holy Place in the heavenly tabernacle and offered his own blood in atonement for our sins (9:24).

The final item in the Most Holy Place was the gold-covered *ark of the covenant* (**9:4b**; Exod 25:10-22), which symbolized the presence of God. Its lid was an 'atonement cover' made of pure gold. Two cherubim made of hammered gold looked down at the atonement cover, which was also called the mercy seat. On the Day of Atonement, the high priest sprinkled some of the blood from the sacrifice on the mercy seat to cover sins that had been committed against the law, symbolized by the stone tablets with the Ten Commandments that were inside the ark (**9:4c-5a**; Exod 40:20; Lev 16:15-16). This ritual symbolized God's promise not to look at the broken law but at the blood that atoned for people's sin.

Three objects were associated with the ark: the stone tablets on which the Ten Commandments were written to remind Israel about the will of God (Exod 25:16); a golden jar of manna, reminding Israel of God's provision in the wilderness (Exod 16:32-34); and Aaron's staff, which reminded Israel both of God's miracles in Egypt and of his choice of Aaron and his descendants as priests (Exod 7:10, 19; Num 17:1-10). All of these objects were no more than symbols and shadows of the new order that would come with Christ Jesus.

Entrance to the earthly tabernacle was restricted. Only priests were admitted to the Holy Place, and the Most Holy Place was hidden by a curtain, and entered only by the high priest on the Day of Atonement (**9:6-7**). The Holy Spirit used these restrictions to show that ordinary people could not gain access to the Most Holy Place as long as the sanctuary stood (**9:8**). This lack of access demonstrated that the sacrifices offered in the temple could not bring about the true holiness needed to enter this sacred area, for they were temporary, imperfect and unable to fully cleanse a guilty conscience (**9:9**). These imperfect ceremonies were only meant to continue until the coming of the new perfect order (**9:10**).

9:11-28 The new tabernacle

The old tabernacle had been constructed on earth by human labour, but the tabernacle in which Christ as the new high priest carries out his redemptive ministry is the true original tabernacle of God in heaven (**9:11**). Such a heavenly sanctuary must be superior to any earthly sanctuary, which is inevitably associated with one geographic location and thus not easily accessible to all.

As the perfect high priest, Jesus did not enter the *Most Holy Place* in that heavenly tabernacle carrying the blood of some earthly animal that had been sacrificed, but rather with an offering of *his own blood* (9:12). This great offering is far more efficient to cleanse us from sin than any ritual involving animal blood (**9:12-13**). We are reminded that our redemption by Christ is not based on our performing ineffective ceremonies but on Christ's great sacrifice. His blood will *cleanse our consciences from acts that lead to death,* that is, from sins, so that we may serve God (**9:14**). He is the final and complete sacrifice for the sins committed against God.

Changing the metaphor slightly, the writer of Hebrews reminds us that Christ died as a sacrifice and to provide a *ransom* that would set people free from their sins. He became the *mediator of a new covenant,* or in other words, he is the Lamb sacrificed to make the covenant effective, and through him many will be set free to inherit eternal life (**9:15a**).

The writer now proceeds to answer the question of why it was necessary for Christ to shed his blood for our salvation. He offers more than one explanation. The first is sparked off by his reference to the *promised eternal inheritance* (**9:15b**) and by the fact that the same Greek word can be translated either 'will' or 'covenant'. An inheritance (or covenant) is something one only receives after the one leaving the inheritance has died (**9:16-17**).

The second reason is that every covenant required blood for it to come into effect (**9:18**). In the ancient world, all covenants were accompanied by sacrifices of animals, whose bodies were cut into two pieces to show the consequences of breaking the covenant (see Jer 34:18). Sprinkling blood on the participants to the covenant marked their commitment to it (**9:19-21**).

But the sprinkling of blood was not only a sign of commitment but also a sign of purification. It showed that a price had been paid for the sin that broke the covenant and thus brought impurity. That is why *the law required that nearly everything be cleansed with blood* because *without the shedding of blood there was no forgiveness* (**9:22**).

The earthly tabernacle was a copy of the heavenly one, and the animal sacrifices offered there were poor imitations of the great sacrifice Jesus Christ made to establish a new covenant and to cleanse the heavenly tabernacle from the pollution that our sins would bring into it (**9:23**). Christ did not make this offering in any human tabernacle, distant from God; instead, he appeared directly before God on our behalf (**9:24**).

The other difference between Christ's sacrifice and those offered by the ot priests was that Christ's redemptive ministry is complete. The Aaronic priests were constantly sacrificing new animals in the old tabernacle. Christ, however, has no need to repeat his sacrifice (**9:25**). His superior heavenly ministry has been completed *once for all* (**9:26**). Humans are not reincarnated time and again, and neither was Christ (**9:27**). He only lived on this earth once, and it

was in that time that he died on the cross as a sacrifice for us. When he comes *a second time* at the end of the age, it will not be to repeat his sacrifice but to bring eternal salvation to those who are *waiting for him,* whether in the sleep of death or in life (**9:28**).

The writer has clearly presented the difference between the heavenly and the earthly tabernacles and shown the superiority of the former and the eternal effectiveness of Christ's sacrifice. The wavering Hebrew believers should have no doubt about where to place their trust.

10:1-25 Superior Sacrifice

Because the sacrificial system was at the heart of the old covenant, the writer to the Hebrews sees a need to elaborate on the change brought about by Christ, whom he presents as the superior, perfect sacrifice. He stresses that Christ's sacrifice has abolished all the other sacrifices of the old covenant, and that the sacrifice of Christ himself has been effective, whereas those offered under the Mosaic law were not. He makes three points about the two types of sacrifices:

- **Animal sacrifices were imperfect copies of the real thing**. The law that required the sacrifices was itself only a *shadow of good things* to come. As shadows, the sacrifices could not make the worshippers *perfect* or permanently cleanse them (**10:1**). The fact that they had to be repeated on an annual basis meant that they served more as an annual reminder of the people's sins than as an effective cleansing from them (**10:2-3**). The blood of animals could never actually take away sins (**10:4**). It was simply a picture of the superior sacrifice that would be offered by Jesus on the cross (Isa 52:13-53:12).

- **Jesus is the superior sacrifice that can take away sins**. The writer quotes Psalm 40:6-8 to prove that God did not want sacrifices and offerings; he was *not pleased* with them (**10:5-6**). They could not make people perfect. Jesus, however, could offer himself and his own body as a superior sacrifice, dying in obedience to the will of God in order to fulfil the requirements of the law. People could thus be *made holy through the sacrifice of the body of Christ* Jesus (**10:9-10a**).

- **There is no need for further sacrifices for sin**. Unlike the priests who had to constantly repeat sacrifices in the imperfect Levitical system, Jesus Christ, as a superior high priest, offered one sacrifice – himself – *once for all* (**10:11-12**). To reinforce Christ's superiority, the writer says that he now waits for *his enemies to be made his footstool* (**10:13**). He has made his people *perfect,* that is, acceptable to God by being set apart for him and living godly lives (**10:14, 18**). Then the writer again quotes from Jeremiah 31:33-34 to show that Christ's sacrificial act is part of God's new covenant with his people (**10:16-17**).

THE PLACE OF TRADITIONAL SACRIFICES

Almost every people group in Africa seems to have had some form of traditional sacrificial system. The things sacrificed were generally cattle, sheep, goats and chickens, although in a few cases (for example, among the Butawa of Nigeria and the Koma of Ethiopia) dogs were also sacrificed. The basic principle seems to have been that what was offered should be a domesticated animal so that there was a close connection between it and the one making the offering. (However, the Akamba of Kenya and the Bakwena of Botswana did at times make offerings using the wild hyrax.)

The animal or bird to be sacrificed had to be carefully chosen. The most important properties governing the choice were as follows:

- *Its source.* Any animal offered on behalf of a whole community had to come from an honourable person. There should be no possibility of that person presenting a stolen animal for sacrifice.

- *Its colour.* The animal offered had to be of a uniform colour. While the exact colour preferred differ from group to group, black, red and white were the most common colours for sacrificial animals.

- *Its quality.* The animal needed to be perfect in every respect, with no birth defects or injuries.

Kola nuts, grains, beer and milk might also be offered in sacrifice, provided that the person supplying them was of good character.

Human sacrifice was not common, but it was sometimes practised in circumstances of extreme need. An event such as the 2004 tsunami that killed more than 200,000 people in Asia might have been thought to require human sacrifice in order to avoid any repetition of the disaster. Similarly, a crisis such as that caused by HIV/AIDS in many villages in Africa might have called for the highest possible sacrifice to appease God so that he would remove the plague. The thinking was that it would be worth sacrificing one human life so as to save many from dying. Such sacrifices should not be confused with the offerings made by some modern cults using human body parts. Their roots are more in demon worship than in any nobler purpose. However, all human sacrifice, no matter what the reason for it, is abhorrent to God (Lev 18:21).

Most traditional sacrifices were linked to common human experiences. Thus they were offered to mark stages in life (conception, birth, naming, circumcision, and so on), the agricultural cycle (planting and harvesting), hunting (as hunters set out and as they returned), and in times of distress resulting from such things as epidemics, droughts, sickness and barrenness. Sacrifices thus seem to have been offered in response to circumstances in people's lives or to request

that some circumstance be changed. They were almost never made simply to worship God for who he is.

But today sacrifices are seldom offered. So are they still of any significance? Should we keep the memory of them alive?

One answer to this question may be based on how these sacrifices relate to the concept of sacrifice in the Bible. The first point to be noted is that they may share the same origin as biblical sacrifices. In general, the Bible gives God's special revelation while African traditional religions (ATR) are based mostly on general revelation. But the practice of offering sacrifices dates back to the start of the OT (Gen 4:3-4; 8:20). Thus when Noah's sons dispersed to repopulate the earth after the flood, all three of them would have taken with them the concept of offering sacrifices.

A second point to note is that there are obvious resemblances between the requirements for sacrifices in ATR and the requirements spelled out in the law of Moses. For example, in both cases the animal offered had to be perfect (in Leviticus 1-9 the instruction, 'without defect' is repeated thirteen times - 1:3, 10; 3:1, 6; 4:3, 23, 28, 32; 5:15, 18; 6:6; 9:2, 3). In Deuteronomy 17:1, an animal with a defect is described as 'detestable to him'. There are also similarities in the types of animals offered, which in the OT included young bulls (Lev 4:3), male and female goats (Lev 4:23, 28), lambs (Lev 4:32), doves or young pigeons (Lev 5:7) and grain (Lev 2:1).

But there are also important differences between sacrifice in ATR and sacrifice as found in the OT. The difference can be traced to the time of Moses, when sacrifices were given a new meaning because of the covenant relationship God had established with Abraham (Gen 17:7) and the covenant demands laid down in Exodus (Exod 19-24). The offering of the sacrifices was now to be done on the basis that the children of Israel were God's chosen people and were expected to conduct themselves in ways that conformed to God's holy nature. What had been offered to express gratitude now also had the dimension of dealing with sin. Burnt offerings (Lev 1:1-17), grain offerings (Lev 2:1-16), fellowship offerings (Lev 3:1-17), sin offerings (Lev 4:1-5:13) and guilt offerings (Lev 5:14-7) become different ways of stressing the focus of an offering. But central to them all was the recognition that God is holy, that men and women fail to meet his standard, and that only God-given rituals can correct the situation.

The rituals that God prescribed in the OT came to their final fulfilment in the supreme sacrifice of Christ as the Lamb of God. The writer of Hebrews relates the OT sacrifices to the work of Christ and shows how he represents the ultimate fulfilment of all that they were meant to accomplish (Heb 9:11-10:18). Christ's blood poured out once is sufficient to take care of the sins of all times. There is no more need to offer daily, weekly, monthly or yearly sacrifices. The needs they sought to meet have been met once and for all by

Christ, 'sacrificed once to take away the sins of many people' (Heb 9:28).

Against this background, we can say that traditional sacrifices have value, limitations and dangers in our presentation of the Christian faith today.

Their greatest value is that they serve as a good beginning point in presenting the Gospel. The good news is that Jesus died to take away our sins (1 Cor 15:3; Gal 1:4), an act without which there would be no fellowship with God. He died as the Lamb of God, who takes away the sins of the world (John 1:29, 36). The concept of a dying sacrifice to take away sin is not 'a stumbling block' or 'foolishness' (1 Cor 1:23) to African hearers, but familiar ground. For mission purposes, the traditional sacrifices then become rich ground from which to draw teachings about Christ as the ultimate sacrifice.

But their usefulness is limited. It is not right, as some have tried to do, to equate sacrifices in ATR with the sacrifices in the ot. Though there were regional differences, the chief reason for offering sacrifices in ATR was to make sure that things would go well. The notion of offering sacrifice just to acknowledge that we are by nature sinners and God is by nature holy, as we find, for example, in the ot fellowship offering, was foreign. In fact, for some African people groups, so long as things are going well, there is no need to disturb God by offering sacrifices. When he sends troubles, appeasing him leads to a physical salvation that is celebrated in terms of newness of life and joy.

It is also often felt that where there is a blessing, it must be acknowledged lest God withhold such blessing in the future. This attitude leads to sacrifices expressing appreciation for benefits. But in both this case and the previous one, fear is the major motive for sacrifice.

The ot sacrificial system also accommodated the need to appease God and to show appreciation for his blessings. But it went beyond that to include sacrifice as a way of worshipping God for who he is. Yes, he has done great things such as rescuing his people from slavery in Egypt, but the reason he does these things is because he is in a relationship with his people. He is 'I am whom I am' (Exod 3:14), meaning that he never changes and is always there for his chosen people. In this sense, the ot sacrifices are richer than the sacrifices offered in African traditional religions.

Just as the ot sacrifices have been replaced by the once-and-for-all sacrifice of Christ, so also the sacrifices in ATR have been replaced. We should not fall for the argument that since our traditional sacrifices are so close to the Bible, they are our way of salvation. All the good in all traditional sacrifices is merely a foreshadowing of the reality that is Christ. He is the God-given way to have fellowship with God.

For practical purposes, we need to know about our heritage, including the sacrifices in our traditional religions. We must, however, always keep the right perspective. These sacrifices are a contact point for the presentation of the supreme sacrifice, that is, Christ. The fact that many of them involved animals whose blood was shed provides a wonderful opportunity to present Christ as sacrifice for sin'. But as Paul says, when he contrasts our now experience to our future full knowledge, 'when perfection comes, the imperfect disappears' (1 Cor 13:10). It is on the basis of the same principle that the writer to the Hebrews wrote, 'He set aside the first to establish the second. And by that will, we have been made holy through the sacrifice of the body of Jesus Christ once for all' (Heb 10:9b-10). Ultimately, this is the message for Africa, as it is also for the whole world, no matter how rich our traditional beliefs and practices may be.

Samuel Ngewa

Actions should flow from the truths the writer has been teaching. Christ, our great high priest, has opened the way for us to enter *the Most Holy Place* (**10:19-21**). We should not miss this opportunity but should *draw near to God*. We should do this with *a sincere heart* and full faith in the completed work of Christ. We are cleansed *from a guilty conscience* because we have had his blood *sprinkled* on our hearts and have been *washed with pure water* (**10:22**).The writer of Hebrews probably wants the readers to think in terms of the symbolism of purification ceremonies such as the one in which the Levites were made ceremonially clean by being sprinkled with water of cleansing (Num 8:6-7). It is not only hearts that are set apart for God but the whole person.

Our traditional African understanding of religion always involves sacrifices and offerings, rituals and ceremonies coupled with prayers to intermediaries for protection, provision for our needs and other blessings. But we have no need

to offer sacrifices, for Christ has offered the only sacrifice that is needed. Nor do we need to pray to intermediaries such as angels, the Virgin Mary and departed saints (Paul, Stephen, John, etc.). We have no need to rely on prayers offered by the clergy, as when Ethiopian Orthodox clergy offer magical prayers associated with the ark (the *tabot*). Christ has opened the door to the holy place, and now we ourselves can draw near to God himself.

The writer of Hebrews exhorts the believers to hold fast to their faith and encourage each other's *love* for the Lord. They are also to encourage each other to do *good deeds* (**10:23-24**). They are not to drift apart and cease *meeting together*, but are to seek to support one another (**10:25**). This is all the more important as the second coming of Christ approaches, because those days will be characterized by more intense persecution (Matt 24:9-11) and increasing evil (Matt 24:12; 2 Tim 3:1-4).

10:26-39 Warning Against Being Unfaithful to Christ

The writer again warns the believers of the danger of deliberately sinning after they have received *knowledge of the truth* in Christ (**10:26**; see 6:4-8; Num 15:22-31; 16:1-3). Anyone who does this has rejected the only available sacrifice for sin and can expect to face God's judgment, which will consume his enemies with fire (**10:27**). He warns them that if rejecting the inferior law of Moses with disdain resulted in death (Num 16:19-35; Deut 17:6), the consequences of rejecting the far superior Son of God will be much more dreadful. Any spurning of the Son of God, disrespect for the blood of Christ, and scornful treatment of the Holy Spirit will be judged severely (**10:28-31**).

The writer encourages the Jewish believers to continue in faith despite opposition and public persecution. He reminds them of how they withstood persecution in the past (**10:32**). They had stood by those who were publicly humiliated, had sympathized with those in prison and had accepted material loss. No wonder they need to continue to meet to 'encourage one another' (**10:33-34**; see also 10:25).

He promises that if they hold on to their confidence, walk by faith in Christ and so do the will of God, they *will receive what he has promised* (**10:35-36**). The waiting for that promise requires patience and perseverance. The writer quotes from Habakkuk 2-3 to emphasize the need to keep believing in God even when we do not comprehend his ways. This calls for faith, which is why the author of Hebrews quotes the verse, *my righteous one will live by faith* (**10:38**; see also Gal 3:11; Rom 1:17). As the readers of Hebrews face some form of persecution, they must have faith in the basis on which God provides justification and in his decisions as he governs the world. God may not remove them from their difficult circumstances, but he is still the Master of these circumstances. At his right time, *He who is coming will come* (**10:37**) and the righteous will be rewarded.

The Jewish believers should not allow their old allegiance to the Jewish tradition, which was based on Mosaic law and the priestly sacrificial system, to weaken their allegiance to Christ, the eternal great high priest, and so to rob them of their promised reward.

Born-again believers today need to heed this warning. We are not to practise syncretism, mixing elements of other faiths with our faith in the work of Christ. It does not matter whether the faith from which we draw is Judaism, as in the Ethiopian Orthodox Church, or the spiritualism of African traditional religion. As pointed out earlier (see comment on 10:22), we should not substitute intermediaries for Christ, whether these intermediaries are traditional church saints or the spirits of ancestors. We should not seek guidance, correction, help or blessings from an ancestor or divinity. In fact, Scripture forbids association with any spirits other than God himself (Deut 18:10-11; 26:14; 32:17; Acts 19:18-19; 1 Cor 10:19-20; Gal 1:6-18).

Nor should we rely on rituals for help, or try to buy God's favour with offerings and sacrifices in the form of alms. The essence of true worship is honouring God by knowing Christ and offering oneself in complete dependence upon him. Such worship may be lacking in some of our churches. It is certainly missing in any faith that involves syncretism.

African believers should learn from the Scriptures how to differentiate between the true worship of God in Christ and deceptive religious philosophies derived from human traditions. No matter how strong our allegiance to our traditional forms of worship, we need to recognize that our allegiance to Christ must be stronger. Faith in Christ does not allow us to cling to other supposed sources of blessings. For African born-again believers, as for the Jewish believers, the sacrificial death of Christ on the cross does not just offer a more powerful way of approaching God than other religious traditions and rituals – it is the only way to approach God. We must discard anything that would interfere with single-hearted commitment to Christ.

11:1-13:21 Superior Faith in Christ

Chapter 10 spoke of the confidence with which the believers could await what was promised, and now the writer gives examples of what it means to live in total confidence in God's word and in anticipation of an unseen future.

11:1-40 Examples of Enduring Faith

The writer starts by defining faith as the ability to be *sure of what we hope for* and certain of things that cannot be seen (**11:1**) and then lists many OT examples of what faith makes possible (**11:2**).

- **Faith sees what others cannot see**. It delights in the reality of future things. It enables believers to understand that by the power of his word God was able to create the visible universe out of things that are invisible and that it belongs to him (**11:3**; see also Ps 19:1-6; 33:6-9). Abel encountered God by faith and was enabled to discern what was an acceptable offering even before the law had been given (**11:4**; Gen 4:3-5). His faith helped him to offer a better sacrifice than Cain and to leave a testimony to others.
- **Faith enables believers to walk closely with God**. Before the flood, Enoch walked with God for three hundred years in the midst of terrible wickedness without wavering in his faith (**11:5-6**; Gen 5:22-24). His upright walk pleased God, who decided to take him away alive to heaven.
- **Faith enables believers to foresee danger and destruction**. Noah was forewarned about the future destruction of the world. He showed his faith by acting on God's warning about the coming flood. His faith enabled him to spend many years building *an ark to save his family*

(**11:7**; Gen 6:8-9:17). The unfaithful and unbelieving people of his day treated God's warning with contempt and were busy eating, drinking, marrying and giving in marriage, buying, selling, planting and building up to the day Noah entered the ark. All those who had rejected God were totally unprepared when the flood came and swept them away (Matt 24:36-42; 2 Pet 2:5).

- **Faith enables believers to obey God when they do not know their way**. Faith in God enabled Abraham to leave his country, his people and his father's household to move to a foreign country (**11:8-10**; Gen 12:1-3). Faith in God does not insist on knowing the future but trusts in him, keeps going, and lives like *a stranger in a foreign country*, while looking ahead for an everlasting city.

- **Faith enables believers to receive God's promise in impossible situations**. It sees the faithful God and not the impossible circumstances. Abraham had his eyes fixed on the faithful God when he was promised a son. Twenty-five years later, Abraham and Sarah's bodies, which were *as good as dead,* were empowered to have a child (**11:11-12**; Gen 17:1-22; 18:10-15; 21:1-7).

- **Faith enables believers to persevere even when the promise is not immediately fulfilled.** Faith in God did not disappoint the men and women of faith even when they did not receive the promise of God in their lifetime but only welcomed its fulfilment from a distance (**11:13-16**). They lived by faith, longing for the superior thing yet to come, and died in faith, trusting that the promise would be fulfilled in the future.

- **Faith enables believers to sacrifice the promise**. Faith in God enabled Abraham to be willing to sacrifice everything, including his only son Isaac upon whom the continuity of his line rested (**11:17-19**; Gen 22:1-18). Denying himself and obeying and following God characterized Abraham's life.

- **Faith enables believers to recognize and pass on the blessing of God**. Faith in God inspired Isaac to bless Jacob and also Joseph's sons (**11:20-21**; Gen 27:1-40; 48:12-20). By faith, Joseph prophesied the exodus and instructed that his bones be taken to the Promised Land (**11:22**; Gen 50:24-25).

- **Faith enables believers to take risks**. Faith in God enlightened Moses' parents to recognize that the baby Moses was not an ordinary child. They perceived the purpose of God in his life and kept him from death for three months (**11:23**; Exod 2:1-4).

- **Faith enables believers to refuse the pleasures of worldly life**. Faith in God inspired Moses to give up his prestigious position of wealth and power in the royal household. His faith guided him to choose to be treated with contempt along with the people of God (**11:24-28**; Exod 2:11-25). He saw the invisible things of God and future reward as though they were visible. Faith sees

disgrace for Christ's sake as of greater value than the pleasures of this world.

- **Faith enables believers to overcome fear and other barriers**. By faith in God, the Israelites had the strength to walk through the water of the Red Sea (**11:29-31**; Exod 14:10-31) and to bring down the fortified walls of the city of Jericho (Josh 6:1-27). By faith, Rahab, a pagan prostitute, took action that saved her life (Josh 2:1-21). She lived to become an ancestor of Jesus.

- **Faith enables believers to endure many other difficulties**. The writer provides many other examples of people who won the favour of God because of their faith in him under impossible circumstances (**11:32-39a**). By faith, believers can live a life of sacrifice and consider mistreatment, torture and abuse from the world as worth suffering for Christ's sake. Faith in Christ does not guarantee a carefree life but a life that is full of trouble and includes many demands to leave behind worldly pleasures and walk with God according to his will.

Then the writer makes his final point: all these heroes of faith had not yet received *what had been promised,* that is, the Messiah (**11:39b**). In that respect, the Jewish believers were more blessed than all those mentioned, for they knew that the Messiah had now come (**11:40**).

12:1-13 Perseverance of Superior Faith

The writer uses the Jewish heroes of the faith, the cloud *host of witnesses* (**12:1a**), as models of perseverance in faith despite difficulties. He encourages the Jewish believers to follow their example. Not only that, but he presents these heroes as *witnesses,* watching the way the Jewish believers are living. It is as if the ancient believers and the people to whom he is writing are all assembled in a stadium for some great marathon. The huge crowd of men and women of faith mentioned in chapter 11 are packed into the tiers of seats. They have come to watch the race and also to inspire those participating in it to run well by attesting to the validity of the contest and by reminding them of the example set by their predecessors.

The believers from previous generations are the former athletes, but the writer and those to whom he was speaking are the competitors today. In order to run well, they need *to throw off everything that hinders* their movement, anything that could slow them down or trip them up (**12:1b**). These hindrances include sins of negligence, unbelief, lethargy and wilfully sinning against the knowledge of God (1 Cor 9:24-27; 2 Tim 2:3-5).

The race they are engaged in is not a sprint but a marathon, and so it is necessary to *run with perseverance the race marked out for us* (**12:1c**). Christ has already marked out the course, and the Jewish believers should not yield to the temptation to try to run a different course. They are to live a disciplined life of Christian discipleship, following the footsteps of Christ who has prepared the way for the contestants by enduring hostile opposition on their behalf.

While running, the contestants should keep their eyes fixed on Jesus (**12:2a**). He is the creator and *perfecter of our faith,* the pioneer runner, our coach and trainer, and the chief organizer of the faith games.

The Jewish believers who are facing persecution (10:32-39) can also look to Jesus. He was despised and rejected but endured the cross and its shame in faithful obedience to the Father (**12:2b**). He experienced sorrow and suffering but persevered, anticipating the glorious joy awaiting him. Contemplation of Jesus' attitude will help them not to grow weary and lose hope (**12:3**; Phil 2:5-11). They will recognize that it may even be necessary for them to shed their own blood while fulfilling the Father's will (**12:4**).

The writer quotes Proverb 3:11-12 as he tells the believers to be like Christ in seeing *hardship as discipline* from the Lord (**12:5-6**). No one enjoys being disciplined. It is often painful and unpleasant. But it is necessary, as any athlete will admit when he looks back at the suffering he underwent while training, and as we realize when we think back to the way our parents dealt with us (**12:7-10**).

The trials that God sends us facilitate character development if perseverance is allowed to finish its work (Rom 5:3-4; Jas 1:2-4). God uses hardships to produce character, maturity and completeness so that his children will not lack anything in Christ. He disciplines believers as his sons and daughters so that they can share in his holiness, in the fullness of Christ's *righteousness* and *peace* (**12:11**).

Instead of rejecting all suffering, African believers must be prepared to embrace divine discipline as of paramount importance for character formation. It gives us an opportunity to acquire staying power and endurance and equips us to live a peaceful and righteous life in Christ.

The writer concludes this portion of his letter by quoting two Scriptures to encourage the Jewish believers to stand firm. He urges them to *strengthen your feeble arms and weak knees* (**12:12**; see Isa 35:3). Weakness in one's limbs limits one's ability to win or even complete a race. The Jewish believers were drooping and tired and tempted to give up – but they should not yield to the temptation to leave Christ's team and rejoin the one following the obsolete Mosaic regulations. They were also to *make level paths for your feet* (**12:13**; Prov 4:26), that is, to choose the right route. The second half of Proverbs 4:26 says 'take only ways that are firm'. Christ, the way, the truth and the life, is the only level and firm path to God.

12:14-29 Warning Against Refusing God's Grace

Spiritual warning is like a bitter medicine that works for our own good. Here the writer issues his final warning in this letter, using Esau as an example to warn his readers of the consequences of careless disregard for Christ. Esau was indifferent to his birthright and lost his blessing (**12:16-17**; Gen 25:29-34; 27:30-40). Similarly, the Jewish believers are in danger of giving up the new covenant for the old Mosaic covenant and thus losing the blessing God intended them to have (**12:15**). They are also warned against letting any *bitter root* grow, that is, anything that will *cause trouble.* The bitter root in Esau was his ungodly nature, which lost him and his descendants his birthright and blessings. But a 'bitter root' can also take the form of sexual immorality, quarrelsomeness and living a godless life, all of which produce bitter results.

The writer contrasts the Jews' lack of access to God at Sinai when God gave Moses the law in the old covenant (**12:18-21**; Exod 19:10-24) to the access they have to God through Christ in the new covenant (12:22-24). The blessings that go with this access include.

- God's presence, symbolized by *coming to Jerusalem,* which was the centre of worship and communion with God (**12:22a**)
- Good company, including angels (**12:22b**) and other believers, both those who are still living (**12:23a**) and those who have gone before (*the spirits of righteous men made perfect* – **12:23c**)
- Fair government, with God as judge (**12:23b**)
- All the benefits that go with Christ's work of redemption (**12:24**)

But all these great blessings go hand in hand with a greater responsibility; hence the warning about the danger of forfeiting the grace of God. The Israelites who refused to listen to Moses were severely punished, as everyone will be who turns away from Christ (**12:25-27**). But true worshippers of God, who are heedful of the heavenly warning given by Christ, will receive the unshakeable everlasting kingdom (**12:28-29**).

13:1-21 Practical Evidence of Faith

In the final pages of his letter, the writer gives the believers a number of specific instructions about the daily practice of faith in Christ.

First, he appeals for fellowship in the local church. He instructs the believers *to keep on loving each other* (**13:1**), to be hospitable (**13:2**), and to take care of those in prison and those who are ill-treated (**13:3**). Loving other believers as brothers and sisters is vital to the organic life of any house church, for love is the greatest evidence of spiritual fellowship in the body of Christ. Where there is true Christian love, there will also be practical hospitality and concern for the needs of those who belong to the family of Christ (13:16).

Showing hospitality to strangers, as Abraham did when he *entertained angels without knowing it* (Gen 18:1-15; 19:1-3), is valued by many African cultures. Tragically, this honourable custom is now being eroded by modern individualism. African believers need to remember that by entertaining strangers they may indeed invite blessing into their homes. The worship that pleases God is not ceremonial church rituals but a lifestyle that is characterized by extending hospitality and love to those in need, such as those who are hungry or thirsty, strangers, the naked, the sick, the imprisoned and the mistreated (Matt 25:31-46; Gal 6:10; 1 John 3:16-18). We are to cultivate a godly hatred of worldly passions and have confidence in God's provision.

The Jewish believers were also instructed that *marriage should be honoured* and *the marriage bed kept pure* (**13:4**). Any sexual relationship outside of marriage is immoral and abhorrent to God. All single men, women, and married couples should learn to understand God's will and purpose for marriage and should preserve his gift of sexual integrity within the marriage relationship. Marriage is a divine institution that requires believers to take heed of divine advice (Gen 2:7, 18, 20b-23; Mal 2:15; Eph 5:21-33). Purity, integrity, loyalty and love are the walls that protect this godly institution against sexual sins. These virtues are not foreign to Africa. For example, one form of marriage in Ethiopia is considered indissoluble, which means that divorce is ruled out unless there is tangible proof of infidelity. This type of marriage is celebrated in the Orthodox Church in a religious ceremony that involves taking Holy Communion. It is called *Kurban* or *Kal Kidan bekurban* (Covenant by Holy Communion). But these virtues need to be guarded lest they are eroded by modernity. They also need to be proclaimed because we still have many African believers who hold to traditional cultural views of marriage rather than developing biblical values from the divine word of God.

The Jewish believers are cautioned to keep their *lives free from the love of money* and be satisfied with what they have (**13:5-6**). The writer quotes Deuteronomy 31:6 and Psalm 118:6-7, to reassure them of the Lord's ability to help and protect them in times of need.

Today in Africa, some preach and teach how to get rich, promising self-centred success and prosperity. Those who embrace their teachings are taught how to name and claim hundredfold financial success for themselves. These preachers and teachers should learn that the love of money is an impediment to cultivating a hospitable lifestyle in the church of Christ. It is time for born-again believers to realize that they are called to be on guard against craving money or wealth, which is a form of idolatry (Matt 6:24; Luke 12:13-21; 16:13-15; 1 Tim 6:6-10). True faith in Christ is costly and involves willingness to pay the price. The quality of our life in Christ is not determined by the abundance of our material possessions but rather by our contentment in the protection of the Lord 'in any and every situation' (Phil 4:11-13).

Then the writer calls the attention of the believers to their relationship with the *leaders who spoke the word of God to you* (**13:7**). These leaders had probably already died, but they were still good models, whose faith and way of life should be imitated. They had set a pattern of taking as their leader the one who is *the same yesterday and today and forever* (**13:8**), and even though these leaders had gone, Jesus Christ is still the unchanging leader. These words challenge those of us who lead the church today. Can our lives be held up as examples for others to follow?

The writer also warns against following strange and destructive teachings. It seems that false leaders were tempting the believers to rely on rituals and ceremonies as a source of strength, rather than relying on the grace of God (**13:9**).

The reference to rituals leads the writer to focus on the worship of the church (**13:10-16**). Once again he emphasizes the necessity of the new covenant, contrasting it with the old one that was filled with useless rules about what foods might or might not be eaten. The stress is on true worship through the atoning blood of Christ outside the camp (**13:10-14**; see also Lev 16:1-34). His statement that *we do not have an enduring city* may be a reference to Jerusalem as the centre of old covenant worship, which he contrasts with their hope of entering the new *city that is to come* (13:14). Rather than animal sacrifices, they now need to offer God *a sacrifice of praise* and thanksgiving. Such praise is the natural fruit of lips that honour him (**13:15**). The only other sacrifice that is called for is *to do good and to share with others*. God now rejects all the ritual sacrifices, as this letter has shown, but sacrifices of praise and service still please him (**13:16**).

Returning to the place of leaders, the writer urges the believers not only to imitate but also to *submit* to leaders (**13:17**). The leaders should be responsible shepherds of God's flock, showing the truth of what they teach by their words, deeds, way of life, teachings, love, purpose, endurance in suffering, integrity and purity (1 Tim 3:1-12). True sheep will find it easy to imitate and obey godly leaders who nurture them in the Lord. If, however, the members of the church disobey such leaders by following strange teachings or acting in ways that make their leadership a burden, then they are also disobeying the supreme shepherd, Christ Jesus (**13:20**).

Given the fact that leaders must submit an account of their service to God and must live lives that are honourable in every way, it is not surprising that the writer requests prayer for himself and his fellow leaders to help them achieve this high ideal.

African church leaders need to examine their own service as shepherds. As a leader, are you willingly and joyfully strengthening those of God's people who are under your care in the grace of Christ, so that they become what God wants them to be? Or are you working for money and power, peddling the word of God for financial gain? A day will come when every African church leader will have to give an account of his or her ministry to the Lord.

Having requested prayer for himself, the writer next prays for the believers to whom he is writing. His prayer begins with a description of the God to whom it is addressed. He is the God who has provided for a new life of peace with himself through the blood of Christ Jesus – the great high priest. Christ's blood established the new eternal covenant that resulted in his being raised from the dead and made the great Shepherd of his redeemed sheep (13:20). The writer then prays in the name of Jesus Christ our Lord, asking the God who has brought the believers all these blessings to do two more things for them. The first is to *equip* them with *everything good* so that they can continue to do God's will. The second is to work in both the writer and the Jewish believers to produce the things that please him (13:21).

13:22-25 Closing Remarks

The writer concludes his message by asking them to *bear with my word of exhortation*, which was full of encouragement and serious warnings (13:22). He gives news of Timothy's release from prison, and again speaks of his desire to visit those to whom he has been writing (13:23; see also 13:19). He finishes with greetings to the leaders and people both from himself and from *those from Italy* (13:24). This may imply that he was writing from Italy, or it may mean that he was writing to Italy and that some expatriates who were with him were sending greetings to their homeland.

The letter concludes with a final blessing, *Grace be with you* (13:25).

Tesfaye Kassa

Further Reading

Ellingworth, Paul. *The Epistle to the Hebrews: A Commentary on the Greek Text*. NIGTC. Grand Rapids: Eerdmans, 1993.

Lane, William L. *Hebrews*. WBC. Dallas: Word, 1991.

JAMES

This letter of James deals with how Christians should behave in the church and in society. It speaks of the conduct that should characterize a Christian. Because of its stress on how Christians should act, some great theologians such as Luther thought that James was teaching salvation by works. This supposed conflict with Paul's teaching that salvation was by faith led them to question the authenticity of this letter. But like the ancient church, these theologians ended up recognizing that James was also divinely inspired. They came to see that the writings of James and Paul complement each other marvellously, for while faith is the requirement for our salvation, works confirm the authenticity of our faith.

Outline of Contents

COMMENTARY

1:1 Greetings

The author identifies himself as *James* (**1:1a**). He cannot be James the son of Zebedee, since he died prematurely (Acts 12:2), nor James the son of Alphaeus, about whom the NT gives little information. It is thus likely that the author is James, the brother of Jesus, who was one of the pillars of the Jerusalem church (Gal 2:9; Acts 15:13-21). He and Peter may be thought of as representing Christians with a Jewish background, while Paul represents those Christians who had come from a pagan background. These two groups of Christians complemented each other rather than opposing one another.

The letter is addressed to *the twelve tribes scattered among the nations* (**1:1b**), that is, to Jewish Christians living outside Palestine. The conquest of Israel and the deportations of Jews had resulted in there being many Jewish communities in the lands surrounding the Mediterranean Sea and even beyond that. It was these communities that had founded the synagogues in which Paul often preached (see, for example, Acts 13:14; 14:1; 17:1). These communities would also have included Jewish Christians who had fled persecution in Palestine. This Jewish audience is apparent in the language the author uses. He writes in Greek, like all the NT authors, but the images and examples he uses and some of the words he chooses remind us of the OT.

The universal quality of the church is already apparent in the distribution of these readers. Like Paul, James could have addressed his letter to 'the church of Jesus Christ in Europe and in Asia Minor'.

1:2-18 Trials

1:2-8 A Requirement for Faith

The author comes across as a preacher, talking to people in front of him, rather than as an author writing a letter. Each time he tackles a new subject, he begins with the expression *my brothers* or *my dear brothers* (see, for example, **1:2, 16**). The first subject he deals with is the problem of temptation and trials. But he does not answer the question of how to resist temptations or how to endure trials. Rather, he simply affirms that resisting temptations and enduring trials is a requirement for faith and results in spiritual growth (**1:4**). It will make us *mature and complete*, he says. This explanation helps us to understand why we must rejoice when we pass through trials (**1:2**).

As far as this author is concerned, faith is not a theoretical matter with a list of dogmas to recite or even beautiful doctrine to defend. He sees it as a practical matter that expresses itself in daily life, and especially in how we respond to trials. We can well imagine that the Christians to whom he was writing were constantly exposed to various temptations, perhaps more so than those who remained in Palestine. They were far from the official church leaders in Jerusalem. Thus the author starts his letter with this subject because falling victim to temptation has dangerous effects on a Christian's daily life.

Living a normal Christian life, especially in the face of temptations, demands wisdom (**1:5**) – that is, the ability to distinguish good from evil, truth from falsehood, and the important from the useless and to make timely decisions that conform to what is right. Wisdom is not natural to human beings; it is learned. Therefore, we must ask for it, without doubting the love of God, who always answers prayer (**1:5**). It goes without saying that, at the heart of this prayer, we must have active faith (**1:6-7**). Will God answer the prayer of the person who hesitates or waffles? Does such a person have true faith?

The reference to wisdom makes us aware that in many ways this letter resembles the wisdom literature in the OT. Books like Proverbs also give advice on how to live. But James is less interested in general advice for living than in helping his readers to relate their faith to everyday situations. While his advice may seem to be disjointed at first glance, on rereading the letter one discovers how the different parts are connected.

1:9-11 Resisting the Temptations of Riches

The first everyday situation to which James speaks is that of concern about social status. Some of those to whom he writes are *in humble circumstances* (**1:9**); that is, they are poor, with low social status, and may be tempted to envy the rich. James reminds these poor believers that their real value is not based on what they have. God has accepted them into his family, and so they occupy a *high position*. They need to remember that those whom the world sees as great are not necessarily great in God's eyes. In fact, riches can be a temptation for Christians because it is easy to trust in them for security rather than in God.

Those who are rich and belong to the upper class of society would be wise to be prepared for a fall and a drop in status. The fall of rich people is very common in Africa. James describes the life of a rich person as being like *a wild flower* that blossoms for a while and then fades for ever (**1:10-11**). The rich will die, just like the poor.

When the author speaks of the raising of the poor and the bringing down of the rich, he is not endorsing a struggle for a classless society. He does not condemn the rich because they are rich. He simply wants to make it clear that

life cannot be based on riches. In the long run, the rich have no advantage over the poor.

1:12-18 Why Does God Allow Temptation?

James next turns to the subject of what is at the root of temptations and why God allows tests. When discussing this subject, it is important to distinguish between two concepts that are both expressed by the same Greek word. The first concept is testing, which God allows to strengthen his children so that they may *receive the crown of life* (**1:12**). The second concept is temptation, which comes from the devil and aims to make God's children fail. It was testing that was being dealt with in **1:2**, where James said that the goal of trials was to make God's children 'mature and complete' (**1:4**).

Tempting, however, is a completely different matter. God may test, but he never tempts. There is no way in which God can be the source of evil or of our misfortunes (**1:13**). On the contrary, he is the source of *every good and perfect gift* (**1:17**). He is faithful and does not change, and so he can be trusted to accomplish his plan for our good (**1:18**).

Temptations come when we entertain evil desires. These desires lead us to commit sin, that is, acts that dishonour God and lead to death (**1:14-15**). We need to seek out and destroy the seeds of envy and lust and create a healthy environment in which the various kinds of evil desires cannot thrive.

Some may doubt the faithfulness of God in moments of testing and trial, so James reminds them that God has chosen *to give us birth through the word of truth* (**1:18**), which means that he has made us his children so that we may *be a kind of firstfruits of all he created*. We will be the peak of his creation, as we were in the time before the fall! What a privilege!

1:19-4:17 From Hearing to Doing the Word

1:19-20 Learning to Listen

Here the author turns to another subject, again introducing it with the expression *my dear brothers* because he wishes to build a trusting relationship with his readers and to address them directly (**1:19**). The subject he is dealing with here is the extremely important one of learning to listen when faced with all kinds of ethical confusion. Most of his advice in this letter centres on this subject.

What they are to listen to is the word (**1:21, 22**), which includes the Law, the Prophets and the Writings. Those who speak quickly are likely slow to listen (**1:19**). They tend to become angry and do not put the word into practice. They do not accomplish what the word teaches. To accomplish the word is to transform into action what we have heard and understood.

1:21-27 True Religion as Opposed to False Religion

The author's theology of listening includes a process: *listen ... get rid of all moral filth ... accept the word* and *do what it says* (**1:21-22**). It is possible to listen to the word without accepting it if we do not pay any attention to what we are hearing or listen only to the parts that please us. The image of a mirror illustrates the point well (**1:23**). When this letter was written, mirrors were made of highly polished metal, not glass, and so a person's reflection was not as clear and sharp as it is in modern mirrors. That is why someone looking at their face in the mirror would have to do so *intently*. Moreover, a mirror only gives a flat image, never a three-dimensional one that shows all sides of the object being reflected. If we only glance at the Scriptures in a superficial manner, we will not be able to see what God is showing us there or get a good enough grasp of what God is really saying to be able to put his will into practice. The same truth applies when we walk out of a church service and say, 'That was a good sermon.' Too often we forget the content of the sermon simply because we make no effort to think about it or understand it thoroughly. We need to make an effort to understand what the word is saying (**1:25**), and after having examined and understood what the word says, we must appropriate it and integrate it into our lives.

If we stop partway through the listening process, we will fail and will live disordered lives. However, if we follow all the steps and put the word that we hear into practice, we will be blessed (**1:25**). After all, God did not give his law to restrict people's freedom or to estrange them but to regulate daily life and make it joyful.

Most of the Jews 'scattered among the nations' were religious, However, James condemns those who claim to be religious but do not concern themselves with putting their beliefs into practice (**1:26**). Without action, good doctrine is useless. Pure religion shows itself in behaviour. He gives an example of the type of behaviour he has in mind: *looking after orphans and widows* (**1:27**). This example derives from the OT, which commanded God's people to care for those who had no one to support them financially. Orphans had no fathers, widows no husbands and foreigners no land to cultivate. James does not mention foreigners in this letter because the Christian Jews to whom this letter is addressed were all foreigners themselves.

But pure religion is not just a non-governmental organization, an NGO doing social work. The work done by believers is the product of their faith and the religion is characterized by the holy lives of its members. Briefly put, the word must produce in us acts that prove our relationship to God and a way of life that glorifies him.

FAVOURITISM

We all regularly encounter favouritism. Sometimes we suffer because of it; sometimes we benefit from it. But it is only when we are the victims that we condemn it. It is easy to benefit from favouritism without even being aware of it.

Favouritism manifests itself in various ways. For example someone may be given something they do not deserve simply because they are relatives of or come from the same village or the same ethnic group as the giver. Such nepotism is frequent in Africa. Unfortunately, it is also evident in the church, where people are sometimes given positions because they are recommended by an authority figure, a political official or even the leader of a denomination.

Favouritism is also happens when people cheat and receive something at someone else's expense. For example, some patients get priority care in public hospitals because they are related to or know the doctor, while others who were there earlier must wait. This is favouritism because it is discrimination. The treatment that is being given to them is being withheld from those who are not associated with a prominent person, or who are simply poor. But everyone should be treated equally. James denounces discrimination and reminds us that God makes no distinction between people but treats us all in the same way (Jas 2:1-13).

Favouritism easily becomes corruption. A favour may be given in exchange for a bribe of money or some other commodity. In this case, favouritism is not just a speck in someone's eye, but a plank (see Matt 7:3-5).

There are also more subtle forms of favouritism. For example, the line between favouritism and honour is not always clear. We owe honour and respect to those whose positions merit it (Rom 13:7). Thus it is right for us in Africa to show respect for the elderly (1 Tim 5:1-2). There is no favouritism when people are given what they are entitled to. But it can be difficult to tell where this justified respect moves over into favouritism. It is all too easy to show favouritism under the pretence that one is merely honouring someone. In the African context, respect for the elderly and for authority may easily lead to this type of favouritism, and the person receiving the favours may enjoy them and see nothing wrong with accepting them. However, those who are in positions of honour and authority need to be aware of the danger that the treatment they are receiving is actually unmerited favouritism.

The fight against favouritism is a major challenge for Christians who are in positions where it is always present. They should make a special effort to live as Christians, in a way that is different from those around them, because they are called to be the light of the world and the salt of the earth (Matt 5:13-16). But what can be done if the salt has lost its saltiness?

Soro Soungalo

2:1-13 Faith and Favouritism

As part of putting the word into practice, the author warns his readers against favouritism (**2:1**). He warns that if they are guilty of discrimination, they are disobeying the word.

The specific issue here is discrimination between the rich and the poor in their meetings (**2:2**). These meetings were probably held in a synagogue rather than in a church, for at that time most converted Jews still probably attended synagogues. This practice continued until the rabbis met at Jamnia in 90 AD and declared a clear and permanent separation between Judaism and Christianity. (Jamnia was also the place where the rabbis finalized the canon of the OT).

The author presents a hypothetical situation in which a rich and a poor man come into a meeting (**2:2**). There would be nothing unusual about this, for there were certainly rich believers (1:10). If the attitude of the leaders was to favour the rich to the detriment of the poor, they were guilty of discrimination, which James condemns as offensive (**2:3-4**). The sin is in the fact that these leaders, whom the author calls *my dear brothers* (**2:5a**), have set themselves up as judges by elevating the rich and insulting the dignity of the poor (**2:6a**). God is on the side of the poor, not because they are poor but because they are responsive to him and are near the Kingdom. If they are *rich in faith*, they *inherit the Kingdom* (**2:5b**). God rejects the rich, not because of their riches but because they commit violent acts: they are *exploiting you … dragging you into court, … slandering the noble name of him to whom you belong* (**2:6b-7**). The 'name' to which James is referring is the name of Jesus Christ. The rich assume that their wealth entitles them to do what they like and that they are not subject to the same rules as others.

Christian communities in Africa are not immune to this sometimes unconscious discrimination in favour of the rich since the power of money is strong when many are poor. The rich are easily noticed and gain the respect of leaders. Then the poor find themselves shoved to one side because, as the proverb says, 'thin cows are not licked by their friends'. They are ignored because they are 'thin' and cannot make a financial contribution to the community.

The solution to discrimination in the Christian community is to practise *the royal law*, the one that says *love your neighbour as yourself* (**2:8**). This law is royal because it is one of the two greatest commandments (Matt 22:39) and also because it was given by Jesus himself. James' emphasis emerges again: he does not tell his readers to 'obey' the law but to *keep* it, or in other words, to put it into practice. If they keep this law, Christians will not discriminate. If they do discriminate, they are disobeying the law (**2:9**). Christians of Jewish origin were eager to keep the law, but had failed to recognize that discrimination is as serious a sin as adultery or murder and that by breaking this one law they were guilty of breaking the whole law (**2:10-11**).

James encourages the believers to be careful in their relationships because one day they will have to give God an account of what they have done, and will be judged not according to the law of Moses, but *by the law that gives freedom* (**2:12**). He warns them that God will judge those who discriminate. Someone who shows favouritism insults the dignity of others and judges them. That person will in turn be judged by God (**2:13**).

2:14-26 Faith in Action in the Face of Nominal Belief

This part of the letter is well known to Christians today and was the section that so troubled the great reformer Martin Luther (see the Introduction). However, in considering whether James is indeed teaching salvation by works in **2:14**, we need to remember when this letter was written. It was probably written towards the end of the first century, by which time Paul's teaching on justification by faith would have been widely known, since Paul's letters had been written decades earlier. However, some Christians in the generation following Paul were misinterpreting the doctrine of justification by faith and even twisting it by claiming that works were no longer important. So James is not opposing Paul. In fact, he places more stress on authentic faith than he is sometimes given credit for. He insists faith is empty and inauthentic if it does not involve putting the word into practice.

The preaching style of this letter appears here more clearly than elsewhere. James addresses his readers as if they were standing before him and sets out to question and persuade them. He uses a concrete example to make his point: What should one do when faced with a brother or sister in need, lacking even the most basic necessities such as clothing and food? (**2:15**). There were certainly many poor people in the churches to which James was writing. Fine-sounding words would not feed them, nor would good wishes (**2:16**). *Faith by itself, if it is not accompanied by action, is dead* (**2:17**). In other words, it needs no enemy to make it disappear.

To drive this point home, James stops using the plural pronoun and changes to the singular in 2:18, as if he were talking to only one person. This type of change is not unusual in the OT, especially in Psalms and Proverbs. As we have said, James' letter could well be a book of wisdom. The author contrasts faith characterized by nice words with the faith that produces works that can be observed. He emphasizes that such works are the result of faith (**2:18**). Faith that is not demonstrated by works is dead in that it is simply a nominal belief, like that of the demons, who also believe in God but do not obey him (**2:19**). The author has good reason to say that the person who advocates such dead faith is a poor man! He is worth very little in spiritual terms (**2:20**).

At this point, the author gives two examples drawn from God's word: Abraham (**2:21**) and Rahab (**2:25**), both of whom became ancestors of our Lord Jesus. *Our ancestor Abraham* was such an example of faith in action that he is called the father of believers (Gal 3:7-9). His faith expressed itself in his willingness to sacrifice his only son to God (Gen 22:1-19). This sacrifice is the action by which Abraham demonstrated his faith (**2:23**). He was not justified by this action, but by the faith that produced it.

Rahab in the second example is the very opposite of Abraham. He is the father of believers, whereas she was only a prostitute (**2:25**). But they shared the same faith, the faith that expresses itself in action. By faith, Rahab risked her life to save the lives of the Israelite spies (Josh 2:1-21).

The author concludes this part of his letter with a metaphor: *as the body without the spirit is dead, so faith without deeds is dead* (**2:26**). This metaphor underscores the importance of putting God's word into practice if we are even to be able to speak about faith.

3:1-18 Considered Versus Hasty Speech

Earlier, James had said that 'everyone should be … slow to speak' (1:19). Now he expands that command beyond speaking in the general sense to apply it to the speaking that is inevitably involved in teaching the people of God: *Not many of you should presume to be teachers* (**3:1b**). The reason that *we who teach will be judged more strictly* is that the more we say, the more likely we are to stumble and make mistakes. Teachers are not perfect and will make mistakes just like everyone else (**3:2**). But their mistakes may have destructive consequences. Thus those who are considering teaching must think carefully before deciding to do so. The judgment of which James speaks will take place when the Lord returns (5:7-9).

James uses three familiar things to illustrate how important it is for Christians, and teachers in particular, to control their tongues. The first two illustrations show how humans can use even small instruments to dominate the world. First, he speaks of how a rider can control and use a strong and dangerous animal like the horse if it has a bit in its mouth (**3:3**). Second, he reminds them that opposing wind and tides will prevent a ship from reaching its destination unless the pilot controls the rudder (**3:4**).

His third example shows how something small and useful can spread great destruction through an entire forest if not carefully controlled (**3:5**). Note that he says *The tongue also is a fire* (**3:6**), not the tongue is like a fire. It is more an identification than a comparison, for the author wants to emphasize how dangerous and destructive the tongue can be. We could translate **3:6** like this: *The tongue is a fire and also a world of injustice. It is a part of the body, but it defiles the whole body, sets the entire created world ablaze, and is itself set ablaze by hell.* This translation is also faithful to the

original Greek, but brings out the extent to which the tongue can do irreparable damage. While it is only one small part of the body, it affects all the other parts. More than that, it can set not only an entire forest on fire (3:5) but also the entire created world! James is using exaggeration, just as the psalmists did (see, for example, Ps 32:3; 42:3, 7) in order to drive home his point that an uncontrolled tongue can cause enormous damage to the body and to everyone around. And 'the body' is a common way of referring to a group of believers. Words can easily cause such groups to fall apart, much to the devil's delight. It is an irony of fate that in the long run the tongue that spreads such destruction will itself be destroyed by the fires of hell.

No matter how successful humans are in controlling the animal world in all its varieties (**3:7**), they have not yet learned to control the tongue (**3:8**). James describes it as an uncontrollable evil that leads inevitably to death. But this is not the whole truth, for the tongue does more than just destroy: we can use it to *praise our Lord and Father* just as we can use it to *curse men* (**3:9**). No wonder he compares it to fire, with which we may cook a meal or burn down the granary. We need to master our tongues so that they can be used for blessing, not cursing.

The fact that even believers use the tongue to say incompatible things is evidence of how difficult it is to control. James urges Christians not to be like a spring of water that produces both fresh and bitter water at the same time. All the fresh water in such a spring would be polluted by the bitter water (**3:10-12**). Christians should take pains that when they speak, their words are like fresh water – that is, kind words that build others up and that honour God.

Mastery of the tongue is a sign of wisdom, for the less one speaks, the fewer serious errors one will make. So James returns to the question of wisdom, which he has already discussed in 1:5-7. Wisdom is characterized by a *good life, by deeds done in the humility that comes from wisdom* (**3:13**). Some of James' readers were no doubt claiming to be wise and intelligent. The author challenges them to prove it. Wisdom is not a philosophical theory but something that has to be demonstrated in daily life. And it, too, follows from applying the truth of the word.

James contrasts two types of wisdom: wisdom that is earthly and the wisdom from heaven. Earthly wisdom rests on lies, and thus on the bad use of the tongue. It divides people and sows hatred and jealousy. When people are not paying sufficient attention to God's word, their actions will spring from earthly motives such as *envy* and *ambition* (**3:14**). Any wisdom they claim to have will be earthly and unspiritual because it is *of the devil* and divides people (**3:15-16**). In contrast to the rivalry that characterizes earthly wisdom, heavenly wisdom fosters healthy human relationships and peace with others (**3:17-18**).

4:1-17 Conflicts and Sin

James has addressed several problems among the Jewish Christians scattered around the world, including discrimination in the churches (2:1-12) and wrong use of the tongue (3:1-18). Now he turns to the *fights and quarrels among you* (**4:1**). Refusal to listen and failure to obey the word are at the root of these conflicts and other sins.

He identifies one particular source of conflict: the pleasures that they desire and allow to dictate their behaviour. Their conflicts are rooted in the envy in their own hearts and their behaviour is self-centred. They think only of themselves. This selfishness is why they neither *have* nor *receive* blessing (**4:2b-3**). What he sees is a vicious circle. The believers allow their desires to excite them and drive them into action, and the action they take only strengthens their desires. Not surprisingly, they do not have what they want because they do not stop to ask for it. Rather than serving God, they serve themselves.

These conflicts can take dramatic form. James speaks as if his readers are at war among themselves, and even killing each other (**4:2a**), which seems unbelievable for a Christian group. No doubt he is exaggerating to force them to recognize the gravity of the situation. While there may not have been any literal war or murder, the tensions and disputes would have left victims. Such use of language was perfectly acceptable in ancient literature, and is often found in the Psalms (for example, Ps 59:6).

James seeks to shock his hearers by bursting out with *adulterous people* (**4:4**)! If we take this literally, it means that some of the readers were guilty of the sin of adultery. But he is speaking like an OT prophet here, and what he is actually speaking of is spiritual infidelity. When the people of Israel turned away from God, they were regarded as an unfaithful wife (Jer 3:20).

Jesus used the same expression when he called the Jews who were demanding miracles 'a wicked and adulterous generation' (Matt 12:39). This type of infidelity is characterized by *friendship with the world*, on the basis of desires and pleasures (**4:4**). James denounces such compromise and duplicity. It is impossible to serve God and the desires of the world at the same time, for one cannot be simultaneously a friend and an enemy of God. A choice must be made. Reading James suggests that there must have been many men and women with divided hearts in the groups to which he was writing. They were no different than those who doubt and who resemble 'a wave of the sea blown and tossed by the wind' (1:6).

The next verse, **4:5**, is difficult to translate and has no exact parallel in either the OT or the NT. James may be alluding to a lost sacred text or to a Jewish tradition. But the point of the sentence is that God is jealous as a husband is. He will not accept Christians living in duplicity, like an unfaithful wife.

Conflicts are the manifestations of subtle sins such as desires or pleasures nourished in the heart. They are also produced by pride (**4:6**) which is not that different from desire, as it is also focused on catering to the flesh. It too is self-centred and self-serving.

In the church, conflicts between people are not necessarily settled through negotiation, as would be the case in the political world. They are settled through repentance. So James invites the people concerned to return to God. They need to separate themselves from the things of the world, which are under the power of the devil, and to draw near to God (**4:7-8**). The verbs used emphasize the importance of repentance – *submit to God, resist the devil* (**4:7**), *wash your hands, purify your hearts* (**4:8**), *mourn and wail* (**4:9**) and *humble yourselves* (**4:10**). There is a clear change in the tone of the author. Whereas he previously addressed them as *brothers* (1:19; 3:1, 12) he now challenges them as *sinners* (**4:8**). He does not mince his words when it comes to dealing with sin.

Another sin that reflects a failure to listen and obey the word is slander. Slanderers enjoy spreading bad reports about other people so that everyone knows their faults and weaknesses (**4:11**). But this is a dangerous game, for they are setting themselves up as judges and are judging others by their own set of standards. Judgment is God's prerogative, and he is the one who makes the laws. Usurping a function that is rightly his is a sin (**4:12**). This sin encourages conflicts and open warfare within the community and clearly shows a failure to obey God's word, especially in relation to what it says about love for our neighbours.

James now gives a specific example of the pride he condemned in 4:6. Addressing a businessman or businesswoman who makes plans without any thought of God, he says something like this: 'You drive yourself hard to succeed in business, but without God. You are very sure of yourself. And yet you are like a mist that appears and disappears' (**4:13-14**). What is the good of making long-term plans when you don't even know what will happen tomorrow? Earlier, he had compared riches to a flower (1:10-11). The rich person who is counting on his riches and the businessperson without God are alike. Both are guilty of the sin of self-sufficiency, of thinking they can succeed on their own. Both will come up short when they confront the brevity of life (**4:15-16**).

At first glance, **4:17** may seem to lack any obvious connection to what James has been saying so far. But we have seen that the thread running through all that has been said is the need to listen to the word of God and then apply it in the way we live. James has been dealing with the implications of God's word ever since the beginning of the letter. Consequently, those who have read this letter will have no excuse for not putting into practice what they have learned. If they do not, they will be sinning by omission.

5:1-6 The Judgment of the Rich

Society has always been characterized by the gulf between the majority who are poor and the handful who are rich. The latter are the powerful ones. They set themselves up above the law. They make demands that are harmful to the interests of the poor. They insult poor people, drag them into court, and slander the noble name of the Lord (2:6-7). James does not call such people 'brothers' because they are not part of the family, even if they attend church (2:2). But God will judge them on that day when everyone will appear before the true judge to account for their behaviour (5:1). That day will be one of weeping and misery for the rich without God. The riches they relied on will evaporate – and will even be used as evidence against them (5:2-3).

The wealth the rich have hoarded should have been used to pay fair wages to their employees (5:4a). This injustice is yet another major addition to the catalogue of wrongs they have committed. But there is irony in the fact that those same rich people who dragged others before courts (2:6) will themselves be judged in court by the *Lord Almighty*, or 'the Lord of Hosts' (that is, armies), who defends his people (5:4b). The poor will be the ones to lay the charge, and the rich will be powerless before this judge, who cannot be manipulated or bribed.

The rich will face judgment on the last day, but some even face judgment now as a result of their overeating and drinking (5:5). In our day, we talk of the illnesses of the rich. Their anxieties and overindulgence lead to stress and shorten their lives. All the thought they have put into their investments will prove useless as they are separated from them by death.

5:7-11 Hope

Endurance, patience and hope are three important themes in this letter. They blend well with the central theme of putting the word into practice. Faith should express itself in concrete action. Society judges Christians not on the faith they profess but on the way they live. For his part, the Lord, who is coming back, will judge us on the works that result from our faith in Jesus Christ. We are not saved by these works, but we will be held accountable for them.

Putting the word into practice requires patience and endurance because we will face many temptations, tests, obstacles and challenges. We must imitate farmers. After having worked hard to get the crop into the soil, they wait patiently for the harvest, which will come at the right time, neither too early nor too late (5:7). Just as the farmer waits for the day of harvest or of reward, so we who serve the Lord must wait patiently for his return (5:8). Patience will help us to avoid both the feverish speculation about the date of his return that characterizes some groups and the lack of

concern shown by those with divided hearts who say that the Lord will never return.

Impatience also shows itself in grumbling about other Christians (and about God), and James warns us against this (5:9). Grumbling is a sign of disorder and misunderstanding, and also reveals a failure to control the tongue, which causes great damage among Christians (see 3:1-10). The Lord will express his displeasure at it when he returns.

While we await that great day, our patience will be tried by suffering, just as the patience of the prophets was (5:10). They spoke out in the name of the Lord despite great opposition. They did not give up and fail in their mission because hope was alive in their hearts. They believed that the day of the Lord was near. We admire people like that.

Another person, not a prophet, who suffered patiently was Job (5:11). He feared God and also endured great suffering. Anyone who loves God may have to face suffering, but by the end of it they will know God better, and have a far deeper understanding of his love and mercy.

5:12 Truth

James tells the believers, *do not swear – not by heaven or by earth or by anything else* (5:12; see also Matt 5:35). In Greek and Jewish culture, when one swore by the heavens or by earth, one was asking a divinity to attest to the truth of what one was saying. James is strongly opposed to this because those who live in truth don't need any further witness, least of all from some divinity! In other words, a believer will always speak only the truth.

5:13-20 True Christian Communities

James is looking forward to real Christian communities whose members put the word of God into practice. Such communities will resist temptations and overcome testing, will take care of the poor, of orphans and of widows, and will be examples of impartiality, endurance and patience.

5:13 Respond to Joy and Sorrow

All believers will experience times of joy and times of sorrow. James made this point clearly at the very beginning of his letter (1:2-3). There will be tests, temptations and sometimes conflicts among fellow Christians. There will also be joy, for James has said that practising the word will bring life and give happiness (1:25).

James' advice on how to respond to different circumstances is simple. In times of suffering, pray (5:13a). Tell God about your physical or spiritual pain and wait for him to deliver you, if that is his will. You should express your dependence on him. In times of joy, there should be thanksgiving and songs of praise (5:13b). By singing, we tell God of our thanksgiving and tell him what he means to us. We could do the same in a prayer, but singing is better because both the words and the rhythm and melody can express our joy, a joy that can come only from God.

5:14-18 Care for the Sick

A community that is faithful to the word also cares for the sick (**5:14**). James recommends calling the *elders,* that is, the people with responsibility for leading the church who thus have some authority. Through their intervention by anointing with oil and praying for the one who is sick, the whole church offers support to that person.

When a member is sick, the whole body is concerned. In other words, the church is a place of healing for the sick. But it is neither the oil nor the elders that heal, but it is the Lord himself, since the anointing is done in his name.

Some in Africa believe it is actually the oil itself that has miraculous power to heal. Others think that healing depends on the quality of the oil used. Such people must stop thinking of the oil as sacred or as possessing special powers and must cling only to the promises of God. That is why the author of this letter recommends prayer (**5:15**). It is the prayer of faith rather than the repetition of special formulas that brings miraculous healing.

The phrase translated *will make the sick person well* can also be translated as 'shall save the sick' (kjv). James then adds, *if he has sinned, he will be forgiven* (**5:15**). This linking of healing and forgiveness has led some to think that healing of the body is an integral part of salvation. The problem with this position is that someone may fall sick several times and be healed as a result of prayer. But one day that person may finally fall ill and die. Such a death does not mean that the person has forfeited salvation. Our salvation is definite and eternal. What this passage is teaching is that the healing of the body is a sign of our redemption. By healing our bodies and forgiving our sins, the Lord shows us that he saves us from eternal death. After all, if he can heal and forgive, how much more can he save!

The session of group prayer is also a time for mutual confession (**5:16a**). Sin is a dangerous enemy of the community. Hence it is important to articulate and express our sins, even the most subtle ones and those we consider insignificant, before God and before other believers. This is the only way to combat them. According to the promise of God's word, mutual confession brings healing because *the prayer*

of a righteous man is powerful and effective (**5:16b**). This is another Semitic expression. In the ot, the righteous were those who feared God and obeyed his word. They would be rewarded by the Lord. In the context of this letter, the righteous are those whose sins have been confessed and forgiven. Their prayers are effective because God listens to them. He cannot listen to anyone who is hard-hearted and lives in sin. James cites the example of Elijah as someone whose prayers were effective (**5:17**; see 1 Kgs 17–18). God listened to his prayer because he was righteous. If God did that for Elijah, why would he not do it for us today?

5:19-20 Care for the Lost

James closes his letter with a sad possibility. The community takes care of the poor and of the needy such as orphans, widows and those who are sick. It should also care for anyone who may *wander from the truth* (**5:19**). He seems to be speaking of a hypothetical case rather than one he has specifically heard of. Some believers may wander away from the word and live in sin. They will follow paths that diverge from the path of walking with God. Unless the community intervenes, such people will die in their sin. This does not mean that they will lose salvation, since that is based on faith. But it is a pity that someone would die without getting spiritual help from the church. The community should not be judgmental but should lovingly seek to lead such a person back into the way of God (**5:20**).

This last paragraph of the letter confirms that James cannot be opposed to Paul (see the Introduction). He does not set works up against faith. Those who are lost are not those who have neglected works but those who have distanced themselves from the truth, that is, from the faith. Africa is fertile ground for new religions and sects, making it more important than ever to be well rooted in biblical truths through reading and studying the word of God. James' focus on truth at the end of his letter undermines any assertion that all he is interested in is works.

Solomon Andria

Further Reading

Adamson, James. *The Epistle of James.* NICNT. Grand Rapids: Eerdmans, 1976.

Moo, Douglas. *James.* TNT. Leicester: Inter-Varsity Press, 1985.

Ralph P. Martin, *James.* WBC. Waco: Word, 1988.

1 PETER

1 Peter was not addressed to a specific group of believers but was a general letter that would have been circulated among a large number of churches (1:1). The references to persecution suggest that it was written from Rome, with Babylon (5:13) being used as a code name for that city.

The letter encourages Christians that *panapo nia njia hupatikana* [Swahili – 'Where there is hope, there is a way']. The hope is in Christ, and what is sought is a way to endure suffering. Peter had witnessed the ministry and suffering of Jesus Christ and his triumphant resurrection and ascension. These experiences had convinced him that there is an eternal home to be enjoyed once this brief life is over. He wrote to encourage scattered groups of young believers to remember this and to testify to the grace of God (5:12). He also gave them practical advice on how to live out the Christian faith in a time of trial and suffering. This message speaks to African Christians who are suffering the ravages of war, famine and disease, and who want to know where God is when they suffer like this. Peter points out that suffering is one way that Satan tempts believers to fall away, but that through following Christ's example, believers will persevere and learn to live in dependence on God alone.

Authorship and Date

The author identifies himself as Peter, Jesus' disciple (1:1). The circumstances described in the letter fit the period of Peter's life, and the terminology and themes reflect those of the Gospels and Acts. Some, however, argue that Peter cannot have been the author because of the excellent Greek in which the letter is written (but see comments on 5:12).

Assuming that the letter was written by Peter and that the tradition regarding his martyrdom by Nero in AD 63–64 is correct, it was probably written in the early AD 60s. This date is supported by the fact that the letter seems to show familiarity with Paul's letters from prison (such as Colossians and Ephesians). It may have been written in two sections, with 1:1-4:6 written when the persecution was not as severe as it appears to be in 4:7-5:14.

Theology

Peter is a practical theologian and constantly relates his theology to the duties of the Christian life. While his major themes are salvation and grace, he also addresses issues of Christian relationships.

God is presented as holy and to be imitated (1:15-16), a father whose children must live up to the family name

(1:17) and a Creator who can be trusted (4:19). His predestination of his chosen people is grounds for assurance and hope.

Jesus Christ is seen as having been predestined by the father's love (1:20, 22) to be a sin offering and a substitute (3:18) to bring about redemption and reconciliation (1:18-19). His death and resurrection encourage Christians to die to sin and live in his risen power (2:24, 4:1), and his sinless obedience and willingness to suffer are an example for Christians (2:21-24).

The Holy Spirit is seen as the agent of sanctification (1:2), the author of Scripture (1:11) and the one who enables preachers of the gospel to carry out their work (1:12).

Peter sees the church as built on the foundation of Christ himself (2:6-8) and as the inheritor of the blessings promised to Israel (2:9-10). The two interwoven functions of the church are to offer worship to God and to witness to others. Because the church is a living institution, composed of individual believers who have publicly confessed their faith in Christ by being baptized, these individuals work together to help each other and to testify to Christ.

Peter has no doubts about the authority of the Bible as the word of God, and he regularly appeals to the OT for support for his positions (1:24, 25; 2:6-8; 3:10-12).

Outline of Contents

It is difficult to create a good outline of 1 Peter because the content of the letter flows from one topic to another without clear divisions.

1:1-2 Greetings

1:3-2:3 Salvation and Holiness

2:4-10 A Chosen People, a Royal Priesthood

2:11-3:7 Believers and Authorities

    2:11-12 Belivers as Outsiders

    2:13-17 All Believers and Civil Authorities

    2:18-25 Believing Slaves and Their Owners

    3:1-7 Believing Wives and Their Husbands

3:8-5:11 Duties and Conduct of All Christians

    3:8-4:6 Witness under Persecution

    4:7-19 Living in the Light of the End

    5:1-11 Encouragement to Leaders and Led

5:12-14 Closing

COMMENTARY

1:1-2 Greetings

In African cultures, greetings involve an inquiry about the well-being of those greeted and an expression of regard for them, their family and their community. For example, among the Mbeere people of Kenya, greetings start with the name or identity of the other person and continue *Ciang'ania! Wĩmwega? Andu aku niega? Ukamakethiaĩĩ!* ['Are you well? Your people are well? Give them my greetings!']. Such greetings are rooted in the belief that individuals are intimately connected with their communities.

Peter's opening words in this letter show a similar sense of community. He starts by introducing himself as *an apostle of Jesus Christ* (**1:1a**) and then goes on to identify those to whom he is writing, namely *strangers in the world* (**1:1b**) or 'exiles of the Dispersion' (RSV). The Dispersion, or Diaspora, was the common way of referring to those Jews who lived outside Palestine. Peter applies this Jewish term to all the scattered Christians, both Jews and Gentiles, whom he describes as 'exiles' or 'strangers'. He uses the same word again in 2:11 and a synonym for it in 1:17. He is reminding them that they are all foreigners, not necessarily because they have been displaced from their homelands, but because their true homeland is in heaven. Wherever they are on earth, they are merely temporary residents. As such, they need encouragement, assurance and constant instruction to help them cope with life in a place where they do not belong.

Many African Christians know what it is like to be a displaced person or a refugee, or have had to leave their communities to search for work. While the issues we face (including AIDS, globalization and denominationalism) may be very different from those faced by the Christians in ancient Asia Minor (the regions of *Pontus, Galatia, Cappadocia, Asia, and Bithynia* (**1:1c**), most of which are in modern Turkey), the reminder that we are all exiles gives us a common bond and a hope of return to our homeland.

Scattered exiles often feel isolated and insignificant, so Peter reminds them that they are *God's elect* (1:1b); they have been specifically *chosen* by God (**1:2a;** see also Matt 24:22). When outside pundits treat Africa as irrelevant and having nothing to contribute, we need to remember that God does not see us in that way! He specifically chose us, and his choice was based on his foreknowledge. While we cannot be certain how this foreknowledge operates, what is clear is that all three persons of the Trinity are active in salvation. The Father foreknew the believers; the Holy Spirit is at work in them, sanctifying them so that they can achieve God's purpose; and this purpose is *obedience to Jesus Christ and sprinkling by his blood* – a reference to the OT sacrifices in which blood was sprinkled on the altar and to the ordination

that set priests apart for God's service (**1:2b**; see also Lev 8:30). Christians have a special place in God's eternal plan, and thus have a special responsibility to live up to their Christian commitment.

As in African greetings, Peter ends the greeting with a prayer for the well-being of his readers, wishing them *grace and peace … in abundance* (**1:2c**). Salvation involves a wholeness in which individuals are at peace with God and with each other.

1:3-2:3 Salvation and Holiness

Peter's readers may wonder how they can possibly enjoy peace when they are 'strangers', far from home (**1:1b**) and suffering *all kinds of trials* (**1:6**). These may have been the normal sufferings of human life, but it must be remembered that Peter was writing at a time when people like the emperor Nero (AD 54–68) saw Christians as useful scapegoats to be blamed for anything that went wrong. They were thus persecuted, with some being burned alive or thrown into arenas to be eaten by wild animals.

African Christians, too, have questions about where peace is to be found as they wrestle with the problems arising from religious pluralism, schism in churches, cultural oppression, poverty, ethnic conflicts, the HIV/AIDS pandemic, gender issues and human animosity, which often translates into violence. They turn to books like 1 Peter to find answers to their questions about how the truths concerning salvation and faith apply in such circumstances. How can they live as Christians in the midst of persecution, poverty and sickness?

Peter encourages despondent Christians with a great shout of praise: *Praise be to the God and Father of our Lord Jesus Christ!* (**1:3a**). Why? Because he has given us *a living hope* and *an inheritance that can never perish, spoil or fade* (**1:3b-4**). Exiles and strangers have often lost hope and have forfeited their inheritance at home. But with God we can be full of enthusiastic hope that our inheritance will be waiting for us in our heavenly home. Here Peter's stress on thanksgiving and hope are similar to Paul's (Eph 2:6-7; Col 1:5). Jesus Christ has restored wholeness to the relationship between God and fallen humanity.

Peter assures the Christians that they *are shielded by God's power until the coming of the salvation that is ready to be revealed at the last time* (**1:5**). But this salvation is not only future, for they are already experiencing some of it. Their present love for Christ and rejoicing (**1:8**) show that they *are receiving the goal of your faith, the salvation of your souls* (**1:9**). Moreover, their sufferings are not pointless, but serve to confirm the genuineness of their faith and will bring them *praise, glory and honour* at Christ's return (**1:7**). He reminds them that even Christ had to endure suffering before he received glory (**1:11**).

Peter also reminds the believers that not only were they chosen (1:2) but they also have the unique privilege of being the beneficiaries of all the work of the OT prophets who foretold the suffering and subsequent glory of Christ. Not only that, but they know things about God's plan of salvation that fascinate even the angels! (1:10-12; see also Eph 3:5, 9). It is worth noting that Peter here describes the OT writers as having been guided by the same Holy Spirit who inspired those who preached the gospel.

The good news of salvation should affect not only believers' emotions but also the practical details of their everyday lives and their relationships with others. Sometimes we hope that this will happen automatically, even though such hope contradicts the African world view that it is not easy to be truly human and truly holy. Peter dashes these hopes and makes it clear that holiness requires work: the believers are told to *prepare your minds for action.* Both preparation and action require self-control and a clear understanding of the reward for action (*the grace to be given you when Jesus Christ is revealed* – 1:13) and of the need to obey God's command to imitate his character (*Be holy because I am holy* – 1:15; see also Matt 5:48). We are God's children, and we are to imitate his character just as a child imitates a loved parent.

God is an impartial father who loves all his children and does not excuse bad behaviour by his favourites while picking on others, and so we all need to live up to the family name (1:17). After all, he loves us so much that he did not simply buy our salvation with material wealth (1:18); rather Christ, his perfect Son, died for us (1:19).

References to God as a father can present some problems, for African Traditional Religions do not think of the Supreme Being as either male or female. It is therefore important to present the notion of fatherhood carefully, recognizing that it is a metaphor that God has given us to help us understand him better. We also need to make it clear that while God is the creator, and is in this sense the father of all, believers have the special honour of being adopted into his close family, and so can call him Father in a more intimate sense. Yet while believers are adopted children, Jesus Christ has always been God's Son, in a unique and eternal relationship with God the Father.

We also need to be aware that not all images of fatherhood are positive. Children of single mothers may never have known a caring father. Others may have suffered violence at the hand of their fathers or have seen their mothers molested by father figures. We must help people understand what the term 'father' means when used to describe the relationship between God and believers.

Imitating Christ also means imitating his love for others. Christ cared for individuals in his encounters with the bereaved, the sick, the hungry and the demon possessed. Christians, too, should *love one another deeply, from the heart*

(1:22). The reason for doing this is that we *have been born ... of imperishable seed* (1:23). We are reminded of the seed that was scattered in the parable of the Sower (Mark 4:1-20), which Jesus identified as 'the word'. Peter's comment that *the word of the Lord stands for ever* (1:25a; see also Isa 40:8) reminds us that though human lives may be brief, our love for our fellow human beings should be steadfast, rooted in the transformation God's imperishable word has produced in us (1:23-25).

God's word had been preached to the believers (1:25b), but human words can express *malice ... deceit, hypocrisy, envy, and slander* (2:1), none of which should be found in those who have God as their Father. Rather than craving status or possessions, Christians should crave *pure spiritual milk* (2:2). They have tasted some of this already, for their joy proves that they *have tasted that the Lord is good* (2:3). Just as babies demand to be fed, so Christians must fervently desire that which will enable them to grow as Christians in order to become more like their Lord. The fruit of the Spirit should be seen both in the faith community and in the lives of individual Christians.

2:4-10 A Chosen People, a Royal Priesthood

Peter now changes the metaphor from fathers and babies to *living stones* (2:5), with Christ supremely as *the living Stone* (2:4a). Each believer is part of a spiritual structure, which is not a dead building but a living edifice made up of people. The community of believers comes into being through individual believers. Mixing his metaphors slightly, Peter points out that not only is the building constructed of believers, but believers also serve within it as *a holy priesthood* whose mission is to offer *spiritual sacrifices acceptable to God* (2:5; see also Rom 12:1). It is clear from both these images that Peter has a high regard for the corporate nature of the people of God. Salvation is not simply an individual matter but involves participation in a community of believers.

Peter then breaks away from his argument to explore the idea that Christ is the living Stone. He cites Isaiah 28:16, and interprets it as referring to Christ as the *chosen and precious cornerstone,* making the point that he is a strong foundation stone, on which it is safe to erect a building: *the one who trusts in him will never be put to shame* (2:6). The church is built on the foundation of Christ himself and for this reason he is precious to believers (2:7)

Unbelievers, however, see things differently. They simply see Christ as an obstacle, as a stone they have no need for. What they fail to recognize is that he is actually *the capstone* or, as the RSV puts it, the 'head of the corner' (2:7; see also Ps 118:22; Matt 21:42). He is the essential stone they need to finish whatever they are building; without him, no project will be complete. Given their blindness to his true function and their refusal to obey his message, it is inevitable that they will stumble and fall over this stone (**2:8**; see also Isa 8:14). This is the probable meaning of the statement that this is *what they were destined for.* The phrase should not be taken as endorsing a full doctrine of predestination.

While the destiny of unbelievers is to break themselves by stumbling over the rock that is Jesus, believers are destined for something far greater. They are *a chosen people, … a holy nation, and a people belonging to God* (**2:9a**). These references suggest that Peter saw the church as inheriting the blessings promised to Israel. His use of 'chosen' repeats his stress in 1:2 and again encourages suffering believers who are *rejected by men* with a reminder that they are *chosen by God and precious to him* (**2:4b**).

To get the full impact of Peter's description of believers as a *royal priesthood* (**2:9b**), we need to remember that in the OT only male members of certain families could be priests. Yet Peter says that all believers, including women, are priests. It is not clear what brought him to this insight. It may be that when the curtain in the temple was torn, Peter recognized that there was nothing to stop both women and men from presenting themselves to God directly. Alternatively, it may have grown out of his understanding of people's individual responsibility for responding to the gospel. Believers are supposed to live a life of holiness and love (1:13-25), growing to maturity as God's people and carrying out their mission of making God known to the world (**2:9c, 11-12**). If all believers have this mission, then all are part of the royal priesthood.

In the contemporary church in Africa, such recognition of women is still a contentious issue. Men and women are recognized as believers and both are baptized in the same way, but in many churches only men can be ordained. Some churches argue that the ordination of women is not biblical, while others only accept it with considerable reservations. Life can be very difficult for a woman who is ordained. When faced with tendencies that prevent God's servants from performing the duties to which God has called them, we should quote this passage from 1 Peter and discourage discrimination on the basis of gender.

Peter's words in 2:9c and 2:11-12 also reveal the two interwoven functions of the church: to *declare the praises of him who called you out of darkness and into this wonderful light.* The church is to offer worship to God and to witness to humanity.

2:11-3:7 Believers and Authorities

2:11-12 Believers as Outsiders
Despite being 'a chosen people' and 'a holy nation' (2:9), believers may have problems in this world, where they do not belong but are merely *aliens and strangers* (**2:11**). Strangers are often treated with hostility, and so they need to live lives that will deflect hostile attacks by making outsiders recognize that what the Christians are doing is actually good. Such recognition will bring praise to God (**2:12**).

Peter spells out what this means in practical terms in the society in which they live, with a strong government, a tradition of slave owning and little respect for women. While he advocates conforming to the public and domestic moral values of this society, he does not endorse them. He does not advocate submission because the systems are just but to enable believers to witness in society. It is clear from his comments on the suffering of slaves (**2:19**) and the fear endured by women (3:6) that his sympathy is with those who are oppressed.

2:13-17 All Believers and Civil Authorities
Everyone is told to submit to the governing authorities *for the Lord's sake* (**2:13**) and *to silence the ignorant talk of foolish people* (**2:15**). The aim is to bear witness and to avoid giving grounds for accusations that Christianity is subversive. God's name must not be brought into disrepute. Peter would agree with Paul that although believers enjoy freedom in God's sight, they are not to abuse their freedom by doing wrong or being rude to others (**2:16**; Gal 5:17). He also makes the point that while Christians are free from the tyranny of the state (after all, they are citizens of heaven), they are also free to uphold the law of the state as God's servants, for the OT associated honouring God with honouring those in authority (Exod 22:28; 1 Kgs 21:10; Prov 24:21). Their lives are to be such that even when they are gossiped about or falsely accused, the accusation will not stand and they will be acquitted.

The application of these instructions to contemporary Africa can be difficult. The believers to whom Peter was writing were living in a strongly centralized state, with Roman governors and local kings subject to the Roman emperor. By contrast, in Africa the power of government is often very localized and patriarchal, under the leadership of local kings, chiefs and heads of households. In interpreting Peter's call for submission, contemporary African readers need to consider the impact of patriarchy and oppressive tendencies. These verses should not be used to justify oppression or to permit the continuation of situations where the human rights of others are undermined.

2:18-25 Believing Slaves and Their Owners
Slaves are told to submit to their owners, following Christ's example. He, too, endured suffering that he did not deserve at the hands of cruel men (**2:21-22**). Just as everyone is exhorted not to abuse their freedom, so slaves are exhorted not to court suffering. There is no merit in enduring deserved punishment (**2:20**). But when suffering is undeserved, Christians are to follow Christ's example and not curse and threaten revenge (**2:23**). They are to

leave the matter in God's just hands and be grateful that Christ endured suffering for them. Rather than being merely a possession of a cruel owner, they are so valuable that Christ died for them (**2:24**). More than that, he is the Good Shepherd, who searched for them as he searched for all his straying sheep, and they have the honour of being members of his flock (**2:25**; see also Luke 15:3-7).

While passages such as this one can be used to encourage Christians on their journey of faith, they should not be used to encourage Christians to passively endure suffering in a situation they could work to resolve. Jesus' suffering and death were not passive and purposeless, but a deliberate sacrifice of himself for the benefit of others. Christians must ask themselves whether their suffering is benefiting others or whether it is merely a stubborn perseverance that allows others to exploit them with no good end in view. It is important to interpret the ethical requirements for living a Christian life contextually.

3:1-7 Believing Wives and Their Husbands

The instructions to wives are modelled on those to slaves. They are told that *in the same way* they should submit to unbelieving husbands in the hopes of winning them to Christ (**3:1-2**). But before there is an outcry about this, it must be noted that Peter later uses exactly the same expression in regard to husbands: *in the same way* they are to be kind and considerate partners, who respect their wives (3:7). Paul makes a similar point when he precedes his instructions to husbands and wives with the instruction 'submit to one another out of reverence for Christ' (Eph 5:21). Thus the term 'submission' does not indicate oppression.

The behaviour of wives is to be modelled on that of *the holy women of the past* (**3:5**), and they must consider their inner character more important than dressing richly and fashionably (**3:3-4**). In applying these passages today, while these central points remain true, we need to remember that the details of what constitutes appropriate behaviour by a wife have changed greatly since Peter's day. Women no longer call their husbands *master*, as Sarah did (**3:6**). And in describing women as *the weaker partner* (**3:7**) Peter may be reflecting a physical reality of his time when many women died in pregnancy and childbirth.

In preaching on these passages in Africa, it needs to be remembered that in Peter's culture husbands were always in the position of authority. Peter's aim was not to add to the oppression of women in the home or in society. Rather, he was encouraging women to live out their faith in a way that would make it attractive to their husbands and to others. Therefore, these passages should not be used to justify oppression of women, or to silence them and exclude them from various leadership roles, or to limit them to the domestic sphere. Unfortunately, the church has often done these things in order to support aspects of African culture that

have a negative effect on women. This reality has led some contemporary theologies of liberation to point out that calling on people to submit tends to result in their eventually being treated as an underclass. This was not Peter's intention, and as part of its witness to society today, the church needs to confront the plight of women.

3:8-5:11 Duties and Conduct of All Christians

In the rest of his letter, Peter encourages the Christians to *live in harmony with one another* (**3:8**) and to practise kindness to one another if they take the virtues that make for peace in all relationships seriously. These virtues include the humility that was called for in 2:13-3:7. They are not to become hostile and resentful when they suffer or are insulted. Instead they are told that just as God has called them into the blessings of fellowship with himself (1:2; 2:9), so he has called them to repay evil with good. They are to give blessings because they themselves have been promised blessings that they did not deserve (**3:9**). Peter reminds them that there is nothing new about this command by citing Psalm 34:16, where the psalmist also spoke of the Lord's approval of those who control their responses and actively avoid evil and *seek peace* (**3:10-12**).

3:8-4:6 Witness under Persecution

A Christian's zeal to do what is right is not likely to lead to persecution, for in the natural course of events one is unlikely to be harmed for being kind (**3:13**). But although being *eager to do good* may disarm many opponents, it is no guarantee that they themselves will be left in peace, as Jesus repeatedly warned (Matt 5:10-12; 10:17-22; 24:9; John 15:18-16:4). Persecution may still come their way, but at least it will be undeserved. More than that, it is a mark of blessing (**3:14a**). How can this possibly be the case? Returning to the same passage in Isaiah from which he drew the image of Christ as the 'stone that causes men to stumble', Peter reminds them that in suffering they will be in the company of God's great prophets, like Isaiah (**3:14b**; Isa 8:12). The injunction *do not fear what they fear* also reminds us of Jesus' repeated encouragement of the disciples: 'Fear not' and 'Do not be afraid of those who kill the body but cannot kill the soul' (Matt 10:28). Jesus himself referred to those who were persecuted for his sake as 'blessed' (Matt 5:11-12). They are to focus on the Lord Jesus Christ and not on their fears (**3:15a**).

Being prepared to endure persecution for Christ's sake does not mean that one has to appear stupid. When given the opportunity, Christians should be able to give a coherent and polite explanation of their assurance of present liberation and hope of future vindication (**3:15b**). The dignified respectfulness of their speech should stand in clear contrast to the malicious slander of those who attack them (**3:16**).

Peter again reminds them that *it is better, if it is God's will, to suffer for doing good than for doing evil* (**3:17**), making the point that suffering on the part of the innocent may be part of the will of God. The supreme example of this, and the best model for the conduct of a Christian, is Jesus Christ. He was innocent but God allowed him to suffer – and his suffering produced benefits for all. By offering himself as a perfect sacrifice for sin, Jesus opened the way to God, dealing with the fundamental problem of the broken relationship between God and humanity (**3:18**; Titus 2:14).

When death separated Christ's spirit from his body, he was enabled to go to preach in the spirit world (**3:19**). This suggests that there is biblical support for the African belief in continued existence after death, whether as the living dead (ancestors who are remembered) or as spirits. While not all spirits will benefit from such preaching, each is accountable for the life lived on earth. It is clear that the spirits referred to here had disobeyed God and were thus in prison (**3:20a**).

Peter refers only to Christ preaching to those who were disobedient *in the days of Noah* (**3:20b**), probably because these were regarded as the ones who had sinned most deeply – after all, God had wiped out all life on earth because of their sins! Peter may also have focused on this group because he wanted to draw a parallel between the flood and baptism. The flood brought death to sinners, and baptism, too, marks a death to sin as we pass under the water (Rom 6:3). But just as God's grace and patience led to the salvation of eight people (Noah, his wife, and his three sons and their wives) so his grace and love manifested in the death and resurrection of Christ have saved the believers to whom Peter is writing and raised them up to the living hope of eternal life (3:20-21). It is no wonder that the believers are not to fear their persecutors, but rather the one *who has gone into heaven … with angels, authorities and powers in submission to him* (**3:22**).

In speaking of the *baptism that now saves you* (**3:21**), Peter is careful not to attach magical powers to the ritual washing with water, as is sometimes done in Africa. It is what baptism symbolizes that is important – namely, the believer's response to God in faith that finds expression in baptism.

Peter urges the believers to regard Christ's death in the body and life in the spirit as the pattern for their own lives (**4:1**). Christ's suffering and death dealt with sin decisively, and the believers should see their own suffering in the same light. After the physical suffering they have endured for Christ, they should have nothing more to do with the sort of sins that had attracted them in the past, even if others despise them for their changed behaviour (**4:2-4**). Today, we see people heaping abuse on Christians because of their stand against sexual immorality and their willingness to label irresponsible sexual behaviour as a sin punishable by God (1 Cor 6:9; Heb 12:14; Rev 21:8, 27). While the church must deal realistically with practical issues such as encouraging the use of condoms by those who have multiple sexual partners, it must also make it clear that unmarried Christians are called to a life of sexual abstinence, while married Christians are called to fidelity.

Peter's reference to *he who has suffered* (**4:1**) does not mean that his words apply only to those who have themselves suffered physical persecution. They also apply to all who have announced their identification with Christ's suffering by accepting baptism. Instead of being drawn into a whirlwind of passions, believers are now to have only one focus, living solely for *the will of God* (**4:2**), that is, trying to please God in all they do. God will be the one to judge the behaviour of their persecutors (**4:5**). Returning to his comment on Christ having preached to 'the spirits in prison' (3:19), Peter reminds them everyone will be judged for what they have done *in regard to the body* and all will die, but all also have the opportunity to hear Christ's preaching and *live according to God in regard to the spirit* (**4:6**). Thus while some Christians may already have died and non-believers may be asking where their hope of life is, Peter reminds them that they live in the spiritual realm. In our African context, people's bodies may waste away because of AIDS, but their spirits live – and will continue to live. Many may also experience injustice of various types. Those who suffer for doing right as followers of Christ, who also suffered (4:1), can be assured that this world's judgment is not the only one. God will judge their case justly and righteously.

4:7-19 Living in the Light of the End

The mention of death reminds Peter that death is not the only form that judgment takes: *the end of all things is near* (**4:7a**), that is, the end of this world at Christ's return. But the word Peter uses for 'end' can also be translated as 'goal' – the world is moving towards its ultimate goal. In the light of this, the believers are to keep in close contact with God in prayer (**4:7c**). A prerequisite for being able to do this is having one's life in order so that one can be *clear minded and self-controlled* (**4:7b**). But the focus on prayer does not mean a withdrawal from the world. Instead, believers are to love one another deeply, without holding grudges against one another (**4:8**; 1Cor 13:4-7). They are to *offer hospitality to one another without grumbling* (**4:9**). Every single one of them is to use whatever gift God has given him to help others (**4:10**; see also 1 Cor 12:7-30). Everything they say (whether in preaching or in daily life) should be the sort of thing that God would say (**4:11a**), and any service they offer (whether in an official role in the church or privately) should be done wholeheartedly, using the gifts God has given them to the full (**4:11b**). This is what it means in practical terms to live for 'the will of God' (4:2).

The aim of living like this is not to earn merit with God or praise from others, but to see God praised because of the lives Christians lead. After all, God is the one to whom belongs *the glory and the power for ever and ever* (**4:11c**). Excited again about the glory of God and what he has called us to, Peter finishes his list with a resounding *Amen*, a wholehearted endorsement of what he has been saying. We should finish our recitation of the Lord's Prayer with similar enthusiasm!

Then Peter returns to earth. Painful suffering is still a present reality for these believers (**4:12-16**). Once again he reminds them that they are privileged to *participate in the sufferings of Christ* (**4:13**; see comments on 3:14-18). Christ's glory will eventually be revealed, but only after God's judgment. If this is what the judgment feels like for believers, how much worse things will be for those who have rejected the gospel (**4:17-18**; Prov 11:31). Christians must leave the last word to God (**4:19**), who watches over both the believers and their persecutors.

But Peter does include one warning to Christians. After pointing out that they should not suffer because they have committed what we would regard as 'major' sins like murder or theft, he adds *or even as a meddler* (**4:15**). Christians sometimes have an urge to meddle in other people's affairs and to cause trouble – and any hostility they experience for doing this is justified, and not a cause for rejoicing!

The only good reason for suffering is to *suffer as a Christian* (**4:16**). This is one of only three uses of the word 'Christian' in the NT (the others are at Acts 11:26 and 26:28). The word means 'a supporter of Christ', or it may have been adopted like a Roman surname, to signal 'I am a member of Christ's family'.

5:1-11 Encouragement to Leaders and Led

Peter closes his letter with an appeal to two groups who will be particular targets for persecution: church leaders and young men. Addressing the elders, Peter identifies himself as *a fellow elder* – someone who knows the responsibilities of their role from the inside. He differs from them in having been an eyewitness to *Christ's suffering*, but he is also like them in living in hope of *the glory to be revealed* (**5:1**).

He then spells out the responsibilities that he and they share. The enemy is like a lion stalking his prey (**5:8**). Just as African herders have to be alert in order to protect their cattle, so the leaders of the church have to watch over those God has entrusted to their care (**5:2a**). They must do this not because it is a duty forced on them, but because this is the way in which God has called them to serve (**5:2b**). They must also not see their position of authority as an opportunity to enrich themselves (**5:2c**). Instead their attitude must be humble and they must try to serve others, rather than expecting to be served themselves (**5:3a**; see also Mark 9:35). Other believers, especially wives, husbands and slaves, have already been called to act with humility

(2:18-3:7); now the leaders are told that it is their job to model these behaviours if they are to be *examples to the flock* (**5:3b**). Their role offers little chance of glory – except when the *Chief Shepherd* (Jesus) evaluates their performance as undershepherds and awards them *a crown of glory that will never fade away* (**5:4**). This unfading crown contrasts with the crowns of laurel leaves awarded to athletes who were the celebrities of the time. A laurel crown soon withers.

The call to submission and holiness is also issued to the young men in the church, who must be prepared to be respectful to those who are older (**5:5a**). Such respect was once common in Africa. *Kîîrira* [Kimbeere, Kenya – 'teaching about values and norms'] was passed on to the young by people of the older generation who had been entrusted with this task on the basis that *Mûûgi nî mûtaare* ['a wise person is the one who is given the teaching']. Knowledge of how to relate to one another, of what behaviour was acceptable and unacceptable, and of religious observances was passed on orally from one generation to the next. This was also the case in Jewish culture and in early Christian culture. Peter is not commanding an uncritical acceptance of everything older people teach, but he is reminding the young that older people have acquired wisdom that should be respected.

Having told the young men not to be proud, Peter realizes that this instruction really applies to every single believer and expands it: *all of you, clothe yourselves with humility towards one another*. He quotes Proverbs 3:34 to back up his command (**5:5b**).

Above all, believers are to submit themselves to God, who may assign them suffering in the present but will undoubtedly exalt them at the appropriate time (**5:6**). Rather than worrying about when trials may come and what to do then, Peter advises them to trust in God, who has their interests at heart (**5:7**). But such trust is not the same as being completely passive. They are called to be *self-controlled and alert* because their enemy is on the prowl (**5:8**; see also Matt 26:41; Mark 14:38). They must stand firm in their faith and not give in when he attacks. They are not alone; other believers *throughout the world are undergoing the same kind of sufferings* (**5:9**). This may at times seem hard to believe when we Africans compare our lot with that of wealthy, Western Christians, but it is certainly true when we think of the sufferings being endured by believers in countries that are not sympathetic to the Christian faith.

Peter started his letter by reminding his readers that they had been chosen (1:2) and had a 'living hope' (1:3) despite their suffering, and he returns to this theme as the letter closes: *God ... called you to his eternal glory* and after a little suffering, he will *make you strong, firm and steadfast* (**5:10**). So sure is Peter of this that he repeats his doxology from 4:11 (**5:11**).

5:12-14 Closing

Peter finishes the letter by acknowledging the role of Silas, who has helped him write it (**5:12**) and may even be the one to deliver it. Silas is probably the same person referred to repeatedly in Acts 15:22-18:5 (see also 2 Cor 1:19; 1 Thess 1:1; 2 Thess 1:1). Silas' help may explain why the Greek in this letter is much better than would be expected of a Galilean fisherman. Silas used his gifts to help Peter communicate his message.

In Peter's farewell, the *she* in **5:13** is probably the church he is currently in (the Greek word for a local church is *ekklesia* – a feminine noun). This church was *in Babylon*, which was probably a code name for Rome. Peter also sends greetings from *my son Mark*, who may have been the Mark whose home he went to when he was delivered from prison (Acts 12:12) and the same Mark who later wrote the gospel that records Peter's account of Christ's life. It is likely that Mark was Peter's spiritual son, rather than his physical son.

He instructs the believers *to greet one another with a kiss of love* (**5:14a**), a gesture of affection that was often used when Christians met (Rom 16:16; 1 Cor 16:20; 2 Cor 13:12; 1 Thess 5:26). Christians in different cultures can substitute other gestures that express our love for each other and our sense that we are members of the same family.

Peter's final words are *Peace to all of you* (**5:14b**). The content of the letter makes it clear that he does not regard peace as the absence of persecution or suffering. Rather, he is referring to the deep spiritual peace that is given by God through Christ (John 14:27). It is the spiritual well-being and blessedness of all who are united to Christ in the church.

Sicily Mbura Muriithi

Further Reading

Keener, C. S. *The IVP Bible Background Commentary: New Testament*. Downers Grove, Ill.: InterVarsity Press, 1993.

Michaels, J. R. *1 Peter*. WBC. Waco: Word, 1988.

Wheaton, D. H. '1 Peter'. In *NBC*. 3d ed. Edited by D. Guthrie and J. A. Motyer. Leicester: Inter-Varsity Press, 1970.

2 PETER

Debates rage about who wrote 2 Peter, where it was written and to whom, its relation to 1 Peter, and why it was not recognized as part of NT canon until the fourth century AD. Many commentators treat the letter as the work of a forger, but this position is untenable in light of the evangelical doctrine of biblical inspiration to which both Peter and Paul subscribe (2 Pet 1:21; 2 Tim 3:16). The author clearly identifies himself as Simon Peter.

1 Peter, which focuses on the issue of Christian suffering, was probably written in response to Emperor Nero's persecution of Christians, which began in AD 63. The lack of any reference to suffering in 2 Peter suggests that it was written before 1 Peter, meaning some time before AD 63.

There is no indication where the recipients of 2 Peter lived. We do know that Peter had personally ministered and written to them (1:16; 3:1) and that they were acquainted with Paul's ministry and letters (3:15-16).

The problem Peter confronts in this letter is identical to the one encountered by Paul (Acts 20:29-31; 2 Thess 2:3; 1 Tim 4:1; 2 Tim 3:1-9). False teachers within the community are introducing destructive heresies that deny the lordship of Christ and his second coming (2:1-3; 3:1-7). Peter urges the believers to resist these heresies and to move beyond conversion to discipleship and fruit bearing (1:5, 10).

The church in Africa has been described as 'a mile long but an inch deep'. If this church is going to make a difference on a continent that is torn apart by all kinds of vices, it has to pay serious attention to the teaching of this epistle.

Outline of Contents

COMMENTARY

1:1-21 Developing One's Faith

1:1-2 Greetings

The author identifies himself as *Simon Peter* (**1:1a**), using both his Jewish and his Gentile names in order to appeal to both Jewish and Gentile readers. The Gospels do the same thing (see Matt 16:16; Luke 5:8; John 21:15-17). Some have suggested that there is also a theological reason for using two names, with Simon (his Jewish name) linking him to the old covenant, while Peter (the name given to him by Christ) connects him to the new covenant.

Among African peoples in general, names are significant, and we thus appreciate why the use of two names was appropriate for Peter's mixed audience. We also know that converts to Christianity have sometimes discarded names associated with African Traditional Religions (such as Ogunseyi – 'god of iron has done it') and have taken names with Christian content (such as Jesuseyi – 'Jesus has done it').

Peter next describes his own relationship to Jesus Christ (**1:1b**). Calling himself a 'bond-servant' (or slave) of Jesus shows that his will is subject to his divine Master. Calling himself an *apostle* emphasizes his authority as one whom Christ commissioned to spread his word (see Matt 28:18-20).

Peter sees no difference between the faith of the apostles and that of their converts, nor between that of a Jewish believer and a Gentile believer. In all cases, their faith is *as precious as ours* (**1:1c**). The faith of all is equal in honour and privilege – a point that is emphasized by Peter's use of a political expression that usually refers to foreigners who have been granted citizenship and that emphasizes believers' unity and equality in Christ (see also Gal 3:28).

Peter's greeting to this unified community is both Greek in wishing them an abundant supply of God's grace (that is, his unmerited favour) and Hebrew in wishing them *shalom* (the Jewish word for harmony and wholeness) as they seek to know God and Jesus Christ more and more (**1:2**). These blessings are much needed amidst the ethnic, tribal and racial strife in Africa.

1:3-4 The Gift of Faith

Before discussing the demands the gospel makes of every believer in 1:5-11, Peter lays out the great privileges given to all believers. He twice repeats the expression *has given us* to emphasize both the availability of these privileges to all believers and the fact that we did not earn them. They are a gift given by God's power (**1:3a**) and through God's promise (**1:4**). These gifts enable us to live a holy life, partake of God's moral excellence and escape the corruption caused by evil desires. The catch is that we can only enjoy them *through our knowledge of him* (**1:3b**). But the church in Africa has only a shallow knowledge of God's word, so that God can say, 'My people are destroyed from lack of knowledge' (Hos 4:6). The church in Africa must disprove the saying 'If you want to hide a treasure from an African, keep it in a book.'

1:5-11 The Growth of Faith

Peter sees salvation as merely an entry point. He mentioned this in 1 Peter 2:2, where he urged his readers, 'Like newborn babies, crave pure spiritual milk so that by it you may grow up in your salvation.' Because of what God has given us (1:3-4) we must make every effort to grow up. There is no room for laziness! He lists seven qualities or virtues that must be added to faith for it to be effective in producing a character that will be commended at the end (**1:8, 11**):

- **Goodness** translates a word that has also been translated as virtue, courage and excellence. It can be used of a land that is fertile and productive. It is the quality that makes a person friendly, courageous a good citizen and skilled in the art of living well.
- **Knowledge** is practical knowledge that enables one to decide rightly and act effectively. Such knowledge contrasts with that of the false teachers of chapter 2, whose actions do not match what they claim to know.
- **Self-control** is more than just the ability to use reason to control one's emotions. Christian self-control is submission to the control of the indwelling Christ and the power of the Holy Spirit (see Gal 5:16-18).
- **Perseverance** has been described as 'the queen of virtues'. It is patience with courage behind it and hope in its front yard. It is the tenacity that refuses to give up when trouble comes but always looks forward to a better tomorrow (see Heb 12:2).
- **Godliness** translates a word that is rarely used in the NT, probably because it was commonly used with reference to pagan religion. Here it refers to piety towards God and practical love for our fellow human beings, especially the most vulnerable and needy (see Jas 1:27).
- **Brotherly kindness** translates what is literally 'love of the brethren'. It is the family affection that naturally provides care, support and solidarity. Such kindness should be a trademark of a Christian community (John 13:35).
- **Love** is *agape*, God's unconditional love for the righteous and the wicked alike. Such love is the nature of God (1 John 4:16), which we inherit when we are born again (1 John 4:7-8). *Agape* desires the highest good of the one loved, which results in sacrificial action for that person's good. It is what God shows for us in John 3:16 and expects us to have for one another in 1 John 3:16.

Preachers across Africa focus on who Jesus is and on the peace or salvation he offers. However, we often neglect to teach the principles that Jesus laid down for our prosperity and success in life. Peter's list of things to be added to faith deals with both the person and the principles of Jesus. If we are to be effective and productive, we need to discover this combination. As a West African proverb says, no bird can fly with just one wing.

1:12-21 The Ground of Faith

Peter wants his readers to be reminded of the facts before he deals with the claims of the false teachers in chapter 2. Thus he first stresses the truth that his readers *know* and in which they are *firmly established* (**1:12**). As he has already reminded them, their salvation is totally free (not earned) and is based on the finished work of Jesus Christ (1:1). Along with this, God has provided them with all that they will ever need for godly living and a glorious ending (1:3-4).

Peter knows that he will soon die, and he wants to leave no doubt about the truth he teaches (**1:13-15**). (He died as a martyr, probably less than three years after writing this letter.)

Peter reminds them that he was an eyewitness of Christ's transfiguration, which he sees as a foretaste of Christ's second coming (**1:16-18**; Matt 17:1-8; Mark 9:2-8; Luke 9:28-36). The historical transfiguration supports the reliability of his prediction for the future. He is not making things up, as the false teachers may be suggesting.

Finally, Peter states that the prophetic Scriptures of the OT also bear witness to the truth (1:19) and that the Holy Spirit has inspired all biblical prophecy (**1:20-21**), including Peter's own prophecy of the return of Jesus Christ (1:16). The Holy Spirit did not suppress the individuality of the human authors of the Scriptures, but he did watch over them as they wrote and made sure that their words did not contain errors. Peter's words regarding the value of the Scriptures still apply to us today: *you will do well to pay attention to it* (**1:19**). God's promised blessing is for those who meditate on his word, to obey and do what it says (Josh 1:8; Ps 1:1-3; John 8:31-32; Jas 1:25).

2:1-22 Denouncing False Teachers

2:1-3 The Certainty of False Teachers

From speaking of the true prophets (1:19-21), Peter swiftly moves on to warn his readers about the inevitable rise of false teachers within their community. Peter based his argument on historical precedent rather than prophetic foresight. What might start as a difference of opinion regarding Christ would quietly turn into a deviation and, eventually, into a denial of Christ as Saviour and Lord (**2:1**). We have seen this happen in Nigeria, where a certain professor started teaching that Christ is not the only way to reach God. Such a position is contrary to the teaching of Christ (John 14:6) and of his apostles (Acts 4:12; Rom 1:16-17). As this man gained disciples and became the head of his denomination, liberal theology took over a denomination that had once had a strong evangelical heritage. Peter warns us that such heresies bring destruction both to those who teach them and to believers (2:1, 3).

2:4-9 The Condemnation of False Teachers

Peter gives three historical examples to prove that false teachers, evil and wickedness will not go unpunished now or in the future. The examples he chooses show that adulterating the truth and denying the uniqueness of Christ is as bad as sexual perversion and other sins.

His first example is the punishment meted out to the angels who sinned by cohabiting with women (2:4; Gen 6:1-4). He is not speaking of Satan's rebellion against God (Rev 12:1-9), for Satan and many of the angels who fell with him are still at large as demons and evil spirits (Matt 17:18; Eph 6:12; 1 Tim 4:1-5; 1 Pet 5:8). By contrast, the culprits in 2:4 and Jude 6 are imprisoned in hell, a place of darkness, awaiting the final judgment. It was an uncommon sin and received a punishment only a step away from the lake of fire, which is the ultimate punishment (Rev 19:20).

Peter's second example is God's punishment of the human wickedness and corruption of Noah's day (2:5). Everyone was destroyed in the flood except Noah and seven others (his wife, his three sons and their wives). Noah was delivered because he was righteous with respect to his belief in and his walk with God (Gen 6:5-13, 18).

Peter's third example is the punishment of the sin-filled cities of Sodom and Gomorrah (2:6-9; Gen 19:1-25). Once again, one righteous man, Lot, was rescued. Just as the Lord protected Noah and rescued Lot in their generations, so he can deliver those of us who have put our trust in Jesus in our generation (2:9). He stands beside believers like the African Anglican bishops who took a stand against the ordination of a gay bishop in the USA in 2003.

2:10-22 The Characteristics of the False Teachers

Peter speaks of false teachers with flaming moral indignation that reminds us of Jesus' condemnation of the Pharisees (Matt 23:13-39). He describes them as indulgent, living to please the flesh (2:10a). In light of Peter's third example in 2:6, many commentators agree that this expression suggests that they practised sodomy.

The false teachers also despise authority, meaning either the Lordship of Christ (see 2:1) or the recognized leadership of Peter and John (as in 3 John 9-11) or some angelic hierarchy (see Jude 8). A proverb in Sierra Leone says 'Rebellion craves recognition.' Rebel leaders, like false teachers, all want to be number one. These men are presumptuous; that is, they show a reckless daring that defies God and oth-

ers (2:10b). They are full of themselves, looking only for personal pleasure and recognition. Their arrogance is such that they revile angelic majesties, belittle their power and speak disrespectfully of them. In contrast with such behaviour, the angels, who are *stronger and more powerful* than the false teachers, do not bring slanderous accusations against them before the Lord (2:11).

Peter compares the false teachers to irrational animals, creatures of instinct, born only to be captured and killed. Like animals, they will die (2:12). Sensuality is self-destructive. The success of Uganda's war against HIV/AIDS has proved that abstinence is the best cure for the disease. In like manner, the antidote to false teaching is the pure spiritual milk of God's word (1 Pet 2:2). But the false teachers don't want what is pure. Instead they delight in drinking parties, fornication and adultery, and they lead inexperienced believers astray (2:14). Like Balaam, a prophet who ignored God's warnings because of his love for money (Num 22:1-34; Jude 11), these false teachers have forsaken the straight and narrow way of truth for the broad road of greed, sex and pride (2:15-16; see also Matt 7:13-16). Many of those who preach a prosperity gospel in our day easily fall into Balaam's error and make a travesty of the gospel. They 'live as enemies of the cross of Christ, their destiny is destruction, their god is their stomach, and their glory is in their shame' (Phil 3:18-19). They are empty – *springs without water* – and worthless like *mists driven by a storm* (2:17). Ironically, they promise freedom while held in bondage by sin (2:19).

Apparently the false teachers had once professed Jesus as their Saviour and Lord. Such knowledge normally frees a sinner from the corruption of this sinful world. But tragically they have renounced their allegiance to Christ and gone back to their former state. A state of ignorance is better than one of apostasy (2:20-21). Peter's two concluding proverbs carry the message that nothing more can be done for them, echoing Jesus' indictment of a wicked generation (Matt 12:43-45; Luke 11:24-26).

3:1-18 Defending the Faith

3:1-2 Restatement of the Purpose for Writing

Peter now gets deeply personal and pastoral. Four times in this closing chapter he addresses his readers as *dear friends* (3:1, 8, 14, 17), using an intimate expression that describes believers' relationship in Christ to one another. As the Lord had commanded him (John 21:15-19), Peter shepherds his flock – feeding them, defending the faith, warning them against heresy– all in a spirit of love (1 Pet 5:1-4). His aim is to encourage *wholesome thinking* (3:10a), which is the best antidote to false teaching and bogus claims. Far too many of our African churches are heavy on emotional experiences but neglect people's minds. Consequently, we have produced 'mindless Christians'. Part of the purpose of this commentary is to reverse this trend.

Wholesome thinking was so important to Peter that he wrote two letters about it (3:1). The first letter referred to here is probably not 1 Peter (although there is disagreement about this). But regardless of which letter he is referring to, he wants his readers to remember what has been said in the Scriptures. In **3:2** he makes it clear that the NT apostles have the same authority as the OT prophets.

3:3-9 Prophecy Regarding Rise of Scoffers

Peter warns the believers that they will inevitably be confronted by mockers who childishly jest and scoff at the Lord's promise to return. The scoffers' question is not a real request for information (**3:3**). It springs from evil desires and caters to their own lusts. These scoffers, who may well be the false teachers of chapter 2, are cynical and self-indulgent and insist that the world will carry on for ever (**3:4**). Peter counters this argument by reminding them that there was a specific time when God created the heavens and the earth (**3:5**; Gen 1:1-31) and that when the world became corrupt, God decisively judged it by the flood (**3:6**; Gen 6–8). Just as God acted in judgment in the past, so he will act again in the future – but then he will use fire instead of flood (3:7).

Peter passionately reminds his readers of God's view of time and his faithfulness to his promise. To one who is eternal, a day is like a thousand years, and vice versa (**3:8**; Ps 90:4). Moreover, if God seems to be slow from a human perspective, it is for our benefit (**3:9**). He is not slow but long-suffering, not impotent but patient, keeping the door of repentance open to all. However, the fact that God does not want anyone to perish does not mean that everyone will be saved, for Peter has just said that the ungodly will be destroyed (**3:7**). Christ has opened the way to salvation for all, but only the repentant benefit.

3:10-13 Promise of the Lord's Return

No one except God knows the date of the Lord's return (Mark 13:32), and we must beware of those who go around making false claims about it. In 2001 one false prophet in Kanungu in Uganda massacred a thousand of his followers to cover up his failed prophecy of Christ's return! Rather than speculate about the date, Peter simply states that it will come *like a thief*, suddenly and unexpectedly (3:10a; Matt 24:43-44; 25:13; Luke 12:39-40) and calls us to be ready for its coming. Heresy has often crept into the church when believers (especially the leaders) are spiritually asleep (Matt 13:25). In our materialistic postmodern society, the call for spiritual alertness is urgent.

When the day does come, everyone will know it! With a thunderous crash the sky, regarded as a canopy over the earth, will disappear, the material elements of the universe will be dissolved by fire, and the earth and all that humanity has constructed will be stripped naked (**3:10,** 12). The destruction will be total.

While we await Christ's return, we should live holy and godly lives (**3:11**). The Yoruba of Western Nigeria call a Christian *onigbagbo* ['one who has received faith']. Faith is regarded as a gift that brings salvation. But accepting this gift has consequences, as a saying that arose among the first generation of Yoruba Christians makes clear: 'We do not receive faith without it taking something away from us. It will take away sorcery, idolatry, adultery, witchcraft and the like.' These uncompromising Christians heard the call to holiness and to separation from the old way of living (as also did the revivalists of East Africa, commonly called *kutenderesas*). Expectation of Christ's return has always served as a moral detergent (1 John 3:3).

The rabbis believed that the sins of the people delayed the coming of the Messiah. Similarly, Peter believes that believers' holy conduct will hasten the coming of the day of God (**3:12**). While the old earth will then be destroyed, the righteous can look forward to enjoying a brand-new heaven and earth (**3:13**). This new creation will be a fulfilment of God's promises in the OT (Isa 65:17; 66:22).

3:14-18 Pastoral Appeal for Readiness

Peter closes his letter with yet another appeal for godly living (compare 3:11). He does not see piety as quiet inactivity in an isolated place. Rather, it is walking the talk, living a life in contact with the marketplace but without being contaminated – *spotless*, *blameless*, and without condemnation (**3:14**).

Peter again states that the Lord is patient for the sake of our salvation and stresses that Paul agrees with him on this point (**3:15**; 3:9). He equates Paul's letters with *the other Scriptures*, by which he means the OT and the NT writings already in circulation (**3:16**; see also 3:2). His readers must have known Paul's letters, especially those like Romans, 1 and 2 Thessalonians and Galatians, that deal with salvation and holy living. Paul's doctrine of justification by faith was being twisted by the false teachers to mean that once saved, believers could do whatever they liked. Paul vigorously refutes this in Romans 3:5-8 and 6:1.

Peter makes two final appeals that sum up his teaching in this letter: Guard your present secure position in Christ and continue to grow in the grace and knowledge of our Lord and Saviour.

Tokunboh Adeyemo

Further Reading

Barclay, William, *The Letters of James and Peter*. DSB. Philadelphia: Westminster Press, 1976.

Green, Michael. *The Second Epistle of Peter and the General Epistle of Jude*. TNT. Grand Rapids: Eerdmans, 1987.

1 JOHN

1 John has many similarities with the Gospel of John, and it is assumed that the Apostle John wrote both. His aim in writing was to assure believers that they have eternal life (5:13) and to exhort them to conduct their lives accordingly. He is interested in both right beliefs and pure conduct.

Outline of Contents

COMMENTARY

1:1-4 The Word Witnessed and Proclaimed

In the opening verse, John makes it clear that his focus is on the *Word of life* (**1:1**). Immediately we are reminded of the references to 'the Word' at the start of the Gospel of John. But this passage seems to treat the Word as impersonal (*that which was from the beginning*) and not as a person ('He was . . . in the beginning' – John 1:1). And yet, John also speaks of having seen and touched the subject of his message, which implies a person. It seems that he is trying to deal with both the message from and about Jesus and with Jesus as a person at the same time. The impersonal message may be heard, but the person exists. We find the same mixture of the abstract and the personal in the next verse, where John speaks of the life *which was with the Father and has appeared to us* (**1:2**). The message is described as the 'word of life', for it is by believing it that one gets eternal life. At the same time, Jesus himself is also the 'Word of life' in that he is the source of life. He gives life to those who hear his message, accept it, and believe in him.

John says that this Word *was from the beginning*. If the 'word' is taken as the message from and about Jesus, the 'beginning' refers to the time when this message was first proclaimed on earth. However, if our focus is on the person of Jesus, this 'beginning' is equivalent to eternity. Jesus, who is eternal, gives eternal life (1:2).

John twice stresses that he and others (probably the other disciples) experienced the 'Word' with all their senses. In **1:1** he says, 'we have heard, we have seen with our eyes, we have looked at, and our hands have touched,' and in **1:3a** he refers to *what we have seen and heard*. He is emphasizing that he was one of those taught by Jesus himself and that this experience qualifies them to be true bearers of Jesus' message.

The purpose for which he is proclaiming this message is *so that you also may have fellowship with us* (**1:3**). The word translated 'fellowship' contains the notions of partnership and sharing. Those who hear this message and put their faith in Jesus come to share in the blessings of God (and particularly in eternal life) along with the proclaimers of the message. More than that, all of them can become partners with *the Father and with his Son* (**1:3b**), making for wonderful, rich fellowship.

At a secondary level, John's purpose in writing this message is *to make our joy complete* (**1:4**). John will rejoice if those who hear and read his message believe it and join him in the fellowship he has just described.

1:5-10 Living in the Light

Having established his credentials and explained his reasons for writing, John proceeds to deliver the message he has been given. He starts off by making two key statements about God's nature: *God is light* and *in him there is no darkness at all* (**1:5**). Darkness stands for error and sin, while light stands for moral purity. The two are incompatible. John is emphasizing that God is holy in his essence and righteous in what he does. He may also be making the point that just as light illuminates a path or exposes things, so God illuminates the hearts of men and women, exposing all that is contrary to his nature.

People who do not understand the nature of God may object to this stress on the holiness of God and make false claims for themselves. John bluntly dismisses the arguments of those who *claim to have fellowship with him yet walk in the darkness* (**1:6**) as a hypocritical lie. These people are not living *by the truth*. Fellowship involves partnership, compatibility and agreement. There can be no compatibility between darkness and light. As the saying goes, *aso funfun on abawon ki ire* [Yoruba, Nigeria – 'a white cloth and a stain never agree']. God is morally pure and has no partnership with anyone who walks in darkness.

But true fellowship is possible, provided *we walk in the light, as God is in the light.* The fellowship starts with God and me, and then moves out to embrace others, so that *we have fellowship with one another* (**1:7**). While fellowship with one another is good (Ps 133:1), it is also something we struggle to maintain. Personality differences and differing perspectives often result in confrontations. God's illumination of my life enables me to see the plank in my eye before I notice the speck of sawdust in someone else's eye (Matt 7:3-5). As we walk (that is, habitually live) in the light, fellowship with one another becomes a reality.

A second group does not admit to walking in darkness. In fact, they *claim to be without sin* (**1:8**), living sinless lives. The problem with such a claim about oneself is that one must either lower God's standard of holiness or redefine sin in order to validate it. People who claim this may also not be allowing God to illuminate their lives and show up the dark spots in need of cleansing. John says that if we make this claim *we deceive ourselves.* But we are the only ones fooled. God is not deceived, nor are others who may know us better than we know ourselves. A claim to have eradicated our sinful nature not only shows that we are prone to self-deception, but also signals an absence of the truth in our lives.

A third group claim *we have not sinned* (**1:10**). These people seem to be denying the truth that sin has universally affected everyone, including them, a truth that is clearly taught in Scripture (Ps 14:2-3; Isa 53:6; Rom 3:23-24). God's whole plan of redemption is based on the fact that all human beings are sinful. To reject God's assessment of humankind is tantamount to an open declaration that God is a liar. Submission to God involves the cry 'I have sinned' (2 Sam 12:13) and not the claim 'I have not sinned'.

John responds to these last two groups by pointing out that we have no need to pretend we are sinless, for *if we walk in the light, as he is in the light . . . the blood of Jesus, his Son, purifies us from all sin* (**1:7**). It is only when we allow God's light to expose areas of darkness in our lives that we feel the need to cry for help. As we continue to walk in that light, it shines ever more brightly within us, exposing more darkness within ourselves and driving us to ask for still more cleansing by Jesus' blood.

Finally, we can trust that *if we confess our sins, he is faithful and just and will forgive us our sins and purify us from all unrighteousness* (**1:9**). Here 'confessing' involves 'calling it as it is'. When God illuminates our lives, we see sin as God sees it and then we turn to him with honest and sincere hearts, wanting to be cleansed from it. The promise that he will forgive us our sins is guaranteed by the fact that he is faithful (he keeps his word) and just (he knows how weak we are). The forgiveness he offers does not merely gloss over sin; rather, it purifies us from every trace of it.

2:1-2 Christ Our Advocate

The discussion of sin prompts John to mention another of his objectives for writing, namely, *that you will not sin* (**2:1a**). Believers who have truly grasped that 'God is light; in him there is no darkness at all' (1:5) will be anxious to avoid sinning, since a sinful act is contrary to the nature of their God. Yet the reality is that even the most determined believers will still find that they have sinned. John reassures them that they have an advocate – *one who speaks to the Father in our defence.* He identifies this advocate as *Jesus Christ, the Righteous One* (**2:1b**).

John may be using Jesus' full title deliberately to emphasize his qualifications for being our advocate. The name 'Jesus' communicates that he is truly human and so can sympathize with us. The title 'Christ' presents him as the one anointed by God and therefore acceptable to God as he pleads the case of someone who has sinned. The fact that he is 'the Righteous One' means that he himself has no need of an advocate, and so is able to represent someone else.

John carried on to describe Jesus as *the atoning sacrifice for our sins* (**2:2a**). The word translated 'atoning sacrifice' in the NIV has been translated as 'propitiation' in some versions, like the NASB, meaning that Jesus appeases God's wrath. Other translations, like the RSV, give it as 'expiation', meaning that he removes our sin. The NIV's translation allows for both ideas. God is affected by the disobedience of his children and, in the context of his righteousness, there is no way to deal with sin but to remove it. Propitiation and expiation are essential parts of the process. Christ does both, not only for our sins *but also for the sins of the whole world* (**2:2b**). His death is sufficient to remove the sins of everyone in the world, appeasing God's anger.

2:3-17 A Life of Obedience

Throughout this epistle, John is preoccupied with Christian living, which he calls our 'walk'. The mention of our need of an advocate with the Father when we sin leads him to comment on how we can test whether we know the Father. He emphasizes that true knowledge of God is always associated with obedience to his commands (**2:3-4**). Claiming to know God while disobeying him is both a lie and a sign of an absence of truth in the person's whole life. Complete love for God is shown by obedience to his word (**2:5**). Then, moving beyond the abstractions of 'commands' and 'word', John summarizes what he means: *Whoever claims to live in him must walk as Jesus did* (**2:6**) – and Jesus has just been identified as 'the Righteous One'. The command to live as Jesus did reminds John of what Jesus called his new commandment: 'Love each other as I have loved you' (John 15:12). John describes this command about love as both *old* (**2:7**) and *new* (**2:8**). It is old because *you have had [it] since the* *beginning* and it *is the message you have heard* (**2:7**). Here the 'beginning' refers to the start of one's Christian life. Salvation is rooted in God's love and demands a response of love to God and his people.

At the same time the commandment is new because *its truth is seen in him and you*. Something new is happening, the reality of which is confirmed by the fact that *the darkness is passing and the true light is already shining* (**2:8**). Jesus lived out this command, and as believers become his disciples, they follow his example. As they do this, the area of light (Christlikeness) expands and the areas in their lives and relationships that are controlled by darkness shrink.

Love for fellow believers confirms that one lives in the sphere of light (**2:9-10**). Love becomes the lens through which one looks at all relationships, and thus one can enjoy a secure footing as one walks the Christian path (2:10). These loving relationships will transcend any distinctions based on race, tribe, clan or class. By contrast, someone who hates a fellow believer is blundering around in darkness and *does not know where he is going, because the darkness has blinded him* (**2:11**; see also John 12:35). Such a person makes no progress in his or her spiritual life.

Recognizing that his readers' understanding and ability to put this into practice will vary, John addresses children, young men and fathers separately. These categories may not reflect the physical age or gender of his readers so much as their different levels of spiritual maturity. John definitely viewed these exhortations as applying to all believers.

He starts by addressing the *children*, telling them that *your sins have been forgiven on account of his name* (**2:12**) and that *you have known the Father* (**2:13**). Their journey of faith began with forgiveness of sin and coming to grips with how it felt to be part of the family of God. It is a wonderful thing to be born again and relate to God as Father! Because this experience is common to all believers, and because John often refers to his readers as *children* (for example, in 2:1, 18, 28), it is possible that this comment is addressed to all believers, and not just to the very young.

Fathers are reminded that *you have known him who is from the beginning* (**2:13a**, **14a**). These readers have long experience of seeing God at work, both in their own lives and in those of others. But John reminds them that God has existed 'from the beginning', implying that no matter how long their spiritual experience, it cannot predate God. He has been there from eternity and is the Father of all his spiritual children.

John tells the young men, *you have overcome the evil one* (**2:13b**) and *you are strong, and the word of God lives in you* (**2:14b**). Struggle with the evil one starts at conversion, but overcoming is possible. In fact, it was the experience of John's readers. Each victory strengthens a believer to deal with the next attack. God's word becomes the source of wisdom for knowing how to resist the evil one (Matt 4:1-11; Luke 4:1-13).

All three groups of believers are called to love one another, but they are also called to hate the things that belong to darkness. This call is stated in the form of a prohibition, *do not love* (2:15). Two objects of the hatred are spelled out, namely, *the world* and *everything in the world* (**2:15**). Here 'the world' stands for the organized system, whether controlled by humans or demons, that is in opposition to God. John identifies three specific categories of behaviour that are in conflict with God's desire that his people walk in the light and love each other: sinful cravings, greed and pride in what one has or does (**2:16**).

There are three reasons why we should hate these things. First, love of the world and love of the Father are mutually exclusive (2:15; see also Matt 6:24). The world is in opposition to the Father, and therefore one has to choose which of them to love; one cannot love both. Moreover, the things of the world all come from a source that is opposed to God (2:16). While God made everything good (Gen 1:31), many things have been perverted by evil. Finally, it is important to remember 'that the world and its desires' will not last (2:17). The system opposed to God only seems to triumph; God is the one who will end it when the time comes (see Rev 20:7-10; 21:1-4).

The heart of the matter is that *the world and its desires pass away, but the one who does the will of God lives forever* (**2:17**). John contrasts the fate of someone who is part of the world system with that of someone who obeys God's command to love. The promise of eternal life is a strong incentive to do God's will.

2:18-27 Recognizing Antichrists

The presence of antichrists is an indication that it is *the last hour* (**2:18**). This 'hour' is the period between Christ's first coming (or possibly the day of Pentecost) and his second coming. It is equivalent to the 'last days'. While there will be one antichrist in the last days (2 Thess 2:3-4), he will be preceded by many of his kind who either imitate Christ (claiming to have his power and authority) or oppose Christ and usurp his place. John writes to warn his readers against them (2:26).

What is particularly confusing about these antichrists, John admits, is that *they went out from us*. Consequently, many may be deceived into thinking that they are true believers, so John hastens to add, *but they did not really belong to us*. He is sure of this, because *if they had belonged to us, they would have remained with us* (**2:19**). The antichrists are not confused believers but people who have deliberately chosen a different, false teaching.

The faithful, however, are not deceived because they are protected by two things: the *anointing from the Holy One* (**2:20**, 27) and knowledge of *the truth* (2:20, 24). The anointing refers to the Holy Spirit and all the blessings that he brings. He is given to believers by the 'Holy One', who could be either the Father or the Son, for John says that both of them send the Holy Spirit (John 14:16, 26; 15:26) and are united in their work (John 14:10). While the false teachers have a spirit that teaches against Christ, believers have the Spirit who bears witness to Christ. So long as they are sensitive to the Spirit's leading, the ones with the spirit of antichrist will not deceive them. The believers also have the word of God, which is the source of true knowledge.

In fact, there is a simple test for telling who is a liar and an antichrist. It centres on the person's response to the statement *Jesus is the Christ*. 'Jesus' is the earthly name given to the One who is eternal but became human (John 1:14) in order to save us. 'Christ' indicates that he is 'anointed', that is, set apart by God as a means of reconciliation with him. Someone who denies that this is the case

is an antichrist. To deny the Son is also to deny the Father who anointed him (**2:22**). On the other hand, someone who acknowledges the truth of the statement enjoys the Father's approval and fellowship (**2:23**).

The believers are to *see that what you have heard from the beginning remains in you* (**2:24**) and to *remain in him* (**2:27**). They have been presented with the gospel centring on the Son of God becoming human, dying in our place, and rising from the dead. John exhorts them not to lose their grip on this truth. They have not only learned it from human lips, but also from *his anointing [that] teaches you about all things*. The truth has also been confirmed by the witness of the Holy Spirit (2:26-27).

RELIGIOUS PLURALISM

The essential message of religious pluralism is that there are many ways of salvation, with salvation defined as reaching God.

Religious pluralism grows out of the diverse sociocultural and religious experiences of human society. It argues that humanity has one face, though that face comes in many different complexions. In the same way, human interpretation of truth varies from place to place, from one generation to another and from one culture to another. But eternal Reality remains the same. Consequently, pluralism says it makes no difference what name people use to address that Reality – Allah, Yahweh, Ngai, Olorun, Brahma, Mungu or God. Diversity must not be taken for difference runs a pluralist's argument.

Pluralists also appeal to the sociological structure of society. In an African family, for example, the grannies may be traditionalists, the parents Muslims and the children Christians. But they live together in harmony. Life is a journey that begins at birth and terminates at death. Whether we travel by road, train, water or air, we reach the same destination.

Baha'ism, which developed from nineteenth-century Islam, is the highest form of religious pluralism. It regards the founders of all religions as divine, including Bahaullah who started the Baha'i movement, and aims to end all religions by accepting all religions. It regards the founders of all religions as divine, including Bahaullah who started the Bahai movement. Bahaullah's is said to be the latest in a series of progressive revelations.

In Africa religious pluralism appeals to politicians, theological liberals and social activists. It was not surprising, therefore, that at the World Conference of Religions held at Cape Town in 2001 the uniqueness of Jesus Christ as the Way, the Truth and the Life was slaughtered on the altar of oneness and togetherness.

If the pluralists' claims are true, then the cross of Jesus is unnecessary and his claim to be the only way to God, 'I am the way ... No-one comes to the Father except through me' (John 14:6), is a hoax. (John 14:6) is a hoax. This raises a question of authority. Pluralists base their claims on fallible human experience. By contrast, Jesus' authority derives from himself, the God-Man, who took on human flesh and was called Emmanuel, meaning 'God is with us'.

The second weakness of pluralism is confusing revelation with salvation. God has revealed himself in nature (Ps 19:1), through his providential activities (Matt 5:45) and by his righteous laws, written on stone tablets (Exod 20) or on people's hearts (Rom 2:15). But mere knowledge that God exists is not enough to save people, for 'although they knew God, they neither glorified him as God nor gave thanks to him, but their thinking became futile and their foolish hearts were darkened' (Rom 1:21).

Finally, pluralists fail to recognize the radical nature of sin and its pervasive consequences, which no human efforts, including religious efforts, can solve. The Bible defines sin as failure to meet God's standards. The just penalty for sin is death, meaning spiritual separation or alienation from God (Rom 6:23a). No one escapes the consequences of sin; '... in this way death came to all people, because all sinned' (Rom 5:12b). However, God's love pays the penalty in the person of Jesus Christ, who died on the cross as a criminal 'so everyone who believes in him might have eternal life' (John 3:16). Thus any sinner who believes in Jesus receives God's free gift of salvation (Rom 6:23b). This rules out the fallacy that all roads lead to the same place.

As Jesus said: 'Enter through the narrow gate. For wide is the gate and broad is the road that leads to destruction, and many enter through it. But small is the gate and narrow the road that leads to life, and only a few find it' (Matt 7:13-14).

Tokunboh Adeyemo

2:28-3:10 Continuing in Christ

John is writing to people who are already in Christ. He exhorts them to *continue in him.* If they do this, they will be *confident and unashamed* when Christ appears (**2:28**). Those who live in obedience will receive a 'well done' from their Lord. They will have something to show – achieved through God's grace to be sure, but also done in obedience as they exercise free will.

One reason for their confidence will be the fact that they will know that they are children of God (John 1:12). When a person's life confirms what they believe, there can be no doubt that they have *been born of him* (**2:29**). John is still awed by this privilege, as is clear from his exclamation about the great love the Father has *lavished on us* (**3:1**). He extended this love to us while we were still his enemies (Rom 5:10). John later spells out how he did this – 'He sent his one and only Son into the world that we might live through him and as an atoning sacrifice for our sins' (4:9-10).

In the meantime, John focuses on what it means to be a child of God. He starts by stressing our great expectation that *we shall be like him* (**3:2**). We may not fully know what this will involve, but it is clearly a glorious state, well worth being excited about! This hope is our motivation for keeping ourselves in continual readiness. Followers of Christ also seek to be pure. As John says, *Everyone who has this hope purifies himself, just as he is pure* (**3:3**) But what does it mean to be pure? In answer, John discusses four overlapping qualities that characterize a child of God.

- **Not being known by the world:** God and the world are polar opposites, so it is no wonder that those who belong to God are seen as strange by the world. The word 'know' as used in 3:1 does not refer merely to intellectual knowledge, but also to emotional appreciation and recognition.
- **Doing what is right:** God who is righteous is the standard of what is right, and his will is expressed in his word, the Scriptures. The degree to which we obey his word determines the degree to which we have been sanctified. While our status as righteous has been settled once and for all by our coming to Christ in faith, we are still called to live righteously, in obedience to him (2:29; 3:7, 10).
- **Loving one's brother:** John reiterates a point he has already made (1:9) and will return to again (3:11-24) when he stresses that *anyone who does not love his brother* is not a child of God (3:10).
- **Not keeping on sinning:** If we are called to be like Christ, there is no place for sin in our lives (**3:6**, 9). Because of our fallen nature, we cannot totally eradicate it, but continual or habitual sin is contrary to the nature of one born of God. Some people may attempt to lead believers astray (**3:7**) by teaching that sin does not really matter, but John gives his readers four reasons why this is not the case. The first relates to the nature of sin

itself. *Sin is lawlessness* (**3:4**), but the believer is called into obedience to the law, not as the basis for salvation but as an expression of love to God. The second is that the whole purpose of Christ's first coming was to *take away our sins* (**3:5**). If they have been taken away, they can no longer be part of our existence. Christ's purpose is also described as *to destroy the devil's work.* Since *the beginning* (**3:8**), the devil's work has been to encourage rebellion against God. The believer cannot be an ally of the one his Lord opposed and destroyed. The final reason why a believer cannot keep on sinning is that God himself planted a seed of Christlikeness in every believer at the moment when he or she trusted in Christ as Saviour (**3:9**). That seed grows and matures. While it will only burst into full bloom in the future, it is growing steadily towards glorification. Believers must not stunt its growth by yielding to sin.

3:11-24 Love Each Another

John next proceeds to expand on his repeated exhortation that *we should love one another.* He says that this is the message his readers have heard from the beginning, that is, ever since they believed in the Lord Jesus Christ (**3:11**; see also 2:7). He then gives them one negative and one positive example that illustrate the meaning of love.

The negative example is Cain, who butchered his own brother, who had done him no wrong (**3:12**). We are reminded of the many men, women and children who have been murdered in Africa, and elsewhere, simply because they belonged to a particular group or tribe. No Christian should be party to such acts! Yet, John warns, his readers can expect to be hated as Abel was hated (**3:13**). The reason for this hatred is that centres of darkness hate those who walk in the light. While Cain demonstrates where hatred can lead, Jesus Christ, who *laid down his life for us*, is our model of *what love is* (**3:16**). Since we have benefited so much from Christ's act, we are expected to show the same kind of love for each other. John makes three points about this love:

- **It derives from Jesus Christ** (3:16, 23). Everyone can show some kind of love, but no one can exercise the love called for here without learning it from Christ. Normally we love others because of something good they have done for us or for good we see in them. Jesus' love enables us to love others in spite of evil done to us and the unpleasantness of the one loved, even when the evil is not a single act but a way of life. Such love is only possible if one takes Christ as one's model and asks him for spiritual strength. Outside Christ, it cannot exist.
- **It is practical.** Jesus' love led him to take on a physical body. We need to express love by sharing our *material possessions* (**3:17**). Our willingness to share indicates whether or not we *have the love of God* – which may mean

either 'God's kind of love' or 'love for God'. If we have the ability to share with the needy but do not do so, we are lacking love in both ways.

- **It is genuine.** We are not to love *with words or tongue but with actions and in truth* (**3:18**). Words and actions are instruments that can be used to express love. But words on their own are not enough. The call to love 'in truth' indicates that our actions and our words must not simply be formalities or attempts to appear in a good light, but must reflect sincere concern for the one loved.

Obedience to the command to love communicates two things about our spiritual state. If we do not love, we are clearly still *in death* (**3:14**) and are equivalent to murderers like Cain (**3:15**; Matt 5:21-22), cut off from eternal life. If we do love our fellow believers, we have clearly passed from death to life. This idea can also be expressed in terms of another contrast that John has used before, the contrast between lies and truth.

Love clearly shows whether we belong to the sphere of the truth or the sphere of lies (3:18-19).

The essence of truth is Jesus himself, who said, 'I am the way, and the truth and the life' (John 14:6). In this epistle, John focuses on the truth that this Jesus is the Christ. He is our advocate before the Father. His blood cleanses our sins. The depth of our appropriation of these beliefs is shown by the extent of our love for one another.

Once we have fulfilled the command to love, we can rest assured that we are children of the truth, even when we are tempted to doubt our status. God is the one who has called us his children, and he knows both the sincerity of our motives and our human weakness (**3:19-20**). Yet, the heart is not useless as a judge. When our consciences are clear, we can approach God boldly and he, in turn, will respond by giving us what we ask (**3:21-22**).

The exercise of love confirms whether we live in Jesus and Jesus lives in us (**3:24**). John's expression *live in him* and *he in them* refers to the union the believer has with Christ by virtue of having become a child of God. Those who have this union have the Holy Spirit in them and he enables them to exercise love.

4:1-6 Discerning Between Spirits

The reference to the Holy Spirit brings John back to the point that this is not the only spirit at work in the world. And so he encourages his readers not to be credulous (*do not believe every spirit*) but to *test the spirits to see whether they are from God* (**4:1**). Both the prohibition 'do not believe' and the command 'test' are in the present tense, indicating that this is not something that can be done once and for all. It must become a habit. Satan is constantly attempting to mislead the people of God (see Gen 3:1-6; Rev 20:7-8). Caution is still needed today.

John outlines a simple test his readers can use to discern where a spirit comes from. If it *acknowledges that Jesus Christ has come in the flesh,* it is *from God* (**4:2**); that is, it has been sent by God and communicates a message God approves.

The reason the test took this particular form seems to be that some people were separating Jesus, the man, from Christ, the Anointed One. They were asserting that Jesus was born a mere man, that he was given God's Spirit at baptism to make him the Christ for his particular mission, and that the Spirit left him before he died. Such teaching denies the incarnation – that is, the truth that Jesus is God's eternally anointed way of salvation who came from heaven and took on human flesh. In the twenty-first century, the exact form of the attack on this truth may be different, but the test still applies: any failure to acknowledge that the Jesus of the Gospels is God's eternal Son in the flesh is a variety of the same error.

Any spirit which does not *acknowledge Jesus* is *not from God* but *is the spirit of the antichrist* (**4:3**). The name 'antichrist' shows that such a spirit is opposed to Christ, and hence it is also opposed to God. Jesus is the Christ and any denial of that truth is not God's message, no matter how intellectually sophisticated the arguments that accompany it.

Believers may be discouraged at the prospect of having to deal with false spirits, so John assures them of victory, based on the fact that *the one who is in you is greater than the one who is in the world* (**4:4**). As John said in 3:24, 'he lives in us.' This 'he' may be God the Father or God the Son – it does not matter which, for where the Father is, the Son is also (John 14:10, 23). In a sense, every believer is indwelt by the Trinity. The Holy Spirit's presence is also the presence of God the Father and God the Son. And any one of them is greater than Satan, who owes his existence to God.

John reminds the believers that there are only two spheres – the sphere of God and the sphere of the world. Anyone who claims to speak or act for God must draw his inspiration from one of these two spheres. Those whose message is in the spirit of the antichrist and contradicts what John says are *from the world* (**4:5a**). Those whose message agrees with that proclaimed by the apostles are *from God* (**4:6a**).

People's responses to the message fall into the same two categories. Those who have refused God's truth and oppose his ways listen to those who promote the spirit of the antichrist because they *speak from the viewpoint of the world*. Their message makes sense to those who do not know God, and so *the world listens to them* (**4:5b**). By contrast, *whoever knows God listens to us* (**4:6b**). John and those who preach the same message operate in the sphere of God, and those who belong to that sphere will hear and appreciate their message.

4:7-21 Living God's Love

The central thrust of this passage is summarized by the exhortation *let us love one another* (**4:7**). If we have been *born of God* we are God's children and will take after him. God 'who is love' gives birth to children who should love. First, we will respond with love for God in return for his love, and then we will extend that love to fellow-believers who are also loved by God.

The love John is calling for is rooted in the love of God. The repetition of the phrase *God is love* (**4:8**, **16**) emphasizes that God's very nature is love. Everything about him proceeds from love. We see his love in what he has done (**4:9**), sending his Son for us even when we were his enemies. The fact that we are the beneficiaries here is stressed by the repetition of 'us', 'we' and 'our' in 4:9-10. His love is not given because we deserve it in any way but because of what he is.

By showing us this love, God has given us a definition of love (**4:10**) and set us an example to follow as we love *one another* (**4:11**). While no one has ever seen God in his essence, we know that his essence is love (4:16). Amazingly, we can even contribute to God's love, as it *is made complete in us* (**4:12**). To understand how this happens, we need to think of love as a triangle. God's love for my fellow-believer and for me form two of the arms. Our love for each other completes the triangle.

John, the other apostles, and all others who have shared in God's love are witnesses to it (4:13-16). This love gives us confidence for the future, for as we pattern our lives after God's nature, *we will have confidence on the day of judgment* (**4:17**). It also gives us confidence in the present, for when our relationship with God is based on love, we no longer need to fear him (**4:18**).

God's love, which we have experienced, is our reason (**4:19**) for loving others. Not everyone around us will deserve our love, yet we must extend love to all. We were equally unlovable when God first loved us. John is prepared to dispute any claim to love God by someone who does not show love to fellow believers (**4:20**, **21**). God's love for us, our love for him, and our love for each other all call for living together harmoniously.

5:1-12 Believing in the Son of God

John now reiterates that true faith centres on Jesus. True believers, those who are *born of God,* must accept that he is *the Christ* – God's anointed – and *the Son of God*, sent from heaven to reveal who God is and to provide an acceptable sacrifice for our sin (**5:1**, 5). But belief and practice are inseparable. The sincerity of one's beliefs about Jesus is demonstrated by one's love for God's other children (**5:2**) and for God and is expressed in obedience (**5:3**). Those who hold true beliefs have victory over the world (**5:4-5**).

Belief is rooted in evidence, and so in 5:6-12 John deals with the testimony to Jesus' status. He emphasizes the agreement in the testimony of *the Spirit, the water and the blood* (**5:6-10**). The reference to the Spirit clearly means that the Holy Spirit lives within believers and provides assurance of the truth about Jesus. The reference to water and blood may point to the sacraments of baptism and the Lord's Supper, or to the water and blood that came from Jesus' side, or to Jesus' baptism and death. The last interpretation seems the most likely. John is stressing that Jesus identified with humankind at his baptism and gave himself to death as our Saviour. Both these actions were done by Jesus Christ (both names are used in 5:6) and not by a Jesus separate from the Christ (see comments on 4:2).

Finally, John stresses the content of the testimony: Jesus (in partnership with God) is the giver of eternal life (**5:11**). Jesus and life are inseparable (**5:12**). Anyone who does not have Jesus does not have eternal life.

5:13-21 Prayer and True God

While unbelievers do not have life, John reassures his readers that if they believe in the name of the Son of God, they can be confident that they do have eternal life (**5:13**). This in turn should give them confidence in approaching God. They can be assured that God will hear them if they ask *according to his will* (**5:14**) and that they will receive what is asked for (**5:15**).

John then discusses one type of prayer that God will certainly hear – prayer for a fellow-believer who sins, provided the sin is the result of ignorance rather than a deliberate sin, or a case of stumbling rather than apostasy. It seems likely that the sin that leads to death (**5:16**) is blasphemy against the Holy Spirit (Matt 12:31-32). The Holy Spirit convicts of sin, and if his work is not acknowledged, there is no point in praying for the sinner. All other sins can be forgiven when the sin is confessed, and prayer is what will bring the sinner to the point of confession.

John closes the letter with a reiteration of the convictions he shares with those to whom he is writing:

- Being *born of God* is incompatible with continuing to sin (**5:18**).
- Jesus will keep those born of God safe from the evil one (5:18).
- Our status is that we are children of God (**5:19**).
- The evil one controls the whole world, but we do not belong to the world (5:19).
- *The Son of God has come* and has already *given us understanding* so that we do not speak out of ignorance but in knowledge (**5:20**).
- The focus of our knowledge is *him who is true,* and so what we speak is the truth (**5:20**).

- We are in the one who is true – both in Jesus Christ and in the true God (5:20).
- This means that we are also in eternal life, for that is what Jesus Christ is (5:20).

Finally, once again addressing his readers as *dear children*, John exhorts them saying, *keep yourselves from idols* (**5:21**). For him, an idol is not just an object one keeps in one's closet. Rather, it is anything that keeps one from living up to one's Christian beliefs. All one needs to do to be an idolater is to choose to believe or do something that is opposed to the will of God.

Samuel Ngewa

Further Reading

Jackman, David. *The Message of John's Letters*. BST. Leicester: Inter-Varsity Press, 1988.

Marshall, I. Howard. *The Epistles of John*. NICNT. Grand Rapids: Eerdmans, 1978.

2 JOHN

This letter was probably written by the Apostle John in the AD 90s, when he would have been an old man. He refers to himself as 'the elder' and addresses the letter to 'the chosen lady and her children' (1). This 'dear lady' (5) is probably a particular congregation, while the 'children of your chosen sister' (13) are another congregation.

COMMENTARY

After naming the author and the recipients of the letter (1), John states that *grace, mercy and peace ... will be with us in truth and love* and names the source of these blessings, *God the Father* and *Jesus Christ, the Father's Son* (3). This statement also expresses a wish that his readers will be blessed with these things. Then he goes on to speak of his joy that some of the chosen lady's children are *walking in the truth* (4). What this means is that they believe that Jesus Christ has come *in the flesh* (7) and that they are following *the teaching of Christ* (9).

John next picks up on his favourite theme of love (1, 3; see also 1 John) and repeats the familiar command to *love one another* (5). Living in love is defined as walking *in obedience to his commands* (6), that is, to the Lord's commands. If we love God, we will obey his commands, and particularly his command to love one another.

John's other great theme is *truth*, which is referred to repeatedly in verses 1, 2, 3 and 4. He contrasts this truth with the lies taught by *deceivers* who do not acknowledge that Jesus Christ has come *in the flesh* (see commentary on 1 John 4:2). John labels anyone who teaches this lie *the deceiver and the antichrist* (7). These people are not the final antichrist, but they share some of the same characteristics in that they oppose Christ by denying his essential nature.

John exhorts his readers to be vigilant and stay on course (8). Though they are walking in the truth, they must be aware that deceivers will attempt to distract them and lure them off the path. He also tells them not to offer hospitality to deceivers (10). False teaching is contagious, and its carriers should be avoided. As the proverb says, *ke osi nme le, eko ya omama mli* [Ga, Ghana – 'If you pound palm nuts, some will stain your cloth']. To welcome such a person is to become a partner *in his wicked work* (11) and only encourages him or her to continue it. Believers should have nothing to do with deceivers, for *nine se ke koto ten yee he gbo* [Ga, Ghana – 'The back of the hand and the palm do not unite'].

John lets his readers know that he has much more to say to them, but would rather speak more to them than write more (12). Visiting them would bring joy to both him and them. He closes with greetings from *the children of your chosen sister* (13), who were probably members of a congregation well known to the recipients of the letter.

Samuel Ngewa

3 JOHN

This letter is also written by 'the elder', who, as in 2 John, is probably the Apostle John. It is addressed to his 'dear friend Gaius', whom he loved deeply (1). Gaius is a common name in the NT. There is a Gaius in Corinth (Rom 16:23; 1 Cor 1:14); another in Macedonia (Acts 19:29) and another in Derbe (Acts 20:4). The letter was probably addressed to the Gaius in Derbe, who, according to tradition, became the first bishop of Pergamum.

COMMENTARY

John's prayer list for Gaius includes *good health* and *that all may go well with you, even as your soul is getting along well* (2). He is praising him and praying that his physical health will match his spiritual health. John acknowledges Gaius' faithfulness to the truth and the good work of hospitality he is already involved in, and encourages him to continue (3-5). In particular, he should help some brothers *on their way in a manner worthy of God* (6). These brothers have two claims on his hospitality: they went out *for the sake of the Name* (that is, the name of Jesus Christ – Acts 5:40-41; Rom 1:5) and they refused to receive *help from the pagans* (7). While 2 John 10 prohibited the welcoming of false teachers, partnership with true brothers amounts to promotion of the truth (8).

Gaius' behaviour contrasts with that of Diotrephes, a man who *loves to be first* (9), wants nothing to do with John and his associates, *refuses to welcome the brothers* and punishes those who do welcome them (10). John warns that *if I come, I will call attention to what he is doing, gossiping maliciously about us* (10). He will condemn what Diotrephes has done.

John exhorts Gaius not to follow Diotrephes' example: *Dear friend, do not imitate what is evil but what is good.* He is to keep God's approval in mind, remembering that *anyone who does what is good is from God. Anyone who does what is evil has not seen God* (11). Gaius is to persevere in doing good. John's words are also a call to African believers to continue to practise hospitality, a value that is rapidly being lost.

Another man, called Demetrius, receives praise from John as being *well spoken of by everyone*, including by John himself. Apart from human witnesses (who can be deceived by appearance) the standard of what is true itself commends Demetrius (12). Good or evil cannot be hidden. As the Nandi (Kenya) say, 'You cannot tie a buck's head in a cloth – the horns will stick out.'

Just as in the previous letter, John tells his readers that he would love to tell them more and hopes to do so when he next sees them (13, 14).

After a prayer for peace, John sends greetings from friends and to friends, asking that they be greeted by name. Here, too, he sets an example regarding warm relationships that includes knowing people's names.

Samuel Ngewa

JUDE

Christianity has always had enemies: false teachers within and fierce persecutors without. Jesus and his apostles encountered them (Luke 20:1-8; Matt 23:13-33; Acts 4:1-3; 9:1-6). Nearly every book of the NT has something to say about them. However, that which was foretold by Paul and Peter (2 Thess 2:3; 2 Pet 2:1-3) had become a historical reality by the time Jude was written in about AD 70. With the deaths of the apostles, their authority had declined and heretics had become bolder. Jude's response is intense, sustained and powerful as he calls on his readers to contend for the apostolic faith.

A lack of respect for the original message is a common among second-generation believers and among the breakaway and independent churches in Africa. In the face of religious pluralism, Christo-paganism, widespread syncretism and theological liberalism that denies the deity of Christ, there is an urgent demand for people ready to defend the Christian message in Africa today. For example, when a resistance movement that is fighting to overthrow an elected government claims to be Christian but mixes witchcraft and magic with the Bible and has a leader who claims to be a messiah, defenders of the faith can and should take him to task.

May the church in Africa heed Jude's call to defend the faith!

Outline of Contents

COMMENTARY

1-4 Purpose

The author introduces himself as *Jude*, the English form of the Hebrew 'Judah' and the Greek 'Judas'. Since Jude, which means 'Praise of Yahweh', was a common name in the first century, he further identifies himself as a *servant of Jesus Christ* (**1a**). A 'servant' is subject to his master, but not a helpless slave. Describing himself in this way places Jude in the great prophetic and apostolic succession with men like Abraham, Moses, David, Peter, Paul and James and confers on his writing corresponding authority (see Ps 105:42; Neh 9:14; Ps 89:3; 2 Pet 1:1; Rom 1:1; Jas 1:1).

Jude also identifies himself as *a brother of James* (1a) who was the head of the church in Jerusalem (Acts 15:13; 21:18) and the author of the Letter of James. Jude and James were half-brothers of our Lord (Matt 13:55; Mark 6:3) and came to believe in him after the resurrection (John 7:1-9; Acts 1:14). The only other biblical allusion to them is in 1 Corinthians 9:5 where it is recorded that 'the other apostles and the Lord's brothers' took their wives along on their missionary journeys. This reference suggests that the letter of Jude has apostolic authority.

Having identified himself, the author goes on to identify his audience. He describes them with three powerful words: *called, loved* and *kept* (**1b**). They are *loved* unconditionally by God the Father (see John 3:16), *kept* or preserved by the Messiah, Jesus the Redeemer (see John 17:2, 3, 12) and *called.* This calling must be by the Holy Spirit, the executive officer of the Godhead, since no one can come to God unless the Spirit draws them (see John 16:8-14).

Jude does not specify the geographical location of his audience, though it seems to be a local assembly (**4, 12**). His greeting, *mercy, peace and love* (**2**), combines the OT concept of the 'mercy seat' or 'atonement cover' (Lev 16:2, 13-16) and the NT concept of the cross (Gal 3:13). These were places where God's unconditional love made it possible for him to meet with believing sinners (Rom 5:8). This greeting is also appropriate for a mixed audience of Jews and Gentiles, whom Jude affectionately calls his *dear friends* (**3, 17, 20**). Jude shares with them the glorious experience of sins forgiven and reconciliation with God, self and others by God's grace. He had intended to write about this salvation, but changed his plans when he became aware of the danger posed by false teachers (**3a**).

As the Yorubas of West Africa say, 'you can go to bed when there is a snake on your thatched roof, but you can't do that when the thatch is on fire' – matters of life and death demand immediate attention. Jude sensed a fire in the congregation and felt constrained to alert the saints and urge them *to contend for the faith* (**3b**). By 'faith' he does not mean an elaborate system of theology, but the simple teaching regarding Christ and the salvation he provides that was presented by Peter (Acts 4:8-12) and Paul (1 Cor 15:3-5). Peter and John defended this teaching before the Sanhedrin in Jerusalem (Acts 4:1-20), Paul and Silas were thrown into jail at Philippi for proclaiming it (Acts 16:16-40), and John was banished to the island of Patmos because of it (Rev 1:9). Standing in the same tradition, Jude calls on his readers to fight for the purity of the faith. It is an ongoing struggle in every age and generation (see 1 Tim 6:12).

Jude does not name the false teachers but describes them as *godless men* (**4**, see 15, 18). They are immoral in life and heretical in faith (4). They falsely assume that grace gives them the right to sin without restraint, or that their sins only magnify the grace of God. Either way they are wrong (see Rom 6:1-4; Titus 2:11-14) and condemned to eternal darkness (4, 13). The question arises, were these men ever saved? Jude would respond with an emphatic 'No!' He does not include them among the *friends* (3, 17, 20), contrasts them with the *saints* (3b), describes them as having *secretly slipped* into the assembly like snakes or thieves (4; see John 10:1) and rains woes upon them (11). They are hypocrites and deceivers (see 2 Pet 2:1).

Jude's call for vigilance still sounds in our churches today, especially when we encounter self-made leaders who bear no resemblance to Christ.

5-13 Judgment of False Teachers

5-7 Three Cases from the Torah

Jude cites three well-known stories from the writings of Moses to support his belief that false teachers will be judged. The cases are not arranged in chronological order as in 2 Peter 2:4-9, but in order of thematic importance.

The first case involved the Israelites. Despite God's gracious deliverance of them from Egypt, many of them despised God's law, slandered his messengers (angelic or human – Exod 32:1-10; Num 12; 16:1-35), and doubted his ability to do what he promised. These sins were expressions of unbelief, and so those who were guilty of them died in the wilderness (**5**; see Num 14:1- 35). Their fate reminds us of the dream in which John Bunyan, the author of *The Pilgrim's Progress*, saw that even from the gates of heaven there was a way to hell. It also reminds us of the warning an elderly African preacher gave his congregation over and over again: 'Make sure you end well!' The fate of the Israelites haunted Paul and the author of Hebrews (1 Cor 10:5-11; Heb 3:12-4:2). It should haunt our minds too, and sober us. The Bible does not condone the infamous saying, 'once saved, ever

saved', which turns the grace of God into licentiousness. While the Bible does say, 'I give them eternal life, and they will never perish' (John 10:28a), it also says that whoever endures to the end will be saved (Matt 10:22).

Jude's second case involved *angels* ('the sons of God' – see Job 1:6; 2:1) who cohabited with the 'daughters of men' (humans) (Gen 6:1-7). Their sin was one of disobedience, not rebellion like that of Lucifer (see Isa 14:12-15). Angels have assigned positions, places and functions (Dan 10:20-22; 12:1; Gen 3:24). As God's messengers (Heb 1:14), they are higher than humans and dwell in the heavenly realm (Dan 9:22; 10:13-20; Luke 2:13-15). However, these angels *did not keep their positions of authority,* but *abandoned their own home* (that is, the heavenly realm) in order to contravene God's law (**6a**). They were immediately imprisoned in darkness awaiting *judgment on the great Day* (**6b**).

Jude's third case was the dramatic punishment *of Sodom and Gomorrah and the surrounding towns* for their *sexual immorality and perversion* (**7**; see Gen 19:4-11). 'Sexual immorality' involves a failure to conform to God's standards, which permit sexual activity only within marriage (Gen 2:24-25; 4:1-2; Exod 20:14; Lev 20:10). 'Perversion' involves an abnormal sexual relationship with someone of the same gender (Lev 18:22; 20:10, 13) or with an animal (Lev 18:23; 20:16). All sin is bad, but sexual immorality seems to be the worst type of sin (see 1 Cor 6:9, 18). In the OT, individuals who committed sexual sins were sentenced to death (Lev 20:13-16), and whole cities like Sodom and Gomorrah were destroyed because of such sins. Paul states categorically that every form of sexual perversion comes under God's wrath (Rom 1:24-27; 1 Cor 6:9-10).

God's social and sexual standards still stand. If he punished violators in Sodom four thousand years ago, Jude argued, he would do so in his own city of Jerusalem two thousand years later, and we can conclude that he will do so in our cities today.

8-10 Three Comparisons with the Present

Jude compares the character of the false teachers of his time to the situations in the three case studies, but in reverse order.

- The false teachers *pollute their own bodies,* a reference to sodomy (8a, 7).
- They defy authority, a reference to the fallen angels (**8b**, 6).
- They show contempt for God's law, a reference to those who didn't believe (8c, 5). Jude probably bases this example on the tradition that God's law was mediated at Sinai by angels (see Acts 7:38, 53; Gal 3:19; Heb 2:2).

All these evils are still common in our day. False leaders in our churches accept gay marriage as 'an alternative lifestyle'. Some liberal theologians dismiss biblical miracles and deny the sovereignty and lordship of Christ. Jude's epistle is as relevant today as it was when it was written in about AD 70.

It is interesting to note that the Bible's account of the death and burial of Moses (Deut 34:5-6) does not mention the drama referred to in **9**. Jude is drawing on some other book that provides a good illustration of his point. He is not saying that the book was divinely inspired.

11 Three Condemnations

Jude likes to put things together in threes. In verse 1 he used three verbs, 'called', 'loved' and 'kept'; in verse 2 he spoke of mercy, peace and love; in verses 5-7 and 8-10 he used three sets of examples. He does the same here, mentioning three individuals from the OT whose disregard for God's word resulted in disaster. He sees the false teachers of his day heading in the same direction and exclaims, *Woe to them!* (**11**).

- The *way of Cain* is referred to as 'evil' in 1 John 3:12 and as showing unbelief (Heb 11:4). It seems that Cain rejected God's law and so was cursed (Gen 4:3-16), just as many in our society reject the cross as the way of salvation and so are subject to the death penalty (Rom 3:23; 6:23; Gal 3:10).
- *Balaam* not only deliberately rebelled against God, but also encouraged others to do the same (Num 22-24). Peter describes him as greedy, a lover of 'wages of wickedness' and mad (2 Pet 2:15-16). Unfortunately there are many in the ministry today for reasons similar to Balaam's.
- *Korah's rebellion* is a fitting climax, for God abruptly ended this insurrection against his authority (see Num 16:1-35).

As far as Jude is concerned, the fate of the false teachers of his day was foretold long ago (4).

12-13 Six Characteristics of False Teachers

Jude describes the false teachers in two graphic triplets that show 'blazing moral indignation at its hottest' (Barclay). The first triplet describes them as *blemishes at your love feast*, implying that they are spreading seeds of hatred and division (**12a**; see also 19; 1 Cor 11:17-22). Next they are described as the type of shepherds condemned by Yahweh, those *who only feed of themselves* (**12b**; Ezek 34:2; see Isa 56:11). Not only are they selfish and irresponsible, they are also as unreliable as *clouds without rain* (**12c**), raising hopes only to dash them.

The second triplet builds on this sense of disappointment, as these teachers are described as *autumn trees, without fruit and uprooted – twice dead* (**12d**). This warning against hypocrisy and spiritual barrenness reminds us of the fig tree Jesus cursed (Matt 21:18-19). Many preachers and tele-evangelists talk big, but their messages lack biblical and spiritual substance. Like *wild waves* they are frothy,

producing only worthless ideas that will bring them *shame* (**13a**). Rather than giving direction and focus to others, they are *wandering stars*, lacking purpose and predictability. These stars shed no light, and will end up in *blackest darkness* (**13b**).

14-16 Doom for False Teachers

As always, Jude looks for an OT example to express the doom of the false teachers. He finds it in the prophecy of Enoch, who lived in the seventh generation after Adam (Gen 5:21-24). But there is a problem – the Bible never mentions this prophecy. Jude was quoting from a book attributed to Enoch that was well known during NT times (see article on the Intertestamental Period). Since the message is true, Jude feels free to quote it, just as Paul felt free to quote heathen poets (Acts 17:28). Enoch was prophesying the second coming of the Lord and the judgment that follows it (**14-15**). There are many other OT and NT passages that agree with his prophesy (see Isa 40:10; 66:15-16; Jer 25:31; Dan 7:10; Hab 3:3-9; Matt 16:27; 24:29-31; 2 Thess 1:6-10; Rev 20:12).

Before leaving the subject of false teachers, Jude uses five other phrases to describe their behaviour: they are *grumblers, fault-finders,* given to *evil desires, boasters* and *flatterers* (**16**). People like this 'will not inherit the kingdom of God' (Gal 5:19-21).

17-23 Duty of Believers in Times of Apostasy

Jude now prescribes an action plan to enable his *dear friends* (**17, 20a**), his brothers and sisters in the Lord, to defend their most holy faith. He contrasts them with the false teachers and offers a loving prescription born of his own experience.

17-19 Remember the Apostles' Teaching

The rise of false teachers and false prophets should not take believers by surprise. Both the Lord himself and his apostles foretold it; and forewarned is forearmed (**17**; Matt 24:5, 11; Acts 20:29; 1 Tim 4:1; 2 Tim 3:1-5; 2 Pet 2:1; 3:3-4). One of the reasons believers quickly succumb to deception is that they don't know what the Bible says. So when the enemy comes to tempt them, often by misquoting Scripture, they fall. Like Jesus we should know the Bible, and be able to use it correctly to defeat the enemy (see Matt 4:4, 7, 10). We are not just to recall the instructions, but to act on them!

False teachers should not be difficult to recognize. Jude has already listed six of their character traits (12-13) and five of their behaviours (16). Here he adds five more. They are *scoffers* marked by pursuit of *ungodly desires* (**18**), they *divide* churches along racial or tribal lines (**19a**) and follow *mere natural instincts* (**19b**). The reason they act this way is simple: they *do not have the Spirit* (**19c**), despite their claiming to be super-spiritual. Anyone who does not have the Spirit is not born again (John 3:3-8).

20a Build One Another Up in Faith

The believers were addressed as 'saints' in 3, and here their faith is described as *most holy* (**20a**), because it is the truth concerning the holy God and his Son, Jesus Christ (1). In order to grow and mature in faith, believers must 'not give up meeting together' (Heb 10:22-25). They should devote themselves continually to the study of the word, to fellowship, to the breaking of bread and to prayer (Acts 2:42).

20b Pray in the Holy Spirit

Jude's first two recommendations focus on the word. His third focuses on prayer, which is the believers' communion with God. There are various interpretations of the expression *in the Holy Spirit*. Some say it means speaking in tongues. But Paul uses the same expression in the context of spiritual warfare (Eph 6:18), and speaks about the Holy Spirit interceding for us when we do not know what to pray for (Rom 8:26-27). In the context of this letter and the war against false teaching, it seems that 'praying in the Spirit' must involve our being filled with the Spirit (Eph 5:18), depending on the Spirit of truth (John 14:17), and realizing that by ourselves we can do nothing (Zech 4:6). If, in the course of doing all this, the Spirit breaks forth in tongues, so be it.

21 Abide in God's Love

The distinguishing mark of Christ's disciples is love (John 13:35). We are first brought into God's family by his love (1). Now Jude says, *keep yourselves in God's love as you wait* (**21**). Love to care for one another, love to support one another, love to correct one another, and love to speak the truth to one another (Eph 4:25).

22 Be Merciful to Doubters

We are often impatient with those who disagree with our viewpoints, and outright unkind to those who doubt what we say. We allow no room for dialogue or reason. Jude

reminds us that 'mercy begets mercy'. We have received eternal life through God's mercy (21), and should in turn be patient and kind to those who doubt as we seek to convince them of the truth.

23a Rescue the Perishing

Probably due to the influence of false teaching, some believers in our day as in Jude's day have gone beyond doubting, and are drifting from the faith into the fire. We must respond urgently. By sharing the word with them, praying in the Spirit for them, and loving them sincerely as Christ loves us, we can snatch back those headed into hell fire and restore them to fellowship.

23b Avoid Corruption

As we engage in the rescue operation, we must be vigilant not to be corrupted by the flesh. Cases abound where sincere counsellors have been carried away by their concern for those they counsel, and have ended up forfeiting their faith and sinking with them. Jude says: Don't compromise! We should have contact without contamination.

24-25 Doxology

Having dealt with the serious danger posed by false teachers and apostasy, Jude turns the spotlight on God and his Son, Jesus Christ, in this magnificent benediction. He ends his letter with prayers of hope that focus on God's power and might.

- He is able to preserve us from falling!
- He is able to present us before his glorious presence without fault and with great joy!
- Hallelujah, what a Saviour! (25). Amen, meaning, 'May it come to pass'.

Tokunboh Adeyemo

Further Reading

Barclay, William. *The Letters of John and Jude.* DSB. Rev. ed. Philadelphia: Westminster Press, 1976.

Lucas, Dick and Christopher Green. *The Message of 2 Peter and Jude.* BST. Leicester, England: Inter-Varsity Press, 1995.

REVELATION

The book of Revelation is unique in the NT. It belongs to a genre known as 'apocalyptic', from the Greek word meaning 'revelation'. Apocalyptic literature is characterized by visions that present the past and the future of heaven and earth in light of the present. Apocalyptic biblical literature describes God's plan in history in visions and symbols in which the ultimate destruction of evil and the triumph of good are inevitable. Such books were often written to encourage God's people when they were undergoing suffering or persecution and were anxious about the present and the future. The seer of these visions was frequently guided by a heavenly being who often interpreted the symbolic meaning of the visions.

Apocalypses usually have a narrative or dramatic structure. Daniel is the best known apocalyptic book in the OT, but other passages of the Bible also have apocalyptic features (for example, Isa 24–27; Ezek 1; 40–48; Zech 9–14; and the 'little apocalypses' of Matt 24; Mark 13; Luke 21). There were also non-biblical Jewish apocalyptic books, such as the book of Enoch and some of the Dead Sea Scrolls, written during NT times.

Writers of apocalypses typically used symbols and coded language to disguise what they were really saying from those who were persecuting them. The codes in Revelation were so effective that few people today agree on exactly what John meant. Some think that many of the predictions in Revelation have not yet been fulfilled. They say that John was writing about events that will come to pass in our own time. Taking that view means that John's writing would have had very little relevance for the people of his time. Others explain Revelation in terms of the first-century Christian church, concluding that many of the events described in it took place during the Roman Empire. John was telling the believers of his day that what was happening to them was a necessary part of the divine plan. Still others find references to the ongoing conflict of evil and good throughout human history – a conflict that will continue until Satan has been finally cast into the lake of fire and the people of God enter the new Jerusalem.

Symbolism in Revelation

Revelation is not only written in symbolic language, but it also presents its message in pictures and images. This approach can sometimes be difficult to understand, especially for Western people, who tend to think in abstract terms. It is more familiar to Africans and people in Near Eastern cultures, who are used to expressing themselves in proverbial or concrete language.

Numbers play an important role in Revelation, but commentators disagree about whether particular numbers should be interpreted literally or symbolically. For example, the number seven (seven churches, seven trumpets, seven seals, seven bowls.) represents wholeness. John writes to seven literal churches, but at the same time he is addressing the whole church. The number four represents earthly things (four corners of the earth, four winds, four creatures.). The number twelve (twelve elders, twelve gates to the holy city) represents both the twelve tribes of the physical Israel in the OT and the twelve apostles, upon whose teaching the church was founded. The number one thousand may symbolize an immense number, and represent something very great, but not necessarily anything numerically precise.

Revelation also includes symbolic images: lampstands, olive trees, stars, horsemen, great cities and a red seven-headed ten-horned dragon all feature in the book. John is merely human, and often when reading Revelation, we feel that he is describing things that lie beyond the power of human language to convey, which is why his images and pictures are often difficult to understand. Once you have come to terms with the author's technique of using visions, imagery and symbolism, which are not commonly used elsewhere in the NT, you will probably have a better grasp of what God wanted the recipients of Revelation to know and do.

Two Extremes to Avoid

Readers are tempted to respond to Revelation in one of two ways. Some find the book so perplexing and weird that they can see no reason to read it and try to understand its message. How can anyone be sure of its meaning? Others fall prey to the opposite danger. They pore over Revelation and conclude that they have discovered the secret explanation of each obscure detail. To the latter group, it may be humbling to learn that every generation since the first century has come up with different interpretations of the meaning and prophecies of Revelation.

Authorship

Both at the beginning and at the end of the book, the author identifies himself as John (1:1, 4, 9; 22:8) and his work as a prophecy (1:3; 22:6-10, 18-19). Widespread testimony attributes the book to the apostle John, who wrote the Gospel of John and the three Letters of John. It must be admitted that this is problematic because the language and grammatical style of this book are somewhat different from that in the other books. Yet these differences may be explained in terms of the very different subject matter of this book. Some images, literary forms, symbolism and the liturgical framework in Revelation are indeed similar to the ones found in the other Johannine books. The placement of the purpose statement at the end of the book also matches John's style (22:6-20; see John 20:30-31; 1 John 5:12-13).

Regardless of whether the author was the Apostle John or some other believer named John, Revelation breathes the spirit of the Lord of life, its author's strong faith, and the triumphant march to victory of God's people in the eventual fulfilment of his saving purpose for mankind.

Occasion and Date

John presents himself as one of the sufferers in a great crisis that had befallen the early church. For nearly the first fifty years of its existence, Christianity enjoyed peace in the Roman world. But eventually emperor worship, which had originally been introduced as a political and religious device to unite the many peoples Rome had conquered, was declared the official religion. Any refusal to worship the emperor drew persecution or death. Because Christians could not worship the Roman emperor and remain true to their Lord, they were persecuted by the political authorities. This persecution lies in the background of Revelation. However, the book does not seem to include any specific reference to Nero's persecution of Christians after the great fire of Rome in AD 64, which suggests that it was written between the reign of Nero (AD 54-68) and that of Domitian (AD 81-96).

Purpose

The purpose of Revelation is stated in 22:6-20. It is to encourage Christians of all times to remain faithful until the end, even if it means martyrdom, since they will also be raised from the dead at the second coming of Christ.

The focus on Jesus Christ's triumph over death through his glorious resurrection means that Revelation is a book that has far more to say about the exercise of power than about the manifestation of divine love. Divine power is demonstrated throughout the book, even in the vindication of the Lamb who was a victim. It is that power of unmasking everything that runs like a thread throughout the vision.

Revelation as a Drama

Revelation is presented as both a letter and a drama. It opens and closes like any other letter of that time. What lies in-between is a drama depicting the events that will lead to the ultimate doom of evil and the ushering in of the eternal 'new Jerusalem'.

Viewing the book as a drama arranged into acts and scenes will help you unpack and understand this difficult book. The suggested outline divides the book into seven acts or visions, each with seven scenes. Some acts have interludes and stage settings. It is best to read Revelation one act at a time, rather than all at once.

Outline of Contents

COMMENTARY

1:1-6 Introduction

Revelation, like every other book in the Bible, was written for a specific group of people with specific needs. Evidently, the writer originally intended his message to be read aloud in the various local churches to which it was addressed (1:3). It can thus be described as a circular letter.

1:1-3 Title

In ancient times, books were written on sheets of parchment or papyrus, which were sewn together at the sides. These sheets were then rolled up to form a scroll. About AD 150 or a little earlier, the codex, which was shaped like a modern book, made its first appearance. At that time, the title that had previously been on a label attached to the outside of the scroll was transferred to the inside first page as a 'title page'. This, it seems, is what produced the opening words found in Revelation 1:1-3.

Just as the Gospel of John (John 1:1-18) and the First Epistle of John (1 John 1:1-4) begin by announcing that Jesus Christ is central to what is contained in those books, so the book of Revelation starts with the announcement *The revelation of Jesus Christ* (**1:1a**). Christ is in the midst of his suffering people and has been involved in human history from the beginning. Though Christ himself is God, he is also the 'mediator between God and men' (1 Tim 2:5). As such, he receives instructions from the Father about what *to show his servants* (**1:1b**). Jesus, in turn, *made it known by sending his angel to his servant John* (**1:1d**). The mediation of an *angel* is in keeping with the visions of OT apocalyptic writers (Ezek 8; Dan 10). In Revelation, as well as communicating God's message, angels worship God the Father and the Lamb (God the Son) and execute God's judgments on the earth whenever necessary. Angels are referred to about sixty-seven times in the book of Revelation.

John is a witness *who testifies to everything he saw* (**1:2**). The main purpose of the revelation he was given was to show God's servants *what must soon take place* (**1:1c**). Historical books like the Pentateuch and the Gospels give us an account of things that have already taken place, whereas apocalyptic writings like Revelation give us an account of present and past events in light of the future. As we read through Revelation, we find that some of these future events are not shown in the clearest light in which God could have set them, but in a light such as he saw most fit and that would best serve his wise and holy purposes.

The blessing in **1:3** is the first of seven contained in the book (14:13; 16:15; 19:9; 20:6; 22:7, 14). It declares the blessedness of one who reads the book or letter of Revelation to a congregation and of those who hear it and take its message to heart. *The one who reads* reflects the early form of worship where a reader would read the Scriptures aloud on the Lord's Day (1:3; 1 Tim 4:13). At that time, only the reader had a copy of the letter or of a particular OT book. Individual possession of Bibles is a very recent privilege. *Those who hear* were the people of the congregations (1:4, 11), who were to hear the written prophecy read. *Prophecy* involves not only future events but also ethical and spiritual exhortations and warnings (Rev 2–3; Isa 1:1-20; Jer 23:1-40). In a sense, it is equivalent to modern exposition of the written word of God.

The reading would also include interpretation to help people understand the written word (Neh 8:8; Mark 4:1-20). Such reading has an impact on people (Heb 4:12; Acts 2:37; 7:54; 10:44). Therefore, any person called by God to public ministry should reverently and thoroughly prepare himself or herself. It is sad to notice that many a public reader of the Scriptures does not familiarize himself or herself adequately with the text before reading in front of a congregation. A divine exhortation for each public reader and preacher of the scriptures is: 'Do your best to present yourself to God as one approved, a workman who does not need to be ashamed, and who correctly handles the word of truth' (2 Tim 2:15).

1:4-6 Greetings

Revelation begins and ends like a typical first-century letter. It opens with the commonly used formula in which a greeting contained three parts: Personal greetings: *John, to the seven churches in Asia* (**1:4a**); a blessing: *Grace and peace...* (**1:4b-5a**); and 'a doxology' or prayer: *To him who loves ... Amen* (**1:5b-6**).

The greetings distinguish this book from all other Jewish apocalyptic works. John writes to actual, historical churches, addressing them in the same way as other NT epistles do. The churches mentioned in chapters 2 and 3 were all in *Asia* (1:4a), which is not the modern continent of Asia but

the Roman province of Asia Minor, in the western part of present-day Turkey.

Like Paul, John combines a Greek greeting ('grace') and a Hebrew greeting ('peace') in the blessing at the opening of this letter (1:4b; see also Rom 1:7; 1 Cor 1:3; 2 Cor 1:2). By 'grace', the Greeks meant something like 'love functioning under adverse conditions.' The noun is derived from a Greek verb that means 'to cheer up'. So what John is saying is this: 'Cheer up because God is in control in spite of the adverse circumstances created by human rebellion'. The standard Hebrew greeting *shalom* or *salaam* literally means 'peace', but it is often used as a synonym for salvation.

The form of the blessing makes it clear that the Trinity is the source of *grace and peace*. John first mentions God the Father, *him who is, and was, and who is to come*, followed by the Holy Spirit, referred to here as *seven spirits*. He mentions Jesus Christ after the Holy Spirit because the following verses and chapters will deal with the person, presence and power of the risen Jesus Christ, God the Son.

The doxology refers to several elements that will be found later in the drama: *freed us ... his blood ... made us to be a kingdom and priests*. This is the language of the sacrificial system of the OT temple. It is good to keep in mind that the teachings of this letter are presented against a background heavily influenced by the OT.

1:7-8 Dramatic Prologue: The Herald

One key to understanding an author's purpose is grasping the literary structure of what he has written. If Revelation is read as a drama that unfolds the history of human suffering, the embodiment and manifestation of evil, and the ultimate triumph of the Lamb and believers, its message will be easier to grasp. The author uses this literary device as a way of presenting his living message in a telling way. His theme can be understood as an account of the working out of God's plan in human affairs, and the consummation of human history with the return and eternal reign of Christ.

The drama opens with the voices of two figures from behind the curtain, so to speak, who announce their parts. One is a herald or a messenger; and the other is the Lord God himself. This is a cosmic stage and the action is related to God's work in the world. The herald is announcing the motif of the play or drama – 'History's most important person is about to appear again on history's stage'. Could anything better enhance our anticipation of the drama's significance than this?

The narrator's introduction to the drama in 1:7-8 is modelled on ancient Greek drama. For example, in Aeschylus' *Agamemnon*, the drama opens with a speech by a 'watchman'. In the biblical tradition, the 'watchman' or 'herald' of good tidings was someone who announced 'peace'. In Isaiah 52:7-8, the watchman announces to Israel, 'Your God reigns!' John, as a herald, is close to the OT messenger's spirit and theme. As a narrator, he alludes to large parts of the OT. So, while his drama has Greek influence and is presented in seven acts of seven scenes each, it proclaims a message in the best Hebrew and Christian prophetic tradition – that of announcing 'good tidings' in the midst of suffering.

While 1:5-6 describe what Christ accomplished on behalf of the believers, **1:7** is a clear reference to Christ's return and his eternal rule over the earth (22:7, 12, 20; Dan 7:13). Christ also introduces himself as *the Alpha and the Omega* (**1:8**), referring to the first and last letters of the Greek alphabet. The meaning is the same as that of 'the First and the Last' in 1:17, and 'the Beginning and the End' in 21:6 and 22:13. Only the book of Revelation refers to God, the Lord Jesus Christ, in this way. God wanted the readers to be encouraged by knowing that God, who knows all things from the beginning to the end, is the absolute source of all creation and history. Nothing lies outside him, just as no other letter of the Greek alphabet lay outside the Alpha and Omega. He is the Lord God of all and is continually present to his people as the Almighty (*pantokrator*, which literally means 'the one who has his hand on everything'). God is in total control (4:8; 11:17; 15:3; 16:7, 14; 19:6, 15; 2 Cor 6:18; Col 1:19).

1:9-3:22 Act I: Vision of the Church on Earth – Jesus Christ in its Midst

Stage Setting: As the curtain is drawn back on this cosmic stage, we see upon it only John (the narrator and seer) and the Son of Man, the Lord Jesus Christ. The centre of the stage is occupied by seven golden lampstands arranged in a circle.

1:9-20 The Narrator and Jesus Christ on the Stage

The stage settings for every act are adapted from OT tabernacle and temple worship. Here the seven lampstands appropriately represent the seven-branched candelabrum of the sanctuary, for the people of God are both the dwelling place of God on earth (Eph 2:19-22) and the light of the world (Matt 5:14-16).

Like the OT prophets, John directs the thoughts of readers and hearers toward the theology of history, which is the theme of his drama. Through it all, we never lose sight of the narrator who is the witness to all these events. John is always that little figure, as it were, by the side of the stage of God's activity – observing keenly and reporting faithfully what he hears (1:10) and sees (1:12).

John tells us that he was on *Patmos*, an island just off the coast of Asia Minor. He was there *because of the word of God and the testimony of Jesus* (**1:9b**). The phrase 'the testimony of Jesus' (see also 12:17; 17:6; 19:10; 20:4) refers to the totality of the earthly life, ministry, death and resurrection of Jesus Christ. It seems that John was not on *Patmos* to preach the Word, but because either persecution or the inner compulsion of the Spirit had led him there. He assures his readers that he is their partner in three things: *suffering*, the *kingdom* and *patient endurance* (**1:9a**). John and his Christian recipients shared with Christ and with one another the suffering and persecution that comes to all believers as a result of their faithfulness to God (John 16:33; Acts 14:22; Col 1:24; 2 Tim 3:12).

The phrase *I was in the Spirit* (**1:10**) is common in apocalyptic literature, but not in any other NT book. It has been understood to indicate some kind of visionary state inspired by the Spirit (see also 4:2; 17:3). The phrase introduces the apocalyptic section of the book (4:2) immediately following the letters to the seven churches, and shows that events of the Spirit as opposed to earthly events are occurring.

John turns in order to *see* as well as to *hear* the one speaking to him (**1:12**). The *voice* could be that of Christ (as in 1:17-18; 4:1; 22:16) or, more likely, that of an angel who appears frequently in Revelation (19:10; 22:8-9). Either of these could appear to John in human form (1:13). John twice mistakenly prostrates himself before an angel, thinking that the angel is the risen Lord Jesus. John compares this voice to *a trumpet* (4:1; Exod 19:16). In chapters 8 and 9, trumpet blasts will herald woes.

The voice like a trumpet commands John to write to the seven churches what he sees and hears (**1:11**). Revelation is unique in the NT in that John functions as a scribe who writes upon command. Events in Revelation unfold in the seer's psychic vision. This does not mean that the events are illusionary or creations of his mind. Instead, this is one form of God's revelation. Often John uses the visionary qualifier *like* (1:9, 10, 13, 14, 15, 16) as he gropes to find language to convey adequately the awesome and stirring images that have confronted him. Sometimes he himself does not even understand the visions (17:6b), and yet he faithfully records everything he sees and hears. If apocalyptic writers like John, Daniel and Ezekiel could not always understand what they had been asked to record, who are we, as modern readers, to claim that we can fully understand and explain every image and symbol in Revelation?

Jesus Christ now reveals himself first to John and then to the seven churches. John's description of the risen and ascended Christ in 1:13-14 uses OT imagery to portray his wisdom, power, steadfastness and penetrating vision. He appears as *someone 'like a son of man'* standing in the middle of the golden lampstands (**1:13**; Dan 7:13). Jesus preferred the title 'Son of Man' for himself throughout his earthly ministry, though he did not deny the appropriate use of 'Son of God' as well (2:18; John 10:36; Mark 14:61). Both titles were used for the Messiah. Thus the person John is seeing is a heavenly Messiah who is also human.

Alluding to Daniel 7:9, John describes Christ's head and hair as *white like wool, as white as snow* (**1:14a**). In ancient Middle Eastern cultures, as in most African traditional cultures, white hair commanded respect and it indicated the wisdom of years. This part of the vision may have shown John something of the deity and wisdom of Christ (Col 2:3). Christ's eyes are like a *blazing fire* (**1:14b**), a detail not found in the vision of the Son of Man in Daniel 7, but occurring in Daniel 10:6. This detail is repeated in the letter to Thyatira (2:18) and in the vision of the anticipated triumphant return of Christ and defeat of his enemies (19:12). It may also portray his penetrating scrutiny and knowledge of hidden things, or his fierce judgment (2 Chr 16:9).

The glory and majesty of Jesus Christ are apparent in the description of his feet being *like bronze glowing in a furnace* (**1:15a**; 2:18) and his voice being *like the sound of rushing waters* (**1:15b**). In Ezekiel and Daniel, God himself is described in similar terms (Ezek 1:13, 24, 27; 8:2; 43:2; Dan 10:6). The glowing bronze feet represent his triumphant trampling over those who are unbelieving and unfaithful to his truth, including the devil, the beast and the false prophet. This vision assures John of Jesus' ultimate victory over ungodly systems and political leaders who are the embodiment of evil throughout human history (Ps 2:1-12).

In Scripture, to be at someone's right hand is to be in a place of power and safety. That is why Hebrews 1:3 speaks of Jesus as seated at the right hand of God the Father in heaven after he accomplished what God the Father had sent him to do on earth. In *his right hand* Jesus is holding *seven stars* (**1:16a**), which are identified as the seven angels of the seven churches. In the Bible, *stars* can also be used to refer to angels (9:1; Job 38:7), the declaration of God's glory (Ps 19:1-4), faithful witnesses to God's truth (Dan 12:3; Matt 2:2; Luke 2:9-10) or God's messengers. The context would determine which one of these is meant.

John sees *a sharp double-edged sword* coming out of the mouth of Christ. This image is used several times in Revelation (**1:16b**; 2:12, 16; 19:15, 21). As a weapon, a sword is a symbol of war, oppression, anguish and political authority. However, John here uses a rare Greek word for sword, which outside Revelation is only used in Luke 2:35. This parallel seems to suggest that Christ conquers the world through his death and resurrection, which is a different type of 'sword'. This is the sword of divine judgment, not of the type of power wielded by the nations (Ps 2:1-12).

Finally, Christ's face is likened to *the sun shining in all its brilliance* (**1:16c**), an image that speaks of his divine glory, pre-eminence and victory (10:1; Matt 13:43; 17:2).

John's encounter with the glorified Christ is such a stupendous experience that he falls to the ground, as did Paul, Ezekiel and Daniel in similar circumstances (**1:17a**; Acts 9:3-4; 22:6-7; Ezek 1:28; 3:23; 43:3; 44:4; Dan 10:7-9). He hears Christ announce that he is *the First and the Last* (**1:17b**). This statement of eternal power and existence belongs only to God (Isa 44:6; 48:12), and so Christ is here presented as God, the Creator and the absolute Lord of history. The words are equivalent to the divine self-identification as *the Alpha and the Omega* (1:8). If the fact that he *was dead* seems to contradict this statement of eternal existence, we need to remember that the purpose of Christ's coming as man was to die the death that was due the entire sinful human race. Therefore he says not only, *I was dead,* but also exclaims, *behold, I am alive for ever and ever* (**1:18a**). Only Jesus who is truly the *Living One* can reveal himself by deeds that verify his claim to be the Lord of life.

Only the Living One could further claim, *I have the keys of death and of Hades* (**1:18b**). 'Hades' is often used to translate Hebrew references to 'the grave'. It sometimes refers to the place of all the departed dead (Acts 2:27, 31), and sometimes to the place of only the departed wicked (Luke 16:23; Rev 20:13-14). Christ's conquest of death and emergence from Hades has given him their 'keys', the symbols that he has the power and authority to enter them. He alone has authority to determine who will enter 'death and Hades' and when they will come out. For the Christian, death is the servant of Christ.

John is told to *write, therefore, what you have seen, what is now and what will take place* (**1:19**). Some commentators see this verse as presenting a chronological outline of the visions in the book, so that it refers to the past ('have seen'), the present ('now') and the future (what will take place). The main problem with adopting such an outline is determining where exactly the breaks should take place in the book.

This first vision is called a *mystery* (**1:20**). In the NT, a mystery is something formerly secret but now revealed. The secret of the stars and lampstands is explained as showing that Jesus, the Lord of human history, is intimately involved with the people of God and is in the midst of his church.

2:1-3:22 The Letters to the Seven Churches

Jesus Christ next reveals himself to and evaluates seven specific churches. The letters were not addressed to these seven churches because they were the only Christian communities in the Roman Empire. Nor were they actually addressed exclusively to them. Rather, seven churches were chosen because seven was the number of completeness, and thus these seven churches represent the whole of the believing community of God. Most of them were experiencing persecution, and some were being tempted to compromise with the systems and powers of evil.

Similar situations face churches throughout the world today. Some are persecuted, with their members being added to the long list of Christian martyrs. Some are living in conditions of social injustice and are involved in a difficult struggle to change those conditions. Others, like the church in Laodicea, are rich, safe and respected, and yet they are spiritually bankrupt. We need to use our ears to 'hear what the Spirit says to the churches' – to all of them, rich and poor, weak and powerful, secure and persecuted; to churches in America, Angola, Bolivia, Britain, Canada, Chad, China, Congo, Namibia, Uganda, Yemen, Zanzibar, and in our own backyard. We should care about what is happening with the Christian church worldwide.

The seven churches were, however, more than just symbols, they were also real churches in real places, situated along a natural ancient travel circuit, beginning at Ephesus and ending at Laodicea. And each of the letters is adapted to the specific situation of the church it addresses.

These letters are all constructed on the same pattern. Each contains some commendation (except the letter to Laodicea), a reproof, an exhortation to correct what is wrong, and a promise to *him who overcomes* (2:7, 11, 17, 26; 3:5, 12, 21). Affirmation is something we find difficult in ministry. It seems much easier to find fault than to compliment. But these letters offer a pattern of affirmation and correction, challenge and comfort. Such a balance is not only biblical but very necessary in pastoral ministry. Weakness and fallibility can be opportunities for spiritual growth and strength (2 Cor 12:9).

The goal of each letter is to encourage the recipients to endure to the end, remaining loyal and faithful to Christ. These letters also suggest that there are limits as to how much Christians should compromise with contemporary culture or political policies. We need to recognize conflicts of interest and to be aware of the extent to which our belief and behaviour are influenced by our own culture. Our reputation in society and culture counts for little if our lifestyle is against God.

We might be inclined to think of these letters as private communications from John to each of the churches, but there is nothing to indicate that they were circulated separately. The book of Revelation was intended to be read as a whole in public in all the churches in the region (1:3). Thus, believers in Ephesus would hear not only the message addressed directly to them but also the messages to Smyrna, Sardis and the rest. This approach makes it clear that there was a common bond uniting all these communities into one. It also means that the message of the whole would have come into sharper focus for each local church because each one would have heard its needs addressed in concrete terms within the context of the wider church.

The unity of all these churches is symbolized by at least three features that appear in all the letters:
• Each letter is addressed to *the angel of the church*. The word 'angel' in Greek means 'a messenger'. This description challenges church leaders to take their work more seriously. In some ways, the pastor of a church embodies the qualities (or lack of them) that characterize that

local church. A pastor, in a sense, distils the character of the belief and behaviour of the individual Christians.
• All the letters begin with a statement about the one whose message is being communicated. Jesus introduces himself to the churches using the same descriptions of himself he used in revealing himself to John in 1:12-20.
• Finally, all the letters end with the same exhortation: *he who has an ear let him hear what the Spirit says to the churches* (2:7, 11, 17, 29; 3:6, 13, 22). This was not just an empty formula. It placed the responsibility on the shoulders of the recipients. The only excuse anyone could have for not responding to what the Spirit had to say was that he or she had no ears! Anyone who had ears had no excuse. This formula is used to link together the messages to all the churches. We might expect the letters to call for each church to hear its own message. But the plural term was used, *churches*. Each local church was to hear and heed the word that was spoken to all the other churches as well as to itself.

2:1-7 Act I, Scene 1: The church at Ephesus

The church at Ephesus could be any local congregation in the history of Christianity. The Lord Jesus' message to it reveals his intimate knowledge of the spiritual condition of all his people. He knows each one of us as we really are inside (1 Sam 16:7; Ps 139:1-24; 2 Tim 2:19; Heb 4:12). Nothing is hidden from his eyes (2 Chr 16:9).

Ephesus was one of the richest cities of the ancient world. Located on a harbour at the tip of Asia Minor, it was a centre of trade and travel. Its people were proud of their city, and especially of the temple of Artemis (also known as Diana), who was worshipped as the source of fertility and abundance. Thus her statue had many breasts. Her temple was one of the great tourist attractions of the ancient Mediterranean world. The city's pride in its trade and religion is clear from the incident in Acts 19:23-41 and the chant 'Great is Artemis of the Ephesians' (Acts 19:34).

Paul has written a letter to the church in Ephesus, but now Jesus Christ reveals himself to them as *him who holds the seven stars in his right hand and walks among the seven golden lampstands* (2:1; 1:13) and brings a message of both praise and warning. The church is praised because, in the midst of such overt idolatry and some persecution, it has *persevered and endured hardships for my name's sake* and *not grown weary* (2:3). As a congregation, the believers have rejected some who had falsely claimed to be apostles (2:2) and they hate *the works of the Nicolaitans* (2:6 – see comment on 2:14-15). On the other hand, they are rebuked for having abandoned the love which originally characterized their lives and warned that if they do not repent, the Lord will take their lampstand from its place (2:4-5). That is, they will no longer be counted among the faithful witnesses of Christ in their own generation.

As far as Christian service was concerned, the members were hard-working. But they lacked devotion to Christ. Believers in every generation are in danger of becoming experts at ministry, simply performing tasks rather than deepening their passion for Christ. If they do, they will become like salt that has lost its saltiness (Matt 5:13). We need to maintain a proper balance.

2:8-11 Act I, Scene 2: The church at Smyrna

Smyrna (now Izmir), situated some thirty-five miles (fifty kilometres) north of Ephesus, was another flourishing city in the Roman province of Asia Minor. How appropriate is the Lord's self-designation as *the First and the Last, who died and came to life again* (**2:8**; 1:8, 17), for a church whose members, as this letter shows, were facing persecution and the threat of death.

Like Ephesus, Smyrna was noted for its pagan worship. Here, however, the worship took forms that were potentially more dangerous for this community of believers. Thus John can only write words of comfort to the church in Smyrna. By being faithful unto death, the church will not be *hurt by the second death* (**2:11**). The *crown of life* that is promised is similar to the laurel wreath worn by an athlete who wins a race, but the emphasis is on finishing the Christian race or pilgrimage well and not on competitive zeal. Persecution has taught the Christians in Smyrna that 'a man's life does not consist in the abundance of his possessions' but in being 'rich towards God' (Luke 12:15, 21). The church in the developing world may not have material wealth, but may it long continue increasing in richness toward God in the midst of persecution and material scarcity.

The reference to *the slander of those who say they are Jews and are not, but are a synagogue of Satan* (**2:9**) may indicate early hostility to true Christians (see comment on 3:9). But the one behind the persecution is really *Satan* or 'the devil' (the terms are used interchangeably – 12:9; 20:2). He may use religious individuals or groups as his instruments in persecuting the faithful. God never promises believers a suffering-free life on this side of eternity. But he promises them his presence in every situation (Ps 23:4; Matt 28:19-20; Heb 13:5).

2:12-17 Act I, Scene 3: The church at Pergamum

The city of Pergamum was located about sixty miles (one-hundred kilometres) north of Smyrna and fifteen miles (twenty-five kilometres) from the coast. It was the headquarters of both the Roman authority and emperor worship in the province of Asia Minor. That is probably why it is called the place *where Satan has his throne* (**2:13a**). However, some interpret this phrase as referring to the temple of Zeus, which was situated on a hill above the city and might be compared to a throne. But it seems more likely that John was thinking of Roman power as the embodiment

of evil during his time, and thus as a symbol of the satanic powers that were upon the earth.

Pergamum was also famous for its magnificent library, which rivalled that of Alexandria. Disputes about which was the best library in the world had resulted in Egypt's stopping all shipments of papyrus to Pergamum. Then the city began copying its books onto animal skins. This material was given the name of *parchment* – that is, 'writing material from Pergamum'. Most of the ancient manuscripts of the NT were written on parchment.

The message to the church in Pergamum is sent from the one *who has the sharp double-edged sword* (**2:12**; 1:16). This is a reference to the coming victory and judgment of Christ. Jesus commends the church for its steadfastness in the very centre of Satan's domain, as exemplified by Antipas, who died for his faith (**2:13b**). God never forgets his martyrs.

However, Jesus also reproves the church for the false doctrines that have spread among them, specifically the teachings of *Balaam* and of *the Nicolaitans* (**2:14-15**). Balaam is an OT prototype of all the false teachers who misled Israel (Num 23–24; 31:16). According to some Jewish writers of the time, both Balaam and Nicolaus mean 'destroyer of the people'. John is saying that, as in times of old, there are those whose teachings destroy people doctrinally and spiritually by inciting them to compromise with idolatry. In this context *sexual immorality* probably has the symbolic meaning, common in the OT, of spiritual adultery, leaving the true God and following idols. The call to repentance is coupled with a warning of judgment on the basis of the Word of God. The community of God's people is no place for compromise.

Christ promises those at Pergamum *who overcome* that he will give them *the hidden manna* and *a white stone with a new name written on it* (**2:17**). 'The hidden manna' probably refers to the manna hidden in the ark of the covenant by Moses (Exod 16:33-34; Heb 9:4), which reminded the children of Israel of God's grace, faithfulness and provision in the wilderness (Ps 78:24). According to apocalyptic Jewish teaching, the messianic era would see the restoration of the hidden wilderness manna: 'And it shall come to pass at that self-same time [in the days when the Messiah comes] that the treasury of manna shall again descend from on high, and they will eat of it in those years' (*2 Baruch* 29:8). The 'manna' may also refer to Holy Communion, which looks to the past, present and future when believers, as citizens of the kingdom, will eat manna at the heavenly banquet. It may also speak of the ever-sufficiency of Jesus Christ in contrast to the allurements of emperor worship.

The 'white stone' probably refers to an invitation or 'admission ticket' that entitled its bearer to attend a banquet. In the ancient world, a *white stone* was a ballot of approval and a token of admission, whereas a black stone denoted rejection and exclusion. Accordingly, the *white stone* promised to the person who overcomes signifies acceptance by the Lord and a place among the company of his redeemed.

Some interpret the 'new name' on the stone as a secret divine name. They cite verses such as 3:12, where the Lord says he will write the name of his God and his own new name on the one who overcomes; and 14:1, where the 144,000 have the name of the Lamb and the name of his Father written on their foreheads; and 22:4, where it is said that the name of the Lord will be on the foreheads of his servants in the new heaven and earth. Those who are thus stamped with the divine name are marked as precious to God and his special possession. But here in 2:17, it is not the person but the white stone that is marked with a name that is *known only to him who receives it*. It thus seems that this verse is not speaking of a divine name, but, rather, of a divinely given name for each person who overcomes. 'Overcoming' involves perseverance in living for God in all life situations. When we fail, we must immediately acknowledge our failure or sin and confess it before the Lord (1 John 1:9). The name known only to the recipient indicates the uniqueness of each individual believer before the Lord, and the distinctness of the relationship each person has with God. There will be no confusion of names in the mind of God. What is revealed to John here is really the fulfilment of the age-old promise 'You shall be called by a new name which the mouth of the Lord will give' (Isa 62:2). The Good Shepherd 'calls his own sheep by name … and the sheep follow him for they know his voice' (John 10:3-4).

2:18-29 Act I, Scene 4: The church at Thyatira

Unlike the previous three cities, Thyatira had no political significance, though it had a few things it could be proud of. It stood at an important crossroads about thirty-five miles (fifty-six kilometres) south-east of Pergamum and was a commercial town with many traders and artisans. Ancient records indicate that it had more craftsmen's guilds than many larger cities. It was the home of Lydia, 'a dealer in purple cloth' (Acts 16:14), who became a disciple of Paul. She must have been a member of the dyers' guild. These guilds wielded significant power. They combined some of the features of our modern trade unions with some religious features. Each guild had its own patron deity, feasts and seasonal festivals. Individuals had to belong to a guild in order to practise a certain trade, and had to participate in their meetings and ceremonies. These guild meetings often took place in pagan temples, where an animal was offered to the gods and then eaten by the members of the guild. This obviously presented Christians with a dilemma. If they did not participate in such feasts and ceremonies, they would be unable to make a living from trading. If they did participate, they were being unfaithful to their Lord. Many African Christians find themselves in similar

situations. Senior members of African families usually expect all family members to cooperate and participate in all pagan rituals and festivals which are aimed at appeasing the spirits of the departed relatives.

This church shows *love, faith, service* and *perseverance* (**2:19**) and was apparently a growing church. However, it has permitted the false teaching of a self-proclaimed prophetess, who may have proposed an easy way out of this dilemma. In the previous letter, people with similar views were likened to Balaam, and here this woman is described as a new *Jezebel* (**2:20**; see 1 Kgs 16:31; 18:4; 19:2; 21:1-25). She leads the people into spiritual adultery and *Satan's so-called deep secrets* (**2:24**). If the congregation does not repent, the Lord will abandon them to sensual ways, so that their judgment will be in accord with their deeds (**2:21-22**). Beware of so-called prophets or apostles who teach 'secret doctrines'!

In contrast, those who hear and obey the words of the one *whose eyes are like a blazing of fire* (**2:18**; 1:14) will receive *authority over the nations* (**2:26**). What is promised here is union with Christ in his universal authority, as is clear from the explanation *just as I have received authority from my Father*. The basis of the promise is the declaration prophetically addressed to the incarnate Son: 'Ask of me, and I will make the nations your inheritance and the ends of the earth your possession. You shall rule them with an iron sceptre; you will dash them to pieces like pottery' (Ps 2:8, 9). The profound blessing of reigning with Christ is exclusively for believers (1 Cor 6:2-3). He can give them this privilege because he is the *Son of God* (**2:18**), a term that appears only here in the entire book, for elsewhere 'Son of Man' is preferred (1:13; 14:14). He may have chosen to use this title here to contrast the glory of the Christ with the pretensions of the emperor cult that hailed Caesar as a god.

The overcomers in Thyatira are promised *the morning star* (**2:28**). This expression may refer to the Son of God in his glory (22:16), or to the resurrection of believers, or both ideas may be combined. In the present night of this fallen world, the light of the eternal day has already dawned in the hearts of those who by faith have received him who is the morning star into their lives. The promise of his return is also like the *morning star* (2 Pet 1:19), which heralds the start of a new day as the darkness of the long night of temptation, persecution, suffering and death is dispelled. Overcomers are promised resurrection and participation in Christ's glory in that kingdom where there will be no night (21:25). Those whose hearts are illumined by divine grace (2 Cor 4:4, 6) will find that 'the path of the righteous is like the first gleam of dawn, shining ever brighter till the full light of day' (Prov 4:18).

This message to the church at Thyatira reminds us that we need to seriously evaluate ourselves as local churches and as individual believers, to see what the Lord is calling us to turn away from. Are our beliefs, behaviour, doctrine, deeds, motives and actions in keeping with what God expects of us as individuals and congregations (1 Cor 11:28)?

3:1-6 Act I, Scene 5: The church at Sardis

Sardis was about thirty miles (fifty kilometres) south of Thyatira and was a prosperous city. Five important roads met there, which made for active trade and gave the city strategic importance. The surrounding area was particularly well-suited to raising sheep, and so Sardis was a centre for the trade in wool and cloth.

The majority of those in the church were spiritually weak. But a few are commended for their faithfulness to the Lord (**3:4**). The Lord knows even those few who are faithful to him (2 Tim 2:19). However, there is very little that is positive in the message to Sardis. It can be summarized in its opening statement: *You have a reputation of being alive, but you are dead* (**3:1**; 2 Tim 3:5). Strikingly, there is no mention of any particular sins as in the other letters, nor is there any reference to persecution, external pressures, or false doctrines within the church. On the contrary, everything seems to be running smoothly. That apparent smoothness seems to have been the great tragedy of the church in Sardis. Its easy life is its greatest indictment. The Lord sees that the church at Sardis is spiritually asleep. Therefore, he exhorts the church to *Wake up!* (**3:3**). The church has to strengthen what remained, or else it will die (**3:2**).

The promise made to overcomers grows out of the reference to white clothing in **3:5**. The faithful Sardian Christians will receive white clothes from Christ, and so will any others who overcome the pollution of pagan society. Furthermore, this pure relationship to Christ is permanently guaranteed: *I will never blot out his name from the book of life.* In ancient times, the names of citizens were recorded in a register. When they died, their names were erased or crossed out of the book of the living. This same idea appears in the OT (Exod 32:32-33; Ps 69:28; Isa 4:3). From this idea of being recorded in God's book of the living (or the righteous) comes the sense of belonging to God's eternal kingdom or possessing eternal life (Dan 12:1; Luke 10:20; Phil 4:3; Heb 12:23; Rev 13:8; 17:8; 20:15; 21:27). For Christ to say that he will never blot out or erase the overcomers' names from the book of life is the strongest possible affirmation that death can never separate believers from Christ (Rom 8:35-39). A person enrolled in the book of life by faith remains in it forever.

Finally, Christ promises *to acknowledge* the names of overcomers *before the Father and his angels.* The word translated 'acknowledge' implies a strong confession before a court. Christ's confession of our names is a statement of our fellowship and oneness with him that assures our heavenly citizenship (Matt 10:32; Luke 12:8). What ultimately counts is not our acceptance by this world's society but that our eternal relationship to Christ is genuine.

3:7-13 Act I, Scene 6: The church at Philadelphia

Philadelphia was about twenty-five miles (forty kilometres) south-east of Sardis on a main highway that connected it to other cities like Smyrna and Pergamum. It was less important than most of the other six cities. Its source of wealth was the flourishing vineyards on the surrounding volcanic plains. Consequently, its main religious allegiance was to Dionysius, the god of wine. Philadelphia was also famous for its many other shrines, though none was as great or as beautiful as the temple of Artemis in Ephesus. According to some authors, there was a custom of inscribing the name of great citizens on the pillars of these temples. This custom may be the background for the promise: *Him who overcomes, I will make a pillar in the temple of my God* (**3:12**).

The letter is free from rebuke, even though the church in Philadelphia would seem not to have been a strong church. The description of the one who speaks as *holy* and *true* (**3:7a**; 6:10) reminds the members of the church that they are called to be holy and obedient to revealed biblical truth (1 Pet 1:15-16).

The further statement that the speaker *has the key of David,* and that *what he opens, no one can shut, and what he shuts, no one can open* (**3:7b**) reminds us of Isaiah 22:22, where very similar words are used of Eliakim, whom God would put in charge of Hezekiah's household (2 Kgs 18:18, 37). Christ, who has been appointed 'head over everything for the church' (Eph 1:22) and invested with 'all authority' (Matt 28:18), is 'faithful … over God's house' (Heb 3:6). *The key* that he holds is a symbol of the trust placed in him and of his authority. It is called *the key of David* because Christ is the promised descendent of David whose kingdom will be established for ever (2 Sam 7:13, 16; Isa 9:7; Luke 1:32; Rev 22:16). The supremacy of his authority is indicated by the assertion that what he opens 'no one can shut' and what he shuts 'no one can open'. Even death, which to us seems so final, is not the end. He wields the key of death and of Hades (1:18) and thus has ultimate power both as redeemer and as judge (John 5:22-29).

As with all the churches, the Lord knows the strengths and weaknesses of the Philadelphian church (**3:8a**; 2 Chr 16:9). Continuing the idea of opening and shutting, he declares that he has opened a door for them, and because he is the one who has opened it, no one else will be able to shut it (**3:8b**). In the past, God had made a similar announcement to Cyrus (Isa 45:1). The door that has opened for the church is not the door through which they can escape their difficult circumstances. Rather, it is a door of opportunity to witness to the power of the gospel (2 Cor 1:4). Paul used a similar metaphor when he explained how God had 'opened

THEOLOGICAL HERESY

The word 'theology' literally means 'God's word'. Christian theology thus involves reflection on our faith and worship in the light of God's word and our contemporary context. Every theology worthy of the name must be deeply rooted in the Scriptures and must not deliberately distort God's word or promote a false interpretation of it that leads to error being accepted as truth.

'Heresy' refers to deviation from the doctrinal beliefs commonly accepted by the Christian church. Most of the theological heresies in church history have had to do with the nature of Jesus Christ, the Trinity, the second coming of Christ and the ethical implications of the Christian message for moral life today. Today, in our African context, common heresies include the teaching that all humans will be saved, the elevation of African traditional religion as equivalent to OT faith, ancestor worship, and the mixing of African traditional religion and Christianity.

Theological heresy was seen by the apostles and the early church fathers as a serious and rebellious departure from established doctrine. In the Pastoral Epistles, the elders are instructed to teach sound doctrine and oppose false teaching (1 Tim 1:3-11; 4:1-16; 2 Tim 1:13-14; 4:1-5; Titus 1:9-2:1). 'False teachers' and 'destructive heresies' are also strongly opposed in 2 Peter 2. Such teachers are described as despising legitimate authority (2 Pet 2:10b-13a) and following the corrupt desires of their sinful nature (2 Pet 2:13b-16). They are said to be dry springs, powerless in dealing with sin (2 Pet 2:19) and destined for judgment (2 Pet 2: 20-22).

Three heretical groups are identified in the NT, namely, Judaizers, Gnostics and Nicolaitans. The Judaizers taught that salvation required both faith in Jesus and obedience to the law of Moses. The Gnostics claimed to possess special insight and taught that Jesus was not really God's Son and that matter was evil and spirit good. Since God was good (and Spirit) he could not personally have created a material world (evil). Also, since spirit and matter could not intermingle, Christ and God could not have united in the person of Jesus (2 Tim 2:17-18). The Nicolaitans practised an extreme form of Gnosticism, claiming that since their bodies were physical (and therefore evil), only what their spirits did was important. They felt free to indulge in promiscuous sexual relationships, to eat food that had been offered to idols and to do anything they pleased with their bodies (1 and 2 John; Rev 2:6,14, 15).

The early church responded strongly to those who deviated from the truth and claimed to have special knowledge outside the biblical text, as can be seen in the epistles and in the action taken in Acts 15:1-31. It barred heretics from its fellowship and prayed for their salvation. It did not, however, call for them to be put to death, and the church was wrong when it later began executing those it considered heretical.

Believers must take care not to label legitimate differences in emphasis within the Christian church as heretical. The differences in theological emphases between, say, Presbyterian and Pentecostal churches do not constitute heresy because both groups can adequately justify their different approaches from Scripture.

James Nkansah-Obrempong

---

the door of faith to the Gentiles' (Acts 14:27; see also 1 Cor 16:9; Col 4:3). The believers in Philadelphia faced fearsome opposition, but this hostility could not shut the door that God had opened.

Those opposing their witness are described as *of the synagogue of Satan* (**3:9**; see 2:9). It seems that there were some Jews who vehemently denied that Jesus was Lord and Messiah and who actively persecuted those who made that claim. They are said to *claim to be Jews though they are not, but are liars*. A true Jew, according to Paul and John, is one who finds forgiveness and life in Jesus, the Messiah.

The word *since* that introduces 3:10 may belong with 3:9, and may thus be saying that the reason for the believers' triumph over the synagogue of Satan is that Christ loves them because they follow his *command to endure patiently* (**3:10a**). This command may be the one to endure until he returns (Luke 21:19; Heb 10:36-38) or it may be the command to endure as patiently as Christ himself did (2 Thess 3:5; Heb 12:1-5).

But the 'since' may also point forward, as in the NIV translation, to a promise of deliverance because of their obedience. This promise has also sparked debate about

what exactly is meant by the phrase *keep you from the hour of trial* (**3:10b**). The Greek may equally well be translated as 'keep you from undergoing the trial' or 'keep you right through the trial'. In other NT passages, the same expression means to be kept from the pollution of the world while still in the world (John 17:15-19; Jas 1:27).

There is also debate about what constitutes 'the hour of trial'. It is clearly a very thoroughgoing test *that is going to come upon the whole world* and apply to all *those who live on the earth*. Some interpret it as the time of intense trouble that will come on the world before the second coming of Christ (Dan 12:1; Joel 2:31; Mark 13:14; 2 Thess 2:1-12). They argue that this trial is the one described in detail in the following chapters of the book of Revelation, and that the Lord is here promising to exempt believers from the fierce persecution yet to come.

Others argue that 'the hour of trial' is the wrath of God from which believers are eternally delivered. Certainly, the book of Revelation as a whole does not promise believers escape from suffering but encourages them to endure it to the end. They have already known suffering, as when Antipas, the faithful witness of Christ, was martyred (2:13).

Martyrdom is, in fact, presented as the means of conquering for both Christ and his followers (5:6). While Christians are not called to seek martyrdom, they are to remain faithful until Christ either calls them home or comes back for them before death. Physical death is not the end of everything for the believer (Matt 10:28; John 14:1-3; 1 Cor 15:51-53; 2 Cor 5:6, 8; 1 Thess 4:13-18). In all their hardships and suffering, they will experience God's shepherding ministry (Ps 23:4; Heb 13:5).

In light of the Lord's anticipated return, the believers should persevere so that they will not lose their promised rewards (**3:11**; 1 Cor 9:24-27). The first reward is becoming a *pillar in the temple of my God* (**3:12a**). Philadelphia suffered frequent earthquakes, and often the only parts of the city left standing were the huge stone columns of temples. These pillars were thus symbols of strength, stability and permanence. Moreover, they were a vital part of the whole building. So the Lord is promising that overcomers will have a place of abiding power and dignity in the coming kingdom of God in which no persecution or trials will ever disturb them again.

Secondly, Christ promises the overcomer, *I will write on him the name of my God and the name of the city of my God, the new Jerusalem, ... and ... my new name* (**3:12b**). The name of the city of Philadelphia had been changed by several rulers in the past, but believers are reminded that the name will come from God himself (not the emperor) and will ensure their citizenship in the new Jerusalem (21:2; Ezek 48:35). Christ's *new name* could be either the name that he alone knows about, signifying his absolute power over all creation (19:12), or the *new name* of Christ given to the believer (Isa 62:2; 65:15). This name is the seal of overcomers' salvation in Christ, who has redeemed them at the infinite cost of his own precious blood, and to whom they therefore belong (1 Cor 6:19; 1 Pet 1:18-19; Rev 7:14-15).

3:14-22 Act I, Scene 7: The church at Laodicea

Laodicea was about forty-five miles (seventy kilometres) south-east of Philadelphia. Like many of the cities mentioned in these two chapters, Laodicea was rich. It was proud of its power and prosperity, and had a famous school of medicine. There were several sources of that prosperity, but two among them seem to be significant in relation to this letter. One was beautiful bluish-black wool, which contrasts with the *white clothes* of sanctification (**3:18b**). The other was a world-famous eye ointment. John refers to this ointment when he counsels the church to buy from Christ *salve to put on your eyes so that you can see* (**3:18c**).

The apathy of this church disgusts the Lord. It's spiritual poverty is extreme. What is that great sin of the Laodiceans tha causes Christ, *the faithful and true witness* (3:14) to say that he will spit them out (**3:16**)? From the text, their sin is not something they do or think. It is rather that they are comfortable, smug, and lukewarm (**3:15**). Thus the Lord says to them: *You say, 'I am rich, I have acquired wealth and do not need a thing.' But you do not realize that you are wretched, pitiable, poor, blind and naked* (**3:17**). Christ encourages the church to seek true riches in him, as well as purity and spiritual sight. There is still hope for Laodicea, for Christ is standing at the door and knocking (**3:20-21**). Some churches today are like the church in Laodicea; rich, safe and respected, and yet they are spiritually bankrupt. If they open their heart to God for meaningful fellowship and spiritual revival, they will enjoy Christ's intimate daily fellowship.

4:1-8:1 Act II: Vision of God in Heaven – The Opening of the Seven Seals

Stage Setting: A great change of scenery is required for act II – *a door standing open in heaven* (4:1). In the middle of the stage appears the throne of God (4:2). Other characters on the stage include the twenty-four elders (4:4), four creatures (4:6) and, on the other side, the narrator (4:1). Before the throne are the Lamb (5:6), the seven lamps (4:5) and a sea of glass (4:6). As in most of the acts of this drama, the description of the activity in heaven forms part of the background for the scenes that will follow. John is saying that the events of history and of man's salvation must be viewed in light of God's redemptive purpose.

4:1-5:14 God in Control

The visionary scenes begin in chapter 4 with an incomparable picture of God's throne in heaven (4:2-8). He is presented as *the Lord God Almighty* (4:8), the one who created the world, and who is totally in control of things. Evil has been allowed, not because God is powerless against it, but because for his own purposes he has given it room to operate within the world for a limited and specified time.

Why has God allowed what appears to be contrary to divine purpose to have free rein in the world? The book of Revelation does not give a direct answer to this question. There are, however, two considerations from the point of view of the whole biblical message. The first is what is often referred to as the divine patience: 'The Lord is merciful and gracious, slow to anger and abounding in steadfast love' (Ps 103:8). 'Do you show contempt for the riches of his kindness, tolerance and patience, not realising that God's kindness leads you towards repentance?' (Rom 2:4). When we recognize ourselves to be sinful, then God's patience is a characteristic we celebrate! However, in a time of great tribulation and persecution God's patience with evil can seem strange. Suffering Christians must then be patient and remain faithful to God until his purpose, already begun in the heavenly realms, is carried out on earth (Jas 1:2-4). The second consideration is that God has created a humanity that could choose to be obedient, and thus could also choose to be disobedient. God did not design human puppets or robots. Thus the message of the Bible stresses the need for each of us to choose to know and obey God's will.

4:1-3 God on his throne

John is summoned by the voice, *like a trumpet,* which he had heard at the beginning (1:10). God and his throne are described in images drawn from Ezekiel's vision of the throne-chariot (**4:2**; see Ezek 1–2; Dan 7:9-10). This scene in heaven is very impressive, but may seem obscure and incoherent when examined in detail. John speaks of things that lie utterly beyond human knowledge. He describes the one sitting on the throne as having *the appearance of jasper and carnelian* (**4:3**). These are precious stones, although we are not certain exactly which stones are referred to. *Jasper* may be the same reddish stone as modern jasper, but John may have been referring to green jade or quartz, or even to diamond because elsewhere it is said to be 'clear as crystal' (21:11). *Carnelian* (or 'sardius' – KJV) was a red stone, and could also have been a ruby. Jasper, carnelian and *emerald* were all precious and costly. The flashes of light from such precious stones are an appropriate symbol of the divine presence, at once restrained as regards detail, but clear as regards majesty. It is interesting to note that sardius and jasper are the first and last of the twelve precious stones in the high priest's breastplate, each of which was inscribed with the name of one of the tribes of Israel (Exod 28:17-21).

Like all apocalypses, the vision overwhelms the reader with a sense of the majesty and awe of God, and serves as a forceful reminder that God, and not any earthly ruler or power, is sovereign over the whole universe and that he alone is worthy of worship.

The throne of God is the focal point of the stage. In both the tent of meeting and the temple in the OT, God's throne was the lid of the ark of the covenant between the worshipping cherubim. The ark stood in the inner part of the sanctuary (the holy of holies). What John sees here is thus the open sanctuary.

4:4-11 God's creatures worship him

In apocalyptic literature, numbers are usually symbolic. Thus the *twenty-four elders* (**4:4**) probably represent the people of God, symbolized by the twelve tribes of Israel and the twelve apostles. They would also remind Jewish readers of the twenty-four orders of Levites appointed to prophesy and praise in the temple (1 Chr 25).

The semicircular arrangement of the *thrones* for the elders around the central throne is similar to that of the Jewish Sanhedrin and the physical phenomena proceeding from the throne express God's power and majesty (Exod 19:16-19). The *seven lamps* (**4:5**) represent the Spirit of

God, as did the seven-branched lampstand in the tabernacle (Exod 25:31-40; Zech 4:2). The *sea of glass* is like the bronze basin in the tabernacle (**4:6a**; Exod 30:17-21) – a symbol of that purity without which man cannot approach God.

The *four living creatures* represent all creation and their *eyes* God's intimate knowledge of all his works (**4:6b**; Ezek 1:5-21). The creatures, one like a lion, one like an ox, one like an eagle and the last with the face of a man, lead the heavenly entourage in continual worship of God. A rabbinic saying says: 'The mightiest among the birds is the eagle, the mightiest among the domestic animals is the bull, the mightiest among the beasts is the lion, and the mightiest among all is man.' The four forms suggest whatever is noblest, strongest, wisest, and swiftest in the natural world, including humankind, is represented before the throne, taking its part in fulfilling the divine will, and worshipping the divine majesty.

We are familiar with the words of worship in the hymn setting: Holy, Holy, Holy, Lord God Almighty (**4:8**; see also Isa 6:3). The twenty-four elders lay their crowns before the throne (**4:10**) and praise the Lord God as creator because he alone is the source of life (**4:11**; 1:8; Pss 33:6-9; 102:25; 136:5-9). Liturgical elements such as these rituals and hymns occur frequently in the book of Revelation. What strikes us is the all-encompassing participation of the worshippers. Worship is more than words. It can be expressed in a variety of ways as long as the focal point is worshipping God and acknowledging his absolute Lordship.

5:1-14 The scroll and Lamb in heaven

Chapter 5 is a pivotal chapter that introduces us to scenes and characters in heaven. Contrary to what we might expect after the majestic introduction, a weak creature with no mark of a victorious triumph, but only the marks of its own slaughter, is the agent of God's purpose.

The chapter starts with John seeing a scroll in the hand of God. The scroll is sealed to guarantee its authenticity and to keep its contents secret. It contains the destiny of the world, the purposes of God for all creation (see Ezek 2:9-10; Dan 10:21). As in many apocalyptic writings, the course of history is already determined. However, the heavenly council is at an impasse because no one in the universe has been found who is able to break the seven seals and open the scroll. The dramatic tension of the scene is heightened by John's beginning to weep (**5:4**). Then, one of the elders informs him that there is indeed one who can open the scroll – the Messiah, described as *the Lion of the tribe of Judah* (**5:5a**; Gen 49:9-10) and *the Root of David* (**5:5b**; 22:16; Isa 11:1, 10; Jer 23:5; 33:15). In Jewish apocalyptic literature, the lion was often used as a symbol of the conquering Messiah.

John looks for the mighty Lion, but all he sees is a *Lamb looking as if it had been slain* (**5:6**), standing in the centre of the throne court. This vision links the sacrificial death of Christ to the OT Passover lamb (Exod 12:5-6; Isa 53:7; John 1:29, 36; Acts 8:32; 1 Pet 1:19). The slain Lamb is the crucified Christ. But this Lamb is more than a victim; he is also powerful and conquering. The Lamb has *seven horns*. In the OT, a horn is a symbol of strength (Deut 33:17) and seven is the number of perfection. Thus the *seven horns* indicate the perfect or absolute power of the Lamb. He is completely adequate for any situation. He also has *seven eyes*, which are explained as *the seven spirits of God sent out into all the earth*. This is probably not a reference to the Holy Spirit, but rather to the omniscience of the Lamb. The *seven eyes* denote perfection of seeing: nothing escapes his eyes (2 Chr 16:9; Zech 4:10).

John uses all these symbols to tell his readers that Christ, of the tribe of Judah and the line of David, is supremely powerful and all-knowing, and that he has won his victory by his atoning and sacrificial death on the cross. There is a striking combination of the utmost power and the utmost self-giving. As Revelation emphasizes, martyrdom is the means of conquering for both Christ and his followers.

The Lamb's act calls forth a hymn of praise from the living creatures and elders (5:8-12). During the hymn, the elders act as priests by offering up *bowls full of incense*, representing the *prayers of the saints* (**5:8**; Ps 141:2). These prayers are petitions similar to those of the martyrs who call on God to judge those who killed them (6:10) and of the redeemed, whose prayers are immediately followed by the trumpets of God's judgment (8:3-5).

Previously the living creatures and the elders sang a hymn to God (4:11), but now they sing a *new song* (**5:9**), unlike anything sung before in heaven. Jesus Christ has introduced the new era of the kingdom of God (Isa 42:9-10) and the hosts of heaven sing his praise. His sacrifice on the cross shows that he is worthy of such honour (4:10-11). Through his death, he *purchased men for God*. The image here is of freeing slaves, as when God liberated Israel from Egypt to become the free people of God in the land of promise. It also points to the greater emancipation for life eternal in the kingdom of God that has been accomplished for all humanity at the cost of the Lamb's blood. The redeemed have become *a kingdom and priests to serve our God* (**5:10**), so fulfilling the vocation to which the ancient people of God were called (Exod 19:6).

Believers, as Jesus' disciples, are called to imitate our master. We need to learn humility from how Christ is introduced to the human race as the slain Lamb, and must learn to die to ourselves and take up our cross and follow him in all aspects of our life (Luke 9:23). This includes such small details as how we wish to be introduced as conference speakers or how we expect members of our congregations to address us. Titles can mean too much to us.

Next, John sees *thousands upon thousands and ten thousands times ten thousands* of angels surrounding the throne (**5:11**). This vision is similar to Daniel's vision of the countless multitudes before 'the Ancient of Days' (Dan 7:9-10). The imagery suggests the infinite honour and power of the one who is at the centre of it all and whose praises are sung in **5:12** – the Lamb.

Whereas the first hymn in this scene is sung only to God (4:10-11), and the next two are songs of praise to the Lamb (5:9-10, 12), the last hymn in **5:13-14** is a grand finale in which all of God's creatures in heaven and earth and in the sea unite in praise to both God the Father and God the Son (5:13; 7:12; Phil 2:6-11). The number of singers has increased from twenty-eight in 5:8 to *every creature in all creation* (5:13). The imagination is staggered by the numbers!

6:1-8:1 Seven Seals in Seven Scenes

When the Lamb has taken the scroll from the hand of God (**6:1**), he begins to undo the seals, and as he breaks them one by one, angels come forth and execute the appointed judgments. The opening of the seven seals (6:1-8:1) is followed by a series of woes marked by the blowing of seven trumpets (8:2-11:18). The woe of the seventh trumpet is followed by the seven bowls of the wrath of God (15:5-16:21).

In the 'seals' section, John speaks of the following disasters in vivid and imaginative language: war, civil dissent, famine, plague, persecution and earthquakes. The 'trumpets' and 'bowls' sections contain little more than a repetition of these calamities. Because John writes in such different ways about all these woes, we can easily overlook how closely the sections resemble each other. We get the impression that the action is moving forward, while for the most part it only repeats itself. One might rightly ask why.

The answer is related to the answer to the question of the place of the seals in the context of Revelation, the church, the history of humankind and the anticipated second coming of Christ. The Lamb is said to open the seals in 6:1, 3, 5, 7, 9, and 12 and 8:1. But has the Lamb already opened the seals? Or is he sequentially opening them? Or will he open them in the future? Different answers to these difficult questions have resulted in many different interpretations of Revelation.

• Some believe that the events accompanying the opening of the seals took place during the Roman Empire. They argue that all the events described in Revelation belong exclusively to the first century when the church was being battered by emperor worship and persecution. All the prophecies in the book are believed to have been fulfilled with the fall of Jerusalem in AD 70, or at least with the fall of Rome in AD 476. The difficulty with this view is that Christ had not returned by these dates, yet his second coming is the book's climax and destination.

- Others hold that these events began to unfold with the inception of the church and will continue as the seals are opened, one by one, until the consummation of history. Revelation is then treated as a forecast of world history from Christ's ascension on. Different passages have been identified as referring to Charlemagne, the French Revolution, various Roman Catholic popes, Mussolini, the European Union and so on. There are enormous disagreements, however, about who equals what. There is also the problem that all these historical interpretations change from age to age, and that they are invariably Eurocentric.
- Still others believe that none of the seals have yet been opened, and that they will only be opened in the final hour of tribulation, just before the return of Christ. They read chapters 4–22 as a guide to what will happen just before and after Christ's return. The problem with this view is that it robs the book of Revelation of its relevance to the readers of John's day for whom it was written.
- Others argue that Revelation is not concerned with historical events in any particular era of church history, but deals with timeless principles in the war between good and evil. The strength of the view is that it recognizes the universal application of Christ's message to the churches, but it overlooks the fact that Revelation was specifically and clearly written to the existing churches of the first century.
- Finally, there is the 'apocalyptic' position, which sees Revelation as focusing on the suffering and persecution of God's people in light of the totality of human history. Since the casting down of Satan to earth, God's creation and his people have been targets of Satan's attacks, and this situation will continue until the second coming of Christ. Writers of apocalypses move backward and forward in human history, and so the disasters recorded in Revelation (seals, trumpets and bowls) should not be squeezed into an artificial chronology.

This last position is the one adopted in this commentary. Revelation is an apocalypse and must be read, studied and interpreted by the rules of that genre. Thus John's account of the seals (and trumpets and bowls) must be read as a working out in detail of the apocalyptic idea that the second coming of Christ will be preceded by periodic historical disasters, which will affect the whole present order in one way or another.

Although John is confident that the Lord Jesus Christ will soon come back and bring ultimate deliverance from this evil world and judgment on it, he does not want to delude his Christian readers with hopes that may be premature. Nothing in the book is more remarkable than the grim honesty with which the writer faces the situation before him. Seeing believers persecuted, he warns them that they must expect periods of sorrow and desolation just as God's

people of previous generations did. And in the midst of all suffering, they should remain faithful to God. He encourages them to face martyrdom with endurance and with the anticipation of joining fellow-martyrs already in the eternal presence of God. Behind the mysteries and the judgments of life on earth, there is the directing hand of the eternal, all-powerful and all-knowing God.

6:1-2 Act II, Scene 1: The rider on the white horse

With the opening of the seals, the scene shifts from heaven to events on earth. A pattern emerges, with a rider on a horse appearing as each of the first four seals is broken. The first to appear is a victorious rider on a *white horse* (**6:2**). Some commentators have identified the rider as Jesus Christ, but the problem with this view is that since the Lamb is the one opening the seals in heaven, he cannot also be one of the riders. Moreover, theologically it would be inappropriate to have an angelic being, a creature, command Christ, the Creator, to do things (6:1). It is thus more likely that this rider, like the riders on the other three horses, is a symbol of the antichrist and the forces of evil and destruction. He may be contrasted with 'Faithful and True', the different rider on a white horse who appears in 19:11-16 and who 'judges and makes war' with justice. The rider in 6:2 is neither faithful nor true, and he wages war simply for the sake of conquest.

While the vision in 6:2 would be sobering for first-century believers, they could take courage in knowing that the Lamb had, for his own beneficent ends, permitted their suffering. So they could trust that despite the seeming victory of the evil one (in their case, through the Roman Empire), they were conquerors in Christ the victor, even if they faced martyrdom (17:14).

6:3-4 Act II, Scene 2: The rider on the red horse

The second horse is more sinister. He rides on a *fiery red* steed whose colour symbolizes slaughter (**6:4**; 2 Kgs 3:22-23). Its colour matches that of the dragon, the devil that persecutes the woman in 12:3, but is ultimately destroyed. First-century Christians may have been reminded of Nero's slaughter of Christians, the martyrdom of Antipas (2:13), or those slain under Domitian's persecutions. But other Christians will know of other slaughters.

6:5-6 Act II, Scene 3: The rider on the black horse

The opening of the third seal heralds the rider on the *black horse* (**6:5**), a colour also used to describe the conditions when the sixth seal is opened and the sun turns black (6:12). The rider holds *a pair of scales*. Elsewhere in the NT this term is translated as 'yoke', and is used metaphorically of a burden laid upon a person: like slavery (Gal 5:1; 1 Tim 6:1), some religious requirements (Acts 15:10), or of the 'yoke' of Christ, which is 'easy and light' (Matt 11:29-30).

Thus while the reference here may be to the scales used for weighing wheat, it is equally possible that it is a metaphor for subjugation to the forces of death-dealing hunger. The prices given for wheat and barley in **6:6** are exceedingly high and may reflect shortages.

6:7-8 Act II, Scene 4: The rider on the pale horse

The fourth seal reveals a rider on a *pale horse,* who is given the name *Death and Hades* (**6:8**). He probably represents death by pestilence or plague. While some may have died of plague in John's time, it is likely that this vision includes all pestilences that have already taken place (for example, in Egypt at the time of the exodus), and those that will take place throughout human history (including HIV/AIDS). As already stated, looking both backward and forward in human history is one of the characteristics of apocalyptic literature.

6:9-11 Act II, Scene 5: The prayer of the martyrs

The fifth seal changes the pattern, and we no longer see horsemen, but rather martyred saints under the altar crying out for justice upon those who killed them (**6:9-10**). They are told to wait a little longer till their fellow servants are also killed (**6:11**). These martyrs are referred to as 'all who have been killed on the earth' (18:24); 'all who refused to worship the image [of the beast and were] killed' (13:15); and 'those who had been beheaded because of their testimony for Jesus' (20:4). These martyred saints are now in heaven (2 Cor 5:6, 8).

Revelation does not dwell on how a loving God can allow so much suffering and even martyrdom. The book leaves us with the problem of Christian suffering, trials and Satan's activities, but encourages us to recognize that God is the one in control, and allows suffering to happen in this life.

6:12-17 Act II, Scene 6: Cosmic catastrophes

After the Lamb has broken the sixth seal, John witnesses certain signs heralding the imminent Day of the Lord (**6:12-14**; see Isa 2:12-21; 13:9-13; Jer 4:23-26; Joel 2:31; 3:15; Zeph 1:14-18; Matt 24:29). The scene in these verses, whether taken literally or figuratively, is one of catastrophes for all the inhabitants of the earth, regardless of their wealth or social class (**6:15-17**). The plea of the people for the rocks and mountains to fall on them occurs in Hosea in the context of God's judgment (6:16; Hos 10:8). Jesus predicted the same reaction from the inhabitants of Jerusalem when God's judgment would fall on them (Luke 23:30). In Revelation, God's wrath on all who refuse to repent of their sinful ways is presented as a past, present and future historical reality (Rom 1:18-25; 2:5). The Bible is consistent in depicting God's punishment of evil and sin from the beginning of human history until its consummation.

7:1-17 First interlude: The sealing of God's people

Between seals six and seven is the first interlude in the drama. In contrast to the awful scenes of the wrath of God portrayed in chapter 6, chapter 7 is a description of the sealing of God's people. It starts with a vision of *four angels standing at the four corners of the earth* (**7:1**). We should not understand this as a statement about the shape of the earth but as an assurance that the four angels watch over the whole world, and none of it is beyond their control. Their function is to hold back *the four winds of the earth* to preventing harmful winds from blowing *on the land or on the sea or on any tree.* The 'winds' may be another way of referring to the four horsemen of the first four seals (6:1-8), for in Zechariah four horses are explicitly interpreted as 'the four spirits [literally 'winds'] of heaven' (Zech 6:5; see also Isa 19:1; 66:15). Whereas Zechariah associates the winds with heaven, stressing their subjection to God in heaven, John refers to them as *winds of the earth* because their destructive activity is connected with the earth. Winds are a natural symbol of destruction (Jer 4:11-12; 49:36).

As is typical of apocalyptic literature, this vision takes us back to answer the question What is the fate of believers during the terrible happenings described in chapter 6? The answer to the question is revealed in the vision of *another angel coming up from the east* (**7:2**). The east is where the day dawns and light is first seen, and thus it often symbolizes a source of blessing. The Garden of Eden was located in the east (Gen 2:8), it was from this direction that the glory came to the temple (Ezek 43:2) and the wise men who came with the news that the Christ was born came from the east (Matt 2:1-2).

The angel has *the seal of the living God.* A seal was basically a mark of ownership (Eph 1:13-14). Here it marks those sealed as God's and thus preserves them from the destruction that will fall on the world (6:1-8; Exod 12:23; Ezek 9:1-6). God's own bear his mark elsewhere in this book (9:4; 14:1; 22:4). This angel shouts to the other four and commands them not to hurt earth, sea or trees until God's servants are sealed on their foreheads (**7:3**). Even when facing persecution and martyrdom, believers can be certain that no plague or persecution can destroy them spiritually but that they will live in God's presence for ever because they are his own possession (3:10; Rom 8:35-39).

The seal on God's servants can be contrasted with the mark of the beast, which identifies those who bear it as beast worshippers and thus objects of God's irreversible wrath (13:16-17; 14:9-11). By contrast, those who have the seal of God are his servants, who worship him with utter devotion and are the objects of his abiding grace. They will not be deluded by the beast (19:20).

God's restraint of the forces of destruction is an important thread that runs through the book of Revelation. Every moment of earth's history is made to serve God's redeeming purpose. The four winds cannot blow and vent their rage as they like, but only as they serve the purposes of God.

John hears the number of those permanently sealed: *144,000 from all the tribes of Israel* (**7:4**). But who are these people? Commentators disagree about whether the 144,000 and the great multitude referred to in 7:9 are the same or different groups, whether the former refers to a literal or spiritual Israel, and whether either or both groups are composed of martyrs. There is little evidence to decide these points, and we must be guided by our understanding of the book of Revelation as a whole. As we have already pointed out, Revelation is an apocalyptic book and not simply an account of the end times.

The problem with interpreting the 144,000 as Jewish believers is that the *great multitude* in **7:9a** also represents those who are saved, but it is said to be composed of people *from every nation, tribe, people and language.* Why would this multitude be saved without sealing, while only the Jews are sealed for protection?

Others argue that the word 'Israel' in 7:4 refers to all believers, regardless of their nationality. They point out that Abraham is 'the father of all who believe' (Rom 4:11), and that believers are thus his children (Gal 3:7) and constitute 'the Israel of God' (Gal 6:16). Believers are the true Jews (2:9; 3:9; see also Rom 2:28-29), the ones God calls his 'very own' people (Titus 2:14) and 'the circumcision' (Phil 3:3).

It could be argued that the specific reference to the twelve tribes in **7:5-8** means that these people are literally of Jewish descent. However, John speaks of the new Jerusalem as the spiritual home of all believers, and it has on its gates the names of the twelve tribes (21:12). There is thus good reason for seeing the 144,000 as all believers. This number is made up of twelve times 12,000, a number that combines the 'twelve' that represents the church (Matt 19:28; Jas 1:1) and the thousand that represents a great number.

This great multitude 'from every nation, tribe, people and language' are clothed in the *white robes* (**7:9b**) that symbolize salvation. 'White' is also the colour of victory, while the *palm branches* they hold were often emblems of triumph (Matt 21:5-8). They are identified by the angel as those *who have come out of the great tribulation* (**7:14**) and who now worship in God's *temple* (**7:15**). God will *spread his tent over them,* meaning that his presence will be amongst them (Exod 40:34-38). Never again will these people endure torment (**7:16**). They will enjoy the supreme protection of the living God himself (Ps 91:1-2). The graciousness of God to those who follow him is brought out in **7:17**, a verse that speaks of a tenderness and comfort not often seen in this book.

8:1 Act II, Scene 7: Silence in heaven

John makes effective use of the element of suspense. After each set of six calamities he withholds the seventh, with a dark hint that when it does come, it will be overwhelming (**8:1**; 10:7; 16:17).

The opening of the seventh seal causes silence in heaven (8:1). The seemingly inevitable process is interrupted, and the pause enables reflection on what is happening, even in heaven. Sometimes silence and reflection are an appropriate response in the midst of the tumult of life. The words of a Shona proverb from Zimbabwe apply here: 'What we cannot speak about we must pass over in silence.' Sometimes, it is tempting to try to explain and justify everything we read in Revelation, when in reality the right response should be silence, awe, fear and dread.

8:2-11:18 Act III: Vision of the Seven Angels – Announcement of God's Wrath

Stage Setting: The stage shows an open sanctuary. Prominently displayed are the altars of sacrifice and of incense. An angel carries a golden censer of incense toward the former as the curtain rises (**8:3**). Before the throne are also seven angels, each with a trumpet in hand (**8:2**). Once again, we are in a worship setting, this time one where the prayers of the saints are heard and acted on (**8:4-6**).

Acts III and IV parallel acts V and VI, and give more details of the events first presented in act II, scene 6. Acts III and V show how believers weather the storm throughout human history, while acts IV and VI depict the failure of non-believers to withstand God's judgment. The events described here as initiated by trumpets may be the same as those initiated by the opening of the seals since their targets are identical (compare 6:1-8; 8:7-12). Similar catastrophes are described in 6:12-17, in this act, and in 16:2-9 in act V, scenes 1-4. Ever since the casting out of the devil from heaven, life on earth has been characterized by cosmic catastrophes and human suffering (Rom 8:20-22), all leading toward the day of final consummation (Isa 2:10-21; 13:9-13; Joel 2:31; 3:15; Zeph 1:14-18; Matt 24:29). In Revelation, God's wrath is presented as both a present historical reality as well as a future judgment.

The first four trumpets (8:7-12) affect four areas of God's creation: earth, sea, fresh water and the heavens (compare 14:7). These are limited judgments aimed at producing repentance (9:20-21). In general, it will be noted that only *a third* of anything is affected. The plagues mentioned in scenes 1, 2 and 4 find their origin in the account of the exodus (Exod 9:23-26; 7:20-21; 10:21).

8:5-7 Act III, Scene 1: Hail and fire fall on the earth

This scene is preceded by *peals of thunder, rumblings, flashes of lightning and an earthquake* (**8:5**). The first angel blows his trumpet, and *hail and fire mixed with blood* rain on earth (**8:7**). A third of the earth, including a third of its plant life, is consumed. Indeed, all the green grass is burnt off. Revelation's grim picture of ecological catastrophe might seem to underline the belief of some that Christianity is not merely world-denying but also indifferent to the cosmos, which is destined for destruction. There are hints in passages like 11:18 and 19:2, however, that the destruction of the earth is a consequence of the sinful behaviour of humankind (Gen 3; Rom 8:20-21).

8:8-9 Act III, Scene 2: A mountain cast into the sea

The second angel blows his trumpet, and *something like a huge mountain, all ablaze* falls into the sea (**8:8**). As a result, a third part of the sea turns bloody, a third of the creatures living in the sea die, and a third of the ships on the sea are destroyed.

8:10-11 Act III, Scene 3: A star falls on rivers and springs

The third angel blows his trumpet and there falls from the sky *a great star burning like a torch.* (**8:10**; see Isa 14:12). For John, a *star* means an angel (1:20; 9:1-2). Whereas the other plagues do not directly affect people, in this passage, the fallen angel is identified with *Wormwood,* a poisonous plant. Its fall affects a third of all rivers and springs of water. So, a third of all waters are poisoned and many creatures die (Jer 9:15; 23:15).

8:12-13 Act III, Scene 4: The sun, moon and stars darken

The fourth angel blows his trumpet, and a third part of the sun, of the moon and of the stars are affected. The result is that daytime is diminished by a third and nighttime likewise.

The effects of the first four trumpet blasts have been terrible, but the effects of the next three will be worse, as they are introduced as 'Woes' (**8:13**). This warning to all people is the negative side of the gospel message (Luke 6:24-26), intended to bring all people to repentance (9:20-21), and is the final demonstration of God's desire to see all people saved (1 Tim 2:3-4).

9:1-12 Act III, Scene 5 (Woe 1): The Abyss is opened

In 7:1-17 we saw the multitude of those who had 'a seal on [their] foreheads'. But we had not yet been told the nature of the 'great tribulation' (7:14) through which they had to pass. John begins to depict this for us here. It is to be a period during which an angel (the *star* of **9:1-2** will permit the release from *the Abyss* of an immoral destructive power, under its leader *Abaddon* or *Apollyon,* names that both mean

'Destroyer' (**9:11**). Spiritual warfare rages from the time Satan or the devil, the destroyer, was thrown out of heaven until the second coming of Christ.

The *locusts* described in 9:3-10 (like the frogs in 16:13) symbolize a demonic force. The imagery of an army of locusts advancing like a cloud, darkening the heavens and sounding like the rattle of chariots, goes back to Joel's vision of an army of locusts that came on Israel as a judgment from God (Joel 1:6; 2:4-10). This, together with the fact that they do not eat plants (**9:4a**), shows that these are no ordinary locusts. Nor are they simply a physical plague, like the locust of Moses' or Joel's day. What these locust-like beings attack is the human spirit. They inflict a non-fatal injury on the beast worshippers who do not have the seal of God on their foreheads (**9:4b**). The locusts are demonic or evil forces (as with the first four trumpets) out of the Abyss from whom the true people of God are spiritually protected. So severe is the torment they inflict that their victims will seek death (**9:5-6**; see Job 3:21; Jer 8:3; Hos 10:8).

This graphic picture of the immoral influences of demonic forces that are constantly at work also reminds us of the limitations of the power of evil. The demons can exercise only the power that is allowed (*given* – 9:5) them by God (see 1 Sam 16:14). On this occasion they have power to torment, but not to kill (Job 1:12; 2:6). The evil of the locusts never gets out of hand, but is under God's sovereign control, and the period of its activity is limited to *five months* (**9:10**), that is, a very short time in the light of eternity.

9:13-21 Act III, Scene 6 (Woe 2): Release of four angels

The action of this scene is set in motion by *a voice coming from … the golden altar* of incense (**9:13**; 8:3). The exactness of the time element suggested by the reference to the *hour and day and month and year* (**9:15**) indicates that the entire drama is within the plan of God (Mark 13:32). The four angels here are those who stood at the four corners of earth in 7:1, where they were presented as the guardians of the earth's four winds. Here they are presented as leaders of a vast army (**9:16**).

These horrific images of destruction look back to the exodus plagues (Exod 7–10) and also forward to eschatological destruction depicted by John in 16:9. The exodus motif that is so prevalent in Revelation drives home the point that even after such devastating plagues, the rest of the people do not repent (**9:20-21**). The people described here respond like Pharaoh. They continue in their idolatrous and rebellious ways. The need for repentance is an insistent theme in the letters to the churches (2:5, 16, 21-22; 3:3, 19). It is as if humanity is brought face to face with the full horror of the wickedness it has created, and yet will do nothing to prevent the consequences of its actions.

10:1-11:13 Second interlude: The little scroll, two witnesses
As was the case between the scenes of the sixth and seventh seals (7:1-17), John inserts an interlude between the sixth and seventh trumpets to provide reassurance to the faithful that they will not be spiritually destroyed by the eschatological woes. This interlude contains two complementary visions: one, an account of a call to John to prophesy (10:1-11) and the other an account of the witness of two figures who prophesy for a time before being killed by the beast from the Abyss (11:1-13).

10:1-11 THE LITTLE SCROLL For the first and last time the seer is drawn away from his observer's corner to the very centre of the stage. This is akin to bringing a member of the audience on stage to act in a play. In **10:1-2**, John sees a *mighty angel* coming down and standing with one foot on the sea and the other on land. The physical description of the angel owes much to Daniel 10:4-6 and the scene draws also upon the vision in Daniel 12 in which two angels appear to Daniel, 'one on this bank of the river and one on the opposite bank' (Dan 12:5). The angel speaks like a roaring lion, causing the seven thunders to break forth. The seven thunders deliver a message that John is about to write down when he is told to *seal up* the message, that is, to keep it secret (**10:4**; 1:19; 22:10; Dan 8:26; 12:4, 9). This refusal to reveal the message of the seven thunders is a way of saying that God's purposes and plans are not all revealed because God is beyond full human comprehension.

Like the contents of the sealed scroll in chapter 5, what the seven thunders utter remains a *mystery* (**10:7**) and thus forms no part of this book of prophecy, which is very much a public text (22:10). However, this mystery will be fulfilled after the seventh trumpet is blown, marking 11:15 as a crucial moment in the narrative. The angel reveals that the mystery which God had proclaimed by *his servants, the prophets* is moving to its climax (10:7; compare Dan 9:6; Amos 3:7; Zech 1:6).

The angel then raises his right hand to heaven and swears by *him who lives forever and ever* (**10:5-6**; Dan 12:7) that there will be no more delay. The time for the fulfilment of God's purposes is near. Soon God will act decisively and will triumph over the evil forces. The cry 'How long?' of saints facing persecution and martyrdom would be answered (Pss 6:3; 13:1; 94:3).

For John, *eating* the scroll is a reinforcement of his commission as prophet. The *scroll is sweet as honey,* but makes his *stomach sour* (**10:9-10**). This scroll, like that of chapters 4–5, contains God's plan for all creation, which John is to make known. *Eating* the scroll is symbolic of taking in the message, of 'consuming' God's word (see Ezek 3:1-2), so that God's message is now John's message. The scroll is both sour and sweet, because it contains judgment and mercy, punishment and blessing. A close parallel with this scroll is found in Daniel 12. There Daniel is told to keep

the 'scroll' or 'book' sealed 'until the time of the end' (Dan 12:4). Now, however, the book is unsealed because there can be no more delay (10:6). The long-awaited time of God's vindication has arrived.

11:1-13 THE TWO WITNESSES John is next commanded to measure the *temple of God and the altar* (**11:1**). In the Bible, measuring has many metaphorical meanings. It may refer to the promise of restoration and rebuilding, with an emphasis on extension or enlargement (Jer 31:38-39; Zech 1:16), or it may mark something for destruction (2 Sam 8:2; 2 Kgs 21:13; Isa 28:17; Lam 2:8; Amos 7:7-9). John's *measuring* of the temple of God, the altar and the worshippers seems to be similar to the *sealing* of believers that protects them from spiritual destruction (7:1-8). Similarly, in 21:15-17 John depicts an angel measuring the heavenly city with a golden rod, apparently to mark it and its inhabitants off from spiritual harm and defilement. As with the sealing, the measuring does not symbolize preservation from physical harm, but the guarantee that none of the faithful worshipers of God will perish even though they may suffer physical death at the hand of the beast (13:7).

Ezekiel was told to 'describe the temple to the people of Israel that they may be ashamed of their sins' (Ezek 43:10). The elaborate description and measurement in Ezekiel 40–48 indicate the glory and holiness of God in Israel's midst and convict Israel of their sin of defiling his sanctuary. Ezekiel was instructed to exclude from the sanctuary 'the foreigners uncircumcised in heart and flesh' (Ezek 44:5-9). Likewise, John is here told not to measure the *outer court* (**11:2**). Those who do not worship the true God are to be excluded from spiritual security and God's blessing. Prophetic ministry calls for a clear separation between those who live for God and those who have defiled themselves with the idolatry of the beast.

The focus now moves to the persecution of the *two witnesses* who represent the believing community in every age (**11:3**). The imagery here is taken from Zechariah 4. The two witnesses are referred to as *two olive trees* or *two lampstands* full of oil, that is, God's Spirit (**11:4**). They witness in the courtyard outside the sanctuary or in the great city, *figuratively called Sodom and Egypt* where *their Lord was crucified* (**11:8**, the only reference to the means of Christ's death in the whole book). In other words, they witness in the evil world, the place of rebellion and persecution.

These witnesses have the same powers as Moses and Elijah (**11:6**; see Exod 7:17-19; 1 Kgs 17:1) and their ministry is variously described as testimony or prophecy (11:3, 6-7). Chapters 10 and 11 issue a direct call to believers to participate in God's ministry as prophets rather than merely as passive spectators. In the midst of superhuman forces, the church as a whole has a prophetic role.

The fate of the two witnesses, who are killed by the beast who *comes up from the Abyss* (**11:7**; 9:11; 13:2; Dan 7:3), reminds us that throughout history God's people are not spared from suffering or tribulation (see 7:14). Prophets, as witnesses of God can expect suffering and even death. Whenever Christians resist evil, they will come under pressure to conform. If they refuse to conform, they may find themselves the target of the anger and retribution of those who seek to maintain the world as it is. Thus the people to whom the witnesses were commanded to prophesy rejoice when they see the corpses lying unburied (**11:9-10**). Those who scorn them are referred to as *inhabitants of the earth,* a phrase with negative connotations (11:10; 6:10; 8:13; 13:8, 12, 14; 17:2, 8).

However, conquest by the beast cannot overcome the true conquest of the Lamb, Jesus Christ. The two witnesses are brought back to life by the *breath of life from God* (**11:11**). That action is followed by a great voice from heaven telling them *Come up here* (**11:12**), the same command that was given to John by the voice 'like a trumpet' (4:1; 10:4; 12:10; 14:13). The ascent of the witnesses to heaven in a cloud echoes the ascension of their Lord (Acts 1:9), and their enemies see them vindicated. A *severe earthquake* follows (**11:13a**; 6:12; 8:5; 16:18), similar to the one which occurred at the resurrection of Jesus (Matt 28:2). The people respond to the earthquake by giving *glory to the God of heaven* (**11:13b**), although they do not truly turn to him. At this point, the second woe has passed.

11:14-18 Act III, Scene 7: Worship in heaven

The absence of any specific mention of the third woe, other than the statement that it *is coming soon* (**11:14**), may be an indication that the final consummation is still awaited. The readers stand in the midst of the drama of human history. It is partly complete, and we are, as it were, offered a preview of the ending. In the midst of the trials and tribulations, we await the climax. We can only watch, wait, witness and worship and not be led astray (Matt 25:1-13; Mark 13:9, 32-37).

The sounding of the seventh trumpet is also related to the events that surround the final consummation of history. But to declare all this now would mean the end of the drama. So what follows next is praise of God by the twenty-four elders. Act III closes as it began, with a picture of the redeemed at prayer as they face the thought of persecution in the last times (**11:15-18**). Praying is one way of staying focused on God when we are going through difficult times.

11:19-15:4 Act IV: Vision of the Church Triumphant

Stage Setting: The setting is like those in acts II and III, except that the sanctuary of God, which is in heaven, is now wholly opened to view. As a result, the ark of the covenant within the sanctuary becomes visible, including its cover, which was regarded as God's throne. Whereas act III the worshipping believers were at the centre of the stage, the view of the ark shows that act IV will deal with God's answer to his people's prayers.

In this act, we are presented with the great conflict between the forces of good and evil, order and chaos, obedience and disobedience, and loyalty and rebellion throughout human history. Evil powers have always rebelled against God's authority and attempted to thwart his purposes. The suffering of the believers of John's day was not an isolated incident. Their struggle was simply another chapter in the ancient story of chaos versus order, obedience versus disobedience, rebellion versus loyalty. God's prophets were persecuted (Jer 38), and those who announced the first coming of Christ were murdered (Acts 7:52-53). John reminds his readers that by their patient endurance and faithful witness, they are contributing to the ultimate overthrow and defeat of the powers of evil.

In acts I, II, III and V, John primarily uses numbers to mark out each scene (for example, there are seven letters, seven seals, seven trumpets and seven bowls). But in acts IV, VI and VII, each new scene is introduced with the words 'I heard' or 'I saw' or 'He showed me' or 'appeared'. A similar approach is used in Ezekiel, Daniel and other apocalyptic literature, but it is not found in any other NT book. Failure to take note of this simple but crucial literary device will result in loss of direction in reading and understanding the rest of the drama.

11:19-13:1a Act IV, Scene 1: The woman and the dragon

John hears *flashes of lightning, rumblings, peals of thunder, an earthquake and a great hailstorm* (**11:19**). Though the sanctuary has stood open on the stage ever since act II, this is the first time that it has occupied such a prominent position. It is not strange that we have not yet been able to look into this holy place. In the OT, only the current high priest was permitted to look upon the ark of the covenant, once a year. It is extraordinary that John should permit us to gaze within this sanctuary at all, and even more so that he should expose it on his cosmic stage. But through the work of Jesus Christ, 'the curtain of the temple was torn in two from top to bottom' (Matt 27:51), and there is now 'a new and living way opened through the curtain' (Heb 10:20) to the throne of God.

12:1-6 THE WOMAN, HER SON AND THE DRAGON In **12:1** John speaks of the appearance of a great sign in heaven, a pregnant woman *clothed with the sun* (see 10:1), with *the moon under her feet* and a *crown* with *twelve stars* on her head (see 1:16). She is crying out in labour pains (**12:2**; see Isa 66:7). The word used to describe her agony is the same word used to describe the experience of the inhabitants of the world as God's judgment comes upon them (9:5; 14:10-11; 18:7, 10,

15; see also Luke 21:23). Thus the woman is not immune from suffering.

The *male child* to whom she gives birth is clearly the Lord Jesus Christ, for he is the one *who will rule all the nations with an iron sceptre* (**12:5**; 2:27; 19:15; Gen 49:9-10; Ps 2:9).

Another sign appears alongside the first (12:3-6): a great dragon, who is identified as Satan in 12:9 and whose influence on earth is depicted in chapter 13. The dragon is *red* (6:4) and its *seven heads, ten horns and seven crowns* resemble the beast in 13:1 (**12:3**; 5:6; Dan 7:7). Its *tail* sweeps *a third of the stars* to earth (**12:4a**; 6:13; 8:12; Dan 8:10). The dragon stands before the woman, echoing the description of the Lamb and the great multitude that stand in God's presence. But the dragon is not worshipping but threatening to devour the woman's child as soon as it is born (**12:4b**; see Gen 4:7). The dragon fails in his attempt to kill the child, who is snatched away, just as the Lord Jesus Christ was taken up to heaven at his ascension.

The woman is pursued by the dragon and she flees into the *desert* (**12:6**), the place where John will later be taken to see Babylon, represented as a very different woman (17:3-4). This desert should not be seen as a harsh and forbidding place. It is a place that God has prepared for the woman, where she will be *taken care of* (12:6). It is unclear who will take care of her. If it is angels, then there is a parallel to the care Jesus Christ received during his temptation in the desert (Mark 1:13). Hagar, too, found relief in the desert after being ill-treated by Sarah (Gen 16:7; 21:4-19), and the prophet Elijah's life was sustained by God when he fled into the desert to escape Jezebel (1 Kgs 19:1-9).

The flight into the desert also reminds us of Joseph and Mary's fleeing to Egypt with the infant Jesus (Matt 2:13-15). But this woman does not represent Mary specifically but rather the whole community of God's people. Throughout their history, the people of God have lived as 'aliens and strangers' in the desert of a fallen and hostile world, while their true home is in heaven (Heb 11:13-16). Yet while they are in the desert, God continues to nurture them and supply their every need 'according to his glorious riches in Christ Jesus' (Phil 4:19)God never forsakes his own people.

The woman is enabled to survive for 1260 days, otherwise defined in 12:14 as 'a time, times and half a time' and in 13:5 as 'forty-two months', that is, for a short period in comparison with the limitless eternity of peace and freedom that will follow in the new heaven and earth.

12:7-12 War in heaven War breaks out in heaven as Michael and his angels fight against the dragon (**12:7**). This is the only reference to the archangel Michael in the NT, apart from Jude 9. In Daniel, Michael is the angelic protector of the people of God (Dan 10:13-21; 12:1), a role that is assumed by the ascended Christ in the NT (Rom 8:34; 1 John 2:1).

This war, though waged in heaven, will have an enormous effect on human history. The dragon and his angels did not prevail and there was no longer any place for them in heaven. As a result, the dragon, *that ancient serpent called the devil or Satan* was cast down to earth with his angels (**12:8-9a**; Gen 3:1, 14). Historically, this speaks of Satan's fall from his former state.

In the Bible, Satan is portrayed as the arch-enemy of God and his people. His enmity underlies the description of him here as the one *who leads the whole world astray* and *the accuser of our brothers* (**12:9b, 10**). His role as deceiver has already been alluded to in the description of Jezebel (2:20-24). There a local church was threatened with deceit; here it is the whole world (13:14; 19:20; 20:3, 8, 10). As we shall see in chapter 13, deceit is a characteristic of the beast, which works through the political and religious (non-Christian) systems of any society.

Believers can easily fall into Satan's traps, and he is eager to accuse them *before our God day and night* (12:10), in contrast to the day-and-night praise of the four living creatures and the martyrs (4:8; 7:15). In giving Satan this role, Revelation is reflecting an OT understanding of Satan as a heavenly prosecutor (Job 1:6-12; 2:1-7; Zech 3:1). In the NT, Satan, as the 'prince of this world' tempts believers to sin and disobey God (John 12:31;1 Pet 5:8). He even tempted Jesus Christ to sin during his earthly life and ministry (Matt 4:1-11).

But powerful as this enemy is, he has been defeated by Christ at the cross. Believers have overcome him *by the blood of the Lamb and by the word of their testimony,* and because *they did not love their lives so much as to shrink from death* (**12:11b**). The Lamb's blood is linked with the victory of the brethren (**12:11a**; see 1:5; 5:9; 19:13). The *word of their testimony* is in harmony with that of the Lamb (2:13) and provokes the same kind of response (11:7).

A voice is heard in heaven announcing that now *the salvation and the power and the kingdom* have come (12:10). The kingdom is now seen to belong to God and the rule to his Messiah (Dan 7:14; Matt 28:18). In 20:1-4, this kingdom is also related to the binding of Satan 'for a thousand years'.

Because of what Christ has done (**12:12a**), and because his victory extends to the believers, the voice calls on the *heavens* and those who live there to rejoice. The term 'heaven' is found fifty-two times in Revelation, but this is the only place it is used as a plural. Heaven speaks of a permanent home (John 14:1-3; 2 Cor 5:6, 8; Phil 1:21).

While the inhabitants of heaven are the ones called to rejoicing, those on earth whose citizenship is in heaven can rejoice too. Although they suffer grievous troubles on earth, their troubles are temporary and triumph is already being savoured in heaven. But for now there is *woe* for them on *earth* and *sea* (**12:12b**). The devil has come down in great anger, knowing that only a little *time* remains before the

PERSECUTION

The church in Africa has long been familiar with persecution. As long ago as the third century AD, the African church father Tertullian was moved to declare that 'the blood of the martyrs is the seed of the church'. The persecution has continued in modern times in countries like Uganda under President Idi Amin, in Chad under President Tombalbaye, and is still continuing in countries like Ethopia and Eritrea. It flares up sporadically in other countries too. Those who convert from Islam to Christianity often face severe discrimination and sometimes even death.

The main aim of persecution is not to destroy the individuals who are persecuted but to eliminate the faith they profess. Persecutors attempt to force Christians to deny their faith in Jesus Christ in order to dislodge Christ from their lives. Thus the real target of persecution is Jesus Christ (Acts 9:4).

Persecution of believers has a long history. The first recorded example in the OT is the killing of Abel by his brother Cain, which is an example of the struggle between the righteous and the unrighteous (Gen 4:3-8). Others who were persecuted include Joseph (Gen 39:19-20), David (1 Sam 18:9; Ps 119:87, 157, 161), Elijah (1 Kgs 19:1-3) and Jeremiah (Jer 26:10-11). Prophets who stood uncompromisingly for the truth sometimes paid with their lives (2 Chr 36:15-16). During the exile, Daniel, Shadrach, Meshach and Abednego were all tested severely for refusing to worship a heathen king (Dan 3 and 6). Readiness to accept suffering and even death for the truth has been carried forward from Judaism to Christianity.

Persecution Predicted

Jesus repeatedly predicted that his followers would face hostility (Matt 5:10-12; 10:16-23, 34-36; Mark 10:29-30; Luke 6:26; 23:28-31). The reason is that they do not belong to the world but to the Kingdom of God (Matt 5:10-12; Mark 13:9-13; John 16:33). One cannot belong to both at the same time, for they are incompatible. The world does not know God (John 16:1-4; Acts 17:23; Rom 1:18-32) and hates Christ (John 15:20). We are thus rejected because we are not members of the same family; we do not share a common father.

Jesus not only expected his followers to be prepared to face persecution but was also prepared to face it himself. He set the example for those who follow him. As John 15:18-25 makes clear, if our Master endured persecution, why should we expect less?

In the Acts of the Apostles, we read of believers being imprisoned, beaten or killed for their faith (Acts 5:17-18, 40; 6:8-7:59). Persecution is also mentioned in the book of Revelation (Rev 1:9; 2:13; 6:9). But God promises that he will avenge the martyred (Rev 19:2). In the midst of persecution, the Christian's vocation is to endure, for through Christ victory is already won (John 16:33).

Persecution is an inescapable part of the true Christian's journey of faith. Yet when it comes, we often ask, "Why me, Lord"? Such questioning can lead to self-pity, doubting and complaining. This response blurs our ability to perceive God's purpose in allowing the adversity, because we are forgetting that God is sovereign. He has the right to rule the universe that he made for his own glory, and we are like clay in the potter's hands. Nothing either good or bad catches God by surprise (Isa 45:7). God can even turn bad circumstances around so that they work for our long-term good (Rom 8:28). Balak's attempt to get Balaam to curse Israel is a good example of this, for instead of curses the Israelites received blessings (Num 22, 23 and 24). No one can disrupt God's promise to his children.

Persecution Refines

James makes the point that persecution has a refining effect on the believer, just as fire purifies gold. Under persecution, our faith is put to the test. He reminds us that trials are inevitable, can take various forms and may arise when we least expect them. We are called to respond properly and to endure the suffering, which will produce fruit such as maturity and completeness in our Christian lives (Jas 1:2-8).

Christians should neither be surprised (John 15:20; 1 Pet 4:12) nor afraid (Isa 41:10-14) when persecuted. Instead they are to rejoice (Jas 1:2). It is a privilege to share in Christ's suffering (Matt 5:11; 1 Pet 4:13-16). Like the apostles, they should see suffering for him as a mark of honour (Acts 5:41) and pray for boldness in the face of persecution (Acts 4:24-30).

Believers are called to pray for their persecutors (Matt 5:44), and even bless them rather than wishing them evil (Rom 12:14). Those who are persecuted are to commit themselves to God (1 Pet 4:19) and rejoice in spite of their suffering (1 Pet 1:6). Their fellow believers are to pray for them (Acts 12:5) and expect great things to happen instead of doubting (Acts 12:15).

Above all, we should all remember that our adversary only attacks believers who are alive. Being persecuted is a sign that you are alive in Christ.

Elias M. Githuka

second coming. The Greek word translated 'time' carries the implication of 'a suitable time' (see 1:3; 11:18). Not much time remains suitable for the activities of the evil one. The righteous do not suffer persecution because Satan is stronger than God but because he is doing all the harm he can while he can, before God stops him. Satan will not be able to do this for much longer. He is a defeated enemy who has limited time.

12:13-13:1a WAR ON EARTH Furious about his failure to devour the woman's male child and about his defeat by Michael, the dragon (Satan) directs his wrath against the woman herself and the rest of her offspring (**12:13**). This image represents the conflict of good and evil throughout human history. It is an account (in metaphorical language) of the persecution and suffering that has been inflicted on God's people since the fall of the devil to earth.

This passage contains the last mention of the woman who first appeared in 12:6. Here, she simultaneously represents Mary the mother of Jesus, Israel from whom the Messiah came, and the people of God of all ages whose descendants are still being persecuted today.

After giving birth, the woman had fled into the desert to be nourished there. She reappears in these verses, but only to be pursued by the dragon. Thus the defeat of Satan is sandwiched between the two parts of the vision of the woman clothed with the sun. Satan is defeated in heaven and cannot conquer the woman and her offspring on earth in spite of repeated, vigorous persecution. The woman is given *the two wings of a great eagle* (**12:14**; Exod 19:4; Isa 40:31) and escapes again to the desert, where she is taken care of (see 12:6). The wider reference of this symbolic language is to the sanctuary the Lord himself provides for his people throughout human history.

The dragon, now referred to as *the serpent,* pours *water like a river* from his mouth *to sweep her away with the torrent* (**12:15**; compare 9:17-19; 11:5; 16:13). She is protected from *the flood* when the earth comes to help her and swallows the water (**12:16**). The earth rises up, as it were, to aid the woman, against those who destroy the earth (11:18). The devil's anger with the woman leads him *to make war against the rest of her offspring* (**12:17**).

John's vision ends abruptly with Satan standing on the seashore on the brink of the Abyss, that place from which the beast will rise to try the faithfulness of the saints of God (11:7).

13:1b-10 Act IV, Scene 2: The beast from the sea

Scene 1 closed with a view of the dragon standing by the sea. He has been thrown from heaven to earth, and stands poised to unleash his fury against God's faithful believers. Scene 2 opens: *And I saw a beast coming out of the sea* (**13:1a**). The sea, which will disappear in the new creation (21:1), is a symbol of chaos (Gen 1:2; Ps 104:7-9). The king-

doms of the world, representing satanic powers, are also described as beasts that come from the sea (Dan 7:3-7).

This beast is like the dragon in having *ten horns* representing power and *seven heads* (**13:1b**; 12:3) signifying the totality of the underworld's wisdom and understanding. The *ten crowns* speak of the dominion of satanic powers, and the *blasphemous name* on each head reveals this beast's opposition to God. John has made reference to it already in 11:7, where it is described as coming 'up from the Abyss' to fight the community of God. It thus seems that act IV is an elaboration of the events already described in scene 6 of act III.

It is very difficult to imagine an animal like the one John describes here. We need to remember that his aim is not to help us draw the beast but to convey an impression of something indescribably horrible. He uses the symbolism that is a common feature of apocalyptic literature and gives the beast the characteristics of the three beasts described in Daniel 7:4-6 – a leopard, a bear and a lion (**13:2a**). In Daniel 7, these beasts represent various world empires, and John may have been thinking in these terms. But John does not see the beast as having any power of its own. The dragon gives it *his power and his throne and great authority* (**13:2b**), making it a formidable enemy.

John says that *one of the heads ... seemed to have had a fatal wound, but the fatal wound had been healed* (**13:3**). John does not say how the beast received its wound, but in 13:14 we find that it was made *by the sword.* He does not even say whether it received the wound after it came to land or how it came to be healed. John's interest is in the fact that a wound that appeared to be mortal had been healed.

Certain features of John's description have led some to identify this head with the Emperor Nero and the beast with the Roman Empire. Nero committed suicide by stabbing himself in the neck, and a legend grew up that he had survived. Against this, it should be observed that the wound is only on one of the beast's heads in 13:3 but has become a wound of the whole beast in 13:12, 14. The self-inflicted wound of the rejected emperor was not a wound inflicted on the whole empire. Moreover, it is difficult to see how the legend about the healing of Nero's throat could have enhanced the authority of the beast or the dragon's war against the saints.

The word translated *fatal wound* is also significant. Elsewhere in Revelation it is translated as 'plague' and refers to a divinely inflicted judgment (9:18, 20; 11:6; 15:1; 16:9, 21; 18:4, 8; 21:9; 22:18). The *sword* in Revelation is a symbol of the divine judgment of the Messiah (1:16; 2:12, 16; 19:15, 21), except in 13:10 where a sword is used against the people of God. It is thus likely that John is not speaking of the sword that caused Nero's death but of the sword as the symbol of God's judgment that has delivered a death blow to the authority of the beast (and the dragon).

This identification of the beast's enemy enables us to understand what event John might have in mind as delivering the death blow. In Revelation, the only conqueror of the beast and the dragon is the slain Lamb, together with his faithful saints (12:11; 19:19-21). The crucifixion, resurrection and exaltation of Jesus Christ dealt the death blow to the dragon and the beast (1:5; 5:9). This thought is paralleled by other NT passages (Luke 10:17-24; 11:14-22; John 12:31-33; Col 2:15). The wound is not a reference to Nero's wound but to Genesis 3:13-15, where God speaks of the serpent's head being bruised.

The same paradox found in chapter 12 also appears here in chapter 13. The dragon in chapter 12 is defeated and cast out of heaven, but he still has time and ability to wage a relentless war against the people of God. Likewise, the beast here in chapter 13 has been dealt a fatal blow by the cross of Christ, and yet he still has time and ability (permitted by God) to wage spiritual warfare against the redeemed. He appears to be alive and in full command; his blasphemies increase (2 Tim 3:1-9). What the sea beast cannot accomplish, he commissions the earth beast to do (13:11-12.). All three, the dragon, the sea beast and the earth beast, though distinguishable, work together to achieve the same purpose: a) deceiving unbelievers so that they worship the dragon and the sea beast, and b) destroying all who oppose them.

There are numerous parallels between John's descriptions of the beast and of Jesus Christ. Both Christ and the beast wield swords; both have their names inscribed on the foreheads of their followers (13:16-14:1); both have horns (5:6; 13:1); both have authority; and both were given (by different authorities) power over every nation, tribe, people and language, as well as over the kings of the earth (1:5; 7:9; 13:7; 17:12). The beast is thus not the Roman Empire or any of its emperors but the great counterpart to Jesus Christ. This theological characterization is far more important than any identification of a specific historical figure.

References to people being manifestations of the antichrist in John's epistles (1 John 2:18, 22; 4:3; 2 John 7) and Paul's description of the coming 'man of lawlessness' (2 Thess 2:3-4, 8-9) have led some past and modern interpreters to conclude that some coming individual will be the antichrist. However, it seems likely that John is not pointing to one particular arch-enemy of God's people, whether in the past or in the future, but to an embodiment of evil that manifests itself in different people throughout human history. This is not to say that John would deny historical manifestations of this satanic reality; but it does prevent us from interpreting his imagery merely in terms of the Roman Empire or limiting it to any single present or future political or religious entity or individual.

The arrogant speech of the beast echoes that of the horn of the fourth beast in Daniel 7:8, 11, 20. But it does not merely speak, it also takes action against the redeemed

(13:5-7; 11:7; 12:7; Dan 7:21), for the dragon gives this beast *his power and his throne and great authority* (13:2b). This transfer of authority suggests that secular and non-Christian religious world systems that oppose God or deny Jesus Christ, at any period in human history, were and are instruments of Satan (13:2-3).

The world's inhabitants fall into line and worship this beast (**13:4**, 8). Those who succumb to the lures of the beast and worship it are the ones whose names are not written in *the book of life,* the register of the citizens of heaven (**13:8**; 3:5). But the saints, whose names are in that book, are the ones on whom the beast makes war (**13:7**). Believers who refuse to worship the beast encounter persecution and even martyrdom. We are reminded of the war of Michael and Satan in heaven (12:7) and the attacks on the two witnesses (11:7). Satan and his cohorts will seem to have the upper hand, but the beast's power is limited and will last for only *forty-two months* (**13:5**), during which time God's servants will have to exercise *patience and faithfulness* (**13:10b**). Ultimately God will assert control and the beast will be allowed to persecute the saints no longer. The quotation in **13:10a** echoes Jeremiah 15:1-2, where God's disgust with rebellious individuals is recorded in the words, 'Send them away from my presence! Let them go!'

13:11-18 Act IV, Scene 3: The beast from the land

John now sees *another beast,* this one *coming up out of the earth,* whereas the first beast had come up out of the sea (**13:11**). This distinction may indicate a still closer association with human society, but not too much should be read into it. In Daniel's vision, the four great beasts that come up out of the sea are explained as four kings who would arise out of the earth (Dan 7:3, 17). The two beasts have a close relationship and they both have a malign influence on human history.

The appearance of this second beast is thoroughly deceptive. It looks *like a lamb* with *two horns,* pretending to be a saviour similar to the Lamb that was slain for our redemption (13:8). But it is a false saviour with a false message of salvation, for its voice is *like a dragon* (13:3) and its lying words are the lying words of the dragon. *It exercised all the authority of the first beast on its behalf,* which implies that it does so under its control (**13:12, 14**). It is thus the agent of the first beast just as the first beast is the agent of the dragon (13:2). Thus both beasts are the instruments of Satan in his warfare against God and his people. Yet because the beast has some of the characteristics of the Lamb, it is easy to understand how people could be deceived and how watchful one has to be to avoid being taken in by what seems plausible and thereby colluding with things or people that are opposed to God.

The primary function of the second beast is to promote the worship of the first beast by *the earth and its inhabitants,* that is, on a worldwide scale. In order to do this, he performs signs and wonders like the prophets of God (**13:13, 15**; compare 1 Kgs 18:38), but he is a false prophet (16:13; 19:20; 20:10; Matt 7:15; Acts 13:6).

This worship that the second beast imposes is not a private matter, for those who worship it will receive a mark on their right hand or on their forehead (**13:15-16**; 14:9, 11; 16:2; 19:20; 20:4). This parody of the sealing of the 144,000 in chapter 7 allows them to buy and sell in the marketplace. Those without the mark are denied access to the economy (**13:17**). The reference here is not so much to a literal mark as to the social ostracism of those who refuse to conform.

For John's original readers, this second beast may have symbolized emperor worship, whose 'god' was the continuing line of emperors deified by decree of the Roman senate. This cult had behind it the authority of the emperor. In the name of that authority, it exercised a priestly function (leading men to worship the emperor's image – 13:15); a prophetic function (performing great miracles to validate the state religion – 13:13); and the power of a grand inquisitor (seeking to brand all people with the mark of the beast without which no one would be able to buy or sell – 13:16-17).

The statement that the number of the beast is 666 is probably an example of the ancient practice of *gematria,* whereby numerical values were assigned to words (**13:18b**). In the ancient world, letters were also used for numbers (in our alphabet, A = 1, B = 2, C = 3, and so on), and one could easily convert a person's name into numbers. Since the numerical value of several names could equal 666, the identification of the person John had in mind is not certain.

But there is another way to approach this number, one that is best exemplified in the RSV rendering, *it is a human number,* which moves away from associating the number with a particular person. Instead it focuses on the fact that in Revelation the number 7 (used of angels, churches, seals, trumpets and bowls) implies completeness, whereas the number 6 falls one short of this. The beast seems to be near perfection and almost messianic; it is, after all, a caricature of the Lamb who was slain (13:3, 11, 13). But it is not perfect, and that makes all the difference. It is actually diabolical and utterly opposed to God (13:4). The number 666 represents a threefold falling short of perfection (dragon: 6, beast: 6, false prophet: 6). But it is close to perfection, and has most of the hallmarks of truth, and so can easily deceive. No wonder wisdom is required! (**13:18a**).

14:1-5 Act IV, Scene 4: The Lamb with the 144,000 martyrs

The dismal picture in scene 3 is deliberately followed by the triumphant one of scene 4. Together, these scenes seem to discount the pre-tribulation rapture, for they contrast those who have *[the Lamb's] name and his Father's name written on their foreheads* with those wearing the mark of the beast (**14:1**; 13:16). Humanity is divided into two camps, and no one can belong to both at the same time.

Scene 3 portrays the martyrdom of God's people. Scene 4 reverses that judgment as John sees the Lamb (Christ) standing on Mount Zion, the centre of the messianic kingdom. With him are *144,000* people who, like the heavenly chorus in 5:8-10, sing a *new song* of praise to God, a song that no one else could learn (**14:2-3**). While it is tempting to interpret the 144,000 as symbolic of all redeemed humanity, a closer reading suggests that they are the martyrs, the ones who have been the victims of the beasts in chapter 13. They are described as *firstfruits* (**14:4b**). This is sacrificial language, appropriate for those who have sacrificed their lives for God. These martyrs maintained their witness even under persecution, *no lie was found in their mouths* (**14:5**).

These with the Lamb *did not defile themselves with women, for they kept themselves pure* (**14:4a**). These words need to be interpreted in terms of the regulations for 'holy war', which required sexual abstinence before battle (Deut 23:9-11; 1 Sam 21:4-5; 2 Sam 11:9-11). John uses this requirement for ceremonial purity to symbolize moral and religious purity. The description is figurative, not literal (2 Cor 11:2). It parallels the use of the imagery of fornication as a metaphor for idolatry (see 2:14, 21) and describes the singularity and lack of compromise that abstinence from sexual intercourse involves, reflecting the profound distaste throughout this book for whatever is ambiguous or mixed (3:15-16).

John's vision offers hope to those who stand firm in God. Those who conform to the ways of the beast may achieve temporary prosperity, but ultimately that cannot continue. This certainty should encourage God's people to remain committed to what they believe even at the risk of public disgrace.

14:6-13 Act IV, Scene 5: The messages of the three angels

Scenes 3 and 4 showed us two multitudes: one made up of those who accepted the secular world system and the other of believers. Now in scene 5 we hear three closely related announcements intended to appeal to the peoples of the world to join the ranks of righteousness and to encourage persecuted believers by saying that God is about to receive them into his rest.

The first announcement proclaims the *eternal gospel* and appeals to all peoples to *fear God,* the Creator and the righteous Judge (**14:6-7**). The second proclaims the impending fall of *Babylon the Great,* or the forces of evil (**14:8**). The third is a warning that eternal torment awaits anyone who *worships the beast* (**14:9-11**). All these declarations represent various aspects of God's message, both negative and positive.

Here we have the first mention of the evil city as *Babylon the Great* (14:8; 16:19; 17:5; 18:2). Babylon's offence is to have caused all the nations to *drink the maddening wine of her adulteries* (14:8; Jer 51:7). This phrase seems to mean that Babylon misled people and caused them to forget their true vocation, which is to worship God and faithfully keep his commandments (compare 17:2; 18:3). Elsewhere, John speaks of Sodom and Egypt combined as the 'great city' (11:8). Revelation speaks of only two cities: the 'holy city' (11:2; 21:2), which is of God, and the evil city, which is of Satan. The city of Satan is anywhere and everywhere that people worship something other than the true and living God.

The overall goal of act IV becomes clear at **14:12-13**: it is to commend the saints for their steadfastness even in persecution. If they *die in the Lord,* they will find *rest* with him.

14:14-20 Act IV, Scene 6: Harvest of sinners and redeemed

The conflict between good and evil that is presented in terms of a battle in 9:13-21, 16:12-16 and 19:19-21 is here graphically portrayed as a harvest. Once again, the emphasis lies on the judgment of sinners and the gathering in of the righteous at the end of human history on earth. The imagery comes from chapter 3 in Joel: 'Swing the sickle, for the harvest is ripe. Come, trample the grapes, for the winepress is full and the vats overflow – so great is their wickedness' (Joel 3:13).

The first reaper is described as *like a son of man* and represents the saving aspect of judgment (**14:15-16**). Jesus also used harvest imagery to explain the gathering in of the redeemed (Mark 4:29; Luke 10:2). The other side of the judgment, condemnation, is apparent in the trampling *in the great winepress of God's wrath* (**14:17-19**). The wine flowing from the vat symbolizes the pouring out of the blood of the guilty who have been executed. The magnitude and severity of God's punishment on the wicked is conveyed by the imagery of blood rising as high as the horses' bridles, for a distance of 1600 stadia [180 miles, 300 kilometres] (**14:20**, Isa 63:1-6). The fact that this blood is shed *outside the city* probably refers merely to ancient warfare when a besieged army was slaughtered at the city walls, and the blood flowed outside the city. The city is the same city that was trampled by unbelievers (11:2).

The scale of the judgment shows that this is no human vengeance, but exclusively that of the Son of Man and his angelic reapers.

15:1-4 Act IV, Scene 7: The song of the Lamb

In acts III and IV, John has been describing the events of the last times and their effect on the community of believers, the redeemed people of God. But in this last scene of act IV, John depicts in a few bold strokes the end of human history and the future of *those who had been victorious,* that is, those who have overcome (**15:2b**; see also 2:7, 11, 17, 26; 3:5, 12, 21). Accordingly, we see only the saved, standing by *a sea of glass mixed with fire* (**15:2a**), which is reminiscent of the 'sea of cast metal' and the ten bronze basins of Solomon's temple (1 Kgs 7:23-39). Like those objects, this sea of glass probably stands for the holiness without which no one can approach God. The saved have passed through it,

even as Israel passed through the Red Sea. The 'fire' of its judgment has served to purify and not to destroy them. So, like Israel after crossing the Red Sea they pause to sing the song of Moses (Exod 15), with modifications of the original as will make it also the *song of the Lamb* (**15:3**).

The redeemed sing as they play upon *harps given them by God* (**15:2c**). They are enjoying constant fellowship with God. They have 'confidence to enter the Most Holy Place', because they have 'full assurance of faith', which they need 'to draw near to God' for 'he who promised is faithful' (Heb 10:19-23).

So, the curtain falls on act IV, leaving us with the confident assurance that those who have God's seal on their foreheads should not fear persecution that may result in martyrdom. God's seal means that they are God's own possession for ever.

15:5-16:21 Act V: Vision of the Seven Angels – God's Wrath Poured Out

Stage Setting: In this act, the sanctuary has been shifted to the back so that the whole tabernacle with its lampstands, altars and the like is visible. More prominently displayed are seven angels carrying seven bowls of God's wrath.

In act III, we saw believers enduring the great suffering of the 'last times'. In act V , we see how the unbelieving world responds to the same suffering. Like those in act III, the first four scenes of act V contain an elaboration of the cosmic catastrophe presented in 6:12-17. This means that the events of both acts are clearly in the same period of the 'last times.' Both the bowl plagues and the trumpet plagues draw upon the plagues inflicted on Egypt.

Another significant difference between acts III and V is the extent to which the sufferings in act V are said to affect humanity. In act III, humans suffer only in scene 3. This is because John's purpose there was to show how the believing community would successfully weather those horrific times. Here, however, stress is laid on the effect of these plagues on those who have on them the mark of the beast and who worship its image. Ungodly people are not capable of dealing with the daily pressure, and in an attempt to cover up their own inadequacies; they 'curse God'. Act V, therefore, presents a picture of human suffering which rises in a crescendo from 'ugly and painful sores' (16:2), to scorching by the fierce heat of the sun (16:8-9) to 'huge hailstones of about a hundred pounds [forty kilograms] each' (16:21). What a picture of unrelieved torment! This exhibition of God's wrath against sin can be described as the gospel message in reverse.

15:5-16:1 Before the tabernacle

In addition to contrasting the reaction of believers and unbelievers to suffering, acts III and V present the angels in contrasting roles. Act III shows the angels as messengers of

God's saving power, while act V show them as messengers of wrath. There is also a contrast with respect to the *tabernacle of the Testimony* (**15:5**). In acts III and IV, we saw the people of God at prayer and the tabernacle fully displayed. Here in act V, the tabernacle is pushed into the background and no one is able to enter it *until the seven plagues of the seven angels were completed* (**15:8**). This recalls Exodus 40:34-35 where 'Moses could not enter the Tent of Meeting, because … the glory of the LORD filled the tabernacle', that is, for the moment the majesty of God's presence was too overpowering for any human to look upon. Here in Revelation it means that nothing can withstand God's wrath against a sinful world. The approach to him is closed and there is no recourse for disobedient humanity during the last judgment. Little wonder that this act closes with the words, 'the plague was so terrible' (16:21).

16:2 Act V, Scene 1: The plague on the earth

The pouring out of the first bowl results in painful sores (compare Exod 9:10, 11; Luke 16:20, 21). This plague specifically affects those *who had the mark of the beast and who worshipped its image* (13:15, 16; 7:3).

16:3 Act V, Scene 2: The plague on the sea

Then the second angel empties his bowl into the sea, and the sea turns bloody like a corpse (**16:3**; Exod 7:19-21). Whereas in the aftermath of the second trumpet, a third of the creatures in the sea were destroyed (8:8-9), here every living thing in the sea dies.

16:4-7 Act V, Scene 3: The plague on rivers and springs

The third angel pours out his bowl into the rivers and springs of water and they turn into blood (Exod 7:17-18). In 8:10-11, these same waters were made 'bitter'; the *angel in charge of the waters* responds by acknowledging God's righteous judgment (**16:5-6**), hailing him as *the Holy One* (as in 15:4) and judge (6:10; 11:17-18; 18:8, 20; 19:11; Ps 119:137). In response, a voice from the altar of sacrifice says, *Yes, Lord God Almighty, true and just are your judgments* (**16:7**).

16:8-9 Act V, Scene 4: The plague on the sun

The fourth angel empties his bowl onto the sun releasing scorching heat on the earth (**16:8**). When people begin burning, they start cursing *the name of God* (**16:9**, 11, 21; 13:6). They recognize that he has ultimate *control over these plagues* but as in 9:20 they give no sign of repentance and do not give God glory (11:13; 14:7).

16:10-11 Act V, Scene 5: The plague on the beast's throne

The first four plagues affected all parts of the cosmos: land, waters, sea and sun. Next, the very citadel of the beast is attacked. The fifth angel pours out his bowl of judgment on the throne of the beast (2:13), and as a result, *his kingdom was plunged into darkness* (**16:10**; compare 8:12; 9:2; Exod 10:22; Matt 24:29; 27:45; Acts 2:20). Despite the great suffering, the people are so hardened against God that nothing is able to bring them to repentance (**16:11**).

16:12-16 Act V, Scene 6: The plague on the Euphrates River

The sixth angel pours forth his bowl upon the Euphrates River. As a result, its waters dry up in preparation for a highway over which the *kings from the East* will travel (**16:12**; 9:13-19). The drying up of the Euphrates River reminds us of the drying up of the Red Sea. The frogs in the scene are reminiscent of the second Egyptian plague (**16:13**; Exod 7:25-8:15), but these are no ordinary frogs. They are demonic spirits who gather together the kings of the earth for a great spiritual battle (**16:14**), one that will be between ideologies and not one of swords and guns.

This is the first time John explicitly mentions the battle of Armageddon, though he has hinted before at its coming. Scenes 6 of this act and of act III describe armies from across the Euphrates who invade the west (9:13-21; 14:14-20; see also 19:19-21). The place where the armies will assemble for battle is called *Armageddon* (**16:16**). The name probably derives from the Hebrew words, *Har Megiddo*, meaning 'the mountain of Megiddo'. Megiddo was an important city guarding the pass through the Jezreel Valley in Israel. Several important battles had been fought there in the past (Judg 5:19). It was the site of the death of Ahaziah (2 Kgs 9:27) and of the defeat of the righteous reforming king Josiah (2 Kgs 23:29). It seems likely that John is not predicting a literal battle at this place, but is using it as a symbol of the final attempt by the forces of evil to defeat God's supremacy. John does not give any description of the confrontation. He will do that in 19:11-21.

Here he gives an admonition from Christ, *Behold, I come like a thief! Blessed is he who stays awake and keeps his clothes with him, so that he may not go naked and be shamefully exposed* (**16:15**). This is a warning against being spiritually unprepared for the coming of Christ, which will occur unexpectedly (Matt 25:1-13). There is no interlude between bowls six and seven, as there was with the seals and trumpets.

Because of the similarities between the scenes of the seals, trumpets and bowls (6:1-16:21), it is possible to treat them as describing one series of suffering. They represent the frequent and intense suffering experienced in different parts of the world throughout human history rather than a chronological series of tribulations just before the second coming of Christ. The emptying of the seventh bowl occuring brings down the curtain on the eschatological drama.

16:17-21 Act V, Scene 7: The plague on the air

The seventh angel empties his bowl into the air and in response, a loud voice comes out of the temple, from the throne, shouting, *It is done!* (**16:17**). This is God's confirmation of the work of the Lamb and echoes the Lamb's own words on the cross (John 19:30). The *earthquake* too is reminiscent of the one after the agony of the Lamb (**16:18**; Matt 27:51). In Revelation earthquakes accompany significant moments: the opening of the sixth seal, which prompted a response of fear on the part of humanity (6:12-16); the ascent of the prayers of the saints to God (8:4); the resurrection of the two witnesses, which prompted fear in the inhabitants of the city (11:13); and following the seventh trumpet blast and the second woe, when God's reign is seen to be effective (11:19).

Here the implication is that the end has fully come; the evil city, *Babylon the Great,* has finally fallen (**16:19**). This scene of terror is in sharp contrast to its counterpart of the 'survivors' giving glory to God in act III (**16:21**; 11:13).

17:1-20:3 Act VI: Vision of the Doom of Evil

Stage Setting: There is no difference from the arrange of the stage in act V, except that the sanctuary is pushed farther to the back of the stage and the Earth's corners become visible. But one of the seven angels still plays a role.

As the curtain fell on act V, we looked forward with trepidation to the filling in of details in the drama of judgment. The motif of judgment runs throughout this Act. But the throne of God, with the worshipping creatures and elders, is still to be seen in the distance. The judgment passed on the 'great harlot' is God's doing, and his all-seeing eye does not fail to observe that judgment carried out.

One of the seven angels who has been pouring out the wrath of God stands alone in the centre of the stage. This angel offers to show John the judgment of Babylon, a theme that will occupy the whole of chapters 17 and 18. These two chapters form an extended appendix, as it were, to the seventh bowl where the judgment on Babylon was first mentioned (16:19). They also expand upon the earlier references to this city (11:8; 14:8) and look forward to the eternal Holy City (21:1–22:5).

It is a characteristic of John's literary technique that he occasionally brings a principal character upon the stage abruptly, without any previous introduction or description. This was true of the beast arising from the Abyss (11:7) and it is true of the woman here. And while the detailed interpretation of this type of vision is common in apocalyptic literature, it is not found in the rest of Revelation. This vision is followed by a sequence of heavenly celebration and earthly laments over Babylon's fate as John shows the city's true character and identity and the reactions both on earth and in heaven to its demise.

17:1-6a Act VI, Scene 1: The woman on the scarlet beast
John is approached by one of the angels who had held the seven bowls of plagues. He is taken into the *desert* by the Spirit (**17:3a**; compare 1:10; 4:2; 21:10; Ezek 8:3), where he comes face to face with Babylon, just as Jesus had come face to face with Satan (Matt 4:1-11). This is the second time *a desert* is stretched before us on the stage (12:6). It seems clear that the events of act VI are to be viewed as depicting the same conflict between good and evil as do the events of act IV. There, God has prepared a place of safety for his people in the desert. As already noted, in Scripture a *desert* can also be a place of temptation or testing (Mark 1:12-13), of rebellion (Exod 17:1-7; Heb 3:8), or of punishment (Num 14:20-23; Heb 3:17).

John is summoned to the desert to witness the judgment of the *great prostitute* (**17:1**). The angel describes this prostitute as one who *sits on many waters,* a phrase that recalls Jeremiah's description of Babylon as 'you who live by mighty waters' (Jer 51:13). The woman John sees here is clearly not the same as the godly woman mentioned in chapter 12. This woman is seated on a scarlet beast that is *covered with blasphemous names* (**17:3b**; Dan 7:24-25). The beast has *seven heads* and *ten horns,* like the beast that arose from the sea (13:1). Unlike the redeemed, who are clothed in white (4:4; 7:9, 13; 19:14), she is *dressed in purple and scarlet* (**17:4a**). She is adorned with gold, precious stones and pearls and holds a golden cup *filled with abominable things and the filth of her impurities* in her hand (**17:4b**). Readers would recall the 'maddening wine' of Babylon (14:8) and now they are seeing its embodiment in the *great prostitute,* Babylon, with whom *the kings of the earth committed adultery* (**17:2a**). She has made all the earth drunk (**17:2b**; 18:3; Jer 51:7) and is herself drunk with *the blood of the saints, the blood of those who bore testimony to Jesus* (**17:6a**).

The imagery here is derived from Ezekiel's dramatic condemnation of Tyre (Ezek 28:1-19), which he presented as a proud city that had amassed great wealth through trade with other nations (Ezek 28:5). But that prosperity would ultimately end in devastation (Ezek 28:18-19). The woman's name is *mystery, Babylon the great, the mother of prostitutes and of the abominations of the earth* (**17:5**).

Solving the 'mystery' of what Babylon represents is important for interpreting the manifestation of evil not only in this chapter but in the whole of Revelation. For the majority of commentators, 'Babylon' stands for the city of Rome, and the beast on which she sits is the Roman Empire with its subject provinces and peoples. But this identification may be inadequate. Babylon cannot be any one historical city. John's description does not neatly fit any particular city; whether the real Babylon, Sodom, Tyre, Nineveh or Rome. Theologically, Babylon is found wherever there is satanic deception. It is defined more by dominant idolatries than by geographic boundaries. Babylon is better understood as the embodiment of all entrenched worldly resistance to God. It is a supernatural mystery that can never be wholly reducible to any individual earthly institution or city. The historical Rome was, therefore, only one of the manifestations of the total system of humankind that excludes God from what it does. As act VI progresses, the lesson that is relentlessly driven home is that evil is always self-destructive and that in the end only God can overcome it.

17:6b-18 Act VI, Scene 2: The beast at war with the woman

The vision of the great prostitute is followed by the interpretation of that vision by an angel who explains the mystery of Babylon and the beast that carries her. Though seldom used in Revelation, such angelic interpretation is a feature of other works of apocalyptic literature (Dan 7–12). The nature of the beast is explained in 17:7-8, then that of its seven heads (17:9-11) and ten horns (17:12-14). The meaning of the waters is explained in 17:15 and of the woman in 17:18.

John is told that the beast *once was, now is not, and will come up out of the Abyss* (**17:8,** 11). These words seem to echo the earlier reference to the fatally wounded beast who was healed (13:3, 12, 14). The tenses: *was ... is not ... will come* indicate that the beast has a three-stage history that can only be understood by *a mind with wisdom* (**17:9**). Satan once had power before his fall, then he was rendered impotent by the death of the Lord Jesus Christ on the cross, and yet he is allowed a *little while* (**17:10b**) to oppose God and his people before finally being sentenced to *destruction* at the second coming of Christ (**17:11**; Matt 7:13; John 17:12; Rom 9:22; 2 Thess 2:3). Thus it seems that this beast is the satanic incarnation of idolatrous power first mentioned in 11:7 and described in 13:1-3, and whose destruction is seen in 19:19-20.

This interpretation links the call for *a mind with wisdom* to the identification of the beast, and not to the issue of the *seven hills* on which Rome was built (17:9; note that the woman also sits on 'many waters' – 17:1, 15 – and on the beast – 17:3). It was common knowledge that Rome was built on seven hills and no particular wisdom would have been required to see that link. It is also difficult to see how this geographic feature of Rome has any real symbolic significance related to the diabolic nature of the beast or the woman. Nor is the actual historical city described as the enemy of the Christian community anywhere else in the NT. Some scholars thus argue that the woman does not represent the city of Rome, but the Roman Empire, but this view is contradicted by the clear statement in 17:18 that the woman represents a city, and by the statement that it is the beast that has seven heads.

The seven heads of the beast are said to represent both seven hills and *seven kings* (**17:10a**). Those who see the city as Rome argue that the *seven kings* represent seven successive Roman emperors. But how are these to be counted? If five Roman emperors *have fallen,* the *one* who *is* should be Galba (Nero's successor), and the one who *has not yet come* should be Otho. But if Galba and his successors (Otho and

Vitellius) who had very short reigns are included (and they should since they appear on the list of legitimate Roman emperors), then the argument for only seven emperors falls apart because the Roman Empire had many more emperors. So some scholars have interpreted the seven kings as a succession of world kingdoms. The first five are said to be Egypt, Assyria, Babylon, Persia and Greece. Rome is understood as a future world kingdom that will oppress the people of God. The problem with this view is that it arbitrarily omits many other kingdoms that have persecuted God's people throughout history, and does not explain how the kings (or kingdoms) it identifies can be seen to have survived the destruction of the prostitute and be pictured as mourning her in 18:9. Nor does the political history of Rome include a Roman emperor turning against the city or empire and destroying her, as implied in 17:16-17.

Any convincing interpretation of the seven kings must do justice to three considerations: First, since the heads belong to the beast, the interpretation must relate their significance to this beast, not to Babylon. Second, since kingship in Revelation often involves conflict between the Lamb and the beast (**17:14**; 19:19), the kind of sovereignty expressed in 17:10 must be the opposite of that exercised by Christ and his followers. And third, since the kings are closely related to the seven hills and to the great prostitute, the nature of the relationship between them must be clarified.

One explanation that does satisfy the criteria one one that recognizes that throughout Revelation, seven is a symbolic number that indicates perfection or fullness. The *seven heads* therefore represent the totality of evil and blasphemy. They represent a quality, not a quantity. The falling of five heads thus represents a significant victory over the beast – and thus God's judgment on the powers of evil throughout human history (14:8; 18:2; Jer 50:23; 51:8-9, 49).

The ten horns (Dan 7:7, 24) are often interpreted as either native rulers of Roman provinces serving under Roman emperors, or native rulers of satellite states, or governors of Palestine. But the number 10 – like most of John's numbers – should be understood symbolically. Ten symbolizes that something is repeated a number of times or an indefinite number (2:10; Neh 4:12; Dan 1:12). Thus the number should not be understood as referring specifically to ten kings or kingdoms, but as indicating the many political sovereignties that enhance the power of the beast throughout human history. These rulers and the beast with which they are allied are the principalities and powers, 'the rulers of the darkness of this world' (Eph 6:12 KJV). To be sure, they use earthly instruments, but their reality is far greater than any specific historical equivalents. These *kings* embody the fullness of Satan's attack against the Lamb and believers worldwide. They are the 'kings from the East' (16:12-14) and the 'kings of the earth' (19:19-21).

The ten kings are said to receive authority for *one hour* (**17:12**). This corresponds to the 'little while' for which the seventh king will reign (17:10). They will reign along with the beast, which is described as an *eighth king* who *belongs to the seven* (17:11). This promise that their reign will be short brings comfort to the persecuted saints.

The influence of the satanic system of Babylon is universal (17:1-2), and it affects all humanity, from the humblest to the proud political leaders of the world, but it is not invincible. The prostitute will be brought *to ruin*, left *naked and* burned *with fire* (**17:16**) by her former lovers, an image that reminds us of the OT prophets' descriptions of the divine judgment falling on Jerusalem, Samaria and Tyre (Ezek 16:39-40; 23:25-27; 28:17-19). The description of the punishment of a convicted prostitute is combined with the picture of judgment against rebellious cities (18:8; Lev 21:9).

The ravaging of the prostitute by the beast and its horns is John's most vivid symbol for the self-destroying power of evil. The attack on the prostitute indicates the final judgment on the kingdom of Satan, for *God has put it into their hearts to accomplish his purpose* (**17:17**). God can use the forces of evil as instruments of his judgment (Jer 25:9-14). Nothing will distract them from their united effort to destroy the prostitute till God's purpose is fulfilled (10:7; 11:18).

The fact that this *woman* is said to be identical to *the great city* shows that this 'city' is not just a historical one (**17:18**). Her other names are 'the great prostitute' (17:1), 'Babylon the Great' (17:5), 'mother of prostitutes' (17:5), 'Sodom' (11:8) and 'Egypt' (11:8). She stands for those in every place and time who seek to oppose and destroy any people of God. Her kingdom *rules over the kings of the earth*, that is, through political and ungodly systems that ignore and exclude God from their belief and behaviour.

18:1-19:10 Act VI, Scene 3: Fallen is Babylon the Great

Scene 3 marks the climax and fulfilment of John's prophecy about the fall of Babylon (17:1). It opens with an announcement of its general theme. This is followed by an appeal to God's people to leave Babylon, a wailing lament, an acted parable and sermon delivered by a mighty angel, and choruses of Hallelujah. This scene contains some of the most beautiful language in the whole book. It draws on OT accounts of the destruction of ancient cities like Babylon (Isa 13:19-22; 47:7-15; Jer 50–51) and Tyre (Ezek 26–28) to create a great funeral dirge (compare 2 Sam 1:17-27; Isa 14:4-21).

So magnificent is the coming event that a dazzling angel of glory bears the divine news (**18:1**). In words very similar to those of the OT prophets the angel announces that *Babylon the Great* has fallen (**18:2**; Isa 21:9). The city is judged because of her *adulteries* and *excessive luxuries* (**18:3; 7,** 9), suggesting that she is guilty of both idolatry and

pride (Ezek 28:4-5, 16-18). John's vision also allows readers some glimpse of how Babylon had gained her wealth at the expense of others (**18:5-6, 13**). A godless system may have great beauty, sophistication and splendour, and its arts, social life and technology may flourish, but these attributes should not be enjoyed at the expense of human life and human rights. All human beings are made in the image of God.

Come out of her, my people (**18:4**) is also Jeremiah's call concerning Babylon (Jer 50:8; 51:6-9; see also Isa 48:20; 52:11; 2 Cor 6:17). Even in its OT setting, this was no mere warning to leave the city of Babylon. John, like the OT prophets, is exhorting God's people to shun the charms and snares of the prostitute city. Babylon exists wherever there is idolatry, prostitution, self-glorification, self-sufficiency, pride and complacency, reliance on luxury and wealth, and violence against life (18:4-8, 24). Believers are to separate themselves from all the forms of Babylon. While they still have to live and work in the world, they also need to claim a distinctive identity and to develop habits of resistance that will enable witness to take place.

Three groups of people lament the city's fall: the *kings of the earth* (**18:9-10**), the *merchants of the earth* who traded with her (**18:11-17a**), and the *sea captains* who became rich from the cargoes they took to the city (**18:17b-20**; see Ezek 27:27-33). With bitter irony, these dirges pronounce 'Woe!' on God's enemies. They are chanted by those who have profited most from the secular systems symbolized by the great prostitute. They are now helpless to save her and can only throw dust on their heads and stand afar off, *weeping and mourning* (18:9-10, 15, 17-19) –traditional symbols of repentance. The suddenness of God's judgment is stressed in the phrase *in one hour* (18:17).

The final fate of Babylon is presented with an image that draws on Jesus' judgment on those who try to deceive his followers. 'If anyone causes one of these little ones who believe in me to sin, it would be better for him to be thrown into the sea with a large millstone tied around his neck' (Mark 9:42). John sees a mighty angel pick up a *boulder the size of a large millstone* (**18:21**). Such a millstone would be around five feet (one and a half metres) in diameter, one foot (thirty centimetres) thick, and would weigh thousands of pounds. With one quick gesture, the angel flings it into the sea. Suddenly the city is gone for ever (Jer 51:64; Ezek 26:21).

This acted parable symbolizes the whole judgment on Babylon. Revelation uses similar prophetic symbolism in the measuring of the sanctuary in 11:1-2, and the sealing of the redeemed in 7:2-8. It is also common in prophetic writings: for example, Jeremiah's linen girdle (Jer 13:1-11), Hosea's adulterous wife (Hos 1–3), and Ezekiel's mimic siege of Jerusalem (Ezek 4:1-3).

This judgment is a death blow to the life of the city (18:21-23a). The reason for such severe judgment is cited again in **18:23-24**: Babylon has led *all the nations ... astray* and she has martyred both the OT *prophets* and some NT *saints* because of their loyalty to the true God (see 17:6; 19:2). Elsewhere in Revelation, the death of martyrs is attributed to the inhabitants of the earth (6:9-10), the beast from the Abyss (11:7; 13:7) and the beast from the earth (13:15). All these have been agents or instruments of Satan.

It is fitting that Babylon's sinfulness and persecution of God's people are reiterated here, for these sins summarize the sins repeated throughout the book of Revelation. John is witnessing God's final judgment on every human institution that opposes God's righteous rule and sovereignty.

The great chorus of the heavenly choir in 19:1-8 opens with a resounding *Hallelujah.* This word, which means 'Praise the Lord!' occurs only in this chapter in the whole NT (19:1, 3, 4, 6). In the OT, it is used mainly in the psalms, especially in Psalms 113–118, which were associated with the Passover. These psalms were used to celebrate the exodus and the destruction of the wicked, exactly as this passage in Revelation does. They would have been sung by Jesus and his disciples after the Passover celebration, before going out to the Mount of Olives the night before his death (Matt 26:30).

The theme of the praise is in the opening words: *salvation and glory and power belong to our God.* First, the choir praise God for the condemnation of the prostitute (**19:1-2**), and then they shout in celebration of the city's eternal destruction (**19:3**). The twenty-four elders and the four living creatures respond with their own praise (**19:4**). Finally, a voice from the throne calls on all the servants of God to praise him (**19:5**).

In 19:6-10, we hear the praises of God's people because *our Lord God Almighty reigns* (Ps 118:24) and *the wedding of the Lamb has come.* The multitude in 19:1 cannot be angelic since it is composed of the redeemed. All the redeemed appear on the cosmic stage, dressed in *fine, bright and clean* linen, which is the court dress demanded in the throne room of the King of kings.

John uses the OT image of Israel as a bride (Ezek 16; Hos 2:19-20), which the NT applies to God's people (2 Cor 11:2; Eph 5:25-26). *Those who are invited to the wedding supper of the Lamb* (**19:9a**; Luke 13:29) are the believers of all ages. To assure John and his readers of the certainty of the end of the great prostitute and the announcement of the wedding supper of the Lamb, the angel adds, *These are the true words of God* (**19:9b**; compare 1:2; 21:5; 22:6).

The closing episode of scene 3 is a bit like that in the interlude at the end of act III (10:1-11). In both scenes, John is drawn into the spotlight and we overhear a conversation between him and an angel. John mistakenly assumes that the angel is a divine being, possibly the Lord Jesus Christ,

and prostrates himself to *worship* the angel, but is quickly prohibited from doing so (**19:10**). In the OT, men prostrate themselves before angels (Num 22:31; 1 Chr 21:16), but they do this in homage, not in worship. There is no place in Christianity for the worship of anyone except God.

Some early Christians were tempted to worship angels (Col 2:18), but this passage rebukes the practice. We need to recognize how easy it is to fall into idolatry. Whenever a Christian gives anyone or anything other than God control of his or her life, he or she has broken the first commandment (Exod 20:1-3).

The angel links himself with John by calling himself *a fellow-servant with you.* Angels and human beings are very different, but they have something important in common. Both are servants of the Lord.

19:11-16 Act VI, Scene 4: The rider on a white horse

The judgment of the wicked city is followed by a vision of the return of Christ and the establishment of the eternal city of God in 19:11-22:5. Christ's coming is portrayed through a series of symbolic pictures, which highlight aspects of the event too great to comprehend in advance.

When heaven is opened the first thing John sees is *Faithful and True* riding a *white horse* (**19:11**). Unlike the similar rider in 6:1-2, this rider comes out of heaven, which stands open. In other words, he emerges from the sanctuary at the back of the stage. The statement that *no one knows* the full name of the rider means that no one can fathom the depth of his person (**19:12**). The rider and those who follow him are dressed for battle and are assembling for the battle of Armageddon (16:12-16; 19:13-14). In 14:1-5 this same group was seen as the Lamb and the 144,000 redeemed people assembled on Mount Zion.

The rider is also called *the Word of God* (**19:13**) and *out of his mouth comes a sharp sword,* which is his answer to the foul lies of the dragon (**19:15**; 1:16). He will win the battle of Armageddon, for he is *Faithful and True,* the one who is destined to carry through the purpose of God to its final conclusion. Therefore, the appropriate title which will eventually be his is *king of kings and lord of lords.*

19:17-18 Act VI, Scene 5: The angel standing in the sun

It seems there is to be another feast. First there was the 'wedding supper' ... for Christ's own people. Now there is the *great supper* of his wrath on the field of Armageddon to which *the birds flying in mid-air* are summoned (**19:17**; Ezek 39:4, 17-20). In his mercy, God has repeatedly given people opportunities to repent of their idolatries, immorality, sorcery and murders and to return to him. Again and again throughout John's drama of human history, they have refused to respond positively to God's mercy and grace (Jer 4:1-2). Although God desires everyone to be saved, he will not force anyone to repent and to turn to him. But the time for his judgment has come.

19:19-21 Act VI, Scene 6: The battle of Armageddon

We are given surprisingly few details about the battle of Armageddon. Ever since it was first mentioned in 16:12-16, we have been anticipating a description of the terrain over which the battle would be fought, the tactics and the nature of the battle itself. However, the lack of detail ought not to surprise us, for this battle is the same one that John has been describing all along. The 'great tribulation' (7:14) seems to be the same as the battle of Armageddon (16:16).

The battle of Armageddon is a war of ideologies, with righteousness opposing evil; 'Faithful and True', 'the Word of God' riding on the 'white horse' (19:11-15) opposing 'the beast' and its 'false prophet' (16:13). The destined result of this long warfare is that *the beast* and its *false prophet* will be cast into *the fiery lake of burning sulphur* (**19:20**), eternally banished from the presence of God.

20:1-3 Act VI, Scene 7: Satan, thrown into the abyss

We have just witnessed the final end of the beast and its false prophet. Now we will witness the judgment of God on the dragon, Satan himself, who has all along been insti-gating rebellion against the rule of God. It is important to resist the temptation to see 20:1-10 as sequentially follow-ing the events described in 19:1-21. The author is not giving the order in which future events will take place.

This scene, like other visions in this section of the drama begins with its own introductory formula: *And I saw* (**20:1a**). An angel with *the key to the Abyss* and *a great chain* (**20:1b**) comes down from heaven and seizes and binds Satan. The evil one is described here by all four titles, *the dragon*, the *ancient serpent, the devil* and *Satan*, so that readers know exactly who the angel is dealing with (**20:2a**).

The Greek word translated *bound* can be used literally (Mark 11:2) and figuratively (Luke 13:11, 16). When used figuratively, it can refer to freeing someone from the power exercised over him or her by a sorcerer, or spirit. To free someone from this power is 'to loose' them. By his death and resurrection Jesus Christ broke the grip of the devil on men and nations and set them free from spiritual bondage (Heb 2:14). Now the gates of hell will not prevail against Christ's church (Matt 16:18).

The *key to the Abyss* and *the great chain* are clearly symbolic for there can be no material key to the immate-rial bottomless abyss. Nor can Satan, a spiritual being, be shackled with a physical chain. We can thus also take the *thousand years* for which Satan is to be bound as symbolic (**20:2b**). As already noted, one thousand symbolizes an immense total. It is the cube of ten, a number of complete-ness. If we take this approach, John is simply saying that

Satan is bound for the complete time that God has deter-mined since his fall from heaven.

While the central thesis of many popular eschatologi-cal positions is that in the future there will be a kingdom lasting *a thousand years*, this passage does not mention any such kingdom. In the gospels, Jesus taught that the king-dom of God was inaugurated with his coming and was now present though not yet fulfilled (Matt 12:28). The presence of Christ is in one sense the kingdom of God invading and transforming human history. Satan is a strong angelic being whose house is 'this present evil age' (Gal 1:4). The vic-tory over Satan by Jesus Christ is the same whether it is described as tying up the strong man (Matt 12:29) or strip-ping him of his armour (Luke 11:21-22).

In this scene, John takes up a rich motif within the Semitic world. For example, in Iranian apocalyptic litera-ture there is an evil serpent, *Azi-Dahaka,* who is chained up at the End. In the apocalyptic sections of the OT, it is also said that the powers of evil 'will be herded together like prisoners bound in a dungeon; they will be shut up in prison and be punished after many days' (Isa 24:21-22). Thus here too the binding of these powers is presented as a holding station, as it were, before the final judgment (2 Pet 2:4; Jude 6).

The three verbs in **20:3** – *threw ... locked and sealed* – have the same ring of finality as our 'signed, sealed, and delivered'. These verbs communicate that Satan is under God's complete control. He is locked up not as a punish-ment, but in order that he may not deceive 'the nations', a word that can mean nations, people (as compared to kings), foreigners, Gentiles, and Gentile Christians (for example, Gal 2:12, 14; Eph 3:1). Satan's activity of deception is also brought under control and restrained.

Theologically, binding Satan does not mean eliminating all his activities in this life, and he remains a dangerous foe who still rages against God's people since his fall from heaven. So the binding of Satan speaks of God's sovereign control over him. Satan has never had free rein to do what-ever he wants (Job 2:6). It is the light of the gospel that exposes the darkness of satanic deception, and the preach-ing of Christ crucified which sets men and women free from the control and power of Satan (Matt 28:19, 20). And Satan is under the sovereign authority and control of Christ until God's purposes for humanity are finished. The power of evil is temporary, and it only operates by divine consent.

20:4-22:5 Act VII: Vision of Eternal Life

Stage Setting: On the stage in heaven are the thrones of Christ and the martyred saints. The following scenes depict the eternal fate of Satan, the beast and the false prophet, all the unbelievers, and 'death and Hades' as well as the eternal state of the kingdom of God for his people.

20:4-10 Act VII, Scene 1: The martyred saints

Although the theme of the binding of Satan (20:1-3) and the thousand year reign (20:4-6) are separate themes in apocalyptic literature, the two events are combined here. This vision seems to draw on Daniel 7:2-14, 23-27, another apocalyptic section of the Bible, so that the restraining of the dragon in Revelation 20:1-3 coincides with the moment when dominion is given to the 'one like a son of man' in Daniel 7:9-14.

This section of Revelation has generated endless debates, and sometimes bitter disputes within the Christian community. Therefore, it is very important to approach it with humility and tolerance, as none of us can claim a definitive and absolutely correct interpretation of this passage. If Peter could openly admit that some of Paul's writings were hard for him to understand (2 Pet 3:15-16), who are we to say we know it all? Moreover, even John, like Daniel, did not always understand what he was actually asked to record (Rev 7:14; 17:6b-7).

The point on which we can all agree is that Jesus Christ promised his followers that he would return. The various views disagree on secondary issues related to the nature and timing of that second coming. Instead of attacking those who hold different views, Christians should try to listen to and learn from each other.

The three main interpretations of this passage can be categorized as premillennial, postmillennial and amillennial. The word 'millennium', comes from the Latin word for one thousand.

- *Premillennialists* ('pre-' means 'before') hold that at Christ's return the Christian dead will be raised and believers still living on earth will be caught up to meet him in the air (1 Thess 4:17). They believe that Christ's second coming will take place before his thousand-year reign on earth and that believers will then reign on earth with Christ for a literal thousand years. Then Satan will be released for a short time. This short period of seven years will be followed by the raising of the rest of the dead. In this way there is an explanation of two resurrections that seem to be mentioned in 20:5. Premillennialists would deny that Satan is bound in this present age since he is so obviously active. They are quick to remind Christians that elsewhere John stresses the devil's present activity (12:12). For premillennialists the symbols and numbers in Revelation are to be interpreted according to their natural meaning unless the context clearly indicates otherwise. But if that were true, then, when John said that Satan would be bound with a chain, did he mean a real chain (though the devil is spirit)? If not, why then should one insist on a literal thousand years? In answer to such questions, premillennialists would insist that if these symbols are not taken in their literal sense, they can be twisted to mean almost

anything, and that while the chains may not be literal, the years could be. In other words, while it would not be natural to say that the devil who is spirit would be tied with a literal chain, there is nothing unnatural in saying one thousand literal years.

- *Postmillennialists* ('post-' means 'after') see the return of Christ as taking place after the millennium. Some of them interpret the millennium as the current triumph of the gospel in this age; others consider it a literal one thousand years of triumph of the gospel before Christ returns at the end of the time. Postmillennialists and premillennialists agree that the events of Revelation 19 occur before those of chapter 20.

- *Amillennialists* ('a-' means 'no') hold that there is no literal millennium, and insist that the thousand-year period is symbolic of the whole time between the life of Jesus on earth and his second coming. They interpret the *first resurrection* (**20:5**) as a reference to the new birth or spiritual regeneration, understood as a resurrection from the spiritual death of sin (Eph 2:1-2). The main weakness of this view is that in context, 'the first resurrection' cannot possibly refer to Christian conversion.

These very different positions show how difficult, and sometimes impossible, it is to impose particular eschatological interpretations on a book that is primarily an apocalyptic book rather than an eschatological exposé.

However, by looking more closely at the context of the book, one finds another way to understand the meaning of 'first resurrection.' John *saw thrones* (**20:4a**; Dan 7:9), which those who expect a literal millennium usually place on earth. But all of John's forty-seven references to 'a throne' or 'thrones' in Revelation locate the throne in heaven, except for Satan's throne (2:13) and that of the beast (13:2; 16:10). John does not say how many thrones there are or who sits on them, but he does immediately go on to speak of those slain for Jesus' sake as reigning for a thousand years. From this one can presume that they are the ones who sit on the thrones with *authority to judge*.

It is interesting to see that John refers to *the souls* of these martyrs, and not to their bodies (**20:4b**; contrast 1 Cor 15:51-57; 1 Thess 4:14-17). The same expression is used with reference to the slain witnesses under the altar (6:9). The term *souls* describes those who have lost their bodily life but are nevertheless still alive and are now in the presence of God in heaven. They will resume their bodily life at the first resurrection.

It is said that the souls of these martyrs *came to life and reigned with Christ for a thousand years* (**20:4c**). The exact translation of these words reflects different eschatological views. The translation 'they came to life and reigned with Christ' implies resurrection, but the Greek can also be translated 'they lived in the presence of Christ', which does not have to imply bodily resurrection. John specifically mentions the presence of *souls* in heaven during 'the one thousand years'.

Of the twenty-two NT occurrences of the Greek verb translated 'to reign', seven are in Revelation. Outside the gospels, the verb refers either to the presence of royalty or to being in presence of royalty rather than to any actual exercise of authority over subjects. For example, in 5:10 and 22:5, 'reign' indicates that at the second coming of Christ, all believers will be in the presence of God eternally in the new Jerusalem. In 11:15 and 19:6 it refers to the presence of the all-powerful God. And here in 20:4, 6, it means that saints who die before the second coming of Christ will have access to his royal presence in heaven with Christ (2 Cor 5:6, 8; 1 Thess 4:13-18). These souls are differentiated from *the rest of dead* who do not live in the presence of the Lord but who are raised at 'the first resurrection' at the end of the thousand years (20:5). John thus speaks of only one resurrection.

The premillennial position assumes a second resurrection, which the text does not mention at all, and also faces the problem that the saints are in heaven, and not on earth, during the one thousand years. When the first resurrection does take place at the end of that time, it will be an experience of all people, including believers of all ages (**20:6, 11-15**). It thus appears that those who reign with Christ for a thousand years are those believers who die before his second coming. This echoes similar teaching elsewhere in the Bible: 'We … would prefer to be away from the body and at home with the Lord' (2 Cor 5:8). For saints, physical death means gaining access to the presence of Christ in heaven.

The 'first resurrection' in 20:5 is contrasted with the 'second death' in 20:6. It seems that here 'first' is not primarily meant to indicate a chronological order but rather a contrast between the first world and the new world order that will last forever. Believers who have lived in the fallen creation will be raised to a second life in God's new world. There will be no death for them in that world. Death in that second world is the final fiery *lake of burning sulphur*, from which there is no resurrection (20:10).

Upon his release, Satan goes out to the ends of the earth to deceive the nations and gather them for battle (**20:7-8**). The fact that he has been released by God shows that the end time is under God's control, not Satan's. Satan is busy, but he is restrained from doing his worst. He cannot spiritually destroy God's people. He cannot even obliterate the souls of martyred saints for they are living in the presence of Christ (20:4).

Where do the nations come from when they have all been destroyed already (19:18, 21)? The answer probably is that John is again not writing chronologically, but is speaking of the same nations associated with the beast and the false prophet throughout human history. *Gog and Magog* were Israel's great enemies to the north (Ezek 38–39), while in

Revelation 20:7, they represent all the nations. In apocalyptic writings, Gog and Magog often symbolize the forces of evil. For John the combination of these two is another way of referring to the hosts of the wicked and depicting the intensity of the attack of evil on the things of God.

God's final judgment of Satan and the nations is certain: *Fire came down from heaven and devoured them* (**20:9**). And the devil, who has deceived them, is thrown into *the lake of burning sulphur, where the beast and the false prophet had been thrown* (**20:10**; 19:20).

20:11-15 Act VII, Scene 2: The last judgment

John sees a *great white throne* (**20:11a**). He does not tell us whether God the Father or Christ is sitting on the throne, but it is probably the Father. Other references tell us that the Father is the Judge through the Son (John 5:22; 2 Cor 5:10). John invests the scene with the greatest solemnity. *Earth and sky fled from his presence* (**20:11b**) and *the dead great and small* are *standing before the throne* (**20:12**).

John does not say which *books were opened*, but it seems that they are books in which the names and deeds of all people are written. *The dead were judged* according to the record of *what they had done* (20:12). John is speaking of the eternal judgment against which there is no appeal. He is probably alluding to Daniel 7:10, 'The court was seated; and the books were opened.'

It is sobering to realize that nothing is forgotten or hidden from God: *each person was judged according to what he had done* (**20:13b**). God's judgment always proceeds on the basis of works (Matt 25:41-46; Rom 2:6; 2 Cor 5:10; Heb 4:12-13) as evidence of belief or unbelief in his Son, Jesus Christ (John 3:16; Rom 8:1). Works are an index of the spiritual condition of a person's heart. We are not told whether these books contain either good and evil works or only the latter. Yet the judgment is not a balancing of good works over bad works. Rather, works are seen as unmistakable evidence of the loyalty of the heart; they express belief or unbelief, faithfulness or unfaithfulness. The judgment will reveal whether or not people's loyalties have been with God and the Lamb or with God's enemies. John's theology of faith and its inseparable relation to works is the same as that of Jesus Christ (John 5:29), Paul (Rom 2:6-8) and James (Jas 2), and that is why the record in another book, the *book of life*, seems to be decisive (20:12, 15; 3:5; 13:8; 17:8; 21:27). Those who have their names in the Lamb's 'book of life' will also have records of righteous deeds. The opposite will also be true. The imagery reflects the delicate balance between grace and sin.

The dead are reported to have come from three places: the sea, death and Hades (**20:13a**). The sea represents the place of unburied bodies, while death and Hades represent the reality of dying and the condition entered into at death (1:18; 6:8). Thus all the dead are included. Death and Hades are personified and in a vivid image are cast into the *lake of fire* to be permanently destroyed (**20:14**; see 19:20; 20:10).

21:1 Act VII, Scene 3: The new heaven and new earth

A new heaven and a new earth now appear on stage (**21:1**; Isa 65:17; 66:22). Creation is being renewed. As the apocalyptic drama nears its end, all evil has been destroyed (17:1-20:15). Not only do the old earth and heaven pass away, but the sea, which is a symbol of chaos, rebellion and evil, no longer exists.

21:2-8 Act VII, Scene 4: The new Jerusalem

John sees the *new Jerusalem* coming down out of heaven. Jerusalem was an accepted symbol of the people of God. It was a tangible sign of the covenant, the focus of Jewish faith and hope. In the OT it was described as the place where God dwelt (Ps 76:2), and it is the place where our redemption was accomplished. But this Jerusalem is different from the old one in that it is *new* and *holy*. This is no human construction. Its origin is God.

John smoothly combines the traditional images of city and bride, saying that the city is *prepared as a bride beautifully dressed for her husband* (**21:2**). The 'great city' of Satan was depicted as a prostitute, but this city is the complete opposite. It will be the place where God eternally dwells with his people, and where there will be no emotional and physical pain or illness (**21:3-5**).

God speaks directly to his people, declaring that the recreation of all things is completed (**21:6-7**). The end has arrived through the actions of the one who is *Alpha and Omega* (1:8). All those who are wicked are excluded from the kingdom of God (**21:8**).

21:9-21 Act VII, Scene 5: Measuring the new Jerusalem

It is significant that the angel who now shows John *the bride, the wife of the Lamb*, is identified in the same way as the angel who showed him the 'great prostitute' (**21:9**; 17:1). The prostitute and the beast were described at length, and so is the city that is the bride in order to bring out the contrast between the rival cities of Babylon and the new Jerusalem.

John's model for the city is Ezekiel's vision of the new temple and the new Jerusalem (Ezek 40–48). In both Ezekiel and Revelation, the seer is led by an angel who shows him the new creation. The presence of the glory of God is central. In Ezekiel, 'the land was radiant with his glory' (Ezek 43:2). In John's vision, God's glory is seen in *brilliance ... like that of a very precious jewel, like a jasper, clear as crystal* (**21:11**; compare Isa 60:1-2, 19).

In ancient times, a wall was an essential feature of a city (Isa 26:1). The wall of the new Jerusalem is very high and is 144 cubits (two hundred feet or sixty metres) thick, symbol-

izing the greatness of the city as well as its impregnability against attack by those described in 21:8 and 27 (**21:12a, 17**). (However, it is also possible that it is the height of the wall that is 144 cubits, in which case the walls are tiny compared to the height of the city, indicating that it is so secure that it scarcely needs a wall.)

In his description of the gates, John follows Ezekiel closely (**21:12b-13**; Ezek 48:30-35). The number twelve figures prominently here. There are twelve gates: three in each wall, with one of the names of the tribes of Israel carved on each (21:12). There are twelve foundations to the city wall, each with the name of one of the twelve apostles of Jesus (**21:14**).

Although the city is measured by the angel, the units of measurement are those commonly used by humans (21:17). The city is a cube: *12,000 stadia* [1500 miles / 2200 kilometres] *in length, and as wide and high as it is long* (**21:16**). This figure (twelve times one thousand) reinforces the earlier reference to the twelve tribes of Israel and the twelve apostles. Again we must not take these numbers literally. What they are communicating is simply that this is an immense city, with room for an enormous number of inhabitants (7:9; John 14:2). There will be room for all believers, of all times.

The city is beautiful and precious beyond all imagination, full of gold and jewels (**21:18-21**). But the central image is of the light, the radiance, the glory that is here because of the presence of God in the midst of the city. The great street itself is made of gold so pure that it is as transparent as glass. This is a description in human language of the great majesty that awaits believers – to be in the presence of God for ever.

21:22-27 Act VII, Scene 6: The lamp of the city

The radical newness of this city of God is seen in the fact that it has no temple (**21:22**). Israel knew that God could not be contained in any human building, but in Solomon's prayer of consecration for the original temple he prayed that 'your eyes may be open towards this temple night and day, this place of which you said, "My Name shall be there"' (1 Kgs 8:29). Ezekiel saw the cloud of glory leave the temple, as a sign that God's presence had left the city and the temple before they were destroyed (Ezek 10:18-19; 11:23). Ezekiel's vision of the restored Jerusalem includes a new temple, but John's vision does not, for God is its sanctuary (and all its inhabitants are priests – 5:10; 20:6).

Just as there is no need of a temple, so there is no need for light. *The city does not need the sun or the moon to shine on it* (**21:23**). God's glory is the illumination for the blessed ones, and God does not depart from the Holy City. The old heaven containing the sun and the moon can be destroyed because it is no long needed.

John sees God bringing *the nations* into the holy city (**21:24, 26**). The gates are never closed, because there is no need for defence and because there is no night, the time when city gates were normally closed (**21:25**). Nothing evil, nothing unclean, will be able to contaminate or corrupt the new Jerusalem (**21:27**).

22:1-5 Act VII, Scene 7: The city's source of life

The concluding chapter of Revelation recalls the creation before the fall. But the redemption of the world is not a simple return to the original creation. All of human history stands in between, with the development of civilization, the enormous growth of population, the creation of cities and all the conflicts of human societies. That is why John sees the future as a city, not as a garden of Eden.

The *river of the water of life* and the *tree of life* are now in the midst of the Holy City (**22:1-2**; see Gen 2:9-10). Now, almost at the end of human history, humans may return and legitimately enjoy the blessing from which they were banished. The river and the tree are reminders that life comes from God. The tree of life is said to bear fruit every month and it is specifically said to bear *twelve crops of fruit* (that is, twelve crops in succession, not twelve kinds of fruit – 22:2a). As there is neither sun nor moon there is of course no 'month', but John's imagery here shows that there is an abundant supply. The image also suggests that life in the new Jerusalem has characteristics of our earthly life – there is food to be eaten, and there are seasons. *The leaves of the tree* are said to be *for the healing of the nations* (22:2b; Ezek 47:12). *Healing* should not be understood in a literal sense because in the new city there is neither sickness nor sin. But the image expresses the truth that in the new city there is enjoyment of life.

The most revealing characteristic of life in the new Jerusalem is that God's people *will see his face* (**22:4**). Life in God's new kingdom is eternal, for *they will reign forever and ever* (**22:5**). It is not said that they will reign over anyone; therefore it is better to take the term *reign* as a reference to being in the royal presence with God. This scene marks the climax of the whole book, the culmination of the process that began in chapters 2 and 3 with the promises made to 'overcomers'. The throne is right in the midst of the new Jerusalem and the believers are now and for ever in the presence of God.

22:6-21 Epilogue

The book concludes with a series of warnings, exhortations and assurances. There are three major emphases in the conclusion: confirmation of the genuineness of the prophecy (22:6-7, 16, 18-19); the imminence of Jesus' second coming (22:7, 12, 20); the warning against idolatry and the invitation to enter the city (22:11, 15, 17).

The reader is returned to the atmosphere at the beginning of the book. It was Jesus who commanded John to write the letter to be sent to the seven churches (1:17-20). Now that the vision is complete, Jesus blesses those who remain faithful (**22:7**). John then adds his own witness that he has indeed written what he saw and heard (**22:8**). He again falls at the feet of his angelic guide to worship him, only to be told again not to do so (22:8-9; 19:10). God alone is to be worshipped. The angel and John, along with the prophets and all faithful believers, are simply servants. John's response shows the overwhelming authority given to the true Word of God. The angel's response shows that the authority given to the Word must not be transferred to the messenger.

The angel (assuming that this is the *he* who speaks) tells John not to seal the book that he has written (**22:10**). By contrast, Daniel was told to seal up his writings because the time for them had not yet come (Dan 8:26). The book John saw in 5:1-9 was sealed with seven seals. It set out the goal of God's creation and the process by which it would be achieved, and could only be opened by 'the Lamb who was slain' (5:12) after his work of redemption had been accomplished.

Jesus now speaks, declaring he will come bringing this reward, which will result in both blessing and punishment (**22:12**). He applies to himself the same titles that have been used for God (**22:13**; 1:8; 21:6). The final blessing of the book is pronounced upon *those who wash their robes* (**22:14**), that is, those who have been redeemed by Christ's death (7:14). They will be able to enter the city of God and eat of the tree of life, which will give them eternal life. The wicked, however, will remain outside the city and not receive its blessed inheritance (**22:15**). These words of Jesus reinforce the words of the angel he has sent to lead John through the vision (**22:16**). The use of a plural *you* in this verse indicates that it is not John, but the readers, who need this added word of authority.

The final section of Revelation (22:17-21) is not only an ending, but also a beginning. There is an invitation issued by the *Spirit and the bride* (**22:17**). The invitation is to come and drink *the water of life*. The invitation is the same as, or at least includes, an invitation to come to the Lord's Table, for similar words were used by first-century Christians at the end of the Lord's Supper: *Come, Lord Jesus!* (**22:20**). Paul concludes his first letter to the Corinthians in the same way (1 Cor 16:22). Clearly, these letters were intended to be read in the worship service.

Between the invitation (22:17) and the conclusion (22:20-21) is a final warning to take seriously what John has written and not to change the words of the book. The accuracy and authenticity of the work are guaranteed by a curse formula (**22:18-19**). Who is the *I* who says these words? Most likely it is John himself. The words parallel the warning given by Jesus in 22:14-15.

John has finished his task. He has faithfully recorded what he has seen and heard in his vision. His words have been authenticated both by the angel and by Jesus himself. Now it is up to those who receive the book to follow its guidance. Will the words be so difficult that some readers will be tempted to tone them down and change them, enabling them to compromise with the powers that be? Difficult as they are, the words are to remain. Those who would change them would be revealing that they are among the unfaithful, and would thus suffer the consequences described in the book.

The final words of Revelation are similar to those in most NT letters: *The grace of the Lord Jesus be with God's people. Amen.*

Onesimus Ngundu

Further Reading

Johnson, Alan F. *Revelation*. EBC. Grand Rapids: Zondervan, 1996.

Keener, Craig S. *Revelation*. NIVAC. Grand Rapids: Zondervan, 2000.

Morris, Leon. *Revelation*. TNT. Leicester: Inter-Varsity Press, 1987.

GLOSSARY

acrostic. A type of poem in which the first line begins with the first letter of the alphabet, the second line with the second letter, and so on. For example: 'All my heart goes out to thee, Lord, in thanksgiving, before the assembly where the just are gathered. Chant we the Lord's wondrous doings, decreed to fulfil all his purposes' (Ps 111:1-2 – KNOX).

acted prophecy. See **symbolic act**

agape. The Greek word used in the NT for the love of God or Jesus for Christians or for the love between Christians. It is different from *eros* (sexual love) and *philos* (friendship).

allegory. An extended piece of writing in which the author is understood to mean something other than what he or she is literally saying. The most famous example is the Song of Songs, which is literally about the love between a man and a woman, but which some interpret as an allegory about the love between Jesus Christ and the church.

allusion. A literary technique in which a text refers to another text or to a person, a place or an event without explicitly mentioning it. The NT contains both direct quotations from the OT and many allusions to it in order to demonstrate how Jesus fulfils OT prophecies (see commentary on Matt 3:1).

amen. A Hebrew word that means 'let it be so'. It is commonly used to mark the end of a prayer.

analogy. A literary technique that involves comparison of the similarities between two things.

antichrist. One who pretends to be Christ, or acts against Christ.

antithetical proverb. A proverb using antithetical parallelism (see **parallelism**).

aphorism. A short pithy statement of the type found in Proverbs 10–30.

apocalyptic. A type of literature describing visions of the past and the future in heaven and on earth, often with an angelic guide. Examples can be found in Isaiah 24–27; Ezekiel 1; 40–48; Daniel 7–12; Zech 9–14; Matt 24; Mark 13; Luke 21; Revelation.

Apocrypha. Books that were included in the Septuagint but are not part of the Hebrew Bible. They are still included in Catholic and Orthodox Bibles (see also **canon; Septuagint**).

ark of the covenant. A chest representing God's throne or footstool and symbolizing his presence with Israel. It was created according to the Lord's instructions and travelled with the Israelites in the desert (Exod 25:10-22). It was kept in the Most Holy Place in the tabernacle and in Solomon's temple. It contained the tablets on which the Ten Commandments were inscribed (see also **Most Holy Place**).

Asherah; Ashtoreth. A goddess worshipped in the ancient Near East.

atonement cover. The lid of the ark of the covenant, thought of as the place where God either sat or rested his feet (see also **ark of the covenant**).

Augustine of Hippo. (AD 354-430) A church father, Christian philosopher and bishop of Hippo in North Africa.

avenger of blood. If a person was killed, a relative had to kill the killer. That person was called the avenger of blood (see also *lex talionis*).

Baal. A Canaanite god associated with storms and with fertility.

2 Baruch. A pseudepigraphical and apocalyptic book, which claims to have been written by Jeremiah's scribe Baruch (see also **apocalyptic; pseudepigrapha**).

Book of the Covenant. See **Book of the Law.**

Book of the Law. The book discovered in the temple during the reign of Josiah in about 622 BC (2 Kgs 22:8-23:24). Either Deuteronomy or the whole Pentateuch (see also **Pentateuch**).

Booths, Feast of. See **Tabernacles, Feast of.**

canon. The collection of books with religious authority found in the Bible. The Jewish canon consists only of the OT and is divided into the Law (the Torah), the Prophets and the Writings (see **Prophets; Torah; Writings**). The Christian canon is divided into the OT and the NT. The OT is further subdivided into the Pentateuch, the Historical Books, the Poetical and Wisdom Books and the Prophets (see **Historical Books; Pentateuch; Poetical Books; Prophets; Wisdom Literature**). Catholic and Orthodox Churches also include various books of the Apocrypha in the canon (see also **Apocrypha; pseudepigrapha**).

cherubim. (sg. **cherub**) Winged creatures that protected the Garden of Eden (Gen 3:24) and were depicted as hovering over the ark of the covenant (Exod 25:18-22). Isaiah and Ezekiel saw them in visions (Isa 6:1-4; Ezek 1–3, 10).

Clement of Alexandria. (died about AD 250) Church father and head of the school for converts in Alexandria, North Africa.

Clement of Rome. (died about AD 100) Church father and third bishop of Rome after Peter.

comparative proverb. A proverb using comparative parallelism (see **parallelism**).

concubine. A woman living with a man in a marriage-like relationship, but of lower status than a wife.

covenant. A binding agreement or treaty. In the Bible, God makes covenants with Noah (Gen 9:1-17), with Abraham (Gen 15:1-21), with all of Israel at Sinai (Exod 24) and with David (2 Sam 7:8-16).

cubit. A measure of length. The distance from the elbow to the knuckle or fingertip (about 18 inches, 45 centimetres).

Davidic dynasty. The descendants of King David who ruled Judah from 1000 BC to the fall of Jerusalem in 587 BC.

Day of Atonement. Also known as Yom Kippur. A day of rest and fasting falling on 10 Tishri (in September/ October). The only day of the year when the high priest entered the Most Holy Place to atone for all the sins of Israel (Lev 16:29-33).

Day of the Lord. Originally any day on which an Israelite festival was celebrated and hence a day of celebration. The prophets' denunciation of the corruption of Israelite religious practices resulted in the Day of the Lord coming to be understood as a day of judgment rather than a day of celebration.

Dead Sea Scrolls. Ancient Hebrew and Aramaic documents discovered along the west coast of the Dead Sea. They include the oldest manuscripts of most biblical books, as well as documents belonging to a Jewish sect, most probably the Essenes (see also **Essenes; Qumran**).

Decalogue. The Ten Commandments, or Ten Words, as given in Exodus 20:1-17 and Deuteronomy 5:6-21.

Diaspora. Derived from the Greek word that means 'scattered'. Refers to all Jews who lived outside the land of Israel.

divided kingdom. The result of the revolt that broke the unified kingdom of Saul, David and Solomon into two smaller kingdoms (see also **northern kingdom; southern kingdom**).

doxology. A formula such as 'Praise the Lord!' that is used in a liturgy (see also **liturgy**).

elohim. A Hebrew word that means 'gods'. When used of the Lord God, it is a plural of majesty – like the royal 'we'. It can also be used to refer to the gods of foreign nations, and sometimes even to people in authority (see also **Yahweh**).

ephah. A measure of volume, a tenth of a homer (about 5 gallons/22 litres) (see also **homer; seah**).

ephod. The 'waistcoat' worn by the high priest, decorated with twelve precious stones representing the twelve tribes of Israel and incorporating a pouch containing the Urim and Thummim (see also **Urim and Thummim**).

epistle. A letter – especially the letters by Paul and others that make up a large part of the NT.

eschatology. The study of what the Bible teaches about the last age of the world and the return of Jesus Christ.

Essenes. A Jewish sect that existed from about 200 BC to AD 100. It was probably Essenes living at Qumran who hid the Dead Sea Scrolls when their community came under attack by the Romans (see also **Dead Sea Scrolls; Qumran**).

eunuch. A man who has been castrated.

Eusebius of Caesarea. (about AD 263-339) Church father and historian. He wrote *The History of the Church*.

exile, the. The seventy years which the Jews spent in Babylonia after being deported to that country by Nebuchadnezzar.

fetish. An object that is believed to possess magical powers.

Firstfruits, Feast of. See **Weeks, Feast of.**

First temple. The temple built by Solomon in about 950 BC and destroyed by the Babylonians in 587 BC (see also **Second temple**).

Former Prophets. In Jewish tradition, Joshua, Judges, 1 and 2 Samuel, 1 and 2 Kings are referred to as the Former Prophets (see also **Historical Books; Latter Prophets**).

genealogy. A list of a person's ancestors or descendants.

Gentile. A non-Israelite. Collectively, the Gentiles are referred to as 'the nations'.

Hades. The Greek name for the place of the dead (see also **Sheol**).

Hallel Psalms. Psalms 113–118, which are psalms of praise recited at the great Jewish festivals.

Hasmoneans. The family name of the Maccabees, who ruled Judea from 142 BC to 63 BC (see also **Maccabees**).

Hellenistic. An adjective that means 'Greek'. It is often used with reference to the spread of Greek culture in the Near East following the campaigns of Alexander the Great (356-323 BC).

Hippolytus of Rome. (died AD 235) Bible commentator and martyr.

Historical Books. The books from Joshua to Esther in the Bible.

Holy of Holies. See **Most Holy Place.**

Holy Place. The space in front of the Most Holy Place in the tabernacle and the temple (see also **Most Holy Place**).

homer. A measure of volume equivalent to a donkey-load of grain (about 50 gallons/220 litres) (see also **ephah; seah**).

Ignatius of Antioch. (about AD 50-110) Church father and bishop of Antioch.

inclusio. A Hebrew literary technique in which a word or phrase is repeated to mark the beginning and end of a passage (see Ps 103:1, 22; Isa 1:21, 26).

Ingathering, Feast of. See **Tabernacles, Feast of.**

Irenaeus of Lyons. (about AD 30–100) Church father and bishop of Lyons, France.

Jehovah. See **Yahweh.**

Jerome. (about AD 340-420) Church father and translator. He translated the whole Bible from Hebrew and Greek into Latin.

Josephus. (about AD 37-100) Jewish politician, general and historian. He wrote *The History of the Jews* and *The Jewish War.*

Jubilee. The name for the fiftieth year in which all property was to be returned to its original owners (Lev 25:8-55).

Justin Martyr. (about AD 100-165) Church father, Christian apologist and martyr.

koine. (Greek: 'common') The common form of Greek spoken throughout the eastern Roman Empire. The language of the NT and the Septuagint (see also **Septuagint**).

Latter Prophets. In Jewish tradition, Isaiah to Malachi (see also **Former Prophets**).

Leviathan. A great beast, probably the crocodile, but also having mythical significance.

levirate marriage. A man's obligation to marry his older brother's widow and 'build up his brother's name'. Children of the marriage would be counted as the children of the older brother (see Deut 25:5-6).

lex talionis. (Latin: 'Law of retaliation') The principle of an eye for an eye and a tooth for a tooth (Lev 24:17-22; Matt 5:38-42).

liturgy. A pattern for formal, organized group worship.

Maccabees. A nickname derived from the Aramaic word for 'hammer'. It was given to the brothers who led the revolt against Syria in 167 BC and founded the Hasmonean dynasty (see also **Hasmoneans**).

Magnificat. Mary's song of praise in Luke 1:46-55. The title comes from the opening words of this poem in the Latin translation.

Major Prophets. Isaiah, Jeremiah, Ezekiel, Daniel. So called because of the length of their books (see also **Minor Prophets**).

mercy seat. See **atonement cover.**

metaphor. A literary technique in which one thing is described in terms of another. For example, 'The Lord is my rock' (Ps 18:2) (see also **simile**).

Minor Prophets. Hosea, Joel, Amos, Obadiah, Jonah, Micah, Nahum, Habakkuk, Zephaniah, Haggai, Zechariah, Malachi. So called because of the shortness of their books (see also **Major Prophets**).

monotheism. The belief that there is only one god.

Most Holy Place. The innermost part of the tabernacle and the temple; also called the Holy of Holies. The ark of the covenant was kept there. It was only entered by the high priest on the Day of Atonement (see also **ark of the covenant; Day of Atonement; Holy Place**).

Nazirites. People who took a special vow never to drink alcohol, cut their hair or touch a dead body (Num 6:1-21).

northern kingdom. The northern part of the divided kingdom, also known as Israel, Samaria and Ephraim. Invaded by the Assyrians in 722 BC, when the population was deported (see also **divided kingdom; southern kingdom**).

oracle. A message from God.

Origen. (about AD 185-254) Christian philosopher and Bible commentator. He was born in Alexandria, North Africa.

papyrus. A writing surface made from the crushed stalks of the papyrus reed.

parable. A story with a moral. Jesus often taught using parables (see Matt 13:3-13).

parallelism. A poetic technique, in which the second of a pair of lines repeats the first line with minor modifications (synonymous parallelism), emphasizes the first line (synthetic parallelism), states the opposite of the first line (antithetical parallelism) or compares something with the thing mentioned in the first line (comparative parallelism). This technique is used a lot in Proverbs (see Prov 10–30).

parchment. A writing surface made from cleaned animal skins.

Passover. One of the three great pilgrim festivals for which all Jewish males were required to go to Jerusalem. It began on 15 Nisan (in March/April) and lasted seven days. The feast celebrated the exodus from Egypt (Exod 12:13) and incorporated the Feast of Unleavened Bread (see also **Tabernacles, Feast of; Weeks, Feast of**).

Pastoral Epistles. 1 and 2 Timothy, Titus. So called because they contain Paul's advice to Timothy and Titus on pastoral issues.

patriarch. A respected ancestor. In the case of the Jews, the patriarchs were Abraham, Isaac and Jacob.

patriarchal. A patriarchal society is one that is ruled by men.

Pauline. Associated with the Apostle Paul.

Pentateuch. The first five books of the Bible: Genesis, Exodus, Leviticus, Numbers and Deuteronomy. They are attributed to Moses.

Pentecost. The fiftieth day after Passover, and thus also after Easter, when the Holy Spirit came upon the disciples (see also **Weeks, Feast of**).

personification. A literary technique in which an abstract concept is spoken of as if it were a person. It is used when Wisdom and Folly are represented as women in Proverbs 8–9, and when Paul addresses death: 'Where, O death, is your victory? Where, O death, is your sting?' (1 Cor 15:55).

Pharisees. A Jewish sect that existed from about 200 BC to AD 100. They were characterized by strict observance of the law, and were the forerunners of rabbinic Judaism.

Poetical Books. Those books of the Bible that are mainly written in poetry, specifically Job, Psalms, and the Song of Songs.

Polycarp. (about AD 70-155) Church father, bishop of Smyrna and martyr.

polytheism. The belief that there are many gods.

post-exilic. Dating from the period after the exile (see **exile, the**).

pre-exilic. Dating from the period before the exile (see **exile, the**).

Prophets. The OT books that contain the words of the prophets. In the Christian tradition, these are the books from Isaiah to Malachi. However, the Jews also include Joshua, Judges, 1 and 2 Samuel, and 1 and 2 Kings in the section they call the Prophets (see also **canon**; **Former Prophets**; **Latter Prophets**; **Major Prophets**; **Minor Prophets**).

pseudepigrapha. There were works produced between about 200 BC and AD 500 that claim to have been written by famous, usually biblical, figures from much earlier (see also **Apocrypha**).

Purim, Feast of. Jewish festival occurring on 14 Adar (in February/March), celebrating the deliverance of the Jews from the plot described in the book of Esther.

Qohelet. The Hebrew title of Ecclesiastes, often used to refer to the author of that book.

Qumran. Site on the north-west coast of the Dead Sea, about fifteen miles (twenty-four kilometres) from Jerusalem where many of the Dead Sea Scrolls were discovered (see also **Dead Sea Scrolls**; **Essenes**).

remnant. Those people who survive the Lord's judgment on his people (see Isa 10:20-23; Zeph 3:9-13; Hag 1:12).

Sabbath. The Sabbath was the seventh day of the week, on which no work was to be done (Exod 20:8-11; Deut 5:12-15).

Sabbath Year. A year in which no agricultural work was to be done, and the people were only to eat what the land produced on its own (Lev 25:1-7) (see also **Jubilee**).

sackcloth. Clothing made of course cloth that is worn as a sign of mourning or repentance.

Sadducees. A Jewish sect that existed from about 200 BC to AD 100 and comprised the political and religious elite.

Samaritans. Descendants of those Jews who did not go into exile and who intermarried with the other groups the Assyrians had settled among them (2 Kgs 17:24-40). Despite their common origin, there were tensions between Jews and Samaritans (see John 4:9).

Sanhedrin. The supreme Jewish religious council in Jerusalem.

scroll. A roll of papyrus or parchment on which books were written.

seah. A measure of volume, a third of an ephah (about 13 pints/7.3 litres) (see also **ephah**; **homer**).

Second temple. The temple built after the exile in about 520 BC, to replace Solomon's Temple and extended by Herod the Great (so also known as Herod's Temple). It was destroyed by the Romans in AD 70 (see also **First temple**).

Septuagint. The Greek translation of the OT, made in Alexandria, North Africa, in the third century BC. Seventy (or seventy-two) translators are said to have been involved in this project.

Servant Songs. Four messianic passages in Isaiah which refer to the servant of the Lord (Isa 42:1-9; 49:1-6; 50:4-9; 52:13-53:12).

shalom. A Hebrew word that means 'peace' or 'wholeness'.

shekel. A measure of weight and hence also of money (about 0.4 ounces, 11.5 grams).

Shema. The Jewish declaration of faith, as given in Deuteronomy 6:4.

Sheol. The Hebrew word for the place of the dead.

simile. A literary technique in which one thing is explicitly said to be like another. For example, 'Your righteousness is like the mighty mountains, your justice like the great deep, O Lord' (Ps 36:6) (see also **metaphor**).

Solomon's Temple. See **First Temple**.

Songs of Ascents. Psalms 120–134. So called because they were sung as pilgrims ascended to Jerusalem during the great Jewish pilgrim festivals.

southern kingdom. The southern part of the divided kingdom, also known as Judah. It was invaded by the Babylonians in 587 BC, when the population was taken into exile. They returned from exile in 537 BC (see also **divided kingdom**; **northern kingdom**).

symbolic act. An act that represents some other act or event. For example, Ezekiel's actions that represented the siege of Jerusalem (see Ezek 4:1-13).

syncretism. The mixing of elements from different religious traditions.

synonymous proverb. A proverb using synonymous parallelism (see **parallelism**).

Synoptic Gospels. The gospels of Matthew, Mark and Luke, which share a lot of common material.

synthetic proverb. A proverb using synthetic parallelism (see **parallelism**).

tabernacle. The portable shrine used by the Israelites during their wanderings in the desert (see Exod 25–30).

Tabernacles, Feast of. One of the three great Jewish pilgrim festivals for which all Jewish males were required to go to Jerusalem. It celebrated the harvest. The feast began on 15 Tishri (in September/October) and lasted eight days.

talent. A measure of weight and hence of money. It was equivalent to 3000 shekels (about 75 pounds/34 kilograms).

Tent of Meeting. The tent used by Moses when he consulted with God during the wandering in the wilderness (see Exod 33:7-11) (see also **tabernacle**).

testament. An agreement or covenant. The Old Testament speaks of God's covenants with Israel. The New Testament speaks of God's new covenant mediated through Jesus Christ to the whole world (see also **covenant**).

theophany. An appearance of God to human beings (see Gen 18:1).

tithe. The portion of their income that Israelites were expected to give for the upkeep of the temple and the support of the poor. It amounted to one tenth of what they earned (see Deut 14:22-29).

Torah. In a narrow sense, the first five books of the Bible, attributed to Moses (see also **Pentateuch**).

Transjordan. Area on the eastern side of the River Jordan, including Bashan, Gilead, Ammon, Moab and Edom. It was where the tribes of Reuben, Gad and half of the tribe of Manasseh settled (see Josh 13:8).

treaty. An agreement, contract or covenant, usually between kings or rulers.

Unleavened Bread, Feast of. See **Passover**.

Urim and Thummim. Two objects that were used to consult the Lord by drawing lots. One of them must have designated a positive response from God and the other a negative response (see Num 27:21; 1 Sam 28:6).

vernacular. The language commonly spoken in a region.

Vulgate. The Latin translation of the Bible, made by Jerome at the end of the fourth century AD (see also **Jerome**).

wadi. A dry river bed that fills with water, often very suddenly, during the wet season.

Weeks, Feast of. One of the three great Jewish pilgrim festivals for which all Jewish males were required to go to Jerusalem. It celebrated the first fruit of the harvest, and came in May/June, fifty days after Passover. In Greek it is called Pentecost (see also **Pentecost**).

Wisdom literature. Job, Proverbs, Ecclesiastes. So called because these books are more concerned with issues of everyday life than with the history of Israel.

Writings. The third division of the Jewish canon. Psalms, Proverbs, Job, Song of Songs, Ruth, Lamentations, Ecclesiastes, Esther, Daniel, Ezra, Nehemiah, 1 and 2 Chronicles (see also **canon**).

Yahweh. The proper name of God. In early Jewish tradition it became too holy to be pronounced. In the oldest Hebrew manuscripts it is written without vowels, YHWH (and is referred to as the Tetragrammaton). In mediaeval Hebrew manuscripts, it was written with the vowels of *adonai* (my lord). The exact pronunciation is uncertain, and most English versions of the Bible represent the name by 'the LORD'.

Zealots. A Jewish movement between about 70 BC and AD 70 that wanted to use violence to get rid of the occupying Roman forces.

ziggurat. Artificial mountain or stepped pyramid on which the Babylonians built their temples.

SOME WEB RESOURCES

Bible Translations and Versions

Bible Gateway:

http://www.biblegateway.com

Includes many version of the Bible that are searchable by passage, keyword or topic. Includes Bibles or New Testaments in Amharic, French, Portuguese, Swahili, Ndebele and Luo. Also includes IVP New Testament Commentaries, encyclopedias and nineteenth-century Bible dictionaries.

International Bible Society

www.ibs.org/index.php

Links to searchable Bible texts in many versions, languages and formats

Bible Commentaries

Bible Gateway

http://www.biblegateway.com

Includes IVP New Testament Commentaries

Classic Bible Commentaries

http://eword.gospelcom.net/comments

Presents fourteen historical commentaries including those by Calvin, Luther and Wesley. Searchable by biblical passage.

Easy English Bible Commentaries

http://www.easyenglish.info

Bible commentaries and Bible studies in Level B Easy English (2800 word vocabulary).

Blue Letter Bible

http://blueletterbible.org

Many Bible versions and commentaries (audio and video), topical essays, concordance, maps, charts.

Biblical History and Geography

Bible History

http://www.bible-history.com/

History of Israel and surrounding nations, with maps articles, timelines, pictures. Some available as free Powerpoint presentations.

Geography of the Bible

http://www.ancientsandals.com/

Pictures, videos and geographical information about sites mentioned in the Bible. Site maintained by Colombia International University

Note: The Web sites listed here are only a few of the many resources available on the Internet. However, when using any Web resource, it is important to remember that the information found is no more reliable than the person or institution managing the Web site. This is not to say that everything that appears in a book is necessarily correct, but at least the information found in books published by reputable companies is more likely to have been screened by a number of people. A Web site may reflect the opinions of just one individual.